...Mach .92
at tree top level flight

The **Fiat G 91 Y** is the modern aircraft to fulfill the requirements in the field
of tactical air support.
2 General Electric J 85 - G.E. -13 A turbojet engines with a total thrust of 3700 kgs.
750 kms of radius in the low-low recce mission at 8700 kg
take off weight. Ferry mission 3500 kg. Take off capabilities,
at operational take off weight, from semi-prepared strips.

FIAT
aviazione

CORSO G. AGNELLI 200 - 10100 TORINO (ITALIA)

2 adv.

THE REMARKABLE NEW SOVIET-BUILT YAK-40

has been designed to carry 27 passengers between grass airfields. For the first time jet performance is offered to millions of new customers who live in areas far from major airports – and the YAK-40 is equally unrivalled for feeder-line services into the big airports. Also available as 8-10 passengers business executive transport.

AVIAEXPORT, Moscow,

can offer a complete range of modern turbine-powered transport aircraft for every purpose. Here are some of them:

ANTONOV An-26 (An-24T with enlarged freight door). Short- to medium-range commercial freight transport. Direct rear loading for freight or vehicles and electrically- or manually-operated conveyor with 4500 kg capacity in floor.

ILYUSHIN Il-62. Long-range commercial airliner. Brings speed and comfort to the longest air routes. Up to 186 passengers can be carried at cruising speed of 900 kmh. Max. range – 9200 km.

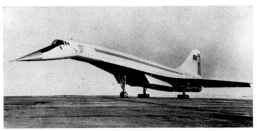

TUPOLEV Tu-144. The world's first long-haul supersonic commercial airliner. Three crew members and up to 120 passengers can be carried at cruising speed of 2500 kmh. Max. range – 6500 km.

TUPOLEV Tu-154. Medium range commercial airliner. Three crew members and up to 164 passengers or 20 tons of freight can be carried at cruising speed of 900-975 kmh. The Tu-154 can take off at full gross weight from "hot and high" airfields and can fly on one engine.

V/O AVIAEXPORT is ready to satisfy all enquiries about Soviet civil aircraft and accessories. It receives representatives of foreign firms in Moscow and sends its own representatives abroad to negotiate transactions.

For more details please apply to V/O "AVIAEXPORT" 32/34 Smolenskaya-Sennaya, Moscow G-200, USSR.

Cables: Aviaexport Moscow.   Telex: Moscow 257.

Telephone: 244-26-86.

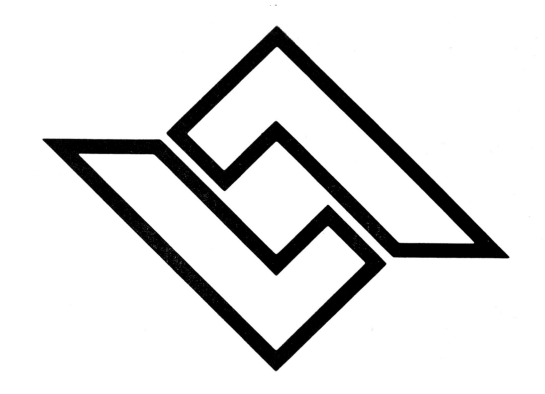

AERITALIA

AERITALIA
the merger into a new company
of Fiat Aircraft Division, Aerfer and Salmoiraghi aerospace activities

AERITALIA
a joint venture of Fiat and Finmeccanica
with equally shared partnership,
ready to face the technological challenge of the 1970's.

AERITALIA
an aerospace enterprise of larger dimension
capable of meeting national and international requirements
in the field of commercial and military aviation

AERITALIA
to day:
six production centers and eight thousand employees

soon:
expanding in Southern Italy with new facilities
supported by a new advanced center
for Aerospace Research and Development

Naples – Italy

Piper Pressurized Navajo makes its entrance at 29,000 feet

The brand new Piper Pressurized Navajo gives you extra power, extra performance, extra payload and extra size—more extra features than you'll find in any other airplane in its class. Take a look at the numbers: **29,000-foot operational altitude with 10,000-foot cabin altitude ■ 5.5 psi pressurization system ■ 266 mph cruise at 24,000 feet ■ 2958-pound useful load ■ 6/8-place capacity ■ Over 1400-mile range ■ 2830-foot accelerate/stop distance ■ Twin turbocharged Lycoming 425 hp engines ■ Full 75% cruise power to 24,000 feet; 65% to 29,000.**

The Piper Pressurized Navajo is packed with features that pilots and passengers appreciate, from its exceptional performance characteristics to its comfortable cabin environment.
For the facts see your local Piper dealer or write for complete information on the Pressurized Navajo to Piper Aircraft Corporation, Lock Haven, Pa. 17745. Dept. PN-2.

PIPER

VSTOL

Dornier believes that VSTOL is the answer to future air traffic problems.

The Dornier VSTOL development group plays an international leading role in the planning and construction of VSTOL aircraft systems. Our Do 31, the first VSTOL jet transport in the world, was a revolutionary development by Dornier. In more than 200 flights, the Do 31 has answered most of the questions asked in this area. Our STOL airplanes, the Do 27, Do 28 and "Skyservant" have now passed the 800th delivery and are in service all over the world.

Dornier teams are presently working on the military and civilian VSTOL transport of tomorrow, developing a new generation of economical STOL and VSTOL jets.

DORNIER AG · P.O. BOX 317
D-799 FRIEDRICHSHAFEN GERMANY

Aircraft (STOL VTOL) · Helicopters · Electronics ·
Process Engineering · Systems Engineering · Logistics

DORNIER SYSTEM GMBH P.O. BOX 648
D-799 FRIEDRICHSHAFEN GERMANY

Space Systems · Missile Systems · Electronic Systems · Ocean
Systems · Operative Research (Consulting Systems Analysis)
Contract Research

JANE'S ALL THE WORLD'S AIRCRAFT

Edited by **John W. R. Taylor**

FRHistS, AFRAeS, FSLAET

Order of Contents

Alphabetical List of Advertisers

Classified List of Advertisers*

List of Editorial Contents

Foreword

Aircraft

Drones

Sailplanes

Military Missiles

Research Rockets and Space Vehicles

Aero Engines

Addenda

Index Section

World Sales Distribution

Jane's Yearbooks,
49/50 Poland St, London W1A 2LG
All the World

except

North, Central and South America:
McGraw-Hill Book Company,
330 West 42nd Street, New York, NY

and

Canada
**McGraw-Hill Company of Canada
Ltd,** 330 Progress Avenue, Scarborough,
Ontario, Canada

Editorial communication to:

The Editor, Jane's All The World's Aircraft,
Jane's Yearbooks, 49/50 Poland Street,
London W1A 2LG, England
Telephone 01-437-0686

Advertisement communication to:

Haymarket Publishing Group,
Gillow House, 5 Winsley Street,
London W1, England
Telephone 01-636-3600

---

*Classified List of Advertisers

The various products available from the advertisers in this edition are listed alphabetically in about 350 different headings. In order to increase the usefulness of the Classified List a section is incorporated, on tinted paper, listing the product headings in French, German, Spanish and Russian, alphabetically in those languages, The identification letter and number corresponding to the English-language listing is shown against each item.

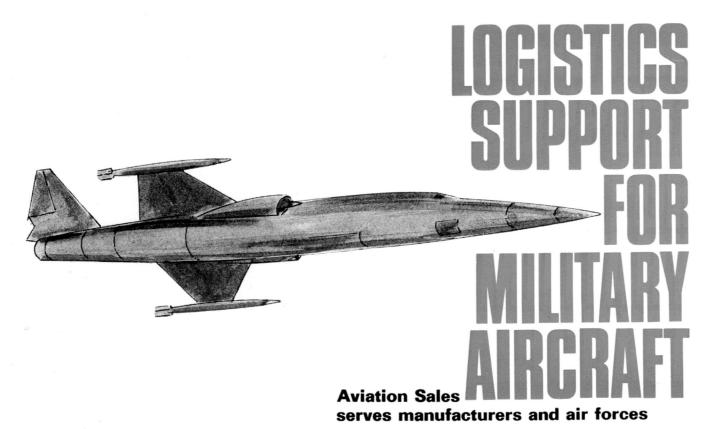

LOGISTICS SUPPORT FOR MILITARY AIRCRAFT

Aviation Sales serves manufacturers and air forces

- ☐ **AIRCRAFT BATTERIES.** SONOTONE nickel-cadmium batteries specified by U.S. and European airforces, major airlines.

- ☐ **BATTERY CHARGER-ANALYZERS** by HYFORE CORP. will service nickel-cadmium aircraft batteries faster, more accurately. . . reduce maintenance.

- ☐ **JET-ENGINE STARTING SYSTEMS** designed by WELLS INDUSTRIES will start any number of jet aircraft simultaneously.

- ☐ **PRINTED CIRCUIT BOARDS** designed to your specifications by AGARD ELECTRONICS. From prototype to quantity production. Rigid quality control. Sophisticated circuity and techniques.

- ☐ **PILOT HEADSETS by TELEX**, including lightweight receivers, microphones, and amplifiers.

- ☐ **COMMUNICATIONS EQUIPMENT** by MELCOR ELECTRONICS. AN/AIC and other types of electronic communications equipment.

- ☐ **LIGHTING EQUIPMENT:** SODERBERG aircraft and marine lights manufactured to AN and MS specifications.

- ☐ **ILLUMINATED PLASTIC CONTROL PANELS** by BODNAR for "heads-up-displays," aircraft instrumentation, and electronic equipment.

- ☐ **JET ENGINE PARTS HANDLING SYSTEMS** by MESCO, including special baskets, stands, fixtures.

- ☐ **HELICOPTER PARTS, COMPONENTS.** types; support for military overhaul and maintenance programs.

- ☐ **METAL STOCKS.** Tubes, sheets, rods, bars, special extrusions.

write for free brochure

Aviation Sales Corporation

115-06 MYRTLE AVENUE
RICHMOND HILL, NEW YORK 11418
Phone 212-441-3100
Cable NYALICE NEWYORK • Telex 620147
Div: **Helicopter Sales Inc.** Sub: **Hyfore Corp.**

BRANCH OFFICES:

England   Aviation & Helicopter Sales (UK) Ltd.
Portsmouth Road • Esher, Surrey
Tel: Esher 62071 or 62072

Italy   "C.T.C." Aviation Sales Italy
Via Eleonora Duse, 5/g • 00197 Rome
Tel: 877007 or 879009

Germany   Aviation & Helicopter Sales (UK) Germany GmbH
Geibelstrasse 8 • 8 Munchen 80
Tel: 0811-443848

ALPHABETICAL LIST OF ADVERTISERS.
1970/71 EDITION.

ALPHABETICAL LIST OF ADVERTISERS—continued.

V/O AVİAEXPORT

V/O AVİAEXPORT

The metal stocks including special extrusions, sheets, tubes, rods, etc., used for manufacturing aviation equipment or any part of aircraft like SST TU-144 are in the export list of V/O ''Aviaexport'', Moscow. Detailed data describing the above products are available from V/O ''Aviaexport'', 32/34, Smolenskaja-Sennaja Sq., Moscow G-200, USSR.

Cable: Aviaexport Moscow   Telephone: 244-26-86   Telex: 257

ALPHABETICAL LIST OF ADVERTISERS—*continued.*

MÜNCHEN

Since the summer of 1969 the firms of Maybach Mercedes-Benz Motorenbau GmbH Friedrichshafen and of M.A.N.-Turbo GmbH in Munich are a combined enterprise under the new names of "Motoren- und Turbinen-Union München GmbH". "Motoren- und Turbinen-Union Friedrichshafen GmbH".

The comprehensive experience of important manufacturers of diesel engines and gas turbines has now been concentrated in the firm of MTU.

MTU-Friedrichshafen develops, manufactures and provides motive power systems equipped with MTU diesel engines, MTU power transmissions and MTU gas turbines.

MTU-Munich develops, manufactures and serves aircraft engines.

Part of the present production programme of MTU-Munich are:

Starfighter Engine J 79-MTU-J1K
A General Electric aero-engine of 7200 kp thrust, further developed by MTU.

Turboprop Engine „Tyne Mk 22"
Installed in the transport aircraft „Transall C 160", built by MTU under licence from Rolls-Royce.

Turbo-Shaft Gas Turbine T 64
General Electric gas turbine built by MTU under licence for the transport helicopter Sikorski CH 53

Airbus Engine
MTU participates in the manufacture of the engines for the European Airbus A 300 B. A great number of the engines required will be assembled in Munich.

Lift-Thrust Engine RB 193
Joint development together with Rolls-Royce for VTOL-aircraft.

Gas Turbine MTU 6022
Own development for helicopter drive and industrial use with an output of 375 HP (metric).

Aero-Engine RB 199 for MRCA-Development
Together with Rolls-Royce and Fiat, MTU is employed in the development and production of this aero-engine of the next generation.

MTU is working already today on the technology of the future.

Motoren- und Turbinen-Union München GmbH
M.A.N. Maybach Mercedes-Benz
8 München 50/Germany, P.O.B. 500 640, Phone (08 11) 5 48 91

The Vought A-7: New world standard for tactical support aircraft.

The Vought A-7 is so versatile it fulfills the tactical support requirements of both the Navy and U. S. Air Force.

The A-7 has been in quantity production since 1965, in service since 1966 and is scheduled for service into the 1980's.

The A-7 is being considered for purchase by a number of other nations.

During two years of operational duty, the A-7 has proved superior in two important ways:

It ranks as one of the world's outstanding weapon systems offering many performance guarantees including its highly accurate navigation and weapon delivery capability.

It is the most cost-effective close-support and interdiction aircraft ever developed. No other aircraft economically neutralizes targets with so few sorties and such a high probability of survival.

The Vought A-7 is the new world standard for tactical support aircraft.

International Office: P. O. Box 5907, Dallas, Texas 75222.

VOUGHT AERONAUTICS

AN LTV AEROSPACE COMPANY

- Le numéro de référence accompagnant chaque rubrique ci-dessous indique la
rubrique anglaise équivalente en page 17 a 43

A 1	Accéléromètres	B 11)		
A 2	Accessoires	L 7)	Ceintures de sécurité	
M 6	Accessoires métalliques	S 1)		
H 15	Accouplements haute pression	D 11	Cibles télécommandées	
A 4	Accumulateurs au cadmium-nickel	V 6	Clapets anti-retour carburant	
A 5	Accumulateurs hydrauliques	V 7	Clapets anti-retour hydrauliques	
S 23	Acier et alliages d'acier	V 9	Clapets de suppression hydrauliques	
S 31	Aciers inoxydables et à preuve de la chaleur et de fluage	R 19	Chariots à extension	
R 8	Aides-radio à la navigation	M 5	Collection de données mésométéorologiques	
B 13	Ailettes de turbines à gaz	P 30	Combinaisons de protection	
A 6	Actionneurs électriques	F 13	Combinaisons de vol	
H 5	Alliages résistant à la chaleur	H 14	Combinaisons pressurisées et casques pour haute altitude	
A 50	Alternateurs	C 17	Commandes de poste de pilotage	
F 22	Aménagements de cabines d'avions	C 3	Commandes de pression cabine	
J 8	Amorceurs de combustible pour réacteurs	P 11	Commandes pneumatiques	
S 7	Amortisseurs oléo-pneumatiques	A 59	Commandes pour vol asymétrique	
A 68	Amplificateurs basse-fréquence	F 23	Commandes et vérins simulateurs de sensation	
A 8	Antennes d'avion	P 12	Commandes servo-motrices d'avions	
E 12	Anti-parasitage de moteurs	C 11	Composants	
S 29	Appareillage de commutation	I 6	Composants d'instruments (Mécaniques)	
R 7	Appareillage radio	P 8	Composants en plastique	
O 4	Appareils à oxygène	P 9	Composants en plastique (renforcés à la fibre de verre)	
A 35	Appareils de mise à l'arrêt d'avions	J 6	Composés de jointoiement	
G 11	Appareils d'entraînement au tir	E 20	Composés résistant à l'érosion	
O 5	Appareils de respiration à oxygène	A 14	Compresseurs d'air	
H 21	Appareils d'essais hydrauliques mobiles et fixes	A 15	Compresseurs d'air cabine	
B 14	Appareils de visée	A 16	Compresseurs d'air pour le démarrage des moteurs	
O 3	Appareils de visée optiques	C 18)	Compresseurs de réfrigération	
M 15	Approvisionnement de métaux	R 12)		
A 56	Armements d'avions	C 14	Connecteurs	
E 22	Assemblages expérimentaux	H 8	Contrôleurs de chauffage pare-brise	
		S 32	Crépines agricoles et chimiques	
G 8	Atelier et équipements de hangars au sol	A 42	Cylindres de moteurs à pistons d'avions	
U 1	Atterrisseurs	B 7	Chargeurs de batteries d'accumulateurs	
U 2	Atterrisseurs escamotables	S 21	Chariots de démarrage au sol	
		F 15	Chariots élévateurs à fourche	
E 3	Auxiliaires électriques de bord	T 17	Chariots élévateurs à fourche et à plate-forme	
V 11	Avions à décollage vertical	F 12	Débitmètres	
A 23	Avions-ambulances	E 9	Débitmètres électroniques	
A 30	Avions commandés par radio	E 13	Démarreur de moteurs	
A 24	Avions commerciaux	S 16	Dispositifs de contrôle de vitesse	
A 25	Avions d'affaires	T 15	Dispositifs d'entraînement au pilotage, à la navigation et au t	
A 28	Avions de l'aéronavale	F 16	Dosificateurs de débit de combustible	
A 32	Avions d'entraînement	F 24	Dispositif de ternissement ; aérosol	
A 33	Avions de transport	D 12	Dynamomètres électriques à courants de Foucault	
A 27	Avions militaires	D 13	Dynamomètres hydrauliques et électriques	
A 22	Avions pour le traitement agricole (saupoudrage et pulvérisation)	H 4	Echangeurs de chaleur	
A 29	Avions privés	L 12	Eclairage de cabine	
A 31	Avions supersoniques	L 14	Eclairage de pistes	
A 34	Avions V/STOL	L 3	Eclairage d'habitacle	
A 44	Balises, lancées d'avions	H 3	Ecouteurs	
H 1	Bancs d'essais de hangar	P 31	Editeurs	
P 26	Bancs d'essais d'hélices	E 10	Electronique et guidage	
		S 10	Electro-vannes	
B 4	Barres en acier inoxydable et résistant à la chaleur	P 13	Energie, panneaux de cellules et ensembles solaires	
P 14	Blocs d'alimentation hydrauliques	G 10	Engins guidés	
B 5	Batteries	M 11	Projectiles téléguidés	
B 6	Batteries, aviation	P 15	Engrenages de précision	
C 5	Câbles électriques	E 6	Ensembles de câbles électriques	
C 6	Câbles H. F.	E 2	Ensembles de libération d'éjecteurs	
T 7	Câbles, thermo-couple	A 46	Ensembles de réfrigération cyclique d'air	
C 12	Calculateurs	V 10	Ensembles de réfrigération moyennant cycle de vapeur	
C 13	Calculateurs aérodynamiques analogiques et numériques	C 16	Equipement de commande pour avions	
A 13	Caméras d'avions	A 19	Equipement de contrôle air cabine	
H 16	Caméras très rapides pour la recherche	E 18	Equipement de contrôle d'ambiance	
P 35	Camions en plateforme	P 20	Equipement de contrôle de pression	
C 7	Canevas	T 6	Equipement de contrôle de température	
D 10	Canons éjecteurs de parachutes	A 21	Equipement de contrôle du trafic aérien	
F 21	Carburants et combustibles	D 6	Equipement de dégivrage	
C 8	Carburateurs	E 13	Equipement de démarrage moteurs	

Die Verweisungszahl bei jedem nachfolgend aufgeführten Gegenstand gibt die entsprechende englische Überschrift auf den Seiten 17 bis 43

A difficult birth

Thirty years ago, the aircraft gas turbine was having a difficult birth.

Materials with properties far superior to anything previously available were needed to save the new infant. Pooling every drop of its knowledge and long experience of nickel alloy manufacture, Henry Wiggin & Company Limited created the first NIMONIC alloys ,and the jet age had dawned. An extra thirty years of exhaustive research and development by Wiggin has extended the range to keep pace with the demands of aircraft gas turbine designers. Now there is a NIMONIC alloy for all the high-temperature components of a gas turbine. And all these alloys are set aside from other products by the one thing that matters—the brand name "NIMONIC".

HENRY WIGGIN & COMPANY LIMITED

Hereford England   telephone 0432 6461   telex 35101

NIMONIC ALLOYS

TRADE MARK

HW8

A1. ACCELEROMETERS

Aeritalia
Aviaexport
Ferranti Limited
Garrett Corporation
Thomson C.S.F.

A2. ACCESSORIES

Avco Lycoming Div. of Avco Corp.
Aviaexport
Aviation Sales Corporation
Garrett Corporation
Hawker Siddeley Group
Mills Equipment Co. Ltd.
Van Dusen Ltd.

A3. AC MOTORS

Aviaexport
Ferranti Ltd.
Garrett Corporation

A4. ACCUMULATORS, CADMIUM-NICKEL

Aviation Sales Corp.
SAFT
Van Dusen Ltd.

A5. ACCUMULATORS, HYDRAULIC

Aviation Sales Corporation

A6. ACTUATORS, ELECTRIC

Aviation Sales Corporation
Garrett Corporation
Hawker Siddeley Group
Hobson Ltd., H. M.
Plessey Company Limited, The
Teleflex
Van Dusen Ltd.

A7. AERIAL SURVEY INSTRUMENTS

Aerospatiale (Div. Systemes
   Balistiques et Spatiaux)
Marconi Co., Ltd.
Vinten Ltd.

A8. AERIALS, AIRCRAFT

Aeritalia
Aviaexport
Aviation Sales Corporation
British Aircraft Corp.
Collins Radio Co.
Dornier AG
Fiat S.p.A.
Hawker Siddeley Group
Marconi Co. Ltd.
Omnipol
S.N.E.C.M.A.
Thomson C.S.F.
Van Dusen Ltd.

A9. AERO AUXILIARY EQUIPMENT

Avco Lycoming Div. of Avco Corp.
Aviaexport
Aviation Sales Corporation
Bendix International
Garrett Corporation
Hawker Siddeley Group
M.L. Aviation Company
Omnipol
Plessey Company Limited, The
Thomson C.S.F.

A10. AERO-ENGINE TEST PLANT

Aviaexport, V/O
Heenan and Froude
S.N.E.C.M.A.

A11. AERONAUTICAL ENGINEERS AND CONSULTANTS

Aviaexport, V/O
Aviation Sales Corporation
BAC
Hawker Siddeley Group
McDonnell Douglas Corp.
M.L. Aviation Co. Ltd.

A12. AIR CAMERAS

Aviation Sales Corporation
McDonnell Douglas Corporation
Vinten Ltd.

A13. AIR COMPRESSORS

Avco Lycoming Div. of Avco Corp.
Aviaexport
Garrett Corporation
Hawker Siddeley Group
Rolls-Royce Limited

A14. AIR COMPRESSORS, CABIN

Garrett Corporation

A15. AIR COMPRESSORS FOR ENGINE STARTING

Avco Lycoming Div. of Avco Corp.
Garrett Corporation
Hawker Siddeley Group
Rolls-Royce Limited

A16. AIR CONDITIONING EQUIPMENT

Garrett Corporation
Hawker Siddeley Dynamics
M.L. Aviation Co. Ltd.
Plessey Company Limited, The
Rolls-Royce Limited

A17. AIR CONDITIONING SYSTEMS

Garrett Corporation
Hawker Siddeley Dynamics
M.L. Aviation Co. Ltd.
S.N.E.C.M.A.

A18. AIR CONTROL EQUIPMENT FOR CABINS

Garrett Corporation
Hawker Siddeley Dynamics

A19. AIR DATA COMPUTER SYSTEMS

Ferranti Ltd.
Garrett Corporation
Hollandse Signaalapparaten N.V.
Marconi Co. Ltd., The

A20. AIR TRAFFIC CONTROL EQUIPMENT

Airmed Limited
Aviaexport, V/O
Ferranti Limited
Hollandse Signaalapparaten N.V.
Marconi Co. Ltd., The
McDonnell Douglas Corporation
S.N.E.C.M.A.
Thomson C.S.F.

A21. AIRCRAFT—AGRICULTURAL (Dusters and Sprayers)

Aeritalia
Aviaexport, V/O
Bell Helicopter
Dornier-Werke G.m.b.H.
Hawker Siddeley Group
Omnipol
Piper Aircraft Corporation
Thomson C.S.F.

A22. AIRCRAFT—AMBULANCE

Aeritalia
Aviaexport, V/O
Bell Helicopter
Dornier AG
McDonnell Douglas Corp.
Omnipol
Piper Aircraft Corporation

A23. AIRCRAFT—COMMERCIAL

Aeritalia
Aerospatiale (S.N.I.A.S.)
Aviaexport, V/O
Bell Helicopter
Boeing Co., The
British Aircraft Corporation
Dornier AG
Fiat S.p.A.
Fokker
Hawker Siddeley Group
McDonnell Douglas Corp.
Omnipol
Piper Aircraft Corporation

GEC-Marconi Electronics

Europe's largest and most comprehensive capital electronics company

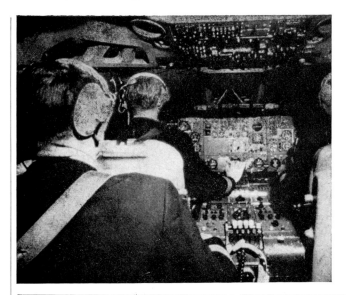

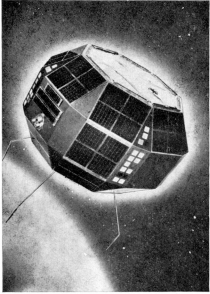

Marconi Radar Systems Limited
Designers and suppliers of complete
ground radar systems for all air
defence, air traffic control and shipborne
defence applications. Product range
includes every type of ground radar
equipment and is the most comprehensive
in the world. Fighting vehicle systems.

The Marconi Company Limited
The principal operating company of
GEC-Marconi Electronics Limited.

**Marconi Communication Systems
Limited**
Designers and suppliers of complete
h.f. point-to-point, microwave and
tropospheric scatter communication
systems ; fixed, mobile and portable
radio telephones ; complete space
communication earth stations ; message
switching systems and digital and data
transmission systems ; mobile
communication systems ; complete sound
and vision broadcasting systems ;
specialised components.

**Marconi-Elliott Avionic Systems
Limited**
Airborne navigation, radar and
communication systems. Electro-optical
systems. Special purpose radars.
Intruder detection systems. Neutron
and X-ray devices. Aircraft tracking
systems. Flight control, engine control,
fuel management and flight
instrumentation systems. Automatic test
equipment.

**Marconi Space and Defence
Systems Limited**
Research, development and production
of advanced electronic equipments.
Satellite communication. Spacecraft,
satellite electronics and launch
vehicle systems. Simulators and
trainers. Military communications. Data
processing for Field Army, Naval and
other shipborne applications. Weapon
guidance and fire control systems.
Fighting vehicle, navigation and
oceanography equipment. Microwave and
electronic counter measure (ECM)
systems. Underwater weapons.

**E-A Space and Advanced
Military Systems Limited (EASAMS)**
Advanced project and system studies and
management for defence, space and
industry.

Marconi Instruments Limited
Designers and manufacturers of a wide
range of electronic measuring
instrumentation from d.c to microwave
frequencies. Signal generators,
response analysers, counters,
voltmeters, power meters, bridges and
oscilloscopes. Programmable automatic
test systems. TV image intensifiers.

GEC-Marconi Electronics Limited
Marconi House, Chelmsford, Essex
England

GMO1 (A)

A24. AIRCRAFT—EXECUTIVE

Aerospatiale (S.N.I.A.S.)
Aviaexport, V/O
Bell Helicopter
British Aircraft Corp.
Dornier AG
Fokker
Hawker Siddeley Group
McDonnell Douglas Corp.
Piper Aircraft Corporation

A25. AIRCRAFT INTEGRATED DATA SYSTEMS

Aviaexport
Garrett Corporation

A26. AIRCRAFT—MILITARY

Aeritalia
Aerospatiale (S.N.I.A.S.)
Bell Helicopter
Boeing Co., The
British Aircraft Corporation
Dornier AG
Fiat S.p.A.
Fokker
Hawker Siddeley Group
McDonnell Douglas Corporation
Saab Aircraft Co.
Westland Helicopters Ltd.

A27. AIRCRAFT—NAVAL

Aeritalia
BAC
Hawker Siddeley Group
McDonnell Douglas Corporation
Westland Helicopters Ltd.

A28. AIRCRAFT—PRIVATE

Aviaexport, V/O
Bell Helocipter
Dornier AG
Hawker Siddeley Group
Omnipol
Piper Aircraft Corporation

A29. AIRCRAFT—RADIO CONTROLLED

BAC

A30. AIRCRAFT—SUPERSONIC

Aeritalia
Aerospatiale (S.N.I.A.S.)
Aviaexport, V/O
Boeing Co., The
British Aircraft Corporation
Fiat S.p.A.
Hawker Siddeley Group
McDonnell Douglas Corporation
Saab Aircraft Co.

A31. AIRCRAFT—TRAINING

Aeritalia
Aviaexport, V/O
Bell Helicopter
British Aircraft Corporation
Dornier AG
Fiat S.p.A.
Hawker Siddeley Group
McDonnell Douglas Corporation
Omnipol
Piper Aircraft Corporation
Saab Aircraft Co.

A32. AIRCRAFT—TRANSPORT

Aeritalia
Aerospatiale (S.N.I.A.S.)
Aviaexport, V/O
Boeing Co., The
British Aircraft Corporation
Dornier AG
Fiat S.p.A.
Fokker
Hawker Siddeley Group
McDonnell Douglas Corporation
Omnipol
Saab Aircraft Co.
Westland Helicopters Ltd.

A33. AIRCRAFT—V/STOL

Aeritalia
Aviaexport, V/O
BAC
Dornier AG
Fiat S.p.A.
Hawker Siddeley Group
McDonnell Douglas Corporation
Westland Helicopters Ltd.

A34. AIRCRAFT ARRESTING GEAR

Anglo American Aviation Company
S.N.E.C.M.A.

A35. AIRCRAFT CANOPIES

Aeritalia
Aviation Sales Corporation
Van Dusen Ltd.

A36. AIRCRAFT ESCAPE SYSTEMS

Aeritalia
Garrett Corporation
G.Q. Parachute Co. Ltd.
M.L. Aviation Co. Ltd.
McDonnell Douglas Corporation

A37. AIRCRAFT FLOATS

Anglo American Aviation Co.
Aviaexport, V/O
Aviation Sales Corporation
Dornier-Werke G.m.b.H.
Edo Commercial Corporation
Garrett Corporation
Van Dusen Ltd.

A38. AIRCRAFT FREIGHT HANDLING EQUIPMENT

Aviaexport, V/O
J. Collins & Sons Ltd.
Dornier-Werke G.m.b.H.
G.Q. Parachute Co. Ltd.
Hawker Siddeley Group
Mills Equipment Co. Ltd.
M.L. Aviation Co. Ltd.

A39. AIRCRAFT MECHANICAL HANDLERS

Dornier-Werke G.m.b.H.
M.L. Aviation Co. Ltd.

A40. AIRCRAFT MODIFICATIONS

Aeritalia
Aviaexport, V/O
BAC
Bell Helicopters
Boeing Co., The
Fokker
Garrett Corporation
Hawker Siddeley Group
McDonnell Douglas Corporation

A41. AIRCRAFT PISTON ENGINE CYLINDERS

Avco Lycoming Div. of Avco Corp.
Aviaexport, V/O
Aviation Sales Corporation
Fiat S.p.A.
Van Dusen

A42. AIRCRAFT PROPELLERS

Aviaexport, V/O
Aviation Sales Corporation
Fiat S.p.A.
Hawker Siddeley Dynamics
Omnipol

A43. AIR DROPPABLE BEACONS

Garrett Corporation

A44. AIRCRAFT SEATS

Aviaexport
M.L. Aviation Co. Ltd.

A45. AIRCRAFT STRETCHERS

G.Q. Parachute Co. Ltd.

A46. AIR CYCLE REFRIGERATION PACKAGES

Garrett Corporation
S.N.E.C.M.A.

A47. AIRFIELD LIGHTING

Aviation Sales Corporation
Standard Wire & Cable Co.

pacing the twenty-mile minute

Supersonic transport aircraft are already flying. Soon they'll be in airline service. With high speed, and high operating costs, they need to be fully flight controlled if they are to operate safely and efficiently.

Today this means fully automated Air Traffic Control Centres—designed for full information correlation and data presentation. Plessey Radar is setting the pace on these systems.

At Bretigny, in France, Plessey Radar Limited, acting in a consortium with Thomson-CSF and AEG-Telefunken, delivered under contract to Eurocontrol a system for accurately simulating supersonic ATC requirements, and generally evaluating procedures and facilities necessary for the control of the Upper Air Space, for the 1970's and beyond. Plessey supplied radar displays, 'pilot' consoles, display drive equipment and buffer stores for this forward thinking project.

Plessey Radar is supplying AR5 long range, L band surveillance radars and an automatic SSR decoding system together with the unique Plessey DIGITRACE Bright Display System for the UK National Air Traffic Control System centred at West Drayton.

Two years ago, Plessey Radar, in conjunction with their consortium partners, was awarded a further contract by Eurocontrol to equip Europe's first fully automated ATC Centre at Maastricht, Holland, which is planned to control European upper airspace by the early 1970's.

Plessey Radar Limited, Addlestone, Weybridge, Surrey, England
Tel: Weybridge 47282.
Telex 262329
Cables: Plessrad Weybridge

PLESSEY RADAR

PE(R)336

A48. AIRPORT MAINTENANCE EQUIPMENT

Aviaexport, V/O

A49. AIRSPEED INDICATORS

Aeritalia
Aviaexport
Aviation Sales Corporation
Dornier Werke G.m.b.H.

A50. ALTERNATORS

Aviation Sales Corporation
Garrett Corporation
Hawker Siddeley Group
Plessey Company Limited, The

A51. ALTITUDE CONTROL SYSTEMS

Aeritalia
Garrett Corporation

A52. AMERICAN SPARES

Aviation Sales Corporation
Garrett Corporation
Van Dusen Ltd.

A53. AMMUNITION BOOSTERS

Garrett Corporation

A54. ANTI-SKID SYSTEMS

Goodyear
S.N.E.C.M.A.

A55. ANTI-SPIN PARACHUTES

G.Q. Parachute Co. Ltd.

A56. ARMAMENTS FOR AIRCRAFT

B.P.D. Division—Snia Viscosa
Hawker Siddeley Dynamics
M.L. Aviation Co. Ltd.

A57. ASSEMBLY AND DRILLING JIGS

A58. ASTRO-INERTIAL NAVIGATION SYSTEMS

Aeritalia
Aerospatiale (Div. Systemes Balistiques et Spatiaux)
Bendix International
Ferranti Ltd.
Thomson C.S.F.

A59. ASYMMETRY CONTROLS

Garrett Corporation

A60. AUTO-SELECTORS

M.L. Aviation Co. Ltd.

A61. AUTOMATIC CHECKOUT SYSTEMS

Aerospatiale (S.N.I.A.S.)
Aviaexport
British Aircraft Corporation
Collins Radio Co.
Ferranti Ltd.
Garrett Corporation
Hawker Siddeley Dynamics

A62. AUTOMATIC PARACHUTE OPENERS

Aviaexport
G.Q. Parachute Co. Ltd.

A63. AUTOMATIC PILOTS

Aeritalia
Aerospatiale (Div. Systemes Balistiques et Spatiaux)
Aviaexport
Collins Radio Co.
Hawker Siddeley Group
Piper Aircraft Corporation
Van Dusen Ltd.

A64. AUTOMATIC VOLTAGE AND CURRENT REGULATORS

Aviaexport
Aviation Sales Corporation
Ferranti Ltd.
Hawker Siddeley Group
Van Dusen Ltd.

A65. AUXILIARY POWER PLANT

Aerospatiale (Div. Systemes Balistiques et Spatiaux)
Avco Lycoming Div. of Avco Corp.
Aviaexport
Aviation Sales Corporation
Garrett Corporation
Hawker Siddeley Group
Rolls Royce Limited

A66. AVIATION LUBRICATING OIL AND SPECIAL PRODUCTS

Van Dusen Ltd.

A67. AGRICULTURAL AIRCRAFT SPRAY AND DUST SYSTEMS AND COMPONENTS

Aviaexport
Dornier Werke G.m.b.H.

A68. AUDIO AMPLIFIERS

Airmed Limited
Collins Radio Co.
Hawker Siddeley Group
Van Dusen Ltd.

B1. BALL SCREWS

Aviation Sales Corporation
Garrett Corporation
Van Dusen Ltd.

B2. BALL SPLINES

B3. BALL TABLES

J. Collins & Sons Ltd.

B4. BARS—STAINLESS AND HEAT-RESISTING STEEL

Aviaexport
Aviation Sales Corporation

B5. BARS—NICKEL ALLOY

Henry Wiggin & Co. Ltd.

B6. BATTERIES

Aerospatiale (Div. Systemes Balistiques et Spatiaux)
Aviation Sales Corporation
S.A.F.T.
Van Dusen Ltd.

B7. BATTERY CHARGERS

Aviation Sales Corporation
Ferranti Ltd.

B8. BATTERY TESTING EQUIPMENT

M.L. Aviation Co. Ltd.

B9. BEARINGS, BALL AND ROLLER

Aviation Sales Corporation
Van Dusen Ltd.

B10. BEARINGS, BRONZE

Aviation Sales Corporation

B11. BEARINGS, SPHERICAL AND ROD ENDS

Baker Perkins Holdings Ltd.,—
Rose Bearings

B12. BELTS, SAFETY

Aviaexport
Aviation Sales Corporation
G.Q. Parachute Co. Ltd.
Mills Equipment Company Ltd.
Teleflex
Van Dusen Ltd.

World's fastest light turbine helicopter. It's a scout ship, a gun ship, an ASW ship.

The 26-foot, four-blade rotor gives much better handling qualities than the usual 35-foot, two-blade system. Permits landing in small clearings...with room to spare.

Room for 42 cubic feet of cargo, plus pilot and two passengers. High payload-to-empty-weight ratio. Aft compartment's level floor lets you skid-in heavy cargo.

Other helicopters also have the Allison 250-C18A engine. But not the 500M's record-breaking top speed (over 150 mph) Nor its life-saving getaway speed (0 to 60 mph in 6 seconds). Nor its trouble-free performance.

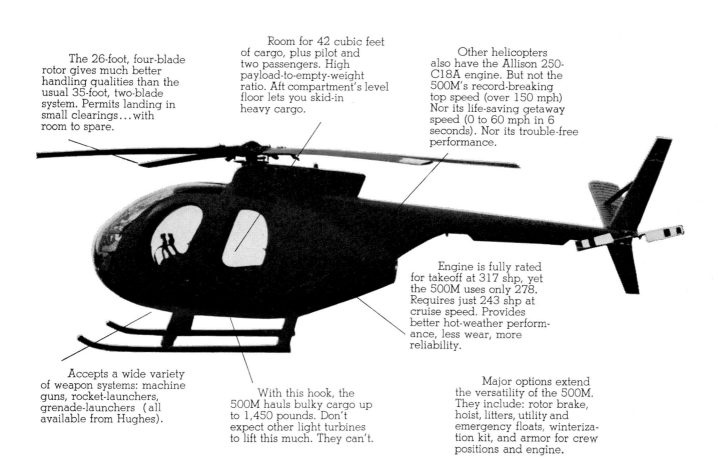

Engine is fully rated for takeoff at 317 shp, yet the 500M uses only 278. Requires just 243 shp at cruise speed. Provides better hot-weather performance, less wear, more reliability.

Accepts a wide variety of weapon systems: machine guns, rocket-launchers, grenade-launchers (all available from Hughes).

With this hook, the 500M hauls bulky cargo up to 1,450 pounds. Don't expect other light turbines to lift this much. They can't.

Major options extend the versatility of the 500M. They include: rotor brake, hoist, litters, utility and emergency floats, winterization kit, and armor for crew positions and engine.

The Hughes 500M is an advanced version of the U. S. Army's OH-6A. It has logged over 750,000 combat hours as scout ship and gun ship. A special model for anti-submarine warfare is available.

For literature on military and civilian models of the Hughes 500, please write: Hughes Helicopters, Box 60688-W Los Angeles, California 90060, U.S.A.

Hughes Helicopters

DISTRIBUTORS: *Belgium:* Sotramat S.A., Brussels; *Germany:* Rietdorf KG, Saffig; *United Kingdom:* Trans World Helicopters Ltd., London; *Italy:* Nardi S.A., Milan; *Sweden:* SAAB Aktiebolag, Norrköping; *Switzerland:* Deltra S.A., Geneva; *Austria:* Manfred J. Harrer, Vienna; *Portugal:* Aviber S.A.R.L., Lisbon; *Spain:* Georges De Sonchen, Madrid (commercial); Compania Aeronautica Espanola S.A., Madrid (government); *Republic of the Congo:* Air Brousse S.P.R.L., Brussels; *Republic of South Africa:* Commercial Air Services (Pty.) Ltd., Johannesburg; *Kuwait:* Specialties Company W.L.L., Kuwait; *Lebanon:* Bardawil & Co., Beirut; *Australia:* Commonwealth Aircraft Corp. Pty., Melbourne; *Republic of China:* China Trade & Development Corp., Taipei; *India:* Cambata Aviation Private Ltd., Bombay; *Japan:* Toyo Menka Kaisha, Ltd., Tokyo; Kawasaki Heavy Industries, Aircraft Div., Tokyo; *New Zealand:* Dalhoff & King, Ltd., Wellington; *Philippines:* Lase International, Inc., Manila; *Singapore:* Maclaine, Watson & Co., Singapore; *Thailand:* L. A. Lewis, Inc., Bangkok; *Argentina:* Cygnus S.A.O.I., Buenos Aires; *Brazil:* S.A. De Commercio Tecnico Aeronautico, Rio de Janeiro; *Chile:* Aeroservicio Limitada, Santiago; *Colombia:* Aero-Merchantil Limitada, Bogota; *Ecuador:* General Victor Suarez, Quito; *Jamaica:* Trans World Helicopters Ltd., Kingston; *Mexico:* Compania Mexicana Aerofoto S.A., Mexico, D.F.; *Nicaragua:* Roger Blandon V., Leon; *Panama:* Agencia Peters, Panama; *Puerto Rico:* Dupre Air Activities, Inc., Mayaguez; *Uruguay:* Aviansa, Montevideo; *Bolivia:* Oil Industry Supply & Service Co., S.A., La Paz; *Peru:* Aeronautica S.A., Lima; *Venezuela:* Aviacion General S.A., Caracas; *Canada:* Helisolair, Ltd., Quebec.

What makes Hawker Siddeley the largest aerospace group in Europe?

B13. BINOCULARS

Barr & Stroud Ltd.

B14. BLADES, GAS TURBINE

Aviaexport, V/O
Fiat S.p.A.
S.N.E.C.M.A.
Thomson C.S.F.

B15. BOMBSIGHTS

Ferranti Limited
Saab Aircraft Co.

B16. BOOKS—AVIATION AND SPACE

B.P.C. Publishing Ltd.
Flight International
Iliffe Books Ltd.
MacDonald & Co. (Publishers) Ltd.
McGraw-Hill Book Company
Pitman, Sir Issaac and Sons Ltd.
Sampson Low, Marston & Co. Ltd.

B17. BRAKE LININGS

Goodyear
S.N.E.C.M.A.
Van Dusen Ltd.

B18. BRAKES FOR AIRCRAFT

Aviaexport
Aviation Sales Corporation
Goodyear
S.N.E.C.M.A.

C1. CABIN COOLING (TROPICAL AIRFIELD EQUIPMENT)

Garrett Corporation
Hawker Siddeley Group
M.L. Aviation Co. Ltd.

C2. CABIN PRESSURE CONTROL SYSTEMS

Aviaexport
Garrett Corporation
Hawker Siddeley Group

C3. CABIN PRESSURE CONTROLS

Aviaexport
Garrett Corporation
Hawker Siddeley Group

C4. CABIN PRESSURISING TEST EQUIPMENT

Garrett Corporation
Hawker Siddeley Group
M.L. Aviation Co. Ltd.

C5. CABLES, ELECTRIC

Fokker
Hawker Siddeley Group
M.L. Aviation Co. Ltd.
Standard Wire & Cable Company
Van Dusen Ltd.

C6. CABLES, R.F.

Hawker Siddeley Group
Standard Wire & Cable Company

C7. CANVAS

Mills Equipment Co. Ltd.
Van Dusen Ltd.

C8. CARBURETTORS

Van Dusen Ltd.

C9. CENTRAL AIR DATA COMPUTERS

Ferranti Ltd.
Garrett Corporation

C10. COATINGS, EROSION RESISTANT

Goodyear

C11. COMPONENTS

Avco Lycoming Div. of Avco Corp.
Aviaexport, V/O
Aviation Sales Corporation
Dornier Werke G.m.b.H.
Ferranti Limited
Fokker
G.E.C. Marconi Electronics Ltd.
M.L. Aviation Co. Ltd.
Standard Wire & Cable Company
Thomson C.S.F.
Van Dusen Ltd.

C12. COMPUTERS

Aerospatiale (Div. Systemes
    Balistiques et Spatiaux)
Collins Radio Co.
Dornier Werke G.m.b.H.
Ferranti Limited
Garrett Corporation
G.E.C. Marconi Electronics Ltd.
Hawker Siddeley Dymanics
Hollandse Signaalapparaten N.V.
Saab Aircraft Co.
S.N.E.C.M.A.
Thomson C.S.F.
Van Dusen Ltd.

C13. COMPUTERS, AERODYNAMIC ANALOGUE AND DIGITAL

Aerospatiale (Div. Systemes
    Balistiques et Spatiaux)
Dornier AG
Ferranti Limited
Garrett Corporation
Hawker Siddeley Dynamics
G.E.C. Marconi Electronics Ltd.
Saab Aircraft Co.
Thomson C.S.F.

C14. CONNECTORS

Aviaexport
Aviation Sales Corporation
Ferranti Ltd.
Garrett Corporation
Thomson C.S.F.
Van Dusen Ltd.

C15. CONSTANT SPEED ALTERNATOR DRIVE UNITS

Avco Lycoming Div. of Avco Corp.
Garrett Corporation
Plessey Company Limited. The

C16. CONTROL EQUIPMENT FOR AIRCRAFT

Aviaexport
Aviation Sales Corporation
Collins Radio Co.
Dornier Systems GmbH
Ferranti Ltd.
Garrett Corporation
Hawker Siddeley Dynamics
Plessey Company Limited, The
Saab Aircraft Co.
S.N.E.C.M.A.
Standard Wire & Cable Company
Teleflex

C17. CONTROLS, COCKPIT

Saab Aircraft Co.
Teleflex
Van Dusen Ltd.

C18. COOLING COMPRESSORS

Garrett Corporation

C19. COOLING TURBINES

Garrett Corporation
S.N.E.C.M.A.

C20. CARGO HANDLING

J. Collins & Sons Ltd.
M.L. Aviation Co. Ltd.

C21. CRYOGENIC TURBINES

Aerospatiale (Div. Systemse
    Balistiques et Spatiaux)
Garrett Corporation
S.N.E.C.M.A.

D1. DATA PROCESSING EQUIPMENT

Aerospatiale (S.N.I.A.S.)
Dornier Werke G.m.b.H.
Ferranti Limited
Garrett Corporation
G.E.C. Marconi Electronics Ltd.
Hollandse Signaalapparaten N.V.
Hawker Siddeley Group
Saab Aircraft Co.
Thomson C.S.F.

D2. DATA PROCESSING EQUIPMENT FOR ATC

Ferranti Ltd.
G.E.C. Marconi Electronics Ltd.
Hollandse Signaalapparaten N.V.
Thomson C.S.F.

D3. DATA RECORDER JETTISON AND RECOVERY SYSTEMS

M.L. Aviation Co. Ltd.

D4. DATA TRANSMISSION EQUIPMENT

Aerospatiale (S.N.I.A.S.)
Bendix International
Collins Radio Co.
Dornier Werke G.m.b.H.
Ferranti Limited
Garrett Corporation
G.E.C. Marconi Electronics Ltd.
Hawker Siddeley Dynamics
S.N.E.C.M.A.
Standard Wire & Cable Company
Thomson C.S.F.

D5. DC MOTORS

Aviaexport
Garrett Corporation

D6. DE-ICING EQUIPMENT

Garrett Corporation
Goodyear
Plessey Company Limited, The

D7. DIRECTION FINDING EQUIPMENT (TRIANGULATION)

Aviaexport
G.E.C. Marconi Electronics Ltd.

D8. DRILLING MACHINES

D9. DRILLS, PORTABLE, PNEUMATIC AND ELECTRIC

D10. DROGUE GUNS

M.L. Aviation Co. Ltd.

D11. DRONES

Aerospatiale (S.N.I.A.S.)
Dornier Systems GmbH

D12. DYNAMOMETERS, ELECTRICAL EDDY-CURRENT

Avco Lycoming Div. of Avco Corp.
Heenan & Froude

D13. DYNAMOMETERS, HYDRAULIC AND ELECTRIC

Avco Lycoming Div. of Avco Corp.
Heenan & Froude

E1. EJECTION SEATS

Aeritalia
Martin-Baker Aircraft Co. Ltd.
Saab Aircraft Co.
S.N.E.C.M.A.

E2. EJECTOR RELEASE UNITS

M.L. Aviation Co. Ltd.

E3. ELECTRIC AUXILIARIES

Aerospatiale (S.N.I.A.S.)
Aviaexport
Aviation Sales Corporation
Garrett Corporation
Hawker Siddeley Group
M.L. Aviation Co. Ltd.
Plessey Company Limited, The
Van Dusen Ltd.

E4. ELECTRICAL EQUIPMENT

Aviaexport
Aviation Sales Corporation
Ferranti Limited
Garrett Corporation
Hawker Siddeley Group
M.L. Aviation Co. Ltd.
Plessey Company Limited, The
Standard Wire & Cable Company

E5. ELECTRICAL PLUGS AND SOCKETS (WATERPROOF)

Ferranti Ltd.
M.L. Aviation Co. Ltd.
Plessey Company Limited, The
Saab Aircraft Co.
Van Dusen Ltd.

E6. ELECTRICAL WIRING ASSEMBLIES

E7. ELECTRO-OPTICAL SYSTEMS

Aeritalia
Aerospatiale (S.N.I.A.S.)
Aviation Sales Corporation
Barr & Stroud Ltd.
Ferranti Ltd.
G.E.C. Marconi Electronics Ltd.
McDonnell Douglas Corp.

E8. ELECTRONIC EQUIPMENT

Aeritalia
Aerospatiale (S.N.I.A.S.)
Airmed Limited
Aviaexport, V/O
Aviation Sales Corporation
Avco Lycoming Div. of Avco Corp.
Barr & Stroud Ltd.
British Aircraft Corporation
Collins Radio Co.
Ferranti Limited
Fiat S.p.A.
Fokker
Garrett Corporation
G.E.C. Marconi Electronics Ltd.
Hawker Siddeley Group
Integral Ltd.
McDonnell Douglas Corporation
M.L. Aviation Co. Ltd.
Saab Aircraft Co.
S.N.E.C.M.A.
Standard Wire & Cable Company
Thomson C.S.F.

E9. ELECTRONIC FLOWMETERS

Kent Meters Ltd.
Integral Ltd.

E10. ELECTRONICS AND GUIDANCE

Aerospatiale (S.N.I.A.S.)
Barr & Stroud Ltd.
Bendix International
British Aircraft Corporation
Collins Radio Co.
Ferranti Limited
Fiat S.p.A.
Hawker Siddeley Group
Marconi Co. Ltd. The
Saab Aircraft Co.
S.N.E.C.M.A.
Standard Wire & Cable Company
Thomson C.S.F.

E11. ENGINE PARTS FABRICATION

Avco Lycoming Div. of Avco Corp.
Aviaexport, V/O
Aviation Sales Corporation
Fiat S.p.A.
S.N.E.C.M.A.

E12 ENGINE PARTS—HANDLING EQUIPMENT

Aviation Sales Corporation

E13. ENGINE STARTING EQUIPMENT

Aviaexport
Avco Lycoming Div. of Avco Corp.
Garrett Corporation
Plessey Company Limited, The
Rolls-Royce Ltd.

E14. ENGINE TESTING EQUIPMENT

Aviaexport
Bendix International
Heenan & Froude
S.N.E.C.M.A.

E15. ENGINES—AIRCRAFT

Avco Lycoming Div. of Avco Corp.
Aviaexport, V/O
Fiat S.p.A.
Garrett Corporation
Omnipol
Rolls-Royce Limited
S.N.E.C.M.A.
Van Dusen Ltd.

E16. ENGINES, AUXILIARY

Avco Lycoming Div. of Avco Corp.
Aviaexport, V/O
Coventry Climax
Garrett Corporation
Rolls-Royce Limited

E17. ENGINES—V/STOL

Avco Lycoming Div. of Avco Corp.
Aviaexport, V/O
Rolls-Royce Limited

E18. ENVIRONMENTAL CONTROL SYSTEMS

Aerospatiale (S.N.I.A.S.)
Garrett Corporation

E19. EROSION RESISTANT COMPOUNDS

Goodyear
Thomson C.S.F.

E20. ESCAPE PODS

McDonnell Douglas Corporation

E21. EXPERIMENTAL ASSEMBLIES

Aviation Sales Corporation
Bell Helicopter
M.L. Aviation Co. Ltd.
Plessey Company Limited, The

E22. EXTRUSIONS, STEEL

Aviation Sales Corporation
Van Dusen Ltd.

E23. ELECTRIC TRACTORS

Coventry Climax Engines Ltd.

F1. FIBRE OPTICS

Barr & Stroud Ltd.
Ferranti Limited

F2. FILTERS, AIR

Aviaexport
Van Dusen Ltd.

F3. FILTERS, ELECTRONIC

Aviaexport
Barr & Stroud Ltd.
Ferranti Ltd.

F4. FILTERS, FUEL AND OIL

Aviaexport
Aviation Sales Corporation

F5. FINISHED MACHINED PARTS IN PHOSPHOR BRONZE AND GUN METAL

Aviation Sales Corporation
Barr & Stroud Ltd.

F6. FIRE PUMPS

Coventry Climax Engines Ltd.

F7. FLIGHT INSTRUMENT TEST SETS

Aviaexport
Garrett Corporation

F8. FLOODLIGHTS

Aviation Sales Corporation
Spectrolab

F9. FLOATATION GEAR

Aviation Sales Corporation
Garrett Corporation

F10. FLOW GAUGES

Aviaexport
Hawker Siddeley Group

F11. FLOWMETERS

Integral Ltd.
Kent Meters Ltd.

F12. FLYING CLOTHING

G.Q. Parachute Co. Ltd.
M.L. Aviation Co. Ltd.

F13. FORGINGS, STEEL

Aviaexport, V/O
Aviation Sales Corporation

F14. FORK LIFT TRUCKS

Coventry Climax Engines Ltd.

F15. FUEL FLOW PROPORTIONERS

Aeritalia
Aviaexport
Flight Refuelling

F16. FUEL PUMPS

Aviaexport
Aviation Sales Corporation
Coventry Climax Engines Ltd.
Flight Refuelling
Garrett Corporation
Plessey Company Limited, The
Van Dusen Ltd.

F17. FUEL SYSTEMS AND REFUELLING EQUIPMENT

Aviaexport
Aviation Sales Corporation
Flight Refuelling
Hawker Siddeley Group
Plessey Company Limited, The

F18. FUEL TANK PRESSURIZATION EQUIPMENT

Eurofoam
Flight Refuelling
Garrett Corporation

F19. FURNISHINGS FOR AIRCRAFT CABINS

Aviaexport
Bell Helicopters
Garrett Corporation
Van Dusen Ltd.

F20. FEEL SIMULATOR CONTROLS & JACKS

Garrett Corporation

G1. GAS TURBINE STARTER SYSTEMS

Garrett Corporation
Plessey Company Limited, The
Rolls-Royce Limited

G2. GAS TURBINES

Avci Lycoming Div. of Avco Corp.
Aviaexport, V/O
Continental Motors Corp.
Fiat S.p.A.
Garrett Corporation
Plessey Company Limited, The
Rolls-Royce Limited
S.N.E.C.M.A.

G3. GAS TURBINES, EQUIPMENT AND ACCESSORIES FOR

Aviaexport, V/O
Aviation Sales Corporation
Garrett Corporation
Hawker Siddeley Group
S.N.E.C.M.A.
Woodward Governor Co.

G4. GENERATORS

Aerospatiale (S.N.I.A.S.)
Aviaexport
Garrett Corporation

G5. GAUGES

Aerospatiale (S.N.I.A.S.)
Aviaexort
Aviation Sales Corporation
Van Dusen Ltd.

G6. GRINDINGS MACHINES

Fokker

G7. GROUND REFUELLING EQUIPMENT

Aviaexport
Aviation Sales Corporation
Hawker Siddeley Group

G8. GROUND WORKSHOP AND HANGAR EQUIPMENT

Aviation Sales Corporation
Garrett Corporation
M.L. Aviation Co. Ltd.

G9. GUIDED MISSILE GROUND HANDLING EQUIPMENT

Aerospatiale (S.N.I.A.S.)
Garrett Corporation
Hawker Siddeley Dynamics
Hollandse Signaalapparaten N.V.
McDonnell Douglas Corp.
M.L. Aviation Co. Ltd.

the world's most advanced escape system

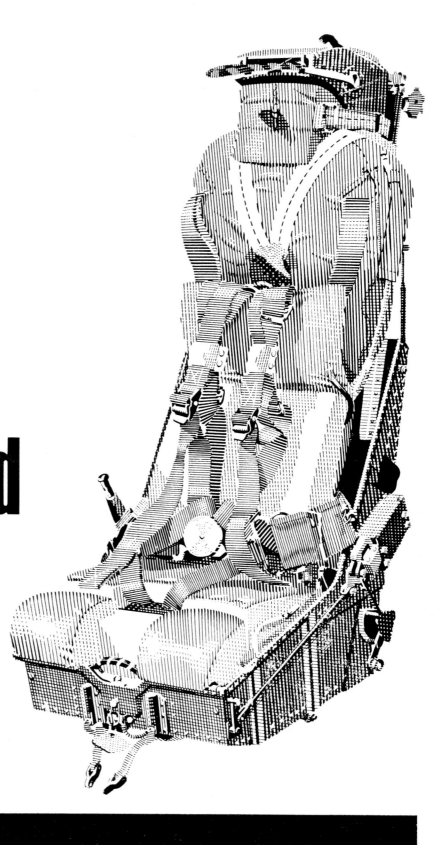

G10. GUIDED MISSILES

Aerospatiale (S.N.I.A.S.)
B.P.D. Division—Snia Viscosa
British Aircraft Corporation
Dornier G.m.b.H.
Fiat S.p.A.
Hawker Siddeley Dynamics
McDonnel Douglas Corporation
Saab Aircraft Co.

G11. GUNNERY TRAINING APPARATUS

Saab Aircraft Co.

H1. HANGAR TEST STANDS

Garrett Corporation
Heenan & Froude

H2. HARNESS, SAFETY

G.Q. Parachute Co. Ltd.
Mills Equipment Co. Ltd.
Teleflex

H3. HEADPHONES

Airmed Limited
Aviaexport
Aviation Sales Corporation
Hawker Siddeley Group
Thomson C.S.F.

H4. HEAT EXCHANGERS

Garrett Corporation
Hawker Siddeley Group

H5. HEAT-RESISTING ALLOYS

Aviation Sales Corporation
Henry Wiggin & Co. Ltd.

H6. HEAT TRANSFER SYSTEMS

Garrett Corporation

H7. HEATED WINDOWS

Barr & Stroud Ltd.

H8. HEATED WINDSCREEN CONTROLLERS

Garrett Corporation
Plessey Company Limited, The

H9. HELICOPTER BUBBLES, DOORS

Aviation Sales Corporation
Bell Helicopters

H10. HELICOPTER WINCHES Etc.

Aviaexport
Aviation Sales Corporation
Garrett Corporation
M.L. Aviation Co. Ltd.
Westland Helicopters Ltd.

H11. HELICOPTERS—COMMERCIAL

Aerospatiale (S.N.I.A.S.)
Agusta, Costruzioni Aeronautiche S.p.A
Aviaexport, V/O
Aviation Sales Corporation
Bell Helicopter
Boeing Co., The
Dornier AG
Fiat S.p.A.
Hughes Tool Company
Saab Aircraft Co.
Westland Helicopters Ltd.

H12. HELICOPTERS—MILITARY

Aerospatiale (S.N.I.A.S.)
Agusta, Costruzioni Aeronautiche S.p.A.
Aviation Sales Corporation
Bell Helicopter
Boeing Co., The
Dornier AG
Fiat S.p.A.
Hughes Tool Company
Saab Aircraft Co.
Westland Helicopters Ltd.

H13. HIGH ALTITUDE TESTING PLANT

Hawker Siddeley Group
Heenan & Froude
McDonnell Douglas Corporation
Plessey Company Limited, The

H14. HIGH ALTITUDE PRESSURE SUITS, HELMETS

Garrett Corporation
M.L. Aviation Co. Ltd.

H15. HIGH PRESSURE COUPLINGS

M.L. Aviation Co. Ltd.
Plessey Company Limited, The

H16. HIGH SPEED RESEARCH CAMERAS

Aviation Sales Corporation
Barr & Stroud Ltd.
McDonnell Douglas Corporation
Thomson C.S.F.

H17. HOSE AND COUPLINGS HYDRAULIC FUEL

Goodyear
Integral Ltd.
Plessey Company Limited, The

H18. HOT AIR BALLOONS

G.Q. Parachute Co. Ltd.

H19. HYDRAULIC EQUIPMENT

Aerospatiale (S.N.I.A.S.)
Aviaexport
Aviation Sales Corporation
Hawker Siddeley Group
Integral Ltd.
Plessey Company Limited, The
Saab Aircraft Co.
S.N.E.C.N.A.

H20. HYDRAULIC PRESSURE PUMPS

Aerospatiale (Div. Systemes Balistiques et Spatiaux)
Aviation Sales Corporation
Garrett Corporation
Integral Ltd.
Plessey Company Limited, The
S.N.E.C.M.A.

H21. HYDRAULIC TEST UNITS, MOBILE AND STATIC

Integral Ltd.

H22. HYDROSKIS

Edo Commercial Corporation

H23. HELICOPTER PARTS AND COMPONENTS

Aeritalia
Aviaexport
Aviation Sales Corporation
Bell Helicopter
Dornier AG
Westland Helicopters Ltd.

H24. HELICOPTER SEARCHLIGHTS

Garrett Corporation
Spectrolab
Teleflex

H25. HELICOPTER SPRAY SYSTEMS AGRICULTURAL

Bell Helicopter

I 1. INERTIAL NAVIGATION SYSTEMS

Aerospatiale (Div. Systemes Balistiques et Spatiaux)
Ferranti Limited
Thomson C.S.F.

I 2. INFLATABLE STRUCTURES

Garrett Corporation
M.L. Aviation Co. Ltd.

I 3. INFRA-RED LINESCAN

Barr & Stroud Ltd.
Hawker Siddeley Group

I 4. INFRA-RED MATERIALS

Barr & Stroud Ltd.

I 5. INFRA-RED SYSTEMS

Barr & Stroud Ltd.
G.E.C. Marconi Electronics Ltd.
Hawker Siddeley Dynamics
Thomson C.S.F.

I 6. INSTRUMENT COMPONENTS (Mechanical)

Aerospatiale (Div. Systemes Balistiques et Spatiaux)
Aviation Sales Corporation
Thomson C.S.F.
Van Dusen Ltd.

E l número de referncia de cada uno de los epígrafos abajo relacionados
indica el equivalente epígrafe en inglés en las páginas..17.a.43.

КЛАССИФИЦИРОВАННЫЙ СПИСОК ОБЪЯВЛЕНИЙ

Ссылочный номер, поставленный перед каждым из нижеперечисленных
названий, указывает эквивалентный заголовок на английском
языке на стр. 17 до 43.

Б19. Автогрузчики, аэродромные	H19. Гидравлическое оборудование
T17. Автогрузчики, вильчатые и платформенные	H22. Гидролыжи
P35. Автогрузчики с подъемной платформой	H3. Головные телефоны
A62. Автоматические открывающие устройства для парашютов	F5. Готовые механически обработанные детали фосфористой бронзы и артиллерийского металла
A64. Автоматические регуляторы для напряжения и мощности тока	B11. Дальномеры
A63. Автопилоты	L9. Дальномеры, лазерные
A60. Автоселекторы	P24. Датчики давления
B5. Аккумуляторы	P18. Датчики перепада давления
B6. Аккумуляторы, авиационные	M1. Датчики числа М
A5. Аккумуляторы, гидравлические	A11. Двигатели, авиационные
A4. Аккумуляторы, кадмие-никелевые	E16. Двигатели, вспомогательные
A1. Акселерометры	M14. Двигатели, гидравлические
A52. Американские запчасти	V14.) Двигатели для самолетов, взлетающих и садящихся
S7. Амортизаторы, масляные-пневматические	E17.) вертикально или с малой длиной пробега и разбега
A8. Антенны, самолетные	M4. Двигатели, морские
D6. Антиобледенительное оборудование	A3. Двигатели переменного тока
I14. Аппаратура внутренних переговорных устройств	D5. Двигатели постоянного тока
A10. Аппаратура для испытания авиационных двигателей	E4. Двигатели, самолетные
C4. Аппаратура для испытания давления в кабине	M12. Двигатели, электрические
E14. Аппаратура для испытания двигателей	H23. Детали и запчасти вертолетов
R16. Аппаратура для испытания ракетных двигателей	I6. Детали приборов (механические)
J2. Аппаратура для испытания реактивных двигателей	J7. Детали реактивных двигателей
T6. Аппаратура для регулирования температуры	D13. Динамометры, гидравлические и электрические
D4. Аппаратура передачи данных	D12. Динамометры, электрические на вихревых токах
C17. Аппаратура управления в кабине летчика	M2. Журналы по авиации и космонавтике
A22. Аппаратура управления воздушным движением	A85. Задерживающее устройство для самолетов
C15. Аппаратура управления самолетами	J6. Замазки для уплотнения соединений
A58. Астро-инерциальные системы навигации	S15. Запчасти для самолетов, построенных в США
W4. Аэродинамические трубы	B7. Зарядные выпрямители
F24. Аэрозоли для предотвращения запотевания	P30. Защитная одежда
A13. Аэрофотокамеры	A68. Звуковые усилители
B12. Бинокли	E11. Изготовление деталей двигателей
B14. Бомбардировочные прицелы	P31. Издатели
L18. Бортовая дальняя радионавигация	S4. Изделия из листового металла
C7. Брезент	P23. Имитаторы усилий в системах управления и загрузочные механизмы
H16. Быстродействующие ночно-исследовательские фото-аппараты	I1. Инерциальные системы навигации
V11. Вертикально взлетающие самолеты	I4. Инфракрасные материалы
H12. Вертолеты, военные	I5. Инфракрасные системы
H11. Вертолеты, гражданские	T8. Испытательное оборудование
F15. Вильчатые автогрузчики	T9. Испытательное оборудование для бортовой радио-аппаратуры
A43. Винты самолетов	T10. Испытательное оборудование для наземной радио-аппаратуры
V12. Вискозиметры	P26. Испытательное оборудование для воздушных винтов
W1. Водоотделители	T11. Испытательное оборудование (металлизация самолетов)
P28. Воздушные винты	M7. Испытательное оборудование на сантиметровых волнах
A14. Воздушные компрессоры	E22. Испытательные комплекты
A15. Воздушные компрессоры в кабине	H1. Испытательные стенды в ангарах
A16. Воздушные компрессоры для запуска двигателей	C6. Кабеля, высокочастотные
F1. Волоконная оптика	T7. Кабеля термоэлементов
A56. Вооружение самолетов	C5. Кабеля, электрические
A9. Вспомогательное авиационное оборудование	C8. Карбюраторы
A65. Вспомогательная силовая установка	E1. Катапультируемые кресла
E3. Вспомогательное электро-оборудование	O4. Кислородная аппаратура
P27. Втулки воздушных винтов	O5. Кислородная аппаратура для дыхания в полете
P7. Выпрессованные изделия, пластические прецизионные	O6. Кислородные системы для дыхания в полете
E23. Выпрессованные изделия, стальные	V1. Клапаны
H13. Высотное испытательное оборудование	V8. Клапаны, гидравлические для определения последовательности
H14. Высотные скафандры, шлемы	V9. Клапаны, гидравлические для регулирования давления
C12. Вычислительные машины	O1. Клапаны для масла
C13. Вычислительные машины, аэродинамические, аналоговые и цифровые	V2. Клапаны и миниатюрные реле
A20. Вычислительные системы для летных данных	V3. Клапаны, контрольные гидравлические
G2. Газовые турбины	V7. Клапаны, обратные гидравлические
G3. Газовые турбины, оборудование и принадлежности	V6. Клапаны, обратные для топлива
H18. Газотурбинные рекуператоры, прогретые	V5. Клапаны, предохранительные гидравлические
G4. Генераторы	P22. Клапаны регулирования давления в жидкостных и газовых системах
M13. Генераторы, моторные	B15. Книги по авиации и космонавтике

J4. Реактивные двигатели
J3. Реактивные стартеры
A59. Регуляторы ассиметрии
C3. Регуляторы давления в кабине
H8. Регуляторы нагрева ветрового стекла
V13. Регуляторы напряжения и мощности тока
F16. Регуляторы подачи топлива
S24. Резервуары
P23. Реле давления
R13. Ремонт и обслуживание самолетов
R14. Ремонт и переборка самолетных двигателей
A48. Ремонтное оборудование на аэропорте
R9. Ремонт радиоаппаратуры
R15. Ремонт самолетных приборов
R1. РЛК для навигации, предупредительного перехвата, управления стрельбой и надсмотра за аэродромами
B3. Роликовые конвейеры
H17. Рукава и муфты для гидравлической жидкости
T13. Ручные инструменты, электрические и пневматические
A66. Самолетное смазочное масло и специальные продукты
A34. Самолеты, взлетающие и садящиеся вертикально или с малой длиной разбега и пробега
A28. Самолеты, военно-морские
A27. Самолеты, военные
A24. Самолеты, гражданские
A25. Самолеты, небольшие пассажирские
A30. Самолеты, радиоуправляемые
A31. Самолеты, сверхзвуковые
A22. Самолеты сельскохозяйственной авиации (опылители и опрыскиватели)
A23. Самолеты скорой помощи
A33. Самолеты, транспортные
A32. Самолеты, учебные
A29. Самолеты, частные
A57. Сборочные приспособления и шаблоны для сверления
D8. Сверлильные станки
D9. Сверлильные станки, портативные, пневматические и электрические
S2. Сервоприводы
A45. Сидения в самолетах
P12. Силовое управление самолетами
P14. Силовой блок, гидравлический
A50. Синхронные генераторы
A37. Системы аварийного покидания
A61. Системы автоматической проверки
E18. Системы кондиционирования воздуха
A18. Системы кондиционирования воздуха
A67. Системы опрыскивания и опыления в сельскохозяйственных самолетах и составные части
S19. Системы предупреждения о срыве потока
A54. Системы противодействия заносу
H25. Системы опыления для сельскохозяйственных вертолетов
A51. Системы регулирования высоты
P21. Системы регулирования давления
C2. Системы регулирования давления в кабине
D3. Системы сброса и спасения самописца
S11. Системы спасения космического летательного аппарата
H6. Системы теплопередачи
S18. Системы увеличения стабилизации
B16. Системы управления пограничным слоем
S27. Системы фотосъемки
E6. Системы электропроводки
M15. Склады металлов
L19. Смазочные вещества
G10. Снаряды, управляемые
M11. Снаряды, управляемые
M5. Собирание мезометеорологических данных
C14. Соединители
S10. Соленоидные клапаны
C11. Составные части
L10. Спасательное оборудование
S28. Спасательное оборудование
E21. Спасательные контейнеры

B1. Спиральные кольца шарикоподшипников
H5. Сплавы, теплостойкие
S14. Спутники, космические
A55. Стабилизирующие парашюты
S23. Стали и стальные сплавы
S31. Стали, нержавеющие, теплостойкие и ползучестойкие
F14. Стальные откованные изделия
N3. Стандартные части (согласно американским стандартам AH, NC, НАС)
M2. Станки
N1. Станки для вырезания из листового металла неправильной формы заготовок
S5. Станки для обработки листового металла
S20. Стартовые контейнеры, бортовые
P29. Схемы наземных поддерживающих операций для самолетов
T1. Тахометры
H4. Теплообменники
T12. Термоэлектрические охладительные системы
T4. Технические публикации
T5. Технические публикации, специальные исследования
W2. Тканая лента
F17. Топливные насосы
F18. Топливные системы и заправочное оборудование
F21. Топливо
B17. Тормозные накладки
L5. Тормозные парашюты
B18. Тормозы для самолетов
T16. Транспортаторы-выпрямители
R20. Транспортеры, роликовые
S9. Тренажеры
T18. Трубки нержавеющей стали
C21. Турбины, низкотемпературные
T19. Турбины с приводом от набегающего воздушного потока
T20. Турбовентиляторные двигатели
E24. Тягачи, электрические
T14. Тягачи, электрические
A49. Указатели скорости полета
A53. Ускорители подачи патронов
H21. Установки для испытания гидравлического давления, передвижные и статические
F10. Устройства для обеспечения плавучести
T15. Устройства для обучения
S15. Устройства для регулирования скорости
J5. Устройства для сбрасывания фонаря
C14. Устройства для привода синхронных генераторов постоянной скорости
L4. Фары для наземных станций
L2. Фары для указания препятствий
L13. Фары, посадочные
L11. Фары, самолетные
F2. Фильтры, воздушные
F4. Фильтры для топлива и масла
S32. Фильтры, химические сельскохозяйственные
F3. Фильтры, электронные
A12. Фирмы инженеров и консультантов по авиационной технике
P10. Формованные изделия из пластмасс
P6. Фотооборудование
M9. Фрезерные станки
A46. Холодильный агрегат, воздушный цикл
V10. Холодильный агрегат, паровой цикл
C9. Центральные вычислители параметров полета
A42. Цилиндры для самолетов с поршневыми двигателями
P4. Части для самолетов, построенных в США
T21. Шины для самолетов
G6. Шлифовальные станки
E12. Экранирующая проводка системы двигателя
E5. Электрические штепселя и розетки (водонепроницаемые)
E4. Электрическое оборудование
E8. Электронная аппаратура
E10. Электроника и наведение
E9. Электронные расходомеры
E7. Электрооптические системы
E18. Эрозиестойкие составы

FOR CIVIL and MILITARY AIRCRAFT

PROVED IN SERVICE

ENGINE RUN·UP STAND

● speeds trouble shooting.

● avoids the need to return engines with only minor defects to the manufacturer or to an overhaul base.

● reduces the number of spare engines needed to ensure maximum aircraft utilisation.

● simple installation requires minimum site preparations.

THE ENGINE RUN-UP STAND IS ONE OF A RANGE OF TEST FACILITIES AVAILABLE FOR THRUST, TORQUE AND GENERAL TESTING OF ANY TYPE OF AERO-ENGINE.

JOHN CURRAN LIMITED

aeronautical and mechanical engineers

G.P.O. Box 72   **CARDIFF**   Cardiff 20641
Curran Road   CF1   1TE   STD: 0222

I 7. INSTRUMENTS, AIRCRAFT

Aeritalia
Aviaexport, V/O
Aviation Sales Corporation
Bendix International
Ferranti Limited
Garrett Corporation
Omnipol
Saab Aircraft Co.
Thomson C.S.F.
Van Dusen Ltd.

I 8. INSTRUMENTS, ELECTRONIC

Aeritalia
Aerospatiale (Div Systemes
   Balistiques et Spatiaux)
Aviaexport, V/O
Bendix International
British Aircraft Corporation
Collins Radio Co.
Ferranti Limited
Fokker
Garrett Corporation
G.E.C. Marconi Electronics Ltd.
Hawker Siddeley Group
Kent Meters Ltd.
M.L. Aviation Co. Ltd.
Thomson C.S.F.
Van Dusen Ltd.

I 9. INSTRUMENTS, FLIGHT SIMULATOR

Aeritalia
Aviation Sales Corporation
G.E.C. Marconi Electronics Ltd.
Thomson C.S.F.

I 10. INSTRUMENTS, NAVIGATION

Aeritalia
Aerospatiale (S.N.I.A.S.)
Aviaexport, V/O
Aviation Sales Corporation
British Aircraft Corporation
Collins Radio Co.
Ferranti Limited
G.E.C. Marconi Electronics Ltd.
Hawker Siddeley Group
Thomson C.S.F.
Van Dusen Ltd.

I 11. INSTRUMENTS, PRECISION

Aeritalia
Avco Lycoming Div. of Avco Corp.
Aviation Sales Corporation
British Aircraft Corporation
Barr & Stroud Ltd.
Ferranti Limited
Garrett Corporation
Hawker Siddeley Group
Thomson S.C.F.

I 12. INSTRUMENTS, TEST EQUIPMENT

Aerospatiale (Div. Systemes
   Balistiques et Spatiaux)
Aviaexport, V/O
British Aircraft Corporation
Collins Radio Co.
Ferranti Limited
Garrett Corporation
Hawker Siddeley Group
Kent Meters Ltd.
McDonnell Aircraft Corporation
Saab Aircraft Co.
Woodward Governor Co.

I 13. INTEGRATED TOTAL PNEUMATIC SYSTEMS

Aerospatiale (Div. Systemes
   Balistiques et Spatiaux)
Garrett Corporation

I 14. INTERCOMMUNICATION EQUIPMENT

Aerospatiale (Div. Systemes
   Balistiques et Spatiaux)
Airmed Limited
Aviaexport
Aviation Sales Corporation
Collins Radio Co.
Hawker Siddeley Group
G.E.C. Marconi Electronics Ltd.
Thomson C.S.F.

I 15. ILLUMINATED PLASTIC CONTROL PANELS AND KNOBS

Aviation Sales Corporation

J1. JACKS

Garrett Corporation

J2. JET ENGINE TEST PLANT

Avco Lycoming Div. of Avco Corp.
Heenan & Froude
Garrett Corporation
S.N.E.C.M.A.

J3. JET FUEL STARTERS

Garrett Corporation

J4. JET PROPULSION ENGINES

Aerospatiale (S.N.I.A.S.)
Aviaexport, V/O
Fiat S.p.A.
Garrett Corporation
Rolls-Royce Limited
S.N.E.C.M.A.

J5. JETTISONABLE CANOPY MECHANISMS

M.L. Aviation Co. Ltd.
Vinten Ltd.

J6. JOINTING COMPOUND

Goodyear
Van Dusen Ltd.

J7. JET ENGINE PARTS

Aviaexport
Aviation Sales Corporation

L1. LAMINATES

Avco Lycoming Div. of Avco Corp.
Aviation Sales Corporation
Fokker

L2. LAMPS—AIRSTRIP, OBSTRUCTION

Aviaexport
Aviation Sales Corporation

L3. LAMPS, COCKPIT

Aviaexport
Aviation Sales Corporation
M.L. Aviation Co. Ltd.

L4. LAMPS FOR GROUND STATIONS

Aviation Sales Corporation

L5. LANDING BRAKE PARACHUTE

G.Q. Parachute Co. Ltd.

L6. LANDING LAMPS

Aviaexport
Aviation Sales Corporation
Teleflex

L7. LAP STRAPS

G.Q. Parachute Co. Ltd.
Mills Equipment Co. Ltd.
Teleflex
Van Dusen Ltd.

L8. LASERS

Aerospatiale (Div. Systemes
   Balistiques et Spatiaux)
Barr & Stroud Ltd.
Ferranti Ltd.
M.L. Aviation Co. Ltd.
Thomson C.S.F.

L9. LASER RANGEFINDER

Aerospatiale (Div. Systemes
   Balistiques et Spatiaux)
Barr & Stroud Ltd.
Ferranti Ltd.

L10. LIFE SAVING EQUIPMENT

Aviaexport
Garrett Corporation
G.Q. Parachute Co. Ltd.
Mills Equipment Co. Ltd.
M.L. Aviation Co. Ltd.
Van Dusen Ltd.

L11. LIGHTS, AIRCRAFT

Aviaexport
Aviation Sales Corporation
Teleflex

L12. LIGHTS, CABIN

Aviation Sales Corporation

L13. LIGHTS, IDENTIFICATION

Aviaexport
Aviation Sales Corporation
Teleflex

Boeing at work: in defence, transportation, space exploration.

Advanced 737

NASA's Apollo/Saturn 5 moon rocket

727-200 trijet airliner

Lunar Rover

Advanced Boeing 737, available next year, will be even more versatile than the outstanding current models. Advanced 737s will fly farther, carry more payload and operate from airports now inaccessible to jet transporters.

Twin turbine Boeing helicopters, built by Vertol Division, are deployed in Vietnam. They serve with U.S. Army, Navy, Marine Corps.

NASA's Apollo/Saturn 5 moon rocket, largest, most powerful in world, launches Americans on spectacularly successful voyages to the moon. Boeing builds the

first-stage booster, integrates Saturn 5 with Apollo command, service and lunar modules, and performs systems engineering, launch and integration support for NASA on entire Saturn 5 system.

Boeing 747 superjet, the world's largest commercial jetliner, is now in service, ushering in an entirely new era of spaciousness and comfort in air travel.

727-200, long-body version of standard 727, world's most popular jet, seats up to 189 for maximum profit on high-density commuter routes.

Lunar Rover. Sometime in 1971, two

astronauts will set off to explore the moon surface in a Boeing two-seater Lunar Rover. The vehicle, one of four now being designed and built by Boeing for NASA, will be carried to the moon in the storage bay of a manned lunar module.

Minuteman is U.S. Air Force's quick-firing, solid-fuel ICBM. Boeing is weapon system integrator, responsible for assembly, test, launch control and ground support systems.

BOEING

Boeing helicopter

747, world's largest commercial jet

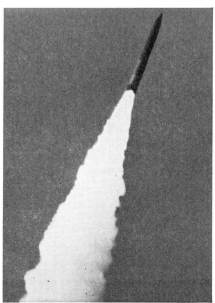

U.S. Air Force Minuteman ICBM

L14. LIGHTS, LANDING

Aviation Sales Corporation
Omnipol
Teleflex

L15. LIGHTS, NAVIGATION

Aviaexport
Aviation Sales Corporation

L16. LINEAR ACTUATORS

Garrett Corporation
Teleflex

L17. LININGS, BRAKE

Goodyear
Van Dusen Ltd.

L18. LORAN, AIRBORNE

Collins Radio Co.
Edo Commercial Corporation

L19. LUBRICANTS

M1. MACH NUMBER TRANSDUCERS

Garrett Corporation

M2. MACHINE TOOLS

Fokker
S.N.E.C.M.A.

M3. MAGAZINES—AVIATION AND SPACE

Flight International
Popular Flying

M4. MARINE ENGINES

Avco Lycoming Div. of Avco Corp.
Rolls-Royce Limited
S.N.E.C.M.A.

M5. MESOMETEOROLOGICAL DATA COLLECTION

Garrett Corporation

M6. METAL FITTINGS

Aviaexport, V/O
Aviation Sales Corp.
G.Q. Parachute Co. Ltd.
Mills Equipment Co., Ltd.
Van Dusen Ltd.

M7. MICRO-WAVE TEST EQUIPMENT

Barr & Stroud Ltd.

M8. MICROPHONES

Aviaexport
Airmed Limited
Aviation Sales Corporation
Hawker Siddeley
G.E.C. Marconi Electronics Ltd.
Thomson C.S.F.

M9. MILLING MACHINES

Fokker

M10. MISSILE RECOVERY PARACHUTES

Aerospatiale (Div. Systemes
Balistiques et Spatiaux)
G.Q. Parachute Co. Ltd.

M11. MISSILES, GUIDED

Aerospatiale (S.N.I.A.S.)
Boeing Co., The
B.P.D. Division—Snia Viscosa
British Aircraft Corporation
Fiat S.p.A.
Hawker Siddeley Group
McDonnell Douglas Corporation
Saab Aircraft Co.

M12. MOBILE PHOTOGRAPHIC UNITS

W. Vinten
Thomson C.S.F.

M13. MOBILE SERVICING VEHICLES

W. Vinten

M14. MOTORS, ELECTRIC

Aerospatiale (S.N.I.A.S.)
Aviaexport
Ferranti Limited
Garrett Corporation
Hawker Siddeley Group
Plessey Company Limited, The

M15. MOTOR GENERATORS

Aerospatiale (Div. Systemes
Balistiques et Spatiaux)
Garrett Corporation
Hawker Siddeley Group

M16. MOTORS, HYDRAULIC

Aerospatiale (Div. Systemes
Balistiques et Spatiaux)
Aviation Sales Corporation
Garrett Corporation
Integral Ltd.

M17. METAL STOCKS

Aviation Sales Corporation

N1. NIBBLING MACHINES

Fokker

N2. NIGHT VISION EQUIPMENT

Barr & Stroud Ltd.

N3. NICKEL ALLOY

Henry Wiggin & Co. Ltd.

O 1. OIL VALVES

Garrett Corporation

O 2. OPTICAL EQUIPMENT

Aerospatiale (Div. Systemes
Balistiques et Spatiaux)
Aviation Sales Corporation
Barr & Stroud Ltd.
Ferranti Ltd.
McDonnell Douglas Corp.
Thomson C.S.F.

O 3. OPTICAL GUN SIGHTS

Barr & Stroud Ltd.
Ferranti Limited
Lockheed Aircraft Corporation
Thomson C.S.F.

O 4. OXYGEN APPARATUS

Aviaexport
Van Dusen Ltd.

O 5. OXYGEN BREATHING APPARATUS

Airmed Limited
Aviaexport
Garrett Corporation

O 6. OXYGEN BREATHING SYSTEMS

Garrett Corporation
M.L. Aviation Co. Ltd.
Van Dusen Ltd.

O 7. OVERHAUL AND MODIFICATION KITS

Aviation Sales Corporation
British Aircraft Corporation
Dornier AG
Woodward Governor Co.

O 8. OVERHAUL PARTS HANDLING BASKETS (STAINLESS STEEL)

Aviation Sales Corporation

P1. PARACHUTES

Aviaexport
G.Q. Parachute Co. Ltd.

P2. PARACHUTES FORCED-DEPLOYMENT

G.Q. Parachutes Co. Ltd.

AGUSTA *HELICOPTERS*

AGUSTA-BELL
AGUSTA-SIKORSKY

FOR ALL PURPOSES

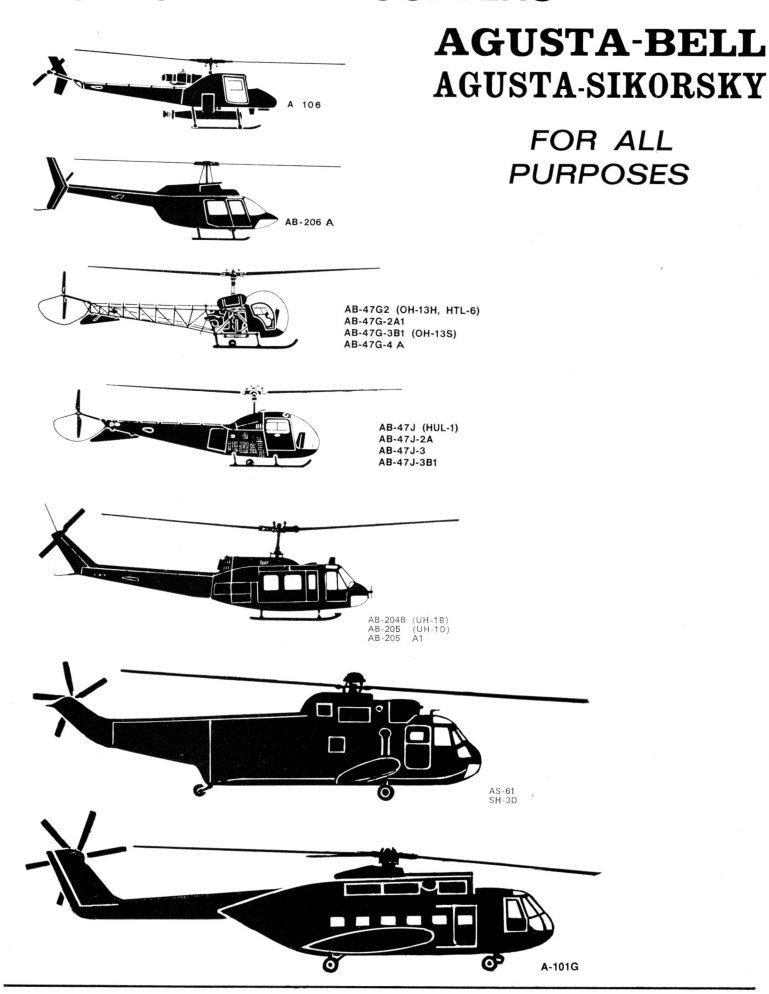

A 106

AB-206 A

AB-47G2 (OH-13H, HTL-6)
AB-47G-2A1
AB-47G-3B1 (OH-13S)
AB-47G-4 A

AB-47J (HUL-1)
AB-47J-2A
AB-47J-3
AB-47J-3B1

AB-204B (UH-1B)
AB-205   (UH-1D)
AB-205   A1

AS-61
SH-3D

A-101G

P3. PARACHUTES—SPECIAL PURPOSE

G.Q. Parachute Co. Ltd.
Omnipol

P4. PARTS FOR U.S. BUILT AIRCRAFT

Aviation Sales Corporation
Bell Helicopter
Ferranti Ltd.
Garrett Corporation
Hawker Siddeley Group
McDonnell Douglas Corporation
M.L. Aviation Co. Ltd.

P5. PERISCOPES

Barr & Stroud Ltd.

P6. PHOTOGRAPHIC EQUIPMENT

Aviation Sales Corporation
McDonnell Douglas Corp.
W. Vinten Ltd.

P7. PLASTIC EXTRUSIONS, PRECISION

Aviation Sales Corporation
B.P.D. Division—Snia Viscosa

P8. PLASTIC FABRICATIONS

Aeritalia
Aerospatiale (Div. Systemes Balistiques et Spatiaux)
Avco Lycoming Div. of Avco Corp.
Aviation Sales Corporation
British Aircraft Corporation
B.P.D. Division—Snia Viscosa
M.L. Aviation Co. Ltd.

P9. PLASTIC FABRICATIONS (re-inforced with fibreglass)

Aeritalia
Aerospatiale (Div. Systemes Balistiques et Spatiaux)
Airmed Limited
Aviation Sales Corporation
British Aircraft Corporation
Fokker

P10. PLASTIC MOULDINGS

Aerospatiale (Div. Systemes Balistiques et Spateuax)
Airitalia
Airmed Limited
B.P.D. Division—Snia Viscosa
British Aircraft Corporation

P11. PNEUMATIC CONTROLS

Garrett Corporation

P12. POWER CONTROL FOR AIRCRAFT

Aviaexport, V/O
Aviation Sales Corpsetion
Garrett Corporation
Hawker Siddeley Group

P13. POWER—SOLCAR CELL PANELS AND ARRAYS

Aerospatiale (Div. Systemes Balistiques et Spatiaux)
British Aircraft Corporation
Spectrolab

P14. POWERPACK, HYDRAULIC

Aviation Sales Corporation
Integral Ltd.

P15. PRECISION GEARS

Barr & Stroud Ltd.

P16. PRECISION POTENTIOMETERS

Aerospatiale (Div. Systemes Balistiques et Spatiaux)
Ferranti Limited

P17. PRESS BRAKES

Fokker
Van Dusen Ltd.

P18. PRESSURE RATIO TRANSDUCERS

Aerospatiale (Div. Systemes Balistiques et Spatiaux)
Garrett Corporation

P19. PRESS TOOL SETS (STANDARDISED)

Saab Aircraft Co.

P20. PRESSURE CONTROL EQUIPMENT

Aviation Sales Corporation
Garrett Corporation

P21. PRESSURE CONTROL SYSTEMS

Aviation Sales Corporation

P22. PRESSURE REGULATING VALVES, FLUIDS AND GASES

Aviation Sales Corporation
Garrett Corporation
S.N.E.C.M.A.

P23. PRESSURE SWITCHES

Aviation Sales Corporation
Hawker Siddeley Group

P24. PRESSURE TRANSDUCERS

Ferranti Ltd.
Garrett Corporation

P25. PROPELLER BALANCING INSTRUMENT

Aviation Sales Corporation
Fokker

P26. PROPELLER TEST STANDS

Aviation Sales Corporation
Hawker Siddeley Dynamics
Heenan & Froude

P27. PROPELLER HUBS

Aviaexport
Aviation Sales Corporation
Hawker Siddeley Dynamics

P28. PROPELLERS

Aviaexport
Aviation Sales Corporation
Hawker Siddeley Dynamics

P29. PROPOSALS FOR AIRCRAFT GROUND SUPPORT OPERATIONS

Aviation Sales Corporation

P30. PROTECTIVE CLOTHING

Garrett Corporation
G.Q. Parachute Co. Ltd.
Mills Equipment Co. Ltd.
M.L. Aviation Co. Ltd.

P31. PUBLISHERS

B.P.C. Publishing Ltd.
Iliffe Transport Publications Ltd.
MacDonald & Co. (Publishers) Ltd.
McGraw-Hill Book Company
Pitman, Sir Isaac, & Sons Ltd.
Sampson Low, Marston & Co. Ltd.

P32. PUMPS, AIR COMPRESSOR

Aviation Sales Corporation
Garrett Corporation
Hawker Siddeley Group

P33. PUMPS, FUEL AND OIL

Aviaexport
Aviation Sales Corporation
Garrett Corporation
Integral Ltd.
Plessey Company Limited, The
S.N.E.C.M.A.
Van Dusen Ltd.

P34. PUMPS, HYDRAULIC

Aviaexport
Aviation Sales Corporation
Garrett Corporation
Integral Ltd.
Plessey Company Limited, The
S.N.E.C.M.A.

P35. PLATFORM TRUCKS

Coventry Climax Engines Ltd.

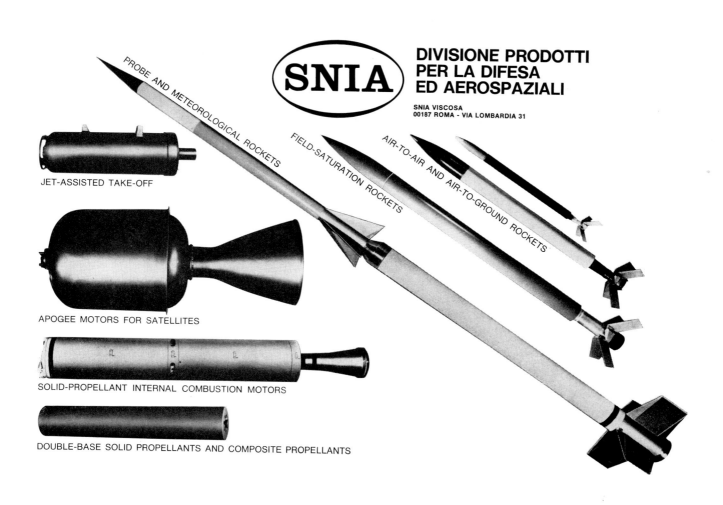

P36. PROVISIONING PARTS BREAKDOWN LIST

Aviation Sales Corporation

P37. PUMPS, AGRICULTURAL SPRAY

Dornier Werke G.m.b.H.

R1. RADAR FOR NAVIGATION WARNING INTERCEPTION, FIRE CONTROL AND AIRFIELD SUPERVISION

Aerospatial (Div. Systemes Balistiques et Spatiaux)
Aviaexport
Collins Radio Co.
Ferranti Limited
G.E.C. Marconi Electronics Ltd.
Hollandse Signaalapparaten N.V.
Omnipol
S.N.E.C.M.A.
Thomson C.S.F.

R2. RADAR REFLECTORS

Aerospatiale (Div. Systemes Balistiques et Spatiaux)
Aviaexport
British Aircraft Corporation
Fokker
G.E.C. Marconi Electronics Ltd.
Thomson C.S.F.

R3. RADAR TOWERS

G.E.C. Marconi Electronics Ltd.
Thomson C.S.F.

R4. RADAR TURNING GEARS AND EQUIPMENT

Aerospatiale (Div. Systemes Balistiques et Spatiaux)
Aviaexport
G.E.C. Marconi Electronics Ltd.
Thomson C.S.F.

R5. RADIO AIRPORT CONTROL EQUIPMENT

Airmed Limited
Aviaexport
G.E.C. Marconi Electronics Ltd.
Hollandse Signaalapparaten N.V.
Standard Wire & Cable Company
Thomson C.S.F.
Van Dusen Ltd.

R6. RADIO ALTIMETERS

Aviaexport
Collins Radio Co.
Standard Telephones & Cables Ltd.
Thomson C.S.F.

R7. RADIO EQUIPMENT

Aerospatiale (Div. Systemes Balistiques et Spatiaux)
Aviaexport
Aviation Sales Corporation
Bendix International
Collins Radio Co.
G.E.C. Marconi Electronics Ltd.
Hawker Siddeley Group
Omnipol
Standard Wire & Cable Company
Thomson C.S.F.

R8. RADIO NAVIGATION EQUIPMENT

Aerospatiale (Div. Systemes Balistiques et Spatiaux)
Aviaexport
Bendix International
Collins Radio Co.
G.E.C. Marconi Electronics Ltd.
Standard Wire & Cable Company
Thomson C.S.F.

R9. RADIO OVERHAUL

Collins Radio Co.
Fokker

R10. RAMJET PROPULSION ENGINES

Aerospatiale (Div. Systemes Balistiques et Spatiaux)
Garrett Corporation
Rolls-Royce Limited

R11. RANGEFINDERS

Aviaexport
Barr & Stroud Ltd.
Ferranti Ltd.
Thomson C.S.F.

R12. RAW MATERIALS

Aviation Sales Corp.

R13. REFRIGERATION COMPRESSORS

Garrett Corporation
M.L. Aviation Co. Ltd.
S.N.E.C.M.A.

R14. REPAIR AND MAINTENANCE OF AIRCRAFT

Aeritalia
Aviaexport
Bell Helicopters
Dornier AG
Fiat S.p.A.
Fokker
Garrett Corporation
Hawker Siddeley Group

R15. REPAIR AND OVERHAUL OF AERO ENGINES

Avco Lycoming Div. of Avco Corp.
Fiat S.p.A.
Rolls-Royce Ltd.
S.N.E.C.M.A.

R16. REPAIR OF AIRCRAFT INSTRUMENTS

Aeritalia
Aviaexport

R17. ROCKET ENGINE TEST PLANT

Aerospatiale (Div. Systemes Balistiques et Spatiaux)
B.P.D. Division—Snia Viscosa
Heenan & Froude

R18. ROCKET PROPULSION

Aerospatiale (Div. Systemes Balistiques et Spatiaux)
British Aircraft Corporation
B.P.D. Division—Snia Viscosa
Rolls-Royce Limited
S.N.E.C.M.A.

R19. ROCKET, SOUNDING

Aerospatiale (Div. Systemes Balistiques et Spatiaux)
British Aircraft Corporation
Dornier Systems GmbH

R20. REACH TRUCKS

Coventry Climax Engines Ltd.

R21. ROLLER CONVEYORS

J. Collins & Sons Ltd.

R22. ROTARY ACTUATORS

Garrett Corporation
Hawker Siddeley Group
Teleflex

S1. SEAT BELTS

Aviaexport
G.Q. Parachute Co. Ltd.
Mills Equipment Co. Ltd.
Teleflex
Van Dusen Ltd.

S2. SERVO ACTUATORS

Avco Lycoming Div. of Avco Corp.
Aviation Sales Corporation
Garrett Corporation
Plessey Company Limited, The
Thomson C.S.F.

S3. SHAPING MACHINES

Aerospatiale (Div. Systemes Balistiques et Spatiaux)
Fokker

S4. SHEET METAL WORK

Aerospatiale (Div. Systemes Balistiques et Spatiaux)
McDonnell Douglas Corp.

S5. SHEET METAL WORKING MACHINES

Aerospatiale (Div. Systemes Balistiques et Spatiaux)
Fokker

S6. SHEETS—NICKEL ALLOY

Henry Wiggin & Co. Ltd.

Who builds a family of turbine engines for small to medium aircraft?

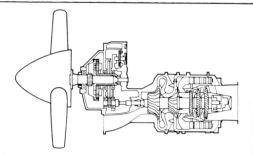

The TPE 331 turboprop has over 1½ million hours in the air.

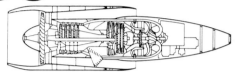

The new ATF 3 turbofan delivers a new low specific fuel consumption of 0.45.

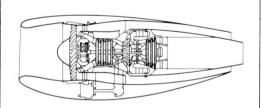

The new TFE 731 turbofan gives 6 to 12-place compact jets longer range.

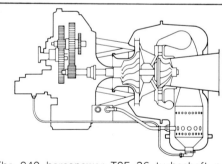

The 240 horsepower TSE 36 turboshaft provides small helicopters with smooth operation.

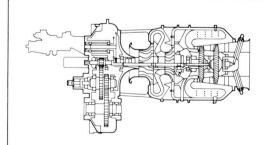

The TSE 231 turboshaft is designed for helicopters and provides 474 shaft horsepower.

Today a great need exists for engines to provide more economical and efficient propulsion for small to medium size transport aircraft.

Garrett is meeting that need with its family of turbine powerplants. These engines include advanced turbofan engines from 2,700 to 8,000 pounds thrust — turboshaft and turboprop engines from 240 to 840 shaft horsepower.

Garrett is totally involved in the aircraft engine business to meet a vital need. And, of course, that goes for worldwide product support, too. The international Garrett support organization is prepared to serve customers anywhere in the world at a moment's notice.

Garrett International, S.A., Headquarters: Geneva; other offices in Paris, Stockholm, Frankfurt, and Slough Bucks, England. **Corporate Offices:** Los Angeles, California, U.S.A.

Garrett International S.A.

one of The Signal Companies

S7. SHEET, STAINLESS AND HEAT-RESISTING STEEL

Aviation Sales Corporation
Van Dusen Ltd.

S8. SIMULATORS

Aerospatiale (Div. Systemes
   Balistiques et Spatiaux)
Dornier Systems GmbH
Ferranti Limited
Garrett Corporation
Hawker Siddeley
McDonnell Douglas Corporation
M.L. Aviation Co. Ltd.
Omnipol
S.N.E.C.M.A.

S9. SOLENOID VALVES

Garrett Corporation
Plessey Company Limited, The

S10. SPACE HARDWARE RECOVERY SYSTEMS

Dornier AG
G.Q. Parachute Co. Ltd.
McDonnell Douglas Corporation

S11. SPACE SYSTEMS

Aerospatiale (S.N.I.A.S.)
Boeing Co., The
British Aircraft Corporation
B.P.D. Division—Snia Viscosa
Dornier Systems GmbH
Ferranti Ltd.
Fiat S.p.A.
Garrett Corporation
Hawker Siddeley Dynamics
McDonnell Douglas Corporation
M.L. Aviation Co. Ltd.
S.N.E.C.M.A.

S12. SPACECRAFT

Aerospatiale (Div. Systemes
   Balistiques et Spatiaux)
Boeing Co., The
Dornier Systemes GmbH
Fokker
Hawker Siddeley Dynamics
McDonnell Douglas Corporation
Thomson C.S.F.

S13. SPACE SATELLITES

Aerospatiale (S.N.I.A.S.)
Aeritalia
British Aircraft Corporation
Dornier Systems GmbH
Hawker Siddeley Group

S14. SPARE PARTS FOR U.S. BUILT AIRCRAFT

Aviation Sales Corporation
Ferranti Ltd.
Garrett Corporation
Hawker Siddeley
McDonnell Douglas Corporation
Standard Wire & Cable Company

S15. SPEED CONTROL DEVICES

Avco Lycoming Div of Avco Corp.
Aviation Sales Corporation
Hawker Siddeley Group
S.N.E.C.M.A.
Woodward Governor Co.

S16. SPRINGS

Integral Ltd.

S17. STABILITY AUGMENTATION SYSTEMS

Aviation Sales Corporation
Dornier Systems GmbH
Ferranti Corporation
Garrett Corporation
Hawker Siddeley Group
Westland Helicopters Ltd.

S18. STALL WARNING SYSTEMS

Ferranti Limited
Van Dusen Ltd.

S20. STARTER PODS AIRBORNE

Garret Corporation
Rolls-Royce Ltd.

S21. STARTER TROLLIES, GROUND

Rolls-Royce Limited

S22. STARTING SYSTEMS, AIRBORNE

Garrett Corporation
Plessey Company Limited, The
Rolls-Royce Limited

S23. STEEL AND STEEL ALLOYS

Aerospatiale (Div. Systemes
   Balistiques et Spatiaux)
Aviaexport
Aviation Sales Corporation

S24. STORAGE TANKS

Aerospatiale (Div Systemes
   Balistiques et Spatiaux)
Garrett Corporation

S25. STRADDLE CARRIERS
   (Materials Handling)

S26. STRAPS, WEBBING

G.Q. Parachute Co. Ltd.
Mills Equipment Co. Ltd.

S27. SURVEILLANCE SYSTEMS

Aerospatiale (Div Systemes
   Balistiques et Spatiaux)
G.E.C. Marconi Electronics Ltd.
S.N.E.C.M.A.
Thomson C.S.F.
Vinten Ltd.

S28. SURVIVAL EQUIPMENT

Aeritalia
Garrett Corporation
G.Q. Parachute Co. Ltd.
Martin-Baker Aircraft Co. Ltd.
M.L. Aviation Co. Ltd.

S29. SWITCHGEAR

Aviaexport
Plessey Company Limited, The
Van Dusen Ltd.

S30. SEARCHLIGHTS

Spectrolab

S31. STEELS, STAINLESS, HEAT AND CREEP RESISTING

Aerospatiale (Div. Systemes
   Balistiques et Spatiaux)

S32. SWITCHES—MINIATURE ELECTRICAL

Aviation Sales Corp.

T1. TACHOMETERS

Aviaexport
Aviation Sales Corporation
Van Dusen Ltd.

T2. TARGET RELEASE AND EXCHANGER MECHANISMS

M.L. Aviation Co. Ltd.

T3. TARGET TOWING WINCHES

Garrett Corporation
M.L. Aviation Co. Ltd.

T4. TECHNICAL PUBLICATIONS

B.P.C. Publishing Ltd.
Dornier Werke G.m.b.H.
Flight International
G.E.C. Marconi Electronics Ltd.
MacDonald & Co. (Publishers) Ltd.
McDonnell Douglas Corp.
McGraw-Hill Book Company
M.L. Aviation Co. Ltd.
Pitman, Sir Isaac, & Sons Ltd.
Sampson Low, Marston & Co. Ltd.

T5. TECHNICAL PUBLICATIONS—SPECIAL STUDIES

Bell Helicopters
Dornier Systems GmbH
Flight International

T6. TEMPERATURE CONTROL EQUIPMENT

Aviaexport
Garrett Corporation
Plessey Company Limited, The
S.N.E.C.M.A.

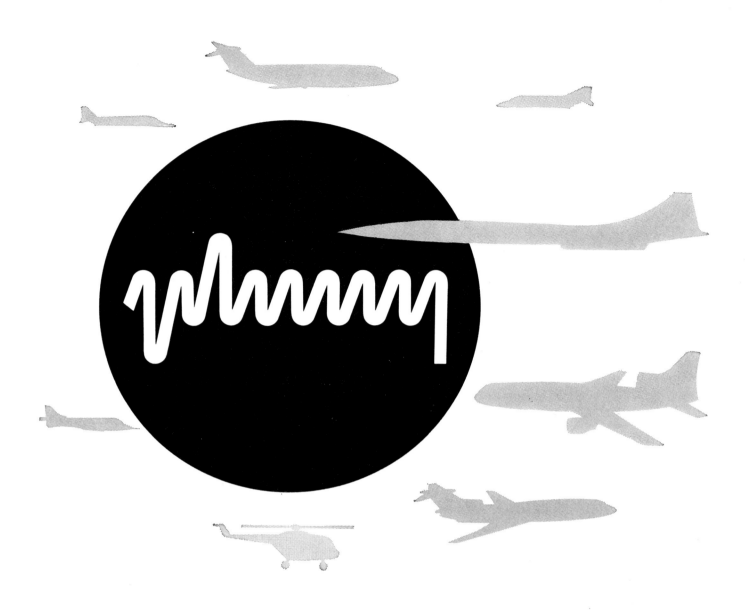

-major resource in international aerospace

The Plessey Company is a major international source of aircraft equipments and systems. The Company's Aerospace Divisions are world leaders in the industry making electrical and mechanical equipments to meet the requirements of modern aircraft. Production, development, research, and product support services are geared to meet all present and future demands.

For information on aerospace equipments and systems – and the new Plessey Airport Lighting System – contact:
Marketing Services Department,
Aerospace Divisions, Dynamics Group,
The Plessey Company Limited,
Eastern Avenue, Chadwell Heath, Essex
RM6 5SD, England. Tel: 01-478 3040 Telex: 23166
or in the USA Plessey Airborne Corporation,
1414 Chestnut Avenue, Hillside, NJ07205
Telephone: (201) 688-0250 Telex: 710-985-4667

PLESSEY DYNAMICS

T7. THERMO-COUPLE CABLES

T8. TEST EQUIPMENT

Aviaexport
Avco Lycoming Div. of Avco Corp.
Collins Radio Co.
Fiat S.p.A.
Garrett Corporation
Hawker Siddeley Group
Heenan & Froude
McDonnell Douglas Corporation
M.L. Aviation Co. Ltd.
S.N.E.C.M.A.

T9. TEST EQUIPMENT, AIRBORNE RADIO

Aviaexport
Collins Radio Co.
Fiat S.p.A.
Standard Wire & Cable Company

T10. TEST EQUIPMENT, AIRFIELD RADIO

Aviaexport
Collins Radio Co.
Fiat S.p.A.
G.E.C. Marconi Electronics Ltd.
Standard Wire & Cable Company

T11. TEST EQUIPMENT (METAL BONDING)

Aviaexport
Fokker

T12. THERMOELECTRIC COOLING SYSTEMS

Garrett Corporation

T13. TOOLS, PNEUMATIC AND ELECTRIC PORTABLE

T14. TRACTORS, ELECTRIC

Coventry Climax Engines Ltd.

T15. TRAINING DEVICES

Bell Helicopters
Ferranti Ltd.
McDonnell Douglas Corporation
M.L. Aviation Co. Ltd.

T16. TRANSFORMER RECTIFIER UNITS

Ferranti Limited
Plessey Company Limited, The

T17. TRUCKS—FORKLIFT AND PLATFORM

Coventry Climax Engines Ltd.

T18. TUBES, STAINLESS STEEL

Aviaexport
Aviation Sales Corporation

T19. TUBES—NICKEL ALLOY

Henry Wiggin & Co. Ltd.

T20. TURBINES—RAM AIR

Garrett Corporation
Rolls-Royce Limited
S.N.E.C.M.A.

T21. TURBOFAN ENGINES

Aviaexport
Garrett Corporation
Rolls-Royce Limited
S.N.E.C.M.A.

T22. TYRES FOR AIRCRAFT

Goodyear

U1. UNDERCARRIAGE EQUIPMENT

British Aircraft Corporation
Hawker Siddeley Group
S.N.E.C.M.A.

U2. UNDERCARRIAGE GEAR RETRACTABLE

British Aircraft Corporation
Hawker Siddeley Group
S.N.E.C.M.A.

V1. VALVES

Aviation Sales Corporation
Garrett Corporation
Plessey Company Limited, The
S.N.E.C.M.A.
Van Dusen Ltd.

V2. VALVES AND MINIATURE RELAYS

Aviaexport
Aviation Sales Corporation
Garrett Corporation

V3. VALVES, CONTROL HYDRAULIC

Aviation Sales Corporation
Goodyear
Hawker Siddeley Group
Integral Ltd.
Plessey Company Limited, The
S.N.E.C.M.A.

V4. VALVES, ELECTRONIC

Ferranti Limited
Garrett Corporation
Saab Aircraft Co.
Van Dusen Ltd.

V5. VALVES, FUSES HYDRAULIC

Aviaexport
Aviation Sales Corporation
Integral Ltd.

V6. VALVES, NON-RETURN, FUEL

Aviaexport
Aviation Sales Corporation
Hawker Siddeley Group
Plessey Company Limited, The

V7. VALVES, NON-RETURN HYDRAULIC

Aviaexport
Aviation Sales Corporation
Hawker Siddeley Group
Integral Ltd.
Plessey Company Limited, The

V8. VALVES SEQUENCE HYDRAULIC

Aviation Sales Corporation
Hawker Siddeley Group
Integral Ltd.
Plessey Company Limited, The

V9. VALVES, RELIEF HYDRAULIC

Aviaexport
Aviation Sales Corporation
Hawker Siddeley Group
Integral Ltd.
Plessey Company Limited, The

V10. VAPOR CYCLE REFRIGERATION PACKAGES

Garrett Corporation

V11. VERTICAL TAKE-OFF AIRCRAFT

Aeritalia
Aerospatiale (S.N.I.A.S.)
Dornier AG
Fiat S.p.A.
Hawker Siddeley Group
Westland Helicopters Ltd.

V12. VISCOMETERS

Ferranti Limited

V13. VOLTAGE AND CURRENT REGULATORS

Aviaexport
Ferranti Limited
Garrett Corporation
Hawker Siddeley Group
Plessey Company Limited, The
Van Dusen Ltd.

W1. WATER SEPARATORS

Garrett Corporation

W2. WEBBING

G.Q. Parachute Co. Ltd.
Mills Equipment Co. Ltd.
Van Dusen Ltd.

W3. WHEELS FOR AIRCRAFT

Aviaexport
Goodyear
S.N.E.C.M.A.
Van Dusen Ltd.

W4. WIND TUNNEL TESTING PLANT

Dornier AG
Ferranti Ltd.
Fiat S.p.A.
Heenan & Froude
Plessey Company Limited, The
Westland Helicopters Ltd.

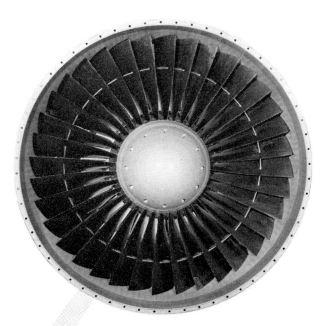

from **1943** Spitfire

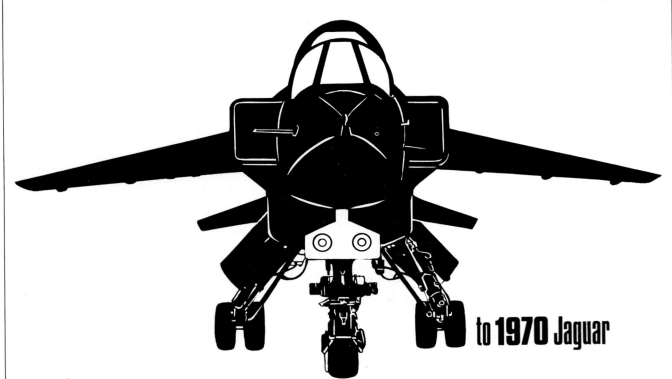

to **1970** Jaguar

Our products (aircrew seats cable tension regulators remote control systems electro-mechanical actuators landing lamps windshield wipers aircrew safety harness) have over 500,000,000 hours flying experience!

As aerospace technology grew, so did Teleflex. Our products are widely used in all types of civil and military aircraft from executive jets to supersonic transports and from light helicopters to advanced strike projects. We would like to tell you more about them — our international aerospace experience means we speak your language.

Teleflex Limited
Basildon, Essex, England.

Téléflex Synéravia,
32 Rue Robert Witchitz,
B.P. 29 Ivry-sur-Seine, France.

Teleflex GmbH,
Heiligenhaus Bezirk,
Dusseldorf,
Deutschland.

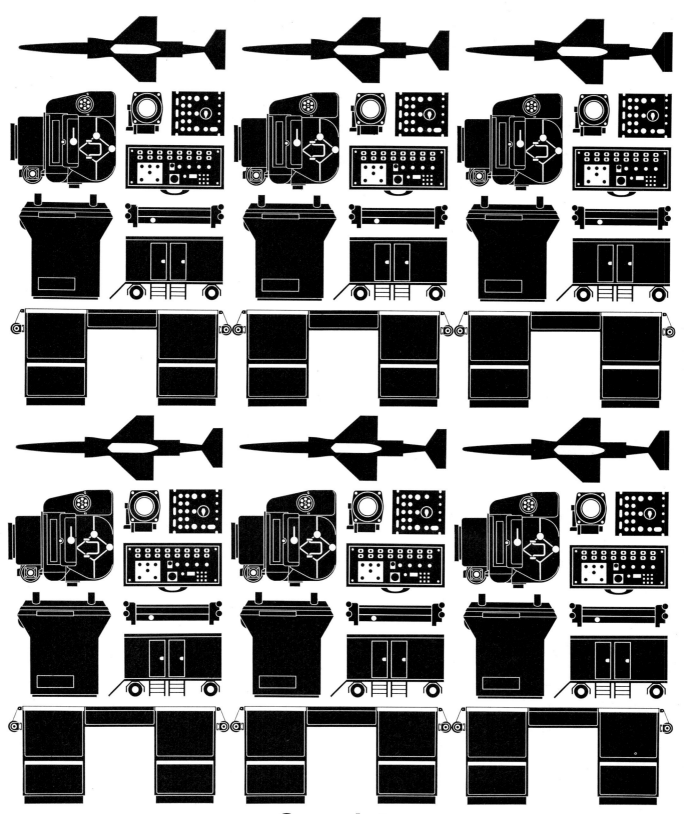

Complete
Photographic reconnaissance
systems

Further information from W Vinten Limited Western Way Bury St Edmunds Suffolk England Telephone Bury St Edmunds 2121 Telex 81176

In these days of lightning technological change, your library must have each and every JANE'S

JANE'S FIGHTING SHIPS
73rd Edition, 1970-1971

Edited by Raymond V. B. Blackman

Comprehensive information, photographs and drawings of over 14,000 ships of 106 countries throughout the world. In addition, a directory section lists naval staff hierarchies, senior command appointments, directors of departments, naval and defense attaches, and commanding officers of major warships and naval establishments of most of the navies of the world.

JANE'S FREIGHT CONTAINERS
3rd Edition, 1970-1971

Edited by Patrick Finlay

The most important development in transportation is covered with usual JANE'S thoroughness. Valuable new addition: index of container identification codes and serial numbers, directory of operational services.

JANE'S SURFACE SKIMMER SYSTEMS
4th Edition, 1970-1971

Edited by Roy McLeavy

Surface skimmers are taking over both from ships and from airplanes. They're fascinating reality, and Jane's reports in detail. List of ACV clubs and associations. Glossary of terms.

JANE'S WORLD RAILWAYS
13th Edition, 1970-1971

Edited by Henry Sampson

A comprehensive encyclopedia of the immense and complex rail industry throughout the world. New features include Containerization and Piggyback and a Directory of Railroad Officials.

JANE'S ALL THE WORLD'S AIRCRAFT
61st Edition, 1970-1971

Edited by John W. R. Taylor

An invaluable reference featuring up-to-date descriptions with specifications and photographs of over 5000 aircraft, apart from missiles and power plants. Included are special sections on aircraft ground equipment, aircraft equipment manufacturers, navigation and control systems and listing of airports.

JANE'S MAJOR COMPANIES OF EUROPE
2nd Edition, 1970-1971

Edited by Lionel F. Gray

This vital reference for the international business world covers 1000 leading companies in 14 European countries. What businessmen, industrialists, brokers, bankers, manufacturers, importers and exporters must know arranged in comparable form, such as the economies, trade, export and import, tax and dividend rates and structures, interest and exchange rates and glossary of international financial terms.

JANE'S WEAPON SYSTEMS
2nd Edition, 1970-1971

Edited by Ronald Pretty and H. R. Archer

This authoritative yearly survey describes the weapon systems for all land, sea and air Defense Services, and their surveillance, guidance, propulsion, "platform" and command elements.

For further information write:
Trade Division
McGraw-Hill Book Company,
330 West 42nd Street, New York, N.Y. 10036

Fly our DC jet 'Family Plan', and go first class all the way.

Flying the McDonnell Douglas "Family Plan" is like having
a one-way ticket to airline profitability. Millions of flight hours in
airline service the world over have proved the first-class
dependability of our family of jetliners: DC-8s, Super DC-8s, and
twinjet DC-9s. And the same engineering excellence, craftsmanship,
and performance that have made "DC" an airline byword for 37
consecutive years will be aboard our new DC-10. This advanced
technology luxury tri-jet is offered in configurations for high-revenue
potential on short, medium, or intercontinental routes.
DC-10. Newest member of our Douglas
Aircraft Company's family of jets.

MCDONNELL DOUGLAS

Pity the Air Traffic Controller when they come in like this

An exaggerated picture perhaps but not for long. Air Traffic is increasing so fast that the controller's job needs an entirely new appraisal. And one of the things we've got to look at is the method of training controllers. Is it adequate to meet the demands of the Seventies?

The flexibility of the Ferranti Radar Simulator provides the answer—now and for the future. It gives the trainee controller practice in Air Traffic Control under conditions so realistic that when he takes over control of real aircraft he'll not only be fully trained but confident too.

Digital techniques readily permit modifications to accommodate changes in a wide range of parameters, including aircraft type and speed, radar and geographical data. Raw radar or fully synthetic output can be provided to drive any type of display. The system can therefore simulate new aircraft and procedural techniques not even envisaged at this stage.

Ferranti have the capability and experience to design and develop a system to suit any individual requirements. If you have an ATC training or evaluation problem talk to Ferranti.

FERRANTI
ATC training systems
**Ferranti Limited,
Digital Systems Department, Bracknell, Berkshire, England. RG12 1RA**

DS21/2

Viggen was here.

Thirty seconds ago a Viggen took off from this stretch of road "somewhere in Sweden". The SAAB 37 Viggen can operate from a runway just 500 metres long, even carrying a typical combat load. *It is the only supersonic STOL combat aircraft being produced in Western Europe.* Today there are six prototypes flying — by 1971 the all-weather, multi-mission Viggen will be in service with the Swedish Air force.

This fine aircraft offers real value for money. With only minor modifications the basic Viggen can fulfil both strike, reconnaissance and interception roles. Maintenance costs are very low and the ground support facilities required are minimal, if need be a start can be made entirely on internal power.

A Viggen pilot is not alone. He's backed up by a powerful digital computer in the belly of the plane. It can be programmed with data on the ground and fed fresh information when airborne. It also tells the pilot all he needs to know in a head-up display on a reflector glass in the pilot's line of view.

The SAAB 37 Viggen is an economical and practical concept for a multipurpose MACH 2 class aircraft designed for the seventies and eighties'. *It is advanced technology in a realistic package!*

SAAB

S-581 88 LINKÖPING SWEDEN

Schiphol.
First airport in Europe with an automatic air traffic control data-processing system:

Schiphol Amsterdam SATCO automatic air traffic control in full operation.

Main features of Signaal flight plan and radar data-processing systems.

Main operational features
flight path calculation
coordination
clearance processing
correlation between radar data and flight plan data
conflict risk detection
conflict resolution
electronic data display
synthetic dynamic display
daylight large screen display
flight progress board
stripprinting
automatic transfer of data via data links to adjacent centres

Programming features
modular design
flexibility
reconfiguration capabilities
on-line real-time programming
software and hardware controlled multi-level programming

Computer features
microminiaturization techniques
high operating speed
1 microsec. memory cycle
mass memories
high reliability
growth potential
continuity of operation
easy servicing.

For further information please apply to N.V. Hollandse Signaalapparaten, P.O. Box 42, Hengelo, The Netherlands.

SIGNAAL

radar, weapon control, data handling and air traffic control systems
N.V. HOLLANDSE SIGNAALAPPARATEN HENGELO

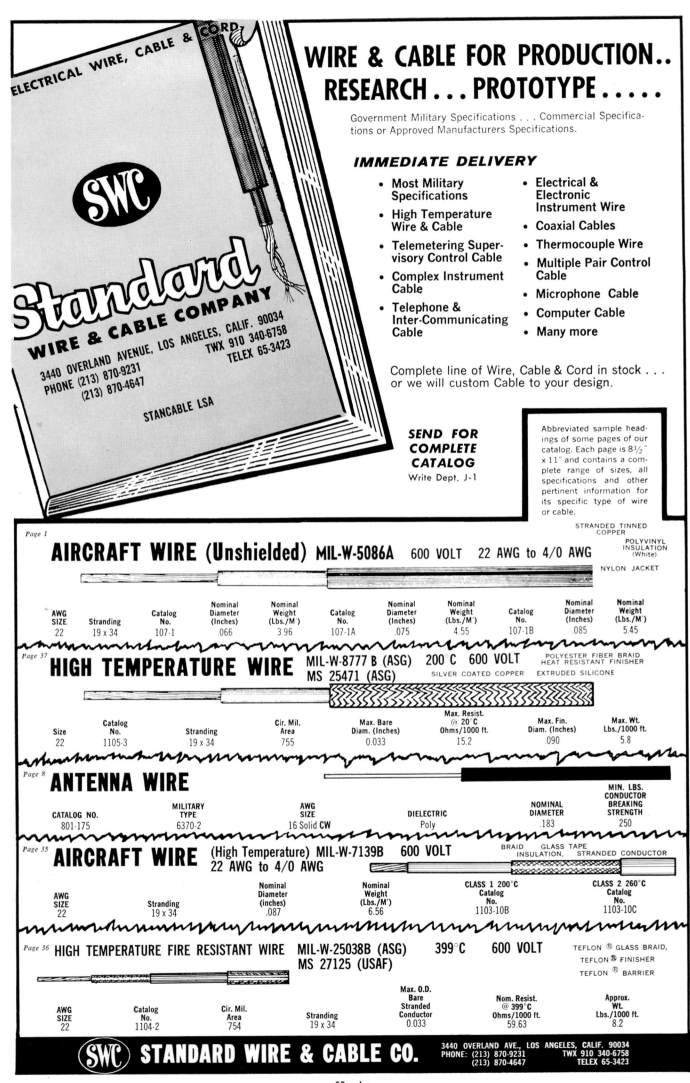

Why

the world's air forces can depend on Rolls-Royce

We built our first military aero engine in 1914. We've been building them ever since. For the last 26 years, gas turbines.

It's a length of experience no other manufacturer can match.

And we have the resources to put our experience to good use. Research and development alone employ over 18,000 of our people. We have more computers than any other company in Europe. Over 180 test beds and rigs. Our altitude chambers can reproduce flight conditions at Mach 2·4 and 80,000 ft. We operate one of the largest and most modern noise research facilities in the world.

To produce the goods, we have nearly nine million sq. ft. of factory floor. With 9,800 machine tools, many of them numerically controlled and a strong, experienced and highly-skilled production force.

This is also true of the 450 plus service engineers who watch over the engines once they go into service. Repair facilities are available at 82 bases strategically situated across the globe. Spares supply is computer controlled. Highly mechanised warehouses ensure prompt supply.

Now you know why the world's air forces can depend on Rolls-Royce. And you won't be surprised to learn that over 70 of them have chosen to do so.

ROLLS-ROYCE LIMITED · DERBY · ENGLAND
Aero Engine Division. Bristol Engine Division. Small Engine Division.

Bofors Flare Bomb Lepus
Photograph made on a night in January at 11.15 p.m.

ILLUMINATING MATERIEL

for all branches of the armed forces

AB BOFORS-BOFORS-SWEDEN

Every hour of every day the performance of aero engines for world-wide service is put to the test on Heenan & Froude test equipment

ten
badges
on the
fuselage

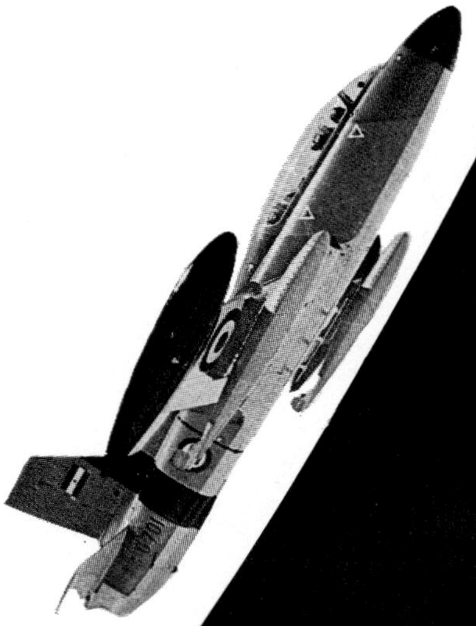

MB 326 aer macchi

The multi-role jet trainer
chosen by 10 operators
in four Continents
has still in the '70
a career of success
and efficient service.

The MB. 326 reached,
in the development of its
versions,
a steady optimation
of performance and systems
which assures
a long life of service
sheltered from a premature
technical obsolescence.

aer macchi

Aeronautica Macchi s.p.a.
Varese, Italia

Bell...First in the air with an Executive Twin!

Bell makes more helicopters than anyone else in the world. And Bell alone offers a full line of models to perform the most complete range of commercial rotorcraft tasks.

This leadership aloft begins with leadership on the ground: in the dreaming room, at the drawing board, in the lab. A leader leads. And so again in 1970 as through the many years till now, there will be more Bells aloft, more models to do more tasks, and more performance from them all, from Bell, the leader.

1 THE 1970s BEGIN WITH BELL'S BRILLIANT NEW TWO-TWELVE TWIN. Never till now a vehicle like this. New dependability from twin-turbine engines, new high performance, new comfort, new convenience: powered by an 1800 H.P. Pratt & Whitney twinpack, the Two-Twelve provides faster door-to-door transportation up to 300 miles than any other ground-air combination.

2 THE MIGHTY 205A. Proven by over 7500 military and commercial craft in this series, it is perhaps the most flexible business-industrial craft ever produced. The 1400 H.P. Lycoming turbine powered 205A is a busy air taxi, a mover of people and cargo over cities, in multi-plant complexes, over swamps, mountains, forests and into remote areas, adapts readily to virtually limitless cabin arrangements. It can carry up to 14 passengers and a pilot, 5000 pounds of external sling, or 4000 pounds in the big 200-cu.-ft. cabin. The mighty 205A is the everything craft.

3 THE SLEEK JETRANGER: SPORTY TRUCK OR HARD-WORKING CHARIOT? The excit-

ing 317 H.P. General Motors turbine-powered JetRanger is personal vehicle for numerous corporate officers, police-vehicle, offshore oil rig worker, helicab — and the fastest selling light turbine helicopter on earth. Eliminates ground snarls from city to city travel, makes corporate jet fleets more useful — and is by far the most beautiful craft of its kind. 140-mph, five places in comfort, 1200 pounds carried externally, 950 inside.

4 THE INTREPID AgMASTER. Its formal name, the 47G-5, identifies it as one of the famous Bell 47s, of which there are still more flying than any rotorcraft of any maker. AgMaster far outworks fixed-wing craft, eliminates turn time, cuts refill time to almost nil, needs no runway — and almost instantly converts to handle any number of other chores from cargo hauling to personnel moving. Easy to fly, inexpensive to buy and to operate.

5 PATROL CAR 47. Low cost, brilliant airworthiness, ease of handling, and availability of many options, make the 47 ideal for police and other public assignments. When "Car 47" is on duty aloft, the fight on the ground is over. Off duty, the car serves as ready firewatch, ambulance, traffic director, or VIP cab.

For more information or for demonstrations, call Bell Helicopter Marketing Services collect now: (817) 280-2142. Or write Bell Helicopter, Ft. Worth 76101

BELL HELICOPTER
A **textron** COMPANY

P. O. BOX 482
FORT WORTH, TEXAS 76101

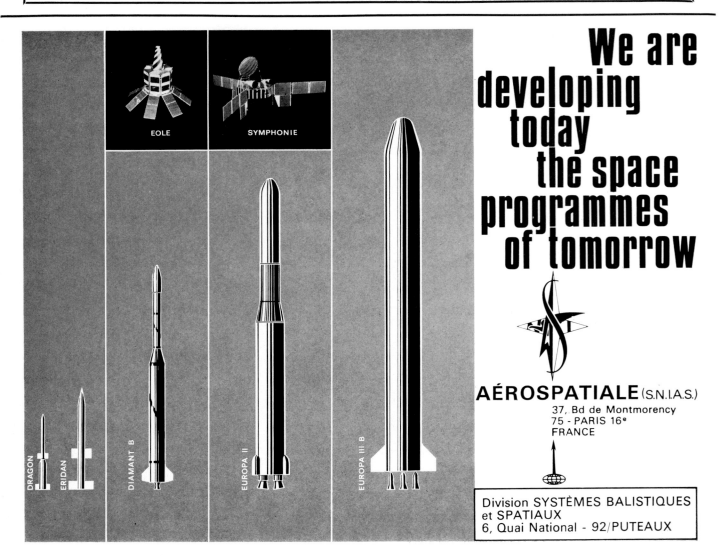

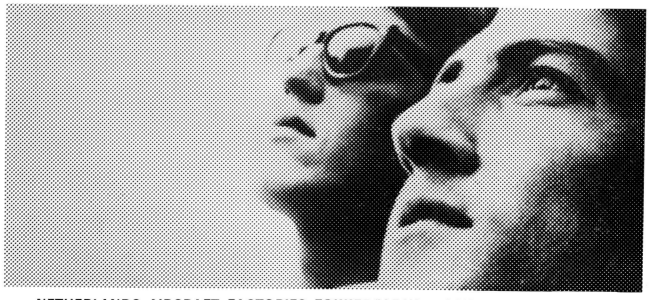

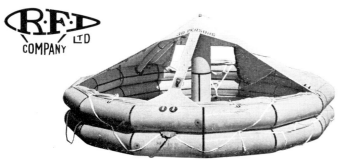
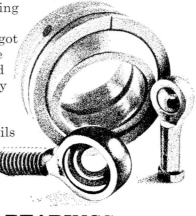

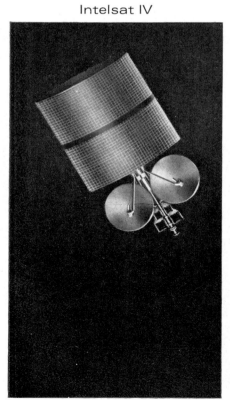

Panavia 200

with Messerschmitt-Boelkow-Blohm, Germany, and Fiat, Italy

Strikemaster

Lightning

RECOGNISES NO BOUNDARIES...

Anti-tank Missiles

British Aircraft Corporation is one of that small elite of international organisations which shape the world's technological progress. BAC has built up for its products and after-sales service a level of international acceptance enjoyed by no other European Aerospace Company. Today its products span the whole range of aerospace technology – from supersonic and subsonic airliners to advanced military aircraft; from defence missile systems to space satellites. Its technical and commercial strength is the keystone of large programmes of international collaboration.

BRITISH AIRCRAFT CORPORATION
the most powerful aerospace company in Europe

100 PALL MALL LONDON SW1

BAC 122

New gas turbines for power-hungry aircraft in the 70's

If your design requires gas turbine power in a range from 2,000 to 10,000 shp or 2,700 to 12,000 lbs. of thrust, you can now turn to the engine source that spans this entire spectrum. Choose from these new power plants of the great Avco Lycoming gas turbine family:

LTC4B-12 is the latest in a series of evolutions of the combat-tested T55, prime mover of the CH-47 Chinook. At virtually no increase in weight, this gas turbine now turns out more than 4,600 hp, is ideally sized for such aircraft as close support fighters, medium V/STOL transports and helicopters.

The advanced technology LTC4V series: a quantum jump in power/weight ratio (9 to 1 in this 5,000 shp demonstrator engine); 25% improvement in specific fuel consumption; remarkable compactness; suitable for adaptation to turboshaft, turboprop, or fan jet; scalable within a 4,000 to 10,000 hp range.

High-bypass turbofans—ALF-501 and ALF-301: advanced performance from a flight-proved team of core engines each one offering high reliability and excellent fuel consumption for its thrust rating. Initial versions of ALF-501 and ALF-301 offer take-off thrust to 5,800 lbs. and 2,730 lbs. respectively, and growth versions are on the way.

The brand new 1,900 shp T53, latest in an already proud line, gives a 35 percent boost in available horsepower over current production models. More than 2,000 hours of testing have already gone into its development.

Power hungry? More power to you—from Avco Lycoming

AVCO LYCOMING DIVISION
STRATFORD, CONNECTICUT, 06497

the multi-role Sea King

* Anti-submarine search and strike
* Search and rescue
* Mine counter measures
* Air to ground and air to sea strike

* Troop lift
* Cargo transport
* Casualty evacuation
* Long range communication

is today's most versatile helicopter

 WESTLAND
HELICOPTERS
LIMITED

YEOVIL SOMERSET ENGLAND Tel. Yeovil (Code 0935) 5222

A SUBSIDIARY OF WESTLAND AIRCRAFT LIMITED

Sure it's ugly.

But this new searchlight for helicopters packs a 20,000-watt wallop.

Beautiful!

Beams 900 feet in diameter and 50 times brighter than full moonlight from an altitude of 3,000 feet—that's the level of performance you can expect from our ugly-but-brilliant Nightsun™ FX-150. It's the most powerful xenon searchlight made for helicopter surveillance and patrol.

FX-150 weighs a compact 160 pounds with remotely controlled two-axis gimbal mount as standard equipment for cockpit control of azimuth and elevation.

Or choose the lightweight Nightsun SX-16—1600 watts in a 25-pound package for light helicopter use.

Both produce illumination so close to natural daylight that color temperature is high enough for night color photography. And both searchlights are available with infrared filter for covert surveillance missions.

Nightsuns are flying now all over the world with Bell, Enstrom, Fairchild Hiller, and other helicopters and fixed wing aircraft. Available for immediate delivery in the U.S. and overseas. For detailed information, write or call Spectrolab/ 12484 Gladstone Avenue, Sylmar, Calif. 91342/ (213) EMpire 5-4611.

LEFT:
Nightsun SX-16. Output, 1600 watts; weight, 25 lbs. Installation kits available for Bell 47G series and 205A(A1), Fairchild Hiller FH-1100 and Hughes OH-6A.

RIGHT:
Nightsun FX-150. Output, 20,000 watts; weight, 160 lbs. Installation kits available for Bell UH1 series and 205A(A1), Sikorsky HH-3E, HH-53B&C, Fairchild C-123 and Lockheed C130 aircraft.

Spectrolab

A Division of Textron Inc.

AN EQUAL OPPORTUNITY EMPLOYER. FOR CAREER OPPORTUNITIES IN SOLAR SIMULATION, WRITE "PERSONNEL".

Nightsun FX150

Nightsun Dealers and Representatives around the world: **AFRITRADE:** Israel, Iran, Kenya, Uganda and Ghana **AGUSTA:** Italy **AIRSERVICES:** Hong Kong, South Korea, Taiwan, Philippine Islands, Burma, Thailand, Laos, Cambodia **AMALGAMATED PACIFIC INDUSTRIES, LTD.:** New Zealand **AVIONIC:** Greece, Cyprus **HELICOPTER SALES:** Australia, New Guinea **HELI-ORIENT:** Singapore, Indonesia, Malaysia **IBERISA:** Spain, Spanish Sahara, Ceuta, Melilla, Canary Islands, Balearic Islands **ITT-EUROPE — STANDARD TELEPHONES AND CABLES LIMITED:** United Kingdom **MOTORFLUG Gmbh:** Germany **OSTERMANS AB:** Sweden, Denmark, Finland, Norway **REPAER:** Republic of South Africa **TRADEWAYS LTD.:** Pakistan **USHIO:** Japan

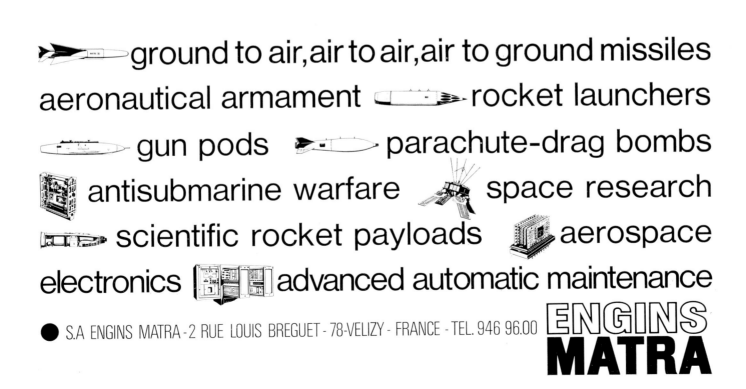

SERVING THE

AEROSPACE INDUSTRY

Nickel-Cadmium Accumulators

VOLTABLOC

SAFT

SOCIÉTÉ DES ACCUMULATEURS FIXES ET DE TRACTION
R.C. Seine 56 B 324 · · · Limited Comp. with a capital of 21.056.000 F · · · Phone : 845-83-47
156, Avenue de Metz - 93 - ROMAINVILLE (France) - Télex : 22.100 - SAFTALCALIN - PARIS

THE SOVIET-BUILT
MI-6 HEAVY TRANSPORT HELICOPTER...

...can carry a 12-ton payload to remote regions difficult for access.

AVIAEXPORT, Moscow,

can offer a range of multipurpose helicopters:

KAMOV KA-26 light utility helicopter is being successfully used in agricultural work, for transporting passengers and cargoes, in prospecting and exploration work, various rescue operations and for erecting jobs. The removable passenger cabin for 6 passengers may be easily replaced by an open platform for bulky cargo loads. An agricultural version can carry 900 kg of dry chemicals or a tank for an equivalent quantity of liquid chemical.

MIL Mi-8 general-purpose commercial transport helicopter is being offered in two versions, one accommodating up to 28 passengers and the other being intended for the freight transportation role with a maximum cargo load of 4000 kg. Both versions are quickly convertible for ambulance duties. A controllable winch and underside cargo hook for lifting slung loads up to 3000 kg may be fitted.

V/O AVIAEXPORT is ready to satisfy all enquiries about Soviet civil aircraft and accessories. It receives representatives of foreign firms in Moscow and sends its own representatives abroad to negotiate transactions.

For more details please apply to V/O "AVIAEXPORT" 32/34 Smolenskaya-Sennaya, Moscow G-200, USSR.

Cables: Aviaexport Moscow.   Telex: Moscow 257.

Telephone: 244-26-86.

Climax handling costs less

Climax fork trucks are speeding airport freight handling in all parts of the world.

It's exacting, tightly scheduled work where smooth, reliable mobility is essential. Speed, lift and reach – with close-in accuracy and manoeuvrability – make Climax the ideal choice for busy airports. Here, as in so many highly organised industries, you'll find the efficiency and experience that make Climax handling cost less.

Coventry Climax Engines Ltd.,
Widdrington Road, Coventry CV1 4DX Telephone: Coventry 21424

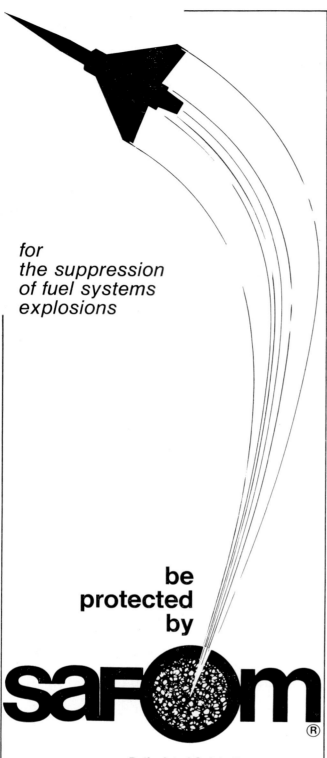

for
the suppression
of fuel systems
explosions

be
protected
by

saf**O**m ®

Reticulated Safety Foam

**Produced
to military specifications**

When fitted into a fuel tank it will
completely suppress the explosion
which follows the ignition
of a fuel/air mixture
in a confined space.

Weight : 30 kg per m3.

Reduction of tank capacity : 3%.

Can be fitted during construction or retrofitted on existing
aircraft fuel-system by our specialised personnel.

PRB s.a.

Division EUROFOAM
12, avenue de Broqueville
1150 Bruxelles
Tél. 02/71.01.40
Telex : 2/23112 Eurofoam Bruxl. B

JANE'S
ALL THE WORLD'S AIRCRAFT

First published in 1909

now has *six* companion volumes

JANE'S FIGHTING SHIPS

Edited by Raymond V. B. Blackman, MBE, C.Eng.,
M.I.Mar.E., M.R.I.N.A.   First published in 1897

JANE'S WORLD RAILWAYS

Edited by Henry Sampson   First published in 1951

JANE'S SURFACE SKIMMERS

Edited by Roy McLeavy   First published in 1967

JANE'S FREIGHT CONTAINERS

Edited by Patrick Finlay   First published in 1968

JANE'S WEAPON SYSTEMS

Edited by Ronald Pretty and Dennis Archer
First published in 1969

JANE'S MAJOR COMPANIES
OF EUROPE

Edited by Lionel F. Gray   First published in 1965

Published by JANE'S YEARBOOKS
49/50 Poland Street, London W1A 2LG, England
and in the Americas by
McGRAW-HILL BOOK COMPANY
330 West 42nd Street, New York, N.Y. 10036, U.S.A.

*Illustrated descriptive prospectuses available on request
from above addresses.*

75 adv.

Cossor-capability

Cossor has land, sea and air – under control, providing a total systems capability.

Instrument landings for the latest civil and military aircraft, airport control systems, etc.

An important link in Cossor control is the large part played by Data Systems pioneered by the Cossor team of experts in research, design and engineering. In fact every control problem receives high level personal supervision by senior executives.

If you want to be in control – talk to Cossor first.

Instrument landing equipment for naval helicopters.

Cossor offer a full range of Airborne and Ramp Test Equipment.

Cossor surface and airborne list

SSR/IFF equipment currently include:
SSR 700 Solid State Transmitter/Receiver – Civil SSR
IFF 750 Solid State Transmitter/Receiver – Military IFF/SSR
IFF 800 Solid State Transmitter/Receiver – Naval IFF
CRI 600 Microminiturised Transmitter/Receiver – Civil-Military

A range of 3 high performance integral aerials 11 to 31 ft.

SSR 2700 Airborne Microminiturised Transponder – Civil SSR
SSR 1600 Airborne Transponder – Civil SSR
SSR 2100 Airborne Microminiturised Transponder – Civil SSR
IFF/SSR 1520 Airborne Transponder – Military IFF/SSR
IFF/SSR 3000 Airborne Microminiturised Transponder –
    Military IFF/SSR
CRM 511 ILS/VOR Audio Frequency Signal Generator
CRM 533 ILS/VOR/COM Radio Frequency Generator
CRM 444 Transponder Ramp Test Set
CRM 555 ILS/VOR Ramp Test Set
CRM 588 Flight Line Test Set

SSR Installation at Ash, Kent.

CSD 1000 High Speed Video Display for Air Traffic Control Rooms

COSSOR Ranging wider every day.

COSSOR ELECTRONICS LIMITED, AVIATION & SURFACE ELECTRONICS DIVISION,
THE PINNACLES, HARLOW, ESSEX, ENGLAND.
TELEPHONE: HARLOW 26862 TELEX: 81228 CABLES: COSSOR, HARLOW.

CONCORDE

AEROSPATIALE ...AN AIRCRAFT FOR EACH STAGE

AIRBUS A 300 B

NORD 262 serie C

NORD 262 SERIES C

THE NORD 262 SERIES C, A NEW 29-PASSENGER PROP-JET TRANSPORT AVAILABLE TODAY FOR COMMUTER REQUIREMENTS OF THE SEVENTIES.
It is backed by the 200,000 operational hours of its predecessor NORD 262 now in airline service in France, the United States and 9 other countries over 4 continents.
This advanced and more powerful version was designed specifically to cope with the rapid growth of 3rd level traffic with the immediate capability of offering profits on low density routes.
Due to its rugged design and remarkable performance (FAR PART 25 certification), the NORD 262 SERIES C is adapted to the most difficult operations and can take off under high altitude/temperature conditions with excellent payloads.
AIRLINES ON THE GO... INVESTIGATE THE NORD 262 SERIES C: IT'S A PROFIT-MAKER RIGHT NOW!

AEROSPATIALE (S.N.I.A.S)
37, Bd. de Montmorency
PARIS · 16e · (FRANCE)

DEPARTEMENT VENTE
AVIONS COMMERCIAUX
2 rue Béranger, CHATILLON (FRANCE)

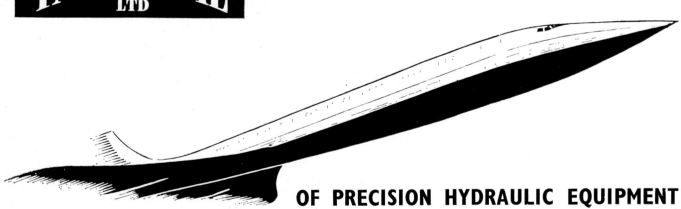

INTRODUCING COLLINS INS-60

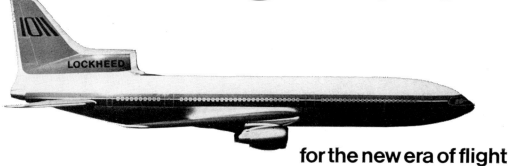

for the new era of flight

Lockheed 1011 operators can be ready for the advanced concepts in Nav/ATC. The INS-60 has been selected for certification on the TriStar.

By starting now with the Collins INS-60 Heading and Attitude System, you can use modular add-ons to keep the L-1011 abreast of developments in area navigation, position reporting, programmed flight plans, high volume waypoint storage, digital integration of avionic capalulities, and Nav system filtering and updating.

This new system provides heading and attitude in just five minutes. After a 15-minute alignment, position readouts are better than 1.5 N.M. per hour C.E.P. The basic system also provides velocity, cross-track, drift angle, and vertical acceleration outputs.

The INS-60 is another example of the engineering and manufacturing excellence achieved with Collins C-System technology.

For more information on this new addition to the most complete line of avionics, contact Collins Radio Company, Cedar Rapids, Iowa 52406.

COLLINS

COMMUNICATION/COMPUTATION/CONTROL

The F-14A's new generator system had to be lightweight and reliable. It's a Bendix IDG.

Our new Integrated-Drive-Generator (IDG) unit is the lightest aircraft generator for its output. Rated 60/75 KVA. Capable of continuous 90 KVA in emergencies. By weight (46 lbs.) and volume, it has the highest specific output of any 400 Hz generator now available. Any wonder this Bendix system was chosen for the Navy/Grumman F-14A?

Our IDG unit is conduction- and spray-cooled by engine oil. Which improves heat transfer 2.5:1 over conventional oil-cooled generators. Reliable? Its test record proves it. Even through a 1,000-hour endurance test.

The Bendix IDG generator for advanced aircraft and helicopter applications. For lightweight, high performance, it has to be Bendix. For complete information, contact: Bendix International, 605 Third Avenue, New York, New York 10016.

The complete F-14A electric power system includes IDG generator; solid state control unit for regulation/control functions; and current transformer assembly which signals feeder faults to control unit.

Bendix International

JANE'S
ALL THE WORLD'S
AIRCRAFT

FOUNDED BY FRED T. JANE IN 1909

COMPILED AND EDITED BY
JOHN W. R. TAYLOR F.R.Hist.S., A.F.R.Ae S., F.S.L.A.E.T.

1970 - 71

S.B.N. 354 000 675

JANE'S YEARBOOKS

LONDON
SAMPSON LOW, MARSTON & Co. LTD.

When you are flying, it is odds we of Philips are helping you travel.

The navigator of your plane may receive traffic control instructions over Philips radio. Probably the stream of messages racing ahead of your plane is routed by Philips switching centres. To keep up with the dizzy growth of aviation, extreme sophistication in electronic equipment is needed. We make that equipment, computers to make your flight safer, to make seat reservation a matter of minutes, to guide you quickly through a crowded departure hall. And switching equipment to organise national weather reporting traffic. After 40 years of cooperation with aviation we feel proud to say: It's Philips telecommunication that keeps things going.

In air communication and aerotronics Philips offer: radio equipment ranging from HF to microwave, multiplex equipment, telegraph and data switchers, telephone exchanges, Mobilophone, computerised equipment for passenger and load handling (AIRLORD), computerised ATC systems (SATCO), and controllers' positions.

It's telecommunication that keeps things going.
N.V. Philips' Telecommunicatie Industrie, P.O. Box 32, Hilversum, Holland.

PHILIPS

It's telecommunication that keeps things going

6940E

JANE'S ALL THE WORLD'S AIRCRAFT
1970-71

The Editor has been assisted in the compilation of this edition as follows:

Kenneth Munson	AIRCRAFT SECTION, THE ARGENTINE TO THE UNITED KINGDOM
David Mondey	AIRCRAFT SECTION, UNITED STATES OF AMERICA, SAILPLANES
W. T. Gunston	AERO-ENGINES
Michael Taylor	METRIC CONVERSIONS
Maurice Allward	SATELLITE DATA

CONTENTS

FOREWORD

AIRCRAFT

DRONES

SAILPLANES

MILITARY MISSILES

RESEARCH ROCKETS AND SPACE VEHICLES

AERO-ENGINES

INDEX

A WIDE RANGE OF PRODUCTS IN USE THROUGHOUT THE WORLD

Single and twin-engined general aviation aircraft; commercial and military trainers; STOL observation aircraft; a fast helicopter; engines — these are the programmes which SIAI has in production or under development today. They cover a wide spectrum of application but all have one thing in common; they were conceived to satisfy the greatest number of users throughout the world.

Markets for training aircraft have been found as far apart as Zambia and Belgium; private aircraft from Australia to America. New-technology products in the course of development will find equally wide application in the years to come. These are some — but not all — of the activities which have made the name of SIAI MARCHETTI famous today. The company is also involved in many other major national aerospace programmes and performs maintenance and overhaul tasks for the armed forces of various countries to keep their aircraft flying. SIAI MARCHETTI is a name steeped in aeronautical history and the value of this tradition is confirmed by its present range of activities.

FOREWORD

SELDOM have so many decisions and events which are vital to the future of the aviation industry been packed into so short a period as the first seven months of 1970. When the year began, many manufacturers in the United States and Britain, in particular, had reason to view the new decade of the 'seventies with foreboding. There was no marked reduction in the demand for transport aircraft to re-equip the airlines; but the Boeing 747, first of the "jumbos", was experiencing a frustrating series of engine problems, traced eventually to insufficiently rigid mountings, while in Britain the Government seemed in no hurry to decide whether or not to order the BAC Three-Eleven airbus into production.

In vain did leaders of the UK industry point out that a commercial project as large as the Three-Eleven was vital to the future of the nation's aviation business. The aircraft industry had never been popular with the Labour Government of Mr Wilson, and the situation was destined to become worse before revealing the slightest sign of improvement.

Hopes that a British lightplane business would be re-established by Beagle were fast disappearing. Outstanding orders on 1 January 1970 were for 16 twin-engined B.206 Series IIs, 267 Pups and 71 Bulldog military trainers, with options on 45 more Bulldogs. This was a pleasing backlog for a small manufacturer on this side of the Atlantic. Unfortunately, according to a speech in Parliament, Pups had been selling at a unit price of £4,350 to £5,350 but cost over £6,000 each to produce. These were not the kind of results HM Government had anticipated when it took over the company in August 1968 to ensure the continuation of light aircraft development and production in the UK. There were more profitable ways of investing official funds and it had been decided in late 1969 to let Beagle die.

In the event, this did not herald the end of all the company's products. The Bulldog programme, for example, was taken over by Scottish Aviation Ltd; but the Beagle facilities at Shoreham were about to be acquired by Miles Aviation and Transport as this edition of *Jane's* closed for press, leaving only 30 Pups and about a dozen B.206s still to be sold before the last traces of Beagle itself were swept away.

Even more sad was the fate of Handley Page, the first company in the world formed specifically for the manufacture of aeroplanes and one of the cornerstones of Britain's aviation industry ever since. Within weeks of celebrating its sixtieth birthday, on 17 June 1969, it was announced that the company was without financial resources and had gone into liquidation. A ray of hope had appeared on 24 October, when the K. R. Cravens Corporation of St Louis, Missouri, USA, formed a new British subsidiary named Handley Page Aircraft Ltd to carry on the former company's activities. With the H.P.137 Jetstream light transport gaining acceptance—and despite cancellation of the projected C-10A military model for the USAF—it seemed that all might yet be well. Work began on new Series 200 and 300 versions of the Jetstream with uprated engines and other improvements. Existing aircraft were modified to serve as prototypes for the new models, with the first production Jetstream 200/300 scheduled to follow in May 1970. Long before then, on 27 February, Handley Page Aircraft Ltd had to announce that it was unable to meet its financial obligations; on 2 March the Radlett works was closed, and on 17 July the majority of the company's machine tools were auctioned off for a modest £250,000. So, yet another old and famous name passed into history.

It was against this background that surviving manufacturers had to await a decision on the BAC Three-Eleven, and wonder how the future of the Concorde might be affected by financial economies in France and the US decision (soon copied elsewhere) that supersonic airline flying over its territory would be forbidden until something had been done to alleviate the problem of the sonic boom.

Other joint programmes were no happier. Of the four original partners in the Panavia multi-role combat aircraft (MRCA) project, the Netherlands had already pulled out. Germany then let it be known that it no longer wanted the single-seater that had been projected in close support and air superiority versions for the *Luftwaffe* and Italy. Instead, it would restrict its initial requirement to a maximum of 420 two-seaters, generally similar to the RAF's interdictor/strike version, of which 385 are planned to be built. This left Italy out on what promised to be a costly limb, unless it switched to the sort of aircraft it did not really want. Nobody was surprised, therefore, when it was announced on 23 July 1970 that only the Governments of Great Britain and the Federal Republic of Germany had signed the Memorandum of Understanding that would initiate the construction of prototypes.

As the old nursery rhyme says, "then there were two". Those who had been critical of the MRCA from the start could well conjecture how long it might be before Germany, too, left the team, so that—with only the RAF's needs to consider—the MRCA could be scaled up into the longer-range, more extensively equipped TSR.2 successor that the British Services *really* wanted from the start. This is unkind. It is believed that Italy will sign the Memorandum later, but will take a smaller number of aircraft than originally planned.

As if this were not enough, the Anglo-French helicopter programme also passed through a difficult period. Chiefly involved was the Westland WG.13, which was being developed in four basic versions, comprising an all-weather general-purpose machine for the British Army, frigate-borne anti-submarine versions for the Navies of both countries, and an extensively-redesigned armed reconnaissance model for the French Army.

The French now cancelled their Army WG.13s, thereby cutting very considerably their involvement in the only one of many Anglo-French aircraft programmes in which a British manufacturer is design leader. Fuel was added to a rather delicate international situation by a report that the head of the French Fleet Air Arm, Vice-Admiral Jacques Thabaud, had told members of the Cercle des Relations Publiques de l'Aéronautique et de l'Espace in Paris that because the needs of the French Navy, Army and Air Force were not compatible, and the British and French Governments had different policies, the WG.13 (of which the French Navy wanted 80) would also prove too expensive, at Fr 12 million (£900,000) per aircraft.

Westland felt constrained to put out an official statement to the effect that "This figure (£900,000) is entirely incorrect. Based on the programme as it now stands, the price of the WG.13 is one quarter of this figure, including allowance for the fixed costs of development and tooling, which vary with the total numbers built".

The boat had, however, been rocked; and hurt feelings in Britain were not improved when a much respected French aviation magazine implied in July that it was unrealistic of the British Government to consider backing development of both the Rolls-Royce RB.211 turbofan engine and the Three-Eleven as a competitor to the A 300B European Airbus, especially at a time when it was negotiating to enter the Common Market. While admitting that it had to recognise the strong international position of Rolls-Royce in the aero-engine field, it proclaimed that the French aerospace industry had become the European pivot so far as airframes, helicopters, certain types of missiles, space research and various categories of equipment are concerned.

If this is the mistaken impression that thirteen disastrous years of indecision and wrong decisions on aerospace matters by successive British Governments have created, one can only hope that it will be remedied quickly by the new Government headed by Mr Heath. Nobody wanted hasty decisions in a first "hundred dynamic days" that would be regretted over the next 1,500 undynamic days; but there is an urgent need for statements on official support for the Three-Eleven, the future of British United Airways as a second-force airline (merged with Caledonian or someone else), the extent of the nation's renewed military commitment "East of Suez", and views on the future need for aircraft carriers equipped with squadrons of fixed-wing aircraft.

Perhaps in the time that will elapse between the writing of this Foreword and its publication some of the questions will be answered. It would be unwise to anticipate which way the decisions will go. Suffice it to say that a visit made by the Editor to the RAF Staff College showed that aircraft carriers continue to be involved as indispensible aids to the success of most of the "war games" studied there—with a carrier-borne version of the VTOL Harrier offering very definite attractions. Nor is it insignificant that the aircraft industries of Germany and France (the European "pivot") felt it essential to retain Hawker Siddeley as subcontractor for the all-important wing of the A 300B Airbus, and as design consultant for the entire A 300B project, with further responsibilities for marketing and after-sales support, after the UK Government withdrew from the programme. There could be no better admission of the unrivalled experience and skill that this British company can contribute to such a transport development project.

Strangely enough, the French themselves are already producing an aircraft that will cut into the A 300B's market. The Dassault Mercure, scheduled to fly early in 1971, is considerably smaller, with a maximum of 155 seats compared with 296 in the European Airbus; but this can only make it more attractive to some airlines. Similarly, Dassault's Mirage G8 must be considered as a potential alternative to the MRCA for countries like Italy and even Germany. Now that the French Air Force have decided that they cannot afford the more sophisticated G4, except as a prototype, Dassault can be relied upon to push the G8 hard in order to perpetuate the success achieved so deservedly by the delta-wing Mirage III and 5 in the world market.

One important decision taken just as this edition of *Jane's* closed for press already foreshadows big future contracts for the Dassault/ Breguet group. Together with Dornier of Germany, they entered their TA 501 Alpha Jet design (see Addenda) in competition with the Aérospatiale/MBB E 650 Eurotrainer and all-German VFW-Fokker VF T 291 to meet *Armée de l'Air/Luftwaffe* requirements for a new subsonic basic and advanced training aircraft. With initial requirements likely to total 400 machines, and about 900 Magisters needing replacement throughout the world in the coming decade, the Alpha Jet should be assured of a good potential market.

Another important European design competition produced its official recommendations at about the same time. This was a wholly-German affair, under which six very different designs had been submitted to meet *Luftwaffe* and Lufthansa specifications for the sort of V/STOL transports they considered they might need in the late 'seventies. The Government committee under Dr Karl Thalau that had been appointed to evaluate the studies eventually chose the Dornier Do 231 (also described in Addenda). This was not altogether surprising, in view of the considerable success

The history of aviation can be reckoned in Flight years. From virtually the beginning—from before even Jane's appeared—Flight has been a crucial part of the flying scene. Its technical authority is such that its features (in particular, the famous cutaway drawings) are used as basic reference material by manufacturers, and the Services airlines the world over. And there is hardly an illustrated magazine anywhere that has not used the Flight photographic library, started when the first aeroplanes flew.

But the contemporary world of aerospace can be reckoned in Flight years too. So many developments have been reported first and fullest in Flight that it has become one of the world's main sources of authoritative information on all areas of space technology and missile development.

Every week Flight carries news and expert opinion from all over the world, and every week, it is read all over the world, in every country where there are aerospace interests, commercial, civil, government or military.

The air age is turning into the space age before our eyes, but Flight International is keeping its readers where they have always been

Flight Years Ahead

FLIGHT INTERNATIONAL
EVERY THURSDAY 2s 6d

already achieved by the earlier Do 31 E. However, this latter aircraft was excruciatingly noisy and considerable research would be needed to make it more acceptable for commercial use. Meanwhile, the *Luftwaffe* has apparently let it be known that it prefers the VFW VC 400/500 tilt-wing concept in certain respects and, anyway, there is considerable doubt that the Federal Government will find money to build any of the contenders.

The Hawker Siddeley Harrier combat aircraft thus remains the only entirely practical V/STOL fixed-wing design in service, or even scheduled for service, anywhere in the world. The prototype of Germany's VFW-Fokker VAK 191B was completed in time for display at the 1970 Hanover Air Show, but had not flown at the time of writing and is currently intended as nothing more than a test-bed for equipment likely to go into the MRCA. The Harrier, on the other hand, is in initial production for the US Marine Corps, and goes from strength to strength in RAF service. Those who predicted its uselessness for anything but short-range hops, around its home base, have been confounded by flights to Cyprus by the aircraft of No 1 Squadron. Weapon firing and dropping trials have gone well, and two Harriers have carried out deck operations from HMS *Eagle* which left little doubt of the future potential of small fast Harrier-carriers on the lines of Russia's *Moskva*.

At the moment, the *Moskva* is equipped only with Kamov Ka-25 helicopters, but there are frequent suggestions in the press that these will give way one day to developments of the crude Yakovlev VTOL aircraft (NATO code-name "Freehand") seen at the 1967 Domodedovo Display. Meanwhile, other rumours of MiG-23s being in squadron service, and even being sent to Egypt, have lacked confirmation.

There has, however, been one interesting newcomer in the Soviet air forces, in the shape of "May", of which details appear for the first time in this edition of *All the World's Aircraft*. No photographs are yet available, but "May" is known to be a maritime patrol version of the Ilyushin Il-18, bearing the same relationship to this airliner as the US Navy's Lockheed P-3 Orion bears to the Electra turboprop transport from which it has evolved. Not many "Mays" are thought to be in service, but, like the AWACS "Moss', illustrated for the first time in *Jane's* last year, it probably reflects growing Soviet capability in the electronics field.

Increasingly complex electronic systems are essential for defence against the missile-carrying nuclear submarines and MRCA type of high-speed low-flying tactical strike aircraft which are the spearheads of modern attack. It is, therefore, no surprise that the US Department of Defense has at last made up its mind to order a counterpart to the Soviet "Moss". The whole original concept of the AWACS (Airborne Warning and Control System) aircraft was, in fact, American and dates back to the early 'fifties; but the USAF took a very long time to choose between the current Boeing and McDonnell Douglas design studies, based on the Model 707 and DC-8 jet transports respectively. Final preference has gone to the Boeing aircraft. No details have yet been released officially, but the basic design study showed a turbofan development of the standard airliner, with a Hawkeye-type "saucer" radome mounted atop sweptforward rhomboidal vertical tail surfaces and a cabin filled with electronic control and reporting stations.

The two main purposes of an AWACS aircraft are (a) to locate an incoming air attack and direct interceptor fighters to deal with it, and (b) to provide airborne control for every kind of tactical air operation, from close support and interdiction to helicopter supply and casevac, and flight refuelling rendezvous.

Boeing will undoubtedly welcome the AWACS contract, as its jet transport assembly lines are at last beginning to run down after fifteen incredible years. It seems only a short while since one US airline chief, alarmed at the costliness and inevitable headaches of the jet transport spending spree initiated by Pan American's pioneer contract for the Boeing 707 in 1955, bemoaned: "We are buying airplanes that haven't yet been fully designed, with millions of dollars we don't have, and are going to operate them off airports that are too small, in an air traffic control system that is too slow, and we must fill them with more passengers than we have ever carried before".

We know now that such fears were unfounded. By the time the 707 and DC-8 entered service, the airlines, airports and air traffic control staff were all capable of coping with the "big jets". As a result, Boeing alone sold well over 2,000 jet transports in fifteen years (exclusive of more than 800 military KC-135s), made up of 691 Model 707s, 154 Model 720s, 837 Model 727s, 270 Model 737s and 200 Model 747s. And, of course, a 747 costs about four times as much as the early 707 and can carry nearly four times as many passengers—although it will have to wait for increased traffic before displaying its full potential. Meanwhile, it is replacing 707s on a one-to-two basis initially.

Big snag in 1970 has been that the delivery of US present-generation airliners has almost overtaken orders. It had to happen eventually. So, although three-quarters of the big 747s remained to be delivered in mid-1970, all but five of the 707/720 family, 38 of the 727s and 21 of the 737s then ordered had already left the Boeing factories. This helps to explain why the AWACS order was such a godsend to the company.

It also explains why Boeing's nationwide payroll declined by about 33,000 to 75,000 between June 1969 and June 1970. This

may still sound a goodly current total, especially with the prospect of increases as the Model 2707-300 supersonic transport programme gathers momentum. The major problem is that the people laid off in tens of thousands do not find it easy to get employment in the aviation industry. McDonnell Douglas's 99,116 employees on 30 June 1970 represented a drop of more than 20,000 in a year and the same kind of story can be told by virtually all the major US companies.

The manufacturers of light aircraft, business-planes and light transports have been hit as hard as the big companies by the general recession in America. Cutbacks in production were supplemented in the first half of 1970 by temporary closure of some production facilities and abandonment of plans to develop certain new projects.

Butler Aviation absorbed Mooney and Ted Smith Aircraft, but decided to relinquish Mooney's licence agreement to assemble and sell the Japanese Mitsubishi MU-2 turboprop business aircraft. The MU-2 will not be lost to the US market as Mitsubishi has a US subsidiary which has taken over Mooney's responsibilities. Other types affected by the recession have been less fortunate. Production of Enstrom's attractive little F-28 helicopter ended early in 1970; Pacaero decided to abandon their PAC-1 twin-turboprop 28-seat commuter airliner, and the possibilities of the General Aircraft Corporation's four-turboprop STOL GAC-100 ever seeing the light of day seem to be diminishing.

As happens so often nowadays, the disappointing news concerning the GAC-100 is having widespread repercussions as far away as Australia, where all seemed clear for the Government Aircraft Factories to manufacture 100 sets of wings and engine nacelles for the aircraft. It was to be a well-organised operation, with the GAF providing all tooling and Qantas flying the finished components to the USA at an initial rate of four sets per month. Coupled with the news in mid-1970 that the Royal Australian Air Force had abandoned further work on the AA-107 advanced trainer/ strike aircraft, proposed jointly by Commonwealth Aircraft Corporation and British Aircraft Corporation, this has left the Australian aircraft industry sorely in need of new programmes.

The attitude of the RAAF is understandable. The AA-107 was intended to supersede the aging Sabre in the gap between the MB.326H basic trainer and combat types. Unfortunately, the RAAF cannot be sure at present what will replace the Mirage as its next interceptor, or what its financial liabilities are likely to be, following problems with the "swing-wing" General Dynamics F-111C which was intended to form its major strike equipment in the 'seventies. Until the F-111 overcomes its setbacks, the RAAF is having to make do with 24 F-4E Phantoms offered by an embarrassed USA to maintain the effectiveness of its South-east Asian ally. But this provides just one more illustration of how difficulties encountered by a major manufacturer can cause serious related problems half a world away.

It is too early to suggest what might be the ultimate fate of the F-111. When the Australian Defence Minister, Mr Frazer, reported to Parliament on 12 May, the greater part of the American F-111 fleet was still grounded because of difficulties with the wing carry-through box and D6AC steel used in the airframe. The Minister said that "Unless these problems are solved, the aircraft will be unacceptable to Australia as a result of the present shortfalls in performance and doubts about structural reliability." There are no doubt daily sighs of relief in Seattle, following Boeing's decision to switch from a "swing-wing" to a delta for its Model 2707-300 SST.

The trump card held by the US industry is that it is so big and so vital to the nation's wellbeing that it can expect to survive virtually any crisis. The worst that ever seems likely to happen is that one of the major concerns (like Douglas in 1967) will build up so many problems that it is compelled to merge with a less troubled or more businesslike partner. If this leads to a group as strong and forward thinking as McDonnell Douglas, nobody has much to complain about.

Latest product of the group, rolled out on 23 July 1970, a few days before this Foreword was written, is the DC-10, first of a new generation of wide-bodied tri-jet or twin-jet transports that will eventually include also the Lockheed TriStar, A 300B, Mercure and, perhaps, the Three-Eleven. With orders and options for 214 DC-10s already received from 12 airlines by that date, the Douglas part of the group can face the future with considerable confidence, despite its loss of the AWACS contract. The McDonnell sector, at St Louis, should be equally happy, with the USAF's F-15 air superiority fighter programme to follow the tremendously successful Phantom, and a licensing link with Hawker Siddeley that gives it the opportunity of building the world's most exciting combat aircraft, the V/STOL Harrier.

The AWACS and F-15 contracts represent only two of the major new programmes that the US Services have been able to launch fairly recently, to ensure the continued maintenance of their present high degree of capability into the 'eighties and, at the same time, to inject a measure of stability into their aircraft industry in a difficult period. The F-15 has its naval counterpart in the Grumman F-14, another twin-jet fighter with the kind of twin-fin tail unit pioneered by the Soviet MiG-23. But whereas the F-15 has a fixed wing reminiscent of that of the Phantom, the F-14 is having another attempt at making the "swing-wing" formula work.

Since 1942, almost 70,000 General Electric jet engines have been built to power 83 different aircraft

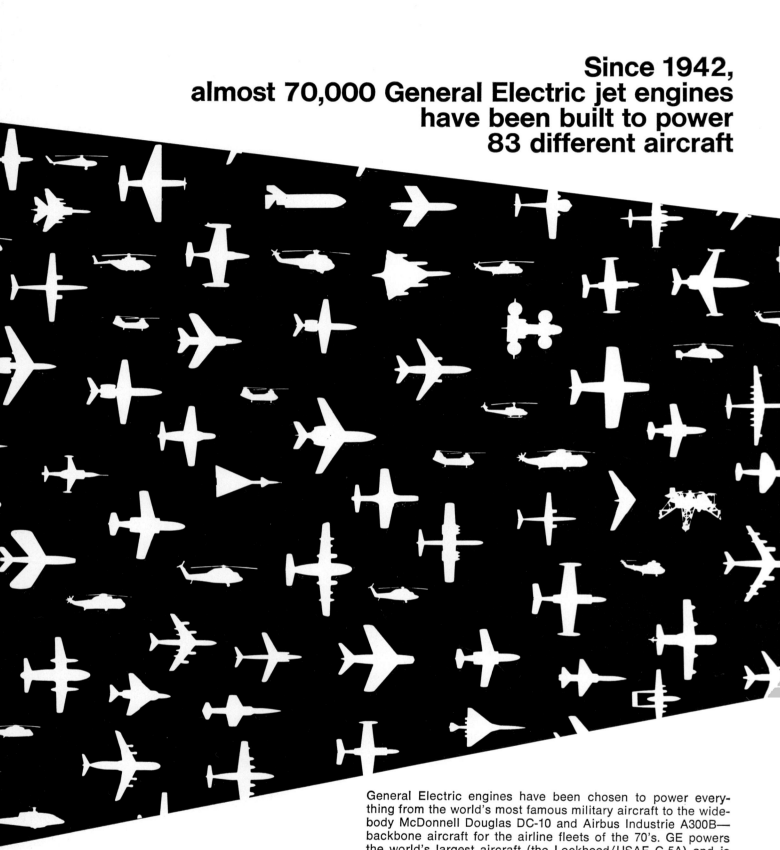

205-73B

General Electric engines have been chosen to power everything from the world's most famous military aircraft to the wide-body McDonnell Douglas DC-10 and Airbus Industrie A300B—backbone aircraft for the airline fleets of the 70's. GE powers the world's largest aircraft (the Lockheed/USAF C-5A) and is the world's leading manufacturer of engines for large turbine-powered helicopters in scheduled airline service and for business jets. And GE engines will power the Boeing-built U.S. SST scheduled to enter airline service in the 1970's. The result? The experience needed to meet any aircraft propulsion requirement. **AIRCRAFT ENGINE GROUP**

GENERAL ELECTRIC
U.S.A.
Reg. Trademark

Both of these fighters will include in their armament new close-range "dogfighting" missiles, proved essential in the air-to-air engagements in Vietnam, and the F-15 at least can be expected to repeat the huge success of the Phantom in the export/licence manufacture field.

Another potential big-seller is the S-3A anti-submarine aircraft which Lockheed are developing to replace the US Navy's S-2 Tracker. But the most exciting new project launched in recent months is the B-1A strategic bomber which the USAF has ordered from North American Rockwell.

The award was so recent, and the project so advanced and complex, that few details have been made available in time for this edition of *All the World's Aircraft*. The only picture which North American has been allowed to release is admitted to be of only a representative design, with "swing-wings", an area-ruled fuselage, conventional tail and diminutive foreplanes. The four General Electric F101 augmented turbofan engines are shown in side-by-side pairs in ducts under the fixed inner portion of each wing; and a crew of four is specified.

Intended to replace the B-52 and B-58, the B-1A project is likely to cost the US taxpayers a total of $12,000 million (£5,000 million) over the next decade. For their money it is said that they will get a force of aircraft each similar in size to a Boeing 707, with a gross weight of about 360,000 lb (163,300 kg), maximum weapon load of more than 50,000 lb (22,700 kg), maximum speed of around Mach 2.2 at 50,000 ft (15,250 m) and maximum unrefuelled range of 5,300 nm (6,100 miles; 9,800 km). Normal cruising speed is given as Mach 0.85 at high altitude, with supersonic over-the-target dash at high or low altitude.

North American experience with the big Mach 3 XB-70A Valkyrie and Mach 6.72 X-15A-2 research aircraft should reap its due rewards in the B-1A programme, which is scheduled to get the first of five flying prototypes (supplemented by two structure test airframes) into the air by the Summer of 1974.

So, during the past two years, the USAF and US Navy have launched programmes that will give them a largely new and extremely formidable range of aircraft for attack and defence in the late 'seventies, to the satisfaction of the US aircraft industry. What, meanwhile, has been happening in the Soviet Union?

At one time, not so very long ago, the Soviet section of *Jane's* seemed to stagnate between massive revelations at Aviation Day displays, several years apart. This is no longer the case, and the diligent seeker of significant facts and figures will find a wealth of important new information in this edition. Dimensions, weights and performance figures for several major front-line combat types are given for the first time. New versions of others have been introduced, including the much-uprated "Fishbed-J" version of the MiG-21 fighter that equips Soviet units operating side-by-side with the home air force in Egypt.

There are references to Be-12 (M-12) maritime amphibians now supplementing Soviet Tu-16 bombers in the same troubled corner of the Mediterranean. What is not made quite so apparent is the gradual hold which the Soviet Union is getting over the Middle East and entire Southern coastline of the Mediterranean, from Morocco to the Red Sea state of Yemen, following the coup in Libya. It is easy to overlook such moves when the USA is so preoccupied in South-east Asia and there are the squabbles on the Sino-Soviet border to distract attention; but they are enormously significant to the future balance of power.

Only in the missile sphere do the current US/Soviet strategic arms limitation talks (SALT) appear to have had the slightest effect so far. Neither nation has progressed greatly with its cripplingly expensive anti-missile defences, despite the continued build-up of ICBM potential by both sides. Photographs taken by US electronic and special reconnaissance aircraft over the Pacific have revealed the progress that Russia, like America, is making towards the perfection of multiple independently-targetable re-entry vehicles (MIRV) for its ICBMs. But the world derives a strange feeling of peace from the fact that the two super powers have available the means to ensure the mutual annihilation of each other, and almost everyone else, at the push of a button. And the US Secretary of Defense can afford to keep projected new weapons like the Navy's advanced undersea long-range missile system (ULMS) as a bargaining item in his "hip pocket" against any lack of enthusiasm for continuation of the SALT meetings.

ULMS, the American "dog-fight" missiles, Israel's effective-looking Gabriel ship-to-ship missile and China's strategic missiles and song-singing satellite all make a first appearance in this edition. So do a host of less warlike products, ranging from the fascinating little control-wing flying-boat of Mr Spratt to the new high-density Il-62M version of Russia's standard long-range jet transport.

The re-alignment of the French aircraft industry, following formation of the Aérospatiale consortium, is reflected for the first time. Similar amalgamations in Italy are underway, with Aeritalia scheduled to become a key national concern in 1971 and new companies like General Avia and Umbra forming to feed and strengthen the industry as a whole.

News-making events of the year, such as the return of the crippled Apollo 13 spacecraft from the Moon, which was followed by an estimated 800 million TV viewers, have their place in this edition.

Comprehensive and authentic coverage of the world's aircraft, missiles and rockets is enhanced by the addition of performance data in knots and nautical miles throughout the book—an innovation which added immensely to the work of Michael Taylor (who again was responsible for all metric conversions) but will be welcomed by technical and professional users of *Jane's*.

Other, smaller changes have been made to improve the quick-reference characteristics of the book, such as transfer of wing chord and aspect ratio figures from the "Wings" descriptive paragraph to the "Dimensions, external" section of each entry.

A more noticeable change is the omission of the sections on the world's airlines, airports, ground equipment, navigation and control systems, and directory of equipment manufacturers which appeared in last year's Diamond Jubilee edition. There are several sound reasons for this. In particular, they made the book too large and heavy for easy everyday use and their continued inclusion would have necessitated an increase in retail price. It is clear that the majority of people who buy *Jane's* are concerned with the "ironmongery" rather than who uses it, where, and the equipment needed to service it at airports, and would prefer not to pay more for information they don't really want. As a result these sections, referred to in last year's book as a "Bonus", have gone—maybe to reappear eventually in a new *Jane's* book for a generally different market, as did the air cushion vehicles which lifted themselves very successfully from *All the World's Aircraft* into *Jane's Surface Skimmers*.

To offset such losses, the reader will find this year greatly increased coverage of aircraft built in parts of the world that have not featured very prominently as aviation design and manufacturing centres in recent years—such as the Argentine, Brazil, Denmark, Finland, New Zealand and Romania. This kind of entry results from the conscientious help given by friends and correspondents like Alex Reinhard in the Argentine, Ronaldo Olive in Brazil, Hans Kofoed in Denmark, Eino Ritaranta in Finland, Wolfgang Wagner of *Deutscher AeroKurier* in Germany and D. P. Henderson in New Zealand.

Increasingly, *Jane's* continues to forge strong links of friendship and co-operation with the aviation press of the entire world. It would be impossible to acknowledge everyone who has supplied facts, figures and photographs this year, but again much help has come from Pierre Sparaco of *Aviation et Astronautique* (Belgium), Janusz Babiejczuk of the *Biuletyn Informacyjny Instytutu Lotnictwa* (Poland), Ann Tilbury of *Flight International* (UK), the Editorial Staffs of *Air et Cosmos* and *Aviation Magazine* (France), *Letectvi Kosmonautika* (Czechoslovakia) and *Aviation Week and Space Technology* (USA), the staff of Tass in Moscow and London, Iris Smith of the Novosti Press Agency, and NASA in the USA. Howard Levy, Jean Seele and Peter Bowers again helped to ensure the fullest possible coverage of US "home-builts". Vico Rosaspina, Eiichiro Sekigawa and Dr Ulrich Haller sent their now customary, highly detailed batches of material to update the Italian, Japanese and Swiss sections respectively. Gordon Swanborough provided a wealth of valuable up-to-the-minute data to help ensure, so far as possible, that nothing relevant was omitted; and Dennis Punnett again coped with incessant demands for new three-view drawings of the highest possible standard in the shortest possible time.

To all of these friends and colleagues go my sincere thanks. Most of all, it gives me pleasure to record my immense gratitude for the enthusiastic and untiring efforts of our little team of Assistant Compilers—Kenneth Munson, David Mondey, Maurice Allward, W. T. Gunston and Michael Taylor. There was so little new in the "Airships" field this year that no reference to lighter-than-air craft appears; but the Lord Ventry has kept in close touch with the Editor throughout the year and there will, undoubtedly, be interesting developments to report in future editions. Parts of the many fine entries on aero-engines produced by Kenneth Fulton for the *Jane's* Supplements to *Flying Review International* have also been embodied in the "Aero-Engines" section of this edition.

As *Jane's All the World's Aircraft* goes to press for the first time in the 'seventies, it is clear that the future already promises much excitement and interest. To new aircraft under development can be added lunar roving vehicles already being produced by Boeing for exploration of the Moon, piggy-back shuttle craft that are being evolved to ferry men and supplies to Earth-orbiting space stations, spacecraft that will photograph Mercury in 1973 and set out later for a nine-year Grand Tour of the most distant planets of our solar system. Who could wish to have been born in any other period of history?

August 1970   J. W. R. T.

PHOTOGRAPHS

The Editor and Publishers receive many requests for prints of photographs that appear in *Jane's*. It is not possible for them to offer any form of photographic service; but photographs of a high proportion of the aircraft described in this edition, as well as of many earlier types, are available at normal trade rates from:—

Flight International, Dorset House, Stamford Street, London SE1

Stephen P. Peltz, 5 Twyford Avenue, East Finchley, London N2.

Air Portraits, 5 Drummond Road, Bordesley Green, Birmingham 9.

AIRCRAFT

(CORRECTED TO 1 AUGUST 1970)

SOME FIRST FLIGHTS MADE DURING THE PERIOD
1 JULY 1969 — 1 JULY 1970

July 1969
11 MFI-15A (SE-301) (Sweden)
14 Hawker Siddeley Harrier T.Mk 2 (2nd aircraft) (UK)
16 Huneault DHC-1B-2 Chipmunk (IO-360 engine; CF-CYT-X) (Canada)
27 Murrayair MA-1 (N101MA) (New Zealand)
29 C.A.A.R.P. CAP 20 (F-WPXU) (France)
31 Jurca M.J.7 Gnatsum (CF-XZI; Falconar-built) (Canada/France)

August
4 Britten-Norman BN-2A Islander (1st Romanian-built)
8 Kawasaki P-2J (1st production; 4702) (Japan)
9 Fairchild Hiller/Republic F-105D (T-Stick II) (USA)
20 FMA IA 58 Pucará (Argentina)
24 Satoh-Maeda SM-OX (Japan)
26 Swearingen FS-226 Metro (USA)

September
4 Reims-Cessna FA-150 Aerobat (France)
13 Cor Dijkman Dulkes Bravo (Netherlands)
15 Cessna Citation (N500CC) (USA)
17 NAMC YS-11A-400 (Japan)
18 Dassault Mirage F1-03 (France)
20 Slingsby Twin Cadet (G-AXMB) (UK)
26 Aérospatiale/Westland SA 330F (F-WRPH) (France)

October
1 Bücker Bü 133F Jungmeister (Germany)
10 Aviation Traders/Vickers Vanguard Merchantman conversion (G-APEM) (UK)

12 SEPECAT Jaguar S-06 (BAC-built; XW560) (International)
19 IPD/PAR-6504 Bandeirante (2nd prototype; 2131) (Brazil)

November
3 Hawker Siddeley Vulcan test-bed (Olympus 593-3B engines) (UK)
14 SEPECAT Jaguar M-05 (French-built) (International)
15 Maj M-20 Kangur (Poland)
26 Conroy CL-44-O Airlifter (N447T) (USA)
27 IAI-101 Arava (4X-IAI) (Israel)
28 National Aerospace Laboratory VTOL test-rig (1st tethered flight) (Japan)

December
11 Hawker Siddeley Trident 3B (G-AWYZ) (UK)

January 1970
8 Hawker Siddeley Buccaneer S.Mk 2 (1st new aircraft for RAF) (UK)
23 Cessna Citation (2nd prototype) (USA)
29 Saab-35XD (Sweden)

February
2 Reims-Cessna FT-337 (France)
17 Saab-105Ö (1101) (Sweden)
19 Canadair CL-84-1 (CX8401) (Canada)
19 Siai-Marchetti S.210 (I-SJAP) (Italy)
21 Dassault Mirage F1-02 (1st flight with Atar 09K-50) (France)
21 Grumman A-6E Intruder (USA)
25 Conroy Turbo Albatross (N16CA) (USA)
26 Reims-Cessna F-337 (France)

March
2 Boeing B-52 test-bed (CF6-6 engine) (USA)
5 Sportavia Avion-Planeur RF7 (Germany)
6 Dassault Mirage 5-BA (France)
6 BAC VC10 test-bed (RB.211 engine; G-AXLR) (UK)
13 Aero Spacelines Guppy-101 (N111AS) (USA)
22 Heintz Zénith (F-WPZY) (France)
25 Robin (Centre Est) DR 300/130 (F-WPXX) (France)
26 Nihon University NM-69 Linnet III (Japan)

April
2 Pilatus PC-6-D/H3 Porter (HB-FFW) (Switzerland)
10 McDonnell Douglas A-4M Skyhawk (USA)
12 Polyt V (OY-DHP) (Denmark)
30 HAL HF-24 Marut Mk IT (BD-888) (India)
30 Britten-Norman BN-2A/IO-540 Islander (UK)

May
20 Revathi Mk II (VT-XAH) (India)
24 Reed 1A Rooivalk (ZS-UDU) (South Africa)
25 Partenavia P.68 (I-TWIN) (Italy)
28 Meridionali/Agusta EMA 124 (Italy)
28 Boeing-Vertol Model 347 (USA)
29 Dassault Milan S-01 (France)

June
10 Robin (Centre Est) HR 100-200 (200 hp) (France)
10 California Airmotive Turbo Star 402 (N32850) (USA)
12 SEPECAT Jaguar S-07 (BAC-built; XW563) (International)
17 Dassault Mirage F1-04 (France)
26 IPD/PAR-6504 Bandeirante (3rd prototype; PP-ZCN) (Brazil)

OFFICIAL RECORDS
Corrected to 1 August 1970

WORLD RECORDS

Six absolute records are classed as World Records by the Fédération Aéronautique Internationale and can be achieved by any type of aircraft.

Distance in a straight line (USA)
Major Clyde P. Evely, USAF, in a Boeing B-52H Stratofortress, on 10-11 January 1962, from Okinawa to Madrid, Spain. 12,532·3 miles (20,168·78 km).

Distance in a closed circuit (USA)
Captain William M. Stevenson, USAF, in a Boeing B-52H Stratofortress, on 6-7 June 1962. Seymour Johnson AFB-Bermuda-Sondrestrom (Greenland)-Anchorage (Alaska)-March AFB-Key West-Seymour Johnson AFB. 11,337 miles (18,245·05 km).

Height (USSR)
Lt Col G. Mossolov in an E-66A, on 28 April 1961, at Podmoskovnœ. 113,892 ft (34,714 m).

Height in sustained horizontal flight (USA)
Col Robert L. Stephens and Lt Col Daniel Andre (USAF) in a Lockheed YF-12A, on 1 May 1965, over a 15/25 km course at Edwards AFB, California. 80,257·91 ft (24,462·596 m).

Speed in a straight line (USA)
Col Robert L. Stephens and Lt Col Daniel Andre (USAF) in a Lockheed YF-12A, on 1 May 1965, over a 15/25 km course at Edwards AFB, California. 2,070·102 mph (3,331·507 km/h).

Speed in a closed circuit (USSR)
M. Komarov in a Mikoyan E-266 (MiG-23), on 5 October 1967, at Podmoskovnœ, over a 500-km (310·7 mile) closed circuit. 1,852·61 mph (2,981·5 km/h).

WORLD RECORDS—MANNED SPACECRAFT

Greatest weight lifted (USA)
F. Borman, J. A. Lovell and W. Anders in Apollo 8, on 21-27 December 1968. 282,147 lb (127,980 kg).

Altitude (USA)
F. Borman, J. A. Lovell and W. Anders in Apollo 8, on 21-27 December 1968. 234,673 miles (377,668·9 km)

Endurance in Earth orbit (USA)
F. Borman and J. A. Lovell in Gemini 7, 4-18 December 1965. 330 hr 35 min.
Awaiting confirmation is a new record of 424 hr set up by Andrian Nikolayev and Vitaly Sevastyanov (USSR) in Soyuz 9 on 1-19 June 1970.

Distance in Earth orbit (USA)
F. Borman and J. A. Lovell in Gemini 7, 4-18 December 1965. 5,719,456 miles (9,204,575 km).
Awaiting confirmation is a new record set up by Andrian Nikolayev and Vitaly Sevastyanov in the Soyuz 9 referred to above.

INTERNATIONAL RECORDS

Following are details of some of the more important international records confirmed by the FAI.

Class C, GROUP I (Aeroplanes with piston-engines)
Distance in a straight line (USA)
Cdr Thomas D. Davies, USN, and crew of three in a Lockheed P2V-1 Neptune, on 29 September-1 October 1946, from Perth, Western Australia, to Columbus, Ohio, USA. 11,235·6 miles (18,081·99 km).

Distance in a closed circuit (USA)
James R. Bede in the Bede BD-2, on 7-10 November 1969, between Columbus, Ohio, and Toledo, Ohio, USA. 8,973·3 miles (14,441·26 km).

Height (Italy)
Mario Pezzi, in a Caproni 161*bis*, on 22 October 1938. 56,046 ft (17,083 m).

Speed in a straight line (USA)
Darryl Greenamyer in a modified Grumman F8F-2 Bearcat, on 16 August 1969, at Edwards AFB, California. 482·462 mph (776·449 km/h).

CLASS C, GROUP III (Aeroplanes with jet engines)
Distance in a straight line, distance in a closed circuit, height, speed in straight line and speed in 500 km closed circuit
See "World Records" above.

Speed in a 100 km (62·14 mile) closed circuit (USSR)
Alexander Fedotov in the Mikoyan E.166, on 7 October 1961. Sidorovo-Essino-Verejia-Kakousevo-Vichniakovo-Sidorovo. 1,491·9 mph (2,401 km/h).

Speed in a 1,000 km (621·4 mile) closed circuit (USSR)
P. Ostapenko in a Mikoyan E-266 (MiG-23), on 27 October 1967, at Podmoskovnoe. 1,814·81 mph (2,920·67 km/h).

CLASS C2, ALL GROUPS (Seaplanes)
Distance in a straight line (UK)
Capt D. C. T. Bennett and First Officer I. Harvey, in the Short-Mayo Mercury, on 6-8 October 1938, from Dundee, Scotland, to the Orange River, South Africa. 5,997·5 miles (9,652 km).

Height (USSR)
Georgi Buryanov and crew of two in a Beriev M-10, on 9 September 1961, over the Sea of Azov. 49,088 ft (14,962 m).

Speed in a straight line (USSR)
Nikolai Andrievsky and crew of two in a Beriev M-10, on 7 August 1961, at Joukovsky-Petrovskoe, over a 15/25-km course. 566·69 mph (912 km/h).

CLASS D, GROUP I (Single-seat sailplanes)
DISTANCE in a straight line (USA)
Alvin H. Parker in a Sisu-1A, on 31 July 1964, from Odessa, Texas, to Kimball, Nebraska. 647·17 miles (1,041·52 km).

Height (USA)
Paul F. Bickle, in a Schweizer SGS 1-23E, on 25 February 1961, at Mojave-Lancaster, California. 46,266 ft (14,102 m).

CLASS D, GROUP II (Two-seat sailplanes)
Distance in straight line (USSR)
J. Kuznetsov and J. Barkhamov in a Blanik, on 3 June 1967. 572·87 miles (921·954 km).

Height (USA)
L. E. Edgar and H. E. Klieforth in a Pratt-Read sailplane, on 19 March 1952, at Bishop, California. 44,256 ft (13,489 m).

CLASS E.1 (Helicopters)
Distance in a straight line (USA)
R. G. Ferry in a Hughes OH-6A, on 6-7 April 1966, 2,213 miles (3,561·55 km).

Height (France)
Jean Boulet in a Sud-Aviation S.E. 3150 Alouette, on 13 June 1958, at Brétigny-sur-Orge. 36,027 ft (10,984 m).

Speed in a straight line (France)
Jean Boulet and Roland Coffignot in a Sud-Aviation SA 3210 Super Frelon, on 23 July 1963, over a 15/25-km course. 217·77 mph (350·47 km/h).

Speed in a 100 km closed circuit (USSR)
Boris Galitsky and crew of five in a Mil Mi-6, on 26 August 1964, at Podmoskovnoe. 211·36 mph (340·15 km/h).

CLASS E.2 (Convertiplanes)
Speed in a straight line (USSR)
D. Efremov and crew of five, in the Kamov Ka-22 Vintokryl, on 7 October 1961, at Joukovski-Petrovskœ, over a 15/25-km course. 221·4 mph (356·3 km/h).

Height (USSR)
D. Efremov and crew of two, in the Kamov Ka-22 Vintokryl, on 24 November 1961 at Bykovo. 8,491 ft (2,588 m).

Speed in a 100 km closed circuit (New Zealand)
Sqd Ldr W. R. Gellatly and J. G. P. Morton, in the Fairey Rotodyne, on 5 January 1959, White Waltham-Wickham-Radley Bottom-Kintbury-White Waltham. 190·90 mph (307·22 km/h).

THE ARGENTINE REPUBLIC

AERO BOERO

AERO TALLERES BOERO SRL

HEAD OFFICE:
Boulevard H. Irigoyen 505, Morteros, Córdoba

DIRECTOR: Hector A. Boero

This company is producing two three-seat all-metal light monoplanes, the Aero Boero 95/115 and Aero Boero 180.

In March 1970 the company was nearing completion of the prototype of a new four-seater, the Aero Boero 210, which will have a tricycle landing gear and a 210 hp Continental fuel-injection engine. This was expected to make its first flight in the Summer of 1970.

All three types are described below.

AERO BOERO 95/115

The earlier versions of the Aero Boero 95, as described in the 1969-70 *Jane's*, are no longer in production. They have been replaced by the Aero Boero 95/115, a more refined development with a 115 hp Lycoming O-235 engine, fairings over the main wheels, a more streamlined cowling made of reinforced plastics and aluminium alloy flaps and ailerons. This aircraft made its first flight in March 1969; a C of A was awarded two months later, and production began in July 1969.

The description below applies to this version.

TYPE: Three-seat light aircraft.

WINGS: Braced high-wing monoplane. Wing section NACA 23012. Dihedral 1° 45′. Incidence 3° at root, 1° at tip. Light alloy structure, Ceconite-covered. Streamline-section Vee bracing strut each side. Aluminium alloy ailerons and flaps.

FUSELAGE: SAE 4130 steel-tube structure, Ceconite-covered.

TAIL UNIT: Wire-braced welded steel-tube structure, Ceconite-covered.

LANDING GEAR: Non-retractable tail-wheel type. Shock-absorption by helicoidal springs inside fuselage. Main wheel tyre size 6·00 × 6, pressure 24 lb/sq in (1·69 kg/cm²). Hayes hydraulic brakes. Fully-castoring steerable tail-wheel.

POWER PLANT: One 115 hp Lycoming O-235-C2A four-cylinder horizontally-opposed air-cooled engine, driving either a McCauley 1C90-7345 or a Sensenich 72 CK propeller. Fuel in two tanks in wings, with total capacity of 24 Imp gallons (110 litres).

ACCOMMODATION: Normal accommodation for pilot and two passengers in enclosed cabin. Baggage compartment on port side, aft of cabin.

ELECTRONICS AND EQUIPMENT: One 40A alternator and one 12V battery. Provision for dual controls, crop-dusting and spraying equipment, night or blind-flying equipment and radio, at customer's option.

DIMENSIONS, EXTERNAL:

Wing span	34 ft 2¼ in (10·42 m)
Wing chord (constant)	5 ft 3½ in (1·61 m)
Wing aspect ratio	6·5
Length overall	22 ft 7½ in (6·90 m)
Height overall	6 ft 10½ in (2·10 m)
Wheel track	6 ft 8¾ in (2·05 m)
Wheelbase	16 ft 8¾ in (5·10 m)

AREAS:

Wings, gross	176·1 sq ft (16·36 m²)
Ailerons (total)	20·45 sq ft (1·90 m²)
Flaps (total)	17·98 sq ft (1·67 m²)
Fin	10·76 sq ft (1·00 m²)
Elevators	27·10 sq ft (2·52 m²)

WEIGHTS AND LOADINGS:

Weight empty, equipped	1,080 lb (490 kg)
Max T-O weight	1,697 lb (770 kg)
Max wing loading	9·65 lb/sq ft (47·1 kg/m²)
Max power loading	14·77 lb/hp (6·7 kg/hp)

PERFORMANCE (at max T-O weight, except where indicated):

Max level speed at S/L	113 knots (130 mph; 210 km/h)
Max cruising speed at S/L	102 knots (117 mph; 188 km/h)
Stalling speed, flaps down	26 knots (30 mph; 48 km/h)
Rate of climb at S/L	1,000 ft (300 m)/min
T-O run, full load	380 ft (115 m)
T-O to 50 ft (15 m), two persons	607 ft (185 m)
Landing from 50 ft (15 m)	500 ft (150 m)
Landing run, heavy braking	150 ft (45 m)
Range with max fuel	429 nm (495 miles; 800 km)

AERO BOERO 180

The three-seat Aero Boero 180 is a light, all-purpose aircraft suitable for a wide range of duties, including agricultural use, glider and banner towing and instrument flight training. The first production example was delivered in December 1969.

TYPE: Three-seat light aircraft.

WINGS: Strut-braced high-wing monoplane. Streamline-section Vee bracing strut each side. Wing section NACA 23012. Dihedral 1° 45′. Incidence 3° at root, 1° at tip. Light alloy structure, covered with Ceconite. Ailerons and flaps of aluminium alloy construction.

Aero Boero 95/115 three-seat light aircraft (115 hp Lycoming O-235 engine)

Aero Boero 180 three-seat light aircraft (180 hp Lycoming O-360-A1A engine)

FUSELAGE: Welded steel-tube structure (SAE 4130), covered with Ceconite.

TAIL UNIT: Wire-braced welded steel-tube structure, covered with Ceconite.

LANDING GEAR: Non-retractable tail-wheel type, with shock-absorption by helicoidal springs inside fuselage. Main wheels and tyres size 6·00 × 6, pressure 24 lb/sq in (1·69 kg/cm²). Hayes hydraulic brakes. Tail-wheel steerable and fully castoring.

POWER PLANT: One 180 hp Lycoming O-360-A1A four-cylinder horizontally-opposed air-cooled engine, driving (according to customer's choice) either a Hartzell constant-speed or McCauley 1A200 or Sensenich 76EM8 fixed-pitch propeller. Fuel in two tanks with total capacity of 30 Imp gallons (136 litres).

ACCOMMODATION: Normal accommodation for pilot and two passengers in enclosed cabin. Baggage compartment on port side, aft of cabin.

ELECTRONICS AND EQUIPMENT: One 40A alternator and one 12V battery. Provision for night or blind-flying instrumentation at customer's option.

DIMENSIONS, EXTERNAL:

Wing span	34 ft 2¼ in (10·42 m)
Wing chord (constant)	5 ft 3½ in (1·61 m)
Wing aspect ratio	6·5
Length overall	22 ft 7½ in (6·90 m)
Height overall	6 ft 10½ in (2·10 m)
Wheel track	6 ft 8¾ in (2·05 m)
Wheelbase	16 ft 8¾ in (5·10 m)

AREAS:

Wings, gross	176·1 sq ft (16·36 m²)
Ailerons (total)	20·45 sq ft (1·90 m²)
Flaps (total)	17·98 sq ft (1·67 m²)
Fin	15·93 sq ft (1·48 m²)
Elevators	30·68 sq ft (2·85 m²)

WEIGHTS AND LOADINGS:

Weight empty, equipped	1,212 lb (550 kg)
Max T-O weight	1,861 lb (844 kg)
Max wing loading	10·7 lb/sq ft (52·0 kg/m²)
Max power loading	10·36 lb/hp (4·7 kg/hp)

PERFORMANCE (at max T-O weight, except where indicated):

Max level speed at S/L	132 knots (152 mph; 245 km/h)
Max cruising speed at S/L	114 knots (131 mph; 211 km/h)
Stalling speed, flaps down	26 knots (30 mph; 48 km/h)
Rate of climb at S/L	1,180 ft (360 m)/min
T-O run	330 ft (100 m)
T-O to 50 ft (15 m) with 1 passenger	615 ft (188 m)
Landing from 50 ft (15 m)	195 ft (60 m)
Range with max fuel	429 nm (495 miles; 800 km)

AERO BOERO 210

Design of the Aero Boero 210 four-seat light aircraft was begun in 1968, and a prototype was nearing completion in March 1970. First flight was scheduled to take place in July 1970. All available details of this aircraft follow.

TYPE: Four-seat light aircraft.

WINGS: Monoplane of mixed metal and wood construction, covered with Ceconite. Wing section NACA 23012. Dihedral 1° 45′. Incidence 2° 30′. Electrically-operated all-metal leading-edge flaps and metal ailerons.

FUSELAGE: Conventional semi-monocoque structure of welded steel tube (SAE 4130), with Ceconite covering.

TAIL UNIT: Conventional single fin and rudder of welded steel tube construction, Ceconite covered. Fixed-incidence tailplane. Trim-tab in elevator.

LANDING GEAR: Non-retractable tricycle type, with rubber shock-absorbers. Main wheel tyre pressure 18 lb/sq in (1·27 kg/cm²). Hayes hydraulic brakes on main wheels.

POWER PLANT: One 210 hp Continental IO-360 six-cylinder horizontally-opposed air-cooled fuel-injection engine, driving a two-blade constant-speed propeller. Fuel in two wing tanks with total capacity of 35·2 Imp gallons (160 litres). Refuelling point on top of each wing.

ACCOMMODATION: Seats for pilot and three passengers in enclosed cabin, access to which is provided by a forward-hinged door on each side. All three passenger seats are removable.

SYSTEMS: One 25A generator and one 12V battery.

ELECTRONICS AND EQUIPMENT: Radio optional.

DIMENSIONS, EXTERNAL:

Wing span	34 ft 2¼ in (10·42 m)
Wing chord (constant)	5 ft 3 in (1·60 m)
Wing aspect ratio	6·7
Length overall	24 ft 3¼ in (7·40 m)
Height overall	8 ft 10¼ in (2·70 m)
Tailplane span	11 ft 7¼ in (3·54 m)
Wheel track	7 ft 2¾ in (2·20 m)
Wheelbase	6 ft 1¾ in (1·875 m)
Passenger doors (each):	
Height	3 ft 0 in (0·91 m)
Width	2 ft 7 in (0·79 m)
Baggage door (port, aft):	
Height	1 ft 8 in (0·51 m)
Width	1 ft 8 in (0·51 m)

DIMENSIONS, INTERNAL:

Cabin:	
Max length	5 ft 8 in (1·73 m)
Max width	3 ft 1 in (0·94 m)
Max height	3 ft 11 in (1·19 m)
Floor area	12 sq ft (1·11 m²)
Volume	52 cu ft (1·50 m³)

AREAS:
Wings, gross   176·5 sq ft (16·40 m²)
Ailerons (total)   16·47 sq ft (1·53 m²)
Leading-edge flaps (total)   19·37 sq ft (1·80 m²)
WEIGHTS AND LOADINGS:
Weight empty, equipped   1,256 lb (570 kg)
Max T-O weight   2,425 lb (1,100 kg)

Max wing loading   13·75 lb/sq ft (67 kg/m²)
Max power loading   11·57 lb/hp (5·25 kg/hp)
PERFORMANCE (estimated, at max T-O weight):
Max cruising speed at 5,900 ft (1,800 m)
    122 knots (140 mph; 225 km/h)
Stalling speed, flaps down
    35 knots (40 mph; 64·5 km/h)

Rate of climb at S/L   1,180 ft (360 m)/min
Service ceiling   19,675 ft (6,000 m)
T-O run   330 ft (100 m)
T-O to 50 ft (15 m)   615 ft (188 m)
Landing run   295 ft (90 m)
Range with max fuel
    429 nm (495 miles; 800 km)

AVEX

ASOCIACION ARGENTINA DE CONSTRUCTORES DE AVIONES EXPERIMENTALES

PRESIDENT: Yves Arrambide

AVEX is an Argentine light aircraft association for amateur constructors, similar in concept to the Experimental Aircraft Association in the US. One of AVEX's members, Ing H. Baserga, completed some years ago an aircraft of his own design, known as the H.B.1.

BASERGA H.B.1

This single-seat racing monoplane was designed by Ing Horacio Baserga, with the assistance of Sr Adolfo Yakstas. Construction began in 1952, and was completed in 1959, but the aircraft has not yet been flown.

WINGS: Cantilever low-wing monoplane. Wings of all-wood construction, with dihedral on outer panels and taper on leading- and trailing-edges.

FUSELAGE: All-wood structure of basically rectangular section, with rounded top-decking.

TAIL UNIT: Cantilever all-wood structure, with dorsal fairing on fin. No tabs in rudder or elevators.

LANDING GEAR: Non-retractable tail-wheel type. Cessna-type spring-steel cantilever legs on main units. Steerable tail-wheel.

POWER PLANT: One 45 hp Praga B-2 engine, driving a two-blade propeller.

ACCOMMODATION: Single seat for pilot under fully-transparent sideways-hinged canopy.

DIMENSIONS, EXTERNAL:
Wing span   20 ft 0¼ in (6·10 m)

Baserga H.B.1 single-seat light aircraft (*Alex Reinhard*)

Length overall   15 ft 7 in (4·75 m)
Height overall   5 ft 5¾ in (1·67 m)
AREA:
Wings, gross   63·5 sq ft (5·90 m²)
WEIGHTS AND LOADING:
Weight empty   523 lb (237 kg)
Max T-O weight   772 lb (350 kg)
Max wing loading   12·1 lb/sq ft (59 kg/m²)

PERFORMANCE (estimated, at max T-O weight):
Max level speed
    110 knots (127 mph; 205 km/h)
Max cruising speed
    104 knots (120 mph; 193 km/h)
Stalling speed   52 knots (59 mph; 94·5 km/h)
Service ceiling   13,125 ft (4,000 m)
Max range   270 nm (310 miles; 500 km)
Endurance   2 hr 30 min

CICARELLI

Sr Cicarelli, a mechanic from Polvaredas, near Buenos Aires, has designed, built and flown two small helicopters, all known details of which appear below. In 1969 construction of a third helicopter, the four-seat Cicaré No. 3, was nearing completion.

CICARÉ No 1

Sr Cicarelli's first design is a lightweight single-seat helicopter with an open steel-tube fuselage frame and skid-type landing gear. The 50 hp four-cylinder engine (originally a 30 hp two-cylinder engine was installed) is also designed by Sr Cicarelli, and drives two contra-rotating co-axial two-blade rotors. The rotor head is of the tilting type, but no details are available of the flight controls, which are different from those of a conventional helicopter and are claimed to make the aircraft much easier to fly.

CICARÉ No 2

The Cicaré No 2 is a more conventional helicopter, with a three-blade main rotor and two-blade tail rotor. Power plant is a Lycoming four-cylinder horizontally-opposed air-cooled engine, installed aft of the cabin. Accommodation is for a pilot and one passenger on side-by-side seats, the cabin being fully enclosed except for the absence of doors. A steel-tube skid-type landing gear is fitted, with a small wheel near the rear of each skid for ground manoeuvring. Initial flight tests were completed during 1968.

The Cicaré No 1 (above) and No 2 (below) single-seat light helicopters (*Alex Reinhard*)

AREA DE MATERIAL CÓRDOBA

AGRUPACIÓN AVIONES-DEPARTAMENTO INGENIERIA, GUARNICION AEREA CÓRDOBA

ADDRESS:
Avenida Fuerza Aérea Argentina Km 5½, Córdoba

DIRECTOR:
Brigadier Abelardo Serafin Sangiácomo

CHIEF DESIGNER AND ENGINEER:
Major Héctor Eduardo Ruiz

The original Fábrica Militar de Aviones (Military Aircraft Factory) was founded in 1927 as a central organisation for aeronautical research and production in the Argentine. Its name was changed to Instituto Aerotécnico in 1943 and then to Industrias Aeronáuticas y Mecánicas del Estado (IAME) in 1952. In 1957 it became a State enterprise under the title of Dirección Nacional de Fabricaciones e Investigaciones Aeronáuticas (DINFIA), but reverted to its original title in 1968. It is now a component of the Area de Material Córdoba division of the Argentine Air Force.

FMA comprises two large divisions. The Instituto de Investigaciónes Aeronáuticas y Espacial (IIAE) is responsible for the design, manufacture and testing of rockets, sounding equipment and other equipment. The Fábrica Militar de Aviones itself controls the manufacturing facilities situated in Córdoba City, in which it manufactures aircraft and, since 1952, motor vehicles in quantity. The laboratories, factories and other buildings belonging to these two divisions of FMA occupy a total covered area of 2,831,000 sq ft (263,000 m²), and a total of 8,000 people is employed.

FMA's head offices are situated in Buenos Aires City. It also controls the Centro de Ensayos en Vuelo (Flight Test Centre), to which all aircraft produced in the Argentine are sent for certification tests.

The major aircraft of national design in current production is the turboprop-powered IA 50 Guarani II twin-engined general-purpose monoplane. The FMA is also producing Cessna 182 aircraft under licence, under a five-year agreement announced in October 1965. First phase called for assembly of 80 aircraft from major assemblies supplied by Cessna. Phase 2 involved assembly of 100 aircraft from detail parts provided by Cessna. Phase 3 involves an estimated 320 aircraft, for which FMA is manufacturing or acquiring in the Argentine as many parts as possible. All aircraft are repurchased by Cessna for sale through its distributors and dealers in Latin America or sold directly by FMA to Argentine government agencies.

The first A182J (Argentine 182) was completed in August 1966 from the initial batch of 12 sets of components supplied by Cessna, and was delivered to its owner on 2 September 1966.

Under current development by FMA are the nationally-designed IA 53 agricultural monoplane and IA 58 Pucará counter-insurgency aircraft.

IA 50 GUARANI II

The original FA1 Guarani I was a twin-turboprop light transport designed and built under the direction of Military Aircraft Engineer Major (then Comandante) Héctor Eduardo Ruiz, head of the design team of the Fábrica Militar de Aviones (Aircraft Factory). It utilised about 20% of the structural components of the earlier IA 35 Huanquero and flew for the first time on 6 February 1962. Full details of the Guarani I can be found in the 1962-63 *Jane's*.

From it was developed, by Major Ruiz, the IA 50 (formerly FA2) Guarani II, the first prototype of which flew for the first time on 23 April 1963 and introduced more powerful engines, de-icing equipment, a single swept fin and rudder and a shorter rear fuselage to save weight. A second prototype was then built, followed by a single pre-production machine.

The Guarani II is in production for the Argentine Air Force (FAA). Initial contracts covered the manufacture of 18 standard models for communications duties, four for photographic operations with the Military Geographic Institute and one furnished as an executive transport for use by the President of Argentina. A contract for a further 10 aircraft was placed in October 1969. These will have redesigned internal furnishings, and many of the steel structural components will be replaced by components made of aluminium alloy, to reduce the aircraft's basic empty weight. Thus, with the prototypes and pre-series aircraft, a total of 36 Guarani II's

Guarani II staff transport in the insignia of the Argentine Navy *(Alex Reinhard)*

Version of the Guarani II equipped with skis for Antarctic operation

is being produced. The first two were in service with I Air Brigade at El Palomar by March 1967.

The pre-series machine was fitted with a Bendix M-4 autopilot, to evaluate this equipment. Production aircraft have flight deck windows of modified size and shape, to meet the US Federal Aviation Agency's CAM4B requirements, and provision for wing-tip auxiliary fuel tanks.

The first 18 production aircraft include one VIP transport (serial TX-110), fourteen troop transports (T-111 to T-124) and two photographic and survey aircraft (F-31 and F-32) for the Argentine Air Force; and one staff transport (5-T-30) for the Argentine Navy. The 19th aircraft (T-125) has been fitted with ski landing gear (also designed by Major Ruiz), for use in the Antarctic.

A version of the Guarani II with pressurised cabin and fully-automatic four-blade propellers is also under consideration.

TYPE: Twin-engined light transport.

WINGS: Cantilever low-wing monoplane. Wing section NACA 63₃218 at root, NACA 63₃212 at tip. Dihedral 7° on outer wings only. Incidence 3° at root, 1° at tip. All-metal single-spar structure. Fabric-covered metal ailerons. All-metal split flaps. Automatic trim-tab in each aileron. Kléber-Colombes de-icing system optional.

FUSELAGE: Duralumin semi-monocoque structure.

TAIL UNIT: Cantilever all-metal structure with 52° 30′ sweepback on fin. Variable-incidence sweptback tailplane, with streamline tip fairings. Trim-tab in rudder and each elevator. Kléber-Colombes leading-edge de-icing system optional.

LANDING GEAR: Retractable tricycle type. Hydraulic actuation, all wheels retracting forward. Oleo-pneumatic shock-absorbers of Argentine manufacture. Each main unit fitted with two Dunlop wheels and tubeless tyres size 750 × 10. Single Dunlop nose-wheel with tubeless tyre size 650 × 10. Tyre pressure 45 lb/sq in (3·16 kg/cm²). Dunlop hydraulic brakes.

POWER PLANT: Two Turboméca Bastan VI-A turboprop engines, each rated at 930 shp plus 165 lb (75 kg) st. Ratier-Figeac FH86 three-blade variable-pitch metal propellers, diameter 9 ft 0¼ in (2·75 m). Water-alcohol injection. Total internal fuel capacity 420 Imp gallons (1,910 litres) in integral tanks in wings. Provision for two wingtip fuel tanks, each with capacity of 77 Imp gallons (350 litres). Oil capacity 4·2 Imp gallons (19 litres) for each engine.

ACCOMMODATION: Crew of two side-by-side on flight deck. Standard seating in main cabin for 10, 12 or 15 passengers. Door with built-in steps at rear of cabin on port side. The 10-passenger executive version has a baggage compartment (port) and bar (starboard) immediately aft of flight deck; two rows of three inward-facing seats at front of main cabin and two pairs of armchair seats facing each other fore and aft with table between; toilet opposite entry door. The utility and paratroop transport has seven inward-facing seats on the port side of the cabin and eight on the starboard side. A navigation and radar training version has six seats and comprehensive equipment in the cabin. An ambulance version carries two pairs of stretchers on the port side of the cabin and one pair on the starboard side, with two seats for attendants. All versions have a forward baggage hold and galley, and a toilet at the rear.

SYSTEMS: SEMCA Type EQ2 air-conditioning equipment. Navigation and landing lights and rotating beacon standard.

ELECTRONICS AND EQUIPMENT: Radio and radar according to military role. Normally two RA-21A VHF receivers, two TA-21A VHF transmitters, one RA-21A-MNA-21B navigation system, one GSA-8A-1 glide slope receiver, one FKA-23-A marker receiver, two DFA-22A ADF installations and two ASA-31A audio panels, all manufactured by Bendix; and one Eldeco 20A HF transceiver. Full blind-flying instrumentation standard. Optional equipment includes Bendix VOR/ILS, automatic pilot, automatic navigation system, weather radar and oxygen equipment.

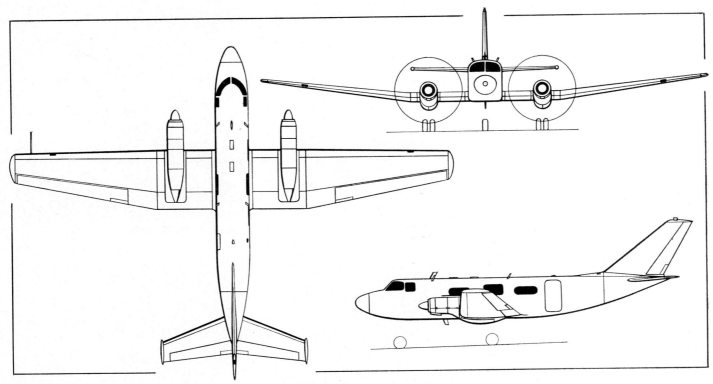

IA 50 Guarani II twin-turboprop light transport

DIMENSIONS, EXTERNAL:
Wing span (without tip-tanks)
                64 ft 1 in (19·53 m)
Wing chord (centre-section) 9 ft 1 in (2·75 m)
Wing aspect ratio   9
Length overall   48 ft 9 in (14·86 m)
Length of fuselage 46 ft 10½ in (14·29 m)
Height over tail   19 ft 0¾ in (5·81 m)
Tailplane span   21 ft 4 in (6·50 m)
Wheel track   15 ft 9½ in (4·82 m)
Wheelbase   11 ft 1¾ in (3·40 m)
Passenger door:
  Height   4 ft 9½ in (1·46 m)
  Width   2 ft 5 in (0·74 m)
AREAS:
Wings, gross   450 sq ft (41·81 m²)
Ailerons (total)   38·2 sq ft (3·55 m²)
Trailing-edge flaps (total) 51·73 sq ft (4·81 m²)
Vertical tail surfaces (total) 60·5 sq ft (5·62 m²)
Horizontal tail surfaces (total)
                 79·0 sq ft (7·34 m²)
WEIGHTS AND LOADING:
Weight empty, equipped 8,650 lb (3,924 kg)
Max payload   3,307 lb (1,500 kg)
Max T-O weight   16,204 lb (7,350 kg)
Max landing weight 14,595 lb (6,620 kg)
Max power loading 7·72 lb/hp (3·5 kg/hp)
PERFORMANCE (at max T-O weight):
Max level speed
      269 knots (310 mph; 500 km/h)
Max permissible diving speed
      277 knots (320 mph; 515 km/h)
Max cruising speed
      265 knots (305 mph; 491 km/h)
Econ cruising speed
      243 knots (280 mph; 450 km/h)
Stalling speed   79 knots (90 mph; 145 km/h)
Rate of climb at S/L   2,640 ft (805 m)/min
Service ceiling   41,000 ft (12,500 m)
Service ceiling, one engine out 11,000 ft (3,350 m)
T-O run   1,380 ft (420 m)
T-O to 50 ft (15 m)   2,200 ft (640 m)
Landing from 50 ft (15 m) 1,970 ft (600 m)
Landing run   820 ft (250 m)
Range with max fuel
     1,389 nm (1,600 miles; 2,575 km)
Range with max payload
     1,076 nm (1,240 miles; 1,995 km)

IA 53

Design work on this small agricultural aircraft was started on 1 October 1964. The first of three prototypes was allocated for a comprehensive programme of static and fatigue testing. The second prototype flew for the first time on 10 November 1966.

No production of the IA 53 has yet been undertaken, but prototype test flying is continuing.

TYPE: Agricultural monoplane.

WINGS: Cantilever low-wing monoplane. Wing section NACA 4412. Dihedral 7° 5′ on outer wings. Incidence 4° 15′. All-metal two-spar structure comprising a constant-chord centre-section and tapered outer panels. Frise metal ailerons. NACA metal slotted flaps.

FUSELAGE: Steel-tube (SAE 4130) structure, covered partly with duralumin panels and partly with glass-fibre reinforced polyester plastic.

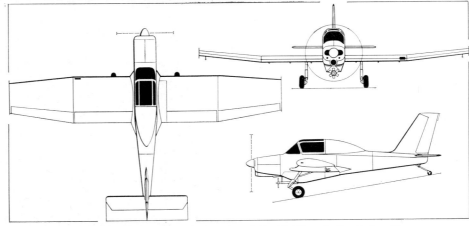

Photograph and three-view drawing of the IA 53 agricultural aircraft

TAIL UNIT: Cantilever all-metal structure, with swept vertical surfaces. Variable-incidence tailplane.

LANDING GEAR: Non-retractable tail-wheel type. Steel ring shock-absorption on main units. Main wheels and tyres size 6·50 × 8. Tail-wheel diameter 8 in (20 cm).

POWER PLANT: One 235 hp Lycoming O-540-B2B5 (optionally 260 hp Continental IO-470-D) six-cylinder horizontally-opposed air-cooled engine, driving a McCauley A 200 FM 9044 or 8648 fixed-pitch propeller, diameter 7 ft 6 in (2·29 m). Fuel in two tanks in wings with total capacity of 39·5 Imp gallons (180 litres), of which 35·2 Imp gallons (160 litres) are usable. Refuelling points above wings. Oil capacity 2·5 Imp gallons (11·5 litres).

ACCOMMODATION: Normal seating for pilot only in enclosed cabin. Provision for carrying second person in tandem on ferry flights.

DIMENSIONS, EXTERNAL:
Wing span	38 ft 0¾ in (11·60 m)
Wing chord at root	6 ft 6¾ in (2·00 m)
Wing chord at tip	4 ft 5½ in (1·36 m)
Wing aspect ratio	6·25
Length overall	26 ft 11 in (8·20 m)
Height overall	10 ft 10 in (3·30 m)
Wheel track	11 ft 5¾ in (3·50 m)
Wheelbase	18 ft 0½ in (5·50 m)

AREAS:
Wings, gross	231·5 sq ft (21·52 m²)
Ailerons (total)	25·40 sq ft (2·36 m²)
Trailing-edge flaps (total)	33·37 sq ft (3·10 m²)
Vertical tail surfaces (total)	20·13 sq ft (1·87 m²)
Horizontal tail surfaces (total)	40·90 sq ft (3·80 m²)

WEIGHTS AND LOADINGS:
Weight empty	1,860 lb (844 kg)
Max T-O weight	3,362 lb (1,525 kg)
Max wing loading	14·54 lb/sq ft (71 kg/m²)
Max power loading	14·95 lb/hp (6·78 kg/hp)

PERFORMANCE (estimated at max T-O weight):
Max level speed at S/L	116 knots (134 mph; 215 km/h)
Max cruising speed	100 knots (115 mph; 185 km/h)
Rate of climb at S/L	755 ft (230 m)/min
Service ceiling	11,800 ft (3,600 m)
T-O run	615 ft (187 m)
T-O to 50 ft (15 m)	1,150 ft (350 m)
Landing from 50 ft (15 m)	1,070 ft (326 m)
Range with max fuel	350 nm (404 miles; 650 km)

IA 58 PUCARÁ
Military designation: A-X2

This twin-turboprop COIN (counter-insurgency) combat aircraft is under development to meet an Argentine Air Force requirement.

As first initiated in August 1966, the IA 58 design had twin tail-booms and a central crew nacelle, in which form it was illustrated in the 1967-68 *Jane's*.

This was superseded by a more conventional aircraft, designed by Comandante (now Major) Héctor Eduardo Ruiz, Chief of the Engineering Group of FMA. An unpowered aerodynamic prototype of this design, with dummy engine nacelles and fixed landing gear, was first flown on 26 December 1967, and was described in the 1968-69 edition of *Jane's*. Detailed design work on the powered version was begun by Comandante Ruiz in February 1968. Construction of the first powered prototype, to which the details below apply, started in September 1968, and this aircraft flew for the first time on 20 August 1969.

Originally known as the Delfin, the IA 58 has now been renamed Pucará. A second prototype, under construction early in 1970, is being fitted with 1,022 eshp Turboméca Astazou XVIG turboprop engines and will offer an all-round improvement in performance.

Military acceptance trials are scheduled for 1971, and a possible AAF requirement for 80 aircraft has been reported.

TYPE: Twin-turboprop counter-insurgency aircraft.

WINGS: Cantilever low-wing monoplane. Wing section NACA 64₂A215 at root, NACA 64₁A212 at tip. Dihedral 7° on outer wing panels. Incidence 2°. No sweepback. Conventional semi-monocoque fail-safe structure of duralumin. Frise-type fabric-covered duralumin ailerons and all-dural slotted trailing-edge flaps. No slats. Balance tab on starboard aileron, electrically-operated trim-tab on port aileron. Kléber-Colombes pneumatic de-icing boots on leading-edges.

FUSELAGE: Conventional semi-monocoque fail-safe structure of duralumin. Door-type air brakes at rear which form tail-cone when closed.

TAIL UNIT: Cantilever semi-monocoque structure of duralumin. Fixed-incidence tailplane and elevators mounted near top of fin. Trim-tab in rudder and each elevator. Kléber-Colombes pneumatic de-icing boots on leading-edges.

LANDING GEAR: Retractable tricycle type, all units retracting forward hydraulically. Shock-absorbers of Kronprinz Ring-Feder type, designed by Comandante Ruiz. Single wheel on nose unit, twin wheels on main units, all with Dunlop tubeless Type III tyres size 7·50-10. Tyre pressures: 41 lb/sq in (2·88 kg/cm²) on main units, 35 lb/sq in (2·46 kg/cm²) on nose unit. Dunlop hydraulic disc brakes. No anti-skid units.

POWER PLANT: First prototype has two 904 ehp Garrett AiResearch TPE 331-U-303 turboprop engines, each driving a Hamilton Standard 33LF/1015-0 three-blade metal propeller of 8 ft 6 in (2·59 m) diameter. Fuel in one fuse-

Powered prototype of the FMA IA 58 Pucará shortly before its first flight

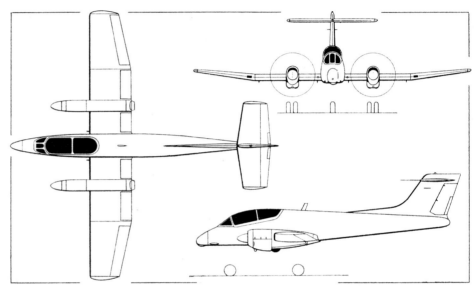
IA 58 Pucará twin-turboprop counter-insurgency combat aircraft

lage tank and three self-sealing tanks in each wing, with total capacity of 313 Imp gallons (1,422 litres). Attachment point beneath each wing at junction of centre and outer panels for external weapons or jettisonable auxiliary fuel tank of 66 Imp gallons (300 litres). Oil capacity 2·6 Imp gallons (11·75 litres).

ACCOMMODATION: Crew of two in tandem on HSA (Folland) 4GT/1 Type 40 ejection seats beneath transparent moulded canopy. Rear seat slightly elevated. Bullet-proof windscreen.

SYSTEMS: Hydraulic system, pressure 3,000 lb/sq in (210 kg/cm²), supplied by two engine-driven pumps, actuates landing gear, flaps, wheel brakes and air brakes. Wing and tail unit de-icing by bleed-air from engines. Electrical system includes two 300A 28V starter-generators for DC power and two 500-750VA rotary inverters for 115V AC power. Two 22Ah Sonotone CA 20-H nickel-cadmium batteries. No APU at present.

ELECTRONICS AND EQUIPMENT: Blind-flying instrumentation standard. Radio equipment includes Bendix DFA-73A-1 ADF, Bendix RTA-42A VHF communications system, Bendix RNA-2bc VHF navigation system, Northern N-420 HF 55B communications system, amplifier and audio-selector system with AS-A-31 panel. Optional equipment includes weather radar, IFF and VHF/FM tactical communications system.

ARMAMENT AND OPERATIONAL EQUIPMENT: Two 20 mm Hispano cannon and four 7·62 mm FN machine-guns in fuselage. One attachment point beneath centre of fuselage and one beneath each wing outboard of engine nacelle for a variety of external stores, including auxiliary fuel tanks. Librascope 335336 gunsight and one AN/AWE programmer.

DIMENSIONS, EXTERNAL:
Wing span	47 ft 6¾ ft (14·50 m)
Wing chord at root	7 ft 4¼ in (2·24 m)
Wing chord at tip	5 ft 3 in (1·60 m)
Wing aspect ratio	6·95
Length overall	45 ft 7¼ in (13·90 m)
Length of fuselage	43 ft 8½ in (13·32 m)
Fuselage: max width	4 ft 0¾ in (1·24 m)
Height overall	17 ft 2¼ in (5·24 m)
Tailplane span	15 ft 5 in (4·70 m)
Wheel track (c/l of shock struts)	13 ft 9¼ in (4·20 m)
Wheelbase	11 ft 5 in (3·48 m)

AREAS:
Wings, gross	326·1 sq ft (30·30 m²)
Ailerons (total)	35·41 sq ft (3·29 m²)
Trailing-edge flaps (total)	38·53 sq ft (3·58 m²)
Fin	37·30 sq ft (3·465 m²)
Rudder, including tab	16·84 sq ft (1·565 m²)
Tailplane	49·51 sq ft (4·60 m²)
Elevators, including tabs	28·11 sq ft (2·612 m²)

WEIGHTS AND LOADINGS (TPE 331 engines):
Basic operating weight	7,826 lb (3,550 kg)
Max T-O weight	13,668 lb (6,200 kg)
Max landing weight	11,023 lb (5,000 kg)
Max wing loading	41·99 lb/sq ft (205 kg/m²)
Max power loading	7·56 lb/hp (3·43 kg/hp)

PERFORMANCE (TPE 331 engines, at max T-O weight except where indicated):
Max level speed at 9,840 ft (3,000 m)	267 knots (308 mph; 495 km/h)
Max permissible diving speed	404 knots (466 mph; 750 km/h)
Max cruising speed at 9,840 ft (3,000 m)	256 knots (295 mph; 475 km/h)
Econ cruising speed at 9,840 ft (3,000 m)	223 knots (257 mph; 414 km/h)
Stalling speed, flaps down	82 knots (94 mph; 151 km/h)
Rate of climb at S/L	2,955 ft (900 m)/min
Service ceiling (at 11,464 lb = 5,200 kg AUW)	29,200 ft (8,900 m)
Service ceiling, one engine out (at 8,818 lb = 4,000 kg AUW and with 15° flap setting)	19,025 ft (5,800 m)
T-O run	1,410 ft (430 m)
T-O to 50 ft (15 m)	1,805 ft (550 m)
Landing from 50 ft (15 m)	3,280 ft (1,000 m)
Landing run	1,895 ft (577 m)
Range with max fuel	1,940 nm (2,235 miles; 3,600 km)

GERMAN BIANCO

GERMAN BIANCO S A

HEAD OFFICE:
Av Roque Sáenz Peña 615, Buenos Aires

Founded in 1898, this large industrial concern established in 1944 a division for aircraft repair and the series production of gliders.

In addition to this work, German Bianco also manufactured the Macchi M.B. 308 three-seat light cabin monoplane, under licence from Aeronautica Macchi of Varese, Italy.

The company has now ceased to manufacture aircraft of any kind.

TURBAY

TURBAY S A

HEAD OFFICE AND WORKS:
Zapiola 1850, Castelar, Buenos Aires
PRESIDENT: Ing Alfredo Turbay

Among early designs by Ing A. Turbay was the T-1B Tucan light aircraft, of which details were given in the 1945-46 *Jane's*. In 1957, he began work on a twin-engined light transport designated T-3A, and Turbay S A was formed in January 1961 to undertake manufacture of this aircraft.

The T-3A prototype (LV-X24), which flew for the first time on 8 December 1964, was described and illustrated in the 1968-69 *Jane's*. The projected production model will have turboprop engines and will incorporate a number of improvements.

AUSTRALIA

AERIAL AGRICULTURE

AERIAL AGRICULTURE PTY LTD

ADDRESS:
Hangar 17, Bankstown Airport, Bankstown, NSW 2200
GENERAL MANAGER:
T. J. Watson
OPERATIONS MANAGER:
C. R. Coote

AERIAL AGRICULTURE DHC-2/A1 WALLAROO 605

Aerial Agriculture Pty Ltd has modified a de Havilland Canada DHC-2 Beaver by replacing the standard Pratt & Whitney Wasp radial piston-engine by a Garrett AiResearch TPE 331 turboprop engine driving a three-blade metal propeller. In this form the aircraft (VH-AAX) is known as the DHC-2/A1 Wallaroo 605. A supplemental type certificate for the aircraft was issued by the Australian Dept of Civil Aviation on 9 December 1969.

A full structural description of the standard DHC-2 Beaver Mark I appeared in the 1968-69 *Jane's*. This is generally applicable to the Wallaroo 605. with the following exceptions:

TYPE: Single-engined agricultural monoplane.
WINGS: As Beaver Mk I, but conventional ribs replaced by ribs of box section to provide bays for fuel cells.
FUSELAGE: Lengthened by 12 in (0·305 m) by insertion of additional section at the natural bulkhead joint immediately aft of cockpit, improving pilot's view and increasing main cabin space.
TAIL UNIT: Main fin and rudder modified to more angular shape and increased in area. Two-section ventral fin added fore and aft of tail-wheel.
POWER PLANT: One 575 shp AiResearch TPE 331-61 turboprop engine, driving a Hartzell three-

Aerial Agriculture DHC-2/A1 Wallaroo 605 (575 shp AiResearch TPE 331-61 turboprop engine)

blade fully-feathering reversible-pitch metal propeller, diameter 8 ft 6 in (2·59 m). Fuel in three tanks in each wing, with total usable capacity of 140 Imp gallons (636 litres).
ACCOMMODATION: Lengthened fuselage increases main cabin volume by approx 16 cu ft (0·45 m³), permitting the addition of two seats to give a total of nine including the pilot. Relocation of fuel supply in wings permits the outlet of solid agricultural chemicals through opening in cabin floor.
DIMENSIONS, EXTERNAL:
Length overall   33 ft 11 in (10·34 m)

WEIGHTS:
Weight empty   2,900 lb (1,315 kg)
Max normal T-O weight   5,100 lb (2,313 kg)
PERFORMANCE (at max normal T-O weight, ISA):
Max level speed at 10,000 ft (3,050 m)
     150 knots (173 mph; 278 km/h)
Rate of climb at S/L   1,200 ft (366 m)/min
Service ceiling   24,500 ft (7,470 m)
T-O to 50 ft (15 m)   1,250 ft (381 m)
Landing from 50 ft (15 m), brakes only
     1,280 ft (390 m)
Landing from 50 ft (15 m), brakes and reverse pitch   1,005 ft (306 m)

AEROSMITH

Aerosmith/Air Parts FU-24/A2 survey aircraft

Aerosmith 400 hp conversion of Air Parts Fletcher FU-24

AEROSMITH

ADDRESS: Bankstown, NSW

This Australian operator has completed two conversions of the Air Parts (New Zealand) Fletcher FU-24 utility aircraft, as illustrated by the adjacent photographs. The aircraft on the left, which is designated FU-24/A2, has been fitted with a magnetometer on top of the fin and is used for aerial survey work. The other aircraft has had the usual 300 hp Rolls-Royce/Continental power plant replaced by an engine of 400 hp and a small dorsal fairing has been added to the fin. No further details were available at the time of writing.

AGRICULTURAL AVIATION

AGRICULTURAL AVIATION PTY LTD

ADDRESS:
Archerfield Aerodrome, Brisbane, Queensland
MANAGING DIRECTOR: M. Witham

AGRICULTURAL AVIATION PA-25B PAWNEE DUAL

This company converted, in 1967, a standard Piper Pawnee 235 aircraft (VH-PEG) into a side-by-side two-seater to provide training facilities for pilots engaged on liquid-spraying agricultural work.

Major modifications involved a 10 in (25·4 cm) widening of the fuselage at the cockpit, the cockpit itself being faired in a straight line back to the base of the fin, and having a new, wider windscreen and bulged windows in the cockpit doors. All flying and agricultural controls are duplicated, and full aileron movement is retained. The battery has been relocated, and the radio sited on the floor beneath the bench seat. Take-off and general performance is said to be superior to that of the standard Pawnee, and the greater keel surface provided by the faired-in rear fuselage decking increases the aircraft's stability in turns.

Piper PA-25B Pawnee converted to two-seat configuration by Agricultural Aviation Pty Ltd
(Queensland Country Life)

A Dept of Civil Aviation Class III C of A was awarded to the aircraft in September 1967, and further similar conversions could be undertaken if required.

CAC

COMMONWEALTH AIRCRAFT CORPORATION PTY, LTD

HEAD OFFICE AND WORKS:
304, Lorimer Street, Port Melbourne, Victoria 3207

DIRECTORS:
Air Chief Marshal Sir Frederick Scherger, KBE, CB, DSO, AFC (Chairman)
M. L. Baillieu
Sir Colin Syme
L. C. Bridgland
H. Flett
W. D. Brookes, DSO
R. R. Law-Smith, CBE, AFC
H. H. Knight (General Manager)

SECRETARY: F. H. Rollason
CHIEF ENGINEER: Ian H. Ring

Commonwealth Aircraft Corporation Pty, Ltd, was formed in 1936 at the invitation of the Commonwealth Government, to establish an aircraft industry to make Australia independent of outside supplies.

The Corporation has an authorised capital of $6,000,000. Shareholders include BHP Nominees Pty, Ltd; The Broken Hill Associated Smelters Pty Ltd (North Broken Hill Ltd); Broken Hill South Ltd; Electrolytic Zinc Co of Australasia Ltd; Rolls-Royce Ltd; Nobel (Australasia) Pty, Ltd and P & O Australian Holdings Pty Ltd.

The company is engaged, as prime contractor, on the manufacture of the Aermacchi M.B.326H

CAC-built Aermacchi M.B. 326H for the Royal Australian Air Force (*S. P. Peltz*)

trainer, both the airframe and the engine being produced under licence, and is also the sole distributor for Australia and New Guinea of the Hughes 300 and 500 (OH-6A) helicopters.

Details of the company's aero-engine activities can be found in the "Aero-engines" section.

COMMONWEALTH M.B.326H

Commonwealth Aircraft Corporation is manufacturing under licence both the airframe and the Viper 11 turbojet engine of the Aermacchi M.B. 326H (CAC project designation CA-30), which has been adopted by the RAAF as its standard

basic trainer. Imported parts are being used for initial production, but will be superseded by locally-produced parts from the 31st aircraft. Certain major components are being subcontracted.

An initial order for 75 aircraft was followed by orders for a further 12 aircraft for the RAAF and 10 for the Royal Australian Navy. Completion of deliveries of these 97 aircraft is scheduled for September 1972.

Details of the M.B.326H can be found under the Aermacchi entry in the Italian section of this edition.

COMMONWEALTH OF AUSTRALIA
DEPARTMENT OF SUPPLY

ADDRESS:
Constitution Avenue, Canberra, ACT 2600

SECRETARY:
A. S. Cooley

DIRECTOR OF PUBLIC RELATIONS:
A. L. Witsenhuysen

Government Aircraft Factories

HEADQUARTERS:
Fishermen's Bend, Melbourne, Victoria 3207

AIRFIELD AND FINAL ASSEMBLY WORKSHOPS:
Avalon, Victoria

MANAGER: G. J. Churcher

The Government Aircraft Factories are units of the Defence Production facilities owned by the Government of the Commonwealth of Australia and operated by the Department of Supply.

The Factories' major recent activity has been responsibility for the production in Australia of the Dassault Mirage III-O fighter and III-D operational trainer for the RAAF as prime contractor. The Commonwealth Aircraft Corporation assisted in the programme, details of which can be found in the 1969-70 Jane's.

Servicing and modification of Mirage III-O fighter aircraft is being undertaken at the Avalon facility, and some spares for Canberra and Mirage aircraft are manufactured.

In current production are the Ikara antisubmarine weapon system and the Jindivik target drone; a target drone version of the Ikara, known as the Turana, is under development. These are described in the appropriate sections of this edition.

Under the terms of a contract between the Australian Government and General Aircraft Corporation of the USA (which see), the GAF are to manufacture wings and engine nacelles for the GAC-100 STOL transport. These activities at the Government Aircraft Factories, including the provision of tooling, will begin when the production phase of the GAC-100 is authorised.

The latest aircraft design to be announced by the GAF is for a twin-turboprop STOL utility transport known as the N2, all available details of which are given below.

GOVERNMENT AIRCRAFT FACTORIES N2

A small, twin-turboprop utility aircraft, known as the N2, is under development at the Fishermen's Bend headquarters of the GAF. Prototype studies began in 1965 for an aircraft powered by a single turboprop engine, but following the development of Australian Armed Services requirements this has now evolved into a twin-engined STOL aircraft suitable for operations in forward military areas. Further development is planned of a simplified higher-capacity commercial model.

The basic N2 design incorporates many features of specifically military interest, including ejection seats, armour protection, self-sealing fuel tanks and duplicated primary controls. Funding was approved in January 1970 for manufacture of two prototype aircraft, the first of which is expected to fly in June 1971. The data below apply to this version.

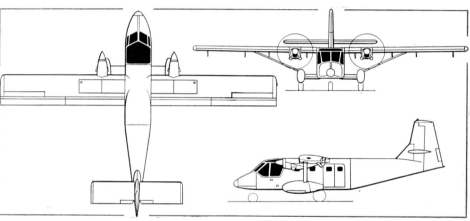

Three-view drawing of the Government Aircraft Factories N2 twin-turboprop utility aircraft

TYPE: Twin-turboprop STOL utility aircraft.

WINGS: Braced high-wing monoplane. Basic NACA 23018 wing section, modified to incorporate increased nose radius and camber. Dihedral 1° from roots. Incidence 2°. No sweepback. Two-spar fail-safe torsion-box structure of light alloy. Full-span double-slotted trailing-edge flaps. All-metal ailerons, which droop with the flaps and transfer their motion progressively to slot-lip ailerons as the flaps extend, resulting in full-span flap. Adjustable trim-tabs. Controls actuated by cables and push-rods. Pneumatic de-icing of leading-edges optional. Small stub wings at cabin floor level support the main landing gear fairings, from which a single strut on each side braces the main wing.

FUSELAGE: Conventional semi-monocoque light alloy structure of stringers and frames. Prototypes will incorporate an optional swing-tail loading facility.

TAIL UNIT: Cantilever all-metal structure. All-moving tailplane, with inset trim and anti-balance tab. Tailplane and rudder actuated by cables. Trim-tab in rudder. Pneumatic de-icing of leading-edges optional.

LANDING GEAR: Retractable tricycle type, with electrical retraction by a single actuator in the fuselage. Emergency free-drop capability. Single aft-retracting nose-wheel, size 8·50 × 6·00. Single wheel, size 29 × 11·00-10, tyre pressure 30 lb/sq in (2·1 kg/cm²), on each main unit. Main wheels retract forward into fairings at extremities of the lower stub-wings. Oleo-pneumatic shock-absorption of GAF design. Hydraulic single-disc brake on each main wheel.

POWER PLANT: Two 400 shp Allison 250-B17 turboprop engines, each driving a 3-blade constant-speed fully-feathering reversible-pitch propeller of 7 ft 0 in (2·13 m) diameter. Fuel in two similar self-sealing bag-type tanks in each wing, with total capacity of 220 Imp gallons (1,000 litres) in military versions. Integral

tanks are planned for commercial version. Refuelling point above outer tank in each wing. Provision for internal auxiliary ferry tanks.

ACCOMMODATION: Crew of two on flight deck, on side-by-side seats with provision for zero/zero escape system. Access to flight deck by forward-opening door on each side. Main cabin has seating for up to 14 passengers, with continuous seat tracks and readily-removable seats which allow rapid rearrangement of the main cabin to suit alternative loads. Access to main cabin by double doors on port side, with single emergency exit door on starboard side. Provision for swing-tail for rear loading. Baggage compartments in nose and rear fuselage. Flight deck and main cabin heated and ventilated; air-conditioning is proposed for later versions.

SYSTEMS: No hydraulic or pneumatic systems normally, but pneumatic airframe de-icing is available optionally. Electrical system comprises a 28V 150A DC starter-generator on each engine, and a 22Ah battery with optional AC inverters. Optional systems include electrical de-icing of engine intakes and propellers, and oxygen supply to crew (demand type) and cabin (continuous flow type).

ELECTRONICS AND EQUIPMENT: Provision is made for a wide range of nav/com equipment to meet specific military requirements. Other optional items include blind-flying instrumentation and a lightweight weather radar. Armour protection will be provided for the crew and vital systems on the military versions which will also be fitted with underwing stores racks.

DIMENSIONS, EXTERNAL:
Wing span	54 ft 0 in (16·46 m)
Wing chord (constant)	5 ft 11¼ in (1·82 m)
Wing aspect ratio	9·1
Length overall	40 ft 10 in (12·45 m)
Height overall	15 ft 11 in (4·85 m)
Tailplane span	17 ft 8½ in (5·36 m)
Wheel track	11 ft 7¾ in (3·55 m)
Wheelbase	12 ft 4 in (3·76 m)
Propeller ground clearance	4 ft 3 in (1·30 m)

Distance between propeller centres
14 ft 4 in (4·37 m)
Cabin double door (port):
Height   4 ft 4 in (1·32 m)
  Width   4 ft 1 in (1·24 m)
  Height to sill   2 ft 10¾ in (0·88 m)
Emergency exit door (stbd):
Height   2 ft 2¼ in (0·67 m)
  Width   2 ft 0 in (0·61 m)

DIMENSIONS, INTERNAL:
Cabin, excl flight deck and rear baggage compartment:
  Length   13 ft 8½ in (4·18 m)
  Max width   4 ft 3 in (1·30 m)
  Max height   5 ft 2½ in (1·59 m)
  Floor area   58 sq ft (5·39 m²)
  Volume   300 cu ft (8·50 m³)
Baggage compartment volume:
  Nose   27 cu ft (0·76 m³)
  Rear   up to 50 cu ft (1·42 m³)

AREAS:
Wings, gross   320 sq ft (29·7 m²)
Ailerons (total)   25·8 sq ft (2·40 m²)
Trailing-edge flaps (total)   102·3 sq ft (9·50 m²)
Fin   55·2 sq ft (5·13 m²)
Rudder, incl tab   24·3 sq ft (2·26 m²)
Tailplane, incl tabs   78·0 sq ft (7·25 m²)
WEIGHTS AND LOADINGS:
Manufacturer's basic weight empty
3,640 lb (1,651 kg)
Max payload, with one pilot, 100 lb = 45 kg avionics allowance and typical interior fitments   2,700 lb (1,224 kg)
Max T-O and landing weight 7,000 lb (3,175 kg)
Max wing loading   21·9 lb/sq ft (106·9 kg/m²)
Max power loading   8·4 lb/shp (3·81 kg/shp)
PERFORMANCE (estimated, at max T-O weight):
Max level speed at S/L
184 knots (212 mph; 341 km/h)
Max permissible diving speed
250 knots (288 mph; 463 km/h)

Max cruising speed at S/L
174 knots (200 mph; 322 km/h)
Econ cruising speed at S/L
143 knots (165 mph; 266 km/h)
Stalling speed, power off, flaps up
64 knots (73 mph; 118 km/h)
Stalling speed, power off, flaps down
42 knots (48 mph; 78 km/h)
Max rate of climb at S/L   2,150 ft (655 m)/min
Rate of climb at S/L, one engine out
800 ft (244 m)/min
Service ceiling   30,000 ft (9,150 m)
Service ceiling, one engine out
12,000 ft (3,650 m)
T-O run   500 ft (152 m)
T-O to 50 ft (15 m)   720 ft (219 m)
Landing from 50 ft (15 m)   670 ft (204 m)
Landing run   360 ft (110 m)
Range with max fuel, 45 min reserves plus allowances for T-O and taxi
920 nm (1,059 miles; 1,704 km)

HAWKER DE HAVILLAND
HAWKER DE HAVILLAND AUSTRALIA PTY, LTD (Member Company of HAWKER SIDDELEY GROUP)

HEAD OFFICE:
Birnie Avenue, Lidcombe, NSW 2141
DIRECTORS:
Sir Aubrey Burke (Chairman: resident in UK)
R. Kingsford-Smith (Deputy Chairman and Managing Director)
L. R. Jones
H. B. M. Vose
M. M. Waghorn
T. W. R. Air
PUBLIC RELATIONS MANAGER:
J. D. S. Keatinge

This company was formed in 1927, when de Havilland Aircraft Pty Ltd, as it was then known, opened a service facility for de Havilland aircraft operating in Australia. During 1939-45, it built Tiger Moths, Dragon Rapides, Mosquitos, military gliders and propeller blades.

At the end of the war, the company proposed a jet fighter production plan to the Australian Government. The first locally-manufactured Vampire flew in June 1948, and the last of 189 Vampire fighters and trainers left the Bankstown production line in June 1961. During this period the company also designed the Drover three-engined bush transport, of which 20 were built.

In 1959, the company took over the Lidcombe premises of the Commonwealth Aircraft Corporation, and in 1962 purchased the Bristol Aeroplane Company (Australia) Pty Ltd and Bristol Aviation Services Pty Ltd. In 1963 the overhaul

responsibilities of the Fairey Aviation Company of Australasia Pty Ltd were taken over. It became a Hawker Siddeley company in 1960, and in 1963 its name was changed to Hawker de Havilland Australia Pty Ltd.

As the major sub-contractor in the Aermacchi M.B.326H production programme for the RAAF and RAN, the company is manufacturing airframe components for this basic trainer at its Aircraft Division, Bankstown, NSW. This Division also undertakes the repair and overhaul of a wide range of civil and military aircraft, including the DHC-4 Caribou and Bell UH-1 Iroquois and OH-13 Sioux helicopters for the Australian Army and RAAF, and DH Sea Venoms, Grumman Trackers and Westland Wessex helicopters for the RAN. Civil types on which overhaul and modification work is undertaken include the Douglas DC-3 and DC-4, Convair 340 and 440, DHC-6 Twin Otter, Hawker Siddeley (DH) 125 and general aviation aircraft.

At Lidcombe, NSW, engine, propeller and accessory overhaul is undertaken, as well as the manufacture of components for Viper turbojet engines to power the licence-built Aermacchi M.B.326H trainer. Also manufactured is the Noelle gas turbine starter for the Atar-powered Mirage III's of the RAAF. Engine types overhauled include the Lycoming T53, Rolls-Royce Viper, Gazelle and Nimbus, Goblin, Ghost and UACL PT6 turbine engines; and the Gipsy, Pratt & Whitney, Wright, Lycoming and Continental series of piston-engines. Recently the company was appointed distributor and approved service organisation for the Allison 250 turbine engine for Australia, south-east Asia and south-west Pacific areas.

The Lidcombe factory has well-equipped machine shops, laboratories and test facilities and has diversified its activities into a wide field of commercial manufacture. In this plant the company has manufactured for some years the stabiliser bearing housing of the Vought A-7 Corsair II strike aircraft, and recently began quantity production of tail rotor hub assemblies for the Bell UH-1 Iroquois helicopter.

The Aviation and Systems Sales Division handles the Australian representation of HS Group aviation products, Rolls-Royce (Bristol) engines, Westland helicopters, British Hovercraft Corporation products and a wide range of British and North American equipment.

The General Aviation Division distributes and supports Beech aircraft throughout Australasia and maintains servicing facilities in all states for all general aviation category aircraft.

Product Support Division supplies aircraft spares to military and civil operators throughout Australia, south-east Asia and the Pacific.

In 1968, the company established the Guildford Division in Perth, Western Australia, to overhaul airframes and maintain piston and turbine engines for the RAAF and the civil market.

A subsidiary of the company, Hawker Siddeley Electronics Ltd, controls the guided weapons activity at Salisbury, South Australia. Its responsibilities include the preparation and firing of the Blue Streak satellite launcher. The company is also involved in the manufacture and overhaul of communications and avionics equipment. In addition, it maintains the NASA deep space tracking station at Tidbinbilla, near Canberra, ACT, and a station at Island Lagoon, Woomera, South Australia.

TRANSAVIA
TRANSAVIA CORPORATION PTY, LTD

HEAD OFFICE:
Transfield House, 102-106 Arthur Street, North Sydney, NSW 2060
WORKS AND SERVICE DIVISION:
73 Station Road, Seven Hills, NSW 2147
CHAIRMAN:
F. Belgiorno-Nettis
DIRECTOR:
C. Salteri
GENERAL MANAGER:
G. Forrester

Transavia Corporation was formed in 1964 as a subsidiary of Transfield Pty, Ltd, one of Australia's largest construction companies.

Its first product is the multi-purpose PL-12 Airtruk agricultural aircraft, of which details are given below.

TRANSAVIA PL-12 AIRTRUK

The Airtruk was designed by Mr Luigi Pellarini, and was originally type-certified in February 1966, for spreading fertilizer and for seeding. Swath width is up to 35 yd (32 m) and of unusual uniformity. A liquid-spraying conversion was developed in 1968 which is capable of covering a 33 yd (30·2 m) swath. This version has an engine-driven spray pump and a liquid chemical capacity of 180 Imp gallons (818 litres).

As can be seen in the adjacent illustration, the PL-12 is unconventional in layout, with two entirely separate tail-booms and tail units. This keeps the tails clear of chemicals, and also permits rapid loading by a vehicle which approaches the aircraft between the tails. The power plant is a 300 hp Continental IO-520-D engine, driving a McCauley type C58 constant-speed propeller, diameter 7 ft 4 in (2·23 m). Standard fuel capacity is 40 Imp gallons (182 litres), with optional total capacity of 80 Imp gallons (364 litres). A cabin for two passengers is located at the rear of the fuselage.

The three-seat prototype Airtruk flew for the first time on 22 April 1965. Delivery of production Airtruks began in December 1966, and a total of 35 was in service by January 1970, in Australia, New Zealand and Africa.

Transavia Airtruk agricultural aircraft fitted with spray bars

DIMENSIONS, EXTERNAL:
Wing span   39 ft 10½ in (12·15 m)
Length overall   21 ft 0 in (6·40 m)
Height overall   9 ft 0 in (2·74 m)
AREA:
Wings, gross   256 sq ft (23·79 m²)

WEIGHTS:
Weight empty   1,750 lb (793 kg)
Payload (agricultural), excluding pilot, fuel and oil   2,000 lb (907 kg)
T-O weight (utility)   3,800 lb (1,725 kg)
Max T-O weight (agricultural) 4,090 lb (1,855 kg)

PERFORMANCE (at max T-O weight, except where indicated):
Max level speed at S/L
119 knots (137 mph; 220 km/h)
Max cruising speed at S/L (75% power)
105 knots (121 mph; 195 km/h)
Average operating speed at S/L
96 knots (110 mph; 177 km/h)
Stalling speed, flaps down:
Max T-O weight 49 knots (56 mph; 90 km/h)
Min T-O weight 36 knots (41 mph; 66 km/h)
Rate of climb at S/L:
Max T-O weight 600 ft (183 m)/min
Min T-O weight 1,760 ft (535 m)/min
Service ceiling:
Max T-O weight 10,500 ft (3,200 m)
Min T-O weight 22,600 ft (6,900 m)
T-O run:
Max T-O weight 780 ft (238 m)
Min T-O weight 195 ft (60 m)
Landing run, min weight 270 ft (82 m)
Range with max payload at S/L
286 nm (330 miles; 530 km)
Range with standard fuel at S/L
330 nm (380 miles; 610 km)

Transavia Airtruk agricultural aircraft fitted with spray bars

AUSTRIA

OBERLERCHNER
JOSEF OBERLERCHNER HOLZINDUSTRIE
HEAD OFFICE:
POB 1, Spittal/Drau

This company was engaged in the design and manufacture of powered aircraft and sailplanes from 1941 and delivered over 4,000 aircraft.

Its most recent product was the JOB 15 four-seat light aircraft. Manufacture of sailplanes was discontinued in 1967.

OBERLERCHNER JOB 15
The JOB 15 can be used as a four-seat touring aircraft or, with only two persons on board, for training and glider towing. The prototype flew towards the end of 1960 and the first production model in 1961.

Twenty-three production aircraft were built, in three versions, as follows:

JOB 15-135. With 135 hp Lycoming O-290 engine. Initial version, with three seats. Three built, one of which was later refitted with 150 hp engine and modified to a four-seater. Details in 1964-65 *Jane's*.

JOB 15-150 and JOB 15-150/2. With 150 hp Lycoming O-320 engine. Production began in 1963. Twenty of the JOB 15-150 version had been built by the Spring of 1969, of which 11 were sold to customers in Germany and one in Switzerland. The developed JOB 15-150/2 is available for licence manufacture.

Oberlerchner JOB 15-150 four-seat light aircraft (150 hp Lycoming O-320-A2B engine)

The JOB 15 received its Austrian type certificate in 1962, its German type certificate in 1963 and its Swiss type certificate in 1966. The JOB 15 has been tested by the Austrian authorities to full aerobatic standard, although no application has yet been made for it to be certificated in this category. Production has been discontinued, but Oberlerchner is offering licence rights to other manufacturers.

A full description of the JOB 15 appeared in the 1969-70 *Jane's*.

BAHAMAS

TRANS-CARIBBEAN
TRANS-CARIBBEAN AIRCRAFT CO
ADDRESS: Freeport, Grand Bahama

TRANS-CARIBBEAN/CONSOLIDATED PBY-5A CANSO CONVERSION
This company is undertaking the conversion of a number of Consolidated PBY-5A Catalina

Canso twin-engined amphibian flying-boats to turbine power, by installing Rolls-Royce Dart turboprop engines in place of the standard radial piston-engines. Reversible-pitch propellers are to be fitted to improve water handling and short-field take-off characteristics.

An optional feature is the provision of a swing-tail, hinged just aft of the waist observation blisters, which gives a roughly semi-circular area of approx 6 × 5 ft (1·8 × 1·5 m) providing direct-loading access to the cabin on land or when the aircraft is beached. Certification flight trials were reported to be underway in the Spring of 1970.

BELGIUM

FAIREY
FAIREY S A
HEAD OFFICE, WORKS AND AERODROME:
6200 Gosselies, near Charleroi
CHAIRMAN:
G. C. D'Arcy Biss
MANAGING DIRECTOR:
T. B. O'Reilly
DIRECTORS:
J. I. Blum
E. R. J. Delville
M. C. A. Holt
A. Talbott
C. C. Vinson
DIRECTOR AND GENERAL MANAGER (Administration and Finance):
J. P. van Gansberghe
GENERAL MANAGER (Manufacturing and Engineering):
R. Legroux
MANAGER, QUALITY ASSURANCE:
D. A. Ross
SALES, PUBLIC RELATIONS AND CONTRACTS:
W. Delbecq

This company, known formerly as Avions Fairey SA, was formed in 1931 as a subsidiary of the English Fairey Aviation Co, Ltd, with the object of producing Fairey fighter aircraft for the Belgian Air Force.

In recent years, Fairey has expanded its facilities very considerably in order to cope with increasing production requirements, including the manufacture of a substantial number of Gloster Meteor, Hawker Hunter and Lockheed F-104G fighters for NATO and the Belgian Air Force.

Following completion of this work, the company is contributing to the Breguet Atlantic programme. In addition, a contract was signed in 1969 between Fairey SA, the Belgian Government, and Avions Marcel Dassault of France, whereby Fairey will undertake a major share in the production of Mirage 5s for the Belgian Air Force. Under the first part of the agreement Fairey is responsible for the detail design tooling and manufacture of rear fuselages for all 106 Mirage 5s so far ordered by Belgium; for the nose-cones of the reconnaissance and single-seat versions; for the manufacture of many accessories; and for build-up and ground testing of the

Atar 09 turbojet engines to power these aircraft. The agreement also covers the manufacture of rear fuselage sections for all Mirage F1 aircraft ordered from Dassault, no matter by whom they are ordered. Other aspects of the agreement provide for participation by Fairey in the production programmes for the Dassault Mirage G variable-geometry strike fighter, and for other aircraft.

The company is also collaborating on an international basis on many other projects, including the VFW-614 transport aircraft, the manufacture of oil tanks for J79 turbojet engines built under licence in Europe, and of special hydraulic equipment.

Overhaul and repair of military aircraft constitute an important part of the company's activities. Currently, Pembroke transports, F-104 Starfighters and F-84F Thunderstreak fighters are passing through the Fairey workshops in large numbers. Important sub-contract work currently in hand includes the manufacture of glass-fibre components for Aérospatiale (Sud-Aviation) helicopters.

Fairey's works cover an area of some 350,000 sq ft (32,516 m²) and employ almost 1,000 people.

SABCA
SOCIÉTÉ ANONYME BELGE DE CONSTRUCTIONS AÉRONAUTIQUES

HEAD OFFICE:
1,470 chaussée de Haecht, 1130 Brussels

WORKS:
Haren/Brussels and Gosselies/Charleroi

CHAIRMAN: A. Dubuisson

DIRECTOR, GENERAL MANAGER:
P. G. Willekens

The Société Anonyme Belge de Constructions Aéronautiques has been since 1920 the largest aircraft manufacturer in Belgium. In addition to building aircraft and aero-engines under licence pre-war for the Belgian Government and the Sabena company, it also built aircraft of its own design.

Avions Marcel Dassault (France) and Fokker-VFW (Nethrelands - Germany) have parity holdings in SABCA, through which the Belgian

company now participates in various European projects.

At Haren, the company has undertaken design work for the Mercure, VFW-614, Mirage F1 and Mirage G4 and is participating in the manufacture of the Breguet Atlantic maritime aircraft, ordered by Dutch and Italian air forces, the Fokker-VFW F.27 and F.28 transports, and the Aérospatiale SA 330 helicopter. It is also manufacturing hydraulic components and tanks for F-104G and TF-104G aircraft in European service.

SABCA is undertaking the maintenance of NATO Hawk surface-to-air missiles, and is preparing to contribute to the production of the successor to the Belgian Air Force's C-119 transports. At Haren, a specially-equipped machine shop is devoted to the production of hydraulic equipment for aircraft and guided missiles.

At Gosselies, SABCA continues to maintain and overhaul F-104G aircraft for the Belgian and German Air Forces and is also setting up the final assembly line of the Mirage 5 chosen to replace the Belgian Air Force's F-84F fighters. Delivery of the first Belgian-built Mirage 5 was due in July 1970. Furthermore, the works

is engaged on overhaul and repair of various military aeroplanes and helicopters for the Belgian and foreign armed forces, including final assembly of the Alouette II Astazou for the Belgian Army.

SABCA's Electronic Division, Cobelda, is manufacturing IFF equipment for the Mirage 5, Doppler equipment for the Breguet Atlantic and a variety of aircraft electronic ground equipment, some of it for the NADGE programmes. It undertakes important work on electronic equipment under F-104G overhaul contracts, and is engaged in the development of a tank fire control system. This Division has also developed ground calibration equipment of its own design for radars, known as CORAPRAN. Its work for the 106 Belgian Mirage 5 aircraft includes functional test procedures in the laboratory before installation of equipment in the aircraft and check-out after such installation.

SABCA is engaged on space activities (ELDO and ESRO), and is a sub-contractor of the CIFAS consortium for the Symphonie satellite.

In 1970 the Haren and Gosselies works occupied a total area of approx 646,000 sq ft (60,000 m²) and between them employed about 2,000 people.

STAMPE ET RENARD
STAMPE ET RENARD S A

This company was formed after World War II by merger of the two pre-war companies Constructions Aéronautiques G. Renard and J.

Stampe et M. Vertongen. It undertook overhaul and repair of the SV-4 biplane, which was designed pre-war by Stampe-et-Vertongen and is still in extensive military and civil service in Belgium and France. In addition, it built the prototype

of a modernised and re-engined version of this aircraft, designated SV-4D, as described and illustrated in the 1968-69 *Jane's*.

It was reported early in 1970 that the company had gone into liquidation.

BRAZIL

AEROTEC
SOCIEDADE AEROTEC LTDA

HEAD OFFICE AND WORKS:
Caixa Postal 286, São José dos Campos, São Paulo State

DIRECTORS:
José Carlos de Souza Reis
Carlos Gonçalves

This company designed and built a light aircraft named the Uirapuru, which, under the military designation T-23, has been ordered by the Brazilian Air Force and for civil flying clubs.

AEROTEC 122 UIRAPURU
Brazilian Air Force designation: T-23

The Uirapuru is a two-seat all-metal light aircraft, designed as a private venture by Engs José Carlos de Souza Reis and Carlos Gonçalves. The prototype (PP-ZTF), with a 108 hp Lycoming O-235-C1 engine, flew for the first time on 2 June 1965 and was described and illustrated in the 1966-67 *Jane's*. It was followed by a second Uirapuru (PP-ZTT), with a 150 hp Lycoming O-320-A engine.

Early in 1968, the Brazilian Air Force placed an order for 30 production machines, powered by 160 hp Lycoming O-320-B2B engines. Two pre-production T-23s (0940 and 0941) were completed early in 1968, making their first flights on 23 January and 11 April respectively. These machines differed from the production version in having 150 hp engines.

The first production T-23 (0942) crashed on 1 November 1968 when its pilot failed to recover from a flat spin. Subsequent flight testing led to the addition of a small auxiliary fin beneath the rear fuselage, to improve spin-recovery characteristics.

In April 1969 the number of T-23's on order by the Brazilian Air Force was increased to 70, and 30 of these had been delivered by February 1970. A possible additional order for Uirapurus by the Brazilian Ministry of Aeronautics, for distribution to civilian flying clubs, has been reported. Current production is at the rate of three aircraft per month.

In Brazilian Air Force service the T-23 Uirapuru is replacing locally-built Fokker S-11 (T-21) and S-12 (T-22) Instructor primary trainers at the Academia da Fôrça Aérea (Air Force Academy) in Rio de Janeiro, and is equipping the recently-created Centro de Instrução de Pilotos Militares (Military Pilots' Training Centre) in Natal, Rio Grande do Norte State.

TYPE: Two-seat primary trainer.

WINGS: Cantilever low-wing monoplane. Wing section NACA 43013. Dihedral 5°. Incidence 2°. Light alloy structure of centre-section and two outer panels. All-metal ailerons and trailing-edge split flaps. Flap settings 0°, 20° and 40°; ailerons deflect 20° up and 13° down. Glass-fibre wingtips.

FUSELAGE: All-metal semi-monocoque structure in 2024-T-3 aluminium, with 4130 steel for critical areas.

Production version of Aerotec T-23 Uirapuru with under-fuselage auxiliary fin (*Ronaldo S. Olive*)

TAIL UNIT: Cantilever all-metal construction. Fin, rudder, tailplane and elevator tips of glass-fibre. Trim-tab in starboard half of elevator. Statically and aerodynamically balanced elevator, aerodynamically balanced rudder. Fixed ventral fin. Vertical and horizontal surfaces of NACA 0009 section. Sweepback 30° on fin leading-edge. Elevator deflects 30° up, 23° down; trim tab 22° up, 40° down; rudder 25° each side.

LANDING GEAR: Non-retractable tricycle type, with nose-wheel steerable 22° to each side. Rubber-cushioned shock-absorbers on main units; oleo shock-absorber on nose unit. All wheels have Goodyear 6·00 × 6 tyres, pressure 26 lb/sq in (1·83 kg/cm²) on main units and 24 lb/sq in (1·69 kg/cm²) on nose unit. Independent hydraulic disc brakes on main units. Parking brake. Legs of 4130 steel, with small fairings on main-wheel legs.

POWER PLANT: One 160 hp Lycoming O-320-B2B four-cylinder horizontally-opposed air-cooled engine, driving a Sensenich M-76-DM-60 two-blade fixed-pitch metal propeller, diameter 6 ft 1½ in (1·87 m). Variable-pitch propeller optional. Two integral fuel tanks in wing leading-edges, with total capacity of 31 Imp gallons (140 litres). Refuelling points above tanks. Optional 11 Imp gallon (50 litre) wingtip tanks.

ACCOMMODATION: Two fully-adjustable seats side-by-side under rearward-sliding transparent canopy. Two-piece windshield. For emergency ejection, canopy separates into two pieces. Seats permit the use of either back-type or seat-type parachutes. Dual controls. Baggage compartment, capacity 66 lb (30 kg), aft of seats with access from cockpit only.

SYSTEMS: Hydraulic system for brakes. Electrical system includes 24V 50A generator, 24V 24Ah generator and electric starter.

ELECTRONICS AND EQUIPMENT: Conventional VFR equipment. Optional items include VHF

transceiver, ADF, artificial horizon and directional gyro. Adjustable-angle 100W landing light in each wing leading-edge.

DIMENSIONS, EXTERNAL:
Wing span	27 ft 10¾ in (8·50 m)
Wing chord (constant)	5 ft 0½ in (1·53 m)
Wing aspect ratio	5·33
Length overall	21 ft 8 in (6·60 m)
Height overall	8 ft 10 in (2·70 m)
Tailplane span	9 ft 2¼ in (2·80 m)
Propeller ground clearance	10¾ in (0·27 m)
Width of fuselage	3 ft 6½ in (1·08 m)
Wheel track	7 ft 10½ in (2·40 m)
Wheelbase	5 ft 0¼ in (1·53 m)

AREAS:
Wings, gross	145·3 sq ft (13·50 m²)
Ailerons (total)	12·81 sq ft (1·19 m²)
Flaps (total)	10·23 sq ft (0·95 m²)
Fin	6·46 sq ft (0·60 m²)
Rudder	5·38 sq ft (0·50 m²)
Tailplane	16·15 sq ft (1·50 m²)
Elevator	11·84 sq ft (1·10 m²)

WEIGHTS AND LOADINGS:
Weight empty	1,191 lb (540 kg)
Max T-O weight	1,825 lb (840 kg)
Max wing loading	13·90 lb/sq ft (63·0 kg/m²)
Max power loading	12·35 lb/hp (5·60 kg/hp)

PERFORMANCE (at max T-O weight, ISA):
Max level speed	122 knots (140 mph; 225 km/h)
Max diving speed	165 knots (190 mph; 307 km/h)
Max design diving speed	181·5 knots (209 mph; 337 km/h)
Max cruising speed at 5,000 ft (1,520 m)	100 knots (115 mph; 185 km/h)
Stalling speed, flaps down	48 knots (55 mph; 88 km/h)
Rate of climb at S/L	787 ft (240 m)/min
Service ceiling	14,760 ft (4,500 m)
T-O run (zero wind)	656 ft (200 m)
Landing run (zero wind)	590 ft (180 m)
Max range	429 nm (495 miles; 800 km)
Endurance	4 hr

CONAL
COMPANHIA NACIONAL DE AVIÕES LTDA
HEAD OFFICE AND WORKS:
Sorocaba, São Paulo State

This company designed and built a prototype light aircraft named the W-151 Sopocaba, described in the 1968-69 *Jane's*. There has been no indication that production is contemplated. Conal also conducts major overhaul of light and medium-sized aircraft.

CTA
CENTRO TÉCNICO DE AERONÁUTICA
HEADQUARTERS:
São José dos Campos, São Paulo

DIRECTOR OF CTA:
Brig do Ar Paulo Victor da Silva

The Centro Técnico de Aeronáutica (Aeronautical Technical Centre) is a Ministry of Aeronautics establishment, charged with conducting aeronautical research, certificating new aircraft types and graduating aeronautical engineers. It is divided into two institutes: the Instituto de Pesquisas e Desenvolvimento (Development and Research Institute) and the Instituto Tecnológico de Aeronáutica (Aeronautical Technological Institute), which is the engineering school.

INSTITUTO DE PESQUISAS E DESENVOLVIMENTO (IPD)
DIRECTOR OF IPD:
Cel Av Paulo Delvaux

The IPD conducts research in several fields, and includes the following departments: PEA (Departamento de Eletrônica) the electronics department; PMR (Departamento de Materiais), the materials department; PAE (Departamento de Assuntos Especiais), the special armaments department; PMO (Departamento de Motôres), the power plant department; and the PAR (Departamento de Aeronaves), the aircraft department.

DEPARTAMENTO DE AERONAVES (PAR)
HEAD OF PAR:
Maj Av Eudes Alves da Costa e Silva

Since 2 January 1970, the PAR's activities have been concentrated upon aircraft certification, flight testing and procurement. Its former work on aircraft development, including that of the IPD/PAR-6504 Bandeirante, has been assigned to a new company known as Embraer (which see).

EMBRAER
EMPRÊSA BRASILEIRA DE AERONÁUTICA SA
HEADQUARTERS:
Av Brig Faria Lima—CTA
PRESIDENT:
Dr Aldo B. Franco da Silva Santos
SUPERINTENDENT DIRECTOR:
Dr Ozires Silva
PRODUCTION DIRECTOR:
Dr Ozilio Carlos da Silva
TECHNICAL DIRECTOR:
Dr Guido Fontegalante Pessotti
INDUSTRIAL RELATIONS DIRECTOR:
Dr Antônio Garcia da Silveira
FINANCIAL DIRECTOR:
Alberto Franco Faria Marcondes
COMMERCIAL DIRECTOR:
Renato José da Silva

With the establishment of this enterprise, in which the Brazilian government is the main shareholder, all the development work previously started at PAR was assigned to Embraer as from 2 January 1970.

Embraer is now responsible for production of the Bandeirante transport aircraft, the licence manufacture of the Aermacchi M.B.326G jet trainer, and project and design work on new prototype aircraft.

IPD/PAR-6504 BANDEIRANTE
Brazilian Air Force designation: C-95

The Bandeirante twin-turboprop light transport was developed by a Brazilian design team under the leadership of M Max Holste, the well-known French aircraft engineer. Construction of the first of four prototypes was started at the PAR in mid-1966. Designated YC-95, and bearing serial number 2130, this aircraft flew for the first time on 26 October 1968. The second aircraft (2131) flew on 19 October 1969. The third and fourth machines are under construction, and production is planned for both the military and the civil market.

The Bandeirante prototypes seat seven to ten passengers. The production version will carry 12 passengers, and the Brazilian Air Force plans currently to use it as a replacement for its fleet of Beechcraft C-45s. Other versions have been projected, including a navigation trainer and an aeromedical evacuation aircraft.

Production will begin with an initial quantity of 20 aircraft, followed by a further series of 80, at an output of two aircraft a month.

The description below applies basically to the prototypes, except where indicated.

TYPE: Twin-turboprop general-purpose transport.

WINGS: Cantilever low-wing monoplane. Dihedral 4° 30' (7° on production version). Incidence 3°. Thickness/chord ratio 16% at root, 12% at tip. All-metal structure, including ailerons and double-slotted flaps. Production models will have leading-edge de-icing system. Trim-tab in port aileron. Landing light in each leading-edge.

FUSELAGE: All-metal semi-monocoque structure. Two upward-hinged doors, one on each side of nose, provide access to avionics equipment.

TAIL UNIT: Cantilever all-metal structure, with sweptback vertical surfaces. Trim-tab in rudder. Production models will have de-icing system for leading-edges of fin and tailplane.

LANDING GEAR: Retractable tricycle type, of ERAM manufacture, with single wheel and oleo-pneumatic shock-absorber on each unit. Main wheels have Kléber-Colombes tyres, size 670 × 210-12, and retract forward into engine nacelles, protruding slightly when up for increased safety in a wheels-up landing. Forward-retracting nose-wheel unit has 420 × 150 Kléber-Colombes tyre and carries an additional GE landing light.

Italian-built Aermacchi M.B.326G of the type to be built in Brazil by Embraer (*Ronaldo S. Olive*)

First prototype IPD/PAR-6504 Bandeirante twin-turboprop utility transport

An additional cabin window identifies the second prototype of the Bandeirante

POWER PLANT: Prototypes have two 550 shp Pratt & Whitney (UACL) PT6A-20 turboprop engines, each driving a Hamilton Standard SK65079-4 three-blade constant-speed fully-feathering propeller of 7 ft 9 in (2·36 m) diameter. Fuel in two bag-type tanks in wings, with total capacity of 220 Imp gallons (1,000 litres). Gravity refuelling point on top of each wing. Production aircraft will be powered by two 680 shp PT6A-27 turboprop engines.

ACCOMMODATION: Two seats side-by-side on flight deck. Cabin seats seven to ten passengers (12 in production version). Conversion into an ambulance for four stretcher patients takes ten minutes. Door on port side, aft of wing, with built-in airstairs. Baggage racks at rear of cabin. Provision for toilet.

ELECTRONICS AND EQUIPMENT: Standard equipment includes one Brazilian-built PEA-Whinner CY-07-04-03A 140-channel VHF transceiver, dual Collins DF-203 radio-compasses, one Collins VOR/LOC 51R-7A receiver, one Collins 51V-5 glide-slope indicator, one Collins 51Z-6 marker beacon, one Northern N414-FR 6-channel HF transceiver, one Bendix RDR-100 weather radar and one Bendix M-4C autopilot. In addition to the above, production aircraft will have an additional transceiver of the Collins 618-M1 type, and the radio-compasses will be Bendix DF A 73A type.

SYSTEMS: Electrical system utilises two starter-generators and a 28V alkaline battery with inverters to supply 115/26V 400 c/s AC. Oxygen and air-conditioning systems standard. Pressurised cabin will be standard in production aircraft.

DIMENSIONS, EXTERNAL:
- Wing span:
  - prototypes — 50 ft 7 in (15·42 m)
  - production — 50 ft 2¼ in (15·30 m)
- Wing chord at root — 7 ft 7½ in (2·32 m)
- Wing chord at tip — 4 ft 5 in (1·35 m)
- Wing aspect ratio (prototypes) — 8·1
- Length overall:
  - prototypes — 41 ft 9½ in (12·74 m)
  - production — 44 ft 3½ in (13·50 m)
- Height overall:
  - prototypes — 16 ft 11½ in (5·17 m)
  - production — 17 ft 8¾ in (5·40 m)
- Tailplane span — 19 ft 0¼ in (5·80 m)
- Wheel track — 15 ft 9 in (4·80 m)

AREAS:
- Wings, gross:
  - prototypes — 314 sq ft (29·17 m²)
  - production — 312 sq ft (29·00 m²)
- Vertical tail surfaces (total) — 58·8 sq ft (5·46 m²)
- Horizontal tail surfaces (total) — 87·2 sq ft (8·10 m²)

WEIGHTS AND LOADINGS:
- Weight empty, equipped:
  - prototypes — 5,620 lb (2,550 kg)
- Max T-O weight:
  - prototypes — 9,920 lb (4,500 kg)
  - production — 10,692 lb (4,850 kg)
- Max wing loading:
  - prototypes — 31 lb/sq ft (154 kg/m²)
  - production — 34·2 lb/sq ft (167 kg/m²)
- Max power loading:
  - prototypes — 9·04 lb/shp (4·10 kg/shp)
  - production — 7·85 lb/shp (3·56 kg/shp)

PERFORMANCE (at max T-O weight, ISA; estimated for production version):
- Max cruising speed:
  - prototypes, at 8,200 ft (2,500 m) — 217 knots (250 mph; 400 km/h)
  - production, at 8,300 ft (2,530 m) — 232 knots (267 mph; 430 km/h)
- Stalling speed — 60 knots (69 mph; 110 km/h)
- Rate of climb at S/L — 1,870 ft (570 m)/min
- Service ceiling — 25,000 ft (7,600 m)
- T-O to 50 ft (15 m) — 1,215 ft (370 m)
- Landing from 50 ft (15 m) — 1,375 ft (420 m)
- Max cruising range, 30 min reserves:
  - prototypes, at 16,400 ft (5,000 m) — 998 nm (1,150 miles; 1,850 km)
  - production, at 10,000 ft (3,280 m) — 1,076 nm (1,240 miles; 2,000 km)

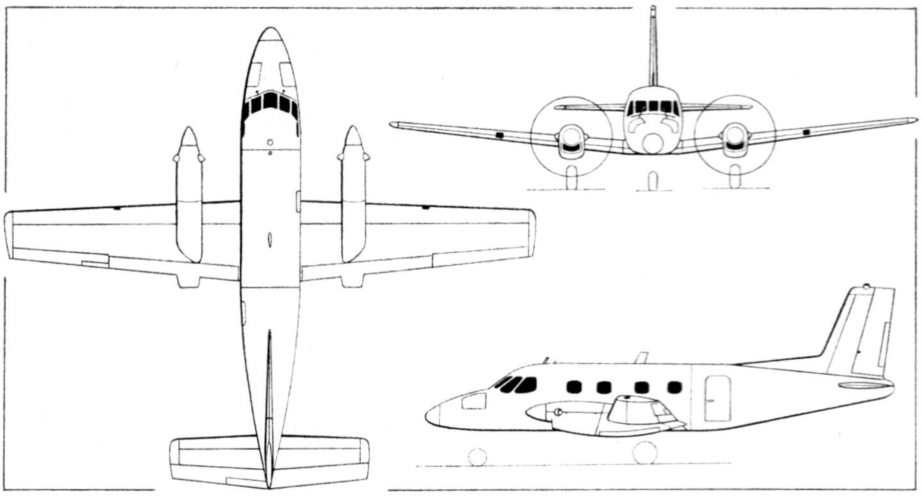

Production configuration of IPD/PAR-6504 Bandeirante twin-turboprop light transport

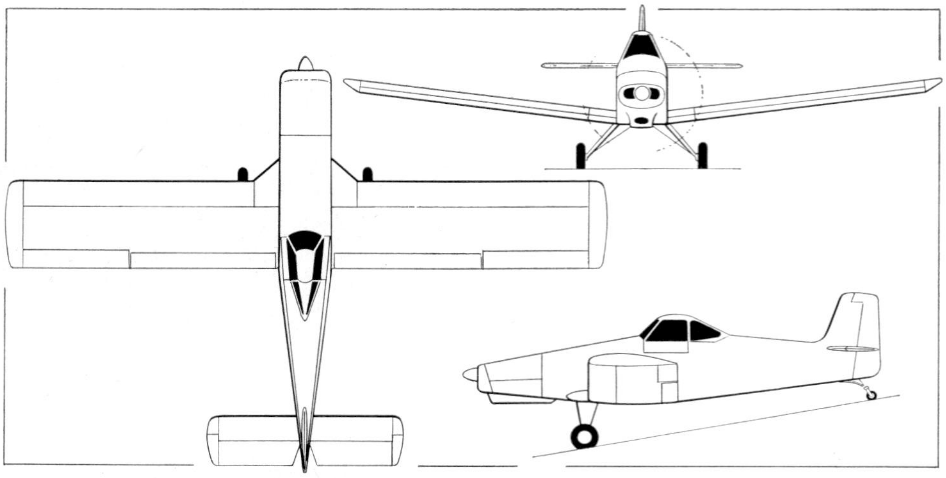

General arrangement drawing of the IPD-6909 Ipanema

IPD-6909 IPANEMA

The IPD-6909 is an agricultural aircraft, designed to specifications laid down by the Brazilian Ministry of Agriculture. A prototype was scheduled to fly in July 1970, and, subject to successful completion of flight and other testing, an initial series of 50 production aircraft is under consideration by the Brazilian Ministry of Agriculture. These will be manufactured jointly by Aerotec and Embraer.

As shown in the adjacent three-view drawing, the IPD-6909 is a single-seat cantilever low-wing monoplane, the wings having 7° dihedral from the roots. It is of all-metal construction, and is powered by a 260 hp Lycoming six-cylinder horizontally-opposed air-cooled engine driving a two-blade propeller of 7 ft 0 in (2·13 m) diameter. Landing gear is of the non-retractable tail-wheel type, with cantilever main-wheel legs.

DIMENSIONS, EXTERNAL:
- Wing span — 36 ft 9 in (11·20 m)
- Wing chord (constant) — 5 ft 3 in (1·60 m)
- Length overall — 24 ft 4½ in (7·43 m)
- Height overall (tail down) — 7 ft 2½ in (2·20 m)
- Fuselage: Max width — 3 ft 0½ in (0·93 m)
- Tailplane span — 11 ft 4¼ in (3·46 m)
- Wheel track — 7 ft 2½ in (2·20 m)

AREAS:
- Wings, gross — 193·75 sq ft (18·00 m²)
- Ailerons (total) — 17·21 sq ft (1·60 m²)
- Flaps (total) — 24·76 sq ft (2·30 m²)
- Fin — 13·02 sq ft (1·21 m²)
- Rudder — 6·78 sq ft (0·63 m²)
- Tailplane — 32·29 sq ft (3·00 m²)
- Elevators — 16·15 sq ft (1·50 m²)

WEIGHT:
- Max T-O weight — 3,086 lb (1,400 kg)

PERFORMANCE (estimated at max T-O weight):
- Design cruising speed — 95 knots (109 mph; 176 km/h)

NEIVA

SOCIEDADE CONSTRUTORA AERONÁUTICA NEIVA, LTDA

HEAD OFFICE AND WORKS:
Rua Santa Clara 260, São José dos Campos, São Paulo State (Caixa Postal 247)

SPECIAL DIVISION: São José dos Campos, São Paulo State

DIRECTORS:
José Carlos de Barros Neiva (General Manager)
Breno A. B. Junqueira (Production Manager)

Neiva has in current production the Regente 420L four-seat AOP aircraft and IPD-6201 Universal basic trainer for the Brazilian Air Force. A modified version of the Regente 420L is under development for the civil market.

NEIVA REGENTE

Brazilian Air Force designations: C-42 and L-42

Design of the Regente was started in 1959 as the Neiva Model 360C, the prototype of which flew for the first time on 7 September 1961. It received its certificate of airworthiness from the Brazilian Ministry of Aeronautics on 12 November 1963.

Two versions have appeared, as follows:

Regente 360C. Initial production version, ordered as four-seat utility aircraft for Brazilian Air Force, by whom it is designated **C-42** (originally U-42). The first production aircraft was flown in February 1965. Total of 80 ordered, all of which had been completed and delivered by the end of 1968.

Regente 420L. Development of Regente 360C for AOP duties with liaison and observation squadrons of the Brazilian Air Force, by whom it is designated **L-42.** Differs from C-42 mainly in having a "stepped-down" rear fuselage, aft of the cabin, for better all-round visibility, and improved controls. The YL-42 prototype flew for the first time in October 1967, and 40 L-42's have been ordered to replace the Brazilian Air Force's Neiva L-6 and Cessna O-1A and O-1E aircraft. The first of these flew in June 1969, and thirty-five had been completed by February 1970; production was planned to end later in that year.

A civil version of the L-42 is under development, and an "intermediate" civil aircraft was undergoing flight trials early in 1970. The production version will have a choice of several power plants, larger front and rear windscreens, improved control surfaces and aerodynamics.

The following description applies generally to both the C-42 and L-42, except where indicated.

TYPE: Four-seat light monoplane, stressed for $+4g$ to $-2{\cdot}5g$.

WINGS: Braced high-wing monoplane. Wing section NACA 4410. Dihedral 1°. Incidence 2° 30′. All-metal single-spar structure. Plain all-metal ailerons on C-42, semi-Fowler type on L-42. All-metal single-slotted semi-Fowler flaps.

FUSELAGE: All-metal semi-monocoque structure.

TAIL UNIT: Cantilever all-metal structure, with sweptback vertical surfaces. Sweepback 33° on fin leading-edge. All-moving tailplane with anti-balance tab.

LANDING GEAR: Non-retractable tricycle type, with steerable nose-wheel. Spring steel main legs. Oleo shock-absorber in nose unit. Main wheel tyres size 7·00 × 6 on C-42, 6·00 × 6 on L-42. Nose-wheel tyre size 6·00 × 6 on C-42, 5·00 × 5 on L-42. Tyre pressures (both versions) 30 lb/sq in (2·10 kg/cm²) on nose units, 27 lb/sq in (1·90 kg/cm²) on main units. Goodyear (L-42) or Brazilian (C-42) hydraulic disc brakes except for early production L-42's which have Goodyear expansion-type brakes.

POWER PLANT (C-42): One 210 hp Continental IO-360-D four-cylinder horizontally-opposed air-cooled engine, driving a Hartzell BHC-C2YF-1B/7663 two-blade constant-speed metal propeller of 6 ft 0 in (1·83 m) diameter. Fuel in two aluminium tanks in wing roots, with total capacity of 38 Imp gallons (172 litres). Oil capacity 1·66 Imp gallons (7·6 litres).

POWER PLANT (L-42): One 180 hp Lycoming O-360-A1D four-cylinder horizontally-opposed air-cooled engine, driving a Hartzell HC-C2YK-1A/A7666 two-blade constant-speed metal propeller of 6 ft 4 in (1·93 m) diameter. Fuel and oil as for C-42.

ACCOMMODATION (C-42): Individual seats for pilot, co-pilot/doctor and navigator/observer. Two of the seats are reversible, and a folding stretcher is permanently carried for instant conversion to an ambulance role. Access to cabin via forward-opening door on each side. Rear baggage door gives access to compartment for up to 40 lb (18 kg) of baggage. Cabin fully ventilated and has glass-fibre sound-proofing.

ACCOMMODATION (L-42): Individual front seats for pilot and one passenger, with bench seat at rear for two more persons. Dual controls standard. Otherwise generally as C-42.

SYSTEMS: Hydraulic system for main wheel braking. 24V battery supplies electrical power.

ELECTRONICS AND EQUIPMENT: Complete IFR equipment standard. Provision for 140-channel Whinner VHF transmitter/receiver, HF transmitter/receiver and Bendix DFA-72. Additionally, L-42 version has provision for ADF transmitter/receiver.

DIMENSIONS. EXTERNAL:

Wing span	29 ft 11½ in (9·13 m)
Wing chord (constant)	4 ft 11 in (1·50 m)
Wing aspect ratio	6·1
Length overall	23 ft 1 in (7·04 m)
Height overall	9 ft 7¼ in (2·93 m)
Tailplane span	10 ft 3 in (3·13 m)
Wheel track:	
C-42	6 ft 6 in (1·98 m)
L-42	6 ft 3½ in (1·92 m)
Wheelbase	7 ft 0 in (2·13 m)
Propeller ground clearance:	
C-42	1 ft 7¾ in (0·50 m)
L-42	1 ft 5¾ in (0·45 m)
Cabin doors (each):	
Height	3 ft 5¼ in (1·05 m)
Width	3 ft 2¾ in (0·98 m)
Height to sill	2 ft 1¼ in (0·64 m)
Baggage door:	
Height	1 ft 6¾ in (0·48 m)
Width	1 ft 5¼ in (0·44 m)

DIMENSIONS, INTERNAL:

Cabin: Max length	6 ft 6¾ in (2·00 m)
Max width	3 ft 3¼ in (1·00 m)
Max height	3 ft 11¼ in (1·20 m)
Floor area	19·4 sq ft (1·80 m²)
Volume	219 cu ft (6·20 m³)

WEIGHTS AND LOADINGS:

Weight empty, equipped:	
C-42	1,410 lb (640 kg)
L-42	1,500 lb (680 kg)
Max T-O and landing weight	2,293 lb (1,040 kg)
Max wing loading	15·77 lb/sq ft (77·3 kg/m²)
Max power loading:	
C-42	12·6 lb/hp (5·70 kg/hp)
L-42	10·8 lb/hp (4·90 kg/hp)

PERFORMANCE (at max T-O weight):

Max level speed at S/L:	
C-42	119 knots (137 mph; 220 km/h)
L-42	129 knots (149 mph; 240 km/h)
Max permissible diving speed	150 knots (173 mph; 280 km/h)
Max cruising speed at S/L:	
C-42	121 knots (139 mph; 223 km/h)
L-42	136 knots (157 mph; 252 km/h)
Econ cruising speed (75% power) at 5,000 ft (1,500 m):	
C-42	115 knots (132 mph; 212 km/h)
L-42	125 knots (144 mph; 231 km/h)
Stalling speed, flaps down	49 knots (56 mph; 90 km/h)
Rate of climb at S/L:	
C-42	690 ft (210 m)/min
L-42	699 ft (213 m)/min
Service ceiling:	
C-42	11,800 ft (3,600 m)
L-42	12,000 ft (3,660 m)
T-O run:	
C-42	1,020 ft (310 m)
L-42	968 ft (295 m)
T-O to 50 ft (15 m):	
C-42	1,150 ft (350 m)
L-42	1,096 ft (334 m)
Landing from 50 ft (15 m):	
C-42	1,510 ft (460 m)
L-42	1,424 ft (434 m)
Landing run:	
C-42, L-42	475 ft (145 m)
Range with max fuel, no reserves:	
C-42	500 nm (576 miles; 928 km)
L-42	512 nm (590 miles, 950 km)
Range with max payload, no reserves:	
C-42	487 nm (651 miles; 904 km)
L-42	498 nm (574 miles; 925 km)

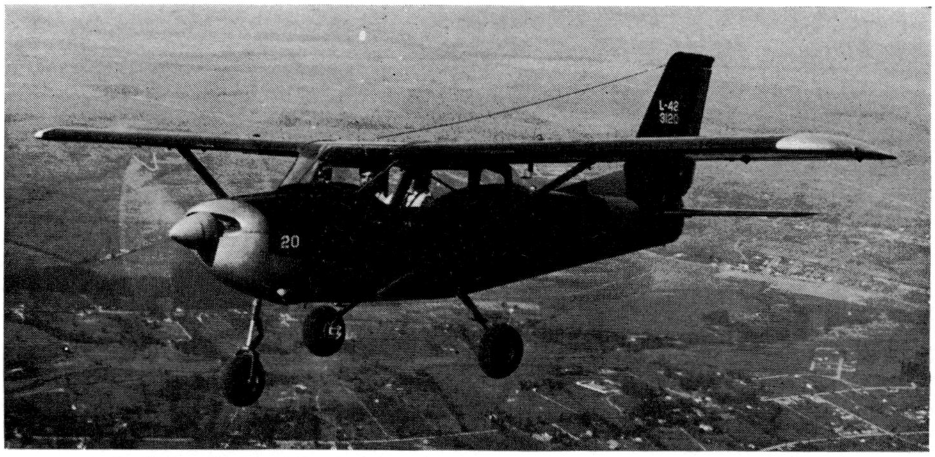

L-42 (Neiva Model 420L) Regente observation aircraft of the Brazilian Air Force

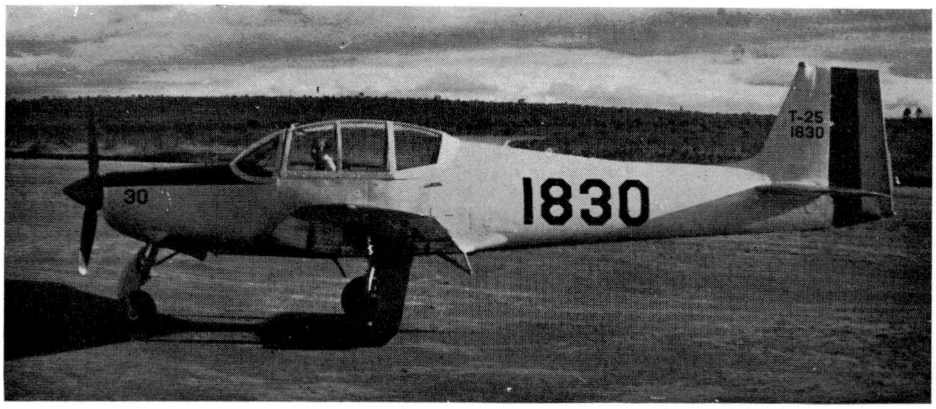

Prototype of the Neiva T-25 Universal basic trainer for the Brazilian Air Force *(Ronaldo S. Olive)*

NEIVA IPD-6201 UNIVERSAL
Brazilian Air Force designation: T-25

The Universal was designed by Mr Joseph Kovacs to meet a Brazilian Air Force requirement for a trainer to replace the Fokker S-11/S-12 Instructors and North American T-6 Texans in current use at its training centres.

Initial design work was started in January 1963. Construction of the prototype began in May 1965, after the Brazilian Air Force Staff had evaluated the project in competition with other proposals, including jet-powered trainers also designed by Mr Kovacs.

The prototype Universal (PP-ZTW) was flown for the first time on 29 April 1966 at the CTA, São José dos Campos, by Neiva's test pilot, Sr Brasílico F. Neto. It has side-by-side seating, to conform with Ministry of Aeronautics preference; other versions currently projected include one with tandem seating and a twin-engined development. Certification by the Brazilian Air Ministry was granted in 1968.

The Brazilian Air Force has ordered 150 Universals, of which the first was scheduled to make its first flight in July 1970.

TYPE: Two/three-seat basic trainer.

WINGS: Cantilever low-wing monoplane. Wing section NACA 632A315 at root, NACA 631212 at tip. Dihedral 6°. Incidence 2°. Single-spar structure of riveted aluminium alloy. All-metal dynamically-balanced slotted ailerons. All-metal split flaps. All controls electrically powered.

FUSELAGE: Welded steel-tube centre fuselage with aluminium skin panels. Semi-monocoque tail-cone of riveted aluminium alloy.

TAIL UNIT: Cantilever all-metal structure, with electrically-controlled tabs on elevators and rudder.

LANDING GEAR: Retractable tricycle type. Hydraulic retraction, main units inward, nose-wheel rearward. ERAM oleo-shock absorbers. Main wheels fitted with Goodyear tyres size 7·50 × 10 and Oldi (Brazil) disc brakes. Nose-wheel steerable and fitted with Goodyear tyre size 6·00 × 6. Tyre pressure (all units) 30 lb/sq in (2·1 kg/cm²).

POWER PLANT: One 300 hp Lycoming IO-540-K1D5 six-cylinder horizontally-opposed air-cooled engine, driving a Hartzell HC-C2YK-4/C8475-2R non-feathering three-blade constant-speed metal propeller, diameter 7 ft 2 in (2·18 m). Fuel in six aluminium tanks in wings, with total capacity of 88·2 Imp gallons (401 litres). Provision for two 16·5 Imp gallon (75·75 litre) wingtip tanks. Refuelling point above wing. Oil capacity 2·5 Imp gallons (11·5 litres).

ACCOMMODATION: Two seats side-by-side, with full dual controls, and optional third seat at rear. Large rearward-sliding transparent canopy. Baggage compartment aft of rear seat.

SYSTEMS: Electrically-actuated hydraulic system, pressure 1,150 lb/sq in (81 kg/cm²), for flaps and landing gear. Manual emergency pump. 24V electrical system.

ELECTRONICS AND EQUIPMENT: 140-channel Brazilian-made VHF radio, HF and ADF. Complete IFR instrumentation. Provision for underwing bombs or rockets.

DIMENSIONS, EXTERNAL:

Wing span	36 ft 1 in (11·00 m)
Wing chord at root	6 ft 9¾ in (2·08 m)
Wing chord at tip	3 ft 7¼ in (1·10 m)
Wing aspect ratio	6·9
Length overall	27 ft 10½ in (8·50 m)
Height overall	10 ft 2 in (3·10 m)
Tailplane span	12 ft 2½ in (3·72 m)
Wheel track	8 ft 10½ in (2·70 m)
Wheelbase	7 ft 4½ in (2·25 m)
Propeller ground clearance	1 ft 1¾ in (0·35 m)

DIMENSIONS, INTERNAL:

Cabin:	
Length	7 ft 2½ in (2·20 m)
Max width	4 ft 1 in (1·25 m)
Max height	4 ft 1 in (1·25 m)
Floor area	32 sq ft (3·0 m²)
Volume	141 cu ft (4·00 m³)
Baggage compartment volume	12·5 cu ft (0·35 m³)

AREAS:

Wings, gross	183 sq ft (17·00 m²)
Ailerons (total)	15·82 sq ft (1·47 m²)
Trailing-edge flaps	17·01 sq ft (1·58 m²)
Fin	6·67 sq ft (0·62 m²)
Rudder, including tab	11·20 sq ft (1·04 m²)
Tailplane	20·23 sq ft (1·88 m²)
Elevators, including tabs	14·85 sq ft (1·38 m²)

WEIGHTS AND LOADINGS:

Weight empty, equipped	2,425 lb (1,100 kg)
Max T-O and landing weight	3,085 lb (1,400 kg)
Max wing loading	16·68 lb/sq ft (82·3 kg/m²)
Max power loading	10·6 lb/hp (4·8 kg/hp)

PERFORMANCE (at max T-O weight):

Max level speed at S/L	175 knots (201 mph; 324 km/h)
Max permissible diving speed	269 knots (310 mph; 500 km/h)
Max cruising speed at 5,000 ft (1,500 m)	165 knots (190 mph; 306 km/h)
Stalling speed, flaps down	54 knots (62 mph; 99 km/h)
Stalling speed, flaps up	60 knots (69 mph; 110 km/h)
Rate of climb at S/L	1,730 ft (528 m)/min
Service ceiling	26,250 ft (8,000 m)
T-O and landing run	495 ft (151 m)
T-O to 50 ft (15 m)	1,155 ft (352 m)
Landing from 50 ft (15 m)	1,330 ft (405 m)
Range with max fuel	538 nm (620 miles; 1,000 km)
Range with max payload	388 nm (447 miles; 720 km)

CANADA

AVIAN

AVIAN AIRCRAFT LTD

HEAD OFFICE:
Georgetown, Ontario

This company was formed in February 1959, with a Dominion Charter, to develop an auto-gyro-type aircraft known as the Avian 2/180 Gyroplane.

AVIAN 2/180 GYROPLANE

Two prototypes of the Avian 2/180 were built. The first began its flight tests in the Spring of 1960. The second made its first controlled flight on 16 February 1961.

The first of three pre-production prototype/demonstrators began its flight tests in January 1962, and more than 300 hours of test flying were completed by the prototypes by the end of 1963.

In July 1964, it was announced that the Canadian Government had approved a $540,000 contract to assist research and development of the 2/180 Gyroplane. The relevant contract was signed in December 1964, enabling Avian to begin work on a modified version, termed the certification prototype. This aircraft was completed in October 1965 and flew for the first time early in the following month. The 2/180 Gyroplane received a provisional Certificate of Airworthiness in April 1968. A full C of A was granted by the Canadian Department of Transport late in 1968, but no further news of the aircraft has been received since that date.

The following details apply to the certification prototype:

TYPE: Two-seat wingless autogyro.

ROTOR SYSTEM: Three-blade rotor, with flapping hinges, but no drag hinges. Conventional control system. Blades are of bonded construction, with extruded aluminium alloy leading-edge and sheet aluminium alloy trailing-edge. Blade section NACA 00135; chord 9·5 in (24·1 cm). Blades do not fold. Rotor brake standard.

ROTOR DRIVE: Shaft-drive from engine by timing belt, through clutch and gearbox, and timing belt at hub, to provide jump take-off capability. Gearbox contains hypoid crown wheel and pinion. Rotor/engine rpm ratio 1 : 5·5. Rotor rpm 263 in auto-rotation at max forward speed at S/L.

FUSELAGE: Box-beam keel, stressed floor and pylon of light alloy. Steel-tube engine and duct mountings. Light alloy secondary structure, with glass-fibre panels in non-structural areas.

TAIL UNIT: Rudder inside light alloy and glass-fibre propeller duct.

LANDING GEAR: Non-retractable tricycle type. Avian biscuit-type shock-absorbers. All-steel cantilever legs, each carrying a single wheel,

Certification prototype of the Avian 2/180 Gyroplane (200 hp Lycoming IO-360 engine)

with Goodyear nylon-reinforced tubeless tyres, size 5·00 × 5. Tyre pressure 34 lb/sq in (2·39 kg/cm²). Castoring nose-wheel. Goodyear hydraulic disc brakes, diameter 5 in (13 cm). Turning circle 20 ft 0 in (6·10 m).

POWER PLANT: One 200 hp Lycoming IO-360 four-cylinder horizontally-opposed air-cooled engine, driving a Hartzell two-blade constant-speed pusher propeller. Propeller is enclosed in a duct, forming efficient ducted fan unit and improving engine cooling. Light alloy fuel tank aft of cabin, with capacity of 30·5 Imp gallons (138·5 litres). Oil capacity 6·7 Imp quarts (7·6 litres).

ACCOMMODATION: Two seats in tandem in enclosed cabin, with dual controls. Door on starboard side, by front seat. Cabin heated by fuel-fired heater or exhaust muff heater.

SYSTEMS: Avian-designed, using off-the-shelf components.

ELECTRONICS AND EQUIPMENT: No blind-flying instruments. Radio optional.

DIMENSIONS, EXTERNAL:
Rotor diameter	37 ft 0 in (11·28 m)

Length overall	16 ft 0 in (4·88 m)
Height overall	7 ft 4 in (2·24 m)
Wheel track	8 ft 0 in (2·44 m)
Wheelbase	7 ft 11 in (2·41 m)

AREAS:
Main rotor blades (each)	14·65 sq ft (1·36 m²)
Rotor disc	1,075 sq ft (99·87 m²)
Rudder	12·4 sq ft (1·15 m²)

WEIGHTS AND LOADINGS:
Weight empty, equipped	1,400 lb (635 kg)
Max T-O and landing weight	2,000 lb (907 kg)
Max disc loading	1·86 lb/sq ft (9·08 kg/m²)
Max power loading	10·0 lb/hp (4·54 kg/hp)

PERFORMANCE (estimated at max T-O weight):
Max level speed	104 knots (120 mph; 193 km/h)
Normal cruising speed	87-96 knots (100-110 mph; 160-177 km/h)
Min level speed	26 knots (30 mph; 48 km/h)
Rate of climb at S/L	870 ft (265 m)/min
Service ceiling	14,000 ft (4,275 m)
T-O to 50 ft (15 m)	300 ft (91 m)
Landing run	0 ft (vertical descent)
Range with normal payload	347 nm (400 miles; 640 km)

CANADAIR

CANADAIR LTD (Subsidiary of General Dynamics Corporation)

HEAD OFFICE AND WORKS:
Cartierville Airport, Montreal, PQ

POSTAL ADDRESS:
PO Box 6087, Montreal 9, PQ

PRESIDENT AND CHIEF EXECUTIVE OFFICER:
Frederick R. Kearns

VICE-PRESIDENTS:
William T. E. Jolliffe
Peter J. Aird (Treasurer and Marketing)
William N. Gagnon (Legal)
Edward H. Higgins (Engineering)
John B. Hunter (Contracts and Finance, and Comptroller)
D. J. Follett (Operations)
J. W. Hughes (Public Relations)

Canadair Limited, the Canadian subsidiary of General Dynamics Corporation of New York, has been engaged in the development and manufacture of commercial and military aircraft since 1944. It also has facilities for research, design, development and manufacture of missile components and systems, electronic equipment and a variety of non-aerospace products.

The company has three plants at Cartierville Airport, Montreal, comprising 2·7 million sq ft

(250,840 m²) of covered floor space, and employed about 8,600 persons in the Spring of 1970.

In current production are the CF-5 and NF-5 tactical support aircraft under Northrop licence for the Canadian Forces and the Netherlands Government, and the CL-215 air tanker/utility amphibious aircraft. Production of the AN/USD-501 drone surveillance system continues for the armies of Canada, Great Britain and the Federal Republic of Germany (see "Drones" section).

Three CL-84 tilt-wing V/STOL aircraft have been built for the Canadian Armed Forces, and a number of CL-91 Dynatrac articulated tracked vehicles are in production for the US Army.

The manufacture of components for F-111, C-5A and F-5 aircraft, submarine components, aero-engine parts and aircraft spares, and the modification, repair and overhaul of aircraft form a substantial part of the current work programme.

Canadair is also building the tooling on the forward mid-assembly and aft tank assembly for the Grumman F-14 fighter for the US Navy.

Canadair has established a subsidiary known as CL Designs (UK) Ltd, at Potters Bar in England, to undertake aircraft tool planning and design, and tool procurement, and another, known as Flextrack-Nodwell, in Calgary, Alberta, for the production of off-road vehicles.

CANADAIR CL-41

Canadian Armed Forces designation: CT-114 Tutor

Two prototypes of the Canadair-designed CL-41 two-seat side-by-side jet trainer were built as a private venture, each powered by a 2,400 lb st Pratt & Whitney JT12A-5 turbojet. The first of these flew for the first time on 13 January 1960.

There were two production versions of the CL-41, as follows:

CL-41A. Ordered for the RCAF (as it was then) in September 1961, with 2,650 lb (1,202 kg) st Orenda-built General Electric J85-Can-40 turbojet. Delivery of 190 completed during 1966. Began to enter service in 1964, and is now employed by the Canadian Armed Forces for basic training. Described fully in 1964-65 *Jane's*.

CL-41G. During production of the CL-41A, development continued to provide two additional rôles—armament and tactical training, and light tactical support. Delivery of 20 of this later production model to the Royal Malaysian Air Force began in 1967 and was completed at the beginning of 1969. Changes include a more powerful 2,950 lb (1,338 kg) st General Electric J85-J4 engine; six stores suspension points capable of carrying up to 4,000 lb (1,815 kg) of gun pods, bombs, rockets, Sidewinder air-to-air missiles or auxiliary fuel tanks; soft-field landing gear; zero-level automatic ejection system and auto intake screens. Provision for variations in avionics, protective armour plate, etc. Described fully in 1968-69 *Jane's*.

CANADAIR CL-84-1
Canadian Armed Forces designation: CX-84

The CL-84 is a twin-engined tilt-wing V/STOL aircraft, produced initially as a private venture and later ordered for evaluation by the Canadian Armed Forces.

Following some seven years of development studies, construction of the original CL-84 prototype was started in November 1963 and completed in December 1964. From its first flight on 7 May 1965 (in the hover mode) to the termination of flight testing in September 1967, this prototype (CF-VTO-X) accumulated 405 operating hours, including 145 flying hours with 151 transitions in 305 flights, before being lost in an accident caused by a malfunction in the control system to the propellers.

In addition to development testing and demonstration flying, the CL-84 prototype underwent a 20-hour tri-Service flight evaluation by the US Army, Air Force, Navy and Marine Corps. During 1966, live simulated rescues over both land and water proved the feasibility of the tilt-wing concept in the hover rescue role. The prototype CL-84 was described fully in the 1967-68 *Jane's*.

Two further versions are being developed, as follows:

CL-84-1 (Canadian Armed Forces designation CX-84). Three examples ordered in February 1968 as evaluation aircraft to determine the operational potential and capabilities of twin-engined tilt-wing V/STOL aircraft in a variety of military roles. First aircraft (CX8401) made its initial flight on 19 February 1970, and all three will be in use by the CAF for evaluation work by the end of 1970. The CL-84-1 is similar to the CL-84 prototype, but has many detailed improvements including additional engine power and avionics.

CL-84-1 Supersedes the previously-announced CL-84-1C (see 1969-70 *Jane's*) as the proposed production version. Externally similar to the CL-84-1, but utilises a growth variant of the Lycoming T53 engine designated T53-19A, rated at 1,800 shp. The fuselage has been modified to increase the passenger/cargo volume by 40 per cent, and a wider-track landing gear provides an enhanced external stores capability. The CL-84-1D can be given a variety of equipment for several specific roles. For aircraft operating in offensive or defensive roles with external ordnance, the wing fuel tanks would not be used, all fuel being carried in foam-filled self-sealing tanks in the fuselage with a max capacity of 3,600 lb (1,632 kg). For utility transport or rescue roles requiring internal volume, fuel would be carried in the wing tanks (max 1,600 lb = 725 kg) and in external drop-tanks as required.

Numerous studies have also been made of growth versions of the CL-84, involving higher-powered engines, more than two engines and more than two propellers. One particular study envisages the use of General Electric T64 engines with larger-diameter propellers and a

5 ft (1·52 m) greater wing span, which would be especially suitable for "hot and high" operation. Roles envisaged for CL-84 variants include tactical armed support, utility tactical transport, helicopter escort, rescue, anti-submarine warfare, liaison and communications, V/STOL training and city-centre-to-city-centre transport.

For vertical take-off, the CL-84's wing is tilted hydraulically; as it tilts upward, the leading-edge and trailing-edge flaps are automatically extended and, simultaneously, the horizontal stabiliser tilts to its optimum position corresponding to the wing angle. There is no separate collective pitch lever, as the engine power is matched automatically by an increase in propeller pitch. Zero-wind vertical take-off is made with the wing at 85°, but the wing may be tilted to a maximum of 102° to permit the aircraft to fly backward at 30·4 knots (35 mph = 56 km/h) or to hover in a 35 mph tail wind with the fuselage horizontal. During transition from the hover mode to forward flight, the horizontal stabiliser tilts with the wing, thus effectively cancelling out trim changes caused by the wing attitude. Transition from stable hovering flight to a forward speed exceeding 100 knots (115 mph = 185 km/h) takes approx 10 sec.

When transition is completed, and the wing locked down, the tail propellers are stopped automatically and aligned fore and aft, where they remain throughout the fixed-wing part of the flight. Transition back to the hover mode is basically the reverse of the above procedure, spin-up of the tail propellers being initiated at the same time as the wing is unlocked, normally at a speed of 125 knots (144 mph = 232 km/h). As the wing approaches the vertical position, the aircraft decelerates to zero forward speed; the onset of positive ground effect as it descends necessitates a slight reduction in power to complete the landing.

With the wing tilted to approx 45°, the CL-84 can make a short take-off, to clear a 50 ft (15 m) obstacle 500 ft (152 m) after brake release, carrying approx twice the VTO payload. Short landings have been carried out at all wing angles between 15° and the vertical.

Low-speed manoeuvring is a feature of the tilt-wing concept. The CL-84 can, for example, maintain a 2g level turn at a speed of 55 knots (63 mph = 102 km/h), resulting in a turning radius of less than 200 ft (61 m), with the wing at 45°. For all ground manoeuvring the wing is positioned at a 15° angle.

The following description applies generally to both the CL-84-1 and the CL-84-1D.

TYPE: Tilt-wing V/STOL aircraft.

WINGS: Cantilever high-set tilting wing. Wing section NACA 63₃-418 (modified). No dihedral or sweep. Variable incidence, from 2° to 102°. Aluminium alloy stressed-skin structure, with extensive use of chemical milling. Full-span slotted trailing-edge flaps of aluminium alloy honeycomb construction, each divided into two sections by engine nacelles and functioning also as ailerons. Flaps operated by tandem hydraulic actuators manufactured by Heroux of Montreal. Full-span Kruger flap under leading-edge of each wing, of aluminium construction, is extended, except with wing fully up or fully down, by a single Heroux actuator each side. Mechanically-controlled Kruger flap over fuselage.

No spoilers, tabs or de-icing equipment. Wing is hinged at the 45 per cent chord station, with tilt actuating jack of electro-hydraulic ball-screw type, by Abex Industries of Canada Ltd, on top of fuselage on starboard side; wing-down lock on port side.

FUSELAGE: Conventional rectangular-section semi-monocoque structure of aluminium skins, frames and longerons, with bonded vertical stiffeners between frames.

TAIL UNIT: Cantilever variable-incidence horizontal surfaces, with sweptback endplate fins. Central sweptback fin and rudder. Conventional aluminium alloy stressed-skin construction. Horizontal surfaces, powered hydraulically by Heroux actuators, are programmed automatically to move with wing to an angle of incidence of about 45° when the wing is in the STOL position, but return to horizontal if wing tilt increases further for VTOL. Elevators and rudder are also hydraulically powered by Heroux actuators, with provision for reversion to manual control.

LANDING GEAR: Retractable tricycle type, designed to permit operation on unprepared terrain. Nose-wheel retracts rearward, main units forward into fairings built on to sides of fuselage. Abex oleo-pneumatic shock-absorbers. Twin wheels on all three units. Goodyear main wheels, size 6.50-8, and tyres, size 7.00-8 type III, pressure 62 lb/sq in (4·36 kg/cm²). Goodyear nose-wheels, size 6.00-6, and tyres, size 6.00-6 type III, pressure 40 lb/sq in (2·81 kg/cm²). Hydraulically-operated Goodyear independent disc brakes on each main unit. Ground steering is by rudder pedal authority over differential propeller pitch and normal use of main-wheel brakes.

POWER PLANT (CL-84-1): Two 1,500 shp Lycoming T53 (LTC1K-4A) turboprop engines, each driving, through an over-running clutch, a Curtiss-Wright reduction gearbox and four-blade lightweight propeller with glass-fibre reinforced plastic blades, diameter 14 ft 0 in (4·27 m). Propellers are handed and are interconnected by a cross-shaft through a central gearbox on top of the fuselage to which the drive shaft to the tail propellers is also linked through a clutch. In the event of one engine failing, or being shut down for economical cruise, the dead engine is declutched automatically from the system, and both main propellers receive equal power from the remaining engine. Horizontal four-blade contra-rotating Servotec tail propellers, diameter 7 ft 0 in (2·13 m), provide pitch control and lift during vertical and low-speed flight. Tail propeller brake fitted. Fuel tanks, each consisting of four inter-connected bladder-type cells, in wing spar box, with total capacity of 206 Imp gallons (936 litres). Provision for two 100 Imp gallon (455 litre) auxiliary drop-tanks beneath the fuselage. Gravity refuelling point above each wing near the tip. Oil capacity 5 Imp gallons (22·75 litres).

POWER PLANT (CL-84-1D): Two 1,800 shp Lycoming T53-19A turboprop engines driving improved propellers; transmission system as for CL-84-1. Provision for auxiliary fuel tanks to be carried in main cargo compartment.

First Canadair CL-84-1 tilt-wing V/STOL aircraft (two 1,500 shp Lycoming T53 turboprop engines)

ACCOMMODATION (CL-84-1): Side-by-side seats on flight deck, for pilot and a check pilot or observer, on North American zero-speed zero-height rocket-ejection seats. Ejection is via twin escape hatches in roof of crew compartment, and can be made at any wing tilt angle. Impact-resistant windshield, and internal and external releases on cockpit side windows. Dual controls standard. Aft of the crew compartment is a passenger/cargo compartment, with single rear-loading door under rear fuselage. This compartment can be furnished with inward-facing troop seats for 12 passengers; alternatively, for the freight role, tie-down rings are provided on a 20 in (51 cm) grid with 1,250 lb (567 kg) capacity.

ACCOMMODATION (CL-84-1D): Enlarged passenger/cargo compartment can accommodate up to 16 persons, on inward-facing troop seats along each side of cabin. Inward-opening loading doors under rear fuselage, with sill 4 ft 0 in (1·22 m) further aft than on CL-84-1. Alternative interior layouts provide for an increased cargo load, six troop seats and three casualty litters, or internal auxiliary fuel tanks. An overhead rail and hoist can be installed for hover rescue operations or to assist the loading of stretchers or freight. When internal auxiliary fuel tanks are carried, all three external fuselage hard-points can be occupied by separate ordnance loads.

SYSTEMS (CL-84-1): Stewart Warner combustion heater. Dual flying, engine and wing tilt controls. Two independent hydraulic systems, max pressure 3,000 lb/sq in (210 kg/cm²), each capable of maintaining essential services. Direct mechanical linkage in flight and engine control systems in case of total hydraulic failure. Primary hydraulic system operates controls; utility system operates controls and utilities. Sperry automatic stability augmentation system provides rate damping about the roll, yaw and pitch axes, as well as attitude stabilisation in pitch. Fire extinguishing system. Mechanical programming unit for entire flight control system provides normal aircraft response under all flight conditions. Electrical power provided by 28V DC system and 115/200V 400 c/s constant-frequency AC system. Primary DC system comprises a main bus powered by two engine-driven 200A 28V starter-generators, a distribution bus powered by the main bus, and a battery bus. One 24V 34Ah nickel-cadmium battery in compartment adjacent to nose-wheel well. AC power provided via a 1500VA single-phase rotary inverter and a 1 to 3 phase adaptor. Automatic changeover permits supply of all AC services from a standby inverter should the primary inverter fail.

ELECTRONICS AND EQUIPMENT (CL-84-1): UHF/AM, UHF/ADF, TACAN, radar altimeter, C14 compass system, and intercom. Provision for installing VHF/AM and VHF/FM. Three hard-points beneath fuselage, each suitable for a 1,000 lb (454 kg) store. Provision for each of the two outer positions to carry a 100 Imp gallon (455 litre) jettisonable auxiliary fuel tank.

DIMENSIONS, EXTERNAL (CL-84-1 and CL-84-1D):
Wing span   33 ft 4 in (10·16 m)
Wing chord (constant)   7 ft 0 in (2·13 m)
Wing aspect ratio   4·76
Span over propeller tips   34 ft 8 in (10·56 m)
Max length   47 ft 3½ in (14·41 m)
Width of fuselage   5 ft 4 in (1·63 m)
Height overall, wing at 0°   14 ft 2⅞ in (4·34 m)
Max propeller arc height, wing tilted 18° 30′
                                   16 ft 1 in (4·90 m)
Height overall, wing tilted 90°
                                   17 ft 1½ in (5·22 m)
Tailplane span   16 ft 8 in (5·08 m)
Wheel track:
  CL-84-1   10 ft 2 in (3·10 m)
  CL-84-1D   11 ft 6 in (3·51 m)
Wheelbase   14 ft 0½ in (4·28 m)
Distance between propeller centres
                                   20 ft 8 in (6·30 m)
Min propeller/ground clearance, wing tilted 15°
                                   2 ft 4 in (0·71 m)
Rear loading door:
  Height   4 ft 3 in (1·29 m)
  Width   3 ft 6 in (1·07 m)
  Height to sill   3 ft 7 in (1·09 m)

DIMENSIONS, INTERNAL:
Cabin, excluding flight deck:
  Length (CL-84-1)   10 ft 0 in (3·05 m)
  Length (CL-84-1D)   14 ft 0 in (4·27 m)
  Max width   4 ft 8 in (1·42 m)
  Max height   4 ft 4 in (1·32 m)
  Floor area (CL-84-1)   46·7 sq ft (4·34 m²)
  Volume (CL-84-1)   200 cu ft (5·66 m³)
  Volume (CL-84-1D)   280 cu ft (7·93 m³)

AREAS:
Wings, gross   233·3 sq ft (21·67 m²)
Trailing-edge flaps (total)
                                   35·3 sq ft (3·28 m²)

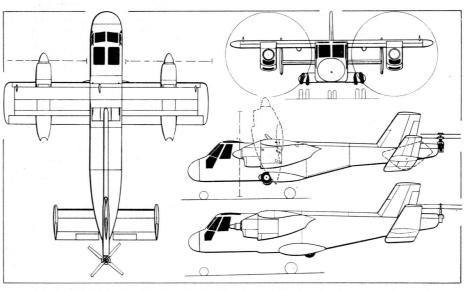

Canadair CL-84-1 tilt-wing V/STOL aircraft. Lower side-view drawing shows CL-84-1D

Leading-edge flaps (total) 21·7 sq ft (2·02 m²)
Fins (total)   59·1 sq ft (5·49 m²)
Rudder   4·1 sq ft (0·38 m²)
Tailplane   87·5 sq ft (8·13 m²)

WEIGHTS AND LOADINGS (estimated:
A=CL-84-1, B=CL-84-1D):
Manufacturer's weight empty:
  A   8,437 lb (3,827 kg)
  B   9,055 lb (4,107 kg)
Operating weight empty (incl one pilot):
  A   8,775 lb (3,980 kg)
  B   9,417 lb (4,271 kg)
Payload with max wing fuel and one pilot (ISA):
  A (VTOL)   2,315 lb (1,050 kg)
  B (VTOL)   3,983 lb (1,806 kg)
  A (STOL)   4,215 lb (1,912 kg)
  B (STOL)   5,783 lb (2,623 kg)
Payload with two 100 Imp gallon (455 litre) drop-tanks and one pilot (ISA):
  B (VTOL)   2,173 lb (985 kg)
  B (STOL)   3,973 lb (1,802 kg)
Max T-O weight at S/L (ISA):
  A (VTOL)   12,600 lb (5,715 kg)
  B (VTOL)   15,000 lb (6,803 kg)
  A (STOL)   14,500 lb (6,577 kg)
  B (STOL)   16,800 lb (7,620 kg)
Max T-O weight at S/L (ISA+15° C):
  A (VTOL)   11,550 lb (5,239 kg)
  A (STOL)   13,300 lb (6,033 kg)
Max wing loading at S/L (ISA weight):
  A (VTOL)   54 lb/sq ft (264 kg/m²)
  B (VTOL)   64 lb/sq ft (312 kg/m²)
  A (STOL)   62 lb/sq ft (303 kg/m²)
  B (STOL)   72 lb/sq ft (351 kg/m²)
Max power loading at S/L (ISA power):
  A (VTOL)   4·20 lb/shp (1·90 kg/shp)
  B (VTOL)   4·17 lb/shp (1·89 kg/shp)
  A (STOL)   4·82 lb/shp (2·19 kg/shp)
  B (STOL)   4·67 lb/shp (2·12 kg/shp)
Cargo floor loading:
  A   100 lb/sq ft (488 kg/m²)

PERFORMANCE (estimated:
A=CL-84-1, B=CL-84-1D):
Max level speed at max VTO weight (ISA):
  A   279 knots (321 mph; 517 km/h)
Max level speed at 10,000 ft (3,050 m) and max VTO weight:
  B   327 knots (376 mph; 606 km/h)
Max continuous speed at 10,000 ft (3,050 m) and max VTO weight:
  B   302 knots (348 mph; 560 km/h)
Max level speed at max VTO weight (ISA+15°C):
  A   266 knots (306 mph; 492 km/h)
Max permissible diving speed:
  A   360 knots (415 mph; 667 km/h)
Max cruising speed at max T-O weight (ISA):
  A (VTOL)   268 knots (309 mph; 497 km/h)
  B (VTOL)   302 knots (348 mph; 560 km/h)
  A (STOL)   261 knots (301 mph; 484 km/h)
  B (STOL)   296 knots (341 mph; 549 km/h)
Rate of climb at S/L (ISA):
  A (VTOL)   4,200 ft (1,280 m)/min
  B (VTOL)   5,600 ft (1,707 m)/min
  A (STOL)   3,300 ft (1,006 m)/min
T-O run:
  A (STOL)   140 ft (43 m)
T-O to 50 ft (15 m):
  A (STOL)   500 ft (153 m)
  B (STOL)   140 ft (43 m)
Landing from 50 ft (15 m):
  A (STOL) at AUW of 12,000 lb (5,440 kg)
                          400 ft (122 m)

Landing run:
  A (STOL)   150 ft (46 m)
Range with max wing fuel, allowances for 2 min at military power and 10% fuel reserve:
  A (VTOL)   365 nm (421 miles; 677 km)
  A (STOL)   356 nm (410 miles; 660 km)
Range with max wing fuel and full payload, cruising at 10,000 ft (3,050 m), 10% fuel reserve:
  A (VTOL)   295 nm (340 miles; 547 km)
  A (STOL)   279 nm (322 miles; 519 km)
Range with max wing fuel, cruising at 10,000 ft (3,050 m), 10% fuel reserve:
  B   319 nm (368 miles; 592 km)
Range with two 100 Imp gallon (455 litre) drop-tanks, cruising at 10,000 ft (3,050 m), 10% fuel reserve:
  B   632 nm (728 miles; 1,171 km)
Ferrying range at 20,000 ft (6,100 m), 10% fuel reserve:
  B   1,919 nm (2,210 miles; 3,558 km)

CANADAIR CL-215

The Canadair CL-215 is a twin-engined amphibian, intended primarily for fire-fighting but adaptable to a wide variety of other duties. It is designed to be as simple as possible to use and maintain, and will operate from small unprepared airstrips, lakes, sheltered bays etc.

The first CL-215, one of 20 originally ordered by the Province of Quebec for forest fire-fighting duties, made its maiden flight on 23 October 1967, and its first take-off from water on 2 May 1968; four more aircraft had flown by 1 March 1969. This order has since been reduced to 15 aircraft, which are expected to incorporate a number of improvements, including a different version of the R-2800 engine.

The Protection Civile of France has ordered 10. Four of these were delivered in 1969 and saw considerable action fighting forest fires in southern France during the year. The remaining six were due to be delivered by the end of May 1970.

The CL-215 has a maximum water load of 1,200 Imp gallons (5,455 litres). Pick-up of this load has been made in 12 sec, while skimming the water at over 70 knots (80 mph; 129 km/h), and the CL-215 can make 75 pick-ups and drops, with only one stop, for refuelling during the course of a single day's operations against a fire 100 miles (161 km) from its base. Pick-up distance from 50 ft (15 m) above the water during landing to 50 ft (15 m) on take-off is 5,450 ft (1,660 m).

The basic version, to which the following description applies, is known as the **CL-215-102.**

TYPE: Twin-engined multi-purpose amphibian.

WINGS: Cantilever high-wing monoplane. No dihedral. All-metal one-piece fail-safe structure, with front and rear spars at 16% and 49% chord. Spars of conventional construction, with extruded caps and web stiffened by vertical members. Aluminium alloy skin, with riveted spanwise extruded stringers, is supported at 30 in (76 cm) pitch by interspar ribs. Leading-edge consists of aluminium alloy skin attached to pressed nose ribs and spanwise stringers. Hydraulically-operated all-metal single-slotted flaps, supported by four external hinges on interspar ribs on each wing. Trim-tab in each aileron, with additional spring tab in port aileron. Detachable glass-fibre wing-tips.

FUSELAGE: All-metal single-step flying-boat hull of conventional fail-safe construction. Length/beam ratio 7·5.

TAIL UNIT: Cantilever all-metal fail-safe structure with horizontal surfaces mounted mid-way up fin. Structure of aluminium alloy sheet, honeycomb panels, extrusions and fittings. Elevators and rudder fitted with dynamic balance, trim-tab (port elevator only) and spring tabs and geared tabs.

LANDING GEAR: Hydraulically-retractable tricycle type. Fully-castoring twin-wheel nose unit retracts rearward into hull and is fully-enclosed by doors. Main gear support structures retract into wells in sides of hull. A plate mounted on each main gear assembly encloses bottom of wheel well. Main wheel tyre pressure 77 lb/sq in (5·4 kg/cm²); nose-wheel tyre pressure 95 lb/sq in (6·68 kg/cm²). Hydraulic disc brakes. Non-retractable stabilising floats are each carried on a pylon cantilevered from wing box structure, with breakaway provision.

POWER PLANT: Two 2,100 hp Pratt & Whitney R-2800-83AM2AH eighteen-cylinder two-row air-cooled radial engines, each driving a Hamilton Standard Hydromatic constant-speed fully-feathering three-blade propeller with 43E60 hub and type 6903 blades of 14 ft 3 in (4·34 m) diameter. Two fuel tanks, each made up of six flexible cells, in wing spar box, with total usable capacity of 950 Imp gallons (4,318 litres). Structural provision for four more cells, increasing total fuel capacity to 1,204 Imp gallons (5,473 litres). Gravity refuelling, through two points, above each tank. Oil in two tanks, with total capacity of 60 Imp gallons (272·75 litres), aft of engine firewalls.

ACCOMMODATION (water bomber version): Crew of two side-by-side on flight deck. Dual controls standard. Two 600 Imp gallon (2,728 litre) water tanks in main fuselage compartment, with retractable pick-up probe in either side of hull bottom. Water-drop door 5 ft 3 in × 2 ft 8 in (1·60 × 0·81 m) in each side of hull bottom. Sliding doors on port side of fuselage forward and aft of wings. Emergency exit 1 ft 8 in × 3 ft 0 in (0·51 × 0·91 m) on starboard side aft of wing trailing-edge. Emergency hatch above starboard cockpit. Mooring hatch on top of hull nose below flight deck windows.

ACCOMMODATION (utility version): Main cabin has standard accommodation for 19 passengers on canvas folding seats. Alternatively, with only minor structural changes, airliner-type seats can be installed at 31 in (79 cm) pitch for 32 passengers.

SYSTEMS: Hydraulic system, pressure 3,000 lb/sq in (210 kg/cm²), utilises two engine-driven pumps to actuate landing gear, flaps, water doors and pick-up probes, and wheel brakes. Electric pump in system provides power for emergency actuation of landing gear and brakes and closure of water doors. Electrical system includes two 250VA single-phase inverters, two 28V 200A DC generators, one 34Ah nickel-cadmium battery and one air-cooled gasoline engine-driven 28V 200A generator GPU.

ELECTRONICS AND EQUIPMENT: Standard installation includes HF, VHF and FM communications equipment, VOR/ILS, glideslope receiver, ADF, radio-compass and marker beacon.

DIMENSIONS, EXTERNAL:

Wing span	93 ft 10 in (28·60 m)
Wing chord (constant)	11 ft 6 in (3·51 m)
Wing aspect ratio	8·15
Length overall	65 ft 0¼ in (19·82 m)
Height over tail (on land)	29 ft 5½ in (8·98 m)
Beam	8 ft 6 in (2·59 m)
Tailplane span	36 ft 0 in (10·97 m)
Wheel track	17 ft 2¾ in (5·25 m)
Wheelbase	23 ft 8½ in (7·23 m)
Forward and rear doors:	
Height	3 ft 8 in (1·12 m)
Width	3 ft 4 in (1·03 m)

Canadair CL-215-102 multi-purpose amphibian in the insignia of the French *Protection Civile*

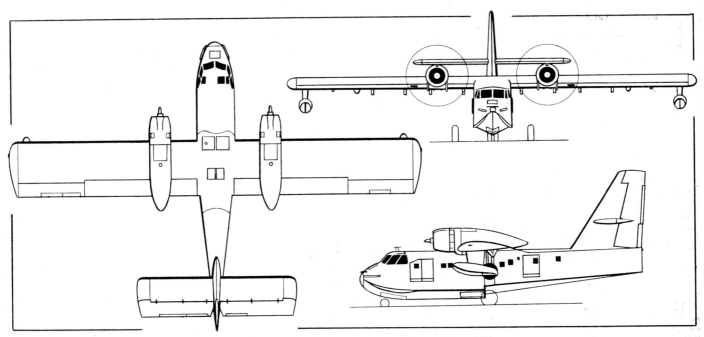

Canadair CL-215 twin-engined multi-purpose amphibian

Single-seat Canadair CF-5A (two General Electric/Orenda J85-15 turbojet engines) in Canadian Armed Forces insignia and camouflage

DIMENSIONS, INTERNAL:
Cabin, excluding flight deck:

Length	30 ft 9½ in (9·38 m)
Max width	7 ft 10 in (2·39 m)
Max height	6 ft 3 in (1·90 m)
Floor area	212 sq ft (19·69 m²)
Volume	1,237 cu ft (35·03 m²)

AREAS:

Wings, gross	1,080 sq ft (100·33 m²)
Ailerons (total)	86·6 sq ft (8·05 m²)
Flaps (total)	241 sq ft (22·39 m²)
Vertical tail surfaces (total)	185·5 sq ft (17·23 m²)
Rudder, incl tabs	64·75 sq ft (6·02 m²)
Horizontal tail surfaces (total)	
	306 sq ft (28·43 m²)
Elevators, incl tabs	84·8 sq ft (7·88 m²)

WEIGHTS AND LOADINGS:

Manufacturer's weight empty	
	25,900 lb (11,748 kg)
Typical operating weight empty	
	27,000 lb (12,247 kg)
Max payload:	
Water bomber	12,000 lb (5,443 kg)
Utility version	6,850 lb (3,107 kg)
Max T-O weight (land):	
Water bomber	43,500 lb (19,731 kg)
Utility version	36,000 lb (16,329 kg)
Max T-O weight (water: both versions)	
	36,000 lb (16,329 kg)
Max zero-fuel weight:	
Water bomber	39,000 lb (17,690 kg)
Utility version	33,800 lb (15,332 kg)
Max landing weight (land and water):	
Water bomber	34,400 lb (15,603 kg)
Utility version	34,400 lb (15,603 kg)
Cabin floor loading	150 lb/sq ft (6·32 kg/m²)

PERFORMANCE (at max T-O weight except where indicated):

Stalling speed, 15° flap, AUW of 43,500 lb
(19,731 kg)   75 knots (86 mph; 138·5 km/h)
Stalling speed, 25° flap, AUW of 34,400 lb
(15,603 kg)   63 knots (72 mph; 116 km/h)
Rate of climb at S/L at AUW of 36,000 lb
(16,329 kg)   943 ft (287 m)/min
T-O to 50 ft (15 m) at AUW of 43,500 lb (19,731
kg) on land   2,650 ft (808 m)
T-O to 50 ft (15 m) at AUW of 36,000 lb (16,329
kg) on water   2,440 ft (744 m)
Landing from 50 ft (15 m) at AUW of 34,400 lb
(15,603 kg):
on land   2,400 ft (732 m)
on water   2,600 ft (792 m)
Range with 3,500 lb (1,587 kg) payload
                    868 nm (1,000 miles; 1,610 km)

Canadair-built two-seat NF-5B's for the Royal Netherlands Air Force

CANADAIR CF-5 AND NF-5 (CL-219 and CL-226)

The **CF-5** is an improved version of the Northrop F-5 fighter aircraft built to Canadian specifications. The improvements are mainly in the areas of performance, navigation and communications equipment, and the CF-5 also has an in-flight refuelling and a high and low level reconnaissance capability not offered by the standard F-5.

In addition, the CF-5 (and NF-5, see below) offers a two-position nose gear for the single-seat model. Other improvements include jettisonable pylons, inlet anti-icing and an arrester hook. The power plant comprises two General Electric/Orenda J85-15 turbojet engines, each rated at 4,300 lb (1,950 kg) st with afterburning.

A total of 115 CF-5s, comprising 89 CF-5A's and 26 two-seat CF-5D's, are being built for the Mobile Command of the Canadian Armed Forces, of which the first (a CF-5A) flew in February 1968; the first two-seat CF-5D was flown on 28 August 1968. Deliveries to the CAF

began in 1968, and 39 CF-5's had been delivered by the end of 1969. The last is due to be delivered in January 1971.

A variant of the CF-5, designated **NF-5**, with manoeuvre flaps, revised nav/radio equipment and capable of carrying 275-US gallon (1,041-litre) underwing fuel tanks, is in production for the Royal Netherlands Air Force, which has ordered 75 NF-5A's and 30 NF-5B's. Centre fuselages, fuel tank compartments, pylons, generators and other components for the NF-5 and CF-5 are being manufactured in the Netherlands.

The first NF-5 was rolled out on 5 March 1969; deliveries to the Royal Netherlands Air Force began in the Autumn of 1969 and 13 NF-5's had been delivered by the end of 1969. Deliveries are scheduled to be completed in September 1971.

Canadair is also manufacturing 25 reconnaissance kits, which can be fitted to any CF-5 model, and 50 flight refuelling kits which can be fitted to any CF-5A. The NF-5 models do not have provision for in-flight refuelling.

DE HAVILLAND CANADA

THE DE HAVILLAND AIRCRAFT OF CANADA, LTD (Member Company of HAWKER SIDDELEY GROUP)

HEAD OFFICE AND WORKS:
Downsview, Ontario
PRESIDENT: B. B. Bundesman
VICE-PRESIDENTS:
F. A. Stanley (Finance and Treasurer)
D. B. Annan (Operations)
W. T. Heaslip (Engineering)
D. L. Buchanan, DFC, BSA (Sales)
PUBLIC RELATIONS AND ADVERTISING MANAGER:
F. de Jersey

The de Havilland Aircraft of Canada, Ltd, was established early in 1928 as a subsidiary of the de Havilland Aircraft Co, Ltd, and is now a member of the Hawker Siddeley Group.

Current facilities in 1970 comprise: main plant at Downsview of 828 385 sq ft (76,959 m²); Malton plant of 199,887 sq ft (18,570 m²); and leased plant (Downsview and Malton) of 286,882 sq ft (26,652 m²). The company has also established a production support facility, known as de Havilland Canada, Inc, at Chicago in the USA.

Until the beginning of World War II, de Havilland Canada acted principally as a sales and servicing organisation for products of the parent company. It became a manufacturing unit during the war and has since produced six original designs.

The first of these was the Chipmunk two-seat *ab initio* trainer, of which a full description has appeared in earlier editions of *Jane's*.

It was followed in 1947 by the DHC-2 Beaver, first of a family of STOL utility aircraft, and

then in 1951, by the Otter. These have been followed into service by three more de Havilland Canada STOL designs, the twin-engined DHC-4 Caribou and DHC-6 Twin Otter utility transports and a turboprop transport, the DHC-5 Buffalo, evolved from the Caribou.

The Los Angeles Division of North American Rockwell Corporation is marketing the Buffalo to US military agencies.

In May 1963 it was announced that de Havilland Canada had been awarded a contract to design and build the prototype of a 200-ton hydrofoil ship for the Royal Canadian Navy, for possible anti-submarine duties. Marine Industries, Ltd, of Sorel, Quebec, was selected as subcontractor responsible for hull assembly. The ship was commissioned HMCS *Bras d'Or* in the Summer of 1968, and attained a speed of 63 knots

de Havilland Canada DHC-4A Caribou STOL utility transport (two 1,450 hp Pratt & Whitney R-2000-7M2 radial engines)

(73 mph = 117 km/h) during calm water trials in 1969. Rough water trials are expected to continue until 1971, when a decision on fitment of the weapons system will be made.

DHC-2 Mark III TURBO-BEAVER

In June 1963, de Havilland Canada began design work on a turboprop version of the Beaver, which they designated DHC-2 Mark III Turbo-Beaver. Construction of a prototype (Beaver airframe No. 1525) was started in the following month and this aircraft flew for the first time on 30 December 1963. Sixty Turbo-Beavers were built, 28 of them for the Ontario Dept of Lands and Forests. These aircraft operate with wheel/ ski landing gear during the Winter months and with integral fire-bombing floats during the Summer. Seventeen other Turbo-Beavers operate in Canada, and most of the remainder under US registry. Two are on Antarctic survey work under British and Australian direction.

The Turbo-Beaver, which is no longer in production, was described in the 1968-69 *Jane's*.

DHC-4A CARIBOU

CAF designation: CC-108

USAF designation: C-7

The decision to proceed with the design of this twin-engined transport was taken in 1955 after nearly two years of study aimed at producing an aircraft combining a load-carrying capacity comparable with that of the DC-3 with the STOL performance of the Beaver and Otter. The prototype was developed with the co-operation of the Canadian Department of Defence Production and an order for one Caribou was placed by the Royal Canadian Air Force. Construction began in 1957 and the prototype flew for the first time on 30 July 1958.

The original DHC-4 Caribou obtained US Type Approval on 23 December 1960, at a gross weight of 26,000 lb (11,793 kg). The DHC-4A was approved on 11 July, 1961, at the current maximum gross weight of 28,500 lb (12,928 kg).

Five Caribou were delivered to the US Army for evaluation in 1959, under the designation YAC-1. As a result of this evaluation, the Caribou was chosen as standard equipment for the US Army, which subsequently awarded de Havilland contracts for a total of 159 production Caribou (originally AC-1). The 134 aircraft still in service on 1 January 1967 were transferred to the USAF under an inter-service agreement.

Versions of the Caribou delivered to the US Army were as follows:

CV-2A. Equivalent to DHC-4.

C-7A (formerly CV-2B). Equivalent to DHC-4A, with higher AUW. Delivery began in 1963. Change of designation followed transfer from US Army to USAF.

One of these Caribou was converted into a flying command post by Collins Radio Company, for operation with the US 1st (Air) Cavalry Division in Vietnam. Nine separate communications positions along one side of the cabin provide commanders with ready contact with ground units as well as long-range communications.

Two US Army Caribou were handed over to the Indian Air Force in January 1963, for evaluation in mountainous terrain.

Other orders include nine of the CAF, of which four serve with United Nations forces in the Middle East, eight for the Republic of Ghana, four for Air Asia of Taiwan, two for the Kuwait Air Force, four for the Zambia Air Force, 20 for the Indian Air Force, 30 for the Royal Australian Air Force, four for the Kenya Air Force, 13 for the Royal Malaysian Air Force, four for the Tanzanian Air Force, 12 for the Spanish Air Force, one for the Uganda Police Air Wing, one for Ansett-MAL for service in Papua and New Guinea, and others for Imperial Oil (one), Pan American Petroleum (one), Pacific Architects (two), Global Associates (four), the Abu Dhabi Defence Force (four) and the Royal Thai Police Force (three).

Altogether 286 Caribou had been delivered by 1 January 1970.

As a first stage in the development programme for the DHC-5 Buffalo (originally Caribou II), the prototype Caribou was fitted with two 2,850 shp General Electric T64-GE-4 turboprops, for which it served as a flying test-bed. The first flight with these engines was made on 22 September 1961.

The following details apply to the standard production Caribou:—

TYPE: Twin-engined all-weather STOL utility transport.

WINGS: Cantilever high-wing monoplane. Wing section NACA $64_2A417\cdot5$ throughout one-piece centre-section, varying to NACA 63_2A615 near tips of outer panels. Dihedral on outer panels 5°. Incidence 3° inboard, 0° outboard. Sweepback at quarter-chord 0°. All-metal two-spar fail-safe structure. Full-span double-slotted flaps, outer trailing portions operated independently as ailerons. Trim-tabs on ailerons. Goodrich flush-mounted inflatable de-icing boots in four sections.

FUSELAGE: All-metal fail-safe semi-monocoque structure. Rear portion is upswept aft of wings, with upward and inward hingeing door forming underside of rear fuselage.

TAIL UNIT: Cantilever all-metal structure. Variable-incidence tailplane. Glass-fibre fairings at top and bottom of rudder. Spring tabs on rudder and elevators. Goodrich inflatable de-icer boots.

LANDING GEAR: Retractable tricycle type. Hydraulic retraction, main units forward, nose unit rearward. Main gear, produced by Jarry Hydraulics, shortens as it retracts. Dual wheels on all units. Hydraulically-steerable nose-wheel. Goodyear wheels and tyres, size $11\cdot00 \times 12$ on main units, $7\cdot50 \times 10$ on nose unit. Tyre pressures (nominal) 40 lb/sq in ($2\cdot81$ kg/cm²). Goodyear four-cylinder single-disc brakes.

POWER PLANT: Two 1,450 hp Pratt & Whitney R-2000-7M2 fourteen-cylinder two-row radial air-cooled engines, driving Hamilton Standard type 43D50-7107A three-blade fully-feathering Hydromatic propellers. Fuel in two wing tanks, each of 10 cells, with total capacity of 690 Imp gallons (3,137 litres). Refuelling point in upper surface of each wing. Oil capacity 50 Imp gallons (227 litres).

ACCOMMODATION: Flight compartment seats two side-by-side. Civil version accommodates 30 passengers, who enter by two doors, at rear of cabin on each side (an air-stair type can be provided) or via the large rear loading ramp, formed by lowering electrically the sloping under-surface of the rear fuselage. The military version carries 32 troops on inward-facing folding seats or 26 fully-equipped paratroops, or, in an ambulance rôle, up to 22 litter patients, 4 sitting casualties and 4 attendants. Typical freight loads are three tons of cargo or two fully-loaded jeeps. The floor is stressed to support distributed loads of 200 lb/sq ft (975 kg/m²) and has tie-down fittings on a 20-in ($0\cdot50$ m) grid pattern over the entire area. Tie-down rings can be fitted at 36 points on the side walls.

SYSTEMS: Flaps, brakes, landing gear retraction and nose-wheel steering actuated by 3,000 lb/sq in (210 kg/cm²) hydraulic system. No pneumatic system. Two engine-driven generators, 24V 300A DC/115V 400-c/s AC.

ELECTRONICS AND EQUIPMENT: To customer's requirements. Blind-flying instrumentation standard.

DIMENSIONS, EXTERNAL:

Wing span	95 ft 7½ in (29·15 m)
Wing chord at root	11 ft 10 in (3·60 m)
Wing chord at tip	5 ft 7¾ in (1·72 m)
Wing aspect ratio	10
Length overall	72 ft 7 in (22·13 m)
Height over tail	31 ft 9 in (9·70 m)
Tailplane span	36 ft 0 in (11·00 m)
Wheel track	23 ft 1½ in (7·05 m)
Wheelbase	25 ft 8 in (7·82 m)

Passenger door (each side):

Height	4 ft 7 in (1·40 m)
Width	2 ft 6 in (0·76 m)

Main cargo door (rear fuselage):

Height	6 ft 3 in (1·90 m)
Width	6 ft 1½ in (1·86 m)
Height to sill	3 ft 9½ in (1·16 m)

DIMENSIONS, INTERNAL:
Cabin, excluding flight deck:

Length	28 ft 9 in (8·76 m)
Max width	7 ft 3 in (2·21 m)
Max height	6 ft 3 in (1·90 m)
Floor area	176 sq ft (16·35 m²)
Volume	1,150 cu ft (32·57 m²)

AREAS:

Wings, gross	912 sq ft (84·72 m²)
Ailerons (total)	91 sq ft (8·45 m²)
Trailing-edge flaps (total)	285 sq ft (26·47 m²)
Fin	127 sq ft (11·80 m²)
Rudder, including tab	84 sq ft (7·80 m²)
Tailplane	144 sq ft (13·37 m²)
Elevators, including tab	86 sq ft (7·99 m²)

WEIGHTS AND LOADINGS:

Basic operating weight (including 2 crew)	18,260 lb (8,283 kg)
Max payload	8,740 lb (3,965 kg)
Normal max T-O weight	28,500 lb (12,928 kg)
Max permissible weight for ferry missions	31,300 lb (14,197 kg)
Max zero-fuel weight	27,000 lb (12,250 kg)
Max landing weight	28,500 lb (12,928 kg)
Normal max wing loading	31·2 lb/sq ft (152·3 kg/m²)
Normal max power loading	9·83 lb/hp (4·45 kg/hp)

PERFORMANCE (at normal max T-O weight):
Max level speed at 6,500 ft (1,980 m)
　　　　　188 knots (216 mph; 347 km/h)
Max diving speed
　　　　　208 knots (240 mph; 386 km/h)
Max and econ cruising speed at 7,500 ft (2,285 m)
　　　　　158 knots (182 mph; 293 km/h)
Stalling speed　　　59 knots (68 mph; 109 km/h)
Rate of climb at S/L　　1,355 ft (413 m)/min
Service ceiling　　　　24,800 ft (7,560 m)
Service ceiling, one engine out 8,800 ft (2,680 m)
T-O run　　　　　　　　725 ft (221 m)
T-O to 50 ft (15 m)　　　1,185 ft (361 m)
Landing from 50 ft (15 m)　1,235 ft (376 m)
Landing run　　　　　　670 ft (204 m)
Range with max fuel
　　　　　1,135 nm (1,307 miles; 2,103 km)
Range with max payload
　　　　　210 nm (242 miles; 390 km)

NOTE: Ranges are for long-range cruising speed
at 7,500 ft (2,285 m), with allowances for
warm-up, taxi, take-off, climb, descent, landing
and 45 min reserve.

DHC-5 BUFFALO
Canadian Armed Forces designation: CC-115
US Army designation: C-8A

Early in May 1962, the US Army invited 25
companies to submit proposals for a new STOL
tactical transport aircraft. De Havilland Canada
won the competition with a developed version of
the Caribou with an enlarged fuselage and two
General Electric T64 turboprop engines. Known
as the Buffalo (originally Caribou II) this aircraft
has a cargo compartment compatible with that
of the US Army's Boeing-Vertol Chinook
helicopter, enabling it to carry loads such as the
Pershing missile, 105 mm howitzer and ¾-ton
truck.

Development costs of the Buffalo have been
shared equally by the US Army, the Canadian
Government and de Havilland Canada.

Four evaluation aircraft were built initially, of
which the first flew for the first time on 9 April
1964. Delivery of these aircraft to the US Army,
for evaluation, began in April 1965. An order
for 15 was placed by the Canadian Ministry of
Defence in December 1964, deliveries of which
began in 1967 and were completed at the end of
1968.

Twenty-four Buffalos were ordered in 1968 by
the Brazilian government. Twelve of these had
been delivered by the end of 1969, and the
remaining 12 are being delivered between March
and October 1970. Sixteen have been ordered by
Peru.

The Ames Research Center of NASA is modifying one aircraft to have Rolls-Royce Spey
turbofan engines and an "augmentor wing flap"
system of boundary layer control.

de Havilland Canada DHC-5 Buffalo STOL utility transport in Canadian Armed Forces insignia

Differences between the US and Canadian
versions are as follows:

C-8A. US model, with 2,850 eshp General
Electric T64-GE-10 turboprops. Overall length
77 ft 4 in (23.57 m). Originally designated
CV-7A.

CC-115. Canadian Armed Forces model, with
3,055 eshp General Electric CT64-820-1 turboprops.
Overall length (with Radome) 79 ft 0 in (24.08 m).
Otherwise similar to C-8A, with only small
differences in performance.

TYPE: Twin-turboprop STOL utility transport.

WINGS: Cantilever high-wing monoplane. Wing
section NACA $64_3A417.5$ (mod) at root,
NACA 63_3A615 (mod) at tip. Dihedral 0° inboard of nacelles, 5° outboard. Incidence 2° 30′.
Sweepback at quarter-chord 1° 40′. Conventional fail-safe multi-spar structure of high-
strength aluminium alloys. Full-span double-
slotted aluminium alloy flaps, outboard sections
functioning as ailerons. Aluminium alloy
slot-lip spoilers, forward of inboard flaps, are
actuated by Jarry Hydraulics unit. Spoilers
coupled to manually-operated ailerons for
lateral control, uncoupled for symmetrical
ground operation. Electrically-actuated trim-
tab in starboard aileron. Geared tab in each
aileron. Rudder-aileron interconnect tab on
port aileron. Outer wing leading-edges fitted
with electrically-controlled flush pneumatic
rubber de-icing boots.

FUSELAGE: Fail-safe structure of high-strength
aluminium alloy. Cargo floor supported by
longitudinal keel members.

TAIL UNIT: Cantilever structure of high-strength
aluminium alloy, with fixed-incidence tailplane
mounted at tip of fin. Elevator aerodynamically and mass-balanced. Fore and trailing
serially-hinged rudders are powered by tandem
jacks operated by two independent hydraulic
systems manufactured by Jarry Hydraulics.
Trim-tab on port elevator, spring-tab on
starboard elevator. Electrically-controlled
flush pneumatic rubber de-icing boot on tailplane leading-edge.

LANDING GEAR: Retractable tricycle type, with
twin wheels on each unit. Hydraulic retraction, nose unit aft, main units forward. Jarry
Hydraulics oleo-pneumatic shock-absorbers.
Goodrich main wheels and tyres, size 37.00 ×
15.00-12, pressure 45 lb/sq in (3.16 kg/cm²).
Goodrich nose wheels and tyres size 8.90 ×
12.50, pressure 38 lb/sq in (2.67 kg/cm²). Goodrich multi-disc brakes.

POWER PLANT: Two General Electric T64 turboprop engines (details under entries for individual versions, above), each driving a
Hamilton Standard 63E60-13 three-blade propeller, diameter 14 ft 6 in (4.42 m). Fuel in one
integral tank in each inner wing, capacity 533
Imp gallons (2,423 litres), and rubber bag tanks

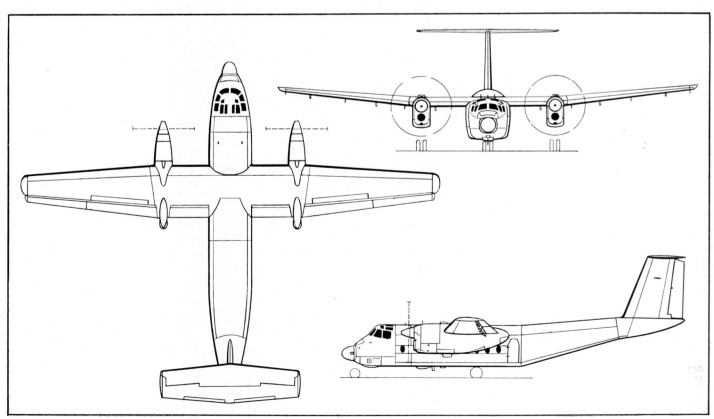

DHC-5 Buffalo twin-turboprop STOL utility transport

in each outer wing, capacity 336 Imp gallons (1,527 litres). Total fuel capacity 1,738 Imp gallons (7,900 litres). Refuelling points above wings and in side of fuselage for pressure refuelling. Total oil capacity 10 Imp gallons (45·5 litres).

ACCOMMODATION: Crew of three, comprising pilot, co-pilot and crew-chief. Main cabin can accommodate roll-up troop seats or folding forward-facing seats for 41 troops or 35 paratroops, or 24 stretchers and six seats. Provision for toilet in forward part of cabin. Door on each side at rear of cabin. Loading height with rear cargo loading door up and ramp down 9 ft 6 in (2·90 m).

SYSTEMS: AiResearch bleed-air cabin heating and cooling system. 3,000 lb/sq in (210 kg/cm²) hydraulic system actuates landing gear, flaps, spoilers, rudders, brakes, nose-wheel steering, winch and APU starting. 50 lb/sq in (3·50 kg/cm²) pneumatic system for engine starting, de-icing and environmental control. Two engine-driven variable-frequency 3-phase 20/30 kVA AC generators with 28V DC and 400-cycle conversion sub-systems. Williams Research Corp WR9-7 APU provides electric, hydraulic and pneumatic power. Brooks & Perkins rail-type cargo handling system, with hydraulic winch and floor rollers.

ELECTRONICS AND EQUIPMENT: Radio and radar to customer's specification. Blind-flying instrumentation standard.

DIMENSIONS, EXTERNAL:
Wing span	96 ft 0 in (29·26 m)
Wing chord at root	11 ft 9¼ in (3·59 m)
Wing chord at tip	5 ft 11 in (1·19 m)
Wing aspect ratio	9·75
Length overall:	
C-8A	77 ft 4 in (23·57 m)
CC-115	79 ft 0 in (24·08 m)
Height overall	28 ft 8 in (8·73 m)
Tailplane span	32 ft 0 in (9·75 m)
Wheel track	30 ft 6 in (9·29 m)
Wheelbase	27 ft 11 in (8·50 m)
Cabin doors (each side):	
Height	5 ft 6 in (1·68 m)
Width	2 ft 9 in (0·84 m)
Height to sill	3 ft 10 in (1·17 m)
Emergency exits (each side, below wing leading-edge):	
Height	3 ft 4 in (1·02 m)
Width	2 ft 2 in (0·66 m)
Height to sill	approx 5 ft 0 in (1·52 m)
Rear cargo loading door and ramp:	
Height	20 ft 9 in (6·33 m)
Width	7 ft 8 in (2·34 m)
Height to ramp hinge	3 ft 10 in (1·17 m)

DIMENSIONS, INTERNAL:
Cabin, excluding flight deck:	
Length, cargo floor	31 ft 5 in (9·58 m)
Max width	8 ft 9 in (2·67 m)
Max height	6 ft 10 in (2·08 m)
Floor area	243·5 sq ft (22·63 m²)
Volume	1,715 cu ft (48·56 m³)

AREAS:
Wings, gross	945 sq ft (87·8 m²)
Ailerons (total)	39 sq ft (3·62 m³)
Trailing-edge flaps (total, including ailerons)	280 sq ft (26·01 m²)
Spoilers (total)	25·2 sq ft (2·34 m²)
Fin	92 sq ft (8·55 m²)
Rudder	60 sq ft (5·57 m²)
Tailplane	151·5 sq ft (14·07 m²)
Elevator, including tabs	81·5 sq ft (7·57 m²)

WEIGHTS AND LOADINGS:
Operating weight empty, including 3 crew at 200 lb (90 kg) each, plus trapped fuel and oil and full cargo handling equipment	23,157 lb (10,505 kg)
Max payload	13,843 lb (6,279 kg)
Max internal fuel	13,598 lb (6,168 kg)
Max T-O weight	41,000 lb (18,598 kg)
Max zero-fuel weight	37,000 lb (16,783 kg)
Max landing weight	39,100 lb (17,720 kg)
Max wing loading	43·4 lb/sq ft (212 kg/m²)
Max power loading	7·2 lb/eshp (3·27 kg/eshp)

PERFORMANCE (C-8A, at max T-O weight):
Max level speed at 10,000 ft (3,050 m)	235 knots (271 mph; 435 km/h)
Max permissible diving speed	290 knots (334 mph; 537 km/h)
Max cruising speed at 10,000 ft (3,050 m)	235 knots (271 mph; 435 km/h)
Econ cruising speed at 10,000 ft (3,050 m)	181 knots (208 mph; 335 km/h)
Stalling speed, 40° flaps at 39,000 lb (17,690 lb) AUW	66 knots (75 mph; 120 km/h)
Stalling speed, flaps up at max AUW	92 knots (105 mph; 169 km/h)
Rate of climb at S/L	1,890 ft (575 m)/min
Service ceiling	30,000 ft (9,150 m)
Service ceiling, one engine out	14,300 ft (4,360 m)
T-O run on firm dry sod	1,040 ft (317 m)

T-O to 50 ft (15 m) from firm dry sod 1,540 ft (470 m)
Landing from 50 ft (15 m) on firm dry sod 1,120 ft (342 m)
Landing run on firm dry sod 610 ft (186 m)
Range with max fuel and 4,000 lb (1,815 kg) payload, with allowances for warm-up, taxying, take-off, climb, descent and 45 min reserve at cruise power 1,885 nm (2,170 miles; 3,490 km)
Range with max payload, reserves as above 440 nm (507 miles; 815 km)

DHC-6 TWIN OTTER

First announced in 1964, the Twin Otter is a STOL transport powered by two Pratt & Whitney (UAC) PT6A series turboprop engines. Design work was started in January 1964, and construction of an initial batch of five aircraft began in November of the same year. The first of these (CF-DHC-X), powered by two 579 eshp PT6A-6 engines, flew for the first time on 20 May 1965.

The fourth and subsequent aircraft of the initial Series 100 version were fitted with PT6A-20 engines, and the first delivery of a production aircraft, to the Ontario Department of Lands and Forests, was made in July 1966, shortly after the Twin Otter received FAA type approval.

By 1 January 1970, 290 Twin Otters had been built, of which 273 had been delivered. Of those delivered at that date, 115 were Series 100, 115 were Series 200 and 43 were Series 300. Military operators of Twin Otters include the Argentine Air Force (five), Army (three) and Navy (one); Chilean Air Force (seven); Jamaica Defence Force (one); Peruvian Air Force (three); the Royal Air Flight, Nepal (one); and the Royal Norwegian Air Force (four).

Three versions of the Twin Otter have so far been announced, as follows:

Twin Otter Series 100. Initial production version, with 579 eshp PT6A-20 engines and short nose; described fully in 1967-68 *Jane's.* Superseded by the Series 200 in April 1968. The Srs 100 was also available with twin-float landing gear, in which configuration boundary fences must be fitted to the outer wing panels and auxiliary finlets added to the upper and lower tailplane surfaces. Max T-O and landing weight of the float version is 11,600 lb (5,261 kg). Wardair of Canada and the Peruvian Air Force are among the operators of this model. In Canada, the Srs 100 floatplane is certificated for use as a water bomber, carrying 225 Imp gallons (1,023 litres) of water in a special compartment in each float. Production complete.

Twin Otter Series 200. Generally similar to Srs 100, but with increased baggage space provided by extending the aft baggage compartment into the rear fuselage and by lengthening the nose, giving a total baggage volume of 126 cu ft (3·57 m³). Available, with short nose, as floatplane.

Twin Otter Series 300. Similar to Srs 200, but with 652 eshp PT6A-27 turboprop engines, increased operating weights and performance. Deliveries began in the Spring of 1969 with the 231st Twin Otter off the line. Available, with short nose, as floatplane.

During the Summer of 1969, the Twin Otter was fitted for certification with a new-type external fire-bombing tank. This completely new forest fire-fighting concept, known as the Membrane Tank System, was designed and built

by Field Aviation Company Ltd. A rectangular tank size 12 ft 0 in × 2 ft 4 in (3·66 × 0·71 m), capable of holding 600 US gallons (500 Imp gallons; 2,273 litres) is mounted on the underside of the aircraft. An expendable fabric membrane supports the fluid, and is jettisoned with the load. It is designed for use on the landplane Twin Otter, using chemical fire retardants. Canadian DoT type approval in the Normal category was received in September 1969.

The following description refers fundamentally to the Srs 300, but is generally applicable also to the Srs 200, except where indicated otherwise.

TYPE: Twin-turboprop STOL transport.

WINGS: Strut-braced high-wing monoplane. Wing section NACA 6A series mean line; NACA 0016 (modified) thickness distribution. Dihedral 3°. No sweepback. All-metal safe-life structure, each wing being attached to the fuselage by two bolts at the front and rear spar fitting and braced by a single streamline-section strut on each side. Light-alloy riveted construction is used throughout except for the upper skin panels, which have spanwise corrugated stiffeners bonded to them. All-metal double-slotted full-span trailing-edge flaps. No spoilers. All-metal ailerons which also droop for use as flaps. Electrically-actuated tab in port aileron, plus geared trim-tabs in both port and starboard ailerons. Optional pneumatic-boot de-icing equipment.

FUSELAGE: Conventional semi-monocoque safe-life structure, built in three sections. Primary structure of frames, stringers and skin of aluminium alloy. Windscreen and cabin windows of acrylic plastic. Cabin floor is of low-density aluminium-faced sandwich construction and is designed to accommodate distributed loads of up to 200 lb/sq ft (976·49 kg/m²).

TAIL UNIT: Cantilever all-metal structure of high-strength aluminium alloys. Fin and fixed-incidence tailplane are bolted to rear fuselage. Manually-operated trim-tabs in rudder and elevators. A geared tab is fitted to the rudder to lighten control forces, and a tab fitted to the starboard elevator is linked to the flaps to control longitudinal trim during flap retraction and extension. Optional pneumatic-boot de-icing of tailplane leading-edge.

LANDING GEAR: Non-retractable tricycle type, with single wheel on each unit. Fully-steerable nose-wheel. Urethane compression-block shock-absorption on main units. Oleo-pneumatic nose-wheel shock-absorber. Goodyear main wheel tyres size 11·00 × 12, pressure 32 lb/sq in (2·25 kg/cm²) on Srs 200, 38 lb/sq in (2·67 kg/cm²) on Srs 300. Goodyear nose-wheel tyre size 8·90 × 12·50, pressure 32 lb/sq in (2·25 kg/cm²) on Srs 200, 33 lb/sq in (2·32 kg/cm²) on Srs 300. Goodrich independent, hydraulically-operated disc brakes on main wheels. Alternatively, high flotation wheels and tyres, for operation in soft-field conditions, are available for Srs 300 at customer's option, size 15·0 × 12·0 for nose-wheel and either 15·0 × 12·0 or 45 × 20-10 for main wheels. Provision for alternative wheel/ski landing gear. Twin-float gear available for Srs 100, and for Srs 200 and 300 without extended nose, with added wing fences and small auxiliary fins.

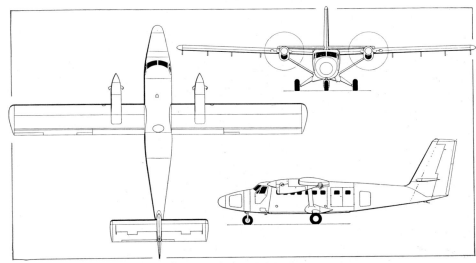

de Havilland Canada DHC-6 Twin Otter Series 300 STOL utility transport

DHC-6 Twin Otter Series 300 STOL transport in the insignia of Mount Cook Airlines of New Zealand

POWER PLANT (Srs 200): Two 579 eshp Pratt & Whitney (UAC) PT6A-20 turboprop engines, each driving a Hartzell three-blade reversible-pitch fully-feathering metal propeller, diameter 8 ft 6 in (2·59 m). Fuel in two tanks (eight cells) under cabin floor, with total capacity of 315 Imp gallons (1,432 litres). Refuelling point for each tank on port side of fuselage. Oil capacity 1·9 Imp gallons (8·7 litres) per engine. Optional electrical de-icing system for propellers and air intakes.

POWER PLANT (Srs 300): Two 652 eshp Pratt & Whitney (UAC) PT6A-27 turboprop engines, each driving a Hartzell HC-B3TN-3D three-blade reversible-pitch fully-feathering metal propeller, diameter 8 ft 6 in (2·59 m). Fuel system as for Srs 200, but with total capacity of 318 Imp gallons (1,446 litres). Oil capacity 2 Imp gallons (9·1 litres) per engine. Optional electrical de-icing system for propellers and air intakes.

ACCOMMODATION: Side-by-side seats for one or two pilots on flight deck, access to which is by a forward-opening car-type door on each side or via the passenger cabin. Windscreen de-misting and defrosting standard. Cabin divided by bulkhead into main passenger or freight compartment and baggage compartment. Seats for up to 19 passengers (Srs 200) or 20 passengers (Srs 300) in main cabin. Standard Srs 300 interior is 20-seat "Commuter" layout, with Douglas track, carpets, double windows, individual air vents and reading lights, and airstair door. Optional layouts include 18- or 19-seat commuter versions, and 13-20 passenger utility version with foldaway seats and double cargo doors with ladder. Access to passenger cabin by door on each side of rear fuselage; optionally, an airstair door may be fitted on the port side. Optional double door for cargo on port side instead of passenger door. Compartments in nose and aft of main cabin, each with upward-hinged door on port side, for 300 lb (136 kg) and 500 lb (227 kg) of baggage respectively; rear baggage hold accessible from cabin in emergency. Emergency exits near front of cabin on each side and (except Srs 300) in cabin roof. Heating of flight deck and passenger cabin by engine-bleed air; ventilation via a ram air intake on the port side of the fuselage nose. Oxygen system for crew and passengers optional. Executive, survey or ambulance interiors can be fitted at customer's choice. Tie-down cargo rings are installed as standard for the freighter role.

SYSTEMS: Hydraulic system, pressure 1,500 lb/sq in (105 kg/cm²), for flaps, brakes, nose-wheel steering and (where fitted) ski retraction mechanism. A hand pump in the crew compartment provides emergency pressure for standby or ground operation if the electric pump is inoperative. Accumulators smooth the system pressure pulses and provide pressure for parking and emergency braking.

Optional low-pressure pneumatic system (18 lb/sq in = 1·27 kg/cm²) for operation of autopilot or wing and tail de-icing boots, if fitted. Primary electrical system is 28V DC, with one 200A starter-generator on each engine. A 22Ah nickel-cadmium battery (optionally 39Ah nickel-cadmium or 36Ah lead-acid battery) for emergency power and engine starting. Separate 3·6Ah battery supplies independent power for engine starting relays and ignition. 65VA (optionally 250VA) main and standby static inverters provide 400 c/s AC power for instruments and avionics. External DC receptacle aft of port side cabin door permits operation of complete system on the ground.

ELECTRONICS AND EQUIPMENT: Navigation and communications equipment, including weather radar, to customer's specification. Dual controls and blind-flying instrumentation standard.

DIMENSIONS, EXTERNAL (Srs 300):
Wing span	65 ft 0 in (19·81 m)
Wing chord (constant)	6 ft 6 in (1·98 m)
Wing aspect ratio	10
Length overall	51 ft 9 in (15·77 m)
Height overall	18 ft 7 in (5·66 m)
Tailplane span	21 ft 0 in (6·40 m)
Wheel track	12 ft 6 in (3·81 m)
Wheelbase	14 ft 9 in (4·50 m)

Passenger door (port side):
Height	4 ft 2 in (1·27 m)
Width	2 ft 6 in (0·76 m)
Height to sill	3 ft 10 in (1·17 m)

Passenger door (starboard side):
Height	3 ft 9½ in (1·15 m)
Width	2 ft 6¼ in (0·77 m)
Height to sill	3 ft 10 in (1·17 m)

Baggage compartment door (nose):
Mean height	2 ft 3¼ in (0·69 m)
Width	2 ft 5¾ in (0·76 m)
Height to sill	3 ft 10 in (1·17 m)

Baggage compartment door (port, rear):
Max height	3 ft 2 in (0·97 m)
Width	2 ft 1½ in (0·65 m)

Cargo double door (port, rear):
Height	4 ft 2 in (1·27 m)
Width	4 ft 8 in (1·42 m)
Height to sill	3 ft 10 in (1·17 m)

DIMENSIONS, INTERNAL (Srs 300):
Cabin, excluding flight deck, galley and baggage compartment:
Length	18 ft 6 in (5·64 m)
Max width	5 ft 3¼ in (1·61 m)
Max height	4 ft 11 in (1·50 m)
Floor area	80·2 sq ft (7·45 m²)
Volume	384 cu ft (10·87 m³)

Baggage compartment (nose):
Volume	38 cu ft (1·08 m³)

Baggage compartment (rear):
Length	6 ft 2 in (1·88 m)
Volume	88 cu ft (2·49 m³)

AREAS (Srs 200 and 300):
Wings, gross	420 sq ft (39·02 m²)
Ailerons (total)	33·2 sq ft (3·08 m²)
Trailing-edge flaps (total)	112·2 sq ft (10·42 m²)

Fin	48·0 sq ft (4·46 m²)
Rudder, including tabs	34·0 sq ft (3·16 m²)
Tailplane	100·0 sq ft (9·29 m²)
Elevators, including tabs	35·0 sq ft (3·25 m²)

WEIGHTS:
Basic operating weight, including pilot (170 lb = 77 kg), radio (100 lb = 45 kg) and full oil:
Srs 200 (13-seat Utility layout)	6,515 lb (2,950 kg)
Srs 300 (20-seat "Commuter" layout)	7,000 lb (3,180 kg)

Max payload for 100 mile (160 km) range:
Srs 200	4,500 lb (2,041 kg)
Srs 300	5,100 lb (2,313 kg)

Max T-O weight:
Srs 200	11,579 lb (5,252 kg)
Srs 300	12,500 lb (5,670 kg)

Max landing weight:
Srs 200	11,400 lb (5,171 kg)
Srs 300 (wheels and skis)	12,300 lb (5,579 kg)
Srs 300 (floats)	12,500 lb (5,670 kg)

PERFORMANCE (at max T-O weight, ISA conditions):
Max cruising speed at 10,000 ft (3,050 m):
Srs 200	165 knots (190 mph; 306 km/h)
Srs 300	182 knots (210 mph; 338 km/h)

Stalling speed, flaps up:
Srs 300	65 knots (74 mph; 119 km/h)

Stalling speed, flaps down:
Srs 300	51 knots (58 mph; 94 km/h)

Rate of climb at S/L:
Srs 200	1,300 ft (396 m)/min
Srs 300	1,600 ft (488 m)/min

Single-engined rate of climb at S/L:
Srs 200	340 ft (104 m)

Service ceiling:
Srs 200	24,300 ft (7,400 m)
Srs 300	26,700 ft (8,138 m)

Service ceiling, one engine out:
Srs 200	8,500 ft (2,590 m)
Srs 300	11,600 ft (3,530 m)

T-O run:
Srs 300, STOL	700 ft (213 m)
Srs 300, CAR Pt 3	860 ft (262 m)

T-O to 50 ft (15 m):
Srs 200, STOL	1,230 ft (375 m)
Srs 200, CAR Pt 3	1,900 ft (579 m)
Srs 300, STOL	1,200 ft (366 m)
Srs 300, CAR Pt 3	1,500 ft (457 m)

Landing from 50 ft (15 m):
Srs 200, STOL	990 ft (302 m)
Srs 200, CAR Pt 3	1,995 ft (608 m)
Srs 300, STOL	1,050 ft (320 m)
Srs 300, CAR Pt 3	1,940 ft (591 m)

Landing run:
Srs 300, STOL	515 ft (157 m)
Srs 300, CAR Pt 3	950 ft (290 m)

Range with max fuel, 30 min reserve:
Srs 200	820 nm (945 miles; 1,520 km)

Range at max cruising speed, 3,250 lb (1,474 kg) payload:
Srs 300	646 nm (745 miles; 1,198 km)

Range with 1 pilot and 13 passengers, 45 min reserve:
Srs 300	677 nm (780 miles; 1,255 km)

DE HAVILLAND CANADA DHC-7

The DHC-7 "Quiet STOL" airliner project was launched by de Havilland Canada after the company had conducted a worldwide market survey of short-haul transport requirements for the 1970s. It is intended as a low noise-level city-centre STOL transport, to complement the DHC-6 Twin Otter by providing greater range, speed and seating capacity for more highly-developed routes. The engine/propeller combination is expected to achieve an exterior noise level of 95 PNdb at 500 ft (152 m) from the take-off path.

Engineering development and marketing of the DCH-7 were continuing during 1970, and a decision on future production was to be taken late in the year. The first flight is planned for early 1972. The DHC-7 will be certificated to FAR Pt 25 regulations and production will begin in 1973, if the go-ahead is given.

TYPE: Four engined short/medium-range quiet STOL transport.

WINGS: Cantilever high-wing monoplane, with dihedral from roots. High-lift devices on trailing-edges and spoilers on wings.

FUSELAGE: Basically circular cross-section with flattened profile under floor level. External diameter 9 ft 2 in (2·79 m).

TAIL UNIT: Cantilever structure with tailplane mounted at top of fin. One-piece elevator.

LANDING GEAR: Retractable tricycle type, with twin wheels on all units. Main units retract into inboard engine nacelles, nose unit into fuselage.

POWER PLANT: Four 1,035 shp Pratt & Whitney (UACL) PT6A-50 turboprop engines, each driving a four-blade propeller of 11 ft 3 in (3·43 m) diameter and of slow-turning type to reduce noise level. Fuel in integral tanks in wings.

ACCOMMODATION: Flight crew of two, plus one cabin attendant. Seats for 48 passengers at 32 in (81 cm) pitch, in pairs on each side of centre aisle. Outward-opening airstair door at rear on port side. Emergency exits on each side at front of cabin and on starboard side at rear. Baggage compartments in nose and rear fuselage. Galley and toilet at rear of cabin. Optional arrangements for mixed freight/passenger loads with forward freight door on port side. Entire accommodation pressurised and air-conditioned. Cabin pressurisation differential 3·6 lb/sq in (0·25 kg/cm²).

DIMENSIONS, EXTERNAL:
Wing span	93 ft 0 in (28·35 m)
Length overall	80 ft 4 in (24·49 m)
Height overall	26 ft 3 in (8·00 m)
Tailplane span	31 ft 0 in (9·45 m)
Min propeller/fuselage clearance	2 ft 4½ in (0·71 m)
Wheel track	23 ft 6 in (7·16 m)
Wheelbase	28 ft 8 in (8·74 m)

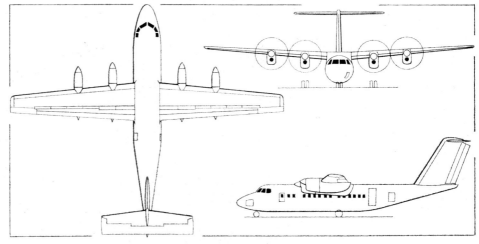

de Havilland Canada DHC-7 four-turboprop STOL utility transport

Passenger door (rear, port):	
Height	5 ft 10 in (1·78 m)
Width	2 ft 6 in (0·76 m)
Height to sill	3 ft 7 in (1·09 m)
Emergency exit door (rear, stbd):	
Height	4 ft 5 in (1·35 m)
Width	2 ft 0 in (0·61 m)
Height to sill	3 ft 7 in (1·09 m)
Emergency exit doors (fwd, each):	
Height	3 ft 0 in (0·91 m)
Width	1 ft 8 in (0·51 m)
Height to sill	5 ft 1 in (1·55 m)
Baggage hold door (rear, port):	
Height	3 ft 0 in (0·91 m)
Width	2 ft 6 in (0·76 m)
Height to sill	4 ft 9 in (1·45 m)
Baggage hold door (nose, port):	
Min height	1 ft 10 in (0·56 m)
Max height	2 ft 3 in (0·69 m)
Width	2 ft 6 in (0·76 m)
Height to sill	3 ft 7 in (1·09 m)
Cargo door (fwd, port, optional):	
Height	4 ft 10 in (1·47 m)
Width	4 ft 0 in (1·22 m)
or	
Height	5 ft 8 in (1·73 m)
Width	5 ft 10 in (1·78 m)

DIMENSIONS, INTERNAL:
Cabin, excluding flight deck:	
Length	40 ft 0 in (12·19 m)
Max width	8 ft 7½ in (2·63 m)
Max height	6 ft 5 in (1·96 m)
Height under wing	6 ft 1 in (1·85 m)
Volume	2,140 cu ft (60·50 m³)

Baggage compartment (rear fuselage):	
Max length	7 ft 4 in (2·24 m)
Volume	220 cu ft (6·23 m³)
Baggage compartment (nose):	
Volume	70 cu ft (1·98 m³)

WEIGHTS:
Max payload (48 passengers and baggage)	9,600 lb (4,355 kg)
Max T-O weight	38,500 lb (17,463 kg)
Max landing weight	36,500 lb (16,556 kg)

PERFORMANCE (estimated at max weights, FAR 25 at S/L, ISA):
Max cruising speed	240 knots (276 mph; 444 km/h)
Stalling speed, flaps down	64 knots (73 mph; 117 km/h)
Rate of climb, en route	1,660 ft (506 m)/min
Rate of climb, one engine out	1,050 ft (320 m)/min
Service ceiling	27,000 ft (8,230 m)
Service ceiling, one engine out	18,500 ft (5,650 m)
T-O run	1,100 ft (335 m)
T-O field length	1,680 ft (512 m)
T-O to 35 ft (10 m)	1,540 ft (469 m)
Landing from 35 ft (10 m)	1,140 ft (347 m)
Landing run	750 ft (229 m)
Landing field length	1,900 ft (579 m)

Range at 15,000 ft (4,570 m) with max (passenger) payload, reserves for 100 nm (115 miles; 185 km) plus 45 min hold
460 nm (530 miles; 852 km)
Range at 15,000 ft (4,570 m) with 6,000 lb (2,722 kg) payload, reserves as above
1,000 nm (1,150 miles; 1,850 km)

FAIREY

FAIREY CANADA LTD

HEAD OFFICE AND PLANTS 1 AND 2:
Eastern Passage, Halifax County, NS
PLANTS 3 AND 4:
Halifax International Airport, NS
BRANCH PLANT:
Victoria International Airport, Sidney, BC
CHAIRMAN:
D. McInnes, QC
PRESIDENT AND GENERAL MANAGER:
D. W. Howell, AMTI (ProdE), MCAI
VICE-PRESIDENT (GOVERNMENT RELATIONS):
H. G. Sager
CHIEF ENGINEER:
J. C. Gibbons, PEng, CEng (UK)
SECRETARY AND TREASURER:
R. Boyd, CA

Fairey Canada Ltd (originally The Fairey Aviation Co of Canada Ltd) was incorporated in November 1948. Initially, its primary rôle was to repair, overhaul and modify RCN and RCAF anti-submarine aircraft. Increased technical capability led to the successful undertaking of complete anti-submarine warfare reconfigurations on all three types of maritime-based aircraft in

Canadian service, the Lockheed P2V-7 Neptune, Canadair CL-28 Argus and, more recently, the de Havilland-built CS2F Tracker.

The CS2F-3 version of the Tracker is equipped with the latest in airborne electronics and systems to extend its navigational, tactical and operational capabilities. This was the third major reconfiguration programme undertaken in recent years by Fairey's engineering and production facilities.

Current projects include Depot Level Repair and Overhaul (DLRO) programmes on the Tracker and Argus aircraft. DLRO represents the latest concept in aircraft maintenance techniques, designed to ensure the continued structural integrity of each airframe.

Parallel with this aircraft activity, Fairey Canada undertook the prototype development of the Helicopter Haul Down and Rapid Securing System known as the "Beartrap". The company achieved a world-wide "first" in successfully proving the concept of hauling down and securing a large helicopter on the deck of a small ship at sea, under adverse conditions. The system is now in production and has been adopted by the

Canadian Armed Forces, the US Navy, the Japanese Navy, the Federal German Navy and the US Coast Guard.

Among recent contracts received by the company is one for the manufacture of "Beartrap" systems to be installed in the Canadian Armed Forces' new DDH-280 destroyer escort vessels which were scheduled to enter service in 1970. The contract calls for the "Twinset" two-helicopter type of installation. "Twinset" represents Fairey Canada's most advanced design concept of the "Beartrap" system.

Fairey Canada's Head Office and Plants 1 and 2 are located at Eastern Passage, Nova Scotia, on the Dartmouth shore of Halifax Harbour. This facility covers 275,000 sq ft (25,550 m²) and consists of a complete engineering and production organisation with a fully-equipped Quality Assurance Laboratory.

Plants 3 and 4, located at Halifax International Airport, are used primarily for the CL-28 Argus DLRO programme. Plant 3 has 52,000 sq ft (4,830 m²) of unobstructed floor space and can accommodate four of these large (142 ft span) aircraft.

FALCONAR

FALCONAR AIRCRAFT LTD

HEAD OFFICE AND WORKS:
Industrial Airport, Edmonton, Alberta
MANAGING DIRECTOR:
C. B. Falconar
SALES MANAGER:
Mel Locke
PUBLIC RELATIONS:
C. B. Falconar

Falconar markets plans and kits of a wide range of light aircraft and sailplanes suitable for amateur construction. These include versions

of the Jodel D.9 and D.11, Druine Turbulent, Piel Emeraude, and Luton Major and Minor; a wide range of single-, two- and three-seat aircraft designated F9, F10, F11 and F12, which are developed from the French Jodel D.9 and D.11 designs and offer a variety of modifications including tricycle landing gear, forward-sliding canopy and sweptback rudder; and the designs of Marcel Jurca. A prototype of the Jurca M.J.7 Gnatsum has been completed and has carried out successfully a full flight test programme. This aircraft is described under the Jurca heading in the French section of this edition.

Two other Falconar products, for which plans and kits are available, are the AMF-S14 and the Model 121 Teal amphibian, details of which are given below.

FALCONAR AMF-S14

The AMF-S14 is a hybrid design, sharing with the Maranda Super Loisir (see 1968-69 Jane's) a common ancestor in the French Adam RA-14 (1956-57 Jane's), although the two Canadian designs are by no means identical.

Design of the first home-built S14 (CF-RDK) began in 1958, and this aircraft was flown in July 1961. By the Spring of 1969 approx 22 had been built in Canada and the US, and plans had been sold for well over 200 more.

All AMF-S14s are now being built with shorter fuselages than the original version.

TYPE: Two-seat sporting and touring aircraft.

WINGS: Braced high-wing monoplane. Wing section NACA 23012. Constant-chord wings, which can be folded back over the fuselage to facilitate storage. Conventional two-spar all-wooden structure, plastic-coated. Bracing struts of steel or dural tube. Slotted flaps and ailerons. No trim-tabs on ailerons.

FUSELAGE: Conventional wooden box-girder structure, covered with plastic-coated synthetic fabric.

TAIL UNIT: Conventional wooden structure covered with plastic-coated synthetic fabric. Wire-braced tailplane. Controllable trim-tab on starboard elevator. Optional ground-adjustable tab on rudder.

LANDING GEAR: Non-retractable tailwheel type. Each main leg is a simple steel-tube Vee-strut, the dural cover of which serves as an entrance step. The axle section of each Vee is connected to a telescopic shock-strut with multiple rubber-pad shock-absorbers. Mechanical or hydraulic braking system at customer's option, though braking may be omitted entirely in grass-field operation if a tail-skid is fitted in place of the tail-wheel. Main wheel tyres may be size 6·00 × 6, 7·00 × 6 or 8·00 × 4. Falconar F30 plastic-coated wooden floats or Federal A1500A ski landing gear optional.

POWER PLANT: A variety of "flat-four" air-cooled engines may be fitted, at customer's option, including Continental, Lycoming or Corvair engines of up to 150 hp, or a 130 hp Franklin. Two-blade wooden or metal propeller. Fuel tank between engine firewall and instrument panel. Provision for auxiliary tank in each wing root.

ACCOMMODATION: For Canadian operation, side-by-side seating for two persons in enclosed cabin with car-type door on each side. Additional passengers or baggage can be carried in aircraft built for US operation. Compartment aft of seats for up to 52 lb (24 kg) of baggage, depending on fuel load. Can be modified to three-seater.

DIMENSIONS, EXTERNAL:
Wing span	31 ft 9 in (9·68 m)
Wing aspect ratio	6·4
Width, wings folded	10 ft 0 in (3·05 m)
Length overall (early models)	23 ft 0 in (7·01 m)
Height overall	7 ft 2 in (2·18 m)
Tailplane span	10 ft 0 in (3·05 m)
Wheel track	7 ft 0 in (2·13 m)

DIMENSION, INTERNAL:
Baggage compartment: Volume 18 cu ft (0·51 m²)

AREA:
Wings, gross   140 sq ft (13·01 m²)

WEIGHTS (landplane):
Weight empty	800 lb (363 kg)
Payload	392 lb (178 kg)
Normal T-O weight (two-seat)	1,300 lb (590 kg)
Max T-O weight (three-seat)	1,500 lb (680 kg)

PERFORMANCE (landplane at normal T-O weight, 150 hp engine):
Max never-exceed speed
          130 knots (150 mph; 241 km/h)
Max cruising speed
          104 knots (120 mph; 193 km/h)
Stalling speed   31 knots (35 mph; 57 km/h)
Rate of climb at S/L   1,200 ft (366 m)/min
Service ceiling   20,000 ft (6,100 m)
Landing run   250 ft (76 m)
Range with standard fuel
          390 nm (450 miles; 724 km)

FALCONAR 121 TEAL

The Teal, design of which was started in 1964, is a two-seat amphibian licensable for amateur construction. It can be fitted with a variety of Continental, Franklin or Lycoming engines from 100 hp to 160 hp; design is to CAM 3 requirements, and the airframe is stressed to withstand 9g at an AUW of 1,500 lb (680 kg).

The prototype (CF-WCZ) first flew in December 1967 and commenced its development trials during the summer of 1968. By the Spring of 1969 a second Teal had been completed, and approx 130 sets of plans had been sold.

Preliminary design studies have been made by Falconar for a glider-towing version of the Teal, and for a projected twin-engined version, the Twin Teal, with simplified wing bracing and other detail improvements.

Details below apply to the prototype Teal.

TYPE: Two-seat light amphibian for amateur construction.

AMF-S14F, modified from Falconar plans by Mr S. Olive of St John, New Brunswick. It has the new shorter fuselage and is fitted with landing gear from a Piper Pacer (*Howard Levy*)

Minicab Hawk built by Mr Mike Hoffman of California from Falconar plans (100 hp Lycoming O-235-C engine) (*Howard Levy*)

Druine D 31 Turbulent built from Falconar plans by Mr Laurence Weishaar of Springfield, Illinois (*Jean Seele*)

WINGS: Strut-braced high-wing monoplane. Wing section NACA 4412 (modified). Dihedral 2°. Incidence 5°. Constant-chord wings of conventional two-spar wood and plywood construction, with plastic coating. Wings supported from wheel/float fairings by a single strut inboard and Vee-strut outboard of each fairing. Wings can be folded back over the fuselage to facilitate storage or transportation. Slotted flaps and ailerons. No tabs.

FUSELAGE: Single-step wooden hull, with ply-wood covering and glass-fibre "second skin" on hull bottom. Glass-fibre cowling. Stabilising floats, into which the main wheels retract, are carried on sponsons on each side of the fuselage, abreast of the cabin. The floats are of wooden construction, with glass-fibre nose and tail sections.

TAIL UNIT: Single fin and rudder, with strut-braced tailplane half-way up fin. Small downward-hinged water rudder below main rudder. Wooden structure, covered with plastic-coated glass-fibre cloth. Trim-tab on each elevator, one being a stick force compensating tab which is actuated when the flaps are lowered.

LANDING GEAR: Retractable tricycle type, which can also serve as beaching gear. Fully castor-ing nose-wheel on prototype, retracting forward into fuselage nose, can be replaced by steerable unit if desired. Main wheels retract rearward into floats. All wheels and tyres same size, 5·00 × 5 on prototype, but size 5·80 × 8 is recommended for nose-wheel and size 6·00 × 6 for main wheels on amateur-built aircraft. Manual retraction on prototype is superseded by hydraulically- or electrically-operated retraction at customer's option. Ski gear optional, in which case the nose-wheel remains retracted and a steerable tail-skid is fitted beneath the rear of the keel, the water rudder being omitted. Main wheels and legs are replaced by short legs bearing the main skis, which have leaf-spring shock-absorbers.

POWER PLANT (prototype): One 160 hp Lycoming O-320-B2A four-cylinder horizontally-opposed air-cooled engine, driving a Hartzell two-blade constant-speed metal or wooden propeller. Fuel in main tank aft of engine firewall, capacity 24 Imp gallons (109 litres). Provision to install additional tank in each wing, increasing total capacity to 54 Imp gallons (245 litres).

ACCOMMODATION: For Canadian operation, side-by-side seats for two persons in fully-enclosed cabin. Additional passengers or baggage can be carried in aircraft built for US operation. Side windows serve as entrance doors, but optional features include a forward-opening car-type door on each side. Dual controls. Baggage compartment aft of seats, accessible via external hatch on top of fuselage or from inside cabin. Forward-hinged emergency hatch on top of fuselage, aft of wing trailing-edge.

SYSTEMS: Starter-generator and propeller governor. Optional electrical system includes alternator or generator, battery and navigation lights.

DIMENSIONS, EXTERNAL:

Wing span	33 ft 0 in (10·06 m)
Wing aspect ratio	6·6
Width, wings folded	10 ft 0 in (3·05 m)
Length overall	24 ft 6 in (7·47 m)
Height overall	7 ft 10 in (2·39 m)
Tailplane span	10 ft 0 in (3·05 m)
Wheel track	9 ft 6 in (2·90 m)

DIMENSIONS, INTERNAL:

Cabin: Max width	3 ft 6 in (1·07 m)
Baggage compartment: Volume	22 cu ft (0·62 m³)

AREA:

Wings, gross	160 sq ft (14·86 m²)

WEIGHTS AND LOADINGS (O-320 engine):

Weight empty, equipped	1,050 lb (476 kg)
Max T-O weight	1,500 lb (680 kg)
Max wing loading	9·735 lb/sq ft (47·52 kg/m²)
Max power loading	9·735 lb/hp (4·415 kg/hp)

Prototype Falconar 121 Teal two-seat light amphibian

PERFORMANCE (at max T-O weight, O-320 engine):

Max level speed	113 knots (130 mph; 209 km/h)
Max permissible diving speed	160·5 knots (185 mph; 297 km/h)
Max cruising speed	109 knots (125 mph; 201 km/h)
Landing speed	36·4 knots (42 mph; 68 km/h)
Stalling speed	32·2 knots (37 mph; 60 km/h)
Rate of climb at S/L	1,100 ft (335 m)/min
Service ceiling	16,400 ft (5,000 m)
T-O run	330 ft (101 m)
Landing run	450 ft (137 m)
Range with standard fuel	390 nm (450 miles; 724 km)
Max range	607 nm (700 miles; 1,125 km)

FOUND
FOUND BROTHERS AVIATION, LTD

Found Brothers Aviation was formed in 1946, and in 1949 produced a light cabin monoplane, the FBA-1A, which was described in contemporary editions of *Jane's*. From this were developed the FBA-2 five-seat cabin monoplane, described fully in the 1967-68 *Jane's*, and the six-seat Centennial 100, described in the 1969-70 *Jane's*. The company closed down at the end of 1968, and its assets (which included three Model 100 Centennial and one FBA-2C aircraft) were put up for sale by auction in the Spring of 1969. No news of the outcome of these proceedings has been received.

HAWKER SIDDELEY

HAWKER SIDDELEY CANADA LTD (Member Company of HAWKER SIDDELEY GROUP)

HEAD OFFICE:
7, King Street East, Toronto 1, Ontario

DIRECTORS:
Sir Arnold Hall, FRS (Chairman)
R. S. Faulkner (President and Chief Executive Officer)
A. A. Bailie (Vice-President, Finance, and Treasurer)
A. S. Kennedy (Vice-Chairman)
G. R. McGregor
A. W. McKenzie

F. P. Mitchell
A. S. Pattillo, QC (Vice-Chairman)
K. L. Phillips, FCA
A. J. Laurence
W. P. Scott
R. G. Smith
C. W. Webster

VICE-PRESIDENTS:
I. E. Bull (Comptroller)
M. E. Davis
R. E. Henderson
J. Grant Mitchell
L. A. Mitten
J. H. Ready (Secretary)

DIRECTOR, EXPORT MARKETING:
R. C. Decker

PUBLIC RELATIONS:
J. F. Painter

Known as A. V. Roe Canada Ltd until 1962, this company controls operating units and subsidiaries in Canada, employing about 8,500 people. Products include naval and commercial ships, off-shore oil-drilling rigs, freight and passenger railway rolling-stock and components, highway trailers, steel castings, towers, bridges, lumbering and sawmill equipment.

The company's chief aviation units are Orenda Limited, the current activities of which are described in the "Aero-engines" section, and the Fort William plant of the Canadian Car Division, which manufactures aircraft components on a sub-contract basis.

HUNEAULT
JEAN PAUL HUNEAULT

ADDRESS:
92 Deslauriers, Pierrefonds, Quebec

Mr Huneault has converted a de Havilland Canada DHC-1 Chipmunk into a specialised aerobatic aircraft, with a more powerful engine and other modifications.

HUNEAULT DHC-1 CHIPMUNK

The basic airframe of Mr Huneault's Chipmunk (CF-CYT-X, c/n 192) is unchanged aft of the firewall, except for replacement of some wing fabric covering (weight 16 lb; 7·3 kg) with metal (weight 20 lb; 9·1 kg).

Principal modification is replacement of the original Gipsy Major engine by a 210 hp Continental IO-360-C six-cylinder horizontally-opposed air-cooled fuel-injection engine, carried on a new dynafocal mounting stressed in excess of DoT requirements. Exhaust and ancillary equipment are regrouped beneath the engine, which drives a McCauley variable-pitch propeller (diameter 6 ft 4 in; 1·93 m) for normal flying or a Hartzell propeller (diameter 6 ft 10 in; 2·08 m) with speed governor for aerobatic flight. New two-piece glass-fibre engine cowlings are carried on rubber anti-vibration mountings.

It is planned to replace the standard fixed landing gear with a retractable type in the near future.

The DHC-1 Chipmunk aircraft modified by Mr Jean Huneault, with Contnental IO-360 engine
(Jean Seele)

The instrumentation in the forward cockpit has been regrouped to meet aerobatic requirements, and the manual flap control has been replaced by an electrical control to save space. Dual flying controls are retained in the rear cockpit, but it now contains no instruments.

Use of a propeller shaft extesion has led to an increase of one inch (2·5 cm) in the length of the fuselage. The empty weight of the modified aircraft is some 8 lb (3·6 kg) less than that of the standard Chipmunk.

During its first flight, on 16 July 1969, CF-CYT-X achieved a maximum cruising speed of 139 knots (160 mph; 257 km/h). Estimated rate of climb is 2,400 ft (731 m)/min with pilot only on board.

NWI
NORTHWEST INDUSTRIES LTD

ADDRESS:
PO Box 517, Industrial Airport, Edmonton, Alberta

NORTHWEST RANGER

Northwest Industries has acquired, from Aermacchi of Italy, a licence to produce for the North American market modified versions of the latter company's AL.60C5 Conestoga bush transport aircraft, under the name Ranger.

The initial version of the Ranger, which underwent certification trials early in 1968, is generally similar to the standard AL.60C5 (see the Italian section of this edition), with a 400 hp

Lycoming IO-720-A1A engine, but has blister fairings over the main landing gear legs and Hoerner wingtips. These modifications result in improvements in cruising speed and landing performance, the Ranger having a power-off landing speed of 54 mph (86 kmh) and a stalling speed of 38 mph (60 kmh). Accommodation is for a pilot and seven passengers.

An uprated version, known as the **Ranger C-6,** has also been developed, with 520 hp Lycoming TIO-720-B1A engine. Optional items include auxiliary fuel tanks and float or ski landing gear.

The description below applied to the Ranger C-6 in 1969, but extensive performance and user trials, and market research, have indicated the desirability of certain changes before the aircraft is made available for sale.

DIMENSIONS, EXTERNAL:

Wing span	39 ft 4 in (11·99 m)
Length overall	28 ft 6 in (8·69 m)
Height overall	9 ft 3 in (2·82 m)

WEIGHTS:

Weight empty	2,848 lb (1,292 kg)
Max T-O weight	4,700 lb (2,132 kg)

PERFORMANCE (at max T-O weight):
Cruising speed (75% power) at 8,500 ft (2,590 m)
144 knots (166 mph; 267 km/h)

Rate of climb at S/L	1,475 ft (450 m)/min
Service ceiling	20,000 ft (6,100 m)
T-O to 50 ft (15 m)	915 ft (279 m)
Landing from 50 ft (15 m)	920 ft (280 m)

Range at econ cruising speed (55% power) at 5,000 ft (1,525 m), standard fuel with 45 min reserve   460 nm (530 miles; 853 km)

PIACL
PIASECKI AIRCRAFT OF CANADA LTD
(Subsidiary of Piasecki Aircraft Corporation, USA)

ADDRESS:
PO Box 1200, Picton, Ontario

PRESIDENT: Frank N. Piasecki

DIRECTORS:
Frank N. Piasecki (President)
D. N. Meyers (Vice-President)
A. J. Kania (Secretary-Treasurer)
H. G. S. Bain
H. J. Bird

This company was established early in 1968 to provide facilities for research, engineering and production in a wide range of aerospace and defence activities covering aircraft, electronics and

related products, and ground handling equipment for aircraft and missiles.

The company has acquired the former Canadian Armed Forces base at Picton, Ontario, amounting to over 700 acres of land and including the airfield with three runways and six hangars. This facility was obtained in conjunction with the certification and production of the 15-seat Pathfinder compound helicopter Model 16H-3J, described under the PiAC heading in the US section.

SAUNDERS
SAUNDERS AIRCRAFT CORPORATION LTD

HEAD OFFICE:
PO Box 185, Postal Station, Montreal AMF, Province of Quebec

WORKS:
Montreal International Airport, Dorval, Province of Quebec

CHAIRMAN:
David Saunders

SAUNDERS ST-27

The Saunders ST-27 is a turboprop conversion of the Hawker Siddeley (de Havilland) D.H.114 Heron Series 2 (see 1966-67 *Jane's*), intended to provide a low-cost short-range light transport for use by third-level and "commuter" airlines. Modifications involve the use of two Pratt & Whitney (UACL) PT6A-27 turboprops, in place of the four Gipsy Queen piston-engines which powered the original Heron, and an 8 ft 6 in (2·59 m) longer fuselage seating up to 24 passengers instead of 14/17 in the original version. The wings and tailplane of the standard Heron are retained (the latter with increased dihedral), and the same landing gear units are used. The rudder has been redesigned, with increased area.

The prototype ST-27 (CF-YBM-X) flew for the first time on 28 May 1969, and the certification programme is being directed by Aviation Traders Ltd of the UK. Subject to successful completion, Saunders proposed similar conversion of 15 more existing Herons before initiating production of the ST-27 as an all-new aircraft. The latter version would have a modified fuselage cross-section with pressurisation available as an optional feature.

In mid-June 1969 one ST-27 had been ordered by Cimber Air of Denmark, and negotiations with British and Canadian operators were under way.

The details below apply to the prototype.

TYPE: Twin-turboprop light transport.

WINGS: Cantilever low-wing monoplane. Aspect ratio 10·5. Conventional two-spar light alloy structure, with light alloy sheet skin. Ailerons and flaps, in three pieces each side, have metal frames and fabric covering. Flaps are operated pneumatically. Trim-tab in each

aileron. Pneumatic de-icing boots on leading-edge.

FUSELAGE: Conventional semi-monocoque light alloy structure. Wing centre-section spar integral with fuselage. Main cabin floor of sandwich construction, stressed for freight carrying. Compared with original Heron Srs 2, an additional 8 ft 6 in (2·59 m) section has been introduced into the centre fuselage, aft of the main spar. A longer nose-cone is fitted.

TAIL UNIT: Cantilever all-metal structure, with marked dihedral on horizontal surfaces. Fixed surfaces are metal-covered, movable surfaces fabric-covered. Trim-tabs in rudder and each elevator. Pneumatic-boot de-icing of leading-edges.

LANDING GEAR: Retractable tricycle type. Pneumatic retraction, nose-wheel rearward into fuselage, main wheels outward into wings. Main legs have rubber shock-absorbers. Nose-wheel has an oleo-pneumatic shock-absorber and is castoring and self-centering. Differentially-operating pneumatic brakes.

POWER PLANT: Two 715 eshp Pratt & Whitney (UACL) PT6A-27 turboprop engines, each driving a Hartzell three-blade constant-speed fully-feathering metal propeller. Electric-boot de-icing of propellers. Fuel in cross-feeding bag-type tanks in each wing, with total capacity of 312 Imp gallons (1,418 litres), with provision for auxiliary tanks increasing max capacity to 412 Imp gallons (1,873 litres). Oil capacity 1·7 Imp gallons (7·7 litres) per engine.

ACCOMMODATION: Crew of two on flight deck, with full dual controls. Non-pressurised main cabin can seat up to 24 persons, 20 of them on individual seats at 30 in (76 cm) pitch on each side of centre aisle, plus four on bench seat at rear. Airstair door at front on port side provides access to flight deck and passenger cabin. Additional airstair door for passengers at rear, on port side. Two emergency exits, one each side of fuselage over wing. Individual passenger seats are removable to permit carriage of freight, the passenger and cargo compartments then being separated by a movable bulkhead. Holds aft of main cabin (with external access door) and in nose for max total baggage load of 960 lb (435 kg). Cabin and

flight deck heated by engine-bleed air. Later production aircraft may have pressurised cabin as an optional feature.

SYSTEMS: Pneumatic system for flap and landing gear actuation and brakes. No hydraulic system. Electrical system includes two 200A starter-generators with primary buss, and independent emergency battery essential buss system. Nickel-cadmium batteries are standard equipment, and emergency battery is maintained at full charge at all times from main system.

ELECTRONICS AND EQUIPMENT: To customer's specification. Provision for dual nav/com equipment, and ADF, with Gables DME and transponder.

DIMENSIONS, EXTERNAL:

Wing span	71 ft 6 in (21·79 m)
Length overall	57 ft 0 in (17·37 m)
Height overall	15 ft 7 in (4·75 m)
Wheel track	16 ft 8 in (5·08 m)

Passenger door (fwd, port):

Height	4 ft 4 in (1·32 m)
Width	2 ft 3 in (0·69 m)

Passenger door (rear, port):

Height	4 ft 4 in (1·32 m)
Width	2 ft 9 in (0·84 m)

DIMENSIONS, INTERNAL:

Cabin:	Max height	5 ft 9 in (1·75 m)
	Max width	4 ft 6 in (1·37 m)
Baggage hold volume (rear)		105 cu ft (2·97 m³)
Baggage hold volume (nose)		22 cu ft (0·61 m³)

WEIGHTS:

Weight empty	7,000 lb (3,175 kg)

Max T-O weight:

FAR	12,500 lb (5,670 kg)
BCAR	13,500 lb (6,124 kg)

PERFORMANCE (at FAR max T-O weight):
Max cruising speed at 7,000 ft (2,125 m)
217 knots (250 mph; 402 km/h)

Stalling speed	64 knots (73 mph; 118 km/h)
Rate of climb at S/L	1,600 ft (488 m)/min
T-O to 50 ft (15 m)	1,600 ft (488 m)
Landing from 50 ft (15 m)	2,000 ft (610 m)
Accelerate-stop distance	3,200 ft (975 m)

Range with 2 + 24 persons and 132 Imp gallons (600 litres) fuel
approx 217 nm (250 miles; 400 km)

Max range with standard fuel, no reserves
738 nm (850 miles; 1,370 km)

Second prototype Saunders ST-27 Heron conversion (two 715 eshp UACL PT6A-27 turboprop engines) at Gatwick Airport, England (*Flight International*)

CHINA (PEOPLE'S REPUBLIC)

STATE AIRCRAFT FACTORY
ADDRESS:
Shen Yang, near Mukden
DIRECTOR: Professor Hsue Shen Tsien

In recent years this State Factory has built aircraft of Russian design, including the MiG-17 and MiG-19 single-seat fighters, MiG-15UTI two-seat jet trainer, Mi-4 general-purpose helicopter, An-2 general-purpose biplane and Yak-18 two-seat basic trainer. It is also producing what is thought to be a simplified version of the MiG-21, not necessarily under licence.

Progress has been made in building up a comprehensive national aircraft industry, complete with its own design teams and research establishments. Several aircraft of national design were flown in the late 1950s, and have been described in previous editions of this work. There has been no news of any subsequent designs, or of series production of non-Russian aircraft, during the past year.

Chinese-built MiG-19 single-seat fighter, in the insignia of the Pakistan Air Force (*John Fricker*)

CHINA (TAIWAN)

CAF/Pazmany PL-1B, Chinese production version of this two-seat primary trainer

AIDC/CAF
AERO-INDUSTRY DEVELOPMENT CENTER, CHINESE AIR FORCE
ADDRESS: Taichung, Taiwan
DIRECTOR: Major General Y. C. Lee
DEPUTY DIRECTORS:
Major General C. Y. Lee (Manufacturing)
Dr T. C. Lee (Engineering and Research)

Early in 1968, the Chinese Air Force was seeking a small aircraft, suitable for the primary training of CAF air cadets, which could be built in Taiwan and serve to revive the country's own aircraft industry. Assisted by Col R. S. Robinson, USAF Senior Adviser to Air Service Command of the CAF, the Chinese Air Force authorities decided to select for this purpose a two-seat amateur-built light aircraft of US design, the Pazmany PL-1.

Construction of the first Chinese-built PL-1A, a slightly modified version of the PL-1, began in June 1968, under the direction of the then Col C. Y. Lee, CAF, at the Aeronautical Research Laboratory at Taichung, and the aircraft was completed in exactly 100 days. It flew for the first time on 26 October 1968, and was officially presented to President Chiang Kai-Shek four days later. Two more prototypes were completed in June 1969, and after a concentrated flight test programme and further modifications the PL-1B production model was evolved. In the Spring of 1970, a production batch of 35 PL-1Bs was being built by AIDC.

The AIDC is also to begin delivery in 1970 of licence-built versions of the Bell UH-1H helicopter (Bell Model 205) for the Chinese Army, under an agreement reached in 1969.

CAF/PAZMANY PL-1A and PL-1B
The following details refer to the prototype PL-1A and the production model PL-1B; the significant improvements in the production type include a wider cockpit, larger rudder and more powerful engine.
TYPE: Two-seat light aircraft.
WINGS: Cantilever low-wing monoplane. Wing section NACA 63₂615. Dihedral 3° from roots. Incidence —1° 20′. All-metal single-spar structure in one piece, with leading-edge torsion box. Plain piano-hinged ailerons and flaps of all-metal construction. No trim-tabs.
FUSELAGE: Conventional all-metal semi-monocoque structure, with flat or single-curvature skins.
TAIL UNIT: Cantilever all-metal structure. One-piece horizontal surface, with anti-servo tab which serves also as a trim-tab.
LANDING GEAR: Non-retractable tricycle type, with all three oleo-pneumatic shock-absorbers interchangeable. Goodyear wheels and tyres size 5·00 × 5; tyre pressure 31 lb/sq in (2·18 kg/cm²). Goodyear brakes. Steerable nosewheel.
POWER PLANT: One 125 hp Lycoming O-290-D (PL-1A) or 150 hp Lycoming O-320-E2A (PL-1B) four-cylinder horizontally-opposed air-cooled engine, driving a McCauley 1A100/MCM 6668 two-blade fixed-pitch metal propeller. Fuel in two glass-fibre wing-tip tanks, each of 10·4 Imp gallons (12·5 US gallons; 47 litres) capacity. Total fuel capacity 20·8 Imp gallons (25 US gallons; 94 litres). Oil capacity 1·7 Imp gallons (2 US gallons; 7·5 litres).
ACCOMMODATION: Two seats side-by-side, under rearward-sliding transparent canopy. Dual controls. Space for 40 lb (18 kg) baggage aft of seats. Heater and air scoops for ventilation.
ELECTRONICS AND EQUIPMENT: VHF radio standard.

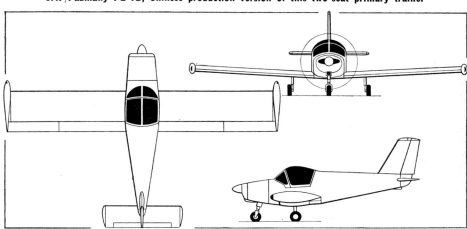

CAF/Pazmany PL-1B two-seat primary training aircraft

DIMENSIONS, EXTERNAL:	
Wing span	28 ft 0 in (8·53 m)
Wing chord (constant)	4 ft 2 in (1·27 m)
Wing aspect ratio	6·72
Length overall:	
PL-1A	18 ft 7 in (5·66 m)
PL-1B	19 ft 8½ in (5·99 m)
Height overall	7 ft 4 in (2·24 m)
Tailplane span	8 ft 0 in (2·44 m)
Wheel track	8 ft 2½ in (2·50 m)
Wheelbase	4 ft 3 in (1·30 m)
DIMENSIONS, INTERNAL:	
Cabin: Length	4 ft 2 in (1·27 m)
Max width:	
PL-1A	3 ft 4 in (1·02 m)
PL-1B	3 ft 6½ in (1·07 m)
Max height	3 ft 4 in (1·02 m)
AREAS:	
Wings, gross	116 sq ft (10·78 m²)
Ailerons (total)	10·54 sq ft (0·98 m²)
Flaps (total)	17·36 sq ft (1·61 m²)
Fin	7·30 sq ft (0·68 m²)
Rudder:	
PL-1A	3·82 sq ft (0·35 m²)
PL-1B	4·20 sq ft (0·39 m²)
Tailplane	18·00 sq ft (1·67 m²)
WEIGHTS AND LOADINGS:	
Weight empty, equipped:	
PL-1A	930 lb (422 kg)
PL-1B	950 lb (431 kg)
Max T-O weight:	
PL-1A	1,400 lb (635 kg)
PL-1B	1,440 lb (653 kg)

Max wing loading:	
PL-1A	12·1 lb/sq ft (59·01 kg/m²)
PL-1B	12·4 lb/sq ft (60·5 kg/m²)
Max power loading:	
PL-1A	11·2 lb/hp (5·1 kg/hp)
PL-1B	9·6 lb/hp (4·35 kg/hp)
PERFORMANCE (at max T-O weight):	
Max level speed at S/L:	
PL-1A	120 knots (138 mph; 222 km/h)
PL-1B	130 knots (150 mph; 241 km/h)
Max permissible diving speed	
	178 knots (205 mph; 330 km/h)
Max cruising speed at S/L:	
PL-1A	100 knots (115 mph; 185 km/h)
PL-1B	113 knots (130 mph; 209 km/h)
Econ cruising speed at S/L:	
PL-1A	90 knots (104 mph; 167 km/h)
PL-1B	100 knots (115 mph; 185 km/h)
Stalling speed, flaps down:	
PL-1A	46 knots (53 mph; 86 km/h)
PL-1B	47 knots (54 mph; 87 km/h)
Rate of climb at S/L:	
PL-1A	1,300 ft (396 m)/min
PL-1B	1,600 ft (488 m)/min
T-O run:	
PL-1A	600 ft (183 m)
PL-1B	560 ft (171 m)
T-O to 50 ft (15 m):	
PL-1A	1,000 ft (305 m)
PL-1B	950 ft (290 m)
Landing from 50 ft (15 m)	1,100 ft (335 m)
Landing run	550 ft (167 m)
Range with max fuel:	
PL-1A	390 nm (450 miles; 724 km)
PL-1B	351 nm (405 miles; 651 km)

CZECHOSLOVAKIA

Central direction of the Czechoslovak aircraft industry is by a body known as the Generální Reditelstvi Aero—Ceskoslovenské Letecke Podniky Trust Aero—Czechoslovak Aeronautical Works, Prague-Letnany, whose General Director is Jan Syrovy. Principal factories concerned with aircraft manufacture are the Aero Vodochody National Corporation, Let National Corporation and Zlin Aircraft-Moravan National Corporation, whose current products appear under the appropriate headings in this section. Other Czechoslovak factories engaged in the production of aero-engines and sailplanes are listed in the relevant sections of this edition.

Sales of all aircraft products outside Czechoslovakia are handled by the Omnipol Foreign Trade Corporation, whose address is given below.

OMNIPOL
OMNIPOL FOREIGN TRADE CORPORATION

ADDRESS:
  Washingtonova 11, Prague 1

GENERAL MANAGER:
  Tomás Marecek, GE

SALES MANAGER:
  Frantisek Rypal, GE

PUBLIC RELATIONS MANAGER:
  Jan Bocek

This concern handles the sales of products of the Czechoslovak aircraft industry outside Czechoslovakia and furnishes all information requested by customers with regard to export goods.

About 29,000 people are employed by the Czechoslovak aircraft industry.

AERO
AERO VODOCHODY NÁRODNÍ PODNIK (Aero Vodochody National Corporation)

ADDRESS:
  Vodochody, p. Odelená Voda, near Prague

MANAGING DIRECTOR:
  Jan Feigel

VICE-DIRECTORS:
  Ing Vlastimil Havelka (Technical)
  Ing Vladimír Flaska (Production)
  Ing Václav Posluh (Sales)
  Oldrich Novák (Works Economy)

CHIEF DESIGNER:
  Ing Jan Vlcek

CHIEF PILOT:
  Vlastimil David

This factory perpetuates the name of one of the three founder companies of the Czechoslovak aircraft industry, which began activities shortly after the end of World War 1 with the manufacture of Austrian Phönix fighters. Subsequent well-known products include the A 11 military general-purpose biplane and its derivatives, and licence manufacture of the French Bloch 200 twin-engined bomber. The present works was established on 1 July 1953, since when it has seven times received the Red Banner award of the Ministry of Engineering and UVOS, as well as many other awards including those of Exemplary Exporting Corporation and the Order of Labour. Its current products include the Aero L-29 and L-39 jet trainers, details of which are given below.

L-29 DELFIN
NATO Code Name: "Maya"

The L-29 was evolved by a team led by K. Tomas and the late Z. Rublic. The first prototype, the XL-29, flew for the first time on 5 April 1959, powered by a Bristol Siddeley Viper turbojet engine. The second prototype, equipped with a Czech M-701 turbojet engine, began its flight trials in July 1960. The pre-production version (third prototype) completed its tests in 1961, and the L-29 was approved for quantity production.

Manufacture is centred at the Vodochody (Aero) and Kunovice plants, which are devoted almost entirely to producing the L-29, to meet large orders from the Czech Air Force, the Soviet Union, Bulgaria, Hungary, the German Democratic Republic, Syria, Egypt, Rumania, Indonesia, Nigeria and Uganda.

The first production aircraft was completed in April 1963, a month ahead of schedule, and by the end of 1969 some 2,500 had been sold. The details below apply to the standard L-29.

A counter-insurgency version, designated L-29R, is available with nose cameras and underwing stores.

A single-seat aerobatic version, the L-29A, is described separately.

TYPE: Two-seat jet basic and advanced trainer.

WINGS: Cantilever mid-wing monoplane. Wing section NACA 64₂A217 at root, NACA 64₂A212 at tip. Dihedral 0° on centre-section, 3° on outer wings. Incidence 1° 30'. All-metal stressed-skin structure with single main spar at 40% chord. All-metal ailerons and hydraulically-operated Fowler flaps. Trim-tab in each aileron.

FUSELAGE: All-metal monocoque structure of circular section. Front portion forms pressurised compartment for the crew, radio equipment and electronics. Centre fuselage is integral with wing centre-section and contains main fuel tanks. Engine mounting is attached to rear bulkhead of centre-fuselage. Rear fuselage is connected to centre portion through eight attachment points, to permit quick removal for engine servicing. Zones of high stress have steel-alloy reinforcement. Hydraulically-operated sideways-opening perforated air-brake on each side of rear fuselage.

TAIL UNIT: All-metal structure with variable-incidence tailplane and elevator mounted at tip of fin. Tailplane incidence is linked with landing flaps. Trim-tabs in elevator. Adjustable tab on rudder.

LANDING GEAR: Retractable tricycle type. Hydraulic retraction, main wheels inward into wing-roots, nose-wheel rearward into fuselage. Oleo-pneumatic shock-absorbers. Single wheel on each unit. Barum low-pressure tyres, size 600 × 180 on main wheels, 420 × 150 on nose-wheel. Pneumatic brakes.

POWER PLANT: One M-701c 500 turbojet engine, rated at 1,960 lb (890 kg) st at 15,400 rpm for take-off. Fuel in two main tanks in fuselage with capacity of 152 Imp gallons (690 litres) and 79 Imp gallons (360 litres) respectively. Total internal fuel capacity 231 Imp gallons (1,050 litres). Total usable capacity 211·5 Imp gallons (962 litres). Provision for two 33 Imp gallon (150 litre) underwing auxiliary tanks. Inverted flying tank in rear main tank permits 15 sec of inverted flight. All tanks of aluminium alloy.

ACCOMMODATION: Crew of two in tandem on synchronised ejection seats in air-conditioned and pressurised cabin. Rear seat raised 6 in (15 cm) higher than front seat. Fittings for g-suits. Canopy over front cockpit opens sideways, to starboard. Rearward-sliding canopy over rear cockpit.

SYSTEMS: Hydraulic system, pressure 1,565 lb/sq in (110 kg/cm²), actuates landing gear, wheel doors, flaps and air-brakes. Emergency manual system for extension of flaps and landing gear. In case of pilot error, flaps retract automatically at an air speed of 168 mph (270 kmh). Pneumatic system for air-brakes and canopy seals. Electrical system includes a 3kW generator on engine and a 28Ah battery which can be used for emergency engine starting.

ELECTRONICS AND EQUIPMENT: Includes VHF radio, radio compass, radio altimeter and marker beacon receiver.

ARMAMENT: Provision for camera gun and gun sight, and either two bombs of up to 220 lb (100 kg), eight air-to-ground rockets or two 7·62-mm machine-gun pods under the wings.

DIMENSIONS, EXTERNAL:

Wing span	33 ft 9 in (10·29 m)
Wing chord at root	8 ft 10 in (2·70 m)
Wing chord at tip	4 ft 7 in (1·40 m)
Wing aspect ratio	5·36
Length overall	35 ft 5½ in (10·81 m)
Height over tail	10 ft 3 in (3·13 m)
Tailplane span	10 ft 11½ in (3·34 m)
Wheel track	11 ft 3½ in (3·44 m)
Wheelbase	12 ft 9½ in (3·90 m)

AREAS:

Wings, gross	213·1 sq ft (19·80 m²)
Ailerons (total)	16·15 sq ft (1·50 m²)
Flaps (total)	30·14 sq ft (2·80 m²)
Air-brakes (total)	5·38 sq ft (0·50 m²)
Fin	14·00 sq ft (1·30 m²)
Rudder	8·61 sq ft (0·80 m²)
Tailplane	23·68 sq ft (2·20 m²)
Elevators	11·84 sq ft (1·10 m²)

WEIGHTS AND LOADING:

Weight empty	5,027 lb (2,280 kg)

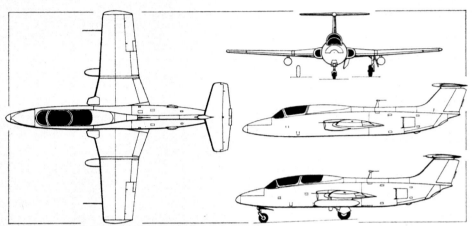

L-29 Delfin tandem two-seat jet trainer, with additional side elevation (*centre*) **of single-seat L-29A aerobatic version**

L-29 Delfin two-seat jet trainer, over 2,000 of which have been built for the Czechoslovak and other air forces (*Martin Fricke*)

Normal T-O weight 7,231 lb (3,280 kg)
Max permissible loaded weight with external
tanks 7,804 lb (3,540 kg)
Max wing loading 36·7 lb/sq ft (179 kg/m²)
PERFORMANCE (at AUW of 7,165 lb = 3,250 kg):
Max level speed at S/L
332 knots (382 mph; 615 km/h)
Max speed at 16,400 ft (5,000 m)
353 knots (407 mph; 655 km/h)
Max permissible speed in dive
442 knots (510 mph; 820 km/h)
Limiting Mach No 0·75
Landing speed 78 knots (90 mph; 145 km/h)
Stalling speed, flaps up
87 knots (100 mph; 160 kmh)
Stalling speed, flaps down
71 knots (81 mph; 130 km/h)
Rate of climb at S/L 2,755 ft (840 m)/min
Service ceiling 36,100 ft (11,000 m)
Take-off run 1,805 ft (550 m)
Landing run 1,444 ft (440 m)
Max range on internal fuel at 16,400 ft (5,000 m)
344 nm (397 miles; 640 km)
Max range with external tanks at 16,400 ft
(5,000 m) 480 nm (555 miles; 894 km)
Endurance on internal fuel at 247 knots (285
mph; 460 km/h) at 16,400 ft (5,000 m)
1 hr 47 min
Endurance with external tanks 2 hr 30 min

L-29A DELFIN AKROBAT

The L-29A is a single-seat version of the
Delfin, intended specifically for military and
sporting aerobatic use. The prototype, shown
in the adjacent photograph, was converted from
a standard production L-29 and completed its
flight trials in November 1967. It was displayed at the Hanover Air Show in May 1968,
and is now available for production to special
order.

The L-29A differs from the standard two-seat
Delfin in having certain avionics and training
equipment removed. The rear crew position is
deleted, the aft canopy being replaced by a rearward-sliding fairing, and the power plant is a
derated version of that fitted to the L-29.
Special attention has been paid to manoeuvrability, safety and ease of control, to make the
L-29A suitable for individual or team aerobatics,
and the aircraft is stressed for both positive and
negative g manoeuvres.

Details of the L-29A are generally similar to
those of the standard L-29, except in the following respects:
TYPE: Single-seat aerobatic and advanced
training aircraft.
POWER PLANT: One M-701 turbojet engine
(1,960 lb = 890 kg st, derated to 1,000 lb = 450
kg st). A modified oil system is fitted, together
with an enlarged inverted-flying fuel tank
which will permit up to 40 sec of inverted
flight. For aerobatic flying, only 88 Imp
gallons (400 litres) of fuel are carried.
ACCOMMODATION: Single seat in air-conditioned
and pressurised cabin. Canopy opens side-
ways, to starboard.
ELECTRONICS AND EQUIPMENT: As for L-29 except
that radio altimeter and marker beacon receiver
are deleted.
ARMAMENT: None.
WEIGHTS:
Normal T-O weight 5,732 lb (2,600 kg)
PERFORMANCE (at normal T-O weight):
Max level speed at S/L
343 knots (395 mph; 635 km/h)
Stalling speed, flaps down
67 knots (78 mph; 125 km/h)
Rate of climb at S/L 3,400 ft (1,040 m)/min
Time to 16,400 ft (5,000 m) 7 min
Service ceiling 43,960 ft (13,400 m)
T-O run 1,085 ft (330 m)
T-O to 80 ft (25 m) 2,415 ft (735 m)
Landing from 80 ft (25 m) 2,120 ft (645 m)
Landing run 1,100 ft (335 m)

L-39

The L-39 was developed in the Aero works at
Vodochody by a team led by the chief designer,
Dipl Ing Jan Vlcek. It is intended for an
advanced jet training rôle, and is an entirely
new design. Two prototype airframes had been
completed by 4 November 1968 when the No 02
aircraft flew for the first time. The 01 airframe
is being used for structural testing. L-39 03,
which is the second flying prototype, had also
flown by the beginning of 1970, at which time
production had not started.
TYPE: Two-seat jet trainer.
WINGS: Cantilever low-wing monoplane, with
slight dihedral from roots. All-metal stressed-
skin structure, with all-metal hydraulically-
operated double-slotted trailing-edge flaps.
Air-brake under each leading-edge. Small
fence above and below each trailing-edge between flap and aileron. Non-jettisonable wing-
tip fuel tanks incorporating landing lights.
FUSELAGE: All-metal semi-monocoque structure,
built in two main sections. Front portion
houses electrical and radio equipment in nose
and pressurised compartment for the crew.
Rear section, aft of crew seats, contains fuel
tanks and engine bay, and can be quickly
removed to provide access for engine servicing.

Aero L-29A Akrobat single-seat aerobatic version of the Delfin jet trainer

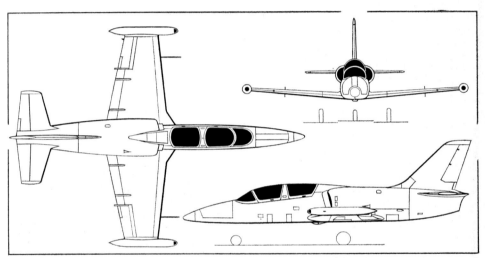

Aero L-39 two-seat jet basic and advanced trainer

Third prototype of the Aero L-39 two-seat jet trainer (one Czechoslovakian-built AI-25W turbofan engine)

TAIL UNIT: Conventional all-metal cantilever
structure, with sweepback on vertical surfaces.
Variable-incidence tailplane. Trim-tab in each
elevator.
LANDING GEAR: Retractable tricycle type, with
single wheel on each unit. Hydraulic retraction, main wheels inward into wings, nose-
wheel rearward into fuselage. Oleo-pneumatic
shock-absorbers and low-pressure tyres on all
units. Hydraulic disc brakes on main wheels.

POWER PLANT: One 3,306 lb (1,500 kg) st Walter
Titan (Motorlet-built Ivchenko AI-25W)
turbofan engine mounted in rear fuselage, with
semi-circular lateral air intakes, fitted with
splitter plates, one each side of fuselage above
wing centre-section. Fuel in rubber bag-type
main tanks aft of cockpit, and non-jettisonable
tank at each wingtip.
ACCOMMODATION: Crew of two in tandem on
zero-height ejection seats beneath individual

transparent canopies which hinge sideways to starboard. Seats ensure safe ejection at speeds above 62 mph (100 km/h).

SYSTEMS: High-pressure hydraulic system for landing gear retraction and control of flaps, air-brakes and wheel brakes.

DIMENSIONS, EXTERNAL:

Wing span	29 ft 10¾ in	(9·11 m)
Length overall	39 ft 8¾ in	(12·11 m)
Height overall	14 ft 4½ in	(4·38 m)

AREA:

Wings, gross	202·4 sq ft	(18·8 m²)

WEIGHTS AND LOADING:

Weight empty	6,283 lb	(2,850 kg)
Max T-O weight	8,377 lb	(3,800 kg)
Max wing loading	41·4 lb/sq ft	(202 kg/m²)

PERFORMANCE (at max T-O weight):
Max level speed 394 knots (454 mph; 730 km/h)
Max limiting Mach number 0·83

Landing speed	81 knots (93 mph; 150 km/h)
Max rate of climb at S/L	3,740 ft (1,140 m)/min
Service ceiling	37,225 ft (11,350 m)
T-O run	1,280 ft (390 m)
T-O to 50 ft (15 m)	2,180 ft (665 m)
Landing from 50 ft (15 m)	2,885 ft (880 m)
Landing run	1,050 ft (320 m)

Range with tip-tanks empty, 5% reserve of main fuel   590 nm (680 miles; 1,100 km)
Max range, tip-tanks full, no reserves
  805 nm (930 miles; 1,500 km)

BRNO

BRNO AERON XA-66

The Aeron XA-66 is a small single-seat autogyro, powered by a 65 hp Walter Mikron III four-cylinder air-cooled in-line engine, driving a two-blade propeller. It was designed by four students at the Transportation Technical Institute at Brno, and made its first flight on 16 May 1968 at Kunovice Airport.

The XA-66 was given the Czechoslovak registration OK-80, and an apparently similar aircraft bearing this registration was displayed by Mr Josef Kunovsky at the Tees-Side Air Pageant in the UK in August 1968, together with an unpowered version described as the KD-67 Idéal. At least six examples of the KD-67 are known to have been built.

The XA-66 was described briefly, and illustrated, in the 1969-70 *Jane's*.

LET

LET NÁRODNÍ PODNIK (Let National Corporation)

ADDRESS:
Kunovice, near Uherské Hradiste

DIRECTORS:
Ing Slavomír Cernocky (Development)
Josef Stuchlík (Production)
Milos Pelech (Sales)
Stanislav Motl (Works Economy)

CHIEF DESIGNER:
Ing Ladislav Smrcek

CHIEF PILOT:
Vladimír Vlk

The Let plant at Kunovice was established in 1950, its early activities including licence production of the Soviet Yak-11 piston-engined trainer under the Czechoslovak designation C-11. It has also contributed to the production of the Aero 45 twin-engined air taxi aircraft and the Z-37 Cmelák agricultural aircraft, and is currently responsible for development and flight testing of the L-410 twin-turboprop light transport.

The factory employed 4,130 workers early in 1969, and in addition to its aircraft manufacturing programme also produces apparatus and equipment for radar and computer technology.

L-410 TURBOLET

The L-410 is a twin-turboprop light transport, intended for use on local passenger and freight services. It is suitable for operation from airfields with a natural grass surface.

Design of the L-410 was started in 1966. The prototype (OK-YKE), powered by Pratt & Whitney (UACL) PT6A-27 turboprop engines, was built by the national corporation of Let, at Kunovice, and flew for the first time on 16 April 1969. Production aircraft, deliveries of which are expected to begin in 1971, will be powered by PT6A-27 engines or M-610 turboprops of Czechoslovakian manufacture. The details below apply to the production version, 20 of which are to be built in 1970-71.

TYPE: Twin-turboprop light passenger and freight transport.

WINGS: Cantilever high-wing monoplane. Wing section NACA 63A418 at root, NACA 63A412 at tip. Dihedral 1° 45′. Incidence +2° 0′ at root, —0° 30′ at tip. No sweepback at front spar. Conventional all-metal two-spar structure, attached to fuselage by four-point suspension. Chemically-machined skin with longitudinal reinforcement. All-metal ailerons with electrically-controlled trim-tab in port aileron. No spoilers. Double-slotted metal flaps, with both slots variable. TKS hydraulic or Kléber-Colombes pneumatic de-icing of leading-edges.

FUSELAGE: Conventional all-metal semi-monocoque structure.

TAIL UNIT: Cantilever all-metal structure of conventional semi-monocoque type. Sweptback vertical surfaces, with small dorsal fin. One-piece tailplane mounted part-way up fin. Manually-controlled trim-tab in each half of elevator. Rudder has electrically-actuated trim-tab on upper half and automatic balance tab on lower half. TKS hydraulic or Kléber-Colombes pneumatic de-icing of leading-edges.

LANDING GEAR: Retractable tricycle type with single wheel on each unit. Hydraulic retraction, nose-wheel forward, main wheels semi-recessed into fairings on each side of fuselage. Technometra Radotin oleo-pneumatic shock-absorbers. Non-braking nose-wheel, fitted with 9·00 × 6 tubeless tyre, pressure 35·6 lb/sq in (2·5 kg/cm²). Main wheels fitted with 12·50 × 10 tubeless tyres, pressure 42·7 lb/sq in (3·0

Let L-410 twin-turboprop 9/17-passenger light transport

Prototype of the Let L-410 Turbolet twin-turboprop light transport (two Pratt & Whitney (UACL) PT6A-27 engines)

kg/cm²). All wheels manufactured by Morovan Otrokovice, tyres by Rudy Rijen, Gottwaldov. Moravan Otrokovice hydraulic disc brakes on main wheels. No anti-skid units. Metal ski landing gear, with plastic undersurface, optional.

Power Plant: Two 730 eshp M-601 turboprop engines, each driving an Avia V-508 three-blade hydraulically-adjustable variable- and reversible-pitch propeller, diameter 8 ft 7¼ in (2·63 m). De-icing systems for propeller blades (electrical) and lower intakes. Six (optionally eight) flexible bag-type fuel tanks in wings, with total capacity (eight tanks) of 290·4 Imp gallons (1,320 litres). Four standard refuelling points above wings, with provision for two extra points when all eight tanks are fitted. Oil capacity 2·2 Imp gallons (10 litres). Alternative installation of two 715 eshp Pratt & Whitney (UACL) PT6A-27 turboprops, with Hamilton Standard LF-23 Type 343 propellers of 8 ft 6 in (2·59 m) diameter. Fuel system as for M-601 version. Oil capacity 1·9 Imp gallons (2·3 US gallons = 8·7 litres).

Accommodation: Crew of one or two on flight deck. Main cabin accommodates from 9 to 17 passengers, with pairs of seats on one side of aisle and single seats opposite. Baggage compartment in nose with two-section access door; toilet and additional baggage compartment at rear. Double upward-opening doors aft on port side, left hand door serving for passenger entrance; both doors open for cargo loading. Downward-opening crew door, forward on starboard side, serves also as emergency exit. Cargo space in rear of cabin. Cabin heated and ventilated by engine bleed-air.

Systems: No air-conditioning or pressurisation systems. Isopressure duplicated hydraulic system, pressure 2,133 lb/sq in (150 kg/cm²), for flap and landing gear actuation. Electrical system includes two 28V 6kW DC generators, three 36V 400 c/s rotary converters, one 115V 400 c/s transformer and two 25Ah storage batteries. No APU or oxygen systems.

Electronics and Equipment: Optional nav/com equipment includes two Mesit (LUN3522) VKDC.1 UKV; two Tesla RKL 41, Collins DF 203 or Bendix ADF 73 ADF; one Collins 51Z6 or MKA208C marker; two Collins 51RV2B VOR/ILS or one Bendix RNA26C and one Bendix RN222BE; and one Bendix M4C autopilot.

Dimensions, external:
- Wing span: 56 ft 1¼ in (17·10 m)
- Wing chord at root: 8 ft 3¾ in (2·534 m)
- Wing chord at tip: 4 ft 1¾ in (1·267 m)
- Wing aspect ratio: 9
- Length overall: 44 ft 7¾ in (13·61 m)
- Length of fuselage: 42 ft 2¾ in (12·89 m)
- Height overall: 18 ft 0½ in (5·50 m)
- Tailplane span: 21 ft 2¾ in (6·47 m)
- Wheel track: 11 ft 11¾ in (3·65 m)
- Wheelbase: 12 ft 2½ in (3·72 m)
- Propeller ground clearance: 3 ft 6½ in (1·08 m)
- Distance between propeller centres: 18 ft 5¼ in (5·62 m)
- Passenger/cargo door (port, aft):
  - Height: 4 ft 3¼ in (1·30 m)
  - Width overall: 4 ft 1¼ in (1·25 m)
  - Width (passenger door only): 1 ft 7¾ in (0·50 m)
  - Height to sill: 2 ft 6¾ in (0·78 m)
- Crew entry/emergency exit door (stbd, fwd):
  - Height: 3 ft 5¼ in (1·05 m)
  - Width: 2 ft 2¼ in (0·665 m)
  - Height to sill: 2 ft 6¾ in (0·78 m)
- Nose baggage compartment doors (each):
  - Height: 1 ft 5 in (0·43 m)
  - Width: 2 ft 5 in (0·74 m)
  - Height to sill: 4 ft 2½ in (1·28 m)

Dimensions, internal:
- Cabin, excluding flight deck:
  - Length: 32 ft 3¾ in (9·85 m)
  - Max width: 6 ft 5¼ in (1·96 m)
  - Max height: 5 ft 5¼ in (1·658 m)
  - Floor area: 150·7 sq ft (14·00 m²)
  - Volume: 635 cu ft (18·00 m³)
- Baggage compartment volume (nose): 38·8 cu ft (1·10 m³)
- Baggage compartment volume (rear):
  - 15 passengers: 109·8 cu ft (3·11 m³)
  - 17 passengers: 59·3 cu ft (1·68 m³)
  - 19 passengers: 31·1 cu ft (0·88 m³)

Areas:
- Wings, gross: 350 sq ft (32·5 m²)
- Ailerons (total): 24·2 sq ft (2·248 m²)
- Trailing-edge flaps (total): 63·7 sq ft (5·92 m²)
- Fin: 40·26 sq ft (3·74 m²)
- Rudder: 29·92 sq ft (2·78 m²)
- Tailplane: 56·05 sq ft (5·208 m²)
- Elevators: 44·04 sq ft (4·092 m²)

Weights and Loadings:
- Basic empty weight, equipped: 6,180 lb (2,803 kg)
- Max payload: 4,085 lb (1,853 kg)
- Max T-O and landing weight: 11,245 lb (5,100 kg)
- Max zero-fuel weight: 10,500 lb (4,764 kg)
- Max wing loading: 32·16 lb/sq ft (157 kg/m²)
- Max power loading:
  - M-601: 8·27 lb/eshp (3·75 kg/eshp)
  - PT6A-27: 7·87 lb/eshp (3·57 kg/eshp)

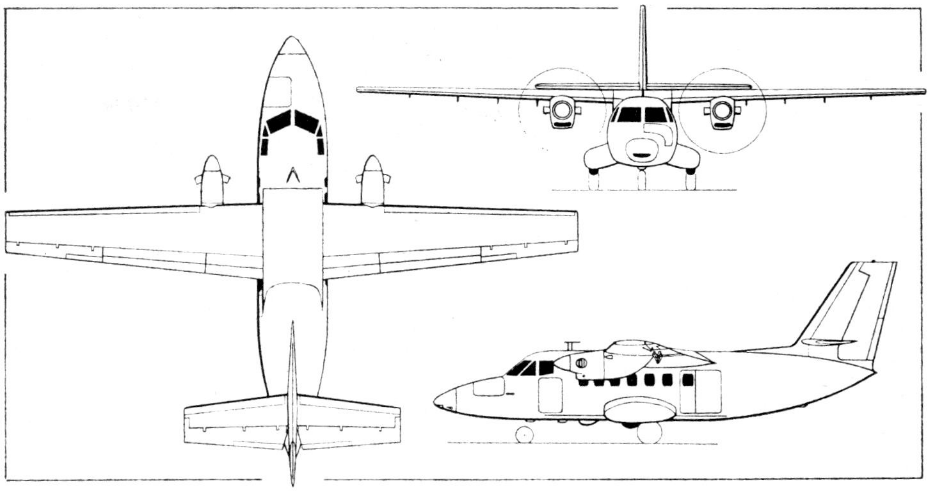

Let L-410 twin-turboprop 9/17-passenger light transport

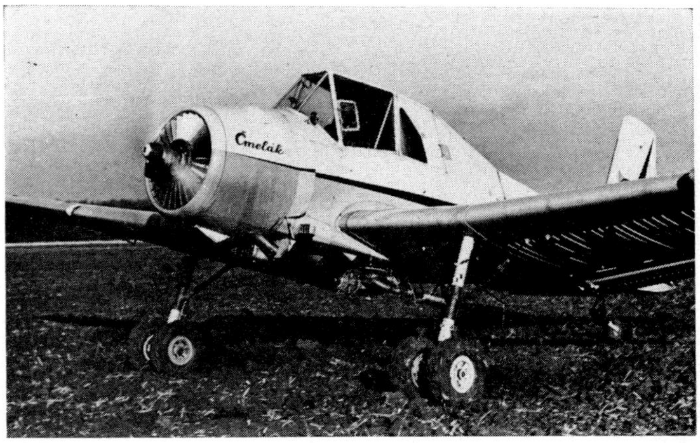

A few Z-37 Cmeláks have been delivered with twin-wheel main landing gear units for operation from muddy ground

Performance (at max T-O weight):
- Max permissible diving speed: 278 knots (321 mph; 518 km/h) EAS
- Max cruising speed at 10,000 ft (3,000 m): 199 knots (229 mph; 369 km/h) TAS
- Econ cruising speed at 10,000 ft (3,000 m): 178 knots (205 mph; 330 km/h)
- Stalling speed, flaps up: 78 knots (90 mph; 145 km/h)
- Stalling speed, flaps down: 61 knots (70 mph; 114 km/h)
- Max rate of climb at S/L: 1,594 ft (486 m)/min
- Rate of climb at S/L, one engine out: 512 ft (156 m)/min
- Service ceiling: 25,500 ft (7,770 m)
- Service ceiling, one engine out: 10,575 ft (3,220 m)
- T-O run, STOL: 689 ft (210 m)
- T-O to 50 ft (15 m), STOL: 1,526 ft (465 m)
- Landing from 50 ft (15 m), STOL: 1,444 ft (440 m)
- Landing run, STOL: 607 ft (185 m)
- Range with max fuel, 45 min reserve: 612 nm (705 miles; 1,140 km)
- Range with max payload, 45 min reserve: 99 nm (115 miles; 185 km)

Z-37 CMELÁK (BUMBLE-BEE)

Design of the Cmelák began in August 1961, and the first XZ-37 prototype of this agricultural aircraft, built in the Let national aircraft works, Kunovice, flew for the first time on 29 March 1963. Ten prototypes were built altogether. Certification in the Normal category, Aerial Work Class D, BCAR, was awarded on 20 June 1966. Additional applications for the production Z-37 Cmelák include mail and cargo transport during the Winter season.

An experimental version of the Z-37 with a 300 hp six-cylinder Continental engine was illustrated in the 1969-70 *Jane's*, as was a two-seat model, the Z-237 (previously referred to as the Z-37-2). Neither of these versions is in production.

The following details refer to the standard production single-seat Z-37, 240 of which had been built by January 1970.

Type: Agricultural monoplane.

Wings: Cantilever low-wing monoplane. Wing section NACA 33015 at root, NACA 43012A at tip. No dihedral on centre-section. Dihedral 7° on outer wing panels. Incidence 3° at root, 0° at tip. All-metal, single-spar fail-safe structure, with auxiliary rear spar, comprising centre-section, built integrally with fuselage, and two outer panels. Fabric-covered aluminium slotted ailerons. Pneumatically-operated double-slotted aluminium flaps. Leading-edge fixed slats of aluminium alloy on outer wings, forward of ailerons.

Fuselage: Welded steel-tube fail-safe structure. Engine, cockpit and under-fuselage covered in dural sheet, remainder fabric-covered.

Tail Unit: Cantilever aluminium alloy structure. Fin and tailplane metal-covered; rudder and elevators fabric-covered. Trim-tabs in elevators and rudder.

Landing Gear: Non-retractable tail-wheel type. Technometra N. C. Semily oleo-pneumatic shock-absorbers. Moravan Otrokovice wheels and Rudy Rijen low-pressure tyres and tubes. Main-wheel tyres size 556 × 163, pressure 32 lb/sq in (2·25 kg/cm²); anti-shimmy tail-wheel tyre size 290 × 110, pressure 40·5 lb/sq in (2·85 kg/cm²). Moravan Otrokovice hydraulic shoe-type brakes on main wheels. Provision for fitting wooden skis, with pneumatically-actuated hydraulic brakes.

Power Plant: One 315 hp M 462 RF nine-cylinder radial air-cooled engine, driving an Avia V-520 two-blade constant-speed metal propeller, diameter 8 ft 10½ in (2·70 m). Two aluminium alloy fuel tanks in port wing centre-section, with total capacity of 55 Imp gallons (250 litres). Solely for carrying replenishment fuel to operating site, two externally-suspended tanks, each of 27·5 Imp gallons (125 litres) capacity, can be carried. Similar tanks can also be used to transport chemicals in concentrated form. Refuelling points above port wing centre-section. Oil capacity 2·97 Imp gallons (13·5 litres). Anti-dust filter in front of carburettor air intake. Provision for pre-heating intake air.

Accommodation: Pilot in enclosed cockpit forward of hopper. One auxiliary seat behind hopper for mechanic or loader. Cabin ventilated and heated by ram air through chemical filter and heat exchanger respectively. Forward-opening door on starboard side.

Systems: Pneumatic system for engine starter, flaps, parking brake and hopper actuation. Electrical power provided by 28V 1500W generator, 24V 10Ah battery and 36V 400 c/s converter.

ELECTRONICS AND EQUIPMENT: ADF and Mesit LUN 3522 optional. Hopper for 143 Imp gallons (650 litres) of spray or 1,320 lb (600 kg) of dust. Spray system and distributor for dry chemicals interchangeable. Total volume available for chemical hopper or cargo 63·5 cu ft (1·8 m³). Effective swath width with the aircraft flying 16 ft (5·0 m) above the ground is 115 ft (35 m) for oily spray, 66 ft (20 m) for aqueous spray, 66·82 ft (20·25 m) for granules and 130 ft (40 m) for dust.

DIMENSIONS, EXTERNAL:

Wing span	40 ft 1¼ in (12·22 m)
Wing chord at root	7 ft 7¼ in (2·32 m)
Wing chord at tip	3 ft 9¾ in (1·16 m)
Wing aspect ratio	6·3
Length overall	28 ft 0½ in (8·55 m)
Length of fuselage	26 ft 8 in (8·12 m)
Height overall	9 ft 6 in (2·90 m)
Tailplane span	14 ft 10½ in (4·53 m)
Wheel track	10 ft 9¾ in (3·30 m)
Wheelbase	18 ft 0½ in (5·50 m)
Propeller ground clearance	1 ft 1¾ in (0·35 m)

AREAS:

Wings, gross	256·2 sq ft (23·8 m²)
Ailerons (total)	22·07 sq ft (2·05 m²)
Trailing-edge flaps (total)	47·04 sq ft (4·37 m²)
Vertical tail surfaces (total)	22·07 sq ft (2·05 m²)
Horizontal tail surfaces (total)	54·14 sq ft (5·03 m²)

WEIGHTS AND LOADINGS:

Weight empty, standard equipment, without agricultural equipment 2,295 lb (1,043 kg)
Max chemicals 1,323 lb (600 kg)
Max T-O weight:
  freight version 3,855 lb (1,750 kg)
  agricultural version 4,080 lb (1,850 kg)
Max wing loading (agricultural)
  15·93 lb/sq ft (77·7 kg/m²)
Max power loading (agricultural)
  13·20 lb/hp (5·99 kg/hp)

PERFORMANCE (at max T-O weight. F=freight version; A=Agricultural version):

Max level speed (without application equipment)
113 knots (130 mph; 210 km/h)

Max permissible diving speed
  145 knots (167 mph; 270 km/h)
Cruising speed at 4,920 ft (1,500 m):
  F 99 knots (114 mph; 183 km/h)
  A 92 knots (106 mph; 170 km/h)
Operating speed, agricultural operations:
  A 65 knots (75 mph; 120 km/h)
Stalling speed, flaps up
  49 knots (56 mph; 90 km/h)
Stalling speed, flaps down
  45 knots (51 mph; 81 km/h)
Rate of climb at S/L:
  F 925 ft (282 m)/min
  A 728 ft (222 m)/min
Service ceiling:
  F 13,125 ft (4,000 m)

T-O run:
  F 410 ft (125 m)
  A 492 ft (150 m)
Landing run:
  F 328 ft (100 m)
  A 400 ft (122 m)
Range, with reserves for 1 hour's flying, plus 10%:
  F 345 nm (398 miles; 640 km)

Z-237 SPARKA

A two-seat conversion trainer model of the Z-37 Cmelák was built. This aircraft, which is correctly designated Z-237 (not Z-37-2 as previously reported), was described briefly and illustrated in the 1969-70 *Jane's*. No production of this version is, however, being undertaken.

Let Z-37 Cmelák single-seat agricultural aircraft (315 hp M 462 RF radial engine)

LETOV

LETOV NÁRODNÍ PODNIK (Letov National Corporation)

ADDRESS:
  Prague 9—Letnany
MANAGING DIRECTOR:
  Bohumil Nemecek
VICE-DIRECTORS:
  Ing Miroslav Vosecky (Engineering)
  Karel Fabián (Production)

Frantisek Cerny (Sales)
Vladislav Nemecek (Works Economy)
CHIEF DESIGNERS:
  Ing Vlastimil Brodsky
  Ing Josef Pokorny
The original Letov company was created on 1 November 1918 from the former Military Air Arsenal, and was best known during the years preceding World War 2 for its two-seat reconnais-

sance/bomber designs, such as the S 1, S 16 and S 328. Since the war its activities have included licence production of the Soviet MiG-15 jet fighter and participation in the production programme for the L-29 Delfin jet trainer. Recently it built the prototype of a small single-seat ultra-light aircraft known as the MK-1 Kocour, details of which were given in the 1969-70 *Jane's*. No production of the Kocour is planned.

VZLU

VYZKUMNY A ZKUSEBNÍ LETECKY USTAV Aeronautical Research and Test Institute

ADDRESS:
  Prague 9—Letnany
MANAGING DIRECTOR:
  Ing Josef Sedlácek
EXECUTIVES:
  Ing Jaroslav Lebduska, CSc (Asst Director of Research)
  Ing Bedrich Typlt (Technical Director)
  Josef Lunácek (Economic Director)
This Institute, whose title is self-explanatory, was founded in 1922 and undertakes a range of activities corresponding broadly to those carried out by the RAE in Britain.

Its low-speed wind tunnel is of conventional continuous-flow type, with a circular test section of 9 ft 10 in (3 m) diameter. The tunnel is equipped with a semi-automatic six-component balance. The maximum speed of the airflow is 11,810 ft/min (60 m/sec). It is further equipped

with a 150kW dynamometer and with high-speed electric motors for propulsion of propeller models. An Eiffel-type aerodynamic tunnel of 5 ft 10¾ in (1·8 m) diameter is used largely to meet the requirements of non-aeronautical industries.

The high-speed aerodynamic laboratory uses a vacuum chamber of 148 cu ft (4·20 m³) capacity for propulsion of the tunnels, with intermittent operation. The high-speed subsonic wind tunnel has a test section of 23·6 × 35·4 in (60 × 90 cm) and is fitted with transonic and supersonic test sections of 23·6 × 23·6 in (60 × 60 cm). A continuous-flow wind tunnel with a test section of 9·8 × 9·8 in (25 × 25 cm) is driven by a compressor.

The structural testing departments verify the static and the fatigue strength of airframes and other structures, investigate the distribution of internal forces, stresses and deformations, and the dynamic properties of structures. The landing gear testing department is equipped with a universal drop tester for dynamic tests of aircraft landing gear.

The propulsion department is engaged in applied research and testing in the field of aircraft propulsion units; in certain instances, development work is involved.

The flight instruments department is engaged primarily in the investigation of new methods and principles associated with the problems of automation and control of some functions performed by aircraft, including the application of results obtained in the investigation and development of flight simulators.

The TL-29 flight simulator for the L-29 Delfin jet trainer simulates the performances and characteristics of the aircraft over the whole range of its operational capabilities, with marginal limits of ±80° in pitch and roll. Also simulated is the entire equipment of the aircraft, including the radio and radio-navigational systems. VFR simulation projects during take-off and landing, by means of TV, pictures of the aerodrome and its vicinity and, during flight over clouds, the upper cloud-base including the horizon on a screen situated in front of the pilot.

ZLIN

MORAVAN NÁRODNÍ PODNIK (Zlin Aircraft Moravan National Corporation)

ADDRESS:
  Otrokovice
MANAGING DIRECTOR:
  Frantisek Kubis
VICE-DIRECTORS:
  Ing Ignác Závrbsky (Technical)
  Oldrich Janecka (Production)
  Ing Milan Svoboda (Sales)
  Frantisek Klapil (Works Economy)
CHIEF DESIGNER:
  Ing Jirí Goldsmíd

CHIEF PILOT:
  Vlastimil Berg

The Moravan works, responsible for production of the famous range of Zlin aerobatic and light touring aircraft, was formed originally on 8 July 1935 as Zlinská Letecká Akciová Spolecnost (Zlin Aviation Joint Stock Co) in Zlin, although manufacture of Zlin aircraft was actually started two years earlier by the Masarykova Letecká Liga (Masaryk League of Aviation). At present, in addition to production of the Zlin 526 series and development of the Zlin 42 and 43, Moravan is building wing assemblies for the L-29 Delfin jet trainer, and fuselages and agricultural equipment for the Z-37 Cmelák. The factory had 1,800 employees early in 1970.

ZLIN 42

The Moravan works at Otrokovice has developed a new series of small sporting and touring aircraft, the first of which is designated Zlin 42. The prototype of this aircraft was first flown in October 1967, and in 1969 began undergoing flight trials prior to certification and subsequent production.

The Z 42 is intended for basic and advanced training, aerobatic training (solo or dual), navigation training, sport, touring and glider towing. Standard power plant is the 180 hp M 137 engine, with which the Z 42 conforms to FAR Pt 23 airworthiness specifications in the aerobatic category and is suitable for service in climates with temperatures between +40° and —40°C.

The first production Z 42, to which the following description applies, was due to fly in 1970.

TYPE: Two-seat light training and touring aircraft.

WINGS: Cantilever low-wing monoplane. Wing section NACA 63₂416·5. Dihedral 6° from roots. Sweep-forward 4° 31' at quarter-chord. All-metal structure with single main spar. All-metal slotted ailerons and flaps all have same dimensions. Flaps operated mechanically by control rods and cables, ailerons mechanically by control rods. Ground-adjustable tab in each aileron.

FUSELAGE: Engine cowlings of sheet metal. Centre fuselage of welded steel-tube truss construction, covered with laminated glass-fibre panels. Rear fuselage is all-metal semi-monocoque structure.

TAIL UNIT: Cantilever all-metal structure. Control surfaces have partial mass and aero-dynamic balance. Trim-tabs on elevator and rudder. Rudder actuated by control cables, elevator by control rods.

LANDING GEAR: Non-retractable tricycle type. Oleo-pneumatic nose-wheel shock-absorber. Main wheels carried on flat spring steel legs. Nose-wheel steering by means of rudder pedals. Single wheel on each unit. Main wheels and Barum tyres size 420 × 150, pressure 27 lb/sq in (1·9 kg/cm²); nose-wheel and Barum tyre size 350 × 135, pressure 35·6 lb/sq in (2·5 kg/cm²). Hydraulic brakes on main wheels can be operated from either seat. Wheel fairings and skis optional.

POWER PLANT: One 180 hp Avia M 137 inverted six-cylinder air-cooled in-line engine, with low-pressure injection pump, driving a two-blade wooden propeller of 6 ft 8¾ in (2·05 m) diameter, or an Avia V 310 two-blade ground-adjustable-pitch metal propeller of 6 ft 4¾ in (1·95 m) diameter. Fuel tanks in each wing leading-edge, with total capacity of 28·5 Imp gallons (130 litres). Provision for fitting wing-tip fuel tanks, each of 12 Imp gallons (55 litres) capacity. Fuel and oil systems permit inverted flying for 2-3 minutes.

ACCOMMODATION: Individual side-by-side seats for two persons, the pilot's seat being to port. Both are adjustable for height and permit the use of back-type parachutes. Baggage space aft of seats. Cabin and windscreen heating and ventilation. Forward-opening door on each side of cabin. Dual controls standard.

SYSTEMS: Electrical system includes a 600W 27V engine-driven generator and 25Ah 27V Varley battery. External power source can be used for starting the engine.

ELECTRONICS AND EQUIPMENT: VHF radio and IFR instrumentation optional.

DIMENSIONS, EXTERNAL:
Wing span	29 ft 10¾ in (9·11 m)
Wing span over tip-tanks	30 ft 1¾ in (9·19 m)
Wing chord (constant)	4 ft 8 in (1·42 m)
Length overall	23 ft 2¼ in (7·07 m)
Height overall	8 ft 10 in (2·69 m)
Tailplane span	9 ft 6 in (2·90 m)
Wheel track	7 ft 7¾ in (2·33 m)
Wheelbase	5 ft 5¼ in (1·66 m)

DIMENSIONS, INTERNAL:
Cabin:	
Length	5 ft 10¾ in (1·80 m)
Width	3 ft 8 in (1·12 m)
Height	3 ft 11¼ in (1·20 m)
Baggage space	7·1 cu ft (0·2 m³)

AREAS:
Wings, gross	141·5 sq ft (13·15 m²)
Ailerons (total)	15·1 sq ft (1·40 m²)
Trailing-edge flaps (total)	15·1 sq ft (1·40 m²)

WEIGHTS AND LOADINGS:
Basic weight, equipped	1,322 lb (600 kg)
Max T-O weight:	
Utility	2,028 lb (920 kg)
Aerobatic	1,851 lb (840 kg)
Max wing loading:	
Utility	14·3 lb/sq ft (70 kg/m²)
Aerobatic	13·1 lb/sq ft (64 kg/m²)
Max power loading:	
Utility	11·29 lb/hp (5·12 kg/hp)
Aerobatic	10·19 lb/hp (4·62 kg/hp)

PERFORMANCE (at AUW of 1,763 lb=800 kg):
Max level speed at S/L	
	124 knots (143 mph; 230 km/h)
Cruising speed	108 knots (124 mph; 200 km/h)
Stalling speed, flaps down, power off	
	48 knots (55 mph; 90 km/h)
Rate of climb at S/L	984 ft (300 m)/min
Service ceiling	18,050 ft (5,500 m)
T-O to 50 ft (15 m)	1,148 ft (350 m)
Landing from 50 ft (15 m)	1,148 ft (350 m)
Range with max internal fuel	
	350 nm (403 miles; 650 km)
Range with wingtip fuel tanks	
	645 nm (745 miles; 1,200 km)

ZLIN 43

The Zlin 43 is the second in the new series of Czechoslovak light sporting and touring aircraft,

Zlin 42 two-seat light trainer and touring aircraft (one 180 hp M 137 engine)

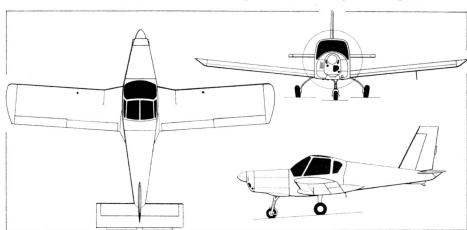

Zlin 42 two-seat light training and touring aircraft

and was first flown in prototype form in November 1968.

It is designed primarily for advanced navigation, night and all-weather flying training, but is also suitable for sports and competitive flying, touring and aerial taxi flying, basic aerobatics (solo or dual) and glider towing. Standard power plant is the 210 hp M 337, with either a two-blade V 310 ground-adjustable metal propeller or an Avia controllable-pitch metal propeller.

The Z 42 and Z 43 have some 80% of their structural components in common, the Z 43 differing principally in power plant and in having an enlarged centre section in the fuselage to accommodate a bigger, four-seat cabin with more comprehensive instrumentation.

Certification under FAR 23, in the utility and normal categories, is scheduled for 1970, with completion of the first production Z 43 to follow in 1971.

TYPE: Two/four-seat light training and touring aircraft.

WINGS: Cantilever low-wing monoplane. Wings are of greater span and area than those of

Z 42, but are otherwise similar except that they have a flat centre-section and no sweep.

FUSELAGE: Similar to that of Z 42, but with additional steel-tube section inserted in centre to permit incorporation of larger cabin.

TAIL UNIT: Similar to Z 42, but with enlarged horizontal surfaces.

LANDING GEAR: As Z 42, but with some reinforcement of the nose-wheel unit and strengthened spring steel legs on main units. Wheel and tyre sizes as Z 42, tyre pressure 35·6 lb/sq in (2·5 kg/cm²) on all units. Hydraulic brakes on main wheels. Optional streamline wheel fairings for all units.

POWER PLANT: One 210 hp Avia M 337 inverted six-cylinder air-cooled in-line engine, with compressor for start and climb, driving an Avia V 310 two-blade adjustable-pitch metal propeller of 6 ft 4¾ in (1·95 m) diameter, or (optionally) an Avia V 500 two-blade constant-speed metal propeller of the same diameter. Fuel tanks in each wing leading-edge, with total capacity of 28·5 Imp gallons (130 litres).

Standard additional tanks in each wing-tip, each of 12 Imp gallons (55 litres) capacity. Fuel and oil systems permit short periods of inverted flying.

ACCOMMODATION: Individual side-by-side seats for two persons in front of cabin, the pilot's seat being to port. Both are adjustable longitudinally and for height, have tilting backs and permit the use of back-type parachutes. Bench seat in rear of cabin for two additional passengers, with baggage space to rear of this seat. Access via forward-opening door on each side of cabin. Cabin and windscreen heating (by heat-exchange system) and ventilation standard. Additional baggage compartment in rear of fuselage, with external access. Dual controls optional.

SYSTEMS: As Z 42.

ELECTRONICS AND EQUIPMENT: Standard Z 43 is equipped with instrumentation for day and night flying under VMC conditions. Optional items include full radio-navigation equipment, and instrumentation for various training roles, and for flight under IFR conditions.

DIMENSIONS, EXTERNAL:
Wing span	32 ft 0¼ in (9·76 m)
Wing chord (constant)	4 ft 8 in (1·42 m)
Length overall	25 ft 5 in (7·75 m)
Height overall	9 ft 6½ in (2·91 m)
Tailplane span	9 ft 10 in (3·00 m)
Wheel track	7 ft 7¾ in (2·33 m)
Wheelbase	5 ft 9 in (1·75 m)

DIMENSIONS, INTERNAL:
Cabin:
Length	8 ft 2½ in (2·50 m)
Width	3 ft 8 in (1·12 m)
Height	3 ft 11¼ in (1·20 m)
Baggage space (inside cabin)	7·1 cu ft (0·2 m³)
Baggage compartment (rear)	8·8 cu ft (0·25 m³)

AREAS:
As for Z 42, except:
Wings, gross	156·1 sq ft (14·50 m²)
Tailplane	27·88 sq ft (2·59 m²)
Elevator, incl tab	13·46 sq ft (1·25 m²)

WEIGHTS AND LOADINGS:
Basic weight, equipped	1,540 lb (700 kg)
Max T-O weight:	
Normal	2,755 lb (1,250 kg)
Utility	2,094 lb (950 kg)
Max wing loading:	
Normal	17·7 lb/sq ft (86·3 kg/m²)
Utility	13·4 lb/sq ft (65·5 kg/m²)
Max power loading:	
Normal	13·12 lb/hp (5·95 kg/hp)
Utility	9·96 lb/hp (4·52 kg/hp)

PERFORMANCE (at AUW of 2,557 lb = 1,160 kg):
Max level speed at S/L	124 knots (143 mph; 230 km/h)
Cruising speed	108 knots (124 mph; 200 km/h)
Stalling speed, flaps down, power off	57 knots (65 mph; 105 km/h)
Rate of climb at S/L	650 ft (198 m)/min
Service ceiling	14,775 ft (4,500 m)
T-O to 50 ft (15 m)	1,540 ft (470 m)
Landing from 50 ft (15 m)	1,540 ft (470 m)
Max range (standard fuel)	325 nm (375 miles; 610 km)
Max range (with wingtip tanks)	590 nm (680 miles; 1,100 km)

ZLIN 526F TRENER-MASTER

A total of more than 1,400 aircraft of the Z 26/126/226/326/526 series have been built at Otrokovice since 1947 and are operating in 36 countries. Sporting successes have included first place in the First, Second, Third and Fifth World Aerobatic Championships in 1960, 1962, 1964 and 1968, first place in the Lockheed Trophy aerobatic competition in Britain in 1957, 1958, 1961, 1963, 1964 and 1965, and first place in the Léon Biancotto Trophée aerobatic competition in France in 1965, 1967 and 1969.

The Z 526F is one of the latest members of this celebrated series. Major modification, compared with the basic Z 526 (see 1968-69 *Jane's*), is in the installation of an Avia M 137 engine in place of the Walter Minor 6-III engine in the Z 526. The prototype was flown in 1968 and the Z 526F was certificated in 1969. Forty had been built by the beginning of 1970.

The Z 526F, to which the description below applies, is intended for ab initio and advanced training, aerobatic flying and training, glider towing etc. Load factors range from +6g to —3g at max aerobatic T-O weight, and the Z 526F is fully aerobatic whether flown dual or solo.

A version with 200 hp Lycoming engine, known as the Z 526L/200, is described separately.

TYPE: Two-seat basic trainer.

WINGS: Cantilever low-wing monoplane. Wings of combined NACA 2418 and NACA 4412 section. Dihedral 4° 30' from roots. Sweepback 6° at quarter-chord. All-metal two-spar structure with flush-riveted light alloy stressed skin. All-metal ailerons, statically and aerodynamically balanced, are operated differentially. All-metal trailing-edge flaps. Flaps and ailerons actuated mechanically by control rods. Ground-adjustable tabs on ailerons.

Zlin 43 four-seat light sporting and touring aircraft (210 hp M 337 engine)

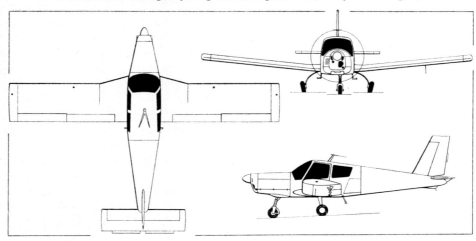
Zlin 43 four-seat light training and touring aircraft

Moravan-built Zlin 526F two-seat basic training and aerobatic aircraft

FUSELAGE: Welded steel-tube structure. Upper and lower surfaces covered with easily-removable metal panels and remainder with fabric.

TAIL UNIT: Cantilever type. Removable tailplane and fin of all-metal stressed-skin construction. Elevator and rudder have metal frames with fabric covering. Trim-tabs on rudder and elevator. Rudder actuated by control cables, elevator by control rods.

LANDING GEAR: Retractable tail-wheel type. Electrical retraction. Oleo-pneumatic shock-absorbers. Main wheels retract backward into wings. Tyres protrude in retracted position to reduce damage in event of wheels-up landing. Fully-castoring self-centering tail-wheel, steerable 30° to either side of centre-line. Barum tyres, main wheels size 420 × 150, pressure 31·3 lb/sq in (2·2 kg/cm²); tail-wheel size 260 × 85, pressure 35·6 lb/sq in (2·5 kg/cm²). Hydraulic brakes on main wheels, actuated from both cockpits.

POWER PLANT: One 180 hp Avia M 137 six-cylinder in-line inverted air-cooled engine, with low-pressure injection pump, driving an Avia V 503 fully-automatic two-blade constant-speed propeller, diameter 6 ft 6¾ in (2·0 m). One fuel tank of 9·9 Imp gallons (45 litres) capacity in each wing root. Fuel and oil installation, designed for aerobatics, permits inverted flying for 3 minutes. Can be fitted with wingtip fuel tanks, with total capacity of 15 Imp gallons (68 litres).

ACCOMMODATION: Tandem seats under continuous sliding canopy which is jettisonable in an emergency. Adjustable seats and rudder pedals in both cockpits. Seat cushions may be replaced by seat-type parachutes. Windscreen frame reinforced as crash pylon. Complete dual controls and instrumentation. Cabin ventilation.

SYSTEMS: Electrical system includes a 600W 27V engine-driven generator and 25Ah 27V Varley battery. External power source can be used for starting the engine.

ELECTRONICS AND EQUIPMENT: Optional equipment includes VKDC-1 radio, and glider towing gear.

DIMENSIONS, EXTERNAL:
Wing span	34 ft 9 in (10·60 m)
Wing span over tip-tanks	35 ft 11½ in (10·96 m)
Wing chord at root	5 ft 0¾ in (1·545 m)
Length overall	26 ft 3 in (8·00 m)
Height overall	6 ft 9 in (2·06 m)
Tailplane span	9 ft 10 in (3·00 m)
Wheel track	5 ft 9¼ in (1·76 m)

DIMENSIONS, INTERNAL:
  Cabin:
    Max length   7 ft 6½ in (2·30 m)
    Max width   2 ft 1½ in (0·65 m)
    Max height   4 ft 11 in (1·50 m)
AREAS:
  Wings, gross   166·3 sq ft (15·45 m²)
  Ailerons (total)   14·77 sq ft (1·372 m²)
  Trailing-edge flaps (total) 14·81 sq ft (1·376 m²)
  Fin   5·27 sq ft (0·49 m²)
  Rudder, incl tab   10·12 sq ft (0·94 m²)
  Tailplane   15·28 sq ft (1·42 m²)
  Elevators, incl tabs   11·52 sq ft (1·07 m²)
WEIGHTS AND LOADINGS:
  Weight empty   1,465 lb (665 kg)
  Max T-O weight:
    aerobatic   2,072 lb (940 kg)
    normal   2,150 lb (975 kg)
  Max wing loading:
    aerobatic   12·5 lb/sq ft (60·8 kg/m²)
    normal   12·9 lb/sq ft (63·1 kg/m²)
  Max power loading:
    aerobatic   11·51 lb/hp (5·22 kg/hp)
    normal   11·95 lb/hp (5·42 kg/hp)
PERFORMANCE (at max normal T-O weight, ISA):
  Max level speed 134 knots (154 mph; 248 km/h)
  Cruising speed 116 knots (133 mph; 214 km/h)
  Stalling speed, flaps down, power off
                  49 knots (56 mph; 90 km/h)
  Max rate of climb at S/L 1,181 ft (360 m)/min
  Service ceiling   19,025 ft (5,800 m)
  T-O run   590 ft (180 m)
  T-O to 50 ft (15 m)   1,122 ft (342 m)
  Landing from 50 ft (15 m) 1,345 ft (410 m)
  Max range with standard fuel
                  255 nm (295 miles; 480 km)
  Max range with wingtip tanks
                  450 nm (520 miles; 840 km)

ZLIN 526A AKROBAT

This is a single-seat version of the Z 526 for
specialised aerobatic use. A version with bulged
one-piece sliding canopy is known as the Z 526
AS Akrobat Special. Descriptions appeared in
the 1969-70 *Jane's*.

ZLIN 526L/200 SKYDEVIL

The Zlin 526L/200 is the latest variant of the
Zlin 526 aerobatic trainer. It is intended for a
similar range of applications to those of the
Z 526F, and differs chiefly in having a 200 hp
Lycoming AIO-360 engine. A prototype began
its flight testing in August 1969, and the first
production aircraft was due to fly in 1970.

It was announced in January 1970 that an
agreement had been signed in Prague under the
terms of which Reims-Aviation in France is to
have exclusive construction and production
licence rights to the Z 526L. An initial batch of
250 will go into production at Reims, for world-
wide sale. Reims-Aviation will have exclusive
marketing rights in France; for all other countries,
the Cessna sales network will distribute these
aircraft.

The description of the Z 526F applies generally
to the Z 526L, with the following exceptions:

Zlin 526L/200 Skydevil (200 hp Lycoming AIO-360-B1B engine)

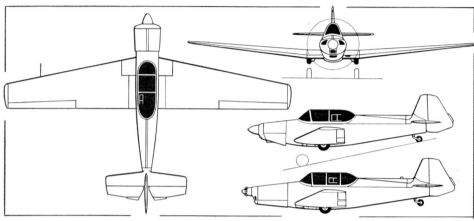

Three-view drawing of the Zlin 526L/200 and (bottom side view) the Z 526F

POWER PLANT: One 200 hp Lycoming AIO-360-
B1B four-cylinder horizontally-opposed air-
cooled fuel-injection engine, fitted with auto-
motive-type alternator and starter, and driving
a Hartzell C2YK-4R/C 7666 A2 two-blade
constant-speed metal propeller of 6 ft 2 in (1·88
m) diameter. Fuel system and capacity as for
Z 526F.

SYSTEMS: Electrical system includes 24V 50A
engine-driven alternator and 27V 25Ah Varley
battery.

DIMENSIONS, EXTERNAL: As Z 526F except:
  Length overall   25 ft 1¼ in (7·65 m)

WEIGHTS AND LOADINGS: As Z 526F, except:
  Weight empty, equipped   1,485 lb (675 kg)
PERFORMANCE (at max normal T-O weight, ISA):
  Max level speed 137 knots (158 mph; 255 km/h)
  Cruising speed 122 knots (140 mph; 225 km/h)
  Stalling speed, flaps down, power off
                  49 knots (56 mph; 90 km/h)
  Max rate of climb at S/L 1,378 ft (420 m)/min
  Service ceiling   22,300 ft (6,800 m)
  T-O to 50 ft (15 m)   1,050 ft (320 m)
  Landing from 50 ft (15 m) 1,345 ft (410 m)
  Max range with standard fuel
                  247 nm (285 miles; 460 km)
  Max range with wingtip tanks
                  380 nm (440 miles; 710 km)

DENMARK

JOHANSEN
DIPL-ING CARL JOHANSEN
ADDRESS:
  405 Mönchengladbach, Uddinger Strasse 15,
  German Federal Republic

Dipl-Ing Johansen, an MSc in mechanical
engineering, designed and built in Denmark a
light twin-engined amphibian which is known as
the CAJO 59. This aircraft, with the Danish
registration OY-DFH, made its first take-off
(from water) in Denmark on 23 July 1967 and
its first take-off from land on 17 April 1968.

Because of the lack of certification facilities in
Denmark, in October 1968 Dipl-Ing Johansen
flew the aircraft to Germany, where he is employed by the RFB company. Bearing the German
registration D-GDFH, it was undergoing, early
in 1970, the necessary flight trials to obtain a
type certificate in the Normal category under
FAR 23 regulations. Once it is certificated, its
designer hopes to find a collaborator for its
eventual production.

JOHANSEN CAJO 59
TYPE: Three/four-seat twin-engined light amphibian.
WINGS: Cantilever gull-winged high-wing monoplane. Wing section NACA 23012. Dihedral
8° 48′ on centre-section, 0° on outer panels.
Incidence 4° at root, 1° at tip. No sweepback.
Conventional two-spar all-wood structure inboard of engines, with single spar outboard of
engines. Fabric-covered wooden full-span
NACA slotted flaps and ailerons, the latter
moving 20° downward when the flaps are fully
extended to 40°.

Johansen CAJO 59 four-seat light amphibian, with German registration for certification trials

FUSELAGE: Conventional hull of wood and glass-
fibre/polystyrol/foam sandwich construction.
No regular step.
TAIL UNIT: Conventional cantilever wooden
structure, with tailplane mounted about one-
third of the way up the fin. Variable-incidence
tailplane. Fabric-covered rudder and elevators,
with trim-tab in rudder.
LANDING GEAR: Mechanically-retractable tricycle type, with main units retracting upward
into fuselage sides. Main wheel tyres size
5·00 × 5, nose-wheel tyre size 3·50 × 3½.
Hydraulic disc brakes of Johansen design.

Non-retractable stabilising float, on single
cantilever strut, near each wing-tip.
POWER PLANT: Two 65 hp Walter Mikron III
four-cylinder in-line inverted air-cooled engines,
each driving a two-blade wooden propeller.
Total of 15 Imp gallons (68 litres) of fuel in
floats and further 15 Imp gallons in tank in
lower part of fuselage.
ACCOMMODATION: Enclosed cabin with seats for
pilot and up to three passengers.
DIMENSIONS, EXTERNAL:
  Wing span   32 ft 1¾ in (9·80 m)

Wing chord at root	5 ft 3 in (1·60 m)	Flaps (total)	21·10 sq ft (1·96 m²)
Wing chord at tip	3 ft 3½ in (1·00 m)	Fin	10·01 sq ft (0·93 m²)
Wing aspect ratio	7·5	Rudder, incl tab	8·07 sq ft (0·75 m²)
Length overall	22 ft 9½ in (6·95 m)	Tailplane	15·07 sq ft (1·40 m²)
Height over tail	9 ft 0¼ in (2·75 m)	Elevators	10·23 sq ft (0·95 m²)
Tailplane span	11 ft 0 in (3·35 m)	

AREAS:

WEIGHTS AND LOADINGS:

Wings, gross	137·8 sq ft (12·80 m²)	Weight empty, equipped	1,278 lb (580 kg)
Ailerons (total)	11·95 sq ft (1·11 m²)	Max T-O weight	1,984 lb (900 kg)
		Max wing loading	14·3 lb/sq ft (70 kg/m²)
		Max power loading	15·2 lb/hp (6·9 kg/hp)

PERFORMANCE (at max T-O weight):

Max level speed
116 knots (134 mph; 215 km/h)
Max cruising speed
108 knots (124 mph; 200 km/h)
Stalling speed, flaps down
33 knots (38 mph; 60 km/h)
Rate of climb at S/L 886 ft (270 m)/min
Range with max fuel
538 nm (620 miles; 1,000 km)

SEREMET

W. SEREMET

ADDRESS: Bredgade 67A, Copenhagen K

Mr Seremet, a Danish engineer and amateur constructor, has designed and built a number of small rotating-wing aircraft, the first trials being carried out in 1962 with two aircraft designated W.S.1 and W.S.2. More recent designs include the W.S.3, W.S.4, W.S.5 and W.S.6, described below, and Mr Seremet has also completed a strap-on autogyro.

SEREMET W.S.3 MINI-COPTER

The W.S.3 is developed from Mr Seremet's earlier designs, referred to above, and is a one-man strap-on helicopter powered by an 18 hp Ydral two-stroke engine. The engine is mounted on an aluminium frame which is strapped on to the pilot's back by means of a shoulder harness. The controls comprise two twist-grips, one for each hand. One of these is the engine throttle, the same hand operating a motor-cycle-type clutch lever; the other changes the tail rotor pitch for directional control. There are no cyclic or collective pitch controls. Height control is obtained simply by increasing or decreasing engine power, while the pilot achieves directional movement by altering his body angle.

By the Spring of 1969 Mr Seremet had made over a dozen flights in the W.S.3, including tethered flights, and interest in the project had been expressed by the Danish Lifeboat Institution. An improved version, the W.S.4, was then under development.

ROTOR SYSTEM: Single main rotor and tail rotor. Three-blade main rotor, with laminated wooden blades of NACA 0012 section. Two-blade anti-torque tail rotor carried on short boom at rear, aft of reduction gearbox.

ROTOR DRIVE: Vertical shaft from engine carries the drive through a reduction gear to the main rotor head, the main rotor being driven through a belt-and-pulley system at approx 800 rpm. Tail rotor is driven from the main shaft.

DIMENSIONS, EXTERNAL:

Diameter of main rotor	11 ft 5¾ in (3·50 m)
Diameter of tail rotor	1 ft 11 in (0·58 m)

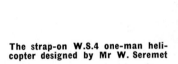

The strap-on W.S.4 one-man helicopter designed by Mr W. Seremet

WEIGHTS:

Weight empty	92 lb (42 kg)
Max T-O weight	220 lb (100 kg)

SEREMET W.S.4 MINI-COPTER

The W.S.4 Mini-Copter strap-on helicopter is a development of the W.S.3 described above, with more powerful engine, larger-diameter rotors and improved controllability. It has a two-blade main rotor, with NACA 0015-section blades, and is powered by a 35 hp Kiekhaefer engine. Flight

testing was due to begin in the early Summer of 1969.

DIMENSIONS, EXTERNAL:

Diameter of main rotor	14 ft 9 in (4·50 m)
Diameter of tail rotor	2 ft 7½ in (0·80 m)

WEIGHTS:

Weight empty	103 lb (47 kg)
Max T-O weight	330 lb (150 kg)

PERFORMANCE:

Endurance	15 min

SEREMET W.S.5 GYRO-GLIDER

The W.S.5 is a single-seat gyro-glider, similar to the Bensen type (see US section), and is designed to be towed into the air behind a motor-car. The basic airframe is constructed of aluminium tubes, bolted together. The rudder and horizontal stabiliser are of water-firmed veneer. A tricycle landing gear is fitted. The tilting free-turning rotor has two blades of NACA 8-H 12 section, and control is effected by an overhead column. Mr Seremet hopes to build an improved version with glass-fibre airframe and rotor blades.

DIMENSIONS, EXTERNAL:

Diameter of rotor	20 ft 8 in (6·30 m)
Length overall	9 ft 4¼ in (2·85 m)
Height overall	5 ft 10¾ in (1·80 m)

WEIGHT:

Weight empty	136 lb (62 kg)

SEREMET W.S.6 AUTOGYRO

The W.S.6, which had made a small number of test flights by the Spring of 1969, has an essentially similar airframe to that of the W.S.5, on which has been installed a 72 hp McCulloch four-cylinder horizontally-opposed air-cooled engine driving a two-blade wooden pusher propeller of 3 ft 6½ in (1·08 m) diameter. There is a fixed tab on each half of the tailplane. Dimensions are the same as for the W.S.5; empty weight is 233 lb (106 kg).

W.S.6 autogyro designed by Mr W. Seremet

EGYPT
(UNITED ARAB REPUBLIC)

HELIOPOLIS AIR WORKS
FACTORY 72, EGYPTIAN GENERAL AERO ORGANISATION

HEAD OFFICE AND WORKS:
Orouba Street, Heliopolis, Cairo
GENERAL MANAGER:
Eng Ibrahim Fahmy Sharawy

CHIEF ENGINEER:
Eng Mohamed Ahmed El-Sirgany

TECHNICAL MANAGER:
Eng Mohamed Mostafa El-Giredly

PRODUCTION MANAGER:
Eng Saad Ahmed Selim

The Heliopolis aircraft factory forms part of the Egyptian General Aero Organisation. It was founded in 1950 and subsequently produced in series several developed versions of the wartime German Bücker Bü 181D Bestmann training monoplane under the name of Gomhouria. Details can be found in the 1966-67 Jane's.

HELWAN AIR WORKS

FACTORY 36, EGYPTIAN GENERAL AERO ORGANISATION

HEAD OFFICE AND WORKS:
Helwan, Cairo

GENERAL MANAGER:
K. H. El-Shishini

This jet aircraft and aero-engine works was inaugurated formally by President Nasser on 25 July 1962. Its first product was a licence-built version of the Spanish Hispano HA-200 Saeta jet trainer.

About 100 Spanish aircraft workers assisted the Egyptians to establish a modern aircraft industry, and were followed by an even larger number of other European designers and engineers at Helwan Air Works. They were engaged primarily on the development of a supersonic fighter, designated HA-300, and the E-300 aero-engine to power this aircraft. This programme was cancelled in May 1969, only six weeks before the scheduled first flight of the HA-300 with an Egyptian engine, and the Helwan works have now been acquired by the Ministry of Industry.

HELWAN AL-KAHIRA

Al-Kahira is the name given to the Hispano HA-200 Saeta tandem two-seat advanced trainer built under licence at Helwan.

Full details of the Saeta can be found under the "Hispano" heading in the Spanish section.

Al-Kahira (HA-200) two-seat jet trainers built under licence by the Helwan Air Works

FINLAND

KOKKOLA

DIPL INGS KALEVI AND SEPPO KOKKOLA

ADDRESS:
Johtokivenkuja 4 B 33, Helsinki 71

The brothers Kalevi and Seppo Kokkola, both graduates of the Helsinki Institute of Technology, began their design studies for light autogyros in 1957. Their first aircraft, the Ko-01, was a towed gyro-glider built to test the efficiency of the rotor system, and was first flown in 1959—the first rotorcraft of Finnish design to be flown in Finland. The Ko-02 second prototype was fitted with a 28 hp Poinsard engine, but was damaged during its first attempted take-off during the Winter of 1960. After being modified and rebuilt as the Ko-03, still with the same Poinsard engine, it made a successful first flight on 9 February 1961 to become the first powered rotorcraft of Finnish design to fly in Finland. The Ko-03 was slightly damaged during adverse weather in the Winter of 1963.

The brothers' latest product is the Ko-04 autogyro, a full description of which is given below.

KOKKOLA Ko-04 SUPER UPSTART

Design of the Ko-04, which is based generally upon that of the earlier Ko-03, was started in 1962, and construction of the prototype began in 1963. This aircraft was completed in the Autumn of 1968 and made its first flight on 12 December 1968. After several test flights, some minor modifications were made during the Winter of 1969-70, and the following description refers to the Ko-04 in this modified form.

TYPE: Single-seat light autogyro.

ROTOR SYSTEM: Two-blade fully-articulated main rotor, with zero offset flapping hinges and drag hinges equipped with friction dampers. Each blade consists of a main spar of laminated wood and rear section of hard plastic foam. Bonded metal leading-edge; rear section covered with bonded plywood. Blade section NACA 8-H-12. Rotor hub and blade attachment parts are of steel construction. Rotor head bearings are of pre-lubricated plastic type, and rotor pivot head is covered with streamlined plastic fairing. Rotor blades have internal mass balance. Rotor pylon encased in streamlined aluminium fairings.

ROTOR DRIVE: Torqueless rotor spin-up device, for take-off and landing, by 30% hydrogen peroxide rocket engine at tip of each blade. Propellant is fed through the blades to these engines from a pressure bottle above the rotor head. A catalyst is located within the rocket engine.

FUSELAGE: Welded steel-tube structure, covered with glass-fibre sheet.

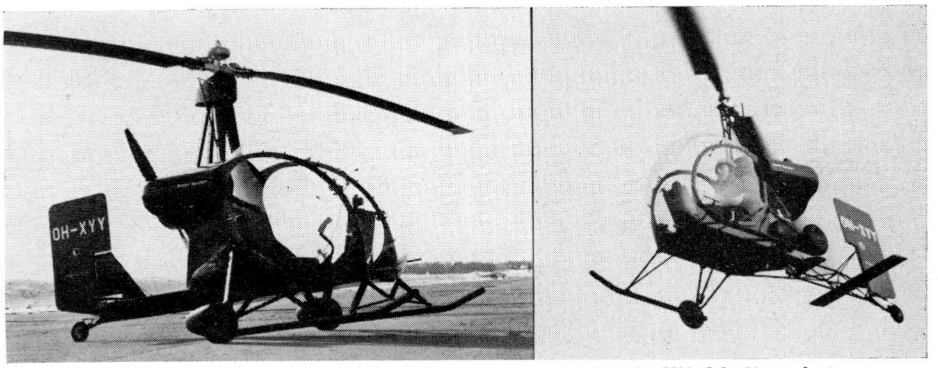

Kokkola Ko-04 Super Upstart autogyro (one 41 hp Agusta MV GA 40 engine)

TAIL UNIT: Cantilever type. Fin and rudder of steel-tube construction, fabric-covered. Adjustable tailplane has sandwich-type structure of plastic foam and plywood.

LANDING GEAR: Non-retractable tricycle type, with steerable tail-wheel, and incorporating steel-tube skids for rough-terrain landing. Rubber shock-absorption on main units, which have 4 × 4 in (10 × 10 cm) tyres, pressure 25·6 lb/sq in (1·8 kg/cm²), and mechanical drum brakes. Tail-wheel size 2 × 4 in (5 × 10 cm). Main gear legs encased in streamlined aluminium fairings.

POWER PLANT: One 41 hp Agusta MV GA 40 two-cylinder horizontally-opposed air-cooled engine, mounted in fully-enclosed glass-fibre cowling aft of rotor pylon and driving a two-blade fixed-pitch wooden propeller of Kokkola design, diameter 4 ft 10¼ in (1·48 m). Cooling fan for engine. Fuel in single aluminium tank aft of cabin, capacity 10 Imp gallons (45 litres). Refuelling point on starboard side. Aircraft is suitable for a variety of power plants, and provision is made for installation of 60 hp 1,600 cc Volkswagen engine.

ACCOMMODATION: Single seat for pilot in fully-enclosed cabin with transparent "bubble" canopy. Entrance by fully-transparent blown plastic door on starboard side with quick-release hinges. Similar door, for emergency exit, on port side. Controllable cabin heating and ventilation, with electrically-driven fan for air circulation.

SYSTEMS AND EQUIPMENT: Battery for radio and auxiliary ignition of engine. PIK-R-2 transistorised VHF radio.

DIMENSIONS, EXTERNAL:

Diameter of main rotor	30 ft 0½ in (9·16 m)
Main rotor blade chord (each, constant)	9¾ in (0·25 m)
Length of fuselage	12 ft 4¾ in (3·78 m)
Width, without rotor and landing gear	2 ft 9¼ in (0·84 m)
Height to top of hydrogen tank	8 ft 2½ in (2·505 m)
Wheel track	5 ft 3 in (1·60 m)
Wheelbase	7 ft 3¼ in (2·22 m)

DIMENSIONS, INTERNAL:

Cabin: Length	4 ft 1¼ in (1·25 m)
Width	2 ft 5½ in (0·75 m)
Height	4 ft 2½ in (1·28 m)

AREAS:

Main rotor blades (each)	10·8 sq ft (1·00 m²)
Rotor disc	710 sq ft (66·00 m²)
Fin	1·83 sq ft (0·17 m²)
Rudder	6·46 sq ft (0·60 m²)
Tailplane	3·01 sq ft (0·28 m²)

WEIGHTS:

Weight empty	430 lb (195 kg)
Max T-O weight	727 lb (330 kg)

PERFORMANCE (at max T-O weight, 41 hp engine):

Normal cruising speed at S/L	54 knots (62 mph; 100 km/h)
Max rate of climb at S/L	295 ft (90 m)/min
T-O run, zero wind	148 ft (45 m)
Landing run, zero wind	10 ft (3 m)
Range	188 nm (217 miles; 350 km)
Endurance	4 hr

PIK

POLYTEKNIKKOJEN ILMAILUKERHO (The Flying Club of the Student Union at the Institute of Technology, Helsinki)

ADDRESS:
Dipoli, Otaniemi

EXECUTIVES:
Pasi Venäläinen (Chairman and Sales Manager)
Visa Hietalahti (Secretary and Public Relations)

This Flying Club was established in 1931 and has since been engaged mainly in the development and construction of high-performance sailplanes.

As an extension of this work (see "Sailplanes" section), it designed and built the single-seat PIK-11, its first powered aircraft, which flew in March 1953, and followed this with a two-seat glider-towing aircraft known as the PIK-15 Hinu, described on page 38.

PIK-15 HINU

The PIK-15 is a side-by-side two-seat light aeroplane, which has been designed for glider-towing duties. Its design, by Kai Mellén, Ilkka Lounamaa and Jussi Rinta, was started in October 1960 and construction of the prototype began in 1962. It flew for the first time on 29 August 1964; since then, five more PIK-15's have been completed and a sixth is under construction.

The airframe is built mainly of Finnish birch plywood and pine, to facilitate construction of the PIK-15 by Finnish clubs. Very effective flaps permit steep and rapid descents after each tow. Excessive engine temperature changes are avoided by the use of a cowl flap system.

The PIK-15 will climb at the rate of 690-880 ft (210-268 m) min towing a single-seat sailplane, or at 490-690 ft (149-210 m) min towing a two-seat sailplane at 75% continuous power, subject to engine limitations. Time to 1,650 ft (500 m) with the single-seat PIK-16C Vasama in tow is 2 min 30 sec. Up to 15 tows per hour can be accomplished.

TYPE: Two-seat glider-towing aircraft.

WINGS: Cantilever low-wing monoplane. Wing section NACA 2415 at root, NACA 4409R at tip. Dihedral on undersurface 5°. Incidence 4° 30' at root. One-piece main box-spar passes through fuselage. Auxiliary spar carries flaps and ailerons. Plywood covering, with fabric overall. Fabric-covered wooden slotted ailerons. Aluminium alloy split flaps function also as air-brakes.

FUSELAGE: All-wood semi-monocoque structure, plywood-covered.

TAIL UNIT: Cantilever wood structure. Fin integral with fuselage. Fixed surfaces plywood covered; rudder and elevators fabric-covered. Controllable trim-tab in starboard elevator.

LANDING GEAR: Non-retractable tail-wheel type. Cantilever spring steel main legs each attached to wing by one bolt. Goodyear main wheels and tubeless tyres, size 6.00 × 6. Scott Model 3-24B steerable tail-wheel. Goodyear 9532181 single-disc hydraulic brakes.

POWER PLANT: One 150 hp Lycoming O-320-A2B or 160 hp O-320-B2B four-cylinder horizontally-opposed air-cooled engine, driving a McCauley 1A175/GM-82-43 (modified) two-blade fixed-pitch propeller. Fuel tank aft of firewall in fuselage, capacity 22.5 Imp gallons (102 litres). Oil capacity 1.66 Imp gallons (7.5 litres). Most of the aircraft now under construction have 160 hp Lycoming engines.

ACCOMMODATION: Two glass-fibre seats side-by-side under rearward-sliding blown Perspex canopy. Steel-tube crash pylon. Baggage compartment aft of seats. Heating, via heat exchanger on port exhaust pipe assembly, and ventilation standard.

ELECTRONICS AND EQUIPMENT: Prototype has 4-channel VHF radio, constructed by PIK, and glider-towing hook.

DIMENSIONS, EXTERNAL:

Wing span	32 ft 9½ in (10·00 m)
Wing chord at root	5 ft 7 in (1·70 m)
Wing chord at tip	3 ft 7¼ in (1·10 m)
Wing aspect ratio	7·15
Length overall	20 ft 8 in (6·30 m)
Height overall	5 ft 6¾ in (1·70 m)
Tailplane span	11 ft 6 in (3·50 m)
Wheel track	9 ft 2¼ in (2·80 m)
Wheelbase	14 ft 10 in (4·52 m)

PIK-15 Hinu two-seat glider-towing aircraft (150 hp Lycoming engine) (*M. J. Hooks*)

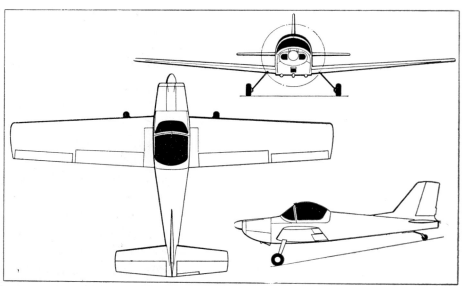

Three-view drawing of the PIK-15 Hinu two-seat glider-towing aircraft

DIMENSIONS, INTERNAL:

Cabin:	
Max width	3 ft 5¾ in (1·06 m)
Baggage compartment volume	7 cu ft (0·20 m³)

AREAS:

Wings, gross	150·7 sq ft (14·0 m²)
Ailerons (total)	12·38 sq ft (1·15 m²)
Trailing-edge flaps (total)	11·30 sq ft (1·05 m²)
Fin	7·00 sq ft (0·65 m²)
Rudder	7·43 sq ft (0·69 m²)
Tailplane	16·58 sq ft (1·54 m²)
Elevators, including tab	15·40 sq ft (1·43 m²)

WEIGHTS AND LOADINGS:

Weight empty, equipped:	
150 hp	1,107 lb (502 kg)
Payload	406 lb (184 kg)
Max T-O and landing weight	1,684 lb (764 kg)
Wing loading	11·16 lb/sq ft (54·5 kg/m²)

Power loading:

150 hp	11·25 lb/hp (5·09 kg/hp)
160 hp	10·58 lb/hp (4·8 kg/hp)

PERFORMANCE (with 150 hp engine, at max T-O weight, with low-pitch propeller, except where indicated):

Max level speed at S/L (high-pitch prop)	129 knots (149 mph; 240 km/h)
Cruising speed at S/L, 75% power (high-pitch prop)	116 knots (134 mph; 215 km/h)
Stalling speed, flaps up (high-pitch prop)	53 knots (60 mph; 95 km/h)
Landing speed, flaps down (high-pitch prop)	45 knots (52 mph; 83 km/h)
Rate of climb at S/L:	
150 hp	1,140 ft (348 m)/min
160 hp	1,234 ft (376 m)/min
Service ceiling	25,000 ft (7,600 m)
Absolute ceiling	26,400 ft (8,050 m)
T-O run	262-295 ft (80-90 m)
Landing run	328 ft (100 m)

TERVAMÄKI-EEROLA

TERVAMÄKI AND EEROLA

ADDRESS:
Tuulimyllyntie 6 D 40, Helsinki 92

Mr Jukka Tervamäki became interested in autogyros in 1956, and built his first machine, powered by an inverted Triumph T 110 engine, in 1958. In 1959 he worked for the Bensen Aircraft Corporation in the USA for two months, to develop an improved Triumph T 110 motor-cycle engine installation for testing on the Bensen B-7M Gyro-Copter.

After returning to Finland, Tervamäki obtained a Diploma in Aeronautical Engineering at the Helsinki Institute of Technology in 1963, and subsequently joined the Finnish Air Force,

working in the helicopter section at its Helsinki headquarters.

In 1964 he was joined by Mr Eerola, at that time a helicopter mechanic at the Finnish Air Force helicopter base at Utti, and together they started to develop a new autogyro. As a first step, they designed rotor blades having an NACA 0012 aerofoil section and made entirely of glass-fibre with a plastic foam core in the trailing-edges. Several sets of blades were produced, test flown and sold.

In May 1966, Tervamäki and Eerola began the design of a new autogyro, and construction of a prototype began in the following September. Designated ATE-3, this machine had a more advanced rotor blade design. An NACA 8-H-12

aerofoil was chosen, for which a completely new blade root attachment system and rotor head were designed. In addition, a low-drag fuselage was developed, of combined steel tube and glass-fibre construction. The prototype (OH-XYV) flew for the first time on 11 May 1968. It had flown a total of 50 hours by the end of February 1970.

In November 1969 the horizontal tail surfaces were removed, and a redesigned vertical tail, made of glass-fibre reinforced plastic with PVC foam ribs, was fitted. Apart from this the structural description of the aircraft, published in the 1969-70 *Jane's*, remains unchanged.

Rotor blades of the type fitted to the ATE-3 are in limited production for amateur builders.

TERVAMÄKI-EEROLA ATE-3

TYPE: Single-seat light autogyro.

DIMENSIONS, EXTERNAL:

Diameter of rotor	22 ft 11½ in (7·0 m)
Length of fuselage	10 ft 6 in (3·2 m)
Height overall	6 ft 2⅝ in (1·9 m)
Wheel track	5 ft 7 in (1·7 m)
Propeller diameter	3 ft 11¼ in (1·20 m)

AREAS:

Main rotor blades (each)	6·78 sq ft (0·63 m²)
Main rotor disc	414·4 sq ft (38·5 m²)

WEIGHTS AND LOADINGS:

Weight empty, equipped	330 lb (150 kg)
Max T-O weight	573 lb (260 kg)
Max disc loading	1·4 lb/sq ft (6·80 kg/m²)
Max power loading	7·72 lb/hp (3·50 kg/hp)

PERFORMANCE (at max T-O weight):

Max level speed at S/L	75·6 knots (87 mph; 140 km/h)
Max permissible diving speed	86 knots (99 mph; 160 km/h)
Max cruising speed at S/L	59 knots (68 mph; 110 km/h)
Econ cruising speed	54 knots (62 mph; 100 km/h)
Rate of climb at S/L	590 ft (180 m)/min
T-O run	165 ft (50 m)
T-O to 50 ft (15 m)	495 ft (150 m)
Landing from 50 ft (15 m)	165 ft (50 m)
Landing run	16 ft (5 m)
Range with max fuel, no reserves	160 nm (185 miles; 300 km)

Tervamäki-Eerola ATE-3 light autogyro, in latest form with tailplane removed   (*Matti Korjula*)

VALMET

VALMET OY TAMPERE WORKS

OFFICE AND WORKS:
Tampere

The Valmet Oy Tampere Works are affiliated to Valmet Oy, a State-owned company consisting of several metal-working factories. The Tampere Works is a direct continuation of the former State Aircraft Factory and belongs to the factory group, Valmet Oy Tampere, which consists of the Tampere Works as the central unit and of the Instrument Works at Tampere and the Kuorevesi Works as subordinate units.

In 1967, the last of 62 CM 170 Magister two-seat jet trainers was completed under licence for the Finnish Air Force.

Present aviation activities are confined mainly to the Kuorevesi Works, which undertakes production of aircraft parts and components, major repairs, overhauls and test flying.

In April 1970 it was announced that Valmet Oy would be responsible for assembly of the 12 Saab-35XS Drakens ordered by the Finnish government, and of other Drakens ordered from Saab.

The Valmet Linnavuori Works at Siuro is directly subordinate to the Head Office of Valmet Oy, Helsinki, and in the aviation field is concerned primarily with aero-engine repairs and overhauls.

FRANCE

AÉROSPATIALE
SOCIÉTÉ NATIONALE INDUSTRIELLE AÉROSPATIALE

HEAD OFFICE
37, Boulevard de Montmorency, 75-Paris 16e

WORKS:
St Aubin de Médoc, St Médard en Jalles, Le Haillan, Bordeaux, Bourges, Cannes, Châteauroux, Châtillon, Les Gâtines, Subdray, Courbevoie, La Courneuve, Les Mureaux, Marignane, Méaulte, Nantes, Puteaux, Suresnes and Toulouse

PRESIDENT-DIRECTOR GENERAL:
Henri Ziegler

VICE-PRESIDENT:
General Jean Crepin

COUNCILLOR:
Charles Cristofini

DIRECTOR GENERAL:
Louis Giusta

DIRECTOR GENERAL ADJOINT:
Jean-François Darteyre

SECRETARY GENERAL:
Pierre Guibert

SECRETARY GENERAL ADJOINT:
Serge Bisone

INSPECTOR GENERAL:
Raymond Brohon

CENTRAL TECHNICAL DIRECTOR:
Roger Chevalier

TECHNICAL DIRECTOR:
Pierre Satre

PRODUCTION DIRECTOR:
Jean Coupain

COMMERCIAL DIRECTOR:
Pierre du Boucheron

FINANCIAL DIRECTOR:
André Gintrand

Aérospatiale SE 210 Caravelle Series 10 R twin-jet transport aircraft in the insignia of UTA

PUBLIC RELATIONS DIRECTOR:
Jean Calmel

DIRECTOR OF TEST FLYING:
André Turcat

DIRECTOR OF CONTRACTS:
René Auriol

DIRECTOR OF INFORMATION:
Pierre Capdeville

DIRECTOR, AIRBUS PROGRAMME:
Roger Beteille

DIRECTOR, CONCORDE PROGRAMME:
Pierre Gautier

DIRECTOR, SN 600 PROGRAMME:
Paul Duvochel

DIRECTOR, V/STOL PROGRAMME:
Maurice Avramito

DIRECTOR, HELICOPTER DIVISION:
François Legrand

DIRECTOR, BALLISTIC SYSTEMS AND SPACE
DIVISION:
Pierre Usunier

DIRECTOR, TACTICAL MISSILES DIVISION:
Emile Stauff

The Société Nationale Industrielle Aérospatiale (SNIAS) was created, with effect from 1 January 1970, by decision of the French government, as a result of the merger of the three companies Sud-Aviation, Nord-Aviation and SEREB. It has the form of a limited company and is managed by a Board of Directors under the Chairmanship of M Henri Ziegler.

Aérospatiale is the biggest aerospace company in the Common Market countries, with a registered capital of 396,500,000 francs, facilities which cover some 80,729,000 sq ft (7,500,000 m²), and a staff of over 42,000 persons. The turnover of the three constituent companies totalled nearly 2·8 thousand million francs including 1·2 thousand million from exports.

Aérospatiale's industrial potential is made up of some twenty separate establishments, with design offices, research and laboratory centres, and ground and flight test facilities, as well as production means which develop and use the most advanced techniques. Its activities extend over all sections of the aerospace industry including aircraft, helicopters, tactical missiles, ballistic missile systems and spacecraft.

In the aircraft field, major activities are the Concorde supersonic transport, developed in co-operation with BAC; the short-to-medium-range subsonic A 300B European Airbus in co-operation with Deutsche Airbus GmbH, Hawker Siddeley Aviation and VFW-Fokker; the Transall twin-turboprop transport in co-operation with VFW-Fokker, the medium-range twin-jet Caravelle, the N 262 transport and the SN 600 Corvette.

In the helicopter field, activities are shared between continued production of the Alouette series, the twin-turbine SA 330 Puma, and the Super Frelon; and development of the SA 341 Gazelle light helicopter to meet Anglo-French requirements. Agreements have been concluded with Westland in the UK for the joint development and production of the SA 330 and SA 341, and for the Westland-designed WG.13, these three types having been chosen to equip the French and British Armed Forces. It is also planned to produce commercial versions of these helicopters.

In the missiles and spacecraft field, the products of Aérospatiale include the Belier, Centaure, Dragon, Dauphin and Eridan research rockets; the AS.30, Entac, SS.11, Milan and Exocet tactical missiles, and the SSBS (surface-to-surface) and MSBS (sea-to-surface) ballistic strategic missiles for military programmes.

The former Sud-Aviation was formed on 1 March 1957, by amalgamation of the two companies Ouest-Aviation and Sud-Est Aviation which, until 1 September 1956, had been known respectively as the Société Nationale de Constructions Aéronautiques du Sud-Ouest (SNCASO) and the Société Nationale de Constructions Aéronautiques du Sud-Est (SNCASE). Both of the original companies had been formed in 1936 by the nationalisation of various private companies. The subsidiary SFERMA was absorbed by Sud-Aviation in January 1965, and in July 1966 Sud-Aviation absorbed Heli-Service. In October 1966, its activities relative to light and business aircraft were regrouped to form a new subsidiary, Socata (which see), which took over from that date the facilities of the former Gérance des Etablissements Morane-Saulnier (GEMS). In April 1967 Sud-Aviation took over the former Potez works at Toulouse-Blagnac.

The former Nord-Aviation was formed in 1936, under the laws for the nationalisation of the aircraft industry, as Société Nationale de Constructions Aéronautiques du Nord (SNCAN). Following the liquidation of the SNCA du Centre in 1949, the Bourges factory of that society was integrated in the Nord group. Towards the end of 1954, the Société Française d'Etudes et de Constructions de Matériels Aéronautiques Spéciaux (SFECMAS, formerly Arsenal de l'Aéronautique) was amalgamated with the Société Nationale de Constructions Aéronautiques du Nord.

AÉROSPATIALE/BAC CONCORDE

Full details of the Concorde programme can be found in the International section of this edition.

AÉROSPATIALE SE 210 CARAVELLE

The Caravelle twin-jet short-to-medium-range airliner was designed by the former SNCA du Sud-Est (later Sud-Aviation), and was ordered in prototype form by the Sécrétariat d'Etat à l'Air in January 1953. The first of two prototypes flew for the first time on 27 May 1955, and the second on 6 May 1956.

The following versions have been produced:

Caravelle I and IA. Initial production series, described in previous editions of *Jane's*. Rolls-Royce Avon RA.29 Mk 522 (Series I) or Mk 522A (Series IA) turbojet engines. First production model flew on 18 May 1958. Entered service in mid-1959. FAA Type Approval 8 April 1959. Nineteen Srs I and thirteen Srs IA built; all except one were later converted to Caravelle III standard.

Caravelle III. Second production version, with 11,400 lb (5,170 kg) st Avon RA.29 Mk 527 turbojets and standard accommodation for 64-80 passengers. First flew on 30 December 1959. First delivery in April 1960 to Alitalia, which later converted its four Series III to VI-N standard. FAA Type Approval 12 July 1960. One Caravelle III, airframe number 42, was fitted with General Electric CJ805-23C turbofan engines. In this form it was designated Caravelle VII, and flew for the first time on 29 December 1960, but was later restored to Srs III standard.

Caravelle VI-N. Two Avon RA.29 Mk 531 engines (each 12,200 lb=5,535 kg st). Accommodation for 16-20 first class and 55-60 economy class passengers, or 80 economy class passengers. First flew on 10 September 1960. First delivery (to Sabena) in January 1961.

Caravelle VI-R. Similar to Series VI-N, but with modified windscreen for improved visibility, Rolls-Royce Avon 533R turbojet engines (each 12,600 lb=5,725 kg st) fitted with thrust reversers, and spoilers in three sections on the trailing-edge of each wing. Prototype flew on 6 February 1961. FAA Type Approval 5 June 1961. Entered service 14 July 1961.

Caravelle 10 R. Similar to Series VI-R, but with Pratt & Whitney JT8D-7 turbofan engines (each 14,000 lb=6,350 kg st) fitted with thrust reversers. Change in fuselage structure gives considerable increase in capacity of lower holds. Prototype flew for the first time on 18 January 1965.

Caravelle 11 R. Mixed passenger/freight version, derived from Series 10 R and also powered by two Pratt & Whitney JT8D-7 turbofan engines.

Increase of 36·6 in (0·93 m) in length of front fuselage. Floor strength increased from 123 lb/sq ft (600 kg/m²) to 205 lb/sq ft (1,000 kg/m²) over a length of 29 ft 6 in (9·0 m). Number of cargo attachment rails increased from four to seven, and a cargo door, size 10 ft 10¾ in × 6 ft 0¼ in (3·32 m × 1·835 m), provided on port side of front fuselage. In addition, various parts of the fuselage have been strengthened.

Typical mixed traffic payloads are: 12 first class passengers and 50 tourist passengers, with 1,642 cu ft (46·5 m³) of cargo space; 50 tourist class passengers and 2,331 cu ft (66·0 m³) of cargo space. In all-freight configuration, the Caravelle 11 R has 4,061 cu ft (115 m³) of cargo space. In all-passenger form, it can be fitted with 89 or 99 seats.

The first Caravelle 11 R flew for the first time on 21 April 1967.

Caravelle 12. Essentially, this is the airframe of the Caravelle Super B (see below), with an even longer fuselage, and powered by 14,500 lb (6,577 kg) st Pratt & Whitney JT8D-9 turbofan engines. Additional 6 ft 6¾ in (2·00 m) section inserted in the fuselage ahead of the wing leading-edge, and a second section 3 ft 11½ in (1·21 m) long added aft of the trailing-edge. Landing gear is in the strengthened form developed for the Super B at its highest operating weight of 123,460 lb (56,000 kg). Wings, engine pods, nose and tail unit, systems and equipment as for the Super B; but there is some strengthening of the central fuselage above the wings, enlargement of two of the emergency exits, and revision of the interior layout. First flight scheduled for November 1970.

Accommodation provides five-abreast seating for 128 tourist-class passengers, arranged as 12 rows at front and 9 rows in rear of cabin with seats at 32 in (81 cm) pitch; three rows in centre, in line with emergency exits; and two four-abreast rows at extreme rear. An alternative tourist layout seating 118 passengers at 34 in pitch (86 cm) is available. A mixed-class layout can be provided for 88 tourist-class passengers at the latter seat pitch and 16 first-class passengers (four-abreast) at 38 in (96 cm) pitch. A passenger/cargo layout is also available, for 100 tourist passengers at 34 in pitch and 250 cu ft (7·10 m³) of cargo space.

Caravelle Super B. The first Caravelle Super B (airframe No 169) flew for the first time on 3 March 1964. It is normally powered by two 14,000 lb (6,350 kg) st Pratt & Whitney JT8D-7 turbofan engines, although the first examples were fitted with JT8D-1 engines. It differs from other Caravelles (except the Srs 11 R and Srs 12) in having a 3 ft 3½ in (1·0 m) longer fuselage, providing accommodation for 68 first-class passengers (four-abreast), 86 mixed-class passengers, or 104 tourist passengers.

Aerodynamic refinements include an extension forward of the wing leading-edge near the root, an increase from 35° to 45° in the operating travel of the flaps, which are of the double-slotted type, the addition of a bullet fairing at the intersection of the rudder and elevators, and a greater tailplane span than any other version except the Srs 12.

First delivery of a Super B, to Finnair, was made on 25 July 1964. The Super B is also sometimes referred to as the Series 10 B.

Production of Caravelles is undertaken by a large group of factories, with final assembly at Toulouse.

All Caravelle versions can be equipped with the Aérospatiale/Lear-Siegler all-weather landing system, which gives significant improvement in airline schedule regularity. Certification of the Cat IIIA installation (50 ft=15 m decision height and 660 ft=200 m RVR) was awarded on 2 March 1967. On 25 November 1968 the French SGAC authorised Caravelles equipped with the system to make Cat IIIA landings in commercial service at adequately-equipped airfields. Up to 1 January 1970, Air Inter Caravelles alone had made over 6,000 automatic landings in scheduled operations, irrespective of weather conditions. A Caravelle of this airline made, for the first time anywhere in the world, an entirely automatic landing in poor visibility conditions (70 ft=21 m ceiling and 650 ft=198 m RVR) on 9 January 1969, during a scheduled passenger-carrying flight from Lyons to Paris.

Studies were under way in 1970 to achieve lower engine noise levels on all Caravelle variants.

Caravelles had been ordered by the following operators up to 1 May 1970:

Series III

Air Algérie	4
Air France	44
Air Inter	9
Finnair	4
Groupe de Liaisons Aérienne	
Ministerielle (France)	1
Royal Air Maroc	5
SAS	21
Swissair	8
Tunis-Air	4
Varig	2

Series VI-N

Aerolineas Argentinas	4
Air Algérie	2
Alitalia	21*
Indian Airlines Corporation	9
JAT (Yugoslavia)	8
Middle East Airlines	3
Sabena	10

*incl 4 converted from Caravelle III

Series VI-R

Austrian Air Lines	5
Cruzeiro do Sul (Brazil)	4
Garrett	1
Iberia	12
Kingdom of Libya Airlines	3
LAN (Chile)	3
Luxair	1
Panair do Brasil	4
TAP (Portugal)	3
United Air Lines	20

Series 10 R

Alia (Jordan)	3
Iberia	7
LTU	4
SATA (Switzerland)	1
Sterling Airways (Denmark)	2
Transeuropa (Spain)	1
UTA	2

Series 11 R

Air Afrique	2
Air Congo	2
Transeuropa (Spain)	2

Series 12

Sterling Airways (Denmark)	7

Super B

Finnair	8
Sterling Airways (Denmark)	12*
Syrian Arab Airlines	2

*includes five of 52,000 kg, four of 54,000 kg and three of 56,000 kg AUW

Of the aircraft listed above, 264 had been delivered by 5 May 1970.

TYPE: Twin-jet medium-range airliner.

WINGS: Cantilever low-wing monoplane. NACA 65,212 wing section with cambered leading-edge. Sweepback at quarter-chord 20°. Dihedral 3°. Incidence at root 2°. Wing in two sections joined on fuselage centre-line. All-metal three-spar structure, with spanwise stringers riveted to skin. Two-piece all-metal ailerons on each wing, operated hydraulically by duplicated Automotive Products actuators, with electric standby power. Hydraulically-actuated Fowler flaps. Air-brakes on upper and lower surfaces ahead of flaps. Three-section spoilers on trailing-edge of each wing of Series VI-R. Thermal de-icing.

FUSELAGE: Circular-section all-metal semi-monocoque structure. Max diameter 10 ft 6 in (3·20 m).

TAIL UNIT: Cantilever all-metal structure. Sweepback on tailplane 30° at quarter-chord. Hydraulically-powered rudder and elevators, using duplicated Automotive Products actuators, with electric standby power. Thermal de-icing.

LANDING GEAR: Retractable tricycle type. Hispano shock-absorbers. Twin nose-wheel unit retracts forward. Each main unit has a four-wheel bogie and retracts inward. Goodyear, Firestone, Kléber-Colombes, Dunlop or Goodrich nose-wheel tyres, size 26 × 7·75-13. Main wheels and tubeless tyres of Goodyear, Dunlop, Firestone or Kléber-Colombes manufacture, size 35 × 9·00-17. Depending on type of tyre and AUW, nose-wheel tyre pressures vary from 85 to 109 lb/sq in (6·0 to 7·6 kg/cm²). Similarly, pressure in front main bogies varies from 100 to 117 lb/sq in (7·0 to 8·2 kg/cm²) and in rear main bogies from 155 to 182 lb/sq in (10·9 to 12·8 kg/cm²). Hydraulic retraction. Maxaret anti-skid brakes on main wheels.

POWER PLANT: Two turbojet or turbofan engines mounted in nacelles on each side of the rear fuselage just ahead of tail unit (details under "Series" descriptions above). Fuel in four integral tanks in wings, with total capacity of 4,180 Imp gallons (19,000 litres). Super B has provision for additional centre tank, increasing total capacity to 4,840 Imp gallons (22,000 litres).

ACCOMMODATION: Crew compartment for two or three persons. Details of passenger accommodation under "Series" descriptions above. Entire accommodation pressurised. Main access to cabin aft through door under rear fuselage with hydraulically-operated integral steps. Steps serve as tail support when lowered. Further door on port side at front of cabin. Two toilets, coat rooms and light baggage racks aft of cabin. Two galleys, one forward and one aft of cabin.

SYSTEMS: Air-conditioning system utilises two turbo-compressors, driven by engine-bleed air, and includes a cold air unit. Pressure differential 8·25 lb/sq in (0·58 kg/cm²). Hydraulic system, pressure 2,500 lb/sq in (175 kg/cm²), for landing gear actuation, nose-wheel steering, brakes, flying controls and air-brakes. Electrical system includes two 30V DC engine-driven generators and inverters for 115V 400 c/s AC. Series 12 and Super B have APU for engine starting, air-conditioning of flight deck and cabin on ground and in flight up to max cruising altitude, and operation of a third 40kVA alternator both on the ground and in the air. Provision for Aérospatiale/Lear automatic landing system for operation in Category IIIA weather conditions.

DIMENSIONS, EXTERNAL:

Wing span	112 ft 6 in (34·30 m)
Wing aspect ratio	8·02
Wing chord at root (except Srs 12 and Super B)	
	20 ft 9 in (6·33 m)
Wing chord at tip	7 ft 4 in (2·23 m)

Length overall:

Srs III, VI, 10 R	105 ft 0 in (32·01 m)
Srs 11 R	107 ft 4 in (32·71 m)
Srs 12	118 ft 10½ in (36·24 m)
Super B	108 ft 3½ in (33·01 m)

Height overall:

except Srs 12 and Super B	28 ft 7 in (8·72 m)
Srs 12 and Super B	29 ft 7 in (9·01 m)

Tailplane span:

except Srs 12 and Super B	
	34 ft 9 in (10·60 m)
Srs 12 and Super B	39 ft 4 in (12·00 m)
Wheel track (c/l of shock-struts)	
	17 ft 0 in (5·21 m)

Wheelbase:

Srs III, VI, 10 R	38 ft 7 in (11·79 m)
Srs 11 R	41 ft 8¾ in (12·72 m)
Srs 12	48 ft 6½ in (14·80 m)
Super B	41 ft 0 in (12·50 m)

Passenger door (fwd, port):

Height	5 ft 6½ in (1·69 m)
Width	3 ft 0 in (0·91 m)
Height to sill	7 ft 8½ in (2·35 m)

Crew door (fwd, stbd):

Height	4 ft 0 in (1·22 m)
Width	2 ft 0 in (0·61 m)

Cargo compartment doors (underfloor, stbd):

Height	3 ft 0 in (0·91 m)
Width	2 ft 6 in (0·76 m)

DIMENSIONS, INTERNAL:

Cabin, excluding flight deck:

Length:

Srs III, VI, 10 R	73 ft 8½ in (22·50 m)
Srs 11 R	76 ft 8½ in (23·37 m)
Srs 12 (incl toilet and rear compartments)	
	86 ft 7 in (26·40 m)
Srs 12 (excl toilet and rear compartments)	
	72 ft 11 in (22·24 m)
Super B	76 ft 11½ in (23·45 m)

Width at floor:

except Srs 12	8 ft 11 in (2·72 m)
Srs 12	8 ft 10 in (2·69 m)
Width at arm-rest	9 ft 9¼ in (3·0 m)
Max height	6 ft 7 in (2·00 m)

Floor area:

Srs III, VI, 10 R	646 sq ft (60·0 m²)
Srs 11 R	670 sq ft (62·25 m²)
Srs 12	767 sq ft (71·28 m²)
Super B	675 sq ft (62·7 m²)

Volume:

Srs III, VI, 10 R	3,885 cu ft (110 m³)
Srs 11 R	4,379 cu ft (124 m³)
Srs 12	5,015 cu ft (142 m³)
Super B	4,414 cu ft (125 m³)

Freight holds (main cabin):

except Super B	201 cu ft (5·70 m³)
Super B	153 cu ft (4·33 m³)

Freight holds (underfloor):

Srs III	339 cu ft (9·60 m³)
Srs VI, 10 R	374 cu ft (10·60 m³)
Srs 12 (rear)	176 cu ft (5·00 m³)
Srs 12 (fwd)	406 cu ft (11·50 m³)
Super B	423 cu ft (12·00 m³)

AREAS:

Wings, gross	1,579 sq ft (146·7 m²)
Ailerons (total)	84·4 sq ft (7·84 m²)
Trailing-edge flaps (total)	265·8 sq ft (24·70 m²)
Fin	107·6 sq ft (10·0 m²)
Rudder	59·2 sq ft (5·5 m²)
Tailplane	232·0 sq ft (21·55 m²)
Elevators	69·4 sq ft (6·45 m²)

WEIGHTS AND LOADINGS:

Manufacturer's weight empty:

Srs III	53,320 lb (24,185 kg)
Srs VI-N	54,922 lb (24,915 kg)
Srs VI-R	57,935 lb (26,280 kg)
Srs 10 R	58,920 lb (26,725 kg)
Srs 11 R	63,585 lb (28,841 kg)
Srs 12	65,050 lb (29,500 kg)
Super B	60,897 lb (27,623 kg)

Basic operating weight:

Srs III	59,985 lb (27,210 kg)
Srs VI-N	60,250 lb (27,330 kg)
Srs VI-R	63,175 lb (28,655 kg)
Srs 10 R	64,100 lb (29,075 kg)
Srs 12	70,100 lb (31,800 kg)
Super B	66,260 lb (30,055 kg)

Max payload:

Srs III	18,520 lb (8,400 kg)
Srs VI-N	17,415 lb (7,900 kg)
Srs VI-R	18,080 lb (8,200 kg)
Srs 10 R	20,720 lb (9,400 kg)
Srs 11 R	20,050 lb (9,095 kg)
Srs 12	29,100 lb (13,200 kg)
Super B	20,060 lb (9,100 kg)

Max T-O weight:

Srs III	101,413 lb (46,000 kg)
Srs VI-N	105,822 lb (48,000 kg)
Srs VI-R	110,230 lb (50,000 kg)
Srs 10 R, 11 R, Super B (standard u/c)	
	114,640 lb (52,000 kg)
Srs 10 R, 11 R, Super B (strengthened u/c)	
	119,050 lb (54,000 kg)
Srs 12	123,460 lb (56,000 kg)
Super B*	123,460 lb (56,000 kg)

*certification at this AUW was imminent in the Spring of 1970.

Max landing weight:

Srs III	96,560 lb (43,800 kg)
Srs VI-N	100,750 lb (45,700 kg)
Srs VI-R	104,990 lb (47,620 kg)
Srs 10 R, 11 R, 12, Super B	
	109,130 lb (49,500 kg)

Max zero-fuel weight:

Srs III, VI-N	78,260 lb (35,500 kg)
Srs VI-R	81,570 lb (37,000 kg)
Srs 10 R	84,880 lb (38,500 kg)
Srs 11 R	88,185 lb (40,000 kg)
Srs 12	99,200 lb (45,000 kg)
Super B	87,080 lb (39,500 kg)

Max wing loading:

Srs III	64·2 lb/sq ft (313 kg/m²)
Srs VI-N	66·8 lb/sq ft (326 kg/m²)

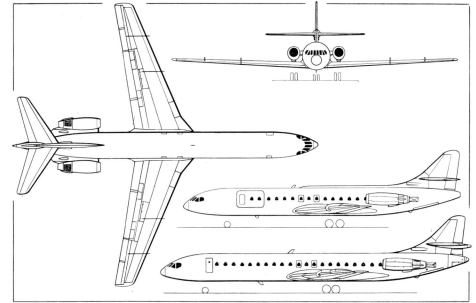

Aérospatiale SE 210 Caravelle 12 medium-range twin-jet airliner, with additional side elevation (upper) of Caravelle 11R

Aérospatiale Caravelle Super B airliner (two Pratt & Whitney JT8D-7 turbofan engines) in the insignia of Syrian Arab Airlines

Srs VI-R	69·8 lb/sq ft (341 kg/m²)
Srs 10 R, 11 R	72·6 lb/sq ft (354 kg/m²)
Srs 12	78·0 lb/sq ft (381 kg/m²)
Super B	75·4 lb/sq ft (368 kg/m²)

Max power loading:

Srs III	4·44 lb/lb st (4·44 kg/kg st)
Srs VI-N	4·33 lb/lb st (4·33 kg/kg st)
Srs VI-R	4·37 lb/lb st (4·37 kg/kg st)
Srs 10 R, 11 R	4·10 lb/lb st (4·10 kg/kg st)
Srs 12, Super B	4·25 lb/lb st (4·25 kg/kg st)

PERFORMANCE:

Max cruising speed at 25,000 ft (7,620 m):
- Srs III at AUW of 90,000 lb (40,820 kg)
  434 knots (500 mph; 805 km/h)
- Srs VI-N at AUW of 92,000 lb (41,730 kg)
  456 knots (525 mph; 845 km/h)
- Srs VI-R at AUW of 94,800 lb (43,000 kg)
  456 knots (525 mph; 845 km/h)
- Srs 10 R at AUW of 104,170 lb (47,250 kg)
  432 knots (497 mph; 800 km/h)
- Srs 11 R at AUW of 114,640 lb (52,000 kg)
  432 knots (497 mph; 800 km/h)
- Srs 12 at AUW of 110,230 lb (50,000 kg)
  437 knots (503 mph; 810 km/h)
- Super B at AUW of 114,640 lb (52,000 kg)
  445 knots (512 mph; 825 km/h)

Best-cost cruising speed at 35,000 ft (10,670 m):
- Srs III at AUW of 94,250 lb (42,750 kg)
  391 knots (450 mph; 725 km/h)
- Srs VI-N at AUW of 96,450 lb (43,750 kg)
  426 knots (490 mph; 790 km/h)
- Srs VI-R at AUW of 100,310 lb (45,500 kg)
  424 knots (488 mph; 785 km/h)
- Srs 10 R at AUW of 104,170 lb (47,250 kg)
  405 knots (466 mph; 750 km/h)
- Super B at AUW of 105,270 lb (47,750 kg)
  432 knots (497 mph; 800 km/h)

T-O distance at max T-O weight:

Srs III	6,000 ft (1,830 m)
Srs VI-N	6,400 ft (1,950 m)
Srs VI-R	6,800 ft (2,073 m)
Srs 10 R (AUW of 114,640 lb=52,000 kg)	
	6,400 ft (1,950 m)

T-O balanced field length at max T-O weight:

Srs 11 R (CAR)	6,400 ft (1,950 m)
Srs 12 (ISA at S/L)	7,345 ft (2,240 m)
Srs 12 (ISA+15°C)	7,805 ft (2,380 m)
Super B (SR 422 B)	6,850 ft (2,090 m)

Landing distance at max landing weight:

Srs III	5,900 ft (1,800 m)
Srs VI-N	6,450 ft (1,965 m)
Srs VI-R	5,650 ft (1,720 m)
Srs 10 R	5,315 ft (1,620 m)
Srs 11 R	5,085 ft (1,550 m)
Super B	5,180 ft (1,580 m)

Landing distance at AUW of 108,025 lb (49,000 kg), ISA at S/L:

Srs 12	5,150 ft (1,570 m)

Range with 16,800 lb (7,620 kg) payload, 260 nm (300 mile; 480 km) diversion and SR 427 reserves:

Srs III	995 nm (1,146 miles; 1,845 km)

Srs VI-N	1,350 nm (1,553 miles; 2,500 km)
Srs VI-R	1,380 nm (1,590 miles; 2,560 km)
Srs 10 R	1,780 nm (2,050 miles; 3,295 km)
Super B	1,758 nm (2,025 miles; 3,260 km)

Range with 18,850 lb (8,550 kg) payload, max fuel, no reserves:

Srs 12	2,055 nm (2,367 miles; 3,810 km)

Range with 18,850 lb (8,550 kg) payload, reserves for 199 nm (230 miles; 370 km) diversion:

Srs 12	1,478 nm (1,702 miles; 2,740 km)

Range with max payload, 260 nm (300 mile; 480 km) diversion and SR 427 reserves:

Srs III	915 nm (1,056 miles; 1,700 km)
Srs VI-N	1,270 nm (1,460 miles; 2,350 km)
Srs VI-R	1,240 nm (1,430 miles; 2,300 km)
Srs 10 R (at 114,640 lb=52,000 kg AUW)	1,565 nm (1,800 miles; 2,900 km)
Srs 10 R (at 119,050 lb=54,000 kg AUW)	1,865 nm (2,145 miles; 3,455 km)
Super B	1,435 nm (1,650 miles; 2,655 km)

Range with max payload, with reserves:

Srs 11 R (at 114,640 lb=52,000 kg AUW)	1,241 nm (1,430 miles; 2,300 km)
Srs 11 R (at 119,050 lb = 54,000 kg AUW)	1,511 nm (1,740 miles; 2,800 km)

Range with max payload, reserves for 199 nm (230 miles; 370 km) diversion:

Srs 12	872 nm (1,005 miles; 1,620 km)

Range with max payload, no reserves:

Srs 12	1,428 nm (1,645 miles; 2,650 km)

AÉROSPATIALE N 262

The N 262 twin-engined pressurised light transport is developed from the earlier unpressurised Nord 260 Super Broussard, of which a limited number only were built, and which are now used for liaison work and for flight testing of Turboméca Astazou turboprop engines.

Design of the N 262 began in the Spring of 1961, and the prototype (F-WKVR) flew for the first time on 24 December 1962. It was followed by three pre-production aircraft, the second of which was later used in airline service by Japan Domestic Airlines before being sold to Air Madagascar in 1966. The pre-production aircraft were built at Châtillon-sous-Bagneux and assembled at Nord's Melun-Villaroche flight test centre, but final assembly of production N 262s (which have a dorsal fin) is undertaken at Bourges.

In the Autumn of 1967 trials began with an N 262 equipped with SFENA-421 automatic landing equipment, enabling landings to be made in Category IIIA weather conditions.

In 1969 two new versions were announced, designated Series C and D, making a total of four versions so far developed, as follows:

Series A. Standard early production version, with Bastan VIC turboprop engines. First

production Series A was airframe number 9 (F-WLHX), delivered to Lake Central Airlines (now Allegheny) on 17 August 1965. Preceded by Series B, as indicated below. Production continues. Described in 1969-70 *Jane's*.

Series B. Designation of first four production aircraft only, built for Air Inter. Same power plant as Series A. First Series B (F-BLHS, airframe number 4) flown for first time on 8 June 1964. Received SGAC certification on 16 July 1964 and FAA Type Approval on 15 March 1965. Entered service 24 July 1964.

Series C. Civil version, with more powerful Bastan VIIA turboprop engines, having improved single-engine ceiling, cruising speed and T-O performance at "hot and high" airfields. New power plant dispenses with water-methanol system of Series A and B and has higher initial TBO. An N 262 (airframe number 36) began flying experimentally with this power plant in July 1968, and has more recently been test-flown with new wing-tips (see general arrangement drawing) which bestow improved low-speed handling. The Series C is to be introduced on to the production line in 1970, alongside the Series A, from the 74th aircraft. First customer for a Series C has not yet been disclosed; delivery is scheduled to begin in late 1970. Described in detail below.

Series D. Military counterpart to Series C. Eighteen ordered for French Air Force in Spring of 1969, for training and liaison duties.

By 27 May 1970 firm orders for N 262s totalled 97, as listed below. Of these, 53 had been delivered.

Series A

Air Ceylon	1
Air Comores	2
Air Madagascar	1
Alisarda (Italy)	2
Allegheny Airlines (USA)*	12
CEV Brétigny (France)	1
Cimber Air (Denmark)	2
Ecole Nationale Supérieure de l'Aéronautique (France)	1
Europe Aéro Service	1
Filipinas Orient Airlines	3
French Air Force	6
French Navy	15
Interregionalflug (W Germany)	2
Linjeflyg (Sweden)	4
Luftfartsdirektoratet (Denmark)	1
Rousseau Aviation (France)	2
SFA (France)	8
Tunis Air	1

Series B

Air Inter (Rousseau Aviation)	4

Series C

Undisclosed	10

Series D

French Air Force	18

Originally purchased by Lake Central before merger with Allegheny; four sold to BC Airlines (Canada).

TYPE: Twin-engined light transport.

WINGS: Cantilever high-wing monoplane. Wing section NACA 23016 (modified) at root, NACA 23012 (modified) at tip. Dihedral 3° from root. Incidence 3°. No sweepback. All-metal two-spar fail-safe structure in conventional light alloys. Sealed all-metal ailerons. Balance tab in starboard aileron. Electrically-controlled hydraulically-actuated all-metal three-position flaps in inner and outer sections on each trailing-edge. Kléber-Colombes (Goodrich licence) pneumatic de-icing boots on outer leading-edges.

FUSELAGE: Semi-monocoque light alloy fail-safe structure, built up from 39 circular main and secondary frames, covered with skin panels arranged circumferentially in sets of four. Max external diameter 8 ft 0½ in (2·45 m).

TAIL UNIT: Cantilever metal structure, built as separate unit and bolted to rear fuselage frame. Fixed-incidence tailplane. Control surfaces fabric-covered. One controllable tab and one balance tab in rudder and each elevator. Kléber-Colombes (Goodrich licence) pneumatic de-icing system on leading-edges.

LANDING GEAR: Retractable tricycle type, designed and manufactured by ERAM, with single wheel on each unit. Electro-hydraulic retraction, nose-wheel forward, main wheels rearward into fairings on sides of fuselage. ERAM oleo-pneumatic nitrogen-filled shock-absorbers. Main wheels have Dunlop or Kléber-Colombes tyres size 12·50 × 16, pressure 59 lb/sq in (4 kg/cm²). Nose-wheel has Dunlop or Kléber-Colombes Type 06 tyre, size 9·00 × 6, pressure 51 lb/sq in (3·5 kg/cm²). Goodyear hydraulic disc brakes, with anti-skid units. Self-centering nose-wheel is fitted with shimmy damper and is steerable hydraulically.

POWER PLANT: Two 1,130 ehp Turboméca Bastan VIIA turboprop engines (Series C and D), each driving a Ratier Forest FH 206-1 four-blade constant-speed variable-pitch fully-feathering metal propeller, diameter 10 ft 6 in (3·20 m). Fuel in six flexible bag-type tanks between wing spars, forming two groups of three tanks with provision for cross-feed and having a total usable capacity of 440 Imp gallons (2,000 litres). Provision for two additional optional bag tanks in wings centre-section, each of 62·5 Imp gallons (285 litres) usable capacity, giving a max usable capacity of 565 Imp gallons (2,750 litres). Refuelling point above outer wing tank on each side. Pressure refuelling point at front of starboard side main landing gear fairing. No fuel dump system. Oil capacity 5 Imp gallons (23 litres). Pneumatic anti-icing of engine intakes and propellers.

ACCOMMODATION: Crew of two on flight deck, with central jump-seat at rear for a third crew member if carried. Standard airline version has seating for 26 passengers at 32 in (81 cm) pitch, maximum seating for 29 at 28 in (71 cm) pitch, in three-abreast rows, with two seats on starboard side of aisle and single seat on port side. Movable forward bulkhead, to cater for variable mixed cargo (in front)/passenger (at rear) layouts. Bulkhead can be located in two intermediate positions, to provide 20 or 14 seats at 32 in pitch in rear of cabin, with 342 cu ft (9·7 m³) or 467 cu ft (13·2 m³) of cargo space respectively in front part of cabin. Galley, toilet and (on 27-seat version) separate coat space at rear of cabin. For quick-change passenger/cargo operation, foldaway seats can be installed which, when folded, give an available width for cargo of 5 ft 6 in (1·68 m) throughout entire cabin length. Alternative layouts include a six-person executive suite forward with 10 passengers aft; ambulance version with accommodation for 12 stretchers and two medical attendants; or aerial survey version with wide range of cameras and survey equipment and fully-equipped darkroom. Army versions can be fitted out to carry 18 paratroops or 29 troops, or as 22-seat transports. Naval versions (Series A) are capable of being fitted out for target towing, artillery and missile observation, radar calibration or crew training duties. Standard transport versions have two-section passenger door at rear on port side, the lower half of which has built-in airstairs, and a large cargo door at front on the port side. Emergency exits at front of cabin on each side, at rear on starboard side, and on port side of flight deck. Standard baggage compartments between flight deck and cabin on each side; on 27-seat version these are smaller, but additional baggage space is provided at rear of cabin on starboard side. All accommodation is pressurised, soundproofed and air-conditioned.

SYSTEMS: SEMCA air-conditioning system using bleed-air from engine. Max pressure differential 4·20 lb/sq in (0·29 kg/cm²). Auxiliary ventilation via ram-air inlet at front of port main landing gear fairing. Hydraulic system, operated by two engine-driven pumps at pressure of 2,900 lb/sq in (200 kg/cm²), actuates landing gear, nose-wheel steering, flaps, brakes and gust locks. Electrically-driven (27V DC) back-up pump and 1,450 lb/sq in (100 kg/cm²) surge accumulator. Hand pump for emergency operation of flaps, landing gear and gust locks. Pneumatic system for de-icing only. Two 24V 40Ah nickel-cadmium batteries, in rear fuselage, and two 9kW engine-driven starter-generators provide 28·5V DC electrical supply for engine starting, feathering pumps and rotary inverters. External 28V DC power receptacle. AC system includes two 12kVA three-phase alternators providing 115/120V 400 c/s power for engine anti-icing, windshield heating and de-icing, and heating for galley. Two single-phase 750VA rotary inverters provide continuous AC supply for flight deck instruments. System also includes four 115/26V 400 c/s auto-transformers. Optional Microturbo Saphir II APU in unpressurised section of rear fuselage provides power for electrical services, engine starting and cabin air-conditioning.

ELECTRONICS AND EQUIPMENT: Standard equipment includes two Collins 618 M 1 VHF, two Collins 51 RV 1 VOR/ILS, Collins 51 Z 4 marker beacon receiver, Collins DF 203 ADF, Collins FD 108 flight director, SFIM A 213 flight recorder, Sperry C 14 gyro compass, two Allen RMI, one Bendix OMI, interphone and public address systems. Emergency equipment includes oxygen masks and cylinders, fire extinguishers, life rafts and radio set. Optional equipment includes HF radio, autopilot, second gyro compass, second ADF, weather radar, ATC transponder, radio altimeter and DME; and alternative choice of flight director/recorder, VHF, VOR/ILS, and marker beacon receiver.

DIMENSIONS, EXTERNAL:
Wing span	71 ft 10 in (21·90 m)
Wing chord at root	10 ft 2 in (3·10 m)
Wing chord at tip	5 ft 11 in (1·80 m)

Aérospatiale N 262 Series A twin-turboprop transport aircraft in French Air Force insignia

Aérospatiale N 262 Series C light transport (two 1,130 ehp Turboméca Bastan VIIA turboprop engines)
(*Air Portraits*)

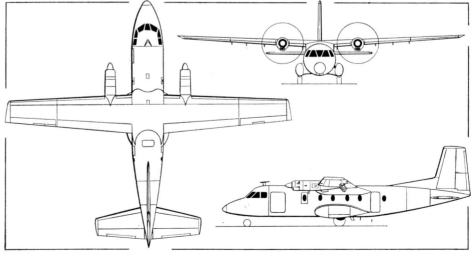
Aérospatiale N 262 Series C twin-turboprop pressurised light transport

Wing aspect ratio 8·72
Length overall 63 ft 3 in (19·28 m)
Height over tail 20 ft 4 in (6·21 m)
Tailplane span 25 ft 9 in (7·84 m)
Wheel track 10 ft 3 in (3·13 m)
Wheelbase 23 ft 9 in (7·23 m)
Passenger door (rear, port):
  Height 5 ft 5¼ in (1·66 m)
  Width 2 ft 3 in (0·68 m)
  Height to sill 3 ft 6½ in (1·08 m)
Cargo door (forward, port):
  Height 5 ft 0¼ in (1·53 m)
  Width 4 ft 2½ in (1·28 m)
  Height to sill 3 ft 6½ in (1·08 m)
Emergency exit doors (fwd, port and stbd):
  Height 3 ft 8¼ in (1·38 m)
  Width 1 ft 8 in (0·51 m)
Emergency exit door (aft, stbd):
  Height 3 ft 0¼ in (0·92 m)
  Width 1 ft 8 in (0·51 m)

Dimensions, internal:
Cabin, including baggage space and toilet:
  Length 34 ft 10 in (10·61 m)
  Max width 7 ft 1 in (2·15 m)
  Width at floor 5 ft 5¼ in (1·66 m)
  Max height 5 ft 11 in (1·80 m)
  Floor area 183 sq ft (17·0 m²)
  Volume 1,146 cu ft (32·5 m³)
Baggage hold (port):
  26 or 29 passengers 67 cu ft (1·9 m³)
  27 passengers 62 cu ft (1·75 m³)
Baggage hold (stbd):
  26 or 29 passengers 92 cu ft (2·6 m³)
  27 passengers 67 cu ft (1·9 m³)
Baggage hold (rear)
  27-passenger version only 46 cu ft (1.3 m³)

Areas:
Wings, gross 592 sq ft (55·0 m²)
Ailerons (total) 43·8 sq ft (4·07 m²)
Trailing-edge flaps (total) 96·6 sq ft (8·98 m²)
Fin 108·7 sq ft (10·1 m²)
Rudder, incl tabs 40·4 sq ft (3·75 m²)
Tailplane 169·0 sq ft (15·7 m²)
Elevators, incl tabs 48·8 sq ft (4·54 m²)

Weights and Loadings:
Basic weight empty 13,613 lb (6,175 kg)
Manufacturer's weight empty, equipped 15,286 lb (6,934 kg)
Basic operating weight 15,873 lb (7,200 kg)
Max payload 6,834 lb (3,100 kg)
Max T-O weight 23,370 lb (10,600 kg)
Max ramp weight 23,480 lb (10,650 kg)
Max zero-fuel and landing weight 22,710 lb (10,300 kg)
Max wing loading 39·5 lb/sq ft (193 kg/m²)
Max power loading 10·4 lb/ehp (4·7 kg/ehp)

Performance (at max T-O weight, except where indicated):
Max level speed 225 knots (260 mph; 418 km/h)
Max and econ cruising speed 220 knots (254 mph; 408 km/h)
Normal operating limit speed 214 knots (247 mph; 397 km/h)
Max speed with landing gear extended 154 knots (177 mph; 285 km/h)
Max speed with 15° flap 143 knots (165 mph; 265 km/h)
Max speed with 35° flap 126 knots (146 mph; 235 km/h)
Final approach speed 90 knots (104 mph; 167 km/h)
Stalling speed, flaps up, at max landing weight 87 knots (100 mph; 160 km/h)
Stalling speed, wheels and flaps down, at max landing weight 72 knots (83 mph; 133 km/h)
Rate of climb at S/L 1,496 ft (456 m)/min
Service ceiling 26,250 ft (8,000 m)
Service ceiling, one engine out 19,500 ft (5,940 m)
T-O run 3,035 ft (925 m)
T-O to 35 ft (10·7 m) 4,050 ft (1,235 m)
Landing from 50 ft (15 m) 1,640 ft (500 m)
Landing run 1,065 ft (325 m)
Range with max fuel, no reserves 1,295 nm (1,490 miles; 2,400 km)
Range with max fuel, FAA reserves 985 nm (1,135 miles; 1,825 km)
Range with max payload of 29 passengers and baggage, no reserves 565 nm (650 miles; 1,050 km)
Range with max payload of 29 passengers and baggage, FAA reserves 350 nm (405 miles; 650 km)

AÉROSPATIALE SN 600 CORVETTE

The Corvette has been designed as a multi-purpose aircraft, powered initially by two rear-mounted JT15D-1 turbofan engines. It is intended to fulfil a variety of roles, including executive transport, air taxi, ambulance, freighter or training aircraft. The initial version is designed to carry up to 13 passengers, plus baggage, and construction of a prototype began early in 1969. This aircraft, to which the details below apply, was scheduled to fly during the third quarter of 1970 and to receive type certification by mid-1971.

Two other versions of the Corvette are currently under consideration, powered respectively by two 2,550 lb (1,156 kg) st JT15D-3 or two flat-rated 2,314 lb (1,050 kg) st SNECMA/Turboméca Larzac turbofan engines. These each have a design max T-O weight of 13,007 lb (5,900 kg), and improved T-O and climb performance, a higher cruising speed of 439 knots (506 mph; 815 km/h) and a greater range with the same max payload as the prototype.

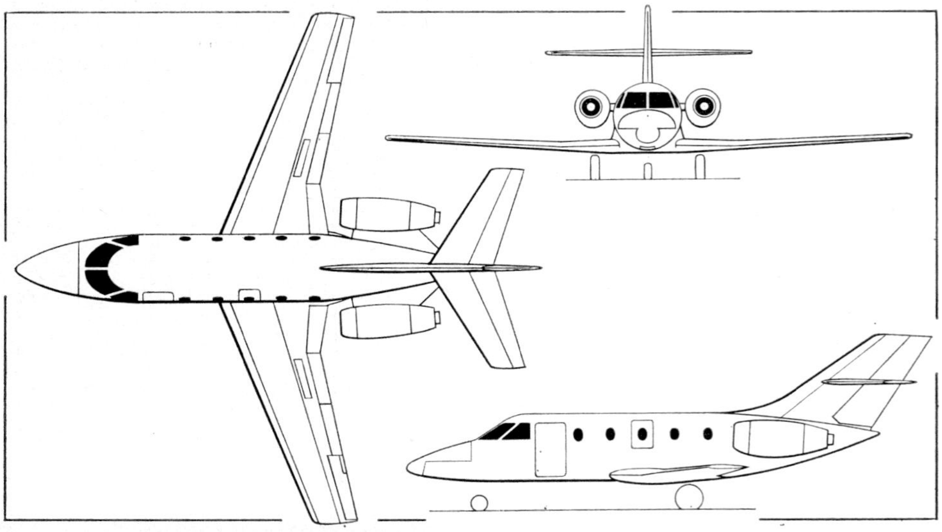

Aérospatiale SN 600 Corvette twin-turbofan multi-purpose transport

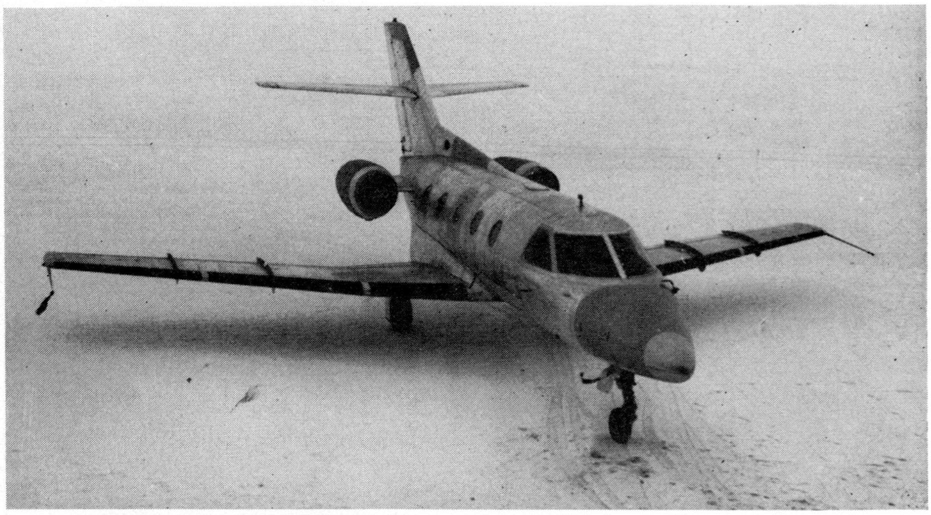

Prototype of the Aérospatiale SN 600 Corvette twin-turbofan multi-purpose transport

Type: Multi-purpose twin-turbofan aircraft.

Wings: Cantilever low-wing monoplane of all-metal construction. Thickness/chord ratio 13·65% at root, 11·5% at tip. Dihedral 3° 6′. Incidence 1° 45′ at root, 0° 31·8′ at tip. Sweepback 22° 39′ on leading-edge. Conventional two-spar fail-safe structure, of aluminium alloy. Manually-operated aluminium alloy ailerons and double-slotted long-travel trailing-edge flaps of aluminium alloy and honeycomb construction. Guillotine-type spoiler forward of each outer flap; air-brakes above and below each wing. Electrically operated trim-tab in port aileron. Pneumatic de-icing of leading-edges.

Fuselage: Aluminium alloy semi-monocoque fail-safe structure of circular cross-section.

Tail Unit: Cantilever aluminium alloy structure, with tailplane mounted half-way up fin. Sweepback on all surfaces. Electrically-actuated variable-incidence tailplane. Manually-operated elevators and rudder. No tabs.

Landing Gear: Retractable tricycle type, with hydraulic shock-absorbers and single wheel on each unit. Main wheels retract inward, nose-wheel forward, into fuselage. Low-pressure tyres on all wheels, nose-wheel pressure 46 lb/sq in (3·26 kg/cm²), main wheel pressure 65 lb/sq in (4·6 kg/cm²). Hydraulic brakes and Maxaret anti-skid units. Nose-wheel steerable.

Power Plant: Two Pratt & Whitney (UACL) JT15D-1 turbofan engines (each 2,200 lb = 1,000 kg st) mounted in pods on each side of rear fuselage. Fuel in two integral wing tanks with total capacity of 370 Imp gallons (1,680 litres). Provision for two auxiliary wing tanks, each of approx 59 Imp gallons (270 litres) capacity.

Accommodation: Crew of one or two on flight deck. Normal seating for 6 to 13 passengers in single seats on each side of centre aisle. Galley, toilet and baggage compartments available to customer's requirements. Up-ward-hinged door, with built-in airstairs, at front on port side. Larger cargo door optional. Cabin heating and air-conditioning standard.

Systems: Cabin pressurisation maintained at a max differential of 8 lb/sq in (0·56 kg/cm²). Hydraulic system for brakes and nose-wheel steering. Main electrical system includes two 9kW 28·5V DC starter-generators, one 40Ah battery and two inverters for 400 c/s AC supply.

Electronics and Equipment: Blind-flying instrumentation standard. Radio, radar or other special equipment to customer's specification.

Dimensions, external:
Wing span 42 ft 0 in (12·80 m)
Wing chord at root 7 ft 9½ in (2·37 m)
Wing chord at tip 3 ft 5¾ in (1·06 m)
Wing aspect ratio 7·45
Length overall 41 ft 11½ in (12·79 m)
Length of fuselage 37 ft 8 in (11·48 m)
Height overall 14 ft 4 in (4·37 m)
Tailplane span 16 ft 4⅞ in (5·00 m)
Wheel track 8 ft 5¼ in (2·57 m)
Wheelbase 16 ft 9½ in (5·12 m)
Passenger door: Height 4 ft 8¾ in (1·44 m)
  Width 2 ft 5½ in (0·75 m)
  Mean height to sill 2 ft 9½ in (0·85 m)
Cargo door (optional): Height 4 ft 8¾ in (1·44 m)
  Width 3 ft 9¼ in (1·15 m)
  Mean height to sill 2 ft 9½ in (0·85 m)

Dimensions, internal:
Cabin, excluding flight deck:
  Max length 18 ft 9½ in (5·73 m)
  Max width 5 ft 1½ in (1·56 m)
  Max height 5 ft 0 in (1·52 m)
  Volume 338 cu ft (9·58 m³)
  Baggage compartment volume (8-passenger layout): 39·5 cu ft (1·12 m³)

AREAS:
Wings, gross   236·8 sq ft (22·00 m²)
Vertical tail surfaces (total) 53·82 sq ft (5·00 m²)
Horizontal tail surfaces (total)
    64·58 sq ft (6·00 m²)

WEIGHTS:
Weight empty, equipped   7,297 lb (3,310 kg)
Max payload   2,493 lb (1,131 kg)
Max T-O weight   12,500 lb (5,670 kg)
Max zero-fuel weight   10,141 lb (4,600 kg)
Max landing weight   11,905 lb (5,400 kg)

PERFORMANCE (estimated, at max T-O weight):
Max level speed at 25,000 ft (7,620 m)
    407 knots (469 mph; 755 km/h)
Max permissible diving speed
    431·5 knots (497 mph; 800 km/h)
Max cruising speed at 25,000 ft (7,620 m)
    405 knots (466 mph; 750 km/h)
Econ cruising speed at 36,100 ft (11,000 m)
    340 knots (391 mph; 630 km/h)
Stalling speed, flaps down
    75 knots (85·5 mph; 137 km/h)
Rate of climb at S/L   3,248 ft (990 m)/min
Service ceiling   39,900 ft (12,160 m)
T-O run (FAR 23, ISA at S/L)
    3,034 ft (925 m)
T-O balanced field length (FAR 25)
    3,839 ft (1,170 m)
Landing run (FAR 25)   1,936 ft (590 m)
Max range with auxiliary tanks, 45 min reserves
    1,526 nm (1,758 miles; 2,830 km)
Range with 13 passengers (max payload), 45
  min reserves   660 nm (760 miles; 1,224 km)

AÉROSPATIALE CM 170 MAGISTER AND SUPER MAGISTER

The Magister is a light two-seat twin-jet trainer, which was developed originally for the French Air Force. The contract for three prototypes was signed on 27 June 1951, and the first of these flew for the first time on 23 July 1952. A pre-production order for ten aircraft was placed in June 1953 and the first aircraft of this order made its maiden flight on 7 July 1954.

The initial series production order for 95 aircraft was signed on 13 January 1954, and the first of these aircraft flew at Toulouse on 29 February 1956. Subsequent contracts have increased the total number of Magister-series aircraft built to 916, as follows:

French Air Force (including prototypes)	400
French Test Centre	5
French Navy (including 2 prototypes)	32
Brazil	7
Germany	250
Israel	52
Austria	18
Finland	82
Belgium and Holland	48
Cambodia	4
Congo, Leopoldville	6
Morocco (handed over by French AF)	8
Lebanon	4

Of the German Magisters, 188 were built under licence by Flugzeug-Union-Süd. Similarly, 62 of the Finnish aircraft were built by Valmet OY and 36 of the Israeli aircraft by Israel Aircraft Industries.

The aircraft for the French Navy are specially equipped for deck operation and are designated CM 175 Zéphyr. Details can be found in the 1962-63 Jane's.

There are two versions of the CM 170, as follows:

CM 170 Magister. Basic version with two 880 lb (400 kg) st Marboré IIA turbojets. Described in 1969-70 Jane's.

CM 170 Super Magister. Similar to Magister, but with 1,058 lb (480 kg) st Marboré VI turbojets. First flown on 28 August 1962. Latest orders for 130 aircraft for French Air Force, included in totals above, and seven for Brazil, are for this model, which continues in production.

The following details refer to the Super Magister.

TYPE: Light twin-jet two-seat trainer.

WINGS: Cantilever mid-wing monoplane. NACA 64 Series wing section, thickness/chord ratio varying from 19% at root to 12% at tip. No dihedral. Incidence 2°. Leading-edge sweepback 13°. Single-spar aluminium-alloy stressed-skin structure. Hydraulically-operated all-metal slotted flaps. Automatic tabs in ailerons. All but early production aircraft have servo-control ailerons. Retractable air-brakes in upper and lower surfaces.

FUSELAGE: All-metal semi-monocoque stressed-skin structure.

TAIL UNIT: Butterfly type, with included angle of 110°. All-metal single-spar structure. Statically and aerodynamically balanced elevators.

CM 170 Super Magister two-seat jet trainer in the insignia of the *Esquadrilha da Fumaca* aerobatic team of the Brazilian Air Force, by whom it is designated T-24 (*Ronaldo S. Olive*)

LANDING GEAR: Messier retractable tricycle type. Hydraulic actuation. Nose-wheel has anti-shimmy device. Messier wheels and hydraulic brakes. Main wheels size 480 × 180 mm. Nose wheel size 350 × 130 mm.

POWER PLANT: Two Turboméca Marboré turbojet engines (details under model descriptions above). Main fuel in two fuselage tanks of 56 Imp gallons (255 litres) and 104 Imp gallons (475 litres) capacity respectively. Total internal fuel capacity 160 Imp gallons (730 litres). Two non-jettisonable wing-tip tanks (27·5 Imp gallons=125 litres each) are standard. For ferrying, two larger wing-tip tanks (50 Imp gallons=230 litres each) may be fitted. Oil capacity 5·37 Imp gallons (24·4 litres).

ACCOMMODATION: Tandem cockpits under transparent canopy. Jettisonable hinged sections over cockpits open upward and rearward. Pupil in front seat, instructor in rear. All flying, brake and engine controls duplicated. Emergency landing gear and air-brake controls in front cockpit only.

SYSTEMS: Cockpits pressurised and air-conditioned by SEMCA turbo-refrigeration equipment driven by air bleeds from engine compressors. Individual oxygen supply with regulator in each cockpit.

ELECTRONICS AND EQUIPMENT: UHF and VHF radio, VOR, IFF, radio compass, inter-phone, and blind-flying equipment standard. Provision for TACAN navigation equipment in place of radio compass.

ARMAMENT: Two 7·5 or 7·62 mm machine-guns (200 rpg) in fuselage nose. Gyro gunsight in each cockpit, that in rear cockpit fitted with additional periscopic sight. Racks for two 55 lb (25 kg) air-to-ground rockets, one type 181 Matra launcher with 18 × 37 mm rockets, one launcher with 7 × 68 mm rockets, one 110 lb (50 kg) bomb or one Nord AS.11 guided missile may be fitted under each wing.

DIMENSIONS, EXTERNAL:
Wing span (with tip tanks) 39 ft 10 in (12·15 m)
Wing span (without tip tanks) 37 ft 5 in (11·4 m)
Wing chord at root   6 ft 6 in (1·98 m)
Wing chord at tip   2 ft 10 in (0·87 m)
Wing aspect ratio   7·42
Length overall   33 ft 0 in (10·06 m)
Height over tail   9 ft 2 in (2·80 m)
Tail span   14 ft 4½ in (4·38 m)
Wheel track   12 ft 6¾ in (3·80 m)
Wheelbase   14 ft 9 in (4·49 m)

AREAS:
Wings, gross   186·1 sq ft (17·30 m²)
Ailerons (total)   11·84 sq ft (1·10 m²)
Flaps (total)   22·6 sq ft (2·10 m²)
Horizontal tail area (projected) 40 sq ft (3·71 m²)
Vertical tail area (projected) 28 sq ft (2·60 m²)

WEIGHTS:
Weight empty with fixed equipment
    5,093 lb (2,310 kg)
Average T-O weight, without external tanks
    6,280 lb (2,850 kg)
Average T-O weight with external tanks
    6,835 lb (3,100 kg)
Max T-O weight   7,187 lb (3,260 kg)

PERFORMANCE:
Max level speed at S/L
    378 knots (435 mph; 700 km/h)
Max level speed at 30,000 ft (9,000 m)
    392 knots (451 mph; 725 km/h)
Max permissible Mach No   0·82
Max permissible diving speed
    399 knots (460 mph; 740 km/h)
Max rate of climb at S/L:

at 2,850 kg AUW   3,935 ft (1,200 m)/min
at 3,100 kg AUW   3,740 ft (1,140 m)/min
Service ceiling at 3,100 kg AUW
    13,125 ft (12,000 m)
T-O run at 3,100 kg AUW   1,970 ft (600 m
T-O to 50 ft (15 m) at 3,100 kg AUW
    2,200 ft (670 m)

Range at 30,000 ft (9,000 m) with 26 Imp gallons (120 litres) fuel reserve:
at 2,850 kg AUW 490 nm (565 miles; 910 km)
at 3,100 kg AUW 755 nm (870 miles; 1,400 km)

Endurance at 30,000 ft (9,000 m) with reserves:
at 2,850 kg AUW   2 hr 0 min
at 3,100 kg AUW   2 hr 50 min

AÉROSPATIALE N 3202-B1B

This is the designation applied to a version of the Nord 3202 two-seat basic trainer (see 1961-62 Jane's) as modified for use in aerobatic competitions by the *Patrouille de l'Aviation Légère de l'Armée de Terre*.

Modifications include an increase in aileron area, the installation of a three-blade variable-pitch propeller, replacement of the original levered main landing gear units with conventional "straight" oleos and a reduction of some 440 lb (200 kg) in the gross weight. The general appearance of the Nord 3202-B1B can be seen in the adjacent illustration.

Aérospatiale N 3202-B1B, modified from the Nord 3202 for aerobatic flying (*Stephen P. Peltz*)

AÉROSPATIALE SA 318C ALOUETTE II ASTAZOU

Developed from the SE 313B Alouette II (described fully in the 1967-68 and 1968-69 editions of *Jane's*), the prototype Alouette II Astazou flew for the first time on 31 January 1961. Extension of the Alouette II airworthiness certificate to the Alouette II Astazou was granted subsequently in France (18 February 1964) and USA (25 November 1964). A total of 1,200 Alouette II's (923 Artouste, 277 Astazou) had been ordered by 21 May 1970. Of these, 1,114 (923 Artouste and 191 Astazou) had been delivered by 1 January 1970, including 450 to French civil operators and the French armed forces. Alouette II helicopters are currently being flown by 101 operators in 45 countries.

TYPE: Turbine-driven general-purpose helicopter.

ROTOR SYSTEM: Three-blade main rotor, two-blade anti-torque rotor. All-metal main rotor blades on articulated hinges, with hydraulic drag-hinge dampers. Blades may be folded towards the rear.

ROTOR DRIVE: Main rotor driven through planetary gearbox, with free-wheel for auto-rotation. Take-off drive for tail rotor at lower end of main gearbox, from where a torque shaft runs to a small gearbox which supports the tail rotor and houses the pitch-change mechanism. Cyclic and collective pitch controls are powered.

FUSELAGE: Glazed cabin has light metal frame. Centre and rear fuselage have a triangulated steel-tube framework.

LANDING GEAR: Skid type, with retractable wheel for ground manoeuvring, or wheel type. Pneumatic floats for normal operation from water and emergency flotation gear, inflatable in the air, are available.

POWER PLANT: One 530 shp Turboméca Astazou IIA turboshaft engine, derated to 360 shp and fitted with a centrifugal clutch. Fuel tank, capacity 127·5 Imp gallons (580 litres), in centre fuselage.

ACCOMMODATION: Glazed cabin seats pilot and passenger side-by-side in front and three passengers behind. Can be adapted, with a raised skid gear, for flying crane (payload 1,322 lb = 600 kg), rescue (hoist capacity 265 lb = 120 kg), liaison, observation, training, agricultural, photographic, ambulance and other duties. As an ambulance can accommodate two stretchers and a medical attendant internally.

DIMENSIONS, EXTERNAL:
Diameter of main rotor	33 ft 5⅝ in (10·20 m)
Diameter of tail rotor	6 ft 3 in (1·91 m)
Length overall, rotors turning	39 ft 8½ in (12·10 m)
Fuselage length, tail rotor turning	31 ft 11¾ in (9·75 m)
Width overall, blades folded	7 ft 6½ in (2·30 m)
Height overall	9 ft 0 in (2·75 m)
Skid track	7 ft 3 in (2·22 m)

WEIGHTS:
Weight empty	1,961 lb (890 kg)
Max T-O weight	3,630 lb (1,650 kg)

PERFORMANCE (at max T-O weight):
Max level speed at S/L	110 knots (127 mph; 205 km/h)
Max cruising speed at S/L	97 knots (112 mph; 180 km/h)
Rate of climb at S/L	1,300 ft (396 m)/min
Service ceiling	10,800 ft (3,300 m)
Hovering ceiling in ground effect	5,085 ft (1,550 m)
Hovering ceiling out of ground effect	2,950 ft (900 m)
Range with max fuel at S/L	388 nm (447 miles; 720 km)
Range with 1,322 lb (600 kg) payload	53 nm (62 miles; 100 km)
Range with 1,058 lb (480 kg) payload	161 nm (186 miles; 300 km)
Max endurance at S/L	5 hr 18 min

AÉROSPATIALE SA 316 ALOUETTE III

The Alouette III helicopter is a development of the Alouette II, with larger cabin capacity, greater power, improved equipment and higher performance. It flew for the first time on 28 February 1959, and a total of 823 had been ordered by 13 May 1970. Of these, 643 had been delivered, including 124 for the French armed forces and French civil operators by 1 January 1970. Alouette III helicopters are currently being flown by 89 operators in 57 countries.

SA 318C Alouette II Astazou helicopters in the insignia of the German Army

Those delivered up to the end of 1969 are now designated **SA 316A**. The **SA 316B**, to which the description below applies, has strengthened main and rear rotor transmissions, higher AUW and increased payload, and first deliveries were made in 1970. For 1971 delivery, the **SA 316C** will have an Artouste IIID turboshaft engine.

The French certificate of airworthiness for the Alouette III was granted on 15 December 1961, and FAA Type Approval on 27 March 1962.

The sale of Alouette III's to the Indian Air Force and Navy includes a licence agreement for manufacture of an initial batch of 80 of these aircraft in India. In addition, 60 are to be built in Switzerland following the award of a licence in November 1969.

In 1960 an Alouette III made unprecedented high-altitude landings and take-offs at a height of 15,780 ft (4,810 m) on Mont Blanc in the French Alps, with seven persons on board, and at a height of 19,698 ft (6,004 m) on Deo Tibaa in the Himalayas, the most elevated platform ever used by a helicopter, with two pilots and a 550 lb (250 kg) payload.

Aérospatiale had also developed an all-weather version of the Alouette III, which flew for the first time on 27 April 1964. With this version, safe landings have been performed down to a minimum ceiling of 100 ft (30 m) and with horizontal visibility limited to 1,000 ft (300 m).

The description below applies generally to all models of the Artouste-powered Alouette III, except where a specific version is indicated.

TYPE: Turbine-driven general-purpose helicopter.

ROTOR SYSTEM: Three-blade main and anti-torque rotors. Main rotor head similar to that of Alouette II. All-metal main rotor blades, with chord of 13·8 in (35 cm), on articulated hinges, with hydraulic drag-hinge dampers. Rotor brake optional.

ROTOR DRIVE: Main rotor driven through planetary gearbox, with free-wheel for autorotation. Take-off drive for tail rotor at lower end of main gearbox, from where a torque shaft runs to a small gearbox which supports the tail rotor and houses the pitch-change mechanism. Cyclic and collective pitch controls are powered.

FUSELAGE: Welded steel-tube centre-section, carrying the cabin at the front and a semi-monocoque tail-boom.

TAIL UNIT: Cantilever all-metal fixed tailplane, with twin endplate fins, mounted on tail-boom.

LANDING GEAR: Non-retractable tricycle type. Nose-wheel is fully-castoring. Provision for pontoon landing gear (unarmed versions only).

POWER PLANT: One 870 shp Turboméca Artouste IIIB turboshaft engine, derated to 550 shp. Fuel in single tank in fuselage centre-section, with capacity of 123 Imp gallons (560 litres).

ACCOMMODATION: Normal accommodation for pilot and six persons, with three seats in front and a four-person folding seat at the rear of the cabin. Two baggage holds in centre-section, on each side of the welded structure and enclosed by the centre-section fairings. Provision for

Installation of 20 mm MG 151 cannon in the cabin of an Alouette III

carrying two stretchers athwartships at rear of cabin, and two other persons, in addition to pilot. All passenger seats removable to enable aircraft to be used for freight-carrying. Provision for external sling for loads of up to 1,650 lb (750 kg). One forward-opening door on each side, immediately in front of two rearward-sliding doors. Dual controls and cabin heating optional.

OPERATIONAL EQUIPMENT (military version): In the assault role, the military Alouette III can be equipped with a wide range of weapons. This range includes a 7·62 mm AA52 machine-gun (with 1,000 rounds of ammunition), mounted athwartships on a tripod behind the pilot's seat and firing to starboard, either through a small window in the sliding door or through the open doorway with the door locked open. The rear seat is removed to allow the gun mounting to be installed. In this configuration, max accommodation is for pilot, co-pilot, gunner and one passenger, although normally only the pilot and gunner would be carried. An alternative to this installation provides for a 20 mm MG 151/20 cannon (with 480 rounds) on an open turret-type mounting on the port side of the cabin. For this installation all seats except that of the pilot are removed, as is the port side cabin door, and the crew consists of pilot and gunner. Instead of these guns, the Alouette III can be equipped with four AS.11 or two AS.12 wire-guided missiles on external jettisonable launching rails with APX-Bézu 260 gyro-stabilised sight; or with two Matra Type 181 or Type 361 rocket launchers containing, respectively, 36 or 72 SNEB 37 mm unguided rockets.

OPERATIONAL EQUIPMENT (naval version): The Alouette III can fulfil a variety of ship-borne roles, and features common to all naval configurations include a quick-mooring harpoon to ensure instant and automatic mooring on landing and before take-off, a nose-wheel locking device, and folding of the main rotor blades. For detecting and destroying small surface craft such as torpedo-boats, it can be equipped with a SFENA three-axis stabilisation system, APX-Bézu 260 gyro-stabilised sight and two AS.12 wire-guided missiles. For the ASW role, the aircraft can carry two Mk 44 homing torpedoes beneath the fuselage, or one torpedo and MAD (magnetic anomaly detection) gear in a streamlined container which is towed behind the helicopter on a 150 ft (50 m) cable. The aircraft can be used for air/sea rescue when the cabin floor is protected by an anti-corrosion covering to prevent sea water from reaching vital components. Rescue hoist (capacity 380 lb = 175 kg) mounted on port side of fuselage.

DIMENSIONS, EXTERNAL:
Diameter of main rotor   36 ft 1¾ in (11·02 m)
Main rotor blade chord (each)   13·8 in (35 cm)
Diameter of tail rotor   6 ft 3¼ in (1·91 m)
Length overall, rotors turning
                                42 ft 1½ in (12·84 m)
Length overall, blades folded
                               32 ft 10¾ in (10·03 m)
Width overall, blades folded 8 ft 6¼ in (2·60 m)

Aérospatiale SA 319 Alouette III Astazou prototype (600 shp Astazou XIV engine)

Height to top of rotor head   9 ft 10 in (3·00 m)
Wheel track   7 ft 10½ in (2·40 m)
WEIGHTS:
Weight empty   2,447 lb (1,110 kg)
Max T-O weight   4,850 lb (2,200 kg)
PERFORMANCE (Standard version, at max T-O weight, except where indicated):
Max level speed at S/L
                              114 knots (131 mph; 210 km/h)
Max cruising speed at S/L
                              97 knots (112 mph; 180 km/h)
Rate of climb at S/L   590 ft (180 m)/min
Service ceiling   10,662 ft (3,250 m)
Hovering ceiling in ground effect
                              5,577 ft (1,700 m)
Range with 1,764 lb (800 kg) payload at S/L
                              91 nm (105 miles; 170 km)
Range with 1,322 lb (600 kg) payload at S/L
                              188 nm (217 miles; 350 km)
Range with max fuel at S/L
                              258 nm (298 miles; 480 km)
Range at best altitude
                              290 nm (335 miles; 540 km)
Range of military version with 2 crew, at average altitude of 1,640 ft (500 m), 15 min reserves:
with 7·62 mm gun
                              259 nm (298 miles; 480 km)
with 20 mm cannon
                              254 nm (292 miles; 470 km)
with four AS.11 missiles
                              247 nm (285 miles; 460 km)

Endurance of ASW version with 2 crew, at average speed of 100 kt (115 mph = 185 kmh), 20 min reserves   2 hr 0 min

Search time of anti-surface vessel version with 2 crew, in area 27 nm (31 miles; 50 km) from base on ship, 30 min reserves   1 hr 30 min

AÉROSPATIALE SA 319 ALOUETTE III ASTAZOU

The SA 319 Alouette III Astazou is a direct development of the SA 316B described above, from which it differs principally in having a more powerful (600 shp) Astazou XIV turboshaft engine with increased thermal efficiency and a 25% reduction in fuel consumption.

A prototype of the SA 319 was completed in 1967. It is now in production for the French Armed Forces, delivery to whom is scheduled to begin late in 1970, as the SA 319A. The SA 319B, with Astazou XVI engine, is planned for introduction in 1971.

WEIGHTS:
Weight empty   2,403 lb (1,090 kg)
Max T-O weight   4,960 lb (2,250 kg)

PERFORMANCE (at max T-O weight):
Max level speed at S/L
                              119 knots (137 mph; 220 km/h)

Aérospatiale SA 321G Super Frelon anti-submarine helicopter of *l'Aéronautique Navale* **(three 1,550 shp Turboméca Turmo III C6 turboshaft engines)**

Max cruising speed at S/L
106 knots (122 mph; 197 km/h)
Rate of climb at S/L 853 ft (260 m)/min
Hovering ceiling in ground effect:
ISA 5,741 ft (1,750 m)
ISA + 20°C 3,280 ft (1,000 m)
Range with 6 passengers (176 lb = 80 kg each),
T-O at S/L 325 nm (375 miles; 605 km)

AÉROSPATIALE SA 321 SUPER FRELON (HORNET)

The Super Frelon is a multi-purpose helicopter, powered by three Turboméca Turmo free-turbine engines which are mounted above the cabin. It is a derivative of the smaller and less powerful SA 3200 Frelon described in the 1961-62 edition of *Jane's*.

Under a technical co-operation contract, Sikorsky Aircraft, USA, provided assistance in the development of the Super Frelon, in particular with the detail specifications, design, construction and testing of the main and tail rotor systems. Under a further agreement, the main gearcase and transmission box are produced in Italy by Fiat.

The first prototype of the Super Frelon (F-ZWWE, originally designated SA 3210-01) flew on 7 December 1962, powered by three 1,320 shp Turmo III C2 engines, and represented the troop transport version. In July 1963 this aircraft set up several international helicopter records, including a speed of 184 knots (212 mph; 341 km/h) over a 3-km course, and a speed of 217·77 mph (350·47 kmh) over a 15/25-km course.

The second prototype (F-ZWWF), flown on 28 May 1963, was representative of the naval version, with stabilising floats on the main landing gear supports.

Four pre-production aircraft (F-ZWWH/I/J/K) followed, and the French government ordered an initial production series of 17, designated SA 321G, in October 1965. A total of 48 Super Frelons had been ordered by 1 January 1970, including 18 for the French Navy, 16 for the South African Air Force, 12 of the transport version for the Israeli Defence Force/Air Force, one for Olympic Airways and one for Kennecott Exploration (Australia) Pty Ltd. Of this total 42 had been delivered.

Passenger and utility versions of the Super Frelon, designated SA 321F and SA 321J respectively, are available, and the main differences between the major versions are summarised below.

SA 321F. Commercial airliner version, designed to carry 34-37 passengers in a standard of comfort comparable to that of fixed-wing airliners, over 108-mile (175-km) stage lengths at a cruising speed of 143 mph (230 km/h), with 20 min reserve fuel. The prototype (F-WMHC) was designed in accordance with the US Federal Aviation Agency's FAR 29 regulations and flew for the first time on 7 April 1967. Type certification granted by the SGAC on 27 June 1968 and by the FAA on 29 August 1968. The aircraft delivered to Olympic Airways is of this type.

SA 321G. Anti-submarine version in service with the *Aéronautique Navale*. Eighteen ordered. This was the first version of the SA 321 to enter production. The first SA 321G flew on 30 November 1965 and deliveries began early in 1966.

SA 321J. Utility and public transport version, intended to fulfil the main roles of personnel and cargo transport. It is designed to carry a maximum of 27 passengers, of 200 lb (90 kg) average weight with baggage, over 338 nm (390 miles = 630 km) stage lengths, cruising at 124 knots (143 mph; 230 km/h) with a 10 per cent safety margin of flight time and a 20 min fuel reserve. External loads of up to 9,920 lb (4,500 kg) can be suspended from the cargo sling and carried 27 nm (31 miles; 50 km), the aircraft returning to base without load. An internal payload of 8,818 lb (4,000 kg) can be carried over 59 nm (68 miles = 110 km) at 124 knots (143 mph = 230 km/h) with 20 min fuel reserves. The SA 321J prototype flew for the first time on 6 July 1967. A French certificate of airworthiness was granted on 20 October 1967.

The description below applies generally to all models of the Super Frelon, except where specific variants are indicated.

TYPE: Three-engined heavy-duty helicopter.

ROTORS: Six-blade main rotor and five-blade anti-torque tail rotor. Main rotor head consists basically of two six-armed star-plates carrying the drag and flapping hinges for each blade. The root of each blade carries a fitting for pitch control and each blade has an individual hydraulic damper to govern movement in the drag plane. Each main blade is 28 ft 2½ in (8·60 m) long, with constant chord and NACA 0012 section. All-metal construction, with D-section main spar forming leading-edge. Tail rotor of similar construction to main rotor, with blades 5 ft 3 in (1·60 m) long. Rearward folding of all six main rotor blades of SA 321G

Close-up of SA 321G anti-submarine helicopter, showing radome and two homing torpedos

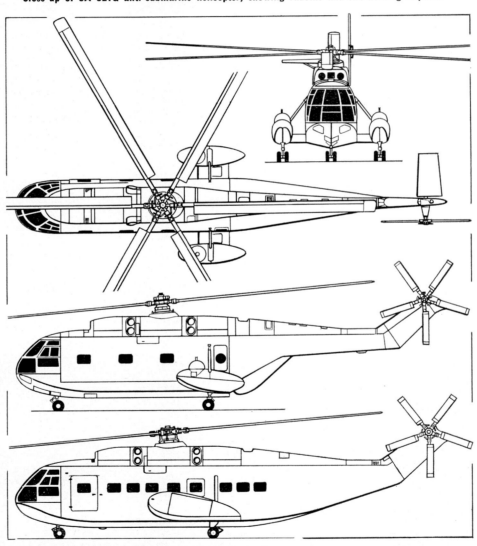

Aérospatiale SA 321G Super Frelon anti-submarine helicopter, with additional side elevation (*bottom*) of SA 321F commercial version

is accomplished automatically by hydraulic jacks simultaneously with automatic folding of the tail rotor pylon.

ROTOR DRIVE: The drive-shaft from the rear engine is geared directly to the shaft from the port forward engine. The two forward engines have a common reduction gear from which an output shaft drives the main rotor shaft through helical gearing. There are two reduction gear stages on the main rotor shaft. The tail rotor shaft is driven by gearing from the shaft linking the rear and port forward engines and incorporates two-stage reduction. The rotor can be stopped within 40 sec by a boosted disc-type rotor brake fitted to this

shaft. Main rotor rpm 207. Tail rotor rpm 990.

FUSELAGE: Boat-hull fuselage of conventional metal semi-monocoque construction, with watertight compartments inside planing bottom. On the SA 321G, there is a small stabilising float attached to the rear landing gear support structure on each side. The tail section of the SA 321G folds for stowage. Small fixed stabiliser on starboard side of the tail rotor pylon. The SA 321F does not have stabilising floats, but large external fairings on each side of the centre fuselage serve a similar purpose and also act as baggage containers.

LANDING GEAR: Non-retractable tricycle type, of Messier design. Twin wheels on each unit. Oleo-pneumatic shock-absorbers can be shortened on the SA 321G to reduce height of aircraft for stowage. Magnesium alloy wheels, all of same size. Tyre pressure 100 lb/sq in (7 kg/cm²). Optionally, low-pressure (50 lb/sq in = 3·5 kg/cm²) tyres may be fitted. Hydraulic disc brakes on main wheels. Nose-wheel unit is steerable and self-centering.

POWER PLANT: Three 1,550 shp Turboméca Turmo III C6 turboshaft engines, two mounted side-by-side forward of main rotor shaft and one aft of rotor shaft. Fuel in flexible tanks under floor of centre fuselage, with total capacity of 874 Imp gallons (3,975 litres). Provision for auxiliary tanks, capacity 440 Imp gallons (2,000 litres), and for in-flight refuelling.

ACCOMMODATION (military versions): Crew of two on flight deck, with dual controls and advanced all-weather equipment. Equipment in the SA 321G, which carries a flight crew of five, includes a tactical table and a variety of devices for anti-submarine detection and attack, towing, mine-sweeping and other duties. Transport version has provision for carrying 27-30 troops, 8,818-9,920 lb (4,000-4,500 kg) of internal or external cargo, or 15 stretchers and two medical attendants. Rescue hoist of 606 lb (275 kg) capacity. Main cabin is ventilated and soundproofed. Access is provided by a sliding door on the starboard side of the front fuselage, and by a rear loading ramp. The ramp is actuated hydraulically and can be opened in flight.

ACCOMMODATION (SA 321F): Airliner-type seats for up to 37 passengers (34 if toilets are installed) in three-abreast rows with centre aisle. Alternative layouts provide for the carriage of 8, 14 or 23 passengers (when toilets are fitted) or 11, 17 or 26 passengers (without toilet facilities), the remainder of the cabin space being blanked off by movable partitions and used for the carriage of freight; in these configurations the unused seats are folded against the cabin wall. All seats and interior furnishings are designed for quick removal when the helicopter is to be used for all-freight services. To cater for operations over marshland or water, the hull and lateral cargo compartments are sufficiently sealed to permit an occasional landing on water.

ACCOMMODATION (SA 321J): Seating for up to 27 passengers in the personnel transport role. As a cargo transport, external loads of up to 9,920 lb (4,500 kg) can be suspended from the cargo sling. Loading of internal cargo (up to 8,818 lb = 4,000 kg) is effected via the rear ramp-doors, with the assistance of a Tirefor hand winch.

OPERATIONAL EQUIPMENT (SA 321G): This version operates normally in tactical formations of three or four aircraft, one helicopter carrying detection and tracking equipment and the others in the group carrying equipment for attack. A central navigational system, Doppler radar and a radio-altimeter are common to all versions. The detection aircraft carries Sylphe panoramic radar with IFF capability and dipping sonar. Four homing torpedoes can be carried in pairs on each side of the main cabin.

DIMENSIONS, EXTERNAL:
Diameter of main rotor 62 ft 0 in (18·90 m)
Main rotor blade chord (each) 1 ft 7¾ in (0·50 m)
Diameter of tail rotor 13 ft 1½ in (4·00 m)
Tail rotor blade chord (each) 11¾ in (0·30 m)
Length overall, rotors turning 75 ft 6⅝ in (23·03 m)
Length of fuselage, incl tail rotor 65 ft 10¾ in (20·08 m)
Length of fuselage 63 ft 7¾ in (19·40 m)
Length overall (SA 321G, blades and tail folded) 56 ft 0 in (17·07 m)
Width overall (SA 321G, blades and tail folded) 17 ft 0¾ in (5·20 m)
Width overall, incl baggage containers (SA 321F) 16 ft 6⅜ in (5·04 m)
Width of fuselage 7 ft 4½ in (2·24 m)
Height at tail rotor (normal) 21 ft 10¼ in (6·66 m)
Height overall (SA 321G, blades and tail folded) 16 ft 2½ in (4·94 m)
Wheel track 14 ft 1 in (4·30 m)
Wheelbase 21 ft 6¼ in (6·56 m)
Cabin door:
Height 5 ft 1 in (1·55 m)
Width 3 ft 11¼ in (1·20 m)
Rear loading ramp:
Length 6 ft 2¾ in (1·90 m)
Width 6 ft 2¾ in (1·90 m)

DIMENSIONS, INTERNAL:
Cabin:
Length (SA 321F) 31 ft 9 in (9·67 m)
Length (SA 321G) 22 ft 11½ in (7·00 m)
Width (SA 321F) 6 ft 5 in (1·96 m)
Width at floor (SA 321G) 6 ft 2¾ in (1·90 m)

Aérospatiale SA 321F Super Frelon in Olympic Airways insignia

Height (SA 321F) 5 ft 11 in (1·80 m)
Height (SA 321G) 6 ft 0 in (1·83 m)
Usable volume (SA 321G) 777 cu ft (22·0 m³)

WEIGHTS:
Weight empty:
SA 321 (standard) 14,420 lb (6,540 kg)
SA 321 G 14,640 lb (6,640 kg)
Weight empty, equipped:
SA 321 F 16,711 lb (7,580 kg)
SA 321 J 15,696 lb (7,120 kg)
Max T-O weight 27,557 lb (12,500 kg)

PERFORMANCE (at max T-O weight):
Max level speed at S/L 129 knots (149 mph; 240 km/h)
Cruising speed at S/L 124 knots (143 mph; 230 km/h)
Cruising speed at S/L, one engine out 122 knots (140 mph; 225 km/h)
Max rate of climb at S/L 1,495 ft (455 m)/min
Rate of climb at S/L, one engine out 705 ft (215 m)/min
Service ceiling 11,475 ft (3,500 m)
Service ceiling, one engine out 5,900 ft (1,800 m)
Hovering ceiling in ground effect 7,380 ft (2,250 m)
Hovering ceiling out of ground effect 1,804 ft (550 m)
Range at S/L 496 nm (572 miles; 920 km)
Range at S/L, one engine out 582 nm (671 miles; 1,080 km)
Range with 5,511 lb (2,500 kg) payload, 20 min reserves 349 nm (403 miles; 650 km)
Ferry range with three 146 Imp gallon (666 litre) ferry tanks 730 nm (840 miles; 1,350 km)
Endurance in ASW role 4 hr
Mean fuel consumption 14·2 lb/mile (4·0 kg/km)

AÉROSPATIALE/WESTLAND SA 330 PUMA

The twin-engined SA 330 was developed initially to meet a French Army requirement for a medium-sized *hélicoptère de manoeuvre*, able to operate by day or night in all weathers and all climates. In 1967, the SA 330 was selected for the RAF Tactical Transport Programme, and is included in the joint production agreement between Aérospatiale and Westland in the UK. The first of two prototypes (F-ZWWN and O) flew on 15 April 1965, and the last of six pre-production SA 330's (F-ZWWP-T and XW241) on 30 July 1968, followed on 12 September 1968 by the roll-out of the first production aircraft.

During 1969 the SA 330-05 (F-ZWWR) was used for flight development trials for the French Army Pumas, while the SA 330-08 (XW 241) has been equipped to British requirements to carry out similar testing of those for the RAF.

Firm orders placed up to 1 January 1970 totalled 163, including 88 for the *Aviation Légerè de l'Armée de Terre* (ALAT), 40 for the Royal Air Force and 35 for export to Algeria, the Ivory Coast, Portugal and South Africa. Deliveries to the French Army began in the Spring of 1969. **SA 330Es** for the RAF are scheduled to enter squadron service in the Autumn of 1970.

The following civil version has also been announced.:

SA 330F. Utility and public transport version, intended primarily as a personnel or cargo transport. Designed to carry 15-17 passengers, with baggage (Commuter version), over 188 nm (217 miles = 350 km) with 20 min fuel reserves, in ISA +20°C conditions at S/L. The prototype SA 330F (F-WRPH) was designed in accordance with FAA FAR Pt 29 regulations, and flew for the first time on 26 September 1969. Trials for SGAC and FAA certification in progress early in 1970.

TYPE: Medium-sized transport helicopter.

ROTOR SYSTEM: Four-blade main rotor, with a compact self-lubricating hub and integral rotor brake. The main rotor head is equipped with drag, flapping and pitch change hinges and with drag hinge dampers. The blade cuffs, equipped with horns, are connected by means of link rods to the swashplate, which is actuated by three hydraulic twin-cylinder servo-control units. The blades, which are of constant chord and twisted, consist of an aluminium alloy extruded spar, milled on the outside to form the leading-edge, and a series of sheet metal pockets hot-bonded to the rear of the spar, to form the trailing-edge. Attachment of the blades to their sleeve by means of two pins enables them to be folded back quickly by a

Aérospatiale SA 321 Super Frelon transport in Israeli Defence Force insignia (*S. P. Peltz*)

semi-automatic device. The five-blade tail rotor has flapping hinges only, and is located on the starboard side of the tail-boom.

ROTOR DRIVE: Each engine is attached at the rear to the main gearbox flange and held at the front by two link rods. Design of the gearbox permits direct coupling of the turbine shafts. The particularly large reduction in rpm between turbine output (23,000 rpm) and the main rotor (265 rpm) requires five reduction stages. The first stage drives, from each engine, an intermediate shaft directly driving the alternator and the ventilation fan, and indirectly driving the two hydraulic pumps. At the second stage the action of the two units becomes synchronised on a single main drive-shaft by means of free-wheeling spur gears. If one or both engines are stopped, this enables the drive gears to be rotated by the remaining turbine or the autorotating rotor, thus maintaining drive to the ancillary systems when the engines are stopped. The hydraulically-controlled rotor brake, installed on the main gearbox, permits stopping of the rotor 15 seconds after engine shut-down.

FUSELAGE: Conventional all-metal semi-mono-coque structure of vertical frames and stressed skin. Local use is made of titanium alloy under the engine installation, which is outside the main fuselage shell. Centre of gravity of the helicopter lies on the centre-line of the main rotor drive-shaft. Rear monocoque tail-boom supports the tail rotor on the starboard side and a horizontal stabiliser on the port side.

LANDING GEAR: Messier semi-retractable tricycle type, with twin wheels on each unit, is standard. Main units retract upward hydraulically into fairings on sides of fuselage, nose unit retracts rearward. When landing gear is down, the nose-wheel jack is extended and the main-wheel jacks are telescoped. Dual-chamber oleo-pneumatic shock-absorbers. All tyres same size, pressure 42·5 lb/sq in (3 kg/cm²) on all units. Hydraulic differential disc brakes, controlled by foot pedals. Lever-operated parking brake.

POWER PLANT: Two 1,320 shp Turboméca Turmo IIIC4 turboshaft engines, mounted side-by-side above cabin forward of the main rotor assembly and separated by a firewall. These are coupled to the main rotor transmission box, with shaft-drive to tail rotor. Fuel in four flexible tanks beneath cargo compartment floor, with total capacity of 341 Imp gallons (1,550 litres). Provision for additional 418 Imp gallons (1,900 litres) in four auxiliary ferry tanks. Each engine is supplied by a pair of interconnected tanks, the lower halves of which have self-sealing walls for protection against small-calibre projectiles and contain the fuel supply pumps. RAF version has fuel flow meters and fuel jettison system.

ACCOMMODATION: Crew of two side-by-side on anti-crash seats on flight deck, with jettison-able doors on starboard side and emergency exit on port side. Internal doorway connects flight deck to cabin, with folding seat in doorway for a third crew member or cargo supervisor. Dual controls standard. Accommodation in main cabin for 16 individually-equipped troops, six litters and four seated patients, or equivalent freight. The number of troops can be increased to 20 in the high-density version. Jettisonable sliding door on each side. Strengthened floor for cargo-carrying, with lashing points. Removable panel on underside of fuselage, aft of main cabin, permits longer loads to be accommodated and also serves as emergency exit. A 3 ft 3¼ in × 2 ft 3¼ in (1·00 × 0·70 m) hatch located in the floor below the centre-line of the main rotor is provided for carrying loads of up to 5,511 lb (2,500 kg) on an internally-mounted cargo sling. A rescue hoist (capacity 606 lb = 275 kg) can be mounted externally on the starboard side of the fuselage and is standard on the RAF version, together with an abseiling beam, cargo hook and full-width main cabin steps. The standard SA 330 can be transformed quickly to a 9/12-seater for VIP transport duties. Cabin and flight deck are heated, ventilated and soundproofed. De-misting, de-icing, washers and wipers for pilot's windscreens.

ELECTRONICS AND EQUIPMENT: Optional communications equipment includes VHF, UHF, tactical HF and SSB HF radio installations and intercom system. Optional flying and navigational equipment includes radio compass, radio altimeter and Doppler. A navigation computer and lane indicator for the aircraft are under development. The SA 330 can also be fitted with an all-weather piloting system which includes a twin-gyro (attitude) data generator and transparent steering-type limited-authority autopilot and ensures automatic stabilisation in all three axes in all weathers, as well as providing maintenance of heading and execution of co-ordinated turns. Standard equipment in the RAF version includes VHF/

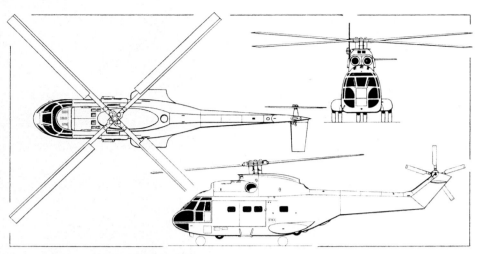

Aérospatiale/Westland SA 330 Puma transport helicopter

SA 330F, prototype of the utility and public transport version of the Puma helicopter

SA 330 Puma, final pre-series aircraft in RAF insignia as XW241

UHF radio, standby UHF, UHF homing, intercom, IFF/SSR, radio altimeter, and Decca navigation system with Flight Log.

SYSTEMS: 115 - 200V AC electrical power supplied by a 20kVA alternator, driven by the port side intermediate shaft from the main gearbox and available on the ground under the same conditions as the hydraulic ancillary systems. 28·5V 10 kW DC power provided from the AC system by two transformer-rectifiers. Main aircraft battery used for self-starting and emergency power in flight. For the latter purpose, an emergency 400VA inverter can supply the essential navigation equipment from the battery, permitting at least 20 min continued flight in the event of a main power failure. Two independent

hydraulic systems are supplied by self-regulating pumps driven by the main gearbox. Reservoirs and control components for each system are located opposite the respective pumps on top of the fuselage. Free-wheels incorporated in the main gearbox ensure that both systems remain in operation, for supplying the servo-controls, if the engines are stopped in flight. Other hydraulically-actuated systems can be operated on the ground from the main gearbox, or by external power through the ground power receptacle. There is also an independent auxiliary system, fed through a hand pump, which can be used in an emergency to lower the landing gear and pressurise the accumulator for the parking brake on the ground.

DIMENSIONS, EXTERNAL:
Diameter of main rotor   49 ft 2½ in (15·00 m)
Diameter of tail rotor   10 ft 3 in (3·12 m)
Ground clearance of tail rotor   6 ft 6¾ in (2·00 m)
Length overall, rotors turning
             59 ft 7¾ in (18·18 m)
Length of fuselage   46 ft 1½ in (14·06 m)
Length, blades folded   48 ft 6¾ in (14·80 m)
Width, blades folded   11 ft 5⅝ in (3·50 m)
Height overall   16 ft 9¾ in (5·12 m)
Height to top of rotor hub   13 ft 8½ in (4·18 m)
Width over wheel fairings   9 ft 10 in (3·00 m)
Wheelbase   13 ft 3 in (4·045 m)
Cabin doors (port and stbd):
   Height   4 ft 5 in (1·35 m)
   Width   4 ft 5 in (1·35 m)
DIMENSIONS, INTERNAL:
Cabin: Length   15 ft 4 in (4·68 m)
   Width at floor   5 ft 5⅝ in (1·72 m)
   Max height   4 ft 10 in (1·47 m)
   Usable volume   353 cu ft (10·00 m³)
   Floor hatch: Length   3 ft 3¼ in (1·00 m)
     Width   2 ft 3½ in (0·70 m)
AREA:
Main rotor disc   1,905 sq ft (177 m²)
WEIGHTS:
Weight empty, basic aircraft 7,561 lb (3,430 kg)
Max T-O weight   14,110 lb (6,400 kg)
PERFORMANCE (at max T-O weight):
Max level speed at S/L
    151 knots (174 mph; 280 km/h)
Max cruising speed at S/L
    143 knots (165 mph; 265 km/h)
Speed range at S/L, on one engine at max power
    59-97 knots (68-112 mph; 110-180 km/h)
Rate of climb at S/L (both engines)
    1,400 ft (426 m)/min
Rate of climb at S/L (one engine out)
    590 ft (180 m)/min
Service ceiling   15,750 ft (4,800 m)
Hovering ceiling in ground effect
    9,186 ft (2,800 m)
Hovering ceiling out of ground effect
    6,233 ft (1,900 m)
Max range at S/L (standard fuel)
    338 nm (390 miles; 630 km)
Ferry range at S/L (with four 104 Imp gallon
= 475 litre ferry tanks)
    751 nm (865 miles; 1,400 km)

AÉROSPATIALE/WESTLAND SA 341 GAZELLE

The SA 341 is an all-purpose lightweight helicopter, designed to replace the Alouette II series from about 1972. Like its predecessors, it is basically a five-seat aircraft, fitted with the same transmission system as the Alouette II Astazou and a Turboméca Astazou IIIN shaft-turbine of 600 shp.

Greater simplicity and improved safety are offered by the use of a three-blade semi-rigid rotor, with laminated glass-fibre blades to eliminate ground resonance, and by shrouding the tail rotor within the tail fin to avoid danger on or near the ground.

Under an Anglo-French agreement signed in 1967, the SA 341 is being developed and produced jointly with Westland Helicopters Ltd. Its main rotor blades were designed and developed in co-operation with Bölkow of Germany.

The first prototype (F-WOFH) made its first flight on 7 April 1967, and was fitted initially with an Astazou IIN2 engine and a standard tail rotor from an Alouette II; in this form it was known as the SA 340, but has since been brought up to SA 341 standard. The second SA 340 prototype (F-ZWRA), which flew for the first time on 17 April 1968, was more representative of the SA 341 production version. It was followed by four pre-production Gazelles (F-ZWRH/L/I/K), of which the third was equipped to British Army requirements and given the British military serial number XW276.

The description below applies to the SA 341 production version.

TYPE: Five-seat light utility helicopter.

ROTOR SYSTEM: Three-blade semi-rigid main rotor and 13-blade tail rotor. Rotor head and rotor mast form a single unit. The main rotor blades each have a single leading-edge spar of plastic material reinforced with glass-fibre, a laminated glass-fabric skin and synthetic foam filler. The anti-torque rotor is completely shrouded in the tail fin. Main rotor blades can be folded for stowage. Rotor brake optional.

ROTOR DRIVE: Main gearbox adjacent to engine, which is mounted above the rear part of the cabin. Transmission system consists of the main gearbox, connected to the engine through a centrifugal clutch and a free-wheel unit, a tail drive shaft and a tail rotor gearbox.

FUSELAGE: Forward section of all-metal semi-monocoque construction, supporting the cabin. Central body structure carrying main gearbox and engine at top and accommodating fuel tank and cargo space aft of cabin. Honeycomb-stabilised stressed-skin tail-cone, incorporating the integral fin within which the tail rotor and gearbox are mounted. Main gearbox and engine cowlings open upwards to provide access to transmission deck and engine.

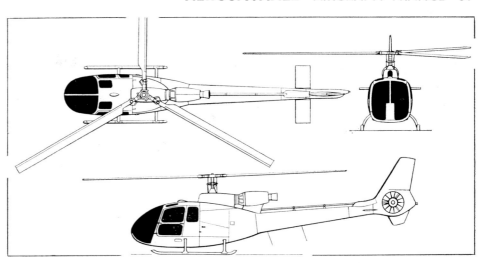

Aérospatiale SA 341 Gazelle five-seat lightweight helicopter

Fourth SA 341 Gazelle helicopter as displayed at Hanover in May 1970, with endplate tail fins
(Brian M. Service)

The Ludion jet-lift VTOL aircraft undergoing tests at Melun-Villaroche

TAIL UNIT: Small horizontal stabiliser on tail-boom, ahead of tail rotor fin.

LANDING GEAR: Steel-tube skid type. Wheel can be fitted at rear of each skid for ground manoeuvring. Provision for alternative pontoon landing gear.

POWER PLANT: One 600 shp Turboméca Astazou IIIN turboshaft engine, installed above fuselage aft of cabin. Fuel in main tank in fuselage, capacity 99 Imp gallons (450 litres).

ACCOMMODATION: Crew of two on side-by-side seats in front of cabin, with bench seat to the rear for a further three persons. The bench seat is in two parts, which can be moved to provide access to a flat deck level with the cargo hold at the rear. Forward-opening jettisonable car-type door on each side of cabin, with smaller cargo-loading door aft of cabin door on port side. Dual controls and cabin heating optional.

EQUIPMENT: Optional communications equipment includes HF (with homing) or VHF radio, intercom and radio compass. A variety of operational equipment can be fitted, according to role, including a 1,322 lb (600 kg) cargo sling, 264 lb (120 kg) rescue hoist, two stretchers (internally), or photographic and survey equipment. Military loads can include two pods of 18 or 36 × 37 mm rockets, four AS.11 wire-guided missiles with APX-Bézu 260 gyro-stabilised sight, an AA52 side-firing 7·62 mm machine-gun or smoke markers. For naval use, provision exists for installing a quick-mooring harpoon developed by the French Navy.

DIMENSIONS, EXTERNAL:
Diameter of main rotor   34 ft 5½ in (10·50 m)
Diameter of tail rotor   2 ft 3½ in (0·70 m)
Length overall, rotor turning
     39 ft 4½ in (12·00 m)
Length of fuselage   31 ft 2¾ in (9·52 m)
Height overall   10 ft 4½ in (3·16 m)
Skid track   6 ft 4 in (1·93 m)
WEIGHTS:
Weight empty   1,873 lb (850 kg)
Max T-O weight   3,747 lb (1,700 kg)
PERFORMANCE (at max T-O weight):
Max level speed at S/L
     143 knots (165 mph; 265 km/h)
Max cruising speed at S/L
     129 knots (149 mph; 240 km/h)
Rate of climb at S/L   1,214 ft (370 m)/min
Service ceiling   16,732 ft (5,100 m)
Hovering ceiling in ground effect
     10,170 ft (3,100 m)
Hovering ceiling out of ground effect
     8,530 ft (2,600 m)
Range with max fuel at S/L
     350 nm (403 miles; 650 km)
Endurance at S/L   4 hr

AÉROSPATIALE ROTOJET

The Rotojet project currently under consideration by Aérospatiale is for a winged compound helicopter employing the cold-jet propulsion system of a tip-driven main rotor.

A by-pass turbine engine is used both for forward propulsion and to provide compressed air for ejection through nozzles situated at approx 40 per cent radius of the main rotor blades. There is no tail rotor.

The initial version envisaged at present is a five-seater, designated SA 350, and the brief details below apply to this model. A much larger Rotojet, employing the same basic propulsion systems, is also being studied. This will have a gross weight of 26,455 lb (12,000 kg) and accommodate 30-36 passengers.

WEIGHTS (SA 350):
Operating weight empty   2,380 lb (1,080 kg)
Max T-O weight   3,858 lb (1,750 kg)
PERFORMANCE (SA 350, estimated):
Max level speed 199 knots (230 mph; 370 km/h)
Best cruising speed
     172 knots (199 mph; 320 km/h)

AÉROSPATIALE LUDION

Displayed for the first time at the 1967 Paris Air Show, the Ludion is an ultra-light jet-lift VTOL aircraft capable of carrying a fully equipped man and a payload of 66 lb (30 kg) up to a height of 500-650 ft (150-200 m) above the ground for a distance of more than 2,300 ft (700 m). Gross weight is approx 440 lb (200 kg) and a max forward speed of 62 mph (100 kmh) is attained.

Developed versions are expected to have commercial applications, but in its present form the project has clear military uses, in enabling heavily-armed troops to overfly natural or combat area obstructions within the aircraft's endurance of some 30 seconds.

The basic structure of the Ludion is of light alloy, with an open seat for the pilot in front and a platform for the payload at the rear. The landing gear consists of a nose-wheel on a long arm, in front of the pilot's footrests, a rear skid carried on a shock-strut, and four lateral balancer skids of glass-fibre.

The Ludion's lifting power is provided by an SEPR rocket motor which operates through decomposition of isopropyl nitrate propellant stored in a cylindrical tank above the load-carrying platform.

A second cylindrical bottle contains compressed nitrogen to pressurise the propellant tank. The rocket-motor consists of a gas generator (decomposing chamber) with propellant flow regulating valve, igniter and two nozzles. The nozzles eject the gases into two Bertin-manufactured "trompes", mounted on each side of the vehicle.

The "trompes" not only augment the thrust, but reduce the temperature and velocity of the gases ejected, as well as the noise level of the power plant. The generator and "trompes"

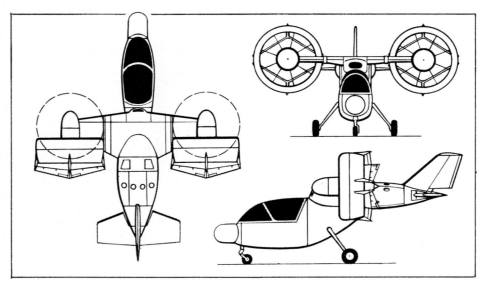

Photograph and three-view drawing of the Aérospatiale N 500 ducted-propeller research aircraft (two 317 shp Allison 250-C18 turboshaft engines)

assembly, which hinges on the upper part of the seat back, can be moved by the pilot to give control in pitch and roll. Directional control is provided by gas-deflection flaps running laterally across the outlet of each "trompe".

Flight tests have demonstrated the good general handling characteristics of the vehicle, which is very stable, and its high manoeuvrability in flight as well as at lift-off and landing.

AÉROSPATIALE N 500

The N 500 is a small single-seat VTOL research aircraft intended primarily to evaluate the flight principles of the tilting-duct concept. It is part of a more general programme which also includes testing of a full-scale 'top fan' system of high static efficiency with variable expansion of the flow from the duct.

The enclosed cabin contains an ejection seat for the pilot. Two 317 shp Allison 250-C18 turboshaft engines are located side-by-side in the rear part of the fuselage and drive the two three-blade ducted pusher propellers through interconnected shafts of Hispano-Suiza design and manufacture, running through the stub-wings. For vertical take-off and landing, the ducts tilt to a horizontal position, complete with the section of the wing to which they are attached.

Cockpit controls are conventional. Control in yaw and roll is by differential thrust and tilt, with a "mixing" process during transition. Control in pitch is by collective tilting of the ducts. There is no provision for attitude control of the fuselage, which is given static stability in hovering flight by pendulum effect.

The first year of testing has been carried out with the aircraft in tethered hovering flight; and is being followed by dynamic stability tests

in wind tunnel and simulator before continuing with further flying.

Development of the full-scale 'top-fan' system is progressing to schedule, using the trap-vortex principle for tip clearance and boundary layer control.

The first prototype was completed in the Spring of 1967 and has been used as a mechanical and aerodynamic test-bed for ground testing only. The second prototype (F-WOFM), to which the details below apply, made its first tethered flight in July 1968, and up to mid-1969 had undergone numerous dynamic stability tests.

In its initial form, the N 500 is intended only for hovering and transition flight trials. Stage 2 development will utilise controlled and variable expansion of the flow from the ducts.

A new version of the N 500 is being designed and is scheduled for completion in 1970; this will have hydraulically-operated controls and will be powered by 370 shp Allison 250-C20 shaft-turbines.

DIMENSIONS, EXTERNAL:
Wing span over ducts   20 ft 1½ in (6·14 m)
Length overall   21 ft 7 in (6·58 m)
Height overall   10 ft 2 in (3·10 m)
Wheel track   6 ft 6¾ in (2·00 m)
Diameter of ducts (each):
   internal   5 ft 2 in (1·58 m)
   external   6 ft 10 in (2·08 m)
WEIGHT:
Max T-O weight   2,760 lb (1,250 kg)
PERFORMANCE (estimated at max T-O weight, with developed ducts):
Max speed at S/L
     188 knots (217 mph; 350 km/h)

BREGUET

BREGUET-AVIATION

HEAD OFFICE, TECHNICAL AND ADMINISTRATIVE
CENTRE:
BP 12, 78-Vélizy-Villacoublay

WORKS:
31-Toulouse and 64-Biarritz

FLIGHT TESTING:
13-Istres

PRESIDENT AND CHAIRMAN:
B. C. Vallières

MANAGEMENT EXECUTIVES:
J. P. Fort (Assistant Managing Director)
G. Ricard (Technical Manager)
J. Barge (Production Manager)
P. Jaillard (Commercial Manager)
M. Tavernier (Asst Commercial Manager)
P. Bergougnan (Personnel and Social Welfare
Manager)
R. Hourcadet (Works Manager, Toulouse)
M. Fraysse (Design Manager, Toulouse)
H. Berrogain (Works Manager, Biarritz)

PUBLIC RELATIONS OFFICER:
Y. Cheyrou-Lagreze

PRESS OFFICER:
C. Raffin

GENERAL SECRETARY:
R. Vivant

The Breguet company was founded in 1911 by
M Louis Breguet, one of the great pioneers of
French aviation, who died on 4 May 1955.

The two main factories of the Breguet company
were incorporated into the nationalised industry
in 1936, but three years later it regained some
measure of independence through the purchase
of the former Latécoère factories at Toulouse.
Bayonne and Biscarosse. In 1970, its works had
a total area of 1,194,790 sq ft (111,000 m²) and it
employed 4,085 people.

A statement issued jointly by Breguet Aviation
and Avions Marcel Dassault, on 28 June 1967,
announced that Dassault had become the major
stockholder in Breguet Aviation, in accordance
with the decision of the French government to
reorganise the aircraft industry. A new Board of
Administration has been formed with B. C.
Vallières of Dassault as President and Chairman.
Breguet Aviation has, however, retained its key
personnel and continues to operate independently.

Breguet's Atlantic maritime reconnaissance
aircraft continues in production under a European
manufacturing programme. In pre-series production is the Breguet 941S STOL transport
employing the deflected slipstream principle of
high lift.

Under a further major agreement, concluded
between the French and British governments in
1965, Breguet and British Aircraft Corporation
are producing jointly a dual-purpose strike-
trainer aircraft named the Jaguar (see "Sepecat",
in the International section of this edition).

Under sub-contracts, Breguet is producing
components for aircraft of the Dassault-Breguet
group, such as the Mirage III, as well as fuselages
for the Fokker-VFW Friendship. It is responsible for overhauling and repairing Super Mystère
B-2 and Mirage III aircraft of the French Air
Force and, under a Dowty Rotol licence, propellers for the Nord 2501 transport and Breguet
Alizé anti-submarine aircraft.

Dassault-Breguet joined forces with Dornier in
the Spring of 1969 to bid for a Franco-German
order for a new jet trainer required by the air
forces of the two countries to replace the Magister,
Lockheed T-33A and Dassault Mystère IV-A.
Breguet designs for this Mach 0·82 aircraft
with two 2,200 lb (1,000 kg) st engines were
initiated as the Breguet 126. The name Alpha
Jet was later adopted for the joint submission,
and a full-scale model of this aircraft was displayed at the Paris Air Show in June 1969.

BREGUET 941

The Breguet 941 is an unpressurised cargo/
passenger transport utilising the deflected-
slipstream STOL technique. In this system the
slipstream of four propellers blows over the
entire span of the wing, the trailing-edge of
which is fitted with extensive slotted flaps. The
four engines are synchronised to maintain uniform
rpm and to ensure that all propellers will continue
to rotate in the event of an engine failure.

A prototype flew for the first time on 1 June
1961. On 29 November 1965, the French
government ordered four Type 941S pre-production aircraft and the setting up of tools and jigs
for full production. The prototype was re-
engined early in 1966 with 1,500 shp Turmo

IIID3 turboprops of the kind that power the
pre-production Breguet 941S.

The first 941S flew on 19 April 1967, followed
by the second on 22 May 1967; all four aircraft
are now flying, and the description below applies
to this version. The pre-series aircraft differ
from the prototype (see 1963-64 *Jane's*) in
having a longer nose accommodating a large
radome, a wider cargo hold and a modified rear
door arrangement. The cockpit has also been
enlarged and visibility improved. Each side
door above the ramp is hinged along its forward
edge instead of along the top edge, to facilitate
the air-dropping of heavy loads. The 941S can
carry 43% of the vehicle types used by a US
airborne division.

Under the auspices of McDonnell Douglas
Corporation, the prototype was demonstrated in
the USA in June 1964 and March 1965, and a
941S was also demonstrated in the USA under
this designation in 1968-69, when it was evaluated
by Eastern and American Airlines, with the
assistance of the US Federal Aviation Agency.
McDonnell Douglas is pursuing further study of
the design, as the McDonnell Douglas 188, and of
developed versions for potential use in both civil
and military fields, one such project being the
Model 210 of increased capacity.

TYPE: Four-engined STOL transport.

WINGS: Cantilever high-wing monoplane. Wing
section NACA 63A416. Thickness/chord ratio
16%. Dihedral 4°. Incidence 3°. Light
alloy fail-safe structure, comprising a torsion
box enclosed by bonded honeycomb panels.
No ailerons or trim-tabs. Full-span double-
slotted flaps, with a fixed slat at the leading-
edge of the rear flap. Flaps operated through
a central hydraulic control box driving four
reversible screw-jacks. Four hinged spoilers
on each wing. Pneumatic de-icing of leading-
edges.

FUSELAGE: Conventional all-metal fail-safe
structure of rectangular section.

TAIL UNIT: Cantilever all-metal construction.
Fixed surfaces covered with light alloy honeycomb panels. Variable-incidence tailplane with
inverted camber profile. All control surfaces
are power boosted by SAMM twin-cylinder
servo-controls and mass-balanced. No trim-
tabs. Pneumatic de-icing of leading-edges.

LANDING GEAR: Retractable tricycle type, of
Messier "Jockey" design. Hydraulic retraction. Each main gear is of the tandem-wheel
type and retracts rearward into a fairing on the
side of the fuselage. The two wheels of each
unit are interconnected hydraulically to
improve behaviour on rough ground. The
twin nose-wheels are steerable and are carried
on a shock-absorber which, like those of the
main gear, can be extended on the ground to
tilt the aircraft and so facilitate loading via the
rear ramp. Kléber-Colombes tubeless tyres,
size 15·00 × 16 on main wheels, size 11·00 × 12
on nose-wheels. Tyre pressures: main wheels
44 lb/sq in (3·1 kg/cm²), nose-wheels 38 lb/sq in
(2·65 kg/cm²). Messier disc brakes and Ministop
anti-skid units on main wheels.

POWER PLANT: Four 1,500 shp Turboméca Turmo
IIID3 shaft-turbines, each driving a Breguet/

Ratier three-blade hydraulically-operated variable-pitch fully-reversible propeller through a
two-stage reduction gear, with one stage at the
rear of the engine and the other at the front. A
bevel-gear drive from the rear of each engine
interconnects the four power plants through a
flexible transmission shaft so that all propellers
remain operative after an engine failure. The
pitch of all four propellers is controlled through
a single constant-speed unit driven by the
transmission shaft. The pitch of the outboard
propellers can be adjusted differentially for
low-speed control. Propeller diameter 13 ft
8½ in (4·5 m). Fuel in five integral and four
bag-type reserve tanks, with total capacity of
2,200 Imp gallons (10,000 litres). Provision
for both pressure and gravity refuelling. Oil
capacity 276 lb (125 kg).

ACCOMMODATION: Crew of three and 57 commercial passengers, 40 fully-equipped troops or 24
stretchers. Doors at front of cabin on port
side and on each side at rear of cabin. Rear
loading ramp.

SYSTEMS: Hydraulic system pressure 3,000
lb/sq in (210 kg/cm²). Electrical system provides
28V DC and 120/208V AC.

ELECTRONICS AND EQUIPMENT: Provision for
VHF, UHF and HF (AM and SSB) radio, ICS,
ADF, TAC, VOR, ILS, radio altimeter,
weather radar and Doppler.

DIMENSIONS, EXTERNAL:

Wing span	76 ft 8½ in (23·4 m)
Wing chord (mean)	12 ft 1 in (3·69 m)
Wing aspect ratio	6·56
Length overall	77 ft 11 in (23·75 m)
Height over tail	31 ft 8 in (9·65 m)
Tailplane span	32 ft 9½ in (10·00 m)
Wheel track	12 ft 2½ in (3·72 m)
Wheelbase	23 ft 8 in (7·22 m)
Passenger door (port, front):	
Height	6 ft 3 in (1·90 m)
Width	3 ft 1½ in (0·95 m)
Rear doors (both):	
Height	6 ft 3 in (1·90 m)
Width	2 ft 11½ in (0·90 m)
Cargo ramp opening:	
Height	7 ft 4½ in (2·25 m)
Width	8 ft 7 in (2·60 m)

DIMENSIONS, INTERNAL:

Cabin: Length	36 ft 7¼ in (11·17 m)
Max width	8 ft 7 in (2·60 m)
Max height	7 ft 4½ in (2·25 m)
Floor area, excluding ramp	312 sq ft (29·0 m²)
Volume (usable)	2,330 cu ft (66 m²)

AREAS:

Wings, gross	902 sq ft (83·78 m²)
Vertical tail surfaces (total)	223 sq ft (20·75 m²)
Horizontal tail surfaces (total)	
	319·5 sq ft (29·68 m²)

WEIGHTS AND LOADINGS:

Weight empty, equipped	32,408 lb (14,700 kg)
Max payload	22,045 lb (10,000 kg)
Max T-O weight:	
assault mission	48,500 lb (22,000 kg)
logistical mission	52,580 lb (23,850 kg)
long range mission	58,420 lb (26,500 kg)

Pre-production Breguet 941S four-engined STOL transport (*Air Portraits*)

Max zero-fuel weight	54,013 lb (24,500 kg)
Max landing weight (exceptional)	
	58,420 lb (26,500 kg)
Max wing loading	65·5 lb/sq ft (320 kg/m²)
Max power loading	9·70 lb/shp (4·4 kg/shp)

PERFORMANCE (at average operating weight):
Max level speed at S/L
  243 knots (280 mph; 450 km/h)
Max permissible diving speed
  274 knots (316 mph; 510 km/h)
Max cruising speed at 10,000 ft (3,050 m)
  225 knots (259 mph; 417 km/h)
Econ cruising speed at 10,000 ft (3,050 m)
  215 knots (248 mph; 400 km/h)
Stalling speed at 44,100 lb (20,000 kg) AUW,
 wheels and flaps down
  46 knots (52 mph; 83 km/h)
Service ceiling 31,170 ft (9,500 m)
Service ceiling, one engine out
  23,000 ft (7,000 m)
T-O run at AUW of 48,500 lb (22,000 kg)
  655 ft (200 m)
T-O to 35 ft (10 m) at AUW of 48,500 lb (22,000 kg)
  1,050 ft (320 m)
Landing from 50 ft (15 m) at AUW of 44,100 lb (20,000 kg) 820 ft (250 m)
Landing run at AUW of 44,100 lb (20,000 kg)
  345 ft (105 m)
Range with max internal fuel
  1,670 nm (1,925 miles; 3,100 km)
Range with max payload
  538 nm (620 miles; 1,000 km)

BREGUET 1150 ATLANTIC

Under the auspices of the NATO Armaments Committee, a specification for a maritime patrol aircraft to supersede the widely-used Lockheed P-2 Neptune was drawn up and published in 1958. A total of 25 design studies were submitted for evaluation, from aircraft manufacturers in several countries. Of these, the Breguet Type 1150 was chosen for development under the name "Atlantic", and two prototypes were ordered in December 1959, followed by an order for two pre-production aircraft.

Responsibility for the supervision and financing of the programme was assumed jointly by the five Governments of the Federal Republic of Germany, Belgium, France, the Netherlands and the USA. The aircraft, both at the prototype and at the series production phases, have been constructed by a consortium formed by Breguet, under the executive supervision of the French *Direction Technique des Constructions Aéronautiques*.

Following its order for Atlantics in 1968, the Italian Government joined the five former associate Governments, and the Italian aircraft industry now participates in the manufacture of engines, airframes and equipment for these aircraft.

Fokker-VFW in the Netherlands are responsible for detail design and manufacture of the centre wing and rear of the engine nacelles. Dornier and MBB in Germany are producing the lower centre and upper rear fuselage and the fin and tailplane. Many airframe components are being supplied by the Belgian ABAP group, made up of Fairey, SABCA and Fabrique Nationale. The outer wings are designed and built by Aérospatiale (Sud-Aviation) in France and the landing gear in Spain by Hispano. From 1969 four Italian manufacturers, led by Aerfer, joined the consortium. These companies are now responsible, inter alia, for most of the wing and tail control surfaces, parts of the fuselage nose and the centre sections of the engine nacelles. Breguet retains responsibility for the main fuselage, final assembly and development.

For the prototypes, Rolls-Royce supplied Tyne RTy.20 turboprop engines from the United Kingdom, and much of the electronic equipment came from the United States. For production aircraft, broader arrangements were made, not only for the airframe but also for engines and equipment. In particular, Hispano are building the Tyne engines under licence in France, assisted by FN (Belgium), MTU (Germany) and (since 1969) Alfa Romeo and Fiat in Italy. Hawker Siddeley Dynamics (UK) and Ratier-Figeac SA (France) manufacture the propellers.

The first prototype flew on 21 October 1961; the second flew on 23 February 1962, but was lost as the result of an accident on 19 April 1962. The first pre-production Atlantic, which flew on 25 February 1963, introduced a 3 ft 0 in (1·0 m) longer front fuselage, to provide more space in the operations control centre.

An initial production series of 40 Atlantics was ordered for the French Navy, and Germany ordered 20. The first of these flew on 19 July 1965, and the first delivery of an operational Atlantic was made to the French Navy on 10 December 1965. All 60 of the initial series were completed by mid-1968; but nine were then ordered for the Royal Netherlands Navy. The first of these was delivered on 26 June 1969.

Breguet 941S STOL transport as demonstrated in the USA under the designation McDonnell Douglas 188

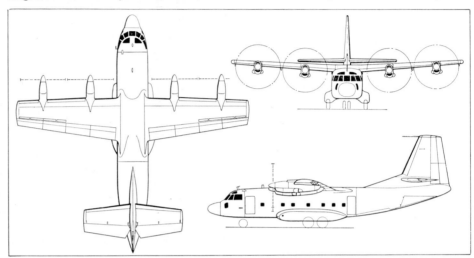

Breguet 941S STOL transport (four 1,500 shp Turboméca Turmo IIID3 turboprop engines)

Production of these and of a subsequent order for 18 for the Italian Navy will maintain production until early 1973. The Dutch order is being fulfilled by the last four aircraft of the initial production series, destined originally for France, and by five from the second production series. These will then be followed by those for Italy, and four further aircraft from the second batch will complete the French order for 40 Atlantics.

TYPE: Twin-engined maritime patrol aircraft.

WINGS: Cantilever mid-wing monoplane. Wing section NACA 64 series. Dihedral on outer wings only. All-metal three-spar fail-safe structure, with bonded light alloy honeycomb skin panels on torsion box and on main landing gear doors. Conventional all-metal ailerons actuated by SAMM twin-cylinder jacks. All-metal slotted flaps, with bonded light alloy honeycomb filling, over 75% of span. Three hinged spoilers on upper surface of each outer wing, forward of flaps. Metal air-brake above and below each wing. No trim-tabs. Kléber-Colombes pneumatic de-icing boots on leading-edges.

FUSELAGE: All-metal "double-bubble" fail-safe structure, with bonded honeycomb sandwich skin on pressurised central section of upper fuselage, weapons bay doors and nose-wheel door.

TAIL UNIT: Cantilever all-metal structure with bonded honeycomb sandwich skin panels on torsion boxes. Tailplane incidence fixed. Control surfaces operated through SAMM twin-cylinder jacks. No trim-tabs. Kléber-Colombes pneumatic de-icing boots on leading-edges.

LANDING GEAR: Retractable tricycle type, manufactured by Hispano-Suiza, with twin wheels on each unit. Hydraulic retraction, nose-wheels rearward, main units forward into engine nacelles. Kléber-Colombes dimpled tyres, size 39 × 13-16 on main wheels, 26 × 7·75-13 on nose-wheels. Tyre pressures: main 138 lb/sq in (9·7 kg/cm²), nose 88 lb/sq in (6·2 kg/cm²). Hispano disc brakes with Maxaret anti-skid units.

POWER PLANT: Two 6,105 ehp Hispano-built Rolls-Royce Tyne RTy.20 Mk 21 turboprop engines, each driving a Ratier-built HSD four-blade constant-speed propeller, diameter 16 ft (4·88 m). Fuel in six integral tanks with total capacity of 4,619 Imp gallons (21,000 litres). Provision for wing-tip tanks to be fitted.

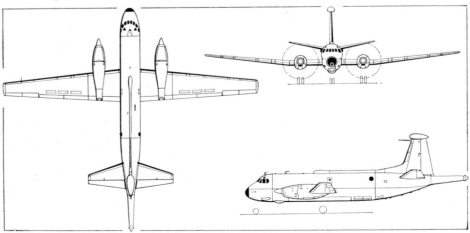

Breguet 1150 Atlantic twin-turboprop maritime patrol aircraft

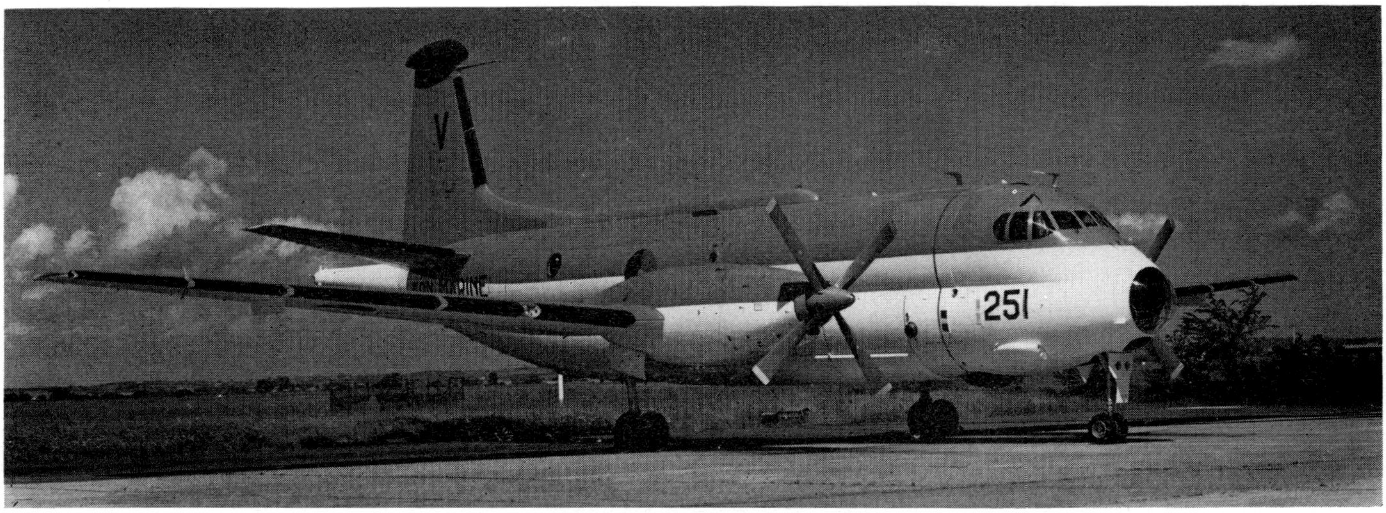

Breguet 1150 Atlantic (two 6,105 ehp Hispano-built Rolls-Royce Tyne RTy.20 turboprop engines) in the insignia of the Royal Netherlands Navy

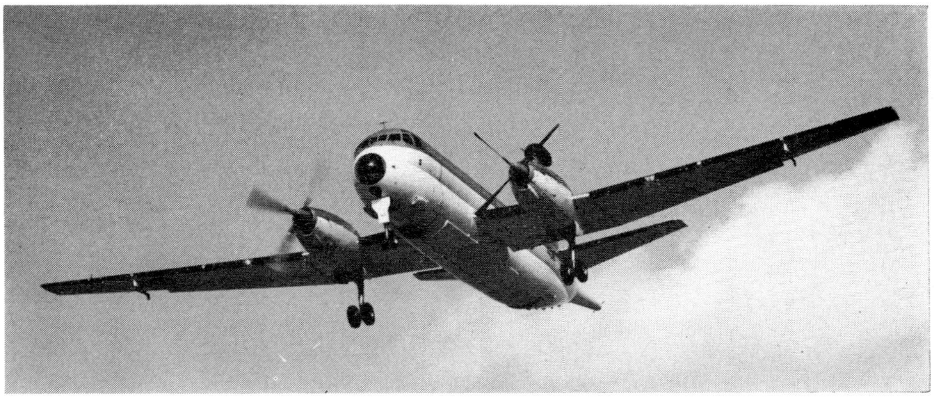

Breguet 1150 Atlantic of the French Navy, with landing gear extended and port propeller feathered (*Air Portraits*)

ACCOMMODATION: Normal flight crew of 12, comprising observer in nose; pilot and co-pilot on flight deck; a tactical co-ordinator, navigator, two sonobuoy operators, and radio, radar and ECM/MAD/Autolycus operators in tactical compartment; and two observers in beam positions. On long-range patrol missions a further 12 would be carried as relief crew. The upper, pressurised section of the fuselage, from front to rear, comprises the nose observer's compartment, flight deck, tactical operations compartment, rest compartment for crew, and beam observers' compartment.

SYSTEMS: SEMCA air-conditioning and pressurisation system. Hydraulic system pressure 3,000 lb/sq in (210 kg/cm²). Electrical system provides 28·5V DC, 115/200V variable-frequency AC and 115/200V stabilised-frequency AC. AiResearch GTCP 85-100 APU in starboard side of front fuselage, adjacent to radar compartment, for engine starting and ground air-conditioning, and can also power one 20 kVA AC alternator and one 4 kW DC generator for emergency electrical power supply.

ARMAMENT AND OPERATIONAL EQUIPMENT: Main weapons carried in bay in unpressurised lower fuselage. Weapons include all NATO standard bombs, 385 lb (175 kg) US or French depth charges, HVAR rockets, homing torpedoes, including types such as the Mk 44 Brush or LX.4 with acoustic heads, or four underwing air-to-surface missiles with nuclear or high-explosive warheads. Electronic equipment includes a retractable CSF radar installation, an MAD tail boom and an electronic countermeasures pod at the top of the tail-fin. Sonobuoys are carried in a compartment aft of the main weapons bay, while the whole of the upper and lower rear fuselage acts as a storage compartment for sonobuoys and marker flares. Compartment for retractable CSF radar 'dustbin' forward of main weapons bay. Forward of this, the lower nose section acts as additional storage for military equipment and the APU. Weapons system includes Plotac optical tactical display 31·5 × 31·5 in (80 × 80 cm) in size, consisting of separate tables for search display and localisation and attack display. At 1/30,000 scale, this gives coverage of an area 24,000 × 24,000 yd (21,950 × 21,950 m) to an accuracy of 1 mm (*ie*, less than 100 ft = 30·5 m at that scale). Heading references provided by duplicated gyroscopic platforms of the 3-gyro (1° of freedom) 4-gimbals type, with magnetic compasses as back-up system. Janus-type Doppler has stabilised antenna and works in the Ke band to provide direct indication of ground speed and drift. In case of failure an automatic switch is made to the Air Data system. The analogue-type navigation computer is accurate to 0·25%. The MAD is of the atomic resonance type and uses light-stimulation techniques. Plotac system has provision to accept additional detectors. Radar has 'sea-return' circuits and stabilised antenna enabling it to detect a submarine snorkel at up to 40 nm (75 km) even in rough seas.

DIMENSIONS, EXTERNAL:

Wing span	119 ft 1 in (36·30 m)
Wing aspect ratio	10·94
Length overall	104 ft 2 in (31·75 m)
Height overall	37 ft 2 in (11·33 m)
Fuselage:	
Max width	9 ft 6 in (2·90 m)
Max depth	13 ft 1½ in (4·00 m)
Tailplane span	40 ft 4½ in (12·31 m)
Wheel track	29 ft 6¼ in (9·00 m)
Wheelbase	31 ft 0 in (9·44 m)

DIMENSIONS, INTERNAL:

Tactical compartment:	
Length	28 ft 2½ in (8·60 m)
Height	6 ft 4 in (1·93 m)
Max width	8 ft 10½ in (2·70 m)
Rest compartment:	
Length	16 ft 8¾ in (5·10 m)
Height	6 ft 4 in (1·93 m)
Max width	8 ft 10½ in (2·70 m)
Beam observers' compartment:	
Length	3 ft 3½ in (1·00 m)
Main weapons bay:	
Length	29 ft 6¼ in (9·00 m)
Height	5 ft 1 in (1·55 m)
Height under wing	3 ft 3½ in (1·00 m)
Max width	7 ft 2½ in (2·20 m)

AREAS:

Wings, gross	1,295 sq ft (120·34 m²)
Ailerons (total)	58·0 sq ft (5·40 m²)
Trailing-edge flaps (total)	288·4 sq ft (26·80 m²)
Spoilers (total)	17·8 sq ft (1·66 m²)
Fin	179·1 sq ft (16·64 m²)
Rudder	64·1 sq ft (5·96 m²)
Tailplane	349·7 sq ft (32·5 m²)
Elevators	89·1 sq ft (8·28 m²)

WEIGHTS:

Useful load	40,900 lb (18,551 kg)
Max zero-fuel weight	76,000 lb (34,473 kg)
Max T-O weight	95,900 lb (43,500 kg)

PERFORMANCE (at max T-O weight):

Max level speed at high altitudes 355 knots (409 mph; 658 km/h)
Cruising speed 300 knots (345 mph; 556 km/h)
Service ceiling 32,800 ft (10,000 m)
T-O to 35 ft (10 m), ISA 4,925 ft (1,500 m)
T-O to 35 ft (10 m), ISA+17°C, 15° flap 5,575 ft (1,700 m)
Max range 4,854 nm (5,590 miles; 9,000 km)
Max endurance at patrol speed of 169 knots (195 mph; 320 km/h) 18 hr

C.A.A.R.P.

COOPÉRATIVE DES ATELIERS AÉRONAUTIQUES DE LA RÉGION PARISIENNE

HEAD OFFICE AND WORKS:
Aérodrome de Beynes, 78-Yvelines

DIRECTOR: Auguste Mudry

This company specialised at first in aircraft modification and repair. It then began the manufacture, under sub-contract, of components for sailplanes, and in 1965 took over from Scintex-Aviation production of the Super Emeraude light aircraft. It also built a prototype of the C.P. 100 side-by-side two-seat aerobatic version of the Emeraude.

C.A.A.R.P. has now ceased production of Emeraude variants and is concentrating on modified versions designated CAP 10 and CAP 20. All available details of these aircraft are given below.

C.A.A.R.P. CAP 10

Developed from the Piel Emeraude two-seat light aircraft (which see), the CAP 10 is intended for use as a training, touring or aerobatic aeroplane. The prototype was flown for the first time in August 1968, and in 1969 completed flight trials for certification in Category A at the Centre d'Essais en Vol at Istres. Construction is to French AIR 2052 (CAR 3) Category A standards for aerobatic flying.

It has been reported that five pre-series CAP 10s have been ordered for the *Armée de l'Air*.

TYPE: Two-seat aerobatic light aircraft.

WINGS: Cantilever low-wing monoplane. Wing section NACA 23012. Dihedral 5° from roots. Incidence 0°. No sweepback. All-spruce single-spar torsion-box structure, with trellis ribs, rear auxiliary spar and okoumé plywood covering. Inner section of each wing is rectangular in plan, outer section semi-elliptical. Wooden trailing-edge plain flaps and slotted ailerons.

FUSELAGE: Conventional spruce girder structure, built in two halves and joined by three main frames. Of basically rectangular section with rounded top-decking. Fabric covering. Forward section also has an inner plywood skin for added strength. Engine cowling panels of non-inflammable laminated plastic.

TAIL UNIT: Conventional cantilever structure. Fin is integral with fuselage and has shallow dorsal fairing. All-wood single-spar fin and tailplane. All surfaces plywood-covered except rudder, which is fabric-covered. Tailplane incidence adjustable on ground. Trim-tab in each elevator.

LANDING GEAR: Non-retractable tail-wheel type. Main-wheel legs of light alloy, with ERAM type 9 270 C oleo-pneumatic shock-absorbers. Single wheel on each main unit, tyre size 380

× 150. Solid tail-wheel tyre, size 6 × 200.
Tail-wheel is steerable by rudder linkage but
can be disengaged for ground manoeuvring.
Hydraulically - actuated main - wheel brakes
and parking brake. Streamline fairings on
main wheels and legs.

POWER PLANT: One 180 hp Lycoming IO-320-B2F
four-cylinder horizontally-opposed air-cooled
engine, with fuel injection, driving a Hoffman
two-blade fixed-pitch wooden propeller. Fuel
in two main tanks in fuselage, one aft of engine
fireproof bulkhead and one beneath baggage
compartment, with total capacity of 33 Imp
gallons (150 litres). Fuel and oil systems
modified to permit periods of inverted flying.

ACCOMMODATION: Side-by-side adjustable seats
for two persons, with provision for back parachutes, under rearward-sliding moulded transparent canopy. Space for 44 lb (20 kg) of
baggage aft of seats in training and touring
models.

SYSTEMS: Electrical system includes Delco-
Remy engine-driven generator and SAFT
12V DC battery.

ELECTRONICS AND EQUIPMENT: CSF 262 12-
channel VHF radio fitted.

DIMENSIONS, EXTERNAL:
Wing span	26 ft 5¼ in (8·06 m)
Wing aspect ratio	5·96
Length overall	21 ft 6¾ in (6·57 m)
Height overall	8 ft 4½ in (2·55 m)
Tailplane span	9 ft 6 in (2·90 m)
Wheel track	6 ft 9 in (2·06 m)

DIMENSIONS, INTERNAL:
Cabin: Max width	3 ft 5½ in (1·054 m)

AREAS:
Wings, gross	116·79 sq ft (10·85 m²)
Ailerons (total)	8·50 sq ft (0·79 m²)
Vertical tail surfaces (total)	14·25 sq ft (1·32 m²)
Horizontal tail surfaces (total)	20·0 sq ft (1·86 m²)

WEIGHTS (A = Aerobatic, U = Utility):
Weight empty, equipped:		
A, U		1,168 lb (530 kg)
Fuel load:		
A		119 lb (54 kg)
U		238 lb (108 kg)
Max T-O weight:		
A		1,666 lb (756 kg)
U		1,829 lb (830 kg)

PERFORMANCE (at max T-O weight):
Max level speed at S/L	146 knots (168 mph; 270 km/h)
Max never-exceed speed	183 knots (211 mph; 340 km/h)
Max cruising speed (75% power)	135 knots (155 mph; 250 km/h)
Stalling speed, flaps up	52 knots (59·5 mph; 95 km/h)
Stalling speed, flaps down	44 knots (50 mph; 80 km/h)
Rate of climb at S/L	over 1,180 ft (360 m)/min
Service ceiling	over 18,050 ft (5,500 m)
Range	approx 538 nm (620 miles; 1,000 km)

C.A.A.R.P. CAP 20

The CAP 20, developed in parallel with the
CAP 10, is essentially a single-seat derivative
of the latter aircraft, although of almost completely new design. Construction of a proto-

Prototype CAP 10 two-seat light training aircraft (180 hp Lycoming engine) (*Air & Cosmos*)

Prototype of the CAP 20 single-seat aerobatic light aircraft (*Air & Cosmos*)

type was financed by the SGAC, and this aircraft
(F-WPXU) flew for the first time on 29 July
1969. Two more prototypes, including one for
evaluation by the *Armée de l'Air*, were under
construction in 1969.

TYPE: Single-seat aerobatic light aircraft.

WINGS: Cantilever low-wing monoplane. All-
wood single-spar wings, of NACA 23012 section,
similar in construction and planform to those
of CAP 10 but with ailerons only on trailing-
edge, and hydraulically-actuated air-brakes.
Dihedral 5° from roots.

FUSELAGE: Conventional all-wood structure,
of basically triangular section with rounded
top-decking. Wooden covering, except for
laminated plastic engine cowling.

TAIL UNIT: Cantilever all-wood structure. Fin
has shallow dorsal fairing. Trim-tab in rudder
and each elevator.

LANDING GEAR: Non-retractable tailwheel type.
Streamline fairings on main wheels and legs.

POWER PLANT: One 200 hp Lycoming AIO-360-
A1A four-cylinder horizontally-opposed air-
cooled engine, driving a Hartzell two-blade
constant-speed metal propeller, diameter 6 ft 0 in
(1·83 m). Fuel in main fuselage tank aft of

cockpit, with system modified to permit periods
of inverted flight. Provision for 16·5 Imp
gallon (75 litre) under-fuselage auxiliary tank
for ferry purposes.

ACCOMMODATION: Single seat for pilot under
transparent moulded canopy which opens
sideways to starboard.

DIMENSIONS, EXTERNAL:
Wing span	26 ft 4¾ in (8·04 m)
Wing aspect ratio	5·96
Length overall	23 ft 7¾ in (7·21 m)

AREA:
Wings, gross	116·79 sq ft (10·85 m²)

WEIGHTS AND LOADING:
Weight empty	1,353 lb (614 kg)
Max T-O weight (aerobatic)	1,675 lb (760 kg)
Max wing loading	14·3 lb/sq ft (70·0 kg/m²)

PERFORMANCE (estimated at max aerobatic T-O
weight):
Max never-exceed speed	202 knots (233 mph; 376 km/h)
Max cruising speed	183 knots (211 mph; 340 km/h)
Max speed for aerobatics	146 knots (168 mph; 270 km/h)
Stalling speed	52·5 knots (60 mph; 96 km/h)

CHASLE
YVES CHASLE

ADDRESS:
rue de la Croix Blanche, 78-Mareil-Marly

M Chasle, a stress engineer with Sud-Aviation,
designed and built a light aircraft named the
YC-12 Tourbillon. Its dimensions were governed
by the maximum size that could be accommodated
in his garage workshop. First flight was made
on 9 October 1965. As a result of the flight tests
leading to its restricted C of A, the height of the
vertical tail surfaces was later increased slightly.
Plans are available to amateur constructors.
More recently, M Chasle has designed a new
tandem two-seat light aircraft known as the
YC-20, details of which are also given below.

CHASLE YC-12 TOURBILLON (WHIRLWIND)

The Tourbillon can be built in a variety of
forms, differing only in the type of engine fitted,
as follows:

YC-121. With 65 hp Continental A65 engine.
Generally similar to prototype except for detail
changes noted below.

YC-122. Similar to YC-121, but with 95 hp
Continental C90 or 100 hp Rolls-Royce/Conti-
nental O-200-A engine.

YC-123. Similar to YC-121, but with 105 hp
Potez 4E-20b engine.

Nine YC-12's were under construction in 1969,
three each in Canada and the US and one each
in France, New Zealand and the UK. Marketing
of the YC-12 in North America is by E. Littner,
546 83rd Avenue, Laval-Chomedey, Quebec,
Canada.

TYPE: Single-seat amateur-built light aircraft.

Prototype Chasle YC-12 Tourbillon single-seat light aircraft (65 hp Continental A65 engine)

WINGS: Cantilever low-wing monoplane. Wing
section NACA Srs 7. Dihedral 6°. Incidence 3° 30'. All-wood structure, with main
box spar of spruce and okoumé, spruce plank
rear spar, girder-type ribs and okoumé plywood
covering. All-wood ailerons and three-position
slotted flaps.

FUSELAGE: Conventional plywood-covered wood
structure, built around four spruce longerons,
four main frames, five secondary frames and
stringers.

TAIL UNIT: Cantilever all-wood structure, with
swept vertical surfaces. Prototype has one-
piece horizontal surfaces with automatic anti-
tab which is controllable in flight. Subsequent
Tourbillons have fixed tailplane and conven-

tional elevators.

LANDING GEAR: Non-retractable tail-wheel type.
Steerable tail-wheel linked with rudder. Main
units have ERAM oleo-pneumatic suspension
(Niemann rubber-band suspension on prototype), Vespa wheels, size 400 × 100, mounted
on "L"-shape legs. Independent mechanical
brakes. Tail-wheel carried on leaf spring.
Provision for changing to a tricycle configuration, by switching main legs port and starboard,
with lower arm of "L" facing rearward, and
mounting nose-unit on firewall.

POWER PLANT: One 65 hp Continental A65 four-
cylinder horizontally-opposed air-cooled engine,
driving an EVRA two-blade propeller, diameter 5 ft 9 in (1·75 m). Fuel tank, capacity

13·3 Imp gallons (60·5 litres), aft of firewall. Oil capacity 0·83 Imp gallons (3·75 litres).

Accommodation: Single-seat. Large transparent rearward-sliding canopy standard. Prototype has sideways-hinged (to starboard) canopy. Baggage space aft of seat.

Electronics and Equipment: Optional items include Radiomaster radio, generator, starter, and night-flying equipment.

Dimensions, external:
Wing span:
prototype 21 ft 0 in (6·40 m)
standard 22 ft 0 in (6·70 m)
Wing chord at root 4 ft 7¼ in (1·40 m)
Wing chord at tip 2 ft 7¼ in (0·79 m)
Wing aspect ratio:
prototype 5·8
standard 6·0
Length overall:
prototype 18 ft 6 in (5·64 m)
YC-121 19 ft 6 in (5·95 m)
YC-122, YC-123 19 ft 2¼ in (5·85 m)
Height overall 7 ft 10½ in (2·40 m)
Tailplane span 6 ft 6¾ in (2·00 m)
Wheel track 5 ft 3 in (1·60 m)
Wheelbase 11 ft 11¾ in (3·65 m)

Areas:
Wings, gross 80·7 sq ft (7·50 m^2)
Ailerons (total) 5·94 sq ft (0·55 m^2)
Flaps (total) 9·69 sq ft (0·90 m^2)
Tailplane, including tab 12·92 sq ft (1·20 m^2)
Tailplane anti-tab 1·42 sq ft (0·13 m^2)
Fin 5·38 sq ft (0·50 m^2)
Rudder 3·77 sq ft (0·35 m^2)

Weights and Loadings:
Weight empty:
YC-121 628 lb (285 kg)
YC-122, YC-123 690 lb (313 kg)
Max T-O weight, without radio:
YC-121 952 lb (432 kg)
YC-122, YC-123 1,015 lb (460 kg)
Max wing loading:
YC-121 11·77 lb/sq ft (57·5 kg/m^2)
YC-122, YC-123 12·55 lb/sq ft (61·3 kg/m^2)
Max power loading:
YC-121 14·64 lb/hp (6·64 kg/hp)
YC-122 10·69 lb/hp (4·85 kg/hp)
YC-123 9·63 lb/hp (4·37 kg/hp)

Performance (estimated):
Max speed at S/L:
YC-121 127 knots (146 mph; 235 km/h)
YC-122 146 knots (168 mph; 270 km/h)
YC-123 151 knots (174 mph; 280 km/h)
Max cruising speed (70% power):
YC-121 110 knots (127 mph; 205 km/h)
YC-122 129 knots (149 mph; 240 km/h)
YC-123 135 knots (155 mph; 250 km/h)
Stalling speed:
YC-121 41 knots (47 mph; 75 km/h)
YC-122, YC-123 44 knots (50 mph; 80 km/h)
Rate of climb at S/L:
YC-121 905 ft (276 m)/min
YC-122 1,380 ft (420 m)/min
YC-123 1,575 ft (480 m)/min
T-O run:
YC-121 855 ft (260 m)
YC-122 660 ft (200 m)
YC-123 593 ft (180 m)
Max range:
YC-121 434 nm (500 miles; 800 km)
YC-122, YC-123 377 nm (435 miles; 700 km)

CHASLE YC-20 RAZ DE MARÉE (TIDAL WAVE)

M Chasle began design of this tandem two-seat light aircraft late in 1967, and in mid-1969 five YC-20's were under construction by amateur builders in France. The first of these was begun in April 1969, and the first flight by a YC-20 was expected to take place in the Summer of 1970.

Type: Two-seat light aircraft.

Wings: Cantilever low-wing monoplane, with NACA Series 7 wing section. Thickness/chord ratio 17% at root, 11% at tip. Dihedral 8°. Incidence 2° 30′. No sweepback. All-wood box-spar structure with false rear spar, plywood-covered. All-wood plain ailerons and three-position slotted flaps.

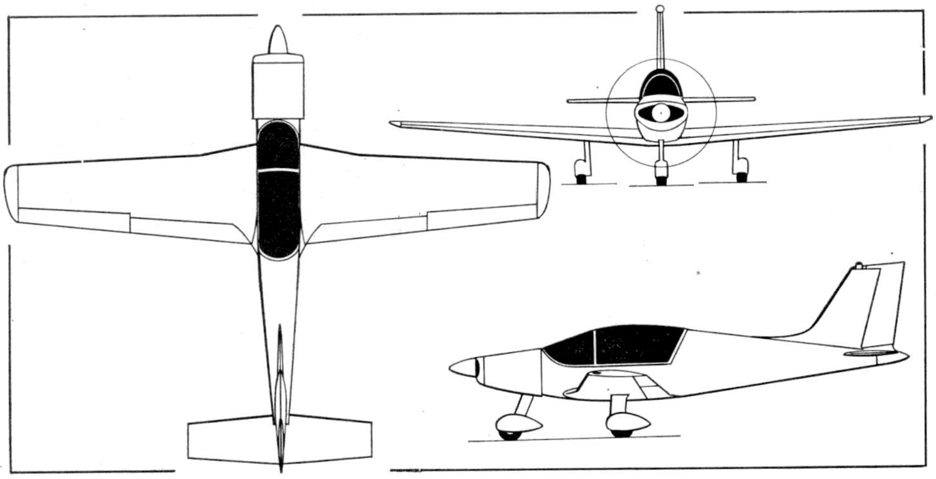

Chasle YC-20 Raz de Marée two-seat amateur-built light aircraft

Fuselage: Structure of five main and five secondary frames, with eight stringers, and plywood stressed-skin covering.

Tail Unit: Cantilever single-spar wooden box structure, plywood covered. Slight sweepback on vertical surfaces. Tailplane incidence adjustable on ground.

Landing Gear: Tricycle type, fixed or retractable at builder's option. Manual retraction, nose-wheel rearward, main wheels inward into wing roots. All three wheels same size, with Goodyear 150 × 380 tyres. Hydraulic brakes.

Power Plant: One 90 hp Rolls-Royce/Continental O-200 or 115 hp Lycoming four-cylinder horizontally-opposed air-cooled engine driving a fixed-pitch propeller. Provision for alternative installation of Lycoming engines of up to 150 hp. Fuel in four metal tanks in wing leading-edges, with total capacity of 26 Imp gallons (120 litres).

Accommodation: Tandem seating for two persons under fully-transparent rearward-opening canopy. Space for up to 33 lb (15 kg) of baggage.

Electronics and Equipment: VHF radio and other equipment to customer's requirements.

Dimensions, external:
Wing span 28 ft 1 in (8·56 m)
Wing chord at root 5 ft 3 in (1·60 m)
Wing chord at tip 3 ft 1¾ in (0·96 m)
Wing aspect ratio 6·7
Length overall (90 or 115 hp engine) 23 ft 7½ in (7·20 m)
Length overall (150 hp engine) 23 ft 3½ in (7·10 m)
Max width of fuselage 2 ft 4 in (0·71 m)
Height overall 8 ft 10¼ in (2·70 m)
Tailplane span 9 ft 3 in (2·82 m)
Wheel track 8 ft 6¼ in (2·60 m)
Wheelbase 6 ft 2¾ in (1·90 m)

Areas:
Wings, gross 118·4 sq ft (11·0 m^2)
Ailerons (total) 9·15 sq ft (0·85 m^2)
Trailing-edge flaps (total) 15·07 sq ft (1·40 m^2)
Fin 10·76 sq ft (1·00 m^2)
Rudder 6·03 sq ft (0·56 m^2)
Tailplane 13·99 sq ft (1·30 m^2)
Elevators 7·53 sq ft (0·70 m^2)

Weights and Loadings (A = 90/115 hp, fixed u/c; B = 90/115 hp, retractable u/c; C = 150 hp, fixed u/c; D = 150 hp, retractable u/c):
Weight empty:
A 855 lb (388 kg)
B 870 lb (395 kg)
C 943 lb (428 kg)
D 959 lb (435 kg)
Max T-O weight:
A 1,439 lb (653 kg)
B 1,455 lb (660 kg)
C 1,527 lb (693 kg)
D 1,543 lb (700 kg)
Max wing loading:
A 12·2 lb/sq ft (59·4 kg/m^2)
B 12·3 lb/sq ft (60·0 kg/m^2)
C 12·9 lb/sq ft (63·0 kg/m^2)
D 13 lb/sq ft (63·6 kg/m^2)
Max power loading:
A 15·98 lb/hp (7·25 kg/hp)
B 16·20 lb/hp (7·35 kg/hp)
C 10·14 lb/hp (4·60 kg/hp)
D 10·25 lb/hp (4·65 kg/hp)

Performance (estimated, at max T-O weight, A = 90/115 hp, fixed u/c; B = 90/115 hp, retractable u/c; C = 150 hp, fixed u/c; D = 150 hp, retractable u/c):
Max level speed:
A 122 knots (140 mph; 225 km/h)
B 132 knots (152 mph; 245 km/h)
C 151 knots (174 mph; 280 km/h)
D 168 knots (193 mph; 310 km/h)
Max cruising speed:
A 110 knots (127 mph; 205 km/h)
B 122 knots (140 mph; 225 km/h)
C 135 knots (155 mph; 250 km/h)
D 151 knots (174 mph; 280 km/h)
Stalling speed:
A, B, C, D, 87 knots (99·5 mph; 160 km/h)
Landing speed:
A, B 40·5 knots (46·6 mph; 75 km/h)
C, D 43·5 knots (50 mph; 80 km/h)
Rate of climb at S/L:
A 885 ft (270 m)/min
B 985 ft (300 m)/min
C 1,380 ft (420 m)/min
D 1,475 ft (450 m)/min
T-O run:
A, B 820 ft (250 m)
C, D 690 ft (210 m)
Landing run:
A, B 590 ft (180 m)
C, D 655 ft (200 m)
Range with max fuel:
A 460 nm (530 miles; 860 km)
B 495 nm (570 miles; 920 km)
C 429 nm (495 miles; 800 km)
D 473 nm (545 miles; 880 km)

CHATELAIN

ANDRÉ CHATELAIN

Address:
c/o Reseau du Sport de l'Air, Café Moderne, 183 Cours Lafayette, Lyons 6e

Details of the AC-9 three/four-seat amateur-built light aircraft designed by M Chatelain of Amiens were given in the 1967-68 *Jane's*.

More recently, M Chatelain has designed and flown the prototype (F-PPPT) of a new side-by-side two-seat light aircraft designated AC-10, all available details of which are given below.

CHATELAIN AC-10

Type: Two-seat light aircraft.

Wings: Cantilever low-wing monoplane, with dihedral from roots. Wing section NACA 23015. Conventional two-spar wood structure, with plywood covering. Mechanically-operated trailing-edge slotted flaps and ailerons.

Fuselage: Steel-tube structure with fabric covering.

Tail Unit: Fabric-covered steel-tube structure with wire-braced tailplane.

Landing Gear: Non-retractable tricycle type, with streamlined fairing on each unit. Telescopic nose-wheel leg, with rubber-block shock-absorption; nose-wheel is steered by linkage with rudder movement. Cantilever rigid-tube legs on main units, hinged at the wing roots and with Weidert rubber-block shock-absorbers.

Power Plant: One 90 hp Rolls-Royce Continental four-cylinder horizontally-opposed air-cooled engine, driving a two-blade fixed-pitch wooden propeller.

Accommodation: Side-by-side seating for two persons under one-piece rearward-sliding transparent moulded canopy taken from a Piel Emeraude.

Dimensions, external:
Wing span 25 ft 7 in (7·80 m)
Wing chord (constant) 4 ft 1¼ in (1·25 m)
Length overall 18 ft 10¼ in (5·75 m)

Area:
Wings, gross 101·2 sq ft (9·40 m^2)

Weights and Loadings:
Weight empty 892 lb (405 kg)
Max T-O weight 1,355 lb (615 kg)
Max wing loading 13·39 lb/sq ft (65·4 kg/m^2)
Max power loading 13·67 lb/hp (6·2 kg/hp)

Performance (at max T-O weight):
Cruising speed 92 knots (106 mph; 170 km/h)
Stalling speed, flaps up 38 knots (43·5 mph; 70 km/h)
Stalling speed, flaps down 28 knots (31·5 mph; 50 km/h)

CROSES
EMILIEN and ALAIN CROSES
ADDRESS:
Route de Davayé, 71-Charnay les Macon

The 1960-61 *Jane's* contained details of the Croses EC-1-02 side-by-side two-seat lightplane of the Mignet tandem-wing type. M Emilien Croses has since built and flown an improved version of this aircraft, known as the EC-6, and a three-seat lightplane/air ambulance development, the B-EC 7 with more powerful engine.

M Croses has also developed the Pouplume, an ultra-light single-seat aeroplane of the same general configuration. Brief details of these types are given below.

CROSES EAC-3 POUPLUME
As in the familiar Mignet designs, the Pouplume single-seat tandem-wing biplane has a fixed rear wing and a pivoted forward wing which dispenses with the need for ailerons and elevators. A conventional rudder is fitted, with a large tail-wheel built into its lower edge.

Construction is conventional, with spruce wing structure and a square-section spruce fuselage covered with okoumé ply. The main landing gear consists of Vespa scooter wheels carried on a wooden cross-member.

The power unit in the prototype (EAC-3-01) is a 10·5 hp Moto 232 cc two-stroke motor-cycle engine, with chain reduction drive to the propeller shaft. The reduction ratio is 3·5 : 1, giving a propeller speed of 1,300 rpm. Fuel capacity is 2·2 Imp gallons (10 litres).

The EAC-3-01 Pouplume took 600 hours to build and flew for the first time in June 1961. This machine was followed, in 1967, by a second prototype (EAC-3-02), with an 8-in (20-cm) longer fuselage. M Croses is offering sets of plans to other amateur constructors and the 1968-69 *Jane's* contained an illustration of a Pouplume built in the Argentine, which introduced several design improvements and attained a speed of 51 knots (59 mph; 95 km/h) with a 232 cc engine.

That shown in the adjacent illustration was built in France by an amateur constructor.

Alternative engines that may be fitted in the Pouplume include the various Volkswagen conversions and the 40 hp de Coucy-Fauvel Pygmée.

DIMENSIONS, EXTERNAL (EAC-3-01):
Span of forward wing	25 ft 7 in (7·8 m)
Span of rear wing	23 ft 0 in (7·0 m)
Length overall	9 ft 10 in (3·0 m)
Height overall	5 ft 11 in (1·8 m)

AREA:
Wings, gross	172 sq ft (16·0 m²)

WEIGHTS:
Weight empty	243-310 lb (110-140 kg)
Max T-O weight	485-573 lb (220-260 kg)

PERFORMANCE (A = 10·5 hp engine; B = 18 hp engine):
Max level speed:
A	38 knots (43·5 mph; 70 km/h)
B	65 knots (75 mph; 120 km/h)

Econ cruising speed:
A	27 knots (31 mph; 50 km/h)
B	38 knots (43·5 mph; 70 km/h)

T-O speed:
A	13·5 knots (15·5 mph; 25 km/h)

Landing speed:
A	9·7 knots (11 mph; 18 km/h)

T-O run:
A	200 ft (60 m)
B	131 ft (40 m)

Landing run:
A	80 ft (24 m)

Fuel consumption:
A	1 Imp gallon (4·5 litres) hr

CROSES EC-6 CRIQUET (LOCUST)
The general appearance of this design by Emilien Croses is shown in the adjacent illustration. It is a development of his earlier EC-1-02 prototype and is a side-by-side two-seater based on the familiar Mignet tandem-wing formula. Construction was started in March 1964 and the EC-6-01 flew for the first time on 6 July 1965.

TYPE: Two-seat tandem-wing light aircraft.

WINGS: Forward wing built in one piece and pivoted on two streamlined supports, giving variable incidence between −2° and +12°. Fixed rear (lower) wing. Wing section NACA 23012 (modified). Both wings have two-spar wooden structure, with plywood leading-edge, overall fabric covering and some components of glass-fibre. No ailerons.

FUSELAGE: Spruce structure, covered with plywood. Glass-fibre engine cowling.

TAIL UNIT: Plywood-covered spruce fin and rudder. No tailplane or elevators.

LANDING GEAR: Non-retractable tail-wheel type. Main wheels, size 420 × 150, carried on single cantilever arch structure made from ash wood on a forme and covered with glass-fibre. Tail-wheel, size 420 × 150, semi-enclosed in bottom of rudder.

POWER PLANT: One 90 hp Continental four-cylinder horizontally-opposed air-cooled engine,

Croses EAC-3 Pouplume light aircraft (10.5 hp Moto engine)

Croses EC-6-01 Criquet two-seat light aircraft (90 hp Continental C90 engine)

driving a modified SIPA two-blade propeller. Fuel capacity originally 13 Imp gallons (60 litres); planned to be increased to 20 Imp gallons (90 litres).

ACCOMMODATION: Two seats side-by-side in enclosed cabin. Door on starboard side.

DIMENSIONS, EXTERNAL:
Span of forward wing	25 ft 7 in (7·80 m)
Span of rear wing	22 ft 11½ in (7·00 m)
Wing chord (constant, each)	
	3 ft 11¼ in (1·20 m)

AREA:
Wings, gross	172 sq ft (16·0 m²)

WEIGHTS:
Weight empty	661 lb (300 kg)
Max T-O weight	1,213 lb (550 kg)

PERFORMANCE (officially certified, at max T-O weight):
Max level speed at S/L
	115 knots (132 mph; 213 km/h)

Econ cruising speed
	86 knots (99 mph; 160 km/h)
Min flying speed	22 knots (25 mph; 40 km/h)

Will not stall

T-O time (max)	6 sec
Climb to 6,560 ft (2,000 m)	6 min 14 sec

BUJON-CROSES B-EC 7 TOUT-TERRAIN
From the EC-6, MM Bujon and Croses have developed the B-EC 7 Tout-terrain, which is a three-seat light touring aircraft or air ambulance, with increased wing span, longer fuselage, more extensively glazed canopy, a rough-field landing gear and a more powerful engine. The prototype (F-PPPM), to which the details below apply, has a 100 hp Rolls-Royce/Continental engine. It is broadly similar to the EC-6, the differences in the B-EC 7 including the following:

TYPE: Three-seat tandem-wing light aircraft or air ambulance.

WINGS: Similar to EC-6, but of tapered planform and with trailing-edge flaps on rear wing. Flaps are linked to movement of forward wing to function as trimming surfaces.

LANDING GEAR: Non-retractable tail-wheel type, suitable for operation from rough terrain. Four main wheels in tandem pairs, each pair carried on a single cantilever wooden arch structure.

Bujon-Croses B-EC 7 Tout-Terrain three-seat lightplane/air ambulance aircraft

Tail-wheel semi-enclosed in bottom of rudder. All five wheels same size. Brakes fitted.

POWER PLANT: One 100 hp Continental four-cylinder horizontally-opposed air-cooled engine, driving a two-blade propeller.

ACCOMMODATION: Pilot and two passengers (or one passenger and a stretcher in ambulance configuration) in enclosed cabin.

DIMENSIONS, EXTERNAL:
Span of forward wing	27 ft 6¾ in (8·40 m)
Span of rear wing	26 ft 3 in (8·00 m)

AREA:
Wings, gross	236·80 sq ft (22·0 m²)

WEIGHTS:
Weight empty	926 lb (420 kg)
Max T-O weight	1,653 lb (750 kg)

PERFORMANCE (at max T-O weight):
Max level speed at S/L	119 knots (137 mph; 220 km/h)
Max cruising speed at S/L	97 knots (112 mph; 180 km/h)
Minimum speed	37·8 knots (43·5 mph; 70 km/h)
Rate of climb at S/L	1,180 ft (360 m)/min
T-O run	490 ft (150 m)
Landing run, brakes on	195 ft (60 m)

DALOTEL (see under "Poulet")

DASSAULT

Dassault Mirage III-E multi-purpose combat aircraft (SNECMA Atar 09C turbojet engine) in Spanish Air Force insignia

AVIONS MARCEL DASSAULT

HEAD OFFICE:
27, Avenue du Prof Pauchet, 92-Vaucresson

PARIS OFFICE:
46 Avenue Kléber, 75-Paris 16e

WORKS:
Saint-Cloud (Hauts de Seine), Melun-Villaroche (Seine-et-Marne), Argenteuil (Val d'Oise), Boulogne (Hauts de Seine), Martignas, Mérignac (Gironde), Talence (Gironde), Cazaux (Gironde), Istres (Bouches du Rhône) and Argonnex (Hte Savoie)

FOUNDER: Marcel Dassault

PRINCIPAL DIRECTOR-GENERAL:
B. C. Vallières

TECHNICAL DIRECTOR-GENERAL:
Henri Deplante

TECHNICAL DIRECTOR: Jean Cabriere

PUBLIC RELATIONS: A. Segura

Avions Marcel Dassault is engaged in the development and production of military and civil aircraft, guided missiles and servo control equipment.

The company's principal current products are the Mirage III multi-purpose fighter, the Mirage 5 ground support aircraft, the Mirage F1 fighter and the Mystère 20 Falcon jet executive transport. Under development are the Mirage G variable-geometry strike aircraft, the Mystère 10 scaled-down development of the Falcon, the MD 320 Hirondelle twin-turboprop aircrew training and transport aircraft, and the Mercure twin-jet short-haul transport.

Co-operation with Aérospatiale (Sud-Aviation) in the supersonic transport, short-haul and executive transport, and vertical take-off fighter fields is continuing.

The two companies have also collaborated in production of the Mystère 20 Falcon and are associated in the Concorde supersonic transport programme.

It was announced in September 1968 that Dassault and LTV Aerospace Corporation, USA, had concluded two technical collaboration agreements. As a first step, Dassault supplied information on its Mirage G variable-geometry aircraft to LTV.

Series production of Dassault aircraft is undertaken under a widespread sub-contracting programme, with the final assembly and flight testing being handled by Dassault.

Dassault is also engaged in the development and manufacture of equipment, mainly hydraulic and hydro-electric powered aircraft controls with "feel" simulation. Its subsidiary, Electronique Marcel Dassault, is engaged on a variety of projects including research and production of weapon systems for air-to-air and surface-to-air missiles, tracking radar for use with missiles, and equipment for supersonic jet aircraft.

The total employment of the Dassault factories is 8,550, while some 30,000 employees of 1,500 other concerns all over France are engaged in the production of Dassault parts and sub-assemblies.

Dassault owns 10 works, covering some 2,045,000 sq ft (190,000 m²) of ground, and operates from 4 flight test centres. The principal works is at Saint-Cloud, where the design office is situated and where most Dassault prototypes are built. Airframes for aircraft and missiles are produced at Argenteuil and Boulogne. Melun-Villaroche is the flight test centre for prototype and pre-production aircraft. Powered controls and electronic equipment are manufactured in quantity at Argonnex, and aircraft components at Talence. Mérignac is the flight test centre for production aircraft and is also engaged in modification and repair work. Martignas is responsible for final assembly of missiles. Cazaux and Istres flight test centres offer facilities for armament testing and continued flight trials throughout the Winter respectively.

In June 1967, Avions Marcel Dassault became the major stockholder in Breguet Aviation (which see). The pooling of the two companies' research, development and production facilities, together with those of Electronique Marcel Dassault, has produced a major group which includes 3,000 engineers and technicians out of a total work force of 13,000, and 17 factories and other premises with an overall floor area of 5,382,000 sq ft (500,000 m²).

Dassault has also invested in the Belgian company SABCA (which see), to which it provides technical, production and commercial assistance.

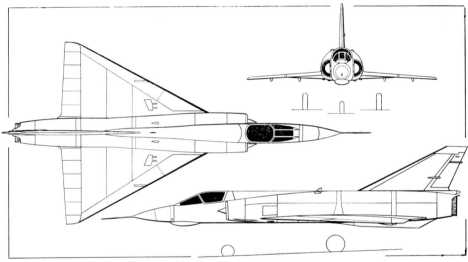

Dassault Mirage III-E single-seat fighter

DASSAULT MIRAGE III

The Mirage III was designed initially as a Mach 2 high-altitude all-weather interceptor, capable of performing ground support missions and requiring only small airstrips. Developed versions include a two-seat trainer, long-range fighter-bomber and reconnaissance aircraft, and a total of 800 Mirage III's of all types had been produced by 30 March 1970, including licence production abroad, out of a total of approx 1,100 ordered.

The experimental prototype flew for the first time on 17 November 1956, powered by a SNECMA Atar 101G turbojet with afterburner (9,900 lb = 4,500 kg st). In this form, on 30 January 1957, in the course of normal testing, it exceeded Mach 1·5 in level flight at an altitude of 36,080 ft (11,000 m). Later it was fitted with an SEPR 66 auxiliary rocket motor (6,610 lb = 3,000 kg st) and reached a speed of Mach 1·9 with this in use, supplementing its turbojet.

Production versions of the Mirage III are as follows:

Mirage III-A. Pre-series of ten aircraft, with SNECMA Atar 09B turbojet (13,225 lb = 6,000 kg) st. First Mirage III-A flew on 12 May 1958, and in a test flight on 24 October 1958 exceeded Mach 2 in level flight at 41,000 ft (12,500 m). Last six equipped to production standard, with CSF Cyrano I*bis* air-to-air radar.

Mirage III-B. Two-seat version of III-A, with tandem seating under one-piece canopy; radar deleted, but fitted with radio beacon equipment. Fuselage 23·6 in (60 cm) longer than that of III-A. Intended primarily as a trainer, but suitable for strike sorties, carrying same air-to-surface armament as Mirage III-C. Prototype flew for first time on 20 October 1959, and first production model on 19 July 1962. Total of 73 two-seaters built, including variants for Brazil, Israel, Lebanon, South Africa (3) and Switzerland (3).

Mirage III-C. All-weather interceptor and day ground attack fighter. Production version of III-A with SNECMA Atar 09B turbojet engine, optional SEPR 841 rocket engine and CSF Cyrano *Ibis* air-to-air radar.

Initial series of 95 for French Air Force, of which the first flew on 9 October 1960. One supplied to Swiss Air Force. Total of 244 built, including variants for Israel and South Africa. Full description in 1968-69 *Jane's*.

Mirage III-D. Two-seat version of the Mirage III-O, built in Australia for the RAAF. First of ten ordered for Mirage OCU was assembled in Australia and delivered in November 1966. Similar models ordered by Lebanon, Pakistan, Peru and South Africa.

Mirage III-E. Long-range fighter-bomber/intruder version, of which 419 have been ordered for the French Air Force and for the air forces of Brazil, Lebanon, Libya, Pakistan, South Africa and Spain.

First of three prototypes flew on 5 April 1961, and the first delivery of a production III-E was made in January 1964. Length increased by 11·8 in (30 cm) compared with III-C, placing pilot further forward of air intakes. First aircraft for Spanish Air Force delivered in April 1970.

Mirage III-O. Version of the Mirage III-E manufactured under licence in Australia. Main differences compared with the standard III-E are fitment of a Sperry Twin Gyro Platform and PHI 5CI navigation unit. First two III-O's assembled in France; first of these handed over on 9 April 1963. Further 98 built in Australia, details of which were given under entry for Commonwealth of Australia, Government Aircraft Factories in 1969-70 *Jane's*.

Mirage III-R. Reconnaissance version of III-E for French Air Force. Set of five OMERA type 31 cameras, in place of radar in nose, can be focused in four different arrangements for very low altitude, medium altitude, high altitude and night reconnaissance missions. Self-contained navigation system and same air-to-surface armament as Mirage III-C. Two prototypes, converted from III-A's, of which the first flew in November 1961. Over 90 production models ordered (including variants for Pakistan, South Africa and Switzerland).

Mirage III-RD. Similar to III-R but with improved Doppler navigation system in fairing under front fuselage, gyro gunsight and automatic cameras. Provision for carrying SAT Cyclope infra-red tracking equipment in ventral fairing, and two 374 Imp gallon (1,700 litre) underwing auxiliary fuel tanks. Twenty ordered for French Air Force.

Mirage III-S. Developed from the Mirage III-E, with a Hughes TARAN electronics fire-control system and armament of HM-55 Falcon missiles. Ordered for Swiss Air Force. The total order was for 36, of which the first two were built in France and the remainder by the Federal Aircraft Factory in Switzerland (which see). The first 24 aircraft were handed over to the Swiss Air Force on 2 March 1968, being allocated in equal quantities to Nos. 16 and 17 Squadrons. Each of these squadrons received a further six aircraft by the end of 1968.

Mirage III-T. Experimental variant with rear fuselage of increased diameter, built as a flying test-bed for the SNECMA TF-106 turbofan engine (19,840 lb = 9,000 kg st) as part of the Mirage III-V experimental VTOL fighter development programme. Fitted initially with a TF-104B turbofan engine, with which it flew for the first time on 4 June 1964. First flight with TF-106 on 25 January 1965.

The following description refers to the Mirage III-E, but is applicable to all versions.

TYPE: Single-seat interceptor, ground attack or reconnaissance aircraft.

WINGS: Cantilever low-wing monoplane of delta planform, with conical camber. Thickness/chord ratio 4·5% to 3·5%. Anhedral 1°. No incidence. Sweepback on leading-edge 60° 34'. All-metal torsion-box structure with stressed skin of machined panels with integral stiffeners. Elevons are hydraulically powered by Dassault twin-cylinder actuators with artificial feel. Air-brakes, comprising small panels hinged to upper and lower wing surfaces, near leading-edge.

FUSELAGE: All-metal structure, "waisted" in accordance with the area rule.

TAIL UNIT: Cantilever fin and hydraulically-actuated powered rudder only. Dassault twin-cylinder actuators with artificial feel.

LANDING GEAR: Retractable tricycle type,

with single wheel on each unit. Hydraulic retraction, nose-wheel rearward, main units inward. Messier shock-absorbers and hydraulic disc brakes. Main wheel tyre pressure 85·5-142 lb/sq in (6-10 kg/cm²). Braking parachute.

POWER PLANT: One SNECMA Atar 09C turbojet engine (13,670 lb = 6,200 kg st with afterburner), fitted with an overspeed system which is engaged automatically from Mach 1·4 and permits a thrust increase of approx 8 per cent in the high supersonic speed range. Optional and jettisonable SEPR 844 single-chamber rocket motor (3,300 lb = 1,500 kg st) or interchangeable fuel tank. Movable half-cone centre-body in each air intake. Total internal fuel capacity 733 Imp gallons (3,330 litres) when rocket motor is not fitted. Provision for this to be augmented by two 132, 285 or 374 Imp gallon (600, 1,300 or 1,700-litre) underwing drop-tanks.

ACCOMMODATION: Single seat under rearward-hinged canopy. Hispano-built Martin-Baker Type RM.4 zero-altitude ejection seat.

SYSTEMS: Two separate air-conditioning systems for cockpit and electronics. Two independent hydraulic systems, pressure 3,000 lb/sq in (210 kg/cm²), for flying controls, landing gear and brakes. Power for DC electrical system from 24V 40Ah batteries and a 26·5V 9kW generator. AC electrical system power provided by one 200V 400 c/s transformer and one 200V 400 c/s 9kVA alternator.

ELECTRONICS AND EQUIPMENT: Duplicated UHF, TACAN, Doppler, CSF Cyrano II fire-control radar in nose, navigation computer, bombing computer, automatic gunsight.

The Mirage III-E has a normal magnetic detector mounted in the fin, and a central gyro and "black boxes" to provide accurate and stabilised heading information. The pilot's equipment determines at any instant the geographical co-ordinates of the aircraft and compares them with the co-ordinates of the target, the differences between the two being presented to the pilot as a "course to steer" and "distance to run". Associated with this facility is a rotative magazine in the cockpit in which it is possible to insert up to 12 plastic punch-cards. Each card represents the co-ordinates of a geographical position. Therefore it is possible before take-off at point A to select point B on the rotating magazine. During take-off, i.e. after reaching 173 mph (278 km/h), the computer will switch on and the heading and distance to point B will be presented to the pilot. When overhead point B (assuming a pure navigational sortie) he can either select point A or the next turning point, or if required this sequence can continue until a maximum of twelve pre-set turning points have been used. Another facility available in the computer is known as the "additional base". Assuming that between points A and B the pilot receives instructions by radio to go to point C (and that there is no punch card in the magazine for point C) the pilot can, by means of setting knobs, "wind on" the bearing and distance of point C from point B; then, when he selects the switch "additional base", the heading to steer and distance to run to point C will be indicated.

Marconi Doppler equipment provides the ground speed and drift information for the above, while TACAN is presented as a "bearing and distance" on the navigation indicator located on the starboard side of the instrument panel.

The Cyrano II installation in the aircraft's nose provides orthodox air-to-air interception radar, and has the additional mode available of control from the ground. In the latter case the pilot simply obeys his gunsight instructions, and radio silence is maintained. Cyrano II also functions in an air-to-ground role for

high-level navigation, presenting a radar picture of the ground; for low-level navigation, presenting the obstacles above a preselected altitude; for blind descent, presenting obstacles that intercept the descent path; for anti-collision, presenting the obstacles that can be avoided by applying a 0·1 *g* "pull-up"; and for distance measuring, by presenting in the sight the oblique aircraft-to-ground distance.

Allied to the Cyrano II installation is the CSF 97 sighting system, of illuminated points, dots, bars and figures, giving air-to-air facility for cannons and missiles, air-to-ground facility for dive-bombing or LABS, and navigation facility for horizon and heading.

ARMAMENT: Ground attack armament consists normally of two 30-mm DEFA cannon in fuselage, each with 125 rounds of ammunition, and two 1,000 lb (454 kg) bombs, or an AS.30 air-to-surface missile under the fuselage and 1,000 lb bombs under the wings. Alternative under-wing stores include JL-100 pods, each with 18 rockets, and 55 Imp gallon (250 litre) fuel tanks. For interception duties, one Matra R.530 air-to-air missile can be carried under fuselage, with optional guns and two Sidewinder missiles.

DIMENSIONS, EXTERNAL:

Wing span	27 ft 0 in (8·22 m)
Wing aspect ratio	1·94
Length overall:	
III-B	50 ft 6½ in (15·40 m)
III-E	49 ft 3½ in (15·03 m)
III-R	50 ft 10½ in (15·50 m)
Height overall	13 ft 11½ in (4·25 m)
Wheel track	10 ft 4 in (3·15 m)
Wheelbase:	
III-E	16 ft 0 in (4·87 m)

AREAS:

Wings, gross	375 sq ft (34·85 m²)
Vertical tail surfaces (total)	48·4 sq ft (4·5 m²)

WEIGHTS AND LOADING:

Weight empty:	
III-B	13,820 lb (6,270 kg)
III-E	15,540 lb (7,050 kg)
III-R	14,550 lb (6,600 kg)
Max T-O weight:	
III-B	26,455 lb (12,000 kg)
III-E, R	29,760 lb (13,500 kg)
Max wing loading:	
III-E, R	75·85 lb/sq ft (370 kg/m²)

PERFORMANCE (Mirage III-E, in 'clean' condition with guns installed, except where indicated):

Max level speed at S/L
756 knots (870 mph; 1,400 km/h)
Max level speed at 39,375 ft (12,000 m)
1,268 knots (1,460 mph; 2,350 km/h) (Mach 2·2)
Cruising speed at 36,100 ft (11,000 m) Mach 0·9
Approach speed
183 knots (211 mph; 340 km/h)
Landing speed 162 knots (187 mph; 300 km/h)
Time to 36,100 ft (11,000 m), Mach 0·9   3 min
Time to 49,200 ft (15,000 m), Mach 1·8
6 min 50 sec
Service ceiling at Mach 1·8 55,775 ft (17,000 m)
Ceiling, using rocket motor 75,450 ft (23,000 m)
T-O run, according to mission (up to max T-O weight)   2,295-5,250 ft (700-1,600 m)
Landing run, using brake parachute
2,295 ft (700 m)

DASSAULT MIRAGE IV

The Mirage IV is a tandem two-seat supersonic delta-wing bomber designed specifically to deliver a nuclear weapon. Its development and production were undertaken in association with many other companies. In particular, Sud-Aviation took responsibility for the wing and rear fuselage, and Breguet for the tail surfaces.

The original prototype Mirage IV, which flew

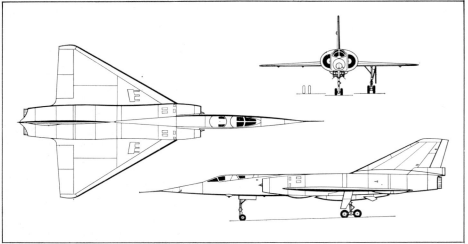

Dassault Mirage IV-A supersonic strategic bomber

for the first time on 17 June 1959, was a scaled-up derivative of the Mirage III fighter, powered by two SNECMA Atar 09 turbojets (each 13,225 lb = 6,000 kg st with afterburner) and with a take-off weight of approximately 55,100 lb (25,000 kg).

The prototype was followed by three pre-production Mirage IV's, of which the first flew on 12 October 1961. Powered by two 14,110 lb (6,400 kg) st Atar 09C's, this aircraft was slightly larger than the first and was more representative of the production Mirage IV-A, with a large circular radome under its centre-fuselage, ahead of the semi-submerged nuclear free-fall bomb. This first pre-production aircraft was used for bombing trials and development at Colomb-Béchar. The second pre-production Mirage IV was similar and was used to develop the navigation system and for flight refuelling trials with a Boeing KC-135F Stratotanker.

The last of the three pre-production aircraft flew on 23 January 1963, and was a completely operational model with Atar 09K's, full equipment, including flight refuelling nose-probe, and armament.

The production Mirage IV-A has advanced electronic navigation and bombing equipment. It has an operational radius of more than 1,000 miles (1,600 km) with a proportion of the flight at a speed of Mach 1·7 at high altitude. The use of flight refuelling, with KC-135F's acting as tankers, extends considerably this radius of action.

The French Air Force ordered a total of 62 production Mirage IV-A's for delivery during the period 1964-67.

A two-year study of the problems of low-altitude penetration showed that the Mirage IV-A could be adapted for a low-level rôle with minor modifications. This was subsequently done.

A full description of the Mirage IV-A appeared in the 1969-70 edition of *Jane's*.

DIMENSIONS, EXTERNAL:
Wing span	38 ft 10½ in (11·85 m)
Length overall	77 ft 1 in (23·50 m)
Height overall	18 ft 6½ in (5·65 m)

AREA:
Wings, gross	840 sq ft (78 m²)

WEIGHTS AND LOADING:
Weight empty	31,965 lb (14,500 kg)
Average T-O weight	69,665 lb (31,600 kg)
Average wing loading	82·9 lb/sq ft (405 kg/m²)

PERFORMANCE:
Max speed at 36,000 ft (11,000 m)	Mach 2·2
Combat speed at high altitude	Mach 1·8
Service ceiling	65,600 ft (20,000 m)

DASSAULT MIRAGE 5

The Mirage 5 is a ground attack aircraft derived from the Mirage III-E, using the same airframe and engine. Basic VFR version has simplified avionics, 110 Imp gallons (500 litres) greater fuel capacity than III-E and considerably extended stores carrying capability. It combines the full Mach 2+ capability of the Mirage III and its ability to operate from semi-prepared airfields with simpler maintenance. In ground attack configuration, up to 8,820 lb (4,000 kg) of weapons and 220 Imp gallons (1,000 litres) of fuel can be carried externally on seven wing and fuselage attachment points. The Mirage 5 can also be flown as an interceptor, with two Sidewinder air-to-air missiles and 1,034 Imp gallons (4,700 litres) of external fuel. At customer's option, any degree of IFR/all-weather operation can be provided for, with reduced fuel or weapons load. The Mirage 5 was flown for the first time on 19 May 1967.

Up to 15 April 1970 more than 230 Mirage 5's had been ordered. The 106 aircraft for the Belgian Air Force will be assembled in Belgium by SABCA (which see).

Dassault Mirage IV-A supersonic strategic bomber, with underwing fuel tanks (*Peter R. March*)

Versions announced so far are as follows:

Mirage 5-BA. Ground-attack model, with more advanced navigation system than basic Mirage 5. For Belgian Air Force. First (Dassault-built) 5-BA flew on 6 March 1970.

Mirage 5-BD. Two-seat version of Mirage 5-BA for Belgian Air Force.

Mirage 5-BR. Reconnaissance version of 5-BA for Belgian Air Force, with five Vinten type 360 cameras installed in nose. Provision to install infra-red photographic equipment is under consideration.

Mirage 5-J. Ordered by Israeli Air Force. Delivery banned by French government.

Mirage 5-P. Twelve ordered by Peru in April 1968. Delivery began in May 1968.

Mirage 5-PD. Two-seat version of Mirage 5-P for Peruvian Air Force.

The structural description of the Mirage III-E is generally applicable to the Mirage 5, with the following exceptions:

SYSTEMS: As Mirage III-E. DC electrical power is provided by two 24V 40Ah batteries only.

ARMAMENT: Ground attack armament consists normally of two 30-mm DEFA cannon in fuselage, each with 125 rounds of ammunition,

First Dassault Mirage 5-BA ground-attack aircraft for the Belgian Air Force

Tandem two-seat cockpit of the Mirage 5-PD for the Peruvian Air Force

Dassault Mirage 5-P multi-purpose combat aircraft in the insignia of the Peruvian Air Force

and two 1,000 lb bombs, or an AS.30 air-to-surface missile under the fuselage and 1,000 lb bombs under the wings. Alternative underwing stores include JL-100 pods, each with 18 × 68-mm rockets and 55 Imp gallons (250 litres) of fuel. For interception duties, one Matra R.530 air-to-air missile can be carried under the fuselage, with optional guns and two Sidewinder missiles.

DIMENSIONS, EXTERNAL:
As III-E, except:
Length overall   51 ft 0¼ in (15·55 m)

WEIGHTS AND LOADING:
As III-E, except:
Weight empty   14,550 lb (6,600 kg)

PERFORMANCE (in 'clean' condition, with guns installed, except where indicated):
As III-E, plus:
Combat radius with 2,000 lb (907 kg) bomb load:
high-low-high   699 nm (805 miles; 1,300 km)
low-low-low   347 nm (400 miles; 650 km)
Ferry range with three external tanks
     2,158 nm (2,485 miles (4,000 km)

DASSAULT MILAN

The Milan is the latest addition to the Mirage III/Mirage 5 family of combat aircraft. It incorporates a number of technical improvements which greatly increase its capabilities in air-to-ground strike, low-speed handling and operation from short airstrips with steep approaches.

The major changes involve the installation of a high-powered Atar 09K-50 turbojet engine, developing 15,875 lb (7,200 kg) st with afterburning; and of a high-lift device consisting of two small retractable foreplane surfaces (known colloquially as "moustaches") housed in the nose. Development of the latter feature was carried out in co-operation with the Swiss aircraft industry, and in particular with the Federal Aircraft Factory at Emmen.

Production aircraft will also have an advanced navigation and weapons system, using electronic equipment already developed for the Anglo-French Jaguar strike aircraft. Other optional features include reinforced landing gear and brakes, arrester hook, rocket-assisted take-off, nose folding and auxiliary fuel tanks.

Work on the prototype Milan, which was modified from a Mirage III-E, was started in mid-1968, and the initial test phase, which ended in March 1969, was conducted with non-retracting foreplanes. The second flight test phase, with retractable foreplanes, began in mid-1969, and the Milan was displayed publicly for the first time at the Paris Air Show in June 1969. The first fully-equipped Milan flew for the first time on 29 May 1970 and production aircraft will be available for delivery early in 1972.

Application of the "moustaches" device to the Concorde supersonic airliner is under consideration. The complete installation on the Milan, including electrical retraction mechanism, weighs 44 lb (20 kg).

DIMENSIONS:
Span of foreplanes, fully extended
         3 ft 3¼ in (1·00 m)
Area of foreplanes   6·35 sq ft (0·59 m²)

WEIGHTS:
Max T-O weight, aircraft 'clean'
         21,384 lb (9,700 kg)
Max T-O weight with external armament
         30,864 lb (14,000 kg)

PERFORMANCE (estimated):
Max level speed at S/L   Mach 1·14
Max level speed at high altitude   Mach 2·2
Max indicated airspeed
     750 knots (863 mph; 1,390 km/h)
Max rate of climb at S/L
      40,157 ft (12,240 m)/min
T-O run at S/L, aircraft 'clean'
        1,970 ft (600 m)
T-O run at S/L, at max T-O weight (armed)
        3,870 ft (1,180 m)

DASSAULT MIRAGE F1

Early in 1964 AMD was awarded a French government contract to develop a replacement for the Mirage III, followed shortly afterwards by an order for a prototype aircraft which was designated Mirage F2. This aircraft was designed as a two-seat low-altitude penetration fighter, and was powered by a Pratt & Whitney TF 306 turbofan engine. It flew for the first time on 12 June 1966 and was described and illustrated in the 1967-68 *Jane's*.

Concurrently with work on the Mirage F2 Dassault also developed, as a private venture, a much smaller single-seat aircraft, the Mirage F1, with a SNECMA Atar 09K turbojet engine. The prototype Mirage F1-01 flew for the first time on 23 December 1966. It exceeded Mach 2 during its fourth flight on 7 January 1967, but was lost in a fatal accident on 18 May 1967.

In September 1967, three pre-series F1 aircraft and a structural test airframe were ordered by the French government. The first pre-series aircraft, the Mirage F1-02, reached Mach 1·15 during its first flight on 20 March 1969, and Mach 2·03 during its third test flight on 24 March. It completed the first phase of its flight test pro-

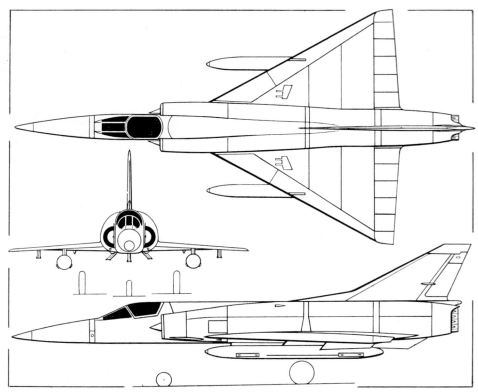

Dassault Mirage 5 single-seat ground attack aircraft

Close-up of the nose housing for the "moustaches" of the Dassault Milan

Dassault Milan in flight with "moustaches" extended

gramme on 27 June 1969. This comprised 62 flights, during which the aircraft was flown at speeds of up to Mach 2·12 (1,200 knots = 1,405 mph = 2,260 km/h) at 36,000 ft (11,000 m) and up to 702 knots (808 mph = 1,300 km/h) at low level; at altitudes of more than 50,000 ft (15,250 m); and with various external military loads, including air-to-air missiles and drop-tanks. Performance was fully up to that anticipated, and the range is likely to be superior to expec-

tations.

During these initial flight tests, the F1-02 was powered by an Atar 09K-31 turbojet engine developing 14,770 lb (6,700 kg) st with afterburning. For the second phase of its test programme, it was re-engined in 1969 with the more powerful Atar 09K-50 turbojet which is specified for the production model.

The Mirage F1-03 flew for the first time on 18 September 1969; by the spring of 1970 the

Dassault Mirage F1-02 first pre-series aircraft (SNECMA Atar 09K-50 afterburning turbojet engine)

prototype and pre-series aircraft had carried out a total of 500 hours of test flying; and had been joined by the F1-04, which is representative of the production version.

Internal fuel capacity is some 40% greater than that of the Mirage III. The installation of a more powerful "Super Atar" engine now under development, will permit the Mirage F1 to fly at speeds of up to Mach 2·5.

The Mirage F1 is dimensionally similar to the Mirage III series, and its swept wing is virtually a scaled-down version of that fitted to the F2, with elaborate high-lift devices which help to make possible take-offs and landings within 1,600-2,600 ft (500-800 m) at average combat mission weight. Operation from semi-prepared, or even sod, runways is possible, and aircraft systems have been improved by comparison with the Mirage III, for increased efficiency and easy servicing.

Primary role of the Mirage F1 is all-weather interception at any altitude, and the standard version, to which the details below apply, utilises the weapon systems of the Mirage III-E, with more advanced systems to follow. It is equally suitable for attack missions, with a variety of external loads carried beneath the wings and fuselage. Dassault have also projected a "utility" version, for operation only under VFR conditions, in which much of the more costly electronic equipment is deleted, the space so vacated being filled with an additional fuel tank.

By the Spring of 1970 orders had been placed for 85 Mirage F1's for the French Air Force. Production of these will be undertaken by AMD in co-operation with the Belgian companies SABCA, in which Dassault has a parity interest, and Fairey SA, which will build rear fuselage sections for all Mirage F1's ordered.

TYPE: Single-seat multi-mission fighter and attack aircraft.

WINGS: Cantilever shoulder-wing monoplane, with anhedral from roots. Sweepback of approx 50° on leading-edge, which has extended chord (saw-tooth) on the outer panels. All-metal two-spar torsion-box structure, making extensive use of mechanically or chemically milled components. Trailing-edge control surfaces of honeycomb sandwich construction. Entire leading-edge can be drooped hydraulically. Two differentially-operating double-slotted flaps and one aileron on each trailing-edge, actuated hydraulically by servo controls. Ailerons are compensated by trim devices incorporated in linkage. Two spoilers on each wing, ahead of flaps.

FUSELAGE: Conventional all-metal semi-monocoque structure. Primary frames are milled mechanically, secondary frames and fuel tank panels chemically. Electrical spot-welding for secondary stringers and sealed panels, remainder titanium flush-riveted or bolted and sealed. Titanium alloy also used for landing gear trunnions, engine firewall and certain other major structures. Central intake bulkheads of honeycomb sandwich construction. High-tensile steel wing attachment points. Nosecone over radar, and antennae fairings on fin, are of plastic. Large hydraulically-actuated door-type air-brake in forward underside of each intake trunk.

TAIL UNIT: Cantilever all-metal two-spar structure, with sweepback on all surfaces. All-moving tailplane mid-set on fuselage, and actuated hydraulically by electrical or manual control. Tailplane trailing-edge panels are of honeycomb sandwich construction. Auxiliary fin beneath each side of rear fuselage.

LANDING GEAR: Retractable tricycle type of Messier design. Hydraulic retraction, nose-

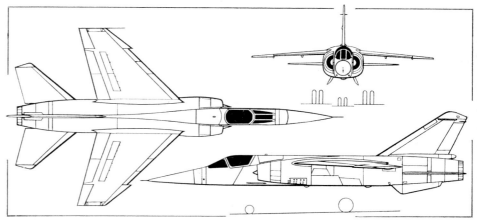

Dassault Mirage F1 single-seat all-weather fighter

Mirage F1 taking off with Matra R.530 air-to-air missile mounted under the fuselage

unit rearward, main units outward and upward into rear of intake trunk fairings. Twin wheels on all units. Nose unit steerable and self-centering. Oleo-pneumatic shock-absorbers. Main wheel tyre pressure 128 lb/sq in (9 kg/cm²), permitting operation from semi-prepared airfields. Brake parachute in bullet fairing at base of rudder.

POWER PLANT: One SNECMA Atar 09K-50 turbojet engine, rated at 15,873 lb (7,200 kg) st with afterburning. Movable conical centre-body in each intake. All internal fuel in integral tanks in fuselage, on each side of intake trunks. Provision for three jettisonable auxiliary fuel tanks (each 286 Imp gallons = 1,300 litres) to be carried on external attachments.

ACCOMMODATION: Single seat for pilot on Martin-Baker Mk 4 ejection seat, under rearward-hinged jettisonable canopy. Cockpit is air-conditioned, and is heated by warm air bled from engine which also heats radar and certain equipment compartments. Liquid oxygen system for pilot.

SYSTEMS: Two independent hydraulic systems, for landing gear retraction, flaps and air-brakes, supplied by pumps similar to those fitted in Mirage III. Electrical system includes two 15kVA variable-speed alternators, either of

which can supply all functional and operational requirements. Emergency and standby power provided by battery and static converter. DC power provided by transformer-rectifiers operating in conjunction with battery.

ELECTRONICS AND EQUIPMENT: Thomson-CSF Cyrano IV fire-control radar in nose permits all-sector interception at any altitude and incorporates system to eliminate "fixed" echoes when following low-flying aircraft. Two UHF transceivers (one UHF/VHF), VOR/ILS, TACAN, IFF, remote-setting interception system, three-axis generator, central air data computer, Bézu Sphere with ILS indicator, Crouzet navigation indicator and SFENA autopilot. CSF sight, with enlarging lens, provides all necessary data for flying and fire control.

ARMAMENT AND OPERATIONAL EQUIPMENT: Standard fixed armament of two 30 mm DEFA cannon, mounted in lower front fuselage. Two stores attachment points under each wing and one under fuselage, plus provision for carrying one Sidewinder air-to-air missile at each wingtip. Max external combat load of 8,818 lb (4,000 kg). Externally-mounted weapons for interception role include up to two Matra R.530 radar homing or infra-red homing missiles and/or two Sidewinders. For ground attack duties, typical loads may include eight 882 lb (400 kg) bombs, five launchers each containing 18 air-to-ground rockets, six 80 US gallon (300 litre) napalm tanks, or two Nord AS.30 air-to-surface missiles. Provision for carrying AS.37 Martel anti-radar missile. Other external loads include two photoflash containers and a reconnaissance pod, or three 286 Imp gallon (1,300 litre) jettisonable auxiliary fuel tanks.

DIMENSIONS, EXTERNAL:
Wing span	27 ft 6¾ in (8·40 m)
Length overall	49 ft 2½ in (15·00 m)
Height overall	14 ft 9 in (4·50 m)
Wheel track	8 ft 2½ in (2·50 m)
Wheelbase	16 ft 4¾ in (5·00 m)

AREA:
Wings, gross	269 sq ft (25·0 m²)

WEIGHTS AND LOADING:
Weight empty	16,314 lb (7,400 kg)
T-O weight, clean	24,030 lb (10,900 kg)
Max T-O weight	32,850 lb (14,900 kg)
Max wing loading	122·2 lb/sq ft (596 kg/m²)

PERFORMANCE:
Max level speed (high altitude)	Mach 2·2
Max level speed (low altitude)	Mach 1·2
Approach speed	141 knots (162 mph; 260 km/h)
Landing speed	122 knots (140 mph; 225 km/h)
Service ceiling	65,600 ft (20,000 m)
Stabilised supersonic ceiling	60,700 ft (18,500 m)
T-O run (AUW of 25,355 lb = 11,500 kg)	1,475 ft (450 m)
Landing run (AUW of 18,740 lb = 8,500 kg)	1,640 ft (500 m)
T-O and landing run (typical intercept mission)	2,035 ft (620 m)
Endurance	3 hr 45 min

DASSAULT MIRAGE G

A contract for one prototype of the Mirage G variable-geometry (swing-wing) experimental fighter was awarded to Dassault by the French government on 13 October 1965, with development of this aircraft intended to proceed simultaneously with work on the now-abandoned Anglo-French V-G fighter programme. The prototype Mirage G was first displayed publicly at the company's Melun-Villaroche flight test centre on 27 May 1967.

First flight took place at Istres on 18 November 1967, the first landing being made at an approach speed of 144 mph (232 kmh) and a touchdown speed of 127 mph (205 kmh). After one week of testing the maximum wing sweep of 70° was attained, and a level flight speed of Mach 2·1 was reached within two months of the first flight. Modifications made since the prototype's first appearance include a shortening of the vertical fin and the addition of two auxiliary fins beneath the rear fuselage.

Dassault claim that, in addition to the advantages inherent in a variable-geometry design, in terms of both high-speed and low-speed performance and handling qualities, the Mirage G will offer improved penetration performance, because of its low sensitivity to turbulence. It is intended to be supersonic at ground level.

By the Spring of 1970 the Mirage G prototype had completed 250 flights, totalling approx 300 hours and achieving all the designed flying limits at low altitudes as well as at high Mach numbers, and had been flown by French, US and Australian pilots.

Late in 1968 the French government ordered two further prototypes, designated Mirage G4. These were to be powered by two Atar 09K-50 engines, but the second aircraft is now to be a lighter-weight version, designated G8 and powered by two Super Atar M53 engines. The Mirage G4 is scheduled to fly in 1971.

Dassault has also proposed a single-seat model, designated Mirage G2, as a potential replacement for the F-8 Crusaders of the French Navy.

The description below applies to the prototype Mirage G in its current form.

TYPE: Two-seat variable-geometry research aircraft.

WINGS: Cantilever shoulder-wing monoplane. The wings have a sweep of 20° in the furthest-forward position and approximately 70° when fully swept. Transition from minimum to maximum sweep, and vice versa, takes approx 15 sec. The wings each pivot from a point on the rear fuselage, just aft of the trailing-edge wing root. The pivots are constructed of maraging steel, and lined with a glass-fibre and Teflon mixture known as Fabroid to reduce friction. High-lift devices include leading-edge flaps (four sections each side) and double-slotted trailing-edge flaps. There are no ailerons. Roll control when the wings are swept back is provided by differential operation of the horizontal tail surfaces. When the wings are forward, the tail surfaces are supplemented by three-section spoilers forward of the flaps on each wing. Movement of the wing is by means of a centrally-mounted actuator, driven hydraulically through two clutch equipped reduction gears.

FUSELAGE: Conventional semi-monocoque all-metal structure, similar in design to that of the

Dassault Mirage G in landing configuration, with wings swept fully forward and leading- and trailing-edge flaps extended

Mirage G variable-geometry aircraft with wings swept fully back

Mirage III, but larger, and making extensive use of chemical milling and spot welding. Two cast magnesium door-type air brakes on each side of rear fuselage.

TAIL UNIT: Sweptback fin and rudder; swept-back all-moving tailplane mid-mounted on rear of fuselage. The tailplane and elevators operate collectively for pitch control. Small auxiliary fin beneath each side of rear fuselage.

LANDING GEAR: Retractable tricycle type, of Messier design, with twin-wheel main units and single wheel on nose unit. Nose-wheel retracts rearward into the fuselage, the main units upward into the air intake trunks. Main-wheel tyre pressure is 85·3 lb/sq in (6 kg/cm²).

POWER PLANT: One SNECMA (Pratt & Whitney) TF-306E turbofan engine, rated at 20,500 lb (9,300 kg) st with afterburning. Fuel in integral tanks in fuselage and wings, total capacity 10,582 lb (4,800 kg).

ACCOMMODATION: Crew of two on tandem-mounted ejection seats in forward fuselage, beneath upward-hinged canopies.

DIMENSIONS, EXTERNAL:
Wing span (min sweep)	42 ft 8 in	(13·00 m)
Length overall	55 ft 1 in	(16·80 m)
Height overall	17 ft 6½ in	(5·35 m)

WEIGHTS AND LOADING (approx):
Weight empty	22,050 lb	(10,000 kg)
Max T-O weight	35,275 lb	(16,000 kg)
Max wing loading	over 123 lb/sq ft	(600 kg/m²)

PERFORMANCE:
Max level speed at height		Mach 2·5
Approach speed		
	125 knots	(144 mph; 232 km/h)
Landing speed	110 knots	(127 mph; 204 km/h)
Service ceiling	65,600 ft	(20,000 m)
T-O run	1,480 ft	(450 m)
Landing run	1,150 ft	(350 m)
Ferry range	3,473 nm	(4,000 miles; 6,500 km)

DASSAULT MYSTÈRE 20/FALCON 20

The Dassault Mystère 20/Falcon is a light twin-jet executive transport, with standard accommodation for 8-10 passengers and a crew of two. An alternative layout offers seats for 14 passengers and the aircraft can be used for a variety of alternative duties such as flight crew training, air ambulance and air route calibration.

Its development was undertaken jointly with Aérospatiale (Sud-Aviation) and construction of the prototype began in January 1962. The fuselage of the prototype was built by Dassault and the wings and tail unit by Sud-Aviation. Dassault were responsible for final assembly. For production aircraft, Dassault are building the wings and Aérospatiale the fuselages and tail units.

The prototype flew for the first time on 4 May 1963, with Pratt & Whitney JT12A-8 turbojets (each 3,300 lb=1,489 kg st). It was re-engined subsequently with General Electric CF700 turbo-fans, which are standard on subsequent aircraft, and flew for the first time with these engines on 10 July 1964.

In August 1963 the Business Jets Division of Pan American World Airways ordered 54 production machines, with an option on 106 more. From the start, these aircraft were marketed by Pan American under the name Fan Jet Falcon, but the original name of Mystère 20 continues to be used in France. The first production machine flew on 1 January 1965, and deliveries had attained the rate of seven aircraft per month by the Spring of 1967. Production continues at the rate of three per month in 1970.

Seven Dassault Falcons were ordered for liaison and communications duties with the Canadian Armed Forces, with an option on 14 more; three have been ordered by the RAAF, and two by the SGAC for radio calibration duties. Two have been ordered by the Spanish government, and one of these also will be used for radio-navigational calibration work. From 20 September 1966, two to three Mystère 20/Falcons were used by Air France to train their jet airliner pilots; these aircraft have since been joined by a further two.

Another Falcon (airframe number 115), fitted with Mirage III-E combat aircraft radar and navigation systems, is in service with the French Air Force for training its Mirage pilots. This version, known as the Falcon SNA, has also been ordered by the Libyan Republic and is being studied by other air forces, as an economical means of training combat aircrew.

The Mystère 20/Falcon received French certifi-cation and US Transport Category Type Approval on 9 June 1965. On the following day, Mme Jacqueline Auriol established a Class C-1-g speed record of 534·075 mph (859·51 km/h) over a 1,000-km closed circuit in a Mystère 20/Falcon. On 15 June she set up a second Class C-1-g record of 508·98 mph (819·13 km/h) over a 2,000-km circuit.

By 27 April 1970 total sales of Mystère 20's had reached 264, of which 76 were for customers in the areas marketed by Dassault, with options on 162 more; of these, 215 had been delivered, including 155 to the Business Jets Division of Pan American, the distributor for the western hemisphere.

The following versions of the Mystère 20/Falcon have so far been announced:

Standard Falcon. Initial production version, with 4,125 lb (1,870 kg) st General Electric CF700-2C turbofan engines and seating for 8-14 passen-gers. Fully described in 1967-68 *Jane's*.

Falcon Series C. As Falcon Series D (see below), but with CF700-2C engines.

Falcon CC. Designation of 73rd production aircraft, built for Business Jets Pty Ltd of Australia. Basically similar to Standard Falcon,

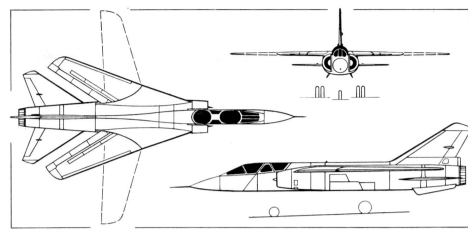
Dassault Mirage G two-seat variable-geometry strike fighter prototype

Dassault Falcon CC, fitted with low-pressure tyres for soft-field operation and under-fuselage fairing

Prototype of the Mystère 20/Falcon F, which has new high-lift devices for improved airfield performance
(*Martin Fricke*)

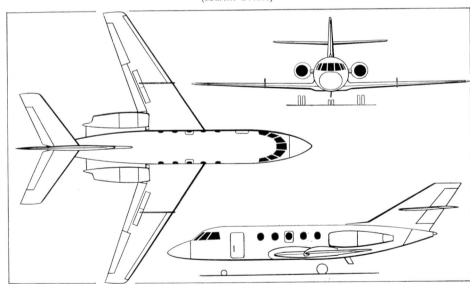
Dassault Mystère 20/Falcon 20 twin-turbofan light executive transport

but with low-pressure tyres for grass-field oper-ation at the same T-O and landing weights. First flown 26 April 1967. Described in 1968-69 *Jane's*.

Falcon Series D. Developed from Standard Falcon, with more powerful CF700-2D turbofan engines (4,250 lb=1,930 kg st each) and fuel capacity increased to 1,120 Imp gallons (5,090 litres). Introduced onto production line from 172nd aircraft. Deliveries began mid-1968. Described in detail below.

Falcon Series E. As Series F (see below), but with wing control surfaces of Series D.

Falcon Series F. Version with new high-lift devices to improve T-O and landing performance. Prototype displayed at Paris Air Show in June 1969. Initial series of 25 being built, to meet firm orders for 20 plus options on a further 80. Deliveries scheduled to begin in July 1970. Com-pared with prototype, production aircraft have slightly increased fuel capacity and range,

E

improved electrical systems and equipment, and will be certificated at a max T-O weight of 28,660 lb (13,000 kg), compared with 27,335 lb (12,400 kg) of the Series D. In 1970 the Series F became the world's first aircraft to receive type approval under the new FAA anti-noise regulations (FARPt 36).

The new high-lift devices introduced on the Series F comprise a leading-edge flap inboard of each wing fence and a slotted leading-edge flap outboard of each fence.

Trailing-edge flaps, which are slightly modified from earlier models, require only a 10° setting for T-O compared with 15° on earlier models; 40° setting for landing remains unchanged. Comparative performances:

T-O balanced field length at S/L at AUW of 26,455 lb (12,000 kg), ISA + 15°C:
Series D 5,955 ft (1,815 m)
Series F 4,790 ft (1,460 m)
Landing balanced field length at S/L at AUW of 22,045 lb (10,000 kg), ISA + 15°C:
Series D 4,200 ft (1,280 m)
Series F 3,640 ft (1,110 m)
Normal range, 8 passengers and baggage, with 45 min LR cruise reserves:
Standard Falcon
1,770 nm (2,040 miles; 3,280 km)
Series D 1,910 nm (2,200 miles; 3,540 km)
Series F 1,927 nm (2,220 miles; 3,570 km)

Falcon SNA. Designation of the 115th production aircraft, ordered in 1967 by the *Armée de l'Air* as an operational trainer for pilots of the Mirage III-E. The complete radar system of the Mirage is installed in the nose and on the flight deck, including the scope and control handle (which are duplicated in the main cabin); together with the sight, with associated weapon and fire mode selector, and the navigation system with its Doppler radar and polar co-ordinate navigation indicator. The yoke and rudder pedals of the Falcon are replaced by the control column and pedals of the Mirage, and an Omera 30 vertical camera is used for target photography. Because of the extra equipment installed, the Falcon's electrical system is extensively modified, and additional power is obtained from two extra hydraulic pumps driven by the engines. For cooling the radar and equipment bays, a second turbo-refrigerator has been added. As well as the second trainee's station and its seat in the main cabin there are four more seats and a work table. The toilet is retained.

In this machine, the trainee is freed from operation of the aircraft, enabling him to concentrate on the technical and navigational aspects of the flight. Exercises "under the hood" are therefore possible, with the pilot (in the port front seat) providing safety watch. The aircraft is being used for a variety of training routines which include ground or contour mapping, and terrain avoidance. On navigation flights, the navigation system provides a target marker showing up on the radar scope; and on air-to-air exercises the sight displays interception orders.

Falcon 30. Long-range version announced in Summer 1969, with deliveries to begin in mid-1972. AiResearch ATF-3A turbofan engines. Range increased to over 2,605 nm (3,000 miles; 4,830 km). Order for 25, plus 25 more on option, announced by PanAm in June 1969.

Falcon 10. Scaled-down version, seating 4-7 passengers, with Larzac, CJ610 or TFE-731-2 turbofans and range comparable to Falcon D or F. First deliveries scheduled for early 1972. Described separately.

Type: Twin-turbofan executive transport.

Wings: Cantilever low-wing monoplane. Thickness/chord ratio varies from 10·5 to 8%. Dihedral 2°. Incidence 1° 30′. Sweepback at quarter-chord 30°. All-metal (copper-bearing alloys) fail-safe torsion-box structure with machined stressed skin. Ailerons are each operated by Dassault twin-body actuators, from dual hydraulic systems, and have artificial feel. Drooping leading-edge. Hydraulically-actuated air-brakes forward of the hydraulically-actuated two-section single-slotted flaps. Leading-edges anti-iced by engine-bleed air.

Fuselage: All-metal semi-monocoque structure of circular cross-section, built on fail-safe principles.

Tail Unit: Cantilever all-metal structure, with electrically-controlled variable-incidence tailplane mounted half-way up fin. Elevators and rudder each actuated by twin hydraulic servos. No trim-tabs.

Landing Gear: Retractable tricycle type, of Messier design, with twin wheels on all three units. Hydraulic retraction, main units inward, nose-wheels forward. Oleo-pneumatic shock-absorbers. Goodyear disc brakes and anti-skid units. Normal tyre pressure 133 lb/sq in (9·35 kg/cm²) on all units. Low-pressure gear (65 lb/sq in = 4·6 kg/cm²) available optionally. Steerable and self-centering nose-wheels. Braking parachute standard.

Power Plant: Two General Electric CF700-2D turbofan engines (each 4,250 lb = 1,930 kg st) mounted in pods on each side of rear fuselage. Fuel in two integral tanks in wings and two auxiliary tanks aft of rear pressure bulkhead in fuselage, with total capacity of 1,120 Imp gallons (1,345 US gallons = 5,090 litres). Separate fuel system for each engine, with provision for cross-feeding. Overwing refuelling points. Single-point pressure refuelling optional.

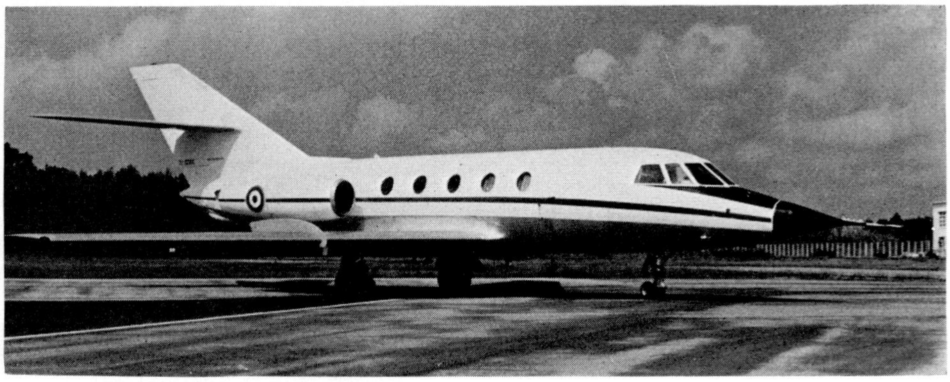

Dassault Falcon SNA radar system trainer in service with the French Air Force

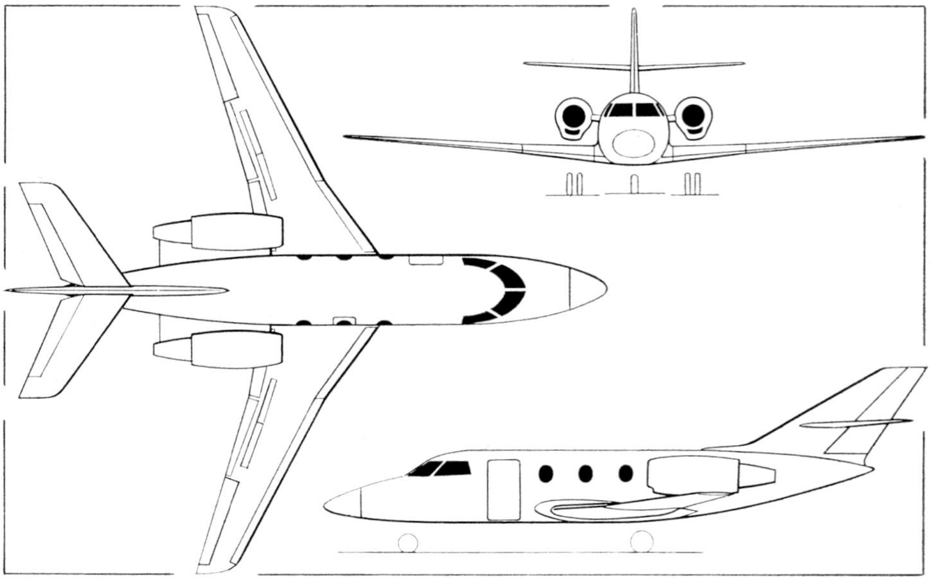

Dassault Falcon 10, a scaled-down version of the Mystère 20/Falcon 20

Accommodation: Crew of two on flight deck, with full dual controls and airline-type instrumentation. Normal seating for eight or ten passengers in individual reclining chairs, with tables between forward pairs of seats and a central "trench" aisle, or 12-14 passengers at reduced pitch without tables. Toilet at rear. Baggage space and wardrobe on starboard side, immediately aft of flight deck opposite entry door, and at rear of cabin. Buffet with ice-box, food and liquid storage at front of cabin on port side. Downward-opening door has built-in steps.

Systems: Duplicated air-conditioning and pressurisation system, supplied with air bled from both engines. Pressure differential 8·3 lb/sq in (0·58 kg/cm²). Two independent hydraulic systems, pressure 3,000 lb/sq in (210 kg/cm²), with twin engine-driven pumps and emergency electric pump, actuate primary flying controls, flaps, landing gear, wheel brakes, air-brakes, and nose-wheel steering. 28V DC electrical system with a 9kW 28V DC starter-generator on each engine, one 1500VA and two 750VA 400 c/s 118/208V inverters and two 40Ah batteries. Automatic emergency oxygen system. 9kW Microturbo Saphir II APU optional.

Electronics and Equipment: Standard equipment includes duplicated VHF and VOR/glideslope, single ADF and DME, marker beacon receiver, ATC transponder, cockpit audio and duplicated blind-flying instrumentation. Optional equipment includes integrated flight instrument system, weather radar, HF communication radio, auto-pilot, second ADF and DME and cabin address system.

Dimensions, external:
Wing span 53 ft 6 in (16·30 m)
Wing chord (mean) 9 ft 4 in (2·85 m)
Wing aspect ratio 6·4
Length overall 56 ft 3 in (17·15 m)
Length of fuselage 51 ft 0 in (15·55 m)
Height over tail 17 ft 5 in (5·32 m)
Tailplane span 22 ft 1 in (6·74 m)
Wheel track 12 ft 1¼ in (3·69 m)
Wheelbase 18 ft 10 in (5·74 m)
Passenger door:
Height 5 ft 0 in (1·52 m)
Width 2 ft 7½ in (0·80 m)
Height to sill 3 ft 7 in (1·09 m)
Emergency exits (each side over wing):
Height 2 ft 2 in (0·66 m)
Width 1 ft 7 in (0·48 m)

Dimensions, internal:
Cabin, including fwd baggage space and rear toilet:
Length 23 ft 2¾ in (7·08 m)
Max width 6 ft 1¾ in (1·87 m)
Max height 5 ft 8 in (1·73 m)
Volume 700 cu ft (20·0 m³)
Baggage compartment (fwd) 24·7 cu ft (0·70 m³)
Baggage compartment (aft) 13·1 cu ft (0·37 m³)

Areas:
Wings, gross 440 sq ft (41·00 m²)
Horizontal tail surfaces (total)
121·6 sq ft (11·30 m²)
Vertical tail surfaces (total) 81·8 sq ft (7·60 m²)

Weights (Series D):
Weight empty, equipped 15,600 lb (7,080 kg)
Max payload 3,050 lb (1,380 kg)
Max T-O and ramp weight 27,335 lb (12,400 kg)
Max zero-fuel weight 18,960 lb (8,600 kg)
Max landing weight 26,040 lb (11,810 kg)

Weights (Series F):
Max T-O and ramp weight 28,660 lb (13,000 kg)
Max zero-fuel weight 19,600 lb (8,900 kg)
Typical landing weight 18,870 lb (8,560 kg)

Performance (Series D):
Max permissible speed at S/L
351 knots (404 mph; 650 km/h) IAS
Max permissible speed at 23,000 ft (7,000 m)
369 knots (426 mph; 685 km/h) IAS
Max cruising speed at 25,000 ft (7,620 m) at AUW of 20,000 lb (9,071 kg)
465 knots (536 mph; 862 km/h)
Econ cruising speed at 40,000 ft (12,200 m)
405 knots (466 mph; 750 km/h)
Stalling speed 87 knots (99 mph; 160 km/h)
Absolute ceiling 42,000 ft (12,800 m)
Service ceiling, one engine out, at AUW of 18,700 lb (8,500 kg) 25,100 ft (7,650 m)
T-O to 35 ft (10·7 m) at AUW of 26,490 lb = 12,015 kg (full tanks, 8 passengers and baggage)
4,560 ft (1,390 m)
ICAO balanced T-O field length, AUW as above 5,610 ft (1,710 m)
ICAO landing field length at AUW of 18,500 lb = 8,392 kg (8 passengers, 45 min reserves)
3,740 ft (1,140 m)

Landing from 35 ft (10·7 m) 2,230 ft (680 m)
Range with max fuel and 1,600 lb (725 kg) payload at econ cruising speed, with reserves for 45 min cruise
1,910 nm (2,200 miles; 3,540 km)

DASSAULT FALCON 10

First announced during the Paris Air Show in June 1969, the Falcon 10 is basically a scaled-down version of the standard Mystère 20/Falcon, incorporating similar wing high-lift devices to those of the Falcon F and powered by two small turbofans in the 2,200 lb (1,000 kg) st class. Like the standard Falcons, it is designed to fail-safe principles and to comply with US FAR 25 transport category requirements.

A prototype, with CJ610-1 engines, was due to fly towards the end of 1970, with deliveries of production aircraft starting in 1972. Pan American's Business Jets Division has placed an initial order for 40, with options on a further 120. At 1 May 1970 total orders amounted to 55 plus 122 options.

Type: Twin-turbofan executive transport.

Wings: Cantilever low-wing monoplane with increased sweepback on inboard leading-edges. All-metal torsion-box structure, with leading-edge slats and double-slotted trailing-edge flaps and plain ailerons.

Landing Gear: Retractable tricycle type with twin wheels on main gear, single wheel on nose gear. Hydraulic retraction, main units inward, nose wheel forward. Oleo-pneumatic shock absorbers. Low-pressure tyres for soft-field operation.

Power Plant: Two AiResearch TFE-731-2 turbofan engines (each 3,230 lb = 1,465 kg) st, mounted in pods on each side of rear fuselage. Fuel in two integral tanks in wings and two feeder tanks aft of rear bulkhead, with total capacity of 660 Imp gallons (790 US gallons = 3,000 litres). Separate fuel system for each engine, with provision for cross-feeding. Pressure refuelling system.

Accommodation: Crew of two on flight deck, with dual controls and airline-type instrumentation. Normal seating for seven passengers (four single seats and three-seat sofa) or for four passengers in single seats. Each pair of seats is separated by a table. Coat compartment on starboard side, immediately aft of flight deck opposite entry door; rear baggage compartment behind sofa. Galley on left of entrance. Optional front toilet compartment. Downward-opening door with built-in steps.

Systems: Duplicated air-conditioning and pressurisation systems supplied with air bled from both engines. Pressure differential 8·8 lb/sq in (0·615 kg/cm²). Two independent hydraulic systems, each of 3,000 lb/sq in (210 kg/cm²) pressure and with twin engine-driven pumps and emergency electric pump, to actuate primary flight controls, flaps, landing gear, wheel brakes, air brakes and nose-wheel steering. 28V DC electrical system with a 9kW DC starter-generator on each engine, three 750VA 400 c/s 115V inverters and two 23Ah batteries. Automatic emergency oxygen system.

Electronics and Equipment: Standard equipment includes duplicated VHF and VOR/glideslope, single ADF, marker beacon receiver, ATC transponder, autopilot, intercom systems and duplicated blind-flying instrumentation. Optional equipment includes duplicated DME and flight director, second ADF, weather radar and radio altimeter.

Dimensions, external:
Wing span 43 ft 0 in (13·10 m)
Wing chord (mean) 6 ft 3 in (1·91 m)
Wing aspect ratio 7·6
Length overall 44 ft 11 in (13·69 m)
Height overall 14 ft 3 in (4·35 m)
Tailplane span 16 ft 5½ in (5·02 m)
Wheel track 9 ft 0 in (2·74 m)
Wheelbase 17 ft 4½ in (5·30 m)
Passenger door:
Height 4 ft 10 in (1·47 m)
Width 2 ft 7 in (0·79 m)
Emergency exit (stbd side, over wing):
Height 2 ft 2 in (0·66 m)
Width 1 ft 7 in (0·48 m)

Dimensions, internal:
Cabin: Length 16 ft 4 in (4·99 m)
Max width 4 ft 9 in (1·46 m)
Max height 4 ft 11 in (1·50 m)

Areas:
Wings, gross 242 sq ft (22·48 m²)
Horizontal tail surfaces (total) 65·7 sq ft (6·10 m²)
Vertical tail surfaces (total) 45·6 sq ft (4·24 m²)

Weights:
Weight empty, equipped 9,710 lb (4,404 kg)
Max payload 1,330 lb (603 kg)
Max T-O weight 16,135 lb (7,319 kg)
Max zero-fuel weight 11,440 lb (5,189 kg)
Max landing weight 15,428 lb (6,970 kg)

Performance (estimated):
Max permissible speed at S/L 351 knots (404 mph; 650 km/h)
Max cruising speed at 25,000 ft (7,620 m) 486 knots (559 mph; 900 km/h)
Stalling speed, landing weight as above 73 knots (84 mph; 135 km/h)
Absolute ceiling 45,200 ft (13,780 m)
FAR 25 T-O field length at 16,135 lb = 7,319 kg AUW (full tanks, 4 passengers and baggage), ISA + 15°C at S/L 4,860 ft (1,480 m)
FAR 25 landing field length at AUW of 11,540 lb = 5,235 kg (4 passengers and baggage, 45 min reserves) 3,500 ft (1,067 m)
Range with max fuel and 760 lb = 345 kg payload (4 passengers and baggage) with 45 min reserves
1,820 nm (2,095 miles; 3,370 km)

DASSAULT MD 320 HIRONDELLE (SWALLOW)

A model of the provisional MD 320 design was exhibited at the 1967 Paris Air Show, and on 28 June 1967 Dassault announced its intention to proceed with development of this aircraft, to be known as the Hirondelle. In September 1967, detail design was completed and construction of an MD 320-01 prototype began; this aircraft (F-WPXB) made its first flight at Bordeaux-Mérignac on 11 September 1968.

Externally, the Hirondelle resembles closely the earlier MD 415 Communauté, which was described and illustrated in the 1960-61 *Jane's*. It is, however, an entirely new design, and has a more spacious cabin. The Hirondelle is intended primarily as a low-cost utility or executive transport, with a capacity similar to that of the more expensive turbofan-powered Mystère 20/Falcon, or as a military aircrew trainer to replace aircraft in the category of the MD 315 Flamant. It conforms to the latest FAA requirements for light transports seating 10 or more passengers.

As a feeder transport, the Hirondelle can be equipped to carry from 8 to 12 passengers in a standard of comfort comparable with that of an airliner, with full pressurisation and air conditioning, coat rack, baggage hold, individual reading lights, and toilets. In liaison or high-density "commuter" configuration, 14 inward-facing seats can be installed along the sides of the cabin. Alternatively, the Hirondelle can be fitted out as a six-passenger executive transport, with armchair seating, tables, galley and toilet; as an all-freight aircraft for up to 3,100 lb (1,400 kg) of freight; or as an ambulance, with space for three stretchers and two attendants.

The details below apply generally to the MD 320-01 prototype. Production aircraft would probably have 1,088 ehp Astazou XVI engines and detail refinements, giving enhanced performance.

Type: Twin-turboprop executive aircraft, utility transport or trainer.

Wings: Cantilever low-wing monoplane. NACA series wing section, with increased chord on inboard sections. All-metal two-spar fail-safe structure, with some use of titanium for the engine cowlings. Split flaps and conventional ailerons. Thermal de-icing of leading-edges.

Fuselage: All-metal semi-monocoque fail-safe structure. Circular cross-section.

Tail Unit: Conventional fin and rudder, with sweepback. Slightly-sweptback horizontal tail surfaces, mounted on top of rear fuselage. All-metal fail-safe structure.

Landing Gear: Retractable tricycle type of Messier design. Main wheels retract inward into the wings and nose-wheel forward into the fuselage. Steerable nose-wheel. Main-wheel legs are interchangeable, right with left. Low-pressure tyres (56·9 lb/sq in = 4 kg/cm²) for rough-field operation.

Power Plant (Prototype): Two 920 ehp Turboméca Astazou XIVD turboprop engines, each driving a Hamilton Standard three-blade propeller of 8 ft 0 in (2·44 m) diameter. Total fuel capacity of 385 Imp gallons (1,750 litres). Production aircraft will be fitted with more powerful turboprop engines (see introductory copy).

Accommodation: Crew of one or two on flight deck, with jump-seat for a third crew member when carried. Airliner-type seating for eight, ten or twelve passengers (those in the ten-seat layout being at 32 in = 81·3 cm pitch), with galley and toilet at rear. Alternative six-seat executive or fourteen-seat high-density layouts available. Access to passenger cabin via door on the port side, aft. A larger cargo door will be an optional feature on production aircraft.

Electronics and Equipment: Wide range of radio and navigation equipment available for production aircraft, according to role, including complete ARINC system.

Systems: Cabin air conditioning, pressurisation, heating and ventilation standard.

Dimensions, external:
Wing span 47 ft 8¾ in (14·55 m)
Length of fuselage 40 ft 2¼ in (12·25 m)
Fuselage: max diameter 5 ft 11¾ in (1·82 m)
Passenger door:
Height 4 ft 5⅛ in (1·35 m)
Width 2 ft 7½ in (0·80 m)
Cargo door (optional):
Height 4 ft 7 in (1·40 m)
Width 4 ft 3¼ in (1·30 m)

Dimensions, internal:
Cabin:
Max height 5 ft 5¾ in (1·67 m)
Max width 4 ft 6½ in (1·49 m)
Volume 700 cu ft (20·0 m³)

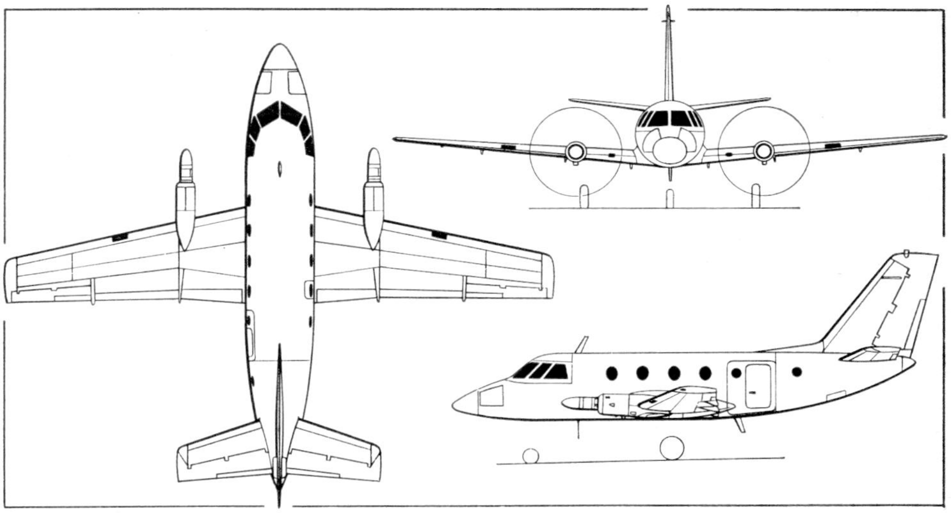

Three-view drawing of the Dassault Hirondelle twin-turboprop utility transport aircraft

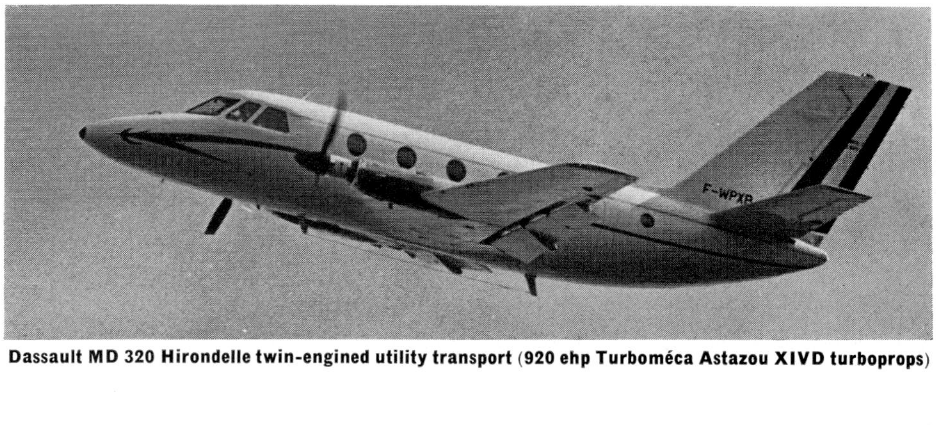

Dassault MD 320 Hirondelle twin-engined utility transport (920 ehp Turboméca Astazou XIVD turboprops)

AREA:
Wings, gross   290·63 sq ft (27·00 m²)
WEIGHTS (A=6-seat executive, B=10 passengers, C=cargo version):
Basic operating weight, empty:
    A   8,200 lb (3,720 kg)
    B   7,716 lb (3,500 kg)
    C   7,341 lb (3,330 kg)
Max payload:
    A   2,160 lb (980 kg)
    B   2,645 lb (1,200 kg)
    C   3,020 lb (1,370 kg)
Max T-O weight   11,905 lb (5,400 kg)

PERFORMANCE (at max T-O weight, except where stated otherwise):
Max cruising speed
     269 knots (310 mph; 500 km/h)
Time to 20,000 ft (6,100 m)   13 min
Service ceiling (all versions) 30,850 ft (9,400 m)
Service ceiling, one engine out (all versions)
     16,400 ft (5,000 m)
T-O to 50 ft (15 m) at AUW of 11,464 lb (5,200 kg)   2,460 ft (750 m)
Landing run at AUW of 9,920 lb (4,500 kg)
     2,297 ft (700 m)

Range with 45 min reserves:
    at 243 knots (280 mph; 450 km/h)
     1,619 nm (1,865 miles; 3,000 km)
    at 269 knots (310 mph; 500 km/h)
     1,081 nm (1,245 miles; 2,000 km)

DASSAULT MERCURE

Dassault is now constructing a prototype of this short-haul large-capacity transport, which is intended to make its first flight early in 1971 and to be available for airline deliveries from the beginning of 1973. Air Inter has an option on 12 Mercures for delivery in 1973-74.

The Mercure is a 116/155-seat twin-engined aircraft optimised for very short ranges of 108-810 nm (125-1,000 miles; 200-1,500 km). The first prototype will have JT8D-11 engines; the second prototype and production aircraft, to which the following description applies, will have the more powerful JT8D-15.

Research has indicated a potential market for up to 1,500 aeroplanes of this size and type by 1980, operating beneath the Airbus level but with greater capacity than is available in the present generation of short-haul twin-jets. The launching programme for the Mercure is estimated to cost 800m Fr (£64m), covering the construction of two prototypes and two static test airframes, certification and production tooling. Of this sum, the French contribution represents 70 per cent; the remaining amount is shared between Fiat in Italy, SABCA in Belgium, CASA in Spain and the Swiss aircraft industry.

All available details of the Mercure follow:

TYPE: Twin-jet short-range transport.

WINGS: Cantilever low-wing monoplane. Special Dassault wing sections. Sweepback at quarter-chord 25°. Two-spar fail-safe structure. Dassault triple-slotted flaps. Five slats on each leading-edge. Spoilers for lateral control and lift dumping. All movable surfaces are hydraulically operated by dual actuators fed by three independent circuits. Engine bleed air for anti-icing of wing leading-edges.

FUSELAGE: Circular-section semi-monocoque fail-safe structure, max diameter 12 ft 9½ in (3·90 m).

TAIL UNIT: Cantilever multi-spar structure. Variable-incidence tailplane for trim and pitch emergency control. Rudder split into two independent parts. No tabs. All control surfaces operated by hydraulic dual actuators fed by three independent circuits.

LANDING GEAR: Twin-wheel tricycle type, hydraulically operated with manual back-up. Nose wheel has ±75° steering. Anti-skid control units on main wheels, which retract inwards. Tyre pressures 128 lb/sq in (9·0 kg/cm²) on main wheels, 107 lb/sq in (7·5 kg/cm²) on nose wheels.

POWER PLANT: Two Pratt & Whitney JT8D-15 turbofan engines, with thrust reversers and Dassault-developed noise absorbers. Take-off thrust 15,500 lb (7,030 kg) each. Engine bleed air for nose cowl de-icing.

ACCOMMODATION: Crew of two side-by-side on flight deck with two extra optional seats. Typical mixed-class accommodation provides 16 seats four-abreast at 38 in (96 cm) pitch and 100 seats six-abreast at 34 in (86 cm) pitch. Basic tourist class accommodation provides 134 seats at 34 in pitch. High-density layouts for up to 155 seats six-abreast at 30 in (76 cm) pitch. Six possible locations of toilets and galleys at front and rear, according to layout. Two passenger entrance doors on port side, two service doors on starboard side, two escape hatches over each wing. Baggage and freight holds beneath cabin floor, front and rear, able to accommodate standard Boeing 727 containers.

SYSTEMS: Air conditioning and pressurisation system uses engine bleed air through duplicated circuits, with automatic regulation. Max differential 8·4 lb/sq in (0·6 kg/cm²). Three independent hydraulic systems for flying controls, flaps, slats, spoilers, tailplane, landing gear, nosewheel steering and brakes; pressure 3,000 lb/sq in (210 kg/cm²). An APU provides electrical emergency power and air for ground conditioning and engine starting.

ELECTRONICS AND EQUIPMENT: To customer's specification. Basic aircraft designed for all-weather (Cat III) operation.

DIMENSIONS, EXTERNAL:
Wing span   100 ft 3 in (30·55 m)
Wing aspect ratio   8
Length overall   111 ft 6 in (34·00 m)
Length of fuselage   108 ft 3 in (33·00 m)
Height overall   37 ft 3¼ in (11·36 m)
Tailplane span   36 ft 1 in (11·00 m)
Wheel track   20 ft 4 in (6·20 m)
Wheelbase   38 ft 5 in (11·71 m)
Passenger and service doors (fwd):
    Height   6 ft 1 in (1·85 m)
    Width   2 ft 8 in (0·81 m)
    Height to sill   9 ft 7 in (2·92 m)
Passenger and service doors (rear):
    Height to sill   10 ft 0 in (3·05 m)

DIMENSIONS, INTERNAL:
Cabin, excluding galleys and toilets:
    Length   67 ft 4 in (20·51 m)
    Max width   11 ft 11 in (3·66 m)
    Max height   7 ft 2¾ in (2·20 m)
    Floor area   818 sq ft (76 m²)
    Volume   4,970 cu ft (141 m³)
Freight hold (forward) volume
     510 cu ft (14·5 m³)
Freight hold (rear) volume   670 cu ft (19 m³)

AREA:
Wings, gross   1,250 sq ft (116 m²)

WEIGHTS AND LOADINGS (estimated):
Manufacturer's weight, empty
     56,383 lb (25,575 kg)
Max payload   36,508 lb (16,560 kg)
Max fuel*   22,930 lb (10,400 kg)
Max T-O weight   114,640 lb (52,000 kg)
Max landing weight   106,924 lb (48,500 kg)
Max zero-fuel weight   99,208 lb (45,000 kg)
Max wing loading   92 lb/sq ft (449 kg/m²)
Max power loading   3·70 lb/lb st (3·70 kg/kg st)
*Can be increased by 13,221 lb (5,997 kg) by use of optional wing centre-section tank

PERFORMANCE (estimated, at max T-O weight, except where indicated):
Max cruising speed at 22,000 ft (6,706 m)
     500 knots (576 mph; 927 km/h) (Mach 0·82)
Max permitted operating speed (V_MO/M_MO)
     379 knots (437 mph; 704 km/h) EAS up to 20,000 ft (6,100 m) and Mach 0·85 above 20,000 ft
Approach speed at normal landing weight (134 passengers and baggage, ATA 67 reserves)
     117 knots (135 mph; 217 km/h)
Take-off field length, ISA at S/L
     6,594 ft (2,010 m)
Landing field length, ISA at S/L, landing weight as above   4,495 ft (1,370 m)
Range at max cruising speed with max fuel (ATA 67 reserves) and 25,397 lb (11,520 kg) payload   898 nm (1,035 miles; 1,667 km)
Range with max payload (ATA 67 reserves)
     387 nm (446 miles; 719 km)

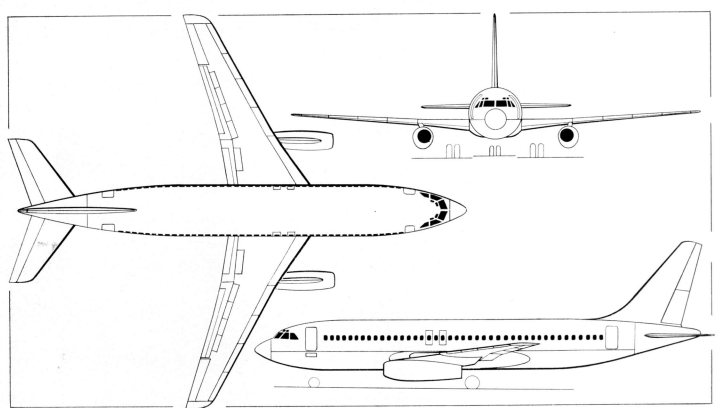

Dassault Mercure twin-turbofan short-range transport aircraft

DORAND
GIRAVIONS DORAND SARL
ADDRESS:
5 rue Jean-Macé, 92-Suresnes
MANAGING DIRECTORS:
Pierre de Guillenchmidt (General Manager)
Claude-Marcel Terret (Financial Manager)
TECHNICAL DIRECTOR:
René Dorand

M René Dorand, well known for his association with Louis Breguet in developing the pre-war Breguet-Dorand *Gyroplane*, which established a series of international rotorcraft records in 1936, formed this present company in 1950. Its activities since then have been limited intentionally and at present are divided into two main categories: research, development and construction of prototype rotorcraft, and the manufac-

ture of precision components required for the company's industrial products. Among the latter have been the DX-50, the world's first helicopter simulator, which was developed for the Aérospatiale Alouette II, and the manufacture of electronic and electro-mechanical sub-assemblies used in simulators for the Mirage III, Etendard IV-M and Transall C-160 fixed-wing aircraft and the SA 330 helicopter. Dorand has also designed and built simulators for several manually guided missiles, and is currently developing prototype simulators for such missiles as the HOT and the MILAN. The company's works occupy a floor area of 27,986 sq ft (2,600 m²), and in 1969 it employed a total of 120 people on aviation activities.

Dorand's rotary-wing department is currently undertaking a development programme on behalf of NASA for a prototype rotor system using jet

flaps, which will enable conventional helicopters to attain speeds of the order of 270 knots (310 mph; 500 km/h). The Dorand system eliminates all mechanical transmission by ejecting the hot engine gases through slots in the trailing-edges of the rotor blades. These gases can be deflected to provide the same effect as flaps on a fixed-wing aircraft, giving lift without the disadvantage of parasitic drag and eliminating the necessary for changes in blade pitch. The prototype rotor system was delivered to NASA in January 1969, and was to be tested in a wind-tunnel at simulated airspeeds of up to 216 knots (350 mph; 400 km/h), the maximum for which it has been designed. In 1966, Dorand signed a technical co-operation agreement with LTV in the United States, under which Dorand will be responsible for developing and building the rotor if an experimental prototype aircraft is ordered.

DRUINE
AVIONS ROGER DRUINE
ADDRESS:
26, Avenue Lamoriciere, Paris 12e

This company was formed by the late Roger Druine, who designed, built and flew his first aircraft at the age of seventeen and died only 20 years later, in 1958. His best-known designs are the Turbulent single-seat monoplane and the Turbi, a two-seat version of the Turbulent, both of which have been built by amateurs throughout the world.

In the United Kingdom the Popular Flying Association, which was delegated by the ARB to administer the simplified procedure for the classification of ultra-light aircraft, is marketing sets of plans and instructions for amateur construction of the Turbulent, Turbi and the more refined Condor.

The Turbulent and Condor are being manufactured by Rollason Aircraft and Engines Ltd of Croydon, England.

DRUINE D.31 TURBULENT
Full details of this single-seat ultra-light monoplane are given under the "Rollason" heading in the UK section.

The example illustrated, built by Mr L. J. Weishaar of Springfield, Illinois, has a modified wing with fixed leading-edge slots. The landing gear has also been modified. Power plant is a converted 30 hp Volkswagen motor-car engine.

DRUINE D.5 TURBI
The prototype Turbi had a 45 hp Beaussier 4 B02 four-cylinder inverted air-cooled engine. Details of this and of the version with 62 hp Walter Mikron II engine can be found in the 1964-65 *Jane's*. The following details refer specifically to the more powerful version built by Mr John Carnwith and shown in the adjacent illustration. Construction took 4½ years at a cost of $2,500, and the aircraft flew for the first time on 15 September 1963.

TYPE: Two-seat light monoplane.

WINGS: Cantilever low-wing monoplane. NACA 23012 wing section. Wood structure, with box-spar and plywood covering. No flaps.

FUSELAGE: Rectangular four-longeron all-wood structure, plywood-covered.

TAIL UNIT: Cantilever wooden structure. Fin built integral with fuselage. Non-adjustable tailplane. All surfaces plywood-covered.

LANDING GEAR: Non-retractable tail-wheel type. Spring shock-absorbers. Steerable tail-wheel. Brakes.

POWER PLANT: 85 hp Continental C85-12 four-cylinder horizontally-opposed air-cooled engine, driving a two-blade fixed-pitch propeller. Glass-fibre cowling. Fuel tank in fuselage in front of forward cockpit.

ACCOMMODATION: Two seats in tandem in open cockpits.

DIMENSIONS, EXTERNAL:
Wing span	28 ft 9 in (8·76 m)
Wing chord (constant)	5 ft 8 in (1·73 m)

Druine Turbulent built in USA by Mr L. J. Weishaar, with modified wings and landing gear and 30 hp Volkswagen engine (*Howard Levy*)

Druine D.5 Turbi, built in Canada with 85 hp Continental engine (*Peter M. Bowers*)

Length overall	22 ft 0 in (6·71 m)
Height overall	5 ft 0 in (1·52 m)

AREA:
Wings, gross	139 sq ft (12·9 m²)

WEIGHTS:
Weight empty	830 lb (376 kg)
Max T-O weight	1,240 lb (562 kg)

PERFORMANCE (at max T-O weight):
Max level speed at S/L:
	104 knots (120 mph; 193 km/h)
Cruising speed	78 knots (90 mph; 145 km/h)
Landing speed	35 knots (40 mph; 64 km/h)
Rate of climb at S/L	500 ft (152 m)/min

Absolute ceiling	10,000 ft (3,050 m)
T-O run	300 ft (91 m)
Landing run	700 ft (213 m)

DRUINE D.61/D.62 CONDOR
The Condor was designed primarily for factory production and incorporates many refinements in design and construction not found in the Turbulent and Turbi. A simplified version is, however, available for amateur construction.

The two standard versions are the D.61 with 65/75 hp Continental engine, and the D.62 with 90/100 hp Continental engine.

A full description of the D.62 is given under the "Rollason" heading in the UK section.

DURUBLE
ROLAND T. DURUBLE
ADDRESS: 40 Rue du Paradis, Les Essarts, 76 Grand-Couronne
M Roland Duruble, with MM Guy Chaunt and Legrand, of Rouen, designed and built a two-seat all-metal light aircraft named the RD-02 Edelweiss, which flew for the first time on 7 July 1962.

DURUBLE RD-02 EDELWEISS
The prototype Edelweiss has a 65 hp Walter Mikron engine, but alternative power plants can be fitted, including a 90 hp Continental flat-four. Plans are available to amateur constructors, and in the Spring of 1970 negotiations were under way for commercial production of the Edelweiss in Belgium.

TYPE: Two-seat amateur-built light aircraft.

WINGS: Cantilever low-wing monoplane. Wing section NACA 23018 at root, NACA 23009 at tip. Dihedral 6° 30'. All-metal two-spar structure, with main spar at 40% root chord and auxiliary front spar. Slotted ailerons and mechanically-operated slotted flaps. No trim-tabs.

FUSELAGE: All-metal semi-monocoque structure, comprising frames, stringers and skin, without longerons. Plastics nose-cowl.

TAIL UNIT: Cantilever all-metal structure, with tailplane set at 6° 30' dihedral. Ground-adjustable tab on rudder. Trim-tab in port elevator.

LANDING GEAR: Retractable tricycle type. Hydraulic retraction, nose-wheel rearward, main units inward into wings. Rubber-block shock-absorption on main units; nose unit has Duruble hydro-air shock absorber. Main wheels and tyres size 330 × 130. Nose-wheel and tyre size 260 × 80. Hydraulic disc brakes.

POWER PLANT: One 65 hp Walter Mikron III four-cylinder in-line inverted air-cooled engine, driving an EVRA two-blade fixed-pitch wooden propeller. Alternative power plants include the 90 hp Continental C90 four-cylinder horizontally-opposed air-cooled engine. Fuel tanks between spars in each wing-root, total capacity 15 Imp gallons (67 litres) with Mikron engine, 26 Imp gallons (120 litres) with C90.

ACCOMMODATION: Two seats side-by-side in enclosed cabin. Entry by raising either half of canopy, which is hinged on centre-line of aircraft.

DIMENSIONS, EXTERNAL:
Wing span	28 ft 3½ in (8·62 m)
Wing chord at root	5 ft 3 in (1·60 m)
Length overall	19 ft 3 in (5·88 m)
Height overall	7 ft 8½ in (2·35 m)

AREA:
Wings, gross	110·6 sq ft (10·25 m²)

WEIGHTS AND LOADINGS:
Weight empty:	
Mikron	680 lb (310 kg)
Max T-O weight:	
Mikron	1,180 lb (535 kg)
C90	1,435 lb (650 kg)
Max wing loading:	
Mikron	10·77 lb/sq ft (52·6 kg/m²)
Max power loading:	
Mikron	18·2 lb/hp (8·25 kg/hp)

PERFORMANCE (at max T-O weight):
Max level speed at S/L:	
Mikron	115 knots (132 mph; 212 km/h)
C90	134 knots (154 mph; 248 km/h)
Max cruising speed:	
Mikron	102 knots (118 mph; 190 km/h)
C90	113 knots (130 mph; 209 km/h)
Stalling speed, power on:	
Mikron	44 knots (50 mph; 80 km/h)
C90	47·8 knots (55 mph; 89 km/h)
Stalling speed, power off:	
Mikron	46 knots (53 mph; 85 km/h)
Rate of climb at S/L:	
Mikron	490 ft (150 m)/min
C90	600 ft (183 m)/min
Service ceiling:	
Mikron	12,000 ft (3,650 m)
C90	15,000 ft (4,575 m)
T-O from grass:	
Mikron	985 ft (300 m)
Range with max fuel:	
Mikron	432 nm (496 miles; 800 km)
C90	540 nm (620 miles; 1,000 km)

DURUBLE RD-03 EDELWEISS

The RD-03 Edelweiss, an enlarged and developed version of the RD-02, has been designed to AIR 2052 (CAR 3) standards, and is projected in three versions, as follows:

RD-03A. With 100 hp Continental O-200 four-cylinder horizontally-opposed air-cooled engine and fuel capacity of 22 Imp gallons (100 litres) in two wing tanks. Can be fitted with 90 hp engine. Side-by-side seats for pilot and one passenger (weight 380 lb = 172 kg) in cabin.

RD-03B. With 115 hp Lycoming engine and same fuel capacity as RD-03A. Seating as RD-03A for Utility category operation, or in "2 + 2" arrangement for pilot and three passengers (340 lb = 154 kg on front seats, 240 lb = 108 kg on rear seats) in Normal category.

RD-03C. With 145 hp Continental engine and additional wing tanks, increasing total fuel capacity to 33 Imp gallons (150 litres). In Utility two-seat form (as RD-03A) or with seating for four adult passengers (total weight 680 lb = 308 kg) in Normal category.

Plans of the RD-03 will be available from the Autumn of 1970.

TYPE: Two/four-seat light aircraft.

WINGS: Cantilever low-wing monoplane. Wing section NACA 23000 series. Thickness/chord ratio 18% at root, 12% at tip. Dihedral 6° 5′ from roots. Incidence 3° at root, 0° at tip. No sweepback. All-metal two-spar duralumin structure, with metal slotted trailing-edge flaps and slotted ailerons. No trim-tabs.

FUSELAGE: Conventional semi-monocoque duralumin structure, of basically rectangular section with curved top-decking.

TAIL UNIT: Cantilever all-metal structure, with sweptback vertical surfaces. Fixed-incidence tailplane. Trim-tab in each elevator, one actuated by flap linkage and the other manually.

LANDING GEAR: Retractable tricycle type. Hydraulic retraction, nose-wheel rearward, main units inward into wings. Duruble hydro-air shock-absorbers on main units. Main wheels and tyres size 355 × 150, nose-wheel and tyre size 330 × 130. Pressure (all tyres) 18 lb/sq in (1·26 kg/cm²). Hydraulic disc brakes.

POWER PLANT: One 100, 115 or 145 hp horizontally-opposed air-cooled engine (see details above). Refuelling point above wing.

ACCOMMODATION: Side-by-side seats for two, three or four persons (see details above) in fully-enclosed cabin.

SYSTEMS: Hydraulic system, pressure 1,000 lb/sq in (70 kg/cm²), for flap and landing gear actuation.

ELECTRONICS AND EQUIPMENT: Radio optional. Blind-flying instrumentation not fitted.

Duruble RD-02 Edelweiss amateur-built light aircraft (65 hp Walter Mikron III engine)

DIMENSIONS, EXTERNAL:
Wing span	28 ft 8½ in (8·75 m)
Wing chord at root	5 ft 7 in (1·70 m)
Wing chord at tip	2 ft 10 in (0·86 m)
Wing aspect ratio	6·95
Length overall (RD-03A)	20 ft 7 in (6·27 m)
Length of fuselage	20 ft 3 in (6·17 m)
Height overall	7 ft 8½ in (2·35 m)
Tailplane span	10 ft 0 in (3·05 m)

DIMENSIONS, INTERNAL:
Cabin: Max length	8 ft 0 in (2·44 m)
Max width	3 ft 10½ in (1·18 m)
Max height	2 ft 6 in (0·76 m)

AREAS:
Wings, gross	118·5 sq ft (11·0 m²)
Ailerons (total)	7·3 sq ft (0·68 m²)
Trailing-edge flaps (total)	17·5 sq ft (1·63 m²)
Fin	7·8 sq ft (0·72 m²)
Rudder	4·9 sq ft (0·46 m²)
Tailplane	12·9 sq ft (1·20 m²)
Elevators, incl tabs	10·0 sq ft (0·93 m²)

WEIGHTS (estimated; A = RD-03A, B = RD-03B, C = RD-03C):
Weight empty, equipped:	
A	840 lb (381 kg)
B	850 lb (385 kg)
C	910 lb (412 kg)
Max T-O and landing weight:	
A (Utility cat)	1,497 lb (679 kg)
B (Utility cat)	1,510 lb (684 kg)
B (Normal cat)	1,688 lb (765 kg)
C (Utility cat)	1,610 lb (730 kg)
C (Normal cat)	1,890 lb (857 kg)
Max wing loading:	
A (Utility)	12·50 lb/sq ft (61·0 kg/m²)
B (Utility)	12·75 lb/sq ft (62·2 kg/m²)
B (Normal)	14·25 lb/sq ft (69·6 kg/m²)
C (Utility)	13·60 lb/sq ft (66·4 kg/m²)
C (Normal)	16·00 lb/sq ft (78·0 kg/m²)
Max power loading:	
A (Utility)	14·97 lb/hp (6·79 kg/hp)
B (Utility)	13·15 lb/hp (5·95 kg/hp)
B (Normal)	4·70 lb hp (6·67 kg/hp)
C (Utility)	11·10 lb/hp (5·03 kg/hp)
C (Normal)	13·00 lb/hp (5·90 kg/hp)

PERFORMANCE (estimated, at max T-O weight):
Max level speed at S/L:	
A (Utility)	139 knots (160 mph; 257 km/h)
B (Utility)	139·4 knots (160·5 mph; 258 km/h)
B (Normal)	138 knots (159 mph; 256 km/h)
C (Utility)	148 knots (170 mph; 274 km/h)
C (Normal)	145 knots (166·5 mph; 268 km/h)

Max permissible diving speed:	
A, B, C (Utility)	184 knots (212 mph; 341 km/h)
B, C (Normal)	203 knots (234 mph; 376·5 km/h)
Max cruising speed at S/L:	
A (Utility)	126·3 knots (145·5 mph; 234 km/h)
B (Utility)	127 knots (146 mph; 235 km/h)
B (Normal)	126 knots (145 mph; 233 km/h)
C (Utility)	134 knots (154·5 mph; 249 km/h)
C (Normal)	131 knots (151 mph; 243 km/h)
Econ cruising speed at S/L:	
A, B (Utility)	121 knots (139 mph; 224 km/h)
B (Normal)	120 knots (138 mph; 222 km/h)
C (Utility)	128 knots (147·5 mph; 237 km/h)
C (Normal)	125 knots (144·5 mph; 233 km/h)
Stalling speed, flaps up:	
A, B (Utility)	48 knots (54·5 mph; 88 km/h)
B (Normal), C (Utility)	49 knots (55 mph; 89 km/h)
C (Normal)	52 knots (59·5 mph; 96 km/h)
Stalling speed, flaps down:	
A, B (Utility)	38 knots (43·5 mph; 70·5 km/h)
B (Normal), C (Utility)	39 knots (45 mph; 72·5 km/h)
C (Normal)	43 knots (49 mph; 79 km/h)
Rate of climb at S/L:	
A	650 ft (198 m)/min
B	700 ft (213 m)/min
C	800 ft (244 m)/min
Service ceiling:	
A, B	15,000 ft (4,570 m)
C	16,500 ft (5,030 m)
T-O run:	
A	820 ft (250 m)
B	900 ft (274 m)
C	1,000 ft (305 m)
T-O to 50 ft (15 m):	
A, B, C	1,500 ft (457 m)
Landing from 50 ft (15 m):	
A	610 ft (186 m)
B	800 ft (244 m)
C	940 ft (287 m)
Landing run:	
A	1,000 ft (305 m)
B	1,100 ft (335 m)
C	1,400 ft (427 m)
Range with max fuel, 30 min reserve:	
A	607 nm (700 miles; 1,125 km)
B	521 nm (600 miles; 965 km)
C	547 nm (630 miles; 1,010 km)

Duruble RD-03C Edelweiss two/four-seat amateur-built light aircraft

GATARD
AVIONS A. GATARD

ADDRESS:
La Devallée, 52 route de Jonzac, 17-Montendre, (Chte Mme)

M Albert Gatard has developed a control system for aeroplanes which involves the use of a variable-incidence lifting tailplane of large area, and has built or is developing a series of aircraft, including the Alouette and Poussin, incorporating his ideas. The Alouette (described in the 1959-60 *Jane's*) was purely experimental, but plans of the Poussin are available to amateur constructors.

Instead of altering the wing angle of attack to increase lift on these aircraft, the pilot lowers full-span slotted aileron/flaps and adjusts the tailplane to maintain pitching equilibrium. In consequence, the aircraft climb with the fuselage datum at no more than 4° to the horizontal, which preserves a good forward view and low body drag.

Early in 1966, M Gatard began work on a prototype of another design, the AG 04. In the Spring of 1969 this aircraft was still under construction. All details which were available at that time are given below, together with particulars of M Gatard's most recent project, the AG 05.

GATARD STATOPLAN AG 02 POUSSIN (CHICK)

M Gatard built two prototypes of the Poussin and the following data apply to the second of these, which incorporated a number of design improvements.

Later modifications included the introduction of a larger rudder, with the hinge-line inclined rearward at an angle of 8°. Flight tests revealed excellent aerobatic qualities and the aircraft was later fitted with special aerobatic harness for the pilot. The power plant was modified to permit up to 20 seconds of inverted flying.

The second prototype was extensively flight-tested at the Centre d'Essais en Vol at Istres, and the performance figures below were also obtained during these tests. As a result of recommendations by the CEV, a 36 hp Rectimo (modified Volkswagen VW 1200) engine is being made available to Poussin customers. Installation of this engine will improve the c.g. position and will make possible a max speed of approx 106 mph (170 km/h), a max cruising speed of approx 96 mph (155 km/h) and a rate of climb at S/L of 689 ft (210 m)/min.

In the Spring of 1969, a further five Poussins were in process of being completed by amateur constructors.

TYPE: Single-seat ultra-light monoplane.

WINGS: Cantilever low-wing monoplane. NACA 23012 wing section. Dihedral 4°. Incidence 3° 30′ at root, 2° at tip. Plywood-covered single-spar all-wood structure. Full-span slotted aileron/flaps, each in two sections which are moved together but at different angles (inboard sections up to 35°, outboard up to 20°) to give the effect of increased aerodynamic twist of the complete wing/aileron/flap assemblies. Aileron/flaps are linked with the variable-incidence tailplane.

FUSELAGE: Plywood-covered wood structure. Perforated air-brake, under fuselage, operates automatically when the main aileron/flaps are lowered at large angles, as during landing.

TAIL UNIT: Braced all-wood structure, with variable-incidence all-moving tailplane of NACA 2309 section. End-plates fitted to tailplane to increase vertical fin area and effective tailplane span. No elevators. Rudder trim-tab actuated by lateral movement of control column, permitting full control by means of the control column only in normal flight.

LANDING GEAR: Non-retractable tail-wheel type. Cantilever levered-suspension main units with rubber-band shock-absorption. Modified Dunlop brakes. Steerable tailwheel.

POWER PLANT: One 24 hp modified Volkswagen four-cylinder horizontally-opposed air-cooled engine, driving Gatard two-blade fixed-pitch wooden propeller. Provision for fitting any alternative engine of up to 40 hp, weighing between 110 and 132 lb (50-60 kg). Fuel tank aft of firewall, capacity 6·6 Imp gallons (30 litres). Oil capacity 0·45 Imp gallons (2 litres).

ACCOMMODATION: Single seat under large rearward-sliding transparent canopy. Baggage space aft of seat. Two map-pockets.

DIMENSIONS, EXTERNAL:
Wing span	21 ft 0 in (6·40 m)
Wing chord (constant)	3 ft 3¼ in (1·00 m)
Length overall	14 ft 10½ in (4·53 m)
Height overall	4 ft 11 in (1·50 m)
Wheel track	4 ft 11 in (1·50 m)
Wheelbase	10 ft 6 in (3·20 m)

AREAS:
Wings, gross	66·2 sq ft (6·15 m²)
Aileron/flaps (total)	21·5 sq ft (2·00 m²)
Fin	0·79 sq ft (0·073 m²)
Rudder	2·80 sq ft (0·26 m²)
Tailplane	18·10 sq ft (1·68 m²)

WEIGHTS:
Weight empty	375 lb (170 kg)
Max T-O weight	617 lb (280 kg)

PERFORMANCE (at max T-O weight):
Max permissible diving speed	116 knots (134 mph; 216 km/h)
Max cruising speed	77 knots (89 mph; 144 km/h)
Max speed for aerobatics	69 knots (80 mph; 130 km/h)
Stalling speed	35 knots (40·3 mph; 65 km/h)
Rate of climb at S/L	435 ft (132 m)/min
T-O run	625 ft (190 m)
T-O to 50 ft (15 m)	1,425 ft (435 m)
Landing from 50 ft (15 m)	1,050 ft (320 m)
Landing run	655 ft (200 m)

GATARD STATOPLAN AG 04 PIGEON

The AG 04, a prototype of which was under construction early in 1969, is a three/four-seat high-wing monoplane, utilising the same control system as its predecessors and powered by a 90 hp Continental engine. The wings are capable of being folded to permit the aircraft to be towed along roads behind a motor car.

GATARD STATOPLAN AG 05 MÉSANGE (TOMTIT)

Design of the AG 05 was under way in the Spring of 1969. Essentially, it is an enlarged development of the Poussin with side-by-side seating for two persons. It is intended primarily as a training or aerobatic aircraft, but will have provision either for seating a third occupant or for installing a supplementary fuel tank aft of the two front seats, to make the aircraft suitable for touring. Control system will be similar to that of the Poussin, but the Mésange will have larger, broader-chord wings without the rounded tips of its predecessor, and will have leading-edge fuel tanks.

TYPE: Two/three-seat light aircraft.

WINGS: Cantilever low-wing monoplane. NACA 23012 wing section. Dihedral 4°. Incidence 3° at root, —1° 30′ at tip. Plywood-covered all-wood structure. Full-span slotted aileron/flaps of similar type to those of Poussin, inboard sections movable between 35° and —20°, outboard sections between 20° and —12°. Aileron/flaps are linked with the variable-incidence tailplane.

FUSELAGE: Plywood-covered steel-tube structure. Air brake beneath centre-section, length 4 ft 11 in (1·50 m), operates automatically in similar manner to that on Poussin.

TAIL UNIT: Plywood-covered all-wood structure. Variable-incidence all-moving tailplane.

LANDING GEAR: Non-retractable tail-wheel type, with rubber-band shock-absorbers on main units. Steerable tail-wheel. Main-wheel brakes and parking brake.

POWER PLANT: Installations envisaged at present are either a 1,600 cc modified Volkswagen horizontally-opposed air-cooled engine or a 90/105 hp Continental flat-four engine. Fuel in two tanks in wing leading-edge, with total capacity of 15 Imp gallons (70 litres). Provision for installing 21·5 Imp gallon (100-litre) auxiliary fuel tank aft of two front seats.

ACCOMMODATION: Normal seating for pilot and one passenger on side-by-side seats in trainer version. For club or private use a third seat may be installed aft of the two front seats when no auxiliary fuselage fuel tank is fitted.

DIMENSIONS, EXTERNAL:
Wing span	28 ft 2½ in (8·60 m)
Wing chord (constant)	4 ft 5¼ in (1·35 m)
Length overall	19 ft 8¼ in (6·00 m)
Wheel track	6 ft 6¾ in (2·00 m)

AREA:
Wings, gross	121·6 sq ft (11·30 m²)

WEIGHTS:
Weight empty	793 lb (360 kg)
Max T-O weight	1,322 lb (600 kg)

PERFORMANCE (estimated, at max T-O weight):
Max cruising speed	95 knots (109 mph; 175 km/h)
Landing speed	39 knots (44·7 mph; 72 km/h)
Rate of climb at S/L	985-1,180 ft (300-360 m)/min
Range (3-seat version)	approx 807 nm (930 miles; 1,500 km)
Max endurance:	
with standard fuel	3 hr 30 min
with auxiliary fuel	8 hr 30 min

Second Gatard Statoplan AG 02 Poussin, with modified tail surfaces

GAZUIT-VALLADEAU
ETABLISSEMENTS GAZUIT-VALLADEAU

ADDRESS:
Aérodrome, 23-Guéret, Saint-Laurent

GAZUIT-VALLADEAU GV 103L

The GV 103L is a two/three-seat light aircraft which has been designed and built by Georges Gazuit, formerly of the design department of Morane-Saulnier, and M Valladeau, who participated in the production of certain Wassmer aircraft as a sub-contractor. Etablissements Gazuit-Valladeau's principal activities have been as a maintenance organisation for light aircraft, particularly those of Jodel or Robin (CEA) design, and its two proprietors embarked upon the design of the GV 103L in January 1968 in an endeavour to produce a low-cost, economical and easy-to-fly light aircraft suitable for use by flying clubs or private pilots. As a two-seater, it can be used for elementary aerobatic training.

A prototype (F-WPZI) flew for the first time on 1 May 1969, and made its first public appearance at the Paris Air Show in June 1969, at which time a second aircraft was under construction. Marketing of the GV 103L, in France and for export, will be undertaken by Eurocraft of Le Bourget.

Construction of the GV 103L is mainly of metal, and is claimed to be extremely simple, needing no special tooling.

TYPE: Two/three-seat light aircraft.

WINGS: Cantilever low-wing monoplane. Wing section NACA 23015. Wings are of constant chord, except for leading-edge roots, which are swept forward. Dihedral from roots. No sweepback. Conventional two-spar structure of AU4G T4 duralumin, with ribs of laminated plastic with metal cappings, and Vascojet root attachment fittings. Skin of sheet duralumin, flush-riveted and bonded. All-metal three-position slotted trailing-edge flaps and plain ailerons. No trim-tabs.

FUSELAGE: Conventional all-metal structure of basically rectangular section. AU4G T4 duralumin stressed skin, flush-riveted and bonded to four main longerons.

TAIL UNIT: Cantilever structure with slight sweepback on vertical surfaces and rectangular-planform horizontal surfaces. Dorsal fin fairing extends to rear of cabin. Of similar construction to wings. No trim tabs in rudder or elevators.

LANDING GEAR: Non-retractable tricycle type, with rubber-block shock-absorbers. Small skid under rear fuselage. Hydraulic disc brakes. Optional streamlined wheel fairings of laminated plastics.

POWER PLANT: One 115 hp Lycoming four-cylinder horizontally-opposed air-cooled engine, driving a two-blade metal fixed-pitch propeller. Fuel in two main tanks in wing leading-edges, with total capacity of 21·1 Imp gallons (96 litres). Provision for auxiliary fuel tank in fuselage beneath rear passenger seat.

ACCOMMODATION: Side-by-side seats for two persons, with a third seat to the rear, in fully enclosed and soundproofed cabin. Dual controls standard for training version, optional in other versions.

DIMENSIONS, EXTERNAL:
Wing span	27 ft 6¾ in (8·40 m)
Length overall	21 ft 9¾ in (6·65 m)
Height overall	8 ft 10¼ in (2·70 m)

AREA:
Wings, gross	129·1 sq ft (12·0 m²)

WEIGHTS AND LOADINGS:
Weight empty:	
Normal cat	1,135 lb (515 kg)
Aerobatic cat	1,113 lb (505 kg)
Max T-O weight	1,862 lb (845 kg)
Max wing loading:	
Normal cat	14·3 lb/sq ft (70·0 kg/m²)
Aerobatic cat	12·3 lb/sq ft (60·0 kg/m²)

PERFORMANCE (at max T-O weight):
Max level speed at S/L	
	122 knots (140 mph; 225 km/h)

Gazuit-Valladeau GV 103L two/three-seat light aircraft (115 hp Lycoming engine) (*Dennis Punnett*)

Cruising speed (75% power) at 4,925 ft (1,500 m)		Range with max payload	
	113 knots (130 mph; 210 km/h)		455 nm (525 miles; 850 km)
Stalling speed	46 knots (53 mph; 85 km/h)	Range with max fuel	
Service ceiling	14,775 ft (4,500 m)		646 nm (745 miles; 1,200 km)

HELICOP-JET

ADDRESS:
4 Avenue de la Porte de Sèvres, 75-Paris 15e

PROPRIETOR:
François Legrand

HELICOP-JET

A full-size mock-up of this "cold-jet" tip-drive light helicopter was exhibited at the Paris Air Show in June 1969. No further news of the aircraft has been received since that time.

The main rotor, of 26 ft 3 in (8·00 m) diameter, has four non-articulated stainless steel blades, containing ducts through which compressed air is channelled from the 260 hp Turboméca Palouste gas-turbine engine to exhaust at the blade tips. Fuel is carried in streamlined external tanks attached to the rear supports of the tubular skid landing gear, aft of the cabin. The cabin itself is extensively glazed, including a fully-transparent car-type door on each side, and seats up to four persons in side-by-side pairs. Tail assembly is of the twin-tailboom type, with an enclosed horizontal surface and endplate fins and rudders.

WEIGHTS:
Weight empty	860 lb (390 kg)
Max T-O weight	1,984 lb (900 kg)

PERFORMANCE (estimated, at max T-O weight):
Max level speed	
	97-108 knots (112-124 mph; 180-200 km/h)
Range	216 nm (250 miles; 400 km)

Mock-up of the Helicop-Jet tip-drive light helicopter (*Stephen P. Peltz*)

HUREL-DUBOIS

SOCIÉTÉ DE CONSTRUCTION DES AVIONS HUREL-DUBOIS S A

HEAD OFFICE AND WORKS:
Route de Verrières, B.P.6, 92-Meudon-la-Forêt (Hts de Seine)

CHAIRMAN: J. Vellutini

PUBLIC RELATIONS MANAGER: S. Montauti

Avions Hurel-Dubois was formed to develop and put into practice the theories of M Hurel regarding the advantages of using wings of high aspect ratio. It is a subsidiary of Compagnie Française d'Entreprises, one of the largest building contractors in Europe.

Its works occupy a floor area of 187,582 sq ft (17,427 m²), and a total of 622 persons were employed on aviation activities in 1970.

Following the construction of three prototype twin-engined transport aircraft, designated HD 31, HD 321-01 and HD 321-02, the company built a series of eight specially-equipped versions of the HD 321, designated HD 34, for photographic duties with the Institut Géographique National. These aircraft continue in service and have been described in previous editions of *Jane's*.

As successors to the HD 321 and HD 34, Hurel-Dubois has been studying various types of light passenger and freight transport aircraft.

Important sub-contract work (design and manufacture) currently in hand includes the

development of components for the Caravelle, Concorde and Mercure jet transports and certain military aircraft; and production of major components of the Mirage III, Mirage IV, Mirage F1 and Mirage G4.

Hurel-Dubois is also engaged in the design and manufacture of commercial furnishings for transport aircraft (Caravelle, Boeing 707, Boeing 727 and Boeing 747), galleys and racks, and mass production of Espace Universel seats.

In addition to these activities Hurel-Dubois is developing, under an agreement with Stanley Aviation Corporation of the USA, applications of the Yankee escape system for military and civil aircraft.

INDRAÉRO

INDRAÉRO SA

HEAD OFFICE AND WORKS:
Usine de Vavre, 36-Argenton sur Creuse

PRESIDENT-DIRECTOR GENERAL:
M. Crepin

Indraéro SA has facilities for the design, construction and overhaul of major aircraft sub-assemblies, and for other non-aviation products.

During the 1950s it provided assistance in the construction of a number of light aeroplanes designed by M Blanchet and M Jean Chapeau, including the Aéro 101 and Aéro 110 described in the 1956-57 *Jane's*.

More recently, Indraéro assisted M Chapeau in the completion of two further prototypes known as the Aéro 20 and Aéro 30. Details of these aircraft are given below.

Indraéro was also engaged, in the Spring of 1969, in the design of a new prototype aircraft of unspecified type.

AÉRO 20

Design of the Aéro 20 was started on 10 July 1965, and construction of a prototype aircraft began on 1 September the same year. This aircraft (F-PKXY) flew for the first time on 11

June 1966, and received certification in the amateur category by the SGAC on 20 August 1968.

TYPE: Tandem two-seat light aircraft.

WINGS: Strut-braced low-wing monoplane. Wing section NACA 23012. Dihedral 5° from roots. Incidence 2° 30'. Fabric-covered wood structure, including ailerons. No flaps. Ailerons are manually controlled by cable linkage. Wings braced by single strut each side, from upper surface to upper fuselage longeron.

FUSELAGE: Conventional structure of wood, with plywood covering.

TAIL UNIT: Cantilever wood and plywood horizontal and vertical surfaces, with fabric covering. Trim-tabs in elevators.

LANDING GEAR: Non-retractable tail-wheel type, with spring-steel shock-absorber struts. Dunlop main wheel tyres, size 420 × 120, pressure 28·5 lb/sq in (2·0 kg/cm²). No brakes.

POWER PLANT: One 90 hp Continental C90-8 four-cylinder horizontally-opposed air-cooled engine, driving a Merville Type 929 two-blade propeller of 5 ft 11¾ in (1·82 m) diameter. Fuel in single main tank in fuselage, capacity 12 Imp

gallons (55 litres). Oil capacity 1·3 Imp gallons (6 litres).

ACCOMMODATION: Seats for two persons in tandem under transparent canopy. Space for 22 lb (10 kg) of baggage aft of rear seat. No radio.

DIMENSIONS, EXTERNAL:
Wing span	28 ft 8½ in (8·75 m)
Wing chord (constant)	4 ft 7 in (1·40 m)
Wing aspect ratio	6
Length overall	19 ft 8¼ in (6·00 m)
Height overall	6 ft 9 in (2·06 m)
Tailplane span	8 ft 6¼ in (2·60 m)
Wheel track	8 ft 0 in (2·435 m)

DIMENSIONS, INTERNAL:
Cabin: Max length	6 ft 10¾ in (2·10 m)
Max width	2 ft 1½ in (0·65 m)
Max height	3 ft 7¼ in (1·10 m)

AREAS:
Wings, gross	114·1 sq ft (10·60 m²)
Ailerons (total)	12·92 sq ft (1·20 m²)
Fin	11·84 sq ft (1·10 m²)
Rudder	7·53 sq ft (0·70 m²)
Tailplane	23·68 sq ft (2·20 m²)
Elevators, including tabs	13·99 sq ft (1·30 m²)

WEIGHTS:
Weight empty	698 lb (317 kg)

Max T-O weight   1,137 lb (516 kg)
Max landing weight   1,047 lb (475 kg)

PERFORMANCE (at max T-O weight):
Max level speed   86 knots (99 mph; 160 km/h)
Max permissible diving speed
          105 knots (121 mph; 195 km/h)
Max cruising speed at 1,640 ft (500 m)
          78 knots (90 mph; 145 km/h)
Stalling speed   30 knots (34·5 mph; 55 km/h)
Rate of climb at S/L   985 ft (300 m)/min
Service ceiling   11,800 ft (3,600 m)
T-O run   425 ft (130 m)
T-O to 50 ft (15 m)   1,050 ft (320 m)
Landing from 50 ft (15 m)   1,150 ft (350 m)
Landing run   525 ft (160 m)
Range with max fuel
          269 nm (310 miles; 500 km)

AÉRO 30

Design of the Aéro 30 was started in October 1967, and construction began in the following month. It flew for the first time on 23 September 1968, and received certification by the SGAC in the amateur category on 23 October 1968.

TYPE: Single-seat light aircraft.

WINGS: Strut-braced biplane. Wing section NACA 23012. Lower wings of equal span. No dihedral or sweepback. Incidence 2° 30′ on upper wings, 3° 30′ on lower wings. Fabric-covered wood structure, including ailerons, which are fitted to both upper and lower wings. No flaps. Ailerons are manually controlled by cable linkage. Single interplane bracing strut on each side.

FUSELAGE: Conventional wooden structure, with plywood covering.

TAIL UNIT: Cantilever all-wood horizontal and vertical surfaces, with plywood covering. Trim-tabs in elevators.

LANDING GEAR: Non-retractable type, with spring-steel shock-absorber struts on main gear legs and tail-skid at rear. Tyres size 400 × 120, pressure 28·5 lb/sq in (2·0 kg/cm²). No brakes.

POWER PLANT: One 45 hp Salmson air-cooled radial engine, driving a Merville 770 two-blade propeller of 6 ft 0¾ in (1·85 m) diameter. Fuel in single tank in fuselage, capacity 8·8 Imp gallons (40 litres). Oil capacity 1·76 Imp gallons (8 litres).

ACCOMMODATION: Single seat for pilot beneath rearward-sliding canopy. Space aft of seat for up to 22 lb (10 kg) of baggage.

DIMENSIONS, EXTERNAL:
Wing span   21 ft 4¾ in (6·52 m)
Wing chord (constant, each)   3ft 3¼ in (1·00 m)
Wing aspect ratio   6
Length overall   18 ft 8½ in (5·70 m)
Height overall   7 ft 11½ in (2·42 m)
Tailplane span   8 ft 10¼ in (2·70 m)
Wheel track   5 ft 3 in (1·60 m)

DIMENSIONS, INTERNAL:
Cabin: Max length   3 ft 11¼ in (1·20 m)
    Max width   2 ft 1½ in (0·65 m)
    Max height   3 ft 7¼ in (1·10 m)

AREAS:
Wings, gross   127·0 sq ft (11·80 m²)
Ailerons (total)   17·22 sq ft (1·60 m²)
Fin   11·84 sq ft (1·10 m²)
Rudder   7·53 sq ft (0·70 m²)
Tailplane   21·53 sq ft (2·00 m²)
Elevators, including tabs   13·99 sq ft (1·30 m²)

Indraéro Aéro 20 two-seat light aircraft (90 hp Continental engine)

Indraéro Aéro 30 single-seat biplane (45 hp Salmson engine)

WEIGHTS:
Weight empty   604 lb (274 kg)
Max T-O weight   850 lb (386 kg)
Max landing weight   784 lb (356 kg)

PERFORMANCE (at max T-O weight):
Max level speed   76 knots (87 mph; 140 km/h)
Max permissible diving speed
      102 knots (118 mph; 190 km/h)
Max cruising speed
      70 knots (81 mph; 130 km/h)

Stalling speed   33 knots (37·5 mph; 60 km/h)
Rate of climb at S/L   590 ft (180 m)/min
Service ceiling   9,850 ft (3,000 m)
T-O run   755 ft (230 m)
T-O to 50 ft (15 m)   1,410 ft (430 m)
Landing from 50 ft (15 m)   1,150 ft (350 m)
Landing run   490 ft (150 m)
Range with max fuel (no aux tank)
       212 nm (245 miles; 400 km)

JODEL

AVIONS JODEL SA

HEAD OFFICE:
36, Route de Seurre, 21-Beaune

DESIGN OFFICE:
21-Darois

PRESIDENT-DIRECTOR GENERAL:
J. Delemontez

The Société des Avions Jodel was formed in March 1946, by MM Jean Delemontez and Edouard Joly, with the former acting as business and technical manager and the latter as test pilot.

Its first activities were concerned with the repair of gliders and light aircraft of the Service d'Aviation Légère et Sportive, on behalf of the State. Simultaneously, the company designed and built the D.9 Bébé Jodel single-seat light monoplane, which made its first flight in January 1948. This aeroplane, which is certificated with various power plants, is intended for amateur construction and can be built in as little as 500 man-hours.

As the result of official tests with the D.9, the French authorities placed an order for the development and construction of two prototypes of a two-seat model, the D.11 fitted with the 45 hp Salmson, and the D.111 with the 75 hp Minié engine. Subsequent developments of the D.11 are the D.112 and D.117, which have a 65 hp and 90 hp Continental engine respectively.

As a result of the success of these basic designs, which are being built in large numbers both commercially and by amateurs, Avions Jodel now devotes its activities mainly to designing advanced developments of its established types and to acting as a consultant to those building and developing its designs.

Several thousand sets of plans of the single-seat Bébé Jodel and of the two-seat models have been delivered to purchasers in all parts of the World.

Sole agents for plans and pre-fabricated components in the British Commonwealth are Phoenix Aircraft Ltd of Cranleigh, Surrey, England (see UK section).

French and foreign companies engaged on licence manufacture of standard or developed versions of the Jodel monoplane include:

Avions Pierre Robin (Centre Est Aéronautique), Dijon (Côte d'Or), France.

Aero-Difusión SL, Santander, Spain.

Details of the current products of these companies are given under their individual entries in this edition.

JODEL D.9 and D.92 BÉBÉ

Designations of current standard models of the Bébé are as follows:—

D.9. With 25 hp Poinsard engine.

D.92. With Volkswagen engine.

The Bébé shown in the adjacent illustration is a D.92 built by Dr Robert Carver of Castalia,

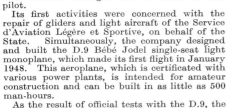

Jodel D.92 built from Falconar plans by Dr Robert Carver of Castalia, Ohio   (Howard Levy)

Ohio, from plans supplied by Falconar in Canada, and was first flown on 15 May 1968. The airframe is fabric-covered throughout, except for metal engine panels, and the power plant is a 36 hp Volkswagen 1,192 cc engine. Max speed at a T-O weight of 750 lb (340 kg) is 75 knots (86 mph; 138 km/h), and normal cruising speed is 65 knots (75 mph; 121 km/h). T-O and landing runs are 800 ft (244 m) and 400 ft (122 m) respectively.

The following details refer to all standard versions of the D.9 Bébé.

TYPE: Single-seat light monoplane.

WINGS: Cantilever low-wing monoplane. Single-spar one-piece wing with wide-span centre-section of constant chord and thickness and two tapering outer portions set at a coarse dihedral angle (14°). Spar and ribs of spruce and plywood, with fabric covering. Ailerons similar in construction.

FUSELAGE: Rectangular spruce and plywood structure.

TAIL UNIT: Cantilever structure of spruce and plywood, with plywood covering on tailplane and fabric-covered rudder and elevators. No fin.

LANDING GEAR: Cantilever main legs with rubber-in-compression springing. Leaf-spring tail-skid or tail-wheel. Cable brakes.

POWER PLANT: Normally one 25 hp Poinsard (D.9) or modified Volkswagen (D.92) flat-four air-cooled engine, but other engines of from 25 to 65 hp may be fitted, including the 36 hp Aeronca JAP, Continental A-40 and Agusta MV G.A.40. Fuel tank in fuselage, capacity 5·5 Imp gallons (25 litres).

ACCOMMODATION: Single seat in open cockpit.

DIMENSIONS, EXTERNAL:
Wing span   22 ft 11 in (7·00 m)
Wing chord (centre-section, constant)
                              4 ft 7 in (1·40 m)
Wing aspect ratio   5·45
Length overall   17 ft 10½ in (5·45 m)
AREA: Wings, gross   96·8 sq ft (9·0 m²)
WEIGHTS:
Weight empty   420 lb (190 kg)
Max T-O weight   705 lb (320 kg)
PERFORMANCE (40 hp engine, at max T-O weight):
Max level speed at S/L
                              87 knots (100 mph; 160 km/h)
Cruising speed   74 knots (85 mph; 137 km/h)
Stalling speed   35 knots (40 mph; 65 km/h)
Rate of climb at S/L   590 ft (180 m)/min
T-O run   360 ft (110 m)
Landing run   330 ft (100 m)
Range with max fuel
                              217 nm (250 miles; 400 km)

JODEL D.11 and D.119

The D.11, with 45 hp Salmson engine, is the basic model in the series of Jodel two-seaters for amateur and commercial production.

The version for amateur construction with 90 hp Continental engine is designated D.119. A typical example is the D.119 built by T. W. Oliver, W. H. Cunningham and R. B. Wilson of Scarborough, Ontario, Canada. Powered by a 90 hp Continental C90-12F flat-four engine, it incorporates a number of modifications, including a redesigned cockpit canopy and engine cowling, and curved vertical tail surfaces instead of the usual square-cut design. Empty weight is 870 lb (395 kg) and gross weight 1,350 lb (612 kg). Max

Jodel D.11 built in Canada from Falconar plans by Mr J. Brenner of Agincourt, Ontario (*Jean Seele*)

Jodel D.9 built by Mr R. Walker of Regina, Saskatchewan, with 65 hp Continental A65-8 engine (*Howard Levy*)

level speed is 122 knots (140 mph; 225 km/h), landing speed 52 knots (60 mph; 97 km/h), rate of climb 700 ft (213 m)/min and range 390 nm (450 miles; 725 km) at 100 knots (115 mph; 185 km/h).

Details of the 65 hp variant of the D.11, designated D.112, are given below.

JODEL D.112 CLUB

The D.112 is a two-seat dual-control version of the D.9. Except for increased overall dimensions, a wider fuselage and enclosed side-by-side cockpit, the D.112 conforms in layout and structure to the D.9, but is fitted normally with a 65 hp Continental flat-four engine. Fuel capacity is 13 Imp gallons (60 litres).

DIMENSIONS, EXTERNAL:
Wing span   26 ft 10 in (8·2 m)
Length overall   20 ft 10 in (6·36 m)
Dihedral on outer wings   19°
AREA:
Wings, gross   137 sq ft (12·72 m²)
WEIGHTS:
Weight empty   600 lb (270 kg)
Max T-O weight   1,145 lb (520 kg)
PERFORMANCE (at max T-O weight):
Max level speed at S/L:
                              102 knots (118 mph; 190 km/h)
Max cruising speed
                              92 knots (105·5 mph; 170 km/h)
Econ cruising speed
                              81 knots (93 mph; 150 km/h)
Stalling speed   38 knots (43 mph; 70 km/h)
Rate of climb at S/L   632 ft (193 m)/min
T-O run   450 ft (137 m)
Landing run   395 ft (120 m)
Range with max fuel
                              323 nm (373 miles; 600 km)

JURCA

MARCEL JURCA

ADDRESS:
2, Rue des Champs Philippe, La Garenne-Colombes (Seine)

WORKS: Constructions Aéronautiques Lorraines, François et Cie, Aérodrôme de Nancy.

M Marcel Jurca, an ex-military pilot and hydraulics engineer, has designed a series of high-performance light aircraft of which plans are available to amateur constructors.

A prototype of his first design, the M.J.1, was built but did not fly. To gain experience, M Jurca next built a two-seat Jodel light aircraft, with the help of members of the Aero Club of Courbevoie, and this flew for the first time in 1954.

The same team then built a prototype of M Jurca's second design, the M.J.2 Tempête single-seat light aircraft, incorporating many Jodel components. It proved so successful that sets of plans were offered to amateur constructors and many more Tempêtes are now flying or under assembly in France and overseas.

M Jurca has developed from the Tempête the single-seat M.J.3 and M.J.4 Shadow, the two-seat M.J.5 Sirocco and the M.J.51 Speroco. Details of all these types are given below, together with all available information on the M.J.6 and M.J.66 Crivat, M.J.7 and M.J.77 Gnatsum, M.J.8 1-Nine-O and M.J.10 Spit.

The M.J.7, M.J.8 and M.J.10 are the first of a series of designs produced by scaling down the basic airframes of World War II fighters to two-thirds or three-quarters of the original size. The M.J.9 will be based on the Messerschmitt Bf 109, the M.J.10 on the Spitfire and the M.J.11 on the P-47 Thunderbolt.

In October 1965, a company named Constructions Aéronautiques Lorraines, François et Cie was founded at Nancy, to produce commercially aircraft of M Jurca's design.

For the North American market, Falconar in Canada (which see) issues kits for all aircraft designed by M Jurca.

JURCA M.J.2 and M.J.20 TEMPÊTE

The prototype Tempête was flown for the first time, by its designer, on 27 June 1956. It obtained its certificate of airworthiness very quickly, and by the Spring of 1970 there were at least twenty Tempêtes flying or under construction in France, Denmark, Portugal, the UK, the United States and Canada, all amateur-built.

The type of engine fitted to a particular aircraft is indicated by a suffix letter in its designation. Suffix letters are A for the 65 hp Continental A65, B for the 75 hp Continental A75, C for the 85 hp Continental C85, D for the 90 hp Continental C90-14F, E for the 100 hp Continental O-200-A, F for the 105 hp Potez 4 E-20, G for the 115 hp Potez 4 E-30, and H for the 125 hp Lycoming.

The standard version is the M.J.2A with A65 engine. The M.J.2D, with 90 hp C90-14F, cruises at 121 mph (195 km/h) and climbs to 3,280 ft (1,000 m) in 3 minutes. It can also perform aerobatics without loss of height. The

Tempête built in Portugal is an M.J.2D with 90 hp Continental; that under construction in Denmark is designated **M.J.20,** and has a 180 hp engine and a strengthened airframe.

The following details apply generally to all M.J.2 models:

TYPE: Single-seat light monoplane.

WINGS: Cantilever low-wing monoplane. NACA 23012 wing section. Incidence 4° at root, 2° at tip. No dihedral. All-wood one-piece single-spar structure with fabric covering. Fabric-covered wooden ailerons.

FUSELAGE: All-wood structure of basic rectangular section, plywood-covered.

TAIL UNIT: Cantilever all-wood structure. Tailplane and fin plywood-covered, elevators and rudder fabric-covered. Trim-tab on starboard elevator.

LANDING GEAR: Non-retractable tail-wheel type. Jodel D.112 cantilever legs with rubber-in-compression springing. Jodel D.112 wheels and Dunlop 420 × 150 tyres. Jodel D.112 tail-skid.

POWER PLANT: One 65 hp Continental A65 four-cylinder horizontally-opposed air-cooled engine, driving Ratier two-blade wooden propeller with ground-adjustable pitch. Provision for fitting 75, 85, 90 or 100 hp Continental, 105 or 115 hp Potez or 125 hp Lycoming engine. Jodel engine-mounting and cowling. Jodel fuel tank, capacity 13·2 Imp gallons (60 litres) aft of firewall in fuselage.

ACCOMMODATION: Single seat under long rearward-sliding transparent canopy.

DIMENSIONS, EXTERNAL:
Wing span   19 ft 8 in (6·0 m)
Wing chord (basic)   4 ft 7 in (1·40 m)
Wing aspect ratio   4·5
Length overall   19 ft 2½ in (5·855 m)
Height over tail   7 ft 10 in (2·4 m)
Tailplane span   8 ft 2 in (2·50 m)
Wheel track   7 ft 6½ in (2·30 m)
AREAS:
Wings, gross   85·90 sq ft (7·98 m²)
Ailerons (total)   10·76 sq ft (1·00 m²)
Fin   6·94 sq ft (0·65 m²)
Rudder   5·81 sq ft (0·54 m²)
Tailplane   9·15 sq ft (0·85 m²)
Elevators   8·61 sq ft (0·80 m²)
WEIGHTS:
Weight empty   639 lb (290 kg)
Max T-O weight   950 lb (430 kg)
PERFORMANCE (65 hp engine):
Max level speed   104 knots (120 mph; 193 km/h)
Cruising speed   89 knots (102 mph; 165 km/h)
Landing speed   43 knots (50 mph; 80 km/h)
Rate of climb at S/L 555 ft (170 m)/min
Service ceiling   11,500 ft (3,500 m)
T-O run   820 ft (250 m)
Endurance   3 hr 20 min

JURCA M.J.3

The M.J.3 is a single-seat sporting aircraft combining the fuselage of the M.J.2 Tempête with a new wing. This wing has an extended leading-edge inboard of the fence on each side and completely new tip shape. The power plant can comprise any flat-four engine of between 85 and 125 hp, the standard engine being the 90 hp Continental C90.

The prototype M.J.3, built in Canada, has a non-retractable landing gear, but a retractable gear is under development. Another M.J.3, built by Mr Denis R. Jacobs of Ohio, was nearing completion in the Spring of 1969.

DIMENSIONS, EXTERNAL:
Wing span   20 ft 5½ in (6·236 m)
Length overall   19 ft 2½ in (5·855 m)
AREA:
Wings, gross   96·9 sq ft (9·0 m²)
WEIGHTS:
Weight empty   727 lb (330 kg)
Max T-O weight   1,058 lb (480 kg)
PERFORMANCE (90 hp engine):
Cruising speed   113 knots (130 mph; 210 km/h)
Stalling speed   44 knots (50 mph; 80 km/h)

JURCA M.J.4 SHADOW

The M.J.4 Shadow is a single-seat sporting aircraft, generally similar to the M.J.3, but with a sweptback fin and rudder. Six are being built in Canada and the United States, one of them by members of Chapter 21 of the US Experimental Aircraft Association at Princeton, Indiana.

DIMENSIONS, EXTERNAL:
Same as for M.J.2
PERFORMANCE (90 hp engine, estimated):
Cruising speed   116 knots (133 mph; 215 km/h)
Stalling speed   41-44 knots (47-50 mph; 75-80 km/h)
Climb to 3,280 ft (1,000 m) 3 min
T-O run   985 ft (250 m)

JURCA M.J.5 SIROCCO

The M.J.5 Sirocco is a tandem two-seat monoplane, developed from the M.J.2 Tempête as a potential club training and touring aircraft. It is fully aerobatic when flown as a two-seater.

The wings are basically similar in planform to those of the M.J.3 and M.J.4 Shadow, although of 4 ft 7 in (1·40 m) chord on outer panels and increased span. The fuselage and tail unit are also similar to those of the M.J.4 except for a slight increase in overall length.

The prototype M.J.5 flew for the first time on 3 August 1962, powered by a 105 hp Potez 4 E-20 engine. It was fitted originally with a non-retractable landing gear, but retractable landing gear and a more powerful engine (160 hp Lycoming O-320) were fitted in 1966. Its fuel capacity is 25·5 Imp gallons (116 litres). In its current form, it will climb to 3,280 ft (1,000 m) in 2½ min.

The version of the Sirocco for amateur construction is generally similar to the prototype, with optional retractable landing gear.

By mid-February 1967, five more Siroccos were flying, one of them factory-built at Nancy. This aircraft, powered by a 100 hp Continental engine, concluded tests at Istres in January 1969, and was awarded a certificate of airworthiness in the Utility category. Since the 100 hp power plant did not permit full exploration of the Sirocco's performance capabilities, supplementary tests were conducted at the CEV with a second Sirocco, powered by a 135 hp Lycoming O-320 engine. These trials were also concluded satisfactorily. A full C of A, covering Aerobatic requirements and unlimited spinning, is applicable only when a power plant of 115 hp minimum rating is installed.

By early 1969, some 35-40 Siroccos were under construction by amateurs, in France, Canada, Germany, Switzerland, England and the US, with various engines. Following certification, M Jurca anticipated an increase in the number of factory-built Siroccos during 1969-70.

The type of engine fitted to a particular aircraft is indicated by a suffix letter in its designation. Suffix letters are A for the 90 hp Continental

Jurca Tempête built in Portugal and owned by Dr J. Fernandes (90 hp Rolls-Royce/Continental C90-8F engine) (*A. Matus*)

French-built Jurca M.J.5H2 Sirocco tandem two-seat aircraft (150 hp Lycoming engine)

C90-8 or -14F, B for the 100 hp Continental O-200-A, C for the 105 hp Potez 4 E-20, D for the Potez 4 E-30, E for the 105 hp Hirth, F for the 125 hp Lycoming, G for the 135 hp Regnier and H for the 160 hp Lycoming. Other Siroccos are now flying with 150 or 180 hp engines. Addition of the numeral 1 indicates a non-retractable landing gear and the numeral 2 indicates a retractable landing gear. Thus, the designation of the original prototype in its latest form is M.J.5H2. The example built at Nancy for certification has a 100 hp Continental engine and so is designated M.J.5B1.

A Sirocco with 115 hp Lycoming O-235-C2B engine and 6 ft 0¾ in (1·85 m) diameter propeller has been completed by Luftsportgruppe Liebherr-Aero-Technik in Germany, and was due to fly for the first time during 1969. This has a modified rudder of reduced height and greater chord, and a jettisonable, sideways-hinged cockpit canopy, and is intended for certification for aerobatic flying. The details below apply to this version, but are generally typical of all versions. A developed version, known as the M.J.51, is described separately.

DIMENSIONS, EXTERNAL:
Wing span   23 ft 0 in (7·00 m)
Wing aspect ratio   4·9
Length overall   20 ft 2 in (6·15 m)
Height overall, tail up:
  standard model   9 ft 2¼ in (2·80 m)
  LAT version   8 ft 6¼ in (2·60 m)
Tailplane span   10 ft 7½ in (3·24 m)
Wheel track   9 ft 2¼ in (2·80 m)
AREA:
Wings, gross   107·64 sq ft (10·00 m²)
WEIGHTS AND LOADINGS:
Weight empty   947 lb (430 kg)
Max T-O weight   1,499 lb (680 kg)
Max wing loading   13·9 lb/sq ft (68·0 kg/m²)
Max power loading   13·03 lb/hp (5·91 kg/hp)
PERFORMANCE (at max T-O weight):
Max level speed   127 knots (146 mph; 235 km/h)
Cruising speed   116 knots (134 mph; 215 km/h)
Stalling speed   44 knots (50 mph; 80 km/h)
Climb to 3,280 ft (1,000 m) 4 min
Service ceiling   16,400 ft (5,000 m)
T-O run   820 ft (250 m)
Landing run   655 ft (200 m)
Endurance   4 hr 20 min

JURCA M.J.51 SPEROCCO

Using knowledge gained from flight experience with the M.J.5 and the Canadian prototype M.J.7, M Jurca has, with the assistance of M J. Lecarme, evolved a new design incorporating some features of each aircraft. It is known as the M.J.51 Sperocco, the name being a contraction of "Special Sirocco", and it is intended for high-performance aerobatics and competition flying. Like other Jurca designs, the M.J.51 is suitable for amateur construction.

The wings, of Habib 64-000 738 laminar-flow profile, are essentially those of the M.J.7 Gnatsum. They are without dihedral, and the angle of incidence is 1° compared with the 4° of the Sirocco. The fuselage is of completely new design, but is of similar construction to the M.J.5. The tail unit consists of M.J.7 horizontal surfaces with a shorter and wider-chord fin and rudder. Landing gear is of the M.J.5 type and is fully retractable.

Any horizontally-opposed engine of 130-240 hp may be installed. Fuel is contained in two wing tanks, each of 12 Imp gallons (55 litres) capacity, and one fuselage tank of 10 or 22 Imp gallons (45 or 100 litres) capacity.

The M.J.51 seats two persons in tandem under a one-piece sliding canopy, the rear seat being 3·9 in (10 cm) higher than the front seat.

With only slight alterations, the standard Sirocco wings can be fitted to the new fuselage, this combination being known as the **M.J.50.** Plans of both versions are available. By January 1970, three sets of M.J.51 plans had been sold to French customers, and the first aircraft was under construction by M Serge Brillant at Melun.

DIMENSION:
Wing span   24 ft 7¼ in (7·50 m)
AREA:
Wings, gross   118 sq ft (11·00 m²)
WEIGHT:
Max T-O weight   1,653 lb (730 kg)
PERFORMANCE (estimated, with 150 hp Lycoming engine):
Max level speed   149 knots (171 mph; 275 km/h)
Max cruising speed (75% power)
                      135 knots (155 mph; 250 km/h)
Stalling speed   49 knots (56 mph; 90 km/h)
Time to 3,280 ft (1,000 m) 1 min 30 sec

JURCA M.J.6 AND M.J.66 CRIVAT

The M.J.6 was the first twin-engined aircraft designed by Marcel Jurca. It is a tandem two-seat low-wing monoplane intended for amateur construction, and its general appearance is shown in the adjacent three-view drawing. A four-seat version with 180 hp engines is designated M.J.66, and a side-by-side two-seat model with 115 or 150 hp engines is known as the M.J.606.

The cabin is enclosed by a large clear-view canopy, and is entered via a door at the front. Baggage lockers are provided in the rear of the engine nacelles, which also house the main wheels of the retractable tricycle landing gear. All versions can be fitted with dual controls.

As currently envisaged, the M.J.6 is intended to be powered by two 150 hp Lycoming O-320 engines, while the M.J.66 will have Lycomings of 180 hp. Fuel is contained in four tanks, two in each leading-edge, with total capacity of 62 Imp gallons (280 litres). Provision is made for auxiliary wingtip tanks, each of 16·5 Imp gallons (75 litres). The wings, of NACA 23012 section, have neither dihedral nor incidence, except for the upturned tip-tanks. Two-section trailing-edge plain flaps and ailerons are fitted. Landing gear is of the fully-retractable tricycle type, with telescopic nose-wheel leg.

Construction of the first M.J.6 (see 1966-67 *Jane's*), which was begun by M P. Pouloux at Egletons, Correze, France, was subsequently suspended. In 1969 another M.J.6 was in process of being completed by Mr Bruce A. Jenkins of Lansing, Michigan, USA. Details below apply to the two-seat M.J.6 in its current form, except where indicated.

DIMENSIONS, EXTERNAL:
Wing span, over tip-tanks	32 ft 1¾ in (9·80 m)
Wing chord	4 ft 7 in (1·40 m)
Length overall	30 ft 8½ in (9·36 m)
Height overall	11 ft 9¾ in (3·60 m)
Distance between propeller centres	13 ft 1½ in (4·00 m)
Tailplane span	13 ft 1½ in (4·00 m)
Wheel track	13 ft 1½ in (4·00 m)

AREAS:
Wings, gross	150·7 sq ft (14·00 m²)
Ailerons (total)	10·75 sq ft (1·00 m²)
Horizontal tail surfaces	40·90 sq ft (3·80 m²)

WEIGHTS AND LOADINGS:
Weight empty:	
M.J.6	1,543 lb (700 kg)
M.J.66	1,587 lb (720 kg)
Max T-O weight:	
M.J.6	2,645 lb (1,200 kg)
M.J.66	3,306 lb (1,500 kg)
Max wing loading:	
M.J.6	17·5 lb/sq ft (85·5 kg/m²)
M.J.66	21·9 lb/sq ft (107·0 kg/m²)
Max power loading:	
M.J.6	8·82 lb/hp (4·0 kg/hp)
M.J.66	9·26 lb/hp (4·2 kg/hp)

PERFORMANCE (estimated at max T-O weight):
Max cruising speed:	
M.J.6	188 knots (217 mph; 350 km/h)
M.J.66	195 knots (224 mph; 360 km/h)
Stalling speed:	
M.J.6	49 knots (56 mph; 90 km/h)
M.J.66	58 knots (66 mph; 105 km/h)
Rate of climb at S/L:	
M.J.6	1,969 ft (600 m)/min
M.J.66	2,165 ft (660 m)/min
Single-engine rate of climb at S/L:	
M.J.6	630 ft (192 m)/min
M.J.66	709 ft (216 m)/min
Service ceiling:	
M.J.6, M.J.66	22,975 ft (7,000 m)
Endurance:	
M.J.6	8 hr
M.J.66	6 hr

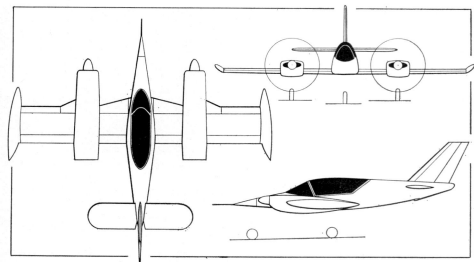

Jurca M.J.6 two-seat twin-engined amateur-built light aircraft

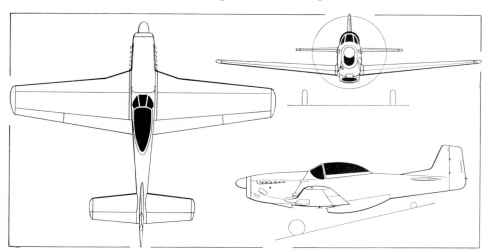

Photograph and three-view drawing of the first Jurca M.J.7 Gnatsum to be completed, with Ranger engine

JURCA M.J.7 and M.J.77 GNATSUM

The Gnatsum is a scale replica, for amateur construction, of the North American P-51D Mustang single-seat fighter of World War II. Its name "Gnatsum" is "Mustang" reversed, and it is available in two versions, as follows:

M.J.7. To two-thirds scale. Prototype (CF-XZI) built in the works of Falconar Aircraft Ltd on the Industrial Airport, Edmonton, Alberta, Canada, and first flown on 31 July 1969. Granted DoT type approval by early 1970. Further examples under construction by Mr J. P. Deloyer of Torrance, California, and three others.

M.J.77. To three-quarters scale. Prototype under construction by Mr J. Carter of Mill Valley, California and Mr Gilbert C. McAdams of Victorville, California.

Unlike previous small-scale replicas of this aircraft, the Gnatsum is scaled down precisely. Use of an in-line engine, such as the 160 hp Walter Minor 6-III or 200 hp Ranger, permits the fuselage cowling lines to follow closely those of the original. Alternative installation of a 100 hp Continental O-200 or Lycoming horizontally-opposed air-cooled engine will require fairing blisters over the cylinders. Sets of plans for both versions are available from M Jurca, and plans and kits from Falconar in Canada (which see).

The M.J.7 built by Falconar has an all-wood airframe, mainly of sitka spruce assembled with a special epoxy glue. The airframe is covered almost completely with thin birch or mahogany plywood, protected internally against moisture by a coating of Hipec Plastithane and covered externally with a thin layer of glass-fibre cloth, with coloured Hipec Plastithane finish. The nose cowling and dorsal fin are made of glass-fibre; the rearward-sliding bubble canopy is of blown acrylic plastic. The few metal parts include the main engine cowlings and wheel fairings door, which are of aluminium.

Power plant of the Falconar-built prototype M.J.7 is a 200 hp Ranger six-cylinder inverted in-line air-cooled engine, of the kind fitted originally to the Fairchild Cornell trainer, and driving a three-blade Hartzell metal propeller. The under-nose air intake matches the carburettor intake of the P-51D, although it is deeper. Dummy exhausts are fitted on each side of the cowling. Standard fuel capacity is 25 Imp gallons (114 litres), which can be doubled by the use of underwing drop-tanks.

Main landing gear, tailwheel and flap actuation is electrical. Cockpit instrumentation is quite extensive, with a VHF radio in the centre of the main panel. The cockpit is upholstered and contains an adjustable seat for the pilot, a jump-seat for a passenger in tandem and a baggage shelf to the rear.

The brief specification details below apply to this prototype aircraft.

DIMENSION:
Wing span	25 ft 10 in (7·87 m)

WEIGHTS:
Weight empty	1,175 lb (533 kg)
Max T-O weight	1,870 lb (848 kg)

PERFORMANCE:
Max level speed	165 knots (190 mph; 305 km/h)
Max cruising speed	152 knots (175 mph; 281 km/h)
Stalling speed, flaps up, power off	66 knots (75 mph; 121 km/h)
Stalling speed, flaps and u/c down, power off	57 knots (65 mph; 105 km/h)
Rate of climb at S/L	1,100 ft (335 m)/min
T-O run	800 ft (244 m)
Landing run	800 ft (244 m)
Range with underwing drop tanks	417 nm (480 miles; 772 km)

JURCA M.J.8 1-NINE-O

The M.J.8 is a single-seat sporting aircraft which has been designed by M Jurca by scaling down to three-quarters of the original dimensions the airframe of the Focke-Wulf Fw 190 fighter.

Its general appearance is shown in the adjacent three-view drawing.

A prototype was near completion by Mr R. Kitchen of Reno, Nevada, early in 1970, and a second machine was under construction by Mr O. Viera of Gardena, California.

The M.J.8 prototype will have a 260 hp Lycoming engine, but the design is suitable for the alternative use of any horizontally-opposed or radial engine in the 100-200 hp range. The landing gear is retractable.

DIMENSIONS, EXTERNAL:

Wing span	25 ft 10 in (7·87 m)
Length overall	21 ft 9 in (6·63 m)
Wing chord at root	5 ft 7 in (1·70 m)
Wing chord at tip	2 ft 11½ in (0·90 m)
Tailplane span	9 ft 4 in (2·84 m)

AREA:

Wings, gross	109·8 sq ft (10·2 m²)

WEIGHTS (160 hp engine):

Weight empty	880 lb (400 kg)
Max T-O weight	1,380 lb (626 kg)

PERFORMANCE (estimated, with 160 hp engine):

Max level speed at S/L	
	139 knots (160 mph; 257 km/h)
Max cruising speed	
	124 knots (143 mph; 230 km/h)
Stalling speed	49 knots (56 mph; 90 km/h)
Rate of climb at S/L	1,650 ft (503 m)/min

JURCA M.J.10 SPIT

The M.J.10 is a single-seat, three-quarter scale representation of the Supermarine Spitfire which can also be modified as a two-seater. It is suitable for any horizontally-opposed or in-line engine of 120-220 hp, although some slight variations from the Spitfire's contours are necessary in the former case. Construction is entirely of wood, except for the glass-fibre engine cowling and fabric covering on the control surfaces.

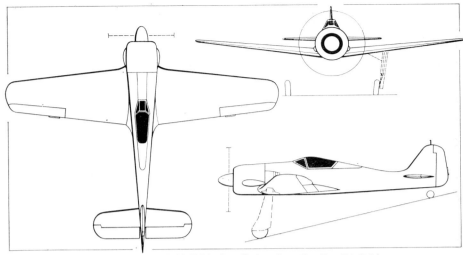

Jurca M.J.8 homebuilt light aircraft, based on the Fw 190 fighter

The single-spar wing is similar in construction to that of the Sirocco. The manually-operated retractable landing gear is fitted with helicoidal spring shock-absorbers.

The range of plans adopts the Spitfire Mk IX as the standard M.J.10 version, but alternative detail plans are available for representing both Merlin- and Griffon-engined models, including the Mks VC and XIV, and for clipped, standard or extended-span wings.

A prototype was nearing completion early in 1970 by Mr Pendlebury of the Chesterfield Air Touring Group at West Bridgford, Nottingham, England.

DIMENSIONS, EXTERNAL:

Wing span	27 ft 6¾ in (8·40 m)
Length overall	23 ft 4½ in (7·125 m)

AREA:

Wings, gross	135·6 sq ft (12·60 m²)

WEIGHTS (160 hp engine):

Weight empty	1,450 lb (658 kg)
Max T-O weight	2,000 lb (907 kg)

PERFORMANCE (estimated, with 160 hp engine):

Max level speed at S/L	
	139 knots (160 mph; 257 km/h)
Cruising speed	124 knots (143 mph; 230 km/h)
Stalling speed	49 knots (56 mph; 90 km/h)
Rate of climb at S/L	1,650 ft (503 m)/min
T-O run	660 ft (200 m)

LEDERLIN
FRANÇOIS LEDERLIN

ADDRESS:
2 rue Charles Peguy, 38-Grenoble

M Lederlin, an architect, has designed and built a two-seat light aeroplane based on the familiar Mignet "Pou-du-Ciel" formula. Although derived from the Mignet HM-380 and designated 380-L, it has retained little of the original except for the wing section. First flight was made on 14 September 1965, a restricted C of A being granted in the following month.

Plans of the 380-L, annotated in English and with both English and metric measurements, are available to amateur constructors.

LEDERLIN 380-L

TYPE: Two-seat amateur-built light aircraft.

WINGS: Tandem-wing biplane. Wing section 3·40-13. Dihedral 3° 30' on outer sections only (both wings). Incidence variable from 0° to 12° (forward wing). Incidence of rear wing 6°. No sweepback. Each wing is made in two parts, bolted together at the centre-line. Construction is conventional, with wooden box-spar and trellis ribs, plywood leading-edge and overall fabric covering. The variable-incidence front wing is pivoted on the cabane structure by ball-joints and on the bracing struts (one each side) by cardan-joints. No ailerons or flaps. Long-span tab on trailing-edge of rear wing, controllable in flight.

FUSELAGE: Welded steel-tube structure, covered with light alloy to front of cabin and with fabric on rear fuselage, over light spruce formers.

TAIL UNIT: Vertical fin and rudder only. Spruce and ply structure, covered with fabric. Ground-adjustable tab in rudder.

LANDING GEAR: Non-retractable tail-wheel type. Cantilever main legs consist of conical spring-steel rods, inclined rearward. Fournier main wheels and tyres, size 380 × 150, with mechanical brakes. Large tailwheel, carried on telescopic leg with spring shock-absorber, can be steered by the rudder controls through a linkage engaged by the pilot.

POWER PLANT: One 90 hp Continental C90-14F four-cylinder horizontally-opposed air-cooled engine, driving a McCauley two-blade metal fixed-pitch propeller, diameter 6 ft 0 in (1·83 m).

Lederlin 380-L two-seat light aircraft (90 hp Continental engine)

Fuel in single tank, capacity 18·75 Imp gallons (85 litres). Oil capacity 1 Imp gallon (4·5 litres).

ACCOMMODATION: Two seats side-by-side in enclosed cabin. Forward-hinged door on each side. Controls comprise a rudder-bar for directional control and a stick, suspended from the roof of the cabin and free laterally, to control the incidence of the forward wing. A further lever, suspended from the roof, controls the tab on the rear wing. Luggage space aft of seats.

DIMENSIONS, EXTERNAL:

Wing span:	
forward	26 ft 0 in (7·92 m)
rear	19 ft 8¼ in (6·00 m)
Wing chord (constant, each)	4 ft 3¼ in (1·30 m)
Length overall	15 ft 7¾ in (4·77 m)
Height overall	6 ft 10 in (2·08 m)
Wheel track	6 ft 8¾ in (2·05 m)
Wheelbase	10 ft 2 in (3·10 m)
Doors (each): Height	2 ft 11½ in (0·90 m)
Width	2 ft 5½ in (0·75 m)
Height to sill	1 ft 7½ in (0·50 m)

DIMENSIONS, INTERNAL:

Cabin:	
Max width	3 ft 6 in (1·07 m)

Max height	3 ft 4 in (1·03 m)
Luggage space	7 cu ft (0·20 m²)

AREAS:

Wings, gross:	
forward	106·8 sq ft (9·92 m²)
rear	80·0 sq ft (7·43 m²)

WEIGHTS AND LOADINGS:

Weight empty	794 lb (360 kg)
Max T-O weight	1,323 lb (600 kg)
Max wing loading	6·96 lb/sq ft (34 kg/m²)
Max power loading	14·8 lb/hp (6·7 kg/hp)

PERFORMANCE (at max T-O weight):

Max level speed at 1,000 ft (305 m)	
	109 knots (125 mph; 201 km/h)
Max permissible diving speed	
	126 knots (145 mph; 233 km/h)
Max cruising speed	
	97 knots (112 mph; 180 km/h)
Econ cruising speed at 2,000 ft (600 m)	
	87 knots (100 mph; 161 km/h)
Stalling speed, power off	
	26 knots (30 mph; 49 km/h)
Rate of climb at S/L	900 ft (275 m)/min
Service ceiling	over 12,000 ft (3,660 m)
T-O run	400 ft (122 m)
Landing run	500 ft (153 m)
Range at econ cruising speed	
	477 nm (550 miles; 885 km)

NICOLLIER
HENRI NICOLLIER

ADDRESS:
c/o Reseau du Sport de l'Air, Café Moderne, 183 Cours Lafayette, Lyons 6e

M Nicollier, who began flying sailplanes and powered aircraft when he was 16 years old, later designed and built a single-seat light aircraft

named the Menestrel, of which plans are available. It flew for the first time on 25 November 1962, and was awarded an official certificate of airworthiness at the end of its flight trials. Its design has required no modification at any time.

A two-seat light aircraft known as the Pacific was under construction in 1969 by M Nicollier and two associates, MM Gehin and Tsilewsky. Its design has been made very simple, so that

other amateurs will find it easy to build. All known details of this aircraft are given below.

NICOLLIER HN 433 MENESTREL

The details below refer to the prototype Menestrel, built by M Nicollier. Several more are under construction by amateurs, including one with flaps and a Porsche engine, but no further news of these had been forthcoming during the past year.

TYPE: Single-seat home-built light aircraft.

WINGS: Cantilever low-wing monoplane. Constant chord to half-span each side; semi-elliptical outer panels. All-wood single-spar structure, fabric-covered. Plain wooden ailerons, fabric-covered. No flaps or tabs.

FUSELAGE: Conventional wooden structure of basic rectangular section, with curved top decking. Fabric-covered.

TAIL UNIT: Cantilever wood structure, fabric-covered. No trim-tabs.

LANDING GEAR: Cantilever main units, with Vespa motor-scooter wheels, and tail-skid.

POWER PLANT: One 30 hp converted Volkswagen 1,300 cc engine, with aluminium pistons and dual ignition. Two-blade fixed-pitch propeller.

ACCOMMODATION: Initially single seat in open cockpit, but a moulded Plexiglas canopy was fitted subsequently.

DIMENSIONS:
Wing span	23 ft 0 in (7·00 m)
Wing aspect ratio	6·4
Length overall	17 ft 2½ in (5·25 m)
Height overall	4 ft 10½ in (1·48 m)

AREA:
Wings, gross	87·7 sq ft (8·15 m²)

WEIGHTS:
Weight empty	385 lb (175 kg)
Max T-O weight	628 lb (285 kg)

PERFORMANCE (at max T-O weight):
Max level speed at S/L	92 knots (106 mph; 170 km/h)
Max cruising speed	81 knots (93 mph; 150 km/h)
Econ cruising speed	78 knots (90 mph; 145 km/h)
Stalling speed	35 knots (40 mph; 65 km/h)
Rate of climb at S/L	590 ft (180 m)/min
Range, with 20 min reserve	230 nm (265 miles; 425 km)

NICOLLIER PACIFIC

TYPE: Two-seat home-built light aircraft.

WINGS: Cantilever low-wing monoplane, with tapered leading- and trailing-edges and dihedral from roots. All-wood structure. Plain wooden ailerons and three-position trailing-edge flaps. All surfaces fabric-covered.

FUSELAGE: Conventional wooden structure of basic rectangular section, with curved top-decking. Fabric-covered.

TAIL UNIT: Cantilever wood structure, with slight sweepback on fin. Trim-tab in each elevator. Fabric-covered.

LANDING GEAR: Non-retractable tail-wheel type,

Nicollier HN 433 Menestrel single-seat home-built aircraft (*Claude Paille*)

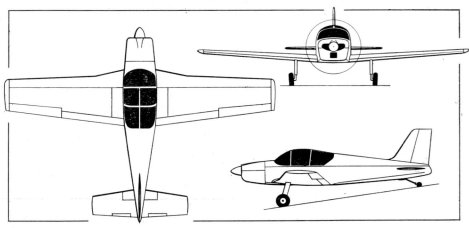

Nicollier Pacific two-seat amateur-built light aircraft

but design permits substitution of non-retractable tricycle landing gear if desired. Cantilever single-strut main-wheel legs.

POWER PLANT: One 90 hp Continental four-cylinder horizontally-opposed air-cooled engine, driving a two-blade propeller.

ACCOMMODATION: Side-by-side seating for two persons in fully-enclosed cockpit.

DIMENSIONS, EXTERNAL:
Wing span	27 ft 0¾ in (8·25 m)
Length overall	20 ft 1 in (6·12 m)

AREA:
Wings, gross	121·6 sq ft (11·30 m²)

WEIGHT AND LOADING:
Max T-O weight	1,388 lb (630 kg)
Max wing loading	11·5 lb/sq ft (56·0 kg/m²)

PERFORMANCE (estimated, at max T-O weight):
Max cruising speed	102 knots (118 mph; 190 km/h)
Endurance	5 hr

NORD-AVIATION (see *Aérospatiale*)

PIEL

AVIONS CLAUDE PIEL

ADDRESS:
Côte de Beulle, Chemin des Alouettes, 78-Maule

M Claude Piel has designed several light aircraft, including the Emeraude, Diamant and Beryl, all of which are described below. Sets of plans of these aircraft are available to amateur constructors.

In addition, M Piel granted licence rights for their manufacture by several commercial concerns. Four French companies, listed in the 1968-69 Jane's, built versions of the Emeraude under licence, as did Binder Aviatik KG (in association with Schempp-Hirth KG) in Germany, Durban Aircraft Corp in South Africa, Aeronasa in Spain and Fairtravel in the UK. Over 200 factory-built Emeraudes were completed by these manufacturers, in addition to those built by amateur constructors.

Authorised distributors of plans for amateur constructors currently include:

E. Littner, 546, 83rd Avenue, Chomedey, Quebec, Canada.

J. Lousberg, 28 C de Grootelaan, Middelkerke, Belgium.

In addition, servicing and constructional facilities for Emeraude variants are available at the works of M Choisel at Abbeville.

PIEL EMERAUDE and SUPER EMERAUDE

There have been several factory-built versions of the Emeraude, but the aircraft is no longer being produced in this form.

The Emeraude and Super Emeraude continue to be available for amateur construction, and the following amateur-built versions have flown:

C.P.301. With 90 hp Continental engine.
C.P.302. With 90 hp Salmson engine.
C.P.303. With 85 hp Salmson engine.
C.P.304. With 85 hp Continental C85-12F engine and wing flaps.
C.P.305. With 115 hp Lycoming engine.

C.P.308. With 75 hp Continental engine.
C.P.320. With Super Emeraude wings and 100 hp Continental engine. C.P.320A has swept-back fin.
C.P.321. As C.P.320, with 105 hp Potez engine.
C.P.323A. With 150 hp Lycoming engine and sweptback fin. C.P.323AB has tricycle landing gear.

The Emeraude is one of the types approved by the Popular Flying Association for amateur construction in the United Kingdom. A three-seat version, known as the Diamant, is described separately.

The following details refer to the basic C.P.301 Emeraude and C.P.320 Super Emeraude, but are generally applicable to all versions.

TYPE: Two-seat light monoplane.

WINGS: Cantilever low-wing monoplane. NACA 23012 wing section. Dihedral 5° 40′. Incidence 4° 10′. Inner half of each wing is rectangular in plan, outer half elliptical. All-wood single-spar structure with fabric covering overall. Slotted ailerons and flaps.

TAIL UNIT: Cantilever wood structure. Fin integral with fuselage. Single-piece all-wood tailplane. Elevators and rudder fabric-covered. Trim-tab in starboard elevator.

LANDING GEAR: Non-retractable tail-wheel type. Cantilever main legs have rubber-in-compression springing. Hydraulic brakes.

POWER PLANT (C.P.301): One 90 hp Continental C90-12F four-cylinder horizontally-opposed air-cooled engine. Two-blade fixed-pitch wooden propeller, diameter 5 ft 11 in (1·80 m). Fuel tank in fuselage behind fireproof bulkhead, capacity 17·6 Imp gallons (80 litres). Provision for auxiliary tank, capacity 8·8 Imp gallons (40 litres).

POWER PLANT (C.P.320): One 100 hp Continental O-200 "flat-four" engine and two-blade fixed-pitch wooden propeller of 5 ft 10 in (1·78 m) diameter. Fuel as for C.P.301.

ACCOMMODATION: Enclosed cockpit seating two side-by-side with dual controls. Sides of

canopy hinge forward for access and exit. Heating and ventilation.

DIMENSIONS, EXTERNAL:
Wing span	26 ft 4½ in (8·04 m)
Wing chord at root	4 ft 11 in (1·50 m)
Wing chord at tip	1 ft 9½ in (0·55 m)
Wing aspect ratio	5·95
Length overall:	
C.P.301	20 ft 8 in (6·30 m)
C.P.320	21 ft 2 in (6·45 m)
Height overall:	
C.P.301	6 ft 0¾ in (1·85 m)
C.P.320	6 ft 2½ in (1·90 m)
Wheel track	6 ft 8¾ in (2·05 m)

AREA:
Wings, gross	116·7 sq ft (10·85 m²)

WEIGHTS AND LOADINGS:
Weight empty:	
C.P.301	838 lb (380 kg)
C.P.320	903 lb (410 kg)
Max T-O weight:	
C.P.301	1,433 lb (650 kg)
C.P.320	1,543 lb (700 kg)
Max wing loading:	
C.P.301	12·3 lb/sq ft (60·0 kg/m²)
C.P.320	13·2 lb/sq ft (64·5 kg/m²)
Max power loading:	
C.P.301	15·87 lb/hp (7·2 kg/hp)
C.P.320	15·43 lb/hp (7·0 kg/hp)

PERFORMANCE (at max T-O weight):
Max level speed:	
C.P.301	110 knots (127 mph; 205 km/h)
C.P.320	124 knots (143 mph; 230 km/h)
Max never-exceed speed:	
C.P.301	118·7 knots (136·7 mph; 220 km/h
C.P.320	149 knots (172 mph; 277 km/h)
Max cruising speed (75% power) at 3,940 ft (1,200 m):	
C.P.301	108 knots (124 mph; 200 km/h)
C.P.320	119 knots (137 mph; 220 km/h)
Econ cruising speed (65% power) at 3,940 ft (1,200 m):	
C.P.301	101 knots (116 mph; 187 km/h)
C.P.320	110 knots (127 mph; 205 km/h)

Approach speed, flaps down:
C.P.301, C.P.320
65 knots (75 mph; 120 km/h)

Stalling speed, flaps up:
C.P.301   51 knots (58 mph; 92 km/h)
C.P.320   53 knots (61 mph; 97 km/h)

Stalling speed, flaps down:
C.P.301   46 knots (53 mph; 85 km/h)
C.P.320   49 knots (56 mph; 90 km/h)

Rate of climb at S/L:
C.P.301   551 ft (168 m)/min
C.P.320   787 ft (240 m)/min

Service ceiling:
C.P.301   13,125 ft (4,000 m)
C.P.320   14,100 ft (4,300 m)

T-O run:
C.P.301   820 ft (250 m)
C.P.320   755 ft (230 m)

T-O to 50 ft (15 m):
C.P.301   1,443 ft (440 m)
C.P.320   1,312 ft (400 m)

Landing from 50 ft (15 m):
C.P.301   1,558 ft (475 m)
C.P.320   1,608 ft (490 m)

Landing run:
C.P.301   820 ft (250 m)
C.P.320   853 ft (260 m)

Range at econ cruising speed:
C.P.301, C.P.320
538 nm (620 miles; 1,000 km)

PIEL DIAMANT and SUPER DIAMANT

The Diamant is essentially a three/four-seat version of the Emeraude, designed for construction by amateurs. There are several versions, as follows:

C.P.60. Prototype, with 90 hp Continental engine.

C.P.601. Standard three-seat version with 100 hp Continental engine.

C.P.602. Similar to C.P.601, but with 115 hp Potez engine.

C.P.604 Super Diamant. Prototype (F-PMEC) flown in Summer of 1964, with a 145 hp Continental engine. Latest version has swept vertical tail surfaces.

C.P.605 Super Diamant. Much modified four-seat ("2+2") version, with 150 hp Lycoming engine and swept vertical tail surfaces.

C.P.605B Super Diamant. Version of C.P.605 with retractable tricycle landing gear.

The following description applies to the C.P.601, C.P.605 and C.P.605B, except where specific versions are indicated.

TYPE: Three/four-seat light monoplane.

WINGS: Cantilever low-wing monoplane. Wing section NACA 23012. Dihedral 5° 40'. Incidence 4° 10'. All-wood single-spar structure, made in one piece, with fabric covering. Slotted ailerons and slotted flaps of wood construction, with fabric covering.

FUSELAGE: Wood structure, covered with fabric.

TAIL UNIT: Cantilever wood structure. Fixed surfaces plywood-covered. Control surfaces fabric-covered. Ground-adjustable tab on each elevator.

LANDING GEAR (C.P.601 and C.P.605): Non-retractable tail-wheel type. Main wheels size 420×150, pressure 24 lb/sq in (1·70 kg/cm²). Hydraulic brakes. Wheel spats. Steerable tail-wheel, size 155×50.

LANDING GEAR (C.P.605B): Retractable tricycle type. Main wheels retract inward. All three wheels and tyres size 400 × 100.

POWER PLANT: One 100 hp Continental O-200 (C.P.601) or 150 hp Lycoming O-320-E2A (C.P.605 and 605B) four-cylinder horizontally-opposed air-cooled engine, driving an EVRA two-blade fixed-pitch wooden propeller, diameter 5 ft 11 in (1·80 m). Fuel tank in fuselage, capacity 18·7 Imp gallons (85 litres). Provision for additional tankage in C.P.605 and 605B, to give total capacity of 35 Imp gallons (160 litres). Oil capacity 0·9 Imp gallons (4 litres).

ACCOMMODATION: Three seats (four, "2+2", in Super Diamants) in enclosed cabin under large rearward-sliding transparent canopy.

DIMENSIONS, EXTERNAL:
Wing span:
C.P.601   30 ft 10 in (9·40 m)
C.P.605, 605B 30 ft 2¼ in (9·20 m)
Wing chord at root 4 ft 11 in (1·50 m)
Wing aspect ratio:
C.P.601   6·5
C.P.605, 605B   6·4
Length overall:
C.P.601   22 ft 3¾ in (6·80 m)
C.P.605, 605B 22 ft 11¾ in (7·00 m)
Height overall:
C.P.601, 605   6 ft 2¾ in (1·90 m)
C.P.605B   6 ft 6¾ in (2·00 m)

Piel C.P.301A Emeraude owned by Mr Gustav Weibe of Newton, Kansas *(Jean Seele)*

Piel C.P.604 Super Diamant three-seat light aircraft (145 hp Continental engine)

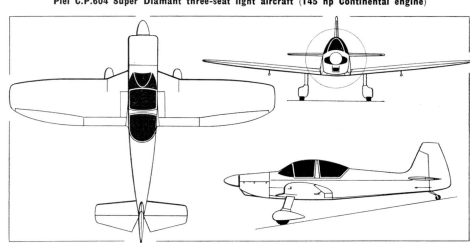

Piel C.P.750 Beryl two-seat light aircraft (150 hp Lycoming O-320-E2A engine)

Wheel track:
C.P.601, 605   6 ft 8¾ in (2·05 m)
C.P.605B   9 ft 10 in (3·00 m)

AREAS:
Wings, gross:
C.P.601   144·8 sq ft (13·45 m²)
C.P.605, 605B 143·2 sq ft (13·30 m²)

WEIGHTS AND LOADINGS:
Weight empty:
C.P.601   992 lb (450 kg)
C.P.605   1,120 lb (508 kg)
C.P.605B   1,146 lb (520 kg)
Max T-O weight:
C.P.601   1,697 lb (770 kg)
C.P.605, 605B 1,873 lb (850 kg)
Max wing loading:
C.P.601   11·7 lb/sq ft (57·25 kg/m²)
C.P.605, 605B 13·1 lb/sq ft (64·00 kg/m²)
Max power loading:
C.P.601   16·97 lb/hp (7·7 kg/hp)
C.P.605, 605B 12·35 lb/hp (5·6 kg/hp)

PERFORMANCE (at max T-O weight):
Max level speed:
C.P.601   116 knots (134 mph; 215 km/h)
C.P.605   132 knots (152 mph; 245 km/h)
C.P.605B   141 knots (162 mph; 260 km/h)
Max never-exceed speed:
C.P.601, 605, 605B
151 knots (174 mph; 280 km/h)

Max cruising speed (75% power) at 3,940 ft (1,200 m):
C.P.601   110 knots (127 mph; 205 km/h)
C.P.605   127 knots (146 mph; 235 km/h)
C.P.605B   132 knots (152 mph; 245 km/h)
Econ cruising speed (65% power) at 3,940 ft (1,200 m):
C.P.601   102 knots (118 mph; 190 km/h)
C.P.605   119 knots (137 mph; 220 km/h)
C.P.605B   124 knots (143 mph; 230 km/h)
Approach speed, flaps down:
C.P.601, 605, 605B
68 knots (78 mph; 125 km/h)
Stalling speed, flaps up:
C.P.601, 605, 605B
49 knots (56 mph; 90 km/h)
Stalling speed, flaps down:
C.P.601, 605, 605B
45 knots (51 mph; 82 km/h)
Rate of climb at S/L:
C.P.601   492 ft (150 m)/min
C.P.605   984 ft (300 m)/min
C.P.605B   1,082 ft (330 m)/min
Service ceiling:
C.P.601   11,810 ft (3,600 m)
C.P.605   15,750 ft (4,800 m)
C.P.605B   16,400 ft (5,000 m)
T-O run:
C.P.601   853 ft (260 m)
C.P.605   590 ft (180 m)
C.P.605B   525 ft (160 m)

T-O to 50 ft (15 m):

C.P.601	1,575 ft (480 m)
C.P.605	1,312 ft (400 m)
C.P.605B	1,247 ft (380 m)

Landing from 50 ft (15 m):

C.P.601	2,133 ft (650 m)
C.P.605	2,231 ft (680 m)
C.P.605B	1,969 ft (600 m)

Landing run:

C.P.601	919 ft (280 m)
C.P.605	984 ft (300 m)
C.P.605B	886 ft (270 m)

Range at econ cruising speed:

C.P.601	387 nm (446 miles; 750 km)
C.P.605	593 nm (683 miles; 1,100 km)
C.P.605B	620 nm (714 miles; 1,150 km)

PIEL C.P.70 and C.P.750 BERYL

The prototype of the **C.P.70 Beryl** tandem two-seat light aircraft was displayed publicly for the first time in August 1965. It retains the wing of the C.P.30 Emeraude virtually unchanged, combining this wing with a modified fuselage and non-retractable tricycle landing gear.

The fuselage of the Beryl is a fabric-covered wooden structure, of slimmer section than that of the Emeraude. Each main landing gear unit is articulated, with the wheel aft of the oleopneumatic shock-absorber. The steerable nosewheel is carried on a conventional fork.

Intended for aerobatic flying, the **C.P.750 Beryl** is also similar in general appearance to the Emeraude but has a longer, steel-tube fuselage seating two persons in tandem, slightly reduced span and other changes.

The C.P.750 has so far been built principally by amateur constructors in Canada, but may also be built in France through the facilities offered by M Choisel at Abbeville.

TYPE: Two-seat aerobatic monoplane.

WINGS: Cantilever low-wing monoplane. Wing section NACA 23012. Dihedral 5° 40'. Incidence 4° 10'. All-wood single-spar structure, made in one piece, with fabric covering. Slotted ailerons and slotted flaps of wood construction with fabric covering.

FUSELAGE: Fabric-covered structure of wood (C.P.70) or welded steel tube (C.P.750).

TAIL UNIT: Cantilever wood structure. Fixed surfaces plywood-covered, control surfaces fabric-covered. Ground-adjustable tab on each elevator.

LANDING GEAR: (C.P.70): Non-retractable tricycle type.

LANDING GEAR (C.P.750): Non-retractable tail-wheel type. Main wheels size 420 × 150, pressure 24 lb/sq in (1·70 kg/cm²). Hydraulic brakes. Wheel spats. Steerable tail-wheel.

POWER PLANT: (C.P.70) One 65 hp Continental C65-8F four-cylinder horizontally-opposed air-cooled engine, driving a two-blade wooden propeller, diameter 5 ft 11 in (1·80 m). Fuel tank in fuselage, capacity 15·4 Imp gallons (70 litres).

POWER PLANT (C.P.750): One 150 hp Lycoming O-320-E2A four-cylinder horizontally-opposed air-cooled engine, driving an EVRA two-blade fixed-pitch wooden propeller, diameter 5 ft 11 in (1·80 m). Fuel tank in fuselage, capacity 15·4 Imp gallons (70 litres), with provision for two auxiliary tanks in wings to give total capacity of 30·75 Imp gallons (140 litres). Oil capacity 1·0 Imp gallon (5 litres).

ACCOMMODATION: Two seats in tandem under rearward-sliding transparent canopy. Rear seat of C.P.70 is wide enough to accommodate one adult and a child, or two children.

DIMENSIONS, EXTERNAL:

Wing span:	
C.P.70	26 ft 4½ in (8·04 m)
C.P.750	26 ft 4 in (8·03 m)
Wing chord at root	4 ft 11 in (1·50 m)
Wing aspect ratio:	
C.P.70	5·95
C.P.750	5·85
Length overall:	
C.P.70	20 ft 10 in (6·35 m)
C.P.750	22 ft 7¾ in (6·90 m)
Height overall:	
C.P.70	5 ft 3 in (1·60 m)
C.P.750	6 ft 10¾ in (2·10 m)
Wheel track:	
C.P.70	6 ft 6¾ in (2·00 m)
C.P.750	7 ft 10½ in (2·40 m)

AREAS:

Wings, gross:	
C.P.70	116·8 sq ft (10·85 m²)
C.P.750	118 sq ft (11·00 m²)

WEIGHTS AND LOADINGS:

Weight empty:	
C.P.70	705 lb (320 kg)
C.P.750	1,058 lb (480 kg)
Max T-O weight:	
C.P.70	1,190 lb (540 kg)
C.P.750	1,675 lb (760 kg)
Max wing loading:	
C.P.70	10·2 lb/sq ft (50·0 kg/m²)
C.P.750	14·1 lb/sq ft (69·0 kg/m²)

Piel C.P.70 Beryl two/three-seat light aircraft (65 hp Continental A65 engine) (*Air et Cosmos*)

Max power loading:

C.P.70	18·3 lb/hp (8·3 kg/hp)
C.P.750	11·0 lb/hp (5·0 kg/hp)

PERFORMANCE (at max T-O weight):

Max level speed:	
C.P.70	95 knots (109 mph; 175 km/h)
C.P.750	151 knots (174 mph; 280 km/h)
Max never-exceed speed:	
C.P.70	118·7 knots (136·7 mph; 220 km/h)
C.P.750	183 knots (211 mph; 340 km/h)
Max cruising speed (75% power) at 3,940 ft (1,200 m):	
C.P.70	84 knots (97 mph; 156 km/h)
C.P.750	143 knots (165 mph; 265 km/h)
Econ cruising speed (65% power) at 3,940 ft (1,200 m):	
C.P.70	78 knots (90 mph; 145 km/h)
C.P.750	135 knots (155 mph; 250 km/h)
Approach speed, flaps down:	
C.P.70	54 knots (62·2 mph; 100 km/h)
C.P.750	70 knots (81 mph; 130 km/h)
Stalling speed, flaps up:	
C.P.70	41 knots (47 mph; 75 km/h)
C.P.750	54 knots (62·2 mph; 100 km/h)
Stalling speed, flaps down:	
C.P.70	39 knots (44 mph; 70 km/h)
C.P.750	52 knots (59 mph; 95 km/h)
Rate of climb at S/L:	
C.P.70	394 ft (120 m)/min
C.P.750	1,280 ft (390 m)/min
Service ceiling:	
C.P.70	9,850 ft (3,000 m)
C.P.750	17,060 ft (5,200 m)
T-O run:	
C.P.70	919 ft (280 m)
C.P.750	623 ft (190 m)
T-O to 50 ft (15 m):	
C.P.70	1,378 ft (420 m)
C.P.750	1,148 ft (350 m)
Landing from 50 ft (15 m):	
C.P.70	919 ft (280 m)
C.P.750	1,706 ft (520 m)
Landing run:	
C.P.70	459 ft (140 m)
C.P.750	919 ft (280 m)
Range at econ cruising speed:	
C.P.70	323 nm (372 miles; 600 km)
C.P.750	593 nm (683 miles; 1,100 km)

PIEL C.P.90 PINOCCHIO

The latest Piel design, the C.P.90 Pinocchio, is essentially a slightly smaller, single-seat development of the basic Emeraude, intended for aerobatic and general sporting flying.

WINGS: Cantilever low-wing monoplane, of similar general planform and construction to Emeraude. Ailerons only, no flaps. Dihedral 5° 40'. Incidence 3°.

FUSELAGE: Fabric-covered wooden structure of basically rectangular cross-section with domed deck.

TAIL UNIT: Cantilever fabric-covered wooden structure, similar to that of Emeraude.

LANDING GEAR: Non-retractable tail-wheel type. Leg fairings and wheel spats on main units.

POWER PLANT: One 100 hp Continental O-200 four-cylinder horizontally-opposed air-cooled engine, driving a two-blade wooden propeller, diameter 5 ft 11 in (1·80 m). Fuel capacity 13·2 Imp gallons (60 litres).

ACCOMMODATION: Single seat under fully-transparent canopy.

DIMENSIONS, EXTERNAL:

Wing span	23 ft 7½ in (7·20 m)
Wing aspect ratio	5·4
Length overall	19 ft 8¼ in (6·00 m)
Height overall	5 ft 11 in (1·80 m)
Wheel track	5 ft 3 in (1·60 m)

AREA:

Wings, gross	103·9 sq ft (9·65 m²)

WEIGHTS AND LOADINGS:

Weight empty	738 lb (335 kg)
Max T-O weight	1,014 lb (460 kg)
Max wing loading	9·8 lb/sq ft (47·7 kg/m²)
Max power loading	10·14 lb/hp (4·6 kg/hp)

PERFORMANCE (estimated, at max T-O weight):

Max level speed	141 knots (162 mph; 260 km/h)
Max never-exceed speed	171 knots (198 mph; 320 km/h)
Max cruising speed (75% power) at 3,940 ft (1,200) m	132 knots (152 mph; 245 km/h)
Econ cruising speed (65% power) at 3,940 ft (1,200 m)	124 knots (143 mph; 230 km/h)
Approach speed	54 knots (62·2 mph; 100 km/h)
Stalling speed	41 knots (47 mph; 75 km/h)
Rate of climb	1,575 ft (480 m)/min
Service ceiling	19,685 ft (6,000 m)
T-O run	590 ft (180 m)
T-O to 50 ft (15 m)	1,312 ft (400 m)
Landing from 50 ft (15 m)	984 ft (300 m)
Landing run	525 ft (160 m)
Range at econ cruising speed	296 nm (341 miles; 550 km)

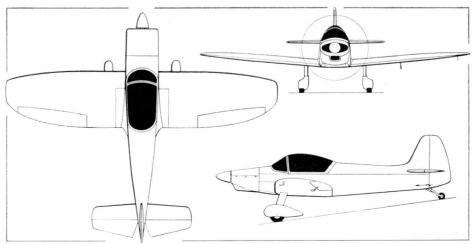

Piel C.P.90 Pinocchio single-seat light sporting aircraft

POTEZ
POTEZ AÉRONAUTIQUE

The original Potez company was formed during the 1914-18 War. In 1937 its aircraft factories at Méaulte (Somme) and Sartrouville (S-et-O)

were incorporated in the nationalised SNCA du Nord, and that at Berre (Bouches-du-Rhône) in the SNCA de Sud-Est.

In 1953, the company returned to aircraft construction after a lapse of seventeen years.

Details of its most recent products, the Potez 94 twin-jet trainer/counter-insurgency aircraft and the Potez 841 and 842 twin-turboprop transport aircraft, were given in the 1968-69 *Jane's*.

POULET
POULET PÈRE ET FILS SARL

ADDRESS:
63 Rue de Varsovie, 92-Colombes

With manufacturing assistance from the Société Poulet, M Michel Dalotel has designed and flown the prototype of a tandem two-seat aircraft, known as the DM-165.

DALOTEL DM-165

The DM-165 has been designed as a tandem two-seat advanced trainer or aerobatic aircraft, and the prototype (F-PPZE) flew for the first time in April 1969. This followed some nine years of design study to develop an aircraft suitable for flying club use at relatively low cost, and series production will depend upon the interest shown by clubs or official organisations. The present wooden wings and tail unit and fabric covering may be replaced in the future by all-metal construction.

TYPE: Tandem two-seat advanced training and aerobatic aircraft.

WINGS: Cantilever low-wing monoplane, with single wooden main spar and stressed plywood covering. Each wing is attached to the lower fuselage by three bolts, and can be dismantled to enable the aircraft to be transported by road. 3° dihedral from roots. Sweepback on leading-edge only. All-wood ailerons along more than half of span of trailing edge, with ±25° of travel; instead of conventional flaps, a sailplane-type air-brake is fitted to each wing. Manual control of ailerons and air-brakes.

FUSELAGE: Welded steel-tube structure, with fabric covering.

TAIL UNIT: Non-swept cantilever wooden surfaces, which can be dismantled for road transportation. Electrically-actuated trim-tab in elevator.

LANDING GEAR: Retractable tail-wheel type. Main wheels retract inward into wings. Electrically-actuated retraction, with manual standby. Steerable Scott tail-wheel.

POWER PLANT: One 165 hp Continental IO-346A four-cylinder horizontally-opposed air-cooled engine with fuel-injection, driving a two-blade fixed-pitch or constant-speed wooden prop-

Prototype Poulet Dalotel DM-165 two-seat light aircraft 165 hp Continental engine) (*Howard Levy*)

eller. Fuel system designed to permit inverted flying. Fuel capacity 18·5 Imp gallons (84 litres).

ACCOMMODATION: Tandem seating for two persons under individual jettisonable cockpit hoods. Hoods are hinged to retractable frame on port side which extends up and over fuselage to starboard to permit access to cockpit. Pilot occupies rear seat.

ELECTRONICS AND EQUIPMENT: Standard equipment includes VHF radio.

DIMENSIONS, EXTERNAL:

Wing span	27 ft 6¾ in (8·40 m)
Length overall	22 ft 10 in (6·96 m)
Height overall, tail down	5 ft 11¾ in (1·82 m)
Tailplane span	9 ft 6 in (2·90 m)

Wheel track	9 ft 0¾ in (2·76 m)
AREAS:	
Wings, gross	132·4 sq ft (12·30 m²)
Ailerons (total)	14·85 sq ft (1·38 m²)
WEIGHTS:	
Weight empty	1,322 lb (600 kg)
Max T-O weight	1,851 lb (840 kg)

PERFORMANCE (at max T-O weight):
Max level speed
162 knots (186 mph; 300 km/h)
Cruising speed 149 knots (171 mph; 275 km/h)
Stalling speed 51·5 knots (59 mph; 95 km/h)
Max rate of climb (constant-speed propeller)
1,969 ft (600 m)/min
Rate of climb (fixed-pitch propeller)
1,378 ft (420 m)/min

REIMS AVIATION
REIMS AVIATION S A

OFFICE AND WORKS:
Reims-Prunay Airport, B.P.533, 51-Reims

GENERAL OFFICE:
18 Quai Alphonse le Gallo, 92-Boulogne Billancourt

PRESIDENT DIRECTOR-GENERAL:
Pierre Clostermann

VICE-PRESIDENT:
Jaques Clostermann

DIRECTOR-GENERAL ADJOINT AND WORKS DIRECTOR: Jean Pichon

FINANCIAL DIRECTOR: Henri Hertz

ADMINISTRATIVE DIRECTOR: Armand Blang

PUBLIC RELATIONS: Frédéric Amanou

Under an agreement signed on 16 February 1960, the Cessna Aircraft Company of Wichita, Kansas, USA, acquired a 49% holding in this company, which was then known as the Société Nouvelle des Avions Max Holste.

Reims Aviation has the right to manufacture under licence Cessna designs for sale in Europe, Africa and Asia. By 23 February 1970 it had assembled a total of 698 Cessna F-172 four-seat aircraft, 585 Cessna F-150 and 35 FA-150 Aerobat two-seat aircraft, 200 Reims Rocket four-seat aircraft and two F-337 six-seat aircraft, all with Rolls-Royce Continental engines. Of this total, 386 aircraft were exported during the 20-month period ending on 1 March 1970. The 1969-70 production programme, which began on 1 August 1969, calls for an output of 360 aircraft, including 109 F-150s, 81 F-150s, 86 F-172s, 72 Rockets, and 12 F-337s and FT-337s.

Reims Aviation was negotiating in the Spring of 1970 for exclusive manufacturing rights to the Zlin 526L aerobatic and training aircraft (see the Czechoslovakian section of this edition).

Reims-Cessna FA-150 Aerobat two-seat aerobatic light aircraft

An initial batch of 250 aircraft would be built, under the designation RAZ-526L, Reims having exclusive sales rights for the aircraft in France. For all other countries it would be distributed through the Cessna sales network. In exchange, Reims-built Cessna types would be distributed in Eastern Europe by an organisation to be appointed by Omnipol.

Reims Aviation is also assisting Aérospatiale (Nord-Aviation) in the series production of the N 262 twin-turboprop light transport, by manufacturing tail units and fuselage tail-cones, wheel fairings, flaps, ailerons, wing leading-edges, wing-tips, engine nacelles and instrument panels. It is a sub-contractor to Dassault in the Mystère 20/Falcon programme, for which it supplies

ailerons and air-brakes, and will participate in the Mirage F1 programme. It is also continuing the overhaul and servicing of M.H.1521 Broussard utility monoplanes.

Reims Aviation employed 390 people at 1 March 1970. Its offices and factories at Reims-Prunay Airport have an area of 215,278 sq ft (20,000 m²).

CESSNA F-150 and FA-150 AEROBAT

Cessna 150 aircraft assembled under licence by Reims Aviation are designated **F-150**. Production is at the rate of 11 aircraft a month in 1969-70. In addition, Reims is producing in 1970 a basic aerobatic version of this aircraft, known as the **FA-150 Aerobat**, with a 100 hp

F

engine. Output of this version is at the rate of eight aircraft per month. Mention has also been made of the **FRA-150,** a more advanced aerobatic two-seater with a 130 hp engine.

Modifications introduced on the 1970 models include tinted skylights (standard on the FA-150, optional on the F-150), a new, contoured cabin roof lining, and an overhead light console.

A full description of the 1970 Cessna 150 and A-150 is given in the US section.

CESSNA F-172

Cessna 172 aircraft assembled under licence by Reims Aviation are designated **F-172.** Production began in 1963 and is at the rate of eight aircraft a month in 1969-70.

The 1970 model, described fully in the US section of this edition, introduces fully-adjustable front seats as an optional extra.

CESSNA FR-172 REIMS ROCKET

First displayed at the 1967 Paris Air Show (as the FR-172E), the Rocket has been developed by Reims Aviation from the F-172.

The Rocket has a 210 hp Rolls-Royce/Continental IO-360-D six-cylinder horizontally-opposed air-cooled fuel-injection engine, driving a constant-speed propeller of 6 ft 4 in (1·93 m) diameter. Capacity of the two wing fuel tanks is increased to 43·3 Imp gallons (197 litres), and the 1970 model has provision for a 14·1 Imp gallon (64 litre) auxiliary fuselage tank, increasing total capacity to 57·4 Imp gallons (261 litres).

As in the standard F-172, the normal four-seat arrangement can be supplemented by a seat for two children in the baggage compartment.

A number of modifications have been made in the 1970 model, to improve passenger comfort and performance and increase the useful load. These include conical-camber wingtips, redesigned seats, improved baggage door hatch and a more flexible electrical system. Optional items include vertically-adjustable, fully-articulated front seats, foldaway child's seat in the baggage area and glider-towing capability. The 10·5 cu ft (0·3 m³) baggage compartment aft of the rear seats holds a maximum of 200 lb (90 kg).

Production was at the rate of seven aircraft a month in 1969-70. Reims Aviation produce the Rocket exclusively, for worldwide sale.

DIMENSIONS, EXTERNAL:

Wing span	35 ft 10 in (10·92 m)
Length overall	26 ft 9 in (8·15 m)
Height overall	8 ft 9½ in (2·68 m)
Tailplane span	11 ft 4 in (3·45 m)
Wheel track	7 ft 2 in (2·18 m)

AREA:

Wings, gross	174 sq ft (16·17 m²)

WEIGHTS AND LOADINGS:

Weight empty	1,410 lb (640 kg)
Max T-O weight	2,550 lb (1,156 kg)
Max wing loading	14·6 lb/sq ft (71·3 kg/m²)
Max power loading	12·1 lb/hp (5·49 kg/hp)

PERFORMANCE (at max T-O weight):

Max level speed at S/L	
	133 knots (153 mph; 246 km/h)
Max cruising speed (75% power) at 5,500 ft	
(1,675 m)	126 knots (145 mph; 233 km/h)
Econ cruising speed at 10,000 ft (3,050 m)	
	91 knots (105 mph; 169 km/h)
Stalling speed, power off, flaps up	
	56 knots (64 mph; 103 km/h)
Stalling speed, power off, flaps down	
	46 knots (53 mph; 86 km/h)
Rate of climb at S/L	880 ft (268 m)/min
Service ceiling	17,000 ft (5,181 m)
T-O run	740 ft (226 m)
T-O to 50 ft (15 m)	1,230 ft (375 m)
Landing from 50 ft (15 m)	1,270 ft (387 m)
Landing run	620 ft (189 m)
Range at max cruising speed, no reserve:	
standard fuel	503 nm (580 miles; 933 km)
with aux tank	690 nm (795 miles; 1,279 km)
Range at econ cruising speed, no reserve:	
standard fuel	642 nm (740 miles; 1,190 km)
with aux tank	877 nm (1,010 miles; 1,625 km)

Reims-Cessna F-172 four-seat light aircraft (150 hp Lycoming O-320-E2D engine)

Cessna Reims Rocket four-seat light aircraft

Reims-Cessna F-337 French-built version of the Super Skymaster for export to Gabon

CESSNA F-337/FT-337

In 1969 Reims Aviation began the assembly under licence of the Cessna 337 Super Skymaster six-seat twin-engined light aircraft. Primary structures are being supplied by Cessna, and engines by Rolls-Royce; smaller components and equipment are French-built. An armed version is available, with underwing stores including Minigun and rocket packs.

Output of the French model is at an initial rate of two aircraft a month in 1970.

The standard Cessna 337 as built by Reims Aviation is designated **F-337;** with a turbocharger system fitted it is known as the **FT-337.**

A full description of the 1970 models of the Cessna 337 appears in the US section of this edition.

RIGAULT-DEPROUX
AVIONS RIGAULT-DEPROUX
PROPRIETORS: MM. Rigault and Deproux

During 1967, MM. Rigault and Deproux completed and tested a single-seat prototype of their projected RD-3 two-seat home-built autogyro. All known details of this aircraft are given below.

RIGAULT-DEPROUX RD-3

The RD-3 is a side-by-side two-seat light autogyro, intended for assembly by amateurs from commercially-built components. In its developed form, shock-absorbers will be fitted to the non-retractable nose-wheel landing gear.

A prototype (F-WNGK) has been completed, and this made its first flight on 25 September 1967, piloted by M Rigault. This aircraft is powered by a 105 hp Potez 4E-20 four-cylinder horizontally-opposed air-cooled engine, driving a Deproux-EVRA two-blade fixed-pitch propeller of 4 ft 11 in (1·50 m) diameter. The main aircraft structure, which is of rectangular-section light alloy, consists of a cruciform-shaped chassis, at the rear of which is a tall single fin and large-area rudder. It is understood that a twin-boom tailplane support has now replaced the single support. The rotor is non-articulated and on the prototype is of 24 ft 3¼ in (7·40 m) diameter. Performance includes an estimated T-O run of 82 ft (25 m).

ROBIN
AVIONS PIERRE ROBIN (CENTRE EST AÉRONAUTIQUE)
HEAD OFFICE AND WORKS:
Aérodrome Dijon-Darois, BP 38, 21-Dijon

PRESIDENT-DIRECTOR GENERAL:
Pierre Robin
SALES: Pierre Robin
This company was formed in October 1957 as Centre Est Aéronautique to design, manufacture and sell touring aircraft.

Its founder, M Pierre Robin, in collaboration with M Jean Delemontez, the engineer responsible for the well-known Jodel series of light aircraft, decided to develop for production a three-seat high-performance lightplane. The result was the Jodel DR 100 Ambassadeur, which was developed in 8½ months and flew for the first time on 14 July 1958. The DR 100 received its certificate of airworthiness on 10 July 1959, by which time a pre-series of eight had been built.

By July 1960, Centre Est had developed a new version designated DR 1050, with a 100 hp Continental engine.

This was followed in 1961 by a version with the 105 hp Potez engine and designated DR 1051. A total of 158 DR 1050/1051 Ambassadeurs were built.

In 1961 and 1962, M Robin gained second place in the Circuit of Sicily international air race in a DR 1051 Ambassadeur. Subsequently Centre Est gave the name Sicile to a further-improved version of the Ambassadeur. This new model took seven of the first nine places in the 1963 Circuit, won by M Robin in the version with a Potez engine.

Further development led to the Sicile Record, and 114 Siciles and 58 Sicile Records were built.

The Sicile Record was followed in turn by the four-seat DR 250, in one of which M Robin achieved his third successive victory in the Circuit of Sicily in 1965. Other DR 250s finished third and fourth.

In 1969 the name of the company was changed to Avions Pierre Robin. For 1970, the Robin (Centre Est) DR 220 "2+2", DR 221, DR 253, DR 315, DR 340, DR 360 and DR 380 remain in production. Flight testing continues of the prototype HR 100, the company's first all-metal aircraft, and a new design, the DR 330, flew for the first time on 26 March 1970.

In addition, following the liquidation of the SAN company (which see), Avions Pierre Robin has acquired manufacturing licences for the Jodel D.140 Mousquetaire and D.140R Abeille previously built by SAN.

In 1969 the company's works covered an area of 75,350 sq ft (7,000 m²) and it employed 74 people. On 16 June 1967, it completed its 500th aeroplane, the first production example of the DR 253 Régent; overall production of aircraft during 1969 reached a total of 121. It was planned to raise output to 155 aircraft during 1970, approx one-third of these being for export.

Robin (CEA) DR 220 "2 + 2" two/four-seat lightplane (100 hp Rolls-Royce/Continental O-200 engine)

Robin (CEA) DR 221 Dauphin three/four-seat light aircraft (108/115 hp Lycoming engine) *(Air Photo Supply)*

ROBIN (CENTRE EST) DR 220 "2 + 2"

First flown on 5 February 1966, this further development of the Ambassadeur/Sicile series was designed for the widest possible range of applications. In economical two-seat form, it offers a high degree of comfort and can be fitted with extensive instrumentation and equipment, including dual nav/com radio and ADF. It conforms with the requirements of the utility category, to permit spinning, and can be used for the complete private pilot training syllabus, from ab initio instruction to navigational training.

Two versions have been built, as follows:

DR 220. Initial production version, as described below. Granted SGAC certification 24 June 1966.

DR 220A. Improved version of the DR 220, with strengthened airframe and a slightly longer landing gear, similar to that fitted in the DR 250.

A total of 3 pre-series and 70 production "2+2's" had been delivered by 1 March 1968, when the rate of production was eight per month.

TYPE: Two/four-seat light monoplane.

WINGS: Cantilever low-wing monoplane. Wing section NACA 23013·5 (modified). Centre-section has constant chord and no dihedral. Outer wings have a dihedral of 14°. All-wood one-piece single box-spar structure. Leading-edge plywood-covered, rest of wing fabric-covered. Fabric-covered wooden flaps and ailerons, interchangeable port and starboard. Manually-operated air-brake under spar outboard of landing gear on each side. Picketing ring under each wing-tip.

FUSELAGE: Wooden semi-monocoque structure of basic rectangular section, plywood-covered.

TAIL UNIT: Cantilever all-wood structure, fabric-covered, with sweptback fin and rudder. All-moving one-piece tailplane.

LANDING GEAR: Non-retractable tail-wheel type. Rubber-in-compression shock-absorbers. Main wheels and tyres size 380 × 150, pressure 25·6 lb/sq in (1·8 kg/cm²). Hydraulically actuated drum brakes can be operated together by hand lever or individually by rudder pedals. SAA Prestige steerable self-centering tail-wheel with solid rubber tyre, size 6 × 2, is carried on a leaf spring. Fairings on main wheels.

POWER PLANT: One 100 hp Rolls-Royce/Continental O-200-A four-cylinder horizontally-opposed air-cooled engine, driving an EVRA two-blade wooden fixed-pitch propeller, diameter 5 ft 9¼ in (1·76 m). Fuel in main tank in fuselage, capacity 24 Imp gallons (110 litres). Provision for auxiliary tank in fuselage, to raise total capacity to 35 Imp gallons (160 litres).

ACCOMMODATION: Normal accommodation for two persons side-by-side, on adjustable seats, in enclosed cabin, with forward-opening canopy door on each side. In addition to being used as a two-seater, the "2 + 2" can, with full tanks, carry one adult or two children on a bench seat in the rear of the cabin. Max load on rear seat, with full tanks, is 198 lb (90 kg). Dual controls standard. Cabin heated and ventilated.

EQUIPMENT: Provision for radio and full blind-flying instrumentation.

DIMENSIONS, EXTERNAL:	
Wing span	28 ft 7½ in (8·72 m)
Wing chord (centre-section, constant)	5 ft 7½ in (1·71 m)
Wing chord at tip	3 ft 0 in (0·90 m)
Wing aspect ratio	5·6
Length overall	22 ft 11½ in (7·00 m)
Height overall	6 ft 0¾ in (1·85 m)
Tailplane span	10 ft 6 in (3·20 m)
Wheel track	8 ft 6⅜ in (2·60 m)
Wheelbase	17 ft 0¾ in (5·20 m)
DIMENSIONS, INTERNAL:	
Cabin: Max length	5 ft 5 in (1·65 m)
Max width	3 ft 5⅜ in (1·05 m)
Max height	3 ft 9¼ in (1·15 m)
AREAS:	
Wings, gross	146·39 sq ft (13·60 m²)
Ailerons (total)	12·38 sq ft (1·15 m²)
Flaps (total)	6·89 sq ft (0·64 m²)
Fin	6·57 sq ft (0·61 m²)
Rudder	6·78 sq ft (0·63 m²)
Horizontal tail surfaces (total)	31·00 sq ft (2·88 m²)
WEIGHTS AND LOADINGS:	
Weight empty, equipped	970 lb (440 kg)
Max T-O weight:	
Normal cat	1,720 lb (780 kg)
Utility cat	1,543 lb (700 kg)
Max wing loading:	
Normal cat	11·75 lb/sq ft (57·35 kg/m²)
Utility cat	10·55 lb/sq ft (51·47 kg/m²)
Max power loading:	
Normal cat	17·2 lb/hp (7·8 kg/hp)
Utility cat	15·4 lb/hp (7·0 kg/hp)
PERFORMANCE (at max T-O weight, Normal category):	
Max level speed at S/L	122 knots (140 mph; 225 km/h)
Max permissible diving speed	145 knots (167 mph; 270 km/h)
Max cruising speed (75% power) at S/L	109 knots (125 mph; 200 km/h)
Econ cruising speed (75% power) at 9,000 ft (2,750 m)	113 knots (130 mph; 210 km/h)
Stalling speed	44 knots (50 mph; 80 km/h)
Rate of climb at S/L	550 ft (168 m)/min
Service ceiling	14,750 ft (4,500 m)
Max range with standard fuel	521 nm (600 miles; 966 km)

ROBIN (CENTRE EST) DR 221 DAUPHIN

Design of the DR 221 began in the Autumn of 1966, and the prototype Dauphin was flown for the first time on 18 February 1967. Following certification by the SGAC in April 1967, an initial production batch of 100 Dauphins was laid down, and 40 of these had been delivered by 1 March 1968.

The structural description and specification of the DR 220 (see above) applies generally to the DR 221, with the following exceptions:

TYPE: Three/four-seat light monoplane.

POWER PLANT: One 108/115 hp Lycoming O-235-C2A four-cylinder horizontally-opposed air-cooled engine, driving an EVRA two-blade wooden fixed-pitch propeller, diameter 5 ft 10⅞ in (1·80 m). Normal fuel capacity as DR 220 but provision for increase to total of 35 Imp gallons (160 litres) when the aircraft is used as a two-seat trainer.

ACCOMMODATION: As DR 220. Front seats adjustable to six positions and rear bench seat capable of accommodating two persons or baggage up to a total weight of 265 lb (120 kg). The instrument panel is large enough to accommodate full airline-standard instrumentation, including an automatic pilot, radio navigation equipment and full blind-flying instrumentation. Special attention has been paid to cabin soundproofing.

WEIGHTS AND LOADINGS:	
Weight empty, equipped	1,047 lb (475 kg)
Max T-O weight:	
Normal cat	1,852 lb (840 kg)
Utility cat	1,720 lb (780 kg)
Max wing loading:	
Normal cat	12·66 lb/sq ft (61·76 kg/m²)
Utility cat	11·75 lb/sq ft (57·35 kg/m²)
PERFORMANCE (at max T-O weight, Normal category):	
Max level speed at S/L	127 knots (146 mph; 235 km/h)
Max permissible diving speed	145 knots (167 mph; 270 km/h)
Max cruising speed (75% power) at S/L	110 knots (127 mph; 205 km/h)
Econ cruising speed (75% power) at 9,000 ft (2,750 m)	119 knots (137 mph; 220 km/h)
Stalling speed	44 knots (50 mph; 80 km/h)
Rate of climb at S/L	650 ft (198 m)/min
Service ceiling	12,800 ft (3,900 m)
Max range with standard fuel	490 nm (565 miles; 910 km)

ROBIN (CENTRE EST) DR 253 RÉGENT

Derived from the DR 250, the Régent has a slightly enlarged fuselage offering spacious accommodation for four persons, with the ability to carry up to five people. It was the first Centre Est production aircraft to have a tricycle landing gear.

Design of the Régent was started in September 1966. The prototype flew on 30 March 1967, followed by the first production DR 253 on 16 June 1967. SGAC certification was granted on 11 July 1967. An initial production of 100 Régents was undertaken, 35 of which had been delivered by mid-July 1968.

Late in 1967 the prototype DR 253 was flown with wings of all-metal construction, as a part of Centre Est's development studies prior to producing a prototype of the HR 100 all-metal light aircraft, described separately.

The description of the DR 220 applies generally to the DR 253, with the following exceptions:

TYPE: Four/five-seat light monoplane.

WINGS: Structure as for DR 220, but of increased area and with longer flaps of aluminium alloy construction. Dihedral on outer sections 16°.

TAIL UNIT: As DR 220, with tailplane tab of aluminium alloy.

LANDING GEAR: Non-retractable tricycle type, with Jodel-Beaune oleo-pneumatic shock-absorbers and Manu hydraulically-actuated drum brakes. All three wheels and tyres are size 420 × 150, pressure 25·6/28·4 lb/sq in (1·8/2·0 kg/cm²). Fairings on all three wheels.

POWER PLANT: One 180 hp Lycoming O-360-A2A four-cylinder horizontally-opposed air-cooled engine, driving a two-blade Sensenich metal fixed-pitch propeller, diameter 6 ft 4 in (1·93 m). Standard fuel capacity of 39·6 Imp gallons (180 litres) in one fuselage tank and two wing leading-edge tanks. Provision for auxiliary fuel tank in fuselage, to increase total capacity to 55 Imp gallons (250 litres). Oil capacity 2 Imp gallons (9·1 litres).

ACCOMMODATION: Side-by-side adjustable front seats for two persons, with rear bench seat accommodating two (optionally three) persons. Baggage compartment aft of rear seat, with external access door.

EQUIPMENT: Provision for automatic pilot, full blind-flying instrumentation and radio and radio navigation equipment for all-weather flying.

SYSTEMS: Electrical system power provided by 12V 35Ah generator.

DIMENSIONS, EXTERNAL: As DR 220, except:
Wing aspect ratio 5·3
Height overall 6 ft 8¾ in (2·05 m)
Wheelbase 5 ft 6⅞ in (1·70 m)

DIMENSIONS, INTERNAL:
Cabin: Max length 5 ft 6⅞ in (1·70 m)
Max width 3 ft 9⅛ in (1·16 m)
Max height 4 ft 1¼ in (1·25 m)
Baggage compartment: Volume 10·6 cu ft (0·3 m³)

AREAS: As for DR 220, except:
Wings, gross 152·85 sq ft (14·20 m²)
Flaps (total) 7·97 sq ft (0·74 m²)

WEIGHTS AND LOADINGS:
Weight empty, equipped 1,323 lb (600 kg)
Max T-O and landing weight 2,425 lb (1,100 kg)
Max wing loading 15·9 lb/sq ft (77·5 kg/m²)
Max power loading 13·4 lb/hp (6·1 kg/hp)

PERFORMANCE (at max T-O weight):
Max level speed at S/L 149 knots (171 mph; 275 km/h)
Max permissible diving speed 167 knots (192 mph; 310 km/h)
Max cruising speed (75% power) at S/L 129 knots (149 mph; 240 km/h)
Econ cruising speed (65% power) at 9,000 ft (2,750 m) 146 knots (168 mph; 270 km/h)
Stalling speed, flaps down 52·5 knots (60 mph; 96 km/h)
Rate of climb at S/L 886 ft (270 m)/min
Service ceiling 16,400 ft (5,000 m)
T-O run 985 ft (300 m)
T-O to 50 ft (15 m) 1,970 ft (600 m)
Landing from 50 ft (15 m) 1,640 ft (500 m)
Landing run 985 ft (300 m)
Max range, standard fuel 647 nm (746 miles; 1,200 m)
Max range with auxiliary fuel tank 864 nm (995 miles; 1,600 km)

Robin (CEA) DR 253 Régent (180 hp Lycoming O-360-A2A engine) (*Air Portraits*)

ROBIN (CENTRE EST) DR 315 CADET

The DR 315, originally known as the Petit Prince, was the second of Centre Est's 1968 models to appear, the prototype (F-WOFT) making its first flight on 21 March 1968. It is a three/four-seat touring and training aircraft, resembling in general appearance and construction the DR 221 Dauphin, although in fact a complete reappraisal of the entire Delemontez/Jodel basic design is a feature of the DR 315, DR 340, DR 360 and DR 380. Thus, although they retain the same overall appearance, features such as wing camber have been improved considerably to enhance general performance and aerodynamic qualities.

By mid-July 1968, 15 DR 315's had been built for French and German customers.

TYPE: Three/four-seat light monoplane.

WINGS: As for DR 220, except that flaps are slightly larger (though not so large as those of the DR 253) and are of aluminium alloy construction.

FUSELAGE: Generally similar to DR 220, but slightly larger cabin.

TAIL UNIT: Similar to DR 220.

LANDING GEAR: Non-retractable tricycle type, similar to that fitted to the DR 253 except that all three wheels and tyres are size 380 × 150, pressure 22·8/25·6 lb/sq in (1·6/1·8 kg/cm²) Fairings over all three legs and wheels.

POWER PLANT: One 108/115 hp Lycoming O-235-C2A four-cylinder horizontally-opposed air-cooled engine, driving a McCauley two-blade fixed-pitch metal propeller, diameter 5 ft 10 in (1·78 m). Standard fuel capacity 22 Imp gallons (100 litres) in main tank in fuselage. Oil capacity 1·25 Imp gallons (5·68 litres).

ACCOMMODATION: Side-by-side adjustable front seats for two persons, with rear bench seat accommodating one or two more persons. Maximum weight on rear seat is 265 lb (120 kg). Baggage compartment aft of rear seat. Particular attention has been paid to cabin sound-proofing.

EQUIPMENT: Provision for radio and full blind-flying instrumentation.

DIMENSIONS, EXTERNAL: As for DR 220 except:
Height overall 6 ft 4¾ in (1·95 m)
Wheelbase 5 ft 6⅞ in (1·70 m)

DIMENSIONS, INTERNAL:
Cabin: Max length 5 ft 6⅞ in (1·70 m)
Max width 3 ft 6⅛ in (1·07 m)
Max height 3 ft 11¼ in (1·20 m)
Baggage compartment: Volume 8·83 cu ft (0·25 m³)

AREAS: As for DR 220, except:
Wings, gross 152·31 sq ft (14·15 m²)
Flaps (total) 7·53 sq ft (0·70 m²)

WEIGHTS AND LOADINGS:
Weight empty, equipped 1,113 lb (505 kg)
Max T-O weight 1,907 lb (865 kg)
Max wing loading 13·04 lb/sq ft (63·6 kg/m²)
Max power loading 16·53 lb/hp (7·5 kg/hp)

PERFORMANCE (at max T-O weight):
Max level speed at S/L 129 knots (148 mph; 238 km/h)
Max permissible diving speed 159·5 knots (183 mph; 295 km/h)
Max cruising speed (75% power) at S/L 110 knots (127 mph; 205 km/h)
Max cruising speed (75% power) at 9,000 ft (2,750 m) 119 knots (137 mph; 220 km/h)
Stalling speed 48 knots (55 mph; 88 km/h)
Rate of climb at S/L 650 ft (198 m)/min
Service ceiling 12,800 ft (3,900 m)
Max range at econ cruising speed 509 nm (587 miles; 945 km)

ROBIN (CENTRE EST) DR 330

Newest member of the Robin range of wood-construction light aircraft, the DR 330 was first flown in prototype form on 25 March 1970. Production was initiated in April, in anticipation of certification of the DR 330 in the Summer of 1970.

The description of the DR 220 is generally applicable to the DR 330, with the following exceptions:

TYPE: Four-seat light monoplane.

WINGS: Of similar configuration and size to DR 220, with NACA 43012 (modified) wing section and 13·5% thickness/chord ratio. Dihedral 14° on outer panels only. Incidence 5°. Ailerons and plain trailing-edge flaps.

TAIL UNIT: All-moving tailplane with anti-tab, otherwise similar to DR 220.

LANDING GEAR: Non-retractable tricycle type, with oleo-pneumatic shock-absorption. All wheels and tyres same size (380 × 150) and pressure (35·6 lb/sq in = 2·5 kg/m²). Hydraulic brakes. Streamlined wheel fairings.

POWER PLANT: One 130 hp Rolls-Royce/Continental O-240-A four-cylinder horizontally-opposed air-cooled engine, driving a fixed-pitch metal propeller of 5 ft 11 in (1·80 m) diameter. Fuel in fuselage tank, capacity 26·4 Imp gallons (120 litres).

ACCOMMODATION: Separate side-by-side front seats and rear bench seat for pilot and three passengers. Forward-opening door on each side of cabin. Heating and ventilation standard.

SYSTEMS AND EQUIPMENT: 12V alternator for electrical power supply. Nav/com equipment optional.

DIMENSIONS, EXTERNAL:
As DR 220, except:
Height overall 6 ft 10¾ in (2·10 m)
Wheelbase 5 ft 3 in (1·60 m)
Propeller ground clearance 10¾ in (0·27 m)

WEIGHTS:
Weight empty 1,168 lb (530 kg)
Max T-O weight 1,984 lb (900 kg)

PERFORMANCE (at max T-O weight):
Max level speed at S/L 135 knots (155 mph; 250 km/h)
Max cruising speed 122 knots (140 mph; 225 km/h)
Econ cruising speed 113 knots (130 mph; 210 km/h)
Stalling speed, flaps up 51·5 knots (59 mph; 95 km/h)
Stalling speed, flaps down 46 knots (53 mph; 85 km/h)

Robin (CEA) DR 315 Cadet three/four-seat light aircraft (115 hp Lycoming engine)

Rate of climb at S/L   787 ft (240 m)/min
Service ceiling   15,420 ft (4,700 m)
T-O and landing run   820 ft (250 m)
T-O to, and landing from, 50 ft (15 m)
     1,968 ft (600 m)
Range with max fuel
     593 nm (683 miles; 1,100 km)

ROBIN (CENTRE EST) DR 340 MAJOR

The prototype of the DR 340 (F-WOFP) was flown for the first time on 27 February 1968, and the aircraft entered production shortly afterwards. Five had been completed by mid-July 1968.

The DR 340 is a full four-seater, and is intended as a family touring aircraft. Otherwise, it is generally similar to the DR 253 and DR 315 described earlier, except in the following respects:

TYPE: Four-seat light monoplane.
WINGS: As for DR 253, except for slightly smaller flaps and reduced gross wing area.
TAIL UNIT: As for DR 253.
LANDING GEAR: As for DR 315.
POWER PLANT: One 140/150 hp Lycoming O-320-E four-cylinder horizontally-opposed air-cooled engine, driving a Sensenich two-blade metal fixed-pitch propeller, diameter 6 ft 0 in (1·83 m). Standard fuel capacity of 34 Imp gallons (155 litres) in one fuselage tank and two wing tanks. Provision for auxiliary tank increasing total capacity to 45 Imp gallons (205 litres).
ACCOMMODATION: Seating for four persons, on two side-by-side adjustable front seats and rear bench seat. Up to 88 lb (40 kg) of baggage can be stowed aft of rear seats when four occupants are carried.
DIMENSIONS, EXTERNAL: As for DR 315.
DIMENSIONS, INTERNAL: As for DR 315.
AREAS: As for DR 315, except:
Flaps (total)   7·53 sq ft (0·70 m²)
WEIGHTS AND LOADINGS:
Weight empty, equipped   1,191 lb (540 kg)
Max T-O weight   2 205 lb (1,000 kg)
Max wing loading   14·49 lb/sq ft (70·67 kg/m²)
Max power loading   14·70 lb/hp (6·67 kg/hp)
PERFORMANCE (at max T-O weight):
Max level speed at S/L
     143 knots (165 mph; 265 km/h)
Max permissible diving speed
     158·5 knots (183 mph; 295 km/h)
Max cruising speed (75% power) at S/L
     124 knots (143 mph; 230 km/h)
Max cruising speed (75% power) at 9,000 ft
(2,750 m)   137 knots (158 mph; 255 km/h)
Stalling speed   49 knots (56 mph; 90 km/h)
Rate of climb at S/L   850 ft (260 m)/min
Service ceiling   15,750 ft (4,800 m)
Max range (75% power) at 8,200 ft (2,500 m)
standard fuel   564 nm (650 miles; 1,050 km)
with auxiliary tank
     738 nm (850 miles; 1,370 km)

ROBIN (CENTRE EST) DR 360 CHEVALIER

The Chevalier is, in essence, a de luxe version of the DR 340 Major, with a hardtop cabin and more powerful engine. The prototype DR 360 (F-WOFS) was flown for the first time on 27 March 1968.

The Chevalier's general configuration is similar to that of the DR 340, from which it can be distinguished by its slightly longer nose and larger spinner.

Five DR 360 Chevaliers had been completed by mid-July 1968.

POWER PLANT: One 160 hp Lycoming O-320-D four-cylinder horizontally-opposed air-cooled engine, driving a Sensenich two-blade metal fixed-pitch propeller, diameter 6 ft 0 in (1·83 m). Fuel capacity as for DR 340. Oil capacity 1·66 Imp gallons (7·55 litres).
WEIGHTS AND LOADINGS: As for DR 340 except:
Max power loading   13·78 lb/hp (6·25 kg/hp)
PERFORMANCE (at max T-O weight):
Max level speed at S/L
     146 knots (168 mph; 270 km/h)
Max permissible diving speed
     159 knots (183 mph; 295 km/h)
Max cruising speed (75% power) at S/L
     127 knots (146 mph; 235 km/h)
Max cruising speed (75% power) at 9,000 ft
(2,750 m)   141 knots (162 mph; 260 km/h)
Stalling speed   49 knots (56 mph; 90 km/h)
Rate of climb at S/L   925 ft (282 m)/min
Service ceiling   16,400 ft (5,000 m)
Max cruising range (75% power) at 9,000 ft
(2,750 m), no reserves:
standard fuel   590 nm (680 miles; 1,090 km)
with auxiliary tank
     777 nm (895 miles; 1,440 km)

ROBIN (CENTRE EST) DR 380 PRINCE

First flown on 15 October 1968, the DR 380 is structurally similar to the DR 360 described above, but has a 180 hp Lycoming O-360-D engine, increased weight and performance figures. It was undergoing SGAC certification trials in the Spring of 1969.

WEIGHTS AND LOADINGS:
Weight empty, equipped   1,256 lb (570 kg)
Max T-O weight   2,358 lb (1,070 kg)
Max landing weight   2,248 lb (1,020 kg)
Max wing loading   1·52 lb/sq ft (7·43 kg/m²)

Prototype of the Robin (CEA) DR 330 four-seat light aircraft (130 hp O-240-A engine) (*Air & Cosmos*)

Robin (CEA) DR 340 Major four-seat light aircraft (140 hp Lycoming O-320-E engine) (*N. B. Rivett*)

Robin (CEA) DR 380 Prince prototype (180 hp Lycoming O-360-D engine) (*Kenneth Munson*)

PERFORMANCE (at max T-O weight):
Max level speed at S/L
     151 knots (174 mph; 280 km/h)
Max permissible diving speed
     167 knots (192 mph; 310 km/h)
Max cruising speed (75% power) at 9,000 ft
(2,750 m)   146 knots (168 mph; 270 km/h)
Max cruising speed (75% power) at S/L
     130 knots (150 mph; 240 km/h)
Rate of climb at S/L   1,043 ft (318 m)/min
Max cruising range (75% power), no reserves:
standard fuel   590 nm (680 miles; 1,090 km)
with auxiliary tank
     777 nm (895 miles; 1,440 km)

ROBIN (CENTRE EST) HR 100

Some years ago Avions Pierre Robin began studies with a view to the eventual production of an all-metal light aircraft similar in concept to its present range of wood-and-fabric designs. As a part of this programme, the prototype DR 253 Régent was flown late in 1967 with all-metal wings, and construction of an all-metal prototype aircraft was begun in 1968. This was known originally as the HR 1, the letters in the designation representing its chief designer, M Heintz, and M Pierre Robin.

The prototype (F-WPXO) was later redesignated HR 100, and flew for the first time on 3 April 1969. In the Spring of 1970 three pre-production aircraft were under construction. Initially these are being fitted with 180 hp four-cylinder engines, for comparative trials with other Robin aircraft of the same power, but production HR 100s will have 200 hp or 260 hp Lycoming IO-540 six-cylinder fuel-injection engines and Hartzell two-blade variable-pitch propellers.

The following details apply to the first prototype HR 100:

TYPE: Four-seat light aircraft.

WINGS: Cantilever low-wing monoplane. Wing section NACA 64 series (modified), with max thickness at 45% chord. Constant chord over most of span, increasing at leading-edge roots. Thickness/chord ratio 15%. Dihedral 6° from roots. No sweepback. All-metal single-spar structure, attached to fuselage by four bolts on each side. Outer skin of flush-riveted Duralinox-Cégédur aluminium alloy. Wing-tips, which incorporate navigation and landing lights, are of polyester. All-metal triple-hinged trailing-edge flaps are actuated electrically and have a max setting of 60°. All-metal mass-balanced ailerons each have a piano-type hinge on the upper surface; they are controlled by rods and cables.

FUSELAGE: All-metal box-girder load-bearing structure, covered mainly with flush-riveted Duralinox-Cégédur aluminium alloy. Top-decking, between engine firewall and front of cabin, and from rear of cabin to fin, is of polyester; the forward panels are removable to provide easy access to instruments and controls.

TAIL UNIT: Cantilever structure, of similar construction to wings, with slight sweepback on fin and rudder. One-piece single-spar all-moving tailplane, with mass-balance and anti-tab. Rudder and tailplane cable-controlled.

LANDING GEAR: Non-retractable tricycle type, with Jodel-Beaune oleo-pneumatic shock-absorbers. Nose-wheel leg is offset to starboard. Single wheel on each unit, all wheels and tyres same size, 420 × 150. Streamlined leg and wheel fairings on all units. Hydraulic disc brakes.

POWER PLANT: One 180 hp Lycoming four-cylinder horizontally-opposed air-cooled engine, driving a two-blade fixed-pitch propeller.

Fuel in two 22 Imp gallon (100 litre) flexible tanks in each leading-edge; total capacity of 88 Imp gallons (400 litres). Refuelling points above each tank.

ACCOMMODATION: Seating for four persons, in pairs, under transparent canopy which slides forward to provide access to all seats. Individual adjustable front seats; bench seat at rear. Baggage space aft of rear seats, accessible internally or by upward-opening external door on port side. Cabin ventilated.

ELECTRONICS AND EQUIPMENT: VHF radio, VOR navigation and landing lights, and rotating anti-collision beacon standard. Provision for installing full IFR equipment, including autopilot.

DIMENSIONS, EXTERNAL:
Wing span	32 ft 9¾ in (10·00 m)
Wing chord (constant)	5 ft 3 in (1·60 m)
Wing aspect ratio	6·1
Length overall	24 ft 3¼ in (7·40 m)
Height overall	7 ft 6½ in (2·30 m)
Tailplane span	10 ft 6 in (3·20 m)
Wheel track	10 ft 6 in (3·20 m)
Wheelbase	5 ft 9 in (1·75 m)

AREAS:
Wings, gross	176·53 sq ft (16·40 m²)
Ailerons (total)	13·89 sq ft (1·29 m²)
Flaps (total)	12·70 sq ft (1·18 m²)
Horizontal tail surfaces (total)	32·72 sq ft (3·04 m²)

WEIGHTS AND LOADINGS:
Weight empty	1,873 lb (850 kg)
Max T-O weight	3,086 lb (1,400 kg)
Max wing loading	17·50 lb/sq ft (85·37 kg/m²)
Max power loading	17·15 lb/hp (7·78 kg/hp)

PERFORMANCE (at max T-O weight):
Cruising speed at 8,000 ft (2,440 m)
162 knots (186 mph; 300 km)
Fuel consumption 11·7 Imp gal/hr (53 litres/hr)
Max range, zero wind, normal reserves
over 1,080 nm (1,245 miles; 2,000 km)
Max endurance   7 hr 30 min

ROBIN (JODEL) D.140E MOUSQUETAIRE IV

The Mousquetaire was developed by the former Société Aéronautique Normande as an economical four-seat light aeroplane for touring or club use, but can be used also as an ambulance for one stretcher patient. The stretcher is loaded easily through the large baggage door on the port side of the fuselage aft of the cabin.

The prototype Mousquetaire flew for the first time on 4 July 1958, and the first production model on 1 November 1958.

The Mousquetaire was built by SAN in eight versions, as described in the 1969-70 edition of *Jane's*.

The latest versions are:

D.140E Mousquetaire IV. Vertical tail surfaces of increased area, all-moving tailplane with anti-tab, increased wing and flap area and improved ailerons. Total of 35 built up to 31 December 1967; subsequent production included 18 for *l'Ecole de l'Air*. Details below apply to this version. When fitted with further-improved ailerons is known as **D.140E1.**

D.140R Abeille. Developed version of D.140E with further modifications to tail surfaces and cabin. Described separately.

TYPE: Four/five-seat cabin lightplane.

WINGS: Cantilever low-wing monoplane. Wing section NACA 23015. Dihedral on outer wings 20°. Incidence 3° 30'. Wings, ailerons and flaps of wood construction with fabric covering.

FUSELAGE: Conventional plywood-covered wooden structure.

TAIL UNIT: Conventional cantilever wood structure with slight sweepback on vertical surfaces. Large trim-tab on port elevator. Ground-adjustable tab on rudder.

LANDING GEAR: Non-retractable type with steerable tail-wheel. Cantilever main units have Silentbloc-Jodel rubber-block shock-absorbers, 500 × 150 wheels and hydraulic brakes. Wheel fairings standard.

POWER PLANT: One 180 hp Lycoming O-360-A2A four-cylinder horizontally-opposed air-cooled engine, driving an EVRA two-blade fixed-pitch wooden propeller. Optional metal constant-speed propeller. Fuel capacity 48·4 Imp gallons (220 litres). Provision for auxiliary fuel tank forward of cabin. Oil capacity 2 Imp gallons (9 litres).

ACCOMMODATION: Two individual front seats, with optional dual controls. Rear bench seat for two or three persons. Entry through canopy side panels which hinge upward on centre-line. Heating and ventilation. Large baggage locker (25 cu ft = 0·70 m³) aft of cabin,

Robin Jodel D.140E Mousquetaire IV four/five-seat light aircraft (180 hp Lycoming O-360-A2A engine)

Robin D.140R Abeille four-seat light aircraft, developed from the Mousquetaire (*Howard Levy*)

Prototype of the Robin HR 100 four-seat all-metal light aircraft (*Howard Levy*)

with upward-hinged door, can be utilised to carry a stretcher in ambulance rôle. Small locker (10 cu ft = 0·28 m³) forward of cabin can be used for baggage, auxiliary fuel tank, emergency equipment or ballast when CG is in aft position. Max baggage capacity 210 lb (96 kg). Baggage capacity with five passengers 44 lb (20 kg).

ELECTRONICS AND EQUIPMENT: Optional equipment includes VHF radio, VOR, radio-compass and full blind-flying instrumentation.

DIMENSIONS, EXTERNAL:
Wing span	33 ft 8¼ in (10·27 m)
Length overall	25 ft 8 in (7·82 m)
Height overall	6 ft 9 in (2·05 m)

AREA:
Wings, gross	199·13 sq ft (18·50 m²)

WEIGHTS AND LOADINGS:
Weight empty	1,367 lb (620 kg)
Max T-O weight	2,645 lb (1,200 kg)
Max wing loading	13·3 lb/sq ft (65 kg/m²)
Max power loading	14·77 lb/hp (6·7 kg/hp)

PERFORMANCE (at max T-O weight):
Max level speed at S/L
137 knots (158 mph; 255 km/h)
Max cruising speed (75% power) at 7,000 ft
(2,300 m)   129 knots (149 mph; 240 km/h)

Econ cruising speed at 9,000 ft (2,750 m)
109 knots (125 mph; 200 km/h)
Rate of climb at S/L   750 ft (230 m)/min
Service ceiling   16,400 ft (5,000 m)
T-O to 50 ft (15 m)   1,000 ft (305 m)
Range with max fuel
755 nm (870 miles; 1,400 km)

ROBIN (JODEL) D.140R ABEILLE

First flown in mid-1965, the D.140R Abeille is a version of the D.140E developed specially for glider and banner towing.

New features include a more extensively-glazed cabin to improve rearward view. Skis can be fitted for operation from snow in mountainous areas.

Specification details are generally similar to those for the D.140E Mousquetaire, except that the Abeille has an empty weight of 1,408 lb (639 kg), max and cruising speeds of 135 knots (155 mph; 250 km/h) and 122 knots (140 mph; 225 km/h) respectively, and a service ceiling of 16,725 ft (5,100 m).

Production of the Abeille began in 1966. Initial orders included one from the *Armee de l'Air* for a number of Abeilles to equip its gliding clubs. A total of 20 had been built up to the end of 1967.

SAN
SOCIÉTÉ AÉRONAUTIQUE NORMANDE

This company was established in 1948 by the late Lucien Querey. Its products included the two-seat Jodel D.150 Mascaret, the four/five-seat Jodel D.140 Mousquetaire and the developed D.140R Abeille.

The company went into liquidation early in 1969. Outstanding contracts are being completed at Beynes by C.A.A.R.P. (which see), and new orders by Avions Pierre Robin, which has acquired licences to build the former SAN-Jodel range of aircraft.

SIPA
SOCIÉTÉ NOUVELLE INDUSTRIELLE POUR L'AÉRONAUTIQUE

This company was formed in 1938. Until 1940 it was engaged in the manufacture of parts and components for aircraft designed by other companies; but since the war it has built many training and light aircraft to its own designs.

SIPA ceased operations on 31 July 1969. The activities upon which it was engaged immediately prior to that date were described in the 1969-70 *Jane's*. They have been taken over by SEMM, a subsidiary of Aérospatiale (which see).

SITAR
SOCIÉTÉ INDUSTRIELLE DE TÔLERIE POUR L'AÉRONAUTIQUE ET MATÉRIEL ROULANT

HEAD OFFICE AND WORKS:
  Zone Industrielle "La Saunière", 89-Saint-Florentin (Yonne)
GENERAL MANAGER:
  Yves Gardan
PRODUCTION MANAGER:
  René Ricordeau

This company is responsible for manufacture of the latest range of light aircraft designed by M Yves Gardan, well known for such earlier types as the SIPA Minicab and Minijet, and for the GY 80 Horizon later produced by Socata (which see). The factory has a floor area of 26,900 sq ft (2,500 m²).

Gardan designs at present being produced by SITAR include the GY 100 Bagheera, GY 110 Sher Khan and GY 90 Mowgli, all of which are described below.

It was reported early in 1969 that the company was also contemplating the development of an all-metal two-seat aerobatic aircraft; and that it was acquiring a single-seat Bücker Jungmeister and a two-seat Jungmann, in which it was proposing to install 200 hp Lycoming fuel-injection engines.

GARDAN GY 100 BAGHEERA

The GY 100 can be operated either as a "2+2" seater for training, or as a three/four-seat touring aircraft. It is aerobatic as a two-seater.

The prototype (F-WOFO), which flew for the first time on 21 December 1967, is powered by a 150 hp Lycoming O-320 engine (derated to 135 hp) and completed its manufacturer's and official flight test programme by the beginning of June 1968. Production began in September 1968, and first deliveries were made in March 1969. It was planned to achieve an output of ten aircraft a month by the end of 1969.

TYPE: Three/four-seat light aircraft.
WINGS: Cantilever low-wing monoplane. Each wing is a separate all-metal single-spar structure, attached to side of fuselage, with constant chord except at leading-edge roots, which are extended forwards. Dihedral 6° from wing-roots. Slotted flaps and ailerons. Wash-out at wing-tips.
FUSELAGE: All-metal semi-monocoque stressed-skin structure. Welded chrome-molybdenum steel-tube engine mounting. Engine cowling of reinforced plastics. Steel-tube overturn structure.
TAIL UNIT: Conventional single fin and rudder, of all-metal construction, with sweepback on both surfaces and tab in rudder. Rectangular one-piece horizontal surfaces, incorporating anti-tab.
LANDING GEAR: Non-retractable tricycle type, with cantilever legs of high-tensile steel and oleo-pneumatic shock-absorbers. Single wheel on each unit. Steerable nose-wheel, linked to rudder bar. All wheels and tyres same size, 380 × 150. Hydraulic disc brakes on main units. Parking brake fitted. Wheel fairings optional.
POWER PLANT (full four-seater): One 150 hp Lycoming O-320-E four-cylinder horizontally-opposed air-cooled engine, derated to 135 hp and driving a two-blade fixed-pitch metal propeller of 6 ft 2 in (1·88 m) diameter. Fuel in two main tanks with total capacity of 33 Imp gallons (150 litres).
POWER PLANT (three/four-seater): One 115 hp Lycoming O-235-C four-cylinder horizontally-opposed air-cooled engine. Propeller and fuel details as above.
ACCOMMODATION: Side-by-side adjustable seats for two persons in front of cabin, with bench seat to rear which will seat two additional passengers. Seat-belts standard. Forward-opening car-type door on starboard side. Dual controls, windshield demisting, cabin heating and ventilation standard.
SYSTEMS: Electrical system includes generator and battery.
ELECTRONICS AND EQUIPMENT: Optional equipment includes VHF radio, VOR, ADF, full blind-flying instrumentation, landing and navigation lights and rotating beacon.

Gardan GY 100 Bagheera four-seat light aircraft (150 hp Lycoming O-320 engine)

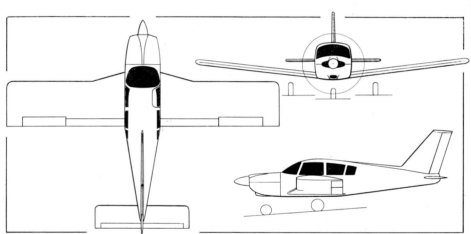

Gardan GY 110 Sher Khan four-seat light aircraft

DIMENSIONS, EXTERNAL:
Wing span	26 ft 10⅞ in (8·20 m)
Wing chord (constant)	4 ft 10¼ in (1·48 m)
Wing aspect ratio	5·5
Length overall	20 ft 0 in (6·10 m)
Height overall	6 ft 6¾ in (2·00 m)
Wheel track	6 ft 7½ in (2·02 m)
Wheelbase	5 ft 3 in (1·60 m)

DIMENSIONS, INTERNAL:
Cabin: Max length	7 ft 2⅝ in (2·20 m)
Max width	3 ft 8 in (1·12 m)
Max height	3 ft 11½ in (1·21 m)

AREA:
Wings, gross	131·32 sq ft (12·20 m²)

WEIGHTS AND LOADINGS:
Weight empty:	
115 hp	1,058 lb (480 kg)
135 hp	1,102 lb (500 kg)
Max T-O weight:	
115 hp	1,851 lb (840 kg)
135 hp	2,023 lb (918 kg)
Max wing loading:	
115 hp	12·4 lb/sq ft (60·6 kg/m²)
135 hp	15·4 lb/sq ft (75·2 kg/m²)
Max power loading:	
115 hp	16·09 lb/hp (7·30 kg/hp)
135 hp	14·99 lb/hp (6·80 kg/hp)

PERFORMANCE (at max T-O weight):
Max level speed at S/L:	
115 hp	119 knots (137 mph; 220 km/h)
135 hp	127 knots (146 mph; 235 km/h)
Cruising speed at S/L:	
115 hp	105 knots (121 mph; 195 km/h)
135 hp	112 knots (129 mph; 207 km/h)
Cruising speed at 5,000 ft (1,500 m):	
115 hp	112 knots (129 mph; 207 km/h)
135 hp	122 knots (140 mph; 225 km/h)

Stalling speed:	
115 hp	43·2 knots (49·7 mph; 80 km/h)
135 hp	46 knots (52·8 mph; 85 km/h)
Rate of climb at S/L:	
115 hp	640 ft (195 m)/min
135 hp	785 ft (240 m)/min
Service ceiling:	
115 hp	9,850 ft (3,000 m)
135 hp	12,450 ft (3,800 m)
T-O run (115 and 135 hp)	490 ft (150 m)
Landing run:	
115 hp	260 ft (80 m)
135 hp	295 ft (90 m)
Max range:	
115 hp	499 nm (575 miles; 930 km)
135 hp	525 nm (605 miles; 980 km)

GY 110 SHER KHAN

The GY 110 is essentially an enlarged and more powerful development of the GY 100, with full seating for four adult passengers and a retractable tricycle landing gear. The wing span and fuselage length are increased, and the GY 110 can be fitted with engines in the 200-300 hp range.

The main features of the GY 110 can be seen in the adjacent three-view drawing.

GARDAN GY 90 MOWGLI

The GY 90 is a smaller, simplified development of the GY 100, seating only two persons side-by-side. It is intended primarily for amateur construction, and can be powered by either a 90 hp or 100 hp Continental flat-four engine. It is of all-metal construction, and is available in the form of plans or kits. There is space behind the seats for 42 lb (19 kg) of baggage.

Transfer of the company's activities to new premises had the effect of delaying the development of this aircraft, but the first amateur-built GY 90 was expected to be completed and flown during 1970.

DIMENSIONS, EXTERNAL:

Wing span	23 ft 7½ in (7·20 m)
Wing aspect ratio	5·2

AREA:

Wings, gross	107·64 sq ft (10·00 m²)

WEIGHTS AND LOADINGS (with 90 hp engine):

Weight empty	840 lb (380 kg)
Max T-O weight	1,390 lb (630 kg)
Wing loading	12·92 lb/sq ft (63 kg/m²)
Power loading	15·43 lb/hp (7 kg/hp)

PERFORMANCE (at max T-O weight, 90 hp engine):

Max level speed at S/L	122 knots (140 mph; 225 km/h)
Cruising speed (75% power)	113 knots (130 mph; 210 km/h)
Rate of climb at S/L	787 ft (240 m)/min
Service ceiling	13,120 ft (4,000 m)
Range	431 nm (497 miles; 800 km)

SOCATA
SOCIÉTÉ DE CONSTRUCTION D'AVIONS DE TOURISME ET D'AFFAIRES (Subsidiary of AÉROSPATIALE)

HEAD OFFICE AND WORKS:
65-Aéroport de Tarbes-Ossun

SALES AND SERVICE CENTRE:
78-Toussus-le-Noble

CHAIRMAN:
Robert Lecamus

SALES DIRECTOR AND PUBLIC RELATIONS:
Lucien Tielès

This company was formed in 1966, as a subsidiary of Sud-Aviation, to undertake development and production of all the Group's light and business aircraft. Main types in the current range are the various versions of the Horizon and Rallye three/four-seat light aircraft, the four-seat ST 10 Diplomate and the seven-seat Rallye 7-300.

During 1969, Socata sold 383 aircraft of all types, approximately 55 per cent of them for export.

Socata also produces wings for the CM 170 Magister jet trainer and components for the Super Frelon helicopter and Mystère 20/Falcon business jet. It is responsible for overhaul and repair of MS 760 Paris and Dassault Flamant aircraft.

In 1970, Socata's works covered an area of 475,230 sq ft (44,150 m²) and employed about 1,000 people.

SOCATA RALLYE-CLUB, RALLYE COMMODORE AND RALLYE MINERVA

The Rallye had its origin in a competition organised by the SFATAT in 1958 and was developed originally by the old-established Morane-Saulnier company. The prototype (90 hp MS 880A) Rallye-Club flew on 10 June 1959, and went into production as the MS 880B and the MS 885 Super Rallye. FAA certification of the design was obtained on 21 November 1961.

Production of the MS 885 (212 built) with 145 hp Continental engine, MS 881 (12 built) with 105 hp Potez engine and MS 886 (3 built) with 150 hp Lycoming engine has ended. Current production versions of the Rallye are as follows:

MS 880B Rallye-Club. Basic 3/4-seat model with 100 hp Rolls-Royce/Continental O-200-A engine. Prototype flew on 12 February 1961. Production of a new series, with improved brakes and more comfortable cabin, was started in 1966. Rate of production 11 per month. Total of 472 built by early 1970.

MS 883 Rallye 115, with 115 hp Lycoming O-235 engine, was flown for the first time on 10 December 1968. Certificated by SGAC on 30 April 1969.

MS 884 Rallye-Minerva 125. Generally similar to MS 880B, but powered by 125 hp Franklin 4A-235 four-cylinder horizontally-opposed air-cooled engine. To be marketed in the USA as the **Waco Minerva 125.** Prototype shown at 1967 Paris Air Show. Five built by early 1970; certification in progress.

MS 892 Rallye Commodore 150. Four-seat version with 150 hp Lycoming O-320-E2A engine, strengthened structure for increased AUW, larger rudder, larger ailerons, fillets of increased size between wing trailing-edges and fuselage, longer nose-wheel leg to give increased propeller clearance, and a luggage compartment. Prototype flew for the first time on 13 February 1964. Rate of production of the Rallye Commodore 150 and 180 is 13 aircraft a month. Rallye Commodore 150 production had reached 214 by early 1970.

MS 893 Rallye Commodore 180. Basically similar to MS 892, but with 180 hp Lycoming O-360-A2A engine, giving extra power for duties such as agricultural spraying and dusting, glider and banner towing. Prototype flew for first time on 7 December 1964. Type approval received on 27 April 1965. Thirty ordered by the SFA for duty as glider tugs at French gliding centres. Glass-fibre wheel fairings, developed as an optional extra in 1966, give a 7·8 knot (9 mph; 15 km/h) increase in max level speed, to 132 knots (152 mph; 245 km/h). Total of 232 built by early 1970.

MS 893 Agricorallye. This is the Rallye Commodore 180 equipped for agricultural duties. Alternative equipment includes Micronair spray-gear and Sorensen dusting installation, in each case with a centre-fuselage chemical hopper of 68 Imp gallons (310 litres) capacity.

MS 894A Rallye Minerva 220. Generally similar to MS 893, but with 220 hp Franklin 6A-350-C1 six-cylinder horizontally-opposed air-cooled engine. Being marketed in the USA by Allied Aero Industries as the **Waco Minerva 220.** Prototype first flown on 12 May 1967. Received FAA Type Approval 29 April 1968. Forty-four built by early 1970. Version with wheel-ski landing gear (**MS 894C,** F-WPXP).

All versions are authorised for use as ambulance aircraft carrying a pilot, one stretcher patient and medical attendant. The MS 892 and 893 can be used for glider towing. Agricultural spray-gear can be fitted and tests have been conducted with various models on ski landing gear.

The 1970 models of the Rallye Commodore have a number of refinements, including a more sloping windscreen, a larger canopy of better aerodynamic form, a cut-back fuselage to improve access to the rear seats, adjustable front seats, a longer dorsal fin carrying the rear canopy rail, and redesigned (optional) wheel fairings.

The 1,000th Rallye, an MS 893 Rallye Commodore 180, was delivered on 10 May 1968; approx 55 per cent of all Rallyes built have been exported, and the total number delivered by 1 January 1970 was 1,378. Of these, some 250 are employed in the glider-towing role, including over 100 in France.

The following details apply to all versions listed above:

Socata MS 883 Rallye 115 (115 hp Lycoming O-235 four-cylinder engine)

Socata Rallye Minerva three/four-seat light monoplane fitted with ski landing gear

MS 893 Rallye Commodore 180 light aircraft (180 hp Lycoming O-360-A2A engine)

TYPE: Three/four-seat light monoplane.

WINGS: Cantilever mid-wing monoplane. Wing section NACA 63A416 (modified). Dihedral 12° 30′. Incidence 4°. All-metal single-spar structure. Wide-chord slotted ailerons. Full-span automatic slats. Long-span slotted flaps. Ailerons and flaps have corrugated metal skin.

FUSELAGE: All-metal monocoque structure.

TAIL UNIT: Cantilever all-metal structure with corrugated skin on the mass-balanced control surfaces. Large trim-tab on elevator.

LANDING GEAR: Non-retractable tricycle type. ERAM oleo-pneumatic shock-absorbers. Castoring nose-wheel. Toe-brakes. Provision for fitting skis or floats.

POWER PLANT: One 4/6-cylinder horizontally-opposed air-cooled engine (details under entries for individual models above), driving a two-blade fixed-pitch metal propeller. Fuel in two tanks in wings, capacity 23 Imp gallons (104 litres) in MS 880B, 37·5 Imp gallons (170 litres) in MS 892 and 48·5 Imp gallons (220 litres) in MS 893. Oil capacity 1·20 Imp gallons (5·0 litres) in MS 880B, 1·75 Imp gallons (8 litres) in other versions.

ACCOMMODATION: Two seats side-by-side in front and bench seat at rear, under large rearward-sliding canopy. Two persons up to a total weight of 242 lb (110 kg) can occupy rear seat of MS 880B; MS 892, 893 and 894A are full four-seaters. Dual controls. Heating and ventilation standard.

ELECTRONICS: VHF radio and Radiostal direction finder optional.

DIMENSIONS, EXTERNAL:
- Wing span: 31 ft 5 in (9·60 m)
- Wing chord (constant): 4 ft 3 in (1·30 m)
- Wing aspect ratio: 7·57
- Length overall:
  - MS 880B: 22 ft $10\frac{1}{2}$ in (6·97 m)
  - MS 892, 893: 23 ft $4\frac{3}{4}$ in (7·13 m)
  - MS 883, 894A: 23 ft $5\frac{3}{4}$ in (7·16 m)
- Height overall:
  - MS 880B, 883: 8 ft $6\frac{1}{4}$ in (2·60 m)
  - MS 892, 893, 894A: 9 ft $2\frac{1}{4}$ in (2·80 m)
- Tailplane span: 10 ft $3\frac{1}{2}$ in (3·13 m)
- Wheel track: 6 ft $6\frac{1}{2}$ in (2·00 m)

DIMENSIONS, INTERNAL:
- Cabin:
  - Length: 7 ft 4 in (2·25 m)
  - Width: 3 ft $8\frac{1}{2}$ in (1·13 m)

AREAS:
- Wings, gross: 132 sq ft (12·28 m²)
- Vertical tail surfaces: 14·96 sq ft (1·39 m²)
- Horizontal tail surfaces: 37·50 sq ft (3·48 m²)

WEIGHTS:
- Weight empty, equipped:
  - MS 880B: 992 lb (450 kg)
  - MS 883: 1,157 lb (525 kg)
  - MS 892: 1,180 lb (535 kg)
  - MS 893: 1,224 lb (555 kg)
  - MS 894A: 1,355 lb (615 kg)
- Max T-O weight:
  - MS 880B: 1,697 lb (770 kg)
  - MS 883: 1,829 lb (830 kg)
  - MS 892: 2,160 lb (980 kg)
  - MS 893: 2,315 lb (1,050 kg)
  - MS 894A: 2,425 lb (1,100 kg)

PERFORMANCE (at max T-O weight):
- Max level speed at S/L:
  - MS 880B: 105 knots (121 mph; 195 km/h)
  - MS 883: 108 knots (124 mph; 200 km/h)
  - MS 892: 113 knots (130 mph; 210 km/h)
  - MS 893: 123 knots (142 mph; 228 km/h)
  - MS 894A: 143 knots (165 mph; 265 km/h)
- Cruising speed (75% power) at 5,000 ft (1,500 m):
  - MS 880B: 93 knots (108 mph; 173 km/h)
  - MS 883: 102 knots (118 mph; 190 km/h)
  - MS 892: 108 knots (124 mph; 200 km/h)
  - MS 893: 122 knots (140 mph; 226 km/h)
  - MS 894A: 135 knots (155 mph; 249 km/h)
- Stalling speed, flaps down:
  - MS 892: 49 knots (56 mph; 90 km/h)
  - MS 893: 51 knots (58 mph; 93 km/h)
  - MS 894A: 52 knots (59·5 mph; 95 km/h)
- Landing speed:
  - MS 880B: 38 knots (44 mph; 70 km/h)
  - MS 892: 44 knots (50 mph; 80 km/h)
  - MS 894A: 44 knots (50 mph; 80 km/h)
- Max rate of climb at S/L:
  - MS 880B: 530 ft (162 m)/min
  - MS 883: 590 ft (180 m)/min
  - MS 892: 630 ft (192 m)/min
  - MS 893: 730 ft (222 m)/min
  - MS 894A: 1,015 ft (310 m)/min
- Service ceiling:
  - MS 880B: 10,500 ft (3,200 m)
  - MS 892: 9,200 ft (2,800 m)
  - MS 893: 12,800 ft (3,900 m)
  - MS 894A: 16,400 ft (5,000 m)
- T-O run:
  - MS 880B: 430 ft (130 m)
  - MS 892: 459 ft (140 m)
  - MS 893: 443 ft (135 m)
  - MS 894A: 393 ft (120 m)

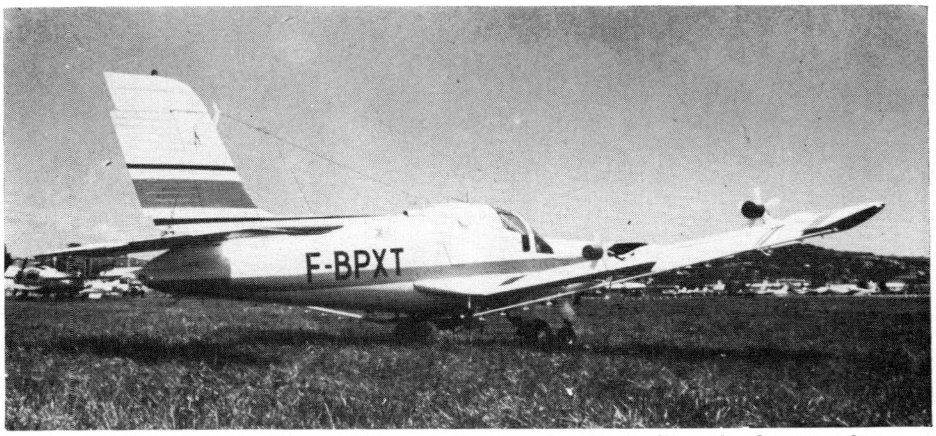

Socata MS 894A Rallye Minerva 220, agricultural version fitted with underwing spray-bars

- T-O to 50 ft (15 m):
  - MS 880B: 1,280 ft (390 m)
  - MS 892: 1,295 ft (395 m)
  - MS 894A: 985 ft (300 m)
- Landing from 50 ft (15 m):
  - MS 880B: 770 ft (235 m)
- Landing run:
  - MS 880B, 883, 894A: 328 ft (100 m)
  - MS 892, 893: 410 ft (125 m)
- Range with max fuel:
  - MS 880B: 460 nm (530 miles; 850 km)
  - MS 883: 780 nm (900 miles; 1,450 km)
  - MS 892, 893: 540 nm (620 miles; 1,000 km)
  - MS 894A: 878 nm (1,012 miles; 1,630 km)

SOCATA ST 60 RALLYE 7-300

As is evident from the adjacent illustrations, the Rallye 7-300 differs considerably from other Rallye models in current production and service. In particular, the centre portion of the fuselage is entirely new, and now embodies a cabin accommodating a pilot and up to six passengers. A new wing centre-section, of increased chord, has been added, and the landing gear is retractable.

A prototype of the Rallye 7-300 (F-BPXN) was flown for the first time on 3 January 1969. The description below applies to the production version.

TYPE: Seven-seat light utility transport.

WINGS: Cantilever low-wing monoplane. All-metal wings of single-spar construction, with three-point attachment to fuselage on each side. Main spar bolt-jointed at centre-section. Constant chord on outer panels, increased chord on inboard leading- and trailing-edges. Full-span all-metal cable-controlled ailerons and inner and outer slotted trailing-edge flaps. Three-section slat on each leading-edge, over nearly whole of span.

FUSELAGE: Conventional all-metal semi-monocoque structure, built in two main sections.

TAIL UNIT: Conventional all-metal structure, with moderately sweptback vertical surfaces and constant-chord non-swept horizontal surfaces. Variable-incidence tailplane. Rudder

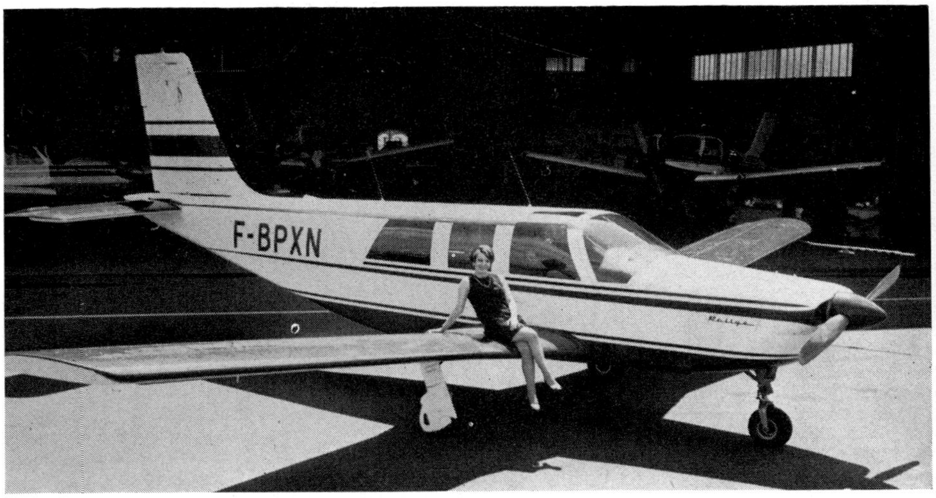

Prototype Socata ST 60 Rallye 7-300 seven-seat light aircraft

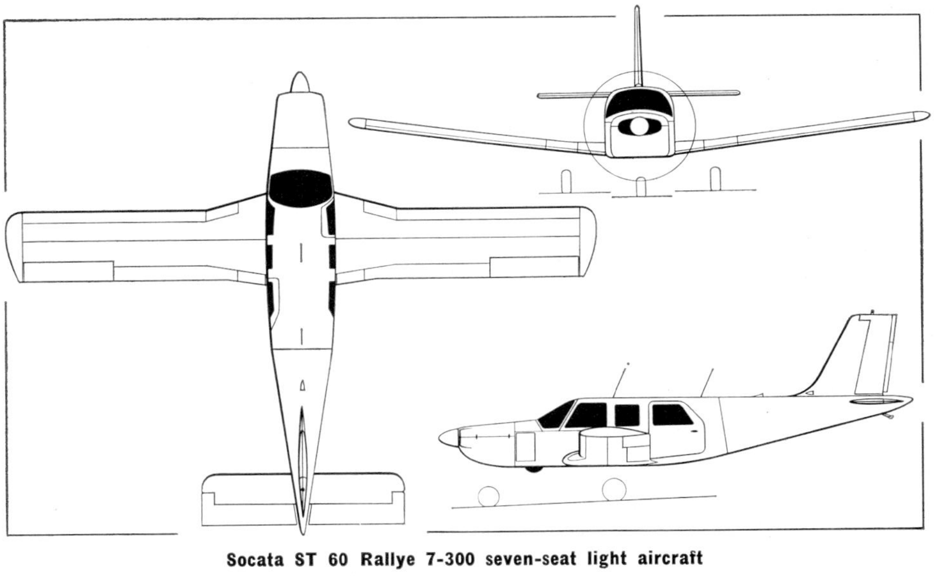

Socata ST 60 Rallye 7-300 seven-seat light aircraft

and elevators mass-balanced. Trim-tab on rudder.

LANDING GEAR: Retractable tricycle type, with single wheel and oleo-pneumatic shock absorber on each unit. All units retract electrically, nose-wheel rearward to lie semi-recessed in fuselage, main wheels inward into wings. Main-wheel tyres, size 440 × 155, pressure 40 lb/sq in (2·80 kg/cm²). Nose-wheel tyre, size 370 × 155, pressure 26 lb/sq in (1·80 kg/cm²). Hydraulic disc brakes on main wheels. Nose-wheel steerable.

POWER PLANT: One 300 hp Lycoming IO-540-K six-cylinder horizontally-opposed air-cooled fuel-injection engine, driving a Hartzell two-blade variable-pitch metal propeller of 6 ft 9¾ in (2·08 m) diameter. Fuel in two main leading-edge tanks and two smaller wing centre-section tanks, with total capacity of 70·4 Imp gallons (320 litres). Refuelling point above each outer wing panel.

ACCOMMODATION: Fully-enclosed cabin with side-by-side seating for two pilots, or one pilot and one passenger, in front. Aft of these seats are a bench seat for three persons, and two separate, staggered seats at the rear. Access to the front and centre seats is by a forward-opening car-type door over the wing on the starboard side; access to rear seats and baggage compartment by a similar door to the rear of the wing on the port side. The rear door has no threshold, to facilitate loading of bulky freight into the flat-floor cabin when the passenger seats are removed. Entire accommodation air-conditioned.

ELECTRONICS AND EQUIPMENT: Prototype equipped with two VHF radios, one VOR, anti-collision beacon and tail navigation light.

DIMENSIONS, EXTERNAL:	
Wing span	36 ft 1 in (11·00 m)
Length overall	28 ft 8½ in (8·75 m)
Height overall	9 ft 2¼ in (2·80 m)
Tailplane span	12 ft 5½ in (3·80 m)
Wheel track	9 ft 2¾ in (2·81 m)
Wheelbase	7 ft 8½ in (2·35 m)
Cabin door (port, rear):	
Height	3 ft 5¼ in (1·05 m)
Width	3 ft 5¾ in (1·06 m)
DIMENSIONS, INTERNAL:	
Cabin: Length	11 ft 9¾ in (3·60 m)
Max width	4 ft 0½ in (1·23 m)
Max height	4 ft 2½ in (1·28 m)
AREAS:	
Wings, gross	165·8 sq ft (15·40 m²)
Ailerons (total)	18·62 sq ft (1·73 m²)
Trailing-edge flaps (total)	25·73 sq ft (2·39 m²)
Fin	9·36 sq ft (0·87 m²)
Rudder, including tab	10·76 sq ft (1·00 m²)
Horizontal tail surfaces (total)	41·55 sq ft (3·86 m²)
WEIGHTS:	
Weight empty	1,962 lb (890 kg)
Max T-O weight	3,946 lb (1,790 kg)
PERFORMANCE (at max T-O weight):	
Max level speed at S/L	162 knots (186 mph; 300 km/h)
Cruising speed (75% power)	151 knots (174 mph; 280 km/h)
Stalling speed, flaps down	54 knots (62 mph; 100 km/h)
Max rate of climb at S/L	985 ft (300 m)/min
Service ceiling	16,400 ft (5,000 m)
T-O run	656 ft (200 m)
Landing run	492 ft (150 m)
Range with max fuel	807 nm (930 miles; 1,500 km)
Endurance	5 hr

SOCATA GY-80 HORIZON

On 10 July 1962, Sud-Aviation obtained the licence to build and market the four-seat all-metal GY-80 Horizon from M Yves Gardan.

The prototype Horizon flew for the first time on 21 July 1960, and was followed by three pre-production models. A total of 260 Horizons were built.

A full description of the Horizon appeared in the 1969-70 edition of *Jane's*.

SOCATA ST 10 DIPLOMATE

The ST 10 was designed by Socata and is based on a certain number of components common to the GY-80 Horizon, from which it differs chiefly in having a longer fuselage and redesigned cabin. A prototype (F-WOFR), known for a time as the Provence, was flown for the first time on 7 November 1967.

Early in 1969, it was modified to flight test refinements that will be standard on production aircraft, including a longer fuselage, a reduction in tailplane span, an increase in rudder area and a shallow "keel" beneath the rear fuselage. In this form the Diplomate received type approval by the SGAC on 26 November 1969.

TYPE: Four-seat light cabin monoplane.

WINGS: Cantilever low-wing monoplane. Wing section NACA 4413-6 (modified) at root and NACA 62A-517 (modified) at tip. Dihedral 7°. Incidence 5° at root, 2° 30′ at tip. All-metal single-spar structure with rear auxiliary spar. Entire trailing-edge made up of two Frise-type slotted ailerons and four electrically-operated Fowler flaps of all-metal construction. Ailerons and flaps are all interchangeable.

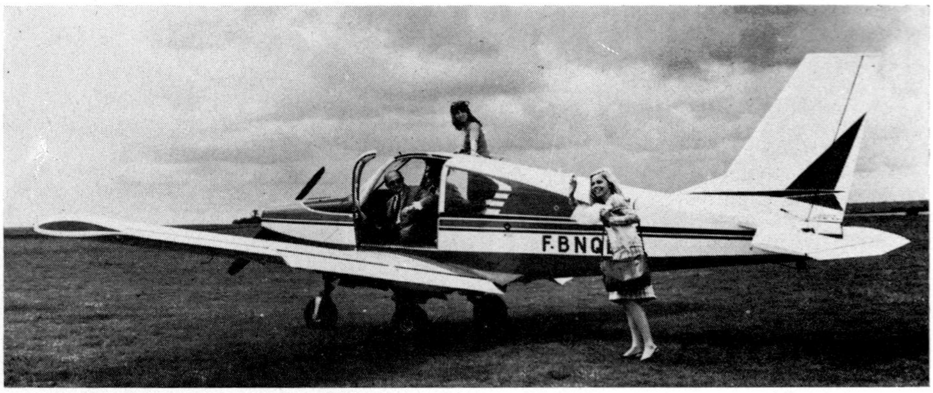

Socata GY-80 Horizon four-seat light monoplane with 180 hp Lycoming O-360-A engine

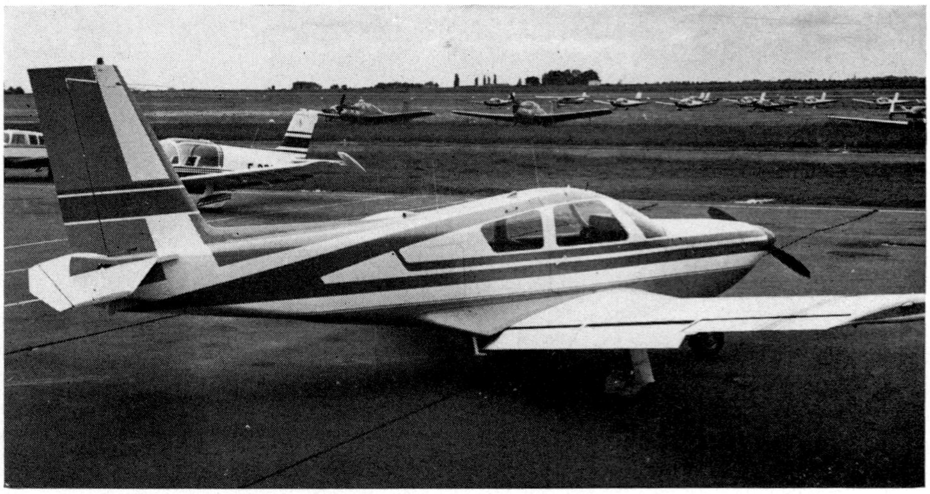

Socata ST 10 Diplomate four-seat light aircraft (200 hp Lycoming IO-360-C engine)

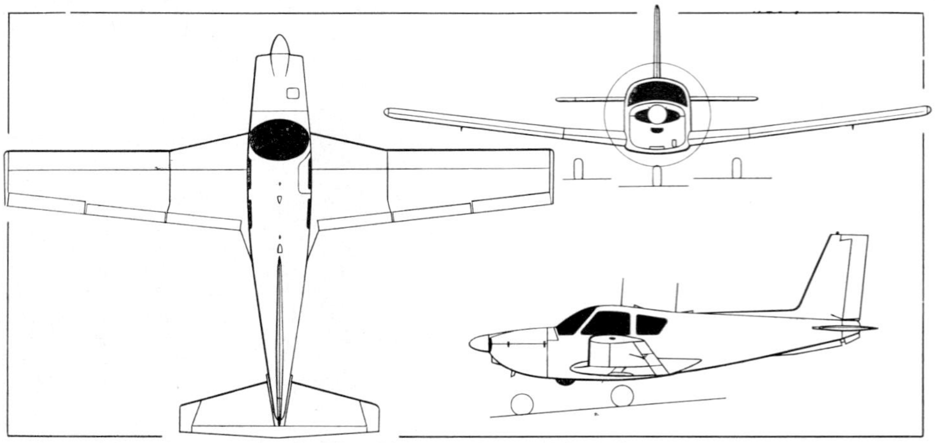

Socata ST 10 Diplomate four-seat light aircraft

FUSELAGE: All-metal structure. Forward section has welded steel-tube structure. Rear section is light alloy semi-monocoque.

TAIL UNIT: Cantilever all-metal structure. All-moving horizontal surfaces with full-span anti-tab. Fin and tailplane halves are interchangeable.

LANDING GEAR: Retractable tricycle type, with single wheel on each unit. Steerable nose-wheel. Electric retraction; nose-wheel retracts rearward to lie semi-recessed in fuselage; main wheels retract inward into wings. Oleo-pneumatic shock-absorbers. All three wheels and tyres size 15 × 6·00 × 6. Main wheel tyre pressure 31·3 lb/sq in (2·2 kg/cm²), nose-wheel tyre pressure 25·6 lb/sq in (1·8 kg/cm²). Parking brake and hydraulically-operated disc brakes.

POWER PLANT: One 200 hp Lycoming IO-360-C four-cylinder horizontally-opposed air-cooled engine, driving a Hartzell constant-speed propeller of 6 ft 2¾ in (1·90 m) diameter. Fuel in two tanks in wing-root leading-edges, with total capacity of 44 Imp gallons (200 litres). Oil capacity 1·75 Imp gallons (8 litres).

ACCOMMODATION: Pilot and three passengers, in pairs, in enclosed cabin. Dual controls standard. Space for 154 lb (70 kg) of baggage aft of rear seat. Large cabin door and baggage access door on starboard side. Cabin heater and windscreen de-froster standard.

ELECTRONICS AND EQUIPMENT: Optional equipment includes VHF and HF radio, VOR, ILS, ADF, blind-flying instrumentation and night-flying equipment.

DIMENSIONS, EXTERNAL:	
Wing span	31 ft 9⅞ in (9·70 m)
Wing chord at root	5 ft 8¾ in (1·75 m)
Wing chord at tip	3 ft 3¼ in (1·00 m)
Wing aspect ratio	7·1
Length overall	23 ft 3½ in (7·10 m)
Height overall	9 ft 5½ in (2·88 m)
Tailplane span	10 ft 4½ in (3·16 m)
Wheel track	9 ft 2¼ in (2·80 m)
Wheelbase	5 ft 9⅝ in (1·77 m)
DIMENSIONS, INTERNAL:	
Cabin: Length	7 ft 4⅝ in (2·25 m)
Max width	3 ft 8⅞ in (1·14 m)
Max height	4 ft 1¼ in (1·25 m)
AREAS:	
Wings, gross	139·93 sq ft (13·00 m²)
Ailerons (total)	7·96 sq ft (0·74 m²)
Trailing-edge flaps (total)	15·93 sq ft (1·48 m²)
Fin	12·92 sq ft (1·20 m²)
Rudder	5·17 sq ft (0·48 m²)

Horizontal tail surfaces (total)
29·17 sq ft (2·71 m²)

WEIGHTS:
Weight empty, equipped   1,594 lb (723 kg)
Max T-O weight   2,690 lb (1,220 kg)

PERFORMANCE (at max T-O weight):
Max level speed at S/L
   151 knots (174 mph; 280 km/h)
Cruising speed (75% power)
   143 knots (165 mph; 265 km/h)
Stalling speed, flaps down
   55 knots (63 mph; 100 km/h)

Rate of climb at S/L   945 ft (288 m)/min
Service ceiling   16,400 ft (5,000 m)
T-O run   886 ft (270 m)
Landing run   820 ft (250 m)
Range with 4 passengers
   703 nm (810 miles; 1,300 km)

SUD-AVIATION (see Aérospatiale)

VB
MM VINTRAS AND BOUILLER
ADDRESS:
c/o Aéro-Club du Béarn, Aérodrome de Pau-Idron, 64-Pau

M Vintras of Pau and M Bouiller of Oloron designed and built a two-seat light aircraft known as the VB-20 Isard, which flew for the first time on 9 August 1965. Certification by the CNRA followed on 17 October 1965. This aircraft was described and illustrated in the 1969-70 *Jane's*. M Vintras is engaged in the construction of five aircraft of a new type, the first of which was due to be completed in 1969-70.

WASSMER
WASSMER-AVIATION SA
HEAD OFFICE AND WORKS:
Route de Parentignat, 63-Issoire

DELIVERY AND AFTER-SALES SERVICE:
Aérodrome d'Issoire-le-Broc

PRESIDENT, DIRECTOR GENERAL:
Jean-Pierre Dumont

This company was founded in 1905 by M Benjamin Wassmer, under the title Société Wassmer, and in its early days was concerned with overhaul and repair of military aircraft and the manufacture of propellers.

When activities were resumed after World War II, Wassmer was again concerned initially with repair work, later building the designs of other manufacturers under licence. In 1955 a design department was created; its first product was the Jodel-Wassmer D.120 Paris-Nice, and subsequently large numbers of Jodel aircraft were built by Wassmer.

Manufacture of Jodel aircraft by this company has now ended (more than 300 having been built) and production is concentrated on aircraft and sailplanes of Wassmer's own design. The main works at Issoire occupy a floor area of 144,236 sq ft (13,400 m²).

Descriptions of the sailplanes appear in the "Sailplanes" section.

In July 1967, Wassmer-Aviation occupied additional premises at the airport of Issoire, with a floor area of 2,690 sq ft (250 m²). Early in 1968 it was producing five aircraft (including one WA-40A and two WA-41) and five sailplanes per month. By the end of the year output also included two WA-4/21's (with 250 hp engines) per month.

WASSMER WA-40A SUPER 4 SANCY
The Super 4 Sancy is a four/five-seat cabin monoplane of Wassmer design, the prototype of which flew for the first time on 8 June 1959. A total of 180 aircraft of this type had been built by the beginning of 1970.

The original WA-40 version (aircraft Nos. 2-52 inclusive) received its French certificate of air-worthiness on 9 June 1960.

The current version is the WA-40A (aircraft No. 53 onward), which introduced a swept fin and rudder, improved engine cowling and optional electric landing gear retraction. The WA-40A flew for the first time in January 1963 and received French certification on 4 March 1963.

The WA-40A is available in standard form with basic engine and flight instrumentation. Radio and navigational equipment, to customer's specification, can be installed as optional extras.

TYPE: Four/five-seat cabin monoplane.

WINGS: Cantilever low-wing monoplane. Wing section NACA 63·618. Dihedral 6°. Wood structure, plywood-covered. Single spar at 35% chord, with a full-span leading-edge torsion box. Plain wooden ailerons. All-wood Fowler flaps. No trim-tabs. Plastic wing-tips containing navigation lights.

FUSELAGE: Welded chrome-molybdenum steel-tube structure, fabric-covered.

TAIL UNIT: Cantilever wooden structure, with swept vertical surfaces. Fin integral with fuselage. One-piece all-moving tailplane. Automatic and controllable trim-tabs.

LANDING GEAR: Retractable tricycle type, with steerable nose-wheel. Nose-wheel retracts rearward, main wheels inward into wing roots. Normal manual retraction is entirely mechanical, requiring only one movement of a lever between the two front seats. Alternative electrical retraction, with Teleflex jack, available optionally. Paulstra rubber-block shock-absorbers. Dunlop or Kléber main wheels and tyres, size 420 × 150, and nose wheel and tyre, size 330 × 130. Tyre pressure 34 lb/sq in (2·4 kg/cm²). SATMO car-type hydraulic brakes. Parking brake. No provision for floats or skis.

POWER PLANT: One 180 hp Lycoming O-360-A2A four-cylinder horizontally-opposed air-cooled

Wassmer WA-40A Super 4 Sancy (180 hp Lycoming O-360-A2A engine)

engine, driving a McCauley 2A36C14-78KM4 two-blade constant-speed propeller, diameter 6 ft 2 in (1·88 m). One flexible fuel tank in each wing. Total fuel capacity 48·5 Imp gallons (220 litres) as four-seater, 37·4 Imp gallons (170 litres) as five-seater. Refuelling point on top of each wing. Provision for auxiliary tanks with total capacity of 48·5 Imp gallons (220 litres). Oil capacity 1·66 Imp gallons (7·5 litres).

ACCOMMODATION: Two adjustable seats at front and rear bench seat for two or three persons, with Dunlopillo upholstery. Starboard front seat removable to permit carriage of a light stretcher on starboard side of cabin. Large rearward-sliding full-vision canopy is removable to facilitate stretcher loading. Individual heating and ventilation at each seat. Sound-proofing. Compartment for up to 221 lb (100 kg) baggage aft of cabin, with external access.

ELECTRONICS AND EQUIPMENT: Delco-Rémy 12V 35A starter-generator standard. Optional equipment includes VHF radio, blind-flying instrumentation, automatic radio-compass and VOR.

DIMENSIONS, EXTERNAL:
Wing span   32 ft 9½ in (10·0 m)
Wing chord (constant)   5 ft 3 in (1·60 m)
Wing aspect ratio   6·2
Length overall   26 ft 6½ in (8·09 m)
Height over tail   9 ft 5 in (2·86 m)
Tailplane span   10 ft 10 in (3·30 m)
Wheel track   10 ft 10 in (3·30 m)
Wheelbase   5 ft 11 in (1·80 m)

Baggage compartment door (port):
Height   1 ft 1½ in (0·34 m)
Width   2 ft 1½ in (0·65 m)

DIMENSION, INTERNAL:
Baggage compartment volume
   8·83 cu ft (0·25 m³)
AREAS:
Wings, gross   172 sq ft (16·0 m²)
Ailerons (total)   13·35 sq ft (1·24 m²)
Trailing-edge flaps (total)   11·84 sq ft (1·10 m²)
Fin   16·15 sq ft (1·50 m²)
Horizontal tail surfaces (total)
   32·30 sq ft (3·00 m²)
WEIGHTS AND LOADING:
Weight empty, equipped (IFR) 1,631 lb (740 kg)
Max T-O and landing weight 2,645 lb (1,200 kg)
Max wing loading   15·36 lb/sq ft (75·0 kg/m²)
PERFORMANCE (at max T-O weight):
Max level speed at S/L
   146 knots (168 mph; 270 km/h)
Max permissible diving speed
   166 knots (192 mph; 310 km/h)
Max cruising speed (75% power) at 7,220 ft
   (2,200 m)   143 knots (165 mph; 265 km/h)
Econ cruising speed (55% power)
   122 knots (140 mph; 225 km/h)
Stalling speed, with flaps
   52 knots (59 mph; 95 km/h)
Rate of climb at S/L   984 ft (300 m)/min
Service ceiling   16,400 ft (5,000 m)
T-O run   607 ft (185 m)
T-O to 50 ft (15 m)   1,740 ft (530 m)
Landing from 50 ft (15 m)   1,315 ft (400 m)
Landing run   656 ft (200 m)
Max range with standard fuel, no reserve, at econ cruising speed at 9,850 ft (3,000 m)
   916 nm (1,055 miles; 1,700 km)
Max range with auxiliary fuel, no reserve, with three persons, at econ cruising speed at 9,850 ft (3,000 m)
   1,830 nm (2,110 miles; 3,400 km)

WASSMER SUPER 4/21
The Super 4/21 differs from the WA-40A in

Wassmer Super 4/21 Prestige (235 hp Lycoming O-540-B2B engine)

having a 250 hp Lycoming IO-540 engine, driving a McCauley variable-pitch constant-speed propeller, an electrically-retractable landing gear with oleo-pneumatic shock-absorbers, and electrically-operated flaps. The 235 hp Lycoming O-540 is available optionally.

The basic Super 4/21 Prestige has VHF radio, blind-flying instruments, a two-axis automatic pilot, night flying lights and a rotating beacon as standard equipment. A version is available with a second VHF radio, radio-compass, VOR and glideslope indicator, and is especially designed for IFR operation.

The prototype Super 4/21 flew for the first time in March 1967 and received its certificate of airworthiness on 15 November 1967. By the beginning of 1970, 25 aircraft of this type had been completed.

A WA-4/21 (F-BOYS, with 250 hp engine), with passengers and baggage, completed a 27,960-mile (45,000-km) round-the-world flight in 45 days piloted by Mme H. Pellissier late in 1968.

Dimensions, external and internal:
Same as for WA-40A, except:
Length overall 25 ft 7 in (7·80 m)

Weights:
Weight empty 1,774 lb (805 kg)
Max T-O weight 3,108 lb (1,410 kg)

Performance (at max T-O weight, 235 hp engine):
Max cruising speed (75% power) at 6,560 ft (2,000 m) 168 knots (193 mph; 310 km/h)
Max range 1,505 nm (1,735 miles; 2,800 km)

WASSMER WA-41 BALADOU

The WA-41 Baladou is a version of the WA-40A Super 4 having a non-retractable landing gear with oleo-pneumatic shock-absorption. Design work was started in 1964 and the prototype flew for the first time in March 1965. Sixty Baladous had been completed by the beginning of 1970, and production continues.

The description of the WA-40A applies also to the Baladou, except for the following details.

Landing Gear: Non-retractable tricycle type. Oleo-pneumatic shock-absorbers built under licence from Hispano-Suiza. Wheel fairings on all three units.

Power Plant: One 180 hp Lycoming O-360-A2A four-cylinder horizontally-opposed air-cooled engine, driving a McCauley two-blade fixed-pitch propeller.

Systems: Electrical system includes Delco-Remy 12V 35Ah generator and 12V battery for engine starting.

Dimension, external:
Length overall 24 ft $11\frac{1}{4}$ in (7·60 m)

Weights:
Weight empty 1,499 lb (680 kg)
Weight empty, equipped 1,565 lb (710 kg)
Max T-O weight 2,645 lb (1,200 kg)

Performance (at max T-O weight):
Max level speed at S/L 139 knots (160 mph; 255 km/h)
Max cruising speed at 6,560 ft (2,000 m) 132 knots (152 mph; 245 km/h)
Cruising speed at S/L 127 knots (146 mph; 235 km/h)
Rate of climb at S/L 885 ft (270 m)/min
T-O run 525 ft (160 m)
Landing run 655 ft (200 m)
Endurance (75% power), no reserves 5 hr 20 min
Max endurance (55% power), no reserves 7 hr 20 min

WASSMER WA-50/51/52/53

First flown on 22 March 1966, the WA-50 is a prototype four-seat light aircraft of which the airframe is made entirely of plastics. Its development was started in 1962, with official support, and the Société du Verre Textile has given considerable help in selecting the most suitable materials for construction.

The airframe is built up of large components moulded in thin layers of glass-fibre, reinforced either by stringers or by a double corrugated skin.

Following flight and ground testing of the prototype WA-50 (see 1969-70 *Jane's*), Wassmer is developing the WA-51, WA-52 and WA-53 production models. The first **WA-51**, known as the **Pacific,** flew for the first time on 17 May 1969; it has a non-retractable landing gear and modifications to the fin and the rear cabin windows. Delivery of production aircraft was anticipated early in 1970.

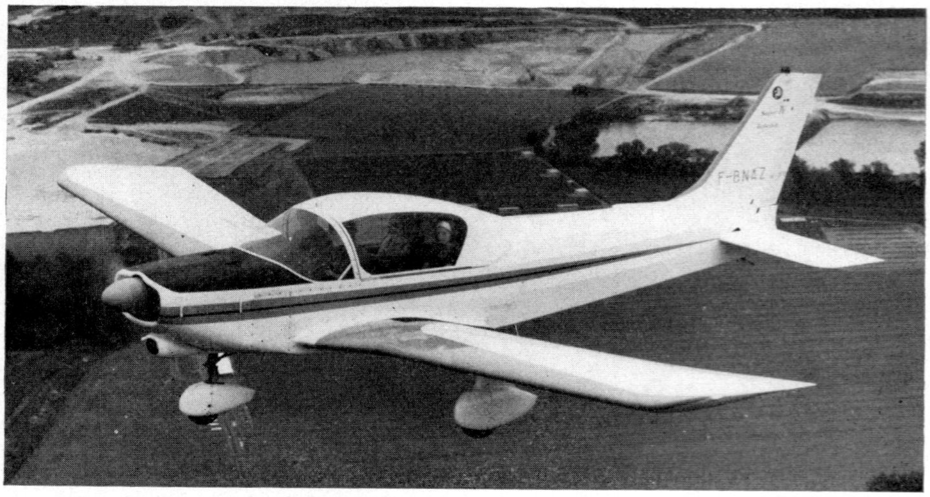

Wassmer WA-41 Baladou, a version of the Super 4 with non-retractable landing gear

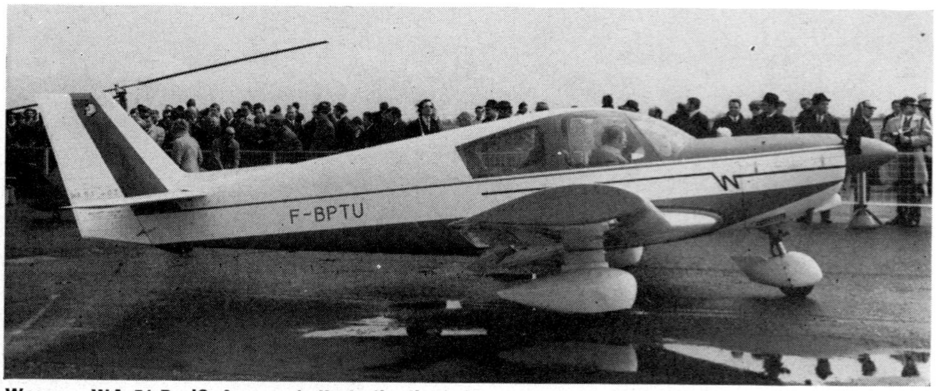

Wassmer WA-51 Pacific four-seat all-plastics light aircraft, third production machine (*J. M. G. Gradidge*)

The following details apply to the prototype WA-51 Pacific;

Type: Four-seat all-plastics light aircraft.

Wings: Cantilever low-wing monoplane. Wing section NACA 63418. Structure of each wing comprises a one-piece top surface and leading-edge moulding, a bottom skin panel, main front spar, auxiliary rear spar, ten ribs and stringers, all of plastics. Each aileron is a simple box structure, with corrugated skin, two end ribs and two internal ribs. Three-position mechanically-operated slotted flaps.

Fuselage: Non-plastic central structure of light alloy, comprising a longitudinal box keel running from the metal firewall to the rear of the cabin, with two cross-members to provide wing pick-ups. Main fuselage shell and integral fin moulded in two halves from glass-fibre, with frames and stringers also of glass-fibre.

Tail Unit: Cantilever all-plastics structure, with swept vertical surfaces. All-moving one-piece tailplane, with anti-tab each side.

Landing Gear: Non-retractable tricycle type. ERAM oleo-pneumatic main wheel shock-absorbers. Steerable nose-wheel on telescopic shock-strut, similar to that of Baladou. Main-wheel brakes and parking brake fitted.

Power Plant: One 150 hp Lycoming O-320-E2A four-cylinder horizontally-opposed air-cooled engine, driving a two-blade fixed-pitch metal propeller. Integral fuel tank in each swept-forward wing root leading-edge, with total capacity of 33 Imp gallons (150 litres).

Accommodation: Four-seats, in pairs, in enclosed cabin. Front two seats are adjustable. Baggage compartment behind rear seats. Upward-hinged door on each side. Cabin heated and ventilated.

Electronics and Equipment: Electrical equipment includes Delco-Rémy 12V engine starter and 12V 50Ah alternator.

Dimensions, external:
Wing span 30 ft 10 in (9·40 m)
Wing aspect ratio 7·1
Length overall 23 ft $5\frac{1}{2}$ in (7·15 m)

Area:
Wings, gross 40·68 sq ft (12·40 m^2)

Weights:
Weight empty 1,320 lb (600 kg)
Max T-O weight 2,245 lb (1,020 kg)

Performance (WA-50, at 2,205 lb = 1,000 kg AUW):
Max permissible speed in dive 193 knots (223 mph; 360 km/h)
Cruising speed 140 knots (161 mph; 260 km/h)
Landing speed 52 knots (59 mph; 95 km/h)
Range with max fuel 535 nm (620 miles; 1,000 km)

GERMANY
(FEDERAL REPUBLIC)

AEROTECHNIK
AEROTECHNIK ENTWICKLUNG UND APPARATEBAU GmbH

Address:
6 Frankfurt/Main 70, Postfach 70 01 65

This German company began work in the early 1960s to develop a low-cost, easy-to-fly helicopter that could be parked or stored in the minimum of space. A prototype, known as the WGM 21, was completed in 1968; all available details of this aircraft are given below.

AEROTECHNIK WGM 21

The prototype WGM 21 (registration D-HIDI) differs essentially from other and more familiar forms of helicopter in having four two-blade rotors, each mounted at the extremity of one of a pair of diametrically-opposed rotor support arms on top of the main rotor column. Aerotechnik claim that by adopting this configuration the entire output of the engine is transmitted directly to the main rotors, and it eliminates the need for tail control surfaces or a tail rotor. This permits the flying controls to be simplified, the pilot being provided with a conventional yoke-type control column and controlling the aircraft about the vertical axis by operating foot pedals which cause the rotor support arms themselves to rotate. The support arms can themselves be folded, so that the helicopter can be stored within an area of only 7 ft $1\frac{3}{4}$ in × 6 ft 6 in (2·18 m × 1·98 m).

The prototype WGM 21 was built primarily to establish the basic soundness of the concept, and its construction has therefore been kept as simple as possible. It has an open-work steel-tube fuselage, a single seat for the pilot and a tricycle landing gear with oleo-pneumatic shock-absorbers on the main units. Power plant is a 54 hp BMW 700 motor-car engine, which has a typical fuel consumption of approx 2·2 Imp gallons (10 litres) an hour at a cruising speed of 62 knots (71 mph; 115 km/h).

The WGM 21 was granted a limited C of A during the Summer of 1968, during which time initial tests were concluded satisfactorily. Further evaluation is to include the ability to hover in ground effect; levelling-out and landing tests; initial tests for autorotation; and acceleration during forward flight. Meanwhile, Aerotechnik is seeking a manufacturer able to produce the aircraft in series.

Dimensions, external:
Diameter of rotor support arms (each) 9 ft $2\frac{1}{4}$ in (2·80 m)
Diameter of rotors (each) 8 ft $6\frac{1}{4}$ in (2·60 m)
Max length, rotors turning 17 ft $8\frac{1}{2}$ in (5·40 m)

Length of fuselage	7 ft 1¾ in (2·18 m)
Max width, rotors turning	17 ft 8½ in (5·40 m)
Max width of fuselage	2 ft 6¼ in (0·77 m)
Height overall	5 ft 8½ in (1·74 m)
Wheel track	6 ft 1½ in (1·87 m)
Wheelbase	3 ft 8 in (1·12 m)

AREA:

Disc area (total)	229·3 sq ft (21·3 m²)

WEIGHTS AND LOADINGS:

Weight empty	540 lb (245 kg)
Max T-O weight	739 lb (335 kg)
Disc loading (total)	3·22 lb/sq ft (15·7 kg/m²)
Blade loading (each)	38·95 lb/sq ft (190 kg/m²)

PERFORMANCE (at max T-O weight):

Max level speed	67 knots (77 mph; 125 km/h)
Cruising speed	62 knots (71 mph; 115 km/h)

Max vertical rate of climb 785 ft (240 m)/min
Max forward rate of climb 1,280 ft (390 m)/min
Hovering ceiling out of ground effect
6,900 ft (2,100 m)
Range, no reserves 135 nm (155 miles; 250 km)

Aerotechnik WGM 21 four-rotor helicopter

BOHNE
HTL-BOHNE
ADDRESS: München

BOHNE EH-102C

HTL-Bohne has completed the prototype of a small four-seat light monoplane, designated EH-102C, which is powered by a 115 hp Lycoming air-cooled engine driving a two-blade propeller. It is intended to install a 150 hp Lycoming in the production version.

The EH-102C is a cantilever low-wing monoplane, with a retractable tricycle landing gear. It has "2 + 2" side-by-side seating for four persons, under a transparent moulded canopy which hinges open to starboard to permit access to the cabin. The tapered wings have plain flaps and ailerons, without tabs. A fixed tailplane is fitted, and there is a trim-tab in the starboard elevator. Both the fin and the rudder have moderate sweepback; there is a small dorsal fairing to the fin and an inset tab in the base of the rudder.

The details below apply to the prototype.

DIMENSIONS, EXTERNAL:

Wing span	27 ft 10¾ in (8·50 m)
Length	20 ft 4 in (6·20 m)
Height	7 ft 0⅝ in (2·15 m)

AREA:

Wings, gross	122·92 sq ft (11·42 m²)

WEIGHTS AND LOADINGS (115 hp engine):

Weight empty	937 lb (425 kg)
Max T-O weight	1,709 lb (775 kg)
Max wing loading	13·9 lb/sq ft (67·8 kg/m²)
Max power loading	14·86 lb/hp (6·74 kg/hp)

PERFORMANCE (at max T-O weight, 115 hp engine):

Max level speed 124 knots (143 mph; 230 km/h)
Max cruising speed
110 knots (127 mph; 205 km/h)
Stalling speed 45 knots (51 mph; 82 km/h)
Rate of climb at S/L 886 ft (270 m)/min
Endurance 5 hr

BÜCKER
AERO TECHNIK CANARY
HEAD OFFICE:
8000 Munich 81, Postfach 81 1129

This company was formed by the late Mr Jack D. Canary to produce under licence the well-known Bücker Bü 133D-1 Jungmeister single-seat sporting biplane. Production was started in March 1967, at the works of Josef Bitz Flugzeugbau in Haunstetten, near Augsburg. The first aircraft flew in mid-1968.

The death of Mr Canary on 19 August 1968, in an accident while flying a BT-13 piston-engined trainer during his work as Technical Adviser for the film *Tora, Tora, Tora!*, caused delays in production. However, by February 1970 four aircraft had been built and sold, and production is to continue as a joint effort by Josef Bitz Flugzeugbau and Wolf Hirth GmbH of Nabern/Teck, near Stuttgart. Mr Carl C. Bücker maintains an interest in this new project, and is assisted by Mr Paul H. Skogstad of Munich, who has taken over Mr Canary's activities.

New spare parts and available major assemblies are being utilised in the remanufacture of the Siemens-Halske Sh-14A4 (Bramo) engines for the Bü 133D-1 Jungmeisters. Due to the limited availability of such engines, as well as a desire by many potential customers to have both a modern engine and more power, a conversion of the Jungmeister has been made by Wolf Hirth GmbH. Designated **Bücker Bü 133F**, this aircraft made its maiden flight in October 1969 with a 220 hp Franklin six-cylinder horizontally-opposed engine and an inverted-flight oil system. This (for all practical purposes) "bolt-on" conversion involves only very minor changes aft of the firewall, and is suitable for easy fitting on existing Jungmeisters.

Aero Technik Canary will continue to offer the Bramo-powered Jungmeister as well as the new Franklin version. A kit will be available later to Jungmeister owners who wish to convert their aircraft.

BÜCKER Bü 133D-1 JUNGMEISTER

To qualify this aircraft for unlimited aerobatics, the structure has been specially stressed and proof-tested, and there is no airspeed limitation. In addition, the power plant installation is arranged to allow constant operation in inverted flight. The flying controls are specially harmonised and balanced to facilitate high-precision co-ordinated air manoeuvres.

The Bü 133D-1 as produced by Aero Technik Canary is entirely standard, with only the substitution of Goodyear tyres, wheels and brakes and American instrumentation.

TYPE: Single-seat fully-aerobatic biplane.

WINGS: Braced single-bay biplane, with parallel interplane struts and N-type centre-section support struts. Fabric-covered wooden-spar wings. Wing section modified Clark "Y". Dihedral 1° 30′ on top wing, 3° 30′ on lower wing. Sweepback at quarter-chord 11°. Aero-

Herr Carl Bücker with one of the Bü 133D-1 Jungmeister aircraft built by Aero Technik Canary

Bü 133F version of the Jungmeister, powered by a 220 hp Franklin 6A-350-C1 engine

dynamically and mass balanced ailerons on both top and bottom wings. No flaps. Fixed tabs on ailerons.

FUSELAGE: Conventional welded chrome-molybdenum steel-tube structure, with fabric covering.

TAIL UNIT: Wire-braced welded chrome-molybdenum steel-tube structure, with fabric cover-ing. Variable-incidence tailplane. Elevators fitted with mechanically-operated trim-tabs.

LANDING GEAR: Non-retractable tail-wheel type. Welded steel-tube main gear assemblies. Oleo-pneumatic shock-absorbers. Goodyear wheels, 6·00 × 6 tyres and disc brakes. Wheel fairing over each main wheel.

POWER PLANT: One 160 hp Siemens Halske Sh-14A4 (Bramo) seven-cylinder air-cooled radial engine, driving a Hoffman HOCO F-H2/R 31-220 115 7 R two-blade fixed-pitch wooden propeller. Fuel tanks in fuselage. Normal fuel capacity 19·5 Imp gallons (88·5 litres), with provision for additional 8·6 Imp gallons (39 litres). Oil capacity 1·76 Imp gallons (8 litres).

ACCOMMODATION: Single seat in open cockpit. Downward-hinged door on each side. Baggage compartment aft of cockpit, with access from port side.

EQUIPMENT: Normal flying and engine instruments standard. Optional extras include an 8·6 Imp gal (39 litre) reserve tank, glider towing hook and custom finishing.

DIMENSIONS, EXTERNAL:
Wing span (both wings)	21 ft 7¾ in	(6·60 m)
Length overall	19 ft 9 in	(6·02 m)
Height overall, tail down	7 ft 2⅝ in	(2·20 m)
Tailplane span	8 ft 2½ in	(2·50 m)

Wheel track	5 ft 3¾ in	(1·62 m)

AREA:
Wings, gross	130 sq ft	(12·0 m²)

WEIGHTS AND LOADINGS:
Weight empty	992 lb	(450 kg)
Max T-O weight	1,410 lb	(640 kg)
Max wing loading	10·9 lb/sq ft	(53·5 kg/m²)
Max power loading	8·8 lb/hp	(4 kg/hp)

PERFORMANCE (at max T-O weight):
Max level speed at 820 ft (250 m)
119 knots (137 mph; 220 km/h)
Max diving speed
156 knots (180 mph; 290 km/h)
Max cruising speed at 820 ft (250 m)
108 knots (124 mph; 200 km/h)
Econ cruising speed at 820 ft (250 m)
76 knots (87 mph; 140 km/h)
Stalling speed 47 knots (54 mph; 86 km/h)
Climb to 3,300 ft (1,000 m) 2 min 30 sec
Service ceiling 19,685 ft (6,000 m)
Range with standard fuel, 6% reserves
269 nm (310 miles; 500 km)

BÜCKER Bü 133F JUNGMEISTER

All dimensional data for this version are as for Bü 133D-1 except that overall length, which is 21 ft 0⅜ in (6·65 m) including propeller spinner. The empty weight has increased slighty to 1,032 lb (468 kg).

Although detailed performance data is not yet available, this new version performs substantially better than earlier versions of the Jungmeister, particularly in climb and in vertical manoeuvres.

First flight of the prototype Bü 133F, modified by Wolf Hirth GmbH, was made on 1 October 1969.

POWER PLANT: One 220 hp Franklin 6A-350-C1 six-cylinder horizontally-opposed air-cooled engine driving a Hoffmann two-blade fixed-pitch wooden propeller. Engine equipped with an FAA-approved modification to the oil system to permit inverted flight. Fuel tank and capacity as for Bü 133D-1. Oil capacity 1·8 Imp gallons (8·3 litres).

DEUTSCHE AIRBUS
DEUTSCHE AIRBUS GmbH

ADDRESS:
D-8 München 19, Leonrodstrasse 68

CHAIRMAN OF THE BOARD OF DIRECTORS:
Bundesminister a.D. Dr Franz Josef Strauss

CHIEF MANAGER:
Dr Bernhard Weinhardt

MANAGEMENT:
Dipl-Ing Felix Kracht
Kurt Lauser
Dipl-Ing Johannes Schaffler

PUBLIC RELATIONS:
Mano Ziegler
This company is the German partner in the consortium for development of the European high-capacity A 300B transport aircraft described under the "Airbus" heading in the International section of this edition.

DORNIER
DORNIER AG

HEAD OFFICE:
Postfach 317, 799 Friedrichshafen/Bodensee

WORKS:
Research and Development: 7759 Immenstaad/Bodensee (near Friedrichshafen)
Production: Postfach 2160, Brunhamstrasse 21, 8000 München 60

AIRFIELD AND FLIGHT TEST CENTRE:
8031 Oberpfaffenhofen, Bavaria

PRESIDENT:
Dr Adalbert Seifriz

BOARD OF DIRECTORS:
Dipl-Ing Claudius Dornier Jr (Chairman)
Dipl-Ing Silvius Dornier
Dipl-Ing Justus Dornier

PUBLIC RELATIONS:
P. Pletschacher

Dornier GmbH, formerly Dornier-Metallbauten, was formed in 1922 by the late Professor Claude Dornier as the successor to the "Do" Division of the former Zeppelin Werke, Lindau, GmbH. It has been operated in the form of an Aktien-Gesellschaft (company limited by shares) since 1 January 1970.

After 1945, when the design and manufacture of aircraft in Germany was forbidden, Prof Dornier established technical offices in Madrid, Spain, where he designed a general-purpose monoplane known as the Do 25.

The advanced development of this aircraft, designated Do 27, was produced in quantity and has been described in earlier editions of this work.

Manufacture of a twin-engined version of the Do 27, known as the Do 28, continued during the past year. In addition, Dornier has in production the Skyservant light utility transport, based on the Do 28. The flight testing of the Do 31 experimental V/STOL transport aircraft ended in April 1970.

In the Summer of 1968 Dornier acquired a 74 per cent holding in Merckle Flugzeugwerke GmbH (which see).

In July 1969 Dornier announced increases in working capital of certain member companies of the Dornier group, raising the total capital liability of the group's member companies to DM 35 million. In 1969 the group employed a total of 6,700 people. Member companies, in addition to Dornier GmbH, include Dornier-Reparaturwerft GmbH at Oberpfaffenhofen (aircraft servicing and maintenance), Dornier-System GmbH of Friedrichshafen (space flight, unmanned flying vehicles and oceanological research) and Lindauer Dornier Gesellschaft mbH of Lindau, which produces machinery for the textile industry and for the manufacture of plastic foils.

Prof Claude Dornier, the founder and head of the company, died on 5 December 1969.

Dornier has developed and flight tested an experimental version of the tethered rotor platform designated Do 32 K "System Kiebitz" (see "Drones" section of this edition), and the development of operational versions has started.

Manufacture of three prototypes of the light five-seat tip-drive helicopter designated Do 132 has begun, and flight tests are scheduled to start in 1971. Dornier is also developing components for compound helicopters, including a helicopter integrated tail rotor system providing both torque control and propulsion, which has already been tested on the ground, and a rotor system with variable rigidity. Other current work includes design studies for the Do 231 V/STOL jet transport for potential civil and military use.

Dornier joined forces with Breguet Aviation (see French section) in the Spring of 1969 to bid for a Franco-German order for a new jet trainer to replace the Magister. Dornier designs for

Dornier Do 28 B-1 twin-engined general-purpose aircraft, prior to delivery to Sudan Airways

Do 28 B-1-S floatplane conversion of the Dornier Do 28 twin-engined light transport

such an aircraft were initiated as the Do P 375; the joint submission, a full-scale model of which was displayed at the Paris Air Show in June 1969, is known as the Alpha Jet and incorporates features of both the Do P 375 and the Breguet 126.

In addition, Dornier is prime contractor for German licence production of the Bell UH-1D helicopter. Current contracts cover the delivery of a total of 387 aircraft of this type, with Dornier being responsible for manufacturing parts of the fuselage and for final assembly and flight testing.

DORNIER Do 27

The prototype Do 27 flew for the first time on 27 June 1955, and the first production aircraft on 17 October 1956.

A total of 680 Do 27's were built, including 428 ordered for the Federal German Air Force and Army and 50 manufactured under licence by CASA, in Spain, as the CASA C.127. The aircraft is not currently in production but all jigs and tools are available for resumed production against further contracts.

Main production models of the Do 27 were described fully in the 1968-69 Jane's.

DORNIER Do 28

The Do 28 is virtually a twin-engined version of the Do 27. The engines are mounted at the extremities of short stub wings which are assembled to the fuselage beneath the pilot's compartment, a new short faired nose taking the place of the single engine of the Do 27. The cantilever main landing gear units are located at the ends of the stub wings behind the engine mountings.

The prototype, which flew for the first time on 29 April 1959, retained the basic structure of the Do 27 almost unchanged and was powered by two 180 hp Lycoming O-360-A1A engines. The wing span and area were increased on the second prototype, which introduced 250 hp Lycoming O-540 engines.

Four versions of the Do 28 have since been produced, as follows:—

Do 28 A-1. Similar to second prototype. Entered production in 1960 and received FAA Type Approval on 20 July 1961. Total of 60 built. Described fully in 1962-63 Jane's.

Do 28 A-1-S. Floatplane conversion of A-1 by the Jobmaster Company, Seattle, Washington, USA, under contract to Hamilton Aviation Ltd, Edmonton, Alberta, Canada. Prototype flew in 1964 and continues in service.

Do 28 B-1. Development of Do 28 A-1 with 290 hp IO-540 engines, increased gross weight and payload. Other innovations include an enlarged tailplane, redesigned aerodynamic control surface balances, more efficient electrically-actuated flaps, auxiliary fuel tanks in wingtips, redesigned instrument panel and many minor detail improvements. Prototype flew in April 1963. Total of 60 built. Production can continue if required. Available also in agricultural version.

Do 28 B-1-S. Floatplane conversion of B-1 by the Jobmaster Company (see A-1-S above). Six in service in Canada.

The designation Do 28D applies to an entirely new design, known as the **Skyservant**, which is described separately.

The following details apply specifically to the Do 28 B-1, a full description of which appeared in the 1969-70 *Jane's*.

DIMENSIONS, EXTERNAL:
Wing span	45 ft 3½ in (13·80 m)
Wing chord (constant)	5 ft 5 in (1·65 m)
Wing aspect ratio	8·5
Length overall	29 ft 6 in (9·00 m)
Height overall	9 ft 2 in (2·80 m)
Span of stub wings	13 ft 1½ in (4·00 m)
Tailplane span	14 ft 5 in (4·40 m)
Wheel track	10 ft 6 in (3·20 m)
Wheelbase	20 ft 8 in (6·30 m)
Flight deck door (each side):	
Height	2 ft 11½ in (0·90 m)
Width	2 ft 5½ in (0·75 m)
Cabin door (each side):	
Height	2 ft 7½ in (0·80 m)
Width	3 ft 5¼ in (1·05 m)
Height to sill	3 ft 7¼ in (1·10 m)
Baggage door (port, aft of cabin):	
Height	1 ft 8½ in (0·52 m)
Width	1 ft 3 in (0·38 m)
Height to sill	2 ft 11½ in (0·90 m)

DIMENSIONS, INTERNAL:
Cabin, excluding flight deck, including baggage
space:	
Length	6 ft 8¾ in (2·05 m)
Max width	4 ft 3¼ in (1·30 m)
Max height	4 ft 7 in (1·40 m)
Floor area	27 sq ft (2·50 m²)
Volume	95·35 cu ft (2·70 m³)
Baggage space	8·83 cu ft (0·25 m³)

AREAS:
Wings, gross (excluding stub wings)	241 sq ft (22·4 m²)
Ailerons (total)	28·42 sq ft (2·64 m²)
Flaps (total)	35·52 sq ft (3·30 m²)
Fin	13·02 sq ft (1·21 m²)
Rudder, including tab and balance	16·57 sq ft (1·54 m²)
Tailplane	32·72 sq ft (3·04 m²)
Elevators, including tab and balance	17·33 sq ft (1·61 m²)

WEIGHTS AND LOADINGS:
Weight empty, equipped:	
Do 28 B-1	3,960 lb (1,800 kg)
Do 28 B-1-S	4,415 lb (2,003 kg)
Max T-O and landing weight	6,000 lb (2,720 kg)
Max wing loading	24·89 lb/sq ft (121·5 kg/m²)
Max power loading	10·34 lb/hp (4·69 kg/hp)

PERFORMANCE (Do 28 B-1 at max T-O weight, except where indicated):
Max level speed at S/L
160 knots (184 mph; 290 km/h)

Dornier Do 28 D-1 Skyservant employed as an air ambulance in Sweden

Max never-exceed speed
179·5 knots (207 mph; 334 km/h)
Max cruising speed at S/L:
Do 28 B-1	148 knots (170 mph; 274 km/h)
Do 28 B-1-S	120 knots (138 mph; 222 km/h)

Econ cruising speed at S/L
130 knots (150 mph; 242 km/h)
Stalling speed 38·5 knots (44 mph; 70 km/h)
Rate of climb at S/L 1,400 ft (426 m)/min
Service ceiling 19,400 ft (5,900 m)
Service ceiling, one engine out
4,900 ft (1,500 m)
T-O run:
Do 28 B-1	570 ft (175 m)
Do 28 B-1-S (10-knot wind)	900 ft (274 m)

T-O to 50 ft (15 m):
Do 28 B-1	980 ft (300 m)
Do 28 B-1-S (10-knot wind)	1,400 ft (427 m)

Landing from 50 ft (15 m):
Do 28 B-1	820 ft (250 m)
Do 28 B-1-S (10-knot wind)	800 ft (244 m)

Landing run 380 ft (115 m)
Normal range with standard fuel and max payload at econ cruising speed, no allowances
666 nm (768 miles; 1,235 km)
Max range with auxiliary tanks at econ cruising speed, no allowances
955 nm (1,100 miles; 1,680 km)

DORNIER Do 28 D-1 SKYSERVANT

The Skyservant is a completely new design, inheriting only the basic configuration of the Do 28. It was developed with the financial assistance of the German Ministry of Economics.

The prototype (D-INTL) first flew on 23 February 1966. Type approval for the Do 28 D was granted on 24 February 1967, and for the Do 28 D-1 on 6 November 1967. Deliveries began in the Summer of 1967.

The two versions of the Skyservant which have been produced differ as follows:

Do 28 D Skyservant. Initial version, described fully in 1967-68 *Jane's*. Seven built, of which two were later converted to Do 28 D-1.

Do 28 D-1 Skyservant. Current production version since 1968, as described below. Detail refinements include a 50-cm increase in wing span and a 150 kg increase in AUW. Meets FAA Pt 135 requirements, particularly with regard to improved climb on one engine.

Production for civil market continues, with some deliveries in 1969. Four others delivered to German Armed Forces, primarily for VIP duties but with provision for adaptation to other work, e.g. ambulance or survey flights. Additional order, for 121 Skyservants for the German Armed Forces, has now been confirmed. Delivery is due to begin at the end of 1970. Modification and re-tooling operations to meet the requirements of the military authorities has had some effect upon the supply position for the civil market.

On 8 January 1970 a Do 28 D-1 Skyservant, piloted by Dornier pilot Frank Tuytjens, set up a new international altitude record in Class C-1-e (landplanes) by flying to a height of 29,528 ft (9,000 m). This record awaits confirmation by the FAI.

TYPE: Twin-engined STOL transport and utility aircraft.

WINGS: Cantilever high-wing monoplane. Wing section NACA 23018 (modified), with nose slot. Dihedral 1° 30. Incidence 4°. All-metal box-spar structure. Ailerons and double-slotted flaps have metal structure, partly Eonnex-covered. Balance tabs on ailerons. Pneumatic de-icing optional.

FUSELAGE: Conventional all-metal stressed-skin structure.

TAIL UNIT: Cantilever all-metal structure, with rudder and horizontal surfaces partly Eonnex-covered. All-moving horizontal surfaces, with combined anti-balance and trim tab. Trim-tab on rudder. Provision for pneumatic de-icing.

LANDING GEAR: Non-retractable tail-wheel type. Dornier oleo-pneumatic shock-absorbers. Main wheel tyres size 8·50-10, pressure 46 lb/sq in (3·23 kg/cm²). Tail-wheel tyre size 5·00-4, pressure 50 lb/sq in (3·50 kg/cm²). Fairings on main legs and wheels standard. Hydraulic brakes. Provision for wheel-ski gear or floats.

POWER PLANT: Two 380 hp Lycoming IGSO-540 six-cylinder horizontally-opposed air-cooled engines, mounted on stub-wings and each driving a Hartzell three-blade constant-speed propeller, diameter 7 ft 9 in (2·36 m). Fuel tanks in engine nacelles, with total usable capacity of 181 Imp gallons (822 litres). Refuelling points above nacelles. Total capacity of separate oil tanks, 7·2 Imp gallons (33 litres).

Dornier Skyservant (two 380 hp Lycoming IGSO-540 six-cylinder engines) as supplied to the German Federal government for VIP transport duties

ACCOMMODATION: Pilot and either co-pilot or passenger side-by-side on flight deck. Dual controls optional. Main cabin accommodates up to 12 seats, with aisle, or 13 inward-facing folding seats, or five stretchers and five folding seats, all layouts including toilet and/or baggage compartment aft of cabin. Second baggage compartment in nose-cone. Alternatively, cabin can be stripped for cargo-carrying. Door on each side of flight deck. Combined two-section passenger and freight door on port side of cabin, at rear. Cabin heating standard.

ELECTRONICS AND EQUIPMENT: IFR instruments and electronics to customer's specification.

DIMENSIONS, EXTERNAL:

Wing span	50 ft 10¼ in (15·50 m)
Wing chord (constant)	6 ft 2¾ in (1·90 m)
Wing aspect ratio	8·4
Length overall	38 ft 0¾ in (11·60 m)
Height overall	12 ft 10 in (3·90 m)
Tailplane span	20 ft 4 in (6·20 m)
Wheel track	11 ft 6 in (3·52 m)
Wheelbase	27 ft 10¾ in (8·50 m)
Passenger door (port rear):	
Height	4 ft 4¾ in (1·34 m)
Width	2 ft 1¼ in (0·64 m)
Height to sill	1 ft 11½ in (0·60 m)
Freight door (port rear):	
Height	4 ft 4¾ in (1·34 m)
Width	4 ft 2½ in (1·28 m)

DIMENSIONS, INTERNAL:

Cabin: Max length	12 ft 9½ in (3·90 m)
Max width	4 ft 6 in (1·37 m)
Max height	4 ft 11⅞ in (1·52 m)
Floor area	56·0 sq ft (5·25 m^2)
Volume	279 cu ft (7·90 m^3)

AREAS:

Wings, gross	308 sq ft (28·60 m^2)
Ailerons (total)	27·6 sq ft (2·56 m^2)
Trailing-edge flaps (total)	51·6 sq ft (4·80 m^2)
Fin	50·0 sq ft (4·65 m^2)
Rudder, including tab	20·0 sq ft (1·85 m^2)
Tailplane, including tab	72·6 sq ft (6·75 m^2)

WEIGHTS AND LOADINGS:

Weight empty	4,775 lb (2,166 kg)
Max T-O and landing weight	8,050 lb (3,650 kg)
Max wing loading	26·11 lb/sq ft (127·5 kg/m^2)
Max power loading	11·6 lb/hp (4·80 kg/hp)

PERFORMANCE (at max T-O weight):

Max level speed at 10,500 ft (3,200 m) 173 knots (199 mph; 320 km/h)

Max cruising speed (75% power) at 10,000 ft (3,050 m) 155 knots (178 mph; 286 km/h)

Econ cruising speed (50% power) at 10,000 ft (3,050 m) 124 knots (143 mph; 230 km/h)

Stalling speed, power off, flaps down 58 knots (66 mph; 106 km/h)

Min speed, power on, flaps down 35 knots (40 mph; 65 km/h)

Rate of climb at S/L	1,180 ft (360 m)/min
Service ceiling	24,300 ft (7,400 m)
Service ceiling, one engine out	9,000 ft (2,750 m)
STOL T-O to 50 ft (15 m)	1,140 ft (347 m)
FAA 23 T-O to 50 ft (15 m)	1,700 ft (518 m)
STOL landing from 50 ft (15 m)	1,220 ft (372 m)
FAA 23 landing from 50 ft (15 m)	1,960 ft (597 m)

Range with max fuel at 10,000 ft (3,050 m), 50% power, no reserves 976 nm (1,125 miles; 1,810 km)

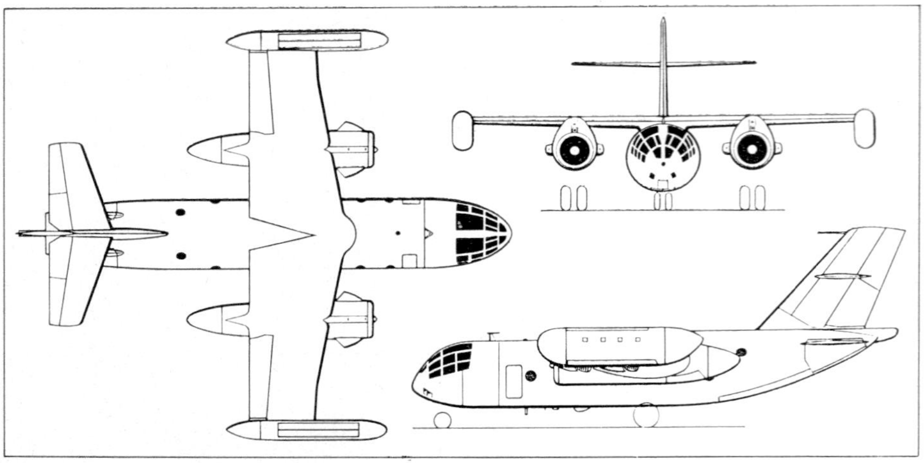

Dornier Do 31 E 1 V/STOL experimental aircraft

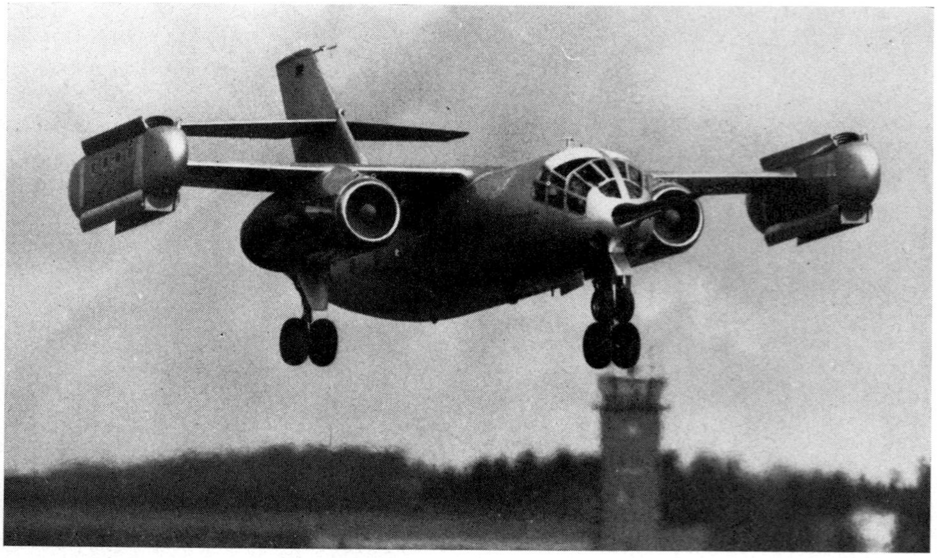

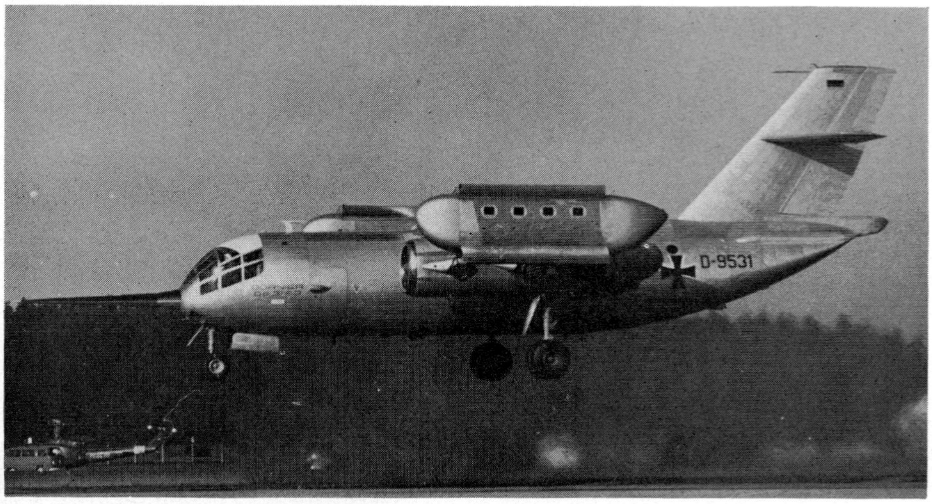

Two views of the Dornier Do 31 E 3 experimental V/STOL transport aircraft

DORNIER Do 31 E

The Dornier Do 31 E is an experimental V/STOL transport aircraft which utilises both deflected thrust and direct jet-lift techniques. It was built with the assistance of Vereinigte Flugtechnische Werke and Hamburger Flugzeugbau.

Initially, two Do 31 E prototypes were constructed under a German Defence Ministry contract, and the first of these, the Do 31 E 1, made its first flight on 10 February 1967. Each of the Do 31 E's has as its primary power plant two Rolls-Royce Bristol Pegasus 5-2 vectored-thrust turbofan engines in nacelles under the wings. In addition there are wingtip pods for two groups of four Rolls-Royce RB 162-4D lift-jets, although these have not been fitted to the Do 31 E 1, which has been used for conventional flight trials only. The second aircraft, the Do 31 E 3, which made its first flight on 14 July 1967, and which has the full complement of engines, was used to carry out an experimental programme of jet-borne flight, which started with successful vertical take-offs and landings and transition flights at the end of 1967. The first transition from vertical take-off to horizontal flight took place on 16 December 1967, and the first transition from horizontal flight to vertical landing on 21 December 1967. A third airframe, for static tests, is designated Do 31 E 2.

During its flight from Munich to Le Bourget on 27 May 1969 to appear at the Paris Air Show, the Do 31 E 3 set up three new international records in Class H (jet-lift aircraft), including an average speed of 277·338 knots (319·36 mph= 513·962 km/h) between Munich and Paris; a height of 29,855 ft (9,100 m); and distance of 367 nm (423 miles; 681 km).

By mid-1969, 200 tests, including 110 take-offs and many transitions, had been made, and testing continued into 1970 with a view to optimising take-off and landing procedures, investigating noise levels, all-weather flying etc., An important phase was the demonstration of the aircraft's STOL capability, with significant increases in payload and max T-O weight.

During 1969-70 the Do 31 E was studied by a team of scientists and engineers from NASA. This evaluation programme stemmed from an agreement between Dornier, NASA and the German Federal Government, and included simulation trials at the NASA Experimental Center in California. The programme ended in April 1970.

The location of the Pegasus engines is determined by the need to protect the fuselage from hot gases ejected from the side nozzles. The lift engines are at the wingtips to ensure effective compensation of the roll moment following a failure of an inboard engine in the vertical flight phase.

For pitch control, high-pressure bleed air from the Pegasus engines is ducted to nozzles at the stern of the aircraft, of which two point up and two down. Roll control is achieved by thrust modulation of the lift engines and yaw control by differential tilting of the lift engine nozzles. Rates of climb and descent are set with the throttle of the lift engines. Control in hovering flight is exercised through an attitude stabiliser developed by Bodenseewerk Perkin Elmer.

TYPE: Experimental V/STOL transport aircraft.

WINGS: Cantilever high-wing monoplane. Wing section NACA 64 (A412)-412·5 at root, NACA 64 (A412)-410 at tip. Sweepback at quarter-chord 8° 30′. No dihedral or incidence. Three-spar riveted light alloy structure. Two-section ailerons, between propulsion engine pod and lift-jet pod on each wing, take form of camber-changing flaps with movement of ±25°. Conventional flap on each wing between fuselage and propulsion engine pod. Ailerons operated by duplicated hydraulic jacks, flaps by a hydraulic motor. No tabs.

FUSELAGE: Conventional all-metal semi-monocoque structure of circular section (diameter 10 ft 6 in = 3·20 m), slightly flattened at bottom. Upswept rear fuselage incorporating rear-loading doors.

TAIL UNIT: Cantilever all-metal structure with vertical surfaces swept back at 40° at quarter-chord. Fixed-incidence tailplane, with sweep of 15°, is mid-set on fin. Elevators in four sections, each with separate hydraulic actuator. Rudders in two sections, each with separate hydraulic actuator. No aerodynamic or mass balancing of control surfaces. No tabs.

LANDING GEAR: Hydraulically-retractable tricycle type with twin wheels on each unit. All units retract rearward, main units into rear of propulsion engine nacelles. Oleo-pneumatic shock-absorbers. Multiple-disc brakes on main wheels. Steerable and fully-castoring nose unit. Brake parachute housed in rear loading ramp and ejected downward, for use during flight testing.

POWER PLANT: Two Rolls-Royce Bristol Pegasus 5-2 vectored-thrust propulsion engines, each rated at 15,500 lb (7,000 kg) st, in pods under wings. Removable lift-jet pod on each wing-tip, each housing four Rolls-Royce RB.162-4D turbojets (each rated at 4,400 lb = 2,000 kg st). Lift-jets are mounted in line astern and are fitted with deflector nozzles enabling thrust to be vectored ±7½° around the installation angle of 15°. Five integral fuel tanks in wings, with total capacity of 1,760 Imp gallons (8,000 litres). Supply to engines is normally from centre-section tank, to which fuel is transferred equally from other tanks to maintain trim.

ACCOMMODATION: Crew of two on flight deck, with dual controls. Folding seats for 36 fully-equipped troops are fitted as standard equipment along cabin side walls. Alternative payloads include 24 stretchers in tiers of four, with centre aisle; two or three jeeps; one Unimog type S or two Unimog type 410 1D vehicles; missiles; and freight on pallets size 5 ft 7 in × 11 ft 6 in (1·7 × 3·5 m). Freight can be air-dropped through open rear doors. Cabin fitted with roller-conveyors, guide rails and winch for freight loading. Air-stair door on port side of cabin at front. Loading ramp which forms undersurface of rear fuselage can be lowered to ground or held horizontal at truck-bed height. Fuselage undersurface aft of ramp hinges up inside fuselage, and each adjacent side panel hinges outward, to provide maximum accessibility for tall vehicles.

SYSTEMS: Two fully-independent hydraulic systems and emergency system, pressure 3,000 lb/sq in (210 kg/cm²). First main system supplies one section of tandem or twin jacks of flying control system, landing gear, flaps, ramp, loading and side doors, nose-wheel steering system, brakes and lift-jet pod doors. Other main system supplies only second section of control jacks. Emergency system supplies flaps, landing gear, ramp loading and side doors when the first main hydraulic system or the electrical system has failed. AC electrical system supplied by four 9kVA three-phase 200/115V 400 c/s generators (two driven by each propulsion engine). DC power supplied by two 3kW 28V transformer/rectifiers. Standby battery fitted.

ELECTRONICS AND EQUIPMENT: Full range of radio and navigation aids, including VOR/ILS and TACAN. Three-axis autostabilisation system by Fluggerätewerk Bodensee GmbH.

DIMENSIONS, EXTERNAL:
Wing span   59 ft 3 in (18·06 m)
Wing aspect ratio   5·05
Length overall   68 ft 6 in (20·88 m)
Height overall   28 ft 0 in (8·53 m)
Wheel track   24 ft 7½ in (7·50 m)
Wheelbase   28 ft 2½ in (8·60 m)

DIMENSIONS, INTERNAL:
Cabin:
Length, with ramp   43 ft 3½ in (13·20 m)
Length, excluding ramp   30 ft 2½ in (9·20 m)
Max height   7 ft 2½ in (2·20 m)
Width at floor   6 ft 11½ in (2·12 m)
Floor area, without ramp 210 sq ft (19·5 m²)
Volume   1,765 cu ft (50 m³)

AREAS:
Wings, gross   613 sq ft (57 m²)
Horizontal tail surfaces (total)
                         176·3 sq ft (16·4 m²)
Vertical tail surfaces (total) 165·7 sq ft (15·4 m²)

WEIGHTS:
Basic design weight   49,500 lb (22,500 kg)
Payload   6,600-11,000 lb (3,000-5,000 kg)
Max T-O weight   60,500 lb (27,500 kg)

PERFORMANCE:
Cruising speed at 20,000 ft (6,000 m)
                347 knots (400 mph; 650 km/h)
Rate of climb at S/L 5,250 ft (1,600 m)/min
Service ceiling   34,500 ft (10,500 m)

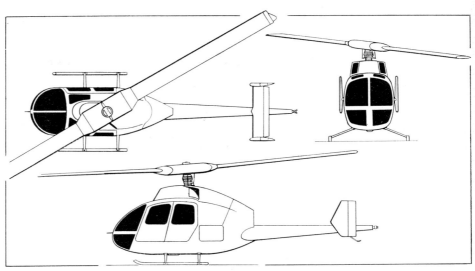

Dornier Do 132 five-seat tip-driven light helicopter

Mock-up of the Dornier Do 132 five-seat tip-drive helicopter

DORNIER Do 132

The Do 132 is a light five-seat tip-drive helicopter suitable for a wide range of civil and military applications. Three prototypes are being built under a Federal Defence Ministry contract, and flight testing is scheduled to begin in the Spring of 1971. The rotor system, including the gas generator and hot gas guidance duct, have already been ground-tested. Costs of modifying the PT6G-20 power plant are being shared between Canada and Germany.

TYPE: Five-seat light multi-purpose helicopter.

ROTOR SYSTEM: Two-blade tip-driven semi-rigid main rotor only. Spherically-shaped head houses central flapping hinge and serves as hot-gas distributor. Blade section NACA 63,021. Leading-edge of each blade consists of a duralumin spar; honeycomb monocoque box-type gas duct. The blade skin is of sheet duralumin. All attachments are bonded. Gas ducts are made of thin-wall welded Nimonic tube which slides inside a special insulating duct in the blade.

ROTOR DRIVE AND CONTROL: Hot gas generated by turbine is fed through holes in the rotor head to the blade ducts, with piston rings sealing the head/blade connection. Gas is ejected through blade-tip nozzles, where it expands. Rotor blade control is conventional, using cyclic and collective pitch control actuated by push-rods via a swashplate. When

yaw control movements are required, rudder pedal movements actuate a hot-gas nozzle at the end of the tail boom.

FUSELAGE: Pod and boom type. The primary structure consists of the main bulkhead, rotor head plate, a vertical beam, and floor longerons. A vertical beam and two struts provide sufficient stiffness against rotor horizontal forces. Longerons on each side of the floor carry the cabin and tailplane loads to the two main bulkheads. Tail-boom is a semi-monocoque structure of aluminium, with ribs and stringers.

TAIL UNIT: Horizontal fixed tailplane, with one-piece full-span elevator and twin endplate fins and rudders. Of aluminium construction, with ribs and stringers. No tabs.

LANDING GEAR: Thin-wall steel-tube skids, with attachments for small ground-handling wheels. Steel cross-members are designed to serve as shock-absorbers. Float landing gear can be substituted for the skids.

POWER PLANT: One Pratt & Whitney (UAC) PT6G-20 modified hot-gas generator mounted by means of pylons to the rear bulkhead. As compared to the standard PT6A-20 turboshaft, the gas generator has no power turbine, the gas energy being directed to work in the blade nozzles. Gas horsepower 720. Generator supplies 5·4 lb (2·46 kg) gas per second at a pressure of 2·41 atmospheres at 750°C. Fuel tank under rear seats.

Dornier-built Bell UH-1D helicopter in German Army insignia

ACCOMMODATION: Two individual seats in front and rear bench seat for three persons. Double doors on each side of cabin, but larger, single doors can be fitted at customer's option. Fittings on each side of fuselage to take stretchers, auxiliary fuel tanks for ferry flights, baggage containers or chemical hoppers for agricultural duties. Dual controls optional.

DIMENSIONS, EXTERNAL:

Rotor diameter	35 ft 1¼ in (10·70 m)
Rotor blade chord (constant)	1 ft 4½ in (0·42 m)
Length overall	24 ft 7¼ in (7·50 m)
Height overall	9 ft 2 in (2·80 m)
Skid track	6 ft 9 in (2·66 m)

DIMENSIONS, INTERNAL:

Cabin:
Max height	5 ft 2¼ in (1·58 m)
Max width	4 ft 5½ in (1·36 m)

WEIGHTS AND LOADING (estimated):
Weight empty	1,488 lb (675 kg)
Normal T-O weight	3,152 lb (1,430 kg)
Max T-O weight	3,637 lb (1,650 kg)
Max (dynamic T-O) weight	3,593 lb (1,630 kg)
Max disc loading	3·25 lb/sq ft (15·9 kg/m²)

PERFORMANCE (estimated):
Max level speed
123 knots (142 mph; 229 km/h)
Cruising speed 119 knots (137 mph; 221 km/h)
Range with 639 lb (290 kg) fuel load
238 nm (275 miles; 450 km)

DORNIER/FIAT G91

Assisted by Messerschmitt-Bölkow-Blohm and VFW-Fokker as sub-contractors, Dornier is building, partly from Fiat-supplied components, a further 22 Fiat G91T/3 two-seat jet trainers for the *Luftwaffe*. These aircraft are scheduled for delivery between March 1971 and January 1972.

DORNIER/BELL UH-1D

Dornier is prime contractor for German licence production of the Bell UH-1D helicopter. Current contracts cover the delivery of a total of 387 aircraft of this type by the end of 1970. Phase I of the programme called for the first 10 aircraft to be assembled and test flown by Bell in the USA, then disassembled and shipped to Dornier. Phase II involved the manufacture by Bell of the major assemblies for 40 aircraft which were sent to Dornier for final assembly and acceptance flights. Phase III calls for complete manufacture in Germany, except for certain dynamic components. The first Phase III UH-1D flew early in 1968 and the 100th was delivered to the German Army in mid-1969.

Full details of the Bell UH-1 series can be found in the US section of this edition.

EWR

ENTWICKLUNGSRING-SÜD GmbH (Subsidiary of Messerschmitt-Bölkow-Blohm GmbH)

ADDRESS:
8 Munich 27, Arabellastrasse 16

BOARD OF DIRECTORS:
Dr Bernhard Weinhardt (Chairman)
Walther Stromeyer (Deputy Chairman)
Hubert Bauer
Dipl-Ing Ludwig Bölkow
Dr Hans-Otto Riedel
Dr Hans Heinrich Ritter von Srbik (Bankhaus Aufhäuser)
Karl Georg Falkenberg (Entwicklungsring-Süd GmbH)

Dipl-Ing Carlhein Mebert
Josef Monat (Entwicklungsring-Süd GmbH)

MANAGEMENT:
Hans Empacher
Kurt Lauser
Dipl-Ing Gero Madelung
Dr Ing Otto-Ernst Pabst

This company was founded on 23 February 1959, when the Bölkow, Heinkel and Messerschmitt companies formed a central design office, at the suggestion of the Federal German Defence Ministry, to undertake the task of developing a Mach 2 VTOL interceptor. Heinkel withdrew from the consortium on 31 December 1964.
On 1 July 1965, EWR was changed from a consortium to a limited liability company. It is now a wholly-owned subsidiary of Messerschmitt-Bölkow-Blohm GmbH.

EWR does not have its own production facilities, the extensive capacity of the parent companies being available to manufacture its designs. Details of the first of these—the two VJ101C experimental VTOL aircraft—appeared in the 1966-67 *Jane's*.

More recently, EWR partnered Fairchild Hiller-FRG Corporation in the now-cancelled US/FRG programme (see International section of the 1967-68 *Jane's*).

EWR has at its disposal a covered area of about 277,700 sq ft (25,800 m²), including a test facility at Manching. It had 1,700 employees in 1967.

HAAK

REINHARD HAAK

ADDRESS: Aachen

Herr Reinhard Haak, an engineer with VFW-Fokker GmbH in Bremen, began in 1967 the design of a tandem two-seat aerobatic aircraft known as the SISA Ha-11. Detail design work has been completed, and construction was expected to begin in 1970.

HAAK SISA Ha-11

The Ha-11 is intended for use as an aerobatic two-seater, although the prototype will be completed initially, for flight test purposes, without certain features specially designed for aerobatic flying. Either a 160 or 200 hp Lycoming engine will be installed for initial testing, with provision for installing a fuel-injection engine at a later date. The Ha-11 has been designed for safe load factors between +8 and —6 g.

TYPE: Two-seat aerobatic light aircraft.

WINGS: Cantilever low-wing monoplane. Two-spar wooden wings, of tapered planform and plywood covered except for wing-tips, which are of glass-fibre and are detachable. Plain trailing-edge flaps and ailerons. On aerobatic version, flaps will be operable in unison with elevators.

FUSELAGE: Welded steel-tube structure, with glass-fibre skin.

TAIL UNIT: Cantilever structure. Steel-tube fin, glass-fibre covered, is welded to fuselage. Remainder of tail unit is of all-wood construction.

LANDING GEAR: Non-retractable tail-wheel type, with rubber shock-absorption.

ACCOMMODATION: Seats for two persons in tandem under fully-transparent rearward-sliding jettisonable canopy. Seats fully adjustable fore and aft and for height.

HAVERTZ

HERMANN HAVERTZ

ADDRESS: Essen, Ladenspelderstrasse 15

Herr Havertz first established an aircraft works in Germany in 1950, and in 1953 he completed the prototype of his first helicopter design, the single-seat HZ-3, powered by a modified Volkswagen engine.

More recently, Herr Havertz has completed two other rotorcraft designs, the HZ-4 and HZ-5; all known details were published in the 1969-70 edition of *Jane's*, together with a photograph of the HZ-5.

HFB (See under "Messerschmitt-Bölkow-Blohm GmbH")

HIRTH

WOLF HIRTH GmbH

ADDRESS: Nabern/Teck

Since early 1967, Wolf Hirth GmbH has been marketing, under the designation KL-35D-160, a modernised and higher-powered version of the well-known pre-war Klemm KL-35D single-seat light aircraft, over 3,000 of which were built between 1936 and 1944.

The company is also to build the prototype of a new single-seat aerobatic aircraft, the Akromaster Mk 2. All known details of these two types are given below.

HIRTH-KLEMM KL-35D-160

The major change in the KL-35D-160 is the substitution, in place of the KL-35D's original 100 hp Hirth engine, of a 160 hp Walter Minor 6-III six-cylinder in-line inverted air-cooled engine driving a two-blade wooden propeller. The fuel system includes a fuselage tank of 6·6 Imp gallons (30 litres) capacity and two wing tanks with a capacity of approx 13·2 Imp gallons (60 litres). Oil capacity is 1·5-2·4 Imp gallons (7-11 litres). The airframe, which makes extensive use of steel tube in its construction, is considerably more robust than that of the original KL-35D.

HIRTH AKROMASTER Mk 2

Wolf Hirth GmbH is undertaking the construction of a new single-seat aerobatic light aircraft known as the Akromaster Mk 2, which was due to fly in the Spring of 1970.

The aircraft has been designed by Ing Meder at the request of a group of German and Swiss aerobatic pilots for an aircraft stressed for flying between the limits of +8 g and —8 g, including prolonged periods of inverted flight. The aircraft's profile is almost symmetrical, so that its aerodynamic properties are virtually identical whether the aircraft is flying right way up or inverted. The tail surfaces are similar to those on several pre-war Arado aircraft, but are located somewhat further forward on the fuselage. Wooden construction is used throughout.

WINGS: Cantilever low-wing monoplane with slight sweepback. Dual-purpose flaps/ailerons.

TAIL UNIT: Conventional type, with single fin and balanced rudder.

LANDING GEAR: Non-retractable type.

POWER PLANT: One 220 hp Franklin 6A-335-C six-cylinder horizontally-opposed air-cooled engine, driving a Hartzell constant-speed propeller. Fuel in three tanks in wings, with total capacity of 22 Imp gallons (100 litres). Fuel and oil systems designed to permit inverted flying.

ACCOMMODATION: Single seat for pilot under rearward-sliding canopy. Space for 22 lb (10 kg) of baggage.

DIMENSIONS, EXTERNAL:
Wing span	26 ft 10¾ in (8·20 m)
Aspect ratio	6·7
Length overall	19 ft 8¼ in (6·00 m)
Height overall	8 ft 2½ in (2·50 m)

AREA:
Wings, gross	107·6 sq ft (10·0 m²)

WEIGHTS AND LOADINGS:
Weight empty	926 lb (420 kg)
Max T-O weight	1,323 lb (600 kg)
Max wing loading	12·3 lb/sq ft (60 kg/m²)
Max power loading	6·6 lb/hp (3·0 kg/hp)

PERFORMANCE (at max T-O weight, estimated):
Max level speed at S/L
167 knots (193 mph; 310 km/h)
Cruising speed at S/L
146 knots (168 mph; 270 km/h)
Landing speed 44 knots (50 mph; 80 km/h)
Rate of climb at S/L
1,970-2,365 ft (600-720 m)/min
Time to 3,280 ft (1,000 m) 1 min 30 sec
Service ceiling 24,600 ft (7,500 m)
T-O run 328 ft (100 m)
Landing run 590 ft (180 m)
Range 325 nm (375 miles; 600 km)
Endurance 2 hr 30 min

KRAUSS

DIPL-ING PETER KRAUSS

ADDRESS:
7 Stuttgart-Stammheim, Freihofstrasse 37

With the assistance of Ing Jürgen Kuntze and Herr Ewald Sammet, Dipl-Ing Krauss, Technical Director of the Kornwestheim Flying Group, has completed and flown a small autogyro known as the TRS-1 (Tragschrauber 1).

KRAUSS TRS-1

Design and construction of the TRS-1 was started in September 1966, and it flew for the first time in September 1968. A certificate of airworthiness in the Experimental class was awarded by the LBA on 11 June 1968. By the Autumn of 1968 the aircraft had completed 49 of the 100 flying hours required before full certification can be granted.

TYPE: Single-seat light autogyro.

ROTOR SYSTEM: Single two-blade all-metal main rotor, with Stan-Zee blades, on Bensen gimbal-type rotor head at top of centrally-located rotor pylon. Rotor can be tilted for fore-and-aft or sideways movement by stick control.

FUSELAGE: Streamlined monocoque pod-and-boom structure, of glass-fibre sandwich construction with a balsa wood core.

TAIL UNIT: Vee-shaped tail surfaces, for lateral control only. These surfaces are of glass-fibre construction, carried on rear tail-boom and consisting of tapered fixed fins and large balanced movable surfaces.

LANDING GEAR: Non-retractable tricycle type, with additional wheel under tail. Glass-fibre cantilever main legs and wheel fairings, the latter housing the bearings of the stub-axles for the main wheels. Main wheel tyres size 4 × 4·00, pressure 35·6 lb/sq in (2·5 kg/cm²). Independent brake on each main wheel. The small tail-wheel, which is the first unit to touch down, has a telescopic shock-absorber.

POWER PLANT: One 72 hp McCulloch four-cylinder two-stroke horizontally-opposed air-cooled engine, mounted on a steel-tube support frame and driving a two-blade propeller of Herr Krauss's own design. Fuel in single main tank, centrally mounted on rotor pylon, with capacity of 4·4 Imp gallons (20 litres).

ACCOMMODATION: Single semi-reclining glass-fibre seat for pilot under one-piece moulded Plexiglas canopy, which hinges sideways to starboard to provide access to cockpit.

ELECTRONICS AND EQUIPMENT: Cockpit instrumentation includes altimeter, ASI, rate of climb indicator, rotor and engine rpm indicators, engine temperature indicator and VHF radio.

DIMENSIONS, EXTERNAL:
Diameter of main rotor	22 ft 7¾ in (6·90 m)
Length overall	12 ft 3½ in (3·75 m)
Height overall	7 ft 2½ in (2·20 m)
Wheelbase	5 ft 7 in (1·70 m)

WEIGHTS:
Weight empty, equipped	335 lb (152 kg)
Max T-O weight	595 lb (270 kg)

PERFORMANCE (at max T-O weight):
Max level speed 92 knots (106 mph; 170 km/h)
Max permissible diving speed
108 knots (124 mph; 200 km/h)
Max cruising speed
76 knots (87 mph; 140 km/h)
Econ cruising speed
59 knots (68 mph; 110 km/h)
Landing speed 7 knots (8 mph; 12 km/h)
Max rate of climb at S/L 590 ft (180 m)/min
Min rate of sink, power off 1,083 ft (330 m)/min

Krauss TRS-1 single-seat light autogyro   (*J. M. G. Gradidge*)

Krauss TRS-3 autogyro shown at the 1970 Hanover Air Show   (*J. M. G. Gradidge*)

T-O run	492 ft (150 m)	Landing run	50 ft (15 m)
T-O to 50 ft (15 m)	820 ft (250 m)	Range with max fuel	
Landing from 50 ft (15 m)	115 ft (35 m)		65 nm (75 miles; 120 km)

LEMBERGER
KARL LEMBERGER
ADDRESS:
74 Tübingen, Wilhelmstrasse 20

In September 1968 Herr Lemberger began the construction of a two-seat all-wood light aircraft of his own design known as the LD 20b. All available details of this aircraft are given below.

LEMBERGER LD 20b
The Lemberger LD 20b is a cantilever biplane, the wings of which are removable to permit the aircraft to be towed behind a motor car. Construction was expected to be completed by the Summer of 1970.

The accompanying drawing shows the general arrangement of the aircraft.

TYPE: Two-seat amateur-built light aircraft.

WINGS: Cantilever biplane wings with considerable stagger, the upper and lower wings having the same planform, dimensions and gross area. Mean wing section NACA 23012. Incidence 1°. Dihedral 2° from roots. Each wing has two closely-spaced full-span spars, which are of T-section out to the sixth rib and then of U-section to form a torsion-box structure with the plywood skin, which covers the leading-edge back to the rear spar. Aft of rear spar, each wing is fabric-covered. Differentially-operated ailerons on lower wings only. Wings can be detached and suspended alongside fuselage when towing the aircraft behind a motor car.

FUSELAGE: All-wood girder structure of basically rectangular section, with curved ply top-decking. Plywood-covered to just aft of pilot's seat; sides and bottom of rear fuselage fabric-covered.

TAIL UNIT: Cantilever all-wood structure, with shallow fin (integral with fuselage) and balanced rudder. Variable-incidence tailplane and dampened elevators. Control surfaces fabric-covered. Horizontal surfaces can be detached for road transportation.

LANDING GEAR: Non-retractable two-wheel type with tail-skid. Glass-fibre fairings will be provided for main units at a later date. Cantilever main-wheel legs. To avoid dismantling rudder assembly for transit, tail-skid is designed for attachment to a framework similar to a car luggage rack, which can be fastened to the car roof. Propeller ground clearance is sufficient to permit this.

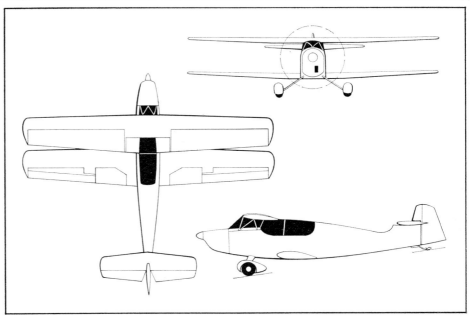

Three-view drawing of the Lemberger LD 20b two-seat biplane

POWER PLANT: One 62 hp Walter Mikron engine, driving a two-blade propeller. Design permits installation of alternative engines of up to 85 hp.

ACCOMMODATION: Tandem seats for two persons in fully-enclosed cabin. Dual controls. Front seat on CG. Ballast tank aft of firewall.

DIMENSIONS, EXTERNAL:
Wing span (each)	23 ft 10½ in (7·28 m)
Length overall	21 ft 10½ in (6·67 m)
Height overall	7 ft 2½ in (2·20 m)

AREAS:
Wings, gross	150·7 sq ft (14·00 m²)
Ailerons (total)	12·92 sq ft (1·20 m²)

Fin	2·15 sq ft (0·20 m²)
Rudder	6·46 sq ft (0·60 m²)
Tailplane	12·92 sq ft (1·20 m²)
Elevators (total)	9·69 sq ft (0·90 m²)

WEIGHTS AND LOADINGS:
Weight empty	661 lb (300 kg)
Max T-O weight	1,186 lb (538 kg)
Max wing loading	7·87 lb/sq ft (38·4 kg/m²)
Max power loading	19·18 lb/hp (8·7 kg/hp)

PERFORMANCE (estimated, at max T-O weight):
Max level speed	96 knots (111 mph; 178 km/h)
Cruising speed	86 knots (99 mph; 160 km/h)
Landing speed	32 knots (37 mph; 60 km/h)
Time to 3,275 ft (1,000 m)	7 min

LFU

LEICHTFLUGTECHNIK-UNION GmbH

(Subsidiary of Messerschmitt-Bölkow-Blohm GmbH)

ADDRESS:
Bonn, Adenauer Allee 68

TECHNICAL AND SCIENTIFIC COMMITTEE:
Ministerialrat von Halem (Chairman)
Dipl-Ing F. Schatt (Deputy Chairman)
Prof Hütter
Dr-Ing Niederstadt

This association was formed in 1963 by Bölkow and its subsidiary Bölkow-Apparatebau GmbH (now part of Messerschmitt-Bölkow-Blohm GmbH); Pützer-Kunststofftechnik GmbH; and Rhein-Flugzeugbau GmbH, each with a one-third share. It is not a commercial undertaking, but a coordinating organisation for research and development of lightweight aircraft. The management of LFU is composed of representatives of the three parent companies, assisted in a consultant capacity by a Technical and Scientific Committee.

LFU's principal activity is the continued research into, and development of, the use of lightweight plastics for aircraft construction. This has resulted in the design and construction of a prototype aircraft, the LFU-205, embodying the results of studies so far undertaken.

All available details of the LFU-205 are given below.

LFU-205

The LFU-205 is a four-seat experimental prototype light aircraft, the entire airframe of which is constructed of glass-fibre reinforced plastics. As well as offering a basic weight some 15 per cent lower than that of a comparable all-metal aircraft, with a consequent improvement in performance, the employment of plastics offers considerable saving of man-hours in production and maintenance. Late in January 1968 an LFU-205 wing was subjected to dynamic loads equivalent to 36,000 flying hours without any evidence of material deterioration.

Development of the LFU-205 has been undertaken by the three constituent companies, additional funds being provided by the Federal Ministries of Defence and Economics and by the Ministries of Economics of Baden-Württemberg and North Rhine-Westphalia.

Construction of the LFU-205 prototype was started early in 1967, Pützer being responsible for manufacturing jigs and fixtures and RFB for the entire wing assembly. Messerschmitt-Bölkow-Blohm, as well as building the fuselage and undertaking final assembly of the prototype, is overall co-ordinator of the programme and is responsible for design, flight testing and certification.

The prototype LFU-205 (D-ELFU) made its first flight on 20 March 1968, and the details below apply to this aircraft.

TYPE: Experimental four-seat light aircraft.

WINGS: Cantilever low-wing monoplane. Eppler 502 wing section. Thickness/chord ratio 15·72% throughout. Dihedral 4° 23′ from roots. Incidence 2°. Wings have 7° sweep-forward from roots. Glass-fibre sandwich structure, consisting of a smooth outer skin and an inner skin laminated, hardened and wet-bonded together to form a rigid structure. Support of the two skins against the sandwich core is provided by a series of small tubes 0·40 in (10 mm) in diameter, wrapped in glass-fibre and running parallel to the ribs. Each wing has three compartments built in this fashion (leading-edge, centre compartment, trailing-edge), the centre compartment being rectangular and extended at the root to enter the fuselage and act as the main spar. The three compartments are then enclosed in a single outer skin to give a smooth exterior. Frise-type ailerons and Fowler-type flaps are also of glass-fibre plastics.

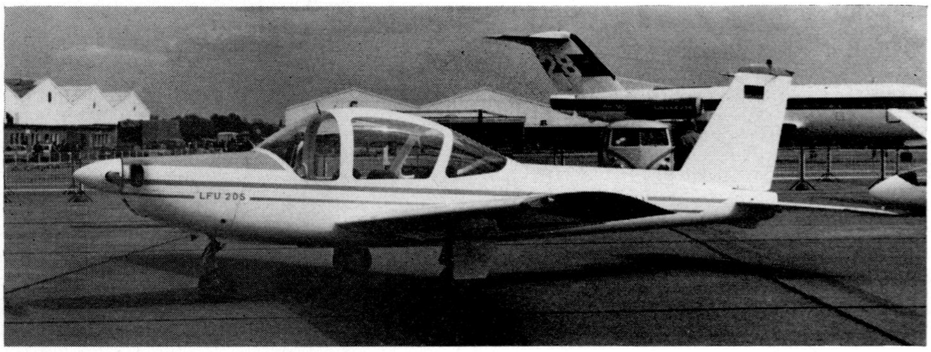

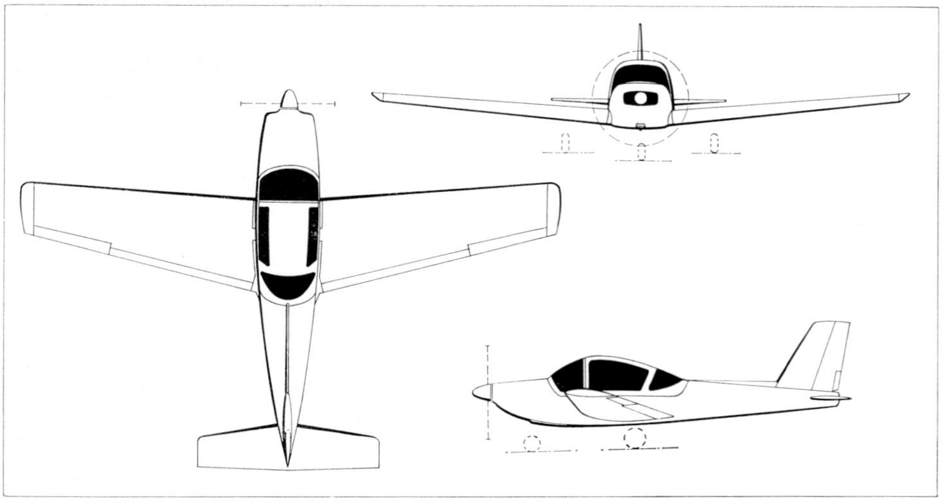

Photograph and three-view drawing of the LFU-205 four-seat light aircraft

FUSELAGE: Semi-monocoque shell of wet-bonded glass-fibre construction, thickness approx 0·60 in (15 mm), with an inner core of glass-fibre covered tubes which lie parallel to the main frames. Each tube is impregnated with epoxy resin and has an inner tube of soft plastic that is inflated to force the outer tube against the inner and outer skins. These skins, of moulded plastic, are laminated in position and then hardened and wet-bonded to give a rigid structure.

TAIL UNIT: Single fin and rudder, with slight sweepback on leading-edge of fin and shallow dorsal fairing from base of fin to rear of cockpit canopy. Trim-tab in rudder and tailplane. One-piece all-moving tailplane mid-mounted on rear fuselage. Similar sandwich construction to that of wings, utilising a foam-plastic core.

LANDING GEAR: Retractable tricycle type, with single wheel on each unit. Main wheels retract inward into wings, nose-wheel rearward into fuselage.

POWER PLANT: One 200 hp Lycoming IO-360-A1C four-cylinder horizontally-opposed air-cooled engine, driving a Hartzell two-blade constant-speed propeller of 6 ft 4 in (1·93 m) diameter. Fuel in two tanks in wings, with total capacity of 42 Imp gallons (192 litres). Refuelling point above each wing. Oil capacity 2 Imp gallons (9 litres).

ACCOMMODATION: Side-by-side seating, in pairs, for four persons beneath rearward-sliding canopy. Space for 88 lb (40 kg) of baggage. Blind-flying instrumentation standard.

DIMENSIONS, EXTERNAL:

Wing span	35 ft 7⅛ in (10·85 m)
Wing chord at root	6 ft 2¼ in (1·885 m)
Wing chord at tip	3 ft 4¾ in (1·035 m)
Wing aspect ratio	7·2
Length overall	25 ft 1¼ in (7·65 m)
Width, wings folded	4 ft 3¼ in (1·30 m)
Height overall	8 ft 0¾ in (2·46 m)
Tailplane span	11 ft 9¾ in (3·60 m)
Wheel track	9 ft 8 in (2·95 m)
Wheelbase	6 ft 9 in (2·06 m)
Propeller ground clearance	11¾ in (0·30 m)

AREAS:

Wings, gross	175·99 sq ft (16·35 m^2)
Ailerons (total)	10·7 sq ft (0·99 m^2)
Trailing-edge flaps (total)	25·2 sq ft (2·34 m^2)
Fin	14·4 sq ft (1·34 m^2)
Rudder, incl tab	5·81 sq ft (0·54 m^2)
Tailplane, incl tab	36·0 sq ft (3·34 m^2)

WEIGHTS AND LOADINGS:

Weight empty	1,543 lb (700 kg)
Max T-O weight	2,645 lb (1,200 kg)
Max wing loading	14·95 lb/sq ft (73·4 kg/m^2)
Max power loading	13·23 lb/hp (6·0 kg/hp)

PERFORMANCE (at max T-O weight):

Max permissible speed at S/L	194 knots (224 mph; 360 km/h)
Cruising speed at S/L	162 knots (186 mph; 300 km/h)
Stalling speed	41 knots (47 mph; 75 km/h)
Landing speed	46 knots (53 mph; 85 km/h)
Rate of climb at S/L	1,083 ft (330 m)/min
Service ceiling	19,685 ft (6,000 m)
T-O run	655 ft (200 m)
T-O to 50 ft (15 m)	1,247 ft (380 m)
Landing from 50 ft (15 m)	1,050 ft (320 m)
Range at 6,560 ft (2,000 m), 75% power, no reserves	755 nm (870 miles; 1,400 km)
Endurance at 154 knots (177 mph; 285 km/h) cruising speed	4 hr 55 min

MERCKLE

MERCKLE FLUGZEUGWERKE GmbH

HEAD OFFICE AND WORKS:
14a Oedheim/Württ., Bad Friedrichshall

Following successful completion of the development programme for its five-seat Model SM 67 turbine-powered helicopter, Merckle began developing a new high-speed helicopter known by the designations E 98D and E 130. Initial wind-tunnel testing was carried out in 1964-66, and the dynamic test version was illustrated in the 1968-69 *Jane's*.

A 74 per cent holding in Merckle was acquired by Dornier GmbH in the Summer of 1968.

MESSERSCHMITT-BÖLKOW-BLOHM

MESSERSCHMITT-BÖLKOW-BLOHM GmbH

HEAD OFFICE:
Ottobrunn bei München, 8 München 80, Postfach 801220

WORKS:
Augsburg, Donauwörth, Hamburg-Finkenwerder, Laupheim, Manching, Munich, Nabern/Teck, Ottobrunn, Schrobenhausen and Stade

CHAIRMAN OF THE BOARD OF DIRECTORS:
Prof Dr Ing e.h. Willy Messerschmitt

PRESIDENT:
Dipl-Ing Ludwig Bölkow

EXECUTIVE VICE-PRESIDENTS:
Dipl-Ing Werner Blohm
Dr e.h. Dipl-Ing Friedrich Drechsler
Johannes Popien

VICE-PRESIDENTS:
Dr Johannes Broschwitz
Sepp Hort

PUBLIC RELATIONS:
Eduard Roth
Helmut Pischel (Commercial Aircraft Division)

EXECUTIVES:
Ernst-Georg Pantel (Aircraft Division)
Werner Blohm (Commercial Aircraft Division)
Günther Kuhlo (Surface Transport Division)

Dr Friedrich Drechsler (Defence Technology Division)
Julius Henrici (Space Division)
Kurt Pfleiderer (Helicopter Division)
Rainer Utecht (Cybernetics Division)
Kyrill von Gersdorff (Administrative Services Division)

In May 1969 the former Messerschmitt-Bölkow GmbH and Hamburger Flugzeugbau GmbH (see 1968-69 *Jane's*) respectively endorsed the merger between their two companies to form a new group known as Messerschmitt-Bölkow-Blohm GmbH. Major shareholder in the new company is the Blohm family, which has a 27·1% interest; other shareholders are Prof Dr Ing e.h. Willy Messerschmitt (23·3%), Dipl-Ing Ludwig Bölkow (14·6%), The Boeing Company and Aérospatiale (9·7% each), and the Bavarian Reconstruction Finance Institute (6·5%). Siemens AG acquired a 9·1% interest in July 1969. The new company is the largest aerospace concern in Germany, with a total work force in 1970 of some 20,000 employees.

The Messerschmitt group had its origin in the Flugzeugbau Messerschmitt of 1923, which became Messerschmitt AG in 1938. The Bölkow company had its origin in a civil engineering office opened by Ludwig Bölkow at Stuttgart in 1948. Hamburger Flugzeugbau GmbH was founded in 1933 by the owners of the great Blohm & Voss shipbuilding company.

HFB and Vereinigte Flugtechnische Werke-Fokker are linked in Entwicklungsring Nord. The first projects of this group included the design and construction of the third stage of the European space booster. HFB is a member of the Franco-German consortium which developed the Transall C-160 military transport, and assists in the manufacture of the Fokker-VFW F.28 Fellowship short-haul jet transport, for which it has exclusive sales rights in the German Federal Republic. It also designed and built the rear fuselage of the Dornier Do 31 E experimental V/STOL transport.

Siebelwerke-ATG (SIAT) was formed on 18 November 1952, by an amalgamation of the Siebel-Flugzeugwerke, successor to the former Klemm-Leichtflugzeugwerke GmbH, and the ATG-Maschinenbau GmbH, which had its origin in the famous 1914-18 War company of Deutsche Flugzeug-Werke (DFW) GmbH. It is now a wholly-owned subsidiary of Messerschmitt-Bölkow-Blohm GmbH.

SIAT is a member of the international consortiums producing the Breguet 1150 Atlantic and Transall C-160; is building the integral wing box assembly, wing leading-edge slats and tip-tanks of the HFB 320 Hansa jet executive transport; and, for Dornier, main rotor blade assemblies for the Dornier/Bell UH-1D helicopter. It has been responsible for complete manufacture of the BO 105 helicopter; and various components for F-104G Starfighters for the German Air Force.

The subsidiary companies, of whose histories more detailed accounts appeared in the 1969-70 edition, are now fully integrated into the eight Divisions listed above.

Current products of MBB include space vehicles, rocket motors, guided missiles, aircraft, helicopters, sailplanes, electronic equipment, and glass-fibre-reinforced plastics.

The company is the German partner in Panavia Aircraft GmbH, Munich, a partner in Deutsche Airbus GmbH, responsible for development of the A 300B European Airbus, and is collaborating with Aérospatiale of France in the Franco-German E 650 Eurotrainer jet trainer project.

Production of the BO 105 five/six-seat twin-turbine helicopter is in progress, and a compound helicopter is under development. The BO 209 Monsun single-engined light aircraft is also in production, together with the BO 208 C Junior.

Under agreements signed in the Summer of 1964, Messerschmitt-Bölkow-Blohm is co-operating with Aérospatiale of France in the field of light military helicopters, including armed helicopters. Its highly successful rigid rotor with glass-fibre blades, as used on the BO 105, is expected to be a feature of these joint programmes and was initially adopted for the SA 341 Gazelle.

In the field of V/STOL aircraft, the BO 140 four-engined tilt-wing transport has been proposed to meet German civil and military requirements for the late 1970s, and the Commercial Aircraft Division has submitted its HFB 600 VTOL project, of which wind-tunnel testing began early in 1970.

Messerschmitt and Bölkow participated in development of the VJ 101C VTOL aircraft, a joint EWR project of 1960-65 described in earlier editions of *Jane's*. Other activities include the design of the Me 408 utility V/STOL transport, utilising two General Electric T58-GE-16 turbofan engines to drive a pair of wing-

Messerschmitt-Bölkow-Blohm BO 208 C Junior (100 hp Rolls-Royce/Continental O-200-A engine)
(J. D. R. Rawlings)

mounted rotors. This aircraft would seat 10-12 passengers, have an AUW for vertical take-off of 11,000 lb (5,000 kg) and a max forward speed of 453 knots (522 mph; 840 km/h). The rotors would be stowable during forward flight, and this would also be a feature of the P-2020, a more advanced project along similar lines with General Electric GE1 turbofans and a VTOL AUW of 52,000 lb (23,600 kg).

MBB BO 208 C JUNIOR

This is the Malmö MFI-9 Junior side-by-side two-seat light aircraft, for which MBB has

licence rights. The first example built by Bölkow flew in April 1962. German certification of the original version was received on 22 April 1963, and FAA certification on 17 January 1964. The current BO 208 C received German certification on 20 May 1965. The 150th Bölkow Junior was delivered in April 1967; by October 1969 German production of Juniors had totalled approx 200. Juniors have been sold in 21 different countries, and Compagnie Aérienne de Transport has acquired the agency for sales of the BO 208 C to French customers. After-sales service of Juniors in France is provided by Aérospatiale.

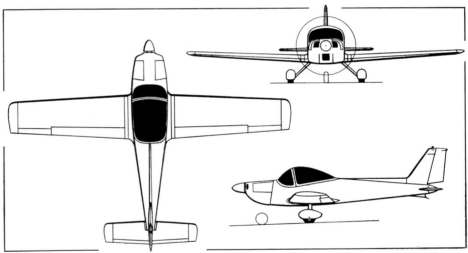

Three-view drawing of the Messerschmitt-Bölkow-Blohm BO 209 Monsun two-seat light aircraft

MBB BO 209 Monsun (prototype, with 115 hp Lycoming engine) with wings folded

The Junior is certificated in both the normal and utility categories and for glider-towing, and in Germany is also certificated for aerobatic use. Only the Swedish-built version can be operated as a floatplane.

TYPE: Two-seat aerobatic light monoplane.

WINGS: Braced shoulder-wing monoplane. Single bracing strut each side. NACA 23009 wing section modified to have leading-edge droop. Dihedral 1°. Incidence 1°. Sweep-forward 3°. All-metal single-spar structure. Wing-tips of glass-fibre reinforced plastics. All-metal ailerons and electrically-operated plain flaps. No trim-tabs.

FUSELAGE: All-metal box structure, with no double curvature. External longerons.

TAIL UNIT: Cantilever all-metal structure of "all-flying" type, with anti-servo and trim-tab on horizontal surface.

LANDING GEAR: Non-retractable tricycle type. Cantilever steel main legs. Steerable nose-wheel, with steel springs and hydraulic damping, is operated by the rudder pedals. Cleveland wheels, size 5·00 × 5 on nose unit and 5·50 × 5 on main units, with Continental tubeless tyres. Main wheel tyre pressure 22·75 lb/sq in (1·60 kg/cm²), nose-wheel tyre pressure 20 lb/sq in (1·40 kg/cm²). Cleveland hydraulic disc brakes and parking brake. With full braking pressure, the Junior can be brought to a halt within 330 ft (100 m) of touchdown. Main wheel fairings available as optional extra.

POWER PLANT: One 100 hp Rolls-Royce/Continental O-200-A four-cylinder horizontally-opposed air-cooled engine, driving a McCauley 1A 100MCM 6758 or 6950 or 6955 two-blade fixed-pitch metal propeller. Fuel tank behind cockpit with normal capacity of 22 Imp gallons (100 litres). Oil capacity 1·0 Imp gallon (4·7 litres).

ACCOMMODATION: Two seats side-by-side in enclosed cabin, with central Y-type control column. Rearward-hinged canopy serves as door. Heating and ventilation standard.

ELECTRONICS AND EQUIPMENT: Optional equipment includes Becker radio and glider and banner towing attachment.

DIMENSIONS, EXTERNAL:
Wing span	26 ft 4 in (8·02 m)
Wing chord (constant)	4 ft 0 in (1·22 m)
Wing aspect ratio	6·9
Length overall	19 ft 0 in (5·79 m)
Height overall	6 ft 6 in (1·98 m)
Tailplane span	9 ft 4 in (2·84 m)
Wheel track	6 ft 4 in (1·94 m)
Wheelbase	4 ft 5½ in (1·36 m)

AREAS:
Wings, gross	100 sq ft (9·37 m²)
Ailerons (total)	4·60 sq ft (0·42 m²)
Flaps (total)	14·00 sq ft (1·30 m²)
Fin	5·13 sq ft (0·48 m²)
Rudder	2·70 sq ft (0·25 m²)
Tailplane	17·00 sq ft (1·57 m²)

WEIGHTS AND LOADINGS:
Weight empty, equipped	837 lb (380 kg)
Max T-O weight:	
Normal	1,390 lb (630 kg)
Utility	1,320 lb (600 kg)
Max wing loading	13·78 lb/sq ft (67·2 kg/m²)
Max power loading	13·90 lb/hp (6·30 kg/hp)

PERFORMANCE (at max T-O weight):
Max level speed at S/L	124 knots (143 mph; 230 km/h)
Max permissible diving speed	152·5 knots (176 mph; 283 km/h)
Max cruising speed	111 knots (127 mph; 205 km/h)
Touchdown speed	43 knots (50 mph; 79 km/h)
Rate of climb at S/L	785 ft (240 m)/min
Service ceiling	14,760 ft (4,500 m)
T-O run	660 ft (200 m)
T-O to 50 ft (15 m)	1,480 ft (450 m)
Landing from 50 ft (15 m)	1,480 ft (450 m)
Landing run	660 ft (200 m)
Range with max fuel	538 nm (620 miles; 1,000 km)
Max endurance	5 hr

MBB BO 209 MONSUN (MONSOON)

This two-seat light aircraft was designed by Dipl-Ing Hermann Mylius, and is now in series production. Its design was started in November 1965, under the designation MHK-101, and the prototype (D-EMHK) flew for the first time on 22 December 1967. This aircraft was described in the 1968-69 edition of *Jane's*. In developed form, it is now known as the BO 209 Monsun (Monsoon).

Construction of a BO 209 prototype started in January 1969, and this aircraft flew for the first time on 28 May 1969. By the Spring of 1970 two prototypes and three production aircraft had been completed, and approx 200 options had been received for production aircraft. German certification to FAR Pt 23 was granted in April 1970.

MBB BO 209 Monsun, production aircraft with non-retractable nose-wheel (*J. M. G. Gradidge*)

Current production versions are as follows:
BO 209-150. With 150 hp Lycoming O-320-E1C four-cylinder horizontally-opposed air-cooled engine, driving a McCauley two-blade fixed-pitch metal propeller or (optionally) a Hartzell two-blade constant-speed propeller. Fuel in two tanks in wings with total capacity of 31 Imp gallons (140 litres). Oil capacity 1·6 Imp gallons (7·4 litres).
BO 209-160. Similar to -150, but with 160 hp Lycoming IO-320-D1A fuel-injection engine and Hartzell constant-speed propeller.

In addition, a version with 125 hp engine and an aerobatic version of the BO 209-160 are under development, together with a three-seat version with fully-retractable landing gear, designated BO 210, which was due to fly in 1970.

The following description applies generally to all versions of the BO 209, except where specific models are indicated.

TYPE: Two-seat light touring, training, aerobatic and glider towing aircraft.

WINGS: Cantilever low-wing monoplane. Wing section NACA 64215 at root, NACA 64212 at tip. Dihedral 2° 30′ from roots. Incidence 2°. Sweepback 1° 24′ at quarter-chord. Single-spar all-metal structure, with glass-fibre tips. All-metal differentially-operated ailerons. Electrically-operated all-metal plain trailing-edge flaps. By removing three bolts on each side, the wings can be folded back alongside the fuselage to facilitate stowage in a confined space or to permit the aircraft to be towed on ordinary roads behind a car. Control lines to flaps and ailerons disconnect and reconnect automatically during folding and unfolding.

FUSELAGE: Conventional semi-monocoque structure, of metal construction except for engine cowlings, which are of glass-fibre.

TAIL UNIT: Single fin and rudder, with sweep-back on fin leading-edge and shallow dorsal fairing from base of fin to rear of cockpit canopy. Vertical tail surfaces are of all-metal construction. All-moving tailplane, of metal construction with glass-fibre tips, has slight taper on leading and trailing edges, and is mid-mounted on extreme rear of fuselage, with cable-controlled full-span anti-servo tab. Tailplane tips are removable during transportation by road.

LANDING GEAR: Tricycle type, with optional rearward-retracting nose-wheel and non-retractable main wheels. Single wheel on each unit. Nose-wheel is steerable by means of the rudder pedals, the controls being disconnected automatically during retraction, which is electrically operated. Nose-wheel extends automatically during landing, and can also be locked in the down position during flight if required. Main gear legs are cantilever steel struts descending at 45° from fuselage main bulkhead. Cleveland wheels size 5·00 × 5; Continental tyres, size 5·00 × 5 on nose gear and 5·50 × 5 on main gear. Streamlined fairings available for main wheels. Cleveland hydraulically-actuated brakes. Small skid under rear fuselage, which can be fitted with an adapter for transport by road.

POWER PLANT: One 150 or 160 hp Lycoming "flat-four" engine (details under model descriptions above). Refuelling point above each wing.

ACCOMMODATION: Side-by-side adjustable seats for pilot and one passenger under rearward-sliding tinted canopy. Space aft of seats for 110 lb (50 kg) of baggage. Cabin heating and ventilation standard.

SYSTEMS: 12V DC electrical system, for flap and landing gear actuation and engine starting, includes 40A alternator and 33Ah battery.

ELECTRONICS AND EQUIPMENT: Optional equipment includes IFR instrumentation, two VOR converter indicators and a radio compass with glide-path and signal receiver. Rotating beacon standard.

DIMENSIONS, EXTERNAL:
Wing span	27 ft 6¾ in (8·40 m)

Wing chord at root	4 ft 7 in (1·40 m)
Wing chord at tip	3 ft 3¼ in (1·00 m)
Wing aspect ratio	6·8
Length overall	21 ft 0 in (6·40 m)
Height overall	7 ft 2½ in (2·20 m)
Tailplane span	9 ft 2¼ in (2·80 m)
Tailplane width with tips removed	8 ft 10¼ in (2·70 m)
Wheel track	6 ft 11½ in (2·12 m)
Wheelbase	4 ft 8¼ in (1·43 m)

DIMENSIONS, INTERNAL:
Cabin: Max length	4 ft 7 in (1·40 m)
Max width	3 ft 3¾ in (1·01 m)
Max height	3 ft 7¾ in (1·11 m)

AREAS:
Wings, gross	110 sq ft (10·22 m²)
Ailerons (total)	4·74 sq ft (0·44 m²)
Trailing-edge flaps (total)	27·99 sq ft (2·60 m²)
Rudder	5·38 sq ft (0·50 m²)
Horizontal tail surfaces (total)	17·87 sq ft (1·66 m²)

WEIGHTS AND LOADINGS:
Weight, empty equipped:	
150 hp	1,045 lb (474 kg)
160 hp	1,067 lb (484 kg)
Max payload	504 lb (229 kg)
Fuel and oil	235 lb (107 kg)
Max T-O and landing weight	1,807 lb (820 kg)
Max wing loading	17·0 lb/sq ft (83·0 kg/m²)
Max power loading:	
150 hp	12·06 lb/hp (5·47 kg/hp)
160 hp	11·29 lb/hp (5·12 kg/hp)

PERFORMANCE (estimated, at max T-O weight):
Max level speed at S/L:	
150 hp	146 knots (168 mph; 270 km/h)
160 hp	148 knots (170 mph; 274 km/h)
Max permissible diving speed	172 knots (198 mph; 320 km/h)
Max cruising speed (75% power) at 8,000 ft (2,450 m):	
150 hp	135 knots (155 mph; 250 km/h)
160 hp	137 knots (158 mph; 255 km/h)
Econ cruising speed (65% power) at 8,000 ft (2,450 m):	
150 hp	129 knots (149 mph; 239 km/h)
160 hp	131 knots (151 mph; 243 km/h)
Stalling speed, flaps down	51 knots (58 mph; 93 km/h)
Rate of climb at S/L:	
150 hp	1,045 ft (318 m)/min
160 hp	1,180 ft (360 m)/min
Time to 3,280 ft (1,000 m):	
150 hp	3 min 6 sec
160 hp	2 min 48 sec
Service ceiling:	
150 hp	16,400 ft (5,000 m)
160 hp	17,050 ft (5,200 m)
T-O run:	
150 hp	625 ft (190 m)
160 hp	590 ft (180 m)
Landing run	655 ft (200 m)
Max range, no reserves (65% power):	
150 hp	538 nm (620 miles; 1,000 km)
160 hp	647 nm (745 miles; 1,200 km)
Max endurance:	
150 hp	4 hr 15 min
160 hp	5 hr 0 min

MBB 223 FLAMINGO

The MBB (originally SIAT) 223 Flamingo won a competition for a standard club and training aircraft, organised by the German Ministry of Economics and the Wissenschaftliche Gesellschaft für Luft- und Raumfahrt, in 1962.

The Flamingo is available in two versions:

SIAT 223A1. Basic two-seat utility version, intended primarily as a training aircraft for airline pilots. Ten ordered by Swissair. The Turkish Air Force is reported to have ordered fifteen. Can also be equipped under Normal Category conditions as a "2+2" three/four-seat touring aircraft.

SIAT 223K1. Single-seat aerobatic version, with specially-modified version of IO-360-C1B engine.

TYPE: Two/four-seat light aircraft.

WINGS: Cantilever low-wing monoplane. Wing section NACA 64_2A215. Dihedral 3°. No sweepback. All-metal two-spar structure. Main spars inserted through fuselage sides and bolted together at centre-line. Rear spars attached to sides of fuselage. Removable plastics wing-tips. All-metal Frise-type ailerons and electrically-operated flaps have corrugated skin and extend over the full span. Trim-tab in starboard aileron.

FUSELAGE: Conventional all-metal semi-monocoque structure of frames and stringers with riveted skin.

TAIL UNIT: Cantilever all-metal structure, with corrugated skin on control surfaces. Trim-tab in port elevator and rudder.

LANDING GEAR: Non-retractable tricycle type. Rubber shock-absorption. Steerable and self-centering nose-wheel. All three wheels and tyres size $6·00 \times 6$. Toe-operated independent hydraulic disc brakes. Parking brake.

POWER PLANT: One 200 hp Lycoming IO-360-C1B four-cylinder horizontally-opposed air-cooled fuel-injection engine (200 hp AIO-300 in aerobatic version), driving a Hartzell two-blade constant-speed propeller, diameter 5 ft 11 in (1·80 m). Fuel in integral tanks in wings with total capacity of 48 Imp gallons (220 litres).

ACCOMMODATION: Two seats side-by-side under large rearward-sliding jettisonable canopy. Removable dual controls. Cabin is soundproofed, heated and ventilated. Space for 200 lb (90 kg) of baggage aft of seats, with internal and external access. Provision for fitting a folding seat for one adult or two children in the baggage area.

SYSTEMS: 24V electrical system, with two 50Ah batteries.

ELECTRONICS AND EQUIPMENT: Provision for radio, radio compass, additional IFR instrumentation and glider-towing attachment.

DIMENSIONS, EXTERNAL:

Wing span	27 ft 2 in (8·28 m)
Wing aspect ratio	6
Length overall	24 ft 4½ in (7·43 m)
Height over tail	8 ft 10¼ in (2·70 m)
Tailplane span	10 ft 6 in (3·20 m)
Wheel track	8 ft 0¼ in (2·70 m)
Wheelbase	5 ft 3 in (1·60 m)

DIMENSIONS, INTERNAL:
Cabin:

Length	7 ft 2½ in (2·20 m)
Width	3 ft 8 in (1·12 m)
Height	3 ft 11¼ in (1·20 m)

AREA:

Wings, gross	123·8 sq ft (11·50 m²)

WEIGHTS AND LOADINGS:

Weight empty, equipped	1,510 lb (685 kg)
Max T-O weight:	
A1 (Normal)	2,315 lb (1,050 kg)
A1 (Utility)	2,160 lb (980 kg)
K1	1,810 lb (821 kg)
Max wing loading:	
A1 (Normal)	18·72 lb/sq ft (91·3 kg/m²)
A1 (Utility)	17·47 lb/sq ft (85·2 kg/m²)
K1	14·64 lb/sq ft (71·4 kg/m²)
Max power loading:	
A1 (Normal)	11·57 lb/hp (5·25 kg/hp)
A1 (Utility)	10·80 lb/hp (4·90 kg/hp)
K1	9·04 lb/hp (4·10 kg/hp)

PERFORMANCE (at max T-O weight):

Max level speed:	
A1 (Normal)	131 knots (151 mph; 243 km/h)
A1 (Utility)	132 knots (152 mph; 245 km/h)
K1	135 knots (155 mph; 249 km/h)
Max permissible diving speed	205 knots (236 mph; 380 km/h)
Cruising speed (75% power):	
A1 (Normal)	116 knots (134 mph; 216 km/h)
A1 (Utility)	118 knots (136 mph; 219 km/h)
K1	120 knots (138 mph; 222 km/h)
Landing speed:	
A1 (Normal)	62 knots (71 mph; 115 km/h)
A1 (Utility)	54 knots (62 mph; 100 km/h)
K1	49 knots (56 mph; 91 km/h)
Rate of climb at S/L:	
A1 (Normal)	846 ft (258 m)/min
A1 (Utility)	886 ft (270 m)/min
K1	1,220 ft (372 m)/min
Service ceiling:	
A1 (Normal)	12,300 ft (3,750 m)
A1 (Utility)	14,100 ft (4,300 m)
K1	17,390 ft (5,300 m)
T-O run:	
A1 (Normal)	722 ft (220 m)
A1 (Utility)	705 ft (215 m)
K1	590 ft (180 m)
T-O to 50 ft (15 m):	
A1 (Normal)	1,312-1,558 ft (400-475 m)
Landing run:	
A1 (Normal)	689 ft (210 m)

MBB 223 Flamingo used by Swissair as a two-seat training aircraft

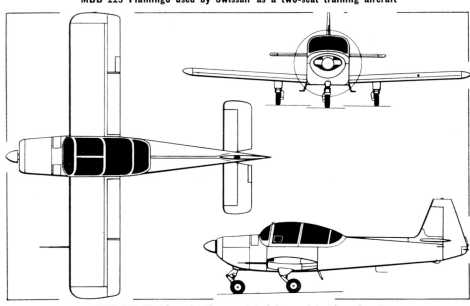

MBB 223 Flamingo two/four-seat training and touring aircraft

Landing from 50 ft (15 m):	
A1 (Normal)	869-1,115 ft (265-340 m)
Range with 30 min reserves:	
A1 (Normal)	475 nm (547 miles; 880 km)
A1 (Utility)	269 nm (310 miles; 500 km)
Range with max fuel:	
A1 (Normal)	620 nm (715 miles; 1,150 km)

MBB BO 105

As a first stage in the development of this light utility helicopter, Bölkow tested a full-size rotor on a ground rig, under German government contract. Design of the aircraft was started in July 1962 and construction of prototypes began in 1964, under a further government contract.

The rotor system is of rigid unarticulated design, with feathering hinges only, based on a concept by Dipl-Ing E. Weiland, and utilises foldable glass-fibre blades. Initial flight tests were made on a Sud-Aviation Alouette II Astazou helicopter, under a programme conducted jointly with Sud-Aviation of France.

The first prototype, fitted with an existing conventional rotor and two Allison 250-C18 turboshaft engines, encountered resonance trouble during ground tests and was destroyed. Subsequent prototypes have had the rigid rotor.

The second BO 105 flew for the first time on 16 February 1967, also powered by two Allison 250-C18 turboshaft engines. The third prototype, with MAN-Turbo 6022 engines, was flown on 20 December 1967. Production aircraft, which will be built by SIAT, can be fitted, at customer's option, with Allison 250-C18, Allison 250-C20, or MTU 6022-A3 engines.

The first two pre-production aircraft (the V4 and V5) were completed in the Spring of 1969, and the V4 (D-HAPE, which is the FAA certification aircraft) flew for the first time on 1 May 1969. The V5 and V7 were purchased by Boeing Vertol, which has purchased three (including one without engines, for modification purposes) and has exclusive rights to produce the BO 105 under licence in the US and other parts of the western hemisphere. One of the Boeing-owned aircraft is remaining in Germany for accelerated endurance tests; another (see illustration overleaf) was equipped to military standards for the US Navy's LAMPS (Light Airborne Multi-Purpose System) competition, but was lost in a crash in June 1970.

Autorotation trials with the BO 105 were successfully concluded in the Autumn of 1969. During the past year, a BO 105 has also been used to flight-test a new MBB-designed "droop-snoot" rotor blade, of NACA 23012 asymmetrical section and having a modified trailing-edge giving improved control in pitching moments.

Total orders and firm options for the BO 105 had reached 48 by early June 1969; production of an initial batch of 70 has been started, the first ten of which were nearing completion early in 1970.

TYPE: Five/six-seat light helicopter.

ROTOR SYSTEM: Four-blade main rotor of rigid unarticulated type, with folding glass-fibre reinforced plastics blades. Titanium rotor hub. Two-blade semi-rigid tail rotor, with blades of glass-fibre reinforced plastics. Rotor brake fitted. WMI (EEC) Spraymat electrical de-icing of main and tail rotor blade leading-edges.

ROTOR DRIVE: Main transmission utilises two stages of spur gears and single stage of bevel gearing. Planetary reduction gear, freewheeling clutch and transmission accessory gear. Tail rotor gearbox on fin. Main rotor/engine rpm ratio 1 : 14·1. Tail rotor/engine rpm ratio 1 : 2·7.

FUSELAGE: Conventional light-alloy semi-monocoque structure of pod-and-boom type. Glass-fibre-reinforced cowling over power plant.

TAIL UNIT: Horizontal stabiliser of conventional light alloy construction.

LANDING GEAR: Normal skids can be replaced by pontoons.

POWER PLANT: Two 375 shp MTU 6022-701-A3 turboshaft engines. Allison 250-C18 or 250-C20 turboshafts can be installed if required. One 125 Imp gallon (570 litre) integral fuel tank under cabin floor, with fuelling point on port side of cabin. Provision for fitting auxiliary tanks in freight compartment for ferrying. Oil capacity: engine 8·8 lb (4 kg), gearbox 15·4 lb (7 kg).

ACCOMMODATION: Pilot and passenger on individual front seats. Removable dual controls. Bench seat for three or four persons. Rear seats removable for cargo and stretcher carrying. Entire rear fuselage aft of seats and under power plant available as freight and baggage space, with access through two clam-shell doors at rear. Two standard stretchers can be accommodated in ambulance rôle. One forward-opening door and one sliding door on each side of cabin. Cabin is ventilated and heated.

SYSTEMS: Hydraulic system for powered controls. 24Ah battery and starter generator, with provision for external connection.

ELECTRONICS AND EQUIPMENT: Provision for radio, rotating beacon, IFR instrumentation and navigation aids, rescue winch, agricultural equipment, autopilot, cargo hook, swivelling seat at front on port side.

DIMENSIONS, EXTERNAL:
Diameter of main rotor   32 ft 1¾ in (9·80 m)
Diameter of tail rotor   6 ft 4¾ in (1·95 m)
Distance between rotor centres
    19 ft 6¼ in (5·95 m)
Length, excl main rotor   28 ft 0½ in (8·55 m)
Overall height   9 ft 9⅝ in (2·98 m)
Skid track   7 ft 10½ in (2·40 m)
Rear loading doors:
  Height   2 ft 1 in (0·64 m)
  Width   4 ft 7 in (1·40 m)
DIMENSIONS, INTERNAL:
Cabin, including cargo compartment:
  Length   14 ft 1 in (4·30 m)
  Max width   4 ft 7 in (1·40 m)
  Max height   4 ft 1 in (1·25 m)
  Floor area (cargo compartment)
    23·68 sq ft (2·20 m²)
  Volume   169 cu ft (4·80 m³)
  Cargo compartment   53 cu ft (1·50 m³)
WEIGHTS AND LOADING:
Weight empty   2,360 lb (1,070 kg)
Normal T-O weight   4,410 lb (2,000 kg)
Overload gross weight   5,070 lb (2,300 kg)
Max disc loading   5·43 lb/sq ft (26·5 kg/m²)
PERFORMANCE estimated, at normal T-O weight):
Max level speed at S/L
    135 knots (155 mph; 250 km/h)
Max cruising speed at S/L
    124 knots (143 mph; 230 km/h)
Max rate of climb at S/L 2,065 ft (630 m)/min
Single-engine climb at S/L 355 ft (108 m)/min
Service ceiling   18,700 ft (5,700 m)
Hovering ceiling in ground effect
    15,090 ft (4,600 m)
Hovering ceiling out of ground effect
    11,480 ft (3,500 m)
Range with standard fuel, no reserves:
  at S/L   324 nm (373 miles; 600 km)
  at 6,560 ft (2,000 m)
    382 nm (440 miles; 710 km)
Max range with auxiliary tanks:
  at S/L   664 nm (765 miles; 1,230 km)
  at 6,560 ft (2,000 m)
    745 nm (858 miles; 1,380 km)
Max endurance with auxiliary tanks 7 hr 12 min

Messerschmitt-Bölkow-Blohm BO 105 light helicopter (two MTU 6022 turboshaft engines) (*B. M. Service*)

MBB BO 105 light helicopter, development aircraft modified by Boeing to carry weapons and other military equipment

MBB HFB 320 HANSA

The HFB 320 Hansa is intended primarily as a 7/12-seat executive transport/feeder-liner, but is available also as a freighter and for a variety of military and civil duties including pilot/navigator training, calibration, aerial survey and target flying and towing.

Design was started in March 1961. The first prototype flew for the first time on 21 April 1964, and was followed by the first production Hansa on 2 February 1966.

An initial series of 50 production Hansas is being built, of which the first 15 had General Electric CJ610-1 engines. Details of this version were given in the 1967-68 *Jane's*.

The next 20 were fitted with more powerful CJ610-5 engines, and this version was described in the 1969-70 *Jane's*.

From the 36th aircraft onwards, production Hansas have the further-uprated CJ610-9 model

Messerschmitt-Bölkow-Blohm HFB 320 Hansa twin-jet transport (two General Electric CJ610-series turbojet engines) (*M. J. Axe*)

of this engine, and the data below apply to this version.

By April 1970, 30 Hansas had been sold, including three of the trainer version to the Netherlands Ministry of Transport for use at the Rijksluchtvaartschool, and eight (of a total of 13 ordered) had been delivered to the Federal German Government; six of these are used as VIP transports. Seven Hansas have been delivered to the USA.

A developed version, the HFB 330 Hansa Fan Jet, with AiResearch ATF-3 turbofan engines and lengthened fuselage, is described separately.

TYPE: Twin-jet executive transport and feeder-liner.

WINGS: Cantilever mid-wing monoplane, with 15° forward sweep at 25% chord to avoid the necessity of taking the main spar through the passenger cabin. Wing section NACA 65A-1·5-13 at root, NACA 63A-1·8-11 (modified) at tip. Dihedral 6°. Incidence 1°. All-metal fail-safe structure, built in three sections. Centre-section is built integrally with fuselage. Removable leading-edges. Load-carrying part of wing designed as a torsion-box, the upper and lower panels of which are made from taper-rolled sheets stiffened by riveted stringers. Mechanically-operated all-metal internally-balanced ailerons. Hydraulically-operated all-metal double-slotted flaps. Air-brakes on upper and lower wing surfaces, forward of flaps, also operated hydraulically. Retractable inboard leading-edge slats. Boundary-layer fence on each wing at approx one-third span. Electrically-actuated trim-tab in port aileron. Electrical de-icing of wings and anti-icing of slats.

FUSELAGE: Conventional all-metal semi-mono-coque fail-safe structure of circular cross-section. Max diameter 6 ft 9 in (2·06 m).

TAIL UNIT: Cantilever all-metal structure, with fixed-incidence tailplane mounted at tip of fin. Tailplane sweepback 20° at quarter-chord; dihedral 3°. Fin sweepback 35° at quarter-chord. Electrically-actuated trim-tab and geared servo-tab in rudder. Electrically and/or manually-actuated trim-tab in each elevator. Goodyear electrical de-icing of fin and tailplane leading-edges.

LANDING GEAR: Retractable tricycle type with single wheel on each unit. Hydraulic retraction, all wheels retracting forward into fuselage. Hydraulically-operated nose-wheel steering and shimmy damper. Lockheed oleo-pneumatic shock-absorbers. Wheels and tyres, size 32 × 8·8 Type VII 12-PR on main units, 18 × 5·5 Type VII 10-PR on nose unit. Tyre pressures: main 120 lb/sq in (8·4 kg/cm²), nose 94 lb/sq in (6·6 kg/cm²). Hydraulic disc brakes with Goodyear anti-skid units. Emergency braking system operated by hand lever. Drag-chute, diameter 9 ft 10 in (3·0 m), stowed in rear fuselage.

POWER PLANT (36th and subsequent aircraft): Two General Electric CJ610-9 turbojet engines (each 3,100 lb = 1,406 kg st) in pods on each side of rear fuselage. Fuel in one tank in centre-section with capacity of 1,212 lb (550 kg), two integral tanks in wings with total capacity of 4,144 lb (1,880 kg) and two non-jettisonable wingtip tanks with total capacity of 1,940 lb (880 kg). Total volume of usable fuel, 915 Imp gallons (4,140 litres). Gravity refuelling points on upper side of wings and tip-tanks. Single pressure refuelling point on upper starboard side of fuselage. Oil capacity, 10·14 lb (4·60 kg) usable.

ACCOMMODATION: Crew of two on flight deck, with full dual controls. Interior arrangement as Executive model (seven passengers), Commuter model (12 passengers, one stewardess, two pilots) or freighter (max payload 4,000 lb = 1,814 kg), with quick-change facility from one version to another. Executive version has two pairs of individual forward and rearward-facing seats, with a folding table between each pair, plus a bench seat for three at the rear. Commuter version for 12 passengers has a four-seat couch at the rear, the remaining eight seats being canted singly at 42° to the centre-line on either side of the cabin. Cargo tie-down rings available in freighter model. All three versions have a toilet compartment immediately aft of the flight deck and forward of the door on the port side, with a pantry opposite. Seven-seat version also has wardrobe at front on starboard side. Trainer version as supplied to the Netherlands accommodates three students, one on the flight deck for flying tuition and two nav/com students in the main cabin, plus three instructors; an additional five students can be seated in the cabin if required. Door is in two halves, opening upward and downward. Lower half of door has built-in airstairs. Size of door is adequate for cargo loading in freighter version. Baggage compartment at rear. Entire accommodation air-conditioned.

SYSTEMS: Normalair air-conditioning system, with pressure differential of 8·25 lb/sq in (0·58 kg/cm²), uses engine-bleed air. Dual hydraulic

MBB HFB 320 Hansa twin-jet executive transport in German military insignia

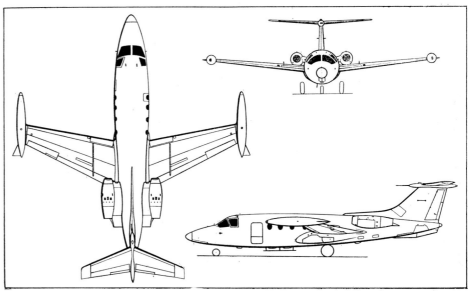

Messerschmitt-Bölkow-Blohm HFB 320 Hansa twin-jet executive transport

systems, pressure 3,000 lb/sq in (210 kg/cm²), operate landing gear retraction, nose-wheel steering, brakes, flaps, slats, elevator trim actuator and air-brakes. One emergency hand-pump system. Two 350A/28V DC starter-generators on engines and two 24Ah batteries. Inverters supply AC power for windscreen, wing and tail de-icing system. Optional AiResearch GTCP 30-142C APU, in rear fuselage, drives a 10·5 kW starter-generator and compressor for ground air-conditioning. Oxygen diluter demand system for crew and continuous flow system with drop-out masks for passengers.

ELECTRONICS AND EQUIPMENT: Choice of 12 different avionics packages. Basic packages comprise a Sperry autopilot and one or two Sperry flight directors, or a Collins autopilot and one or two Collins flight directors. The Collins packages can be equipped to Cat. II specifications or have provision for Cat. II. Typical installation comprises Sperry SP40 autopilot, two Sperry IIS flight directors, two Sperry C9 compass systems, two Collins 618 M-1 VHF communications installations, two Collins 51 RV-1 VHF navigation systems, Collins 313 N-3 VHF control panel, two Collins DF 203 ADF, Collins 51 Z-4 marker, RCA AVQ-75 DME, RCA AVQ-65 ATC transponder, RCA AVQ-20 weather radar and Collins 346 B-3 interphone. Fully-duplicated IFR instrumentation. FD 109 flight director in trainer.

DIMENSIONS, EXTERNAL:
Wing span over tip tanks	47 ft 6 in (14·49 m)
Wing chord at root	11 ft 0¼ in (3·36 m)
Wing chord at tip	3 ft 8 in (1·12 m)
Wing aspect ratio	6
Length overall	54 ft 6 in (16·61 m)
Length of fuselage	51 ft 0 in (15·56 m)
Height over tail	16 ft 2 in (4·94 m)
Tailplane span	20 ft 10 in (6·35 m)
Wheel track	7 ft 9 in (2·36 m)
Wheelbase	22 ft 1½ in (6·74 m)

Passenger door (forward, port):
Height	4 ft 3 in (1·30 m)
Width	2 ft 3½ in (0·70 m)

DIMENSIONS, INTERNAL:
Total pressurised volume	670 cu ft (19·00 m³)

Cabin, excluding flight deck, but including toilet, pantry and wardrobe:
Length	15 ft 0 in (4·58 m)
Max width	6 ft 2¾ in (1·90 m)
Max height	5 ft 9 in (1·75 m)
Floor area	71·0 sq ft (6·6 m²)
Volume	435 cu ft (12·32 m³)
Wardrobe (forward) volume	9·4 cu ft (0·265 m³)
Baggage hold (rear) volume	35 cu ft (1·00 m³)

AREAS:
Wings, gross	324·4 sq ft (30·14 m²)
Ailerons (total)	14·75 sq ft (1·37 m²)
Trailing-edge flaps (total)	55·50 sq ft (5·16 m²)
Slats (total)	11·04 sq ft (1·02 m²)
Air-brakes (total)	6·45 sq ft (0·60 m²)
Vertical tail surfaces (total)	55·00 sq ft (5·11 m²)
Horizontal tail surfaces (total)	78·04 sq ft (7·25 m²)

WEIGHTS AND LOADING:
Operating weight, empty:
Passenger version	11,960 lb (5,425 kg)
Freighter version	11,874 lb (5,386 kg)

Max payload:
Passenger version	3,913 lb (1,775 kg)
Freighter version	4,000 lb (1,814 kg)
Max taxi weight	20,460 lb (9,300 kg)
Max T-O weight	20,280 lb (9,200 kg)
Max zero-fuel weight	15,875 lb (7,200 kg)
Max landing weight	19,400 lb (8,800 kg)
Max wing loading	62·3 lb/sq ft (305 kg/m²)

PERFORMANCE (at max T-O weight except where stated otherwise):
Max permissible diving speed:
below 19,000 ft (5,800 m)
378 knots (435 mph; 700 km/h) EAS
above 19,000 ft (5,800 m) Mach 0·83
Max cruising speed at 25,000 ft (7,620 m) at mean weight of 16,530 lb (7,500 kg)
446 knots (513 mph; 825 km/h)
Econ cruising speed at 35,000 ft (10,670 m) at AUW of 16,530 lb (7,500 kg)
365 knots (420 mph; 675 km/h)
Stalling speed:
with T-O flap 107 knots (123 mph; 198 km/h)
landing configuration
97 knots (111 mph; 178 km/h)
Rate of climb at S/L at AUW of 16,530 lb (7,500 kg) 4,250 ft (1,295 m)/min
Time to 25,000 ft (7,600 m) 12 min
Max operating altitude 40,000 ft (12,200 m)
T-O run at 17,640 lb (8,000 kg) AUW
2,182 ft (665 m)
T-O to 50 ft (15 m) at 17,640 lb (8,000 kg) AUW 2,740 ft (835 m)

FAA balanced field length at max T-O weight 4,757 ft (1,450 m)
FAA landing field length at max landing weight 4,429 ft (1,350 m)
Range with 6 passengers and baggage (1,200 lb = 545 kg payload), 45 min reserves 1,278 nm (1,472 miles; 2,370 km)

MBB HFB 330 HANSA FAN JET

First announced in September 1969, the HFB 330 is basically a "stretched" version of the HFB 320 Hansa, with which it has a large number of components in common. The wings remain the same, but the fuselage is lengthened to accommodate up to 14 passengers (16 in high-density layout) and the power plant consists of two rear-mounted Garrett AiResearch ATF-3 turbofan engines. The HFB 330 will be available in the same three-way QC (quick-change) executive, commuter or freighter configurations as the HFB 320, but will have considerably better performance, including improved airfield characteristics and a substantially greater range.

Work on the construction of a prototype has begun, and flight testing of the Hansa Fan Jet is scheduled to begin in 1971, with certification anticipated by the Autumn of 1972. Deliveries are scheduled to begin at the rate of one aircraft a month in November 1972, rising to two a month by the Spring of 1973. Production of the HFB 320 is expected to continue after the introduction of the HFB 330.

TYPE: Twin-turbofan executive transport, feeder-liner and freight transport.

WINGS: As HFB 320.

FUSELAGE: Cross-sectional dimensions and construction as HFB 320, but lengthened by 2 ft 3½ in (0·70 m) to increase internal capacity.

TAIL UNIT: Of similar appearance to HFB 320, but with variable-incidence tailplane and elevator, both being actuated hydraulically. Modified bullet fairing.

LANDING GEAR: Improved landing gear and braking system to cater for increased operating weights.

POWER PLANT: Two AiResearch ATF-3 turbofan engines (each 4,050 lb = 1,840 kg st and fitted with thrust reversers) in pods on each side of rear fuselage. Fuel system and capacity (total of 915 Imp gallons = 4,140 litres usable) as for HFB 320, but with pressure refuelling.

ACCOMMODATION: Crew of two on flight deck with full dual controls. Interior arrangement as executive model (7-10 passengers) or feeder-liner (14-16 passengers), with toilet and luggage compartment at front on port and starboard sides respectively; or in all-freight configuration. Executive versions have four or six forward- and rearward-facing seats, on either side of centre aisle, with rear bench seat for three/four persons. Feeder-liner version has five or six seats on either side, canted at an angle to the centre-line, plus the bench seat at the rear. When in use as a freighter, a glass-fibre polyester protective cover can be provided for the cabin lining, and a barrier net installed at the front of the cabin capable of taking a strain equivalent to nine times the design cabin payload of 3,340 lb (1,515 kg). All versions have a large luggage compartment aft of the main cabin, over the wing leading-edge. Entry door forward on port side; emergency exit in forward part of main cabin on starboard side. Entire accommodation pressurised and air-conditioned.

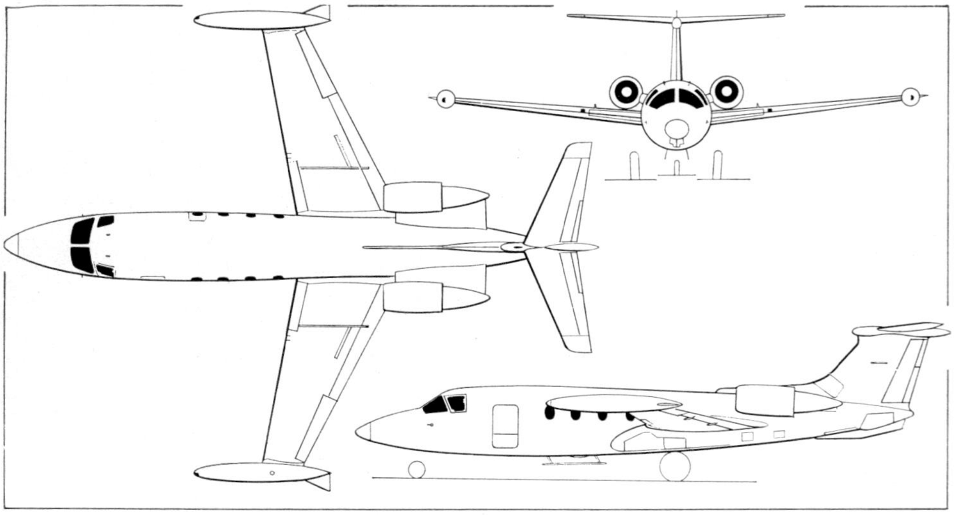

MBB HFB 330 fan-engined version of the Hansa

SYSTEMS: Air conditioning system using engine bleed-air, with pressure differential of 8·58 lb/sq in (0·605 kg/cm²), giving at 43,000 ft (13,100 m) a cabin pressure equivalent to an altitude of 7,900 ft (2,400 m). Cabin air-conditioning on ground supplied by AiResearch GTCP 30-142C APU, which also provides power on the ground for engine starting and other electrical equipment. Dual hydraulic systems as in HFB 320. Electrical system includes two 12kW starter-generators and one APU-supplied 15kW emergency starter-generator, and a 25Ah battery for DC power. Constant-frequency AC system includes 2·5VA main inverter, 2·5VA emergency inverter and 250VA static inverter. Variable-frequency AC system includes two 20kVA generators. Standard oxygen equipment includes automatic system for passengers and separate manually-operated system for crew.

ELECTRONICS AND EQUIPMENT: Autopilot and anti-stall system standard. Other radio and electronic equipment to customer's requirements.

DIMENSIONS, EXTERNAL:
As HFB 320, except:
Length overall 56 ft 9½ in (17·31 m)
Length of fuselage 53 ft 4¼ in (16·26 m)
Wheel track 8 ft 0 in (2·44 m)
Wheelbase 24 ft 7¼ in (7·50 m)
Emergency exit door (forward, stbd):
Height 3 ft 0 in (0·915 m)
Width 1 ft 8 in (0·51 m)

DIMENSIONS, INTERNAL:
As HFB 320, except:
Total pressurised volume 735 cu ft (20·82 m³)
Cabin excluding flight deck and rear luggage compartment, but including toilet, pantry and wardrobe):
Length 17 ft 3¾ in (5·28 m)
Floor area 80·62 sq ft (7·49 m²)
Volume 438·6 cu ft (12·42 m³)
Luggage compartment, rear:
Length 5 ft 10¾ in (1·80 m)
Floor area 25·30 sq ft (2·35 m²)
Volume 35·3 cu ft (1·00 m³)
Freight compartment (freighter version, including rear luggage bay):
Length 18 ft 2½ in (5·55 m)
Floor area 82·24 sq ft (7·64 m²)
Volume 343·3 cu ft (9·72 m³)

AREAS: As HFB 320.

WEIGHTS AND LOADINGS:
Basic operating weight, empty:
Passenger versions 13,670 lb (6,200 kg)
Freight version 13,230 lb (6,000 kg)
Max payload 4,000 lb (1,815 kg)
Max fuel load 7,295 lb (3,310 kg)
Max T-O and landing weight 22,485 lb (10,200 kg)
Max ramp weight 22,595 lb (10,250 kg)
Max zero-fuel weight 17,195 lb (7,800 kg)
Max wing loading 69·4 lb/sq ft (339 kg/m²)
Max power loading 2·78 lb/lb st (2·78 kg/kg st)

PERFORMANCE (estimated, at max T-O weight, ISA):
Max level speed 322 knots (370 mph; 595 km/h) EAS
Max permissible diving speed 380 knots (434·5 mph; 700 km/h) EAS
Max permissible Mach number in dive Mach 0·85
Max cruising speed 477 knots (550 mph; 885 km/h)
Max cruising Mach number Mach 0·8
Time to 25,000 ft (7,620 m) 8 min
Service ceiling at 18,500 lb (8,390 kg) AUW 42,980 ft (13,100 m)
Service ceiling, one engine out, at 18,500 lb (8,390 kg) AUW 26,900 ft (8,200 m)
Balanced field length for T-O (S/L) 4,790 ft (1,460 m)
Landing run (S/L) 2,870 ft (875 m)
Range with 45 min reserves:
4 passengers and max fuel 2,431 nm (2,800 miles; 4,510 km)
7 passengers and max fuel 2,296 nm (2,645 miles; 4,260 km)
14 passengers 1,758 nm (2,025 miles; 3,260 km)
4,000 lb (1,815 kg) payload 1,402 nm (1,615 miles; 2,600 km)

PÖSCHEL

PÖSCHEL AIRCRAFT GmbH

ADDRESS: D-7901, Ulm-Allewind

PRESIDENT: Günter Pöschel

In 1969, Pöschel Aircraft had under construction the prototype of a five/six-seat light executive STOL amphibian known as the P-300 Equator. All available details of this aircraft appear below.

PÖSCHEL P-300 EQUATOR

The Equator is a pressurised light executive STOL amphibian with standard accommodation for five or six persons, although up to eight can be carried when required. The single Lycoming engine is installed aft of the passenger cabin and drives a two-blade tractor propeller mounted on a fairing at the top of the vertical tail assembly. Extensive use is made in the construction of epoxy resins and glass-fibre, which give an exceptionally clean aerodynamic exterior finish. The Equator is fully amphibious, the land undercarriage retracting into the fuselage, which is completely watertight. When not in use, the outboard stabilising floats retract to form streamlined wingtip fairings. The Equator will be capable of operating from water with a wave height of up to 3 ft 3 in (1·00 m).

Construction of a prototype aircraft was begun in 1968, but in January 1970 the aircraft had yet to make its first flight. A number of options to purchase eventual production models have been received by Pöschel.

TYPE: Five/six-seat light executive STOL amphibian.

WINGS: Cantilever high-wing monoplane. Wings of Wortmann laminar-flow section. Full-span Fowler-type trailing-edge flaps, with spoiler forward of each flap. Conventional two-spar structure with outer skin of resin-bonded glass-fibre.

FUSELAGE: Conventional semi-monocoque structure, with outer skin of resin-bonded glass-fibre.

TAIL UNIT: "T" tail surfaces, the fin being integral with the fuselage. At the top of the fin is a streamlined "acorn" fairing, on which the tailplane and elevators are mounted and whose forward section is formed by the spinner encasing the hub of the propeller. Construction similar to that of wings.

LANDING GEAR: Retractable tricycle type, with single wheel on each unit. All units retract into fuselage. Streamlined stabilising floats, for use during operation on water, are mounted on single unbraced struts and retract, when not in use, to form wing-tip fairings.

POWER PLANT: One 310 hp Lycoming TIO-541 turbosupercharged six-cylinder horizontally-opposed air-cooled engine, mounted in the fuselage aft of the cabin and driving, by means of extension shafts, a two-blade Hartzell constant-speed reversible-pitch propeller, of 7 ft 9 in (2·36 m) diameter, mounted at the forward end of a small "acorn" fairing at the intersection of the fin and tailplane. Fuel in single main tank in fuselage, capacity 110 Imp gallons (500 litres).

ACCOMMODATION: Side-by-side seating for pilot and one passenger in front of pressurised cabin, with seats in two rows behind them to accommodate four, five or six additional passengers. Cabin heating, lighting and air-conditioning standard.

ELECTRONICS AND EQUIPMENT: Optional equipment includes IFR panel, autopilot and weather radar.

DIMENSIONS, EXTERNAL:
Wing span (over floats) 38 ft 7¼ in (11·60 m)
Length overall 26 ft 10¾ in (8·20 m)
Height overall 10 ft 2 in (3·10 m)

AREA:
Wings, gross 172·2 sq ft (16·0 m²)

WEIGHTS (estimated):
Weight empty 1,874 lb (850 kg)
Max T-O weight (A = Normal category, B = Utility category):
A 3,968 lb (1,800 kg)
B 3,307 lb (1,500 kg)

PERFORMANCE (estimated at max T-O weight, ISA conditions; A = Normal category, B = Utility category):

Max level speed at S/L:
A   208 knots (239 mph; 385 km/h)
B   209 knots (241 mph; 388 km/h)
Cruising speed (75% power) at S/L:
A   199 knots (229 mph; 369 km/h)
B   201 knots (232 mph; 373 km/h)
Cruising speed (75% power) at 23,950 ft
(7,300 m):
A   248 knots (286 mph; 460 km/h)
B   250 knots (288 mph; 464 km/h)
Stalling speed:
A   40 knots (46 mph; 74 km/h)
B   36 knots (41·5 mph; 66 km/h)
Max rate of climb:
A   1,705 ft (519 m)/min
B   2,030 ft (618 m)/min
Service ceiling:
A   29,525 ft (9,000 m)
B   32,800 ft (10,000 m)
T-O run:
A   380 ft (116 m)
B   255 ft (78 m)
T-O to 50 ft (15 m):
A   655 ft (200 m)
B   510 ft (155 m)
Landing from 50 ft (15 m):
A   520 ft (159 m)
B   445 ft (135 m)

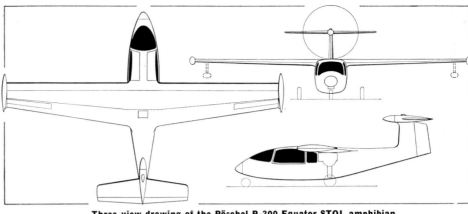

Three-view drawing of the Pöschel P-300 Equator STOL amphibian

Landing run:
A   165 ft (51 m)
B   140 ft (43 m)
Max range (75% power) at 23,950 ft (7,300 m):

A   1,985 miles (3,200 km)
B   2,015 miles (3,250 km)
Max endurance (75% power):
A, B   7 hr 0 min

RFB

RHEIN-FLUGZEUGBAU GmbH (Subsidiary of VFW-Fokker GmbH)

HEAD OFFICE AND MAIN WORKS:
405 Mönchengladbach, Flugplatz an der Niersbrücke, Postfach 408

OTHER WORKS:
505 Porz-Wahn, Flughafen Köln-Bonn, Halle 6; and 2401 Lübeck-Blankensee, Flugplatz

RFB is engaged on the development and construction of airframe structural components, with particular reference to wings made entirely of glass-fibre reinforced resins. Research and design activities include studies for the Federal German Ministry of Defence.

Current manufacturing programmes include series and individual production of aircraft components and assemblies, made of light alloy, steel and glass-fibre reinforced resin, for aircraft in quantity production by other German companies, as well as spare parts and ground equipment.

Under contract to the German government, RFB is servicing certain types of military aircraft. It operates a factory-certified service centre for all types of Piper aircraft and the Hawker Siddeley 125 and Mitsubishi MU-2 turbine-powered business aircraft. General servicing of other types of all-metal aircraft is undertaken, together with the servicing, maintenance, repair and testing of all kinds of flight instruments, engine instruments and navigation and communications electronics.

In the aircraft propulsion field, RFB is developing specialised applications for ducted propellers. It undertakes servicing and maintenance of Lycoming engines, Rolls-Royce Bristol Viper turbojets and AiResearch TPE 331-25A turboprop engines.

RFB is an equal partner with Messerschmitt-Bölkow-Blohm and Pützer in the LFU Leichtflugtechnik Union GmbH (which see). Development, design and construction of the wings of the LFU-205 was carried out by the engineering staff of RFB.

In 1968, 65% of the shares of RFB were acquired by VFW-Fokker GmbH. In 1969, RFB acquired a percentage holding in the Sportavia company (which see).

SIAT (see under "Messerschmitt-Bölkow-Blohm")

SPORTAVIA

SPORTAVIA-PÜTZER GmbH u Co KG

HEAD OFFICE AND WORKS:
Flugplatz Dahlemer Binz, D-5377 Post Schmidtheim

SALES MANAGER: Alfons Pützer

PUBLIC RELATIONS MANAGER: Manfred Küppers

This company was formed in 1966 by Comte Antoine d'Assche, director of the French company Alpavia SA, and Mr Alfons Pützer, to take over from Alpavia manufacture of the Avion-Planeur series of light aircraft designed by M René Fournier.
In 1969, RFB (which see), a subsidiary of VFW-Fokker GmbH, acquired a percentage holding in Sportavia.

SPORTAVIA AVION-PLANEUR RF4D

Designed by M René Fournier, the RF4 combines to a remarkable degree the characteristics of a small sporting aeroplane and a training sailplane, its performance being so high that it should not be regarded merely as a powered sailplane. It is fully aerobatic, with a safety factor of 13 at full loading.
The engine is a simple conversion of the standard Volkswagen motor car engine, by Rectimo Co of Chambery, France. The only modifications are the fitting of a special Zenith carburettor, propeller shaft, and a Bendix magneto of the type used on the 65 hp Continental aero-engine. The engine can be stopped and re-started in flight.
The prototype Avion-Planeur, designated Fournier RF01, flew for the first time on 6 July 1960, and was described fully in the 1960-61 edition of Jane's. The subsequent RF2 (two built) and RF3 (95 built) were described in the 1966-67 edition.
The current production RF4D has a main spar built in laminated pine, giving increased structural strength for aerobatics. The ailerons are aerodynamically compensated and the fuselage has a rounded undersurface. All ply-wood covering is Finnish birch.
By the Spring of 1970, a total of 160 RF4D's had been built and delivered, to customers in most countries in Western Europe and several countries overseas. One of these, flown by M. J. Slovak, crossed the Atlantic in May 1969 in 175 hr 42 min 7·11 sec to win the £1,000 prize

Sportavia Avion-Planeur RF4D light aircraft (40 hp converted Volkswagen engine) *(Jean Seele)*

offered by the *Evening News* newspaper for the best performance in the *Daily Mail* air race by a light aircraft of under 5,000 lb (2,268 kg) AUW.

TYPE: Single-seat light aircraft.

WINGS: Cantilever low-wing monoplane. Wing section NACA 23015 at root, NACA 23012 at tip. Dihedral 4°. Incidence 3° 30′ at root, 0° at tip. All-wood single-spar structure, with plywood and fabric covering, built in one piece and attached to fuselage by four bolts. Frise-type fabric-covered wood ailerons. No flaps. Three-section metal-skinned spoilers on each wing, extended from slot in upper surface inboard of ailerons.

FUSELAGE: All-wood structure, plywood-covered.

TAIL UNIT: Cantilever wood structure. Trim-tab in rudder.

LANDING GEAR: Single main wheel is retracted forward manually into a glass-fibre cowling. Rubber cord shock-absorption. Dunlop 420 × 150 main wheel and tyre, pressure 28·7 lb/sq in (2·0 kg/cm²). Steerable tail-wheel. Balancer skid of 6 mm steel wire under each wing. Manually-operated brake on main wheel.

POWER PLANT: One 40 hp converted Volkswagen 1,200 cc four-cylinder motor-car engine, with single ignition and carburettor. Hoffmann two-

blade fixed-pitch wooden propeller of 4 ft 4 in (1·32 m) diameter. Single fuel tank in fuse-lage with capacity of 7·7 Imp gallons (35 litres). Oil capacity 0·5 Imp gallons (2·5 litres).

ACCOMMODATION: Single seat under moulded transparent canopy which opens sideways to starboard.

EQUIPMENT: Optional equipment includes radio, electric turn and bank indicator and oxygen system.

DIMENSIONS, EXTERNAL:
Wing span   36 ft 11¼ in (11·26 m)
Wing chord at root   4 ft 7 in (1·40 m)
Wing chord at tip   1 ft 11½ in (0·60 m)
Wing aspect ratio   11·2
Length overall   19 ft 10¼ in (6·05 m)
Height overall (tail down)   5 ft 1¾ in (1·57 m)
Tailplane span   9 ft 2 in (2·80 m)

AREA:
Wings, gross   120.6 sq ft (11·20 m²)

WEIGHTS AND LOADING:
Weight empty   584 lb (265 kg)

Max T-O weight:
aerobatic 804 lb (365 kg)
utility 859 lb (390 kg)
Max wing loading 7·11 lb/sq ft (34·7 m^2)

Performance (at max T-O weight):
Max permissible diving speed:
134 knots (155 mph; 250 km/h)
Max cruising speed
97 knots (112 mph; 180 km/h)
Econ cruising speed
87 knots (100 mph; 160 km/h)
Stalling speed 38 knots (43·5 mph; 70 km/h)
Rate of climb at S/L 690 ft (210 m)/min
Service ceiling 19,700 ft (6,000 m)
Min rate of sink, power off 4·27 ft (1·30 m)/sec
Best glide ratio, power off 20 : 1
T-O run 427 ft (130 m)
T-O to 50 ft (15 m) 875 ft (270 m)
Landing from 50 ft (15 m) 755 ft (230 m)
Landing run 328 ft (100 m)
Range with max fuel
360 nm (415 miles; 670 km)
Fuel consumption at 105 mph (170 kmh)
2·0 Imp gallons (9·0 litres)/hr
Fuel consumption at cruising speed of 68 mph (110 kmh) 0·88 Imp gallons (4·0 litres)/hr

SPORTAVIA AVION-PLANEUR RF5

This tandem two-seat version of the Avion-Planeur differs from the single-seaters mainly in having wings of increased span, with folding outer sections to facilitate hangarage, and a more powerful engine. It is fitted with dual controls.

The pupil sits in the forward seat during dual instruction, which is the pilot's seat when the aircraft is flown solo.

Construction of the prototype RF5 (D-KOLT) was started in the Summer of 1967, and this aircraft flew for the first time in January 1968. Production began late in 1968. The RF5 received domestic type certification by the LBA in March 1969, in accordance with German airworthiness requirements for powered sailplanes. Sixty RF5's had been delivered by the end of February 1970, when a further 30-40 were on order.

Type: Two-seat light aircraft.

Wings: Cantilever low-wing monoplane. Wing section NACA 23015 at root, NACA 23012 at tip. Dihedral 3° 30′ at main spar centre-line. Incidence 4°. No sweepback. All-wood single-spar structure, with plywood and fabric covering. Fabric-covered wooden ailerons. Three-section metal-skinned spoilers on each wing at 50% chord, extended from slot in upper surface inboard of ailerons. Outer wing panels fold inward to facilitate hangarage. No flaps or tabs.

Fuselage: All-wood structure of bulkheads and stringers, plywood and fabric covered.

Tail Unit: Cantilever all-wood structure, plywood and fabric covered. Fixed-incidence tailplane. Flettner trim-tab in port elevator.

Landing Gear: Single TOST main wheel, with twin oleo-pneumatic shock-absorbers, manually retracted forward, with spring assistance, into front fuselage. Dunlop tyre, size 6·00 × 6, pressure 28·4 lb/sq in (2·0 kg/cm^2), on main wheel, which has manually-operated brake. Single Rhombus 160-80 tail-wheel, with Doetsch oleo-pneumatic shock-absorber, is steerable in conjunction with rudder movement. Outriggers beneath each wing, just inboard of fold line.

Power Plant: One 68 hp (max cont rating 63 hp) Sportavia-Limbach SL 1700 E Comet four-cylinder four-stroke engine, driving a Hoffmann two-blade fixed-pitch metal propeller of 4 ft 9¾ in (1·47 m) diameter. Fuel in two metal tanks in wing-root leading-edges, with total capacity of 13·2 Imp gallons (60 litres). Refuelling point on top of port wing. Oil capacity 0·55 Imp gallons (2·5 litres).

Accommodation: Adjustable seats in tandem for pilot and one passenger under one-piece sideways-hinged Plexiglas canopy. Space for 22 lb (10 kg) of baggage aft of rear seat. Cabin heated and ventilated. Adjustable rudder pedals and canopy emergency release standard.

Systems: Electrical system includes alternator and 25Ah battery.

Electronics and Equipment: Optional equipment includes radio nav/com equipment, artificial horizon, VOR, ADF, oxygen, navigation and landing lights and rotating beacon.

Dimensions, external:
Wing span 45 ft 1 in (13·74 m)
Wing chord at root 5 ft 2¾ in (1·59 m)
Wing chord at tip 1 ft 11½ in (0·60 m)
Wing aspect ratio 12·25

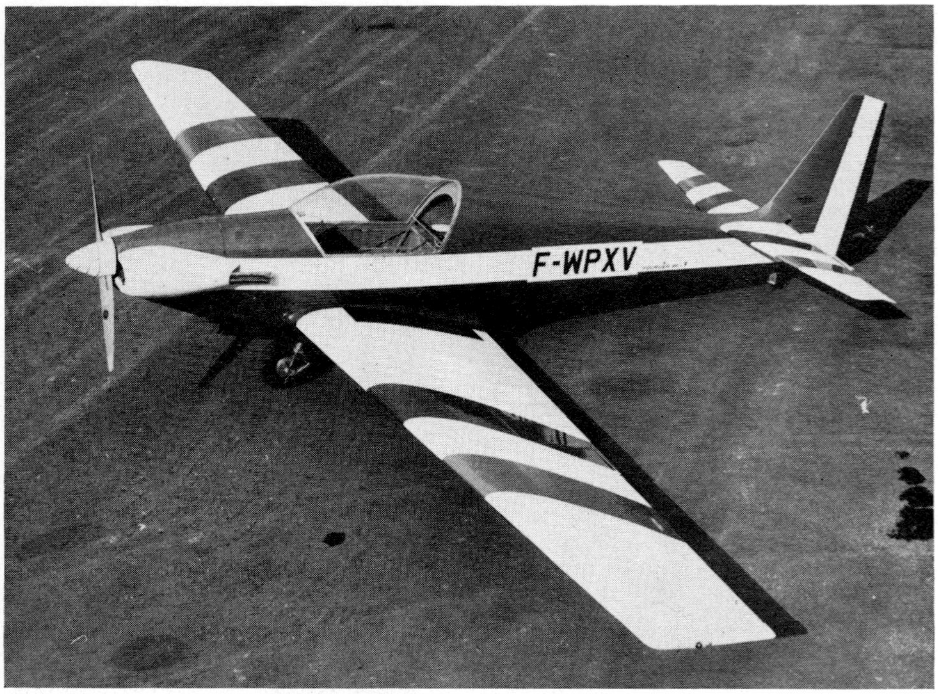

Prototype of the Sportavia Avion-Planeur RF7 single-seat light aircraft

Length overall 25 ft 7¼ in (7·80 m)
Width, wings folded 28 ft 8 in (8·74 m)
Height overall (tail down) 6 ft 5 in (1·96 m)
Tailplane span 12 ft 2½ in (3·72 m)
Distance between outriggers 28 ft 6½ in (8·70 m)

Areas:
Wings, gross 162·75 sq ft (15·12 m^2)
Ailerons (total) 16·15 sq ft (1·50 m^2)
Spoilers (total) 8·07 sq ft (0·75 m^2)
Fin 5·49 sq ft (0·51 m^2)
Rudder 8·50 sq ft (0·79 m^2)
Tailplane 17·44 sq ft (1·62 m^2)
Elevators, including tab 10·55 sq ft (0·98 m^2)

Weights and Loadings:
Weight empty, equipped 925 lb (420 kg)
Max T-O weight 1,433 lb (650 kg)
Max wing loading 8·77 lb/sq ft (42·8 kg/m^2)
Max power loading 21·05 lb/hp (9·55 kg/hp)

Performance (at max T-O weight):
Max level speed at S/L
102 knots (118 mph; 190 km/h)
Max permissible diving speed
134 knots (155 mph; 250 km/h)
Max cruising speed at S/L
100 knots (115 mph; 185 km/h)
Econ cruising speed
65 knots (75 mph; 120 km/h)
Stalling speed 40 knots (45·5 mph; 73 km/h)
Rate of climb at S/L 590 ft (180 m)/min
Min rate of sink, power off 4·59 ft (1·4 m)/sec
Service ceiling 16,400 ft (5,000 m)
T-O run 655 ft (200 m)
T-O to 50 ft (15 m) 1,575 ft (480 m)
Landing from 50 ft (15 m) 1,245 ft (380 m)
Landing run 590 ft (180 m)
Range with max fuel
376 nm (434 miles; 700 km)

SPORTAVIA AVION-PLANEUR RF7

The RF7 is of basically similar configuration and construction to the RF4D, with shorter wing span, increased tailplane span and a power plant similar to that of the RF5.

Construction of a prototype began in July 1969 and this aircraft flew for the first time on 5 March 1970.

Type: Single-seat light aircraft.

Wings: Cantilever low-wing monoplane. Details as for RF4D except that overall span is reduced.

Fuselage, Tail Unit and Landing Gear: As for RF4D, except that tailplane span is increased and there is no rudder tab.

Power Plant: One 68 hp (max cont rating 63 hp) Sportavia-Limbach SL 1700 D dual-ignition four-cylinder four-stroke engine, driving a Hoffmann two-blade fixed-pitch metal propeller of 4 ft 9¾ in (1·47 m) diameter. Fuel and oil as for RF4D.

Accommodation: As for RF4D.

Equipment: As for RF4D.

Dimensions, external:
Wing span 30 ft 10 in (9·40 m)
Wing chord at root 4 ft 7 in (1·40 m)
Wing chord at tip 2 ft 5¼ in (0·74 m)
Wing aspect ratio 8·8
Length overall 19 ft 10¼ in (6·05 m)
Tailplane span 9 ft 10 in (3·00 m)
Propeller ground clearance 9 in (0·23 m)

Areas:
Wings, gross 108 sq ft (10·00 m^2)
Fin 3·77 sq ft (0·35 m^2)
Rudder 5·27 sq ft (0·49 m^2)
Tailplane 12·90 sq ft (1·20 m^2)
Elevators 6·03 sq ft (0·56 m^2)

Weights and Loading:
Weight empty 661 lb (300 kg)
Max T-O weight 981 lb (445 kg)
Max wing loading 9·1 lb/sq ft (44·5 kg/m^2)

Performance (at max T-O weight):
Max cruising speed at S/L
119 knots (137 mph; 220 km/h)
Stalling speed 47 knots (54 mph; 86·5 km/h)
Service ceiling 23,000 ft (7,000 m)
T-O run 410 ft (125 m)
T-O to 50 ft (15 m) 876 ft (267 m)
Landing from 50 ft (15 m) 679 ft (207 m)
Landing run 338 ft (103 m)
Range with max fuel
350 nm (403 miles; 650 km)

SPORTAVIA SFS 31 MILAN

The SFS 31 is, essentially, the combination of the Avion-Planeur RF4D fuselage and tail unit with the wings of the Scheibe SF-27M sailplane (which see). Its designation is formed by adding together the manufacturers' initial letters and the digits in the designations of these two aircraft, and the SFS 31 is produced jointly by the two companies.

The first SFS 31 prototype (D-KORO) flew for the first time on 8 January 1969, and by February 1970 a total of 16 had been ordered, of which four had been completed.

Type: Single-seat light aircraft.

Wings: Cantilever low-wing monoplane. Wing section Wortmann FX 61-184 at root, FX 60-126 at tip. Dihedral 4° from roots. Wooden structure, with pine box-spar at about 43% chord. Plywood ribs. Wings covered with birch plywood and fabric (see description of SF-27M in "Sailplanes" section). Wooden ailerons, glass-fibre/metal air brakes.

Fuselage and Tail Unit: As for RF4D.

Landing Gear: Similar to RF4D, but with spring-assisted retraction of single main wheel, which is of size 380 × 150.

Power Plant: One 39 hp Rectimo (converted VW) 4 AR 1200 four-cylinder four-stroke engine, driving a Hoffman two-blade fixed-pitch or fully-feathering wooden propeller, diameter 4 ft 4 in (1·32 m) or 4 ft 5½ in (1·36 m) respectively. Fuel in single fuselage tank, capacity 7·7 Imp gallons (35 litres). Oil capacity 0·55 Imp gallons (2·5 litres).

Accommodation: As for RF4D.

Equipment: Optional equipment includes radio, electrical turn-and-bank indicator and oxygen supply.

Dimensions, external:
Wing span 49 ft 2½ in (15·00 m)
Wing chord at root 3 ft 7 in (1·094 m)
Wing chord at tip 1 ft 5½ in (0·44 m)
Wing aspect ratio 18·6
Length overall 19 ft 10¼ in (6·05 m)
Height overall, tail down 5 ft 1¾ in (1·57 m)
Tailplane span 9 ft 10 in (3·00 m)

AREAS:
Wings, gross 129 sq ft (12·00 m²)
Fin 3·77 sq ft (0·35 m²)
Rudder 5·27 sq ft (0·49 m²)
Tailplane 12·9 sq ft (1·20 m²)
Elevators 6·03 sq ft (0·56 m²)
WEIGHTS AND LOADING:
Weight empty 661 lb (300 kg)
Max T-O weight 948 lb (430 kg)
Max wing loading 7·3 lb/sq ft (35·8 kg/m²)
PERFORMANCE (at max T-O weight):
Max permissible diving speed 118 knots (136 mph; 220 km/h)
Max cruising speed at S/L 97 knots (112 mph; 180 km/h)
Econ cruising speed at S/L 87 knots (100 mph; 160 km/h)
Stalling speed 38 knots (43·5 mph; 70 km/h)
Rate of climb at S/L 590 ft (180 m)/min
Service ceiling 19,700 ft (6,000 m)
T-O run 690 ft (210 m)
Range with max fuel 360 nm (415 miles; 670 km)

VFW-FOKKER

VFW-FOKKER GmbH (Subsidiary of ZENTRALGESELLSCHAFT VFW-FOKKER mbH)

HEAD OFFICE:
Hünefeldstrasse 1-5, 28 Bremen 1 (Postfach 1206)

WORKS:
Bremen, Einswarden, Hoykenkamp, Lemwerder, Speyer and Munich

EXECUTIVE DIRECTORS:
Dr Werner Knieper (Chairman)
Prof Gerhard Eggers
Dipl-Ing Albert Niehus
Dipl-Ing Hans Pasche
Dr Otto Proksch
Dr Ing Fritz Wenck

SALES MANAGERS:
Dr Hans Rico Büssgen and Frithjof Lindemann (Civil Aircraft)

PUBLIC RELATIONS MANAGER: Franz Cesarz

The Vereinigte Flugtechnische Werke GmbH (VFW) was formed at the end of 1963 by a merger of the two Bremen-based aircraft companies of Focke-Wulf GmbH and "Weser" Flugzeugbau GmbH. They were joined in 1964 by Ernst Heinkel Flugzeugbau GmbH. The capital stock is DM 75 million. Organisations with a major interest in the company were Fried Krupp GmbH, Essen (35·1%), United Aircraft Corporation, USA (26·4%); Hanseatische Industrie-Beteiligungen GmbH (26·4%); Frau Lisa Heinkel, Stuttgart (9·0%) and Ernst Heinkel Maschinenbau GmbH, Karlsruhe (3·1%). It had a total of 12,000 employees at the end of 1969.

In 1968-69, VFW acquired 65% of the shares of RFB (Rhein-Flugzeugbau GmbH, which see) and a 50% holding in Henschel Flugzeugwerke AG of Kassel.

With effect from 1 January 1969, VFW became an equal partner with Fokker of the Netherlands in a new company known as Zentralgesellschaft VFW-Fokker mbH, with headquarters in Dusseldorf. The two partners continue to operate independently, as subsidiaries of Zentralgesellschaft VFW-Fokker. The name of the VFW company was changed to VFW-Fokker GmbH as a consequence of the amalgamation.

Details of the history and products of the former Focke-Wulf, "Weser" and Heinkel companies can be found in earlier editions of *Jane's*.

Current activities of VFW-Fokker include manufacture of major components for the Transall C-160 at its Lemwerder factory, as the prime contractor for the series production of this type. In addition, VFW participated in design and construction of the Dornier Do 31 E VTOL transport and is a partner in the Fokker F.28 jet transport programme. It is developing a family of light autogyros which includes the H3, H5, H7 and H9. The Fk 3 high-performance glider, described in the "Sailplanes" section, is also in production.

Aircraft at the prototype development stage include the VAK 191B VTOL research aircraft and the VFW 614 twin-turbofan light passenger and freight transport.

Other work includes the overhaul and repair of Noratlas, Albatross, JetStar and Piaggio P.149D aircraft, together with modification work on the F-104G.

Through the ERNO Raumfahrttechnik GmbH, in which it has a 60% interest, VFW-Fokker is engaged on studies of high-energy propellants. Study and project work is also in progress in connection with the national space programme and the third stage of the European satellite launcher. VFW-Fokker is also participating in development and manufacturing programmes for the MRCA 75 and A 300 B European Airbus (see International section), and for the Bell UH-1D and Sikorsky CH-53A helicopters.

VFW-FOKKER VFW 614

Development of this twin-turbofan short-haul jet transport has been undertaken with the financial backing of the Federal German Government. Construction of the first of three prototypes was started on 1 August 1968 and is expected to be completed late in 1970. First flight is scheduled for June 1971 and certification by the end of 1972. In addition, two airframes are being completed for static testing. The following options had been announced by early 1970, with deliveries to begin late in 1972: Sterling Airways (five), Filipinas Orient Airways (two), Bavaria Fluggesellschaft (three), General Air (two), Transportes Aereos Buenos Aires (two), Cimber-Air (three) and Yemen Airlines (three).

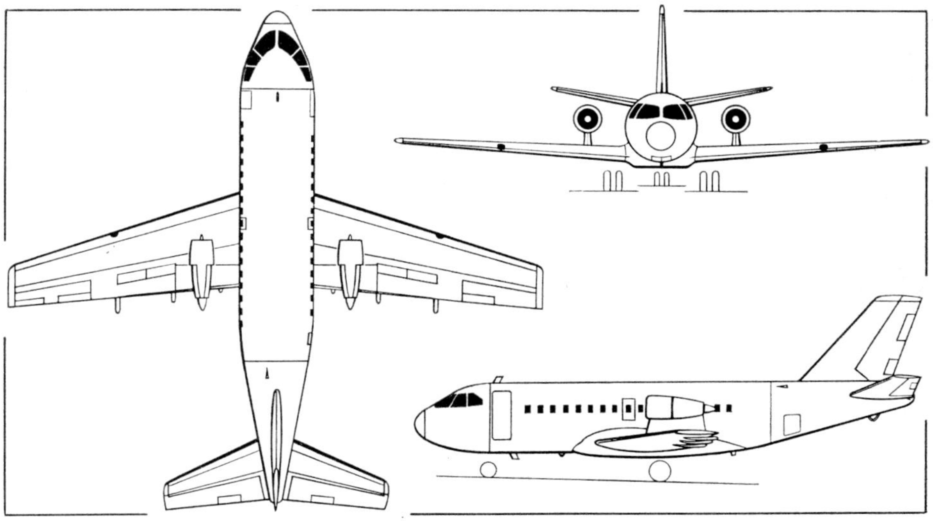

VFW-Fokker VFW 614 twin-turbofan short-haul passenger transport

Manufacture of the VFW 614 will be a collaborative venture under the leadership of VFW-Fokker, with participation in the development and production programme by SIAT (now a Messerschmitt-Bölkow-Blohm subsidiary) in Germany, by Fokker-VFW in the Netherlands, and by SABCA and Fairey in Belgium.

The details below apply to the prototype.

TYPE: Twin-turbofan short-haul transport.

WINGS: Cantilever low-wing monoplane. Wing section NACA 63₂A-015 at root, NACA 65₁A-012 at tip. Dihedral 3°. Incidence 3°. Sweepback 15° at quarter-chord. Continuous two-spar fail-safe torsion-box dural structure, consisting of a centre-section integral with the fuselage, and two outer wings. Manually-operated Flettner-type bonded duralumin ailerons, with trim-tabs. Hydraulically-operated single-slotted Fowler-type trailing-edge flaps of bonded dural construction. Four split-type flight spoilers and four ground spoilers, of bonded dural construction. Honeycomb structure trim-tab in each aileron. TKS liquid de-icing system.

FUSELAGE: Conventional semi-monocoque fail-safe pressurised structure of circular section, built of high-strength aluminium alloys.

TAIL UNIT: Part-bonded all-swept all-metal structure, with variable-incidence dihedral tailplane. All control surfaces operated manually, rudder with optional hydraulic boost. Electrically-operated tailplane trim, with mechanical back-up system. Control tabs in elevators and rudder; trim-tab in rudder. TKS liquid de-icing system for leading-edges.

LANDING GEAR: Hydraulically retractable tricycle type of Dowty Rotol design, with twin wheels on each unit. Steerable nose-wheel unit retracts forward. Main units retract inward into fuselage. Oleo-pneumatic telescopic shock-absorbers. All tyres of BF Goodrich manufacture, nose-wheels size 7·50-10 with 8·50-10 tyres; main wheels and tyres size 34 × 12-12. Tyre pressure 57 lb/sq in (4 kg/cm²) on nose unit, 65 lb/sq in (4·57 kg/cm²) on main units. Goodrich 12 × 4 disc brakes on main units. Hytrol Mk III/Hydro-Aire anti-skid units.

POWER PLANT: Two Rolls-Royce (Bristol)/SNECMA M45H turbofan engines, each rated at 7,511 lb (3,410 kg) st, mounted on overwing pylons aft of the wing rear spar. Fuel in integral wing tanks, with total capacity of 1,390 Imp gallons (6,330 litres). Single-point pressure refuelling point in starboard outer wing. Provision for over-wing gravity refuelling. Oil capacity 1·75 Imp gallons (8 litres).

ACCOMMODATION: Crew of two on flight deck, with foldable third seat to rear. Full dual controls and instruments. Alternative configurations provide 36, 40 or 44 passenger seats at 32-33 in (81-84 cm) pitch in main cabin, in rows of four with 16 in (41 cm) wide centre aisle. Passenger door, with built-in stairs, at front of cabin on port side. Cargo door for cabin baggage compartment at front on starboard side. Catering service door beside pantry at rear of cabin on starboard side. Cabin baggage compartment at front of cabin (stbd). Toilet on port side, at rear of cabin. Underfloor baggage holds fore and aft of wing. Cabin pressurised and air-conditioned.

SYSTEMS: Garrett-Normalair double air-cycle air-conditioning system, using engine bleed air. Pressure differential 6·55 lb/sq in (0·46 kg/cm²). Hydraulic system, pressure 3,000 lb/sq in (210 kg/cm²), utilises a pump on each engine and electrically-powered (DC) auxiliary hydraulic pump, with Skydrol 500B fluid, for nose-wheel steering, landing gear, speed-brakes, spoilers, flaps and brakes. Constant-frequency three-phase 200/115V 400 c/s AC electrical system. Two transformer-rectifiers provide 28V DC power, with batteries for emergency supply. Priority oxygen supply system for flight crew, with second oxygen system for passengers and cabin staff. TKS liquid de-icing system for wings and tail. APU provides air supply for engine starting and air-conditioning on ground, and electrical power for pre-flight check of avionics and systems without running engines.

ELECTRONICS AND EQUIPMENT: Standard equipment includes two VHF communications installations, two VHF navigation aids, marker, ADF, two compass systems, intercom system, flight data recorder, autopilot/flight director, DME, ATC transponder, weather radar and voice recorder. Optional items include an additional ADF, HF communications installation, Decca Type 72 Doppler navigator, radio altimeter, Cat II autopilot with flight attitude reference system and radio altimeter. Blind-flying instrumentation standard.

DIMENSIONS, EXTERNAL:
Wing span 70 ft 6½ in (21·50 m)
Wing chord at root 13 ft 11¼ in (4·25 m)
Wing chord at tip 5 ft 7¼ in (1·71 m)
Wing aspect ratio 7·22
Length overall 67 ft 7 in (20·60 m)
Length of fuselage 66 ft 1¼ in (20·15 m)
Height overall 25 ft 8 in (7·84 m)
Tailplane span 29 ft 6¼ in (9·00 m)
Wheel track 12 ft 9½ in (3·90 m)
Wheelbase 23 ft 0¼ in (7·02 m)
Passenger door (fwd, port):
Height 6 ft 10¾ in (2·10 m)
Width 2 ft 5½ in (0·75 m)
Height to sill 6 ft 1¼ in (1·86 m)
Freight door (fwd, stbd):
Height 3 ft 10 in (1·17 m)
Width 3 ft 8⅞ in (1·14 m)
Height to sill 6 ft 1¼ in (1·86 m)
Catering service door (rear of cabin, stbd):
Height 5 ft 0¼ in (1·53 m)
Width 2 ft 0 in (0·61 m)
Height to sill 6 ft 6 in (1·98 m)
Underfloor baggage door (fwd):
Height 2 ft 6¾ in (0·78 m)
Width 2 ft 9½ in (0·85 m)
Height to sill 3 ft 10 in (1·17 m)
Underfloor baggage door (rear):
Height 2 ft 6¾ in (0·78 m)
Width 2 ft 9½ in (0·85 m)
Height to sill 4 ft 0¾ in (1·24 m)

DIMENSIONS, INTERNAL:
Cabin, excluding flight deck:
 Length 36 ft 9¼ in (11·21 m)
 Max width 8 ft 8¾ in (2·66 m)
 Max height 6 ft 4¾ in (1·95 m)
 Floor area 248·75 sq ft (23·11 m²)
 Volume 1,748 cu ft (49·50 m³)
Baggage compartment volume:
 Front fuselage 91·5 cu ft (2·59 m³)
 Underfloor (fwd) 67·5 cu ft (1·91 m³)
 Underfloor (aft) 51·0 cu ft (1·45 m³)

AREAS:
 Wings, gross 688·89 sq ft (64·00 m²)
 Ailerons (total) 36·38 sq ft (3·38 m²)
 Trailing-edge flaps (total) 124·86 sq ft (11·60 m²)
 Spoilers (total) 54·5 sq ft (5·06 m²)
 Fin 63·08 sq ft (5·86 m²)
 Rudder 38·64 sq ft (3·59 m²)
 Tailplane 140·79 sq ft (13·08 m²)
 Elevators 52·96 sq ft (4·92 m²)

WEIGHTS AND LOADINGS:
 Operating weight, empty 26,896 lb (12,200 kg)
 Max structure-limited payload
  8,598 lb (3,900 kg)
 Max design T-O and landing weight
  41,006 lb (18,600 kg)
 Max design taxi weight
  41,226 lb (18,700 kg)
 Max design zero-fuel weight
  35,494 lb (16,100 kg)
 Max wing loading 59·4 lb/sq ft (290 kg/m²)
 Max power loading 0·366 lb/lb st (0·366 kg/kg st)

PERFORMANCE (estimated, at max design T-O weight):
 Max level speed at 21,000 ft (6,400 m)
  397 knots (457 mph; 735 km/h) TAS
 Max permissible diving speed
  330 knots (380 mph; 613 km/h) EAS
 Max cruising speed at 25,000 ft (7,620 m)
  390 knots (449 mph; 722 km/h) TAS
 Stalling speed, flaps up
  114 knots (131 mph; 210 km/h)
 Stalling speed, flaps down
  98 knots (112 mph; 180 km/h)
 Max rate of climb at S/L 3,248 ft (990 m)/min
 Rate of climb at S/L, one engine out
  827 ft (252 m)/min
 Service ceiling 24,925 ft (7,600 m)
 Service ceiling, one engine out
  14,725 ft (4,490 m)
 T-O run 3,346 ft (1,020 m)
 T-O to 35 ft (10 m) 2,756 ft (840 m)
 Landing from 50 ft (15 m) 2,395 ft (730 m)
 Landing run 1,562 ft (476 m)
 Range with max fuel, FAR Pt 121 reserves
  995 nm (1,146 miles; 1,845 km)
 Range with max payload, reserves as above
  339 nm (391 miles; 630 km)

VFW-FOKKER VAK 191B

To meet the German Requirement VAK 191B for a subsonic VTOL tactical reconnaissance-fighter to replace the Fiat G91, the former Focke-Wulf company produced a design study under the designation FW 1262. A development of this project was initiated jointly by VFW and Fiat of Italy under an agreement signed by the German and Italian Defence Ministers early in 1964. In 1968, the Italian government withdrew from the programme, which is now being continued by VFW-Fokker, with Fiat as associate sub-contractor responsible for the previously-agreed portions of the airframe.

The number of prototypes to be completed has been reduced from six to three. The first of these was rolled out on 24 April 1970 and was due to begin flight testing in November 1970, following several weeks of tethered hovering trials. By 1971, it is expected that the three VAK 191B prototypes wil be available as system test-beds in connection with the Panavia MRCA-75 programme.

TYPE: Single-seat V/STOL experimental reconnaissance fighter.

WINGS: Cantilever shoulder-wing monoplane. Sweptback wings of NACA 63A005 section at aircraft centre-line, NACA 65A006 section at centre-line of outrigger pods. Wings have 12° 30′ anhedral from roots. Incidence 1° 30′. Sweepback at quarter-chord approx 40°. Multi-spar fail-safe structure of aluminium alloy, including ailerons and trailing-edge flaps. Exhaust door of forward lift engine extends to act as air-brake. Lockheed AIR 46176 actuators for flaps and AIR 48830 actuators for ailerons.

FUSELAGE: Semi-monocoque fail-safe structure of aluminium and copper alloy.

TAIL UNIT: Cantilever sweptback surfaces, constructed of aluminium-copper and aluminium-zinc alloys with titanium bolts. One-piece all-moving tailplane, fitted with Lockheed AIR 48594 actuator. Rudder fitted with Lockheed AIR 48832 actuator.

LANDING GEAR: Tandem type, with single nose-wheel and zero-track twin main wheels retracting rearward hydraulically into fuselage, plus outrigger wheels retracting rearward into pod-type fairings near the wingtips. Hawker Siddeley Dynamics oleo-pneumatic shock-

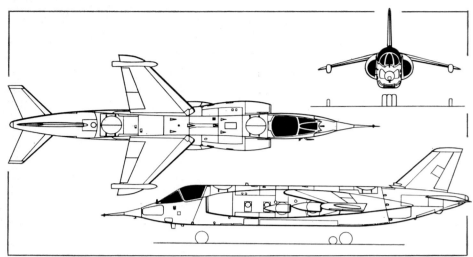

VFW-Fokker VAK 191B single-seat V/STOL experimental reconnaissance fighter

First VFW-Fokker VAK 191B experimental V/STOL aircraft (one Rolls-Royce/MTU RB.193 vectored-thrust turbojet and two RB.162 lift-jets)

Model of the VFW-Fokker VC 400 VTOL transport (*Flight International*)

absorbers on main units. All three main wheel tyres Type III, size 9·00 × 6, of 1 ft 10¾ in (584 mm) diameter. Single wheel on each outrigger, with Goodyear Type VIII tyres, size 12 1/2 × 4 1/2, diameter 1 ft 1 in (328 mm). Tyre pressures: nose-wheel 94 lb/sq in (6·6 kg/cm²); main wheels 67 lb/sq in (4·7 kg/cm²); outriggers 60 lb/sq in (4·2 kg/cm²). Goodyear multiple disc brakes and anti-skid units.

POWER PLANT: Two MTU RB.162-81 lift-jets (each 5,577 lb = 2,530 kg st) mounted vertically in the fuselage, one immediately aft of the cockpit and the other aft of the wing, and one MTU RB.193-12 vectored-thrust turbojet of approx 9,920 lb (4,500 kg) st for forward propulsion. Stabilisation is by "puffer-jets" at nose,

tail and wing-tips. Fuel in seven main tanks in centre-fuselage and one in rear fuselage, with total capacity of 4,365 lb (1,980 kg). Refuelling point in centre-fuselage. Oil capacity 1 Imp gallon (4·55 litres) for cruise engine, 0·34 Imp gallons (1·55 litres) for each lift engine.

ACCOMMODATION: Pilot on Martin-Baker Mk 9 ejection seat under upward-hinged canopy. Internal weapons bay in underside of centre-fuselage. Cockpit is air-conditioned.

SYSTEMS: Separate Normalair-Garrett air-conditioning systems for cockpit and electronics compartment. Hydraulic system, pressure 4,000 lb/sq in (280 kg/cm²), for flight controls, cruise-engine starting and emergency operation.

Two 15/20kVA generators provide 200/115V 400 c/s AC electrical power; one 22Ah battery for DC power. Klöckner-Humbold-Deutz T112 APU supplies hydraulic and electrical power.

DIMENSIONS, EXTERNAL:
Wing span 20 ft 2½ in (6·16 m)
Wing chord at aircraft c/l 11 ft 4½ in (3·47 m)
Wing chord at outrigger c/l 3 ft 11¼ in (1·20 m)
Wing aspect ratio 2·3
Length overall (incl probe) 53 ft 7 in (16·335 m)
Length overall (without probe) 48 ft 3½ in (14·72 m)
Length of fuselage (without probe) 48 ft 1½ in (14·67 m)
Max width of fuselage 7 ft 0¼ in (2·14 m)
Height overall 14 ft 1 in (4·295 m)
Tailplane span 11 ft 2¾ in (3·42 m)
Outrigger wheel track 17 ft 7 in (5·36 m)
Distance between rear twin-wheel centre-lines 1 ft 4 in (0·405 m)
Wheelbase (main gear) 20 ft 8¼ in (6·306 m)

AREAS:
Wings, gross 134·5 sq ft (12·50 m^2)
Ailerons (total) 11·84 sq ft (1·10 m^2)
Trailing-edge flaps (total) 8·83 sq ft (0·82 m^2)
Fin 60·1 sq ft (5·58 m^2)
Rudder 8·87 sq ft (0·824 m^2)
Tailplane 41·5 sq ft (3·86 m^2)

WEIGHT:
Max T-O weight 16,535-19,840 lb (7,500-9,000 kg)

VFW-FOKKER VC 400

The VC 400 is a tilting-wing V/STOL passenger or utility cargo transport intended for service in the late 1970s. Project definition was completed in 1968, and construction of a ground test rig began in 1969. Development phase 1, involving development and construction of the propeller/gear system, was completed in February 1969 by the Hamilton Standard Division of United Aircraft Corporation in the US, and phase 2 provides for the delivery of this system to VFW-Fokker in July 1971. The shaft system and centre gear development and construction are being undertaken by Hispano-Suiza in France and Zahnradfabrik Friedrichshafen in Germany. First flight is scheduled to take place in 1973, with 3,925 shp T64-GE-7 engines in the prototype.

An enlarged version, designated VC 500, was one of three VFW-Fokker designs submitted for the joint military and civil V/STOL transport competition late in 1969.

TYPE: Tilting-wing V/STOL passenger or military cargo transport.

WINGS: Two cantilever high-mounted tilting wings (foreplane and rear main wing), having special sections with RAE 102 thickness distribution. Thickness/chord ratios 15·3% (foreplane), 18% (main wing centre-section) and 16% (main wing outer panels). 15° anhedral on outer panels of main wing only. Foreplane has 2° 24′ incidence, main wing 5° 42′, in down position. Both wings can be tilted to an angle of 90°, and are of conventional two-spar duralumin construction. Main wing is fitted with nearly full-span elevons for lateral and longitudinal control and trim. These control surfaces act as simple flaps for small deflection angles; at larger angles of deflection in either direction they have the characteristics of a slotted flap. During transitional flight the elevons are extended to +20°. The deflection range is +60° in this speed range. The foreplane is fitted with a double-slotted trailing-edge flap, with fixed vane, the flap being programmed to extend up to 60° during transitional flight. Both the foreplane and the main wing are fitted with full-span leading-edge slats. All controls are actuated hydraulically. There are no trim-tabs. Leading-edges have electrical de-icing.

FUSELAGE: Conventional fail-safe pressurised structure, of basically circular cross-section, built of light alloy with spars and profiles.

TAIL UNIT: Large sweptback central fin above fuselage, and two smaller ventral fins set at 45° anhedral angle on sides of rear fuselage. Leading-edge of main fin has electrical de-icing.

LANDING GEAR: Retractable four-leg type, consisting of two separate nose-wheels and two main wheels. All units retract inward hydraulically into centre-fuselage, and have oleo-pneumatic telescopic shock-absorption. One steerable and one self-centering nose-wheel. Nose-wheels and tyres size 750 × 270-14, pressure 77 lb/sq in (5·41 kg/cm^2); main wheels and tyres size 48 × 18·00-18, pressure 52 lb/sq in (3·66 kg/cm^2). Brakes and anti-skid units to be selected.

POWER PLANT: Four General Electric T64-GE-S5C-1 turboshaft engines, each developing 5,260 shp and mounted two on each of the front and rear wings, driving three-blade Hamilton Standard AF-141 lightweight propellers of 23 ft 0 in (7·01 m) diameter. Blades have NACA section and consist of a glass-fibre reinforced plastic shell bonded to a titanium spar; they are governed by an hydraulically-operated mechanical blade pitch actuator with pitch lock unit, and are attached to propeller shaft by quick-disconnect ball-bearings with integral raceway blade retention. In addition to individual nacelle drive systems there is an inter-connecting cross-shaft system, with two-speed reduction planetary gearbox, which ensures that all propellers remain operative in the event of engine failure. Fuel is contained in four flexible bag-type tanks beneath fuselage floor (self-sealing in military version), with total capacity of 1,640 Imp gallons (7,455 litres). Central pressure refuelling point on port side of fuselage. Oil capacity 33 Imp gallons (150 litres).

ACCOMMODATION: Seats for two pilots side by side on flight deck, with foldable seat for third crew member when required. Passenger version can seat up to 60 persons, in five-abreast arrangement at 32-in (81-cm) pitch, plus two cabin attendants. Galley and toilet at rear of cabin. Entry to main cabin via hydraulically-operated integral airstair door at rear. One type I and one Type II emergency exit on each side of fuselage. Baggage compartment at front. Cargo door on starboard side. Military version can carry up to 82 troops or equivalent freight load.

SYSTEMS: Cabin air-conditioned and pressurised to maintain pressure equivalent to an altitude of 8,000 ft (2,438 m). Two independent hydraulic systems, each of 3,000 lb/sq in (210 kg/cm^2). No pneumatic system. Two 60kVA generators, with CSD, provide 115/220V 400 c/s AC power. Plessey Solent Mk 2 APU for engine starting, ground operation and standby power.

ELECTRONICS AND EQUIPMENT: Standard equipment includes VHF/VHF, VHF/AM, HF/SSB, UHF/ADF, LF/ADF, VOR/DME, flight data control equipment, gyro compasses, intercom, navigation computer, weather and terrain-avoidance radar, ATC transponder, audio control centre and loudspeaker.

DIMENSIONS, EXTERNAL:
Wing span (main wing) 62 ft 8 in (19·10 m)
Distance between wing-tilt axes (front and rear) 30 ft 0 in (9·144 m)
Distance between propeller centres (each pair) 36 ft 1 in (11·00 m)
Length overall 73 ft 6 in (22·40 m)
Length of fuselage 68 ft 10¾ in (21·00 m)
Max fuselage width 11 ft 0¼ in (3·36 m)
Max fuselage width over main wheel fairings 11 ft 9¾ in (3·60 m)
Height overall 25 ft 3¼ in (7·70 m)
Nose-wheel track 9 ft 10 in (3·00 m)
Main wheel track 14 ft 9¼ in (4·50 m)
Wheelbase 25 ft 1⅝ in (7·662 m)
Passenger door (aft):
Height 6 ft 6¾ in (2·00 m)
Width 2 ft 1½ in (0·65 m)
Height to sill 4 ft 7 in (1·40 m)
Crew entry door (port):
Height 3 ft 0¼ in (0·92 m)
Width 2 ft 1½ in (0·65 m)
Height to sill 2 ft 11½ in (0·90 m)
Baggage door (stbd):
Height 3 ft 3¼ in (1·00 m)
Width 3 ft 3¼ in (1·00 m)
Height to sill 4 ft 1¼ in (1·25 m)
Galley servicing door (stbd):
Height 3 ft 3¼ in (1·00 m)
Width 1 ft 5¾ in (0·45 m)
Height to sill 4 ft 1¼ in (1·25 m)
Emergency exit (Type I):
Height 4 ft 0 in (1·22 m)
Width 2 ft 0 in (0·61 m)
Height to sill 4 ft 1¼ in (1·25 m)
Emergency exit (Type II):
Height 3 ft 8 in (1·12 m)
Width 1 ft 8 in (0·51 m)
Height to sill 4 ft 1¼ in (1·25 m)

DIMENSIONS, INTERNAL:
Cabin, excluding flight deck:
Length 38 ft 4¾ in (11·70 m)
Max width 7 ft 6½ in (2·30 m)
Max height 6 ft 6¾ in (2·00 m)

Prototype of the VFW-Fokker H3 Sprinter three-seat cabin rotorcraft

Floor area 323 sq ft (30·0 m^2)
Volume 2,260 cu ft (64·0 m^3)
Baggage hold (fwd), volume 212 cu ft (6·0 m^3)

AREAS:
Main wing, gross 480 sq ft (44·60 m^2)
Foreplane, gross 214·2 sq ft (19·90 m^2)
Elevons (rear wing, total) 144·2 sq ft (13·40 m^2)
Flaps (rear wing, total) 144·2 sq ft (13·40 m^2)
Flaps (foreplane, total) 34·4 sq ft (3·20 m^2)
Main fin 187·3 sq ft (17·40 m^2)
Ventral fins (total) 55·97 sq ft (5·20 m^2)

WEIGHTS AND LOADINGS (for VTOL operation at 984 ft = 300 m, 29°C; C = civil, M = military version):
Basic operating weight, empty
C 42,659 lb (19,350 kg)
M 38,713 lb (17,560 kg)
Max payload:
C 10,714 lb (4,860 kg)
M 15,211 lb (6,900 kg)
Max T-O and landing weight (C, M) 61,729 lb (28,000 kg)
Max ramp weight (C, M) 61,949 lb (28,100 kg)
Max zero-fuel weight:
C 53,373 lb (24,210 kg)
M 53,925 lb (24,460 kg)
Max disc loading (C, M) 37·3 lb/sq ft (182 kg/m^2)
Max power loading (C, M) 3·75 lb/shp (1·70 kg/shp)

PERFORMANCE (estimated, at max T-O weight):
Max cruising speed at 10,825 ft (3,300 m) 410 knots (472 mph; 760 km/h)
Max permissible diving speed 388 knots (447 mph; 720 km/h)
Econ cruising speed at 26,250 ft (8,000 m) 378 knots (435 mph; 700 km/h)
Max rate of climb at S/L 650 ft (198 m)/min
Service ceiling 30,000 ft (9,140 m)
Range with max payload 317 nm (366 miles; 590 km)
Max ferry range 960 nm (1,106 miles; 1,780 km)

VFW-FOKKER H3 SPRINTER

This cabin rotorcraft is the first in a family of compound helicopters being developed by VFW-Fokker, embodying experience gained from the experimental WFG-H2 (see 1968-69 *Jane's*), and utilises the same basic design principles. Among advantages claimed for the design are its simplicity, both to fly and to maintain, and improvements in safety, cost-effectiveness and noise reduction compared with conventional rotorcraft.

The VFW-H3 is intended for use as a three-seat executive transport, two-seat dual control trainer, ambulance aircraft (with room for pilot, doctor and two stretcher patients in an enlarged cabin), or as an agricultural aircraft with a payload of up to 685 lb (310 kg).

For vertical take-off, landing and hovering flight, a turbo-compressor provides compressed air to tip-drive the three-blade rotor, the H3 in these modes functioning as a conventional helicopter. For transition to forward flight, the power is transferred progressively to shrouded propellers on each side of the fuselage, the rotor autorotating once the aircraft is in horizontal flight. This method of propulsion eliminates the need for conventional transmission and drive-shaft systems, hydraulic systems, clutches and torque compensation (i.e., tail rotor). Full rotor autorotation is maintained in the event of engine failure.

Two prototypes of the VFW-H3 were completed in 1968, and underwent extensive ground testing. First flight was due to take place in the Spring of 1970.

TYPE: Three-seat light compound helicopter.

ROTOR SYSTEM: Three-blade fully-articulated main rotor, developed by VFW-Fokker, with interchangeable constant-chord blades of NACA 23015 section. No tail rotor. Blades are attached to hub by means of single spherical bearings and do not fold. Fairings over rotor hub and pylon. Rotor brake fitted. Rotor rpm range 280-480. For operation in extreme climatic conditions, blades of optimum design can be fitted without additional modification.

ROTOR DRIVE: During VTOL and hovering flight, compressed air generated by a mechanically-driven compressor is ducted through the rotor blades and expelled through cut-out nozzles at the blade tips. For transition to forward flight, power is switched to the lateral propellers, the rotor then autorotating.

FUSELAGE: Built around aluminium alloy load-bearing box-beam keel, which supports cabin floor at front, main landing gear cross-tube, nose-wheel leg, central bulkheads and engine-bay structure and light alloy circular-section semi-monocoque tail-boom. Non-structural cabin skin of glass-fibre-reinforced plastic laminate, with filling of foam plastics.

TAIL UNIT: Vee tail surfaces, each half with separate elevator, are carried at extreme rear of tail boom and are of conventional light alloy construction. Control surface actuation (used for directional control only) is by means of foot-pedals.

LANDING GEAR: Non-retractable tricycle type. Main wheels mounted under stub-wing fairings on fuselage sides. High-impact oleo-rubber shock-absorbers. All wheels same size with 5·00 × 5 Continental 6PR nylon-reinforced tyres, pressure 36·4 lb/sq in (2·56 kg/cm²). Wheel brakes can be operated individually by foot pedals or jointly by lever in cabin. Protective tail-skid under rear of tail-boom.

POWER PLANT: One Allison 250-C20 (-C18 in prototypes) with max cont rating of 346 hp and T-O rating of 400 hp, mounted in rear upper part of main fuselage, with overhead plenum-type suction chamber for intake air. According to flight manoeuvre required, the engine supplies compressed air to drive the three-blade rotor and/or two seven-blade shrouded propellers mounted on stub wings at the fuselage sides. Propulsion system reduces the number and size of gearboxes required. Fuel in two bladder-type tanks aft of cabin, with total capacity of 70 Imp gallons (320 litres). Refuelling point aft of bulkhead on starboard side. Oil capacity 1·76 Imp gallons (8 litres).

ACCOMMODATION: Single seat for pilot in front of cabin, with side-by-side seating for two persons at rear. Forward-hinged car-type doors adjacent to pilot's seat on starboard side and to passenger seats on port side. Provision for modifying to crop-spraying or rescue configuration. Separate baggage door. Cabin heating and ventilation standard. Bleed air from engine compressors for cabin heating and windshield de-icing systems.

SYSTEMS: Electrical system includes 3·5 kW generator and 24V 24Ah battery. De-icing system for engine air intakes and propeller shrouds; de-icing system for rotor blades is unnecessary, due to hot compressed air within the blades. Design eliminates the need for a hydraulic system.

Full-size mock-up of the VFW-Fokker H5 five-seat cabin rotorcraft

ELECTRONICS AND EQUIPMENT: Radio and radar available at customer's option.

DIMENSIONS, EXTERNAL:

Diameter of rotor	28 ft 6½ in (8·70 m)
Rotor blade chord	10 in (25·4 cm)
Diameter of propeller shrouds (each)	
	2 ft 11 in (0·89 m)
Length overall, rotor turning	
	30 ft 5¾ in (9·29 m)
Length of fuselage	24 ft 2¼ in (7·37 m)
Height to top of rotor hub	8 ft 2½ in (2·50 m)
Max width over propeller shrouds	
	10 ft 6 in (3·20 m)
Max width of fuselage	4 ft 0½ in (1·23 m)
Wheel track	6 ft 6¾ in (2·00 m)
Wheelbase	7 ft 5¾ in (2·28 m)

DIMENSIONS, INTERNAL:

Cabin: Max length	7 ft 6½ in (2·30 m)
Max width	3 ft 9¾ in (1·16 m)
Max height	3 ft 11¾ in (1·21 m)

AREAS:

Main rotor blades (each)	11·73 sq ft (1·09 m²)
Rotor disc	639·91 sq ft (59·45 m²)

WEIGHTS AND LOADING:

Weight empty	1,091 lb (495 kg)
Payload	595 lb (270 kg)
Max T-O and landing weight	2,134 lb (968 kg)
Max zero-fuel weight	1,713 lb (777 kg)
Max disc loading	3·33 lb/sq ft (16·28 kg/m²)

PERFORMANCE (estimated at max T-O weight, ISA conditions):

Max permissible diving speed	
	161 knots (186 mph; 300 km/h)
Max and econ cruising speed at S/L	
	135 knots (155 mph; 250 km/h)

Max rate of climb at S/L	1,280 ft (390 m)/min
Vertical rate of climb at S/L	195 ft (60 m)/min
Dynamic vertical rate of climb at S/L	
	1,380 ft (420 m)/min
Service ceiling	13,120 ft (4,000 m)
Hovering ceiling in ground effect	
	5,070 ft (1,540 m)
Hovering ceiling out of ground effect	
	1,500 ft (455 m)
Range with max fuel, 10% reserves	
	425 nm (490 miles; 790 km)
Range with max payload, 10% reserves	
	260 nm (300 miles; 480 km)
Max endurance (as autogyro)	3 hr
Max endurance (as helicopter)	2 hr

VFW-FOKKER H5

Development has begun of an enlarged version of the H3, designated H5. This will utilise essentially the same components as the H3, but will have increased engine power and seats for five persons. Like the H3, it will have no hydraulic system.

VFW-FOKKER H4, H7 and H9

Preliminary design work has been completed on the H7, which will be a five/seven-seat compound helicopter. It is basically a new design, but will utilise some cabin components of the H5 and will have slightly modified H5 flying controls.

The H4 project has a folding rotor; the projected H9 is a much larger aircraft, with a 50 ft 0 in (15·25 m) main rotor and AUW of approx 12,000 lb (5,450 kg).

WAGNER
WAGNER HELICOPTER-TECHNIK

ADDRESS:
799 Friedrichshafen-Flugplatz
DIRECTOR: Josef Wagner
CHIEF ENGINEER: Alfred Vogt

Development of the Wagner helicopter was started in 1960, the objective being to develop a torque-free basic vehicle which could be fitted with a variety of cabins and specialised equipment for different applications.

A contra-rotating rotor system is retained in the current Wagner Sky-trac 1 and 3 helicopters described below, but the rotary engine is replaced by a conventional drive from a standard horizontally-opposed six-cylinder aero-engine.

The four-seat roadable version, known as the Aerocar, underwent tests in 1968 fitted with a shaft-turbine engine (see below).

WAGNER SKY-TRAC

The two versions of the Sky-trac differ in the cabin structure fitted to the basic airframe. The single-seat Sky-trac 1 was first flown in July 1965. The Sky-trac 3 is a three-seater, with the pilot seated centrally at the front of the cabin and two passengers to the rear, on each side of the rotor pylon.

It is claimed that the Sky-trac will lift and transport more than its own empty weight. It can be fitted with an under-body cargo hook, on the CG, for hauling external freight loads. For agricultural duties, it can be fitted with spray-bars and a tank for approximately 143 Imp gallons (650 litres) of chemicals. As an ambulance, it will carry a stretcher patient inside the cabin, on the starboard side, in addition to the pilot and a medical attendant.

TYPE: Light multi-purpose helicopter.

Prototype Wagner Aerocar roadable helicopter as shown at the 1970 Hanover Air Show
(Brian M. Service)

ROTOR SYSTEM: Two identical two-blade contra-rotating rotors of composite construction. Each blade consists of a stressed light alloy leading-edge spar and a glass-fibre/epoxy resin laminate shell with honeycomb core. The rotor heads are of welded sheet steel, the blades being attached via ball sockets which serve as flapping and drag hinges. A rotor brake is fitted.

ROTOR DRIVE: Power input to special angle gearbox is transmitted through a drive clutch, sprag clutch and torsional damper. Rotor rpm 311.

FUSELAGE: Basic structure is a simple steel-tube truss framework, supporting the cabin at the front, rotor pylon centrally and power plant at the rear.

TAIL UNIT: Vee tail surfaces carried on open steel-tube boom.

LANDING GEAR: Tubular skid landing gear with retractable ground handling wheels. Height and track of gear are variable to accommodate bulky loads or to facilitate installation of special equipment. Pontoons can be attached to the skids for amphibious operation.

POWER PLANT: One 260 hp Franklin 6AS-335-B six-cylinder horizontally-opposed air-cooled engine, with exhaust-driven turbosupercharger, mounted horizontally aft of rotor pylon. Single fuel tank aft of pilot's seat, capacity 21 Imp gallons (95 litres). Provision for auxiliary tank.

ACCOMMODATION: Sky-trac 1 has single seat for pilot inside a transparent plastic enclosure, open at the rear. Sky-trac 3 has two additional seats at rear of widened cabin structure, inclined slightly inward. Conventional controls.

DIMENSIONS, EXTERNAL:
Diameter of rotors (each)   32 ft 9¾ in (10·00 m)
Length overall   23 ft 3½ in (7·10 m)
Length of fuselage   6 ft 10¾ in (2·10 m)
Height overall (Sky-trac 3)   11 ft 9¾ in (3·60 m)
Skid track   7 ft 4 in (2·23 m)

AREA:
Main rotor disc   846 sq ft (78·60 m²)

WEIGHTS (designed):
Weight empty, less cabin enclosure
                                 1,675 lb (760 kg)
Weight empty, equipped (Sky-trac 1)
                                 1,808 lb (820 kg)
Max T-O weight   3,300 lb (1,500 kg)

PERFORMANCE (estimated at max T-O weight):
Max speed at S/L 86 knots (99 mph; 160 km/h)
Max cruising speed
                         76 knots (87 mph; 140 km/h)
Max rate of climb at S/L   1,180 ft (360 m)/min
Vertical rate of climb at S/L 785 ft (240 m)/min
Max range, standard fuel
                         108 nm (125 miles; 200 km)
Max endurance, standard fuel   1 hr 18 min

WAGNER AEROCAR

Although the Aerocar helicopter looks very different from the Sky-trac, it is based on the same principle. The only major difference is that it is fitted with a roomy enclosed cabin, seating the pilot and up to four passengers, and is roadable, with the rotor blades folded back and anchored. The road wheels are powered through a hydraulic drive from the main engine.

The prototype Aerocar was completed in 1965, originally having a 260 hp Franklin 6AS-335-A engine, and gave good results during its initial flight tests. It was later re-engined with a 420 shp version of the Turboméca Oredon 4 shaft-turbine engine, in which form max T-O weight is 3,300 lb (1,500 kg).

Wagner Sky-Trac 1 helicopter fitted with external cargo sling

Wagner Sky-Trac 3 helicopter fitted with pontoon landing gear (*Brian M. Service*)

INDIA

CIVIL AVIATION DEPARTMENT

TECHNICAL CENTRE, CIVIL AVIATION DEPARTMENT

HEAD OFFICE:
Civil Aviation Department, R. K. Puram, New Delhi 22

DIRECTOR GENERAL: G. C. Arya

WORKS:
Technical Centre, Safdarjung, New Delhi-3

DEPUTY DIRECTOR GENERAL:
S. Ramamritham

DEPUTY DIRECTOR (R&D): K. B. Ganesan

In addition to its work on the design and development of sailplanes, described in the appropriate section of this work, the Civil Aviation Department has designed and is developing a 2/3-seat light aircraft named the Revathi, of which details follow.

REVATHI

The prototype Revathi Mk I, described and illustrated in the 1969-70 *Jane's*, flew for the first time on 13 January 1967, and was Type

Prototype of the Revathi light aircraft in modified Mk II form with constant-chord metal wings

Certificated in January 1969 after satisfactory completion of flight trials at the Indian Institute of Technology, Kanpur.

It has subsequently been further developed into the Revathi Mk II, and the description below applies to the aircraft in this form. Major changes are the introduction of constant-chord metal wings, and increased fuel capacity and AUW. First flight of the Mk II was made on 20 May 1970.

The Revathi is intended for use by civil flying clubs as a two-seat basic trainer able to provide all training necessary for a private pilot's licence, including spinning, night flying, instrument flying and cross-country navigation. As a touring aircraft it can accommodate three persons.

TYPE: Two/three-seat light aircraft.

WINGS: Cantilever low-wing monoplane. Wing section NACA 23015 at root and up to 60·6% of each half-span, NACA 4412 at tip. Dihedral 5°. Incidence 4°. Two-spar stressed-skin structure. The nose cell and, at root, the rear cell also, are covered with aluminium alloy sheet; the remainder of the wing is fabric-covered. Bottom-hinged slotted wooden ailerons with plywood leading-edge and fabric covering. All-wood slotted trailing-edge flaps. Landing light in each leading-edge.

FUSELAGE: Welded steel-tube truss structure, covered with sheet aluminium alloy to rear of cockpit and fabric elsewhere.

TAIL UNIT: Cantilever horizontal surfaces of wood, with plywood covering on tailplane and fabric-covered elevators. Swept vertical surfaces of steel-tube construction, covered with fabric. Fin integral with fuselage. Trim-tab in starboard elevator. Elevator incorporates shielded horn balance; the rudder has an unshielded horn balance.

LANDING GEAR: Non-retractable tail-wheel type. Rubber rings in tension provide shock-absorption in main units. Dunlop main wheels, size 6·00 × 6·5, pressure 25-35 lb/sq in (1·75-2·45 kg/cm²). Dunlop hydraulic disc brakes. Castoring tail-wheel, with solid tyre, carried on leaf springs, coupled flexibly to rudder.

POWER PLANT: One 145 hp Rolls-Royce/Continental O-300-C six-cylinder horizontally-opposed air-cooled engine, driving a Sensenich M74 DC54 two-blade fixed-pitch metal propeller, diameter 6 ft 2 in (1·88 m). Fuel in two integral tanks, one in each wing, with total capacity of 32·6 Imp gallons (148 litres). Auxiliary tank, capacity 11 Imp gallons (50 litres), installed aft of cockpit. Oil capacity 1·6 Imp gallons (7·5 litres).

ACCOMMODATION: Enclosed cabin, seating two persons in front and one to the rear. Dual controls standard, including duplicated wheel brake and throttle controls. Jettisonable door on each side. Baggage compartment, capacity 3 cu ft (·085 m³).

ELECTRONICS AND EQUIPMENT: Blind- and night-flying instrumentation standard, as is Bendix RT-221A-14 380-channel VHF transceiver. Bendix RN-222 VHF navigation receiver, with glide-slope supplement, IN-224 VOR/ILS, and 204A marker receiver optional.

DIMENSIONS, EXTERNAL:

Wing span	30 ft 10 in (9·40 m)
Wing chord (constant)	4 ft 11 in (1·50 m)
Wing aspect ratio	6·27
Length overall	24 ft 10 in (7·58 m)
Height overall in flying attitude	9 ft 8¾ in (2·97 m)
Tailplane span	9 ft 0 in (2·74 m)
Wheel track	6 ft 5 in (1·96 m)
Wheelbase	17 ft 6 in (5·33 m)
Propeller ground clearance	9½ in (0·24 m)
Cabin doors (each):	
Height	4 ft 0 in (1·22 m)
Width	2 ft 10½ in (0·88 m)

DIMENSIONS, INTERNAL:

Cabin: Length	7 ft 2½ in (2·20 m)
Max width	3 ft 1½ in (0·95 m)
Max height	3 ft 11¾ in (1·21 m)

AREAS:

Wings, gross	151·7 sq ft (14·09 m²)
Ailerons (total)	9·9 sq ft (0·92 m²)
Trailing-edge flaps (total)	15·1 sq ft (1·40 m²)
Fin	8·65 sq ft (0·804 m²)
Rudder	8·40 sq ft (0·78 m²)
Tailplane	13·1 sq ft (1·22 m²)
Elevators, including tab	13·9 sq ft (1·29 m²)

WEIGHTS AND LOADINGS:

Weight empty, equipped	1,353 lb (614 kg)
Max T-O and landing weight:	
normal	2,120 lb (962 kg)
utility	1,832 lb (831 kg)
Max wing loading:	
normal	13·98 lb/sq ft (68·2 kg/m²)
utility	12·08 lb/sq ft (58·95 kg/m²)
Max power loading:	
normal	14·62 lb/hp (6·63 kg/hp)
utility	12·61 lb/hp (5·72 kg/hp)

PERFORMANCE (estimated, at max T-O weight):

Max level speed at S/L	104 knots (120 mph; 193 km/h)
Max permissible diving speed	140 knots (161 mph; 260 km/h)
Max cruising speed (75% power) at 6,000 ft (1,830 m)	91 knots (105 mph; 169 km/h)
Stalling speed, flaps down:	
normal	45·5 knots (52 mph; 83 km/h)
utility	41·7 knots (48 mph; 77 km/h)
Rate of climb at S/L:	
normal	732 ft (223 m)/min
utility	899 ft (274 m)/min
Service ceiling	15,000 ft (4,570 m)
T-O run	750 ft (227 m)
Landing run	660 ft (200 m)
Range with max fuel (incl auxiliary tank), no reserve	434 nm (500 miles; 800 km)
Range with wing fuel tanks, no reserve	347 nm (400 miles; 640 km)

HAL
HINDUSTAN AERONAUTICS LTD

ADDRESS:
 Indian Express Building, Vidhana Veedhi,
  Bangalore 1

CHAIRMAN:
 Air Chief Marshal P. C. Lal

DIRECTORS:
 Dr S. Dhawan
 J. P. Kacker
 K. T. Satarawala
 Air Marshal Shivdev Singh
 V. N. Sukul
 P. L. Tandon
 Dr V. M. Ghatage
 Air Vice-Marshal A. S. Rikhy (Managing Director, Bangalore Division)
 Air Cdre C. R. Kurpad (Managing Director, MiG Complex)

GENERAL MANAGERS OF DIVISIONS:
 Kanpur Division: Gp Capt P. D. Chopra
 Nasik Division: Air Cdre M. Bhaskaran
 Koraput Division: G. Nara Simhan
 Hyderabad Division: R. M. Nayahr

Hindustan Aeronautics Ltd (HAL) was formed on 1 October 1964, amalgamating the former Hindustan Aircraft Ltd (formed 1940) and Aeronautics India Ltd (formed 1963), and now has six Divisions, at Bangalore, Kanpur, Nasik, Koraput, Hyberabad and Lucknow. Of these, the oldest, the Bangalore Division, is directly under the control of one of the Managing Directors and is engaged in the manufacture of civil and military aircraft and aero-engines both, under licence and of indigenous design. This Division also has a large organisation undertaking repair and overhaul of airframes, engines, and allied instruments and accessories.

The Kanpur Division is engaged mainly in the manufacture of Hawker Siddeley HS 748 transport aircraft under licence. It also produces the Rohini and ITG-3 sailplanes, of which details can be found in the "Sailplanes" section.

Nasik, Koraput and Hyderabad form the MiG Complex, undertaking the manufacture of MiG-21FL fighters with the collaboration of the USSR.

The Lucknow Division, formed late in 1969, is in the detailed project planning stage and is at present intended to produce aircraft accessories under licence from various manufacturers in the UK, France and the USA.

BANGALORE DIVISION

ADDRESS:
 Bangalore-17 (Mysore State)

The Bangalore Division of HAL consists essentially of the former Hindustan Aircraft Limited, the activities of which, since its formation in 1940, were described in previous editions of Jane's.

The Division is engaged in developing and building aircraft and aero-engines of its own design, and also manufactures various aircraft and aero-engines under licence. The first aircraft of its own design to enter production was the HT-2 piston-engined primary trainer (described in 1965-66 Jane's), followed by two lightplanes named the Pushpak and Krishak, with two and three seats respectively. Development of the HF-24 Marut jet fighter and HJT-16 Kiran jet trainer were undertaken towards the end of 1956 and 1959 respectively.

The Bangalore Division is currently manufacturing under licence the Aérospatiale Alouette III helicopter. Production of the Hawker Siddeley Gnat fighter (see 1969-70 Jane's) has ended.

Orpheus 701 and 703 turbojet engines to power the Gnat and HF-24 fighters are being produced under licence from Rolls-Royce Ltd (Bristol Division). Also produced under licence are Rolls-Royce Dart turboprop engines to power Kanpur-built Hawker Siddeley 748's and Turboméca Artouste turboshaft engines for the Division's own Alouette programme.

In addition to engines manufactured under licence, the company has developed a four-cylinder 90 hp piston-engine which has been type certified and flight tested in the Pushpak.

Prototype of the HAL HF-24 Mk IT two-seat training version of the Marut twin-jet fighter

Currently under development are the 2,500 lb (1,135 kg) st HJE-2500 turbojet and the six-cylinder 250 hp PE-2 piston-engine. The PE-2 is intended as a power plant for the HA-31 agricultural aircraft.

The Bangalore Division is a repair and overhaul agency for Hawker Siddeley (de Havilland) Dove/Devon aircraft, DHC-4 Caribou, Fairchild C-119 Packet transports and English Electric Canberra bombers. Various piston-engines and jet engines are also overhauled at Bangalore. The branch factory in Calcutta is continuing to concentrate on the repair and overhaul of DC-3's belonging to the Indian Air Force and non-scheduled operators.

HAL HUL-26 PUSHPAK

To meet the requirement for an inexpensive ultra-light training aircraft for Indian flying clubs, Hindustan Aircraft undertook the development of the Pushpak, a two-seat high-wing monoplane of simple and robust construction.

Work on the project began in early 1958 and the prototype flew for the first time on 28 September the same year. The prototype and current production Pushpaks are powered by a 90 hp Rolls-Royce/Continental engine.

A total of 150 Pushpaks had been delivered by January 1969.

A full description of the Pushpak appeared in the 1969-70 edition of *Jane's*.

POWER PLANT: One 90 hp Continental C90-8F four-cylinder horizontally-opposed air-cooled engine. Two-blade fixed-pitch wood propeller, diameter 6 ft 0 in (1·83 m). Normal fuel capacity 12·5 Imp gallons (56 litres). Provision for auxiliary tank, capacity 6·75 Imp gallons (30·7 litres).

DIMENSIONS, EXTERNAL:

Wing span	36 ft 0 in (10·97 m)
Wing chord (constant)	5 ft 0 in (1·52 m)
Length overall	21 ft 0 in (6·40 m)
Height overall in flying attitude	
	9 ft 1 in (2·77 m)
Tailplane span	10 ft 0 in (3·05 m)
Wheel track	5 ft 9½ in (1·75 m)
Wheelbase	15 ft 10 in (4·83 m)

WEIGHTS AND LOADINGS:

Weight empty	870 lb (395 kg)
Max T-O weight	1,350 lb (613 kg)
Max wing loading	7·15 lb/sq ft (34·9 kg/m²)
Max power loading	15 lb/hp (6·8 kg/hp)

PERFORMANCE (at max T-O weight):

Max level speed	78 knots (90 mph; 114 km/h)
Cruising speed	
	61-74 knots (70-85 mph; 112-136 km/h)
Rate of climb at S/L	500 ft (152 m)/min
Service ceiling	14,000 ft (4,270 m)
Absolute ceiling	15,400 ft (4,697 m)
Range in still air	
	217 nm (250 miles; 400 km)
Endurance	3 hours

HAL HAOP-27 KRISHAK Mk 2

The Krishak Mk 2 (HAOP-27) was designed to meet the operational requirements for AOP duties. Normally, it carries a crew of two, but there is a swivelling seat for a third person in the rear of the cabin.

Work on the Krishak began in mid-1958. The first prototype flew for the first time in November 1959, followed by a second in November 1960. An initial order was placed for 30 Krishaks for air observation post duties with the Indian Army, and delivery of these began in December 1964. The total on order was later increased to 68, all of which have now been completed.

A full description appeared in the 1969-70 *Jane's*.

HAL HF-24 MARUT (WIND SPIRIT)

The HF-24 Marut single-seat fighter has been developed by HAL under the design leadership of Dr Kurt Tank, who was responsible for the wartime Focke-Wulf aeroplanes.

Work on the project began in 1956, to meet an Indian Air Force requirement. An unpowered full-scale wooden flying model of the HF-24 was flight tested extensively. It flew for the first time on 21 March 1959, and was normally released from its two-plane at a height of 12,000-15,000 ft (3,660-4,570 m).

The first prototype HF-24 Mk I, powered by two Rolls-Royce Bristol Orpheus 703 turbojet engines, flew for the first time on 17 June 1961. It was followed by the second Mk I prototype in October 1962.

Sixty production HF-24's are being manufactured to Mk I standards as ground attack fighters, with Orpheus 703 engines. The first Mk I flew in March 1963 and four were delivered to the Indian Air Force on 10 May 1964. The Mk I continues in production.

Variants of the Marut under development include the Mk IR, fitted with a reheated version of the Orpheus 703 engine, and the Mk IT tandem two-seat trainer without reheat.

The prototype Mk IT (BD 888) made its first flight on 30 April 1970, in the hands of Wg Cdr R. D. Sahni, chief test pilot of the Bangalore Division of HAL. This version has full dual controls, and a wide choice of systems enables the aircraft to be used for several advanced training roles, including instrument and armament training. Development of the Mk IT, and of other versions of the HF-24. have been the responsibility of an all-Indian design team under Mr S. C. Das since the departure of Dr Kurt Tank and his German team in 1967.

An HF-24 was sent to Egypt in mid-1966 to serve as a flying test-bed for the Helwan-developed E-300 turbojet, the aircraft being fitted with one E-300 and one Orpheus 703. It flew for the first time on 29 March 1967. The Egyptian development programme for this engine was cancelled in 1969.

TYPE: Single-seat supersonic fighter.

WINGS: Cantilever low-wing monoplane of thin section. Slight anhedral. Extended leading-edge on outer wings. Conventional torsion-box structure. Hydraulically-actuated ailerons and trailing-edge flaps, with provision for reversion to manual control. No de-icing system.

FUSELAGE: Conventional all-metal semi-monocoque structure, narrowed in accordance with area rule in region of wing trailing-edge. Two hydraulically-operated box-type air-brakes on fuselage, opening outward. Engine air-intakes on each side of cockpit, with central shock-cones.

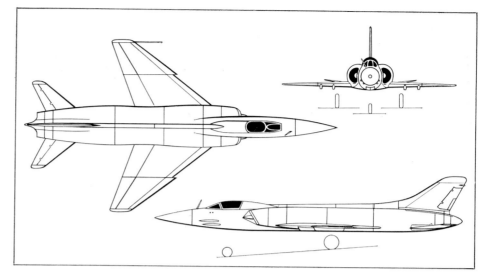

Photograph and three-view drawing of the HAL HF-24 Marut Mk I twin-jet fighter

TAIL UNIT: Cantilever all-metal structure with sweepback on all surfaces. Hydraulically-operated low-set variable-incidence tailplane with emergency trim. Hydraulically-actuated elevators, with provision for reversion to manual control. Manually-operated rudder, with trim-tab.

LANDING GEAR: Retractable tricycle type, with single wheel on each unit. Hydraulic retraction, nose-wheel forward, main units inward into fuselage. Steerable nose-wheel.

POWER PLANT (Mk I): Two Rolls-Royce Bristol Orpheus 703 turbojet engines, each rated at 4,850 lb (2,200 kg) st, side-by-side in rear fuselage. Fuel in main fuselage collector tank, wing centre-section supply tank and two integral wing tanks, with total usable capacity of 567 Imp gallons (2,577 litres). Provision for four underwing drop tanks and internal auxiliary tank.

ACCOMMODATION: Pilot only, on Martin-Baker Mk S4 zero-altitude ejection seat, under rearward-sliding blister canopy. Windscreen heated by sandwiched gold-film electrode. Side screens and canopy demisted by warm air from air-conditioning system.

SYSTEMS: Air-conditioning system includes two air-cycle heat exchangers and cold air unit. Cockpit pressurised to differential of 3·5 lb/sq in (0·25 kg/cm²) between 24,000 and 40,000 ft (7,300-12,200 m). Hydraulic system, pressure 4,000 lb/sq in (281 kg/cm²), supplied by two engine-driven pumps, for all services. Nitrogen system, pressure 3,000 lb/sq in (210 kg/cm²), to provide emergency power for landing gear, air-brakes and flaps. 24V DC single-wire earth return electrical system, with two 24V 25Ah batteries and 4Ah emergency supply battery.

ARMAMENT: Four 30-mm Aden guns in nose, with about 120 rounds per gun, and retractable pack of 48 air-to-air rockets in lower fuselage aft of nose-wheel unit. Attachments for four 1,000 lb (454 kg) bombs, drop tanks or other stores under wings.

DIMENSIONS, EXTERNAL:

Wing span	29 ft 6¼ in (9·00 m)
Length overall	52 ft 0¾ in (15·87 m)
Height overall	11 ft 9¾ in (3·60 m)
Wheel track	9 ft 2 in (2·80 m)

AREA:

Wings, gross	273·9 sq ft (25·45 m²)

WEIGHTS:

Weight empty	13,658 lb (6,195 kg)
T-O weight, clean	19,734 lb (8,951 kg)

PERFORMANCE:

Max level speed attained at 40,000 ft (12,200 m)	
	Mach 1·02
Min flying speed, clean	
	132 knots (152 mph; 245 km/h)

HAL HJT-16 Mk II Kiran jet basic trainer (2,500 lb st Rolls-Royce Bristol Viper 11 turbojet)

HAL HJT-16 Mk II KIRAN

In December 1959, the Government of India approved the design and development by HAL of a side-by-side two-seat jet basic trainer designated HJT-16 Mk II. This aircraft is powered by a Rolls-Royce Bristol Viper 11 turbojet.

Detailed design work on the HJT-16 Mk II began in 1961 under the leadership of Dr V. M. Ghatage. The first prototype flew for the first time on 4 September 1964. It was followed by a second aircraft in August 1965.

A contract for 24 pre-production and 36 production examples of the HJT-16 Mk II has been placed by the Indian Defence Ministry, with further orders to follow. Initial deliveries to the IAF, of six aircraft, were made in March 1968.

TYPE: Two-seat jet basic trainer.

WINGS: Cantilever low-wing monoplane. Wing section NACA 23015 at root, NACA 23012 at tip. Dihedral 4° from roots. Incidence 0° 30′ at root. Conventional all-metal three-spar structure. Frise-type differential ailerons. Hydraulically-actuated split trailing-edge flaps.

FUSELAGE: All-metal semi-monocoque structure. Hydraulically-actuated door-type air-brake under centre-fuselage.

TAIL UNIT: Cantilever all-metal structure. Electrically-operated variable-incidence tailplane. No trim-tabs.

LANDING GEAR: Retractable tricycle type of HAL design. Hydraulic actuation. Main units retract inward into fuselage; self-centering twin-contact non-steerable nose-wheel retracts forward. Oleo-pneumatic shock-absorbers. Main wheel tyres size 506 × 164 mm. Nose-wheel tyre size 391 × 160 mm. Hydraulic brakes.

POWER PLANT: One 2,500 lb (1,135 kg) st Rolls-Royce Bristol Viper 11 turbojet engine. Internal fuel in main saddle tanks in fuselage (2 × 44 Imp gallons), wing centre-section collector tank (62 Imp gallons) and outboard wing tanks (2 × 50 Imp gallons), with total capacity of 250 Imp gallons (1,137 litres). Provision for two underwing tanks with total capacity of 100 Imp gallons (454 litres). System permits 30 sec of inverted flight.

ACCOMMODATION: Crew of two side-by-side in air-conditioned and pressurised cockpit, on Martin-Baker Mk H4HA zero-altitude fully-automatic ejection seats. Clamshell-type canopy has replaced the original rearward-sliding type. Dual controls and duplicated blind-flying instruments.

SYSTEMS: Air-conditioning system has max pressure differential of 3·5 lb/sq in (0·25 kg/cm²). Hydraulic system for landing gear, flaps and dive-brake, pressure 3,000 lb/sq in (210 kg/cm²). Accumulator for manual emergency system. Electrical system is of 24V DC single-wire earth return type, with two 24V 25Ah batteries. Normalair pressure-demand oxygen system.

ELECTRONICS AND EQUIPMENT: STR 9X/M 10-channel VHF transmitter-receiver and TR 2002 single-channel VHF standby set. Marconi AD 722 ADF standard.

DIMENSIONS, EXTERNAL:
Wing span	35 ft 1¼ in (10·70 m)
Wing aspect ratio	6
Length overall	34 ft 9 in (10·60 m)
Height overall	11 ft 11 in (3·64 m)
Tailplane span	12 ft 9½ in (3·90 m)
Wheel track	7 ft 11 in (2·42 m)
Wheelbase	11 ft 6 in (3·50 m)

AREAS:
Wings, gross	204·5 sq ft (19·00 m²)
Ailerons (total)	16·68 sq ft (1·55 m²)
Flaps (total)	23·47 sq ft (2·18 m²)
Vertical tail surfaces (total)	22·60 sq ft (2·10 m²)
Rudder	7·05 sq ft (0·66 m²)
Horizontal tail surfaces (total)	40·90 sq ft (3·80 m²)
Elevators	12·27 sq ft (1·14 m²)

WEIGHTS:
Weight empty	5,362 lb (2,432 kg)
Normal T-O weight	7,712 lb (3,498 kg)
Max T-O weight	8,660 lb (3,928 kg)

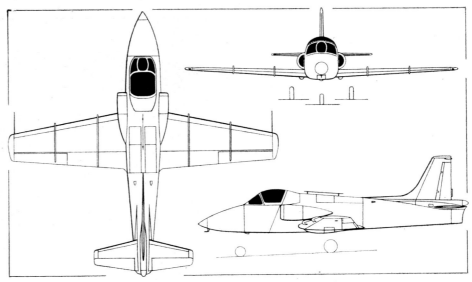

HAL HJT-16 Mk II Kiran jet basic trainer

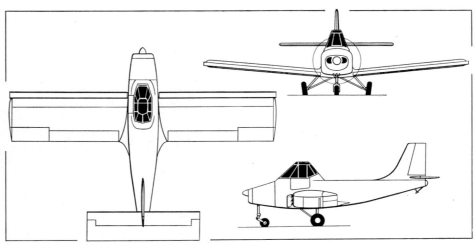

HAL HA-31 agricultural and utility monoplane (250 hp Rolls-Royce/Continental IO-470 engine)

PERFORMANCE (at normal T-O weight):
Max level speed at S/L
387 knots (446 mph; 718 km/h)
Max level speed at 30,000 ft (9,150 m)
383 knots (441 mph; 709 km/h)
Stalling speed, flaps up
80 knots (92 mph; 149 km/h)
Stalling speed, flaps down
70 knots (80 mph; 129 km/h)
T-O run   1,475 ft (450 m)
Endurance on internal fuel at 200 knots (230 mph; 370 km/h) at 20,000 ft (6,100 m)
2 hr 10 min

HAL HA-31

Work on this agricultural aircraft began in mid-1968, and the prototype was completed in 1969. The HA-31 is intended primarily for aerial application of pesticides and fertilisers. It can also be used for aerial survey, fire/patrol duties and cloud-seeding.

The HA-31 is a single-seat low-wing monoplane with a non-retractable tricycle undercarriage.

The cockpit is designed to withstand 40 g impact forces without buckling in the event of a crash. The prototype is powered by a 250 hp Rolls-Royce /Continental engine, but it is planned to fit the P.E.2 piston-engine, under development by HAL, in production aircraft. A 1,200 lb (544 kg) payload can be carried in a hopper located just above the wing centre-section and below the cockpit.

DIMENSIONS, EXTERNAL:
Wing span	39 ft 4½ in (12·00 m)
Wing aspect ratio	6

Length overall	26 ft 10¾ in (8·20 m)
Height overall	12 ft 0½ in (3·67 m)

AREA:
Wings, gross	258 sq ft (24·0 m²)

WEIGHTS:
Weight empty	2,314 lb (1,050 kg)
Max T-O weight	3,792 lb (1,720 kg)

PERFORMANCE (at max T-O weight):
Max level speed at S/L	108 knots (124 mph; 200 km/h)
Min flying speed	35 knots (40 mph; 64 km/h)
Rate of climb at S/L	748 ft (228 m)/min
Service ceiling	14,108 ft (4,300 m)
T-O to 50 ft (15 m)	1,017 ft (310 m)
Landing from 50 ft (15 m)	676 ft (206 m)
Range	463 nm (534 miles; 860 km)

HAL/HAWKER SIDDELEY GNAT

Development of this single-seat lightweight fighter was started in the UK by the former Folland Aircraft, Ltd, as a private venture in 1951. British-built Gnat Mk 1 fighters were supplied subsequently to the Ministry of Aviation (6), India (25 plus 15 sets of components), Finland (12) and Yugoslavia (2).

Production of the Gnat Mk 1 fighter, under licence at the Bangalore Division of Hindustan Aeronautics Ltd, has now ended. A description appeared in the 1969-70 edition of *Jane's*.

KANPUR DIVISION

ADDRESS:
Chakeri, Kanpur

When the decision was taken to build the Hawker Siddeley 748 twin-turboprop transport in India, as a replacement for the Dakotas of the Indian Air Force, four hangars at Kanpur were taken over, on 23 January 1960, as the IAF Aircraft Manufacturing Depot. The Depot was incorporated in Aeronautics (India) Ltd in June 1964 and subsequently became the Kanpur Division of Hindustan Aeronautics Ltd.

HAL/HAWKER SIDDELEY 748

The first set of jigs for the 748 was set up in the Depot by mid-1960, and the first Indian-built 748 flew on 1 November 1961, followed by the second one on 13 March 1963.

The first four Indian 748's were Srs 1 aircraft, utilising components imported from the UK. The first Indian-built Srs 2 flew for the first time on 28 January 1964. Series production of the Srs 2 is now under way, at a current production rate of nine aircraft a year; by May 1970, 22 Srs 2 aircraft had been built and delivered. Most of the airframe components are manufactured by HAL from raw materials, although some components are still being imported from the UK.

The aircraft's Dart 531 turboprop engines are built by the Bangalore Division of HAL. Some HF, VHF and other radio equipment is being manufactured by Bharat Electronics Ltd of Bangalore.

Indian Airlines Corporation placed an initial order for 14 Srs 2 aircraft; the first of these was delivered on 28 June 1967 and the last in March 1970. A further 10 aircraft ordered by the airline are due to be delivered in 1971-72.

HAL is also producing the aircraft in several versions for the Indian Air Force, which ordered five Srs 1's and 22 Srs 2's. Some of these have already been delivered as executive transports, and delivery of others for pilot, navigator and signaller training duties was due to begin during 1970.

HAL-built Hawker Siddeley HS 748 twin-turboprop airliner in the insignia of Indian Airlines Corporation

INDONESIA

LIPNUR

DEPARTEMEN ANGKATAN UDARA REPUBLIK INDONESIA, LEMBAGA INDUSTRI PENERBANGAN NURTANIO (Department of the Indonesian Air Force, Nurtanio Aircraft Industry)

Address:
Lanuma Husein Sastranegara (Husein Sastranegara AFB), Bandung

General Director:
Colonel Ind AF Sugito Ir

To honour the service of the late Air Marshal Nurtanio Pringgoadisurjo, who was largely responsible for establishing an aircraft industry in Indonesia, the Department of the Air Force of Indonesia named after him the former Institute for Aero Industry Establishment.

The Institute had come into being in August 1961, as a successor to the Indonesian Air Force Design, Development and Production Depot. Of the products of the Depot and Institute, designed under Air Marshal Nurtanio's leadership, the X-03 Belalang 85 and Belalang 90 (1966-67 *Jane's*) are in service; the X-05 Super Kunang 35 (1966-67 *Jane's*), the B-8m Kolentang and the X-07 Kunang 50 are flying; the Kunang 60 is under design, and the X-08 Manjang helicopter is 95% completed.

LIPNUR has facilities for training aircraft factory workers. Its engineering and production facilities are being used at the present time for the manufacture under licence of the Polish PZL-104 utility aircraft, under the Indonesian name "Gelatik".

Indonesian-built PZL-104 Gelatik agricultural aircraft (225 hp Continental O-470 engine)

PZL-104 GELATIK (RICE BIRD)

The Gelatik is a licence-built version of the Polish PZL-104 Wilga utility aircraft, with a Continental engine and detail changes compared with the current Polish production model.

Work on the design modifications was started in 1962, and assembly of the first Indonesian PZL-104 began in 1963; this aircraft flew for the first time in 1964, and Gelatiks assembled in Indonesia from knocked-down components were in service during 1966. Present plans entail production of a total of 56 aircraft, of which delivery was continuing in 1970. These are employed chiefly as passenger, ambulance or agricultural aircraft, or at flying clubs. The agricultural version received Indonesian certification to BCAR standards on 23 December 1965, and the passenger and ambulance versions on 5 July 1966.

Type: STOL general utility aircraft.

Wings: Cantilever high-wing monoplane. Wing section NACA 2415. Dihedral 1°. Incidence 4° 30′. All-metal single-spar structure, with leading-edge torsion box. Each wing attached to fuselage by three bolts, two at spar and one at forward fitting. All-metal slotted ailerons, which can be drooped to supplement flaps during landing. Mechanically-operated single-slotted all-metal flaps in two sections on each wing. Full-span fixed slots on leading-edges. Ground-adjustable tab on aileron.

Fuselage: All-metal stressed-skin semi-monocoque structure.

Tail Unit: Cantilever all-metal structure, with fixed-incidence tailplane. Elevator and rudder are aerodynamically and statically balanced. Ground-adjustable tab in elevator.

Landing Gear: Non-retractable tail-wheel type. Semi-cantilever main units have oleo-pneumatic shock-absorbers. Castoring and self-centering tail-wheel with oleo-pneumatic shock-absorber. Tyres size 500 × 150 mm on main wheels and size 255 × 110 mm on tail-wheel. Tyre pressure: main wheels 39·8 lb/sq in (2·80 kg/cm²); tail-wheel 25 lb/sq in (1·70 kg/cm²). Hydraulic brakes. Streamline fairings optional for main wheels and legs.

Power Plant: One 225 hp Continental O-470-13A or 230 hp O-470-L six-cylinder horizontally-opposed air-cooled engine, driving a McCauley type 2A 34C-50/90A-2 two-blade constant-speed metal propeller, diameter 7 ft 2½ in (2·20 m). Two fuel tanks in wings, with total capacity of 42 Imp gallons (192 litres). Refuelling points in wings. Oil capacity 2·5 Imp gallons (11·5 litres).

Accommodation: Pilot and three passengers in pairs, or equivalent cargo. Upward-hinged door on each side. Cabin has strengthened honeycomb floor. Baggage compartment aft of seats.

Electronics and Equipment: Motorola or Nova Star VHF transceiver standard. 24V 10Ah battery for lights, instruments and radio system.

Dimensions, external:	
Wing span	36 ft 9 in (11·20 m)
Wing chord (constant)	4 ft 7 in (1·40 m)
Wing aspect ratio	8
Length overall	27 ft 2¾ in (8·30 m)
Height overall	9 ft 2¼ in (2·80 m)
Tailplane span	13 ft 1½ in (4·00 m)
Wheel track	6 ft 11½ in (2·12 m)
Wheelbase	19 ft 10½ in (6·06 m)
Propeller ground clearance	2 ft 2¾ in (0·68 m)
Passenger doors (each):	
Height	3 ft 1 in (0·94 m)
Width	4 ft 11 in (1·50 m)
Dimensions, internal:	
Cabin: Length	7 ft 2½ in (2·20 m)
Max width	3 ft 9¼ in (1·15 m)
Max height	4 ft 11 in (1·50 m)
Floor area	23 sq ft (2·20 m²)
Volume	85 cu ft (2·40 m³)
Baggage space	17·5 cu ft (0·50 m³)
Areas:	
Wings, gross	166·6 sq ft (15·50 m²)
Ailerons (total)	17·2 sq ft (1·60 m²)
Flaps (total)	21·6 sq ft (2·00 m²)
Fin	15·9 sq ft (1·48 m²)
Rudder	9·8 sq ft (0·91 m²)
Tailplane	17·8 sq ft (1·65 m²)
Elevators (total)	16·7 sq ft (1·55 m²)
Weights and Loadings:	
Weight empty	1,567 lb (711 kg)
Max T-O and landing weight	2,535 lb (1,150 kg)
Max zero-fuel weight	2,259 lb (1,025 kg)
Max wing loading	15·2 lb/sq ft (74 kg/m²)
Max power loading	11·2 lb/hp (5·1 kg/hp)
Performance (at max T-O weight):	
Max level speed at S/L	109 knots (126 mph; 203 km/h)
Max permissible diving speed	146 knots (169 mph; 273 km/h)
Max cruising speed	97 knots (112 mph; 180 km/h)
Econ cruising speed	81 knots (93 mph; 150 km/h)
Stalling speed	27 knots (31 mph; 49 km/h)
Rate of climb at S/L	905 ft (276 m)/min
Service ceiling	15,800 ft (4,850 m)
T-O run	395 ft (120 m)
T-O to 50 ft (15 m)	705 ft (215 m)
Landing from 50 ft (15 m)	920 ft (280 m)
Landing run	490 ft (150 m)
Range with max fuel	269 nm (310 miles; 500 km)
Range with max payload	212 nm (245 miles; 400 km)

LIPNUR X-08 MANJANG

TYPE: Single-seat light helicopter.

ROTOR SYSTEM: Two-blade see-saw type main rotor, with cyclic-pitch control. Blade chord 8 in (20·3 cm). Two-blade tail rotor driven by flexible shaft from reduction gearbox. Blade chord 4 in (10·2 cm). Main rotor/engine rpm ratio 1 : 5. Tail rotor/engine rpm ratio 1 : 1.

LANDING GEAR: Twin skids, with ground handling wheels.

POWER PLANT: One 100 hp vertically-installed Continental flat-four engine, with reduction gear, starting clutch and freewheel.

ACCOMMODATION: Single seat in enclosed cabin.

DIMENSIONS, EXTERNAL:
Diameter of main rotor	21 ft 0 in (6·40 m)
Diameter of tail rotor	4 ft 0 in (1·22 m)
Length overall	25 ft 6 in (7·77 m)
Height overall	8 ft 3 in (2·51 m)
Width overall	6 ft 6 in (1·98 m)

WEIGHTS (designed):
Weight empty	850 lb (385 kg)
Max T-O weight	1,150 lb (522 kg)

PERFORMANCE (estimated):
Max level speed at S/L	78 knots (90 mph; 145 km/h)
Rate of climb at S/L	1,500 ft (460 m)/min

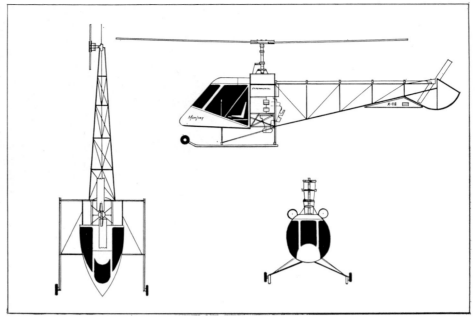

LIPNUR X-08 Manjang single-seat light helicopter

INTERNATIONAL PROGRAMMES

AIRBUS

AIRBUS INDUSTRIE

HEAD OFFICE:
37 Boulevard de Montmorency, Paris 16e, France

AIRFRAME PRIME CONTRACTORS:
Aérospatiale (SNIAS), 37 Boulevard de Montmorency, Paris 16e, France
Deutsche Airbus GmbH, 8 München 19, Leonrodstrasse 68, Postfach 47, German Federal Republic

SALES ORGANISATION:
Airbus International, 37 Boulevard de Montmorency, Paris 16e, France

Aérospatiale of France, Deutsche Airbus of Germany, Hawker Siddeley Aviation of the UK and Fokker-VFW of the Netherlands are co-operating in the design, development and production of the so-called European Airbus, a large-capacity short/medium-range transport aircraft to enter airline service from the middle 1970s. Aérospatiale is design leader, and controls the programme through a co-ordinating company known as Airbus Industrie.

Work on such a design dates back to June 1965, when discussions began between industry representatives from Britain and France. Almost simultaneously, an Airbus study group was formed in Germany, and in January 1966 preliminary negotiations were held between government representatives of the three countries. The first official agreement for joint development of an Airbus was reached in September 1966, and on 15 October 1966 a basic specification was submitted for official approval. Designated A 300, it was the subject of formal presentations to airline operators in March 1967. Details of this original design appeared in previous editions of *Jane's.*

On 26 September 1967, the three governments gave the Airbus consortium authority to continue design studies and project definition. This agreement nominated Hawker Siddeley Aviation, Sud-Aviation and Deutsche Airbus as the airframe partners, and Rolls-Royce, SNECMA and MAN-Turbo (now MTU) as the engine partners. Airframe design leadership went to Sud-Aviation (now Aérospatiale) and power plant leadership to Rolls-Royce.

The original A 300 design was superseded in December 1968 by a new design, the A 300B, described in detail below. The decision to allocate funds for the further development of this aircraft was taken by the French and German governments in May 1969; in addition, Hawker Siddeley Aviation is financing separately a part of the development. A levy on sales of the A 300B will be imposed to defray the development costs.

Hawker Siddeley has total design responsibility for the wings, and is working in collaboration with Fokker-VFW, who are building the wing moving surfaces under a participation agreement with the Dutch government.

AIRBUS A 300B

The Airbus A 300B is basically a single-deck aircraft with underwing pods for two turbofan engines. It is currently being offered with two alternative power plants—the 49,000 lb (22,226 kg) st General Electric CF6-50A, or the 51,000 lb (23,133 kg) st Rolls-Royce RB.211-52—but the underwing location of the power plant enables the A 300B to use any large advanced-technology turbofan engine. Both the engines at present offered have considerable development potential, and are installed in pods interchangeable with those of the McDonnell Douglas DC-10 Series 30 (CF6) or Lockheed L-1011-8 TriStar (RB.211).

Four aircraft will be built for flight testing and certification trials. Construction of the first of these began in September 1969 and had reached the sub-assembly stage by early 1970. This aircraft will be powered by CF6-50A engines. First flight is scheduled for mid-1972 and certification by mid-1973. Four aircraft will be available for delivery at the time of certification, and in the Spring of 1970 Airbus Industrie was reported to have received letters of intent covering 50 aircraft.

In addition to the flight test aircraft, one fatigue test airframe and one for static tests are being built.

Design of the A 300B ensures an easy stretch to take full advantage of future development of the power plant. For example, the maximum permissible fuselage stretch would permit up to 325 passengers to be carried in a typical layout. Alternatively, with the existing seating capacity, a version with a 2,300 nm (2,650 mile; 4,260 km) range could be available for delivery at the end of 1974.

The details below apply to the standard A 300B now under construction.

TYPE: Large-capacity short/medium-range transport.

WINGS: Cantilever mid-wing monoplane. Thickness/chord ratio 10·5%. Sweepback 28° at quarter-chord. Primary two-spar box-type structure, integral with fuselage and incorporating fail-safe principles, built of high-strength aluminium alloy. Third spar across inboard sections. Machined skin with open-sectioned stringers. Each wing has three-section leading-edge slats, and three tabbed Fowler-type double-slotted flaps on trailing-edge; an all-speed aileron between inboard flap and outer pair; and a low-speed aileron outboard of the outer pair of flaps. Lift dump facility by combination of two spoilers (outboard) and three air-brakes (inboard) on each wing, forward of outer pair of flaps, plus two additional surfaces forward of inboard flap. The flaps extend over 84% of each half-span, and increase the wing chord by 25% when fully extended. The datum of the all-speed aileron is deflected downward by up to 10° with flap operation to maintain continuity. Drive mechanisms for flaps and slats are similar to one another, each powered by twin motors driving ball screw-jacks on each surface with built-in protection against asymmetric operation. The low-speed aileron is centralised and locked at speeds above 190 knots (219 mph; 352 km/h), while the spoilers operate only when aileron

deflection reaches 5°. Pre-selection of the air-brake/lift dump lever allows automatic extension of the lift dumpers on touch-down. All flight controls actuated hydraulically, with no manual reversion. Anti-icing of wing leading-edges, outboard of engine pods, is by hot air bled from engines.

FUSELAGE: Semi-monocoque structure of open Z-section frames and stringers, of circular cross-section and built mainly of high-strength aluminium alloy with steel or titanium for some major components. Primary structure incorporates fail-safe principles. Resinated glass-fibre laminates under consideration for secondary structure.

TAIL UNIT: Cantilever all-metal structure, with sweepback on all surfaces. Variable-incidence tailplane and separately-controlled elevators. Tailplane powered by two motors driving a fail-safe ball screw-jack.

LANDING GEAR: Retractable tricycle type. Twin-wheel nose unit retracts forward and main units inward into fuselage. Each four-wheel main unit comprises two tandem-mounted bogies, with tyres size 46 × 16-20, pressure 158 lb/sq in (10·8 kg/cm²). Nose-wheel tyres size 39 × 13-16, pressure 140 lb/sq in (9·8 kg/cm²). Low-pressure main-wheel tyres (size 49 × 17-20, pressure 138 lb/sq in = 9·43 kg/cm²) optional. Hydraulic disc brakes on all main wheels. Anti-skid units fitted.

POWER PLANT: Two turbofan engines (see details in introductory copy) in underwing pods, fitted with thrust reversers which are actuated pneumatically by engine-bleed air. Fuel in two integral tanks in each wing, with total usable capacity of 9,460 Imp gallons (43,000 litres). Two refuelling points standard beneath starboard wing; two additional points beneath port wing available at customer's option.

ACCOMMODATION: Crew of three on flight deck, with provision for two-man operation. Fourth seat for observer. Electrical de-icing and demisting of windscreen. Up to 261 passengers normally in main cabin in eight-abreast layout with 34 in (86 cm) seat pitch. Typical mixed-class layout has 36 first-class (six abreast with two aisles, 40 in = 102 cm seat pitch) and 203 tourist-class (eight abreast with two aisles, 34 in = 86 cm seat pitch). This layout includes one galley and two toilets forward, with two more galleys and three toilets aft. Up to 296 passengers can be carried at 30 in (76 cm) seat pitch in single-class high-density layout. Two outward-opening plug-type passenger entry doors ahead of wing leading-edge on each side, and one on each side at rear. Underfloor baggage/cargo holds fore and aft of wings, with doors on starboard side. The forward hold will accommodate four 88 × 125 × 64 in (224 × 317 × 163 cm) pallets or ten LD2 containers; the rear hold will accommodate six LD2 containers each of 150 cu ft (4·25 m²) capacity. Bulk loading of freight provided for in rear hold. In an all-cargo layout, the main cabin can accommodate standard 8 × 8 ft (2·44 × 2·44 m) containers. Entire accommodation is pressurised, including freight, baggage and electronics compartments.

SYSTEMS: Air for air-conditioning system can be provided from engines, the APU or a high pressure ground source. Supply is controlled by separate and parallel bootstrap-type units, each of which includes a flow limiting unit, primary and secondary cooler units, water separator and temperature control unit. In addition, air from each engine passes through a pressure control pre-cooler unit. The equipment is supplied by Garrett. Two independent automatic systems, with manual override, control the cabin altitude, its rate of change and the differential pressure. Only one system operates at any one time, the second being a standby before manual control has to be used. Cabin differential pressure for normal operations is 8·25 lb/sq in (0·58 kg/cm²), i.e. sea-level cabin conditions can be maintained up to 21,000 ft (6,400 m), while at 35,000 ft (10,675 m) the cabin altitude is about 6,000 ft (1,830 m). The rate of change of cabin altitude can be controlled between 200 and 2,000 ft (61 and 610 m)/min. Valves limit the maximum differential pressure to 9·25 lb/sq in (0·65 kg/cm²) if the pressure control and air-conditioning system fails. Hydraulic system comprises three fully-independent circuits, operating simultaneously. Fluid used is a fire-resistant phosphate-ester type, working at a pressure of 3,000 lb/sq in (210 kg/cm²). The three circuits provide triplex power for primary flying controls; if any circuit fails, full control of the aircraft is retained without any necessity for action by the crew. All three circuits supply the all-speed and low-speed ailerons, air-brakes, rudder and elevator; "blue" circuit additionally supplies tail trim, spoilers, slats and rudder variable-gear unit; "green" circuit additionally supplies spoilers, slats, elevator artificial feel unit, flaps, steering, wheel-brakes and normal landing gear requirements; "yellow" circuit additionally supplies tail trim, lift dumpers, rudder variable-gear unit, elevator artificial feel unit, flaps and steering. Each circuit is normally powered by engine-driven self-regulating pumps, one on each engine for the green circuit and one each for the blue and yellow circuits. The pumps are manufactured by Vickers of the US. Power loss in any circuit can be restored through motor/pump transfer units without any fluid having to change circuit. In the event of a double engine failure, power in the yellow circuit can be restored by a drop-out ram-air turbine driving a hydraulic pump. Two parallel electric pumps in the green circuit provide either in-flight emergency power or, by utilising the transfer units, power to enable ground checks to be carried out on the entire hydraulic system. The emergency wheel braking system is completely isolated by a non-return valve and has a separate accumulator. A third electric pump recharges this accumulator for towing and parking, and also operates the cargo doors and the emergency lowering of the landing gear. The hydraulic power equipment is installed in the main landing gear wells, with guards to protect it from damage. The equipment is grouped in modules to permit removal without interference with piping or associated equipment. Main electrical power is supplied by two three-phase constant-frequency AC generators mounted on the engines. A third identical generator, driven by the APU, can supply power both in flight, to replace a failed engine-driven generator, and on the ground. Supply frequency is 400 c/s and voltage is 115/200V. Any one generator can supply sufficient power to operate all equipment and systems necessary for take-off and landing. No load-monitoring is required when an engine-driven generator is inoperative. Take-offs are permitted with any two generators functioning. Two alternative generating systems are offered in the A 300B, depending on engine type, to provide maximum commonality of power plant with other aircraft types in an operator's fleet. With General Electric engines, a conventional generator-CSD system, with Westinghouse generators, is installed, the two units being mounted on opposite sides of the engine gearbox with the CSD driving an air-cooled generator at a constant 8,000 rpm. Each generator is rated at 90kVA, with overload ratings of 135kVA for 5 minutes and 180kVA for 5 seconds. The APU generator is driven at constant speed through a gearbox. The system used in conjunction with the Rolls-Royce engines involves the use of a Lear-Siegler integrated drive generator (IDG), the constant-speed drive mechanism and generator being combined in an integrated package. Lubrication and oil-cooling systems and interface bearings are shared between the drive and the generator. The latter, which rotates at 12,000 rpm, is rated at 60kVA but can deliver 90kVA continuously. The APU generator is driven at constant frequency through a sandwich gearbox which supplies oil for cooling and lubrication. Three unregulated transformer-rectifier units (TRUs) supply 28V DC power, and are cooled by natural ventilation which is

fan-assisted if half load is exceeded. Normal DC power is supplied by two TRUs, with the third retained for essential services. No DC load-shedding is required after the loss of one TRU. 24V batteries are used for APU starting and fuel control, engine starter control, standby lights and, by selection, emergency busbar. This busbar and a 115V 400 c/s static inverter provide standby power in flight if normal power is unavailable. This system is separated completely from the main system. Oxygen distribution throughout the cabin will be provided, from bottles, through pipes to outlets distributed uniformly in the cabin. Various options are offered, including automatic drop-out masks. Hot air protection is provided for the engine intakes and the slat sections on the wings outboard of the engines. The necessity to protect other zones, such as the tailplane and the slat sections inboard of the engines, is the subject of further testing. The Garrett TSCP 700-5 APU is installed in the tail-cone, exhausting upward. Fire protection system is self-contained, and firewall panels protect main structure from an APU fire. The APU can be operated on the ground, in flight up to 35,000 ft (10,675 m), and in icing conditions. Relights are possible up to 25,000 ft (7,620 m). Aircraft is completely independent of ground power sources, since all major services can be operated by using the APU.

ELECTRONICS AND EQUIPMENT: Standard communications equipment includes two VHF sets and one Selcal system, plus interphone and passenger address systems. An accident recorder and voice recorder are also installed. Standard navigation equipment includes two VOR, two ILS, two radio altimeters, one marker beacon, two ADF, two DME, two ATC transponders and a weather radar. Most other electronic equipment will be to customer's requirements, only those related to the blind landing system (VOR/ILS and radio altimeter) being selected and supplied by the manufacturer. Additional optional equipment includes an HF set, third VHF, second marker beacon, third VOR/ILS, second radar, Doppler system, navigation computer and pictorial display, and Harco system. Both the pilot and co-pilot have an integrated instrument system combining heading, attitude, flight director and radio information. The automatic flight control system includes a comprehensive range of en-route facilities such as rate of descent, height acquire and Mach locks in addition to the normal height, speed and pitch attitude locks. Standard specification includes coupled approach facility suitable for Category 2 operation. Optional specifications include a complete range of equipment standards up to multiplex autoland developed to Category 3B. The A 300B is being designed for Category 3B automatic landing capability. It is intended that the necessary systems will be certificated to control the aircraft for a landing on one engine, and with this in mind the systems have been designed specifically to provide the redundancy required to maintain the overall safety level. The possible need for an over-shoot capability only 10 ft (3 m) above the runway, even on one engine, is being anticipated in the design, and trade-offs between flap setting, flap raising technique, climb gradient and obstacle clearance are being thoroughly explored.

DIMENSIONS, EXTERNAL:
Wing span	147 ft 1¼ in (44·84 m)
Wing aspect ratio	7·71
Length overall	167 ft 2¼ in (50·96 m)

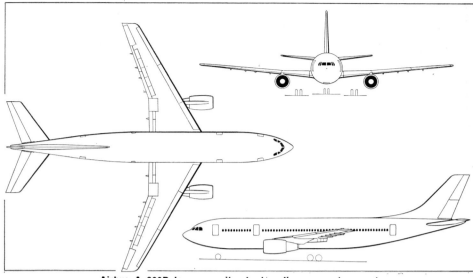

Airbus A 300B large-capacity short/medium-range transport

Length of fuselage	162 ft 0 in (49·38 m)
Fuselage max diameter	18 ft 6 in (5·64 m)
Height overall	54 ft 4 in (16·56 m)
Tailplane span	55 ft 7 in (16·94 m)
Wheel track	31 ft 6 in (9·60 m)
Wheelbase	57 ft 7½ in (17·57 m)
Passengers doors (each):	
Height	6 ft 4 in (1·93 m)
Width	3 ft 6 in (1·07 m)
Height to sill:	
(fwd)	14 ft 8¾ in (4·49 m)
(centre)	15 ft 2 in (4·62 m)
(rear)	17 ft 2 in (5·23 m)
Underfloor cargo door (fwd):	
Height	5 ft 7 in (1·70 m)
Width	8 ft 0 in (2·44 m)
Height to sill	8 ft 4¾ in (2·56 m)
Underfloor cargo door (rear):	
Height	5 ft 7 in (1·70 m)
Width	5 ft 11¼ in (1·81 m)
Height to sill	9 ft 8½ in (2·96 m)
Underfloor cargo door (extreme rear):	
Height	3 ft 1 in (0·95 m)
Width	3 ft 1 in (0·95 m)
Height to sill	10 ft 2 in (3·10 m)

DIMENSIONS, INTERNAL:
Cabin, excl flight deck:	
Length	119 ft 7¾ in (36·50 m)
Max width	17 ft 7 in (5·35 m)
Max height	8 ft 4 in (2·54 m)
Underfloor cargo hold volume:	
forward	2,401 cu ft (68·0 m²)
rear	1,271 cu ft (36·0 m²)
extreme rear	671 cu ft (19·0 m²)
Max total volume for bulk loading	
	4,343 cu ft (123·0 m²)

AREAS:
Wings, gross	2,799 sq ft (260·0 m²)
Vertical tail surfaces (total)	
	486·5 sq ft (45·2 m²)
Horizontal tail surfaces (total)	
	748·1 sq ft (69·5 m²)

WEIGHTS (GE=General Electric, RR=Rolls-Royce engines):
Manufacturer's weight empty	
	153,510 lb (69,630 kg)
Operating weight empty:	
GE	179,250 lb (81,300 kg)
RR	181,825 lb (82,474 kg)
Max payload:	
GE	61,050 lb (27,690 kg)
RR	58,475 lb (26,525 kg)
Max T-O weight	291,000 lb (132,000 kg)
Max landing weight	264,550 lb (120,000 kg)
Max zero-fuel weight	241,400 lb (109,500 kg)

PERFORMANCE (estimated, at max T-O weight except where indicated):
Max operating speed (VMO)	
	360 knots (415 mph; 668 km/h) CAS
Max operating Mach number (MMO):	
	Mach 0·84
Max cruising speed at 25,000 ft (7,620 m)	
	505 knots (582 mph; 937 km/h)
Typical approach speed	
	128 knots (147 mph; 237 km/h)
Max operating altitude	40,000 ft (12,200 m)
T-O run at S/L (ISA +18°C):	
GE	6,988 ft (2,130 m)
RR	6,700 ft (2,042 m)
Landing run at S/L at typical AUW:	
GE, RR	5,643 ft (1,720 m)

Range with max payload, reserves for 200 nm (230 mile = 370 km) diversion, 45 min hold at 5,000 ft (1,525 m) and 5% en-route burn-off:
GE	1,116 nm (1,286 miles; 2,070 km)
RR	1,219 nm (1,404 miles; 2,260 km)

Range with max fuel, reserves as above:
GE	2,104 nm (2,423 miles; 3,900 km)
RR	2,250 nm (2,591 miles; 4,170 km)

CONCORDE

CONCORDE SUPERSONIC TRANSPORT PROG-RAMME

AIRFRAME PRIME CONTRACTORS:

British Aircraft Corporation Ltd, 100 Pall Mall, London S.W.1, England

Aérospatiale (SNIAS), 37 Boulevard de Mont-morency, 75-Paris 16e, France

POWER PLANT PRIME CONTRACTORS:

Rolls-Royce Ltd, Bristol Engine Division, GPO Box 3, Filton, Bristol, England

Société Nationale d'Etude et de Construction de Moteurs d'Aviation, 150 Boulevard Hauss-mann, Paris 8e, France

AIRFRAME DIRECTORS' COMMITTEE (1970-71):

Henri Ziegler (Chairman)
Dr A. E. Russell (Vice-Chairman)
J. Coupain
P. du Boucheron
G. T. Gedge
L. Giusta
A. H. C. Greenwood
G. Hanby
P. Satre
Handel Davies
Dr W. J. Strang
G. Bourdaud'hui (Secretary)
J. Haas (Secretary)

SALES MANAGER:

E. H. Burgess (BAC)

Anglo-French negotiations concerning the development of a supersonic transport aircraft culminated on 29 November 1962 in the signing of two agreements, one between the French and British governments, the other between the manufacturers listed above, to whom the project was entrusted. The agreements provide for a fair division of the work, responsibility and development costs among the partners, and cover the manufacture of two prototypes of the aircraft, which is named Concorde, followed by two pre-production aircraft and two complete airframes for static and fatigue testing.

Overall policy is controlled by an Anglo-French Concorde Directing Committee, who are advised by a Concorde Management Board composed of British and French government nominees. The industrial management of the project is in the hands of two Anglo-French committees of directors, comprising executives of the two air-frame companies and executives of the two engine companies, respectively.

A list of executives concerned with the Concorde power plant programme can be found in the "Aero-Engines" section, together with a description of the Rolls-Royce (Bristol Division)/SNECMA Olympus 593 turbojet which powers the Concorde.

CONCORDE

Development of the airframe of the Concorde supersonic transport is being undertaken jointly by Aérospatiale and BAC and there will be two final assembly lines, at their Toulouse and Filton works respectively. There will, however, be no duplication of main production jigs.

Construction of the two prototypes began in February 1965. The first of these, Concorde 001 (F-WTSS), assembled by Aérospatiale, was rolled out in December 1967, and underwent engine running tests during the early part of 1968. It made its first flight on 2 March 1969, and was followed by the Concorde 002 prototype (G-BSST) on 9 April 1969. The planned test programme, involving the two prototypes, two pre-production and the first three production Concordes, will total some 4,300 hr, including 750 hr during certification trials and 1,500 hr on route-proving flights.

BAC are assembling the first pre-production Concorde (G-AXDN), scheduled to fly early in 1971, followed shortly afterwards by the second, assembled in France. The first production Concorde is scheduled to fly in France early in 1972, followed a few months later by the second,

in the UK, and by two more production Con-cordes at the end of that year. Deliveries will begin in 1973.

Delivery positions for 74 Concordes have so far been reserved as follows:

Air Canada	4
Air France	8
Air-India	2
American Airlines	6
BOAC	8
Braniff	3
Continental Air Lines	3
Eastern Air Lines	6
Japan Air Lines	3
Lufthansa	3
Middle East Airlines	2
Pan American	8
Qantas	4
Sabena	2
TWA	6
United Air Lines	6

Changes announced for the production version include alterations to the wing leading-edge contours, wingtips and the extreme rear of the fuselage, to reduce drag; increase in total fuel capacity; and modification of the engine air intakes. Some of these alterations are to be introduced on the pre-production aircraft and others early in the production line.

The Concorde is powered by four Olympus 593 turbojet engines, produced jointly by Rolls-Royce Ltd (Bristol Engine Division) and SNECMA. These engines will each develop 38,050 lb (17,260 kg) st with 17% reheat in their initial in-service form, rising to 38,400 lb (17,420 kg) st with 9% reheat soon afterwards. The prototypes have an overall length of 184 ft 6 in (56·30 m) and gross weight of 326,000 lb (148,000 kg), but are generally similar in other respects to the longer and heavier pre-production and production models.

When the max T-O weight was increased from 350,000 lb (158,750 kg) to 385,000 lb (175,000 kg), the maximum permissible structure temperature was slightly restricted from 426°K to 400°K to ensure that the increased loadings imposed on the structure by the higher weight did not pre-judice the design airframe life target of 45,000 hours (equivalent to 12/15 years of intensive airline operation).

Thus, although on many route sectors the Concorde is still capable of a max cruising speed of Mach 2·2, on some sectors cruising speed will be

restricted slightly, within the range of Mach 2·2/Mach 2·0. The effect on block times on these sectors will, however, be marginal, because the engine manufacturers have made available a modest degree of thrust augmentation on the Concorde's engines for use during take-off and transonic acceleration. On the London to New York sector, for example, the new block time will normally be 3 hr 22 min against the previous 3 hr 17 min.

A detailed review of all potential Concorde operations shows that on 37 per cent of the world's routes the maximum cruising speed will be Mach 2·2, and on 60 per cent it will be Mach 2·1 or above.

When sonic boom considerations preclude use of the normal climb technique, sufficient power is available to increase the transonic acceleration height to over 40,000 ft (12,200 m). Normally, however, the aircraft will accelerate and climb from 200 knots (230 mph; 370 km/h) CAS at S/L to 400 knots (460 mph; 740 km/h) CAS at 5,000 ft (1,500 m), then climb at a constant CAS of 400 knots (460 mph; 740 km/h) to 36,900 ft (11,000 m) where its speed will be Mach 1·15, climb and accelerate to Mach 1·8 (530 knots; 610 mph; 980 km/h CAS) at 45,300 ft (13,800 m) and continue climbing at this CAS until the cruise Mach number is reached, finally climbing to cruising height at cruising Mach number.

As its share of the programme Aérospatiale is responsible for development and production of the rear cabin section, wings and wing control surfaces, hydraulic system, flying controls, navi-gation systems, radio and air-conditioning system. BAC is responsible for the three forward sections of the fuselage, the rear fuselage and ver-tical tail surfaces, the engine nacelles and ducting, the electrical system, sound and thermal insula-tion, oxygen system, fuel system, engine installa-tion, and fire warning and extinguishing systems.

Both the 001 and 002 prototypes completed the second phase of their flight development programmes in the Summer of 1969. This included T-O and landing tests; handling during climb and approach at a wide range of subsonic speeds; engine reheat and re-lighting at various altitudes up to 40,000 ft (12,200 m); functioning of all systems; noise measurements during flight at low level; flying qualities at subsonic speeds throughout the CG range; and exploration of the speed range up to Mach 0·95. The 001 and 002 had, at this stage, made 39 and 24 flights respec-tively, totalling 104 flying hours.

In September 1969, Concorde 001 (powered by Olympus 593-2A engines) began to explore the

French-built 001 prototype of the BAC/Aérospatiale Concorde supersonic transport

British-built Concorde 002 prototype, shown just after take-off from RAF Fairford in March 1970 (*Brian M. Service*)

transonic speed range beyond Mach 1, while 002 resumed flight testing early in 1970 with 32,900 lb (14,923 kg) st Olympus 593-2B engines; these were being replaced with 34,700 lb (15,740 kg) st 593-3B's later in the year to explore the supersonic flight regime up to Mach 2. Concorde 001 achieved Mach 1·50 (500 knots; 434 mph; 698 km/h CAS) in December 1969, having made its first supersonic flight (at Mach 1·05) on 1 October 1969, on its 45th flight; and had completed the third phase of the overall test programme by the Spring of 1970.

The following details apply to the production aircraft, construction of which is under way.

TYPE: Four-jet supersonic transport.

WINGS: Cantilever low wing of ogival delta planform. Thickness/chord ratio 3% at root, 2·15% from nacelle outboard. Slight anhedral. Continuous camber. Multi-spar torsion box structure, manufactured mainly from RR-58 or AU2GN aluminium alloy. Integrally-machined components used for highly loaded members and skin panels. In centre wing, spars are continuous across fuselage, the spars and associated frames being built as single assemblies extending between the engine nacelles. Forward wing sections built as separate components attached to each side of fuselage, spar loads being transferred to cross-members in lower part of main fuselage frames. Three elevons on trailing-edge of each wing, of aluminium alloy honeycomb construction. Each elevon is independently operated by a tandem jack, each half supplied from an independent hydraulic source and controlled by a separate electrical system. Power control units are supplied by Dowty Boulton Paul. Hydraulic artificial feel units protect the aircraft against excessive aerodynamic loads induced by pilot through over-control. Auto-stabilisation is provided. Autopilot control is by signals fed into normal control circuit. No high-lift devices. (Air-brakes on prototypes, but not on production aircraft.) Leading-edges ahead of air intakes are electrically de-iced.

FUSELAGE: Mainly-conventional pressurised aluminium alloy semi-monocoque structure of constant cross-section, with unpressurised nose and tail cones. Hoop frames at approx 21·5 in (0·55 m) pitch support shell of skin panels and closely-pitched longitudinal stringers. Window surrounds in passenger cabins formed of integral skin-stringer panels machined from aluminium alloy planks. Nose is drooped hydraulically to improve forward view during take-off, initial climb, approach and landing. Retractable visor is raised hydraulically to fair in windscreen in cruising flight.

TAIL UNIT: Vertical fin and rudder only. Fin is multi-spar torsion box of similar construction to wing. Aerodynamic reference chord at base 34 ft 9 in (10·59 m). Two-section aluminium rudder controlled in same way as elevons. No de-icing system.

LANDING GEAR: Hydraulically-retractable tricycle type. Main units manufactured by Hispano-Suiza, nose unit by Messier, with Dunlop or Kléber wheels and tyres. Twin-wheel steerable nose unit retracts forward. Four-wheel bogie main units retract inward. Oleo-pneumatic shock-absorbers. Main wheels and tyres size 47 × 15·75-22, pressure 180 lb/sq in (12·65 kg/cm²). Nose-wheels and tyres size 31 × 10·75-14, pressure 174 lb/sq in (12·25 kg/cm²). Dunlop segmented disc brakes. Hispano-Suiza SPAD anti-skid units. Retractable tail bumper.

ENGINE NACELLES: Each consists of hydraulically-controlled variable-area (by ramp) air intake, engine bay and nozzle support structure. Intakes are of RR.58 or AU2GN aluminium alloy with steel leading-edges. The engine bay has an Ineal centre wall with aluminium alloy forward doors and titanium rear doors. The nozzle bay, aft of the rear spar, is of nimonic material. Leading-edges of intake walls, rear ramp sections and intake auxiliary door are electrically de-iced. Engine nose-bullet and inlet guide vanes are de-iced by hot engine-bleed air.

POWER PLANT: Four turbojet engines (see above) with silencers and thrust reversers. Fuel system is used also as heat sink and as a means of maintaining aircraft trim. All tanks are of integral construction and are in two groups, with total usable capacity of about 25,800 Imp gallons (117,285 litres). Main group comprises five tanks in each wing and four tanks in fuselage and maintains CG automatically in cruising flight. Trim tank group (four tanks) comprises three tanks at the front and a tank of 2,800 Imp gallons (12,730 litres) capacity in fuselage beneath tail fin. This group maintains correct relationship between CG and aerodynamic centre of pressure by transferring fuel rearward during acceleration and forward during return to subsonic flight. Four pressure refuelling points in bottom fairing, two forward of each main landing gear unit. Oil capacity 4·5 Imp gallons (20 litres) per engine.

ACCOMMODATION: Pilot and co-pilot side-by-side on flight deck, with third crew member behind, on starboard side. Provision for supernumerary seat behind pilot. Wide variety of four-abreast seating layouts to suit individual requirements of airlines. With all normal toilet and galley service facilities, up to 128 economy class passengers can be carried with 34 in (86 cm) seat pitch. A version with 144 passenger seats at 32 in (81 cm) pitch is available. Toilets at centre and/or rear of cabin. Baggage space under forward cabin and aft of cabin. Passenger doors forward of cabin and amidships on port side, with service doors opposite. Baggage door aft of cabin on starboard side. Emergency exits in rear half of cabin on each side. Two galleys.

ELECTRONICS: Primary navigation system comprises three identical inertial platforms, each coupled to a digital computer to form three self-contained units, two VOR/ILS systems, one ADF, two DME systems, one marker, two weather radars and two radio altimeters. Provision for supplementary system including a long-distance radio fixing system of the Loran 'C' type. Optional equipment includes a second ADF. Basic communications equipment consists of two VHF and two HF transmitter receivers, one Selcal decoder and two ATC transponders. Nose radome by Reinforced Microwave Plastics. Provision for a third VHF transmitter-receiver and data link equipment.

SYSTEMS: Hawker Siddeley Dynamics air-conditioning system, comprising four independent sub-systems, with Hamilton Standard heat exchangers. Pressure differential 10·7 lb/sq in (0·75 kg/cm²). In each sub-system the air passes through a primary ram-air heat exchanger to an air cycle cold-air unit, and then through secondary air/air and air/fuel heat exchangers. The air is then mixed with hot air and fed to cabins, flight deck, baggage holds, landing gear, equipment and radar bays. Hydraulic services utilise two primary and one standby system, pressure 4,000 lb/sq in (281 kg/cm²). Temperature of the Oronite M.2V fluid is limited by heat exchangers. Main systems actuate flying control surfaces, artificial feel units, landing gear, wheel brakes, nose-wheel steering, windshield visor, nose-cone droop, engine intake ramps and fuel pumps in forward transfer tank. Electrical system powered by four 60kVA brushless alternators giving 200/115V AC at 400 c/s. Four 150A transformer-rectifiers and two 25Ah batteries provide 28V DC supply.

DIMENSIONS, EXTERNAL:

Wing span	84 ft 0 in (25·60 m)
Wing aerodynamic reference chord at root	90 ft 9 in (27·66 m)
Wing aspect ratio	1·7
Length overall	203 ft 8¾ in (62·10 m)
Height overall	39 ft 10¼ in (12·15 m)
Wheel track	25 ft 4 in (7·72 m)
Wheelbase	59 ft 8¼ in (18·19 m)
Passenger doors (each):	
Height	5 ft 6 in (1·68 m)
Width	2 ft 6 in (0·76 m)
Height to sill: fwd	16 ft 4 in (4·98 m)
amidships	15 ft 6 in (4·72 m)
Service doors (each):	
Height	4 ft 0 in (1·22 m)
Width	2 ft 0 in (0·61 m)
Height to sill: fwd	16 ft 4 in (4·98 m)
amidships	15 ft 6 in (4·70 m)
Baggage hold door (underfloor):	
Length	3 ft 3 in (0·99 m)
Width	2 ft 9 in (0·84 m)
Height to sill	11 ft 5 in (3·50 m)

DIMENSIONS, INTERNAL:

Cabin:	
Length, flight deck door to rear pressure bulkhead, including galley and toilets	129 ft 0 in (39·32 m)
Width	8 ft 7½ in (2·63 m)
Height	6 ft 5 in (1·96 m)
Volume	8,440 cu ft (238·5 m³)
Baggage/freight compartments:	
Underfloor	237 cu ft (6·70 m³)
Rear fuselage (total)	475 cu ft (13·42 m³)

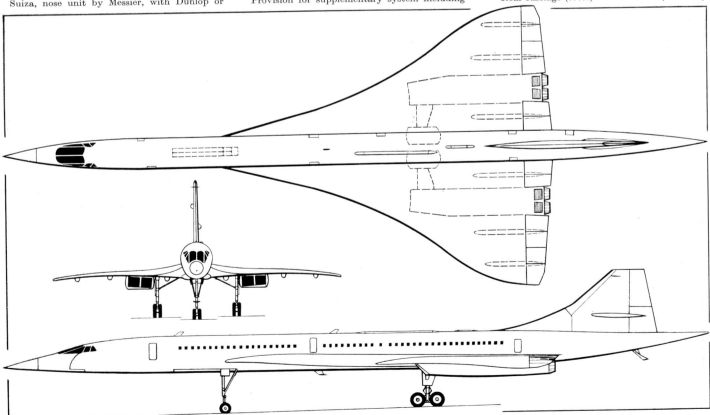

Pre-production version of the BAC/Aérospatiale Concorde four-jet supersonic transport aircraft

AREAS:
Wings, gross 3,856 sq ft (358·25 m²)
Elevons (total) 344·44 sq ft (32·00 m²)
Fin (less dorsal fin) 365 sq ft (33·91 m²)
Rudder 112 sq ft (10·40 m²)
WEIGHTS AND LOADINGS:
Operating weight, empty 169,000 lb (76,650 kg)
Design payload 28,000 lb (12,700 kg)
Max T-O weight 385,000 lb (175,000 kg)
Considered limit zero-fuel weight
200,000 lb (90,720 kg)

Max landing weight 240,000 lb (108,860 kg)
Max wing loading approx 100 lb/sq ft (488 kg/m²)
Max power loading approx
2·5 lb/lb st (2·5 kg/kg st)
PERFORMANCE (estimated at max T-O weight):
Max cruising speed at 54,500 ft (16,600 m)
Mach 2·2 or 530 knots CAS, whichever is the
lesser, equivalent to TAS of
1,259 knots (1,450 mph; 2,333 km/h)
Max range speed approx Mach 2·05
Rate of climb at S/L 5,000 ft (1,525 m)/min

Service ceiling approx 65,000 ft (19,800 m)
T-O to 35 ft (10·7 m) 9,850 ft (3,000 m)
Landing from 35 ft (10·7 m) 7,800 ft (2,380 m)
Range with max fuel, FAR reserves and 17,000
lb (7,710 kg) payload
3,820 nm (4,400 miles; 7,080 km)
Range with max payload, FAR reserves:
at Mach 0·93 at 30,000 ft (9,100 m)
3,125 nm (3,600 miles; 5,790 km)
at Mach 2·05, cruise/climb
3,490 nm (4,020 miles; 6,470 km)

PANAVIA
PANAVIA AIRCRAFT GmbH

HEAD OFFICE:
8 München 86, Postfach 8606 29, Arabellastrasse 16, German Federal Republic

DIRECTORS:
Ludwig Bölkow (Chairman)
A. H. C. Greenwood
F. Forster-Steinberg
Dr F. Giura
F. W. Page
Dr C. Raffagni

PROGRAMME DIRECTORS:
G. Madelung (Managing)
E. Loveless (Deputy Managing)
H. Langfelder (System Engineering, Munich)
B. O. Heath (System Engineering, Warton)
H. J. Klapperich (Finance and Contracts)
Dr E. Delmastro (Production)
G. Althusius (Procurement)
J. K. Quill (Marketing)

PUBLICITY EXECUTIVE:
F. Oelwein

In July 1968, representatives of the governments of the German Federal Republic, Italy,
the Netherlands and the UK indicated a mutual
requirement for a supersonic strike and reconnais-
ssance aircraft for service in the late 1970s.
This aircraft is known as the MRCA (Multi-Role
Combat Aircraft). The Netherlands government indicated subsequently that the MRCA
did not meet its requirements, though it may
participate industrially in the manufacturing
programme.

The German, British and Italian governments
have set up a joint organisation known as
NAMMO (NATO MRCA Management Organisation). This has its executive agency NAMMA
(NATO MRCA Management Administration)
in Munich in the same building as Panavia
GmbH, the industrial company responsible for
design, development and production of the
aircraft.

Panavia was formed on 29 March 1969, and
following a redistribution in September 1969 its
120,000 DM capital was distributed between
Messerschmitt-Bölkow-Blohm (50%), British
Aircraft Corporation (33%) and Fiat (17%).

An inter-governmental Memorandum of Understanding concerning the project definition phase
was signed by the German, British and Italian
governments in May 1969. This was to last
for one year, after which a full development
contract was to be placed involving the construction of prototype aircraft.

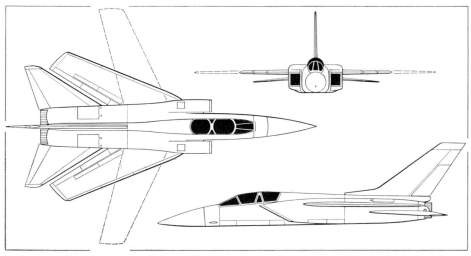

Three-view drawing (provisional) of the two-seat Panavia 200 combat aircraft

PANAVIA 100 and 200

The European MRCA is projected initially for
three combat roles: single-seat close air support,
single-seat air superiority fighter, and two-seat
interdictor/strike aircraft. In addition, a
requirement exists for a two-seat training version. The single-seat version is designated
Panavia 100, and the two-seat version **Panavia
200.** Initial indicated requirements were for 600
single-seaters (480 for Germany and 120 for Italy)
and 505 two-seaters (120 for Germany and 385
for the UK); subsequently Germany indicated
that it would no longer require the single-seat
version, and that its maximum requirement
for the two-seat version would be 420.

No dimensions, weights or performance data
for the MRCA had been released up to the Spring
of 1970, but the aircraft has been described
officially as "a medium-sized aircraft no larger
than the Mirage G and substantially lighter
than the Phantom". Its general appearance
can be seen in the accompanying illustration.
The aircraft will have variable-geometry wings
and will be powered by two 14,500 lb (6,577 kg)
st Rolls/Royce-MTU RB.199-34R afterburning
turbofan engines mounted side-by-side in the
fuselage.

Germany is to be responsible for manufacturing
the centre fuselage section, including the engine

installation and the wing pivot mechanism.
Britain will build the rear fuselage, including the
tail unit, and will share with Germany the production of the front fuselage, forward of the
engine air intakes. The outer wing panels may
be manufactured in Italy. The engines will be
developed and manufactured by Turbo-Union
Ltd (Rolls-Royce and MTU 40% each, Fiat
20%). Avionica Systems Engineering GmbH,
formed in Munich on 28 August 1969, will work
under contract from Panavia, and in close collaboration with the avionics teams of the airframe
companies, to develop the various avionics
systems for the aircraft. The parent companies
of Avionica are Elliott Automation (UK), Elek-
tronik System Gesellschaft (Germany) and SIA
(Italy).

Two full-scale mock-ups have been completed,
one of which was being used in the Spring of
1970 for external vision tests.

An initial development batch of 13 aircraft
(seven single-seat and six two-seat) was originally scheduled to be built, but the total has
been reduced to seven as a result of Germany's
requirement for only the two-seater. Approval
for the construction of these aircraft to begin
was due to be given by mid-1970, and the first
is scheduled to fly early in 1973.

SEPECAT
SOCIÉTÉ EUROPÉENNE DE PRODUCTION DE L'AVION ÉCOLE DE COMBAT ET APPUI TACTIQUE

MAJOR AIRFRAME COMPANIES:
British Aircraft Corporation, 100 Pall Mall,
London SW1, England
Breguet Aviation, BP12, 78 Velizy-Villa-
coublay, France

DIRECTORS:
B. C. Vallières (alternate chairman)
F. W. Page (alternate chairman)
Raoul Vivant (Finance)
Paul Jaillard (Sales)
A. H. C. Greenwood
H. R. Baxendale (Finance)
Jeffrey Quill (Sales)
Pierre François

MANAGEMENT COMMITTEE:
Directors as above, plus:
J. Barge (Production)
G. Ricard (Engineering Project Manager)
T. O. Williams (Production)
I. Yates (Engineering Project Manager)

MILITARY LIAISON OFFICER (UK):
John Teague (BAC)

This Anglo-French company was formed in
May 1966 by Breguet Aviation and British
Aircraft Corporation, the two partners in the
design and production of the Jaguar supersonic
light strike fighter/trainer which will equip both
the French Services and Royal Air Force from
1971.

The Jaguar project was initiated by a Memorandum of Understanding signed by the Defence
Ministries of Britain and France on 17 May 1965.

The governments of the two countries appointed
a Jaguar Management Committee to look after
their interests. SEPECAT is the complementary
industrial organisation.

SEPECAT JAGUAR

The Jaguar, which was evolved from the
Breguet Br 121 project, was designed by Breguet
and BAC to meet a common requirement of the
French and British Air Forces laid down early
in 1965. This requirement called for a dual-
rôle aircraft, to be used as an advanced trainer
and tactical support aircraft of light weight
but high performance, to enter service in early
1971. The Jaguar is also being developed for
naval operations from aircraft carriers.

The following versions of the Jaguar are projected:

Jaguar A. French single-seat tactical support
aircraft.

Jaguar B. British two-seat training version.

Jaguar E. French two-seat training version.

Jaguar M. French single-seat naval tactical
version.

Jaguar S. British single-seat tactical support
aircraft. More advanced electronics than
Jaguar A.

Breguet and BAC also have under consideration
a specialised reconnaissance version of the
Jaguar, able to carry a variety of different sensory
systems in a standard low-drag, under-belly
pack. This was described in the 1968-69 *Jane's*.

The Jaguar prototype manufacturing programme was divided into two phases. Phase 1
called for the production of two trainer proto-

types (E-01 and E-02), two tactical prototypes
(A-03 and A-04) and one airframe for static tests.
Construction of the E-01 began in the Summer
of 1966, and this aircraft flew for the first time on
8 September 1968, followed by the E-02 on 11
February 1969. The single-seat A-03 and A-04
prototypes flew for the first time on 29 March
1969 and 27 May 1969 respectively. The E-01
flew supersonically within five flying hours of its
first flight, and considerable supersonic flight
experience was subsequently obtained, before
this prototype was lost on 26 March 1970. The
pilot ejected safely after experiencing power
failure during landing approach.

Phase 2 covered the production of a single prototype of the French naval version (M-05, which
first flew on 14 November 1969), two prototypes
of the British strike version (S-06, first flight 12
October 1969, serial number XW560, and S-07)
and one airframe for fatigue tests. An eighth
prototype will represent the British two-seat
model. By the end of February 1970 the first
six prototypes had completed a total of 326
flying hours. The S-07 flew on 12 June 1970;
the B-08 is due to fly in early 1971. The S-06
is fitted with the Elliott modular air data computer, and the S-07 with the Elliott E.3R digital
inertial navigation and weapon aiming system,
incorporating a Marconi-Elliott 920M computer,
which will equip RAF versions of the Jaguar.

Flight testing in 1970 is devoted mainly to
weapons trials and flutter investigation. The
M-05 completed initial deck landing and T-O
trials at RAE Bedford in Spring 1970; these
were to be followed by trials aboard the French
aircraft carrier *Clémenceau* later in the year.

SEPECAT Jaguar S-07 prototype (XW563) in RAF markings with underwing bombs and rocket pods and ventral drop-tank

Under the terms of a production agreement signed by the British and French Defence Ministers on 9 January 1968, an initial series of 400 Jaguars is to be built, 200 for the Royal Air Force and 200 for the *Armée de l'Air* and *Aéronavale*. The first formal production contract, placed in the Autumn of 1969, covers 50 Jaguars for France; the second is for 30 for the RAF. Authorisation has also been given for long-dated materials to be purchased to meet future production commitments.

Deliveries of production Jaguars to the *Armée de l'Air* are scheduled to begin in early 1971, followed by deliveries to the RAF in 1972.

Breguet factories at Toulouse and Biarritz are responsible for the front and centre fuselage, including the air intakes and landing gear. The Preston Division of BAC has responsibility for the rear fuselage, wings and tail unit. There will be final assembly lines for complete aircraft in both Britain and France.

Great emphasis has been placed on simple design and sturdy construction, for operation from unprepared airstrips. The Jaguar makes full use of research and development work performed on other BAC and Breguet tactical aircraft, notably the Lightning, TSR 2 and Taon.

The powered flying controls of the Jaguar are being developed and supplied by Fairey Hydraulics Ltd and are the most advanced yet designed for a European aircraft, with all functions contained within a single assembly. The Jaguar is fully power-controlled in all three axes and is automatically stabilised as a weapons platform by gyros which sense disturbances and feed appropriate correcting data through a computer to the power control assemblies, in addition to the human pilot manoeuvre demands. The power controls are all of duplex tandem arrangement, with both mechanical and electrical servo-valves of the established Fairey platen design.

Carrying tactical loads, the Jaguar will operate from grass strips less than 3,280 ft (1,000 m) long. Training versions will be able to operate from conventional runways only 6,560 ft (2,000 m) long, with full provision for safety in the event of an engine failure at the critical point of take-off.

The performance data below refer to the Jaguar in its initial form. With development, the maximum speed at high altitude will exceed Mach 2.

TYPE: Medium-weight single-seat tactical support aircraft (Jaguar A and S), carrier-based naval tactical aircraft (Jaguar M) and two-seat advanced trainer (Jaguar B and E).

WINGS: Cantilever shoulder-wing monoplane. Anhedral 3°. Sweepback 40° at quarter-chord. Outer panels fitted with slat which also gives effect of extended chord "dog-tooth" leading-edge. All-metal two-spar torsion-box structure, the skin of which is machined from solid aluminium alloy, with integral stiffeners. No conventional ailerons. Lateral control by two-section spoilers, forward of outer flap on each wing, in association (at low speeds) with differential tailplane. Hydraulically-operated full-span double-slotted trailing-edge flaps. Leading-edge slats. Entire wing unit is British-built.

FUSELAGE: All-metal structure, mainly aluminium, built in two main sections and making use of sandwich panels and, around the cockpits, honeycomb panels. Local use of titanium alloy in engine bay area. Entire forward and centre fuselage, up to and including the main under-carriage bays, and including cockpit(s), air intakes, main systems installations and landing gear, is of French construction. Entire section aft of main-wheel bays, including engine installation and complete tail assembly, is British-built. Two door-type air-brakes under rear fuselage, immediately aft of each main-wheel

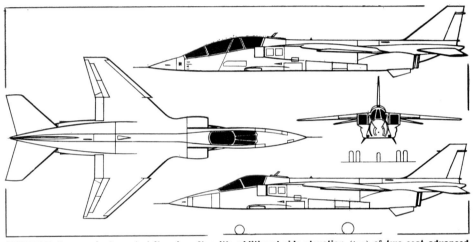

SEPECAT Jaguar single-seat strike aircraft, with additional side elevation (*top*) of two-seat advanced training version

well. Structure and systems, aft of cockpit(s), are identical for single-seat and two-seat versions.

TAIL UNIT: Cantilever all-metal two-spar structure, covered with aluminium alloy sandwich panels. Rudder and outer panels and trailing-edge of tailplane have honeycomb core. One-piece slab-type all-moving tailplane, with 10° of anhedral. 40° sweepback on horizontal, and 43° on vertical surfaces, at quarter-chord. For initial test flights, at least, the two halves of the tailplane can operate differentially to supplement the spoilers. Auxiliary fins beneath the rear fuselage, aft of the jet-pipes, are fitted to some prototypes.

LANDING GEAR: Messier-designed retractable tricycle type, all units having Dunlop wheels and low-pressure tyres for rough-field operation. Hydraulic retraction, with oleo-pneumatic shock-absorbers. Forward-retracting main units each have twin wheels, tyre size 615 × 225-10, tyre pressure 56 lb/sq in (3·94 kg/cm²). Wheels pivot during retraction to stow horizontally in bottom of fuselage. Single rearward-retracting nose-wheel, with tyre size 550 × 250-6 and pressure of 40 lb/sq in (2·81 kg/cm²). Dunlop hydraulic brakes. Land-based models

are fitted with an arrester hook, and a brake parachute housed in fuselage tail-cone. Jaguar M has strengthened undercarriage, with single main wheels and twin-nose-wheels, a strengthened arrester hook, and catapult gear for carrier operation.

POWER PLANT: Two Rolls-Royce Turboméca Adour turbofan engines (each 4,620 lb = 2,100 kg st dry, and 6,950 lb = 3,150 kg st with afterburning). Lateral-type air intakes, on each side of fuselage aft of cockpit. These are of fixed geometry. Fuel in eight tanks, one in each wing and six in fuselage. Armour protection will be provided for critical fuel system components. In the basic tactical sortie the loss of fuel from one tank at the half-way point would not prevent the aircraft from regaining its base. Provision for carrying three auxiliary drop-tanks, each of 264 Imp gallons (1,200 litres) capacity. Jaguar A, M and S will be equipped for the "buddy" system of flight refuelling, with a retractable probe forward of cockpit on starboard side.

ACCOMMODATION (Jaguar B and E): Crew of two in tandem on Martin-Baker Mk 9 zero-altitude zero-speed ejection seats or Mk 4 zero-altitude seats under individual rearward-hinged canopies.

Jaguar M-05, prototype of the French naval strike version, with single-wheel main landing gear

Rear seat is 15 in (38 cm) higher than front seat. Front of cockpit is armoured. Windscreen bullet-proof against 7·5-mm rifle fire.

Accommodation (Jaguar A, M and S): Enclosed cockpit for pilot with rearward-hinged canopy and Martin-Baker Mk 9 zero-altitude zero-speed ejection seat, or Mk 4 zero-altitude 90-knot seat. Front and underside of cockpit are armoured against light ground fire. Bullet-proof windscreen, as in two-seat version.

Systems: Air-conditioning and pressurisation systems maintain automatically, throughout the flight envelope, comfortable operating conditions for the pilot, and also control the temperature in certain equipment bays. Electrical power provided by two 15kVA AC generators. DC power provided by two 4kW transformer-rectifiers. Emergency AC power for essential instruments provided by 15Ah battery and static inverter. Two independent hydraulic systems, powered by two Vickers engine-driven pumps. Hydraulic pressure 3,000 lb/sq in (210 kg/cm²). First system (port engine) supplies one channel of each actuator for the flying controls, the hydraulic motors which actuate the flaps and slats, the landing gear retraction and extension system, the brakes and anti-skid units. The second system supplies the other half of each flying control actuator, two further hydraulic motors actuating the slats and flaps, the air-brake and landing gear extension jacks, nose-wheel steering system and the wheel brakes. De-icing, rain clearance and demisting standard. Liquid oxygen system installed, which also pressurises pilot's anti-*g* suit.

Electronics: Standard equipment includes VHF/UHF radio, VOR/ILS, TACAN and air data computer on all versions. Wide variety of navigation equipment according to mission, ranging from a standard gyro-compass to a fully-automatic inertial system with digital computer. Depending on type of navigation equipment installed, a choice of attack systems is available, from a standard gunsight to an entirely self-computing system with head-up display. The Jaguar B and S will have an inertial nav/attack system, with a digital weapon-aiming computer, moving-map and head-up displays, HF/UHF radio, IFF and (S only) panoramic camera. Jaguar E will have a twin-gyro platform and CSF sighting head. Jaguar A will have same equipment as E plus Decca RDN 72 Doppler radar, manufactured in France by Electronique Marcel Dassault, navigation computer and panoramic camera. Jaguar M will have same equipment as A plus weapon aiming computer and laser ranging device.

The Jaguar E-01, first prototype of the French two-seat training version

Armament (Jaguar A, M, and S): Two 30 mm cannon (Aden type in Jaguar S, DEFA 553 type in Jaguar A and M) in lower fuselage aft of cockpit. One attachment point on fuselage centre-line and two under each wing. Provision for wingtip attachments for air-to-air missiles. Centre-line and inboard wing points can each carry up to 2,000 lb (1,000 kg) of weapons, and the outboard underwing points up to 1,000 lb (500 kg) each. Typical alternative loads include four Nord AS.30 air-to-surface missiles; two Martel AS.37 anti-radar missiles and a drop-tank; four Sidewinder air-to-air missiles (for interception missions); three 1,000 lb (454 kg) bombs and two rocket launchers; various unguided air-to-air or air-to-surface rockets, including the 68 mm SNEB rocket; or a reconnaissance-camera pack with two photo-flare pods or two drop-tanks.

Armament (Jaguar B and E): Two 30 mm cannon (Aden type in Jaguar B, DEFA 553 in Jaguar E), as in tactical models. The two-seat versions have similar weapons capability to the tactical models, and can be employed for operational missions as required.

Dimensions, external:

Wing span	27 ft 10¼ in (8·49 m)
Wing chord at root	11 ft 9 in (3·58 m)
Wing chord at tip	3 ft 8½ in (1·13 m)
Wing aspect ratio	3
Length overall:	
A, M and S	50 ft 11 in (15·52 m)
B and E	53 ft 11 in (16·42 m)
Height overall	15 ft 1½ in (4·64 m)
Tailplane span	14 ft 10⅜ in (4·53 m)
Wheel track (B and E)	7 ft 10½ in (2·40 m)
Wheelbase (B and E)	18 ft 7¼ in (5·67 m)

Areas:

Wings, gross	258·33 sq ft (24·00 m²)
Leading-edge slats (total)	11·30 sq ft (1·05 m²)
Trailing-edge flaps (total)	44·35 sq ft (4·12 m²)
Spoilers (total)	11·09 sq ft (1·03 m²)
Vertical tail surfaces (total)	39·83 sq ft (3·70 m²)
Horizontal tail surfaces (total)	83·96 sq ft (7·80 m²)

Weights:

Normal T-O weight	22,046 lb (10,000 kg)
Max T-O weight	30,865 lb (14,000 kg)

Performance (estimated, at max T-O weight):

Max level speed at S/L
729 knots (840 mph; 1,350 km/h) (Mach 1·1)
Max level speed at 36,000 ft (11,000 m)
972 knots (1,120 mph; 1,800 km/h) (Mach 1·7)
Landing speed 115 knots (132 mph; 213 km/h)
T-O run with typical tactical load
1,480 ft (450 m)
T-O to 50 ft (15 m) with typical tactical load
2,365 ft (720 m)
Landing from 50 ft (15 m) with typical tactical load
2,825 ft (860 m)
Landing run with typical tactical load
1,545 ft (470 m)
Typical attack radius, internal fuel only
hi-lo-hi 675 nm (775 miles; 1,250 km)
low altitude throughout
350 nm (405 miles; 650 km)
Typical attack radius, with external fuel
hi-lo-hi 890 nm (1,025 miles; 1,650 km)
low altitude throughout
460 nm (530 miles; 850 km)
Ferry range, with external fuel
2,430 nm (2,800 miles; 4,500 km)
Max high-altitude endurance at subsonic speed (B and E) 3 hr 0 min

TRANSALL

ARBEITSGEMEINSCHAFT TRANSALL

Address (including export office):
Hünefeldstrasse 1-5, 28 Bremen 1

Transall (Transporter Allianz) is the name of a group formed in January 1959 by French and German aircraft companies to undertake the joint development and production of a turboprop military transport designated the Transall C-160. Participating companies are Messerschmitt-Bölkow-Blohm GmbH, Aérospatiale (Nord Aviation) and VFW-Fokker GmbH. They retain their separate status for other activities.

TRANSALL C-160

The Transall C-160 was developed to meet the specific requirements of the Federal German and French governments. Italian requirements were also borne in mind from the early stages of the programme. The aircraft is intended for military transport duties, carrying troops, freight, supplies and vehicles, and is capable of operating from semi-prepared surfaces. It is powered by two Rolls-Royce Tyne turboprop engines, with provision for fitting two turbojet engines in underwing pods to provide auxiliary power for STOL operations.

VFW-Fokker GmbH is overall project manager and is responsible for design and manufacture of the main fuselage, including the main landing gear fairings, the engine nacelles for some aircraft and horizontal tail unit. Messerschmitt-Bölkow-Blohm GmbH (originally Hamburger Flugzeugbau GmbH) has responsibility for the front and rear fuselage. Dornier is building the vertical tail surfaces, and Messerschmitt-Bölkow-Blohm the wing centre-section. Production of landing gear units is shared between Messier in France and Liebherr in Germany. The outer wing units and power plant assemblies are the responsibility of Aérospatiale (Nord Aviation), who also assembled the first prototype. This flew for the first time on 25 February 1963.

The second prototype, which flew on 25 May 1963, was assembled at VFW's Lemwerder works, where the third airframe underwent static testing. The fourth airframe was assembled by Hamburger Flugzeugbau and flew as the third prototype on 19 February 1964. This aircraft was equipped with a Smiths Flight Control System capable of extension to provide auto-landing capability. The fifth airframe was fatigue tested by EAT, in Toulouse, France. The flight test programme was completed during 1967.

The Tyne turboprop engines for the prototypes and pre-series aircraft were supplied by Rolls-Royce. Those for production C-160's are being produced under licence by MTU in association with Hispano-Suiza (France) and FN (Belgium).

The following versions of the C-160 have been announced:

C-160 A. Pre-series aircraft with 20 in (50 cm) longer fuselage which is standard on subsequent aircraft. Three for French air force; three for German air force, each participating company building two aircraft. First C-160 A, completed by Nord, flew on 21 May 1965. These aircraft were built for joint German-French operational trials at Mont-de-Marsan, France. Production completed in July 1968.

C-160 D. Designation of the 110 production models for the *Luftwaffe*. First example flown 2 November 1967; 30 completed and delivered (eight by Aérospatiale (Nord Aviation), twelve by HFB and ten by VFW-Fokker) by February 1970. First delivery 26 April 1968. The first *Luftwaffe* unit to be equipped was LTG.63, based at Hohn, Schleswig-Holstein. Six in use early in 1970 to fly German relief to Nigeria.

C-160 F. Designation of the 50 production models for the French Air Force. First example flown 13 April 1967, and delivered on 2 August 1967; 22 completed and flown by February 1970 (six by Aérospatiale (Nord Aviation), nine by HFB and seven by VFW-Fokker). First delivery 26 April 1968. The first French Transall squadron was formed during 1968 at Orléans-Bricy, and became operational in 1969-70.

C-160 Z. Designation of the nine aircraft ordered by the South African Air Force. First example flown 28 February 1969. Four aircraft, all built by Aérospatiale (Nord Aviation), had been delivered by February 1970.

The following details refer to the standard C-160 D/F, production of which was stepped up in May 1968 from one to four aircraft per month.

Type: Twin-engined turboprop transport.

Wings: Cantilever high-wing monoplane. Dihedral on outer wings 3° 26′. All-metal two-spar structure designed on fail-safe principles. Wing in three sections, comprising a centre-section, which carries the engines, and two outer sections. All-metal ailerons and hydraulically-operated double-slotted flaps. Hydraulically-operated air-brakes (inboard) and spoilers (outboard) forward of flaps on each wing. Electrical anti-icing of leading-edge.

Fuselage: All-metal semi-monocoque structure of circular basic section, flattened at the bottom, and designed on fail-safe principles. Underside of upswept rear fuselage lowers to form loading ramp for vehicles.

Tail Unit: Cantilever all-metal structure. Electrical anti-icing of tailplane leading-edge.

Landing Gear: Retractable tricycle type of Messier design. Hydraulic retraction. Each main unit comprises two pairs of wheels in tandem and is mounted inside a fairing on the side of the fuselage. Wheels can be raised to lower the fuselage for loading. Steerable twin-wheel nose unit. Main wheel tyres size 15·00 × 16; nose-wheel tyres size 12·50 × 16. Tyre pressure 42·7-47·0 lb/sq in (3·0-3·3 kg/cm²). Messier brakes.

Power Plant: Two 6,100 eshp Rolls-Royce Tyne RTy.20 Mk 22 turboprop engines, each driving a Ratier Figeac-built HSD Type 4/8000/6, DB244 Re-15 four-blade constant-speed fully-feathering reversible-pitch propeller, 18 ft 0 in (5·486 m) diameter. Single-point pressure refuelling. Fuel in wing tanks with total capacity of 3,625 Imp gallons (16,500 litres). Water-methanol capacity 71·5 Imp gallons (325 litres). Provision for mounting two auxiliary turbojet engines (Rolls-Royce RB.162 or others), with thrust reversers, under the outer wings.

Accommodation: Pressurised accommodation for crew of four, comprising pilot, co-pilot, navigator and flight engineer. Typical payloads include 93 troops or 61-81 fully-equipped paratroops; 62 litters and four attendants; armoured vehicles, tanks and tractors not exceeding 35,270 lb (16,000 kg) total weight; one empty five-ton truck and crew; two empty three-ton trucks and crews; or three jeeps with partially-loaded trailers and crews. Flight deck and cargo compartment air conditioned and pressurised in flight and on the ground. Power-assisted controls. Cargo

Transall C-160 Z built by Aérospatiale for delivery to the South African Air Force

compartment is provided with a freight door at the front on the port side, a paratroop door on each side immediately aft of the landing gear fairings and a hydraulically-operated rear loading ramp. The floor and all doors are at truck-bed height. The floor is provided with lashing points of 11,025 lb (5,000 kg) and 26,460 lb (12,000 kg) capacity, arranged in a 20 in (50·8 cm) grid, and is stressed to carry large military vehicles. Loads which cannot be driven in can be taken on board rapidly by a winch and system of roller conveyors. Individual loads of up to 17,640 lb (8,000 kg) can be air-dropped.

SYSTEMS: Normalair pressurisation and air-conditioning system, differential 4·59 lb/sq in (0·32 kg/cm²). Two separate primary hydraulic systems, pressure 2,500 lb/sq in (175 kg/cm²), for flying controls, loading ramp, landing gear, wheel brakes, flaps, spoilers, air-brakes, nose-wheel steering and other auxiliaries. Two more systems for emergency and ground services, as well as a hand-pump driven emergency system. Three-phase AC electrical systems, 115/200V 400-580 c/s and 115/200V 400 c/s. 28VDC system and 40Ah battery. AiResearch GTCP-85 APU in forward part of port main undercarriage fairing. An automatic landing system for installation in the C-160 is being developed by VFW-Fokker.

ELECTRONICS AND EQUIPMENT: Sperry SP40 autopilot and Doppler radar standard. Wide range of radio and electronic equipment standard, including VOR/ILS, radio compass, radio altimeter, UHF-homing, TACAN, Doppler, nav computer, Rebecca, navigation and weather radar, IFF, VHF, UHF, HF communication systems.

DIMENSIONS, EXTERNAL:

Wing span	131 ft 3 in (40·0 m)
Wing chord (mean)	13 ft 8½ in (4·176 m)
Wing aspect ratio	10

Transall C-160 D transport aircraft (two Rolls-Royce Tyne RTy.20 turboprop engines)

Length overall	106 ft 3½ in (32·40 m)	Width	3 ft 0 in (0·90 m)
Height over tail	38 ft 5 in (11·65 m)	Cargo door (front, port side):	
Tailplane span	47 ft 7 in (14·50 m)	Height	5 ft 11 in (1·80 m)
Wheel track	16 ft 9 in (5·10 m)	Width	6 ft 6 in (1·98 m)
Wheelbase	34 ft 4½ in (10·48 m)	Rear loading ramp:	
Paratroop door (each side):		Length	12 ft 1½ in (3·70 m)
Height	6 ft 2½ in (1·90 m)	Width	10 ft 3½ in (3·15 m)

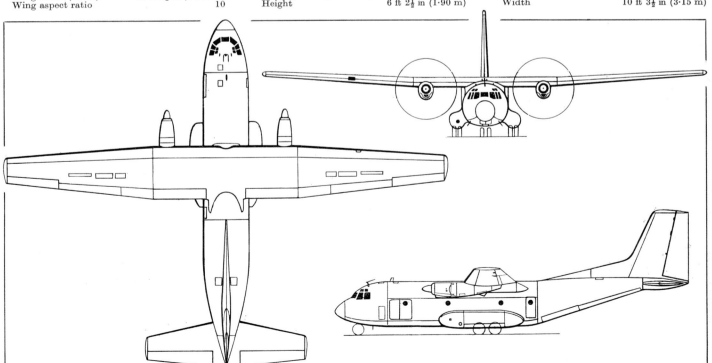

Transall C-160 twin-turboprop medium-range military transport

DIMENSIONS, INTERNAL:
Cabin, excluding flight deck and ramp:
Length 44 ft 4 in (13·51 m)
Max width 10 ft 3½ in (3·15 m)
Max height 9 ft 8½ in (2·98 m)
Floor area 458·5 sq ft (42·6 m²)
Volume 4,072 cu ft (115·3 m³)
Cabin, including ramp:
Length 56 ft 6 in (17·21 m)
Floor area 584 sq ft (54·25 m²)
Volume 4,940 cu ft (139·9 m³)
AREAS:
Wings, gross 1,722·7 sq ft (160·1 m²)
Ailerons (total) 76·39 sq ft (7·1 m²)
Trailing-edge flaps (total) 366·92 sq ft (34·1 m²)
Vertical tail surfaces (total) 387·5 sq ft (36·0 m²)
Horizontal tail surfaces (total)
473·6 sq ft (44·0 m²)
WEIGHTS:
Weight empty, equipped 63,400 lb (28,758 kg)

Basic operating weight, empty
63,815 lb (28,946 kg)
Normal payload 17,640 lb (8,000 kg)
Max payload 35,270 lb (16,000 kg)
Normal T-O and landing weight
97,450 lb (44,200 kg)
Max T-O and landing weight
108,250 lb (49,100 kg)
PERFORMANCE (at AUW of 90,390 lb = 41,000 kg
except where otherwise indicated, ISA con-
ditions):
Max level speed at 14,760 ft (4,500 m)
289 knots (333 mph; 536 km/h)
Max cruising speed at 18,050 ft (5,500 m)
277 knots (319 mph; 513 km/h)
Max cruising speed at 26,250 ft (8,000 m) at
AUW of 93,696 lb (42,500 kg)
266 knots (306 mph; 492 km/h)
Rate of climb at S/L at max T-O weight
1,440 ft (440 m)/min

Service ceiling at AUW of 99,225 lb (45,000 kg)
27,900 ft (8,500 m)
Single-engine ceiling 13,600 ft (4,150 m)
T-O run at max T-O weight (S/L, 20° flap)
2,600 ft (795 m)
T-O to 35 ft (10 m) at 99,208 lb (45,000 kg) AUW
(S/L, 20° flap) 2,067-2,362 ft (630-720 m)
Landing from 50 ft (15 m) at AUW of 90,389 lb
(41,000 kg) (S/L, 60° flap) 1,903 ft (580 m)
Landing run at AUW of 97,450 lb (44,200 kg)
(S/L, 60° flap) 1,160 ft (360 m)
Range with 17,640 lb (8,000 kg) payload, 10%
fuel reserves and allowance for 30 min at
13,120 ft (4,000 m)
2,459 nm (2,832 miles; 4,558 km)
Range with 35,270 lb (16,000 kg) payload, 10%
fuel reserves and allowance for 30 min at
13,120 ft (4,000 m)
634 nm (730 miles; 1,175 km)

ZENTRALGESELLSCHAFT VFW-FOKKER mbH

ADDRESS:
Düsseldorf

In May 1969 it was announced that NVKNV
Fokker of the Netherlands and Vereinigte
Flugtechnische Werke GmbH of Germany had
decided to combine their activities. To accomplish this, a new central company named Zentral-

gesellschaft VFW-Fokker mbH, with headquarters in Düsseldorf, was created, in which
each company has a 50% holding. This company has a Board of Management comprising
three directors from each company, and its first
task has been to determine future policy. The
effective operating date of the association was
made retrospective to 1 January 1969.
The two participating companies are equal
and wholly-owned subsidiaries of Zentralgesellschaft VFW-Fokker mbH, and are continu-

ing their existing activities under the new titles
of Fokker-VFW NV and Vereinigte Flugtechnische Werke-Fokker GmbH respectively (see the
Netherlands and German sections of this edition).
They have already collaborated, since 1960, in
the Northgroup consortium to produce 350 Lockheed F-104G Starfighters for their respective air
forces, and in development of the F.28 Fellowship
and VFW-614 transport aircraft. Fokker-VFW
and Avions Marcel Dassault of France each have
a parity interest in the Belgian company SABCA.

ISRAEL

IAI

ISRAEL AIRCRAFT INDUSTRIES LTD

HEAD OFFICE AND WORKS:
Lod Airport

PRESIDENT:
A. W. Schwimmer
EXECUTIVE VICE-PRESIDENT:
A. Ben-Yoseph
VICE-PRESIDENTS:
Prof M. Arens (Gen Manager, Engineering
Division)
Z. Mendes (Marketing)
A. Ostrinsky (Personnel and Administration)
Z. Yaari (Central Services)
S. N. Ariav (Gen Manager, Aircraft Manufac-
turing Division)
S. Yoran (Gen Manager, Bedek Aviation)
A. Avitzur (Finance)
M. Doron (Corporate Planning)
COMMERCIAL DIRECTOR, COMMODORE JET:
S. Samach
DIRECTOR OF INFORMATION:
Elkana Galli
This company was established in 1953 as Bedek
Aircraft Ltd. The change of name, to Israel
Aircraft Industries, was made on 1 April 1967.
IAI employs over 11,000 people in all its facili-
ties. It is licensed by the Israel Civil Aviation
Administration, US Federal Aviation Adminis-
tration, British Air Registration Board and the
Israeli Air Force as an approved repair station
and maintenance organisation.
Israel Aircraft Industries Ltd is composed of
several divisions, plants and subsidiary companies
as follows:
Bedek Aviation, comprising three directorates
concerned with Aircraft, Engines and Accessories. The approved services range from turnaround servicing to complete rebuilding of airframes, engines, components, accessories, equipment and systems. This Division is capable of
maintaining, handling, inspecting and overhauling any aircraft from a Piper Cub to a Boeing
707 transport and helicopters, including many
categories of military aircraft. It specialises
in US, British and French equipment. The
test cells can accommodate engines from 500 to
50,000 lb (227-22,700 kg) st. Design and refitting of aircraft interiors is a speciality.
The **Aircraft Manufacturing Division** and its
specialised subsidiaries produce a wide range of
jigs and tooling, primary parts, and spare parts
for jet engines and aircraft. It produced the
French CM 170 Magister jet trainer under licence,
from primary components manufactured by
IAI, and incorporated a number of modifications
and improvements. It is currently responsible
for production of the company's Arava and
Commodore Jet aircraft, which are described
below.
The experimental refitting of an Israeli Air
Force Mirage III-CJ with a General Electric J79
turbojet engine was reported in 1970.
Among other items, flap assemblies for the
Dassault Mystère 20/Falcon executive aircraft are
built by this Division, which also produces a
complete range of ground support equipment for
many aircraft. Currently in production are
several cargo loading systems.
The **Engineering Division** is engaged in a variety
of aircraft design and development programmes.
It has originated many major aircraft part
modifications in support of the Bedek Aviation

and Aircraft Manufacturing Divisions, such as
those for the Magister and for the conversion of
Boeing Stratocruisers. One of the major under-
takings of this division was the development of
an indigenous design, the Arava twin-turboprop
STOL transport. Design development of the
Arava by the division is continuing.
Following acquisition of the tooling and production rights for the former Aero Commander
Jet Commander, the Engineering Division evolved
a number of modifications for incorporation into
the IAI production models of this aircraft, which
is now known as the Commodore Jet.
The company's electronics subsidiary, **ELTA,**
although wholly owned, is fully autonomous.
Its current research, design and production
programmes are concerned with airborne avionics
and medical electronics.
Other IAI subsidiary plants include: Orlite
(manufacturing aviation glass-fibre products);
PML and TAMAM (manufacturing precision
gears and electro-mechanical and hydrometric
instruments); and Servo-Hydraulics Ltd (manufacturing servo-controls, precision and electro-
hydraulic components and systems).

IAI-101 ARAVA

The Arava was designed to fulfil the need for a
light transport with STOL performance and
rough-field landing capabilities.
Design work started in 1966 and construction
of a prototype began towards the end of the
same year. This airframe was used for structural

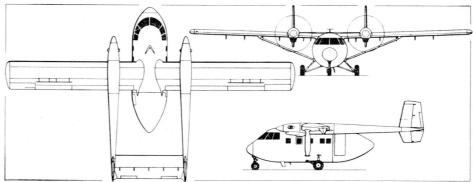
IAI Arava twin-turboprop STOL light transport

Prototype of the IAI-101 Arava light STOL transport (two 715 eshp PT6A-27 turboprop engines)

testing; it was followed by a flying prototype
(4X-IAI), which made its first flight on 27
November 1969, and in early 1970 was undergoing
flight trials for Israeli and FAA (FAR 23) type
certification. An initial batch of 10 production
aircraft is being built.
In addition to the standard production version
described below, the aircraft is also being offered
at an AUW of 13,500 lb 6,123 kg) and further
growth versions are under consideration. Deliveries are expected to begin early in 1972, and
systems are being developed for special-purpose
operations which include utility, police, reconnaissance and rescue work. The commuter
version can carry 20 passengers or 4,410 lb (2,000
kg) of freight.
TYPE: Twin-turboprop STOL light transport.
WINGS: Braced high-wing monoplane, with
single streamline-section bracing strut each side.
Wing section NACA 63(215)A 417 (modified).
Thickness/chord ratio 17%. Dihedral 1° 30'.
Incidence 0° 27'. No sweepback. Light
alloy two-spar torsion-box structure. Frise-
type light alloy ailerons. Double-slotted light
alloy flaps. Scoop-type light alloy spoilers
for lateral control above wing at 71% chord.
Trim-tab in port aileron. Pneumatic de-icing
boots optional.
FUSELAGE: Conventional semi-monocoque light
alloy structure of stringers, frames and single-
skin panels.
TAIL UNIT: Cantilever light alloy structure, with
twin fins and rudders, carried on twin booms

extending rearward from engine nacelles. Fixed-incidence tailplane. Geared tab and trim-tab in elevator and geared trim-tab in each rudder. Pneumatic leading-edge de-icing boots optional.

LANDING GEAR: Non-retractable tricycle type, with single wheel on each unit. Main wheels carried on twin struts, incorporating oleo-pneumatic shock-absorbers. Main wheels size 11·00 × 12. Nose-wheel size 9·00 × 6. Tyre pressure (all) 40 lb/sq in (2·81 kg/cm²). Disc brakes. Anti-skid units, low-pressure tyres (28 lb/sq in = 1·97 kg/cm²), floats or skis optional.

POWER PLANT: Two 715 eshp Pratt & Whitney (UACL) PT6A-27 turboprop engines, each driving a Hamilton Standard 23LF-361 three-blade fully-feathering reversible-pitch metal propeller, diameter 8 ft 6 in (2·59 m). Two integral fuel tanks in each wing, with total usable capacity of 322·5 Imp gallons (1,466 litres). Four overwing refuelling points. Optional pressure refuelling point in fuselage/strut fairing.

ACCOMMODATION: Crew of one or two on flight deck. Main cabin fitted out for up to 20 passengers, in four-abreast rows. Alternative configurations include executive layouts for 6-8 persons and casualty evacuation version for 12 stretcher patients and attendants. Easily convertible to all-freight rôle, carrying mixed cargo, vehicles or agricultural equipment. Downward-hinged door, with built-in airstairs, at rear of cabin on port side for passengers. Opposite this door, at floor level, is an emergency exit door which may be hinged and used optionally for baggage loading. Aft fuselage section is hinged to swing sideways through more than 90° to provide unrestricted access to cabin. Crew door at starboard side of flight deck. Cabin heated and ventilated. Air-conditioning optional.

SYSTEMS: Hydraulic system for brakes and nose-wheel steering only. Electrical system includes two 28V 200A (optionally 250A) DC engine-driven starter-generators, a 28V 25Ah (optionally 40Ah) battery and two 250VA 115/26V 400 c/s static inverters.

ELECTRONICS AND EQUIPMENT: Blind-flying instrumentation standard. Optional equipment includes VHF, VOR/ILS, ADF, marker beacon, DME, ATC transponder, autopilot, weather radar and PA system.

DIMENSIONS, EXTERNAL:
Wing span	69 ft 6 in (20·88 m)
Wing chord (constant)	6 ft 10½ in (2·09 m)
Wing aspect ratio	10
Length overall	42 ft 7½ in (12·99 m)
Length of fuselage pod	30 ft 7¼ in (9·33 m)
Height overall	17 ft 0¾ in (5·20 m)
Propeller ground clearance	5 ft 9 in (1·75 m)
Tailplane span	17 ft 1 in (5·21 m)
Wheel track	13 ft 1½ in (4·00 m)
Wheelbase	15 ft 2 in (4·62 m)

Crew door (fwd, stbd):
Height	2 ft 11 in (0·89 m)
Width	1 ft 8¾ in (0·53 m)

Passenger door (rear, port):
Height	5 ft 3 in (1·60 m)
Width	2 ft 1¼ in (0·64 m)

Emergency/baggage door (rear, stbd):
Height	3 ft 9 in (1·14 m)
Width	2 ft 1¼ in (0·64 m)

Emergency window exits (each):
Height	2 ft 2 in (0·66 m)
Width	1 ft 6¾ in (0·48 m)

DIMENSIONS, INTERNAL:
Cabin, excluding flight deck and hinged tail cone:
Length	12 ft 8¼ in (3·87 m)
Max width	7 ft 8 in (2·33 m)
Max height	5 ft 8½ in (1·74 m)
Floor area	77·1 sq ft (7·16 m²)
Volume	466·2 cu ft (13·2 m³)
Baggage holds (volume inside hinged tail cone):	113 cu ft (3·2 m³)

AREAS:
Wings, gross	470·2 sq ft (43·68 m²)
Ailerons (total)	18·84 sq ft (1·75 m²)
Trailing-edge flaps (total)	94·72 sq ft (8·80 m²)
Spoilers (total)	9·04 sq ft (0·84 m²)
Fins (total)	52·31 sq ft (4·86 m²)
Rudders (total incl tabs)	37·03 sq ft (3·44 m²)
Tailplane	100·75 sq ft (9·36 m²)
Elevator, including tabs	30·03 sq ft (2·79 m²)

WEIGHTS AND LOADINGS:
Weight empty	7,789 lb (3,533 kg)
Max payload	4,410 lb (2,000 kg)
Max T-O and landing weight	12,500 lb (5,670 kg)
Max ramp weight	12,676 lb (5,750 kg)
Max zero-fuel weight	11,684 lb (5,300 kg)
Max wing loading	26·63 lb/sq ft (130 kg/m²)
Max power loading	8·75 lb/eshp (3·97 kg/eshp)

PERFORMANCE (estimated at max T-O weight):
Max level speed at 10,000 ft (3,050 m)	188 knots (217 mph; 350 km/h)
Max diving speed (structural)	251 knots (290 mph; 466 km/h)
Max and econ cruising speed at 10,000 ft (3,050 m)	182 knots (209 mph; 337 km/h)
Stalling speed, flaps up	75 knots (86 mph; 137 km/h)
Stalling speed, flaps down, power off	57 knots (65 mph; 105 km/h)
Rate of climb at S/L	1,715 ft (522 m)/min
Rate of climb at S/L, one engine out	445 ft (135 m)/min
Service ceiling	28,550 ft (8,700 m)
Service ceiling, one engine out	11,150 ft (3,400 m)
STOL T-O run	590 ft (180 m)
STOL T-O to 50 ft (15 m)	1,000 ft (305 m)
STOL landing from 50 ft (15 m)	870 ft (265 m)
STOL landing run	395 ft (120 m)
Range with max fuel and 1,774 lb (805 kg) payload, 30 min reserve	753 nm (867 miles; 1,395 km)
Range with max payload, 30 min reserve	261 nm (301 miles; 486 km)

IAI COMMODORE JET 1123

In 1967, Israel Aircraft Industries acquired all production and marketing rights for the North American Rockwell Corporation (formerly Aero Commander) Jet Commander executive jet transport. The version now being developed for production in Israel is known as the **Commodore Jet 1123.**

The first of two prototype Jet Commanders (N601J) was flown for the first time in the US on 27 January 1963. The US production line was phased out between 1967 and mid-1969. By February 1970 more than 130 Jet Commander/Commodore Jet aircraft (mostly US production) had been delivered. These were of three basic models: the 1121, 1121A and 1121B.

Many modifications and improvements were incorporated by IAI into the original Jet Commander/Commodore Jet 1121, resulting chiefly in increased fuel capacity and performance.

By June 1971 IAI will have in production its new Commodore Jet 1123, to which the description below applies. This version is 1 ft 10 in (0·56 m) longer than the Model 1121, and improvements incorporated as standard include wingtip auxiliary fuel tanks, more powerful engines, an APU, strengthened landing gear, modified electrical system, double-slotted flaps, and a redesigned interior incorporating toilet facilities. Up to January 1970, 96 of this model had been ordered. The prototype flew for the first time in that month, but was destroyed on 21 January after the crew had escaped by parachute.

Sales and service of the Commodore Jet in Europe and the western hemisphere are undertaken by Commodore Jet Sales and Commodore Aviation Corporation of Washington, DC, USA.

TYPE: Twin-jet light executive transport.

WINGS: Cantilever mid-wing monoplane. Wing section NACA 64A212. Dihedral 2°. Incidence 1° at root, —1° at tip. Sweepback 4° 37' at quarter-chord. All-metal flush-riveted fail-safe structure. Manually-operated all-metal ailerons. Hydraulically-operated all-metal double-slotted trailing-edge flaps. Electrically-operated trim-tab in port aileron. Hydraulically-actuated spoiler and two lift dumpers above each wing, forward of flap. Pneumatic anti-icing boots standard.

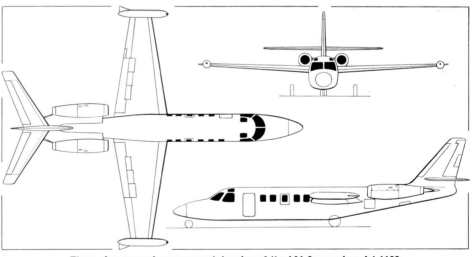

Three-view general arrangement drawing of the IAI Commodore Jet 1123

IAI Commodore Jet 1123, a lengthened development by Israel Aircraft Industries of the original US-designed Jet Commander

FUSELAGE: All-metal semi-monocoque flush-riveted structure with pressurised fail-safe cabin and baggage compartment.

TAIL UNIT: Cantilever all-metal structure, with 28° sweepback at quarter-chord. Variable-incidence tailplane, actuated electrically. Manually-operated elevators and rudder. Trim-tab in rudder. Pneumatic anti-icing boots standard.

LANDING GEAR: Hydraulically-retractable tricycle type, main wheels retracting outward into wings, twin nose-wheels rearward. Oleo-pneumatic shock-absorbers. Single wheel on each main unit, pressure 155 lb/sq in (10·9 kg/cm^2). Nose-wheel tyre pressure 50 lb/sq in (3·5 kg/cm^2). Goodyear brakes. Anti-skid units fitted.

POWER PLANT: Two 3,100 lb (1,406 kg) st General Electric CJ610-9 turbojet engines, mounted in pod on each side of rear fuselage. Max internal fuel load of 8,500 lb (3,855 kg), plus wingtip tanks each containing an additional 730 lb (331 kg). Refuelling points in wingtips and fuselage.

ACCOMMODATION: Standard seating for two pilots and up to 10 passengers in pressurised cabin. Interior layout to customer's requirements, with galley and toilet standard. Separate pressurised baggage compartment. Passenger door at front on port side, and two emergency exits. Entire accommodation heated, ventilated and air-conditioned.

SYSTEMS: GEC electrical system. Goodyear anti-icing boots, and bleed-air heating of engine intakes. Microturbo APU.

EQUIPMENT: Full blind-flying instrumentation standard.

DIMENSIONS, EXTERNAL:
- Wing chord at root: 10 ft 6 in (3·20 m)
- Wing chord at tip: 3 ft 6 in (1·07 m)
- Wing aspect ratio: 6·19
- Length of fuselage: 52 ft 3 in (15·93 m)
- Height overall: 15 ft 9½ in (4·81 m)
- Tailplane span: 19 ft 4 in (5·89 m)
- Wheel track: 12 ft 0 in (3·66 m)
- Passenger door:
  - Height: 4 ft 4 in (1·32 m)
  - Width: 2 ft 0 in (0·61 m)

DIMENSIONS, INTERNAL:
- Cabin, excluding flight deck:
  - Length: 15 ft 8 in (4·78 m)
  - Max width: 4 ft 11 in (1·50 m)
  - Max height: 4 ft 11½ in (1·51 m)

AREAS:
- Wings, gross: 303·3 sq ft (28·18 m^2)
- Ailerons (total): 15·39 sq ft (1·43 m^2)
- Trailing-edge flaps (total): 41·58 sq ft (3·86 m^2)
- Fin: 48·60 sq ft (4·51 m^2)
- Rudder, including tab: 10·69 sq ft (0·99 m^2)
- Tailplane: 52·42 sq ft (4·87 m^2)
- Elevators: 17·66 sq ft (1·64 m^2)

WEIGHTS:
- Basic operating weight: 11,070 lb (5,021 kg)
- Max T-O weight: 20,500 lb (9,298 kg)
- Max ramp weight: 20,800 lb (9,434 kg)
- Max zero-fuel weight: 13,000 lb (5,896 kg)
- Max landing weight: 19,000 lb (8,618 kg)

PERFORMANCE (estimated, at max T-O weight):
- Max level and cruising speed at 19,500 ft (5,944 m): 470 knots (541 mph; 871 km/h)
- Max permissible diving speed: Mach 0·765
- Econ cruising speed at 41,000 ft (12,500 m): 365 knots (420 mph; 676 km/h)
- Stalling speed, flaps and landing gear down: 75 knots (86 mph; 139 km/h)
- Max rate of climb at S/L: 4,100 ft (1,250 m)/min
- Rate of climb at S/L, one engine out: 935 ft (285 m)/min
- Service ceiling: 45,000 ft (13,715 m)
- Service ceiling, one engine out: 29,800 ft (8,800 m)
- T-O run: 3,045 ft (928 m)
- T-O to 35 ft (10·7 m): 4,012 ft (1,223 m)
- Landing from 50 ft (15 m): 3,045 ft (928 m)
- Landing run: 2,100 ft (640 m)
- Range with max fuel (45 min reserve): 1,736 nm (2,000 miles; 3,218 km)
- Range with 2,000 lb (907 kg) payload (45 min reserve): 1,259 nm (1,450 miles; 2,333 km)

ITALY

AERFER

AERFER—INDUSTRIE AEROSPAZIALI MERIDIONALI SpA

REGISTERED OFFICE:
Via Medina 40, Naples

HEAD OFFICE AND WORKS:
80038 Pomigliano d'Arco, Naples

OTHER WORKS:
Capodichino Airport, Naples

PRESIDENT:
Gen SA(r) Mario Porru

DIRECTORS:
Dr Ing Oscar Cinquegrani (Managing Director)
Dr Ing Amilcare Porro (General Manager)
Dr Ing Tiziano Fortunati (Vice-General Manager)
Gen Adolfo Varini (Commercial)
Dr Ing Costantino Berti (Quality Control)
Dr Giuseppe Pozzolo (Accounting)
Dr Guido Machera (Personnel)
Dr Ing Mario Orlando (Production)
Prof Ing Mario Calcara (Planning)

Aerfer was formed in 1955 by the merger of the Officine di Pomigliano per Costruzioni Aeronautiche e Ferroviarie-Aerfer and Industrie Meccaniche e Aeronautiche Meridionali-IMAM, builders of the well-known wartime Ro-37, Ro-41 and Ro-57 aircraft. Its activities expanded subsequently to include the overhaul and repair of aircraft on a very large scale, component manufacture and the design and production of prototypes such as the Sagittario 2 light fighter, first all-Italian aircraft to exceed Mach 1. It is a member of the Finmeccanica financial group which, in turn, belongs to the Istituto per la Ricostruzione Industriale (IRI). The Pomigliano d'Arco works is engaged primarily in the design and manufacture of aircraft and space vehicles, while that at Capodichino is concerned with aircraft reconditioning and overhaul.

Aerfer is to combine its activities with Fiat in the new company Aeritalia (which see), which will become fully operational under this new title in the second half of 1971.

Under a production agreement with McDonnell Douglas Corporation, USA, Aerfer is manufacturing basic fuselage structural skin panels for the DC-9 jet transport, as sole source, as well as fins and rudders for the DC-10 three-engined jet transport. Aerfer is sharing with General Dynamics (Convair Division) the manufacture of DC-10 fuselages, and has been appointed by Boeing to build nacelle support fittings for the Boeing 747. Aerfer is also the leading manufacturer of Italian-built components for the Breguet Atlantic maritime patrol aircraft.

The centre fuselage and wing panels for Italian licence-built Lockheed F-104S Starfighters are being manufactured by Aerfer. The company is also engaged in the joint programme for design and development of the G222 military STOL transport (described under Fiat entry), with responsibility for the complete fuselage aft of the flight deck, and has a large share in building the Fiat G91Y for the Italian Air Force.

In co-operation with Aermacchi, Aerfer has developed the AM.3C observation, training and utility monoplane for the Italian Army and will be responsible for production of this type.

Aerfer is manufacturing spare parts for the Republic F-84G and F-84F. IRAN inspection and overhaul work, under Italian and US Air Force contracts, is concerned mainly with F-84G and F-84F aircraft. US Navy contracts involve repair, reconditioning and modification of A-1 Skyraider, A-3 Skywarrior, F-1 Fury, F-3 Demon, F-4 Phantom II, F-8 Crusader, C-54 Skymaster, S-2 Tracker and other aircraft. Commercial aircraft overhaul and inspection includes work on the Caravelles and Friendships of Italian and foreign airlines.

In the field of space activities, Aerfer is participating in the ELDO/ESRO programmes. It is responsible for the locking system between the satellite and the final stage of the launch vehicle, and for manufacture of the separation device. Aerfer has also manufactured the satellite structure, in collaboration with another Italian company, as well as special equipment for static and dynamic operating tests.

AERFER/AERMACCHI AM.3C

First shown in model form at the 1965 Paris *Salon*, the AM.3 (originally M.B.335) is a three-seat monoplane designed to meet an Italian Air Force requirement. It utilises the basic wing of the Aermacchi-Lockheed AL.60. Duties for which it is suitable include forward air control, observation, liaison, transport of passengers and cargo, casualty evacuation, tactical support of ground forces and general duties.

Development is being undertaken jointly by Aerfer and Aermacchi.

The first of three prototypes (assembled at Varese by Aermacchi) flew for the first time on 12 May 1967, followed by the second (assembled by Aerfer) on 22 August 1968. The third airframe is for static testing.

The two flying prototypes were each powered originally by a 340 hp Continental GTSIO-520-C engine, in which form they were described in the 1969-70 *Jane's*. In 1969 both were refitted with Lycoming GSO-480-B1B6 engines; the description below applies to this version, which is designated AM.3C.

Early in 1970 the AM.3C was undergoing evaluation on behalf of the Italian Army, and an initial production order for 20 aircraft was under negotiation.

TYPE: Three/four-seat general-purpose monoplane.

WINGS: Strut-braced high-wing monoplane, with one bracing strut each side. Wing section NACA 23016 at root, NACA 4412 at tip. Dihedral 2°. Incidence 1° at root, —1° 54′ at tip. All-metal D-spar torsion-box structure. All-metal piano-hinged ailerons. Manually-operated Fowler flaps of all-metal two-spar construction.

FUSELAGE: Welded chrome-molybdenum steel-tube centre fuselage structure, covered with light alloy skin at front. but with much of the cabin covered with glass-fibre-reinforced plastic panels. Light alloy semi-monocoque rear fuselage, attached to centre portion at three points for easy removal.

TAIL UNIT: Conventional cantilever all-metal structure. Variable-incidence tailplane for trimming. Spring-tab in rudder.

LANDING GEAR: Non-retractable tail-wheel type. Each main leg consists of a tubular strut hinged to lower side of fuselage, with oleo-pneumatic shock-absorber between top of strut and wing-strut pick-up point on fuselage. Cast light alloy main wheels, each fitted with a size 6·50 × 8 4PR type III tyre, pressure 24 lb/sq in (1·69 kg/cm^2). Steerable tail-wheel, with oleo-pneumatic shock-absorber. Tail-wheel tyre size 10·00-6PR type I, pressure 30 lb/sq in (2·11 kg/cm^2). Single-disc hydraulic brakes. Provision for fitting floats or Fluidyne Fli-lite MK3000 hydraulically-actuated main wheel-skis and tail ski.

POWER PLANT: One 340 hp Piaggio-built Lycoming GSO-480-B1B6 six-cylinder horizontally-opposed air-cooled engine, driving a Piaggio P1033-G4-AD/0691/245 three-blade metal propeller. Two light alloy fuel tanks in each wing, near root. Total fuel capacity 52·5 Imp gallons (238 litres).

ACCOMMODATION: Normal accommodation for two persons in tandem, with dual controls. Provision for two additional seats at rear, or a stretcher or freight in place of both rear seats. Forward-hinged door by pilot's seat. Large upward-hinged door immediately aft of pilot's door, to open up entire starboard side of cabin. Third door on port side.

ELECTRONICS AND EQUIPMENT: Blind-flying instrumentation standard, also ARINC 546 680-channel VHF transceiver, Collins AN/ARC-54 800-channel VHF-FM transceiver with homing group, AN/ARN-83 ADF, and RMI.

ARMAMENT: Standard version has two underwing pylons, each capable of carrying up to 375 lb (170 kg) of external stores, including a Matra pod containing two 7·62-mm machine-guns and 2,000 rounds of ammunition, a General Electric Minigun pod and 1,500 rounds of ammunition, a Matra 125 pack of six 2·75-in rockets, a Matra 122 pack of seven BPD 50-mm rockets, a 250-lb GP bomb, an AN/M1A2 cluster of six 20-lb fragmentation bombs, an AN/M4A1 cluster of three 23-lb parachute-retarded fragmentation bombs, an M28A2 cluster of twenty-four 4-lb "butterfly" bombs, a Nord AS.11 or AS.12 wire-guided missile, an M84A1 target marker, an M46 photoflash or M26A1 parachute-flare, or a 250-lb supply container. Alternatively, a Vinten 70-mm automatic three-camera reconnaissance pack can be carried under the fuselage; or two 70-mm cameras or a three-lens CA-103 camera can be carried inside the fuselage.

DIMENSIONS, EXTERNAL:
- Wing span: 38 ft 6 in (11·73 m)
- Wing chord at root: 5 ft 8 in (1·73 m)
- Wing chord at tip: 4 ft 2½ in (1·28 m)
- Wing aspect ratio: 7·2
- Length overall: 28 ft 8 in (8·73 m)
- Height overall (tail down): 8 ft 11 in (2·72 m)
- Tailplane span: 14 ft 11 in (4·55 m)
- Wheel track: 8 ft 7 in (2·62 m)
- Propeller ground clearance: 2 ft 3¼ in (0·695 m)
- Pilot's door (starboard):
  - Mean height: 3 ft 1½ in (0·95 m)
  - Max width: 2 ft 1¼ in (0·64 m)
- Rear door (starboard):
  - Height: 2 ft 10⅝ in (0·88 m)
  - Max width: 5 ft 10⅞ in (1·80 m)

DIMENSIONS, INTERNAL:
- Cabin: Length: 8 ft 2 in (2·50 m)
  - Max width: 2 ft 8 in (0·81 m)
  - Max height: 5 ft 3 in (1·60 m)

WEIGHTS AND LOADINGS:
- Weight empty: 2,380 lb (1,080 kg)
- Normal T-O weight (2 crew only): 3,306 lb (1,500 kg)
- Max T-O weight (underwing weapons): 3,750 lb (1,700 kg)
- Max wing loading: 18·3 lb/sq ft (89·3 kg/m^2)
- Max power loading: 11·0 lb/hp (5·00 kg/hp)

PERFORMANCE (at normal T-O weight):
Max level speed at 8,000 ft (2,438 m)
    150 knots (173 mph; 278 km/h)
Max level speed at S/L
    141 knots (162 mph; 260 km/h)
Max cruising speed (75% power) at 8,000 ft
  (2,438 m) 133 knots (153 mph; 246 km/h)
Rate of climb at S/L   1,378 ft (420 m)/min
Service ceiling   27,550 ft (8,400 m)
T-O run   280 ft (85 m)
T-O to 50 ft (15 m)   558 ft (170 m)
Landing from 50 ft (15 m)   571 ft (174 m)
Landing run   217 ft (66 m)
Max range at 5,000 ft (1,524 m), 30 min reserves
    534 nm (615 miles; 990 km)
Endurance at 5,000 ft (1,524 m), 30 min reserves
    5 hr 45 min

Right: **Aerfer/Aermacchi AM.3 three-seat general-purpose monoplane**

AERITALIA
HEAD OFFICE:
Naples
CHAIRMAN:
Gen S. A. (r) Gastone Valentini

This is the title of a new stock company formed on 12 November 1969 by a joint shareholding of Fiat and Finmeccanica (IRI) to combine the activities of the Aircraft Section of Fiat's Aviation Division, Aerfer, and the avionics company Salmoiraghi. It will not, however, become fully operational under the new title until the second half of 1971; meanwhile Aerfer and Fiat (which see) continue activities under their existing titles.

AERMACCHI
AERONAUTICA MACCHI SpA
HEAD OFFICE:
Corso Vittorio Emanuele 31, Milan
OFFICES AND WORKS:
Via Sanvito Silvestro 80, Casella Postale 246, 21100 Varese
PRESIDENT:
Dott Ing Paolo Foresio
TECHNICAL DIRECTOR AND CHIEF ENGINEER:
Ing Ermanno Bazzocchi
SALES MANAGER:
Dott Ing Giorgio Marlia
PUBLIC RELATIONS MANAGER:
Dott Fabrizio Foresio

The Macchi company was founded in 1912 in Varese and its first aeroplane was built in 1913. Its factory area is now 397,200 sq ft (36,900 m²) and it has 1,500 employees.

Lockheed Aircraft International acquired a substantial minority interest in Aermacchi in December 1959, and Aermacchi is producing the Lockheed 60 light utility transport as the Aermacchi-Lockheed AL.60. Also in production is one of Aermacchi's own designs, the M.B. 326 jet trainer. A prototype of the single-seat M.B. 336B, developed from the M.B. 326, was due to fly in mid-1970.

Under development, in association with Aerfer, is a military AOP and liaison monoplane designated AM.3C, which utilises the basic wing structure of the AL.60. This aircraft is described under the Aerfer entry above.

AERMACCHI M.B. 326
(except M.B.326G and GB)
The first prototype of the Aermacchi M.B. 326 jet trainer flew for the first time on 10 December 1957, powered by a Rolls-Royce Bristol Viper 8 turbojet engine. The second prototype had a more powerful Viper 11 and this engine, built in Italy by Piaggio, is fitted in production M.B. 326 trainers built for the air forces of Italy, Australia, Ghana, Tunisia and South Africa. The higher-rated Viper 20 is used in some armed versions of the M.B. 326, including those for the Argentine Navy, Brazilian Air Force and Congolese Air Force.

Eight versions have been built, as follows:

M.B. 326. Basic trainer with Viper 11 turbojet, rated at 2,500 lb (1,135 kg) st. First of 100 for Italian Air Force flew on 5 October 1960. In service at Italian Air Force flying schools since January 1962.

M.B. 326B. Trainer/ground attack version, with six attachment points under wings for external stores. Typical operational loads include (a) two 0·50-in machine-gun pods, with 300 rpg, and four Matra 122 packs each with seven 68-mm air-to-air rockets, (b) one 0·50-in machine-gun pod, four Matra 122 packs and one pod containing four 70-mm Vinten reconnaissance cameras, (c) twelve 5-in HVAR rockets, (d) six 260-lb (118-kg) bombs, (e) one camera pod, one machine-gun pod, two underwing fuel tanks and larger tip-tanks. For weapon training, Practice Aero 4B canisters can be carried, each containing eight 3-lb (1·4-kg) practice bombs. The M.B.326B is flown normally as a single-seater when carrying weapons, but can be adapted quickly into a standard two-seat trainer and can also be used for target towing. Power plant, dimensions and

performance are similar to those of the M.B. 326. For operation from rough airstrips or grass, oversize tyres may be fitted on all three wheels. Eight built for Tunisian Air Force; deliveries began in Summer of 1965.

M.B. 326D. Similar to M.B. 326, but with airline-type electronic and navigation equipment, including two VHF communications sets, one VOR/ILS, one ADF and one marker beacon receiver. Four delivered to Alitalia for *ab initio* training at the airline's pilot training centre. First delivered on 27 May 1963.

M.B. 326F. Armed version, similar to M.B. 326B, except for different electronics and equipment. Delivery of seven for Ghana Air Force began in Summer of 1965.

M.B. 326G. Dual-rôle training/counter-insurgency attack version, powered by Viper 20 Mk 540 engine of 3,410 lb (1,547 kg) st. This version, and a single-seat development designated **M.B.336B**, are described separately.

M.B. 326GB. Armed version, generally similar to M.B. 326G, with Viper 20 engine. Six ordered for Argentine Navy, which has a total requirement for up to 24, 112 for the Brazilian Air Force and 17 for the Congolese Air Force. Described separately.

M.B. 326H. Similar to M.B. 326 for "all-through" training duties with the Royal Australian Air Force. Special equipment includes TACAN (RT.384/ARN.52(V)), UHF (718B-8) and ADF (DFA-73A). Initial order for 75, with option for 25 more. First 12 delivered from Aermacchi production; remainder being produced in Australia by Commonwealth Aircraft Corporation, with Hawker de Havilland as the major sub-contractor.

M.B. 326M. Dual-role training/light attack version, being produced under licence for the South African Air Force by Atlas Aircraft Corporation of South Africa Ltd, as the **Impala**. More than 50 had been delivered by the beginning of 1969, beginning in the first half of 1966 with aircraft assembled from Italian components. The proportion of locally-produced components is being increased progressively, and eventually some 80% of each Impala will be of South African manufacture. Using a prototype retained in Italy, Aermacchi has more recently been developing and clearing for operational use various armament configurations. Alternative underwing loads of the M.B. 326M include two 12·7 mm gun packs, two SUU-11 General Electric Minigun 7·62-mm machine-gun packs with 1,500 rounds, and two rocket packs each containing six 80-mm SURA rockets; two Miniguns, two 500-lb (227-kg) bombs and two Matra 361 packs each containing thirty-six 37-mm FFAR rockets; two Miniguns and two napalm tanks; two Nord AS.11 missiles; or two Del Mar towed targets.

In December 1967, an M.B. 326, piloted by Cdte Massimo Ralli, set up four international records in Class C-1-d. Details of these were given in the 1969-70 *Jane's*.

The following data apply to the M.B. 326 and M.B. 326D, but are generally applicable to the M.B. 326B, M.B. 326F and M.B. 326H also, except in the details noted above.

TYPE: Two-seat jet trainer, stressed for flight load factors of +8g and −4g and for fatigue life of at least 15,000 hours.

WINGS: Cantilever mid-wing monoplane. Wing section NACA 6A series. Thickness/chord ratio 13·7% at root, 12% at tip. Dihedral 2° 55′. Incidence 2° 30′. All-metal two-spar stressed-skin structure in three sections, of which the centre-section is integral with the fuselage. Servo-tab operated all-metal ailerons and hydraulically-operated slotted flaps. Electrically-actuated balance and trim tab in port aileron. Geared balance tab in starboard aileron.

FUSELAGE: All-metal semi-monocoque structure. Hydraulically-operated dive-brake under centre fuselage.

TAIL UNIT: Cantilever all-metal structure. Electrically-actuated trim-tab in each elevator.

LANDING GEAR: Hydraulically-retracted tricycle type, with oleo-pneumatic shock-absorbers. Nose-wheel retracts forward, main units outward into wings. Pirelli main wheels and tyres, size 6·50 × 10 8-ply. Dunlop twin-contact nose-wheel tyre size 5 × 4·5. Hydraulic disc brakes. Steerable and self-centering nose-wheel with anti-shimmy device.

POWER PLANT: One Rolls-Royce Bristol Viper 11 Mk 22 turbojet engine (2,500 lb = 1,135 kg st). Fuel in twin rubber-cell fuselage tank and two fixed wingtip tanks with total capacity of 225 Imp gallons (1,023 litres), or 304 Imp gallons (1,382 litres) with optional larger tip-tanks. Provision for two 57 Imp gallon (257 litres) underwing jettisonable tanks. Pressure refuelling point on starboard side of fuselage. Gravity fuelling point above each tank.

ACCOMMODATION: Crew of two in tandem under a one-piece moulded Perspex canopy which hinges sideways to starboard. Pressurised cabin. Dual controls and instruments. Blind flying screens for pupil. Martin-Baker Mk 04A lightweight ejection seats.

SYSTEMS: Hydraulic system, pressure 2,500 lb/sq in (175 kg/cm²), for landing gear and doors, flaps, air-brake and wheel brakes. Independent manually-operated hydraulic system for emergency landing gear extension. DC electrical supply from 30V 150A starter generator and two 24V 25Ah batteries. 7Ah emergency battery. Two 100VA 115V three-phase inverters for AC supply. Transformer for 26V single-phase AC.

ELECTRONICS AND EQUIPMENT: M.B. 326, as supplied to Italian Air Force, has UHF system, including AN/ARC-52 transceiver and D.103/ITAL emergency transceiver. Alternative VHF system employs two Collins 618M-1A transceivers. An AN/AIC-18 interphone is standard. Optional equipment includes ARN-65 TACAN; Collins 51RV-1 VHF VOR/ILS with Bendix MKA-28A marker beacon receiver; Marconi AD.722 or Collins DF-203 ADF; and Bendix TRA-61C IFF.

ARMAMENT (optional): Two 7·7-mm machine-guns in fuselage, with gun-camera. Four 13·2 lb (6 kg) or 16·7 lb (7·5 kg) rockets and four 33 lb (15 kg) or 100 lb (45 kg) bombs under wings.

DIMENSIONS, EXTERNAL:
Wing span:
  without tip-tanks   32 ft 11¼ in (10·04 m)
  with tip-tanks   34 ft 8 in (10·56 m)
Wing chord (mean)   6 ft 3 in (1·90 m)
Wing aspect ratio   5·26

I

Length overall 34 ft 11¼ in (10·65 m)
Height overall 12 ft 2½ in (3·72 m)
Tailplane span 13 ft 4½ in (4·08 m)
Wheel track 7 ft 9¼ in (2·37 m)
Wheelbase 13 ft 7¼ in (4·15 m)

AREAS:
Wings, gross 204·52 sq ft (19·0 m²)
Ailerons (total) 14·21 sq ft (1·32 m²)
Flaps (total) 28·20 sq ft (2·62 m²)
Fin 18·19 sq ft (1·69 m²)
Rudder 8·07 sq ft (0·75 m²)
Tailplane 28·96 sq ft (2·69 m²)
Elevators 11·52 sq ft (1·07 m²)

WEIGHTS:
Weight empty:
M.B. 326 4,930 lb (2,237 kg)
Crew (2) 355 lb (160 kg)
Fuel and oil 1,880 lb (853 kg)
Electronic equipment:
M.B. 326 155 lb (70 kg)
Max T-O weight:
M.B. 326:
small tip-tanks 7,600 lb (3,450 kg)
large tip-tanks 8,300 lb (3,765 kg)
M.B. 326B:
normal 9,480 lb (4,300 kg)
max 10,000 lb (4,535 kg)

PERFORMANCE (at max T-O weight, except where indicated):
Max level speed:
M.B. 326 at S/L at AUW of 7,500 lb (3,400 kg) 415 knots (478 mph; 770 km/h)
M.B. 326 at 15,000 ft (4,575 m) at AUW of 7,500 lb (3,400 kg) 435 knots (501 mph; 806 km/h)
M.B. 326B at 20,000 ft (6,000 m) with 50% fuel 340 knots (392 mph; 631 km/h)
Max permissible diving speed:
M.B. 326 Mach 0·8
M.B. 326B Mach 0·7
Stalling speed, clean:
M.B. 326 at AUW of 7,400 lb (3,355 kg) 88 knots (101 mph; 163 km/h)
M.B. 326B at AUW of 8,800 lb (3,990 kg) 97 knots (111 mph; 178 km/h)
Stalling speed, wheels and flaps down:
M.B. 326 at AUW of 7,400 lb (3,355 kg) 79 knots (91 mph; 146 km/h)
M.B. 326B at AUW of 8,800 lb (3,990 kg) 87 knots (100 mph; 161 km/h)
Rate of climb at S/L:
M.B. 326, clean, at AUW of 7,500 lb (3,400 kg) 4,400 ft (1,340 m)/min
M.B. 326B 2,300 ft (700 m)/min
Service ceiling:
M.B. 326, clean 41,000 ft (12,500 m)
T-O run:
M.B. 326 at AUW of 7,500 lb (3,400 kg) 1,370 ft (420 m)
M.B. 326B at AUW of 10,000 lb (4,535 kg) 2,690 ft (820 m)
T-O to 50 ft (15 m):
M.B. 326 at AUW of 7,500 lb (3,400 kg) 1,970 ft (600 m)
M.B. 326B at AUW of 10,000 lb (4,535 kg) 3,760 ft (1,145 m)
Landing from 50 ft (15 m):
M.B. 326 2,100 ft (640 m)
M.B. 326B 2,600 ft (793 m)
Range, with reserve for 10 min at 1,000 ft (300 m) and 5% final reserve:
M.B. 326 with small tip-tanks at 40,000 ft (12,200 m) 614 nm (708 miles; 1,140 km)
M.B. 326 with large tip-tanks at 38,000 ft (11,500 m) 898 nm (1,035 miles; 1,665 km)
M.B. 326 with large tip-tanks and underwing tanks at 33,000 ft (10,000 m) 1,080 nm (1,245 miles; 2,000 km)
Combat radius, with armament and 10% fuel reserve, 3 min over target:
M.B. 326B with 2,420 lb (1,100 kg) armament at S/L 100 nm (115 miles; 185 km)
M.B. 326B with 2,520 lb (1,145 kg) armament at 5,000 ft (1,500 m) 100 nm (115 miles; 185 km)
M.B. 326B with 1,500 lb (680 kg) armament at 30,000 ft (9,150 m) 250 nm (290 miles; 460 km)

AERMACCHI M.B. 326G and M.B. 326GB

These dual-role training and counter-insurgency attack versions of the M.B. 326 differ from other versions primarily in having a more powerful Viper turbojet engine. The prototype M.B. 326G flew for the first time in the Spring of 1967, and the similar M.B. 326GB is now in production.

Six have been ordered by the Argentine Navy (which has an eventual requirement for 24), and 17 by the Congolese Air Force. In addition, 112 are to be assembled in Brazil under licence by Embraer (which see) for the Brazilian Air Force.

The general description above of the M.B. 326 applies equally to the M.B. 326G and M.B. 326GB with the following exceptions:

TYPE: Two-seat basic trainer and tactical ground-attack aircraft.

WINGS: Generally similar to M.B. 326. Wing section NACA 6A series (modified). Manually-operated ailerons.

TAIL UNIT: Cantilever all-metal structure. Electrically-actuated trim-tab in rudder and each elevator.

LANDING GEAR: Generally similar to M.B. 326.

POWER PLANT: One Rolls-Royce Bristol Viper 20 Mk 540 turbojet engine, rated at 3,410 lb (1,547 kg) st. Fuel in flexible rubber main tank in fuselage, capacity 172 Imp gallons (782 litres), and two fixed wing-tip tanks with combined capacity of 134 Imp gallons (610 litres). Total standard fuel capacity 306 Imp gallons (1,392 litres). Provision for two 73 Imp gallon (332 litre) jettisonable underwing tanks, to give total capacity of 452 Imp gallons (2,056 litres). Single-point pressure refuelling receptacle under fuselage. Fuel dump valves permit quick emptying of tip-tanks.

ACCOMMODATION: Generally similar to M.B. 326.

SYSTEMS: Air-conditioning and pressurisation system, differential 3 lb/sq in (0·21 kg/cm²), uses air bled from engine compressor and incorporates turbo-refrigerator unit. Hydraulic system, pressure 2,500 lb/sq in (175 kg/cm²), for landing gear and doors flaps air-brake and wheel brakes. Independent manually-operated hydraulic system for emergency landing gear extension. DC electrical supply from 30V 9kW starter-generator and two 24V 22Ah batteries. Fixed-frequency AC system powered by 750VA main inverter, with 250VA stand-by unit. 6kVA alternator supplies engine air intake anti-icing system and can feed primary electrical system, via transformer-rectifier, in event of DC generator failure.

ELECTRONICS AND EQUIPMENT: To customer's specification. Standard configuration includes UHF transmitter-receiver type AN/ARC-51BX with 3,500 channels or 26 preset channels, auxiliary UHF system with 5-channel Collins 718B-8C transmitter-receiver, AN/AIC-18 interphone, AN/ARN-52(V) TACAN with USAF type AQU-4/A horizontal situation indicator, and AN/ARN-83 ADF, AN/ARA-50 UHF/DF, Collins 51RV-1 (ARINC 547) VOR/ILS and CPU-76/A flight director computer. Standard AN/APX-72 IFT transponder can be replaced by Bendix-FIAR TRA-62A, AN/APX-68 or AN/APX-77 IFF/SIF system.

ARMAMENT (optional): Up to 4,000 lb (1,814 kg) of armament can be carried on six underwing attachments. Typical weapon loads include those listed above for the M.B. 326M, plus the following alternatives: two LAU-3/A packs each containing nineteen 2·75-in FFAR rockets and two packs each containing eight Hispano-Suiza SURA 80-mm rockets; two 12·7-mm gun pods and four packs each containing six SURA 80-mm rockets; one 7·62-mm Minigun, one 12·7-mm gun pod, two Matra 122 rocket packs and two packs each containing six SURA 80-mm rockets; two 500-lb bombs and eight 5-in HVAR rockets; two Nord AS.12 missiles; one 12·7-mm gun pod, one reconnaissance pack containing four Vinten cameras and two 600-lb (272-kg) drop tanks, or two Matra SA-10 packs each containing a 30-mm Aden gun and 150 rounds. SFOM type 83 fixed gun-sight or Ferranti LFS 5/102A gyro-sight. Gun-camera in nose.

DIMENSIONS:
As for M.B.326, except:
Wing span:
without tip-tanks 33 ft 3¾ in (10·15 m)
with tip tanks 35 ft 7 in (10·85 m)
Wing aspect ratio 6·08

AREAS:
Wings, gross 208·3 sq ft (19·35 m²)
Fin 16·7 sq ft (1·55 m²)
Rudder 7·6 sq ft (0·71 m²)
Tailplane 28·2 sq ft (2·62 m²)
Elevators 9·5 sq ft (0·88 m²)

WEIGHTS (T=Trainer, A=Attack):
Basic operating weight, excluding crew:
T 5,920 lb (2,685 kg)
A 5,640 lb (2,558 kg)*
Max zero-fuel weight:
T 6,280 lb (2,849 kg)
A 5,820 lb (2,640 kg)*
Max T-O weight (full internal fuel, wingtip and underwing tanks):
T 10,090 lb (4,577 kg)
A, no armament 9,805 lb (4,447 kg)
A, with 1,695 lb (769 kg) armament 11,500 lb (5,216 kg)
Max T-O weight (max armament):
A, with fuel in fuselage tank only and 4,325 lb (1,962 kg) armament 11,500 lb (5,216 kg)*
* *Without tip-tanks and aft ejection seat*

PERFORMANCE (T=Trainer at typical weight of 8,680 lb (3,937 kg), representing max T-O weight without underwing tanks; AC=Attack version at combat weight of 10,500 lb (4,763 kg); AM=Attack version at max T-O weight):
Max level speed:
T 468 knots (539 mph; 867 km/h)
Max permissible diving speed:
T Mach 0·82 or 469 knots (541 mph; 871 km/h) EAS
AC Mach 0·75 or 419 knots (483 mph; 778 km/h) EAS
Max cruising speed:
T 430 knots (495 mph; 797 km/h)
Rate of climb at S/L:
T 6,050 ft (1,844 m)/min
AC 3,550 ft (1,082 m)/min
AM 3,100 ft (945 m)/min
Time to 10,000 ft (3,050 m):
AC 3 min 10 sec
AM 4 min 0 sec

Aermacchi M.B.326GB armed jet trainer/attack aircraft in the insignia of the Congolese Air Force

Time to 20,000 ft (6,100 m):
T	4 min 10 sec
AC	8 min 0 sec
AM	9 min 20 sec

Time to 30,000 ft (9,150 m):
T	7 min 40 sec
AC	15 min 0 sec
AM	18 min 40 sec

Time to 40,000 ft (12,200 m):
T	13 min 5 sec

Service ceiling:
T	47,000 ft (14,325 m)
AC	39,000 ft (11,900 m)

T-O run, standard day:
T	1,350 ft (412 m)
AC	2,100 ft (640 m)
AM	2,770 ft (845 m)

T-O run, ISA + 25°C:
T	1,660 ft (506 m)
AC	2,640 ft (805 m)
AM	3,280 ft (1,000 m)

T-O to 50 ft (15 m), standard day:
T	1,820 ft (555 m)
AC	2,840 ft (866 m)
AM	3,740 ft (1,140 m)

T-O to 50 ft (15 m), ISA + 25°C:
T	2,310 ft (704 m)
AC	3,650 ft (1,113 m)
AM	4,630 ft (1,411 m)

Landing from 50 ft (15 m), standard day:
T at landing weight of 7,000 lb (3,175 kg)
     2,070 ft (631 m)
AC at landing weight of 9,250 lb (4,195 kg)
     2.630 ft (802 m)

Landing from 50 ft (15 m), ISA + 25°C:
T at landing weight of 7,000 lb (3,175 kg)
     2,200 ft (671 m)
AC at landing weight of 9,250 lb (4,195 kg)
     2,810 ft (857 m)

Range (T, with 25 Imp gallons = 113 litres reserve):
Fuselage and tip tanks
     998 nm (1,150 miles; 1,850 km)
Fuselage, tip and underwing tanks
     1,320 nm (1,520 miles; 2,445 km)
Combat radius (A at max AUW):
Max fuel, 1,695 lb (769 kg) armament, 200 lb (90 kg) fuel reserve, out at 20,000 ft (6,100 m), return at 25,000 ft (7,620 m)
     350 nm (403 miles; 648 km)
Fuselage tank only, 4,000 lb (1,814 kg) armament, 200 lb (90 kg) fuel reserve, cruise at 10,000 m (3,050 m), five minutes over target
     69 nm (80 miles; 130 km)
Max fuel, 1,700 lb (771 kg) armament, 200 lb (90 kg) fuel reserve, cruise at 10,000 ft (3,050 m), 1 hr 50 min patrol at 500 ft (150 m) over target
     49·5 nm (57 miles; 92 km)

AERMACCHI M.B. 336B

The M.B. 336B is a single-seat ground attack aircraft developed from, and based upon the airframe of, the M.B. 326G, retaining most of the structure and systems of the latter aircraft. Logistic problems, and the transition of pilots to the new type, are thus simplified for air forces already using the basic M.B. 326 for training purposes.

Offensive capabilities are, however, greatly enhanced by the installation of two 30 mm Aden or DEFA cannon in the fuselage, with 150 rpg, leaving the six underwing stations free for bombs, rockets or additional fuel. Survivability can be improved by the installation of self-sealing fuel tanks, with anti-explosive reticulated foam filling, and of armour protection for the pilot and the most vulnerable systems.

Major differences in the M.B. 336B, compared with the M.B. 326G, include the installation of a more powerful 4,000 lb (1,814 kg) st Rolls-Royce Bristol Viper 600 turbojet engine; deletion of the rear pilot's station; single-seat front cockpit, which is pressurised and has provision for armour protection from small-arms fire; and an auxiliary fuel tank in the fuselage. Provision is made for complete instrumentation for navigation and armament delivery systems, and for self-sealing fuel tanks and armour protection for critical fuel system areas.

The M.B. 336B has a max T-O weight of 12,000 lb (5,443 kg), as compared with the 11,500 lb (5,216 kg) of the M.B. 326G. A prototype was due to fly in the Summer of 1970.

AERMACCHI-LOCKHEED AL.60F5 AND AL.60C5 CONESTOGA

Aermacchi has exclusive manufacturing rights, outside the United States, for the Lockheed 60 light utility transport.

The first Aermacchi-built machine flew on 19 April 1961. The current production versions are as follows:

AL.60F5 Conestoga. Basic current version with tricycle landing gear. Described in detail below.

AL.60C5 Conestoga. Basically the same as the AL.60F5, but with a tail-wheel undercarriage. First four delivered to Canada in early 1968. Ten have been delivered to the Central African

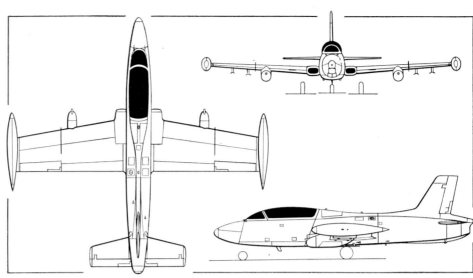

Aermacchi M.B.326G basic training and light tactical attack aircraft

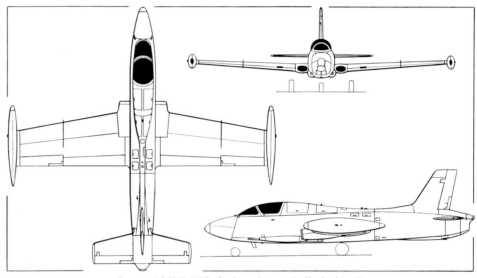

Aermacchi M.B.336B single-seat ground attack aircraft

Federation. In Canada, NWI (which see) is developing a modified version known as the **Ranger.**

A version of the Conestoga with 520 hp turbo-supercharged engine was under development in 1969. Details of earlier versions, with different power plants, can be found in previous editions of *Jane's.*

TYPE: Single-engined cabin monoplane.

WINGS: Strut-braced high-wing monoplane. Wing section NACA 23016 at root, NACA 4412 at tip. Dihedral 2°. Incidence 1° at root, —1° 54' at tip. All-metal D-spar torsion-box structure. All-metal piano-hinged ailerons. Hand-operated Fowler flaps, of two-spar sheet metal construction, are interchangeable right/left.

FUSELAGE: All-metal semi-monocoque structure built in three sections; power plant section, cabin section and rear fuselage.

TAIL UNIT: Cantilever all-metal structure. Adjustable tailplane. Servo-tab in elevators.

LANDING GEAR (AL.60F5): Non-retractable tricycle type. Cantilever steel-tube main legs are inclined rearward and are connected to an oleo-pneumatic shock-absorber mounted horizontally under the cabin floor. Nose unit has oleo-pneumatic shock-absorber and is steerable. Main wheel tyre size 7·00 × 8-6PR type III, pressure 32 lb/sq in (2·25 kg/cm²). Nose-wheel tyre size 6·00 × 6-6PR type III, pressure 30 lb/sq in (2·11 kg/cm²). Single-disc hydraulic brakes.

POWER PLANT: One 400 hp Lycoming IO-720-A1A eight-cylinder horizontally-opposed air-cooled engine, driving a Hartzell HC-A3VK three-blade constant-speed metal propeller, diameter 7 ft 0½ in (2·15 m). Three metal fuel tanks in each wing. Total capacity of six tanks 75·75 Imp gallons (345 litres).

ACCOMMODATION: Enclosed cabin seating six to eight in standard version. Pilot and co-pilot side-by-side, with four individual seats in pairs, or two three-place bench seats to rear. Alternative parachutists' seats without backrest

Aermacchi-Lockheed AL.60C5 Conestoga in military markings of the Central African Federation

available. Provision for two-seat bench in luggage compartment. Rear seats can be removed to provide space for 1,440 lb (653 kg) of cargo. Heating and ventilation standard. Front access door on port side, by pilot's seat, hinges forward. Main cabin door, on starboard side, is in two sections: forward section opens forward and is used to embark passengers and light cargo; rear section opens rearward to supplement forward section when loading bulky cargo. Provision for sliding door at rear of cabin on port side, which can be opened in flight to permit dropping of parachutists or supplies. Ambulance version has accommodation for two stretchers, one sitting casualty and medical attendant.

SYSTEMS: Hydraulic system for wheel brakes only. 28V DC electrical system supplied by engine-driven generator and battery type AN3154-1A.

ELECTRONICS AND EQUIPMENT: Standard equipment includes instrument, cabin, navigation and landing lights and rotating beacon. Instrumentation and electronic equipment to customer's specification, including duplicated VHF transceivers, interphone, HF transceiver, ADF, VOR/LOC, glideslope receiver and marker beacon receiver.

DIMENSIONS, EXTERNAL:

Wing span	39 ft 4 in (11·99 m)
Wing chord at root	5 ft 8 in (1·73 m)
Wing chord at tip	4 ft 2½ in (1·28 m)
Wing aspect ratio	7·2
Length overall (AL.60F5)	28 ft 10½ in (8·80 m)
Height overall (AL.60F5)	10 ft 10 in (3·30 m)
Tailplane span	15 ft 0½ in (4·59 m)
Wheel track	9 ft 4 in (2·84 m)
Pilot's door (fwd, port):	
Height	3 ft 6 in (1·07 m)
Width	1 ft 11½ in (0·60 m)
Passenger door (stbd):	
Height	3 ft 6 in (1·07 m)
Width	2 ft 8 in (0·82 m)
Cargo door (stbd):	
Height	3 ft 6 in (1·07 m)
Width (total opening, including passenger door)	4 ft 9 in (1·45 m)

Aermacchi-Lockheed AL.60F5 Conestoga utility aircraft, with tricycle landing gear

Sliding door (optional):	
Height	3 ft 6 in (1·07 m)
Width	2 ft 4½ in (0·72 m)

DIMENSIONS, INTERNAL:

Cabin: Length (instrument panel to aft bulkhead)	10 ft 3 in (3·12 m)
Max width	3 ft 9 in (1·14 m)
Max height	4 ft 3 in (1·30 m)

AREAS:

Wings, gross	210·4 sq ft (19·55 m²)
Ailerons (total)	23·5 sq ft (2·18 m²)
Trailing-edge flaps (total)	39·9 sq ft (3·71 m²)
Vertical tail surfaces (total)	23·12 sq ft (2·15 m²)
Horizontal tail surfaces (total)	55·40 sq ft (5·15 m²)

WEIGHTS AND LOADING (AL.60F5):

Weight empty	2,395 lb (1,086 kg)
Basic operating weight, empty (8 seats)	2,732 lb (1,239 kg)
Max payload (cargo)	1,440 lb (653 kg)

Max T-O weight	4,500 lb (2,041 kg)
Max landing weight	4,275 lb (1,941 kg)
Max wing loading	21·4 lb/sq ft (104 kg/m²)

PERFORMANCE (AL.60F5, at max T-O weight):

Max speed at S/L	135 knots (156 mph; 251 km/h)
Max permissible speed in dive	178 knots (205 mph; 330 km/h) CAS
Max cruising speed (280 hp at 10,000 ft = 3,050 m)	126 knots (145 mph; 233 km/h)
Econ cruising speed (200 hp at 5,000 ft = 1,525 m)	94 knots (108 mph; 174 km/h)
Rate of climb at S/L	1,080 ft (330 m)/min
Service ceiling	13,600 ft (4,150 m)
T-O run	645 ft (196 m)
T-O to 50 ft (15 m)	1,100 ft (335 m)
Landing from 50 ft (15 m)	846 ft (258 m)
Range with max fuel, no reserve	560 nm (645 miles; 1,037 km)
Endurance with max fuel, no reserve	5 hr 52 min

AGUSTA
COSTRUZIONI AERONAUTICHE GIOVANNI AGUSTA SpA

HEAD OFFICE:
Cascina Costa, Gallarate

PRESIDENT AND GENERAL MANAGER:
Cav del Lavoro Domenico Agusta

VICE-PRESIDENT AND SALES MANAGER:
Corrado Agusta

PUBLIC RELATIONS MANAGER:
E. Guerra

This company was established in 1907 by Giovanni Agusta and built many experimental and production aircraft before World War II.

In 1952 Agusta acquired a licence to manufacture the Bell Model 47 helicopter and the first Agusta-built Model 47G made its maiden flight on 22 May 1954.

In addition to versions of the Model 47, Agusta is now producing under exclusive licence the Bell Iroquois Models UH-1B and UH-1D, as the Agusta-Bell 204-B and 205 respectively, the twin-engined Model 212, and the light turbine-powered Model 206A JetRanger helicopter.

Under licence from Sikorsky, production of 24 SH-3D Sea King helicopters for the Italian Navy was started in 1967.

Details of these aircraft are given hereafter, together with descriptions of helicopters designed by Agusta.

Early in 1970, Agusta acquired 30% of the share capital of Siai-Marchetti, with an option on a further 30% which it was expected to take up later in the year.

AGUSTA A 101G

The Agusta A 101G three-engined helicopter is suitable for a wide variety of military and civil applications, including passenger, troop and freight transport, with internal or external freight loads, rescue and anti-submarine duties. The prototype, built for the Italian Air Force, flew for the first time on 19 October 1964, and two further prototypes have since been built.

Agusta is developing a civil transport version known as the A 101H. This aircraft is described separately.

TYPE: Three-engined multi-purpose helicopter.

ROTOR SYSTEM: Single main rotor and tail rotor. Five-blade fully-articulated main rotor; blades of NACA 0012 section, fitted with lag and flapping hinges. Six-blade anti-torque rotor on port side of fin. All blades are of aluminium alloy bonded construction, attached to steel hubs by aluminium alloy grips. Rotor brake fitted to main rotor.

ROTOR DRIVE: Transmission from all three engines via main, intermediate and 90° tail rotor gearboxes. Main rotor/engine rpm ratio 1 : 32·6. Tail rotor/engine rpm ratio 1 : 6·92.

FUSELAGE: Pod-and-boom structure of aluminium alloy semi-monocoque construction.

TAIL UNIT: Vertical fin and strut-braced starboard horizontal stabiliser carried at extreme rear of tail-boom. Structure of aluminium alloy.

LANDING GEAR: Non-retractable tricycle type, with Magnaghi shock-absorbers. Single Goodyear main wheels, size 9·50 × 16, and twin self-centering nose-wheels, size 24 × 7·7. Pressure 85·3 lb/sq in (6·0 kg/cm²) on all tyres.

Agusta A 101G medium-size general-purpose helicopter (three 1,400 shp Rolls-Royce Bristol Gnome H.1400 turboshaft engines)

Magnaghi hydraulic disc brakes fitted on rear wheels.

Power Plant: Three 1,400 shp Rolls-Royce Bristol Gnome H.1400 turboshaft engines (max cont rating 1,250 shp), mounted above main cabin. Fuel in three tanks, in fairings on fuselage sides, with total capacity of 440 Imp gallons (2,000 litres). Three refuelling points. Oil capacity 15·39 Imp gallons (70 litres).

Accommodation: Crew of two on flight deck, access to which is provided by a forward-opening car-type door on each side. Main cabin can accommodate up to 36 passengers or paratroops, 18 stretcher patients and 5 attendants, or up to 11,025 lb (5,000 kg) of freight. Access to main cabin is by sliding door on each side, or via a rear loading ramp which can be left open in flight. Bulky freight can be carried externally on an under-fuselage hook. Cabin can be heated by warm air from engines.

Systems: Dual hydraulic systems; primary system (pressure 2,500 lb/sq in = 175 kg/cm^2) for flight controls and secondary system (pressure 3,000 lb/sq in = 210 kg/cm^2) for brakes and rear ramp operation. 28V DC electrical system includes two batteries and two generators.

Electronics and Equipment: Fully equipped for both VFR and IFR flying. Provision for installing autopilot and autostabilisation equipment. External cargo sling or other operational equipment according to role.

Dimensions, external:
Diameter of main rotor 66 ft 11¼ in (20·40 m)
Main rotor blade chord (constant, each) 1 ft 9 in (0·533 m)
Diameter of tail rotor 13 ft 1½ in (4·00 m)
Distance between rotor centres 40 ft 8 in (12·40 m)
Length of fuselage (including tail rotor) 66 ft 3 in (20·19 m)
Width, rotors folded 15 ft 2¾ in (4·64 m)
Height to top of rotor head 21 ft 6¼ in (6·56 m)

Dimensions, internal:
Cabin: Length 20 ft 4 in (6·20 m)
Max width 8 ft 2 in (2·50 m)
Max height 6 ft 6 in (1·98 m)

Weights:
Weight empty 15,100 lb (6,850 kg)
Normal T-O weight 27,340 lb (12,400 kg)
Max T-O weight 28,440 lb (12,900 kg)

Performance (A = AUW of 23,150 lb = 10,500 kg; B = AUW of 25,350 lb = 11,500 kg; C = AUW of 27,560 lb = 12,500 kg; D = max T-O weight):
Max level speed at S/L:
A 130 knots (150 mph; 241 km/h)
B 126 knots (145 mph; 233 km/h)
C 122 knots (140 mph; 225 km/h)
D 117 knots (135 mph; 217 km/h)
Max cruising speed:
A 117 knots (135 mph; 217 km/h)
B, C 113 knots (130 mph; 209 km/h)
D 109 knots (125 mph; 201 km/h)
Max rate of climb at S/L:
A 2,860 ft (872 m)/min
B 2,420 ft (738 m)/min
C 2,070 ft (631 m)/min
D 1,910 ft (582 m)/min
Service ceiling:
A 15,090 ft (4,600 m)
B 12,960 ft (3,950 m)
C 10,660 ft (3,250 m)
D 9,680 ft (2,950 m)
Hovering ceiling in ground effect:
A 11,320 ft (3,450 m)
B 8,530 ft (2,600 m)
C 5,740 ft (1,750 m)
D 4,600 ft (1,400 m)
Hovering ceiling out of ground effect:
A 9,190 ft (2,800 m)
B 6,070 ft (1,850 m)
C 3,280 ft (1,000 m)
D 1,970 ft (600 m)
Range:
A 217 nm (250 miles; 402 km)
B 212 nm (245 miles; 394 km)
C 208 nm (240 miles; 386 km)
D 204 nm (235 miles; 378 km)

AGUSTA A 101H

The Agusta A 101H is a projected version of the A 101G, designed for passenger and cargo transport duties. The main cabin can accommodate up to 36 passengers, in four-abreast seating, and their baggage; or 24 stretchers if used as an ambulance. The crew consists of two pilots and a cabin steward.

Power plant of the A 101H would be three Rolls-Royce Bristol Gnome H.1800 turboshaft engines, giving 1,750 hp each for take-off and having a max combined continuous power rating of 4,000 hp. Alternatively, three General Electric T58-16 turboshaft engines (each 1,870 hp) may be installed. Dimensions, weights and performance data and a three-view drawing appeared in the 1969-70 *Jane's*.

AGUSTA A 106

The A 106 light turbine-powered helicopter is a high-performance single-seat aircraft, particularly suitable for armed operation. It was designed originally for ASW attack duties, carrying two Mk 44 torpedoes and equipment for contact identification.

Comprehensive instrumentation and electronic equipment make possible operation of the A 106 in reduced visibility conditions.

Design of the A 106 began in July 1965, and a prototype was flown for the first time in November 1965. Development of the aircraft for Army roles was being studied in 1970.

Production of the proposed A 106B version, described in the 1969-70 *Jane's*, is no longer contemplated.

Type: Single-seat light helicopter.

Rotor System: Two-blade teetering main rotor, with stabiliser bar. Blade section NACA 0015. Two-blade tail rotor. Both main and tail rotor blades are of aluminium alloy bonded construction, and each is attached to its steel hub by means of an aluminium alloy grip. For stowage, main rotor blades fold rearward about drag hinges, and steel-tube support structure for tail rotor folds forward over tail-boom. Rotor brake fitted. Tab on each main rotor blade, near tip.

Rotor Drive: Rotors driven through steel shafting. Primary gearbox for main rotor, 90° gearbox for tail rotor. Main rotor/engine rpm ratio 1 : 6·72. Tail rotor engine/rpm ratio 1 : 1.

Fuselage: Conventional stressed-skin semi-monocoque structure of aluminium alloy. Front section forms the cabin and fuel tank bays. Rear section is a tapered monocoque boom of sandwich construction, at the rear of which is a steel-tube structure which supports the tail rotor.

Tail Surfaces: Elevator, of inverted aerofoil section, on each side of tail-boom at rear. Fixed vertical surfaces above and below tail rotor support strut.

Landing Gear: Fixed tubular skid-type, with removable ground manoeuvring wheels. Provision for auxiliary flotation gear to be installed.

Power Plant: One Turboméca-Agusta TAA 230 turboshaft engine, derated to 330 hp for T-O and a max continuous rating of 280 hp. Fuel in two main tanks, one in each side of forward fuselage aft of cabin, with total capacity of 44 Imp gallons (200 litres). Provision for external auxiliary tank on each side of front fuselage, aft of cabin, raising total capacity to 132 Imp gallons (600 litres). Refuelling point on each side aft of cabin. Oil capacity 2·2 Imp gallons (10 litres).

Accommodation: Single seat for pilot in fully-enclosed cabin, with forward-hinged car-type door on each side.

Systems: Hydraulic system, pressure 430 lb/sq in (30·2 kg/cm^2), for flight controls. Electrical system includes one starter-generator and one 28V DC battery.

Electronics and Equipment: Operational equipment includes Julie active acoustic echo ranging, and provision for two Mk 44 homing torpedoes on carrier beneath rear part of forward fuselage.

Dimensions, external:
Diameter of main rotor 31 ft 2 in (9·50 m)
Main rotor blade chord (constant, each) 11 in (27·94 cm)
Diameter of tail rotor 4 ft 7 in (1·40 m)
Distance between rotor centres 18 ft 1¼ in (5·525 m)
Length overall, rotors turning 36 ft 0 in (10·975 m)
Length of fuselage, tail rotor turning 28 ft 6½ in (8·70 m)
Width, rotors folded 6 ft 2 in (1·88 m)
Height to top of rotor hub 8 ft 2½ in (2·50 m)
Elevator span 6 ft 6¼ in (1·99 m)
Width over skids 6 ft 2 in (1·88 m)

Areas:
Main rotor blades (each) 14·28 sq ft (1·327 m^2)
Tail rotor blades (each) 1·02 sq ft (0·095 m^2)
Main rotor disc 762·95 sq ft (70·88 m^2)
Tail rotor disc 16·54 sq ft (1·537 m^2)

Weights:
Weight empty (standard) 1,300 lb (590 kg)
Weight empty, with instruments and electronic equipment 1,520 lb (690 kg)
Normal T-O weight 2,954 lb (1,340 kg)
Max T-O weight 3,086 lb (1,400 kg)

Performance (at AUW of 2,954 lb = 1,340 kg):
Max level speed at S/L 96 knots (110 mph; 177 km/h)
Max cruising speed at S/L 91 knots (105 mph; 169 km/h)
Max rate of climb at S/L 1,230 ft (375 m)/min
Hovering ceiling in ground effect 8,350 ft (2,545 m)
Hovering ceiling out of ground effect 3,700 ft (1,127 m)
Range, max internal fuel at S/L 134 nm (155 miles; 249 km)
Range, max internal and external fuel at S/L 399 nm (460 miles; 740 km)
Max endurance at S/L, internal fuel 1 hr 40 min
Max endurance at S/L, with external tanks 4 hr 30 min

AGUSTA A 109C

This twin-engined helicopter is a development of the single-engined A 109 design of which details were given in the 1966-67 *Jane's*. It is intended to accommodate a pilot and seven passengers in its basic form, with a large luggage compartment at the rear of the fuselage. Alternatively, it can be adapted for freight-carrying, or as an ambulance.

A prototype is under construction, and is scheduled to fly in late 1970/early 1971.

Type: Twin-engined general-purpose helicopter.

Rotor System and Drive: Fully-articulated four-blade single main rotor and two-blade semi-rigid delta-hinged tail rotor. Main transmission assembly is housed in fairing above the passenger cabin, driving the main rotor through a coupling gearbox and main reduction gearbox, and the tail rotor through a 90° gearbox. Main rotor/engine rpm ratio 1 : 15·64. Tail rotor/engine rpm ratio 1 : 1·02.

Fuselage and Tail Unit: Pod-and-boom type, of all-metal construction, built in four main sections: nose, cockpit, passenger cabin and tail-boom. Sweptback vertical fin and non-swept elevators mounted on rear of tail-boom. Tail rotor on port side.

Landing Gear: Retractable tricycle type, with single main wheels and self-centering steerable nose-wheel. Hydraulic retraction, nose-wheel forward, main wheels upward into fuselage. Brakes on main wheels, locking mechanism on nose-wheel. All wheels size 5·00 × 5.

Power Plant: Two 400 shp Allison 250-C20 turboshaft engines (max cont rating 346 shp), mounted side-by-side in upper rear fuselage and separated from passenger cabin and from each other by firewalls. Fuel in single main tank in lower rear fuselage, capacity 121 Imp gallons (550 litres). Oil capacity 1·2 Imp gallons (5·5 litres) for each engine and 1·6 Imp gallons (7·5 litres) for transmission.

Accommodation: Crew of one or two on flight deck, which has access door on each side. Dual controls. Main cabin seats up to six passengers, in two rows of three, with large space at rear for baggage. A seventh passenger can be carried in lieu of second crew member. Passenger door on each side. First row of seats removable to permit use as freight transport. Ambulance version can accommodate two stretchers and

Agusta A 106 light anti-submarine helicopter, in Italian Navy insignia

two medical attendants, in addition to the pilot, when the forward cabin bulkhead is removed. Cabin heating and ventilation standard.

SYSTEMS: Primary hydraulic system for landing gear operation, wheel and rotor braking and nose-wheel locking. Secondary hydraulic system provides for flight servo-controls. 28V DC electrical system, using two 150A starter-generators and one 28V 23Ah battery. 115V 400 c/s AC power supplied by 250VA static inverter.

EQUIPMENT: Standard flight instrumentation, VHF transceiver and ADF. Additional instrumentation and equipment to customer's requirements.

DIMENSIONS, EXTERNAL:
Diameter of main rotor	36 ft 1 in (11·00 m)
Diameter of tail rotor	6 ft 6¾ in (2·00 m)
Length of fuselage, tail rotor turning	36 ft 0½ in (10·99 m)
Height to top of rotor hub	9 ft 6 in (2·90 m)
Width over main wheels	8 ft 0½ in (2·45 m)
Passenger doors (each):	
Width	3 ft 7 in (1·10 m)

DIMENSIONS, INTERNAL:
Cabin, excluding flight deck:
Length	5 ft 3¾ in (1·62 m)
Width	4 ft 5½ in (1·36 m)
Height	4 ft 2½ in (1·28 m)
Volume	approx 100 cu ft (2·82 m³)
Baggage compartment:	
Volume	approx 18 cu ft (0·52 m³)

WEIGHTS:
Weight empty	2,535 lb (1,150 kg)
Design max T-O weight	5,070 lb (2,300 kg)

PERFORMANCE (estimated, at 4,850 lb = 2,200 kg AUW, ISA):
Max level speed at S/L
  149·5 knots (172 mph; 277 km/h)
Max level speed at 6,560 ft (2,000 m)
  148·5 knots (171 mph; 275 km/h)
Econ cruising speed at S/L
  120·5 knots (139 mph; 223 km/h)
Rate of climb at S/L 2,060 ft (630 m)/min
Rate of climb at S/L, one engine out
  460 ft (138 m)/min
Service ceiling 17,400 ft (5,300 m)
Service ceiling, one engine out
  8,850 ft (2,700 m)
Hovering ceiling in ground effect
  11,810 ft (3,600 m)
Hovering ceiling out of ground effect
  9,190 ft (2,800 m)
Max range at S/L 337 nm (388 miles; 625 km)
Max range at 6,560 ft (2,000 m)
  397 nm (457 miles; 735 km)
Max endurance at S/L 3 hr 28 min

AGUSTA-BELL MODEL 47 SERIES

Latest versions of the Bell Model 47 in production by Agusta include the standard Models 47G-3B-1 and -3B-2, 47G-4A, 47J-2A and 47G-5. In addition, Agusta is building two special variants of its own design, derived from the series 47J, designated 47J-3 and 47J-3B-1.

The 47J-3 differs from the standard 47J-2A in having a modified main transmission able to absorb greater power input, i e 270 hp for take-off and a max continuous output of 260 hp, in lieu of the normal 260 hp and 220 hp respectively. Performance remains similar to that of the 47J-2A, as described under the Bell entry in the US section of the 1966-67 *Jane's*.

A special ASW version of the 47J-3 was evolved for the Italian Navy, for operation from the decks of ships. This version has instrumentation for over-sea operation in reduced visibility, and a high-efficiency rotor brake. Its armament comprises one Mk 44 torpedo.

The 47J-3B-1 is a high-altitude four-seat helicopter, powered by a Lycoming TVO-435-B1A engine, rated at 270 hp for take-off and 220 hp for continuous operation. The engine is equipped with an exhaust-driven supercharger, fitted with an automatic control which maintains sea level conditions up to at least 14,000 ft (4,300 m). The 47J-3B-1 also has a high-inertia rotor and servo-control on both the cyclic and collective pitch control systems.

All versions can be fitted with the full range of optional equipment offered by Bell, including pontoons, litters, etc. A total of more than 1,000 had been built in Italy by the end of 1967 and production continues.

WEIGHTS:
Weight empty:
47J-3	1,819 lb (825 kg)
47J-3B-1	1,863 lb (845 kg)
Max T-O weight:	
47J-3 and 3B-1	2,950 lb (1,340 kg)

PERFORMANCE (47J-3B-1, at max T-O weight):
Max level speed at S/L
  91 knots (105 mph; 169 km/h)
Normal cruising speed at 5,000 ft (1,525 m)
  75 knots (86 mph; 138 km/h)
Max rate of climb at S/L 905 ft (276 m)/min
Max rate of climb at 14,000 ft (4,300 m)
  785 ft (240 m)/min
Service ceiling 17,500 ft (5,340 m)
Hovering ceiling in ground effect
  16,500 ft (5,030 m)

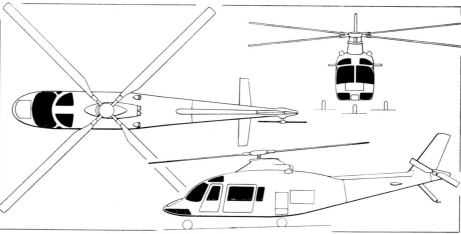

Agusta A 109C high-performance eight-seat helicopter

Agusta-Bell 47J-3B-1 (270 hp Lycoming TVO-435-B1A engine)

Hovering ceiling out of ground effect
  12,200 ft (3,720 m)
Range with max fuel at 5,000 ft (1,525 m), no reserves 182 nm (210 miles; 338 km)
Max endurance at 5,000 ft (1,525 m), no reserves 3 hr 30 min

AGUSTA-BELL 204B

The Agusta-Bell 204B is a medium-size utility helicopter, similar to the Bell UH-1B Iroquois. Since 1961 some hundreds have been built for the armed services of Italy, Spain, Sweden, Holland, Austria, Turkey and Saudi Arabia, and for commercial operators in Italy, Norway, Sweden, Switzerland and Lebanon. Versions of the AB 204B have been built with 44 ft (13·41 m) and 48 ft (14·63 m) main rotors and with Bristol Siddeley Gnome, Lycoming T53 and General Electric T58 shaft-turbine engines.

Current production machines have a 48 ft main rotor and are powered by a 1,100 shp Lycoming T53-11A turboshaft engine or, on request, by a Rolls-Royce (Bristol Division) Gnome H.1200 or a General Electric T58-GE-3.

Agusta has designed and built a special version of the AB 204B for ASW operation. This carries dipping sonar gear and special electronic equipment for automatic stabilisation and automatic approach to hovering, in addition to all-weather flight instrumentation. The AB 204B ASW helicopter has been designed for individual or dual-rôle search and attack missions. The armament consists of two Mk 44 torpedoes. It is in service with both the Italian and Spanish navies.

The AB 204B can be equipped with a hoist, external auxiliary fuel tanks and emergency flotation gear.

The following data apply to the standard AB 204B, with 48 ft main rotor, Lycoming T53-11A engine and 242 US gal (916 litre) fuel tanks.

WEIGHTS:
Weight empty (standard)	4,600 lb (2,090 kg)
Normal T-O weight	8,500 lb (3,860 kg)
Max T-O weight with external cargo	9,500 lb (4,310 kg)

PERFORMANCE (at AUW of 8,500 lb = 3,860 kg):
Max level speed at S/L
  104 knots (120 mph; 193 km/h)
Cruising speed 96 knots (110 mph; 177 km/h)
Max rate of climb at S/L 1,400 ft (427 m)/min
Hovering ceiling in ground effect
  10,000 ft (3,050 m)
Hovering ceiling out of ground effect
  4,500 ft (1,370 m)
Max range, no reserve
  340 nm (392 miles; 630 km)
Max endurance, no reserve 4 hr

Agusta-Bell 204B anti-submarine helicopter of the Italian Navy

AGUSTA-BELL 205 and 205A-1

The Agusta-Bell Model 205 is a multi-purpose utility helicopter, corresponding to the UH-1D/UH-1H versions adopted by the US armed forces. It can be used to transport passengers, equipment and troops, or for casualty evacuation, tactical support, rescue or other missions. Various special installations such as litters, floats, snow skids, armament or a rescue hoist can be fitted according to role. The cabin will accommodate a pilot and 14 passengers, and has a clear volume of 220 cu ft (6·2 m³) when stripped for cargo carrying. The AB 205 is fitted with IFR and night flying instruments, and for normal operation only one pilot is carried.

Several hundred AB 205's have been built, the latest production version having a Lycoming T53-L-13 turboshaft engine, developing a maximum of 1,400 hp for take-off.

The AB 205 is in service with the Italian armed forces and with those of Iran, Kuwait, Morocco, Saudi Arabia, Spain, Turkey, Zambia and other countries.

In 1969 Agusta began production of a developed version known as the **AB 205A-1**, certificated for commercial and passenger transport operation. The Agusta-Bell 205A-1 can accommodate up to 14 passengers and has a 28·3 cu ft (0·8 m³) luggage compartment in the tail boom. A wide variety of equipment can be fitted to fulfil a number of other roles. Power plant is a 1,400 shp Lycoming T53-L-13A turboshaft engine, derated to 1,250 shp for take-off.

DIMENSIONS, EXTERNAL:

Main rotor diameter	48 ft 0 in (14·63 m)
Tail rotor diameter	8 ft 6 in (2·59 m)
Fuselage length	41 ft 11 in (12·78 m)
Width overall	9 ft 0½ in (2·76 m)
Height overall	14 ft 8 in (4·48 m)

WEIGHTS (AB 205):

Weight empty (standard)	4,800 lb (2,177 kg)
Normal T-O weight	8,500 lb (3,860 kg)
Max T-O weight	9,500 lb (4,310 kg)

WEIGHTS (AB 205A-1):

Weight empty (standard)	5,195 lb (2,356 kg)
Max T-O weight (FAA cert):	
internal load	9,500 lb (4,309 kg)
external load	10,500 lb (4,762 kg)

PERFORMANCE (AB 205 at AUW of 8,500 lb = 3,860 kg, with T53-L-13 engine):

Max level speed at S/L	120 knots (138 mph; 222 km/h)
Cruising speed	115 knots (132 mph; 212 km/h)
Max rate of climb at S/L	1,800 ft (548 m)/min
Hovering ceiling in ground effect	17,000 ft (5,180 m)
Hovering ceiling out of ground effect	11,000 ft (3,350 m)
Max range, standard tanks, no reserves	312 nm (360 miles; 580 km)
Max endurance, standard tanks, no reserves	3 hr 48 min

PERFORMANCE (AB 205A-1, at max T-O weight with internal load):

Max level speed	120 knots (138 mph; 222 km/h)
Max cruising speed	109 knots (126 mph; 203 km/h)
Max rate of climb at S/L	2,030 ft (619 m)/min
Hovering ceiling in ground effect	11,000 ft (3,355 m)
Hovering ceiling out of ground effect	6,800 ft (2,075 m)
Max range, standard tanks, no reserve	287 nm (331 miles; 532 km)
Max endurance, standard tanks, no reserve	3 hr 18 min

AGUSTA-BELL 206A JETRANGER

The Agusta-Bell 206A JetRanger, manufactured under licence from Bell, is a turbine-powered high-performance helicopter, particularly suitable for light transport duties. Sixty are being built for the Italian Air Force, a further 50 for the Turkish Army and police force, and substantial orders have been placed by other military and commercial operators, including the armed forces of Austria, Iran, Saudi Arabia and Sweden.

The cabin can accommodate four persons in addition to the pilot; the luggage compartment has a capacity of 250 lb (113 kg) and a usable volume of 16 cu ft (0·45 m³).

The Agusta-Bell 206A is powered by an Allison 250-C18 turboshaft engine, with a T-O rating of 317 shp and max continuous rating of 270 shp.

Agusta is also building, for the Italian Army, substantial numbers of a developed version known as the **AB 206A-1**. Basically similar to the OH-58A Kiowa US model, this has a larger-diameter main rotor, main transmission with a different reduction ratio, and other minor changes. The fuel tank is of the self-sealing type and has a capacity of 73 US gallons (61 Imp gallons = 276 litres). The present production version of the AB 206A-1, described below, has an Allison 250-C18 engine, but installation of the more powerful Allison 250-C20 engine in later aircraft is being considered.

Agusta-Bell 205 multi-purpose helicopter in the insignia of the Royal Saudi Air Force

Civil passenger version of the Agusta-Bell 205A-1 fourteen-seat helicopter (*Stephen P. Peltz*)

DIMENSIONS, EXTERNAL (AB 206A-1):
As AB 206A, except:

Main rotor diameter	35 ft 4 in (10·77 m)
Length overall, rotors turning	40 ft 11¾ in (12·49 m)
Length of fuselage	32 ft 3½ in (9·84 m)

WEIGHTS:

Weight empty, standard	
206A	1,431 lb (649 kg)
206A-1	1,520 lb (690 kg)
Max T-O weight:	
206A (civil, internal load) and 206A-1	3,000 lb (1,361 kg)
206A (civil, underslung load, and military)	3,350 lb (1,520 kg)

PERFORMANCE (Allison 250-C18 engine at AUW of 2,600 lb = 1,180 kg, ISA):

Max level speed at S/L:	
206A, 206A-1	130 knots (150 mph; 241 km/h)
Cruising speed:	
206A	119 knots (137 mph; 220 km/h)
206A-1	116 knots (134 mph; 215 km/h)
Max rate of climb at S/L:	
206A	2,010 ft (613 m)/min
206A-1	1,930 ft (588 m)/min
Hovering ceiling in ground effect:	
206A	13,800 ft (4,200 m)
206A-1	15,500 ft (4,720 m)
Hovering ceiling out of ground effect:	
206A	8,500 ft (2,590 m)
206A-1	10,800 ft (3,290 m)
Max range, standard tank, no reserve:	
206A	356 nm (410 miles; 660 km)
206A-1	330 nm (381 miles; 613 km)
Max endurance, standard tank, no reserve:	
206A	4 hr 24 min
206A-1	4 hr 40 min

PERFORMANCE (AB 206A-1, estimated with Allison 250-C20 engine at AUW of 2,600 lb = 1,180 kg, ISA):
As above, except:

Hovering ceiling in ground effect	18,000 ft (5,490 m)

Agusta-Bell 206A JetRanger turbine-powered light helicopter in Swedish Police Force insignia

Agusta-Sikorsky SH-3D Sea King anti-submarine helicopter in the insignia of the Italian Navy

Hovering ceiling out of ground effect
14,000 ft (4,270 m)
Max range, standard tank, no reserve
352 nm (406 miles; 648 km)
Max endurance, standard tank, no reserve
4 hr 18 min

AGUSTA-BELL 212

The Agusta-Bell Model 212 medium-sized twin-engined transport helicopter is basically similar, except for its power plant, to the AB 205A-1, having the same seating capacity and a similar variety of applications.

Power plant is the UACL PT6T-3 Turbo Twin Pac, consisting of two turbine engines mounted side-by-side above the cabin and having a common reduction gearbox. This unit has a max rating of 1,800 hp, but is derated in the AB 212 to 1,250 shp for T-O and a max cont rating of 1,100 shp. Fuel capacity 225 US gallons (187 Imp gallons = 850 litres).

Standard accommodation is for a pilot and up to 14 passengers, but the helicopter is readily adaptable to alternative roles, including VIP transport, freighter, aerial crane, ambulance and rescue.

DIMENSIONS, EXTERNAL:
Diameter of main rotor   48 ft 0 in (14·63 m)
Diameter of tail rotor   8 ft 6 in (2·59 m)
Length overall, rotors turning
57 ft 1½ in (17·41 m)
Fuselage length   46 ft 1¼ in (14·05 m)
Height to top of cabin roof   7 ft 8 in (2·34 m)
Height overall   14 ft 4¾ in (4·39 m)
Elevator span   9 ft 4 in (2·84 m)
Width over skids   8 ft 8 in (2·64 m)
WEIGHTS:
Weight empty (standard)   5,560 lb (2,522 kg)

Max T-O weight (FAR 29)   10,000 lb (4,536 kg)
Max T-O weight (FAR 133) 10,500 lb (4,763 kg)
PERFORMANCE (at 10,000 lb = 4,536 kg AUW, ISA):
Cruising speed at S/L
105 knots (121 mph; 195 km/h)
Max rate of climb at S/L   1,457 ft (444 m)/min
Max vertical rate of climb at S/L
787 ft (240 m)/min
Service ceiling   12,150 ft (3,700 m)
Hovering ceiling in ground effect
12,150 ft (3,700 m)
Hovering ceiling out of ground effect
9,900 ft (3,020 m)
Max range at S/L with standard tanks, no reserve:
on two engines   253 nm (292 miles; 470 km)
on one engine   296 nm (341 miles; 550 km)
Max range at 5,000 ft (1,524 m), with standard tanks, no reserve:
on two engines   258 nm (298 miles; 480 km)

AGUSTA-SIKORSKY SH-3D SEA KING

During 1967, Agusta began the construction under licence of 24 Sikorsky SH-3D Sea King anti-submarine helicopters for the Italian Navy. Manufacture of the S-61N civil transport helicopter is being considered.

Full details of the SH-3D and S-61N can be found under the Sikorsky heading in the US section of this edition.

AGUSTA A 120B

The Agusta A 120B is a project for a high-speed medium-range compound transport helicopter, powered by three General Electric T64-GE-12 turboshaft engines, each with a max rating of 3,435 hp. Two of these are installed in pylon-mounted nacelles beneath the high-mounted

wings, driving the five-blade main rotor, and each also drives a four-blade tractor propeller through a supplementary gearbox. The third engine, installed on top of the fuselage, has direct drive to the main transmission. A retractable tricycle landing gear is fitted, each main unit consisting of two wheels in tandem.

The entire accommodation, including flight deck, is pressurised, and a flight crew of two is carried, plus two cabin stewards. Main cabin can accommodate 65 passengers and their baggage.

Dimensions, weights and performance data were given in the 1969-70 *Jane's*.

AGUSTA A 123

The Agusta A 123 is a project for a medium-sized compound helicopter, powered by two Lycoming T53 turboshaft engines, each with a max rating of 1,800 hp; these are mounted side-by-side on top of the fuselage and drive four-blade main and tail rotors and a four-blade pusher propeller at the extreme rear of the aircraft. The helicopter is fitted with high-mounted wings, to off-load the main rotor during cruising flight, and has a fully retractable tricycle landing gear.

The main cabin has standard accommodation for 14-17 passengers, with a spacious baggage compartment, or for six stretchers and three sitting casualties when used as an ambulance. A flight crew of two is carried. The A 123 is also suitable for use as an armed helicopter, or as a military transport or freighter. An external load of up to 8,300 lb (3,765 kg) can be carried on an under-fuselage cargo hook.

Dimensions, weights and performance data were given in the 1969-70 *Jane's*.

AMBROSINI

SOCIETÀ AERONAUTICA ITALIANA ING A. AMBROSINI & C

HEAD OFFICE:
Viale Castro Pretorio 25, Rome
COMMERCIAL OFFICE:
Viale Maino 23, Milan
WORKS:
Passignano sul Trasimeno
AIRPORT:
Castiglione del Lago
PRESIDENT:
Ing Angelo Ambrosini
TECHNICAL DIRECTOR:
Dr Ing Goffredo Buglione
COMMERCIAL MANAGER:
Albino Carmine
WORKS MANAGER:
p.i. Emilio Mariotti
TECHNICAL MANAGER:
Dr Ing Camillo Silva
ADMINISTRATIVE MANAGER:
Silvio Spaccapelo

The Società Aeronautica Italiana was incorporated into the Ambrosini group in 1934. Since that time it has designed and built a number of touring and training aircraft, as well as the pre-war S.A.I.7 series of lightweight racing and fighter-trainer monoplanes and the post-war

S.7 and Super S.7. It was also responsible for the Sagittario experimental lightweight jet fighter, the first Italian-designed aircraft to exceed the speed of sound.

Ambrosini has acquired from Procaer the prototype of the F15E Picchio four-seat light aircraft designed by Ing Stelio Frati, and is completing the flight testing and certification of this aircraft, under the designation NF 15, with a view to eventual production. The company has also received RAI type approval for the four-seat NF 409, all available details of which are given below, and is working on the design of a new STOL aircraft known as the AS 408. Manufacture of the Aero Subaru light aircraft, under licence from Fuji of Japan, is under consideration.

AMBROSINI NF 15

This is the former F15E version of the Picchio aerobatic light aircraft, designed by Ing Stelio Frati and described and illustrated under the Procaer heading in the 1969-70 edition of *Jane's*.

The NF 15 prototype (I-PROM) flew for the first time on 16 December 1968. It was subsequently acquired by Ambrosini, which is carrying out final flight testing prior to certification and production. The structural description below applies to this prototype; the dimensions, weights and performance data are for the production version.

TYPE: Four-seat light monoplane.

WINGS: Cantilever low-wing monoplane. NACA 64·215/64·210 wing sections. Dihedral 6°. Incidence 4°. One-piece wood structure with single main spar, rear spar carrying aileron and flap hinges, and short front spar to carry landing gear loads. Plywood covering, with outer skin of thin aluminium sheet bonded on to the plywood. All-metal Frise ailerons and Fowler flaps.

FUSELAGE: Semi-monocoque wood structure with plywood covering and outer skin of thin aluminium sheet bonded on to the plywood.

TAIL UNIT: Cantilever type. Fixed surfaces have wood structure with plywood covering and outer skin of aluminium sheet bonded to the plywood. All-metal control surfaces. Trim-tab on elevator.

LANDING GEAR: Retractable tricycle type. Electro-mechanical retraction. Oleo-pneumatic shock-absorbers. Main wheels size 6·00 × 6. Steerable nose-wheel size 5·00 × 5. Hydraulic disc brakes.

POWER PLANT: One 300 hp Continental IO-520-F six-cylinder horizontally-opposed air-cooled engine, driving a two-blade constant-speed metal propeller. Fuel in two tanks in wings, and two wing-tip tanks, giving a total capacity of 70·8 Imp gallons (322 litres). Oil capacity 2·5 Imp gallons (11·5 litres).

ACCOMMODATION: Four persons in pairs in enclosed cabin. One forward-opening door on starboard side. Space for 88 lb (40 kg) of baggage behind rear bench seat.

ELECTRONICS AND EQUIPMENT: Blind-flying instruments and radio optional.

DIMENSIONS, EXTERNAL:

Wing span over tip-tanks	32 ft 5¾ in (9·90 m)
Wing chord at root	5 ft 8 in (1·72 m)
Wing chord at tip	2 ft 9 in (0·85 m)
Wing aspect ratio	7·37
Length overall	24 ft 7¼ in (7·50 m)
Height overall	9 ft 2½ in (2·80 m)
Tailplane span	11 ft 8 in (3·55 m)
Wheel track	9 ft 1¼ in (2·78 m)
Wheelbase	5 ft 8½ in (1·73 m)

DIMENSIONS, INTERNAL:

Cabin: Length	9 ft 0 in (2·75 m)
Max width	3 ft 11¼ in (1·20 m)
Max height	4 ft 5¼ in (1·35 m)

AREAS:

Wings, gross	143·2 sq ft (13·30 m²)
Ailerons (total)	12·81 sq ft (1·19 m²)
Flaps (total)	18·50 sq ft (1·72 m²)
Fin	9·50 sq ft (0·88 m²)
Rudder	5·27 sq ft (0·49 m²)
Tailplane	17·97 sq ft (1·67 m²)
Elevators, incl tab	13·67 sq ft (1·27 m²)

WEIGHTS:

Basic weight empty	1,856 lb (842 kg)
Weight empty, equipped	1,948 lb (884 kg)
Max T-O weight	2,998 lb (1,360 kg)

Procaer-built prototype of the Ambrosini NF 15 four-seat light aircraft

PERFORMANCE (at max T-O weight):

Max level speed at S/L
186 knots (214 mph; 345 km/h)

Max cruising speed (75% power) at 5,500 ft (1,675 m) 175 knots (202 mph; 325 km/h)

Econ cruising speed (65% power) at 10,000 ft (3,050 m) 168 knots (194 mph; 312 km/h)

Rate of climb at S/L 1,558 ft (475 m)/min

T-O to 50 ft (15 m) 1,345 ft (410 m)

Landing run 1,476 ft (450 m)

Max range at max cruising speed
798 nm (919 miles; 1,480 km)

Max range at econ cruising speed
1,067 nm (1,229 miles; 1,979 km)

AMBROSINI NF 409

The Ambrosini NF 409, which received RAI type approval early in 1970, is a four-seat all-metal light aircraft, designed by Ing Stelio Frati and powered by a 280 hp Continental six-cylinder horizontally-opposed air-cooled engine. Construction of the prototype was initiated by Procaer, but production aircraft are to be built by Ambrosini.

The NF 409 is slightly larger than the NF 15, but no additional details had been received at the time of closing for press.

BUCCIERO

RENATO BUCCIERO

ADDRESS:

via Giovanni Prati 7-B2, Rome

Captain Bucciero, an airline pilot with Alitalia, designed a two-seat all-metal light training and touring aircraft known as the SVIT (Studio per un Velivolo da Istruzione e Turismo), which was built with the assistance of Mr Gastone Canal, an Alitalia engineer.

BUCCIERO SVIT

Design of the SVIT was started in January 1966, and construction began on 1 July 1966. This aircraft (I-FANI) flew for the first time on 2 July 1968, and was certificated by the RAI in the FAR 23 Utility category in April 1969. Initially, the SVIT was fitted with an 85 hp Continental C85 piston-engine, and this version was described in the 1969-70 *Jane's*.

In April 1969 it was refitted with a 100 hp Continental O-200-A engine, with which it began further certification flights. These were interrupted due to an oil leakage, and the prototype has not yet been certificated with the 100 hp engine. The description below applies to it in this form.

In May 1969 Capt Bucciero began, with the financial help of seven other Alitalia pilots and two flight engineers, to build three examples of a developed version with the 100 hp engine. These are generally similar to the SVIT prototype except for modified landing gear, a sliding cockpit canopy and rounded fuselage top-decking. All three were due to be completed during 1970.

TYPE: Two-seat light training and touring aircraft.

WINGS: Cantilever mid-wing monoplane. Wing section NACA 65_2415 (modified). Thickness/chord ratio 16%. Dihedral 2° 30′ from roots. Incidence 2°. No sweepback. Metal-skinned two-spar torsion-box structure of 2024-T3. Slotted trailing-edge flaps and ailerons of 2024-T3.

FUSELAGE: All-metal (2024-T3) structure, built in four main sections: engine bay, front fuselage, cabin and rear fuselage. Engine bay has a steel-tube basic structure, with cowling panels of non-inflammable plastic. Front fuselage is of steel-tube construction with aluminium alloy covering. Cabin section and rear fuselage are light alloy semi-monocoque structures. Fuselage is of circular section at front, rectangular at rear.

TAIL UNIT: Cantilever all-metal (2024-T3) structure, with all-moving tailplane and full-span anti-tab. Small dorsal fin fairing and auxiliary fin beneath rear fuselage.

LANDING GEAR: Non-retractable tricycle type, with cantilever spring-steel main legs. Nose-wheel unit has steel spring shock-absorption. Same size (5·00-5) wheels and Continental tubeless tyres (pressure 34 lb/sq in = 2·39 kg/cm²) on all units. Hydraulic disc brakes on main wheels. Nose-wheel is steerable.

Bucciero SVIT two-seat aerobatic light aircraft (100 hp Continental O-200-A engine)

POWER PLANT: One 100 hp Continental O-200-A four-cylinder horizontally-opposed air-cooled engine, driving a two-blade McCauley metal propeller, diameter 6 ft 1 in (1·85 m). Fuel tank in each wing, with total capacity of 25·5 Imp gallons (116 litres).

ACCOMMODATION: Side-by-side seating for two persons under transparent Plexiglas canopy, the port half of which hinges upward from the centre-line to give access to the cockpit. Dual controls fitted. Baggage compartment aft of cabin, with door on port side.

SYSTEMS: Hydraulic system for actuation of wheel brakes. 12V electrical system includes 20A generator and 24Ah battery.

EQUIPMENT: Standard cockpit instrumentation for VFR flying.

DIMENSIONS, EXTERNAL:

Wing span	24 ft 7¼ in (7·50 m)
Wing chord (constant)	4 ft 3½ in (1·31 m)
Wing aspect ratio	5·84
Length overall	18 ft 2½ in (5·55 m)
Height overall	7 ft 5¾ in (2·28 m)
Tailplane span	9 ft 5½ in (2·88 m)
Wheel track	6 ft 8¾ in (2·05 m)
Wheelbase	6 ft 11½ in (2·12 m)

AREAS:

Wings, gross	103·76 sq ft (9·64 m²)
Ailerons (total)	9·04 sq ft (0·84 m²)
Trailing-edge flaps (total)	17·22 sq ft (1·60 m²)
Fin	9·15 sq ft (0·85 m²)
Rudder	3·34 sq ft (0·31 m²)
Horizontal tail surfaces (total)	20·45 sq ft (1·90 m²)

WEIGHTS (100 hp engine):

Weight empty	925 lb (420 kg)
Max T-O and landing weight	1,488 lb (675 kg)

PERFORMANCE (at max T-O weight, 100 hp engine):

Max level speed at S/L
109 knots (125 mph; 201 km/h)

Max permissible diving speed
154 knots (177 mph; 286 km/h)

Max cruising speed at 8,200 ft (2,500 m)
95 knots (109 mph; 175 km/h)

Stalling speed, flaps up
37 knots (42 mph; 68 km/h)

Stalling speed, flaps down
32 knots (36 mph; 58 km/h)

Rate of climb at S/L 750 ft (229 m)/min

Service ceiling 13,000 ft (3,962 m)

FIAT
SOCIETÀ PER AZIONI FIAT
HEAD OFFICE:
Corso Giovanni Agnelli 200, Turin
CHAIRMAN:
Dott Gianni Agnelli
VICE-CHAIRMAN AMD MANAGING DIRECTOR:
Dott Ing Gaudenzio Bono
VICE-CHAIRMAN:
Dott Ing Giovanni Nasi
GENERAL MANAGER:
Dott Ing Niccolò Gioia
AVIATION DIVISION DIRECTOR (INTERIM):
Dott Ing Franco Giura
AVIATION DIVISION SALES MANAGER:
Dott Cesare Raffagni
AVIATION DIVISION PUBLIC RELATIONS OFFICER:
Renzo Storace

The Aircraft Section of Fiat's Aviation Division is, with Aerfer (which see), a shareholder in the Aeritalia company formed on 12 November 1969. Aeritalia will become fully operational under the new title in the second half of 1971.

Currently, the sections of the Fiat organisation which are engaged in the design, production and testing of aircraft, aero-engines and electronic equipment are known as:

SEZIONE VELIVOLI (Aircraft Factory)
WORKS: Corso Marche 41, Turin
SEZIONE MOTORI AVIO (Aero-Engine Factory)
WORKS: Via Nizza 312, Turin
OFFICINE DI CASELLE (Caselle Works), including an Aviation Electronics Centre
WORKS: Caselle Torinese
OFFICINE DEL SANGONE (Sangone Works)
WORKS: Strada del Drosso, Turin

The direction and technical and commercial departments of the central organisation co-ordinate the activities of the four above-mentioned establishments, each of which has its own managerial staff.

The company is engaged at the present time on the design, development and production of military aircraft, electronic equipment and components for space vehicles.

Series production of its G91R/T series of light jet ground attack and reconnaissance fighters and operational trainers has been completed (see 1966-67 Jane's) although Dornier is building 22 more G91T/3's for the Luftwaffe. Fiat is building for the Italian Air Force a twin-engined tactical derivative, designated G91Y, and is also prime contractor for the 82 Lockheed F-104S Starfighters ordered for the Italian Air Force, and for the engines to power these aircraft. First F-104S deliveries were made in the Spring of 1969; follow-on production of a further 83 aircraft is planned.

The Italian Ministry of Defence-Air Force has awarded Fiat orders for two prototypes of the G222 military transport.

Fiat is building major components for the three development prototypes of the VAK 191B V/STOL experimental aircraft, under sub-contract to the German company VFW-Fokker (see the German section of this edition).

It is also building for the French Aérospatiale company components of the SE 210 Caravelle twin-jet airliner. In collaboration with the same company, it has designed and is building the main transmission gearbox for the SA 321 Super Frelon and SA 330 Puma helicopters.

Early in 1969 an agreement was concluded whereby Fiat will be responsible for producing rear fuselages and tail units for the French Dassault Mercure twin-jet transport, representing a 10% share by Fiat in the Mercure programme.

Other activities include the continued overhaul and repair of F-104G Starfighter, G91 and F-86 aircraft.

Details of Fiat's aero-engine activities are given in the "Aero-Engines" section.

FIAT G91Y
Announced in the Spring of 1965, the G91Y is a twin-engined development of the earlier single-engined Fiat G91 (see 1966-67 Jane's); its structure is based upon the airframe of the G91T.

Compared with the original G91, the G91Y has approximately 60% greater take-off thrust at the cost of only a relatively small increase in power plant weight. This makes possible a considerable increase in military load and/or fuel. It is possible to cruise with one engine stopped to extend endurance.

The J85-GE-13A engines are interchangeable with the projected J85-J5 version which will develop 2,920 lb (1,325 kg) st dry and 4,300 lb (1,950 kg) st with afterburning, without increase in weight. With two J85-J5's, the take-off distance and time-to-height of the G91Y would be reduced by 5% and the maximum speed increased by approximately 1%. The normal T-O distance can be reduced by approx 50% by the use of JATO rockets, and an under-fuselage arrester hook enables the aircraft to be used in SATS (Short Airfield for Tactical Support) conditions.

Two prototypes of the G91Y were built, of which the first flew for the first time on 27

Fiat-built F-104S Starfighter for the Italian Air Force

December 1966. The second prototype, first flown in September 1967, was completed to full operational standard, including armament and navigational equipment. In the Spring of 1969 work was progressing on the completion of a pre-series batch of 20 G91Y's for the Italian Air Force, the first of which was flown in July 1968. An initial production order for 35 has been placed by the Italian Air Force, and a two-seat advanced and operational training version, designated G91YT, has also been designed.

The details below apply to the production G91Y.

TYPE: Lightweight single-seat tactical fighter-bomber and reconnaissance aircraft.

WINGS: Cantilever low-wing monoplane. Laminar-flow section. Sweepback at quarter-chord 37° 40' 38". All-metal two-spar structure, with milled skin panels and detachable leading-edge. All-metal ailerons with hydraulic servo-control. Electrically-actuated slotted trailing-edge flaps. Automatic full-span leading-edge slats.

FUSELAGE: All-metal semi-monocoque structure. Rear fuselage detachable for engine replacement. Two door-type air-brakes under centre-fuselage.

TAIL UNIT: Cantilever all-metal structure. Electrically-actuated variable-incidence tailplane. Auxiliary fins beneath each side of rear fuselage.

LANDING GEAR: Retractable tricycle type. Hydraulic actuation. Main wheel tyre pressure 57 lb/sq in (4·0 kg/cm²). Hydraulic brakes. Brake-chute housed at base of rudder. Arrester hook under rear fuselage.

POWER PLANT: Two General Electric J85-GE-13A turbojet engines (each 2,720 lb = 1,235 kg st dry, 4,080 lb = 1,850 kg st with afterburning), mounted side-by-side in rear fuselage. Provision for JATO units for assisted take-off. Fuel in main tanks in fuselage and inner wing panels with total capacity of 703 Imp gallons (3,200 litres). Provision for underwing auxiliary tanks.

ACCOMMODATION: Pilot only, on fully-automatic zero-zero ejection seat, under electrically actuated rearward-hinged jettisonable canopy. Cockpit armoured, pressurised and air-conditioned.

ARMAMENT AND OPERATIONAL EQUIPMENT: Two 30 mm DEFA cannon and cameras in nose.

Four underwing attachments for 1,000 lb bombs, 750 lb napalm tanks, 7 × 2 in rocket packs, 28 × 2 in rocket packs or 4 × 5 in rocket containers. Nav/attack system includes Computing Devices of Canada 5C-15 position and homing indicator, Sperry SYP twin-axis gyro platform, Bendix RDA-12 Doppler radar and AiResearch air data computer. Ferranti ISIS B gyro-gunsight, Honeywell AN/APN-171 radar altimeter, Specto head-up display and Marconi AD 370 automatic direction-finding equipment.

DIMENSIONS, EXTERNAL:
Wing span	29 ft 6½ in (9·01 m)
Wing aspect ratio	4·475
Length overall	38 ft 3½ in (11·67 m)
Height overall	14 ft 6 in (4·43 m)
Tailplane span	13 ft 1½ in (4·00 m)
Wheel track	9 ft 8 in (2·94 m)
Wheelbase	11 ft 8 in (3·56 m)

AREA:
Wings, gross	195·15 sq ft (18·13 m²)

WEIGHTS AND LOADINGS:
Weight empty	8,598 lb (3,900 kg)
Normal T-O weight	17,196 lb (7,800 kg)
Max T-O weight (semi-prepared surface)	15,432 lb (7,000 kg)
Max T-O weight (hard runway)	19,180 lb (8,700 kg)
Max wing loading	98·3 lb/sq ft (480 kg/m²)
Max power loading	2·35 lb/lb st (2·35 kg/kg st)

PERFORMANCE (at max T-O weight):
Max level speed at 30,000 ft (9,145 m)	Mach 0·95
Max level speed at S/L	599 knots (690 mph; 1,110 km/h)
Stalling speed, flaps down	125 knots (143 mph; 230 km/h)
Max rate of climb at S/L (with afterburning)	17,000 ft (5,180 m)/min
Max rate of climb at S/L (without afterburning)	7,000 ft (2,134 m)/min
Time to 40,000 ft (12,200 m) with afterburning	4·5 min
Time to 40,000 ft (12,200 m) without afterburning	11 min
Service ceiling	41,000 ft (12,500 m)
Single-engine ceiling (with afterburning)	35,000 ft (10,700 m)
T-O run: hard runway	4,000 ft (1,219 m)

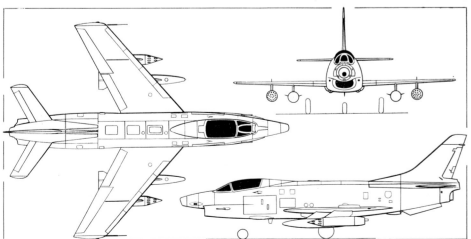

Fiat G91Y single-seat twin-engined tactical reconnaissance-fighter

Fiat G91Y twin-engined combat aircraft of the Italian Air Force

semi-prepared surface	3,000 ft (914 m)
semi-prepared surface, with JATO	
	1,500 ft (457 m)
T-O to 50 ft (15 m):	
hard runway	6,000 ft (1,829 m)
semi-prepared surface	4,500 ft (1,372 m)
semi-prepared surface, with JATO	
	2,500 ft (762 m)
Landing from 50 ft (15 m)	1,970 ft (600 m)
Typical combat radius at S/L	
	404 nm (466 miles; 750 km)
Ferry range with max fuel	
	1,890 nm (2,175 miles; 3,500 km)

FIAT G222

The G222 was originally conceived in four separate configurations, as described in the 1969-70 edition of *Jane's*. Three of these—the V/STOL medium-range transport, the civil conventional transport and the anti-submarine version—have been halted at the research project stage, but Fiat has an Italian Defence Ministry contract to complete two prototypes of the military conventional transport version, to which the following description applies. An additional airframe is being completed for static and fatigue testing.

The first of these prototypes was rolled out on 14 May 1970 and made its first public appearance at the Turin Air Show later that month. This aircraft was scheduled to fly for the first time in the Summer of 1970.

Most major Italian airframe companies are sharing in construction of the aircraft, including Aerfer, Aermacchi, Piaggio and Siai-Marchetti.

TYPE: Twin-engined general-purpose military transport aircraft.

WINGS: Cantilever high-wing monoplane. Thickness/chord ratio 15%. Light alloy three-spar fail-safe structure in three portions. One-piece centre-section fits in recess in top of fuselage and is secured by bolts at six main points. All-metal ailerons and double-slotted trailing-edge flaps. Controls are hydraulically-powered.

FUSELAGE: Stressed-skin aluminium alloy fail-safe structure of circular cross-section.

TAIL UNIT: Cantilever aluminium alloy two-spar structure, with sweptback vertical surfaces. Variable-incidence tailplane. Elevators hydraulically-powered.

LANDING GEAR: Hydraulically-retractable tricycle type, suitable for use from prepared runways or grass fields. Tandem-wheel main units retract rearward into fairings on sides of fuselage. Twin-wheel nose unit retracts forward. Oleo-pneumatic shock-absorbers. Hy-

draulic multi-disc brakes. No anti-skid units.

POWER PLANT: Two 3,400 shp General Electric T64-P-4C turboprop engines, each driving a three-blade reversible-pitch metal propeller. JATO rockets can be fitted to shorten T-O run.

ACCOMMODATION: Crew of three or four on flight deck. Seats for 44 fully-equipped troops or 40 parachute troops. Alternative payloads include 36 stretcher patients, two jeeps or equivalent freight. Crew entry door forward of cabin on port side. Doors at front and rear of main cabin on starboard side and at rear on port side. Underside of upswept rear fuselage lowers to form loading ramp, which can be opened in flight for air-drop operations. Entire accommodation pressurised and air-conditioned.

SYSTEMS: Doppler PHI navigation system, independent of ground radio navigational aids.

DIMENSIONS, EXTERNAL:

Wing span	94 ft 2 in (28·70 m)
Length overall	74 ft 5½ in (22·70 m)
Height overall	32 ft 1¾ in (9·80 m)
Tailplane span	41 ft 0 in (12·50 m)
Wheel track	12 ft 7¼ in (3·84 m)

DIMENSIONS, INTERNAL:

Main cabin:	
Length	27 ft 11½ in (8·52 m)
Width	8 ft 0½ in (2·45 m)
Height	7 ft 4½ in (2·25 m)
Volume	1,660 cu ft (47·0 m²)

AREA:

Wings, gross	883 sq ft (82 m²)

WEIGHTS:

Weight empty	28,000 lb (12,700 kg)
Max payload	19,840 lb (9,000 kg)
Normal T-O weight	54,000 lb (24,500 kg)
Max T-O weight	58,420 lb (26,500 kg)

PERFORMANCE (estimated, at normal T-O weight):

Max level speed at S/L	
	281 knots (323 mph; 520 km/h)
Cruising speed at 14,750 ft (4,500 m)	
	216 knots (249 mph; 400 km/h)
Time to 14,750 ft (4,500 m)	10 min 30 sec
Service ceiling	29,500 ft (9,000 m)
T-O run	1,085 ft (330 m)
T-O to 50 ft (15 m)	1,870 ft (570 m)
Landing from 50 ft (15 m)	1,312 ft (400 m)
Landing run	590 ft (180 m)
Basic mission range with 14,330 lb (6,500 kg)	
payload	1,075 nm (1,240 miles; 2,000 km)
Range with max fuel	
	2,690 nm (3,100 miles; 5,000 km)

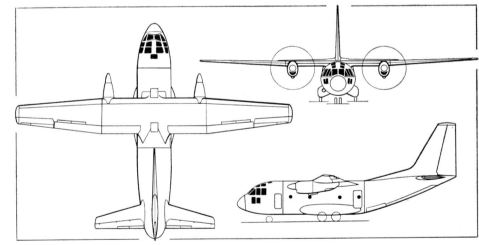

Photograph (*F. G. Swanborough*) **and three-view drawing of the Fiat G222 general-purpose military transport**

GENERAL AVIA
COSTRUZIONI AERONAUTICHE GENERAL AVIA

ADDRESS:
Via Trieste 24, 20096 Pioltello, Milan

PROPRIETOR:
Dott Ing Stelio Frati

Dott Ing Frati is well known for the many successful light aircraft which, as a freelance designer, he has evolved since 1950.

These have been built in prototype and production series by several Italian manufacturers, and have included such aircraft as the two-seat F.4 and three-seat F.7 Rondone, built by Ambrosini; the Caproni F.5 two-seat light jet aircraft and the twin-engined F.6 Airone built for Pasotti; the Aviamilano F.8 Falco and F.14 Nibbio; the Procaer F.15 Picchio, F.400 Cobra and F.480; and the F.250.

Of these, the Picchio has now been acquired by Ambrosini as the NF 15, and the 260 hp developed version of the F.250 is manufactured by Siai-Marchetti as the SF.260; both of these aircraft are described under the appropriate headings in this section.

Dott Ing Frati's designs have all possessed considerable aesthetic appeal, and all have been capable of full aerobatic flying, including spinning.

Early in 1970, Dott Ing Frati established the new company of General Avia, of which he is the proprietor and sole director, and has acquired extensive and well-equipped workshops where, from April 1970, further prototypes of his current designs are to be built. The latest of these is the F.20 Pegaso light business twin, of which details are given below. The next design to follow the F.20 will probably be a business executive jet aircraft.

GENERAL AVIA F.20 PEGASO (PEGASUS)

The F.20 Pegaso is a five/six-seat light business twin, of all-metal construction, with non-swept parallel-chord wings and tailplane and swept-back vertical tail surfaces. Its appearance can be seen from the accompanying three-view general arrangement drawing.

Design of the Pegaso started in January 1970, and construction of a prototype was begun in June 1970. This aircraft is scheduled to make its first flight in July 1971.

TYPE: Twin-engined five/six-seat light executive transport.

WINGS: Cantilever low-wing monoplane. Wing section NACA 65_2-415. Dihedral 5°. Incidence 1° 45'. All-metal single-spar structure in light alloy, with flush-riveted stressed skin. Differentially-operated all-metal ailerons and electrically-operated double-slotted metal flaps.

FUSELAGE: All-metal semi-monocoque structure, with bulkheads and stringers, and flush-riveted aluminium alloy skin.

TAIL UNIT: Cantilever all-metal structure with flush-riveted skin. Trim-tabs in rudder and each elevator.

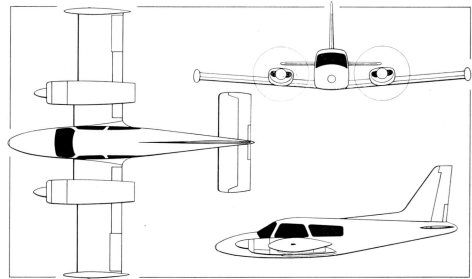

General Avia F.20 Pegaso light twin-engined executive aircraft

LANDING GEAR: Retractable tricycle type, with single main wheels. Nose-wheel steerable 18° to left and right. Electrical retraction, with manual standby. Oleo-pneumatic shock-absorbers. Main wheels size 7·00 × 6, nose-wheel size 5·00 × 5.

POWER PLANT: Two 285 hp Continental IO-520-F six-cylinder horizontally-opposed air-cooled engines with fuel injection, each driving a Hartzell fully-feathering constant-speed propeller. Fuel in two tanks in wings, each of 22 Imp gallons (100 litres), and two wingtip tanks each of 33 Imp gallons (150 litres) capacity. Total capacity 110 Imp gallons (500 litres).

ACCOMMODATION: Normal seating, in fully-enclosed cabin, for five or six persons, with space for 180 lb (82 kg) of baggage at rear. Access to cabin via large door on each side. Normal IFR instrumentation and dual controls.

DIMENSIONS, EXTERNAL:
Wing span over tip-tanks	31 ft 2¾ in (9·52 m)
Wing chord at root	5 ft 5 in (1·65 m)
Wing chord at tip	4 ft 11 in (1·50 m)
Wing aspect ratio	6·3
Length overall	27 ft 2¾ in (8·30 m)
Height overall	11 ft 5¾ in (3·50 m)
Tailplane span	11 ft 1¾ in (3·40 m)
Wheel track	11 ft 5¾ in (3·50 m)
Wheelbase	7 ft 10½ in (2·40 m)

AREAS:
Wings, gross	155·0 sq ft (14·40 m²)
Ailerons (total)	12·06 sq ft (1·12 m²)

Trailing-edge flaps (total)	18·08 sq ft (1·68 m²)
Fin	15·07 sq ft (1·40 m²)
Rudder, incl tab	8·07 sq ft (0·75 m²)
Tailplane	22·60 sq ft (2·10 m²)
Elevators, incl tabs	17·76 sq ft (1·65 m²)

WEIGHTS AND LOADINGS:
Weight empty, equipped	2,645 lb (1,200 kg)
Max T-O weight	4,409 lb (2,000 kg)
Max wing loading	28·5 lb/sq ft (139 kg/m²)
Max power loading	7·72 lb/hp (3·5 kg/hp)

PERFORMANCE (estimated, at max T-O weight):
Max level speed at S/L	232 knots (267 mph; 430 km/h)
Max cruising speed (75% power)	216 knots (249 mph; 400 km/h)
Econ cruising speed (60% power)	194 knots (224 mph; 360 km/h)
Stalling speed, flaps down	60 knots (69 mph; 110 km/h)
Rate of climb at S/L	2,165 ft (660 m)/min
Rate of climb at S/L, one engine out	492 ft (150 m)/min
Service ceiling	23,775 ft (7,250 m)
Service ceiling, one engine out	9,500 ft (2,900 m)
T-O run	853 ft (260 m)
Landing run	820 ft (250 m)
Max range at max cruising speed	1,050 nm (1,210 miles; 1,950 km)
Max range at econ cruising speed	1,215 nm (1,400 miles; 2,250 km)

ITAL-AIR

ADDRESS:
Via Monte di Pietà 24, Milan

PRINCIPAL EXECUTIVES:
Dr Gianni Mazzocchi (President)
Dott Ing Stelio Frati
Dott Ing Paulo Barbaro
Dott Ing Alessandro Baj

Dr Mazzocchi, a well-known Italian publisher, has initiated the formation of this new Italian aircraft manufacturing company intended primarily to develop, build and market a range of light aircraft and twin-engined executive aircraft. His plans were announced in the February 1970 issue of the magazine *Quattrosoldi*, of which Dr Mazzocchi is the proprietor, when an appeal was launched for the subscription of funds toward the initial working capital of the new company.

Among well-known figures in Italian aviation to join with Dr Mazzocchi in this venture are Dott Ing Paulo Barbaro, formerly Managing Director of Siai-Marchetti, and Dott Ing Stelio Frati, whose most successful recent designs have been the Ambrosini (ex-Procaer) NF 15 and Siai-Marchetti SF.260 light aircraft (which see). Dott Ing Frati is no longer associated with either Procaer or Siai-Marchetti. Instead, he has formed the new company General Avia (which see) at Pioltello, where prototypes of his new designs are being constructed. Series production of such aircraft would be undertaken by Ital-Air in collaboration with General Avia.

JANNOTTA

DR ING ORLANDO JANNOTTA

ADDRESS:
Via Lieti 51, 80131 Naples

Dr Ing Jannotta has completed the design and construction of a single-seat ultra-light high-wing monoplane (I-IANN), known as the I-66 San Francesco. Design work was started in 1966, and the aircraft took approx 900 man-hours to complete. Three small firms have taken part in building some of the parts, and the final assembly and static testing were carried out by monks belonging to the Order of St Francis, from which the aircraft takes its name.

Test flying of the I-66 took place between the Spring and Autumn of 1969. Dr Ing Jannotta does not intend to build further examples, but hopes to make the aircraft available on a wider basis either by a licence production arrangement or by the sale of plans to flying clubs or other amateur constructors.

All available details of the I-66 are given below.

JANNOTTA I-66 SAN FRANCESCO

TYPE: Single-seat amateur-built ultra-light aircraft.

WINGS: Strut-braced high-wing monoplane. Wing section NACA 23012. Constant chord. Incidence 4° 20' at root, 0° at tip. Dihedral 1°. No sweepback. All-wood two-spar structure, with steel attachments to fuselage.

Jannotta I-66 San Francesco light aircraft (40 hp modified Volkswagen engine) (*Vico F. Rosaspina*)

All-wood ailerons. No flaps. Single Vee-strut bracing each side.

FUSELAGE: Fabric-covered steel-tube structure, of basically rectangular section.

TAIL UNIT: Cantilever steel-tube structure, with fabric covering. Trim-tab on rudder.

LANDING GEAR: Non-retractable tail-wheel type, with rubber shock-absorbers.

POWER PLANT: One 40 hp modified Volkswagen 1,200 cc engine, with dual ignition, driving a two-blade propeller. Fuel in single tank in fuselage, capacity approx 6·6 Imp gallons (30 litres).

ACCOMMODATION: Single seat for pilot in enclosed cabin, with forward-opening door on each side.

DIMENSIONS, EXTERNAL:
Wing span	29 ft 6¼ in (9·00 m)
Wing chord (constant)	4 ft 11 in (1·50 m)
Wing aspect ratio	6
Length overall	19 ft 0¼ in (5·80 m)
Fuselage max width	1 ft 11¾ in (0·60 m)
Fuselage max depth	3 ft 7 in (1·09 m)

AREAS:

Wings, gross	144 sq ft (13·37 m²)
Ailerons (total)	15·3 sq ft (1·42 m²)
Fin	2·26 sq ft (0·21 m²)
Rudder	5·17 sq ft (0·48 m²)
Tailplane	11·1 sq ft (1·03 m²)
Elevators	8·18 sq ft (0·76 m²)

WEIGHTS AND LOADING:

Weight empty	441 lb (200 kg)
Max T-O weight	661 lb (300 kg)
Max wing loading	4·59 lb/sq ft (22·4 kg/m²)

PERFORMANCE (at max T-O weight):
Cruising speed at two-thirds power
54 knots (62 mph; 100 km/h)

Best glide ratio
11 : 1 at 41 knots (47 mph; 76 km/h)
Min sinking speed
5·77 ft (1·76 m)/sec at 33·4 knots (38·5 mph; 62 km/h)
Landing speed (with ground effect)
24·3 knots (28 mph; 45 km/h)

MERIDIONALI
ELICOTTERI MERIDIONALI SpA

HEAD OFFICE:
Via Poggio Laurentino, Rome
WORKS:
Frosinone
PRESIDENT:
Gen Ettore Pellacci
SALES AND PUBLIC RELATIONS MANAGER:
Dr Franco Ostini
SECRETARY GENERAL:
Gen Ernesto Caprioglio
TECHNICAL MANAGER:
Ing Mario Sala

In April 1968 it was announced that an agreement had been concluded between this Italian company and The Boeing Company in the US, whereby Elicotteri Meridionali acquired rights to undertake co-production, marketing and servicing of the Boeing-Vertol CH-47C Chinook transport helicopter for customers in Italy, Austria, Switzerland and the Middle East.

Manufacture of the Chinook began in the Spring of 1970, to meet initial orders for 26 for the Italian Army and 20 for the Iranian Air Force.

In addition, Meridionali announced in April 1970 that it was to undertake the series production of a new helicopter known as the EMA 124. This aircraft has been designed by Agusta, and will be built under a licence agreement between the two companies, which are sharing the development work. All available details of the EMA 124 are given below.

MERIDIONALI/AGUSTA EMA 124

The three-seat EMA 124 has been designed by Costruzioni Aeronautiche Giovanni Agusta, and conforms to FAR Part 27 airworthiness requirements. It is suitable for a variety of duties, including passenger or goods transport, pilot training, survey, reconnaissance, agricultural or other aerial work, policing duties and casualty transportation. The general appearance of the aircraft, which is derived from the Bell 47, can be seen from the adjacent illustration.

TYPE: Three-seat light helicopter.
ROTOR SYSTEM: Semi-rigid two-blade main rotor, with provision for blade folding. Semi-rigid delta-hinged two-blade tail rotor.
ROTOR DRIVE: Transmission system consists of a main rotor reduction gearbox, tail rotor gearbox and drive shafting. Main gearbox in-

Artist's impression of the Meridionali/Agusta EMA 124 three-seat light helicopter

corporates a centrifugal clutch and a roller-type free-wheeling unit. Collective pitch control is exercised through rigid linkage; cyclic pitch control through rigid linkage with hydraulic boost.
FUSELAGE: Basic welded-tube structure, built in three sections; cabin, centre-section and tail-boom.
TAIL UNIT: One-piece elevator mid-mounted on tail-boom. Small ventral fin.
LANDING GEAR: Fixed tubular-skid type, with two removable ground-handling wheels.
POWER PLANT: One 305 shp (derated to 250 shp) Lycoming VO-540-B1B3 six-cylinder horizontally-opposed air-cooled engine, mounted aft of cabin. Fuel in two interconnected metal tanks above engine, with total capacity of 33 Imp gallons (150 litres).
ACCOMMODATION: Side-by-side seating for pilot and two passengers in fully-enclosed and fully-transparent cabin. Provision for dual controls.
SYSTEMS: Single hydraulic system, including pump, reservoir, filter, pressure relief valve and irreversible valves, powers the servo-control

cylinders. 28V DC electrical system supplied by one 24V 11Ah battery and a 28V 50A generator.
ELECTRONICS AND EQUIPMENT: Provision for installing Narco Mk XII or King KY-95 VHF communications sets, or alternatives to customer's requirements.
DIMENSIONS, EXTERNAL:

Main rotor diameter	31 ft 2 in (9·50 m)
Tail rotor diameter	4 ft 7 in (1·40 m)

WEIGHTS:

Weight empty	1,543 lb (700 kg)
Max T-O weight	2,535 lb (1,150 kg)

PERFORMANCE (estimated, at max T-O weight, ISA):

Max level speed at S/L	92 knots (106 mph; 170 km/h)
Cruising speed at S/L	78 knots (90 mph; 145 km/h)
Max rate of climb at S/L	827 ft (252 m)/min
Service ceiling	14,100 ft (4,300 m)
Hovering ceiling in ground effect	8,200 ft (2,500 m)
Hovering ceiling out of ground effect	5,575 ft (1,700 m)
Max range at S/L	225 nm (260 miles; 420 km)

NARDI
NARDI S A PER COSTRUZIONI AERONAUTICHE

HEAD OFFICE AND WORKS:
Aeroporto Forlanini, Milan
PRESIDENT:
Dr Ing Luigi Nardi
VICE-PRESIDENT, MANAGING DIRECTOR AND COMMERCIAL MANAGER:
Dr Elto Nardi

This company was established by the four Nardi brothers in 1933. Their first product, the FN-305, flew in 1935, and subsequently more than 600 of these aircraft were built by Nardi and, under licence, by Piaggio. They were followed by other Nardi designs, produced in large numbers.

The Nardi factory at Loreto was almost completely destroyed during World War II, but the Milan factory was rebuilt and the prototype of the company's first post-war aircraft, the FN-333 all-metal amphibian, flew there for the first time on 4 December 1952.

Nardi has manufacturing and marketing rights in Italy for the Hughes 300 three-seat light helicopter and Hughes 500 five-seat helicopter. Initially, it is assembling Hughes 500's from US-built components. The first three are military Hughes 500M's and were due to be delivered to the Italian Border Guard in September-October 1969. Thereafter, Nardi was to begin delivery of Italian-assembled civil Hughes 500's, for which it had received orders for 40 by June 1969. It will graduate to complete manu-

facture of both Hughes types in Italy by 1971. Details of both the Hughes 300 and Hughes 500 can be found in the US section of this edition.

In 1969, Nardi was also engaged in studies of helicopters of its own design for possible future development.

In addition to aircraft manufacture, Nardi has specialised in the production of wheels, brakes, retractable landing gear, hydraulic and electric aircraft controls, fuel pumps, armament installations and aircraft accessories generally. Among the more recent of these activities, still continuing in 1970, is the production of landing gear, flaps and other accessories for F-104G Starfighters and other NATO combat aircraft and for the domestic F-104S programme.

PARTENAVIA
PARTENAVIA COSTRUZIONI AERONAUTICHE SpA

HEAD OFFICE AND WORKS:
PO Box 2179, Via Rettifilo al Bravo, 3, 80022 Arzano, Naples
PRESIDENT:
Prof Ing Luigi Pascale

This company has built a series of light aircraft to the designs of Prof Ing Luigi Pascale.

Its current products are the P.64B Oscar-B four-seat light aircraft, the two-seat P.66B Oscar-100, developed from the P.64, and the three-seat P.66B Oscar-150.

Series production of both the P.64B and the P.66B began in September 1967, and initial

production lines were laid down for 50 of each version.

Under development is a new light twin-engined aircraft, designated Partenavia P.68.

PARTENAVIA P.64B OSCAR-B

Design of this improved version of the P.64 Oscar four-seat light aircraft (see 1966-67 Jane's) was started in November 1966 and construction of the prototype began in January 1967. The prototype flew in the first half of 1967. Fifty-four Oscar-B's had been built by the end of January 1970, and production continues.

Improvements introduced in the Oscar-B include a "stepped-down" rear fuselage and panoramic rear cabin window, giving an all-round field of vision.

In addition to production by the parent company, the Oscar-B is being produced by AFIC (Pty) Ltd of Johannesburg as the **RSA 200 Falcon** (see the South African section of this edition).

The two-seat P.66B Oscar-100 is described separately.

TYPE: Four-seat light monoplane.
WINGS: Braced high-wing monoplane with single streamline-section bracing strut each side. Wing section NACA 63 series. Thickness/chord ratio 15%. Dihedral 1° 10'. Incidence at root 1° 40'. No sweepback. Stressed-skin single-spar torsion-box structure of aluminium alloy, with glass-fibre reinforced leading-edges. Ailerons and manually-operated slotted trailing-edge flaps of similar construction to wings.

FUSELAGE: Conventional all-metal semi-mono-coque stressed-skin structure.

TAIL UNIT: Cantilever stressed-skin metal structure with sweptback vertical surfaces. All-moving tailplane in two symmetrical halves joined by steel cross-tube. Anti-balance tab in trailing-edge of tailplane, over 80% of span.

LANDING GEAR: Non-retractable tricycle type, with steerable nose-wheel. Cantilever spring steel main legs. Oleo nose-wheel shock-absorber. Cleveland main wheels type 40-28, with Pirelli tyres size 6·00 × 6. Goodyear nose-wheel tyre size 5·00 × 5. Cleveland type 30-18 hydraulic disc brakes.

POWER PLANT: One 180 hp Lycoming O-360-A1A four-cylinder horizontally-opposed air-cooled engine, driving a Hartzell HC-C2YK-1A two-blade variable-pitch constant-speed metal propeller, diameter 6 ft 2 in (2·26 m), or a Sensenich fixed-pitch propeller. Two fuel tanks in wing roots, total capacity 44 Imp gallons (200 litres). Refuelling points above wings. Oil capacity 1·66 Imp gallons (7·5 litres).

ACCOMMODATION: Enclosed cabin seating four persons in pairs with dual controls; front seats are of the adjustable sliding type. Three forward-hinged doors: one by each front seat and on starboard side at rear. Baggage space aft of rear seats, with separate access door on starboard side. Heating, ventilation and sound-proofing standard.

ELECTRONICS AND EQUIPMENT: Optional items include full IFR instrumentation, Grime rotating beacon, VHF radio, VOR and ADF.

DIMENSIONS, EXTERNAL:
Wing span	32 ft 9¼ in (9·99 m)
Wing chord (constant)	4 ft 5½ in (1·36 m)
Wing aspect ratio	7·45
Length overall	23 ft 8¾ in (7·23 m)
Height overall	9 ft 1 in (2·77 m)
Tailplane span	10 ft 2 in (3·10 m)
Wheel track	6 ft 10½ in (2·10 m)

AREAS:
Wings, gross	144·2 sq ft (13·40 m²)
Ailerons (total)	13·88 sq ft (1·29 m²)
Trailing-edge flaps (total)	18·40 sq ft (1·71 m²)
Fin	7·86 sq ft (0·73 m²)
Rudder	4·84 sq ft (0·45 m²)
Tailplane, including tab	23·36 sq ft (2·17 m²)

WEIGHTS AND LOADINGS:
Weight empty	1,477 lb (670 kg)
Max T-O weight	2,546 lb (1,155 kg)
Max landing weight	2,425 lb (1,100 kg)
Max wing loading	16·86 lb/sq ft (77·39 kg/m²)
Max power loading	13·89 lb/hp (6·3 kg/hp)

PERFORMANCE (at max T-O weight):
Max level speed at S/L
141 knots (162 mph; 260 km/h)
Max permissible diving speed
202 knots (233 mph; 376 km/h)
Max cruising speed (75% power) at 7,000 ft (2,150 m) 129 knots (149 mph; 240 km/h)
Econ cruising speed at 11,000 ft (3,300 m)
126 knots (145 mph; 233 km/h)
Stalling speed, flaps down
48 knots (55 mph; 87 km/h)
Rate of climb at S/L 1,025 ft (312 m)/min
Service ceiling 17,400 ft (5,300 m)
T-O run 804 ft (245 m)
Landing run 656 ft (200 m)
Range with max fuel
647 nm (746 miles; 1,200 km)
Endurance (75% power) 5 hr

PARTENAVIA P.66B OSCAR-100 AND OSCAR-150

These all-metal light aircraft are two- and three-seat counterparts of the P.64B Oscar-B described above. Many airframe components of the three types are interchangeable, and the structural description of the P.64B applies equally to the P.66B, except for details given below.

The P.66B is available in two versions, as follows:

Oscar-100. Two-seater, with 115 hp Lycoming O-235-C1B engine, as described below. Sixty-four built by the end of January 1970; production continues.

Oscar-150. Similar to Oscar-100, but with seating for three persons. Power plant is a 150 hp Lycoming O-320-E2A four-cylinder horizontally-opposed air-cooled engine, driving a two-blade Sensenich 74DM6S5-2-60 metal propeller. Twelve built by the end of January 1970; production continues.

TYPE: Two-seat light monoplane.

WINGS: As for Oscar-B.

FUSELAGE: Forward portion, to rear of cabin, is a welded steel-tube structure, covered with light alloy panels. Rear fuselage is of conventional light alloy stressed-skin construction.

POWER PLANT: One 115 hp Lycoming O-235-C1B four-cylinder horizontally-opposed air-cooled engine, driving a Sensenich 76AM6-2-46 two-blade fixed-pitch metal propeller, diameter 6 ft 2 in (1·88 m). Two fuel tanks in wings, with total capacity of 22 Imp gallons (100 litres). Provision for auxiliary tank of 17·5 Imp gallons (80 litres) capacity. Refuelling point above wing.

Partenavia P.64B Oscar-B four-seat light aircraft (180 hp Lycoming O-360-A1A engine)

Partenavia P.66B Oscar-150 (150 hp Lycoming O-320-E2A engine)

ACCOMMODATION: Two adjustable sliding seats side-by-side in enclosed cabin, with forward-hinged door on each side. Dual stick-type controls standard (starboard one quickly removable). Dual wheel-type controls optional. Provision for fitting rear seat for a child weighing up to 90 lb (40 kg). Luggage space aft of seats. Cabin heated, ventilated and soundproofed.

ELECTRONICS AND EQUIPMENT: Provision for full blind-flying instrumentation, VHF nav/com radio, VOR and ADF.

DIMENSIONS, EXTERNAL:
As for P.64B Oscar-B, except:
Length overall 23 ft 3⅛ in (7·09 m)

WEIGHTS AND LOADINGS (Oscar-100):
Weight empty	1,235 lb (560 kg)
Max T-O weight	1,808 lb (820 kg)
Max wing loading	12·53 lb/sq ft (61·2 kg/m²)
Max power loading	15·74 lb/hp (7·14 kg/hp)

PERFORMANCE (Oscar-100 at max T-O weight):
Max level speed at S/L
116 knots (134 mph; 215 km/h)
Max cruising speed (75% power) at 7,000 ft (2,150 m) 102 knots (118 mph; 190 km/h)
Stalling speed, flaps up
49 knots (56 mph; 90 km/h)
Stalling speed, flaps down
41 knots (47 mph; 75 km/h)
Rate of climb at S/L 735 ft (225 m)/min
Service ceiling 13,125 ft (4,000 m)
T-O run 720 ft (220 m)
Landing run 394 ft (120 m)
Endurance at max cruising speed 3 hr 30 min

PARTENAVIA P.68

Designed by Prof Ing Luigi Pascale, the P.68 is a twin-engined high-wing monoplane for private or business flying, air taxi, training or third-level transport duties. The first prototype entered the static test stage early in 1970, and made its first flight on 25 May 1970. FAA and RAI certification was anticipated by the end of 1970.

TYPE: Six-seat light transport and trainer.

WINGS: Cantilever high-wing monoplane. Wing section NACA 63 series. Thickness/chord ratio 15%. Dihedral 1°. Incidence 1° 30'. No sweepback. Stressed-skin single-spar torsion-box structure, of aluminium alloy except for approx 30% of each leading-edge, which is of glass-fibre. All-metal ailerons and electrically-operated slotted trailing-edge flaps.

FUSELAGE: Conventional all-metal semi-mono-coque structure of frames and longerons with stressed-skin covering.

TAIL UNIT: Cantilever stressed-skin metal structure. All-moving tailplane, in two symmetrical halves joined by steel cross-tube and of constant chord except for increase at leading-edge roots. Balance tab in tailplane trailing-edge, over 80% of span. Sweptback fin and rudder, with small dorsal fin. No tab on rudder.

LANDING GEAR: Non-retractable tricycle type, with steerable nose-wheel, on first prototype. Cantilever spring steel main legs. Oleo-pneumatic shock-absorber on nose-wheel. Cleveland main wheels, type 40-96, with Pirelli tyres size 6.00 × 6. Goodyear nose-wheel tyre, size 5.00 × 5. Cleveland type 30-61 hydraulic disc brakes. Second prototype will have hydraulically-retractable tricycle landing gear, with oleo-pneumatic shock-absorbers.

POWER PLANT: Two 200 hp Lycoming IO-360-A1A four-cylinder horizontally-opposed air-cooled engines, each driving a Hartzell HC-C2YK-2/C-666A-2 two-blade variable-pitch constant-speed fully-feathering propeller of 6 ft 2 in (1·88 m) diameter. Fuel in two integral tanks in outer wings, with total capacity of 107 Imp gallons (485 litres). Oil capacity 3·3 Imp gallons (15 litres).

ACCOMMODATION: Seating for six persons in cabin, including pilot, in three rows of two, with space for baggage aft of rear pair. Front seats are of the adjustable sliding type. Access to all seats via large car-type door in port side of cabin. Access to baggage compartment via separate door on starboard side. Dual controls, cabin heating, ventilation and soundproofing standard.

ELECTRONICS AND EQUIPMENT: Optional equipment includes full IFR instrumentation, Grimes rotating beacon, VHF radio, VOR and ADF.

DIMENSIONS, EXTERNAL:
Wing span	39 ft 4½ in (12·00 m)
Wing chord (constant)	5 ft 1 in (1·55 m)
Wing aspect ratio	7·75
Length overall	29 ft 11 in (9·12 m)
Height overall	10 ft 8 in (3·25 m)
Tailplane span	14 ft 9 in (4·50 m)
Wheel track (1st prototype)	7 ft 10½ in (2·40 m)
Wheel track (2nd prototype)	6 ft 6¾ in (2·00 m)
Wheelbase	11 ft 5¾ in (3·50 m)

DIMENSIONS, INTERNAL:
Cabin:
Length	10 ft 0 in (3·05 m)
Max width	4 ft 0 in (1·22 m)
Max height	4 ft 0 in (1·22 m)
Baggage space	37 cu ft (1·05 m³)

AREAS:
Wings, gross	200·2 sq ft (18·60 m²)
Ailerons (total)	19·27 sq ft (1·79 m²)
Trailing-edge flaps (total)	25·51 sq ft (2·37 m²)
Fin	17·11 sq ft (1·59 m²)
Rudder	4·74 sq ft (0·44 m²)
Tailplane, including tab	47·47 sq ft (4·41 m²)

WEIGHTS AND LOADINGS:
Weight empty	2,337 lb (1,060 kg)
Max T-O and landing weight	3,880 lb (1,760 kg)
Max wing loading	19·4 lb/sq ft (94·62 kg/m²)
Max power loading	10·78 lb/hp (4·89 kg/hp)

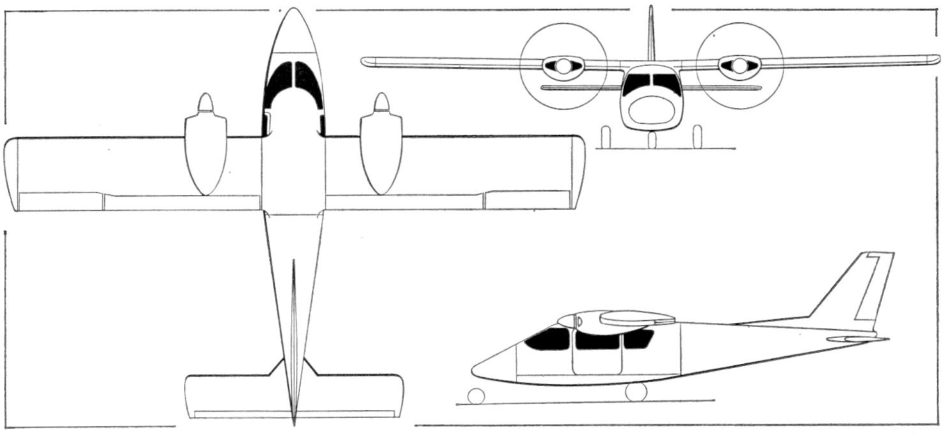

Partenavia P.68 six-seat light transport and trainer

PERFORMANCE (estimated at max T-O weight):
Max level speed at S/L (fixed landing gear)
168 knots (193 mph; 311 km/h)
Max level speed at S/L (retractable landing gear)
180 knots (207 mph; 333 km/h)
Stalling speed, flaps up
66 knots (75 mph; 120 km/h)
Stalling speed, flaps down
54 knots (62 mph; 100 km/h)
Rate of climb at S/L   1,475 ft (450 m)/min

Rate of climb at S/L, one engine out
315 ft (96 m)/min
Service ceiling   23,300 ft (7,100 m)
Service ceiling, one engine out
7,225 ft (2,200 m)
T-O to 50 ft (15 m), both engines
1,310 ft (400 m)
T-O to 50 ft (15 m) one engine out (balanced)
2,295 ft (700 m)

PIAGGIO
INDUSTRIE AERONAUTICHE E MECCANICHE RINALDO PIAGGIO, SpA
HEAD OFFICE:
Viale Brigata Bisagno 14, Genoa (426)
BRANCH OFFICE:
Via A. Gramsci 34, Rome
WORKS:
Finale Ligure and Genoa-Sestri
CHAIRMAN AND MANAGING DIRECTOR:
Ing Armando Piaggio
TECHNICAL DIRECTORS:
Ing Alberto Faraboschi
Ing Guido Ferraris (Engine Division)
TECHNICAL CONSULTANT:
Ing Giovanni P. Casiraghi
SALES MANAGER:
Dr Bruno Canevali
PUBLIC RELATIONS MANAGER:
Dr Alceo Gerli

This company was formed on 29 February 1964, and has since operated as an independent concern, after assuming control of the Aeronautical Division and Rolling Stock and Industrial Vehicles Division embodied previously in Piaggio & C, SpA. It employs about 1,200 people.
Piaggio began the construction of aeroplanes in its Genoa-Sestri plant in 1916, and later in the Finale Ligure works. A second large plant covering approx 430,000 sq ft (40,000 m²) has recently been built at Genoa-Sestri, on the edge of Genoa's Christopher Columbus Airport, for the assembly and overhaul of the P166 trio of twin-engined aircraft and of the PD-808 light twin-jet utility aircraft.
Piaggio's main activity at present is concentrated upon development and production of the PD-808. This aircraft resulted from an agreement between Piaggio and McDonnell Douglas calling for the joint design of an aircraft for both military and commercial use to be manufactured in Piaggio's works at Finale Ligure.
The Aero-Engine Division of Rinaldo Piaggio is manufacturing the Viper 11, 526 and 540 turbojets under licence from Rolls-Royce Ltd (Bristol Division) for installation in the Aermacchi M.B.326, PD-808 and M.B.326G respectively. Also in production are the Lycoming GSO-480 and VO-435 piston-engines and T53 turboshaft engine under licence from the Avco Lycoming Division of Avco.

PIAGGIO P166
The P166 is produced in three versions, as follows:
P166. Major production version with two 340 hp Lycoming engines and normal accommodation for 6-8 people. Prototype flew on 26 November 1957. FAA Type Approval obtained on 31 July 1958, following certification by the RAI. Production includes a total of 51 for the Italian Air Force for training, ambulance and communications duties; these aircraft are designated **P166M**. Total of 94 built up to March 1970.
P166B Portofino. Developed version with two 380 hp Lycoming engines, longer nose and restyled cabin with accommodation for 6-10 people. Prototype flew on 27 March 1962. Five built by March 1970.
P166C. Basically similar to P166B, but with seats for a pilot and up to 12 passengers. First P166C flew on 2 October 1964. Two built by March 1970.

The majority of commercial P166 models so far built have been for export.
The following details apply to the P166B and P166C:
TYPE: Twin-engined light transport.
WINGS: Shoulder gull-wing cantilever monoplane. NACA 230 wing section. Dihedral 21° 30' on inner portion, 2° 8' on outer wings. Incidence 2° 43'. All-metal aluminium alloy flush-riveted structure. All-metal slotted ailerons, with geared and trim-tab on starboard aileron. All-metal slotted flaps. Rubber boot de-icing of leading-edges optional.
FUSELAGE: All-metal aluminium alloy flush-riveted semi-monocoque structure.
TAIL UNIT: Cantilever all-metal aluminium alloy flush-riveted structure. Geared and trim-tab on elevators; trim-tab in rudder.
LANDING GEAR: Retractable tricycle type. Magnaghi oleo-pneumatic shock-absorbers. Hydraulic retraction. Nose-wheel retracts rearward. Main units retract outboard and up on P166B, inboard and up on P166C. Goodyear 24 × 7·7 main wheels with 8·50-10 tyres, pressure 50 lb/sq in (3·50 kg/cm²) on P166B, 52 lb/sq in (3·65 kg/cm²) on P166C. Goodyear 6·00 × 7·7 nose-wheel and tyre, pressure 42 lb/sq in (2·95 kg/cm²). Goodyear or Magnaghi hydraulic brakes.
POWER PLANT: Two 380 hp Lycoming IGSO-540-AIC six-cylinder horizontally-opposed air-cooled engines, each driving a Hartzell type HC-BZ30-2 BL/L10151-8 three-blade feathering constant-speed pusher propeller. Fuel in two internal tanks in outer wings (each 46·6 Imp gallons = 212 litres). P166B has also two external wingtip tanks (each 45·8 Imp gallons = 208 litres). Total fuel capacity: P166B 184·8 Imp gallons (840 litres), P166C 93·2 Imp gallons (424 litres). Total oil capacity 7·5 Imp gallons (34 litres).
ACCOMMODATION (P166B): Standard seating for pilot and five passengers in individual seats, with toilet and bar at rear. Alternative layouts include an 8-seat executive version, with two rows of three seats in cabin, facing each other; high-density 10-seat version with three

Piaggio P166M twin-engined tactical transport of the South African Air Force (340 hp Lycoming engines)
(Lewis G. Pain)

individual seats on each side of central aisle in cabin, and curved rear twin-seats in place of toilet and bar; cargo version with stripped cabin; ambulance and air survey versions. Main door in centre of cabin on port side. Separate door to flight deck on starboard side. Outside door to baggage compartment aft of cabin on port side. Dual controls standard.
ACCOMMODATION (P166C): Seats for two pilots, or pilot and passenger, at front, with dual controls. Six individual seats in pairs in forward cabin, with centre aisle. Rear cabin contains two individual rearward-facing seats and forward-facing bench seat for three persons. Doors and rear baggage compartment as for P166B.
SYSTEMS: Hydraulic system, pressure 1,840 lb/sq in (125 kg/cm²) on P166B, 1,900 lb/sq in (133·6 kg/cm²) on P166C, operates landing gear, flaps and brakes. 28V engine-driven DC generators for electrical system.
ELECTRONICS AND EQUIPMENT: Optional equipment includes VHF radio, VOR, ADF, marker beacon receiver, glideslope receiver and autopilot.
DIMENSIONS, EXTERNAL:
Wing span:
P166B without tip tanks	44 ft 4 in (13·51 m)
P166B with tip tanks	46 ft 9 in (14·52 m)
P166C	47 ft 2 in (14·33 m)
Wing chord at root	7 ft 10½ in (2·40 m)
Wing chord at tip	3 ft 9¼ in (1·15 m)
Wing aspect ratio	7·3
Length overall	39 ft 3 in (11·90 m)
Height over tail, wheels down	16 ft 5 in (5·00 m)
Tailplane span	16 ft 9 in (5·10 m)

Wheel track:
P166B	8 ft 9 in (2·66 m)
P166C	7 ft 5 in (2·27 m)
Wheelbase	15 ft 5½ in (4·71 m)

Passenger door (port side):
Height	4 ft 10 in (1·47 m)
Width	2 ft 2 in (0·66 m)

DIMENSIONS, INTERNAL:
Cabin: Length:
P166B	11 ft 8 in (3·55 m)

Piaggio-Douglas PD-808 twin-jet light utility aircraft (two 3,360 lb st Rolls-Royce Bristol Viper Mk 526 turbojet engines)

P166C	15 ft 10 in (4·84 m)
Max width	5 ft 2 in (1·57 m)
Max height	5 ft 9 in (1·76 m)
Floor area:	
P166B	55·3 sq ft (5·14 m²)
P166C	68·1 sq ft (6·33 m²)
Volume:	
P166B	234·1 cu ft (6·63 m³)
P166C	340·1 cu ft (9·63 m³)
Baggage hold (front), P166B only	27·2 cu ft (0·77 m³)
Baggage hold (rear):	
P166B	63·6 cu ft (1·80 m³)
P166C	53·5 cu ft (1·52 m³)

AREAS:
Wings, gross	285·9 sq ft (26·56 m²)
Ailerons (total)	21·00 sq ft (1·95 m²)
Trailing-edge flaps (total)	25·60 sq ft (2·38 m²)
Fin	17·44 sq ft (1·62 m²)
Rudder, including tab	13·24 sq ft (1·23 m²)
Tailplane	37·67 sq ft (3·50 m²)
Elevators, including tab	13·88 sq ft (1·29 m²)

WEIGHTS AND LOADINGS:
Weight empty, equipped:	
P166B	5,556 lb (2,520 kg)
P166C	5,820 lb (2,640 kg)
Max payload (both)	2,204 lb (1,000 kg)
Max T-O and landing weight:	
P166B	8,377 lb (3,800 kg)
P166C	8,708 lb (3,950 kg)
Max wing loading:	
P166B	29·3 lb/sq ft (143 kg/m²)
P166C	30·45 lb/sq ft (148·7 kg/m²)
Max power loading:	
P166B	11·02 lb/hp (5·00 kg/hp)
P166C	11·46 lb/hp (5·20 kg/hp)

PERFORMANCE (P166B and P166C at max T-O weight, except where indicated otherwise):
Max level speed at 11,300 ft (3,450 m):	
*P166B	214 knots (246 mph; 396 km/h)
**P166C	213 knots (245 mph; 394 km/h)
Max permissible diving speed:	
P166B	169 knots (195 mph; 476 km/h)
P166C	242 knots (279 mph; 450 km/h)
Max cruising speed (75% power):	
*P166B at 15,000 ft (4,550 m)	194 knots (223 mph; 359 km/h)
**P166C at 14,000 ft (4,265 m)	193 knots (222 mph; 357 km/h)
Econ cruising speed (45% power):	
*P166B at 15,000 ft (4,550 m)	153 knots (176 mph; 283 km/h)
**P166C at 14,000 ft (4,265 m)	139 knots (160 mph; 257 km/h)
Stalling speed, flaps and wheels down:	
P166B	65·5 knots (75 mph; 120 km/h)
P166C	66 knots (76 mph; 122 km/h)
Rate of climb at S/L:	
Both	1,415 ft (430 m)/min
Service ceiling:	
P166B	29,100 ft (8,870 m)
P166C	27,000 ft (8,230 m)
Service ceiling, one engine out:	
P166B	13,500 ft (4,115 m)
P166C	11,500 ft (3,505 m)
T-O run:	
P166B	935 ft (285 m)
P166C	1,320 ft (402 m)
T-O to 50 ft (15 m):	
P166B	1,800 ft (548 m)
P166C	1,930 ft (588 m)
Landing from 50 ft (15 m):	
*P166B	1,400 ft (427 m)
**P166C	1,860 ft (567 m)
Landing run:	
*P166B	920 ft (280 m)
**P166C	1,280 ft (390 m)
Range with max fuel, no reserve:	
P166B	1,300 nm (1,500 miles; 2,410 km)
P166C	630 nm (725 miles; 1,170 km)

Range with max payload, no reserve:	
P166B	337 nm (388 miles; 626 km)
P166C	406 nm (468 miles; 754 km)

*at intermediate flying weight of 7,715 lb (3,500 kg)
**at intermediate flying weight of 8,346 lb (3,785 kg)

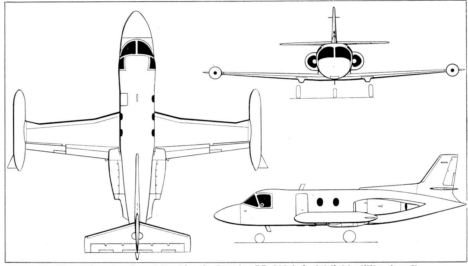

Three-view drawing of the Piaggio-Douglas PD-808 twin-jet light utility aircraft

PIAGGIO-DOUGLAS PD-808

The PD-808 is a 6/10-seat light jet utility aircraft suitable for both civil and military use. Projected rôles for the military version include Government VIP transport, navigation training, airways aids checking and photographic reconnaissance.

The Italian Defence Ministry assisted Piaggio by purchasing the two prototypes and providing test facilities. The first prototype flew on 29 August 1964 and the second on 14 June 1966. Both of these aircraft were powered by two 3,000 lb (1,360 kg) st Bristol Siddeley Viper Mk 525 turbojet engines. Both Italian RAI and American FAA type certificates were received on 29 November 1966.

In mid-1965, the Italian Defence Ministry ordered 25 production PD-808's. These aircraft, to which the details below apply, have more powerful Viper Mk 526 engines and differ from the original prototype in having larger tip-tanks, longer dorsal fin and forward-sliding nose fairing. Production in both executive and military configurations is now under way, and eight aircraft had been delivered by early April 1970.

TYPE: Twin-jet light utility aircraft.

WINGS: Cantilever low-wing monoplane. Wing section DES 0010-1·1-40/11° Mod. at root, DES 0008-1·1-40/9° Mod. at tip. Dihedral 3°. Incidence 1°. Sweepback 1° 50' at quarter-chord. All-metal aluminium alloy fail-safe three-spar structure. All-metal ailerons, each with geared and trim tab. Hydraulically-operated single-slotted trailing-edge flaps. Hydraulically-operated spoilers on top of each wing operate on nose-wheel contact during landing.

FUSELAGE: Circular-section all-metal fail-safe structure with machined frames. Hydraulically-operated air-brakes under fuselage.

TAIL UNIT: Cantilever all-metal structure, with fixed-incidence tailplane mounted on base of fin. Trim and geared tab on elevator, trim-tab on rudder.

LANDING GEAR: Retractable tricycle type with single wheel on each unit. Hydraulic retraction, all units retracting forward. Oleo-pneumatic shock-absorbers. Goodyear main wheels and tyres size 24 × 7·14, (P7R) pressure 98 lb/sq in (6·87 kg/cm²). Goodyear nose-wheel and tyre, size 18 × 5·5 (8 PD), pressure 88 lb/sq in (6·19 kg/cm²). Messier hydraulic brakes. Hydraulic nose-wheel steering.

POWER PLANT: Two Rolls-Royce Bristol Viper Mk 526 turbojet engines (each rated at 3,360 lb = 1,524 kg st) mounted on sides of rear fuselage. Fuel in two integral tanks in wings, with total capacity of 425·5 Imp gallons (1,935 litres), and two integral wing-tip tanks with total capacity of 394 Imp gallons (1,792 litres). Total fuel capacity 819·5 Imp gallons (3,727 litres). Refuelling points on tip-tanks. Oil capacity 28 lb (13 kg).

ACCOMMODATION (Civil version): Crew of one or two on flight deck, with dual controls. Standard seating for five passengers in individual chairs, with bar and toilet at front of cabin and baggage space aft of rear seats. Further stowage space in nose, with access by sliding nose forward. Up to eight seats in cabin in high-density version. Executive interiors styled by Pininfarina available. Ambulance version has accommodation for two litters, two sitting casualties and medical attendant. With cabin stripped, there is space for 185 cu ft (5·24 m³) of freight, survey camera stations, navigation training equipment etc. Downward-opening plug-type door, with built-in steps, at front of cabin on port side. Cabin air-conditioned and pressurised.

ACCOMMODATION (Military versions): In addition to standard transport roles, the aircraft can be used for training and combat duties. The NASARR radar-navigational trainer has one main student station in the co-pilot's seat, with two or three more student stations in the cabin.

SYSTEMS: AiResearch simple air-cycle air-conditioning and pressurisation system, using engine-bleed air. Pressure differential 8·8 lb/sq in (0·62 kg/cm²). Hydraulic system, pressure 3,000 lb/sq in (210 kg/cm²), operates landing gear, flaps, spoilers, air-brakes, nose-wheel steering and wheel brakes. Pneumatic de-icing and anti-icing. Electrical system includes two DC generators, three inverters, two AC generators and two batteries.

ELECTRONICS AND EQUIPMENT: Standard equipment includes VHF radio, ADF, glideslope and marker beacon receivers. DME and weather radar optional.

DIMENSIONS, EXTERNAL:
Wing span 37 ft 6 in (11·43 m)
Wing span over tip-tanks 43 ft 3½ in (13·20 m)
Wing chord (mean) 8 ft 0 in (2·438 m)
Wing aspect ratio 6·25
Height overall 15 ft 9 in (4·80 m)
Tailplane span 17 ft 9½ in (5·43 m)
Wheel track 12 ft 0¾ in (3·68 m)
Wheelbase 14 ft 9 in (4·50 m)
Passenger door (forward, port):
Height 4 ft 1⅛ in (1·26 m)
Width 2 ft 1½ in (0·65 m)

DIMENSIONS, INTERNAL:
Cabin: Length 14 ft 8 in (4·47 m)
Max width 5 ft 4½ in (1·64 m)
Max height 4 ft 9 in (1·45 m)
Floor area 50·16 sq ft (4·66 m²)
Volume 291 cu ft (8·24 m³)

AREAS:
Wings, gross 225 sq ft (20·9 m²)
Ailerons (total) 12·10 sq ft (1·12 m²)
Trailing-edge flaps (total) 25·00 sq ft (2·32 m²)
Spoilers (total) 13·45 sq ft (1·25 m²)
Air-brakes 6·00 sq ft (0·56 m²)
Fin 36·0 sq ft (3·34 m²)
Rudder, including tab 5·81 sq ft (0·54 m²)
Tailplane 70·0 sq ft (6·50 m²)
Elevators, including tab 18·9 sq ft (1·75 m²)

WEIGHTS AND LOADING (seven-seat version):
Weight empty, equipped 10,650 lb (4,830 kg)
Max payload 1,600 lb (726 kg)
Max T-O weight 18,000 lb (8,165 kg)
Max ramp weight 18,300 lb (8,300 kg)
Max zero-fuel weight 12,500 lb (5,670 kg)
Max landing weight 16,000 lb (7,257 kg)
Max wing loading 80 lb/sq ft (390·6 kg/m²)

PERFORMANCE (at max T-O weight, except where indicated):
Max level speed at 19,500 ft (5,945 m) 459 knots (529 mph; 852 km/h)
Max permissible diving speed 425 knots (489 mph; 788 km/h) EAS between S/L and 14,000 ft (4,260 m); Mach 0·85 above 14,000 ft (4,260 m)
Max cruising speed above 36,000 ft (11,000 m) 432 knots (497 mph; 800 km/h)
Econ cruising speed at 41,000 ft (12,500 m) 390 knots (449 mph; 722 km/h)
Stalling speed, landing configuration, at landing weight of 13,023 lb (5,907 kg) 100 knots (115 mph; 185 km/h)
Rate of climb at S/L at AUW of 15,821 lb (7,176 kg) 5,400 ft (1,650 m)/min
Service ceiling 45,000 ft (13,715 m)
Service ceiling, one engine out 26,000 ft (7,925 m)
T-O run 2,905 ft (885 m)
T-O to 50 ft (15 m) 3,350 ft (1,020 m)
Landing from 50 ft (15 m) 3,800 ft (1,158 m)
Landing run 2,700 ft (822 m)
Range with max fuel, 45 min fuel reserve 1,100 nm (1,270 miles; 2,045 km)

PROCAER

PROGETTI COSTRUZIONI AERONAUTICHE SpA

HEAD OFFICE:
Via Cardinale Ascanio Sforza 85, Milan
WORKS:
Strada Alzaia Naviglio Pavese 78, Milan
PRESIDENT: Dott Ing Rico Neeff

Production by this company in recent years was concentrated on various versions of the Picchio F15 four-seat light aircraft. These have been described in earlier editions of *Jane's*.

During the past year the prototype F15E Picchio light aircraft has been acquired by Ambrosini, and is described under that heading in this edition.

The Procaer F.480 Cobra four-seat jet-powered light aircraft was described in the 1969-70 edition of *Jane's*. Its designer, Ing Stelio Frati, now directs his own company, General Avia, and is a director of the new Ital-Air company formed by Dr Mazzochi (see under appropriate headings in this section).

SIAI-MARCHETTI

SIAI-MARCHETTI SOCIETA PER AZIONI

MANAGEMENT AND WORKS:
21018 Sesto Calende (Varese)
AERODROME: Vergiate (Varese)
ROME OFFICE: Via Barberini, 36, 00187 Rome
PRESIDENT:
Dr Maria Luisa Rippa Protto
DIRECTORS:
Dr Ing Ado Bonuti
Dr Ing Alessandro Brena
Dr Nando Cucciniello

Founded in 1915, the Siai-Marchetti company was known originally as Savoia-Marchetti. It has produced a wide range of military and civil landplanes and flying-boats.

Current products of the company's own design are the S.205 four-seat light aircraft, which is built in seven different versions, the five-seat S.208 and twin-engined six-seat S.210. In addition, a two-seat light training aircraft known as the SA.202 Bravo is being developed in collaboration with FFA in Switzerland (which see). The last three types all incorporate S.205 components.

Siai-Marchetti acquired from Aviamilano all rights in the SF.260 three/four-seat aerobatic aircraft and is a stock-holder in the Silvercraft company (which see), responsible for the SH-4 three-seat helicopter.

In 1968, a Vertical Flight Division was formed, under the direction of Dr Ing Emilio Bianchi, to design and produce VTOL aircraft and/or their components. At the same time, laboratory facilities were increased in order to carry out fatigue testing of dynamic components, endurance testing of transmission components and similar activities. The Division's pre-design group has begun the study of light single-engined and medium-sized twin-engined rotorcraft, from which was evolved a project for a twin-engined high-speed helicopter known as the SV-20. Details of this project are given below.

Siai-Marchetti is engaged on the overhaul and repair of various types of aircraft for the Italian Air Force and for military and private customers in other countries. It employs a total of approximately 2,000 people.

Early in 1970, 30% of the share capital of Siai-Marchetti was acquired by Agusta (which see), together with an option on a further 30% which it was expected to take up later in the year.

Italian-built prototype of the SA.202 Bravo light training aircraft (115 hp Lycoming engine)

SIAI-MARCHETTI/FFA SA.202 BRAVO

The SA.202 is a two-seat light training aircraft, designed by Siai-Marchetti and currently being developed and produced jointly by the Italian company and FFA in Switzerland, with whom an agreement was concluded in 1967.

Siai-Marchetti will manufacture wings, landing gear and engine installations for both Swiss and Italian Bravos, while FFA will contribute complete fuselages (including cabin and controls) and tail units, and both Swiss- and Italian-assembled Bravos will incorporate certain features of the Siai-Marchetti S.205 (which see). Aircraft assembled in Italy will be designated SA.202, and those assembled in Switzerland AS.202.

The first Bravo to fly was the Swiss-built prototype (HB-HEA), which flew for the first time on 7 March 1969; this aircraft is powered by a 150 hp Lycoming engine. The Italian-built second prototype, powered by a 115 hp Lycoming O-235-C2A engine, flew on 7 May 1969. Two Italian- and two Swiss-built prototypes have been completed. Swiss certification was expected in mid-1970, and a prototype with 160 hp engine was due to fly later in the year. The third (FFA-built) prototype now has a taller fin and rudder and enlarged dorsal fin fairing.

The first 50 production aircraft, to which the description below applies, will be of the SA.202/15 version, with 150 hp Lycoming O-320-E2A engines.

TYPE: Three-seat light training aircraft.

WINGS: Cantilever low-wing monoplane. Wing section NACA 63_2618 (modified) at centre-line, 63_2415 at tip. Thickness/chord ratio 17·63% at root, 15% at tip. Dihedral 5° 43′ from roots. Incidence 3°. Sweepback at quarter-chord 0° 40′. Conventional aluminium single-spar fail-safe structure, with honeycomb laminate skin. Aluminium single-slotted flaps and single-slotted ailerons. Ground-adjustable tab on port aileron.

FUSELAGE: Conventional aluminium semi-monocoque fail-safe structure, with several glass-fibre fairings.

TAIL UNIT: Cantilever aluminium single-spar structure with sweptback vertical surfaces. Rudder mass-balanced, with provision for anti-collision beacon. Fixed-incidence tailplane. One-piece elevator with full-span trim-tab on starboard half, full-span Flettner tab on port half. Ground-adjustable tab on rudder.

LANDING GEAR: Non-retractable tricycle type, with steerable nose-wheel. Rubber-cushioned shock-absorber struts of Siai-Marchetti design. Main wheel tyres size 6·00 × 6; nose-wheel tyre size 5·00 × 5. Tyre pressure (all units) 35 lb/sq in (2·5 kg/cm²). Independent hydraulically-operated disc brake on each main wheel.

POWER PLANT: One 150 hp Lycoming O-320-E2A four-cylinder horizontally-opposed air-cooled engine, driving a McCauley 1C172 MGM two-blade fixed-pitch metal propeller, diameter 6 ft 2 in (1·88 m). Fuel in two leading-edge wing tanks with total capacity 31·7 Imp gallons (144 litres). Refuelling point above each wing. Oil capacity 1·8 Imp gallons (8 litres).

ACCOMMODATION: Seats for two persons side-by-side, in aerobatic version, under rearward-sliding jettisonable transparent canopy. Third seat at rear in utility version. Space for 176 lb (80 kg) of baggage aft of seats (Utility category). Dual controls, cabin ventilation and heating standard.

SYSTEMS: Hydraulic system, of Siai-Marchetti manufacture, for brake actuation. One 12V 60A engine-driven alternator and one 25Ah battery provide electrical power for engine starting, lighting, instruments, communications and navigation installations.

ELECTRONICS AND EQUIPMENT: Provision for VHF radio, VOR, ADF, blind-flying instrumentation or other special equipment at customer's option. Clutch-and-release mechanism for glider-towing optional.

DIMENSIONS, EXTERNAL:
Wing span 31 ft 2 in (9·50 m)
Wing chord at c/l 6 ft 1¼ in (1·86 m)
Wing chord at root 3 ft 9½ in (1·16 m)
Wing aspect ratio 6·51
Length overall 21 ft 5½ in (6·54 m)
Length of fuselage 20 ft 3 in (6·17 m)
Height overall 9 ft 1 in (2·77 m)
Tailplane span 12 ft 0½ in (3·67 m)
Wheel track 7 ft 4¼ in (2·24 m)
Wheelbase 5 ft 0½ in (1·54 m)
Propeller ground clearance 8¾ in (0·23 m)

DIMENSIONS, INTERNAL:
Cabin: Max length 7 ft 0½ in (2·15 m)
Max width 3 ft 4¼ in (1·02 m)
Max height 3 ft 7¼ in (1·10 m)
Floor area 23·14 sq ft (2·15 m²)

AREAS:
Wings, gross 149 sq ft (13·86 m²)
Ailerons (total) 11·7 sq ft (1·09 m²)
Trailing-edge flaps (total) 16·57 sq ft (1·54 m²)
Fin 14·1 sq ft (1·31 m²)
Rudder 5·70 sq ft (0·53 m²)
Tailplane 29·0 sq ft (2·69 m²)
Elevator, including tab 8·72 sq ft (0·81 m²)

WEIGHTS AND LOADINGS:
Weight empty, equipped 1,336 lb (606 kg)
Max payload:
Aerobatic 386 lb (175 kg)
Utility 595 lb (270 kg)
Max T-O and landing weight:
Aerobatic 1,873 lb (850 kg)
Utility 2,204 lb (1,000 kg)
Max wing loading 14·8 lb/sq ft (72·2 kg/m²)
Max power loading 1·36 lb/hp (6·66 kg/hp)

PERFORMANCE (Utility version at max T-O weight):
Max level speed at S/L 122 knots (140 mph; 225 km/h)
Max permissible diving speed 186 knots (215 mph; 345 km/h)
Max cruising speed (75% power) 113 knots (130 mph; 209 km/h)
Econ cruising speed 78 knots (90 mph; 145 km/h)

Stalling speed, flaps up 55 knots (63 mph; 101 km/h)
Stalling speed flaps down 46 knots (52 mph; 84 km/h)
Rate of climb at S/L 820 ft (250 m)/min
Service ceiling 13,000 ft (4,000 m)
T-O run 850 ft (260 m)
T-O to 50 ft (15 m) 1,600 ft (490 m)
Landing from 50 ft (15 m) 1,210 ft (370 m)
Landing run 590 ft (180 m)
Range with max fuel, no reserves: 595 nm (685 miles; 1,100 km)

SIAI-MARCHETTI S.205

This four-seat all-metal light aircraft has been so designed that it can be powered by engines of from 180 to 300 hp and can be fitted with either a retractable or non-retractable landing gear. Its potential versions range, therefore, from the most economical touring aircraft to a high-performance sporting machine.

Honeycomb panels are used widely in the air-frame, giving a very rigid structure.

Design of the S.205 was started in March 1964 and construction of the prototype began in July of the same year. Three examples were completed by April 1965. These all had a 180 hp Lycoming engine, but a wide range of versions have since become available, with different engines and equipment, as follows:

S.205-18/F. Basic version, with 180 hp Lycoming O-360-A1A engine, Hartzell constant-speed propeller, diameter 6 ft 2 in (1·88 m), and non-retractable landing gear. First production model flew in February 1966. Certificated by Italian authorities and FAA.

S.205-18/R. Same as 18/F, but with retractable landing gear.

S.205-20/F. With 200 hp Lycoming IO-360-A1A engine, Hartzell constant-speed propeller and non-retractable landing gear.

S.205-20/R. Same as 20/F, but with retractable landing gear.

S.205-22/R. With 220 hp Franklin 6A-350-C1 engine, McCauley constant-speed propeller and retractable landing gear. The S.205-22/R has been assembled and marketed in the USA, by Allied Aero Industries, as the **Waco S.220 Vela.**

S.205 components are utilised in other Siai-Marchetti designs, including the SA.202, S.208 and S.210.

The following description applies to all versions, of which a total of 450 (including 62 Waco S.220) had been built by the end of 1969.

Type: Four-seat light aircraft.

Wings: Cantilever low-wing monoplane. Wing section NACA 63_3618 on aircraft centre-line, NACA 63_2415 at tip. Dihedral 5° 42′. Incidence 2° at root, —1° at tip. Sweepback at quarter-chord 2° 1′. All-metal structure, with large honeycomb skin panels. All-metal ailerons and slotted flaps.

Fuselage: All-metal semi-monocoque stressed-skin structure.

Tail Unit: Cantilever all-metal structure. Trim-tab in port elevator.

Landing Gear: Electrically-retractable or non-retractable tricycle type according to version (see above). Oleo-pneumatic shock-absorbers. Main wheel tyres size 6·00-6 6-ply rating: nose-wheel tyre size 5·00-5. Tyre pressure 25 lb/sq in (1·75 kg/cm²). Goodyear hydraulic disc-brakes. Wheel fairings standard on 18/F and 20/F.

Power Plant: Details of engine and propeller given under individual model descriptions. Fuel in two wing tanks, with total capacity of 47 Imp gallons (215 litres). Optional wing-tip tanks for all versions, increasing total fuel capacity to 98 Imp gallons (446 litres). Oil capacity 1.66 Imp gallons (7·5 litres).

Accommodation: Enclosed cabin, seating two side-by-side in front and two on rear bench seat. Rear seats removable for freight-carrying. Forward-opening cabin door and baggage door on starboard side. Cabin ventilated and heated.

Electronics and Equipment: Variety of HF, VHF, VOR and ADF equipment can be installed. Electric turn-and-bank indicator standard. Optional items include gyro-horizon, directional gyro, two-axis autopilot and navigation coupler system.

Dimensions, external:
Wing span 35 ft 7½ in (10·86 m)
Wing chord at root 5 ft 3½ in (1·61 m)
Wing chord at tip 3 ft 10 in (1·17 m)
Wing aspect ratio 7·04
Length overall 26 ft 3 in (8·00 m)
Height overall 9 ft 5¾ in (2·89 m)
Tailplane span 11 ft 2½ in (3·42 m)
Wheel track 11 ft 8 in (3·55 m)
Wheelbase 6 ft 2¾ in (1·90 m)
Cabin door:
Height 3 ft 2¼ in (0·97 m)
Width 3 ft 2¼ in (0·97 m)
Baggage compartment door:
Height 1 ft 8¾ in (0·53 m)
Width 1 ft 9¼ in (0·54 m)
Height to sill 2 ft 3½ in (0·70 m)

Dimensions, internal:
Cabin: Length 5 ft 10¼ in (1·78 m)
Max width 3 ft 8¾ in (1·14 m)
Max height 4 ft 4 in (1·32 m)
Floor area 21·8 sq ft (2·03 m²)
Volume 88·0 cu ft (2·5 m³)

Areas:
Wings, gross 173 sq ft (16·09 m²)
Ailerons (total) 16·66 sq ft (1·55 m²)
Trailing-edge flaps (total) 23·32 sq ft (2·51 m²)
Fin 12·50 sq ft (1·16 m²)
Rudder 6·24 sq ft (0·58 m²)
Tailplane 24·11 sq ft (2·24 m²)
Elevators, including tab 13·24 sq ft (1·23 m²)

Weights and Loadings:
Weight empty:
18/F, 18/R 1,565 lb (710 kg)
20/F 1,598 lb (725 kg)
20/R 1,630 lb (740 kg)
22/R 1,653 lb (750 kg)
Max T-O and landing weight:
18/F, 18/R 2,645 lb (1,200 kg)
20/F, 20/R 2,866 lb (1,300 kg)
22/R 2,976 lb (1,350 kg)
Max wing loading:
18/F, 18/R 15·28 lb/sq ft (74·6 kg/m²)
20/F, 20/R 16·5 lb/sq ft (80·8 kg/m²)
22/R 17·2 lb/sq ft (83·9 kg/m²)
Max power loading:
18/F, 18/R 14·7 lb/hp (6·66 kg/hp)
20/F, 20/R 14·33 lb/hp (6·50 kg/hp)
22/R 13·54 lb/hp (6·14 kg/hp)

Performance (at max T-O weight):
Max level speed at S/L:
18/F 127 knots (146 mph; 235 km/h)
18/R 141 knots (162 mph; 260 km/h)
20/F 135 knots (155 mph; 250 km/h)
20/R 151 knots (174 mph; 280 km/h)
22/R 159 knots (183 mph; 295 km/h)
Max permissible diving speed:
All versions 174 knots (201 mph; 323 km/h)
Max cruising speed:
18/F 116 knots (134 mph; 215 km/h)
18/R 130 knots (150 mph; 240 km/h)
20/F 122 knots (140 mph; 226 km/h)
20/R 138 knots (159 mph; 255 km/h)
22/R 152 knots (175 mph; 281 km/h)
Stalling speed, flaps and landing gear down:
All versions 46 knots (52·5 mph; 84 km/h)
Rate of climb at S/L:
18/F 690 ft (210 m)/min
18/R 767 ft (234 m)/min
20/F 770 ft (235 m)/min
20/R 865 ft (264 m)/min
22/R 1,160 ft (354 m)/min
Service ceiling:
18/F 14,750 ft (4,500 m)
18/R 16,900 ft (5,150 m)
20/F 16,000 ft (4,880 m)
20/R 17,650 ft (5,380 m)
22/R 20,330 ft (6,200 m)
T-O run:
18/F, 18/R, 20/F, 20/R 780 ft (238 m)
22/R 720 ft (220 m)
T-O to 50 ft (15 m):
18/F, 18/R 1,410 ft (430 m)
20/F, 20/R 1,340 ft (408 m)
22/R 1,240 ft (378 m)
Landing from 50 ft (15 m):
18/F, 18/R 1,510 ft (460 m)
20/F, 20/R, 22/R 1,540 ft (470 m)
Landing run:
18/F, 18/R 607 ft (185 m)
20/F, 20/R, 22/R 620 ft (190 m)
Range with max internal fuel* and max payload:
18/F 664 nm (765 miles; 1,230 km)
18/R 772 nm (890 miles; 1,430 km)
20/F 720 nm (830 miles; 1,335 km)
20/R 816 nm (940 miles; 1,500 km)
22/R 714 nm (823 miles; 1,325 km)
*with wing-tip auxiliary fuel tanks range is increased by approx 430 nm (495 miles; 800 km) in each case.

Siai-Marchetti S.205-20/F four-seat light aircraft, with fixed landing gear

SIAI-MARCHETTI S.208

First flown on 22 May 1967, the S.208 utilises many components of the S.205 but has a more powerful engine and is able to carry up to five persons. Production began in the Spring of 1968. Current orders include 24 of a version, designated **S.208M,** for the Italian Air Force. These have a jettisonable cabin door, and will be used for liaison and training duties.

The description of the S.205 applies equally to the S.208, except in the following details:

Type: Five-seat light aircraft.

Landing Gear: Retractable type only. Otherwise as for S.205.

Power Plant: One 260 hp Lycoming O-540-E4A5 six-cylinder horizontally-opposed air-cooled engine, driving a Hartzell two-blade constant-speed metal propeller, diameter 6 ft 2 in (1·88 m). Two fuel tanks in wings, with total capacity of 47 Imp gallons (215 litres), and two auxiliary wingtip tanks (each 25·4 Imp gallons = 115·5 litres), bringing total fuel capacity to 98 Imp gallons (446 litres). Oil capacity 2·5 Imp gallons (11·35 litres).

Accommodation: Enclosed cabin seating pilot and up to four passengers. Forward-opening cabin door on starboard side (jettisonable on S.208M). Second door, on port side, available optionally. Access to baggage compartment, aft of seats, from inside or outside. Eight warm air outlets, four of which are individual, and two windscreen defroster outlets.

Electronics and Equipment: Provision for full range of HF, VHF, VOR and ADF equipment,

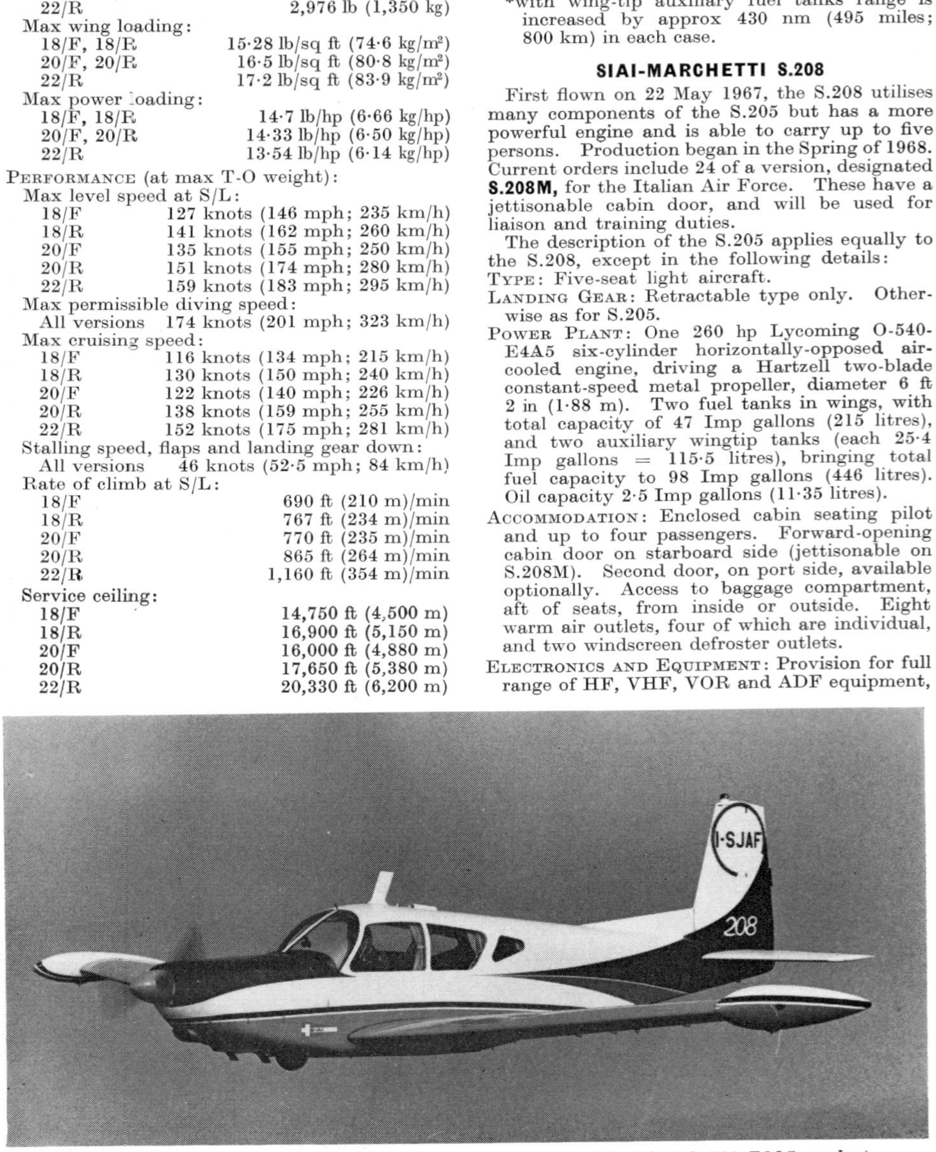

Siai-Marchetti S.208 four/five-seat light aircraft (260 hp Lycoming O-540-E4A5 engine)

to customer's specification. Blind-flying instrumentation, two-axis autopilot and navigation systems optional.

DIMENSIONS, EXTERNAL AND INTERNAL:
Same as for S.205

AREAS:

Wings, gross	173 sq ft (16·09 m²)
Ailerons (total)	11·67 sq ft (1·08 m²)
Trailing-edge flaps (total)	23·36 sq ft (2·17 m²)
Fin	12·1 sq ft (1·12 m²)
Rudder	6·6 sq ft (0·61 m²)
Tailplane	24·1 sq ft (2·24 m²)
Elevators, including tab	13·2 sq ft (1·23 m²)

WEIGHTS AND LOADINGS:

Weight empty, equipped	1,720 lb (780 kg)
Max T-O weight	2,976 lb (1,350 kg)
Max wing loading	17·2 lb/sq ft (84 kg/m²)
Max power loading	11·6 lb/hp (5·19 kg/hp)

PERFORMANCE (at max T-O weight):
Max level speed at S/L
173 knots (199 mph; 320 km/h)
Max cruising speed
162 knots (187 mph; 300 km/h)
Range with max internal fuel
647 nm (746 miles; 1,200 km)
Range with max fuel (incl tip-tanks)
1,085 nm (1,250 miles; 2,000 km)

SIAI-MARCHETTI S.210

This is a twin-engined version of the S.205 series, embodying many components of the latter. The prototype (I-SJAP) made its first flight on 19 February 1970.

The description of the S.205 applies also to the S.210, except in the following details:

TYPE: Six-seat twin-engined light aircraft.

WINGS: Wing section at tip NACA 63_3618. Modified as necessary to carry engines on wings.

TAIL UNIT: Additional trim-tab, in rudder.

LANDING GEAR: Retractable type only.

POWER PLANT: Two 200 hp Lycoming TIO-360-A horizontally-opposed air-cooled and turbo-supercharged engines, each driving a Hartzell HC-C2YK-1B/8468-10R two-blade constant-speed metal propeller, diameter 6 ft 2 in (1·88 m). Four fuel tanks in wings, with total capacity of 79·2 Imp gallons (360 litres). Total oil capacity 3·33 Imp gallons (15 litres).

ACCOMMODATION: Pilot and five passengers in enclosed cabin. One forward-hinged door on each side. Six individual warm air outlets and two windscreen defroster outlets.

ELECTRONICS: Provision for full range of HF, VHF, VOR and ADF equipment to customer's specification. Optional equipment includes blind-flying instrumentation, two-axis autopilot and navigation aids.

DIMENSIONS, EXTERNAL:

Wing span	38 ft 2 in (11·63 m)
Length overall	29 ft 0 in (8·83 m)
Height overall	10 ft 11¼ in (3·33 m)
Tailplane span	15 ft 5 in (4·70 m)
Wheel track	11 ft 8¼ in (3·56 m)
Wheelbase	8 ft 10 in (2·69 m)
Passenger doors (each):	
Height	3 ft 2¼ in (0·97 m)
Width	3 ft 2¼ in (0·97 m)

DIMENSIONS, INTERNAL:

Cabin:	
Length	7 ft 7¾ in (2·33 m)
Max width	3 ft 8¾ in (1·14 m)
Max height	4 ft 4 in (1·32 m)

AREAS:

Wings, gross	185·5 sq ft (17·23 m²)
Ailerons (total)	11·69 sq ft (1·09 m²)
Trailing-edge flaps (total)	23·36 sq ft (2·17 m²)
Fin	12·25 sq ft (1·14 m²)
Rudder, including tab	9·28 sq ft (0·86 m²)
Tailplane	27·56 sq ft (2·56 m²)
Elevators, including tab	20·88 sq ft (1·94 m²)

WEIGHTS AND LOADINGS:

Weight empty, equipped	2,271 lb (1,030 kg)
Max T-O weight	4,078 lb (1,850 kg)
Max wing loading	21·97 lb/sq ft (107·3 kg/m²)
Max power loading	10·33 lb/hp (4·62 kg/hp)

PERFORMANCE (estimated, at max T-O weight):
Max level speed at S/L
193 knots (222 mph; 357 km/h)
Max cruising speed at 8,000 ft (2,400 m)
183 knots (211 mph; 340 km/h)
Econ cruising speed at 8,000 ft (2,400 m)
169 knots (195 mph; 314 km/h)

Rate of climb at S/L	1,980 ft (603 m)/min
Service ceiling	26,500 ft (8,100 m)
Service ceiling, one engine out	14,400 ft (4,400 m)
T-O run	920 ft (280 m)
T-O to 50 ft (15 m)	1,310 ft (400 m)
Landing from 50 ft (15 m)	1,800 ft (550 m)
Landing run	770 ft (235 m)

Range with max payload
1,024 nm (1,180 miles; 1,900 km)

SIAI-MARCHETTI SF.260

Designed by Ing Stelio Frati, the SF.260 is a low-wing monoplane, and is certificated for aerobatic flying.

The prototype, known as the F.250, was built by Aviamilano, with a 250 hp Lycoming engine (see 1965-66 *Jane's*), and flew for the first time on 15 July 1964.

The version developed for production was manufactured, initially under licence from Aviamilano, by Siai-Marchetti, and is therefore designated SF.260. When Aviamilano ceased its aeronautical activities, Siai-Marchetti became official holder of the type certificate and of all manufacturing rights in the SF.260. The aircraft received FAA type approval on 1 April 1966.

Prototype of the Siai-Marchetti S.210 twin-engined six-seat light aircraft

Following delivery of the first 50 production aircraft, a second series of 50 civil SF.260's has entered production, to fulfil orders from Air France, Sabena and other customers.

Concurrently with these aircraft, Siai-Marchetti is also building an initial quantity of 56 of a military version, the **SF.260M**, for the Belgian (36), Congolese (12) and Zambian Air Forces (8). The SF.260M has an enlarged rudder and internal equipment applicable to its role as a basic military training aircraft.

An SF.260 set up an FAI speed record in Class C-1-c on 17 October 1968, by flying from Las Vegas to Los Angeles at an average speed of 214·08 mph (344·51 kmh).

TYPE: Three-seat cabin monoplane.

WINGS: Cantilever low-wing monoplane. Wing section NACA 64212 at root, NACA 64210 at tip. Dihedral 5°. All-metal single-spar structure in two portions. All-metal Frise-type ailerons and electrically-operated slotted flaps.

FUSELAGE: All-metal semi-monocoque structure, with comparatively thick skin and few stringers.

TAIL UNIT: Cantilever all-metal structure with swept vertical surfaces. Rudder and elevators statically and dynamically balanced. Controllable trim-tab in elevator.

LANDING GEAR: Retractable tricycle type. Electrical retraction with manual emergency actuation. Oleo-pneumatic shock-absorbers. Steerable nose-wheel with tyre size 5·00 × 5. Main wheels and tyres size 6·00 × 6. Cleveland single-disc hydraulic brakes.

POWER PLANT: One 260 hp Lycoming O-540-E4A5 six-cylinder horizontally-opposed air-cooled engine, driving a two-blade Hartzell type HC-C2YK-1B/8467-8R or HC-C2YK-1B/8477-8R metal constant-speed propeller, diameter 7 ft 6 in (1·93 m). Fuel in four tanks, two in wings, with total capacity of 22 Imp gallons (100 litres), and two on wingtips, with total capacity of 31 Imp gallons (140 litres). Total fuel capacity 53 Imp gallons (240 litres).

ACCOMMODATION: Three seats in enclosed cockpit, two in front, one at rear. Two children with a weight not exceeding 250 lb (113 kg) may use rear seat. Rearward-sliding transparent canopy. Baggage compartment capacity 88 lb (40 kg). Cabin sound-proofed with glass-fibre, heated and ventilated.

EQUIPMENT: Optional equipment includes blind-flying instrumentation, communications radio and oxygen system.

DIMENSIONS, EXTERNAL:

Wing span over tip tanks	26 ft 11¾ in (8·25 m)
Wing chord at root	5 ft 3 in (1·60 m)
Wing chord at tip	2 ft 6¾ in (0·78 m)
Wing aspect ratio	6·4

Siai-Marchetti SF.260 three-seat light aircraft (260 hp Lycoming engine) *(Stephen P. Peltz)*

Siai-Marchetti SF.260M, military trainer version of this three-seat light monoplane

Length overall	23 ft 0 in (7·02 m)
Height overall	8 ft 6 in (2·60 m)
Tailplane span	9 ft 9¾ in (3·00 m)
Wheel track	7 ft 5 in (2·26 m)
Wheelbase	5 ft 3½ in (1·62 m)

AREAS:

Wings, gross	108·5 sq ft (10·10 m²)
Ailerons (total)	8·50 sq ft (0·79 m²)
Flaps (total)	12·7 sq ft (1·19 m²)
Fin	8·05 sq ft (0·75 m²)
Rudder	5·38 sq ft (0·50 m²)
Tailplane	14·9 sq ft (1·39 m²)
Elevators	10·0 sq ft (0·93 m²)

WEIGHTS AND LOADINGS:

| Weight empty, equipped | 1,543 lb (700 kg) |

Max T-O weight:

Utility	2,430 lb (1,102 kg)
Aerobatic	2,205 lb (1,000 kg)
Max wing loading	22·4 lb/sq ft (109 kg/m²)
Max power loading	9·33 lb/hp (4·23 kg/hp)

PERFORMANCE (at max utility T-O weight):

Max level speed at S/L
    204 knots (235 mph; 375 km/h)

Max cruising speed at 10,000 ft (3,050 m)
    186 knots (214 mph; 345 km/h)

Stalling speed, flaps down
    57 knots (65 mph; 104 km/h)

Rate of climb at S/L	1,770 ft (540 m)/min
Service ceiling	21,370 ft (6,500 m)
T-O run on runway	820 ft (250 m)
T-O run on grass	950 ft (290 m)
T-O to 50 ft (15 m)	1,390 ft (425 m)
Landing from 50 ft (15 m)	1,610 ft (490 m)
Landing run	790 ft (240 m)

Range with max fuel (two persons)
    1,107 nm (1,275 miles; 2,050 km)

SIAI-MARCHETTI SM.1019

The Siai-Marchetti SM.1019 is a light STOL aircraft suitable for military observation, light ground attack or utility duties. It is based very largely upon the airframe of the American Cessna L-19/O-1 Bird Dog (see 1964-65 *Jane's*), from which it differs basically in having an Allison 250-B15G turboprop engine in a lengthened nose, and redesigned, angular vertical tail surfaces of greater area. The main fuselage, wings, landing gear and cabin have been extensively modified to meet current operational requirements.

Design of the SM.1019 was started in January 1969, and construction of a prototype began two months later. This aircraft flew for the first time on 24 May 1969, and was granted certification by the RAI on 25 October 1969. Early in 1970 it was undergoing evaluation by the Italian Armed Forces, with the prospects of an order for between 100 and 200 aircraft with production beginning early in 1971.

TYPE: Two-seat STOL aircraft.

WINGS: Braced high-wing monoplane. Wing section NACA 2412. Incidence 1° 30'. No dihedral or sweepback. Wing braced by single strut on each side. Conventional all-metal structure, with metal ailerons and trailing-edge slotted flaps, the latter being actuated electrically. Trim-tab on starboard aileron.

FUSELAGE: Conventional all-metal stressed-skin structure.

TAIL UNIT: Conventional cantilever all-metal structure, with horizontal surfaces mounted on top of fuselage and dorsal fairing to fin. Ground-adjustable trim-tab on rudder. Manually-operated mechanically actuated trim-tab in starboard elevator.

LANDING GEAR: Non-retractable tail-wheel type, with cantilever leaf-type spring-steel main-wheel legs. Main wheels have low-pressure tyres, size 7·00-6, pressure 30 lb/sq in (2·11 kg/cm²); tail-wheel and tyre of 8 in (20·3 cm) diameter, pressure 35 lb/sq in (2·46 kg/cm²). Goodyear hydraulic single-disc brake on each main wheel. Provision for fitting ski landing gear.

POWER PLANT: One 317 shp Allison 250-B15G (T63) turboprop engine, driving a Hartzell HC-A3VF-5 constant-speed three-blade metal propeller, diameter 7 ft 6 in (2·29 m). Fuel in four tanks in wings, with total capacity of 68·3 Imp gallons (82 US gallons=310 litres). Refuelling points on top of wings. Oil capacity 1·75 Imp gallons (2·1 US gallons=8 litres).

ACCOMMODATION: Pilot and one passenger (or co-pilot) seated in tandem in fully-enclosed and extensively glazed cabin, access to which is provided by two doors on starboard side. Cabin heated and ventilated. Dual controls optional.

SYSTEMS: No hydraulic or air-conditioning systems. Electrical power is provided by an engine-driven 150A starter-generator and a 24V 24Ah nickel-cadmium battery. Auxiliary receptacle for use with external power source.

ELECTRONICS AND EQUIPMENT: Equipment of prototype includes VHF nav/com, UHF, VHF/FM communications set, ADF and marker beacon. Production aircraft will be equipped to customer's requirements. Twin landing lights in outer port wing leading-edge.

ARMAMENT AND OPERATIONAL EQUIPMENT: Two MA-4A bomb racks are installed beneath each wing, and the aircraft's armament system is

Siai-Marchetti SM.1019 prototype development of the Cessna Bird Dog light aircraft

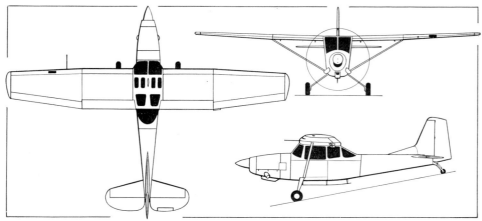

Three-view drawing of the SM.1019 two-seat STOL light military aircraft

capable of accommodating rockets, flares or minigun pods in various combinations, up to a maximum external load of 500 lb (227 kg).

DIMENSIONS, EXTERNAL:

Wing span	36 ft 0 in (10·97 m)
Wing chord at root	5 ft 4 in (1·63 m)
Wing chord at tip	3 ft 7 in (1·09 m)
Wing aspect ratio	7·44
Length overall	27 ft 8 in (8·43 m)
Height overall	7 ft 9¾ in (2·38 m)
Tailplane span	10 ft 6½ in (3·215 m)
Wheel track	7 ft 6½ in (2·30 m)
Wheelbase	19 ft 10½ in (6·06 m)
Propeller ground clearance	9 in (0·23 m)

Baggage door: Height 1 ft 6½ in (0·47 m)

| Width | 1 ft 9 in (0·53 m) |
| Height to sill | 2 ft 0¼ in (0·62 m) |

DIMENSIONS, INTERNAL:

Cabin: Max length 5 ft 7¾ in (1·72 m)

Max width	2 ft 0¾ in (0·63 m)
Max height	4 ft 1¼ in (1·25 m)
Floor area	11·63 sq ft (1·08 m²)
Volume	47·67 cu ft (1·35 m²)

AREAS:

Wings, gross	173·94 sq ft (16·16 m²)
Ailerons (total)	18·30 sq ft (1·70 m²)
Trailing-edge flaps (total)	21·10 sq ft (1·96 m²)
Fin	10·22 sq ft (0·95 m²)
Rudder, incl tab	12·38 sq ft (1·15 m²)
Tailplane	19·27 sq ft (1·79 m²)
Elevators, incl tab	13·35 sq ft (1·24 m²)

WEIGHTS AND LOADINGS (operational mission, without external stores):

Weight empty, equipped	1,480 lb (672 kg)
Max payload	510 lb (231 kg)
Max T-O weight	2,513 lb (1,140 kg)
Max zero-fuel weight	1,990 lb (903 kg)
Max landing weight	2,403 lb (1,090 kg)
Max wing loading	14·4 lb/sq ft (70·54 kg/m²)
Max power loading	7·93 lb/shp (3·6 kg/shp)

PERFORMANCE (prototype flight test data):

Max level speed at 6,000 ft (1,830 m)
    163 knots (188 mph; 302 km/h) TAS

Max permissible diving speed
    168 knots (194 mph; 313 km/h) IAS

Max cruising speed at 6,000 ft (1,830 m)
    150 knots (173 mph; 278 km/h) TAS

Econ cruising speed at 10,000 ft (3,050 m)
    117 knots (135 mph; 217 km/h) TAS

Max rate of climb at S/L 1,625 ft (495 m)/min

Service ceiling (estimated) 30,000 ft (9,150 m)

Range with max fuel, 10 min reserves
    665 nm (765 miles; 1,230 km)

Range with external stores, 10 min reserves
    280 nm (320 miles; 515 km)

SIAI-MARCHETTI SV-20A and SV-20C

The SV-20A is a twin-engined high-speed winged helicopter, which has been evolved by Siai-Marchetti's Vertical Flight Division.

The SV-20C is a compound helicopter version, with a 5 ft 3 in (1·60 m) diameter three-blade constant-speed pusher propeller, driven through two sets of bevel gears, aft of the starboard engine nacelle.

In December 1968 work was started on the manufacture of dynamic components and major dynamic assemblies, as well as a number of airframes, for fatigue and transmission system tests as a preparatory step to the further development of the design. All available details of the two versions, which are basically similar, are given below. General appearance of the aircraft can be seen from the accompanying three-view drawing.

TYPE: High-speed winged helicopter.

ROTOR SYSTEM: Single two-blade tapered main rotor and two-blade tail rotor. Main rotor of semi-rigid teetering type, the blades being mounted on roller bearings for pitch change, connected by a laminated strap which resists the centrifugal loads, and attached to mast by flapping hinges. Rotor brake is optional. Both the main and tail rotor blades have an extruded aluminium spar, and are covered with impregnated glass-fibre with a plastic honeycomb core.

ROTOR DRIVE: Gearbox consists of a single-stage helical gear combined with two spiral bevel gears. Main rotor has a two-stage planetary gearbox combined with a bevel gear driven from the turbines. Main rotor rpm 349. Main rotor/engine rpm ratio 0·0435 : 1. Tail rotor/engine rpm ratio 0·2269 : 1.

WINGS: Cantilever high-mounted wings, of NACA 64-A-421 section at root, NACA 64-A-418 at tip. Thickness/chord ratio 18% at root, 12% at tip. Aluminium honeycomb sandwich construction.

FUSELAGE: All-metal semi-monocoque structure of aluminium honeycomb sandwich.

TAIL UNIT: Aluminium alloy monocoque tail boom supports the horizontal stabiliser, vertical fin and tail rotor, including transmission and controls.

LANDING GEAR: Tubular skid type, of aluminium alloy. Lock-on wheels can be fitted for ground manoeuvring. Provision for floats, skis or other landing gear according to role.

POWER PLANT: Two wing-mounted Pratt & Whitney (UACL) PT6A-40 turboshaft engines, each developing 1,100 shp max for T-O. Turboméca Astazou XIVA or Rolls-Royce RR.360 engines can be installed, to customer's choice. Fuel in two interconnected flexible tanks installed in vapour-tight compartments in fuselage, with total capacity of 338 US gallons (281 Imp gallons = 1,280 litres). System has been designed to avoid CG displacement due to fuel consumption in flight. Provision for auxiliary fuel tanks to be carried on wing pylons. Oil capacity 2·4 US gallons (2 Imp gallons = 9 litres).

ACCOMMODATION: Crew of two pilots on flight deck. Typical loads in main cabin include 12 passengers or troops; four stretcher cases and a medical attendant; or approx 2,750 lb (1,250 kg) of freight. External cargo or military loads can be carried on six underwing pylons or on an under-fuselage cargo hook. Doors on each side of flight deck and at front and rear of passenger cabin on port side.

SYSTEMS: Hydraulic system supplies boosted controls. Electrical system is of 28V DC single-conductor type, with negative leads earthed to airframe. Electrical power is supplied by a starter-generator on each engine, a third generator connected to and driven by the main rotor gearbox, and a battery. System is provided with external power receptacle. Heating and air-conditioning systems optional.

ELECTRONICS AND EQUIPMENT: Standard VFR and IFR instrumentation, radio, ADF and VOR.

DIMENSIONS, EXTERNAL:
- Diameter of main rotor — 42 ft 2¼ in (12·86 m)
- Main rotor blade chord (at 75% radius) — 2 ft 1¼ in (0·643 m)
- Diameter of tail rotor — 7 ft 10½ in (2·40 m)
- Distance between rotor centres — 25 ft 8¼ in (7·83 m)
- Wing span — 19 ft 8¼ in (6·00 m)
- Wing chord at root — 3 ft 10 in (1·166 m)
- Wing chord (mean) — 2 ft 8¾ in (0·833 m)
- Wing chord at tip — 1 ft 7½ in (0·50 m)
- Length overall, rotors turning — 51 ft 0¾ in (15·562 m)
- Length of fuselage — 39 ft 3½ in (11·98 m)
- Height to top of rotor hub — 11 ft 7¾ in (3·55 m)
- Wheel track — 7 ft 2¾ in (2·20 m)

DIMENSIONS, INTERNAL:
- Cabin: Length — 12 ft 7½ in (3·85 m)
- Max width — 4 ft 11 in (1·50 m)
- Max height — 4 ft 3¼ in (1·30 m)
- Floor area — 55·97 sq ft (5·20 m²)
- Volume — 238·37 cu ft (6·75 m³)

AREAS:
- Main rotor blades (each) — 44·52 sq ft (4·136 m²)
- Tail rotor blades (each) — 3·36 sq ft (0·312 m²)
- Main rotor disc — 1,397·36 sq ft (129·82 m²)
- Tail rotor disc — 48·65 sq ft (4·52 m²)
- Fin — 19·27 sq ft (1·79 m²)
- Stabiliser — 33·58 sq ft (3·12 m²)

WEIGHTS AND LOADINGS:
- Weight empty — 4,122 lb (1,870 kg)
- Max payload — 2,037 lb (924 kg)
- Max T-O weight — 8,818 lb (4,000 kg)
- Max disc loading — 6·31 lb/sq ft (30·80 kg/m²)
- Max power loading — 4·01 lb/shp (1·82 kg/shp)

PERFORMANCE (estimated, at max T-O weight):
- Max cruising speed at S/L:
  - SV-20A — 175 knots (202 mph; 324 km/h)
  - SV-20C — 210 knots (242 mph; 389 km/h)
- Econ cruising speed at S/L (both) — 160 knots (184 mph; 296 km/h)
- Max rate of climb at S/L:
  - SV-20A — 1,900 ft (579 m)/min
  - SV-20C — 2,300 ft (701 m)/min
- Hovering ceiling in ground effect (both) — 23,000 ft (7,010 m)
- Hovering ceiling out of ground effect (both) — 17,500 ft (5,334 m)
- Range with max fuel (both) — 416 nm (480 miles; 890 km)

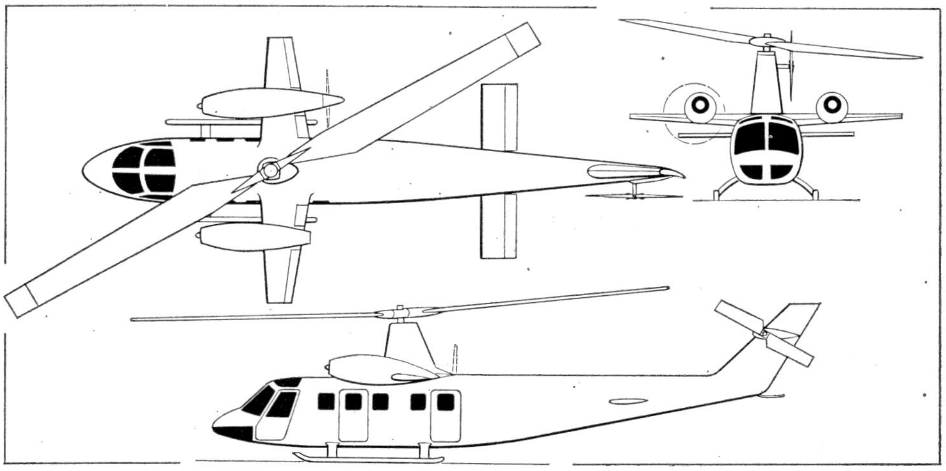

Siai-Marchetti SV-20C, a compound version of the SV-20A with pusher propeller

SILVERCRAFT

SILVERCRAFT SpA

HEAD OFFICE AND WORKS:
Strada del Sempione 114, 21018 Sesto Calende (Varese)

PUBLIC RELATIONS MANAGER:
Dott Ing Pier Maria Pellò

SILVERCRAFT SH-4

Developed in co-operation with Siai-Marchetti SpA, which remains a stockholder in the Silvercraft company, the SH-4 is a three-seat light helicopter suitable for pilot training, utility, agricultural, survey, police, ambulance, military liaison and observation duties.

The prototype flew for the first time in March 1965, and five pre-production models had been completed by the end of 1967. On 4 September 1968 the SH-4 became the first all-Italian helicopter to receive both FAA and RAI certification.

Production of an initial series of 50 aircraft is under way in the Silvercraft works at Sesto Calende. Twenty SH-4's had been built by the end of 1969, and deliveries began early in 1970.

The following versions of this helicopter have been announced:

SH-4. Standard general-purpose version. May be fitted with either a 200 hp Franklin 6A-350-D1 or 235 hp Franklin 6A-350-D1A engine, in each case derated to 170 hp.

SH-4A. Agricultural version, powered by Franklin 6A-350-D1 engine (see above). Fitted with 35 ft 5¼ in (10·80 m) spray bars capable of covering a 108 ft (33 m) swath width with liquid chemicals. Max capacity of chemical tanks 50·6 Imp gallons (230 litres) up to a max weight of 441 lb (200 kg). Max rate of distribution 19·8 Imp gallons (90 litres)/min; chemical tanks can be replenished in 1 minute. Total weight (empty) of spray installation 82 lb (37 kg).

SH-4C. As standard SH-4, but powered by Franklin 6AS-350-D1 engine fitted with AiResearch exhaust-driven supercharger. Also available as two-seater or with pontoon landing gear.

TYPE: Three-seat light helicopter.

ROTOR SYSTEM: Two-blade semi-rigid main and tail rotors. Blades constructed of laminated wood, with glass-fibre covering and (on main rotor) steel weights at blade tips to augment the inertia of the rotor. Aluminium alloy attachment fittings and steel hubs.

ROTOR DRIVE: Rotors driven through steel shafting. Primary gearbox, consisting of two sets of planetary gears (reduction ratio 1 : 0·89), mounted aft of engine; secondary bevel gearboxes at base of main rotor drive-shaft (reduction ratio 1 : 0·164) and in rear of tail boom for main and tail rotors respectively. Rotor design eliminates need for stabilisation bars and dampers, and rotor is controlled directly without hydraulic servo-command system. Main rotor/engine rpm ratio (235 hp engine), 418 : 2,850. Tail rotor/engine rpm ratio (235 hp engine), 2,434 : 2,850.

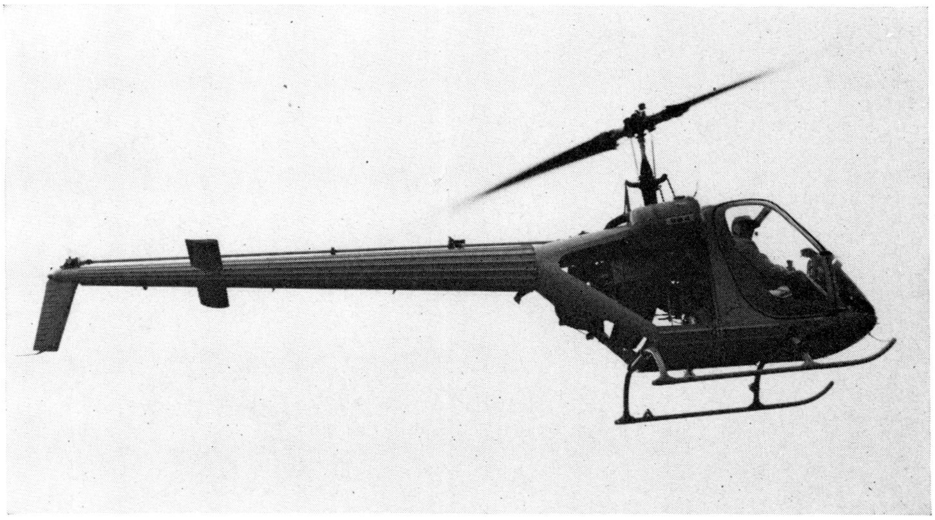

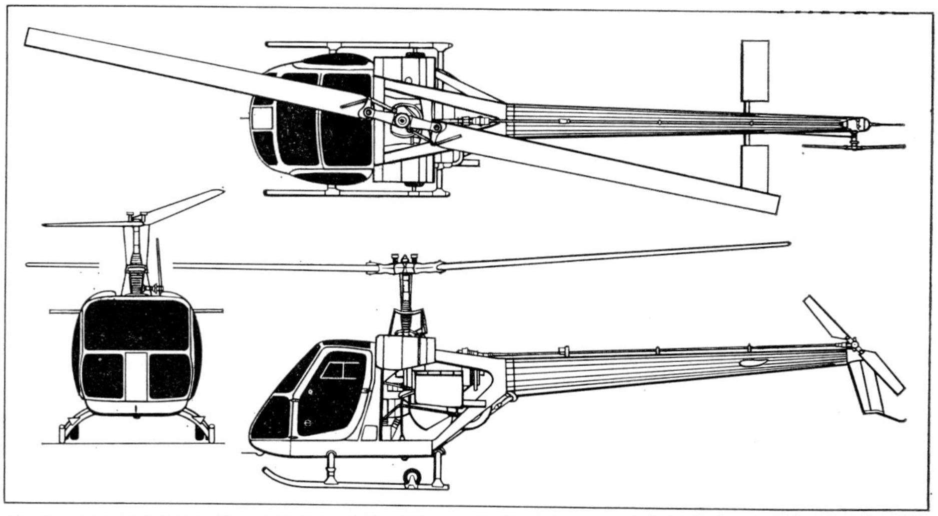

Photograph and three-view drawing of the Silvercraft SH-4 three-seat light helicopter (170 hp Franklin 6A-350-D engine)

FUSELAGE: Central structure of aluminium alloy, except engine fireproof bulkheads which are of titanium alloy. Semi-monocoque cabin at front and semi-monocoque tail boom are also of aluminium construction. Cabin door frames and window frames of reinforced glass-fibre.

TAIL UNIT: Horizontal stabiliser mid-mounted on tail boom. Ventral stabilising fin beneath tip of tail boom.

LANDING GEAR: Tubular skid type, with provision to fit ground manoeuvring wheels or skis. Tail-skid at base of ventral stabilising fin, to protect tail rotor. Alternative pontoon gear available for amphibious operation.

Power Plant: One 235 hp (derated to 170 hp) Franklin 6A-350-D1A six-cylinder horizontally-opposed air-cooled engine in aircraft intended for operation at altitude, or one 200 hp (derated to 170 hp) Franklin 6A-350-D1 engine in agricultural SH-4A. Engine installed horizontally, offset to port. Fuel in two main tanks, one on each side of base of pylon, with total capacity of 28·6 Imp gallons (130 litres). For short-range missions, one tank may be omitted, the remaining tank containing enough fuel for up to 1 hour's flight. Oil capacity 2 Imp gallons (9 litres).

Accommodation: Bench seat for pilot and two passengers side-by-side in enclosed cabin. Forward-hinged, easily removable car-type door on each side. Roof panels of blue-tinted Plexiglas. Large baggage compartment. Agricultural version normally flown as single-seater.

Systems: 12V electrical system includes generator, 24Ah battery and engine starter.

Optional Equipment: Dual controls; radio; cabin heating system; navigation, landing and cabin lights. External cargo hook under engine platform for 441 lb (200 kg) slung load. Baggage container on starboard side of engine platform, aft of cabin. Provision in ambulance version for an enclosed stretcher pannier to be mounted externally on brackets on port side of cabin. Agricultural installation of 35 ft 5¼ in (10·80 m) spray boom and twin tanks, one mounted externally each side of cabin and each containing 22 Imp gallons (100 litres) of liquid chemical.

Dimensions, external:
- Diameter of main rotor: 29 ft 7½ in (9·03 m)
- Diameter of tail rotor: 4 ft 6¾ in (1·39 m)
- Length overall, main rotor fore and aft: 34 ft 4¼ in (10·47 m)
- Length of fuselage, incl tail skid: 25 ft 1¼ in (7·65 m)
- Span of horizontal stabiliser: 6 ft 8¾ in (2·05 m)
- Max width of fuselage: 5 ft 0¾ in (1·54 m)
- Height to top of cabin roof: 5 ft 8⅛ in (1·73 m)
- Height overall: 9 ft 9¼ in (2·98 m)
- Width over skids: 5 ft 8½ in (1·74 m)

Dimensions, internal:
- Cabin:
  - Length: 4 ft 9¾ in (1·47 m)
  - Max height: 4 ft 0¾ in (1·24 m)

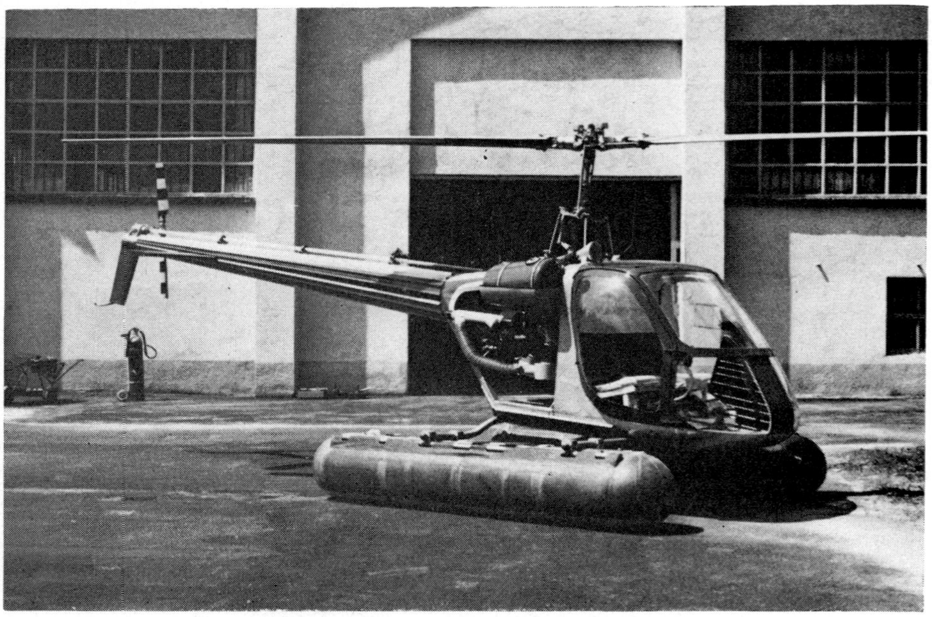

Silvercraft SH-4 helicopter fitted with pontoon landing gear

Areas:
- Main rotor blades (each): 12·61 sq ft (1·17 m²)
- Tail rotor blades (each): 0·97 sq ft (0·09 m²)
- Main rotor disc: 689·32 sq ft (64·04 m²)
- Tail rotor disc: 16·32 sq ft (1·52 m²)

Weights and Loadings:
- Weight empty:
  - SH-4: 1,124 lb (510 kg)
  - SH-4C: 1,157 lb (525 kg)
- Max T-O weight (Normal cat): 1,900 lb (862 kg)
- Max disc loading: 2·76 lb/sq ft (13·36 kg/m²)
- Max power loading: 11·2 lb/hp (5·07 kg/hp)

Performance (at max T-O weight, 235 hp engine):
- Max level speed at S/L: 87 knots (100 mph; 161 km/h)
- Max cruising speed: 70 knots (81 mph; 130 km/h)
- Econ cruising speed: 49 knots (56 mph; 90 km/h)
- Max rate of climb at S/L: 1,180 ft (360 m)/min
- Service ceiling:
  - SH-4: 15,090 ft (4,600 m)
  - SH-4C: 24,600 ft (7,500 m)
- Hovering ceiling in ground effect:
  - SH-4: 9,845 ft (3,000 m)
  - SH-4C: 20,500 ft (6,250 m)
- Hovering ceiling out of ground effect:
  - SH-4: 7,875 ft (2,400 m)
  - SH-4C: 13,950 ft (4,250 m)
- Range with max fuel: 173 nm (200 miles; 320 km)
- Max endurance: 3 hr

UMBRA

AERONAUTICA UMBRA SpA

Head Office and Works:
Via Piave 12, 06034 Foligno

Rome Office:
Via Scarpellini 20, Rome

Other Works:
Rome, Perugia and Varese

President and General Manager:
Muzio Macchi

Vice-President:
Avv Amilcare Ottaviani

Planning Director:
Ing Fernando Monti

Commercial Director:
Dott Giulio Macchi

Aeronautica Umbra was founded in 1935 by Sr Muzio Macchi, former General Manager of the Aeronautica Macchi works at Varese. Prior to World War 2 it employed some 2,400 workers and built several hundred S.M.79 bombers and torpedo-bombers for the Italian Services. It also manufactured aircraft components, notably propellers and landing gears, and designed two experimental aircraft, including the AUT-18 fighter prototype.

Since the war, other precision engineering items, such as large-diameter roller-bearings, have been manufactured, and the original factory at Foligno has been rebuilt and modernised to provide facilities for the building of prototype and production-series aircraft.

Currently, Umbra is manufacturing under licence the German Scheibe SF-25B Falke powered sailplane (see "Sailplanes" section), for which it has exclusive marketing rights in Italy and North Africa; and in 1968 began the design of a three-engined STOL light transport aircraft, the A.U.M.903, of which details are given below.

UMBRA A.U.M. 903

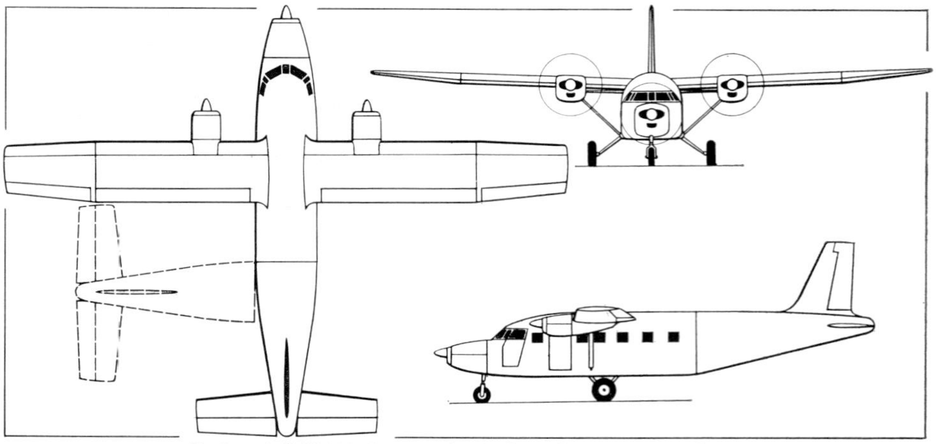

Umbra A.U.M.903 three-engined high-wing transport aircraft

Type: Three-engined STOL light transport.

Wings: Braced high-wing monoplane, with single streamline-section bracing strut each side. Wing section NACA 23015 at root, NACA 4412 at tip. Dihedral 2°. Incidence 3° at root, 0° at tip. Light alloy two-spar torsion-box structure. All-metal ailerons and all-metal hydraulically-operated slotted flaps. Trim-tab in port aileron. Pneumatic de-icing boots optional.

Fuselage: Conventional semi-monocoque light alloy structure. Swing-tail rear fuselage turning through 90° to port side to permit direct loading of bulky cargo.

Tail Unit: Cantilever aluminium alloy structure. Variable-incidence tailplane. Servo-tabs in rudder and each elevator. Pneumatic de-icing boots optional.

Landing Gear: Non-retractable tricycle type, with steerable nose-wheel. Single wheel on each unit. Oleo-pneumatic shock-absorbers. Main wheel tyres size 11·00-12, pressure 45 lb/sq in (3·15 kg/cm²). Nose-wheel tyre size 9·00-6, pressure 43 lb/sq in (3·0 kg/cm²). Hydraulic brakes.

Power Plant: Three 500 hp Lycoming TIO-720-B1A turbocharged eight-cylinder horizontally-opposed air-cooled engines, each driving a three-blade variable-pitch propeller, diameter 7 ft 2¾ in (2·20 m). Fuel in three tanks in each wing, with total capacity of 297 Imp gallons (1,350 litres).

Accommodation: Crew of one or two on flight deck. Accommodation in main cabin for up to 18 passengers, or eight stretcher patients and medical attendants, or 4,410 lb (2,000 kg) of freight, vehicles or agricultural equipment. The cabin is divided into two compartments by a bulkhead to permit mixed passenger/cargo loads to be carried, five passengers being accommodated in the forward compartment. Swing-tail permits loading of freight pallets, cars etc. Cabin heated and ventilated.

Systems: Hydraulic system for actuation of flaps, brakes and nose-wheel steering. No pneumatic system. Electrical system includes three self-rectifying alternators, two batteries, one main and one emergency inverter.

Electronics and Equipment: Standard equipment includes dual VHF radio, dual VOR/ILS, marker beacon and ADF. Blind-flying instrumentation standard.

Dimensions, external:
- Wing span: 62 ft 3½ in (18·99 m)
- Wing chord at root: 6 ft 10¾ in (2·10 m)
- Wing chord at tip: 5 ft 3 in (1·60 m)
- Wing aspect ratio: 9·4
- Length overall: 49 ft 5¼ in (15·07 m)
- Height overall: 18 ft 10 in (5·74 m)
- Tailplane span: 19 ft 8¼ in (6·00 m)
- Wheel track: 13 ft 1½ in (4·00 m)
- Wheelbase: 13 ft 5½ in (4·10 m)
- Crew door:
  - Height: 4 ft 4¾ in (1·34 m)
  - Width: 2 ft 2 in (0·66 m)
  - Height to sill: 3 ft 11¼ in (1·20 m)
- Passenger door (port):
  - Height: 4 ft 9½ in (1·46 m)
  - Width: 2 ft 2 in (0·66 m)
  - Height to sill: 3 ft 9½ in (1·16 m)
- Rear door (stbd):
  - Height: 4 ft 2¼ in (1·28 m)
  - Width: 2 ft 0 in (0·61 m)
  - Height to sill: 4 ft 9½ in (1·46 m)

Dimensions, internal:
- Front cabin, excluding flight deck:
  - Length: 6 ft 6¾ in (2·00 m)
  - Max width: 6 ft 2¾ in (1·90 m)

Max height	5 ft 11¾ in (1·82 m)	
Floor area	40·9 sq ft (3·80 m²)	
Volume	212 cu ft (6·00 m³)	
Rear cabin:		
Length	11 ft 5¾ in (3·50 m)	
Max width	6 ft 2¾ in (1·90 m)	
Max height	6 ft 1¼ in (1·86 m)	
Floor area	71·6 sq ft (6·65 m²)	
Volume	406 cu ft (11·50 m³)	
AREAS:		
Wings, gross	409 sq ft (38·00 m²)	
Trailing-edge flaps (total)	63·1 sq ft (5·86 m²)	
Horizontal tail surfaces (total)		
	88·5 sq ft (8·22 m²)	
Vertical tail surfaces (total)		
	49·8 sq ft (4·625 m²)	

WEIGHTS AND LOADING (estimated):
Basic operating weight, incl 2 pilots, full oil, radio (100 lb = 45 kg) and fuel for 45 min reserve at cruise conditions
7,685 lb (3,486 kg)
Max payload 4,410 lb (2,000 kg)
Max T-O and landing weight
12,500 lb (5,670 kg)
Max wing loading 30·5 lb/sq ft (149 kg/m²)

PERFORMANCE (estimated, at max T-O weight):
Max level speed at 10,000 ft (3,050 m)
188 knots (216 mph; 348 km/h)
Cruising speed (75% power) at 10,000 ft
172 knots (198 mph; 318 km/h)

Cruising speed (60% power) at 10,000 ft
155 knots (178 mph; 287 km/h)
Rate of climb at S/L 1,722 ft (540 m)/min
Rate of climb at S/L, one engine out
866 ft (264 m)/min
T-O to 50 ft (15 m):
STOL 1,050 ft (320 m)
FAR 23 1,493 ft (455 m)
Landing from 50 ft (15 m):
STOL 1,410 ft (430 m)
FAR 23 1,740 ft (530 m)
Range with max payload, 45 min reserves
108 nm (125 miles; 200 km)
Range with max fuel, 45 min reserves
673 nm (776 miles; 1,250 km)

JAPAN

FUJI

FUJI JUKOGYO KABUSHIKI KAISHA (Fuji Heavy Industries Ltd)

HEAD OFFICE:
Subaru Building, No 7, 1-chome, Nishi-shinjyuku, Shinjuku-ku, Tokyo
AIRCRAFT FACTORY:
Utsunomiya City, Tochigi Prefecture
PRESIDENT:
Nobuo Yokota
VICE-PRESIDENT:
Eiichi Ohara
MANAGING DIRECTORS:
Tameharu Yamada
Yoshio Inoue
Masaru Iino
Sukemitsu Irie
Nobuhiro Sakata
DIRECTOR OF AIRCRAFT OPERATION DIVISION:
Iwao Shibuya
MANAGER OF AIRCRAFT DEPARTMENT:
Atsushi Kasai
SUPERINTENDENT OF UTSUNOMIYA AIRCRAFT FACTORY:
Shiro Aizaki
PUBLIC RELATIONS MANAGER:
Tadaaki Ohkuma

Fuji Heavy Industries Ltd was established on 15 July 1953. It is a successor to the Nakajima Aircraft Company, which was established in 1914 and built 30,000 aircraft up to the end of World War II.
Under a licence and technical assistance agreement with the Beech Aircraft Corporation, concluded in 1953, Fuji built the Beechcraft Mentor at the Utsunomiya plant. Deliveries began in August 1954, and Fuji supplied a total of 124 Mentors to the Japan Air Self-Defence Force, a further 36, with spares, to the Philippine Air Force and one to the Indonesian Air Force. Japanese production of the Mentor ceased in April 1960.
Several modified versions of the Mentor, designated LM-1 Nikko, LM-2, KM and KM-2, were also built by Fuji. Details of these can be found in earlier editions of Jane's.
Simultaneously, under licence from Cessna, Fuji produced for the Japan Ground Self-Defence Force 22 L-19E Bird Dog observation aircraft, the first of which flew in December 1957. The last of these aircraft was completed in 1959.
Under another major agreement, the company is producing in Japan the Bell Model 204B helicopter. The first 204B covered by the agreement arrived in Japan in kit form in May 1962 for assembly by Fuji. The Japan Ground Self-Defence Force plans to purchase a total of 89 of the UH-1B military version and several are used by civil operators.
First aircraft designed entirely by Fuji was the T1 intermediate two-seat jet trainer, described fully in the 1967-68 Jane's. It has been followed by a four-seat light aeroplane known as the FA-200 Aero Subaru, details of which are given below.
Early in 1970, Fuji began design studies for a twin-engined six/eight-seat aircraft, known as the FA-300, intended as a light business aircraft or for military or civil crew trainer duties.
Fuji was also responsible for construction of the VTOL flying test-bed designed by the National Aerospace Laboratory (which see). Since completing the rig, in May 1968, Fuji has co-operated with the NAL in a series of functional tests.

FUJI KM-2

The KM-2 is a side-by-side two- or four-seat intermediate trainer, developed from the Model KM prototype (see 1965-66 Jane's), under a Japanese Maritime Self-Defence Force contract. The first KM-2 flew on 16 July 1962. Delivery of the main series of 25 production aircraft for the JMSDF began in September 1962 and was completed in May 1965. A JMSDF contract

Fuji KM-2 intermediate trainer of the Japan Maritime Self-Defence Force

for three more KM-2's was received in 1968, and delivery of these was completed by February 1970.
A full description of the KM-2 appeared in the 1969-70 Jane's.

FUJI FA-200 AERO SUBARU

Fuji began detail design of this light aircraft in 1964 and the prototype flew for the first time on 12 August 1965. Since then refinements have been made to the aircraft, and the following versions have been built:
FA-200-160. Basic four-seat light aircraft, with 160 hp Lycoming engine. Received Japan Civil Aviation Bureau Normal Category Type Certificate as a four-seater on 1 March 1966, Utility Category certification as a three-seater on 6 July 1966 and Aerobatic Category certification as a two-seater on 29 July 1967. FAA Type Approval in all three categories followed on 26 September 1967.
FA-200-180. Developed version with 180 hp Lycoming engine. Certification by JCAB in Normal, Utility, and Aerobatic categories was received on 28 February 1968, and FAA Type Approval in all three categories on 25 April 1968.
FA-203S. STOL research aircraft used by National Aerospace Laboratory. Generally similar to FA-200-180, but with leading-edge slats and full-span trailing-edge 'flaperons'. BLC suction system operated by a converted motor-car engine. Conversion to STOL configuration carried out April-November 1967. One only produced.
Production began in March 1968, and 80 aircraft had been completed by the end of February 1970. Production in 1970 was at the rate of eight aircraft per month.
The description below applies generally to both the FA-200-160 and FA-200-180, except where a specific version is indicated.
TYPE: Four-seat light monoplane.

WINGS: Cantilever low-wing monoplane. Dihedral 7°. Incidence 2° 30'. All-metal structure, with single extruded main spar at 42% chord. All-metal riveted ailerons and single-slotted flaps. Trim-tab on each aileron.
FUSELAGE: All-metal semi-monocoque structure.
TAIL UNIT: Cantilever all-metal structure, with swept vertical surfaces. One-piece horizontal surface. Trim-tab in port elevator. Manually-adjustable tab on rudder.
LANDING GEAR: Non-retractable tricycle type. Oleo-pneumatic shock-absorbers. Tube-type 4-ply tyres size 6·00-6 on main wheels, 5·00-5 on nose-wheel. Hydraulic disc brakes. Parking brake.
POWER PLANT: One 160 hp Lycoming O-320-D2A (180 hp Lycoming IO-360-B1B in FA-200-180) four-cylinder horizontally-opposed air-cooled engine, driving a McCauley IC 172/MGM 7656 two-blade fixed-pitch metal propeller, diameter 6 ft 4 in (1·93 m) in FA-200-160 (McCauley B2D34C 53/74E-0 constant-speed two-blade metal propeller, diameter 6 ft 2 in (1·88 m) in FA-200-180). Fuel in two integral tanks in inner wings with total capacity of 45 Imp gallons (204·5 litres). Oil capacity 1·5 Imp gallons (7 litres).
ACCOMMODATION: Four seats, in pairs, in enclosed cabin. Large rearward-sliding canopy. Compartment for 88 lb (40 kg) of baggage in FA-200-160, 176 lb (80 kg) in FA-200-180.
ELECTRONICS AND EQUIPMENT: Optional extras include radio, full blind-flying instrumentation, landing and navigation lights, cabin lights and rotating beacon.
DIMENSIONS, EXTERNAL:
Wing span 30 ft 11 in (9·42 m)
Wing chord (constant) 5 ft 0 in (1·525 m)
Length overall 26 ft 1 in (7·96 m)
Height overall 8 ft 7½ in (2·63 m)
Tailplane span 11 ft 4½ in (3·47 m)
Wheel track 5 ft 5½ in (1·66 m)
Wheelbase 8 ft 7½ in (2·63 m)

Fuji FA-200-160 Aero Subaru four-seat light aircraft (160 hp Lycoming O-320-D2A engine)

AREAS:
Wings, gross⁕   150·7 sq ft (14·0 m²)
Ailerons (total)   12·11 sq ft (1·13 m²)
Fin   16·11 sq ft (1·50 m²)
Rudder   9·58 sq ft (0·89 m²)
Tailplane   35·74 sq ft (3·32 m²)

WEIGHTS (N=Normal Category; A=Aerobatic Category):
Weight empty:
   FA-200-160   1,366 lb (620 kg)
   FA-200-180   1,410 lb (640 kg)
Max payload:
   N (FA-200-160)   970 lb (440 kg)
   N (FA-200-180)   1,125 lb (510 kg)
   A (FA-200-160)   573 lb (260 kg)
   A (FA-200-180)   661 lb (300 kg)
Max T-O weight:
   N (FA-200-160)   2,337 lb (1,060 kg)
   N (FA-200-180)   2,535 lb (1,150 kg)
   A (FA-200-160)   1,940 lb (880 kg)
   A (FA-200-180)   2,072 lb (940 kg)

PERFORMANCE (N = Normal Category, A = Aerobatic Category, at max T-O weight):
Max level speed at S/L:
   N (FA-200-160)   120 knots (138 mph; 222 km/h)
   N (FA-200-180)   126 knots (145 mph; 233 km/h)
   A (FA-200-160)   122 knots (140 mph; 225 km/h)
   A (FA-200-180)   128 knots (147 mph; 237 km/h)
Max cruising speed (75% power) at 5,000 ft (1,500 m):
   N (FA-200-160)   106 knots (122 mph; 196 km/h)
   N (FA-200-180)   110 knots (127 mph; 204 km/h)
   A (FA-200-160)   109 knots (126 mph; 203 km/h)
   A (FA-200-180)   112 knots (129 mph; 208 km/h)
Econ cruising speed (55% power) at 5,000 ft (1,500 m):
   N (FA-200-160)   89 knots (102 mph; 164 km/h)
   N (FA-200-180)   90 knots (104 mph; 167 km/h)
   A (FA-200-160)   98 knots (113 mph; 182 km/h)
   A (FA-200-180)   101 knots (116 mph; 187 km/h)
Stalling speed, flaps down:
   N (FA-200-160) 49 knots (56 mph; 90 km/h)
   N (FA-200-180) 53 knots (60 mph; 97 km/h)
   A (FA-200-160) 45 knots (51 mph; 82 km/h)
   A (FA-200-180) 48 knots (55 mph; 88 km/h)
Rate of climb at S/L:
   N (FA-200-160)   680 ft (207 m)/min
   N (FA-200-180)   760 ft (232 m)/min
   A (FA-200-160)   950 ft (290 m)/min
   A (FA-200-180)   1,120 ft (341 m)/min
Service ceiling:
   N (FA-200-160)   11,400 ft (3,480 m)
   N (FA-200-180)   13,700 ft (4,175 m)
   A (FA-200-160)   15,600 ft (4,760 m)
   A (FA-200-180)   17,300 ft (5,270 m)
T-O to 50 ft (15 m):
   N (FA-200-160)   1,530 ft (465 m)
   N (FA-200-180)   1,476 ft (450 m)
   A (FA-200-160)   1,020 ft (310 m)
   A (FA-200-180)   985 ft (300 m)
Landing from 50 ft (15 m):
   N (FA-200-160)   1,115 ft (340 m)
   N (FA-200-180)   1,150 ft (350 m)
   A (FA-200-160)   1,017 ft (310 m)
   A (FA-200-180)   1,050 ft (320 m)
Range with max fuel:
   N (FA-200-160)   607 nm (700 miles; 1,125 km)
   N (FA-200-180)   534 nm (615 miles; 970 km)
   A (FA-200-160)   777 nm (895 miles; 1,440 km)
   A (FA-200-180)   647 nm (745 miles; 1,200 km)

FUJI-BELL 204B/UH-1B

Fuji is manufacturing Bell Model 204B and UH-1B helicopters under sub-licence from Mitsui and Co Ltd, Bell's Japanese legal licensee. By the end of February 1970, four Fuji-built 204B's were in service with Asahi Helicopter Company, two with All Nippon Airways, two with Tokyo Metropolitan Police Board Headquarters and two with Japan Domestic Airlines.

Initial orders for the UH-1B, from the Japan Ground Self-Defence Force, totalled 36, all of which were delivered by December 1967. By 31 March 1970, 57 UH-1B's had been delivered to the JGSDF, which is to purchase a further 33 by 1973.

The Fuji-Bell 204B and UH-1B are identical with the versions of these aircraft built by Bell Helicopter Company (see US section).

Fuji was also flight testing during 1970 one aircraft fitted with door-hinged rotor blades and is modifying another 204B for trials as a winged helicopter.

Fuji FA-200-180 Aero Subaru light aircraft (180 hp Lycoming IO-360-B1B engine)

Fuji-Bell 204B helicopter in the insignia of All Nippon Airways

The Bell 204B which Fuji is modifying for trials as a winged helicopter   (*Press Association*)

ITOH

ITOH CHU KOKU SEIBI KABUSHIKI KAISHA (C. Itoh Aircraft Maintenance and Engineering Co Ltd)

HEAD OFFICE AND WORKS:
1060 Tobitakyu-machi, Chofu, Tokyo

PRESIDENT: Manzo Saito

MANAGING DIRECTOR: Kizo Takeishi

This company was established in December 1952, to undertake the maintenance and repair of small and medium-size aircraft. In 1960, it built the N-58 Cygnet light cabin monoplane in association with students of Nihon University, where the aircraft was designed. As a follow-up to this venture it collaborated with the University in the development and construction of a prototype four-seat light aircraft known as the N-62 Eaglet. The production version of this aircraft was described and illustrated in the 1968-69 *Jane's*.

Late in 1968, Itoh undertook the conversion of a number of T-6 Texan aircraft to represent Nakajima B5N ("Kate") torpedo-bombers for the film *Tora, Tora, Tora!* Details of this work are given in the Addenda.

Itoh had no plans for new products in early 1970. The company name was changed on 29 May 1970 (see Addenda).

JEAA

JAPAN EXPERIMENTAL AIRCRAFT ASSOCIATION (Chapter 306 of EAA International)

ADDRESS: c/o Asahi Miyahara, 27, 2-chome, Uehara, Shibuya-ku, Tokyo

Various fixed- and rotating-wing aircraft are currently being designed and built by members of the JEAA. Among these are a single-seat monoplane under construction by Mr Otani, shown in the accompanying photograph. This has a non-retractable tricycle landing gear and is powered by a 1,200 cc Volkswagen engine.

Another member, Mr Asahi Miyahara, has designed a two-seat motor glider, and a single-seat ultra-light aircraft for amateur construction, of which all available details follow. It was hoped that both of these aircraft would make their first flights during 1970.

Single-seat home-built aircraft under construction by Mr Otani of the JEAA (*Asahi Miyahara*)

JEAA (MIYAHARA) MOTOR GLIDER

POWER PLANT: One 50-60 hp 1,600 cc Volkswagen engine, driving a two-blade propeller.

DIMENSIONS, EXTERNAL:

Wing span	45 ft 11¼ in (14·00 m)
Length overall	25 ft 3 in (7·70 m)

Two-seat motor glider (1,600 cc Volkswagen engine) designed by Mr Asahi Miyahara

JEAA-S1

POWER PLANT: One 40 hp engine, driving a two-blade propeller.

DIMENSIONS, EXTERNAL:

Wing span	26 ft 10¾ in (8·20 m)
Length overall	20 ft 2¼ in (6·15 m)
Height overall	8 ft 6¼ in (2·60 m)

JEAA-S1 single-seat ultra-light monoplane, designed by Mr Asahi Miyahara

---

KAWASAKI

KAWASAKI JUKOGYO KABUSHIKI KAISHA (Kawasaki Heavy Industries Ltd)

HEAD OFFICE:
2-16-1 Nakamachi-Dori, Ikuta-ku, Kobe

TOKYO AND AIRCRAFT GROUP OFFICE:
World Trade Center Building, 3-5 Shiba Hamamatsu-cho, Minato-ku, Tokyo

PRESIDENT:
Kiyoshi Yotsumoto

VICE-PRESIDENTS:
Riichi Kato
Kenji Hasegawa

WORKS:
Gifu

GENERAL MANAGER, AIRCRAFT GROUP:
Michio Nakaminami

ASST GENERAL MANAGER, AIRCRAFT GROUP:
Kenji Uchino

The former Kawasaki Kikai Kogyo Kabushiki Kaisha and Kabushiki Kaisha Kawasaki Gifu Seisakusho were amalgamated under the name Kawasaki Kokuki Kogyo Kabushiki Kaisha (Kawasaki Aircraft Co, Ltd) on 15 March 1954.

With effect from 1 April 1969, this company was amalgamated with the Kawasaki Dockyard Co, Ltd, and the Kawasaki Rolling Stock Mfg Co, Ltd, to form a new company known as Kawasaki Heavy Industries Ltd. The Aircraft Division of the former Kawasaki Aircraft Co, Ltd, which employs some 8,000 people, continues its existing activities unchanged as the Aircraft Group of the new company.

In addition to extensive overhaul work, Kawasaki has built many US aircraft under licence since 1955. It began by delivering 210 Lockheed T-33A jet trainers in 1955-59. Subsequently, it modified one T-33A as a launch aircraft for the Kawasaki KAQ-5 rocket-powered target drone and another as an ECM trainer, carrying ASQ-1 equipment.

In 1959, Kawasaki received a contract to manufacture 42 Lockheed P2V-7 (P-2H) Neptune anti-submarine aircraft for the Japanese Maritime Self-Defence Force. The first was completed in September 1959 and the last was delivered on 27 March 1963. Six more Neptunes were

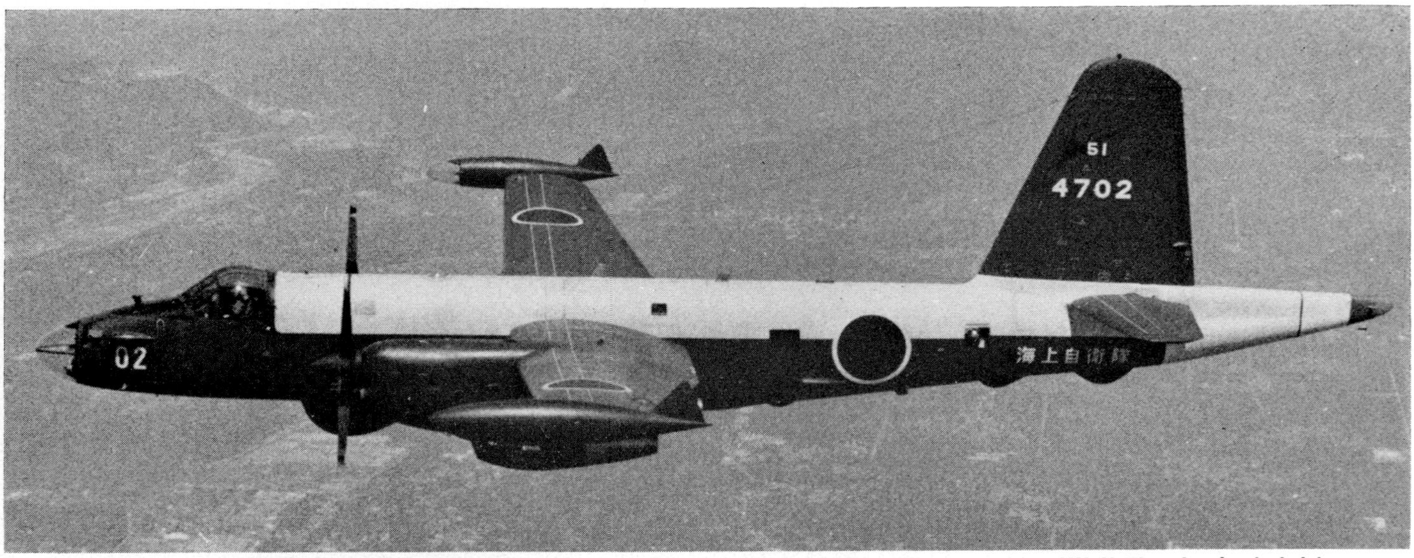

Production Kawasaki P-2J maritime patrol aircraft (two 2,850 ehp General Electric T64 turboprops and two IHI J3-7C underwing turbojets

ordered subsequently and were delivered in 1965. Kawasaki has since developed from the Neptune a new anti-submarine aircraft designated P-2J, and details of this are given below.

Kawasaki has been producing the Bell Model 47 helicopter under licence since 1953 and had built a total of 419 by 1 March 1970, made up of 11 Model 47D's, 15 Model 47G's, 179 Model 47G-2's, 32 Model 47G-2A's and 171 Model KH-4's developed from the Model 47 by its own design staff. Of this total, 100 helicopters were delivered to the JGSDF, 10 to the JMSDF, 255 to Japanese civil operators, 13 to Burma, 16 to Thailand, two each to Taiwan, Korea and Brazil and one to the Philippines. Current rate of production is four Model 47G-2A's and KH-4's per month.

Kawasaki has exclusive rights to manufacture and sell the larger Boeing-Vertol 107 Model II and IIA helicopters in Japan; the Hughes Model 369HM (500M) light observation helicopter is also being manufactured by Kawasaki under a licence agreement concluded in October 1967.

Kawasaki is responsible for manufacture of main wings and nacelle structures, including installation of the landing gear, for the NAMC YS-11 turboprop transport and will assemble the new XC-1A transport for the JASDF. Basic design studies are being undertaken for a new ASW aircraft, provisionally designated PX-L, to succeed the JMSDF's P2V-7 (P-2H) Neptunes. Kawasaki is also engaged on research in the field of tilting-propeller VTOL aircraft under the Ministry of International Trade and Industry's joint V/STOL research programme.

Kawasaki's aero-engine, drone and missile activities are described in the appropriate sections of this work.

KAWASAKI P-2J

JMSDF designation: P-2J

The P-2J was developed by Kawasaki, originally under the designation GK-210, to meet a JMSDF requirement for a new anti-submarine aircraft to replace its P2V-7 Neptunes in service during the 1970s. Design is based very closely upon that of the P2V-7 (P-2H), and began in October 1961. Work on the conversion of a standard P2V-7 as the P-2J prototype began in June 1965, and this aircraft flew for the first time on 21 July 1966.

As compared with the original P2V-7, the wings and tail of the P-2J remain virtually unchanged, apart from an increase in rudder area, but the fuselage has been lengthened by inserting an additional section between the wing leading-edge and the cockpit, to accommodate improved electronic equipment. The main landing gear has also been redesigned and now has twin wheels on each unit. The original piston-engines are replaced by two Japanese-built General Electric turboprop engines, the underwing turbojets are Japanese J3-IHI-7C's, and the total fuel capacity has been substantially increased.

The first production example of the P-2J was flown on 8 August 1969, and was delivered to the JMSDF on the following 7 October. A second aircraft was also delivered before the end of the year, and present contracts cover the completion and delivery of 13 P-2J's by March 1971. The JMSDF will purchase a total of 46 under the third national defence programme.

Type: Four-engined anti-submarine and maritime patrol aircraft.

Wings: Cantilever all-metal mid-wing monoplane, with taper on outer panels. Wing section NACA 2419 (modified) at root, NACA 4410·5 at tip. Dihedral 5° on outer panels. Incidence 3° 30′ at root. No sweepback. Wing was designed to give temporary flotation in event of ditching. Centre-section box beam is continuous through fuselage. All-metal ailerons, each incorporating a controllable trim-tab. Fowler-type all-metal inboard and outboard trailing-edge flaps. All-metal spoilers in upper surface of outer wing panels, inboard of ailerons. Thermal de-icing of leading-edges.

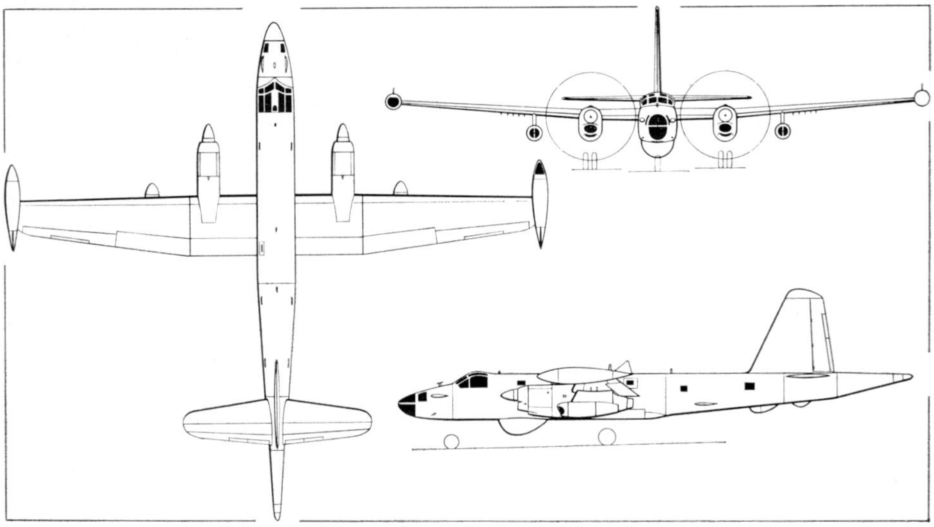

Production version of the Kawasaki P-2J twin-turboprop development of the Lockheed Neptune

Fuselage: Conventional all-metal unpressurised semi-monocoque structure, basically as P2V-7 (P-2H) but with extra 4 ft 2 in (1·27 m) section inserted between wing leading-edge and cockpit.

Tail Unit: Cantilever all-metal structure, incorporating "Varicam" (variable camber), a movable trimming surface between the fixed tailplane and each elevator which is operated by hydraulically-driven screw-jack. Spring tab and trim-tab in rudder, balance tab and spring tab in elevators. Tail unit has no de-icing, but is otherwise virtually unchanged from P2V-7 except for an increase in rudder area by extending the chord by 1 ft (0·30 m) at the top.

Landing Gear: Retractable tricycle type, with single steerable nose-wheel and twin-wheel main units. Hydraulic retraction, nose-wheel forward, main wheels rearward into inboard engine nacelles. Sumitomo Precision oleo-pneumatic shock-absorbers. Goodyear Type VII tubeless tyres on all units, size 9·9 × 34-14 on nose-wheel and 13 × 39-16 on main wheels. Tyre pressures 90 lb/sq in (6·3 kg/cm²) on nose-wheel, 100 lb/sq in (7·0 kg/cm²) on main wheels. Goodyear disc brakes and on/off-type anti-skid units on main units.

Power Plant: Two 2,850 ehp General Electric T64-IHI-10 turboprop engines, mounted on wing centre-section and each driving a Sumitomo Precision 63E60-19 three-blade variable-pitch metal propeller, diameter 14 ft 6¼in (4·43 m). Outboard of these engines, on pylons beneath the outer wing panels, are two pod-mounted Ishikawajima J3-IHI-7C turbojets, each rated at 3,085 lb (1,400 kg) st. Fuel in inboard and outboard wing tanks with total capacity of 2,515 Imp gallons (3,020 US gallons = 11,433 litres), plus 333 Imp gallons (400 US gallons = 1,514 litres) in port wingtip tank. For ferry purposes a 583 Imp gallon (700 US gallon = 2,650 litre) auxiliary tank can be installed in the weapons bay. Oil capacity 5·2 Imp gallons (6·2 US gallons = 23·6 litres) for each turboprop and 2·4 Imp gallons (2·9 US gallons = 11·0 litres) for each turbojet engine.

Accommodation: Crew of twelve, including two pilots on flight deck and ten men in tactical compartment in forward fuselage. Aft of this compartment, in centre fuselage, are an ordnance room, galley and toilet. Crew escape hatches in flight deck, tactical and ordnance compartments. All accommodation heated, ventilated and air-conditioned.

Systems: Primary hydraulic system, pressure 3,000 lb/sq in (210 kg/cm²), for Varicam (tail unit), landing gear and nose-wheel steering. Secondary system, pressure 1,500 lb/sq in (105 kg/cm²), for flaps, spoilers, jet pod doors, main wheel brakes and propeller braking. Two 40kVA generators provide 115/200V AC power at 400 c/s. DC power from three 28V 200A transformer-rectifiers.

Electronics and Equipment: Standard equipment includes HRC-6 VHF radio, HRC-7 HF, AN/ARC-552 UHF and APS-80J search radar. Details of operational equipment are classified, but this is of comparable standard to that carried by the Lockheed P-3 Orion and includes a smoke detector and MAD in the elongated tail cone. Searchlight in starboard wingtip pod.

Dimensions, external:

Wing span	97 ft 8½ in (29·78 m)
Wing span over tip-tanks	101 ft 3½ in (30·87 m)
Wing chord at root	14 ft 7¼ in (4·45 m)
Wing chord at tip	7 ft 3½ in (2·22 m)
Wing aspect ratio	10
Length overall	95 ft 10¾ in (29·23 m)
Height overall	29 ft 3½ in (8·93 m)
Tailplane span	34 ft 0 in (10·36 m)
Wheel track	25 ft 0 in (7·62 m)
Wheelbase	29 ft 0 in (8·84 m)
Distance between propeller centres	25 ft 0 in (7·62 m)

Areas:

Wings, gross	1,000 sq ft (92·9 m²)
Ailerons (total)	63·2 sq ft (5·87 m²)

Trailing-edge flaps (total) 179·6 sq ft (16·70 m²)
Spoilers (total)   15·2 sq ft (1·41 m²)
Fin   190·0 sq ft (17·65 m²)
Rudder, incl tabs   43·5 sq ft (4·04 m²)
Tailplane   231·0 sq ft (21·50 m²)
Elevators, incl tabs and Varicam
                            91·0 sq ft (8·45 m²)
WEIGHTS:
Weight empty   42,500 lb (19,277 kg)
Max T-O weight   75,000 lb (34,019 kg)
Max zero-fuel weight   50,900 lb (23,087 kg)
Max landing weight   62,000 lb (28,122 kg)
PERFORMANCE (at max T-O weight):
Max permissible diving speed
                350 knots (403 mph; 649 km/h)
Max cruising speed
                217 knots (250 mph; 402 km/h)
Econ cruising speed at 10,000 ft (3,050 m)
                200 knots (230 mph; 370 km/h)
Stalling speed, flaps down
                90 knots (103 mph; 166 km/h)
Max rate of climb at S/L 1,800 ft (550 m)/min
Service ceiling   30,000 ft (9,150 m)
T-O to 50 ft (15 m)   3,600 ft (1,100 m)
Landing from 50 ft (15 m) 2,880 ft (880 m)
Range with max fuel
                2,400 nm (2,765 miles; 4,450 km)

KAWASAKI KH-4
JGSDF designation: H-13KH

Developed by Kawasaki from the three-seat Bell Model 47G-3B, the KH-4 is a four-seat light general-purpose helicopter powered by a 270 hp Lycoming TVO-435-B1A or -D1A six-cylinder horizontally-opposed air-cooled engine. The prototype flew for the first time in August 1962 and the KH-4 received JCAB Normal category type approval on 9 November 1962.

A total of 171 KH-4's had been built by 1 January 1970. Of this total, 133 were delivered to civil operators, 19 to the JGSDF, 16 to Thailand, 2 to Korea and 1 to the Philippines.

In addition to changes in the cabin, to accommodate one extra person, the Kawasaki KH-4 has a new instrument layout, modified control system and larger fuel capacity, totalling 46 Imp gallons (209 litres). Kits are available to equip the aircraft with agricultural dusting and spray gear, granular distributor, pontoons, auxiliary fuel tank, cargo sling, litters, cabin heater and loud-speaker.

DIMENSIONS, EXTERNAL:
Diameter of main rotor   37 ft 1½ in (11·32 m)
Diameter of tail rotor   5 ft 10½ in (1·78 m)
Distance between rotor centres
                         21 ft 11¼ in (6·69 m)
Length overall (main rotor fore and aft)
                         43 ft 2⅓ in (13·17 m)
Length of fuselage   32 ft 7¼ in (9·93 m)
Width overall (main rotor fore and aft)
                         9 ft 5½ in (2·88 m)
Height to top of rotor hub 9 ft 3½ in (2·84 m)
Skid track   7 ft 6 in (2·29 m)
AREAS:
Main rotor blades (each) 17·14 sq ft (1·59 m²)
Tail rotor blades (each) 1·12 sq ft (0·10 m²)
Main rotor disc   1,083 sq ft (100·61 m²)
Tail rotor disc   25·6 sq ft (2·38 m²)
WEIGHTS AND LOADINGS:
Weight empty   1,890 lb (857 kg)
Max T-O and landing weight
                         2,850 lb (1,292 kg)
Max disc loading   2·63 lb/sq ft (12·8 kg/m²)
Max power loading   11·0 lb/hp (4·99 kg/hp)
PERFORMANCE (at max T-O weight):
Max level and diving speed
                91 knots (105 mph; 169 km/h)
Cruising speed
                76 knots (87 mph; 140 km/h)
Max rate of climb at S/L
                850 ft (260 m)/min
Service ceiling   18,500 ft (5,640 m)
Hovering ceiling in ground effect
                         18,000 ft (5,485 m)
Hovering ceiling out of ground effect
                         15,000 ft (4,570 m)
Range with max fuel
                186 nm (214 miles; 345 km)
Max endurance   4 hr

KAWASAKI KHR-1

The KHR-1 experimental helicopter was modified from the KH-4 to test a rigid-rotor system under development by Kawasaki. It retained essentially the airframe of the KH-4, but had a three-blade rigid main rotor system. The rotor control system and main rotor shaft were redesigned, the stabilising bar deleted, and the centre fuselage and main transmission members strengthened to transmit increased rotor moment to the fuselage.

This aircraft flew for the first time on 25 April 1968, and flight testing was completed successfully on 8 November 1968, flights being made both with and without an electro-mechanical stability augmentation system. Total flying time was 68 hr 56 min.

ROTOR SYSTEM: Three-blade main rotor, with blades of NACA 0012 section to which trim-tabs were fitted, as on KH-4. Blades rigidly attached to strengthened rotor shaft by flexible hub-plates, with feathering freedom only. Tail

Kawasaki KH-4 four-seat helicopter (270 hp Lycoming TVO-435-B1A engine)

Kawasaki KHR-1 experimental rigid-rotor helicopter, developed from the KH-4

Kawasaki-Boeing KV-107/II-3 helicopter of the JMSDF, with mine countermeasures gear

rotor as KH-4. Main rotor/engine rpm ratio =1·9 : 1. Tail rotor/engine rpm ratio= 0·6 : 1.

ACCOMMODATION: Seat for pilot in centre of cabin at front, with observer's seat behind and to starboard. Instrumentation to rear of pilot on port side.

SYSTEMS AND EQUIPMENT: Hydraulic system for main rotor control and stability augmentation system. Type 6R-303 VHF radio.

DIMENSIONS, EXTERNAL: As KH-4, except:
Diameter of main rotor   34 ft 0 in (10·36 m)
WEIGHTS:
Weight empty   2,194 lb (995 kg)
Max T-O weight   2,850 lb (1,292 kg)

KAWASAKI/BOEING-VERTOL KV-107/II and IIA

Kawasaki has exclusive rights to manufacture and sell the Boeing-Vertol 107 Model II helicopter in Japan. The first KV-107 produced by Kawasaki under this licence agreement flew for the first time in May 1962, and by 1 January 1970 orders totalled 74, of which 50 had been delivered.

Deliveries have included two for Air Lift Inc of Japan, four for Thailand, two for the JMSDF, one for New York Airways and two for Pan American, for operation by New York Airways. Twenty-four have been delivered to the JGSDF, twelve to the JASDF and two to the JMSDF. Another 25 KV-107's are included in the Japan Defence Agency's five-year defence programme covering fiscal years 1967-71. Eighteen of these are being delivered to the JGSDF as troop transports, four to the JMSDF for minesweeper duties and three to the JASDF for rescue duties.

In 1965, Kawasaki obtained world-wide sales rights in the KV-107 from the Boeing Company's Vertol Division. In November 1965, it was awarded a type certificate for the KV-107 by the FAA. To meet various requirements, it offers the aircraft in seven versions, as follows:

KV-107/II-1. Basic utility helicopter. None yet built.

KV-107/II-2. Basic airline helicopter. Ten built by 31 March 1968, for Thailand (three), Pan American (three, for operation by New York Airways) and Air Lift Inc of Japan (formerly Kanki Airlines, two). Remaining two used as company test aircraft.

KV-107/II-3. (RH-46 series). Mine counter-measures (MCM) helicopter for JMSDF with additional fuel tanks, towing winch and cargo sling. Six ordered, of which two had been delivered by 31 March 1969. One of these was fitted with minesweeping and retrieval equipment, for evaluation by the JMSDF during the financial year ending on 31 March 1970.

KV-107/II-4. (CH-46 series). Tactical cargo/troop transport for JGSDF, with foldable seats for 26 troops or 15 casualty litters. Strengthened floor for carrying heavy vehicles. Orders for 42 planned, of which 24 had been delivered by the beginning of 1970. Production scheduled to continue until 1973.

KV-107/II-5. Long-range search and rescue helicopter for JASDF. Orders for 15 planned, of which 12 had been delivered by early 1970. Large additional fuel tank each side of fuselage, with total capacity of 833 Imp gallons (3,787 litres). Extensive nav/com equipment, four searchlights, domed observation window and rescue hoist.

KV-107/II-6. De luxe transport version. None yet built.

KV-107/II-7. De luxe VIP transport with 6-11 seats. One sold to Thailand in 1964.

The KV-107 is powered by two 1,250 shp CT58-110 shaft-turbine engines built by either General Electric in the USA or IHI in Japan. Details of its structure and performance can be found under the Boeing entry in the US section.

In addition, Kawasaki has completed for demonstration purposes one example of the **KV-107/IIA**, an improved model powered by two 1,500 shp General Electric CT58-140-1 turboshaft engines (max cont rating 1,250 shp), which give improved performance during VTOL and in "hot and high" conditions. Fuel capacity 350 US gallons=1,323 litres (standard), 1,000 US gallons =3,785 litres (max). Prototype first flown 3 April 1968. Awarded type approval by JCAB on 26 September 1968 and by FAA on 15 January 1969.

The following data apply to the KV-107/IIA.

WEIGHTS:
Weight empty:

Utility model	10,118 lb (4,589 kg)
Airliner model	11,024 lb (5,000 kg)
Max T-O weight	19,000 lb (8,618 kg)

PERFORMANCE (at max T-O weight, standard day):
Max level speed at S/L
   146 knots (168 mph; 270 km/h)
Max permissible diving speed
   175 knots (202 mph; 325 km/h)

Max cruising speed at S/L
   141 knots (162 mph; 261 km/h)
Econ cruising speed at S/L
   130 knots (150 mph; 241 km/h)
Max rate of climb at S/L 2,080 ft (634 m)/min
Max vertical rate of climb at S/L
   1,250 ft (381 m)/min
Service ceiling   14,000 ft (4,265 m)
Service ceiling, one engine out
   5,700 ft (1,740 m)
Hovering ceiling out of ground effect
   8,900 ft (2,715 m)
Min landing area:
  Length   126 ft (38 m)
  Width   75 ft (23 m)
T-O to 50 ft (15 m)   430 ft (131 m)
Landing from 50 ft (15 m), one engine out
   275 ft (84 m)
Range with standard fuel
   192 nm (222 miles; 357 km)
Range with max fuel
   592 nm (682 miles; 1,097 km)

KAWASAKI/HUGHES 369 SERIES

A total of 19 Model 369HM helicopters, assembled by Kawasaki Heavy Industries under licence from the Hughes Tool Company's Aircraft Division, had been delivered to the JGSDF by January 1970. The first commercial Model 369HS was delivered to the Yomiuri Press in September 1969.

MITSUBISHI

MITSUBISHI JUKOGYO KABUSHIKI KAISHA (Mitsubishi Heavy Industries, Ltd)

HEAD OFFICE:
  5-1, Marunouchi 2-Chome, Chiyoda-ku, Tokyo 100
NAGOYA AIRCRAFT WORKS:
  No 10 Oye-cho, Minato-ku, Nagoya 455
CHAIRMAN OF BOARD OF DIRECTORS:
  Fumihiko Kono
PRESIDENT:
  Yoichiro Makita
EXECUTIVE VICE-PRESIDENTS:
  Shigeichi Koga
  Yuji Satoh
  Gakuji Moriya
  Seiji Watanabe
SENIOR MANAGER OF AIRCRAFT AND SPECIAL VEHICLE DIVISION:
  Hirotsugu Hirayama
DEPUTY SENIOR MANAGER OF AIRCRAFT AND SPECIAL VEHICLE DIVISION:
  Yoshitoshi Sone
ASSISTANT SENIOR MANAGER OF AIRCRAFT AND SPECIAL VEHICLE DIVISION:
  Tetsuro Hikida
MANAGER OF AIRCRAFT DEPARTMENT:
  Tadatoshi Suzuki
MANAGER OF SPECIAL VEHICLE DEPARTMENT:
  Yoshitoshi Sone
MANAGER OF SPACE SYSTEM DEPARTMENT:
  Tetsuro Hikida
GENERAL MANAGER OF NAGOYA AIRCRAFT WORKS:
  Teruo Tojo
MANAGER OF PUBLICITY CENTRE:
  Shinichi Kuroda

Mitsubishi began the production of aircraft in the present Oye plant of its Nagoya Engineering Works in 1921, and manufactured a total of 18,000 aircraft of approximately one hundred different types during the 24 years prior to the termination of World War II in 1945.

The company was also one of the leading aero-engine manufacturers in Japan, and produced a total of 52,000 engines in the 1,000-2,500 hp range.

The conclusion of the Peace Treaty in 1952 enabled the aircraft industry in Japan to recommence, and in December of that year the company constructed its present Komaki aircraft plant.

This factory, together with Mitsubishi's Oye and Daiko plants, has since been separated from the original Nagoya Engineering Works and consolidated as the Nagoya Aircraft Works, with a combined floor area of some 1,765,000 sq ft (163,975 m²).

Like other Japanese companies, Mitsubishi re-started with overhaul work for the USAF. Contracts to overhaul F-86 Sabre fighters led, in June 1955, to the selection of Mitsubishi as the company to manufacture 300 F-86F fighters for the Japan Air Self-Defence Force under a licence agreement with North American Aviation, Inc.

It subsequently received a letter of intent for the production of 230 Lockheed F-104J and F-104DJ Starfighters, in co-operation with Kawasaki.

In May 1969 it received a letter of intent for the production of F-4EJ Phantom fighters under licence from McDonnell Douglas Corporation. The first contract was due to be finalised in March 1970, and delivery of the aircraft is due to begin in the Summer of 1971. A total of 104 F-4EJ's is to be produced.

Similarly, overhaul work on Sikorsky S-55 helicopters, started in 1954, led in December 1958 to a licence agreement for the manufacture of this type in the Oye and Komaki plants, and 44 were delivered for civil and military use. Subsequently, Mitsubishi assembled 20 S-58/HSS-1's for the JMSDF (17), Maritime Safety Agency (2) and Asahi Helicopter Ltd (1).

Today, Mitsubishi holds licence agreements to manufacture the Sikorsky S-61, SH-3A and S-62 helicopters. By 31 March 1970, Mitsubishi had built two S-61A's (for the JMSDF, for use in support of the Japanese Antarctic Expedition) and two S-61N's for civil operators, and had delivered 29 of an order for 54 SH-3A's (HSS-2's) to the JMSDF for anti-submarine duties. Mitsubishi had also delivered 25 S-62A's by 31 March 1970: 9 to the JASDF, 8 to the JMSDF, 5 to civil operators, two to the Philippines and one to Thailand. One more S-62 is on order for the

JMSDF which, like the JASDF, uses the type for rescue duty.

Mitsubishi has developed and is producing a twin-turboprop utility transport designated MU-2. It is responsible for producing the front and centre fuselage sections of the YS-11 transport (see NAMC entry) and for final assembly of this aircraft.

Current activities at the Daiko plant include the manufacture of components for piston-engines and jet engines, the overhaul of piston and turboprop engines for domestic and foreign airlines, and production and repair of the Mitsubishi gas-turbine compressor (GCM-1) for the air starter of the F-104J and the Mitsubishi multi-purpose gas-turbine power unit (GPM-1).

Mitsubishi is also producing under licence Allison T63 turboshaft engines to power the Hughes 369HM (500 M) helicopters being manufactured by Kawasaki for the JGSDF, and will produce the Pratt & Whitney JT8D-9 turbofan engines to power the NAMC XC-1 military transport aircraft.

In September 1967 the Japan Defence Agency nominated Mitsubishi as prime contractor for development of the XT-2 supersonic trainer for the JASDF, with Fuji, Kawasaki and Shin Meiwa as principal sub-contractors. Mitsubishi is also a sub-contractor in the XC-1A production programme.

MITSUBISHI MU-2
JASDF designation: MU-2S
JGSDF designation: LR-1

The MU-2 is a twin-turboprop STOL utility transport, the basic design of which was begun in 1960. Prototype construction began in 1962 and the first aircraft was completed in July 1963. Seven versions have been announced, as follows:

MU-2A. Powered by two 562 shp Turboméca Astazou IIK turboprop engines. Prototype flown on 14 September 1963. Three built, one later converted to MU-2B. Full description in 1965-66 *Jane's*.

MU-2B. Powered by AiResearch TPE 331-25AB turboprops. Otherwise generally similar to

Mitsubishi MU-2E twin-turboprop search and rescue aircraft of the Japan Air Self-Defence Force, with Doppler nose radar

MU-2A. First MU-2B flew on 11 March 1965. Japanese Type Approval received on 15 September 1965; FAA Type Approval on 4 November 1965. Thirty-four built (one converted from MU-2A), including 28 for customers in the USA, 1 for Switzerland, 2 for Sweden, 1 for Itogumi and 2 others for Japanese customers. Production completed. Full description in 1967-68 *Jane's*.

MU-2C. Unpressurised liaison and reconnaissance/support version for JGSDF, which has ordered two. First flown on 11 May 1967, and first production aircraft delivered on 30 June 1967. A further eight are to be purchased during 1970-72. Of this total of 10, five will be equipped with photographic equipment and five with side-looking airborne radar. JGSDF designation is **LR-1.** Wingtip fuel tanks replaced by fuselage tank aft of cabin. One vertical and one swing-type oblique camera in photographic version. Optional equipment includes two 13 mm nose guns, bombs and rockets.

MU-2D. Superseded MU-2B as standard commercial model. First flown on 5 March 1966. Differs from MU-2B only in having integral fuel tanks instead of bladder type, and additional metal tanks in outer wings. Eighteen built. Production completed. Described in 1968-69 *Jane's*.

MU-2E. Search and rescue version for Japan Air Self-Defence Force. Doppler radar in nose "thimble", bulged observation window on each side of rear fuselage, and port-side sliding door to allow a lifeboat to be dropped. Unpressurised cabin. Extensive nav/com equipment, increased fuel capacity of 305·6 Imp gallons (1,389 litres), and max T-O weight increased to 10,053 lb (4,560 kg). First flight on 15 August 1967; eight aircraft delivered to JASDF by 31 March 1970. Present order is for 9 more aircraft (JASDF designation **MU-2S**) to be completed by March 1973.

MU-2F. Commercial version developed from MU-2D, with uprated AiResearch TPE 331-1-151A turboprop engines of 705 eshp and extra fuel in enlarged wing-tip tanks. First flown on 6 October 1967, MU-2F received its JCAB Type Certificate on 3 April 1968 and FAA Type Certificate on 6 August 1968. Seventy delivered by March 1970.

MU-2G. "Stretched" version, developed from MU-2F and retaining the same power plant. Interior cabin length increased by 9 ft 1½ in (2·78 m), and overall length by 6 ft 2¾ in (1·90 m), by adding external fairings on fuselage sides into which the main landing gear units retract. Nose-wheel unit repositioned further aft and retracts forward instead of rearward as on other MU-2 models. Other modifications include increase in fin height and area. Prototype (JA 8737) first flown on 10 January 1969; JCAB Type Certificate received on 2 June 1969 and FAA Type Certificate on 14 July 1969. Described in detail below.

By 1 April 1970, total orders for the MU-2 (all versions) had reached 176, including 146 for export and 30 for Japanese customers. Of these, 150 had been delivered (138 for export and 12 in Japan).

A subsidiary company, Mitsubishi Aircraft International, Inc, in San Angelo, Texas, was established on 1 October 1967 for final assembly in the US of semi-finished MU-2's shipped from Japan and for marketing of the aircraft in the western hemisphere.

In Europe, the MU-2 is distributed by Pilatus Aircraft Ltd in Switzerland and AB May-Flyg in Sweden; and in Australia by Forrester Stephen Pty Ltd.

TYPE: Twin-turboprop utility transport.

WINGS: Cantilever high-wing monoplane. Wing section NACA 64A415 at root, NACA 63A212 (modified) at tip. No dihedral. Incidence 2°. One-piece two-spar all-metal structure of light alloy. Spoilers for lateral control, between rear spar and flaps. Electrically-actuated full-span double-slotted flaps of aluminium alloy and plastics construction. Outboard flap section each side incorporates trim aileron. All primary controls manually-operated. Pneumatic de-icing boots.

FUSELAGE: Circular-section aluminium alloy semi-monocoque structure.

TAIL UNIT: Cantilever structure of aluminium alloy, except for top of fin, which is of reinforced plastics. Small auxiliary fin beneath each side of rear fuselage. Trim-tab in rudder and each elevator. Pneumatic de-icing boots.

LANDING GEAR: Retractable tricycle type with single wheel on each main unit and twin-wheel steerable nose unit. All wheels retract electrically, nose-wheel forward, main wheels upward into fairings on fuselage sides. Oleo-pneumatic shock-absorbers. Main wheel tyres Type III, size 8·50—10 8-ply. Nose-wheel tyres Type III, size 5·00—5 6-ply. Tyre pressure 40-60 lb/sq in (2·81-4·22 kg/cm²) on all units. Goodrich single-disc nine-spot hydraulic brakes.

POWER PLANT (MU-2F and MU-2G): Two 705 eshp AiResearch TPE 331-1-151A turboprop engines, each driving a Hartzell HC-B3TN-5/T10178HB-11 fully-feathering three-blade reversible-pitch constant-speed propeller of 7 ft 6 in (2·29 m) diameter. Total internal fuel capacity of 155 Imp gallons (706 litres) and two fixed wingtip tanks with total capacity of 150 Imp gallons (682 litres). Max total fuel capacity of 305 Imp gallons (1,388 litres).

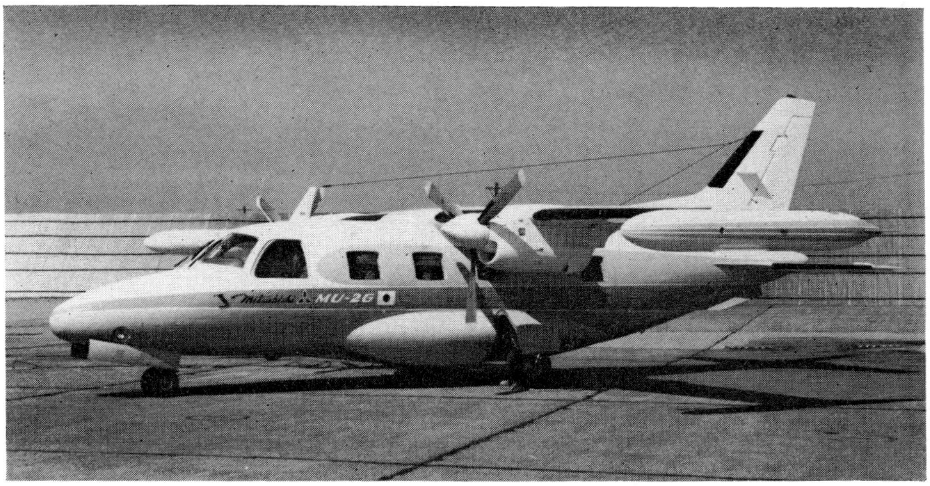

Mitsubishi MU-2G six/fourteen-seat utility transport aircraft

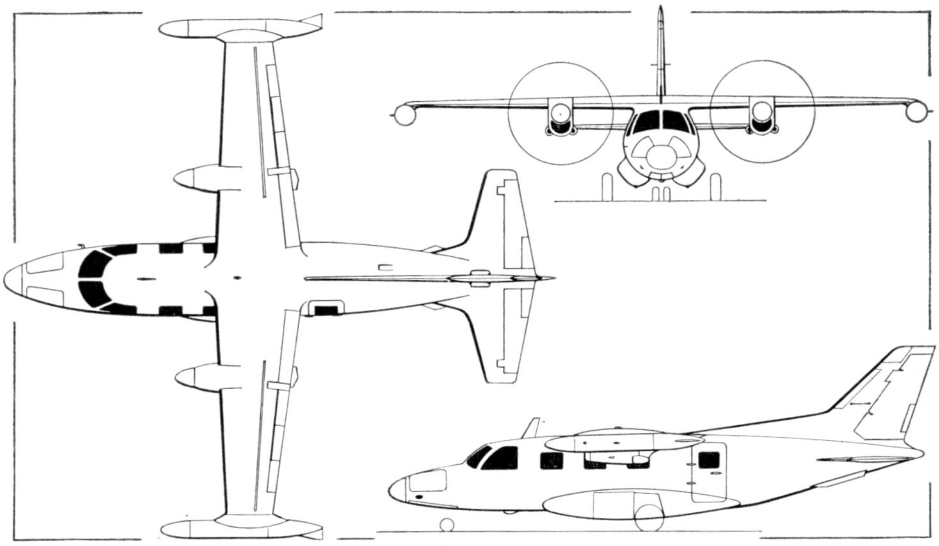

Mitsubishi MU-2G twin-turboprop utility transport

ACCOMMODATION (MU-2G): Seats for pilot and co-pilot or passenger on flight deck. Optional dual controls. Seating in main cabin, on rearward- and forward-facing seats, for from 4 to 12 persons. Separate compartment at rear of main cabin provides coat locker and 38 cu ft (1·08 m³) baggage compartment. Door at rear of cabin on port side with built-in airstair. Emergency exit door under wing leading-edge on starboard side.

SYSTEMS: AiResearch air-cycle pressurisation and air-conditioning system. Differential 5·0 lb/sq in (0·35 kg/cm²). No hydraulic system. 28V DC electrical system. Oxygen system standard.

ELECTRONICS AND EQUIPMENT: Blind-flying instrumentation standard. Radio and radar to customer's requirements.

DIMENSIONS, EXTERNAL:
- Wing span, over tip-tanks: 39 ft 2 in (11·95 m)
- Wing chord (mean): 5 ft 0¾ in (1·54 m)
- Wing aspect ratio: 7·71
- Length overall: 39 ft 5¾ in (12·03 m)
- Length of fuselage: 38 ft 10 in (11·84 m)
- Height overall: 13 ft 8¼ in (4·17 m)
- Tailplane span: 15 ft 9 in (4·80 m)
- Wheel track: 7 ft 10½ in (2·40 m)
- Wheelbase: 14 ft 5¼ in (4·40 m)
- Distance between propeller centres: 14 ft 9 in (4·50 m)
- Cabin door: Height: 4 ft 0 in (1·22 m)
  - Width: 2 ft 5½ in (0·76 m)
- Emergency exit door:
  - Height: 2 ft 4½ in (0·72 m)
  - Width: 2 ft 3½ in (0·70 m)

DIMENSIONS, INTERNAL:
- Cabin: Length: 19 ft 8¼ in (6·00 m)
  - Max width: 4 ft 11 in (1·50 m)
  - Max height: 4 ft 3¼ in (1·30 m)
- Baggage compartments (total): 38 cu ft (1·08 m³)

AREAS:
- Wings, gross: 178 sq ft (16·55 m²)
- Flaps (total): 42·0 sq ft (3·90 m²)
- Spoilers (total): 5·82 sq ft (0·54 m²)
- Fin: 30·68 sq ft (2·85 m²)
- Rudder, including tab: 12·60 sq ft (1·17 m²)
- Tailplane: 43·26 sq ft (4·02 m²)
- Elevators, including tabs: 15·04 sq ft (1·39 m²)

WEIGHTS AND LOADINGS:
- Weight empty, equipped: 6,563 lb (2,977 kg)
- Max T-O weight: 10,802 lb (4,900 kg)
- Max landing weight: 10,262 lb (4,655 kg)
- Max wing loading: 60·6 lb/sq ft (296 kg/m²)
- Max power loading: 7·67 lb/eshp (3·48 kg/eshp)

PERFORMANCE (at AUW of 9,170 lb = 4,160 kg):
- Max permissible diving speed: 330 knots (380 mph; 611 km/h)
- Max cruising speed at 10,000 ft (3,050 m): 283 knots (326 mph; 525 km/h)
- Econ cruising speed at 20,000 ft (6,100 m): 261 knots (300 mph; 482 km/h)
- Stalling speed, flaps up: 103 knots (118 mph; 189 km/h)
- Stalling speed, flaps down: 79 knots (91 mph; 145 km/h)
- Rate of climb at S/L: 2,592 ft (790 m)/min
- Rate of climb at S/L, one engine out: 728 ft (222 m)/min
- Service ceiling: 27,000 ft (8,230 m)
- Service ceiling, one engine out: 11,600 ft (3,540 m)
- T-O to 50 ft (15 m): 1,890 ft (576 m)
- Landing from 50 ft (15 m): 1,673 ft (510 m)
- Max range with wingtip tanks full, at 23,000 ft (7,000 m) with 30 min reserves: 1,346 nm (1,550 miles; 2,500 km)

MITSUBISHI XT-2

In September 1967 Mitsubishi was named prime contractor for the development of a new supersonic jet trainer and light attack aircraft, the XT-2, for the JASDF. Basic design studies were completed during 1968 and were followed by detail design later that year and by construction of a mock-up early in 1969. This is being followed by the construction of two prototypes, the first of which is scheduled to fly in mid-1971, and a structural test airframe. The contract for production T-2's will be placed in 1972, and JASDF pilots will begin training on the aircraft in 1974.

The XT-2, Japan's first domestically-developed supersonic aircraft, is being designed by a team led by Dr Kenji Ikeda. It is of shoulder-wing monoplane configuration, with two seats in tandem, and will be adaptable for ground-support duties as a possible replacement for the F-86F. Tentative plans are for the eventual purchase of 100 of the ground support version, and 50-60 trainers. Under consideration is a short-range photographic reconnaissance version as a potential replacement for the JASDF's Republic RF-86F aircraft. Fuji, Kawasaki, Nippi and Shin Meiwa will be major sub-contractors in the programme.

TYPE: Two-seat supersonic jet trainer.

WINGS: Cantilever shoulder-wing monoplane, with anhedral from roots. Increased sweep-back on inboard leading-edges, and extended chord ("dog-tooth") outer leading-edges. Trailing-edge flaps over nearly whole of span. Lateral control by two-section spoilers ahead of flaps. No conventional ailerons.

FUSELAGE: Conventional semi-monocoque structure.

TAIL UNIT: Cantilever structure, with sweptback horizontal surfaces. One-piece all-moving tail-plane, with marked anhedral.

LANDING GEAR: Retractable tricycle type, with single wheel on each unit. All units retract into fuselage. Oleo-pneumatic shock-absorption.

POWER PLANT: Two licence-built Rolls-Royce/Turboméca Adour turbofan engines (each 6,950 lb = 3,150 kg st with afterburning), mounted side-by-side in centre fuselage. Lateral air intake trunks on each side of fuse-lage, aft of cockpit, with splitter plates.

ACCOMMODATION: Crew of two in tandem on Weber ejection seats under individual rearward-hinged canopies.

OPERATIONAL EQUIPMENT: Provision for two fixed cannon in lower front fuselage. General Electric SR-3 attitude/heading reference system.

DIMENSIONS (approximate):
Wing span	26 ft 3 in	(8·00 m)
Length overall	55 ft 9 in	(17·00 m)
Height overall	16 ft 6 in	(5·00 m)

WEIGHT (approximate):
Normal T-O weight	21,000 lb	(9,500 kg)

PERFORMANCE (estimated):
Max level speed at 33,000 ft (10,000 m) Mach 1·6
T-O and landing field length 5,000 ft (1,525 m)
Max range for ferrying
1,390 nm (1,600 miles; 2,575 km)

Mock-up of the Mitsubishi XT-2 supersonic trainer for the Japan Air Self-Defence Force

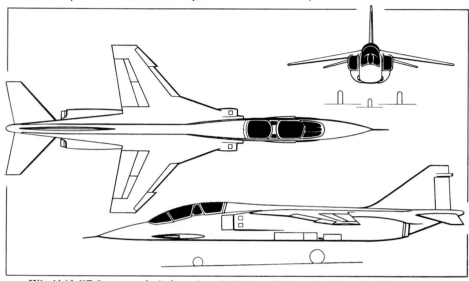

Mitsubishi XT-2 supersonic trainer (two Rolls-Royce/Turboméca Adour turbofan engines)

NAKAMURA
EIJI NAKAMURA
ADDRESS: Tokyo

NAKAMURA MP-X-6
The MP-X-6 is an experimental man-powered aircraft, designed by Mr Nakamura and com-pleted in 1969. It is of twin-boom configuration, of wooden construction, covered with styrene paper, and weighs 132 lb (60 kg). Wing span is 68 ft 10¾ in (21·0 m), overall length 19 ft 8¼ in (6·0 m) and wing area 226 sq ft (21·0 m²). Two attempts at take-off were made in September 1969, but both were unsuccessful.

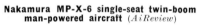

Nakamura MP-X-6 single-seat twin-boom man-powered aircraft (*AiReview*)

NAMC
NIHON KOKUKI SEIZO KABUSHIKI KAISHA
(Nihon Aeroplane Manufacturing Co, Ltd)

HEAD OFFICE:
Toranomon Daiichi Building, No. 1, Kotohira-cho, Shiba, Minato-Ku, Tokyo

ACTING PRESIDENT:
Atsushi Miyamoto

DIRECTORS:
Kohei Nagatani
Mitsuo Ohtani
Hiroshi Itoh
Teruo Tojo
Joji Yusa

MANAGERS:
Kiyoshi Tamaki (General Affairs Dept)
Daizo Ohash (Financing Dept)
Takeshi Kobayash (Sales Dept)
Mitsuo Mizutani (Service Dept)
Yoshiro Nozaki (Procurement Dept)
Fumio Shima (First Engineering Dept)
Yoshio Minoda (Second Engineering Dept)
Takeshi Mikami (XC-1 Administration Dept)

AUDITORS:
Hisao Tada
Katsuo Sato

CONSULTANTS:
Kikuji Sekiguchi
Minoru Ohta

The manufacture of a medium-sized passenger airliner of Japanese design was first advocated by the Ministry of International Trade and Industry in 1956.

In 1957, with financial assistance from the Japanese Government, basic design work was started as a joint effort by six companies:—Mitsubishi, Kawasaki, Fuji, Shin Meiwa, Nippi and Showa.

In order to promote the project more efficiently, the Transport Aircraft Development Association (TADA, Yusoki Sekkei Kenkyu Kyokai) was established in May 1957. It was succeeded in June 1959 by the NAMC, the capital for which was subscribed jointly by the Japanese Government and a number of private companies. This concern is now responsible for development and production of the airliner, which is designated YS-11.

Manufacture of the YS-11 is divided between the six private companies listed above, assisted by other component, accessory and equipment manufacturers in Japan. For example, Mitsubishi is responsible for manufacture of the fuselage and its equipment, as well as for final assembly; Kawasaki provides the wings and engine nacelles, Fuji the tail unit, Shin Meiwa the rear fuselage, Nippi the ailerons and flaps, and Showa Aircraft the honeycomb structural components. NAMC retains responsibility for design work, overall control of production and quality, and sales of the aircraft.

In 1967, the Japanese Ministry of International Trade and Industry decided to initiate research on a transport aircraft to succeed the YS-11.

The project work is being undertaken by the Society of Japanese Aerospace Constructors, and it was decided that construction of a proto-type of this aircraft, known as the Y-X, should be the responsibility of NAMC.

NAMC is also engaged in developing a new military transport, the XC-1A, for the JASDF. A mock-up was completed in March 1968. The XC-1A is intended to become the ASDF's standard freight transport, replacing the Curtiss C-46 in the early 1970's.

NAMC YS-11
Construction of the first of two prototypes of this twin-turboprop short/medium-range trans-port began in March 1961 and it flew for the first time on 30 August 1962. Two other airframes were used for structural testing. The first production YS-11 flew on 23 October 1964.

The YS-11 received its Type Certificate from the Japan Civil Aviation Bureau on 25 August 1964. FAA Certification was granted on 18 October 1965, under the agreement on reciprocal acceptance of airworthiness certification.

NAMC expects to produce at least 180 YS-11's by 1971, to meet domestic and export orders, notably from North and South America. By 1 March 1970, the following orders had been received:

YS-11-100
All Nippon Airways	3	Type 102
	4	Type 111
	2	Type 117
Filipinas Orient Airlines	2	Type 107
	1	Type 116
	1	Type 121
Japan Air Academy	2	Type 115

NAMC YS-11A-200 short/medium-range twin-turboprop airliner in the insignia of the Brazilian airline VASP (*Ronaldo S. Olive*)

Japan Air Self-Defence		
Force	2	Type 103
	2	Type 105
Japan Civil Aviation Bureau	1	Type 104
	1	Type 110
	1	Type 118
Japan Domestic Airlines	2	Type 106
	3	Type 108
	3	Type 109
	2	Type 120
	1	Type 124
	1	Type 125
Japan Maritime Self-		
Defence Force	2	Type 112
Korean Airlines	3	Type 125*
LANSA	1	Type 120
	1	Type 126
Toa Airways	2	Type 101
	2	Type 114
	1	Type 123
	1	Type 127
	1	Type 128
	1	Type 129

YS-11A-200

All Nippon Airways	3	Type 208
	19	Type 213
China Airlines	2	Type 219
Cruzeiro	8	Type 202
Japan Air Self-Defence		
Force	1	Type 218
Japan Domestic Airlines	1	Type 217
Japan Maritime Safety		
Agency	1	Type 207
Japan Maritime Self-Defence		
Force	4	Type 206
Olympic Airways	5	Type 220
Piedmont Airlines	21	Type 205

South West Airlines	2	Type 209
	1	Type 214
Toa Airways	1	Type 221
VASP	2	Type 211
	4	Type 212

YS-11A-300

ALA/Austral	3	Type 309
Japan Air Self-Defence		
Force	1	Type 305
Japan Domestic Airlines	1	Type 307
Korean Airlines	1	Type 310*
Olympic Airways	1	Type 312*
	1	Type 315*
Toa Airways	1	Type 313
Trans Air (Canada)	2	Type 306

YS-11A-400

Japan Air Self-Defence		
Force	8	Type 402

*Leased from NAMC

Deliveries to operators began in March 1965, and the 130th YS-11 was delivered on 9 January 1970.

The designations YS-11P, YS-11M and YS-11T are no longer in use for the military versions, which are included by their respective type numbers in the list above.

The current YS-11A series are developed from the original YS-11-100, which they superseded from the 50th production aircraft onward. They differ from the YS-11 mainly in offering an increased payload and a variety of configurations.

The following versions of the YS-11 have been announced:

YS-11-100. Basic passenger transport, with standard seating for 60 passengers. Two proto-types and 47 production aircraft built, including four for JASDF as 32/48-seat VIP transports and two for JMSDF as cargo transports. Pro-duction completed October 1967. Described in 1967-68 *Jane's*.

YS-11A-200. Passenger version of YS-11A, with standard seating for 60 passengers. Max payload increased by 2,970 lb (1,350 kg). First example flown on 27 November 1967, and delivered to Piedmont Airlines in Spring 1968. By 1 March 1970, 75 had been ordered, of which 63 had been delivered. Total includes four for JMSDF for use on anti-submarine training duties. Certification by the Japan Civil Aviation Bureau granted in January 1968.

YS-11A-300. Mixed traffic version of YS-11A, with standard accommodation for 46 passengers, total of 540 cu ft (15·3 m³) of cargo space, and an 8 ft 1½ in × 6 ft 0 in (2·48 × 1·83 m) cargo door in port side of forward fuselage. First flown in Summer 1968. Eleven ordered and delivered by 1 March 1970.

YS-11A-400. All-cargo configuration, with max available cargo space of 2,860 cu ft (81 m³), reinforced floor and a 10 ft 0 in × 6 ft 0 in (3·05 × 1·83 m) cargo door in port side of aft fuselage. Eight ordered by JASDF. First flight took place on 17 September 1969 and first two aircraft delivered to JASDF by the end of February 1970.

NAMC also has in the design stage the all-passenger **YS-11A-500** and the mixed-traffic **YS-11A-600.** These are respectively similar to the -200 and -300 models, but have a 1,100 lb (500 kg) increase in max T-O weight. A four-turboprop STOL development, designated **YS-11S,** is also under consideration.

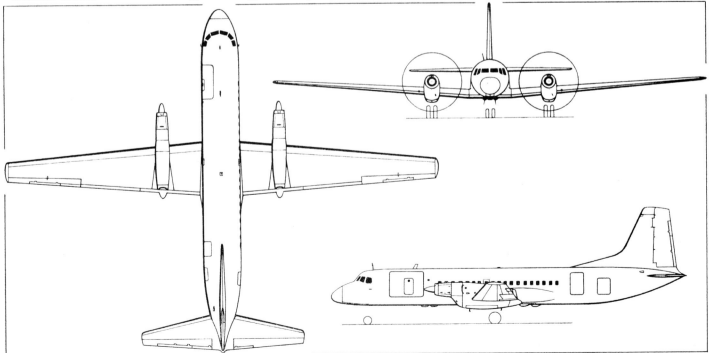

NAMC YS-11A-300 twin-turboprop short/medium-range transport for mixed traffic

The following details apply to all civil versions in current production:

TYPE: Twin-engined short/medium-range transport.

WINGS: Cantilever low-wing monoplane. Wing section NACA 64A-218 (modified) at root, NACA 64A-412 (modified) at tip. Dihedral 6° 19′. Incidence 3°. Sweepback at quarter chord 3° 11′. Aluminium alloy two-spar stressed-skin fail-safe structure. Aluminium alloy internally-sealed ailerons and hydraulically-operated Fowler flaps. Spring tab and trim tab in port aileron; spring tab in starboard aileron. Rubber boot de-icing system.

FUSELAGE: Circular-section stressed-skin aluminium alloy fail-safe structure, diameter 9 ft 5½ in (2·88 m).

TAIL UNIT: Cantilever aluminium alloy stressed-skin structure. Fixed-incidence tailplane. Spring-trim tab in rudder. Balance tab and trim tab in port elevator; balance tab in starboard elevator. Rubber boot de-icing system from aircraft No 41 onwards.

LANDING GEAR: Retractable tricycle type with twin wheels on each unit. All wheels retract forward hydraulically. Sumitomo Precision oleo-pneumatic shock-absorbers. Goodyear main wheel tyres (tubeless) size 12·50-16 Type III. Goodyear steerable nose-wheels and tyres (tubeless) size 24 × 7·7 Type VII. Tyre pressures: main wheels 75 lb/sq in (5·27 kg/cm²), nose-wheels 50 lb/sq in (3·52 kg/cm²). Goodyear single-disc hydraulic brakes, with Hydro Aire Mk I anti-skid units.

POWER PLANT: Two Rolls-Royce Dart Mk 542-10K (R.Da10/1) turboprop engines, each giving 3,060 ehp with water-methanol injection for take-off. Rotol four-blade propellers, diameter 14 ft 6 in (4·42 m). Fuel in wing tanks: two bag-type tanks inboard of engines with total capacity of 490 Imp gallons (2,230 litres), two integral tanks outboard of engines with total capacity of 1,110 Imp gallons (5,040 litres). Total fuel capacity 1,600 Imp gallons (7,270 litres). Gravity fuelling points above wing; pressure refuelling points under wing. Total oil capacity 13·75 Imp gallons (62 litres).

ACCOMMODATION (YS-11A-200): Flight crew of two, plus two cabin attendants. Seats for up to 60 passengers at 34 in (86 cm) pitch, in pairs on each side of centre aisle. Outward-opening main door at front on port side. Cargo compartment at rear of cabin. Baggage and freight holds forward of cabin and under floor, forward of wings. Galley and toilet aft of cabin.

ACCOMMODATION (YS-11A-300): Flight crew of two, plus two cabin attendants. Passenger cabin, aft of propeller plane, has 46 seats at 34 in (86 cm) pitch, in pairs on each side of centre aisle, and a rear row of 2 seats on starboard side only. Galley and toilet aft of cabin. Outward-opening passenger door on port side, aft of cabin. Main cargo door forward of wing on port side. Cargo and baggage holds forward of main cabin and under floor.

ACCOMMODATION (YS-11A-400): Two pilots on flight deck. Entire cabin normally clear for cargo carrying, supplemented by underfloor hold. Provision for 42 troop seats along walls of main cabin. Main cargo door at rear of cabin on port side. Crew entry door at front of cabin on port side.

SYSTEMS: Two engine-driven 12kW 28V DC generators and constant-frequency AC electrical system. Hydraulic system, pressure 3,000 lb/sq in (210 kg/cm²), actuates landing gear retraction, nose-wheel steering, brakes and flaps. AiResearch heating, cooling and pressurisation systems, with two Godfrey blowers, differential 4·16 lb/sq in (0·29 kg/cm²). Optional equipment includes AiResearch GTCP 36-16 APU for cabin air-conditioning, main engine starting and alternative source of electrical and hydraulic power on the ground.

ELECTRONICS AND EQUIPMENT: Standard installation comprises Collins or NEC VHF and VOR/ILS, Collins or Bendix ADF, Bendix, Collins or Toshiba marker beacon. Sperry or Tokyo Keiki ILS. Blind-flying instrumentation standard. Provision for Collins or Mitsubishi HF, Toshiba or Bendix weather radar, Bendix autopilot, Collins DME, Collins voice recorder, Collins ATC transponder, Fairchild flight recorder.

DIMENSIONS, EXTERNAL:

Wing span	104 ft 11¾ in (32·00 m)
Wing chord at root	13 ft 9½ in (4·20 m)
Wing chord at tip	4 ft 11 in (1·50 m)
Wing aspect ratio	10·8
Length overall	86 ft 3½ in (26·30 m)
Height overall	29 ft 5½ in (8·98 m)
Tailplane span	39 ft 4½ in (12·00 m)
Wheel track	28 ft 2½ in (8·60 m)
Wheelbase	31 ft 2½ in (9·52 m)

Passenger door (forward, port, YS-11A-200):

Height	5 ft 9 in (1·75 m)
Width	3 ft 4 in (1·00 m)
Height to sill	7 ft 3½ in (2·22 m)

Passenger door (aft, port, YS-11A-300):

Height	5 ft 9 in (1·75 m)
Width	3 ft 4 in (1·00 m)

Crew door (forward, port, YS-11A-400):

Height	5 ft 9 in (1·75 m)
Width	3 ft 4 in (1·00 m)

Baggage hold door (fwd, stbd, YS-11A-200):

Height	4 ft 0 in (1·22 m)
Width	2 ft 8 in (0·80 m)

Cargo hold door (aft, stbd, all versions):

Height	4 ft 0 in (1·22 m)
Width	2 ft 8 in (0·80 m)

Servicing door (aft, port, YS-11A-200):

Height	4 ft 0 in (1·22 m)
Width	2 ft 0 in (0·61 m)

Servicing door (aft, stbd, YS-11A-300):

Height	4 ft 0 in (1·22 m)
Width	2 ft 8 in (0·80 m)

Cargo door (fwd, port, YS-11A-300):

Height	6 ft 0 in (1·83 m)
Width	8 ft 2 in (2·48 m)

Forward entrance door, within cargo door (YS-11A-300):

Height	4 ft 0 in (1·22 m)
Width	2 ft 0 in (0·61 m)

Cargo door (aft, port, YS-11A-400):

Height	6 ft 0 in (1·83 m)
Width	10 ft 0 in (3·05 m)

Aft entrance door, within cargo door (YS-11A-400):

Height	4 ft 0 in (1·22 m)
Width	2 ft 1 in (0·64 m)

DIMENSIONS, INTERNAL (YS-11A-200):

Cabin, excluding flight deck, galley and toilets:

Length	44 ft 1 in (13·44 m)
Max width	8 ft 10 in (2·70 m)
Max height	6 ft 6 in (1·99 m)
Floor area	400 sq ft (37·33 m²)
Volume	2,150 cu ft (61·0 m³)

Baggage compartment (fwd of cabin) 94 cu ft (2·66 m³)
Freight hold (aft of cabin) 213 cu ft (6·03 m³)
Freight hold (under floor) 70 cu ft (1·98 m³)

DIMENSIONS, INTERNAL (YS-11A-300):

Cabin, excluding flight deck, fwd cargo hold, galley and toilet:

Length	36 ft 4 in (11·07 m)
Max width	8 ft 10 in (2·70 m)
Max height	6 ft 6 in (1·99 m)
Floor area	273 sq ft (25·40 m²)
Volume	1,715 cu ft (48·57 m³)

Baggage compartment (aft of cabin) 90 cu ft (2·55 m³)
Freight hold (fwd of cabin) 360 cu ft (10·19 m³)
Freight hold (under floor) 70 cu ft (1·98 m³)

DIMENSIONS, INTERNAL (YS-11A-400):

Main freight hold, excluding flight deck:

Length	59 ft 0 in (17·98 m)
Max width	8 ft 10 in (2·70 m)
Max height	6 ft 2 in (1·88 m)
Floor area	443 sq ft (41·19 m²)
Volume	2,790 cu ft (78·90 m³)

Underfloor freight hold 70 cu ft (1·98 m³)

AREAS (all versions):

Wings, gross	1,020·4 sq ft (94·8 m²)
Ailerons (total)	63·80 sq ft (5·92 m²)
Trailing-edge flaps (total)	202·20 sq ft (18·78 m²)
Fin	104·95 sq ft (9·75 m²)
Rudder, including tab	51·13 sq ft (4·75 m²)
Tailplane	180·50 sq ft (16·76 m²)
Elevators, including tabs	57·40 sq ft (5·33 m²)

WEIGHTS AND LOADINGS:

Operating weight, empty:

YS-11A-200	33,942 lb (15,396 kg)
YS-11A-300	34,855 lb (15,810 kg)
YS-11A-400	32,595 lb (14,785 kg)

Max payload:

YS-11A-200	14,559 lb (6,604 kg)
YS-11A-300	13,646 lb (6,190 kg)
YS-11A-400	15,906 lb (7,215 kg)
Max T-O weight:	54,010 lb (24,500 kg)
Max zero-fuel weight:	48,500 lb (22,000 kg)
Max landing weight:	52,910 lb (24,000 kg)
Max wing loading:	52·8 lb/sq ft (258 kg/m²)
Max power loading:	8·83 lb/ehp (4·00 kg/ehp)

PERFORMANCE (at max T-O weight):

Max permissible diving speed (all versions):

Below 15,400 ft (4,695 m)	295 knots (340 mph; 546 km/h)
Above 15,400 ft (4,695 m)	Mach 0·601

Max cruising speed at 15,000 ft (4,575 m) 253 knots (291 mph; 469 km/h)
Econ cruising speed at 20,000 ft (6,100 m) 244 knots (281 mph; 452 km/h)
Stalling speed at max landing weight, flaps down 76 knots (87 mph; 140 km/h)
Rate of climb at S/L 1,220 ft (372 m)/min
Service ceiling 22,900 ft (6,980 m)
Service ceiling, one engine out 9,000 ft (2,740 m)
T-O to 35 ft (10 m) (SR 422B) 3,650 ft (1,110 m)
Landing from 50 ft (15 m) at max landing weight (SR 422B) 2,170 ft (660 m)

Range with max fuel, no reserves:
without bag tanks 1,137 nm (1,310 miles; 2,110 km)
with bag tanks 1,736 nm (2,000 miles; 3,215 km)

Range with max payload, no reserves: 590 nm (680 miles; 1,090 km)

NAMC XC-1A

The XC-1A is a medium-sized troop and freight transport designed to meet the JASDF's C-X requirement for a replacement for its present fleet of Curtiss C-46 transports during the early 1970s. Preliminary design work was started by NAMC in 1966, and in September 1967 a prototype development contract was awarded. Following the completion of a full-sized mock-up in March 1968, construction began in the following Autumn of two flying prototypes and one airframe for static tests. The first flying prototype, which is being built at Kawasaki's Gifu factory, was scheduled to make its first flight in October 1970, with the second aircraft following some three months later. Series production will begin in 1971, the first flight of a production C-1A being scheduled for 1972 and first delivery to the JASDF in 1973.

Present JASDF plans call for 44 examples of the transport version, three others for weather reconnaissance and five for ECM duties. Another five will be purchased by the JMSDF for minelaying and AEW. The JASDF is also considering a stretched version of the XC-1A, a prototype of which is tentatively planned to fly in 1978, as a long-range over-water transport.

Major sub-contractors in the C-1A programme will be Fuji, who will be responsible for manufacturing the outer wing panels, pylons and engine pods; Kawasaki, who will build the front fuselage and wing centre-section and undertake final assembly and flight testing; Mitsubishi (who also built the mock-up) will manufacture the centre and aft fuselage sections and the tail surfaces; and Nihon Hikoki (Nippi) will produce the flaps, ailerons and engine pods. The palletised cargo loading system is to be produced by Shin Meiwa, and the landing gear by Sumitomo.

TYPE: Twin-turbofan medium-range transport.

WINGS: Cantilever high-wing monoplane. Wings have moderate sweepback, with slightly increased leading-edge sweep inboard of the engine pylons. 20° sweepback at quarter-chord. Thickness/chord ratio 12% at root, 11% at tip. Anhedral 5° 30′ from roots. Conventional two-spar fail-safe structure of aluminium alloy, including control surfaces. Two four-stage Fowler-type flaps on each trailing-edge, with 75° travel. Forward of these, on each wing, are three flight spoilers and a ground spoiler. Drooping leading-edge slats, in four sections, on each wing. Aileron outboard of each outer flap. Flaps are operated hydraulically, ailerons manually. Thermal anti-icing of leading-edges, using engine-bleed air.

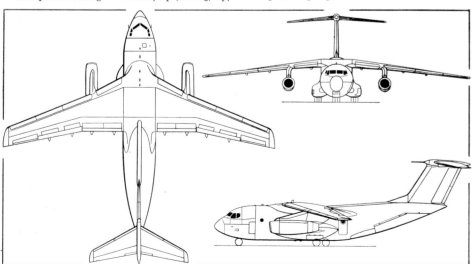

NAMC XC-1A twin-turbofan medium-range transport

FUSELAGE: Conventional semi-monocoque fail-safe structure of aluminium alloy, with a circular cross-section.

TAIL UNIT: "T" type cantilever structure, with sweepback on all surfaces (30° on fin leading-edge, 20° at tailplane quarter-chord). Tail-plane has 5° anhedral. Conventional aluminium alloy structure. Variable-incidence tail-plane, fitted with elevators, mounted at top of fin. Trim-tabs in elevators (one each) and rudder (two). Elevators and rudder are each operated by two independent hydro-actuator systems; the elevators can be operated manually in an emergency. Thermal anti-icing of tailplane, using engine-bleed air.

LANDING GEAR: Hydraulically-retractable tri-cycle type, of Sumitomo design. Each main unit has two pairs of wheels in tandem, retracting into fairings built on to the sides of the fuselage. Nose unit has twin wheels. Oleo shock-absorbers. Kayaba wheels with Dunlop tyres, which on main units have pressure of 75 lb/sq in (5·27 kg/cm²). Kayaba hydraulic brakes and anti-skid units.

POWER PLANT: Two 14,500 lb (6,575 kg) st Pratt & Whitney JT8D-9 turbofan engines, installed in pylon-mounted underwing pods and fitted with thrust reversers. Fuel in four integral wing tanks with total capacity of 3,344 Imp gallons (15,200 litres). Single pressure-refuelling point for all tanks.

ACCOMMODATION: Crew of five on flight deck, comprising pilot, co-pilot, navigator, flight engineer and load supervisor. Flight deck and main cabin pressurised and air-conditioned. Standard complements are as follows: troops (max) 60, paratroops (max) 45, litters 36 plus attendants. As a cargo carrier, loads can include a 2½-ton truck, a 105 mm howitzer, two ¾-ton trucks or three jeeps. Up to three pre-loaded freight pallets, 7 ft 2½ in (2·20 m) square by 8 ft 10¼ in (2·70 m) long, designed by Shin Meiwa, can be carried. Floor is stressed for loads of up to 99·6 lb/sq in (7 kg/cm²). Access to flight deck via forward door on port side of fuselage. Paratroop door on each side of fuselage, aft of trailing-edge. Rear-loading ramp-door at rear of cabin opens to the full cabin cross-section.

SYSTEMS: Hydraulic system for landing gear actuation. APU in front section of starboard landing gear fairing.

ELECTRONICS AND EQUIPMENT: Standard equipment includes Bendix autopilot, Doppler radar, radio altimeter, dual HF and single VHF and UHF radio, two ADF transponders, UHF/DF, VOR/ILS, TACAN, and SIF. Optional equipment includes LORAN and weather radar.

DIMENSIONS, EXTERNAL (approximate):

Wing span	101 ft 8¼ in (31·00 m)
Wing chord at root	20 ft 8 in (6·30 m)
Wing chord at tip	6 ft 6¾ in (2·00 m)
Wing aspect ratio	7·8
Length overall	95 ft 1¾ in (29·00 m)
Length of fuselage	86 ft 11 in (26·50 m)
Height overall	32 ft 9¾ in (10·00 m)
Tailplane span	38 ft 0¾ in (11·60 m)
Wheel track	14 ft 5¼ in (4·40 m)
Wheelbase	30 ft 6 in (9·30 m)
Rear-loading ramp-door:	
Length	9 ft 10 in (3·00 m)
Width	8 ft 6¼ in (2·60 m)
Height to sill	4 ft 1¼ in (1·25 m)

DIMENSIONS, INTERNAL (approximate):

Cabin: Max length	34 ft 9¼ in (10·60 m)
Max width	10 ft 4 in (3·15 m)
Max height	8 ft 2½ in (2·50 m)
Floor area	296·654 sq ft (27·57 m²)
Volume	3,108 cu ft (88·00 m³)

AREAS (approximate):

Wings, gross	1,291·7 sq ft (120·0 m²)
Ailerons (total)	75·3 sq ft (7·0 m²)
Trailing-edge flaps (total)	247·6 sq ft (23·0 m²)
Spoilers (total)	96·9 sq ft (9·0 m²)
Fin	172·2 sq ft (16·0 m²)
Rudder, including tabs	64·6 sq ft (6·0 m²)
Tailplane	193·7 sq ft (18·0 m²)
Elevators, including tabs	75·3 sq ft (7·0 m²)

WEIGHTS (estimated):

Weight empty, equipped	50,706 lb (23,000 kg)
Normal payload	17,637 lb (8,000 kg)
Max T-O weight	85,980 lb (39,000 kg)

PERFORMANCE (estimated, at max T-O weight):

Max level speed at 23,200 ft (7,600 m) 440 knots (507 mph; 815 km/h)

Max cruising speed at 35,100 ft (10,700 m) 380 knots (438 mph; 704 km/h)

Rate of climb at S/L 3,806 ft (1,160 m)/min

Service ceiling 39,370 ft (12,000 m)

T-O run (with 17,637 lb = 8,000 kg payload) 2,200 ft (670 m)

T-O to 50 ft (15 m) 3,940 ft (1,200 m)

Landing run (with 17,637 lb = 8,000 kg payload and reverse thrust) 1,215 ft (370 m)

Range with max fuel (payload of 5,732 lb = 2,600 kg) 1,800 nm (2,073 miles; 3,336 km)

Range with 17,637 lb (8,000 kg) payload 700 nm (806 miles; 1,297 km)

NAMC Y-X

In July 1969, NAMC announced the basic configuration of a short/medium-range, 116/149-passenger STOL transport aircraft as a successor to the YS-11, with the project designation Y-X. This design, which had the provisional manufacturer's designation YS-33, had two underwing Rolls-Royce RB.203-08 Trent engines and a third Trent engine in the rear of the fuselage. Later in 1969, however, this configuration was cancelled, and NAMC is currently developing a new and more advanced design to meet the Y-X requirement, possibly using the RB.203-12 variant of the Trent engine and having a provisional first flight date of 1974.

NATIONAL AEROSPACE LABORATORY

NATIONAL AEROSPACE LABORATORY

ADDRESS:
1880 Jindaiji-cho, Chofu City, Tokyo

The Kakuta branch of the National Aerospace Laboratory has carried out a series of trials of a test rig installed in a tower as a first step towards the completion of a nationally designed and built VTOL aircraft. The test rig, design of which began in 1967, was constructed by Fuji Heavy Industries Ltd and was completed in May 1968. It is powered by two 3,373 lb (1,530 kg) st Ishikawajima-Harima JR-100F lift-jet engines and made its first hovering test flight on 28 November 1969 tethered to 28 ft (8·5 m) high guide rails. The first free-flight test was scheduled to take place in September 1970. The rig has two fuel tanks, each with a capacity of 66 Imp gallons (300 litres).

DIMENSIONS (approximate):

Span	23 ft 0 in (7·00 m)
Length	32 ft 9½ in (10·00 m)
Height	9 ft 10 in (3·00 m)

WEIGHT:

Max T-O weight	4,190 lb (1,900 kg)

PERFORMANCE:

Max hovering duration	10 min

NIHON UNIVERSITY

COLLEGE OF SCIENCE AND ENGINEERING (DEPARTMENT OF MECHANICAL ENGINEERING), NIHON UNIVERSITY

ADDRESS:
Kanda-Surugadai, Chiyoda-ku, Tokyo

CHIEF PROFESSOR: Dr Hidemasa Kimura

Under the leadership of Dr Kimura, the students of Nihon University designed and built two light aeroplanes known as the Okamura N-52 and N-58 Cygnet. They next designed a STOL lightplane designated N-62, in collaboration with the C. Itoh Aircraft Engineering Co, who built the prototype. This aircraft was put into production by Itoh, as the N-62 Eaglet, and was described under their entry in the 1968-69 *Jane's*.

Recent products of this design team were two successful man-powered aircraft named the NM-63 Linnet and the NM-66 Linnet II, which were described fully in the 1966-67 and 1967-68 *Jane's* respectively. Construction of a third man-powered design, the Linnet III, was begun late in 1969; this is described below.

NIHON UNIVERSITY NM-69 LINNET III

Dr Kimura and his team began design studies for this single-seat man-powered aircraft in April 1969. Construction of the Linnet III began in October 1969, and it made its first flight on 26 March 1970. A lightweight flight recorder was being installed for a second phase of flight testing beginning in September 1970.

TYPE: Single-seat man-powered aircraft.

WINGS: Cantilever low/mid-wing monoplane. Wing section NACA 8418 at root, NACA 8415 at tip. Dihedral 6° from roots. Incidence 5° 7'. One-piece wooden structure. Single spar with American spruce flanges and balsa webs. Each half contains 63 balsa ribs. Sheet balsa, 1 mm thick, on leading-edges. Whole structure covered with 0·75 mm thick styrene-paper. Wing-tips of hollowed-out acrylic foam plastic, each with rattan skid. Ground-adjustable trim-tab over approx one-third of each half-span, instead of ailerons. No flaps.

FUSELAGE: Welded aluminium-tube basic truss structure, with balsa-wood stringers and fairings. Nose-cap is made of styrene foam plastic, the entire remainder of the structure being covered with styrene paper 0·5-0·75 mm thick.

TAIL UNIT: Cantilever structure, of similar construction to wings. All-flying horizontal tail surfaces, with inverted NACA 4412 aerofoil section.

Two views of the Nihon University NM-69 Linnet III man-powered aircraft in flight on 26 March 1970

Landing Gear: Two non-retractable bicycle wheels, mounted in tandem. Front wheel size 18 × $1\frac{3}{8}$ in (457 × 35 mm), rear wheel $12\frac{1}{2}$ × $2\frac{1}{4}$ in (318 × 57 mm). No shock-absorbers. Tyre pressure 28·5 lb/sq in (2·0 kg/cm²) for both wheels. No brakes.

Power System: Man-power on bicycle pedals, transmitted to the pusher propeller by a duralumin torque shaft, and to the front wheel by a chain. Estimated power developed = 0·4 hp at take-off, and 0·3 hp for three minutes in level flight. Two-blade propeller, diameter 9 ft 10 in (3·00 m), made of FRP. Blades have RAF 6 section ribs, with a pitch of 36° at 75% radius. Normal rpm 125.

Accommodation: Pilot only, on bicycle saddle in a cabin with a bubble-type canopy.

Dimensions, external:

Wing span	83 ft 0 in (25·30 m)
Wing chord at root	5 ft $11\frac{1}{4}$ in (1·81 m)
Wing chord at tip	2 ft 0 in (0·61 m)
Wing aspect ratio	21·2
Length overall	19 ft $2\frac{3}{4}$ in (5·86 m)
Height overall	13 ft 7 in (4·14 m)
Tailplane span	19 ft $0\frac{1}{4}$ in (5·80 m)
Wheelbase	2 ft $7\frac{1}{2}$ in (0·80 m)

Areas:

Wings, gross	325·1 sq ft (30·2 m²)
Trim-tabs (total)	6·89 sq ft (0·64 m²)
Fin	16·68 sq ft (1·55 m²)
Rudder	4·84 sq ft (0·45 m²)
Horizontal tail surfaces (total)	36·60 sq ft (3·40 m²)

Weights and Loading (estimated):

Weight empty	110·7 lb (50·2 kg)
T-O weight	220-230 lb (100-105 kg)
Wing loading	0·68-0·72 lb/sq ft (3·3-3·5 kg/m²)

Performance (estimated):

Cruising speed	14 knots (16 mph; 26 km/h)
Cruising lift coefficient	1·0
Stalling speed	12·7 knots (14·6 mph; 23·5 km/h)
Max flying height	6 ft (1·8 m)
T-O run	260 ft (80 m)

NIPPI

NIHON HIKOKI KABUSHIKI KAISHA (Japan Aircraft Manufacturing Company Ltd)

Head Office:
No. 8, 3-Chome, Choja-machi, Naka-ku, Yokohama

Works: Sugita and Atsugi

President: Masami Takasaki

Executive Vice-Presidents:
Masatoshi Takasaki
Makoto Watanabe
Takahide Aioi

Managing Directors:
Kenzo Cogo (Contracts, Marketing)
Shigeru Kato (Production, Engineering, Planning)

Directors:
Toshiharu Baba (Aircraft Engineering)
Matsuo Ishiwata (Production, Atsugi Works)
Masanao Morita (Production, Sugita Works)
Yoshimoto Tajima (Engineering)

Public Relations Manager:
Taketoshi Kitamura

Nihon Hikoki (Nippi) is engaged chiefly on overhaul, repair and maintenance of US Navy carrier-based aircraft, the S2F anti-submarine aircraft operated by the Japan Maritime Self-Defence Force and other aircraft of the Japan Defence Agency.

Other current programmes include detail design and production of wings, ailerons, flaps, etc, in support of Shin Meiwa's PS-1 flying-boat programme, NAMC XC-1 cargo transport programme, and a VTOL project under contract from the Technical Research and Development Institute of the Japan Defence Agency, study of high-lift devices and the manufacture of structural components and equipment for a wide range of Japanese aircraft, including the NAMC YS-11 transport and licence-built versions of the Sikorsky S-62, Bell UH-1B and Boeing-Vertol 107 Model II helicopters.

Nippi has also been engaged in developing a new anti-submarine aircraft, the PX-L, and modernising the S2F anti-submarine aircraft for the JMSDF.

OHNISHI

YUICHI OHNISHI

Address:
c/o Tatebayashi Aero, Ohaza-Kondo 760, Tatebayashi, Gunma Prefecture

Mr Ohnishi, an engineer and designer, has built and flown a single-engined ultra-light aircraft of his own design known as the OG-2. All available details of this aircraft are given below.

OHNISHI OG-2

Design of the OG-2 was started in August 1966, and construction began two months later. The aircraft (JA0143) flew for the first time in February 1967, and was certificated by the JCAB in November 1968, shortly after it had been exhibited at the Tokyo Air Show.

Originally, it was powered by a 40 hp Toyura Pabrica two-stroke engine driving a pusher propeller, and in this form was described and illustrated in the 1969-70 *Jane's*.

In its latest form, the OG-2 is powered by a 55 hp modified Sparu motor-car engine driving a tractor propeller, and the description below applies to it in this form.

Type: Single-seat ultra-light aircraft.

Wings: Strut-braced high-wing monoplane. Wing section Clark Y series. Thickness/chord ratio 12%. Dihedral 4°. Incidence 4°. No sweepback. Two-spar all-wood structure, fabric-covered. Plain wooden ailerons, with fabric covering. No flaps or tabs. Braced to chassis by Vee strut on each side.

Fuselage: Open-work structure, front portion of square-section aluminium alloy supports engine, pilot's seat and landing gear; rear portion, of welded steel-tube construction, supports tail unit.

Tail Unit: All-wood structure, fabric-covered. Strut-braced one-piece tailplane, set on top of fin, with large rudder to rear. No tabs in elevators or rudder. Tailplane incidence can be adjusted on ground.

Landing Gear: Non-retractable tricycle type, nose-wheel having leaf-spring shock-absorber. Main wheel tyres size 300 × 80, nose-wheel tyre size 200 × 60. Pressure (all tyres) 28·5 lb/sq in (2·0 kg/cm²). Steel belt plate acts as brake on nose-wheel.

Power Plant: One 55 hp Fuji-built Sparu 1,000 cc four-stroke four-cylinder horizontally-opposed water-cooled motor-car engine, driving a two-blade wooden propeller of 3 ft 5 in (1·04 m) diameter. Fuel in single main tank, capacity 4·4 Imp gallons (20 litres). Oil capacity 0·4 Imp gallons (1·8 litres).

Ohnishi OG-2 single-seat ultra-light monoplane in latest form, with tractor propeller (*Asahi Miyahara*)

Accommodation: Single open seat for pilot at front of fuselage, beneath the wing.

Dimensions, external:

Wing span	40 ft $0\frac{1}{4}$ in (12·20 m)
Wing chord (constant)	4 ft 7 in (1·40 m)
Wing aspect ratio	8·5
Length overall	20 ft 4 in (6·20 m)
Height overall	7 ft $6\frac{1}{2}$ in (2·30 m)
Tailplane span	4 ft 7 in (1·40 m)
Wheel track	3 ft $3\frac{1}{4}$ in (1·00 m)
Wheelbase	8 ft $2\frac{1}{2}$ in (2·50 m)

Areas:

Wings, gross	180·83 sq ft (16·80 m²)
Rudder	10·8 sq ft (1·00 m²)
Horizontal tail surfaces (total)	35·5 sq ft (3·30 m²)

Weights and Loading:

Weight empty	536 lb (243 kg)
Max T-O weight	668 lb (303 kg)
Max wing loading	3·69 lb/sq ft (18·0 kg/m²)

Performance (at max T-O weight):

Max level speed at S/L	52 knots (60 mph; 96 km/h)
Max cruising speed	35 knots (40 mph; 65 km/h)
Stalling speed	22 knots (25 mph; 40 km/h)
Rate of climb at S/L	276 ft (84 m)/min
T-O run	197 ft (60 m)
Landing run	260 ft (80 m)

SATOH-MAEDA

DR HIROSHI SATOH and MR KEN-ICHI MAEDA

SATOH-MAEDA SM-OX

Designed by Dr Satoh and Mr Maeda, the SM-OX man-powered aircraft was built by students of the Fukuoka high school. Construction began in 1966 and was completed in November 1968. The SM-OX flew for the first time on 24 August 1969, travelling a distance of 100 ft (30 m) and reaching a height of 5 ft (1·5 m).

Type: Single-seat man-powered aircraft.

Wings: Cantilever low-wing monoplane. Styrene-paper covered two-spar structure with slight forward sweep. Wing section NACA 4418 at root, NACA 4415 at tip.

Fuselage: Paper-covered wooden structure with oval section. A basic frame and two bicycle wheels are integrated in the bottom of cockpit to accelerate take-off run.

Tail Unit: Paper-covered wooden cruciform

Satoh-Maeda SM-OX single-seat man-powered aircraft during early flight trials in 1969 (*AiReview*)

structure, with 12% thickness ratio in horizontal plane.

POWER SYSTEM: 5 ft 10 in (1·8 m) diameter three-blade propeller at rear of the fuselage. Power is transmitted from bicycle pedals to propeller via a drive-shaft made from FRP fishing rod.

DIMENSIONS, EXTERNAL:

Wing span	70 ft 10½ in (21·60 m)
Wing aspect ratio	16·8
Length overall	19 ft 3 in (5·87 m)
Height overall	8 ft 4¾ in (2·56 m)

AREA:

Wings, gross	299 sq ft (27·78 m²)

WEIGHTS:

Weight empty	119·3 lb (54·1 kg)
Max T-O weight	242·5 lb (110·0 kg)

SHIN MEIWA

Second prototype of the Shin Meiwa PX-S anti-submarine flying-boat, which has been ordered into production for the JMSDF

SHIN MEIWA INDUSTRY Co., Ltd

HEAD OFFICE:
1-5-25, Kosone-Cho, Nishinomiya City, Hyogo Prefecture

TOKYO OFFICE:
c/o Shin Ohtemachi Building, 5th Floor, 4-2 Chome, Ohtemachi, Chiyoda-ku

WORKS:
Kobe, Itami and Takarazuka

PRESIDENT:
Toshio Itoh

VICE-PRESIDENT:
Teruo Watanabe

EXECUTIVE MANAGING DIRECTOR:
Hiroshi Kohno

SUPERINTENDENT, AIRCRAFT DIVISION:
Tadao Uno

SALES MANAGER AND PUBLIC RELATIONS:
Kazuo Kubota

The former Kawanishi Aircraft Company became Shin Meiwa in 1949 and has established itself as a major overhaul centre for Japanese and US military and commercial aircraft.

Shin Meiwa is also engaged in the manufacture of components for helicopters and fixed-wing aircraft. In particular, it produces fuselage and tail assemblies for the P-2J (Neptune development) maritime patrol aircraft built in Japan by

Kawasaki, and it is one of the companies collaborating in the manufacture of the NAMC YS-11 turboprop transport.

Under development by Shin Meiwa for the JMSDF is a medium-range STOL flying-boat designated PS-1, of which details are given below.

As part of the development programme for this aircraft, the company completely rebuilt a Grumman UF-1 Albatross as a dynamically-similar flying scale model of the new design, under the designation UF-XS. The flight test programme for this aircraft was completed in September 1964. It was described and illustrated in the 1964-65 *Jane's*.

SHIN MEIWA PX-S and PS-1

After seven years of basic study and research, Shin Meiwa was awarded a contract to develop a new anti-submarine flying-boat for the Japanese Maritime Self-Defence Force in January 1966. The first prototype (5801), designed by a team headed by Dr Shizuo Kikuhara, was completed in August 1967 and flew for the first time on 5 October 1967. This aircraft was delivered to the JMSDF on 31 July 1968 after completing manufacturer's flight testing. The second prototype, which flew on 14 June 1968, was handed over on 30 November 1968. These two aircraft

were delivered to the 415th Flight Test Squadron of the JMSDF, and by the end of 1969 had completed 220 and 325 hours of flying respectively. A third and fourth aircraft were ordered by the JMSDF on 29 March 1969. These will be pre-series aircraft, and will be designated PS-1. Deliveries are scheduled for September 1971 and January 1972 respectively. The description below applies to this version.

In the meantime, production contracts are to be negotiated for the remaining 12 aircraft required by the JMSDF, with delivery of all 16 to be completed by 1973. Purchase of a further 20 by 1976 is planned.

A further version, designated SS-2, has also been announced, for the air/sea rescue role. The fuselage would be lengthened by approx 6½ ft (2·0 m), but would otherwise be basically similar to the PS-1, retaining the search radar but equipped to carry up to 36 stretchers and five medical attendants. Further variants are under consideration, including an early warning version, and amphibious and pressurised STOL civil transport models.

To make possible very low landing and take-off speeds, the PS-1 has both a boundary layer control system and extensive flaps for propeller slipstream deflection. Improved seaworthiness

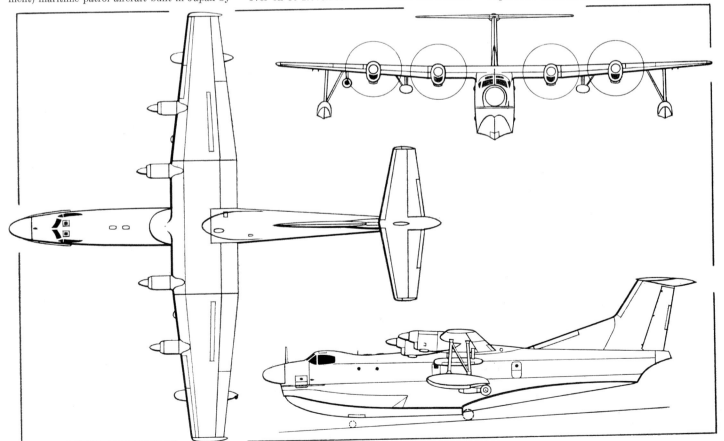

Three-view drawing of the PS-1 production version of the Shin Meiwa PX-S STOL maritime reconnaissance flying-boat

results from the use of a high length-to-beam ratio hull, with specially-developed spray suppression strakes on the nose. Control and stability in low-speed flight are enhanced by "blowing" the rudder, flaps and elevators, and by use of an automatic stabilisation system.

The PS-1 is designed to dip its large sonar deep into the sea during repeated landings and take-offs, and for this purpose was designed to be able to land on very rough water, in winds of up to 29 mph (47 kmh). In its early tests, the prototype PX-S carried out take-offs and landings in seas with wave heights of up to 13 ft (4 m). Such operations are facilitated by its STOL characteristics, and in particular by its low landing speed.

TYPE: Four-turboprop STOL anti-submarine flying-boat.

WINGS: Cantilever high-wing monoplane. Conventional all-metal, two-spar structure with rectangular centre-section and tapered outer panels. High-lift devices include leading-edge slats extending over nearly 34% of the span and large outer and inner blown trailing-edge flaps extending 60° and 80° respectively. Two spoilers are located in front of the outer flap on each wing. Powered ailerons. Leading-edge de-icing boots.

FUSELAGE: All-metal semi-monocoque hull structure. Vee-shaped single-step planing bottom, with curved anti-spray chine fairing along sides of nose and spray suppressor slots in lower fuselage sides aft of inboard propeller line. Double-deck interior.

TAIL UNIT: Cantilever all-metal structure, with tailplane mounted on top of sweptback fin. Large dorsal fin. Tailplane has slats and de-icing boots on leading-edge. Blown rudder and elevators.

LANDING GEAR: Hull; with fixed stabilising floats near wingtips. Retractable tricycle-type beaching gear installed, with aft-retracting single-wheel main gear unit on each side of hull and forward-retracting twin steerable nose-wheels, making aircraft independent of ground beaching aids.

POWER PLANT: Four 2,850 ehp Ishikawajima-built General Electric T64-IHI-10 turboprop engines, each driving a Hamilton Standard 63E60-15 three-blade constant-speed reversible-pitch propeller of 14 ft 6 in (4·42 m) diameter. Additionally, one 1,250 shp Ishikawajima-built General Electric T58-IHI-8B gas-turbine is housed in the upper centre portion of the fuselage to provide power for boundary-layer control system on rudder, flaps and elevators. Fuel in two rear-fuselage tanks and five wing tanks, with total usable capacity of 1,925 Imp gallons (8,750 litres). Oil capacity 30·8 Imp gallons (140 litres).

ACCOMMODATION: Two pilots and flight engineer on flight deck, which has wide-visibility bulged windows at sides. Aft of this on the upper deck is a tactical compartment, housing two sonar operators, a navigator, MAD operator, radar operator, radio operator and a tactical co-ordinator. Electronic, magnetic and sonic equipment is installed on starboard side, with crew's rest area and bunks on port side. Aft of tactical compartment is the weapons compartment. On the lower deck, from nose to rear, are the electronics compartment, oxygen-bottle bay, main gear bay and two fuel tanks. Door on port side of rear fuselage.

ARMAMENT AND OPERATIONAL EQUIPMENT: Weapons bay on upper deck, aft of tactical compartment, in which are stored a large dipping sonar, AQA-3 Jezebel passive long-range acoustic search equipment with 20 sonobuoys and their launchers, Julie active acoustic echo ranging with 30 explosive charges, four 330 lb (150 kg) anti-submarine bombs, and smoke bombs. External armament includes two underwing pods, mounted between each pair of engine nacelles and each containing two homing torpedoes, and a launcher beneath each wingtip for three 5 in (12·7 cm) air-to-surface rockets. Large search radar in fairing on nose of hull, and retractable ASQ-10 MAD (magnetic anomaly detector) tail 'sting'. Searchlight below starboard outer wing. Other equipment includes an automatic flight

control system, including automatic stabilisation equipment, electronic countermeasures equipment and a specially-developed wave-height meter.

DIMENSIONS, EXTERNAL:
Wing span	108 ft 8¾ in (33·14 m)
Length overall	109 ft 10⅞ in (33·50 m)
Height overall	31 ft 10½ in (9·715 m)
Tailplane span	40 ft 6½ in (12·36 m)
Wheel track	10 ft 2 in (3·10 m)
Wheelbase	26 ft 10¾ in (8·20 m)

AREAS:
Wings, gross	1,462 sq ft (135·8 m²)
Ailerons (total)	68·9 sq ft (6·40 m²)
Inner flaps (total)	101·18 sq ft (9·40 m²)
Outer flaps (total)	152·85 sq ft (14·20 m²)
Leading-edge slats (total)	64·7 sq ft (6·01 m²)
Spoilers (total)	22·60 sq ft (2·10 m²)
Fin	189 sq ft (17·56 m²)
Rudder	75·5 sq ft (7·01 m²)
Tailplane	248 sq ft (23·05 m²)
Elevators	94·5 sq ft (8·78 m²)

WEIGHTS:
Weight empty	51,852 lb (23,520 kg)
Payload	5,578 lb (2,530 kg)
Normal T-O weight	71,871 lb (32,600 kg)
Max T-O weight	86,862 lb (39,400 kg)

PERFORMANCE (at max T-O weight):
Max level speed at 5,000 ft (1,500 m)	
	295 knots (340 mph; 547 km/h)
Cruising speed at 5,000 ft (1,500 m)	
	170 knots (196 mph; 315 km/h)
Approach speed	47 knots (54 mph; 87 km/h)
Touchdown speed	41 knots (47 mph; 76 km/h)
Stalling speed	40 knots (46 mph; 75 km/h)
Rate of climb at S/L	2,264 ft (690 m)/min
Service ceiling	29,500 ft (9,000 m)
Time to 10,000 ft (3,000 m)	5 min
T-O run (calm water)	820 ft (250 m)
T-O to 50 ft (15 m)	968 ft (295 m)
Landing from 50 ft (15 m)	787 ft (240 m)
Landing run	590 ft (180 m)
Normal range	1,169 nm (1,347 miles; 2,168 km)
Max range for ferrying	
	2,560 nm (2,948 miles; 4,744 km)
Endurance	15 hr

SHOWA

SHOWA HIKOKI KOGYO KABUSHIKI KAISHA (Showa Aircraft Industry Co, Ltd)

HEAD OFFICE:
No 3, 3-Chome, Nihonbashi-Muromachi, Chuo-ku, Tokyo

SALES OFFICE:
No 1, 2-Chome, Nihonbashi-Muromachi, Chuo-ku, Tokyo

WORKS:
No 600, Tanaka-cho, Akishima-shi, Tokyo

PRESIDENT: Hidesuke Noda
EXECUTIVE DIRECTOR:
Katsumi Yoshimura
MANAGING DIRECTORS:
Tsuneo Okai
Kunio Nishi

Showa, which before the war was responsible for the manufacture of the Douglas DC-3 under licence, was the first Japanese aircraft manufacturing company to resume post-war operations when it undertook the overhaul and repair of aircraft of the US Air Force.

The company's present activities comprise mainly the manufacture of honeycomb sandwich floor panels, partition panels, doors and crew seats for the NAMC YS-11 twin-turboprop transport aircraft; manufacture of wingtip floats, tail fin, partition and other doors, torpedo pods and hatches for the Shin Meiwa PS-1 flying-boat; and the supply of aluminium and non-metal honeycomb and honeycomb sandwich panels for aircraft construction. Showa also manufactures a variety of airborne equipment, including galleys, trolleys and containers.

TACHIKAWA

SHIN TACHIKAWA KOKUKI KABUSHIKI KAISHA (New Tachikawa Aircraft Co, Ltd)

HEAD OFFICE:
841, Sunakawa-machi, Tachikawa City, Tokyo

FACTORIES:
Tachikawa and Sunagawa
PRESIDENT: Yoshio Kawasaki
CHIEF ENGINEER: Shigeru Motoo
The New Tachikawa Aircraft Company was established on 15 November 1949.

As soon as the Air Law permitting the manufacture of aircraft was published on 15 July 1952, the company began the design of its first aeroplane, the R-52. This aircraft and its revised version, the R-53, have been described in previous editions of *Jane's*.

NETHERLANDS

AVIOLANDA

AVIOLANDA MAATSCHAPPIJ VOOR VLIEG-TUIGBOUW NV (Subsidiary of Fokker-VFW NV)

HEAD OFFICE:
Veerdam 44, Papendrecht (Postbus 1)

WORKS:
Papendrecht

MANAGERS:
N. G. J. W. van Marle

A. Brasser
Ir A Dijk (sub-manager Papendrecht)

SALES MANAGER:
Ir L. G. Drenthen

Founded in 1927, this company built Dornier flying-boats and Curtiss Hawk fighters under licence before World War II and has produced major components for Gloster Meteor and Hawker Hunter fighters since the war. It became a

wholly-owned Fokker subsidiary in 1967. Aviolanda's current activities include the production of components and sub-assemblies for the Canadian-built (Northrop) NF-5 and components for the Lockheed F-104G Starfighter, and production of Aviobridge telescopic passenger ramps and nose-loaders, electrical and electronic equipment, licensed production of ground apparatus for missiles, radio-telescopes, radomes and aircraft containers.

DULKES

COR DIJKMAN DULKES

ADDRESS: Beverwijk, near Haarlem

DULKES BRAVO

Mr Dulkes, a craftsman, and his brother, a metal-worker, completed in 1969 a small, strut-braced high-wing monoplane which they named Bravo. The aircraft took some 3½ years to build, and was completed without previous aircraft construction experience by either brother. It has a welded steel-tube fuselage, covered in fabric, and all-wooden wings. Many of the components were acquired from scrapyards, and the power plant is a well-worn 35 hp engine from a DAF motor car.

Neither brother possessed a pilot's licence, and, since the aircraft had not been inspected during construction, it had no authority to fly. However, on 13 September 1969 it was taken on to a local beach by a qualified pilot, to carry out taxi trials. With the aircraft at high speed, the pilot then took off, but was unable to land owing to the crowds that had gathered on the beach below. He flew on to land at Rotterdam Airport, where the aircraft was impounded and further flights subsequently forbidden.

Dulkes Bravo single-seat home-built light aircraft (*B. van der Klaauw*)

FOKKER-VFW

FOKKER-VFW NV (Subsidiary of Zentralgesell-schaft VFW-Fokker mbH)

HEAD OFFICE AND MAIN FACTORY:
PO Box 7600, Schiphol-Oost (Amsterdam-Airport)

OTHER FACTORIES:
Fokker-Dordrecht, at Dordrecht
Avio-Diepen, at Ypenburg, near The Hague
Aviolanda, at Papendrecht and Woensdrecht
Aviobridge NV, at Papendrecht
Lichtwerk NV, at Hoogeveen
SABCA, at Haren and Gosselies, Belgium

BOARD OF MANAGEMENT:
F. J. L. Diepen
Ir H. C. van Meerten
Dr G. C. Klapwijk

The Fokker works at Amsterdam were founded in 1919 by the late A. H. G. Fokker, the well-known aircraft designer, who died on 23 December 1939.

The factory in the north of Amsterdam was destroyed in World War II. Although it was rebuilt, a new factory was built in 1951 on Schiphol Airport.

In 1954 the Fokker company enlarged its facilities by acquisition of the Avio-Diepen Industrie Mij NV at Ypenburg and the former Aviation Section of the De Schelde factory at Dordrecht. In 1966, the SABCA company of Belgium was taken over by Fokker, which now has a parity holding in the company with Avions Marcel Dassault of France. In 1967 Aviolanda at Papendrecht became a wholly-owned Fokker subsidiary. In turn, Northrop Corporation of USA acquired a holding in Fokker. Lichtwerk NV at Hoogeveen was taken over in 1969.

In May 1969 it was announced that NVKNV Fokker (Royal Netherlands Aircraft Factories Fokker) had decided to combine activities with VFW of Germany. With effect from 1 January 1969, a new central company was created (Zentralgesellschaft VFW-Fokker mbH: see International section), in which the Dutch and German holding companies each have a 50% interest. Each formed an operating company which became a wholly-owned subsidiary of Zentralgesellschaft, and Fokker continues its existing activities under the new title of Fokker-VFW NV.

In current production for commercial operators are the F.27 Friendship twin-turboprop and F.28 Fellowship twin-turbofan airliners. The Fairchild Hiller Corporation of Hagerstown, Maryland, USA, is manufacturing the F.27 under licence for the Western hemisphere, and is responsible for sales of the F.28 in the US, Canada and Mexico; it has ordered an initial batch of 10 F.28's.

In co-operation with other Dutch and German companies, including VFW, Fokker manufactured 350 Lockheed F-104G Starfighters for the Royal Netherlands and German air forces. It also designed in detail and builds in series the wing centre-section of the Breguet Atlantic maritime patrol aircraft, in collaboration with companies in France, Belgium, Italy and Germany.

Fokker-VFW is now manufacturing 190 sets of components of the Canadian-built Northrop F-5, which has been selected as the replacement for F-84F and T-33 aircraft currently in service with the Royal Netherlands Air Force. A total of 73 NF-5A's and 29 two-seat NF-5B's have been ordered.

Other current work includes the repair and overhaul of military and civil aircraft, and modification of these aircraft at Ypenburg and Woensdrecht and by SABCA. A variety of industrial products manufactured.

Fokker-VFW is also engaged in the Dutch ANS satellite programme, together with Philips, and studies are also made for satellites proposed by other groups, such as EST.

In 1970, Fokker-VFW employed about 8,000 people.

FOKKER F.27 FRIENDSHIP

The Friendship is a medium-sized airliner suitable for short/medium-range traffic. Two prototypes were built. The first made its first flight on 24 November 1955, and was designed to accommodate 28 passengers in a 73 ft (22·3 m) long fuselage. It was powered originally by two Rolls-Royce Dart 507 turboprops and later re-engined with Dart 511 turboprops. In 1958 it was equipped with the more powerful Dart 528 for certification purposes. The second prototype, which flew on 31 January 1957, was representative of Series 100 production aircraft, with Dart 511 engines and 32 seats in a 76 ft (23·1 m) fuselage. Two further prototype airframes were built for structure and fatigue testing.

The F.27 has been in series production for several years, both by Fokker and by Fairchild Hiller in the United States. Deliveries by Fokker began in November 1958, and the sale of the 500th Friendship was announced on 30 December 1968. Up to mid-June 1970 the following orders had been announced by Fokker-VFW:

Aer Lingus	7
Aero Trasporti Italiani	14

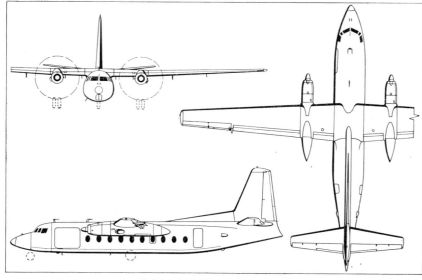

Fokker F.27 Mk 400 Combiplane

Air Congo	8
Air France	2
Air Inter	10
Alia, Royal Jordanian Airlines	1
All Nippon Airways and Fujita Airlines	25
ALM Dutch Antillean Airlines	2
Ansett-ANA, Airlines of NSW, Airlines of South Australia, Ansett Mandated Airlines (New Guinea), MacRobertson Miller Airlines, Queensland Airlines	23
Aramco	2
Argentine Air Force	10
Australian Dept of Civil Aviation	2
Balair (see also Swissair)	1
Braathens	8
Caltex Pacific (Indonesia)	1
Condor Flugdienst GmbH (Lufthansa)	2
Danish Aero Lease	2
DETA (Mozambique)	3
DTA (Angola)	4
East African Airways	4
East-West Airlines	5
French Ministère des Postes et Télécommunications (Air France)	15
Garuda Indonesian Airways	11
Gulf Aviation Company	1
Helmut Horten (Germany)	1
Iberia	8
Icelandair	3
Indian Airlines Corp	15
Iranian Oil Consortium	1
KLM Royal Dutch Airlines	2
Korean Air Lines	6
LTU (Germany)	3
Luxair	3
Malaysia-Singapore Airlines	17
A. P. Møller (Denmark)	5
Netherlands Dept of Civil Aviation	1
Royal Netherlands Air Force	12
New Zealand Dept of Civil Aviation	2
New Zealand National Airways Corp	9
Nigeria Airways	7
Oasis Oil Co (Libya)	1
Occidental of Libya Inc	1
Pakistan Directorate General of Civil Aviation	1
Pakistan International Airlines	13
Permina	3
Philippine Air Force	1
Philippine Air Lines	17
Philips Gloeilampenfabrieken (Holland)	1
Royal Air Maroc (Royal Air Inter)	2
Royal Nepal Airlines	1
Schreiner Airways	3
Sobelair (Sabena)	1
HIM the Shah of Iran	1
Sterling Airways (Denmark)	2
Sudanese Air Force	4
Sudan Airways	4
Swissair (for operation by Balair)	3
Trans-Australia Airlines	18
Turkish Airlines	5
Union of Burma Airways	7

Fairchild-built F-27's and FH-227's have been ordered by the following airlines:

Aerovias Ecuatorianas	1
Aerovias Venezolanas	5
Allegheny Airlines	10
Aloha Airlines	6
Bonanza Airlines	13
Lloyd Aéreo Boliviano	2
Mohawk Airlines (stretched version)	23
Northeast Airlines (stretched version)	7
Northern Consolidated Airlines	3
Ozark Airlines (21 stretched version)	25
Pacific Airlines	10
Paraense Transportes Aéreos SA (Brazil)	5
Piedmont Airlines	18
Quebecair	3

Trans Mar de Cortes	1
Turkish Airlines	5
West Coast Airlines	6
Wien Alaska Airlines	2

In addition 51 aircraft have been sold to corporate and private owners by Fairchild Hiller. Total sales on 31 May 1970 were 543 (Fokker-VFW 347 and Fairchild Hiller 196).

Fokker is standardising currently on the Mks 500 and 600, but any of the following five versions of the F.27 are available to order:

F.27 Mk 200 (Fairchild F-27A). Current basic airliner or executive model with Dart RDa.7 Mk 532-7 turboprops.

F.27 Mk 400 Combiplane. Cargo or combined cargo/passenger version of Mk 200.

F.27 Mk 400M. Military version, with accommodation for 45 parachute troops, 12,836 lb (5,834 kg) of freight or 24 litters and 8 attendants. Large cargo door and enlarged parachuting door on each side. Nine of the 12 RNAF aircraft, the four ordered by the Sudanese Air Force and eight by the Argentine Air Force are of this type.

F.27 Mk 500. Similar to F.27 Mk 200, but with lengthened fuselage and large cargo door. The 15 aircraft for the CEP (Air France) are of this type, with special "para-dropping" type large doors on both sides. Air Inter, ALM, A. P. Møller and Sterling Airways have also ordered the Mk 500. First example flown on 15 November 1967.

F.27 Mk 600. Similar to Mk 200, but with a large 7 ft 7½ in × 5 ft 10 in (2·32 × 1·78 m) cargo door. Does not have the reinforced and watertight flooring of the Combiplane. 47 of this version have been sold and delivered to 17 airlines. Can be fitted with quick-change interior, featuring roller tracks and palletised seats.

Components for the F.27 variants are produced by Fokker-Dordrecht and by SABCA in Belgium. Breguet at Biarritz is manufacturing the fuselage aft of the front section.

Present rate of production by Fokker-VFW is two aircraft per month.

TYPE: Twin-turboprop medium-range airliner.

WINGS: Cantilever high-wing monoplane. Wing section NACA 64-421 at root, 64-415 at tip. Dihedral 2° 30′. Incidence 3° 30′. All-metal riveted and metal-bonded two-spar stressed-skin structure, consisting of centre-section and two detachable outer sections. Detachable honeycomb-core sandwich leading-edges with rubber-boot de-icers. Glass-fibre reinforced plastic trailing-edges. Electrically-operated single-slotted flaps, divided by engine nacelles. Electrically-operated trim-tab in each aileron. Pneumatic-boot anti-icing of leading edges.

FUSELAGE: All-metal stressed-skin structure, built to fail-safe principles, with cylindrical portions metal bonded and conical parts riveted. Fuselage is pressurised between rear bulkhead of nose-wheel compartment and circular pressure bulkhead aft of the luggage compartment. Length of pressurised section 53 ft (16·16 m), except for Series 500 which the pressurised section is 57 ft 11 in (17·66 m) long. The slightly flattened fuselage bottom is reinforced by under-floor members.

TAIL UNIT: Cantilever all-metal stressed-skin structure. Fin and tailplane, as well as leading-edges of surfaces, are detachable. Trim-tab in each elevator. Pneumatic-boot anti-icing.

LANDING GEAR: Retractable tricycle type. Pneumatic retraction. Dowty oleo-pneumatic shock-absorber struts. Twin-wheel main units

Fokker F.27 Mk 400M twin-turboprop transport aircraft, one of eight delivered to the Argentine Air Force

retract backward into engine nacelles. Single-wheel steerable nose unit retracts forward into non-pressurised nose-cone. Main wheel tyre pressure 80 lb/sq in (5·62 kg/cm²), nose-wheel tyre pressure 50 lb/sq in (3·51 kg/cm²). Pneumatic brakes on main wheels, with Dunlop Maxaret automatic anti-skid system.

Power Plant (Mks 200, 400, 500 and 600): Two Rolls-Royce Dart Mk 532-7 (RDa.7 rating) turboprop engines, each developing 2,050 shp plus 525 lb (238 kg) st for take-off. Four-blade Rotol propellers, diameter 11 ft 6 in (3·50 m). Integral fuel tanks in outer wings, capacity 1,130 Imp gallons (5,140 litres). Overwing fuelling, but pressure refuelling optional. Provision for carrying two 200 Imp gallon (910 litre) external fuel tanks under wings. Methyl-bromide fire-prevention system with flame detectors.

Accommodation: (Mks 200 and 600): Flight compartment seats two pilots side-by-side, with folding seat for third crew member if required. Main cabin has standard capacity for 40 passengers, but alternative arrangements allow this number to be increased to 52. Passenger door at rear of cabin, on port side, with toilet opposite. Standard cargo door at front of Mk 200 on port side; large cargo door in same position on Mk 600, with sill at truck-bed level. Cargo holds forward and aft of main cabin, size dependent on interior arrangement.

Accommodation (executive and VIP versions): Can be furnished to customer's specification, but a basic layout is available. In this, the cabin is divided into three sections: a conference room with six seats, a rest room with settee and divan, and a lounge with four seats. Toilet, galley, wardrobe, luggage space and seat for attendant in forward fuselage. Second toilet and luggage space at rear.

Accommodation (Mk 400 Combiplane): Principal features of this version are a large cargo loading door forward of the wings on the port side, with the sill at truck-bed height, and a reinforced cargo floor, with tie-down rings. Typical layouts include 40 passengers four abreast at 35 in (90 cm) seat pitch, plus 218 cu ft (6·17 m³) of cargo space; 28 passengers at same seat pitch in rear of cabin, plus 588 cu ft (16·65 m³) cargo space; or all-cargo version with 1,715 cu ft (48·56 m³) of cargo space.

Accommodation (Mk 500): Same as Mk 200 airliner, except for having large cargo door. Main cabin has standard seating for 52 passengers; alternative layouts enable up to 56 passengers to be carried.

Systems: Pressurisation and air-conditioning system utilises two Rootes-type engine-driven blowers. Choke heating and air-to-air heat exchanger; optional bootstrap cooling system. Pressure differential 4·16 lb/sq in (0·29 kg/cm²). Pneumatic system, pressure 3,300 lb/sq in (232 kg/cm²), for landing gear retraction, nose-wheel steering and brakes. Emergency pneumatic circuits for landing gear extension and brakes. No hydraulic system. Primary 28V electrical system supplied by two 375A 30V DC engine-driven generators. Secondary system supplied via two 115V 400 c/s AC constant-frequency inverters. Variable-frequency AC power supply, from 120/208V 15kVA engine-driven alternators, for anti-icing and heating. Two 24V 40Ah nickel-cadmium batteries. 38·4 cu ft (1·08 m³) oxygen system for pilots.

Electronics and Equipment: Standard equipment includes VHF and HF receiver/transmitters, automatic D/F radio-compass, ILS and intercommunications system. Provision for weather radar, autopilot, etc.

Fokker F.27 Friendship (two 2,050 shp Rolls-Royce Dart Mk 532-7 turboprop engines) in the insignia of Air Congo

Dimensions, external:
Wing span: 95 ft 2 in (29·00 m)
Wing chord at root: 11 ft 4 in (3·45 m)
Wing chord at tip: 4 ft 7 in (1·40 m)
Wing aspect ratio: 12
Length overall:
except Mk 500: 77 ft 3½ in (23·56 m)
Mk 500: 82 ft 2½ in (25·06 m)
Height overall:
except Mk 500: 27 ft 11 in (8·50 m)
Mk 500: 28 ft 7¼ in (8·71 m)
Tailplane span: 32 ft 0 in (9·75 m)
Wheel track (c/l shock-struts): 23 ft 7½ in (7·20 m)
Wheelbase:
except Mk 500: 28 ft 8 in (8·74 m)
Mk 500: 31 ft 11¼ in (9·74 m)
Passenger door (aft, port):
Height: 5 ft 5 in (1·65 m)
Width: 2 ft 5 in (0·74 m)
Service/emergency door (aft, stbd):
Height: 3 ft 8 in (1·12 m)
Width: 2 ft 5 in (0·74 m)
Cargo door (Mk 200):
Height: 3 ft 11 in (1·19 m)
Width: 3 ft 5 in (1·04 m)
Cargo door (Mks 400, 500 and 600):
Height: 5 ft 10 in (1·78 m)
Width: 7 ft 7½ in (2·32 m)

Dimensions, internal:
Cabin, excluding flight deck:
Length:
except Mk 500: 47 ft 5 in (14·46 m)
Mk 500: 52 ft 4 in (15·96 m)
Max width: 8 ft 4½ in (2·55 m)
Max height: 6 ft 7½ in (2·02 m)
Volume:
except Mk 500: 2,136 cu ft (60·5 m³)
Mk 500: 2,360 cu ft (66·8 m³)
Freight hold (fwd) max:
Mk 200: 169 cu ft (4·78 m³)
Mks 400, 500, 600: 197 cu ft (5·58 m³)
Freight hold (aft) max:
all versions: 100 cu ft (2·83 m³)

Areas:
Wings, gross: 754 sq ft (70·0 m²)
Ailerons (total): 37·80 sq ft (3·51 m²)
Trailing-edge flaps (total): 136·90 sq ft (12·72 m²)
Vertical tail surfaces (total): 153 sq ft (14·20 m²)
Horizontal tail surfaces (total): 172 sq ft (16·00 m²)

Weights and Loadings:
Manufacturer's weight, empty:
Mk 200, 48 seats: 24,000 lb (10,885 kg)
Mk 400, 48 seats: 24,790 lb (11,244 kg)
Mk 400, all-cargo: 23,310 lb (10,573 kg)
Mk 400M: 23,850 lb (10,818 kg)
Mk 500, 56 seats: 25,300 lb (11,475 kg)
Mk 600, 48 seats: 24,360 lb (11,049 kg)
Operating weight empty:
Mk 200, 48 seats: 24,870 lb (11,280 kg)
Mk 400, 48 seats: 25,660 lb (11,639 kg)
Mk 400, all-cargo: 23,848 lb (10,817 kg)
Mk 400M, all-cargo: 24,637 lb (11,175 kg)
Mk 400M, medical evacuation: 25,509 lb (11,570 kg)
Mk 400M, paratrooper: 25,075 lb (11,373 kg)
Mk 500: 26,190 lb (11,879 kg)
Mk 600: 25,230 lb (11,444 kg)
Maximum payload (weight limited):
Mk 200: 12,630 lb (5,728 kg)
Mk 400, 48 seats: 11,840 lb (5,370 kg)
Mk 400, all-cargo: 13,652 lb (6,192 kg)
Mk 400M, all-cargo: 12,863 lb (5,834 kg)
Mk 400M, medical evacuation: 11,991 lb (5,439 kg)
Mk 400M. paratrooper: 12,425 lb (5,635 kg)
Mk 500: 12,310 lb (5,583 kg)
Mk 600: 12,270 lb (5,565 kg)
Payload with 29 cu ft (0·82 m³) pantry:
Mk 200, 48 passengers: 10,276 lb (4,661 kg)
Mks 400 and 600, 48 passengers: 10,556 lb (4,788 kg)
Mk 500, 56 passengers: 11,876 lb (5,387 kg)
Max T-O weight:
Mks 200, 400, 400M and 600: 43,500 lb (19,730 kg)
Mk 500: 45,000 lb (20,411 kg)
Max landing weight:
Mks 200, 400, 400M, 500 and 600: 41,000 lb (18,600 kg)
Max zero-fuel weight:
except Mk 500: 37,500 lb (17,010 kg)

Mk 500   38,500 lb (17,463 kg)
Max wing loading:
Mks 200, 400 and 600 57·7 lb/sq ft (282 kg/m²)
Mk 500   59·6 lb/sq ft (291 kg/m²)
PERFORMANCE (at max T-O weight, except where indicated):
Normal cruising speed at 20,000 ft (6,100 m):
Mks 200, 400 and 600 at 38,000 lb (17,237 kg)
256 knots (295 mph; 474 km/h)
Mk 500 at 38,000 lb (17,237 kg)
254 knots (292 mph; 470 km/h)
Rate of climb at S/L:
Mks 200, 400 and 600 1,270 ft (387 m)/min
Mk 500 1,200 ft (366 m)/min
Service ceiling:
Mks 200, 400, 500 and 600 at 38,000 lb (17,237 kg) 28,500 ft (8,690 m)
Service ceiling, one engine out:
Mks 200, 400, 500 and 600 at 38,000 lb (17,237 kg) 11,600 ft (3,545 m)
T-O run with water/methanol:
Mks 200, 400, 500 and 600 at 42,000 lb (19,051 kg) 4,100 ft (1,250 m)
Range with max space-limited payload, including 45 min holding at 10,000 ft (3,050 m), 199 nm (230 miles; 370 km) diversion and 5% fuel reserves:
Mk 200 (at 24,000 ft = 7,315 m)
915 nm (1,059 miles; 1,705 km)
Mk 400 (at 20,000 ft = 6,100 m)
665 nm (770 miles; 1,240 km)
Mk 500 (at 20,000 ft = 6,100 m)
599 nm (690 miles; 1,110 km)
Mk 600 (at 20,000 ft = 6,100 m)
745 nm (858 miles; 1,380 km)
Range with max payload, limited by landing weight, reserves as above:
Mk 200 498 nm (574 miles; 925 km)
Mk 400 461 nm (531 miles; 855 km)
Mk 400, all-cargo
498 nm (574 miles; 925 km)
Mk 500 579 nm (667 miles; 1,075 km)
Mk 600 468 nm (540 miles; 870 km)
Range with max fuel, reserves as above:
Mk 200, with 9,524 lb (4,320 kg) payload
1,065 nm (1,227 miles; 1,975 km)
Mk 400, all-cargo with 10,560 lb (4,790 kg) payload 1,065 nm (1,227 miles; 1,975 km)
Mk 400, with 8,732 lb (3,961 kg) payload
974 nm (1,122 miles; 1,805 km)
Mk 500, with 9,680 lb (4,390 kg) payload
954 nm (1,099 miles; 1,770 km)
Mk 600, with 9,661 lb (4,382 kg) payload
974 nm (1,122 miles; 1,805 km)

FOKKER F.28 FELLOWSHIP

Announced in April 1962, the F.28 Fellowship is a twin-turbofan short-haul transport with accommodation for up to 65 passengers. It has been developed in collaboration with other European aircraft manufacturers and with the financial support of the Netherlands Government. One half of the Dutch share of the development cost has been supplied through the Netherlands Aircraft Development Board, the other half being made available through a loan guaranteed by the government.

Under agreements signed in the Summer of 1964, the design and construction of two prototypes, development and flight testing, and series production are being undertaken by Fokker-VFW in association with Messerschmitt-Bölkow-Blohm GmbH (formerly HFB) and VFW-Fokker of Germany and Short Bros and Harland of Belfast, N Ireland.

Fokker-VFW are responsible for the front fuselage, to a point just aft of the flight deck, the centre fuselage and wing root fairings. Messerschmitt-Bölkow-Blohm are responsible for the section of fuselage from the wing trailing-edge to the rear pressure bulkhead and for the engine nacelles and support stubs. VFW-Fokker are responsible for the rear fuselage and tail unit, and for the cylindrical fuselage section between the wing leading-edge and flight deck. Short Bros and Harland are responsible for the outer wings and other components including the main wheel and nose-wheel doors.

First flight of the first prototype F.28 (PH-JHG) was made on 9 May 1967, and the second prototype, PH-WEV, flew on 3 August 1967. These aircraft have Rolls-Royce RB.183-2 Spey Mk 555 turbofans, as specified for production aircraft. The third F.28 (PH-MOL) flew for the first time on 20 October 1967 and was brought up to production standard in the early Summer of 1968.

The first order for an F.28 was received in November 1965 from LTU (Germany), and in June 1968 Fairchild Hiller Corporation in the US placed an initial order for ten, following its decision not to proceed with its own "Americanised" F-228 version of the Fellowship.

The Dutch RLD granted a C of A to the F.28 on 24 February 1969, and the first delivery (of the fourth aircraft, to LTU) was made on the same day. The aircraft received FAA Type Approval on 24 March 1969 and German certification on 30 March 1969.

A total of 31 Fellowships had been ordered by 22 January 1970, as follows:

Aerolinee Itavia (Italy)	3
Ansett Airlines of Australia (MacRobertson-Miller Airlines)	3
Braathens (Norway)	5
Fairchild Hiller Corpn	10
Iberia	3
LTU (Germany)	5
Martinair (Holland)	1
Undisclosed	1

First F.28 commercial service was flown by Braathens on 28 March 1969.

Two versions of the Fellowship have been announced, as follows:

Mk 1000. Initial version, in production and service, with seating for up to 65 passengers.

Mk 2000. Similar to Mk 1000 except for lengthened fuselage, permitting an increase in accommodation for up to 79 passengers in all-tourist layout. Higher operating weights and revised performance. F.28 prototype being modified to Mk 2000 standard for first flight in early 1971. Certification scheduled for early 1972.

The details below apply to both versions, except where a specific model is indicated:

TYPE: Twin-turbofan short-range airliner.

WINGS: Cantilever low-wing monoplane. Wing section NACA 0000-X 40Y series with camber varying along span. Thickness/chord ratio up to 14% on inner wing, 10% at tip. Dihedral 2° 30'. Sweepback at quarter-chord 16°. Single-cell two-spar light alloy torsion-box structure, comprising centre-section, integral with fuselage, and two outer wings. Fail-safe construction. Lower skin made of three planks. Taper-rolled top skin. Forged ribs in centre-section, built-up ribs in outer panels. Double-skin leading-edge with ducts for hot-air de-icing. Irreversible hydraulically-operated ailerons. Emergency manual operation of ailerons, through tabs. Hydraulically-operated Fowler double-slotted flaps over 70% of each half-span with electrical emergency extension. Five-section hydraulically-operated lift dumpers in front of flaps on each wing. Trim-tab in each aileron.

FUSELAGE: Circular-section semi-monocoque light alloy structure, made up of skin panels with Redux-bonded Z-stringers. Redux doubler plates at door and window cut-outs. Quickly-detachable sandwich (metal/end grain balsa) floor panels. Hydraulically-operated petal air-brakes form aft end of fuselage. Max external diameter 10 ft 10 in (3·30 m).

TAIL UNIT: Cantilever light alloy structure, with hydraulically-actuated variable-incidence tailplane mounted near tip of fin. Electrical emergency actuation of tailplane. Hydraulically-boosted elevators with tabs. Irreversible hydraulically-operated rudder with duplicated actuators and emergency manual operation. Honeycomb sandwich skin panels used extensively, in conjuction with multiple spars. Double-skin leading-edges for hot-air de-icing.

LANDING GEAR: Retractable tricycle type of Dowty-Rotol manufacture, with twin wheels on each unit. Hydraulic retraction, nose-wheels forward, main units inward into fuselage. Oleo-pneumatic shock-absorbers. Goodyear wheels, tyres and electronically-controlled braking system. Steerable nose-wheel. Main wheel tyres size 39 × 13 type VII, pressure 97 lb/sq in (6·8 kg/cm²) on Mk 1000, 100 lb/sq in (7·0 kg/cm²) on Mk 2000. Nose-wheel tyres size 24 × 7·7 type VII, pressure 80 lb/sq in (5·6 kg/cm²). Low-pressure tyres optional on all units.

POWER PLANT: Two Rolls-Royce RB.183-2 Spey Mk 555-15 turbofan engines with blade-cooling (each 9,850 lb = 4,468 kg st) mounted in pods on sides of rear fuselage. No water injection or thrust reversers. Thermal anti-icing for air intakes. Integral fuel tank in each outer wing panel with total usable capacity of 2,143 Imp gallons (9,740 litres). Optional seven tank units in wing centre-section with total usable capacity of 726 Imp gallons (3,300 litres). Single refuelling point under port wing, near root.

ACCOMMODATION: Crew of two side-by-side on flight deck, with jump-seat for third crew member on Mk 2000. Pantry/luggage space immediately aft of flight deck on starboard side, followed by entrance lobby with hydraulically-operated airstair door on port side, service

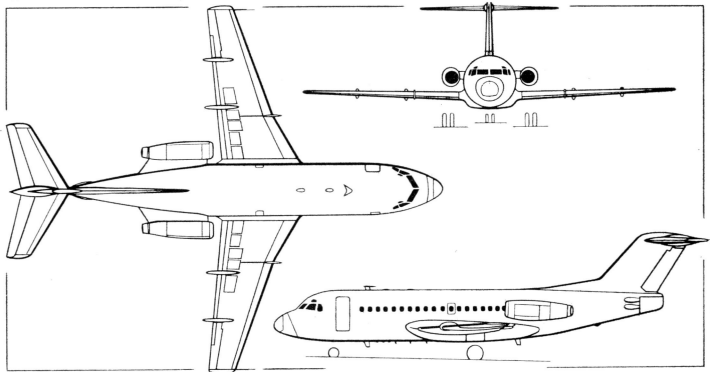

Fokker F.28 Fellowship Mk 1000 twin-turbofan short-range jet transport

Fokker F.28 Fellowship Mk 1000 (two 9,850 lb st Rolls-Royce Spey Mk 555-15 turbofan engines) in the insignia of Martinair Holland

and emergency door on starboard side and seat for stewardess. Additional emergency door on each side of main cabin, over wing. Main cabin layout of Mk 1000 can be varied to accommodate 40 four-abreast or 60 or 65 passengers five-abreast at 38/41, 32/33 or 31 in (97/104, 81/84 or 79 cm) seat pitch respectively. In Mk 2000, layout can be varied to accommodate 48, 75 or 79 passengers at 39/40, 33/31 or 31 in (99/102, 84/79 or 79 cm) seat pitch. Aft of cabin are a wardrobe (port), luggage compartment (centre) and toilet compartment (starboard), with luggage door on port side. Underfloor cargo compartments fore and aft of wing, with single door on starboard side of forward hold of Mk 1000 and two doors on Mk 2000, with one door on rear hold of each version.

SYSTEMS: AiResearch air-conditioning system, using engine-bleed air. Pressure differential 6·55 lb/sq in (0·46 kg/cm²); optional pressure differential of 7·45 lb/sq in (0·52 kg/cm²). Two independent hydraulic systems, pressure 3,000 lb/sq in (210 kg/cm²). Primary system for flight controls, landing gear, nose-wheel steering and brakes, secondary system for duplication of certain essential flight controls. Flying control hydraulic components supplied by Jarry Hydraulics. Electrical system utilises two 20 kVA Westinghouse engine-driven generators to supply three-phase 115/200V 400 c/s AC power, with transformer-rectifiers for DC supply. One 25Ah battery for starting APU and for emergency DC power, with inverter for AC supply. AiResearch GTCP-36-3 APU, mounted aft of rear pressure bulkhead, for engine starting, ground air conditioning and to drive a third AC generator for standby use on essential services.

ELECTRONICS AND EQUIPMENT: Radio and radar to customer's specification. Smiths SEP6 automatic flight control system standard, with provision for flight director, auto-throttle, radar altimeter, para-visual director, flare computer and go-around system.

DIMENSIONS, EXTERNAL:

Wing span	77 ft 4¼ in (23·58 m)
Wing aspect ratio	7·27
Length overall:	
1000	89 ft 10¾ in (27·40 m)
2000	97 ft 1¾ in (29·61 m)
Length of fuselage:	
1000	80 ft 6½ in (24·55 m)
2000	87 ft 9½ in (26·76 m)
Height overall	27 ft 9½ in (8·47 m)
Tailplane span	28 ft 4¼ in (8·64 m)
Wheel track (c/l of shock struts)	
	16 ft 6½ in (5·04 m)
Wheelbase:	
1000	29 ft 2½ in (8·90 m)
2000	33 ft 11½ in (10·35 m)

Passenger door (fwd, port):

Height	6 ft 4¼ in (1·93 m)
Width	2 ft 10 in (0·86 m)
Height to sill	6 ft 10½ in (2·10 m)
Service/emergency door (fwd, stbd):	
Height	4 ft 2 in (1·27 m)
Width	2 ft 0 in (0·61 m)
Emergency exits (centre, each):	
Height:	
1000	3 ft 0 in (0·91 m)
2000	3 ft 1½ in (0·95 m)
Width:	
1000	1 ft 8 in (0·51 m)
2000	2 ft 11½ in (0·90 m)
Luggage door (port, aft):	
Height	1 ft 11½ in (0·60 m)
Width	1 ft 8 in (0·51 m)
Freight hold doors (each):	
Height	3 ft 1½ in (0·95 m)
Width (fwd, each)	2 ft 11½ in (0·90 m)
Width (aft)	2 ft 7½ in (0·80 m)
Height to sill (fwd, each)	4 ft 5¼ in (1·35 m)
Height to sill (aft)	5 ft 2¼ in (1·58 m)

DIMENSIONS, INTERNAL:
Cabin, excluding flight deck:

Length:	
1000	43 ft 0 in (13·10 m)
2000	50 ft 3 in (15·31 m)
Max length of seating area:	
1000	35 ft 2¾ in (10·74 m)
2000	42 ft 6¾ in (12·95 m)
Max width	10 ft 2 in (3·10 m)
Max height	6 ft 7¼ in (2·02 m)
Floor area:	
1000	413·3 sq ft (38·4 m²)
2000	482·2 sq ft (44·8 m²)
Volume:	
1000	2,525 cu ft (71·5 m³)
2000	2,931 cu ft (83·0 m³)
Freight hold (underfloor, fwd):	
1000	245 cu ft (6·90 m³)
2000	342 cu ft (9·70 m³)
Freight hold (underfloor, rear)	
	135 cu ft (3·80 m³)
Luggage hold (aft of cabin) max	
	81·2 cu ft (2·30 m³)

AREAS:

Wings, gross	822 sq ft (76·4 m²)
Vertical tail surfaces (total)	132·4 sq ft (12·3 m²)
Horizontal tail surfaces (total)	
	210 sq ft (19·5 m²)

WEIGHTS AND LOADINGS:

Manufacturer's weight empty:	
1000	31,263 lb (14,180 kg)
2000	32,832 lb (14,893 kg)
Typical operating weight empty:	
1000	34,500 lb (15,650 kg)
2000	36,400 lb (16,510 kg)
Max payload:	
1000	14,500 lb (6,580 kg)
2000	18,100 lb (8,210 kg)

Max T-O weight:	
1000	63,000 lb (28,580 kg)
2000	65,000 lb (29,480 kg)
Max zero-fuel weight:	
1000	49,000 lb (22,230 kg)
2000	54,500 lb (24,720 kg)
Max landing weight:	
1000	54,000 lb (24,490 kg)
2000	59,000 lb (26,760 kg)
Max wing loading:	
1000	76·6 lb/sq ft (374 kg/m²)
2000	79·1 lb/sq ft (386 kg/m²)
Max power loading:	
1000	3·2 lb/lb st (3·2 kg/kg st)
2000	3·3 lb/lb st (3·3 kg/kg st)

PERFORMANCE (at max landing weight, ISA, except where indicated; Mk 2000 estimated):

Max permissible operating speed	Mach 0·75
Max permissible diving speed	Mach 0·83
Max cruising speed at 21,000 ft (6,400 m):	
1000, 2000	
	458 knots (528 mph; 849 km/h) TAS
Best-cost cruising speed:	
1000 at 25,000 ft (7,620 m)	
	451 knots (519 mph; 836 km/h) TAS
2000 at 30,000 ft (9,150 m)	
	441 knots (508 mph; 817 km/h) TAS
Long-range cruising speed at 30,000 ft (9,150 m):	
1000	371 knots (427 mph; 687 km/h) TAS
2000	367 knots (423 mph; 680 km/h) TAS
Approach speed:	
1000	114 knots (131 mph; 211 km/h) TAS
2000	119 knots (137 mph; 220 km/h) TAS
Max cruising altitude	30,000 ft (9,150 m)

Balanced T-O field length (SR 422B), max T-O weight at S/L:

1000	5,030 ft (1,533 m)
2000	5,500 ft (1,676 m)

Balanced T-O field length (SR 422B), max T-O weight at S/L, ISA + 15°C:

1000	5,740 ft (1,750 m)
2000	6,150 ft (1,874 m)

Balanced T-O field length (SR 422B), max T-O weight at 3,000 ft (915 m):

1000	5,900 ft (1,798 m)
2000	6,320 ft (1,926 m)

Balanced landing field length (SR 422B) at S/L:

1000	3,300 ft (1,006 m)
2000	3,540 ft (1,079 m)

Balanced landing field length (SR 422B) at 5,000 ft (1,525 m):

1000	3,720 ft (1,134 m)
2000	4,000 ft (1,219 m)

Range:

1000 with 60 passengers	
	1,100 nm (1,266 miles; 2,038 km)
2000 with 75 passengers	
	735 nm (846 miles; 1,362 km)
Max range with outer-wing fuel only:	
1000	1,160 nm (1,336 miles; 2,149 km)
2000	1,055 nm (1,215 miles; 1,955 km)

NEW ZEALAND

AESL
AERO ENGINE SERVICES LTD

HEAD OFFICE AND WORKS:
Hamilton Airport, R.D.2, Hamilton
DIRECTORS:
A. M. Coleman (Managing Director)
O. G. James
T. S. Robinson
R. Seabrook
D. McLeod

ENGINEERING MANAGER:
H. W. Robertson
COMPANY SECRETARY:
J. L. Slater

This company was established in 1954, and until 1966 concentrated on the repair and overhaul of light aircraft engines. More recently, airframe facilities were established, and early in 1967 AESL acquired world rights to manufacture the Victa Airtourer light aircraft, from Victa Ltd of Australia, which it is now producing, as the AESL Airtourer, in six separate models. Details of these appear below.

AESL is the major facility in New Zealand for the overhaul of light aircraft engines, and is also engaged in the maintenance and repair of fixed-wing aircraft and helicopters.

Glos-Air Ltd of Staverton Airport, Cheltenham, England, were appointed the sole UK distributors for the Airtourer early in 1968. Aircraft are received by Glos-Air in a "partially knocked-down" condition and are assembled, painted and test-flown at Staverton prior to delivery to UK operators.

AESL is also to assemble and distribute in Australasia the Britten-Norman Nymph lightplane (see UK section). Parts for one hundred Nymphs (the first orders placed for this aircraft) were ordered during the Paris Air Show in May/June 1969.

AESL AIRTOURER

The Airtourer was designed by Henry Millicer, then Chief Aerodynamicist of the Australian Government Aircraft Factories, as an entry for a competition for a light two-seat aircraft held in 1953 by the Royal Aero Club of Great Britain. It won the competition, against 103 other designs.

A prototype Airtourer, built mainly of wood and powered by a 65 hp Continental engine, flew for the first time on 31 March 1959, and was described fully in earlier editions of *Jane's*.

Production Airtourers, built initially by Victa Ltd of Milperra, NSW, Australia, and since October 1967 by the Airtourer Division of AESL in New Zealand, have an all-metal airframe.

Seven versions have so far been announced, as follows:

Airtourer 100. Basic model with 100 hp Continental O-200-A engine. Prototype (with 95 hp engine) flew on 12 December 1961, and the first production model on 20 June 1962. The Airtourer 100 received Australian DCA Type Approval on 4 July 1962. No longer in production. Described in 1969-70 *Jane's*.

Airtourer T1. Similar to Airtourer 100 except for its 115 hp Lycoming O-235-C2A engine. Prototype flew on 17 September 1962 and first production model on 22 February 1963. DCA Type Approval received on 6 July 1963. Full aerobatics permissible under limit flight loads of 6 *g* at AUW of 1,650 lb (748 kg). Stressed to ultimate load factor of 9 *g* for Normal category operation. Previously known as Airtourer 115.

Airtourer T2. Similar to T1, but structure reinforced to cater for increased AUW and aerobatic weight for 150 hp Lycoming O-320-E2A engine.

Airtourer T3. As T2, but with 130 hp engine. Production due to start in 1970.

Airtourer T4. Redesigned by Air New Zealand Ltd and previously known as Airtourer 150. Similar to T2, with 150 hp O-320-E2A engine. Prototype flew in September 1968; first production model delivered to UK in January 1969.

Airtourer T5. Previously known as Super 150. Similar to T4, but with O-320-E1A engine, constant-speed propeller and needle-type spinner. Prototype flew in November 1968; first production model delivered in January 1969.

Airtourer T6. As T5, but military configuration.

A total of 170 Airtourer 100's and 115's had been completed by Victa Ltd when production by that company was suspended late in 1966.

Up to mid-February 1970, 50 Airtourers had been built and delivered by AESL, including twenty-five T1's, seven T2's, two T4's and sixteen T5's. Of this total, 27 had been exported, to Glos-Air in the UK, to Australia, Fiji and South Africa. Four T6's were due to be delivered to the Royal New Zealand Air Force by mid-1970.

TYPE: Two-seat fully-aerobatic light monoplane.

WINGS: Cantilever low-wing monoplane. NACA 5 digit series wing sections. Thickness/chord ratio 12%. Dihedral 6°. Incidence 3° at root, 0° at tip. Taper 3° 26′ on leading-edge. Single-spar light alloy stressed-skin structure, foam-reinforced in tank bay. Light alloy ailerons and flaps of NACA type, with fluted skins. Ailerons and flaps are interconnected by rod and mechanical linkages, so that both function simultaneously as ailerons and flaps. Adjustable trim-tab on aileron.

FUSELAGE: All-metal stressed-skin semi-monocoque type, reinforced with foam plastic in cockpit area. Split flap under fuselage.

TAIL UNIT: Cantilever light alloy structure. Ground-adjustable tabs in rudder and elevator. Control of rudder by rod and cable linkage, of elevator by rod and mechanical linkage.

LANDING GEAR: Non-retractable tricycle type. Cantilever spring-steel main legs. Nose-wheel is carried on automotive coil spring and shock-absorber, and is steerable. All three wheels are identical, with Dunlop Australia wheels and tubeless tyres size 5·00 × 5. Tyre pressure 23 lb/sq in (1·62 kg/cm²) on main units, 16 lb/sq in (1·12 kg/cm²) on nose unit. Dunlop Australia single-disc dual hand-operated hydraulic brakes with parking lock. Landing gear designed to shear prior to any excess impact loading being transmitted to wing, to minimise structural damage in the event of a crash-landing.

POWER PLANT (Airtourer T1 and T2): One 115 hp Lycoming O-235-C2A four-cylinder horizontally-opposed air-cooled engine, driving a McCauley two-blade metal propeller, diameter 5 ft 10½ in (1·79 m). Fuel in single rubber bag tank centrally placed in wing, with usable capacity of 29 Imp gallons (132 litres). Refuelling point in side of fuselage above wing. Oil capacity 1·25 Imp gallons (5·7 litres).

AESL Airtourer T4 two-seat light monoplane (150 hp Lycoming O-320-E2A engine) (*Air Portraits*)

AESL Airtourer T5, with Lycoming O-320-E1A engine and needle-type spinner (*Kenneth Munson*)

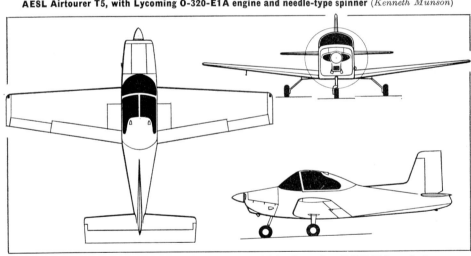

AESL Airtourer T1 two-seat light aircraft (115 hp Lycoming O-235-C2A engine)

POWER PLANT (Airtourer T4, T5 and T6): One 150 hp Lycoming O-320 four-cylinder horizontally-opposed air-cooled engine (details under model descriptions above) driving a McCauley or Sensenich two-blade metal propeller (Airtourer T4) or Hartzell two-blade constant-speed propeller (T5 and T6), diameter 6 ft 0½ in (1·84 m). Fuel tankage as for Airtourer T1 and T2. Oil capacity 1·75 Imp gallons (8 litres).

ACCOMMODATION: Two seats side-by-side in enclosed and soundproofed cabin, under rearward sliding Perspex canopy. Dual controls. Heating and ventilation standard. Luggage compartment aft of seats with capacity of 100 lb (45 kg) and luggage tie-down provision.

SYSTEMS: Heating from engine muffler. Hydraulic system, pressure 700 lb/sq in (49 kg/cm²), for brakes. Engine-driven generator, 35A × 12V. Alternator fitted on Airtourer T4, T5 and T6.

ELECTRONICS AND EQUIPMENT: Optional equipment includes blind-flying instrumentation, Bendix or AWA Skyphone VHF, or AWA Skyranger HF, and Bendix ADF radio. Rotating beacon.

DIMENSIONS, EXTERNAL:	
Wing span	26 ft 0 in (7·92 m)
Wing chord at root	5 ft 9 in (1·75 m)
Wing chord at tip	3 ft 1¾ in (0·96 m)
Wing aspect ratio	5·65
Length overall:	
T1, T2, T4	21 ft 5⅞ in (6·55 m)
T5, T6	22 ft 0 in (6·71 m)
Height overall	7 ft 0 in (2·13 m)
Max fuselage width	3 ft 5¾ in (1·06 m)
Tailplane span	10 ft 10 in (3·30 m)
Wheel track	9 ft 6 in (2·90 m)
Wheelbase	5 ft 0⅛ in (1·52 m)
DIMENSIONS, INTERNAL:	
Cabin: Length	5 ft 8 in (1·73 m)
Max width	3 ft 6 in (1·07 m)
Max height	4 ft 2 in (1·27 m)
Baggage space	8 cu ft (0·23 m²)
AREAS:	
Wings, gross	120 sq ft (11·15 m²)
Full-span ailerons/flaps:	
as ailerons (total)	26·5 sq ft (2·46 m²)
as flaps (total)	30·5 sq ft (2·83 m²)
Fin	6·60 sq ft (0·61 m²)
Rudder, including tab	5·60 sq ft (0·52 m²)

Tailplane	17·20 sq ft (1·60 m²)
Elevators, including tab	13·80 sq ft (1·28 m²)

WEIGHTS AND LOADINGS:
Weight empty, equipped:

T1, T2	1,080 lb (490 kg)
T4	1,165 lb (528 kg)
T5, T6	1,175 lb (532 kg)

Max T-O weight (aerobatic):

T1, T2	1,550 lb (703 kg)
T4, T5	1,650 lb (748 kg)
T6	1,750 lb (793 kg)

Max T-O weight (Normal cat):

T1, T2	1,650 lb (748 kg)
T4, T5	1,750 lb (793 kg)
T6	1,850 lb (839 kg)

Max landing weight:

T1, T2	1,650 lb (748 kg)
T4, T5 (aerobatic)	1,650 lb (748 kg)
T4, T5 (Normal)	1,750 lb (793 kg)
T6 (Normal)	1,850 lb (839 kg)

Max wing loading:

T1, T2	13·3 lb/sq ft (64·9 kg/m²)
T4, T5	14·6 lb/sq ft (71·3 kg/m²)
T6	15·4 lb/sq ft (75·2 kg/m²)

Max power loading:

T1, T2	14·3 lb/hp (6·50 kg/hp)
T4, T5	11·7 lb/hp (5·31 kg/hp)
T6	12·3 lb/hp (5·58 kg/hp)

PERFORMANCE (at max T-O weight):
Max level speed at S/L:

T1, T2	123 knots (142 mph; 230 km/h)
T4	130 knots (150 mph; 241 km/h)
T5, T6	142 knots (164 mph; 264 km/h)

Max permissible diving speed (structural):

T1, T2	175 knots (202 mph; 325 km/h)
T4, T5, T6	203 knots (234 mph; 376 km/h)

Max cruising speed at 4,000 ft (1,220 m):

T1, T2	114 knots (131 mph; 230 km/h)
T4	122 knots (140 mph; 225 km/h)
T5, T6	130 knots (150 mph; 241 km/h)

Econ cruising speed (65% power) at 5,000 ft (1,525 m):

T1, T2	108 knots (124 mph; 200 km/h)
T4	109 knots (125 mph; 201 km/h)
T5, T6	116 knots (134 mph; 216 km/h)

Stalling speed:

T1, T2	46 knots (53 mph; 85 km/h)
T4, T5, T6	49 knots (56 mph; 90 km/h)

Rate of climb at S/L:

T1, T2	900 ft (274 m)/min
T4	1,050 ft (320 m)/min
T5, T6	1,150 ft (351 m)/min

Time to 10,000 ft (3,050 m):

T1, T2	14 min
T4, T5, T6	11 min

Service ceiling:

T1	14,000 ft (4,275 m)
T4, T5, T6	18,000 ft (5,485 m)

T-O run:

T1, T2, T5, T6	700 ft (213 m)
T4	750 ft (229 m)

T-O to 50 ft (15 m):

T1, T2	1,250 ft (380 m)
T4	1,200 ft (366 m)
T5, T6	1,150 ft (351 m)

Landing from 50 ft (15 m):

T1, T2	1,200 ft (366 m)
T4	1,340 ft (408 m)
T5, T6	1,220 ft (372 m)
Landing run (all versions)	706 ft 215 m)

Range with max fuel, no allowances:

T1, T2	616 nm (710 miles; 1,140 km)
T4	542 nm (625 miles; 1,005 km)
T5, T6	581 nm (670 miles; 1,075 km)

AIR NEW ZEALAND
AIR NEW ZEALAND LTD

HEAD OFFICE:
Airways House, 101-103 Customs Street East, Auckland 1
WORKS: Mangere (Auckland)
GENERAL MANAGER: C. J. Keppel
ENGINEERING MANAGER: G. Kemp
PRESS OFFICER: A. S. Francis

Under contract to Murrayair of Hawaii, Air New Zealand engineers began in November 1968 the construction of a two-seat agricultural aircraft using as a basis the pre-war Boeing-Stearman Model 75 Kaydet biplane trainer. This aircraft (N101MA) first flew on 27 July 1969. Subsequently it was dismantled and shipped to Honolulu to complete its trials for FAA certification, and once this is granted Murrayair plans to complete further aircraft of the same type to this configuration. FAA (Pt 8) Type Approval was pending in February 1970.

The new aircraft, which is known as the Murrayair MA-1, is described below.

MURRAYAIR MA-1

The principal differences between the MA-1 and the original Stearman 75 are the installation of a much more powerful engine, a substantial increase in total wing area, strengthening of the landing gear, and redesign of the forward fuselage to accommodate the crew and the dust hopper. The only unmodified Stearman components are the tail surfaces. The main landing gear wheels and brakes are those of the North American Harvard trainer.

Wing area is increased by some 35 per cent, from the original 297·4 sq ft (27·63 m²), by the insertion of a new aluminium centre-section, incorporating the fuel tank, in the upper wing; the original flying wires are replaced by aerofoil-shaped struts. Wing stagger is increased.

To accommodate the new engine (which, unlike the uncowled installation on the original aircraft, has a shaped cowling) and the hopper, the fuselage has been lengthened and strengthened; glass-fibre panels replace the former fabric side panels. The hopper forms an integral part of the front fuselage, in the position occupied formerly by the Stearman's front cockpit; the rear cockpit, which is now fully enclosed, has a bench seat for the pilot and a loader/driver. The seat is raised slightly to improve visibility.

The main landing gear, in addition to being strengthened, has a wider track than formerly, to improve stability on the ground.

These modifications permit an increase in max T-O weight of nearly 3,500 lb (1,588 kg).

TYPE: Two-seat agricultural biplane.
WINGS: Strut-braced biplane with forward-staggered wings of unequal span. NACA 4412 wing section. Dihedral 1° 30′ on upper wings, 3° on lower wings. Incidence 4° 30′ on upper wings, 4° on lower wings. No sweepback. Stagger 31°. Upper wing carried on streamline steel-tube struts. Conventional two-spar structure. Centre-section of upper wing is of aluminium construction. Outer panels of top wing, and both lower wing panels, have spruce laminated spars and ribs, with duralumin channel-section compression struts

The prototype Murrayair MA-1, completed by Air New Zealand

and steel tie-rod internal bracing, and fabric covering. Ailerons, of aluminium construction with fabric covering, on both upper and lower wings linked by struts. No trim-tabs or slats.
FUSELAGE: Rectangular welded chrome-molybdenum steel-tube framework, with glass-fibre side panels except over engine, which has a metal cowling.
TAIL UNIT: Conventional single fin and rudder, of welded chrome-molybdenum steel-tube construction with fabric covering. Wire-braced fixed-incidence tailplane and fin. Trim-tab in each elevator.
LANDING GEAR: Non-retractable tail-wheel type, with single wheels on main units. Each main-wheel leg incorporates a torque-resisting oleo, hydraulically damped pneumatic spring, enclosed in a streamlined metal fairing. Harvard main wheels, with 27 SG 10-ply nylon tyres, pressure 30 lb/sq in (2·11 kg/cm²). No wheel fairings. Harvard hydraulic main-wheel brakes. Steerable tail-wheel.
POWER PLANT: One 600 hp Pratt & Whitney R-1340-AN1 Wasp nine-cylinder radial air-cooled engine, on a steel-tube mounting, driving a Hamilton Standard 12.D.40 two-blade adjustable-pitch metal propeller, diameter 9 ft 0 in (2·74 m). Fuel tank in upper wing centre-section, capacity 91·6 Imp gallons (110 US gallons; 416 litres). Refuelling point above upper wings. Oil capacity 8·3 Imp gallons (10 US gallons; 37·7 litres).
ACCOMMODATION: Side-by-side seating for pilot and loader/driver in fully-enclosed ventilated cockpit in centre of fuselage. Sliding side-screens of cockpit canopy retract into cockpit wall.
OPERATIONAL EQUIPMENT: Between the cockpit and the engine is mounted a 55 cu ft (1·56 m³) dust or liquid hopper, the largest of its kind ever fitted to a single-engine aircraft. The hopper, designed by Air New Zealand and manufactured by Kendricks Plastiglass of Wanganui, is of glass-fibre construction. It is

built around the fuselage tubing, which in this area is of stainless steel to resist chemical corrosion. As a further precautionary measure, the hollow steel support struts for the hopper, and all other fuselage tubes, are filled with linseed oil. Any sign of oil seeping from the tubes provides an early warning of a potential corrosion problem.

DIMENSIONS, EXTERNAL:

Wing span (upper)	41 ft 8 in (12·70 m)
Wing span (lower)	35 ft 0 in (10·67 m)
Wing chord (both, constant)	5 ft 3 in (1·60 m)
Wing aspect ratio (upper)	7·9
Wing aspect ratio (lower)	6·7
Wing stagger	3 ft 11 in (1·19 m)
Wing gap	6 ft 6 in (1·98 m)
Length overall (tail up)	28 ft 8 in (8·74 m)
Height overall (tail down)	11 ft 0 in (3·35 m)
Propeller ground clearance (tail up)	1 ft 2 in (0·36 m)
Tailplane span	12 ft 6 in (3·81 m)
Wheel track	8 ft 8 in (2·64 m)
Wheelbase	22 ft 0 in (6·71 m)

Hopper opening, above fuselage:

Length	2 ft 0 in (0·61 m)
Width	1 ft 6 in (0·46 m)

AREAS:

Wings, gross (both)	402·95 sq ft (37·43 m²)
Upper wings (total)	219·2 sq ft (20·36 m²)
Lower wings (total)	183·75 sq ft (17·07 m²)
Ailerons (total)	55·2 sq ft (5·13 m²)
Fin	3·14 sq ft (0·29 m²)
Rudder	11·83 sq ft (1·10 m²)
Tailplane	21·16 sq ft (1·97 m²)
Elevators, incl tabs	14·14 sq ft (1·31 m²)

WEIGHTS AND LOADINGS:

Weight empty	3,746 lb (1,699 kg)
Hopper load	2,334 lb (1,058 kg)
Max T-O and landing weight (FAR Pt 8)	6,250 lb (2,834 kg)
Max wing loading	15·5 lb/sq ft (75·7 kg/m²)
Max power loading	10·4 lb/hp (4·72 kg/hp)

PERFORMANCE:
Max permissible diving speed
142 knots (164 mph; 263 km/h)

AIR PARTS
AIR PARTS (N.Z.) LTD

HEAD OFFICE:
135 Ward Street, Hamilton
BASE:
Hamilton Airport, R.D.2, Hamilton
CHAIRMAN: Trevor P. Baron
MANAGING DIRECTOR: G. M. Robertson
GENERAL MANAGER: G. Scheltema
SECRETARY: B. Sheridan

In 1957, this company acquired the Australasian sales rights for the Fletcher FU-24 utility aircraft. In 1964, it purchased all manufacturing and sales rights for the FU-24 from the Sargent-Fletcher Company of El Monte, California, and this aircraft is now being produced in Air Parts' works at Hamilton, New Zealand.

Air Parts has also produced two turboprop-powered developments of the FU-24, designated Fletcher 1060 and 1160; all three types are described below.

AIR PARTS FLETCHER FU-24

The FU-24 was designed initially for agricultural top-dressing work in New Zealand. The prototype flew in July 1954, followed by the first production aircraft five months later.

The initial production series of 100 was delivered to New Zealand operators for top-dressing work. Since then, another 39 have been produced, some of them for customers in Australia and South America. Over half of the aerial agricultural work in New Zealand is currently undertaken by FU-24 aircraft.

Two standard versions are available, as follows:

FU-24. Basic agricultural version, with side-by-side seating, 230 Imp gallon (1,045 litre) hopper for chemicals, and 300 hp Continental engine.

FU-24A. As FU-24, but fitted with dual controls.

In addition, Air Parts is producing a utility cargo/passenger version of the FU-24, powered by a 300 hp Rolls-Royce/Continental engine and capable of carrying four or five passengers or 1,680 lb (762 kg) of cargo. Production of a turboprop-powered version of this model is also under consideration.

A version with a 310 hp Continental GIO-470-A engine received FAA type approval on 28 October 1964, but there are no plans for its production.

During the second half of 1969 a further version of the FU-24 was developed, with a 400 hp Lycoming IO-720 eight-cylinder horizontally-opposed engine. Conversion was carried out on an existing FU-24 belonging to an NSW top-dressing company, with whom it is now back in operation. Certification of the 400 hp model was expected early in 1970, and new aircraft with this power plant are in production.

The following details refer to the standard 300 hp model:

TYPE: General-utility cabin monoplane.

WINGS: Cantilever low-wing monoplane. NACA 4415 wing section. Dihedral (outer wings) 8°. Incidence 2°. All-metal two-spar structure. All-metal plain-hinged ailerons. All-metal slotted flaps.

FUSELAGE: All-metal semi-monocoque structure. Cockpit area stressed for 40 g impact.

TAIL UNIT: Cantilever all-metal structure. All-movable horizontal tail with anti-servo tab.

LANDING GEAR: Non-retractable tricycle type. Fletcher air-oil shock-absorber struts. Goodrich wheels and tyres, size 8·50 × 6, pressure 18 lb/sq in (1·27 kg/cm²). Goodrich hydraulic expander brakes on main wheels.

POWER PLANT: One 300 hp Rolls-Royce/Continental IO-520-F six-cylinder horizontally-opposed air-cooled engine, driving a McCauley two-blade constant-speed variable-pitch metal propeller, diameter 7 ft 2 in (2·18 m). Fuel tank in each wing-root leading-edge, with total usable capacity of 44 US gallons (166 litres). Oil capacity 3 US gallons (11·4 litres).

ACCOMMODATION: Enclosed cabin for pilot and six passengers or equivalent freight. Rearward-sliding hood over front two seats. Large door on port side of fuselage gives access to five rear seats or cargo space in utility version.

ELECTRONICS AND EQUIPMENT: Optional equipment includes King KX100 radio, blind-flying instruments, agricultural spraying and dusting equipment.

DIMENSIONS, EXTERNAL:

Wing span	42 ft 0 in (12·81 m)
Wing chord (constant)	7 ft 0 in (2·13 m)
Wing aspect ratio	6
Length overall	31 ft 10 in (9·69 m)
Height over tail	9 ft 4 in (2·84 m)
Tailplane span	13 ft 9½ in (4·20 m)
Wheel track	12 ft 2 in (3·71 m)
Wheelbase	7 ft 6 in (2·28 m)
Passenger door (rear cabin roof):	
Length	3 ft 4 in (1·02 m)
Width	3 ft 8½ in (1·14 m)

DIMENSIONS, INTERNAL:

Cabin: Length	3 ft 9 in (1·14 m)
Max width	4 ft 0 in (1·22 m)
Max height	4 ft 2 in (1·27 m)
Floor area	16 sq ft (1·49 m²)

AREAS:

Wings, gross	294 sq ft (27·31 m²)
Ailerons (total)	19·6 sq ft (1·82 m²)
Trailing-edge flaps (total)	34·0 sq ft (3·16 m²)
Fin	13·6 sq ft (1·26 m²)
Rudder	6·9 sq ft (0·64 m²)
Tailplane	43·1 sq ft (4·00 m²)
Tailplane tab	4·9 sq ft (0·45 m²)

WEIGHTS AND LOADINGS:

Weight empty, equipped	2,000 lb (907 kg)
Max payload (agricultural)	1,610 lb (730 kg)
Normal max T-O weight	3,500 lb (1,588 kg)
Special T-O weight	4,000 lb (1,815 kg)
Normal wing loading	11·9 lb/sq ft (58·07 kg/m²)
Normal power loading	13·4 lb/hp (6·08 kg/hp)

PERFORMANCE (at normal max T-O weight):

Max level speed at S/L	124 knots (143 mph; 230 km/h)
Max permissible diving speed	145 knots (167 mph; 269 km/h)
Max cruising speed (75% power)	110 knots (127 mph; 204 km/h)
Stalling speed	42 knots (48 mph; 77 km/h)
Rate of climb at S/L	900 ft (275 m)/min
Service ceiling	17,000 ft (5,180 m)
T-O run	500 ft (152 m)
T-O to 50 ft (15 m)	950 ft (290 m)

Air Parts Fletcher FU-24 agricultural aircraft, fitted with underwing spray bars

Prototype of the Air Parts Fletcher FU-24 utility aircraft fitted with a 400 hp Lycoming IO-720 engine

Utility cargo/passenger version of the Air Parts Fletcher FU-24 single-engined cabin monoplane

Landing from 50 ft (15 m)	900 ft (275 m)
Landing run	500 ft (152 m)
Range with max fuel	322 nm (371 miles; 597 km)

AIR PARTS FLETCHER 1060

The Fletcher 1060 is essentially an enlarged development of the piston-engined FU-24, powered by a Pratt & Whitney PT6A-20 turboprop engine and capable of carrying an increased agricultural load with an improved performance. It retains substantially the same airframe as the FU-24, but an additional section has been introduced into the fuselage aft of the cabin, to provide room for a 47 cu ft (1·33 m³) hopper, and the cockpit is thus forward of the wing leading-edge. The wings themselves have been lengthened and strengthened to provide space for considerably increased fuel tankage.

Redesign of the basic FU-24 into the 1060 was started in June 1966; construction of a prototype began in November 1966, and this aircraft flew for the first time in July 1967. In June 1969, certification was granted by the New Zealand Department of Civil Aviation, but there are no plans for production of this version at present.

A description of the prototype appeared in the 1969-70 Jane's.

AIR PARTS FLETCHER 1160

The Fletcher 1160 is essentially similar to the 1060, except for the weight and performance variations resulting from the installation of an AiResearch TPE 331 turboprop engine in place of the PT6A-20.

The prototype Fletcher 1160 (unlike that of the 1060, which was built from the outset as a prototype) was produced by converting an existing FU-24 airframe which had already been in service for several years. Work on the conversion began in August 1967, and the prototype flew for the first time in December 1967.

In 1968, the prototype 1160 began certification trials by the New Zealand Department of Civil Aviation. Unfortunately, this aircraft crashed prior to certification, although by that time it had given ample evidence of being highly successful.

The original prototype is being replaced by an improved and more powerful version with a 615 shp AiResearch turboprop engine, with which it was due to fly in February/March 1970. It will have a max T-O weight of nearly 6,500 lb (2,945 kg) and an agricultural payload approaching 1½ tons. It is expected to be available in both agricultural and cargo/passenger versions.

The description below applies to the original prototype:

TYPE: Agricultural and general utility cabin monoplane.

WINGS: Cantilever low-wing monoplane. NACA 4415 wing section. Thickness/chord ratio

15%. Dihedral 8° on outer sections. Incidence 2°. Two-spar aluminium-alloy structure. Horn-balanced plain ailerons with beaded alloy skin. Half-span slotted flaps with beaded alloy skin.

FUSELAGE: All-metal semi-monocoque stringer and frame type with aluminium alloy skin.

TAIL UNIT: Conventional two-spar structure with aluminium alloy skin. One-piece all-moving tailplane with full-span anti-servo tab acting also as trim-tab.

LANDING GEAR: Non-retractable tricycle type. Fletcher oleo-pneumatic shock-absorber struts. Single steerable nose-wheel. Cleveland twin main wheels and tyres, size 8·00 × 6 or 8·50 × 6, pressure 11 lb/sq in (0·77 kg/cm²). Cleveland disc brake on each main wheel.

POWER PLANT: One AiResearch TPE 331 turboprop engine, derated to 530 shp and driving a Hartzell three-blade fully-feathering reversible-pitch propeller of 8 ft 0 in (2·44 m) diameter. Fuel tank in each wing-root leading-edge, with total capacity of 136 Imp gallons (618 litres). Refuelling point above each inboard leading-edge. Oil capacity 1·46 Imp gallons (7·62 litres).

ACCOMMODATION: Forward bench seat in agricultural version for pilot and, when necessary, one passenger. Enclosed cabin with rearward-sliding hood over front seats. Passenger version accommodation as for FU-24, with space provision for baggage hold.

SYSTEMS: DC electrical power for engine starting, external lights and fuel pump provided by four 12V 25Ah batteries.

ELECTRONICS AND EQUIPMENT: Agricultural spraying and dusting equipment. Radio and blind-flying instrumentation optional.

DIMENSIONS, EXTERNAL:
Wing span	44 ft 0 in (13·41 m)
Wing chord (constant)	7 ft 0 in (2·13 m)
Wing aspect ratio	6·3
Length overall	35 ft 2½ in (10·73 m)
Height overall	9 ft 4 in (2·84 m)
Tailplane span	13 ft 9½ in (4·20 m)
Wheel track	10 ft 11 in (3·33 m)
Wheelbase	8 ft 6 in (2·59 m)

Air Parts Fletcher 1060 (500 shp PT6A-20 turboprop engine) operated by James Aviation Ltd

Air Parts Fletcher 1160 (530 shp AiResearch TPE 331 turboprop engine) carrying out crop-dusting activities

AREAS:
Wings, gross	308 sq ft (28·61 m²)
Ailerons (total)	13·90 sq ft (1·29 m²)
Trailing-edge flaps (total)	16·50 sq ft (1·53 m²)
Fin	14·13 sq ft (1·31 m²)
Rudder	6·37 sq ft (0·59 m²)
Tailplane (excl tab)	43·10 sq ft (4·00 m²)
Tailplane tab	4·90 sq ft (0·45 m²)

WEIGHTS AND LOADING:
Weight empty	2,810 lb (1,275 kg)
Hopper capacity	3,000 lb (1,316 kg)
Max payload with full fuel	1,940 lb (880 kg)

Max T-O weight (Special category)	5,450 lb (2,472 kg)
Max landing weight (Normal category)	4,860 lb (2,204 kg)
Max power loading	10·3 lb/shp (4·67 kg/shp)

PERFORMANCE (at max T-O weight, except where indicated):
Rate of climb at S/L	1,050 ft (320 m)/min
T-O run	800 ft (244 m)
T-O to 50 ft (15 m)	1,200 ft (366 m)
Landing from 50 ft (15 m) at max landing weight, full reverse pitch	980 ft (299 m)

POLAND

BORZECKI
JOZEF BORZECKI
ADDRESS:
Wroclaw

Mr Borzecki's first home-built design was a single-seat all-metal powered glider named the Stratus, which he completed in 1965. He was also co-designer of the Pterodaktyl-1 amateur-built flexible-wing paraglider, completed and tested in 1967. In the same year he completed the Cirrus powered monoplane. His latest design is the Altostratus, which is a modified version of the Stratus powered by a 25 hp engine.

BORZECKI CIRRUS
The Cirrus is a single-seat powered monoplane of wooden construction evolved from the well-known Salamandra training glider. It flew for the first time on 22 May 1968, piloted by Mr Borzecki, some 18 months after he began its design.

Like the Stratus, the Cirrus has a control system of Mr Borzecki's own design, in which the control column actuates both the aileron and rudder controls, thus eliminating the need for rudder pedals.

TYPE: Single-seat sporting monoplane.

WINGS: Braced high-wing monoplane adapted from that of the Salamandra sailplane. Tapering single-spar structure, with short diagonal auxiliary spar, plywood D-section leading-edge and fabric covering overall. Single bracing strut each side. Air-brakes on upper and lower surfaces.

FUSELAGE: Pilot's nacelle and Salamandra open rear frame, of wooden construction.

TAIL UNIT: Wire-braced wooden structure, unchanged from Salamandra.

LANDING GEAR: Cantilever spring-steel main legs, with low-pressure tyres on wheels.

POWER PLANT: One 28 hp modified Volkswagen engine, driving a small two-blade wooden propeller made by Mr Borzecki. Fuel tank, capacity 6·6 Imp gallons (30 litres), in compartment aft of pilot's seat.

DIMENSIONS, EXTERNAL:
Wing span	41 ft 0 in (12·50 m)
Wing aspect ratio	9·2
Length overall	21 ft 4 in (6·50 m)
Height overall	6 ft 4¾ in (1·95 m)

AREA:
Wings, gross	180·75 sq ft (16·8 m²)

WEIGHTS:
Weight empty	440 lb (200 kg)
Normal T-O weight	approx 661 lb (300 kg)

PERFORMANCE:
Max level speed at S/L	75·5 knots (87 mph; 140 km/h)

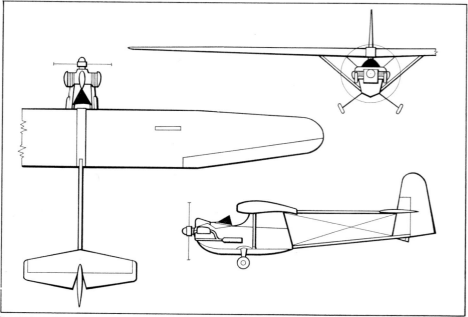

Photograph and three-view drawing of the Borzecki Cirrus single-seat sporting monoplane

Max cruising speed at S/L	64 knots (74 mph; 120 km/h)
Landing speed	24 knots (28 mph; 45 km/h)
Min sinking speed, power off	4·27 ft (1·3 m)/sec
Max rate of climb at S/L	394 ft (120 m)/min

Service ceiling	16,400 ft (5,000 m)
T-O run	460 ft (140 m)
Landing run	328 ft (100 m)
Fuel consumption	1·54 Imp gall (7 litres)/hour

IL
INSTYTUT LOTNICTWA
ADDRESS:
Warsaw: 21 Okecie, Al. Krakowska 129

SCIENTIFIC DIRECTOR: Dr Czeslaw Skoczylas
HEAD OF TECHNICAL INFORMATION DIVISION:
Jerzy Grzegorzewski, MSc(Eng)
The Instytut Lotnictwa (IL) or Aviation

Institute in Warsaw conducts scientific research, including investigation of the problems associated with supersonic speeds and the technology of aviation materials.

JANOWSKI
JAROSLAW JANOWSKI
ADDRESS:
Lodz

Mr Janowski, assisted by Mr Witold Kalita, has designed and completed a light single-seat amateur-built aircraft, the J-1 Don Kichot, of which details are given below. Its power plant, the 25 hp Saturn two-cylinder engine, was also designed by Mr Janowski, and built by Mr S. Polawski, and is described in the "Aero-Engines" section of this edition.

JANOWSKI J-1 DON KICHOT (DON QUIXOTE)
Design and construction of the J-1 was started in 1967, and it was expected to fly for the first time in the Spring of 1970. The aircraft is also known by the name Przasniczka.

TYPE: Single-seat ultra-light monoplane.

WINGS: Strut-braced high-wing monoplane. Clark Y wing section. Thickness/chord ratio 13%. Single-spar wooden structure, with plywood D-section leading-edge, fabric covering and additional glass-fibre covering on centre-section. Braced by single steel strut on each side. Fabric-covered wooden ailerons. No flaps.

FUSELAGE: Pod-and-boom type. Main central part of fuselage is of welded steel-tube construction, rear portion of wood construction. Plywood covering overall except for nose, which is of plywood and plastic foam sandwich construction.

TAIL UNIT: Wooden structure, with non-swept constant-chord horizontal surfaces and swept-back vertical surfaces. All fixed surfaces plywood-covered, movable surfaces fabric-covered. Trim-tab in elevator.

LANDING GEAR: Non-retractable tail-wheel type. Cantilever spring-steel main legs, each with single wheel and 300 × 125 low-pressure tyre. Self-castoring tail-wheel, diameter 4·72 in (120 mm). Mechanical brakes.

POWER PLANT: One 25 hp Janowski Saturn two-stroke two-cylinder horizontally-opposed air-cooled engine, mounted at top of fuselage aft of cabin and driving a two-blade fixed-pitch wooden pusher propeller designed by Mr Janowski. Fuel capacity 4·4 Imp gallons (20 litres).

ACCOMMODATION: Single seat in enclosed cabin in forward part of fuselage.

DIMENSIONS, EXTERNAL:
Wing span	24 ft 7¼ in (7·50 m)
Wing chord (constant)	3 ft 3¼ in (1·00 m)
Wing aspect ratio	7·5
Length overall	16 ft 4¾ in (5·00 m)
Height overall	4 ft 5¼ in (1·35 m)
Wheel track	3 ft 9¼ in (1·15 m)

AREA:
Wings, gross	80·7 sq ft (7·50 m²)

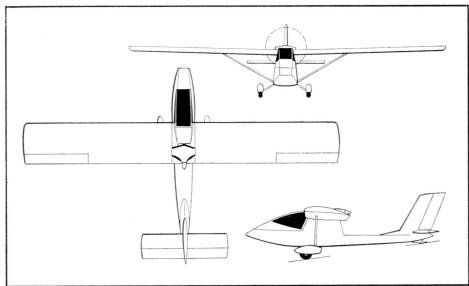

Photograph and three-view drawing of the Janowski J-1 single-seat light aircraft

WEIGHTS:
Weight empty	286 lb (130 kg)
Normal T-O weight	496 lb (225 kg)
Max T-O weight	551 lb (250 kg)

PERFORMANCE (estimated, at max T-O weight):
Max level speed at S/L	89 knots (103 mph; 165 km/h)
Cruising speed	65 knots (75 mph; 120 km/h)
Stalling speed	36 knots (41 mph; 65 km/h)
Rate of climb at S/L	394 ft (120 m)/min
Service ceiling	8,200 ft (2,500 m)
T-O run	328 ft (100 m)
Landing run	164 ft (50 m)
Range	215 nm (248 miles; 400 km)
Fuel consumption	1·5 Imp gallons (7 litres) per hour

MAJ
MARIAN MAJ
ADDRESS: Radom

Mr Maj has designed, built and flown a single-seat amateur-built light aircraft known as the M-20 Kangur, details of which are given below.

MAJ M-20 KANGUR (KANGAROO)
Design and construction of the M-20 Kangur was started in 1965, and the aircraft flew for the first time on 15 November 1969.

TYPE: Single-seat sporting monoplane.

WINGS: Braced high-wing monoplane. Clark Y wing section. Constant chord. Thickness/chord ratio 13%. Two-spar all-wood structure, with plywood D-section leading-edge and fabric covering. Fabric-covered wooden plain ailerons. No flaps. Duralumin Vee bracing strut on each side.

FUSELAGE: Plywood-covered wooden structure of basically rectangular section.

TAIL UNIT: Braced structure of welded steel-tube with fabric covering.

LANDING GEAR: Non-retractable tail-wheel type. Welded steel-tube side Vees, faired over with fabric, and two half-axles. Rubber-cord shock-absorbers. Low-pressure tyres, size 300 × 125, on main units. Steel tail-skid.

POWER PLANT: One 28 hp modified 1,131 cc Volkswagen engine, driving a two-blade fixed-pitch wooden propeller of Maj design, diameter 4 ft 4 in (1·32 m). Fuel tank, capacity 3·5 Imp gallons (16 litres), in port wing.

ACCOMMODATION: Single seat in enclosed cockpit.

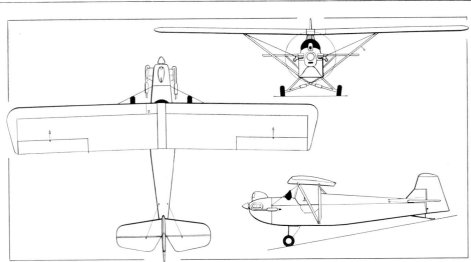

Maj M-20 Kangur single-seat light aircraft (28 hp Volkswagen engine)

DIMENSIONS, EXTERNAL:
Wing span	26 ft 6¾ in (8·10 m)
Wing aspect ratio	6·6
Length overall	17 ft 4¾ in (5·30 m)
Height overall	6 ft 2¾ in (1·90 m)
Wheel track	4 ft 5¼ in (1·35 m)

AREA:
Wings, gross   102 sq ft (9·50 m²)

WEIGHTS:
Weight empty   485 lb (220 kg)
Normal T-O weight   683 lb (310 kg)
Max T-O weight   705 lb (320 kg)

PERFORMANCE (at max T-O weight):
Max level speed at S/L
                       69 knots (80 mph; 129 km/h)
Cruising speed   50 knots (58 mph; 93 km/h)
Landing speed   36 knots (42 mph; 67 km/h)
Rate of climb at S/L   295 ft (90 m)/min
Service ceiling   8,858 ft (2,700 m)
T-O run   262 ft (80 m)
Landing run   295 ft (90 m)
Range   107·5 nm (124 miles; 200 km)
Fuel consumption
                       1·8 Imp gallons (8 litres) per hour

Maj M-20 Kangur single-seat light sporting monoplane (28 hp modified Volkswagen engine)

PZL

POLSKIE ZAKLADY LOTNICZE (Polish Aviation Works)

HEAD OFFICE:
Warsaw, 5 Miodowa Str.

The Polish aircraft industry is controlled and administered by the Zjednoczenie Przemyslu Lotniczego (Aircraft Industry Union). All aircraft factories are incorporated in this union, though each remains responsible for its own range of products.

The Polish aircraft industry manufactures the Soviet Antonov An-2 utility biplane under licence, and is responsible for development and production of the Mil Mi-2 turbine-powered helicopter. Several aircraft of Polish origin are also in production. The Szybowcowy Zaklad Doswiadczalny (SZD) or Experimental Glider Institute at Bielsko-Biala is the leading glider and sailplane development and manufacturing centre.

When represented on foreign markets, the entire Polish aircraft industry appears under the traditional name of Polskie Zaklady Lotnicze (PZL), and some of the latest Polish designs carry PZL designations.

The export sales of all Polish aviation products are handled exclusively by a state-controlled enterprise:

Motoimport, 26 Przemyslowa, Warsaw

WSK-MIELEC

WYTWORNIA SPRZETU KOMUNIKACYJNEGO-MIELEC (Transport Equipment Manufacturing Centre, Mielec)

HEAD OFFICE AND WORKS: Mielec

Largest and best-equipped aircraft factory in Poland, the WSK at Mielec was engaged mainly on licence production of MiG single-seat jet-fighters for several years. These aircraft carry the Polish designation of LiM, meaning apparently Licence MiG.

It is believed that, after completion of the production order for LiM-5's (MiG-17's) for the Polish Air Force, licence production of MiG fighters ceased completely in Poland in about 1959.

Following a reduction in orders for combat aircraft in 1955, the WSK obtained other work. In 1956 it began quantity production of the TS-8 Bies two-seat piston-engined basic trainer which was described fully in the 1962-63 edition of Jane's. Three years later, the Soviet-designed An-2 general-utility biplane also went into production at Mielec. The first ten Polish-built An-2's were completed in 1960, and the Mielec factory has since built considerable numbers of this aircraft in several versions, including a twin-float variant, and has exported them to the USSR, Bulgaria and Yugoslavia. Orders have also been received from Czechoslovakia and the German Democratic Republic.

In 1968, series production was started of the An-2P, a feeder-liner version developed in Poland and equivalent to the An-2M built in the USSR. In comparison with its Soviet counterpart, the An-2P has a redesigned and more attractive passenger cabin layout incorporating glass-wool soundproofing. There are 12 upholstered forward-facing seats for passengers, plus two foldable seats for children in the centre aisle and an infant's cradle. Other modifications include a new propeller and spinner, a reduction in the weight of the radio, removal of non-essential equipment, to save weight, and improved cabin lighting, heating and ventilation systems. Performance and other basic data remain unchanged from earlier versions, which remain in production in Poland.

In parallel production is the TS-11 Iskra jet trainer.

There is a design office at the factory for development of original aircraft. The latest known product of this design team, the M-4 Tarpan two-seat light training and sporting aircraft, was described in the 1964-65 Jane's.

TS-11 ISKRA (SPARK)

Developed by the OKL under the supervision of Docent Ing T. Soltyk, the TS-11 Iskra two-seat jet trainer was produced as a replacement for the piston-engined TS-8 Bies. The prototype, built at the WSK Warsaw-Okecie, began flight trials on 5 February 1960. Quantity production commenced at the WSK Mielec in 1962. The formal handing over of the first Iskra for service with the Polish Air Force took place in March 1963. The Iskra was still in production in 1970, and deliveries to military training centres continue.

In September 1964 the Iskra set up four international records in Class C-1-d, by achieving speeds of 452·7 knots (521·33 mph; 839 km/h) over a 15/25-km course, 386·2 knots (444·71 mph; 715·691 km/h) over a 100-km closed circuit and 394·3 knots (454·03 mph; 730·701 km/h) over

Antonov An-2P transport biplane, built under licence by WSK at Mielec

a 500-km closed curcuit, and a distance of 275·3 nm (317·02 miles; 510·194 km) in a closed circuit.

TYPE: Fully-aerobatic jet primary and basic trainer.

WINGS: Cantilever mid-wing monoplane. Thickness/chord ratio 9%. Marked dihedral. All-metal torsion-box structure with steel main spar and duralumin stressed skin. Hydraulically-servo-assisted ailerons. Two-section double-slotted flaps and air-brakes fitted. One boundary layer fence on each wing.

FUSELAGE: All-metal semi-monocoque structure of pod-and-boom type.

TAIL UNIT: Cantilever all-metal structure. Fin integral with fuselage. Mass- and aerodynamically-balanced elevators and rudder.

LANDING GEAR: Retractable tricycle type with single wheel on each unit. Nose-wheel retracts forward, main wheels inward into wing-root air intake extensions. Hydraulic retraction. Low-pressure tyres.

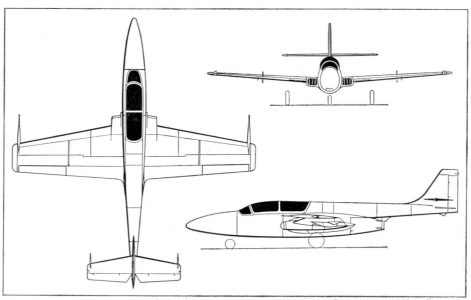

Three-view drawing of the WSK-Mielec TS-11 Iskra jet trainer

POWER PLANT: One Type HO-10 axial-flow turbojet of Polish design, rated at 1,760 lb (800 kg) st, in early aircraft and one SO-1 turbojet rated at 2,205 lb (1,000 kg) st in current production aircraft. Engine mounted in fuselage aft of cockpit, with nozzle under tailboom. Fuel in integral tanks in wings and in a fuselage tank.

ACCOMMODATION: Crew of two in tandem on lightweight ejection seats, under a one-piece hydraulically-actuated rearward-hinged jettisonable canopy. Cockpit pressurised and air-conditioned. Rear seat slightly raised.

ELECTRONICS AND EQUIPMENT: Complete dual controls and instrumentation, including blind-flying panels. R/T, intercom and oxygen equipment standard. Position and homing indicator.

ARMAMENT: Forward-firing armament in nose of fuselage, with gun camera. Attachments for a variety of underwing stores, including bombs and rockets.

DIMENSIONS, EXTERNAL:
Wing span	33 ft 0 in (10·06 m)
Length overall	36 ft 7 in (11·15 m)
Height overall	11 ft 0½ in (3·37 m)

AREA:
Wings, gross	770 sq ft (71·5 m²)

WSK-Mielec TS-11 Iskra jet trainer (1,760 lb st HO-10 turbojet engine)

WEIGHTS:
Weight empty	5,400 lb (2,450 kg)
Normal T-O weight	6,835 lb (3,100 kg)
Max T-O weight	7,935 lb (3,600 kg)

PERFORMANCE (at max T-O weight):
Max level speed at 20,000 ft (6,000 m)	432 knots (497 mph; 800 km/h)
Max permissible diving speed	Mach 0·9

Normal cruising speed	324 knots (373 mph; 600 km/h)
Landing speed	92 knots (106 mph; 170 km/h)
Rate of climb at S/L	4,135 ft (1,260 m)/min
Service ceiling	42,650 ft (13,000 m)
T-O run	1,640 ft (500 m)
Landing run	2,133 ft (650 m)
Range with max fuel	538 nm (620 miles; 1,000 km)

WSK-OKECIE
WYTWORNIA SPRZETU KOMUNIKACYJNEGO-OKECIE (Transport Equipment Manufacturing Centre. Okecie)

HEAD OFFICE AND WORKS:
Warsaw 21 Okecie, Al. Krakowska 110/114

MANAGERS:
Jan Staszek, Eng MSc (General Manager)
Jerzy Milczarek, Eng (Technical)
Zenon Orzanowski, MSc (Sales)

PUBLIC RELATIONS:
Jerzy Pasterski, Eng MSc

The former Osrodek Konstrukcji Lotniczych (OKL: see 1968-69 *Jane's*) has been replaced by a design office, and since 1965 has been incorporated in WSK-Okecie, which is responsible for research and development both for its own designs and for licence-built products. The Okecie factory is responsible for light aircraft development and production, and for the design and manufacture of associated agricultural equipment for its own aircraft and for those built at other factories in the Aircraft Industry Union.

PZL-101A GAWRON (ROOK)
The PZL-101 has been developed from the Yak-12, several versions of which were licence-produced in the WSK at Warsaw-Okecie. The prototype flew for the first time in April 1958 and the first production Gawron flew in February 1960.

Following extensive evaluation trials in the countries of eastern Europe, including the Soviet Union, the PZL-101 was approved by these countries as the standard agricultural aircraft for the period beginning in 1961. In addition to orders from these countries and domestic orders, a number of PZL-101's have been sold to Austria, Finland, India, Spain, Turkey, the USSR and Vietnam.

There are three current production versions of the Gawron, all designated PZL-101A. The standard version, with 260 hp AI-14R engine, is equipped for agricultural duties. The ambulance and utility models are conversions of the standard airframe.

In addition, a version designated **PZL-101AF** was developed. This has a 300 hp AI-14RF engine and increased payload; it was first flown on 30 August 1966 but is not in production.

The following details apply to all three production variants of the PZL-101A Gawron:

TYPE: Single-engined agricultural, ambulance and utility monoplane.

WINGS: Braced high-wing monoplane. Clark Y wing section. Thickness/chord ratio 11%. Dihedral 2° 15'. Incidence 3° 30'. Sweepback at quarter-chord 4° 30'. Two-spar all-metal structure with fabric covering. Aircraft produced since 1969 have laminar-flow wing-tips instead of the former large end-plates. Vee duralumin bracing struts with auxiliary support struts. Fabric-covered metal slotted ailerons and pneumatically-operated slotted flaps on trailing-edge. Full-span fixed slats on leading-edge. Trim-tab in each aileron.

FUSELAGE: Rectangular welded steel-tube structure. Front portion metal-covered, rear portion fabric-covered.

TAIL UNIT: Braced duralumin structure covered with sheet duralumin on leading-edges and with fabric covering aft. Tailplane incidence adjustable on ground. Mass-balanced elevators. Trim-tab in starboard elevator and balance tab in port elevator.

WSK-Okecie PZL-101A Gawron agricultural version with original end-plate wingtips

WSK-Okecie PZL-101A Gawron, current production model without end-plate wingtips

LANDING GEAR: Non-retractable tail-wheel type. Welded steel-tube side Vees faired over with fabric, and two half-axles hinged to bottom of fuselage. Rubber cord shock-absorbers and hydraulic dampers. Fully castoring, self-centering tail-wheel with oleo-pneumatic shock-absorber. Low-pressure tyres, size 595 × 185 on main wheels, 255 × 110 on tail-wheel. Tyre pressure 40 lb/sq in (2·8 kg/cm²). Pneumatic brakes. Wire-cutters on leading-edges of side Vees. Ski gear optional.

POWER PLANT: One 260 hp AI-14R nine-cylinder radial air-cooled engine in clam-shell cowling. Pneumatic starting. Two-blade Type W530-D-11/N constant-speed wooden propeller, diameter 9 ft 0½ in (2·75 m). Two fuel tanks in wings, with total capacity of 39·6 Imp gallons (180 litres). Provision for two under-wing auxiliary tanks with total capacity of 35 Imp gallons (160 litres). Oil capacity 5·0 Imp gallons (23 litres).

ACCOMMODATION AND EQUIPMENT (Standard agricultural model): Adjustable seat for pilot. Second seat for mechanic or loader. Door on each side of cabin. The hopper, made of glass-fibre, has a dust-proof hatch and can carry 1,100 lb (500 kg) of dust and a distributor, or an equivalent weight of liquid chemicals and spray bars, although the max capacity for liquid chemicals is 175 Imp gallons (800 litres). Dusting gear can be adjusted to discharge from 0 to 1,323 lb (0-600 kg) of dust per hectare and has three settings to give swath widths of 50-300 ft (15-100 m). The spray pump can discharge up to 2·2 Imp gallons (10 litres) of liquid chemicals per second.

ACCOMMODATION AND EQUIPMENT (Ambulance and utility models): Accommodation for pilot and two stretcher patients and attendant, or for a pilot and three passengers, in heated and ventilated cabin. Door on each side. Upward-hinged triangular door on port side for stretcher loading. Dual controls optional. With passenger seats removed, utility model can carry 660 lb (300 kg) of cargo.

ELECTRONICS AND EQUIPMENT: VHF radio and blind-flying instrumentation standard in ambulance version. Provision for glider towing hook.

DIMENSIONS, EXTERNAL:
Wing span	41 ft 7½ in (12·68 m)
Wing chord (constant)	7 ft 6½ in (2·30 m)
Wing aspect ratio	6·7
Length overall	29 ft 6½ in (9·00 m)
Height overall	9 ft 2¾ in (2·81 m)
Tailplane span	14 ft 11 in (4·53 m)
Wheel track	7 ft 2½ in (2·20 m)
Wheelbase	20 ft 7½ in (6·28 m)

Doors (each):
- Height 3 ft 3¼ in (1·00 m)
- Width 3 ft 3¼ in (1·00 m)

Dimensions, internal:
- Cabin: Floor area 24·2 sq ft (2·25 m^2)
- Volume 90 cu ft (2·55 m^3)

Areas:
- Wings, gross 256·8 sq ft (23·86 m^2)
- Ailerons (total) 30·14 sq ft (2·80 m^2)
- Flaps (total) 30·14 sq ft (2·80 m^2)
- Fin 13·45 sq ft (1·25 m^2)
- Rudder 10·01 sq ft (0·93 m^2)
- Tailplane 21·64 sq ft (2·01 m^2)
- Elevators 32·40 sq ft (3·01 m^2)

Weights and Loading:
- Weight empty, equipped:
  - Agricultural 2,260 lb (1,025 kg)
  - Ambulance 2,354 lb (1,068 kg)
- Max T-O and landing weight 3,660 lb (1,660 kg)
- Max zero-fuel weight:
  - Agricultural 3,527 lb (1,600 kg)
  - Ambulance 3,373 lb (1,530 kg)
- Max wing loading 14·34 lb/sq ft (70·0 kg/m^2)

Performance (agricultural version, at max T-O weight):
- Max level speed at S/L 92 knots (106 mph; 171 km/h)
- Max permissible diving speed 115 knots (133 mph; 215 km/h)
- Max cruising speed 70 knots (81 mph; 130 km/h)
- Econ cruising speed 65 knots (75 mph; 120 km/h)
- Dusting and spraying speed 59-69 knots (68-80 mph; 110-130 km/h)
- Landing speed 36 knots (41 mph; 65 km/h)
- Rate of climb at S/L 530 ft (162 m)/min
- Service ceiling 11,100 ft (3,380 m)
- T-O run 330 ft (100 m)
- T-O to 50 ft (15 m) 1,050 ft (320 m)
- Landing from 50 ft (15 m) 853 ft (260 m)
- Landing run 460 ft (140 m)
- Range with max internal fuel 356 nm (410 miles; 660 km)
- Range with external tanks 614 nm (708 miles; 1,140 km)

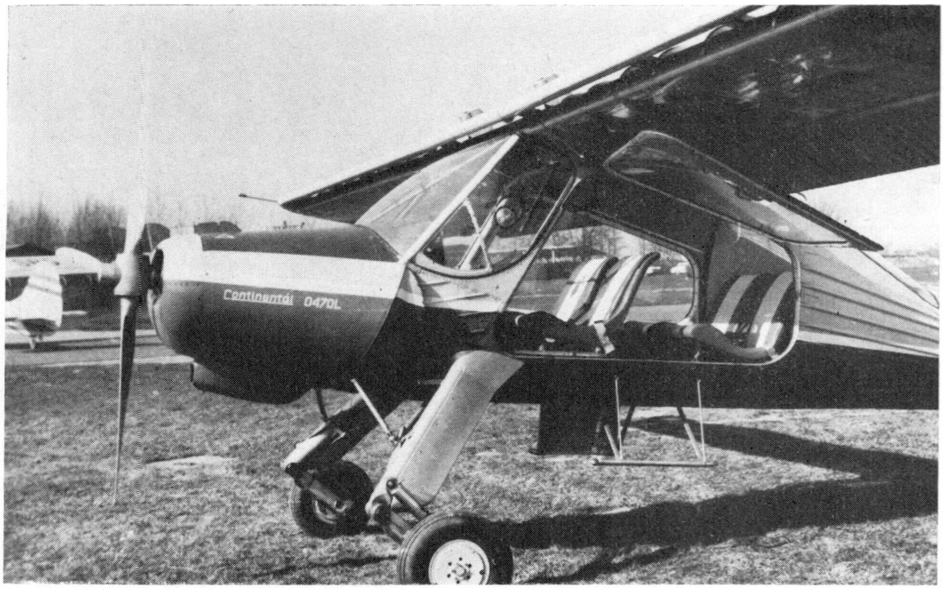

WSK-Okecie PZL-104 Wilga 32, with Continental O-470-L engine and short-stroke landing gear

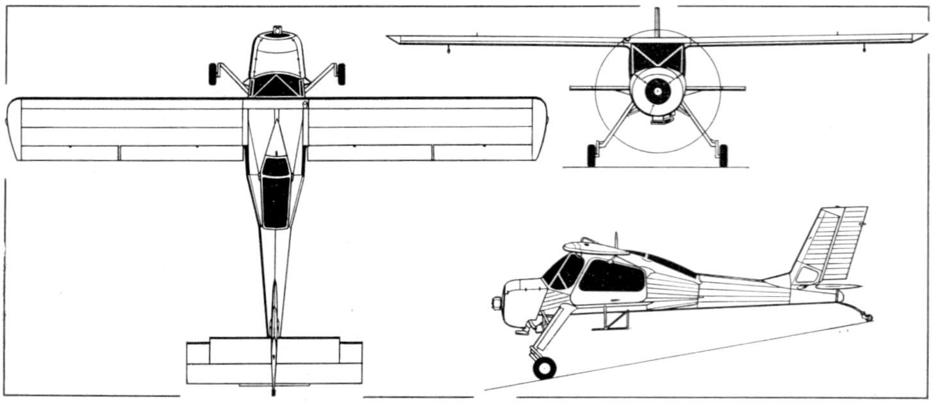

PZL-104 Wilga 35 general-purpose monoplane

PZL-104 WILGA (THRUSH)

The PZL-104 Wilga is a light general-purpose aircraft intended for a wide variety of general aviation and flying club duties. The original prototype (SP-PAZ), known as the Wilga 1, with a 180 hp WN-6B engine, flew for the first time on 24 April 1962.

It was followed by the prototype of the Wilga 2, with a completely redesigned fuselage and tail unit. Design of the Wilga 2 was started in March 1962, and construction of the prototype began in December 1962. It first flew, as SP-PAR, on 1 August 1963, powered by a 195 hp WN-6RB engine. This prototype was fitted out at first as a four-seat passenger aircraft (Wilga 2P) but was converted later to the agricultural configuration (Wilga 2R). The second prototype, with a 225 hp Continental O-470 engine (Wilga C), flew as SP-PCD on 30 December 1963. On 8 May 1964, this aircraft established a Polish national height record for its class by climbing to 22,428 ft (6,836 m). The Wilga C received Polish certification on 18 March 1964.

A modified version of the Wilga C is in production in Indonesia as the Lipnur Gelatik (which see).

On 31 December 1965 the prototype was flown of the **Wilga 3,** a version powered by a 260 hp AI-14R radial engine. Small quantities of this model were built as the **Wilga 3A** for flying club use, and as the **Wilga 3S** for ambulance duties. The **Wilga 3CA** was a variant developed in 1966, having similar landing gear and horizontal tail surfaces to the Wilga 3, but powered by a Continental O-470-L engine. These and other early models were described in the 1968-69 edition of *Jane's*.

In 1967 the basic design was further modified, with improved cabin comfort, redesigned landing gear and glass-fibre laminated tail-wheel leg. This version is known as the **Wilga 35** (first flight 28 July 1967) when fitted with a 260 hp AI-14R engine, and as the **Wilga 32** (first flown 12 September 1967) with a 230 hp Continental O-470-L or O-470-R engine and shorter landing gear. Both the Wilga 32 and Wilga 35 received a Polish type certificate on 31 March 1969, having entered production in 1968. A British C of A has been granted for the import of the Wilga 32 into the UK. Initial production models are the **32A and 35A** (indicating Aeroclub version) for paratroop training and glider towing, and some have been sold to Bulgaria and Romania. Passenger/liaison (**Wilga 32P and 35P**) and ambulance (**Wilga 32S and 35S**) models are also available.

The following description applies to the Wilga 32 and 35.

Type: Single-engined general-purpose monoplane.

Wings: Cantilever high-wing monoplane. Wing section NACA 2415. Thickness/chord ratio 15%. Dihedral 1°. All-metal single-spar structure, with leading-edge torsion box and beaded metal skin. Each wing attached to fuselage by three bolts, two at spar and one at forward fitting. All-metal aerodynamically and mass-balanced slotted ailerons, with beaded metal skin. Ailerons can be drooped to supplement flaps during landing. Manually-operated all-metal slotted flaps with beaded metal skin. Fixed metal slat on the leading-edge along the full span of the wing and over the fuselage.

Fuselage: All-metal semi-monocoque structure in two portions, riveted together. Forward section incorporates main wing-spar carry-through structure. Rear section is in the form of a tail cone. Beaded metal skin. Floor in cabin is of sandwich construction, with a paper core, covered with foam rubber.

Tail Unit: Braced all-metal structure, with sweptback vertical surfaces. Stressed-skin single-spar tailplane attached to fuselage by a single centre fitting and supported by a single aluminium alloy strut on each side. Stressed-skin two-spar fin structure of semi-monocoque construction. Rudder and one-piece elevator are aerodynamically horn-balanced and mass-balanced, with counterweights in the form of metal slats attached to the front section of the elevator. Controllable trim-tab in centre of elevator trailing-edge.

Landing Gear: Non-retractable tail-wheel type. Semi-cantilever main units, of rocker type, have PZL oleo-pneumatic shock-absorbers. Stomil low-pressure tyres size 500 × 150 on main wheels. Hydraulic brakes. Steerable tail-wheel, size 200 × 80, carried on sprung leg of glass-fibre reinforced resin. Retractable metal ski landing gear optional.

Power Plant (Wilga 32): One 230 hp Continental O-470-L or O-470-R six-cylinder horizontally-opposed air-cooled engine, driving a McCauley 2A346-050-90A two-blade constant-speed metal propeller, diameter 7 ft 4 in (2·24 m). Two removable fuel tanks in each wing, with total capacity of 43 Imp gallons (196 litres). Refuelling point on each side of fuselage, at junction with wing. Oil capacity 2·5 Imp gallons (11·5 litres).

Power Plant (Wilga 35): One 260 hp Ivchenko AI-14R nine-cylinder air-cooled radial engine, driving a US-122000 two-blade constant-speed wooden propeller, diameter 8 ft 8 in (2·65 m). Fuel capacity as for Wilga 32; oil capacity 3·5 Imp gallons (16 litres).

Accommodation: Passenger version accommodates four persons in pairs, with adjustable front seats. Baggage compartment aft of seats. Upward-opening door on each side of cabin, jettisonable in emergency. In the parachute training version the starboard door is removed and replaced by two tubular uprights with a central connecting strap, and the starboard front seat is rearward-facing. Back-rests of the rear seats are removable, and jumps are facilitated by a step on the starboard side and by a parachute hitch. A controllable towing hook can be attached to the tail landing gear permitting the Wilga, in this role, to tow a single glider of up to 1,433 lb (650 kg) weight or two or three gliders with a total combined weight of 2,480 lb (1,125 kg).

Systems: Hydraulic system pressure 570 lb/sq in (40 kg/cm^2) in both models. In the Wilga 32, the electrical system includes a Delco-Rémy generator, 10Ah battery and Eclipse Pioneer electrical starter. In the Wilga 35, engine starting is effected pneumatically by a built-in system of 7 litres capacity with a pressure of 710 lb/sq in (50 kg/cm^2); electrical system includes GSK-1500 generator and a 10Ah battery for 24V DC power.

Electronics and Equipment: Standard equipment of Wilga 32's for the UK includes ARK-9 radio compass, directional gyro and stall-warning signal, but these items are optional on all other Wilga 32's. Standard equipment of Wilga 35 includes R 860 VHF radio and blind-flying instrumentation.

Dimensions, external:
- Wing span 36 ft 4⅞ in (11·14 m)
- Wing chord (constant) 4 ft 7¼ in (1·40 m)
- Wing aspect ratio 8
- Length overall 26 ft 6¾ in (8·10 m)
- Height overall:
  - Wilga 32 8 ft 2½ in (2·50 m)
  - Wilga 35 9 ft 7¾ in (2·94 m)
- Tailplane span 12 ft 1¾ in (3·70 m)
- Wheel track:
  - Wilga 32 8 ft 1¼ in (2·47 m)
  - Wilga 35 9 ft 4¼ in (2·85 m)
- Wheelbase:
  - Wilga 32 21 ft 3¾ in (6·50 m)
  - Wilga 35 21 ft 11¾ in (6·70 m)

Passenger doors (each):
Height	3 ft 3¼ in (1·00 m)
Width	4 ft 11 in (1·50 m)

DIMENSIONS, INTERNAL:
Cabin: Length	7 ft 2½ in (2·20 m)
Max width	3 ft 10 in (1·20 m)
Max height	4 ft 11 in (1·50 m)
Floor area	23·8 sq ft (2·20 m²)
Volume	85 cu ft (2·40 m³)
Baggage compartment	17·5 cu ft (0·50 m³)

AREAS:
Wings, gross	166·8 sq ft (15·5 m²)
Ailerons (total)	17·0 sq ft (1·60 m²)
Trailing-edge flaps (total)	21·6 sq ft (2·00 m²)
Fin	15·9 sq ft (1·48 m²)
Rudder	9·8 sq ft (0·91 m²)
Tailplane	13·24 sq ft (1·23 m²)
Elevator, including tab	23·36 sq ft (2·17 m²)

WEIGHTS AND LOADINGS:
Weight empty, equipped:
Wilga 32	1,624 lb (737 kg)
Wilga 35	1,829 lb (830 kg)
Max T-O and landing weight	2,711 lb (1,230 kg)
Max wing loading	16·3 lb/sq ft (79·4 kg/m²)

Max power loading:
Wilga 32	11·79 lb/hp (5·35 kg/hp)
Wilga 35	10·41 lb/hp (4·72 kg/hp)

PERFORMANCE (at max T-O weight):
Max level speed:
Wilga 32	110 knots (127 mph; 205 km/h)
Wilga 35	113 knots (130 mph; 210 km/h)
Max permissible diving speed:	
	150 knots (173 mph; 279 km/h)

Max cruising speed:
Wilga 32	81 knots (93 mph; 150 km/h)
Wilga 35	104 knots (120 mph; 193 km/h)

Econ cruising speed:
Wilga 32	73 knots (84 mph; 135 km/h)
Wilga 35	69 knots (79 mph; 127 km/h)
Stalling speed	50 knots (57·5 mph; 92 km/h)

Rate of climb at S/L:
Wilga 32	865 ft (264 m)/min
Wilga 35	1,245 ft (380 m)/min

Service ceiling:
Wilga 32	12,075 ft (3,680 m)
Wilga 35	15,025 ft (4,580 m)

T-O run:
Wilga 32	280 ft (85 m)
Wilga 35	410 ft (125 m)

T-O to 50 ft (15 m):
Wilga 32	625 ft (190 m)
Wilga 35	770 ft (235 m)

PZL-104 Wilga 35A general-purpose aircraft with AI-14R radial engine

Landing from 50 ft (15 m):
Wilga 32	780 ft (238 m)
Wilga 35	1,070 ft (326 m)

Landing run:
Wilga 32	430 ft (131 m)
Wilga 35	690 ft (210 m)

Range with max fuel, 30 min reserve:
Wilga 32	338 nm (390 miles; 630 km)
Wilga 35	356 nm (410 miles; 660 km)

PERFORMANCE AS GLIDER TUG (at max T-O weight):
Rate of climb at S/L towing 1 glider:
Wilga 32A	785 ft (240 m)/min
Wilga 35A	770 ft (234 m)/min

Rate of climb at S/L towing 2 gliders:
Wilga 32A	670 ft (204 m)/min
Wilga 35A	750 ft (228 m)/min

Rate of climb at S/L towing 3 gliders:
Wilga 32A	435 ft (132 m)/min
Wilga 35A	395 ft (120 m)/min

Service ceiling with 1 glider:
Wilga 32A	14,800 ft (4,510 m)

Wilga 35A	13,125 ft (4,000 m)

Service ceiling with 2 gliders:
Wilga 32A	10,900 ft (3,320 m)
Wilga 35A	12,800 ft (3,900 m)

Service ceiling with 3 gliders:
Wilga 32A, 35A	8,200 ft (2,500 m)

Time to reach service ceiling:
Wilga 32A: (1 glider)	45 min
(2 gliders)	44 min
(3 gliders)	42 min
Wilga 35A: (1 glider)	37 min 12 sec
(2 gliders)	43 min 12 sec
(3 gliders)	36 min 36 sec

Range:
Wilga 32A:
(1 glider)	333 nm (383 miles; 617 km)
(2 gliders)	282 nm (324 miles; 522 km)
(3 gliders)	226 nm (259 miles; 418 km)

Wilga 35A:
(1 glider)	344 nm (395 miles; 637 km)
(2 gliders)	272 nm (313 miles; 504 km)
(3 gliders)	227 nm (260 miles; 420 km)

WSK - SWIDNIK

WYTWORNIA SPRZETU KOMUNIKACYJ-NEGO Im. ZYGMUNTA PULAWSKIEGO-SWIDNIK (Zygmunt Pulawski's Transport Equipment Manufacturing Centre, Swidnik)

HEAD OFFICE AND WORKS:
Swidnik

In 1955, when the manufacture of combat aircraft was drastically reduced in Poland, the WSK at Swidnik began licence production of the Soviet-designed Mi-1 helicopter, which was built under the designation of SM-1. A small design office was formed subsequently at the factory to work on variants and developments of the basic SM-1 design and on original projects, including the SM-4 Latka helicopter prototype, of which brief details were given in the 1967-68 *Jane's*.

Production of the SM-1 series, and the developed SM-2, has ended. Details of these types can be found in the 1966-67 *Jane's*. Production at Swidnik is now concentrated on various versions of the Soviet-designed Mil Mi-2 turbine-powered helicopter.

The WSK design office is also considering proposals for a new, lightweight general-purpose helicopter with four/five seats and an AUW of about 3,750 lb (1,700 kg). It will have a max speed of 108-135 knots (125-155 mph; 200-250 km/h), and a range of about 270 nm (310 miles; 500 km). Initially, it will have a single Isotov GTD-350 turboshaft engine of the type that powers the Mi-2, but eventually a developed version of this engine, of 500-700 shp, is likely to be used.

In September 1957, the WSK Swidnik works were named after the famous pre-war PZL designer Zygmunt Pulawski.

WSK/MIL Mi-2

The Mil Mi-2, announced in the Autumn of 1961, was designed in the USSR by the Mikhail L.Mil bureau. It retains the basic configuration of the earlier Mi-1 helicopter, but instead of the latter's single piston-engine has two Isotov turboshaft engines mounted side-by-side above the cabin.

Development of the Mi-2 prototype, usually referred to in the Soviet Union as the V-2, continued in the USSR until the helicopter had completed its initial State trials programme of flying. Then, in accordance with an agreement signed in January 1964, further development, production and marketing of the Mi-2 were assigned exclusively to the Polish aircraft industry.

Production of the Mi-2 by WSK began in 1966, and this factory has since built the helicopter in liaison-passenger, cargo, agricultural and ambu-

Agricultural version of the WSK-Swidnik (Mil) Mi-2 helicopter, with spray tanks and bars (*BIIL*)

lance versions. It has planned a considerable development programme to improve the Mi-2 during the period up to 1975. As a first stage, it is intended to replace the present metal stabiliser, tail rotor blades and main rotor blades with similar components made of plastics, to simplify production and improve performance. Stage two will involve improvement of the cabin heating and ventilation system and introduction of skid landing gear to improve performance and versatility. Stage three will see the introduction of a training version and the switch to a larger cabin on the major production versions.

TYPE: Twin-turbine general-purpose light helicopter.

ROTOR SYSTEM: Three-blade main rotor fitted with hydraulic blade vibration dampers. All-metal blades of NACA 230-13M constant section. Flapping, drag and pitch hinges on each blade. Main rotor blades and those of three-blade tail rotor each consist of an extruded duralumin spar with bonded honeycomb trailing-edge pockets. Rotors do not fold. Electric blade de-icing system for main and tail rotors. Rotor brake fitted.

ROTOR DRIVE: Main rotor shaft driven via gearbox on each engine (reduction ratio 0·246 : 1), three-stage main gearbox, intermediate gearbox and tail rotor gearbox. Main rotor/engine rpm ratio 247 : 24,000; tail rotor/engine rpm ratio 1,445 : 24,000.

FUSELAGE: Conventional semi-monocoque structure of pod-and-boom type, made up of three main assemblies: the nose (including cockpit), central section and tail boom. Construction is of sheet duralumin, bonded and spot-welded or riveted to longerons and frames. Main load-bearing joints are of steel alloy.

TAIL UNIT: Variable-incidence horizontal stabiliser controlled by collective-pitch lever.

LANDING GEAR: Non-retractable tricycle type. Twin-wheel nose unit. Single wheel on each main unit. Oleo-pneumatic shock-absorbers. Main shock-absorbers designed to cope with both normal operating loads and possible ground resonance. Main-wheel tyres, size 600 × 180, pressure 64 lb/sq in (4·5 kg/cm²). Nose-wheel tyres, size 300 × 125, pressure 50 lb/sq in (3·5 kg/cm²). Pneumatic brakes on main wheels.

POWER PLANT: Two 437 shp Isotov GTD-350 turboshaft engines, mounted side-by-side above cabin. Fuel in single flexible tank, capacity 131 Imp gallons (600 litres) under cabin floor. Provision for carrying a 52·5 Imp gallon (238 litre) external tank on each side of cabin. Refuelling point in starboard side of fuselage. Oil capacity 5·4 Imp gallons (25 litres).

ACCOMMODATION: Normal accommodation for one pilot on flight deck and six to eight passengers in air-conditioned cabin, there being back-

L

to-back bench seats for three persons each, with optional extra starboard side seat at the front and another at the rear. All seats are removable for carrying up to 1,543 lb (700 kg) of internal freight. Access to cabin via forward-hinged doors on starboard side at front of cabin and aft on port side. Ambulance version has accommodation for four stretchers and a medical attendant. Side-by-side seats and dual controls can be installed for pilot training. Cabin heating and ventilation standard.

OPERATIONAL EQUIPMENT: As an agricultural aircraft, the Mi-2 carries a hopper on each side of the fuselage (total capacity 220 Imp gallons = 1,000 litres) and either two parallel spraybars to the rear of the cabin or a distributor for dry chemicals under each hopper. Swath width covered by the spraying version is 130-150 ft (40-45 m). As a search and rescue aircraft, an electric hoist, capacity 265 lb (120 kg), is fitted. In the freight role an under-fuselage hook can be fitted for suspended loads of up to 1,765 lb (800 kg).

SYSTEMS: Cabin heating system by engine-bleed air; heat exchangers also provide warm air for ventilation system during cold weather. Hydraulic system, pressure 855-1,140 lb/sq in (60-80 kg/cm²), for cyclic and collective pitch control boosters. Pneumatic system, pressure 710 lb/sq in (50 kg/cm²), for main-wheel brakes. Electrical system includes two batteries and two generators.

ELECTRONICS AND EQUIPMENT: Standard equipment includes two radio transceivers and blind-flying panel.

DIMENSIONS, EXTERNAL:
- Diameter of main rotor: 47 ft 6¾ in (14·50 m)
- Main rotor blade chord (constant, each): 1 ft 3¾ in (0·40 m)
- Diameter of tail rotor: 8 ft 10¼ in (2·70 m)
- Length overall, rotors turning: 57 ft 2 in (17·42 m)
- Length of fuselage: 37 ft 4¾ in (11·40 m)
- Height to top of rotor hub: 12 ft 3½ in (3·75 m)
- Wheel track: 10 ft 0 in (3·05 m)
- Wheelbase: 8 ft 7½ in (2·63 m)
- Passenger door (port, rear):
  - Height: 3 ft 5¾ in (1·065 m)
  - Width: 3 ft 8 in (1·115 m)
- Passenger door (stbd, front):
  - Height: 3 ft 7¾ in (1·11 m)
  - Width: 2 ft 5½ in (0·75 m)

DIMENSIONS, INTERNAL:
- Cabin:
  - Length, including flight deck: 13 ft 4¼ in (4·07 m)
  - Length, excluding flight deck: 7 ft 5½ in (2·27 m)
  - Mean width: 3 ft 11¼ in (1·20 m)
  - Mean height: 4 ft 7 in (1·40 m)

AREAS:
- Main rotor blades (each): 25·83 sq ft (2·40 m²)
- Tail rotor blades (each): 2·37 sq ft (0·22 m²)
- Main rotor disc: 1,776 sq ft (165·0 m²)
- Tail rotor disc: 61·35 sq ft (5·7 m²)
- Horizontal stabiliser: 7·53 sq ft (0·7 m²)

WEIGHTS AND LOADINGS:
- Basic operating weight, empty: 5,180 lb (2,350 kg)
- Max payload, excluding pilot: 1,765 lb (800 kg)
- Max T-O weight (normal): 7,826 lb (3,550 kg)
- Max T-O weight (overload): 8,157 lb (3,700 kg)
- Max disc loading: 4·3 lb/sq ft (21·0 kg/m²)
- Max power loading: 8·82 lb/hp (4·0 kg/hp)

PERFORMANCE (at max normal T-O weight):
- Max level speed at 1,640 ft (500 m): 113 knots (130 mph; 210 km/h)
- Max cruising speed at 1,640 ft (500 m): 108 knots (124 mph; 200 km/h)
- Econ cruising speed for max range at 1,640 ft (500 m): 102 knots (118 mph; 190 km/h)
- Econ cruising speed for max endurance at 1,640 ft (500 m): 54 knots (62 mph; 100 km/h)
- Max rate of climb at S/L: 885 ft (270 m)/min
- Service ceiling: 13,755 ft (4,200 m)
- Hovering ceiling in ground effect: 6,550 ft (2,000 m)
- Hovering ceiling out of ground effect: 3,275 ft (1,000 m)
- Minimum landing area: 100 × 100 ft (30 × 30 m)
- Range at 1,640 ft (500 m) with max fuel, 30 min reserve: 313 nm (360 miles; 580 km)
- Range at 1,640 ft (500 m) with max payload, 5% fuel reserve: 91 nm (105 miles; 170 km)

SOBKOW

STANISLAW SOBKOW

Mr Stanislaw Sobkow of Warsaw has designed and constructed a two-seat amateur-built light helicopter. Earlier, he was responsible for a single-seat light aircraft known as the WS-3 Czajka (Lapwing) which was built and flown in 1956.

WS-4 SWIERSZCZ (CRICKET)

Design of the WS-4 was started in 1959 and construction in 1960. Its ground testing began in 1968.

TYPE: Two-seat light helicopter.

ROTOR SYSTEM: Two-blade contra-rotating co-axial rotor system. Each blade has a wooden leading-edge and duralumin aft ribs, with fabric skin. Mass balance on each blade, on an outrigger. Blade section NACA 23012. Twist 6°. Conventional cyclic-pitch and collective-pitch control.

ROTOR DRIVE: Mechanical drive through two-stage gearbox. Main rotor/engine rpm ratio 1 : 12·7.

FUSELAGE: In two sections: cabin and tail-boom. Forward section is a welded steel-tube structure, carrying the engine and Plexiglas cabin. Rear section is also a steel-tube structure, triangular in cross-section.

TAIL SURFACES: Small synchronized elevator at rear end of fuselage responds to fore and aft movement of the cyclic-pitch control. Rudder actuated by the pilot.

LANDING GEAR: Tubular skid-type, with small ground handling wheels. Skids fitted with rubber-cord shock-absorbers.

POWER PLANT: One 75 hp Praga D four-cylinder horizontally-opposed fan-cooled engine, mounted horizontally. Fuel tank of 8·8 Imp gallons (40 litres) capacity.

ACCOMMODATION: Two individual seats side-by-side in Plexiglas cabin. Dual controls.

DIMENSIONS, EXTERNAL:
- Diameter of main rotors: 26 ft 3 in (8·0 m)
- Main rotor blade chord (constant, each): 9 in (0·23 m)
- Length of fuselage: 14 ft 1 in (4·3 m)
- Width over skids: 3 ft 7 in (1·1 m)
- Height to top of rotor hub: 9 ft 0 in (2·74 m)

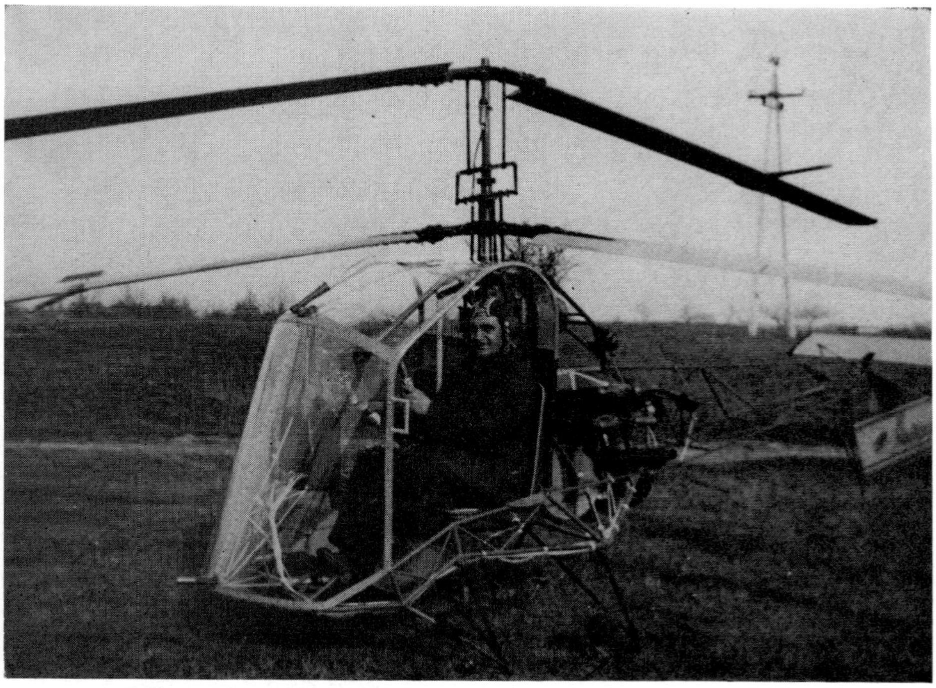

Sobkow WS-4 Swierszcz two-seat light helicopter (75 hp Praga D engine)

AREAS:
- Main rotor blades (each): 8·9 sq ft (0·83 m²)
- Main rotor disc (each): 538 sq ft (50 m²)

WEIGHTS AND LOADINGS:
- Weight empty: 528 lb (240 kg)
- Max T-O weight: 990 lb (450 kg)
- Max disc loading: 0·92 lb/sq ft (4·5 kg/m²)
- Max power loading: 13·2 lb/hp (6 kg/hp)

PERFORMANCE (at max T-O weight):
- Max level speed at S/L: 65 knots (75 mph; 120 km/h)
- Econ cruising speed: 49 knots (56 mph; 90 km/h)
- Max rate of climb at S/L: 415 ft (126 m)/min
- Service ceiling: 7,500 ft (2,300 m)
- Range with max fuel: 189 nm (218 miles; 350 km)

PORTUGAL

OGMA

OFICINAS GERAIS DE MATERIAL AERONÁUTICO (GENERAL AERONAUTICAL MATERIAL WORKSHOPS)

WORKS:
Alverca do Ribatejo

DIRECTOR:
Brigadier Engineer Alberto Fernandes

ASSISTANT DIRECTOR:
Colonel Engineer Rui do Carmo da Conceição Espadinha

OGMA was first organised in 1918 and has been in continuous operation since then. It is a department of the Secretary of State for Aeronautics and is charged with the responsibility of maintaining and repairing all flying equipment, ground equipment, communications and radar equipment of the Portuguese Air Force. It also undertakes the manufacture of training aircraft and spare parts.

OGMA has a total floor space of 1,031,722 sq ft (95,847 m²), to which are being added new installations totalling 116,117 sq ft (10,706 m²). It has a personnel strength of 3,700.

OGMA is currently engaged on considerable conversion and re-manufacturing work, and performs IRAN inspection of F-86F, Fiat G91, T-33, T-37C, C-45, C-54, P-2E, Noratlas, Broussard, Dornier Do 27 and DC-6 aircraft and Alouette III helicopters.

Sizeable installations have been established for the repair of F-104G Starfighter aircraft and the overhaul of J79 turbojet engines. As a preliminary step, a new training centre was built and equipped with a complete F-104G mock-up.

In addition to major overhaul and IRAN work on aircraft, aero-engines and components for the Portuguese Air Force, OGMA performs maintenance work on Noratlas transport aircraft for the Federal German Air Force. Under a contract signed in 1959, it also undertakes periodic inspection, minimum essential depot level maintenance, IRAN, rehabilitation, fuel tank deseal/reseal work on C-47 and C-54 aircraft and refurbishing and painting of C-118, T-29, C-131 and T-39 aircraft of the USAF in the European area.

OGMA is established as an industrial organisation operating on private industry principles. Initial funds were provided for self-contained administration, but the Air Force and other contractors are charged for work done.

RHODESIA

RAABA
RHODESIAN AMATEUR AIRCRAFT BUILDERS' ASSOCIATION
ADDRESS: Salisbury
CHAIRMAN: J. Battershill

This association was formed in 1969 by pilots John Battershill and Douglas Elliot. Its first manufacturing venture was the completion of a Rhodesian prototype of the British Taylor Titch light aircraft, full details of which can be found under the "Taylor" heading in the UK section of this edition. Construction was undertaken by Mr Victor Ginn, a Salisbury aircraft engineer, and the aircraft flew for the first time early in 1970. Original plans to produce the Titch commercially in Rhodesia have now been abandoned.

ROMANIA

IRMA
INTREPRINDEREA DE REPARAT MATERIAL AERONAUTIC
WORKS:
Bucharest (Baneasa Airport) and Brasov

Before World War II the principal aircraft and aero-engine manufacturing organisation in Romania was the Regia Autonoma Industria Aeronautica Romana, a state establishment controlled by the Ministers of War and Marine. Apart from building aircraft of its own design, under the initials IAR, it also manufactured aircraft and engines under licence.

After the war the IAR factory at Brasov was de-militarised by the Soviet occupation authorities; later, a Russo-Romanian commercial agreement provided for conversion of the establishment into a general engineering works under joint Russo-Romanian ownership, with the name Sovromtractor. Russian interests were subsequently withdrawn but this factory continues as a general engineering concern, the aviation spares and repairs plant at Brasov now being known as URMV-3.

In 1968 it was announced that the Britten-Norman BN-2 Islander (see UK section) was to be manufactured under licence in Romania, and the aircraft is now in production by IRMA.

The initial agreement with IRMA was for the production of 215 Islanders, and the first Romanian-built example flew for the first time at Baneasa Airport, Bucharest, on 4 August 1969. Rate of production in 1970 was five Islanders per month, and completion of the initial quantity is scheduled for 1974.

Several types of light aircraft have been developed at Brasov since the war. The latest of these are the IAR-821, IAR-822 and IS-23, described below.

IAR-821 and IAR-822
This single-seat light agricultural and utility monoplane was designed by Ing Radu Manicatide, chief of the aircraft design bureau of IRMA. The prototype was flown for the first time in 1967, by "Master of Sport" Constantin Manolaches, a well-known Romanian aerobatic pilot.

Few constructional details of the IAR-821 are available, but its general appearance is shown in the adjacent illustrations. The basic structure is of metal tube, with fabric covering. Layout is conventional, with a low wing of constant chord, a strut-braced tailplane and non-retractable tailwheel landing gear. The power plant comprises a 300 hp Ivchenko AI-14RF nine-cylinder radial air-cooled engine, driving a two-blade controllable-pitch propeller of 8 ft 10¼ in (2·7 m) diameter.

The pilot sits in an enclosed cockpit, fitted with a steel-tube overturn structure and jettisonable upward-hinged glazed side panels. For agricultural duties, a chemical hopper is installed immediately forward of the cockpit, with a capacity of 176 Imp gallons (800 litres) or 1,323 lb (600 kg).

A tandem two-seat version for training and glider-towing duties, first flown in 1968, is known as the **IAR-821B**. In 1969, the prototype of the **IAR-822** made its first flight. This is a single-seat agricultural aircraft, similar to the IAR-821 but powered by a 290 hp Lycoming IO-540-G1D5 engine; it is described in the Addenda.

DIMENSIONS, EXTERNAL (IAR-821, IAR-821B and IAR-822):
Wing span (all)   42 ft 0 in (12·80 m)
Length overall:
821, 821B   30 ft 2 in (9·20 m)
822   30 ft 10 in (9·40 m)
Height overall (all)   9 ft 2¼ in (2·80 m)
AREA (IAR-821, IAR-821B and IAR-822):
Wings, gross   280 sq ft (26·0 m²)
WEIGHTS:
Weight empty:
821 (agricultural)   2,380 lb (1,080 kg)
821B   2,270 lb (1,030 kg)
Max T-O weight:
821 (agricultural)   4,189 lb (1,900 kg)
821B   2,535 lb (1,150 kg)
PERFORMANCE (at max T-O weight):
Max level speed at S/L:
821 (agricultural)
                                92 knots (106 mph; 170 km/h)
821B   119 knots (137 mph; 220 km/h)

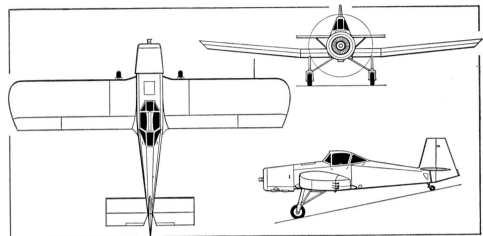

Three-view drawing and photograph (retouched) of the IAR-821

Max cruising speed at 5,000 ft (1,500 m):
821 (agricultural)
                                97 knots (112 mph; 180 km/h)
Econ cruising speed:
821 (agricultural)
                                86 knots (99 mph; 160 km/h)
821B   110 knots (127 mph; 204 km/h)
Min flying speed:
821 (agricultural)
                                39-41 knots (45-47 mph; 72-76 km/h)
Service ceiling:
821 (agricultural)   18,372 ft (5,600 m)
821B   21,325 ft (6,500 m)
T-O run:
821B   295 ft (90 m)
Range at econ cruising speed:
821 (agricultural)
                                215 nm (248 miles; 400 km)
821B   350 nm (403 miles; 650 km)

Endurance:
821 (agricultural)   2 hr 30 min
821B   3 hr 30 min

IS-23
First flown in Romania in prototype form in 1967, the IS-23 is an experimental light STOL utility aircraft suitable for ambulance, agricultural, glider-towing and other duties. It was designed to an officially-issued specification, by Ing Josif Silimon, who is best known as a designer of medium- and high-performance sailplanes. An agricultural version, designated IS-23A, has been reported.

TYPE: Light STOL utility aircraft.

WINGS: Cantilever high-wing monoplane, with rectangular centre-section and tapered outer

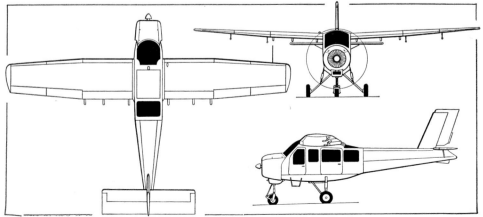

Three-view drawing of IS-23 STOL utility aircraft

panels. Marked dihedral from roots. Extensive high-lift devices include two-section aileron and slotted Fowler-type flap on each wing. All-metal construction.

FUSELAGE: All-metal, pod and boom type.

TAIL UNIT: All-metal structure, with braced tailplane. Sweptback vertical surfaces. Adjustable tab on rudder.

LANDING GEAR: Non-retractable tricycle type, with steerable nose unit. Telescopic shock-absorber on each main unit. Wheels may be replaced by floats or skis.

POWER PLANT: One 300 hp Ivchenko AI-14RF nine-cylinder radial air-cooled engine. Prototype has a two-blade propeller, but production version will have a three-blade propeller, diameter 9 ft 6¼ in (2·90 m). All fuel in wing tanks, capacity 22 Imp gallons (100 litres).

ACCOMMODATION: Enclosed cabin, accommodating up to five persons, or a pilot, two stretcher patients and a medical attendant. Passenger seats may be removed for cargo carrying. Forward-hinged door on each side at front. Wide forward-hinged cargo door on port side at rear of cabin.

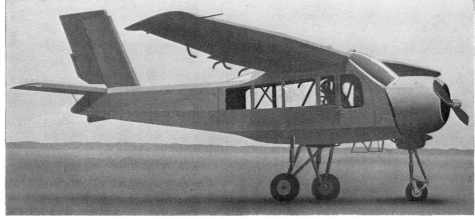

Photograph (retouched) of the IS-23 utility aircraft

DIMENSIONS, EXTERNAL:
Wing span	40 ft 8¼ in (12·40 m)
Length overall	29 ft 10¼ in (9·10 m)
Height overall	11 ft 9¾ in (3·60 m)

WEIGHTS:
Weight empty	2,976 lb (1,350 kg)
Max T-O weight	4,630 lb (2,100 kg)

PERFORMANCE:
Max level speed at S/L
110 knots (127 mph; 205 km/h)
Max cruising speed at 5,000 ft (1,500 m)
97 knots (112 mph; 180 km/h)
Econ cruising speed
83 knots (96 mph; 155 km/h)

Rate of climb at S/L at max T-O weight
787 ft (240 m)/min
Service ceiling, at AUW of 4,520 lb (2,050 kg)
15,750 ft (4,800 m)
T-O run 395-610 ft (120-185 m)
Landing run 197-265 ft (60-80 m)

SOUTH AFRICA

AFIC
AFIC (PTY) LTD

HEAD OFFICE:
PO Box 8816, Johannesburg

WORKS:
"L" Hangar, c/o Atlas Aircraft Corporation of South Africa, Kempton Park, Transvaal

DIRECTORS:
P. Henman-Laufer
A. G. Mechin
D. P. Hewartson (Sales Manager)

PUBLIC RELATIONS MANAGER:
H. Hodgson

This company was formed in 1967 to produce a modified version of the Italian Partenavia P.64B Oscar-B, designated RSA 200, of which details follow. Plans are also in hand to introduce, in 1971, the twin-engined P.68.

AFIC RSA 200 FALCON

The all-metal RSA 200 was developed in 1966-67 by Partenavia Costruzioni Aeronautiche SpA of Italy from their original partly-fabric-covered P.64 Oscar four-seat light aircraft under a contract from AFIC. Its Italian counterpart is the P.64B Oscar-B, from which it differs mainly in interior design, instrument layout and internal equipment.

AFIC (Pty) Ltd has selling rights for the aircraft in all countries of the world except Italy, the German Federal Republic and Switzerland.

A prototype of the RSA 200 (ZS-FCH) was flown in South Africa late in 1967, and the first South African assembled RSA 200 (ZS-FGA) flew early in 1968. Certification by the South African Dept of Civil Aviation was granted early in 1968.

With detail exceptions, as noted below, the standard RSA 200 utilises the same basic airframe and 180 hp Lycoming engine as the P.64B Oscar-B, and the first South African aircraft were assembled from Italian-built components. A version with 200 hp fuel-injection engine is also available.

By early May 1969, a total of 40 RSA 200's had been ordered by customers in South and South-West Africa and Zambia, and a demonstration model has since been ordered for delivery to the UK. Twenty-two RSA 200's had been completed by the end of 1969. It was planned to increase output to 25 aircraft per year in 1970. Interior and other improvements have been made during the past year, and the aircraft has now been named Falcon.

The description of the P.64B Oscar-B, given under the Partenavia heading in the Italian section of this edition, applies also to the RSA 200 with 180 hp engine, except in the following respects:

LANDING GEAR: Non-retractable heavy-duty tricycle type with directly-steerable nose-wheel. Oleo-helical spring shock-absorber, with hydraulic damper, on nose unit; cantilever steel leaf spring main legs. Goodyear wheels and tyres, nose-wheel size 5·00 × 5—6-ply, pressure 26

AFIC RSA 200 Falcon licence-built version of the Partenavia P.64B Oscar-B light aircraft

lb/sq in (1·83 kg/cm²), main wheels size 6·00 × 6—6-ply, pressure 30 lb/sq in (2·11 kg/cm²). Cleveland 30-18 hydraulic disc brakes on main units, operated by hand brake (toe brake optional). Streamlined fairings on all three wheels optional.

POWER PLANT: One 180 hp Lycoming O-320-A1A engine (as in P.64B), driving a Hartzell HC-C2YK-1A two-blade propeller, diameter 6 ft 2 in (1·88 m). Optionally, one 200 hp Lycoming IO-360-A1A fuel-injection engine. Fuel in two main tanks in wings, with total capacity of 40 Imp gallons (181 litres). Oil capacity 2 Imp gallons (9 litres).

ACCOMMODATION: Enclosed tubular steel-framed cabin, seating four persons in two adjustable side-by-side front seats (with arm rests) and rear bench seat. Dual controls optional. Space for 200 lb (90 kg) of baggage when only two passengers are carried.

SYSTEMS: Hydraulic system for brakes only. Electrical system has 12V 35Ah battery with transistorised voltage regulator, battery charging diode, ammeter and 35A generator.

ELECTRONICS: Skycrafter, King KY 90A, King KX-160-1, King KX 150B VHF/VOR, Narco MK III or Narco MK 12 VHF/VOR VHF radio; PaceAire 5-Channel, Sunaire T-5-DA (with CU 500 A fixed antenna tuning unit) or Pancom DX 10-DA (with electric reel) HF radio; Polaris, King KR 80 A or Bendix T-12-C ADF; Positive-Flite Wings Leveller autopilot with electric turn co-ordinator. Blind-flying instrumentation standard.

DIMENSIONS, EXTERNAL:
Wheelbase	7 ft 0 in (2·13 m)
Passenger doors (each):	
Height	3 ft 4 in (1·02 m)
Width	2 ft 3 in (0·69 m)
Height to sill	2 ft 5 in (0·74 m)
Baggage door (stbd, rear):	
Height	1 ft 5 in (0·43 m)
Width	2 ft 2 in (0·66 m)
Height to sill	2 ft 9 in (0·84 m)

DIMENSIONS, INTERNAL:
Cabin: Length	6 ft 0 in (1·83 m)
Max width	3 ft 7 in (1·09 m)
Max height	3 ft 10 in (1·17 m)
Floor area	20 sq ft (1·86 m²)
Volume	80 cu ft (2·27 m³)
Baggage compartment:	
Volume	14 cu ft (0·40 m³)

WEIGHTS:
Weight empty	1,500 lb (680 kg)
Max T-O weight	2,546 lb (1,155 kg)
Max landing weight	2,425 lb (1,100 kg)

PERFORMANCE (at max T-O weight):
Max level speed at S/L
146 knots (168 mph; 270 km/h)
Max permissible diving speed
169 knots (195 mph; 313·5 km/h)
Max cruising speed (75% power) at 7,000 ft (2,150 m) 136 knots (157 mph; 253 km/h)
Econ cruising speed (65% power) at 11,000 ft (3,300 m) 126 knots (145 mph; 233 km/h)
Stalling speed, flaps up
50 knots (57 mph; 92 km/h)
Stalling speed, flaps down
43 knots (49 mph; 79 km/h)
T-O run 750 ft (229 m)
T-O to 50 ft (15 m) 1,600 ft (488 m)
Landing from 50 ft (15 m) 1,550 ft (472 m)
Landing run 656 ft (200 m)
Max range, no reserves (75% power)
645 nm (746 miles; 1,200 km)

ALLEN

ROY ALLEN

ADDRESS:
Cape Province

ALLEN SAFARI

Mr Roy Allen, an engineer, has designed a small twin-engined utility transport aircraft suitable for production in South Africa, where a local group is reported to be interested in financing the project. Known as the Safari, it is an all-metal high-wing "bush" transport, with a rectangular-section fuselage of 530 cu ft (15 m³) capacity. Access to the hold is provided by a large loading door on the port side of the fuselage, below the wing trailing-edge, or by a rear-loading ramp for vehicles or larger items of freight. It has a non-retractable tricycle landing gear, with oleo-pneumatic shock-absorption, and low-pressure tyres for rough-field operation. Probable power plant would be two 450 hp Pratt & Whitney R-985 Wasp nine-cylinder radial air-cooled engines, ample stocks of which are available in South Africa. Designed payload is 15 passengers or 4,000 lb (1,814 kg) of freight.

DIMENSIONS, EXTERNAL:

Wing span	37 ft 0¾ in (11·30 m)
Length overall	37 ft 0¾ in (11·30 m)
Height overall	16 ft 4¾ in (5·00 m)

PERFORMANCE (estimated, at max T-O weight):

Cruising speed 148 knots (170 mph; 275 km/h)	
Service ceiling	10,000 ft (3,050 m)
T-O to 50 ft (15 m)	1,200 ft (365 m)
Max range	521 nm (600 miles; 965 km)

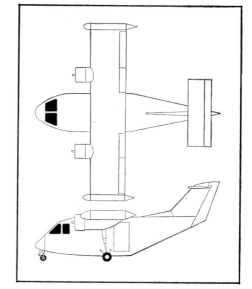

The projected Allen Safari "bush" transport

ATLAS

ATLAS AIRCRAFT CORPORATION OF SOUTH AFRICA (PTY) LIMITED

HEAD OFFICE AND WORKS:
PO Box 11, Atlas Road, Kempton Park, Transvaal

DIRECTORS:
V. R. Verster (Chairman)
Maj Gen G. T. Moll (alternate Chairman)
C. F. Hafele
A. W. Schumann (alternate)
N. Bestbier (Acting Managing Director)
D. G. Malan
H. R. Malan
Dr G. S. J. Kuschke
H. H. L. Abrahamse
L. W. Dekker
A. E. G. Trollip
Dr W. J. de Villiers
J. E. K. Tucker
Prof M. A. du Toit Meyer

MARKETING MANAGER:
Brig J. W. Willers

This company was founded in January 1965 by Bonuscor South Africa in collaboration with the Industrial Development Corporation, to establish an aircraft industry in South Africa. In 1969 the entire share capital of Atlas was purchased by the Armaments Development and Production Corporation of South Africa Ltd. As a result of this change of ownership, all activities in respect of civil aircraft maintenance and overhaul have been terminated.

Impala (Aermacchi M.B.326) jet trainer of the South African Air Force

The present programme entails licence construction of the Aermacchi M.B.326 jet trainer. In addition, Atlas undertakes the maintenance and overhaul of South African Air Force aircraft. Manufacturing and servicing operations began in the company's new works at Jan Smuts International Airport early in 1967.

ATLAS IMPALA

"Impala" is the name given to the South African version of the Aermacchi M.B.326M currently being produced for delivery to the SAAF. Beginning with aircraft assembled from imported components, the proportion of locally-produced components is being increased rapidly, and about 80 per cent of each aircraft will eventually be of South African manufacture. Full structural and performance details of the M.B. 326M can be found in the Italian section of this edition.

GRAHAM/van NIEKIRK

ADDRESS:
Jankempdorp

Mr H. C. Graham and Mr J. van Niekirk have designed and built a small single-seat autogyro (ZS-UDL), all known details of which are given below.

TYPE: Single-seat autogyro.

ROTOR SYSTEM: Two-blade semi-rigid main rotor, attached to hub by a series of flat plates. Blades are of all-metal construction, with leading-edge spars of extruded aluminium alloy to which the sheet-alloy trailing-edges are bonded and riveted. Spars are rebated to thickness of trailing-edge sheets to give smooth surface finish. Blade section NACA 8 H 12 series. Trim-tab in each blade, near tip.

ROTOR CONTROL AND DRIVE: Rotor head is controlled by stick movement and is mounted on a universal joint assembly at the forked upper end of the rotor mast. Control rods linking stick to head are moved in unison for fore-and-aft control or differentially for lateral control. Rotor spin-up is provided via flexible drive from the propeller boss and is disengaged before take-off.

TAIL UNIT: Steerable rudder only, mounted at rear end of cruciform chassis.

LANDING GEAR: Non-retractable tricycle type, with steerable spring-suspension nose-wheel. Main wheels are taken from a Piper Cub.

POWER PLANT: One 72 hp McCulloch engine, mounted on steel-tube framework aft of pilot and driving a two-blade pusher propeller. Fuel in single gravity tank mounted above the engine.

DIMENSIONS, EXTERNAL:

Rotor diameter	approx 21 ft 0 in (6·40 m)
Rotor blade chord (constant)	7 in (0·18 m)

REED/UNIVERSITY OF NATAL

ADDRESS:
Dept of Mechanical Engineering, King George V Avenue, Durban, Natal Province

HEAD OF DEPARTMENT:
Prof Maitland Reed

Prof Maitland Reed, with Capt J. H. Rautenbach as consultant on flight matters, and assisted by seven final-year students, began in 1965 the design of an aerobatic biplane named the Rooivalk, intended specifically for inverted-flight manoeuvres.

Construction of the prototype, which started in 1968, has been a University of Natal project, and has been conducted by University technicians with materials and money provided by the people of Durban. The aircraft is to be controlled by the Durban Aerobatic Group, the South African aerobatic trust formed for the purpose.

REED 1A ROOIVALK (KESTREL)

The Rooivalk, which has similar overall dimensions to the Bücker Jungmann biplane, has low wing and power loadings, and a deep fuselage for knife-edge stability. Provision is made for a second cockpit in prototype, so that the aircraft can be used for training.

The aircraft will be used for training South African pilots in aerobatics and for national and international competitions.

The Rooivalk prototype (ZS-UDU) made its first flight on 24 May 1970, and flight testing is continuing during 1970.

TYPE: Single-seat aerobatic or two-seat training biplane.

WINGS: Strut-braced biplane. Wing section NACA 0012 (symmetrical). Dihedral 2° 30′ on upper wings, 4° 30′ on lower wings. Incidence 4°. Outer wing sections, which have 10° sweepback, are braced by parallel interplane struts. Wings have Sitka spruce main spars, with aluminium alloy ribs and leading-edges and 4130 steel-tube drag struts; they are braced by drag wires and are fabric-covered. Aluminium alloy ailerons on upper and lower wings. Fixed metal balance tab on each upper aileron. Wings stressed to 13·5 g. All controls statically and dynamically balanced.

FUSELAGE: Welded chrome-molybdenum steel-tube (4130) safe-life structure, stressed to 13·5 g, covered with Dacron fabric.

TAIL UNIT: Single fin and rudder, with cantilever adjustable-incidence tailplane. Welded steel-tube structure, fabric-covered. Fixed tabs on rudder and each elevator.

LANDING GEAR: Non-retractable tail-wheel type. Cantilever spring steel main legs, with glass-fibre dampers. Goodyear wheels and tyres;

main wheels Type IIIC (6 ply), size 5·00 × 5, self-centering tailwheel size 8·00. No wheel brakes.

POWER PLANT: One 210 hp Continental IO-360-C six-cylinder horizontally-opposed air-cooled engine with fuel injection, driving a Hartzell HC-A2VF-3/V7636D two-blade constant-speed reversible-pitch propeller of 6 ft 4 in (1·93 m) diameter. Fuel in glass-fibre tank in fuselage with total capacity of 13 Imp gallons (59 litres). Refuelling point in engine cowling. Fuel system modified to permit sustained inverted flying.

ACCOMMODATION: Single open cockpit in aerobatic version, with Perspex observation panel in floor. Provision for installing a second cockpit forward of this when required for training role.

ELECTRONICS AND EQUIPMENT: Lightweight VHF radio. Blind-flying instrumentation not fitted.

DIMENSIONS, EXTERNAL:
Wing span   25 ft 0 in (7·62 m)
Wing chord (upper and lower, constant)
                             3 ft 10 in (1·17 m)
Wing aspect ratio (upper and lower)   6·53
Length overall   22 ft 0 in (6·71 m)
Length of fuselage   19 ft 8 in (5·99 m)
Height overall   7 ft 9 in (2·36 m)
Tailplane span   10 ft 0 in (3·05 m)
Wheel track   6 ft 2 in (1·88 m)
Wheelbase   17 ft 0 in (5·18 m)

AREAS:
Wings, gross   182 sq ft (16·91 m²)
Ailerons (total)   20·00 sq ft (1·86 m²)
Fin   3·20 sq ft (0·30 m²)

WEIGHTS AND LOADINGS:
Weight empty (both versions)   980 lb (444 kg)
Max T-O weight (single-seat)   1,300 lb (590 kg)
Max T-O weight (two-seat)   1,500 lb (680 kg)
Max wing loading (single-seat)
                             7·14 lb/sq ft (34·8 kg/m²)
Max wing loading (two-seat)
                             8·20 lb/sq ft (40·0 kg/m²)

Rooivalk single/two-seat aerobatic biplane

Max power loading (single-seat)
                             6·19 lb/hp (2·81 kg/hp)
Max power loading (two-seat)
                             7·14 lb/hp (3·24 kg/hp)

PERFORMANCE (estimated at max T-O weight, two-seat):
Max level speed at S/L
                             108 knots (124 mph; 200 km/h)

Stalling speed   45 knots (51 mph; 83 km/h)
Rate of climb at S/L   2,200 ft (671 m)/min
Service ceiling   25,000 ft (7,620 m)
T-O run   150 ft (46 m)
T-O to 50 ft (15 m)   350 ft (107 m)
Landing from 50 ft (15 m)   730 ft (223 m)
Landing run   450 ft (137 m)
Range with max fuel, 1 Imp gallon (4·5 litres)
reserve   130 nm (150 miles; 241 km)

ROTORCRAFT

ROTORCRAFT S A (Pty) LTD

ADDRESS:
PO Box 5095, Cape Town

DIRECTORS:
C. Kramer
J. Solomon

TECHNICAL CONSULTANT: G. A. Ford

Rotorcraft SA was registered in February 1963 to develop and produce the Minicopter single-seat ultra-light autogyro.

ROTORCRAFT MINICOPTER

Two versions of the Minicopter were made available as follows:

Minicopter Mk 1. Basic single-seat model with an open-sided cabin made of glass-fibre and Perspex.

Minicopter Mk 1A. Similar to Mk 1 but without canopy.

Following the production and sale of a number of aircraft of this type in South Africa, the company investigated the possibility of licence manufacture of the basic single-seat model in Europe and the USA. In addition, plans and associated technical data were prepared for the purpose of manufacturing the Minicopter in kit form for assembly by amateurs.

A full description and illustration of the Minicopter appeared in the 1969-70 edition of Jane's.

SPAIN

AERO-DIFUSIÓN

AERO-DIFUSIÓN, SL

HEAD OFFICE AND WORKS:
Aerodromo de la Albericia, Apartado 198, Santander

PRESIDENT: Fernando de Caralt
GENERAL MANAGER: Jaime de Caralt

After building experimentally a French-designed Jodel D.112 lightplane in 1954, this company was registered on 6 May 1955, to manufacture, overhaul and repair aircraft.

Its first products were licence-built versions of the Jodel D.112, of which it sold 64 under the name Popuplane. Details of these aircraft can be found in the 1963-64 Jane's.

In 1962, the company was taken over by a new management and subsequently developed a fully-approved and much-refined new light aircraft, named the Jodel D.1190.S Compostela, of which details follow.

AERO-DIFUSIÓN JODEL D.1190.S COMPOSTELA

This is a development of the standard French-designed Jodel D.119, developed in collaboration with the original designer, M Delemontez, to conform with US CAR Pt 3 requirements. It received French certification on 12 February 1963, FAA certification on 20 June 1963, Spanish certification on 6 November 1963, and German certification on 30 July 1965.

TYPE: Two-seat light cabin monoplane.

WINGS: Cantilever low-wing monoplane. Wing section NACA 23013·5. Dihedral 12° on outer wing panels only. Incidence 4° 20′ at root. All-wood structure, with single one-piece box-spar, fabric-covered. Fabric-covered wooden ailerons. No flaps or tabs.

FUSELAGE: All-wood structure with plywood skin.

TAIL UNIT: Cantilever wood structure with dorsal fin but no primary fin. Tailplane plywood-covered. Rudder and elevators fabric-covered. Trim-tab in elevators.

Aero-Difusión Jodel D.1190.S Compostela (90 hp Continental C90-14F engine)

LANDING GEAR: Non-retractable tail-wheel type. Main wheels size 420 × 150 on cantilever legs with Jodel rubber shock-absorption. Tyre pressure 21·5 lb/sq in (1·5 kg/cm²). Jodel brakes. Open-sided wheel fairings standard.

POWER PLANT: One 90 hp Rolls-Royce/Continental C90-14F four-cylinder horizontally-opposed air-cooled engine driving an EVRA two-blade fixed-pitch wooden propeller. Glass-fibre cowling. Fuel tank aft of cabin, capacity 24 Imp gallons (110 litres). Refuelling point on port side of fuselage aft of windows.

ACCOMMODATION: Two seats side-by-side in enclosed cabin, with dual controls. Forward-hinged door on each side. Heating and ventilation standard. Baggage space aft of seat.

ELECTRONICS AND EQUIPMENT: Optional items include King KX-150-B VHF/VOR, King KR-80 ADF, and blind-flying instrumentation.

DIMENSIONS, EXTERNAL:
Wing span   26 ft 11 in (8·20 m)
Wing chord (centre-section, constant)
                            5 ft 7 in (1·70 m)
Wing chord at tip   2 ft 11½ in (0·90 m)
Wing aspect ratio   5·3
Length overall   20 ft 6½ in (6·26 m)
Height over tail   6 ft 9 in (2·05 m)
Tailplane span   8 ft 10¼ in (2·70 m)
Wheel track   5 ft 10¾ in (1·80 m)
Wheelbase   15 ft 1 in (4·60 m)
Doors (each):
Height   3 ft 3¼ in (1·00 m)
Width   2 ft 1½ in (0·65 m)

DIMENSIONS, INTERNAL:

Cabin: Length	6 ft 0¾ in (1·85 m)
Max width	3 ft 4 in (1·02 m)
Max height	3 ft 7¼ in (1·10 m)
Baggage space	8·8 cu ft (0·25 m³)

AREAS:

Wings, gross	136·7 sq ft (12·70 m²)
Ailerons (total)	11·63 sq ft (1·08 m²)
Rudder	7·53 sq ft (0·70 m²)
Tailplane	16·15 sq ft (1·50 m²)
Elevators, including tab	15·61 sq ft (1·45 m²)

WEIGHTS AND LOADINGS:

Weight empty, equipped	882 lb (400 kg)
Max T-O and landing weight:	
Normal category	1,455 lb (660 kg)
Utility category	1,190 lb (540 kg)
Max wing loading	10·65 lb/sq ft (52 kg/m²)
Max power loading	16·1 lb/hp (7·3 kg/hp)

PERFORMANCE (at max T-O weight):

Max level speed at S/L	124 knots (143 mph; 230 km/h)
Max permissible diving speed	151 knots (174 mph; 280 km/h)

Max cruising speed at 5,000 ft (1,500 m)	113 knots (130 mph; 210 km/h)
Econ cruising speed at 5,000 ft (1,500 m)	108 knots (124 mph; 200 km/h)
Stalling speed	44 knots (50 mph; 80 km/h)
Rate of climb at S/L	985 ft (300 m)/min
Service ceiling	13,000 ft (4,000 m)
T-O run	330 ft (100 m)
Landing run	360 ft (110 m)
Range with max fuel and max payload, 20 min reserve	590 nm (680 miles; 1,100 km)
Max endurance	5 hr 30 min

AISA

AERONAUTICA INDUSTRIAL, SA

HEAD OFFICE:
Plaza de las Cortes 2, Apartado 984, Madrid 14

WORKS AND AERODROME:
Cuatro Vientos (Carabanchel Alto), Madrid 19

PRESIDENT:
Manuel Loring, Conde de Mieres

COUNSELLOR DEPUTY:
Fernando Beltrán Rojo

DIRECTOR GENERAL (Technical):
José A. Delgado

SALES MANAGER:
Rodrigo García

PUBLIC RELATIONS MANAGER:
Ramón Prieto

This concern has since 1923 been engaged in the manufacture, repair and maintenance of fixed-wing aircraft and helicopters.

During recent years, the AISA design office has been responsible for several liaison, training and sporting aircraft, including the I-11, I-11B, AVD-12 (in collaboration with M Dewoitine) and I-115.

AISA is also engaged in IRAN repair and maintenance of several types of US aircraft, in particular the North American T-6 trainers operated by the Spanish Air Force.

Since 1962, AISA has been awarded several US government contracts for IRAN and repair work on Sikorsky S-55 (H-19) and S-58 (H-34) helicopters. It is also engaged on the repair and overhaul of Bell 47 and Hughes 300 helicopters.

In 1967, AISA concluded an agreement with Siai-Marchetti of Italy to co-produce and market the latter company's S.205 four-seat light aircraft, and production of this aircraft (described in Italian section) began in 1968.

AISA I-11B

Spanish Air Force designation: L.8C

The prototype I-11 had a tricycle landing gear and first flew in 1950. The I-11B, with tail-wheel landing gear, was developed in response to the request of would-be owners for a traditional layout, and the prototype of this version flew on 16 October 1953. The first 70 production I-11B's had only basic flying instruments; the second series of 110 aircraft have a full blind-flying panel. Some are used by the Spanish Air Force for liaison and training duties, under the designation L.8C.

Some aircraft of this type are powered by the 93 hp ENMA Flecha engine.

TYPE: Two-seat touring or training monoplane. Fully-aerobatic when flown as a single-seater.

WINGS: Cantilever low-wing monoplane. NACA 23015/23009 wing section. Dihedral 7°. Incidence 3°. Two-spar wood structure with plywood skin. Ailerons have wood structure and fabric covering. Two-position flaps.

FUSELAGE: Wood monocoque structure, plywood-covered.

TAIL UNIT: Cantilever all-wood structure. Fixed surfaces plywood-covered, movable surfaces fabric-covered. Single-piece elevator has semi-automatic trim-tabs. Rudder tab adjustable on ground only.

LANDING GEAR: Non-retractable tail-wheel type. Oil/spring shock-absorbers. Hydraulic brakes. Steerable tail-wheel.

AISA I-11B two-seat touring and training light aircraft (90 hp Continental C90-12F engine)

AISA-built Siai-Marchetti S.205-20/R four-seat light cabin monoplane

POWER PLANT: One 90 hp Continental C90-12F four-cylinder horizontally-opposed air-cooled engine driving a two-blade Aeromatic or fixed-pitch wood propeller. Total fuel capacity 17·6 Imp gallons (80 litres).

ACCOMMODATION: Two seats side-by-side, with dual controls, under "blister" type canopy. Baggage space aft of seats.

DIMENSIONS, EXTERNAL:

Wing span	30 ft 7 in (9·34 m)
Wing chord at root	5 ft 8 in 1·74 m)
Wing chord at tip	3 ft 9 in (1·14 m)
Length overall	21 ft 3 in (6·47 m)
Height (tail down)	6 ft 3 in (1·90 m)
Tailplane span	10 ft 0 in (3·04 m)
Wheel track	8 ft 10 in (2·70 m)

AREAS:

Wings, gross	144 sq ft (13·40 m²)
Ailerons (total)	11·60 sq ft (1·12 m²)

Flaps (total)	15·00 sq ft (1·40 m²)
Fin	6·76 sq ft (0·63 m²)
Rudder	5·11 sq ft (0·48 m²)
Tailplane	17·16 sq ft (1·60 m²)
Elevators	9·62 sq ft (0·89 m²)

WEIGHTS:

Weight empty	926 lb (421 kg)
Normal T-O weight	1,417 lb (644 kg)
Max permissible weight:	
semi-aerobatic	1,474 lb (670 kg)
fully-aerobatic	1,257 lb (570 kg)

PERFORMANCE (at normal T-O weight):

Max level speed	108 knots (124 mph; 200 km/h)
Cruising speed	96 knots (110 mph; 177 km/h)
Min speed	41 knots (47·2 mph; 76 km/h)
Rate of climb at S/L	726 ft (200 m)/min
Service ceiling	15,415 ft (4,700 m)
Range with max fuel	349 nm (403 miles; 650 km)

CASA

CONSTRUCCIONES AERONAUTICAS S A

HEAD OFFICE:
Rey Francisco, 4 Madrid (8)

WORKS:
Madrid, Getafe, Seville and Cadiz

PRESIDENT:
José Ortiz-Echagüe

GENERAL DIRECTOR:
Eugenio Aguirre Castillo

CHIEF ENGINEER, PRODUCTION:
José María Román Arroyo

CHIEF ENGINEER, PROJECTS:
Ricardo Valle Benítez

This company was formed in March 1923 for the primary purpose of producing metal aircraft for the Spanish Air Force. It began by building under licence the Breguet XIX and has since manufactured many other aircraft of foreign design. The latest of these is the Northrop F-5 fighter, for which the company received a contract early in 1966.

CASA's own Project Office has designed and produced several transport aircraft under contract to the Spanish Air Ministry. Of these,

the CASA-207 Azor (see 1969-70 *Jane's*) was built in both troop and military cargo transport versions. The latest transport design is the C.212 Aviocar, described overleaf.

The Project Office also undertakes design and development work for foreign companies and has, for example, collaborated with Hamburger Flugzeugbau GmbH in the design of the HFB 320 Hansa light twin-jet executive transport. CASA is participating in the manufacture of this aircraft, and HFB (now a part of Messerschmitt-Bölkow-Blohm-GmbH) in turn acts as sub-contractor in the Aviocar production programme, building the wing centre-section, flaps and engine nacelles.

CASA has a 6% participation share in the manufacture of the prototype Dassault Mercure short/medium-range jet transport, and is building part of the fuselage. It has four factories, employing a total of 5,000 people in 1969, and had produced almost 1,700 aircraft by the beginning of 1970.

CASA has carried out maintenance and modernisation work for the Spanish Air Force and, since 1954, for the US Air Force in Europe. The types of aircraft concerned include the Lockheed F-104, T-33 and C-130, North American F-86 and F-100, Convair F-102, Republic F-105, McDonnell Douglas C-47, C-54 and F-4, Sikorsky H-19B and Bell 47G.

CASA 207 AZOR

Spanish Air Force designation: T.7

Following the production of 10 of the basic C.207-A (T.7A) 30-passenger transport version of the Azor for the Spanish Air Force, CASA completed a further 10 C.207-C (T.7B) Azors equipped for troop and cargo carrying. A full description of the Azor appeared in the 1969-70 edition of *Jane's*.

CASA (NORTHROP) SF-5A and SF-5B

Spanish Air Force designations: C.9 and CE.9

Under a contract received in 1966, CASA is building under licence for the Spanish Air Force single- and two-seat versions of the American Northrop F-5 jet fighter. Present arrangements involve the manufacture of 70 of these aircraft, comprising 36 single-seat SF-5A's (C.9) and 34 two-seat SF-5B's (CE.9). The first five of these aircraft had been completed by the end of 1968, and delivery of the first 10 took place in June 1969.

Manufacture of the SF-5's is being carried out by CASA's Seville and Getafe factories. The Seville plant is building the front and centre fuselage sections and the landing gear, and is also responsible for final assembly, flight testing and delivery.

A full description of the F-5 can be found under the "Northrop" heading in the US section.

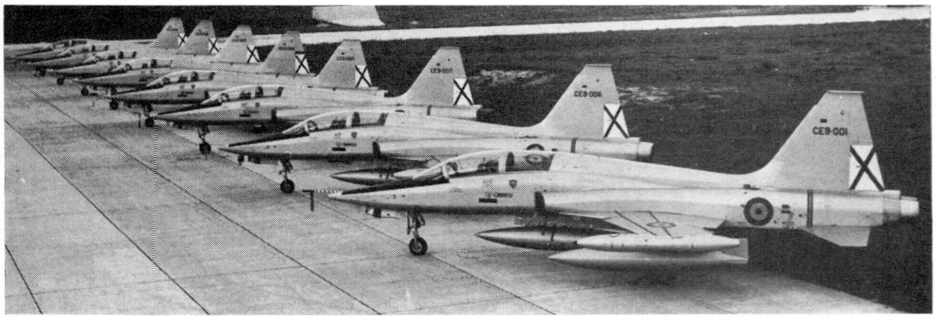

Line-up of CASA (Northrop) SF-5B's (CE.9's) for the Spanish Air Force

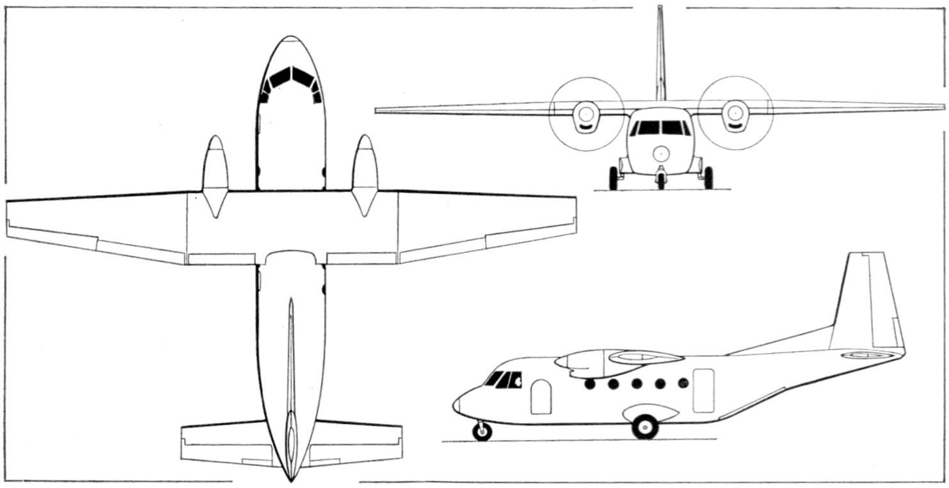

CASA C.212 Aviocar twin-turboprop light transport aircraft

CASA C.212 AVIOCAR

The Aviocar is a twin-turboprop light utility STOL transport, which has been evolved by CASA to fulfil a variety of military or civil rôles, but primarily to replace the mixed fleet of Junkers Ju 52/3m (T.2), Douglas DC-3 (T.3) and CASA-207 Azor (T.7) transport aircraft currently in service with the Spanish Air Force. The latest available details of the Aviocar are given below.

The C.212 is at present proposed in four main versions—as a 16-seat paratroop transport, ambulance, military freighter or 18-seat passenger transport—and will be certificated to joint military and civil standards laid down by the Instituto Nacional de Técnica Aeroespecial (INTA), which will also be responsible for the flight testing. It will have a STOL capability that will enable it to use unprepared landing strips of about 1,310 ft (400 m) in length, and other applications at present envisaged include those of forest fire patrol and (with a hopper installed) of dispensing chemicals for pest control.

On 24 September 1968, CASA was awarded a contract by the Ministerio del Aire for the development and construction of two flying prototypes and one airframe for structural testing. During the first year after the award of this contract, detail design was finalised, over 500 hours of wind-tunnel tests were carried out, and a full-size fuselage mock-up was built to evaluate such features as cabin vision, accessibility and location of the principal items of equipment. CASA has a co-operative agreement with HFB of Germany (a Division of the Messerschmitt-Bölkow-Blohm group) whereby the German company is contributing to the development and will manufacture the wing centre-section for the Aviocar, including the engine nacelles, flaps and flap controls.

By early 1970, construction of the main sub-assemblies (wings, fuselage, tail unit and landing gear) for the first prototype was well advanced. The first flight was scheduled to take place in September 1970; the second prototype is expected to fly for the first time in March 1971.

Type: Twin-turboprop STOL utility transport.

Wings: Cantilever high-wing monoplane. Wing section NACA 65_3-218. Incidence 2° 30′. No dihedral or sweepback. All-metal light alloy fail-safe structure. All-metal ailerons and double-slotted trailing-edge flaps. Rubber-boot de-icing of leading-edges.

Fuselage: Semi-monocoque fail-safe structure of light alloy construction.

Tail Unit: Cantilever two-spar all-metal structure, with dorsal fairing forward of fin. Tailplane mid-mounted on rear of fuselage. Trim-tab in rudder and each elevator. Rubber-boot de-icing of leading-edges.

Landing Gear: Non-retractable tricycle type, with single main wheels and single steerable nose-wheel. CASA oleo-pneumatic shock-absorbers. Dunlop wheels and tyres, main units size 11·00 × 12 8-ply Type III, nose unit size 8·00 × 7 Type III. Tyre pressure (all units) 45 lb/sq in (3·16 kg/cm²). Dunlop hydraulic disc brakes on main wheels.

Power Plant: Two 755 eshp AiResearch TPE 331-201 turboprop engines, each driving a Hartzell HC-B3TN-5D three-blade constant-speed metal propeller, diameter 8 ft 6 in (2·59 m). Fuel in two tanks in each outer wing panel, with total capacity of 418 Imp gallons (1,900 litres). Oil capacity 1·32 Imp gallons (6 litres) per engine.

Accommodation: Crew of two on flight deck. For the paratroop rôle, the main cabin can be fitted with 16 inward-facing seats along the cabin walls, to accommodate 15 paratroops and an instructor/jumpmaster. As an ambulance, the cabin would normally be equipped to carry 10 stretcher patients and 3 sitting casualties, plus medical attendants, but an alternative layout provides for up to 18 stretchers to be carried if necessary. As a freighter, the Aviocar can carry up to 4,410 lb (2,000 kg) of cargo in the main cabin, including light vehicles. The civil passenger transport version of the Aviocar has standard seating for 18 persons in five rows of three (one to port and two to starboard of centre aisle) at 33 in (83 cm) pitch, plus three seats side by side at rear of cabin, but can seat up to 21 persons in a high-density layout. Entry to cabin is via two large doors on the port side, one aft of (and providing access to) the flight deck and one aft of the wing trailing-edge. In addition, there is a two-section under-fuselage loading ramp/door aft of the main cabin; and this door is openable in flight for the discharge of paratroops or cargo. All versions have a toilet at the forward end of the main cabin on the starboard side, with a baggage compartment opposite on the port side. In the civil transport version, the interior of the rear-loading door can be used for additional baggage stowage.

Systems: Unpressurised cabin. Hydraulic system, pressure 2,000 lb/sq in (140 kg/cm²), operates main-wheel brakes, flaps and nose-wheel steering. Electrical system is supplied by two 3kW starter generators.

Electronics and Equipment: Radio and radar equipment includes Bendix RTA 41B VHF, AN/ARC 34C UHF, VOR/ILS and one ADF. Blind-flying instrumentation standard. Optional equipment includes TACAN, SIF/IFF, Collins 618S-4 HF and a second ADF.

Dimensions, external:

Wing span	62 ft 4 in (19·00 m)
Wing chord at root	8 ft 2½ in (2·50 m)
Wing chord at tip	4 ft 1¼ in (1·25 m)
Wing aspect ratio	9
Length overall	49 ft 8½ in (15·15 m)
Height overall	20 ft 8¾ in (6·32 m)
Tailplane span	24 ft 3¼ in (7·40 m)
Wheel track	10 ft 2 in (3·10 m)
Wheelbase	17 ft 10½ in (5·45 m)
Passenger door (port, aft):	
Max height	5 ft 2¼ in (1·58 m)
Max width	2 ft 3½ in (0·70 m)
Crew and servicing door (port, fwd):	
Max height	3 ft 7¼ in (1·10 m)
Max width	1 ft 11⅝ in (0·60 m)
Rear-loading door:	
Max length	13 ft 1½ in (4·00 m)
Max width	5 ft 7 in (1·70 m)

Dimensions, internal:

Wings, gross	430·56 sq ft (40·0 m²)
Ailerons (total)	26·37 sq ft (2·45 m²)
Trailing-edge flaps (total)	79·44 sq ft (7·38 m²)
Fin	45·75 sq ft (4·25 m²)
Rudder, incl tab	31·74 sq ft (2·02 m²)
Tailplane	75·35 sq ft (7·00 m²)
Elevators, incl tabs	42·18 sq ft (3·92 m²)

Weights and Loadings:

Weight empty, equipped	7,160 lb (3,250 kg)
Max payload	4,410 lb (2,000 kg)
Max T-O weight	13,230 lb (6,000 kg)
Max zero-fuel weight	11,980 lb (5,435 kg)
Max landing weight	12,680 lb (5,750 kg)
Max wing loading	30·75 lb/sq ft (150 kg/m²)
Max power loading	8·75 lb/eshp (3·97 kg/eshp)

Performance (estimated, at max T-O weight except where indicated):

Max level speed at 12,000 ft (3,660 m)
205 knots (236 mph; 380 km/h)

Max permissible diving speed
252 knots (290 mph; 467 km/h) EAS

Max cruising speed at 12,000 ft (3,660 m)
198 knots (228 mph; 367 km/h)

Econ cruising speed at 10,000 ft (3,050 m)
154 knots (177 mph; 285 km/h)

Stalling speed, flaps up
81 knots (94 mph; 150 km/h)

Stalling speed, flaps down
64 knots (73 mph; 117 km/h)

Max rate of climb at S/L 1,675 ft (510 m)/min

Service ceiling 23,950 ft (7,300 m)

Service ceiling, one engine out
8,700 ft (2,650 m)

T-O run (normal)	1,215 ft (370 m)
T-O run (STOL)	820 ft (250 m)
T-O to 50 ft (15 m)	1,640 ft (500 m)
Landing from 50 ft (15 m)	1,560 ft (475 m)
Landing run (normal)	805 ft (245 m)
Landing run (STOL)	425 ft (130 m)

Range at 9,840 ft (3,000 m) with max fuel and 2,095 lb (950 kg) payload, 5% and 20 min reserves 1,035 nm (1,195 miles; 1,920 km)

Range at 9,840 ft (3,000 m) with max payload, reserves as above
390 nm (445 miles; 720 km)

HISPANO
LA HISPANO-AVIACIÓN SA
HEAD OFFICE:
General Mola, 11-2°, Madrid-1
AIRCRAFT WORKS:
Calle San Jacinto 102-106, Seville
Aeropuerto de Sevilla, Seville
PRESIDENT:
Emilio González Garcia
VICE-PRESIDENT:
Fernando Orduña Gómez
MANAGING DIRECTOR:
Enrique de Gusmán de Ozamiz
PUBLIC RELATIONS MANAGER:
Domingo Balaguer

The main interests in Hispano-Aviacion SA are held by the Instituto Nacional de Industria and CASA: a 27% interest is held by Messerschmitt-Bölkow-Blohm of Germany.

The company's current product is the HA-200 jet training aircraft, which is being built in series for the Spanish Air Force. A derivative of the HA-200 E, designated HA-220, is being developed as a ground attack aircraft.

HISPANO HA-200 SAETA
Military designation: E-14
Design and construction of the prototype HA-200 began in 1954 and it flew for the first time on 12 August 1955. A second prototype was also built, followed by five pre-production models, before series production of the original HA-200A version (30 built) was started.

There are three current production versions of the HA-200, as follows:

HA-200 B. Two Turboméca Marboré IIA turbojet engines. Equipped with a 20-mm Hispano cannon, Ferranti gyroscopic predictor gun-sight and Lear ADF. First of ten preproduction models (all supplied to Egypt) flew on 21 July 1960.

Licence production of the HA-200 B is under way in Egypt, where the aircraft is known as the Al-Kahira. Ninety are being built.

HA-200 D. All systems generally modernised, new wheels and brakes and heavier armament. Production of 55 for Spanish Air Force completed in Winter of 1967-68; 40 are being fitted with the armament installations specified for the HA-200 E. Described in 1968-69 Jane's.

HA-200 E Super Saeta. Basically as HA-200 D, but with more powerful Marboré VI turbojets, more extensive and modern electronic equipment of Bendix design, and two Matra type 38 attachments for the air-launched weapons. Described below.

TYPE: Two-seat twin-jet advanced flying and armament trainer.

WINGS: Cantilever low-wing monoplane. Wing section is combination of NACA 63₂A (2·5) and 64₂A (2·5) laminar-flow sections. Thickness/chord ratio 15% at root, 13·5% at tip. Dihedral 5°. Incidence 4° at root. Sweepback 4° 30′ at quarter-chord. Single-spar light-alloy structure. Statically and aerodynamically balanced all-metal ailerons. Hydraulically-operated slotted flaps. Automatic trim-tabs in ailerons. All controls manually operated. No de-icing equipment.

FUSELAGE: Conventional light alloy semi-monocoque structure. Hydraulically-operated all-metal ventral fan-type dive-brakes.

TAIL UNIT: Cantilever all-metal structure, with tailplane mounted part-way up fin. Variable-incidence tailplane. Fixed tabs on elevators.

LANDING GEAR: Retractable tricycle type with non-steerable nose-wheel. Hydraulic retraction. Nose-wheel retracts rearward, main units inward. Hispano oleo-pneumatic shock-absorbers. HA-200 D and E have Dunlop main wheels and tubeless tyres, size 20 × 5·25 × 11, pressure 85 lb/sq in (6·00 kg/cm²) and Hispano nose-wheel with Pirelli tyre size 12 × 6·00 × 8, pressure 64 lb/sq in (4·50 kg/cm²), and Dunlop hydraulic plate brakes.

POWER PLANT: Two Turboméca Marboré VI turbojets (each 1,058 lb = 480 kg st). Fuel in two tanks in fuselage and two in wings, with total capacity of 164 Imp gallons (745 litres), and two fixed wing-tip tanks with total capacity of 140 Imp gallons (644 litres). Refuelling points on each tip-tank and on port side of centre-fuselage. Oil capacity 2·5 Imp gallons (12 litres).

ACCOMMODATION: Instructor and pupil in tandem in pressurised cabin, with dual controls. Heating and air conditioning systems. Windscreen de-iced by hot air blast. Jettisonable sideways-hinged (to starboard) canopy section over each cockpit.

SYSTEMS: Normalair-Garrett pressurisation system, differential 2·75-3·13 lb/sq in (0·19-0·22 kg/cm²). Hydraulic system, max pressure 1,135 lb/sq in (80 kg/cm²), actuates flaps, dive brakes and landing gear retraction. Pneumatic system, pressure 1,850-2,135 lb/sq in (130-150 kg/cm²), actuates landing gear emergency release. Generator and battery for 28V DC electrical system. 110V 400 c/s AC system.

Hispano HA-200 E Super Saeta jet advanced trainer (two Turboméca Marboré VI turbojet engines)

ELECTRONICS AND EQUIPMENT: Bendix electronics include type RTA-41 VHF, ADF-72 ADF, RNA-26C VOR, 5C PHI and TRA-62 IFF(SIF)/ATC. Sperry Gyrosyn compass. Other equipment includes emergency cockpit lighting, oxygen equipment and fire detection system.

OPERATIONAL EQUIPMENT AND ARMAMENT: Normal fixed armament of two 7·7 mm Breda machine-guns in nose. Can be equipped with a variety of guns, rockets and bombs and photographic and reconnaissance equipment. The HA-200 E has two Matra type 38 universal attachments able to carry a wide variety of rocket launchers, bomb racks, containers, etc; Maurer type P-2 camera for photographing the results of ground attack missions; a Maurer type N-6 camera gun; and a VRM Zeus reflector sight.

DIMENSIONS, EXTERNAL:
Wing span	34 ft 2 in (10·42 m)
Wing span over tip-tanks	35 ft 10 in (10·93 m)
Wing chord at root	6 ft 6 in (1·99 m)
Wing chord at tip	4 ft 2 in (1·27 m)
Wing aspect ratio	6·22
Length overall	29 ft 5 in (8·97 m)
Height over tail	9 ft 4 in (2·85 m)
Tailplane span	11 ft 9½ in (3·60 m)
Wheel track	10 ft 7 in (3·22 m)
Wheelbase	8 ft 0 in (2·45 m)

AREAS:
Wings, gross	187·2 sq ft (17·40 m²)

Ailerons (total)	11·25 sq ft (1·05 m²)
Trailing-edge flaps (total)	24·44 sq ft (2·27 m²)
Fin	14·10 sq ft (1·31 m²)
Rudder, including tab	7·43 sq ft (0·69 m²)
Tailplane	23·68 sq ft (2·20 m²)
Elevators, including tabs	10·12 sq ft (0·94 m²)

WEIGHTS:
Basic operating weight	4,453 lb (2,020 kg)
Max T-O weight	7,937 lb (3,600 kg)
Max zero-fuel weight	5,190 lb (2,355 kg)
Max landing weight	5,840 lb (2,650 kg)

PERFORMANCE (at max T-O weight):
Max level speed at S/L	359 knots (413 mph; 665 km/h)
Max level speed at 23,000 ft (7,000 m)	373 knots (429 mph; 690 km/h)
Max permissible diving speed	Mach 0·75 or 425 knots (490 mph; 790 km/h)
Max cruising speed at 19,700 ft (6,000 m)	313 knots (360 mph; 579 km/h)
Stalling speed, flaps up	81 knots (93 mph; 150 km/h)
Stalling speed, flaps down	71 knots (81 mph; 130 km/h)
Rate of climb at S/L at AUW of 5,840 lb (2,650 kg)	3,050 ft (930 m)/min
Service ceiling	42,650 ft (13,000 m)
Service ceiling, one engine out	26,250 ft (8,000 m)
T-O run	2,625 ft (800 m)
T-O to 50 ft (15 m)	3,545 ft (1,080 m)
Landing from 50 ft (15 m)	2,300 ft (700 m)

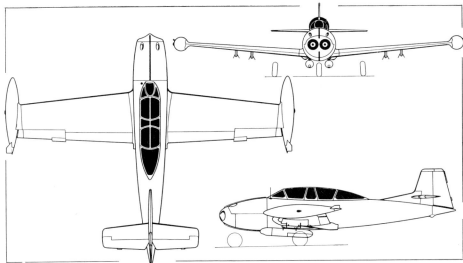

Hispano HA-220 light attack aircraft, developed from the HA-200

Prototype of the Hispano HA-220 ground attack aircraft developed from the Super Saeta

Landing run   1,310 ft (400 m)
Range with max fuel at 29,500 ft (9,000 m)
                    807 nm (930 miles; 1,500 km)

HISPANO HA-220

Hispano has begun design work on a ground
attack aircraft designated HA-220. This is a
development of the HA-200 E, with Marboré VI
turbojet engines, but converted to single-seat

configuration. All fuel tanks are of the self-
sealing type, and an additional self-sealing tank
is installed in the second cockpit. The cockpit
area and various other parts of the HA-220 have
armour protection, and electronics and equipment appropriate to the ground attack role is
installed.

The HA-200 can have two under-fuselage and
four underwing points on which external stores

can be carried. A typical load would be four
Hispano or Matra 38 underwing attachments for
air-to-surface weapons, with two 0·50-in machine-
gun pods (250 rpg) or 7·62-mm Minigun pods
(1,500 rpg) under the fuselage. A gun camera
is installed under the fuselage.

Twenty-five ordered for Spanish Air Force in
December 1967. The first of these was due to
make its first flight in the Spring of 1970.

SWEDEN

ANDREASSON
BJÖRN ANDREASSON
ADDRESS:
c/o AB Malmö Flygindustri, Bulltofta Flygplats, Box 463, 201 24 Malmö 1

Mr Andreasson has designed seven different
types of light aircraft. Best known of these is the
BA-7, which is being built in series by AB Malmö
Flygindustri (whose Aircraft Division is headed
by Mr Andreasson), as the MFI-9B Trainer/Mili-
trainer, and by Messerschmitt-Bölkow-Blohm in
Germany, as the BO 208 C Junior.

An earlier design, the BA-4 biplane, was
modernised by Mr Andreasson for members of the
Swedish branch of the Experimental Aircraft
Association, and a prototype was built by
apprentices of the MFI apprentice school as part
of their training programme. To distinguish it
from the original BA-4, it is designated BA-4B.

ANDREASSON BA-4B

The prototype BA-4B, built by MFI apprentices, was of all-metal constuction. The design
provides for alternative all-wooden wings.

TYPE: Single-seat fully-aerobatic light biplane.

WINGS: Braced biplane type, with a single
streamline-section interplane strut each side.
A streamline-section bracing strut runs from
the bottom fuselage longeron on each side to
the top of the interplane strut, and an N-type
cabane structure supports the centre-section.
Incidence, upper wing 3°, lower wing 4°.
Stagger 20°. Dihedral, upper wing 2°, lower
wing 4°. Alternative all-metal structure or
all-wood structure, with solid spars, covered
with heavy plywood skin. Pop-riveted
ailerons, of simplified sheet metal construction,
on lower wings only. No flaps. Provision for
fitting detachable plastics wing-tips.

FUSELAGE: Sheet metal structure, with external
stringers, making extensive use of pop riveting.
Turtle-deck either sheet metal or reinforced
plastic.

TAIL UNIT: Cantilever structure of pop-riveted
sheet metal construction.

LANDING GEAR: Non-retractable tail-wheel type.
Cantilever spring steel main legs. Main wheels
size 5·00 × 4 or 5·00 × 5. Hydraulic brakes.
Steerable tail-wheel carried on leaf-spring.

Andreasson BA-4B single-seat amateur-built light aircraft (*Air Portraits*)

POWER PLANT: Prototype has 100 hp Rolls-Royce/
Continental O-200-A four-cylinder horizontally-
opposed air-cooled engine. Provision for other
engines, including Volkswagen conversions.
Standard fuel tank, capacity 11 Imp gallons
(50 litres), forward of cockpit. Provision for
carrying external "bullet" tank of 11 Imp
gallons (50 litres) capacity under fuselage.

ACCOMMODATION: Single seat in open cockpit.

ELECTRONICS AND EQUIPMENT: Provision for
battery, VHF radio and IFR instrumentation.

DIMENSIONS, EXTERNAL:
Wing span:
  upper   17 ft 7 in (5·34 m)
  lower   16 ft 11 in (5·14 m)
Wing chord (upper and lower, constant)
                       2 ft 7½ in (0·80 m)
Wing aspect ratio (upper and lower)   6
Length overall   15 ft 0 in (4·60 m)
Tailplane span   6 ft 6 in (2·00 m)

AREAS:
Wings, total   90 sq ft (8·3 m²)
Fin   3·25 sq ft (0·3 m²)
Rudder   3·25 sq ft (0·3 m²)
Tailplane   6·5 sq ft (0·6 m²)
Elevators   5·4 sq ft (0·5 m²)

WEIGHT:
Max T-O weight   827 lb (375 kg)

PERFORMANCE (prototype, at max T-O weight):
Max level speed
                122 knots (140 mph; 225 km/h)
Max cruising speed
                104 knots (120 mph; 193 km/h)
Min flying speed   35 knots (40 mph; 64 km/h)
Rate of climb at S/L   2,000 ft (600 m)/min
T-O and landing run   less than 330 ft (100 m)
Range with standard fuel
                152 nm (175 miles; 280 km)

ERICSON
HUGO ERICSON
ADDRESS: Box 78, Tandsbyn

Mr Hugo Ericson, leader of the Swedish Chapter of the Experimental Aircraft Association,
has with the help of Ing Hjalmar Larsson designed a single-engined pusher amphibian. The
aircraft has been based broadly upon the Woods
Woody Pusher (see US section of this edition)
but with an entirely new hull-type fuselage
made of glass-fibre plastics with a plastic foam
filling. Initially, the aircraft is to be powered
by an 85 hp engine, driving a pusher propeller
of approx 5 ft 10 in (1·78 m) diameter. The
details below apply to the aircraft in this form,
which is still under construction.

DIMENSIONS, EXTERNAL:
Wing span   30 ft 6¼ in (9·30 m)
Wing aspect ratio   6·8
Length overall   23 ft 9½ in (7·25 m)
Height overall   7 ft 10½ in (2·40 m)
AREA:
Wings, gross   150·7 sq ft (14·00 m²)
WEIGHTS:
Weight empty   794 lb (360 kg)
Max T-O weight   1,323 lb (600 kg)
PERFORMANCE (estimated, at max T-O weight):
Max level speed
                108 knots (124 mph; 200 km/h)
Min safe flying speed
                38 knots (43·5 mph; 70 km/h)

Model of the Ericson two-seat light amphibian, based on the Woods Woody Pusher

MFI
AB MALMÖ FLYGINDUSTRI (Subsidiary of Saab Aktiebolag, Linköping)
HEAD OFFICE AND WORKS:
Bulltofta Flygplats, Box 463, 201 24 Malmö 1
MANAGING DIRECTOR:
Rudolf Abelin
MANAGER:
Ove Dahlén
DESIGN AND DEVELOPMENT:
E. A. Wohlberg
SPECIAL PROJECTS:
B. Andreasson

This company manufactures airframe and
missile components, glass-fibre reinforced plastics
and laminated structures, and offers aircraft
maintenance facilities.

In charge of special projects is Mr. Björn
Andreasson, who had already designed and built
seven different types of light aircraft before
joining the company. One of his designs, the
BA-7, is in production as the MFI-9B Trainer.
Another version is built under licence in Germany
by Messerschmitt-Bölkow-Blohm as the BO 208
Junior.

To meet a Swedish Army requirement, AB

Malmö Flygindustri also developed a four-seat
observation monoplane known as the MFI-10
Vipan.

More recently, MFI has developed and built
a new design known as the MFI-15. Based
upon the MFI-9, this is intended as a fully-aerobatic training aircraft, and is also suitable for
light attack or agricultural duties.

MFI-9B TRAINER/MILI-TRAINER

The prototype of this two-seat light monoplane
was designed and built by Mr Björn Andreasson
in the United States, as the BA-7. When it was
first flown, on 10 October 1958, it had one-piece

all-moving vertical and horizontal tail surfaces, but a fixed fin and smaller rudder were fitted during 1960 and are also a feature of the production models, which have the Malmö designation MFI-9.

Three production prototypes were constructed at Bulltofta, and various versions of the MFI-9 are now being built in quantity by Malmö Flygindustri for sale in Scandinavia and by Messerschmitt-Bölkow-Blohm in Germany.

The production aircraft have a 100 hp Rolls-Royce/Continental O-200 engine instead of the 75 hp Continental A75 fitted in the original BA-7. There are three versions, as follows:

MFI-9 Junior. Basic version. First production prototype flew on 17 May 1961, followed by first production MFI-9 on 9 August 1962. Total of 25 built by Malmö. In quantity production by Messerschmitt-Bölkow-Blohm as BO 208 (which see).

MFI-9B Trainer. Developed version, first flown in 1963 and in current production by Malmö. Enlarged cabin with seats moved rearward and provision for parachutes. Enlarged vertical tail surfaces, electrically-operated flaps and other changes. Total of 45 built by MFI (including Mili-Trainers) by 1 March 1970. Described in detail below.

MFI-9B Mili-trainer. Military primary trainer counterpart of Trainer. Can carry a variety of weapons, including air-to-surface missiles, equipment or cameras for tactical reconnaissance, artillery spotting, radioactive sampling, limited convoy escort, target spotting and marking, close support or helicopter interception duties. Two prototypes were evaluated by the Swedish Air Force in the Summer of 1964.

TYPE: Two-seat light monoplane, stressed for flight load factors of $+4.4\ g$ and $-1.76\ g$.

WINGS: Braced shoulder-wing monoplane. Single bracing strut each side. NACA 23008·5 (modified) section. Dihedral 1°. Incidence 2°. Sweep-forward 3° at quarter-chord. Heavy aluminium skin, with extruded main spar at 30% chord and bent-up sheet metal rear spar at 75% chord. Wings fold by undoing spar attachment bolts. Mass-balanced all-metal ailerons hinged to top surface of wings. All-metal plain flaps. Drooped leading-edge. No tabs.

FUSELAGE: All-metal box structure, with no double curvature. External longerons and prefabricated skin panels.

TAIL UNIT: Cantilever all-metal structure comprising swept fin and rudder and one-piece mass-balanced horizontal "stabilator" with large anti-servo and trimming tab.

LANDING GEAR: Non-retractable tricycle type. Main legs comprise tapered steel rods in rubber bushings. Nose unit of swing-axle type with oleo damping. Cleveland wheels and tyres, size 5·00 × 5 on all three units. Cleveland hydraulic disc brakes. Provision for fitting skis or Pee-Kay 1500 floats.

POWER PLANT: One 100 hp Rolls-Royce/Continental O-200-A four-cylinder horizontally-opposed air-cooled engine, driving a McCauley MCM 6758 two-blade metal propeller. Fuel in tank behind cockpit, capacity 17·5 Imp gallons (80 litres). Refuelling point above rear canopy. Oil capacity 1·0 Imp gallon (4·5 litres).

ACCOMMODATION: Two seats side-by-side in enclosed cabin, with central control column. Front portion of canopy hinges rearward to serve as door. Ventilation and heating standard. Space for 44 lb (20 kg) baggage aft of seats.

ELECTRONICS AND EQUIPMENT: Provision for radio and blind-flying instrumentation for VFR and IFR flying by day or night.

ARMAMENT AND OPERATIONAL EQUIPMENT (Mili-trainer): Attachment point under each wing for either six 7·5-cm Bofors Frida air-to-surface rockets, one or two Bofors Bantam air-to-surface wire-guided missiles, three Frida rockets plus one Bantam, one Matra 181 rocket launcher containing eighteen 37-mm SNEB rockets, grenades or special weapons. Camera window is standard, and for reconnaissance missions a Vinten 70-mm side-looking camera can be installed in the port side of the fuselage aft of the pilot's seat.

DIMENSIONS, EXTERNAL:

Wing span	24 ft 4 in (7·43 m)
Wing chord (constant)	4 ft 0 in (1·22 m)
Wing aspect ratio	6
Length overall:	
landplane	19 ft 2 in (5·85 m)
seaplane	20 ft 0 in (6·10 m)
Height over tail:	
landplane	6 ft 7 in (2·00 m)
seaplane	7 ft 6½ in (2·30 m)
Tailplane span	9 ft 5 in (2·84 m)
Wheel track	6 ft 7 in (2·00 m)
Float track	6 ft 3 in (1·90 m)

DIMENSIONS, INTERNAL:

Cabin: Length	3 ft 11¼ in (1·20 m)
Max width	3 ft 5¼ in (1·05 m)

AREA:

Wings, gross	93 sq ft (8·70 m²)

Malmö MFI-9 "minicon", fitted with two underwing pods each containing six rockets

Malmö Flygindustri MFI-9B Trainer two-seat light monoplane

WEIGHTS:

Weight empty:	
landplane	750 lb (340 kg)
seaplane	882 lb (400 kg)
Max T-O weight:	
landplane (utility)	1,270 lb (575 kg)
seaplane	1,378 lb (625 kg)

PERFORMANCE (at max T-O weight):

Max level speed at S/L:	
landplane	129 knots (149 mph; 240 km/h)
Max permissible diving speed:	
landplane	165 knots (190 mph; 305 km/h)
Max cruising speed:	
landplane	126 knots (145 mph; 236 km/h)
seaplane	100 knots (115 mph; 185 km/h)
Econ cruising speed at S/L:	
landplane	113 knots (130 mph; 210 km/h)
Stalling speed, power off:	
landplane	44 knots (50 mph; 80 km/h)
Rate of climb at S/L:	
landplane	900 ft (270 m)/min
seaplane	710 ft (216 m)/min
Service ceiling:	
landplane	15,000 ft (4,500 m)
seaplane	13,800 ft (4,200 m)
T-O run:	
landplane	490 ft (150 m)
Landing run:	
landplane	425 ft (130 m)
Range with max payload:	
landplane	434 nm (500 miles; 800 km)
seaplane	364 nm (420 miles; 680 km)
Endurance at 70% power:	
landplane	4 hr

MFI-10 VIPAN (PEEWIT)

The Vipan was designed to meet a joint specification by the Royal Swedish Aero Club and the Swedish Defence Board for an aircraft suitable for operation as a low-cost four-seat civil touring and utility aircraft and as a sturdy military AOP and casualty evacuation aircraft with short-field capability. It has flown in two forms, as follows:

MFI-10. Original prototype, with 160 hp Lycoming O-320 engine, first flown early in 1961.

MFI-10B. Second and third prototypes, produced under Swedish Army contract, with 180 hp Lycoming O-360 engine. First flown on 27 June 1962.

A full description of the Vipan was given in the 1969-70 edition of *Jane's*. Early in 1970 it was planned to refit the aircraft with a more powerful engine.

MFI-15

The MFI-15 was designed to fulfil a Swedish Air Force and Army requirement, and is available in two main versions, as follows:

MFI-15A. For pre-selection training. Fitted with non-retractable tricycle landing gear.

Construction of prototype (SE-301) began in 1968, and this aircraft flew for the first time on 11 July 1969. Subsequently, its original low-mounted horizontal tail surfaces were replaced by new ones, mounted at the top of the fin to prevent interference or damage by snow and debris when operating in winter from rough airfields. Can be (and has been) converted easily to MFI-15B standard, without modification to basic airframe structure.

MFI-15B. Artillery spotting version, capable of miscellaneous army aviation duties. Generally similar to MFI-15A, but has a tailwheel landing gear and a supplementary high-lift flap aft of the main flap on each wing to improve T-O and landing performance at short, unprepared airstrips. Prototype (SE-301), first flown early in 1970, was the MFI-15A prototype converted to MFI-15B standard.

The description below is generally applicable to both versions, except where indicated.

TYPE: Two/three-seat light aircraft, stressed for flight load factors of $+4.4\ g$ and $-1.76\ g$ (Utility cat) and $+6.0\ g$ and $-3.0\ g$ (Aerobatic cat.)

WINGS: Braced shoulder-wing monoplane, with single bracing strut each side. Thickness/chord ratio 10%. Dihedral 1° 30′. All-metal structure, swept forward 5° from roots. Mass-balanced all-metal Frise-type ailerons. Electrically-operated all-metal plain flaps and (MFI-15B only) additional high-lift trailing-edge flap below and to rear of main flap. No tabs.

FUSELAGE: All-metal box structure.

TAIL UNIT: Cantilever all-metal "T" tail comprising swept fin and rudder and one-piece mass-balanced horizontal "stabilator" with large anti-servo and trimming tab. No tabs in rudder.

LANDING GEAR: Non-retractable tricycle type on MFI-15A; non-retractable tail-wheel type on MFI-15B. Cantilever spring steel main legs on both versions. Cleveland 5·50 × 5 main wheels and 5·00 × 5 nose wheel on MFI-15A; Goodyear 6·00 × 5 main wheels and Scott 8-in tail wheel on MFI-15B. Cleveland disc brakes on main units. Landes or Fluidine skis, or Edo floats, optional on both versions.

POWER PLANT (both models): One 160 hp Lycoming IO-320-B20 four-cylinder horizontally-opposed air-cooled engine with fuel injection, driving a McCauley MGM 7660 two-blade fixed-pitch metal propeller. Fuel in single main tank in fuselage, aft of cockpit, with total capacity of 30·8 Imp gallons (140 litres). Oil capacity 1·65 Imp gallons (7·5 litres).

ACCOMMODATION: Side-by-side adjustable seats, with provision for back-type parachutes, for two persons beneath fully-transparent rearward-sliding canopy. Space aft of front seats for 220 lb (100 kg) of baggage or, optionally, a third (rearward-facing) seat. Upward-hinged door on port side of cabin. Heated and ventilated. Dual controls standard.

SYSTEMS: 28V 50A DC electrical system.

ELECTRONICS AND EQUIPMENT: Provision for full blind-flying instrumentation and radio.

DIMENSIONS, EXTERNAL:
Wing span	28 ft 6½ in (8·70 m)
Wing chord (outer panels, constant)	4 ft 5½ in (1·36 m)
Length overall:	
MFI-15A	22 ft 1¾ in (6·75 m)
MFI-15B	22 ft 5¾ in (6·85 m)
Height overall:	
MFI-15A	8 ft 6¼ in (2·60 m)
MFI-15B (tail down)	6 ft 2¾ in (1·90 m)
Tailplane span	8 ft 4½ in (2·55 m)
Wheel track:	
MFI-15A	7 ft 1½ in (2·17 m)
MFI-15B	6 ft 7¾ in (2·025 m)
Wheelbase:	
MFI-15A	5 ft 0½ in (1·54 m)
MFI-15B	15 ft 7 in (4·75 m)
Cabin door (port):	
Height	2 ft 6¾ in (0·78 m)
Width	1 ft 8½ in (0·52 m)

DIMENSIONS, INTERNAL:
Cabin: Max width	3 ft 7¼ in (1·10 m)
Max height (from seat squab)	3 ft 3¼ in (1·00 m)

AREAS:
Wings, gross:	
MFI-15A	127 sq ft (11·80 m²)
MFI-15B	134·5 sq ft (12·50 m²)
Fin	8·72 sq ft (0·81 m²)
Rudder	6·46 sq ft (0·60 m²)
Horizontal tail surfaces (total)	17·54 sq ft (1·63 m²)

WEIGHTS AND LOADINGS:
Weight empty, min VFR equipped (all categories)	1,153 lb (523 kg)
Max T-O weight:	
Normal	1,929 lb (875 kg)
Utility	1,763 lb (800 kg)
Aerobatic	1,708 lb (775 kg)
Max zero-fuel weight:	
Normal	1,708 lb (775 kg)
Utility	1,543 lb (700 kg)
Aerobatic	1,488 lb (675 kg)
Max wing loading:	
MFI-15A, Normal	15·3 lb/sq ft (74·6 kg/m²)
MFI-15A, Utility	14·0 lb/sq ft (68·3 kg/m²)
MFI-15A, Aerobatic	13·6 lb/sq ft (66·2 kg/m²)
MFI-15B, Normal	14·3 lb/sq ft (70·0 kg/m²)
MFI-15B, Utility	13·1 lb/sq ft (64·0 kg/m²)
Max power loading:	
MFI-15A, B, Normal	12·06 lb/hp (5·47 kg/hp)
MFI-15A, B, Utility	11·02 lb/hp (5·00 kg/hp)
MFI-15A, Aerobatic	10·69 lb/hp (4·85 kg/hp)

PERFORMANCE (at max T-O weight, Utility category):
Max level speed at S/L:	
MFI-15A	138 knots (159 mph; 256 km/h)
MFI-15B	130 knots (150 mph; 241 km/h)
Max permissible diving speed (MFI-15A, B)	197 knots (227 mph; 365 km/h)
Cruising speed:	
MFI-15A	126 knots (145 mph; 226 km/h)
MFI-15B	112 knots (129 mph; 213 km/h)
Stalling speed, flaps down:	
MFI-15A	50 knots (57·2 mph; 92 km/h)
MFI-15B	45 knots (51 mph; 82 km/h)
Max rate of climb at S/L:	
MFI-15A	1,043 ft (318 m)/min
MFI-15B	1,083 ft (330 m)/min
Time to 6,560 ft (2,000 m):	
MFI-15A	9 min
MFI-15B	8 min
Service ceiling:	
MFI-15A	4,435 ft (4,400 m)
MFI-15B	4,765 ft (4,500 m)
T-O to 50 ft (15 m):	
MFI-15A	1,181 ft (360 m)
MFI-15B	820 ft (250 m)
Landing from 50 ft (15 m):	
MFI-15A	1,148 ft (350 m)
MFI-15B	984 ft (300 m)
Endurance (MFI-15A, B)	4 hr

Prototype of the MFI-15 in MFI-15A configuration (*above*), and (*below*) in MFI-15B form with tail-wheel landing gear

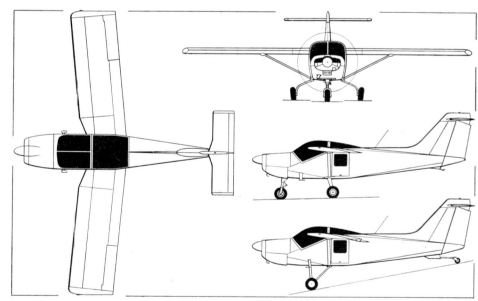

MFI-15A pre-selection trainer, with additional side view (*bottom*) of MFI-15B

SAAB-SCANIA

SAAB AKTIEBOLAG

HEAD OFFICE:
S-581 88 Linköping

WORKS:
Linköping, Jönköping, Norrköping, Malmö, Stockholm, Södertälje, Katrineholm, Oskarshamn, Trollhättan and Gothenburg

PRESIDENT:
Curt Mileikowsky

DEPUTY AND FIRST EXECUTIVE VICE-PRESIDENT:
B. Johnson

EXECUTIVE VICE-PRESIDENTS:
H. E. Löfkvist
A. Rydberg
T. Gullstrand
G. Lindström
E. Nilsson
B. Akerlind
S. Sjöström

INFORMATION:
N. M. von Arbin

AEROSPACE GROUP
GROUP DIRECTOR: T. Gullstrand
DIRECTOR, AIRCRAFT DIVISION: B. Wassgren
CHIEF ENGINEER, MISSILE & AVIONICS DIVISION: I. K. Olsson
DIRECTOR, MALMÖ FLYGINDUSTRI: R. Abelin
NORRKÖPING DEPARTMENT: Captain B. Bjernekull
INFORMATION: Hans G. Andersson

COMPUTER AND ELECTRONICS GROUP
GROUP DIRECTOR: G. Lindström

AUTOMOTIVE GROUP
GROUP DIRECTOR: E. Nilsson

NORDARMATUR GROUP
GROUP DIRECTOR: B. Hökby

The original Svenska Aeroplan AB was founded at Trollhättan in 1937 for the production of military aircraft. In 1939 this company was amalgamated with the Aircraft Division (ASJA) of the Svenska Järnvägsverkstäderna rolling stock factory in Linköping, which had been manufacturing and developing military and civil aircraft since 1930. Following this merger, Saab moved its head office and engineering departments to Linköping, which has since become the company's main factory.

In 1950, Saab acquired a factory at Jönköping for development and manufacture of airborne equipment. Other post-war expansions include a bomb-proof underground factory in Linköping, as well as important new production and engineering facilities in Linköping, Jönköping, Trollhättan and Gothenburg. The Gothenburg factory is engaged mainly on producing transmissions for the motor-car production at Trollhättan, which began in 1949-50. Current rate of production is approximately 80,000 cars per year.

To reflect the growing diversity of the company's activities, its name was changed to Saab Aktiebolag in May 1965. During 1967, AB Malmö Flygindustri (MFI) became a Saab subsidiary.

During 1968 a decision was taken to merge the company with another large Swedish automotive concern, Scania-Vabis, to strengthen the two companies' position in automotive product development, production and export. To broaden the basis for expansion into the industrial equipment field, another major Swedish company, Nordarmatur (NAF), was also acquired.

The new Saab-Scania company has a total of approximately 25,000 employees. Since January 1970 it has been organised in four separate groups, as shown above.

Saab's current aerospace products include the Saab-35 Draken family of single-seat all-weather fighter-bombers, the Saab-105 twin-jet trainer and light attack aircraft and the Saab-37 Viggen multi-mission combat aircraft, now in quantity production under a Kr 1,690 m Air Force contract signed in April 1968. During 1968-69 the company also received two major export orders, one from Denmark for 46 Drakens and one from Austria for 40 Saab-105XT's.

The company's Norrköping department handles sales of Cessna aircraft, Rolls-Royce light aircraft engines and Hughes helicopters.

Saab is carrying out design studies on a number of different commercial transport aircraft, but a decision to proceed with actual design and development remains to be taken.

Saab has greatly expanded its activities in the electronics field and has more than 1,800 people engaged on this work. Current production items include general-purpose computers, automatic pilots and fire control and bombing systems for piloted aircraft, and components for guided missiles. A major production programme is the airborne computer for the Saab-37, and many toss bomb sights have been bought by the United States, France, Switzerland and Denmark.

Saab is main contractor to the Swedish Air Board for licence production of the Falcon RB08 coastal defence and ship-to-ship guided missile. It is also developing the new Saab 305 (RB05) air-to-surface missle for the Swedish Air Force and a modernised version of the Air Force RB04 homing anti-shipping missile to be carried by the AJ 37 Viggen.

SAAB-35 DRAKEN
Swedish Air Force designations: J 35, S 35 and SK 35

The Saab-35 Draken single-seat fighter, which has a high supersonic speed, was designed mainly to intercept bombers in the transonic speed range, and carries radar equipment to accomplish this under all weather conditions. It is, however, able to carry also substantial weapon loads for attack duties or cameras for photographic reconnaissance.

The Draken is of the "double delta" configuration, developed exclusively in Sweden, which provides large space for fuel, armament and equipment in combination with low structure weight, low drag and a high air intake efficiency.

The first of three prototypes of the Saab-35 made its maiden flight on 25 October 1955. During 1956 the aircraft was ordered into quantity production, and the first production Saab-35A (J 35A) made its first flight on 15 February 1958.

The following versions of the J 35 have been announced:

J 35A. Initial production version, with Svenska Flygmotor RM6B turbojet giving

Saab S 35E reconnaissance version of the Draken, with nose-mounted cameras

approximately 11,000 lb (5,000 kg) st without and 14,400 lb (6,520 kg) st with afterburner. Saab S6 fire control equipment. Lear autopilot. Entered service with Swedish Air Force early in 1960. Production completed. Some converted into SK 35C's; most of the others converted to J 35B standard. Described in 1969-70 *Jane's*.

J 35B. Development of J 35A with Saab S7 collision-course fire control system and electronic equipment designed especially for integration with Sweden's semi-automatic air defence control system. The J 35B first flew on 29 November 1959, and is in service with the Swedish Air Force. Production completed.

SK 35C. Two-seat dual-control trainer version of J 35A, with different front fuselage. Instructor and pupil in tandem under a long canopy, with the instructor's seat raised slightly to improve forward vision past the pupil. No radar. Same weapons capability as tactical versions. First SK 35C flew on 30 December 1959. Production completed.

J 35D. Development of J 35B with more powerful Flygmotor RM6C turbojet engine. Saab FII5 autopilot. Increased fuel capacity. First flew on 27 December 1960. Production completed.

S 35E. Reconnaissance version based on J 35D. One wide-angle and four other cameras in pressurised nose compartment for 180° low-altitude photography, plus three long focal length cameras (one in nose and one in each gun compartment) for high-altitude or distant low-altitude use. Camera windows fitted with defrosting equipment. Fuselage nose slides forward for easy access to cameras. Equipment includes new Swedish camera sight and modernised navigation aids. First S 35E flew for first time on 27 June 1963. In service since late 1965. Production completed.

J 35F. Development of J 35D with improved Saab S7B collision-course fire-control system, radar and normal armament of two Saab-produced

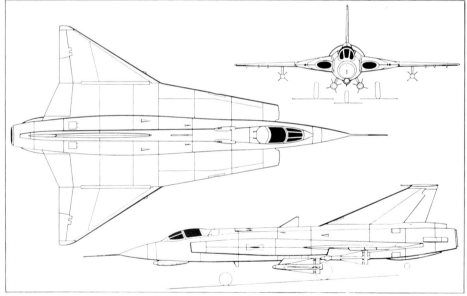

Saab J 35F Draken armed with RB27 and RB28 missiles

Saab J 35F Draken all-weather fighter, with Hughes Falcon underwing missiles and under-nose infra-red target seeker

RB27 Falcon HM-55 (radar-guided) and two RB 28 Falcon HM-58 (infra-red) air-to-air missiles. Infra-red target seeker in fairing under nose. One 30 mm Aden M/55 cannon in starboard wing. Ordered in greater numbers than any other version. Several hundred currently in production with deliveries scheduled until 1971. In service.

35X. Long-range attack/reconnaissance version developed for the export market. Externally similar to the J 35F, but has greatly increased attack capability and range. For reconnaissance duties, a nose similar to that of the S 35E is fitted. T-O run with nine 1,000 lb bombs is 4,030 ft (1,210 m).

On 29 March 1968 the Danish Defence Ministry ordered 20 aircraft of this type, designated **Saab 35XD**, for the Royal Danish Air Force, plus three **Saab 35XT** two-seat trainers. Purchase of a further 23 Drakens was approved on 18 June 1968; these comprise 20 more Saab 35XD's and three Saab 35XT's. These aircraft will be designated **F-35** (fighter/bomber), **RF-35** (reconnaissance/fighter) and **TF-35** (trainer/fighter) in RDAF service. The first production Saab 35XD flew for the first time on 29 January 1970; the first unit to receive Drakens will be No 725 Squadron RDAF.

In April 1970, 12 Drakens (designated **Saab-35XS**) were ordered by Finland. These will be assembled in Finland by Valmet Oy (which see), for delivery between 1974-75, but existing Drakens may be leased to Finland before that date for familiarisation purposes.

The total number of Drakens built or on order for Sweden, Denmark and Finland is approx 600.

The description below refers to the Saab 35XD, but is generally applicable also to the J 35D and J 35F.

Type: Single-seat supersonic all-weather fighter, reconnaissance and attack aircraft.

Wings: Cantilever "double delta" mid-wing monoplane. Sweepback on centre wing leading-edge 80°, on outer wing leading-edge 57°. Thickness/chord ratio 5%. Central wing integral with fuselage. All-metal stressed-skin structure. with some bonding. Outer wing panels, attached to centre wing with a bolt joint, have relatively thick skin on a framework of spars and ribs and can be detached for transportation by road.

Fuselage: All-metal structure, in front and rear main sections, connected to each other by a bolt joint. Fuselage front section integral with front of centre wing structure. Two pairs of air-brakes, above and below rear fuselage.

Control Surfaces: Conventional delta-shape fin and rudder. Elevons on wing trailing-edge comprise two inboard and two outboard surfaces, the latter being mass-balanced. Each control surface servo-operated by two hydraulic tandem jacks, fed by two separate hydraulic systems. No part of load on control surfaces is fed into stick and rudder pedals. Stick forces are generated artificially. Three-axis stabilisation system.

Landing Gear: Retractable tricycle type. Hydraulic actuation. Main units retract outward, the legs shortening during retraction to reduce the space required inside wing. Nose-wheel retracts forward and is steerable. Tyre pressures 142-185 lb/sq in (10-13 kg/cm²) on nose unit, 171-242 lb/sq in (12-17 kg/cm²) on main units. Goodyear double-disc brakes and Dunlop anti-skid brake units. Dual retractable tail-wheels. Brake parachute in fairing above rear fuselage. Arrester hook optional.

Power Plant: One Svenska Flygmotor (Rolls-Royce licence) Avon 300-series engine (Swedish Air Force designation RM 6C) with Swedish-developed afterburner. Static thrust approximately 12,790 lb (5,800 kg) dry and 17,650 lb (8,000 kg) with afterburner. Internal fuel in integral tanks in inner wings and fuselage bag tanks. Total internal fuel capacity 880 Imp gallons (4,000 litres). Provision for external tanks under fuselage and wings, increasing total capacity to 1,980 Imp gallons (9,000 litres) in Saab 35XD and approx 1,650 Imp gallons (7,500 litres) in J 35D and J 35F. Additional internal tanks can be fitted in place of guns for ferry purposes. Single-point pressure fuelling system, capacity 185 Imp gallons (840 litres) per minute.

Accommodation: Pressurised and air-conditioned cockpit, with fully-automatic Saab 73SE-F rocket-assisted ejection seat and GQ parachute system permitting ejection within the normal flight envelope and down to 54 knots (62 mph; 100 km/h) on the ground. Rearward-hinged canopy.

Systems: Duplicated hydraulic system, with two independent pumps, for control surface and landing gear actuation. Third pump, for emergency use, is driven by ram air in case of engine failure. Three-phase AC electrical system supplies 200/115V 400 c/s power via a 20kVA engine-driven generator or, in emergency, via a 3·5kVA generator in emergency power unit. Equipment requiring DC power is fed from these AC systems via two rectifiers giving 2·2 kW at 29V. One 24V 22Ah accumulator acts as a buffer. The power permits three engine starting attempts.

First Saab-35XD production Draken for the Danish Air Force

Electronics and Equipment: Complete radar equipment with nose scanner and pilot's scope, as well as Saab S7 collision-course fire-control equipment. Saab FH5 autopilot, with air data system, stick-steering and various following modes. Vertical tape instruments. Aga FR 21 VHF. DME.

Armament: Nine attachment points (each 1,000 lb = 454 kg) for external stores: three under each wing and three under fuselage. Stores can consist of air-to-air missiles and unguided air-to-air rocket pods (19 × 7·5-cm), 12 × 13·5-cm Bofors air-to-ground rockets, nine 1,000 lb or fourteen 500 lb bombs, or fuel tanks. Two or four RB24 Sidewinder air-to-air missiles can be carried under wings and fuselage. Two 30-mm Aden cannon (one in each wing) can be replaced by extra internal fuel tanks. With two 280 Imp gallon (1,275 litre) and two 110 Imp gallon (500 litre) drop tanks, two 1,000 lb (454 kg) or four 500 lb (227 kg) bombs can be carried.

Dimensions, external:
- Wing span: 30 ft 10 in (9·40 m)
- Wing aspect ratio: 1·77
- Width, outer wing panels removed: 14 ft 5 in (4·40 m)
- Length overall: 50 ft 4 in (15·35 m)
- Height overall: 12 ft 9 in (3·89 m)
- Wheel track: 8 ft 10½ in (2·70 m)
- Wheelbase: 13 ft 1 in (4·00 m)

Area:
- Wings, gross: 529·6 sq ft (49·2 m²)

Weights:
- T-O weight clean: 25,130 lb (11,400 kg)
- T-O weight with two 1,000-lb bombs and two 280 Imp gallon drop tanks: 32,165 lb (14,590 kg)
- Max T-O weight:
  - J 35D, F: 33,070 lb (15,000 kg)
  - 35XD: 35,275 lb (16,000 kg)
- Max overload T-O weight: 35,275 lb (16,000 kg)
- Normal landing weight: 19,400 lb (8,800 kg)

Performance (A=AUW of 25,130 lb; B=AUW of 32,165 lb):
- Max level speed with afterburning:
  - A: Mach 2
  - B: Mach 1·4
- Rate of climb at S/L with afterburning:
  - A: 34,450 ft (10,500 m)/min
  - B: 22,650 ft (6,900 m)/min
- Time to 36,100 ft (11,000 m) with afterburning:
  - A: 2 min 36 sec
- Time to 49,200 ft (15,000 m) with afterburning:
  - A: 5 min 0 sec
- T-O run, with afterburning:
  - A: 2,130 ft (650 m)
  - B: 3,840 ft (1,170 m)
- T-O to 50 ft (15 m) with afterburning:
  - A: 3,150 ft (960 m)
  - B: 5,080 ft (1,550 m)
- Landing run at normal landing weight:
  - A and B: 1,740 ft (530 m)
- Radius of action (high-low-high) internal fuel only:
  - A: 343 nm (395 miles; 635 km)
- Radius of action (high-low-high) with two 1,000 lb bombs and two drop-tanks:
  - B: 541 nm (623 miles; 1,003 km)
- Ferry range with max internal and external fuel: 1,754 nm (2,020 miles; 3,250 km)

SAAB-37 VIGGEN (THUNDERBOLT)

Swedish Air Force designations: AJ 37, JA 37, S 37 and SK 37

The Saab-37 Viggen multi-mission combat aircraft is the major component in System 37, the next manned weapon system for the Swedish Air Force.

In brief, System 37 comprises the Saab-37 aircraft with power plant, airborne equipment, armament, ammunition and photographic equipment; special ground servicing equipment, including test equipment; and special training equipment, including simulators. Particular attention is paid to the optimum adaptation of System 37 to the SwAF base organisation and air defence control system (STRIL 60).

The Saab-37 is designed as a basic "platform" which can be readily adapted to fulfil the four primary rôles of attack, interception, reconnaissance and training. It has an extremely advanced aerodynamic configuration, using a foreplane, fitted with flaps, in combination with a main delta wing to confer STOL characteristics.

By employing a Swedish supersonic development of the American Pratt & Whitney JT8D turbofan engine, with a very powerful Swedish-designed afterburner, the Saab-37 can cruise economically at extremely low altitudes and, at the same time, possesses the acceleration and climb performance required for interception duties. The combination of advanced aerodynamic features with this powerful engine, thrust reverser, automatic speed control during landing and head-up display, enables the aircraft to operate from narrow runways of about 1,640 ft (500 m) length.

The first of seven prototypes of the Saab-37 flew for the first time on 8 February 1967, followed by the second aircraft on 21 September 1967 and the third on 29 March 1968. By April 1969 all six single-seat prototypes were flying, the sixth aircraft being fully representative of the AJ 37 initial production version. External modifications introduced since the first prototype began flight testing include a "dog-tooth" wing leading-edge and a flat (instead of dihedral) foreplane. The seventh Viggen, prototype for the two-seat SK 37 trainer, was flown for the first time on 2 July 1970. A number of airframe parts have also been completed for static testing.

Four versions have so far been announced, as follows:

AJ 37. Single-seat all-weather attack version, with secondary interceptor capability. Initial production version, which will begin to replace the A 32A Lansen from mid-1971. Original order for 83, announced on 20 March 1967, was followed by a further contract announced on 5 April 1968, bringing total so far ordered to 150.

JA 37. Single-seat interceptor version, with secondary capability for attack missions. Intended to replace the J 35 Draken from the mid-seventies.

S 37. Single-seat reconnaissance version, intended to replace the S 32C version of the Lansen.

SK 37. Tandem two-seat training version, due to enter service simultaneously with the AJ 37. Rear cockpit takes the place of some electronics and forward fuselage fuel tank, and is fitted with bulged hood and periscope. Orders, placed at same time as those for AJ 37, so far total 25.

The following details refer specifically to the AJ 37 version of the Viggen.

Type: Single-seat all-weather attack aircraft, stressed for ultimate load factor of 12 *g*.

Wings: Tandem arrangement of canard foreplane, with trailing-edge flaps, and a rear-mounted delta main wing with two-section hydraulically-actuated powered elevons on each trailing-edge, which can be operated differentially or in unison. Main wing has compound sweep on leading-edge. Outer sections have extended ("dog-tooth") leading-edge. Extensive use of metal-bonded honeycomb panels in wing and for foreplane flaps and main landing gear doors.

Fuselage: Conventional all-metal semi-monocoque structure, of similar construction to that of Draken, using light metal forgings and heat-resistant plastic bonding. Local use of titanium for engine firewall and other selected areas. Four plate-type air-brakes, one on each side and two below fuselage, are of metal-bonded honeycomb construction, which is also used for other selected areas of centre fuselage. Quick-release handle permits nose-cone to be pulled forward on tracks to give access to radar compartment.

Tail Unit: Vertical surfaces only, comprising main fin and powered rudder, supplemented by a small ventral fin. Rudder of metal-bonded honeycomb construction. The main fin can be folded downward to port.

Landing Gear: Retractable tricycle type of Saab origin, designed for a max rate of sink of

First and second Saab-37 Viggen prototypes, the nearer aircraft fitted with Saab RB05 missiles and rocket pods under the wings and fuselage

985 ft (300 m)/min. Power-steerable twin-wheel nose unit retracts forward. Each main unit has two main wheels in tandem and retracts inward into main wing. Main oleos shorten during retraction. Nose-wheel tyres size 18 × 5·5, pressure 155 lb/sq in (10·9 kg/cm²). Main wheel tyres size 26 × 6·6, pressure 215 lb/sq in (15·1 kg/cm²).

Power Plant: One Svenska Flygmotor RM8 (supersonic development of the Pratt & Whitney JT8D-22, turbofan engine) fitted with a Swedish-developed afterburner and thrust reverser. This engine has a static thrust, with afterburning of approx, 26,450 lb (12,000 kg). Thrust reverser doors are actuated automatically by the compression of the oleos as the main landing gear strikes the runway, the thrust being deflected forward via three annular slots in the ejector wall. The ejector is normally kept open at subsonic speeds to reduce fuselage base drag; at supersonic speeds, with the intake closed, the ejector serves as a supersonic nozzle. Fuel is contained in one tank in each wing, a saddle tank over the engine, one tank in each side of the fuselage, and one aft of the cockpit. Electrically-powered pumps deliver fuel to the engine from the central fuselage tank, which is kept filled continuously from the peripheral tanks. Pressure refuelling point beneath starboard wing. Provision for jettisonable external auxiliary tank on centre pylon under fuselage.

Accommodation: Pilot only, on Saab fully-adjustable rocket-assisted ejection seat beneath rearward-hinged clamshell canopy. Cockpit pressurisation, heating and air-conditioning by engine bleed-air via heat exchangers, cooling turbines and water separator. Bird-proof windscreen.

Systems: Two independent hydraulic systems, of 3,000 lb/sq in (210 kg/cm²) pressure, each with engine-driven pump and with auxiliary electrically-operated standby pump for emergency use. Three-phase AC electrical system supplies 210/115V 400 c/s power via a 60kVA liquid-cooled brushless generator, which also provides 28V DC power via batteries and rectifier. Emergency standby power from 6kVA turbo-generator, which is extended automatically into the airstream in the event of a power failure or when the landing gear is extended. External power receptacle on port side of fuselage.

Electronics and Flight Equipment: Altogether, about 50 "black boxes", with a total weight of approx 1,323 lb (600 kg), are installed in the Saab-37. Flight equipment includes an automatic speed control system, SRA head-up display system, AGA aircraft attitude instruments and radio, Philips air data unit and instruments, L. M. Ericsson radar, STC radar altimeter, Doppler navigation equipment and AIL Tactical Instrument Landing System (TILS), a microwave scanning beam landing guidance system. Most of the electronic equipment in the Saab-37 is connected to the CK-37 airborne digital computer, which is programmed to check out and monitor these systems both on the ground and during flight.

Armament and Operational Equipment (AJ 37): All armament is carried externally on seven permanent attachment points, three under the fuselage and two under each wing, with standard 30 in (75 cm) store ejection racks, and one beneath each wing for missiles only. Wings can be fitted with two additional hard-points if required. Primary armament will be the Swedish RB04 air-to-surface homing missile for use against naval targets or the Saab RB05 air-to-surface missile for use against both ground and naval targets, plus various types of air-to-surface rockets, bombs, 30-mm Aden guns and mines. The attack version can be adapted to perform interception missions armed with air-to-air missiles. Computations in connection with various phases of an attack, including navigation, target approach and fire control calculations, are handled by a Saab CK-37 miniaturised digital computer. This computer, which performs 48 specific tasks within the aircraft and is capable of 200,000 calculations per second, also provides data to the head-up display in the cockpit, thus freeing the pilot for concentration on other aspects of a flight. For a typical attack mission, the pilot would feed into the computer the position of the target and flight-path way-points; the exact time of the attack; details of intended and alternative landing bases; and the type and method of delivery of the weapons to be carried. The CK-37 computer would then calculate and present to him information regarding engine start and take-off times, navigation and approach to the target (including any deviations from the time schedule), weapon aiming and release, climb-out, return flight path and landing. Continuous monitoring of the flight paths and fuel situation is provided throughout the mission, and the computer can also, when required, release the weapons automatically.

Saab-37 Viggen carrying two RB04 air-to-surface missiles beneath the wings

Dimensions, external:
- Main wing span: 34 ft 9¼ in (10·60 m)
- Length overall (incl probe): 53 ft 5¾ in (16·30 m)
- Length of fuselage: 50 ft 8¼ in (15·45 m)
- Height overall: 18 ft 4½ in (5·60 m)
- Height overall, main fin folded: 13 ft 1½ in (4·00 m)
- Wheel track: 15 ft 7½ in (4·76 m)
- Wheelbase (c/l of shock struts): 18 ft 2 in (5·54 m)

Weight:
- T-O weight with normal armament: approx 35,275 lb (16,000 kg)

Performance:
- Max level speed:
  - at high altitude: Mach 2
  - at 330 ft (100 m): above Mach 1·1
- Approach speed: approx 119 knots (137 mph; 220 km/h)
- Time to 36,000 ft (11,000 m) from brakes off: approx 2 min
- T-O run: approx 1,310 ft (400 m)
- Landing run: 1,310-1,475 ft (400-450 m)
- Required landing field length:
  - conventional landing: 4,920 ft (1,500 m)
  - with reverse thrust: 3,280 ft (1,000 m)
  - with auto-throttle: 2,300 ft (700 m)
  - no-flare landing using head-up display: 1,640 ft (500 m)
- Tactical radius with external armament:
  - high-low-high: over 540 nm (1,000 km)
  - low altitude throughout: over 270 nm (500 km)

SAAB-105

Swedish Air Force designation: SK 60

The first of two prototypes of the Saab-105 flew for the first time on 29 June 1963, and the second on 17 June 1964. The Swedish Air Board ordered 130 production aircraft early in 1964, the first of which flew on 27 August 1965. A follow-up order for 20 more was placed in 1965. All 150 have been delivered. A full description appeared in the 1969-70 *Jane's*.

Designation of the Swedish Air Force versions are as follows:

SK 60A. Basic training and liaison version, of which deliveries to Ljungbyhed Air Base began in the Spring of 1966. Two Turboméca Aubisque turbofan engines (each 1,640 lb = 743 kg st). All have certain provisions for conversion to attack configuration.

SK 60B. SK 60A with completed provision for ground attack use. These aircraft are still used mainly as trainers, but can be changed very quickly to light attack configuration, with rockets, gun pods or guided missiles.

SK 60C. A number of SK 60B aircraft will have a permanent reconnaissance camera installation in the nose, in addition to attack capability. The camera is of panoramic type. A special tape recorder may also be carried on reconnaissance missions. Prototype flew on 18 January 1967.

SAAB-105XT

First flown on 29 April 1967, the Saab-105XT is a development of the SK 60B version of the Saab-105, with improved performance and armament load capacity resulting from the installation of two General Electric J85-17B turbojet engines. To cater for the higher fuel consumption, compared with the Saab-105, internal fuel capacity has been increased.

The wing structure has been strengthened and permits a weapon load of up to 4,410 lb (2,000 kg) to be carried. Max T-O weight is also increased, but the Saab-105XT retains the ability to take off on one engine. It can be used for training, ground attack, liaison, interception or photo-reconnaissance duties. Provision is made for target towing reel and launcher to be installed beneath the port wing.

Forty are being built for the Austrian Air Force, and delivery of these began in the Spring of 1970. They are designated **Saab-105Ö**.

A developed version, designated **Saab-105XH**, has been designed to meet the needs of the Swiss Air Force; this is described in the Addenda.

TYPE: Multi-purpose light twin-jet monoplane.

WINGS: Cantilever shoulder-wing monoplane. Sweepback 12° 48' at quarter-chord. Anhedral 6°. Thickness/chord ratio 10·3% at root, 12% at tip. One-piece stressed-skin structure with two continuous spars. Ailerons of bonded honeycomb construction, statically and aerodynamically balanced and with boosted control. Geared servo-tab in each aileron; starboard tab adjustable mechanically for trimming. Hydraulically-operated single-slotted flaps of honeycomb construction. Two small fences on upper surface of each wing.

FUSELAGE: All-metal stressed-skin semi-monocoque structure. Hydraulically-operated perforated airbrakes pivoted in transverse slots in lower fuselage aft of landing gear.

TAIL UNIT: Cantilever all-metal structure, with tailplane mounted at tip of fin. Control surfaces of bonded honeycomb construction, statically and aerodynamically balanced. Electrically-operated trim-tab in rudder. A pneumatic yaw-damper is also fitted. Geared servo-tab in each elevator, adjustable electrically for trimming. Small ventral fin.

LANDING GEAR: Retractable tricycle type. Hydraulic actuation. Main units retract into fuselage. Forward-retracting hydraulically-steerable nose-wheel. Oleo-pneumatic shock-absorbers. Hydraulic disc brakes with anti-skid system.

POWER PLANT: Two General Electric J85-17B turbojet engines, each rated at 2,850 lb (1,293 kg) st. Engine starting by internal battery. Fuel in two fuselage tanks and two wing tanks with total capacity of 451 Imp gallons (2,050 litres). Pressure refuelling point in starboard wingtip. Provision for overwing refuelling to a total of 310 Imp gallons (1,400 litres). Provision for two 110 Imp gallon (500 litres) underwing drop tanks.

ACCOMMODATION: Two side-by-side ejection seats. Alternative provision for four fixed seats. Bird-proof windscreen. Electrically-actuated rearward-hinged canopy of double-curved acrylic glass. Dual controls standard.

SYSTEMS: Air-conditioning system includes refrigeration unit. Nominal cabin pressure differential of 3·4 lb/sq in (0·24 kg/cm²). Hydraulic system, pressure 3,000 lb/sq in (210 kg/cm²), has two pumps (one on each engine) and actuates landing gear, nose-wheel steering, brakes, flaps, air-brakes and aileron boost. DC electrical system has two 300A 29V starter-generators and two 22Ah batteries. External power connector installed. AC system provides 3-phase power at 200/115V 400 c/s from two 250A converters. G-suit connections. Oxygen system, with two 5-litre bottles.

ELECTRONICS AND EQUIPMENT: A wide range of navigational and communications equipment can be installed. The standard installation includes one VHF and one UHF unit with audio control, one VOR/ILS with marker beacon, one ADF, one transponder and one DME.

ARMAMENT AND OPERATIONAL EQUIPMENT: Three attachment points under each wing, the inner and outer points each capable of supporting a

Saab-105XT multi-purpose military aircraft with underwing camera pod

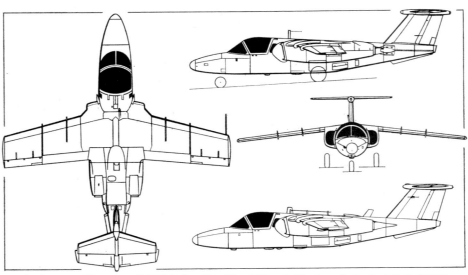

Saab-105 multi-purpose light jet aircraft, with additional side view (*bottom*) **of Saab-105XT**

610 lb (275 kg) load and the centre points each capable of supporting 1,000 lb (450 kg). Total weapons load 4,410 lb (2,000 kg). Wide range of weapons includes two 1,000 lb (454 kg) and four 500 lb (227 kg) bombs; ten 250 lb (113 kg) bombs; twelve 176 lb (80 kg) Lepus flare bombs; four 500 lb bombs and two 30-mm gun pods; four 500 lb (227 kg) napalm bombs and two Minigun pods; twelve 13·5-cm rockets; six pods each containing four 5-in rockets; twenty-two 7·5-cm rockets; two Saab RB05 air-to-surface and two infra-red (Sidewinder) air-to-air missiles and two Minigun pods; or a camera pod, flash pod, two Minigun pods and two drop tanks. Ferranti Isis F-105 gyro gun-sight standard.

DIMENSIONS, EXTERNAL:

Wing span	31 ft 2 in (9·50 m)
Length overall	34 ft 5 in (10·50 m)
Height overall	8 ft 10 in (2·70 m)
Wheel track	6 ft 7 in (2·00 m)
Wheelbase	12 ft 9½ in (3·90 m)

AREA:

Wings, gross	175 sq ft (16·3 m²)

WEIGHTS:

Weight empty	5,655 lb (2,565 kg)
Max T-O weight, trainer	9,987 lb (4,530 kg)
Max T-O weight, with armament	14,330 lb (6,500 kg)

PERFORMANCE (at max T-O weight):

Max speed at S/L
    524 knots (603 mph; 970 km/h)

Max speed at 33,000 ft (10,000 m)
    472 knots (544 mph; 875 km/h)

Max permissible diving speed   Mach 0·86

Time to 33,000 ft (10,000 m):
    trainer   4-5 min

T-O run (trainer)   1,181 ft (360 m)

Landing run   1,890 ft (575 m)

Range at 43,000 ft (13,100 m) at 378 knots (435 mph; 700 km/h), 20 min reserves
    1,294 nm (1,491 miles; 2,400 km)

Range at 36,000 ft (11,000 m) at 378 knots (435 mph; 700 km/h) with external tanks and 30 min reserves
    1,629 nm (1,876 miles; 3,020 km)

Typical attack radius, including reserves, with 3,000 lb (1,360 kg) bomb load:
    hi-lo-hi mission 446 nm (514 miles; 827 km)
    low altitude throughout
    174 nm (201 miles; 324 km)

Typical attack radius, including reserves, with 2,000 lb (907 kg) bomb load and 2 drop tanks:
    hi-lo-hi mission 732 nm (844 miles; 1,360 km)
    low altitude throughout
    283 nm (326 miles; 523 km)

First production Saab-105Ö (two 2,850 lb st General Electric J85-17B turbojet engines) in the insignia of the Austrian Air Force

SWITZERLAND

AFU

AKTIENGESELLSCHAFT FÜR FLUGZEUG-UNTERNEHMUNGEN ALTENRHEIN

HEAD OFFICE AND WORKS:
Altenrhein bei Rorschach

MANAGING DIRECTOR:
Dr J. Riedener

CHIEF ENGINEER:
Dipl Ing P. Spalinger

This company was formed in the Spring of 1959 to undertake the manufacture, sales, development testing, repair and maintenance of aircraft. It subsequently took over from the FFA responsi-

bility for the P-16 strike fighter, a full description of which appeared in the 1961-62 *Jane's*.

AFU proposed a new version of the P-16, for COIN duties, with a more powerful turbojet or turbofan engine. This aircraft was described fully in the 1968-69 *Jane's*.

The company has no current aviation activities.

DÄTWYLER

MAX DÄTWYLER & CO

HEAD OFFICE AND WORKS:
Flugplatz, 4900 Langenthal-Bleienbach BE

Dätwyler & Co is a servicing organisation which has specialised in the repair and modification of Piper aircraft, particularly war-surplus Cubs. In 1960, it produced a specialised glider-tug known as the MDC-Trailer, using standard Super Cub components, and details of this aircraft can be found in the 1966-67 *Jane's*.

A new version of the Bücker Jungmann, named the Lerche, built by Dätwyler to the design of Ing Fritz Dubs, was described in the 1969-70 *Jane's*.

Other current activities of this company include the manufacture of components for the Pilatus Porter and development of a simple two-seat trainer of original design, of which all available details are given below.

DÄTWYLER SWISS TRAINER

After some two years of study, Dätwyler announced during 1967-68 some preliminary details of a new two-seat basic training aircraft called the Swiss Trainer. Designed by Hans Farner, in collaboration with the Swedish designer Bjorn Andreasson, a prototype of the Swiss Trainer is under construction.

A single-seat glider-towing version, powered by a 180 hp Franklin air-cooled engine, is also projected.

The details below apply to the prototype two-seat training version.

TYPE: Two-seat basic training aircraft.

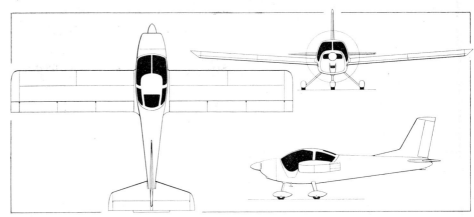

Dätwyler Swiss Trainer two-seat basic training aircraft

WINGS: Cantilever mid-wing monoplane. Constant-chord wings, with full-span flaps and ailerons.

FUSELAGE: Semi-monocoque structure.

TAIL UNIT: Single sweptback fin and rudder. Tailplane, set at base of fin, has sweepback on leading-edge. One-piece elevator, with balance tab.

LANDING GEAR: Non-retractable tricycle type. Single wheel, with streamlined fairing, on each unit.

POWER PLANT: One 115-160 hp Lycoming hori-

zontally-opposed air-cooled engine, driving a two-blade propeller.

ACCOMMODATION: Side-by-side seats for two persons, under large rearward-hinged transparent moulded canopy.

DIMENSIONS, EXTERNAL:
Wing span	32 ft 1¾ in (9·80 m)
Length overall	22 ft 5¼ in (6·84 m)

AREA:
Wings, gross	158·23 sq ft (14·70 m²)

WEIGHTS (estimated):
Weight empty	1,014 lb (460 kg)
Max T-O weight	1,587 lb (720 kg)

FEDERAL AIRCRAFT FACTORY

**EIDGENÖSSISCHES FLUGZEUGWERK —
FABRIQUE FEDERALE D'AVIONS —
FABBRICA FEDERALE D'AEROPLANI**

HEAD OFFICE AND WORKS:
CH-6032 Emmen

DIRECTOR: Lucien Othenin-Girard

CHIEF DESIGNER: J. Branger

The F+W is the Swiss Government's official aircraft establishment for research, development and production of military aircraft. It was prime contractor for the production of the Swiss-built Dassault Mirage III-S and III-RS aircraft (details under Dassault entry in French section), and now has similar responsibility for production of the Aérospatiale (Sud-Aviation) SE 316S Alouette III helicopter (details under Aérospatiale entry in French section).

The first Mirage III-S manufactured in Switzerland and assembled at the Federal Aircraft Factory was flown in October 1965. Production of both the III-S and III-RS has been completed.

Since 1967, the F+W has been evolving a turboprop conversion of a pre-war design by EKW (forerunner of F+W), the C-3603. This aircraft, redesignated C-3605, flew for the first time on 19 August 1968, and is described below.

F+W C-3605

The C-3605 is a turboprop conversion of the EKW C-3603 fighter-bomber, which has been in Swiss Air Force service since 1942 and of which 144 were built up to 1944.

In 1967 the basic airframe of the C-3603's still in service was assessed as having a further 10 years of useful life, and work began at the Federal Aircraft Factory under Ing Jean-Pierre Weibel later that year with a view to replacing the aircraft's original 1,020 hp Saurer/SLM-built Hispano-Suiza 12Y-51 piston-engine with a Lycoming T5307A turboprop engine. Fundamentally, the modification involved the insertion of an additional section in the front fuselage to maintain the original CG position, the remainder of the airframe being basically unchanged.

Prototype conversion was carried out on the 102nd production C-3603 which, with the new engine, was redesignated C-3605 and flew for the first time on 19 August 1968. A third, central, tail fin was added subsequently.

Following the successful completion of flight testing, the conversion of 20 aircraft to C-3605 standard is currently in progress.

TYPE: Two-seat target-towing aircraft.

WINGS: Cantilever low-wing monoplane. Aluminium alloy single-spar structure, with flush-riveted light alloy stressed skin, attached to fuselage by five bolts on each side. Trailing-edge slotted metal flaps and mass-balanced metal ailerons, all fabric-covered. Trim-tab on each aileron.

FUSELAGE: Conventional aluminium alloy semi-monocoque structure.

TAIL UNIT: Cantilever variable-incidence tailplane mounted on rear of fuselage, with twin endplate fins and rudders. Third, central, fin added subsequent to first flight. Aluminium alloy structure. Tailplane and fins metal-covered, rudders and one-piece elevator fabric-covered. Trim-tab on each rudder.

F+W C-3605 turboprop-engined target towing aircraft, with additional central tail fin

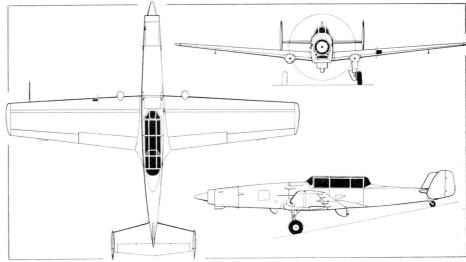

Federal Aircraft Factory (F+W) C-3605 turboprop-powered target towing aircraft

M

LANDING GEAR: Retractable tail-wheel type. Hydraulic retraction. Oleo-pneumatic shock-absorbers. Main units retract rearward and turn through 90°, the wheels into wells to lie flush with underside of wing aft of main spar and the main legs into "knuckle" type fairings beneath the wing. Retractable tail-wheel. Single wheel on each unit. BF Goodrich main wheels size 24 × 7·7 and tyres size 8·50-10, pressure 51 lb/sq in (3·58 kg/cm²). BF Goodrich multiple-disc brakes.

POWER PLANT: One 1,100 shp Lycoming T5307A turboprop engine, driving a Hamilton Standard 53C51 three-blade reversible-pitch metal propeller of 10 ft 0 in (3·05 m) diameter. Fuel in four wing tanks with total capacity of 112 Imp gallons (510 litres). Single refuelling point in fuselage. Provision for two 48·4 Imp gallon (220 litre) underwing drop-tanks. Oil capacity 3 Imp gallons (13·6 litres).

ACCOMMODATION: Crew of two in tandem cockpits under continuous transparent enclosure with individual canopy over each cockpit. Heating and ventilation of both cockpits standard.

SYSTEMS: Hydraulic system, pressure 3,200 lb/sq in (225 kg/cm²), for landing gear, flap and brake actuation and drive for the towing winch. Pneumatic system for brakes. 28V DC electrical system includes 9kW starter-generator and battery.

ELECTRONICS AND EQUIPMENT: Blind-flying instrumentation standard. Provision for VHF and UHF radio. Special equipment includes SZW 52 target-towing winch, with 6,560 ft (2,000 m) towing cable, in rear cockpit.

DIMENSIONS, EXTERNAL:
Wing span	45 ft 1 in (13·74 m)
Wing aspect ratio	6·58
Length overall	39 ft 5¾ in (12·03 m)
Height overall	13 ft 3½ in (4·05 m)
Tailplane span	12 ft 8 in (3·86 m)
Wheel track	10 ft 1¼ in (3·08 m)
Wheelbase	21 ft 10½ in (6·67 m)

AREA:
Wings, gross	308·9 sq ft (28·70 m²)

WEIGHTS AND LOADINGS:
Weight empty	5,806 lb (2,634 kg)
Normal T-O weight	7,275 lb (3,300 kg)
Max T-O weight, with drop-tanks	8,192 lb (3,716 kg)

Wing loading (normal T-O weight)
23·6 lb/sq ft (115 kg/m²)
Wing loading (max T-O weight)
26·4 lb/sq ft (129 kg/m²)
Power loading (normal T-O weight)
6·61 lb/shp (3 kg/shp)
Power loading (max T-O weight)
7·45 lb/shp (3·38 kg/shp)

PERFORMANCE (at max T-O weight):
Max level speed at 10,000 ft (3,050 m)
233 knots (268 mph; 432 km/h)
Max permissible diving speed
323 knots (372 mph; 600 km/h)
Max cruising speed at 10,000 ft (3,050 m)
227 knots (261 mph; 420 km/h)
Econ cruising speed at 20,000 ft (6,100 m)
188 knots (217 mph; 350 km/h)
Stalling speed, flaps down
53 knots (61 mph; 98 km/h)
Rate of climb at S/L 2,470 ft (753 m)/min
Service ceiling 32,800 ft (10,000 m)
T-O and landing run 590 ft (180 m)
T-O to 50 ft (15 m) 1,005 ft (307 m)
Landing from 50 ft (15 m) 1,695 ft (516 m)
Range with max fuel, clean aircraft, 10% reserve 525 nm (605 miles; 980 km)

FFA

FLUG- & FAHRZEUGWERKE AG

HEAD OFFICE AND WORKS:
Altenrhein, near Rorschach

PRESIDENT: Dr C. Caroni

WORKS DIRECTOR: O. Wick

CHIEF ENGINEER:
Dipl-Ing P. Spalinger

This company, known formerly as AG für Dornier Flugzeuge, was originally the Swiss branch of the German Dornier company. It is now an entirely Swiss company.

Until 1959 it was responsible for the design and development of the P-16 single-seat strike fighter, which was produced to meet a Swiss Air Force requirement. All further work on the P-16 was taken over subsequently by Aktiengesellschaft für Flugzeugunternehmungen Altenrhein.

More recently, FFA has developed a new 15 m glass-fibre sailplane named the Diamant, of which details are given in the "Sailplanes" section, and has participated in the licence production of components for the Swiss Mirage III programme. Current activities include the co-production, with Siai-Marchetti of Italy, of the latter company's SA.202 Bravo light aircraft, details of which are given below, and the overhaul, modification and servicing of military and civil aircraft.

The company has altogether about 1,300 employees, approximately half of whom are engaged on its aviation activities. The remainder are employed in the manufacture of railway rolling stock, motor vehicle bodies, and anodised aluminium sheeting for the domestic building industry.

Third prototype (second Swiss-built prototype) of the AS.202 Bravo two-seat light aircraft, with modified vertical tail surfaces

FFA/SIAI-MARCHETTI AS.202 BRAVO

Following an agreement concluded in 1967 with Siai-Marchetti of Italy, FFA is now engaged in co-production and marketing of the latter company's SA.202 Bravo two-seat light trainer and sporting aircraft, under the Swiss designation AS.202.

The FFA contribution consists of complete fuselages (including the cabin and controls) and tail units, the carrying out of wind tunnel and static load tests, and the flight testing and certification of the aircraft. Siai-Marchetti is completing the wings, landing gear and engine installation. Both Swiss- and Italian-assembled Bravos incorporate certain features and components of the Siai-Marchetti S.205.

Two Swiss versions have been announced, as follows:

AS.202/10. Two-seat version, with 115 hp Lycoming O-235-C2A engine.

AS.202/15. Two-seat version, with 150 hp Lycoming O-320-E2A engine. Optional third seat.

The first Bravo to fly was a Swiss-assembled AS.202/15 prototype (HB-HEA), which flew for the first time on 7 March 1969; the third aircraft, also Swiss-built, was displayed at the 1969 Paris Air Show. Swiss certification of the Bravo was anticipated in mid-1970, to be followed by FAA certification.

A full structural description of the Bravo will be found under the "Siai-Marchetti" heading in the Italian section of this edition.

PILATUS
PILATUS FLUGZEUGWERKE AG
HEAD OFFICE AND WORKS:
CH-6370, Stans, near Lucerne
GENERAL MANAGER: Dr E. Schaerer
MANAGERS:
E. Della Casa (Sales)
Dr E. Muller (Technical)
Dr K. Zimmermann (Management Services)
PUBLIC RELATIONS MANAGER:
R. Danis

Pilatus Flugzeugwerke AG was formed in December 1939, with a capital of two million Swiss francs, and began work in September 1941. A founder's syndicate had been formed in 1938 under the leadership of M. E. Bührle, the Swiss industrialist and owner of the Oerlikon company, of which the Pilatus company is now a subsidiary.

The current Pilatus products are the PC-6 Porter and PC-6-A1, B1 and C1 Turbo-Porter single-engined utility transports, of which full details follow.

PILATUS PC-6 PORTER

The Pilatus PC-6 Porter is a single-engined utility aircraft. STOL characteristics permit operations from small airfields, and a combination wheel/ski gear or floats may be fitted as alternatives to the standard wheel landing gear. A spacious cabin, with wide non-structural double doors or sliding door, permits rapid conversion from a pure freighter to a passenger transport. The Porter can also be adapted for ambulance duties (two stretchers and seats for five persons, including crew), aerial photography, supply dropping, parachute training, agricultural dusting and spraying, etc.

Design work began in 1957 and the first of five prototype Porters made its first flight on 4 May 1959. Swiss certification of the basic PC-6/340, with 340 hp Lycoming engine, was received in August 1959, and the entire pre-series of 20 aircraft was delivered by the Summer of 1961.

Further series have since been laid down, and a total of 59 had been built by December 1968. These include the PC-6/340-H2, with higher AUW than the original PC-6/340, which was described and illustrated in the 1969-70 *Jane's*.

All aircraft delivered up to mid-1966 had double doors without central pillar, on the starboard side of the cabin; these doors were non-structural and the aircraft could be flown without them. A further door on the port side was optional.

Current production machines have a forward-opening door on each side of the cockpit, a large rearward-sliding door on the starboard side of the cabin and a double door on the port side of the cabin.

The latest version is the **PC-6/D-H3,** distinguishable from previous Porter models by its larger, sweptback vertical tail surfaces and modified wingtips. This version (HB-FFW), which flew for the first time on 2 April 1970, has a 500 hp Lycoming TIO-720 engine, increased payload and range, and was due to be certificated in mid-1970, with first deliveries following in late 1970 or early 1971. Wing and tail modifications may be made available for converting existing Porter airframes.

The details below apply to the PC-6/D-H3.

Pilatus-built variants of the Porter with turboprop engines are known as **Turbo-Porters.** These are described separately.

TYPE: Single-engined STOL utility transport.

WINGS: Braced high-wing monoplane, with single streamline-section bracing strut each side. Wing section NACA 64-514. Dihedral 1°. Incidence 2°. Single-spar all-metal structure. Entire trailing-edge hinged, inner sections consisting of all-metal double-slotted flaps and outer sections of all-metal single-slotted ailerons. No air-brakes, trim-tabs or de-icing equipment.

FUSELAGE: All-metal semi-monocoque structure.

TAIL UNIT: Cantilever all-metal structure. Variable-incidence tailplane. Flettner tabs.

LANDING GEAR: Non-retractable tail-wheel type. Oleo shock-absorbers of Pilatus design and Thommen manufacture on all three units. Steerable tail-wheel. Goodyear main wheels and tyres size 7·50 × 10 (pressure 32 lb/sq in = 2·2 kg/cm²) or 11·00 × 12 (pressure 12·8 lb/sq in = 0·90 kg/cm²). Goodyear disc brakes. May be fitted with Pilatus wheel-skis or Edo 39-4000 or 58-4580 floats.

POWER PLANT: One 500 hp Lycoming TIO-720-C1A six-cylinder horizontally-opposed air-cooled engine. Lycoming TIGO-541-A1A or Rolls-Royce/Continental Tiara series engines may be available as alternative. Refuelling points above wings.

ACCOMMODATION: Cabin has pilot's seat forward on port side with one passenger seat alongside, and is normally fitted with six quickly removable seats for passengers, in pairs. Up to ten persons can be carried in high-density seating.

Floor is level, flush with door sill and is provided with rails for the seats. Forward-opening door beside each of the two front seats. Large rearward-sliding door on starboard side of main cabin. Double doors without central pillar, on port side. Hatch in floor 1 ft 10¾ in × 2 ft 11½ in (58 × 90 cm), openable from inside cabin for installation of aerial camera or for supply dropping. Hatch in cabin rear wall 1 ft 7 in × 2 ft 7 in (50 × 80 cm) permits stowage of six passenger seats or accommodation of freight items up to 16 ft 5 in (5 m) in length. Walls lined with lightweight sound-proofing and heat-insulation material and adjustable heating and ventilation systems provided.

SYSTEMS: Cabin heated by air from exhaust heat exchanger. Bendix 30B-24-1A 1500W engine-driven generator.

ELECTRONICS AND EQUIPMENT: Blind-flying instruments are standard equipment. Radio is optional.

DIMENSIONS, EXTERNAL:
- Wing span: 49 ft 8 in (15·13 m)
- Wing span over navigation lights: 49 ft 10½ in (15·20 m)
- Wing chord (constant): 6 ft 3 in (1·90 m)
- Wing aspect ratio: 7·96
- Length overall: 33 ft 5½ in (10·20 m)
- Height overall: 10 ft 6 in (3·20 m)
- Elevator span: 16 ft 9½ in (5·12 m)
- Wheel track: 9 ft 10 in (3·00 m)
- Wheelbase: 25 ft 10 in (7·87 m)
- Cabin double-door (port), and sliding door (stbd):
  - Height: 3 ft 5 in (1·04 m)
  - Width: 5 ft 2¼ in (1·58 m)

DIMENSIONS, INTERNAL:
- Cabin, from back of pilot's seat to rear wall:
  - Length: 7 ft 6½ in (2·30 m)
  - Max width: 3 ft 9½ in (1·16 m)
  - Max height (at front): 4 ft 2½ in (1·28 m)
  - Height at rear wall: 3 ft 10½ in (1·18 m)
  - Floor area: 28·6 sq ft (2·67 m²)
  - Volume: 107 cu ft (3·28 m³)

AREAS:
- Wings, gross: 310 sq ft (28·8 m²)
- Ailerons (total): 40·05 sq ft (3·72 m²)
- Trailing-edge flaps (total): 40·05 sq ft (3·72 m²)
- Tailplane: 43·40 sq ft (4·03 m²)
- Elevators: 45·40 sq ft (4·22 m²)

WEIGHTS:
- Basic operating weight, empty: 2,938 lb (1,288 kg)
- Min flying weight: 3,141 lb (1,425 kg)
- Max T-O weight,: 5,511 lb (2,500 kg)

PERFORMANCE (estimated, at max T-O weight):
- Max cruising speed: 129 knots (149 mph; 240 km/h)
- Econ cruising speed (60% power) at 1,000 ft (305 m): 108 knots (124 mph; 200 km/h)
- Max flying speed, flaps down: 82 knots (94 mph; 150 km/h)
- Stalling speed, flaps up: 49 knots (56 mph; 90 km/h)
- Stalling speed, flaps down: 37 knots (42 mph; 67 km/h)
- T-O run: 528 ft (161 m)
- T-O to 50 ft (15 m): 1,099 ft (335 m)
- Landing from 50 ft (15 m): 722 ft (220 m)
- Landing run: 308 ft (94 m)
- Max range, with reserves: 727 nm (838 miles; 1,350 km)

PILATUS PC-6-A1/H2 TURBO-PORTER

This version of the Turbo-Porter is basically similar to the PC-6, described above, but is powered by a 700 eshp Astazou XII turboprop engine, driving an hydraulically-actuated variable-pitch propeller. 46 built by December 1968.

On 15 November 1968 a Turbo-Porter powered by a 922 shp Turboméca Astazou XIV turboprop engine set a new world altitude record in Class C-1-c of 44,242 ft (13,485 m).

DIMENSIONS, EXTERNAL AND INTERNAL, AND AREAS:
- As for PC-6 Porter except:
  - Length overall: 36 ft 4¼ in (11·08 m)

WEIGHTS:
- Weight empty: 2,410 lb (1,093 kg)
- Max T-O weight: 4,850 lb (2,200 kg)

PERFORMANCE (at max T-O weight):
- Max cruising speed at 10,000 ft (3,050 m): 143 knots (165 mph; 265 km/h)
- Rate of climb at S/L: 1,400 ft (425 m)/min
- Service ceiling: 32,000 ft (9,750 m)
- T-O run: 380 ft (115 m)
- T-O to 50 ft (15 m): 790 ft (240 m)
- Landing from 50 ft (15 m): 590 ft (180 m)
- Landing run: 220 ft (67 m)
- Range with max fuel: 590 nm (680 miles; 1,095 km)
- Endurance with max fuel: 4 hr 36 min

PILATUS PC-6-B1/H2 TURBO-PORTER

This version of the Turbo-Porter is fitted with a 550 shp Pratt & Whitney (UACL) PT6A-20 turboprop engine, driving a Hartzell HC-B3TN-3 or -5C three-blade fully-feathering reversible-pitch constant-speed metal propeller, diameter 8 ft 5 in (2·56 m). Fuel capacity 106·6 Imp gallons (485 litres) normal, 141·6 Imp gallons (644 litres) maximum. It flew for the first time in May 1966, and is in production by both Pilatus and Fairchild Hiller in America. Total of 112 built by December 1968, including 73 by Pilatus and 39 by Fairchild Hiller.

The aircraft built by Fairchild Hiller are known simply as Porters.

LANDING GEAR: Goodyear 24 × 7 Type II main wheels and tyres and 5·00-4 tailwheel. Oversize Goodyear 11·00-12 Type III main wheels and tyres optional.

DIMENSIONS, INTERNAL AND EXTERNAL: As for PC-6 Porter, except:
- Length overall: 36 ft 1 in (11·00 m)

AREAS:
- Wings, gross: 310 sq ft (28·80 m²)
- Ailerons (total): 41·2 sq ft (3·83 m²)
- Flaps (total): 40·5 sq ft (3·76 m²)
- Fin: 18·3 sq ft (1·70 m²)
- Rudder: 10·3 sq ft (0·96 m²)
- Tailplane: 43·40 sq ft (4·03 m²)
- Elevators: 45·40 sq ft (4·22 m²)

WEIGHTS AND LOADINGS:
- Weight empty, equipped: 2,650 lb (1,202 kg)
- Basic operating weight empty: 2,843 lb (1,290 kg)
- Max T-O and landing weight: 4,850 lb (2,200 kg)
- Max wing loading: 15·57 lb/sq ft (76 kg/m²)
- Max power loading: 8·8 lb/shp (4·0 kg/shp)

PERFORMANCE (at max T-O weight):
- Max level speed: 151 knots (174 mph; 280 km/h)
- Econ cruising speed: 135 knots (155 mph; 250 km/h)
- Stalling speed, flaps up: 46 knots (53 mph; 85 km/h)
- Stalling speed, flaps down: 35 knots (40 mph; 64 km/h)
- Rate of climb at S/L: 1,339 ft (408 m)/min
- Service ceiling: 25,590 ft (7,800 m)
- T-O run: 381 ft (116 m)
- T-O to 50 ft (15 m): 623 ft (190 m)
- Landing from 50 ft (15 m): 568 ft (173 m)
- Landing run: 240 ft (73 m)
- Range with standard fuel: 485 nm (559 miles; 900 km)
- Range with max fuel: 593 nm (683 miles; 1,100 km)

PILATUS PC-6-C1/H2 TURBO-PORTER

Design work on this version of the Turbo-Porter was started on 19 November 1964. Construction of a prototype began on 1 March 1965, and it flew for the first time at the Fairchild Hiller works in America in October 1965. The first Pilatus-built PC-6-C1/H2 flew on 4 March 1966. A total of nine had been built by the end of 1968.

The PC-6-C1/H2 differs from the PC-6-B1/H2 Turbo-Porter only in having a 575 shp AiResearch TPE 331-25D turboprop engine, driving a Hartzell HC-B3TN-5C/T 10178CH three-blade variable-pitch metal propeller.

Early in 1969 a Turbo-Porter (HB-FEG) was undergoing certification trials fitted with a 600 shp AiResearch TPE 331-1-100 turboprop engine.

DIMENSIONS, INTERNAL AND EXTERNAL, AND AREAS: As for PC-6-B1 Turbo-Porter, except:
- Length overall: 35 ft 9 in (10·90 m)

WEIGHTS:
- Weight empty, equipped, without radio: 2,480 lb (1,125 kg)
- Max payload: 1,638 lb (745 kg)
- Max T-O weight: 4,850 lb (2,200 kg)

Pilatus PC-6 Porter (340 hp Lycoming GSO-480-B1A6 engine) with twin-float landing gear

Pilatus PC-6 Porter in current production form, with 500 hp Lycoming TIO-720 engine, modified wingtips and sweptback fin and rudder (*J. M. G. Gradidge*)

Pilatus PC-6-B1/H2 Turbo-Porter in the insignia of the Royal Australian Army (*Howard Levy*)

PERFORMANCE (at max T-O weight):
Max permissible diving speed
    151 knots (174 mph; 280 km/h)
Max cruising speed at 10,000-12,000 ft (3,000-
    3,650 m)   136 knots (157 mph; 253 km/h)
Stalling speed, flaps down
    45·5 knots (52 mph; 83 km/h)
Stalling speed, flaps up
    51 knots (58 mph; 94 km/h)
Rate of climb at S/L   1,500 ft (450 m)/min
Service ceiling   25,500 ft (7,775 m)
T-O run   340 ft (104 m)
T-O to 50 ft (15 m)   600 ft (183 m)
Landing from 50 ft (15 m)   510 ft (155 m)
Landing run   220 ft (670 m)
Range with max fuel
    521 nm (600 miles; 965 km)

PILATUS TURBO-PORTER (AGRICULTURAL VERSION)

The Turbo-Porter can be made available, if required, equipped for agricultural duties, the necessary equipment being easily removable when not required to permit the use of the aircraft for other work.

For liquid spraying, a stainless steel tank (capacity 249 Imp gallons = 1,133 litres) is installed behind the two front seats, and 62-nozzle spray booms are fitted beneath the wings. In this configuration the aircraft can cover a swath width of 148 ft (45 m). Ultra-low volume system, using four to six atomisers, also available.

For dusting with powders or granulated materials, a tank of similar capacity is installed in the fuselage, the lower part of the tank in this case being replaced by a discharge and dispersal door. Effective swath width of this version is from 42-82 ft (13-25 m), the optimum width being approx 66 ft (20 m).

Both versions are fitted with small doors in the fuselage sides, giving access to the tank/hopper for servicing, removal or replenishment, and

Pilatus PC-6-C1/H2 Turbo-Porter with AiResearch TPE 331 turboprop engine

two single seats or a bench seat for three persons can be installed aft of the tank. Optional items include an engine air intake screen and a loading door for chemicals in the top of the fuselage.

WEIGHTS (L = liquid spray system; D = dry chemicals system):
Weight empty:
L, D   2,579 lb (1,170 kg)
Agricultural installation:
L   293 lb (133 kg)
D   231 lb (105 kg)
Chemical:
L   2,592 lb (1,176 kg)

D   2,665 lb (1,209 kg)
Fuel, oil and pilot:
L, D   630 lb (286 kg)
Max T-O weight:
L, D   6,106 lb (2,770 kg)
Max landing weight:
L, D   4,850 lb (2,200 kg)

PERFORMANCE (liquid spray version, PT6A-20 engine, at max T-O weight):
Operating speed
    approx 86 knots (99 mph; 160 km/h)
Operating height   20-26 ft (6-8 m)
Spraying duration with full spray tank   6 min

TRANSAIR

TRANSAIR S A

HEAD OFFICE AND WORKS:
Neuchâtel Airport, 2013 Colombier
PRESIDENT AND GENERAL MANAGER:
Olivier de Coulon
TECHNICAL DIRECTOR:
Jean-Pierre Kohli
ADMINISTRATION MANAGER:
Georges Croisy
SALES MANAGER:
Philippe Bujard

Transair S A was formed just after World War II, with six employees. Today it is a major maintenance and repair centre, employing 115 people and certificated by the Swiss Federal Air Office, British ARB, German LBA and American FAA.

Its major activities are maintenance, repair, overhaul and modification of Swiss and US Army military aircraft, civil aircraft and components. It is also distributor or agent for Beechcraft aeroplanes, the Hawker Siddeley HS 125 executive transport, Lycoming and Continental engines, Hartzell and McCauley propellers and a wide range of electronic and other equipment.

Among the modification schemes developed by Transair is one which involves fitting the Piper Super Cub with a more powerful engine, as described below.

TRANSAIR/PIPER PA-18-180 SUPER CUB

This re-engined Piper Super Cub conforms with FAR Pt 23 requirements in both the Normal and Utility categories. It is specially suited for

Transair/Piper PA-18-180 Super Cub 180 with wheel-ski landing gear

transport in mountainous regions when fitted with ski landing gear, and has also been sold in Switzerland, Austria and Italy for glider-towing.

The general description of the Piper PA-18-150 Super Cub, in the US section, applies also to this aircraft, except in the following details.
POWER PLANT: One 180 hp Lycoming O-360-A2A four-cylinder horizontally-opposed air-cooled engine, driving a two-blade fixed-pitch metal propeller. Fuel capacity 30 Imp gallons (136 litres).
WEIGHTS AND LOADINGS:
Weight empty   970 lb (440 kg)
Max T-O weight   1,750 lb (794 kg)

Max wing loading   9·8 lb/sq ft (47·85 kg/m²)
Max power loading   9·7 lb/hp (4·4 kg/hp)
PERFORMANCE (at max T-O weight):
Max level speed at S/L
    113 knots (130 mph; 209 km/h)
Normal cruising speed
    91 knots (105 mph; 169 km/h)
Stalling speed   38 knots (43 mph; 69 km/h)
Rate of climb at S/L, ski landing gear
    1,300 ft (395 m)/min
Service ceiling   20,000 ft (6,100 m)
T-O to 50 ft (15 m), flaps up   600 ft (183 m)
Landing from 50 ft (15 m), flaps down
    525 ft (160 m)

THE UNITED KINGDOM

AIRMARK

AIRMARK LTD

ADDRESS:
1, Stewart's Grove, London SW3
DIRECTORS:
D. A. Hood
K. Platt
T. M. Storey, ACA

This company was formed early in 1969, and acquired all rights in the T.S.R.3 racing monoplane. It is investigating various potential projects in the light aviation field and has built a modified version of the American Cassutt I racing monoplane, which is intended to form a nucleus for the introduction of American Formula I-type racing into the UK. Design studies so far undertaken include a six-seat light twin-engined utility transport known as the AM.21. Up to the Spring of 1970 no decision had been taken as to the future of this project.

AIRMARK T.S.R.3

The T.S.R.3 (T. Storey Racer 3) was designed by Mr Tom Storey in April-May 1967, and construction of a prototype began in June 1967. This aircraft (G-AWIV) flew for the first time on 25 July 1968. A small dorsal fin was added later.

The T.S.R.3 was described and illustrated in the 1969-70 *Jane's*. No further work has been done on the aircraft during the past year.

AIRMARK/CASSUTT 111M

Airmark undertook to complete three slightly modified examples of the Cassutt Special I (No 111) racing monoplane, the first of which flew in the Summer of 1969. It holds the European agency for plans and kits of this aircraft, and also has a manufacturing agreement with Capt T. K. Cassutt.

The Airmark/Cassutt 111M is generally similar

to the single-seat Cassutt Special I (described in the US section of this edition), with the following exceptions and a small modification to the rear wing spar.

POWER PLANT: One 95 hp Rolls-Royce/Continental C90-8F four-cylinder horizontally-opposed air cooled-engine, driving a two-blade fixed-pitch wooden propeller, diameter 4 ft 10 in (1·47 m). Fuel capacity 10 Imp gallons (45·5 litres) in tank aft of engine firewall.
ACCOMMODATION: As Cassutt Special I, but with seat-back moved 4 in (10 cm) to rear to improve ease of entry. One-piece canopy, opening sideways to port.
EQUIPMENT: Bendix CNS 220-A VHF radio.
WEIGHT:
Max T-O weight   830 lb (376 kg)
PERFORMANCE (at max T-O weight):
Max level speed
    170 knots (196 mph; 315 km/h)

Max permissible diving speed
      216 knots (249 mph; 400 km/h)
Max cruising speed
      145 knots (167 mph; 269 km/h)
Econ cruising speed
      125 knots (144 mph; 232 km/h)
Stalling speed
      54 knots (62·5 mph; 100·5 km/h)
Max rate of climb   2,000 ft (610 m)/min

Airmark/Cassutt 111M single-seat racing monoplane (95 hp Rolls-Royce/Continental C90-8F engine) (*Air Portraits*)

AVIATION TRADERS
AVIATION TRADERS (ENGINEERING) LTD

HEAD OFFICE:
Portland House, Stag Place, London, SW1

WORKS:
Southend and Stansted Airports, Essex

DIRECTORS:
R. L. Cumming, CA (Chairman)
J. Wiseman, ARAeS, MSLAET (Managing Director)
J. R. Batt, AFRAeS, MSLAET
C. W. Murrell, CEng, AFRAeS, AMSLAET
M. S. F. Mula, AACCA, ACCS

CHIEF DESIGNER: A. C. Leftley, CEng, FRAeS

Aviation Traders (Engineering) Ltd was formed in 1949 and became a member company of Air Holdings Ltd in 1961. It operates as both an aircraft overhaul and a manufacturing company.

With extensive and fully-equipped overhaul shops, the company is both AID and ARB approved, undertaking work for major aircraft constructors and airlines on specification, design and manufacturing contracts, and also carries out manufacturing to customer design.

The design and construction of cargo doors and air transportation pods for the carriage of replacement engines on the VC10, design of air intake dump doors for the Concorde, design and installation of interiors for various transport, executive and passenger aircraft, including the Britannia, BAC One-Eleven and Herald, illustrate the company's diversity.

In 1967 Aviation Traders was awarded a major contract to design and manufacture the conversion of Vanguard 953 aircraft into palletised freight transports for BEA. The first of these converted Vanguards (G-APEM) flew for the first time on 10 October 1969.

Aviation Traders also undertook the redesign and reconstruction of a Heron Mk 2 as a 23-seat twin-turboprop commuter airliner on behalf of Saunders Aircraft Co of Canada (which see).

Aviation Traders also has extensive manufacturing facilities for airport and airline ground support equipment. It holds manufacturing and distribution licences from Aviobridge in the Netherlands, relating to various models of covered passenger gangways, and from Cochran-Western

Aviation Traders/Vickers Vanguard Merchantman, first converted aircraft (*Brian M. Service*)

Corporation in the USA embracing a wide range of airline ground support equipment, including new equipment for the Boeing 747, McDonnell Douglas DC-10 and Lockheed L-1011. It has received a major order for Boeing 747 container handling devices from a leading European airline.

AVIATION TRADERS/VICKERS VANGUARD MERCHANTMAN CARGO CONVERSION

This cargo conversion of the Vanguard 953 for British European Airways introduces an hydraulically-operated freight door 11 ft 7 in long × 6 ft 8 in deep (3·48 × 2·03 m), incorporated in a replacement structural panel in the forward fuselage. This panel is jig-manufactured as a separate item before the aircraft is withdrawn from service, thereby ensuring that the aircraft is out of service only long enough for installation of the panel, the new strengthened floor and the mechanised cargo handling system, including Pelco Rolamat roller-conveyors. This system

is similar to that employed in the Britannia conversion (see 1969-70 *Jane's*), with the load secured by pallet locks. A crash net, retractable sill guard and detachable tail prop are also installed.

Up to eleven pallets measuring 9 ft 0 in × 7 ft 4 in (2·74 × 2·23 m), or eight of these pallets plus two pallets measuring 10 ft 5 in × 7 ft 4 in (3·17 × 2·23 m) can be carried. The maximum freight load, limited by zero-fuel weight, is approx 43,000 lb (19,504 kg).

Work on the first Vanguard conversion for BEA began in 1968, and the first aircraft flew for the first time on 10 October 1969. It was being followed by a second aircraft, after which the next three conversions will be undertaken by BEA in their engineering base at Heathrow Airport, using kits supplied by Aviation Traders. Up to 14 Vanguards will eventually be converted for freighting, in which form they are named Merchantman.

BAC
BRITISH AIRCRAFT CORPORATION (HOLDINGS) LTD

HEAD OFFICE:
100, Pall Mall, London, SW1

DIRECTORS:
Sir Reginald Verdon-Smith, LLD, BCL, MA (Chairman)
Marshal of the Royal Air Force Sir Dermot A. Boyle, GCB, KCVO, KBE, AFC (Vice Chairman)
Sir George R. Edwards, CBE, FRS, BSc(Eng), Hon DSc, CEng, Hon FRAeS, Hon FAIAA (Managing Director)
A. D. Marris, CMG
W. Masterton, CA (Financial Director)
The Rt Hon Lord Nelson of Stafford, MA, Hon DSc, CEng, MInstCE. MIMechE, FIEE, FRAeS (Deputy Chairman)
G. A. Riddell, BCom, CA
Sir Leslie Rowan, KCB, CVO (Deputy Chairman)
R. P. H. Yapp

SECRETARY: B. Cookson, LLB

TREASURER: T. B. Pritchard, FCA

British Aircraft Corporation Ltd was formed in February 1960 and brought together the aircraft and guided weapon interests of The Bristol Aeroplane Co, Ltd, The English Electric

Co, Ltd, and Vickers Ltd. The shares of the Corporation are held by the three principals in the following proportions: the General Electric and English Electric Companies Ltd 40 per cent, Vickers 40 per cent, and Rolls-Royce (who acquired The Bristol Aeroplane Co in 1966) 20 per cent.

The Corporation had originally four wholly-owned subsidiaries in Bristol Aircraft Ltd, English Electric Aviation Ltd, Vickers-Armstrongs (Aircraft) Ltd and British Aircraft Corporation (Guided Weapons) Ltd, and a controlling share interest in Hunting Aircraft Ltd. But a new wholly-owned subsidiary company known as British Aircraft Corporation (Operating) Ltd was formed to take over, from 1 January 1964, the whole of the business formerly carried out by the subsidiaries. Simultaneously, all remaining shares of Hunting Aircraft, Ltd, were acquired by BAC.

From 1 August 1968, British Aircraft Corporation Ltd became British Aircraft Corporation (Holdings) Ltd, and the former British Aircraft Corporation (Operating) Ltd was renamed British Aircraft Corporation Ltd.

The Board of the latter company is as follows:

BRITISH AIRCRAFT CORPORATION LTD

DIRECTORS:
Sir George R. Edwards, CBE, FRS, BSc(Eng), Hon DSc, CEng, Hon FRAeS, Hon FAIAA (Chairman and Managing Director)

W. Masterton, CA (Deputy Chairman)
A. H. C. Greenwood, JP, FRAeS (Deputy Managing Director)
J. E. Armitage, FCWA (Commercial Director)
E. G. Barber, BSc, CEng, AFRAeS (Director of Personnel and Training)
Handel Davies, CB, MSc, CEng, FRAeS, FAIAA (Technical Director)
G. T. Gedge, CEng, FIProdE (Managing Director, BAC (Filton) Ltd)
G. R. Jefferson, CBE, BSc, CEng, MIMechE, FRAeS (Chairman and Managing Director, BAC (Guided Weapons) Ltd)
G. E. Knight, CBE (Chairman, BAC (Filton) Ltd and BAC (Weybridge) Ltd)
F. W. Page, CBE, MA, CEng, FRAeS (Chairman and Managing Director, BAC (Preston) Ltd)
T. B. Pritchard, FCA (Financial Director)
Dr A. E. Russell, CBE, DSc, FRAeS, FAIAA
J. Ferguson Smith, FCA (Managing Director, BAC (Weybridge) Ltd)

SECRETARY: B. Cookson, LLB

PUBLICITY MANAGER: C. J. T. Gardner

DEPUTY PUBLICITY MANAGER: F. H. Kelly

PRESS OFFICER: A. S. C. Lumsden

The former Bristol Aircraft Ltd is now the Filton Division (British Aircraft Corporation (Filton) Ltd); the former English Electric Aviation Ltd is the Preston Division (British Aircraft Corporation (Preston) Ltd); and the former

Vickers-Armstrongs (Aircraft) Ltd is the Weybridge Division (British Aircraft Corporation (Weybridge) Ltd). The former Hunting Aircraft Ltd continued to operate as the Luton Division (British Aircraft Corporation (Luton) Ltd) until December 1966, when this Division was closed: its BAC One-Eleven work was transferred to Weybridge Division and its work on developments of the Jet Provost was taken over by Preston Division.

A fifth subsidiary, the Guided Weapons Division (British Aircraft Corporation (Guided Weapons) Ltd), was formed in April 1963 to manage the guided weapons activities of the Corporation. (See "Military Missiles" section).

Each Division is managed by an individual management company, with its own Board of Directors.

Overseas subsidiaries of BAC are: British Scandinavian Aviation AB of Sweden (formerly Svensk-Engelsk Aero-Service AB); British Aircraft Corporation (Australia) Pty Limited; and British Aircraft Corporation (USA) Inc.

British Aircraft Corporation (AT) Limited, owned jointly and equally by BAC and Fairey Engineering Ltd, was formed in February 1962 to take over the Fairey guided weapon interests.

In addition to development and production of the aircraft described on the following pages, BAC has a design study contract for a variable-geometry aircraft from the British Government.

In May 1966, BAC and Breguet Aviation of France formed jointly the SEPECAT company (see International section) to control the development and production programme for the Jaguar light strike fighter and trainer.

A similar international company, Panavia Aircraft GmbH (which see), was formed in March 1969 (the present shareholders being BAC, Messerschmitt-Bölkow-Blohm and Fiat) to foster the development and production of a European multi-role combat aircraft.

Notable among other BAC collaborative projects is that with Aérospatiale of France in the development of the Concorde supersonic airliner, also described in the International section of this edition.

FILTON DIVISION
BRITISH AIRCRAFT CORPORATION (FILTON) LTD

DIRECTORS:
G. E. Knight, CBE (Chairman)
G. T. Gedge, CEng, FIProdE (Managing Director)
D. J. Farrar, OBE, MA, FRAeS (Director, Project Administration)
G. Hanby, FCA, FCWA (Financial Director)
J. T. Jeffries, FIProdE (General Manager)
R. P. Matthews
F. H. Pollicutt, CEng, FRAeS, AFAIAA (Chief Engineer, Structures and Systems)
J. Ferguson Smith, FCA
Dr W. J. Strang, PhD, BSc, CEng, FRAeS (Technical Director)
E. B. Trubshaw, OBE, MVO (General Manager, Flight Operations, and Chief Test Pilot)

M. G. Wilde, BSc, DipAe, CEng, AFRAeS (Chief Engineer, Aerodynamics, Pre-Design and Power Plant)

SPECIAL DIRECTORS:
E. H. Burgess, MBE, DFC (Director of Marketing)
H. Giddings, CEng, FRAeS, AMIMechE (Chief Development Engineer)
J. M. Hahn, BSc(Eng), FBCS, AFRAeS, GMIMechE
E. A. Hyde (Assistant General Manager, Flight Test and Ground Support Organisation)
J. Longley, CEng, FIProdE (Assistant General Manager, Manufacturing Services)
D. Wynne, FCWA

SECRETARY: H. T. Fream

PUBLICITY MANAGER (FILTON):
F. G. Clark

Filton Division, with 7,000 employees (excluding those on guided weapon work), is responsible for design and development of the Concorde supersonic transport, in partnership with Aérospatiale of France; for production of the rear fuselage and tail unit of the BAC One-Eleven jet transport; and for continued after-sales service for operators of Bristol 170 and Britannia aircraft.

Under Ministry of Aviation contract, the Filton Division of BAC redesigned and almost completely rebuilt the Fairey Delta 2 research aircraft as the BAC 221, for use by the Royal Aircraft Establishment, Bedford, in a basic research programme. This aircraft was described fully in the 1967-68 *Jane's*.

BAC/AÉROSPATIALE CONCORDE
Details of the Concorde programme can be found in the International section of this edition.

PRESTON DIVISION
BRITISH AIRCRAFT CORPORATION (PRESTON) LTD

DIRECTORS:
F. W. Page, CBE, MA, CEng, FRAeS (Chairman and Managing Director)
H. R. Baxendale, OBE, ACWA (Deputy Chairman)
A. F. Atkin, OBE, BSc(Hons), DipAe, CEng, FRAeS, FIMechE
Wing Cdr R. P. Beamont, CBE, DSO, DFC, DFC(USA), FRAeS (Director of Flight Operations)
R. F. Creasey, OBE, BSc(Eng) (Director of Advanced Systems and Technology)
F. D. Crowe, BSc, CEng, FRAeS (Chief Engineer)
B. O. Heath, BSc, DIC, CEng, AFRAeS
F. E. Roe, DIC, BSc, CEng, ACGI, FRAeS (Director of Resources)
R. H. Sawyer, FCA, FCWA (Financial Director)
T. O. Williams, MA, CEng, MIMechE, MIEE (Production Director)

SPECIAL DIRECTORS:
R. Dickson, MA(Cantab), CEng, FRAeS (Chief of Aerodynamics and Research)
G. M. Hobday, OBE, AFRAeS (Sales and Service Manager)
R. Hothersall
I. R. Yates, BEng, CEng, AIMechE, FRAeS

SECRETARY: A. C. Buckley, BSc

PUBLICITY MANAGER:
A. F. Johnston

Preston Division includes the Warton and Samlesbury works and has 9,500 employees. It is responsible for production of the Lightning single-seat fighter and two-seat trainer; development and production of the Jet Provost/BAC 145/BAC 167 series of aircraft; Canberra refurbishing for overseas customers and after-sales service for operators of this bomber. In

November 1969 the Samlesbury works was rebuilding over 25 Canberras to meet existing orders, the largest number of these aircraft ever to be rebuilt at any one time.

Current programmes in the design and development stage include the Anglo-French Jaguar combat aircraft (see International section), classified projects for the British Government, and the European multi-role combat aircraft (see "Panavia" entry in the International section).

It was announced in July 1969 that BAC and Aermacchi of Italy had signed a preliminary agreement whereby the two companies will collaborate in the joint development of two new military jet trainer aircraft for service in the second half of the 1970s. BAC (Preston) is to conduct feasibility studies for a new advanced trainer, while Aermacchi will carry out similar studies for a basic jet trainer. Each company will provide the other with technical and marketing support for the two aircraft, and it is possible that other companies may be invited to join the programme at a later date.

BAC 145 JET PROVOST
Two prototypes of this pressurised development of the Jet Provost trainer were ordered by the former Ministry of Aviation, and the first of these began its flight trials on 28 February 1967. These prototypes were the last two production examples of the Jet Provost T.Mk 4 (see 1968-69 *Jane's*), which were retained at the factory for conversion to T. Mk 5 standard.

Two versions have so far been announced, as follows:

Jet Provost T.Mk 5. Designation of version for the RAF, over 100 of which have been ordered. These will all be produced as newly-manufactured aircraft.

First aircraft delivered, to CFS at Little Rissington, on 4 September 1969.

Jet Provost Mk 55. Armed version for Sudan Air Force, which ordered an unspecified number in 1967. Increased AUW and modified hydraulic and other systems.

Although the BAC 145 bears an obvious resemblance to the Jet Provost T.Mk 4, it is almost completely redesigned. The new front fuselage introduces a pressurised cabin for the crew, a lengthened nose containing an enlarged compartment for radio and equipment, and a redesigned windscreen and sliding canopy, giving improved all-round view from the cabin. The wings are redesigned for a fatigue life of more than 5,000 hours and to provide greater internal fuel capacity, so that tip-tanks are not normally required. The new wing is also capable of carrying a greatly increased underwing load in the weapons training or strike rôle. There are engine tappings for the pressurisation system, the jet pipe is 10 in (0·25 m) longer than that of the T.Mk 4 and the tailcone is redesigned.

The description below of the Jet Provost T.Mk 5 is generally applicable to the Mk 55 armed version, except where a particular model is specified.

TYPE: Two-seat jet primary and basic trainer.

WINGS: Cantilever low-wing monoplane. Wing section NACA 23015 (modified) at root, NACA 4412 (modified) at tip. Dihedral 6°. Incidence 3° at root, 0° at tip. All-metal structure, with main and subsidiary spars, having three-point attachment to fuselage. Metal-covered ailerons with balance tabs. Hydraulically-operated slotted flaps. Hydraulically-operated air-brakes and lift spoilers on wings at rear spar position ahead of flaps. Air-brakes and flaps hydraulically-operated.

FUSELAGE: All-metal semi-monocoque stressed-skin structure, built in two parts, comprising bulkheads, built-up frames and longerons covered with light alloy panels. Two sections

BAC 145 Jet Provost T.Mk 5 jet trainer (2,500 lb st Rolls-Royce Bristol Viper Mk 202 turbojet engine) in Royal Air Force insignia

are joined in line with wing subsidiary spar. Hinged nose-cap provides access to pressurisation, oxygen, radio and electrical equipment.

TAIL UNIT: Cantilever all-metal structure. One-piece tailplane, interchangeable elevators, fin and rudder. Fixed surfaces covered with smooth and movable surfaces with fluted alloy skin. Combined trim and balance tab in starboard elevator, balance tabs in port elevator and rudder.

LANDING GEAR: Hydraulically-retractable tricycle type. Main wheels retract inward into wings, nose-wheel forward. Dowty oleo-pneumatic shock-absorbers. Dunlop wheels and tubeless tyres. Dunlop hydraulic disc brakes.

POWER PLANT: One Rolls-Royce Bristol Viper Mk 202 turbojet engine (2,500 lb = 1,134 kg st) in fuselage aft of cockpit. Lateral intakes on each side of forward fuselage. Internal fuel capacity (one integral tank outboard and three bag tanks inboard in each wing) is 262 Imp gallons (1,191 litres). Refuelling point near each wingtip. Two wingtip fuel tanks, total capacity 96 Imp gallons (436 litres), are standard on Mk 55 aircraft but are used for ferry purposes only on RAF Mk 5's. All tanks in wings are interconnected. System designed to permit 30 sec of inverted flight. Oil capacity 1·75 Imp gallons (8 litres).

ACCOMMODATION: Two persons side-by-side in pressurised cabin, on Martin-Baker automatic ejection seats suitable for use down to ground level and 90 knots (104 mph = 167 km/h). Power-operated rearward-sliding canopy. Dual controls standard in T.Mk 5.

SYSTEMS: Pressurisation and air-conditioning system by Normalair and Tiltman Langley, differential 3 lb/sq in (0·21 kg/cm²), using engine-bleed air. Hydraulic system, pressure 1,500 lb/sq in (105 kg/cm²), for landing gear, flaps, air-brakes, lift spoilers and wheel brakes. Engine-driven generator provides 28V DC supply. Two 25Ah batteries. Two inverters supply phased AC to flight instruments and fire warning system. Automatically-controlled gaseous oxygen system for each crew member.

ARMAMENT (optional): Thirty T.Mk 5 aircraft are each fitted with two GM Mk 2L reflector gun-sights; remainder have SFOM sights. Provision for camera recorder, two 7·62-mm FN machine-guns (with 550 rounds per gun) in nose of each engine air intake duct, and strong points on each wing for carriage of external stores. Underwing stores for Mk 55 include two 50 Imp gallon (227 litre) fuel tanks, 12 × 8-cm Oerlikon 9·7-kg rockets, 18 × 8-cm Hispano-Suiza 11·9-kg rockets, 72 × 37-mm SNEB rockets in four Matra launchers, four FN 7·62-mm machine-guns in two pods (500 rounds per gun), 48 × 2-in rockets in two White & Riches launchers, 24 × 2·75-in rockets in four Matra launchers, four Nord AS.11 wire-guided missiles, 6 × 3-in Mk 6 rockets with 60-lb heads or twelve with 25-lb heads, six Type T.10 rockets with 28-kg heads, four HVAR rockets with 35-lb or 52-lb heads, 28 × 68-mm SNEB rockets in four Matra launchers, two Beagle reconnaissance packs, each with one F.95 camera, eight 25-lb practice bombs, four 540-lb bombs, two 500-lb GP bombs or eight 19-lb fragmentation bombs.

DIMENSIONS, EXTERNAL:

Wing span (Mk 5)	35 ft 4 in (10·77 m)
Wing span over tip-tanks (Mk 55)	
	36 ft 11 in (11·25 m)
Wing chord at root	7 ft 8 in (2·33 m)
Wing chord at tip	4 ft 4 in (1·31 m)
Wing aspect ratio	5·84
Length overall	34 ft 0 in (10·36 m)
Height overall	10 ft 2 in (3·10 m)
Tailplane span	13 ft 6 in (4·11 m)
Wheel track	10 ft 8·9 in (3·27 m)
Wheelbase	9 ft 7·4 in (2·93 m)

AREAS:

Wings, gross	213·7 sq ft (19·80 m²)
Ailerons (total)	19·06 sq ft (1·77 m²)
Flaps (total)	24·80 sq ft (2·30 m²)

WEIGHTS (T.Mk 5):
T-O weight:

2 crew, fuel for one hour	6,989 lb (3,170 kg)
2 crew, full internal fuel	7,629 lb (3,460 kg)
2 crew, full internal fuel and tip-tanks	
	8,524 lb (3,866 kg)
Overload max T-O weight	9,200 lb (4,173 kg)

PERFORMANCE (T.Mk 5):
Max level speed at AUW of 6,400 lb (2,900 kg):

at S/L	355 knots (409 mph; 658 km/h)
at 25,000 ft (7,620 m)	
	382 knots (440 mph; 708 km/h)

Rate of climb at S/L:

AUW 6,900 lb (3,130 kg)	4,000 ft (1,220 m)/min
AUW 7,600 lb (3,447 kg)	3,550 ft (1,082 m)/min

Service ceiling:

AUW 6,900 lb (3,130 kg)	36,750 ft (11,200 m)
AUW 7,600 lb (3,447 kg)	34,500 ft (10,500 m)

T-O run:

AUW 6,900 lb (3,130 kg)	1,070 ft (325 m)
AUW 7,600 lb (3,447 kg)	1,340 ft (410 m)

T-O to 50 ft (15 m):

AUW 6,900 lb (3,130 kg)	1,650 ft (503 m)
AUW 7,600 lb (3,447 kg)	2,070 ft (630 m)

Landing from 50 ft (15 m):

AUW 6,400 lb (2,900 kg)	2,360 ft (720 m)
AUW 7,200 lb (3,266 kg)	2,560 ft (780 m)

Landing run:

AUW 6,400 lb (2,900 kg)	1,540 ft (470 m)
AUW 7,200 lb (3,266 kg)	1,740 ft (530 m)

Max range with tip tanks, at 160 knots (184 mph; 296 km/h) EAS at 35,000 ft (10,670 m): With 288 lb (130 kg) reserve fuel
780 nm (900 miles; 1,450 km)

BAC 167 STRIKEMASTER

This version of the new series of aircraft developed from the Jet Provost has a BAC 145 airframe, but is powered by a Rolls-Royce Bristol Viper Mk 535 turbojet engine (3,410 lb = 1,547 kg st) and has eight underwing hard points enabling it to carry up to 3,000 lb (1,360 kg) of stores. This makes it particularly suitable for counter-insurgency combat operations, for which it can also be fitted with two 7·62-mm FN machine-guns, self-sealing fuel tanks and armour plate.

The max T-O weight of 11,500 lb (5,215 kg) includes one pilot only, full usable internal fuel (270 Imp gallons = 1,227 litres), two 48 Imp gallon (218 litre) wingtip tanks and 2,650 lb (1,200 kg) of external stores, including pylons. Typical under-wing loads include 12 × 3-in Mk 6 rockets with 60-lb warhead, 32 Hispano-Suiza Sura Type 3 rockets, 96 × 2-in Mk 1 rockets with 3¼-lb war-heads in four pods, four 500-lb bombs, two 50-gallon napalm tanks and 72 × 2-in rockets in two pods, or two Bristol 50-gallon overload fuel tanks and two Beagle reconnaissance pods, each containing a Vinten F.95 70-mm camera.

For ferrying, a similar T-O weight of 11,500 lb (5,215 kg) is permitted, including full internal fuel, two 48 Imp gallon (218 litre) wingtip tanks, two 73 Imp gallon (332 litre) and two 48 Imp gallon (218 litre) underwing tanks.

The first BAC 167 (G27-8) was flown for the first time on 26 October 1967, and the aircraft is now in production.

A total of 80 Strikemasters had been ordered by the end of 1969, as follows:

Mk 80. For Saudi Arabian Air Force. First order for BAC, placed in 1967. Deliveries began in 1968.

Mk 81. For South Yemen People's Republic Air Force.

Mk 82. For Sultan of Muscat and Oman's Air Force. Original order increased during 1968.

Mk 83. Six for Kuwait Air Force, ordered in October 1968. Deliveries began in 1969.

Mk 84. Sixteen for Singapore Air Defence Command.

WINGS, FUSELAGE AND TAIL UNIT: As for BAC 145.

LANDING GEAR: Tyre pressures 98 lb/sq in (6·89 kg/cm²) on main units; 90 lb/sq in (6·33 kg/cm²) on nose unit.

POWER PLANT: One Rolls-Royce Bristol Viper Srs 20 F-20 Mk 535 turbojet engine (details in introductory copy). Oil capacity 1·63 Imp gallons (7·4 litres).

SYSTEMS: Hydraulic system pressure increased to 2,100 lb/sq in (147·6 kg/cm²).

DIMENSIONS, EXTERNAL, AND AREAS: As for BAC 145.

WEIGHTS:

Operating weight empty, equipped, including crew	6,195 lb (2,810 kg)

Normal T-O weight:

pilot training (tip tanks empty)	
	8,355 lb (3,789 kg)
navigation training (tip tanks full)	
	9,143 lb (4,147 kg)
armament training (tip tanks full, weapons)	
	10,500 lb (4,762 kg)
Max T-O weight	11,500 lb (5,216 kg)

PERFORMANCE (at max T-O weight except where indicated):
Max level speed, with 50% fuel, clean:

at S/L	391 knots (450 mph; 724 km/h)
at 20,000 ft (6,100 m)	
	410 knots (472 mph; 760 km/h)

Stalling speed at 9,500 lb (4,309 kg) AUW:

flaps up	98·5 knots (113 mph; 182 km/h)
flaps down	85·5 knots (98 mph; 158 km/h)

Rate of climb at S/L (training, full internal fuel)
5,250 ft (1,600 m)/min

Time to height (training, full internal fuel):

to 30,000 ft (9,150 m)	8 min 45 sec
to 40,000 ft (12,200 m)	15 min 30 sec

T-O to 50 ft (15 m):

at 7,930 lb (3,579 kg) AUW (training)	
	1,900 ft (579 m)
at 11,500 lb (5,216 kg) AUW (combat)	
	3,500 ft (1,067 m)

Landing from 50 ft (15 m):

at 6,500 lb (2,948 kg) AUW (training)	
	2,400 ft (732 m)
at 11,250 lb (5,103 kg) AUW (aborted armed sortie)	
	4,250 ft (1,295 m)

Range with 200 lb (91 kg) fuel reserve:

at 8,355 lb AUW (training)	
	629 nm (725 miles; 1,166 km)

BAC 167 Strikemaster Mk 84 in the insignia of Singapore Air Defence Command

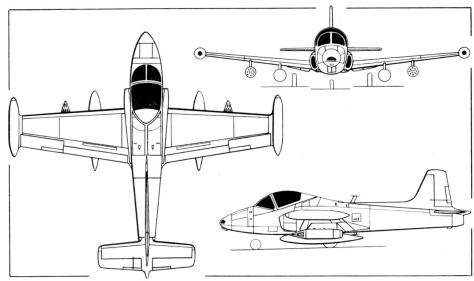

BAC 167 Strikemaster light attack aircraft

at 10,500 lb AUW (combat):
      1,075 nm (1,238 miles; 1,992 km)
at 11,500 lb AUW (max T-O)
      1,260 nm (1,382 miles; 2,224 km)

BAC LIGHTNING

The Lightning had its origin in a specification for a manned supersonic research aircraft issued by the Ministry of Supply in 1947 under the designation E.R.103. English Electric submitted their proposal in 1949, having designed their project so that it would be capable of development into a fighter, and were awarded a prototype contract on 1 April 1950. In 1954 work began on re-engineering the Lightning as a complete weapons system.

The Lightning was built subsequently for the Royal Air Force as a supersonic (Mach 2+) all-weather day and night interceptor. Production and delivery of RAF Lightning variants were completed in 1967, but developed versions are being manufactured as multi-rôle ground attack fighters for overseas air forces.

The Lightning can cruise economically on one engine up to about 25,000 ft (7,600 m), and can fly on one engine up to much higher altitude. It is inherently stable over a 13 : 1 speed range, and can be flown hands-off and rolled at Mach 1·8 without auto-stabilisation. At any height, Mach 1 can be attained without reheat.

The following versions have appeared:

P.1A. Three research prototypes only, each powered by two Bristol Siddeley Sapphire ASSa.5 turbojets and with elliptical air intake. Two for intensive flying trials and one for structure testing to destruction in ground rig. First flight (WG760) 4 August 1954.

P.1B. This was the company designation given to the three operational prototype P.1 aircraft with Rolls-Royce Avon turbojets and centre-body air intakes. First flight (XA847) 4 April 1957. The Air Ministry adopted the name Lightning in October 1958.

Lightning F. Mk 1 and 1A. Operational version of P.1B. The twenty pre-production aircraft were of this basic type, which was also built in series. Two Rolls-Royce Avon RA.24R turbojets with reheat. Air intake with pointed centre-body containing Ferranti Airpass Mk 1 interception and fire-control radar. Two 30-mm Aden cannon and Hawker Siddeley Firestreak air-to-air weapons. The Firestreaks and their control equipment were carried on a self-contained weapon pack which could be replaced by an alternative pack containing a further two Aden guns.

First production F.Mk 1 (XM134) flew on 29 October 1959. Deliveries of Mk 1 to No 74 Squadron began in Summer of 1960; Mk 1A's, with provision for flight refuelling, UHF radio and other changes, were supplied to Nos 56 and 111 squadrons. These versions, which were described fully in the 1968-69 *Jane's*, are no longer in first-line service.

Lightning F.Mk 2 and 2A. Development of F.Mk 1A, with improved reheat system, longer range, higher speed and ceiling, more advanced electronic equipment, liquid oxygen breathing system, etc. First F.Mk 2 (XN723) flew for the first time on 11 July 1961. Aircraft still in service with Nos 19 and 92 Squadrons in Germany have been modified almost to F.Mk 6 standard, with square-tip fin, larger ventral pack, cambered wing leading-edge and arrester hook, in which form they are redesignated F.Mk 2A. Total of seven F.Mk 2 and T.Mk 4 Lightnings supplied to Saudi Arabia in 1966/67. Production completed.

Lightning F.Mk 3. Further development, powered by Avon 300-series turbojets (each 16,360 lb = 7,420 kg st with reheat). Hawker Siddeley Red Top air-to-air missiles as alternative to Firestreak. No guns. Larger, square-top tail-fin. For long-range ferrying, provision was made for two large jettisonable overwing fuel tanks (each 260 Imp gallons = 1,182 litres) to be carried, with flight refuelling probe under port wing. These tanks were not adopted as standard on the Mk 3, but are in use on the F.Mk 6. First development aircraft for Mk 3 (XG310) was flown in November 1961. First production F.Mk 3 (XP693) flew for the first time on 16 June 1962. Production Lightning Mk 3's entered service with No 74 Squadron in April 1964 and subsequently re-equipped also Nos 23, 29, 56 and 111 Squadrons. Nos 23 and 74 now have the F.Mk 6. Production completed.

Lightning T.Mk 4. Two-seat trainer for RAF. Supplied also to Saudi Arabia as interim trainer. Complementary to F.Mk 1. Described separately.

Lightning T.Mk 5. Fully-operational two-seat trainer. Complementary to F.Mk 3. Described separately.

Lightning F.Mk 6. Known originally (but unofficially) as the F.Mk 3A, this fully-developed version has outer portion of wing leading-edge extended to incorporate camber, which materially reduces subsonic drag and hence improves range, and new ventral fuel pack with more than double the capacity of the former pack. New pack can carry two 30 mm Aden cannon in the forward section and has two fins to maintain

Current models of the BAC Lightning multi-purpose combat aircraft. Top to bottom: Mk 53 export version, RAF F. Mk 6, and two-seat T. Mk 55 of the Royal Saudi Air Force

directional stability at supersonic speeds. An arrester hook is fitted for emergency use at airfields equipped with certain types of arrester gear. The prototype for this version (XP697) flew for the first time on 17 April 1964. First flight of production F.6 (XR752) on 16 June 1965. First Squadron to receive F.6 was No 5, which began to re-equip in December 1965. It was followed by Nos 11, 23 and 74 Squadrons. Production completed.

Lightning F.Mk 53. Developed multi-role version of F.Mk 6 for Saudi Arabia and Kuwait. First F.53 (53-666) flown 1 November 1966. First delivery to Royal Saudi Air Force (53-667) on 4 December 1967. Described in detail below.

Lightning T.Mk 55. Export version of T.Mk 5 (described separately) for Saudi Arabia and Kuwait.

The following details apply to the Lightning F.Mk 53, but are generally applicable to other late versions, for which similar data are classified:

TYPE: Single-seat supersonic all-weather interceptor, strike and reconnaissance aircraft.

WINGS: Cantilever mid-wing monoplane. English Electric ASN/P1/3 basic wing section. Mean sweepback 60° on leading-edge, 52° on trailing-edge. Thickness/chord ratio approximately 5%. All-metal five-spar structure made in two panels, joined on centre-line. Upper and lower skins generally 0·2 in (0·5 cm) thick light alloy. Corrugated-sandwich skin over main-wheel bays. Hydraulically-powered mass-balanced ailerons, which extend across wing-tips at right angles to fuselage, have metal honeycomb sandwich tips with large horn-balance. Fore-and-aft notches in leading-edge in lieu of fences. Large hydraulically-operated one-piece plain flaps serve as integral fuel tanks.

FUSELAGE: Conventional all-metal structure. Hydraulically-operated air-brakes on upper part of fuselage near junction with fin leading-edge.

TAIL UNIT: Cantilever all-metal structure. Rudder and tips of tailplane of metal honeycomb sandwich. Low-set one-piece all-moving tailplane follows approximate shape of wing. Cropped-delta shape fin and rudder, without trim-tab. Control surfaces hydraulically-powered.

LANDING GEAR: Retractable tricycle type, of joint English Electric/British Messier design, with single wheel on each unit. Main units retract outward into wings. Non-steerable nose-wheel, with shimmy damper and centering unit, retracts forward into fuselage. Dunlop wheels, tyres and multi-cylinder plate brakes, with Maxaret anti-skid units. 16 ft (4·88 m) Irving ribbon braking parachute in bottom of rear fuselage. Provision for arrester hook under rear fuselage.

POWER PLANT: Two Rolls-Royce Avon 302-C turbojet engines (each 16,300 lb = 7,393 kg st with reheat), staggered one above the other in the fuselage, and with variable-area nozzles. Lower engine is well forward of upper one. Integral fuel tanks in wings and flaps. Additional fuel in all compartments of ventral pack, including gun-pack portion. Two 260 Imp gallon (1,182 litre) jettisonable tanks can be carried on overwing pylons in lieu of tanks. Main tanks pressure-fuelled through adaptor under port wing trailing-edge. Provision for flight refuelling for ferrying, with detachable probe under port wing.

ACCOMMODATION: Enclosed cockpit for pilot, fitted with rearward-hinged canopy and Martin-Baker Type BS4.C Mk 2 ejection seat which operates down to 90 knots (104 mph = 167 km/h) at zero altitude. Cockpit pressurised and refrigerated.

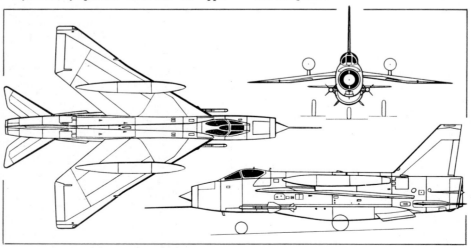

BAC Lightning F.Mk 6 interceptor with overwing ferry tanks

SYSTEMS AND EQUIPMENT: Normalair pressure control and emergency oxygen systems. Pressure differential 4·0 lb/sq in (0·28 kg/cm²). Electrical system includes 29kVA alternator, 28V DC generator and 28V battery. Elliott's autopilot, with attitude hold and ILS coupling. Equipment includes UHF/VHF transceiver, standby UHF, TACAN, UHF homing, IFF Mk 10 with SIF, ILS localiser and glide-slope indicator. Alternative choices of radio/navigation equipment, VHF, VOR and radio compass available. Ferranti Airpass A123S fire-control radar in intake centre-body. Light fighter sight standard.

ARMAMENT: Large ventral pack is in three portions: centre and rear portions are fuel tanks; forward hatch tank can contain all fuel, or some fuel plus two 30 mm Aden guns with 120 rounds per gun. Forward of this pack is a weapon bay capable of accommodating any one of a variety of operational packs. These include a twin-Firestreak or twin-Red Top air-to-air missile pack, a rocket pack with two retractable launchers for a total of 44 × 2-in spin-stabilised rockets, a reconnaissance pack housing five Vinten Type 360 70-mm cameras, or a night reconnaissance pack containing both cameras and line-scan equipment (in conjunction with underwing flares). Two pylons beneath outer wings, each capable of carrying two 1,000 lb

(454 kg) HE, retarded or fire bombs, two Matra 155 launchers for 18 SNEB 68-mm rockets apiece, two flare pods or two machine-gun pods. Two further pylons above inner wings, each carrying one 1,000 lb HE, retarded or fire bomb, one Matra 155 launcher, two Matra 100 launchers (each with 18 SNEB rockets and 50 Imp gallons = 227 litres of fuel) or one 260 Imp gallon (1,182 litre) ferry tank. Total possible over- and under-wing loads of 144 rockets or six 1,000 lb bombs. Retarded bombs on overwing pylons are blown upward on release by an ejector cartridge to permit release at very low levels.

DIMENSIONS, EXTERNAL:

Wing span	34 ft 10 in (10·61 m)
Length overall	55 ft 3 in (16·84 m)
Height overall	19 ft 7 in (5·97 m)
Tailplane span	14 ft 6 in (4·42 m)
Wheel track	12 ft 9·3 in (3·89 m)

AREA (Lightning F.1A):

Wings, net	380·1 sq ft (35·31 m²)

PERFORMANCE:

Max level speed at operational height	above Mach 2
Time to operational height and speed of Mach 0·9 (clean condition)	2 min 30 sec
Acceleration from Mach 1 to Mach 2+ (clean condition)	3 min 30 sec

BAC LIGHTNING TRAINER

This operational trainer version of the Lightning interceptor (known originally as the English Electric P.11) is generally similar to the fighter, except that the front fuselage has been widened by 11½ in (29 cm) to accommodate two Martin-Baker Type BS4.B Mk 2 ejection seats side-by-side. The Airpass radar and missile armament are retained, and the Lightning Trainer can be used for two-seat combat duties. All flying and fire controls and instruments are duplicated.

Three versions have been announced, as follows:

Lightning T.Mk 4. Complementary to F.Mk 1. First of two prototypes (XL628) flew for first time on 6 May 1959. First flight of production T.4 (XM966) on 15 July 1960. Entered service with No 226 OCU, RAF, in June 1962. Supplied also to Saudi Arabia as interim trainer in 1966. Production completed.

Lightning T.Mk 5. Complementary to F.Mk 3, with similar square-tip fin. First T.Mk 5 (XM967) flew for first time on 29 March 1962. Deliveries began in March 1965. Production completed.

Lightning T. Mk 55. Export development of T.Mk 5 for Saudi Arabia and Kuwait, with the modified wings and extra fuel capacity of the F.Mk 53. First T.55 (55-710) flown on 3 November 1966. First delivery to Royal Saudi Air Force (55-711) on 18 December 1967.

WEYBRIDGE DIVISION

BRITISH AIRCRAFT CORPORATION (WEYBRIDGE) LTD

DIRECTORS:

G. E. Knight, CBE (Chairman)
Sir Geoffrey Tuttle, KBE, CB, DFC, FRAeS (Vice Chairman)
J. Ferguson Smith, FCA (Managing Director)
E. S. Allwright, BSc(Eng), MIMechE, CEng, ACGI, DIC, AMInstCE, FRAeS (Project Director, Concorde)
W. R. Coomber (General Manager, Hurn)
Dr H. H. Gardner, BSc, Hon DSc, CEng, FRAeS
G. T. Gedge, CEng, FIProdE
R. C. Handasyde
D. James, BSc, CEng, FRAeS (Deputy Technical Director)
E. E. Marshall, CEng, AFRAeS (Technical Director)
J. A. Pull (Works Director)
H. Smith, FCA (Financial Director)
E. B. Trubshaw, OBE, MVO (Manager, Flight Operations)
H. Zeffert, CEng, FRAeS, MIEE, MAIEE (Director of Systems Engineering)

SPECIAL DIRECTORS:

K. Bentley, MA, CEng, AFRAeS (Asst Technical Director)
R. H. Botterill, CEng, AFRAeS, AFAIAA (Service Controller)
F. H. J. Denning (Assistant General Manager)
P. G. Hall
R. Heeks
P. D. Imlach (Production Manager)
K. S. Lawson, BSc(Eng), DIC, AFRAeS
D. Parker, CEng, AFRAeS (Asst Technical Director)
J. Prothero Thomas, CEng, AFRAeS
K. M. G. Upham (Personnel Manager)
Sir Barnes Wallis, CBE, DSc(Hon), FRS, RDI, MInstCE, CEng, HonFRAeS (Chief of Aeronautical Research and Development)
R. H. White-Smith, MA (Oxon) (Administration Manager)

SECRETARY: L. F. Trueman, FACCA

DIRECTOR OF SALES (Commercial Aircraft): D. J. John

DIRECTOR OF MARKETING: J. Prothero Thomas

SALES PUBLICITY MANAGER: J. H. Motum

Weybridge Division, with 13,500 employees, is responsible for after-sales service for the VC10 and Super VC10; for manufacture of major components of the BAC One-Eleven jet transport and its final assembly at Hurn; for part of BAC's commitment on the Concorde SST programme; for design studies for new subsonic transports; and for after-sales service of earlier aircraft of Vickers design, including the Viscount and Vanguard, of which details can be found in the 1964-65 *Jane's*, and the Hunting Prince/Pembroke series.

BAC VC10 (SERIES 1100)

The first announcement of BOAC's intention to place an order for VC10's was made in May 1957. Design work was started in March 1958 and construction of the prototype (G-ARTA) began in January 1959.

G-ARTA flew for the first time on 29 June 1962. ARB Certification was received on 23 April 1964, and the VC10 entered service on BOAC's route to West Africa on 29 April 1964.

Production of the VC10 is now completed. Variants built are listed below; a full description appeared in the 1969-70 *Jane's*.

Model 1100. Prototype only (originally G-ARTA). Wing span originally 140 ft 2 in (42·72 m) and wing area 2,808 sq ft (260·9 m²). AUW 299,000 lb (135,625 kg). Thrust reversers on all four engines. Brought up to airline standard in 1967 and sold to Laker Airways. See Model 1109 below.

Model 1101. Twelve for BOAC. First one (G-ARVA) flew on 8 November 1962, last one on 8 July 1964. Küchemann wingtips added, increasing span to 146 ft 2 in (44·55 m) and area to 2,851 sq ft (264·9 m²). AUW 314,000 lb (142,430 kg). Equipped to carry 16 first-class, 93 economy passengers. Thrust reversers on outboard engines only. Production completed.

Model 1102. Two for Ghana Airways. Second has large hydraulically-operated cargo door between the two standard passenger doors. Otherwise as Model 1101 except for a 4% chord leading-edge extension from wing root to fence,

giving wing area of 2,936 sq ft (272·8 m²). Associated with the leading-edge extension are a new fence, near the root, and re-contoured tips incorporating built-in droop on the leading-edge. First one flew on 14 November 1964. Production completed.

Model 1103. Three for British United Airways, with cargo door and extended leading-edge. Dimensions and weights as for Model 1102. Production completed.

Model 1106. Fourteen for RAF Air Support Command, with cargo door, folding hatracks, machined cargo floor with 20-in (50 cm) grid of 10,000-lb (4,535-kg) lashing points overall, and extended leading-edge. Conway RCo.43 engines and fin fuel tank as for Super VC10. Thrust reversers on outboard engines only; nose probe for flight refuelling. Rolls-Royce (Bristol) Artouste Mk 526 APU in tail-cone for ground electrics and engine starting, in addition to standard ram-air turbine for emergencies. AUW 323,000 lb (146,510 kg). Max landing weight 235,000 lb (106,600 kg). Range with max payload of 57,400 lb (26,030 kg) is 3,900 miles (6,275 km), cruising at 369 knots (425 mph; 683 km/h) at 30,000 ft (9,145 m). Standard seating for 150 passengers in rearward-facing seats. Dimensions as for Model 1102 except wing area, which is 2,932 sq ft (272·4 m²). First one (XR806) flew for the first time on 26 November 1965. Deliveries to No 10 Squadron began on 7 July 1966, and were completed in early 1968. RAF aircraft are designated VC10 C.Mk 1, and are named after holders of the Victoria Cross.

One aircraft, re-registered G-AXLR, flew for the first time on 6 March 1970 with the two port-side Conway engines replaced by a single Rolls-Royce RB.211 turbofan engine. This aircraft, which is on lease to Rolls-Royce from the Ministry of Defence for the purpose of flight-testing this engine, also incorporates a number of other airframe modifications, as well as a thrust reversal and spoiler system and a two-position noise attenuating nozzle.

Model 1109. New designation of prototype, following sale to Laker Airways (see under Model 1100 above). Now has same wing as Model 1106 and AUW of 312,000 lb (141,520 kg).

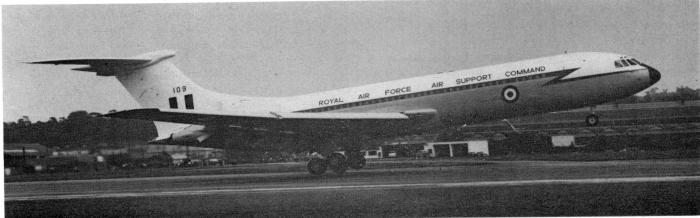

BAC VC10 C. Mk 1 (four Rolls-Royce Conway RCo.43 turbofan engines) in the insignia of RAF Air Support Command

BAC SUPER VC10 (SERIES 1150)

The Super VC10 was designed to carry larger payloads than the standard VC10, for a relatively small increase in take-off distance. The fuselage is 13 ft (4·27 m) longer than that of the VC10 and will accommodate 163-174 economy class passengers or a mixed payload such as 32 first-class and 99 economy-class passengers. A sixth toilet is provided, with the standard four galleys.

Apart from the additional fuselage length and associated strengthening, the most important changes compared with the VC10 are repositioning of the rear cabin door aft of the wing, transfer of the rear freight hold door from port to starboard side, and the addition of a fuel tank in the fin. The Super VC10 has the 4% chord leading-edge extension as fitted to many VC10's and is powered by four 21,800 lb (9,888 kg) st Rolls-Royce Conway RCo.43 turbofan engines. Total fuel capacity is 19,365 Imp gallons (88,032 litres).

Two versions of the Super VC10 have been built as follows:

Model 1151. Basic passenger transport. Seventeen for BOAC, each equipped to carry 16 first-class, 123 economy passengers. First one (G-ASGA) flew for the first time on 7 May 1964. Entered service with BOAC on 1 April 1965. Deliveries completed by early 1969. This version has four thrust reversers (basic Srs 1150 specification calls for only two, on outboard engines).

Model 1154. Five for East African Airways. Basically as Model 1151, but with large freight door forward of wing on port side and strengthened floor forward of wing leading-edge to permit mixed passenger/freight operation. Size of freight door is 11 ft 8 in × 7 ft (3·56 m × 2·13 m) with sill height of 10 ft 4 in (3·15 m). A split pallet system is used, to provide a centre aisle for access between the first and economy class cabins. A typical payload is 12 pallets, carrying 20,000 lb (9,070 kg) of freight, and 111 economy class passengers on seats with 33 in (84 cm) pitch. Dimensions as for Model 1151. Payload (12-pallet configuration) 62,434 lb (28,320 kg). Thrust reversers on outboard engines only. First Model 1154, of initial order for four, handed over on 30 September 1966. A fifth aircraft, ordered in June 1969 and delivered in February 1970, was the last of 54 VC10's and Super VC10's to be built.

Automatic landing trials with a Super VC10 (G-ASGG) began in latter part of 1965. Fully-equipped and operational aircraft entered service with BOAC in May 1968, and received certification on 14 January 1970 to operate in Category 2 weather minima. All 17 BOAC Super VC10's were due to be fitted with the system by Spring 1970, and extension to achieve Category 3A operation is under active development. The system used has been developed jointly by BAC and Elliott-Automation. On 16 May 1969 a BOAC Super VC10 made the first fully-automatic landing in commercial service using this system.

A full description of the Super VC10 Srs 1150 appeared in the 1969-70 edition of *Jane's*.

BAC ONE-ELEVEN

Details of the One-Eleven were announced on 9 May 1961, simultaneously with the news that British United Airways had ordered ten. Design and manufacture are shared between three BAC factories, at Weybridge, Filton and Hurn.

There are five commercial versions, as follows:

Modified BAC VC10 Model 1106 used as flying test-bed for the Rolls-Royce RB.211-22 turbofan engine for the Lockheed TriStar airliner

Series 200. First production model, for applications demanding both short and medium range. Two 10,330 lb (4,686 kg) st Rolls-Royce Spey-25 Mk 506 turbofan engines. The BAC-owned prototype One-Eleven Srs 200 flew for the first time on 20 August 1963, followed by the first production Model 201 on 19 December 1963 and the first Model 203 on 9 June 1964. ARB certification received on 6 April 1965, and FAA type approval on 20 April 1965. First services operated by BUA and Braniff on 9 and 25 April 1965 respectively. Total of 56 ordered by 1 March 1970.

Series 300. Physically similar to Series 200 but developed for applications demanding range with high payload. Two 11,400 lb (5,171 kg) st Rolls-Royce Spey Mk 511 turbofan engines in 4 in (10 cm) longer nacelles. Increased standard fuel tankage (centre-section tank). Heavier wing planks and shear webs and strengthened landing gear to cater for increased AUW. Enlarged capacity wheel brakes. Nine ordered by 1 March 1970.

Series 400. Generally similar to Series 300, but modified to meet the requirements of US operators. Standard items as for Series 300, plus lift dumpers and drop-out oxygen systems. First Srs 400 flew for first time on 13 July 1965. FAA type approval received 22 November 1965 and ARB certification on 10 December 1965. Total of 70 ordered by 1 March 1970.

Series 475. Combines the standard fuselage and accommodation of the Series 400 with the wings and power plant of the Series 500. The Srs 400/500 development aircraft (G-ASYD) is being converted to serve as prototype and was due to fly in late 1970. Certification and first production deliveries scheduled for June 1971.

Series 500. Derived from 300/400 Series, this version incorporates a lengthened fuselage (100 in = 2·54 m fwd of wing, 62 in = 1·57 m aft) which accommodates 97-119 passengers, with a flight crew of two. Wingtip extensions increase the span by 5 ft (1·52 m). Take-off performance is improved by the increased wing area and by the installation of two Rolls-Royce Spey Mk 512 DW turbofans, each rated at 12,550 lb (5,692 kg) st. The main landing gear is strengthened and heavier wing plank stringers are used to cater for the increased AUW.

Prototype, converted from Srs 400 development aircraft (G-ASYD), flew for first time on 30 June 1967.

The first Srs 500 production aircraft (G-AVMH) flew on 7 February 1968, ten weeks ahead of schedule. ARB certification of the Srs 500 was received on 15 August 1968. Deliveries to BEA began on 29 August 1968, more than one month ahead of schedule, and regular services were started on 17 November 1968. A total of 55 Srs 500's had been ordered by 10 June 1970.

Executive and freighter versions of the One-Eleven are also available.

Orders for 190 One-Elevens had been received up to 10 June 1970, of which 169 had been delivered. These orders are as follows:

Series 200	
British United Airways	10 Model 201
Braniff International Airways (USA)	14 Model 203
Mohawk Airlines (USA)	18 Model 204
Zambia Airways	2 Model 207
Aer Lingus	4 Model 208
Aloha Airlines (Hawaii)	3 Model 215
Series 300	
British Eagle International (to be transferred)	3 Model 301
Quebecair (Canada)	2 Model 304
Laker Airways	4 Model 320L

BAC Super VC10 Model 1151 (four Rolls-Royce Conway RCo.43 turbofan engines) in the insignia of **BOAC** (*Brian M. Service*)

BAC One-Eleven Series 400 twin-turbofan transport aircraft in the insignia of Gulf Aviation

Series 400

American Airlines	30	Model 401
Philippine Air Lines	4	Model 402
TACA International (El Salvador)	2	Model 407
Channel Airways	3	Model 408
LACSA (Costa Rica)	2	Model 409
LANICA (Nicaragua)	1	Model 412
Bavaria Fluggesellschaft	4	Model 414
Court Line	5	Model 416
Austral/ALA (Argentina)	4	Model 420
VASP (Brazil)	2	Model 422
Tarom (Romania)	6	Model 424
Gulf Aviation	2	Model 432

Series 475

Faucett (Peru)	1	Series 475

Series 500

British United Airways	8	Model 501
Caledonian Airways	4	Model 509
BEA	18	Model 510
Paninternational (Germany)	3	Model 515
Bahamas Airways	3	Model 517
Court Line	7	Model 518
SADIA (Brazil)	3	Model 520
Austral/ALA (Argentina)	3	Model 521
British Midland Airways	2	Model 520
	1	Model 523
Germanair	3	Model 524

Executive versions

Helmut Horten GmbH (Germany)	1	Model 201
Tenneco Inc	2	Model 212
RAAF	2	Model 217
Victor Comptometer Corp	1	Model 410
Engelhard Industries (USA)	1	Model 419
Brazilian Air Force	2	Model 423

TYPE: Twin-engined short/medium-range jet transport.

WINGS: Cantilever low-wing monoplane. Modified NACA cambered wing section. Thickness/chord ratio 12½% at root, 11% at tip. Dihedral 2°. Incidence 2° 30'. Sweepback 20° at quarter-chord. All-metal structure of copper-based aluminium alloy, built on fail-safe principles. Three-shear-web torsion box with integrally-machined skin/stringer panels. Ailerons of Redux-bonded light alloy honeycomb, manually operated through servo-tabs. Port servo-tab used for trimming. Light alloy Fowler flaps hydraulically-operated through Hobson actuators. Light alloy spoiler/air-brakes on upper surface of wing, operated hydraulically through Boulton Paul actuators. Hydraulically-actuated lift-dumpers, inboard of spoilers, are standard on Srs 400, 475 and 500; structural provision for them on Srs 300. Thermal de-icing of wing leading-edges with hot air tapped from engine HP compressors.

FUSELAGE: Conventional circular-section all-metal fail-safe structure with continuous frames and stringers. Skin made from copper-based aluminium alloy.

TAIL UNIT: Cantilever all-metal fail-safe structure, with variable-incidence tailplane mounted at tip of fin. Fin integral with rear fuselage. Tailplane controlled through duplicated hydraulic units of Hobson manufacture. Elevators and rudder actuated hydraulically through tandem jacks of Boulton Paul manufacture. Leading-edges of fin and tailplane de-iced by hot air tapped from engine HP compressors.

LANDING GEAR: Retractable tricycle type, with twin wheels on each unit. Hydraulic retraction, nose unit forward, main units inward. Oleo-pneumatic shock-absorbers manufactured by BAC. Hydraulic nose-wheel steering. Dunlop wheels, tubeless tyres and 4 plate heavy-duty hydraulic disc brakes. Maxaret anti-skid units on Srs 200 and 300. Hytrol Mk III anti-skid units on Srs 400, 475 and 500. Main wheel tyres size 40 × 12, pressure (Srs 200) 128 lb/sq in (9·00 kg/cm²); (Srs 300, 400) 141 lb/sq in (9·92 kg/cm²); (Srs 500) 148 lb/sq in (10·4 kg/cm²). Dunlop 44 × 16 tyres on Srs 475, pressure 81 lb/sq in (5·7 kg/cm²). Nose-wheel tyres size 24 × 7·25, pressure (Srs 200) 100 lb/sq in (7·03 kg/cm²); (Srs 300, 400, 500) 110 lb/sq in (7·73 kg/cm²). Dunlop 24 × 7·25 tyres on Srs

475, pressure 115 lb/sq in (8·0 kg/cm²). All tyre pressures are given for aircraft at mid CG position and operating at max taxi weight.

POWER PLANT: Two turbofan engines, mounted in pods on each side of rear fuselage (details under "series" descriptions). Fuel in integral tank in each wing, with total capacity of 2,240 Imp gallons (10,183 litres) on Srs 200 and 3,085 Imp gallons (14,024 litres) on Srs 300, 400, 475 and 500. Centre-section tanks with capacity of 850 Imp gallons (3,864 litres) are optional on Srs 200, and standard on Srs 300, 400 and 500. Pressure refuelling point in fuselage forward of wing on starboard side. Provision for gravity refuelling. Fuel jettison system optional. Oil capacity (total engine oil) 3 Imp gallons (13·66 litres).

ACCOMMODATION (all versions except Srs 500): Crew of two on flight deck and up to 89 passengers in main cabin. Single-class or mixed-class layout, with movable divider bulkhead to permit any first/tourist ratio. Typical mixed-class layout has 16 first-class (four abreast) and 49 tourist (five abreast) seats. Galley units normally at front on starboard side. Coat space available on port side aft of flight deck and, on Srs 200 and 300, at rear vestibule. One toilet at rear on stbd side in Srs 200. Two toilets in Srs 300, 400 and 500, in front and rear combinations (Srs 300 has 1 front port, 1 rear stbd; Srs 400 and 500 have one each side at rear). Ventral entrance with hydraulically-operated airstair. Forward passenger door on port side now incorporates power operated air-stair; in Srs 475, there is structural provision only for this feature. Galley service door forward on starboard side. Two baggage and freight holds under floor, fore and aft of wings, with doors on starboard side. Entire accommodation air-conditioned.

ACCOMMODATION: (Srs 500): Crew of two on flight deck and up to 119 passengers in main cabin. Two additional overwing emergency exits, making two on each side. Otherwise generally similar to other versions.

SYSTEMS: Fully-duplicated air-conditioning and pressurisation systems with main components by Normalair and AiResearch. Air bled from engine compressors through heat exchangers. Max pressure differential 7·5 lb/sq in (0·53 kg/cm²). Hydraulic system, pressure 3,000 lb/sq in (210 kg/cm²), operates flaps, spoilers, rudder, elevators, tailplane, landing gear, brakes, nose-wheel steering, ventral and forward airstairs and windscreen wipers. No pneumatic system. Electrical system utilises two 30kVA Westinghouse AC generators, driven by Plessey constant-speed drive and starter units, plus a similar generator mounted on the APU and shaft-driven. AiResearch

gas-turbine APU in tail-cone to provide ground electrical power, air-conditioning and engine starting, also some system check-out capability. APU is run during take-off to eliminate performance penalty of bleeding engine air for cabin air-conditioning.

ELECTRONICS AND EQUIPMENT: Communications and navigation equipment generally to customers' individual requirements. Typical installation includes dual VHF communications equipment to ARINC 546, dual VHF navigation equipment to ARINC 547A, including glide-slope receivers, marker receiver, flight/service interphone system, Marconi AD 370, Bendix DFA 73 or Collins DF 203 ADF, ATC transponder to ARINC 532D, Collins 860 E2 DME, Ekco E 190 or Bendix RDR 1E weather radar. Sperry CD or CL11 compass systems and Collins FD 108 Flight Director system (dual) are also installed. The autopilot is the Elliott 2000 Series system and provision is made for additional equipment, including automatic throttle control for low weather minima operation.

DIMENSIONS, EXTERNAL:

Wing span:	
Srs 200, 300, 400	88 ft 6 in (26·97 m)
Srs 475, 500	93 ft 6 in (28·50 m)
Wing chord at root	16 ft 5 in (5·01 m)
Wing chord at tip	5 ft 3½ in (1·61 m)
Wing aspect ratio:	
Srs 200, 300, 400	8
Srs 475, 500	8·5
Length overall:	
except Srs 500	93 ft 6 in (28·50 m)
Srs 500	107 ft 4 in (32·72 m)
Length of fuselage:	
except Srs 500	83 ft 10 in (25·55 m)
Srs 500	97 ft 4 in (29·67 m)
Height overall	24 ft 6 in (7·47 m)
Tailplane span	29 ft 6 in (8·99 m)
Wheel track	14 ft 3 in (4·34 m)
Wheelbase:	
except Srs 500	33 ft 1 in (10·08 m)
Srs 500	41 ft 5 in (12·62 m)
Passenger door (fwd, port):	
Height	5 ft 8 in (1·73 m)
Width	2 ft 8 in (0·82 m)
Height to sill	7 ft 0 in (2·13 m)
Ventral entrance:	
Height	6 ft 0 in (1·83 m)
Width	2 ft 2 in (0·66 m)
Height to sill	7 ft 0 in (2·13 m)
Freight door (fwd, starboard):	
Height (projected)	2 ft 7 in (0·79 m)
Width	3 ft 0 in (0·91 m)
Height to sill	3 ft 7 in (1·09 m)
Freight door (rear, starboard):	
Height (projected)	2 ft 2 in (0·66 m)

Photographic impression of the BAC One-Eleven Series 475

BAC One-Eleven Series 500 transport aircraft (two Rolls-Royce Spey Mk 512 DW turbofan engines) in the insignia of Court Line

Width	3 ft 0 in (0·91 m)
Height to sill	4 ft 3 in (1·30 m)
Galley service door (fwd, starboard):	
Height (projected)	4 ft 0 in (1·22 m)
Width	2 ft 3 in (0·69 m)
Height to sill	7 ft 0 in (2·13 m)

DIMENSIONS, INTERNAL (except Srs 500):
Cabin, excluding flight deck:

Length	56 ft 10 in (17·31 m)
Max width	10 ft 4 in (3·16 m)
Max height	6 ft 6 in (1·98 m)
Floor area	approx 506 sq ft (47·0 m²)
Freight hold, fwd	354 cu ft (10·02 m³)
Freight hold, rear:	
Srs 200, 300, 400	180 cu ft (5·10 m³)
Srs 475	156 cu ft (4·42 m³)

DIMENSIONS, INTERNAL (Srs 500):
Cabin, excluding flight deck:

Length	70 ft 4 in (21·44 m)
Total floor area	approx 665 sq ft (61·78 m²)
Freight hold (total volume)	711 cu ft (20·13 m³)

AREAS:
Wings, gross:

except Srs 475, 500	1,003 sq ft (93·18 m²)
Srs 475, 500	1,031 sq ft (95·78 m²)
Ailerons (total)	30·8 sq ft (2·86 m²)
Flaps (total)	175·6 sq ft (16·30 m²)
Spoilers (total)	24·8 sq ft (2·30 m²)
Vertical tail surfaces (total)	117·4 sq ft (10·90 m²)
Rudder, with tab	32·8 sq ft (3·05 m²)

Horizontal tail surfaces (total)	257·0 sq ft (23·90 m²)
Elevators, with tab	70·4 sq ft (6·55 m²)

WEIGHTS AND LOADINGS:
Basic operating weight:

Srs 200	46,405 lb (21,049 kg)
Srs 300	48,722 lb (22,100 kg)
Srs 400	49,587 lb (22,493 kg)
Srs 475	51,814 lb (23,502 kg)
Srs 500	54,807 lb (24,860 kg)

Max payload:

Srs 200	17,595 lb (7,981 kg)
Srs 300	22,278 lb (10,105 kg)
Srs 400	21,413 lb (9,713 kg)
Srs 475	21,186 lb (9,609 kg)
Srs 500	26,193 lb (11,880 kg)

Max T-O weight:

Srs 200	79,000 lb (35,833 kg)
Srs 300, 400	87,000 lb (39,463 kg)
Srs 475	92,000 lb (41,730 kg)
Srs 500	99,650 lb (45,200 kg)

Max ramp weight:

Srs 475	92,500 lb (41,957 kg)
Srs 500	100,000 lb (45,359 kg)

Max landing weight:

Srs 200	69,000 lb (31,298 kg)
Srs 300, 400	78,000 lb (35,381 kg)
Srs 475	84,000 lb (38,101 kg)
Srs 500	86,000 lb (39,009 kg)

Max zero-fuel weight:

Srs 200	64,000 lb (29,030 kg)
Srs 300, 400	71,000 lb (32,206 kg)
Srs 475	73,000 lb (33,112 kg)
Srs 500	81,000 lb (36,741 kg)

Max wing loading:

Srs 200	78·3 lb/sq ft (382 kg/m²)
Srs 300, 400	86·7 lb/sq ft (423 kg/m²)
Srs 475	89·23 lb/sq ft (436 kg/m²)
Srs 500	96·7 lb/sq ft (472 kg/m²)

Max power loading:

Srs 475	3·66 lb/lb st (3·66 kg/kg st)

PERFORMANCE (at max T-O weight, Srs 475 estimated):
Max level speed at 21,000 ft (6,400 m)

Srs 200, 300, 400, 475, 500	476 knots (548 mph; 882 km/h)

Max permissible diving speed (structural):

Srs 200	399 knots (460 mph; 740 km/h) EAS
Srs 300, 400, 475, 500	410 knots (472 mph; 760 km/h) EAS

Max cruising speed at 21,000 ft (6,400 m):

Srs 200, 300, 400, 475, 500	476 knots (548 mph; 882 km/h)

Econ cruising speed at 25,000 ft (7,620 m):

Srs 200, 300, 400, 475, 500	440 knots (507 mph; 815 km/h)

Stalling speed (T-O flap setting):

Srs 200	109 knots (125 mph; 201 km/h)
Srs 300, 400	114 knots (131 mph; 211 km/h)

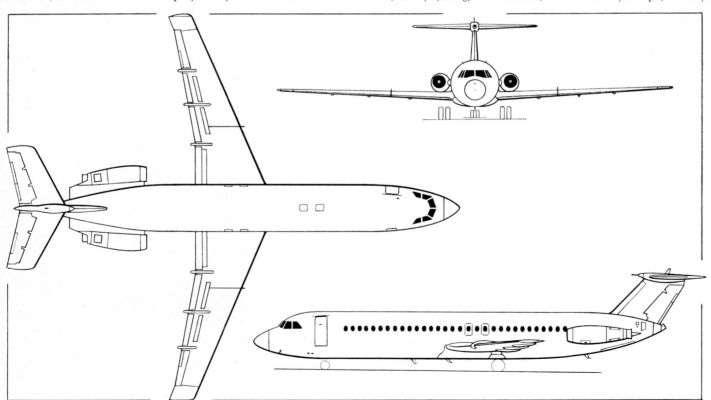

BAC One-Eleven Series 500 twin-turbofan airliner, with lengthened fuselage and extended wingtips

Srs 475	111 knots (128 mph; 206 km/h) EAS
Srs 500	120 knots (138 mph; 222 km/h)

Rate of climb at S/L at 300 knots (345 mph; 555 km/h) EAS:

Srs 200	2,500 ft (762 m)/min
Srs 300, 400	2,580 ft (786 m)/min
Srs 475	2,350 ft (716 m)/min
Srs 500	2,150 ft (655 m)/min

Max cruising height:

Srs 200, 300, 400, 475, 500	35,000 ft (10,670 m)

T-O run at S/L, ISA:

Srs 200	6,500 ft (1,981 m)
Srs 300	7,500 ft (2,286 m)
Srs 400	7,450 ft (2,270 m)
Srs 475	5,400 ft (1,646 m)
Srs 500	6,880 ft (2,097 m)

Balanced T-O to 35 ft (10·7 m) at S/L, ISA:

Srs 200	6,850 ft (2,088 m)
Srs 300	8,000 ft (2,438 m)
Srs 400	7,800 ft (2,377 m)
Srs 475	5,880 ft (1,792 m)

Srs 500	7,505 ft (2,288 m)

Landing distance (BCAR) at S/L, ISA, at max landing weight:

Srs 475	4,650 ft (1,417 m)

Landing run at S/L, ISA at max landing weight:

Srs 475	2,710 ft (826 m)

Still-air range with max fuel, ISA, with reserves for 200 nm (230 miles; 370 km) diversion and 45 min hold:

Srs 200	1,849 nm (2,130 miles; 3,430 km)
Srs 300, 400	1,954 nm (2,250 miles; 3,620 km)
Srs 475	1,820 nm (2,095 miles; 3,371 km)
Srs 500	1,780 nm (2,050 miles; 3,300 km)

Still-air range with typical capacity payload, ISA, reserves as above:

Srs 200	759 nm (875 miles; 1,410 km)
Srs 300, 400	1,241 nm (1,430 miles; 2,300 km)
Srs 475	1,380 nm (1,589 miles; 2,557 km)
Srs 500	990 nm (1,140 miles; 1,834 km)

BAC THREE-ELEVEN

Announced at the SBAC Display in September 1968, the projected BAC Three-Eleven is currently in the design development/market evaluation stage at the Weybridge Division of BAC, for short/medium-range airline service from the mid-1970's.

Typical configuration is for 220 passengers to be carried in a wide cabin layout seating from six to nine abreast. The power plant at present proposed is two rear-mounted Rolls-Royce RB.211 turbofans, of the type chosen for the Lockheed 1011 TriStar transport. Range will be of the order of 2,000 miles (3,200 km), cruising at Mach 0·8 at an AUW of approx 270,000 lb (122,500 kg). Runway requirements will be approx 6,000-7,000 ft (1,830-2,135 m).

Proposals were submitted to the British government in December 1969 covering both the technical and commercial aspects of the Three-Eleven, and detailed discussions were continuing in 1970.

BEAGLE
BEAGLE AIRCRAFT LTD

HEAD OFFICE AND WORKS:
Shoreham Airport, Shoreham-by-Sea, Sussex

RECEIVER AND MANAGER:
K. R. Cork

DIRECTORS:
P. G. Masefield, MA(Eng), CEng, FRAeS, MInstT, Hon FAIAA (Chairman)
K. N. Myer (Managing Director)
T. N. Ritchie, TD
J. B. MacKirdy (Production Director)
D. W. Gray (Marketing Director)
G. C. J. Larroucau, DLC(Hons), AFRAeS, DCAe (Director of Engineering)
Margaret V. Lawrence (Secretary)

Beagle Aircraft Ltd was a private company owned by the Ministry of Technology. The company was acquired by the State in August 1968, in order to ensure continuation of light aircraft development and manufacture in Britain. Formed in 1962, as a subsidiary of British Executive and General Aviation Ltd (itself a subsidiary of Pressed Steel Company), Beagle Aircraft had earlier absorbed and replaced both Beagle-Auster Aircraft Ltd, Rearsby, and Beagle-Miles Aircraft Ltd, Shoreham.

Beagle Aircraft subsequently disposed of its entire interests in Auster Aircraft to Hants and Sussex Aviation Ltd of Portsmouth (which see).

Following the British Government's decision to withdraw its financial backing of Beagle "because of higher priorities for available funds," Mr K. R. Cork was appointed Receiver and Manager of Beagle Aircraft Ltd on 2 December 1969. The company was put into members' voluntary liquidation on 27 February 1970.

On 30 May 1970 it was announced that manufacture of the Bulldog military trainer was being taken over by Scottish Aviation Ltd (which see).

Up to 31 December 1969, Beagle Aircraft Ltd had delivered 62 B.206 Series I and Series II aircraft, including 20 Bassets to the RAF and two other aircraft to the Ministry of Technology, and a total of 128 Pups. Outstanding orders at that time, for home and overseas customers, were for 16 B.206 Series II, 267 Pups, and 71 Bulldogs, with options on a further 45 Bulldogs.

BEAGLE B.121 PUP

Three versions of the two/three-seat Pup were produced initially, as follows:

Pup-100 (B.121 Series 1). Fully-aerobatic light aircraft with accommodation for two adults. Powered by 100 hp Rolls-Royce/Continental O-200-A four-cylinder engine, driving a McCauley type 1A105/SCM 7053 two-blade fixed-pitch metal propeller, diameter 5 ft 10 in (1·78 m). Fuel capacity 24 Imp gallons (109 litres). Design of this version began in August 1966. Construction of the first prototype (G-AVDF) was started in the following month and it flew for the first time on 8 April 1967. The first production Pup-100 (G-AVZM) was flown on 23 February 1968, and deliveries of this version began in April 1968.

Pup-150 (B.121 Series 2). Generally similar to Pup-100, with standard accommodation for two, but optional seating provides for either a third adult or two children. Powered by 150 hp Lycoming O-320-A2B four-cylinder engine, driving a Sensenich type M.74 DMS-0-60 two-blade fixed-pitch metal propeller, diameter 6 ft 2 in (1·88 m). Standard fuel capacity 24 Imp gallons (109 litres), with optional increase to 34 Imp gallons (155 litres). To improve aerobatic qualities, including unlimited spinning, a larger rudder was fitted initially to this version, and has since been adopted as standard for both versions. Third prototype Pup (G-AVLN), made its first flight on 17 January 1968 as the prototype Pup-150.

Pup-160 (B.121 Series 3). Designation of six aircraft produced to requirements of Iranian

Beagle B.121 Series 3 Pup-160 for delivery to Iran, with 160 hp Lycoming O-320-D2C engine

customer, with 2+2 seating, 160 hp Lycoming O-320-D2C engine, and standard fuel capacity of 36 Imp gallons (164 litres) with no optional increase.

A total of 128 Pups had been delivered by 31 December 1969, at which time there were outstanding orders for a further 267 aircraft.

The **Bulldog** military trainer version of the Pup is described under the "Scottish Aviation" heading in this section.

The following details apply to the Pup-100 and Pup-150:

TYPE: Two/three-seat light aircraft.

WINGS: Cantilever low-wing monoplane. Wing section NACA 63_2-615. Thickness/chord ratio 15%. Dihedral 6° 30'. Incidence 1° 30' at root, —1° at tip. Sweepback 1° 30' at quarter-chord. Conventional single-spar two-cell structure of copper-bearing light alloy. Slotted ailerons and trailing-edge flaps of similar material. No tabs.

FUSELAGE: Conventional all-metal semi-monocoque fail-safe structure.

TAIL UNIT: Cantilever two-spar light alloy structure. Fixed-incidence tailplane. Full-span trim-tab on starboard elevator. Fixed ventral fin.

LANDING GEAR: Non-retractable tricycle type, with single wheel on each unit. Steerable nose-wheel, with Lockheed Air 49006 oleo-pneumatic shock-absorber. Main gear utilises Lockheed Air 48688 cantilever shock-struts with dampers. Dunlop type AH52599 nose-wheel assembly. Dunlop type AH52595 main wheel assembly. All wheels same size, with Dunlop OR5966 tyres, size 5·00 × 5. Pup-100 tyre pressure 29 lb/sq in (2·04 kg/cm²); Pup-150 tyre pressure 35 lb/sq in (2·46 kg/cm²). Dunlop type AH52596 disc brakes. Parking brake.

POWER PLANT: One horizontally-opposed air-cooled engine (details under model descriptions). Two metal fuel tanks, one in each wing, capacity as given under model descriptions. Refuelling points above wing. Oil capacity (Pup-100) 1·25 Imp gallons (5·75 litres); (Pup-150 and -160) 1·675 Imp gallons (7·61 litres).

ACCOMMODATION: Pup-100 has two seats side-by-side. Pup-150 is basically a two-seater, with an optional third seat for an adult passenger on the starboard side, aft of the front seats, or for two children on occasional seats. Both front seats are adjustable for rake in three positions and hinge forward for access to baggage compartment. Dual controls standard. Forward-hinged door over wing on each side. Baggage compartment aft of seats. Heating and ventilation standard.

SYSTEMS: Cabin heating and cooling by heat exchanger and ducting. Hydraulic system for brakes only; toe-operated brakes for pilot only. Electrical equipment includes 12V 60A alternator and 12V 25Ah battery. 17Ah aerobatic battery optional.

ELECTRONICS AND EQUIPMENT: An extensive range of Bendix, Elliott and King communications and navigation radios to customers' requirements. Standard equipment includes windscreen demister, map holder, ash trays, cabin fire extinguisher. Optional equipment includes full blind-flying instrumentation, stop-watch/clock, PW-74 AM altimeter, accelerometer, ambient temperature gauge, Brittain turn co-ordinator, toe-brake for co-pilot, sun visors, first aid kit, jettisonable doors, map stowages, windscreen defrosting, blind-flying screens, cabin lights, landing lights, navigation lights, taxi lights, rotating beacon, heated pitot head and external supply socket. Auxiliary fuel tanks are also available for the Pup-150.

Beagle Pup-150 aerobatic light aircraft (150 hp Lycoming O-320-A2B engine)

DIMENSIONS, EXTERNAL:

Wing span	31 ft 0 in (9·45 m)
Wing chord at root	4 ft 11½ in (1·51 m)
Wing chord at tip	2 ft 9 in (0·84 m)
Wing aspect ratio	8·04
Length overall:	
Pup-100	22 ft 11 in (6·99 m)
Pup-150	23 ft 2 in (7·06 m)
Pup-160	23 ft 2¼ in (7·07 m)
Height overall	7 ft 6 in (2·29 m)
Tailplane span	11 ft 0 in (3·35 m)
Wheel track	7 ft 0 in (2·13 m)
Wheelbase	4 ft 7 in (1·40 m)
Cabin door (each):	
Height (mean)	3 ft 0 in (0·91 m)
Width (mean)	2 ft 9 in (0·84 m)
Height to sill	3 ft 6 in (1·07 m)

DIMENSIONS, INTERNAL:

Cabin: Length	6 ft 6 in (1·98 m)
Max width	3 ft 9 in (1·14 m)
Max height	3 ft 6 in (1·07 m)
Floor area	29 sq ft (2·69 m²)
Volume	85 cu ft (2·41 m³)
Baggage space	15 cu ft (0·42 m³)

AREAS (Pup-100, -150):

Wings, gross	119·5 sq ft (11·10 m²)
Ailerons (total)	9·2 sq ft (0·85 m²)
Trailing-edge flaps (total)	10·7 sq ft (0·99 m²)
Fin	21·7 sq ft (2·02 m²)
Rudder	6·76 sq ft (0·63 m²)
Tailplane	27·5 sq ft (2·55 m²)
Elevators, incl tab	10·9 sq ft (1·01 m²)

WEIGHTS AND LOADINGS:

Weight empty, equipped:	
Pup-100	985 lb (447 kg)
Pup-150	1,090 lb (494 kg)
Pup-160	1,175 lb (533 kg)
Max T-O, zero-fuel and landing weight:	
Pup-100	1,600 lb (725 kg)
Pup-150	1,925 lb (873 kg)
Pup-160	1,950 lb (884 kg)
Max wing loading:	
Pup-100	13·40 lb/sq ft (65·42 kg/m²)
Pup-150	16·1 lb sq ft (78·6 kg/m²)
Pup-160	16·25 lb/sq ft (79·3 kg/m²)
Max power loading:	
Pup-100	16·00 lb/hp (7·26 kg/hp)
Pup-150	12·85 lb/hp (5·83 kg/hp)
Pup-160	12·2 lb/hp (5·53 kg/hp)

PERFORMANCE (at max T-O weight):

Max level speed at S/L:	
Pup-100	110 knots (127 mph; 204 km/h)
Pup-150	120 knots (138 mph; 222 km/h)
Pup-160	128 knots (147 mph; 237 km/h)
Max diving speed:	
Pup-100, -150, -160	169 knots (195 mph; 314 km/h)
Cruising speed (75% power):	
Pup-100 at 7,000 ft (2,150 m)	102 knots (118 mph; 190 km/h)
Pup-150 at 7,500 ft (2,290 m)	114 knots (131 mph; 211 km/h)
Pup-160 at 4,000 ft (1,220 m)	112 knots (129 mph; 208 km/h)
Econ cruising speed (60% power) at 8,000 ft (2,450 m):	
Pup-100	94 knots (108 mph; 174 km/h)
Econ cruising speed (55% power) at 8,000 ft (2,450 m):	
Pup-150	100 knots (115 mph; 185 km/h)
Pup-160	96 knots (111 mph; 179 km/h)
Stalling speed, flaps up:	
Pup-100	54 knots (62 mph; 100 km/h)
Pup-150	56 knots (64 mph; 103 km/h)
Pup-160	50 knots (58 mph; 94 km/h)
Stalling speed, flaps down:	
Pup-100	46 knots (53 mph; 86 km/h)
Pup-150	49 knots (56 mph; 91 km/h)
Pup-160	46 knots (53 mph; 86 km/h)

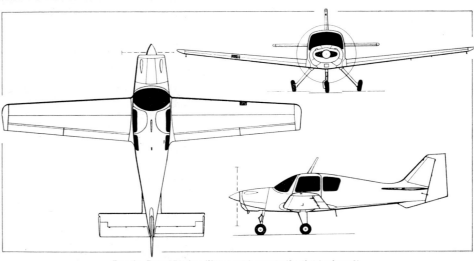

Beagle Pup-150 two/three-seat aerobatic light aircraft

Rate of climb at S/L:	
Pup-100	575 ft (175 m)/min
Pup-150	800 ft (244 m)/min
Pup-160	880 ft (268 m)/min
Service ceiling:	
Pup-100	11,200 ft (3,410 m)
Pup-150	14,700 ft (4,480 m)
Pup-160	15,000 ft (4,570 m)
T-O run:	
Pup-100	720 ft (220 m)
Pup-150	890 ft (271 m)
Pup-160	885 ft (270 m)
T-O to 50 ft (15 m):	
Pup-100	1,260 ft (384 m)
Pup-150, -160	1,480 ft (451 m)
Landing from 50 ft (15 m):	
Pup-100	1,060 ft (323 m)
Pup-150	1,410 ft (430 m)
Pup-160	1,420 ft (433 m)
Landing run:	
Pup-100	407 ft (124 m)
Pup-150	620 ft (189 m)
Pup-160	640 ft (195 m)
Still-air range with max fuel:	
Pup-100	494 nm (569 miles; 915 km)
Pup-150, standard fuel	382 nm (440 miles; 710 km)
Pup-150, optional fuel	549 nm (633 miles; 1,020 km)
Pup-160 (45 min reserve)	455 nm (524 miles; 843 km)
Pup-160 (no reserve)	525 nm (604 miles; 972 km)

BEAGLE B.206
RAF Name: Basset CC.Mk 1

The B.206 is a twin-engined light transport with standard accommodation for five to eight persons. The following versions were produced:

B.206X. Prototype (G-ARRM). Flew for the first time on 15 August 1961. Smaller than subsequent B.206's, with a span of 38 ft 0 in (11·58 m) and max T-O weight of 6,310 lb (2,862 kg). Powered by two 260 hp Continental IO-470-A engines.

B.206Y. Prototype (G-ARXM) of developed B.206, with 310 hp Rolls-Royce/Continental GIO-470-A engines and increased dimensions.

First flew on 12 August 1962. Lost in a flying accident on 25 May 1964.

B.206Z1. Pre-production aircraft (XS742) for MoA, built at Shoreham and first flown on 24 January 1964. Delivered to A and AEE, Boscombe Down, for performance and tropical trials.

B.206Z2. Second pre-production aircraft (XS743) for MoA. First flew on 20 February 1964. Prototype for military B.206R. Delivered to A and AEE for radio and installation trials.

B.206 Series I (B.206C). Initial commercial production version. First B.206C flew at Rearsby on 17 July 1964. Early aircraft built with overwing cabin door. Later aircraft have passenger/cargo door aft of wings. Production completed.

B.206 Series I (B.206R). Military production version. First of 20 ordered for communications and ferrying duties with RAF, under name of **Basset CC.Mk 1**, flew on 24 December 1964. Overwing cabin door. Production completed.

One aircraft allocated to the Queen's Flight in 1969 for the personal use of HRH The Prince of Wales.

B.206 Series II (B.206-S). Development of Series I with supercharged engines and other changes. Design started in December 1963. Construction of prototype began in June 1964 and it flew for the first time on 23 June 1965. Later production version has extended cabin with additional rear window and large passenger/cargo door aft of wings on port side. Aircraft delivered include two ambulance models for the Royal Flying Doctor Service of New South Wales, Australia.

A developed version (G-AWLN), known as the **Series III**, was also flown, which introduced dorsal and ventral fins, small tabs on the fin, and an extended tailplane trailing-edge, and could accommodate ten passengers.

By 31 December 1969, Beagle had delivered a total of 40 B.206 Series I and II aircraft, plus 20 Bassets to the RAF and the two B.206Z aircraft for the Ministry of Technology (formerly MoA).

A full description of the Series I and II appeared in the 1969-70 edition of *Jane's*.

BOULTON PAUL (see "Dowty Boulton Paul")

BRITTEN-NORMAN
BRITTEN-NORMAN SALES LTD
HEAD OFFICE:
Bembridge Airport, Isle of Wight
DIRECTORS:
A. F. Bartlett
F. R. J. Britten
N. D. Norman
W. Oppenheimer, FCA

Britten-Norman has developed and put into production a small twin-engined feeder-line aircraft known as the BN-2 Islander and a four-seat light aircraft designated the BN-3 Nymph.

BRITTEN-NORMAN BN-2A ISLANDER
The Islander is intended as a modern replacement for aircraft in the class of the de Havilland Dragon Rapide. Detail design work began in April 1964 and construction of the prototype (G-ATCT) was started in September of the same year. It flew for the first time on 13 June 1965, powered by two 210 hp Rolls-Royce/Continental IO-360-B engines and with wings of 45 ft (13·72 m) span. Subsequently, the prototype was re-engined with more powerful Lycoming O-540 engines, with which it flew for the first time on 17 December 1965. The wing span was also increased by 4 ft (1·22 m) to bring the prototype to production standards.

The production prototype BN-2 Islander (G-ATWU) flew for the first time on 20 August 1966, in the livery of Loganair, a company which operates two such aircraft on services in the Scottish islands. The Islander received its domestic C of A on 10 August 1967 and an FAA type certificate on 19 December 1967.

On 28 May 1968 an Islander (G-AVUB) demonstrated its STOL characteristics by landing on and taking off from the deck of the aircraft carrier HMS *Hermes* without using either arrester wires or catapult.

Also during 1968 an Islander was converted for forestry control, locust control and crop spraying in the Far East. It was fitted with four Micronair AU-3000 rotary atomisers, and the floor was specially modified to carry a 250 Imp gallon (1,136 litre) chemical tank, or aerial survey camera equipment. The Desert Locust Control Organisation at Asmara, Ethiopia, have ordered a similarly equipped Islander for locust reconnaissance and control in East Africa.

The current production version of the Islander is as follows:

BN-2A Srs 2. Basic version, with Lycoming O-540-E4C5 engine. Described in detail below. The Series 2 model, which superseded the Srs 1 on 1 June 1969, has a number of new standard features, including a side-loading baggage compartment door, new fuel gauge system, forced draught ventilation intakes, carburettor charge temperature indicator, fully-variable carburettor heat control, intercom system including second head set, passenger address system, alternate static source, two sun visors, provision for combustion monitor and ramshorn control yoke.

Delivery of Islanders began in August 1967, and by February 1970 a total of 280 had been ordered by operators in 40 countries. To meet increasing demands, Britten-Norman placed a contract for manufacture of an initial series of 236 Islanders with British Hovercraft Corporation, who took over complete responsibility for production up to final assembly stage. Deliveries in 1970 are at the rate of 12 a month, and 135 Islanders had been delivered by 1 March 1970.

Islanders are also being produced by IRMA in Romania (which see).

Development of the basic design continues, and many new features have been introduced or will be made available during 1970. Streamlining of the leg fairings and engine nacelles has improved the cruising speed, and the Islander has now been cleared to a max T-O weight of 6,300 lb (2,857 kg), giving a 300 lb (136 kg) increase in disposable load. Provision of two 21 Imp gallon (99·7 litre) auxiliary tanks in extended-span wingtips will almost double the full-load range.

All of the above features will become available for fitting retrospectively to Islanders already in service.

An Islander fitted with 300 hp Lycoming IO-540-K fuel-injection engines was flown for the first time on 30 April 1970.

TYPE: Twin-engined feeder-line transport.

WINGS: Cantilever high-wing monoplane. NACA 23012 wing section. Thickness/chord ratio 12%. No dihedral. Incidence 2°. No sweepback. Conventional riveted two-spar torsion-box structure in one piece, using aluminium-clad aluminium alloys. Flared-up wingtips of Britten-Norman design. Slotted ailerons and electrically-operated single-slotted flaps of metal construction. Ground-adjustable tab on starboard aileron. BTR-Goodrich pneumatic de-icer boots optional.

FUSELAGE: Conventional riveted four-longeron semi-monocoque structure of pressed frames and stringers and metal skin, using L72 aluminium-clad aluminium alloys.

TAIL UNIT: Cantilever two-spar structure, with pressed ribs and metal skin, using aluminium-clad aluminium alloys. Fixed-incidence tailplane. Trim-tabs in rudder and elevator. Pneumatic de-icing of tailplane and fin optional.

LANDING GEAR: Non-retractable tricycle type, with twin wheels on each main unit and single steerable nose-wheel. Cantilever main legs mounted aft of rear spar. All three legs fitted with Lockheed oleo-pneumatic shock-absorbers. All five wheels and tyres size 600 × 6, supplied by Goodyear. Tyre pressure: main 35 lb/sq in (2·46 kg/cm²); nose 27 lb/sq in (1·90 kg/cm²). Foot-operated Goodyear hydraulic brakes.

POWER PLANT (BN-2A): Two 260 hp Lycoming O-540-E4C5 six-cylinder horizontally-opposed air-cooled engines, each driving a Hartzell HC-C2YK-2B two-blade metal constant-speed feathering propeller, diameter 6 ft 8 in (2·03 m). Integral fuel tank between spars in each wing, outboard of engine. Total fuel capacity 111 Imp gallons (505 litres). Refuelling point above wing. Total oil capacity 5 Imp gallons (22·75 litres).

ACCOMMODATION: Up to ten persons in pairs on bench seats. Centre aisle omitted to keep down width of fuselage. Backs of seats fold forward. Access to all seats provided by three forward-hinged doors, forward of wing and at rear of cabin on port side and forward of wing on starboard side. Baggage area at rear of cabin. Special executive layouts available. Can be operated as freighter with single seat for pilot only on port side. In ambulance rôle, two stretchers and attendants can be accommodated.

SYSTEMS: Southwind cabin heater optional. Electrical system includes one or two 24V 50A self-rectifying alternators, supplying instruments, lighting and radio. No hydraulic or pneumatic systems, except for self-contained hydraulic brakes.

ELECTRONICS AND EQUIPMENT: Optional items include blind-flying instrumentation, autopilot, and a wide range of VHF or HF communications and navigation equipment.

DIMENSIONS, EXTERNAL:

Wing span	49 ft 0 in (14·94 m)
Wing chord (constant)	6 ft 8 in (2·03 m)
Wing aspect ratio	7·4
Length overall	35 ft 8 in (10·87 m)
Height overall	13 ft 8 in (4·16 m)
Tailplane span	15 ft 5 in (4·70 m)
Wheel track	11 ft 3¼ in (3·45 m)
Wheelbase	12 ft 10½ in (3·93 m)
Cabin door (front, port):	
Height	3 ft 8 in (1·12 m)
Width	2 ft 2 in (0·66 m)
Height to sill	1 ft 11¼ in (0·59 m)
Cabin door (front, starboard):	
Height	3 ft 8 in (1·12 m)
Width	2 ft 10 in (0·86 m)
Height to sill	1 ft 10½ in (0·57 m)
Cabin door (rear, port):	
Height	3 ft 8 in (1·12 m)
Width:	
top	2 ft 1 in (0·64 m)
bottom	4 ft 0 in (1·22 m)
Height to sill	1 ft 8½ in (0·52 m)

DIMENSIONS, INTERNAL:

Passenger cabin, aft of pilot's seat:	
Length	10 ft 0 in (3·05 m)
Max width	3 ft 7 in (1·09 m)
Max height	4 ft 0 in (1·22 m)
Floor area	32 sq ft (2·97 m²)
Volume	130 cu ft (3·68 m³)
Baggage space aft of passenger cabin	
	36 cu ft (1·02 m²)
Freight capacity:	
Aft of pilot's seat, incl baggage space	166 cu ft (4·70 m²)
With four bench seats folded into baggage space	130 cu ft (3·68 m²)

AREAS:

Wings, gross	325 sq ft (30·2 m²)
Ailerons (total)	25·6 sq ft (2·38 m²)
Flaps (total)	39·0 sq ft (3·62 m²)
Fin	36·64 sq ft (3·41 m²)
Rudder, incl tab	17·2 sq ft (1·60 m²)
Tailplane	73·0 sq ft (6·78 m²)
Elevators, incl tabs	33·16 sq ft (3·08 m²)

The Britten-Norman BN-2A Islander which won outright the BP England-Australia Air Race in 1969

BN-2A Islander in the insignia of Suburban Airlines, after take-off from La Guardia Airport

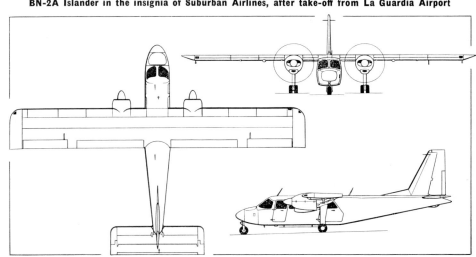

Britten-Norman BN-2A Islander twin-engined light transport

WEIGHTS AND LOADINGS:

Weight empty, with basic equipment	3,550 lb (1,610 kg)
Typical basic operating weight, incl pilot, oil and radio	4,122 lb (1,870 kg)
Max T-O and landing weight	6,300 lb (2,857 kg)
Max zero-fuel weight	5,800 lb (2,630 kg)
Max wing loading	19·4 lb/sq ft (94·7 kg/m²)
Max power loading	12·1 lb/hp (5·49 kg/hp)

PERFORMANCE (at max T-O weight):

Max level speed at S/L	147 knots (170 mph; 273 km/h)
Max permissible diving speed	182 knots (210 mph; 335 km/h)
Cruising speed, 75% power at 7,000 ft (2,135 m)	139 knots (160 mph; 257 km/h)
Cruising speed, 67% power at 9,000 ft (2,745 m)	137 knots (158 mph; 254 km/h)
Cruising speed, 59% power at 13,000 ft (3,960 m)	133 knots (153 mph; 246 km/h)

Stalling speed, flaps down	43 knots (49 mph; 79 km/h)
Stalling speed, flaps up	50 knots (57 mph; 92 km/h)
Rate of climb at S/L	1,050 ft (320 m)/min
Rate of climb, one engine out at S/L	190 ft (58 m)/min
Absolute ceiling	16,200 ft (4,940 m)
Service ceiling	14,600 ft (4,450 m)
Service ceiling, one engine out	5,600 ft (1,707 m)
T-O run	560 ft (171 m)
T-O to 50 ft (15 m)	1,090 ft (332 m)
Landing from 50 ft (15 m), ISA, S/L	960 ft (293 m)
Landing run	450 ft (137 m)
Range with max fuel at 59% power, 30 min reserve	703 nm (810 miles; 1,300 km)
Range with max payload at 59% power, 30 min reserve	369 nm (425 miles; 670 km)

Britten-Norman Islander with extended-span wingtips containing additional fuel tanks

BRITTEN-NORMAN BN-3 NYMPH

The Britten-Norman Nymph, although to all outward appearances a conventional four-seat light aircraft, represents an interesting new approach to making such aircraft available at minimum cost to the widest possible market.

Britten-Norman aims to achieve this by an arrangement known as GDP (Grand Design Partnership), whereby it will, instead of building complete aircraft, supply them in kit form for assembly under licence by specially-approved maintenance and repair organisations and other agencies. The kits will be supplied with all metal shaped and cut to size, and with pre-drilled master holes and jig-bored drilling strips to facilitate assembly, together with a complete Kardex system for stock control of spares. Licensees will therefore be able to participate in both the manufacture and after-sales service of the aircraft, and in countries where (for example) there is no import duty on aircraft components this system will enable the Nymph to compete favourably with ready-made domestic and foreign aircraft.

No special jigs or tools will be required, and assembly plans and other visual aids will be made available. In addition, Britten-Norman is to set up an Assembly School at Bembridge, to train licensees' representatives in assembly and inspection techniques. An incidental by-product of this school may be a few completed aircraft available for sale, but otherwise Britten-Norman does not intend to manufacture the aircraft itself in the normal way.

Design of the Nymph was started in September 1968, and the first prototype was built and flown in less than eight weeks, construction having started on 25 March 1969. The prototype (G-AXFB) flew for the first time on 17 May 1969 and made its first public appearance at the Paris Air Show in the following month. A second airframe is under construction for structural testing.

During the Paris Show 100 Nymphs were ordered for the Australian and New Zealand markets. These will be assembled in New Zealand by AESL (which see), with deliveries beginning in mid-1970.

Production Nymphs will be offered with a choice of 115 or 160 hp Lycoming, or 130 hp Rolls-Royce/Continental engine, and it is expected that certification will be achieved in time for deliveries of the first aircraft to begin in September 1970. It is estimated that the Nymph can be assembled in 250-500 man-hours, dependent on the licensees' annual output of the aircraft and the skill of the labour available.

TYPE: Four-seat light aircraft.

WINGS: Strut-braced high-wing monoplane. Wing section NACA 23012. Dihedral 1° 30' from roots. Incidence 3° 30'. No sweepback. Conventional two-spar all-metal structure of Alclad light alloy, including trailing-edge flaps and ailerons. Braced on each side by single strut from fuselage floor line. No trim-tabs. Optional wing-folding to facilitate stowage.

FUSELAGE: Conventional semi-monocoque structure of basically rectangular section, with frames and stringers and Alclad light alloy sheet covering. Glass-fibre engine cowling.

TAIL UNIT: Cantilever all-metal structure, with sweepback on vertical surfaces and rectangular horizontal surfaces. Small dorsal fin fairing. No trim-tabs in rudder or elevators.

LANDING GEAR: Non-retractable tricycle type with single wheel on each unit. Cessna-type spring steel main legs on prototype. Goodyear tyres, all size 6·00 × 6. Tyre pressure 22 lb/sq

in (1·55 kg/cm²) on main wheels, 15 lb/sq in (1·05 kg/cm²) on nose wheel. Goodyear disc brakes.

POWER PLANT (prototype): One 115 hp Lycoming O-235-C1B four-cylinder horizontally-opposed air-cooled engine, driving a Sensenich two-blade fixed-pitch metal propeller of 6 ft 2 in (1·88 m) diameter. Fuel tank in each wing root, total capacity 30 Imp gallons (136 litres). Refuelling point above each wing. Alternative 130 hp Rolls-Royce/Continental engine or 160 hp Lycoming O-320 engine available at customer's option.

ACCOMMODATION: Side-by-side individual seats, in pairs, for pilot and up to three passengers in fully-enclosed cabin, access to which is via forward-hinged door on port side. Similar door optional on starboard side. Baggage space aft of rear seats, which can be folded or removed to give extra stowage space. Cabin heating and ventilation standard.

SYSTEMS: Hydraulic system, pressure 500 lb/sq in (35·15 kg/cm²), for main wheel brakes. DC electrical system includes 14V 40A alternator and 25Ah battery. Exhaust-mounted heater with punka louvres for cabin heating.

ELECTRONICS AND EQUIPMENT: Normal instrumentation for VFR and IFR flying. General Aviation Class I radio equipment optional.

DIMENSIONS, EXTERNAL:

Wing span	39 ft 3·9 in (11·98 m)
Wing chord (constant)	4 ft 4 in (1·32 m)
Wing aspect ratio	9·1
Length overall	23 ft 7·7 in (7·20 m)
Width, wings folded	12 ft 0 in (3·66 m)
Height overall	9 ft 6 in (2·90 m)
Tailplane span	12 ft 0 in (3·66 m)
Wheel track	7 ft 2 in (2·18 m)
Wheelbase	6 ft 10 in (2·08 m)
Passenger door (port):	
Height	3 ft 0 in (0·91 m)
Width	2 ft 10 in (0·86 m)
Height to sill	2 ft 6 in (0·76 m)

DIMENSIONS, INTERNAL:

Cabin:	
Length	8 ft 4 in (2·54 m)
Max width	3 ft 5 in (1·04 m)
Max height	4 ft 0 in (1·22 m)

AREAS:

Wings, gross	169 sq ft (15·70 m²)
Ailerons (total)	14·9 sq ft (1·38 m²)
Trailing-edge flaps (total)	20·0 sq ft (1·86 m²)
Fin	7·74 sq ft (0·72 m²)
Rudder	5·66 sq ft (0·53 m²)
Tailplane	21·6 sq ft (2·01 m²)
Elevators	13·4 sq ft (1·24 m²)

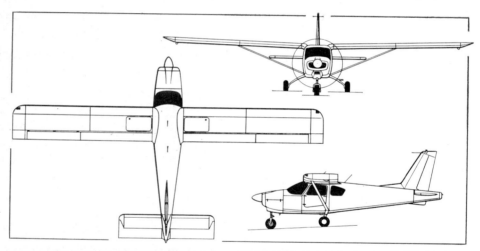

Photograph and three-view drawing of the prototype Britten-Norman BN-3 Nymph four-seat light aircraft (115 hp Lycoming O-235-C1B engine)

WEIGHTS AND LOADINGS (A = 115 hp engine, B = 130 hp, C = 160 hp):

Weight empty:

A	1,140 lb	(517 kg)
B	1,180 lb	(535 kg)
C	1,250 lb	(566 kg)

Max T-O and landing weight:

A	1,925 lb	(873 kg)
B	2,100 lb	(952 kg)
C	2,350 lb	(1,065 kg)

Max wing loading:

A	11·38 lb/sq ft	(55·6 kg/m²)
B	12·42 lb/sq ft	(60·6 kg/m²)
C	13·91 lb/sq ft	(67·9 kg/m²)

Max power loading:

A	16·70 lb/hp	(7·57 kg/hp)
B	16·15 lb/hp	(7·33 kg/hp)
C	14·70 lb/hp	(6·67 kg/hp)

PERFORMANCE (at max T-O weight; B and C estimated):

Max level speed at S/L:

A	102 knots	(117 mph; 188 km/h)
B	107 knots	(123 mph; 198 km/h)
C	117 knots	(135 mph; 217 km/h)

Max cruising speed at 7,500 ft (2,285 m):

A	98 knots	(113 mph; 182 km/h)
B	102·4 knots	(118 mph; 190 km/h)
C	113 knots	(130 mph; 209 km/h)

Rate of climb at S/L:

A	600 ft	(183 m)/min
B	630 ft	(192 m)/min
C	700 ft	(213 m)/min

Service ceiling:

A	11,200 ft	(3,415 m)
B	11,500 ft	(3,505 m)
C	12,000 ft	(3,660 m)

T-O run:

A	875 ft	(267 m)
B	850 ft	(259 m)
C	830 ft	(253 m)

T-O to 50 ft (15 m):

A	1,550 ft	(472 m)
B	1,520 ft	(463 m)
C	1,480 ft	(451 m)

Landing from 50 ft (15 m):

A	950 ft	(290 m)
B	1,020 ft	(311 m)
C	1,110 ft	(338 m)

Landing run:

A	500 ft	(152 m)
B	520 ft	(158 m)
C	540 ft	(165 m)

Range with max fuel:

A	521 nm	(600 miles; 965 km)
B	503 nm	(580 miles; 930 km)
C	451 nm	(520 miles; 835 km)

BROOKLAND (see "Gyroflight")

CAMPBELL

CAMPBELL AIRCRAFT LTD

HEAD OFFICE AND WORKS:
Membury Airfield, Lambourn, Newbury, Berks

DIRECTORS:
J. V. Campbell, ARAeS
A. M. W. Curzon-Herrick
J. P. Metcalfe (Sales)
G. Whatley, MInstPI

SECRETARY:
C. G. Horwood, ACA

In 1959, this company acquired sole rights to manufacture and sell in the UK the complete range of products and kits designed by Bensen Aircraft Corporation of Raleigh, NC, USA. Its first licence-built aircraft flew on 19 August 1960.

In addition to building the full range of complete Gyro-Gliders and Gyro-Copters, on wheels and floats, Campbell Aircraft marketed sets of drawings, kits of parts and individual components for these rotor-kites and light autogyros.

During 1969 company policy was changed, and Campbell now markets only the Cricket single-seat autogyro, of which all available details are given below. The Curlew two-seat autogyro, described briefly and illustrated in the 1969-70 *Jane's*, is no longer being developed.

CAMPBELL CRICKET

The Cricket is a single-seat light autogyro of Campbell design. Construction of a prototype began in June 1969, and it flew for the first time during the following month. By early 1970 orders had been received for 32 Crickets, of which eight had been completed. These are flyable under a Board of Trade permit issued on 14 November 1969.

TYPE: Single-seat light autogyro.

ROTOR SYSTEM: Two-blade auto-rotating main rotor. All-metal blades of hollow section with solid extruded leading-edge, bonded and flush-riveted, and attached to hub by blocks and four bolts on each blade. Rotor brake fitted.

ROTOR DRIVE: Mechanical drive from engine for rotor spin-up only (under development).

FUSELAGE: All-metal structure, with engine mounts of T45 tube, argon arc-welded, and high-tensile alloy main frame.

TAIL UNIT: Fin and rudder only, of Aerolam alloy sandwich construction, supported by single-spar tail-boom. Automatic rudder offset.

LANDING GEAR: Non-retractable tricycle type,

Prototype of the Campbell Cricket single-seat autogyro (75 hp modified Volkswagen engine)

with small tail-wheel. No shock-absorbers. Same size (5 in = 12·7 cm) nylon wheels, with Avon tyres and tubes, on each unit. Tyre pressure (all units) 14 lb/sq in (68 kg/cm²). Campbell drum brake on nose-wheel. Steerable nose-wheel, linked to rudder control.

POWER PLANT: One 75 hp modified Volkswagen 1,600 cc engine, driving a Hordern-Richmond fixed-pitch propeller of 4 ft 2 in (1·27 m) diameter. Single fuel tank, capacity 7·25 Imp gallons (33 litres) aft of pilot's seat. Oil capacity 4·25 Imp pints (2·4 litres).

ACCOMMODATION: Single seat for pilot in open cockpit. Glass-fibre nose nacelle and windscreen afford adequate protection from elements.

EQUIPMENT: Radio optional. Special camera mount available for aerial photographic work.

DIMENSIONS, EXTERNAL:

Diameter of main rotor	21 ft 9 in	(6·63 m)
Main rotor blade chord (each)	7 in	(17·8 cm)
Length of fuselage	11 ft 3 in	(3·43 m)

Height to top of rotor hub	6 ft 10 in	(2·08 m)
Wheel track	5 ft 2½ in	(1·59 m)

WEIGHTS AND LOADING:

Weight empty, less rotors	295 lb	(133·5 kg)
Max T-O and landing weight	650 lb	(294·5 kg)
Max disc loading	1·9 lb/sq ft	(9·3 kg/m²)

PERFORMANCE (at max T-O weight):

Max level speed at S/L	69 knots	(80 mph; 129 km/h)
Max cruising speed at S/L	56 knots	(65 mph; 105 km/h)
Econ cruising speed at S/L	52 knots	(60 mph; 97 km/h)
Max rate of climb at S/L	740 ft	(226 m)/min
Service ceiling	11,000 ft	(3,353 m)
T-O run	105 ft	(32 m)
T-O to 50 ft (15 m)	330 ft	(101 m)
Landing from 50 ft (15 m)	50 ft	(15 m)
Landing run	3 ft	(1 m)
Range with max fuel	220 nm	(253 miles; 407 km)
Endurance	2 hr	

CIERVA

CIERVA ROTORCRAFT LTD

ADDRESS:
South Block, Redhill Aerodrome, Surrey

DIRECTORS:
J. G. Weir, CMG, CBE (Chairman)
N. M. Niven (Deputy Chairman)
Lord Kindersley, CBE, MC
Dipl Ing J. S. Shapiro (Technical Director)
G. R. L. Weir

Cierva Rotorcraft, formerly the Cierva Autogiro Company, has acquired the whole of the share capital of Rotorcraft Ltd, the company which was set up by the Mitchell Engineering Group to back the development of the Servotec-designed Grasshopper helicopter.

Servotec Ltd, headed by Mr J. S. Shapiro, continues to be the design group within the company.

CIERVA ROTORCRAFT Mk III GRASSHOPPER

This developed version of the Grasshopper is a four-seat commercial utility helicopter, powered by two 135 hp Rolls-Royce/Continental O-300 flat-four engines. The rotor system comprises two co-axial contra-rotating two-blade rotors.

The first of two prototypes had begun ground tests by mid-1969. No news of the aircraft has been received since that date.

DIMENSIONS, EXTERNAL:

Rotor diameter (each)	32 ft 0 in	(9·75 m)
Length overall, rotors turning	34 ft 5 in	(10·49 m)

Height overall	9 ft 3 in	(2·82 m)
Width across skids	6 ft 2½ in	(1·89 m)
Max width at cabin	5 ft 2½ in	(1·59 m)

PERFORMANCE (estimated at AUW of 3,050 lb = 1,383 kg, for single-engine 100 ft = 30 m/min climb in forward flight):

Max level speed	120 knots	(138 mph; 222 km/h)
Cruising speed (75% power)	101 knots	(116 mph; 187 km/h)
Max rate of climb at S/L	1,100 ft	(335 m)/min
Service ceiling	12,000 ft	(3,660 m)
Hovering ceiling out of ground effect	4,000 ft	(1,220 m)
Range	217 nm	(250 miles; 402 km)

CLUTTON-TABENOR
ERIC CLUTTON

ADDRESS:
92, Newlands Street, Shelton, Stoke-on-Trent, Staffordshire

Mr E. Clutton and Mr E. Sherry designed and built, over a six-year period, a single-seat light aircraft designated FRED, of which details were given in the 1967-68 *Jane's*. In mid-1967, Mr Clutton began modifying it to Series 2 standard, in partnership with Mr Tabenor, and the details below apply to this latest model.

Also described below is a new aeroplane, the Easy Too, designed by Mr Clutton and Mr Tabenor to make full use of a geared Volkswagen engine flight-tested in FRED Series 2 and described briefly in the "Aero-Engines" section of this edition.

CLUTTON-TABENOR FRED SERIES 2

FRED (Flying Runabout Experimental Design) was designed as a powered aircraft that could be flown by any reasonably experienced glider pilot without further training. Other aims were that it should be able to operate from small, rough fields and be roadable.

First flight was made on 3 November 1963, with a 27 hp 500-cc Triumph 5T motor-cycle engine, driving the propeller through a 2·5 : 1 reduction gear. This was replaced by a Scott A2S engine from a pre-war Flying Flea and many local circuits were made with this, although it would not develop its rated power of 34 hp and proved unreliable. In mid-1966, an American-built Lawrance radial engine from an APU was converted for installation in FRED, which was designated Series 2 after the engine change.

Another change made after the first flights was replacement of the original bungee-in-tension landing gear shock-absorbers by steel springs.

During 1968 the Lawrance engine was replaced by a 66 hp Volkswagen 1,500 cc engine, modified by the provision of a toothed belt to drive the propeller at half engine speed. Development of the geared VW engine continued during 1969, and early in 1970 it was running with a reduction ratio of 2 : 1, driving a 5 ft 8 in (1·73 m) American-style propeller. Ignition is by two Lucas SR4 magnetos, chain-driven from the clutch end of the crankshaft.

FRED is described by its builders as being virtually unstallable with power on. Stall warning is a pronounced Dutch roll. It can be rigged in 20 minutes and has been road-towed behind a motor-cycle combination.

To meet numerous requests, sets of plans for FRED have been available to amateur constructors since February 1970.

TYPE: Single-seat amateur-built light aircraft.

WINGS: Wire-braced parasol monoplane. Wing section. Göttingen 535. Thickness/chord ratio 17·2%. No dihedral or incidence. 1° washout on tips. Spruce and plywood structure, with torsion-box leading-edge, auxiliary rear spar and drag spar, fabric-covered. Non-differential ailerons. No flaps or trim-tabs.

FUSELAGE: Spruce longerons. Plywood covered to rear of cockpit, except for aluminium top decking. Fabric covering on rear fuselage, except for plywood top decking, front portion of which is removable for access to baggage locker.

TAIL UNIT: Cantilever structure of spruce and plywood. No fixed fin. Tailplane incidence adjustable on ground. Pushrod-operated elevators. No tabs.

LANDING GEAR: Non-retractable main wheels and tail-skid. Main units sprung with motor-cycle rear suspension springs. Industrial truck wheels. Tyre pressure 26 lb/sq in (1·83 kg/cm²). No brakes.

POWER PLANT: One 66 hp Volkswagen 1,500 cc motor-car engine, modified for aviation use by provision of toothed belt reduction gear and

Clutton-Tabenor FRED Series 2 in latest form, with geared Volkswagen engine

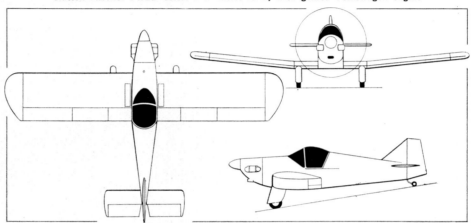
E.C.2 (Easy Too) light aircraft designed by Mr Eric Clutton

dual ignition, and driving a two-blade fixed-pitch propeller, diameter 6 ft 0 in (1·83 m). Single fuel tank in centre-section, capacity 7·5 Imp gallons (34 litres). Provision for second centre-section tank. Oil capacity 0·75 Imp gallons (3·5 litres).

ACCOMMODATION: Single seat in open cockpit.

DIMENSIONS, EXTERNAL:
Wing span	22 ft 6 in (6·86 m)
Wing chord (constant)	5 ft 0 in (1·52 m)
Wing aspect ratio	4·4
Length overall	17 ft 0 in (5·18 m)
Height overall	6 ft 0 in (1·83 m)
Tailplane span	9 ft 0 in (2·74 m)
Wheel track	4 ft 0 in (1·22 m)
Wheelbase	10 ft 6 in (3·20 m)

AREAS:
Wings, gross	110 sq ft (10·22 m²)
Ailerons (total)	12 sq ft (1·11 m²)
Rudder	13·5 sq ft (1·25 m²)
Tailplane	11·25 sq ft (1·04 m²)
Elevators	12 sq ft (1·11 m²)

WEIGHTS:
Weight empty	533 lb (242 kg)
Max T-O weight	773 lb (350 kg)

PERFORMANCE (at max T-O weight):
Max cruising speed
65 knots (75 mph; 120 km/h)
Econ cruising speed
55 knots (63 mph; 101 km/h)
Approach speed 45 knots (52 mph; 84 km/h)
Stalling speed
approx 35 knots (40 mph; 63 km/h)

Range with max fuel
173 nm (200 miles; 320 km)

CLUTTON-TABENOR E.C.2 EASY TOO

The Easy Too is a new aeroplane whose design was started in 1969 to utilise the geared Volkswagen power plant developed by Mr Clutton and Mr Tabenor. It is a single-seat aircraft, plywood-covered with a polyester resin finish and having foldable wings. A prototype was nearing completion in the early part of 1970, and was expected to fly in the Summer. It is stressed for aerobatics.

The general appearance of Easy Too can be seen in the accompanying three-view drawing. The prototype is powered by the new geared 1,500 cc Volkswagen engine, but the aircraft is equally suited to a direct-drive VW engine. The outer wing panels can be folded back by one person, by withdrawing pins and replacing them by an irreversible screw-jack arrangement which locks them in position. The ailerons and flaps are coupled automatically. The folding hinge and support is entirely separate from the flying fittings, and the aeroplane can be towed on the road behind a motor-car. The wing-tips, of glass-fibre, are of similar type and size to those fitted to the Rollason Turbulent and the Taylor Monoplane. A one-piece sliding cockpit canopy is fitted. Wing span of Easy Too is 23 ft 4 in (7·11 m) and the estimated empty weight is 485 lb (220 kg). It is intended to make plans of the aircraft available after the successful conclusion of flight testing.

DOWTY BOULTON PAUL
DOWTY BOULTON PAUL LTD (Subsidiary of Dowty Rotol Ltd)

HEAD OFFICE, WORKS AND AERODROME:
Pendeford Lane, Wolverhampton WV9 5EW

DIRECTORS:
R. F. Hunt, CEng, FRAeS (Chairman)
A. W. Turner (Managing Director)
T. D. H. Andrews, AMCST, CEng, FIMechE, FRAeS
D. J. Millard, CEng, FIMechE, FRAeS
G. A. Woolsey, FCA (Executive Director, Finance)
F. A. Hewitt, CEng, MIMechE, AFRAeS (Executive Director, Production)
A. S. Watson

AIRCRAFT SALES MANAGER:
P. E. N. Smith, CEng, MIMechE, ARAeS
PUBLIC RELATIONS OFFICER:
C. C. Morris

The former Boulton Paul Aircraft Ltd was formed in June 1934 to take over the old-established Aircraft Department of Boulton & Paul Ltd of Norwich which began the manufacture of aircraft in 1915. It became a member of the Dowty Group in 1961. The company name was changed to Dowty Boulton Paul Ltd in January 1970.

The last aircraft of Boulton Paul design were the P.111 and P.120 delta-wing high-speed research monoplanes, of which descriptions can be found in earlier editions of *Jane's*.

The company has also been concerned with development of the Canberra and Lightning

military aircraft, and in producing major assemblies for the Beagle B.206.

Dowty Boulton Paul now specialises in the design and manufacture of power-operated flying controls and associated equipment. These range from the unique self-contained packaged units fitted to the VC10 and Vulcan aircraft, to the valve ram units in the BAC One-Eleven, Buccaneer and Concorde. The Concorde is the first civil aircraft to use electrical signalling for primary control.

Since its successful initial flight test programme on the Tay Viscount in 1957, the company has been actively engaged in the design of equipment for complete electric control of aircraft. Current development is in multiplex systems incorporating quadruplex and quintuplex units into the design philosophy.

FAIRTRAVEL
FAIRTRAVEL LTD

HEAD OFFICE:
Deepwood, Farnham Royal, Bucks

WORKS:
Blackbushe Airport, Camberley, Surrey, and Denham, Bucks

CHAIRMAN:
Air Vice-Marshal D. C. T. Bennett, CB, CBE, DSO, FRAeS

Fairtravel Ltd was responsible for producing the Linnet two-seat light aircraft, a description of which appeared in the 1968-69 *Jane's*.

It is unlikely that production will be resumed, but a final decision on this has not yet been taken.

GYROFLIGHT
GYROFLIGHT LTD

HEAD OFFICE:
Dean and Chapter, Ferryhill, Co Durham

MANAGING DIRECTOR:
C. Golightly, DSC

PROJECT MANAGER AND TEST PILOT:
B. R. Luesley

After successfully converting a Volkswagen engine to power his home-built Druine Turbulent light aircraft (G-APOL), in 1960, Mr Ernest Brooks began development of an ultra-light gyroplane fitted with a similar power plant. He was killed when this aircraft, known as the Mosquito Gyroplane, crashed on 9 March 1969. A subsequent enquiry established that the crash was not caused by any fault in the aircraft.

Since his death, a number of business changes and expansions have taken place, and the new company Gyroflight Ltd has been formed to foster the design, development and other aspects of aircraft built by Brookland Rotorcraft Ltd. Production of the Brookland Mosquito has ended during the past year. Gyroflight began manufacture in December 1969, in its new factory at Ferryhill, of a new range of aircraft which includes the Hornet single-seat gyroplane, and the single-seat Gnat and two-seat Midge gyrogliders. Prefabricated kits for the Midge are also marketed.

BROOKLAND MOSQUITO GYROPLANE

Construction of the original prototype Brookland Mosquito Mk 1 Gyroplane was started on 7 May 1962, and it flew for the first time on 30 August 1962. Described in 1967-68 *Jane's*.

A prototype of the improved Mosquito Mk 2 Gyroplane was built and flown in 1967, powered by a developed version of Mr Brooks' 1,200-cc Volkswagen conversion, developing 90 hp and giving improved performance. Simplified control system. Described in 1969-70 *Jane's*.

A total of 11 Mosquito Mk 2's were built. Production ended in October 1969.

GYROFLIGHT HORNET

The Hornet is a developed version of the Mosquito, of which design was started in December 1969. The first aircraft flew for the first time in January 1970, and by late February 1970 four had been completed and a further eight were partially completed. A full C of A was anticipated by the end of 1970.

TYPE: Single-seat ultra-light autogyro.

ROTOR SYSTEM: Two-blade auto-rotating main rotor. Blade section Clark Y (modified). All-metal blades of L65 and L71 light alloy, glued and riveted, and attached to hub by bolts. Blades do not fold, but can be quickly unbolted and rebolted when required. Fixed tab on each blade, near tip. No rotor brake.

ROTOR DRIVE: Gearbox for pre-rotation spin-up only, to approx 200 rpm.

FUSELAGE: Primary structure of L65 and L71 light alloy, with welded steel fittings bolted to keel, axle and rotor mast.

TAIL UNIT: Glass-fibre fin and rudder only.

LANDING GEAR: Non-retractable tricycle type, with offset sprung axle. Same-size wheels and tyres (300 × 5) on all units, pressure 10 lb/sq in (0·70 kg/cm²). Brookland brakes. Nose-wheel steering integrated with rudder controls.

POWER PLANT: One 70 hp Brookland Aero Engine Mk II, driving a two-blade fixed-pitch propeller of 4 ft 0 in (1·22 m) diameter. Single fuel tank aft of seat, capacity 5 Imp gallons (23 litres). Larger tank of 7 Imp gallons (32 litres) capacity optional. Oil capacity 6 Imp pints (27 litres).

ACCOMMODATION: Single seat for pilot behind glass-fibre windshield.

SYSTEMS AND EQUIPMENT: Stabilflyte system (mechanical, offset head with trim device) for "hands-off" stabilisation. Ultra-light VHF radio set. Optional "Mini-Map" moving map display.

DIMENSIONS, EXTERNAL:
Diameter of main rotor	22 ft 0 in (6·71 m)
Main rotor blade chord (each)	7 in (17·8 cm)
Length overall	12 ft 0 in (3·66 m)
Height to top of rotor hub	6 ft 0 in (1·83 m)
Wheel track	5 ft 4 in (1·63 m)
Wheelbase	3 ft 5 in (1·04 m)

WEIGHTS:
Weight empty, equipped	310 lb (140 kg)
Max T-O weight	600 lb (272 kg)

PERFORMANCE (at max T-O weight):
Max level speed at S/L	69 knots (80 mph; 129 km/h)
Max cruising speed at S/L	61 knots (70 mph; 113 km/h)
Econ cruising speed at S/L	52 knots (60 mph; 97 km/h)
Max rate of climb at S/L	750 ft (229 m)/min
Service ceiling	10,000 ft (3,050 m)
T-O run, still air	180 ft (55 m)
Landing run, still air	30 ft (9 m)
Range with max fuel	147 nm (170 miles; 273 km)

GYROFLIGHT SPRITE

The Sprite is basically a scaled-up version of the Hornet, some 25% greater in size and having a more powerful engine. Design started in January 1970, and the first Sprite was expected to make its first flight in mid-1970. It is suitable for use as a side-by-side two-seat trainer, or can be flown as a single-seater with increased fuel load.

POWER PLANT: One 85 hp Brookland Aero Engine Mk III, driving a 4 ft 9 in (1·45 m) diameter propeller. Main fuel tank of 5 or 7 Imp gallons (23 or 32 litres) capacity, with secondary tank of 3 Imp gallons (14 litres) capacity.

DIMENSIONS, EXTERNAL:
Diameter of main rotor	25 ft 0 in (7·62 m)
Main rotor blade chord (each)	7 in (17·8 cm)
Length overall	13 ft 6 in (4·11 m)
Height overall	7 ft 6 in (2·29 m)
Wheel track	5 ft 4 in (1·63 m)
Wheelbase	3 ft 11 in (1·19 m)

WEIGHTS:
Weight empty	350 lb (159 kg)
Normal max T-O weight	750 lb (340 kg)

PERFORMANCE (at max T-O weight):
Max range, with limited reserve:
8 gallons	139 nm (160 miles; 257 km)
10 gallons	156 nm (180 miles; 289 km)
Max endurance	4 hr

HANDLEY PAGE

Handley Page Ltd was associated with flying in all its aspects from the time of its foundation on 17 June 1909. It thus had the distinction of being the first limited company incorporated in Great Britain for the purpose of manufacturing aircraft. Its founder, and Chairman and Managing Director until his death on 21 April 1962, was Sir Frederick Handley Page.

Handley Page (Reading) Ltd was formed in June 1948, when Handley Page Ltd took over Miles Aircraft Ltd.

On 8 August 1969, it was announced that Handley Page Ltd no longer possessed the financial resources to continue in its present form, and had gone into voluntary liquidation. Following this announcement the appointed receiver and manager, Mr Kenneth Cork, arranged the formation of a new company called Handley Page Aircraft Ltd to carry on the activities of the former company as a subsidiary of the K. R. Cravens Corporation of St Louis, Missouri, USA. Terravia Trading Services negotiated a sales agreement with the new company for worldwide marketing rights in the Jetstream light transport aircraft in areas not covered by previous agreements with International Jetstream Corporation (sales in the US) or Bavaria Fluggesellschaft (sales in Austria, Federal Germany and Switzerland).

However, on 27 February 1970 a further announcement was made, to the effect that Handley Page Aircraft Ltd was not able to meet its financial obligations, and on 2 March 1970 the Radlett works was closed and all except a small force of essential maintenance and security personnel were given notice.

The contract for conversion work on Victor Mk 2 tanker aircraft for the RAF, on which Handley Page had begun initial development work, has now been taken over by Hawker Siddeley Aviation.

Handley Page's most recent commercial aircraft designs were the H.P.R.7 Herald and H.P. 137 Jetstream, of which brief summaries are given below. Full descriptions of both aircraft appeared in the 1969-70 *Jane's*.

HANDLEY PAGE H.P.R.7 HERALD

The prototype Dart-engined Herald made its first flight on 11 March 1958. The second prototype flew on 17 December 1958, and the first production Herald on 30 October 1959. Main production versions were the Series 200 and 400, as indicated below. A full description of the Herald appeared in the 1969-70 *Jane's*.

Herald Series 200. Basic model seating up to 56 passengers. The second prototype of the Dart-engined Herald was converted to Series 200 standard early in 1961.

Herald Series 400. Developed from the Series 200 as a side-loading military troop/freight transport or ambulance aircraft. Incorporates strengthened floor, and fuselage door openable in flight for dropping of supplies and paratroops.

HANDLEY PAGE H.P.137 JETSTREAM

Handley Page announced this twin-turboprop executive, feeder-line and military transport on 19 January 1966, simultaneously with the news that the first batch of 20 production aircraft had been ordered by International Jetstream Corporation (USA).

A prototype, four pre-production Jetstreams and a static test airframe were built initially, and the prototype (G-ATXH) flew for the first time on 18 August 1967, with Astazou XII turboprop engines fitted temporarily. It was followed by the second Mk 1 aircraft (G-ATXJ) on 28 December 1967, and the third (G-ATXI) on 8 March 1968. These aircraft were used for an intensive flying programme and obtained full British and US type approval by March 1969.

Four versions of the Jetstream had been announced as follows:

Jetstream Mk 1. Civil version with Turboméca Astazou XIV turboprop engines, described in 1969-70 *Jane's*. Total of 29 delivered by 1 February 1970.

Jetstream Mk 3M. Military version with Ai-Research TPE 331 turboprop engines and detail changes. Two prototypes (G-AWBR and G-ATXI) were flown for certification of airframe and military avionics. Eleven ordered for USAF, by whom they were designated C-10A. These were in an advanced state of construction when this order was cancelled.

Jetstream Series 200 and Series 300. Developed versions of Mk 1, with 993 eshp Turboméca Astazou XVI C turboprop engines and max T-O weights of 12,500 lb (5,670 kg) and 14,000 lb (6,350 kg) respectively. Flight test programme was initiated using the second prototype (G-ATXJ) and a production Jetstream Mk 1 (G-AXFV). The original Jetstream prototype (G-ATXH) was also refitted with Astazou XVI engines for intensive development. First production aircraft was due to have flown in May 1970.

HANTS & SUSSEX AVIATION
HANTS & SUSSEX AVIATION LTD

ADDRESS: The City Airport, Portsmouth, Hants

DIRECTORS:
Gen J. Desmond Smith (Chairman)
A. E. Hawes (Managing Director)
R. W. Fox

This company purchased from Beagle Aircraft Ltd the entire assets of the former Auster company, together with the registered name Auster. It intends to provide support for all Auster types, including modification and the supply of spares.

HAWKER SIDDELEY
HAWKER SIDDELEY GROUP, LTD

REGISTERED OFFICE:
18, St James's Square, London SW 1

DIRECTORS:
Sir Arnold Hall, FRS (Chairman and Managing Director)
Sir Aubrey Burke, OBE, MInstT, FRSA (non-executive Vice Chairman)
J. T. Lidbury, FRAeS (Deputy Managing Director)
Air Marshal Sir Harry Broadhurst, GCB, KBE, DSO, DFC, AFC, RAF (Retd)
H. G. Herrington, CBE, FRAeS
R. R. Kenderdine
A. Stewart Kennedy
A. J. Laurence, FCA (Finance)
Sir Joseph Lockwood
C. D. MacQuaide
Sir Halford Reddish, FCA
J. F. Robertson, CA
The Rt Hon Lord Shawcross, PC, QC

Sir Thomas Sopwith, CBE, Hon FRAeS (Founder and President)
SECRETARY: C. B. White, MA

Following a major reorganisation, which became effective on 1 July 1963, the principal interests and operations of the Hawker Siddeley Group, Ltd, other than in Canada, were integrated into seven major subsidiaries and operating divisions. These are: Hawker Siddeley Aviation Ltd, Hawker Siddeley Dynamics Ltd, Hawker Siddeley Holdings Ltd, Hawker Siddeley Diesels Ltd, Hawker Siddeley Electric Ltd, the Metals Companies and Hawker Siddeley International Ltd.

Hawker Siddeley Aviation (which see) is responsible for all aircraft design, development, production and supply. Hawker Siddeley Dynamics (see appropriate sections) is responsible for the design, development and production of the Group's guided weapons, space-launch vehicles, satellites, propellers, air conditioning systems, electronic fuel control systems, alternators and static inverter power supply systems, hydraulic and pneumatic systems, automatic check-out systems (TRACE), electrical and electronic systems.

Hawker Siddeley Holdings is the holding company for several companies which were, in the main, formerly part of Hawker Siddeley Aviation, but whose products do not fall within the categories mentioned above. Hawker Siddeley Diesels Ltd and Hawker Siddeley Electric Ltd are the holding companies for the Group's industrial power interests. The Metals Companies include High Duty Alloys Ltd, which produces many aviation components, including Hiduminium RR.58 (French designation A-U2GN) aluminium-alloy components for the Anglo-French Concorde supersonic transport. It has also forged more than 30 million gas-turbine compressor blades of this material. Hawker Siddeley International co-ordinates the export sales promotion of all Group products.

Overseas subsidiaries include The de Havilland Aircraft of Canada, Ltd, Hawker de Havilland Australia Pty, Ltd, and Hawker Siddeley Canada.

HAWKER SIDDELEY AVIATION LTD

HEAD OFFICE:
Richmond Road, Kingston upon Thames, Surrey

DIRECTORS:
Sir Arnold Hall, FRS (Chairman)
J. T. Lidbury, FRAeS (Deputy Chairman and Managing Director)
Sir Aubrey Burke, OBE, MInstT, FRSA
A. Stewart Kennedy
Air Chief Marshal Sir Harry Broadhurst, GCB, KBE, DSO, DFC, AFC, RAF (Retd) (Deputy Managing Director)
A. J. Laurence, FCA (Finance Director)
R. L. Lickley, BSc, DIC, CEng, FIMechE, FRAeS (Assistant Managing Director)
Capt E. D. G. Lewin, CB, CBE, DSO, DSC, AFRAeS, RN (Retd) (Sales Director)
E. G. Rubython (Commercial Director)
J. L. Thorne (Director and General Manager, Hatfield)
J. T. Stamper, MA, CEng, FRAeS (Technical Director)
P. Jefferson, CEng, AFRAeS, MIMechE (Production Director)
J. H. A. Wood, MA (Director and General Manager, Manchester)
J. P. Smith, ECng, FRAeS (Director and Chief Engineer, Civil)
B. P. Laight, MSc, MIMechE, FRAeS (Director and Chief Project Engineer, Military)
W. J. Heasman, FCA (Financial Director)

EXECUTIVE DIRECTORS:
R. G. Adolphus, BSc, CEng, AFRAeS (Production, Kingston)
C. F. Bethwaite (Deputy Chief Engineer, Hatfield)
R. D. Boot, BSc(Eng), FRAeS (Chief Engineer, Brough)
M. J. Brennan, BSc, FIMechE, FRAeS (Special Projects, Head Office)
R. A. Courtman, MIProdE (Manufacturing, Head Office)
D. M. Craik, ACIS (Commercial, Hatfield)
J. Cunningham, CBE, DSO, DFC, DL (Chief Test Pilot, Hatfield)
R. H. Francis, MSc, FRAeS, FBIS, FIMechE (Research, Head Office)
J. Garston (Manager, Chester)
J. L. Glasscock, BA, FCIS, JP (Manager, Kingston)
R. S. Hooper, DCAe, DAe, CEng, MIMechE, AFRAeS (Chief Engineer, Kingston)
E. C. T. Humberstone, FInstPS (Purchasing, Head Office)
W. B. Irvine, CA (Financial Control, Head Office)
E. F. T. Jenkins, BCom (Contracts, Head Office)
J. A. Johnstone (Marketing, Hatfield)
W. Lambert, FCA (Finance, Hatfield)
J. McGregor Smith, ACWA (Finance, Manchester)
F. Murphy, OBE, DFC, AFRAeS (Military Sales, Head Office)
P. R. Owen (Chief Designer, Hatfield)
A. G. T. Peters, CEng, AFRAeS (Airbus, Hatfield)
A. Sewart, OBE, FIProdE, FRAeS, JP (Manchester)
A. S. Watson (Marketing, Manchester)
J. White, MIProdE (Manager, Brough)
G. A. Whitehead, CBE, FIMechE, CEng, FRAeS, AMCT (Chief Engineer, Manchester)
L. G. Wilgoss (Accounting, Head Office)
G. R. Wilkinson (Production, Hatfield)

SECRETARY: R. D. Smith Wright, FCA

Hawker Siddeley Aviation Ltd is responsible for all aircraft design, development, production and supply activities of the Hawker Siddeley Group.

The Aviation Head Office at Kingston upon Thames administers company policy and co-ordinates the activities of the eleven establishments in the United Kingdom. At present three civil aircraft types, the HS 125 business jet, the HS 748 turboprop feeder-liner and the Trident short/medium-range jet airliner; and three military aircraft types, the Harrier V/STOL strike fighter, the Buccaneer low-level strike/reconnaissance aircraft and the Nimrod jet-powered maritime reconnaissance aircraft, are in quantity production.

Two separate agreements have been made by Hawker Siddeley Aviation and McDonnell Douglas Corporation in the US. In these, the American company has responsibility for licence production and support of the Harrier in the United States, and Hawker Siddeley, as weapon system sister design company, has responsibility for in-service support and modification of the McDonnell Douglas F-4K and F-4M Phantoms serving with the Royal Navy and Royal Air Force.

In addition, Hawker Siddeley Aviation and Beech Aircraft Corporation in the US have joined forces to design, build and market a family of business jet aircraft. This agreement was initiated by the transfer to Beech of all marketing for the HS 125 in North America, where it is now known as the Beechcraft Hawker 125. The prototype of a larger, faster business jet, the Beechcraft Hawker 600, is currently under construction, and a new-generation business jet, the Beechcraft Hawker 200, is in the advanced project stage.

Hawker Siddeley Aviation is also working in close conjunction with Airbus Industrie, the European company designing and manufacturing the A 300B high-capacity short-haul airliner. Under the participation agreement Hawker Siddeley has responsibility for the design of the wing and the manufacture of its main structure, and is working in close co-operation with Fokker-VFW in the Netherlands, which manufactures the wing moving surfaces.

HAWKER SIDDELEY 125 (DH 125)
RAF name: Dominie T. Mk 1

The Hawker Siddeley (formerly de Havilland) 125 twin-jet executive aircraft is designed to meet the requirement for a fast, economical private aircraft to serve the needs of industry. It is also suitable for use by the armed forces in the communications rôle, as a troop carrier for 10 men, as an ambulance aircraft, for photographic survey and as an economical trainer for pilots, navigators and specialised radio and radar operators. All Series of HS 125's can operate off unpaved runways without modification.

The first HS 125 flew for the first time on 13 August 1962, and deliveries to customers began in the Autumn of 1964. The 100th aircraft came off the assembly line at Hawker Siddeley Aviation's Chester factory in July 1966. Following the devaluation of the pound sterling late in 1967, sales of the HS 125 increased to a rate of approx one a week, and by 1 February 1970 a total of 226 HS 125's had been sold, 186 of them for export. Four corporations have each bought three HS 125's; six others have two each.

In December 1969 it was announced that Hawker Siddeley Aviation and Beech Aircraft Corporation of the US (which see) had joined forces to design, build and market a family of jet executive aircraft, starting with the joint marketing of the HS 125 (which in America is now known as the **Beechcraft Hawker 125**).

The companies announced two further types in prospect. The first of these is a larger, faster executive jet aircraft to be known as the BH 600, powered by two R-R Bristol Viper 600 engines; the second is a smaller, "second-generation" business jet, with outstanding short-field capability and operating economics, to be known as the BH 200.

The following versions of the HS 125 have been announced:

HS 125 Srs 1. First 8 production aircraft only, built before end of 1964. Two Viper 520 turbojets, each rated at 3,000 lb (1,360 kg) st. Max T-O weight 20,000 lb (9,070 kg). Max landing weight 18,100 lb (8,210 kg).

HS 125 Srs 1A. In production from beginning of 1965. "North American" airframe with modifications to meet FAA requirements. Total of 62 built, 30 with Viper 521 engines and 32 with Viper 522's. Described in 1965-66 *Jane's*.

HS 125 Srs 1B. For sale throughout world except where FAA regulations apply. Max T-O weight 21,200 lb (9,615 kg). Otherwise same as Srs 1A. Total of 15 built, 5 with Viper 521 engines and 10 with Viper 522's.

HS 125 Srs 2. Navigational trainer version; 20 built for RAF as **Dominie T.Mk 1.** First Dominie T.Mk 1 flew on 30 December 1964. In service with No 1 Air Navigation School, at RAF Stradishall. Basically as Srs 1A/B. Production completed. Viper 520 engines (each 3,000 lb = 1,360 kg st). Max T-O weight 21,200 lb (9,615 kg). Max landing weight 19,550 lb (8,865 kg). Described in 1969-70 *Jane's*.

HS 125 Srs 3. Two Srs 3 aircraft were built for Qantas for airline pilot training, with extensive additional equipment to simulate Boeing airliners operated by this company.

Hawker Siddeley 125 Dominie T. Mk 1 of No 1 Air Navigation School, RAF

Viper 522 engines. Max T-O weight 21,000 lb (9,530 kg). Max landing weight 20,000 lb (9,072 kg). Max zero-fuel weight 13,500 lb (6,125 kg).

HS 125 Srs 3A. Produced for North American market. Powered by two 3,360 lb (1,525 kg) st Viper 522 turbojets, the Srs 3A offers improvements in performance and general passenger comfort. AiResearch air-conditioning and pressurisation system is fitted, enabling an APU to be installed for ground power and cabin air conditioning. Srs 3A meets FAA transport category requirements. Production completed.

HS 125 Srs 3B. Similar to Srs 3A, but intended for world markets except USA and Canada or where FAA regulations apply. Srs 3B carries a max payload of 2,000 lb (907 kg) for stages of up to 1,275 nm (1,470 miles; 2,365 km), with reserves. Production completed. Described in 1968-69 *Jane's*.

HS 125 Srs 3A-RA and 3B-RA. Versions with increased AUW and fuel capacity, these can fly up to 1,475 nm (1,700 miles; 2,736 km) with reserves. The additional fuel is carried in a tank faired into the underside of the rear fuselage. Production completed.

HS 125 Srs 400A and 400B. Current versions in production, with new integral airstair door, and improvements to flight deck cabin, vestibule and exterior appearance. Increased T-O weight. First announced in September 1968. Described in detail below.

TYPE: Light jet executive transport.

WINGS: Cantilever low-wing monoplane. Thickness/chord ratio 14% at root, 11% at tip. Dihedral 2°. Incidence 2° 6' at root, —24' at tip. Sweepback at quarter-chord 20°. Wings are built in one piece and dished to pass under fuselage, to which they are attached by four vertical links, a side link and a drag spigot. All-metal two-spar fail-safe structure, with partial centre spar of approx two-thirds span, sealed to form integral fuel tankage which is divided into two compartments by centre-line rib. Skins are single-piece units on each of the upper and lower semi-spans. Ailerons manually operated by cable linkage. Tabs in each aileron. Large four-position double-slotted flaps are actuated hydraulically via a screw-jack on each flap. Mechanically-operated hydraulic cut-out prevents asymmetric operation of the flaps. Flat-plate spoilers above and below each wing, forming part of flap shrouds, provide lift dumping facility during landing, and have interconnected controls to prevent asymmetric operation. TKS liquid system, using porous stainless steel leading-edge panels, for de-icing or anti-icing of wings.

FUSELAGE: One-piece all-metal semi-monocoque fail-safe structure, making extensive use of Redux bonding. Constant circular cross-section over much of its length.

TAIL UNIT: Cantilever all-metal structure, with fixed-incidence tailplane mounted near top of fin. Small triangular ventral fin. Control surfaces operated manually via cable linkage. Tabs in rudder and each elevator. TKS liquid de-icing or anti-icing of fin and tailplane leading-edges.

LANDING GEAR: Retractable tricycle type, with twin wheels on each unit. Hydraulic retraction of all units into fuselage, nose-wheels forward, main wheels inward. Oleo-pneumatic shock-absorbers. Steerable and fully-castoring nose unit. Dunlop main wheels and tyres, size 23 × 7-12, pressure 112 lb/sq in (7·87 kg/cm²). Dunlop nose-wheels and tyres size 18 × 4¼-10, pressure 75 lb/sq in (5·26 kg/cm²). Main wheel tyre pressures can be reduced to 75 lb/sq in (5·26 kg/cm²) at 21,500 lb (9,752 kg) AUW if required when using runways of low bearing strength. Dunlop double-disc hydraulic brakes with Maxaret anti-skid units on all main wheels.

POWER PLANT: Two Rolls-Royce Bristol Viper 522 turbojet engines (each 3,360 lb = 1,525 kg st) mounted in pods on sides of rear fuselage. Hot-air anti-icing of intake lips, bullet and inlet vanes. Integral fuel tanks in wings, with total capacity of 1,025 Imp gallons (4,660 litres). Over-wing refuelling point near each wing-tip. Rear under-fuselage tank of 112 Imp gallons (509 litres) capacity, with refuelling point on starboard side of rear fuselage, raising overall total capacity to 1,137 Imp gallons (5,170 litres). Oil capacity 23 Imp pints (13 litres).

ACCOMMODATION: Crew of two on flight deck, which is fully soundproofed, insulated and air-conditioned. Optional foldaway seat for third crew member. Luxury seating for seven passengers, with baggage, is standard. Alternative interior layouts will accommodate from six to twelve passengers. Cabin is unobstructed and is fully pressurised and air-conditioned. Armchair seats or divans on each side of well-type centre aisle. Cloakroom and toilet at rear. Entrance vestibule at front, with space for food and drink cabinets and a cupboard for coats or baggage. Outward-opening door at front on port side, with integral airstairs. Emergency exit over wing on starboard side.

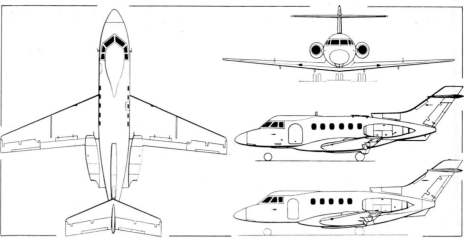

Hawker Siddeley HS 125 Srs 400A twin-jet executive transport. Additional side elevation (centre right) shows the Dominie T. Mk 1 navigational trainer

Hawker Siddeley 125 of the Malaysian Air Force

Windshield demisting by engine-bleed air; electrical windshield anti-icing with methanol spray back-up.

SYSTEMS: Air-conditioning and pressurisation system by AiResearch. Maximum differential 8·36 lb/sq in (0·58 kg/cm²). Oxygen system standard, with drop-out masks for passengers. Hydraulic system, pressure 2,300-3,000 lb/sq in (160-210 kg/cm²), for operation of landing gear, main wheel doors, flaps, air-brakes, nose-wheel steering, main wheel brakes and anti-skid units. Two accumulators provide emergency hydraulic power for wheel brakes in case of a main system failure. Independent auxiliary system for lowering landing gear and flaps in event of a main system failure. DC electrical system utilises two 9kW engine-driven starter-generators and two 24V 25Ah batteries. A 24V 3·5Ah battery provides separate power for igniter and starter control circuits. AC electrical system includes two 115V 2·5kVA 400 c/s three-phase rotary inverters for avionics and one engine-driven 115V 3kVA frequency-wild alternator for windscreen anti-icing. External power socket for 28V external DC supply. AiResearch GTCP-30-92 auxiliary power unit and emergency static inverter of 115V 400 c/s are optional. Engine ice protection system supplied by engine-bleed air. Graviner triple FD Firewire fire warning system and two BCF engine fire extinguishers.

ELECTRONICS AND EQUIPMENT: Comprehensive electronics are available to customer's requirements, including an automatic flight system comprising autopilot (typically, Sperry SP40C or Bendix PB60 for US models, Collins AP104 in US and UK models), flight director and compass; dual VHF nav/com; HF com; dual ADF; marker; ATC transponder; DME; and weather radar. Doppler, Decca Navigator, flight data recorder, passenger address system and tape reproducer may also be installed. Equipment for ICAO Category II low weather minima operation is also available as an option. Standard equipment includes dual controls, full blind-flying instrumentation, complete ice protection system, stick-shaker stall warning, and electrically-heated rudder auto-bias to apply corrective rudder during asymmetric engine power conditions. A spring

and *g* weight are included in the elevator circuit to reduce variations in stick force to a minimum over a wide CG range.

DIMENSIONS, EXTERNAL:

Wing span	47 ft 0 in (14·33 m)
Wing chord (mean)	7 ft 6¼ in (2·29 m)
Wing aspect ratio	6·25
Length overall	47 ft 5 in (14·45 m)
Height overall	16 ft 6 in (5·03 m)
Tailplane span	20 ft 0 in (6·10 m)
Wheel track (c/l of shock struts)	9 ft 2 in (2·79 m)
Wheelbase	18 ft 9 in (5·72 m)
Passenger door (fwd, port):	
Height	4 ft 3 in (1·30 m)
Width	2 ft 3 in (0·69 m)
Height to sill	3 ft 6 in (1·07 m)
Emergency exit (stbd):	
Height	3 ft 0 in (0·91 m)
Width	1 ft 8 in (0·51 m)

DIMENSIONS, INTERNAL:

Cabin: Length	19 ft 4 in (5·90 m)
Max width	5 ft 11 in (1·80 m)
Max height	5 ft 9 in (1·75 m)
Baggage hold (opposite door)	26 cu ft (0·74 m³)
Baggage hold (aft)	10 cu ft (0·28 m³)

AREAS:

Wings, gross	353 sq ft (32·8 m²)
Vertical tail surfaces (total) incl dorsal fin	56·7 sq ft (5·27 m²)
Horizontal tail surfaces (total)	100 sq ft (9·29 m²)

WEIGHTS AND LOADING:

Weight empty, equipped	11,275 lb (5,115 kg)
Typical operating weight	12,310 lb (5,584 kg)
Max payload	1,890 lb (857 kg)
Max T-O and ramp weight	23,300 lb (10,568 kg)
Max zero-fuel weight	14,200 lb (6,441 kg)
Max landing weight	20,000 lb (9,071 kg)
Max wing loading	66·0 lb/sq ft (322 kg/m²)

PERFORMANCE (at max T-O weight except where indicated):

Max design diving speed	Mach 0·825 or 370 knots (426 mph; 686 km/h) IAS
Max cruising speed at 31,000 ft (9,450 m)	443 knots (510 mph; 821 km/h)
Econ cruising speed above 37,000 ft (11,300 m)	391 knots (450 mph; 724 km/h)
Stalling speed at max landing weight, flaps down	87 knots (100 mph; 161 km/h)

Rate of climb at S/L   3,700 ft (1,128 m)/min
Service ceiling   41,000 ft (12,500 m)
Service ceiling, one engine out
     22,000 ft (6,700 m)
T-O run   3,440 ft (1,049 m)
T-O to 35 ft (10·7 m)   4,090 ft (1,247 m)
Landing from 50 ft (15 m) at 14,500 lb (6,575 kg)
   AUW   1,960 ft (597 m)
Landing run at 14,500 lb (6,575 kg) AUW
     1,015 ft (310 m)
Range with 1,000 lb (454 kg) payload, 45
   min hold   1,530 nm (1,762 miles; 2,835 km)
Range with max fuel and max payload, no
   reserves   1,997 nm (1,940 miles; 3,120 km)

HAWKER SIDDELEY 748
RAF name: Andover CC.Mk 2

The Hawker Siddeley (formerly Avro) 748 is a short/medium-range turboprop airliner, the design of which was started in January 1959. The prototype flew on 24 June 1960, followed by a second prototype on 10 April 1961.

There are three basic versions of the HS 748:

748 Series 1. Initial production version with 1,880 ehp Dart RDa.6 Mk 514 engines. First production 748 Series 1 (G-ARMV) flew on 30 August 1961, and received its C of A in January 1962. Production completed.

748 Series 2. Developed version with 2,105 ehp Dart RDa.7 Mk 531 engines but otherwise similar to Series 1. The second prototype Series 1 was re-engined with Dart 7's and first flew as a Series 2 on 6 November 1961. It was subsequently fitted out as a demonstration aircraft and was sold in August 1967. First production Series 2 flew in August 1962. C of A received in October 1962.

748 Series 2A. Superseded Series 2 in production from mid-1967. Differs only in having 2,280 ehp Dart RDa.7 Mk 532-2L turboprop engines, giving improved performance.

In addition to commercial and foreign military orders for these versions, the RAF has a specially-equipped version, as follows:

Andover CC.Mk 2. This version of the HS 748 Series 2 was ordered for The Queen's Flight and for special passenger-carrying duties with the RAF. The two Queen's Flight aircraft were delivered in July-August 1964, and were described in the 1969-70 *Jane's*.

The HS 748 is the subject of a manufacturing agreement with the Indian Government and is in production for the Indian Air Force. The first five IAF machines were delivered unassembled from England and the first of these flew on 1 November 1961.

A further 64 aircraft, all Series 2's, are being assembled, from British-built components, by the Kanpur Division of Hindustan Aeronautics Ltd (which see). Twenty-four of these are for Indian Airlines Corporation and the remainder for the Indian Air Force. The first fourteen IAC aircraft had been delivered by the end of March 1970.

Orders for the HS 748 by 1 February 1970, excluding Indian production, were as follows:

748 Series 1

Aerolineas Argentinas	12
BKS Air Transport	2
Skyways Coach Air	3
Smith's Aviation Division	1

748 Series 2 and 2A

Air Ceylon	1
Air Malawi	2
AerO Maya (Mexico)	2
Amoco Canada Petroleum	1
Austrian Airlines	2
Avianca (Colombia)	2
Bahamas Airways	4
BKS Air Transport	1
Board of Trade (CAFU)	2
Brazilian Air Force	6

Hawker Siddeley HS 748 Srs 2A airliner in the insignia of Varig *(Ronaldo S. Olive)*

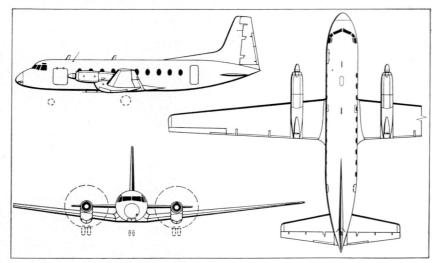

Hawker Siddeley 748 twin-engined turboprop transport

BWIA	1	Venezuelan Ministry of Defence	1
Channel Airways	4	Zambia Air Force (Presidential	
Court Line	2	Flight)	1
Compania Panamena de Aviacion	2	Zambia Airways	2
Department of the Presidency,		**Andover CC.Mk 2**	
Argentina	1	RAF Air Support Command	4
Ecuadorean Air Force	1	The Queen's Flight	2
Falcks Flyvetjeneste	1		
Fiji Airways	3		

The following details apply to the HS 748 Series 2 and 2A.

Type: Twin-engined 40/58-passenger airliner.

Wings: Cantilever low-wing monoplane. Wing section NACA 23018 at root, NACA 4412 at tip. Dihedral 7°. Incidence 3°. Sweepback 2° 54′ at quarter-chord. All-metal two-spar fail-safe structure. No cut-outs in spars for engines or landing gear. All-metal set-back hinge, shielded horn-balance, manually-operated ailerons and electrically-actuated Fowler flaps. Geared tab in each aileron. Trim-tab in starboard aileron. Pneumatic de-icer boots on leading-edge.

Fuselage: All-metal semi-monocoque riveted fail-safe structure, of circular section.

Tail Unit: Cantilever all-metal structure. Fixed-incidence tailplane. Manually-operated controls. Trim-tabs in elevators and rudder. Spring tab in rudder.

German Federal Government	
(Bundesanstalt für Flugsich-	
erung)	1
Ghana Airways	2
LAN-Chile	9
Leeward Islands Air Transport	2
Linea Aeropostal Venezolana	6
Midwest Airlines (Canada)	1
Mount Cook Airlines	1
Philippine Air Lines	12
Rousseau Aviation (France)	1
Royal Australian Air Force	10
Royal Nepal Airlines	2
SAESA (Mexico)	3
TAME (Ecuador)	1
Thai Airways	6
Thai Royal Flight	1
Varig (Brazil)	10

Hawker Siddeley HS 748 Srs 2A twin-turboprop transport in the insignia of Fiji Airways

LANDING GEAR: Retractable tricycle type, with hydraulically-steerable nose-wheel. All wheels retract forward hydraulically. Main wheels retract into bottom of engine nacelles forward of front wing spar. Dowty Rotol shock-absorbers. Twin wheels on all units. Main wheels size 32 × 10·75-14. Nose-wheels 25·65 × 8·5-10. Tyre pressures: main wheels 73 lb/sq in (5·13 kg/cm²), nose-wheels 55 lb/sq in (3·87 kg/cm²). Dunlop disc brakes with Maxaret anti-skid units.

POWER PLANT: Two Rolls-Royce Dart RDa.7 Mk 531 turboprop engines (Srs 2), each developing 2,105 eshp, or Rolls-Royce Dart RDa.7 Mk 532-2L turboprop engines (Srs 2A), each developing 2,290 ehp and driving Dowty Rotol four-blade constant-speed fully-feathering propellers, diameter 12 ft 0 in (3·66 m). Fuel in two integral tanks, one in each wing, with total capacity of 1,140 or 1,440 Imp gallons (5,182 or 6,550 litres). Underwing pressure refuelling and overwing gravity refuelling. Oil capacity 25 Imp pints (14·2 litres) per engine.

ACCOMMODATION: Crew of two on flight deck, and cabin attendant. Normal accommodation for 40-58 passengers in paired seats on each side of central gangway. Baggage compartment forward of cabin, with provision for steward's seat. Galley, toilet and baggage compartment aft of cabin. Forward baggage compartment and steward's seat can be replaced by freight hold with moving partition between hold and passenger cabin. Main passenger entrance door, on port side at rear, with smaller door on starboard side to serve as baggage door and emergency exit. Crew entrance and freight door on port side at front. Provision for power-operated entrance stairs.

SYSTEMS: Normalair pressurisation and air-conditioning system, giving equivalent altitude of 8,000 ft (2,440 m) at 25,000 ft (7,600 m). Hydraulic system, pressure 2,500 lb/sq in (175 kg/cm²), for landing gear retraction, nose-wheel steering, brakes and propeller brakes. No pneumatic system. APU available. One 9kW 28V DC generator and one 22 kVA alternator on each engine. Three or four 115V AC 3-phase 400 c/s inverters.

ELECTRONICS AND EQUIPMENT: Collins or Bendix solid-state radio and radar. Blind-flying instrumentation and weather radar standard. Provision for Smiths autopilot.

DIMENSIONS, EXTERNAL:

Wing span	98 ft 6 in (30·02 m)
Wing chord at root	11 ft 5¼ in (3·49 m)
Wing chord at tip	4 ft 5 in (1·34 m)
Wing aspect ratio	11·967
Length overall	67 ft 0 in (20·42 m)
Height over tail	24 ft 10 in (7·57 m)
Tailplane span	36 ft 0 in (10·97 m)
Wheel track	24 ft 9 in (7·54 m)
Wheelbase	20 ft 8 in (6·30 m)
Propeller ground clearance	2 ft 0 in (0·61 m)
Passenger door (port, rear):	
Height	5 ft 2 in (1·57 m)
Width	2 ft 6 in (0·76 m)
Height to sill	6 ft 0½ in (1·84 m)
Fwd freight and baggage door:	
Height	4 ft 6 in (1·37 m)
Width	4 ft 0 in (1·22 m)
Height to sill	6 ft 0½ in (1·84 m)
Baggage door (rear, stbd):	
Height	4 ft 1 in (1·24 m)
Width	2 ft 1 in (0·64 m)
Height to sill	6 ft 0½ in (1·84 m)

DIMENSIONS, INTERNAL:

Cabin, excluding flight deck:	
Length	46 ft 6 in (14·17 m)
Max width	8 ft 1 in (2·46 m)
Max height	6 ft 3½ in (1·92 m)

Floor area	296 sq ft (27·5 m²)
Volume	1,936 cu ft (54·82 m³)
Max total freight holds	337 cu ft (9·54 m³)

AREAS:

Wings, gross	810·75 sq ft (75·35 m²)
Ailerons (total)	42·90 sq ft (3·98 m²)
Trailing-edge flaps (total)	159·80 sq ft (14·83 m²)
Fin	105·64 sq ft (9·81 m²)
Rudder, including tabs	39·36 sq ft (3·66 m²)
Tailplane	188·9 sq ft (17·55 m²)
Elevators, including tabs	54·10 sq ft (5·03 m²)

WEIGHTS AND LOADINGS (Srs 2A):

Basic operating weight, including crew	25,988 lb (11,787 kg)
Max payload	11,512 lb (5,221 kg)
Max T-O weight	44,495 lb (20,182 kg)
Max zero-fuel weight	37,500 lb (17,010 kg)
Max landing weight	42,100 lb (19,096 kg)
Max wing loading	54·9 lb/sq ft (267 kg/m²)
Max power loading	9·75 lb/eshp (4·42 kg/eshp)

PERFORMANCE (Srs 2A):

Max permissible diving speed at 15,000 ft (4,570 m) 328 knots (378 mph; 608 km/h)
Max cruising speed (at AUW of 40,000 lb = 18,145 kg) 249 knots (287 mph; 461 km/h)
Rate of climb at S/L (at AUW of 40,000 lb = 18,145 kg) 1,290 ft (393 m)/min
Service ceiling (at AUW of 40,000 lb = 18,145 kg) 25,000 ft (7,600 m)
T-O run (at max T-O weight) 2,750 ft (838 m)
T-O to 50 ft (15 m) (at max T-O weight) 3,300 ft (1,006 m)
Landing from 50 ft (15 m) at max landing weight 1,980 ft (605 m)
Landing run at max landing weight 1,255 ft (383 m)
Range with max fuel, with reserves for 230 miles (370 km) diversion and 45 min hold 1,617 nm (1,862 miles; 2,996 km)
Range with max payload, reserves as above 599 nm (690 miles; 1,110 km)

HAWKER SIDDELEY TRIDENT

The Hawker Siddeley (formerly de Havilland D.H. 121) Trident was ordered into production initially to meet BEA's requirements for a short-haul 600 mph airliner for service from 1963-64 onwards. Design was started in 1957 and construction of the first airframe began on 29 July 1959. The first Trident (G-ARPA), a production aircraft for BEA, flew for the first time on 9 January 1962.

Four versions of the Trident have been ordered, as follows:

Trident 1. Initial version with three Rolls-Royce RB.163/1 Mk 505/5 Spey turbofans, each rated at 9,850 lb (4,468 kg) st, and seats for up to 103 passengers. Received C of A on 18 February 1964. Twenty-four built for BEA, with whom it made its first revenue flight on 11 March 1964, and entered full scheduled service on 1 April 1964. Details in 1968-69 *Jane's*.

Trident 1E. Basically similar to Trident 1, but with Rolls-Royce RB.163-25 Mk 511-5 Spey turbofans, each rated at 11,400 lb (5,170 kg) st, and wing of increased span incorporating full-length leading-edge slats in place of the drooping leading-edge of the Trident 1. Integral fuel tankage in wing increased. Revised entry door permits smaller vestibule, giving maximum accommodation for 115 passengers. AUW increased. First Trident 1E flew for the first time on 2 November 1964. Certificate of Airworthiness received in November 1965. Fifteen built. Four aircraft (2 for Channel Airways, 2 for BKS) embody an extra emergency exit, permitting a high-density seating layout (up to 139 seats).

Trident 2E. Developed version; 15 ordered by BEA in August 1965, with accommodation for up to 115 passengers. Overall length unchanged. Fuel capacity increased, enabling the aircraft to operate non-stop over BEA's longest routes,

between London and the Middle East. Max T-O weight increased considerably, but take-off performance improved by use of more powerful (11,930 lb = 5,411 kg st) Rolls-Royce Spey RB.163-25 Mk 512-5W turbofan engines. Landing distances reduced by use of leading-edge slats, as in Trident 1E, and by increased wing span. Low-drag (Küchemann) wing-tips. Some strengthening of undercarriage, and of wing and fuselage by use of thicker panels, is offset by other weight savings including greater use of titanium. BEA machines are furnished to carry 97 tourist class passengers, compared with 88 in this operator's Trident 1's, and are fitted with automatic landing equipment. The first Trident 2E (G-AVFA) flew for the first time on 27 July 1967, and the first aircraft for BEA (G-AVFC) was delivered on 15 February 1968. BEA refers to this variant as the Trident Two, and scheduled services began on 18 April 1968.

A high-density version is available, having a maximum of 149 seats.

Trident 3B. High-capacity short-haul development of Trident 1E, with fuselage lengthened by 16 ft 5 in (5·00 m) to accommodate from 128 to 179 passengers. Wing span same as for Trident 2E, but wing area increased, wing incidence increased by 2° 30' and flap span increased. Powered by same mark of Spey turbofan as Trident 2E, but with Rolls-Royce RB.162 turbojet in tail for improved T-O performance. First flight, on 11 December 1969, was made by G-AWYZ without an operational RB.162 engine fitted, as were the next 44 flights up to the end of January 1970, totalling more than 70 hours. The RB.162 was fitted in February and first flight with this engine operating was made on 22 March 1970. Scheduled to enter service with BEA (which has ordered 26, with options on 10 more) in early 1971.

Orders for the Trident announced by 28 February 1970 were as follows:

Trident 1
BEA	24

Trident 1E
Air Ceylon	1
British Air Services, BKS	2
Channel Airways	2
Iraqi Airways	3
Kuwait Airways	3
*Pakistan Int Airlines	4

Trident 2E
BEA	15
Cyprus Airways	2

Trident 3B
BEA	26

*Three of the four aircraft operated formerly by Pakistan International Airlines were sold to the Chinese People's Republic early in 1970.

On 10 June 1965, a BEA Trident 1 made the first automatic touch-down on a commercial airline service, at London Airport, using its Smiths Autoflare equipment. Subsequently, under ARB approval, BEA Tridents on regular service amassed considerable experience of the equipment at duplex level and working to Category 1 normal weather limits.

All BEA Trident 1's have been modified for autoland. Trident 2E's are delivered with autoland installed at triplex level and were the first airliners in the world with complete all-weather-operation instrumentation of this kind. ARB certification for Trident autolands in Category 2 weather (100 ft decision height, 400 metres RVR) was received in September 1968 for Trident 1's and February 1969 for Trident 2's. Full Category 2 operation was scheduled for the Winter of 1969. Trident 3B operations down to 12 ft decision height and 300 m RVR is planned for Winter 1971/72.

Hawker Siddeley Trident 2E medium-range airliner in the insignia of Cyprus Airways

Hawker Siddeley Trident 3B airliner, with lengthened fuselage and auxiliary turbojet, in BEA insignia (*Brian M. Service*)

The following details apply generally to the Trident 2E and 3B:

TYPE: Short/medium-range jet airliner.

WINGS: Cantilever low-wing monoplane. Wing sections designed with high critical drag rise Mach number for economical operation at ultimate subsonic cruising speeds. Mean thickness/chord ratio approx 9·8%. Dihedral 3°. Incidence 6° 30′ at root, 1° 30′ at tip. Sweepback at quarter-chord 35°. Main wing is continuous from wingtip to wingtip, and comprises a six-cell centre-section box extending across the fuselage, a two-cell box from the wing root out to 40% of the semi-span, and from there a single-cell box to the wingtip. The entire wing box is subdivided to form integral fuel tanks. Skins and stringers are of aluminium alloy, as are the leading-edge and trailing-edge flaps. Extensive use is made of Reduxing between skins and stringers. Structure is fail-safe, except for slat and flap tracks which are safe-life components tested to at least six times the aircraft life. Conventional all-metal ailerons actuated by triplexed power control system without manual reversion. Three independent hydraulic systems work continuously in parallel and power three separate jacks of Fairey manufacture at each primary flying control surface. Two all-metal double-slotted trailing-edge flaps on each wing. Krueger leading-edge flap at each wing-root. All flaps operated by screw jacks and hydraulic motors of Hobson manufacture. One all-metal spoiler on 2E, two on 3B, forward of outer flap on each wing, act also as airbrakes/lift dumpers. Lift dumpers forward of inner flaps. No trim-tabs. Srs 2E and 3B have full-span leading-edge slats, in four sections per wing, operated by screw-jacks and extending on curved titanium tracks. Thermal anti-icing system.

FUSELAGE: Consists of a pressure shell extending back to the engines and a rear fuselage carrying the engines and tail unit. Semi-monocoque fail-safe structure of aluminium-copper alloys, using Redux bonding to attach stringers to skin throughout the pressure cell. No structural bulkheads in pressure cell. Unpressurised cut-outs for nose and main landing gear and wing centre-section.

TAIL UNIT: Cantilever all-metal structure, with tailplane mounted at tip of fin. All-moving tailplane with geared slotted flap on trailing-edge to assist in providing high negative lift coefficient for take-off and landing. No trim-tabs. Power control system as for ailerons. Thermal anti-icing of leading-edges.

LANDING GEAR: Retractable tricycle type. Hydraulic retraction. Hawker Siddeley (main units) and Lockheed (nose) oleo-pneumatic shock-absorbers. Each main unit consists of two twin-tyred wheels mounted on a common axle: during retraction the leg twists through nearly 90° and lengthens by 6 in (15 cm), enabling wheels to stow within the circular cross-section of the fuselage. Nose unit has twin wheels and is offset 2 ft 0 in (61 cm) to port, retracting transversely. Dunlop wheels, tyres and multi-plate disc brakes, with Maxaret anti-skid units. Trident 3B has main wheel tyres size 36 × 10, pressure 165 lb/sq in (11·60 kg/cm²), and nose-wheel tyres size 29 × 8, pressure 124 lb/sq in (8·72 kg/cm²).

POWER PLANT: Three Rolls-Royce Spey turbofan engines (details under "Series" descriptions). Two in pods, one on each side of rear fuselage; one inside rear fuselage. Additionally, Trident 3B has a 5,250 lb (2,381 kg) st Rolls-Royce RB.162-86 turbojet installed in tail, below the rudder, to boost T-O and climb-out. Five integral fuel tanks, four in wings and one in centre-section. Total usable fuel capacity: Trident 2E, 6,400 Imp gallons (29,094 litres); Trident 3B, 5,620 Imp gallons (25,548 litres). One pressure refuelling point under each wing. Oil capacity 3 Imp gallons (13·5 litres) per engine.

ACCOMMODATION (Trident 2E): Crew of three on flight deck. Mixed-class version has galley (stbd) and toilet (port) at front, then a 12-seat first-class compartment, with seats in pairs on each side of central aisle, two galleys (port), 79-seat tourist-class cabin with three-seat units on each side of aisle, and two toilets at rear. All-tourist version in BEA service has 97 seats, six-abreast, with galley and toilet at front and two toilets at rear. Provision can be made for 132 passengers in high-density seating arrangement, or 149 passengers with some seven-abreast. Two inward-opening plug-type passenger doors, at front and centre of cabin on port side, with provision for built-in air-stairs. Doors for crew and servicing at front and amidships on starboard side. Large under-floor baggage holds forward and aft of wing. All crew and passenger accommodation air-conditioned. Provision for air-conditioning forward part of forward baggage hold for animals.

ACCOMMODATION (Trident 3B): Basically as for Trident 2E, with four-abreast first-class seats at 38-in (96·5-cm) pitch and six-abreast tourist seating at 31-in (79-cm) pitch. Mixed-class version has toilet (port) and two galleys (port and stbd) at front, 14-seat first-class cabin, and 122-seat tourist cabin, with two galleys and two toilets (one each port and stbd) at rear. All-tourist version has 152 seats at 30-in (76-cm) pitch, no coat stowage and only one galley (stbd) instead of two at rear, but is otherwise similar. High-density versions can have up to 179 seats (with seven-abreast seating in centre fuselage) at 28-in (71-cm) pitch and no rear galley, but are otherwise similar to the 152-seat version.

SYSTEMS: Hawker Siddeley Dynamics air-conditioning and pressurisation system, differential 8·25 lb/sq in (0·58 kg/cm²). Two independent supplies, each capable of maintaining full cabin pressurisation, with emergency ram

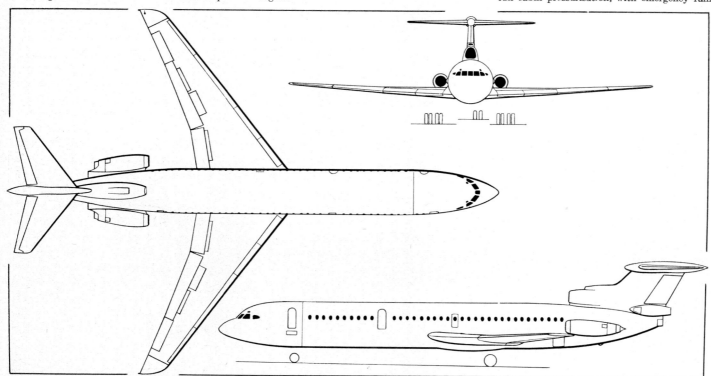

Hawker Siddeley Trident 3B high-capacity short-haul airliner, with lengthened fuselage and auxiliary turbojet

RB.162 booster engine in tail of Trident 3B

air system for use below 8,000 ft (2,440 m). Three independent hydraulic systems operating all flying controls, landing gear, nose-wheel steering, brakes and windscreen wipers. Each system powered by separate engine-driven pump, operating continuously in parallel at 3,000 lb/sq in (210 kg/cm²), using Skydrol fluid. Back-up hydraulic power supplied by two electrically - driven pumps, and emergency power from drop-out air turbine, capable of feeding any one system. Pneumatic system for toilet flushing, forward water system, stall recovery system and for pressurising hydraulic reservoirs. Electrical system comprises three separate channels, supplied by three 27·5 kVA brushless generators. Emergency 30-min AC and DC supply available from 24V battery. AiResearch GTCP 85C APU for engine starting and cabin air-conditioning, driving generator to provide 40 kVA of electrical power from which hydraulic systems can also be actuated through standby pumps.

ELECTRONICS AND EQUIPMENT: To customer's specification. Provision for duplicated VOR/ILS, including a third localiser for three-channel automatic landing guidance; integration of navigational aids with flight system, providing coupling facilities for all flight modes except take-off; duplicated ADF, VHF and HF with selective calling; C- or X-band weather radar; triplicated radio altimeters for automatic landing; Doppler; DME and transponder.

DIMENSIONS, EXTERNAL:
Wing span (Srs 2E, 3B)	98 ft 0 in (29·87 m)
Wing geometric mean chord:	
Srs 3B	15 ft 2¾ in (4·65 m)
Wing aspect ratio:	
Srs 3B	6·43
Length of fuselage:	
Srs 3B	119 ft 11 in (36·55 m)
Length overall:	
Srs 2E	114 ft 9 in (34·97 m)
Srs 3B	131 ft 2 in (39·98 m)
Height overall:	
Srs 2E	27 ft 0 in (8·23 m)
Srs 3B	28 ft 3 in (8·61 m)
Tailplane span	34 ft 3 in (10·44 m)
Wheel track (centres of shock-struts)	
	19 ft 1¼ in (5·83 m)
Wheelbase:	
Srs 2E	44 ft 0 in (13·41 m)
Srs 3B	52 ft 6½ in (16·01 m)

Passenger doors (both):		
Height	5 ft 10 in (1·78 m)	
Width	2 ft 4 in (0·71 m)	
Min height to sill	9 ft 5 in (2·87 m)	
Max height to sill	10 ft 3 in (3·12 m)	

Crew and service doors (fwd stbd on Srs 2E; fwd, centre and rear stbd on Srs 3B. Optional fourth door rear port side on high-density Srs 3B):
Height	4 ft 0¼ in (1·22 m)
Width	2 ft 0 in (0·61 m)
Height to sill	approx 9 ft 0 in (2·74 m)

Emergency exits (above centre-section port and stbd):
Height	3 ft 4 in (1·03 m)
Width	1 ft 8 in (0·51 m)

Baggage hold doors (fwd, stbd):
Height (vertical)	2 ft 11 in (0·89 m)
Width	4 ft 0 in (1·22 m)
Height to sill	4 ft 6 in (1·37 m)

Baggage hold door (rear, port):
Mean height (vertical)	2 ft 8 in (0·81 m)
Width	2 ft 11 in (0·89 m)
Height to sill	4 ft 6 in (1·37 m)

DIMENSIONS, INTERNAL:
Cabin, excluding flight deck:	
Length:	
Srs 2E	67 ft 1½ in (20·46 m)
Srs 3B	83 ft 5 in (25·43 m)
Max width	11 ft 3½ in (3·44 m)
Max height:	
Srs 2E	6 ft 7½ in (2·02 m)
Srs 3B	6 ft 8 in (2·03 m)
Floor area:	
Srs 2E	708 sq ft (65·77 m²)
Srs 3B	1,043 sq ft (96·9 m²)
Volume:	
Srs 2E	4,440 cu ft (125·7 m³)
Srs 3B	5,600 cu ft (158·57 m³)
Freight hold (fwd):	
Srs 2E	490 cu ft (13·88 m³)
Srs 3B	633 cu ft (17·92 m³)
Freight hold (rear):	
Srs 2E	270 cu ft (7·65 m³)
Srs 3B	477 cu ft (13·51 m³)

AREAS:
Wings, gross:	
Srs 2E	1,461 sq ft (135·73 m²)
Srs 3B	1,493 sq ft (138·7 m²)
Ailerons (total)	52·5 sq ft (4·89 m²)
Trailing-edge flaps (total):	
Srs 3B	291·9 sq ft (27·12 m²)
Spoilers	15·3 sq ft (1·42 m²)
Fin	202 sq ft (18·76 m²)
Rudder	52·1 sq ft (4·84 m²)
Tailplane	310 sq ft (28·80 m²)

WEIGHTS AND LOADINGS:
Operating weight, empty:	
Srs 2E	73,200 lb (33,203 kg)
Srs 3B (128-seat)	83,473 lb (37,863 kg)
Srs 3B (152-seat)	83,104 lb (37,695 kg)
Max payload:	
Srs 2E	26,800 lb (12,156 kg)
Srs 3B (128-seat)	32,027 lb (14,527 kg)
Srs 3B (152-seat)	32,396 lb (14,695 kg)
Max T-O weight:	
Srs 2E	143,500 lb (65,090 kg)
Srs 3B	150,000 lb (68,040 kg)
Max ramp weight:	
Srs 3B	150,500 lb (68,267 kg)
Max zero-fuel weight:	
Srs 2E	100,000 lb (45,359 kg)
Srs 3B	115,500 lb (52,395 kg)
Max landing weight:	
Srs 2E	113,000 lb (51,261 kg)
Srs 3B	128,500 lb (58,285 kg)
Max wing loading:	
Srs 3B	100·5 lb/sq ft (490·7 kg/m²)

Max power loading:	
Srs 3B	3·65 lb/lb st (3·65 kg/kg st)

PERFORMANCE (Srs 2E at max T-O weight):
Max diving speed (design limit)   Mach 0·95
Typical high-speed cruise Mach 0·88 at 27,000 ft (8,230 m) = 525 knots (605 mph; 972 km/h)
Econ cruising speed Mach 0·88 at 30,000 ft (9,150 m) = 518 knots (596 mph; 959 km/h)
T-O field length for 1,000 miles (1,610 km) stage, with 21,378 lb (9,697 kg) payload
        6,400 ft (1,950 m)
Range with max fuel* and 16,020 lb (7,266 kg) payload   2,171 nm (2,500 miles; 4,025 km)
Range with typical space-limited payload* of 21,378 lb (9,679 kg)
        2,110 nm (2,430 miles; 3,910 km)

PERFORMANCE (Srs 3B, estimated at max T-O weight except where stated):
Max diving speed (design limit)   Mach 0·95
Max cruising speed at 28,300 ft (8,625 m)
        522 knots (601 mph; 967 km/h)
Econ cruising speed at 29,000-33,000 ft (8,800-10,000 m)   463 knots (533 mph; 858 km/h)
Stalling speed (at max landing weight, flaps down)   111 knots (128 mph; 206 km/h) EAS
T-O to 35 ft (10 m)   7,500 ft (2,290 m)
Landing from 30 ft (9 m) at max landing weight
        5,920 ft (1,805 m)
Range with max fuel* and 23,500 lb (10,660 kg) payload   1,439 nm (1,658 miles; 2,668 km)
Range with max payload*
        950 nm (1,094 miles; 1,761 km)

*Reserves for 217 nm (250 mile = 450 km) diversion, 45 min hold at 15,000 ft (4,570 m), final reserve, 4·5% en route allowance and allowances for taxi prior to take-off, circuit approach and land at destination, and taxi after landing.

HAWKER SIDDELEY HARRIER
RAF designations: Harrier GR.Mk 1 and T.Mk 2

The Harrier is the western world's only operational fixed-wing V/STOL strike fighter. Developed from six years of operating experience with the P.1127/Kestrel series of aircraft (see 1968-69 Jane's), the Harrier is an integrated V/STOL weapons system, incorporating the Ferranti FE 541 inertial navigation and attack system and Specto head-up display. The first of six single-seat prototypes flew for the first time on 31 August 1966.

The major production version is the single-seat Harrier GR. Mk 1. A two-seat operational version, the T. Mk 2, retains the full combat capability of the GR. Mk 1. Export versions of the single- and two-seat models, which have a more powerful Rolls-Royce Bristol Pegasus 11 engine, are designated Mk 50 and Mk 51 respectively. This engine can also be fitted in the GR. Mk 1/T. Mk 2 airframes. Details of all four models appear below.

In May 1969 Royal Air Force Harriers, flight-refuelled by Victor tankers, made four non-stop Atlantic crossings during the Daily Mail Trans-Atlantic Air Race. The New York-bound Harrier set a world record between the centres of London and New York, its flight time for the 3,030 nm (3,490 miles; 5,615 km) trip being 5 hr 57 min.

By February 1970, 50 aircraft of the Harrier family had been built, and had made some 17,000 lift-offs and landings from a variety of surfaces such as grass, tarmac, concrete, dirt and gravel strips, snow- and ice-covered runways. They had also operated from the decks of nine ships, including US, Argentine and British aircraft carriers, Italian and British cruisers, and US amphibious support ships. The aircraft had been

Hawker Siddeley Harrier GR. Mk 1 V/STOL aircraft, one of two which carried out operational test-flying from the aircraft carrier HMS Eagle in 1969

flown by more than 70 Air Force, Navy, Marine and Army pilots form the UK, the US and the German Federal Republic.

Harrier GR. Mk 1. Single-seat close-support and tactical reconnaissance version, in quantity production for the Royal Air Force. First of 77 production aircraft currently on order (XV738) flew on 28 December 1967. Entered service, with No 1 Squadron of RAF Air Support Command at Wittering, on 1 April 1969.

The flight development programme has covered the carriage and delivery of the principal weapon loads, and successful flights have been made with two 330 Imp gallon (1,500 litre) ferry tanks which give the aircraft a ferry range of 2,000 nm (2,300 miles; 3,700 km). A four-Sidewinder installation will be provided to give the aircraft an effective air-to-air capability in conjunction with the two 30 mm Aden guns.

Tropical trials were carried out in Sicily in August 1967, and winterisation trials in Canada in January/February 1970.

The Harrier is designed to be self-contained at forward bases, needing a minimum of ground personnel and equipment. Design emphasis has aimed at ease of maintenance in the field, and a complete engine change has been carried out in 5½ hours at a typical field location, without recourse to any permanent facilities.

Harrier T. Mk 2. Two-seat version, retaining the full combat capability of the GR. Mk 1 in terms of equipment fit and weapon carriage. There is a large degree of commonality in structure and system components, ground support equipment and flight and ground crew training. Differences include a new, longer nose section forward of the wing leading-edge, with two cockpits in tandem; a tail-cone approx 6 ft (1·83 m) longer than that of the single-seat model; and enlarged fin surfaces. First of the development aircraft flew on 24 April 1969, followed by the second on 14 July 1969 and the first production aircraft on 3 October 1969. Tropical trials took place in Sicily in August 1969. Current orders are for 13 of this version (including two development aircraft), which was due to enter RAF service in 1970.

Harrier Mk 50. Single-seat close-support and tactical reconnaissance version for export. Dimensionally the same as GR. Mk 1, but with 21,500 lb (9,752 kg) st Rolls-Royce Bristol Pegasus 11 engine and internal modifications to customer's specification. Initial quantity of 12 ordered in 1969 for US Marine Corps; additional funds have been requested to purchase 18 more during 1971 fiscal year. McDonnell Douglas have licence rights to manufacture "any significant numbers" of Harriers ordered under future US government contracts.

Harrier Mk 51. Two-seat version for export, with Pegasus 11 engine and internal modifications to suit customer requirements for both operational and training capability.

The details below apply generally to the Harrier GR. Mk 1 and T. Mk 2, except where a specific version is indicated.

TYPE: V/STOL close-support and reconnaissance aircraft.

WINGS: Cantilever shoulder-wing monoplane. Aerofoil section of HSA design. Thickness/chord ratio 10% at root, 5% at tip. Anhedral 12°. Incidence 1° 45′. Sweepback at quarter-chord 34°. One-piece aluminium alloy three-spar safe-life structure with integrally-machined skins, manufactured by Brough Division of HSA, with six-point attachment to fuselage. Plain ailerons and flaps, of bonded aluminium-alloy honeycomb construction, with trim-tab in each aileron. Ailerons irreversibly operated by Fairey tandem hydraulic jacks. Jet reaction control valve built into front of each outrigger wheel fairing. Entire wing unit removable to provide access to engine. For

Hawker Siddeley Harrier GR. Mk 1 in ferry configuration, with extended wingtips, underwing drop-tanks and refuelling probe

ferry missions, the normal "combat" wingtips can be replaced by bolt-on extended tips to increase ferry range.

FUSELAGE: Conventional semi-monocoque safe-life structure of frames and stringers, mainly of aluminium alloy, but with titanium skins at rear and some titanium adjacent to engine and in other special areas. Access to power plant through top of fuselage, with wing removed. Jet reaction control valves in nose and in extended tail-cone. Large forward-hinged dive brake under fuselage, aft of main-wheel well.

TAIL UNIT: One-piece variable-incidence tail-plane, with 15° of anhedral, irreversibly operated by Fairey tandem hydraulic jack. Rudder and trailing-edge of tailplane are of bonded aluminium honeycomb construction. Rudder is operated manually. Trim-tab in rudder. Ventral fin under rear fuselage. Fin tip carries suppressed VHF aerial and dorsal fairing carries HF notch aerial.

LANDING GEAR: Retractable bicycle type of Dowty Rotol manufacture, permitting operation from rough unprepared surfaces of CBR as low as 3% to 5%. Hydraulic actuation, with nitrogen bottle for emergency extension of landing gear. Single steerable nose-wheel retracts forward, twin coupled main wheels rearward, into fuselage. Small outrigger units retract rearward into fairings slightly inboard of wingtips. Nose-wheel leg is of levered-suspension Liquid Spring type. Dowty-Rotol telescopic oleo-pneumatic main and outrigger gear. Dunlop wheels and tyres, size 26·00 × 8·75-11 (nose unit), 26·00 × 7·75-13 (main units) and 13·50 × 6·4 (outriggers). GR. Mk 1 tyre pressures 90 lb/sq in (6·33 kg/cm²) on nose wheel and main units, 95 lb/sq in (6·68 kg/cm²) on outriggers. T. Mk 2 tyre pressures 100 lb/sq in (7·03 kg/cm²) on nose unit, 95 lb/sq in (6·68 kg/cm²) on main and outrigger units. Dunlop multi-disc brakes and Dunlop-Hytrol adaptive anti-skid system.

POWER PLANT: One Rolls-Royce Bristol Pegasus Mk 101 vectored-thrust turbofan engine (19,000 lb = 8,620 kg) st, with four exhaust nozzles of the two-vane cascade type, rotatable through approx 100° from fully-aft position. Engine-bleed air from HP compressor used for jet reaction control system and to power duplicated air motor for nozzle actuation. The low-drag intake cowls, with inward-cambered lips, each have 8 automatic suction relief doors aft of the leading-edge to improve intake efficiency by providing extra air for the engine at low forward or zero speeds. Fuel in five integral tanks in fuselage and two in wings, with total capacity of approx 650 Imp gallons (2,955 litres). This can be supplemented by two 100 Imp gallon (455 litre) jettisonable combat tanks or two 330 Imp gallon (1,500 litre) ferry tanks on the inboard wing pylons. Ground refuelling point in port rear nozzle fairing. Provision for in-flight refuelling probe above the port intake cowl.

ACCOMMODATION: Crew of one (Mk 1) or two (Mk 2) on Martin-Baker Type 9A Mk 1 zero-zero rocket ejection seats in a pressurised, heated and air-conditioned cockpit. Manually-operated canopy, rearward-sliding on Mk 1, sideways-opening (to starboard) on Mk 2. Bird-proof windscreen, with hydraulically-actuated wiper. Windscreen de-icing.

SYSTEMS: Pressurisation system of HSA design, with Normalair-Garrett and Marston major components, max pressure differential 3·5 lb/sq in (0·25 kg/cm²). Duplicated hydraulic systems, each of 3,000 lb/sq in (210 kg/cm²), actuate flying controls, landing gear and nose-wheel steering and include a retractable ram-air turbine inside top of rear fuselage, driving a small hydraulic pump for emergency power. AC electrical system with transformer-rectifiers to provide required DC supply. Two 4kVA Plessey alternators. Two 28V 25Ah batteries, one of which energises a 24V motor to start Rotax gas-turbine starter/APU. This unit

Production Hawker Siddeley Harrier T. Mk 2 two-seat V/STOL fighter trainer for the Royal Air Force

can drive a 2kVA auxiliary alternator for ground readiness servicing and standby. Normalair-Garrett liquid oxygen system of 1 Imp gallon (5 litres) capacity. Bootstrap-type cooling unit for equipment bay, with intake at base of dorsal fin.

ELECTRONICS AND EQUIPMENT: Plessey U/VHF, Ultra standby UHF, Marconi HF/Tac VHF, Hoffman TACAN and IFF. Ferranti FE541 inertial navigation and attack system, with Specto head-up display of all flight information and Smiths air data computer.

ARMAMENT AND OPERATIONAL EQUIPMENT: Optically-flat panel in nose, on port side, for F.95 oblique camera, which is carried as standard. No built-in armament. Combat load is carried on four underwing and one under-fuselage pylon, all with ML ejector release units. The inboard wing points and the fuselage point are stressed for loads of up to 1,200 lb (544 kg) each, and the outboard under-wing pair for loads of up to 650 lb (295 kg) each; the two strake fairings under the fuselage can each be replaced by a 30-mm Aden gun pod and ammunition. At present, the Harrier is cleared for operations with a maximum external load exceeding 5,000 lb (2,270 kg). The Harrier is able to carry 30-mm guns, bombs, rockets and flares, and in addition to its fixed recon-naissance camera, can also carry a five-camera reconnaissance pod on the under-fuselage pylon. A typical combat load comprises a pair of 30-mm Aden gun pods, a 1,000 lb (454 kg) bomb on the under-fuselage pylon, a 1,000 lb (454 kg) bomb on each of the inboard under-wing pylons, plus a Matra launcher with 19 × 68-mm SNEB rockets on each outboard under-wing pylon.

DIMENSIONS, EXTERNAL:
Wing span, combat configuration
    25 ft 3 in (7·70 m)
Wing span, ferry configuration
    29 ft 8 in (9·04 m)
Wing chord at root   11 ft 8 in (3·56 m)
Wing chord at tip   4 ft 1½ in (1·26 m)
Wing aspect ratio:
  combat   3·175
  ferry   4·08
Length overall:
  GR.Mk 1   45 ft 6 in (13·87 m)
  T.Mk 2   55 ft 9½ in (17·00 m)
Height overall:
  GR.Mk 1   approx 11 ft 3 in (3·43 m)
  T.Mk 2   approx 12 ft 2 in (3·71 m)
Tailplane span   13 ft 11 in (4·24 m)
Outrigger wheel track   22 ft 2 in (6·76 m)
Wheelbase, nose-wheel to main wheels
    approx 11 ft 4 in (3·45 m)

AREAS:
Wings, gross, combat configuration
    201 sq ft (18·67 m²)
Wings, gross, ferry configuration
    216 sq ft (20·1 m²)
Ailerons (total)   10·5 sq ft (0·98 m²)
Trailing edge flaps (total)   13·9 sq ft (1·29 m²)
Fin (excluding ventral fin):
  GR.Mk 1   25·8 sq ft (2·40 m²)
  T.Mk 2   33·0 sq ft (3·07 m²)
Rudder, including tab   5·3 sq ft (0·49 m²)
Tailplane   47·50 sq ft (4·41 m²)

WEIGHTS AND LOADING:
Basic operating weight, empty, with crew:
  GR.Mk 1   12,200 lb (5,533 kg)
  T.Mk 2 (solo for combat) 13,000 lb (5,896 kg)
  T.Mk 2 (dual)   13,600 lb (6,168 kg)
Max T-O weight (GR.Mk 1)
    over 22,000 lb (9,979 kg)
Max wing loading (GR.Mk 1)
    112·4 lb/sq ft (549 kg/m²)

PERFORMANCE:
The Harrier has been flown to the following conditions:
Level speed
  over 640 knots (737 mph; 1,186 km/h) EAS
Mach number   approaching 1·3
Ceiling   over 50,000 ft (15,240 m)
Endurance, with one in-flight refuelling
    over 7 hr
Range, with one in-flight refuelling
  over 3,000 nm (3,455 miles; 5,560 km)
Ferry range, unrefuelled
  approaching 2,000 nm (2,300 miles; 3,700 km)

HAWKER SIDDELEY BUCCANEER

The Hawker Siddeley (formerly Blackburn B.103) Buccaneer is a strike aircraft, designed for sustained flight at near-sonic speed at sea level. A development batch of 20 aircraft was ordered in July 1955, and the first of these (XK486) flew for the first time on 30 April 1958.

Two versions were produced for the Royal Navy, as follows:

Buccaneer S.Mk 1. Initial production version with two Bristol Siddeley Gyron Junior turbojet engines. Production order for a "substantial number" announced in October 1959. First production S.Mk 1 flew on 23 January 1962. Deliveries, to 700Z Flight, began in March 1961. The first Buccaneer squadron, No 801, was commissioned at RNAS Lossiemouth on 17 July 1962. This squadron embarked in HMS *Ark Royal* in February 1963. The second squadron, No 809, commissioned in January 1963

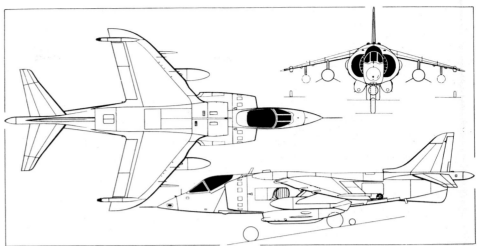

Hawker Siddeley Harrier GR.Mk 1 (Rolls-Royce Bristol Pegasus vectored-thrust turbofan)

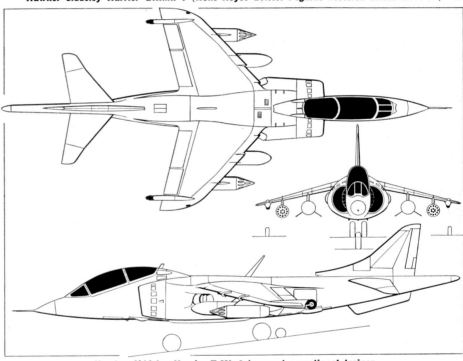

Hawker Siddeley Harrier T.Mk 2 two-seat operational trainer

and the third, No 800, in March 1964. Nos 801 and 809 were later re-equipped with the Bucc-aneer S.Mk 2.

Buccaneer S.Mk 2. Developed version with two Rolls-Royce RB.168 Spey turbofan engines, greatly increased performance and operational range. Production order for Royal Navy announced in January 1962. Prototype, converted from a Mk 1, flew for the first time on 17 May 1963, and the first production S.Mk 2 flew on 6 June 1964. This version has slightly extended wingtips compared to the S.Mk 1.

The S.Mk 2 entered service with the Royal Navy in 1965. Aircraft of the second production phase incorporate modifications enabling them to carry the Martel air-to-surface missile. Some Buccaneer S.Mk 2's of the earlier phase are undergoing modification to confer the same capability.

Eventually all Royal Navy S.Mk 2's will be taken over by the RAF, and the first four were delivered to No 12 Squadron at RAF Honington on 1 October 1969.

Basically, all Buccaneers operated by the Royal Navy are Mk 2's. Those operated by the RAF will be known as **S. Mk 2A** (without Martel capability) and **S. Mk 2B** (with Martels). Other airframe and equipment differences will exist between these models, but the capability to carry Martel air-to-ground missiles is the fundamental definition of aircraft standard. Mk 2A's will eventually be brought up to Mk 2B standard.

The RAF, in addition to the ex-RN aircraft, has ordered 26 new-production Buccaneers, the first of which flew on 8 January 1970. Deliveries were due to commence later in the year, and the first squadron formed with new aircraft will be based in Germany.

In addition, the following land-based export version has been built:

Buccaneer S.Mk 50. Basically similar to S.Mk 2, but fitted with a Rolls-Royce Bristol BS.605 twin-chamber retractable rocket engine (8,000 lb = 3,630 kg st for 30 seconds) in the rear fuselage,

to boost take-off performance from hot and high airfields. Sixteen delivered to South African Air Force, beginning in January 1965.

The following details apply to the Buccaneer S.Mk 2.

TYPE: Two-seat strike and reconnaissance aircraft.

WINGS: Cantilever mid-wing monoplane. Sweep-back at quarter-chord: 40° at root, decreasing first to 38° 36' and then to 30° 12'. Thin section. No dihedral. Incidence 2° 30'. Structure is of all-metal multi-spar design with integrally-stiffened thick skins machined from the solid. Inner wings each have an aluminium alloy auxiliary spar and two steel main spars which are bolted to three spar rings in centre fuselage. Outer wings have two aluminium alloy spars. Electrically-actuated ailerons, powered by Dowty Boulton Paul duplicated tandem actuators, can be drooped in conjunction with the inboard flaps to provide a full-span trailing-edge flap system. No trim-tabs. Resin-bonded glass-fibre tips on wings and ailerons. "Super-circulation" boundary layer control, with air outlet slots near leading-edges and forward of the drooping ailerons and plain flaps. This system also provides thermal de-icing of the engines and intakes; use of the boundary layer system supplies sufficient heat to de-ice the wing and tailplane leading-edges under most operational conditions. Outer wings fold upward hydraulically for stowage.

FUSELAGE: All-metal semi-monocoque structure, bulged at rear end in conformity with "area rule". Built in three main sections, comprising cockpit, centre fuselage and rear fuselage, plus nose-cone and tail-cone. Upper section of centre fuselage contains the fuel tanks, lower section contains the weapons bay. Engine and jet-pipe firewalls and heat shields are titanium. Equipment bay in rear fuselage has strengthened floor to absorb stresses when arrester hook is used and transfer them to main

Hawker Siddeley Buccaneer S. Mk 2 strike aircraft (two 11,100 lb st Rolls-Royce RB.168-1A Spey turbofan engines) in Royal Air Force insignia

structure. Tail-cone is made up of two petal-type air-brakes, hydraulically actuated to hinge sideways into the airstream; these can be opened fully or to any intermediate position. For stowage the resin-bonded glass cloth nose-cone hinges sideways to port and the air brakes are fully opened.

TAIL UNIT: Cantilever all-metal structure, with tailplane mounted on top of fin. Large dorsal fin faired into fuselage dorsal fairing. All-moving tailplane attached to tip of fin, which is pivoted to move with it. Electrically-actuated tailplane trim flap is used only when ailerons are deflected. Flying control surfaces powered by Boulton Paul duplicated tandem actuators. "Super-circulation" boundary layer control system, with air outlet slots in under-skin of tailplane, just aft of leading-edge.

LANDING GEAR: Retractable tricycle type of Dowty manufacture. Hydraulic retraction, main wheels inward into jet-pipe nacelles, nose-wheel rearward into front fuselage. Oleo shock-absorbers and single wheels on all units. Goodyear or Dunlop wheels and tubeless tyres, size 24 × 6·6 on nose unit, 35 × 10 on main units. Hydraulically steerable nose-wheel. Goodyear or Dunlop double-disc hydraulic brakes, with anti-skid system. Sting-type arrester hook under rear fuselage.

POWER PLANT: Two 11,100 lb (5,035 kg) st Rolls-Royce RB.168-1A Spey turbofan engines (S.Mk 2 and S. Mk 50), housed in nacelles on each side of the fuselage. Standard internal fuel (S. Mk 2) in eight integral tanks in upper part of centre fuselage, total capacity 1,560 Imp gallons (7,092 litres), with provision for cross-feed of all fuel to either engine. In addition, a 425 Imp gallon (1,932 litre) bomb-door fuel tank can be fitted, without detriment to the aircraft's bomb-carrying capability. Provision for additional 440 Imp gallon (2,000 litre) auxiliary tank in weapons bay, and/or two 250 or 430 Imp gallon (1,136 or 1,955 litre) underwing drop-tanks on the inboard pylons. Detachable flight refuelling probe standard. In the tanker rôle (max capacity 2,570 Imp gallons = 11,683 litres) the inboard starboard pylon is occupied by a 140 Imp gallon (636 litre) Mk 20B or 20C refuelling pod which is fed continuously from the main fuel system.

ACCOMMODATION: Crew of two in tandem on Martin-Baker Type 4MS ejection seats in pressurised cockpit under single electrically-actuated rearward-sliding blown Perspex canopy. Seats in S. Mk 2 fitted retrospectively with rocket assistance to provide zero-speed, zero-altitude ejection. S. Mk 2 also has separate underwater escape system. Canopy can be jettisoned separately, if necessary, by explosive charge. Windscreen anti-icing by gold film electrical heating system.

SYSTEMS: Liquid oxygen breathing system. Normalair pressurisation and air-conditioning system. Main hydraulic system pressure 4,000 lb/sq in (281·2 kg/cm²); secondary system, for flying controls, pressure 3,300 lb/sq in (232 kg/cm²). Two 30kVA alternators, one driven by each engine, provide 200V 400 c/s three-phase AC electrical power. For certain equipment this is phased through a 115V 400 c/s transformer. Two 4·5 kW rectifiers supply a 28V battery to provide DC power for certain other systems. Emergency battery provides 20 min of power in the event of failure of main generating system.

ELECTRONICS, ARMAMENT AND OPERATIONAL EQUIPMENT: Equipment specified for RAF aircraft is still classified.

DIMENSIONS, EXTERNAL:
Wing span	44 ft 0 in (13·41 m)
Wing chord at root	13 ft 7 in (4·14 m)
Wing chord at tip	8 ft 0 in (2·44 m)
Wing chord (mean)	11 ft 11½ in (3·65 m)

Wing aspect ratio	3·55
Width folded	19 ft 11 in (6·07 m)
Length overall	63 ft 5 in (19·33 m)
Length folded	51 ft 10 in (15·79 m)
Height overall	16 ft 3 in (4·95 m)
Height folded	16 ft 8 in (5·08 m)
Tailplane span	14 ft 3 in (4·34 m)
Wheel track	11 ft 10½ in (3·59 m)
Wheelbase	20 ft 8 in (6·30 m)

AREAS:
Wings, gross	514·70 sq ft (47·82 m²)
Ailerons (total)	54·80 sq ft (5·09 m²)
Trailing-edge flaps (total)	23·30 sq ft (2·16 m²)
Fin	68·60 sq ft (6·37 m²)
Rudder	10·74 sq ft (1·00 m²)
Tailplane, gross	75·52 sq ft (7·02 m²)
Tailplane trim flap	22·20 sq ft (2·06 m²)

WEIGHTS:
Typical take-off weights
46,000 lb (20,865 kg) to 56,000 lb (25,400 kg)
Max T-O weight	62,000 lb (28,123 kg)
Typical landing weight	35,000 lb (15,876 kg)

PERFORMANCE:
T-O run at S/L, ISA conditions:
At 46,000 lb (20,865 kg) AUW
2,360 ft (720 m)
At 56,000 lb (25,400 kg) AUW
3,800 ft (1,160 m)
At 56,000 lb (25,400 kg) AUW with rocket
assistance (S.Mk 50)   2,470 ft (755 m)
Landing run at S/L, ISA conditions:
At 35,000 lb (15,876 kg) landing weight
3,050 ft (930 m)
Typical strike range
2,000 nm (2,300 miles; 3,700 km)
Endurance, with two in-flight refuellings 9 hr

HAWKER SIDDELEY HS 801 NIMROD
RAF designation: Nimrod MR.Mk 1

The Nimrod is a derivative of the Comet 4C, and is in production to replace the Shackleton MR.Mk 2 reconnaissance aircraft of RAF Strike Command. It has a 6 ft 6 in (1·98 m) shorter, modified fuselage with a new unpressurised, underslung pannier for operational equipment and weapons.

Design of the Nimrod began in June 1964. It is intended basically to fly at high subsonic speed and high altitude to the search area, make a low-speed low-level patrol and a fast return to base. When required, it can loiter over search areas with two of the four Spey turbofan engines shut down. Airfield performance is well within the limits of existing Strike Command airfields. A wide range of weapons can be carried.

In addition to its reconnaissance and ASW roles, the Nimrod can carry out day or night

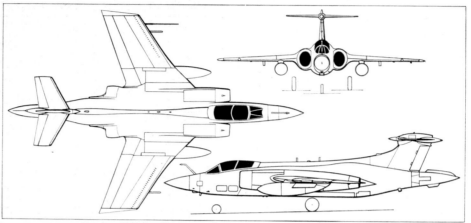

Hawker Siddeley Buccaneer S.Mk 2A twin-engined strike aircraft

photography and can carry conventional bombs and air-to-surface missiles, including the HSD/Matra Martel. The aircraft can also carry up to 45 troops, and for long-range ferry duties additional fuel can be accommodated in the weapons bay.

The two prototypes utilised modified Comet 4C airframes; but production aircraft are completely new. The first prototype, which flew on 23 May 1967, has Spey engines and was used for aerodynamic investigations. The second, powered by the original Avon engines of the Comet, was flown on 31 July 1967 and was used for development of the special maritime equipment. The first of 38 production Nimrod MR. Mk 1 aircraft flew on 28 June 1968 and deliveries began on 2 October 1969.

TYPE: Four-jet maritime reconnaissance aircraft.

WINGS: Cantilever mid-wing monoplane, of metal construction. Sweepback 20° at quarter-chord. All-metal two-spar structure, comprising a centre-section, two stub-wings and two extension planes. Extensive use of Redux metal-to-metal bonding. All-metal ailerons, operated through duplicated hydraulic and mechanical units. Plain flaps outboard of engines, operated hydraulically. Hot-air anti-icing system.

FUSELAGE: Basically, the all-metal semi-monocoque structure of the Comet 4C is retained, shortened by 6 ft 6 in (1·98 m). The circular-section pressurised cabin remains unbroken, with an additional underslung, unpressurised pannier providing space for operational equipment and weapons. Segments of this pannier are free to move relative to each other, so that structural loads in weapons bay are not transmitted to main pressure-cell. A glass-fibre nose radome and tail boom are provided.

TAIL UNIT: Cantilever all-metal structure, similar to that of the Comet 4C, with the addition of a dorsal fin. Rudder and elevators operated through duplicated hydraulic and mechanical units. A glass-fibre pod on top of the fin houses ECM equipment. Hot-air anti-icing system.

LANDING GEAR: Retractable tricycle type, similar to that of the Comet 4C, with strengthened main leg and axle beams. Stronger wheels and new tyres with a higher ply rating, of the same overall size as those fitted to the Comet 4C, are operated at higher pressures. Hydraulic brakes of increased capacity.

POWER PLANT: Four Rolls-Royce RB.168 Spey Mk 250 turbofan engines (each approx 11,500 lb = 5,217 kg st). Reverse thrust fitted on outboard engines. Extra fuel tanks in weapons bay.

Hawker Siddeley Nimrod MR. Mk 1 maritime reconnaissance aircraft of RAF Strike Command (four Spey turbofan engines) (*Air Portraits*)

ACCOMMODATION: Normal crew of twelve, with three on flight deck, and two navigators and seven sensor operators in forward cabin. Flight deck has greater field of view than that of the Comet, with larger side windows and new "eyebrow" windows. Main cabin is fitted out as a tactical compartment, containing detection equipment. Hemispherical observation windows, giving 180° field of view, are provided. Galley and rest quarters in centre section of fuselage; ordnance area in rear cabin. Bomb-bay may be utilised for the carriage of freight. Provision is made for a trooping rôle, and in this configuration 45 passengers can be accommodated. Two normal doors, an emergency door and four emergency exits are provided, as in the Comet.

SYSTEMS: Air-conditioning by engine-bleed air; Smith-Kollsman pressurisation system, max differential 8·75 lb/sq in (0·61 kg/cm²). Anti-icing and bomb-bay heating by engine-bleed air. Hydraulic system, pressure 2,500 lb/sq in (175 kg/cm²), for duplicated flying control power units, landing gear retraction, wheel brakes, nose-wheel steering, flaps, bomb-doors and camera doors. Rover APU provides high-pressure air for engine starting. Electrical system utilises four 60kVA engine-driven alternators, with English Electric constant-speed drives, to provide 200V 400 c/s three-phase AC supply. Secondary AC comes from two 115V three-phase static transformers, with duplicate 115/26V two-phase static transformers which also feed a 1kVA frequency changer providing a 115V 1,600 c/s single-phase supply for radar equipment. Emergency supplies for flight instruments are provided by a 115V single-phase static inverter. DC supply is by four 28V transformer/rectifier units backed up by two cadmium-nickel batteries.

ELECTRONICS AND EQUIPMENT: Routine navigation by Doppler/inertial system incorporating data computer and twin-gyro compass, and operating in conjunction with Ferranti vertical projector. Tactical navigation by Elliott nav/attack system, utilising Elliott 920B computer and data processing equipment. ASW equipment includes IC sonar and a new long-range sonar system, ASV 21 air-to-surface vessel detection radar, Autolycus ionisation detector, and ECM gear. MAD (magnetic anomaly detector) in extended tail "sting". Searchlight in starboard external wing fuel tank. Smith's SFS.6 flight system and SEP.6 autopilot. VHF and Marconi AD 470 HF radio and ILS glide-slope indicator. Yaw damper and Mach trim standard.

ARMAMENT: Bay for active and passive sonobuoys in pressurised part of rear fuselage. Ventral weapons bay, approx 50 ft (15 m) long, can accommodate full range of ASW weapons including bombs, mines, depth charges and torpedoes. Pylon beneath each wing at approx one-third span, on which can be carried an AS.12 or Martel air-to-surface missile.

DIMENSIONS, EXTERNAL:

Wing span	114 ft 10 in (35·00 m)
Wing chord at root	29 ft 6 in (9·00 m)
Wing chord at tip	6 ft 9 in (2·06 m)
Length overall	126 ft 9 in (38·63 m)
Height overall	29 ft 8½ in (9·01 m)
Tailplane span	47 ft 7¼ in (14·51 m)
Wheel track	28 ft 2½ in (8·60 m)
Wheelbase	46 ft 8½ in (14·24 m)

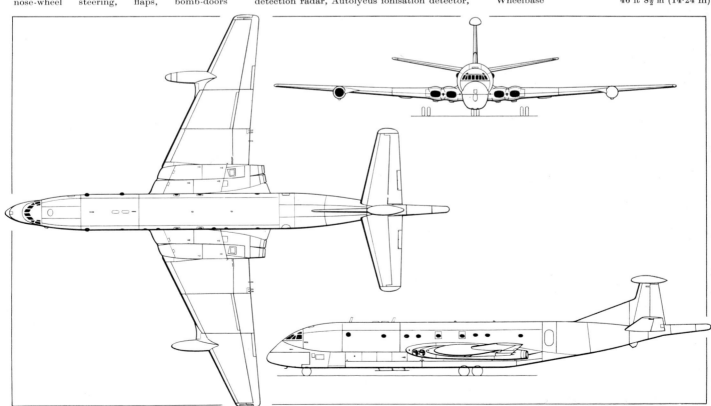

Hawker Siddeley Nimrod MR.Mk 1 four-turbofan maritime reconnaissance aircraft

DIMENSIONS, INTERNAL:
Cabin (including flight deck, navigation and ordnance areas, galley and toilet):
Length 88 ft 0 in (26·82 m)
Max width 9 ft 8 in (2·95 m)
Max height 6 ft 10 in (2·08 m)
Volume 4,384 cu ft (124·14 m³)

AREAS:
Wings, gross 2,121 sq ft (197·0 m²)
Ailerons (total) 60·6 sq ft (5·63 m²)
Trailing-edge flaps (total) 251·6 sq ft (23·37 m²)
Fin and rudder (above tailplane centre line) 118 sq ft (10·96 m²)
Dorsal fin 61 sq ft (5·67 m²)

Tailplane 435 sq ft (40·41 m²)
Elevators (including tab) 135·3 sq ft (12·57 m²)

PERFORMANCE:
Max cruising speed over 434 knots (500 mph; 805 km/h)

ISAACS
JOHN O. ISAACS
ADDRESS:
42 Landguard Road, Southampton SO1 5DP, Hants

Mr. Isaacs has designed and built a single-seat light aircraft, the airframe of which is basically a $\frac{7}{10}$th scale wooden version of that of the Hawker Fury fighter of the 1930's. Constructional drawings are available to amateur builders.

He has also designed an all-wood scaled-down version of the Supermarine Spitfire single-seat fighter of World War 2. Construction of the prototype began in the Summer of 1969, and work on it continues. The first flight is not expected to take place before 1971. It is stressed to meet the aerobatic requirements of +9g and —4½g (factored) as laid down in BCAR.

ISAACS FURY II
Design of the Isaacs Fury was started in January 1961 and construction of the aircraft began in April 1961. It flew for the first time on 30 August 1963, powered by a 65 hp Walter Mikron engine (see 1965-66 Jane's).

The design was revised in 1966-67 to permit installation of more readily-available flat-four engines of up to 125 hp. Simultaneously, the entire airframe was restressed to allow an increased all-up weight of up to 1,000 lb (450 kg).

Mr Isaacs modified the Fury prototype to this new Mk II standard, by the trial installation of a 125 hp Lycoming O-290 four-cylinder horizontally-opposed air-cooled engine, and flew the aircraft in this form in the Summer of 1967.

Three more Furies are being constructed by amateurs in the UK, and one in Canada. The Canadian Fury was expected to fly during the Summer of 1970.

The following details apply to the Fury in its restressed Mk II form.

TYPE: Single-seat ultra-light biplane, stressed to 9g for aerobatics.

WINGS: Staggered biplane, with N-type interplane struts each side and two N-strut assemblies supporting centre-section of top wing above fuselage. Conventional wire bracing. Wing section RAF 28. Thickness/chord ratio 9·75%. Dihedral 1° on top wing, 3° 30′ on bottom wings. Incidence 3° 20′ on top wing, 3° 50′ on bottom wings. Spruce "plank" spars and Warren girder ribs, with fabric covering. Fabric-covered spruce ailerons on top wing only. No flaps.

FUSELAGE: Spruce structure, covered with birch plywood.

TAIL UNIT: Strut-braced spruce structure of "plank" spars and girder ribs, fabric-covered. Ground-adjustable tab in port elevator.

LANDING GEAR: Non-retractable gear, with tailskid. Cross-axle tied to Vees with rubber-cord for shock-absorption. Main wheels consist of WM.2 14 in (35·5 cm) rims spoked to home-made hubs. Dunlop tyres, size 3·25-14, pressure approx 33 lb/sq in (2·32 kg/cm²). No brakes.

POWER PLANT: One four-cylinder horizontally-opposed air-cooled engine of 90-125 hp. Fury II prototype has a 125 hp Lycoming O-290 engine. Two-blade fixed-pitch propeller. Fuel tank in fuselage, aft of fireproof bulkhead, capacity 10 Imp gallons (45·5 litres) or 12 Imp gallons (54·5 litres). Oil capacity varies with type of engine fitted.

ACCOMMODATION: Single seat in open cockpit. Small door above top longeron on port side opens downward. Space for light luggage aft of seat. Radio optional.

DIMENSIONS, EXTERNAL:
Wing span:
top 21 ft 0 in (6·40 m)
bottom 18 ft 2 in (5·54 m)
Wing chord (both, constant) 3 ft 6 in (1·07 m)
Wing aspect ratio (upper) 6
Length overall 19 ft 3 in (5·87 m)
Height over tail (flying altitude) 7 ft 0 in (2·13 m)
Tailplane span 7 ft 0 in (2·13 m)
Wheel track 4 ft 2 in (1·27 m)

AREAS:
Wings, gross 123·8 sq ft (11·50 m²)
Ailerons (total) 10·56 sq ft (0·98 m²)

Isaacs Fury II prototype G-ASCM (125 hp Lycoming engine) in mock RAF insignia

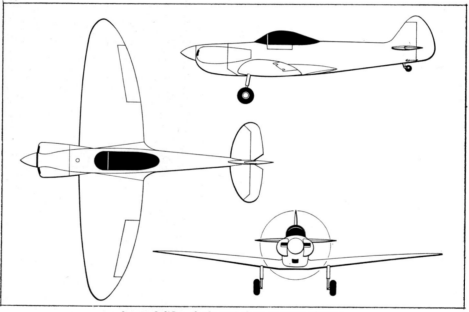

Isaacs Spitfire single-seat light sporting aircraft

Fin 2·90 sq ft (0·27 m²)
Rudder 4·83 sq ft (0·45 m²)
Tailplane 10·50 sq ft (0·98 m²)
Elevators 5·70 sq ft (0·53 m²)

WEIGHTS AND LOADINGS (125 hp Lycoming):
Weight empty 710 lb (322 kg)
Max permissible T-O weight 1,000 lb (450 kg)
Normal wing loading 8·05 lb/sq ft (39·3 kg/m²)
Normal power loading 8·00 lb/hp (3·63 kg/hp)

PERFORMANCE (with uncowled 125 hp engine):
Max level speed 100 knots (115 mph; 185 km/h)
Stalling speed 33 knots (38 mph; 61 km/h)
Rate of climb at S/L 1,600 ft (488 m)/min

ISAACS SPITFIRE
TYPE: Single-seat amateur-built sporting aircraft.

WINGS: Cantilever low-wing monoplane of semi-elliptical planform. Wing section NACA 2200 series. Thickness/chord ratio 13·2% at root, 6% at tip. Dihedral 6°. Incidence 2° at root, —30′ at tip. Two-spar wing built in one piece, mainly of spruce but with birch plywood leading-edge and fabric covering.

FUSELAGE: Spruce structure, covered with birch plywood.

TAIL UNIT: Cantilever structure of spruce; fixed surfaces plywood-covered, control surfaces fabric-covered.

LANDING GEAR: Non-retractable tail-wheel type on prototype. Cantilever main legs.

POWER PLANT: One 100 hp Continental O-200 four-cylinder horizontally-opposed air-cooled engine, or alternative engine in same category.

ACCOMMODATION: Single seat under blister-type transparent canopy.

DIMENSIONS, EXTERNAL:
Wing span 22 ft 1½ in (6·75 m)
Wing chord at root 5 ft 0 in (1·52 m)
Length overall 19 ft 3 in (5·88 m)
Height overall 5 ft 3 in (1·60 m)
Tailplane span 6 ft 3½ in (1·92 m)
Wheel track 5 ft 10 in (1·78 m)

AREA:
Wings, gross 87 sq ft (8·08 m²)

WEIGHTS AND LOADINGS:
Max T-O weight 1,000 lb (454 kg)
Max wing loading 11·5 lb/sq ft (56 kg/m²)
Max power loading 10 lb/hp (4·54 kg/hp)

PERFORMANCE (estimated at max T-O weight):
Max level speed 130 knots (150 mph; 240 km/h)
Stalling speed 49 knots (56·5 mph; 90 km/h)

MARSHALL

MARSHALL OF CAMBRIDGE (ENGINEERING) LTD

HEAD OFFICE AND WORKS:
Airport Works, Cambridge CB5 8RX

DIRECTORS:
A. G. G. Marshall, OBE (Managing)
M. M. Fry
R. Lane
J. H. Huntridge
M. J. Marshall
R. D. Horsbrough
M. St Clair Marshall
P. D. N. Hedderwick

SALES MANAGER:
J. F. H. du Boulay

The Aircraft Division of this company (known as Marshalls Flying School Ltd until 1962) has specialised for many years in the modification, overhaul and repair of military and commercial aircraft, including the design and installation of interior furnishing for executive transports.

The company's design department is both ARB and AID approved. As the appointed service and repair centre for the Grumman Gulfstream and Lockheed C-130 transport aircraft, Marshall of Cambridge also has FAA approval covering most types of American aircraft. The company's conversion, modification and overhaul facilities, which include some of the largest heated hangars in England, with workshop support to full aircraft factory standard, have enabled it to undertake numerous major programmes of work on Viscounts, Britannias, Comets, VC10's and a vast number of other civil and military aircraft.

In 1966, Marshall of Cambridge was appointed the Designated Centre for the Royal Air Force Hercules C.Mk 1 transport aircraft, being responsible for controlling all technical data, special modifications and development, together with the preparation of these aircraft and painting before delivery to the Service. In the same year, the company was appointed by Lockheed as the service and repair centre for Hercules aircraft in Europe, the Middle East and Africa.

During 1966 also, Marshall of Cambridge was selected to design and manufacture the new variable-geometry nose and visor for the pre-production Concorde aircraft, and to design and manufacture the Concorde flight deck and associated electrics, and ground equipment.

Recent additions to the factory include a separate hangar for specialised painting of the largest aircraft, and a sculpture milling shop for manufacture of major aircraft components. Current activities include furnishing and finishing of all Britten-Norman Islanders.

McCANDLESS

McCANDLESS AVIATION LTD

HEAD OFFICE AND WORKS:
Newtownards Aerodrome, County Down, Northern Ireland

DIRECTOR: Rex McCandless

This company operates an ARB-approved aircraft maintenance, repair and design organisation at Newtownards. Its Director, Mr Rex McCandless, bought a proprietary gyroplane in 1961, to gain experience before developing a powered light autogyro of his own design. With the technical assistance of Mr Frank Robertson, Chief of Preliminary Design for Short Brothers and Harland, he brought this aircraft to the production stage, as described in the 1969-70 *Jane's*. Production is undertaken by the W. H. Ekin (Engineering) Co Ltd, of Crumlin, Co Antrim, which had completed six of these aircraft by the beginning of 1970.

McCANDLESS M4 GYROPLANE

Although similar in general configuration to other single-seat ultra-light autogyros, the McCandless Gyroplane incorporates many important innovations.

In its original test-bed form, it retained a proprietary fuselage, and was powered by a Triumph motor-cycle engine of about 35 hp. This prototype made a number of short hops in 1961.

During the following year, Mr McCandless built a new welded tubular space-frame fuselage of mild steel, so designed that it would break up progressively, without injury to the pilot, in a really heavy landing. At the same time, he evolved a vibration-free power plant installation, with the engine mounted on links and shock-absorbers beneath the pilot's seat, with its crankshaft vertical behind the seat. From the crankshaft, a shaft drive with flexible couplings at each end drove the propeller through a right-angled bevel gearbox which was attached rigidly to the airframe. A powered spin-up device was introduced simultaneously, using a slipping belt drive and 10 : 1 reduction gear.

Powered by the original Triumph engine, the new prototype flew successfully for more than a year, and was then re-engined with a Norton motor-cycle engine of about 45 hp. When a suitable Volkswagen engine became available in 1965, this was substituted for the Norton. Its vibration-free flat-four arrangement has made it possible to dispense with gears and to use a flat-toothed belt-drive to the propeller on the production version of the McCandless Gyroplane. A hand lever and ratchet arrangement is used for engine starting.

More recent developments have included the

Side-by-side two-seat version of the McCandless Gyroplane (*Helicopter World*)

design of a new cockpit, to which a fully-enclosed canopy can be fitted later; and an open-fuselage, side-by-side two-seat version (G-ATXY) for training purposes, equipped with full dual controls.

The details below apply to the single-seat production version:

ROTOR SYSTEM: Two-blade fixed-pitch teetering rotor, with direct control by rotor tilt. Wooden blades. Cruise autorotation speed 360 rpm.

ROTOR SPIN-UP DRIVE: Belt drive from engine, tensioned by idler pulley, driving rotor through worm reduction and freewheel up to 300 rpm. Spin-up lever moved automatically to "off" position by opening throttle.

FUSELAGE: Space-frame of T.45 and T.26 steel tube, assembled by Sifbronze welding.

TAIL UNIT: Fixed fin and tailplane and movable rudder only.

LANDING GEAR: Non-retractable tricycle type. Main wheels carried on light alloy tubular axle. Nose-wheel is steerable and has rubber suspension. Brake on nose-wheel.

POWER PLANT: One 60 hp 1600 cc Volkswagen four-cylinder horizontally-opposed air-cooled engine, mounted behind the pilot's seat and fitted with twin Amal motor-cycle carburettors and single Scintilla magneto. Two-blade fixed-pitch propeller. Main fuel tank, capacity 4·5 Imp gallons (20·5 litres), below engine.

ACCOMMODATION: Single seat in open cockpit. Aluminium alloy cockpit fairing and Perspex windshield standard.

DIMENSION, EXTERNAL:

Diameter of rotor	22 ft 0 in (6·71 m)
Length overall	12 ft 6 in (3·81 m)
Height overall	8 ft 6 in (2·59 m)
Width	6 ft 0 in (1·83 m)

WEIGHTS:

Weight empty	310 lb (141 kg)
Max T-O weight	510 lb (231 kg)

PERFORMANCE (at max T-O weight):

Normal cruising speed at up to 1,000 ft (300 m)	69·5 knots (80 mph; 130 km/h)
Rate of climb at S/L	850 ft (259 m)/min
T-O run	180 ft (55 m)
Landing run	45 ft (14 m)
Range	195 nm (225 miles; 362 km)

MITCHELL-PROCTER

The Mitchell-Procter team was dissolved in October 1968. The prototype Mitchell-Procter Kittiwake I light aircraft, described below, is now owned by Procter Aircraft Associates, which is marketing sets of plans for this design. Mr C. G. B. Mitchell retains design rights in the Kittiwake I and of the developed Kittiwake II.

MITCHELL-PROCTER KITTIWAKE I

The Kittiwake I light aircraft was designed to make full use of modern materials and constructional techniques while retaining a simplicity of design that makes it possible for the aircraft to be built without special tooling. The wings attach directly to the sides of the fuselage, so that construction and storage can take place in a normal-sized garage.

Design of the Kittiwake I was started in February 1965. Construction of the prototype (G-ATXN) began in June 1965 and it flew for the first time on 23 May 1967. The details that follow apply to this prototype.

Plans of the Kittiwake I are obtainable from Procter Aircraft Associates Ltd (which see), and in 1970 a number of these aircraft were under construction by amateur builders.

Mitchell-Procter Kittiwake I (100 hp Rolls-Royce/Continental O-200-A engine) (*Lorna Minton*)

TYPE: Single-seat glider-towing and sporting light aircraft.

WINGS: Cantilever low-wing monoplane. Wing section NACA 3415. Dihedral 5°. Incidence 2° 30′. No washout. All-metal (L.72 and L.64 aluminium alloys) structure, with single main spar at 30% chord and light false spar at 66%. Multiple ribs. No spanwise stiffeners. Wings attach at fuselage sides; centre-section is integral with fuselage. All-metal (L.72) NACA single-slotted flaps.

FUSELAGE: All-metal (L.72) structure. Four-longeron box with flat sides and bottom, and single-curvature top decking. Integral wing centre-section forms seat and landing gear attachment structure.

TAIL UNIT: Cantilever all-metal (L.72) structure. Fixed-incidence tailplane. Manually-operated tab on elevator trailing-edge.

LANDING GEAR: Non-retractable tricycle type. Cantilever spring steel main legs. Nose unit has rubber torsion bush shock-absorption. All three units fitted with Goodyear wheels and tyres, size 5·00-5. Tyre pressure 25 lb/sq in (1·75 kg/cm²). Goodyear hydraulically-operated disc brakes on main wheels.

POWER PLANT: One 100 hp Rolls-Royce/Continental O-200-A four-cylinder horizontally-opposed air-cooled engine, driving a McCauley 69CM52 two-blade fixed-pitch metal propeller of 5 ft 9 in (1·75 m) diameter for general use or a McCauley 76CM36 two-blade fixed-pitch metal propeller of 6 ft 4 in (1·93 m) diameter for glider-towing. Two integral fuel tanks in wing leading-edges, with total capacity of 22 Imp gallons (100 litres). Space for fuel tank forward of instrument panel, capacity 12 Imp gallons (54·5 litres). Oil capacity 1·5 Imp gallons (7 litres).

ACCOMMODATION: Single seat under rearward-sliding canopy.

ELECTRONICS AND EQUIPMENT: Prototype has full blind-flying instrumentation and electrical system, but no radio.

DIMENSIONS, EXTERNAL:
Wing span	24 ft 0 in (7·32 m)
Wing chord (constant)	4 ft 6½ in (1·38 m)
Wing aspect ratio	5·28
Length overall	19 ft 7 in (5·97 m)
Height overall	7 ft 6 in (2·29 m)
Tailplane span	8 ft 0 in (2·44 m)
Wheel track	5 ft 9 in (1·75 m)
Wheelbase	5 ft 0 in (1·52 m)

DIMENSIONS, INTERNAL:
Cabin: Length	5 ft 0 in (1·52 m)
Max width	2 ft 1 in (0·64 m)
Max height, seat to canopy	3 ft 5 in (1·04 m)

AREAS:
Wings, gross	105 sq ft (9·75 m²)
Ailerons (total)	9·30 sq ft (0·86 m²)
Trailing-edge flaps (total)	14·00 sq ft (1·30 m²)
Fin	14·30 sq ft (1·33 m²)
Rudder	5·20 sq ft (0·48 m²)
Tailplane	21·50 sq ft (2·00 m²)
Elevators, including tab	10·00 sq ft (0·93 m²)

WEIGHTS AND LOADINGS (prototype, incl some test equipment):
Weight empty, equipped	910 lb (413 kg)
Max T-O and landing weight	1,350 lb (612 kg)
Max aerobatic weight	1,250 lb (567 kg)
Max wing loading	12·9 lb/sq ft (63·0 kg/m²)
Max power loading	13·5 lb/hp (6·12 kg/hp)

PERFORMANCE (at AUW of 1,250 lb = 567 kg):
Max level speed 114 knots (131 mph; 211 km/h)	
Max cruising speed (75% power)	
	106 knots (122 mph; 196 km/h)

Rate of climb at S/L:
69CM52 propeller	850 ft (259 m)/min
76CM36 propeller	1,050 ft (320 m)/min
Range at 100 knots (115 mph; 185 km/h)	
	425 nm (490 miles; 790 km)
Range at 80 knots (92 mph; 148 km/h)	
	468 nm (540 miles; 870 km)

MITCHELL

C. G. B. MITCHELL

ADDRESS: "Clouds" 17 Tavistock Road, Fleet, Hants

Mr C. G. B. Mitchell, formerly associated with Mr Roy G. Procter in Mitchell-Procter Aircraft Ltd, is now concentrating on the development of the Kittiwake II light sporting aircraft.

MITCHELL KITTIWAKE II

Construction of the prototype Kittiwake II was started in March 1968 by Robinson Aircraft Ltd of Blackbushe, Hants, and the structure was completed in April 1969. A Rolls-Royce/Continental O-240 engine has been installed in place of the Lycoming O-290-A originally selected, and it was anticipated that the aircraft would fly for the first time in 1970.

Plans are available to amateur constructors, and sets have been sold in North America.

The details of the Mitchell-Procter Kittiwake I (above) are generally applicable to the Kittiwake II, with the following exceptions:

TYPE: Two-seat sporting light aircraft.

WINGS: Incidence 2° 30′.

POWER PLANT (Prototype): One 130 hp Rolls-Royce/Continental O-240 four-cylinder horizontally-opposed air-cooled engine, driving a two-blade fixed-pitch metal propeller, diameter 6 ft 0 in (1·83 m). Alternative installation of Continental or Lycoming engines from 90 to 150 hp will be permissible. Two non-integral fuel tanks in wing-roots, with total capacity of 22 Imp gallons (100 litres). Oil capacity 1·5 Imp gallons (7 litres).

ACCOMMODATION: Two side-by-side seats under rearward-sliding canopy.

DIMENSIONS, EXTERNAL:
Wing span	25 ft 6 in (7·77 m)
Wing aspect ratio	5·7
Length of fuselage	20 ft 5 in (6·22 m)
Height overall	7 ft 8 in (2·34 m)
Tailplane span	8 ft 0 in (2·44 m)
Wheel track	7 ft 8 in (2·34 m)
Wheelbase	4 ft 9 in (1·45 m)

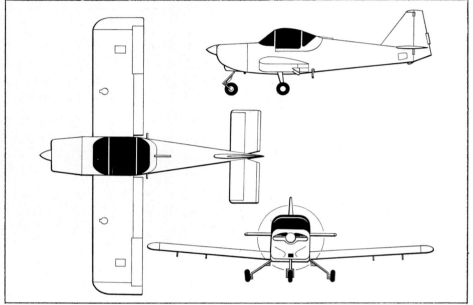

Mitchell Kittiwake II two-seat light aircraft for amateur construction

DIMENSIONS, INTERNAL:
Cabin: Length	5 ft 0 in (1·52 m)
Max width	3 ft 5 in (1·04 m)
Max height, seat to canopy	3 ft 2 in (0·96 m)

AREAS:
As for Kittiwake I, except:
Wings, gross	113 sq ft (10·50 m²)

WEIGHTS AND LOADINGS (prototype, estimated):
Weight empty, equipped	1,000 lb (454 kg)

Max T-O weight:
normal	1,600 lb (726 kg)
aerobatic	1,500 lb (680 kg)
Max wing loading	14·15 lb/sq ft (69·75 kg/m²)
Max power loading	12·3 lb/hp (5·58 kg/hp)

PERFORMANCE (estimated, at max T-O weight):
Max level speed at S/L	
	120 knots (138 mph; 222 km/h)
Max cruising speed	
	109 knots (125 mph; 201 km/h)
Econ cruising speed	
	91 knots (105 mph; 169 km/h)
Stalling speed, flaps up	
	59 knots (68 mph; 110 km/h)
Stalling speed, flaps down	
	47 knots (54 mph; 87 km/h)
Rate of climb at S/L	1,000 ft (305 m)/min
Range with max fuel, no reserves	
	434 nm (500 miles; 805 km)

NIPPER

NIPPER AIRCRAFT LTD

HEAD OFFICE:
East Midlands Airport, Castle Donington, Derby

MANAGING DIRECTOR: D. P. L. Antill

This British company purchased the complete world-wide rights for the Nipper aircraft from Belgium in 1966.

The Nipper has a full C of A in the UK. More than half of those being built are for export.

Nipper Aircraft have developed and are now marketing a 24-channel solid-state transceiver for light aircraft, known as the Model 20/4 Nipper radio; this may be powered by dry batteries or from an aircraft's 14V DC supply.

Nipper Aircraft operate a light aircraft hangar for permanent and temporary visitors to the East Midlands Airport, and have an approved maintenance bay for light aircraft. They have also acquired the agency for Siai-Marchetti aircraft in the northern and midland regions of the UK.

NIPPER Mk III and IIIA

During the past two years many improvements have been made to the standard Nipper Mk III, including a wider cockpit and larger canopy to increase pilot comfort. This also permits a bigger and more comprehensive instrument

Nipper Mk III single-seat ultra-light aircraft (45 hp Rollason Ardem X engine)

panel. There is now a full-width cockpit floor, improved pilot's seat, and the engine exhaust system has been redesigned to point downwards, halving the cockpit noise level. Screened ignition is fitted, and there is wing-root provision for installation of the Nipper radio and a glove and accessories locker. Existing aircraft can be modified to this standard.

The Mk III Nipper can be supplied at customer's option with either the 1,500-cc Rollason Ardem engine or, as the Mk IIIA, with the 1,600-cc Ardem engine. Either is available with a full C of A. The Nipper is also available with wing-tip fuel tanks which almost double the standard fuel capacity. With these tanks fitted, but empty, the aircraft remains aerobatic. Flutter tests have been completed satisfactorily at speeds up to 156 knots (180 mph; 290 km/h).

In addition to the above factory-built aircraft, Nippers are available in the form of several stages of kits for amateur construction, and can be built at home for operation on a Permit to Fly basis. Twelve kits have been sold and are in various stages of completion; two of these aircraft were expected to be competing in flying-club events by mid-1970.

TYPE: Single-seat ultra-light monoplane.

WINGS: Cantilever shoulder-wing monoplane. Modified NACA 43012A wing section. Dihedral 5° 30'. Incidence 2°. All-wood one-piece single-spar structure, with plywood-covered leading-edge and overall fabric covering. Wooden ailerons with fabric covering. No flaps. Portion of port wing-root trailing-edge is made of light alloy and hinged, with built-in footrest, so that it can be folded down to assist access to cockpit. Wing is quickly removable, to permit aircraft to be towed behind a motor car.

FUSELAGE: Welded steel-tube structure. Under-fuselage fairing of glass-fibre. Rear fuselage fabric-covered.

TAIL UNIT: Braced tailplane and elevators of wood construction. No fin. Rudder of steel-tube construction with fabric covering.

LANDING GEAR: Non-retractable tricycle type. Nieman transverse rubber-ring shock-absorbers. Steerable nose-wheel. Continental tyres, size 4·00 × 4, pressure 26 lb/sq in (1·8 kg/cm²). Disc brakes.

POWER PLANT: Standard power plant is one 45 hp Rollason Ardem X four-cylinder horizontally-opposed air-cooled engine, driving a two-blade fixed-pitch wooden propeller with glass-fibre spinner. More powerful versions of Ardem engine are available optionally. Fuel tank between engine and cockpit, capacity 7·5 Imp gallons (34 litres). Provision for two 3·625 Imp gallon (16·5 litre) wing-tip fuel tanks. Oil capacity 0·77 Imp gallons (3·5 litres).

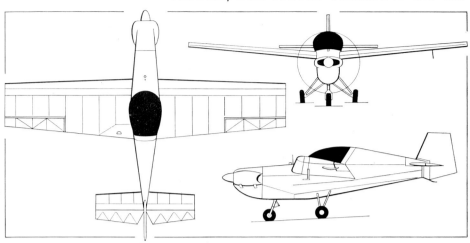

Nipper Mk IV single-seat ultra-light aircraft

ACCOMMODATION: Single seat under blown Perspex sliding canopy. Small baggage space aft of seat.

ELECTRONICS: Nipper, Pye Bantam, Bayside BEI 990P and various other radio installations available.

DIMENSIONS:
Wing span (without tip-tanks)
19 ft 8 in (6·00 m)
Wing span (with tip-tanks)   20 ft 6 in (6·25 m)
Wing chord at c/l   4 ft 7¼ in (1·40 m)
Wing chord at tip   3 ft 7¼ in (1·10 m)
Wing aspect ratio   4·8
Length overall   15 ft 0 in (4·56 m)
Height overall   6 ft 3½ in (1·90 m)
Tailplane span   7 ft 0 in (2·14 m)
Wheel track   4 ft 7 in (1·40 m)
Wheelbase   3 ft 8 in (1·13 m)

AREAS:
Wings, gross   80·70 sq ft (7·50 m²)
Ailerons (total)   8·93 sq ft (0·83 m²)
Rudder   7·50 sq ft (0·70 m²)
Tailplane   9·30 sq ft (0·86 m²)
Elevators   5·80 sq ft (0·54 m²)

WEIGHTS AND LOADINGS:
Weight empty   458 lb (208 kg)
Max T-O weight:
aerobatic category   660 lb (300 kg)
Max wing loading   9·0 lb/sq ft (44 kg/m²)
Max power loading   16·1 lb/hp (7·3 kg/hp)

PERFORMANCE (at max T-O weight):
Max permissible speed
126 knots (146 mph; 235 km/h)

Max level speed at S/L:
without tip-tanks
93 knots (107 mph; 173 km/h)
with tip-tanks
83 knots (96 mph; 155 km/h)
Max cruising speed (75% power) at S/L:
without tip-tanks
82·5 knots (95 mph; 153 km/h)
Econ cruising speed at S/L
78 knots (90 mph; 145 km/h)
Stalling speed, power off
33 knots (38 mph; 61 km/h)
Rate of climb at S/L   650 ft (198 m)/min
Service ceiling   12,000 ft (3,660 m)
T-O run   280 ft (85 m)
Landing run   360 ft (110 m)
Range with max internal fuel, 30 min reserve,
173 nm (200 miles; 320 km)
Range with tip-tanks
390 nm (450 miles; 720 km)

NIPPER Mk IV

In the Spring of 1970, plans were well advanced for the approval and construction of the prototype Nipper Mk IV. This retains the basic airframe of the Mk III/IIIA, but with a lengthened nose to cater for installation of a lighter 48 hp Nelson H-63CP four-cylinder two-stroke horizontally-opposed air-cooled engine, with electric starter and alternator.

DIMENSIONS, EXTERNAL, AND AREAS:
As Mk III/IIIA, except:
Length overall   16 ft 6 in (5·03 m)

ORD-HUME
ARTHUR W. J. G. ORD-HUME

ADDRESS:
"Mirador", Rose Mead, Lake, Sandown, IoW, and 14 Elmwood Road, Chiswick, London W4

Mr Ord-Hume was a co-founder and (until 1962) a director of Phoenix Aircraft Ltd, which was responsible for redesigning the pre-war Luton Minor and Luton Major aircraft. As an amateur aircraft constructor, he was one of the first in the UK to construct his own aircraft after World War 2 and has since built or restored 11 aeroplanes.

Following the dissolution of the French company Constructions Aéronautiques du Béarn (see 1956-57 Jane's), Mr Ord-Hume acquired the original drawings for the GY-20 Minicab and spent three years redrafting the plans and translating them into English. Several examples of the Minicab built to the English plans, for which Mr Ord-Hume holds the exclusive rights, are currently flying in Australia, Canada, the US, the UK and Europe, and many more are under construction.

Mr Ord-Hume has also designed an all-wood ultra-light aircraft, the O-H 7, for amateur construction, and a prototype of this aircraft is under construction.

Details of both of these aircraft appear below.

ORD-HUME GY-20 MINICAB

The original GY-20 Minicab was designed in France by M Yves Gardan (see SITAR) and flew for the first time in February 1949. Production Minicabs were built by Constructions Aéronautiques du Béarn, until that company's dissolution following the death of its Chief Engineer and General Manager. Mr Ord-Hume subsequently acquired original drawings for the GY-20 and redrafted them to make the aircraft suitable for amateur construction. They were first introduced in this revised form in 1963, and amateur construction of Minicabs to Mr Ord-Hume's plans is now approved in the US, Canada, Australia, New Zealand and the UK. The standard Ord-Hume GY-20 embodies as standard the so-called GY-201 and JB-01 modifications for increased fuel capacity and spar strengthening for increased AUW.

Ord-Hume GY-20 Minicab, one of five built and flown in the United Kingdom

Five Ord-Hume Minicabs have been built and flown in the UK, and a further 16 were under construction during 1970.

A full structural description of the Béarn GY-20 Minicab was given in the 1956-57 edition of Jane's; the following new data apply to the Ord-Hume version in its current form.

TYPE: Two-seat light monoplane.

POWER PLANT: One 65 hp Continental four-cylinder horizontally-opposed air-cooled engine. Modified plans also available for installation of 90 hp Continental engine. Fuel capacity 11 Imp gallons (50 litres) in fuselage tank aft of engine firewall. Provision for auxiliary fuel tank.

ACCOMMODATION: Side-by-side seating for two persons under forward-hinged canopy. Space for 25 lb (11 kg) of baggage aft of seats.

DIMENSIONS, EXTERNAL:
Wing span   25 ft 0 in (7·62 m)
Length overall   17 ft 10 in (5·44 m)
Height overall   5 ft 5 in (1·65 m)

AREA:
Wings, gross   107·6 sq ft (10·0 m²)

WEIGHTS AND LOADINGS:
Weight empty   595 lb (270 kg)
Max T-O weight   1,069 lb (485 kg)
Max wing loading   9·84 lb/sq ft (48·5 kg/m²)
Max power loading   16·28 lb/hp (7·38 kg/hp)

PERFORMANCE:
Max level speed at S/L
108 knots (124 mph; 200 km/h)
Cruising speed at S/L
97 knots (112 mph; 180 km/h)

Stalling speed, flaps up
        41 knots (47 mph; 76 km/h)
Rate of climb at S/L   680 ft (207 m)/min
Service ceiling   13,100 ft (4,000 m)
Range with standard fuel
      404 nm (466 miles; 750 km)

ORD-HUME O-H 7 COUPÉ

The O-H 7 Coupé, designed by Mr Ord-Hume, is an ultra-light high-wing monoplane of all-wood construction, and is intended for amateur building. It is a development of the Luton L.A.4a Minor, which was redesigned by Mr Ord-Hume. Design of the O-H 7 Coupé began in 1963 and construction in 1967. First flight of the prototype and certification under the Restricted Category C of A was scheduled for the Summer of 1969, but was unavoidably postponed due to the closing of Mr Ord-Hume's Sandown Airport workshop. Completion was, however, anticipated during 1970.

TYPE: Single-seat ultra-light monoplane.

WINGS: Cantilever high-wing monoplane. Wing section NACA 23015. Dihedral 3°. Incidence 3°. No sweepback. All-wood two-spar structure, with built-up lattice or routed ribs. Main spar is a built-up I-section beam, rear spar has two booms and a single side web; fabric covering. All-wood slotted ailerons. Wooden trailing-edge flaps optional. Wings removable for storage or transport.

FUSELAGE: All-wood structure, consisting of four principal longerons with stressed plywood covering. Turtleback comprised of stringers with fabric covering. Fuselage underside fully sealed for when aircraft operates as seaplane.

TAIL UNIT: All-wood fabric-covered structure. Tailplane has two spars with routed plywood ribs; elevator a single spar with lattice ribs. Incidence of tailplane ground-adjustable. Trim-tab on port elevator.

LANDING GEAR: Prototype has non-retractable tail-wheel landing gear, but airframe is designed for alternative tricycle gear or floats. All shock-absorption by rubber in compression. Tension struts attached to Vee-frame fixed between main legs.

POWER PLANT: Prototype has a 62 hp Walter Mikron four-cylinder inverted in-line air-cooled engine, driving a two-blade fixed-pitch wooden propeller with glass-fibre sheath, diameter 5 ft 3 in (1·60 m). Fuel contained in two glass-fibre tanks, one in each wing root, usable capacity 7·2 Imp gallons (32·7 litres). Total capacity 14·4 Imp gallons (65·4 litres). Refuelling point on top surface of each wing root. Oil capacity 7 Imp pints (3·98 litres). Design will ultimately be offered for amateur construction with installation drawings for 1,600 cc and 1,700 cc converted Volkswagen engines.

ACCOMMODATION: Single seat in enclosed cabin. Upward-opening door on port side. Door can be kept open in flight. Lockable compartment for baggage aft of pilot's seat. Additional stowage for hand baggage in turtleback.

ELECTRONICS AND EQUIPMENT: Blind-flying instrumentation standard. Provision for installation of light aircraft transceiver.

DIMENSIONS, EXTERNAL:
Wing span   25 ft 9 in (7·85 m)
Wing chord (constant)   5 ft 0 in (1·52 m)
Wing aspect ratio   5
Length overall   20 ft 3 in (6·17 m)
Width, wings removed   4 ft 6 in (1·37 m)
Height overall   6 ft 4 in (1·93 m)
Tailplane span   8 ft 0 in (2·44 m)
Wheel track   4 ft 0 in (1·22 m)
Wheelbase   4 ft 6 in (1·37 m)

AREAS:
Wings, gross   128·7 sq ft (12·0 m²)
Ailerons (total)   approx 12 sq ft (1·11 m²)
Optional trailing-edge flaps (total)
     7 sq ft (0·65 m²)
Fin   1·5 sq ft (0·14 m²)
Rudder   5·2 sq ft (0·48 m²)
Tailplane   9·8 sq ft (0·91 m²)
Elevators, including tab   5·9 sq ft (0·55 m²)

WEIGHTS AND LOADINGS:
Weight, empty   430 lb (195 kg)
Max T-O and landing weight   750 lb (340 kg)
Max wing loading   5·8 lb/sq ft (28·3 kg/m²)
Max power loading   12 lb/hp (5·44 kg/hp)

PERFORMANCE (estimated, at max T-O weight):
Max level speed at S/L
     80 knots (92 mph; 148 km/h)
Max diving speed
     96 knots (111 mph; 178·5 km/h)
Max cruising speed at S/L
     69 knots (80 mph; 129 km/h)
Econ cruising speed
     59-62·5 knots (68-72 mph; 109-116 km/h)
Stalling speed, flaps up
     22 knots (25 mph; 40·5 km/h)
Stalling speed, flaps down
     20 knots (22 mph; 35·5 km/h)
Rate of climb at S/L   1,050 ft (320 m)/min
Service ceiling   11,000 ft (3,355 m)
T-O run, 5 mph wind   150 ft (46 m)
T-O to 50 ft (15 m)   480 ft (146 m)
Landing run   210 ft (64 m)
Range with max fuel
     512 nm (590 miles; 945 km)

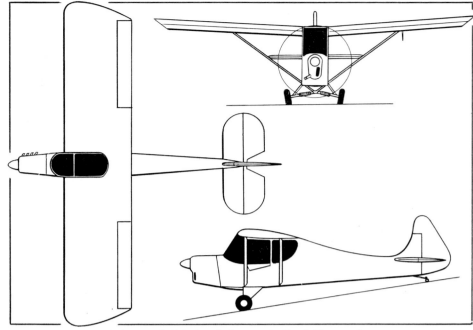

Ord-Hume O-H 7 Coupé single-seat ultra-light monoplane

PHOENIX

PHOENIX AIRCRAFT LTD

HEAD OFFICE:
St James's Place, Cranleigh, Surrey

DIRECTORS:
David Rendel, BA, CEng, MIMechE, AFRAeS (Managing)
Derek Page, BSc, MP
Dr John Urmston, BA(Cantab), MRCS, LRCP
James L. Bainbridge (Executive)

Phoenix Aircraft Ltd was formed in 1958 to produce light aircraft and engines. It has acquired licence rights in the pre-war designs of Luton Aircraft Ltd and has brought up-to-date the designs of the Luton Minor and Major. It has also evolved a two-seat version of the former aircraft known as the Phoenix Minor III.

Other recent designs, by Sqn Ldr Darrol Stinton, include the S34 Majorette and a project known as the S31, which is for a single-seat aircraft, powered by a 55 hp Ardem engine and having Hall-Warren wings of rhomboidal shape. Detail design of the S31 is being continued in collaboration with the College of Aeronautics at Cranfield, and Phoenix hoped to begin construction of a prototype at Cranleigh in 1970.

The company specialises in the supply of sets of plans and instructions, kits of materials and components for amateur constructors who wish to build either the Luton Minor or Major, and the Currie Wot light biplane. It has been appointed sole agent for the British Commonwealth for the supply of drawings of the French Jodel D.9 and D.11 and American EAA Biplane light aircraft, and is the only stockist of spares for the Aeronca-JAP J.99 engine. These components are interchangeable with those of the US Aeronca engine.

LUTON L.A.4a MINOR

The first Luton Minor flew in 1936 and proved entirely suitable for construction and operation by amateur builders and pilots. Examples were built pre-war in England and other parts of the world.

In 1960, the design was modernised and re-stressed completely to the latest British Airworthiness Requirements, allowing for a power increase to 55 hp and a maximum flying weight of 750 lb (340 kg).

By December 1969, 149 sets of plans for the Luton Minor had been sold. Minors are under construction in many parts of the world, and several amateur-built examples have been completed and flown successfully since mid-1962. At least one of them, built in Australia by R. A. Pearman and H. Nash, has obtained a full Certificate of Airworthiness.

TYPE: Single-seat light monoplane.

WINGS: Strut-braced parasol monoplane. Wing section RAF 48. No dihedral. Wooden two-spar structure in two halves, attached to the fuselage by tubular centre-section pylons and braced by parallel lift struts of streamline-section steel tubing. Wings removable for ground transport and storage. Leading-edge and tips plywood-covered, remainder fabric-covered. Plain ailerons of wood construction, fabric-covered. No flaps.

FUSELAGE: Rectangular all-wood structure. Sides and bottom plywood-covered. Curved decking aft of cockpit fabric-covered.

TAIL UNIT: Cantilever all-wood structure, fabric-covered. Fixed fin on current version. Aerodynamically-balanced rudder.

LANDING GEAR: Non-retractable tail-wheel type with divided main legs of tubular-steel construction. Rubber disc shock-absorbers. Brakes and wheel fairings optional. Fully-castoring tail-wheel.

POWER PLANT: One air-cooled engine in the 37-55 hp range, driving a two-blade fixed-pitch wooden propeller. Fuel tank forward of cockpit, capacity 6·5 Imp gallons (29·5 litres). Provision for additional tanks in wings.

ACCOMMODATION: Single seat in open cockpit. Coupé top optional. Luggage space aft of seat.

Phoenix Luton L.A.4a Minor single-seat light aircraft (*Air Portraits*)

DIMENSIONS, EXTERNAL:
Wing span	25 ft 0 in (7·62 m)
Wing chord (constant)	5 ft 3 in (1·60 m)
Wing aspect ratio	5
Length overall	20 ft 9 in (6·32 m)

AREA:
Wings, gross	125 sq ft (11·6 m²)

WEIGHTS:
Weight empty	390 lb (177 kg)
Max T-O weight	750 lb (340 kg)

PERFORMANCE (37 hp Aeronca-JAP J.99 engine, at normal T-O weight):
Max level speed at S/L	74 knots (85 mph; 137 km/h)
Max cruising speed	65 knots (75 mph; 121 km/h)
Stalling speed	25 knots (28 mph 45 km/h)
Rate of climb at S/L	450 ft (137 m)/min
T-O run	240 ft (73 m)
Landing run	120 ft (36·5 m)
Range with standard fuel	155 nm (180 miles; 290 km)
Range with auxiliary tanks	340 nm (400 miles; 645 km)

PHOENIX MINOR III

The Minor III is a developed version of the L.A.4a Minor with side-by-side seating for two persons. Differences from the L.A.4a include increased wing span, a 65 hp engine and an AUW of 950 lb (430 kg). Construction of a prototype began in 1969, and this aircraft was expected to fly for the first time in 1970.

LUTON L.A.5a MAJOR

The prototype Luton Major flew on 12 March 1939, and was demonstrated at several pre-war flying displays. Phoenix Aircraft Ltd has brought the design up-to-date, including re-stressing to current British Airworthiness Requirements, and is offering sets of plans to amateur constructors. A total of 53 sets had been sold by the end of 1969, and several Majors are now being built throughout the world. The first was completed in February 1965 by S. G. and T. G. Stott of Wincanton, Somerset.

TYPE: Two-seat cabin monoplane.

WINGS: Braced high-wing monoplane wings of similar construction to those of Luton Minor. Vee bracing struts. RAF 48 wing section. Dihedral 2°. Wings fold back along sides of fuselage.

FUSELAGE: Wooden structure with plywood covering.

TAIL UNIT: Cantilever wooden structure, fabric-covered. Trim-tab in elevators.

LANDING GEAR: Fixed tail-wheel type with divided main legs. Rubber disc shock-absorbers. Fully-castoring tail-wheel. Brakes optional.

POWER PLANT: Normally one 62 hp Walter Mikron Series II four-cylinder in-line air-cooled engine. Alternative engines include 83 hp Agusta G.A.70, 55 hp and 65 hp Lycoming, 65 hp Continental A65 and 85 hp Continental C85. Fuel capacity 11 Imp gallons (50 litres).

ACCOMMODATION: Enclosed cabin seating two persons in tandem, with dual controls. Door on starboard side.

DIMENSIONS, EXTERNAL:
Wing span	35 ft 2 in (10·72 m)
Wing chord (constant)	5 ft 3 in (1·60 m)
Wing aspect ratio	7·55
Length overall	23 ft 9 in (7·24 m)
Width, wings folded	11 ft 8 in (3·55 m)

AREA:
Wings, gross	163 sq ft (15·14 m²)

WEIGHTS:
Weight empty	700 lb (318 kg)
Max T-O weight	1,300 lb (590 kg)

PERFORMANCE (at max T-O weight):
Max level speed at S/L	87 knots (100 mph; 161 km/h)
Max cruising speed	80 knots (92 mph; 148 km/h)
Stalling speed	33 knots (38 mph; 61 km/h)
Rate of climb at S/L	650 ft (198 m)/min
T-O run	250 ft (76 m)
Landing run	160 ft (49 m)
Range with max fuel	260 nm (300 miles; 483 km)

PHOENIX S34 MAJORETTE

The Majorette was designed as a four-seat all-metal aircraft for amateur construction. Its design was evolved by Sqn Ldr Darrol Stinton from the pre-war two-seat Luton Major, and was described in the 1969-70 Jane's.

Development of the Majorette has been postponed during the building of a prototype of the two-seat Phoenix Minor III.

CURRIE WOT

This aircraft was designed originally by Mr J. R. Currie in 1937. Two examples were built at

Phoenix Luton L.A.5a Major two-seat cabin monoplane (62 hp Walter Mikron Series II engine)

Currie Wot (65 hp Walter Mikron III engine) built by Dr J. H. B. Urmston (A. Dunn)

Lympne in that year, but were destroyed in a wartime bombing raid. Mr V. H. Bellamy took over the design after the war, at the Hampshire Aeroplane Club, and the first Wot built by members of this club (G-APNT) flew for the first time on 11 September 1958. Like the pre-war machines, it was powered originally by a 35 hp Aeronca-JAP twin-cylinder air-cooled engine, but has since been re-engined with a flat-four Lycoming.

The second machine built at the Club (G-APWT) was powered by a 60 hp Walter Mikron four-cylinder in-line air-cooled engine, in which form it was known as the "Hot Wot". When fitted temporarily, and unsuccessfully, with twin-float landing gear in 1959, it became the "Wet Wot". Subsequently, it reverted to a wheel landing gear and was re-engined temporarily with a 60 hp Rover T.P.60 turboprop, as a flying test-bed for this engine. Known as the "Wizz Wot", it was the smallest turboprop-powered aircraft flown up to that time.

Further Wots have since been completed, including Dr Urmston's G-ARZW with a 65 hp Walter Mikron III engine ("Hotter Wot").

Dr Urmston purchased all rights in the design from Mr Bellamy and subsequently had the aircraft re-stressed, in anticipation of meeting the British Aerobatic requirement of 6g at an AUW of 900 lb (408 kg). He has since become a Director of Phoenix Aircraft Ltd, which now markets drawings of the Wot and was preparing kits early in 1970.

The following details refer to Dr Urmston's Wot, built to standard plans. Data on the versions with Aeronca-JAP and 60 hp Mikron engines can be found in the 1961-62 Jane's.

TYPE: Single-seat fully-aerobatic light biplane.

WINGS: Braced biplane type, with two parallel interplane struts each side and N-type centre-section support struts. Wing section Clark Y. Dihedral (both wings) 3°. No incidence. Conventional spruce and plywood structure, with fabric covering. Fabric-covered ailerons on lower wings only. No flaps.

FUSELAGE: All-wood structure. Plywood-box construction, with overall fabric covering.

TAIL UNIT: Cantilever structure of spruce and plywood, with fabric covering. Fixed-incidence tailplane. Adjustable tab on rudder. Trim-tab in port elevator.

LANDING GEAR: Non-retractable two-wheel type. Rubber-cord shock-absorption. Main wheels fitted with Dunlop tyres, size 400 × 8, pressure 18 lb/sq in (1·27 kg/cm²). No brakes.

POWER PLANT: One 65 hp Walter Mikron III four-cylinder in-line air-cooled engine, driving a two-blade fixed-pitch wooden propeller. Fuel tank aft of firewall, capacity 12 Imp gallons (54·5 litres). Oil capacity 1·5 Imp gallons (7 litres).

ACCOMMODATION: Single seat in open cockpit.

DIMENSIONS, EXTERNAL:
Wing span (both)	22 ft 1 in (6·73 m)
Wing span (both, constant)	3 ft 6 in (1·07 m)
Wing aspect ratio	6·3
Length overall	18 ft 3½ in (5·58 m)
Height overall	6 ft 9 in (2·06 m)
Wheel track	4 ft 6½ in (1·38 m)

AREA:
Wings, gross	140 sq ft (13·0 m²)

WEIGHTS:
Weight empty	550 lb (250 kg)
Max T-O weight	900 lb (408 kg)

PERFORMANCE (at max T-O weight):
Max level speed at 2,000 ft (600 m)	83 knots (95 mph; 153 km/h)
Max permissible diving speed	112 knots (130 mph; 209 km/h)
Max cruising speed at 2,000 ft (600 m)	78 knots (90 mph; 145 km/h)
Econ cruising speed at 2,000 ft (600 m)	69 knots (80 mph; 129 km/h)
Stalling speed	35 knots (40 mph; 65 km/h)
Rate of climb at S/L	600 ft (183 m)/min
Range with max fuel	208 nm (240 miles; 385 km)

PRACTAVIA
PRACTAVIA LTD

ADDRESS:
57 Redstone Hill, Redhill, Surrey

This company has been formed to market plans and kits of a two-seat all-metal aerobatic aircraft known as the Sprite, the design of which was initiated by Pilot magazine, under whose heading it was first described in the 1969-70 Jane's.

PILOT SPRITE

Initial design work on the Sprite was started by the staff of Pilot magazine early in 1968, after consultation with many experienced light aircraft constructors. The concept excited so much enthusiasm that a design and development panel was set up to ensure the success of the project. Detailed design began in November 1968. Mr Brian Healey, editor of *Pilot* magazine, is project executive, and Mr Lloyd Jenkinson and Mr Peter Sharman, lecturers at Loughborough University, are the designers.

Two prototypes are being constructed by BEA apprentices, under the direction of their instructor, Mr Bert Page, at London Airport. The first of these was expected to fly in mid-1970. Plans are already available for amateur construction, and in addition to the BEA-built prototypes more than 30 aircraft were under construction by individuals early in 1970. Kits are also being made available.

TYPE: Two-seat all-metal aerobatic aircraft, suitable for amateur construction.

WINGS: Cantilever low-wing monoplane. Wing section NACA 64315. Dihedral 6° on outer panels only. No incidence or sweepback. All-metal structure of aluminium alloy. Single main spar with light rear spar forming central tiorson box. Skins and ribs of L72 alloy, extrusions of L65 alloy and spar caps of L73 alloy. Single-slotted full-span flaps and ailerons of L72 alloy. No trim-tabs. Outer wing panels detachable for transit.

FUSELAGE: All-metal semi-monocoque structure, with no double curvature. Longerons of L65 aluminium alloy, skins and frames of L72 alloy. Sides and top curved to avoid drumming.

TAIL UNIT: Cantilever all-metal structure with swept vertical surfaces, constructed of L72 alloy. Fixed-incidence tailplane. Trim-tab in centre of elevator trailing-edge, of one-third span; outer one-third on each side comprises anti-balance tab.

LANDING GEAR: Non-retractable tricycle type standard, although design of wing structure will allow for fitment of retractable gear as a future development. Shock absorption by rubber in compression. Wheels and tyres size 500 × 5. Hydraulic disc brakes.

POWER PLANT: One 100 hp Rolls-Royce/Continental O-200-A, or 115 hp Lycoming O-235 four-cylinder horizontally-opposed air-cooled engine, driving a two-blade fixed-pitch propeller. Other suitable power plants include a 125 or 150 hp Lycoming or a 135 hp Rolls-Royce/Continental engine. Fuel contained in one fuselage tank, aft of firewall, capacity 12 Imp gallons (54·5 litres). Wing-tip fuel tanks optional, capacity 12 Imp gallons (54·5 litres) each. Maximum total capacity 36 Imp gallons (163·5 litres). Oil capacity 1 Imp gallon (4·5 litres).

ACCOMMODATION: Two seats, side-by-side, in enclosed cockpit, with rearward-sliding transparent canopy. Space for baggage behind seats.

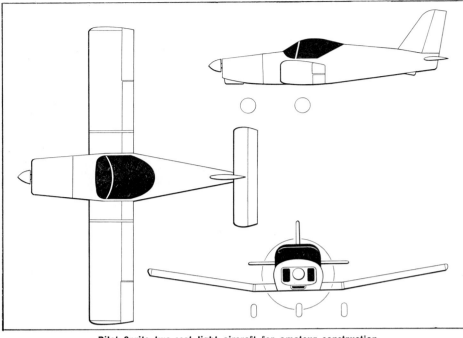

Pilot Sprite two-seat light aircraft for amateur construction

SYSTEMS: Air conditioning. Hydraulic system for brakes only. 12V electrical system.

ELECTRONICS AND EQUIPMENT: Radio, blind-flying instrumentation and special equipment to individual builder's requirements.

DIMENSIONS, EXTERNAL:

Wing span	24 ft 0 in (7·32 m)
Wing span over tip tanks	27 ft 0 in (8·23 m)
Wing chord (constant)	4 ft 0 in (1·22 m)
Wing aspect ratio	6
Length overall	20 ft 0 in (6·10 m)
Width, outer panels removed	8 ft 0 in (2·44 m)
Height overall	8 ft 3 in (2·51 m)
Tailplane span	8 ft 0 in (2·44 m)
Wheel track	7 ft 6 in (2·29 m)
Wheelbase	4 ft 7 in (1·40 m)

DIMENSIONS, INTERNAL:
Cabin:

Max width	3 ft 10 in (1·17 m)
Max height	3 ft 2 in (0·97 m)

AREAS:

Wings, gross	96 sq ft (8·92 m²)
Ailerons (total)	8 sq ft (0·74 m²)
Trailing-edge flaps (total)	16 sq ft (1·49 m²)
Fin	10·5 sq ft (0·98 m²)
Rudder	3·5 sq ft (0·33 m²)
Tailplane	18·0 sq ft (1·67 m²)
Elevator, including tabs	9·0 sq ft (0·84 m²)

WEIGHTS AND LOADINGS (100 hp engine):

Weight empty	850 lb (385 kg)
Max T-O weight	1,400 lb (635 kg)
Max wing loading	14·6 lb/sq ft (71·2 kg/m²)
Max power loading	12·2 lb/hp (5·53 kg/hp)

PERFORMANCE (estimated, at max T-O weight with 125 hp engine):

Max diving speed	212 knots (245 mph; 394 km/h)
Max cruising speed	111 knots (128 mph; 206 km/h)
Stalling speed, flaps down	48 knots (55 mph; 89 km/h)

PROCTER

PROCTER AIRCRAFT ASSOCIATES LTD

HEAD OFFICE:
"Greenball", Crawley Ridge, Camberley, Surrey

DIRECTORS:
Roy G. Procter
Roger H. White-Smith
Mrs Barbara Alexander

SECRETARY:
Mrs Ann Procter

This company changed its name from Mitchell-Procter Aircraft Ltd in November 1968. The latter company comprised a group of enthusiasts who designed and built the prototype Kittiwake I (see under "Mitchell-Procter" heading), which is owned and operated by the new company.

Procter Aircraft Associates have designed and are developing a larger aircraft on the same lines, known as the Petrel.

Sets of plans for construction of the Kittiwake I are available to amateur constructors from the above address and those for the Petrel will be available as soon as the prototype has been completed. It is planned to market materials, kits of parts and completed aircraft.

PROCTER PETREL

This two-seat light aircraft is based upon the Kittiwake I single-seat lightplane (which see), with increased wing area, but has many components in common with the single-seater and has also been optimised for glider towing. The opportunity is also being taken to make a number of improvements and simplifications to the detail mechanical design, compared with the Kittiwake I.

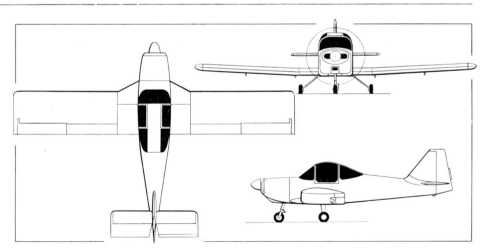

Procter Petrel two-seat light aircraft for amateur construction in its latest form, with revised landing gear and other changes

Procter has sub-contracted construction of the prototype Petrel to Miles Aviation and Transport (R and D) Ltd at Ford Aerodrome, Sussex. In March 1970 this aircraft was approx 50% completed and was expected to fly during the Summer of 1970. It has a fuel capacity of 16 Imp gallons (73 litres).

Plans for eventual series production of the Petrel will depend upon finance, and upon the

outcome of flight trials, which are intended to clear the aircraft for full aerobatic flying.

DIMENSIONS, EXTERNAL:

Wing span	30 ft 0 in (9·14 m)
Length overall	20 ft 9 in (6·32 m)
Height overall	7 ft 8 in (2·33 m)

WEIGHTS:

Weight empty	1,137 lb (515·5 kg)
Max T-O weight	1,680 lb (762 kg)

ROLLASON

ROLLASON AIRCRAFT AND ENGINES LTD

HEAD OFFICE AND WORKS:
Croydon Airport, Croydon, Surrey

AIRCRAFT SALES DEPARTMENT:
Redhill Aerodrome, Surrey

DIRECTORS:
Norman Jones (Chairman)
R. F. Thompson (General Manager)

D. M. Jones (Sales Manager)
Mrs M. Harriott (Secretary)

Well-known for many years as an aircraft overhaul, repair and sales organisation, this company entered the manufacturing field in 1957. It is building under licence the French Druine Turbulent, and has also undertaken conversion of the Ardem 4CO2 engine for this aircraft. The first Rollason-built Turbulent flew on 1 January

1958, and 30 had been built by the Spring of 1970. In addition, the company manufactures Turbulent components to assist amateur constructors of this aircraft.

Also flying are 38 Rollason-built Druine Condor two-seat light aircraft, and the Condor is now Rollason's main production type.

Development and construction of the Luton Beta light aircraft continues.

ROLLASON (DRUINE) D31 TURBULENT

In general, the Rollason-built Turbulent is similar to the standard Druine design. Main differences are that it has wheels of slightly greater size and a tail-skid instead of a tail-wheel, although a tail-wheel is available as an optional extra.

Other optional extras include a hand-starter, wheel spats, taxying and parking brakes and a sliding canopy which increases the speed of the Turbulent by about 8 mph (13 kmh). VHF radio has been fitted to two aircraft.

A Turbulent was operated successfully on skis from Redhill Aerodrome in the Winter of 1962-63, and subsequently, and a seaplane version was constructed early in 1968 for use on land or water.

The standard Rollason-built D31 Turbulent is powered by a 45 hp 1,500 cc Ardem (Volkswagen) Mk IV or 55 hp Ardem Mk V (racing) four-cylinder horizontally-opposed air-cooled engine, the conversion of which from a standard motor car engine is undertaken by Rollason. It operates with a Permit to Fly. Production continues, to order, during 1970.

Rollason built a slightly modified (D31A) Turbulent, registered G-ARLZ, which was awarded a full Certificate of Airworthiness in 1966. Only major modification is an improved wing main spar, but D31A's intended for C of A approval must be fitted, like G-ARLZ, with an ARB-approved 45 hp 1,500 cc Ardem Mk X engine, with which the max T-O weight is 700 lb (317 kg). One of them (G-AWPA) is shown in the adjacent illustration.

The following data apply to the D31 "Permit" Turbulent.

TYPE: Single-seat ultra-light monoplane.

WINGS: Cantilever low-wing monoplane. Wing section NACA 23012. Dihedral 4°. Incidence 3° 40'. All-wood two-spar structure of grade A spruce and birch ply, covered with fabric. Built-in leading-edge slot on outer 45% of half-span. Wooden slotted ailerons with fabric covering. No flaps or tabs.

FUSELAGE: Conventional rectangular four-longeron spruce structure with domed decking. Plywood-covered.

TAIL UNIT: Cantilever wooden structure of spruce and plywood. Fixed surfaces plywood-covered, movable surfaces fabric-covered. No tabs.

LANDING GEAR: Non-retractable two-wheel type, with tailskid. Rollason compression-spring shock-absorbers. Dunlop or Goodyear main wheels and tyres, size 14 × 3, pressure 28 lb/sq in (1·97 kg/cm²). Vespa mechanical brakes. Skis may be fitted as alternative to wheels.

POWER PLANT: One 45 hp Rollason Ardem 4CO2 Mk IV or 55 hp Ardem Mk V (racing) four-cylinder horizontally-opposed air-cooled engine, driving a type Z/3405 two-blade fixed-pitch wooden propeller manufactured by Airscrew & Weyroc Ltd. Fuel tank in fuselage forward of cockpit, capacity 8·5 Imp gallons (39 litres). Oil capacity 0·5 Imp gallons (2·25 litres).

ACCOMMODATION: Pilot only, in open cockpit. Sliding canopy available as optional extra. Luggage locker aft of seat, capacity 25 lb (11·5 kg).

ELECTRONICS: Provision for installation of lightweight radio.

DIMENSIONS, EXTERNAL:
Wing span	21 ft 7 in (6·58 m)
Wing chord (constant)	3 ft 11 in (1·90 m)
Wing aspect ratio	5·4
Length overall	17 ft 6 in (5·33 m)
Height overall	5 ft 0 in (1·52 m)
Tailplane span	6 ft 6 in (1·98 m)
Wheel track	5 ft 8 in (1·73 m)
Wheel/tailskid base	12 ft 6 in (3·81 m)

AREAS:
Wings, gross	77·5 sq ft (7·20 m²)
Ailerons (total)	7·6 sq ft (0·71 m²)
Fin	1·3 sq ft (0·12 m²)
Rudder	3·2 sq ft (0·30 m²)
Tailplane	6·1 sq ft (0·57 m²)
Elevators	5·5 sq ft (0·51 m²)

WEIGHTS AND LOADINGS (D31):
Weight empty	395 lb (179 kg)
Max T-O weight	620 lb (281 kg)
Max wing loading	8·0 lb/sq ft (39·1 kg/m²)
Max power loading	13·8 lb/hp (6·25 kg/hp)

PERFORMANCE (D31 with 45 hp engine, at max T-O weight):
Max level speed	95 knots (109 mph; 176 km/h)
Max permissible diving speed	
	108 knots (125 mph; 202 km/h)
Max cruising speed	
	87 knots (100 mph; 161 km/h)
Econ cruising speed	
	76 knots (87 mph; 141 km/h)
Stalling speed	39 knots (44 mph; 71 km/h)
Rate of climb at S/L	450 ft (137 m)/min
Service ceiling	9,000 ft (2,740 m)
T-O run from grass	310 ft (95 m)
T-O to 50 ft (15 m) from grass	410 ft (125 m)
Landing from 50 ft (15 m) on grass	
	320 ft (98 m)
Landing run on grass	170 ft (52 m)
Range with max fuel, normal allowances	
	217 nm (250 miles; 400 km)

Rollason-built Druine D31A Turbulent (45 hp Ardem Mk X engine) (*Roy Davis*)

ROLLASON (DRUINE) D62 CONDOR

Rollason have developed a slightly modified version of the Druine D62 Condor two-seat light aircraft, which has flown in the following forms:

D62. Prototype Rollason Condor (G-ARHZ) with 90 hp Continental C90 engine. First flew in May 1961. Operated on a Permit to Fly.

D62A. Two examples built, with 100 hp Rolls-Royce/Continental O-200-A engine. G-ARVZ first flew in August 1963; G-ASEU flew in February 1964 and qualified subsequently for a Transport Category (Club) C of A.

D62B. Two examples, G-ASRB and G-ASRC, built originally as D62A's and modified into D62B's. Main changes are a 4 in (10 cm) reduction in overall length, 30 lb (14 kg) reduction in empty weight and use of an Airscrew-Weyroc propeller instead of the EVRA propeller of the D62A. G-ASRB flew in December 1964, G-ASRC in January 1965. Two more (G-ATAU and G-ATAV) flew in August and October 1965 respectively. These first four aircraft were without flaps, but subsequent D62B's are fitted with flaps.

A total of 38 Condors of all marks had been delivered by the Spring of 1970, and flight development has resulted in clearances for spinning and glider towing.

Further developments for 1970 include a version with Rolls-Royce/Continental O-240 engine, intended specifically for glider towing; and one with removable auxiliary fuel tanks for long-distance ferrying or touring.

The following details refer specifically to the D62B:

TYPE: Two-seat light monoplane.

WINGS: Cantilever low-wing monoplane. Dihedral 3° 10' on top of spar booms. Incidence 5° at root, 3° 6' at tip. All-wood two-spar structure of grade A spruce and birch ply, covered with fabric. Frise ailerons and flaps of wooden construction, with fabric covering.

FUSELAGE: Conventional rectangular four-longeron spruce structure with domed decking. Plywood-covered.

TAIL UNIT: Cantilever wooden structure of spruce and plywood. Fin plywood-covered. Tailplane and movable surfaces fabric-covered. Controllable tab in port elevator. Fixed tab on rudder.

LANDING GEAR: Non-retractable tail-wheel type. Jodel-Rollason cantilever main legs. Dunlop main wheels and tyres, size 16·38 × 5·75, pressure 24 lb/sq in (1·69 kg/cm²). Lockheed hydraulic twin-shoe brakes.

POWER PLANT: One 100 hp Rolls-Royce/Continental O-200-A four-cylinder horizontally-opposed air-cooled engine, driving an Airscrew-Weyroc Z 5793 two-blade fixed-pitch propeller. Fuel tank in fuselage forward of cabin, capacity 16 Imp gallons (73 litres). Oil capacity 1 Imp gallon (4·5 litres).

ACCOMMODATION: Pilot and passenger side-by-side in enclosed cabin. Door on each side, hinged to open upward. Luggage shelf at rear of cabin.

ELECTRONICS AND EQUIPMENT: Blind-flying instrumentation and full night flying equipment standard. Narco radios to customer's requirements.

DIMENSIONS, EXTERNAL:
Wing span	27 ft 6 in (8·38 m)
Wing chord at root	5 ft 7½ in (1·72 m)
Wing chord at tip	3 ft 3½ in (1·00 m)
Wing aspect ratio	6·3
Length overall	22 ft 6 in (6·86 m)
Height overall	7 ft 9 in (2·36 m)
Tailplane span	10 ft 8 in (3·25 m)
Wheel track	10 ft 6 in (3·20 m)
Wheelbase	16 ft 6 in (5·03 m)
Cabin doors:	
Height	2 ft 3 in (0·69 m)
Width	2 ft 2 in (0·66 m)
Height of sill above wing	1 ft 3 in (0·38 m)

AREAS:
Wings, gross	119·8 sq ft (11·13 m²)
Ailerons (total)	9·8 sq ft (0·91 m²)
Trailing-edge flaps (total)	18·4 sq ft (1·71 m²)
Fin	5·8 sq ft (0·54 m²)
Rudder, including tab	6·6 sq ft (0·61 m²)
Tailplane	15·3 sq ft (1·42 m²)
Elevators, including tab	9·75 sq ft (0·91 m²)

WEIGHTS AND LOADINGS:
Weight empty	920 lb (417 kg)
Max T-O weight	1,475 lb (670 kg)
Max wing loading	14·6 lb/sq ft (71·3 kg/m²)
Max power loading	14·75 lb/hp (6·70 kg/hp)

PERFORMANCE (at max T-O weight):
Max level speed	
	110 knots (127 mph; 204 km/h)
Max permissible diving speed	
	146 knots (169 mph; 272 km/h)
Max cruising speed	
	100 knots (115 mph; 185 km/h)
Econ cruising speed	
	93 knots (107 mph; 172 km/h)
Stalling speed	40 knots (46 mph; 74 km/h)
Rate of climb at S/L	610 ft (185 m)/min
Service ceiling	12,000 ft (3,650 m)
T-O run from grass	410 ft (125 m)
T-O to 50 ft (15 m) from grass	580 ft (177 m)
Landing from 50 ft (15 m) on grass	
	450 ft (137 m)
Landing run on grass	280 ft (85 m)
Range with max fuel and max payload, normal allowances	300 nm (350 miles; 560 km)

ROLLASON/LUTON GROUP BETA

The Luton Group, which designed the Luton Beta light aircraft (see 1966-67 *Jane's*) has since dispersed. Development and construction of the

Rollason (Druine) D62B Condor (100 hp Rolls-Royce/Continental O-200-A engine) (*Air Photo Supply*)

Beta was taken over by Rollason and the following versions have been announced:

Beta B1. With 65 hp Continental A65 engine. Prototype, built by Rollason and first flown on 21 April 1967, was of this version, but has since been converted to B2 standard. Further development of this aircraft, which has taken place during the past year, includes fitting of a new streamlined cowling and nose extension, which adds approx 8·7 knots (10 mph; 16 km/h) to the max level speed. This has been done to assist the promotion of Formula I racing in the UK, and can be incorporated in production aircraft if required.

Beta B2. With 90 hp Continental C90 engine. Construction of three Beta B2s was started by Rollason during 1968, and the first of these (G-AWHV) flew for the first time on 15 February 1969. All three were expected to be flying by Spring 1970. Production Beta B2's have a cleaner canopy line, shorter main gear with wheel fairings and improved interior and exterior finish.

Rollason had sold 30 sets of Beta plans to amateur constructors by the beginning of 1970.

Beta B3. With 55 hp Rollason Ardem 4CO2 Mk V engine.

Beta B4. With 100 hp Continental O-200 engine, starter-generator and radio. One expected to be flying by Spring 1970.

TYPE: Single-seat ultra-light sporting aircraft.

WINGS: Cantilever low-wing monoplane. Wing section NACA 23012. Dihedral 7° on outer wings. Incidence 3° at root, 1° at tip. All-wood torsion-box structure in three sections: constant-chord centre-section and detachable tapered outer wings. Single main spar and auxiliary rear spar. Plywood-covered. Mass-balanced wooden ailerons, covered with fabric aft of spar. Optional plain flaps of similar construction to ailerons. No tabs.

FUSELAGE: All-wood semi-monocoque structure with frames, stringers and plywood covering. Welded steel-tube engine mounting.

TAIL UNIT: Cantilever all-wood structure with sweptback vertical surfaces. Fin and tailplane plywood-covered; rudder and elevators fabric-covered aft of spar.

LANDING GEAR: Non-retractable tail-wheel type, with steerable tail-wheel. Cantilever main legs, with rubber-in-compression shock-absorption. Goodyear tyres size 5·00 × 5 type III, pressure 28 lb/sq in (1·97 kg/cm²). Goodyear brakes. Main wheel fairings standard.

POWER PLANT: One four-cylinder horizontally-opposed air-cooled engine (details under individual model descriptions), driving a two-blade

Rollason/Luton Group Beta B2 single-seat racing aircraft (90 hp Continental C90 engine) (*Air Portraits*)

fixed-pitch propeller. One metal fuel tank in fuselage aft of firewall, capacity 10·5 Imp gallons (48 litres).

ACCOMMODATION: Single seat in enclosed cockpit. Side-hinged canopy. Baggage compartment aft of seat.

DIMENSIONS, EXTERNAL:

Wing span	20 ft 5 in (6·22 m)
Wing chord at root	3 ft 9 in (1·14 m)
Wing chord at tip	2 ft 3½ in (0·70 m)
Wing aspect ratio	6·15
Length overall	16 ft 8 in (5·08 m)
Width with outer wings removed for road transport	6 ft 8 in (2·03 m)
Height overall	6 ft 3 in (1·91 m)
Tailplane span	6 ft 0 in (1·83 m)
Wheel track	4 ft 10 in (1·47 m)
Wheelbase	11 ft 2 in (3·40 m)

AREAS:

Wings, gross	66 sq ft (6·13 m²)
Ailerons (total)	9·6 sq ft (0·89 m²)
Trailing-edge flaps (optional; total):	5·4 sq ft (0·50 m²)
Fin	2·9 sq ft (0·27 m²)
Rudder	4·4 sq ft (0·41 m²)
Tailplane	10·5 sq ft (0·98 m²)
Elevators	5·0 sq ft (0·46 m²)

WEIGHTS AND LOADINGS:

Weight empty:	
B1, B2	560 lb (254 kg)
B3	500 lb (227 kg)
Max T-O and landing weight	850 lb (385 kg)
Max wing loading	13·1 lb/sq ft (64·0 kg/m²)
Max power loading:	
B1	13·1 lb/hp (5·94 kg/hp)

PERFORMANCE (at max T-O weight; data for B3 and B4 estimated):

Max level speed at S/L:		
B1	129 knots	(149 mph; 240 km/h)
B2	169 knots	(195 mph; 314 km/h)
B3	123 knots	(142 mph; 229 km/h)
B4	160 knots	(185 mph; 298 km/h)
Max permissible diving speed		
	195 knots	(225 mph; 362 km/h)
Max cruising speed at 7,000 ft (2,150 m):		
B1	122 knots	(140 mph; 225 km/h)
B2, B4	139 knots	(160 mph; 257 km/h)
B3	114 knots	(131 mph; 211 km/h)
Stalling speed:		
B1, B2 without flaps		
	53 knots	(60 mph; 97 km/h)
B3 without flaps 52 knots		(59 mph; 95 km/h)
Rate of climb at S/L:		
B1	1,000 ft (305 m)/min	
B2, B4	1,800 ft (548 m)/min	
B3	700 ft (213 m)/min	
Service ceiling:		
B1	15,000 ft (4,575 m)	
B2	20,000 ft (6,100 m)	
T-O run, without flaps:		
B1	900 ft (274 m)	
B2	600 ft (183 m)	
B3	990 ft (302 m)	
Landing run, without flaps:		
B1, B2	1,000 ft (305 m)	
Range with max fuel at max cruising speed, no reserves:		
B1	217 nm	(250 miles; 400 km)
B2	277 nm	(320 miles; 515 km)
B3	260 nm	(300 miles; 480 km)

SCOTTISH AVIATION

SCOTTISH AVIATION LTD (Member Company of CAMMELL LAIRD GROUP)

HEAD OFFICE AND WORKS:
Prestwick International Airport, Ayrshire

LONDON OFFICE:
6 Bolton Street, London W1

DIRECTORS:
The Duke of Hamilton, PC, GCVO, AFC, FRGS (President)
T. D. M. Robertson (Chairman)
H. W. Laughland, CA (Managing Director)
T. Draper Williams
G. S. Nelson
R. W. Johnson, CBE
Dr W. G. Watson
W. Willis
J. R. Woods

SECRETARY: W. L. Denness, CA
CHIEF ENGINEER: Dr W. G. Watson
PRODUCTION MANAGER: W. H. Ward
COMMERCIAL MANAGER: D. McConnell
WORKS ACCOUNTANT: J. Baird
MARKETING MANAGER: R. L. Porteous

Scottish Aviation Ltd was formed in 1935 to provide opportunities for employment in the various branches of aviation in Scotland. In doing so, the company developed Prestwick International Airport and on it established an aircraft design and manufacturing industry.

The company's five-seat Prestwick Pioneer first flew in 1950 and was followed by the 16-seat Twin Pioneer in 1955. A total of 150 aircraft of these types were built before production was completed. Details of both designs can be found in earlier editions of *Jane's*.

Under the name SALchek, Scottish Aviation operates a complete aviation service, including component and special installation design and manufacture; and conversion, rebuild, repair and maintenance of civil and military aircraft.

Present long-term contracts include maintenance, repair and modification of CF-104 Starfighters for the Canadian Armed Forces; production of components for, and the rebuilding of, Rolls-Royce piston and jet engines, manufacture of major airframe components, including large fuselage sections for the Lockheed C-130 Hercules transport aircraft. Other recent contracts have included freighter conversions and the complete refurbishing of various transport aircraft.

The company's design facilities are ARB- and AQD-approved and the aircraft production, conversion and maintenance services are covered by ARB, AQD and FAA approvals.

A subsidiary company, Scottish Air Engine Services Ltd, also based at Prestwick Airport, undertakes the repair and rebuilding of Pratt & Whitney and Lycoming piston-engines.

Following the liquidation of Beagle Aircraft Ltd, it was announced on 30 May 1970 that Scottish Aviation Ltd would assume responsibility for production of the Bulldog military training aircraft, a description of which is given below.

SCOTTISH AVIATION/BEAGLE B.125 BULLDOG

Beagle Aircraft announced on 2 October 1968 that, following discussions with the UK Ministry of Defence, as well as with representatives of other major air forces, they had decided to introduce a military trainer version of the Beagle Pup. This was allocated the manufacturer's designation B.125 Series 1, and was later named Bulldog. The airframe is basically the same as that of the Pup, but as the description below shows there are a number of detail changes from the B.121 Series (described on page 205).

First flight of the prototype (G-AXEH) was made on 19 May 1969. Total orders for Bulldogs, all outstanding at 31 December 1969, amounted to 71. Largest single order was for 58 aircraft, with options on 45 more, for the Swedish Air Board, with initial deliveries scheduled for August 1970. Eight were ordered for the Zambian Air Force and five for the Kenya Air Force. The Zambian Air Force was later reported to have cancelled its order.

Evaluation of the prototype in Sweden has included extensive operation from snow, on ski landing gear.

Following the voluntary liquidation of Beagle Aircraft Ltd, manufacture of the Bulldog has been taken over by Scottish Aviation Ltd.

TYPE: Two-seat primary trainer.

WINGS: Cantilever low-wing monoplane. Wing section NACA 63₂615. Dihedral 6° 30'. Incidence 1° 30' at centre-line of aircraft. Sweepback 2° 56' at leading-edge. Conventional single-spar two-cell riveted stressed-skin structure of light alloy. Electrically-operated slotted trailing-edge flaps and slotted ailerons of similar construction. No trim-tabs.

FUSELAGE: Conventional all-metal semi-monocoque fail-safe structure.

TAIL UNIT: Cantilever two-spar light alloy structure. Fixed-incidence tailplane. Full-span trim-tab on starboard elevator. Manually-operated trim-tab on rudder. Fixed ventral fin.

LANDING GEAR: Non-retractable tricycle type, with single wheel on each unit. Steerable nose-wheel with Lockheed oleo-pneumatic shock-absorber and Dunlop wheel and tyre size 5 × 500, pressure 35 lb/sq in (2·46 kg/cm²). Main gear has Lockheed oleo-pneumatic shock-absorbers and Dunlop wheels and tyres size 6 × 600, pressure 25 lb/sq in (1·76 kg/cm²). Dunlop hydraulic disc brakes. Optional ski landing gear.

POWER PLANT: One 200 hp Lycoming IO-360-A1C four-cylinder horizontally-opposed air-cooled engine, driving a Hartzell two-blade constant-speed metal propeller, diameter 6 ft 2 in (1·88 m). Two metal fuel tanks, one in each wing leading-edge, each with usable capacity of 17 Imp gallons (77 litres). Total usable capacity 34

Imp gallons (154 litres). Refuelling point on upper surface of each wing. Oil capacity 1·665 Imp gallons (7·58 litres).

ACCOMMODATION: Enclosed cabin seating two side-by-side with dual controls. Rearward-sliding jettisonable transparent canopy. Cabin heated and ventilated.

SYSTEMS: Hydraulic system for brakes only. 28V DC electrical power provided by engine-driven alternator. 28V storage battery.

ELECTRONICS AND EQUIPMENT: As required by individual customers.

DIMENSIONS, EXTERNAL:

Wing span	33 ft 0 in (10·06 m)
Wing chord at root	4 ft 7½ in (1·41 m)
Wing chord at tip	2 ft 9 in (0·84 m)
Wing aspect ratio	8·46
Length overall	23 ft 2½ in (7·07 m)
Height overall	7 ft 5¾ in (2·28 m)
Tailplane span	11 ft 0 in (3·35 m)
Wheel track	6 ft 8 in (2·03 m)
Wheelbase	4 ft 7 in (1·40 m)

DIMENSIONS, INTERNAL:

Cabin: Length	6 ft 11 in (2·11 m)
Max width	3 ft 9 in (1·14 m)
Max height	3 ft 4 in (1·02 m)

AREAS:

Wings, gross	128·5 sq ft (11·94 m²)
Ailerons (total)	9·4 sq ft (0·87 m²)
Trailing-edge flaps (total)	13·95 sq ft (1·30 m²)
Fin	21·27 sq ft (1·98 m²)
Rudder, including tab	7·89 sq ft (0·73 m²)
Tailplane	27·3 sq ft (2·54 m²)
Elevators, including tab	10·88 sq ft (1·01 m²)

WEIGHTS AND LOADINGS:

Basic empty weight	1,398 lb (634 kg)
Max T-O and landing weight	2,350 lb (1,065 kg)
Max wing loading	18·3 lb/sq ft (89·3 kg/m²)
Max power loading	11·8 lb/hp (5·35 kg/hp)

PERFORMANCE (at max T-O weight):

Max level speed, S/L, ISA conditions
141 knots (162 mph; 261 km/h)

Max diving speed
209 knots (241 mph; 387·5 km/h) IAS

Max cruising speed at 5,000 ft (1,525 m)
133 knots (153 mph; 246 km/h)

Econ cruising speed, 55% power at 15,000 ft (4,570 m) 129 knots (148 mph; 238 km/h)

Stalling speed, flaps down
57 knots (65 mph; 105 km/h)

Rate of climb at S/L	1,100 ft (335 m)/min
Service ceiling	over 20,000 ft (6,100 m)
T-O run	750 ft (229 m)
T-O to 50 ft (15 m)	1,095 ft (334 m)
Landing from 50 ft (15 m)	1,200 ft (366 m)
Landing run	600 ft (183 m)

Range with max fuel and max payload, 55% power at 4,000 ft (1,220 m), ISA
545 nm (628 miles; 1,010 km)

SCOTTISH AVIATION/VICKERS VISCOUNT FREIGHTER CONVERSION

A convertible freighter/passenger configuration has been designed by Scottish Aviation for Viscount Series 800 and 810 aircraft. Several have been modified for Aer Lingus, and incorporate the major changes detailed below.

The 89 in (2·26 m) wide door installed in the

Beagle-built Bulldog two-seat military training aircraft in Swedish insignia (*James Waddington*)

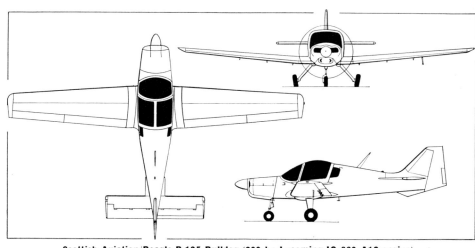

Scottish Aviation/Beagle B.125 Bulldog (200 hp Lycoming IO-360-A1C engine)

forward fuselage is made in two halves, the forward half only being used for passenger operations. Structural strengthening of the forward fuselage and floor members, and the installation of a freight handling system, are included in the conversion scheme. Designed by Brownline Corporation, the freight handling system utilises a ballmat at the door, for man-oeuvring pallets, and roller trays along the cabin floor, with side guides to ensure smooth transfer of the pallets. Floor-mounted locks and nets

secure the load. A galley is installed at the rear, together with two hostess seats, and a pneumatic tail support is fitted to maintain a level floor when loading pallets to the rear. Mixed pay-loads are possible, utilising a movable bulkhead to separate passengers from freight.

Up to nine pallets can be carried, each measuring 53 in × 88 in (1·35 m × 2·24 m) and with a load capacity of 2,368 lb (1,074 kg). Max freight load, limited by zero-fuel weight, is 14,900 lb (6,750 kg).

SHORT
SHORT BROTHERS & HARLAND LTD

HEAD OFFICE, WORKS AND AERODROME:
Queen's Island, Belfast 3, N Ireland

OTHER FACTORIES:
Newtownards (2), Castlereagh, Belfast (2)

LONDON OFFICE:
Berkeley Square House, Berkeley Square, W1

CHAIRMAN:
Air Marshal Sir Edouard Grundy, KBE, CB

MANAGING DIRECTOR:
P. F. Foreman

DIRECTORS:
D. S. Scoffham (Sales)
F. F. H. Charlton
D. W. G. L. Haviland, CB
Dr Llewellyn Smith, CBE
J. F. Mallabar
T. L. Metcalfe
C. C. Simpson

SECRETARY:
E. W. A. Woolmer, BA, FCA

GENERAL MANAGER, AIRCRAFT DIVISION:
H. Gomes

COMMERCIAL AND ADMINISTRATIVE MANAGER:
D. N. B. McCandless

SKYVAN DIVISION MANAGER:
A. F. C. Roberts

CHIEF TEST PILOT:
D. B. Wright

PUBLIC RELATIONS:
R. R. Rodwell

First manufacturer of aircraft in the United Kingdom, the original firm of Short Brothers was established at Leysdown in 1909, with a contract to build six Wright biplanes. It later transferred its works to Rochester.

In June, 1936, Short Brothers, in collaboration with Harland & Wolff Ltd, the well-known ship-builders, formed a new company known as Short & Harland Ltd to build aircraft in Belfast.

In 1947, in accordance with Government policy,

Short & Harland Ltd purchased the undertaking of Short Brothers (Rochester & Bedford) Ltd and concentrated its activities at Belfast. Consequently, Short & Harland Ltd altered its name to Short Brothers & Harland Ltd.

In 1954 the Bristol Aeroplane Co, Ltd acquired a financial interest in Short Brothers & Harland Ltd. With the subsequent acquisition of the Bristol Aeroplane Co by Rolls-Royce, Short Brothers & Harland is now owned by the British Government, Rolls-Royce and Harland & Wolff, with the Government holding the controlling interest.

The company's current products include the Belfast heavy transport, which is in service with RAF Air Support Command, and a turboprop STOL light transport, the Skyvan, which was developed as a private venture and is now in use throughout the world for passenger, freight, survey, military and miscellaneous operations.

Development flying of the SC.1 VTOL research aircraft (see 1968-69 *Jane's*) continues.

In addition to this work, Shorts are collaborating with Fokker-VFW, Messerschmitt-Bölkow-Blohm and VFW-Fokker in the design and production of the F.28 Fellowship jet transport, with responsibility for the wings; and they hold a contract worth over £5 million from the Avco Corporation of Nashville, Tennessee, to produce ailerons, spoilers, wingtips and landing gear doors for the Lockheed L-1011 TriStar. During 1967, Shorts began the design and manufacture of pods for Rolls-Royce jet engines, and now have an £18 million agreement for podding the RB.211 turbofan engines which Rolls-Royce are supplying to power the Lockheed TriStar. Deliveries of engines podded by Shorts, direct to Lockheed at Palmdale, began in the early Summer of 1970. To cope with their involvement in the TriStar programme, Shorts have installed some of Europe's most advanced facilities for the hot-forming of titanium and the manipula-

tion of high-temperature creep-resistant alloys. They are producing M45H turbofan pods for the VFW-Fokker VFW 614 transport aircraft. Production of fuselage components for the Boeing 747, under an £800,000 contract awarded in 1969, began early in 1970.

In addition to their activities in the field of piloted aircraft, Shorts are engaged on missile development and production, as described in the "Military Missiles" section and production of supersonic target drones.

SHORT SC.5/10 BELFAST
RAF designation: Belfast C.Mk 1

The SC.5/10 Belfast military transport was designed specifically for the carriage of heavy freight, including the largest types of guns, vehicles, guided missiles and miscellaneous loads with which the RAF and the British Army are concerned. It has "beaver-tail" rear loading doors capable of permitting the unhindered passage of any load that the fuselage can contain.

As a troop transport, the Belfast can carry more than 200 men, after fitting the removable upper floor for which provision can be made in the basic transport. As a missile carrier it is able to carry all types of guided weapons, from strategic offensive missiles to light support weapons. Small missiles such as the Thunderbird and Bloodhound can be crated and stowed in quantity. RAF Belfasts have been much used carrying helicopters in quantity between the UK and theatres overseas, and have carried the largest-ever payloads of any RAF aircraft.

Design started in February 1959. Construction of the first Belfast began in October 1959 and this aircraft flew for the first time on 5 January 1964. The second Belfast flew on 1 May 1964. These aircraft formed part of an order for 10 for RAF Air Support Command. The first was delivered to No 53 Squadron, at RAF Brize Norton, on 20 January 1966. Production has now ended, but modification of Belfasts continues at Shorts' works.

In June 1966 a Belfast (XR364) became the largest aircraft yet to make a fully automatic landing, using the Autoland system, at RAE Bedford. In January 1970 the Belfast became the world's first military transport cleared for "hands-off" automatic landings in fully-operational conditions.

A detailed description of the Belfast appeared in the 1969-70 *Jane's*.

TYPE: Four-engined heavy transport.

POWER PLANT: Four 5,730 ehp Rolls-Royce Tyne RTy.12 turboprops, each driving a Hawker Siddeley type 4/7000/6 fully-feathering propeller with four aluminium alloy blades, diameter 16 ft (4·88 m). Fuel in three integral tanks in each wing, with capacities (inner to outer) of 2,865, 1,860 and 425 Imp gallons (13,024, 8,455 and 1,932 litres) respectively. Total fuel capacity 10,300 Imp gallons (46,822 litres). Refuelling point in port landing gear fairing. Usable oil capacity 2¾ Imp gallons (12·5 litres) per engine. Provision for flight refuelling probe over flight deck.

ACCOMMODATION: Crew of four on flight deck, plus air quartermaster. Basically a freighter, with simple conversion to carry 150 troops in trooping role. Provision of a complete upper deck increases accommodation to 250 troops. Air-conditioned and pressurised throughout. "Beaver-tail" rear loading doors and large door on port side at forward end of hold. Passenger door on each side immediately forward of ramp. Floor provided with lashing points of 10,000 lb (4,540 kg) and 25,000 lb (11,340 kg) capacity, arranged in standard 20 in (50·8 cm) grid and stressed to carry most of the largest military vehicles without the use of load-spreaders. Loads which cannot be driven into hold can be taken on board by winch and a system of roller conveyers.

DIMENSIONS, EXTERNAL:

Wing span	158 ft 9½ in (48·42 m)
Wing chord at root	24 ft 6 in (7·47 m)
Wing chord at tip	6 ft 7 in (2·01 m)
Wing aspect ratio	10·22
Length overall	136 ft 5 in (41·69 m)
Height over tail	47 ft 0 in (14·30 m)
Tailplane span	65 ft 0 in (19·81 m)
Wheel track	19 ft 4 in (5·89 m)
Wheelbase	48 ft 11½ in (14·91 m)
Passenger doors (port and stbd, rear):	
Height	6 ft 4 in (1·93 m)
Width	2 ft 10½ in (0·88 m)
Height to sill	5 ft 4 in (1·63 m)
Main rear entrance over ramp:	
Height (ramp horizontal)	10 ft 0 in (3·05 m)
Width	12 ft 0 in (3·66 m)
Height to sill	5 ft 4 in (1·63 m)
Freight door (port, front):	
Height	6 ft 6 in (1·98 m)
Width	8 ft 0 in (2·44 m)
Height to sill	5 ft 4 in (1·63 m)

DIMENSIONS, INTERNAL:

Hold:	
Length, incl ramp	84 ft 4 in (25·70 m)
Max width	16 ft 1 in (4·90 m)
Max height	13 ft 5 in (4·09 m)
Volume	11,000 cu ft (311·5 m³)

AREAS:

Wings, gross	2,466 sq ft (229 m²)
Ailerons (total)	141·9 sq ft (13·19 m²)
Trailing-edge flaps (total)	487·4 sq ft (45·29 m²)
Spoilers (total)	36·65 sq ft (3·40 m²)
Fin	376·5 sq ft (34·97 m²)
Rudder, including tab	119·3 sq ft (11·08 m²)
Tailplane	741·5 sq ft (68·89 m²)
Elevators, including tabs	230·0 sq ft (21·37 m²)

Short Belfast C. Mk 1 heavy military transport (**XR369** *Spartacus*) of No 53 Squadron, RAF Air Support Command (*Stephen P. Peltz*)

WEIGHTS AND LOADINGS:

Basic operating weight	127,000 lb (57,600 kg)
Max payload	78,000 lb (35,400 kg)
Max T-O weight	230,000 lb (104,300 kg)
Max zero-fuel weight	205,000 lb (93,000 kg)
Max landing weight	215,000 lb (97,520 kg)
Max wing loading	93·2 lb/sq ft (455·1 kg/m²)
Max power loading	10·03 lb/hp (4·55 kg/hp)

PERFORMANCE (at max T-O weight):

Never-exceed speed
269 knots (310 mph; 500 km/h) EAS up to 24,000 ft (7,300 m); Mach 0·65 above 24,000 ft (7,300 m)

Max cruising speed at 200,000 lb (90,720 kg) AUW   306 knots (352 mph; 566 km/h)

Econ cruising speed at 200,000 lb (90,720 kg) AUW at 24,000 ft (7,300 m)
292 knots (336 mph; 540 km/h)

Stalling speed at max landing weight
98 knots (112 mph; 180 km/h)

Rate of climb at S/L   1,060 ft (323 m)/min

Service ceiling   30,000 ft (9,145 m)

Service ceiling, one engine out, at 180,000 lb (81,650 kg) AUW   26,000 ft (7,925 m)

T-O to 35 ft (10·7 m) (BCAR balanced field length)   7,200 ft (2,195 m)

Landing from 50 ft (15 m) at max landing weight   5,000 ft (1,525 m)

Landing run at max landing weight
3,500 ft (1,065 m)

Range with max fuel, 20% reserve
4,600 nm (5,300 miles; 8,530 km)

Range with max payload, 20% reserve
870 nm (1,000 miles; 1,610 km)

SHORT SC.7 SKYVAN

Design of the SC.7 Skyvan was started as a private venture in 1959, and construction of the first prototype began in 1960. This aircraft (G-ASCN) flew for the first time on 17 January 1963, with two 390 hp Continental GTSIO-520 piston-engines, and completed its flight trials by mid-1963. It was then re-engined with 520 shp Astazou II turboprops and first flew in its new form on 2 October 1963.

In February 1964, Shorts received authorisation from the British government to proceed with production of the Skyvan. An initial batch of 20 was laid down, and the first of these flew on 29 October 1965, with 730 eshp Astazou XII turboprop engines. In April 1966 a further batch of 30 Skyvans was laid down.

The following versions of the Skyvan have been announced:

Skyvan Srs 1 and Srs 1A. Designation of first prototype, as described above, with Continental (Srs 1) and later with Astazou II engines (Srs 1A).

Skyvan Srs 2. Designation of three development aircraft (G-ASCO/ASZI/ASZJ) and initial production version, with Astazou XII engines as described above. Early in 1967 it was announced that Srs 2 Skyvans fitted with these engines could not meet performance specifications under hot and high altitude conditions and that an alternative power plant was being considered. On 26 May 1967 this was named as the AiResearch TPE 331-201, which now powers the current civil Srs 3 and military Srs 3M production versions. Production of the Srs 2 has now ended, and several of those originally ordered as Srs 2's have subsequently been re-engined to Srs 3 standard. The first eight Skyvans each have a total fuel capacity of 175 Imp gallons (796 litres). This was increased to 225 Imp gallons (1,024 litres) in Srs 2 Skyvans from the ninth aircraft onward. A full description of the Srs 2 appeared in the 1968-69 *Jane's*.

Skyvan Srs 3. Current civil production version, described in detail below. Superseded Srs 2 in production in 1968. First Skyvan Srs 3 to fly was the second development aircraft, G-ASZI, which had been equipped originally with Astazous. The first flight with AiResearch engines was made on 15 December 1967, and a second machine (G-ASZJ) re-engined with TPE 331's flew on 20 January 1968.

Skyvan Srs 3M. Military version of Srs 3, with Bendix RDR-100 weather radar in nose radome and modified internal equipment as described below. Prototype (G-AXPT) flew for the first time early in 1970. Suitable for paratrooping and supply dropping, assault landing,

Short Skyvan Series 3 light utility transport (two 715 shp AiResearch TPE 331-201 turboprop engines) in the insignia of the Canadian operator Selkirk Air

troop transport, casualty evacuation, staff transport, and vehicle or ordnance transport. Initial order for two placed in February 1969 by the Austrian Air Force, and one ordered in Spring 1970 by the Sultan of Muscat & Oman's Air Force).

In addition to the above models, Shorts released details in May 1969 of an executive version of the Skyvan, accommodating nine passengers. This has four fully-reclining armchairs, one three-seat and one two-seat couch, cocktail cabinet, desk, galley unit and baggage space.

Total orders for Skyvans had reached 37 (including three Srs 3M's) by 7 July 1970, of which 33 had been delivered. In February 1970 the Skyvan became the first aircraft to be certificated under the British Air Registration Board's new Civil Airworthiness Requirements for STOL operations. One aircraft, for the Royal Air Flight of Nepal, is being fitted out as a VIP transport.

The description below applies to the standard civil Srs 3 and military Srs 3M in current production.

TYPE: Light civil or military STOL utility transport.

WINGS: Braced high-wing monoplane. Wing section NACA 63A series (modified). Thickness/chord ratio 14%. Dihedral 2° 2'. Incidence 2° 30'. Light alloy structure consisting of a two-cell box with wing skins made up of a uniform outer sheet bonded to a corrugated inner sheet. All-metal single-slotted ailerons. Geared tabs on port and starboard ailerons, with manual trim on starboard aileron. All-metal single-slotted flaps. Provision for sintered leading-edge de-icing system.

FUSELAGE: Light alloy structure. Nose and crew cabin section is of conventional skin-stringer design. Elsewhere, the fuselage structure consists of double-skin panels (flat outer sheets bonded to inner corrugated sheets), stabilised by frames.

TAIL UNIT: Cantilever all-metal two-spar structure, with twin fins and rudders. Fixed-incidence tailplane. Geared trim-tabs in outer elevators and rudders. Provision for sintered leading-edge de-icing system.

LANDING GEAR: Non-retractable tricycle type. Single wheel on each unit. Main units carried on short sponsons. Electro-Hydraulics oleo-pneumatic shock-absorbers. Main wheel tyres size 11·00-12, pressure 40 lb sq/in (2·81 kg/cm²). Steerable nose-wheel, tyre size 7·50-10, pressure 40 lb/sq in (2·81 kg/cm²). Hydraulically-operated disc brakes, with differential braking for steering. Provision for fitting skis and low-pressure tyres.

POWER PLANT: Two 715 shp Garrett AiResearch TPE 331-201 turboprop engines, each driving a Hartzell HC-B3TN-5/T10282H three-blade variable-pitch propeller of 8 ft 6 in (2·59 m) diameter. Fuel in four tanks in pairs on top of fuselage between wing roots, each pair consisting of one tank of 40 Imp gallons (182 litres) capacity and one of 106·5 Imp gallons (484 litres) capacity. Total fuel capacity of 293 Imp gallons (1,332 litres). Provision for increase in total fuel capacity to 400 Imp gallons (1,818 litres) by installing four specially-designed tanks in spaces between fuselage frames on each side, beneath main fuel tank. Oil capacity 1·7 Imp gallons (7·73 litres).

ACCOMMODATION: Crew of one, with provision for two. Accommodation (Srs 3) for up to 19 passengers, or 12 stretcher patients and attendants, or 4,600 lb (2,085 kg) of freight, vehicles or agricultural equipment. Srs 3M can accommodate 22 equipped troops; 16 paratroopers and a despatcher; 12 stretcher cases and two medical attendants, or 5,000 lb (2,270 kg) of freight. It carries its own lightweight vehicle loading ramps and has a one-piece military door which leaves the fuselage threshold entirely clear of appendages. Executive version provides luxury accommodation and equipment for nine passengers. Full-width rear loading door and forward door on each side of crew compartment. Rear door can be opened in flight to permit the parachuting of loads up to 4 ft 6 in (1·37 m) in height. Cockpit and cabin heated by engine bleed air mixed with fresh air from intake in nose. Cabin unpressurised. Some aircraft fitted with Rolamat cargo loading equipment.

SYSTEMS: Hydraulic system, pressure 2,500 lb/sq in (175 kg/cm²), operates flaps and wheel brakes. No pneumatic system. Electrical system utilises two busbars, operating independently, each connected to a 28V 125A DC starter-generator, a battery and a 115V 400 c/s static inverter. General services are 28V DC; some radio and instruments 115V AC.

ELECTRONICS AND EQUIPMENT: Radio optional. Typical installation for operations in Europe and USA consists of duplicated VHF, duplicated VOR/ILS, marker beacon and ADF. Provision for HF, DME, transponder, autopilot and weather radar. Blind-flying instrumentation standard.

EQUIPMENT (Srs 3M): Bendix RDR-100 weather radar, with nose radome; a port-side blister

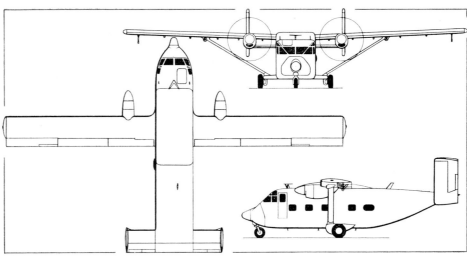

Short Skyvan, military Series 3M version with nose radome

Prototype Skyvan Series 3M military transport aircraft

window for an air despatcher; two anchor cables for parachute static lines; a guard rail beneath the tail to prevent control surface fouling by the static lines; inward-facing paratroop seats with safety nets; parachute signal light; mounts for NATO-type stretchers; and roller conveyors for easy loading and paradropping of pallet-mounted supplies.

DIMENSIONS, EXTERNAL:

Wing span	64 ft 11 in (19·79 m)
Wing chord (constant)	5 ft 10 in (1·78 m)
Wing aspect ratio	11
Length overall:	
civil Srs 3	40 ft 1 in (12·21 m)
military Srs 3M	41 ft 4 in (12·60 m)
Height over tail	15 ft 1 in (4·60 m)
Tailplane span	17 ft 4 in (5·28 m)
Wheel track	13 ft 10 in (4·21 m)
Wheelbase	14 ft 10 in (4·52 m)
Propeller ground clearance	5 ft 0 in (1·52 m)
Crew and passenger doors (fwd, port and stbd):	
Height	5 ft 3 in (1·60 m)
Width	1 ft 8 in (0·51 m)
Height to sill	3 ft 9 in (1·14 m)
Rear loading door:	
Height	6 ft 6 in (1·98 m)
Width	6 ft 6 in (1·98 m)
Height to sill	2 ft 6 in (0·76 m)

DIMENSIONS, INTERNAL:

Cabin, excluding flight deck:	
Length	18 ft 7 in (5·67 m)
Max width	6 ft 6 in (1·98 m)
Max height	6 ft 6 in (1·98 m)
Floor area	120 sq ft (11·15 m²)
Volume	780 cu ft (22·05 m³)

AREAS:

Wings, gross	373 sq ft (34·65 m²)
Ailerons (total)	32·3 sq ft (3·00 m²)
Trailing-edge flaps (total)	63·1 sq ft (5·86 m²)
Fins	82·0 sq ft (7·62 m²)
Rudders, including tabs	26·0 sq ft (2·42 m²)
Tailplane	81·0 sq ft (7·53 m²)
Elevators, including tabs	39·0 sq ft (3·62 m²)

WEIGHTS AND LOADINGS (with 293 Imp gallons = 1,332 litres of fuel):

Basic operating weight:	
civil Srs 3	7,289 lb (3,306 kg)
military Srs 3M	7,400 lb (3,356 kg)
Typical operating weight as freighter:	
civil Srs 3	7,600 lb (3,447 kg)
military Srs 3M	7,620 lb (3,456 kg)
Typical operating weight with passengers or troops:	
civil Srs 3	8,100 lb (3,674 kg)

military Srs 3M	8,330 lb (3,778 kg)
Max payload for normal T-O weight:	
civil Srs 3	4,600 lb (2,086 kg)
military Srs 3M	5,000 lb (2,267 kg)
Max payload for overload T-O weight:	
military Srs 3M	6,000 lb (2,721 kg)
Max T-O and landing weight:	
civil Srs 3, normal	12,500 lb (5,670 kg)
military Srs 3M, normal	13,500 lb (6,123 kg)
military Srs 3M, overload	14,500 lb (6,577 kg)
Max wing loading:	
civil Srs 3	33·5 lb/sq ft (163·6 kg/m²)
military Srs 3M	36·2 lb/sq ft (176·7 kg/m²)

PERFORMANCE (at max T-O weight, with 293 Imp gallons = 1,332 litres of fuel):

Max permissible diving speed	
2·0 knots (277 mph; 445 km/h) EAS	
Max cruising speed at 10,000 ft (3,050 m):	
max cont power	
175 knots (201 mph; 323 km/h) TAS	
cruise power	
168 knots (193 mph; 311 km/h) TAS	
Econ cruising speed at 10,000 ft (3,050 m)	
150 knots (173 mph; 278 km/h) TAS	
Stalling speed, flaps down:	
civil Srs 3 60 knots (69 mph; 111 km/h) TAS	
military Srs 3M	
63 knots (72 mph; 116 km/h) TAS	
Rate of climb at S/L:	
civil Srs 3	1,640 ft (500 m)/min
military Srs 3M	1,520 ft (463 m)/min
Service ceiling (100 ft = 30 m/min climb):	
civil Srs 3	22,500 ft (6,858 m)
military Srs 3M	21,000 ft (6,400 m)
Service ceiling, one engine out (50 ft = 15 m/min climb):	
civil Srs 3	12,500 ft (3,810 m)
military Srs 3M	10,000 ft (3,050 m)
T-O run, STOL, unfactored:	
civil Srs 3	850 ft (259 m)
military Srs 3M	770 ft (235 m)
T-O run (normal):	
civil Srs 3 (BCAR)	1,680 ft (512 m)
T-O to 50 ft (15 m), STOL, unfactored:	
civil Srs 3	1,260 ft (384 m)
military Srs 3M	1,250 ft (381 m)
T-O to 50 ft (15 m):	
civil Srs 3 (BCAR, normal)	2,000 ft (610 m)
civil Srs 3 (BCAR, STOL)	1,580 ft (482 m)
civil Srs 3 (FAR Pt 23)	1,600 ft (488 m)
Landing from 50 ft (15 m):	
civil Srs 3 (BCAR, normal)	2,040 ft (622 m)
civil Srs 3 (BCAR, STOL)	1,860 ft (567 m)

civil Srs 3 (FAR Pt 23)   1,480 ft (451 m)
military Srs 3M (STOL, unfactored)
                             1,390 ft (424 m)
Landing from 30 ft (9 m):
civil Srs 3 (STOL, unfactored)
                             1,150 ft (351 m)
civil Srs 3 (BCAR, STOL)   1,640 ft (500 m)

Landing run:
military Srs 3M (STOL, unfactored)
                             690 ft (210 m)
Range with max fuel at long-range cruising
speed, 45 min reserves:
civil Srs 3   577 nm (665 miles; 1,070 km)
military Srs 3M 573 nm (660 miles; 1,062 km)

Range (typical freighter) at long-range cruising
speed, 45 min reserves:
civil Srs 3 with 4,000 lb (1,814 kg) payload
                          159 nm (184 miles; 296 km)
military Srs 3M with 5,000 lb (2,268 kg)
payload   144 nm (166 miles; 267 km)

SLINGSBY

HEAD OFFICE AND WORKS:
Kirkbymoorside, Yorkshire

OFFICERS: See "Sailplanes" section

In addition to its activities as a sailplane design and manufacturing company, Slingsby Aircraft Co Ltd had in recent years undertaken work on powered aircraft.

On behalf of film companies, Slingsby built a series of ·83-scale S.E.5A replicas based on the Currie Wot airframe (see 1968-69 *Jane's*), and two replicas of the Rumpler C IV (1969-70 *Jane's*).

The company was also commissioned by Central American Manufacturing Company in the USA to build a prototype of their unique Camco V-Liner advertising aircraft (see 1969-70 *Jane's*), but work on this was subsequently abandoned.

Late in 1969 the assets of Slingsby Aircraft Co Ltd were acquired by Vickers Ltd after the former company had been placed in the hands of a receiver. Under its earlier title of Slingsby Sailplanes Ltd it has now resumed the manufacture of sailplanes, and these activities are described in the appropriate section of this edition.

TAYLOR

Mrs. JOHN F. TAYLOR

ADDRESS: 25, Chesterfield Crescent, Leigh-on-Sea, Essex SS9 5PD

The late Mr John Taylor, AMIED, an amateur constructor, designed and built the prototype of a single-seat ultra-light sporting monoplane. His object was to produce the airframe for a cost of not more than £100. Its size was governed by the fact that it had to be built in a room measuring 16 ft × 11 ft, and the fuselage and wings had to be passed through an upstairs window after completion. Construction took about 14 months, and it flew for the first time in June 1960.

Plans of the Taylor Monoplane have been made available to amateur constructors and many sets have been sold to customers in the United Kingdom, the United States, Canada, Australia, South Africa, Finland and New Zealand.

Aircraft currently flying and under construction are fitted with a variety of engines, including the 40 hp Aeronca E 113, 65 hp Continental A65, 65 hp Lycoming and 72 hp two-stroke McCulloch. Aircraft with the 65 hp engines have a 4 in (10 cm) longer nose and 10 in (25 cm) longer rear fuselage to maintain the correct CG position.

A second design by Mr Taylor, named the Titch, was awarded second prize in the Midget Racer Design Competition organised by Mr Norman Jones of the Rollason company in 1964. A prototype was built and flown successfully, but crashed on 16 May 1967, killing its designer.

Mrs J. F. Taylor is continuing to market plans of both these aircraft to amateur constructors.

TAYLOR MONOPLANE J.T.1

The prototype of this small fully-aerobatic single-seat monoplane was designed for, and originally fitted with, a British-built JAP engine. The basically-similar US Aeronca E.113 engine is equally suitable and the design can be modified slightly to take 65 hp Continental and Lycoming engines. Any of the modified Volkswagen engines now on the market can also be fitted and the prototype was, in fact, re-engined with the latest type of 1,500cc Ardem engine, by Rollason Aircraft, in the Spring of 1964. It has also been fitted with a one-piece sideways-hinged (to starboard) windscreen-canopy assembly.

The first Taylor Monoplane completed overseas was built by Mr Hugh Beckham, of Wichita, Kansas. Named *Fifinella*, it originally had a 30 hp converted Volkswagen engine and flew for the first time on 8 August 1964. With a max T-O weight of 640 lb (290 kg), it has a cruising speed of 105 mph (169 km/h), and take-off and landing run of 600 ft (183 m). No flaps are fitted.

A description of it in its latest form, with a 56 hp Porsche engine, appears in the Addenda.

TYPE: Single-seat ultra-light monoplane.

WINGS: Cantilever low-wing monoplane. Wing section RAF 48. Constant chord. Dihedral on outer panels 4°. Wood two-spar structure, comprising centre-section and outer panels. Plywood and fabric covering. Differential ailerons. Split trailing-edge flaps.

FUSELAGE: Conventional plywood-covered wood structure of four main longerons and curved formers. Centre-section integral with fuselage.

TAIL UNIT: Cantilever fin and tailplane are plywood-covered wood structures. Elevators and rudder are fabric-covered wood structures.

LANDING GEAR: Non-retractable two-wheel type. Cantilever main legs, with coil-spring shock-absorption. Wheels fitted with tail-wheel tyres from an Avro Anson aircraft. Leaf-spring tail-skid with steerable skid-pad.

POWER PLANT: One 38 hp JAP two-cylinder horizontally-opposed air-cooled engine, driving a modified Flottorp two-blade wood fixed-pitch propeller. Fuel tank aft of firewall, capacity 6 Imp gallons (27 litres).

Taylor J. T. 1 Monoplane built by Mr James Fordyce of Fielding, New Zealand, with VW engine and fuselage 10 in longer than standard

Taylor Monoplane built by Mr Yvan Bougie of Valleyfield, Quebec, powered by a Volkswagen engine
(Howard Levy)

ACCOMMODATION: Single seat under transparent Perspex canopy. Aerobatic harness. Small locker aft of seat.

DIMENSIONS, EXTERNAL:
Wing span	21 ft 0 in (6·40 m)
Wing aspect ratio	6
Length overall	15 ft 0 in (4·57 m)
Height over tail	4 ft 10 in (1·47 m)
Tailplane span	6 ft 6 in (1·98 m)

AREAS:
Wings, gross	76 sq ft (7·06 m²)
Ailerons (total)	8 sq ft (0·74 m²)
Fin	1·48 sq ft (0·14 m²)
Rudder	4·56 sq ft (0·42 m²)
Tailplane	6 sq ft (0·56 m²)
Elevators	5·75 sq ft (0·51 m²)

WEIGHTS AND LOADINGS:
Weight empty	410 lb (186 kg)
Max T-O weight	620 lb (281 kg)
Max wing loading	8 lb/sq ft (39 kg/m²)
Max power loading	16 lb/hp (78 kg/hp)

PERFORMANCE:
Max level speed at S/L	91 knots (105 mph; 169 km/h)
Max never-exceed speed	113 knots (130 mph; 209 km/h)
Cruising speed	78 knots (90 mph; 145 km/h)
Never-exceed speed with flaps down	56 knots (65 mph; 105 km/h)
Stalling speed, flaps up	40 knots (46 mph; 75 km/h)
Stalling speed, flaps down	33 knots (38 mph; 62 km/h)
Rate of climb at S/L	950 ft (290 m)/min
Range	200 nm (230 miles; 370 km)

TAYLOR J.T.2 TITCH

Construction of the prototype Titch was started in February 1965 and it flew for the first time on 22 January 1967.

Many flight tests indicated that the prototype was pleasant to fly as an aerobatic aircraft. The stall was found to occur at a very high angle of attack and to be straightforward, with no wing drop and a height loss of only 50 ft (15 m).

Several more examples of the Titch have been completed or are in the course of construction in the USA, Canada, France and the UK.

The following details apply to the prototype. The example built and flown by Mr Z. H. Graves of Littleton, Colorado, USA, has a 65 hp Lycoming engine.

TYPE: Single-seat light monoplane.

WINGS: Cantilever low-wing monoplane. Taylor-modified NACA 23012 wing section. Dihedral 5° on top surface. Incidence 3° 30′. Spruce structure with main box-spar and "plank" auxiliary spar. Plywood and fabric covering. Plain manually-operated ply-covered flaps over half-span and fabric-covered differential ailerons.

FUSELAGE: All-wood structure, with four main longerons, four secondary longerons and double-curvature ply covering. Aluminium cockpit side-panels.

TAIL UNIT: All-wood structure, with fixed-incidence tailplane. Fixed surfaces plywood-covered, control surfaces fabric-covered.

LANDING GEAR: Non-retractable tail-wheel type. Steerable tail-wheel. Chrome-vanadium compression spring shock-absorbers. Wheels of own manufacture, with tyres size 5 × 4 and two expanding shoe brakes per wheel.

POWER PLANT: One 85 hp Continental C85-12F four-cylinder horizontally-opposed air-cooled engine, driving a Hegy wooden two-blade scimitar propeller, diameter 5 ft 0 in (1·52 m). Glass-fibre fuel tank between firewall and instrument panel, capacity 10 Imp gallons (45·5 litres).

ACCOMMODATION: Single seat, with aerobatic harness, under bubble canopy hinged along starboard side.

DIMENSIONS, EXTERNAL:
Wing span	18 ft 9 in (5·72 m)
Wing chord at root	4 ft 6 in (1·37 m)
Wing chord at tip	3 ft 0 in (0·91 m)
Wing aspect ratio	5·14
Length overall	16 ft 1½ in (4·91 m)
Height overall	4 ft 8 in (1·42 m)
Tailplane span	6 ft 6 in (1·98 m)
Wheel track	5 ft 0 in (1·52 m)

AREAS:
Wings, gross	68 sq ft (6·32 m²)
Ailerons (total)	7·00 sq ft (0·65 m²)
Trailing-edge flaps (total)	3·40 sq ft (0·32 m²)
Fin	1·53 sq ft (0·14 m²)
Rudder	2·70 sq ft (0·25 m²)
Tailplane	4·60 sq ft (0·43 m²)
Elevators	4·70 sq ft (0·44 m²)

Taylor J.T.2 Titch single-seat light aircraft (85 hp Continental C85-12F engine)

WEIGHTS (A = Continental or Lycoming engine, B = Volkswagen engine):
Weight empty:
A	455 lb (206 kg)
B	410 lb (185 kg)

Max T-O weight:
A	710 lb (322 kg)
B	640 lb (290 kg)

PERFORMANCE (prototype, except where indicated):
Normal cruising speed
    135 knots (155 mph; 250 km/h)
Econ cruising speed
    95·5 knots (110 mph; 177 km/h)

Best approach speed
    65 knots (75 mph; 121 km/h)
Stalling speed, flaps up:
  Continental engine
    52 knots (59 mph; 95 km/h)
  VW engine 46 knots (53 mph; 86 km/h)
Stalling speed, flaps down:
  Continental engine
    42 knots (48 mph; 78 km/h)
  VW engine 40 knots (46 mph; 74 km/h)
Unstick speed 54 knots (62 mph; 100 km/h)
Touchdown speed 48 knots (55 mph; 89 km/h)
Rate of climb at S/L 1,100 ft (335 m)/min

WALLIS

WALLIS AUTOGYROS LTD

HEAD OFFICE:
121, Chesterton Road, Cambridge

DIRECTORS:
Wing Cdr K. H. Wallis, CEng, AFRAeS
G. V. Wallis
P. M. Wallis

By adopting a completely new design approach to the mechanical details of the single-seat ultra-light autogyro, Wing Cdr Wallis has produced a much-refined aircraft which can be flown quite safely "hands and feet off". The Wallis prototype (G-ARRT, flown for first time in August 1961) introduced many patented features, including a rotor head with offset gimbal system to provide hands and feet off stability and to eliminate pitch-up and "tuck-under" hazards; a high-speed flexible rotor spin-up shaft with positive disengagement during flight; an automatic system of controlling rotor drive on take-off which allows power to be applied until the last moment; centrifugal stops to control rotor blade teetering; and a novel safe starting arrangement.

A pre-production development of G-ARRT, known as the WA-116, was produced by Beagle Aircraft Ltd in 1962 for evaluation by the British Army, and was described and illustrated in the 1963-64 *Jane's*. G-ARRT was used for all initial strain-gauge testing and handling trials, and a Certificate of Airworthiness was granted in August 1962. Owing to the use of an uncertificated engine, intended originally for target drone applications, the C of A is necessarily restricted.

The WA-116 is not readily suitable for fitment of a fully-certificated engine and this design will, therefore, be built only for special requirements, for operation by the manufacturer and selected users.

The design was amended and simplified, retaining the well-proven structural integrity of the prototype, as the WA-116-A, in an attempt to meet world-wide requests from amateur constructors wishing to build an autogyro of Wallis design. However, after a most careful study the company has decided that amateur construction is unlikely to reach a sufficiently high standard of airworthiness, even when key components are factory made and fully airworthy. It has decided, therefore, that amateur construction of such craft is not in the public interest, and that no requests for plans, parts or assistance can now be entertained.

The aircraft now intended for full certification is the WA-117, an advanced design powered by a 100 hp Rolls-Royce/Continental O-200-B engine. Under development are a very high-performance light autogyro, known as the WA-118 Meteorite, and an experimental model known as the WA-119, with a modified motor car engine.

WALLIS WA-116 AGILE AND WA-116-T

The pre-production prototype WA-116, built by Beagle Aircraft Ltd, flew for the first time on 10 May 1962. Its max certificated T-O weight is 550 lb (250 kg), but the prototype Wallis

Wallis WA-116 autogyro, with SFIM recorder on port undercarriage leg, after altitude record attempt

autogyro, G-ARRT, has been flown at an AUW of 655 lb (297 kg), carrying a useful load of 420 lb (190 kg).

A standard Wallis WA-116 (G-ARZB) was modified and fitted with dummy armament (see 1969-70 *Jane's*) for use in the James Bond film *You only live twice*.

On 11 May 1968 the prototype WA-116, G-ARRT, more than doubled the previous world altitude record for autogyros. The attempt was made with the prototype in its original form, except for the addition of a pilot's cockpit nacelle. An altitude of 15,220 ft (4,639 m) was attained before the flight was terminated due to the cold and the need to conserve fuel for descent through cloud. World records in Class E3 (all autogyros) and E3a (autogyros under 500 kg) were confirmed by the FAI. G-ARRT has since been fitted with a Wallis-modified 90 hp McCulloch engine for further attempts on world speed, distance and altitude records. On 12 May 1969 it attained a speed of 96·5 knots (111 mph; 179 km/h) which made the WA-116 also the fastest autogyro in the world.

A WA-116-T two-seat trainer version has been developed, to allow dual control training and pilot conversion. Using a very close tandem

seating arrangement, only the rudder pedals need to be duplicated, other controls being usable by either front or rear pilot. An extension control column has now been provided, to give comfortable dual control of this item. The prototype (G-AXAS) has no cockpit nacelle, but it is anticipated that production models would be so equipped. Basic weight is similar to that of the single-seater and, with a 90 hp Wallis-McCulloch engine, good performance is retained. Flights during the past year have been made carrying a 230 lb (104 kg) passenger.

The **WA-116-A** is similar to the WA-116 but is simplified.

TYPE: Single-seat ultra-light autogyro.

ROTOR SYSTEM: Two-blade teetering autorotative rotor, built of wood, with metal reinforcing and with considerable internal mass balance. Blade section changes toward inboard stations. Offset-gimbal rotor head designed from the outset for a rotor spin-up drive, combined with rotor brake and tacho-generator drive. Centrifugal teeter stops to restrict teetering during spin-up while permitting safe teetering for all flight conditions. Blades do not fold.

ROTOR DRIVE: Initial rotor spin-up only, by flexible shaft and engine clutch.

FUSELAGE: Basic structure of aluminium alloy tube, with cockpit nacelle.

TAIL UNIT: Fin and rudder are hollow plywood-covered structures, finished in Madapolam.

LANDING GEAR: Non-retractable tricycle type. Main legs have compression spring shock-absorption. Nose unit has compression rubber shock-absorption. Drum brake on all three wheels. All tyres size 260 × 85 mm, pressure 25 lb/sq in (1·76 kg/cm²). Alternatively, 8·00 × 2 tyres may be fitted to all three wheels for use on relatively smooth ground. On very rough ground, size 300 × 100 tyres are recommended for main wheels.

POWER PLANT: One 72 hp McCulloch Model 4318A four-cylinder horizontally-opposed air-cooled two-stroke engine, mounted aft of rotor pylon and driving a two-blade propeller diameter 3 ft 10 in (1·17 m). Fuel tank aft of pilot, capacity 8 Imp gallons (36 litres).

ACCOMMODATION: Single seat in cockpit nacelle. Trainer version has dual seating in tandem and dual rudder pedals. Radio optional.

DIMENSIONS, EXTERNAL:
- Diameter of rotor: 20 ft 4 in (6·20 m)
- Length of fuselage, to nose of nacelle: 11 ft 1 in (3·38 m)
- Length of fuselage, including pitot-static source: 12 ft 4 in (3·76 m)
- Width, rotors and wheels folded: 3 ft 0 in (0·91 m)
- Height to top of rotor head: 6 ft 1 in (1·85 m)
- Wheel track: 5 ft 4 in (1·63 m)
- Wheelbase: 3 ft 6 in (1·07 m)

DIMENSIONS, INTERNAL:
- Cockpit nacelle: Length: 4 ft 8 in (1·42 m)
  - Max width: 1 ft 6 in (0·46 m)
  - Max height: 3 ft 0 in (0·91 m)

AREAS:
- Rotor blades (each): 10 sq ft (0·93 m²)
- Rotor disc: 324 sq ft (30·1 m²)
- Fin: 3 sq ft (0·28 m²)
- Rudder: 4 sq ft (0·37 m²)

WEIGHTS:
- Weight empty, equipped: 255 lb (116 kg)
- Max certificated T-O weight: 550 lb (250 kg)

PERFORMANCE (at AUW of 500 lb = 227 kg):
- Max level speed at S/L: 100 knots (115 mph; 185 km/h)
- Max cruising speed at S/L: 69 knots (80 mph; 129 km/h)
- Econ cruising speed at S/L: 52 knots (60 mph; 97 km/h)
- Max rate of climb at S/L: 1,350 ft (410 m)/min
- Service ceiling: over 10,000 ft (3,050 m)
- T-O run: under 90 ft (27 m)

Wallis WA-116-T two-seat trainer prototype (90 hp Wallis-McCulloch engine)

- T-O to 50 ft (15 m): 300 ft (91 m)
- Landing from 50 ft (15 m): 210 ft (64 m)
- Landing run: 10 ft (3 m)
- Range with standard fuel: 121 nm (140 miles; 225 km)
- Range with max payload: 78 nm (90 miles; 145 km)

WALLIS WA-117

The WA-117 is an advanced model of the Wallis Autogyro, employing proven features of the WA-116 airframe and powered by a 100 hp Rolls-Royce/Continental O-200-B flat-four engine. Construction of an experimental test vehicle (G-ATCV) began in 1964 and this aircraft began flight trials in March 1965.

A pre-production prototype WA-117 (G-AVJV) has been flying since May 1967, and a third machine has also flown.

The WA-117, in its definitive form, will be available with a fully-enclosed cockpit and other new design features resulting from the operation of Wallis autogyros in all parts of the world, under extreme conditions of climate and terrain.

By the Spring of 1970, development of the WA-117 was virtually completed; production of the aircraft was still under discussion.

Under construction in early 1970 was a version with a Rolls-Royce/Continental O-240 engine, known provisionally as the WA-117-S. This is not, at present, intended for production, but will be used by Wg Cdr Wallis for record attempts and other work.

A two-seat dual-control trainer version is also being designed.

WALLIS WA-118 METEORITE

Design of the WA-118 Meteorite was started in April 1965. Construction began in October 1965 and it flew for the first time on 6 May 1966. It is intended for a long-term test programme, with the emphasis on high-speed and high-altitude research.

The 120 hp Italian Meteor Alfa engine of this research aircraft has been brought up to the latest modification standards during the past year, and has been further modified by Wallis Autogyros Ltd to fit it for autogyro operation.

A second Meteorite airframe (G-AVJW) has been built, and this aircraft made its first flight with a modified Meteor Alfa 1 engine on 9 August 1969; flight tests will continue on an opportunity basis. All available details of the WA-118 were given in the 1967-68 edition of *Jane's*.

WALLIS WA-119 IMP

The WA-119 is an experimental autogyro, powered by a much-modified version of the water-cooled, ohc Hillman Imp motor car engine, and has a performance adequate for short field operation. Development is proceeding at low priority, but the WA-119 is not intended for commercial exploitation.

WARD

M. WARD

ADDRESS:
4 Eagle Road, North Scarle, Lincs

Mr M. Ward, a joiner by trade and a keen aero-modeller, has designed and built an exceptionally small single-seat monoplane, named the Gnome, to which he holds the exclusive rights for construction and the sale of drawings. It has been registered G-AXIE during the past year and is operated on a Permit to Fly basis by its current owner, who is believed to have replaced the original power plant by a Sachs-Wankel engine.

Design of the Gnome began in April 1966 and construction on 5 June 1966. First flight was made on 4 August 1967 after an earlier "lift-off" by Mr Ward. He is planning to build an improved version of this aircraft.

Ward Gnome single-seat ultra-light aircraft (14 hp Douglas motor-cycle engine)

WARD P46 GNOME

TYPE: Single-seat ultra-light aircraft.

WINGS: Braced low-wing monoplane with single bracing strut on each side. Wing section Clark Y. Thickness/chord ratio 12½%. Dihedral 3°. Incidence 2°. All-wood structure with box spars, D-section leading-edge box and built-up ribs. Wooden ailerons. No trim-tabs. No flaps. Wings detachable for transit.

FUSELAGE: All-wood structure, with four basic longerons of $\frac{3}{4}$ in square section and $\frac{3}{4}$ in by $\frac{3}{8}$ in diagonals. Formers constructed of $\frac{1}{2}$ in and $\frac{1}{4}$ in plywood. Curved top decking. Entire structure covered with $\frac{1}{16}$ in plywood skin.

TAIL UNIT: All-wood cantilever structure. Fixed-incidence tailplane. Tailplane and fin have $\frac{1}{16}$ in plywood skins. Elevators and rudder are fabric-covered. No trim-tabs.

LANDING GEAR: Non-retractable tail-wheel type. Main gear of steel tube with rubber-in-compression shock-absorption. Go-Kart wheels and tyres, size 4·00 × 5, pressure 16 lb/sq in (1·12 kg/cm²). No brakes.

POWER PLANT: Originally one 14 hp Douglas two-cylinder horizontally-opposed air-cooled motor-cycle engine of 1925 vintage, driving a fixed-pitch two-blade wooden propeller, diameter 3 ft 10 in (1·17 m), with spinner. One plastic fuel tank in forward fuselage, capacity 1 Imp gallon (4·5 litres). Refuelling point in top of fuselage nose decking, forward of windscreen. Oil capacity 4 Imp pints (2·27 litres).

ACCOMMODATION: Single seat in open cockpit.

DIMENSIONS, EXTERNAL:
- Wing span: 15 ft 9 in (4·80 m)
- Wing chord at root: 4 ft 0 in (1·22 m)
- Wing chord at tip: 3 ft 0 in (0·91 m)
- Wing aspect ratio: 2
- Length overall: 11 ft 6 in (3·51 m)
- Width, wing detached: 2 ft 10 in (0·86 m)
- Height overall: 4 ft 6 in (1·37 m)
- Tailplane span: 6 ft 0 in (1·83 m)
- Wheel track: 4 ft 0 in (1·22 m)
- Wheelbase: 6 ft 6 in (198 m)

DIMENSIONS, INTERNAL:
- Cockpit:
  - Length: 3 ft 6 in (1·07 m)
  - Max width: 1 ft 9 in (0·53 m)
  - Floor area: 5·9 sq ft (0·55 m²)

AREAS:
- Wings, gross: 49 sq ft (4·55 m²)
- Ailerons (total): 6 sq ft (0·56 m²)
- Fin: 1·5 sq ft (0·14 m²)
- Rudder: 4 sq ft (0·37 m²)
- Tailplane: 6 sq ft (0·56 m²)
- Elevators: 7 sq ft (0·65 m²)

WEIGHTS AND LOADING:
- Weight empty: 210 lb (95 kg)
- Max T-O and landing weight: 380 lb (172 kg)
- Max wing loading: 7·75 lb/sq ft (37·8 kg/m²)

PERFORMANCE (Douglas engine, at max T-O weight at height of 10 ft = 3·05 m):
- Max level speed: 48 knots (55 mph; 88·5 km/h)
- Cruising speed: 43 knots (50 mph; 80·5 km/h)
- Stalling speed: 26 knots (30 mph; 49 km/h)
- Rate of climb: approx 300 ft (91 m)/min
- T-O run: 600 ft (183 m)
- Landing run: 300 ft (91 m)
- Range: approx 43 nm (50 miles; 80 km)

WARD EAGLET

Mr Ward has reached the preliminary design stage of a new project known as the Eaglet, although further development had been deferred temporarily early in 1970 owing to pressure of other work. As envisaged at that time, the design of the Eaglet was for a single-seat high-wing monoplane with a fully-enclosed cabin and powered by a 1,300 cc Volkswagen engine. Wing span is 22 ft 0 in (6·71 m), length 15 ft 6 in (4·72 m) and wing area 80 sq ft (7·43 m²). Max design T-O weight of the Eaglet is 720 lb (326 kg), and max wing loading 9 lb/sq ft (43·9 kg/m²).

WESTLAND
WESTLAND AIRCRAFT LTD

HEAD OFFICE, WORKS AND AERODROME:
Yeovil, Somerset
LONDON OFFICE:
8, The Sanctuary, Westminster, SW1
CHAIRMAN:
E. C. Wheeldon, CBE, CEng, FIProdE, FRAeS, FInstD
VICE-CHAIRMAN:
Sir Eric Mensforth, CBE, MA, Hon DEng, CEng, FIMechE, FRAeS, FIProdE
CHIEF EXECUTIVE:
D. C. Collins, CBE, CEng, FIMechE, FIProdE, FRAeS
FINANCE DIRECTOR:
W. Oppenheimer, FCA
COMMERCIAL DIRECTOR:
B. D. Blackwell, MA, BSc(Eng), CEng, FIMechE, FRAeS
DIRECTORS:
The Rt Hon Lord Aberconway

WESTLAND HELICOPTERS LTD

HEAD OFFICE, WORKS AND AERODROME:
Yeovil, Somerset
CHAIRMAN:
D. C. Collins, CBE, CEng, FIMechE, FIProdE, FRAeS
MANAGING DIRECTOR:
G. S. Hislop, PhD, BSc, CEng, ARCST, FIMechE, FRAeS, FRSA
ASSISTANT MANAGING DIRECTOR (FINANCE):
W. Oppenheimer, FCA

YEOVIL DIVISION

CHIEF DESIGNER: V. A. B. Rogers

WORKS MANAGER: F. Martin

Helicopters in current production at this headquarters division of Westland include the Wessex

L. Boddington, CBE, MF, CEng, FIMechE, FRAeS
SECRETARY:
A. R. B. Hobbs, FACCA

Westland Aircraft Ltd was formed in July 1935, to take over the aircraft branch of Petters Ltd, previously known as the Westland Aircraft Works, which had been engaged in aircraft design and construction since 1915.

Westland entered the helicopter industry in 1947 by acquiring the licence to build the Sikorsky S-51, of which it produced 133 under the name Westland Dragonfly. This technical association with Sikorsky has continued, and it was decided subsequently to concentrate the company's resources on the design, development and construction of helicopters.

In 1959, Westland acquired Saunders-Roe Ltd. In 1960, it further acquired the Helicopter Division of Bristol Aircraft Ltd and Fairey Aviation Ltd, as a result of which it is the only major organisation engaged in helicopter design

ASSISTANT MANAGING DIRECTOR (WORKS):
H. W. D. Winkworth, CEng, FIProdE

ASSISTANT MANAGING DIRECTOR (COMMERCIAL):
B. D. Blackwell, MA, BSc(Eng), CEng, FIMechE, FRAeS

SALES DIRECTOR:
M. H. C. Gordon, CEng, FRAeS

ENGINEERING DIRECTOR:
J. Speechley, DCAe, CEng, FRAeS

60, with twin turbine power plants; the Agusta-Bell 47G-3B, which is built under licence for the British Army as the Sioux, and the Sikorsky Sea King, which is being produced under licence for the Royal Navy. Under development is the new WG.13 twin-turbine light utility helicopter, which is the subject of an Anglo-French

and manufacture in the United Kingdom.

As from 1 October 1966, the company's helicopter business has been conducted through a new wholly-owned company named Westland Helicopters Ltd.

Through the British Hovercraft Corporation Ltd, Westland is continuing development of the Hovercraft type of vehicle pioneered by Saunders-Roe, in association with the National Research Development Corporation.

One of Westland's subsidiary companies, Normalair-Garrett Ltd, specialises in the design, development and production of aircraft pressure control, air-conditioning and oxygen breathing systems. Able to supply complete aircraft installations, Normalair-Garrett Ltd is recognised as the foremost European authority in this field. All British pressurised aircraft, both civil and military, use Normalair-Garrett equipment, as do many aircraft of foreign design. In addition, this latter company produces data loggers, trace readers and hydraulic equipment for aircraft flying controls.

FINANCE DIRECTOR:
A. R. B. Hobbs, FACCA

WORKS DIRECTOR:
D. D. G. Frankland

RESEARCH DIRECTOR:
J. P. Jones, PhD, BSc(Eng), CEng, FRAeS

Westland Helicopters Ltd is responsible for all the helicopter business of the Westland Group. Its current products are described below.

joint programme. Production of the turbine-engined Whirlwind Series 3 (see 1969-70 *Jane's*) ended in the Summer of 1969.

Stemming from earlier projects, designated WE-01 and WE-02, Westland has moved to a range of convertible rotorcraft projects which could meet present inter-city VTOL requirements.

WESTLAND WESSEX

The Wessex is a turbine-powered development of the Sikorsky S-58. Ten versions were produced, and details of these can be found in the 1969-70 *Jane's*. A full structural description appeared in the 1968-69 edition.

Only the Wessex 60 remained in production in 1970.

Wessex Mk 60. Civil development of Mk 2, with two coupled Rolls-Royce Bristol Gnome turboshaft engines. Designed to carry 10 passengers to airline standards, up to 16 for aerial work duties, or eight stretcher patients, two sitting casualties and a medical attendant, or 15 survivors in a rescue role. Eleven delivered to Bristow Helicopters Ltd. Details below apply to this version.

DIMENSIONS, EXTERNAL:
Diameter of main rotor — 56 ft 0 in (17·07 m)
Diameter of tail rotor — 9 ft 6 in (2·90 m)
Length overall — 65 ft 9 in (20·03 m)
Length of fuselage — 48 ft 4½ in (14·74 m)
Length, blades and tail folded — 38 ft 6 in (11·73 m)
Width, rotors folded — 13 ft 4 in (4·06 m)
Height to top of rotor hub — 14 ft 5 in (4·39 m)
Height overall — 16 ft 2 in (4·93 m)
Wheel track — 12 ft 0 in (3·66 m)

Cabin door: Height — 4 ft 0 in (1·22 m)
Width — 4 ft 0 in (1·22 m)
Height to sill — approx 3 ft 0 in (0·91 m)

DIMENSIONS, INTERNAL:
Main cabin: Length — 13 ft 8 in (4·16 m)
Max width — 5 ft 6 in (1·68 m)
Max height — 6 ft 0 in (1·83 m)

AREAS:
Main rotor blades (each) — 38·25 sq ft (3·55 m²)
Tail rotor blades (each) — 2·90 sq ft (0·27 m²)
Main rotor disc — 2,463 sq ft (228·8 m²)
Tail rotor disc — 71 sq ft (6·60 m²)

WEIGHTS AND LOADING:
Weight empty, equipped — 8,657 lb (3,927 kg)
Max T-O weight — 13,600 lb (6,169 kg)

PERFORMANCE (at max T-O weight):
Max level speed at S/L — 116 knots (133 mph; 214 km/h)
Max cruising speed — 105 knots (121 mph; 195 km/h)
Max rate of climb at S/L — 1,540 ft (470 m)/min
Vertical rate of climb at S/L — 620 ft (190 m)/min
Service ceiling — 10,000 ft (3,050 m)
Range with standard fuel — 290 nm (334 miles; 538 km)

WESTLAND SEA KING

The Sea King was developed by Westland to meet the Royal Navy's requirement for an advanced anti-submarine helicopter with prolonged endurance. In addition to this, it is capable of fulfilling the alternative primary rôles of MCM (mine counter-measures) and air-to-surface strike. The Sea King can also undertake a number of secondary rôles, including search and rescue, tactical troop transport, casualty evacuation, cargo carrying and long-range self-ferry. Other rôles are under consideration, and Westland has proposed a lightweight land-based general-purpose version capable of carrying a 9,600 lb (4,355 kg) payload over a 22 nm (25 mile; 40 km) radius with normal fuel reserves.

The Sea King development programme stemmed from a licence agreement for the S-61 helicopter concluded originally with Sikorsky in 1959. This permitted Westland to utilise for the Royal Navy Sea King the basic airframe and rotor system of the Sikorsky SH-3D, of which a description can be found in the US section. Considerable changes have been made in the power plant and in specialised equipment, to meet British requirements.

The fuselage is essentially similar to that of the basic Sikorsky aircraft, and is of the watertight-

Westland Wessex Mk 60 twin-turbine utility helicopter in service with Bristow Helicopters Ltd

hull type which allows water landing in an emergency. The main landing gear, which is retractable, is housed in sponsons braced to the fuselage by fixed struts. To improve the lateral stability and flotation capability of the helicopter with the rotor stopped, inflatable buoyancy bags are fitted to the outside of each sponson.

To meet Royal Navy specific requirements, the Sea King is powered by two Rolls-Royce Bristol Gnome H.1400 turboshaft engines, which feature the full authority electronic engine governing system currently fitted to Gnome 1200 engines. This provides precise control of rotor speed in steady-state and transient manoeuvres.

A £24 million order for Sea Kings for the Royal Navy was placed in 1967, and a pattern aircraft was imported from the USA for conversion to Sea King prototype standard as XV370. Four sets of components were also imported, and assembled by Westland as pre-production aircraft.

The first production Sea King HAS Mk 1 (XV642) was flown for the first time on 7 May 1969 and by the Summer of 1969 six production aircraft had been delivered to RNAS Culdrose to equip the Royal Navy's first Sea King unit, No 700S Intensive Flying Trials Squadron, which was commissioned on 19 August 1969. On 23 April 1969 HMS *Blake* was commissioned after conversion to the rôle of command helicopter cruiser. It is intended that she will accommodate eventually a squadron of four Sea Kings.

The first operational Sea King squadron was No 824, and a second squadron, No 826, was due to be commissioned in June 1970.

On 20 June 1969 Westland announced a further order, worth £15 million, to supply 22 Sea Kings to the Federal German Navy, primarily for search and reconnaissance duties. Four have also been ordered for the Indian Navy, for anti-submarine duties, with two more on option.

POWER PLANT: Two 1,500 shp (max cont rating 1,250 shp) Rolls-Royce Bristol Gnome H.1400 turboshaft engines, as described above. Standard fuel system has a maximum capacity of 704 Imp gallons (3,200 litres), contained in bag tanks beneath the cabin floor, arranged to provide two completely independent main systems and an auxiliary system. The system may be pressure or gravity refuelled and defuelled and provision is made for fuel jettison. An increased-capacity system of 818 Imp gallons (3,719 litres) is available, involving the addition of an extra underfloor tank. An externally-mounted long-range system, comprising two 100 Imp gallon (454·5 litre) tanks, is also available, and one or two long-range ferry tanks can be accommodated in the main cabin. Each of these has a maximum fuel capacity of 1,500 lb (680 kg), but as this system utilises cabin space it is intended primarily for the self-ferry rôle.

SYSTEMS: Three main hydraulic systems. Primary and auxiliary systems operate main rotor control. Utility system (3,000 lb/sq in = 210 kg/cm²) for main landing gear, sonar and rescue winches, blade folding and windscreen wipers. Electrical system includes two 20kVA 200V three-phase 400 c/s engine-driven generators, a 26V single-phase AC

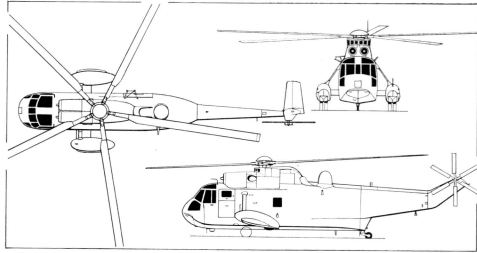

Westland Sea King multi-purpose helicopter (two Rolls-Royce Bristol Gnome H.1400 engines)

supply fed from the aircraft's 22Ah nickel-cadmium battery through an inverter, and DC power provided as a secondary system from two 200A transformer-rectifier units.

OPERATIONAL EQUIPMENT (ASW model): As equipped for this rôle, the Sea King is a fully-integrated all-weather hunter-killer weapons system, capable of operating independently of surface vessels, and has the following equipment and weapons to achieve this task: Plessey Type 195 dipping sonar, AW.96 Doppler navigation system, AW.391 search radar in dorsal radome and AW.391 transponder beneath rear fuselage, STR.70 radio altimeter, Sperry Mk 7B compass system, Louis Newmark Mk 31 automatic flight control system, two No 4 marine markers, four No 2 Mk 2 smoke floats, up to four Mk 44 homing torpedoes, or four Mk 11 depth charges or one Clevite simulator. Observer/navigator has tactical display on which sonar contacts are integrated with search radar and navigational information. Radio equipment comprises AN-ARC.52 UHF and homer, Ultra D.403 standby UHF, HF radio, Ultra UA.60M intercom, Telebrief system and IFF provisions. For secondary rôle a mounting is provided on the aft frame of the starboard door for a general-purpose machine-gun. The Mk 31 AFCS provides radio altitude displays for both pilots; artificial horizon displays; three-axis stabilisation in pilot-controlled manoeuvres; attitude hold, heading hold and height hold in cruising flight; controlled transition manoeuvres to and from the hover; automatic height control and plan position control in the hover; and an auxiliary trim facility.

OPERATIONAL EQUIPMENT (MCM model): This model retains the Doppler navigation system and large ground-stabilised radar system of the ASW version, and carries a five-man crew

comprising two pilots, two crewmen and a radar operator/observer. Special MCM equipment includes a tow boom, tow winch, and Vermoor sweeping gear which, with its associated dual winch and gear stowage, enables the Sea King to achieve a higher sweep rate than is possible by surface vessels. Measures under development will also permit shallow-moored or acoustic mines to be destroyed by an aircraft using specialised mine-sweeping equipment. The addition of air-to-surface missiles on this and other versions greatly increases the attack potential of the helicopter.

OPERATIONAL EQUIPMENT (Search and rescue and transport models): Sea Kings equipped for search and rescue retain the Doppler and, optionally, search radar, and have in addition a Breeze BL.10300 variable-speed hydraulic rescue hoist of 600 lb (272 kg) capacity mounted above the starboard-side cargo door. Automatic main rotor blade folding and spreading is standard with this version, and for shipboard operation the tail pylon can also be folded. With search radar fitted, a total of 22 survivors and medical staff can be carried; this total can be increased to 25 if the search radar is omitted. In the casualty evacuation rôle, the Sea King can accommodate up to 12 stretchers and two medical attendants, or intermediate combinations of seats and stretchers; a typical layout might provide for 16 seats and two stretchers. In the troop transport rôle, the Sea King can accommodate 25 troops, with the majority of seats at 17·5 in (70 cm) pitch, and can carry this load over a range of 400 nm (460 miles; 737 km) under ISA sea level conditions. As a cargo transport, the aircraft has an internal capacity of 6,000 lb (2,720 kg) or a max external load capacity of 8,000 lb (3,630 kg) when a low-response sling is fitted.

Westland Sea King HAS. Mk 1 anti-submarine helicopter for the Royal Navy, equipped with four homing torpedoes

DIMENSIONS, EXTERNAL:
Diameter of main rotor   62 ft 0 in (18·90 m)
Diameter of tail rotor   10 ft 4 in (3·16 m)
Length overall (rotors turning)
                           72 ft 8 in (22·15 m)
Length of fuselage (incl tail rotor)
                           57 ft 2 in (17·42 m)
Length overall (rotors folded)
                           55 ft 9¾ in (17·01 m)
Length overall (rotors and tail folded)
                           47 ft 3 in (14·40 m)
Height overall (rotors turning)
                           16 ft 10 in (5·13 m)
Height overall (rotors spread and stationary)
                           15 ft 11 in (4·85 m)
Height to top of rotor hub
                           15 ft 6 in (4·72 m)
Width overall (rotors folded):
  with flotation bags   16 ft 4 in (4·98 m)
  without flotation bags   15 ft 8 in (4·77 m)
Wheel track (c/l of shock struts)
                           13 ft 0 in (3·96 m)
Cabin door (port):
  Height   5 ft 6 in (1·68 m)
  Width   3 ft 0 in (0·91 m)
Cargo door (stbd):
  Height   5 ft 0 in (1·52 m)
  Width   5 ft 8 in (1·73 m)
  Height to sill   3 ft 9 in (1·14 m)
DIMENSIONS, INTERNAL:
Cabin: Length   19 ft 3 in (5·87 m)
  Max width   6 ft 6 in (1·98 m)
  Max height   6 ft 3½ in (1·92 m)
WEIGHTS   (A=anti-submarine,   B=MCM,
C=missile/ASW, D=missile/troops, E=troop
transport, F=search and rescue, G=casualty
evacuation, H=lightweight version, I=internal
cargo):
Basic weight:
  A, E, F, G, I   12,700 lb (5,760 kg)
  B   14,406 lb (6,534 kg)
  C   16,384 lb (7,431 kg)
  D   15,583 lb (7,068 kg)
  H   10,750 lb (4,876 kg)
Weight, empty, equipped:
  A   15,474 lb (7,019 kg)
  B   15,431 lb (6,999 kg)
  C   16,999 lb (7,710 kg)
  D   16,198 lb (7,347 kg)
  E   12,491 lb (5,666 kg)
  F   13,784 lb (6,253 kg)
  G   14,418 lb (6,540 kg)
  H   12,228 lb (5,545 kg)
  I   13,430 lb (6,092 kg)
Max T-O weight (all)   21,500 lb (9,751 kg)
PERFORMANCE (at AUW of 20,500 lb=9,298
kg, ISA):
Max permissible diving speed
                  124 knots (143 mph; 230 km/h)
Normal operating speed
                  113 knots (131 mph; 211 km/h)
Max endurance speed
                  75 knots (86 mph; 138 km/h)
Max rate of climb at S/L, 1,770 ft (540 m)/min
Max rate of climb at S/L, one engine out
                           324 ft (99 m)/min
Approved ceiling   10,000 ft (3,050 m)
Ferry/transit range (MCM model):
  standard fuel   600 nm (690 miles; 1,110 km)
  auxiliary fuel 700 nm (805 miles; 1,295 km)
Max self-ferry range, with max internal and
  external fuel at 5,000 ft (1,525 m)
                  960 nm (1,105 miles; 1,778 km)

WESTLAND WG.13

The WG.13 is one of three types of aircraft
covered by the Anglo-French helicopter agreement which was first proposed in February 1967
and confirmed on 2 April 1968. Westland has
design leadership in the WG.13, which is a
medium-sized helicopter intended to fulfil general-
purpose, naval and civil transport rôles. Its
partner in the programme is Aérospatiale.
Five development aircraft are being built,
plus two airframes for ground testing. The
semi-rigid main rotor was to be test-flown on a
Scout helicopter during the Summer of 1970.
The first WG.13 was expected to fly in
late 1970/early 1971. Initial production will be
concentrated upon the following versions:
All-weather general-purpose version for the
British Army, with advanced avionics;
Advanced frigate-borne anti-submarine search
and strike versions for the Royal Navy (as a
Wasp replacement) and French Navy, with
armament of two homing torpedoes or other
weapons, carried on sides of fuselage. Two of
this version have also been ordered for the Argentine Navy.
In addition, a training version for the Royal
Air Force is proposed. The projected armed
reconnaissance version for the French Army (see
1969-70 Jane's) has been cancelled.
To meet the military requirements of the two
countries, it is anticipated that production of the
WG.13 will total several hundreds of aircraft.
Westland also plans to market civil models of
the general-purpose version, including an eight-
seat executive transport version.
The following details apply generally to the two
basic military versions, except where stated
otherwise.
TYPE: Twin-engined multi-purpose helicopter.
ROTOR SYSTEM: Single four-blade semi-rigid main

Artist's impression of the Royal Navy anti-submarine version of the WG.13, with homing torpedoes

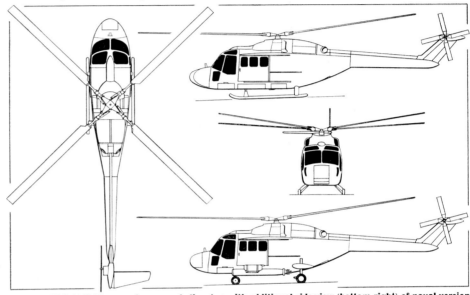

Westland WG.13 light general-purpose helicopter, with additional side view (bottom right) of naval version

rotor and four-blade tail rotor. Main rotor
blades, which are interchangeable, are of
cambered aerofoil section and embody mass
taper. Each blade consists of a two-piece
two-channel stainless steel D-shaped box-spar,
to which is bonded a glass-fibre reinforced
plastic rear skin with a plastic honeycomb
core. Blade tips are of moulded glass-fibre
reinforced plastic, with a stainless steel anti-
erosion sheath forward of the 50% chord
line. Each blade is attached to the main rotor
hub by titanium root attachment plates and a
flexible arm; the inboard portion of each arm
accommodates most of the flapping movement
of each blade, while the outer portion provides
freedom in the lag plane. The rotor hub and
inboard portions of the flexible arms are built as
a complete unit, in the form of a titanium
monobloc forging. Each of the tail rotor
blades has a light alloy spar, machined integrally with the root attachment, which forms
the nose portion of the aerofoil section and has
a flush-fitting stainless steel sheath on the
leading-edge. Rear section of each blade is of
similar construction to that of main rotor
blades. The tail rotor hub has conventional
flapping and feathering hinges, and incorporates
torsionally flexible tie bars which carry the
centrifugal loads inboard to the flapping hinges.
Each tail rotor blade is attached to the hub
by the outboard tie bar pin and a six-bolt root
end flanged joint. Main rotor brake is fitted as
standard. Main rotor blades of both versions,
and tail section of naval version, can be folded
for stowage.
ROTOR DRIVE: Power from each engine is passed
via the first-stage reduction of the main gearbox, which utilises two involute-form spiral
bevel pinions and gears to transmit vertical
drive to the main rotor. Each of these first-
stage outputs is coupled to the main rotor
shaft through individual conformal pinions,
one meshing on each side of a large output
gear. By this means, power is supplied to the
main shaft at two diametrically-opposed points,
producing a balanced drive. There is an accessory gearbox drive shaft from each of the spiral
bevel gears. Free-wheel units are mounted
in each engine/gearbox shaft, and also within
the accessory drive chain of gears. Rotor head
controls are actuated by three identical servo-
jacks, trunnion-mounted from the main rotor
gearbox. The collective jack is mounted
centrally on the forward gearbox, with the

cyclic jacks positioned at 45° on each side.
Autostabiliser valves are incorporated on
the jack bodies. Cyclic and collective inputs
from the three control jacks are translated to
the lower bearing housing of a four-armed
spider which is located within, and rotates
with, the main rotor shaft. The spider is
mounted universally within a splined section
of the main shaft, above its bearing housing,
and is linked to the blade pitch-change levers
by four adjustable-length track rods. Provision is made for in-flight blade tracking. A
full-authority rotor speed governing system is
employed, pilot control being limited to
selection of the desired rotor speed range. In
the event of an engine failure, this system
will restore power up to single-engine maximum
contingency rating to maintain rotor speed
within the prescribed limits. A lock-out free-
wheel unit can be selected manually, to isolate
the main rotor transmission from the port
engine input drive. This leaves only the
accessory drive connected, allowing ground
running of accessories without turning the
rotors. On naval version, main rotor can
provide negative thrust to increase stability
on deck after touchdown. Tail rotor drive
is taken from the main gearbox by a conformal
pinion and through a spiral bevel gear to the
tail shaft. A conventional rotor brake is
mounted on the main gearbox at the tail
drive shaft coupling, the shaft continuing aft
to the intermediate and final tail rotor gearboxes. Pitch variation of the tail rotor blades
is controlled by a spider, actuated by hydraulic
jack via a shaft which extends through the
centre of the tail rotor gearbox.
FUSELAGE AND TAIL UNIT: Conventional semi-
monocoque pod-and-boom structure of light
alloy, including a cantilever floor structure
with unobstructed surface. The forward end is
free from bulkheads, giving an unrestricted field
of view. Large windows in each of the side
sliding doors. Provision for internally-
mounted defensive armament, and for universal
flange mountings on each side of the exterior
to carry external stores and weapons. Tail-
boom is a light alloy monocoque structure
bearing the sweptback vertical fin, which has
a half-tailplane on the starboard side.
LANDING GEAR: (utility version): Non-retractable
tubular skid type. Provision for a pair of
adjustable ground handling wheels on rear of
each skid. Flotation gear optional.

Landing Gear: (naval version): Non-retractable tricycle type, with single-wheel main units and twin-wheel nose unit. Designed for high shock-absorption to facilitate take-off from and landing on small decks under severe sea and weather conditions. Flotation gear, and hydraulically-actuated harpoon deck securing system, optional.

Power Plant: Two Rolls-Royce BS.360-07-26 turboshaft engines. Each has a max continuous rating of 750 shp, a take-off and inter-contingency rating of 830 shp and a max contingency rating of 900 shp. Engines are mounted side-by-side on top of the fuselage upper decking, aft of the main rotor shaft and gearbox. Fuel in five bag-type tanks, all within the fuselage structure, comprising two main bag tanks each of 480 lb (218 kg) capacity, two side-by-side collector tanks each of 170 lb (77 kg) capacity, and a 300 lb (136 kg) capacity underfloor tank situated at the forward end of the cabin. Total fuel capacity 1,600 lb (726 kg). Two overload tanks, total capacity 1,600 lb (726 kg), can be carried in the cabin for increased ferry range. Engine oil tank capacity 1·5 Imp gallons (6·82 litres). Main rotor gearbox oil capacity 4 Imp gallons (18·1 litres). Pressure refuelling and fuel jettison capability on general-purpose version. Provision for self-sealing of both collector tanks to provide protection against small-arms fire.

Accommodation: General-purpose version carries crew of one or two pilots, according to role, on side-by-side seats which are adjustable for height. Individual crew entry door on each side. Maximum high-density passenger configuration for one pilot and 12 fully-equipped troops on lightweight bench seats in sound-proofed cabin. Standard bench seating can be removed quickly to permit the carriage of up to 2,471 lb (1,120 kg) of freight internally. Tie-down rings are provided. Alternatively, loads of up to 3,000 lb (1,361 kg) can be carried externally on a freight hook mounted below the cabin floor. In an ambulance role, three standard stretchers and up to three seated casualties (or two plus a medical attendant) can be carried. Naval version will have secondary capability for passenger or supply transport duties, or for air/sea search and rescue. An eight-seat executive transport version is under consideration.

Systems: Two independent hydraulic systems in all versions, with third system in naval version to supply extra ancillary equipment. Pumps are powered by accessory drive from main rotor gearbox, enabling full power to be drawn from both main systems in the event of an engine failure. If either No 1 or No 2 main system fails, the other maintains adequate flying control. Tail rotor operation reverts to mechanical control if No 1 system fails. No pneumatic system. 28V DC electrical power supplied by two engine-driven starter-generators, with 24V 23Ah nickel-cadmium battery for standby use and engine starting. 200V three-phase AC power is available at a nominal 400 c/s from two transmission-driven generators. This feeds the avionics and the anti-icing system, and also provides 28V DC standby supply via a transformer-rectifier. When transmission AC supply is not available for use on the ground, an additional AC power source is supplied from a static inverter powered from the DC system. Printed circuits are employed in all consoles and instrument panels. Design of electrical system permits installation of additional equipment modules. Autostabilisation system standard. Optional cabin heating and ventilation by mixing unit combining engine bleed-air with outside air.

Electronics and Flight Equipment: Main equipment bays are in nose and at rear of cabin. Standard equipment in all versions includes duplex flight stabiliser and autopilot; and in general-purpose version includes windscreen wipers, navigation lights, adjustable landing light, anti-collision beacon, and cabin and engine fire extinguishers. Provision for dual controls on all versions, to customer's requirements. Optional radio/navigation equipment includes Plessey PTR 377 UHF/VHF transceiver, IFF, VHF Omni-Range receiver, Doppler navigation computer and display (including TAS transmitter), Decca Mk 19 flight log, HSI, radio altimeter and crew intercom in all versions; tactical map display (instead of Decca Mk 19) and external intercom system in general-purpose version; and Ultra D 403M standby UHF, Telebrief, search radar and X-band transponder in naval version. Other optional equipment (all versions) includes vortex-type intake and filters, signal pistol and cartridges, Schermuly flare installation and emergency kit.

Armament and Operational Equipment: For search and rescue role, the general-purpose version can be fitted with flotation gear, a waterproof floor, and a 600 lb (272 kg) capacity hoist in the starboard side of the cabin. Hoist can be swung back into the cabin when not in use, permitting the sliding door to be closed. For anti-tank or air-to-surface strike missions, the general-purpose version can be equipped with one 20 mm Hispano Hurricane or AME 621 cannon, one 20 mm GEC Vulcan three-barrelled cannon or two GEC Miniguns mounted inside the cabin; or with external racks on each side of the cabin for a variety of stores, including two Minigun or other self-contained gun pods, two pods of 14 and two of 7 2-in rockets, or up to six AS.11 or four AS.12 or alternative air-to-surface missiles. The general-purpose version can also be equipped for other duties, including fire-fighting and crash rescue, military command post, staff liaison, customs and border control, offshore oil-drilling support, air charter, and pilot and operational training. The naval version can carry out a number of these roles, but has specialised equipment for its primary duties. For the ASW role, this includes two Mk 44 homing torpedoes or alternative weapons, mounted externally one each side of the cabin, and retractable detection/classification gear, with provision for internal stowage of sono-buoys and classified equipment. Radar for surface search can be provided, together with homing missiles for attacking light surface craft; alternatively, AS.12 or similar wire-guided missiles can be employed in conjunction with a stabilised optical sighting system. The naval version is also suitable for carrier plane-guard duties, carrying a rescue winch and one or more frogmen.

Dimensions, external (A=general-purpose version, N=naval version):
Diameter of main rotor 42 ft 0 in (12·80 m)
Diameter of tail rotor 7 ft 3 in (2·21 m)
Main rotor blade chord (constant, each) 1 ft 3½ in (0·39 m)
Tail rotor blade chord (constant, each) 7·1 in (0·18 m)
Length overall, rotors turning 49 ft 9 in (15·16 m)
Length overall:
A, blades folded 41 ft 10¾ in (12·77 m)
N, blades and tail folded 34 ft 0 in (10·36 m)
Length of fuselage, nose to tail rotor centre 38 ft 3¼ in (11·665 m)
Width overall, folded:
A 7 ft 2 in (2·18 m)
N 9 ft 7¾ in (2·93 m)
N, main wheels castored 10 ft 0 in (3·05 m)
Height overall, tail rotor turning:
A 12 ft 0 in (3·66 m)
N 12 ft 3 in (3·73 m)
Height overall, tail rotor stopped:
A 11 ft 3 in (3·43 m)
N 11 ft 6 in (3·505 m)
Height over folded main rotor:
A 10 ft 3 in (3·12 m)
N 10 ft 6 in (3·20 m)
Tail rotor ground clearance:
A 4 ft 9 in (1·45 m)
N 5 ft 0 in (1·52 m)
Skid track (A) 6 ft 8 in (2·03 m)
Wheel track (N) 9 ft 1¼ in (2·775 m)
Wheelbase (N) 9 ft 10¾ in (3·01 m)
Cabin door openings (each):
Mean height 3 ft 11 in (1·19 m)
Mean width 4 ft 6 in (1·37 m)

Dimensions, internal:
Cabin, from back of pilots' seats:
Length 6 ft 9 in (2·06 m)
Max width between doors 5 ft 10 in (1·78 m)
Max width aft of doors 4 ft 7½ in (1·40 m)
Max width at floor 5 ft 7½ in (1·71 m)
Max height 4 ft 8 in (1·42 m)

Weights (A=general-purpose version, N=naval version):
Manufacturer's bare weight empty (A) 5,175 lb (2,347 kg)
Manufacturer's basic weight empty:
A 5,299 lb (2,403 kg)
N 5,712 lb (2,591 kg)
Operating weight empty, equipped:
A, freighter 5,529 lb (2,508 kg)
A, ferry 5,584 lb (2,533 kg)
A, troop transport 5,611 lb (2,545 kg)
A, command post 5,867 lb (2,661 kg)
A, search and rescue 5,927 lb (2,688 kg)
A, ambulance 5,941 lb (2,695 kg)
A, strike (six AS.11) 6,265 lb (2,842 kg)
N, freighter 5,902 lb (2,677 kg)
N, search and rescue 6,670 lb (3,025 kg)
N, strike (two AS.12) 6,739 lb (3,057 kg)
N, anti-submarine 7,487 lb (3,396 kg)
Search and rescue T-O weight:
A 7,527 lb (3,414 kg)
N 8,270 lb (3,751 kg)
Max T-O weight:
A 8,000 lb (3,629 kg)
N 8,550 lb (3,878 kg)
Max overload T-O weight (A, ferry) 8,784 lb (3,984 kg)

Performance (estimated, at max T-O weight, ISA; A=general-purpose version, N= naval version):
Max cruising speed at S/L (A) 160 knots (184 mph; 296 km/h)
Max cruising speed at 16,000 ft (4,875 m) (A) 100 knots (115 mph; 185 km/h)
Max level speed at S/L, one engine out (A) 146 knots (168 mph; 271 km/h)
Econ cruising speed for max range (A) 138 knots (159 mph; 256 km/h)
Endurance speed at S/L (A) 70 knots (81 mph; 130 km/h)
Min speed at S/L, max contingency, one engine out (A) 5 knots (6 mph; 9 km/h)
Max vertical rate of climb at S/L (A) over 1,200 ft (365 m)/min
Max forward rate of climb at S/L (A) over 2,500 ft (762 m)/min
Max forward rate of climb at S/L, one engine out (A) 1,210 ft (369 m)/min
Range at S/L with max fuel and typical mission payload, 5% reserves:
A, with one pilot + 10 passengers 150 nm (173 miles; 278 km)
A, with one pilot + internal cargo load 425 nm (489 miles; 788 km)
A, with one pilot and slung cargo load 300 nm (345 miles; 556 km)
A, as ambulance with two pilots 395 nm (455 miles; 732 km)
Typical radius at S/L with crew of two, fuel for 15 min loiter and 5% reserves:
A, search and rescue 178 nm (205 miles; 328 km)
Typical radius at S/L with crew of two and 5% reserves:
N, anti-submarine (no loiter) 130 nm (150 miles; 241 km)
N, anti-submarine (40 min loiter) 80 nm (92 miles; 148 km)
N, anti-submarine (80 min loiter) 30 nm (34·5 miles; 56 km)

HAYES DIVISION

Works:
Hayes, Middlesex

The current activities of this Division include production of the Wasp and Scout helicopters, developed by Westland's Cowes Division, and of the SA 330 helicopter for the RAF.

WESTLAND/AÉROSPATIALE SA 330 PUMA

In the Spring of 1968, production began of the Aérospatiale SA 330 Puma air-transportable logistic helicopter. One of three new types being manufactured under the 1967 Anglo-French helicopter agreement, the SA 330 is to be supplied to the RAF and also to the French Armed Forces. It is currently in joint production at Westland's Hayes Division and at the Marignane factory of Aérospatiale. French-built components are used in British production, and vice versa. The first joint production SA 330 flew in September 1968. Final assembly of the RAF machines, the first of which are scheduled to enter service in the Autumn of 1970, is undertaken at Hayes.

WESTLAND WASP/SCOUT

The Scout is a compact five/six-seat turbine-powered general-purpose helicopter. Project work on the design was started by the former Saunders-Roe company in November 1957, and the first of two prototypes began ground running less than six months later, on 19 June 1958. It made its first flight on 20 July 1958, and was followed by the second prototype on 30 September 1958.

The prototype (G-APVL) of the production version, designated P.531-2 Mk 1, flew for the first time on 9 August 1959. It was powered by a Rolls-Royce Bristol Nimbus free-turbine engine, which superseded the 400 shp (derated to 325 shp) Blackburn-Turboméca Turmo used in the earlier versions.

The Scout is intended for a variety of military and civil duties, including liaison, light freighting, casualty evacuation, air/sea rescue, reconnaissance, training in turbine techniques and as a weapon carrier. In its passenger-carrying form it has two seats in front and a rear bench-type seat for three persons. In the ambulance rôle, the rear of the cabin is utilised for carrying two stretchers; two further casualties can be carried in external panniers. A lightweight Lucas air-operated hoist can be fitted for rescue operations. Full blind-flying equipment and instruments are available, including autopilot/autostabiliser gear. Cabin heating/demisting and rotor de-icing can be provided. Dual controls and basic flying instrument panels can be fitted for training duties.

The following versions are currently in production and service:

Scout AH.Mk 1. Version for British Army, with 685 shp (derated) Rolls-Royce Bristol Nimbus 101 or 102 turboshaft engine. First pre-production example (XP165) flew on 4 August 1960. First Scout with now-standard powered controls (XP190) flew on 6 March 1961 and the type entered service with the Army in the Spring of 1963. A total of 66 had been built by July 1964, with production continuing. Repeat order for between 35 and 40 aircraft for Army announced in September 1964. Two delivered to Royal Australian Navy for operation from survey ships. Three supplied to Royal

Jordanian Air Force, including one for service as VIP transport for King Hussein. Two sold to Government of Uganda for police work, and two to Bahrain State Police. Production ended early 1970.

Wasp HAS.Mk 1. Version for Royal Navy, developed directly from Scout, with 710 shp (derated) Rolls-Royce Bristol Nimbus 503. Basically as Scout AH.Mk 1, but with folding tail and special landing gear for deck operations. Intended primarily for operation from small platforms on frigates and destroyers in anti-submarine weapon-carrying rôle, the normal load being two Mk 44 torpedoes. Two to be carried by the Navy's new ice patrol ship, for survey, ice reconnaissance and personnel ferrying duties. Also to be employed for search and rescue, training and other subsidiary duties. First Wasp HAS. Mk 1 for Royal Navy flew on 28 October 1962, and deliveries began in second half of 1963. Total of 36 built by July 1964, with production continuing. More than 200 landings made during trials on frigate *Nubian* in February 1963, in all degrees of wind and sea, by day and night. Wasp is fully operational with Royal Navy. Other countries which have Wasps for naval duty are South Africa (10), Brazil (3), New Zealand (3) and the Netherlands (12).

All versions have a constant-speed rotor/turbine control system, with pre-select facility.

The following details apply to both the Wasp HAS.Mk 1 and Scout AH.Mk 1:

TYPE: Five/six-seat general-purpose helicopter.

ROTOR SYSTEM: Four-blade main rotor, with all-metal blades, carried on fully-articulated hub with drag and flapping hinges. Torsion-bar blade-suspension system. Two-blade tail rotor with wooden blades (Scout AH.Mk 1) or metal blades (Wasp HAS.Mk 1) and single central flapping hinge. Main rotor blades fold for stowage. Rotor brake standard.

ROTOR DRIVE: Rotors driven through steel shafting. Primary gearbox at rear of engine, secondary gearbox at base of pylon, angle gearbox at base of fin, tail rotor gearbox at top of fin. Main rotor/engine rpm ratio 1 : 71. Tail rotor/engine rpm ratio 1 : 15.

FUSELAGE : Conventional aluminium alloy stressed-skin structure, manufactured in two main sections. Front section forms the cabin, fuel tank bays and aft compartment. Rear section is a tapered boom terminating in a fin which carries the tail rotor.

TAIL SURFACE: Horizontal stabiliser, of light alloy construction, mounted under rear of tail-boom on Scout; and on starboard side of fin, opposite tail rotor, on Wasp.

LANDING GEAR (Scout AH.Mk 1): Tubular-skid type, with removable ground manoeuvring wheels. Single-acting recoil damper shock-absorption.

LANDING GEAR (Wasp HAS.Mk 1): Non-retractable four-wheel type. All four wheels castor and are carried on Lockheed shock-absorber struts. All wheels and tubeless tyres are Dunlop, size 15 × 4·75-6·5, pressure 60 lb/sq in (4·22 kg/cm²). Dunlop dog clutch brakes. Flotation gear standard.

POWER PLANT: One Rolls-Royce Bristol Nimbus turboshaft engine (see under individual versions above), mounted above fuselage to rear of cabin. Fuel in three interconnected flexible tanks in fuselage below main rotor, with total capacity of 155 Imp gallons (705 litres). Refuelling point on starboard side of decking. Oil capacity 1·5 Imp gallons (7 litres).

ACCOMMODATION: Two seats side-by-side at front of cabin, with bench seat for three persons at rear. Four doors, by front and rear seats on each side of cabin. Rear seats removable for cargo carrying. Heater standard.

SYSTEMS: Delaney Galley/Westland 1kW cabin heating and windscreen demisting system. Hydraulic system, pressure 1,050 lb/sq in (74 kg/cm²), operating servo jacks for rotor head controls and rotor brake. No pneumatic system. 28V DC electrical supply from engine-driven generator. Limited supply by 25Ah or 35Ah battery in Scout, 15Ah or 23Ah battery in Wasp. Three-phase 115V 400 c/s AC provided by inverter.

ELECTRONICS AND EQUIPMENT (Scout AH.Mk 1): PTR.161F and TR.1998A VHF radio and Army B.47/48 radio. Ultra U.A.60 intercom and station box control. Blind-flying instrumentation standard. No special equipment.

ELECTRONICS AND EQUIPMENT (Wasp HAS.Mk 1): PTR.170 and PV.141 UHF and UHF homing radio, and stand-by UHF. Intercom taken from side tone of UHF T/R. Blind-flying instrumentation standard. Equipment includes autostabilisation/autopilot system, with radio altimeter.

Westland Scout helicopter of the British Army (Rolls-Royce Nimbus turboshaft engine)

Westland Wasp HAS. Mk 1 general-purpose helicopter of the Royal Navy

DIMENSIONS, EXTERNAL:

Diameter of main rotor	32 ft 3 in (9·83 m)
Diameter of tail rotor	7 ft 6 in (2·29 m)
Distance between rotor centres	20 ft 5½ in (6·24 m)
Length overall, rotors turning	40 ft 4 in (12·29 m)
Length of fuselage	30 ft 4 in (9·24 m)
Width, rotors folded:	
Scout	8 ft 6 in (2·59 m)
Wasp	8 ft 8 in (2·64 m)
Height to top of rotor hub	8 ft 11 in (2·72 m)
Overall height, tail rotor turning	11 ft 8 in (3·56 m)
Wheel track: Wasp	8 ft 0 in (2·44 m)
Skid track: Scout	8 ft 6 in (2·59 m)
Wheelbase: Wasp	8 ft 0 in (2·44 m)
Cabin doors (fwd, each):	
Height	3 ft 8½ in (1·13 m)
Width	3 ft 1 in (0·94 m)
Height to sill	2 ft 5 in (0·74 m)
Cabin doors (rear, each):	
Height	3 ft 8½ in (1·13 m)
Width	3 ft 6 in (1·07 m)
Height to sill	2 ft 5 in (0·74 m)

DIMENSIONS, INTERNAL:

Cabin: Length	6 ft 0½ in (1·84 m)
Max width	5 ft 1 in (1·55 m)
Max height	4 ft 5 in (1·35 m)

AREAS:

Main rotor blades (each)	15·5 sq ft (1·44 m²)
Tail rotor blades (each)	1·82 sq ft (0·17 m²)
Main rotor disc	816·86 sq ft (75·90 m²)
Tail rotor disc	44·16 sq ft (4·10 m²)
Tailplane:	
Scout	8·23 sq ft (0·76 m²)
Wasp (semi-span)	3·32 sq ft (0·31 m²)

WEIGHTS AND LOADINGS:

Manufacturer's empty weight (Wasp	
	3,452 lb (1,566 kg)
Basic operating weight (Scout)	
	3,232 lb (1,465 kg)

Max payload, external cargo	1,500 lb (680 kg)
Max fuel load (Wasp)	1,240 lb (562 kg)
Max T-O and landing weight:	
Scout	5,300 lb (2,405 kg)
Wasp	5,500 lb (2,495 kg)
Max disc loading:	
Scout	6·48 lb/sq ft (31·64 kg/m²)
Wasp	6·70 lb/sq ft (32·71 kg/m²)

PERFORMANCE (at max T-O weight):

Max level speed at S/L:	
Scout	114 knots (113 mph; 211 km/h)
Wasp	104 knots (120 mph; 193 km/h)
Max permissible diving speed:	
Scout	114·5 knots (132 mph; 212 km/h)
Wasp	109 knots (126 mph; 203 km/h)
Max cruising speed:	
Scout	106 knots (122 mph; 196 km/h)
Wasp	96 knots (110 mph; 177 km/h)
Econ cruising speed:	
Scout	106 knots (122 mph; 196 km/h)
Wasp	96 knots (110 mph; 177 km/h)
Max rate of climb at S/L:	
Scout	1,670 ft (510 m)/min
Wasp	1,440 ft (439 m)/min
Vertical rate of climb at S/L:	
Scout and Wasp	600 ft (183 m)/min
Practical manoeuvring ceiling:	
Scout:	13,400 ft (4,085 m)
Wasp	12,200 ft (3,720 m)
Hovering ceiling in ground effect:	
Wasp	12,500 ft (3,810 m)
Hovering ceiling out of ground effect:	
Wasp	8,800 ft (2,682 m)
Max range with standard fuel (Wasp)	
	263 nm (303 miles; 488 km)

Range with max fuel, including allowances of 5 min for T-O and landing, and 15 min cruising at best cruising height, with 4 passengers:

Scout	273 nm (315 miles; 510 km)
Wasp	234 nm (270 miles; 435 km)

P

WESTON DIVISION

WORKS:
Oldmixon Works, Weston-super-Mare, Somerset

GENERAL MANAGER: E. Gilberthorpe

After completing a programme of Whirlwind conversion work, this Division has undertaken production of Sea King components, and also units for the Britten-Norman Islander (which see) under sub-contract. Joint production with Aérospatiale of the SA 341 Gazelle light military helicopter for the British Army and the French armed forces will also be undertaken by the Weston Division.

Third pre-production (French-built) SA 341 Gazelle helicopter in British Army markings as XW276

THE UNITED STATES OF AMERICA

AAC
AMERICAN AVIATION CORPORATION

HEAD OFFICE:
318 Bishop Road, Cleveland, Ohio 44143

PRESIDENT: Russell W. Meyer, Jr

DIRECTOR OF MARKETING: Larry K. Kelly

SALES MANAGER: Robert L. Staib

PUBLIC RELATIONS MANAGER: R. Stephan Harman

American Aviation Corporation was formed in 1964 to develop, certify and manufacture the AA-1 Yankee (known formerly as the Bede BD-1) a low-cost two-seat sport or utility aircraft, incorporating aluminium honeycomb construction in the fuselage and metal-to-metal bonding throughout the airframe. The AA-1 received FAA Type Certification on 29 August 1967 and is currently in production at the company's manufacturing plant, adjacent to Cuyahoga County Airport, Cleveland, Ohio.

AMERICAN AVIATION AA-1 YANKEE

Design of this two-seat light aircraft was initiated in June 1962, and construction of the prototype began in October of the same year. It was intended to offer low-cost flying by utilising advanced constructional techniques and a simplified design. The prototype flew for the first time on 11 July 1963 and FAA Type Certification was granted on 29 August 1967; an amended Certificate for the production version was issued on 16 July 1968.

First production aircraft flew on 30 May 1968, and a total of 345 had been completed by February 1970.

Details of the production version are as follows:

TYPE: Two-seat sporting or utility monoplane.

WINGS: Cantilever low-wing monoplane. Wing section NACA 64$_2$415 (modified). Dihedral 5°. Incidence 3° 30'. No sweep. Alclad aluminium skin and ribs, attached to main spar by adhesive bonding. Tube-type circular-section main spar serves as integral fuel tank. Plain ailerons of bonded construction, with honeycomb ribs and Alclad aluminium skin. Electrically-actuated plain trailing-edge flaps of bonded construction, with honeycomb ribs and aluminium skin, and RAE Motors Corporation actuators. Ground-adjustable trim-tab on each aileron.

FUSELAGE: Aluminium honeycomb cabin section and aluminium semi-monocoque rear fuselage structure, utilising adhesive bonding. The use of honeycomb eliminates false floors, resulting in greater usable cabin space relative to cross-sectional area.

TAIL UNIT: Cantilever adhesive-bonded all-metal structure. Movable surfaces built up of honeycomb ribs bonded to sheet aluminium. All three fixed surfaces interchangeable. Combined trim and anti-servo tab in starboard elevator.

LANDING GEAR: Non-retractable tricycle type. Nose gear of E6150 tubular steel, with large free-swivelling fork. Main legs are cantilever leaf springs of glass-fibre. US Royal main wheels and tyres Type VI, size 15 × 6.0-6, pressure 26 lb/sq in (1.83 kg/cm²). US Royal nose-wheel tyre Type III LP, size 5.00 × 5, pressure 22 lb/sq in (1.55 kg/cm²). Cleveland single-disc hydraulic brakes. Optional wheel fairings.

POWER PLANT: One 108 hp Lycoming O-235-C2C four-cylinder horizontally-opposed air-cooled engine, driving a McCauley two-blade fixed-pitch propeller, type 1A105/5CM 7157, diameter 5 ft 11 in (1.80 m), with spinner. Two integral fuel tanks in wings, with total capacity of 24 US gallons (91 litres). Refuelling points at wing tips. Oil capacity 1.5 US gallons (5.7 litres).

AAC AA-1 Yankee two-seat sporting or utility aircraft (108 hp Lycoming O-235-C2C engine)

ACCOMMODATION: Two individual seats side-by-side in enclosed cabin, under large transparent sliding canopy. Optional seat for child. Cabin heated and ventilated. Centre console, between seats, accommodates trim wheel, electric flap operating switch and ashtray. Space for 100 lb (45 kg) baggage aft of seats.

SYSTEMS: Hydraulic system for brakes only. Electrical system includes 40A 14V engine-driven alternator and 25Ah battery to supply flap motor, lights, navigation equipment and flight instrumentation.

ELECTRONICS AND EQUIPMENT: Standard equipment includes windshield defroster, cabin heating system, air ventilators, cargo tie-down rings, instrument panel glare shield, ashtray, map holder, glove compartment and removable hat-shelf. Optional items include sensitive altimeter, blind flying instrumentation, engine-driven vacuum pump and suction gauge, eight-day or electric clock, outside air temperature gauge, hour recorder, dual controls, fire extinguisher, pitot heating system, landing light, omniflash beacon, de luxe propeller spinner, canopy sun curtain, tinted windows, cigarette lighter and winterisation kit. Optional electronics include Genave Alpha/200 nav/com 100-channel VHF transceiver; Narco Mk 12B 90-channel VHF transceiver plus 100-channel VOR/ILS; Mk 12B 360-channel VHF transceiver plus 100-channel VOR/ILS; Mk 16 360-channel VHF transceiver plus 100-channel VOR/ILS; Genave Beta 4096 transponder; MBT marker beacon; DME 70; UGR-2 glide-slope; ADF-31A and associated antennae and equipment.

DIMENSIONS, EXTERNAL:
Wing span	24 ft 6 in (7.47 m)
Wing chord (constant)	4 ft 0 in (1.22 m)
Wing aspect ratio	6.06
Length overall	19 ft 2¾ in (5.86 m)
Height overall	6 ft 9¾ in (2.08 m)
Tailplane span	7 ft 8¼ in (2.34 m)
Wheel track	8 ft 3 in (2.45 m)
Wheelbase	4 ft 5 in (1.35 m)
Propeller ground clearance	8¼ in (0.21 m)

DIMENSIONS, INTERNAL:
Cabin: length	4 ft 6 in (1.37 m)
Max width	3 ft 5 in (1.04 m)
Max height	3 ft 9¼ in (1.15 m)
Floor area	16.7 sq ft (1.55 m²)

AREAS:
Wings, gross	98.11 sq ft (9.11 m²)
Ailerons (total)	5.20 sq ft (0.48 m²)
Trailing-edge flaps (total)	5.44 sq ft (0.50 m²)

Fin	4.74 sq ft (0.44 m²)
Rudder	3.50 sq ft (0.32 m²)
Tailplane	11.70 sq ft (1.09 m²)
Elevators, including tab	7.00 sq ft (0.65 m²)

WEIGHTS AND LOADINGS:
Weight empty	947 lb (429 kg)
Max T-O and landing weight	1,500 lb (680 kg)
Max zero fuel weight	1,368 lb (620 kg)
Max wing loading	15.3 lb/sq ft (74.7 kg/m²)
Max power loading	13.9 lb/hp (6.30 kg/hp)

PERFORMANCE (at max T-O weight):
Max level speed at S/L	125 knots (144 mph; 232 km/h)
Max diving speed	169 knots (195 mph; 313 km/h)
Max cruising speed 75% power at 8,000 ft (2,440 m)	116 knots (134 mph; 215 km/h)
Econ cruising speed at 10,000 ft (3,050 m)	99 knots (114 mph; 183 km/h)
Stalling speed, flaps down	58 knots (66 mph; 106.5 km/h)
Stalling speed, flaps up	60 knots (69 mph; 111.5 km/h)
Rate of climb at S/L	810 ft (247 m)/min
Service ceiling	11,250 ft (3,430 m)
T-O run, paved runway	900 ft (274 m)
T-O to 50 ft (15 m) paved runway	1,615 ft (492 m)
Landing from 50 ft (15 m) paved runway	1,245 ft (379 m)
Landing run paved runway	490 ft (149 m)
Range with max fuel, no reserves, at 10,000 ft (3,050 m)	445 nm (516 miles; 830 km)

AMERICAN AVIATION AA-2

Design work on this high-performance four-seat low-wing monoplane, utilising similar construction techniques to the AA-1, was started in 1968 and the prototype of the AA-2 made its first flight early in 1970. Flight testing was in progress at the time of writing, with FAA certification anticipated late in 1970 and production scheduled to begin early in 1971. It is reported that the production model will have a wing span of 30 ft 0 in (9.14 m), overall length of 23 ft 3 in (7.09 m) and gross weight of 2,400 lb (1,089 kg). Power plant of the AA-2 is a 180 hp Lycoming O-360-A1A four-cylinder engine. No further details were available at the time of writing, but maximum level speed has been estimated at 135 knots (155 mph; 249 km/h) and cruising speed at 75% power at 126 knots (145 mph; 233 km/h).

ACE
ACE AIRCRAFT MANUFACTURING CO

ADDRESS:
106 Arthur Road, Asheville, North Carolina 28806

OWNER: Thurman G. Baird

SALES AND PUBLIC RELATIONS MANAGER: V. P. Baird

This company is the successor to the original Corben Aircraft Company, which was established in 1923 and began manufacturing the Baby Ace

single-seat ultra-light monoplane in kit form in 1931.

The Corben assets were acquired in 1953 by Mr Paul Poberezny, President of the Experimental Aircraft Association. With Mr S. J. Dzik, a former WACO engineer, he completely redesigned the Baby Ace, with the intention of offering it in the form of plans and kits of parts for amateur construction. All rights in the new version, known as the Model C, were sold to Mr Cliff DuCharme of West Bend, Wisconsin, to dispel any suggestions of the Experimental Aircraft Association being concerned with a profit-making venture. Again the Baby Ace was redesigned, as

the Model D, and special tools were built to produce Baby Ace components in quantity. At the same time, the side-by-side two-seat Junior Ace was redesigned as the Junior Ace Model E.

In 1961, the company was acquired by Mr Edwin T. Jacob of McFarland, Wisconsin, from whom all rights were purchased by the present owner in 1965. Plans, kits and parts are available to amateur builders.

It is estimated that there are about 350 Baby Aces flying today and hundreds more being built. Ace Aircraft Manufacturing Co also has full rights in the American Flea Ship and Heath Parasol light aircraft, of which plans are available.

The company had two more aircraft under development in the Spring of 1969, one of which was a small single-seat biplane with a span of 21 ft (6·40 m). The second, a single-seat wire-braced parasol-wing monoplane with a span of 32 ft (9·75 m), is intended to be powered by a Volkswagen engine. No other details were available at the time of writing.

BABY ACE MODEL D

The prototype of the redesigned Baby Ace Model D flew for the first time on 15 November 1956. Large numbers have since been built by amateurs, some of whom have introduced authorised refinements to the basic design. At least one Baby Ace is flying with a float landing gear.

TYPE: Single-seat ultra-light monoplane.

WINGS: Braced parasol monoplane. Wing section Clark Y (modified). Dihedral 1°. Incidence 1°. Fabric-covered two-spar wood structure. Fabric-covered wood ailerons. No flaps.

FUSELAGE: Welded steel-tube structure, fabric-covered.

TAIL UNIT: Wire-braced steel-tube structure, fabric-covered.

LANDING GEAR: Non-retractable tail-wheel type. Combination special tubing and spring shock-absorption. Goodrich 8·00 × 4 main wheels. Scott hydraulic brakes. Wheel spats optional. Steerable tail-wheel. Alternatively Edo 1140 floats on seaplane version.

POWER PLANT: One Continental A65, A85, C65 or C85 four-cylinder horizontally-opposed air-cooled engine of 65-85 hp driving two-blade wood fixed-pitch propeller. Fuel in tank aft of firewall with capacity of 16·8 US gallons (63·6 litres). Oil capacity 1 US gallon (3·8 litres).

ACCOMMODATION: Single seat in open cockpit. Wide door on starboard side. Space for 10 lb (4·5 kg) baggage.

DIMENSIONS, EXTERNAL:

Wing span	26 ft 5 in (8·05 m)
Wing chord (constant)	4 ft 6 in (1·37 m)
Wing aspect ratio	5·95
Length overall	17 ft 8¾ in (5·40 m)
Height overall	6 ft 7¾ in (2·02 m)
Tailplane span	7 ft 0 in (2·13 m)
Wheel track	6 ft 0 in (1·83 m)
Wheelbase	13 ft 0 in (3·96 m)

DIMENSION, INTERNAL:

Baggage space	2·2 cu ft (0·06 m³)

AREAS:

Wings, gross	112·3 sq ft (10·43 m²)
Ailerons (total)	10·2 sq ft (0·95 m²)
Fin	3·5 sq ft (0·33 m²)
Rudder	4·5 sq ft (0·42 m²)
Tailplane	10·75 sq ft (1·00 m²)
Elevators	6·5 sq ft (0·60 m²)

WEIGHTS:

Weight empty, equipped	575 lb (261 kg)

Max T-O weight:

65 hp	950 lb (431 kg)
85 hp landplane or seaplane	1,150 lb (522 kg)

PERFORMANCE (65 hp engine at max T-O weight):

Max level speed at S/L	
	96 knots (110 mph; 177 km/h)
Max cruising speed	
	87-91 knots (100-105 mph; 160-169 km/h)
Stalling speed	30 knots (34 mph; 54·7 km/h)
Rate of climb at S/L	1,200 ft (365 m)/min
Service ceiling	16,000 ft (4,875 m)
T-O run	200 ft (60 m)
Landing run	250 ft (76 m)
Range with max fuel	
	303·5 nm (350 miles; 560 km)

JUNIOR ACE MODEL E

The Junior Ace Model E differs from the Baby Ace Model D in being a side-by-side two-seater. It is powered usually by an 85 hp Continental C85 four-cylinder horizontally-opposed air-cooled engine, and the data below refer to an aircraft with this type of power plant that has been built by Mr Louis C. Seno of Melrose Park, Illinois.

Baby Ace Model D (65 hp Continental A65 engine) built by Mr Robert Morris of Erie, Pennsylvania
(Jean Seele)

Junior Ace Model E (65 hp Continental A65-8F engine) built by Mr Alfred Hagel of Montello, Wisconsin
(Jean Seele)

First flown on 2 August 1966, it has a cockpit 3 in (7·5 cm) wider and 4 in (10 cm) deeper than that of the standard Model E, full electrical system and increased fuel capacity of 22·5 US gallons (85 litres).

DIMENSIONS:

Wing span	26 ft 0 in (7·92 m)
Wing chord (constant)	4 ft 6 in (1·37 m)
Wing aspect ratio	5·95
Length overall	18 ft 0 in (5·50 m)
Height overall	6 ft 7 in (2·00 m)

WEIGHTS:

Weight empty	809 lb (367 kg)
Max T-O weight	1,335 lb (606 kg)

PERFORMANCE:

Max level speed at S/L	
	113 knots (130 mph; 209 km/h)
Cruising speed	91 knots (105 mph; 169 km/h)
Landing speed	57 knots (65 mph; 105 km/h)
Service ceiling	10,000 ft (3,050 m)

T-O run	400 ft (122 m)
Landing run	600 ft (183 m)
Range with max fuel	
	303·5 nm (350 miles; 560 km)

AMERICAN FLEA SHIP

This small single-seat triplane was originally sold in ready-to-fly and kit form by Universal Aircraft Company of Fort Worth, Texas, immediately prior to World War 2. All rights to the drawings and patents applicable to the American Flea Ship have been acquired by Mr Thurman Baird of Ace Aircraft Manufacturing Co, who also owns the example shown in the illustration on this page. He is offering sets of plans to amateur constructors.

The construction of the American Flea Ship is extremely simple. All wing panels are of similar dimensions, to permit interchangeability, and each has only a single spar. The ribs are made mainly of plywood. A novel feature is that the entire lower wings are pivoted to function as ailerons, with a range of movement of ±4° 30′.

The American Flea Ship (*left*) and Heath Parasol Model V, of which plans are available from Ace Aircraft Manufacturing Co

The fuselage is made of welded steel tubing and the landing gear is welded "solidly" in place, with the oversize tyres acting as shock-absorbers.

Mr Baird's American Flea Ship has a 65 hp Continental flat-four engine, but a variety of other engines of 30-70 hp can be fitted. Fuel capacity is 7·5 US gallons (28·5 litres).

DIMENSIONS, EXTERNAL:
Wing span	20 ft 10 in (6·35 m)
Wing chord (constant)	2 ft 4 in (0·71 m)
Length overall	13 ft 0 in (3·96 m)
Height overall	6 ft 6 in (1·98 m)

AREA:
Wings, gross	140 sq ft (13·0 m²)

WEIGHTS (typical):
Weight empty	460 lb (210 kg)
Max T-O weight	670 lb (305 kg)

PERFORMANCE (typical):
Max level speed at S/L	78-83 knots (90-95 mph; 145-153 km/h)
Cruising speed	65-69 knots (75-80 mph; 120-129 km/h)
Landing speed	26 knots (30 mph; 48 km/h)
Rate of climb at S/L	600 ft (183 m)/min
Service ceiling	12,000 ft (3,650 m)

AEROCAR

AEROCAR, INC

HEAD OFFICE AND WORKS:
Box 546, Longview, Washington 98632

PRESIDENT AND GENERAL MANAGER:
Moulton B. Taylor

Aerocar, Inc has been developing since February 1948 a flying automobile designed by Mr M. B. Taylor. The prototype Aerocar, with a Lycoming O-290 engine, was completed in October 1949. It was followed by a pre-production Aerocar Model I, with Lycoming O-320 engine, and this was used for tests which led to FAA Airworthiness Certification of the Aerocar on 13 December 1956.

Four additional Model I Aerocars have been completed for demonstration tours of the United States and for sale to customers. One of these is fitted with the more powerful Lycoming O-360 engine and has also been certificated by the FAA.

The accumulated road mileage on the six Model I Aerocars is well over 200,000 miles and they have logged a total of more than 5,000 flying hours. No further production of this model is planned.

Development of the Aerocar is continuing and many changes have been made to the hand-built models, enhancing both the flight performance and the road operation. Production of the refined Model III Aerocar will begin when sufficient capital has been raised to make this possible.

In 1966 Aerocar built the prototype of a light flying-boat for a private customer. At the time of writing, it was completing two additional machines on similar lines but in this case amphibious, with a tricycle landing gear. Details of this aircraft, known as the Coot, are given on page 246. Many sets of plans for the Coot have also been sold to potential amateur constructors.

AEROCAR MODEL III

The Aerocar is a "flying automobile" which incorporates a number of features not previously introduced in craft of this type. It is completely roadable, being able to tow its wing-tail assembly as a trailer behind the automobile section.

The four-wheel automobile section accommodates two persons side-by-side and encloses in the rear portion a Lycoming piston-engine which provides front-wheel automobile drive and drives a pusher propeller aft of the tail unit. The engine is of a low-compression type, so that automotive fuel can be used in an emergency.

The road wheels are driven through a special "fluid drive" system, and the propeller shaft is also driven through a unique "dry fluid drive" which uses steel shot as the energy transmitting medium. The latter results in smooth and vibration-free operation of the long propeller shaft. Noise is reduced to a minimum by use of a concentric rubber drive element.

A three-control flight system is combined with the automobile controls, the same wheel being used for both. Conventional clutch and foot brake pedals are provided, together with three forward speeds and reverse in the wheel drive. When the control wheel is used in flight to operate the ailerons, it also applies rudder co-ordination by means of an aerodynamic tab mounted in the rudder.

The flight section consists of a pair of wings and a rear fuselage section which carries the tail and encloses the shaft for the pusher propeller. When the flight section is detached from the body, the wings, which have retractable trailer wheels inset in the leading-edges of the roots, may be folded to each side of the tail section and the

T-O run	50-100 ft (15-30 m)
Range	195 nm (225 miles; 360 km)

HEATH PARASOL MODEL V

This single-seat ultra-light parasol monoplane dates back to 1926, when the first Heath Parasol, with 27 hp Henderson motorcycle engine, was designed and built by Mr Edward B. Heath and Mr Clair Linsted. Several developed versions were put into large-scale production, complete and in kit form, in the Heath Aircraft Company's works at Chicago, the final version being the Model V, introduced in 1931.

In 1941, some years after Heath Aircraft Company went out of the aircraft business, the J. W. Peterson Aircraft Company of Grand Rapids, Michigan, began producing an aircraft known as the Peterson Sportster. This was the Heath Parasol Model V with the tail unit redesigned on more modern lines, the wing-tip shape revised to match the tail unit, and a new type of landing gear utilising spring-loaded shock-struts.

Mr Thurman Baird of Ace Aircraft Manufacturing Co owns one of the very few Peterson Sportsters that were built. Shown in the illustration

Aerocar Model III, with wing-tail assembly in tow

Aerocar Model III in flight configuration

flight section towed tail-first behind the automobile section. The change-over from road transportation to aircraft can be accomplished without special equipment by one person in 5 minutes and all component locks are fool-proof. It is impossible to start the engine until all components have been properly engaged.

Extensive field testing of the pre-production Model I Aerocars (described in the 1963-64 *Jane's*) has led the company to develop the considerably improved Aerocar Model III, on which it is hoped to concentrate production. The new version is essentially the same as its predecessors except that the automobile section has a three-position electrically-retractable landing gear. The fully-extended position is used for take-off, landing and to facilitate attachment or removal of the wings/tail unit. Partial retraction is intended for normal road travel, and the wheels can be fully retracted in flight.

The Model III has a much refined glass-fibre body, giving a more conventional appearance on the road. The opportunity has been taken to incorporate more than 600 additional modifications to improve the Aerocar.

The following description applies to the Aerocar Model III of which a prototype has been produced by conversion of an Aerocar Model I; this flew for the first time in June 1968. The FAA static test programme was completed on 15 January 1969 and Type Inspection Authorisation has been issued. Final certification has been delayed by the necessity to prove recent engine modifications, but was expected in the Spring of 1970.

TYPE: Two-seat roadable aircraft.

WINGS: Braced high-wing monoplane. Single streamline-section bracing strut each side. NACA 43012 wing section. Dihedral 2°. Incidence 6°. Conventional light alloy all-metal structure. Wings are detachable for towing and have retractable towing wheels in roots. Balanced metal ailerons. No flaps.

on page 244, it has a 40 hp Continental A40 engine. Plans of this version are available from Mr Baird and can be adapted to make use of a 30 hp Heath-B4 or 35 hp Aeronca engine. At least one similar aircraft is flying with a 65 hp Lycoming engine. Standard fuel capacity is 6 US gallons (23 litres).

Construction is orthodox, with a welded steel-tube fuselage and wooden wings, with fabric covering overall. The main wheels are fitted with 4·00 × 8 tyres. There are no brakes.

DIMENSIONS, EXTERNAL:
Wing span	25 ft 0 in (7·62 m)
Wing chord (constant)	4 ft 6 in (1·37 m)
Length overall	17 ft 3 in (5·26 m)

AREA:
Wings, gross	110 sq ft (10·22 m²)

WEIGHT (40 hp Continental):
Weight empty	350 lb (159 kg)

PERFORMANCE (40 hp Continental):
Cruising speed	74 knots (85 mph; 137 km/h)
Landing speed	30 knots (35 mph; 56 km/h)
Range	173 nm (200 miles; 320 km)

FUSELAGE: Aluminium alloy structure, covered with glass-fibre. Rear portion detachable. Forward portion capable of operation as automobile.

TAIL UNIT: Cantilever all-metal structure of "Y" configuration, with sweptback ventral fin. Trim-tab in each elevator. Rudder trim-tab interconnected with ailerons.

LANDING GEAR: Electrically-retractable four-wheel type, with steerable front wheels. Three positions: fully-extended for aircraft ground operation, partially retracted for automobile operation and fully retracted in flight. Independent torsion bar suspension. Gabriel automotive hydraulic shock-absorbers. Goodrich expanding brakes on rear wheels, Airheart disc brakes on front wheels. Tyre size 5·60 × 12. Tyre pressures 22 lb/sq in (1·55 kg/cm²).

POWER PLANT: One 143 hp (de-rated) Lycoming O-320-A1A four-cylinder horizontally-opposed air-cooled engine, driving a Hartzell Type HA12 UF two-blade pusher propeller, diameter 6 ft 0 in (1·83 m). Fuel in one glass-fibre tank, capacity 34 US gallons (128 litres). Refuelling point in side of car. Oil capacity 1 US gallon (3·75 litres).

ACCOMMODATION: Two automobile bucket seats side-by-side in car-type cabin. Door on each side. Baggage space aft of cabin, above engine.

ELECTRONICS AND EQUIPMENT: Genave VHF radio, solid-state AM radio and blind-flying instrumentation to customer's requirements.

DIMENSIONS, EXTERNAL (Aircraft):
Wing span	34 ft 0 in (10·36 m)
Wing chord (constant)	5 ft 8 in (1·73 m)
Wing aspect ratio	6
Length overall	23 ft 0 in (7·01 m)
Height overall	7 ft 0 in (2·13 m)
Tailplane span	8 ft 0 in (2·44 m)

DIMENSIONS, EXTERNAL (Automobile):
Length	11 ft 0 in (3·35 m)
Height	4 ft 4 in (1·32 m)

Wheel track	4 ft 4 in (1·32 m)
Wheelbase	6 ft 8 in (2·03 m)
Doors (each): Height	3 ft 1 in (0·94 m)
Width	2 ft 6 in (0·76 m)
Height to sill 1 ft 0 in to 1 ft 8 in (0·30-0·50 m)	
Trailer length	15 ft 0 in (4·57 m)
Overall car/trailer length	26 ft 6 in (8·07 m)
Max width of trailer	8 ft 0 in (2·44 m)
Max height of trailer	8 ft 0 in (2·44 m)

DIMENSIONS, INTERNAL:

Cabin: Length	3 ft 11 in (1·19 m)
Max width	3 ft 11 in (1·19 m)
Max height	3 ft 7 in (1·09 m)
Baggage space	14 cu ft (0·40 m²)

REAS:

Wings, gross	190 sq ft (17·65 m²)
Ailerons (total)	21 sq ft (1·95 m²)
Fin	3 sq ft (0·28 m²)
Rudder	4 sq ft (0·37 m²)
Tailplane (total)	28 sq ft (2·60 m²)
Elevators (total)	9 sq ft (0·84 m²)

WEIGHTS AND LOADINGS:

Weight empty (auto)	1,100 lb (500 kg)
Weight empty (aircraft)	1,500 lb (680 kg)
Trailer (wing and tail)	400 lb (181 kg)
Max T-O weight	2,100 lb (953 kg)
Max wing loading	11 lb/sq ft (53·7 kg/m²)
Max power loading	14·7 lb/hp (6·67 kg/hp)

PERFORMANCE (Aircraft, estimated):

Max speed at 7,000 ft (2,135 m)	
	119 knots (137 mph; 220 km/h)
Max permissible diving speed	
	138 knots (159 mph; 256 km/h)
Econ cruising speed (60% power) at 5,000 ft	
(1,524 m) 109 knots (125 mph; 201 km/h)	
Stalling speed	44 knots (50 mph; 80 km/h)
Rate of climb at S/L	650 ft (198 m)/min
Service ceiling	12,000 ft (3,660 m)
T-O run	650 ft (198 m)
T-O to 50 ft (15 m)	1,250 ft (380 m)
Landing from 50 ft (15 m)	1,100 ft (335 m)
Landing run	300 ft (91 m)
Range with max fuel and max payload, no	
allowances 430 nm (500 miles; 805 km)	

PERFORMANCE (Automobile, estimated):

Max road hp	40
Road speed at 2,700 rpm	
	58 knots (67 mph; 108 km/h)
Practical road cruising speed	
	61 knots (70 mph; 112 km/h)
Practical speed with wings in tow	
	44-52 knots (50-60 mph; 80-96 km/h)
Road range	260 nm (300 miles; 480 km)
Road turning radius	15 ft 0 in (4·57 m)
Road fuel consumption	
	15 miles/US gallon (5·3 km/litre)

AEROCAR COOT MODEL B

The prototype of this small side-by-side two-seat amphibian was completed in June 1969. Its general appearance is shown in the adjacent three-view drawing. A variant, the Coot Model A, is similar except that it has a conventional rear fuselage and single fin instead of the twin-boom configuration of the Model B.

The "float-wing" configuration permits rough-water operation and, since the close proximity of the wings to the water forms a "pressure wedge", unusually low take-off and landing speeds are possible without recourse to flaps or other lift-enhancing devices.

The structure is basically of wood, with the exception of the twin-boom tail of the Coot-B, which must necessarily be of all-metal construction. The conventional single tail of the Coot-A, however, can be of steel-tube and fabric, wood monocoque or all-metal construction. The rear-ward-folding wings, of NACA 4415 section, can be folded by one person. The fabric-covered ailerons are of metal construction and statically balanced. No tip floats. Construction of the hull, which has only seven bulkheads, is straight-forward without the complication of wheel-well doors. Tailplane and elevators of Coot-A fold, and tailplane incidence is variable. Coot-B has elevator trim-tabs. All control surfaces are statically balanced. Tricycle type landing gear is manually retractable.

The Coot has been designed to use any engine of 100-150 hp, and the prototype Coot-B, built by Dick Liljegren of Kelso, Washington, is powered by a 125 hp Continental C-125 four-cylinder horizontally-opposed air-cooled engine. Maximum fuel capacity is 50 US gallons (189 litres). The first two Coot-As built by Aerocar have 125 hp Franklin engines.

Certain component parts, including the glass-

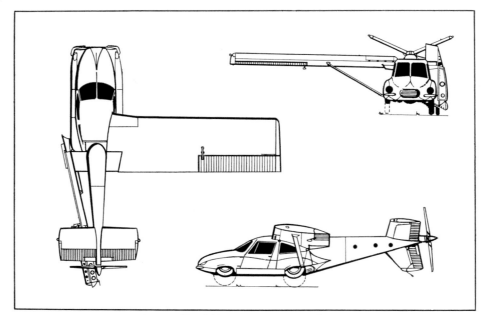

Aerocar Model III two-seat roadable aircraft

First Coot Model B, built by Mr R. E. Liljegren of Kelso, Washington

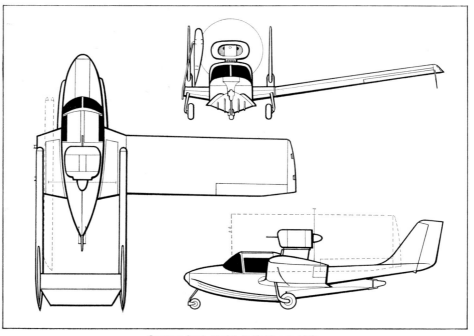

Aerocar Coot Model B light amphibian

fibre engine cowls, fore-deck, instrument panel, tail fairings, engine cooling-fan blades and spring steel main landing gear legs, and plans are available to amateur constructors.

DIMENSIONS, EXTERNAL:

Wing span (Model A)	36 ft 0 in (10·97 m)
Wing span (Model B)	37 ft 0 in (11·28 m)
Wing chord (constant)	5 ft 0 in (1·52 m)
Length overall	20 ft 0 in (6·10 m)
Height overall	8 ft 0 in (2·44 m)
Width folded	8 ft 0 in (2·44 m)
Tailplane span (Model A)	10 ft 0 in (3·04 m)
Tailplane span (Model B)	8 ft 0 in (2·44 m)

AREA:

Wings, gross	180 sq ft (16·72 m²)

WEIGHTS (prototype):

Weight empty	1,200 lb (544 kg)
Max T-O weight	1,900 lb (861 kg)

PERFORMANCE

Cruising speed 100 knots (115 mph; 185 km/h)	
Rate of climb at S/L 600-800 ft (183-245 m)/min	
Water T-O	12 sec

AEROMOD

AEROMOD, INC

ADDRESS:
2 Theresa Drive, North Little Rock, Arkansas 72118

PRESIDENT: E. W. Moore

CHIEF ENGINEER: William G. Dorsch

CHIEF PILOT: William E. Findley

In 1965, William G. Dorsch designed a biplane conversion of the Piper PA-18 Super Cub, under the name Loadstar Model 100, to provide greatly increased payload, reduced stalling speed and STOL capability. A prototype conversion flew for the first time in August 1966, and received FAA Supplementary Type Approval on the 23rd of that month. With the aid of William E. Findley, Mr Dorsch produced a total of four such conversions by the beginning of 1967, plus a similar conversion of a J-3 Cub.

Although the conversion was conceived originally for agricultural applications, it has since become popular for many different uses. As a result, Aeromod Inc was incorporated in April 1967 to manufacture and market the conversion in kit form.

Aeromod have also developed an engine mounting to permit the 180 hp Lycoming O-360 engine to be fitted in a PA-18 Super Cub.

AEROMOD LOADSTAR MODEL 100

This aircraft is basically a Piper PA-18 Super Cub or J-3 Cub, to which an additional all-metal lower wing has been fitted. Each new lower wing panel weighs 38 lb (17·25 kg), but the conversion offers a net 600 lb (272 kg) of additional lift.

Once the fittings are installed on an aircraft, the lower wings can be fitted or removed in 30 minutes or less, permitting operation with or without the lower wings, as best suited to each particular operation.

Apart from agricultural applications, Loadstar Model 100 conversions have been used for glider and advertising banner towing, pipeline and wireline patrol, traffic patrol, aerial photography and all types of bush and sport flying.

Loadstar Model 100 conversions differ from standard PA-18 Super Cubs and J-3 Cubs only in the following details:

WINGS: The all-metal lower wings are attached to the fuselage and upper wings through 4130 chrome-molybdenum steel fittings, supported by additional stiffeners, with N-type interplane struts. Wing section is of original design with thickness/chord ratio of 10·5%. Incidence 3°. No dihedral or sweep. No ailerons on lower wings.

POWER PLANT: Any four-cylinder horizontally-opposed air-cooled engine of 105 to 180 hp on PA-18 conversion, or 85 to 150 hp on J-3 conversion.

DIMENSIONS, EXTERNAL:

Wing span (lower)	21 ft 0 in (6·40 m)
Wing chord (constant)	3 ft 10¼ in (1·18 m)
Wing aspect ratio	4·64

AREAS:

Lower wings, gross	69 sq ft (6·41 m²)

WEIGHTS AND LOADINGS:

Weight empty (agricultural):

125 hp J-3	964 lb (437 kg)
150 hp PA-18	1,210 lb (549 kg)

Max T-O weight (standard):

85 hp J-3	1,220 lb (553 kg)
150 hp PA-18	1,750 lb (794 kg)

Max T-O weight (agricultural):

125 hp J-3	2,364 lb (1,072 kg)
150 hp PA-18	2,610 lb (1,184 kg)

Aeromod Loadstar Model 100, a biplane conversion of a Piper PA-18 Super Cub

Max wing loading (standard):

150 hp PA-18	7·2 lb/sq ft (35·2 kg/m²)

Max wing loading (agricultural):

125 hp J-3	10 lb/sq ft (48·82 kg/m²)
150 hp PA-18	10·2 lb/sq ft (49·80 kg/m²)

PERFORMANCE (standard conversion, at max T-O weight):

Cruising speed:

85 hp J-3	69 knots (80 mph; 129 km/h)
150 hp PA-18	83 knots (95 mph; 153 km/h)

Landing speed:

85 hp J-3	24 knots (28 mph; 45 km/h)
150 hp PA-18	26 knots (30 mph; 48 km/h)

Minimum flying speed, partial flap, power on at 2,100 rpm, constant altitude:

150 hp PA-18	22 knots (25 mph; 40 km/h)

Stalling speed, power off, no flaps:

150 hp PA-18	29 knots (33 mph; 53 km/h)

Stalling speed, power off, full flaps:

150 hp PA-18	25 knots (28 mph; 45 km/h)

Stalling speed, power on at 2,150 rpm, no flaps:

150 hp PA-18	26 knots (30 mph; 49 km/h)

Stalling speed, power on at 2,150 rpm, full flaps:

150 hp PA-18	20 knots (23 mph; 37 km/h)

Rate of climb at S/L:

85 hp J-3	800 ft (244 m)/min
150 hp PA-18	1,200 ft (365 m)/min

T-O run:

85 hp J-3; 150 hp PA-18	125 ft (38 m)

T-O to 50 ft (15 m):

150 hp PA-18	375 ft (114 m)

Landing from 50 ft (15 m):

150 hp PA-18	380 ft (116 m)

Landing run:

85 hp J-3; 150 hp PA-18	125 ft (38 m)

PERFORMANCE (agricultural aircraft, from sod strip, 100°F/37·8°C, no wind, 1,100 lb = 499 kg payload):

Stalling speed 39 knots (44 mph; 71 km/h)

T-O run:

125 hp J-3	725 ft (221 m)
150 hp PA-18	750 ft (229 m)

AERO SPACELINES

Aero Spacelines B-377PG Pregnant Guppy (four Pratt & Whitney R-4360-B6 engines)

AERO SPACELINES INC (Subsidiary of Unexcelled Inc)

HEAD OFFICE AND WORKS:
P.O. Drawer B, Santa Barbara Airport, Santa Barbara, California 93102.
CHAIRMAN OF THE BOARD:
A. M. "Tex" Johnston
PRESIDENT:
W. C. Lawrence
VICE-PRESIDENTS:
Dan McKinnon (Operations)
J. J. Laferty (Finance)
Joseph H. Andrews (Sales)
DIRECTOR OF PUBLIC RELATIONS AND ADVERTISING:
John Kemp

This company was responsible for the development and construction of two conversions of Boeing Stratocruiser/C-97 transport aircraft, under the names of Pregnant Guppy and Super Guppy respectively, to provide specialised transportation of large booster stages and other items used in America's national space programmes. The conversions were performed entirely with private capital and with no prior contracts or other commitments. The US government subsequently contracted for the exclusive use of both aircraft, and heavy utilisation by NASA and the Department of Defense has precluded their use for commercial transportation of outsize cargoes.

To meet a potential commercial requirement, Aero Spacelines subsequently built the prototype of a third Stratocruiser conversion, known as the Mini Guppy.

New advanced versions of the Super Guppy and Mini Guppy were announced late in 1968, and the first three of an eventual mixed fleet of ten or twelve of these two types are now in production and scheduled to be in service during 1970. The final fleet of aircraft is expected to be made up of equal numbers of Super Guppies and Mini Guppies.

Aero Spacelines' parent company, Unexcelled, Inc, of New York, formed a new company early in 1968, known originally as Tex Johnston, Inc and since changed to TIFS Inc, to produce Total Inflight Simulation (TIFS) trainers. TIFS are variable-stability aircraft designed to train aircrews by computerised simulation of the control response characteristics of any given aircraft. The first TIES aircraft, based on a Convair Model 580, is available for demonstration during 1970.

AERO SPACELINES B-377PG PREGNANT GUPPY

Following the formation of Aero Spacelines at Van Nuys, California, in 1961, it initiated the conversion of a Boeing B-377 Stratocruiser into a transport for large booster rockets of the kind being produced under US space programmes. The converted aircraft flew for the first time on 19 September 1962, and was given the designation B-377PG Pregnant Guppy.

The first stage that was flight tested involved lengthening the rear fuselage of the Stratocruiser, by inserting a 16 ft 8 in (5·08 m) section aft of the wing trailing-edge. The much more ambitious second stage entailed building a huge circular-section "bubble" structure over the top of the fuselage. This new structure has an inside height of 19 ft 9 in (6·02 m), compared with a normal headroom of just under 9 ft 0 in (2·74 m) for the upper deck of the aircraft, enabling it to accept cargo up to 19 ft 9 in (6·02 m) in diameter.

Initial flight tests of some 60 hours proved the B-377PG to be stable and controllable in all flight regimes. As a result, the conversion was

Aero Spacelines Super Guppy, a conversion of the Boeing C-97J (four Pratt & Whitney T34-P-7WA turboprop engines)

completed in the Spring of 1963, when the original upper fuselage structure (inside the new structure) was removed and the tail of the aircraft was made removable, for straight-in loading of the booster rockets, carried on oversize pallets, through the medium of a bolt-joint aft of the wing. Volume of the cabin is now 29,187 cu ft (826·5 m²), which was larger than the cabin space available in any other aircraft in the world at the time of the conversions.

Test flying was resumed on 16 May and the B-377PG received FAA Supplemental Type Approval under Part 8 (special purpose) CAR on 10 July 1963. Immediately afterwards, it flew from Los Angeles to Cape Kennedy carrying an inert Saturn S-IV stage manufactured by Douglas Aircraft. This operation and subsequent regular flights have been made under NASA-Marshall Space Flight Center contracts awarded to Aero Spacelines.

The basic power plant consists of four Pratt & Whitney R-4360-B6 radial engines, each driving a Hamilton Standard Model 34E60-387 constant-speed propeller. Early in 1968, these engines were supplemented by attachments for four Aerojet-General 15KS-1000-A1 assisted take-off rockets, and flight tests have shown that these offer a considerable improvement in take-off performance from short runways.

DIMENSIONS, EXTERNAL:
Wing span	141 ft 3 in (43·05 m)
Length overall	127 ft 0 in (38·71 m)
Height to top of fuselage	31 ft 3 in (9·53 m)
Height overall	38 ft 3 in (11·66 m)

DIMENSIONS, INTERNAL:
Cargo compartment:
Total length	80 ft 0 in (24·38 m)
Length of constant-section portion	
	30 ft 0 in (9·14 m)
Max width	19 ft 9 in (6·02 m)
Max height	19 ft 9 in (6·02 m)
Floor width	8 ft 7 in (2·62 m)

WEIGHTS:
Max payload	29,000 lb (13,155 kg)
Max T-O weight	133,000 lb (60,328 kg)*

This will be increased to 145,000 lb (65,770 kg) after programmed modification.

PERFORMANCE:
Normal cruising speed
195 knots (225 mph; 362 km/h)

AERO SPACELINES B-377SG SUPER GUPPY

Shortly after completion of the B-377PG Pregnant Guppy, Aero Spacelines put in hand the construction of an even larger aircraft, capable of accommodating the S-IVB third stage of the Saturn V launch vehicle and the Apollo Lunar Module adapter, neither of which could be carried by any existing aircraft.

The resulting aircraft, known as the B-377SG Super Guppy, utilises the wing, flight deck and forward fuselage of a Boeing C-97J (one of two C-97's that were powered by Pratt & Whitney T34 turboprop engines), and incorporates a hinged nose section (including the flight deck) for straight-in loading of bulky cargoes on oversize pallets.

Sections from four Stratocruisers have been embodied in the Super Guppy. The wing span has been increased by 15 ft (4·57 m) and the fuselage has been lengthened by 30 ft 10 in (9·40 m). The upper lobe of the fuselage is large enough to house cylindrical loads with a diameter of 25 ft (7·62 m) and has a volume of 49,790 cu ft (1,410 m²).

The power plant comprises four 7,000 eshp Pratt & Whitney T34-P-7WA turboprop engines, each driving a Model CT735S-B312 propeller.

The Super Guppy flew for the first time on 31 August 1965, eight months after conversion started, and immediately joined the B-377PG in service under contract to NASA.

DIMENSIONS, EXTERNAL:
Wing span	156 ft 3 in (47·63 m)
Length overall	141 ft 3 in (43·05 m)
Height to top of fuselage	36 ft 6 in (11 13 m)
Height overall	46 ft 5 in (14·15 m)

DIMENSIONS, INTERNAL:
Cargo compartment:
Length (constant section)	30 ft 8 in (9·35 m)
Length overall	108 ft 10 in (33·17 m)
Max width	25 ft 0 in (7·62 m)
Max height	25 ft 6 in (7·77 m)
Floor width	8 ft 7 in (2·62 m)

WEIGHTS:
Operating weight empty	105,000 lb (47,625 kg)
Max T-O weight	175,000 lb (79,378 kg)
Max payload	41,000 lb (18,597 kg)

PERFORMANCE:
Normal cruising speed
261 knots (300 mph; 483 km/h)

AERO SPACELINES GUPPY-201

The new Guppy-201 is powered by four Allison 501-D22C turboprop engines, with water injection, each driving a Hamilton Standard propeller. Fuel capacity totals 59,000 lb (27,035 kg). It utilises the lower fuselage, wings, tail unit and cockpit of existing B-377/C-97 airframes, portions of the lower fuselage of several aircraft being joined to provide a larger cabin.

To facilitate loading, this version has a 110° swing nose, and features an air-transportable cargo loader. It can accommodate oversize pallets on rails 65 ft (19·81 m) long. A cabin pressurisation system provides the equivalent of 8,000 ft (2,440 m) altitude at 20,000 ft (6,100 m). Systems and equipment include complete anti-icing, closed-circuit television for cargo monitoring, four 60KVA 115V 400 c/s 3-phase alternators, all-weather international avionics and provision for JATO.

This new aircraft is to be utilised for the air transportation of fuselage sections of the McDonnell Douglas DC-10 airliner from General Dynamics

Artist's impression of Aero Spacelines Guppy-201 (four Allison 501-D22C turboprop engines)

Aero Spacelines B-377MG Mini Guppy commercial transport (four Pratt & Whitney R-4360-B6 engines)

Corporation's Convair division plant at San Diego, California, to McDonnell Douglas Corporation's Aircraft Division plant at Long Beach, California, where final assembly of DC-10 subassemblies and components takes place.

Convair is responsible for the production of five fuselage sections of the DC-10, totalling 128 ft (39·48 m) in length, and each almost 20 ft (6·10 m) in diameter. Prior to loading, the two aft fuselage sections will be joined into a single 38 ft 9¾ in (11·83 m) element and this, together with the 33 ft (10·06 m) fuselage centre section, will comprise one load. The two forward fuselage sections, joined into a single 54 ft (16·46 m) element, will also comprise a single load, and thus an entire fuselage will be carried in two flights.

It was announced subsequently that Guppy-201s will also be utilised to transport Lockheed L-1011 TriStar wings from the Avco Corporation's Aerostructures Division at Nashville, Tennessee, to Lockheed-California's new commercial aircraft plant at Palmdale, California. The 25-ft (7·62-m) diameter cargo compartment of the Guppy-201 can accommodate both wings of an L-1011 in a nearly complete built-up configuration, although the weight of these assemblies exceeds 40,000 lb (18,145 kg).

The following details were available at the time of writing:

DIMENSIONS, EXTERNAL:
Wing span	156 ft 8 in (47·75 m)
Length overall	143 ft 10 in (43·84 m)
Height to top of fuselage	36 ft 6 in (11·13 m)
Height overall	45 ft 10 in (13·97 m)

DIMENSIONS, INTERNAL:
Cargo compartment:
Max width	25 ft 1 in (7·65 m)
Max height	25 ft 6 in (7·77 m)
Floor width	13 ft 0 in (3·96 m)
Length of constant-section portion	32 ft 0 in (9·75 m)
Max length	111 ft 6 in (33·99 m)

WEIGHTS:
Operating weight, empty	101,075 lb (45,847 kg)
Max payload	52,925 lb (24,006 kg)
Max T-O weight	170,000 lb (77,110 kg)
Max zero-fuel weight	154,000 lb (69,854 kg)
Max landing weight	160,000 lb (72,570 kg)

PERFORMANCE (estimated):
Cruising speed at 20,000 ft (6,100 m)
240 knots (280 mph; 450 km/h)

AERO SPACELINES B-377MG MINI GUPPY

Following purchase of the company by Unexcelled Inc, in 1965, Aero Spacelines moved its main office and base of operations from Van Nuys to Santa Barbara, California. There it developed the first of several large aircraft intended to satisfy a rapidly developing commercial market for the airlift of large aircraft sections, helicopters, jet-engine power plants, oil drilling equipment and other cargoes too large to be accommodated by any existing commercial aircraft.

This first aircraft, known as the B-377MG Mini Guppy, utilises a basic B-377 fuselage, lengthened by 22 ft 6 in (6·86 m ʃ. It has a new wing centre-section, increasing the span by 15 ft 0 in (4·57 m), and a floor width of 13 ft 0 in (3·96 m), the widest of any existing US aircraft. It has been expanded laterally, to accommodate cargo up to 18 ft 2 in (5·54 m) in width and 15 ft 5 in (4·70 m) in height. Loading is facilitated by a swing tail.

The modification was started in December 1966 and completed in May 1967. The aircraft made its maiden flight on 24 May and, just two days and nineteen hours later, flew to Paris for display at the 1967 Paris Air Show.

Power plant of this version comprises four Pratt & Whitney R-4360-B6 piston-engines, driving Hamilton Standard Model 34E60-387 propellers.

DIMENSIONS, EXTERNAL:
Wing span	156 ft 3 in (47·63 m)
Length overall	132 ft 10 in (40·49 m)
Height to top of fuselage	27 ft 6 in (8·38 m)
Height overall	38 ft 3 in (11·66 m)

DIMENSIONS, INTERNAL:
Cargo compartment:
Max width	18 ft 2 in (5·54 m)
Max height	15 ft 5 in (4·70 m)
Floor width	13 ft 0 in (3·96 m)

Prototype Aero Spacelines Guppy-101 (four Allison 501-D22C turboprop engines) with swing-nose open for loading

Length (constant section) 75 ft 10 in (23·11 m)
Max length 99 ft 0 in (30·18 m)
WEIGHTS:
Max gross weight 142,800 lb (64,770 kg)
Max payload 32,000 lb (14,515 kg)
PERFORMANCE:
Normal cruising speed
208 knots (240 mph; 386 km/h)

AERO SPACELINES GUPPY-101

This swing-nose turboprop version of the B-377MG Mini Guppy is expected to be in service late in 1970, although the prototype, which made a first flight on 13 March 1970, was destroyed

in an accident, reportedly as the result of an engine failure shortly after take-off, on 12 May 1970. The power plant, fuel capacity and systems are identical to those of the Guppy-201 already described. The specification of this aircraft differs as follows:

DIMENSIONS, EXTERNAL:
Wing span 156 ft 8 in (47·75 m)
Length overall 135 ft 6 in (41·30 m)
Height to top of fuselage 26 ft 8 in (8·13 m)
Height overall 40 ft 9 in (12·42 m)
DIMENSIONS, INTERNAL:
Cargo compartment:
Max width 18 ft 4 in (5·59 m)

Max height 15 ft 6 in (4·72 m)
Floor width 13 ft 4 in (4·06 m)
Length of constant-section portion
73 ft 2 in (22·30 m)
Max length 103 ft 2 in (31·45 m)
WEIGHTS:
Operating weight, empty 91,075 lb (41,311 kg)
Max payload 62,925 lb (28,542 kg)
Max T-O weight 180,000 lb (81,650 kg)
Max zero-fuel weight 154,000 lb (69,854 kg)
Max landing weight 160,000 lb (72,570 kg)
PERFORMANCE (estimated):
Cruising speed at 20,000 ft (6,100 m)
270 knots (311 mph; 500 km/h)

AGRINAUTICS

AGRICULTURAL AVIATION ENGINEERING COMPANY

POSTAL ADDRESS:
PO Box 5045, McCarran Airport, Las Vegas, Nevada 89111
WORKS:
1333 Patrick Lane, McCarran Airport, Las Vegas, Nevada 89109
GENERAL MANAGER:
George S. Sanders
SPECIAL PROJECTS MANAGER:
Phillip R. Pickell
SALES MANAGER:
L. R. Ferguson

Agricultural Aviation Engineering Company is one of the leading companies engaged in engineering, design and manufacture of aerial dispersal systems for both fixed and rotary-wing aircraft. Established for more than ten years, it has completed military R & D contracts and has designed and built systems for military use.

As a designer and manufacturer of components and systems for the major agricultural aircraft manufacturers in the USA, the company has designed and carried out conversions of many different aircraft, including the Sikorsky H-19, Bell UH-1, and Cessna Agwagon, for domestic users and for foreign governments. Most recent project has been the development of a spray system for installation on Douglas C-47's for use in Greece.

The company's current range of equipment includes liquid and powder dispersal systems, spray booms and accessories, ground loading pumps, bottom loading and quick-disconnect

Douglas C-47 equipped with agricultural spray system developed by Agrinautics

valves, spray-pump packs and wind-driven pumps. Its engineering facilities are sited in

40,000 sq ft (3,715 m²) of factory accommodation at McCarran Airport, Las Vegas.

AIR-MOD

AIR-MOD ENGINEERING COMPANY

POSTAL ADDRESS:
PO Box 82516, Oklahoma City, Oklahoma
WORKS:
Will Rogers World Airport, Oklahoma City, Oklahoma

Air-Mod Engineering Company announced on 28 June 1968 that they had completed negotiations with Doyn Aircraft, Inc, of Wichita,

Kansas, for the exclusive manufacturing and distribution rights for the two latest Doyn conversions.

The first conversion, to be known as the Super Cardinal, is a 180 hp version of the stock Cessna Cardinal, available with either constant-speed or fixed-pitch propeller and offering a cruising speed of 135 knots (155 mph; 249 km/h). The second conversion, the Super 150, consists of the basic Cessna 150 re-engined with a 150 hp Lycoming O-320 engine, permitting a 1,000 ft (305 m)/min rate of climb and cruising speed of

122 knots (140 mph; 225 km/h).

Other Doyn/Cessna conversions which Air-Mod are producing include a 180 hp power package for the Cessna 170, 172 and 175, all of which are available on an engine exchange basis. Air-Mod are also offering a 180 hp conversion for the Piper Apache and a 250 hp conversion for the Beechcraft Travel Air. All of these power package conversions are available in kit form, or may be installed at the Air-Mod works. No further information had been received from this company at the time of writing.

ALLISON

ALLISON DIVISION OF GENERAL MOTORS CORPORATION

HEAD OFFICE AND WORKS:
Indianapolis, Indiana 46206

OFFICERS:
See "Aero-Engines" section
In May 1969, Pacific Airmotive Corporation of Burbank, California (which see) became prime contractor for the Convair 580 conversion programme, managed until that time by the

Allison Division of General Motors. Under the programme, piston-powered Convair 340/440s could be converted to 580s, using Allison gas-turbine engines. PAC directed all conversion operations; Allison continued to supply the aircraft engines and propellers.

AMERICAN JET INDUSTRIES

AMERICAN JET INDUSTRIES, INC (a subsidiary of CALIFORNIA AIRMOTIVE CORPORATION)

HEAD OFFICE AND WORKS:
3021 Airport Avenue, Santa Monica, California 90405
PRESIDENT: Allen E. Paulson

American Jet Industries has produced the prototype of a two-seat primary jet trainer/COIN aircraft, designated T-610 Super Pinto, which flew for the first time on 28 June 1968. It is a development of the TT-1 Pinto jet primary trainer, built by Temco Electronics and Missiles Company, the prototype of which made its first flight on 26 March 1956. A production batch of 14 Pintos was subsequently bought by the US Navy to study the feasibility of Naval Cadets starting their primary flying training in jet aircraft. Full details of the TT-1 Pinto can be found in the 1960-61 *Jane's*.

The Super Pinto has many design refinements by comparison with the Pinto of twelve years earlier. Most significant feature is the increase in performance resulting from the installation of a General Electric turbojet engine producing 2,850 lb (1,292 kg) st, compared with the 920 lb (417 kg) st Continental J69-T-9 turbojet which powered the Pinto. A five-seat executive version is projected.

American Jet Industries T-610 Super Pinto (one General Electric CJ610-4 turbojet engine)

AMERICAN JET INDUSTRIES T-610 SUPER PINTO

TYPE: Two-seat jet primary trainer or COIN aircraft.

WINGS: Cantilever mid-wing monoplane. Three different wing sections are used to preserve airflow over the outer wings long after the roots have stalled, to maintain aileron control well into the stall: 64₃A118 at root, 64₂A215 at station 88·50, and 64₂A415 at tip. Incidence 3° at root, 0° 30′ at station 88·50, and —1° 30′ at tip. Dihedral 6°. Ailerons have spring tabs and electrically-operated trim-tabs. Hydraulically-operated flaps, mechanically interlocked to ensure synchronous action.

FUSELAGE: All-metal forward structure, with moulded glass-fibre tail-cone. A thrust-diverter/speed brake mounted on a 30-in (0·76 m) fuselage extension can be actuated on the ground to attenuate thrust or can be deployed in flight as an air-brake.

TAIL UNIT: Cantilever all-metal structure. Swept vertical surface with small dorsal fin. Elevator has electrically-operated trim-tab. Rudder has ground-adjustable trim-tab.

LANDING GEAR: Hydraulically-retractable tricycle type, with single wheel on each unit. Main wheels retract inward into under-surface of wing. Heavy duty multiple-disc brakes.

POWER PLANT: One General Electric CJ610-4 turbojet engine, rated at 2,850 lb (1,292 kg) st. Fuel in fuselage and wing tanks, with single-point refuelling in each wing. Total fuel capacity 202 US gallons (764 litres). Oil capacity 4 US pints (2·27 litres).

ACCOMMODATION: Two seats in tandem in enclosed cabin; rear seat raised for improved forward visibility. Single bubble-type canopy, hinged at rear. Dual controls and automatically-sequenced ejection seats standard. Cockpit heating, windshield and canopy defogging by engine-bleed air.

SYSTEMS: Hydraulic system, pressure 3,400 lb/sq in (239 kg/cm²), supplies landing gear, wing flaps, speed brakes and seat adjustment. 28V DC electrical system. AC power provided by two 115V three-phase inverters.

ELECTRONICS: Installed to customer's requirements.

DIMENSIONS, EXTERNAL:

Wing span	29 ft 10 in (9·09 m)
Wing chord at tip	3 ft 4 in (1·02 m)
Length overall	33 ft 10¾ in (10·33 m)
Height overall	10 ft 10 in (3·30 m)
Tailplane span	13 ft 3 in (4·04 m)
Wheel track	13 ft 3½ in (4·05 m)
Wheelbase	12 ft 2¼ in (3·71 m)

AREAS:

Wings, gross	163·4 sq ft (15·18 m²)
Ailerons (total)	10·0 sq ft (0·93 m²)
Trailing-edge flaps (total)	15·65 sq ft (1·45 m²)
Air brakes (total)	1·9 sq ft (0·18 m²)
Vertical tail surfaces (total)	30·10 sq ft (2·80 m²)
Rudder, including tab	5·10 sq ft (0·47 m²)
Horizontal tail surfaces (total)	40·9 sq ft (3·80 m²)
Elevators, including tab	11·6 sq ft (1·08 m²)

WEIGHTS:

Weight empty, equipped	3,200 lb (1,451 kg)
Max T-O weight	5,300 lb (2,404 kg)

PERFORMANCE (at max T-O weight):

Max level speed (at 25,000 ft = 7,620 m)	450 knots (518 mph; 843 km/h)
Max diving speed (at 15,000 ft = 4,570 m)	Mach 0·8
Econ cruising speed (at 25,000 ft = 7,620 m)	375 knots (432 mph; 695 km/h)
Stalling speed, flaps down	63 knots (72 mph; 116 km/h)
Rate of climb at S/L	10,000 ft (3,050 m)/min
Service ceiling	over 50,000 ft (15,240 m)
T-O run	500 ft (152 m)
Landing from 50 ft (15 m)	800 ft (363 m)
Range with max fuel	846 nm (975 miles; 1,570 km)

ANDERSON

EARL ANDERSON

Mr Earl Anderson, a Boeing 707 captain flying for Pan American World Airways, has designed and built an original light amphibian which he has named EA-1 Kingfisher. The project occupied a period of nine years from start of design to completion, at a cost of around $5,500, and the first flight was made on 24 April 1969. After completing 50 hours of flight, as required by FAA regulations, Mr Anderson has flown the Kingfisher to Canada and back on a fishing trip and is currently experimenting with strakes to minimise spray thrown up during take-off and landing.

All available details follow:

ANDERSON EA-1 KINGFISHER

TYPE: Two-seat light amphibian.

WINGS: Braced high-wing monoplane with streamline-section Vee bracing struts each side (Standard Piper Cub wing). Stabilising floats mounted beneath wings, adjacent to wingtips, are constructed of ⅜ in square mahogany stringers, covered with 1/16 in mahogany plywood coated with glass-fibre. Each float weighs 4¼ lb (2 kg).

FUSELAGE: Conventional flying-boat hull of wooden construction with spruce frames and longerons, covered with 1/16 in and ¼ in mahogany plywood coated with glass-fibre.

TAIL UNIT: Conventional strut-braced tail unit.

LANDING GEAR: Retractable tail-wheel type. Each main unit is retracted forward, manually and individually, with spring-loaded assist mechanism.

Anderson EA-1 Kingfisher homebuilt light amphibian (100 hp Continental O-200 engine)
(Howard Levy)

POWER PLANT: One 100 hp Continental O-200 four-cylinder horizontally-opposed air-cooled engine, driving a fixed-pitch two-blade tractor propeller. Single fuel tank in hull, immediately forward of windshield, capacity 20 US gallons (76 litres).

ACCOMMODATION: Two seats, side-by-side, in enclosed cabin. Piper Tri-Pacer windshield.

DIMENSIONS, EXTERNAL:

Wing span	36 ft 1 in (11·00 m)
Length overall	23 ft 6 in (7·16 m)
Height overall	8 ft 0 in (2·44 m)
Wheel track	5 ft 0 in (1·52 m)

WEIGHTS:

Weight empty	1,032 lb (468 kg)
Max T-O weight	1,500 lb (680 kg)

PERFORMANCE (at max T-O weight):

Cruising speed	74 knots (85 mph; 136 km/h)
Rate of climb at S/L	500-600 ft (150-180 m)/min
Service ceiling	10,000 ft (3,050 m)

ARDC

AERONAUTICAL RESEARCH & DEVELOPMENT CORPORATION

HEAD OFFICE:
87 Terrace Hall Avenue, Burlington, Massachusetts.

POSTAL ADDRESS:
PO Box 8246, Boston, Massachusetts 02114

CHAIRMAN OF THE BOARD AND ACTING PRESIDENT:
George E. Fryer

DIRECTORS:
George E. Fryer
Louis F. Freitas
Jack D. Gateman
William F. Sentner
Richard V. Tino

This company announced early in 1969 that it had acquired from Lear Jet Industries their Brantly Helicopter Corporation division and this is now known as the Brantly Division of ARDC.

The former Brantly B-2B is being updated and improved and will be re-designated B-2E in its new production form.

Production of the former Brantly Model 305 continues, as well as the ARDC/Omega RP-440 flying-crane helicopter. ARDC are also involved in a research and development programme for the Omega TP-900 three-turbine helicopter, an advanced version of the RP-440, for use with a detachable pod. In an all-passenger configuration the pod would accommodate 14 persons and baggage, but ARDC consider that other potential uses might include the carriage of freight, refrigerated cargo and pre-sorted mail, or that the pod could become a complete medical treatment container with its own electrical power source, oxygen, litters and equipment.

ARDC announced early in 1970 their intention to develop a lightweight single-seat helicopter to be known as the ARDC-Fryer Flyer Dash I. Powered by a 100 hp engine and with a gross T-O weight of 820 lb (372 kg), it is estimated that the Dash I will have a maximum level speed at S/L of 95·5 knots (110 mph; 177 km/h).

ARDC/OMEGA RP-440

The original prototype of this helicopter, known as the BS-12, was flown for the first time on 26 December 1956, and received its FAA Type Certificate in April 1961. It was powered by two 225 hp Franklin 6VS-335 engines and was followed by a second machine, known as the BS-12D1, with 260 hp Lycoming O-540 engines and a number of detail refinements. Two pre-production models, designated BS-12D3S, flew in 1963 with supercharged Franklin engines. The production version now offered by ARDC reverts to Lycoming engines, as described below.

TYPE: Twin-engined general-purpose helicopter.

ROTOR SYSTEM: Four-blade fully-articulated main rotor. Blades have laminated birch spar, spruce and balsa afterbody, stainless steel leading-edge and glass-fibre covering. Blades attached to hub through horizontal and vertical hinges and friction dampers. Two-blade teetering tail rotor of similar construction to main rotor. Rotor blades do not fold.

ROTOR DRIVE: Both engines connected to a single gear-box through a flexible drive consisting of 13 nylon-cored full-wedge rubber belts. Centrifugal clutch in drive-shaft from each engine engages at specified rpm through action of flywheel-mounted brake linings. Spiral jaw clutch disengages engine from drive in case of failure. Final drive from belt to rotor shaft

through spiral bevel gear. Tail rotor shaft-driven at constant velocity, through universal joints, from main transmission. Main rotor rpm 280 min, 350 max.

FUSELAGE: Semi-monocoque cabin structure. Uncovered welded steel-tube rear fuselage.

LANDING GEAR: Non-retractable tricycle type, with twin nose-wheels and single wheel on each main unit.

POWER PLANT: Two 290 hp Lycoming IO-540-F1B5 six-cylinder horizontally-opposed air-cooled engines, mounted on steel-tube outrigger structures. Complete power plants can be removed as units on their mountings. Fuel tanks in fuselage, with total capacity of 76 US gallons (288 litres). Separate fuel system for each engine.

ACCOMMODATION: Enclosed cabin for pilot and passenger side-by-side in front. Room for two or three persons on rear bench seat. Payload carried under rear fuselage, directly under rotor shaft.

DIMENSIONS, EXTERNAL:

Diameter of main rotor	38 ft 5 in (11·71 m)
Main rotor blade chord	10 in (25·4 cm)
Diameter of tail rotor	7 ft 11 in (2·41 m)
Tail rotor blade chord	4 in (10 cm)
Length overall	48 ft 4 in (14·73 m)
Height overall	13 ft 0 in (3·96 m)
Wheel track	13 ft 9 in (4·19 m)

AREAS:

Main rotor blade (each)	14·3 sq ft (1·33 m²)
Main rotor disc	1,194·6 sq ft (110·98 m²)
Tail rotor disc	48·0 sq ft (4·46 m²)

WEIGHTS:

Weight empty	3,260 lb (1,479 kg)
Payload	1,250 lb (567 kg)
Normal T-O weight	5,150 lb (2,336 kg)

PERFORMANCE (at max T-O weight):
Max level speed at S/L
    83 knots (95 mph; 153 km/h)
Max cruising speed
    74 knots (85 mph; 137 km/h)
Max rate of climb at S/L 950 ft (290 m)/min
Service ceiling   12,400 ft (3,780 m)
Hovering ceiling in ground effect
    6,000 ft (1,830 m)
Range with max fuel
    112 nm (130 miles; 209 km)

ARDC/BRANTLY MODEL B-2B and B-2E

The B-2E is an updated version of the B-2B, with a de-rated 205 hp Lycoming engine, improved door closures and cabin heating system, solid-state instrumentation and other minor internal improvements.

Detailed information on the B-2E was not available at the time of writing, and the description below applies to the B-2B, which is no longer in production.

A combined total of approximately 400 B-2s of all types had been completed at the beginning of February 1970.

TYPE: Two-seat light helicopter.

ROTOR SYSTEM: Three-blade main rotor. Articulated inboard flapping hinges offset 2·67 in (67·8 mm) from hub, and coincident flap and lag hinges offset 51·85 in (1,317 mm) from hub. Symmetrical blade section with 29% thickness ratio on inboard portion; NACA 0012 section outboard of hinge. Inboard portion of each blade is rigid, built around a steel spar blade. Outboard portion is flexible, with an extruded aluminium leading-edge spar and polyurethane core; aluminium skin is bonded to core and riveted to spar. Blades are attached to hub by flapping links and do not fold. A rotor brake is standard equipment. Two-blade tail anti-torque rotor of all-metal construction.

ROTOR DRIVE: Through centrifugal clutch and planetary reduction gears. Bevel gear take-off from main transmission with flexible coupling to tail rotor drive-shaft. Main rotor/engine rpm ratio 1 : 6·158. Anti-torque rotor/engine rpm ratio 1 : 1.

FUSELAGE: Stressed-skin all-metal structure with conical tail section. Tail rotor on swept-up boom extension.

LANDING GEAR: Alternative skid or wheel landing gear. Skid type has small retractable wheels for ground handling, fixed tail-skid and four oleo shock-absorbers with rubber-disc taxying springs. Tyres size 10 × 3½, pressure 60 lb/sq in (4·22 kg/cm²). The wheel gear has two main wheels and twin nose-wheels, all on oleo-pneumatic shock-absorbers. Inflatable pontoons, which attach to the standard skids, are available to permit operation from water.

POWER PLANT: One 180 hp Lycoming IVO-360-A1A four-cylinder, horizontally-opposed air-cooled engine, mounted vertically, with induction cooling system. Fuel in rubber bag-type tank under engine, capacity 31 US gallons (117 litres). Refuelling point on port side of fuselage. Oil capacity 1·5 US gallons (5·7 litres).

ACCOMMODATION: Totally-enclosed circular cabin for two persons seated side-by-side. Forward-hinged door on each side. Dual controls. Cabin heater and demisting fan standard. Compartment for 50 lb (22·7 kg) baggage in forward end of tail section.

ELECTRONICS AND EQUIPMENT: Provision for Narco Mk 12, King KY 90 or King KX 150A radio. Twin landing lights in nose.

DIMENSIONS, EXTERNAL:
Diameter of main rotor	23 ft 9 in (7·24 m)
Main rotor blade chord:	
inboard	8·85 in (22·48 cm)
outboard	8·0 in (20·32 cm)
Diameter of tail rotor	4 ft 3 in (1·29 m)
Length overall	21 ft 9 in (6·62 m)
Height overall	6 ft 9 in (2·06 m)
Skid track	5 ft 8¼ in (1·73 m)
Passenger doors (each):	
Height	2 ft 7 in (0·79 m)
Width	2 ft 9¾ in (0·86 m)
Baggage compartment door:	
Mean height	9¾ in (0·25 m)
Length	1 ft 9¾ in (0·55 m)

DIMENSIONS, INTERNAL:
Max width of cabin	4 ft 2 in (1·27 m)
Baggage compartment	6 cu ft (0·17 m²)

AREAS:
Main rotor blade (each)	7·42 sq ft (0·69 m²)
Main rotor disc	442 sq ft (41·06 m²)
Tail rotor disc	13 sq ft (1·21 m²)

WEIGHTS AND LOADINGS:
Weight empty with skids	1,020 lb (463 kg)
Weight empty with floats	1,060 lb (481 kg)
Max T-O weight	1,670 lb (757 kg)
Max disc loading	3·77 lb/sq ft (18·4 kg/m²)
Max power loading	9·27 lb/hp (4·20 kg/hp)

Model of the proposed ARDC/Omega TP-900 three-turbine helicopter

Pre-production version of the Omega RP-440 flying crane helicopter *(Howard Levy)*

ARDC/Brantly Model B-2B two-seat helicopter (180 hp Lycoming IVO-360-A1A engine)

PERFORMANCE (at max T-O weight):
Max level speed at S/L
    87 knots (100 mph; 161 km/h)
Max cruising speed (75% power)
    78 knots (90 mph; 145 km/h)
Rate of climb at S/L 1,900 ft (580 m)/min
Service ceiling   10,800 ft (3,290 m)
Hovering ceiling in ground effect
    6,700 ft (2,040 m)
Range with max fuel, with reserve
    217 nm (250 miles; 400 km)

ARDC/BRANTLY MODEL 305

The Model 305 is a five-seat helicopter of similar configuration to the Model B-2B described above, but larger in every respect. Design work began in September 1963 and the prototype flew for the first time in January 1964. FAA type approval of the Model 305 was received on 29 July 1965 and deliveries began in the following month. A total of approximately 50 Model 305s had been built at the beginning of February 1970.

TYPE: Five-seat light helicopter.

ROTOR SYSTEM: Three-blade main rotor. Articulated inboard flapping hinges offset 3·625 in (9·21 cm) from hub, and coincident flap and lag hinges outboard. Inboard portion of each blade is rigid, built around a steel spar blade. All-metal outboard portion has a D-spar and is foam-filled. Two-blade all-metal tail rotor. Each blade has a forged aluminium leading-edge spar, ribs and riveted aluminium skin. Main rotor blades do not fold. Rotor brake is standard.

ROTOR DRIVE: Main rotor shaft-driven through centrifugal clutch and planetary reduction gears. Bevel gear take-off from main transmission, with flexible coupling, through tail rotor drive-shaft and intermediate gearbox to tail gearbox. Main rotor/engine rpm ratio 1 : 6·666. Tail rotor/engine rpm ratio 1 : 0·998.

FUSELAGE: Stressed-skin all-metal structure, with conical tail section. Tail rotor carried on swept-up boom extension.

TAIL UNIT: Small variable-incidence horizontal stabiliser of all-metal stressed-skin construction.

LANDING GEAR: Alternative skid, wheel or float gear. Skid landing gear has four oleo struts, two on each side, and small retractable ground handling wheels. The wheel gear has two main wheels and twin nose wheels, all on oleo-pneumatic shock-absorbers. Goodyear main wheels and tyres size 6·00 × 6, pressure 30 lb/sq in (2·10 kg/cm²). Goodyear nose-wheels and tyres size 5·00 × 5, pressure 28 lb/sq in (1·97 kg/cm²). Goodyear single-disc hydraulic brakes on main wheels.

POWER PLANT: One 305 hp Lycoming IVO-540-A1A six-cylinder horizontally-opposed air-cooled engine. Fuel in one rubber-cell tank located under engine, capacity 43 US gallons (163 litres). Refuelling point in port side of fuselage. Oil capacity 2·5 US gallons (9·5 litres).

ACCOMMODATION: Two individual seats side-by-side in front, with dual controls. Rear bench seat for three persons. Door on each side. Rear compartment for 250 lb (113 kg) of baggage, with downward-hinged door on starboard side.

ELECTRONICS AND EQUIPMENT: King or Narco radio, to customer's specification. Blind-flying instrumentation is available, but helicopter is not certificated for instrument flight.

DIMENSIONS, EXTERNAL:
Diameter of main rotor	28 ft 8 in (8·74 m)
Main rotor blade chord (constant)	
	10 in (25·4 cm)
Diameter of tail rotor	4 ft 3 in (1·30 m)
Length overall, rotor turning	32 ft 11 in (10·03 m)
Length of fuselage	24 ft 5 in (7·44 m)
Overall height	8 ft 0⅛ in (2·44 m)
Wheel track	6 ft 10¾ in (2·10 m)
Wheelbase	7 ft 0½ in (2·15 m)
Passenger doors (each):	
Height	2 ft 8¼ in (0·82 m)
Width	3 ft 3⅜ in (1·02 m)
Baggage compartment door:	
Height, mean	1 ft 0¼ in (0·30 m)
Width	2 ft 3 in (0·69 m)

DIMENSIONS, INTERNAL:
Cabin: Length	7 ft 6½ in (2·30 m)
Max width	4 ft 6¾ in (1·39 m)
Max height	4 ft 0½ in (1·22 m)
Baggage compartment	16·7 cu ft (0·47 m³)

ARDC/Brantly Model 305 five-seat light helicopter (305 hp Lycoming IVO-540-A1A engine)

AREAS:
Main rotor blade (each)	11·79 sq ft (1·09 m²)
Tail rotor blade (each)	0·50 sq ft (0·05 m²)
Main rotor disc	35·8 sq ft (3·33 m²)
Tail rotor disc	14·18 sq ft (1·32 m²)

WEIGHTS AND LOADINGS:
Weight empty	1,800 lb (817 kg)
Max T-O and landing weight	2,900 lb (1,315 kg)
Max zero-fuel weight	2,700 lb (1,224 kg)
Max disc loading	4·65 lb/sq ft (22·7 kg/m²)
Max power loading	9·84 lb/hp (4·46 kg/hp)

PERFORMANCE (at max T-O weight):
Max level speed at S/L	104 knots (120 mph; 193 km/h)
Max cruising speed at S/L	96 knots (110 mph; 177 km/h)
Max rate of climb at S/L	975 ft (297 m)/min
Service ceiling	12,000 ft (3,660 m)
Hovering ceiling in ground effect	4,080 ft (1,245 m)
Range with max fuel and max payload, with 15 min reserve	191 nm (220 miles; 354 km)

AVIATION SPECIALTIES

AVIATION SPECIALTIES INC

HEAD OFFICE:
4930 East Falcon Drive, Falcon Field, Mesa, Arizona 85201

GENERAL MANAGER:
Floyd D. Stilwell

Aviation Specialties have developed a turbine-powered conversion of the Sikorsky S-55 helicopter, and this was scheduled for FAA certification early in 1970. Production of at least 100 conversions is anticipated.

AVIATION SPECIALTIES/SIKORSKY S-55-T

The S-55-T flight test airframe is powered by a Garrett-AiResearch TSE 331-3 turboshaft engine, rated at 840 shp.

The conversion entails removing the existing Wright R-1300 piston-engine and replacing it with the turboshaft engine, which is mounted at an angle of approximately 35°, with the exhaust facing down and forward. The new engine is connected to the engine mount by three gearbox mount fittings, and this in turn mates to the original attachment fittings on the firewall of the helicopter structure. The output-flange of the turbine connects directly to the existing fluid-drive clutch unit. The throttle-collective interconnection system has been redesigned to eliminate the interconnection, so that the throttle can be connected to the underspeed governor shaft of the engine's fuel control.

A weight saving of approximately 900 lb (408 kg) is made by the conversion, and it is expected that the S-55-T will have a useful load of approximately 3,000 lb (1,360 kg) at a rated gross weight of 7,200 lb (3,265 kg). The basic CG envelope of the S-55 is retained by re-arrangement of equipment in the aircraft.

Aviation Specialties S-55-T, a turbine-powered conversion of the Sikorsky S-55

BANNICK

BANNICK COPTERS, INC

ADDRESS:
3760 Campus Drive, Newport Beach, California 92660

VICE-PRESIDENT:
Lester J. Bannick

Mr Lester J. Bannick designed a single-seat light autogyro known as the Model T Copter, and made plans and kits of parts available to amateur constructors. He has now discontinued this model and is producing instead a single-seat autogyro powered by a 1,600 cc Volkswagen engine, designated Bannick Copter Model VW. Plans and kits of parts to enable amateur constructors to build a similar aircraft are available from Bannick Copters, Inc. Under development is a very clean two-seat light autogyro known as the Model C Copter.

BANNICK COPTER MODEL VW

The Model VW has a two-blade main rotor constructed of 6061 T6 aluminium and provided with a rotor brake and clutch for pre-rotation of rotor. Fuselage structure is built up from 6061 T6 aluminium angle-section of 0·125 in thickness. The tail unit consists of a vertical fin and rudder of plywood. The tricycle landing gear comprises three aluminium wheels with tyres 5 in (12·7 cm) in diameter. Power plant consists of one 64 hp Volkswagen 1,600 cc four-cylinder horizontally-opposed air-cooled engine driving a two-blade fixed-pitch pusher propeller. Fuel tank under pilot's seat, capacity 9 US gallons (34 litres). Oil capacity 1 US gallon (3·8 litres).

Five Model VWs had been completed by March 1969.

DIMENSIONS, EXTERNAL:
Diameter of main rotor   23 ft 0 in (7·01 m)

PERFORMANCE:
Max diving speed
86·5 knots (100 mph; 160 km/h)
Max cruising speed 52 knots (60 mph; 97 km/h)
T-O to 50 ft (15 m)   100 ft (30 m)
Landing from 50 ft (15 m)   50 ft (15 m)
Landing run   20 ft (6 m)

BANNICK MODEL C COPTER

Design of the Model C was started in 1964, and the first flight was made in 1967. The rotor is similar to that of the Bannick Model T Copter, described in the 1968/69 *Jane's*, and pre-rotation is achieved through a flexible drive and friction clutch. The 135 hp Lycoming engine is mounted in a mid-position on the main pylon and drives a two-blade pusher propeller. Fuselage is of welded steel-tube construction, completely faired-in with glass-fibre. The horizontal stabiliser is streamlined into the fuselage, and the tail unit is completed with a conventional fin and rudder. Landing gear is of the non-retractable nose-wheel type. Fuel capacity is 16·5 US gallons (62·5 litres).

It is known that research and development of the Model C was continuing in 1969, but no further details of this model had been made available at the time of writing.

Bannick Model C Copter two-seat autogyro (135 hp Lycoming engine)

BEDE

BEDE AIRCRAFT, INC

HEAD OFFICE: 355 Richmond Road, Cleveland, Ohio 44143

As a successor to the former Bede Aviation Corporation, Mr James Bede formed Bede Aircraft Inc, to continue development of plans and kits of parts for construction of his BD-4 two/four-seat light aircraft, which are marketed by Bede Homebuilts from the above address.

Mr Bede is continuing development of his BD-2 Love One aircraft for an attempted non-stop un-refuelled round-the-world flight, and full details of this may be found under the heading of World Flight Incorporated in this section.

The Bede BD-4 has evolved from the original BD-1 design, which was acquired by American Aviation Corporation (which see) and developed as the AA-1 Yankee. A total of 233 BD-4's were under construction and over 1,000 sets of plans had been sold by January 1970.

Bede BD-4 two/four-seat light aircraft (108 hp Lycoming O-235-C1 engine)

BEDE BD-4

TYPE: Two/four-seat sporting and utility monoplane for amateur construction.

WINGS: Cantilever high-wing monoplane. Wing section NACA 64 415. No dihedral. Incidence 3°. Each wing is built around 24 glass-fibre "panel-ribs" which are slid over a 6¼ in (16·5 cm) diameter extruded aluminium tubular spar, to which they are secured by epoxy resin, and large-diameter tube clamps. Each 10 ft (3·05 m) wing section then slides for 1 ft (0·30 m) over a smaller-diameter 2024-T3 centre-section tube. Identical and interchangeable trailing-edge flaps and ailerons are attached to the trailing-edge of the ribs. Design allows for either removable or folding wings.

FUSELAGE: All-metal structure of bolt-together design. Formed 2024-T3 aluminium angle-sections, made from 0·063 in sheet stock in 2 in × 2 in, 1½ in × 1½ in and 1 in × 1 in sizes, are used for the basic structure of the fuselage. Simple metal gussets are used to form joints, bolted together with AN3 flush screws and nuts. Skin of either aluminium sheet or glass-fibre panels can be pop-riveted or bonded to the primary structure. Access door to cabin on each side, under wing.

TAIL UNIT: Cantilever all-metal structure with swept vertical surfaces. All-moving tailplane, consisting of a single 2¼ in (5·85 cm) diameter tubular spar, with six metal ribs and aluminium skin. Fin and rudder are constructed on U-section metal spars, with aluminium skin. Rudder pivots on a one-piece piano-hinge. All control surfaces statically mass-balanced.

LANDING GEAR: Non-retractable tricycle type. Each main leg is formed from a single piece of 2024-T3 aluminium plate, which rotates on a pivot point inside the fuselage. Shock loads are absorbed by rubber in compression. Main wheels size 6·00 × 6 with 15 in (0·38 m) diameter tubed tyres. Non-steerable fully-castoring nose-wheel carried on a 1½ in (3·81 cm) diameter 4130 steel tube which pivots on the fuselage and has similar shock-absorption to the main legs. Nose-wheel of either 8 in or 10 in (0·20 m

or 0·25 m) diameter. Hydraulic brakes. Optional wheel fairings increase maximum speed by 8·5 knots (10 mph; 16 km/h).

POWER PLANT: One 108 hp Lycoming O-235-C1 four-cylinder horizontally-opposed air-cooled engine, driving a McCauley 1B-90/CM two-blade fixed-pitch propeller, diameter 5 ft 9 in (1·75 m) for two-seat configuration; or one 180 hp Lycoming O-360 engine, driving a Hartzell 7663-A4 constant-speed propeller, diameter 6 ft 4 in (1·93 m), for four-seat configuration. Alternative engines of up to 200 hp, and McCauley or Hartzell constant-speed propellers, are optional. Propeller spinner standard. Simple three-piece cowling with glass-fibre nose section. Engine mounting of swing-out type for easy maintenance. Fuel contained between wing panel ribs, with standard capacity of 25·8 US gallons (97 litres) in each wing. Total standard fuel capacity 51·6 US gallons (195 litres). Max fuel capacity 85 US gallons (322 litres). Refuelling points above each wing.

ACCOMMODATION: Two or four seats, in pairs, in enclosed cabin.

SYSTEMS: Hydraulic system for brakes only. Electrical system includes engine-driven generator, 12V battery and navigation lights.

DIMENSIONS, EXTERNAL:
Wing span	25 ft 6 in (7·77 m)
Wing chord (constant)	4 ft 0 in (1·22 m)
Wing aspect ratio	6·1
Length overall	21 ft 10½ in (6·67 m)
Width, wings folded	7 ft 2½ in (2·20 m)
Height overall	6 ft 2½ in (1·89 m)
Tailplane span	7 ft 1¼ in (2·17 m)
Wheel track	7 ft 0 in (2·13 m)

DIMENSIONS, INTERNAL:
Cabin:
Length	7 ft 5 in (2·26 m)
Max width	3 ft 5 in (1·04 m)
Max height	3 ft 5 in (1·04 m)

AREAS:
Wings, gross	102 sq ft (9·48 m²)
Ailerons, total	3·6 sq ft (0·33 m²)
Trailing-edge flaps, total	8·0 sq ft (0·74 m²)
Fin	6·9 sq ft (0·64 m²)
Rudder	1·5 sq ft (0·14 m²)
Tailplane	21·3 sq ft (2·00 m²)

WEIGHTS AND LOADINGS (A = 108 hp, B = 180 hp):
Empty weight:		
A		840 lb (381 kg)
B		880 lb (399 kg)
Max T-O weight:		
A		1,400 lb (635 kg)
B		1,800 lb (816 kg)
Max wing loading:		
A		14·6 lb/sq ft (71·3 kg/m²)
B		16·7 lb/sq ft (81·5 kg/m²)
Max power loading:		
A		13·0 lb/hp (5·90 kg/hp)
B		10·0 lb/hp (4·54 kg/hp)

PERFORMANCE (at max T-O weight, A = 108 hp, B = 180 hp):
Max level speed at S/L:		
A		135 knots (156 mph; 251 km/h)
B		156 knots (180 mph; 290 km/h)
Cruising speed at 75% power:		
A		126 knots (145 mph; 233 km/h)
B		152 knots (175 mph; 282 km/h)
Cruising speed at 65% power:		
A		123 knots (142 mph; 229 km/h)
B		148 knots (170 mph; 274 km/h)
Stalling speed, flaps down:		
A		47 knots (54 mph; 87 km/h)
B		51 knots (58 mph; 94 km/h)
Stalling speed, flaps up:		
A		53 knots (60 mph; 97 km/h)
B		54 knots (62 mph; 100 km/h)
Max rate of climb at S/L:		
A		900 ft (274 m)/min
B		1,400 ft (427 m)/min
T-O run:		
A		600 ft (183 m)
B		525 ft (160 m)
Landing run:		
A		500 ft (152 m)
B		600 ft (183 m)
Max range:		
A, B		1,042 nm (1,200 miles; 1,930 km)

BEECHCRAFT
BEECH AIRCRAFT CORPORATION

HEAD OFFICE AND MAIN WORKS:
Wichita, Kansas 67201

BRANCH DIVISIONS:
Liberal, Kansas; Salina, Kansas; and Boulder, Colorado

CHAIRMAN OF THE BOARD AND CHIEF EXECUTIVE OFFICER:
Mrs O. A. (Walter H.) Beech

PRESIDENT:
Frank E. Hedrick

SENIOR VICE-PRESIDENT:
George T. Humphrey

VICE-PRESIDENTS:
L. E. Bowery (Bell Programmes)
Ed C. Burns (Operations)
Seymour Colman (Production)
Leddy L. Greever (Corporate Director)
Wyman L. Henry (Marketing)
James N. Lew (Engineering)
Jack L. Marinelli (Aircraft Research and Development)
Roy H. McGregor (Aerospace Marketing and Contracts)
M. G. Neuburger (Export Sales)
Austin Rising (Corporate Planning and Special Services)
L. L. Pechin (Manufacturing)

SECRETARY-TREASURER:
John A. Elliott

ASSISTANT SECRETARIES:
L. Winters
R. W. Fisher

ASSISTANT TREASURER:
P. M. Vann

MANAGER, ADVERTISING AND SALES PROMOTION:
R. James Yarnell

DIRECTOR, PUBLIC RELATIONS:
Bill Robinson

Founded in 1932 by the late Walter H. Beech, pioneer designer and builder of light aeroplanes in the United States, the Beech Aircraft Corporation is currently engaged in the production of civil and military aircraft, missile targets, aircraft and missile components and cryogenic equipment for spacecraft.

Production of the Beechcraft Model H18 Super H18 (total of 9,388 built) has now ended; details of this may be found in the 1969-70 *Jane's*.

Earlier, the Model E95 Travel Air and Queen Air 88 were taken out of production, after manufacture of 719 and 45 aircraft respectively.

Deliveries by Beech in 1969 were made up of 10 Super H18s, 344 Bonanzas, 70 Queen Airs, 239 Barons, 170 Musketeers, 81 King Airs, 85 Dukes and 62 Beechcraft Airliners.

Details of the 21 types of civil aircraft in current production are given below.

Production continues under the $75 million contract awarded by Bell Helicopter Company in 1968 for the manufacture of airframes for the turbine-powered Bell JetRanger helicopter. The contract, covering production of airframes for both military and commercial JetRangers, was additional to a contract under which Beech aircraft was already delivering JetRanger airframes to Bell.

The JetRanger airframe programme, which is likely to exceed 4,000 units over a five-year period, was assigned to Beech Aircraft's Wichita Plant III. Included in the contract are airframes for the Bell light observation helicopter (OH-58A). Beech Aircraft is responsible for fuselage, skid gear, tail boom, spar, stabiliser and two rear fairing assemblies. Initial deliveries of JetRanger airframes began in October 1968, with first deliveries of OH-58A airframes following in November. Units are shipped to Fort Worth, where Bell completes assembly.

Beech also produces sub-assemblies for the Bell UH-1 Iroquois, and manufacture of assemblies for the McDonnell Douglas F-4 Phantom II has entered its eighth consecutive year.

Beech Aircraft and Hawker Siddeley Aviation Ltd, of Kingston upon Thames, England, announced in December 1969 a combining of their efforts to design, develop, manufacture and market a family of next-generation corporate jet aircraft.

Under this arrangement Beech Aircraft assumed marketing responsibilities in the US, and other areas of the world, for the Hawker Siddeley 125, which is now known as the Beechcraft Hawker 125 (BH 125). A full description of this aircraft may be found in the "UK Aircraft" section of this edition.

The joint programme provided for Beech Aircraft to purchase the aviation assets of Hawker Siddeley International Ltd, including the spare parts inventory for the BH 125, the de Havilland Dove and the de Havilland Heron.

Business executive jet aircraft produced by the two companies will all be known as Beechcraft Hawker types, and will include a new larger and faster version of the BH 125, designated BH 600,

which is now undergoing analysis and development and is scheduled for initial delivery in 1971. A new-generation jet aircraft designated BH 200 is projected, retaining the interior layout and comfort of the BH 125 series, and combining high and more economical performance with outstanding short-field capability.

Beech is also developing and manufacturing target drones for the US military services and details of these can be found in the "Drones" section of this work.

Beech Aircraft occupies over 2,300,000 sq ft (213,680 m²) of plant area at its four major facilities in Wichita, Liberal and Salina, Kansas, and Boulder, Colorado.

The Salina division supplies all wings used in Wichita production and is responsible for manufacture and final assembly of the six-seat Beechcraft Duke. It also produces the Model 1025 Cardinal target drone.

All assembly, flight testing and delivery of Beechcraft Musketeers is carried out at the Liberal Division.

Work at Boulder involves orbital satellite, space vehicle or missile applications, including design, development, final assembly and testing of the cryogenic gas storage system for the National Aeronautics and Space Administration's Apollo spacecraft. Boulder also produces aircraft assemblies for other Beech divisions and the AQM-37A missile target system for the US Navy. (See "Drones" section).

Wholly-owned subsidiaries of the parent company include Beech Acceptance Corporation, Inc, which is engaged in business aircraft retail finance and leasing; Beechcraft Research & Development Inc, which is concerned with military work of a classified nature in the advanced fields of aircraft, missiles and astronautics; Beechcraft AG, which has its headquarters in Zurich, Switzerland, and supports in Europe the sales, liaison and other activities of the parent company; Beech Holdings, Inc, a supporting company to assist the needs of the parent company, particularly in marketing; and the following product distributorships: Houston-Beechcraft, Inc, Houston, Texas; Denver-Beechcraft, Inc, Denver, Colorado; United Beechcraft, Inc, Wichita, Kansas; and Beechcraft West, Oakland and Van Nuys, California.

BEECHCRAFT MODEL H18 SUPER H18

With delivery in November 1969 of three Super H18's to Japan Air Lines, production of the Model 18 series ended. More than 32 years had elapsed since the first Model 18 made its initial flight on 15 January 1937, representing the

longest continuous production record of any aircraft. A total of 756 Super H18's had been delivered since 1954. Details of this model may be found in the 1969-70 *Jane's*.

BEECHCRAFT MUSKETEER

First flown on 23 October 1961, the Musketeer is a low-cost all-metal two-to-six-seat light aircraft. The original Model 23 Musketeer received FAA certification on 20 February 1962 and first deliveries were made in the Autumn of 1962. In October 1965 Beech introduced a new range of Musketeers. A more powerful engine was introduced on the Custom version in March 1967, and an optional aerobatic kit was made available for the Sport and Custom models in 1968. The Musketeer Super R, with retractable landing gear, was introduced in late 1969.

Details of the current models are as follows:

Custom. Standard four-seat Musketeer with 180 hp Lycoming O-360-A2G engine and non-retractable landing gear. Aerobatic version is approved for rolls, Immelmann turns, loops, spins, chandelles, limited inverted flight and other manoeuvres, carrying two persons.

Sport. Two-seat (optional four-seat) sporting and training version with 150 hp Lycoming O-320-E2C engine and non-retractable landing gear. Aerobatic version is approved for rolls, Immelmann turns, loops, spins, chandelles, limited inverted flight and other manoeuvres, carrying two persons.

Super. Generally similar to Custom version, but with 200 hp Lycoming IO-360-A2B engine and optional constant-speed propeller.

Super R. Generally similar to the Super version, but has a constant-speed propeller as standard and retractable tricycle type landing gear. Electrically-actuated hydraulic system based on a self-contained unit in the rear fuselage, comprising electrically-driven hydraulic pump, fluid reservoir and valves. An emergency valve, sited adjacent to the pilot's feet, allows selection of the landing gear to free-fall within three seconds. Main wheels retract inward into wings, nose-wheel turns through 90° as it retracts rearwards. Four windows standard on each side of cabin.

Production of the Musketeer is centred in Beech's Liberal, Kansas, plant. A total of 2,079 Musketeers of all models had been delivered by the end of 1969.

TYPE: Two/six-seat cabin monoplane.
WINGS: Cantilever low-wing monoplane. Wing section NACA 63₂A415. Dihedral 6° 30'. Incidence 3° at root, 1° at tip. Single extruded main spar at 50% chord. Aluminium skin and stringers are bonded to honeycomb Trussgrid ribs on forward 50% of wing; rear 50% of wing is riveted. Slotted all-metal riveted ailerons

Aerobatic version of the Beechcraft Musketeer Custom

Beechcraft Musketeer in service with the Mexican Air Force

and mechanically-controlled (optionally electrically-actuated) flaps have corrugated skin. No trim-tabs. Plastic wing-tips.

FUSELAGE: Cabin section has basic keel formed by floor and lower skin, with rolled skin side panels, stringers, a minimum number of bulkheads and structural top. Conventional semi-monocoque rear fuselage.

TAIL UNIT: Cantilever all-metal structure, with swept vertical surfaces. One-piece all-moving horizontal surface with full-span anti-servo tab. Optional electric tailplane trim. Rudder and aileron controls interconnected for easy cross-country flying.

LANDING GEAR (Custom, Sport, Super): Non-retractable tricycle type. Beech rubber-disc shock-absorbers. Tube-type tyres size 6·00-6 × 15 (optionally 6·00-6 × 17·5), pressure 40 lb/sq in (2·81 kg/cm²), on all wheels. Goodyear hydraulic brakes. Steerable nose-wheel. Parking brake.

LANDING GEAR (Super R): Retractable tricycle type with electrically-actuated hydraulic retraction. Main units retract outwards and upwards into wing wells, nose-wheel unit turns through 90° and retracts rearward to fold flat into a fairing behind the nose-wheel strut. Steerable self-centering nose-wheel. Beech rubber-disc shock absorbers. Main wheels with tube-type tyres size 6·00-6 × 17·5; nose-wheel tyre size 5·00-5 × 14·2. Goodyear hydraulic brakes with toe-operated control. Parking brake.

POWER PLANT: One four-cylinder horizontally-opposed air-cooled engine (details under model listings above), driving Sensenich two-blade fixed-pitch metal propeller, diameter 6 ft 4 in (1·93 m). Fuel in two tanks in inboard wing leading-edges, with total capacity of 60 US gallons (227 litres). Refuelling points above tanks. Oil capacity 2 US gallons (7·5 litres).

ACCOMMODATION (Custom, Super and Super R): Pilot and three to five passengers, in pairs, in enclosed cabin. Door on starboard side; optional port door available. Compartment for 140 lb (63 kg) baggage, with external door on starboard side. In-flight adjustable seats, ash trays, cigarette lighter, pilot's storm window, windshield defroster, instrument panel glare shield, sun visors, air vents, map stowage, wall-to-wall carpeting. Optional aerobatic kit for Custom includes "g" meter, quick-release door, inertia reel and shoulder harnesses.

ACCOMMODATION (Sport): Generally as for other versions except pilot and one to three passengers in pairs. Optional aerobatic kit includes "g" meter, quick-release door, inertia reel and shoulder harnesses.

SYSTEMS: Electrical system supplied by 60A self-exciting alternator, 12V 25Ah battery. Hydraulic system for brakes only, except on Super R which has electro-hydraulic retraction system for landing gear. Vacuum system for instruments optional.

ELECTRONICS AND EQUIPMENT: Standard equipment includes vertical read-out engine gauges, 8-day clock; outside air temperature gauge; stall warning system; ventilation, heating and defrosting system; landing light; navigation lights; rotating beacon; cabin dome light; overhead instruments and map light; cabin boarding step; tow bar; tie-down rings; control lock and pitot cover. Standard avionics comprise Narco Mark 8 nav/com with VOR/LOC indicator, microphone, cabin speaker and antennae. A wide range of optional equipment includes Beechcraft "New-Matic" flight control system; blind flying instrumentation; vacuum system; dual controls; mixture indicator; heated pitot tube; electrically-operated tailplane trim; electrically-operated flaps; tinted windshield and cabin windows; rear "family-seat" installation; headrests; 35Ah battery; heavy-duty tyres (except for Super R); fire extinguisher; instrument post lights; wing-mounted taxi light; internal corrosion proofing and optional paint schemes. An extensive range of Bendix, King, Narco, Polaris and Sunair avionics is available optionally to customer's requirements.

DIMENSIONS, EXTERNAL:
Wing span	32 ft 9 in (9·98 m)
Wing chord (constant)	4 ft 4¾ in (1·34 m)
Wing aspect ratio	7·5
Length overall	25 ft 0 in (7·62 m)
Height overall	8 ft 3 in (2·51 m)
Tailplane span	10 ft 8 in (3·25 m)
Wheel track	11 ft 10 in (3·61 m)
Wheelbase	6 ft 4 in (1·93 m)
Passenger door: Height	3 ft 2 in (0·97 m)
Width	3 ft 4 in (1·03 m)
Baggage compartment door:	
Height	1 ft 6½ in (0·47 m)
Width	1 ft 11¾ in (0·60 m)

DIMENSIONS, INTERNAL:
Cabin, aft of instrument panel:
Length:
Custom, Super, Super R	7 ft 11 in (2·41 m)
Sport	5 ft 11 in (1·80 m)
Max width	3 ft 5 in (1·04 m)
Max height	4 ft 0½ in (1·22 m)

Floor area:
Custom, Super, Super R	24·2 sq ft (2·25 m²)

Volume:
Custom, Super, Super R	109 cu ft (3·09 m³)

Baggage compartment:
Custom, Super, Super R	19·5 cu ft (0·55 m³)
Sport	28·8 cu ft (0·82 m³)

AREAS:
Wings, gross	146 sq ft (13·57 m²)
Ailerons (total)	9·9 sq ft (0·92 m²)
Flaps (total)	18·7 sq ft (1·74 m²)
Fin	10·61 sq ft (0·99 m²)
Rudder	4·62 sq ft (0·43 m²)
Tailplane, incl anti-servo tab	27·0 sq ft (2·51 m²)

WEIGHTS AND LOADINGS:
Weight empty, equipped:
Custom	1,365 lb (619 kg)
Sport	1,350 lb (612 kg)
Super	1,410 lb (639 kg)
Super R	1,625 lb (737 kg)

Max T-O weight:
Custom	2,450 lb (1,111 kg)
Sport	2,250 lb (1,020 kg)
Super	2,550 lb (1,156 kg)
Super R	2,750 lb (1,247 kg)

T-O weight, utility category:
Custom, Sport	2,030 lb (920 kg)
Super	2,200 lb (997 kg)
Super R	2,375 lb (1,077 kg)

Max wing loading:
Custom	16·78 lb/sq ft (81·9 kg/m²)
Sport	15·14 lb/sq ft (73·9 kg/m²)
Super	17·47 lb/sq ft (85·3 kg/m²)
Super R	18·84 lb/sq ft (91·9 kg/m²)

Max power loading:
Custom	13·61 lb/hp (6·17 kg/hp)
Sport	15·00 lb/hp (6·8 kg/hp)
Super	12·75 lb/hp (5·78 kg/hp)
Super R	13·75 lb/hp (6·24 kg/hp)

PERFORMANCE (at max T-O weight):
Max speed at S/L:
Custom	131 knots (151 mph; 243 km/h)
Sport	122 knots (140 mph; 225 km/h)
Super	137 knots (158 mph; 254 km/h)
Super R	148 knots (170 mph; 274 km/h)

Max cruising speed (75% power) at 7,000 ft (2,135 m):
Custom	124 knots (143 mph; 230 km/h)
Sport	114 knots (131 mph; 211 km/h)
Super	130 knots (150 mph; 241 km/h)
Super R	141 knots (162 mph; 261 km/h)

Econ cruising speed (55% power) at 10,000 ft (3,050 m):
Custom	107 knots (123 mph; 198 km/h)
Sport	98 knots (113 mph; 182 km/h)
Super	107 knots (123 mph; 198 km/h)
Super R	122 knots (140 mph; 225 km/h)

Stalling speed, flaps down, power off:
Custom	52 knots (59 mph; 95 km/h)
Sport	49 knots (56 mph; 91 km/h)
Super	53 knots (61 mph; 98 km/h)
Super R	55 knots (63 mph; 102 km/h)

Rate of climb at S/L:
Custom	820 ft (250 m)/min
Sport	700 ft (213 m)/min
Super	880 ft (268 m)/min
Super R	910 ft (277 m)/min

Service ceiling:
Custom	13,650 ft (4,160 m)
Sport	11,100 ft (3,380 m)
Super	14,850 ft (4,525 m)
Super R	15,000 ft (4,572 m)

T-O run:
Custom	950 ft (290 m)
Sport	885 ft (270 m)
Super	950 ft (290 m)

T-O to 50 ft (15 m):
Custom	1,380 ft (420 m)
Sport	1,320 ft (402 m)
Super	1,380 ft (420 m)

Landing from 50 ft (15 m):
Custom	1,275 ft (389 m)
Sport	1,220 ft (372 m)
Super	1,300 ft (396 m)

Landing run:
Custom	640 ft (195 m)
Sport	590 ft (180 m)
Super	660 ft (201 m)

Range with max fuel, allowances for warm-up, T-O, climb and 45 min fuel reserve:
at 75% power:
Custom	594 nm (685 miles; 1,102 km)
Sport	666 nm (767 miles; 1,235 km)
Super	547 nm (630 miles; 1,015 km)
Super R	570 nm (657 miles; 1,057 km)

at 55% power:
Custom	746 nm (860 miles; 1,384 km)
Sport	766 nm (883 miles; 1,420 km)
Super	714 nm (823 miles; 1,325 km)
Super R	764 nm (880 miles; 1,416 km)

BEECHCRAFT BONANZA MODEL V35B and TURBO BONANZA MODEL V35B TC

The prototype Bonanza flew for the first time on 22 December 1945 and the type went into production in 1947. Beech had delivered a total of 9,073 V-tail Bonanzas by 1 January 1970.

There are two current versions of this design with four/six seats and V-tail as follows:

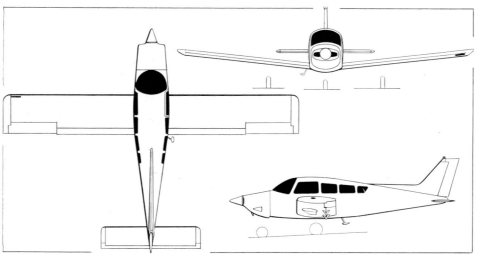

General arrangement drawing of the Beechcraft Musketeer Super R

Beechcraft Musketeer Super R, which has a retractable landing gear

Model V35B. Standard version, as described below.

Model V35B TC. Generally similar to V35B but fitted with turbocharger and oxygen system as standard equipment.

The Bonanza Model A36 utility aircraft, and Model F33 series with conventional tail unit, are described separately.

Optional extras available on the current Bonanza include the Beech-designed "Magic Hand" introduced in May 1965. Designed to eliminate the possibility of wheels-up landing or inadvertent retraction of the landing gear on the ground, it lowers the gear automatically on approach when the engine manifold pressure falls below approximately 20 in (50 cm) and airspeed has been reduced to 120 mph (193 kmh). On take-off, it keeps the gear down until the aircraft is airborne and has accelerated to 90 mph (145 kmh) IAS. The system can be switched off by the pilot at will.

TYPE: Four/six-seat light cabin monoplane.

WINGS: Cantilever low-wing monoplane. Wing section Beech modified NACA 23016·5 at root, modified NACA 23012 at tip. Dihedral 6°. Incidence 4° at root, 1° at tip. Sweepback 0° at quarter-chord. Each wing is a two-spar semi-monocoque box-beam of conventional aluminium alloy construction. Symmetrical-section ailerons and single-slotted flaps of aluminium alloy construction. Ground-adjustable trim-tab in each aileron.

FUSELAGE: Conventional aluminium alloy semi-monocoque structure. Hat-section longerons and channel-type keels extend forward from cabin section, making the support structure for the engine and nose-wheel an integral part of the fuselage.

TAIL UNIT: "Butterfly" type, consisting of tail-plane and elevators set at 33° dihedral angle. Semi-monocoque construction. Fixed surfaces have aluminium alloy structure and skin. Control surfaces, aft of the light alloy spar, are primarily of magnesium alloy, with large trim-tab in each. Tail surfaces are interchangeable port and starboard, except for tabs and actuator horns.

LANDING GEAR: Electrically-retractable tricycle type, with steerable nose-wheel. Main wheels retract inward into wings, nose-wheel aft. Beech oil-air shock-absorbers on all units. Goodyear main wheels and tyres, size 7·00 × 6, pressure 30 lb/sq in (2·11 kg/cm²). Goodyear nose wheel and tyre, size 5·00 × 5, pressure 40 lb/sq in (2·81 kg/cm²). Goodyear ring-disc hydraulic brakes. Parking brake.

POWER PLANT: One 285 hp Continental IO-520-B six-cylinder horizontally-opposed air-cooled engine (turbocharged TSIO-520-D in Model V35B TC), driving a McCauley two-blade metal constant-speed propeller, diameter 7 ft 0 in (2·13 m). Three-blade Hartzell propeller, diameter 6 ft 8 in (2·03 m), available optionally. Manually-adjustable engine cowl flaps. Two standard fuel tanks in wing leading-edges, with total usable capacity of 49·5 US gallons (187 litres). Optionally, these can be replaced by tanks with total usable capacity of 80 US gallons (303 litres). Refuelling points above tanks. Oil capacity 3 US gallons (11·5 litres).

ACCOMMODATION: Enclosed cabin seating four, five or six persons on individual seats. Centre windows open for ventilation on ground and have release pins to permit their use as emergency exits. Cabin structure reinforced for protection in turn-over. Space for up to 270 lb (122·5 kg) of baggage aft of seats. Passenger door and baggage access door both on starboard side.

SYSTEMS: Electrical system supplied by 70A alternator, 12V 35Ah battery. Hydraulic system for brakes only. Oxygen system standard on V35B TC.

ELECTRONICS AND EQUIPMENT: Standard equipment includes heating, ventilation and defrosting system; 8-day clock; outside air temperature gauge; flap position indicator; electroluminescent sub-panel lighting; two landing lights; navigation lights; cabin dome and instrument lights; ultra-violet proof windshield and windows; wall-to-wall carpeting; glove compartment; sun visors; ash trays; cigarette lighters; pilot's foul weather window; coat hangar strap; coat hook; arm rests; two headrests; assist straps; utility shelf; tow bar; pitot tube cover; control lock and winterisation kit. Standard avionics comprise Narco Mark 16 nav/com with IN-5/4R converter-indicator, microphone, headset, cabin speaker and Beechcraft B11-1 nav/com/ GS antenna. Optional items include nav/com equipment by ARC, Bendix, King, Narco, Sunair and Wilcox, including marker beacon receiver, ADF, DME, VOR/LOC transmitter-receiver and glide slope receiver, Beechcraft B-VII autopilot, dual controls, rotating beacons and fifth and sixth seats.

Beechcraft Bonanza Model V35B (285 hp Continental IO-520-B engine)

DIMENSIONS, EXTERNAL:

Wing span	33 ft 5½ in (10·20 m)
Wing chord at root	7 ft 0 in (2·13 m)
Wing chord at tip	3 ft 6 in (1·07 m)
Wing aspect ratio	6·1
Length overall	26 ft 4½ in (8·04 m)
Height over tail	6 ft 6½ in (1·99 m)
Tailplane span	10 ft 1½ in (3·08 m)
Wheel track	9 ft 7 in (2·93 m)
Wheelbase	7 ft 0 in (2·13 m)
Passenger door:	
Height	3 ft 0 in (0·91 m)
Width	3 ft 1 in (0·94 m)
Baggage compartment door:	
Height	1 ft 8 in (0·51 m)
Width	2 ft 0 in (0·61 m)

DIMENSIONS, INTERNAL:

Cabin, aft of instrument panel:	
Length	8 ft 6 in (2·59 m)
Max width	3 ft 6 in (1·07 m)
Max height	4 ft 2 in (1·27 m)
Volume	118 cu ft (3·34 m³)
Baggage space	35 cu ft (0·99 m³)

AREAS:

Wings, gross	181 sq ft (16·80 m²)
Ailerons (total)	11·4 sq ft (1·06 m²)
Trailing-edge flaps (total)	21·3 sq ft (1·98 m²)
Fixed tail surfaces	23·8 sq ft (2·20 m²)
Movable tail surfaces, including tabs	14·4 sq ft (1·34 m²)

WEIGHTS AND LOADINGS:

Weight empty, equipped:	
V35B	1,972 lb (894 kg)
V35B TC	2,035 lb (923 kg)
Max T-O and landing weight	3,400 lb (1,542 kg)
Max wing loading	18·80 lb/sq ft (91·8 kg/m²)
Max power loading	11·96 lb/hp (5·42 kg/hp)

PERFORMANCE (Both versions, except where stated otherwise, at max T-O weight):

Max level speed:	
V35B at S/L	182 knots (210 mph; 338 km/h)
V35B TC at 19,000 ft (5,790 m)	217 knots (250 mph; 402 km/h)
Max cruising speed (75% power) at 6,500 ft (1,980 m)	176 knots (203 mph; 327 km/h)
Max cruising speed (75% power) at 24,000 ft (7,315 m):	
V35B TC	200 knots (230 mph; 370 km/h)
Econ cruising speed (45% power):	
V35B at 12,000 ft (3,660 m)	142 knots (164 mph; 264 km/h)
V35B TC at 16,000 ft (4,875 m)	144 knots (166 mph; 267 km/h)

Stalling speed, wheels and flaps down	55 knots (63 mph; 102 km/h)
Stalling speed, wheels and flaps up	65 knots (74 mph; 119 km/h)
Rate of climb at S/L:	
V35B	1,136 ft (346 m)/min
V35B TC	1,225 ft (373 m)/min
Service ceiling:	
V35B	17,500 ft (5,335 m)
V35B TC	29,500 ft (8,990 m)
T-O run:	
V35B	965 ft (295 m)
V35B TC	950 ft (290 m)
T-O to 50 ft (15 m)	1,320 ft (402 m)
Landing from 50 ft (15 m)	1,177 ft (360 m)
Landing run	647 ft (197 m)
Range with standard fuel, with allowances for warm-up, T-O, climb and 45 min fuel reserve:	
V35B	520 nm (599 miles; 963 km)
V35B TC	498 nm (574 miles; 923 km)
Range with max fuel, reserves as above:	
V35B	964 nm (1,111 miles; 1,788 km)
V35B TC	939 nm (1,082 miles; 1,741 km)

BEECHCRAFT BONANZA MODEL F33, F33A, and F33C

These versions of the Bonanza are four-to-five-seat single-engined executive aircraft, similar in general configuration to the rest of the Bonanza line, but distinguished by a conventional tail unit with swept-back vertical surfaces. The prototype flew for the first time on 14 September 1959, and the production models were known as Debonairs until 1967.

There are three current versions, as follows:

Model F33. With 225 hp Continental IO-470-K engine. Received FAA Type Approval on 2 December 1964.

Model F33A. Similar to F33 but with 285 hp Continental IO-520-B engine.

Model F33C. Announced originally on 18 June 1968, this aerobatic version of the Bonanza, now known as the F33C, differs from the standard F33A only in embodying structural changes that were necessary for certification in the Aerobatic Category under FAA regulations. The changes include the addition of structural members in the rear fuselage and modifications to the ailerons, tailplane, fin and rudder to increase their strength, plus the use of heavier rudder cables. Standard equipment includes shoulder harness for both front seats, a quick-release cabin door and a "g" meter. The standard four/five-

Beechcraft Turbo Bonanza Model V35B TC (285 hp Continental TSIO-520-D engine)

Q

seat interior is retained, but operation in the Aerobatic Category is limited to a pilot and one passenger. Permitted manoeuvres include rolls, inside loops, Immelmann turns, Cuban eights, split "S" turns, snap rolls, spins and limited inverted flight.

A total of 1,522 Model 33's had been built by the end of 1969. Twenty-one are used for pilot training by Lufthansa German Airlines.

Optional extras include the "Magic Hand" automatic landing gear control system described under the Model V35B Bonanza entry.

TYPE: Four-to-five-seat cabin monoplane.

WINGS: As for V35B Bonanza, but not square-tipped.

FUSELAGE: As for Bonanza V35B series.

TAIL UNIT: Conventional cantilever all-metal stressed-skin structure, primarily of aluminium alloy but with corrugated magnesium skin on elevators. Large trim-tab in each elevator. Fixed tab in rudder.

LANDING GEAR: As for Bonanza V35B series, except for main wheel tyres size 6·00 × 6.

POWER PLANT: One six-cylinder horizontally-opposed air-cooled engine (details under model listings above), driving a McCauley two-blade metal constant-speed propeller, diameter 7 ft 0 in (2·13 m). Fuel in two wing tanks with total capacity of 50 US gallons (189·5 litres). Optional long-range tanks giving total capacity of 80 US gallons (303 litres). Oil capacity 2½ US gallons (9·5 litres).

ACCOMMODATION: Enclosed cabin seating four to five in two pairs plus an optional side-facing fifth seat. Baggage compartment and hat shelf aft of seats. Passenger and baggage compartment doors both on starboard side. Heater standard.

SYSTEMS: Electrical system supplied by 70A alternator, 12V 35Ah battery. Aerobatic fuel boost pump for F33C only. Hydraulic system for brakes only.

ELECTRONICS AND EQUIPMENT: As described for V35B and V35B TC Bonanzas, except "g"-meter, pilot and co-pilot shoulder harness, easily-removable seat back cushions and quick-release door on F33C only.

DIMENSIONS, EXTERNAL:
Wing span	32 ft 10 in (10·01 m)
Wing chord at root	7 ft 0 in (2·13 m)
Wing chord at tip	3 ft 6 in (1·07 m)
Wing aspect ratio	6·1
Length overall	25 ft 6 in (7·77 m)
Height over tail	8 ft 3 in (2·51 m)
Tailplane span	12 ft 2 in (3·71 m)
Wheel track	9 ft 6¾ in (2·91 m)
Wheelbase	7 ft 5¼ in (2·27 m)
Passenger door:	
Height	3 ft 0 in (0·91 m)
Width	3 ft 1 in (0·94 m)
Baggage compartment door:	
Height	1 ft 8 in (0·51 m)
Width	2 ft 0 in (0·61 m)

DIMENSIONS, INTERNAL:
Cabin, aft of instrument panel:	
Length	6 ft 11 in (2·11 m)
Max width	3 ft 6 in (1·07 m)
Max height	4 ft 2 in (1·27 m)
Volume	103 cu ft (2·92 m³)
Baggage compartment	20 cu ft (0·57 m³)

AREAS:
Wings, gross	177·6 sq ft (16·5 m²)
Ailerons (total)	11·4 sq ft (1·06 m²)
Trailing-edge flaps (total)	21·3 sq ft (1·98 m²)
Fin	9·1 sq ft (0·85 m²)
Rudder, including tab	4·6 sq ft (0·43 m²)
Tailplane	18·82 sq ft (1·75 m²)
Elevators, including tabs	13·36 sq ft (1·24 m²)

WEIGHTS AND LOADINGS:
Weight empty:	
F33	1,885 lb (855 kg)
F33A	1,933 lb (876 kg)
F33C	1,936 lb (878 kg)
Max T-O and landing weight:	
F33	3,050 lb (1,383 kg)
F33A	3,400 lb (1,542 kg)
F33C standard	3,400 lb (1,542 kg)
F33C aerobatic	2,800 lb (1,270 kg)
Max wing loading:	
F33	17·2 lb/sq in (84·0 kg/m²)
F33A	19·1 lb/sq ft (93·3 kg/m²)
Max power loading:	
F33	13·5 lb/hp (6·12 kg/hp)
F33A	11·6 lb/hp (5·26 kg/hp)

PERFORMANCE:
Max level speed at S/L:	
F33	169 knots (195 mph; 314 km/h)
F33A, F33C	181 knots (208 mph; 335 km/h)
Max cruising speed (75% power):	
F33 at 7,000 ft (2,135 m)	
	161 knots (185 mph; 298 km/h)
F33A, F33C at 6,500 ft (1,980 m)	
	174 knots (200 mph; 322 km/h)

Beechcraft Bonanza Model F33 (225 hp Continental IO-470-K engine)

Econ cruising speed at 10,000 ft (3,050 m):
F33, (50% power)	
	134 knots (154 mph; 248 km/h)
F33A, F33C (45% power):	
	135 knots (156 mph; 251 km/h)
Stalling speed, wheels and flaps down:	
F33	52·5 knots (60 mph; 97 km/h)
F33A, F33C	53 knots (61 mph; 98·5 km/h)
Stalling speed, wheels and flaps up:	
F33	62 knots (71 mph; 114·5 km/h)
F33A, F33C	63 knots (72 mph; 116 km/h)
Rate of climb at S/L:	
F33,	930 ft (283 m)/min
F33A, F33C	1,200 ft (365 m)/min
Service ceiling:	
F33,	17,800 ft (5,425 m)
F33A, F33C	18,300 ft (5,575 m)
T-O run:	
F33	982 ft (300 m)
F33A, F33C	880 ft (268 m)
T-O to 50 ft (15 m):	
F33	1,288 ft (393 m)
F33A, F33C	1,225 ft (373 m)
Landing from 50 ft (15 m):	
F33	1,298 ft (396 m)
F33A, F33C	1,150 ft (350 m)
Landing run:	
F33	643 ft (196 m)
F33A, F33C	625 ft (190 m)

Range at econ cruising speed, with allowances for warm-up, T-O, climb and 45 min reserve:
Standard fuel:	
F33	564 nm (650 miles; 1,045 km)
F33A, F33C	516 nm (595 miles; 957 km)
Max fuel:	
F33	1,016 nm (1,170 miles; 1,880 km)
F33A, F33C	937 nm (1,080 miles; 1,738 km)

BEECHCRAFT BONANZA MODEL A36

This version of the Bonanza, introduced in mid-1968, is a six-seat utility aircraft developed from the Bonanza Model V35B. It is generally similar to that of the V35B, but is distinguished by a conventional tail unit with swept-back vertical surfaces, similar to that of the F33 series of Bonanzas (formerly known as Debonairs) and has large double doors on the starboard side of the fuselage aft of the wing root, to facilitate loading and unloading of bulky cargo when used in a utility rôle. The cabin area is increased by 6 cu ft (0·17 m³) compared with the V35B.

The Model A36, as all Bonanza models, is licensed in the FAA Utility Category at full gross weight, with no limitation of performance. A total of 188 had been built by the end of 1969.

The details given for the Model V35B Bonanza apply also to the Model A36, except in the following respects:

TYPE: Six-seat/utility light cabin monoplane.

TAIL UNIT: Conventional cantilever all-metal stressed-skin structure, primarily of aluminium alloy but with corrugated magnesium skin on elevators. Large trim-tab in each elevator. Fixed tab in rudders.

LANDING GEAR: Electrically-retractable tricycle type, similar to that of Baron. Main units retract inward into wings, nose-wheel rearward. Beech air-oil shock-absorbers. Steerable nose-wheel. Goodyear wheels. Twin-spot hydraulic brakes.

ACCOMMODATION: Enclosed cabin seating six persons on individual seats in pairs. Two removable seats and two folding seats permit rapid conversion to utility configuration. Double doors of bonded aluminium honeycomb construction on starboard side facilitate loading of cargo. Used as an air ambulance, one stretcher can be accommodated with ample room for a medical attendant and/or members of the patient's family. Extra windows provide improved visibility for passengers. Stowage for 400 lb (181 kg) of baggage.

SYSTEMS: Electrical system supplied by 70A alternator, 12V 35Ah battery. Hydraulic system for brakes only.

ELECTRONICS AND EQUIPMENT: Standard equipment includes Narco Mark 16 nav/com, with VOA-40 Omni conv/ind and Beechcraft antenna. Optional items include instrument flight equipment, auto-pilot or Beechcraft Constant Co-Pilot wing levelling device, Magic Hand landing gear system, oxygen system and various interior refinements.

DIMENSIONS, EXTERNAL:
Wing span	32 ft 10 in (10·01 m)
Length overall	26 ft 4 in (80·3 m)
Height overall	8 ft 5 in (2·57 m)
Wheel track	9 ft 6¾ in (2·91 m)
Wheelbase	9 ft 1¼ in (2·78 m)

Beechcraft Bonanza Model A36 (285 hp Continental IO-520-B engine)

Forward passenger door:
| Height | 3 ft 4 in (1·02 m) |
| Width | 3 ft 1 in (0·94 m) |

Rear passenger/cargo door:
| Height | 3 ft 4 in (1·02 m) |
| Width | 3 ft 9 in (1·14 m) |

AREA:
| Wings, gross | 177·6 sq ft (16·50 m²) |

WEIGHTS AND LOADINGS:
Weight empty, equipped	2,023 lb (917 kg)
Max T-O weight	3,600 lb (1,633 kg)
Max wing loading	20·2 lb/sq ft (98·6 kg/m²)
Max power loading	12·6 lb/hp (5·7 kg/hp)

PERFORMANCE:
Max speed at S/L
177 knots (204 mph; 323 km/h)
Cruising speed (75% power) at 6,500 ft (1,980 m)
169 knots (195 mph; 314 km/h)
Cruising speed (65% power) at 10,000 ft (3,050 m)
162 knots (187 mph; 301 km/h)
Cruising speed (55% power) at 10,000 ft (3,050 m)
145 knots (167 mph; 269 km/h)
Stalling speed, power off, undercarriage down and 30° flaps   66 knots (64 mph; 103 km/h)
Stalling speed, power off, undercarriage and flaps up   56 knots (75 mph; 121 km/h)
Rate of climb at S/L   1,015 ft (309 m)/min
Service ceiling   16 000 ft (4,875 m)
Absolute ceiling   17,800 ft (5,425 m)
T-O run   1,112 ft (339 m)
T-O to 50 ft (15 m)   1,525 ft (465 m)
Landing from 50 ft (15 m)   1,240 ft (368 m)
Landing run   683 ft (208 m)
Range with standard fuel, with allowance for warm-up, T-O, climb and 45 min fuel reserve:
55% power at 10,000 ft (3,050 m)
460 nm (530 miles; 853 km)
65% power at 10,000 ft (3,050 m)
447 nm (515 miles; 829 km)
75% power at 6,500 ft (1,980 m)
421 nm (485 miles; 780 km)
Range with max fuel, reserves as above:
55% power at 10,000 ft (3,050 m)
851 nm (980 miles; 1,577 km)
65% power at 10,000 ft (3,050 m)
820 nm (945 miles; 1,521 km)
75% power at 6,500 ft (1,980 m)
760 nm (875 miles; 1,408 km)

BEECHCRAFT BARON MODEL B55 and E55

US Army designation: T-42A

The Baron, introduced in November 1960, is a development of the Travel Air with more power, greater all-weather capability and airframe refinements that include a swept tail-fin. It first flew in prototype form on 29 February 1960.

The original Model 95-55 Baron was a four/five-seater, but optional five-seat and six-seat layouts are available on the following current versions:

Model B55. With two 260 hp Continental IO-470-L engines. Received FAA Type Approval in September 1963.

Model E55. With two 285 hp Continental IO-520-C engines.

The turbocharged Turbo Baron is described separately.

It was announced in February 1965 that the US Army had selected the B55 Baron as winner of its competition for a twin-engined fixed-wing instrument trainer. Subsequently, 65 Barons were ordered, under the designation T-42A.

A total of 2,242 Barons had been built by the end of 1969.

TYPE: Four, five or six-seat cabin monoplane.

WINGS: Cantilever low-wing monoplane. Wing section B55: NACA 23016·5 at root, NACA 23012 at tip; E55: NACA 23017·5 at root, NACA 23010·5 at tip. Dihedral 6°. Incidence 4° at root, B55 1° at tip, E55—1° at tip. Each wing is a semi-monocoque box beam of aluminium alloy construction. Plain ailerons of aluminium construction. Electrically-operated single-slotted aluminium alloy flaps. Manually-operated trim-tab in each aileron. Pneumatic rubber de-icing boots optional.

FUSELAGE: Semi-monocoque aluminium alloy structure. E55 has nose extended by 11·6 in (0·29 m).

TAIL UNIT: Cantilever all-metal structure. Two trim-tabs in elevators, one in rudder. Pneumatic rubber de-icing boots optional.

LANDING GEAR: Electrically-retracted tricycle type. Main units retract inward into wings, nose-wheel rearward. Beech air-oil shock-absorbers. Steerable nose-wheel with shimmy damper. Goodyear wheels. Main tyres size 6·50 × 8, pressure 50 lb/sq in (3·52 kg/cm²). Nose-wheel tyre size 5·00 × 5, pressure 50 lb/sq in (3·52 kg/cm²). Goodyear twin-spot hydraulic brakes. Parking brake.

Beechcraft Baron Model B55 (two 260 hp Continental IO-470-L engines)

POWER PLANT: Two six-cylinder horizontally-opposed air-cooled engines (details under model listings above), driving McCauley Type 2AF36C-39 fully-feathering propellers, diameter 6 ft 6 in (1·98 m). Optional Hartzell three-blade propellers. Electrically-operated cowl flaps. Fuel in four tanks in wings with total usable capacity of 112 US gallons (424 litres). Different wing tanks can be fitted to give total usable capacity of 142 US gallons (536 litres). Oil capacity 6 US gallons (23 litres).

ACCOMMODATION: Standard model has four individual seats in pairs in enclosed cabin, with door on starboard side. Fifth and sixth seats optional. Baggage compartments forward and aft of cabin, each with outside door.

SYSTEMS: Cabin heated by Janitrol 50,000 BTU heater. Electrical system includes two 25A 24V alternators (50A 24V on E55), one 17Ah 24V battery. Hydraulic system for brakes only. Vacuum system for flight instruments.

ELECTRONICS AND EQUIPMENT: Standard equipment includes alternate static air source; blind-flying instrumentation; electric turn co-ordinator; outside air temperature gauge; 8-day clock; flap position indicator; heated pitot tube; silent ventilation system; ultra-violet proof windshield and windows; sound proofing; wall-to-wall carpeting; glove compartment; sun visors; in-flight storage pockets; ash trays; cigarette lighter; pilot's foul-weather window; coat hangar strap; coat hook; arm rests; head rests; two landing lights; navigation lights; entrance door courtesy light; cowl flap position light; cabin dome, instrument and map lights; two cabin reading lights; tow bar; control locks and winterisation kit. Standard avionics comprise Narco Mark 16 nav/com; Narco VOA-40 VOR/LOC converter indicator; Bendix T-12C ADF; microphone; headset; cabin speaker and Beechcraft B-11-1 nav/com/GS antennae. Optional avionics include a wide range of nav/coms by ARC, Collins, King, Narco, RCA and Sunair, ADF and DME. Optional equipment includes rotating beacons, dual controls, executive writing desk, Zep oxygen installation, Beechcraft B-VII or H-14 autopilot, latter with heading lock, altitude hold, automatic pitch trim, and VOR/ILS coupling, and RCA radar.

DIMENSIONS, EXTERNAL:
Wing span	37 ft 10 in (11·53 m)
Wing chord at root	7 ft 0 in (2·13 m)
Wing chord at tip	2 ft 11·6 in (0·90 m)
Wing aspect ratio	7·16

Length overall:
| B55 | 27 ft 0 in (8·23 m) |
| E55 | 29 ft 0 in (8·84 m) |

Height over tail:
| B55 | 9 ft 7 in (2·92 m) |
| E55 | 9 ft 2 in (2·79 m) |

Tailplane span:
B55	13 ft 9¼ in (4·20 m)
E55	15 ft 11¼ in (4·86 m)
Wheel track	9 ft 7 in (2·93 m)

Wheelbase:
| B55 | 7 ft 0 in (2·13 m) |
| E55 | 8 ft 0 in (2·44 m) |

Passenger door:
Height	3 ft 1 in (0·94 m)
Width	3 ft 0 in (0·91 m)
Height to step	1 ft 1 in (0·33 m)

Baggage door (fwd):
| Height | 1 ft 10 in (0·56 m) |
| Width | 2 ft 1 in (0·64 m) |

Baggage door (rear):
Height	1 ft 10½ in (0·57 m)
Width	1 ft 6½ in (0·47 m)
Height to sill	2 ft 4 in (0·71 m)

DIMENSIONS, INTERNAL:
Cabin: length   8 ft 6 in (2·59 m)
| Max width | 3 ft 6 in (1·07 m) |
| Max height | 4 ft 2 in (1·27 m) |

Baggage compartment (fwd):
B55	12 cu ft (0·34 m³)
E55	18 cu ft (0·51 m³)
Baggage compartment (rear)	35 cu ft (0·99 m³)

AREAS:
Wings, gross	199·2 sq ft (18·50 m²)
Ailerons (total)	11·40 sq ft (1·06 m²)
Trailing-edge flaps (total)	25·70 sq ft (2·39 m²)
Fin	11·00 sq ft (1·02 m²)
Rudder, including tab	11·60 sq ft (1·08 m²)
Tailplane: B55	31·80 sq ft (2·95 m²)

Elevators, including tabs:
| B55 | 16·20 sq ft (1·51 m²) |

WEIGHTS AND LOADINGS:
Weight empty:
| B55 | 3,073 lb (1,393 kg) |
| E55 | 3,092 lb (1,402 kg) |

Max T-O and landing weight:
| B55 | 5,100 lb (2,313 kg) |
| E55 | 5,300 lb (2,405 kg) |

Max wing loading:
| B55 | 25·6 lb/sq ft (120·5 kg/m²) |
| E55 | 26·6 lb/sq ft (130·0 kg/m²) |

Max power loading:
| B55 | 9·8 lb/hp (4·45 kg/hp) |
| E55 | 9·3 lb/hp (4·22 kg/hp) |

PERFORMANCE (at max T-O weight):
Max level speed at S/L:
| B55 | 205 knots (236 mph; 380 km/h) |
| E55 | 210 knots (242 mph; 390 km/h) |

Max cruising speed (75% power) at 7,000 ft (2,135 m):
| B55 | 195 knots (225 mph; 362 km/h) |
| E55 | 200 knots (230 mph; 370 km/h) |

Econ cruising speed (50% power) at 10,000 ft (3,050 m):
| B55, E55 | 169 knots (195 mph; 314 km/h) |

Stalling speed (wheels and flaps down):
| B55 | 68 knots (78 mph; 26 km/h) |
| E55 | 67 knots (77 mph; 124 km/h) |

Rate of climb at S/L:
| B55, E55 | 1,670 ft (510 m)/min |

Rate of climb at S/L, one engine out:
| B55 | 320 ft (98 m)/min |
| E55 | 335 ft (102 m)/min |

Service ceiling:
| B55 | 19,700 ft (6,000 m) |
| E55 | 20,900 ft (6,370 m) |

Service ceiling, one engine out:
| B55 | 7,000 ft (2,135 m) |
| E55 | 7,100 ft (2,165 m) |

T-O run:
| B55 | 910 ft (277 m) |
| E55 | 596 ft (182 m) |

T-O to 50 ft (15 m):
| B55 | 1,255 ft (382 m) |
| E55 | 968 ft (295 m) |

Landing from 50 ft (15 m):
| B55 | 1,370 ft (418 m) |
| E55 | 1,414 ft (431 m) |

Landing run:
| B55 | 840 ft (256 m) |
| E55 | 868 ft (265 m) |

Range with max fuel, allowances for warm-up, T-O, climb and 45 min fuel reserve:
| B55 | 1,063 nm (1,225 miles; 1,970 km) |
| E55 | 992 nm (1,143 miles; 1,840 km) |

BEECHCRAFT TURBO BARON A56TC

This turbocharged version of the Baron received FAA Type Approval on 19 May 1967, and deliveries began in September 1967. It is claimed to be the first production light twin-engined aircraft to offer air-conditioning as an optional extra. A total of 81 had been built by the end of 1969.

The details given for the Baron Model E55 apply also to the Turbo Baron, except in the following respects.:

POWER PLANT: Two 380 hp Lycoming TIO-541-E1B4 six-cylinder horizontally-opposed air-cooled turbocharged engines, each driving a Hartzell three-blade metal constant-speed propeller. Standard usable fuel capacity 142 US gallons (536 litres). Optional additional tankage raises total usable capacity to 204 US gallons (772 litres).

ELECTRONICS AND EQUIPMENT: Generally as for Baron, but 66 cu ft oxygen supply is standard equipment. Optional equipment includes 114 cu ft oxygen supply, a 16,500 BTU air-conditioning unit, weather radar and transponder.

DIMENSIONS, EXTERNAL AND INTERNAL:
As for E55 Baron, except:
Wheelbase 8 ft 2¼ in (2·50 m)

WEIGHTS AND LOADINGS:
Weight empty, equipped 3,700 lb (1,678 kg)
Max T-O weight 5,990 lb (2,717 kg)
Max wing loading 30·0 lb/sq ft (146·5 kg/m²)
Max power loading 7·8 lb/hp (3·54 kg/hp)

PERFORMANCE (at max T-O weight):
Max cruising speed, 79% power at 25,000 ft (7,620 m) 252 knots (290 mph; 467 km/h)
Cruising speed, 75% power at 25,000 ft (7,620 m) 247 knots (284 mph; 457 km/h)
Cruising speed, 65% power at 25,000 ft (7,620 m) 231 knots (266 mph; 428 km/h)
Econ cruising speed, 45% power at 25,000 ft (7,620 m) 189 knots (218 mph; 351 km/h)
Stalling speed, flaps and landing gear down, power off 73 knots (84 mph; 136 km/h)
Max rate of climb at S/L 2,020 ft (616 m)/min
Max rate of climb at S/L, one engine out 410 ft (125 m)/min
Service ceiling 32,200 ft (9,814 m)
Service ceiling, one engine out 18,600 ft (5,670 m)
Absolute ceiling 33,100 ft (10,090 m)
Absolute ceiling, one engine out 20,300 ft (6,190 m)
T-O run 1,005 ft (306 m)
T-O to 50 ft (15 m) 1,420 ft (433 m)
Landing from 50 ft (15 m) 2,080 ft (634 m)
Landing run 1,285 ft (392 m)
Range, with max fuel, including allowance for warm-up, taxi, take-off, climb to altitude and 45 min reserve at 45% power:
75% power at 25,000 ft (7,620 m) 929 nm (1,070 miles; 1,722 km)
65% power at 25,000 ft (7,620 m) 1,027 nm (1,183 miles; 1,903 km)
45% power at 25,000 ft (7,620 m) 1,128 nm (1,299 miles; 2,090 km)

BEECHCRAFT BARON 58

In December 1969 Beech added to their twin-engined 4/6-seat Baron series of aircraft a new model designated Baron 58. It differs from the earlier versions by having the forward fuselage extended by 10 in (25·40 cm), double passenger/cargo doors on the starboard side of the fuselage, a fourth window on each side of the cabin and redesigned engine nacelles. By moving forward the instrument panel, cabin door and two front seats, it has been possible to provide a more spacious cabin without disturbing the wing location and main spar. The wheelbase has also been extended and gives improved ground handling.

Other improvements include the introduction of more contoured seats, a new pilot's storm window, extended propeller hubs to improve engine cooling, re-siting of starter and magneto switches on the pilot's sub-panel, a three-deck circuit breaker console on the pilot's sidewall, colour-coded switches, a simplified fuel selector and a number of new paint schemes and interior trims.

Design of this version started on 16 August 1968. Construction of the first prototype began in March 1969 and first flight was made in June 1969. First flight of a production aircraft was made in November and FAA Certification was granted on 19 November 1969.

At the end of March 1970 orders for the Baron 58 totalled 49, of which 17 had been built.

TYPE: Four, five or six-seat cabin monoplane.

WINGS: Cantilever low-wing monoplane. Wing section NACA 23016·5 at root, NACA 23010·5 at tip. Dihedral 6°. Incidence 4°. No sweepback. Each wing is a two-spar semi-monocoque box beam of aluminium alloy construction. Plain ailerons with corrugated aluminium skins. Trim and balance tab in port aileron. Electrically-operated single-slotted trailing-edge flaps with corrugated aluminium skins. Pneumatic rubber de-icing boots optional.

FUSELAGE: Semi-monocoque aluminium alloy structure, with nose extended 10 in (25·40 cm) more than on the Model E55. Avionics compartment in nose, capacity 7 cu ft (0·20 m³).

TAIL UNIT: Cantilever all-metal structure. Two trim-tabs in elevator, one in rudder. Pneumatic rubber de-icing boots optional.

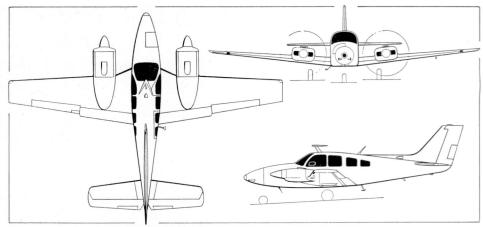

General arrangement drawing of the Beechcraft Baron Model 58

Beechcraft Baron 58, showing new windows and passenger/cargo doors of this model

LANDING GEAR: Electrically-retractable tricycle type. Main units retract inward into wings, nose-wheel rearward. Beech air-oil shock-absorbers. Steerable nose-wheel. Cleveland main wheels Type 40-87; main wheel tyres size 6·50 × 8, pressure 50 lb/sq in (3·52 kg/cm²). Goodyear nose-wheel Type 9532102 or 9532669; nose-wheel tyre size 5·00 × 5, pressure 65 lb/sq in (4·57 kg/cm²). Cleveland 30-66 twin-spot hydraulic brakes.

POWER PLANT: Two 285 hp Continental IO-520-C six-cylinder horizontally-opposed air-cooled engines, each driving a McCauley metal two-blade constant-speed fully-feathering propeller, diameter 6 ft 6 in (1·98 m). McCauley three-blade propeller, diameter 6 ft 4 in (1·93 m) optional. Electrically-operated cowl flaps. Fuel in four tanks in wings with standard usable capacity of 142 US gallons (536 litres). Two optional fuel tanks may be fitted to provide total usable capacity of 168 US gallons (636 litres). Single refuelling point in each wing, just inboard of tip. Oil capacity 6 US gallons (23 litres). Electric or fluid propeller de-icing optional.

ACCOMMODATION: Standard model has four individual seats in pairs in enclosed cabin. Folding fifth and sixth seats optional. Club seating with aft-facing third and fourth seats optional. Forward-hinged door at front of cabin on starboard side. Double passenger/cargo doors on starboard side, aft of wing trailing-edge, forward door hinged to open forward, aft door hinged to open aft. Forward baggage compartment, capacity 300 lb (136 kg) with external access door in nose, forward of windshield. Rear baggage compartment, capacity 400 lb (181 kg), and space for 120 lb (54 kg) baggage in extended rear compartment. Window adjacent to third and fourth seats can be used as emergency exit. Cabin heated and ventilated.

SYSTEMS: Electrical system supplied by two 50A 24V alternators; 24V 17Ah battery. Hydraulic system for brakes only. Cabin heated by Janitrol 50,000 BTU heater. Pneumatic system for instrument gyros and optional surface de-icing boots. Oxygen system of either 49 cu ft (1·39 m³) or 65 cu ft (1·84 m³) capacity optional.

ELECTRONICS AND EQUIPMENT: Standard equipment includes blind-flying instrumentation, outside air temperature gauge, 8-day clock, heated pitot tube, two landing lights, ultra-violet proof windshield and windows, sound-proofing, carpeted floor, sun visors, in-flight storage pockets, ash trays, cigarette lighter, arm rests, head rest, tow bar, control lock assembly, winterisation kit. Standard avionics include Narco Mark 16 nav/com with VOA-40 VOR/LOC indicator, Bendix T-12C ADF, microphone, headset, cabin speaker and Beechcraft B11-1 nav/com/GS antenna. A wide range of optional equipment and avionics is available to customer's requirements.

DIMENSIONS, EXTERNAL:
Wing span 37 ft 10 in (11·53 m)
Wing chord at root 7 ft 0 in (2·13 m)
Wing chord at tip 2 ft 11·6 in (0·90 m)
Wing aspect ratio 7·16
Length overall 29 ft 9 in (9·07 m)
Height overall 9 ft 6 in (2·90 m)
Tailplane span 15 ft 11 in (4·85 m)
Wheel track 9 ft 7 in (2·92 m)
Wheelbase 8 ft 11 in (2·72 m)
Forward passenger door:
Height 3 ft 4 in (1·02 m)
Width 3 ft 1 in (0·94 m)
Rear passenger/cargo door:
Height 3 ft 4 in (1·02 m)
Width 3 ft 9 in (1·14 m)
Nose baggage door:
Height 1 ft 10 in (0·56 m)
Width 2 ft 1 in (0·64 m)
Emergency exit window:
Height 1 ft 9 in (0·53 m)
Width 2 ft 0 in (0·61 m)

DIMENSIONS, INTERNAL:
Cabin, including rear baggage area:
Length 12 ft 7 in (3·84 m)
Max width 3 ft 6 in (1·07 m)
Max height 4 ft 2 in (1·27 m)
Floor area 40 sq ft (3·72 m²)
Volume 135·9 cu ft (3·85 m²)
Baggage compartment (fwd) 17·2 cu ft (0·49 m²)
Baggage compartment (aft) 37 cu ft (1·05 m²)
Extended rear baggage compartment 10 cu ft (0·28 m²)

AREAS:
Wings, gross 199·2 sq ft (18·50 m²)
Ailerons (total) 11·40 sq ft (1·06 m²)
Trailing-edge flaps (total) 25·70 sq ft (2·39 m²)
Fin 11·00 sq ft (1·02 m²)
Rudder, including tab 11·60 sq ft (1·08 m²)
Tailplane 53·3 sq ft (4·95 m²)
Elevators, including tab 19·8 sq ft (1·84 m²)

WEIGHTS AND LOADINGS:
Weight empty 3,194 lb (1,449 kg)
Max T-O and landing weight 5,400 lb (2,449 kg)
Max wing loading 27·1 lb/sq ft (132·3 kg/m²)
Max power loading 9·5 lb/hp (4·3 kg/hp)

PERFORMANCE (at max T-O weight):
Max level speed at S/L 210 knots (242 mph; 390 km/h)
Max diving speed 223 knots (257 mph; 414 km/h)
Max cruising speed, 75% power at 7,000 ft (2,135 m) 200 knots (230 mph; 370 km/h)
Econ cruising speed, 45% power at 12,000 ft (3,660 m) 141 knots (162 mph; 300 km/h)
Stalling speed, landing gear and flaps down, power off 72 knots (83 mph; 134 km/h)
Rate of climb at S/L 1,694 ft (516 m)/min
Rate of climb at S/L, one engine out 382 ft (116 m)/min
Service ceiling 17,800 ft (5,425 m)
Service ceiling, one engine out 7,150 ft (2,180 m)
T-O run 899 ft (274 m)
T-O to 50 ft (15 m) 1,093 ft (333 m)
Landing from 50 ft (15 m) 1,469 ft (448 m)

Landing run   1,044 ft (318 m)
Range with max fuel, 45 min reserve
                  993 nm (1,143 miles, 1,839 km)

BEECHCRAFT DUKE A60

Design work on this 4/6-seat pressurised and turbosupercharged light twin-engined transport started early in 1965. Construction of the prototype began in January 1966, and the first flight was made on 29 December 1966. FAA Type Approval was granted on 1 February 1968. A total of 116 Dukes had been produced by 1 January 1970.

TYPE: Four/six-seat cabin monoplane.

WINGS: Cantilever low-wing monoplane. Wing section NACA 23016·5 at root, NACA 23010·5 at tip. Thickness-chord ratio 13·7% at root, 10·5% at tip. Dihedral 6°. Incidence 4° at root, 1° at tip. Each wing is a two-spar semi-monocoque box-beam of conventional aluminium alloy construction. Overhang-balance ailerons constructed of aluminium alloy. Conventional hinged trim-tab in port aileron. Electrically-operated single-slotted aluminium alloy flaps. Pneumatic rubber de-icing boots optional.

FUSELAGE: Semi-monocoque aluminium alloy structure. Heavy-gauge chemically-milled aluminium alloy skins.

TAIL UNIT: Cantilever all-metal structure. Aluminium spars and end ribs; magnesium alloy skins reinforced with metal bonded honeycomb stiffeners running chordwise. Dorsal fin. Swept vertical and horizontal surfaces. Tailplane dihedral 10°. Trim-tabs in rudder and port elevator. Pneumatic rubber de-icing boots optional.

LANDING GEAR: Electrically-retractable tricycle type. Main units retract inward, nose-wheel aft; all three units have fairing doors. Beechcraft air-oil shock-absorbers. Goodyear main wheels and tyres, size 6·50 × 8·0, pressure 70 lb/sq in (4·92 kg/cm²). Goodyear steerable nose-wheel with shimmy damper, tyre size 6·00 × 6, pressure 48 lb/sq in (3·37 kg/cm²). Goodyear multiple-disc hydraulic brakes.

POWER PLANT: Two 380 hp Lycoming TIO-541-E1A4 six-cylinder horizontally-opposed air-cooled turbosupercharged engines, each driving a Hartzell three-blade metal constant-speed and fully-feathering propeller, diameter 6 ft 2 in (1·88 m). Propeller feathering accumulators and electric anti-icing optional. Two interconnected fuel cells in each wing containing 71 US gallons (269 litres); total capacity 142 US gallons (538 litres). Optionally, four interconnected fuel cells in each wing containing 102 US gallons (386 litres); total capacity 204 US gallons (772 litres). Refuelling points in leading-edge of each wing, near wing-tip. Oil capacity 8 US gallons (30 litres), of which 6·5 US gallons (24·5 litres) are usable.

ACCOMMODATION: Standard model has four individual seats in pairs, with centre aisle, in enclosed cabin. Door, hinged at forward edge, on port side at rear of cabin. Baggage hold in the nose, capacity 32 cu ft (0·91 m³), with external access door on port side of nose. Additional stowage for 28·25 cu ft (0·80 m³) of baggage at rear of cabin. Optional extras include fifth and sixth seats, rearward-facing third and fourth seats, headrests, translucent panels separating passenger and pilot seating, writing desks, refreshment cabinets, toilet, windshield electric de-icing, urethane paint scheme and cabin fire extinguishers.

SYSTEMS: Cabin pressurisation system, differential 4·6 lb/sq in (0·32 kg/cm²), supplied by engine turbosupercharger bleed air, maintains cabin altitude equivalent to 10,000 ft (3,050 m) at 24,800 ft (7,559 m). Optional electrically-driven vapour-cycle air-conditioning system of 14,000 BTU and combustion heater of 45,000 BTU. Hydraulic system for brakes only. Pneumatic system for pressure-operated instruments and de-icing boots only. 28V 60A alternators standard; 125A generators optional.

ELECTRONICS AND EQUIPMENT: Blind-flying instrumentation, heated pitot tube and electric fuel vent anti-icing standard. Optional extras include de luxe instrument panel carrying duplicate blind-flying instruments, instantaneous vertical speed indicator, tachometer with synchroscope, flight hour recorder, engine hour recorder, clock, map light, electrically-operated elevator trimming, "Magic Hand" landing gear extension system. Standard avionics package comprises Narco Mark 24 VHF Nav/Com (360 channel) with VOA-9 VOR/ILS converter/indicator, B3 com antenna and B12 nav antenna, Narco Mark 24 standby VHF nav/com (360 channel) with VOA-8 VOR/LOC converter/indicator and B6 com antenna, Bendix T-12C ADF with 551-A indicator and OECO voice-range filter, Narco MBT-24R marker beacon with B16 antenna, Narco UGR-2 glideslope with A-326A GS antenna. Beech metal radio panel and static wicks with microphone key button in pilot's control wheel. Dual microphones and headsets. White lighting. An extensive range of optional avionics equipment is available to customer's requirements.

Beechcraft Duke 4/6-seat pressurised transport (two 380 hp Lycoming TIO-541-E1A4 engines)

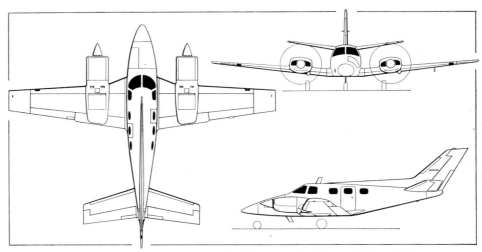

Three-view drawing of the Beechcraft Duke pressurised transport (two 380 hp Lycoming TIO-541-E1A4 engines)

DIMENSIONS, EXTERNAL:
Wing span	39 ft 3 in (11·96 m)
Wing chord at fuselage C/L	9 ft 2¼ in (2·80 m)
Wing chord at tip	2 ft 11⅜ in (0·90 m)
Wing aspect ratio	7·243
Length overall	33 ft 10 in (10·31 m)
Height overall	12 ft 4 in (3·76 m)
Tailplane span	17 ft 0 in (5·18 m)
Wheel track	11 ft 0 in (3·35 m)
Wheelbase	9 ft 3 in (2·82 m)
Passenger door:	
Height	3 ft 11½ in (1·21 m)
Width	2 ft 2½ in (0·67 m)
Height to sill	2 ft 8 in (0·81 m)
Baggage compartment door:	
Height	1 ft 11½ in (0·60 m)
Width	3 ft 1¼ in (0·96 m)
Height to sill	3 ft 1½ in (0·95 m)

DIMENSIONS, INTERNAL:
Cabin:	
Length	11 ft 10 in (3·61 m)
Max width	4 ft 2¼ in (1·28 m)
Max height	4 ft 4 in (1·32 m)
Floor area	45 sq ft (4·18 m²)
Volume	171·6 cu ft (4·86 m³)

AREAS:
Wings, gross	212·9 sq ft (19·78 m²)
Ailerons (total)	11·4 sq ft (1·06 m²)
Trailing-edge flaps (total)	25·7 sq ft (2·39 m²)
Fin	17·5 sq ft (1·63 m²)
Rudder, including tab	12·4 sq ft (1·15 m²)
Tailplane	45·6 sq ft (4·24 m²)
Elevators, including tab	16·4 sq ft (1·52 m²)

WEIGHTS AND LOADINGS:
Weight empty, equipped	4,175 lb (1,893 kg)
Max T-O, ramp, zero-fuel and landing weight	
	6,775 lb (3,073 kg)
Max wing loading	31·8 lb/sq ft (155·3 kg/m²)
Max power loading	8·9 lb/hp (4·04 kg/hp)

PERFORMANCE (at max T-O weight):
Max level speed at 23,000 ft (7,010 m)
                  248 knots (286 mph; 460 km/h)
Max diving speed
         234 knots (270 mph; 434 km/h) CAS
Max cruising speed:
  79% power at 25,000 ft (7,620 m)
                  241 knots (278 mph; 447 km/h)
  79% power at 20,000 ft (6,100 m)
                  229 knots (264 mph; 425 km/h)
  79% power at 15,000 ft (4,570 m)
                  219 knots (252 mph; 406 km/h)
Cruising speed:
  75% power at 25,000 ft (7,620 m)
                  235 knots (271 mph; 436 km/h)
  75% power at 20,000 ft (6,100 m)
                  224 knots (258 mph; 415 km/h)
  75% power at 15,000 ft (4,570 m)
                  214 knots (246 mph; 396 km/h)
  65% power at 25,000 ft (7,620 m)
                  221 knots (255 mph; 410 km/h)
  65% power at 20,000 ft (6,100 m)
                  211 knots (243 mph; 391 km/h)
  65% power at 15,000 ft (4,570 m)
                  201 knots (232 mph; 373 km/h)
  45% power at 25,000 ft (7,620 m)
                  182 knots (210 mph; 338 km/h)
  45% power at 20,000 ft (6,100 m)
                  177 knots (204 mph; 328 km/h)
  45% power at 15,000 ft (4,570 m)
                  171 knots (197 mph; 317 km/h)
Stalling speed, wheels and flaps down, power off
                  76 knots (87 mph; 140 km/h)
Stalling speed, wheels and flaps up, power off
                  86 knots (98 mph; 157 km/h)
Rate of climb at S/L   1,601 ft (488 m)/min
Rate of climb at S/L, one engine out
                  307 ft (94 m)/min
Service ceiling   30,800 ft (9,387 m)
Service ceiling, one engine out
                  15,100 ft (4,600 m)
T-O run   1,278 ft (390 m)
T-O to 50 ft (15 m)   1,691 ft (515 m)
Landing from 50 ft (15 m)   2,380 ft (725 m)
Landing run   1,318 ft (402 m)
Range, with max optional fuel and allowances for warm-up, taxi, take-off, climb to altitude and 45-min fuel reserve:
  75% power at 25,000 ft (7,620 m)
                  844 nm (973 miles; 1,566 km)
  75% power at 20,000 ft (6,100 m)
                  824 nm (949 miles; 1,527 km)
  75% power at 15,000 ft (4,570 m)
                  802 nm (924 miles; 1,487 km)
  65% power at 25,000 ft (7,620 m)
                  931 nm (1,073 miles; 1,727 km)
  65% power at 20,000 ft (6,100 m)
                  922 nm (1,062 miles; 1,709 km)
  65% power at 15,000 ft (4,570 m)
                  891 nm (1,027 miles; 1,653 km)
  45% power at 25,000 ft (7,620 m)
                  1,020 nm (1,175 miles; 1,891 km)

45% power at 20,000 ft (6,100 m)
1,018 nm (1,173 miles; 1,888 km)
45% power at 15,000 ft (4,570 m)
1,008 nm (1,161 miles; 1,868 km)

BEECHCRAFT QUEEN AIR A65 AND QUEEN AIRLINER A65

US Army designation: U-8F Seminole

First flown in prototype form on 28 August 1958, four months after its design was started, the standard Queen Air is a six/nine-seat business aeroplane incorporating the features of a modern airliner. It may also be operated as a cargo transport by removal of bulkheads and passenger seating, giving 266 cu ft (7·53 m³) of cargo space.

Compared with the Model 65, the first production version of the Queen Air, the current A65 has swept vertical tail surfaces and increased fuel capacity. It is instrumented for all-weather operation and is designed to accommodate the latest electronic equipment, including weather-avoidance radar.

In addition to commercial deliveries, Beech has produced Queen Airs for the US Army under the designation U-8F. The Japanese Maritime Self-Defence Force also chose the Queen Air 65 as its standard navigation trainer and command transport.

The Queen Air received FAA Type Approval on 1 February 1959. A total of 329 of the original Model 65's and current Model A65's and 71 U-8F's had been built by the end of 1969.

The more powerful Queen Air B80 and the new Queen Air 70, introduced in 1968, are described separately. All three models are available in 11-seat high-density airliner versions.

TYPE: Six/eleven-seat business and utility aircraft.

WINGS: Cantilever low-wing monoplane. Wing section NACA 23018 at root, NACA 23016·5 at joint of tip and outer panel, NACA 23012 at tip. Dihedral 7°. Incidence 4° 48′ at root, 0° at tip. Two-spar all-metal structure of aluminium alloy. All-metal ailerons of magnesium, each with a trim-tab. Single-slotted aluminium alloy flaps. Pneumatic rubber de-icing boots optional.

FUSELAGE: Aluminium alloy semi-monocoque structure.

TAIL UNIT: Cantilever all-metal structure of aluminium alloy, with sweptback vertical surfaces. Tailplane dihedral 7°. Trim-tabs in rudder and elevators, Pneumatic rubber de-icing boots optional.

LANDING GEAR: Electrically-retractable tricycle type. Main units retract forward, nose-wheel aft. Beechcraft air-oil shock-absorbers. Goodyear main wheels, size 8·50 × 10, pressure 47 lb/sq in (3·30 kg/cm²). Goodyear steerable nose-wheel, size 6·50 × 10, pressure 35 lb/sq in (2·46 kg/cm²). Goodyear single-disc hydraulic brakes. Parking brakes.

POWER PLANT: Two 340 hp Lycoming IGSO-480-A1E6 six-cylinder horizontally-opposed air-cooled geared and supercharged engines. Hartzell three-blade fully-feathering constant-speed propellers, diameter 7 ft 9 in (2·36 m). Fuel in two 44 US gallon (166 litre) inboard tanks and four outboard tanks totalling 126 US gallons (477 litres) in wings, giving standard capacity of 214 US gallons (811 litres). Provision for optional auxiliary wing tanks to bring total capacity to 264 US gallons (1,000 litres). Refuelling points above wings. Oil capacity 8 US gallons (30 litres).

ACCOMMODATION: Crew of one or two on flight deck and four to nine passengers in cabin. Basic layout has five commuter passenger seats; executive layout has four lounge chairs, fore and aft partitions and lavatory; airliner layout has seven commuter and two folding passenger seats, extended aft baggage compartment and door, map case, cabin fire extinguisher and fourth cabin window. Door on port side of cabin at rear; optionally double-width cargo doors. Optional toilet and baggage compartment opposite door, capacity 350 lb (160 kg). Other optional items include sofa, tables, refreshment cabinets and external cargo pod.

SYSTEMS: Optional electrically-driven vapour-cycle air-conditioning system with combustion heater. Standard model has 100,000 BTU heater and ventilating system. Hydraulic system for brakes only. Two 28V 150A DC engine-driven generators and 24V 13Ah nickel-cadmium battery for electrical system.

ELECTRONICS AND EQUIPMENT: Standard avionics comprise Narco Mark 16 nav/com with VOA-50M VOR/ILS converter-indicator, B3 com antenna, B17 nav/GS antenna, Narco Mark 16 standby nav/com with VOA-40 VOR/LOC converter-indicator, B3 com antenna, Bendix T-12C ADF with 551A indicator and OECO 20128 filter, Narco MBT-24R remote marker beacon with B16 marker antenna, Narco UGR-2 glide slope, Beech metal radio panel and accessories, static wicks, single audio switch panel, white lighting, two microphones, two headsets, cockpit speaker, OECO 20119 speaker amplifier. Standard equipment includes dual controls, blind flying instrumentation, outside air temperature gauge, 8-day clock, flap position indicator, dynamic brake on landing gear, landing gear warning system, heated stall warning system, dual heated pitot heads, cabin door "unlocked" warning light, external power socket, two landing lights, navigation lights, dual rotating beacons, cabin door and indirect overhead lighting, reading lights for each passenger, map light, aft compartment dome light, primary and secondary instrument light systems, windshield defroster, dual storm windows, sun visors, map pockets, four-way adjustable pilot and co-pilot seats, ash trays, cigarette lighters, "No Smoking-Fasten seat belt" sign, carpeted floor, provisions for removable cabin partitions and toilet, window curtains, emergency exit, coat rack, tow bar, control lock assembly and heated fuel vents. A wide range of avionics and equipment is available to customer's requirements, including ARC, Collins, King, Bendix, Sunair, Narco, Pantronics or RCA radar and radio packages; Bendix, Collins or RCA weather-avoidance radar; oxygen equipment; H14 autopilot and additional soundproofing.

Beechcraft Queen Air 70 (two 340 hp Lycoming IGSO-480-A1E6 engines)

DIMENSIONS, EXTERNAL:

Wing span	45 ft 10½ in (13·98 m)
Wing chord at root	7 ft 0½ in (2·15 m)
Wing chord at tip	3 ft 6 in (1·07 m)
Wing aspect ratio	7·51
Length overall	35 ft 6 in (10·82 m)
Height overall	14 ft 2½ in (4·33 m)
Tailplane span	17 ft 2¾ in (5·25 m)
Wheel track	12 ft 9 in (3·89 m)
Wheelbase	12 ft 3½ in (3·75 m)
Standard passenger door:	
Height	4 ft 3¾ in (1·31 m)
Width	2 ft 3 in (0·69 m)
Height to sill	3 ft 10 in (1·17 m)
Optional cargo door:	
Height	4 ft 3¾ in (1·31 m)
Width	4 ft 6 in (1·37 m)
Height to sill	3 ft 10 in (1·17 m)

DIMENSIONS, INTERNAL:

Cabin, including flight deck and baggage area:	
Length	19 ft 7 in (6·97 m)
Max width	4 ft 4 in (1·32 m)
Max height	4 ft 9 in (1·45 m)
Volume	331 cu ft (9·37 m³)
Baggage compartment	22 cu ft (0·62 m³)

AREAS:

Wings, gross	277·06 sq ft (25·73 m²)
Ailerons (total)	13·90 sq ft (1·29 m²)
Trailing-edge flaps (total)	29·30 sq ft (2·72 m²)
Fin	23·67 sq ft (2·20 m²)
Rudder, including tab	14·00 sq ft (1·30 m²)
Tailplane	47·25 sq ft (4·39 m²)
Elevators, including tabs	17·87 sq ft (1·66 m²)

WEIGHTS AND LOADINGS:

Weight empty	4,980 lb (2,258 kg)
Max T-O weight	7,700 lb (3,493 kg)
Max landing weight	7,350 lb (3,334 kg)
Max wing loading	27·8 lb/sq ft (135·7 kg/m²)
Max power loading	12·03 lb/hp (5·45 kg/hp)

PERFORMANCE (at max T-O weight):

Max level speed at 12,000 ft (3,600 m)
208 knots (239 mph; 385 km/h)
Max permissible diving speed
234 knots (270 mph; 435 km/h)
Max cruising speed (70% power) at 15,200 ft (4,633 m) 186 knots (214 mph; 344 km/h)
Econ cruising speed (45% power) at 15,000 ft (4,570 m) 149 knots (171 mph; 275 km/h)
Stalling speed (wheels and flaps down)
70 knots (80 mph; 129 km/h)
Stalling speed (wheels and flaps up)
82 knots (94 mph; 152 km/h)
Rate of climb at S/L 1,300 ft (396 m)/min
Rate of climb at S/L, one engine out
245 ft (75 m)/min
Service ceiling at 6,500 lb (2,950 kg) AUW
31,300 ft (9,540 m)
Service ceiling, one engine out, at 6,500 lb (2,950 kg) AUW 15,500 ft (4,725 m)
Absolute ceiling at 6,500 lb (2,950 kg) AUW
32,700 ft (9,967 m)
Absolute ceiling at 6,500 lb (2,950 kg) AUW, one engine out 16,300 ft (4,968 m)
T-O run 1,180 ft (360 m)
T-O to 50 ft (15 m) 1,560 ft (475 m)
Landing from 50 ft (15 m) 1,750 ft (533 m)
Landing run 1,330 ft (405 m)
Range with auxiliary fuel, with allowances for warm-up, T-O, climb and 45 min fuel reserve at:
70% power at 15,000 ft (4,570 m)
968 nm (1,115 miles; 1,794 km)
65% power at 17,000 ft (5,180 m)
1,094 nm (1,260 miles; 2,027 km)
45% power at 15,000 ft (4,570 m)
1,419 nm (1,635 miles; 2,631 km)

BEECHCRAFT QUEEN AIR 70 AND QUEEN AIRLINER 70

In 1968, Beech introduced a new twin-engined aircraft, known as the Queen Air 70, which oined the Queen Air A65 and Queen Air B80 as the third in the current series of 6/11-seat business and utility aircraft. With the same power plant as the A65 and extended wing of the B80, the Queen Air 70 has an operating economy comparable with the A65, while carrying a useful load over ten per cent greater.

A total of 30 Queen Air 70's had been delivered by 31 December 1969.

The description of the Queen Air A65 applies also to the Queen Air 70 and Queen Airliner 70, except in the following details:

WINGS: Wing section NACA 23020 at root, NACA 23012 outboard of joint between outer panel and wing-tip. Incidence 3° 55′ at root, 0° 1′ at tip.

DIMENSIONS, EXTERNAL:

As for Queen Air A65, except:

Wing span	50 ft 4 in (15·34 m)
Wing aspect ratio	8·7

AREAS:

As for Queen Air A65, except:

Wings, gross	293·9 sq ft (27·3 m²)

WEIGHTS AND LOADINGS:

Weight empty, equipped	5,000 lb (2,267 kg)
Max T-O weight	8,200 lb (3,720 kg)
Max wing loading	27·89 lb/sq ft (136 kg/m²)
Max power loading	12·8 lb/hp (5·8 kg/hp)

PERFORMANCE:

Max speed, at 12,000 ft (3,655 m)
208 knots (239 mph; 385 km/h)
Cruising speed, 70% power, at 15,200 ft (4,630 m) 186 knots (214 mph; 344 km/h)
Cruising speed, 70% power, at 10,000 ft (3,050 m) 178 knots (205 mph; 330 km/h)
Cruising speed, 65% power, at 16,800 ft (5,120 m) 182 knots (210 mph; 338 km/h)
Cruising speed, 65% power, at 10,000 ft (3,050 m) 174 knots (200 mph; 322 km/h)
Cruising speed, 45% power, at 15,000 ft (4,570 m) 149 knots (171 mph; 275 km/h)

Cruising speed, 45% power, at 10,000 ft (3,050 m) 144 knots (166 mph; 267 km/h)
Stalling speed, power off, flaps and wheels down 69 knots (79·5 mph; 128 km/h)
Stalling speed, power off, flaps and wheels up 83 knots (95·5 mph; 157 km/h)
Rate of climb at S/L, 8,200 lb (3,719 kg) AUW 1,375 ft (419 m) min
Rate of climb at S/L, 7,000 lb (3,175 kg) AUW 1,730 ft (527 m) min
Rate of climb at S/L, one engine out
  8,200 lb (3,719 kg) AUW 230 ft (70 m) min
  7,000 lb (3,175 kg) AUW 343 ft (104 m) min
Service ceiling at 7,000 lb (3,175 kg) AUW 30,000 ft (9,145 m)
Service ceiling, one engine out at 7,000 lb (3,175 kg) AUW 14,900 ft (4,540 m)
Absolute ceiling at 7,000 lb (3,175 kg) AUW 31,300 ft (9,540 m)
Absolute ceiling, one engine out at 7,000 lb (3,175 kg) AUW 15,500 ft (4,725 m)
T-O run 1,269 ft (387 m)
T-O to 50 ft (15 m) 1,675 ft (510 m)
Landing from 50 ft (15 m) 2,107 ft (642 m)
Landing run 1,244 ft (379 m)
Range with 264 US gallons fuel, including warm-up, taxi, take-off and climb to altitude with 45 min reserve:
  70% power at 15,000 ft (4,570 m) 968 nm (1,115 miles; 1,794 km)
  70% power at 10,000 ft (3,050 m) 972 nm (1,120 miles; 1,802 km)
  70% power at 5,000 ft (1,525 m) 950 nm (1,095 miles; 1,762 km)
  65% power at 17,000 ft (5,180 m) 1,094 nm (1,260 miles; 2,028 km)
  65% power at 10,000 ft (3,050 m) 1,098 nm (1,265 miles; 2,036 km)
  65% power at 5,000 ft (1,525 m) 1,076 nm (1,240 miles; 1,996 km)
  45% power at 15,000 ft (4,570 m) 1,419 nm (1,635 miles; 2,631 km)
  45% power at 10,000 ft (3,050 m) 1,441 nm (1,660 miles; 2,671 km)
  45% power at 5,000 ft (1,525 m) 1,437 nm (1,655 miles; 2,663 km)

BEECHCRAFT QUEEN AIR B80 AND QUEEN AIRLINER B80

The prototype of the original Queen Air 80, which introduced more powerful engines than those of the A65, flew for the first time on 22 June 1961 and received its FAA Type Certificate on 20 February 1962. It was followed in January 1964 by the Queen Air A80, with increased wing span and AUW, new interior styling, increased fuel capacity and redesigned nose compartment, giving more space for radio. The A80 has been followed in turn by the improved B80 and eleven-seat Queen Airliner B80, to which the details below apply.

By the end of 1969 Beech had built a total of 429 Queen Air 80's, A80's, B80's and Queen Airliner B80's.

TYPE: Six/eleven-seat business aircraft, commuter airliner and utility aircraft.

WINGS, FUSELAGE, TAIL UNIT AND LANDING GEAR: Same as for Queen Air 70.

POWER PLANT: Two 380 hp Lycoming IGSO-540-A1D six-cylinder horizontally-opposed air-cooled geared and supercharged engines, each driving a Hartzell three-blade fully-feathering constant-speed propeller, diameter 7 ft 9 in (2·36 m). Fuel in two inboard wing tanks, each with capacity of 44 US gallons (166 litres) and two outboard tanks, each 63 US gallons (238·5 litres). Total standard fuel capacity 214 US gallons (809 litres). Provision for two optional auxiliary tanks in wings to bring total capacity to 264 US gallons (1,000 litres). Refuelling points above wings. Oil capacity (total) 8 US gallons (30 litres).

SYSTEMS, ELECTRONICS AND EQUIPMENT: Same as for Queen Air A65.

DIMENSIONS, EXTERNAL AND INTERNAL:
As for Queen Air A65, except:
  Wing span 50 ft 3 in (15·32 m)
  Baggage compartment 53 cu ft (1·50 m³)

AREAS:
As for Queen Air A65, except:
  Wings, gross 293·9 sq ft (27·3 m²)

WEIGHTS AND LOADINGS:
  Weight empty, equipped 5,060 lb (2,295 kg)
  Max T-O and landing weight 8,800 lb (3,992 kg)
  Max wing loading 29·9 lb/sq ft (146·0 kg/m²)
  Max power loading 12·2 lb/hp (5·53 kg/hp)

PERFORMANCE (at max T-O weight, except where indicated):
  Max level speed at 11,500 ft (3,500 m) at average AUW 215 knots (248 mph; 400 km/h)
  Max cruising speed (70% power) at 15,000 ft (4,570 m) at average AUW 195 knots (224 mph; 360 km/h)
  Econ cruising speed (45% power) at 15,000 ft (4,570 m) at average AUW 159 knots (183 mph; 294 km/h)
  Stalling speed, wheels and flaps down 72 knots (82 mph; 132 km/h)

Beechcraft Queen Air B80 (two 380 hp Lycoming IGSO-540-A1D engines)

Beechcraft U-21A military utility transports in US Army service

Rate of climb at S/L 1,275 ft (388 m)/min
Rate of climb at S/L, one engine out 265 ft (80 m)/min
Service ceiling 26,800 ft (8,168 m)
Service ceiling, one engine out 11,800 ft (3,596 m)
T-O run 1,372 ft (418 m)
T-O to 50 ft (15 m) 1,800 ft (549 m)
Landing from 50 ft (15 m) at max landing weight 2,311 ft (704 m)
Landing run at max landing weight 1,340 ft (408 m)
Range with max fuel, with allowances for warm-up, T-O, climb and 45 min fuel reserve 1,354 nm (1,560 miles; 2,510 km)

BEECHCRAFT MODEL 65-A90-1
US Army designation: U-21A

This twin-turboprop unpressurised utility aircraft is a development of the NU-8F, a turboprop conversion of a Queen Air 80 which Beech produced for the US Army in 1963 (see 1964-65 Jane's). The NU-8F was a six-passenger transport powered by two 500 shp Pratt & Whitney (UACL) PT6A-6 engines. By comparison, the U-21A has 550 shp PT6A-20 engines, as fitted in the King Air, and is capable of accommodating up to 10 combat troops or six command personnel in varied interior arrangements, plus a crew of two. It can be adapted quickly for air evacuation ambulance or cargo carrying duties, and is also used for special missions on behalf of the Army Security Agency.

Design of the U-21 began in October 1966, and in the following month construction of the prototype started. Only four months later, in March 1967, the prototype made its first flight, and FAA certification was granted on 27 April 1967.

An initial contract for the U-21A was placed by the US Army in October 1966, covering the manufacture of 48 aircraft and the training of 20 instructor pilots and 20 instructor mechanics by Beech. Subsequent contracts raised the number of U-21A's ordered to 129. The first of these was delivered on 16 May 1967, and deliveries were completed in the Spring of 1969. For latest orders see Addenda.

TYPE: Military utility transport.

WINGS: Cantilever low-wing monoplane. Wing section NACA 23014.10 (modified) at root, NACA 23016.22 (modified) at junction of centre-section and outer panel, NACA 23012.00 (modified) at tip. Dihedral 7°. Incidence 4° 48' at root, 0° at tip. Two-spar structure of aluminium alloy. All-metal ailerons of magnesium, each with anti-servo trim-tab; port tab is also manually adjustable. Single-slotted aluminium alloy flaps. Pneumatic de-icing boots are installed on the wing leading-edges.

FUSELAGE: All-metal semi-monocoque structure, mainly of 2024 aluminium alloy.

TAIL UNIT: Cantilever all-metal structure, mainly of 2024 aluminium alloy, but with magnesium

Beechcraft King Air Model B90 (two 550 shp Pratt & Whitney (UACL) PT6A-20 turboprop engines)

alloy skin on control surfaces. Sweptback vertical surfaces. Controllable trim-tabs in rudder and elevators. Pneumatic de-icing boots on fin and tailplane leading-edges.

LANDING GEAR: Electrically-retractable tricycle type. Main units retract forward, nose-wheel aft. Beechcraft air-oil shock-absorbers. Goodyear main wheels size 7·50×10 and tyres size 8·50×10, pressure 55 lb/sq in (3·87 kg/cm²). Goodyear steerable nose-wheel and tyre size 6·50×10, pressure 50-55 lb/sq in (3·52-3·87 kg/cm²). Goodyear multiple-disc hydraulic brakes.

POWER PLANT: Two 550 shp Pratt & Whitney (UACL) PT6A-20 turboprop engines, driving Hartzell three-blade fully-feathering and reversible constant-speed propellers. Main fuel cell of 58 US gallons (219·5 litres) in each aft nacelle section, plus four interconnected auxiliary cells containing 131 US gallons (496 litres), in each wing. Total capacity 378 US gallons (1,427 litres). The nacelle and inboard wing tanks are self-sealing, the remaining three cells in each wing are conventional bladders. Refuelling points above each nacelle and at the outboard point of each wing. Oil capacity 4·6 US gallons (17 litres) of which 3 US gallons (11 litres) are usable.

ACCOMMODATION: Crew of two, seated side-by-side and separated from the main cabin by a removable half-curtain. The cabin accommodates ten combat-equipped troops on centre-facing bench seats. An alternative ambulance arrangement will accommodate three litter patients, plus three ambulatory patients or medical attendants. A staff transport version accommodates six passengers in forward-facing chairs. With all seats removed, the cabin can hold up to 3,000 lb (1,360 kg) of cargo. Cargo tie-down fittings are installed in the floor. A double door on the port side of the fuselage, aft of the wing, facilitates loading of bulky items. Both doors are removable. Cabin heated by 100,000 BTU combustion heater. A 22 cu ft (0·62 m³) compartment, forward of the flight deck, houses electronic equipment.

SYSTEMS: Hydraulic system for brakes only. Pneumatic system uses engine bleed-air at 16 lb/sq in (1·12 kg/cm²) to operate air-driven instruments and pneumatic de-icer boots. Bleed-air pressure and vacuum are cycled to the single de-icer inflation system through a valve. A selector switch allows automatic single-cycle operation or manual operation. Electrical system utilises two Beech 250A starter-generators. A BB-433A battery is used with an inverter installed in each wing.

ELECTRONICS: Standard avionics comprise complete all-weather nav/com system, utilising Collins, Bendix, RCA, Sperry and Beechcraft equipment, including weather radar and transponder.

EQUIPMENT: Dual controls and wing icing lights are standard.

DIMENSIONS, EXTERNAL:

Wing span	45 ft 10½ in (13·98 m)
Wing aspect ratio	7·51
Length overall	35 ft 6 in (10·82 m)
Height overall	14 ft 2½ in (4·33 m)
Tailplane span	17 ft 2¾ in (5·25 m)
Wheel track	12 ft 9 in (3·89 m)
Wheelbase	12 ft 3½ in (3·75 m)

Passenger and/or cargo doors:

Height	4 ft 3¾ in (1·31 m)
Width	4 ft 6 in (1·37 m)
Height to sill	3 ft 10 in (1·17 m)

DIMENSIONS, INTERNAL:
Cabin:

Length	17 ft 10 in (5·44 m)
Max width	4 ft 7 in (1·40 m)
Max height	4 ft 9 in (1·45 m)
Floor area	70 sq ft (6·50 m²)
Volume	371·5 cu ft (10·52 m³)

AREAS:

Wings, gross	279·7 sq ft (25·98 m²)
Ailerons (total)	13·90 sq ft (1·29 m²)
Trailing-edge flaps (total)	29·30 sq ft (2·72 m²)
Fin	23·67 sq ft (2·20 m²)
Rudder, including tab	14·00 sq ft (1·30 m²)
Tailplane	46·21 sq ft (4·30 m²)
Elevators, including tab	17·87 sq ft (1·66 m²)

WEIGHTS AND LOADINGS:

Weight empty, equipped	5,434 lb (2,464 kg)
Max payload	3,936 lb (1,785 kg)
Max T-O weight	9,650 lb (4,377 kg)
Max landing weight	9,168 lb (4,158 kg)
Max wing loading	34·48 lb/sq ft (168·35 kg/m²)
Max power loading	8·77 lb/shp (3·97 kg/shp)

PERFORMANCE (at max T-O weight):

Max level speed at 10,000 ft (3,050 m)	230 knots (265 mph; 426 km/h) TAS
Max permissible diving speed	259 knots (299 mph; 481 km/h) CAS
Max cruising speed at 10,000 ft (3,050 m)	213 knots (245 mph; 395 km/h) TAS
Econ cruising speed at 10,000 ft (3,050 m)	178 knots (205 mph; 328 km/h) TAS
Stalling speed (flaps and wheels down)	80 knots (92 mph; 148·5 km/h) CAS
Stalling speed (flaps and wheels up)	96 knots (110 mph; 178 km/h) CAS
Rate of climb at S/L	2,160 ft (658 m)/min
Service ceiling	26,150 ft (7,970 m)
Service ceiling, one engine out	12,000 ft (3,660 m)
T-O run	1,618 ft (493 m)
T-O to 50 ft (15 m)	1,923 ft (586 m)
Landing from 50 ft (15 m)	2,453 ft (748 m)
Landing run	1,280 ft (390 m)

Range with max fuel (allowances for climb to and cruise at 25,000 ft = 7,620 m, 30 min reserve at altitude, 2,457 lb = 1,114 kg fuel before engine start, one crew member at 200 lb = 90 kg):
1,455 nm (1,676 miles; 2,697 km)

Range with max payload (allowances for climb to and cruise at 25,000 ft = 7,620 m, 30 min reserve at altitude, 2,120 lb = 961 kg fuel before engine start, one crew member at 200 lb = 90 kg plus 2,000 lb = 907 kg cargo):
1,056 nm (1,216 miles; 1,956 km)

BEECHCRAFT KING AIR MODEL B90
USAF designation: VC-6A

This latest model of the King Air is a pressurised 6/10-seat business aircraft powered by two Pratt & Whitney (UACL) PT6A-20 turboprop engines. It has superseded the original Models 90 and A90 King Air, of which deliveries began in the last quarter of 1964 and in 1966 respectively.

A total of 486 King Airs had been delivered by the end of 1969, including one for the USAF's 1,254th Special Air Missions Squadron at Andrews AFB, Maryland, for VIP transport duties under the designation VC-6A.

TYPE: Six/ten-seat twin-turboprop business aircraft.

WINGS: Cantilever low-wing monoplane. Wing section NACA 23014·1 (modified) at root, NACA 23016.22 (modified) at outer panel of centre-section, NACA 23012 at tip. Dihedral 7°. Incidence 4° 48′ at root, 0° at tip. Sweepback at quarter-chord 0°. Two-spar aluminium alloy structure. All-metal ailerons of magnesium, each with anti-servo tab; port tab adjustable. Single-slotted aluminium alloy flaps. Automatic pneumatic de-icing boots on leading-edges standard.

FUSELAGE: Aluminium alloy semi-monocoque structure.

TAIL UNIT: Cantilever all-metal structure with sweptback vertical surfaces. Fixed-incidence tailplane, with 7° dihedral. Trim-tabs in rudder and each elevator. Automatic pneumatic de-icing boots on leading-edges of fin and tailplane.

LANDING GEAR: Electrically-retractable tricycle type. Nose-wheel retracts rearward, main wheels forward into engine nacelles. Main wheels protrude slightly beneath nacelles when retracted, for safety in a wheels-up emergency landing. Steerable nose-wheel with shimmy damper. Beech air-oil shock-absorbers. BF Goodrich main wheels size 24 × 7·7 and tyres size 8·50-10, pressure 55 lb/sq in (3·87 kg/cm²). BF Goodrich nose-wheel and tyre size 6·50-10, pressure 52 lb/sq in (3·66 kg/cm²). BF Goodrich multiple disc brakes. Parking brakes.

POWER PLANT: Two 550 shp Pratt & Whitney (UACL) PT6A-20 turboprop engines, each driving a Hartzell three-blade constant-speed fully-feathering propeller, diameter 7 ft 9 in (2·36 m). Fuel in two tanks in engine nacelles, each with capacity of 61 US gallons (231 litres) and bladder-type auxiliary tanks in outer wings, each with capacity 131 US gallons (496 litres). Total fuel capacity 384 US gallons (1,454 litres). Refuelling points in top of each engine nacelle and in wing leading-edge outboard of each nacelle. Oil capacity 4·6 US gallons (17·5 litres).

ACCOMMODATION: Two seats side-by-side in cockpit. Normally, four reclining seats are provided in the main cabin, in pairs facing each other fore and aft. Optional arrangements seat up to eight persons, some with two- or three-place couch and refreshment cabinets. Baggage racks at rear of cabin on starboard side, toilet on port side. Door on port side aft of wing, with built-in airstairs. Entire accommodation pressurised and air-conditioned.

SYSTEMS: Pressurisation system utilises a Roots-type supercharger driven by a hydraulic motor in the port nacelle. Air can be heated by an 80,000 BTU combustion heater or refrigerated by an automatically-controlled 16,000 BTU air-conditioning system. Pressure differential 4·6 lb/sq in (0·32 kg/cm²). Electrical system utilises two 200 A starter-generators, 24V 40Ah nickel-cadmium battery. Oxygen system (22 cu ft = 0·62 m³) standard. Vacuum system for flight instruments.

ELECTRONICS AND EQUIPMENT: Standard avionics include Collins 618M-2B VHF transceiver and B3 antenna, Collins 51RV-2B automatic Omni No. 1 with glide slope, 331A-3G indicator and B17 nav/GS antenna, dual omni range filters, Collins dual 356F-3 audio amplifiers with dual 356C-4 isolation amplifiers, Collins DF-203 ADF with voice range filter and Beech flush antenna, Collins 51Z-6 marker beacon with dual marker lights and B16 antenna, Collins 51RV-2B automatic Omni No. 2 with glide slope, 331A-3G indicator, Collins 618M-2B standby transceiver and B3 antenna, RCA AVQ-55 radar with 12 in antenna and bright scope, Sperry C-14-3 compass system (pilot's), Collins PN-101 electric nav system (co-pilot's), Allen 2105D-B-6 RMI with nav and ADF switching, Wilcox 1014A transponder and B18 antenna, RCA AVQ-75 DME with MI-591085-3 indicator, B18 antenna and Nav 1 and 2 switching, DME hold for AVQ-75, dual 600VA OECO 20139 inverters, AIM 500E electric gyro horizon (pilot's), AIM 3 in vacuum gyro horizon (co-pilot's), associated radio accessories including microphone keys in pilot and co-pilot's control wheels, static wicks and lighting. Standard equipment includes heated stall warning system, dual heated pitot heads, external power socket, wing ice lights, two landing lights, taxi light, navigation lights, dual rotating beacons, dual map lights, indirect cabin lighting, reading lights, entrance door light, aft compartment dome light, primary and secondary instrument light systems, white cockpit lighting, fresh air outlets, ash trays, cigarette lighters, double glazed windows, curtains, soundproofing, carpeted floor, "No smoking-fasten seat belt" sign, toilet, coat rack, windshield defroster, dual storm windows, sun visors, map pockets, windshield wipers, tow bar and control lock assembly. A wide range of optional avionics and equipment is available to customer's requirements.

DIMENSIONS, EXTERNAL:

Wing span	50 ft 3 in (15·32 m)
Wing chord at root	7 ft 0½ in (2·15 m)
Wing chord at tip	3 ft 6 in (1·07 m)
Wing aspect ratio	7·51
Length overall	36 ft 6 in (11·13 m)
Length of fuselage	34 ft 6 in (10·52 m)
Height over tail	14 ft 8 in (4·47 m)
Tailplane span	17 ft 2½ in (5·25 m)
Wheel track	12 ft 9 in (3·89 m)
Wheelbase	12 ft 3½ in (3·75 m)
Passenger door:	
Height	4 ft 3¾ in (1·31 m)
Width	2 ft 4 in (0·71 m)
Height to sill	3 ft 10 in (1·17 m)

DIMENSIONS, INTERNAL:

Cabin, including baggage compartment:	
Length	17 ft 10 in (5·43 m)
Max width	4 ft 6 in (1·37 m)
Max height	4 ft 9 in (1·45 m)
Floor area	70 sq ft (6·50 m²)
Volume	314 cu ft (8·89 m³)
Baggage compartment	26·5 cu ft (0·75 m³)

AREAS:

Wings, gross	293·90 sq ft (27·30 m²)
Ailerons (total)	13·90 sq ft (1·29 m²)

Trailing-edge flaps (total)	29·30 sq ft (2·72 m²)
Fin	23·67 sq ft (2·20 m²)
Rudder, including tab	14·00 sq ft (1·30 m²)
Tailplane	47·25 sq ft (4·39 m²)
Elevators, including tabs	17·87 sq ft (1·66 m²)

WEIGHTS AND LOADINGS:

Weight empty, equipped	5,685 lb (2,578 kg)
Max T-O weight	9,650 lb (4,377 kg)
Max ramp weight	9,705 lb (4,402 kg)
Max wing loading	32·8 lb/sq ft (160·1 kg/m²)
Max power loading	8·8 lb/shp (3·99 kg/shp)

PERFORMANCE (at max T-O weight, except where stated otherwise):

Max level speed at 21,000 ft (6,400 m)
    234 knots (270 mph; 434 km/h)
Max cruising speed at 16,000 ft (4,875 m) at AUW of 8,365 lb (3,794 kg)
    222 knots (256 mph; 412 km/h)
Stalling speed, wheels and flaps up
    89 knots (102 mph; 164 km/h)
Stalling speed, wheels and flaps down
    74 knots (85 mph; 137 km/h)
Rate of climb at S/L
    2,000 ft (610 m)/min
Rate of climb at S/L, one engine out
    555 ft (169 m)/min
Service ceiling 27,200 ft (8,290 m)
Service ceiling, one engine out
    14,100 ft (4,298 m)
T-O run 1,750 ft (533 m)
T-O to 50 ft (15 m) 2,180 ft (664 m)
Landing from 50 ft (15 m), with propeller reversal 1,680 ft (512 m)
Landing from 50 ft (15 m) without propeller reversal 2,010 ft (613 m)
Landing run, with propeller reversal
    640 ft (195 m)
Landing run, without propeller reversal
    980 ft (299 m)
Range, at max cruising speed, including fuel allowance for starting, taxi, take-off, climb, descent and 45 min reserve at max cruising power, at:
21,000 ft (6,400 m)
    1,114 nm (1,283 miles, 2,064 km)
16,000 ft (4,880 m)
    963 nm (1,110 miles; 1,770 km)
12,000 ft (3,660 m)
    857 nm (987 miles; 1,588 km)
Max range at econ cruising power, allowances as above, at:
21,000 ft (6,400 m)
    1,273 nm (1,466 miles, 2,359 km)
16,000 ft (4,880 m)
    1,187 nm (1,367 miles; 2,200 km)
12,000 ft (3,660 m)
    1,082 nm (1,246 miles; 2,005 km)

BEECHCRAFT 99 AIRLINER

Largest aircraft yet to be marketed by Beech, the 17-seat twin-turboprop 99 Airliner has been designed specifically for the scheduled airline and scheduled air taxi market. The prototype flew for the first time in July 1966 and the first delivery of a production aircraft was made on 2 May 1968. Production was scheduled to attain a rate of 100 units per annum by mid-1968 to meet world-wide orders for $30 million worth of the Beech 99. These came from 15 US regional and scheduled commuter airlines and from 10 airlines in nine foreign countries. First US deliveries were to Commuter Airlines, Inc, with initial foreign deliveries going to Australia and Canada, and by 1 February 1970 a total of 125 of these aircraft were in service with 38 airlines.

Installation of an optional forward-hinged cargo door forward of the standard air-stair door permits the 99 Airliner to be used for all-cargo or combined cargo-passenger operations, with a movable bulkhead separating freight and passengers in the latter configuration.

Three versions are available:

99 Airliner. Standard model with two 550 shp Pratt & Whitney (UACL) PT6A-20 turboprop engines, as described below.

99A Airliner. Identical to the standard model except for installation of two 680 shp Pratt & Whitney (UACL) PT6A-27 turboprop engines, flat-rated to 550 shp, for improved high-altitude and single-engine performance.

99 Executive. Basically the same as the standard model, but offering optional seating arrangements for eight to 17 persons and various corporate interiors.

A Beechcraft 99A Airliner, piloted by a British crew, won three awards in the England-Australia air race in December 1969. Subject to FAI confirmation the 99A Airliner also set a new record time of 48 hr 15 min 50 sec for the flight, beating by 32 hr 40 min 10 sec the class record set in March 1938 by a D.H.88 Comet.

TYPE: Twin-turboprop light passenger, freight or executive transport.

WINGS: Cantilever low-wing monoplane. Wing section NACA 23018 at root, NACA 23016·5 at centre-section joint with outer panel, NACA 23012 at tip. Dihedral 7°. Incidence 4° 48′ at root, 0° at tip. Two-spar all-metal aluminium alloy structure. All-metal ailerons of magnesium. Single-slotted aluminium alloy flaps. Optional automatic pneumatic de-icing boots.

FUSELAGE: All-metal semi-monocoque structure.

TAIL UNIT: Cantilever all-metal structure, with sweptback vertical surfaces and a ventral stabilising fin. Trim-tabs in elevators and rudder. Pneumatic de-icing boots optional.

LANDING GEAR: Retractable tricycle type with single steerable nose-wheel and twin wheels on each main unit. Electrical retraction, nose-wheel rearward, main units forward into engine nacelles. Beech oleo-pneumatic shock-absorbers. Goodrich wheels, tyres and multiple disc brakes. Shimmy damper on nose-wheel.

POWER PLANT: Two Pratt & Whitney (UACL) PT6A turboprop engines (in accordance with model listings above), each driving a Hartzell three-blade fully-feathering and reversible-pitch constant-speed propeller, diameter 6 ft 7½ in (2·02 m). Automatic feathering system standard. Rubber fuel tanks in wings, with total capacity of 374 US gallons (1,415 litres).

ACCOMMODATION: Crew of two side-by-side on flight deck, with full dual controls and instruments. Half-curtain or bulkhead between flight deck and cabin. Standard version has 15 removable high-density cabin chairs, two-abreast with centre aisle (single chair opposite door). Executive version has six standard seats in cabin, the two forward seats facing rearwards. Baggage space aft of rear seats, with external door. Nose baggage compartment with two external doors. An optional under-fuselage baggage/cargo pod with a volume of 35·5 cu ft (1·01 m³) and structural capacity of 800 lb (363 kg) is available, and this

Beechcraft 99A Airliner (two 680 shp Pratt & Whitney (UACL) PT6A-27 turboprop engines) in Air Cape insignia

does not affect speed appreciably. Airstair door on port side of cabin at rear. Optional forward-hinged cargo door forward of passenger door, to give wide unobstructed opening for cargo loading. A wide selection of corporate interiors and removable chemical or electric flushing toilet optional.

SYSTEMS: Automatic 80,000 BTU heating system and high-capacity ventilation system, with individual fresh air outlets, standard. Hydraulic system for brakes only. 28V DC electrical system, with two 200A generators, 40Ah nickel-cadmium battery and dual solid-state inverters.

ELECTRONICS AND EQUIPMENT: Standard electronics include dual 360-channel nav/com systems, dual VOR/ILS converter-indicators, three-light marker beacon with Beechcraft B-16 marker antenna, ADF with amplifier, glide-slope receiver, DME and transponder, with dual blind-flying instrumentation. Optional export electronics package comprises dual 360-channel nav/com systems with Beechcraft B-2 and B-3 antennae, dual VOR/LOC converter-indicators, marker beacon with Beechcraft B-16 antenna, dual ADF with amplifier and HF transceiver with fixed antenna. Standard equipment includes electric propeller anti-icing, landing and taxi lights, wing ice lights, cabin, instrument and map lights, dual rotating beacons, and fire detector system. Optional equipment includes high-pressure oxygen system, air-conditioning system with Freon compressor, engine fire extinguishing system, weather radar, propeller synchronisers, high-intensity anti-collision lights, autopilot and electrical windscreen anti-icing system.

DIMENSIONS, EXTERNAL:
Wing span	45 ft 10½ in (14·00 m)
Wing chord at root	7 ft 0½ in (2·15 m)
Wing chord at tip	3 ft 6 in (1·07 m)
Wing aspect ratio	7·51
Length overall	44 ft 6¾ in (13·58 m)
Height overall	14 ft 4¼ in (4·38 m)
Tailplane span	22 ft 4½ in (6·82 m)
Wheel track	13 ft 0 in (3·96 m)
Wheelbase	17 ft 11¾ in (5·48 m)
Passenger door:	
Height	4 ft 3½ in (1·31 m)
Width	2 ft 4 in (0·71 m)
Cargo double-door (optional):	
Height	4 ft 3½ in (1·31 m)
Width	4 ft 5½ in (1·36 m)

DIMENSIONS, INTERNAL:
Cabin, including flight deck:	
Length	25 ft 4 in (7·72 m)
Max width	4 ft 7 in (1·40 m)
Max height	4 ft 9 in (1·45 m)
Volume	423·6 cu ft (12·0 m³)
Baggage space (nose) volume	43·9 cu ft (1·24 m³)
Baggage space (rear) volume	21·1 cu ft (0·60 m³)

WEIGHTS:
Weight empty, equipped	5,780 lb (2,621 kg)
Basic operating weight	5,875 lb (2,665 kg)
Max T-O weight	10,400 lb (4,717 kg)

PERFORMANCE (at max T-O weight, unless stated otherwise. A = 99 Airliner, B = 99A Airliner):
Max cruising speed at AUW of 10,000 lb (4,535 kg):
A at 10,000 ft (3,050 m)
    221 knots (254 mph; 409 km/h)
B at 12,000 ft (3,650 m)
    247 knots (284 mph; 457 km/h)

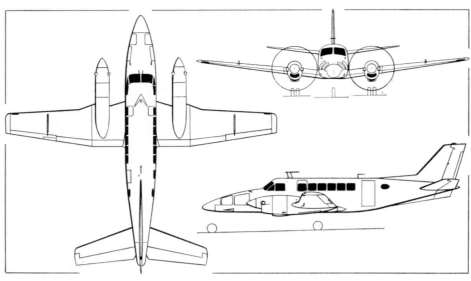

Beechcraft 99 Airliner seventeen-seat light transport

Normal cruising speed:
A at 12,000 ft (3,650 m)
    219 knots (252 mph; 406 km/h)
Normal cruising speed at AUW of 10,000 lb (4,535 kg):
B at 12,000 ft (3,650 m)
    247 knots (284 mph; 457 km/h)
Rate of climb at S/L: A   1,700 ft (518 m)/min
Service ceiling:
A   23,650 ft (7,210 m)
B   26,200 ft (7,986 m)
Service ceiling, one engine out:
A   8,100 ft (2,470 m)
B   13,200 ft (4,025 m)
T-O run: A   1,800 ft (549 m)
Accelerate/stop distance: A   3,850 ft (1,173 m)
Landing from 50 ft (15 m), with propeller reversal: A   2,220 ft (677 m)
Range with max fuel and 1,800 lb (816 kg) payload: A   955 nm (1,100 miles; 1,770 km)
Range with 16 passengers and 480 lb (218 kg) baggage, 45 min reserve:
A   325 nm (375 miles; 603 km)

BEECHCRAFT KING AIR 100

Beech Aircraft announced on 26 May 1969 the addition of a new version of the King Air to its fleet of corporate transport aircraft. Designated King Air 100, this is a pressurised transport with increased internal capacity and more powerful engines, enabling it to carry a useful load of more than two short tons. By comparison with the King Air 90 series, it has a fuselage 4 ft 2 in (1·27 m) longer, reduced wing span, larger rudder and elevator and dual-wheel main landing gear.

It is available in a variety of interior configurations, including a 15-seat commuter layout, and introduces a number of new features. These include fences on the wing upper surface; fluorescent strip lighting in the cabin; polarised cabin windows with rotatable interior panes to allow passengers to reduce external light intensity and glare; a revised control pedestal incorporating electric elevator trim, autopilot, cabin pressurisation controls and electric circuit breakers. De-icing and anti-icing systems are standard equipment, as is a full complement of avionics, ncluding transponder and weather-avoidance radar. Flame-arresters are incorporated into each non-icing flush fuel vent for added protection in the event of a lightning strike.

A new fuel system has been developed for the King Air 100, jet pumps replacing transfer pumps. Boost pumps in each engine nacelle provide fuel pressure to the engine and fuel flow to the jet pumps, which operate on a venturi principle. Back-up pumps allow continued operation in the event of primary pump failure.

A new pressurisation and heating system has been developed for the King Air 100, utilising engine-bleed air, and electric heating coils in the nose of the aircraft allow the cabin to be pre-heated prior to engine start. The system uses jet pumps, operating on the venturi principle, located forward of the firewall behind each engine and is such that the quantity and temperature of the air supplied to the cabin is controlled as a function of ambient temperature and altitude. Check-valves retain pressurisation in the event of single-engine operation, and either engine can provide adequate pressure and heat for full systems operation.

The King Air 100 has been approved for Category II landing minima by the FAA. Initial deliveries were made in August 1969, following FAA Certification. A total of 21 King Air 100's had been built at the beginning of January 1970.

TYPE: Twin-turboprop light passenger, freight or executive transport.

WINGS: As for Beechcraft 99 Airliner. Pneumatic de-icing boots standard.

FUSELAGE: As for King Air B90, except length extended by 2 ft 6 in (0·76 m) forward of the wing, and 1 ft 8 in (0·51 m) aft of the wing.

Beechcraft 99A Airliner with optional under-fuselage baggage/cargo pod in place

TAIL UNIT: Generally as for King Air B90, but tailplane span and fin height increased, and rudder and elevators of increased area.

LANDING GEAR: As for Beechcraft 99 Airliner. Main wheels and tubeless tyres size 18 × 5·5, 8-ply rating, pressure 92 lb/sq in (6·47 kg/cm²). Nose-wheel and tyre size 6·50 × 10, pressure 50 lb/sq in (3·52 kg/cm²).

POWER PLANT: Two 680 shp Pratt & Whitney (UACL) PT6A-28 turboprop engines, each driving a Hartzell three-blade fully-feathering and reversible-pitch constant-speed propeller, diameter 7 ft 9½ in (2·37 m). Rubber fuel cells in wings, with total capacity of 374 US gallons (1,415 litres). Automatic fuel heating systems; inertial engine inlet de-icing system; engine inlet lips de-iced by electro-thermally heated boots. Goodrich electric propeller anti-icing system.

ACCOMMODATION: Crew of two side-by-side on flight deck, with full dual controls and instruments. Easily-removable partition with sliding door between flight deck and cabin. Six fully-adjustable individual cabin chairs standard, with removable head rests, with a variety of possible layouts. Fully-carpeted floor. External access door to forward radio compartment. Plug-type emergency exit at forward end of cabin on starboard side. Passenger door at rear of cabin on port side, with integral airstair. Easily-removable aft cabin partition with sliding doors. Lavatory installation and stowage for up to 510 lb (231 kg) luggage in aft fuselage. Other standard cabin equipment includes ash trays, two cigarette lighters, fresh air outlets for all passengers, cabin coat rack, coat hangers and dual "No Smoking-Fasten Seat Belt" signs. Electro-thermally heated windshield, hot air windshield defroster and windshield wipers standard. Optional equipment includes cabin fire extinguisher, additional cabin window, flush toilet and a variety of interior cabinets.

SYSTEMS: Cabin pressurised to a maximum differential of 4·6 lb/sq in (0·32 kg/cm²). Oxygen system for flight deck and 22 cu ft (0·62 m³) oxygen system for cabin standard. Cabin oxygen system of 49·2 cu ft (1·39 m³) or 65·6 cu ft (1·86 m³) optional. Dual vacuum system for instruments. Hydraulic system for brakes only. Pneumatic system for wing and tail unit de-icing only. Two 250A starter/generators. Nickel-cadmium 28V 40Ah battery.

EQUIPMENT: Standard equipment includes stall warning system, heated pitot heads, overhead floodlight for flight deck, full blind flying instrumentation, wing ice lights, dual landing lights, nose gear taxi light, adjustable cabin reading lights, entrance door, baggage compartment and map lights, blue-white cockpit lighting, primary and secondary instrument lights, navigation lights, dual rotating beacons, map pockets and dual adjustable sun visors. Optional items include a variety of interior layouts and seating, engine fire extinguisher system propeller synchrophaser, smoke detection system for radio compartment, flight hour meter, Twilighter Mk III strobe lights, Foxboro fuel totaliser system and automatic propeller feathering with synchrophaser.

ELECTRONICS: Standard system comprises one Collins 618M-2B VHF com receiver; one Collins 51RV-2B Auto Omni with Glideslope, 331-A-3G indicator, B-17 Nav/GS antenna and voice filter; Collins dual 356F-3 with dual 356C-4

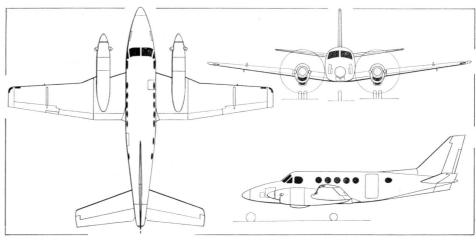

Beechcraft King Air 100 twin-turboprop pressurised transport

amplifiers; Collins DF-203 ADF, with voice filter and flush antenna; Collins 51Z-6 marker beacon with dual lights and B-16 antenna; Auto Omni No. 2 with glide slope and 331A-3G indicator; Collins 618M-2B standby transceiver; RCA AVQ-75 DME with M1591085-3 indicator, and B-18 antenna; Allen 2105D-B-6 RMI with Nav and ADF switching; Sperry C-14-3 and Collins PN-101 compasses; RCA AVQ-55 radar with bright scope and 12-in antenna; dual OECO 20139 inverters with failure lights; Wilcox 1014A transponder with B18 antenna; and one 500E G.H.; DME hold for AVQ-75 and one 3-in G.H. gyro. An extensive range of optional Collins, Bendix and ARC electronics is available to customers' requirements.

DIMENSIONS, EXTERNAL:

Wing span	45 ft 10½ in (13·98 m)
Wing chord at root	7 ft 0½ in (2·15 m)
Wing chord at tip	3 ft 6 in (1·07 m)
Wing aspect ratio	7·51
Length overall	39 ft 11¼ in (12·17 m)
Height overall	15 ft 4¼ in (4·68 m)
Tailplane span	22 ft 4½ in (6·81 m)
Wheel track	13 ft 0 in (3·96 m)
Wheelbase	14 ft 11 in (4·55 m)

WEIGHTS:

Weight empty	6,405 lb (2,905 kg)
Max ramp weight	10,668 lb (4,838 kg)
Max T-O weight	10,600 lb (4,808 kg)

PERFORMANCE (estimated at max T-O weight unless detailed otherwise):
Cruising speed, high cruise power, at 9,500 lb (4,309 kg) AUW:
At 21,000 ft (6,400 m)
239 knots (275 mph; 443 km/h)
At 16,000 ft (4,875 m)
245 knots (282 mph; 454 km/h)
At 10,000 ft (3,050 m)
248 knots (285 mph; 459 km/h)
Cruising speed, low cruise power, at 9,500 lb (4,309 kg) AUW:
At 21,000 ft (6,400 m)
226 knots (260 mph; 418 km/h)

At 16,000 ft (4,875 m)
234 knots (269 mph; 433 km/h)
At 12,000 ft (3,660 m)
237 knots (273 mph; 439 km/h)
Stalling speed, power off, wheels and flaps down
73 knots (84 mph; 135·5 km/h)
Stalling speed, power off, wheels and flaps up
89 knots (102 mph; 165 km/h)
Max rate of climb at S/L
2,200 ft (671 m)/min
Max rate of climb at S/L, one engine out
608 ft (185 m)/min
Service ceiling 25,900 ft (7,895 m)
Service ceiling, one engine out 11,800 ft (3,595 m)
T-O run 1,452 ft (443 m)
T-O to 50 ft (15 m) 1,729 ft (527 m)
Landing from 50 ft (15 m), without propeller reversal 2,138 ft (652 m)
Landing from 50 ft (15 m), with propeller reversal 1,410 ft (430 m)
Landing run, without propeller reversal
1,159 ft (353 m)
Landing run, with propeller reversal
750 ft (229 m)
Range, at high cruise power, including allowances for starting, taxi, take-off, climb, descent and 45 min reserve:
At 21,000 ft (6,400 m)
945 nm (1,089 miles; 1,752 km)
At 16,000 ft (4,875 m)
830 nm (956 miles, 1,538 km)
At 10,000 ft (3,050 m)
706 nm (813 miles, 1,308 km)
Range at low cruise power, including allowances for starting, taxi, take-off, climb, descent and 45 min reserve:
At 21,000 ft (6,400 m)
1,005 nm (1,158 miles; 1,863 km)
At 16,000 ft (4,875 m)
895 nm (1,031 miles; 1,659 km)
At 10,000 ft (3,050 m)
762 nm (878 miles; 1,413 km)
Max range, allowances as above:
At 21,000 ft (6,400 m)
1,087 nm (1,252 miles; 2,014 km)
At 16,000 ft (4,875 m)
1,022 nm (1,177 miles; 1,894 km)
At 10,000 ft (3,050 m)
911 nm (1,050 miles; 1,689 km)

Beechcraft King Air 100 8/15-seat pressurised light transport (two 680 shp Pratt & Whitney (UACL) PT6A-28 turboprop engines)

BELL

BELL AEROSPACE COMPANY DIVISION OF TEXTRON INC

HEAD OFFICE AND WORKS:
Buffalo, New York 14240
PRESIDENT:
William G. Gisel
EXECUTIVE VICE-PRESIDENT:
Dr Richard M. Hurst
VICE-PRESIDENTS:
Don R. Ostrander (Planning)
Lawrence P. Mordaunt (Manager, Minuteman III Programme)
Joseph R. Piselli (Marketing)
Dr Clifford F. Berninger (Engineering)
John H. van Lonkhuyzen (Research)
Peter J. Wacks (Industrial Relations)
Norton C. Willcox (Finance)
William S. Nochisaki (Manufacturing)
Edward W. Virgin (Eastern Region)
John M. Schweizer, Jr (Western Region)
John F. Gill (Product Assurance)
Ramon J. Hartung (Project and Systems Management)
William M. Smith (SES-New Orleans)
SECRETARY: Joseph E. Conners

On 3 January 1970 the former Bell Aerospace Corporation was merged into Textron Inc. Simultaneously, the former Bell Aerosystems Company assumed its new name of Bell Aerospace Company Division of Textron Inc.

Bell Aerospace Company is active in aircraft, missile, propulsion and electronics systems development and advanced technology for US aerospace and defence programmes. Its research and development programmes in the VTOL-STOL field include air cushion vehicles, rocket and jet-powered back-pack individual mobility systems, with which Bell test pilots have flown to heights of up to 80 ft (25 m) and travelled forward at up to 60 mph (96 km/h), and a two-man "pogo-stick" rocket transport device evolved from the rocket-belt concept. The company has also initiated development of a pilot self-rescue system for the US Air Force.

Two major current programmes are devoted to development and testing of the X-22A tilting-duct VTOL research aircraft for the US Navy and of the Lunar Landing Training Vehicles which NASA is using to explore the procedures associated with landings on the Moon and to train astronauts in the techniques involved.

The company is also engaged in design studies of lightweight rocket-powered lunar exploration flying vehicles capable of propelling astronauts over the Moon's surface and of jet-powered individual back-pack flying systems for military use.

Production of liquid-propellant rocket engines for Lockheed's Agena satellite programme continues and is described in the "Aero-Engines" section. Other space contracts have included the manufacture of reaction controls for the North American X-15A research aircraft, Minuteman, and Centaur launch vehicle. Major research and development programmes cover the investigation of high-energy propellants, advanced structural materials and positive-expulsion rocket-propellant tank devices.

The Bell automatic All-Weather Carrier Landing System (AWCLS) is now in production for the US Navy and is being installed on 13 aircraft carriers and at five land bases for pilot familiarization. This system, capable of providing completely automatic landing facilities for two aircraft per minute, has been evaluated by the FAA and USAF.

Other electronics work is concerned with precision inertial guidance/navigation equipment and airborne target location, fire control and satellite communication systems.

BELL MODEL D2127
US military designation: X-22A

Under a US Navy contract, awarded in November 1962, Bell Aerospace Company has built and flown two prototypes of a tri-service tilting-duct V/STOL research aircraft known as the X-22A. The first was rolled out on 25 May 1965. It flew for the first time on 17 March 1966, making four vertical flights to a height of 25 ft (7·6 m) and turning through 180°. Subsequently, it made a number of STOL take-offs, with the ducts at an angle of 30°, followed by forward flights at speeds of over 86 knots (100 mph; 169 km/h), before suffering severe damage in a heavy landing following hydraulic system failure on 8 August 1966. It was considered to be beyond practical repair, and had logged just over three flying hours at the time of the accident.

The second X-22A flew for the first time on 26 January 1967, and by May 1969 had accumulated a total flight time of 110 hours. During this time the X-22A had made 386 vertical and 216 short-take offs, 405 vertical and 197 short landings, and 185 transitions from vertical to horizontal flight, and vice-versa. Flights have been made at speeds up to 221 knots (255 mph; 412 km/h).

On 30 July 1968 the X-22A made a sustained hover at an altitude of 8,020 ft (2,445 m), believed to be a world record for V/STOL aircraft.

Head-on view of Bell X-22A tilting-duct research aircraft in vertical flight

Bell X-22A in transition phase (four 1,250 shp General Electric YT58-GE-8D turboshaft engines)

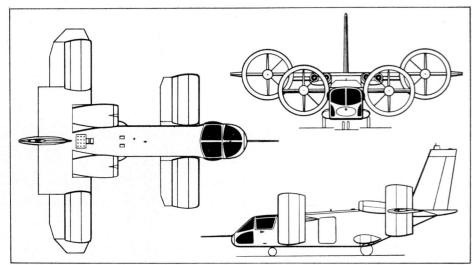

Bell X-22A research aircraft with tilting ducts in cruise position

In the Spring of 1968, a variable stability system (VSS), designed and built by Cornell Aeronautical Laboratory was installed. The VSS enables the X-22A to change its flight characteristics automatically while airborne, making it a suitable test bed for studying a whole range of V/STOL flight problems, as well as providing the ability to simulate other V/STOL configurations.

A major component of the VSS is a Low Range Airspeed System, which can measure accurately speed in any direction, from zero to ± 156 knots (180 mph; 290 km/h). A sensing element, comprising a 2 ft (0·61 m) long tube, is mounted at the top of the fin. Spinning at 1,560 rpm, this tube detects variations in pressure as it turns, from which electronic equipment determines the actual airspeed and direction of flight.

The X-22A has a tandem layout, with the four ducted propellers mounted near the tips of the foreplane and wings. For take-off, the ducts tilt upwards through 90° so that the propellers function as helicopter rotors.

On 19 May 1969 the X-22A was formally delivered to the US government and will be used in continuing research for the US Navy, Army and Air Force as well as for the FAA and NASA.

TYPE: Tilting-duct V/STOL research aircraft.

WINGS: Cantilever wings mounted at rear of fuselage, each with a tilting duct built into leading-edge. Wing section outboard of ducts NACA 64A-415. No dihedral. Elevon control surface in each wing, in slipstream from duct. Aluminium alloy structure of skins, beams and stringers.

FUSELAGE: Conventional all-metal semi-monocoque structure of basically square section. Fairing on each side of rear fuselage to house main landing gear units when retracted.

TAIL SURFACES: Fixed vertical fin at tail, with no rudder. Foreplane at front of fuselage, carrying two forward ducts. Elevon control surface in slipstream from each duct. Construction similar to that of wings.

LANDING GEAR: Retractable tricycle type, supplied by Loud Company. Hydraulic retraction. Twin wheels on nose unit; single wheel on each main unit. Goodyear wheels, tyres and brakes.

POWER PLANT: Four 1,250 shp General Electric YT58-GE-8D shaft-turbine engines mounted in pairs at root of each wing. Cross-shafting ensures that all ducted propellers continue to be powered in the event of an engine failure. Propellers are constant-speed units by Hamilton Standard, diameter 7 ft 0 in (2·13 m), each with three lightweight blades consisting of a glass-fibre shell over a steel load-carrying core. Fuel in single tank in fuselage at aircraft's centre of gravity.

ACCOMMODATION: Crew of two side-by-side on flight deck, on Douglas Aircraft zero-altitude zero-speed ejection seats. Cabin is designed to carry 1,500 lb (680 kg) of payload, made up of passengers, cargo, instrumentation or mixed loads. Six passengers can be carried in folding troop-type seats, or up to ten passengers in high-density seating.

CONTROL SYSTEM: Control is achieved at the ducts through the use of thrust modulation, obtained by propeller pitch change, and by means of the four elevons, in the slipstream of each duct. These controls are integrated for both vertical and level flight. Altitude control in vertical flight is by increasing and decreasing engine power. Propeller pitch and elevons are controlled by duplicated hydraulic power systems. Pilot's controls consist of conventional stick and rudder pedals, plus a removable collective pitch stick for certain test phases in which engine speed control is used. During transition, when the ducts are at angle locations between those used for hover and level flight, the control stick and pedals produce mixed propeller pitch and elevon deflections in proportions dependent upon the angular position of the ducts, in order to produce uncoupled, or pure, roll and yaw moments. This is accomplished by a mixing box employing variable-ratio bellcranks. The relative location of the pilot's control inputs and the propeller pitch and elevon control outputs of the variable-ratio bellcranks are determined by the angular position of the duct. A variable stability and control system, supplied by Cornell Aeronautical Laboratory, is provided in addition to the primary mechanical-hydraulic system described above. Its purpose is to provide the capability to simulate other V/STOL aircraft, to evaluate handling requirements and simulate changes in the aircraft to evaluate different concepts and modifications. In addition, it provides the autopilot function.

ELECTRONICS AND EQUIPMENT: Collins UHF radio and ADF. ITT Federal Laboratories TACAN. Honeywell radar altimeter.

DIMENSIONS, EXTERNAL:
Wing span	39 ft 3 in (11·96 m)
Span across front ducts	23 ft 0 in (7·01 m)
Length overall (excl boom)	39 ft 7 in (12·07 m)
Height overall	20 ft 8 in (6·31 m)
Wheel track	8 ft 0 in (2·44 m)
Wheelbase	16 ft 0 in (4·88 m)

WEIGHTS:
VTOL gross weight	16,274 lb (7,381 kg)
Max T-O weight (VTOL and STOL)	18,016 lb (8,171 kg)

PERFORMANCE (estimated):
Max level speed at S/L
275 knots (316 mph; 510 km/h)
Cruising speed 185 knots (213 mph; 342 km/h)
Cruising height
11,000-15,000 ft (3,350-4,575 m)
Rate of climb at S/L 6,400 ft (1,950 m)/min
Short T-O to 50 ft (15 m) 700 ft (213 m)
Range 386 nm (445 miles: 715 km)
Endurance at S/L, including 10 min hovering
2 hours

BELL/LAKE LA-4 ACLS CONVERSION

Bell Aerospace is developing an air cushion landing system (ACLS), which started as a company-funded research project in December 1963. In 1966 the company was awarded a $99,000 contract by the USAF Flight Dynamics Laboratory for wind-tunnel testing of the project.

Lake LA-4, fitted with Bell Aerospace's ACLS, taking off from Lake Erie

Bell Aerospace's LLTV making a simulated Moon-landing during astronaut training

Subsequent Air Force contracts included a $99,500 feasibility study in 1966, a $98,700 model test programme in 1967 and a $66,300 flight test programme in 1968.

The initial intention was to find the best way of providing an ACLS for cargo transports, following flight tests carried out with a modified Lake LA-4 four-seat amphibian.

A small auxiliary engine is installed in the rear fuselage of the LA-4, and this drives a 2 ft (0·61 m)-diameter fan to inflate an air cushion "bag" on the underside of the aircraft. When the nylon-cloth-and-rubber bag is inflated to a pressure of 50 lb/sq ft (244·1 kg/m²), the air escapes through hundreds of jet nozzles circling the underside of the bag, thus creating the air cushion. In flight the bag is deflated, hugging the aircraft tightly to reduce aerodynamic drag. Gross weight of the LA-4 in this configuration is 2,400 lb (1,088 kg).

The auxiliary engine can be shut down in flight; alternatively, its airflow can be diverted through louvres in the sides of the fuselage to provide supplementary forward thrust to increase the aircraft's performance.

When landing with the ACLS, the aircraft's forward speed is checked by a skid brake system activated by inflatable air pillows. These are brought into contact with the ground by a braking control.

During a three-month test programme carried out over land surfaces in the early part of 1969, the ACLS completed 18·5 operating hours, during which take-offs and landings were made on snow, ice, concrete and grass surfaces. Practical experience has shown the system to be suitable for operation in high crosswind conditions. Taxying tests were conducted successfully over snow, grass, sand, mud, ploughed land, ditches and land hazards such as tree-stumps. This programme was conducted under contracts from the Air Force Systems Command's Flight Dynamics Laboratory at Wright-Patterson AFB.

In August 1969 a further series of tests began to determine the practicallity of the system for operations on and from water. On 11 September 1969 the aircraft took off from Lake Erie in choppy conditions, with a 22 knots (25 mph; 40 km/h) wind, requiring only 650 ft (198 m) for its T-O run. After landing, the aircraft taxied over the lake and straight on to the shore, demonstrating the transition capability of this system.

When fully developed, the ACLS is expected to have military and commercial applications, permitting deployment over a very wide range of surface conditions. In addition, preliminary studies have established that the Air Cushion Landing concept is applicable to both the booster and orbiter stages of the proposed Space Shuttle System.

BELL LUNAR LANDING RESEARCH VEHICLE (LLRV) AND LUNAR LANDING TRAINING VEHICLE (LLTV)

In the Spring of 1964 Bell Aerospace Company delivered to NASA two Lunar Landing Research Vehicles (LLRV's) which were ordered as part of the support programme for the Apollo project (which see).

These vehicles were first used in an extensive research programme, at the NASA Flight Research Center, Edwards, California, to provide a realistic simulation on Earth of landing operations in a lunar environment. Purposes of this programme were to explore the problems associated with landing on the Moon and to provide test data for designers of the Apollo Lunar Module (LM) (described under the "Grumman" entry in the "Research Rockets" section). The LLRV's were then transferred to NASA's Manned Spacecraft Center, Houston, Texas, and converted for use in training astronauts in the correct procedures of approach, hover and touchdown on the lunar surface.

The first flight test of an LLRV was made by NASA project pilot Joseph A. Walker, at Edwards on 30 October 1964. When fully loaded with fuel and instruments, the vehicle weighed about 3,710 lb (1,683 kg). It was designed so that various sections, such as the legs, pilot display panel and controls, could be removed and replaced eventually by actual LM components.

On 6 May 1968, at Ellington AFB, Texas, an LLRV crashed after an in-flight failure. The pilot/astronaut, Neil A. Armstrong, ejected and landed safely by parachute.

A new vehicle, designated Lunar Landing Training Vehicle (LLTV) and designed specifically for the training function, was developed subsequently by Bell and three examples were delivered late in 1967, to allow expansion of the training programme. First flight of an LLTV was made at Ellington AFB, Texas, on 3 October 1968. One was lost in an accident at Ellington AFB on 11 December 1968, but the pilot ejected safely.

On 14 June 1969 the LLTV was first used by astronauts selected to make Moon landings, and Apollo 11 and 12 commanders, Neil Armstrong and Charles Conrad respectively, each made up to 50 LLTV practice landings prior to their successful journeys to the Moon in 1969. Astronaut James Lovell also completed extensive LLTV training before the start of the Apollo 13 mission.

The LLTV is a vertical take-off and landing machine that is designed to fly to altitudes of up to 1,000 ft (305 m), to hover and to fly horizontally at speeds of up to 60 ft/sec (18 m/sec). It is 11 ft 4 in (3·45 m) in height and is carried on four welded aluminium alloy truss legs with a spread of 13 ft 4 in (4·06 m). The legs support a platform for the pilot and his controls. A General Electric CF700-2V turbofan engine (4,200 lb = 1,905 kg st) and Bell Aerospace hydrogen peroxide rockets provide the thrust which enables the vehicle to take off, hover and then drop gently to Earth in simulated lunar landings. Max vertical velocity is 30 ft/sec (9 m/sec) and nominal T-O weight is 4,051 lb (1,837 kg), including 200 lb (90 kg) of instrumentation. Latter includes a Flight Data System, designed by Ryan Aeronautical Company, comprising a radar altimeter and velocity sensor which gives information on the LLTV's position and rate of motion in any direction.

Two basic differences between the Moon and Earth had to be considered in the design of the LLRV and LLTV. These are the low lunar gravity, which is about one-sixth that of the Earth, and the Moon's low atmospheric pressure which produces virtually no aerodynamic forces on the vehicle. However, a variable-stability autopilot system, developed by Bell, enables astronauts to fly the LLRV and LLTV on Earth and get virtually the same reactions and sensations as if they were operating in a lunar environment.

The turbofan engine, modified for vertical operation and installed on a gimbal mounting behind the cockpit, is controlled automatically and provides lift equal to five-sixths of the vehicles' gross weight. Thus, this engine counteracts five-sixths of the Earth's gravity. The remaining one-sixth Earth gravity is comparable to the gravity on the Moon.

Lift for the remaining one-sixth of the vehicle's weight is provided by two Bell rocket motors of 500 lb (225 kg) st each. Controlled by the pilot, these rockets are throttleable and simulate those that are used in the LM for lunar landings. Each vehicle has six additional 500 lb (225 kg) st Bell rocket motors as a back-up landing system in case of failure of the turbofan engine.

Sixteen Bell reaction control rockets, similar to those used on all US manned space flights to date, are mounted on the LLTV for attitude control, and the flying controls on the LLTV simulate those of the LM.

BELL "POGO" VEHICLES AND LUNAR FLYING VEHICLE

In the early 1960s, as a follow-up to its original one-man back-pack rocket-belt lift devices, Bell Aerosystems began development and testing of a variety of flying platform configurations designed to evaluate the handling qualities and control techniques for Lunar Flying Vehicles and various Earth mobility systems.

Designed to carry both one and two men, these "Pogo" vehicles consist of a simple open platform mounted on four castoring wheels. They are powered by hydrogen peroxide propulsion systems which provide a maximum flight duration of 21 seconds. In the one-man "Pogo" the single propulsion system weighs approximately 80 lb (36 kg), with a thrust level of about 300 lb (136 kg). The two-man "Pogo" has two of these systems.

Bell is currently evaluating kinesthetic control, a concept which virtually eliminates all manual control and allows the operator to simply lean in

First free flight of Bell's one-man kinesthetically controlled "Pogo"

Artist's impression of the Bell Lunar Flying Vehicle on a lunar exploration mission

the direction he wishes to travel. Earlier "Pogo" vehicles were equipped with a thrust vector control system which the operator manipulated with hand-held grips. First free flight of a one-man kinesthetically-controlled "Pogo" was made late in 1968 and flight tests of a similarly controlled two-man "Pogo" were initiated early in 1969.

As a result of its "Pogo" work, Bell received in 1968 a $250,000 contract from NASA for preliminary design of a Lunar Flying Vehicle, which is under study for the transportation of astronauts on lunar exploration missions, and which would have also a payload pallet mounted behind the astronaut. Such a vehicle, using as fuel residual propellants from the Lunar Module descent stage, must be capable of minimum flight ranges of 10-15 miles (16-24 km) and be able to perform at least 30 sorties. It would be powered by two rocket-engines and have motor-cycle-type hand grips for control of thrust and attitude.

BELL JET FLYING BELT

Currently under development for the US Army, under a $3 million contract sponsored by DOD's Advanced Research Projects Agency, this is an experimental one-man back-pack flying system powered by a miniature jet-engine.

A total of 430 lb (195 kg) thrust is provided by a single Williams Research Corporation WR-19 high-bypass turbojet engine measuring approximately 1 ft (0·30 m) in diameter by 2 ft (0·61 m) in length, and which features a high thrust-to-weight ratio and low specific fuel consumption.

The bypass concept, in which a proportion of engine intake air is diverted through a chamber around the core of the engine and mixed with the primary flow of hot exhaust gases, insulates the operator and fuel tanks from primary engine heat.

The system burns standard JP-4 fuel, carried in transparent plastic tanks which wrap around the engine. A helmet vibrator warns the pilot when fuel contents have been consumed to a reserve level.

Ignition is achieved with a solid-propellant

cartridge which, when triggered by the operator, exhausts into the engine, spinning the turbine and igniting the fuel. Thrust from the engine is channeled equally through two gimballed thrust nozzles directed downward behind the operator's shoulders.

Flight control is achieved through manipulation of manually actuated hand controls and arm motions, giving the operator complete freedom of flight, including vertical axis rotation and hovering manoeuvres. Range and flight duration of the Jet-Belt will be measured in miles and minutes, instead of the feet and seconds to which flights of rocket-powered predecessors have been limited.

Bell Aerospace Jet Flying Belt in free flight

Weight of the system is distributed comfortably on the operator's hips by means of a specially-developed glass-fibre corset. A two-way radio communications system is an integral part of the Jet Flying Belt, as is an operator recovery system consisting of a paratrooper's standard parachute deployed by a drogue gun. Stowed in a container on top of the Jet Flying Belt, this has demonstrated an ability to effect safe recovery during hovering flight as low as 65 ft (20 m).

The first of a series of manned free flight tests began on 7 April 1969, these being of a "low and slow" nature to explore the flight envelope and handling qualities. To date, speeds of up to 26 knots (30 mph; 48 km/h) at altitudes of up to 45 ft (14 m) have been attained, with a max duration of 4 min 40 sec. It is anticipated that development will allow speeds up to 86 knots (100 mph; 161 km/h), range of 26 nm (30 miles; 48 km) and duration of 25 min.

Empty weight of the Jet Flying Belt is 124 lb (56 kg) and gross take-off weight 365 lb (165 kg). Approximately 60 lb (27 kg) of the weight supported by the operator is offset by the engine at a "ground idle" setting. Fuel capacity is about 6 US gallons (22·7 litres). The cartridge start system and rapid acceleration characteristics of the WR-19 engine permit lift-off within ten seconds of initiating engine start.

Potential military applications for this new mobility system include flying over barbed-wire and mine-fields, reconnaissance, counter-guerilla warfare, perimeter guard and amphibious landings. Some potential civil applications are for riot control, powerline and pipeline patrols, photographic news coverage, rescue operations, traffic surveillance and microwave tower inspections.

On 26 January 1970, Bell announced that the company had granted to the Williams Research Corporation, Walled Lake, Michigan, a licence to manufacture, use and sell certain small lift device systems, including the Jet Flying Belt.

BELL PILOT SELF-RESCUE SYSTEM

Bell Aerospace Company has built and is flight testing an experimental aircrew self-rescue system, designed to investigate the feasibility of using a jet-powered parawing to carry an ejection seat and its occupant clear of hostile territory. Bell believe that results of early tests may lead to development of an escape system comprising an ejection seat, a packaged self-deploying parawing, turbojet engine, associated controls and fuel tanks. Following ejection from a disabled aircraft, the parawing would be deployed and the jet engine ignited automatically. After escaping from the danger area, at a speed of 87 knots (100 mph; 161 km/h) or more, the occupant would jettison the seat and parachute to the ground. An operating range of 43 nm (50 miles; 80·4 km) is envisaged.

This research is being carried out under contract to the USAF Flight Dynamics Laboratory, as part of its Integrated Air Crew Escape/Rescue Systems Capability (AERCAB) programme.

The Bell design for a feasibility model to evaluate this concept stemmed from a company-funded programme initiated in 1967. This, designated the Discretionary Descent Device, was made up of a 170-lb (77-kg) thrust Bell Rocket Belt, an aircraft ejection seat and a non-rigid parawing with a gross area of 800 sq ft (74·3 m²), the entire system being mounted on a four-wheeled frame.

A series of 24 unmanned/manned, unpowered/powered drop tests were made during 1968 from a helicopter flying at altitudes ranging from 3,500-9,000 ft (1,070-2,745 m) and Bell claim that they achieved the first manned free flight of a powered non-rigid parawing in this period.

Bell's current feasibility model under the AERCAB programme consists of a parawing rigidly mounted to an ejection seat, housing a modified Continental T65 turbojet engine, and

has also a special recovery parachute and a landing impact attenuator.

Under the terms of the contract, all flight tests will be unmanned and controlled remotely. The feasibility model, with its parawing already deployed, will be dropped from a helicopter, the programme calling for both unpowered and powered drops for evaluation of glide and powered free flight characteristics.

Artist's impression of Bell's jet-powered self-rescue system

BELL HELICOPTER COMPANY

HEAD OFFICE:
PO Box 482, Fort Worth, Texas 76101

PRESIDENT:
Edwin J. Ducayet

EXECUTIVE VICE-PRESIDENT:
James F. Atkins

VICE-PRESIDENTS:
Roy Coleman (Manufacturing)
Bartram Kelley (Engineering)
Hans Weichsel, Jr (Military Marketing)
Edwin L. Farmer (Finance)
Gen H. H. Howze (Product Planning)
M. R. Barcellona (Management Engineering)
John Finn (Industrial Relations)
James C. Fuller (Public Relations)
William L. Humphrey (General Manager, Overhaul Modification Centre, Amarillo)
Joseph Mashman (Special Projects)
Warren T. Rockwell (Washington Operations)
Dwayne K. Jose (Commercial Marketing)
Frank M. Sylvester (International Marketing)

TREASURER: T. R. Treff

Bell Helicopter Company is the largest operating division of Textron Inc.

Present production at Fort Worth is concerned primarily with military and commercial versions of the turbine-powered UH-1 Iroquois, the AH-1 HueyCobra armed helicopter developed from the UH-1, military and commercial versions of the Model 206A JetRanger, and the latest models of the Bell 47, which has been in continuous production since receiving the first helicopter Approved Type Certificate from the CAA on 8 March 1946.

A co-production contract between Bell and the Federal Republic of Germany is expected to provide approximately 350 UH-1Ds to the armed forces of that nation by the end of 1970. Prime contractor in West Germany is Dornier GmbH. Other versions of the UH-1 are built under licence by Agusta in Italy and Fuji in Japan. Bell also has a licence agreement with the Republic of China covering co-production of an unspecified number of Model 205 general-purpose helicopters.

By the end of 1969, Bell had built and delivered 13,000 production helicopters, including more commercial helicopters than all other US manufacturers combined.

It was in 1958 that Bell's Model XV-3 pioneer tilt-rotor research aircraft achieved the first full in-flight conversion by a machine of this configuration. In following years more than 120 similar conversions were achieved successfully by Bell, US Army, USAF and NASA test pilots.

Since that time Bell engineers have continued research on this concept and hold currently six USAF/NASA contracts to investigate prop-rotor and folding prop-rotor technology. The contracts include manufacture and wind-tunnel testing of examples of both these rotors, and a successful termination of these tests could lead to development of a transport aircraft capable of speeds in excess of 347 knots (400 mph; 644 km/h), while retaining VTOL capability.

It is proposed that prop-rotors would be mounted at the tips of a medium-span high-mounted tilt-wing. For take-off the rotors (shaft-driven by convertible turboshaft/turbofan engines) would be used as those of a conventional helicopter. Once airborne, the wing would be tilted forward through 90 degrees until the rotors served as propellers, allowing forward speeds of 239-261 knots (275-300 mph; 443-483 km/h) for short/medium-range flights. Speeds in excess of this figure, the prop-rotors would be stopped and folded back to a minimum drag configuration, forward propulsion being provided by the engines operating as turbofans and lift being developed by the tilt-wing.

Also under investigation, and already tested extensively, is a method of varying a rotor's diameter in flight. Maximum diameter would provide lift for vertical take-off and climb, with minimum diameter being used when the rotor was serving as a conventional tractor propeller, thus increasing cruise efficiency.

In October 1969, the US Army Aviation Systems Command (AVSCOM) awarded Bell a contract to act as technical advisor for AVSCOM's Automatic Inspection Diagnostic and Prognostic System (AIDAPS) test-bed programme. This is intended to investigate the capability of off-the-shelf diagnostic equipment to detect malfunctions, identify faulty components and, to a limited degree, provide malfunction or failure prediction. AVSCOM will test the systems on Bell UH-1D helicopters after preliminary evaluation in test cells.

More than 10,500 people were employed by Bell during 1969.

BELL MODEL 47G-3B-2, 47G-4A, 47G-5 AND Ag-5

USAF designation: UH-13
US Army designation: OH-13 Sioux and TH-13T
US Navy/Marine Corps designation: TH-13 (formerly HTL)
British Army designation: Sioux AH.Mk 1 and 2

Current commercial production versions of the Bell Model 47 are as follows:—

Model 47G-3B-2. Three-seater with outstanding high-altitude performance over a wide range of temperatures. Basically similar to earlier Model 47G-3, but Lycoming TVO-435-G1A supercharged engine uprated to 280 hp, fuel capacity increased to 57 US gallons (216 litres), cabin widened by 8 in (20 cm) to 5 ft 0 in (1·52 m), and AUW increased by 100 lb (45 kg). A 10 lb (4·5 kg) weight has been added to each blade-tip to improve autorotation characteristics and manoeuvrability. FAA Type certificate issued 17 January 1968. A similar version, manufactured by Agusta in Italy and Westland in the UK, is standard equipment in the British Army, under the name Sioux AH.Mk 1. The Royal New Zealand Air Force has ordered seven 47G-3B-2s for delivery during 1970.

Model 47G-4A. Basic three-seat utility helicopter with 305 hp (derated to 280 hp) Lycoming VO-540-B1B3 engine. Cyclic and collective flying controls are hydraulically-boosted. Airframe approved for 1,200 hours between overhauls. Dynamic components, cabin and centre-frame interchangeable with 47G-3B-2. Deliveries began in December 1965.

Between 6 and 11 May 1969 a Bell 47G-4A owned by Pacific Southwest Airlines established an unofficial endurance record for helicopters of 121 hours, piloted by C. E. Keough and L. Dolan.

Model 47G-5. Low-cost model in which non-essential structures and components have been eliminated to reduce initial price and increase max useful load to 1,191 lb (540 kg). Powered by 265 hp Lycoming VO-435-B1A engine. Standard items on current version include tinted Plexiglas canopy, doors, heavy-duty battery, 70 amp 12V alternator, synchronised elevator and twin 28·5 US gallon (108 litre) fuel tanks. A rotating beacon, landing light and full range of Model 47 optional extras are available. The standard Model 47 rotor system, with stabilising bar, and hydraulically-boosted controls are retained. Features include an automotive electrical system and compact low-profile instrument pedestal. Available as two-seat agricultural model (**Ag-5**), with Bell AgMaster chemical application system, or three-seat utility model. Deliveries began in January 1966.

Bell's AgMaster chemical application system is manufactured by Transland Aircraft and weighs about 200 lb (90·7 kg). Standard equipment includes two 60 US gallon (227 litre) glass-fibre hoppers, both of which can be loaded from either side of the aircraft. Able to be installed by two persons in 25 minutes, the AgMaster system is available with a choice of spray-boom lengths and up to 120 nozzle locations. Two removable outboard sections provide for controlled swath widths of from 20 ft to 200 ft (6-60 m). Flying at 60 mph (96 kmh) a helicopter fitted with this equipment can spray up to 14·4 acres per minute.

Military versions of the Model 47 include the following:—

OH-13S. US Army observation version of 47G-3B, of which production continues during 1970. Powered by 260 hp Lycoming TVO-435-25 engine.

TH-13T. Two-seat instrument training version of standard 47G-3B-1 with additional avionics equipment, including VOR, ADF, marker beacon receiver, ILS glideslope, gyro-magnetic compass and attitude gyro system, and blind-flying hood for pupil pilot. Order for 103 for US Army announced in June 1964, followed by further orders for 26 on 17 August 1965, 91 on 15 October 1965, 54 on 16 June 1966 and 141 on 22 June 1967, making a total of 415 ordered. First delivery made in December 1964; deliveries completed in 1968. Powered by 270 hp Lycoming TVO-435-D1B engine.

Bell Ag-5 two-seat agricultural helicopter with AgMaster spray equipment

The description which follows refers specifically to the Model 47G-4A.

TYPE: Three-seat general-utility helicopter.

ROTOR SYSTEM: Two-blade semi-rigid main rotor, with interchangeable blades of all-metal bonded construction and stabilising bar below and at right-angles to blades. Conventional swashplate assembly for cyclic-pitch and collective-pitch control. Blades do not fold. Two-blade all-metal tail rotor. Brake on main rotor optional.

ROTOR DRIVE: Through centrifugal clutch and two-stage planetary transmission. Shaft-drive to tail rotor. Main rotor rpm 333-370.

FUSELAGE: In three sections: centre, tail and cabin. Centre section has a welded steel-tube structure to carry the engine and cabin. Rear section is also a steel-tube structure, is triangular in cross-section and serves as a support for the tail rotor drive-shaft.

TAIL SURFACE: Small synchronised elevator at rear end of fuselage responds to the fore and aft motion of the cyclic-pitch control, to provide better stability and allow a greatly increased CG travel.

LANDING GEAR: Tubular skid type with small ground handling wheels and tie-down and towing attachments. Cross-tubes serve as supports for external loads such as litters or cargo bins. For amphibious operation, two air-inflated nylon floats are easily attached.

POWER PLANT: One vertically-mounted 305 hp (derated to 280 hp) Lycoming VO-540-B1B3 six-cylinder horizontally-opposed fan-cooled engine with clutch, drive shaft and rotor assembly in an integral unit. Two interconnected saddle-mounted fuel tanks (57 US gallons=216 litres total capacity) on CG and with gravity feed.

ACCOMMODATION: Side-by-side seats for three in cabin enclosed by a blue-tinted free-blown Plexiglas canopy. Door on each side, with sliding windows. For fair weather or specialised operations the doors are quickly removable. Can carry 1,000 lb (455 kg) cargo externally on under-fuselage hook.

ELECTRONICS AND EQUIPMENT: Standard equipment includes complete VFR flight and engine instruments, hydraulic boost controls, 28-volt/50 amp generator, electric starter, ground handling wheels, heavy-duty battery, etc. Additional accessories available in FAA-approved kits include pontoons, night flying equipment, dusting and spraying equipment, cargo carriers, litters, dual controls, heater-defroster, rotor brake, inertial reel and shoulder harness, ARC, King or Narco 360-channel VHF transceivers, fire extinguisher, first aid kit, etc.

DIMENSIONS, EXTERNAL:
Diameter of main rotor	37 ft 1½ in (11·32 m)
Main rotor blade chord	11 in (28 cm)
Diameter of tail rotor	5 ft 10 in (1·78 m)
Length overall (main rotor fore and aft)	43 ft 2½ in (13·17 m)
Length of fuselage	32 ft 6 in (9·90 m)
Width, rotors fore and aft	8 ft 6 in (2·59 m)
Width over skids	7 ft 6 in (2·29 m)
Height to top of rotor hub	9 ft 3 in (2·82 m)

DIMENSIONS, INTERNAL:
Cabin: Length	4 ft 11 in (1·50 m)
Max width	5 ft 0 in (1·52 m)
Max height	4 ft 6 in (1·37 m)

AREAS:
Main rotor blade (each)	17·14 sq ft (1·59 m²)
Tail rotor blade (each)	1·20 sq ft (0·11 m²)
Main rotor disc	1,083 sq ft (100·61 m²)
Tail rotor disc	26·8 sq ft (2·49 m²)

WEIGHTS:
Weight empty, with oil and equipped:
47G-3B-2	1,892 lb (858 kg)
47G-4A	1,843 lb (836 kg)

Bell OH-13S US Army observation helicopter (260 hp Lycoming TVO-435-25 engine)

47G-5	1,659 lb (752 kg)
OH-13S	2,203 lb (999 kg)
TH-13T	2,550 lb (1,156 kg)

Max T-O weight:
OH-13S, Ag-5, 47G-5	2,850 lb (1,293 kg)
47G-3B-2, 47G-4A, TH-13T	2,950 lb (1,338 kg)

PERFORMANCE (at max T-O weight, except where indicated. 47G-5 figures for aircraft with synchronised elevator and second fuel tank):

Max level speed at S/L:
all except Ag-5	91 knots (105 mph; 169 km/h)
Ag-5	78 knots (90 mph; 145 km/h)

Recommended cruising speed at 5,000 ft (1,525 m):
OH-13S, TH-13T, 47G-3B-2	72 knots (83 mph; 133 km/h)
47G-4A	77 knots (89 mph; 143 km/h)
47G-5, Ag-5	74 knots (85 mph; 137 km/h)

Max rate of climb at S/L:
47G-3B-2	1,065 ft (325 m)/min
47G-4A	800 ft (244 m)/min
OH-13S	550 ft (168 m)/min
TH-13T	900 ft (274 m)/min

Service ceiling:
47G-3B-2	17,600 ft (5,365 m)
47G-4A	11,200 ft (3,415 m)
Ag-5, 47G-5	10,500 ft (3,200 m)
OH-13S	18,500 ft (5,640 m)
TH-13T	16,800 ft (5,120 m)

Hovering ceiling in ground effect:
47G-3B-2	16,600 ft (5,060 m)
47G-4A	7,700 ft (2,347 m)
Ag-5, 47G-5	5,900 ft (1,800 m)
OH-13S	18,000 ft (5,500 m)
TH-13T	16,000 ft (4,875 m)

Hovering ceiling out of ground effect:
47G-3B-2	14,700 ft (4,480 m)
47G-4A	3,900 ft (1,190 m)
47G-5, Ag-5	1,350 ft (412 m)
OH-13S	14,800 ft (4,510 m)

TH-13T	10,500 ft (3,200 m)

Range with max fuel at 5,000 ft (1,525 m), no reserves:
47G-3B-2, OH-13S, TH-13T	217 nm (250 miles; 402 km)
47G-4A	225 nm (259 miles; 416 km)
47G-5, Ag-5	222 nm (256 miles; 411 km)

BELL MODEL 206A JETRANGER
US Navy designation: TH-57A SeaRanger
US Army designation: OH-58A Kiowa

Design of this five-seat turbine-powered general-purpose helicopter was started in April 1965. Construction of a prototype began in July 1965 and this aircraft was first flown on 10 January 1966. It received a provisional Type Certificate within four months, at which time two further examples had joined the flight test programme. Full certification was received on 20 October 1966, and deliveries began early in 1967. By December 1968, a total of 361 commercial models had been built, excluding Jet-Rangers produced under licence by Agusta in Italy.

In addition to the standard commercial version, there are two military versions of the JetRanger, as follows:

TH-57A SeaRanger. Primary light turbine training helicopter, of which 40 were ordered by the US Navy on 31 January 1968, to replace Bell TH-13M's used by Naval Air Training Command at Pensacola, Florida. Basically similar to Model 206A, with naval electronics and control equipment. Intended initially for VFR operation. Dual controls standard. All 40 were delivered during 1968.

OH-58A Kiowa. Light observation helicopter version of the Model 206A for the US Army; described separately.

Seven JetRangers have been supplied to the Brazilian Air Force which has designated them OH-4. Four of these machines, used by the BAF for COIN operations, are armed with a four-tube M2A2 launcher for 2·75-in folding-fin air-to-ground rockets, mounted at the aft edge of the port door, and a ·50-in calibre machine-gun on a flexible mount by the starboard door.

Under a five-year programme, covered by contracts valued at more then $75 million, Beech Aircraft is producing airframes for both the commercial and the military versions of the Model 206A. The work involves manufacture of the fuselage, skid gear, tail-boom spar, stabiliser and two rear fairing assemblies. The first Beech-produced airframe was delivered to Bell on 1 March 1968.

TYPE: Turbine-powered general-purpose light helicopter.

ROTOR SYSTEM: Two-blade semi-rigid see-saw type main rotor, employing pre-coning and underslinging to ensure smooth operation. Blades are of standard Bell "droop-snoot" section. They have a D-shape aluminium spar, bonded aluminium alloy skin, honeycomb core and a trailing-edge extension. Each blade is connected to the hub by means of a grip, pitch-change bearings and a tension-torsion strap

Bell TH-13T instrument trainer helicopter (270 hp Lycoming TVO-435-D1B engine)

assembly. Two tail rotor blades have bonded aluminium skin but no core. Main rotor blades do not fold, but modification to permit manual folding is possible. Rotor brake available as optional kit.

ROTOR DRIVE: Rotors driven through tubular steel alloy shafts with spliced couplings. Initial drive from engine through 90° spiral bevel gear to single-stage planetary main gearbox. Shaft to tail rotor single-stage bevel gearbox. Free-wheeling unit ensures that main rotor continues to drive tail rotor when engine is disengaged. Main rotor/engine rpm ratio 1:15; main rotor rpm 374-394. Tail rotor/engine rpm ratio 1:2·?.

FUSELAGE: Forward cabin section is made up of two aluminium alloy beams and 1 in (2·5 cm) thick aluminium honeycomb sandwich. Rotor, transmission and engine are supported by upper longitudinal beams. Upper and lower structure are interconnected by three fuselage bulkheads and a centre-post to form an integrated structure. Intermediate section is of aluminium alloy semi-monocoque construction. Aluminium monocoque tail-boom.

TAIL UNIT: Fixed stabiliser of aluminium monocoque construction, with inverted aerofoil section. Fixed vertical tail-fin in sweptback upper and ventral sections, made of aluminium honeycomb with aluminium alloy skin.

LANDING GEAR: Aluminium alloy tubular skids bolted to extruded cross-tubes. Tubular steel skid on ventral fin to protect tail rotor in tail-down landing. Special high-skid gear (10 in = 25 cm greater ground clearance) available for use in areas with high brush. Inflated bag-type pontoons or stowed floats capable of in-flight inflation available as optional kits.

POWER PLANT: One 317 shp Allison 250-C18A turboshaft engine. Fuel tank below and behind passenger seat, capacity 76 US gallons (288 litres). Refuelling point on starboard side of fuselage, aft of cabin. Oil capacity 5·5 US quarts (5·2 litres).

ACCOMMODATION: Two seats side-by-side in front and rear bench seat for three persons. Two forward-hinged doors on each side, made of formed aluminium alloy with transparent panels. Baggage compartment aft of rear seats, capacity 250 lb (113 kg), with external door on port side.

SYSTEMS: Hydraulic system, pressure 600 lb/sq in (42 kg/cm²), for cyclic, collective and directional controls. Electrical supply from 150A starter-generator. One 24V 13Ah nickel-cadmium battery.

ELECTRONICS: Full range of electronics available in form of optional kits, including VHF communications and omni navigation kit, glideslope kit, ADF, DME, marker beacon, transponder and intercom and speaker system.

EQUIPMENT: Standard equipment includes night lighting equipment, dynamic flapping restraints, door locks, fire extinguishers and first aid kit. Optional items include dual controls, custom seating, external cargo sling with 1,200 lb (545 kg) capacity, heater, high-intensity night lights, turn and slip indicator, clock, engine oil vent, fire detection system, engine fire extinguisher, fairing kit, camera access door, engine hour meter, internal litter kit and stability and control augmentation system.

DIMENSIONS, EXTERNAL:
Diameter of main rotor	33 ft 4 in (10·16 m)
Main rotor blade chord	13 in (33 cm)
Diameter of tail rotor	5 ft 2 in (1·57 m)
Distance between rotor centres	19 ft 6½ in (5·96 m)
Length overall, blades turning	39 ft 1 in (11·91 m)
Length of fuselage	31 ft 2 in (9·50 m)
Height overall	9 ft 6½ in (2·91 m)
Stabiliser span	6 ft 5¼ in (1·96 m)
Width over skids	6 ft 3½ in (1·92 m)

DIMENSIONS, INTERNAL:
Cabin: Length	7 ft 0 in (2·13 m)
Max width	4 ft 2 in (1·27 m)
Max height	4 ft 3 in (1·28 m)
Baggage compartment	16 cu ft (0·45 m³)

AREAS:
Main rotor blades (total)	36·1 sq ft (3·35 m²)
Tail rotor blades (total)	2·26 sq ft (0·21 m²)
Main rotor disc	873 sq ft (81·1 m²)
Tail rotor disc	20·97 sq ft (1·95 m²)
Stabiliser	9·65 sq ft (0·90 m²)

WEIGHTS AND LOADING:
Weight empty, including oil	1,425 lb (646 kg)
Max T-O and landing weight	3,000 lb (1,360 kg)
Max zero-fuel weight	2,510 lb (1,138 kg)
Max disc loading	3·44 lb/sq ft (16·79 kg/m²)

PERFORMANCE:
Max level speed at S/L:
at 2,100 lb (953 kg) AUW
130 knots (150 mph; 241 km/h)
at 3,000 lb (1,360 kg) AUW
130 knots (150 mph; 241 km/h)
Max permissible diving speed
130 knots (150 mph; 241 km/h)
Max cruising speed:
at 2,100 lb (953 kg) AUW
122 knots (140 mph; 225 km/h)

Bell 206A JetRanger light utility helicopter (317 shp Allison 250-C18A turboshaft engine)

Armed version of the Bell 206A, operated by the Brazilian Air Force and designated OH-4 (*Ronaldo S. Olive*)

at 3,000 lb (1,360 kg) AUW
114 knots (131 mph; 211 km/h)
Max rate of climb at S/L:
at 2,100 lb (953 kg) AUW
2,740 ft (835 m)/min
at 3,000 lb (1,360 kg) AUW
1,450 ft (442 m)/min
Service ceiling:
at 2,100 lb (953 kg) AUW
over 20,000 ft (6,100 m)
at 3,000 lb (1,360 kg) AUW
over 17,700 ft (5,395 m)
Hovering ceiling in ground effect (standard day):
at 2,100 lb (953 kg) AUW 19,300 ft (5,880 m)
at 3,000 lb (1,360 kg) AUW 7,900 ft (2,410 m)
Hovering ceiling out of ground effect (standard day):
at 2,100 lb (953 kg) AUW 15,400 ft (4,695 m)
at 3,000 lb (1,360 kg) AUW 3,350 ft (1,020 m)
Maximum range at S/L:
at 2,100 lb (953 kg) AUW
313 nm (361 miles; 581 km)
at 3,000 lb (1,360 kg) AUW
304 nm (351 miles; 564 km)
Maximum range at 8,000 ft (2,440 m)
at 2,100 lb (953 kg) AUW
399 nm (460 miles; 740 km)
at 3,000 lb (1,360 kg) AUW
340 nm (392 miles; 630 km)
Max endurance at S/L:
at 2,100 lb (953 kg) AUW   4 hr 42 min
at 3,000 lb (1,360 kg) AUW   4 hr 0 min
Max endurance at 8,000 ft (2,440 m)
at 2,100 lb (953 kg) AUW   5 hr 24 min
at 3,000 lb (1,360 kg) AUW   4 hr 36 min

BELL KIOWA
US Army designation: OH-58A

On 8 March 1968 the US Army named Bell as winner of its reopened light observation helicopter competition. The first increment of a planned total order for 2,200 aircraft generally similar to the Model 206A was placed. Subsequent orders brought the total purchased by the end of 1969 to 1,200, with deliveries scheduled for the period 1969 to mid-1972. The first OH-58A was delivered to the US Army on 23 May 1969 and deployment in Vietnam began in the early Autumn of 1969.

On 1 May 1970 it was announced that 74 OH-58As had been ordered for the Canadian Armed Forces, for delivery at the rate of five per month from mid-1971.

Major difference between the OH-58A Kiowa and JetRanger concerns the main rotor, which has an increased diameter. There are also differences in the internal layout and electronics.

TYPE: Turbine-powered light observation helicopter.

ROTOR SYSTEM, ROTOR DRIVE: As for Model 206A, except main rotor/engine rpm ratio 1:17.44; main rotor rpm 354. Tail rotor/engine rpm ratio 1:2.353.

FUSELAGE, TAIL UNIT AND SKID LANDING GEAR: As for Model 206A.

POWER PLANT: One 317 shp Allison T63-A-700 turboshaft engine. Fuel tank below and behind the aft passenger seat, total usable capacity 73 US gallons (276 litres). Refuelling point on starboard side of fuselage, aft of cabin. Oil capacity 1·5 US gallons (5·64 litres).

ACCOMMODATION: Forward crew compartment seats pilot and co-pilot/observer side-by-side. Entrance to this compartment is provided by one entrance door on each side of fuselage. The cargo/passenger compartment, which has its own access doors, one on each side, provides approximately 40 cu ft (1·13 m²) of cargo area, or provisions for two passengers by installation of two seat cushions, seat belts and shoulder harnesses.

SYSTEMS: As Model 206A, except that directional controls are not hydraulically-powered.

ELECTRONICS: C-6533/ARC intercommunication subsystem, AN/ARC-114 VHF-FM, AN/ARC-115 VHF-AM, AN/ARC-116 UHF-AM, AN/ARN-89 ADF, AN/ASN-43 gyro magnetic compass, AN/APX-72 transponder, TSEC/KY-28 communications security set, C-8157/ARC control indication, MT-3802/ARC mounting, TS-1843/APX transponder test set and mounting, KIT-1A/TSEC computer and mounting, and duplicate AN/ARC-114.

ARMAMENT: Standard equipment is the XM-27 armament kit, utilising the 7·62-mm Minigun.

R

DIMENSIONS, EXTERNAL:
As Model 206A except:
Diameter of main rotor   35 ft 4 in (10·77 m)
Length overall, blades turning
    40 ft 11¾ in (12·49 m)
Length of fuselage   32 ft 3½ in (9·84 m)
AREAS:
As Model 206A except:
Main rotor blades (total) 38·26 sq ft (3·55 m²)
Main rotor disc   978·8 sq ft (90·93 m²)
WEIGHTS AND LOADINGS:
Weight empty   1,583 lb (718 kg)
Operating weight   2,305 lb (1,045 kg)
Max T-O and landing weight
    3,000 lb (1,360 kg)
Max zero-fuel weight   2,525 lb (1,145 kg)
Max disc loading   30·7 lb/sq ft (14·9 kg/m²)
PERFORMANCE (estimated at observation mission
gross weight of 2,760 lb=1,251 kg, standard
day, except where indicated otherwise):
Max permissible speed at S/L
    120 knots (138 mph; 222 km/h)
Cruising speed for max range
    102 knots (117 mph; 188 km/h)
Loiter speed for max endurance
    49 knots (56 mph; 90·5 km/h)
Max rate of climb at S/L 1,780 ft (543 m)/min
Service ceiling   19,000 ft (5,790 m)
Hovering ceiling, in ground effect
    13,600 ft (4,145 m)
Hovering ceiling, out of ground effect
    8,800 ft (2,682 m)
Hovering ceiling, out of ground effect (armed
scout mission at 3,000 lb = 1,360 kg)
    6,000 ft (1,828 m)
Max range at S/L, no reserves
    302 nm (348 miles; 560 km)
Max range at S/L, armed scout mission at
3,000 lb (1,360 kg), no reserves
    309 nm (356 miles; 572 km)
Endurance at S/L, no reserves   3 hr 30 min

BELL MODEL 204
US Military designations: UH-1A/B/C/E/F/L, HH-1K and TH-1F/L Iroquois.

In 1955 the Bell Model 204 won a US Army design competition for a utility helicopter suitable for front-line casualty evacuation, general utility and instrument training duties. The production version was originally designated HU-1, giving rise to the nickname "Hueycopter" or "Huey", which survived the change of designation to UH-1. Official US Army name for the UH-1 series is Iroquois.

The following versions of the Model 204 have appeared:

XH-40. Three prototypes, of which the first flew on 20 October 1956.

YH-40. Six service test models.

UH-1. Nine pre-production models.

UH-1A. Initial production version, incorporating changes requested as a result of service testing. Six-seater, powered by an 860 shp Lycoming T53-L-1A turboshaft engine, derated to 770 shp. Deliveries to US Army began on 30 June 1959 and were completed in March 1961. Thirteen operated by Utility Tactical Transport Helicopter Company in Vietnam were modified to carry 16 × 2·75-in air-to-surface rockets and two 0·30-in machine-guns. Fourteen were delivered for use as helicopter instrument trainers with dual controls and a device for simulated instrument instruction.

UH-1B. Development of the UH-1A, initially with 960 shp T53-L-5 turboshaft. Subsequent deliveries with 1,100 shp T53-L-11. Crew of two and seven troops, or three litters, two sitting casualties and medical attendant, or 3,000 lb (1,360 kg) of freight. Rotor diameter 44 ft (13·41 m). Normal fuel capacity 165 US gallons (625 litres); overload capacity 330 US gallons (1,250 litres). For armed support duties, a rocket pack and electrically-controlled machine-gun can be mounted on each side of cabin. Other armament installations tested on UH-1B included General Electric M-5 nose-mounted 40-mm grenade launcher and XM-30 armament system, consisting of two side-mounted XM-140 30-mm cannon with central ammunition reservoir and fire-control system. Deliveries began in March 1961. This version was superseded by the UH-1C on the Bell assembly line, but continues in production by Fuji in Japan, where delivery of 89 to the JGSDF will be completed in 1973.

Model 204B. Commercial and military export version of UH-1B, with ten seats, 1,100 shp T5311A turboshaft and 48 ft (14·63 m) rotor. Tail boom incorporates a 35 cu ft (0·99 m²) baggage compartment. Cabin doors with jettisonable emergency exits, passenger steps on each side of cabin, improved outside lights, commercial radio equipment, fire detection and extinguishing systems. Received FAA certification on 4 April 1963. More than 60 delivered for commercial service up to end 1967. Military deliveries included 24 for RAAF and 8 for RAN. Deliveries from licence manufacture by Fuji in Japan have included 2 for Asahi Helicopter Company, 2 for All-Nippon Airways, 1 for Tokyo Metropolitan Police and 7 for Bell to meet US civil orders. Licence-built

Bell OH-58A Kiowa turbine-powered light observation helicopter for the US Army

Bell TH-1L, training version of the Model 204 for the US Navy

Bell UH-1L, a utility version of the TH-1L for the US Navy

versions (AB 204B) by Agusta SpA in Italy can have Rolls-Royce Bristol Gnome H.1200 or General Electric T58-GE-3 turboshaft as alternative to T5311A and have standard 242 US gallon (916 litre) fuel tanks. Military versions have been supplied to the armed services of Italy, Spain, Sweden, the Netherlands, Austria, Turkey and Saudi-Arabia; commercial AB 204B's are flying in Italy, Norway, Sweden, Switzerland and Lebanon. A special ASW version supplied to the Italian and Spanish Navies is designed for individual or dual-role search and attack missions, with armament of two Mk 44 torpedoes. Equipment includes dipping sonar, automatic stabilisation and automatic approach to hover and all-weather instrumentation.

UH-1C. In September 1965, Bell introduced its Model 540 "door-hinge" rotor, with blades of increased (27 in = 69 cm) chord, on this developed version of the UH-1B, offering some increase in speed and a substantial increase in manoeuvrability through resistance to blade stall. Through reduced vibration and stress levels, the 540 rotor eliminates previous limitations on max level flight speed. T53-L-11 turboshaft, accommodation and armament as for UH-1B. Normal fuel capacity 242 US gallons (916 litres); overload capacity 592 US gallons (2,241 litres). Superseded UH-1B in production for US Army, but is itself superseded by AH-1G HueyCobra.

UH-1E. In March 1962, Bell won a design competition for an assault support helicopter for the US Marine Corps, to replace Cessna O-1B/C fixed-wing aircraft and Kaman OH-43D helicopters. Designated UH-1E, this version is generally similar to the UH-1B/C, but has a personnel hoist, rotor brake and Marine electronics. The 540 rotor and increased fuel capacity (as UH-1C) were introduced in 1965.

Payload consists of a pilot and eight passengers or 4,000 lb (1,815 kg) of freight. Initial small purchase was made in 1962 for evaluation, and first UH-1E flew in February 1963. Larger contracts have followed; the latest for 48 in November 1966 and 18 in early 1967 extended production until the Summer of 1968. First delivery to an operational unit, Marine Air Group 26 at New River, NC, was made on 21 February 1964. UH-1E's operational on troop-carrying and escort duties in Vietnam have two fixed 7·62-mm M-60 machine-guns, on pylons on each side of the cabin, and two pods, each containing seven or eighteen 2·75-in rockets, also one on each side.

UH-1F. Following a design competition, it was announced in June 1963 that an initial batch of 25 UH-1F helicopters, based on the UH-1B, were to be built for the USAF in 1963-64, and many more later, for missile site support duties. Each has a 1,272 shp General Electric T58-GE-3 turboshaft (derated to 1,100 shp), a 48 ft (14·63 m) rotor, normal fuel capacity of 250 US gallons (945 litres) and overload capacity of 410 US gallons (1,552 litres). This version can handle up to 4,000 lb (1,815 kg) of cargo at missile site silos, or carry a pilot and 10 passengers. The first UH-1F flew on 20 February 1964. Subsequent contracts for a further 121 aircraft were completed in 1967. First delivery to an operational unit was made to the 4486th Test Squadron at Eglin AFB in September 1964. This model has been used for classified psychological warfare missions in Vietnam.

TH-1F. Training version of UH-1F for USAF. Production completed.

HH-1K. Sea-air rescue version for US Navy, which placed letter contract for 27 late in 1968, with deliveries to be made in 1970. Has UH-1E airframe, T53-L-13 turboshaft engine (derated to 1,100 shp) and revised avionics.

TH-1L. Training version for US Navy. Similar to UH-1E but with 1,400 shp Lycoming T53-L-13 turboshaft (derated to 1,100 shp) and improved electronics. Contract for 45 received on 16 May 1968; the first of these was delivered to the USN at Pensacola, Florida, on 26 November 1969.

UH-1L. Utility version of TH-1L for US Navy. Eight ordered, and delivered during 1969.

UH-1M. US Army version fitted with Hughes Aircraft Iroquois night fighter and night tracker (Infant) system to detect and acquire ground targets under low ambient lighting conditions. Two sensors mounted on nose of cabin serve a low-light-level TV system with three cockpit displays and a direct-view system using an image intensifier at cockpit/gunner's station. Three UH-1Ms deployed with hunter-killer helicopter groups in Vietnam in early 1970 to evaluate system.

RH-2 (Research Helicopter 2). One UH-1A was used as a flying laboratory for new instrument and control systems. Installations included an electronic control system and high-resolution radar in a large fairing above the flight deck, enabling the pilot to detect obstacles ahead of the aircraft in bad visibility.

HueyTug. It was announced on 3 September 1968 that a UH-1C had been retrofitted with a 2,850 shp Lycoming T55-L-7C turboshaft and 50 ft (15·24 m) "door-hinge" rotor as the prototype of a new flying crane version able to lift a three-ton external payload. Associated modifications all of which can be applied retrospectively to existing UH-1s, include substitution of a 2,000 hp transmission and larger tail rotor, reinforcement of the airframe and fitment of a larger tail boom, and use of a stability control and augmentation system instead of the normal stabiliser bar. The HueyTug is designed to hover out of ground effect at 4,000 ft (1,220 m), 95°F, at 14,000 lb (6,350 kg) max T-O weight. Max level speed, clean, is 140 knots (161 mph; 259 kmh).

Dimensions, external (HH-1K, TH-1L, UH-1C, E and L):
Diameter of main rotor	44 ft 0 in (13·41 m)
Diameter of tail rotor	8 ft 6 in (2·59 m)
Length overall (main rotor fore and aft)	53 ft 0 in (16·15 m)
Length of fuselage	38 ft 5 in (11·70 m)
Overall height	12 ft 7¼ in (3·84 m)

Dimensions, internal (204B):
Cabin:
Length	8 ft 6 in (2·59 m)
Max width	7 ft 10 in (2·39 m)
Max height	4 ft 10 in (1·47 m)
Baggage compartment	30 cu ft (0·85 m²)

Areas (HH-1K, TH-1L, UH-1C, E and L):
Main rotor disc	1,520 sq ft (141·2 m²)
Tail rotor disc	56·8 sq ft (5·27 m²)

Weights and Loadings:
Weight empty:
UH-1C (incl 2 armoured crew seats)	5,071 lb (2,300 kg)
UH-1E	5,055 lb (2,293 kg)

Operating weight, including two crew:
HH-1K	5,775 lb (2,620 kg)
TH-1L	5,643 lb (2,560 kg)
UH-1F	4,902 lb (2,224 kg)
UH-1L	5,921 lb (2,685 kg)

Mission weight:
HH-1K, TH-1L, UH-1L	6,600 lb (2,993 kg)
UH-1F	8,524 lb (3,866 kg)

Bell HueyTug, flying-crane version of the UH-1C with uprated turboshaft engine

Max gross weight (military qualified):
HH-1K, TH-1L, UH-1L	8,500 lb (3,855 kg)
UH-1F	9,000 lb (4,082 kg)

Max overload weight:
HH-1K, TH-1L, UH-1C, E, L	9,500 lb (4,309 kg)

Max zero-fuel weight:
UH-1C	7,927 lb (3,596 kg)

Max disc loading:
UH-1C	6·25 lb/sq ft (30·5 kg/m²)

Max power loading:
UH-1C	8·63 lb/hp (3·91 kg/hp)

Performance (at max overload weight, except where stated otherwise):
Max level speed:
HH-1K, TH-1L, UH-1L	125 knots (144 mph; 231 km/h)
UH-1C	128 knots (148 mph; 238 km/h)
UH-1E	140 knots (161 mph; 259 km/h)
UH-1F	100 knots (115 mph; 185 km/h)

Max permissible speed at mission weight:
HH-1K, TH-1L, UH-1L	140 knots (161 mph; 259 km/h)
UH-1F	103 knots (119 mph; 191 km/h)

Max cruising speed at S/L:
UH-1C	128 knots (148 mph; 238 km/h)
UH-1E	120 knots (138 mph; 222 km/h)

Econ cruising speed at 5,000 ft (1,525 m):
UH-1C	124 knots (143 mph; 230 km/h)

Max rate of climb at S/L:
HH-1K, TH-1L, UH-1L	1,160 ft (353 m)/min
UH-1C	1,400 ft (425 m)/min
UH-1E	1,849 ft (563 m)/min
UH-1F	1,360 ft (415 m)/min

Vertical rate of climb at S/L:
UH-1C at 8,500 lb (3,855 kg) AUW	540 ft (165 m)/min

Service ceiling:
HH-1K, TH-1L, UH-1L	10,200 ft (3,110 m)
UH-1C	11,500 ft (3,500 m)
UH-1E	21,000 ft (6,400 m)
UH-1F	12,400 ft (3,780 m)

Hovering ceiling in ground effect:
HH-1K, TH-1L, UH-1L	10,400 ft (3,170 m)
UH-1C	10,600 ft (3,230 m)
UH-1E	15,800 ft (4,815 m)
UH-1F	9,600 ft (2,925 m)

Hovering ceiling, out of ground effect:
HH-1K, TH-1L, UH-1L at 8,500 lb (3,855 kg) AUW	7,400 ft (2,255 m)
UH-1C at 8,500 lb (3,855 kg) AUW	10,000 ft (3,050 m)
UH-1E	11,800 ft (3,595 m)
UH-1F at 9,000 lb (4,082 kg) AUW	5,800 ft (1,765 m)

Range with max fuel, no allowances:
HH-1K, TH-1L, UH-1L	275 nm (317 miles; 510 km)
UH-1C	331 nm (382 miles; 615 km)
UH-1E	248 nm (286 miles; 460 km)
UH-1F	305 nm (352 miles; 566 km)

BELL MODEL 205
US Military designations: UH-1D/H Iroquois
Canadian Military designation: CUH-1 Iroquois

Although basically similar to the Model 204, the Model 205 introduced a longer fuselage, increased cabin space to accommodate a much larger number of passengers, and other changes. The following military versions have been built:

UH-1D. This US Army version of the Model 205 Iroquois had a 1,100 shp Lycoming T53-L-11 turboshaft, 48 ft (14·63 m) rotor, normal fuel capacity of 220 US gallons (832 litres) and overload capacity of 520 US gallons (1,968 litres). Relocation of the fuel cells increases cabin space to 220 cu ft (6·23 m²), providing sufficient room for a pilot and twelve troops, or six litters and a medical attendant, or 4,000 lb (1,815 kg) of freight. A contract for a service test batch of seven YUH-1Ds was announced in July 1960 and was followed by further very large production orders from the US Army and from Australia (6), Brazil (12), Chile (2) and New Zealand (5). First YUH-1D flew on 16 August 1961 and deliveries to US Army field units began on 9 August 1963, when the second and third production UH-1Ds went to the 11th Air Assault Division at Fort Benning, Georgia. The UH-1D has been superseded in production for the US Army by the UH-1H, but UH-1Ds are being built under licence in Germany for the German services. Prime contractor is Dornier.

UH-1H. Following replacement of the original T53-L-11 turboshaft by the 1,400 shp T53-L-13, the version of the Model 205 currently in production by Bell for the US Army is designated UH-1H. Deliveries began in September 1967. The latest contracts received will extend production into 1972; they include 319 aircraft for the US Army, the contract for which carries an initial funding of $23·4 million, and nine aircraft for the RNZAF.

CUH-1H. Similar to UH-1H, for Mobile Command, Canadian Armed Forces. First of ten delivered on 6 March 1968.

The commercial Model 205A-1 is described separately.

The 4,000th Model 205/205A helicopter, a UH-1H, was completed in March 1969.

The following details refer specifically to the military UH-1H, except where stated otherwise.

Type: Single-rotor general-purpose helicopter.

Rotor System: Two-blade all-metal semi-rigid main rotor with interchangeable blades built up of extruded aluminium spars and laminates. Usual Bell stabilising bar above and at right angles to main rotor blades. Underslung feathering axis hub. Two-blade all-metal tail rotor of honeycomb construction. Blades do not fold.

Rotor Drive: Shaft-drive to both main and tail rotors. Transmission rating 1,100 shp. Main rotor rpm 294-324.

Fuselage: Conventional all-metal semi-monocoque structure.

Tail Surface: Small synchronised elevator on rear fuselage is connected to the cyclic control to increase allowable CG travel.

Landing Gear: Tubular skid type. Lock-on ground handling wheels and inflated nylon float-bags available.

Power Plant: One 1,400 shp Lycoming T53-L-13 turboshaft mounted aft of the transmission on top of the fuselage and enclosed in cowlings. Five interconnected rubber fuel cells, total capacity 220 US gallons (832 litres). Overload fuel capacity of 520 US gallons obtained by installation of kit comprising two 150 US gallon (568 litre) internal auxiliary fuel tanks interconnected with the basic fuel system.

Accommodation: Cabin space of 220 cu ft (6·23 m²) provides sufficient room for pilot and 11-14 troops, or six litters and a medical attendant, or 3,880 lb (1,759 kg) of freight. Crew doors open forward and are jettisonable. Two doors on each side of cargo compartment; front door is hinged to open forward and is removable, rear door slides aft. Forced air ventilation system.

Equipment: Bleed-air heater and defroster, comprehensive range of engine and flight instruments, power plant fire detection system, 30V 300A DC starter-generator, navigation, landing and anti-collision lights, controllable searchlight, hydraulically-boosted controls.

Bell UH-1F helicopter equipped experimentally with an antenna for the detection of low-flying aircraft. Suspended below the aircraft, the antenna pedestal is attached to the reinforced section of the helicopter on the port side of the cargo compartment. Retraction and rotation of the antenna are performed by two electric motors

Optional equipment includes external cargo hook, auxiliary fuel tanks, rescue hoist, 150,000 BTU muff heater.

ELECTRONICS: FM, UHF, VHF radio sets, IFF transponder, Gyromatic compass system, direction finder set, VOR receiver and inter-communications set standard. Optional nav/com systems.

DIMENSIONS, EXTERNAL:
Diameter of main rotor	48 ft 0 in (14·63 m)
Main rotor blade chord	21 in (53·3 cm)
Diameter of tail rotor	8 ft 6 in (2·59 m)
Tail rotor blade chord	8·4 in (21·3 cm)
Length overall (main rotor fore and aft)	57 ft 1 in (17·40 m)

Length of fuselage:
UH-1D, UH-1H	41 ft 10¾ in (12·77 m)

Overall height:
UH-1D, UH-1H	14 ft 6 in (4·42 m)

AREAS:
Main rotor disc	1,809 sq ft (168·06 m²)
Tail rotor disc	56·7 sq ft (5·27 m²)

WEIGHTS AND LOADINGS:
Weight empty:
UH-1D	4,939 lb (2,240 kg)
UH-1H	4,973 lb (2,255 kg)

Basic operating weight:
UH-1H (troop carrier mission)	5,319 lb (2,413 kg)

Mission weight:
UH-1H	9,039 lb (4,100 kg)

Max T-O and landing weight:
UH-1D, H	9,500 lb (4,309 kg)

Max zero-fuel weight:
UH-1D, H	8,070 lb (3,660 kg)

Max disc loading:
UH-1D, H	5·25 lb/sq ft (25·6 kg/m²)

Max power loading:
UH-1D, H	8·63 lb/hp (3·91 kg/hp)

PERFORMANCE (UH-1H, at max T-O weight):
Max level speed
    110 knots (127 mph; 204 km/h)
Max permissible diving speed
    110 knots (127 mph; 204 km/h)
Max cruising speed
    110 knots (127 mph; 204 km/h)
Econ cruising speed at 5,700 ft (1,735 m)
    110 knots (127 mph; 204 km/h)
Rate of climb at S/L   1,600 ft (488 m)/min
Service ceiling   12,600 ft (3,840 m)
Hovering ceiling in ground effect
    13,600 ft (4,145 m)
Hovering ceiling out of ground effect
    1,100 ft (335 m)
Range with max fuel, no allowances, no reserves, at S/L at 9,500 lb (4,309 kg) AUW
    276 nm (318 miles; 511 km)

BELL MODEL 205A-1

The Model 205A-1 is a fifteen-seat commercial utility helicopter, developed from the UH-1H, with 1,400 shp Lycoming T5313A turboshaft, derated to 1,250 shp for take-off. It is designed for rapid conversion for alternative air freight, flying crane, ambulance, rescue and executive roles. Total cargo capacity is 248 cu ft (7·02 m²) including baggage space in tail-boom, with 7 ft 8 in (2·34 m) by 4 ft 1 in (1·24 m) door openings on each side of the cabin to facilitate loading of bulky freight. External load capacity in flying crane role is 5,000 lb (2,268 kg). The ambulance version can accommodate six stretcher patients and one or two medical attendants.

Normal fuel capacity is 215 US gallons (814 litres); optional capacity 395 US gallons (1,495 litres).

The Model 205A-1 is produced under licence in Italy by Agusta as the AB 205 for military operators, including the armed services of Italy, Morocco, Saudi-Arabia and Spain. It is also being produced under licence in the Republic of China, with a proportion of the manufacturing and assembly work being done at Taichung, Taiwan. Deliveries were scheduled to begin in 1970 and to extend over several years.

Two twin-engined versions, corresponding to the Bell Model 212, have been tested in prototype form by Agusta. These are the AB 205TA with Turbomeca Astazou turboshafts (no further development planned) and the AB 205BG with coupled Rolls-Royce Bristol Gnome H.1200 engines.

The description of the Bell UH-1H applies also to the Model 205A-1, except for the following details:—

TYPE: Fifteen-seat commercial utility helicopter.

ELECTRONICS AND EQUIPMENT: Standard equipment includes vertical gyro system, 5 in Gyro attitude indicator, gyro compass, master caution panel, bleed air heater, force trim hydraulic boost controls, sound-proof headliner, dual windscreen wipers, cabin and engine fire extinguishers, map case and retractable passenger boarding steps. Optional items include dual controls, float landing gear, rotor brake, external cargo suspension, rescue hoist, auxiliary fuel tanks, litter installations, high-output cabin heater, protective covers and

Bell UH-1D operated by the SAR unit of the Brazilian Air Force (*Ronaldo S. Olive*)

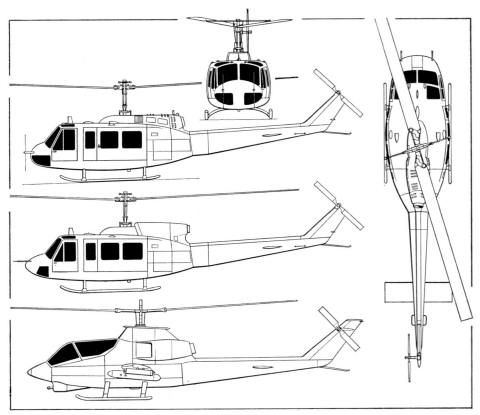

Bell UH-1H general arrangement drawing, with side views of Bell 212 (centre) and Bell AH-1G (bottom)

customised interiors. Standard electronics comprise 360-channel VHF transceiver and intercom system. An extensive range of nav/com systems is available as optional items.

DIMENSIONS, EXTERNAL:
Length of fuselage	41 ft 6 in (12·65 m)
Height overall	14 ft 4¾ in (4·39 m)

WEIGHTS:
Weight empty, equipped	5,082 lb (2,305 kg)
Normal T-O weight	9,500 lb (4,309 kg)
Max T-O weight, external load	10,500 lb (4,763 kg)

PERFORMANCE (at normal T-O weight):
Max level speed at S/L
    110 knots (127 mph; 204 km/h)
Max level speed at 3,000 ft (915 m)
    110 knots (127 mph; 204 km/h)
Max cruising speed at S/L
    110 knots (127 mph; 204 km/h)
Max cruising speed at 8,000 ft (2,440 m)
    96 knots (111 mph; 179 km/h)
Max rate of climb at S/L 1,680 ft (512 m)/min
Max vertical rate of climb at S/L
    1,020 ft (311 m)/min
Service ceiling   14,700 ft (4,480 m)
Hovering ceiling, in ground effect
    10,400 ft (3,170 m)
Hovering ceiling, out of ground effect
    6,000 ft (1,830 m)

Range at S/L, at max cruising speed
    270 nm (311 miles; 500 km)
Range at 8,000 ft (2,440 m) at max cruising speed, no reserves
    298 nm (344 miles; 553 km)

BELL MODEL 208 TWIN DELTA

First flown on 27 April 1965, the Bell Model 208 is basically a UH-1D Iroquois re-engined with a Continental XT67-T-1 free-turbine power plant, comprising two T72-T-2 Model 217 turboshafts coupled to a common reduction gearbox and output shaft. The complete power plant has a T-O rating of 1,400 shp and max continuous rating of 1,200 shp and is capable of developing 1,540 shp for 2½ minutes.

The Model 208 was the first twin-turbine helicopter built by Bell and was intended to evaluate the use of multi-engine power plants in a comparatively small helicopter. The programme was company funded.

BELL MODEL 212 TWIN TWO-TWELVE
US Military designation: UH-1N
Canadian Military designation: CUH-1N

Bell announced on 1 May 1968 that the Canadian government had approved development of a twin-engined UH-1 helicopter to be powered by a Pratt & Whitney (UACL) PT6T power plant. Subsequently, on 19 September 1969, Bell stated that the Canadian government had ordered 50 of these aircraft (designated **CUH-1N**) for the Canadian Armed Forces, with options on 20 more.

Simultaneously, orders totalling 141 aircraft for the United States services were announced, comprising 79 for the USAF, 40 for the USN and 22 for the USMC, all having the designation **UH-1N.**

Initial deliveries for the USAF were scheduled to begin in 1970, while the USN, USMC and CAF will have their aircraft in operation early in 1971.

A commercial version, to be known as the Twin Two-Twelve, is also to be built, and full-scale production was scheduled to follow FAA type certification which was anticipated by mid-1970.

The Model 212/UH-1N utilises a Bell 205A/UH-1H airframe, and civil and military versions have basically the same configuration, but differ in mission kits and avionics. They each accommodate a pilot and 14 passengers or, in cargo configuration, provide 220 cu ft (6·23 m³) of internal capacity, with the capability of carrying an external load of 4,000 lb (1,814 kg).

Power plant is a Pratt & Whitney (UACL) PT6T-3 Turbo "Twin-Pac", which consists of two PT6 turboshaft engines coupled to a combining gearbox with a single output shaft. Producing 1,800 shp, the "Twin Pac" is flat-rated to 1,250 shp for T-O and 1,100 shp for continuous operation. In the event of an engine failure, the remaining engine is capable of delivering 900 shp for 30 minutes or 765 shp continuously, which is adequate to maintain cruise performance at maximum gross weight.

The description given for the Bell UH-1H applies generally to the Model 212, but the twin-engined power plant makes considerable changes to the specification which is detailed below for the UH-1N:

DIMENSIONS, EXTERNAL:
Diameter of main rotor (with tracking tips)
    48 ft 2⅛ in (14·69 m)
Main rotor blade chord   21 in (53·3 cm)
Diameter of tail rotor   8 ft 6 in (2·59 m)
Tail rotor blade chord   11·5 in (35·0 cm)
Length overall (main rotor fore and aft)
    57 ft 0 in (17·37 m)
Length of fuselage   42 ft 10¾ in (13·07 m)
Height overall   14 ft 4¾ in (4·39 m)
WEIGHTS:
Operating weight (including 215 lb = 97·5 kg crew)   6,169 lb (2,798 kg)
Max T-O weight and mission weight
    10,000 lb (4,535 kg)
PERFORMANCE (at max T-O weight):
Max level speed
    105 knots (121 mph; 194 km/h)
Max permissible speed
    105 knots (121 mph; 194 km/h)
Max rate of climb at S/L
    1,460 ft (445 m)/min
Service ceiling   11,500 ft (3,505 m)
Hovering ceiling, in ground effect
    17,100 ft (5,212 m)
Hovering ceiling, out of ground effect
    9,900 ft (3,020 m)
Max range at S/L, no reserves
    257 nm (296 miles; 476 km)

BELL MODEL 533

The Model 533 is a YUH-1B Iroquois helicopter which Bell have modified, under US Army Transportation Research Command contract, for service as a high-performance research vehicle to evaluate various rotor systems and methods of drag reduction.

For the initial flight trials, major changes included the addition of aerodynamic fairings on the fuselage, the use of a cambered vertical tail surface to unload the tail rotor, and the introduction of a tilting rotor mast inside a fairing structure. In this form the Model 533 flew for the first time on 10 August 1962. It was modified subsequently into a winged jet compound helicopter by the addition of a small swept wing and two Continental J69-T-29 turbojets, rated at 1,700 lb (771 kg) st, mounted in pods on each side of the fuselage.

These made possible even higher speeds, and on 15 October 1964 the Model 533 became the first rotorcraft to exceed a speed of 200 knots, by attaining 236 mph (380 km/h) during a test flight. On 6 April 1965, it became the first to reach 250 mph (402 km/h) in level flight. During the same test flight, it attained 254 mph (409 km/h) in a slight dive and demonstrated its manoeuvrability by performing 2G turns and 60° banks at speeds of around 200 mph (320 km/h). A Mach number of 0·985 was achieved at the tips of the advancing blades of the two-blade rotor, which has special tapered tips. Take-off weight of the aircraft was 8,600 lb (3,900 kg).

Early in 1968, the Model 533 was again modified to take more powerful auxiliary turbojets, this time two wing-tip-mounted Pratt & Whitney JT12A-3's, each rated at 3,300 lb (1,498 kg) st, for further testing in the 250 knot (285 mph=460 km/h) speed range. It was announced in May 1969 that the Model 533 had attained a speed of 274 knots (316 mph; 509 km/h).

Since then, the two-blade main rotor has been replaced by a four-blade flex-beam rotor system, but no details of performance in this configuration had been released at the time of writing.

TYPE: High-performance compound helicopter.

Bell Model 212 Twin Two-Twelve twin-engined medium-size commercial helicopter

ROTOR SYSTEM: Normally fitted with a standard UH-1B two-blade semi-rigid rotor with modified blade-tips.
ROTOR DRIVE: Normal shaft-drive to main and tail rotors. Main rotor/engine rpm ratio 1:20·383. Tail rotor/engine rpm ratio 1:3·99.
FUSELAGE: Conventional metal semi-monocoque structure with glass-fibre honeycomb external fairings.
LANDING GEAR: Tubular skid type, with faired cross-tubes.
POWER PLANT: One 1,400 shp Lycoming T53-L-13 turboshaft engine. Oil capacity 1·6 US gallons (6·0 litres).
ACCOMMODATION: Normal accommodation for a pilot and co-pilot.
DIMENSIONS, EXTERNAL:
Same as for UH-1B, except:
Diameter of main rotor   44 ft 0 in (13·41 m)
WEIGHT:
Normal T-O weight for flight tests
    9,200 lb (4,173 kg)
PERFORMANCE:
See above.

BELL MODEL 209 HUEYCOBRA (single-engined)
US Army designation: AH-1G

First flown on 7 September 1965, six months after its development was started, the Model 209 HueyCobra is a development of the UH-1B/C Iroquois intended specifically for armed helicopter missions. It combines the basic transmission and rotor system and (in its standard form) the power plant of the UH-1C with a new streamlined fuselage designed for maximum speed, armament load and crew efficiency.

The prototype was sent to Edwards AFB for US Army evaluation in December 1965. On 11 March 1966, the Army announced its intention to order the HueyCobra into production.

Two production versions have been announced so far, as follows:

AH-1G. Standard version for US Army, powered by 1,400 shp (derated to 1,100 shp) Lycoming T53-L-13 turboshaft, driving a two-blade wide-chord Model 540 "door-hinge" rotor of the kind fitted to the UH-1C. Main rotor rpm is 294-324. A development contract for two pre-production prototypes was placed on 4 April 1966, followed on 13 April by an initial contract for 110 production aircraft plus long lead-time spares. Subsequent contracts had raised the total on order to 838 by October 1968. Most of these had been delivered by the Autumn of 1969, but on 30 January 1970 the US Army ordered a further 170 AH-1G's for delivery between July 1971 and August 1972. Deliveries of the original production series began in June 1967 and operational deployment to Vietnam began in the early Autumn of 1967. The US Marine Corps acquired 38 AH-1Gs during 1969, for transition training and initial

deployment, pending delivery of the AH-1J; these are included in the above totals.

AH-1J. Twin-turbine version for US Marine Corps. Described separately.

Relatively small, the HueyCobra has a low silhouette and narrow profile, with a fuselage width of only 36 in (0·91 m). These features make it easy to conceal with small camouflage nets or to move under cover of trees. Tandem seating for the crew of two provides maximum field of view for the pilot and forward gunner. The skid landing gear is non-retractable. Stub-wings carry armament and help to offload the rotor in cruising flight.

Emerson Electric designed and developed for the HueyCobra the TAT-102A tactical armament turret, which was faired into the front fuselage undersurface and housed a GAU2B/A (formerly XM-134) Minigun six-barrel 7·62-mm machine-gun, with 8,000 rounds. This turret has been superseded on the AH-1G by the XM-28 subsystem, mounting either two Miniguns, with 4,000 rounds each; two XM-129 (similar to the XM-75) 40-mm grenade launchers, each with 300 rounds; or one Minigun and one XM-129. Two rates of fire are provided for the TAT-102A and XM-28 Miniguns, namely 1,600 and 4,000 rounds per minute. The lower rate is for searching or registry fire, while the higher rate is used for attack, the rate of fire being controlled by the gunner's trigger. The XM-129 fires at a single rate of 400 rounds per minute. Structural provisions have been incorporated in the airframe to accept a turret subsystem capable of firing the M-61A1 20-mm Vulcan gun at a firing rate of 750 rounds per minute, the XM-197 three-barrel 20-mm gun, or a three-barrel 30-mm gun.

Four external stores attachments under the stub-wings accommodate various loads, including a total of 76 2·75-in rockets in four XM-159 packs, 28 similar rockets in four XM-157 packs, two XM-18E1 Minigun pods, an XM-35 20-mm gun kit, or (when fully developed) two pods each containing four TOW wire-guided missiles.

In normal operation, the co-pilot/gunner controls and fires the turret armament, using a hand-held pantograph-mounted sight to which the turret is slaved. The gunner can fire throughout a field of 230° (± 115° both sides of the aircraft centreline) and can depress the turreted weapons 50° and elevate them 25°. Velocity jump compensation automatically computes the lead angle with respect to the relative motion of aircraft and target. In addition, the gunner has the capability of firing the wing stores.

The pilot can fire the turreted weapons only in the stowed position, dead ahead. The turret returns to the stowed position automatically when the gunner releases his grip on the slewing switch.

The pilot normally fires the wing stores, utilizing the XM-73 adjustable rocket sight. Rockets

Bell Model 533 high-performance research helicopter which attained a speed of 274 knots (316 mph; 509 km/h) in this configuration

are fired in pairs, made up of one rocket from each opposing wing station. Any desired number of pairs from one to nineteen can be preselected on the cockpit-mounted intervalometer. The inboard wing stores are equipped to fire either the XM-18 or XM-18E1 Minigun pod. All wing stores are symmetrically or totally jettisonable.

Late in 1969 an XM-35 20-mm cannon kit was added to the weapons available for the AH-1G and six aircraft were equipped with the XM-35 and delivered to the US Army in December 1969. A total of 350 of these kits have been ordered by the Army.

Designed jointly by Bell and General Electric, the XM-35 armament subsystem consists of a six-barrel 20-mm automatic cannon, two ammunition boxes and certain structural and electrical modifications. Mounted on the inboard stores attachment of the port stub-wing, the XM-35 has a firing rate of 750 rounds per minute. Two ammunition boxes faired flush to the fuselage below the stub wings accommodate 1,000 rounds. Total installed weight of the system is 1,172 lb (531 kg).

The crew are protected by seats and side panels made of NOROC armour, manufactured by the Norton Company. Other panels protect vital areas of the aircraft.

On missions of 57-mile (92-km) radius, the HueyCobra can reach the target area in half the time taken by a UH-1B and operate in the target area for three times as long. During flight tests it has been dived at a speed of 246 mph (397 kmh). Normal fuel capacity is 247 US gallons (1,345 litres).

DIMENSIONS, EXTERNAL:
Diameter of main rotor	44 ft 0 in (13·41 m)
Main rotor blade chord	27 in (68·6 cm)
Diameter of tail rotor	8 ft 6 in (2·59 m)
Tail rotor blade chord	8·4 in (21·3 cm)
Wing span	10 ft 4 in (3·15 m)
Length overall (main rotor fore and aft)	
	52 ft 11¼ in (16·14 m)
Length of fuselage	44 ft 5 in (13·54 m)
Overall height	13 ft 5½ in (4·10 m)
Width over skids	7 ft 0 in (2·13 m)

AREAS:
Main rotor disc	1,520·4 sq ft (141·2 m²)
Tail rotor disc	56·8 sq ft (5·27 m²)

WEIGHTS:
Operating weight	6,096 lb (2,765 kg)
Mission weight	9,254 lb (4,197 kg)
Max T-O and landing weight	9,500 lb (4,309 kg)

PERFORMANCE (at max T-O weight):
Max level speed	
	190 knots (219 mph; 352 km/h)
Max permissible speed	
	190 knots (219 mph; 352 km/h)
Max rate of climb at S/L	1,580 ft (482 m)/min

Bell AH-1J SeaCobra attack helicopter of the US Marine Corps

Service ceiling	12,700 ft (3,870 m)
Hovering ceiling in ground effect	
	9,900 ft (3,015 m)
Max range at S/L, max fuel, no reserves	
	336 nm (387 miles; 622 km)

BELL MODEL 209 HUEYCOBRA (twin-engined)
US Marine Corps designation: AH-1J SeaCobra

This is a modified version of the Bell AH-1G, initially for the US Marine Corps. A first batch of 49 AH-1Js was ordered for the USMC in May 1968, and a pre-production aircraft was displayed to a conference of representatives of the US armed forces at Enless, Texas, on 14 October 1969; this aircraft was later moved to the Bell Flight Test Center at Arlington. Subsequently, on 31 March 1970, the US Army placed a contract with Bell, worth almost $1·2 million, for the supply of spare rotor blades and drive mechanisms. Delivery of the first AH-1Js was scheduled to begin in mid-1970.

The SeaCobra differs from the single-engined AH-1G in having Marine avionics and an 1,800 shp Pratt & Whitney (UACL) T400-CP-400 coupled free-turbine turboshaft power plant (a military version of the UACL PT6T-3 Turbo "Twin Pac" power plant as described for the Model 212/UH-1N). Engine and transmission are flat-rated for 1,100 shp continuous output, with increase to 1,250 shp for take-off or 5 min emergency power. To cater for the increased power, the tail rotor pylon has been strengthened and the tail rotor blade chord increased.

An electrically-driven 20-mm turret system, developed by the General Electric Company, is faired into the forward lower fuselage, and houses an XM-197 three-barrel weapon, which is a lightweight version of the General Electric M-61 cannon. The firing rate is 750 rounds per minute, but a 16-round burst limiter is incorporated

in the firing switch. The gun has a tracking capability of 220° in azimuth, 50° depression and 18° elevation, and can be slewed at a rate of 80° per second. A barrel length of 5 ft (1·52 m) makes it imperative that the XM-197 is centralised before wing stores are fired. An ammunition container of 750-round capacity is located in the fuselage directly aft of the turret. Four external stores attachment points under the stub-wings can accommodate various loads, including XM-18E1 7·62-mm Minigun pods as well as 2·75-in folding-fin rockets in either seven-tube (XM-157) or 19-tube (XM-159) packs.

DIMENSIONS, EXTERNAL:
As for AH-1G except:
Tail rotor blade chord	11·5 in (29·2 cm)
Length overall (main rotor fore and aft)	
	53 ft 4 in (16·26 m)
Length of fuselage	44 ft 7 in (13·59 m)
Width of fuselage	4 ft 2½ in (1·28 m)
Height overall	13 ft 8 in (4·15 m)

WEIGHTS:
Operating weight, including 400 lb (181 kg) crew:	6,918 lb (3,137 kg)
Mission weight	9,616 lb (4,361 kg)
Max T-O and landing weight	
	10,000 lb (4,535 kg)

PERFORMANCE (at max T-O weight, except as detailed):
Max level speed	
	180 knots (207 mph; 333 km/h)
Max permissible diving speed	
	180 knots (207 mph; 333 km/h)
Max rate of climb at S/L	1,090 ft (332 m)/min
Service ceiling	10,550 ft (3,215 m)
Hovering ceiling in ground effect	
	12,450 ft (3,794 m)
Hovering ceiling out of ground effect, at mission weight	3,500 ft (1,066 m)
Max range, no reserves	
	311 nm (359 miles; 577 km)

BELLANCA
BELLANCA AIRCRAFT ENGINEERING, INC

HEAD OFFICE:
165 New York Avenue, Lindenhurst, New York 11757

PRESIDENT: August T. Bellanca

The original Bellanca Aircraft Corporation of New Castle, Delaware, merged with companies not engaged in aircraft manufacture and lost its identity in 1959. This new company, formed by Mr August Bellanca and his father, the late G. M. Bellanca, bought all of the original Bellanca aircraft designs with the exception of the Model 14-19.

Since 1956, Bellanca Aircraft Engineering has carried out extensive research into the use of glass-fibre composite materials for airframe construction. Following the successful testing of full-scale structures, embodying a variety of different design and fabrication techniques, it is now developing the prototype of an aircraft known as the Bellanca Model 25, constructed of high-strength glass-fibre-epoxy laminates. Construction of the first aircraft was well advanced at the beginning of 1970, as can be seen by the accompanying photograph. The company intends to produce both single and twin-engined versions, later models being powered by turboprop engines.

Bellanca plans to erect an 80,000 sq ft factory adjacent to an airport on Maryland's eastern shore in which to manufacture the Model 25, but a final decision on its location had not been made at the time of writing.

BELLANCA MODEL 25

Research and design of this aircraft was initiated in 1956 by the late G. M. Bellanca and his son, August T. Bellanca. Construction of a prototype began in 1962 and development and testing of this aircraft is continuing in consultation with the FAA. Complete aerodynamic testing in a 7 ft by 10 ft (2·13 m by 3·05 m) wind tunnel was completed successfully in 1967. Production tooling was 90% complete in March 1968, and the prototype is expected to fly for the first time during 1970.

Prototype of the Bellanca Model 25, nearing completion

The early decision to fabricate this aircraft from glass-fibre composites resulted from much research and testing. Basically, the advantages are that smooth aerodynamic surfaces are obtained, together with high strength. The materials used in the Bellanca Model 25 have a higher strength-to-weight ratio than aluminium, with better durability and fatigue resistance.

TYPE: Five-seat light cabin monoplane.

WINGS: Cantilever low-wing monoplane. Laminar-flow wing section. Incidence 2°. Moulded as two half-shells, with two glass-fibre spars.

FUSELAGE: Semi-monocoque structure of glass-fibre epoxy laminate. Glass-fibre stringers. Fuselage is to be moulded in two halves, each with an integral wing root, vertical fin half and tailplane root.

TAIL UNIT: Cantilever glass-fibre epoxy laminated structure. Variable-incidence tailplane. No trim-tabs.

LANDING GEAR: Retractable tricycle type, hydraulically-operated. Oleo-pneumatic shock-absorbers. Main wheels and tyres size 15 × 6·00-6.

POWER PLANT: One 400 hp Lycoming IO-720-A1A eight-cylinder horizontally-opposed air-cooled engine, driving a Hartzell three-blade propeller, diameter 6 ft 8 in (2·03 m). Integral fuel tank in each wing, capacity 45 US gallons (170 litres). Total fuel capacity 90 US gallons (340 litres).

ACCOMMODATION: Pilot and four passengers in enclosed cabin. Door on starboard side. Stowage for 200 lb (90·7 kg) of baggage.

WEIGHT (estimated):
Max T-O weight	3,775 lb (2,712 kg)

PERFORMANCE (estimated):
Max speed at S/L	
	226 knots (260 mph; 418 km/h)
Stalling speed	57 knots (65 mph; 105 km/h)
Range	over 955 nm (1,100 miles; 1,770 km)

BELLANCA

BELLANCA SALES COMPANY (Subsidiary of MILLER FLYING SERVICE, INC)

HEAD OFFICE:
PO Box 776, Plainview, Texas 79072
WORKS:
Box 624, Alexandria, Minnesota
CHAIRMAN: J. K. Downer
PRESIDENT: James M. Miller
VICE-PRESIDENTS:
Chuck Wolfe
John McCarten
SECRETARY: Marge Mitchell
TREASURER: Warren A. Wilbur III

Known formerly as International Aircraft Manufacturing, Inc (Inter-air), Bellanca Sales Company is a subsidiary of Miller Flying Service. It is manufacturing several new versions of the well-known Bellanca 14-19 four-seat business aircraft at the rate of one aircraft every two working days.

BELLANCA 260C MODEL 14-19-3C

This considerably refined version of the Bellanca 14-19 series can be identified by the single swept-back vertical tail assembly which replaces the original triple-fin tail unit.

TYPE: Four-seat light business aircraft.

WINGS: Cantilever low-wing monoplane. Bellanca B wing section. Dihedral 4° 30'. Incidence 0° at root, —3° at tip. Structure consists of two laminated Sitka spruce spars, mahogany plywood and spruce ribs and mahogany plywood skin, covered with Plasticote and painted with synthetic enamel. Ailerons and electrically-actuated flaps are Plasticote-covered wooden structures.

FUSELAGE: Welded 4130 steel-tube structure, covered with Plasticote. Two-piece glass-fibre engine cowling, suspended from firewall.

TAIL UNIT: Strut-braced welded 4130 steel-tube structure, covered with Plasticote. Sweptback vertical surfaces. Trim tab in elevator.

LANDING GEAR: Tricycle type, with Auto-Axtion electro-hydraulic retraction, which lowers gear automatically during approach if pilot omits to do so, and prevents accidental retraction on ground. Manual emergency extension. All wheels protrude slightly in "up" position to reduce damage in a wheels-up landing. Nose-wheel retracts rearward, main wheels forward. Spring-air-oil shock-absorbers. Main wheel tyres size 6·00 × 6 6-ply. Steerable nose-wheel. Goodyear type 2-747 hydraulic disc-brakes.

POWER PLANT: One 260 hp Continental IO-470-F six-cylinder horizontally-opposed air-cooled engine, driving a Hartzell HC-C2YF-1A two-blade metal constant-speed propeller, diameter 6 ft 8 in (2·03 m). Fuel in two tanks in wings and one tank in fuselage, aft of cabin, each with capacity of 20 US gallons. Total fuel capacity 60 US gallons (227 litres). Refuelling points above each wing and on starboard side of fuselage. Oil capacity 3 US gallons (11·5 litres).

ACCOMMODATION: Four seats in pairs in enclosed cabin. Dual controls standard, with brakes on port side only. Moulded glass-fibre door on starboard side of cabin. Tinted glass. Baggage space, capacity 186 lb (84 kg), aft of rear seats, with glass-fibre external door and in-flight access. Heating and ventilation standard.

SYSTEMS: 12V electrical system, with Prestolite alternator, solid-state regulator and 33Ah battery.

ELECTRONICS AND EQUIPMENT: Standard equipment includes blind-flying instrumentation, Bellanca Aero-Guide autopilot, landing and navigation lights and compass. Optional equipment includes wide range of radio transceivers by King and Narco, Narco ADF, glideslope receiver, DME and marker beacon receiver, King DME and marker beacon receiver, Kett Polaris X with KoursePointer and marker beacon, rotating beacon and curtains.

DIMENSIONS, EXTERNAL:

Wing span	34 ft 2 in (10·41 m)
Length overall	22 ft 11 in (6·98 m)
Height overall	6 ft 4 in (1·93 m)
Tailplane span	12 ft 2 in (3·71 m)
Wheel track	9 ft 0 in (2·74 m)
Wheelbase	6 ft 8 in (2·03 m)

Lycoming-engined version of the Bellanca Viking 300

Cabin door:	
Height	2 ft 10 in (0·86 m)
Max width	2 ft 9 in (0·84 m)
Baggage compartment door:	
Height	2 ft 0 in (0·61 m)
Width	1 ft 8¼ in (0·51 m)

DIMENSIONS, INTERNAL:

Cabin: Length, firewall to rear wall	10 ft 2 in (3·10 m)
Max width	3 ft 7 in (1·09 m)
Max height	3 ft 11 in (1·19 m)
Baggage compartment volume	12·08 cu ft (0·34 m³)

AREAS:

Wings, gross	161·5 sq ft (15·00 m²)
Ailerons (total)	11·77 sq ft (1·09 m²)
Trailing-edge flaps (total)	16·16 sq ft (1·50 m²)

WEIGHTS AND LOADINGS:

Weight empty, equipped	1,850 lb (839 kg)
Max T-O and landing weight	3,000 lb (1,360 kg)
Max wing loading	18·58 lb/sq ft (90·7 kg/m²)
Max power loading	11·5 lb/hp (5·2 kg/hp)

PERFORMANCE (at max T-O weight):

Max level speed at S/L	170 knots (196 mph; 315 km/h)
Max permissible diving speed	196 knots (226 mph; 363 km/h)
Max cruising speed (75% power) at 8,000 ft (2,440 m)	162 knots (186 mph; 299 km/h)
Econ cruising speed (63% power) at 10,000 ft (3,050 m)	156 knots (180 mph; 290 km/h)
Stalling speed, flaps and wheels down	54 knots (62 mph; 100 km/h)
Rate of climb at S/L	over 1,500 ft (457 m) min
Service ceiling	22,500 ft (6,860 m)
T-O run	340 ft (104 m)
T-O to 50 ft (15 m)	1,000 ft (305 m)
Landing from 50 ft (15 m)	800 ft (244 m)
Landing run	400 ft (122 m)
Range with max fuel and max payload	868 nm (1,000 miles; 1,610 km)

BELLANCA VIKING 300 SERIES

The three aircraft comprising the Viking 300 Series have an identical airframe to the Bellanca 200C. Each is available in Standard or Super versions, the latter offering more luxurious appointments and increased fuel capacity. The three standard models differ as follows:

Standard Viking 300 (Continental-engined version). Powered by a 300 hp Continental IO-520-D six-cylinder horizontally-opposed air-cooled engine, driving a Hartzell three-blade constant-speed propeller. McCauley two- or three-blade propeller optional. Standard fuel capacity 58 US gallons (220 litres). Super Viking 300 has standard fuel capacity of 72 US gallons (272·5 litres). Optional fuel tanks for long range provide maximum capacity of 92 US gallons (348 litres). Oxygen system optional.

Standard Viking 300 (Lycoming-engined version). This is identical to the foregoing version except for the installation of a Lycoming IO-540 engine. McCauley propellers not optional for this model.

Standard Turbo Viking 300. Powered by a 310 hp TIO-540 turbocharged engine. Fuel capacity of 72 US gallons (272·5 litres) standard; optional maximum capacity of 92 US gallons (348 litres). McCauley propellers not optional. Oxygen system standard.

The description of the Bellanca 260C applies also to the Viking 300 Series, except as detailed below:

ELECTRONICS AND EQUIPMENT: Standard equipment includes artificial horizon, directional gyro, electric turn co-ordinator, rate of climb indicator, vacuum gauge, 8-day clock, outside air temperature gauge, tinted glass, sun visor, cigar lighter, tow bar, stall warning device, vernier throttle, mixture and propeller controls, soundproofing, custom interior, cushions, tie-down straps, entrance step. With factory-installed radio equipment the following additional equipment is standard: Narco omni antenna, electroVoice microphone, power cable, Narco VP-10 broad-band transmitting antenna and microphone jacks. Bellanca Aero-Guide autopilot is standard equipment and this may be upgraded by the addition of Mitchell Century II or III exchange options, and optional accessories which include Aero-Guide as back-up for Century II or III, radio tracker for Aero-Guide, radio coupler and automatic trim for Century II or III, glideslope coupler for Century III, electric trim and switch kits. Optional radio and navigation equipment includes Bendix, King and Narco VHF transceivers, transponders and marker beacon receivers, Bendix, King, Kett and Narco ADF radio receivers, King and Narco DME and Narco course line computer. Miscellaneous optional equipment includes E6T meter, heated pitot tube, auxiliary power source, stereo tape player, oxygen system, propeller spinners, true air speed indicator, alternative paint schemes, 3 in gyros, strobes, quick oil drain, alternative static source and wheel doors for main landing gear.

DIMENSIONS, EXTERNAL AND INTERNAL, AND AREAS:
Same as for Bellanca 260C, except:

Length overall	23 ft 6 in (7·16 m)
Height overall	7 ft 4 in (2·24 m)

WEIGHTS (A = IO-520, B = IO-540, C = TIO-540):
Weight empty:

A	1,900 lb (862 kg)
B	1,950 lb (884 kg)
C	2,010 lb (911 kg)
Max T-O weight	3,200 lb (1,451 kg)

PERFORMANCE (at max T-O weight, A = IO-520, B = IO-540, C = TIO-540):
Max permissible speed:

A, B, C,	196 knots (226 mph; 363 km/h) IAS

Max cruising speed:

A	163 knots (188 mph; 303 km/h) TAS
B	168 knots (194 mph; 312 km/h) TAS
C	204 knots (235 mph; 378 km/h) TAS

Max rate of climb at S/L:

A	1,840 ft (561 m)/min
B, C	1,800 ft (549 m)/min

Service ceiling:

A	21,000 ft (6,400 m)
B	21,600 ft (6,584 m)
C	24,000 ft (7,315 m)

T-O run:

A	450 ft (137 m)
B, C	460 ft (140 m)

Landing run:

A, B, C	575 ft (175 m)

Landing from 50 ft (15 m):

A	1,050 ft (320 m)
B, C	1,100 ft (335 m)

BENSEN

BENSEN AIRCRAFT CORPORATION

HEAD OFFICE AND WORKS:
Raleigh-Durham Airport, Raleigh, North Carolina 27602
PRESIDENT: Igor B. Bensen

The Bensen Aircraft Corporation was formed by Mr Igor B. Bensen, formerly Chief of Research of the Kaman company, to develop a series of lightweight helicopters and rotary-wing gliders suitable for production in kit form for amateur construction as well as in ready-to-fly condition.

Production is now centred on the B-8M/V Gyro-Copter powered autogyro, the B-8MA Agricopter agricultural spraying version and various land and water-borne versions of the B-8 rotor-kite.

Bensen is also developing the B-12 Sky-mat multi-rotor ground effect machine.

Work on the B-11M Kopter-Kart multi-engined version of the Gyro-Copter has ended, but details of this aircraft can be found in the 1969-70 *Jane's*.

BENSEN MODEL B-8 GYRO-GLIDER
USAF designation: X-25

The Gyro-Glider is a simple unpowered rotor-kite which can be towed behind even a small motor car and has achieved free gliding with the towline released. It is available as either a completed aircraft or kit of parts for amateur construction. Alternatively, would-be constructors can purchase a set of plans, with building and flying instructions. No pilot's licence is required to fly it in the United States and many hundreds of kits and plans have been sold. Application has been made for an Approved Type Certificate.

The original Model B-7 Gyro-Glider was described in the 1958-59 edition of this work. It has been followed by the Model B-8, which is offered as either a single-seater or two-seater, the latter version being suitable for use as a pilot trainer.

Under contract to the USAF, Bensen have delivered a single-seat and a two-seat Gyro-Glider to the USAF Flight Dynamics Laboratory at Wright-Patterson AFB, Dayton, Ohio, where, designated X-25, they are being used to explore the feasibility of using tilting rotors on a Discretionary Descent Vehicle (DDV).

A new concept in rescue devices, the DDV would have a set of rotor blades folded into an ejection system, in addition to the normal parachute, enabling a pilot to attain any pre-selected site within gliding range. Current tests are designed to determine pilot reaction to, and evaluation of, the new concept.

The Model B-8 consists basically of an inverted square-section tubular aluminium T-frame structure, of which the forward arm supports the lightweight seat, towing arm, rudder bar and landing gear nose-wheel. The rear arm supports a large stabilising fin and rudder, with the main landing gear wheels carried on a tubular axle near the junction of the T-frame. The free-turning two-blade rotor is universally-mounted at the top of the T-frame and is normally operated directly by a hanging-stick control. A floor-type control column is available as optional equipment. A movable rudder with pedal controls is standard equipment.

The standard Gyro-Glider rotor is of laminated plywood construction, with steel spar. Factory-built all-metal rotor blades, and metal tail surfaces, are available as optional items.

The two-seat trainer version of the Gyro-Glider is fitted with castoring cross-wind landing gear and has an extra-wide wheel track. It will maintain level flight down to 19 mph (30·5 kmh).

DIMENSIONS, EXTERNAL:
Diameter of rotor	20 ft 0 in (6·10 m)
Length of fuselage	11 ft 4 in (3·45 m)
Height overall	6 ft 3 in (1·90 m)

BENSEN MODEL B-8W HYDRO-GLIDER

The basic structure of this floatplane rotor-kite is similar to that of the B-8 Gyro-Glider and conversion from one to the other is simple. Main changes are that the nose-wheel landing gear is replaced by two floats. The original round-type floats have been superseded by flat-bottomed pontoons of polyurethane foam covered by glass-fibre, which give better planing, with less spray.

The Hydro-Glider is towed by a motorboat.

BENSEN MODEL B-8M AND B-8V GYRO-COPTER AND B-8MW HYDRO-COPTER

First flown on 6 December 1955, the Gyro-Copter is a powered autogyro conversion of the Gyro-Glider, designed for home construction from kits or plans. When fitted with floats it is known as a Hydro-Copter.

The current **B-8M** version of the Gyro-Copter has a more powerful engine than the original B-7M and can be equipped with an optional mechanical rotor drive. By engaging this drive, the rotor can be accelerated to flying speed while the aircraft is stationary. Then by transferring the power to the pusher propeller, it is possible to take off in only 50 ft (15 m), with the rotor auto-rotating normally. Alternatively, a 1 hp Ohlsson & Rice Compact III two-stroke engine can be attached to the rotor for pre-rotation, automatically disengaging itself at take-off rpm.

Other non-standard items available optionally include a 90 hp engine instead of the normal 72 hp engine, a larger-diameter rotor, an offset gimbal rotor head, a floor-type control column instead of the normal overhead type of column, dual ignition, nose-wheel arrester and Bensen-manufactured pontoons of polyurethane foam covered with glass-fibre. All-metal rotor blades and tail surfaces are available as alternatives to the standard wooden components.

The prototype Model B-8M Gyro-Copter flew for the first time on 8 July 1957 and the first production model on 9 October 1957. The aircraft illustrated is Mr Bensen's own B-8M

One of two Bensen B-8 Gyro-Gliders supplied to the USAF. In May 1968 one was converted into a powered Gyro-Copter, designated X-25A. The other is a two-seat Gyro-Glider, designated X-25B

Spirit of Kitty Hawk, which incorporates many improvements and optional items such as the Ohlsson & Rice auxiliary engine for rotor spin-up.

On this aircraft, Mr Bensen set up (with FAI confirmation) a series of international records on 15 May 1967. They include a distance of 74·3 miles (119·58 km) in a closed circuit, distance of 82·8 miles (133·2 km) in a straight line, speed of 51·35 mph (82·64 kmh) over a 100-km closed circuit and altitude of 7,275 ft (2,217 m). In June 1967 new records were gained by Mr Bensen, flying his own B-8M, when he attained officially-recorded speeds of 73·3 mph (117·97 kmh) and 79·0 mph (127·15 kmh) over 3-km and 15-km courses respectively. These were confirmed by the FAI as new world speed records in October

Bensen Model B-8MW Hydro-Copter (72 hp McCulloch 4318E or 90 hp 4318G engine)

Igor Bensen and his B-8M Gyro-Copter *Spirit of Kitty Hawk*, fitted with 1 hp Ohlsson & Rice auxiliary engine to start rotor (*Peter M. Bowers*)

1967. Each of these records applied to both class E.3 (all autogyros) and class E.3a (autogyros weighing less than 500 kg). The records for altitude and speed over 3 km have since been exceeded by the British Wallis WA-116.

The B-8M is roadable, requiring no removal of, or changes in its equipment for transition from air to ground travel. The rotor is merely stopped in a fore-and-aft position by a lock. Gyro-Copters have been driven on highways and have negotiated heavy city traffic with ease in a number of public demonstrations in the USA.

The **B-8V**, which flew for the first time in the autumn of 1967, is basically a standard B-8M, but is powered by a 1600 cc Volkswagen engine. In unmodified form the VW1600 yields just adequate flight performance at 600 lb (272 kg) gross weight. Since Bensen engineers considered that most Gyro-Copters would not have a gross weight as high as 600 lb, the VW engine justified inclusion as an alternative power plant to the standard McCulloch engine.

Kits and parts for the B-8V, excluding engine and mounting, are available, as are plans and an instruction manual for converting the B-8M to a B-8V, or for mounting a VW engine on a standard B-8 airframe.

Versions of the B-8 are being built under licence in the UK by Campbell Aircraft Ltd (which see).

TYPE: Single-seat light autogyro.

ROTOR SYSTEM: B-8M has single two-blade rotor of laminated plywood construction, with steel spar (Optional all-metal rotor). Blade section Bensen G2. Teetering hub, with no lag hinges or collective-pitch control. A similar rotor, of all-metal construction, is provided for the B-8V. A larger-diameter rotor is not available as an alternative for this latter model. No anti-torque rotor. Rotor speed 400 rpm.

ROTOR DRIVE (optional): An auxiliary 1 hp Ohlsson & Rice engine is available to spin-up the rotor.

FUSELAGE: Square-section tubular 6061-T6 aluminium structure.

TAIL SURFACES: Vertical fin and rudder of ¼ in plywood. (Optional all-metal tail surfaces).

LANDING GEAR: Non-retractable tricycle type, with auxiliary tail-wheel. No shock-absorbers. Steerable nose-wheel. General Tire wheels, size 12 in × 4 in (30·5 × 10·15 cm). Tyre pressure 10 lb/sq in (0·70 kg/cm²). Brake on nose-wheel.

POWER PLANT: One 72 hp McCulloch Model 4318E four-cylinder horizontally-opposed air-cooled two-stroke engine (or, optionally, a 90 hp McCulloch 4318G engine of similar weight and dimensions), driving a two-blade wooden fixed-pitch Aero Prop Model BA 48-A2 pusher propeller, diameter 4 ft 0 in (1·22 m), with leading-edges covered with stainless steel. Alternatively, one 64 hp Volkswagen 1,600 cc four-cylinder horizontally-opposed air-cooled four-stroke engine, driving a Troyer Model 50-24-65 two-blade wooden fixed-pitch pusher propeller, diameter 4 ft 2 in (1·27 m). Fuel tank under pilot's seat, capacity 6·0 US gallons (22·75 litres). Can be fitted with auxiliary tank for ferrying.

ACCOMMODATION: Open seat for pilot, with overhead azimuth stick and rudder pedal controls. Optional floor-type control column. Safety belt.

DIMENSIONS, EXTERNAL:
Diameter of rotor:		
standard	20 ft 0 in (6·10 m)	
optional (on B-8M and B-8MW)		
	22 ft 0 in (6·70 m)	
Rotor blade chord	7 in (18·8 cm)	
Length of fuselage	11 ft 4 in (3·45 m)	
Height overall	6 ft 3 in (1·90 m)	
Wheel track	5 ft 0 in (1·52 m)	

AREAS (Standard rotor):
Rotor blade (each)	5·83 sq ft (0·54 m²)
Rotor disc	314 sq ft (29·17 m²)

WEIGHTS (Standard rotor):
Weight empty:	
B-8M	247 lb (112 kg)
B-8V	348 lb (158 kg)
Max T-O weight:	
B-8M	500 lb (227 kg)
B-8V	600 lb (272 kg)

PERFORMANCE (at max T-O weight, with standard rotor):
Max level speed at S/L:	
B-8M	74 knots (85 mph; 137 km/h)
B-8V	52 knots (60 mph; 96·5 km/h)
Max cruising speed at S/L:	
B-8M	52 knots (60 mph; 96·5 km/h)
B-8V	43 knots (50 mph; 80·5 km/h)
Economical cruising speed:	
B-8M, B-8V	39 knots (45 mph; 72·5 km/h)
Min speed in level flight:	
B-8M	13 knots (15 mph; 24 km/h)
B-8V	17·4 knots (20 mph; 32 km/h)
T-O speed at S/L:	
B-8M	17·4 knots (20 mph; 32 km/h)
B-8V	22 knots (25 mph; 40 km/h)
Landing speed:	
B-8M	6 knots (7 mph; 11·5 km/h)
B-8V	9 knots (10 mph; 16 km/h)
Max rate of climb:	
B-8M	1,000 ft (305 m)/min

Bensen B-8MA Agricopter (90 hp McCulloch 4318G engine)

Bensen B-8V Gyro-Copter with 1,600 cc Volkswagen engine

B-8V	650 ft (198 m)/min
Service ceiling:	
B-8M	12,500 ft (3,800 m)
B-8V	8,000 ft (2,440 m)
T-O run, unpowered rotor, zero wind:	
B-8M	300 ft (92 m)
B-8V	400 ft (122 m)
T-O run, powered rotor, zero wind:	
B-8M	50 ft (15·2 m)
Landing run in 10 mph (16 km/h) wind:	
B-8M, B-8V	0 ft
Landing run in zero wind:	
B-8M	20 ft (6 m)
B-8V	25 ft (7·5 m)
Normal range:	
B-8M	86 nm (100 miles; 160 km)
B-8V	130 nm (150 miles; 241 km)
Ferry range:	
B-8M	260 nm (300 miles; 482 km)
B-8V	345 nm (400 miles; 643 km)
Endurance:	
B-8M	1·5 hrs
B-8V	2·25 hrs

BENSEN MODEL B-8MA AGRICOPTER

Bensen has announced introduction of an agricultural version of the B-8M Gyro-Copter. Known as the B-8MA Agricopter, this is basically the same as the B-8M but has a 5 US gallon (19 litre) tank for chemicals mounted beneath the engine and a micro-spray system developed by the Bensen company. Introduction of ultra low volume insecticides has made it possible for this small-capacity system to offer effective cover of an area of from 160 to 400 acres during a single 40-minute flight.

At the time of writing, the Agricopter had received FAA Certification only in an Experimental Category. Operators of such aircraft in the USA must hold an agricultural aircraft operator's certificate.

First flight of the prototype was made in September 1969 and production aircraft were scheduled to fly in March 1970.

The description of the B-8M applies also to the Model B-8MA except in the following details:

POWER PLANT: One 90 hp McCulloch 4318G four-cylinder horizontally-opposed air-cooled two-stroke engine, driving an Aerial Prop Model BA 48-A8-90 two-blade wooden fixed-pitch propeller, diameter 4 ft 0 in (1·22 m).

Kit of parts for Bensen B-8M Gyro-Copter and completed aircraft

DIMENSIONS, EXTERNAL:
Diameter of rotor   21 ft 8 in (6·60 m)
Length of fuselage   13 ft 3 in (4·04 m)
WEIGHT:
Max T-O and landing weight   600 lb (272 kg)
PERFORMANCE (at AUW of 500 lb = 227 kg):
As for the Model B-8M with standard rotor.

BENSEN B-11M KOPTER-KART
Production of the B-11M Kopter-Kart has
ended; details of this model may be found in the
1969-70 *Jane's*.

BENSEN B-12 SKY-MAT
First flown on 2 November 1961, the B-12
Sky-mat is a VTOL aircraft, intended primarily
for agricultural spraying operations. It is of
all-metal construction, to allow permanent storage
out of doors, and had eight rotors in its original
form. Now, as can be seen in the illustrations
on this page, it has ten two-blade rotors, each
driven by a 10 hp West Bend engine, running on
automotive fuel.
Normal operating height of the B-12 is 3 ft
(0·91 m) above the ground, but it is capable of
hopping over obstacles up to 50 ft (15·24 m) high.
This model is not yet in production.
DIMENSIONS:
Rotor diameter (each)   5 ft 0 in (1·52 m)
WEIGHTS:
Weight empty   400 lb (181 kg)
Max T-O weight   800 lb (362 kg)
PERFORMANCE:
Max level speed   56 knots (65 mph; 105 kmh)
Cruising speed   39 knots (45 mph; 72 kmh)

**Two views of the Bensen B-12 Sky-Mat, with ten rotors, each powered
by a 10 hp West Bend engine.**   (*Howard Levy*)

BERLIN DOMAN
BERLIN DOMAN HELICOPTERS, INC
HEAD OFFICE AND WORKS:
New Garden Flying Field, Toughkenamon,
Pennsylvania 19374
CHAIRMAN AND CHIEF EXECUTIVE OFFICER:
Dr Don R. Berlin
PRESIDENT:
Glidden S. Doman
Doman Helicopters, Inc ceased production in
1961, and subsequently transferred its assets to
Caribe Doman Helicopters, Inc, of San Juan,
Puerto Rico (see under Puerto Rico heading in
1967-68 *Jane's*), where development of the Doman
D-10B helicopter was continued.
Following a meeting of stockholders of Doman
Helicopters, Inc, on 27 September 1967, the
company's name was changed to Berlin Doman
Helicopters, Inc, to reflect the active interest of
Dr Don R. Berlin, the company's Chairman and
Chief Executive officer.
The new company does not intend to produce
the D-10B at its Toughkenamon factory. Instead,
it is developing a new nine-seat transport helicop-
ter which it has designated BD-19.

BERLIN DOMAN BD-19
Following a market survey, Berlin Doman
have decided to produce initially a nine-seat
helicopter, to which they have given the designation BD-19, and which will be powered by
two 317 shp Allison Model 250-C18 turboshaft
engines. The BD-19 will have a retractable
landing gear and water-landing capability.
The company intends later to produce developed
versions of this helicopter, with greater capacity,
powered by more powerful or additional engines.
All available details follow:
TYPE: Nine-seat utility transport helicopter.

**Mock-up of Berlin Doman BD-19 nine-seat transport helicopter (two 317 shp Allison
Model 250-C18 turboshaft engines)**

ROTOR: Four-blade rigid main rotor mounted
on tilting hub. Blades of plastic laminates.
Blade chord 10·2 in (25·9 cm). Three-blade
tail rotor of similar construction.
TAIL UNIT: Small horizontal stabiliser. Vertical
fin fairing around tail rotor support structure.
LANDING GEAR: Retractable nose-wheel type.
Nose and main units each carry twin wheels
and tyres. Hull sealed for operation from
water.
POWER PLANT: Two 317 shp Allison Model 250-C18
turboshaft engines.

WEIGHTS:
Weight empty   3,000 lb (1,360 kg)
Max T-O weight   6,500 lb (2,948 kg)

PERFORMANCE (estimated at max T-O weight):
Cruising speed 126 knots (145 mph; 233 km/h)
Rate of climb at S/L, without water injection
                        1,200 ft (366 m)/min
Hovering ceiling in ground effect, with water
injection   4,500 ft (1,370 m)
Range with standard fuel, 15 min reserves
                  390 nm (450 miles; 724 km)

BIRD

The Bird Innovator, a four-engined conversion of the PBY-5A Catalina amphibian

BIRD CORPORATION
ADDRESS:
Mark 3 Respirator Lane, Palm Springs, Cal-
ifornia 92262
Bird Corporation, best known as the world's
largest manufacturers of medical respirators,
evolved a conversion scheme for the PBY-5A
Catalina amphibian, with the initial aim of

improving the performance of their own PBY-5A.
This was originally a basic "Landseair" conversion and re-conversion, and was acquired for use
as a flying classroom, office, hotel and transport
for medical teaching teams. Special air evacuation equipment pioneered aboard this aircraft,
known as the *Wandering Albatross*, now serves
Allied forces throughout the world.

The power of the original PBY was limited
intentionally, to provide extreme long-range
capability, resulting in marginal performance if
one engine failed. One scheme for performance
improvement adopted by other operators involves
replacement of the standard 1,250 hp Pratt &
Whitney radial engines by two more powerful
engines. Instead of following suit, the Bird
Corporation studied the feasibility of converting

their own PBY-5A to a four-engined configuration, to avoid the greater noise and vibration experienced with larger engines and to permit the use of reversible-pitch propellers.

Fuel economy dictated the use of piston-engines and the final choice was two 340 hp Lycoming engines, driving Hartzell fully-feathering propellers, for installation outboard of the standard Pratt & Whitney engines.

FAA Supplemental Type Certificate was received on 20 December 1968, and Bird Corporation are now accepting orders for this conversion, known as the Bird Innovator, from PBY operators throughout the world.

BIRD INNOVATOR

This four-engined conversion of the PBY-5A Catalina (for details of which see 1945-46 *Jane's*) involves installation of two 340 hp Lycoming GSO-480-B2D6 geared and supercharged horizontally-opposed six-cylinder air-cooled engines in the outer wing panels, on a centre line 2 ft 1 in (0·64 m) from the wing splices. The new engines are aligned with the chord line, with a 3° outboard cant. The top of the nacelle is clean and flush with the top skin of the wing, while frontal area is minimal, slightly exceeding the maximum thickness of the aerofoil. Dual augmenter exhausts discharge from the bottom of the nacelle.

An additional 375 US gallons (1,419 litres) of fuel is contained in three interconnecting bladder tanks in the wings, and a 15 US gallon (58 litre) oil tank is installed, together with a CO_2 bottle for fire protection. A unique fuel boost and transfer system allows fuel to be transferred in either direction between auxiliary and main fuel

tanks. A rapid fuel dump system is integrated into the master fuel dump chutes.

Additional stringers and stress plates are built into the wing to maintain original structural integrity. Aileron cables are re-routed and Flettner tabs are installed on each aileron to boost control. With the exception of the ailerons, the whole wing trailing-edges are now metal skinned. A square-tipped fin and rudder assembly, of increased area, is installed.

The new Hartzell 83XF-3A reversible-pitch fully-feathering propellers are controlled through two Hamilton Standard synchronising boxes. Auxiliary engine feathering is accomplished by toggling back on synchronising control switches. Two-second reversing is obtained by retarding the engine throttles and then moving them over a detention stop. Further rearward movement applies thrust to the reversed propeller blades.

The original PBY propeller controls are used as throttles for the auxiliary engines. All other engine controls, such as mixture, carburettor heating, etc., are electrically operated via control switches adjacent to their counterparts for the main engines. Auxiliary engine instruments are mounted in a straight line across the top of the panel. The special heavy-duty battery pack is installed as far aft as possible in the fuselage, to help adjust weight and balance.

The entire conversion adds approximately 3,500 lb (1,588 kg) to the aircraft's weight.

Special hoists lift two 14 ft 0 in (4·27 m) boats up under each wing, where they are locked automatically into position, serving as cargo containers as well as for transportation on the water. An airstair door allows easy passenger

access, and a projected cargo conversion has large doors for easy loading of freight.

The new auxiliary engines provide excellent handling on both land and water, and a performance in the air which exceeded design expectations.

PERFORMANCE:
Max cruising speed
174 knots (200 mph; 322 km/h)
Cruising speed (34,000 lb = 15,422 kg gross weight at 5,000 ft = 1,525 m)
137 knots (158 mph; 254 km/h)
Cruising speed (64% power at 11,000 ft = 3,350 m):
All engines 132 knots (152 mph; 244 km/h)
Starboard auxiliary feathered
125 knots (144 mph; 231 km/h)
Port auxiliary feathered
124 knots (143 mph; 229 km/h)
Both auxiliaries feathered
112 knots (129 mph; 207 km/h)
Starboard main engine feathered
110 knots (127 mph; 204 km/h)
Port main engine feathered
108 knots (124 mph; 199 km/h)
Rate of climb at 73% power at S/L
750 ft (228 m)/min
Service ceiling, one main engine out
15,000 ft (4,570 m)
Service ceiling, both port engines feathered
10,000 ft (3,050 m)
T-O run at 34,000 lb (15,422 kg)
approx 1,000 ft (305 m)
T-O run at 85% T-O power at 34,000 lb (15,422 kg)
under 2,000 ft (610 m)

BOEING
THE BOEING COMPANY

HEAD OFFICE:
PO Box 3707, Seattle, Washington 98124

ESTABLISHED: July 1916

CHAIRMAN OF THE BOARD:
William M. Allen

PRESIDENT AND CHIEF EXECUTIVE OFFICER:
T. A. Wilson

SENIOR VICE-PRESIDENTS:
E. C. Wells
G. Stoner (Operations)
J. E. Prince (Administration)
H. W. Haynes (Finance)

VICE-PRESIDENTS:
G. C. Martin (Engineering)
H. W. Neffner (Contracts)
L. P. Mickelwait (Industrial and Public Relations)
E. A. Ochel (Manufacturing)
George S. Schairer (Research and Development)
M. L. Pennell (Product Development)
R. J. Murphy Jr (Washington Representative)
Other Vice-Presidents are listed under Divisions.

TREASURER: J. B. L. Pierce

CONTROLLER: V. F. Knutzen

PUBLIC RELATIONS AND ADVERTISING DIRECTOR:
R. P. Bush

Commercial Airplane Group:

ADDRESS:
PO Box 707, Renton, Washington 98055

GROUP VICE-PRESIDENT:
E. H. Boullioun

VICE-PRESIDENTS:
J. B. Connelly (CAG Asst General Manager)
C. E. Dillon (General Manager, 737 Division)
D. J. Euler (CAG Marketing Plans)
T. E. Gamlem (General Manager, Fabrication and Services Division)
K. F. Holtby (Chief Engineer)
H. E. Hurst (SST Division Assistant General Manager)
W. M. Maulden (Manager, Group Programmes)
G. D. Nible (General Manager, 747 Division)
G. Snyder (Engineering, 707/727 Division)
M. T. Stamper (CAG General Manager)
J. E. Steiner (CAG General Manager, 707/727/737 Divisions)
R. W. Welch (Finance and Contracts)
B. M. Wheat (Administration)
C. F. Wilde (CAG Commercial Sales)
H. W. Withington (General Manager, SST Division)

Aerospace Group:

ADDRESS:
PO Box 3999, Seattle, Washington 98124

VICE-PRESIDENTS:
G. H. Stoner (Group Vice-President)
O. C. Boileau (General Manager, Missile Division)
R. H. Jewett (General Manager, Aerospace Systems Division)
G. H. Hage (Manager, Space Shuttle Team)

MANAGER SPACECRAFT BRANCH:
R. B. Hildebrand

MANAGER, ASMS BRANCH:
R. A. Montgomery

GENERAL MANAGER, AEROSPACE OPERATIONS:
R. H. Nelson

MANAGER, MARINE BRANCH:
A. M. Gonnella

GENERAL MANAGER, SOUTHEAST DIVISION:
H. J. McClellan

Wichita Division:

ADDRESS:
3801 South Oliver, Wichita, Kansas 67210

VICE-PRESIDENT AND GENERAL MANAGER:
O. H. Smith

Military Aircraft Systems Division:

ADDRESS:
PO Box 3707, Seattle, Washington 98124

VICE-PRESIDENT AND GENERAL MANAGER:
R. W. Taylor

Vertol Division:

ADDRESS:
Boeing Centre, PO Box 16858, Philadelphia Pa, 19142

VICE-PRESIDENT AND GENERAL MANAGER:
R. W. Tharrington

VICE-PRESIDENT (OPERATIONS):
T. C. Pitts

In May 1961 The Boeing Airplane Company changed its proprietary name to The Boeing Company as a recognition of the Company's diversified interests. The change did not imply any decreased interest in the design and manufacture of aircraft and, in most respects, Boeing remains the largest single aeronautical company in the world, with a total of approximately 90,000 employees in March 1970.

The Commercial Airplane Group, with headquarters at the company's Renton, Washington, facility just south of Seattle, has six divisions. The 707/727 Division, 737 Division and 747 Division all continue to manufacture aircraft of those series; the SST Division will develop and build two SST prototypes; the Fabrication and Services Division handles central fabrication services from its Auburn, Washington, plant, and other services such as CAG facilities; and the Engineering and Operations Division is responsible for such functions as technology, quality control and flight operations.

The 737 Division has its headquarters at Plant Two, near the company's head offices in South Seattle; the SST Division is located just south of Plant Two at the Developmental Centre; the 747 Division is at Everett, Washington, 30 miles north of Seattle; and the 707/727 and E and O Divisions are based at Renton.

The Wichita Division at Wichita, Kansas, continues modification programmes, 737 and 747 parts fabrication, research, programmes on military aircraft currently in use with the armed forces (B-52 and KC-135) and other support functions for the company.

The Vertol Division, based near Philadelphia, produces the CH-46 Sea Knight helicopter for the US Navy and Marine Corps, and the CH-47 Chinook for the US Army. Research and development work on heavy-lift helicopters is being carried out and the Division has demonstrated the BO 105 light helicopter to the US Navy. Boeing has marketing rights for this aircraft in the United States and other parts of the Western Hemisphere, and has an option to manufacture it in the US. The BO 105 was developed and is manufactured in Germany by Messerschmitt-Bölkow-Blohm GmbH (which see), the largest German aerospace company, in which Boeing has a holding of just under 10%.

Formation of a Military Aircraft Systems Division (MASD) was announced in December 1968. Intended to bring Boeing into a competitive position for potential new military systems incorporating aircraft, the Division is staffed with specialists in weapon system analysis, electronic systems, advanced systems management techniques and aircraft design. MASD's major effort during 1969 was concerned with the design competition for the B-1 advanced manned supersonic bomber for the USAF.

The other of the company's two major groups, the Aerospace Group, has its headquarters at the company's space centre at Kent, Washington, some 12 miles south of Seattle. This group consists of the Aerospace Systems Division, Missile Division, Aerospace Operations, Spacecraft Branch, Navy Systems Branch and AWACS Branch. Responsibilities include assembly and testing of the Minuteman ICBM and development of the SRAM short-range attack missile for the USAF, as well as work on other missile systems. The group is a prime contractor for NASA on the Apollo programme, including responsibility for production of the first stage of Saturn V.

In 1969 the Aerospace Group was awarded a NASA contract to develop and build the Lunar Rover vehicle, to be used for transporting astronauts on the Moon's surface. The Group is also one of two competitors for the USAF Airborne Warning and Control Systems (AWACS). Another important activity involves development of hydrofoil marine vessels and the Boeing-built *Tucumcari*, a hydrofoil gunboat using completely submerged foils and water-jet propulsion, is in service with the US Navy.

BOEING MODEL 707
US Air Force designation: VC-137

The prototype of the Boeing Model 707 was the first jet transport to be completed and flown in the United States. It made its first flight on 15 July 1954 and was still in use as a test vehicle in 1969.

Designated Model 367-80, it was built as a private venture and was used to demonstrate the potential of commercial and military developments of the design. During its early test programme, it was fitted with a flight-refuelling boom, to prove the capability of this type of aircraft for refuelling present and future jet bombers, fighters and reconnaissance aircraft at or near their operational altitudes and speeds. As a result, a developed version was ordered in

Boeing Model 707-366C (four Pratt & Whitney JT3D-3B turbofan engines) in the insignia of United Arab Airlines

large numbers for the USAF under the designation KC-135.

On 13 July 1955 Boeing was given clearance by the USAF to build commercial developments of the prototype concurrently with the production of military KC-135 tanker-transports. These transport aircraft have the basic designations of Boeing 707 and 720, but are available in many different versions, of which a total of 845 had been sold and 840 delivered by 30 June 1970. These totals include four specially-equipped aircraft delivered to the USAF under the designations VC-137A (now VC-137B) and VC-137C.

The basic versions of the 707 are as follows:—

367-80. The prototype tanker-transport, flown on 15 July 1954. Powered originally by Pratt & Whitney JT3P turbojets (each 9,500 lb = 4,300 kg st), with max T-O weight of 160,000 lb (72,570 kg). Wing span 130 ft 0 in (39·60 m). Length 128 ft 0 in (39·01 m), Height 38 ft 3 in (11·6 m).

This aircraft has been in continuous use for development flying, with the emphasis on testing various boundary layer control systems since 1960. In its latest form, as the 367-80B, it is powered by JT3D-1 turbofan engines (each 17,000 lb=7,718 kg st). Test equipment currently installed includes three segments of single-hinge trailing-edge flaps on each wing, between the fuselage and outboard aileron; a Krueger flap on the leading-edge of each wing, between the fuselage and inboard engine pylon; and two segments of slats from that point to the wingtip.

The leading-edge of the tailplane is fitted with a full-span inverted slat. The wing trailing-edge flaps are blown by air bled from turbofan engines, the system utilising up to 30% of the total thrust. Approach speeds of under 100 mph (160 kmh) have been made practicable by this equipment.

The 367-80B is also fitted currently with a computer and power-operated controls of such a type that it can be used as a variable-stability aircraft. It was operated by NASA in December 1964, to study low-speed flight problems of large passenger jet transports, and during mid-1965 to duplicate configurations of supersonic transports as programmed by NASA. Soft-field landing gear was fitted subsequently in connection with the Boeing 747 development programme, but has now been removed.

In 1968, the 367-80 completed a lengthy study for NASA of a direct-lift control system (DLC), which could make possible steeper landing approaches in order to reduce noise at airports.

This aircraft is being used currently for the development of an automatic landing system offering increased confidence to the pilot, and of a monitor system independent of ILS, termed Independent Landing Monitor (ILM).

707-020. Alternative designation for Model 720 (which see).

707-120. First production version. Intended primarily for continental use, but capable of full-load over-ocean operation on many routes. Four Pratt & Whitney JT3C-6 turbojet engines (each 13,500 lb=6,124 kg st). Longer fuselage

than prototype. Fuselage width increased by 16 in (0·41 m) to 12 ft 4 in (3·76 m). Accommodation for up to 181 passengers. First production aircraft, a 707-121 for Pan American World Airways, flew for the first time on 20 December 1957 and made the first US commercial jet flight on 26 October 1958. FAA Type Approval received 23 September 1958. Production completed.

The 707-138 for Qantas was the only version of the 707-120 with the optional shorter fuselage (134 ft 6 in=41·00 m) and received FAA Type Approval on 24 June 1959. Production completed.

707-120B. Development of 707-120, with four 17,000 lb (7,718 kg) st Pratt & Whitney JT3D-1 or 18,000 lb (8,165 kg) st JT3D-3 turbofan engines and design improvements incorporated originally in the Boeing 720. These include a new inboard wing leading-edge and four additional segments of leading-edge flaps, which lessen runway requirements and raise the max cruising speed to Mach 0·91. First 707-120B flew for the first time on 22 June 1960. FAA Type Approval was received on 1 March 1961.

The 707-138B for Qantas was the only model with the optional shorter fuselage (see 707-138 above). It first flew in July 1961 and received FAA Type Approval on 24 July 1961. Production completed.

707-220. Airframe and accommodation identical with those of 707-120 but powered by four Pratt & Whitney JT4A-3 engines (each 15,800 lb

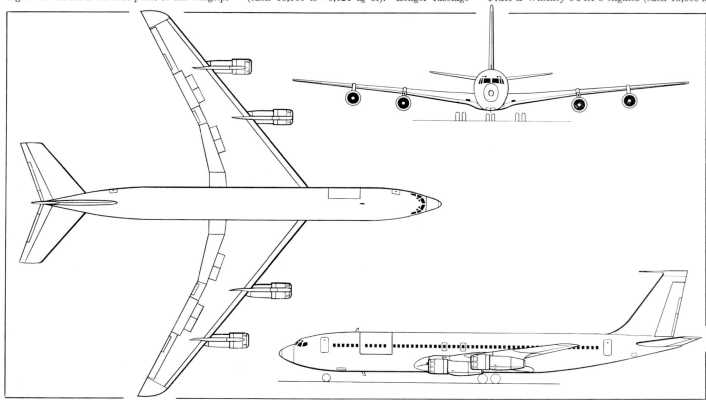

Boeing 707-320C four-turbofan passenger/cargo transport

Boeing Model 707-311C (four Pratt & Whitney JT3D-3B turbofan engines) in service with Wardair

=7,167 kg st). Received FAA Type Approval on 5 November 1959. Production completed.

707-320 Intercontinental. Long-range over-ocean version with increased wing span and longer fuselage. Four Pratt & Whitney JT4A-3 or -5 (each 15,800 lb=7,167 kg st), or JT4A-9 (each 16,800 lb=7,620 kg st), or JT4A-11 (each 17,500 lb=7,945 kg st) turbojet engines. Accommodation for up to 189 passengers. The 16th production 707 was the first 707-320 and flew for the first time on 11 January 1959. Received FAA Type Approval on 15 July 1959. Production completed.

707-320B Intercontinental. Development of 707-320 with four Pratt & Whitney JT3D-3 or -3B turbofan engines (each 18,000 lb = 8,165 kg st), fitted with double thrust reversers. New leading and trailing-edge flaps, low-drag wing-tips and other refinements. First 707-320B flew on 31 January 1962. FAA Type Approval received on 31 May 1962, and the type entered service with Pan American in June 1962.

707-320C Convertible. Cargo or mixed cargo-passenger version of 707-320B with 91 in × 134 in (2·31 m × 3·4 m) forward cargo door and Boeing-developed cargo loading system, using pallets or containers. Cargo space comprises 7,415 cu ft (210 m²) on full upper deck and 1,700 cu ft (48 m²) in two lower-deck holds. Accommodation for up to 215 passengers. Received FAA Type Approval on 30 April 1963, and first entered service with Pan American in June 1963.

707-320C Freighter. All-cargo version of the Convertible. Passenger facilities eliminated, increasing payload by 2,736 lb (1,241 kg). The full upper deck will accommodate 7,612 cu ft (215·5 m²) of cargo, and 1,770 cu ft (50 m²) can be loaded on two lower decks. The cargo system can carry thirteen 88 in × 125 in (2·24 m × 3·68 m) or 88 in × 108 in (2·24 m × 2·74 m) "A" Type containers. There is a crew rest area aft of the flight deck.

707-420 Intercontinental. As 707-320 but powered by four Rolls-Royce Conway Mk 508 turbofan engines (each 17,500 lb=7,945 kg st). Received FAA Type Approval 12 February 1960. Production completed.

VC-137A. Three Model 707-120's delivered to USAF for use by VIP personnel. Same as 707-120, except for interior furnishing and electronic equipment installed. Forward area of cabin contains communications centre, galley, toilet and 8-seat compartment. Centre portion is designed as an airborne HQ, with conference table, swivel chairs, projection screen for films and two convertible sofa/bunks. Aft cabin contains 14 double reclining passenger seats, two tables, three galleys, two toilets and closets. First VC-137A flew for the first time on 7 April 1959. All three have since been re-engined with JT3D turbofans and are now designated VC-137B.

VC-137B. This is the current designation of the three USAF VC-137A's following their conversion to turbofan power. They continue in service with the 89th Military Airlift Wing of Military Airlift Command, carrying a crew of seven or eight and 40 passengers. Max T-O weight 258,000 lb (117,025 kg).

VC-137C. One 707-320B, with JT3D-3 turbofan engines and internal furnishing similar to VC-137B. Crew of seven or eight and 49 passengers. Delivered to Special Air Missions Squadron of the USAF Military Airlift Command, but now with 89th Military Airlift Wing. Used to carry government officials, including the President, and visiting dignitaries of foreign countries. Max T-O weight 322,000 lb (146,055 kg).

The following orders for the Boeing 707 have been announced:—

Model 707-120

Continental Air Lines	5	707-124
TWA	15	707-131

Model 707-120B

Pan American	6**	707-121B
American Airlines	56†	707-123B
TWA	41	707-131B
Qantas	13*	707-138B
Pan American	2**	707-139B
USAF	3***	707-153B
		(VC-137B)

Model 707-220

Braniff	5°	707-227

Model 707-320

Pan American	26	707-321
Air France	21	707-328
Sabena	7	707-329
TWA	12	707-331
South African Airways	3	707-344

Model 707-320B

Malaysia-Singapore Airlines	3	707-312B
Pan American	60	707-321B
American Airlines	10	707-323B
Air France	8	707-328B
Lufthansa	12	707-330B
TWA	38	707-331B
BOAC	2	707-336B
Air India	3	707-337B
South African	2	707-344B
Northwest Orient	10	707-351B
USAF	1	707-353B
		(VC-137C)
El Al	3	707-358B
Avianca (Colombia)	2	707-359B
TAP (Portugal)	7	707-382B
Olympic Airways	2	707-384B
Aerolineas Argentinas	4	707-387B

Model 707-320C

Federal Republic of Germany	4	707-307C
China Air	2	707-309C
Wardair	2	707-311C
Pan American	34	707-321C
American Airlines	37	707-323C
Continental	13	707-324C
Braniff	9	707-327C
Air France	9	707-328C
Sabena	7	707-329C
Lufthansa	5	707-330C
TWA	17	707-331C
BOAC	7	707-336C
Air-India	2	707-337C
Qantas	21	707-338C
Pakistan International	4	707-340C
VARIG	6	707-341C
South African Airways	5	707-344C
Seaboard World Airlines	2	707-345C
Western Air Lines	5	707-347C
Canadian Armed Forces	4	707-347C
Irish International	4	707-348C
Flying Tiger	4°	707-349C
Northwest Orient	26	707-351C
Executive Jet Aviation	2	707-355C
El Al	2	707-358C
Ethiopian	2	707-360C
British Eagle	1	707-365C
United Arab Airlines	4	707-366C
Saudi Arabian Airlines	2	707-368C
Kuwait Airways	3	707-369C
Airlift International	3	707-372C
World Airways	9	707-373C
Olympic Airways	4	707-384C
LAN-Chile	1	707-385C
Iran National Airlines	2	707-386C
Aerolineas Argentinas	2	707-387C
Caledonian Airways	2	707-399C
Middle East Airlines	4	707-3B4C

Model 707-420

Lufthansa	5	707-430
BOAC	19****	707-436
Air-India	6	707-437
VARIG	3	707-441
El Al	3	707-458
Cunard-Eagle	1§	707-465

† 25 converted from Model 707-123 by fitting turbofans.

* 7 converted from Model 707-138 by fitting turbofans.

** Converted from Models 707-121 and 707-139 by fitting turbofans.

*** Converted from Model 707-153 by fitting turbofans.

**** Includes one delivered originally to Cunard Eagle.

§ Second aircraft ordered but delivered direct to BOAC.

° One destroyed prior to delivery

The following description applies in general to all models of the Boeing 707:—

TYPE: Four-engined jet airliner.

WINGS: Cantilever low-wing monoplane. Dihedral 7°. Incidence 2°. Sweepback at quarter-chord 35°. All-metal two-spar fail-safe structure. Centre-section continuous through fuselage. Normal outboard aileron and small inboard aileron on each wing, built of aluminium honeycomb panels. Two Fowler flaps and one split fillet flap of aluminium alloy construction on each wing. Two-segment hydraulically-operated leading-edge flap inboard of outer engine pylon on each wing of 707-120, -220, -320, -420. Full-span leading-edge flaps on 707-120B, -320B and -320C. Two hydraulically-operated aluminium alloy spoilers on each wing, forward of ailerons. Primary flying controls are aerodynamically balanced and manually - operated through spring - tabs. Lateral control at low speeds by all four ailerons, supplemented by spoilers which are interconnected with the ailerons. Lateral control at high speeds by inboard ailerons and spoilers only. Operation of flaps adjusts linkage between inboard and outboard ailerons to permit outboard operation only with extended flaps. Spoilers may also be used symmetrically as speed brakes. Thermal anti-icing of wing leading-edges.

FUSELAGE: All-metal semi-monocoque fail-safe structure with cross-section made up of two circular arcs of different radii, the larger above, faired into smooth-contoured ellipse.

TAIL UNIT: Cantilever all-metal structure. Anti-balance tab and trim-tab in rudder. Trim and control tabs in each elevator. Electrically and manually operated variable-incidence tailplane. Powered rudder. Small ventral fin (except on 707-320B and C).

LANDING GEAR: Hydraulically-retractable tricycle type. Main units are four-wheel bogies which retract inward into underside of thickened wing-root and fuselage. Dual nose-wheel unit retracts forward into fuselage. Landing gear doors close when legs fully extended. Gear can be extended in flight to give maximum rate of descent of 15,000 ft/min (4,570 m/min) when used in conjunction with spoilers. Boeing oleo-pneumatic shock-absorbers. Main wheels and tyres size 46 × 16. Nose-wheels and tyres size 39 × 13. Tyre pressures (707-120, -120B): main wheels 135 lb/sq in (9·50 kg/cm²), nose-wheels 90 lb/sq in (6·33 kg/cm²). Tyre pressures (707-220): main wheels 160 lb/sq in (11·25 kg/cm²), nose-wheels 90 lb/sq in (6·33 kg/cm²). Tyre pressures (707-320, -420): main wheels 160 lb/sq in (11·25 kg/cm²), nose-wheels 115 lb/sq in (8·10 kg/cm²). Tyre pressures (707-320B): main wheels 170 lb/sq in (11·95 kg/cm²), nose-wheels

115 lb/sq in (8·10 kg/cm²). Tyre pressures (707-320C): main wheels 180 lb/sq in (12·66 kg/cm²), nose-wheels 115 lb/sq in (8·10 kg/cm²). Multi-disc brakes by Bendix on 707-120, -120B, -220, by Goodrich on 707-320, -320B, -420, and by Goodyear on 707-320C. Hydro-air flywheel detector type anti-skid units.

POWER PLANT: Four turbojet or turbofan engines mounted in pods under wings (details under "series" descriptions). Fuel in four main, two reserve and one centre main integral wing tanks. Total fuel capacity varies with individual model, but max standard capacities given by Boeing are: 707-120, -220 13,478 US gallons (51,020 litres); 707-120B 17,334 US gallons (65,616 litres); 707-320, -320B, -320C, -420 23,855 US gallons (90,299 litres). Provision for both pressure and gravity refuelling. Total oil capacity; 707-120, -120B, -220 24 US gallons (91 litres); 707-320, -420 48 US gallons (182 litres); 707-320B, -320C 30 US gallons (114 litres).

ACCOMMODATION (707-120, -120B, -220): Flight compartment seats pilot and co-pilot side-by-side, with stations for flight engineer and navigator behind. Main cabin, free of structural obstructions, can seat up to 181 passengers in six-abreast economy configuration. Typical arrangement has 36 first-class and 95 coach class seats, with four galleys and four toilets. Two passenger doors, forward and aft on port side. Galley servicing doors forward and aft on starboard side. Baggage compartments fore and aft of wing in lower segment of fuselage below cabin floor. Entire accommodation, including baggage compartments, air-conditioned and pressurised.

ACCOMMODATION (707-320, -320B, -320C, -420): Basically as for 707-120. Max accommodation for 189 economy class passengers in all except 707-320C which can seat up to 215 passengers due to provision of two extra emergency exits aft of wing. Typical arrangement has 14 first-class seats, a 4-seat lounge and 133 coach class seats, with four galleys and five toilets.

SYSTEMS: Air-cycle vapour-cycle air-conditioning and pressurisation system, using three (two on -320C Freighter) AiResearch engine-driven turbo-compressors. Pressure differential 8·6 lb/sq in (0·60 kg/cm²). Hydraulic system, pressure 3,000 lb/sq in (210 kg/cm²), for landing gear retraction, nose-wheel steering, brakes, flaps, flying controls and spoilers. Electrical system includes four 30kVA or 40kVA 115/200V 3-phase 400 c/s AC alternators and four 75A transformer-rectifiers giving 28V DC. No APU.

ELECTRONICS AND EQUIPMENT: To customer's specification.

DIMENSIONS, EXTERNAL:

Wing span:	
120, 120B, 220	130 ft 10 in (39·87 m)
320, 420	142 ft 5 in (43·41 m)
320B, 320C	145 ft 9 in (44·42 m)
Wing chord at root:	
120, 220	28 ft 0 in (8·53 m)
120B	28 ft 2 in (8·58 m)
320, 320B, 320C, 420	33 ft 10·7 in (10·33 m)
Wing chord at tip:	9 ft 4 in (2·84 m)
Wing aspect ratio:	
120, 120B, 220	7·065
320, 320B, 320C, 420	7·056
Length overall:	
120, 220	144 ft 6 in (44·04 m)
120B	145 ft 1 in (44·22 m)
320, 320B, 320C, 420	152 ft 11 in (46·61 m)
Length of fuselage:	
120, 120B, 220	138 ft 10 in (42·31 m)
320, 320B, 320C, 420	145 ft 6 in (44·35 m)
Width of fuselage	12 ft 4 in (3·76 m)
Height overall:	
120, 120B, 220	42 ft 0 in (12·80 m)
320	41 ft 8 in (12·70 m)
320B, 320C, 420	42 ft 5 in (12·93 m)
Tailplane span:	
120, 220	39 ft 8 in (12·09 m)
120B	43 ft 4 in (13·21 m)
320, 320B, 320C, 420	45 ft 9 in (13·95 m)
Wheel track	22 ft 1 in (6·73 m)
Wheelbase:	
120, 120B, 220	52 ft 4 in (15·95 m)
320, 320B, 320C, 420	59 ft 0 in (17·98 m)
Passenger doors (each):	
Height	6 ft 0 in (1·83 m)
Width	2 ft 10 in (0·86 m)
Height to sill:	
fwd	10 ft 6 in (3·20 m)
aft	10 ft 8 in (3·25 m)
Cargo door (707-320C only):	
Height	7 ft 7 in (2·31 m)
Width	11 ft 2 in (3·40 m)
Height to sill	10 ft 6 in (3·20 m)
Forward baggage compartment door:	
Height	4 ft 2 in (1·27 m)
Width	4 ft 0 in (1·22 m)
Height to sill	5 ft 1 in (1·55 m)
Rear baggage compartment door (fwd):	
Height	4 ft 1 in (1·24 m)
Width	4 ft 0 in (1·22 m)
Height to sill	5 ft 3 in (1·60 m)
Rear baggage compartment door (aft):	
Height	2 ft 11 in (0·89 m)

Width	2 ft 6 in (0·76 m)
Height to sill	6 ft 5 in (1·96 m)

DIMENSIONS, INTERNAL:

Cabin, excluding flight deck:	
Length: 120, 120B, 220	104 ft 10 in (31·95 m)
320, 320B, 320C, 420	111 ft 6 in (33·99 m)
Max width	11 ft 8 in (3·55 m)
Max height	7 ft 7 in (2·31 m)
Floor area:	
120, 120B, 220	1,093 sq ft (101·54 m²)
320, 320B, 320C, 420	1,143 sq ft (106·18 m²)
Volume: 120, 120B, 220	7,484 cu ft (211·9 m³)
320, 320B, 420	7,983 cu ft (226 m³)
320C Convertible	8,074 cu ft (228·6 m³)
320C Freighter	9,470 cu ft (268 m³)
Baggage compartment (fwd):	
120	680 cu ft (19·25 m³)
120B, 220	755 cu ft (21·38 m³)
320, 320B, 420	870 cu ft (24·65 m³)
320C Convertible	835 cu ft (23·65 m³)
320C Freighter	865 cu ft (24·50 m³)
Baggage compartment (rear):	
120, 120B, 220	910 cu ft (25·75 m³)
320, 320B, 420	905 cu ft (25·62 m³)
320C Convertible	865 cu ft (24·50 m³)
320C Freighter	905 cu ft (25·62 m³)

AREAS:

Wings, gross:	
120, 220	2,433 sq ft (226·04 m²)
120B	2,521 sq ft (234·2 m²)
320, 420	2,892 sq ft (268·68 m²)
320B, 320C	3,010 sq ft (279·64 m²)
Ailerons (total):	
120, 120B, 220	120 sq ft (11·15 m²)
320, 320B, 320C, 420	121 sq ft (11·24 m²)
Trailing-edge flaps (total):	
120, 120B, 220	362 sq ft (33·63 m²)
320, 420	436 sq ft (40·51 m²)
320B, 320C	476 sq ft (44·22 m²)
Leading-edge flaps:	
120, 220, 320, 420	27 sq ft (2·51 m²)
120B	38 sq ft (3·53 m²)
320B, 320C	154 sq ft (14·31 m²)
Fin	328 sq ft (30·47 m²)
Rudder, including tabs	102 sq ft (9·48 m²)
Tailplane:	
120, 220	500 sq ft (46·45 m²)
120B	545 sq ft (50·63 m²)
320, 320B, 320C, 420	625 sq ft (58·06 m²)
Elevators, including tabs:	
120, 120B, 220	118 sq ft (10·95 m²)
320, 320B, 320C, 420	151 sq ft (14·03 m²)

WEIGHTS AND LOADINGS:

Basic operating weight, empty:	
120	118,000 lb (53,520 kg)
120B	123,151 lb (55,861 kg)
220	122,000 lb (55,340 kg)
320	135,000 lb (61,235 kg)
320B	138,385 lb (62,771 kg)
320B (optional)	140,524 lb (63,740 kg)
320C (Passenger)	138,323 lb (62,742 kg)
320C Freighter	133,119 lb (60,381 kg)
420	133,000 lb (60,330 kg)
Max payload:	
120	52,000 lb (23,590 kg)
120B	46,849 lb (21,250 kg)
220	48,000 lb (21,770 kg)
320	55,000 lb (24,950 kg)
320B	51,615 lb (23,413 kg)
320B (optional)	54,476 lb (24,709 kg)
320C Convertible	83,996 lb (38,099 kg)
320C Freighter	91,839 lb (41,657 kg)
420	57,000 lb (25,855 kg)
Max T-O weight:	
120, 120B	257,000 lb (116,575 kg)
220	247,000 lb (112,037 kg)
320, 420	312,000 lb (141,520 kg)
320B	327,000 lb (148,325 kg)
320B (optional)	333,600 lb (151,315 kg)
320C Freighter	332,000 lb (150,590 kg)
Max ramp weight:	
120, 120B	258,000 lb (117,025 kg)
220	248,000 lb (112,490 kg)
320, 420	316,000 lb (143,335 kg)
320B	328,000 lb (148,780 kg)
320B (optional)	336,000 lb (152,405 kg)
320C Freighter	336,000 lb (152,405 kg)
Max zero-fuel weight:	
120, 120B, 220	170,000 lb (77,110 kg)
320, 320B, 420	190,000 lb (86,180 kg)
320C	230,000 lb (104,330 kg)
Max landing weight:	
120, 120B	190,000 lb (86,180 kg)
220	185,000 lb (83,915 kg)
320, 320B, 420	207,000 lb (93,895 kg)
320B (optional)	215,000 lb (97,520 kg)
320C	247,000 lb (112,037 kg)
Max wing loading:	
120	105·6 lb/sq ft (515·5 kg/m²)
120B	101·9 lb/sq ft (497·5 kg/m²)
220	101·5 lb/sq ft (495·6 kg/m²)
320, 420	107·9 lb/sq ft (526·8 kg/m²)
320B	108·6 lb/sq ft (530·2 kg/m²)
320C	110·0 lb/sq ft (537·1 kg/m²)
Max power loading:	
120	4·76 lb/lb st (4·76 kg/kg st)
120B	3·57 lb/lb st (3·57 kg/kg st)
220	3·91 lb/lb st (3·91 kg/kg st)
320, 420	4·46 lb/lb st (4·46 kg/kg st)
320B	4·54 lb/lb st (4·54 kg/kg st)
320C	4·59 lb/lb st (4·59 kg/kg st)

PERFORMANCE (at average cruising weight):

Max level speed:	
120, 220, 320, 420	541 knots (623 mph; 1,002 km/h)
120B, 320B, 320C	545 knots (627 mph; 1,010 km/h)
Max permissible diving speed	Mach 0·95
Max cruising speed at 25,000 ft (7,620 m):	
120	496 knots (571 mph; 919 km/h)
120B	537 knots (618 mph; 995 km/h)
220, 320	523 knots (602 mph; 969 km/h)
320B, 320C	521 knots (600 mph; 966 km/h)
420	515 knots (593 mph; 954 km/h)
Econ cruising speed:	
120	477 knots (549 mph; 884 km/h)
120B	484 knots (557 mph; 897 km/h)
220	467 knots (538 mph; 865 km/h)
320	473 knots (545 mph; 876 km/h)
320B, 320C	478 knots (550 mph; 886 km/h)
420	461 knots (531 mph; 854 km/h)
Stalling speed (flaps down, at max landing weight):	
120, 220	112 knots (128 mph; 206 km/h)
120B	107 knots (123 mph; 198 km/h)
320, 420	110 knots (126 mph; 203 km/h)
320B	97 knots (111 mph; 179 km/h)
320C	105 knots (121 mph; 195 km/h)
Rate of climb at S/L:	
120	2,400 ft (731 m)/min
120B	5,050 ft (1,539 m)/min
220	4,300 ft (1,310 m)/min
320	3,500 ft (1,067 m)/min
320B	3,550 ft (1,082 m)/min
320C	2,940 ft (896 m)/min
420	2,900 ft (884 m)/min
Service ceiling:	
120	37,500 ft (11,430 m)
120B, 220, 320, 320B, 420	42,000 ft (12,800 m)
320C	38,500 ft (11,735 m)
CAR T-O to 35 ft (10·7 m):	
120	10,550 ft (3,215 m)
120B	7,450 ft (2,270 m)
220	8,220 ft (2,505 m)
320, 420	10,650 ft (3,245 m)
320B	10,350 ft (3,155 m)
320C	10,620 ft (3,240 m)
CAR landing from 50 ft (15 m):	
120	6,320 ft (1,925 m)
120B	6,550 ft (1,995 m)
220	6,230 ft (1,900 m)
320, 420	7,280 ft (2,220 m)
320B	5,930 ft (1,807 m)
320C	6,250 ft (1,905 m)
Landing run:	
120	2,760 ft (840 m)
120B	3,035 ft (925 m)
220	2,825 ft (860 m)
320, 420	2,990 ft (910 m)
320B	2,455 ft (750 m)
320C	2,575 ft (785 m)
Range with max fuel, allowances for climb and descent, no reserves:	
120	4,038 nm (4,650 miles; 7,485 km)
120B	5,397 nm (6,215 miles; 10,002 km)
220	4,115 nm (4,739 miles; 7,626 km)
320	5,748 nm (6,620 miles; 10,654 km)
320B	6,608 nm (7,610 miles; 12,250 km)
320C	6,521 nm (7,510 miles; 12,086 km)
420	5,848 nm (6,735 miles; 10,840 km)
Range with max payload, allowances for climb and descent, no reserves:	
120	2,793 nm (3,217 miles; 5,177 km)
120B	3,677 nm (4,235 miles; 6,820 km)
220	2,831 nm (3,260 miles; 5,245 km)
320	4,154 nm (4,784 miles; 7,700 km)
320B	5,349 nm (6,160 miles; 9,915 km)
320C	3,408 nm (3,925 miles; 6,317 km)
420	4,224 nm (4,865 miles; 7,830 km)

BOEING MODEL 720

Production of the Boeing 720 intermediate-range member of the Boeing four-jet transport family has now ended.

Although a completely different design from the weight and structural strength standpoints, the 720 is almost identical to the 707-120 in external outline and main dimensions, aerodynamic design and control systems. This made possible the use of 707 passenger cabin interiors, flight deck, systems components and most 707 interchangeable and replaceable parts and spares.

The most important aerodynamic change compared with the 707-120 was a refinement to the wing leading-edge, which increased the angle of sweepback and decreased the thickness/chord ratio, with consequent improvement in take off performance and cruising speed. These modifications were incorporated subsequently on the Boeing 707-120B.

Major weight saving was achieved by lightening the structure to the extent made possible by reducing the standard fuel load.

There were two versions, as follows:

720. Basic model, powered by four Pratt & Whitney JT3C-7 (each 12,500 lb=5,670 kg st) or JT3C-12 (each 13,000 lb=5,902 kg st) turbojets. The first 720 flew on November 23, 1959. FAA Type Approval received on June 30, 1960, and the type entered service with United Air Lines on July 5, 1960.

720B. Developed version, powered by four Pratt & Whitney JT3D-1 (each 17,000 lb=7,710

Boeing Model 727-17 three-turbofan commercial transport aircraft in the insignia of CP Air

Boeing Model 727-81 (three Pratt & Whitney JT8D-7 turbofan engines) in the insignia of All Nippon Airways

kg st) or JT3D-3 (each 18,000 lb = 8,165 kg st) turbofan engines. First 720B flew on 6 October 1960. FAA Type Approval received on 3 March 1961.

Full details of the Model 720 may be found in the 1968/69 *Jane's*.

BOEING MODEL 727

On 5 December 1960, Boeing announced its intention to produce a short/medium-range jet transport designated Boeing 727. Design work had been under way since June 1959 and component manufacture had been started in October 1960.

Simultaneously with the Boeing announcement, Eastern and United Air Lines each signed agreements to purchase 727's.

A major innovation, compared with this company's earlier designs, was the choice of a rear-engined layout, with two Pratt & Whitney JT8D engines mounted on the sides of the rear fuselage and a third at the base of the T-tail assembly.

In other respects the 727 bears a resemblence to the 707 and 720 series. It has an identical upper fuselage section and many parts and systems are interchangeable between the three types.

On 22 April 1969 Boeing announced that a 727-200 delivered to TWA was the 1,500th jet-powered airliner produced by the company at its Renton, Washington, factory.

Four versions of the Model 727 are currently available, as follows:

727-100. Standard transport for up to 131 passengers. Three JT8D-7 turbofans, each flat-rated at 14,000 lb (6,350 kg) st to 84° F are standard, with JT8D-9s flat-rated at 14,500 lb (6,577 kg) st optional. AUW of basic model is 142,000 lb (64,410 kg), but 727-100 is available with AUW of 152,000 lb (68,947 kg), 160,000 lb (72,570 kg) and 169,000 lb (76,655 kg).

727-100C. Convertible cargo-passenger version, with standard AUW of 160,000 lb (72,570 kg) and optional AUW of 169,000 lb (76,655 kg). Announced on 22 July 1964. Identical with 727-100 except for installation of heavier flooring and floor beams and same large cargo door as on Boeing 707-320C. Effective opening is 7 ft 2 in (2·18 m) high by 11 ft 2 in (3·40 m) wide, and 727-100C is able to utilise same cargo pallets and handling system as 707-320C. Galleys and seats quickly removable and hatracks stowable, permitting conversion for mixed passenger/cargo or all-cargo services in under two hours. Typical

payloads are 94 mixed-class passengers; 52 passengers and baggage, plus 22,700 lb (10,295 kg) of cargo on four pallets; or 38,000 lb (17,236 kg) of cargo on eight pallets. The full eight-pallet payload can be carried more than 1,700 miles (2,737 km). A 30,000 lb (13,605 kg) payload can be carried 2,300 miles (3,700 km).

727-100QC. Same as 727-100C, except that, by using palletized passenger seats and galleys, and advanced cargo loading techniques, complete conversion from all-passenger to all-cargo configuration can be made in less than half an hour. All-cargo, high-AUW version has ramp weight of 170,000 lb (77,110 kg), max T-O weight of 169,000 lb (76,655 kg) and max landing weight of 142,500 lb (64,640 kg).

727-200. "Stretched" version announced on 5 August 1965 with basic accommodation for 163 passengers and maximum capacity of 189 passengers. Fuselage extended by 10 ft (3·05 m) both forward and aft of main undercarriage wheel well. Structural modification corresponding to higher loads. Revised centre engine air intake. Three JT8D-7 turbofans, each flat rated at 14,000 lb (6,350 kg) st to 84°F, are standard. Optionally, JT8D-9's, rated at 14,500 lb (6,577 kg) st or JT8D-11s rated at 15,000 lb (6,804 kg) st can be fitted. Construction began in September 1966 and the first flight was made on 27 July 1967. FAA Certification was awarded on 30 November 1967.

The following orders for the 727 series had been announced by 30 April 1970:

Icelandair	1	727-08C
China Air	2	727-09
China Air	1	727-09C
Wardair	1	727-11
Ariana	2	727-113C
Pacific Southwest	8	727-14
Pacific Southwest	21	727-214
LAN-Chile	2	727-16
LAN-Chile	2	727-16C
CP Air	4	727-17
Pan American	21	727-21
Pan American	6	727-21QC
Piedmont	1	727-22
United Air Lines	88*	727-22
United Air Lines	38†	727-22QC
United Air Lines	28	727-222
American Airlines	58	727-23
American Airlines	41	727-223
Continental	1	727-24C
Continental	19	727-224
Eastern Air Lines	50	727-25

Eastern Air Lines	25	727-25QC
Eastern Air Lines	26	727-225
Braniff	7	727-27
Braniff	18	727-27QC
Braniff	3	727-227
Air France	17	727-228
Sabena	2	727-29
Sabena	3	727-29QC
Lufthansa	16	727-30
Lufthansa	2	727-230
Lufthansa	11	727-30QC
TWA	27	727-31
TWA	8	727-31QC
TWA	35	727-231
Transair (Sweden)	2	727-34
Transair (Sweden)	1	727-34C
National Airlines	13	727-35
National Airlines	25	727-235
South African Airways	6	727-44
South African Airways	3	727-44C/QC
Japan Air Lines	12	727-46
Western Air Lines	6	727-247
Northwest Orient Airlines	20	727-51
Northwest Orient Airlines	12	727-51C
Northwest Orient Airlines	24	727-251
Executive Jet Aviation	2	727-55C
Avianca (Colombia)	4	727-59
FAA	1	727-61
Faucett	1	727-61
Trans International	2	727-71C
Airlift International	4	727-72C
World Airways	6	727-73QC
Mexicana	3	727-74
Mexicana	3	727-274
Trans-Australia Airlines	6	727-76
Ansett-ANA	4	727-77
Ansett-ANA	2	727-77C
BWIA	3	727-78
All Nippon Airways	8	727-81
TAP (Portugal)	3	727-82
TAP (Portugal)	2	727-82C
Olympic Airways	5	727-284
American Flyers	2	727-85C
Iran Air	4	727-86
Japan Domestic	2	727-89
Alaska Airlines	3	727-90C
Frontier Airlines	4	727-91
Frontier Airlines	3	727-291
Air Asia (CAT)	2	727-92C
Southern Air Transport	1	727-92C
Pacific Air Lines	1	727-93
Air West	2	727-193
GATX-Armco-Boothe	6	727-293
Northeast Airlines	8	727-95
Northeast Airlines	11	727-295

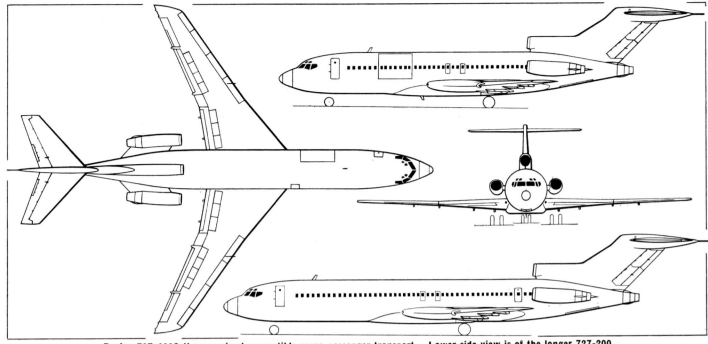

Boeing 727-100C three-engined convertible cargo-passenger transport. Lower side view is of the longer 727-200

LAB-Bolivia	1	727-1AO
Trans Caribbean	1	727-1A7C
Royal Air Moroc	1	727-2B6
Allegheny	2	727-2B7
Air Algerie	2	727-2D6
Cruzeiro do Sul	3	727-100

† Includes 15 leased from Boeing
* Includes 13 leased from Boeing
** Includes 1 leased from Boeing
° Leased from Boeing

The first 727-100, a production model, flew for the first time on 9 February 1963; the second followed on 12 March 1963 and four aircraft were used for an intensive 1,100-hour test flying programme that led to FAA certification of the 727-100 on 24 December 1963. Deliveries for airline crew training had begun two months earlier, under a provisional Type Certificate, and scheduled services with 727's were started by Eastern Air Lines on 1 February 1964, followed five days later by United Air Lines. The 727-100C received type approval on 13 January 1966.

From a total of 837 727s on order, 799 had been delivered by 30 June 1970.

TYPE: Three-engined jet airliner.

WINGS (727-100): Cantilever low-wing monoplane. Special Boeing aerofoil sections. Thickness/chord ratio from 9% to 13%. Dihedral 3°. Incidence 2°. Sweepback at quarter-chord 32°. Primary structure is a two-spar aluminium alloy box with conventional ribs. Upper and lower surfaces are of riveted skin-stringer construction. There are no chordwise splices in the primary structure from the fuselage to the wingtip. Structure is fail-safe. Hydraulically-powered aluminium ailerons, in inboard (high speed) and outboard (low speed) units, operate in conjunction with flight spoilers. Triple-slotted trailing-edge flaps constructed primarily of aluminium and aluminium honeycomb. Four aluminium leading-edge slats on outer two-thirds of wing. Three Krueger leading-edge flaps on inboard third of wing, made from magnesium or aluminium castings. Seven aluminium (plus some magnesium) spoilers on each wing, consisting of five flight spoilers outboard and two ground spoilers inboard. Spoilers function also as airbrakes. Balance tab on each outboard aileron; control tab on each inboard aileron. Controls are hydraulically-powered dual systems with automatic reversion to manual control. Actuators manufactured primarily by Weston, National Water Lift and Bertea. Thermal anti-icing of wing leading-edges by engine-bleed air.

WINGS (727-200): Same as 727-100, except for modified trailing-edge flap support structure and redesigned wing-to-fuselage fairing.

FUSELAGE: Semi-monocoque fail-safe structure, with aluminium alloy skin reinforced by circumferential frames and longitudinal stringers.

TAIL UNIT: Cantilever structure, built primarily of aluminium alloys, with tailplane mounted near tip of fin. Dual-powered variable-incidence tailplane, with direct manual reversion. Hydraulically-powered dual elevator control system with control tab manual reversion. Hydraulically-powered rudders, utilising two main systems with back-up third system for lower rudder. Anti-balance tabs; rudder trim by displacing system neutral.

LANDING GEAR: Hydraulically-retractable tricycle type, with twin wheels on all three units. Nose-wheels retract forward, main gear inward into fuselage. Boeing oleo-pneumatic shock-absorbers. B.F. Goodrich nose-gear wheels, tyres and brakes are standard on all models. Goodrich main-gear wheels, tyres and brakes are standard on the 727-100 and 727-100C. Bendix main-gear wheels, tyres and brakes are standard on the 727-200. Goodrich and Bendix are both approved suppliers of main-gear wheels, tyres and brakes for all Model 727s. Nose-wheels and tyres are size 32 × 11·5 Type VIII. Main gear wheels and tyres size 49 × 17 Type VII are standard on all models, with Goodrich size 50 × 20 optional on the 727-100 and -100C.

POWER PLANT: Three Pratt & Whitney JT8D turbofan engines (details under individual model listings) with thrust reversers. Each has individual fuel system fed from integral tanks in wings, but all three tanks are interconnected. Standard total fuel capacity 7,174 US gallons (27,158 litres): optional capacity 7,680 US gallons (29,070 litres) or 7,980 US gallons (30,207 litres). Fuelling point near leading-edge on underside of starboard wing at midspan. Total usable oil capacity 12 US gallons (45·5 litres).

ACCOMMODATION (727-100): Crew of three on flight deck. Max accommodation for 131 passengers in six-abreast seats. Basic 94-passenger layout has 28 first-class passengers, four-abreast, in forward cabin and 66 tourist passengers six-abreast in rear cabin, two central galleys and wardrobes, toilets at front (one) and rear (two). Other layouts to customer's specification. Entry via hydraulically-operated integral aft stairway under centre engine and door at front on port side with optional Weber Aircraft electrically-operated airstairs. Two heated and pressurised baggage and freight compartments under floor, forward and aft of main landing gear bay.

ACCOMMODATION (727-200): Crew of three on flight deck. Basic accommodation for 163 passengers, six-abreast. Max capacity 189 passengers. Two galleys forward and/or aft. One toilet forward and two aft. Other layouts to customer's specification. Passenger doors as on 727-100, except for two Type III emergency exits in mid-cabin on each side and aft service door on each side. Both fore and aft cargo compartments have one outward-opening cargo door; a second cargo door is optional for the aft compartment.

SYSTEMS: AiResearch air-conditioning and pressurisation system, using engine-bleed air combined with air-cycle refrigeration. Pressure differential 8·6 lb/sq in (0·60 kg/cm²). Three independent 3,000 lb/sq in (210 kg/cm²) hydraulic systems, utilising Boeing Material Specification BMS 3-11 hydraulic fluid, provide power for flying controls, landing gear and aft airstairs. Electrical system includes three 40 kVA 400 c/s constant-frequency AC generators, three 50A transformer-rectifier units, one 22Ah battery. Optional AiResearch APU provides electrical power and compressed air for engine starting, air-conditioning and electrical systems on ground.

ELECTRONICS AND EQUIPMENT (727-100): Standard equipment includes two ARINC 546 VHF

communications installations, Collins selcal, flight and service attendants interphone, passenger address system, ARINC 542 flight recorder with remote encoder, one ARINC 547 VHF navigation system with glideslope, two ARINC 550 ADF, two ARINC 521D DME, one ARINC 532D ATC, Collins marker beacon receiver, Bendix RDR-1E X-band weather radar, Sperry SP-50 Single-channel Mod. Blk. IV autopilot, two yaw dampers, two vertical gyros, two Sperry C-9D compasses, without latitude correction, ARINC 557 voice recorder, ARINC 552 radio altimeter, instrument comparison and warning system, central air data system, variable instrument switching and two Collins FD-108 flight directors (with glideslope gain programming). Optional equipment includes dual ARINC 540 and 543 Doppler, dual ARINC 552 radio altimeters, Loran, dual HF, third vertical gyro, third VHF navigation unit, third VHF transceiver, auto throttles, speed command, engine failure warning light and automatic bleed air shut-off, and Sperry SP-50 Mod Blk.IV autopilot with dual pitch channels, roll monitor and flare coupler.

ELECTRONICS AND EQUIPMENT (727-200): Essentially the same as for the Model 727-100.

DIMENSIONS, EXTERNAL:

Wing span	108 ft 0 in (32·92 m)
Wing chord at root	25 ft 3 in (7·70 m)
Wing chord at tip	7 ft 8 in (2·34 m)
Wing aspect ratio	7·67
Length overall:	
727-100	133 ft 2 in (40·59 m)
727-200	153 ft 2 in (46·69 m)
Length of fuselage:	
727-100	116 ft 2 in (35·41 m)
727-200	136 ft 2 in (41·51 m)
Height overall	34 ft 0 in (10·36 m)
Tailplane span	35 ft 9 in (10·90 m)
Wheel track	18 ft 9 in (5·72 m)
Wheelbase:	
727-100	53 ft 3 in (16·23 m)
727-200	63 ft 3 in (19·28 m)
Passenger door (ventral):	
Height	6 ft 4 in (1·93 m)
Width	2 ft 8 in (0·81 m)
Passenger door (fwd):	
Height	6 ft 0 in (1·83 m)
Width	2 ft 10 in (0·86 m)
Height to sill	8 ft 9 in (2·67 m)
Service door (727-200, each):	
Height	5 ft 0 in (1·52 m)
Width	2 ft 6 in (0·76 m)
Baggage hold door (727-100, each):	
Height	2 ft 11 in (0·89 m)
Width	4 ft 0 in (1·22 m)
Height to sill:	
fwd	4 ft 9 in (1·45 m)
aft	5 ft 2 in (1·57 m)
Baggage hold door (727-200, fwd):	
Height	3 ft 6 in (1·07 m)
Width	4 ft 6 in (1·37 m)
Baggage hold door (727-200, aft):	
Height	3 ft 8 in (1·12 m)
Width	4 ft 6 in (1·37 m)

DIMENSIONS, INTERNAL:
Cabin (aft of flight deck to rear pressure bulkhead):

Length:	
727-100	72 ft 8 in (22·15 m)
727-200	92 ft 8 in (28·24 m)
Max width	11 ft 8 in (3·55 m)
Max height	7 ft 2 in (2·18 m)

Floor area:
727-100   766 sq ft (71·17 m²)
727-200   980 sq ft (91·05 m²)
Volume:
727-100   5,174 cu ft (146·5 m³)
727-200   6,652 cu ft (188·4 m³)
Baggage hold (fwd):
727-100   425 cu ft (12·03 m³)
727-200   690 cu ft (19·54 m³)
Baggage hold (aft):
727-100   475 cu ft (13·45 m³)
727-200   760 cu ft (21·52 m³)

AREAS:
Wings, gross   1,700 sq ft (157·9 m²)
Ailerons (total)   57 sq ft (5·30 m²)
Trailing-edge flaps, retracted (total)
  281 sq ft (26·10 m²)
Trailing-edge flaps, extended (total)
  388 sq ft (36·04 m²)
Flight spoilers (total)   79·8 sq ft (7·41 m²)
Fin   356 sq ft (33·07 m²)
Rudder, including tabs   66 sq ft (6·13 m²)
Tailplane   376 sq ft (34·93 m²)
Elevators, including tabs   95 sq ft (8·83 m²)

WEIGHTS AND LOADINGS (A=AUW of 142,000 lb (64,410 kg); B=AUW of 152,000 lb (68,950 kg); C=AUW of 160,000 lb (72,575 kg); D=AUW of 169,000 lb (76,655 kg); E=AUW of 172,000 lb (78,015 kg); F=AUW of 175,000 lb (79,378 kg):
Operating weight empty (basic specification):
727-100 (A)   86,237 lb (39,116 kg)
727-100 (B)   86,598 lb (39,280 kg)
727-100 (C)   86,623 lb (39,291 kg)
727-100 (D)   86,719 lb (39,335 kg)
727-100C (C, D)   89,537 lb (40,613 kg)
727-200 (E, F)   94,757 lb (42,981 kg)
Operating weight empty (typical airline):
727-100 (A, B, C, D)   89,000 lb (40,370 kg)
727-100C (C, D, all-passenger configuration)   92,000 lb (41,730 kg)
727-100C (C, D, all-cargo configuration)   88,000 lb (39,916 kg)
727-200 (E, F)   98,000 lb (44,452 kg)
Max payload (structural, based on airline OWE):
727-100 (A)   22,000 lb (9,979 kg)
727-100 (B)   25,000 lb (11,340 kg)
727-100 (C)   29,000 lb (13,154 kg)
727-100 (D)   34,500 lb (15,649 kg)
727-100C (C, all-passenger configuration)   31,500 lb (14,288 kg)
727-100C (C, all-cargo configuration)   35,500 lb (16,102 kg)
727-100C (D, all-passenger configuration)   40,000 lb (18,144 kg)
727-100C (D, all-cargo configuration)   44,000 lb (19,958 kg)
727-200 (E)   38,000 lb (17,236 kg) or 40,000 lb (18,144 kg)
727-200 (F)   40,000 lb (18,144 kg)
Max T-O weight:
727-100 (A)   142,000 lb (64,410 kg)
727-100 (B)   152,000 lb (68,950 kg)
727-100 (C)   160,000 lb (72,575 kg)
727-100 (D)   169,000 lb (76,655 kg)
727-100C (C)   160,000 lb (72,575 kg)
727-100C (D)   169,000 lb (76,655 kg)
727-200 (E)   172,000 lb (78,015 kg)
727-200 (F)   175,000 lb (79,380 kg)
Max ramp weight:
727-100 (A)   143,000 lb (64,865 kg)
727-100 (B)   153,000 lb (69,400 kg)
727-100 (C)   161,000 lb (73,025 kg)
727-100 (D)   170,000 lb (77,110 kg)
727-100C (C)   161,000 lb (73,025 kg)
727-100C (D)   170,000 lb (77,110 kg)
727-200 (E)   173,000 lb (78,470 kg)
727-200 (F)   176,000 lb (79,830 kg)
Max zero-fuel weight:
727-100 (A)   111,000 lb (50,350 kg)
727-100 (B)   114,000 lb (51,710 kg)
727-100 (C)   118,000 lb (53,525 kg)
727-100 (D)   123,500 lb (56,020 kg)
727-100C (C)   123,500 lb (56,020 kg)
727-100C (D)   132,000 lb (59,875 kg)
727-200 (E)   136,000 lb (61,690 kg) or 138,000 lb (62,595 kg)
727-200 (F)   138,000 lb (62,595 kg)
Max landing weight:
727-100 (A, B)   135,000 lb (61,235 kg)
727-100 (C)   137,500 lb (62,370 kg) or 142,500 lb (64,635 kg)
727-100 (D)   142,500 lb (64,635 kg)
727-100C (C)   137,500 lb (62,370 kg) or 140,000 lb (63,505 kg) or 142,500 lb (64,635 kg)
727-100C (D)   142,500 lb (64,635 kg)
727-200 (E, F)   150,000 lb (68,040 kg)
Max wing loading:
727-100 (A)   83·5 lb/sq ft (407·7 kg/m²)
727-100 (B)   89·4 lb/sq ft (436·5 kg/m²)
727-100 (C)   94·1 lb/sq ft (459·4 kg/m²)
727-100 (D)   99·4 lb/sq ft (485·3 kg/m²)
727-100C (C)   94·1 lb/sq ft (459·4 kg/m²)
727-100C (D)   99·4 lb/sq ft (485·3 kg/m²)
727-200 (E)   101·2 lb/sq ft (494·1 kg/m²)
727-200 (F)   102·9 lb/sq ft (502·4 kg/m²)
Max power loading:
727-100 (A)   3·4 lb/lb st (3·4 kg/kg st)
727-100 (B)   3·6 lb/lb st (3·6 kg/kg st)
727-100 (C)   3·8 lb/lb st (3·8 kg/kg st)
727-100 (D)   4·0 lb/lb st (4·0 kg/kg st)

727-100C (C)   3·8 lb/lb st (3·8 kg/kg st)
727-100C (D)   4·0 lb/lb st (4·0 kg/kg st)
727-200 (E)   4·1 lb/lb st (4·1 kg/kg st)
727-200 (F)   4·2 lb/lb st (4·2 kg/kg st)

PERFORMANCE (727-100 and 727-100C at AUW of 160,000 lb = 72,575 kg and 727-200 at AUW of 172,000 lb = 78,015 kg, except where indicated):
Max level speed:
727-100, 727-200 at 21,600 ft (6,585 m)   547 knots (630 mph; 1,014 km/h)
Max permissible diving speed   Mach 0·95
Max cruising speed:
727-100 at 19,000 ft (5,800 m)   525 knots (605 mph; 974 km/h)
727-200 at 21,600 ft (6,585 m)   517 knots (595 mph; 958 km/h)
Econ cruising speed at 30,000 ft (9,150 m):
727-100   495 knots (570 mph; 917 km/h)
727-200   493 knots (568 mph; 914 km/h)
Stalling speed at S/L, flaps up:
727-100   156 knots (179 mph; 288 km/h)
727-200   164 knots (188 mph; 302 km/h)
Stalling speed at S/L, flaps down:
727-100   95 knots (109 mph; 176 km/h)
727-200 at AUW of 150,000 lb (68,040 kg)   102 knots (117 mph; 188 km/h)
Rate of climb at S/L:
727-100   3,150 ft (960 m)/min
727-200   2,600 ft (793 m)/min
Service ceiling:
727-100   37,400 ft (11,400 m)
727-200   35,200 ft (10,730 m)
T-O run:
727-100   4,980 ft (1,518 m)
727-200   5,820 ft (1,774 m)
CAR T-O distance to 35 ft (10·5 m):
727-100   7,450 ft (2,271 m)
727-200   8,000 ft (2,438 m)
CAR landing distance from 50 ft (15 m):
727-100 at AUW of 137,500 lb (62,370 kg)   4,700 ft (1,433 m)
727-200 at AUW of 150,000 lb (68,040 kg)   5,100 ft (1,554 m)
Landing run:
727-100 at AUW of 137,500 lb (62,370 kg)   1,900 ft (579 m)
727-200 at AUW of 150,000 lb (68,040 kg)   2,000 ft (610 m)
Range with max fuel:
727-100 at long-range cruising speed, with 7,980 US gallons (30,207 litres) fuel, ATA domestic reserves, AUW of 169,000 lb (76,655 kg) and payload of 19,000 lb (8,618 kg)   2,300 nm (2,650 miles; 4,265 km)
727-200 at long-range cruising speed, with 7,980 US gallons (30,207 litres) fuel, ATA domestic reserves, AUW of 175,000 lb (79,380 kg) and payload of 25,000 lb (11,340 kg)   1,867 nm (2,150 miles; 3,460 km)
Range with max payload:
727-100 at long-range cruising speed, ATA domestic reserves and AUW of 169,000 lb (76,655 kg)   1,650 nm (1,900 miles; 3,058 km)
727-200 at long-range cruising speed, ATA domestic reserves and AUW of 175,000 lb (79,380 kg)   1,120 nm (1,290 miles; 2,076 km)

BOEING MODEL 737

The decision to build this twin-jet short-range transport was announced by Boeing on 19 February 1965. Simultaneously, a first order for 21 aircraft was placed by Lufthansa.

Five versions are available, as follows:

737-100. To carry normally 103 passengers and baggage with 34″ pitch seating, or up to 115 passengers in 31″ pitch seating with no reduction in cabin facilities. JT8D-7 engines (each 14,000 lb = 6,350 kg st). Optionally JT8D-9 engines (each 14,500 lb = 6,575 kg st).

737-200. Generally similar to 737-100, but with fuselage lengthened by 6 ft 4 in (1·93 m). Accommodates normally 115 passengers and baggage with 34″ pitch seating, or up to 125 passengers in 31″ pitch seating with no reduction in cabin facilities. JT8D-9 engines standard; JT8D-7 engines optional.

737-200C. Convertible passenger/cargo version of 737-200.

737-200QC. Same as 737-200C, except that conversion is made much quicker by use of palletized passenger seats.

737-200 Business Jet. Version of the 737-200 with custom styled luxury interior. Additional fuel tankage in lower cargo compartment for extended range.

Continuous refinement of the Boeing 737 has led the Boeing Company to introduce a number of improvements in stages from 1969 to 1971. The first series of modifications to improve performance was made on the production line during 1969; the second series will come into effect in 1971 and further optional improvements will be offered at that time. The 1971 aircraft is identified as the **Advanced Model 737-200**.

The 1969 refinements were effective from the 135th production aircraft and were concerned with improving the specific range by decreasing drag, and improving the effectiveness of the thrust reversers. Target-type reversers replaced the earlier clam-shell type and this change was accompanied by a 45-in (1·14 m) aft extension of the engine pod, which helped to reduce drag. Small changes were made to the wing vortex

generators, and the sealing of the lower leading-edges of the flaps and slats, when retracted, was improved. In addition to being introduced on the production line, these modifications have been offered in kit form to operators of the first 134 aircraft, free of charge.

An additional change introduced on the production line at this time allows Model 737-200 aircraft to use an increased take-off flap setting of 25°, and strengthening of the flap tracks allows unrestricted use of a 40° setting for landing. Previously, Series 200 aircraft with landing weights of below 98,000 lb (44,450 kg) could not use this setting.

The three Advanced 737 versions are scheduled to become available from May 1971, to permit short-field operation. Similar to current 737-200 series aircraft, the Advanced 737s will have an improved high-lift system, comprising modified leading-edge slats, Krueger flaps and engine nacelle fairings, as well as better stopping capabilities which will include automatic brakes, a new anti-skid system and a revised metering pin in the main landing gear shock strut. In addition, new Pratt & Whitney JT8D-15 turbofan engines, rated at 15,500 lb (7,030 kg) st, are scheduled to become available in September 1971. Introduction of these improvements will allow the Advanced 737s to operate from airfields as short as 4,000 ft (1,220 m). The models are identified as follows:

Advanced 737-200. Basic model with max ramp weight of 110,000 lb (49,885 kg), with JT8D-7 turbofan engines as standard. JT8D-9 or JT8D-15 engines optional. Basic fuel capacity 2,861 US gallons (10,830 litres). Optional fuel capacity up to 4,232 US gallons (16,020 litres). Alternative high-weight model will have max ramp weight of 116,000 lb (52,605 kg), with JT8D-9 engines standard or JT8D-15 engines optional and basic fuel capacity of 4,783 US gallons (18,105 litres). Either model accommodates normally 115 passengers and baggage, with 34 in (86 cm) pitch seating, or up to 125 passengers in 31 in (79 cm) pitch seating with no reduction in cabin facilities.

Advanced 737-200C/QC. High gross weight convertible passenger/cargo model with strengthened fuselage and floor, and a large two-position upper deck cargo door, size 7 ft 2 in × 11 ft 2 in (2·18 m × 3·40 m). The quick-change (QC) feature will allow more rapid conversion by using palletised passenger seating and other special interior furnishings.

Advanced 737-200 Business Jet. Same as the high-weight model of the 737-200, except certain airline-type furnishings will not be installed to allow post-delivery installation of luxury interior to customer's requirements. Additional fuel capacity offered by installation of fuel cells in lower cargo compartments. With max fuel this model could carry 20 passengers up to 4,000 miles (6,437 km).

Orders announced by 30 June 1970 were as follows:

Model 737-100

Malaysia-Singapore Airlines	5	737-112
Lufthansa	22	737-130
Avianca (Colombia)	2	737-159

Model 737-200

Piedmont Airlines	12	737-201
Britannia Airways	6	737-204
Braathens	3	737-205
Malaysia-Singapore Airlines	1	737-212
Pacific Southwest	10	737-214
CP Air	7	737-217
NAC (New Zealand)	3	737-219
United Air Lines	75	737-222
South African Airways	6	737-244
Western Airlines	30	737-247
Irish International Airlines	5	737-248
Pacific Western	2	737-275
All Nippon	10	737-281
Aerolineas Argentinas	4	737-287
Frontier Airlines	5	737-291
Air California	2	737-293
GATX-Boothe*	15	737-293/2C0
Aloha	2	737-297
VASP	5	737-2A1
PLUNA	1	737-2A3
Business Jet	1	737-2A6
Indian Airlines	7	737-2A8
DETA	2	737-2B1
Air Madagascar	1	737-2B2
Eastern Provincial	2	737-2E1

Model 737-200C/QC

Wien Consolidated	4	737-202C/210C
Britannia Airways	2	737-204C
Lufthansa	6	737-230C
Nordair	3	737-242C
Irish International Airlines	3	737-248C
Pacific Western	1	737-275C
Aerolineas Argentinas	2	737-287C
Aloha	1	737-293C
Transair	2	737-2A9C

*Leased from Boeing

The Model 737 was designed to utilise many components and assemblies already in production for the Boeing 727. Design work began on 11 May 1964, and the first Model 737 flew for the

Boeing Model 737-2B1 twin-turbofan airliner in the insignia of the Mozambique airline DETA

first time on 9 April 1967. Deliveries began before the end of 1967, following FAA certification on 15 December, and 249 had been delivered by 30 June 1970.

Boeing has developed a gravel runway kit for the Model 737, and has obtained FAA Certification for operation of this aircraft from unpaved or gravel runways.

The kit comprises a vortex dissipator for each engine, a gravel deflection "ski" on the nose-wheel, deflectors between the main landing gear wheels, protective shields over hydraulic tubing and speed brake cable on the main gear strut, glass-fibre reinforcement of lower inboard flap surfaces, application of teflon-base paint to fuselage and wing undersurfaces and provision of more robust DME, ATC and VHF antennae and a retractable rotating beacon on the lower fuselage.

The kit includes a vortex dissipator for each engine, which consists of a short hollow boom protruding from under each engine's forward edge. The boom is capped by a plug with downward-facing orifices. Pressurised engine-bleed air forced through these orifices destroys any ground-level vortex and prevents small pieces of gravel being ingested by the engines.

TYPE: Twin-jet short-range transport.

WINGS: Cantilever low-wing monoplane. Special Boeing wing sections. Average thickness/chord ratio 12·89%. Dihedral 6°. Incidence 1° at root. Sweepback at quarter-chord 25°. Aluminium alloy dual-path fail-safe two-spar structure. Ailerons of aluminium honeycomb construction. Boeing-developed triple-slotted trailing-edge flaps, all of aluminium with trailing-edges of aluminium honeycomb. Aluminium alloy Krueger flaps on leading-edge, inboard of nacelles. Three leading-edge slats of aluminium alloy with aluminium honeycomb trailing-edge on each wing from engine to wing-tip.

Two-section aluminium honeycomb flight spoilers on each outer wing serve as both air-brakes in the air and for lateral control, in association with ailerons. Two section aluminium honeycomb ground spoilers on each wing inboard of engine, are used only during landing. Ailerons are hydraulically powered by two hydraulic systems with manual reversion. Trailing-edge flaps are hydraulically-powered, with electrical back-up. Leading-edge slats and Krueger flaps are symmetrically powered by two hydraulic systems each. Flight spoilers are symmetrically powered by the two main individual hydraulic systems. Engine bleed air for anti-icing supplied to engine nose cowls and all wing leading-edge slats.

FUSELAGE: Aluminium alloy semi-monocoque fail-safe structure.

TAIL UNIT: Cantilever aluminium alloy multi-spar structure. Variable-incidence tailplane. Elevator has dual hydraulic power, with manual reversion. Rudder is powered by a dual actuator from two main hydraulic systems, with a standby hydraulic actuator and system. Tailplane trim has dual electric drive motors, with manual back-up. Elevator control tabs for manual reversion are locked out during hydraulic actuation.

LANDING GEAR: Hydraulically-retractable tricycle type, with free-fall extension. Nose-wheels retract forward, main units inward. No main gear doors: wheels form wheel-well seal. Twin wheels on each main and nose unit. Boeing oleo-pneumatic shock-absorbers. Main wheels and tyres size 40 × 14. Nose-wheels and tyres size 24 × 7·7. Bendix multi-disc brakes. Goodyear anti-skid units standard.

POWER PLANT: Two Pratt & Whitney JT8D

turbofan engines (details under individual model listings), in underwing pods. High-performance target-type thrust reversers installed on all aircraft delivered after February 1969, in place of a thrust reverser of earlier design. Fuel in two integral wing tanks with total capacity of 2,861 US gallons (10,830 litres) is standard on the basic gross weight model. Optional centre wing cells increase capacity to 4,232 US gallons (16,020 litres). High gross weight models have additional capacity up to 4,783 US gallons (18,105 litres) by utilising bladder cells in centre wing. Single-point pressure refuelling through leading-edge of starboard wing. Fuelling rate 300 US gallons (1,135 litres)/min. Auxiliary overwing fuelling points. Total oil capacity 11 US gallons (41·5 litres).

ACCOMMODATION: Crew of two side-by-side on flight deck. Details of passenger accommodation given under individual model descriptions. Passenger versions are equipped with forward airstair; an aft airstair is optional. Convertible passenger/cargo versions have the aft airstair as standard and forward airstair optional. One plug-type door at each corner of cabin, of which passenger doors are on port side and service doors on starboard side. Overwing escape hatches on each side. Basic passenger cabin has two lavatories aft and two galleys forward, opposite passenger door, or lavatories and galleys forward and aft. Flexibility is provided for a large variety of interior arrangements. Freight holds forward and aft of wing, under floor.

SYSTEMS: Air-conditioning and pressurisation system utilises engine-bleed air. Max differential 7·5 lb/sq in (0·53 kg/cm²). Two independent hydraulic systems, using fire-resistant hydraulic

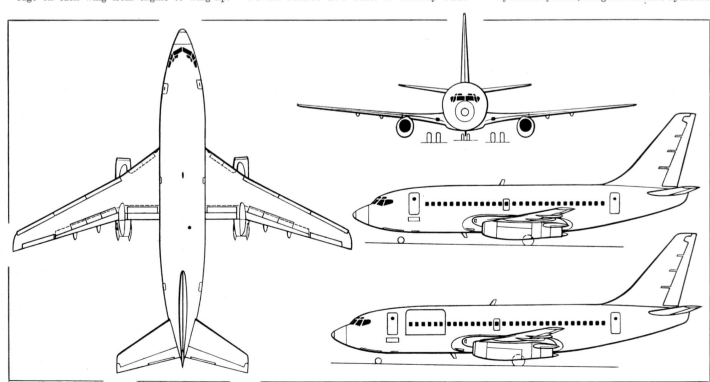

Boeing 737-100 twin-jet transport. Lower side view is of the longer 737-200C

fluid, for flying controls, flaps, slats, landing gear, nose-wheel steering and brakes; pressure 3,000 lb/sq in (210 kg/cm²). No pneumatic system. Electrical supply provided by engine-driven generators. AiResearch APU for air supply and electrical power in flight and on the ground, as well as engine starting.

ELECTRONICS AND EQUIPMENT: Equipment to satisfy FAA category II low weather minimum criteria is standard. Autopilot specially designed for ILS localiser and glideslope control features control wheel steering.

DIMENSIONS, EXTERNAL:

Wing span	93 ft 0 in (28·35 m)
Wing chord at root	15 ft 5·6 in (4·71 m)
Wing chord at tip	5 ft 3 in (1·60 m)
Wing aspect ratio	8·83
Length overall	
737-100	94 ft 0 in (28·65 m)
737-200	100 ft 0 in (30·48 m)
Length of fuselage:	
737-100	90 ft 7 in (27·61 m)
737-200	96 ft 11 in (29·54 m)
Height overall	37 ft 0 in (11·28 m)
Tailplane span	36 ft 0 in (10·97 m)
Wheel track	17 ft 2 in (5·23 m)
Wheelbase:	
737-100	34 ft 4 in (10·46 m)
737-200	37 ft 4 in (11·38 m)
Main passenger door (port, front):	
Height	6 ft 0 in (1·83 m)
Width	2 ft 10 in (0·86 m)
Height to sill	8 ft 7 in (2·62 m)
Passenger door (port, rear):	
Height	6 ft 0 in (1·83 m)
Width	2 ft 6 in (0·76 m)
Width with airstair	2 ft 10 in (0·86 m)
Height to sill	8 ft 11 in (2·72 m)
Galley service door (stbd, front):	
Height	5 ft 5 in (1·65 m)
Width	2 ft 6 in (0·76 m)
Height to sill	8 ft 7 in (2·62 m)
Service door (stbd, rear):	
Height	5 ft 5 in (1·65 m)
Width	2 ft 6 in (0·76 m)
Height to sill	8 ft 11 in (2·72 m)
Freight hold door (stbd, fwd):	
Height	4 ft 3 in (1·30 m)
Width	4 ft 0 in (1·22 m)
Height to sill	4 ft 3 in (1·30 m)
Freight hold door (stbd, rear):	
Height	4 ft 0 in (1·22 m)
Width	4 ft 0 in (1·22 m)
Height to sill:	
737-100	5 ft 0 in (1·52 m)
737-200	4 ft 9 in (1·45 m)

DIMENSIONS, INTERNAL:

Cabin, including galley and toilet:

Length:	
737-100	62 ft 2 in (18·95 m)
737-200	68 ft 6 in (20·88 m)
Max width	11 ft 6½ in (3·52 m)
Max height	7 ft 2 in (2·18 m)
Floor area:	
737-100	619 sq ft (57·5 m²)
737-200	687 sq ft (63·8 m²)
Volume:	
737-100	4,187 cu ft (118·56 m³)
737-200	4,636 cu ft (131·28 m³)
Freight hold (forward) volume:	
737-100	280 cu ft (7·93 m³)
737-200	370 cu ft (10·48 m³)
Freight hold (rear) volume:	
737-100	370 cu ft (10·48 m³)
737-200	505 cu ft (14·30 m³)

AREA:

Wings, gross	980 sq ft (91·05 m²)

WEIGHTS AND LOADINGS (A=AUW of 100,500 lb; B=AUW of 104,000 lb; C=AUW of 110,000 lb; D=AUW of 109,000 lb; E=AUW of 114,500 lb):

Operating weight, empty:

737-100 (A,B)	56,893 lb (25,800 kg)
737-100 (C)	62,026 lb (28,130 kg)
737-200 (D)	58,607 lb (26,580 kg)
737-200 (E)	59,651 lb (27,050 kg)
737-200C(E):	
all-passenger configuration	62,436 lb (28,315 kg)
all-cargo configuration	59,109 lb (26,805 kg)
737-200QC (E):	
all-passenger configuration	65,313 lb (29,620 kg)
all cargo configuration	60,120 lb (27,265 kg)
Business Jet (E)	54,126 lb (24,545 kg)

Max payload:

737-100 (A, B)	28,107 lb (12,745 kg)
737-100 (C)	27,974 lb (12,685 kg)
737-200 (D)	29,393 lb (13,330 kg)
737-200 (E)	35,349 lb (16,030 kg)
737-200C (E):	
all-passenger configuration	32,564 lb (14,770 kg)
all-cargo configuration	35,891 lb (16,275 kg)
737-200QC (E):	
all-passenger configuration	29,687 lb (13,465 kg)
all-cargo configuration	34,880 lb (15,820 kg)
Business Jet (E)	40,874 lb (18,535 kg)

Max T-O weight:

737-100 (A)	100,500 lb (45,575 kg)
737-100 (B)	104,000 lb (47,165 kg)
737-100 (C)	110,000 lb (49,885 kg)
737-200 (D)	109,000 lb (49,435 kg)
737-200 (E)	114,500 lb (51,925 kg)
737-200C, 737-200QC in either all-passenger or all-cargo configuration and Business Jet:	114,500 lb (51,925 kg)

Max ramp weight:

737-100 (A)	100,800 lb (45,715 kg)
737-100 (B)	104,000 lb (47,165 kg)
737-100 (C)	111,000 lb (50,340 kg)
737-200 (D)	110,000 lb (49,885 kg)
737-200 (E)	116,000 lb (52,605 kg)
737-200C and 737-200QC in either all-passenger or all-cargo configuration and Business Jet (E):	116,000 lb (52,605 kg)

Max zero-fuel weight:

737-100 (A, B)	85,000 lb (38,550 kg)
737-100 (C)	90,000 lb (40,815 kg)
737-200 (D)	88,000 lb (39,910 kg)
737-200 (E)	95,000 lb (43,085 kg)
737-200C and 737-200QC in either all-passenger or all-cargo configuration and Business Jet (E):	95,000 lb (43,085 kg)

Max landing weight:

737-100 (A, B)	98,000 lb (44,445 kg)
737-100 (C)	99,000 lb (44,895 kg)
737-200 (D)	98,000 lb (44,445 kg)
737-200 (E)	103,000 lb (46,710 kg)
737-200C and 737-200QC in either all-passenger or all-cargo configuration and Business Jet (E):	103,000 lb (46,710 kg)

Max wing loading:

737-100 (A)	102·5 lb/sq ft (500·4 kg/m²)
737-100 (B)	106·1 lb/sq ft (518·0 kg/m²)
737-100 (C)	112·2 lb/sq ft (547·8 kg/m²)
737-200 (D)	111·2 lb/sq ft (543·4 kg/m²)
737-200 (E)	116·8 lb/sq ft (570·2 kg/m²)
737-200C and 737-200QC in either all-passenger or all-cargo configuration and Business Jet (E)	116·8 lb/sq ft (570·2 kg/m²)

Max power loading:

737-100 (A)	3·46 lb/lb st (3·46 kg/kg st)
737-100 (B)	3·58 lb/lb st (3·58 kg/kg st)
737-100 (C)	3·79 lb/lb st (3·79 kg/kg st)
737-200 (D)	3·76 lb/lb st (3·76 kg/kg st)
737-200 (E)	3·95 lb/lb st (3·95 kg/kg st)
737-200C and 737-200QC in either all-passenger or all-cargo configuration and Business Jet (E):	3·95 lb/lb st (3·95 kg/kg st)

PERFORMANCE (Standard day, with JT8D-9 engines):

Max level speed, all models, at 23,500 ft (7,165 m)   509 knots (586 mph; 943 km/h)

Max permissible diving speed, all models, at 20,000 ft (6,095 m)   545 knots (628 mph; 1,010 km/h)

Max cruising speed:

737-100, at an average cruise weight of 90,000 lb (40,823 kg) at 22,100 ft (6,735 m)   495 knots (570 mph; 917 km/h)

737-200, at an average cruise weight of 90,000 lb (40,823 kg) at 21,900 ft (6,675 m)   493 knots (568·5 mph; 915 km/h)

Econ cruising speed at 30,000 ft (9,145 m)   Mach 0·78

Stalling speed, flaps down, at max landing weight:

737-100	103 knots (118 mph; 190 km/h)
737-200	102 knots (117 mph; 189 km/h)

Rate of climb at S/L, all models at 100,000 lb (45,355 kg) AUW   3,319 ft (1,012 m)/min

FAR T-O distance to 35 ft (10·5 m):

737-100 at 100,500 lb (45,585 kg) AUW   5,630 ft (1,716 m)

737-200 at 109,000 lb (49,440 kg) AUW   7,100 ft (2,164 m)

FAR landing distance from 50 ft (15 m) at max landing weight:

737-100	4,800 ft (1,463 m)
737-200	4,660 ft (1,420 m)

Range with max fuel, cruising at 30,000 ft (9,145 m), including reserves for 200 miles (321 km) flight to alternate airport and 45 min continued cruise, 737-100 at 104,000 lb (47,170 kg) taxi weight, 737-200 at 114,500 lb (51,710 kg) taxi weight:

737-100 with 92 passengers   1,815 nm (2,090 miles; 3,360 km)

737-200 with 112 passengers   1,919 nm (2,210 miles; 3,555 km)

Range with max payload, cruising at 30,000 ft (9,145 m), including reserves for 174 nm (200 miles; 321 km) flight to alternate airport and 45 min continued cruise, 737-100 at 104,000 lb (47,170 kg) taxi weight, 737-200 at 114,000 lb (51,710 kg) taxi weight:

737-100 with 103 passengers   1,597 nm (1,840 miles; 2,960 km)

737-200 with 115 passengers   1,854 nm (2,135 miles; 3,435 km)

BOEING MODEL 747

First details of this very large commercial transport were announced on 13 April 1966, simultaneously with the news that Pan American World Airways had placed a $525 million contract for 25 Boeing 747's, including spares.

There was no prototype and the first 747 was rolled-out from the factory on 30 September 1968, making its first flight on 9 February 1969 from Paine Field, 20 miles north of Seattle. The certification flight programme was completed and FAA certification granted on 30 December 1969. More than 1,400 flight test hours were flown by five 747s at several test

Boeing Model 737-242C of Nordair, fitted with nose-wheel gravel deflector and vortex dissipators on lower leading-edge of engine inlets for operation from unimproved runways

sites, including Boeing Field, adjacent to the company's headquarters in Seattle. Grant County Airport, Eastern Washington; Roswell, New Mexico; and Edwards AFB, California.

The first 747 to be delivered was received by Pan American late in 1969, and this company inaugurated commercial service with the type on its New York/London route on 22 January 1970. Thirty-two aircraft had been delivered by mid-May 1970, of a total of 200 ordered.

The initial version of the 747 has a gross ramp weight of 713,000 lb (323,400 kg), with a max T-O weight of 710,000 lb (322,050 kg).

In late November 1968, Boeing announced an improved model, with a max T-O weight of 775,000 lb (351,540 kg), to be produced in passenger (747B), convertible (747C) and freighter (747F) versions and available from 1971. Four versions of the Boeing 747 are, therefore, available as follows:

747. Initial version with seats for up to 490 passengers. Typical load is 374, or 66 first class and 308 tourist passengers. Referred to as **Series 100.**

747B. Passenger version with accommodation as 747. Increased max T-O weight and fuel capacity. 747B/C/F referred to as **Series 200.**

747C. Convertible passenger/cargo version. Nose hinged just below the cockpit to open forward and up for direct cargo loading onto the main deck. In all-cargo rôle will carry up to 30 containers measuring 10 ft long, 8 ft high and 8 ft wide (3·05 × 2·44 × 2·44 m), plus 30 lower-lobe containers of 173 cu ft (4·90 m³) capacity and 800 cu ft (22·65 m³) of bulk cargo.

747F. All-cargo version, similar to 747C, capable of delivering 200,000 lb (90,720 kg) of containerised and palletised cargo over a range of 4,312 miles (6,940 km).

Orders announced by 30 June 1970 were as follows:

KLM	7	747-06B
Pan American	33	747-21
United Air Lines	18	747-22
American Airlines	16	747-23
Continental	4	747-24
Eastern Air Lines	4	747-25
Braniff	2	747-27
Air France	8	747-28
Sabena	2	747-29
Lufthansa	3	747-30
Lufthansa	1	747-30B
Lufthansa	1	747-30F
TWA	15	747-31
Delta Air Lines	5	747-32
Air Canada	3	747-33
National Airlines	2	747-35
BOAC	12	747-36
Air-India	3	747-37B
Qantas	4	747-38B
Alitalia	5	747-43/43B
South African Airways	3	747-44B
Japan Air Lines	3	747-46
Japan Air Lines	8	747-46B
Irish International	2	747-48
Northwest Orient	15	747-51
Iberia	3	747-56
Swissair	2	747-57B
El Al	2	747-58B
World Airways	3	747-73C
SAS	2	747-83B
Universal Airlines	2*	747-2D5C
Condor	1	747-230B
Korean Air Lines	1	747F
Unannounced orders	6	747B

*To be leased from GATX-Boothe

The following details apply specifically to the basic Model 747 passenger airliner.

TYPE: Four-turbofan heavy commercial transport.

WINGS: Cantilever low-wing monoplane. Special Boeing wing sections. Thickness/chord ratio 13·44% inboard, 7·8% at mid-span, 8% outboard. Dihedral 7°. Incidence 2°. Sweepback 37° 30′ at quarter-chord. Aluminium alloy dual-path fail-safe structure. Low-speed outboard ailerons; high-speed inboard ailerons. Triple-slotted trailing-edge flaps. Six aluminium honeycomb spoilers on each wing, comprising four flight spoilers outboard and two ground spoilers inboard. Ten variable-camber leading-edge flaps outboard and three-section Krueger flaps inboard on each wing leading-edge. All controls fully powered.

FUSELAGE: Conventional semi-monocoque structure, consisting of aluminium alloy skin, longitudinal stiffeners and circumferential frames. Structure is of fail-safe design, utilising riveting, bolting and structural bonding.

TAIL UNIT: Cantilever aluminium alloy dual-path fail-safe structure. Variable-incidence tailplane. No trim-tabs. All controls fully powered.

LANDING GEAR: Hydraulically-retractable tricycle type. Twin-wheel nose unit retracts forward. Main gear comprises four four-wheel bogies: two mounted side-by-side under fuselage at wing trailing-edge, retract forward: two mounted under wings retract inward. Cleveland Pneumatic oleo-pneumatic shock-absorbers. All 18 wheels and tubeless tyres of model 747 are size 46 × 16 Type VII. Tyre pressure: main wheels 204 lb/sq in (14·34 kg/cm²), nose-wheels 165 lb/sq in (11·6 kg/cm²). Main wheels and tyres size 49 × 17 on 747B model, pressure 185 lb/sq in (13·0 kg/cm²). Disc brakes on all main wheels, with individually-controlled anti-skid units.

POWER PLANT: Four Pratt & Whitney JT9D-3 turbofan engines, each rated at 43,500 lb (19,730 kg) st, in pods pylon-mounted on wing leading-edges. All four versions of the 747 will be structurally capable of accepting JT9D-3, JT9D-3W, JT9D-7 or JT9D-7W engines and will have QEC capability. Corresponding thrust for the above engines is 43,500, 45,000, 45,500 and 47,000 lb (19,730, 20,410, 20,635 and 21,320 kg). The JT9D-7W engine will be available from 1972. Fuel in seven integral tanks. Capacity of centre-wing tank varies according to version: 747 12,890 US gallons (48,790 litres); 747B, C 16,680 US gallons (63,139 litres); 747F 8,830 US gallons (33,422 litres). Remaining tanks common to all versions: two inboard main tanks, each 12,240 US gallons (46,333 litres); two outboard main tanks, each 4,420 US gallons (16,731 litres); two outboard reserve tanks, each 500 US gallons (1,892 litres). Total capacity, 747 47,210 US gallons (178,702 litres); 747B, C 51,000 US gallons (193,051 litres); 747F 43,150 US gallons (163,334 litres). Refuelling point on each wing between inboard and outboard engines. Total usable oil capacity 5 US gallons (19 litres).

ACCOMMODATION: Normal operating crew of three, on flight deck above level of main deck. Observer station and provision for second observer station are provided. Basic accommodation for 374 passengers, made up of 66 first class and 308 economy class, with multi-seat lounge. Alternative layouts accommodate 447 economy class passengers in nine-abreast seating or 490 ten-abreast. All versions have two aisles. Five passenger doors on each side, of which two forward of wing on each side will normally be used. Freight holds under floor, forward and aft of wing, with doors on starboard side. One door on forward hold, two on rear hold. Aircraft is designed for fully-mechanical loading of baggage and freight.

SYSTEMS: Air-cycle air-conditioning system. Pressure differential 8·9 lb/sq in (0·63 kg/cm²). Electrical supply from four air-cooled 60kVA generators mounted one on each engine. Two 60kVA generators (supplemental cooling allows 90kVA each) mounted on APU for ground operation and to supply primary electrical power when engine-mounted generators are not operating. Three-phase 400 c/s constant-frequency AC generators, 115/200V output. 28V DC power obtained from transformer-rectifier units. 24V 30A/hr nickel-cadmium battery for selected ground functions and as in-flight back-up. Gas-turbine APU for pneumatic and electrical supplies.

ELECTRONICS AND EQUIPMENT: Standard avionics include two ARINC 566 VHF communications systems, two ARINC 566 satellite communications systems, ARINC 531 selcal, two ARINC 547 VOR/ILS navigation systems, two ARINC 550 ADF, marker beacon, two ARINC 521D DME, two ARINC 532D ATC, two ARINC 552 low-range radio altimeters, weather radar, two ARINC 561 inertial navigation systems, two heading reference systems, ARINC 412 interphone, passenger address system, passenger entertainment system, ARINC 542 flight recorder, ARINC 557 cockpit voice recorder, integrated electronic flight control system to provide automatic stabilisation, path control and pilot assist functions for category II and III landing conditions, two ARINC 565 central air data systems, stall warning system, central instrument warning system, attitude and navigation instrumentation, and standby attitude indication. Provision for two ARINC 533A HF communications systems.

DIMENSIONS, EXTERNAL:

Wing span	195 ft 8 in (59·64 m)
Wing chord at root	54 ft 4 in (16·56 m)
Wing chord at tip	13 ft 4 in (4·06 m)
Wing aspect ratio	6·96
Length overall	231 ft 4 in (70·51 m)
Length of fuselage	225 ft 2 in (68·63 m)
Height overall	63 ft 5 in (19·33 m)
Tailplane span	72 ft 9 in (22·17 m)
Wheel track	36 ft 2 in (11·02 m)
Wheelbase	83 ft 11½ in (25·59 m)

Passenger doors (ten, each):

Height	6 ft 4 in (1·93 m)
Width	3 ft 6 in (1·07 m)
Height to sill approx	16 ft 0 in (4·88 m)

Baggage door (front hold):

Height	5 ft 8 in (1·73 m)
Width	8 ft 8 in (2·64 m)
Height to sill approx	8 ft 6 in (2·59 m)

Baggage door (forward door, aft hold):

Height	5 ft 8 in (1·73 m)
Width	8 ft 8 in (2·64 m)
Height to sill approx	8 ft 10 in (2·69 m)

Bulk loading door (rear door on aft hold):

Height	4 ft 0 in (1·22 m)
Width	3 ft 8 in (1·12 m)
Height to sill approx	9 ft 6 in (2·90 m)

DIMENSIONS, INTERNAL:

Cabin, including toilets and galleys:

Length	185 ft 0 in (56·39 m)
Max width	20 ft 0 in (6·10 m)
Max height	8 ft 4 in (2·54 m)
Floor area, passenger deck	3,316 sq ft (308·1 m²)
Volume, passenger deck	27,860 cu ft (789 m³)

Baggage hold (fwd, containerised) volume
2,800 cu ft (79·3 m³)

Baggage hold (aft, containerised) volume
2,450 cu ft (69·4 m³)

Bulk volume	1,000 cu ft (28·3 m³)

AREAS:

Wings, reference area	5,500 sq ft (511 m²)

Boeing Model 747-43 in Alitalia insignia, in landing configuration with flaps and landing gear extended

Boeing Model 747-51 (four Pratt & Whitney JT9D-3 turbofan engines) in the insignia of Northwest Orient Airlines

Ailerons (total)	222 sq ft (20·6 m²)
Trailing-edge flaps (total)	847 sq ft (78·7 m²)
Leading-edge flaps (total)	518 sq ft (48·1 m²)
Spoilers (total)	331 sq ft (30·8 m²)
Fin	830 sq ft (77·1 m²)
Rudder	247 sq ft (22·9 m²)
Tailplane	1,470 sq ft (136·6 m²)
Elevators	350 sq ft (32·5 m²)

WEIGHTS (747 with JT9D-3 engines, 747B, C and F with JT9D-7W engines):
Operating weight, empty:

747	348,816 lb (158,220 kg)
747B	361,216 lb (163,844 kg)
747C passenger	370,816 lb (168,199 kg)
*747C cargo	347,072 lb (157,429 kg)
747F	332,142 lb (150,657 kg)

*Includes pallets on main deck and containers in lower compartments.
Max payload:

747	177,684 lb (80,596 kg)
747B	165,284 lb (74,971 kg)
747C passenger	155,684 lb (70,617 kg)
747C cargo	242,928 lb (110,189 kg)
747F	257,858 lb (116,962 kg)

Max T-O weight:

747	710,000 lb (322,050 kg)
747B, C, F	775,000 lb (351,540 kg)

Max ramp weight:

747	713,000 lb (323,400 kg)
747B, C, F	778,000 lb (352,895 kg)

Max zero-fuel weight:

747, 747B, C passenger	526,500 lb (238,815 kg)
747C cargo, F	590,000 lb (267,615 kg)

Max landing weight:

747, 747B, C passenger	564,000 lb (255,825 kg)
747C cargo F	630,000 lb (285,760 kg)

*PERFORMANCE (estimated at max T-O weight):
Max level speed:
747 at 30,000 ft (9,150 m) at AUW of 600,000 lb (272,155 kg)
517 knots (595 mph; 958 km/h)

747B, C, F at 30,000 ft (9,150 m) at AUW of 600,000 lb (272,155 kg)
528 knots (608 mph; 978 km/h)
Cruise ceiling, all versions 45,000 ft (13,715 m)
FAR T-O distance to 35 ft (10·5 m) at S/L, standard day:

747	10,400 ft (3,170 m)
747B, C, F	10,900 ft (3,322 m)

FAR landing field length, at max landing weight:

747, 747B, C passenger	6,750 ft (2,057 m)
747C cargo, F	7,270 ft (2,216 m)

Range (long-range cruise, FAR 121.645 reserves):
747 with 374 passengers and baggage
5,028 nm (5,790 miles; 9,138 km)
747B with 79,618 lb (36,114 kg) payload
5,748 nm (6,620 miles; 10,650 km)
747C passenger with 79,618 lb (36,114 kg) payload 5,419 nm (6,240 miles; 10,040 km)
747C cargo with 236,025 lb (107,059 kg) payload 2,501 nm (2,880 miles; 4,630 km)
747F with 257,858 lb (116,962 kg) payload
2,501 nm (2,880 miles; 4,630 km)
Range with max fuel (long-range cruise, FAR 121.645 reserves):
747B, 747C passenger
6,157 nm (7,090 miles; 11,410 km)
747C cargo, 747F
4,850 nm (5,585 miles; 8,985 km)

*Flight test performance figures were being evaluated at the time of writing; they indicate better performance figures than estimated for all parameters.

BOEING MODEL 2707-300 SST

After several years of preliminary study, Boeing established a permanent company-sponsored supersonic transport programme in January 1958. On 31 December 1966 the company was named winner of the US SST design competition, together with General Electric which was awarded responsibility for power plant development. The winning Boeing design was of variable-geometry configuration and known as the Model 2707-200. In October 1968 Boeing announced that it had abandoned this proposal in favour of a fixed gull-wing design, the Model 2707-300, and by the following February activity on all other configurations had ceased.

The General Electric GE4 engines specified for the variable-geometry design have been retained and the target take-off thrust figure has gone up from 50,600 lb (22,952 kg) st to a guaranteed 68,600 lb (31,116 kg) st in the GE4/J5P prototype engines.

Much of the original systems design has also been carried over to the Model 2707-300, but a major structural change is that the wings will now use sandwich skins instead of machined panels.

Go-ahead for the construction of two prototypes was approved by President Nixon on 23 September 1969, and it is planned to fly the first of these in late 1972/early 1973. In January 1970 it was announced that the first engineering drawings of a prototype part, a wing leading-edge flap, had been released. A full-scale structures mock-up is due to be completed in 1970.

The development contract awarded to Boeing calls for 100 hours of flight testing on each prototype. Production of a definite version is planned to begin in 1975. Certification of the GE4 engine is at present scheduled for 1976, with aircraft certification two years later, in 1978, and with deliveries beginning immediately after this. To date, deposits have been paid on 122 SST production-line positions by 26 airlines.

The US government is funding 90 per cent (currently some $1,300 m), less risk money provided by airlines, of the design, building and

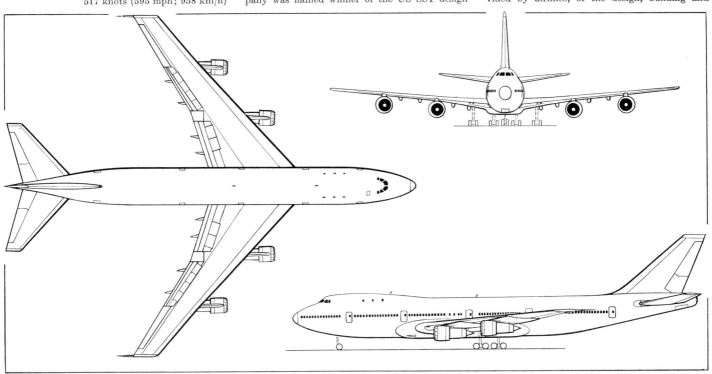

Boeing 747 heavy transport aircraft (four Pratt & Whitney JT9D-3 turbofan engines)

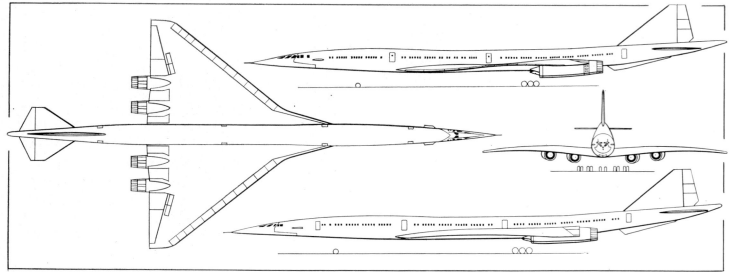

Three-view drawing of the production version of the Boeing 2707-300 and side view (top) of the prototype

flight testing of the two Model 2707-300 prototypes. This will be repaid through royalties on
sales of approximately the first 300 aircraft. An
additional $1,000 m could be paid by the 500th
aircraft, if sales reach this figure. Boeing and
General Electric will contribute 10 per cent
(some $300m) to the programme, and nine US
airlines and one foreign carrier have invested
$58·5m risk capital, besides paying, like all
prospective customers, $200,000 for each
delivery position reserved. The present reservation schedule calls for the first four production
aircraft to be delivered to TWA (Nos 1 and 3)
and Pan American (Nos 2 and 4). The first
foreign carrier to get delivery will be Alitalia
(No 5). The delivery rate target is five aircraft
per month.

In terms of weight, it is estimated that more
than 60 per cent of the prototype aircraft will be
provided by sub-contractors, and the following
risk-sharing companies have been named
provisionally; Aeronca, Middletown, Ohio,
wing trailing-edge flaps and flaperons; Fairchild
Hiller Corporation, Farmingdale, New York,
and Hagerstown, Maryland, aft fuselage section,
ventral and vertical fin, and tailplane primary
structure; LTV Aerospace Corporation, Dallas,
Texas, fuselage section and forward wing strake;
North American Rockwell Corporation, Los
Angeles, California, outboard wing, wingtip
and wing leading-edge flaps; Northrop Corporation, Hawthorne, California, cabin and nose
sections; and Rohr Corporation, Chula Vista,
California, engine pods. Final assembly will be
by Boeing at Seattle.

Boeing envisages that production versions of
the Model 2707-300 will comprise a family of
aircraft with fuselages of different widths and
lengths and with varying payload/range performance. These would be somewhat larger than
the prototypes, with a maximum design taxi
weight of 750,000 lb (340,190 kg).

The various models at present under study
include a long-range version with the same fuselage size as the prototypes and accommodating
250 passengers in a five-abreast cabin layout; a
version seating a maximum of 321 passengers in
a seven-abreast/twin-aisle arrangement, with a
fuselage length of 296 ft (90·21 m), for New
York-London or Los Angeles-Hawaii stage
lengths; and another seating 281-298 passengers within a fuselage length of 298 ft (90·82 m).
Early production models will have a full-pay-
load Paris-New York range, which the SST,
cruising at Mach 2·7, would cover in a block
time of 2 hours 45 minutes.

The aircraft will be equipped with a Category
3B automatic landing system, permitting landings in zero ceiling, 200 ft (61 m) runway visual
range conditions.

The following description applies to the prototypes:
TYPE: Long-range supersonic transport aircraft.
WINGS: Cantilever low-wing delta planform.
Special wing sections. Thickness/chord ratio
3·7% at root, 3% at tip. Gull-wing design,
with 4° dihedral from root to outboard engine,
3° anhedral from outboard engine to tip.
Sweepback at leading-edge 50°. Titanium
(Ti-6A1-4v) fail-safe structure of multiple
built-up spars, beams and ribs. Majority
of wing covered with titanium alloy sandwich.
Stainless steel skins in engine bays. Stainless
steel leading-edge and tip sections. Full-
span trailing-edge flaps of simple hinged type,
of which two sections operate also as ailerons
(flaperons) in low-speed flight. Simple hinged
leading-edge flaps. Slot deflector upper and
lower spoilers at mid-span. No trim-tabs.
All control surfaces hydraulically powered by
redundant systems. No anti-icing equipment.

FUSELAGE: Conventional semi-monocoque fail-
safe structure, with skin panels, stringers and
frames of titanium alloy.
TAIL UNIT: Conventional tail unit of similar
construction to wings, except that trailing-
edges are also of stainless steel. Variable-
incidence tailplane, with elevators. Three-
segment rudder, of which top segment is
locked at supersonic speed. All control surfaces hydraulically powered by redundant
systems. No trim-tabs or anti-icing equipment.
LANDING GEAR: Retractable tricycle type in
cooled wheel wells. Hydraulic actuation, all
units retracting forward. Conventional oleo
shock-absorbers. Each main unit consists of a
bogie with six dual wheels carrying twelve
tyres size 40 × 12. Twin-wheel nose unit with
tyres size 35 × 15. Main wheel tyre pressure
200 lb/sq in (14·kg/cm²). Individual wheel
anti-skid control.
POWER PLANT: Four General Electric GE4/J5P
turbojet engines in individual underwing pods.
Fuel in four main tanks, with auxiliaries. Fuel
trim system. Total potential fuel capacity
440,000 lb (199,580 kg).
ACCOMMODATION: Prototype will carry flight
crew of three. Plug-type side-hinged doors.
Forward and aft freight holds under passenger
cabin floor.
SYSTEMS: Air-cycle air-conditioning and pressurisation system, differential 11 lb/sq in (0·77
kg/cm²). Four independent hydraulic systems
for flying controls and landing gear, pressure
4,000 lb/sq in (281 kg/cm²). Pneumatic
engine starting system. Variable-speed constant-frequency electrical system, supplied by
four 75kVA engine-driven generators.
ELECTRONICS AND EQUIPMENT: Advanced instrumentation, radio and radar to customers'
specification.

DIMENSIONS, EXTERNAL:

Wing span	141 ft 8 in	(43·18 m)
Wing chord at root	98 ft 5 in	(30·0 m)
Wing chord at tip	12 ft 6 in	(3·81 m)
Wing aspect ratio	2·55	
Length overall	286 ft 8 in	(87·38 m)
Height overall	50 ft 1 in	(15·27 m)
Tailplane span	33 ft 4 in	(10·16 m)
Wheel track	20 ft 4 in	(6·20 m)
Wheelbase	104 ft 8 in	(31·90 m)
Passenger doors (forward):		
Height	6 ft 0 in	(1·83 m)
Width	3 ft 6 in	(1·07 m)
Height to sill	15 ft 2 in	(4·62 m)
Passenger doors (centre):		
Height	6 ft 0 in	(1·83 m)
Width	3 ft 6 in	(1·07 m)
Height to sill	14 ft 9 in	(4·50 m)
Passenger doors (rear):		
Height	6 ft 0 in	(1·83 m)
Width	2 ft 8 in	(0·81 m)
Height to sill	17 ft 6 in	(5·33 m)
Baggage and freight door (forward):		
Height	3 ft 10 in	(1·17 m)
Width	5 ft 4 in	(1·63 m)
Height to sill	10 ft 8 in	(3·25 m)
Baggage and freight doors (rear, two):		
Height	2 ft 7 in	(0·79 m)
Width	2 ft 5 in	(0·74 m)
Height to sill: fwd	12 ft 7 in	(3·84 m)
rear	14 ft 0 in	(4·27 m)

DIMENSIONS, INTERNAL:

Cabin (passenger section, including galleys and toilets):		
Length	183 ft 0 in	(55·78 m)
Max width	10 ft 10 in	(3·30 m)
Max height	7 ft 0 in	(2·13 m)
Baggage holds:		
Fwd belly, containerised	1,053 cu ft	(29·82 m²)
Aft belly, bulk	300 cu ft	(8·50 m²)

AREAS:

Wings, gross, incl ailerons and flaps		
	8,497 sq ft	(789 m²)
Vertical tail surfaces, total incl ventral fin		
	783 sq ft	(72·74 m²)
Horizontal tail surfaces, total		
	591 sq ft	(54·90 m²)

WEIGHT:

Max ramp weight	635,000 lb	(288,030 kg)

PERFORMANCE (estimated):

Max level speed at 73,000 ft (22,250 m)		Mach 2·7
Max permissible diving speed		Mach 2·9
Max cruising speed at 60,000-70,000 ft (18,300-21,350 m)		Mach 2·7
Lift-off speed	197 knots	(227 mph; 365 km/h)

BOEING-VERTOL MODEL 107
**US Navy and Marine Corps designation: CH-46/
UH-46 Sea Knight**
RCAF designation: CH-113 Labrador
Canadian Army designation: CH-113A Voyageur
Swedish Service designation: HKP-4

In 1956, Vertol began preliminary design and
engineering of a twin-turbine transport helicopter
for commercial and military use. The main
objective was to take full advantage of the high
power, small size and light weight of the shaft-
turbine engines then becoming available. To
achieve the best possible hovering performance,
the traditional Vertol tandem-rotor layout was
retained, and the turbines were mounted above
the rear of the cabin, on each side of the aft
rotor pylon. This results in maximum unobstructed cabin area and permits the use of a
large rear ramp for straight-in loading of vehicles
and bulky freight.

Construction of a prototype, designated Model
107, was started in May 1957, and this aircraft
flew for the first time on 22 April 1958, powered
by two 860 shp Lycoming T53 shaft-turbine
engines. It was designed for water landing
capability, without the addition of special
flotation gear or boat hull design, and was intended to carry 23-25 passengers in normal airline
standard accommodation.

As a result of experience with this prototype,
including extensive demonstration tours in North
America, Europe and the Far East, several
advanced versions were developed. Those in
current service or under development are as
follows:

107 Model II. Standard commercial version,
with two 1,250 shp General Electric CT58 shaft-
turbines. Available as an airliner with roll-out
rear baggage container or utility model with rear
loading ramp. A prototype, modified at company
expense from one of the three YHC-1A (CH-46C)
military helicopters built for evaluation by the
US Army, flew for the first time on 25 October
1960, followed by the first production model on
19 May 1961. FAA certification was received on
26 January 1962. Seven, with 25-seat interior,
were delivered subsequently to New York Airways, who introduced the 107 Model II on to
their scheduled services on 1 July 1962. Of the
seven, three were purchased by Pan American
World Airways, who leased them to New York
Airways. Ten were ordered by Kawasaki Air-
craft Company, Vertol's licensee in Japan, prior to production in Kawasaki's works.
In December 1965, Kawasaki (which see) was
given world-wide licence to sell the 107
Model II, except to Canadian and US military
agencies. Commercial models are now available
from Kawasaki, who hold the US Type Certificate.
Military versions continue to be built by The
Boeing Company's Vertol Division.

107 Model IIA. In the Spring of 1968, Kawasaki and The Boeing Company were certifying
the 107 Model IIA airliner, with 1,400 shp
General Electric CT58-140-1 shaft-turbine engines,

to increase performance at high operating temperatures. Maximum certified weights now current will not be increased. Instead, advantage will be taken of the additional horsepower available at temperatures above standard to increase the payload under such conditions.

CH-46A (formerly HRB-1) **Sea Knight.** This US Marine Corps assault transport version of the 107 Model II has the specified military mission of carrying a crew of 3 and 17-25 fully-equipped troops or 4,000 lb (1,814 kg) of cargo over a combat radius of 115 miles (185 km) at 150 mph (240 kmh). An initial batch of 14 was ordered in February 1961, followed by annual repeat orders which brought the total number ordered to 462 by the end of 1966, including CH-46D's (see below). An integrated loading system permits rapid loading, by one man, under field conditions. A powered blade-folding system enables the rotor blades to be folded quickly by a pilot-operated control, to simplify handling on board aircraft carriers. The CH-46A is powered by two 1,250 shp General Electric T58-GE-8B shaft-turbine engines, and has all-weather capabilities. In a rescue rôle, it can retrieve 20 persons up to 105 miles (168 km) from its base, and can carry 15 litter patients and two attendants. First CH-46A flew on 16 October 1962. The US Navy Board of Inspection and Survey tests required for fleet release were completed in November 1964, and four Marine Squadrons were operating CH-46A's by June 1965. In September 1965, the US Department of Defense ordered Boeing to increase production of the CH-46A/D by 100%. The CH-46 has been in service in Vietnam since March 1966, and had exceeded 100,000 combat flight hours by August 1968.

CH-46D Sea Knight. Generally similar to CH-46A, but with 1,400 shp General Electric T58-GE-10 shaft-turbines and cambered rotor blades. All CH-46's delivered since September 1966 are of this version. A total of 425 CH-46/UH-46 Sea Knights had been delivered by 2 May 1968. A CH-46D Sea Knight handed over to the US Marine Corps in August 1968 was the 1,000th twin-turbine tandem-rotor helicopter to be completed by Boeing-Vertol. The 500th CH-46 Sea Knight was delivered to the US Marine Corps in June 1969.

UH-46A Sea Knight. Similar to CH-46A. Ordered by US Navy for operation from AFS or AOE combat supply ships. UH-46A's are utilised to transfer supplies, ammunition, missiles and aviation spares from these ships to combatant vessels under way at sea. Secondary tasks include transfer of personnel, search and rescue. First deliveries to Utility Helicopter Squadron One, Ream Field, California in July 1964, followed by deliveries to Utility Helicopter Squadron Four at Norfolk in December 1964. Total of 24 delivered. Since mid-1965, UH-46A's have been deployed in the Mediterranean and South China Sea.

The war in Vietnam has led to innovations in ship resupply by UH-46A, including bad weather VERTREP (vertical replenishment) and night VERTREP with the aid of small signal lights.

UH-46D Sea Knight. Generally similar to UH-46A, but with 1,400 shp General Electric T58-GE-10 shaft-turbine engines and cambered rotor blades. UH-46's delivered since September 1966 are of this version.

CH-113 Labrador. Six utility models delivered to RCAF in 1963-64 for search and rescue duties. Generally similar to CH-46A. Two 1,250 shp General Electric T58-GE-8B shaft-turbines. Larger-capacity fuel tanks (total of 900 US gallons = 3,408 litres), giving a range of over 650 miles (1,050 km).

CH-113A Voyageur. Twelve aircraft, in a configuration very similar to that of CH-46A, were delivered to the Canadian Army in 1964-65. They are used as troop and cargo carriers in logistical and tactical missions.

HKP-4. Built for Royal Swedish Navy (three) and Air Force (ten), in 1962-63, with Bristol Siddeley Gnome H.1200 shaft-turbine engines and fuel tanks of 1,000 US gallons (3,786 litres) capacity. Naval version has equipment for anti-submarine and mine countermeasures operations, plus a retractable hook for towing surface vessels and minesweeping gear. The Air Force version is fitted with special search and rescue equipment, including a retractable rescue boom in the forward door. First HKP-4 flew on 19 April 1963.

Basic 107-II. This basic utility version of the 107-CH-46 helicopter has been projected primarily for export sales. It is basically the CH/UH-46 aircraft, as produced for the US Marine Corps and US Navy. General Electric T58-GE-5 shaft-turbines of 1,500 shp are standard, together with two increased-capacity fuel tanks, totalling 1,000 US gallons (3,784 litres). Certain special items of equipment, such as power-folding rotor heads, blade de-icing, cabin heater and heated windshields, are not included as standard but are available as optional equipment.

The basic 107-II helicopter has symmetric aerofoil blades on a manual blade-folding rotor head. Improvements developed for the CH-UH-46D helicopters are incorporated directly into the airframe of this model.

Boeing-Vertol UH-46D Sea Knight of HC-6 Squadron US Navy *(Brian M. Service)*

The following details apply to both the standard commercial 107 Model II and the Sea Knight.

Type: Twin-engined transport helicopter.

Rotor System: Two three-blade rotors in tandem, rotating in opposite directions. Each blade on 107 Model II aircraft delivered to New York Airways and Kawasaki is made up of a steel "D" spar to which is bonded a trailing-edge box constructed of aluminium ribs and glass-fibre skin. CH-113, CH-113A and HKP-4 have manually-folding blades and the CH/UH-46 has power-operated blade folding.

Rotor Drive: Power is transmitted from each engine through individually-overrunning clutches into the aft transmission, which combines the engine outputs, thereby providing a single power output to the interconnecting shaft which enables both rotors to be driven by either engine. Rotor/engine rpm ratio: CH-46A 73·722 : 1, CH-113 73·770 : 1.

Fuselage: Square-section stressed-skin semi-monocoque structure built primarily of high-strength bare and alclad aluminium alloy. Transverse bulkheads and built-up frames support transmission, power plant and landing gear. Loading ramp forms undersurface of upswept rear fuselage on utility and military models. Baggage container replaces ramp on airliner version. Fuselage is sealed to permit operation from water.

Landing Gear: Non-retractable tricycle type, with twin wheels on all three units. Oleo-pneumatic shock-absorbers manufactured by Loud (main gear) and Jarry Ltd (nose gear). Goodyear tubeless tyres, size 8 × 5·5, pressure 150 lb/sq in (10·55 kg/cm^2), on all wheels. Goodyear disc brakes.

Power Plant (107 Model II-10): Two 1,250 shp General Electric CT58-110-1 shaft-turbine engines, mounted side-by-side at base of rear rotor pylon. Alternatively, two Bristol Siddeley Gnome H.1200 shaft-turbines (in HKP-4). Fuel tanks in sponsons, capacity 350 US gallons (1,323 litres). New model with 1,400 shp CT58-140 engines under development.

Power Plant (CH-46/UH-46). Two General Electric T58 shaft-turbine engines (details under model listings above). Two self-sealing fuel tanks in sponsons, with total capacity of 380 US gallons (1,438 litres). Refuelling points above tanks. Total oil capacity 4·2 US gallons (15·9 litres).

Accommodation (107 Model II): Standard accommodation for two pilots, stewardess and 25 passengers in airliner. Seats in eight rows, in pairs on port side and single seats on starboard side (two pairs at rear of cabin) with central aisle. Airliner fitted with parcel rack and a roll-out baggage container, with capacity of approximately 1,500 lb (680 kg), located in underside of rear fuselage. Ramp of utility model is power-operated on the ground or in flight and can be removed or left open topermit carriage of extra-long cargo.

Accommodation (CH/UH-46): Crew of three, 25 troops and troop commander. Door at front of troop compartment on starboard side. Door is split type; upper half rolls on tracks to stowed position in fuselage crown, lower half is hinged at the bottom and opens outward, with built-in steps. Loading ramp and hatch at rear of fuselage can be opened in flight or on the water. Floor has centre panel stressed for 300 lb/sq ft (1,464·6 kg/m^2). A row of rollers is installed on each side for handling standard military pallets or wire baskets. Outer portion of floor is vehicle treadway stressed for 1,000 lb (454 kg) rubber-tyred wheel loads. Cargo and personnel hoist system includes a variable-speed winch capable of 2,000 lb (907 kg) cable pull at 30 ft (9 m) min for cargo loading or 600 lb (272 kg) cable pull at 100 ft (30 m) min for personnel hoisting, and can be operated by one man. A 10,000 lb (4,535 kg) capacity hook for external loads is installed in a cargo hatch in the floor.

Systems (CH/UH-46): Cabin heated by Janitrol combustion heater. Hydraulic system provides 1,500 lb/sq in (105 kg/cm^2) pressure for flying control boost, 3,000 lb/sq in (210 kg/cm^2) for other services. Electrical system includes two 40kVA AC generators and a Leland 200A DC generator. Solar APU provides power for starting and systems check-out.

Electronics and Equipment: Blind-flying instrumentation standard. CH-46 has dual stability augmentation systems and automatic trim system.

Dimensions, external:
Diameter of main rotors (each):
107-II, CH-113, CH/UH-46A and Basic 107-II 50 ft 0 in (15·24 m)
CH/UH-46D 51 ft 0 in (15·54 m)
Distance between rotor centres 33 ft 4 in (10·16 m)
Length overall, blades turning:
107-II, CH-113, CH/UH-46A and Basic 107-II 83 ft 4 in (25·40 m)
CH/UH-46D 84 ft 4 in (25·70 m)
Length of fuselage:
107-II, CH-113 44 ft 7 in (13·59 m)
CH/UH-46A and D and Basic 107-II 44 ft 10 in (13·66 m)
Width, rotors folded 14 ft 6¼ in (4·42 m)
Height to top of rear rotor hub 16 ft 8½ in (5·09 m)
Wheel track 12 ft 10½ in (3·92 m)
Wheelbase 24 ft 10 in (7·57 m)
Passenger door (fwd):
Height 5 ft 3 in (1·60 m)
Width 3 ft 0 in (0·91 m)

Dimensions, internal:
Cabin, excluding flight deck:
Length 24 ft 2 in (7·37 m)
Normal width 6 ft 0 in (1·83 m)
Max height 6 ft 0 in (1·83 m)
Floor area:
107-II 145 sq ft (13·47 m^2)
CH/UH-46A and D, CH-113 and Basic 107-II (including ramp) 180 sq ft (16·72 m^2)
Volume (usable):
107-II, CH-113, CH/UH-46A and D and Basic 107-II 865 cu ft (24·5 m^3)

Areas:
Main rotor blade (each):
107-II, CH-113, CH/UH-46A and Basic 107-II 37·50 sq ft (3·48 m^2)
CH/UH-46D 39·85 sq ft (3·70 m^2)
Main rotor discs (total):
107-II, CH-113, CH/UH-46A and Basic 107-II 3,925 sq ft (364·6 m^2)
CH/UH-46D 4,086 sq ft (379·6 m^2)

Weights and Loadings:
Weight empty, equipped:
107-II 10,732 lb (4,868 kg)
CH-113 11,251 lb (5,104 kg)
CH/UH-46A 12,406 lb (5,627 kg)
CH/UH-46D 13,067 lb (5,927 kg)
Basic 107-II 11,585 lb (5,240 kg)
Mission T-O weight: CH-113 19,394 lb (8,797 kg)
Max T-O and landing weight:
107-II 19,000 lb (8,618 kg)
CH-113, CH/UH-46A, Basic 107-II 21,400 lb (9,706 kg)
CH/UH-46D 23,000 lb (10,433 kg)
Max disc loading:
107-II 4·84 lb/sq ft (23·60 kg/m^2)
CH-113, CH/UH-46A, Basic 107-II 5·45 lb/sq ft (26·61 kg/m^2)
CH/UH-46D 5·63 lb/sq ft (27·48 kg/m^2)
Max power loading:
107-II 7·8 lb/shp (3·54 kg/shp)
CH-113, CH/UH-46A 8·77 lb/shp (3·98 kg/shp)
CH/UH-46D 8·84 lb/shp (4·00 kg/shp)
Basic 107-II 8·24 lb/shp (3·73 kg/shp)

Performance (107-II and CH/UH-46A at AUW of 19,000 lb = 8,618 kg; CH-113 at AUW of 18,700 lb = 8,482 kg; CH/UH-46D at AUW of 20,800 lb = 9,434 kg; Basic 107-II at AUW of 20,800 lb = 9,434 kg):
Max permissible speed:
107-II, CH-113 145 knots (168 mph; 270 km/h)
CH/UH-46A 138 knots (159 mph; 256 km/h)
CH/UH-46D 144 knots (166 mph; 267 km/h)

Basic 107-II
          120·5 knots (139 mph; 224 km/h)
Max cruising speed:
107-II, CH-113
          136 knots (157 mph; 253 km/h)
CH/UH-46A
          135 knots (155 mph; 249 km/h)
CH/UH-46D
          140 knots (161 mph; 259 km/h)
Basic 107-II
          120·5 knots (139 mph; 224 km/h)
Average cruising speed:
107-II, CH-113, CH/UH-46A
          130 knots (150 mph; 241 km/h)
CH/UH-46D
          140 knots (161 mph; 259 km/h)
Basic 107-II
          120·5 knots (139 mph; 224 km/h)
Econ cruising speed:
107-II, CH-113
          130 knots (150 mph; 241 km/h)
CH/UH-46A
          131 knots (151 mph; 243 km/h)
CH/UH-46D
          134 knots (154 mph; 248 km/h)
Basic 107-II
          120·5 knots (139 mph; 224 km/h)
Max rate of climb at S/L:
107-II   1,515 ft (462 m)/min
CH-113   1,548 ft (472 m)/min
CH/UH-46A   1,374 ft (419 m)/min
CH/UH-46D   1,660 ft (506 m)/min
Basic 107-II   1,920 ft (585 m)/min
Service ceiling (normal rated power):
107-II   13,000 ft (3,960 m)
CH-113   11,250 ft (3,430 m)
CH/UH-46A   13,000 ft (3,960 m)
CH/UH-46D   14,000 ft (4,265 m)
Basic 107-II   14,000 ft (4,265 m)
Service ceiling (normal rated power), one engine
out:
107-II   350 ft (107 m)
CH-113   1,200 ft (366 m)
CH/UH-46A   S/L
CH/UH-46D   850 ft (259 m)
Hovering ceiling in ground effect:
107-II   8,400 ft (2,560 m)
CH-113   9,800 ft (2,985 m)
CH/UH-46A   9,070 ft (2,765 m)
CH/UH-46D   9,500 ft (2,895 m)
Basic 107-II   10,000 ft (3,048 m)
Hovering ceiling out of ground effect:
107-II, CH-113   6,600 ft (2,012 m)
CH/UH-46A   5,600 ft (1,707 m)
CH/UH-46D   5,750 ft (1,753 m)
Basic 107-II   7,100 ft (2,165 m)
Ranges:
107-II utility with 6,600 lb (3,000 kg) payload,
   10% fuel reserve
          94 nm (109 miles; 175 km/h)
CH-113 with 2,000 lb (907 kg) payload to hover
   IGE at 10,150 ft (3,090 m), 10% fuel reserve
          577 nm (665 miles; 1,070 km)
CH-113 with 5,000 lb (2,270 kg) payload to
   hover IGE at 13,350 ft (4,070 m), 10% fuel
   reserve   405 nm (467 miles; 751 km)
CH/UH-46A at AUW of 19,229 lb (8,722 kg)
   with 4,000 lb (1,815 kg) payload, 10% fuel
   reserve   199 nm (230 miles; 370 km)
CH/UH-46A at AUW of 21,400 lb (9,706 kg)
   with 6,070 lb (2,753 kg) payload, 10% fuel
   reserve   199 nm (230 miles; 370 km)
CH/UH-46D at AUW of 20,800 lb (9,435 kg)
   with 4,550 lb (2,064 kg) payload, 10% fuel
   reserve   206 nm (238 miles; 383 km)
CH/UH-46D at AUW of 23,000 lb (10,433 kg)
   with 6,750 lb (3,062 kg) payload, 10% fuel
   reserve   198 nm (228 miles; 366 km)
Basic 107-II (T58-GE-5 engines) with 2,400 lb
   (1,088 kg) payload, 30 minutes fuel reserve
   at best endurance speed
          549 nm (633 miles; 1,020 km)

BOEING-VERTOL MODEL 114
US Army designation: CH-47 Chinook

Development of the CH-47 (formerly YHC-1B) Chinook series of helicopters began in 1956, when the Department of the Army announced its intention to replace its piston-engined transport helicopters with a new generation of turbine-powered helicopters. As a result of a systems capability analysis by a joint Army/Air Force Selection Board, the Vertol Division of the Boeing Company was awarded an initial contract for five YCH-47A's by the US Army in June 1959. The first YCH-47A was completed on 28 April 1961. The first hovering flight was made on 21 September 1961. Since then, the effectiveness of the CH-47 has been increased by successive product improvement programmes. A total of 550 Chinooks had been delivered by February 1969, at which time US Army CH-47's had flown more than 500,000 hours; of this total more than two-thirds had been accumulated under combat conditions in South-East Asia.

The CH-47 was designed to meet the US Army's requirement for an all-weather medium transport helicopter and, depending upon the series model, is capable of transporting specified payloads under severe combinations of altitude and temperature conditions. The primary mission radius criteria established by the US Army is 115 miles (185 km). The primary mission take-off gross weight is based on the capability of hovering out of ground effect at 6,000 ft/95°F (1,830 m/ 35°C). The CH-47 has demonstrated its ability to hover out of ground effect with a useful load of 20,800 lb (9,435 kg) at sea level under standard atmospheric conditions.

Boeing-Vertol announced that a CH-47 Chinook had flown on 30 April 1969 with composite material rotor blades. These 60 ft (18·29 m) diameter blades, constructed of glass-fibre with an aluminium honeycomb core, are the largest composite material blades yet built.

Three versions of the Chinook have been announced:

CH-47A. Initial production version, powered by two 2,200 shp Lycoming T55-L-5 or 2,650 shp T55-L-7 shaft-turbine engines.

CH-47B. Developed version with 2,850 shp T55-L-7C shaft-turbines, redesigned rotor blades with cambered leading-edge, blunted rear rotor pylon, and strakes along rear ramp and fuselage for improved flying qualities. First of two prototypes flew for the first time in early October 1966. Deliveries began on 10 May 1967.

CH-47C. This latest model achieves its increased performance from a combination of strengthened transmissions, two 3,750 shp T55-L-11 engines and increased integral fuel capacity totalling 1,129 US gallons (4,273 litres). First flight of the CH-47C was made on 14 October 1967, and deliveries of production aircraft began in the Spring of 1968. They were first deployed in Vietnam in September 1968.

In April 1968, The Boeing Company and Elicotteri Meridionali of Italy reached an agreement for the co-production, marketing and servicing of the CH-47C Chinook, covering Italy, Austria, Switzerland and the Middle East.

Following delivery of the CH-47A to the US Army in December 1962, for service testing and pilot training, the helicopter participated in the Army's team exercises for the evaluation of air mobility and became fully operational with the First Cavalry Division (Air Mobile), formerly the 11th Air Assault Division. The Chinook was classified in October 1963 as Standard A (the US Army's designation for its standard medium transport helicopter). It is the only type so designated in this size category.

By the beginning of 1969, more than 270 CH-47 Chinooks had been deployed in Vietnam, and had logged more than 360,000 hours of combat flight. On one occasion, no fewer than 147 refugees and their possessions were evacuated by

a single aircraft; and more than 5,700 disabled aircraft worth more than $1·5 billion had been recovered by Chinooks and flown to repair bases by January 1969.

Boeing-Vertol announced, at the beginning of April 1970, receipt of a $46·3 million contract from the US Army Aviation Systems Command for an additional 36 CH-47 Chinooks, as well as a contract worth $232,428 to study and evaluate the effects of various manufacturing processes for finishing and surfacing spiral bevel gears.

TYPE: Twin-engined medium transport helicopter.

ROTOR SYSTEM (CH-47A): Two three-blade rotors, rotating in opposite directions and driven through interconnecting shafts which enable both rotors to be driven by either engine. Blades have a steel "D" spar, to which trailing-edge boxes constructed of aluminium ribs and glass-fibre skin are bonded. They have a modified NACA 0012 section, and have provision for a chemical de-icing system. Two blades of each rotor can be folded manually. Rotor heads are fully-articulated, with pitch, flapping and drag hinges. All bearings are submerged completely in oil.

ROTOR SYSTEM (CH-47B/C): Blades have cambered leading-edge, a strengthened steel spar structure, honeycomb-filled trailing-edge boxes and are approximately ·6 in (15 cm) longer than those of the CH-47A.

ROTOR DRIVE: Power is transmitted from each engine through individual overrunning clutches, into the combiner transmission, thereby providing a single power output to the interconnecting shafts. Rotor/engine rpm ratio 66 : 1 for the A and B models, and 64 : 1 for the CH-47C.

FUSELAGE: Square-section all-metal semi-monocoque structure. Loading ramp forms undersurface of upswept rear fuselage. Fairing pods under bottom of each side are made of metal honeycomb sandwich and are sealed and compartmented, as is the under-floor section of the fuselage, for buoyancy during operation from water.

LANDING GEAR: Non-retractable quadricycle type, with dual wheels on each forward unit and single wheels on each rear unit. Oleo-pneumatic shock-absorbers on all units. Rear units fully castoring and steerable; power steering installed on starboard rear unit. All wheels are government-furnished size 24 × 7·7-VII, with tyres size 8·50-10-III, pressure 67 lb/sq in (4·71 kg/cm²). Two single-disc hydraulic brakes. Provision for fitting detachable wheel-skis.

POWER PLANT: Two Lycoming T55 shaft-turbine engines (details under model listings above), mounted on each side of rear rotor pylon. Self-sealing fuel tanks in external pods on sides of fuselage. Total fuel capacity of CH-47A/B is 621 US gallons (2,350 litres) and 1,129 US gallons (4,273 litres) for the CH-47C. Refuelling points above tanks. Total oil capacity 3·7 US gallons (14 litres).

ACCOMMODATION: Two pilots on flight deck, with dual controls. Jump seat is provided for crew chief or combat commander. Jettisonable door on each side of flight deck. Depending on seating arrangement, 33 to 44 troops can be accommodated in main cabin, or 24 litters plus two attendants, or vehicles and freight. Typical loads include a complete artillery section with crew and ammunition, and missile systems such as Littlejohn. All components of the Pershing missile system are transportable by Chinooks. Extruded magnesium floor designed for distributed load of 300 lb/sq ft (1,465 kg/m²) and concentrated load of 2,500 lb (1,136 kg) per wheel in tread portion. Floor contains eighty-three 5,000 lb (2,270 kg) tie-down fittings and eight 10,000 lb (4,540 kg) fittings. Rear loading ramp can

Boeing CH-47 Chinook with detachable wheel-skis fitted *(Stephen P. Peltz)*

Boeing CH-47C Chinook twin-engined medium transport helicopter

be left completely or partially open, or can be removed to permit transport of extra-long cargo and in-flight parachute or free-drop delivery of cargo and equipment. Main cabin door, at front on starboard side, comprises upper hinged section which can be opened in flight and lower section with integral steps. Lower section is jettisonable.

SYSTEMS: Cabin heated by 200,000 BTU heater-blower. Hydraulic system provides pressures of 3,000 lb/sq in (210 kg/cm²) for flying controls, and 4,000 lb/sq in (280 kg/cm²) for engine starting. Electrical system includes two 20kVA alternators driven by transmission drive system. Solar T62 APU runs accessory gear drive, thereby operating all hydraulic and electrical systems.

ELECTRONICS AND EQUIPMENT: All government furnished, including UHF communications and FM liaison sets, transponder, intercom, omni-receiver, ADF and marker beacon receiver. Blind-flying instrumentation standard. Special equipment includes dual electro-hydraulic stability augmentation system, automatic/manual speed trim system, hydraulically-powered winch for rescue and cargo handling purposes, cargo and rescue hatch in floor, external cargo hook of 20,000 lb (9,072 kg) capacity, integral work stands and steps for maintenance, rear view mirror, provisions for paratroops' static lines and for maintenance davits for removal of major components.

DIMENSIONS, EXTERNAL:
Diameter of rotors (each):
CH-47A   59 ft 1¼ in (18·02 m)
CH-47B/C   60 ft 0 in (18·29 m)
Main rotor blade chord:
CH-47A   1 ft 11 in (58·4 cm)
CH-47B/C   2 ft 1¼ in (63·5 cm)
Distance between rotor centres
                39 ft 2 in (11·94 m)
Length overall, rotors turning:
CH-47A   98 ft 1·3 in (29·90 m)
CH-47B/C   99 ft 0 in (30·18 m)
Length of fuselage   51 ft 0 in (15·54 m)
Width, rotors folded 12 ft 5 in (3·78 m)
Height to top of rear rotor hub
                18 ft 7 in (5·67 m)
Wheelbase   22 ft 6 in (6·86 m)
Passenger door (fwd, stbd):
Height   5 ft 6 in (1·68 m)
Width   3 ft 0 in (0·91 m)
Height to sill 3 ft 7 in (1·09 m)
Rear loading ramp entrance:
Height   6 ft 6 in (1·98 m)
Width   7 ft 7 in (2·31 m)
Height to sill 2 ft 7 in (0·79 m)
DIMENSIONS, INTERNAL:
Cabin, excluding flight deck:
Length   30 ft 2 in (9·20 m)

Condition 1 Criteria: Take-off gross weight equals gross weight to hover out of ground effect at 6,000 ft/95°F (1.830 m/35°C). Radius of action of 100 nm (115 miles; 185 km). Fuel reserve of 10%. Payload is carried internally.

Condition 2 Criteria: Take-off gross weight equals design gross weight. Radius of action of 100 nm (115 miles; 185 km). Fuel reserve of 10%. Payload is carried internally.

Condition 3 Criteria: Take-off gross weight equals alternative design gross weight. Radius of action of 20 nm (23 miles; 37 km). Fuel reserve of 10%. Payload is carried externally. Except for the mission average cruise speed, all other performance is predicated on internal loading of cargo.

Width   7 ft 6 in (2·29 m)
Height   6 ft 6 in (1·98 m)
Floor area   226 sq ft (21·0 m²)
Usable volume   1,474 cu ft (41·7 m³)

AREAS:
Rotor blade (each):
CH-47A   56·6 sq ft (5·26 m²)
CH-47B/C   63·1 sq ft (5·86 m²)

Main rotor discs (total):
CH-47A   5,486 sq ft (509·6 m²)
CH-47B/C   5,655 sq ft (525·3 m²)

BOEING-VERTOL MODEL 347

First flown in late May 1970, the Model 347 is a research helicopter developed with company funds under US Army sponsorship. It is an enlarged CH-47A with increased diameter four-blade rotors and a stretched fuselage. Wings will be added later for improved manoeuvrability.

CH-47 CHINOOK WEIGHTS AND PERFORMANCE

	Condition 1	Condition 2	Condition 3
Take-off weight:			
CH-47A	28,400 lb (12,882 kg)	28,550 lb (12,950 kg)	33,000 lb (14,969 kg)
CH-47B	31,350 lb (14,220 kg)	33,000 lb (14,969 kg)	40,000 lb (18,144 kg)
CH-47C	39,200 lb (17,781 kg)	33,000 lb (14,969 kg)	46,000 lb (20,865 kg)
Weight empty:			
CH-47A	17,932 lb (8,133 kg)	17,932 lb (8,133 kg)	18,112 lb (8,216 kg)
CH-47B	19,375 lb (8,788 kg)	19,375 lb (8,788 kg)	19,555 lb (8,870 kg)
CH-47C	20,378 lb (9,243 kg)	20,378 lb (9,243 kg)	20,547 lb (9,320 kg)
Payload:			
CH-47A	6,000 lb (2,722 kg)	6,150 lb (2,790 kg)	13,400 lb (6,078 kg)
CH-47B	7,200 lb (3,266 kg)	8,850 lb (4,014 kg)	18,600 lb (8,437 kg)
CH-47C	13,450 lb (6,101 kg)	7,500 lb (3,402 kg)	23,450 lb (10,637 kg)
Mission radius:			
CH-47A	100 nm (115 miles; 185 km)	100 nm (115 miles; 185 km)	20 nm (23 miles; 37 km)
CH-47B	93 nm (107 miles; 172 km)	92 nm (106 miles; 171 km)	20 nm (23 miles; 37 km)
CH-47C	100 nm (115 miles; 185 km)	100 nm (115 miles; 185 km)	20 nm (23 miles; 37 km)
Average cruising speed:			
CH-47A	130 knots (150 mph; 241 km/h)	130 knots (150 mph; 241 km/h)	115 knots (132 mph; 212 km/h)
CH-47B	141 knots (162 mph; 261 km/h)	141 knots (162 mph; 261 km/h)	119 knots (137 mph; 220 km/h)
CH-47C	139 knots (160 mph; 257 km/h)	137 knots (158 mph; 254 km/h)	114 knots (131 mph; 211 km/h)
Max speed at S/L, normal rated power:			
CH-47A	130 knots (150 mph; 241 km/h)	130 knots (150 mph; 241 km/h)	110 knots (127 mph; 204 km/h)
CH-47B	156 knots (180 mph; 290 km/h)	155 knots (178 mph; 286 km/h)	125 knots (144 mph; 232 km/h)
CH-47C	155 knots (178 mph; 286 km/h)	165 knots (190 mph; 306 km/h)	123 knots (142 mph; 229 km/h)
Max rate of climb at S/L, standard temperature, normal rated power:			
CH-47A	2,180 ft (644 m)/min	2,160 ft (658 m)/min	1,595 ft (486 m)/min
CH-47B	2,225 ft (678 m)/min	2,010 ft (613 m)/min	1,285 ft (392 m)/min
CH-47C	2,045 ft (623 m)/min	2,880 ft (878 m)/min	1,320 ft (402 m)/min
Hovering ceiling out of ground effect, max power, standard temperature:			
CH-47A	12,500 ft (3,810 m)	12,300 ft (3,750 m)	7,300 ft (2,225 m)
CH-47B	12,400 ft (3,780 m)	10,700 ft (3,260 m)	1,700 ft (520 m)
CH-47C	9,600 ft (2,925 m)	14,750 ft (4,495 m)	Sea Level
Service ceiling, normal rated power, standard temperature:			
CH-47A	11,900 ft (3,625 m)	11,900 ft (3,625 m)	9,200 ft (2,805 m)
CH-47B	15,000 ft (4,570 m)	14,000 ft (4,265 m)	9,000 ft (2,745 m)
CH-47C	10,200 ft (3,110 m)	15,000 ft (4,570 m)	8,000 ft (2,440 m)
Max ferry range (integral and internal auxiliary fuel only). Cruise at optimum altitude and standard temperature. No payload. 10% Fuel reserve			
CH-47A	—	—	835 nm (962 miles; 1,548 km)
CH-47B	—	—	1,086 nm (1,250 miles; 2,021 km)
CH-47C	—	—	1,233 nm (1,420 miles; 2,285 km)

BOWERS

PETER M. BOWERS

ADDRESS:

13826 Des Moines Way South, Seattle, Washington 98168

Mr Peter Bowers, an aeronautical engineer with Boeing in Seattle, is a principle source of detailed information on vintage aircraft in the United States, and has provided much of the data for a number of replicas of 1914-18 War aircraft now under construction or flying.

Among several aircraft built by Mr Bowers is a full-scale replica of the Wright Model EX of 1911, the first aeroplane to cross the American continent. This machine was tested as a towed sailplane in the Autumn of 1961 and during 1967/68 was converted into a replica of the Wright Model "A", the US Army's first aeroplane. Powered by a 25 hp Ford Model "T" engine, it was intended to take part in celebrations to mark the anniversary of the 1908/09 flights of the original machine.

In addition to this work on replicas, Mr Bowers has designed and built a single-seat light aircraft known as the Fly Baby, of which full details are given below.

Mr Bowers is building the prototype of a new two-seat light aircraft of his own design. It will be of all-wood construction with a tapered cantilever wing of inverted-gull shape. When arranged as a tandem two-seater, with a 108-125 hp engine, this aircraft will be known as the Bowers Little Stuka. The side-by-side version will have a 150 hp engine and will be named Namu II, after Seattle's famous captive whale, because of its more bulky appearance.

BOWERS FLY BABY 1-A

The prototype Fly Baby monoplane was produced to compete in an Experimental Aircraft Association design contest, organised to encourage the development of a simple, low-cost, easy-to-fly aeroplane that could be built by inexperienced amateurs for recreational flying. It was built in 720 working hours, at a cost of $1,050, and flew for the first time on 27 July 1960. As only one other aircraft was completed by the specified closing date, the contest was postponed for two years.

Following a crash in April 1962, when a pilot borrowed the Fly Baby and became lost in mountain country in bad weather, an entirely new fuselage was built. This is 6 in (15 cm) longer than the original and features minor structural improvements. In addition, the original Continental A65 engine, converted to give 75 hp, has been replaced by a C75 engine converted to give 85 hp, and the capacity of the fuel tank has been increased from 12 to 16 US gallons (60·5 litres).

When the EAA contest was finally held in the Summer of 1962, Fly Baby was placed first and won a prize of $2,500. Home construction plans of the aircraft are available and 2,431 sets had been sold by 1 May 1970. In May 1970, 481 Fly Babies were known to be under construction and 77 had been completed by early May 1970, including some based on detailed drawings and instructions published in *Sport Aviation*, journal of the EAA.

The Fly Baby monoplane has been tested as a twin-float seaplane, in which configuration it has a max AUW of 1,000 lb (454 kg) and cruising speed of 97 mph (156 kmh).

During 1968, Mr Bowers designed and built interchangeable biplane wings for the Fly Baby, and he has since designated the monoplane version as the Fly Baby 1-A, and the biplane as the Fly Baby 1-B.

The Fly Baby 1-A shown in an illustration above differs from those built to the original plans by having an enclosed cabin; it was constructed by Mr Thomas J. Newall of Troy, Michigan.

The following description applies to the Fly Baby 1-A. The Fly Baby 1-B biplane is described separately.

TYPE: Single-seat light monoplane.

WINGS: Wire-braced low-wing monoplane. Double ½ in 1 × 19 stainless steel bracing wires. Wing section NACA 4412. Wooden two-spar structure, covered with Dacron fabric and finished with two coats of nitrate dope and one coat of automotive enamel. Wings rotate about a special fitting to fold back alongside the fuselage for towing.

FUSELAGE: Conventional plywood-covered wood structure of rectangular section. Decking behind cockpit, including pilot's head-rest, is removable and can be replaced with higher transparent section matched with a sliding transparent cockpit canopy for enclosed cockpit operation.

TAIL UNIT: Wire-braced wood structure, fabric-covered.

LANDING GEAR: Non-retractable tail-wheel type. Main landing gear struts of laminated wood, braced by crossed steel wires. Steel-tube straight-across axle faired with streamline-section steel tube. Ends of axles project beyond wheel hubs to serve as anchor points

Modified Bowers Fly Baby 1-A built by Mr Thomas J. Newall of Troy, Michigan (*Jean Seele*)

Bowers Fly Baby 1-A (85 hp Continental C85 engine) built by Mr Francis Londo of Bothell, Washington. The non-standard canopy adds 7 mph to cruising speed

for wing bracing wires. Shock-absorption by low-pressure 8·00 × 4 tyres, carried on Piper Cub wheels, with hydraulic brakes.

POWER PLANT: One 85 hp Continental C75 four-cylinder horizontally-opposed air-cooled engine, driving a two-blade fixed-pitch propeller. Fuel tank from Piper J-3 Cub, capacity 16 US gallons (60·5 litres).

ACCOMMODATION: Single seat in open or enclosed cockpit. Baggage in under-fuselage "tank" which can be removed and carried like a suitcase.

DIMENSIONS, EXTERNAL:

Wing span	28 ft 0 in (8·53 m)
Wing chord (constant)	4 ft 6 in (1·37 m)
Length overall	18 ft 6 in (5·64 m)
Height, wings folded	6 ft 6 in (1·98 m)

WEIGHTS:

Weight empty	605 lb (274 kg)
Max T-O weight	924 lb (419 kg)

PERFORMANCE (at max T-O weight):

Max level speed at S/L	over 104 knots (120 mph; 193 km/h)
Cruising speed	91-96 knots (105-110 mph; 169-177 km/h)
Landing speed	39 knots (45 mph; 72·5 km/h)
Rate of climb at S/L	1,100 ft (335 m)/min
T-O run	250 ft (76 m)
Landing run	250 ft (76 m)
Range with max fuel	277 nm (320 miles; 515 km)

BOWERS FLY BABY 1-B

During 1968 Mr Bowers designed and built a set of interchangeable biplane wings for the original prototype Fly Baby and with these fitted it flew for the first time on 27 March 1969.

The new wings have the same aerofoil section and incidence as those of the monoplane version, but the rib webs are made of ⅟₁₆ in instead of ⅛ in plywood and the wingtip bows are formed from ¼ in aluminium tube instead of laminated wood strips. This lightweight construction limits weight increase to only 46 lb (20 kg) for an increase of 30 sq ft (2·79 m²) in wing area. Span is reduced by 6 ft (1·83 m) and chord by 1 ft (0·30 m). Ailerons are fitted to the lower wings only.

To facilitate entry to the cockpit the upper wing has been located well forward, and in order to bring the new centre of lift in line with the original CG, both planes have been given 11° of sweep-back. Change-over from monoplane to

Biplane conversion of the Fly Baby, designated Bowers Fly Baby 1-B (*Chuck Billingsly*)

biplane configuration can be accomplished by two people in approximately one hour.

The description of the Fly Baby 1-A applies also to the 1-B, except in the following details.

TYPE: Single-seat light biplane.

WINGS: Forward-stagger single-bay biplane with N-type interplane and centre-section struts. Landing and flying bracing wires. Sweepback 11°. Wooden structure with Dacron covering. Rib webs constructed of $\frac{1}{8}$ in plywood, wingtip

bows formed of $\frac{1}{2}$ in aluminium tube. Ailerons on lower wings only.

POWER PLANT: One 65 hp Continental A65 engine, currently being replaced by one 108 hp Lycoming O-235 engine.

DIMENSIONS, EXTERNAL:
Wing span   22 ft 0 in (6·71 m)
Wing chord, both wings (constant)
     3 ft 6 in (1·07 m)
Height overall   6 ft 10 in (2·08 m)

AREA:
Wings, gross   150 sq ft (13·94 m²)

WEIGHTS AND LOADING:
Weight empty   651 lb (295 kg)
Max T-O weight   972 lb (440 kg)
Max wing loading   6·5 lb/sq ft (31·74 kg/m²)

PERFORMANCE (at max T-O weight):
Cruising speed   67 knots (77 mph; 124 km/h)
Rate of climb at S/L   600 ft (183 m)/min

BRANTLY (see under Aeronautical Research and Development Corporation)

BUSHBY
BUSHBY AIRCRAFT INC

ADDRESS:
848 Westwood Drive, Glenwood, Illinois 60425

Mr Robert W. Bushby, a research engineer with Sinclair Oil Co, began by building a Midget Mustang single-seat sporting monoplane, using drawings, jigs and certain components produced by the aircraft's designer, the late David Long. He is now producing the aircraft in kit form and is also offering sets of plans of the Midget Mustang and a two-seat derivative known as the Mustang-II to amateur constructors.

BUSHBY/LONG MIDGET MUSTANG

The prototype of the Midget Mustang was completed in 1948 by David Long, then chief engineer of the Piper company. He flew it in the National Air Races that year, and in 1949 was placed fourth in the Continental Trophy Race at Miami.

Two versions have been developed by Robert Bushby, as follows:

MM-1-85. Powered by 85 hp Continental C85-8FJ engine. Flew for first time on 9 September 1959.

MM-1-125. Powered by 135 hp Lycoming O-290-D2 engine. Otherwise similar to MM-1-85. Flew for first time in July 1963.

At least 48 Midget Mustangs had been completed by the Spring of 1970 and there were 450 more under construction throughout the world.

The following details apply to both versions:

TYPE: Single-seat fully-aerobatic sporting monoplane.

WINGS: Cantilever low-wing monoplane. Wing section NACA 64A212 at root, NACA 64A210 at tip. Dihedral 5°. Incidence 1° 30'. Two-spar flush-riveted stressed-skin aluminium structure. Aluminium statically-balanced ailerons and plain trailing-edge flaps.

FUSELAGE: Aluminium flush-riveted stressed-skin monocoque structure.

TAIL UNIT: Cantilever all-metal structure. Controllable trim-tab in port elevator.

LANDING GEAR: Non-retractable tail-wheel type. Cantilever spring steel main legs. Steerable tail-wheel. Goodyear wheels and tyres, size 5·00 × 5, pressure 18 lb/sq in (1·27 kg/cm²). Goodyear hydraulic disc brakes.

POWER PLANT (MM-1-85): One 85 hp Continental C85-8FJ or -12 four-cylinder horizontally-opposed air-cooled engine, driving a McCauley two-blade metal fixed-pitch propeller. Fuel tank aft of firewall, capacity 15 US gallons (57 litres). Optional wing-tip tanks, each with capacity of 7 US gallons (26·5 litres). Oil capacity 1 US gallon (3·75 litres).

POWER PLANT (MM-1-125): One 135 hp Lycoming O-290-D2 four-cylinder horizontally-opposed air-cooled engine, driving a Sensenich two-blade metal fixed-pitch propeller. Fuel tank aft of firewall, capacity 15 US gallons (57 litres). No provision for wing-tip tanks. Oil capacity 1·5 US gallons (5·75 litres).

ACCOMMODATION: Single seat in enclosed cabin. Canopy hinged on starboard side. Space for 12 lb (5·5 kg) of baggage aft of seat. Room for back parachute.

ELECTRONICS AND EQUIPMENT: Radio optional. No provision for blind-flying instrumentation. Electrical system available on MM-1-85 only.

DIMENSIONS, EXTERNAL:
Wing span   18 ft 6 in (5·64 m)
Span over tip tanks (MM-1-85)
     19 ft 8 in (5·99 m)
Wing chord at root   5 ft 0 in (1·53 m)
Wing chord at tip   2 ft 6 in (0·76 m)
Wing aspect ratio   4
Length overall   16 ft 5 in (5·00 m)
Height overall   4 ft 6 in (1·37 m)
Tailplane span   6 ft 6 in (1·98 m)
Wheel track   5 ft 1 in (1·55 m)

DIMENSIONS, INTERNAL:
Cabin: length   3 ft 11 in (1·19 m)
Max width   1 ft 10 in (0·56 m)
Max height   4 ft 0 in (1·22 m)
Baggage space   2 cu ft (0·057 m²)

AREAS:
Wings, gross   68 sq ft (6·32 m²)
Ailerons (total)   4·8 sq ft (0·45 m²)
Trailing-edge flaps (total) 7·5 sq ft (0·70 m²)
Fin   3·5 sq ft (0·33 m²)
Rudder   3·36 sq ft (0·31 m²)
Tailplane   8·78 sq ft (0·82 m²)
Elevators, including tab   5·12 sq ft (0·48 m²)

Bushby/Long Midget Mustang (85 hp Continental C85-8FJ engine) built by Mr Dennis Simpson of Anderson, Indiana (*Jean Seele*)

WEIGHTS AND LOADINGS:
Weight empty:
MM-1-85   575 lb (261 kg)
MM-1-125   590 lb (268 kg)
Max T-O and landing weight:
MM-1-85   875 lb (397 kg)
MM-1-125   900 lb (408 kg)
Max wing loading:
MM-1-85   12·9 lb/sq ft (63·00 kg/m²)
MM-1-125   13·2 lb/sq ft (64·45 kg/m²)
Max power loading:
MM-1-85   10·0 lb/hp (4·53 kg/hp)
MM-1-125   7·2 lb/hp (3·26 kg/hp)

PERFORMANCE (at max T-O weight):
Max level speed at S/L:
MM-1-85   165 knots (190 mph; 306 km/h)
MM-1-125   182 knots (210 mph; 338 km/h)
Max permissible diving speed
   243 knots (280 mph; 450 km/h)
Max cruising speed:
MM-1-85   152 knots (175 mph; 281 km/h)
MM-1-125   165 knots (190 mph; 306 km/h)
Econ cruising speed:
MM-1-85   129 knots (148 mph; 238 km/h)
MM-1-125   143 knots (165 mph; 265 km/h)
Stalling speed, flaps down:
MM-1-85   50 knots (57 mph; 92 km/h)
MM-1-125   53 knots (60 mph; 97 km/h)
Rate of climb at S/L:
MM-1-85   1,750 ft (533 m)/min
MM-1-125   2,200 ft (670 m)/min
Service ceiling:
MM-1-85   over 16,000 ft (4,875 m)
MM-1-125   19,000 ft (5,790 m)
T-O run:
MM-1-85   450 ft (137 m)
MM-1-125   400 ft (122 m)
T-O to 50 ft (15 m):
MM-1-85   900 ft (274 m)
MM-1-125   700 ft (213 m)
Landing from 50 ft (15 m)   1,200 ft (365 m)
Landing run   500 ft (152 m)
Range with max fuel:
MM-1-85   347 nm (400 miles; 640 km)
MM-1-125   325 nm (375 miles; 603 km)
Range with max fuel and tip-tanks:
MM-1-85   651 nm (750 miles; 1,200 km)

BUSHBY M-II MUSTANG-II

Design of this side-by-side two-seat derivative of the Midget Mustang was started in 1963. Construction of a prototype began in 1965 and it flew for the first time on 9 July 1966. During 1968 Mr Bushby designed an alternative non-retractable tricycle landing gear for the Mustang II, and amateur constructors have the option of either configuration. Some 300 examples are being built by amateurs in the Spring of 1970, at which time at least three Mustang IIs were flying.

The details below apply to the de luxe model, and the empty weight quoted includes IFR instrumentation and nav/com equipment. The M-II can also be operated as an aerobatic aircraft in what Bushby Aircraft call the "Sport" configuration. This is identical to the de luxe model except that the electrical system, radio and additional IFR instrumentation are deleted.

The "Sport" model has an empty weight of 750 lb (340 kg) and T-O weight of 1,250 lb (567 kg).

TYPE: Two-seat amateur-built light aircraft.

WINGS: Cantilever low-wing monoplane. Outer wings similar to those of Midget Mustang, attached to new constant-chord centre-section of short span. Wing section NACA 64A212 at root, NACA 64A210 at tip. Dihedral 5° on outer wings only. Incidence 1° 30'. Two-spar flush-riveted stressed-skin aluminium structure. Aluminium statically-balanced ailerons and plain trailing-ege flaps. No trim-tabs.

FUSELAGE: Aluminium flush-riveted stressed-skin monocoque structure.

TAIL UNIT: Cantilever all-metal structure. Fixed-incidence tailplane. Controllable trim-tab in starboard elevator.

LANDING GEAR: Standard version has non-retractable tail-wheel type. Cantilever spring steel main legs. Goodyear 5·00 × 5 main wheels and tyres, pressure 20 lb/sq in (1·41 kg/cm²). Goodyear hydraulic disc brakes. Steerable tail-wheel. Alternatively, non-retractable tricycle type. Cantilever spring steel main legs. Cleveland or Goodyear wheels and tyres size 5·00 × 5. Non-steerable nose-wheel, mounted on oleo-pneumatic shock strut and free to swivel up to 16° either side. Goodyear wheel and tyre size 5·00 × 5. Goodyear or Cleveland hydraulic disc brakes. Wheel fairings optional on either type of landing gear.

POWER PLANT: Normally one 160 hp Lycoming O-320 four-cylinder horizontally-opposed air-cooled engine, driving a two-blade fixed-pitch metal propeller, diameter 6 ft 0 in (1·82 m). Provision for other engines including a 125 hp Lycoming O-290 engine, driving a two-blade fixed-pitch metal propeller 5 ft 8 in (1·73 m) in diameter. Fuel tank aft of firewall, capacity 25 US gallons (94·6 litres). Refuelling point on starboard side of fuselage aft of firewall. Provision for wingtip tanks. Oil capacity 2 US gallons (7·5 litres).

ACCOMMODATION: Two seats side-by-side, under large rearward-sliding transparent canopy. Dual controls. Baggage space aft of seats, capacity 75 lb (34 kg).

SYSTEMS: 12V electrical system, supplied by Delco-Remy 15A generator and Exide 33A battery.

ELECTRONICS AND EQUIPMENT: Provision for full IFR instrumentation and dual nav/com system.

DIMENSIONS, EXTERNAL:
Wing span   24 ft 2 in (7·37 m)
Wing chord at root   4 ft 10 in (1·47 m)
Wing chord at tip   2 ft 7 in (0·79 m)
Wing aspect ratio   5·5
Length overall   19 ft 6 in (5·94 m)
Height overall   5 ft 3 in (1·60 m)
Tailplane span   7 ft 6 in (2·29 m)
Wheel track   6 ft 10 in (2·08 m)

DIMENSIONS, INTERNAL:
Cabin:
Length, incl baggage compartment
     5 ft 2 in (1·57 m)
Max width   3 ft 4 in (1·02 m)
Max height   3 ft 5 in (1·04 m)
Baggage space   5·5 cu ft (0·16 m²)

AREAS:

Wings, gross	97·12 sq ft (9·02 m²)
Ailerons (total)	4·8 sq ft (0·45 m²)
Flaps (total)	9·1 sq ft (0·85 m²)
Fin	4·25 sq ft (0·39 m²)
Rudder	4·1 sq ft (0·38 m²)
Tailplane	9·28 sq ft (0·86 m²)
Elevators, incl tab	5·42 sq ft (0·50 m²)

WEIGHTS AND LOADINGS:

Weight empty, equipped (N = nose-wheel, T = tail-wheel landing gear):

N 125 hp engine	911 lb (413 kg)
T 125 hp engine	900 lb (408 kg)
N 160 hp engine	938 lb (425 kg)
T 160 hp engine	927 lb (420 kg)
Max T-O and landing weight	1,450 lb (658 kg)
Max wing loading	14·9 lb/sq ft (72·75 kg/m²)
Max power loading	11·6 lb/hp (5·26 kg/hp)

PERFORMANCE (with tail-wheel, at max T-O weight):

Max level speed at S/L:

125 hp	148 knots (170 mph; 274 km/h)
160 hp	171 knots (197 mph; 317 km/h)

Max permissible diving speed:

125 hp	173 knots (200 mph; 322 km/h)
160 hp	211 knots (243 mph; 391 km/h)

Max cruising speed at 7,500 ft (2,285 m):

125 hp	152 knots (175 mph; 282 km/h)
160 hp	161 knots (185 mph; 297 km/h)

Stalling speed, flaps down:

125 hp	47 knots (54 mph; 87 km/h)
160 hp	51 knots (58 mph; 94 km/h)

Stalling speed, flaps up:

125 hp	51 knots (58 mph; 94 km/h)
160 hp	53 knots (60 mph; 96 km/h)

Bushby M-II Mustang-II with newly-developed tricycle landing gear (*Jean Seele*)

Rate of climb at S/L:

125 hp	1,000 ft (305 m)/min
160 hp	1,400 ft (425 m)/min

Service ceiling:

125 hp	16,000 ft (4,875 m)
160 hp	18,000 ft (5,485 m)

T-O run	650 ft (198 m)

T-O run to 50 ft (15 m):

125 hp	1,050 ft (320 m)
160 hp	1,000 ft (305 m)

Landing from 50 ft (15 m):

125 hp	950 ft (290 m)
160 hp	1,000 ft (305 m)

Landing run:

125 hp	700 ft (215 m)
160 hp	750 ft (228 m)

Range with standard fuel (75% power):

125 hp	416 nm (480 miles; 770 km)
160 hp	373 nm (430 miles; 692 km)

Range with optional wingtip tanks:

160 hp	542 nm (625 miles; 1,005 km)

BUSHMASTER

Bushmaster 2000 (three 450 hp Pratt & Whitney R-935-AN-14B engines), a modernised version of the Ford Tri-Motor

AIRCRAFT HYDRO-FORMING, INC

HEAD OFFICE:
131 East Gardena Boulevard, Gardena, California 90247

PRESIDENT: Ralph P. Williams

Aircraft Hydro-Forming, Inc, is a major subcontractor to the aircraft industry. Employing nearly 200 people, it supplies wing leading-edges and engine pods for the Douglas DC-8 and components for many other types, including the DC-9, Boeing 707, Northrop F-5 and Republic F-105.

In addition, it is continuing a programme to market a modernised version of the Ford Tri-Motor transport aircraft, which was initiated by the original designer of the Tri-Motor, the late Mr William B. Stout. A prototype of the new version has been built as the Bushmaster 2000. All available details follow.

BUSHMASTER 2000

The original Ford Tri-Motor was first produced in the 1920's by the Stout Metal Airplane Company, a division of the Ford Motor Company. After more than 35 years of service, several Tri-Motors are still in commercial operation.

Some years ago, the original designer of the type, the late Mr William B. Stout, conceived the idea of modernising the design and putting it back into production as a simple and economical transport aircraft able to operate from grass surfaces. The Bushmaster 2000, of which the prototype was completed in 1966, is the end product of this programme.

New features compared with the original Tri-Motor include more powerful and lighter Pratt & Whitney R-985-AN-1 or AN-14B engines, each

rated at 450 hp, with improved cowlings for better engine temperature control; Hartzell HC-B3R30-2E fully-feathering three-blade constant-speed propellers; 24V 50A engine-driven generator; aileron, elevator and rudder trim-tabs; oleo-pneumatic main landing gear shock-absorbers; B.F. Goodrich main wheels and tubeless tyres, size 15·00 × 10-ply rating; Hayes Industries tail-wheel and US Rubber tyre, size 17·00 × 8-ply rating; B.F. Goodrich single-disc brakes; modernised cockpit with larger windows; fully-swivelling tail-wheel; re-routing of control cables internally; addition of a large cargo door; strengthened floor for concentrated loads; a larger tail fin; and redesigned elevators which are now interchangeable with each other and with rudder. Later production models will be fitted with wing flaps.

Construction remains all-metal, but the corrugated skin panels are now made of new, lighter and stronger aluminium sheet, riveted to the flanges of structural members. The wing is built around three main spars, with five auxiliary spars to reinforce the corrugated skin. Inter-spar stress distribution is accomplished by struts and diagonals instead of ribs.

The Bushmaster normally accommodates 15 passengers, or equivalent freight, and a crew of two, but can be operated by a single pilot; a high-density seating arrangement will accommodate a pilot and 23 passengers. Optional items include a 600 US gallon (2,272 litre) tank for fire-fighting, forest dusting, etc, and a large floor hatch for loading extra-long items such as oil rig equipment. The normal wheel landing gear can be replaced by floats or skis. Standard fuel capacity is 360 US gallons (1,363 litres), with provision for auxiliary tanks.

FAA certification at a max T-O weight of 12,500 lb (5,670 kg) has been received, but Bushmaster is exploring the possibility of a variation in the Type Certificate to allow domestic operation above 12,500 lb gross weight.

DIMENSIONS, EXTERNAL:

Wing span	77 ft 10 in (23·72 m)
Length overall	49 ft 6 in (15·09 m)
Height overall	13 ft 9 in (4·19 m)
Wheel track	21 ft 0 in (6·40 m)

Cabin door (stbd, rear):

Width	5 ft 0 in (1·52 m)
Height	5 ft 0 in (1·52 m)

DIMENSIONS, INTERNAL:

Cabin: length 20 ft 0 in (6·10 m)

Average width	5 ft 0 in (1·52 m)
Average height	7 ft 0 in (2·13 m)
Volume	720 cu ft (20·4 m³)

AREA:

Wings, gross	900 sq ft (83·6 m²)

WEIGHTS:

Weight empty	7,500 lb (3,401 kg)
Max T-O weight	12,500 lb (5,670 kg)

PERFORMANCE (at max T-O weight):

Max cruising speed 113 knots (130 mph; 209 km/h)

Econ cruising speed 96-100 knots (110-115 mph; 177-185 km/h)

Landing speed	52 knots (60 mph; 97 km/h)
T-O run	580 ft (177 m)
T-O to 50 ft (15 m)	820 ft (250 m)
Landing from 50 ft (15 m)	1,083 ft (330 m)
Landing run	673 ft (205 m)

Range with max fuel 607 nm (700 miles; 1,125 km)

BUTLER
BUTLER AIRCRAFT COMPANY
HEAD OFFICE AND WORKS:

7949 Woodley Avenue, Van Nuys, California 91406

On 16 February 1970 Butler Aviation International acquired the entire assets of Ted Smith Aircraft Company from its former parent, American Cement Corporation. The new company name of Butler Aircraft Company has been adopted.

The Ted Smith Aircraft Company designed and began production of the first two of a series of small twin piston-engined business aircraft known as Aerostars. Design studies are under way for follow-up series of single piston-engined aircraft and turbojet-powered business aircraft.

Limited production began in the Spring of 1967 in the company's research and development facility. A new production factory, with an initial work area of 60,000 sq ft, was occupied on 5 January 1968, at Van Nuys Airport, Van Nuys, California. In the Spring of 1968 production of the Models 600 and 601 had begun. The first delivery of a Model 600 was made in August 1968, and that of a Model 601 in the Summer of 1969.

Butler Aviation International has also acquired Mooney Aircraft Corporation (which see).

BUTLER AEROSTAR 600/601/620

The name "Aerostar" has been given to the initial series of three twin-engined business aircraft being produced by Butler Aircraft Company. All versions have the same basic airframe, with different power plants, and seat up to six persons.

It is claimed that the Aerostar airframe contains only 25% as many components as are used in designs of comparable size. Construction involves the extensive use of monocoque assemblies, in which unstiffened sections of the skin carry loads. The vertical and horizontal fixed tail surfaces are interchangeable, as are the three tail control surfaces.

Current versions of the Aerostar are as follows:

Model 600. Powered by two 290 hp Lycoming IO-540 six-cylinder horizontally-opposed air-cooled engines. Oil capacity 6 US gallons (22·7 litres). In production.

Model 601. As Model 600, but with 290 hp Lycoming IO-540 turbocharged engines. In production.

Model 620. As Model 600, but with 310 hp turbocharged Lycoming TIO-541 engines, and pressurised cabin. Under development.

Design work on the series was started in November 1964. Construction of the prototype began in December 1965 and this aircraft (Model 360/400 prototype) flew for the first time in November 1966. The Model 600/601 prototype flew for the first time in October 1967, the first production Model 600 on 20 December 1967 and the first production Model 601 on 9 July 1968.

The Aerostar Model 360 received FAA type approval in May 1967 and the Model 400 in October 1967. FAA type approval of the Model 600 under FAR Part 23 was awarded on 27 March 1968. The Model 601 was awarded an FAA Type Certificate in November 1968.

TYPE: Twin-engined executive transport.

WINGS: Cantilever mid-wing monoplane. Wing section NACA 64₁A212. Dihedral 2°. Incidence 1°. No sweep. All-metal structure, utilising heavy skin attached to three spars, several bulkheads and several stringers. Entire wing assembly, excluding attachments for ailerons and flaps, contains fewer than 50 detail parts. Ailerons and flaps each comprise a spar, ribs, nose skin and one-piece wrap-around aluminium skin aft of spar.

FUSELAGE: All-metal fail-safe monocoque structure. Skin composed of large segments of aluminium alloy sheet over stringers and frames. Entire fuselage contains fewer than 100 parts, including skin panels. All fuselage assemblies designed basically for pressurisation.

TAIL UNIT: Cantilever all-metal structure. Fin and tailplane swept back at angle of 30° at 25% chord. Electrically-operated trim-tabs in rudder and elevators.

LANDING GEAR: Retractable tricycle type, with single wheel on each unit. Hydraulic retraction, main units inward, nose-wheel forward. Steerable nose-wheel. Hydraulic multiple-disc brakes.

POWER PLANT: Two Lycoming engines (details under individual model listings above), each driving a Hartzell three-blade metal fully-feathering constant-speed propeller, diameter 6 ft 6 in (1·98 m). Fuel in integral wing tanks and fuselage tank, total capacity 177 US gallons (669 litres), of which 170 US gallons (643 litres) are usable.

ACCOMMODATION: Cabin seats six people in track-mounted individual reclining seats. Clamshell type door on port side by pilot's seat. Emergency escape windows at rear of cabin. Tinted windshield and cabin windows. Large utility shelf in aft cabin. Baggage compartment, capacity 240 lb (109 kg), aft of cabin,

with external access. Individual air vents, reading lights and ash trays are provided for each seat as standard equipment.

SYSTEMS: Air-conditioning system incorporates a 30,000 BTU Janitrol heater (Model 601, 35,000 BTU). Electrical systems for all models are 28V single-buss systems, each using two engine-driven 50A alternators. Two 12V 24Ah batteries. Model 620 fuselage structure is modified to withstand a cabin pressure differential of 5·0-5·5 lb/sq in (0·35-0·39 kg/cm²). Pressurisation system utilises engine turbo-supercharging bleed air. Hydraulic pressure of 1,000 lb/sq in (70·3 kg/cm²), provided by engine-driven pump, is used to actuate landing gear and wing flaps. Model 601 has oxygen system with individual outlets at each seat as standard.

ELECTRONICS: Standard avionics includes two Narco MK-12B nav/com systems (Model 601 has Narco MK-24); Narco VOA-8 VOR/ILS converter indicator; Narco VOA-9 VOR/ILS converter indicator; Narco ADF-31A ADF with BFO; Narco UGR-2 glideslope receiver; Narco MBT-R-28 Marker Beacon receiver; Narco UDI-4/300 DME with GS indicator; Bendix TPR 610 transponder (Model 601 has Narco UAT-1 transponder). Installation includes all related antennae, filters, cabin speaker and microphone.

EQUIPMENT: Dual controls, blind-flying instrumentation, external power receptacle, two rotating beacons, landing and taxi lights, navigation lights, instrument panel lights and heated pitot static source.

DIMENSIONS, EXTERNAL:

Wing span	34 ft 2½ in (10·43 m)
Wing chord at root	7 ft 2 in (2·18 m)
Wing chord at tip	2 ft 10·4 in (0·87 m)
Wing aspect ratio	6·83
Length overall	34 ft 9¾ in (10·61 m)
Height overall	12 ft 1½ in (3·70 m)
Tailplane span	14 ft 4 in (4·37 m)
Wheel track	10 ft 2¼ in (3·11 m)
Passenger door:	
Height	3 ft 9 in (1·14 m)
Width	2 ft 4 in (0·87 m)
Baggage compartment door:	
Height	2 ft 0 in (0·61 m)
Width	1 ft 10 in (0·56 m)

DIMENSIONS, INTERNAL:

Cabin: Length	12 ft 6 in (3·81 m)
Width	3 ft 10 in (1·17 m)
Height	4 ft 0 in (1·22 m)
Baggage space	30 cu ft (0·85 m²)

AREAS:

Wings, gross	170 sq ft (15·8 m²)
Tailplane	45·2 sq ft (4·20 m²)

WEIGHTS AND LOADINGS:

Weight empty, equipped:

600	3,425 lb (1,553 kg)
601	3,700 lb (1,678 kg)

Max T-O and landing weight:

600	5,500 lb (2,495 kg)
601	5,700 lb (2,585 kg)
620	6,000 lb (2,720 kg)

Max wing loading:

600	32·3 lb/sq ft (157·7 kg/m²)
601	33·5 lb/sq ft (163·6 kg/m²)
620	35·3 lb/sq ft (172·3 kg/m²)

Max power loading:

600	9·5 lb/hp (4·30 kg/hp)
601	9·8 lb/hp (4·45 kg/hp)
620	9·7 lb/hp (4·40 kg/hp)

PERFORMANCE (at max T-O weight, estimated for Model 620):

Max level speed at S/L:

600	226 knots (260 mph; 418 km/h)
620	228 knots (263 mph; 423 km/h)

Max cruising speed:

600, 70% power at 10,000 ft (3,050 m)
    217 knots (250 mph; 402 km/h)
601, at 25,000 ft (7,620 m)
    271 knots (312 mph; 502 km/h)
601, at 20,000 ft (6,100 m)
    260 knots (300 mph; 483 km/h)
601, at 15,000 ft (4,570 m)
    251 knots (289 mph; 465 km/h)
620, at 20,000 ft (6,100 m)
    249 knots (287 mph; 462 km/h)

Cruising speed:

600, 65% power at 10,000 ft (3,050 m)
    208 knots (240 mph; 386 km/h)
600, 55% power at 10,000 ft (3,050 m)
    195 knots (225 mph; 362 km/h)
601, 75% power at 25,000 ft (7,620 m)
    255 knots (294 mph; 473 km/h)
601, 75% power at 20,000 ft (6,100 m)
    243 knots (280 mph; 451 km/h)
601, 75% power at 15,000 ft (4,570 m)
    232 knots (267 mph; 430 km/h)

First production Butler Aerostar 600 (two 290 hp Lycoming IO-540 engines)

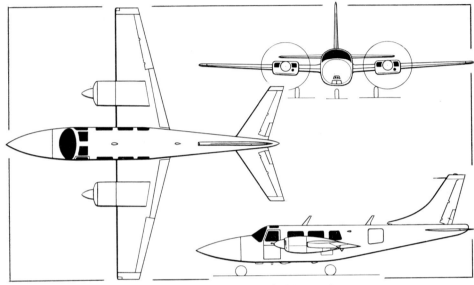

Butler Aerostar Model 600 light transport

601, 70% power at 25,000 ft (7,620 m)
    247 knots (285 mph; 459 km/h)
601, 70% power at 20,000 ft (6,100 m)
    236 knots (272 mph; 438 km/h)
601, 70% power at 15,000 ft (4,570 m)
    225 knots (259 mph; 417 km/h)
601, 65% power at 25,000 ft (7,620 m)
    239 knots (275 mph; 443 km/h)
601, 65% power at 20,000 ft (6,100 m)
    228 knots (263 mph; 423 km/h)
601, 65% power at 15,000 ft (4,570 m)
    218 knots (251 mph; 404 km/h)
620, 60% power at 20,000 ft (6,100 m)
    226 knots (260 mph; 418 km/h)
Stalling speed, wheels and flaps down:
600   67 knots (77 mph; 124 km/h)
601   69 knots (79 mph; 128 km/h)
620   70 knots (81 mph; 131 km/h)

Rate of climb at S/L:
600   1,850 ft (564 m)/min
601   1,800 ft (549 m)/min
620   1,690 ft (515 m)/min
Rate of climb at S/L, one engine out:
600   450 ft (137 m)/min
601   400 ft (122 m)/min
Service ceiling:
600   22,000 ft (6,705 m)
601, 620   over 30,000 ft (9,145 m)
Service ceiling, one engine out:
600   6,300 ft (1,920 m)
601   over 14,000 ft (4,265 m)
T-O run:
601   1,095 ft (334 m)
T-O to 50 ft (15 m):
600   1,025 ft (312 m)
601   1,520 ft (463 m)

620   1,100 ft (335 m)
Landing from 50 ft (15 m):
600   1,100 ft (335 m)
601   1,800 ft (549 m)
620   1,250 ft (381 m)
Landing run:
601   932 ft (284 m)
Range:
600 (65% power at 10,000 ft = 3,050 m with max fuel, 30 min reserve)
    1,216 nm (1,400 miles; 2,250 km)
601 (70% power at 20,000 ft = 6,100 m with max fuel, 30 min reserve at 50% power)
    1,225 nm (1,410 miles; 2,265 km)
620 (at 20,000 ft = 6,100 m with max fuel, 45 min reserve)
    1,244 nm (1,433 miles; 2,306 km)

CAMAIR
CAMAIR AIRCRAFT CORPORATION
HEAD OFFICE:
PO Box 231, Remsenburg, Long Island, New York 11960
PRESIDENT:
Fred Garcia, Jr

This company manufactures a twin-engined version of the North American/Ryan Navion light aircraft, known as the Twin Navion.

CAMAIR TWIN NAVION
The Camair Twin Navion embodies structural modifications to cater for the increased power and weight, together with design and aerodynamic refinements which provide improved performance, comfort and styling. It has been built in the following versions:

Camair Model "A". Single prototype only. Built and flown in 1953 with two 225 hp Continental engines.

Camair Model "B". Powered by two 240 hp Continental O-470-B engines. First flown in early 1954. Total of 28 delivered between 1955-59.

Camair Model "C". First flown in 1960. Production aircraft powered by two 260 hp Continental IO-470-D engines.

Camair Model "D". A single prototype of this version was completed, powered by two 260 hp Continental TSIO-470-B six-cylinder horizontally-opposed air-cooled turbo-supercharged engines. Fuel capacity and gross weight were increased. Refinements included a new instrument panel and one-piece canopy windows. Camair do not intend to put this version into production: the prototype will be retained by the company for flight testing modifications to be introduced on the Models "B" and "C".

The following details apply specifically to the Camair Model "C".

TYPE: Twin-engined four-seat cabin monoplane.
WINGS: Cantilever low-wing monoplane. Wing section NACA 4415R at root, NACA 6410R at tip. Dihedral 7° 30'. Incidence 2° at root, —1° at tip. All-metal structure. All-metal mass-balanced ailerons and hydraulically-operated flaps.
FUSELAGE: All-metal semi-monocoque structure.
TAIL UNIT: Cantilever all-metal structure. Port and starboard tailplane and elevator assemblies interchangeable. Controllable trim-tabs on rudder and elevators. Fin and rudder are larger than those of the Navion to provide additional area required for twin-engine certification.

Camair Twin Navion Model "C" (two 260 hp Continental IO-470-D engines)

LANDING GEAR: Hydraulically-retractable tricycle type. Oleo-pneumatic shock-absorbers. Main wheel tyres size 7·00 × 8, Type III. Steerable nose-wheel, tyre size 6·00 × 6, Type III. Goodyear hydraulic disc brakes.
POWER PLANT: Two 260 hp Continental IO-470-D six-cylinder horizontally-opposed air-cooled engines, each driving a Hartzell constant-speed fully-feathering propeller, diameter 6 ft 10 in (2·08 m). Two 19·5 US gallon (74 litre) aluminium alloy fuel tanks in wing roots and two 35 US gallon (131·5 litre) wingtip tanks. Total fuel capacity 109 US gallons (411 litres).
ACCOMMODATION: Enclosed cabin seating pilot and co-pilot on individual bucket seats and two passengers on bench-type rear seat. Rearward-sliding Plexiglas canopy with transverse web which seals the luggage compartment and provides a shelf when the canopy is closed. Dual controls. Cabin sound-proofing and heating. Windshield de-fogger. Baggage compartment aft of cabin, with outside access, for 180 lb (82 kg) and forward compartment for equipment and baggage in nose, capacity 100 lb (45 kg). Total baggage capacity 280 lb (127 kg).
ELECTRONICS AND EQUIPMENT: Optional items include complete radio, full IFR instrumentation and oxygen system.
DIMENSIONS, EXTERNAL:
Wing span   34 ft 8 in (10·57 m)

Wing chord at root   7 ft 2½ in (2·20 m)
Wing chord at tip   3 ft 11 in (1·19 m)
Wing aspect ratio   6·04
Length overall   28 ft 0 in (8·53 m)
Height overall   10 ft 8 in (3·25 m)
Wheel track   8 ft 8½ in (2·65 m)
Wheelbase   7 ft 8½ in (2·35 m)
AREAS:
Wings gross,   184·34 sq ft (17·13 m²)
Ailerons (total)   10·32 sq ft (0·96 m²)
Trailing-edge flaps (total)   29·23 sq ft (2·72 m²)
Fin   18·20 sq ft (1·69 m²)
Rudder   8·20 sq ft (0·76 m²)
Tailplane   43·05 sq ft (4·0 m²)
Elevators   14·10 sq ft (1·31 m²)
WEIGHTS AND LOADING:
Weight empty   2,950 lb (1,338 kg)
Max T-O wieght   4,323 lb (1,961 kg)
Wing loading   23·45 lb/sq ft (114·5 kg/m²)
PERFORMANCE (at AUW of 3,500 lb = 1,590 kg):
Max level speed
    174 knots (200 mph; 322 km/h)
Max cruising speed (75% power) at 6,000 ft (1,830 m) 165 knots (190 mph; 306 km/h)
Stalling speed   57 knots (65 mph; 105 km/h)
Rate of climb at S/L   1,800 ft (550 m)/min
Single-engine climb at S/L 500 ft (152 m)/min
Service ceiling   22,000 ft (6,700 m)
Single-engine ceiling   9,000 ft (2,750 m)
T-O run   400 ft (122 m)
Landing run   600 ft (183 m)

CARSTEDT
CARSTEDT, INC
HEAD OFFICE AND WORKS:
Long Beach International Airport, California
Carstedt have designed and are manufacturing a "stretched" version of the D.H.104 Dove light transport, powered by two turboprop engines, primarily for 3rd-level airline operation. All available details follow.

CARSTEDT JET LINER 600
The Jet Liner 600 is a turboprop conversion of the Hawker Siddeley (D.H.104) Dove light transport, with a "stretched" fuselage able to accommodate a crew of two and 18 passengers. The prototype flew for the first time on 18 December 1966.

To provide the additional seating, a new 87 in (2·21 m) section is inserted in the rear fuselage. The cockpit canopy is lowered to reduce drag, the loss of headroom being offset by lowering the crew seats and moving the panel 8 in (20 cm) forward. Passenger comfort is improved by the installation of a simple AiResearch air-cycle refrigeration system.

Power plant of the Jet Liner 600 consists of two 605 ehp Garrett AiResearch TPE 331 turboprop engines, each driving a Hartzell three-blade constant-speed fully-feathering and reversible-pitch propeller. Fuel capacity on the prototype has been more than doubled by the installation of tanks with a total capacity of 225 US gallons (850 litres) outboard of the nacelles. These are optional on production conversions.

At the time of writing, max T-O weight of the Jet Liner 600 was limited to 9,150 lb (4,150 kg), but an increase to 10,500 lb (4,760 kg) was awaited.

DIMENSIONS, EXTERNAL:
As for D.H.104 Dove, except:
Length overall   46 ft 6 in (14·17 m)
WEIGHTS:
Weight empty (average)   4,700 lb (2,130 kg)
Max T-O weight   9,150 lb (4,150 kg)
PERFORMANCE (at max T-O weight):
Max cruising speed at 10,000 ft (3,050 m)
    261 knots (300 mph; 482 km/h)

Econ cruising speed at 10,000 ft (3,050 m)
    248 knots (285 mph; 459 km/h)
Stalling speed, wheels and flaps down
    55 knots (63 mph; 102 km/h)
Rate of climb at S/L over 3,000 ft (915 m)/min
Service ceiling   34,000 ft (10,350 m)
Single-engine ceiling   18,000 ft (5,500 m)
T-O to 50 ft (15 m)   under 2,500 ft (760 m)
Landing run with reverse thrust 1,000 ft (305 m)
Range with 18 passengers, with reserves
    434 nm (500 miles; 805 km)
Range with max fuel, reduced payload
    2,344 nm (2,700 miles; 4,340 km)

Carstedt Jet Liner 600, a "stretched" Dove with 605 ehp AiResearch TPE 331 turboprops, in service with Apache Airlines (T. R. Waddington)

CASSUTT
THOMAS K. CASSUTT
ADDRESS:
38 Westcliff Drive, Huntington Station, N.Y.
Capt Tom Cassutt, an airline pilot, designed and
built in 1954 a small single-seat racing monoplane
known as the Cassutt Special I (No 111), in which
he won the 1958 Championships. In 1959, he
completed a smaller aircraft on the same lines,
known as the Cassutt Special II (No 11).
Plans of both aircraft, and of a sporting version
of No 111 with a larger cockpit, are available to
amateur constructors. As a result, many Cassutt
Specials are flying and under construction, and
brief details of a number of these are given in
the table.

CASSUTT SPECIAL I
The original Cassutt Special I (No 111), named
Jersey Skeeter. is described in detail below. The
example which was illustrated in the 1969-70
Jane's is a variant of the Cassutt Special I
built by Mr Ken Conrad of Clarence, Iowa,
which has been flying since 24 December 1966.
It took him 11 months to build at a cost of
$1,500, and differs from standard by having a
lowered turtle deck, swept vertical tail surface,
cantilever aluminium alloy main legs and glass-
fibre wing covering. Powered by a 90 hp Continental engine, Mr Conrad's Cassutt has an empty
weight of 520 lb (236 kg), max T-O weight of
750 lb (340 kg), cruising speed of 150 mph (241
kmh), landing speed of 80 mph (129 kmh) and
max range of 1,000 miles (1,609 km).
At least one Cassutt Special I, built by Mr J.
Coughlin, is powered by a 100 hp Continental
O-200 engine.
Airmark Ltd in the UK (which see) has built
three slightly modified examples of the Cassutt
Special 1, and these are known as Airmark/
Cassutt 111M's in Britain.
TYPE: Single-seat racing monoplane.
WINGS: Cantilever mid-wing monoplane. Wing
section Cassutt 1107. No incidence or dihedral.
All-wood two-spar structure with spruce
ribs, solid spars and plywood skin, fabric
covered. Ailerons are of welded steel-tube
construction, fabric covered. No flaps.
FUSELAGE: Steel-tube structure, fabric-covered.
TAIL UNIT: Cantilever steel-tube structure, with
fabric covering.
LANDING GEAR: Non-retractable tail-wheel type.
Wittman cantilever spring steel main legs.
Main wheel tyres size 5·00 × 5. Wheel fairings
standard.
POWER PLANT: One Continental C85-8F four-
cylinder horizontally-opposed air-cooled engine,
rated normally at 85 hp but capable of developing 112-115 hp in racing trim. Sensenich two-
blade fixed-pitch propeller. Fuel capacity 15
US gallons (57 litres). Oil capacity 1 US gallon
(3·8 litres).
ACCOMMODATION: Single seat in enclosed cockpit.
DIMENSIONS, EXTERNAL:

Wing span	14 ft 11 in (4·54 m)
Wing chord (mean)	4 ft 6 in (1·37 m)
Wing aspect ratio	3·37
Length overall	16 ft 0 in (4·88 m)
Height overall	4 ft 3 in (1·30 m)
Tailplane span	3 ft 11 in (1·19 m)
Wheel track	4 ft 6 in (1·37 m)

AREAS:

Wings, gross	66·0 sq ft (6·13 m²)
Ailerons (total)	7·5 sq ft (0·70 m²)
Fin	2·4 sq ft (0·22 m²)
Rudder	2·1 sq ft (0·195 m²)

A modified Cassutt Special I built by Mr Clair Meyer of Fort Dodge, Iowa (*Jean Seele*)

Tailplane	5·3 sq ft (0·49 m²)
Elevators	3·1 sq ft (0·29 m²)

WEIGHTS:

Weight empty	516 lb (234 kg)
Max T-O weight	730 lb (331 kg)

PERFORMANCE (at max T-O weight):

Max level speed	200 knots (230 mph; 370 km/h)
Max cruising speed	165 knots (190 mph; 306 km/h)
Stalling speed	61 knots (70 mph; 113 km/h)
Rate of climb at S/L	2,000 ft (610 m)/min
Endurance with max fuel	3 hours

CASSUTT SPECIAL II
TYPE: Single-seat racing monoplane.
WINGS: Cantilever mid-wing monoplane. Wing
section Cassutt 13106. No incidence or dihedral.
All-wood structure. No flaps.
FUSELAGE: Steel-tube structure, fabric-covered.
TAIL UNIT: Cantilever steel-tube structure,
fabric-covered. The prototype (No 11) has
small centre fin and auxiliary fins on the tail-
plane tips.
LANDING GEAR: Non-retractable tail-wheel type.
Wittman cantilever spring steel main legs.
Main wheel tyre size 5·00 × 5. Wheel fairings
standard.

POWER PLANT AND ACCOMMODATION: As for
Cassutt Special I.
DIMENSIONS, EXTERNAL:

Wing span	13 ft 8 in (4·16 m)
Wing chord (constant)	4 ft 10 in (1·47 m)
Wing aspect ratio	2·83
Length overall	16 ft 0 in (4·88 m)
Height overall	3 ft 10 in (1·16 m)
Tailplane span	3 ft 9 in (1·14 m)
Wheel track	3 ft 2 in (0·97 m)

AREAS:

Wings, gross	66 sq ft (6·13 m²)
Ailerons (total)	6 sq ft (0·56 m²)
Fin	1·0 sq ft (0·09 m²)
Rudder	1·6 sq ft (0·15 m²)
Tailplane	4·3 sq ft (0·40 m²)
Elevators	2·4 sq ft (0·22 m²)

WEIGHTS:

Weight empty	433 lb (196 kg)
Max T-O weight	800 lb (363 kg)

PERFORMANCE (at max T-O weight):

Max level speed at S/L	204 knots (235 mph; 378 km/h)
Max cruising speed	174 knots (200 mph; 322 km/h)
Stalling speed	54 knots (62 mph; 100 km/h)
Rate of climb at S/L	3,000 ft (915 m)/min
Endurance with max fuel	3 hours

Builder (B) Owner (O)	Name of A/C	Racing Number	Wing Span	Length Overall	Height Overall	Normal Loaded Weight	Max Speed
(B, O) Marion Baker & Associates	Boo-Ray	81	15 ft 0 in (4·57 m)	16 ft 8 in (5·08 m)	4 ft 0 in (1·22 m)	750 lb (340 kg)	210 mph (337 km/h)
(B, O) Ken Burmeister	Firefly	4	13 ft 8 in (4·17 m)	17 ft 1 in (5·21 m)	4 ft 3 in (1·30 m)	738 lb (335 kg)	N.A.
(B) R. Grieger (O) E. E. Stover	Ole Yaller	58	15 ft 0 in (4·57 m)	16 ft 6 in (5·03 m)	4 ft 11 in (1·50 m)	834 lb (378 kg)	N.A.
(B) D. Hoffman R. Philbrick (O) Harold Lund	Chabasco	76	13 ft 8 in (4·17 m)	16 ft 6½ in (5·04 m)	N.A.	774 lb (351 kg)	210 mph (337 km/h)
(B, O) Ray O. Morris	Miss A-Go-Go	12	14 ft 11 in (4·55 m)	16 ft 0 in (4·88 m)	4 ft 6 in (1·37 m)	642 lb (291 kg)	225 mph (362 km/h)
(B, O) Fred Wofford	Gold Dust	7	14 ft 4 in (4·37 m)	17 ft 3 in (5·26 m)	4 ft 3½ in (1·31 m)	787 lb (357 kg)	195 mph (314 km/h)
(B, O) James H. Wilson	Snoopy	—	14 ft 6 in (4·42 m)	16 ft 9 in (5·11 m)	4 ft 2 in (1·27 m)	800 lb (363 kg)	240 mph (386 km/h)

CAVALIER
CAVALIER AIRCRAFT CORPORATION
HEAD OFFICE AND WORKS:
Sarasota-Bradenton Airport, Box 1719, Sara-
sota, Florida 33578
PRESIDENT:
David B. Lindsay Jr
VICE-PRESIDENTS:
E. T. Kiser (Marketing)
G. E. Tyler (Operations)
H. B. B. Barron (Public Relations)
Cavalier Aircraft Corporation, which incorpor-
ates the former Trans-Florida Aviation, Inc,
holds ownership of the F-51 Mustang Type
Certificate and the name "Mustang" is its regis-
tered trade mark.
In addition to marketing a tandem two-seat
business and sporting conversion of the North
American F-51D Mustang as the Cavalier, it has
contracts to supply the USAF, and other air
forces which receive MAP assistance from the
United States, with new F-51D Mustang II
counter-insurgency fighters and trainers and to
provide associated support programmes. It has
also developed a new turbine-powered counter-
insurgency and close-support fighter, known as
the Turbo Mustang III, which Cavalier are
marketing under a Minimax programme, implying minimum investment associated with
maximum operational flexibility.

Cavalier Mustang II counter-insurgency patrol and attack aircraft

Other activities include the development and
production of two-seat conversion kits, wingtip
tank kits, L-shape and rectangular internal wing
fuel cell kits, modified baggage compartment
doors, modernised Aeroquip fuel system kits,
anti-collision beacon kits, high-pressure oxygen
installations, anti-icing installations and Brittain

B5 auto-pilot installations for Mustang aircraft.

CAVALIER F-51D MUSTANG
Cavalier has been awarded a USAF contract
to deliver F-51D Mustang two-seat fighter aircraft
for counter-insurgency duties with air forces
which receive MAP assistance from the United

States. This is not simply a remanufacturing programme. The aircraft are assembled from component parts, some manufactured as new and the others taken from stocks. The completed Mustangs are being delivered as 1967/68 aircraft, with many updated features, including Bendix solid-state electronics and revised armament.

There are three versions of the Cavalier F-51D:

The basic F-51D two-seat fighter for MAP countries has standard Mustang wings and fuselage, but the height of the fin is increased by 14 in (35 cm) to improve stall characteristics and provide a more stable gun platform. The new Bendix electronics include a T-12C ADF, RN-222A VHF/VOR receiver and dual RT-221A-28 VHF transceivers. Power plant is a Packard V-1650-7 (Rolls-Royce Merlin) piston-engine. In addition to carrying the standard fixed armament of six 0·50-in machine-guns, the wings have been reinforced to permit the carriage of external stores on four hard-points under each wing. Each inboard hard-point can carry a 1,000 lb (454 kg) bomb or 110 US gallon (415 litre) fuel tank: the other six hard-points carry 5 in (12·7 cm) air-to-surface rockets. A Type N-4 or N-6 gun camera is mounted in the port wing. The pilot's gun sight is a British Mk IIIN type. Controls are fitted in only the front cockpit, the rear seat being occupied by an observer.

The TF-51D training version is basically similar to the two-seat fighter, but has dual controls, a longer and higher canopy over the two cockpits and only four guns in the wings.

Two Cavalier Mustangs have been supplied to the US Army as unarmed "chase" aircraft for use during the Lockheed AH-56A Cheyenne helicopter flight test programme. Dual controls are not fitted. A primary duty for these aircraft is air photography; additional equipment includes flight test instrumentation and an extra 400 US gallons (1,515 litres) of fuel in wingtip tanks.

CAVALIER MUSTANG II

Cavalier have developed this new two-seat version of the F-51D Mustang as a private venture specifically for counter-insurgency patrol and attack duties. Installation of a 1,760 hp Rolls-Royce Merlin 620 engine and further reinforcement of the wings and fuselage has made possible increases in max T-O weight and armament. The standard installed armament of six 0·50-in machine guns, with 2,000 rounds of ammunition, is supplemented by external stores on six underwing hard-points. The two inboard points can each carry a 1,000 lb (454 kg) bomb; each of the others can carry up to 750 lb. A typical underwing load comprises six LAU-3/A pods containing a total of 114 2·75-in rockets. Underwing fuel tanks will not normally be carried; instead, the Mustang II is fitted with two non-jettisonable 110 US gallon (415 litre) wingtip tanks, giving it a maximum endurance of over 7½ hours.

An advanced type of armament control panel has been developed specially for the Mustang II, and this allows unusual flexibility of weapon selection. For example, it permits use of the gun camera alone, or the selection and firing of up to 114 rockets, or can be set to drop various kinds of external stores in the manner best suited for the particular mission requirements.

The prototype Mustang II flew for the first time in December 1967, and is being cleared for a max T-O weight of 13,700 lb (6,215 kg).

CAVALIER TURBO MUSTANG III

Following development of the 1967/68-model F-51D Mustang and Mustang II, Cavalier have produced as a private venture the prototype of a modified version re-engined initially with a Rolls-

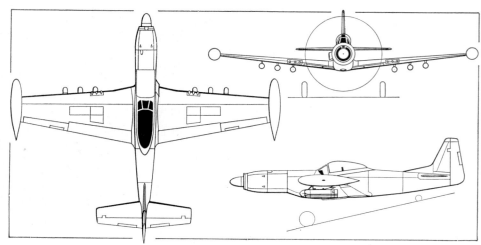

Cavalier Turbo Mustang III, a turboprop conversion of the basic F-51D Mustang

Royce Dart Mk 510 turboprop power plant. The purpose of this prototype development programme was to evaluate the operation of a turboprop power plant in a lightweight, simple, and inexpensive aircraft for possible use as a counter-insurgency, close air support aircraft by the USAF. This aircraft was designated Turbo Mustang III.

The basic airframe is similar to that of the Cavalier F-51D Mustang, with a number of structural modifications to allow the Mustang III to perform effectively a low-level close air support mission. These include a redesigned tail unit providing increased fin height to improve directional stability; design and installation of chord-line tip tanks; re-design of fuselage to provide optional one- or two-seat configuration, together with strengthened longerons between cockpit and tail unit; and installation of internal spars and webs in the wing to give the necessary stress reserve for armament hard-points and tip tanks.

The aircraft was designed to incorporate structural plastic armour for engine cowling, on the underside of the fuselage, and around the cockpit area. For this purpose Cavalier designers have allotted 1,500 lb (680 kg) of airframe weight for the armour installation. Armour being considered for use would provide protection against 14·7-mm armour piercing projectiles at a velocity of 4,000 fps and at zero-degree obliquity. Other design features are the planned use of the North American LW-3B pilot ejection system, providing a zero-zero escape capability, and the incorporation of reticulated foam in all permanently-installed fuel tanks for fire suppresion.

Following flight testing of this Rolls-Royce powered prototype, which produced excellent performance data, Cavalier is proceeding with the development of a version powered with the Avco Lycoming T55-L-9 turboprop power plant, rated at 2,535 eshp for take-off and 2,178 cruise eshp. Flight at these higher power ratings has already been performed with the prototype powered by a military version of the Dart RDa.7 turboprop engine. Weighing approximately 800 lb (362 kg) less than the Mk 510 and already widely used in the US military inventory, the T55 would greatly simplify logistics support of the aircraft should it be produced in appreciable numbers.

Two of the Lycoming power plants are being supplied to Cavalier under a lease agreement with the USAF. They are being installed in a production-configured single-seat aircraft and in a

dual-control two-seat trainer. Utilising this modern lightweight power plant design, these aircraft will be evaluated for production in significant quantities for possible sales on a world-wide basis. Initial tactical use of the aircraft will probably be by recipient nations under the MAP to augment the fire-power of fixed-wing aircraft and helicopter gunships currently employed in combat team operations in southeast Asia.

Presently lacking a specific designation, the Lycoming-powered aircraft will possess performance sufficiently improved over previous Cavalier-developed derivatives of the F-51 design to warrant a designation other than merely another variant of the Mustang series. Mission profiles for the aircraft, particularly with respect to range and endurance capabilities, are predicted by Cavalier officials to exceed those of the Turbo Mustang III by approximately 15 per cent.

The following details apply to the prototype:

TYPE: Single-turboprop close-support fighter.

WINGS: Cantilever low-wing monoplane. Laminar-flow wing section.

FUSELAGE: All-metal semi-monocoque structure.

TAIL UNIT: Cantilever all-metal structure.

LANDING GEAR: Hydraulically-retractable tail-wheel type. Main wheels retract inward into wing, tail-wheel forward. Main wheels have 27 in 10-ply rating, smooth contour tyres; tail-wheel tyre is 12·50 × 4·5 in, 10-ply rating. Tyre pressures: main 60 lb/sq in (4·22 kg/cm²), tail 75 lb/sq in (5·27 kg/cm²). Multiple disc brakes. Production models to have anti-skid units.

POWER PLANT (previously installed): One Rolls-Royce Dart Mk 510 turboprop, rated at 1,740 ehp for take-off and 1,490 max cruise hp, driving a Dowty-Rotol four-blade variable-pitch propeller, diameter 11 ft 6 in (3·51 m). Propeller pitch and power were both controlled by linkage to a single pilot control that automatically synchronised power settings with propeller pitch position. A separate protected switch enabled the propeller to be set in a maximum drag, or flat pitch position, to provide controlled decelleration to reduce ground roll on landing. Engine installed in clam-shell cowling. Planned installation of the Lycoming T55-L-9 turboprop will not entail the use of a lengthened engine cowling as required for the Rolls-Royce engine but will be accommodated within the original cowling dimensions of the basic aircraft design. This feature will enable virtually the same handling qualities as the original aircraft design to be retained in the

The prototype Cavalier Turbo Mustang III single/two-seat close-support fighter (1,740 ehp Rolls-Royce Dart Mk 510 turboprop engine)

turboprop-powered version. Propeller pitch and power control will be exercised by linkage to two pilot controls: a Main Power Lever for actuating the primary power control element of an automatic fuel and power control system and a Pitch Control Lever providing propeller rpm control. Propeller, diameter 11 ft 6 in (3·51 m), under consideration for use with the Lycoming engine, can be produced by Hamilton Standard, Allison Division of General Motors, or Dowty-Rotol. Fuel in two wing root tanks each 92 US gallons (348 litres) and two chord-line tip tanks, each 120 US gallons (454 litres). Total installed fuel capacity 424 US gallons (1,604 litres). A 110-US gallon (416-litre) jettisonable fuel tank can be carried under each wing on the inboard hard-point.

ACCOMMODATION: One- or two-seat configuration optional, under rearward-sliding transparent canopy.

ELECTRONICS AND EQUIPMENT: ARN 52 series TACAN, ARN 80 series VOR/ILS, AN/ARQ 50 UHF/ADF, ARC 109 UHF/AM, ARC 114 UHF/FM, ARC 115 VHF/AM, ARC 123 HF/SSB, KY 28 A security and IFF transponder. Eye-level mounted armament control panel in cockpit houses all arming and selector switches for internal armament and external stores.

ARMAMENT: Six underwing hard-points for external stores, the two inboard points each able to carry a load of 1,000 lb (453 kg), with 750 lb (340 kg) on each of the other four points. These permit a wide range of external stores to be carried, including SUU-7A bomblet dispensers, BLU-1/B (M-116) or BLU-11/B fire bombs, SUU-11/A or SUU-12/A 0·5-in gun pods, M-117 or M6-4/A1 general-purpose bombs, MK-81 or MK-82 low-drag bombs, XM-75 grenade launchers and LAU-3A (19-tube), AERO-6A (7-tube) or LAU-59 (7-tube) rocket launchers. Six M2 or M3 0·50-in machine-guns installed in wing. Cavalier Mk 1 illuminated non-computing gunsight. For photographic reconnaissance a number of strike, horizon-to-horizon, continuous film strip and framing cameras are available.

DIMENSIONS, EXTERNAL:
Wing span   37 ft 0 in (11·28 m)
Wing aspect ratio   5·8
Length overall   36 ft 9½ in (11·20 m)
Height overall   14 ft 10¾ in (4·54 m)

AREA:
Wings, gross   233·0 sq ft (21·6 m²)

WEIGHTS:
Weight empty, equipped   7,396 lb (3,355 kg)
Armament allowance, incl guns
                             4,000 lb (1,815 kg)
Max T-O weight   14,000 lb (6,350 kg)

PERFORMANCE (estimated, with T55 engine):
Max speed, clean
                 470 knots (541 mph; 870 km/h)
Stalling speed, clean
                   75 knots (86 mph; 138 km/h)
T-O run at AUW of 10,000 lb (4,581 kg), including 2,000 lb (907 kg) armament
                             750 ft (229 m)
T-O to 50 ft (15 m) at AUW of 10,000 lb (4,581 kg), including 2,000 lb (907 kg) armament
                             1,200 ft (365 m)
Landing run   950 ft (289 m)
Mission radius at AUW of 10,000 lb (4,581 kg), with 2,000 lb (907 kg) armament, 2½-hr loiter and fuel reserves
              over 134 nm (155 miles; 250 km)
Ferry range   1,997 nm (2,300 miles; 3,700 km)

CAVALIER 2000

This remanufactured two-seat conversion of the F-51D Mustang fighter is available in five forms, as follows:

Cavalier 750. As basic Cavalier 2000 but without auxiliary fuel tanks. This version has two internal wing tanks, each of 92 US gallons (348 litres) capacity.

Cavalier 1200. As Cavalier 750, but with two additional L-shape fuel bladder tanks, each of 48 US gallons (182 litres) capacity.

Cavalier 1500. As Cavalier 750, but with two additional rectangular fuel bladder tanks, each of 63 US gallons (238·5 litres) capacity.

Cavalier 2000. Basic Cavalier, with two 110 US gallon (416·5 litre) wingtip fuel tanks.

Cavalier F-51D, two-seat version of the Mustang fighter in US Army service

Cavalier 2500. Basically as Cavalier 2000, but with two 60 US gallon (227 litre) internal wing cells added to 184 US gallon (696 litre) basic fuel capacity.

TYPE: Two-seat high-speed business and sporting aircraft.

WINGS: Cantilever low-wing monoplane. Laminar-flow wing section. Mean aerodynamic chord 6 ft 7·6 in (2·02 m). Dihedral 5°. All-metal (24ST) stressed-skin structure. Sealed metal ailerons, each with trim-tab. Plain trailing-edge flaps containing step to facilitate entry into cockpit.

FUSELAGE: All-metal (24ST) semi-monocoque structure.

TAIL UNIT: Cantilever all-metal (24ST) structure. Trim-tabs in elevators and rudder.

LANDING GEAR: Hydraulically-retractable tailwheel type. Main wheels retract inward in wings, tail-wheel forward. Bendix oleo-pneumatic shock-absorbers. Goodyear wheels and 27-in smooth contour tyres on main wheels. Tyre pressure: main 46-73 lb/sq in (3·23-5·13 kg/cm²), tail 62-89 lb/sq in (4·36-6·26 kg/cm²). Goodyear multi-disc brakes.

POWER PLANT: One 1,595 hp Packard-built Rolls-Royce Merlin V-1650-7 twelve-cylinder liquid-cooled engine with two-stage supercharger and Hamilton Standard 24D50-65 four-blade constant-speed propeller. Basic fuel in two tanks in wing roots, each with capacity of 92 US gallons (348 litres). Cavalier 750, 1200, 1500 and 2500 have additional internal wing fuel cells as described under notes on these versions. Cavalier 2000 and 2500 have wing-tip tanks. Max total installed fuel capacity 184 US gallons (696 litres) in Cavalier 750, 280 US gallons (1,060 litres) in Cavalier 1200, 310 US gallons (1,173 litres) in Cavalier 1500, 374 US gallons (1,416 litres) in Cavalier 2000 and 484 US gallons (1,832 litres) in Cavalier 2500. Provision for two 110 US gallon (416·5 litre) underwing jettisonable tanks when optional internal wing fuel cells are not installed. Oil capacity 12·5 US gallons (47 litres).

ACCOMMODATION: Two persons in tandem under one-piece rearward-sliding transparent canopy. Pilot in front cockpit. Baggage space behind rear seat or in wings, depending on required fuel tankage. Cabin and seats have de luxe ribbed upholstery, with foam rubber cushions. Other refinements include a completely redesigned instrument panel, floor carpets, new cabin sound-proofing and insulation, and modified heating and ventilation systems installed in the canopy.

SYSTEMS: Hydraulic system, pressure 1,200 lb/sq in (84 kg/cm²), for landing gear and flaps. One 100A electrical generator. Independent demand-type oxygen regulators for pilot and passenger, supplied by oxygen bottles in rear fuselage or, optionally, from high-pressure oxygen system.

ELECTRONICS AND EQUIPMENT: Blind-flying instrumentation standard. Optional instrumentation includes a Sperry H6-B electro gyro,

Sperry C4 gyrosyn compass system, Regency 505 transponder, Collins PN 101 system, Bendix T12C ADF, DME, and Safe-Flight SC24 speed control system. Radio equipment is installed either in the instrument panel or aft of passenger seat, to meet individual requirements. Brittain B5 auto-pilot can also be installed.

DIMENSIONS, EXTERNAL:
Wing span:
  Cavalier 2000, 2500, over tip-tanks
                        40 ft 1½ in (12·22 m)
  Cavalier 750, 1200, 1500 37 ft 0½ in (11·29 m)
Length overall   32 ft 2¼ in (9·81 m)
Height overall   12 ft 2½ in (3·72 m)
Tailplane span   13 ft 2¼ in (4·02 m)
Wheel track   11 ft 10 in (3·60 m)

AREA:
Wings, gross   272·3 sq ft (25·29 m²)

WEIGHTS AND LOADINGS:
Average weight empty:
  Cavalier 750, 1200, 1500   7,000 lb (3,175 kg)
  Cavalier 2000, 2500   7,500 lb (3,400 kg)
Max payload:
  Cavalier 750, 1200, 1500   3,500 lb (1,588 kg)
  Cavalier 2000, 2500   3,000 lb (1,360 kg)
Max T-O weight   10,500 lb (4,763 kg)
Max landing weight   9,200 lb (4,175 kg)
Max wing loading   38·5 lb/sq ft (188 kg/m²)
Max power loading   7·0 lb/hp (3·18 kg/hp)

PERFORMANCE (at max T-O weight):
Max level speed at 28,000 ft (8,535 m)
                 397 knots (457 mph; 735 km/h)
Max permissible speed in dive at 10,000 ft
  (3,050 m)   438 knots (505 mph; 810 km/h)
Max cruising speed at 30,000 ft (9,145 m)
                 368 knots (424 mph; 682 km/h)
Normal cruising speed at 25,000 ft (7,620 m)
                 321 knots (370 mph; 595 km/h)
Econ cruising speed at 20,000 ft (6,100 m)
                 274 knots (316 mph; 509 km/h)
Econ cruising speed at 10,000 ft (3,050 m)
                 226 knots (260 mph; 418 km/h)
Approach speed
     100-104 knots (115-120 mph; 185-193 km/h)
Stalling speed, wheels and flaps down
                   75 knots (86 mph; 138 km/h)
Max rate of climb at S/L   2,550 ft (777 m)/min
Service ceiling   42,000 ft (12,800 m)
T-O run   1,000 ft (305 m)
T-O to 50 ft (15 m)   1,850 ft (565 m)
Landing from 50 ft (15 m) 1,750 ft (535 m)
Landing run   925 ft (282 m)
Range with max installed fuel, no reserve:
  Cavalier 750   651 nm (750 miles; 1,205 km)
  Cavalier 1200
            1,042 nm (1,200 miles; 1,930 km)
  Cavalier 1500
            1,302 nm (1,500 miles; 2,415 km)
  Cavalier 2000
            1,736 nm (2,000 miles; 3,200 km)
  Cavalier 2500
            2,171 nm (2,500 miles; 4,020 km)

CESSNA
CESSNA AIRCRAFT COMPANY
HEAD OFFICE AND WORKS:
Wichita, Kansas 67201
CHAIRMAN OF THE BOARD AND CHIEF EXECUTIVE
OFFICER:
Dwane L. Wallace
PRESIDENT:
Delbert L. Roskam
SENIOR VICE-PRESIDENTS:
Frank A. Boettger

R. L. Lair (Aircraft Operations)
R. P. Bauer (Treasurer and Controller)
VICE-PRESIDENTS:
Pierre Clostermann (President, Reims Aviation)
Frank Martin (Commercial Aircraft Marketing)
James B. Taylor (Citation)
VICE-PRESIDENTS AND GENERAL MANAGERS:
V. G. Weddle (Commercial Aircraft Marketing)
Burt L. Whitlock (Industrial Products Division)
Vernon W. Deinzer (Aircraft Radio Corporation)
Derby Frye (Military Relations)

GENERAL MANAGER:
John Dussault (McCauley Industrial Corporation)
SECRETARY: Vincent E. Moore
PUBLIC RELATIONS MANAGER:
Jerry Kell
Cessna Aircraft Company was founded by the late Clyde V. Cessna, a pioneer in US aviation in 1911, and was incorporated on 7 September 1927. It had delivered more than 85,000 aircraft by January 1970.

Cessna has four plants in Wichita engaged on the production of commercial and military aircraft, and an Industrial Products Division in Hutchinson, Kansas, which manufactures fluid power systems.

Subsidiary companies owned by Cessna are Aircraft Radio Corporation at Boonton, New Jersey, the McCauley Industrial Corporation of Dayton, Ohio, Cessna Industrial Products Ltd of Glenrothes, Fife, Scotland, and National Aero Finance in Wichita. It has a 49% interest in Reims Aviation of France.

Total employment in all Cessna divisions and companies averaged 12,738 during 1969.

Early in 1970 Cessna had in production 35 types of commercial aircraft, as described below. In addition, it is continuing to produce the T-37B twin-engined jet trainer and A-37 strike aircraft for the USAF and the T-37C for the US Military Assistance Programme.

During 1969 Cessna commercial sales totalled 5,887 aircraft.

Military sub-contract programmes include manufacture of assemblies, including bomb and missile ejection racks, wing tank and missile pylons, for the McDonnell F-4 Phantom II, and ammunition dispenser containers under US Army ordnance contract. Acceptance of Cessna's defence products and components by both US and overseas governments resulted in sales totalling more than $74 million during 1969.

CESSNA MODEL 150

The prototype of the Model 150 flew for the first time in September 1957, and Cessna re-entered the two-seat light aircraft market by putting it into production in August 1958. By January 1970 a total of 14,172 model 150s had been delivered.

The Model 150 is also built in France by Reims Aviation as the F-150.

The current American-built Model 150K is available in standard, trainer and commuter versions, on wheels or floats. The trainer has as standard equipment dual controls, a Cessna 300 series 90-channel nav-com installation, rate of climb indicator, a turn co-ordinator that provides visual presentation of turn information and landing lights.

The commuter has the same equipment as the trainer, plus a vacuum system with directional and horizon gyros, wheel fairings, individual seats, heated pitot and "omni-flash" beacon.

Most noticeable external change in the 1970 Model 150K involves the introduction of conical camber glass-fibre wing tips, offering increased stability, and improved styling. Other new external features include provision of a ground-adjustable rudder trim-tab, easily-adjusted door stops and the choice of ten paint schemes.

Internal changes include headroom increased by 2½ in (6·35 cm), resulting from the introduction of a new contoured cabin ceiling, concealing an expanded insulation material to improve sound absorption. An overhead lighting console is embodied in the ceiling and this, together with a grey instrument panel finish, offers better instrument visibility. New seat backs to the individual seats increase leg room; a split-type rocker switch is introduced to improve flexibility of the electrical system; re-location of the radio speaker adjacent to the pilot's head improves its audibility.

The original Model 150 received FAA Type Approval on 10 July 1958.

TYPE: Two-seat cabin monoplane.

WINGS: Braced high-wing monoplane. Wing section NACA 2412 (tips symmetrical). Dihedral 1°. Incidence 1° at root, 0° at tip. All-metal structure, with conical camber glass-fibre tips. Modified Frise all-metal ailerons. Electrically-actuated NACA single-slotted all-metal flaps.

FUSELAGE: All-metal semi-monocoque structure.

TAIL UNIT: Cantilever all-metal structure, with sweptback vertical surfaces. Trim-tab in starboard elevator.

LANDING GEAR: Non-retractable tricycle type. "Land-o-Matic" spring-steel cantilever main legs. Steerable nose-wheel on oleo-pneumatic shock-absorber strut. Size 6·00 × 6 wheels, with nylon tube-type tyres, on main wheels; size 5·00 × 5 nose-wheel, with nylon tube-type tyre. Tyre pressure 30 lb/sq in (2·11 kg/cm²). Toe-operated single-disc hydraulic brakes. Optional wheel fairings for all three units (standard on commuter). Floats optional.

POWER PLANT: One 100 hp Continental O-200-A four-cylinder horizontally-opposed air-cooled engine. McCauley two-blade metal fixed-pitch propeller, diameter 5 ft 9 in (1·75 m) on landplane, 6 ft 3 in (1·90 m) on floatplane version. Two all-metal fuel tanks in wings. Total standard fuel capacity 26 US gallons (98 litres), of which 22·5 US gallons (85 litres) are usable on land-

Cessna Model 150K two-seat cabin monoplane (100 hp Continental O-200-A engine)

plane, 21·5 US gallons (81·5 litres) on floatplane; optional long-range tanks increase total capacity to 38 US gallons (143·8 litres), of which 35 US gallons (132·5 litres) are usable on landplane, 33·5 US gallons (127 litres) on floatplane. Oil capacity 1·5 US gallons (5·7 litres).

ACCOMMODATION: Enclosed cabin seating two side-by-side. Dual controls standard in trainer and commuter, optional in standard model. Baggage compartment behind seats, backs of which hinge forward for access. Baggage capacity 120 lb (54 kg). Alternatively, "family seat" can be fitted in baggage space, for two children not exceeding 120 lb (54 kg) total weight. Door on each side. Heating and ventilation standard. Winterisation kit optional.

ELECTRONICS AND EQUIPMENT: Optional equipment includes Cessna 90-channel nav/com 300 installation (standard on trainer and commuter); nav/omni 300 with full VOR/LOC/glideslope receiver and optional marker beacon; nav/com 300R; ADF 300; blind-flying instrumentation (standard on commuter model); dual controls (standard in trainer and commuter); and "omni-flash" beacon (standard on commuter). Optional extras include a wing levelling stability augmentation system, winterisation kit, control-wheel mounted map light, advanced-design dry vacuum pump, ground service plug for external battery connection, handle and step for easier refuelling and a quick-drain oil system.

DIMENSIONS, EXTERNAL:

Wing span	32 ft 8½ in (9·97 m)
Wing chord at root	5 ft 4 in (1·63 m)
Wing chord at tip	3 ft 8½ in (1·12 m)
Wing aspect ratio	7·0
Length overall:	
Standard	23 ft 0 in (7·01 m)
Trainer, Commuter	23 ft 9 in (7·24 m)
Floatplane	24 ft 1 in (7·34 m)
Height overall:	
Landplane	8 ft 7½ in (2·63 m)
Floatplane	9 ft 1 in (2·77 m)
Tailplane span	10 ft 0 in (3·05 m)
Wheel track	6 ft 6½ in (1·99 m)
Wheelbase	4 ft 10 in (1·47 m)
Passenger doors (each):	
width	2 ft 10 in (0·86 m)

AREAS:

Wings, gross	157 sq ft (14·59 m²)
Ailerons (total)	17·88 sq ft (1·66 m²)
Trailing-edge flaps (total)	18·56 sq ft (1·72 m²)
Fin	7·55 sq ft (0·70 m²)
Rudder	6·50 sq ft (0·60 m²)
Tailplane	17·06 sq ft (1·58 m²)
Elevators, including tab	11·46 sq ft (1·06 m²)

WEIGHTS AND LOADINGS:

Weight empty, equipped, standard tanks:	
Standard	975 lb (442 kg)
Trainer	1,005 lb (456 kg)
Commuter	1,060 lb (481 kg)
Floatplane	1,135 lb (515 kg)
Max T-O weight:	
Landplane	1,600 lb (726 kg)
Floatplane	1,650 lb (748 kg)
Max wing loading:	
Landplane	10·2 lb/sq ft (49·8 kg/m²)
Floatplane	10·5 lb/sq ft (51·3 kg/m²)
Max power loading:	
Landplane	16·0 lb/hp (7·26 kg/hp)
Floatplane	16·5 lb/hp (7·49 kg/hp)

PERFORMANCE (all models, on wheels and floats, at max T-O weight):

Max level speed at S/L:	
Landplane	106 knots (122 mph; 196 km/h)
Floatplane	89 knots (103 mph; 166 km/h)
Max permissible diving speed:	
Landplane	140 knots (162 mph; 261 km/h)
Max cruising speed (75% power) at 7,000 ft (2,133 m):	
Landplane	102 knots (117 mph; 188 km/h)
Floatplane	85 knots (98 mph; 158 km/h)
Econ cruising speed at 10,000 ft (3,050 m):	
Landplane	81 knots (93 mph; 149 km/h)
Floatplane	68 knots (78 mph; 126 km/h)
Stalling speed, flaps down, power off	
Landplane, Floatplane	42 knots (48 mph; 78 km/h)
Rate of climb at S/L:	
Landplane	670 ft (204 m)/min
Floatplane	560 ft (171 m)/min
Service ceiling:	
Landplane	12,650 ft (3,850 m)
Floatplane	10,700 ft (3,260 m)
T-O run:	
Landplane	735 ft (224 m)
Floatplane	1,310 ft (399 m)
T-O to 50 ft (15 m):	
Landplane	1,385 ft (422 m)
Floatplane	2,075 ft (632 m)
Landing from 50 ft (15 m):	
Landplane	1,075 ft (328 m)
Floatplane	850 ft (259 m)
Landing run:	
Landplane	445 ft (136 m)
Floatplane	415 ft (126 m)
Range at econ cruising speed, normal tankage, no reserve:	
Landplane	490 nm (565 miles; 909 km)
Floatplane	369 nm (425 miles; 685 km)
Range at econ cruising speed, long-range tanks, no reserve:	
Landplane	764 nm (880 miles; 1,416 km)
Floatplane	581 nm (670 miles; 1,075 km)
Range at max cruising speed, normal tankage, no reserve:	
Landplane	412 nm (475 miles; 767 km)
Floatplane	330 nm (380 miles; 610 km)
Range at max cruising speed, long-range tanks, no reserve:	
Landplane	630 nm (726 miles; 1,168 km)
Floatplane	512 nm (590 miles; 950 km)

CESSNA MODEL A150K AEROBAT

Introduced in 1970, the Model A150K Aerobat has been designed to provide the economy and versatility of the standard Model 150, together with aerobatic capability. Structural changes allow the Aerobat to perform "unusual attitude" manoeuvres and it is licensed in the aerobatic category for load factors of plus six and minus three g at full gross weight, permitting the performance of barrel and aileron rolls, snap rolls, loops, Immelmann turns, Cuban eights, spins, vertical reversements, lazy eights and chandelles.

Equipment of the Aerobat differs only slightly from the standard aircraft. Quick-release cabin doors, removable seat cushions and backs, quick-release lap belts, and shoulder harnesses are standard, as are two tinted skylights which offer extra visibility; a ground-adjustable rudder trim-tab is fitted and distinct external styling provides immediate recognition of the A150's aerobatic role. Optional equipment includes an accelerometer, 3-in lightweight non-tumbling gyros, conical-camber glass-fibre wing-tips, steps and handles to simplify refuelling and a quick oil drain valve.

Structural changes have increased the empty weight slightly, by comparison with the standard Model 150, and all available details of specification and performance of the Aerobat are given below:

DIMENSIONS, EXTERNAL:

Wing span	33 ft 2 in (10·11 m)
Length overall	23 ft 9 in (7·01 m)
Height overall	8 ft 7½ in (2·63 m)

AREA:

Wings, gross	159·5 sq ft (14·82 m²)

WEIGHTS AND LOADINGS:

Weight empty, equipped, standard tanks:	
	1,030 lb (467 kg)

Max T-O weight   1,600 lb (726 kg)
Max wing loading   10·0 lb/sq ft (48·9 kg/m²)
Max power loading   16·0 lb/hp (7·26 kg/hp)

PERFORMANCE (at max T-O weight):
Max level speed at S/L
      104 knots (120 mph; 193 km/h)
Max cruising speed (75% power) at 7,000 ft
(2,133 m)   100 knots (115 mph; 185 km/h)
Econ cruising speed
      78 knots (90 mph; 146 km/h)
Stalling speed, flaps up, power off
      48 knots (55 mph; 89 km/h)
Stalling speed, flaps down, power off
      42 knots (48 mph; 77 km/h)
Rate of climb at S/L   670 ft (204 m)/min
Service ceiling   12,650 ft (3,856 m)
T-O run   735 ft (224 m)
T-O to 50 ft (15 m)   1,385 ft (422 m)
Landing from 50 ft (15 m) 1,075 ft (328 m)
Landing run   445 ft (136 m)
Range at max cruising speed, standard tanks,
no reserve   408 nm (470 miles; 756 km)
Range at max cruising speed, optional long-
range tanks, no reserve
    621 nm (715 miles; 1,151 km)
Range at econ cruising speed, at 7,000 ft
(2,133 m), standard tanks, no reserve
    482 nm (555 miles; 893 km)
Range at econ cruising speed, at 10,000 ft
(3,050 m), optional long-range tanks, no
reserve   742 nm (855 miles; 1,376 km)

CESSNA MODEL 172
USAF designation: T-41A

The current version of the Model 172, designated 172K, is available in two commercial forms:

Model 172K. Standard version, described
below.

Skyhawk. de luxe version of 172K, described
separately.

In addition, a version designated F-172 is being
produced in France by Reims Aviation.

On 31 July 1964, the USAF ordered 170
earlier-type Model 172's, under the designation
T-41A, for delivery between September 1964 and
July 1965. USAF student pilots complete about
30 hours of basic training on the T-41A before
passing on to the T-37B jet primary trainer.
Eight T-41A's have been bought by the Ecuador-
ian Air Force, and 26 by the Peruvian government.
The USAF ordered 34 more in July 1967. The
more powerful T-41B/C/D (R172E) are described
separately.

A total of 16,348 aircraft in the Model 172/
Skyhawk series had been built by January 1970.

The 1970 Model 172K introduces re-designed
and more comfortable seating, new grey instrument panel to reduce eye strain, new split-type
master rocker switch to by-pass the alternator
and voltage regulator if necessary, conical-
cambered glass-fibre wingtips, improved baggage
door latch, door stop and control knobs on lower
panel. New optional items include fully-
articulating front seats with headrests, a fold-
away seat for two children, allowing an unobstructed baggage area when not in use, a new
10-channel single sideband HF transceiver and
a quick oil drain valve.

TYPE: Four-seat cabin monoplane.

WINGS: Braced high-wing monoplane. NACA
2412 wing section. Dihedral 1° 44'. Incidence
1° 30' at root, —1° 30' at tip. All-metal
structure, except for conical-camber glass-
fibre wingtips. Single bracing strut on each
side. Modified Frise all-metal ailerons.
Electrically-controlled NACA all-metal single-
slotted flaps inboard of ailerons.

FUSELAGE: All-metal semi-monocoque structure.

TAIL UNIT: Cantilever all-metal structure.
Sweepback on fin 35° at quarter-chord. Trim-
tab in starboard elevator. Ground-adjustable
trim-tab in rudder.

LANDING GEAR: Non-retractable tricycle type.
Cessna "Land-o-Matic" cantilever spring steel
main legs. Nose-wheel is carried on an oleo-
pneumatic shock-strut and is steerable with
rudder up to 10° and controllable up to 30° on
either side. Cessna main wheels size 6·00 ×
6 and nose-wheel size 5·00 × 5 (optionally
6·00 × 6), with nylon cord tube-type tyres.
Tyre pressure: main wheels 23 lb/sq in (1·62
kg/cm²), nose-wheel 26 lb/sq in (1·83 kg/cm²).
Hydraulic disc brakes. Optional wheel fairings.
Alternative float and ski gear.

POWER PLANT: One 150 hp Lycoming O-320-E2D
four-cylinder horizontally-opposed air-cooled
engine. Two-blade fixed-pitch metal propeller,
diameter 6 ft 4 in (1·93 m) on landplane. Propeller diameter 6 ft 8 in (2·03 m) on floatplane.
One fuel tank in each wing, total capacity 42
US gallons (159 litres). Usable fuel 38 US
gallons (143·8 litres). Provision for long-range
tanks, giving total capacity of 52 US gallons
(197 litres). Oil capacity 2 US gallons (7·5
litres).

ACCOMMODATION: Cabin seats four in two pairs.
Baggage space aft of rear seats, capacity 120
lb (54 kg). An optional fold-away seat can

Cessna Model A150K Aerobat, aerobatic version of the standard Model 150

be fitted in baggage space, for one or two
children not exceeding 120 lb (54 kg) total weight.
Door on each side of cabin giving access to all
seats and to simplify loading if rear seats are
removed and cabin used for freight. Baggage
door on port side. Combined heating and
ventilation system. Glass-fibre sound-proofing.

SYSTEMS: Electrical system includes a 60A
alternator and electric starter.

ELECTRONICS AND EQUIPMENT: Optional extras
include Cessna 300 90-channel nav/com, 300
nav/omni with full VOR/LOC/glideslope receiver and optional marker beacon, 300R nav/com,
ADF 300, Cessna 10-channel HF transceiver,
Cessna Nav-o-Matic 300 single-axis autopilot
or Nav-o-Matic 400 two-axis autopilot, dual
controls, omni-flash beacon, blind flying instrumentation, smaller-case 3-in gyros, a turn
co-ordinator that provides visual presentation
of turn information (replacing former turn and
bank indicator), a wing-levelling stability
system that automatically maintains a wings-
level attitude, fully-articulating front seats
with head rests, quick oil drain valve and map
light.

DIMENSIONS, EXTERNAL (L=landplane; F=
floatplane):
Wing span   35 ft 9½ in (10·90 m)
Wing chord at root   5 ft 4 in (1·63 m)
Wing chord at tip   3 ft 8½ in (1·12 m)
Wing aspect ratio   7·52
Length overall: L   26 ft 11 in (8·20 m)
    F   27 ft 0 in (8·23 m)
Height overall: L   8 ft 9½ in (2·68 m)
    F   9 ft 11 in (3·02 m)
Tailplane span   11 ft 4 in (3·45 m)
Wheel track: L   7 ft 2 in (2·18 m)
Wheelbase: L   5 ft 4 in (1·63 m)
Passenger doors (each):
Height   3 ft 3¾ in (1·01 m)
Width   2 ft 11 in (0·89 m)

AREAS:
Wings, gross   174 sq ft (16·16 m²)
Ailerons (total)   18·3 sq ft (1·70 m²)
Trailing-edge flaps (total) 21·20 sq ft (1·97m²)
Fin   11·24 sq ft (1·04 m²)
Rudder   7·30 sq ft (0·68 m²)
Tailplane   20·16 sq ft (1·87 m²)
Elevators, including tab 16·15 sq ft (1·50 m²)

WEIGHTS AND LOADINGS (L=landplane; F=
floatplane):
Weight empty, equipped:
L   1,245 lb (565 kg)
F   1,405 lb (637 kg)
Max T-O weight:
L   2,300 lb (1,043 kg)
F   2,220 lb (1,007 kg)
Max wing loading:
L   13·2 lb/sq ft (64·45 kg/m²)
F   12·7 lb/sq ft (62·0 kg/m²)
Max power loading:
L   15·3 lb/hp (6·94 kg/hp)
F   14·8 lb/hp (6·71 kg/hp)

PERFORMANCE (L=landplane; F=floatplane, at
max T-O weight):
Max level speed at S/L:
L   121 knots (139 mph; 224 km/h)
F   94 knots (108 mph; 174 km/h)
Max permissible diving speed:
L   151 knots (174 mph; 280 km/h)
Max cruising speed (75% power):
L at 9,000 ft (2,743 m)
    114 knots (131 mph; 211 km/h)
F at 6,500 ft (1,980 m)
    92 knots (106 mph; 171 km/h)
Econ cruising speed at 10,000 ft (3,050 m):
L   102 knots (117 mph; 188 km/h)
F   84 knots (97 mph; 156 km/h)
Stalling speed, flaps up:
L   50 knots (57 mph; 92 km/h)
F   51·5 knots (59 mph; 95 km/h)

Cessna Skyhawk, de luxe version of the Model 172K (150 hp Lycoming O-320-E2D engine)

Stalling speed, flaps down:
L 43 knots (49 mph; 79 km/h)
F 45·5 knots (52 mph; 84 km/h)
Rate of climb at S/L:
L 645 ft (196 m)/min
F 580 ft (177 m)/min
Service ceiling:
L 13,100 ft (3,995 m)
F 12,000 ft (3,660 m)
T-O run:
L 865 ft (264 m)
F 1,620 ft (494 m)
T-O to 50 ft (15 m):
L 1,525 ft (465 m)
F 2,390 ft (729 m)
Landing from 50 ft (15 m):
L 1,250 ft (381 m)
F 1,345 ft (410 m)
Landing run:
L 520 ft (158 m)
F 590 ft (180 m)
Range with standard fuel at max cruising speed, no reserve:
L 534 nm (615 miles; 990 km)
F 434 nm (500 miles; 805 km)
Range with standard fuel at econ cruising speed, no reserve:
L 555 nm (640 miles; 1,030 km)
F 460 nm (530 miles; 855 km)

CESSNA SKYHAWK

The Skyhawk is a de luxe version of the Model 172K, to which it is generally similar. Standard equipment includes full blind-flying instrumentation, including the new turn co-ordinator and lightweight 3-in gyros, sun visors, landing and taxi lights, electric clock, speed fairings on the wheels, all-over paint scheme including racing stripes, and tow-bar.

The Skyhawk is certificated for operation as a floatplane, and can be fitted with skis.

DIMENSIONS:
Same as for Model 172K

WEIGHTS AND LOADINGS:
Same as for Model 172K, except:
Weight empty, equipped 1,315 lb (596 kg)

PERFORMANCE (at max T-O weight):
Same as for Model 172K, except
Max level speed at S/L
L 122 knots (140 mph; 225 km/h)
Max cruising speed (75% power) at 9,000 ft (2,743 m): L 115 knots (132 mph; 212 km/h)
Econ cruising speed at 10,000 ft (3,050 m):
L 102 knots (118 mph; 190 km/h)
Range with standard fuel at max cruising speed, no reserve 538 nm (620 miles; 995 km)
Range with standard fuel at econ cruising speed, no reserve 568 nm (655 miles; 1,050 km)

CESSNA MODEL R172E
US Army designation: T-41B
US Air Force designations: T-41C and T-41D

The Cessna Model R172E is a more powerful version of the 172. Its design was started in late 1963, and a prototype was then built, with a 180 hp Continental O-360 engine. Type approval was received in 1964, but the original power plant has been replaced in the production Model R172E by a fuel-injection IO-360 engine, as described below.

In August 1966, the US Army ordered 255 aircraft of this type, under the designation **T-41B**, for training and installation support duties. Delivery of these was completed in March 1967.

In October 1967, the US Air Force ordered 45 of these aircraft, with a fixed-pitch propeller, under the designation **T-41C**, for cadet flight training at the USAF Academy in Colorado. Thirty **T-41D's**, with a constant-speed propeller and 28V electrical system, have been ordered for the Colombian Air Force.

In addition, a version known as the Reims Rocket is being produced by Reims Aviation in France (which see).

The description of the Model 172K applies also to the R172E, except for the following details.

POWER PLANT: One 210 hp Continental IO-360-D six-cylinder horizontally-opposed air-cooled engine, driving a McCauley D2A34C67/76S metal constant-speed propeller, diameter 6 ft 4 in (1·93 m). Two metal fuel tanks in wings with total capacity of 52 US gallons (197 litres), of which 46 US gallons (174 litres) are usable. Refuelling points above wing. Oil capacity 10 US quarts (9·5 litres).

ACCOMMODATION: Basically as for Model 172K. T-41B has special crew seat backs and shoulder harness, with forward-hinged door on each side of cabin by crew seats.

ELECTRONICS AND EQUIPMENT: The T-41B, C and D have variations in their electronics and other equipment consistent with their intended rôles.

WEIGHTS AND LOADINGS:
Weight empty, equipped 1,550 lb (703 kg)
Max T-O and landing weight 2,500 lb (1,135 kg)
Max wing loading 14·3 lb/sq ft (69·8 kg/m²)
Max power loading 11·9 lb/hp (5·40 kg/hp)

PERFORMANCE (at max T-O weight):
Max level speed at S/L
133 knots (153 mph; 246 km/h)
Max permissible diving speed
158 knots (182 mph; 293 km/h)
Max cruising speed at S/L
126 knots (145 mph; 233 km/h)
Econ cruising speed at 5,500 ft (1,675 m)
128 knots (147 mph; 236 km/h)
Stalling speed, flaps down
46 knots (53 mph; 85 km/h)
Rate of climb at S/L 910 ft (277 m)/min
Service ceiling 17,500 ft (5,335 m)
T-O run 635 ft (195 m)
T-O to 50 ft (15 m) 1,045 ft (318 m)
Landing from 50 ft (15 m) 860 ft (262 m)
Landing run 400 ft (122 m)
Range with max fuel at econ cruising speed at 10,000 ft (3,050 m)
695 nm (800 miles; 1,285 km)

CESSNA MODEL 177

On 30 September 1967, Cessna introduced their Model 177, a single-engined four-seat aircraft powered by a 150 hp Lycoming engine and intended as a luxury addition to their range of single-engined two and four-seat models.

Among many new features, the 1969 Model 177A introduced a 180 hp Lycoming engine with a between-overhauls life of 2,000 hours, a redesigned induction air system and relocated carburettor air filter offering better access for maintenance.

The 1970 Model 177B introduced a new wing leading-edge of gull-wing concept, and this made necessary new wing-to-cabin-top fairings; wing fairing seals and conical-camber glass-fibre wingtips are standard. A different version of the 180 hp Lycoming engine has been fitted, driving a constant-speed propeller; the engine has a new lower cowl incorporating cowl flaps and a new exhaust tail-pipe. The improved performance resulting from the foregoing has necessitated a number of detail changes which include a re-designed tailplane mounting plate and rear bulkhead, a stronger push-rod for the tailplane trim-tab, new static ports and pitot head, new tachometer, airspeed indicator and fuel pressure gauge. Introduction of a rudder trim system has caused the central pedestal to be re-designed to accommodate the rudder trim wheel and the cowl flap control.

A total of 1,413 Model 177/Cardinals had been sold by January 1970. Two commercial versions are currently available.

Model 177B. Standard version, described below.

Cardinal. de luxe version of 177B, described separately.

TYPE: Four-seat cabin monoplane.

WINGS: Cantilever high-wing monoplane. Wing section modified NACA 2400 series. Dihedral 1° 30'. Incidence 3° 30' at root, 0° 30' at tip. All-metal structure except for conical camber glass-fibre wingtips. Modified Frise all-metal ailerons. Electrically-operated wide-span all-metal slotted flaps.

FUSELAGE: All-metal semi-monocoque structure of low profile.

TAIL UNIT: Cantilever all-metal structure. Sweepback on fin 35° at quarter-chord. All-moving tailplane, with large controllable trim-tab. Controllable rudder trim-tab.

LANDING GEAR: Non-retractable tricycle type. Improved Cessna Land-O-Matic cantilever main legs, each comprising a one-piece machined conically-tapered steel tube. Nose-wheel is carried on a short-stroke oleo-pneumatic shock-strut, with hydraulic damper, and is steerable

with rudder up to 12° each side and controllable up to 45° on either side. Cessna main wheels size 6·00 × 6 and nose-wheel size 5·00 × 5, with nylon cord tube-type tyres. Tyre pressure 30 lb/sq in (2·11 kg/cm²). Single-caliper hydraulic disc brakes. Parking brake locks both main wheels. Wheel fairings optional.

POWER PLANT: One 180 hp Lycoming O-360-A1F four-cylinder horizontally-opposed air-cooled engine, driving a two-blade constant-speed metal propeller, diameter 6 ft 4 in (1·93 m). Pointed aluminium spinner. Fuel is carried in a 24·5 US gallon (93 litre) integral fuel tank in each wing, vented at the wingtip. Total usable fuel 48 US gallons (182 litres). Refuelling point on top of each wing. Oil capacity 2 US gallons (7·5 litres).

ACCOMMODATION: Cabin seats four in two pairs. Optional seat for two children aft of rear seats. Baggage compartment in rear fuselage, capacity 120 lb (54 kg) with large forward-hinged external access door in port side of fuselage. Forward-hinged door on each side of cabin, forward of main landing gear. Combined heating and ventilation system. Glass-fibre sound-proofing.

SYSTEMS: Electric supply from 12V 60A alternator. 12V 25Ah battery. Optional wing-levelling stability augmentation system.

ELECTRONICS AND EQUIPMENT: Optional items include Cessna 300 series nav/com radio, HF transceiver, ADF, Nav-O-Matic 300 autopilot, blind-flying instruments and landing light. Standard equipment includes omni-flash beacon, wind-shield defroster, stall warning indicator and navigation lights.

DIMENSIONS, EXTERNAL:
Wing span 35 ft 6 in (10·82 m)
Wing chord at root 5 ft 6 in (1·68 m)
Wing chord at tip 4 ft 0 in (1·22 m)
Wing aspect ratio 7·31
Length overall 26 ft 11½ in (8·22 m)
Height overall 9 ft 1 in (2·77 m)
Tailplane span 11 ft 10 in (3·61 m)
Wheel track 8 ft 3½ in (2·53 m)
Wheelbase 6 ft 4½ in (1·94 m)
Passenger doors (each):
Height 3 ft 8 in (1·12 m)
Width 4 ft 0 in (1·22 m)
Height to sill 2 ft 3 in (0·69 m)

DIMENSIONS, INTERNAL:
Cabin:
Length 14 ft 7½ in (4·46 m)
Maximum width 4 ft 0 in (1·22 m)
Maximum height 3 ft 8½ in (1·13 m)

AREAS:
Wings, gross 174·0 sq ft (16·2 m²)
Ailerons (total) 18·86 sq ft (1·75 m²)
Trailing-edge flaps (total) 29·50 sq ft (2·74 m²)
Fin 11·02 sq ft (1·02 m²)
Rudder 6·41 sq ft (0·60 m²)
Tailplane, including tab 35·01 sq ft (3·25 m²)

WEIGHTS AND LOADINGS:
Weight empty, equipped 1,365 lb (619 kg)
Max T-O weight 2,500 lb (1,133 kg)
Max wing loading 14·5 lb/sq ft (70·8 kg/m²)
Max power loading 13·9 lb/hp (6·30 kg/hp)

PERFORMANCE (at max T-O weight):
Max level speed at S/L
128 knots (147 mph; 237 km/h)
Max cruising speed (75% power) at 9,500 ft (2,895 m) 117 knots (135 mph; 217 km/h)
Econ cruising speed at 10,000 ft (3,050 m)
101 knots (116 mph; 187 km/h)
Rate of climb at S/L 760 ft (232 m)/min
Service ceiling 15,800 ft (4,815 m)
T-O run 845 ft (258 m)
T-O to 50 ft (15 m) 1,575 ft (480 m)
Landing from 50 ft (15 m) 1,220 ft (372 m)
Landing run 435 ft (133 m)

Cessna Cardinal, de luxe version of the Model 177B (180 hp Lycoming O-360-A1F engine)

Range at max cruising speed, no reserve
        551 nm (635 miles; 1,021 km)
Range at econ cruising speed, no reserve
        655 nm (755 miles; 1,215 km)

CESSNA CARDINAL

The Cardinal is a de luxe version of the Model 177B, to which it is generally similar. Standard equipment includes sensitive altimeter, electric clock, speed fairings on the wheels, external air temperature gauge, full blind flying instrumentation, rate of climb indicator, turn co-ordinator, special interior appointments, landing light, all-over two-tone paint scheme, sun visors and tow bar.

DIMENSIONS:
  Same as for Model 177B.
WEIGHTS AND LOADINGS:
  Same as for Model 177B, except:
    Weight empty, equipped   1,440 lb (653 kg)
PERFORMANCE (at max T-O weight):
  Same as for Model 177B, except:
    Max level speed at S/L
        130 knots (150 mph; 241 km/h)
    Max cruising speed (75% power) at 9,500 ft
    (2,895 m) 120 knots (138 mph; 222 km/h)
    Econ cruising speed at 10,000 ft (3,050 m)
        102 knots (118 mph; 190 km/h)
    Range at max cruising speed, no reserve
        564 nm (650 miles; 1,045 km)
    Range at econ cruising speed, no reserve
        668 nm (770 miles; 1,235 km)

CESSNA MODEL 180 SKYWAGON

The Model 180 Skywagon features the typical Cessna braced high-wing monoplane layout, but has a tail-wheel type of landing gear.

The 1970 Model 180 introduces a split-type master rocker switch, improved instrument panel control knobs, vinyl floor mats, conical camber glass-fibre wingtips, more comfortable seating and a wider choice of interior trims. New optional items include fully articulating front seats, a fold-away child's seat for the rear cabin, quick oil drain valve, 10-channel single sideband HF transceiver, Cessna anti-precipitation ADF sense antenna and control wheel microphone switch.

A total of 5,088 Model 180's had been built by January 1970.

TYPE: One/six-seat cabin monoplane.
WINGS: Generally similar in construction to those of Model 172. Dihedral 1° 45'.
FUSELAGE: All-metal semi-monocoque structure. Identical to fuselage of Cessna 185, except for firewall and mounting brackets for dorsal fin.
TAIL UNIT: Unswept cantilever all-metal structure with adjustable-incidence tailplane. Normally, no trim-tabs; but manually-operated rudder trim is optionally available.
LANDING GEAR: Non-retractable tail-wheel type. Cessna cantilever spring steel main legs. Tail-wheel has tapered tubular spring. Main wheels and nylon tube-type tyres size 6·00 × 6 (optionally 8·00 × 6). Scott tail-wheel with 8 in (20 cm) tyre. Tyre pressure, main wheels 28 lb/sq in (1·97 kg/cm²), tail-wheel 55-65 lb/sq in (3·87-4·57 kg/cm²) according to load. Hydraulic disc brakes. Parking brake. Alternative Edo Model 628-296 floats, snow ski or amphibian gear.
POWER PLANT: One 230 hp Continental O-470-R six-cylinder horizontally-opposed air-cooled engine, driving McCauley 2A34C50/90A8 constant-speed metal propeller, diameter 6 ft 10 in (2·08 m) on landplane, 7 ft 4 in (2·24 m) on floatplane. Fuel in two tanks in wings, with total standard capacity of 65 US gallons (246 litres) and usable capacity of 60 US gallons (227 litres). Optional long-range tanks with total capacity of 84 US gallons (318 litres), of which 79 US gallons (299 litres) are usable. Oil capacity 3 US gallons (11·5 litres).
ACCOMMODATION: Standard seating is for a pilot only, with a choice of three optional arrangements. Maximum seating is for six persons in three pairs, without baggage space, With fewer seats there is space at rear of cabin for up to 400 lb (181 kg) of baggage. Door on each side of cabin, plus optional cargo door and baggage compartment door on port side. Starboard door has quick-release hinge pins so that it can be removed when loading bulky cargo. Passenger seats can all be removed when aircraft is to be used for freight carrying. Heating and ventilation standard.
ELECTRONICS AND EQUIPMENT: Wide range of optional electronics includes VHF and HF radio, ADF, VOR/LOC, VOR/ILS, Series 300 HF transceiver, Series 300 ATC transponder and other navigation aids by Cessna. Optional extras include blind-flying instruments, Cessna Nav-o-Matic 300 single-axis autopilot, dual controls, oxygen system, castoring landing gear, stretcher kit, omni-flash beacon, wing levelling stability augmentation system and turn co-ordinator.

DIMENSIONS, EXTERNAL:
Wing span	36 ft 2 in (11·02 m)
Wing chord at root	5 ft 4 in (1·63 m)
Wing chord at tip	3 ft 7 in (1·09 m)
Wing aspect ratio	7·52

Cessna Model 180 Skywagon one/six-seat cabin monoplane (230 hp Continental O-470-R engine)

Length overall:		
Landplane, skiplane	25 ft 9 in (7·85 m)
Floatplane	27 ft 0 in (8·23 m)
Amphibian	27 ft 6 in (8·38 m)
Height overall:	
Landplane, skiplane	7 ft 9 in (2·36 m)
Floatplane	12 ft 2 in (3·71 m)
Amphibian	12 ft 8 in (3·86 m)
Tailplane span	10 ft 10 in (3·30 m)
Wheel track, landplane	7 ft 8 in (2·33 m)
Passenger doors (each):	
Height	3 ft 3¾ in (1·01 m)
Width	2 ft 11 in (0·89 m)

AREAS:
Wings, gross	174 sq ft (16·16 m²)
Ailerons (total)	18·3 sq ft (1·70 m²)
Trailing-edge flaps (total)	21·23 sq ft (1·97 m²)
Fin	9·01 sq ft (0·84 m²)
Dorsal fin	2·04 sq ft (0·19 m²)
Rudder	7·29 sq ft (0·68 m²)
Tailplane	20·94 sq ft (1·94 m²)
Elevators	15·13 sq ft (1·40 m²)

WEIGHTS AND LOADINGS:
Weight empty, equipped:
Landplane	1,545 lb (700 kg)
Floatplane	1,855 lb (841 kg)
Skiplane	1,690 lb (766 kg)
Amphibian	2,100 lb (952 kg)

Max T-O weight:
Landplane, skiplane	2,800 lb (1,270 kg)
Floatplane	2,950 lb (1,338 kg)
Amphibian	2,950 lb (1,338 kg)

Max wing loading:
Landplane, skiplane	16·1 lb/sq ft (78·6 kg/m²)
Floatplane	17·0 lb/sq ft (83·0 kg/m²)
Amphibian	17·0 lb/sq ft (83·0 kg/m²)

Max power loading:
Land plane, skiplane	12·2 lb/hp (5·53 kg/hp)
Floatplane, amphibian	12·8 lb/hp (5·80 kg/hp)

PERFORMANCE (at max T-O weight):
Max level speed at S/L:
Landplane	148 knots (170 mph; 274 km/h)
Floatplane, amphibian, skiplane	
	129 knots (149 mph; 240 km/h)

Max permissible speed in dive:
Landplane	167 knots (192 mph; 309 km/h)

Max cruising speed (75% power) at 6,500 ft (1,980 m):
Landplane	141 knots (162 mph; 261 km/h)
Floatplane, amphibian	
	128 knots (147 mph; 237 km/h)
Skiplane	125 knots (144 mph; 232 km/h)

Econ cruising speed at 10,000 ft (3,050 m):
Landplane	105 knots (121 mph; 195 km/h)
Floatplane	99 knots (114 mph; 183 km/h)
Amphibian	99 knots (114 mph; 183 km/h)
Skiplane	88 knots (101 mph; 162 km/h)

Stalling speed, flaps up:
All versions	57 knots (65 mph; 105 km/h)

Stalling speed, flaps down:
All versions	51 knots (58 mph; 93·5 km/h)

Rate of climb at S/L:
Landplane	1,090 ft (332 m)/min
Floatplane	990 ft (302 m)/min
Amphibian	990 ft (302 m)/min

Service ceiling:
Landplane	19,600 ft (5,975 m)
Floatplane	16,000 ft (4,877 m)
Amphibian	16,000 ft (4,877 m)

T-O run:
Landplane	625 ft (190 m)
Floatplane	1,280 ft (390 m)
Amphibian, on land	1,360 ft (415 m)
Amphibian, on water	1,280 ft (390 m)

T-O to 50 ft (15 m):
Landplane	1,205 ft (367 m)
Floatplane	2,070 ft (631 m)
Amphibian, on land	2,185 ft (666 m)
Amphibian, on water	2,070 ft (631 m)

Landing from 50 ft (15 m):
Landplane	1,365 ft (416 m)
Floatplane	1,720 ft (524 m)
Amphibian, on land	1,490 ft (454 m)
Amphibian, on water	1,720 ft (524 m)

Landing run:
Landplane	480 ft (146 m)
Floatplane	735 ft (224 m)
Amphibian, on land	1,025 ft (312 m)
Amphibian, on water	735 ft (224 m)

Range at econ cruising speed, with long-range tanks, no reserve:
Landplane	1,055 nm (1,215 miles; 1,955 km)
Floatplane	946 nm (1,090 miles; 1,754 km)
Amphibian	946 nm (1,090 miles; 1,754 km)
Skiplane	829 nm (955 miles; 1,537 km)

Range at max cruising speed, standard fuel, no reserve:
Landplane	603 nm (695 miles; 1,118 km)
Floatplane, amphibian	
	547 nm (630 miles; 1,014 km)
Skiplane	538 nm (620 miles; 998 km)

Range at max cruising speed, with long-range tanks, no reserve:
Landplane	803 nm (925 miles; 1,489 km)
Floatplane, amphibian	
	725 nm (835 miles; 1,344 km)
Skiplane	712 nm (820 miles; 1,320 km)

CESSNA MODEL 182

The 1970 version of the Model 182 introduces many new features, including an increase of 145 lb (65 kg) in gross weight, fully-articulating front seats and improved suspension of all seating, grey-finish instrument panel to reduce eye

Cessna Skylane, de luxe version of the Model 182 (230 hp Continental O-470-R engine)

strain, a new low control wheel and new elevator control system to lower stick forces, transistorised dimming for incandescent and electroluminescent panel lights, colour-matched rocker switches, a split-type master switch, press-to-reset circuit breakers for stall warning, alternator and turn-coordinator, a new eyebrow panel housing lights to illuminate the upper panel, flight instruments grouped in the standard "T" arrangement, radio speaker in a new centre-ceiling console which contains also red and white panel flood-lighting plus provisions for optional oxygen system controls, increased choice of interior trims, improved front cowling design and re-location of outside air temperature gauge. New options include ground manoeuvring assist handles in the tail cone, heavy duty exterior door handles, a quick drain oil valve and a fold-away child's seat for the baggage area.

A new optional item for the Model 182, pre-viously available only for the Models 185, 206 and 207 Skywagons, is an under-fuselage detach-able glass-fibre Cargo-Pack, more than 9 ft long and 2 ft 7 in wide (2·75 m × 0·79 m), with a volume of 21·5 cu ft (0·61 m³) and capacity of 300 lb (136 kg). The Pack incorporates loading doors on the side and at the rear.

A total of 11,097 Model 182/Skylanes had been delivered by January 1970.

The Model 182 is built also, under licence, by DINFIA in the Argentine (which see).

TYPE: Four-seat cabin monoplane.

WINGS: Similar to those of Model 172.

FUSELAGE: All-metal semi-monocoque structure.

TAIL UNIT: Cantilever all-metal structure with swept fin and rudder. Trim-tab in starboard elevator.

LANDING GEAR: Non-retractable tricycle type. Land-O-Matic cantilever spring steel main legs. Oleo-pneumatic nose unit. Cessna main wheels and tyres size 6·00 × 6, pressure 32 lb/sq in (2·25 kg/cm²). Cessna nose-wheel and tyre size 5·00 × 5, pressure 45 lb/sq in (3·16 kg/cm²). Main wheel tyres size 8·00 × 6 and nose-wheel tyre size 6·00 × 6 are optional. Cessna hydraulic disc brakes. Optional wheel fairings.

POWER PLANT: Similar to that of Model 180, except for McCauley propeller type 2A36C/90M-8, diameter 6 ft 10 in (2·08 m).

ACCOMMODATION: Generally similar to Model 172.

ELECTRONICS AND EQUIPMENT: Optional equip-ment includes a wide range of VHF transceivers and navigation receivers, with VOR/LOC indicator, by Cessna, ADF, marker beacon, ILS receiver, Cessna Series 300 HF transceiver and Series 400 solid-state ADF, Cessna Nav-O-Matic 300 or 400 auto-pilot, blind-flying instrumentation, dual controls, glider towing hook, omni-flash beacon, oxygen system, stretcher kit, turn co-ordinator to replace turn and bank indicator, wing levelling stability augmentation system, 3 in (7·5 cm) boom microphone, map light, ground manoeuvring assist handles, heavy duty exterior handles, quick drain oil valve and a fold-away child's seat.

DIMENSIONS, EXTERNAL:
Wing span	35 ft 10 in (10·92 m)
Length overall	28 ft 0½ in (8·55 m)
Height overall	8 ft 10½ in (2·71 m)
Tailplane span	11 ft 8 in (3·55 m)
Wheel track	7 ft 11½ in (2·43 m)
Wheelbase	5 ft 6½ in (1·69 m)
Passenger doors (each):	
Height	3 ft 4¼ in (1·02 m)
Width	2 ft 11¼ in (0·90 m)

AREAS:
Wings, gross	174 sq ft (16·16 m²)
Ailerons (total)	18·3 sq ft (1·70 m²)
Trailing-edge flaps (total)	21·20 sq ft (1·97 m²)
Fin	11·62 sq ft (1·08 m²)
Rudder	6·95 sq ft (0·65 m²)
Tailplane	22·96 sq ft (2·13 m²)
Elevators	15·85 sq ft (1·47 m²)

WEIGHTS AND LOADINGS:
Weight empty, equipped	1,580 lb (716 kg)
Max T-O weight	2,950 lb (1,338 kg)
Max landing weight	2,800 lb (1,270 kg)
Max wing loading	16·1 lb/sq ft (78·6 kg/m²)
Max power loading	12·2 lb/hp (5·53 kg/hp)

PERFORMANCE (at max T-O weight):
Max level speed at S/L
143 knots (165 mph; 266 km/h)
Max cruising speed, 75% power at 6,500 ft
(1,980 m)   136 knots (157 mph; 253 km/h)
Econ cruising speed at 10,000 ft (3,050 m)
97 knots (112 mph; 180 km/h)
Stalling speed, flaps down
48 knots (55 mph; 88·5 km/h)
Rate of climb at S/L	980 ft (300 m)/min
Service ceiling	18,900 ft (5,760 m)
T-O run	625 ft (190 m)
T-O to 50 ft (15 m)	1,205 ft (367 m)
Landing from 50 ft (15 m)	1,350 ft (411 m)
Landing run	590 ft (180 m)

Range at max cruising speed, standard fuel,
no reserve   594 nm (685 miles; 1,100 km)
Range at max cruising speed, with long-range tanks, no reserve
785 nm (905 miles; 1,455 km)
Range at econ cruising speed, standard fuel, no reserve   785 nm (905 miles; 1,455 km)
Range at econ cruising speed, with long-range tanks, no reserve
1,033 nm (1,190 miles; 1,915 km)

CESSNA SKYLANE

The Skylane is a *de luxe* version of the Model 182 and was first introduced in January 1958. The current model has full blind-flying instru-mentation, lightweight 3 in (7·5 cm) attitude gyros, turn co-ordinator replacing turn and bank indicator, wheel fairings, tinted glass and all-over paint scheme as standard equipment in addition to the refinements incorporated in the Model 182. Optional items include a wide range of radio and navigation aids, a wing levelling stability augmentation system, boom micro-phone and map light.

DIMENSIONS, EXTERNAL:
Same as for Model 182.

WEIGHTS AND LOADINGS:
Same as for Model 182, except:
Weight empty, equipped	1,640 lb (744 kg)
Max wing loading	16·9 lb/sq ft (82·5 kg/m²)
Max power loading	12·8 lb/hp (5·81 kg/hp)

PERFORMANCE (at max T-O weight):
Max level speed at S/L
146 knots (168 mph; 270 km/h)
Max cruising speed, 75% power at 6,500 ft
(1,980 m)   139 knots (160 mph; 257 km/h)
Econ cruising speed at 10,000 ft (3,050 m)
100 knots (115 mph; 185 km/h)
Stalling speed, flaps up
58 knots (66 mph; 107 km/h)
Stalling speed, flaps down
50 knots (57 mph; 92 km/h)
Max rate of climb at S/L	890 ft (271 m)/min
Service ceiling	17,700 ft (5,395 m)
T-O run	705 ft (215 m)
T-O to 50 ft (15 m)	1,350 ft (411 m)
Landing from 50 ft (15 m)	1,350 ft (411 m)
Landing run	590 ft (180 m)

Range at max cruising speed, standard fuel,
no reserve   599 nm (690 miles; 1,110 km)
Range at max cruising speed, with long-range fuel tanks, no reserve
790 nm (910 miles; 1,464 km)
Range at econ cruising speed, with long-range fuel tanks, no reserve
1,007 nm (1,160 miles; 1,866 km)

CESSNA MODEL 185 SKYWAGON
US Military designation: U-17

The prototype of the Model 185 Skywagon flew for the first time in July 1960 and the first production model was completed in March 1961.

The 1970 Model 185 Skywagon introduced the same new features as the Model 180.

Cessna has received important contracts to supply U-17 Skywagons to the US Air Force for delivery to overseas countries, under the US Military Assistance Programme. The latest order, placed in October 1967, was for 24 U-17B's.

A total of 1,612 Model 185 Skywagons, including U-17A/B's, had been built by January 1970.

The Model 185 Skywagon can be fitted with Edo 628-2960 floats, or Edo Model 597 amphibious floats, or Fli-Lite skis, and is suitable for agri-cultural duties, using quickly-removable Sorensen spray-gear. It can carry under its fuselage a detachable glass-fibre Cargo-Pack, more than 9 ft long and 2 ft 7 in wide (2·75 m × 0·79 m), with a volume of 21·5 cu ft (0·61 m³) and capacity of 300 lb (136 kg). The Pack incorporates loading doors on the side and at the rear.

TYPE: One/six-seat cabin monoplane.

WINGS AND FUSELAGE: Similar to Model 180.

TAIL UNIT: Same as for Model 180, except for fin of increased area.

LANDING GEAR: Similar to Model 180, except for tyre pressures: main wheels (6·00 × 6) 35 lb/sq in (2·46 kg/cm²), main wheels (8·00 × 6) 25 lb/sq in (1·76 kg/cm²), tail-wheel 55-70 lb/sq in (3·87-4·92 kg/cm²) depending on load. Optional amphibian, float or ski gear.

POWER PLANT: One 300 hp Continental IO-520-D six-cylinder horizontally-opposed air-cooled engine, driving a McCauley constant-speed metal propeller, diameter 6 ft 10 in (2·08 m) on landplane version, 7 ft 2 in (2·18 m) on float-plane and amphibian versions. Fuel in two tanks in wings, total capacity 65 US gallons (246 litres), of which 62 US gallons (235 litres) are usable. Extended-range tanks available as optional equipment in place of standard tanks, total capacity 84 US gallons (318 litres), of which 81 US gallons (306·5 litres) are usable. Oil capacity 3 US gallons (11·4 litres).

ACCOMMODATION, ELECTRONICS AND EQUIPMENT: Same as for Model 180.

DIMENSIONS:
Same as for Model 180.

AREAS:
Same as for Model 180, except:
Fin	13·86 sq ft (1·29 m²)

WEIGHTS AND LOADINGS:
Weight empty, equipped:
Landplane	1,575 lb (714 kg)
Floatplane	1,890 lb (857 kg)
Amphibian	2,135 lb (968 kg)
Skiplane	1,725 lb (782 kg)

Max T-O weight:
Landplane, skiplane	3,350 lb (1,519 kg)
Floatplane	3,320 lb (1,506 kg)
Amphibian, land take-off	3,265 lb (1,481 kg)
Amphibian, water take-off	3,100 lb (1,406 kg)

Max wing loading:
Landplane, skiplane	19·3 lb/sq ft (94·2 kg/m²)
Floatplane	19·1 lb/sq ft (93·3 kg/m²)
Amphibian	18·8 lb/sq ft (91·8 kg/m²)

Max power loading:
Landplane, skiplane	11·2 lb/hp (5·08 kg/hp)
Floatplane	11·1 lb/hp (5·0 kg/hp)
Amphibian	10·9 lb/hp (4·9 kg/hp)

PERFORMANCE (at max T-O weight):
Max level speed at S/L:
Landplane	155 knots (178 mph; 286 km/h)
Floatplane	141 knots (162 mph; 261 km/h)
Amphibian	135 knots (156 mph; 251 km/h)
Skiplane	136 knots (157 mph; 252 km/h)

Max permissible diving speed:
Landplane	182 knots (210 mph; 338 km/h)

Max cruising speed (75% power) at 7,500 ft= 2,285 m:
Landplane	147 knots (169 mph; 272 km/h)
Floatplane	135 knots (155 mph; 249 km/h)
Amphibian	129 knots (149 mph; 240 km/h)
Skiplane	130 knots (150 mph; 241 km/h)

Econ cruising speed at 10,000 ft (3,050 m):
Landplane	112 knots (129 mph; 208 km/h)
Floatplane	94 knots (108 mph; 174 km/h)
Amphibian	88 knots (101 mph; 162 km/h)
Skiplane	109 knots (126 mph; 203 km/h)

Stalling speed, flaps up:
Landplane, skiplane
58·5 knots (67 mph; 108 km/h)
Floatplane, amphibian
57 knots (65 mph; 105 km/h)
Stalling speed, flaps down:
Landplane, skiplane
51·5 knots (59 mph; 95 km/h)
Floatplane, amphibian
50 knots (57 mph; 92 km/h)
Rate of climb at S/L:
Landplane	1,010 ft (308 m)/min
Floatplane	960 ft (293 m)/min
Amphibian	970 ft (296 m)/min

Cessna Agwagon "B" agricultural aircraft (230 hp Continental O-470-R or 300 hp Continental IO-520-D engine)

Service ceiling:
Landplane 17,150 ft (5,229 m)
Floatplane 16,400 ft (5,000 m)
Amphibian 15,300 ft (4,663 m)
T-O run:
Landplane 770 ft (235 m)
Floatplane 1,105 ft (337 m)
Amphibian, on land 670 ft (204 m)
Amphibian, on water 885 ft (270 m)
T-O to 50 ft (15 m):
Landplane 1,365 ft (416 m)
Floatplane 1,740 ft (530 m)
Amphibian, on land 1,275 ft (389 m)
Amphibian, on water 1,430 ft (436 m)
Landing from 50 ft (15 m):
Landplane 1,400 ft (427 m)
Floatplane 1,530 ft (466 m)
Amphibian, on land 1,240 ft (378 m)
Amphibian, on water 1,480 ft (450 m)
Landing run:
Landplane 480 ft (146 m)
Floatplane 640 ft (195 m)
Amphibian, on land 780 ft (238 m)
Amphibian, on water 600 ft (183 m)
Range at econ cruising speed at 10,000 ft (3,050 m), long-range tanks, no reserve:
Landplane 933 nm (1,075 miles; 1,730 km)
Floatplane 842 nm (970 miles; 1,561 km)
Amphibian 790 nm (910 miles; 1,464 km)
Skiplane 807 nm (930 miles; 1,497 km)
Range at max cruising speed, standard tanks, no reserve:
Landplane 573 nm (660 miles; 1,062 km)
Floatplane 521 nm (600 miles; 965 km)
Amphibian 499 nm (575 miles; 925 km)
Skiplane 503 nm (580 miles; 933 km)
Range at max cruising speed, long-range tanks, no reserve:
Landplane 746 nm (860 miles; 1,384 km)
Floatplane 681 nm (785 miles; 1,263 km)
Amphibian 655 nm (755 miles; 1,215 km)
Skiplane 660 nm (760 miles; 1,223 km)

CESSNA AGWAGON "B"

First flown in prototype form on 19 February 1965, the Agwagon is a specialised agricultural aircraft which Cessna decided to develop after an extensive survey into the requirements of the operators of such aircraft.

On 5 December 1969 Cessna announced a new version of this aircraft known as the Agwagon "B", incorporating many design changes and a number of new optional items.

New features include increased wing dihedral for improved stability, wing fences immediately outboard of the wing bracing strut attachment points, aileron leading-edge gap seals, cockpit canopy with all-round vision, tinted windows, a pair of tinted top windows for improved visibility while turning, Land-O-Matic cantilever spring-steel main landing gear with special shims at the fuselage attachment points to reduce maintenance, a vertically-adjusting seat with a lower cushion front, press-to-reset circuit breakers for the stall warning indicator, turn and bank indicator and alternator regulator, a split-type master switch for separate control of battery and alternator circuits, a universal dispersal control system, new wire cutters, bullet-style spinner for constant-speed propeller installations, control column lock, navigation lights, retractable tail-cone lift handles, quick-release canopy door hinges, quick-removable engine induction air filter and a quick oil drain valve.

Exclusive to the Agwagon is an optional engine-driven hydraulic spray system, the internally-mounted pump of which conserves engine horse-power and reduces drag. Other new options include an electrically-operated spray valve for remote pump spray systems, a spring-loaded check valve to prevent dry material in the hopper from entering the pipelines of the optional side loading system, and a windshield defogging system.

Optional liquid or dry dispersal systems designed for the Agwagon "B" include low or high-volume liquid systems with either a fan-driven angle pump or the engine-driven low-drag hydraulic pump, low or high-volume quick-change liquid or dry system with either a strut-mounted pump or the engine-driven hydraulic pump, medium-volume spreader dry dispersal system or vane-type low-drag high-volume dry spreader.

A dual system of landing lights is available, to improve depth perception and ground visibility for night-spraying and dusting operations, together with a 24V electrical system.

The standard 230 hp engine and fixed-pitch propeller can be replaced optionally by a 300 hp fuel-injection engine and constant-speed propeller.

The Agwagon received FAA Type Approval on 14 February 1966, and deliveries began in March 1966. A total of 572 Agwagons had been delivered by January 1970.

TYPE: Single-seat agricultural monoplane.

WINGS: Braced low-wing monoplane, with single streamline-section bracing strut each side. Wing section NACA 2412 from root to inboard tip, symmetrical tip. Dihedral 0° on centre-section, 9° on top surface of outer wings.

Incidence 1° 30' at root, —1° 30' at tip. All-metal structure with mechanically-operated NACA all-metal single-slotted flaps inboard of Frise all-metal ailerons. Aileron leading-edge gaps sealed. Wing fences immediately outboard of bracing strut attachment points. Conical-camber tips optional.

FUSELAGE: Rectangular-section welded steel-tube structure with removable metal skin panels forward of cabin. All-metal semi-monocoque rear fuselage.

TAIL UNIT: Cantilever all-metal structure. Fixed-incidence tailplane. Trim-tab in starboard elevator.

LANDING GEAR: Non-retractable tail-wheel type. Land-O-Matic spring steel cantilever main legs. Tapered tubular tail-wheel spring shock-absorber. Main wheels and tyres size 8·00 × 6 (optionally 8·50 × 10). Hydraulic disc brakes and parking brake.

POWER PLANT: One 230 hp Continental O-470-R six-cylinder horizontally-opposed air-cooled engine, driving either a McCauley 1A200AOM/9044 two-blade fixed-pitch aluminium propeller, diameter 7 ft 6 in (2·29 m), or a McCauley 2A34C50/90A2 two-blade constant-speed propeller, diameter 7 ft 4 in (2·24 m). Optionally one 300 hp Continental IO-520-D six-cylinder horizontally-opposed air-cooled engine, with fuel injection, driving a McCauley D2A34C58/90AT-4 two-blade constant-speed propeller, diameter 7 ft 2 in (2·18 m). This latter power plant installation includes combined fuel flow and manifold pressure gauge, propeller governor and electric auxiliary fuel pump. Metal fuel tank aft of firewall, capacity 37 US gallons (140 litres) or, optionally, 56 US gallons (212 litres) for 300 hp engine installation. Oil capacity 3 US gallons (11·4 litres).

ACCOMMODATION: Pilot only, on vertically and longitudinally adjustable seat, in enclosed cabin. Steel overturn structure. Combined window and door on each side, hinged at bottom. Heating and ventilation standard. Baggage space beneath fuel tank. Windshield defogging system optional.

ELECTRONICS AND EQUIPMENT: Optional items include radio transceiver and omni equipment, position lights, instrument lights, rotating beacon, dual landing lights and 24V electrical system. Standard agricultural equipment includes a 200 US gallon (757 litres) or 1,800 lb (816 kg) capacity glass-fibre hopper, located approximately in the centre of the CG range and suitable for dust or liquids. A variety of optional spray and dust equipment is available. Spray booms are located slightly aft and below wing trailing-edges and give effective swath width of up to 70 ft (21·3 m). Wire-cutting cable from cockpit canopy to top of fin. Optional rear canopy window, foul weather windows and landing gear-mounted wire-cutters.

DIMENSIONS, EXTERNAL:
Wing span 41 ft 2 in (12·55 m)
Wing chord at root 5 ft 4 in (1·63 m)
Wing chord at tip 3 ft 8 in (1·12 m)
Wing aspect ratio 8·1
Length overall 25 ft 3 in (7·70 m)
Height overall 7 ft 4½ in (2·25 m)
Tailplane span 10 ft 10 in (3·30 m)
Wheel track 7 ft 10½ in (2·41 m)
Wheelbase 20 ft 10 in (6·35 m)
AREAS:
Wings, gross 202 sq ft (18·8 m²)
Ailerons (total) 27·7 sq ft (2·57 m²)
Flaps (total) 21·2 sq ft (1·97 m²)
Fin 11·1 sq ft (1·03 m²)
Rudder 7·3 sq ft (0·68 m²)
Tailplane 20·9 sq ft (1·94 m²)
Elevators, including tab 15·1 sq ft (1·40 m²)
WEIGHTS AND LOADINGS (FP=fixed-pitch propeller; CS=constant-speed propeller):

Weight empty:
230FP 1,815 lb (823 kg)
230CS 1,830 lb (830 kg)
300 1,845 lb (837 kg)
Max T-O weight, normal category:
230, 300 3,300 lb (1,497 kg)
Max T-O weight, agricultural:
230 3,800 lb (1,722 kg)
300 4,000 lb (1,814 kg)
Wing loading (normal category):
230, 300 16·3 lb/sq ft (86·7 kg/m²)
Power loading (normal category):
230 14·3 lb/hp (6·5 kg/hp)
300 11·0 lb/hp (5·0 kg/hp)
PERFORMANCE (at AUW of 3,300 lb=1,497 kg, without dispersal equipment):
Max level speed at S/L:
230FP 103 knots (119 mph; 192 km/h)
230CS 120 knots (138 mph; 222 km/h)
300 131 knots (151 mph; 240 km/h)
Max cruising speed:
230FP (70% power) at 5000 ft (1,525 m)
 101 knots (116 mph; 188 km/h)
230CS (75% power) at 6,500 ft (1,980 m)
 111 knots (128 mph; 206 km/h)
300 (75% power) at 6,500 ft (1,980 m)
 122 knots (141 mph; 227 km/h)
Stalling speed, flaps up:
230/300 54 knots (62 mph; 100 km/h)
Stalling speed, flaps down:
230/300 51 knots (58 mph; 94 km/h)
Rate of climb at S/L:
230FP 710 ft (215 m)/min
230CS 755 ft (230 m)/min
300 940 ft (285 m)/min
Service ceiling:
230FP 13,000 ft (3,960 m)
230CS 13,700 ft (4,175 m)
300 15,700 ft (4,785 m)
T-O run:
230FP 845 ft (257 m)
230CS 805 ft (245 m)
300 610 ft (186 m)
T-O to 50 ft (15 m):
230FP 1,365 ft (416 m)
230CS 1,320 ft (402 m)
300 970 ft (296 m)
Landing from 50 ft (15 m):
230/300 1,265 ft (386 m)
Landing run: 420 ft (128 m)
Range at cruising speeds quoted above, no reserves:
230FP 282 nm (325 miles; 523 km)
230CS 291 nm (335 miles; 539 km)
300 278 nm (320 miles; 515 km)
300, with optional fuel
 412 nm (475 miles; 764 km)

CESSNA MODEL U206 and TU206 SKYWAGON 206

In spite of its name, this aircraft differs considerably from the Model 185 Skywagon. It has swept vertical tail surfaces, a tricycle landing gear, a tailplane of greater span, new wide-span flaps, and double cargo doors on the starboard side of the fuselage which permit the easy loading and unloading of a crate more than 4 ft long, 3 ft wide and 3 ft deep (1·22 m × 0·91 m × 0·91 m).

There are four current versions of the Cessna Model 206, as follows:

U206 Skywagon 206. Standard cargo utility model with 300 hp Continental IO-520-F engine and double loading doors, as described in detail above and below.

TU206 Turbo-Skywagon 206. Similar to U206 but with 285 hp Continental TSIO-520-C turbocharged engine in modified cowling and provided with a manifold pressure relief valve to prevent overboost.

P206 and TP206 Super Skylane. De luxe six-seat versions, described separately.

Cessna Turbo-Skywagon 206 cargo/utility aircraft (285 hp Continental TSIO-520-C engine)

A number of refinements have been introduced on the 1970 models, including a split-type master rocker switch, improved instrument panel control knobs, vinyl floor mats, an extended choice of interior trims, a streamlined lower engine cowl, re-location of the outside air temperature gauge, fore and aft adjustment of the fifth and sixth seats, improved suspension of all seating, pilot's control wheel set in a lower position, grey finish instrument panel to reduce eye strain and transistorised instrument lighting controls. New optional items include fully-articulating front seats, quick oil drain valve, 10-channel single-sideband HF transceiver, Cessna anti-precipitation ADF sense antenna and a new central overhead speaker console when optional radios are ordered.

A Model 206 Skywagon has been flown with various underwing weapon loads by pilots of the TAC Special Air Warfare Center to evaluate its potential for light COIN strike missions. Typical loadings have included a 7·62-mm six-barrel Minigun pod under each wing, plus an SUU/14A bomblet dispenser under the port wing.

A total of 1,413 Model 206 Skywagons had been built by January 1970.

TYPE: Single-engined cargo utility aircraft.

WINGS: Braced high-wing monoplane. Single streamline-section bracing strut each side. Wing section NACA 2412 from root to just inboard of tip, wingtip is symmetrical. Dihedral 1° 44′. Incidence 1° 30′ at root, —1° 30′ at tip. All-metal structure. Glass-fibre conical camber tips. Modified Frise-type wide-chord ailerons. Electrically-operated long-span NACA single-slotted flaps. No tabs.

FUSELAGE: Conventional all-metal semi-monocoque structure.

TAIL UNIT: Cantilever all-metal structure, with sweptback vertical surfaces. Large trim-tab in starboard elevator. Electrical operation of trim-tab optional.

LANDING GEAR: Non-retractable tricycle type. Cessna "Land-o-Matic" cantilever spring steel main legs. Oleo-pneumatic nose-wheel shock-absorber. Cessna wheels, tubeless tyres and hydraulic disc brakes. Main wheels and tyres size 15·00 × 6·00-6, pressure 42 lb/sq in (2·95 kg/cm²). Nose-wheel and tyre size 5·00 × 5, pressure 45 lb/sq in (3·16 kg/cm²). Optional 8·00 × 6 main wheel tyres, 6·00 × 6 nose-wheel tyre. Available with floats and hydraulically-operated wheel-skis.

POWER PLANT: One Continental six-cylinder horizontally-opposed air-cooled engine (details under model listings above), driving a McCauley D2A34C58/90AT-8 two-blade metal constant-speed propeller, diameter 6 ft 10 in (2·08 m) on landplane; propeller diameter 7 ft 2 in (2·18 m) on floatplane (several different three-blade propellers optional). Two fuel tanks in wings, with total standard capacity of 65 US gallons (246 litres), of which 63 US gallons (238·5 litres) are usable. Optional capacity of 84 US gallons (318 litres), of which 80 US gallons (302·8 litres) are usable. Oil capacity 3 US gallons (11·4 litres).

ACCOMMODATION: Pilot's seat only standard. Optional individual seats for up to five passengers. Pilot's door on port side. Large double cargo doors on starboard side; forward door hinged to open forward, rear door hinged to open rearward. Aircraft can be flown with cargo doors removed for photography, air dropping of supplies or parachuting. Glass-fibre cargo pack, capacity 300 lb (136 kg), can be carried under the fuselage.

ELECTRONICS AND EQUIPMENT: Optional extras include a complete range of radio and navigation equipment, including the Cessna 300 nav/com, ADF and marker beacon receiver, Cessna 500 nav/com VHF transmitter, ADF, nav/omni and transceiver, Cessna Series 300 HF transceiver, Series 300 ATC transponder, 10-channel single-sideband HF transceiver, anti-precipitation ADF sense antenna and audio selector switch system. When radios are installed, Cessna's new printed-circuit junction box, low-drag VHF antennae and new central overhead console to house the dual heavy-magnet radio speakers are included in the package. Other options include Cessna Nav-O-Matic 300 or 400 autopilot, blind-flying instrumentation, instrument panel white lighting, omni-flash beacon, dual controls, glider towing hook, oxygen system, agricultural spray gear (tank capacity 110 or 160 US gallons = 416 or 605 litres), survey camera installation in cabin floor, stretcher kit, casket-carrying provisions, wing levelling stability augmentation system, fully-articulating front seats, quick oil drain valve and sky diving kit.

DIMENSIONS, EXTERNAL (L=landplane; F=floatplane; S=skiplane):

Wing span	35 ft 10 in (10·92 m)
Wing chord at root	5 ft 4 in (1·63 m)
Wing chord at tip	3 ft 7 in (1·09 m)
Wing aspect ratio	7·63
Length overall:	
L, S	28 ft 0 in (8·53 m)
F	28 ft 5½ in (8·67 m)
Length of fuselage	25 ft 8¼ in (7·82 m)
Height over tail:	
L, S	9 ft 7½ in (2·93 m)
F	13 ft 11½ in (4·25 m)
Tailplane span	13 ft 0 in (3·96 m)
Wheel track: L	8 ft 1¾ in (2·48 m)
Pilot's door (port):	
Height, mean	3 ft 4 in (1·03 m)
Width	2 ft 10½ in (0·88 m)
Cargo double door (stbd):	
Height	3 ft 2½ in (0·98 m)
Width	3 ft 6½ in (1·08 m)
Height to sill	2 ft 1 in (0·64 m)

DIMENSIONS, INTERNAL:

Cabin: Length	11 ft 5 in (3·48 m)
Max width	3 ft 8 in (1·12 m)
Max height	4 ft 1½ in (1·26 m)
Volume available for payload	98·8 cu ft (2·80 m³)
Under-fuselage cargo pack	12 cu ft (0·34 m³)

AREAS:

Wings, gross	174·0 sq ft (16·17 m²)
Ailerons	17·32 sq ft (1·60 m²)
Trailing-edge flaps	28·35 sq ft (2·63 m²)
Fin	11·62 sq ft (1·08 m²)
Rudder, including tab	6·95 sq ft (0·65 m²)
Tailplane	24·84 sq ft (2·31 m²)
Elevators, including tab	20·08 sq ft (1·86 m²)

WEIGHTS AND LOADINGS (L=landplane; F=floatplane; S=skiplane):

Weight empty, one seat only:	
U206: L	1,710 lb (776 kg)
F	2,070 lb (939 kg)
S	1,940 lb (880 kg)
TU206: L	1,810 lb (821 kg)
F	2,170 lb (984 kg)
S	2,040 lb (925 kg)
Max T-O and landing weight:	
U206: L	3,600 lb (1,633 kg)
F	3,500 lb (1,588 kg)
S	3,300 lb (1,496 kg)
TU206: L, F	3,600 lb (1,633 kg)
S	3,300 lb (1,496 kg)
Max wing loading:	
U206: L	20·7 lb/sq ft (101 kg/m²)
F	20·1 lb/sq ft (98 kg/m²)
S	19·0 lb/sq ft (93 kg/m²)
TU206: L, F	20·7 lb/sq ft (101 kg/m²)
S	19·0 lb/sq ft (93 kg/m²)
Max power loading:	
U206: L	12·0 lb/hp (5·4 kg/hp)
F	11·7 lb/hp (5·3 kg/hp)
S	11·0 lb/hp (4·99 kg/hp)
TU206: L, F	12·6 lb/hp (5·7 kg/hp)
S	11·6 lb/hp (5·26 kg/hp)

PERFORMANCE (L=landplane; F=floatplane; S=skiplane):

Max level speed:	
U206 at S/L:	
L	151 knots (174 mph; 280 km/h)
F	135 knots (156 mph; 251 km/h)
S	121 knots (139 mph; 224 km/h)
TU206 at 19,000 ft (5,790 m):	
L	174 knots (200 mph; 322 km/h)
F	157 knots (181 mph; 291 km/h)
S	145 knots (167 mph; 269 km/h)
Max cruising speed (75% power):	
U206 at 6,500 ft (1,980 m):	
L	142 knots (164 mph; 264 km/h)
F	131 knots (151 mph; 243 km/h)
S	119 knots (137 mph; 270 km/h)
TU206: L at 24,000 ft (7,320 m)	160 knots (184 mph; 296 km/h)
F at 20,000 ft (6,100 m)	142 knots (164 mph; 264 km/h)
S at 20,000 ft (6,100 m)	132 knots (152 mph; 245 km/h)
Econ cruising speed:	
U206 at 10,000 ft (3,050 m):	
L	114 knots (131 mph; 211 km/h)
F	98 knots (113 mph; 182 km/h)
S	92 knots (106 mph; 171 km/h)
TU206 at 15,000 ft (4,575 m):	
L	121 knots (139 mph; 224 km/h)
F	111 knots (128 mph; 206 km/h)
S	102 knots (118 mph; 190 km/h)
Stalling speed, flaps up:	
U206: L	61 knots (70 mph; 113 km/h)
F	58·5 knots (67 mph; 108 km/h)
S	60 knots (69 mph; 111 km/h)
TU206: L	61 knots (70 mph; 113 km/h)
F	59 knots (68 mph; 110 km/h)
S	60 knots (69 mph; 111 km/h)
Stalling speed, flaps down:	
U206: L	53 knots (61 mph; 98 km/h)
F, S	52·5 knots (60 mph; 96 km/h)
TU206: L, F	53 knots (61 mph; 98 km/h)
S	52·5 knots (60 mph; 96 km/h)
Rate of climb at S/L:	
U206: L	920 ft (280 m)/min
F	855 ft (260 m)/min
S	800 ft (244 m)/min
TU206: L	1,030 ft (314 m)/min
F	950 ft (290 m)/min
S	920 ft (280 m)/min
Service ceiling:	
U206: L	14,800 ft (4,511 m)
F	13,900 ft (4,237 m)
S	11,500 ft (3,505 m)
TU206: L	26,300 ft (8,020 m)
F	24,200 ft (7,375 m)
S	23,500 ft (7,163 m)
T-O run:	
U206:	
L	900 ft (274 m)
F	1,445 ft (440 m)
TU206:	
L	910 ft (277 m)
F	1,400 ft (427 m)
T-O to 50 ft (15 m):	
U206	
L	1,780 ft (543 m)
F	2,475 ft (754 m)
TU206:	
L	1,810 ft (552 m)
F	2,400 ft (731 m)
Landing from 50 ft (15 m):	
U206:	
L	1,395 ft (425 m)
F	1,570 ft (479 m)
TU206:	
L	1,395 ft (425 m)
F	1,610 ft (491 m)
Landing run:	
U206:	
L	735 ft (224 m)
F	695 ft (212 m)
TU206:	
L	735 ft (224 m)
F	710 ft (216 m)
Range, 75% power at 6,500 ft (1,980 m), normal fuel, no reserve:	
U206: L	564 nm (650 miles; 1,045 km)
F	521 nm (600 miles; 966 km)
S	473 nm (545 miles; 877 km)
TU206:	
L at 24,000 ft (7,320 m)	607 nm (700 miles; 1,127 km)
F at 20,000 ft (6,100 m)	538 nm (620 miles; 998 km)
S at 20,000 ft (6,100 m)	495 nm (570 miles; 917 km)
Range, 75% power at 6,500 ft (1,980 m), long-range tanks, no reserve:	
U206: L	720 nm (830 miles; 1,335 km)
F	664 nm (765 miles; 1,231 km)
S	603 nm (695 miles; 1,118 km)
TU206:	
L at 24,000 ft (7,320 m)	772 nm (890 miles; 1,432 km)
F at 20,000 ft (6,100 m)	686 nm (790 miles; 1,311 km)
S at 20,000 ft (6,100 m)	642 nm (740 miles; 1,190 km)
Range at econ cruising speed, long-range tanks, no reserve:	
U206 at 10,000 ft (3,050 m):	
L	885 nm (1,020 miles; 1,640 km)
F	872 nm (1,005 miles; 1,617 km)
S	725 nm (835 miles; 1,343 km)
TU206 at 15,000 ft (4,575 m):	
L	911 nm (1,050 miles; 1,690 km)
F	768 nm (885 miles; 1,424 km)
S	703 nm (810 miles; 1,303 km)

CESSNA MODEL P206 and TP206 SUPER SKYLANE

The Super Skylane is a de luxe six-seat version of the Model 206 series. It retains the ability to carry the Super Skywagon's under-fuselage cargo pack, but does not have the double loading doors of the U206 and TU206. Instead, it has a door on each side of the cabin at the front and a third door on the port side at the rear.

There are two current versions, as follows:

P206 Super Skylane. Standard version. Counterpart of the U206, with 285 hp Continental IO-520-A engine.

TP206 Turbo-System Super Skylane. Generally similar to P206, but with same 285 hp Continental TSIO-520-C turbocharged engine as TU206.

Specification and performance figures are generally similar to those for the U206 and TU206 respectively, with the following exceptions.

DIMENSIONS, EXTERNAL:

Length overall:	
P206/TP206	28 ft 3 in (8·61 m)
Height overall:	
P206/TP206	9 ft 7½ in (2·93 m)

WEIGHTS AND LOADINGS:

Weight empty, 6-seater:	
P206	1,835 lb (833 kg)
TP206	1,935 lb (878 kg)

CESSNA SKYWAGON 207 AND TURBO-SKYWAGON T207

On 19 February 1969 Cessna announced two new seven-seat versions of its Skywagon utility aircraft. Generally similar to the earlier Model 206 Super Skywagon, the new Skywagon had been "stretched" to provide improved load-carrying ability while retaining the single engine and operating economy of the Model 206.

In addition to the longer fuselage, new features included a door for the co-pilot or passenger on the starboard side at the front of the cabin, and a separate baggage compartment forward of the cabin, accessible through an external door, also on the starboard side of the fuselage.

Design of this model started in November 1967 and the prototype flew for the first time on 11 May 1968. The first production aircraft, a Model 207, was completed on 13 December 1968 and made its first flight on 3 January 1969, followed three days later by the first flight of a T207 Turbo-Skywagon. Both models received FAA Certification on 31 December 1968. A total of 123 Model 207's had been completed by January 1970.

The 1970 Model 207 introduces a number of improvements, including improved suspension for all seats, all of which have reclining backs and fore and aft adjustment, a split-type master rocker switch, improved instrument panel control knobs, vinyl floor mats, wider choice of interior trims, pilot's control wheel lowered, grey-finish instrument panel to reduce eye strain and transistorised instrument lighting controls. New options include quick oil drain valve, 10-channel single-sideband HF transceiver, Cessna anti-precipitation ADF sense antenna and courtesy lights, including a new forward baggage compartment light.

There are two current versions of the Cessna Model 207, as follows:

Skywagon 207. Standard passenger/cargo utility model with 300 hp Continental IO-520-F engine, as described in detail below.

Turbo-Skywagon T207. Generally similar to Skywagon 207, but with 300 hp Continental TSIO-520-G turbosupercharged engine driving a McCauley D2A34C78/90AT-8·5 two-blade metal constant-speed propeller, diameter 6 ft 9½ in (2·07 m). Three-blade propeller optional. Oxygen system standard.

The following description applies to the Skywagon 207, except where stated otherwise:

Type: Single-engined utility aircraft.

Wings: Braced high-wing monoplane. Single streamline-section bracing strut each side. Wing section NACA 2412 from root to just inboard of tip; wingtip is symmetrical. Dihedral 1° 44′. Incidence 1° 30′ at root, —1° 30′ at tip. All-metal structure. Glass-fibre conical-camber tips. Modified Frise-type all-metal wide-chord ailerons. Electrically-operated long-span NACA single-slotted all-metal flaps. No trim-tabs.

Fuselage: Conventional all-metal semi-monocoque structure.

Tail Unit: Cantilever all-metal structure, with sweptback vertical surfaces. Tailplane fixed with —3° incidence. Large trim-tab in starboard elevator. Electrical operation of trim-tab optional. Rudder trimmed by adjustment of rubber bungee.

Landing Gear: Non-retractable tricycle type. Improved Cessna "Land-O-Matic" cantilever main legs of one-piece tapered steel tube. Cessna oleo-pneumatic nose-wheel shock-absorber with hydraulic shimmy damper. Cessna wheels, tubeless tyres and hydraulic disc brakes. Main wheels and tyres size 6·00 × 6, pressure 55 lb/sq in (3·87 kg/cm²). Nose-wheel and tyre size 5·00 × 5, pressure 49 lb/sq in (3·45 kg/cm²). Optional 8·00 × 6 main wheel tyres, pressure 35 lb/sq in (2·96 kg/cm²), nose-wheel tyre size 6·00 × 6, pressure 29 lb/sq in (2·04 kg/cm²), and wheel fairings.

Power Plant: One 300 hp Continental IO-520-F six-cylinder horizontally-opposed air-cooled engine, driving a McCauley D2A34C58/90AT-8 two-blade metal constant-speed propeller, diameter 6 ft 10 in (2·08 m). McCauley D3A32-C90/82NC-2 three-blade metal constant-speed propeller, diameter 6 ft 8 in (2·03 m) optional. A bladder-type fuel tank, capacity 32·5 US gallons (123 litres), is located in the inboard section of each wing. Total fuel capacity 65 US gallons (246 litres) of which 58 US gallons (220 litres) are usable. Optional tankage increases capacity to 42 US gallons (159 litres) in each wing, giving a total capacity of 84 US gallons (318 litres) of which 77 US gallons (292 litres) are usable. Refuelling points in upper surface of each wing. Oil capacity 3 US gallons (11·4 litres).

Accommodation: Pilot's seat only standard. Optional individual seats for up to six passengers, arranged in three pairs, two-abreast, with a single seat at the rear of cabin. Pilot's door on port side, co-pilot's door on starboard side at front. Large double cargo doors on starboard side of rear cabin; forward door hinged to open forward, rear door hinged to open rearward. Aircraft can be flown with cargo doors removed for photography, air dropping of supplies or parachuting; optional equipment includes a spoiler for use when the aircraft is flown in this configuration. Separate baggage compartment, forward of cabin, capacity 120 lb (54 kg), accessible through top-hinged door on

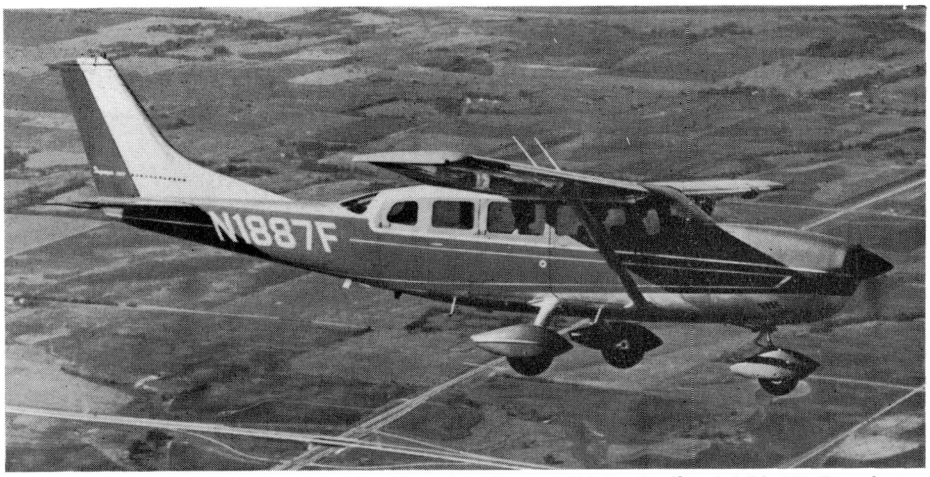

The seven-seat Cessna Skywagon 207 utility aircraft (one 300 hp Continental IO-520-F engine)

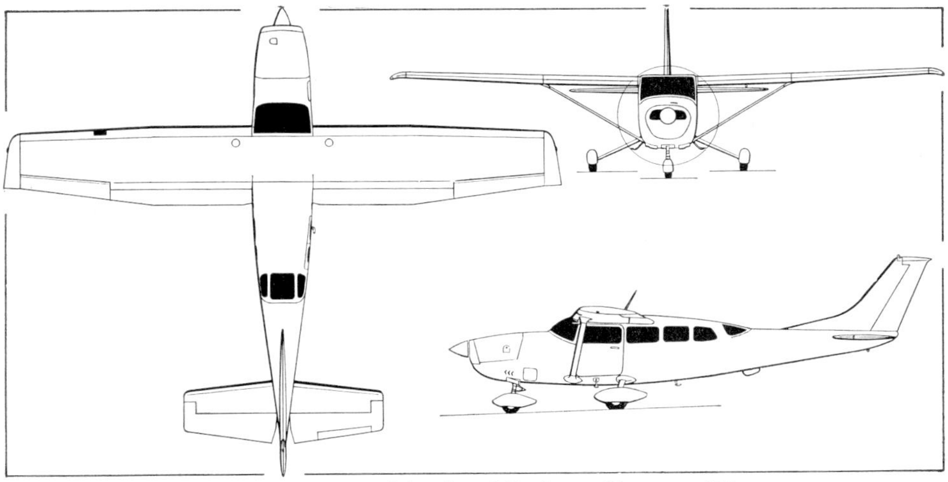

General arrangement drawing of the Cessna Skywagon 207

starboard side. External glass-fibre cargo pack, capacity 300 lb (136 kg), carried beneath the fuselage, is available as an optional extra.

Systems: Hydraulic system for brakes. Engine-driven 60A alternator and storage battery to supply electrical services.

Electronics and Equipment: Optional extras include a complete range of radio and navigation equipment, including the Cessna 300 series transceiver, nav/com, ADF, marker beacon, DME, HF transceiver and transponder; Cessna 400 series transceiver, nav/com, ADF, glideslope and transponder, 10-channel single sideband HF transceiver, anti-precipitation ADF sense antenna, Cessna 300 or 400 Nav-O-Matic autopilot, blind-flying instrumentation, dual controls, wing levelling system, instrument panel white lighting, oxygen system, courtesy lights, quick oil drain valve, ambulance kit (including stretcher, oxygen and attendant's seat), aerial camera installation, skydiving kit, glider tow hook and portable stretcher.

Dimensions, external:
- Wing span — 35 ft 10 in (10·92 m)
- Wing chord at root — 5 ft 4 in (1·63 m)
- Wing chord at tip — 3 ft 8 in (1·12 m)
- Wing aspect ratio — 7·46
- Length overall — 31 ft 9 in (9·68 m)
- Height overall — 9 ft 6½ in (2·91 m)
- Tailplane span — 13 ft 0 in (3·96 m)
- Wheel track — 10 ft 0 in (3·05 m)
- Wheelbase — 6 ft 11¼ in (2·11 m)
- Forward cabin doors (each):
  - Height — 3 ft 5½ in (1·05 m
  - Width — 2 ft 11½ in (0·89 m)
  - Height to sill — 2 ft 4 in (0·71 m)
- Cargo double doors (stbd):
  - Height — 3 ft 2 in (0·97 m)
  - Width — 3 ft 8½ in (1·13 m)
  - Height to sill — 2 ft 6 in (0·76 m)
- Baggage door (stbd):
  - Height — 2 ft 0 in (0·61 m)
  - Width — 1 ft 1½ in (0·34 m)
  - Height to sill — 3 ft 4 in (1·02 m)

Dimensions, internal:
- Cabin:
  - Length — 14 ft 0 in (4·27 m)
  - Max width — 3 ft 8½ in (1·13 m)
  - Max height — 4 ft 1 in (1·24 m)
  - Floor area — 47·1 sq ft (4·38 m²)
  - Volume — 155·5 cu ft (4·40 m³)
- Forward baggage compartment:
  - Length — 1 ft 5 in (0·43 m)
  - Max width — 3 ft 5½ in (1·05 m)
  - Max height — 2 ft 3 in (0·69 m)
  - Floor area — 4·9 sq ft (0·46 m²)
  - Volume — 9·5 cu ft (0·27 m³)
- Under-fuselage cargo pack — 12·0 cu ft (0·34 m³)

Areas:
- Wings, gross — 174·0 sq ft (16·17 m²)
- Ailerons — 17·32 sq ft (1·60 m²)
- Trailing-edge flaps — 26·60 sq ft (2·66 m²)
- Fin — 9·04 sq ft (0·84 m²)
- Rudder — 6·95 sq ft (0·65 m²)
- Tailplane — 24·84 sq ft (2·31 m²)
- Elevators, including tab — 20·08 sq ft (1·86 m²)

Weights and Loadings:
- Weight empty, one seat only:
  - 207 — 1,880 lb (852 kg)
  - T207 — 1,980 lb (898 kg)
- Max T-O and landing weight:
  - 207 and T207 — 3,800 lb (1,724 kg)
- Max wing loading:
  - 207 and T207 — 21·8 lb/sq ft (106·4 kg/m²)
- Max power loading:
  - 207 and T207 — 12·7 lb/hp (5·7 kg/hp)

Performance (at max T-O weight and with optional wheel fairings):
- Max level speed:
  - 207 at S/L — 146 knots (168 mph; 270 km/h)
  - T207 at 17,000 ft (5,180 m) — 164 knots (189 mph; 304 km/h)
- Max diving speed:
  - 207 and T207 — 182 knots (210 mph; 338 km/h)
- Normal cruising speed (75% power):
  - 207 at 6,500 ft (1,980 m) — 137 knots (158 mph; 254 km/h)
  - T207 at 10,000 ft (3,050 m) — 142 knots (163 mph; 262 km/h)
  - T207 at 20,000 ft (6,100 m) — 153 knots (176 mph; 283 km/h)
- Econ cruising speed:
  - 207 at 10,000 ft (3,050 m) — 114 knots (131 mph; 211 km/h)
  - T207 at 20,000 ft (6,100 m) — 135 knots (156 mph; 251 km/h)
- Stalling speed, flaps up:
  - 207 and T207 65·3 knots (75 mph; 121 km/h)
- Stalling speed, 30° flaps:
  - 207 and T207 58·5 knots (67 mph; 108 km/h)
- Rate of climb at S/L:
  - 207 — 810 ft (247 m)/min
  - T207 — 885 ft (270 m)/min
- Service ceiling:
  - 207 — 13,300 ft (4,054 m)
  - T207 — 24,200 ft (7,376 m)
- T-O run:
  - 207 and T207 — 1,100 ft (335 m)
- T-O to 50 ft (15 m):
  - 207 and T207 — 1,970 ft (600 m)

Landing from 50 ft (15 m):
207 and T207   1,500 ft (457 m)
Landing run:
207 and T207   765 ft (233 m)
Range (at normal cruising speed, no reserves, standard fuel):
207 at 137 knots (158 mph; 254 km/h) at 6,500 ft (1,980 m)
508 nm (585 miles; 941 km)
T207 at 151 knots (174 mph; 280 km/h) at 20,000 ft (6,100 m)
529 nm (610 miles; 982 km)
T207 at 140 knots (161 mph; 259 km/h) at 10,000 ft (3,050 m)
490 nm (565 miles; 909 km)
Range (at normal cruising speed, no reserves, auxiliary fuel):
207 at 137 knots (158 mph; 254 km/h) at 6,500 ft (1,908 m)
673 nm (775 miles; 1,247 km)
T207 at 151 knots (174 mph; 280 km/h) at 20,000 ft (6,100 m)
712 nm (820 miles; 1,320 km)
T207 at 140 knots (161 mph; 259 km/h) at 10,000 ft (3,050 m)
655 nm (755 miles; 1,215 km)
Range (at econ cruising speed, no reserves, auxiliary fuel):
207 at 114 knots (131 mph; 211 km/h) at 10,000 ft (3,050 m)
803 nm (925 miles; 1,489 km)
T207 at 135 knots (156 mph; 251 km/h) at 20,000 ft (6,100 m)
790 nm (910 miles; 1,445 km)

CESSNA MODEL 210

The original prototype Model 210, which flew in January 1957, followed the general formula of the Cessna series of all-metal high-wing monoplanes, but was the first to have a retractable tricycle landing gear.

Later versions of the Model 210 have a fully-cantilever wing, eliminating the bracing struts used on earlier models. Their design was started on 24 October 1964 and construction of a prototype began on 29 November 1964. The first T210 with the new wing flew on 18 June 1965.

The 1970 versions of the Model 210 feature a change from four to six-seat accommodation, made possible by a complete re-design of the landing gear to provide a flat floor area for the entire cabin. The front four seats are of the fully-articulating type and fore and aft adjustment is provided. Vertical adjustment of the co-pilot's seat is optional. The fifth and sixth seats have backs which can be folded forward to add substantial baggage space and provide accommodation for articles up to 6 ft 7 in (2·01 m) in length. The rear baggage area has a volume of 16·25 cu ft (0·46 m³) and an increase in useful load of 300 lb (136 kg) has been achieved without a major decrease in performance. The new main landing gear is constructed of chrome vanadium tapered steel-tube, has a wider track to improve ground handling, and the hydraulic pipe-lines for the disc brakes now pass within the tubular steel legs.

Other improvements include provision of 3 ft (0·91 m) long picture windows on each side of the cabin immediately aft of the entrance doors, a 29-in (0·74-m) wide baggage door on the port side of the fuselage, a wide selection of interior trims, grey-finish instrument panel to reduce eye strain, transistorised dimming controls for instrument lighting, lower mounting of the pilot's control wheel, a new split-type master rocker switch and an overhead console containing pilot and co-pilot air vents, floodlighting for instruments and provisions for radio speaker and oxygen controls.

There are two current production versions as follows:

210 Centurion. Standard model, with 285 hp Continental IO-520-A six-cylinder horizontally-opposed air-cooled engine, rated at 300 hp for T-O or 5 min emergency power, driving a McCauley E2A34C73/90AT-8 two-blade metal propeller or, optionally a McCauley D3A32C88/82NC-2 three-blade metal propeller.

T210 Turbo-System Centurion. Identical to 210, but powered by a 285 hp Continental TSIO-520-C turbosupercharged engine, driving a McCauley E2A34C70/90AT-8 two-blade metal propeller or, optionally, a McCauley D3A32C88/82NC-2 three-blade metal propeller. Manifold pressure relief valve to prevent overboosting.

The Turbo-System Centurion holds an international altitude record for aircraft of this class with a height of 43,699 ft (13,320 m).

Both versions received FAA Type Approval on 23 August 1966. A total of 2,622 Model 210s had been delivered by January 1970.

TYPE: Six-seat cabin monoplane.

WINGS: Cantilever high-wing monoplane. Wing section NACA 64₂A215 at root, NACA 64₁A412 (A=0·5) at tip. Dihedral 1° 30′. Incidence 1° 30′ at root, —1° 30′ at tip. All-metal structure, except for glass-fibre conical-camber tips. All-metal Frise-type ailerons. Electrically-

Cessna Model T210 Turbo-System Centurion (285 hp Continental TSIO-520-C engine)

actuated all-metal Fowler-type flaps. Ground-adjustable tab in each aileron. Pneumatic de-icing system optional.

FUSELAGE: All-metal semi-monocoque structure.

TAIL UNIT: Cantilever all-metal structure with 36° sweepback on fin. Fixed-incidence tailplane. Controllable trim-tabs in rudder and starboard elevator. Electric operation of elevator tab optional. Pneumatic de-icing system optional.

LANDING GEAR: Hydraulically-retractable tricycle type with single wheel on each unit. Nose unit retracts forward, main units aft and inward. Wheel-doors close when wheels are up or down. Chrome vanadium tapered steel-tube main legs. Oleo-pneumatic nose-wheel shock-absorber. Cessna main wheels and tube-type tyres, size 6·00 × 6, pressure 42 lb/sq in (2·95 kg/cm²). Cessna nose-wheel and tyre, size 5·00 × 5, pressure 45 lb/sq in (3·16 kg/cm²). Cessna hydraulic disc brakes.

POWER PLANT: One six-cylinder horizontally-opposed air-cooled engine, as described under model listings above. Propeller diameter 6 ft 10 in (2·08 m). Electric de-icing system for propeller optional. Integral fuel tanks in wings, with max total capacity of 90 US gallons (340 litres). Refuelling points above wing. Wing fuel drains optional. Oil capacity 3 US gallons (11·4 litres) in 210, 3¼ US gallons (12·3 litres) in T210.

ACCOMMODATION: Six persons in pairs in enclosed cabin. Optional four-seat executive interior with a fully-reclining couch-type rear seat. Forward-hinged door on each side of cabin. Baggage space aft of rear seats, with outside door on port side. Combined heating and ventilation system.

SYSTEMS: Hydraulic system, pressure 1,500 lb/sq in (105 kg/cm²), actuates landing gear. Electrical supply from 12V 60A alternator.

ELECTRONICS AND EQUIPMENT: Standard equipment includes rudder and aileron interconnect system, glare-resistant finish on upper engine cowling, electroluminescent instrument panel lighting, ashtrays and courtesy lights. Optional items include Cessna Series 300 and 400 VHF transceivers, nav/com radios, ADF, DME, marker beacon receiver, transponders, glide-slope receiver, HF transceiver, and Nav-O-Matic 300 or 400 autopilot, Narco UGR-2 glide-slope receiver, King KA-25C isolation amplifier, 10-channel single-sideband HF transceiver, 90-channel or 360-channel Narco Mark 12B nav/com, oxygen system (standard on T210), blind flying instrumentation, dual controls, wing levelling stability augmentation system, de-icing system, boom microphone, omni-flash beacon, map light, white instrument post lighting, economy mixture indicator, flight hour recorder, vertically-adjustable co-pilot's seat, corrosion proofing, oil filter (standard on T21) and oil dilution system, adjustable headrests for each seat, armrests, underwing courtesy lights and rear view mirror.

DIMENSIONS, EXTERNAL:

Wing span	36 ft 9 in	(11·20 m)
Wing chord at root	5 ft 6 in	(1·68 m)
Wing chord at tip	4 ft 0 in	(1·22 m)
Wing aspect ratio	7·66	
Length overall	28 ft 3 in	(8·61 m)
Height overall	9 ft 8 in	(2·95 m)
Tailplane span	13 ft 0 in	(3·96 m)
Wheel track	8 ft 6 in	(2·59 m)
Wheelbase	5 ft 9 in	(1·75 m)
Passenger doors (each):		
Height	3 ft 4¼ in	(1·02 m)
Width	2 ft 11¼ in	(0·90 m)
Height to sill	3 ft 0 in	(0·91 m)
Baggage compartment door:		
Height	1 ft 10½ in	(0·57 m)
Width	2 ft 5 in	(0·74 m)

DIMENSIONS, INTERNAL:

Cabin:		
Length	11 ft 6 in	(3·50 m)
Max width	3 ft 6½ in	(1·08 m)
Max height	4 ft 0½ in	(1·23 m)
Floor area	29·0 sq ft	(2·69 m²)
Volume	139·9 cu ft	(3·96 m³)
Baggage space	16·25 cu ft	(0·46 m³)

AREAS:

Wings, gross	176·0 sq ft	(16·35 m²)
Ailerons (total)	18·86 sq ft	(1·75 m²)
Trailing-edge flaps (total)	29·50 sq ft	(2·74 m²)
Fin, including dorsal fin	10·26 sq ft	(0·95 m²)
Rudder, including tab	6·95 sq ft	(0·65 m²)
Tailplane	18·57 sq ft	(1·73 m²)
Elevators, including tab	20·08 sq ft	(1·87 m²)

WEIGHTS AND LOADINGS:

Weight empty (approx):		
210	2,080 lb	(943 kg)
T210	2,180 lb	(989 kg)
Max T-O and landing weight:		
210, T210	3,800 lb	(1,723 kg)
Max wing loading:		
210, T210	21·6 lb/sq ft	(105 kg/m²)
Max power loading:		
210	12·7 lb/hp	(5·76 kg/hp)
T210	13·3 lb/hp	(6·03 kg/hp)

PERFORMANCE (at max T-O weight):

Max level speed:
210 at S/L   174 knots (200 mph; 322 km/h)
T210 at 19,000 ft (5,800 m)
200 knots (230 mph; 370 km/h)
Max cruising speed:
210, 75% power at 7,500 ft (2,285 m)
163 knots (188 mph; 303 km/h)
T210, 75% power at 24,000 ft (7,300 m)
190 knots (219 mph; 352 km/h)
Econ cruising speed:
210 at 10,000 ft (3,050 m)
134 knots (154 mph; 248 km/h)
T210 at 24,000 ft (7,300 m)
152 knots (175 mph; 282 km/h)
Stalling speed, flaps up:
210, T210   66 knots (75 mph; 121 km/h)
Stalling speed, flaps down:
210, T210   57 knots (65 mph; 105 km/h)
Max rate of climb at S/L:
210   860 ft (262 m)/min
T210   930 ft (283 m)/min
Service ceiling:
210   15,500 ft (4,724 m)
T210   28,500 ft (8,686 m)
T-O run
210   1,100 ft (335 m)
T210   1,170 ft (357 m)
T-O to 50 ft (15 m):
210   1,900 ft (579 m)
T210   2,030 ft (619 m)
Landing from 50 ft (15 m):
210, T210   1,500 ft (457 m)
Landing run:
210, T210   765 ft (233 m)
Range at max cruising speed, standard fuel, no reserves:
210   664 nm (765 miles; 1,231 km)
T210   734 nm (845 miles; 1,360 km)
Range at max cruising speed, long-range fuel, no reserves:
210   925 nm (1,065 miles; 1,713 km)
T210   1,016 nm (1,170 miles; 1,882 km)
Range at econ cruising speed, long-range fuel, no reserves:
210   1,085 nm (1,250 miles; 2,011 km)
T210   1,155 nm (1,330 miles; 2,140 km)

CESSNA MODEL 310 and T310
USAF designation: U-3

The Model 310 is a twin-engined five or six-seat cabin monoplane, the prototype of which flew on 3 January 1953. It went into production in 1954 and 3,032 had been built by January 1970. A new Turbo-System Model 310 was introduced in late 1968, and the first production model was delivered in December 1968.

There are two current versions of the Model 310, as follows:

310Q. Standard model as described in detail below:

Turbo-System T310Q. Similar to 310Q but with two 285 hp Continental TSIO-520-B turbocharged engines, with electric propeller synchronisation as standard.

Improvements in the 1970 Model 310 include an increase in max T-O weight, provision of an Accru-Measure fuel monitoring system, re-design of the instrument panel with grey finish to reduce eye-strain and improve contrast, instrument dials which are larger and of a standard type, instrument pointer lengths matched to scale markings, larger lettering and numerals, blue lettering for secondary information, elimination of all unnecessary information from instrument dials, and provision of instrument white post lighting and electroluminiscent switch-panel lighting as standard. All flight instruments are in the conventional "T" arrangement and a large centre panel can accommodate a full range of optional avionics, including weather radar. A new overhead console houses radio speaker, dome lights, pilot and co-pilot oxygen outlets (optional), and provide stowage for an optional boom microphone. Cabin improvements include seating with improved suspension and side-panel arm rests, and exterior styling now offers a choice of ten three-colour schemes.

The Cessna 310 has been in service with the USAF since 1957, when it won a competition for a light twin-engined administrative liaison and cargo aircraft. Initial orders for a total of 160 "off-the-shelf," under the designation U-3A (formerly L-27A), were followed by a contract for 35 later models, designated U-3B, which were delivered between December 1960 and June 1961, and a number of these are operational in Vietnam.

TYPE: Twin-engined five or six-seat cabin monoplane.

WINGS: Cantilever low-wing monoplane. Wing section NACA 23018 at centre-line, NACA 23009 at tip. Dihedral 5°. Incidence 2° 30′ at root, —0° 30′ at tip. All-metal structure. Electrically-operated split flaps. Trim-tab in port aileron. Pneumatic de-icing system optional.

FUSELAGE: All-metal semi-monocoque structure.

TAIL UNIT: Cantilever all-metal structure, with 40° sweepback on fin at quarter-chord. Small ventral fin. Trim-tabs in rudder and starboard elevator. Electrically-operated elevator trim optional. Pneumatic de-icing system optional.

LANDING GEAR: Retractable tricycle type. Electro-mechanical retraction. Cessna oleo shock-absorber struts. Nose-wheel steerable to 15° and castoring from 15° to 55° in both directions. Main wheels size 6·50 × 10, tyre pressure 60 lb/sq in (4·22 kg/cm²). Nose-wheel size 6·00 × 6, tyre pressure 24 lb/sq in (1·69 kg/cm²). Goodyear single-disc hydraulic brakes.

POWER PLANT: Two 260 hp Continental IO-470-VO six-cylinder horizontally-opposed air-cooled engines. (Turbo-System 310 detailed in model listings above). Manually-adjustable cowl flaps. Propeller and windshield de-icing, electric propeller synchronisation (standard on T310), automatic propeller unfeathering, oil filters (standard on T310), and oil dilution system optional. McCauley two-blade metal constant-speed fully-feathering propellers, diameter 6 ft 9 in (2·06 m). Standard fuel in two permanently attached canted wing-tip tanks, each holding 50 US gallons (189 litres). Cross-feed fuel system. An optional 40 US gallon (151 litres) auxiliary fuel system consists of two 20 US gallon (75·5 litres) rubber fuel cells which are installed between the wing spars outboard of each engine nacelle and connected to the main fuel system. Additional auxiliary fuel can be accommodated in two optional wing locker fuel tanks, each containing 20 US gallons (75·5 litres), bringing total fuel capacity to 180 US gallons (682 litres). Oil capacity 6 US gallons (22·7 litres).

ACCOMMODATION: Cabin normally seats five, two in front and three on cross-bench behind. Four alternative seating arrangements are available, with up to six individual seats in pairs, all of which can tilt and have fore and aft adjustment, individual air vents, reading lights, magazine pockets and ash trays. Cabin windows are double-glazed to reduce noise level. Janitrol 35,000 BTU thermostatically-controlled blower-type heater. Large door on starboard side giving access to all seats. Optional 3 ft 4 in (1·02 m) long cargo door for loading of bulky items. Baggage compartment at rear of cabin, capacity 360 lb (163 kg), with internal and external access. Locker for a further 120 lb (54·5 kg) of baggage in the rear of each engine nacelle. Total baggage capacity 600 lb (272 kg). Optional cabin accessories include writing desk, window curtains, electrical adjustment of pilot and co-pilot seats, all-leather seats, oxygen system and photographic survey provisions.

Cessna Turbo-System T310Q five/six-seat cabin monoplane (two 285 hp Continental TSIO-520-B engines)

SYSTEMS: Electrical supply from two 50A (optionally 100A) alternators. Hydraulic system for brakes only. Goodrich pneumatic de-icing system optional.

ELECTRONICS AND EQUIPMENT: Standard equipment includes blind-flying instrumentation, rotating beacon, and landing lamp in port wing. Optional items include a wide range of avionics, comprising Cessna Series 300, 400 and 800 nav/com, ADF, marker beacon receiver, HF transceiver, DME, transponder, glide slope receiver, radio magnetic indicator, two- and three-axis autopilot, AVQ-45 or -46 weather radar, PN-101 pictorial navigation system indicator, 10- or 22-channel HF transceiver, single sideband HF transceiver. Other optional items comprise dual controls, boom microphone, economy mixture and instantaneous rate-of-climb indicators, flight hour recorder, Goodrich pneumatic de-icing system, oxygen system, fuselage ice impact panels, corrosion proofing, taxi lights, and courtesy lights.

DIMENSIONS, EXTERNAL:
Wing span	36 ft 11 in (11·25 m)
Wing chord at root	5 ft 7½ in (1·72 m)
Wing chord at tip	3 ft 10¼ in (1·18 m)
Wing aspect ratio	7·3
Length overall	29 ft 6 in (8·99 m)
Height overall	9 ft 11 in (3·02 m)
Tailplane span	17 ft 0 in (5·18 m)
Wheel track	12 ft 0 in (3·66 m)
Wheelbase	9 ft 6 in (2·90 m)

DIMENSIONS, INTERNAL:
Luggage compartment (fuselage)	41 cu ft (1·16 m³)
Luggage compartments (nacelles, total)	14·9 cu ft (0·42 m³)

AREAS:
Wings, gross	179 sq ft (16·63 m²)
Ailerons (total)	11·44 sq ft (1·06 m²)
Trailing-edge flaps (total)	22·9 sq ft (2·13 m²)
Fin	14·30 sq ft (1·33 m²)
Rudder	11·76 sq ft (1·09 m²)
Tailplane	32·15 sq ft (2·99 m²)
Elevators	22·10 sq ft (2·05 m²)

WEIGHTS AND LOADINGS:
Weight empty:	
310	3,190 lb (1,446 kg)
T310	3,292 lb (1,493 kg)
Max T-O and landing weight:	
310	5,300 lb (2,404 kg)
T310	5,500 lb (2,494 kg)
Max wing loading:	
310	29·6 lb/sq ft (145 kg/m²)
T310	30·73 lb/sq ft (150 kg/m²)
Max power loading:	
310	10·2 lb/hp (4·63 kg/hp)
T310	9·65 lb/hp (4·38 kg/hp)

PERFORMANCE (at max T-O weight):
Max level speed:	
310 at S/L	205 knots (236 mph; 380 km/h)
T310 at 16,000 ft (4,875 m)	238 knots (274 mph; 441 km/h)
Max cruising speed:	
310, 75% power at 6,500 ft (1,980 m)	192 knots (221 mph; 356 km/h)
T310, 75% power at 20,000 ft (6,100 m)	225 knots (259 mph; 417 km/h)
Econ cruising speed:	
310 at 10,000 ft (3,050 m)	159 knots (183 mph; 295 km/h)
T310 at 25,000 ft (7,620 m)	201 knots (231 mph; 372 km/h)
Stalling speed:	
310	63 knots (72 mph; 116 km/h) IAS
T310	68 knots (78 mph; 126 km/h) IAS
Max rate of climb at S/L:	
310	1,495 ft (456 m)/min
T310	1,790 ft (546 m)/min
Max rate of climb at S/L, one engine out:	
310	327 ft (100 m)/min
T310	408 ft (124 m)/min
Service ceiling:	
310	19,500 ft (5,943 m)
T310	28,200 ft (8,595 m)
Service ceiling, one engine out:	
310	6,680 ft (2,036 m)
T310	17,550 ft (5,350 m)

T-O run:	
310	1,519 ft (463 m)
T310	1,306 ft (398 m)
T-O to 50 ft (15 m):	
310	1,795 ft (547 m)
T310	1,662 ft (507 m)
Landing from 50 ft (15 m):	
310	1,697 ft (517 m)
T310	1,790 ft (546 m)
Landing run:	
310	582 ft (177 m)
T310	640 ft (195 m)
Range at max cruising speed, 600 lb (272 kg) usable fuel, no reserves:	
310	672 nm (774 miles; 1,245 km)
T310	662 nm (763 miles; 1,227 km)
Range at max cruising speed, 840 lb (381 kg) usable fuel, no reserves:	
310	939 nm (1,082 miles; 1,741 km)
T310	926 nm (1,067 miles; 1,717 km)
Range at max cruising speed, 1,080 lb (489 kg) usable fuel, no reserves:	
310	1,207 nm (1,390 miles; 2,236 km)
T310	1,320 nm (1,521 miles; 2,447 km)
Max range at econ cruising speed, 1,080 lb (489 kg) usable fuel, no reserves:	
310	1,501 nm (1,729 miles; 2,782 km)
T310	1,675 nm (1,929 miles; 3,104 km)

CESSNA MODEL 318
USAF designation: T-37

The T-37 was the first jet trainer designed as such from the start to be used by the USAF. The first of two prototype XT-37's made its first flight on 12 October 1954, and the first of an evaluation batch of 11 T-37A's flew on 27 September 1955.

A total of 1,176 T-37's had been delivered by January 1970, with production continuing. In addition to aircraft supplied to the USAF, there have been substantial deliveries to foreign governments by direct purchase, or through the Military Assistance Programme.

Three versions have been built in quantity:

T-37A. Initial production version with Continental J69-T-9 turbojets (each 920 lb = 417 kg st). 416 built. Converted to T-37B standard by retrospective modification.

T-37B. Two Continental J69-T-25 turbojets (each 1,025 lb = 465 kg st). New Omni navigational equipment, UHF radio and instrument panel. First T-37B was accepted into service with the USAF in November 1959. The T-37B has also been supplied to the Royal Hellenic Air Force, the Royal Thai Air Force and the Turkish, Cambodian, Chilean and Pakistan Air Forces. Forty-seven ordered by the Federal German government are being used to train Luftwaffe pilots at Sheppard AFB in Texas.

It was announced in December 1961 that equipment can be added to the T-37B to enable it to perform military surveillance and low-level attack duties, in addition to training. Details are given in the paragraph on "Armament and Equipment" below. At the same time, it was stated that the range of this aircraft can be extended by the addition of two 65 US gallon (245 litre) wing-tip fuel tanks. Two armed T-37B's were evaluated at the USAF Special Air Warfare Center, and were followed by two prototypes of the more powerful and more heavily armed YAT-37D (see entry on A-37). Thirty-nine T-37B's have been converted to A-37A standard. To replace these and to meet further requirements, the USAF placed further contracts for the T-37B in 1967 and again in 1968, with deliveries extending to January 1970.

T-37C. Basically similar to T-37B, but with provision for both armament and wing-tip fuel tanks. Initial order for 34 placed by USAF for supply to foreign countries under Military Assistance Programme. Portugal has 30, of which 18 were supplied under this Programme, Peru has 15 and others have been supplied to Cambodia, Chile, Greece, Pakistan, Thailand and Turkey. Brazil has ordered 65 and Colombia 10, with deliveries extending until March 1970.

The following details refer to the T-37B.

TYPE: Two-seat primary trainer.

WINGS: Cantilever low-wing monoplane. Wing section NACA 2418 at root, NACA 2412 at tip. Dihedral 3°. Incidence at root 3° 30'. Two-spar aluminium alloy structure. Hydraulically-operated all-metal high-lift slotted flaps inboard of ailerons.

FUSELAGE: All-metal semi-monocoque structure. Hydraulically-actuated speed brake below forward part of fuselage in region of cockpit.

TAIL UNIT: Cantilever all-metal structure. Fin integral with fuselage. Tailplane mounted one-third of way up fin. Movable surfaces all have electrically-operated trim-tabs.

LANDING GEAR: Retractable tricycle type. Bendix air-oil shock-absorbers. Hydraulic actuation. Steerable nose-wheel. Tyres and multiple disc brakes by General Tire and Rubber Co. Main wheel tyres size 20 × 4·4. Nose-wheel tyre size 16 × 4·4. Wheel brakes operated by separate hydraulic system controlled by dual rudder and brake pedals.

POWER PLANT: Two Continental J69-T-25 turbojet engines (each 1,025 lb = 465 kg st). Six rubber-cell interconnected fuel tanks in each wing, feeding main tank in fuselage aft of cockpit. Total usable fuel capacity 309 US gallons (1,170 litres). Automatic fuel transfer by engine-driven pumps and submerged booster pumps. Provision for two 65 US gallon (245 litre) wing-tip fuel tanks on T-37C only. Oil capacity 3·12 US gallons (11·8 litres).

ACCOMMODATION: Enclosed cockpit seating two side-by-side with dual controls. Ejector seats and jettisonable clam-shell type canopy. Standardised cockpit layout, with flaps, speed brakes, trim-tabs, radio controls, etc, positioned and operated as in standard USAF combat aircraft.

ELECTRONICS: Standard USAF UHF radio; Collins VHF navigation equipment; IFF may be fitted retrospectively.

ARMAMENT AND EQUIPMENT: Provision for two jettisonable underwing armament pods, manufactured by General Electric, each containing an 0·50 in machine-gun with 200 rounds, two 2·75 in folding-fin rockets and four 3 lb practice bombs. Alternatively two 250 lb bombs or four Sidewinder missiles can be fitted in place of armament pods. Associated equipment includes K14C computing gun sight and AN-N6 16-mm gun camera. For reconnaissance duties, KA-20 or KB-10A cameras, or HC217 cartographic camera, can be mounted in fuselage.

DIMENSIONS, EXTERNAL:

Wing span	33 ft 9·3 in (10·3 m)
Wing chord (mean)	5 ft 7 in (1·70 m)
Wing aspect ratio	6·2
Length overall	29 ft 3 in (8·93 m)
Height overall	9 ft 2 in (2·8 m)
Tailplane span	13 ft 11½ in (4·25 m)
Wheel track	14 ft 0½ in (4·28m)
Wheelbase	7 ft 9 in (2·36 m)

AREAS:

Wings, gross	183·9 sq ft (17·09 m²)
Ailerons (total)	11·30 sq ft (1·05 m²)
Trailing-edge flaps (total)	15·10 sq ft (1·40 m²)
Fin	11·54 sq ft (1·07 m²)
Rudder, including tab	6·24 sq ft (0·58 m²)
Tailplane	34·93 sq ft (3·25 m²)
Elevators, including tabs	11·76 sq ft (1·09 m²)

WEIGHT AND LOADINGS:

Max T-O weight	6,574 lb (2,982 kg)
Max wing loading	35·7 lb/sq ft (174·3 kg/m²)
Max power loading	3·21 lb/lb st (3·21 kg/kg st)

PERFORMANCE (at max T-O weight):

Max level speed at 20,000 ft (6,100 m)
369 knots (425 mph; 684 km/h)
Normal cruising speed at 35,000 ft (10,670 m)
313 knots (360 mph; 579 km/h)
Stalling speed 74 knots (85 mph; 137 km/h)
Rate of climb at S/L 3,370 ft (1,027 m)/min
Service ceiling 39,200 ft (11,948 m)
Service ceiling, one engine out
25,000 ft (7,620 m)
T-O to 50 ft (15 m) 2,000 ft (610 m)
Landing from 50 ft (15 m) 2,545 ft (775 m)
Range at 313 knots (360 mph; 579 km/h), standard tankage
755 nm (870 miles; 1,400 km)
Range at 289 knots (333 mph; 536 km/h) at 35,000 ft (10,670 m), standard tankage, with 5% reserves 809 nm (932 miles; 1,500 km)

CESSNA MODEL 318
USAF designation: A-37

The A-37 is a development of the T-37 trainer, intended for armed counter-insurgency (COIN) operations from short unimproved airstrips. Two YAT-37D prototypes were produced initially, for evaluation by the USAF, by modifying existing T-37 airframes. The first of these flew for the first time on 22 October 1963, powered by two 2,400 lb (1,090 kg) st General Electric J85-GE-5 turbojets. There are two production versions, as follows:

Cessna T-37B two-seat primary jet trainer (two 1,025 lb st Continental J69-T-25 turbojet engines)

Cessna A-37B two-seat light strike aircraft (two General Electric J85-GE-17A turbojet engines)

A-37A. First 39 aircraft, with de-rated (2,450 lb = 1,111 kg st) engines. Converted from T-37B trainers under letter contract received from USAF Systems Command in August 1966. Deliveries began on 2 May 1967 and have been completed. In the Summer of 1967 a squadron of 25 A-37As arrived in South Vietnam to begin a four-month computerised evaluation of their ability to perform six basic missions: close air support; armed escort for Army troop-carrying helicopters; combat air patrol for truck convoys; armed reconnaissance; forward air control; and night interdiction. At the end of the test period a very favourable report on the A-37A was returned, the computer data giving high ratings on all six types of mission. After termination of the test period, the A-37As remained in service with the 604th Air Commando Squadron at Bien Hoa air base, and early in 1968 they completed their 10,000th combat sortie in Vietnam.

A-37B. (Model 318E). The A-37B is the new production version, design of which began in January 1967. Construction of the prototype started in the following month and it flew for the first time in September 1967. The A-37B has two General Electric J85-GE-17A turbojets which offer more than double the take-off power available for the T-37, permitting an almost-doubled take-off weight. A total of 180 had been delivered by the end of 1969.

The following details apply to the production A-37B:

TYPE: Two-seat light strike aircraft.

WINGS: Cantilever low-wing monoplane. Wing section NACA 2418 (modified) at root, NACA 2412 (modified) at tip. Dihedral 3°. Incidence 3°38' at root, 1° at tip. No sweep at 22½% chord. Two-spar aluminium alloy structure. Conventional all-metal ailerons, with forward skin of aluminium alloy and aft skin of magnesium alloy. Electrically-operated trim-tab on port aileron with force-sensitive boost tabs on both ailerons, plus hydraulically-operated slot-lip ailerons forward of the flap on the outboard two-thirds of flap span. Hydraulically-operated all-metal slotted flaps of NACA 2h type. No de-icing equipment.

FUSELAGE: All-metal semi-monocoque structure. Hydraulically-operated speed brake, measuring 3 ft 9 in (1·14 m) by 1 ft 0 in (0·30 m), below forward fuselage immediately aft of nose-wheel well. Mountings for removable probe for in-flight refuelling on upper fuselage in front of cockpit. Windshield defrosting by engine bleed air.

TAIL UNIT: Cantilever all-metal structure. Fin integral with fuselage. Fixed incidence tailplane mounted one-third of way up fin. Electrically-operated trim-tabs in port elevator and rudder. No de-icing equipment.

LANDING GEAR: Retractable tricycle type. Cessna oleo-pneumatic shock-absorber struts on all three units. Hydraulic actuation, main wheels retracting inboard, nose-wheel forward. Steerable nose-wheel. Goodyear tyres and single disc brakes. Main wheel tyres size 7·00 × 8-14PR. Nose-wheel tyre size 6·00 × 6-6PR. Tyre pressure: main wheels 110 lb/sq in (7·73 kg/cm²), nose-wheel 37 lb/sq in (2·60 kg/cm²).

POWER PLANT: Two General Electric J85-GE-17A turbojet engines, each rated at 2,850 lb (1,293 kg) st. Fuel tank in each wing, each with capacity of 113 US gallons (428 litres); two non-jettisonable tip-tanks, each of 95 US gallons (360 litres) capacity; sump tank in fuselage, aft of cockpit, capacity 91 US gallons (344 litres). Total standard usable fuel capacity 507 US gallons (1,920 litres). Single-point refuelling through in-flight refuelling probe, with adaptor. Alternative refuelling through flush gravity filler cap in each wing and each tip-tank. Four 100 US gallon (378 litre) auxiliary tanks can be carried on underwing pylons. Provision for inflight refuelling through nose-probe. Total oil capacity 2·25 US gallons (9 litres).

ACCOMMODATION: Enclosed cockpit seating two side-by-side, with dual controls, dual throttles, full flight instrument panel on port side, partial panel on starboard side, engine instruments in between. Full blind-flying instrumentation. Jettisonable canopy hinged to open upward and rearward. Standardised cockpit layout as in standard USAF combat aircraft. Cockpit air-conditioned but not pressurised. Flak-curtains of layered nylon are installed around the cockpit.

SYSTEMS: AiResearch air-conditioning system of expansion turbine type, driven by engine bleed air. Hydraulic system, pressure 1,500 lb/sq in (105·5 kg/cm²), operates landing gear, main landing gear doors, flaps, thrust attenuator, nose-wheel steering system, speed-brake, stall spoiler, inlet screen. Pneumatic system, pressure 2,000 lb/sq in (140·6 kg/cm²), utilises nitrogen-filled 50 cu in (819 cm²) air bottle for emergency landing gear extension. Electrical system includes two 28V DC 300 amp starter-generators, two 24V nickel-cadmium batteries, and provision for external power source. One main inverter (2,500VA 3-phase 115V 400 c/s), and one standby inverter (750VA 3-phase 115V 400 c/s), to provide AC power.

ELECTRONICS: Radio and radar installations include UHF communications (AN/ARC-34C), FM communications (FM-622A), TACAN (AN/ARN-65), ADF (AN/ARN-83), IFF (AN/APX-64), direction finder (AN/ARA-50) and interphone (AIC-18).

ARMAMENT AND OPERATIONAL EQUIPMENT: GAU-2B/A 7·62 mm minigun installed in forward fuselage. Each wing has four pylon stations, the two inner ones carrying 800 lb (363 kg) each, the intermediate one 600 lb (272 kg) and the outer one 500 lb (227 kg). The following weapons, in various combinations, can be carried on these underwing pylons: SUU-20 bomb and rocket pod, MK-81 or MK-82 bomb, BLU/32/B fire bomb, SUU-11/A gun pod, CBU-24/B or CBU-25/A dispenser and bomb, M-117 demolition bomb, LAU-3/A rocket pod, CBU-12/A, CBU-14/A or CBU-22/A dispenser and bomb, BLU-1C/B fire bomb, LAU-32/A or LAU-59/A rocket pod, CBU-19/A cannister cluster and SUU-25/A flare launcher. Associated equipment includes an armament control panel, Chicago Aerial Industries CA-503 non-computing gun sight, KS-27C gun camera and KB-18A strike camera.

DIMENSIONS, EXTERNAL:
Wing span, over tip tanks	35 ft 10½ in (10·93 m)
Wing chord at root	6 ft 7·15 in (2·01 m)
Wing chord at tip	4 ft 6 in (1·37 m)
Wing aspect ratio	6·2
Length overall	29 ft 3½ in (8·93 m)
Height overall	8 ft 10½ in (2·70 m)
Tailplane span	13 ft 11½ in (4·25 m)
Wheel track	14 ft 0½ in (4·28 m)
Wheelbase	7 ft 10 in (2·39 m)

AREAS:
Wings, gross	183·9 sq ft (17·09 m²)
Ailerons (total)	11·30 sq ft (1·05 m²)
Trailing-edge flaps (total)	15·10 sq ft (1·40 m²)
Fin	11·54 sq ft (1·07 m²)
Rudder, including tab	6·24 sq ft (0·58 m²)
Tailplane	34·93 sq ft (3·25 m²)
Elevators, including tab	11·76 sq ft (1·09 m²)

WEIGHTS AND LOADINGS:
Weight empty, equipped	5,843 lb (2,650 kg)
Max T-O and landing weight	14,000 lb (6,350 kg)
Max zero-fuel weight	10,710 lb (4,858 kg)
Max wing loading	65·4 lb/sq ft (319·3 kg/m²)
Max power loading	2·1 lb/lb st (2·1 kg/kg st)

PERFORMANCE (at max T-O weight):
Max level speed at 16,000 ft (4,875 m)	440 knots (507 mph; 816 km/h)
Max diving speed (Mach limitation)	455 knots (524 mph; 843 km/h)
Max cruising speed at 25,000 ft (7,620 m)	425 knots (489 mph; 787 km/h)
Stalling speed, wheels and flaps down	98·5 knots (113 mph; 182 km/h)
Rate of climb at S/L	6,990 ft (2,130 m)/min
Service ceiling	41,765 ft (12,730 m)
Service ceiling, one engine out	25,000 ft (7,620 m)
T-O run	1,245 ft (379 m)
T-O to 50 ft (15 m)	2,030 ft (619 m)
Landing from 50 ft (15 m)	6,600 ft (2,012 m)
Landing run	4,150 ft (1,265 m)

Range with max fuel, including four 100 US gallon (378 litre) drop tanks at 25,000 ft (7,620 m) with reserves 878 nm (1,012 miles; 1,628 km)
Range with max payload, including 4,100 lb (1,860 kg) ordnance 399 nm (460 miles; 740 km)

CESSNA MODEL 337 SUPER SKYMASTER AND TURBO-SYSTEM SUPER SKYMASTER
USAF designation: O-2

This unique all-metal 4/6-seat business aircraft resulted from several years of study by Cessna aimed at producing a twin-engined aeroplane that would be simple to fly, low in cost, safe and comfortable, while offering all the traditional advantages of two engines. Construction of a full-scale mock-up was started in February 1960 and completed two months later. The prototype flew for the first time on 28 February 1961, followed by the first production model in August 1962. FAA Type Approval was received on 22 May 1962 and deliveries of the original Model 336 Skymaster, with non-retractable landing gear, began in May 1963.

A total of 195 Model 336 Skymasters had been built by January 1965. In the following month, this version was superseded by the Model 337 Super Skymaster, with increased wing incidence, retractable landing gear, and other changes, making it virtually a new aeroplane. A total of 898 Super Skymasters had been built by January 1969.

Improvements in the 1970 versions of the Model 337 include an increase in max T-O weight, higher permitted speed with landing gear extended, provision of an Accru-Measure fuel

Cessna O-2A, a forward air control military version of the Super Skymaster

monitoring system, introduction of conical camber glass-fibre wingtips, re-design of the instrument panel with grey finish to reduce eye-strain and improve contrast, new control knobs and switches, and all flight instruments are mounted in the professional "T" arrangement. Cabin seating has improved suspension and pilot and co-pilot seats are of the fully-articulating type with vertical adjustment of the pilot's seat as standard. Options available include fully-articulating passenger seats, matching headrests, over-size wheels and heavy-duty brakes, snap-action microphone switch, anti-precipitation ADF sense antenna and 10-channel single side-band HF transceiver.

Model 337 Super Skymaster. Standard model, with two 210 hp Continental IO-360-C six-cylinder horizontally-opposed air-cooled engines.

Model 337 Turbo-System Super Skymaster. Identical to standard model, but powered by two 210 hp Continental TSIO-360-A turbosupercharged engines. A manifold pressure relief valve is provided on both engines to prevent overboosting. Six-outlet oxygen system standard.

In addition, two military versions have been ordered by the USAF, as follows:

O-2A. Equipped for forward air controller missions, including visual reconnaissance, target identification, target marking, ground-air coordination and damage assessment. Dual controls standard. Four underwing pylons for external stores, including rockets, flares or other light ordnance, such as a 7·62-mm Minigun pack. Modified 60A electrical system to support special electronics systems, including UHF, VHF, FM, ADF, TACAN and APX transponder.

Initial contract, dated 29 December 1966, called for 145 O-2A's; a follow-on contract awarded in June 1967 brought the total on order to 192, all of which had been delivered early in 1968. A further contract was announced on 26 June 1968, for the provision of 45 more O-2A's, together with modification services and spares, and this was amended in September 1968 to increase the quantity to 154 aircraft. The additional 109 O-2A's have new lightweight electronics. Early in 1970 Cessna delivered 12 O-2A's to the Imperial Iranian Air Force and these are being used for training, liaison and observation duties.

O-2B. Generally similar to the commercial version, but equipped for psychological warfare missions. Advanced communications system and high-power air-to-ground broadcasting system, supplied by University Sound division of LTV Ling Altec and utilising three 600W amplifiers

with highly directional speakers. Manual dispenser fitted, for leaflet dropping. Initial contract for 31 placed on 29 December 1966, and the programme was initiated by the repurchase of 31 commercial aircraft, six of which were used for pilot training at Eglin AFB, Florida. First O-2B accepted by USAF on 31 March 1967 and was assigned to Vietnam. A combined total of 397 O-2A's and O-2B's had been delivered by January 1970.

The following details apply to the commercial versions of the Super Skymaster.

TYPE: Tandem-engined cabin monoplane.

WINGS: Braced high-wing monoplane, with single streamlined bracing strut each side. Wing section NACA 2412 at root, NACA 2409 at tip. Dihedral 3°. Incidence 4° 30' at root, 2° 30' at tip. Conventional all-metal two-spar structure. All-metal Frise ailerons. Electrically-operated all-metal single-slotted flaps. Ground-adjustable tab in port aileron. Pneumatic de-icing system optional.

FUSELAGE: Conventional all-metal semi-monocoque structure.

TAIL UNIT: Cantilever all-metal structure with twin fins and rudders, carried on two slim metal booms. Trim-tab in elevator, with optional electric actuation. Optional pneumatic de-icing system.

LANDING GEAR: Retractable tricycle type. Cantilever spring steel main legs. Oleo-pneumatic steerable nose leg. Main wheels and tyres size 6·00 × 6. Nose wheel and tyre size 15·00 × 6·00 × 6. Tyre pressure 45 lb/sq in (3·16 kg/cm²). Hydraulic disc brakes. Over-size wheels and heavy-duty brakes optional.

POWER PLANT: Two Continental six-cylinder horizontally-opposed air-cooled engines, each driving a McCauley two-blade fully-feathering constant-speed metal propeller, diameter 6 ft 4 in (1·93 m). Electrically-operated cowl flaps. Propeller de-icing optional. Fuel in two main tanks in each outer wing, with total usable capacity of 92 US gallons (348 litres), and two optional auxiliary tanks in inner wings with total usable capacity of 36 US gallons (136 litres). Total usable capacity with auxiliary tanks 128 US gallons (484 litres). Refuelling points above wings. Total oil capacity 5 US gallons (19 litres).

ACCOMMODATION: Standard accommodation for pilot and co-pilot on fully-articulating individual seats, with rear bench seat for two passengers. Alternative arrangements utilise four, five or six individual seats. Space for 365 lb

Cessna Model 337 Super Skymaster (two 210 hp Continental IO-360-C engines)

(165 kg) of baggage in four-seat version. Cabin door on starboard side. Baggage door at rear of cabin on starboard side. Cabin is heated, ventilated and soundproofed. Ash trays, adjustable air vents and reading lights available to each passenger. Provision for carrying glass-fibre cargo pack, with capacity of 300 lb (136 kg), under fuselage; this reduces cruising speed by only 3 mph (5 km/h).

SYSTEMS: Electrical system supplied by engine-driven generators. Hydraulic system for brakes only.

ELECTRONICS AND EQUIPMENT: Optional equipment includes dual controls, boom microphone, economy mixture indicator, flight hour recorder, corrosion proofing, oil filter (standard on Turbo Skymaster), automatic propeller synchronisation, unfeathering accumulator, fully-articulating seats for passengers, arm rests, headrests, oxygen system (standard on Turbo Skymaster), provisions for aerial survey cameras, wing courtesy lights and instrument white post lighting. Optional avionics include Cessna Series 300 or 400 nav/com transceiver, ADF, marker beacon receiver, DME, HF transceiver, glide slope receiver, transponder, one- or two-axis autopilot, King isolation amplifier, Narco Mark 12B 360-channel nav/com, Narco glide slope receiver, Sunair single sideband HF transceiver and factory-installed partial provisions for additional avionics.

DIMENSIONS, EXTERNAL:
Wing span	38 ft 2 in (11·63 m)
Wing chord at root	6 ft 0 in (1·83 m)
Wing chord at tip	4 ft 0 in (1·22 m)
Wing aspect ratio	7·18
Length, overall:	
Standard	29 ft 9 in (9·07 m)
Turbo-System	29 ft 10 in (9·09 m)
Height overall	9 ft 4 in (2·84 m)
Tailplane span	10 ft 0⅜ in (3·06 m)
Wheel track	8 ft 2 in (2·49 m)
Wheelbase	7 ft 10 in (2·39 m)
Passenger door:	
Height	3 ft 10 in (1·17 m)
Width	3 ft 0 in (0·91 m)
Baggage door:	
Height	1 ft 9½ in (0·55 m)
Width	1 ft 7 in (0·48 m)

DIMENSIONS, INTERNAL:
Cabin: Length	9 ft 11 in (3·02 m)
Max width	3 ft 8¼ in (1·12 m)
Max height	4 ft 3¼ in (1·30 m)
Volume	138 cu ft (3·91 m³)
Baggage space	17 cu ft (0·50 m³)

AREAS:
Wings, gross	201 sq ft (18·67 m²)
Ailerons (total)	15·44 sq ft (1·43 m²)
Trailing-edge flaps (total)	36·88 sq ft (3·43 m²)
Fins (total)	30·68 sq ft (2·85 m²)
Rudders (total)	10·70 sq ft (0·99 m²)
Tailplane	36·27 sq ft (3·37 m²)

WEIGHTS AND LOADINGS:
Weight empty, equipped:	
Standard	2,660 lb (1,206 kg)
Turbo-System	2,850 lb (1,292 kg)
Max T-O weight:	
Standard	4,440 lb (2,013 kg)
Turbo-System	4,630 lb (2,100 kg)
Max landing weight:	
Both versions	4,400 lb (1,995 kg)
Max wing loading:	
Standard	21·9 lb/sq ft (107 kg/m²)
Turbo-System	22·9 lb/sq ft (112 kg/m²)
Max power loading:	
Standard	10·6 lb/hp (4·8 kg/hp)
Turbo-System	11·0 lb/hp (4·99 kg/hp)

PERFORMANCE (A= standard model; B= Turbo-System model, at max T-O weight):
Max level speed:	
A at S/L	173 knots (199 mph; 320 km/h)
B at 20,000 ft (6,100 m)	
	200 knots (230 mph; 370 km/h)
Max cruising speed:	
A, 75% power at 5,500 ft (1,675 m)	
	166 knots (191 mph; 307 km/h)
B, 75% power at 24,000 ft (7,300 m)	
	194 knots (223 mph; 359 km/h)
Econ cruising speed:	
A at 10,000 ft (3,050 m)	
	125 knots (144 mph; 232 km/h)
B at 24,000 ft (7,300 m)	
	150 knots (173 mph; 278 km/h)
Stalling speed, flaps up:	
A	68 knots (78 mph; 126 km/h)
B	70 knots (80 mph; 129 km/h)
Stalling speed, flaps down:	
A	60 knots (69 mph; 111 km/h)
B	61 knots (70 mph; 113 km/h)
Max rate of climb at S/L:	
A	1,180 ft (360 m)/min
B	1,105 ft (337 m)/min
Rate of climb at S/L, front engine only:	
A	285 ft (87 m)/min
B	295 ft (90 m)/min
Rate of climb at S/L, rear engine only:	
A	370 ft (113 m)/min
B	375 ft (114 m)/min
Service ceiling:	
A	19,300 ft (5,880 m)
B	29,300 ft (8,930 m)

Service ceiling, front engine only:	
A	6,500 ft (1,980 m)
B	14,400 ft (4,390 m)
Service ceiling, rear engine only:	
A	8,500 ft (2,590 m)
B	17,200 ft (5,240 m)
T-O run:	
A	910 ft (277 m)
B	1,000 ft (305 m)
T-O to 50 ft (15 m):	
A	1,565 ft (477 m)
B	1,675 ft (510 m)
Landing from 50 ft (15 m):	
A, B	1,650 ft (503 m)
Landing run:	
A, B	700 ft (213 m)
Range at max cruising speed, standard fuel, no reserves:	
A	660 nm (760 miles; 1,223 km)
B	746 nm (860 miles; 1,384 km)
Range at max cruising speed, long-range fuel, no reserves:	
A	920 nm (1,060 miles; 1,705 km)
B	1,033 nm (1,190 miles; 1,915 km)
Range at econ cruising speed, long-range fuel, no reserves:	
A	1,168 nm (1,345 miles; 2,164 km)
B	1,346 nm (1,550 miles; 2,494 km)

CESSNA MODEL O-2TT

It is not intended to produce the Model O-2TT and all available details of this aircraft may be found in the 1969-70 *Jane's*.

CESSNA MODEL 401

Announced on 1 November 1966, the Model 401 is a medium-priced six/eight-seat executive transport.

The prototype flew for the first time on 26 August 1965 and type approval was received on 20 September 1966. A total of 308 had been built by January 1970.

The current production version is known as the Model 401B, and introduces a number of improvements, including Accru-Measure fuel monitoring system, new seats which have tapered backs, headrests and more comfortable armrests, and a re-designed instrument array with flight instruments in the basic "T" arrangement, standard instrument faces with larger lettering and figures, grey finish instrument panel to reduce eye-strain and increase contrast and provision of instrument white post lighting, a systems annunciator panel and a lighting management console with linear adjustment for precise lighting control. New optional items include a dual heated pitot system, cabin ground ventilation system and a high-intensity strobe light system.

TYPE: Six/eight-seat executive transport.

WINGS: Cantilever low-wing monoplane, with "Stabila-tip" fixed wingtip fuel tanks. Wing section NACA 23018 at aircraft centre-line, NACA 23015 at centre-section/outer wing junction, NACA 23009 at tip. Dihedral 5° on outer panels. Incidence 2° at root, —0° 30′ at tip. All-metal two-spar structure. All-metal ailerons and electrically-actuated split flaps. Trim-tab in port aileron. Optional pneumatic de-icing system.

FUSELAGE: All-metal semi-monocoque structure.

TAIL UNIT: Cantilever all-metal structure, with 40° sweepback on fin at quarter-chord. Fixed-incidence tailplane. Trim-tabs in rudder and starboard elevator. Electric operation of trim-tabs optional. Optional Goodrich pneumatic de-icing system.

LANDING GEAR: Retractable tricycle type, with single wheel on each unit. Electro-mechanical retraction, main units inward into wings, nose

unit rearward. Cessna oleo-pneumatic shock-absorbers. Cleveland Aircraft Products wheels, with Cessna tyres size 6·50 × 10 on main wheels, size 6·00 × 6 on nose-wheel. Tyre pressures: main, 62 lb/sq in (4·36 kg/cm²); nose, 40 lb/sq in (2·81 kg/cm²). Cleveland single-disc hydraulic brakes.

POWER PLANT: Two 300 hp Continental TSIO-520-E six-cylinder horizontally-opposed air-cooled engines, each driving a McCauley three-blade constant-speed fully-feathering propeller, diameter 6 ft 4½ in (1·94 m). Propeller synchronisation and automatic unfeathering optional. Optional propeller and windshield de-icing system. Two wingtip fuel tanks, each with capacity of 50 US gallons (189·25 litres). Four optional auxiliary tanks, two in wings and two in nacelles, each with capacity of 20 US gallons (75·75 litres). Standard fuel capacity 100 US gallons (378·5 litres). Capacity with auxiliary tanks 140 or 180 US gallons (530 or 681·5 litres). Refuelling points on top inner surface of each wingtip tank, in top surface of each wing between nacelle and wingtip tank, and forward of baggage door in each nacelle. Oil capacity 6 US gallons (22·75 litres). Manifold pressure relief valves to prevent engine overboosting are standard equipment.

ACCOMMODATION: Two seats side-by-side in pilot's compartment. Nine different standard interior layouts, for four, five or six passengers in main cabin, with reading light, ventilator and oxygen outlet by each seat, and ash trays and cigarette lighters within reach. Main cabin can be separated from pilot's compartment by optional solid divider, with door. Area aft of cabin can be partitioned off to include an optional baggage compartment and wardrobe, with dressing table, refreshment bar and toilet. Door with built-in airstair on port side of cabin at rear. An emergency escape hatch is provided on the starboard side of the cabin. Optional cargo door available. Cabin windows have double glazing to reduce noise level; inward-opening foul weather windows on each side of flight deck. Carpeted nose baggage compartment, accessible from either side, has capacity of 350 lb (159 kg). Wing lockers, at rear of each engine nacelle, each have capacity of 120 lb (54 kg). Total baggage capacity 930 lb (422 kg).

SYSTEMS: Electrical power supplied by 28V system, utilising two 50A (optionally 100A) gear-driven alternators and 24Ah battery. Hydraulic system for brakes only.

ELECTRONICS AND EQUIPMENT: Optional electronics include Cessna Series 300, 400 or 800 nav/com, ADF, marker beacon receiver, transponder, DME, HF transceiver, glide slope receiver, radio magnetic indicator, audio amplifier, two- or three-axis autopilot, PN-101 pictorial navigation system, T-22RA HF transceiver, T-10R HF transceiver, single sideband HF transceiver, AVQ-45, AVQ-46 or AVQ-55 weather radar. Optional equipment includes fuselage ice impact panels, corrosion proofing, taxi lights, cabin intercom system, beverage units, shaver converters, toilet, writing tables, stereo equipment, hat shelf, thermos and refreshment bar, executive table, oxygen system, all-leather seats, aft cabin speakers, electric adjustment of pilot's and co-pilot's seat, dual controls, blind flying instrumentation for co-pilot, boom microphone, flight hour recorder, economic mixture and instantaneous rate-of-climb indicators, dual heated pitot system, cabin ground ventilation and high-intensity strobe light system. A 250-watt landing light which retracts into the bottom of the tip-tank is standard.

Cessna Model 401B six/eight-seat executive transport (two 300 hp Continental TSIO-520-E engines)

DIMENSIONS, EXTERNAL:
Wing span over tip tanks 39 ft 10¼ in (12·15 m)
Wing chord at root   5 ft 7½ in (1·71 m)
Wing chord at tip   3 ft 9½ in (1·16 m)
Wing aspect ratio   7·5
Length overall   33 ft 9 in (10·29 m)
Height overall   11 ft 8 in (3·56 m)
Tailplane span   17 ft 0 in (5·18 m)
Wheel track   14 ft 8 in (4·47 m)
Wheelbase   10 ft 5½ in (3·19 m)
Passenger door (standard):
  Height   3 ft 11½ in (1·21 m)
  Width   1 ft 11 in (0·58 m)
  Height to sill   3 ft 11½ in (1·21 m)
Cargo door (optional):
  Height   3 ft 11½ in (1·21 m)
  Width   3 ft 3½ in (1·00 m)
  Height to sill   3 ft 11½ in (1·21 m)
Nose baggage door (each):
  Height   1 ft 0 in (0·30 m)
  Width   2 ft 0½ in (0·62 m)
Nacelle baggage door (each):
  Height   1 ft 0 in (0·30 m)
  Width   2 ft 0½ in (0·62 m)
DIMENSIONS, INTERNAL:
Cabin:
  Length   14 ft 6 in (4·42 m)
  Max width   4 ft 8 in (1·42 m)
  Max height   4 ft 3 in (1·30 m)
  Volume   222·4 cu ft (6·30 m³)
AREAS:
Wings, gross   195·72 sq ft (18·18 m²)
Ailerons (total)   11·44 sq ft (1·06 m²)
Trailing-edge flaps (total) 22·90 sq ft (2·13 m²)
Fin   37·89 sq ft (3·52 m²)
Rudder, including tab   17·77 sq ft (1·65 m²)
Tailplane   60·70 sq ft (5·64 m²)
Elevators, including tab   17·63 sq ft (1·64 m²)
WEIGHTS AND LOADINGS:
Weight empty   3,665 lb (1,662 kg)
Max T-O weight   6,300 lb (2,858 kg)
Max landing weight   6,200 lb (2,812 kg)
Max wing loading   32·20 lb/sq ft (157·2 kg/m²)
Max power loading   10·5 lb/hp (4·76 kg/hp)
PERFORMANCE (at max T-O weight):
Max level speed at S/L
                       198 knots (228 mph; 367 km/h)
Max level speed at 16,000 ft (4,875 m)
                       227 knots (261 mph; 420 km/h)
Max permissible diving speed
                  231 knots (266 mph; 428 km/h) CAS
Max cruising speed (75% power) at 10,000 ft
(3,050 m)   189 knots (218 mph; 351 km/h)
Max cruising speed (75% power) at 20,000 ft
(6,100 m)   208 knots (240 mph; 386 km/h)
Econ cruising speed at 25,000 ft (7,620 m)
                   187 knots (215 mph; 346 km/h)
Stalling speed, wheels and flaps down
                  69 knots (79 mph; 127·5 km/h) IAS
Rate of climb at S/L   1,610 ft (491 m)/min
Single-engine rate of climb at S/L
                              255 ft (78 m)/min
Service ceiling   26,180 ft (7,980 m)
Service ceiling, one engine out 11,700 ft (3,565 m)
T-O run   1,695 ft (517 m)
T-O to 50 ft (15 m)   2,220 ft (677 m)
Landing from 50 ft (15 m)   1,765 ft (538 m)
Landing run   777 ft (237 m)
Range at max cruising speed at 10,000 ft
(3,050 m), 600 lb (272 kg) usable fuel, no
reserves   573 nm (660 miles; 1,062 km)
Range at max cruising speed at 10,000 ft
(3,050 m), 1,080 lb (489 kg) usable fuel, no
reserves   1,030 nm (1,186 miles; 1,908 km)
Range at max cruising speed at 20,000 ft
(6,100 m), 600 lb (272 kg) usable fuel, no
reserves   602 nm (694 miles; 1,116 km)
Range at max cruising speed at 20,000 ft
(6,100 m), 1,080 lb (489 kg) usable fuel, no
reserves   1,083 nm (1,248 miles; 2,008 km)
Max range, econ cruising speed at 10,000 ft
(3,050 m), 1,080 lb (489 kg) usable fuel, no
reserves   1,261 nm (1,453 miles; 2,338 km)
Max range, econ cruising speed at 25,000 ft
(7,620 m), 1,080 lb (489 kg) usable fuel, no
reserves   1,262 nm (1,454 miles; 2,339 km)

CESSNA MODEL 402

The Model 402 was announced simultaneously with the Model 401 and the two types have a similar airframe and power plant. Main difference is that the 402 has been designed for the third-level airline market and has a convertible cabin, enabling it to be changed quickly from a ten-seat commuter to a light cargo transport. The reinforced cabin floor is of bonded crushed honeycomb construction, and the 402 has the same optional cargo door as the 401.

The same prototype served for both models and the FAA type certificate, awarded on 20 September 1966, also covered both types. A total of 251 Model 402's had been built by January 1970.

The current Model 402B introduces a number of new features, including an extended nose section to accommodate up to 250 lb (113 kg) of electronics in addition to 350 lb (159 kg) of baggage, Accru-Measure fuel monitoring system, a redesigned instrument array with flight instruments in the basic "T" arrangement, standard instrument faces with larger lettering and figures, grey finish instrument panel to reduce eye-strain and increase contrast, provision of

Cessna 402B, showing nose baggage compartment, crew and passenger access doors

instrument white post lighting, a systems annunciator panel and a lighting management console with linear adjustment for precise lighting control. New optional items include a dual heated pitot system, cabin ground ventilation system, and a high-intensity strobe light system.

The description of the Model 401 applies also to the Model 402, except in the following details which apply specifically to the current Model 402B:

TYPE: Ten-seat (nine-seat optional) convertible passenger and freight transport.

FUSELAGE: As for Model 401 except nose extended by 2 ft 4 in (0·71 m).

LANDING GEAR: As for Model 401 except for optional oversize multiple disc brakes and nose-wheel fender.

ACCOMMODATION: Two seats side-by-side in pilot's compartment. Four individual seats in pairs and two bench seats, each accommodating two passengers, in main cabin. Passenger reading lights optional. Door with built-in airstair on port side of cabin at rear. An emergency escape hatch is provided on the starboard side of cabin. Optional cargo door and crew access door available. Nose baggage compartment, with optional carpeting, is accessible from either side and has a capacity of 350 lb (159 kg). Articles up to 6 ft 5 in (1·96 m) in length may be carried in the nose compartment. Avionics or baggage compartment in nose, separate from forward baggage compartment, and accessible through an "over the top" 180° cam-locked door, has a capacity of 250 lb (113 kg). Optional side access door. Wing lockers, at rear of each engine nacelle, each have capacity of 120 lb (54 kg). Total baggage capacity 840 lb (381 kg), if no avionics are carried in the forward nose compartment.

ELECTRONICS AND EQUIPMENT: Optional electronics as for Model 401. Optional equipment includes fuselage ice impact panels, de-icing equipment, double cargo doors for cabin, separate crew door, cargo barriers, dual heated pitot system, cabin ground ventilation system, high-intensity strobe light system and "Fasten seat belts" and "No smoking" signs in English and Spanish for cabin.

DIMENSIONS, EXTERNAL:
As for Model 401 except:
  Length overall   36 ft 3 in (11·05 m)
  Nose baggage door (each):
    Height   1 ft 8 in (0·51 m)
    Width   2 ft 7½ in (0·8 m)
WEIGHTS AND LOADINGS:
As for Model 401 except:
  Weight empty   3,719 lb (1,686 kg)

PERFORMANCE (at max T-O weight):
As for Model 401 except:
  Single-engine rate of climb at S/L
                              225 ft (69 m)/min
  Service ceiling, one engine out
                           11,320 ft (3,450 m)
Range at max cruising speed (75% power) at
10,000 ft (3,050 m), no reserves:
  with 100 US gallons (378 litres) usable fuel
                     573 nm (660 miles; 1,060 km)
  with 140 US gallons (530 litres) usable fuel
                     802 nm (924 miles; 1,487 km)
  with 180 US gallons (680 litres) usable fuel
                     1,030 nm (1,186 miles; 1,908 km)
Range at max cruising speed (75% power) at
20,000 ft (6,100 m), no reserves:
  with 100 US gallons (378 litres) usable fuel
                     602 nm (694 miles; 1,116 km)
  with 140 US gallons (530 litres) usable fuel
                     844 nm (972 miles; 1,564 km)
  with 180 US gallons (680 litres) usable fuel
                     1,083 nm (1,248 miles; 2,008 km)
Max range at 25,000 ft (7,620 m) at 187 knots
(215 mph; 346 km/h), no reserves:
  with 180 US gallons (680 litres) usable fuel
                     1,261 nm (1,453 miles; 2,338 km)

CESSNA MODEL 414

Cessna announced on 10 December 1969 introduction of the new pressurised twin-engined Model 414, intended as a "step-up" aircraft for owners of Cessna or other light unpressurised twins.

It combines the basic fuselage and tail unit of the Model 421 with the wing of the Model 401 and has 310 hp turbocharged Continental engines. Newly-developed flush intakes in the engine cowlings provide improved air cooling of the engine installation, and cabin heating and pressurisation are provided by a new Garrett AiResearch engine-bleed air system, either engine being able to maintain full pressurisation down to 60 per cent power. A "radiant heating" system circulates heated air beneath the cabin floor and up the side walls, and an optional 45,000 BTU heater is available to provide heating on the ground or for use during extremely low temperatures. The aircraft is equipped with Cessna's new Accru-Measure fuel monitoring system which provides a linear readout in both pounds and gallons to an accuracy of plus or minus 3 per cent.

A choice of eight seating layouts provides accommodation for up to seven persons, including crew, and seats incorporate armrests, tapered backs and headrests.

The prototype of the Model 414 flew for the

Cessna Model 414 six/seven-seat pressurised light transport (two 310 hp Continental TSIO-520-J engines)

first time on 1 November 1968 and FAA Certification was granted on 18 August 1969.

TYPE: Six/seven-seat pressurised light transport.

WINGS: Cantilever low-wing monoplane, with "Stabila-tip" fixed wingtip fuel tanks. Wing section NACA 23018 (modified) at aircraft centre-line, NACA 23015 (modified) at centre-section/outer wing junction, NACA 23009 (modified) at tip. Dihedral 5° on outer panels. Incidence 2° at root. All-metal two-spar structure with stamped ribs and surface skins reinforced with spanwise stringers. All-metal ailerons and electrically-actuated split-flaps. Trim-tab in starboard aileron. Optional pneumatic de-icing system.

FUSELAGE: Conventional all-metal semi-monocoque structure, with fail-safe structure in the pressurised section.

TAIL UNIT: Cantilever all-metal structure, with sweptback vertical surfaces. Fixed-incidence tailplane. Trim-tabs in rudder and starboard elevator. Optional pneumatic de-icing system.

LANDING GEAR: Retractable tricycle type. Electro-mechanical retraction, main units inward into wings, nose-wheel unit rearward. Manual system for emergency retraction or extension. Oleo-pneumatic shock-absorbers. Steerable nose-wheel. Magnesium wheels. Main wheel tyres size 6·50 × 10, 8-ply rating, nose-wheel tyre size 6·00 × 6, 6-ply rating. Goodyear single-disc hydraulic brakes. Parking brakes.

POWER PLANT: Two 310 hp Continental TSIO-520-J six-cylinder horizontally-opposed air-cooled turbocharged engines, each driving a McCauley 3AF32C93/82NC metal three-blade constant-speed fully-feathering propeller, diameter 6 ft 4½ in (1·94 m). Unfeathering pressure accumulator and electrical blade de-icing system optional. Standard fuel in two "Stabila-tip" fixed wingtip tanks, each of 50 US gallons (189·25 litres) capacity. Optional auxiliary wing tanks raise total capacity to 140 US gallons (530 litres). Optional auxiliary wing locker fuel tanks available to provide maximum total capacity of 180 US gallons (681·5 litres). Oil capacity 6·5 US gallons (24·6 litres).

ACCOMMODATION: Two seats side-by-side in pilot's compartment. Optional curtain, or solid divider with curtain, to separate pilot's compartment from main cabin. Optional arrangements provide for front passenger seats to face aft and a forward-facing seventh seat. Individual consoles each include reading light and ventilator. Optional items include executive writing desk, tables, hat shelf, stereo equipment, dual aft cabin speakers, electrically-adjustable pilot and co-pilot seats, refreshment and Thermos units, 11 cu ft (0·31 m³) emergency or 114·9 cu ft (3·25 m³) standard oxygen system, fore-and-aft cabin dividers, electric shaver converter, all-leather seats, passenger instrument console (clock, true airspeed indicator and altimeter) and intercom. Door is two-piece type with built-in airstairs in bottom portion, on port side of cabin at rear. Plug-type emergency escape hatch on starboard side of cabin. Foul-weather windows for pilot and co-pilot on each side of fuselage. Electrically de-iced windshield optional. Baggage accommodated in nose compartment with external access doors, capacity 350 lb (159 kg), two wing lockers, capacity 120 lb (54·5 kg) each, and in rear cabin area, capacity 340 lb (154 kg). Total baggage capacity 930 lb (422 kg).

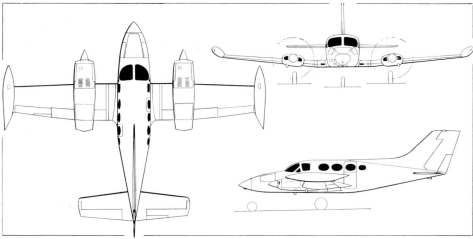

General arrangement drawing of the Cessna Model 414

SYSTEMS: Cabin pressurisation system, max differential 4·2 lb/sq in (0·30 kg/cm²). Electrical system of 28V supplied by dual 50A alternator rectifiers (100A alternators optional). 24V 25Ah battery. Hydraulic system for brakes only.

ELECTRONICS AND EQUIPMENT: Standard equipment includes blind flying instrumentation, dual controls, and blue-white post lights for instrument panel. Optional equipment includes propeller and windshield de-icing systems, fuselage ice impact panels, corrosion proofing, propeller synchronisers and automatic unfeathering systems, taxi light, co-pilot flight instruments, boom microphone, flight hour recorder, mixture and instantaneous rate-of-climb indicators. Optional avionics include Cessna 300, 400 and 800 series radios, including ADF, radio magnetic indicator, omni receiver, weather radar, DME, ATC transponder, HF transceiver, marker beacon, glideslope receiver, and series 400 and 800 Nav-o-Matic autopilot.

DIMENSIONS, EXTERNAL:

Wing span over tip tanks	39 ft 10¼ in (12·15 m)
Wing chord, c/l to nacelles (constant)	5 ft 7½ in (1·71 m)
Wing chord at tip	3 ft 9½ in (1·16 m)
Wing aspect ratio	7·5
Length overall	33 ft 9 in (10·29 m)
Height overall	11 ft 10 in (3·61 m)
Tailplane span	17 ft 0 in (5·18 m)
Wheel track	14 ft 8¼ in (4·48 m)
Wheelbase	10 ft 5¾ in (3·19 m)
Passenger door:	
Height	3 ft 11½ in (1·21 m)
Width	1 ft 11 in (0·58 m)
Height to sill	3 ft 11½ in (1·21 m)

DIMENSIONS, INTERNAL:

Cabin:	
Length	14 ft 6 in (4·42 m)
Max width	4 ft 7 in (1·40 m)
Max height	4 ft 3 in (1·29 m)
Volume	215·6 cu ft (6·11 m³)

AREAS:

Wings gross	195·72 sq ft (18·18 m²)
Ailerons (total)	11·44 sq ft (1·06 m²)
Trailing-edge flaps (total)	22·90 sq ft (2·13 m²)
Fin	37·89 sq ft (3·52 m²)
Rudder, including tab	17·77 sq ft (1·65 m²)
Tailplane	60·70 sq ft (5·64 m²)
Elevators, including tab	17·63 sq ft (1·64 m²)

WEIGHTS AND LOADINGS:

Weight empty	4,039 lb (1,832 kg)
Max T-O weight	6,350 lb (2,880 kg)
Max landing weight	6,200 lb (2,812 kg)
Max wing loading	32·49 lb/sq ft (159 kg/m²)
Max power loading	10·24 lb/hp (4·64 kg/hp)

PERFORMANCE (at max T-O weight):

Max level speed at S/L:	197 knots (227 mph; 365 km/h)
Max level speed at 20,000 ft (6,100 m)	236 knots (272 mph; 438 km/h)
Cruising speed, 75% power at 25,000 ft (7,260 m)	219 knots (252 mph; 405 km/h)
Cruising speed, 75% power at 10,000 ft (3,050 m)	191 knots (220 mph; 354 km/h)
Rate of climb at S/L	1,580 ft (482 m)/min
Rate of climb at S/L, one engine out	240 ft (73 m)/min
Service ceiling	30,100 ft (9,175 m)
Service ceiling, one engine out	11,350 ft (3,460 m)
T-O run	1,695 ft (517 m)
T-O to 50 ft (15 m)	2,350 ft (716 m)
Landing from 50 ft (15 m)	1,865 ft (568 m)
Landing run	805 ft (245 m)

Range, max fuel, no reserves:
75% power at 20,000 ft (6,100 m)
  1,103 nm (1,271 miles; 2,045 km)
75% power at 25,000 ft (7,620 m)
  1,149 nm (1,323 miles; 2,129 km)
Max range at 10,000 ft (3,050 m)
  1,206 nm (1,389 miles; 2,235 km)

CESSNA MODEL 421

On 28 October 1965, Cessna announced a new pressurised twin-engined business aircraft designated Model 421, the prototype of which had flown for the first time on 14 October 1965. FAA type approval was received on 1 May 1967 and deliveries began in the same month.

Subsequently two new versions of the Model 421 were introduced:

Model 421B Golden Eagle. First announced on 10 December 1969 this is an improved version of the Model 421A. Principal changes from the earlier model comprise an increase of 2 ft 4 in (0·71 m) in overall length as a result of enlarging the nose section of the fuselage to provide more baggage and avionics capacity, an extension of

Cessna Model 421B pressurised transport (two 375 hp Continental GTSIO-520-D engines)

2 ft 0 in (0·61 m) in wing span to maintain take-off and cruise performance without the need to increase engine power, and strengthening of the landing gear to cater for a gross weight which has increased from 6,840 lb (3,102 kg) to 7,250 lb (3,289 kg). Other improvements include introduction of an Accru-Measure fuel monitoring system; flight instruments mounted in the basic "T" arrangement; new easy-to-read instruments with standard faces, larger lettering and numerals; instrument white post lighting; new lighting console providing precise control of all cockpit lighting; a systems annunciator panel and more comfortable seating. New optional equipment includes a high-intensity strobe light system; ARB conversion for UK operators; crew shoulder harnesses and dual heated pitot system.

Model 421B Executive Commuter. First announced on 16 February 1970, this is a ten-seat version of the above model, designed specifically for the commuter airline, commercial and corporate flying markets. It differs by having lightweight, easily-removable seating to provide alternative passenger/cargo configuration; standard fuel capacity of 175 US gallons (662 litres), with optional tanks to allow a maximum fuel capacity of 225 US gallons (852 litres); and deleted rear cabin baggage area, resulting in a total avionics and baggage capacity of 1,000 lb (453 kg).

A total of 331 Model 421's had been delivered by January 1970.

The description which follows applies to the Model 421B Golden Eagle:

TYPE: Six/eight-seat pressurised light transport.

WINGS: Generally the same as for Model 414, except different aspect ratio and chord at root.

FUSELAGE, TAIL UNIT AND LANDING GEAR: As for Model 414.

POWER PLANT: Two 375 hp Continental GTSIO-520-D six-cylinder horizontally-opposed air-cooled geared and turbocharged engines, each driving a McCauley three-blade metal fully-feathering constant-speed propeller, diameter 7 ft 6 in (2·29 m). Standard fuel capacity is 170 US gallons (643 litres) contained in "Stabila-tip" fixed wingtip fuel tanks and two auxiliary wing tanks. Optional auxiliary wing tanks raise total capacity to 248 US gallons (939 litres). Oil capacity 6·5 US gallons (24·6 litres).

ACCOMMODATION: Generally the same as for Model 414, except passenger cabin will accommodate up to six passengers; seats have tapered backs and headrests. The nose compartment will contain a total of 600 lb (272 kg) of baggage and avionics, and two wing lockers an additional 200 lb (91 kg) each, plus 340 lb (154 kg) in the rear cabin area, making a total capacity of 1,340 lb (608 kg).

SYSTEMS, ELECTRONICS AND EQUIPMENT: Generally as for Model 414.

DIMENSIONS, EXTERNAL:
As for Model 414, except:
Wing span over tip tanks 41 ft 10¼ in (12·76 m)
Wing chord at root 5 ft 9·86 in (1·77 m)
Wing aspect ratio 7·37
Length overall 36 ft 1 in (11·00 m)
Wheel track 16 ft 11 in (5·16 m)

WEIGHT:
Max T-O weight 7,250 lb (3,289 kg)

PERFORMANCE:
Max cruising speed
226 knots (260 mph; 418 km/h)
Service ceiling 26,500 ft (8,077 m)
Range, with six passengers, baggage and 45 min fuel reserve
over 868 nm (1,000 miles; 1,609 km)

CESSNA MODEL 500 CITATION

On 7 October 1968 Cessna announced that it was developing a new eight-seat pressurised executive jet aircraft named the Fanjet 500, designed to operate from most airfields now used by light and medium twin-engined aircraft.

Following the first flight of the prototype on 15 September 1969, Cessna announced that the aircraft was to be known as the Citation. Since the earlier announcement, the gross weight has been increased from 9,500 lb (4,310 kg) to 10,350 lb (4,695 kg) and several other changes have been made. These include a lengthened front fuselage, engine nacelles further aft, larger vertical tail, and lowered tailplane, now with dihedral. A second prototype of the Citation flew on 23 January 1970, and two fuselage sections will be used for structural and pressurisation testing.

The Citation is designed to fly from runways as little as 2,500 ft (762 m) in length, and will also be able to fly into and out of many unpaved airfields which are not suitable for other commercial jet aircraft. It is to be offered on a direct company-to-customer basis in the basic standard configuration or as a complete business aircraft package, including factory-installed interior and avionics, ground and flight training, and one year of computerised maintenance service. Cessna states that factory installation of interior and avionics will allow greater payload and will also ensure that proper attention is given to the weight distribution of installed equipment.

Initial deliveries of production models of the Citation are scheduled for late 1971. These will be certificated to FAR Pt 25 for transport category aircraft.

TYPE: Twin-jet executive transport.

WINGS: Cantilever low-wing monoplane without sweepback. Aspect ratio 6·568. All-metal fail-safe structure with two primary spars, an auxiliary spar, three fuselage attachment points and conventional ribs and stringers. Manually-operated ailerons, with manual trim. Electrically-operated flaps. Aerodynamic speed brakes.

FUSELAGE: All-metal pressurised structure of circular section. Fail-safe design, providing multiple load paths.

TAIL UNIT: Cantilever all-metal structure. Horizontal surfaces mounted part-way up fin, with dihedral of 9°. Large dorsal fin. Manually-operated control surfaces. Electric elevator trim with manual override; manual rudder trim.

LANDING GEAR: Retractable tricycle type, with single wheel on each unit. Pneumatic emergency extension. Individual main wheel brakes and parking brake.

POWER PLANT: Two Pratt & Whitney JT15D-1 turbofan engines, each rated at 2,200 lb (998 kg) st for take-off, mounted in pods on each side of rear fuselage. Integral fuel tanks in wings.

ACCOMMODATION: Crew of two on separate flight deck. Fully-carpeted main cabin equipped with four forward-facing reclining chairs, with headrests, in pairs, plus a fifth corner lounge chair at rear of cabin. Toilet compartment and main baggage area at rear of cabin. Second baggage area in nose. Cabin is pressurised, heated and ventilated. Individual reading lights and air inlets for each passenger. Plug-type door with integral airstair at front on port side and two emergency exits. Doors on each side of nose baggage compartment. Tinted windows, each with curtains. Optional eight-seat layout for crew of two and six passengers.

SYSTEMS: Pressurisation system supplied with engine-bleed air; max pressure differential 7·5 lb/sq in (0·53 kg/cm²). Skydrol hydraulic system, or equivalent, with two pumps to operate landing gear and speed brakes. Electrical system supplied by two 250A starter-generators, with two 400 c/s inverters and nickel-cadmium battery. 110V converter optional. Oxygen system includes two crew demand masks and five drop-out constant-flow masks for passengers.

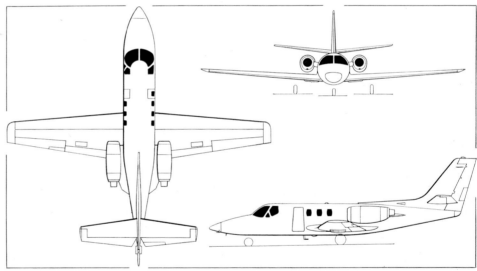

Three-view drawing of the Cessna Citation executive transport

Cessna Citation eight-seat twin-jet executive transport (two Pratt & Whitney JT15D-1 turbofan engines)

ELECTRONICS AND EQUIPMENT: Provision for advanced instrumentation and avionics, to customer's specification. Standard equipment includes automatic engine start system; engine fire-warning and extinguishing systems; inlet anti-icing; birdproof windscreen with de-fog system, windscreen anti-icing and wiper on port side only; gust locks; stall warning system; two anti-collision beacons; wing ice, taxi, navigation and landing lights; external power receptacle; flight deck sunshades; baggage tie-down kit; cabin fire extinguisher; and standard blind-flying instruments. Optional items include refrigeration air conditioner, high-capacity oxygen system, surface de-icing system, ice detection system, anti-skid warning system, windscreen anti-icing and wiper for starboard side, strobe lights, angle-of-attack indicator, dual heated pitot and static sources, crew shoulder harness, weather radar and stereo equipment.

DIMENSIONS, EXTERNAL:

Wing span	43 ft 8½ in (13·32 m)
Length overall	44 ft 0¾ in (13·43 m)
Height overall	14 ft 3½ in (4·36 m)

DIMENSIONS, INTERNAL:
Cabin:

Length, front to rear bulkhead	17 ft 6 in (5·33 m)
Max width	4 ft 11¼ in (1·51 m)
Max height	4 ft 4 in (1·32 m)
Baggage space:	
Cabin	61 cu ft (1·73 m³)
Nose	22 cu ft (0·62 m³)

WEIGHTS AND LOADINGS:

Weight empty (excluding avionics)	5,408 lb (2,453 kg)
Max ramp weight	10,500 lb (4,762 kg)
Max T-O weight	10,350 lb (4,695 kg)
Wing loading	36·5 lb/sq ft (178·2 kg/m²)
Power loading	2·16 lb/lb st (2·16 kg/kg st)

PERFORMANCE (estimated at AUW of 10,350 lb = 4,695 kg):

Max operating speed	287 knots (330 mph; 531 km/h) CAS or Mach 0·7
Max level speed at 26,400 ft (8,046 m)	349 knots (402 mph; 647 km/h)
Max cruising speed at 25,400 ft (7,740 m)	347 knots (400 mph; 644 km/h)
T-O safety speed (V₂=1·2Vs)	104 knots (120 mph; 193 km/h) CAS

Max gear and flap extension speed

	174 knots (200 mph; 321 km/h) CAS
Approach speed	109 knots (125 mph; 201 km/h) CAS
Stalling speed, wheels and flaps down	83 knots (95 mph; 153 km/h) CAS
Rate of climb at S/L	3,260 ft (994 m)/min
Service ceiling	38,400 ft (11,704 m)
Service ceiling, one engine out	21,400 ft (6,522 m)
T-O to 35 ft (10·7 m)	3,350 ft (1,021 m)
FAA balanced field length	4,020 ft (1,225 m)
Landing from 50 ft (15 m)	2,080 ft (634 m)

Range, with crew and six passengers and baggage, with allowances for T-O, climb and 45 min reserve at cruise altitude:
at max cruise thrust at 35,000 ft (10,670 m)
1,146 nm (1,320 miles; 2,124 km)
at 90% cruise thrust at 35,000 ft (10,670 m)
1,213 nm (1,397 miles; 2,248 km)
Range with max fuel, two persons and baggage, allowances as above:
at max cruise thrust at 35,000 ft (10,670 m)
1,230 nm (1,416 miles; 2,279 km)
at 90% cruise thrust at 35,000 ft (10,670 m)
1,304 nm (1,502 miles; 2,417 km)

CHAMPION
KENNETH R. CHAMPION
ADDRESS:
Route 1, Gobles, Michigan

Mr Champion has designed and built two light aircraft, of which plans are available to amateur constructors. The first was the single-seat J-1 Jupiter, which flew for the first time on 1 July 1959 and, one month later, won first prize for outstanding design at the 1959 International Fly-in of the Experimental Aircraft Association. Details of this prototype can be found in the 1961-62 Jane's. An amateur-built J-1 Jupiter, based on Mr Champion's plans, is described below.

Details of Mr Champion's second prototype, the two-seat Jupiter K-2, can be found in the 1965-66 Jane's.

CHAMPION J-1 JUPITER
The Jupiter single-seat light aircraft shown in the adjacent illustration was built from Mr Champion's plans by Mr James Mann, a fireman of Columbus, Ohio, and flew for the first time in May 1965. It differs from the original design in having a built-up turtle-deck, aft of the cockpit, and endplates on the wings.

Construction is of wood. The wing has Douglas fir spars and spruce ribs, with glass-fibre covering. The tail unit is also glass-fibre covered and the engine cowling is of formed glass-fibre. Power plant is a 65 hp Continental A65 four-cylinder horizontally-opposed air-cooled engine.

Champion Jupiter (65 hp Continental A65-85 engine) built by Mr James Mann (*Peter M. Bowers*)

DIMENSIONS, EXTERNAL:

Wing span	20 ft 0 in (6·10 m)
Wing chord (constant)	4 ft 0 in (1·22 m)
Length overall	17 ft 4 in (5·28 m)
Height overall	5 ft 0 in (1·52 m)

WEIGHTS:

Weight empty	650 lb (295 kg)
Max T-O weight	950 lb (430 kg)

PERFORMANCE (at max T-O weight):

Max level speed at S/L	130 knots (150 mph; 241 km/h)
Max cruising speed at S/L	109 knots (125 mph; 201 km/h)
Landing speed	57 knots (65 mph; 105 km/h)
Rate of climb at S/L	850 ft (260 m)/min
T-O run	800 ft (245 m)
Landing run	600 ft (183 m)
Endurance with max fuel	3 hours

CHAMPION
CHAMPION AIRCRAFT CORPORATION
HEAD OFFICE:
12750 Main, Stillwater, Minnesota 55082
WORKS:
Osceola, Wisconsin 54020
PRESIDENT AND CHAIRMAN OF BOARD:
Robert DePalma
VICE-PRESIDENTS:
W. A. Flickinger (Sales)
L. G. Nelson (Engineering)
SECRETARY:
C. R. Bentley
TREASURER:
Russel Wilson

The Champion Aircraft Corporation was formed by Flyers Service, Inc to build and market the Model 7 Champion light two-seat training and agricultural monoplane, the manufacturing rights of which were bought from the Aeronca Manufacturing Corporation in June 1954.

Production of the Champion Model 7EC by Champion Aircraft began in late 1954 and the first aircraft came off the assembly line in February 1955. Since then, several different versions have been produced as described in previous editions of Jane's. Current production is centred on a model known as the Citabria.

CHAMPION MODEL 7ECA/7GCAA/7GCBC/ 7KCAB CITABRIA
The Citabria ("airbatic" spelled backwards) is Champion Aircraft's latest development of the Model 7 Champion airframe. There are four current versions, as follows:

Model 7ECA. Basic version, with 108 hp Lycoming O-235-C1 engine and standard wings. Design and prototype construction started on 1 January 1964. Prototype flew for first time on 1 May 1964 and first production model on 18 August 1964. FAA certification received 5 August 1964. During 1969 the Model 7ECA received FAA certification for operation with Edo floats.

Model 7GCAA. Generally similar to Model 7ECA but with 150 hp Lycoming O-320-A2B

engine. Design started 15 February 1965. Construction of prototype began on 1 May 1965, and it flew on 30 May, followed by the first production model on 20 July 1965. FAA certification received 30 July 1965.

Model 7GCBC. Generally similar to Model 7ECA but with 150 hp Lycoming O-320-A2B engine as standard power plant (108 hp Lycoming O-235-C1 optional) and wings of increased span, fitted with flaps. Construction of prototype started 30 November 1965, and it flew for the first time on the next day, followed by first production machine on 10 January 1966. FAA type approval received on 3 December 1965. During 1967 the 150 hp Model 7GCBC received FAA certification for operation with Edo Model 89-2000 floats.

Model 7KCAB. Generally similar to Model 7ECA but with 150 hp Lycoming IO-320-E219 engine. This is claimed to be the only aerobatic aircraft currently certificated with a special fuel and oil system for prolonged inverted flying.

A total of 865 Citabrias of all types had been produced by early 1968.

TYPE: Two-seat light cabin monoplane.

WINGS: Braced high-wing monoplane. NACA 4412 wing section. Dihedral 2°. Incidence 1°. Two wood spars, aluminium ribs, fabric covering. Steel-tube Vee bracing struts. Single-spar fabric-covered metal ailerons. Fabric-covered metal flaps on 7GCBC only. Glass-fibre reinforced polyester wing-tips.

FUSELAGE: Welded chrome-molybdenum steel-tube structure, covered with fabric.

TAIL UNIT: Wire-braced welded steel-tube structure, with fabric covering. Fixed-incidence tailplane. Counter-balanced elevators. Controllable trim-tab in elevator.

LANDING GEAR: Non-retractable tail-wheel type. Champion oil-spring shock-absorbers. Main wheels and tyres size 7·00 × 6 6-ply on all models. Tyre pressure 24 lb/sq in (1·69 kg/cm²). Cleveland disc brakes. Wheel fairings standard. Dee Kay 1800 floats available on 7ECA.

Federal A-2000-A skis available on Models 7ECA and 7GCBC. Edo floats available on Models 7ECA and 7GCBC.

POWER PLANT: One four-cylinder horizontally-opposed air-cooled engine, as described under model listings above. McCauley two-blade fixed-pitch metal propeller; type 1C90ALM on 108 hp models and type 1C172AGM on 150 hp models. Two aluminium fuel tanks in wings, standard total capacity 26 US gallons (98 litres) with 108 hp engine, 39 US gallons (148 litres) with 150 hp engine. The larger tanks are optional with 108 hp engine. Refuelling points above tanks. Oil capacity 6 US quarts (5·75 litres) on versions with 108 hp engine, 8 US quarts (7 litres) on 150 hp versions.

ACCOMMODATION: Enclosed cabin seating two persons in tandem. Dual controls. Heater standard. Quick-jettison door on starboard side. Space for 100 lb (45 kg) baggage.

ELECTRONICS AND EQUIPMENT: Wide range of King and Narco radio equipment optional, including omni, ILS and ADF. Blind-flying instrumentation optional. Standard equipment includes landing and navigation lights.

DIMENSIONS, EXTERNAL:
Wing span:

7ECA, 7GCAA, 7KCAB	33 ft 5 in (10·19 m)
7GCBC	34 ft 5·4 in (10·50 m)
Wing chord (constant)	5 ft 0 in (1·52 m)

Wing aspect ratio:

7ECA, 7GCAA	6·72
7GCBC	6·97

Length overall:

7ECA, 7GCBC (108 hp)	22 ft 7 in (6·88 m)
7GCAA, 7GCBC (150 hp), 7KCAB	22 ft 8 in (6·91 m)
Height overall	6 ft 7¾ in (2·02 m)
Wheel track	6 ft 4 in (1·93 m)
Wheelbase	16 ft 1 in (4·90 m)
Cabin door: Height	3 ft 1 in (0·94 m)
Width	3 ft 1 in (0·94 m)
Height to sill	1 ft 5½ in (0·44 m)

AREAS:
Wings, gross:
7ECA, 7GCAA, 7KCAB 165 sq ft (15·33 m²)
7GCBC 170·2 sq ft (15·81 m²)
Ailerons (total) 16·5 sq ft (1·53 m²)
Flaps: 7GCBC 18·4 sq ft (1·71 m²)
Fin 7·02 sq ft (0·65 m²)
Rudder 6·83 sq ft (0·63 m²)
Tailplane 13·05 sq ft (1·21 m²)
Elevators, including tab 13·78 sq ft (1·28 m²)
WEIGHTS AND LOADINGS:
Weight empty, equipped:
7ECA 980 lb (444 kg)
7GCAA 1,037 lb (470 kg)
7GCBC (150 hp) 1,075 lb (488 kg)
7GCBC (108 hp) 1,025 lb (465 kg)
7KCAB 1,100 lb (499 kg)
Max T-O and landing weight:
landplanes 1,650 lb (748 kg)
7GCBC seaplane 1,800 lb (816 kg)
Max wing loading:
7ECA, 7GCAA, 7KCAB 10 lb/sq ft (48·8 kg/m²)
7GCBC 9·69 lb/sq ft (47·3 kg/m²)
Max power loading:
7ECA, 7GCBC (108 hp) 15·3 lb/hp (6·94 kg/hp)
7GCAA, 7GCBC (150 hp), 7KCAB
  11·0 lb/hp (5·00 kg/hp)
PERFORMANCE (at max T-O weight):
Max level speed at S/L:
7ECA 102 knots (117 mph; 188 km/h)
7ECA seaplane 75 knots (86 mph; 138 km/h)
7GCAA 113 knots (130 mph; 209 km/h)
7GCBC (150 hp)
  111 knots (128 mph; 206 km/h)
7GCBC (108 hp)
  101 knots (116 mph; 187 km/h)
7GCBC seaplane
  96 knots (110 mph; 177 km/h)
7KCAB 116 knots (133 mph; 214 km/h)
Max permissible diving speed
  140 knots (162 mph; 261 km/h)
Max cruising speed (75% power)
7ECA, 7GCBC (108 hp) at 7,500 ft (2,285 m)
  97 knots (112 mph; 180 km/h)
7GCBC seaplane
  89 knots (103 mph; 166 km/h)
7GCAA, 7GCBC (150 hp) 7KCAB at 8,000 ft
(2,440 m) 109 knots (125 mph; 201 km/h)
Stalling speed:
All models, without flaps
  44 knots (50 mph; 81 km/h)
7GCBC, flaps down
  39 knots (45 mph; 73 km/h)
Rate of climb at S/L:
7ECA 725 ft (221 m)/min
7ECA seaplane 515 ft (157 m)/min
7GCAA, 7KCAB 1,120 ft (341 m)/min
7GCBC (108 hp) 775 ft (236 m)/min
7GCBC (150 hp) 1,145 ft (348 m)/min
7GCBC seaplane 800 ft (243 m)/min
Service ceiling:
7ECA, 7GCBC (108 hp) 12,000 ft (3,660 m)
7GCAA, 7GCBC (150 hp), 7KCAB
  17,000 ft (5,180 m)
T-O run:
7ECA 450 ft (137 m)
7GCAA, 7KCAB 375 ft (114 m)
7GCBC (150 hp) 296 ft (90 m)
7GCBC (108 hp) 425 ft (129 m)

Champion Model 8KCAB Citabria two-seat cabin monoplane (150 hp Lycoming IO-320 engine)

T-O to 50 ft (15 m):
7ECA 890 ft (271 m)
7GCAA, 7KCAB 630 ft (192 m)
7GCBC (150 hp) 525 ft (160 m)
7GCBC (108 hp) 860 ft (262 m)
Landing from 50 ft (15 m):
7ECA, 7GCAA, 7KCAB 755 ft (230 m)
7GCBC 690 ft (210 m)
Landing run:
7ECA, 7GCAA, 7KCAB 400 ft (121 m)
7GCBC 310 ft (94 m)
Range at max cruising speed (39 US gallons
fuel):
7ECA, 7GCBC (108 hp)
  630 nm (728 miles; 1,172 km)
7GCAA, 7GCBC (150 hp), 7KCAB
  465 nm (537 miles; 865 km)

CHAMPION MODEL 8KCAB CITABRIA

The parasol-wing open-cockpit Champion Model 8KCAB Citabria Pro described in the 1969/70 *Jane's* is not to become a production model. Instead, Champion have built a two-seat light cabin monoplane to which this designation has been re-applied, and for which FAA Certification under FAR 23 was anticipated early in 1970. Generally similar to the 150 hp Model 7 Citabrias. All available details follow:

TYPE: Two-seat light cabin monoplane.
WINGS: Braced high-wing monoplane. Wing section NACA 1412 modified. Dihedral 1°. Incidence 1° 30'. Steel-tube Vee bracing struts.
FUSELAGE: Welded steel-tube structure, fabric covered.
TAIL UNIT: Wire-braced welded steel-tube structure. Fixed-incidence tailplane. Trim-tab in elevator.
LANDING GEAR: Non-retractable tail-wheel type. Fairings on main wheels.

POWER PLANT: One 150 hp Lycoming IO-320 four-cylinder horizontally-opposed air-cooled engine, driving a Hartzell type HC-C2YL-2 two-blade metal propeller. Fuel contained in two wing tanks, with total usable capacity of 41 US gallons (155 litres). Oil capacity 2 US gallons (7 litres).
ACCOMMODATION: Enclosed cabin seating two persons in tandem. Door on starboard side. Space for 100 lb (45 kg) baggage.
DIMENSIONS, EXTERNAL:
Wing span 32 ft 0 in (9·75 m)
Wing chord (constant) 5 ft 4 in (1·63 m)
Length overall 22 ft 8 in (6·91 m)
Height overall 7 ft 8 in (2·34 m)
Wheel track 6 ft 4 in (1·93 m)
Wheelbase 16 ft 4 in (4·98 m)
AREAS:
Wings, gross 169 sq ft (15·7 m²)
Ailerons (total) 10·34 sq ft (0·96 m²)
Fin 7·02 sq ft (0·65 m²)
Rudder 6·83 sq ft (0·63 m²)
Tailplane 12·25 sq ft (1·14 m²)
Elevators, including tab 14·58 sq ft (1·35 m²)
WEIGHTS AND LOADINGS:
Weight, empty 1,225 lb (555 kg)
Max T-O weight 1,800 lb (815 kg)
Max wing loading 10·7 lb/sq ft (52·2 kg/m²)
Max power loading 12·0 lb/hp (5·44 kg/hp)
PERFORMANCE (at max T-O weight):
Max level speed
  120 knots (138 mph; 222 km/h)
Cruising speed, 75% power at 8,000 ft (2,450 m)
  109 knots (125 mph; 201 km/h)
Stalling speed 46 knots (53 mph; 86 km/h)
Rate of climb at S/L 1,025 ft (312 m)/min
Service ceiling 16,000 ft (4,875 m)
Range, 75% power at 8,000 ft (2,450 m)
  490 nm (565 miles; 909 km)

CONROY
CONROY AIRCRAFT CORPORATION

HEAD OFFICE:
114 William Moffett Place, Santa Barbara Airport, Goleta, California 93017
PRESIDENT AND GENERAL MANAGER:
John M. Conroy
VICE-PRESIDENTS:
F. R. Atkins (Administration and Finance)
R. W. Lillibridge (Engineering and Manufacturing)
P. G. Smith (Assistant to President, Marketing)
DIRECTOR OF RESEARCH AND DEVELOPMENT:
R. R. Kirby
DIRECTOR OF MARKETING AND PUBLIC RELATIONS:
D. L. Batten

The Conroy Aircraft Corporation has been founded by Mr J. M. Conroy, developer of the original Pregnant Guppy and its successors, the Super and Mini Guppy aircraft, to provide specialised aircraft and services, particularly for the petroleum industry which is faced with the carriage of bulky and heavy cargo to undeveloped sites.

The company is currently producing an outsize cargo transport version of the Canadair CL-44; a turboprop conversion of the Fairchild C-119; a turboprop conversion of the Douglas DC-3, and a STOL aircraft utilising the basic Cessna 337 airframe. It has also converted a Grumman Albatross amphibian to be powered by Rolls-Royce Dart turboprop engines in place of the normal piston-engined power plant. Under evaluation at the time of writing was a modification of the Sikorsky S-64 Skycrane, to enable it to carry fuselage sections of new large transport aircraft; as well as development of an Aquafoil float. This float has an aerodynamic shape which produces additional lift, increasing an aircraft's payload, and will be available as a

Conroy Turbo Three, a conversion of the Douglas DC-3 (two Rolls-Royce Dart Mk 510 turboprop engines)

standard float or with retractable landing gear, thus enabling an aircraft operator to convert readily from land to floatplane or an amphibious configuration.

CONROY/DOUGLAS TURBO THREE

The Conroy turboprop conversion of the DC-3, known as the Turbo Three, provides for the installation of two Rolls-Royce Dart Mk 510 engines in new nacelles, and driving Rotol four-blade propellers with automatic feathering and electrical de-icing. The Dart engines have FAA Certification at 1,600 shp, but may be torque-limited to 1,350 shp to match DC-3 certification and performance limits. Conroy intend to analyse the DC-3 engine mounting and support structure to obtain certification at 1,600 shp. Electric engine starters standard; water-methanol injection system optional.

No change in landing gear is anticipated for

The Conroy CL-44-O conversion of a Canadair CL-44D on an early test flight

operation in compliance with DC-3 service bulletins for normal T-O and landing weights. Conversion to heavy weight (26,900 lb = 12,201 kg) landing gear optional. The standard inboard wing fuel system with a capacity of 822 US gallons (3,111 litres) is retained, but optional conversions for the installation of 400, 800 or 1,100 US gallon (1,513, 3,028, or 4,163 litre) outboard wing fuel tanks will be available. A fuel jettison system will be provided for aircraft in which T-O weight is greater than 105% of the approved landing weight.

Following certification at 26,900 lb (12,201 kg), which will take the form of an FAA Supplemental Type Certificate, it is proposed to certificate the aircraft at 32,000 lb (14,515 kg) max T-O weight. Zero fuel weight will be established at 26,500 lb (12,020 kg) and max landing weight will remain at 26,900 lb (12,201 kg).

The first Turbo Three conversion was completed by Conroy in the spring of 1969, using engines and nacelles from a surplus Viscount. Following its first flight on 13 May this aircraft was flown to the Paris Air Show and subsequently completed a 28-nation demonstration tour.

Conversion of the standard DC-3 to turboprop power will take approximately 30 days at the Conroy plant at Santa Barbara Airport, or will be available in kit form for installation elsewhere.

PERFORMANCE (estimated):
Max level speed, at up to 32,000 lb (14,515 kg) AUW
    187 knots (215 mph; 346 km/h)
Max permissible dive speed, at up to 32,000 lb (14,515 kg) AUW
    248 knots (285 mph; 458 km/h)
Continuous cruising speed at up to 32,000 lb (14,515 kg) AUW
    187 knots (215 mph; 346 km/h)
T-O run, at 26,900 lb (12,201 kg) S/L, standard day   1,487 ft (455 m)
T-O to 50 ft (15 m), at 26,900 lb (12,201 kg) S/L, standard day   3,118 ft (950 m)
Landing from 50 ft (15 m), at 26,900 lb (12,201 kg) S/L, standard day   2,118 ft (645 m)
Landing run, at 26,900 lb (12,201 kg) S/L, standard day   1,126 ft (345 m)
Range with standard fuel, no reserves:
    816 nm (940 miles; 1,510 km)
Range, with 1,922 US gallons fuel, no reserves:
    1,954 nm (2,250 miles; 3,620 km)

CONROY CL-44-O

Conroy has carried out a conversion of the Canadair CL-44 long-range freighter to increase the volumetric capacity of the cargo compartment by almost 100%. This involved removal of the upper half of the standard fuselage, which has been replaced by a new pressurised structure, using prefabricated frames and stringers to increase the maximum inside diameter to 13 ft 11 in (4·24 m).

As in the original CL-44D-4, described in the 1964-65 *Jane's*, the entire rear fuselage is hinged to swing sideways to starboard for direct in-loading of freight from the rear.

The CL-44-O, which is able to transport large jet engines, airframes and other bulky items over intercontinental range, was flown for the first time on 26 November 1969, and is currently undergoing a flight test programme. The aircraft, in its original form, was purchased from Flying Tiger Line, and Conroy holds options on three more CL-44s.

DIMENSIONS, INTERNAL:
Cargo compartment, length overall
    98 ft 1 in (29·90 m)
Length, constant section   84 ft 0 in (25·60 m)
Max width, floor level   10 ft 9 in (3·28 m)
Max width   13 ft 11 in (4·24 m)
Max height   11 ft 4 in (3·45 m)
WEIGHTS (estimated):
Operating weight   97,500 lb (44,225 kg)
Max payload   62,500 lb (28,349 kg)
Max T-O weight   210,000 lb (95,250 kg)

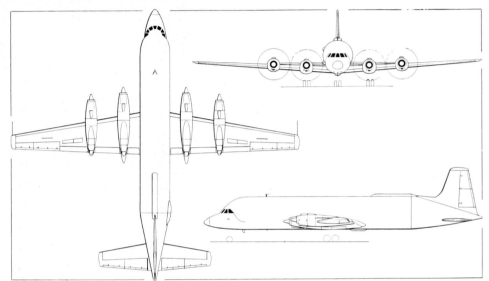

General arrangement drawing of the Conroy CL-44-O

Max zero-fuel weight   160,000 lb (72,570 kg)
Max landing weight   165,000 lb (74,840 kg)
PERFORMANCE (estimated):
Cruising speed   282 knots (325 mph; 523 km/h)

CONROY STOLIFTER

The Stolifter, developed by Conroy Aircraft Corporation, is an extensively-modified Cessna Model 337 Super Skymaster, intended for passenger/cargo operations in civil use, or as a light utility military aircraft suitable for varying roles, including cargo or troop transport, air evacuation and reconnaissance.

Primary difference between the Stolifter and Skymaster is the deletion of the latter's rear-mounted engine, and the installation of a 575 shp Garrett AiResearch TPE 331-25A turboprop engine in the nose of the Stolifter in place of the usual piston-engine. Fuel capacity is 140 US gallons (530 litres).

The fuselage has been extended rearward, and has an upward-opening aft section to facilitate straight-in loading of cargo; the cubic capacity of this aircraft is almost double that of the Skymaster.

In an all-passenger configuration, the Stolifter can accommodate a crew of one or two and seven

The Conroy Stolifter conversion of the Cessna 337 (575 shp AiResearch TPE 331-25A turboprop engine)

or six passengers respectively; a combination passenger/cargo interior is possible. The company is planning to introduce a "stretched" version, with the fuselage extended 1 ft 6 in (0·46 m) in length, to permit the carriage of two additional passengers.

Short take-off and landing characteristics have been given to this model by incorporation of the Robertson Aircraft Corporation's new wing high-lift systems, as described in that company's entry in this volume (which see).

The following details were available at the time of writing:
WEIGHTS:
Weight empty   2,600 lb (1,179 kg)
Max T-O weight   4,700 lb (2,132 kg)
PERFORMANCE (at max T-O weight):
Cruising speed at 20,000 ft (6,100 m)
    217 knots (250 mph; 402 km/h)
Cruising speed at 15,000 ft (4,570 m)
    208 knots (240 mph; 386 km/h)
Cruising speed at 10,000 ft (3,050 m)
    195 knots (225 mph; 362 km/h)
Cruising speed at 5,000 ft (1,525 m)
    182 knots (209 mph; 336 km/h)
Landing speed   39 knots (44 mph; 71 km/h)

Rate of climb at S/L	1,700 ft (518 m)/min
Service ceiling	40,000 ft (12,200 m)
T-O run	250 ft (76 m)
T-O to 50 ft (15 m)	450 ft (137 m)
Landing run	200 ft (61 m)
Endurance (at 75% power, no reserve) 4 hours	

CONROY TURBO ALBATROSS

Conroy, in conjunction with Viscount International Corporation of Salisbury, Maryland, has designed a turboprop-engined conversion of the Grumman HU-16 Albatross amphibian, last described in the 1964/65 *Jane's*. Some 400 of these aircraft are still in service and Conroy is offering the new installation to owners of these piston-engined aircraft at a cost of around $150,000.

The conversion entails replacing the original Wright R-1820 engines with Rolls-Royce Dart RLa.6 Mk 510 turboprop engines, each of 1,740 ehp, complete with nacelle cowling and engine mounting designed for the Vickers Viscount 700 Series aircraft. Each main engine mounting is affixed to the original hardpoints of the Albatross through the medium of a Conroy-designed steel-tube interconnection mounting. This has been designed so that the engine is canted 3° outboard and 5° down to compensate for the increased thrust during single-engine conditions and ensure optimum centre-line of thrust in flight.

Each engine has an electric starter, de-icing system and water-methanol injection system to enhance take-off power under high ambient temperature conditions, and drives a Dowty-Rotol fully-feathering four-blade metal propeller, diameter 10 ft 0 in (3·05 m). These propellers have electrical de-icing.

Two glass-fibre fairings of aerodynamic form complete the engine installation; one for the lower nacelle cowling, the other for the tail-pipe which is carried over the wing. This latter fairing is a one-piece unit that houses also the water-methanol tank system, and has two inspection covers to provide access to the engine accessory section and electrical junction box. The one-piece tail-pipe has stainless steel fireproof insulation, with a stainless steel shroud beneath it, to protect the wing and embodying augmented cooling air ducts.

The majority of the turboprop electrical units are located together near the rear main electrical junction-box in the fuselage, and the main aircraft batteries have been re-located to form a part of this assembly. The cockpit installation

Conroy Turbo Albatross, a Dart-engined conversion of the Grumman HU-16A amphibian

includes instrumentation for the new engines, electric circuit protection, conversion of existing throttles to provide single-lever interconnection between engine speed and propeller control, and provision of a 'ground fine' feature that provides zero thrust to facilitate manoeuvring on water.

Construction of the prototype started in September 1969. This aircraft, originally an HU-16A Albatross, made its first flight in its new form on 25 February 1970, and completed its amphibious flight test programme on 13 March 1970. The lighter-weight and more powerful engines have resulted in a 28% performance improvement compared with the original piston-engined model. It is anticipated that a similar conversion of the HU-16B Albatross will offer a performance increase of at least 10-15%.

The following details were available at the time of writing.

WEIGHT:
Weight empty, equipped
approx 21,800 lb (9,888 kg)

PERFORMANCE (prototype conversion):
Max cruising speed at 10,000 ft (3,050 m)
174 knots (200 mph; 322 km/h)
Max cruising speed at 20,000 ft (6,100 m)
148 knots (170 mph; 274 km/h)
Stalling speed, flaps and wheels down
78 knots (90 mph; 144 km/h)
Max rate of climb at S/L 1,275 ft (389 m)/min
Max rate of climb at S/L, one engine out
250 ft (76 m)/min
Service ceiling 25,000 ft (7,620 m)
Service ceiling, one engine out 9,000 ft (2,745 m)
T-O run on land 1,900 ft (579 m)
Range with max fuel
1,632 nm (1,880 miles; 3,025 km)

CONTINENTAL COPTERS
CONTINENTAL COPTERS, INC

ADDRESS:
PO Box 13284, Cardinal Road, Fort Worth, Texas 76118

PRESIDENT: John L. Scott

Continental Copters has developed and is producing a specialised single-seat agricultural conversion of the Bell Model 47 helicopter, under the name El Tomcat. Design work on the conversion began in 1959 and the original prototype El Tomcat Mk II flew in April of that year, receiving an FAA Supplementary Type Certificate shortly afterwards.

The prototype of the improved El Tomcat Mk III flew for the first time in April 1965. Further refinement of the design produced the El Tomcat Mk IIIA in January 1966; details and a picture of this version can be found in the 1966-67 *Jane's*. It was superseded in 1967 by the El Tomcat Mk IIIB, which introduced a number of improvements and was described in the 1968-69 *Jane's*.

In 1968 Continental Copters produced the El Tomcat Mk IIIC, an improved version of the IIIB with cleaner nose profile, "wrap-around" side windows in the roof of the cabin for rear-quarter visibility and refuelling capability from either side of the aircraft. Also in 1968 the company delivered its first El Tomcat Mk V, generally similar to the IIIC but with a change in power plant.

Since that time, production of the Mk V has ended, this model being superseded by the Mk V-A which has a 260 hp Lycoming VO-435-A1F engine and a 24V electrical system as standard.

At the time of writing a prototype of an advanced version, designated El Tomcat Mk VI, was under construction. This will have a turbocharged Lycoming TVO-435-B1A engine, developing 270 hp, and will introduce Bell 47-110-250-23 main rotor blades. The increased length of these will necessitate extension of the fuselage centre frame at both front and rear to compensate for the rearward movement of the CG. This version will, in general, utilise components of the Bell Model 47G-3B-1, and the company has already received a firm order for one Mk VI.

A total of three El Tomcat Mk V-A's were delivered during 1969, and by the end of that year 22 Bell Model 47's had been converted.

In addition, Continental Copters has for some years been producing passenger helicopters conforming to the Bell 47G and G-2 types. These are assembled from spare and/or surplus parts and are listed in the FAA Helicopter Specification H-1. Other helicopters, not included in this list, have been delivered to Latin America.

CONTINENTAL COPTERS EL TOMCAT Mk IIIC and Mk V-A

The El Tomcat is basically a Bell Model 47G-2 helicopter which has been converted into a specialised single-seat agricultural aircraft. Payload is increased by deletion of unnecessary structure and equipment. In particular, the original cabin is replaced by a simple functional cab for the pilot.

Two generally similar versions are currently available, each with a fuel capacity of 29 US gallons (109 litres):

El Tomcat Mk IIIC. Powered by either a 200 hp Franklin 6V4-200-C32, 210 hp 6V-335-A or 235 hp 6V-350-A engine. Standard Bell Model 47D-1 fuel system. Refuelling points at each side of aircraft. Oil capacity 4 US gallons (15 litres). First flown in May 1968.

El Tomcat Mk V-A. Powered by 260 hp Lycoming VO-435-A1F engine. Oil capacity 3 US gallons (11 litres). Has the 24V electrical system of the Bell Model 47G-2. First flown in June 1968.

In the current El Tomcat Mk IIIC and V-A, the

El Tomcat Mk IIIC single-seat agricultural helicopter conversion of the Bell Model 47

windshield has been further reduced in area and moved closer to the pilot compared with earlier versions. The glass-fibre nose has been modified to ensure easy accessibility to all instruments, the battery and other equipment. It provides a flush mounting for two 600-Watt landing lights which are controllable in elevation by the pilot during flight, landing-light switches being mounted on the collective stick, immediately below the throttle. The cabin roof is of glass-fibre, lower than on earlier versions of El Tomcat, and incorporates wrap-round side windows for rear-quarter visibility. Standard equipment includes hydraulic boost controls and pilot's shoulder harness.

El Tomcat has a revised control system. The collective control has been altered to conform to standard collective geometry, but Continental retains ball bearings in the collective jack shaft, instead of brass bushings, to provide smoother operation. A Harley Davidson throttle control is fitted. The flying controls are hydraulically-boosted.

The chemical hoppers now take the form of two streamlined blister tanks which fit flush against the sides of the fuselage immediately aft of the cabin. A fan-driven pump is mounted adjacent to each tank, aft of the spray-bar supports. A filtered ventilation system for the cockpit minimises toxic spray ingress during spraying operations. Types of spray-gear fitted include the Bell Agmaster, Simplex Lo Profile and special designs developed by customers.

Apart from the changes noted above, the basic structural description of the standard Bell Model 47 applies also to El Tomcat.

Deliveries in 1969 totalled three Mk V-A's.

DIMENSIONS:
As for standard Bell Model 47G-2.

WEIGHTS:
Weight empty, less specialised equipment
IIIC   1,200 lb (544 kg)
V-A   1,375 lb (623 kg)
Max T-O weight:
IIIC, V-A   2,450 lb (1,111kg)

PERFORMANCE:
As for standard Bell Model 47G-2 except:
Range (with fuel reserve for 30 min):
IIIC   112 nm (130 miles; 209 km)
V-A   86 nm (100 miles; 160 km)

CUSTER

CUSTER CHANNEL WING CORPORATION

HEAD OFFICE: 604 North Grand, Enid, Oklahoma 73701

RESEARCH AND DEVELOPMENT CENTRE:
Hagerstown, Maryland, 21740

CHAIRMAN OF THE BOARD: Dr Jack Kough

VICE-PRESIDENT AND CHIEF EXECUTIVE OFFICER:
Sam Stoner.

SECRETARY-TREASURER: Earl P. Zepp

This company was founded by Mr Willard R. Custer, who spent 45 years developing a unique form of STOL aircraft utilising what is known as a channel wing. In this, the power plant is suspended in a channel section in the wing, with the propeller at the trailing-edge. By drawing air through the channel at high velocities, pressures over the wing are decreased to a greater degree than in conventional wing configurations, creating increased lift.

In February 1968, Mr Custer retired, but is retained as engineering consultant. The new Board has obtained additional finance and is continuing with the programme to complete FAA certification of the Corporation's Model CCW-5 aircraft.

It is claimed that the Custer Channel Wing aircraft has demonstrated power-on lift co-efficients of 5, whereas conventional aircraft, by combining the most complicated of high-lift devices, can obtain lift coefficients of approximately 3. This makes possible good STOL performance and the CCW-5 prototype has attained minimum level flight speeds as low as 45 mph (72.5 kmh).

The DeVore Aviation Service Corporation has the prime responsibility of securing the type certification of the CCW-5 and, in addition, of promoting the design of additional Custer aircraft, leading to the development of a high-performance STOL aircraft. Present recommendations are for the development of an 8/9-seat STOL passenger/cargo aircraft powered by a 317 shp turboprop version of the Allison T63 engine, and this would have almost identical performance to that of the CCW-5.

Details of the Custer CCW-5 channel-wing aircraft may be found in the 1969-70 Jane's.

CVJETKOVIC

ANTON CVJETKOVIC

ADDRESS:
624 Fowler Avenue, PO Box 323, Newbury Park, California 91320.

When living in Yugoslavia, Mr Anton Cvjetkovic designed a single-seat light aeroplane designated CA-51 and powered by a modified Volkswagen engine. A prototype was built by members of Zagreb Aeroclub in 1951, and was followed by five more aircraft of the same type. (Details and photograph in 1967-68 Jane's).

After moving to the United States, Mr Cvjetkovic began work, in May 1960, on the design of an improved light aircraft which he designated CA-61. Construction of a prototype was started in February 1961 and it flew for the first time in August 1962. Plans of both single-seat and two-seat all-wood versions are available to amateur constructors, together with plans of a two-seat aircraft designated CA-65, of which the prototype was completed in 1965. Since then Mr Cvjetkovic has completed the design of an all-metal version of the same aircraft, designated CA-65A, and plans of this are also available.

CVJETKOVIC CA-61 MINI ACE

The CA-61 can be built as a single-seat or side-by-side two-seat light aircraft, with any Continental engine of between 65 and 85 hp. Alternatively, the single-seater can be fitted with a modified Volkswagen engine. Construction takes less than 1,000 hours.

The following details refer specifically to the single-seat prototype.

TYPE: Single-seat light aircraft.

WINGS: Cantilever low-wing monoplane. Wing section NACA 4415. Dihedral 3°. No incidence. Structure consists of two spruce spars, each built in one piece, built-up spruce girder-type ribs and plywood-covered leading-edge torsion box, with fabric covering overall. Fabric-covered spruce ailerons. No flaps.

FUSELAGE: Conventional wooden structure of basic square section, plywood-covered.

TAIL UNIT: Cantilever wooden structure, covered with plywood. Fixed-incidence tailplane. Trim-tab in elevator.

LANDING GEAR: Non-retractable tail-wheel type. Cantilever main legs, with helical spring shock-absorption. Goodyear main wheels and tyres, size 5·00 × 5 Type III and Model L5 brakes. Steerable tail-wheel.

POWER PLANT: One 65 hp Continental A65 four-cylinder horizontally-opposed air-cooled engine, driving a Flottorp 63-55 two-blade fixed-pitch propeller. Fuel in two steel tanks in fuselage, with capacities of 12 US gallons and 5 US gallons respectively. Total fuel capacity 17 US gallons (64 litres). Oil capacity 1¼ US gallons (4·5 litres).

ACCOMMODATION: Single seat in enclosed cockpit.

ELECTRONICS AND EQUIPMENT: Prototype fitted with Nova Star radio and omni.

DIMENSIONS, EXTERNAL:
Wing span   27 ft 6 in (8·38 m)
Wing chord (constant)   4 ft 7 in (1·40 m)
Wing aspect ratio   6·0
Length overall   18 ft 11 in (5·77 m)
Height overall (in flying position)
                              6 ft 10 in (2·08 m)
Wheel track:
Single-seat   8 ft 2 in (2·49 m)
Two-seat   8 ft 7 in (2·62 m)

AREA:
Wings, gross   126·5 sq ft (11·75 m²)

WEIGHTS AND LOADINGS:
Weight empty:
Single-seat   606 lb (275 kg)
Two-seat   800 lb (363 kg)
Max T-O weight:
Single-seat   950 lb (430 kg)
Two-seat   1,300 lb (590 kg)
Max wing loading:
Single-seat   7·5 lb/sq ft (36·6 kg/m²)
Two-seat   10·25 lb/sq ft (50·0 kg/m²)

PERFORMANCE:
Max level speed at S/L
                     104 knots (120 mph; 193 km/h)
Normal cruising speed
                      87 knots (100 mph; 161 km/h)
Min flying speed:
Single-seat   37 knots (42 mph; 67·5 km/h)
Two-seat   44 knots (50 mph; 80·5 km/h)
Range with max fuel:
Single-seat   369 nm (425 miles; 685 km)
Two-seat   321 nm (370 miles; 595 km)

CVJETKOVIC CA-65

Design work on this side-by-side two-seat light aircraft was started in September 1963. Construction of the prototype began in March 1964

Cvjetkovic CA-61 single-seat light aircraft (65 hp Continental A65 engine)

and it flew for the first time in July 1965. Plans are available to other constructors, and the illustration on page 327 shows a CA-65 built by Mr John Hickle.

The CA-65 closely resembles the CA-61 in general appearance, but has a more powerful engine and retractable landing gear. A folding-wing version was introduced during 1967.

TYPE: Two-seat light aircraft.

WINGS: Cantilever low-wing monoplane. Modified NACA 4415 wing section. Dihedral 0° on centre-section, 3° on outer wings. Structure consists of two spruce spars, each built in one piece, and built-up spruce girder-type ribs, completely plywood-covered. Fabric-covered spruce ailerons. On the folding-wing version, the outer wings fold upward from their junction with the centre-section.

FUSELAGE: Conventional wooden structure of basically square section, plywood-covered. Manually-operated landing flap under fuselage.

TAIL UNIT: Cantilever wooden structure. Fixed surfaces covered with plywood. Elevator and rudder fabric-covered. Fixed-incidence tailplane.

LANDING GEAR: Mechanically-retractable tail-wheel type. Main wheels retract inward. Goodyear main wheels and tyres, size 5·00 × 5 Type III. Goodyear type L5 brakes. Steerable tail-wheel.

POWER PLANT: One 125 hp Lycoming O-290-G four-cylinder horizontally-opposed air-cooled engine, driving a Sensenich 66-68 two-blade fixed-pitch propeller, diameter 5 ft 8 in (1·73 m). Two aluminium fuel tanks in fuselage, each with capacity of 14 US gallons. Total fuel capacity 28 US gallons (106 litres).

ACCOMMODATION: Two seats side-by-side in enclosed cockpit, with dual controls; although hydraulic brakes can be operated only by the pilot. Forward-opening canopy.

RADIO: Bayside BEI-990 radio fitted in prototype.

DIMENSIONS, EXTERNAL:
Wing span	25 ft 0 in (7·62 m)
Width, wings folded	9 ft 0 in (2·74 m)
Length overall	19 ft 0 in (5·79 m)
Height overall (in flying position)	7 ft 4 in (2·24 m)
Height, wings folded	10 ft 0 in (3·05 m)
Wheel track	6 ft 11 in (2·11 m)

AREA:
Wings, gross	108 sq ft (10·03 m²)

WEIGHTS AND LOADINGS:
Weight empty	900 lb (408 kg)
Max T-O weight	1,500 lb (680 kg)
Max wing loading	13·9 lb/sq ft (67·9 kg/m²)
Max power loading	12·0 lb/hp (5·44 kg/hp)

PERFORMANCE (at max T-O weight):
Max level speed	139 knots (160 mph; 257 km/h)
Normal cruising speed	117 knots (135 mph; 217 km/h)
Stalling speed	48 knots (55 mph; 89 km/h)
Rate of climb at S/L	1,000 ft (305 m)/min
Service ceiling	15,000 ft (4,575 m)
Take-off run	450 ft (137 m)
Landing run	600 ft (183 m)
Range with max fuel	434 nm (500 miles; 804 km)

CVJETKOVIC CA-65A

This is essentially similar to the all-wood CA-65; it differs by having a tail unit with a swept vertical surface and is of all-metal construction. It is designed for +9 and —6 g ultimate loading.

The general description of the CA-65 applies also to the CA-65A, except in the following details.

WINGS: The wing structure consists of a single main spar and an auxiliary wing spar, with aluminium sheet ribs and skin riveted throughout. The main wing spar cap is made of extruded and bent-up sheet aluminium angles,

Cvjetkovic CA-65 two-seat light aircraft (125 hp Lycoming O-290-G engine)

tapered towards the tip to produce a wing of uniform bending strength. Ribs are formed from 0·025 in aluminium sheet. Wing skin is of 2024-T3 aluminium alloy sheet.

FUSELAGE: All-metal structure with four aluminium angle longerons and built-up frames. Fuselage skin is of 0·025-0·032 in 2024-T3 aluminium alloy sheet. To simplify formation of the curvature on the upper fuselage, the skins are broken up into small sections of flat panels.

TAIL UNIT: Cantilever all-metal structure, with swept vertical surfaces. Construction similar to that of the wings.

POWER PLANT: The structure is designed to accommodate a Lycoming engine of 108-150 hp.

DIMENSIONS, EXTERNAL: As for Model CA-65 except:
Wing span	25 ft 5 in (7·75 m)
Length overall	19 ft 8 in (5·99 m)
Height overall	7 ft 6 in (2·29 m)

AREA:
Wings, gross	109·4 sq ft (10·16 m²)

LOADING:
Max wing loading	13·7 lb/sq ft (66·9 kg/m²)

PERFORMANCE (150 hp engine):
Max level speed	151 knots (174 mph; 280 km/h)
Normal cruising speed	130 knots (150 mph; 241 km/h)
Stalling speed	48 knots (55 mph; 89 km/h)
Rate of climb at S/L	1,530 ft (466 m)/min
Service ceiling	15,000 ft (4,570 m)
T-O run	325 ft (99 m)
Landing run	600 ft (183 m)
Range with max fuel	460 nm (530 miles; 853 km)

D'APUZZO

NICHOLAS E. D'APUZZO

ADDRESS:
704 Booth Lane, Ambler, Pennsylvania 19002

Mr D'Apuzzo, who is employed by the Naval Air Development Center, Johnsville, Warminster, Pennsylvania, as a project manager on specialised projects, has designed several sporting aircraft for amateur construction. Among the best known of these are the Denight Special midget racer, described in the 1962-63 *Jane's*, and the PJ-260 single-seat aerobatic biplane described under the "Parsons-Jocelyn" heading in this edition.

His other designs include the Senior Aero Sport, which is a two-seat version of the PJ-260, and the smaller single-seat Junior Aero Sport.

D'APUZZO D-260 SENIOR AERO SPORT

This is a two-seat dual-control version of the PJ-260 aerobatic biplane described under the "Parsons-Jocelyn" heading in this section.

At the time of writing, a total of 16 PJ-260's and Senior Aero Sports were known to have been completed and flown by amateur constructors in the United States, with a further 56 under construction.

At the 1968 EAA International Fly-in at Rockford, Illinois, a Senior Aero Sport (N4030Q) built by Mr Tom Luckey of Maple Glen, Pennsylvania, was selected as the "Grand Champion" homebuilt, and a similar aircraft (N112JF), built by Mr Jim Frankenfield of Hatfield, Pennsylvania, was runner-up.

There are three basic versions of the Senior Aero Sport, as follows:

D-260 (1). With Lycoming O-435 series engine.

D-260 (2). With Continental O-470/E-185 series engine. Construction of prototype started by Mr C. L. McHolland of Sheridan, Wyoming, in May 1962 and first flight made on 17 July 1965, with a 225 hp E-185 (modified) engine, driving an Aeromatic F-200H-O-85 propeller. Fuel in one 16 US gallon (60·5 litre) tank in fuselage and one 21 US gallon (79·5 litre) streamlined external tank under fuselage.

D-260(3). With Lycoming GO-435 series engine. Construction of prototype started by Mr G. A. Shallbetter of Minneapolis in April 1961 and first flight made on 17 July 1965, with a 260 hp GO-435-C2 engine, driving a Hartzell controllable-pitch propeller of 7 ft 6 in (2·29 m) diameter. Four fuel tanks in fuselage, with total capacity of 36 US gallons (136 litres). Second D-260(3), completed by Mr Alfred Fessenden of Lafayette, New York, is fitted with a Hartzell constant-speed propeller.

The general description of the PJ-260 applies equally to all three versions of the Senior Aero Sport, with the following exceptions:

D'Apuzzo D-260 (2) Senior Aero Sport built by Mr J Frankenfield of Hatfield, Pennsylvania

TYPE: Two-seat sporting biplane.

LANDING GEAR: Non-retractable tail-wheel type. Cantilever spring steel main units. Goodyear 6·00 × 6 main wheels and tyres, pressure 20 lb/sq in (1·41 kg/cm²). Goodyear disc brakes.

POWER PLANT: One six-cylinder horizontally-opposed air-cooled engine. Details under individual model listings above.

ACCOMMODATION: Two seats in tandem in open cockpits. Luggage space behind headrest.

SYSTEM: 12V electrical system, with optional starter and navigation lights.

ELECTRONICS: Prototypes fitted with two-way radio and omni.

DIMENSIONS, EXTERNAL:
Same as PJ-260, except:
Wheel track	8 ft 5 in (2·57 m)
Wheelbase	15 ft 9 in (4·80 m)

AREAS:
Same as PJ-260, except:
Wings, gross	185 sq ft (17·2 m²)

WEIGHTS AND LOADINGS:
Normal T-O weight:
D-260 (2)	2,050 lb (930 kg)
D-260 (3)	2,150 lb (975 kg)
Max T-O and landing weight:	
All versions	2,150 lb (975 kg)
Max wing loading:	
All versions	11·5 lb/sq ft (56·1 kg/m²)

Max power loading:
D-260 (2)	9·77 lb/hp (4·43 kg/hp)
D-260 (3)	9·00 lb/hp (4·08 kg/hp)

PERFORMANCE (D-260 (3) at max T-O weight. D-260 (2) comparable):
Max level speed at 7,000 ft (2,135 m)	135 knots (155 mph; 250 km/h)
Max permissible diving speed	165 knots (190 mph; 305 km/h)
Max cruising speed at 7,000 ft (2,135 m)	122 knots (140 mph; 225 km/h)
Econ cruising speed at 7,000 ft (2,135 m)	113 knots (130 mph; 209 km/h)
Stalling speed	48 knots (55 mph; 89 km/h)
Rate of climb at S/L	2,000 ft (610 m)/min
Service ceiling	20,000 ft (6,100 m)
T-O run	400 ft (122 m)
T-O to 50 ft (15 m)	700 ft (213 m)
Landing from 50 ft (15 m)	900 ft (275 m)
Landing run	600 ft (183 m)
Range with max fuel and max payload	434 nm (500 miles; 805 km)

D'APUZZO D-200 JUNIOR AERO SPORT

The Junior Aero Sport is a smaller single-seat version of the PJ-260. Its design was started in September 1963 and construction of two prototypes began in September 1964. The first of these was still under construction early in 1970.

TYPE: Single-seat sporting biplane.

WINGS: Conventional braced biplane type. Wing section NACA M-12 (mod). Dihedral 0° on top wing, 0° 30′ on bottom wing. Incidence 2° on both wings. No sweepback. Spruce spars, wooden ribs and light alloy nose skin, with fabric covering. Fabric-covered aluminium alloy ailerons. No flaps.

FUSELAGE: Welded steel-tube structure, with aluminium alloy panels forward of cockpit and fabric covering aft.

TAIL UNIT: Wire-braced welded steel-tube structure with fabric covering. Fixed-incidence tailplane. Trim-tab in each elevator.

LANDING GEAR: Non-retractable tail-wheel type. Cantilever spring steel main legs. Goodrich-Hayes main wheels and tyres, size 5·00 × 4, pressure 20 lb/sq in (1·40 kg/cm²). Goodrich-Hayes brakes.

POWER PLANT: One 180 hp Lycoming O-360 four-cylinder horizontally-opposed air-cooled engine, driving a Hartzell two-blade constant-speed metal propeller. Fuel tank in fuselage, capacity 20 US gallons (75 litres). Oil capacity 2 US gallons (7·5 litres).

ACCOMMODATION: Single seat in open cockpit.

DIMENSIONS, EXTERNAL:

Wing span (both)	21 ft 8 in (6·60 m)
Wing chord (constant)	3 ft 4 in (1·02 m)
Wing aspect ratio	4·2
Length overall	18 ft 3 in (5·56 m)
Height overall	6 ft 4 in (1·93 m)
Tailplane span	7 ft 2 in (2·18 m)
Wheel track	5 ft 0 in (1·52 m)
Wheelbase	13 ft 6 in (4·11 m)

AREAS:

Wings, gross	140 sq ft (13·00 m²)
Ailerons (total)	16·5 sq ft (1·53 m²)
Fin	5·0 sq ft (0·46 m²)
Rudder	5·0 sq ft (0·46 m²)

WEIGHTS:

Weight empty	840 lb (381 kg)
Max T-O and landing weight	1,275 lb (578 kg)

PERFORMANCE (estimated at max T-O weight):

Max level speed at 7,000 ft (2,135 m)	139 knots (160 mph; 257 km/h)
Max permissible diving speed	191 knots (220 mph; 354 km/h)
Max cruising speed at 7,000 ft (2,135 m)	122 knots (140 mph; 225 km/h)
Stalling speed	48 knots (55 mph; 89 km/h)

Artist's impression of D'Apuzzo Junior Aero Sport

Rate of climb at S/L	2,500 ft (762 m)/min
Service ceiling	20,000 ft (6,100 m)
T-O run	400 ft (122 m)
T-O to 50 ft (15 m)	650 ft (198 m)
Landing from 50 ft (15 m)	850 ft (260 m)
Landing run	550 ft (168 m)
Range with max fuel	260 nm (300 miles; 480 km)

DAVIS

LEEON D. DAVIS

ADDRESS:

3501 Baumann Avenue, Midland, Texas 79701

Mr Davis, an experimental mechanic with Aero Commander, designed and built his first light aircraft, the DA-1A five-seat high-wing monoplane, ten years ago. Details can be found in the 1960-61 *Jane's*.

He has since completed prototypes of a two-seat low-wing monoplane designated DA-2A, and a four-seat development designated DA-3. All available details of these follow.

DAVIS DA-2A

This side-by-side two-seat light aircraft was flown for the first time on 21 May 1966, after 18 months of spare-time work and an expenditure of $1,600. At the Experimental Aircraft Association's annual fly-in a few weeks later, it gained the awards for both the most outstanding design and the most popular aircraft. Plans are available to other amateur constructors.

The DA-2A is of simple all-metal construction and has an all-moving Vee-tail (included angle 100°), like Mr Davis's earlier DA-1A. The wings are of constant chord, without flaps. Aspect ratio 4·48. Dihedral is 5°. The non-retractable tricycle landing gear has cantilever spring steel main legs and a steerable nose-wheel. Power plant is a 65 hp Continental A65-8 four-cylinder horizontally-opposed air-cooled engine; but the DA-2A is stressed for engines of up to 100 hp. Total fuel capacity is 20 US gallons (76 litres) and oil capacity 1 US gallon (3·75 litres).

There is baggage space aft of the side-by-side seats, or alternatively, a child's seat may be located in this position.

DIMENSIONS, EXTERNAL:

Wing span	19 ft 2¾ in (5·86 m)
Wing chord (constant)	4 ft 3½ in (1·31 m)
Length overall	17 ft 10¼ in (5·44 m)
Height overall	5 ft 5 in (1·65 m)

DIMENSIONS, INTERNAL:

Cabin:

Length	4 ft 6¾ in (1·49 m)
Max width	3 ft 5 in (1·04 m)
Max height	3 ft 8¾ in (1.14 m)

AREAS:

Wings, gross	82·5 sq ft (7·66 m²)
Tail surfaces (total)	12·75 sq ft (1·18 m²)

WEIGHTS AND LOADINGS:

Weight empty	610 lb (277 kg)
Max T-O weight	1,125 lb (510 kg)
Max wing loading	14·5 lb/sq ft (70·7 kg/m²)
Max power loading	17·3 lb/hp (7·8 kg/hp)

PERFORMANCE (at max T-O weight):

Max level speed at S/L	104 knots (120 mph; 193 km/h)
Cruising speed	100 knots (115 mph; 185 km/h)
Landing speed	54 knots (62 mph; 100 km/h)
Range with max fuel	390 nm (450 miles; 725 km)

DAVIS DA-3

This four-seat light aircraft is basically a scaled-up development of the DA-2A. It is of similar all-metal construction and has the same type of all-moving Vee-tail as Mr Davis' earlier designs.

Davis DA-2A two-seat amateur-built light aircraft (65 hp Continental A65-8 engine)

Davis DA-3 four-seat amateur-built light aircraft (65 hp Continental A65 engine)

Power plant of the prototype is a 65 hp Continental A65 four-cylinder horizontally-opposed air-cooled engine; but the DA-3 is stressed for power plants up to 100 hp. Plans are expected to be made available to amateur constructors at a later date.

DIMENSIONS, EXTERNAL:

Wing span	22 ft 3 in (6·78 m)
Wing chord at root	5 ft 2 in (1·63 m)
Wing chord at tip	4 ft 3½ in (1·31 m)
Length overall	19 ft 8 in (5·99 m)
Height overall	5 ft 7 in (1·70 m)

WEIGHTS:

Weight empty	700 lb (317 kg)
Max T-O weight (65 hp)	1,300 lb (590 kg)
Max T-O weight (100 hp)	1,600 lb (725 kg)

PERFORMANCE:

Max level speed	96 knots (110 mph; 177 km/h)
Cruising speed	87 knots (100 mph; 161 km/h)
Landing speed	56 knots (65 mph; 105 km/h)

DEL MAR

DEL MAR ENGINEERING LABORATORIES

HEAD OFFICE AND WORKS:
International Airport, 6901, Imperial Highway, Los Angeles, California 90045

PRESIDENT: Bruce Del Mar

VICE-PRESIDENT: Fred M. Kuykendall Jr (Sales and Service)

Del Mar is engaged primarily on the design and production of weapons support and training systems for the armed forces of the United States, Canada and other nations.

Its current products include the Whirlymite family of ultra-light helicopters, suitable for a wide variety of piloted or drone applications, with the basic dynamic components common to all versions. Development of the DH-20 Whirlymite Tandem, described in the 1969/70 *Jane's*, has been suspended.

DEL MAR DH-2 WHIRLYMITE

The prototype DH-1A Whirlymite Scout, which flew for the first time on 15 June 1960, was an ultra-light single-seat helicopter powered by a 56 hp Kiekhaefer Mercury piston-engine. During 1962-63 the design was revised extensively, to make it suitable for production, and a new production prototype was built.

The following developed versions are currently available:

DH-2A Whirlymite Scout. Generally similar to the production prototype DH-1A, but with a shaft-turbine engine, in which form the helicopter can lift a useful load equal to its own empty weight. The original 65 shp Solar T-62 engine specified for this version has now been superseded by the more powerful AiResearch GTP30-91. Design was started in December 1962 and the prototype DH-2A flew for the first time in May 1963.

DH-2C Whirlymite Target Drone. Minimum-size low-cost destructible target for use in development of anti-helicopter missiles and for training personnel in their use. Basically similar to DH-2A. Described in "Drones" section of 1969-70 *Jane's*.

DEL MAR DHT-2A WHIRLYMITE HELICOPTER PILOT TRAINER

The DHT-2A Whirlymite is a second-generation pilot training system developed from the DHT-1, described in the 1965-66 *Jane's*. Like the earlier model, it is a fully flyable one-man helicopter, mounted on an air cushion platform. It duplicates completely and preserves the handling characteristics and sensations of actual helicopter flight, thus enabling the student pilot to sense the true "feel" and response of a helicopter. As a result, the student acquires rapidly and develops basic control skills through practical experience in a realistic but completely safe flight environment.

In its original form, as the DHT-2 (see 1968-69 *Jane's*), it differed from the DHT-1 in introducing a gas-turbine power plant in the helicopter and an improved method of platform tethering. The tethering cable incorporated telephone communication lines for two-way conversation and provision for emergency shut-down of the trainer by an instructor. Now, following modification to DHT-2A standard, it retains these new features of the DHT-2, plus a protective canopy for the pilot.

The improvements made to the DHT-2/2A result in part from two evaluations by the US Army. Operation of its gas-turbine engine is similar to that for the power plants of turbine-powered utility and light observation helicopters in current service with the US Army and other Services.

The helicopter, described below, is swivelled on the upper end of a free-rising structural arm which is mounted through a four-bar linkage to the mobile base platform. The base platform itself is an air cushion vehicle of the plenum chamber type, with flexible skirt. The air cushion, which raises the platform a small distance above the ground, is produced and maintained by two electric fans flush-mounted in the top deck of the platform: these fans derive their power supply from the starter/generator of the gas-turbine engine. Extending from the periphery of the platform is a series of outrigger arms, with fully-swivelling castors at their ends, which act as tilt-limiting bumpers to prevent the trainer from exceeding the limits of safe operation.

The details below refer to the DHT-2A, of which production was suspended in the Spring of 1969, pending closer definition of military requirements.

Del Mar DHT-2A helicopter pilot trainer

TYPE: Helicopter pilot trainer.

ROTOR SYSTEM: Three-blade main rotor. Each blade is a two-piece all-aluminium structure with NACA 0015 section and constant chord of 3·5 in (8·9 cm). Blades fold for storage and transport. Fully-articulated hub with friction lag-hinge dampers. No rotor brake. Two-blade teetering all-metal tail anti-torque rotor.

ROTOR DRIVE: Belt drive to main transmission, and spiral bevel gearing. Main rotor/engine rpm ratio: 700 : 8,900. Tail rotor/engine rpm ratio: 3,600 : 8,900.

CONTROL SYSTEM: Conventional floor-mounted cyclic control stick, collective-pitch lever with twist-grip throttle and anti-torque control pedals.

FUSELAGE: Consists simply of a steel-tube and aluminium alloy " backbone " carrying the rotor systems, transmission, fuel tank, engine, and cockpit.

TAIL UNIT: All-metal ventral fin.

LANDING GEAR: Rigid strut type of aluminium alloy with four pads.

POWER PLANT: One 100 shp AiResearch GTP-30-100 turboshaft engine. Fuel tank above engine and aft of main rotor drive shaft, capacity 12·5 US gallons (47·3 litres). Refuelling point at top of tank. Oil capacity 0·5 US gallon (1·86 litres).

ACCOMMODATION: Single seat for pilot in an enclosed cabin, with door on each side.

SYSTEMS: Engine-driven DC generator.

DIMENSIONS, EXTERNAL:
Diameter of main rotor 16 ft 0 in (4·88 m)
Diameter of tail rotor 3 ft 0 in (0·91 m)

Distance between rotor centres	9 ft 8 in (2·94 m)
Length overall	19 ft 3¾ in (5·89 m)
Length of fuselage	16 ft 6 in (5·03 m)
Width overall	5 ft 4 in (1·63 m)
Height overall	7 ft 8½ in (2·35 m)
Cabin doors, each:	
Height	3 ft 8 in (1·12 m)
Width	3 ft 1 in (0·94 m)
Height to sill	1 ft 5½ in (0·44 m)

DIMENSIONS, INTERNAL:
Cabin, length	3 ft 1 in (0·94 m)
Max width	2 ft 0 in (0·61 m)
Max height	4 ft 4 in (1·32 m)
Floor area	6·17 sq ft (0·57 m²)
Volume	21·5 cu ft (2·0 m³)

AREAS:
Main rotor blades (each)	2·0 sq ft (0·19 m²)
Tail rotor blades (each)	0·33 sq ft (0·03 m²)
Main rotor disc	200 sq ft (18·58 m²)
Tail rotor disc	7·1 sq ft (0·66 m²)
Tail fin	2·0 sq ft (0·19 m²)

WEIGHTS AND LOADINGS (in flight configuration without air cushion platform):
Weight empty	479 lb (217 kg)
Max T-O weight	715 lb (324 kg)
Max zero-fuel weight	395 lb (179 kg)
Max disc loading	3·58 lb/sq ft (17·5 kg/m²)
Max power loading	7·15 lb/shp (3·24 kg/shp)

PERFORMANCE:
Max level speed at S/L
  39 knots (45 mph; 72 km/h)
Hovering ceiling in ground effect
  8,600 ft (2,620 m)
Endurance with max fuel, no allowances
  1 hr 15 min

DEMPSEY

T. DEMPSEY

ADDRESS:
2023E 8th, c/o "M" System, Odessa, Texas 79761

Mr Tom Dempsey, a jeweller by profession, has constructed three light aircraft. His first machine was a Loving Love, after which he designed and built an original four-seater known as the TD-162 (TD-2). This fully-aerobatic high-wing monoplane, powered by a 150 hp Lycoming engine, was described and illustrated in the 1966-67 *Jane's*.

Experience gained with the TD-162, which has logged 650 hours of flight to date, encouraged Mr Dempsey to embark on the design and construction of an advanced home-built project which he has designated the TD-3 Beta Lightning. All available details follow:

DEMPSEY TD-3 BETA LIGHTNING

The TD-3 Beta Lightning follows the general lines of the Lockheed P-38 Lightning fighter of WWII. Other than a few brief sketches and calculations for high-stress points, loading and CG positions, no engineering drawings exist and the machine was constructed step by step with co-operation from the local FAA inspection representative. The first flight and subsequent FAA certification, comprising 50 hours' flying, were completed at Ector during the late summer of 1969, after which the aircraft was flown to Lubbock for final clearance. Construction time was 2 years 8 months and the total cost was approximately $10,000.

TYPE: Twin-engined fully-aerobatic sporting and touring aircraft.

Dempsey TD-3 Beta Lightning (two 160 hp Lycoming IO-320 engines)

WINGS: Cantilever mid-wing monoplane, utilising a conventional spruce and plywood box main spar and plywood ribs. The centre-section carries the seat pick-up points as well as the cockpit floor; its outboard extremities carry both engine bearers, landing gear attachments and tail-boom fixings. The outer wing panels are 10 ft (3·05 m) in length and are of ply-skinned wooden construction. Four-position flaps (giving settings of 10, 20, 30 and 40°) and ailerons are of all-metal construction.

FUSELAGE: Welded steel-tube structure, covered with glass-fibre panels clipped to lugs attached to the primary structure.

TAIL UNIT: Tailplane and fins of glass-fibre-covered wooden construction. Rudders and elevators are all-metal structures. The tail assembly is carried on two tubular welded steel booms, glass-fibre-covered, attached to the centre-section and faired in to the lines of the engine cowlings.

LANDING GEAR: Retractable tricycle type. Hydraulically - operated with emergency hand-pump. Nose unit retracts into fuselage pod. Main units retract rearwards into engine nacelles, with spring-loaded wheel-well doors. All wheels are interchangeable and have 6 × 615 low-profile tyres from a Cessna 210.

POWER PLANT: Two 160 hp Lycoming IO-320 four-cylinder horizontally-opposed air-cooled

engines, driving fully-feathering Hartzell metal propellers. Four integral fuel tanks in wings, total capacity 72 US gallons (272 litres).

ACCOMMODATION: Crew of two seated side-by-side in enclosed cabin, with space for an occasional third person. Canopy opens upward and rearward. Full dual controls. Large baggage space.

EQUIPMENT: Full equipment for IFR conditions, plus full blind-flying panel. Narco Mk 12A VOR 4-channel omni.

DIMENSIONS, EXTERNAL:
Wing span   30 ft 0 in (9·14 m)

Length overall	19 ft 6 in (6·00 m)
Height overall	6 ft 0 in (1·83 m)

WEIGHTS:
Weight empty	1,896 lb (860 kg)
Max T-O weight	2,896 lb (1,314 kg)

PERFORMANCE:
Max level speed
234 knots (270 mph; 434 km/h)
Approach speed 83 knots (95 mph; 153 km/h)
Stalling speed 65 knots (75 mph; 105 km/h)
Rate of climb at 95 knots (110 mph; 177 km/h)
at S/L   2,000 ft (610 m)/min
Range (normal configuration)
846 nm (975 miles; 1,569 km)

DISTRIBUTOR WING
AERIAL DISTRIBUTORS, INC

ADDRESS:
PO Box 218, Robbins, California 95676
PRESIDENT: LeRoy Lampson
VICE-PRESIDENT: Phillip Wagner
SECRETARY-TREASURER: Harold Moore

This company has built the prototype of a new agricultural aircraft known as the Distributor Wing DW-1, which results from research studies by NASA and the Universities of Wichita and Robbins, California.

DISTRIBUTOR WING DW-1

A unique feature of this aircraft is that the equipment it carries for agricultural duties is built into the airframe as an integral part of the aircraft, instead of being attached in the usual way. Power for the spraying and dusting systems is supplied by a separate Lycoming four-cylinder engine mounted under and slightly to the rear of the aircraft's main power plant, in the nose. When the aircraft is used for dusting, this auxiliary power plant drives through multiple Vee-belts a fan mounted in the lower part of the aircraft's deep nose. Air from the fan is ducted rearward to where a valve under the hopper releases chemical dust into the duct. The mixture of air and dust is then ducted into each wing, between the spars, and ejected rearward from a variable-orifice slot immediately forward of the flaps. At the time same, a quantity of clean air is ducted to the outer part of each wing and ejected over the small ailerons to increase their effectiveness.

In a spraying rôle, the auxiliary power plant drives a pump through a system of pulleys and a shaft, and this pumps the liquid chemicals out of nozzles built into the trailing-edges of the flaps.

The first Distributor Wing DW-1 flew on 30 January 1965. It was illustrated in its original form in the 1965-66 *Jane's*. Since then, its cowling lines have been revised, as shown in the adjacent illustration.

The following data apply to the projected production version, with the new cowling and different engines.

Distributor Wing DW-1 agricultural aircraft (350 hp Lycoming IGO-540 engine)

TYPE: Single-seat agricultural aircraft.

WINGS: Braced low-wing monoplane, with single short streamline-section bracing strut each side. Two-spar wing of all-metal construction, with "blown" ailerons and flaps along entire trailing-edge. Forward-hinged access doors over inter-spar dust-ducts.

FUSELAGE: Welded steel-tube structure covered with light alloy panels, some of which are removable for access to interior.

TAIL UNIT: Cantilever all-metal structure with sweptback vertical surfaces. One-piece all-moving horizontal surfaces.

LANDING GEAR: Non-retractable tail-wheel type. Cantilever main legs.

POWER PLANT: One 350 hp Lycoming IGO-540 six-cylinder horizontally - opposed air-cooled engine, driving a three-blade Hartzell variable-pitch propeller, diameter 8 ft 8 in (2·64 m). One 108 hp Lycoming O-235 four-cylinder horizontally-opposed air-cooled engine used solely to power agricultural spraying and dusting gear (see above). Two fuel tanks in wing leading-edges with total capacity of 60 US gallons (225 litres).

ACCOMMODATION: Pilot only in enclosed cockpit. Canopy has integral steel-tube overturn structure. Light pressurisation prevents ingress of chemicals.

EQUIPMENT: Spraying and dusting equipment is described above. Hopper, forward of cockpit, has two loading doors in top, actuated hydraulically under control of the pilot. Its capacity is 39·9 cu ft (1·13 m³).

DIMENSIONS, EXTERNAL:
Wing span	43 ft 10 in (13·36 m)
Length overall	28 ft 4 in (8·63 m)

Height to top of cockpit canopy
8 ft 2 in (2·49 m)
Tailplane span	14 ft 3 in (4·34 m)
Wheel track	12 ft 2 in (3·71 m)

AREA:
Wings, gross   240 sq ft (22·30 m²)

WEIGHT:
Max T-O weight   5,200 lb (2,360 kg)

PERFORMANCE:
Operating speed
61-130 knots (70-150 mph; 115-240 km/h)
Stalling speed, empty
40 knots (46 mph; 74 km/h)
Stalling speed at max AUW
50 knots (57 mph; 92 km/h)

DOUGLAS (*see under "McDonnell Douglas"*)

DUMOD
THE DUMOD CORPORATION

HEAD OFFICE AND WORKS:
PO Box 425, Building 147, Wright Road, Opa-Locka Airport, Opa-Locka, Florida 33054
PRESIDENT: Willis H. duPont
VICE-PRESIDENT: Mirem duPont
SECRETARY/TREASURER: Harold Gray

This company has produced a modernisation scheme for the Beechcraft 18, which offers a considerable improvement in performance and standard of accommodation.

No recent information has been received from The Dumod Corporation; but it is reported that Broome County Aviation, parent organisation of Commuter Airlines, Broome County Airport, Binghampton, New York, has acquired all rights, jigs, etc of the Dumod Corporation.

DUMOD I

The Dumod I (known originally as the Infinité I) is a modernised Beechcraft 18 with Volpar tricycle landing gear, Hamilton Standard propellers, high-performance wing-tips and new glass-fibre control surfaces. Refinements to the cabin include the installation of larger double-glazed windows, an accordion-type door between the cabin and flight deck, a three-step flush-fitting air-stair door and improved soundproofing.

The flight deck is enlarged by 6 cu ft (0·17 m³) and fitted with a panoramic wrap-around windshield. Interior arrangements of the main cabin include an executive layout with two rearward-facing armchair seats, two tables, two forward-facing armchair seats, and two inward-facing seats on the starboard side, with restroom at the rear; a standard passenger layout with seven forward-facing armchair seats and rear bench-type seat for two persons; and a cargo layout with seven folding seats and the rear bench seat.

Dumod Liner 15-seat conversion of the Beechcraft Model 18 (*Howard Levy*)

In all cases, there is provision for a crew of two, with dual controls, and a baggage compartment aft, which is accessible in flight.

Optional extras include fuel-injection engines, radar, autopilot, individual oxygen supply and landing lights.

By the Spring of 1966 a total of 37 Beechcraft 18's had been converted to Dumod I standard.

WEIGHTS:
Useful load	over 4,000 lb (1,815 kg)
Max T-O weight	10,200 lb (4,627 kg)
Max landing weight	9,772 lb (4,433 kg)

PERFORMANCE (at max T-O weight):
Max level speed at S/L
210 knots (242 mph; 390 km/h)
Max cruising speed (60% power) at 10,000 ft
(3,050 m)   191 knots (220 mph; 354 km/h)
Single-engine ceiling over 10,000 ft (3,050 m)
T-O to 50 ft (15 m)   1,850 ft (564 m)
Range with max fuel at normal cruising speed
1,736 nm (2,000 miles; 3,220 km)

DUMOD LINER

This aircraft (known originally as the Infinité II) is basically similar to the Dumod I, but the forward fuselage has been lengthened by 6 ft 3 in (1·90 m). making the Dumod Liner 8 ft 2½ in (2·50 m) longer than a standard Beechcraft 18. It can accommodate up to 15 persons.

The prototype conversion was completed in 1964. Since then, further changes have been made, and the current version has an additional centre tail-fin, with dorsal and ventral fins. Other improvements include a new recessed instrument panel and multi-disc wheel brakes. The standard 450 hp R-985 engines and three-blade fully-feathering Hartzell propellers are unchanged.

By mid-1966, one Dumod Liner had been delivered, to Empire State Airlines, and ten more had been ordered.

DIMENSIONS, EXTERNAL:
Wing span   47 ft 7 in (14·50 m)

Length overall	43 ft 5 in (13·23 m)	Max T-O weight	10,200 lb (4,625 kg)	Rate of climb at S/L, one engine out	
Height overall	9 ft 9 in (2·97 m)	Max landing weight	9,772 lb (4,432 kg)		185 ft (56 m)/min
Wheel track	19 ft 2 in (5·84 m)			Service ceiling	16,500 ft (5,030 m)
AREA:		PERFORMANCE (at max T-O weight):		Service ceiling, one engine out	9,500 ft (2,900 m)
Wings, gross	349 sq ft (32·42 m²)	Cruising speed (60% power) at 10,000 ft (3,050		T-O to 50 ft (15 m)	2,230 ft (680 m)
WEIGHTS:		m) 191 knots (220 mph; 354 km/h)		Landing run	2,520 ft (770 m)
Weight empty	6,400 lb (2,900 kg)	Stalling speed 66 knots (76 mph; 122 km/h)		Range with 202 US gallons (764 litres) fuel	
		Rate of climb at S/L 1,325 ft (405 m)/min			868 nm (1,000 miles; 1,600 km)

EAA

EXPERIMENTAL AIRCRAFT ASSOCIATION INC

ADDRESS:
PO Box 229, Hales Corners, Wisconsin 53130

PRESIDENT: Paul H. Poberezny

VICE-PRESIDENT: Ray Scholler

SECRETARY: S. H. Schmid

TREASURER: Art Kilps

As a service to its members, the EAA decided in 1955 to develop a modern single-seat sporting biplane suitable for home construction by amateurs. The design drawings were prepared by Mr J. D. Stewart and Mr T. Seely of the Allison Division, General Motors Corporation, with the assistance of Mr Paul H. Poberezny, President of the EAA.

EAA BIPLANE

The prototype of the EAA Biplane was built between 1957 and May 1960 as a class-room project by students of St Rita's High School, Chicago, under the supervision of Mr Robert Blacker. It flew for the first time on 10 June 1960. Flight tests showed the need for changes in the incidence of the upper wing and in the design of the tailplane to improve control and reduce vibration. After modification, flight testing was resumed on 26 November 1960.

Subsequently, a new metal propeller was fitted, the engine cooling was improved and a cockpit canopy was installed. The prototype was then taken over by the EAA, and further changes were made, including removal of the cockpit canopy, reduction in size of the cockpit opening, raising of the engine cowling, installation of a new turtle deck and headrest and fitting of a new instrument panel.

Mr Poberezny subsequently introduced further modifications, including lighter wing spars and fittings, which have reduced the empty weight of the aircraft, together with increases in the area of the tail surfaces and many other improvements. This modified version is known as the EAA Biplane Model P.

Over 6,250 sets of drawings of the EAA Biplane had been sold by February 1970 and many are flying and under construction.

The adjacent illustration shows an EAA Biplane built by Mr Paul Hanson of Albert Lea, Minnesota, and which is powered by an 85 hp Continental C85 engine.

The 1969/70 *Jane's* shows a version built by Mr Carlton H. Mann of Mineral Wells, Texas. Construction occupied 26 months and cost $1,900, and first flight was made on 7 June 1968. Modifications comprise a raised and widened forward fuselage, glass-fibre fuel tank, bungee-type trim system using an additional horn on the elevator in place of trim-tab, Y-duct on top of engine to

EAA Biplane (85 hp Continental C85 engine) built by Mr Paul Hanson of Albert Lea, Minnesota (*Jean Seele*)

improve cooling, recessed oil cooler box, adjustable rear N-strut, changed windshield and different tail construction and configuration. The cockpit is mahogany lined and a full electrical system and landing lights have been installed. Fabric is replaced by the "Poly-Fibre" type of covering developed by Stits Aircraft Corporation (which see).

Powered by a 125 hp Lycoming O-290-D engine, Mr Mann's aircraft has an empty weight of 824 lb (374 kg), max T-O weight of 1,200 lb (544 kg). max speed of 160 mph (257 kmh), cruising speed of 130 mph (209 kmh), landing speed of 70 mph (113 kmh), rate of climb of 1,000 ft (305 m) min, T-O run of 400 ft (122 m), landing run of 600 ft (183 m) and range with max fuel of 300 miles (483 km).

The following details apply to the standard EAA Biplane Model P:

TYPE: Single-seat sporting biplane.

WINGS: Braced biplane, with N-shape streamline-section cabane and interplane struts. Dihedral 0° on upper wing, 2° on lower wings. Incidence 2° on upper wing, 2° on lower wings. All-wood two-spar structure, with aluminium leading-edge and overall fabric covering. Ailerons of similar construction to wings, on lower wings only. No flaps.

FUSELAGE: Welded steel-tube structure, fabric-covered.

TAIL UNIT: Wire-braced welded steel-tube structure, fabric-covered.

LANDING GEAR: Non-retractable tail-wheel type, modified from standard Piper J3 components.

Rubber cord shock-absorption. Brakes on main wheels. Wheel fairings optional. Piper J3 steerable tail-wheel.

POWER PLANT: One 85 hp Continental C85-8 four-cylinder horizontally-opposed air-cooled engine, driving two-blade fixed-pitch propeller. Provision for fitting more powerful engines, including 125 hp Lycoming O-290-G. Piper J3 fuel tank aft of fire-wall in fuselage, capacity 18 US gallons (68 litres).

ACCOMMODATION: Single seat in open cockpit.

DIMENSIONS, EXTERNAL:
Wing span	20 ft 0 in (6·10 m)
Wing chord, both (constant)	3 ft 0 in (0·91 m)
Length overall	17 ft 0 in (5·18 m)
Height overall	6 ft 0 in (1·83 m)

AREA:
Wings, gross	108 sq ft (10·03 m²)

WEIGHTS (85 hp engine):
Weight empty	710 lb (322 kg)
Max T-O weight	1,150 lb (522 kg)

PERFORMANCE (85 hp engine, at max T-O weight):
Max level speed at S/L	109 knots (125 mph; 201 km/h)
Econ cruising speed	96 knots (110 mph; 177 km/h)
Stalling speed	44 knots (50 mph; 80 km/h)
Rate of climb at S/L	1,000 ft (305 m)/min
Service ceiling	11,500 ft (3,500 m)
T-O run	500 ft (152 m)
Landing run	800 ft (245 m)
Range with max fuel	304 nm (350 miles; 560 km)

EDO

EDO CORPORATION

HEAD OFFICE AND WORKS:
College Point, Long Island, New York 11356.
This company is a leading manufacturer of alighting gear for water-based aircraft, including not only floats, but high-performance components such as hydro-skis and hydrofoils.

Much of its development work on hydro-skis and hydrofoils is conducted under the sponsorship of the US Navy. This work, conducted over the past 20 years, has resulted in the establishment of a number of practical configurations of hydro-skis and hydrofoils for hulled seaplanes. Most recently, the Thurston Aircraft Corporation HRV-1 was equipped with an Edo-designed

hydrofoil. Currently, a survey of hydro-ski seaplane design technology is being conducted for the Office of Naval Research.

Aircraft floats now in production range in size from the types suitable for the Piper Super Cub to others large enough for the Beechcraft 18 series.

ELMENDORF

LEONARD C. ELMENDORF

ELMENDORF SPECIAL

Mr Leonard C. Elmendorf, a sheet-metal worker by trade, has designed and built an original single-seat biplane in a period of 8½ months, at a cost of about $5,000. The engine has been modified for inverted flight and a smoke generating system is installed. All available details follow:

TYPE: Single-seat sporting biplane.

WINGS: Single-bay biplane. Wings of equal span, with N-type interplane and centre-section struts. Lift and landing bracing wires. All wooden structures.

FUSELAGE: Welded steel-tube structure with fabric covering.

TAIL UNIT: Conventional braced tail unit of welded steel-tube construction, fabric covered.

LANDING GEAR: Non-retractable tail-wheel type. Wheel fairings on main units.

POWER PLANT: One 125 hp Lycoming O-290-G

Elmendorf Special single-seat homebuilt biplane (125 hp Lycoming O-290-G engine) (*Howard Levy*)

four-cylinder horizontally-opposed air-cooled engine, driving a two-blade fixed-pitch propeller.

ACCOMMODATION: Single seat for pilot in open cockpit.

DIMENSIONS, EXTERNAL:		
Wing span	20 ft 0 in (6·10 m)	
Length overall	16 ft 0 in (4·88 m)	
WEIGHT:		
Max T-O weight	1,250 lb (567 kg)	

PERFORMANCE (at max T-O weight):
Cruising speed	113 knots (131 mph; 210 km/h)
Landing speed	60 knots (69 mph; 111 km/h)
Max rate of climb at S/L	1,200 ft (365 m)/min
Range	260 nm (300 miles; 480 km)

ENSTROM

R. J. ENSTROM CORPORATION (Subsidiary of Purex Corporation Ltd, Pacific Airmotive Group)

HEAD OFFICE AND WORKS:
PO Box 349, Menominee County Airport, Menominee, Michigan 49858

SALES OFFICE:
PO Box 687, Reston, Virginia 22070

VICE-PRESIDENTS:
Paul L. Shultz (Engineering)
Andreas Aastad (Sales)

GENERAL MANAGER:
Martin Vale

This company was formed in 1959 to develop a light helicopter, designed and built by Rudy J. Enstrom. The experimental version flew for the first time on 12 November 1960. It was followed by two production prototypes, designated F-28, and this model was put into production. It was later followed in production by the improved F-28A, and a turbine-powered version, designated T-28, was to be introduced during 1970. Work on the turbocharged F-28B (see 1969-70 *Jane's*) had been suspended, pending availability of a more suitable engine.

During 1969 Anhembi Aviacao Ltd of Sao Paulo, Brazil, and G. M. Guevara and Sons Inc, in Manila, the Philippines, became distributors of Enstrom helicopters. A licence to manufacture the F-28A was being negotiated by Twyford Moors (Helicopters) Ltd of the UK (which see). The British-built version was to be known as the F-28A Solent.

In October 1968 Enstrom Corporation was acquired by the Purex Corporation Ltd, and was operated as a part of the Pacific Airmotive Aerospace Group. It is reported to have closed down all operations on 13 February 1970.

ENSTROM F-28A

The first experimental Enstrom helicopter had a simple uncovered steel-tube fuselage and two-blade main rotor. A change to a three-blade rotor was made on the F-28 production version, which has a fully-enclosed fuselage and tail-boom. A further change involves the use of a fully-articulated main rotor in place of the earlier rigid-in-plane type.

The first of the F-28 production prototypes flew on 27 May 1962, and the second on 15 May 1963. Enstrom obtained a Provisional Type Certificate for the F-28 on 14 November 1963 and production reached the rate of one per month in mid-1967.

The current production model, designated F-28A, is generally similar to the F-28, with the exception of a modified drive ratio, which turns the rotor more slowly and allows the engine to run at 205 hp at 2,900 rpm. This has increased the aircraft's useful load by 200 lb (91 kg). Improvements in visibility, accessibility and convenience are incorporated in this new model, of which deliveries began in April 1968, and FAA Type Certification for the F-28A was awarded on 28 May 1968. During 1969 production averaged three aircraft per month, and a total of 63 aircraft had been completed by January 1970.

The following details refer to the F-28A:

TYPE: Three-seat light helicopter.

ROTOR SYSTEM: Three-blade fully-articulated main rotor of bonded construction, each blade comprising an extruded aluminium spar and two heavy-gauge aluminium alloy skins. Weight and complexity of system reduced by mounting swashplate beneath gearbox, so that only small rocker arms on the hub are exposed to the airflow. Offset flapping hinges. Laminated elastomeric feathering axis bearing. Blade section NACA 00135. Blades do not fold. Two-blade teetering tail anti-torque rotor of bonded aluminium alloy construction. No rotor brake.

ROTOR DRIVE: Main rotor driven by single "Poly-V" belt from engine to ring and pinion reduction gear. Shaft-drive to tail rotor. Main rotor/engine rpm ratio 1 : 8·7879. Tail rotor/engine rpm ratio 1 : 1·2262.

FUSELAGE: Made in three basic sections: forward cabin, centre pylon and aft tail-cone. Welded steel-tube pylon structure carries the landing gear, engine, gear box and drive system. The cabin shell is of glass-fibre and sheet aluminium construction, and is an integral unit which can be removed easily from the airframe. The tail cone, attached to the centre pylon at three points, is a sheet aluminium alloy semi-monocoque structure, carrying the tail rotor system and a small fixed horizontal stabiliser at the tail end. A tubular steel tail rotor guard protects the tail assembly from damage in a tail-down landing.

Enstrom F-28A three-seat helicopter with float landing gear

LANDING GEAR: Aluminium and steel-tube skid type with oleo-pneumatic shock-absorbers and two small wheels for ground handling. The wheels may be retracted or removed for flight. Hard-surfaced skid shoes protect the skid tubes from abrasion and can be replaced when worn. Alternative float gear.

POWER PLANT: One 205 hp Lycoming HIO-360-C1B four-cylinder horizontally-opposed air-cooled engine. Fuel in two glass-fibre tanks, with total capacity of 30 US gallons (114 litres). Oil capacity 2 US gallons (7·5 litres).

ACCOMMODATION: Pilot and two passengers side-by-side on bench seat, with removable door on each side. Alternative seating for two, with dual control, in training role. Windshield and all windows of tinted Plexiglas. Poly-foam cabin insulation. Ventilation and heating systems. Fully-enclosed compartment for 60 lb (27 kg) baggage aft of engine bay available as an optional extra.

SYSTEMS: Electrical system supplied by 12V DC engine-driven generator; 24V DC system optional.

ELECTRONICS AND EQUIPMENT: Bendix RT221B-14 or King KY 95 360-channel VHF radio, and cargo hook available as optional items.

DIMENSIONS, EXTERNAL:
Diameter of main rotor	32 ft 0 in (9·75 m)
Diameter of tail rotor	4 ft 8 in (1·42 m)
Main rotor blade chord	9·5 in (24 cm)
Tail rotor blade chord	3·375 in (8·57 cm)
Length overall	29 ft 4 in (8·94 m)
Length of fuselage	28 ft 1 in (8·56 m)
Height overall	9 ft 0 in (2·74 m)
Skid track	7 ft 4 in (2·23 m)
Cabin doors (each):	
Height	4 ft 0 in (1·22 m)
Width	3 ft 1 in (0·94 m)
Height to sill	1 ft 8 in (0·51 m)

Baggage compartment door:
Height	1 ft 9 in (0·53 m)
Width	1 ft 5½ in (0·44 m)
Height to sill	2 ft 8 in (0·81 m)

DIMENSIONS, INTERNAL:
Cabin: Length	5 ft 0 in (1·52 m)
Max width	5 ft 4 in (1·63 m)
Max height	4 ft 2 in (1·27 m)
Volume	95 cu ft (2·70 m²)
Baggage compartment	7·0 cu ft (0·20 m²)

AREAS:
Main rotor disc	804 sq ft (74·7 m²)
Tail rotor disc	17·1 sq ft (1·59 m²)

WEIGHTS AND LOADINGS:
Weight empty	1,450 lb (657 kg)
Max T-O and landing weight	2,150 lb (975 kg)
Max disc loading	2·67 lb/sq ft (13·04 kg/m²)
Max power loading	10·5 lb/hp (4·76 kg/hp)

PERFORMANCE (at max T-O weight):
Max level speed at S/L	97 knots (112 mph; 180 km/h)
Max cruising speed (at 75% power)	87 knots (100 mph; 161 km/h)
Max rate of climb at S/L	1,050 ft (320 m)/min
Service ceiling	12,000 ft (3,650 m)
Hovering ceiling in ground effect	6,000 ft (1,825 m)
Hovering ceiling out of ground effect	3,400 ft (1,025 m)

ENSTROM T-28

Following flight tests of an F-28A fitted experimentally with a 240 shp Garrett AiResearch TSE 36-1 turboshaft engine, Enstrom decided to build a production version of this aircraft, under the designation T-28.

Development of the T-28 began in January 1968 and the prototype made its first flight four months later. The version that was intended to enter production in mid-1970 retains the basic airframe and main rotor system of the F-28A,

Enstrom T-28 three-seat light helicopter (240 shp Garrett-AiResearch TSE 36-1 turboshaft engine)

but has a larger diameter tail rotor to offset increased main rotor torque, a new transmission system, manufactured by the Buehler Corporation and certified for the increased power rating, and fuel capacity increased to 72 US gallons (273 litres).

A military version was under development early in 1970 to meet a requirement for a small turbine-powered training helicopter.

The description of the F-28A applies also to the T-28, except in the following details.

POWER PLANT: One 240 shp Garrett AiResearch TSE 36-1 turboshaft engine. Fuel in two glass-fibre tanks, with total capacity of 72 US gallons (273 litres). Oil capacity 1·5 US gallons (5·7 litres).

DIMENSIONS, EXTERNAL:
Tail rotor diameter	4 ft 8 in (1·42 m)

WEIGHTS:
Weight empty	1,300 lb (589 kg)
Max T-O weight	2,300 lb (1,043 kg)

PERFORMANCE:
Max permissible speed	112 knots (129 mph; 207 km/h)
Cruising speed	96 knots (110 mph; 177 km/h)
Max rate of climb at S/L	1,400 ft (427 m)/min
Service ceiling	15,000 ft (4,575 m)
Hovering ceiling in ground effect	10,400 ft (3,170 m)
Range	286 nm (330 miles; 531 km)
Max endurance	4 hr

EVANS

W. SAMUEL EVANS

ADDRESS: 645 Arenas Street, La Jolla, California

Mr W. S. Evans, a design engineer with the Convair division of General Dynamics Corporation, set out to design for the novice homebuilder an all-wood aircraft that would be easy to build and safe to fly. He was prepared to sacrifice both appearance and performance to achieve this aim. Two years of spare-time design and a year of construction have produced a strut-braced low-wing monoplane with an all-moving tail unit, powered by a 40 hp Volkswagen engine, which Mr Evans has called the Volksplane.

All available details follow:

EVANS VOLKSPLANE

TYPE: Single-seat homebuilt aircraft.

WINGS: Strut-braced low-wing monoplane. Two streamline-section bracing struts on each side. Wing section NACA 4412. Square tips. Dihedral 5°. Conventional wood structure with two rectangular spar beams, internal wooden compression struts and diagonal wire bracing, dispensing with the need for a complicated box spar. Fabric covering. Ailerons of wooden construction, fabric covered. No trim-tabs. No flaps.

FUSELAGE: Rectangular-section all-wood stressed-skin structure, consisting essentially of three bulkheads, four longerons and plywood skin. Stressed-skin design eliminates the need for any diagonal bracing. Glass-fibre fairing aft of pilot's seat.

TAIL UNIT: No fixed fin. The rudder is constructed of plywood ribs clamped to a 2-in (5·08-cm) aluminium tube which is mounted vertically through the rear fuselage and pivots in two nylon bushes. Leading- and trailing-edges are of wood and the whole unit is fabric covered. The fabric-covered all-moving tailplane is a wooden cantilever structure, comprising ply ribs blocked and glued to

Evans Volksplane single-seat homebuilt monoplane (40 hp Volkswagen engine) (*Howard Levy*)

a simple constant-section box spar. Both rudder and tailplane have anti-servo tabs.

LANDING GEAR: Non-retractable main wheels and tail skid. Main wheels carried on a bent section of heavy-gauge 24ST-3 aluminium bar, wire-braced by diagonal cables. Shock-absorption by low-pressure tyres. Main wheels and tyres size 6·00 × 6. Tyre pressure 12 lb/sq in (0·84 kg/cm²). Hydraulic brakes operated by single hand lever.

POWER PLANT: One 40 hp, 53 hp or 65 hp modified Volkswagen motor car engine, driving a Hegy two-blade propeller, diameter 4 ft 6 in (1·37 m), with pitch of 24 in for 40 hp engine, 30 in for 53 hp and 36 in for 65 hp. Glass-fibre fuel tank aft of firewall and integral with the forward fuselage cowlings, capacity 8 US gallons (30 litres). Filling point on top of fuselage, forward of windshield.

ACCOMMODATION: Single seat in open cockpit. No luggage stowage.

DIMENSIONS, EXTERNAL:
Wing span	24 ft 0 in (7·32 m)
Wing chord (constant)	4 ft 2 in (1·27 m)
Length overall	18 ft 0 in (5·49 m)
Height overall	5 ft 1½ in (1·56 m)
Tailplane span	7 ft 0 in (2·13 m)
Wheel track	4 ft 9 in (1·45 m)

AREAS:
Wings, gross	100 sq ft (9·29 m²)
Rudder	7·6 sq ft (0·71 m²)
Tailplane	15·0 sq ft (1·39 m²)

WEIGHTS:
Weight empty	440 lb (200 kg)
Max T-O weight	750 lb (340 kg)

PERFORMANCE (at T-O weight of 650 lb; 295 kg):
Max diving speed	104 knots (120 mph; 193 km/h)
Stalling speed	40 knots (46 mph; 74 km/h)
Rate of climb at S/L	400 ft (122 m)/min
T-O run (average breeze)	450 ft (137 m)
Landing run (average breeze)	200 ft (61 m)

FAIRCHILD HILLER

FAIRCHILD HILLER CORPORATION

EXECUTIVE OFFICE:
Germantown, Maryland 20767

CHAIRMAN OF THE BOARD:
Sherman M. Fairchild

PRESIDENT AND CHIEF EXECUTIVE OFFICER:
Edward G. Uhl

EXECUTIVE VICE-PRESIDENT:
Charles Collis

VICE-PRESIDENTS:
Ralph Bonafede
Stanley Demain
Paul R. Fitez
Coleman Raphael
John Stack
Thomas Turner
John F. Dealy
Norman Grossman
Don Strait
Earl R. Uhlig

TREASURER: Joseph H. Dugan

COMPTROLLER: Franklin M. Beall

SECRETARY: John L. Grabber

Aircraft Division
DIVISIONAL OFFICE AND WORKS:
Hagerstown, Maryland 21740
GENERAL MANAGER AND VICE-PRESIDENT: Ralph Bonafede

Aircraft Service Division
DIVISIONAL OFFICE AND WORKS:
St Augustine, Florida 32084
VICE-PRESIDENT AND ACTING GENERAL MANAGER:
C. Collis
CRESTVIEW, FLORIDA FACILITY, ACTING GENERAL MANAGER:
T. J. Vincent
ST. AUGUSTINE, FLORIDA FACILITY, GENERAL MANAGER:
H. Meltzer

ST. PETERSBURG, FLORIDA FACILITY, GENERAL MANAGER:
C. Stathis

Republic Aviation Division
DIVISIONAL OFFICE AND WORKS:
Farmingdale, Long Island, New York 11735
GENERAL MANAGER AND VICE PRESIDENT:
Donald J. Strait

Space and Electronics Systems Division
DIVISIONAL OFFICE AND WORKS:
Germantown, Maryland 20767
VICE-PRESIDENT AND GENERAL MANAGER:
Dr Coleman Raphael
Winston-Salem, North Carolina Facility
PLANT MANAGER: Charles K. Craggs

Fairchild Aircraft Marketing Company, Inc
Germantown, Maryland 20767
PRESIDENT:
George Attridge

Technical Services Division
DIVISIONAL OFFICE AND WORKS:
Riverdale, Maryland 20840
GENERAL MANAGER:
Bernard S. Tabish

Stratos Group
DIVISIONAL OFFICE AND WORKS:
Bay Shore, Long Island, New York 11706
VICE-PRESIDENT AND GENERAL MANAGER:
Stanley Demain

Stratos Bay Shore
Bay Shore, Long Island, New York 11706
GENERAL MANAGER:
Robert C. Iwans

Stratos—Western
Manhattan Beach, California 90266
GENERAL MANAGER:
Irwin D. Miller

Industrial Products
Winston-Salem, North Carolina 27107
GENERAL MANAGER:
Ralph Huston

Burns Aero Seat Company, Inc
Burbank, California 91502
PRESIDENT:
Jerry Goldress

S. J. Industries, Inc
Alexandria, Virginia 22304
PRESIDENT:
R. F. Julius

Primary work at the Fairchild Hiller Aircraft Division is production of FH-227 and F-27 twin-turboprop transport aircraft, under licence from Fokker of the Netherlands. The company also markets and provides support for the Fokker F.28 Fellowship in the USA. Final preparations for engineering and installation of a large cargo door on the F-27/FH-227 transports was a 1969 programme of this division.

Helicopter production in the Aircraft Division is concentrated on the five-seat turbine-powered FH-1100. The Division is also producing the Porter eight-seat STOL aircraft under licence from Pilatus of Switzerland.

Current government contract work at the Hagerstown facility includes the manufacture of pylons for F-105 aircraft and modification of C-119 and C-123 transport aircraft. Commercial subcontract work on the Boeing 707, 727, 737 and 747 production programmes continues and Fairchild Hiller have been awarded a $34·5 million contract by The Boeing Company to build the aft fuselage section and empennage for the Boeing SST, with the first sections for delivery late in 1971. In addition, subcontract work on the twin fin and rudder structures for the Grumman F-14A and wing structures for the Swearingen Metro transport is under way.

The Florida-based Aircraft Service Division is engaged on inspection, repair, overhaul and modification of a wide variety of aircraft, including the C-119G and C-119K gunships, the C-123 twin-engined transport, C-130 four-turboprop transport, KC-135 jet tanker, HU-16 air-sea rescue amphibian, McDonnell Douglas DC-9 jet transport, F-102 and F-105 tactical fighters.

Republic Aviation Division is responsible for design and manufacture of high-performance military aircraft and for the company's manned spacecraft activities. Production of its F-105 fighter-bomber was completed in 1964, but the Division continues to develop advanced systems for this aircraft to meet changing requirements, particularly in Vietnam.

To improve the capabilities of the F-105 a new automatic bombing system, known as the T-Stick II, has been developed and prototype testing is currently being carried out.

Republic Aviation Division manufactures under subcontract aft fuselages, fin and tail-cone assemblies, rudders, tailplanes and engine access doors for the F-4 Phantom II tactical fighter. Most of this work involves fabrication in titanium.

The Division is a participant in the Boeing 747 and supersonic transport programmes, the latter also involving the use of large quantities of titanium. Aft fuselage sections for the Grumman F-14A will be fabricated at Farmingdale.

The newly-formed Fairchild Aircraft Marketing Company, Inc, of Germantown, Maryland, is responsible for all sales of Fairchild Hiller commercial aircraft, including the Swearingen Metro (which see) for which more than 60 orders had been received by 28 January 1970.

The Space and Electronics Systems Division directs the company's efforts in the design, development and manufacture of missile and unmanned space projects and electronic systems. It is a major supplier of deployable/retractable tubular structures and their mechanisms of the kind used as antennae and gravity stabilisation booms for spacecraft. Its other programmes have included development of lightweight structures for use in the OGO, Imp, RAE, Tiros, OAO and Nimbus programmes.

The Division designed and manufactured the Space Support Unit (SSU) of the SERT II satellite successfully launched in February 1970, and now in orbit testing the feasibility of electric propulsion for future space travel. The SSU is its first major space programme since the highly successful Pegasus project. A major effort of the division during 1969 has been concerned with NASA's ATS F and G competition. This advanced communications satellite will be placed in stationary orbit 19,365 nm (22,300 miles; 35,890 km) above the equator and will deploy a 30-foot (9·14 m) diameter antenna to transmit and receive communications from a wide variety of ground terminals.

The Division is active in the design and manufacture of search and weather radar, and in intelligence data acquisition and management. Its auxiliary data annotation systems (ADAS) are in use in the RF-4, RF-101, P-3 and OV-IC aircraft. Its pioneering in reconnaissance photo interpretation has led to the Automatic Picture Transmission System (APTS), continuous enlargers, automatic film titlers, automatic film incinerators and code matrix readers. A stores management system developed by the Division will provide F-111D pilots with an inventory control and monitoring unit by integrating, on only two cockpit panels, the displays and controls of all the various weapons and stores.

The acquisition of S.J. Industries, a wholly-owned subsidiary, has strengthened considerably the facilities of the Space and Electronics Systems Division, as it is one of the few companies in the US that install solar cells on space vehicle panels.

The Stratos Group specialises in the development and manufacture of aerospace and industrial accessories and components such as compressors, heat exchangers, high-speed turbo machinery, air-conditioning equipment and high-temperature pneumatic valves and controls. Products for the US space programme include waste disposal locks for the Apollo manned space vehicles. The Division also manufactures cooling systems for military and executive jet aircraft.

Stratos Western manufactures intricate valves and regulators required for space vehicles. Current contracts include about 50 different components for the Saturn space booster. Self-sealing disconnects pioneered by the Division are used on the Lunar Module (LM). Commercial products to be manufactured will include lower lobe galley modules for Boeing 747's and McDonnell Douglas DC-10's. A newly-designed food and beverage dispensing system has been demonstrated successfully. Stratos Western is also a major producer of sonobuoy launch systems and underwater sound source dispensers for the US Navy's anti-submarine aircraft, and automatic flare launch/ejector systems and specialised flares for the USAF.

The Industrial Products Division, with its commercial line of gears and control valves, specialises in products for industrial machinery, including pressure regulators, pneumatic controls and multi-speed transmissions.

Burns Aero Seat Company, a wholly-owned subsidiary, is America's largest manufacturer of aircraft seats for airlines and custom seating for executive aircraft.

In addition to Burns Aero Seat Company and S. J. Industries, the company has the following subsidiaries: Fairchild Arms International, Ltd (Germantown, Maryland); Fairchild Aviation (Holland) NV (Amsterdam, Netherlands); and Fairchild Hiller-FRG Corporation (Munich, Germany).

FAIRCHILD HILLER F-27 and FH-227

Fairchild Hiller continues, to special order, limited production of the F-27 and FH-227 series of twin-turboprop airliners. Since the first production Fairchild F-27 flew on 15 April 1958, an extensive series of new models has been developed, and details of these are given below. The latest improvement, offered as a retrofit on all models, consists of a large cargo door in the forward fuselage, permitting easy operation in convertible cargo/passenger configuration.

F-27. Original Fairchild-built version with Rolls-Royce Dart RDa.6 Mk 511 engines and AUW of 35,700 lb (16,195 kg). Among subsequent modifications, the Mk 511-7E engine with increased hot day max cont power was certificated for the F-27. Production completed, but modernisation kits are available to utilise the increased power of the "wet boosted" Mk 514-7 engine, giving a maximum permissible AUW of 40,500 lb (18,370 kg). Received FAA Type Approval on 16 July 1958.

F-27A. Same as F-27 but fitted with more-powerful Dart RDa.7 engines. Original version of the engine was the Mk 528, which now carries an increase in hot day max cont power, as the Mk 528-7E. All currently certificated structural weight increases are applicable to the F-27A, with a maximum permissible AUW of 42,000 lb (19,050 kg). It can be supplied with RDa.6 engines for operators wishing to supplement existing fleets of the Model F-27. Received FAA Type Approval 31 December 1958.

F-27B. Basically the F-27 but with large cargo door forward of the wings, and convertible cargo and/or passenger interior. Max AUW limited currently to 38,500 lb (17,464 kg). Received FAA Type Approval 25 October 1958. Production completed, but modernisation kits based on Dart Mk 514-7 engine are available.

F-27F. Business transport version of F-27A. Utilises increased power of Dart RDa.7 Mk 529-7E to improve take-off performance and climb capability under emergency conditions. Capable of extremely long flights when optional extended-range fuel tankage is installed. Received FAA Type Approval 24 February 1961.

F-27J. Most recent version of F-27 for airline and business use. Utilises increased power of 2,250 eshp Dart RDa.7 Mk 532-7 engine. Max weights raised to 42,000 lb (19,050 kg) for T-O and 40,000 lb (18,145 kg) for landing. In production.

F-27M. Special high-altitude version of F-27, certified for airports with elevations up to 15,000 ft (4,575 m), using 2,250 eshp Dart RDa.7 Mk 532-7N engines. Max T-O and landing weights as for F-27J. In production.

FH-227. "Stretched" version of the F-27J, with a 6 ft longer fuselage, giving increased cabin space for additional passengers and freight, with second cargo section aft. 2,250 eshp Dart RDa.7 Mk 532-7 engines. Max weights raised to 43,500 lb (19,730 kg) for T-O and 43,000 lb (19,500 kg) for landing. Modernisation kits available to convert existing FH-227s to FH-227C or FH-227E standard.

FH-227B. Development of FH-227 with increased max operating speed and weights. Redesigned windshield, heavier wing skin and stringers, strengthened rear fuselage frames and heavy-duty landing gear. Dart RDa.7 Mk 532-7 engines, driving propellers of increased diameter. Max weights raised to 45,500 lb (20,640 kg) for T-O and 45,000 lb (20,410 kg) for landing. Accommodation for up to 56 passengers. First order, for 10, received from Piedmont Airlines in April 1966. FAA Certification received June 1967. Modification kit available to convert to FH-227D.

FH-227C. Modernisation of the FH-227, utilising propeller and performance improvements of the FH-227B, but retaining max T-O weight of 43,500 lb (19,730 kg) and max operating speed of the FH-227. Conversion kit available.

FH-227D. Latest development of 227 series. Improved anti-skid braking units, added intermediate flap position for T-O and 2,300 take-off power of Dart RDa.7 Mk 532-7L engines as applied to FH-227B. Certificated December 1967. In production.

FH-227E. Modernisation of the FH-227C, introducing the improvements of the FH-227D but retaining the structure of the FH-227C. Conversion kit available.

The following details refer to all the production models listed above.

TYPE: Twin-turboprop transport aircraft.

WINGS: Cantilever high-wing monoplane. Wing section NACA 64-421 (modified) at root, NACA 64-415 (modified) at tip. Dihedral 0° on centre-section, 2° 30′ on outer wings. Incidence 3° 28′ at root. Torsion-cell fail-safe structure of two spars, stressed skin and stringers. Centre-section integral with fuselage. Outer wings have detachable tips. Main torsion box structure partially bonded, partially riveted. Leading-

Fairchild Hiller FH-227B twin turboprop transport aircraft (two 2,250 eshp Rolls-Royce Dart Mk 532-7 turboprop engines)

edges of metal honeycomb construction with Goodrich pneumatic de-icer boots. Trailing-edge of reinforced glass-fibre skin, with glass-fibre and metal ribs, riveted to rear spar. Manually-operated metal ailerons with glass-fibre leading-edge. All-metal single-slotted flaps in two interconnected sections on each wing, divided by nacelles. Spring tab (inboard) and trim tab (outboard) in each aileron.

FUSELAGE: All-metal semi-monocoque fail-safe structure except for glass-fibre nose cap.

TAIL UNIT: Cantilever all-metal structure, except for glass-fibre leading-edge on control surfaces. Fixed-incidence tailplane. Manually-operated control surfaces. Trim-tab in port elevator. Balance tab (lower) and trim-tab (upper) in rudder. Goodrich pneumatic de-icer boots on leading-edge of fin and tailplane.

LANDING GEAR: Pneumatically-retractable tri-cycle type with twin-wheel main units and single pneumatically-steerable nose-wheel. Nose unit retracts forward, main units rearward into engine nacelles. Main gear is certificated for use as an air-brake. Dowty-Rotol oleo-pneumatic shock-absorbers. Goodyear main wheels and 9·50 × 16 12-ply tyres, pressure 93 lb/sq in (6·54 kg/cm²) on F-27 series; 99 lb/sq in (6·96 kg/cm²) on FH-227, FH-227C and FH-227E; and 107 lb/sq in (7·52 kg/cm²) on FH-227B and FH-227D. Goodyear nose-wheel and 8·50 × 10 10-ply tyre, pressure 64 lb/sq in (4·50 kg/cm²) on F-27 series; 65 lb/sq in (4·57 kg/cm²) on FH-227, FH-227C and FH-227E; and 70 lb/sq in (4·92 kg/cm²) on FH-227B and FH-227D. Goodyear pneumatic brakes with Westinghouse and/or Dunlop anti-skid system on all models except FH-227D and FH-227E which use a Goodyear fully-modulated electronic anti-skid system.

POWER PLANT: Two Rolls-Royce Dart turboprop engines (details under "Series" descriptions), each driving a Rotol four-blade fully-feathering constant-speed propeller, diameter 12 ft 0 in (3·66 m) on F-27 and F-27B or 11 ft 6 in (3·50 m) on F-27A, F-27F, F-27J, F-27M and FH-227, or 12 ft 6 in (3·81 m) on FH-227B, FH-227C, FH-227D and FH-227E. Standard tankage on F-27 and FH-227 series comprises one integral tank in each outer wing, with combined usable capacity of 1,336 US gallons (5,054 litres), and nacelle collector tanks with total usable capacity of 28 US gallons (106 litres), giving overall total of 1,364 US gallons (5,160 litres). Optional extended-range tanks consist of (a) centre-wing bladder cells with total extra usable capacity of 699 US gallons (2,650 litres) or (b) these centre-wing tanks plus two outer wing bladder cells, giving extra usable capacity of 1,004 US gallons (3,800 litres). Centre-wing tanks are standard on F-27F, which has total standard usable capacity of 2,063 US gallons (7,810 litres). Pressure refuelling points in nacelle wheel wells; (single point fuel and water/methanol pressure refuelling system in FH-227 series). Gravity fuelling points in top surface of outer wings. Oil capacity 3·98 US gallons (15 litres).

ACCOMMODATION: Pilot and co-pilot on flight deck, plus stewardess in all models. Seats for 40-44 passengers in F-27; 40-48 in F-27A and F-27M; 20-48 in convertible interior of F-27B; 10-40, dependent on customers requirements, in F-27F; 44-52 in FH-227 series. Airliner versions have seats four-abreast, in pairs on each side of centre aisle. Forward of main cabin is compartment for heavy baggage and freight, with upward-sliding plug-type service door on port side. Aft of cabin is rear compartment, with carry-on baggage space, and, in FH-227 series with standard interior arrangement, an additional cargo compartment with plug-type door on starboard side, sliding forward. The pneumatically-operated airstairs, on port side of fuselage, open into rear compartment. Galley and/or toilet can be located in either forward or aft compartment. F-27B has large electrically actuated cargo door, with integral crew entry door, in place of forward service door. A similar large cargo door is now available as a retrofit kit for all models.

SYSTEMS: Pressurisation system supplied by Godfrey Roots blower on each engine. Stratos air cycle and vapour-cycle cooling systems. Janitrol 150,000 BTU/hr combustion heater and AiResearch choke valve heating systems. Pressure differential 5·46 lb/sq in (0·38 kg/cm²). No hydraulic system. Pneumatic system, pressure 3,300 lb/sq in (232 kg/cm²), operates landing gear, airstairs, nose-wheel steering, brakes, and propeller brakes. Additional emergency system for landing gear and brakes. Power for primary electrical system provided by 24-28V DC single-wire negative ground system. In secondary system, power is provided by a 115V 400 c/s AC constant-frequency single-phase system. Instrument power supply is provided by a 26V and a 115V 400 c/s AC three-phase system. De-icing equipment power supply provided by 208V three-phase AC

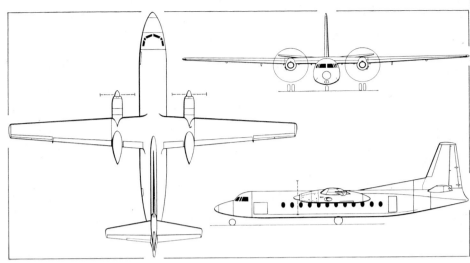

Fairchild Hiller FH-227 long-fuselage development of the F-27/Friendship series

system. Gas-turbine APU drives 28V 500A or 750A DC generator and can be used for ground and air operation of aircraft systems.

ELECTRONICS AND EQUIPMENT: Blind-flying instrumentation standard on all models. Other installed equipment on F-27, F-27A, F-27B and F-27F includes Collins VOR, VHF transmitter and VHF receiver, Bendix intercom and Sperry Gyrosyn compass, the VOR and VHF equipment being supplied on a loan basis, to be returned in operating condition. There are space and structural provisions for two glide-slope receivers, two ADF, HF, DMET, marker beacon and 18 in weather radar. A high-pressure oxygen system is installed for the pilot and co-pilot, with one or three portable oxygen bottles for passengers. Provision for Safe-Flight stall warning indicator.

DIMENSIONS, EXTERNAL:

Wing span	95 ft 2 in (29·0 m)
Wing chord at root	11 ft 4½ in (3·45 m)
Wing chord at tip	4 ft 7 in (1·40 m)
Wing aspect ratio	12·0
Length overall:	
F-27 series	77 ft 2 in (23·50 m)
FH-227 series	83 ft 8 in (25·50 m)
Height over tail:	
F-27 series	27 ft 6 in (8·40 m)
FH-227 series	27 ft 7 in (8·41 m)
Tailplane span	32 ft 0 in (9·75 m)
Wheel track	23 ft 7½ in (7·20 m)
Wheelbase:	
F-27 series	28 ft 8 in (8·73 m)
FH-227 series	34 ft 6¼ in (10·53 m)
Passenger door (port, aft):	
Height	5 ft 5 in (1·65 m)
Width	2 ft 5 in (0·74 m)
Height to sill:	
F-27 series	3 ft 11 in (1·19 m)
FH-227 series	4 ft 0 in (1·22 m)
Service door (port, fwd):	
Height	3 ft 11 in (1·19 m)
Width	3 ft 5 in (1·04 m)
Height to sill:	
F-27 series	3 ft 7 in (1·09 m)
FH-227 series	3 ft 6 in (1·07 m)
Service door (FH-227 series, stbd, aft):	
Height	4 ft 1 in (1·24 m)
Width	2 ft 5 in (0·74 m)
Height to sill	4 ft 0 in (1·22 m)
Cargo door (F-27B, port, fwd):	
Height	7 ft 7½ in (2·32 m)
Width	5 ft 11 in (1·80 m)

DIMENSIONS, INTERNAL:
Cabin, excluding flight deck, including baggage compartments, toilet and galley:

Length:	
F-27 series	47 ft 4 in (14·43 m)
FH-227 series	53 ft 3 in (16·32 m)
Max width	8 ft 4 in (2·54 m)
Max height	6 ft 8 in (2·03 m)
Floor area:	
F-27 series	304·1 sq ft (28·25 m²)
FH-227 series	344·8 sq ft (32·03 m²)
Volume:	
F-27 series	2,000 cu ft (56·63 m³)
FH-227 series	2,260 cu ft (63·99 m³)
Freight hold (fwd):	
F-27 series (except F-27B)	200 cu ft (5·66 m³)
F-27B	variable up to 2,000 cu ft (56·63 m³)
FH-227 series	variable up to 2,260 cu ft (63·99 m³)

AREAS:

Wings, gross	754 sq ft (70·0 m²)
Ailerons (total)	75·20 sq ft (6·98 m²)
Trailing-edge flaps (total)	136·90 sq ft (12·72 m²)
Fin, including dorsal fin	189·40 sq ft (17·60 m²)
Rudder, including tabs	33·40 sq ft (3·10 m²)
Tailplane	172·00 sq ft (16·00 m²)
Elevators, including tab	34·10 sq ft (3·17 m²)

WEIGHTS AND LOADINGS:
Weight empty (excludes interior fittings and avionics):

F-27	20,664 lb (9,373 kg)
F-27A, F	21,353 lb (9,685 kg)
F-27B	20,927 lb (9,492 kg)
F-27J, M	21,400 lb (9,707 kg)
FH-227	22,736 lb (10,313 kg)
FH-227B	23,200 lb (10,523 kg)
FH-227C	22,736 lb (10,313 kg)
FH-227D	23,261 lb (10,551 kg)
FH-227E	22,923 lb (10,398 kg)
Max payload (approx, depending upon configuration):	
F-27J	11,000 lb (4,990 kg)
FH-227, 227C, 227E	11,200 lb (5,080 kg)
FH-227B, 227D	12,600 lb (5,715 kg)
Max T-O weight:	
F-27	40,500 lb (18,370 kg)
F-27A, F, J, M	42,000 lb (19,050 kg)
F-27B	38,500 lb (17,464 kg)
FH-227, 227C, 227E	43,500 lb (19,730 kg)
FH-227B, 227D	45,500 lb (20,640 kg)
Max zero-fuel weight:	
F-27 series	36,300 lb (16,465 kg)
FH-227, 227C, 227E	39,000 lb (17,690 kg)
FH-227B, 227D	41,000 lb (18,600 kg)
Max landing weight:	
F-27, A, F, J, M	40,000 lb (18,145 kg)
F-27B	36,700 lb (16,647 kg)
FH-227, 227C, 227E	43,000 lb (19,500 kg)
FH-227B, 227D	45,000 lb (20,410 kg)
Max wing loading:	
F-27	53·71 lb/sq ft (262·2 kg/m²)
F-27A, F, J, M	55·70 lb/sq ft (272 kg/m²)
F-27B	51·06 lb/sq ft (249·3 kg/m²)
FH-227, 227C, 227E	57·69 lb/sq ft (281·7 kg/m²)
FH-227B, 227D	60·34 lb/sq ft (294·6 kg/m²)
Max power loading:	
F-27	12·06 lb/eshp (5·41 kg/eshp)
F-27A	9·98 lb/eshp (4·53 kg/eshp)
F-27B	10·32 lb/eshp (4·68 kg/eshp)
F-27F	9·61 lb/eshp (4·36 kg/eshp)
F-27J, M	9·33 lb/eshp (4·23 kg/eshp)
FH-227, 227C	9·67 lb/eshp (4·38 kg/eshp)
FH-227B	10·11 lb/eshp (4·59 kg/eshp)
FH-227D	9·89 lb/eshp (4·49 kg/eshp)
FH-227E	9·46 lb/eshp (4·29 kg/eshp)

PERFORMANCE (at demonstration AUW of 34,000 lb = 15,420 kg):

Max level speed:

F-27, F-27B	249 knots (287 mph; 462 km/h)
F-27A	263 knots (303 mph; 488 km/h)
F-27F	281 knots (324 mph; 521 km/h)

Max permissible speed in dive (all speeds EAS):
F-27, FH-227, 227C, 227E
   287 knots (331 mph; 532 km/h) = Mach 0·616
FH-227B, 227D
   307 knots (354 mph; 570 km/h)

Max cruising speed at 20,000 ft (6,100 m):

F-27, F-27B	237 knots (273 mph; 439 km/h)
F-27A, F	261 knots (300 mph; 483 km/h)

Max cruising speed at 15,000 ft (4,570 m):

F-27J, M	258 knots (297 mph; 478 km/h)
FH-227 series	255 knots (294 mph; 473 km/h)

Econ cruising speed at 25,000 ft (7,620 m):

F-27, F-27B	224 knots (258 mph; 415 km/h)
F-27A, F	232 knots (267 mph; 430 km/h)
F-27J, M	234 knots (270 mph; 435 km/h)
FH-227 series	234 knots (270 mph; 435 km/h)

Stalling speed, flaps up, at max landing weight:

F-27, A, F, J, M	93 knots (106·4 mph; 172 km/h)
F-27B	89 knots (102·1 mph; 165 km/h)
FH-227, 227C, 227E	97 knots (110·7 mph; 179 km/h)
FH-227B, 227D	99 knots (113·4 mph; 183 km/h)

Stalling speed, flaps down, at max landing weight:

F-27, A, F, J, M	73 knots (84·0 mph; 135·5 km/h)
F-27B	70 knots (80·6 mph; 130·0 km/h)
FH-227, 227C, 227E	76 knots (87·3 mph; 140·5 km/h)
FH-227B, 227D	78 knots (89·4 mph; 144·0 km/h)

Rate of climb at S/L:

F-27A	2,200 ft (670 m)/min
F-27F	2,380 ft (725 m)/min
F-27J	1,580 ft (482 m)/min
FH-227	1,560 ft (475 m)/min

Rate of climb at S/L, one engine out:

F-27A	635 ft (194 m)/min
F-27F	690 ft (210 m)/min

Service ceiling:

All models	28,000 ft (8,535 m)

FAA en-route ceiling, one engine out at max AUW:

F-27	4,000 ft (1,220 m)
F-27A	6,400 ft (1,950 m)
F-27B	6,000 ft (1,830 m)
F-27J, M	6,400 ft (1,950 m)
FH-227	6,000 ft (1,830 m)
FH-227B	5,700 ft (1,740 m)
FH-227C	7,800 ft (2,380 m)
FH-227D	5,700 ft (1,740 m)
FH-227E	7,800 ft (2,380 m)

FAA T-O field length, at max AUW:

F-27	5,600 ft (1,707 m)
F-27A	5,740 ft (1,750 m)
F-27B	4,900 ft (1,494 m)
F-27F	5,400 ft (1,646 m)
F-27J, M	5,180 ft (1,579 m)
FH-227	5,530 ft (1,686 m)
FH-227B	5,730 ft (1,747 m)
FH-227C	4,400 ft (1,341 m)
FH-227D	4,630 ft (1,411 m)
FH-227E	3,950 ft (1,204 m)

FAA landing field length, at max landing weight:

F-27 series (except F-27B)	3,775 ft (1,151 m)
F-27B	3,580 ft (1,091 m)
FH-227, 227C, 227E	4,100 ft (1,250 m)
FH-227B, 227D	4,360 ft (1,329 m)

Range with max fuel, 45 min reserve at 10,000 ft (3,050 m):

F-27 with 6,411 lb (2,908 kg) payload	1,568 nm (1,806 miles; 2,906 km)
F-27A	1,580 nm (1,820 miles; 2,930 km)
F-27B with 4,436 lb (2,012 kg) payload	1,629 nm (1,876 miles; 3,020 km)
F-27F*	2,448 nm (2,820 miles; 4,535 km)
F-27J*	2,431 nm (2,800 miles; 4,505 km)
FH-227	1,402 nm (1,615 miles; 2,595 km)
FH-227B, 227D	1,372 nm (1,580 miles; 2,540 km)
FH-227C, 227E	1,437 nm (1,655 miles; 2,660 km)

*with optional long-range fuel tankage

Range with max payload, 45 min reserve, at 10,000 ft (3,050 m):

F-27	297 nm (343 miles; 552 km)
F-27A, F	792 nm (912 miles; 1,468 km)
F-27B	155 nm (179 miles; 288 km)
F-27J	790 nm (910 miles; 1,465 km)
FH-227	533 nm (614 miles; 988 km)
FH-227B, 227D	526 nm (606 miles; 975 km)
FH-227C, 227E	569 nm (656 miles; 1,055 km)

FAIRCHILD HILLER/PILATUS PORTER AND ARMED PORTER

Fairchild Hiller is producing an initial series of 100 Pilatus Turbo-Porters, under licence from Pilatus Flugzeugwerke AG of Switzerland. These aircraft, known as Porters, are available with a 575 shp AiResearch TPE331-25D(A) or -25D(B), a 550 shp Pratt & Whitney (UACL) PT6A-20, or a 680 shp Pratt & Whitney (UACL) PT6A-29 (flat rated to 550 shp) turboprop engine. Flat rating is adopted on the latter engine in order to obtain improved hot-day and/or high-altitude performance. For further details see the "Pilatus" entry.

The first production Fairchild Hiller Porter (with PT6A-20 engine) was rolled out on 3 June 1966.

Intermountain Aviation Inc, of Marana, Arizona, include three Porters in their fleet of 16 aircraft and these are used to carry smoke-jumpers of the Forest Service of the US Department of Agriculture, on a dawn-to-dusk call basis.

An Armed Porter has been developed for counter-insurgency operations, including transport, light armed and photographic-reconnaissance, leaflet dropping and loudspeaker broadcasting. This version has an under-fuselage hard-point capable of carrying a 590 lb (268 kg) store, and four underwing hard-points, of which the inboard pair can carry 510 lb (231 kg) each, and the outboard pair 350 lb (159 kg) each. However, total external load on each wing may not exceed 700 lb (318 kg).

Powered by the TPE 331-25D engine, the Armed Porter has a complete military nav/com system, including VHF, UHF, HF and FM electronics, an armament control system, Navy Mk 20 Mod 4 gunsight, dual throttles, additional

Armed Porter version of the Fairchild Hiller/Pilatus Porter

Fairchild Hiller/Pilatus PC-6/B1-H2 Porter of Alaska Air Guides, Inc, with wheel-ski landing gear
(Norman E. Taylor)

windows at floor level and above the cockpit, and low-pressure tyres for rough-field operation.

Alternative installations include two MXU-A70/A side-firing Miniguns, with 2,000-round magazines, in the main cabin; SUU-11A/A Minigun pods on the inner underwing attachments and LAU-32B/A rocket pods (each 7 × 2·75-in rockets) or 250-lb general-purpose bombs on the outer wing attachments; M19-19A6 machine-guns on fixed side-firing mounts; pintle-mounted GAU-ZB/A Minigun with belt feed; an AEM-SYS-ZA 1,400-Watt 20-speaker broadcasting pod on an inner wing hard-point; a pod containing three P-2 70-mm cameras, and universal 5-in store dispensers each carrying eight flares of two million candlepower.

FAIRCHILD HILLER MODEL FH-1100

The FH-1100 is a refined development of the OH-5A helicopter which Hiller designed for the US Army's LOH (light observation helicopter) competition.

Design of the OH-5A was started on 13 November 1961. Construction began in May 1962 and the first prototype flew on 26 January 1963. FAA certification was received on 20 July 1964. The decision to put the FH-1100 into immediate production was announced in February 1965 and the first production model was rolled out on 3 June 1966. An initial series of 250 is being built.

The FH-1100 is suitable for a wide range of civil and military duties and one of the OH-5A's was used for a series of trials at sea, from a helicopter platform on the USS *Bausell*, in April 1965, to demonstrate the anti-submarine weapons-delivery potential of the FH-1100 to representatives of the Royal Netherlands Navy. Sixteen have been ordered for the Thailand Royal Border Police, and on 14 December 1967 the company announced an order for 30 FH-1100s from Okanagan Helicopters Ltd, of Vancouver, Canada, for delivery extending into 1969. This represented the largest number of helicopters ordered at one time by a commercial operator.

An ambulance version, test-flown in 1968, carries a pilot, two stretcher patients and attendant.

Fairchild Hiller announced in March 1969 that they had developed a reverse scoop inlet for the FH-1100, to permit operation in snow conditions. At the same time they introduced an automatic engine re-ignition system that re-lights the engine automatically immediately after a flame-out. This system utilises loss of engine torque to indicate flame-out. Both systems are in production in kit form at the company's Aircraft Division at Hagerstown, Maryland, and may be fitted retrospectively; they were incorporated as standard equipment on production aircraft in 1969.

TYPE: Turbine-powered five-seat utility helicopter.

ROTOR SYSTEM: Two-blade semi-rigid main rotor of all-metal construction, with each blade attached to hub by single main retention bolt and drag strut. Each blade has a rolled stainless steel leading-edge spar bonded to an aluminium-covered honeycomb trailing section. Two-blade tail rotor of bonded aluminium sheet. Main rotor blades fold. Rotor brake kit available.

ROTOR DRIVE: Mechanical drive through single-stage bevel and two-stage planetary main transmission, with intermediate tail rotor gearbox and tail rotor gearbox. Main rotor/engine rpm ratio 1 : 16·30. Tail rotor/engine rpm ratio 1 : 2·75.

FUSELAGE: Aluminium alloy semi-monocoque structure of pod-and-boom type. Rearward-sliding aluminium alloy engine cowling.

TAIL UNIT: Vertical fin of aluminium-covered honeycomb. Horizontal stabiliser of glass-fibre-covered honeycomb.

LANDING GEAR: Skid type with torsion-tube suspension. Skids foldable for stowage. Two removable ground handling wheels. Certificated for operation from water on quick-attach inflatable floats produced by Garrett's Air Cruisers Division.

POWER PLANT: One 317 shp Allison 250-C18 shaft-turbine engine, derated to 274 shp for take-off and a maximum continuous rating of 233 shp. Single bladder fuel tank in bottom of centre fuselage, capacity 69 US gallons (261 litres). Refuelling point on starboard side of rear fuselage. Oil capacity 2·75 US quarts (2·6 litres) in engine, 2·75 US quarts (2·6 litres) in transmission.

ACCOMMODATION: Pilot and passenger side-by-side in front. Rear seats for three passengers in standard utility model. Four-seat executive layout available. Rear seats fold to provide flush cargo deck. Four forward-hinged doors, two on each side of cabin. Ambulance version carries two stretcher patients and attendant, and has aft-hinged rear door on port side to provide double-door width opening for easy loading. Baggage compartment under engine deck, capacity 150 lb (68 kg), with door on starboard side.

ELECTRONICS AND EQUIPMENT: Radio optional.

SYSTEMS: Dual hydraulic systems, pressure 900 lb/sq in (63·3 kg/cm²), for cyclic and collective pitch controls. Boost cylinders manufactured by Conair Inc. 28V electrical system, with 100A starter/generator and 24Ah battery. Hamilton-Standard stability augmentation system to maintain automatically aircraft attitude in pitch and roll.

ARMAMENT: Provision for wide range of weapons, including anti-submarine weapons, or two weapon packs each containing two 7·62-mm machine-guns with 300 rpg or two grenade launchers, or one of each, mounted on each side of cabin.

DIMENSIONS, EXTERNAL:

Diameter of main rotor	35 ft 4¾ in (10·79 m)
Diameter of tail rotor	6 ft 0 in (1·83 m)
Length overall, rotors fore and aft	
	39 ft 9½ in (12·13 m)
Length of fuselage	29 ft 9½ in (9·08 m)
Width of fuselage	4 ft 4 in (1·32 m)
Height overall	9 ft 3⅓ in (2·83 m)
Skid track	7 ft 2¼ in (2·20 m)

DIMENSIONS, INTERNAL:

Cabin: Length	7 ft 8½ in (2·35 m)
Max width	4 ft 3⅓ in (1·31 m)
Max height	4 ft 7 in (1·40 m)

AREAS:

Main rotor blade (each)	15·08 sq ft (1·40 m²)
Tail rotor blade (each)	1·02 sq ft (0·095 m²)
Main rotor disc	981 sq ft (91·14 m²)
Tail rotor disc	28·27 sq ft (2·63 m²)

WEIGHTS AND LOADING:

Weight empty	1,396 lb (633 kg)
Max T-O weight	2,750 lb (1,247 kg)
Max disc loading	2·80 lb/sq ft (13·7 kg/m²)

PERFORMANCE (at max T-O weight):

Max cruising speed at 5,000 ft (1,525 m)
110 knots (127 mph; 204 km/h)
Econ cruising speed
106 knots (122 mph; 196 km/h)
Max rate of climb at S/L 1,600 ft (488 m)/min
Vertical rate of climb at S/L 800 ft (244 m)/min
Service ceiling 14,200 ft (4,325 m)
Hovering ceiling in ground effect
13,400 ft (4,085 m)
Hovering ceiling out of ground effect
8,400 ft (2,560 m)
Range with standard fuel and max payload at S/L, no reserve 302 nm (348 miles; 560 km)

FAIRCHILD HILLER M473
USAF designation: C-123K

To meet a USAF requirement, Fairchild Hiller has developed a modification scheme to increase the payload capacity of the C-123B Provider tactical transport aircraft and to improve its take-off performance.

Starting in May 1962, under USAF contract, the prototype YC-123H (built originally in 1957, and having a wider-track landing gear than the production C-123B) was fitted with two auxiliary engines in underwing pods, supported by pylons. A drag parachute system was also installed to provide a steeper approach angle for landing on short tree-lined airstrips. This version flew for the first time on 30 July 1962.

In 1966 Fairchild Hiller was awarded a USAF contract to modify 183 C-123B aircraft to the auxiliary jet configuration. Design of the modification began in February 1966. Basically, it involved the addition of two pylon-mounted General Electric J85-GE-17 auxiliary turbojet engines (each 2,850 lb = 1,293 kg st) in low-drag nacelles with integral intake doors, outboard of the standard piston-engines. New Goodyear high-capacity wheels, brakes and anti-skid units, and a new stall warning system were installed.

Commercial version of the Fairchild Hiller FH-1100 five-seat utility helicopter

The first modified aircraft, redesignated C-123K, flew on 27 May 1966. The last of the 183 aircraft which were modified was delivered in September 1969.

Since 1962 C-123's have been the principal USAF intra-theatre transport aircraft in South Vietnam. Several squadrons equipped with C-123K's are currently operating there, performing many special missions in addition to regular transport duties. These include insect spraying, delivery of rubberised nylon bladders filled with bulk fuel and air-drop of troops, ammunition and livestock.

Details of the standard C-123B last appeared in the 1958-59 *Jane's*.

WEIGHTS:

Weight empty	35,366 lb (16,042 kg)
Basic operating weight	36,576 lb (16,590 kg)
Max payload	15,000 lb (6,800 kg)
Max T-O weight	60,000 lb (27,215 kg)
Max landing weight	60,000 lb (27,215 kg)

PERFORMANCE (at max T-O weight):

Max level speed at 10,000 ft (3,050 m)
198 knots (228 mph; 367 km/h)
Max cruising speed at 10,000 ft (3,050 m)
150 knots (173 mph; 278 km/h)
Stalling speed, wheels and flaps down
83 knots (95 mph; 152 km/h)
Rate of climb at S/L, one engine out
1,220 ft (372 m)/min
Service ceiling, one engine out
21,100 ft (6,430 m)

T-O run	1,167 ft (356 m)
T-O to 50 ft (15 m)	1,809 ft (551 m)
Landing from 50 ft (15 m)	1,800 ft (549 m)

FAIRCHILD HILLER M484
USAF designation: C-119K

Fairchild Hiller modified a C-119 military transport to YC-119K standard, by adding two pylon-mounted auxiliary turbojets and installing a more powerful version of the existing piston-engines. Design of the conversion was started in May 1966 and the prototype aircraft flew for the first time in February 1967.

The YC-119K is powered by two 3,700 hp (wet) Wright R-3350-999 TC18EA2 engines and two General Electric J85-GE-17 auxiliary turbojets, each rated at 2,850 lb (1,293 kg) st.

Fairchild Hiller announced on 26 February 1970 that they had received a contract from the USAF to modify five C-119G aircraft to the C-119K configuration, including inspection and repair, and installation of anti-skid braking units.

Details of the standard C-119 last appeared in the 1957-58 *Jane's*.

WEIGHTS:

Weight empty	44,747 lb (20,300 kg)
Basic operating weight	45,435 lb (20,610 kg)
Max payload	20,000 lb (9,070 kg)
Max T-O weight	77,000 lb (34,925 kg)
Max landing weight	77,000 lb (34,925 kg)

PERFORMANCE (at max T-O weight):

Max level speed at 10,000 ft (3,050 m)
211 knots (243 mph; 391 km/h)

Fairchild Hiller C-123K Provider, a conversion of the C-123B with General Electric J85-GE-17 auxiliary turbojet engines (*Denis Hughes*)

Fairchild Hiller AC-119K Gunship, an armed conversion of the C-119 transport aircraft

Max cruising speed at 10,000 ft (3,050 m)
162 knots (187 mph; 300 km/h)
Stalling speed, wheels and flaps down
98 knots (112 mph; 180 km/h)
Rate of climb at S/L, one engine out
1,050 ft (320 m)/min
Service ceiling, one engine out
18,100 ft (5,515 m)
T-O run 1,501 ft (458 m)
T-O to 50 ft (15 m) 2,100 ft (640 m)
Landing from 50 ft (15 m) 3,200 ft (975 m)
Ferry range with four 500 US gal (1,890 litre)
Benson tanks
3,004 nm (3,460 miles; 5,570 km)
Range with max payload
859 nm (990 miles; 1,595 km)

FAIRCHILD HILLER AC-119 GUNSHIP
USAF designations: AC-119G and AC-119K

To meet an Air Force requirement, Fairchild Hiller's Aircraft Service Division has modified 52 C-119 aircraft into gunships, with the designations AC-119G and AC-119K. Both models are now operating in Vietnam where the concept of arming large transport aircraft for interdiction and suppression of enemy ground attack has proved very effective. Such gunships have the advantage of long endurance and an ability to carry a large load of equipment, sensors, guns and ammunition needed to locate and attack enemy material and personnel.

The first series of 26 AC-119G aircraft retain two Wright R-3350-89B engines and are fitted with four side-firing 7·62-mm General Electric Miniguns, a pallet-mounted airborne illuminator light set housed in the rear fuselage on the port side, with a LAU 74/A flare launcher on the starboard side. A light-intensifying night observation system is carried on the port side of the fuselage, forward of the wing, and other equipment includes a 60-kVA auxiliary power unit, pilot's gunsight, analogue gunfire control computer system and protective armour for the crew.

The second series of 26 AC-119K's have all the equipment of the AC-119G's, plus two General Electric J-85 auxiliary jet engines each rated at 2,850 lb (1,293 kg) st to improve performance, reduce take-off run and increase payload. Additional equipment includes a forward-looking infra-red sensor, side- and forward-looking radar and more nav/com. Armament is strengthened by the addition of two 20-mm cannon.

FAIRCHILD HILLER MODEL 616 AERCAB

The Fairchild Hiller Stratos-Western Division is one of two companies under contract to the US Navy to investigate an integrated aircrew escape/rescue capability (AERCAB) for combat aircraft. A ¼-scale model of the Fairchild Hiller Model 616 has been successfully tested by the Navy in a wind tunnel, a full-scale prototype model has been built and negotiations have been concluded for construction of a full-scale flying prototype.

The US Navy issued a work objective for the AERCAB on 27 August 1968 through the Naval Air Development Center. The purpose of AERCAB is to permit recovery of aircrew who eject from their aircraft over enemy territory and to provide capability to fly the ejection seat up to a distance of 50 miles (80 km) at up to 100 knots (115 mph; 185 km/h) prior to vertical descent by personal parachute.

A summary of the NADC requirements lists the following points:

Safe ejection at velocities up to 600 knots (691 mph; 1,112 km/h) ;
Sequencing to provide automatic deployment after ejection;
A climb rate of 1,000 ft (305 m) per minute for three minutes after deployment;
Cruise at 100 knots (115 mph; 185 km/h) for 30 minutes;
Operating altitudes from sea level to 10,000 ft (3,050 m);
Man/AERCAB separation and vertical descent by personal parachute at end of flight;
Completely automatic operation from time of aircraft ejection to man/AERCAB separation (with provision for manual override);
Minimum packaged or folded volume to allow for installation in the A-7 and F-4 aircraft with minimum aircraft modifications;
Uncompromised normal ejection mode if conditions warrant (automatically sensed by on-board equipment);
Incorporation of all normal aircrew survival equipment.

The AERCAB would be used in situations where the disabled aircraft was at more than 800 ft (243 m) and in an upright attitude. Below this height, or in an adverse attitude, conventional seat ejection would be used; an on-board ejection sequencer would automatically select the correct mode.

Fairchild Hiller's concept can be considered basically as a powered glider. It consists of a seat, tail boom, wing, jet engine and inflatable nose fairing. The seat, of conventional design

including catapult thrusters and sustainer rockets, forms the basic structure for the entire vehicle.

The nose fairing is a double-walled inflatable structure which when deflated stows under the pilot's legs against the front of the seat. It protects the occupant from the airstream and provides a low drag profile for the vehicle. A

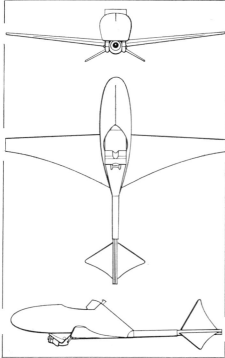

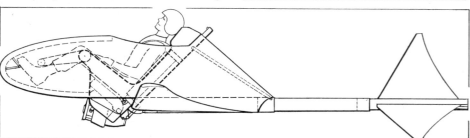

Three-view general arrangement drawing of the Fairchild Hiller Model 616 fully deployed (top), and detailed fuselage view showing the basic structure

tank in the seat provides a source of compressed air to inflate the nose structure and a tubular framework extends forward from the seat to support it when inflated.

Three tubular telescoping sections make up the tail boom and position the tail surfaces far enough aft for aerodynamic stability. The outer section of the boom is fixed and forms the primary structural member and the innermost boom section contains and carries the tail surfaces.

The wing of the Model 616 is designed on the Princeton sailwing principal, with a rigid spar to support the leading-edge and tip, and the trailing-edge tensioned by wire. Top and bottom surfaces are covered by a fabric of dacron sailcloth. Wing lift is gained from the predictable deformation of the fabric between the leading-edge and the tensioned trailing-edge catenary. Fuel is stored in the leading-edge spar, which is of NACA symmetrical aerofoil section; when stowed, the spar folds in the middle and hinges back.

A small turbofan engine, of the type developed by Continental Motors or Williams, is proposed as the power plant. The required thrust is 160 lb (72·5 kg).

A wholly-automatic deployment and recovery sequence is planned, with provision for pilot override at all times. Initiation of deployment starts with stabilization of the seat by the drogue chute in the airstream, and as soon as the seat has slowed to 150 knots (172 mph; 277 km/h) IAS. Deployment is achieved through mechanical linkages to the drogue chute line and the AERCAB will be in the climb condition at full engine thrust, in 6-10 seconds after ejection.

An autopilot will fly the AERCAB to a pre-determined altitude and will then trim it to cruise at 100 knots (115 mph; 185 km/h) on a pre-selected heading, programmed into the autopilot prior to the start of the mission. After engine shut-down, the AERCAB glides to a pre-set altitude, sensed by radar altimeter, and the pilot is then ejected by deploying his personal

parachute. Using manual override or in the event of engine malfunction, the pilot can fly the Model 616 as a glider, when its best gliding L/D ratio is 8 : 1.

DIMENSIONS (Deployed):

Span	15 ft 5½ in (4·70 m)
Length	15 ft 0¼ in (4·57 m)
Height	2 ft 6½ in (0·77 m)
Tailplane span	4 ft 2 in (1·27 m)
Aspect ratio	6·9
Wing dihedral	6°
Tailplane anhedral	30°

AREAS:

Wings, gross	36 sq ft (3·34 m²)
Tailplane area	6·68 sq ft (0·62 m²)
Vertical fin area	3·34 sq ft (0·31 m²)

WEIGHTS AND LOADINGS:

Empty weight	304 lb (138 kg)
Useful load	296 lb (134 kg)
Max gross weight	600 lb (272 kg)
Wing loading	16·6 lb/sq ft (81·1 kg/m²)
Power loading	3·75 lb/lb st (3·75 kg/kg st)

REPUBLIC AVIATION DIVISION of Fairchild Hiller Corporation

DIVISIONAL OFFICE AND WORKS:
Farmingdale, Long Island, New York 11735

VICE PRESIDENT AND GENERAL MANAGER: D. J. Strait

F-15 PROGRAMME MANAGER: Dr N. Grossman

CHIEF ENGINEER: J. Williamson

DIRECTOR OF MARKETING: L. W. Helmuth

DIRECTOR OF OPERATIONS: N. Harris

DIRECTOR OF EMPLOYEE RELATIONS: B. Gottsch

DIRECTOR OF PUBLIC RELATIONS: R. Wendell

DIRECTOR OF CONTRACTS: K. Posch

CONTROLLER: D. Crane

Founded on 17 February 1931, as the Seversky Aircraft Company, Republic operated as Republic Aviation Corporation from 1939 until 1965. On 8 July 1965, it was announced that the Directors of Fairchild Hiller had transmitted to the Directors of Republic a proposal for the acquisition by Fairchild Hiller of Republic's operating assets. This proposal was accepted in September 1965, and Republic became a division of Fairchild Hiller Corporation.

Production of the F-105 Thunderchief supersonic fighter-bomber has been completed, but Republic has important contracts to improve the operational capabilities of F-105's in service, and has developed a new bombing system for the F-105D, known as the T-Stick II.

Major sub-contracts cover the manufacture of assemblies for the McDonnell F/RF-4 Phantom II fighter and the Boeing 747 and supersonic transport (SST) aircraft. For the 747, the Division is manufacturing all the wing control surfaces, including ailerons, spoilers, leading-edge flaps and trailing-edge flaps. Its part in the SST programme involves production of a major portion of the fuselage structure and the tail unit.

In partnership with EWR-Süd of West Germany, Republic Division was selected to proceed with the project definition phase of the US/FRG V/STOL tactical fighter programme; but this work has now terminated. (see International section).

Republic is producing the waste management system for the USAF Manned Orbiting Laboratory programme. It has been investigating, under various USAF contracts, for several years, the possibilities of a hypersonic vehicle.

Republic is producing the Bikini drone surveillance system for the US Marine Corps and is involved in several space environment and life sciences programmes. It has developed and is producing a pump system under contract to New York University to treat Hydrocephalic patients. The New York State Motor Vehicle Bureau awarded Republic a contract for the design of a Safety Car.

Under project FIRE, Republic built for NASA two spacecraft for lunar re-entry studies. The first was launched successfully in April 1964; the second, launched in May 1965, was equally successful. In February 1963, Republic was awarded a contract by NASA to study overall requirements for a synchronous meteorological satellite (SMS).

The Republic Power Conversion Laboratory announced in 1960 that it had developed the world's first continuously-operating experimental pinch plasma engine. Republic's achievement has been recognized by several subsequent contracts from the USAF and Navy. An operational model of the pinch plasma engine was developed for flight testing and is currently operating successfully on the LES 6 satellite which was placed in orbit in 1968. This laboratory is also developing a thermionic diode for the direct conversion of nuclear energy into electrical power.

REPUBLIC AP-63-31 THUNDERCHIEF
USAF designation: F-105

The F-105 was developed to meet USAF requirements for a supersonic single-seat fighter-bomber able to deliver nuclear weapons, as well as heavier loads of conventional bombs and rockets, at very high speeds and over long ranges.

Design work began in 1951 and construction of two YF-105A prototypes began in 1954. The following versions have been built:

YF-105A. The first of two YF-105A's exceeded Mach 1 during its initial test flight on 22 October 1955, powered by a Pratt & Whitney J57 turbojet engine.

F-105B. Single-seat day fighter-bomber with Pratt & Whitney J75-P-3 or -5 turbojet engine (15,000 lb=6,810 kg st dry, approx 25,000 lb= 11,350 kg with afterburner). Introduced swept-forward air intakes. The first example of this developed version flew on 22 May 1956, and was delivered to the USAF Flight Test Center shortly afterwards. The first production aircraft was delivered to USAF Tactical Air Command on 27 May 1958. The 335th Tactical Fighter Squadron, Fourth Tactical Fighter Wing, Eglin AFB, Florida, was first squadron to be equipped with F-105B. Production was completed in 1959 in favour of F-105D after 75 had been built.

JF-105B. Three aircraft of initial test batch of 15 were started as RF-105B's with cameras in nose. When this rôle was dropped, they were redesignated JF-105B for special tests. The first of them flew for the first time on 18 July 1957.

F-105D. Single-seat all-weather fighter-bomber with Pratt & Whitney J75-P-19W turbojet, NASARR monopulse radar system and Doppler for night or bad weather operation. NASARR provides all radar functions for both low and high level missions—air search, automatic tracking, ground mapping and terrain avoidance. First F-105D flew on 9 June 1959, and deliveries to the 4th Tactical Fighter Wing began in May 1960. Over 600 built. Max T-O weight 52,546 lb (23,832 kg). Max level speed Mach 1·11 at sea level, Mach 2·1 above 36,000 ft (11,000 m). Some 30 aircraft of this version are being modified to carry the newly-developed T-Stick II bombing system. The external appearance of these aircraft is changed considerably by the addition of a 'saddle-back' from aft of the cockpit to the base of the fin to house additional avionics.

F-105F. Two-seat dual-purpose trainer/tactical fighter version of F-105D. Only major design

changes are an increase in the length of the fuselage and a proportionate increase in the height of the tail fin. Unspecified number ordered for USAF in Autumn of 1962, in lieu of equal number of F-105D's, for service with all F-105D units. First F-105F flew for the first time on 11 June 1963.

Contracts awarded by the USAF in 1968 covered installation in F-105 aircraft of a new bombing system, adaptation of the F-105 to carry the latest missiles, and the design and production of new advanced electronic countermeasures equipment for the F-105.

The following details refer to the F-105F:

TYPE: Two-seat dual-purpose trainer/tactical fighter.

WINGS: Cantilever mid-wing monoplane. Wing section NACA 65A-005·5 at root, NACA 65A-003·7 at t p. Anhedral 3° 30'. No incidence. Sweepback at quarter-chord 45°. Unique swept-forward air intake ducts in wing root leading-edges to provide double shock-wave to slow compressor air and to reduce turbulence in way of tailplane. All-metal stressed-skin structure. Conventional ailerons, of aluminium alloy construction, are used only at low subsonic speeds. Primary roll control is by five sections of hydraulically-actuated aluminium spoiler forward of flaps on each wing. Single-slotted aluminium alloy trailing-edge flaps. Full-span plain aluminium alloy leading-edge flaps, with conical camber. Control surfaces actuated by fully-powered irreversible tandem jacks. No trim-tabs or de-icing system.

FUSELAGE: Semi-monocoque structure of aluminium and magnesium with "wasp-waist" in way of wings in accordance with Area Rule. Radar in nose. Large internal weapons bay under wing position. Hydraulically-operated "clover-leaf" speed brakes, made of titanium and stainless steel, form last 3 ft (0·91 m) of fuselage around tail-pipe.

TAIL UNIT: Cantilever structure of aluminium and magnesium. All surfaces highly swept. Ram air-intake in base of fin to provide cooling air for rear end of aircraft. One-piece "flying tail" and mass-balanced rudder, with flutter-damper, are actuated hydraulically by irreversible tandem jacks. No trim-tabs. Ventral stabilising fin under rear fuselage.

LANDING GEAR: Hydraulically-retractable tricycle type, with single wheel on each unit. Main units retract inward into thickened area of wing-roots created by main air intake

Republic F-105D Thunderchief with 'saddle back' housing avionics for the T-Stick II bombing system

ducts. Nose-wheel retracts forward. Bendix oleo-pneumatic shock-absorbers. Main wheel tyres size 36 × 11, pressure 205 lb/sq in (14·4 kg/cm²). Nose-wheel tyre size 24 × 7·7, pressure 140 lb/sq in (9·85 kg/cm²). Multi-pad Goodyear brakes, with anti-skid units.

POWER PLANT: One Pratt & Whitney J75-P-19W turbojet engine (26,500 lb = 12,030 kg st with water injection and afterburning). Fuel in three flexible tanks in fuselage (forward, main and aft) with total capacity of 770 US gallons (2,915 litres) and one 390 US gallon (1,477 litre) bomb-bay tank. Provision for one 650 US gallon (2,460 litre) or 750 US gallon (2,840 litre) external tank under fuselage and two under-wing tanks on inboard pylons, each of 450 US gallons (1,705 litres). Refuelling point on port side of fuselage, aft of wing. Provision for both flying boom and probe-and-drogue flight refuelling. Retractable refuelling probe on port side of forward fuselage. Oil capacity 6·5 US gallons (24·5 litres).

ACCOMMODATION: Crew of two, in tandem, on ejection seats, in separate pressurised and air-conditioned cockpits. Electrically - operated rearward-hinged canopies.

SYSTEMS: Hamilton Standard air-conditioning and pressurisation system, differential 5 lb/sq in (0·35 kg/cm²). Hydraulic system, pressure 3,000 lb/sq in (210 kg/cm²), operates landing gear, speed brakes, primary flying controls, leading-edge flaps, flight refuelling probe and bomb-bay doors. No pneumatic system. Electrical system includes air-turbine motor for AC supply and engine-driven DC generator.

EQUIPMENT: General Electric FC-5 flight-control system connects with AN/APN-131 Doppler for automatic navigation. AN/ARC 70 UHF radio. AN/ASG-19 "Thunderstick" integrated armament control system consisting of NASARR radar, General Electric automatic lead computing sight, toss-bomb computer and associated equipment.

ARMAMENT: Fixed armament consists of one General Electric M-61 20-mm Vulcan auto-matic multi-barrel gun with 1,029 rounds. Typical alternative loads are (1) 650 gal centre-line tank, 450 gal tank on one inner wing pylon, nuclear store on other inner pylon, (2) 650 gal centre-line tank and four GAM-83B Bullpup nuclear missiles, (3) 450 gal tanks on centre-line and inner wing pylons, nuclear weapon in bomb-bay, (4) 650 gal centre-line tank, two 3,000 lb bombs on inner wing pylons, (5) 650 gal centre-line tank, two 450 gal tanks on inner wing pylons, four Sidewinder missiles on outer wing pylons, (6) Three rocket packs on centre-line, two on each inner wing pylon and one on each outer pylon, (7) Nine BLU-1/B fire-bombs or nine MLU-10/B mines in similar arrangement to rocket packs, or sixteen leaflet bombs, 750 lb bombs, or MC-1 toxic bombs.

DIMENSIONS, EXTERNAL (F-105F):
Wing span	34 ft 11·2 in (10·65 m)
Wing chord (mean)	11 ft 6 in (3·50 m)
Wing aspect ratio	3·18
Length overall	69 ft 1·18 in (21·06 m)
Length of fuselage	66 ft 11·85 in (20·42 m)

Republic F-105F Thunderchief two-seat trainer/tactical fighter

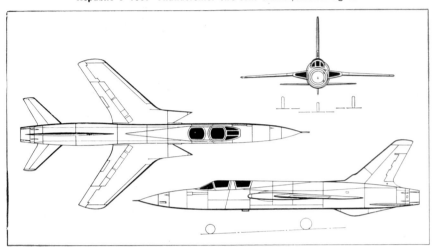

Republic F-105F Thunderchief two-seat trainer/tactical fighter

Height over tail	20 ft 1·96 in (6·15 m)	Max wing loading	140 lb/sq ft (683·5 kg/m²)
Tailplane span	17 ft 4·72 in (5·30 m)	Max power loading	4·54 lb/lb st (4·54 kg/kg st)
Wheel track	17 ft 3·2 in (5·26 m)		
Wheelbase	21 ft 1·18 in (6·43 m)	PERFORMANCE (F-105F):	
		Max level speed at 38,000 ft (11,600 m)	
AREAS (F-105F):			Mach 2·25
Wings, gross	385 sq ft (35·77 m²)	Max level speed at S/L	Mach 1·25
Ailerons (total)	15·37 sq ft (1·43 m²)	Max cruising speed	Mach 0·95
Trailing-edge flaps (total)	61·40 sq ft (5·70 m²)	Econ cruising speed, depending on altitude	
Leading-edge flaps (total)	22·70 sq ft (2·11 m²)		Mach 0·4-0·88
Spoilers (total)	18·70 sq ft (1·74 m²)	Stalling speed (minimum)	
Fin	61·52 sq ft (5·72 m²)		155 knots (178 mph; 287 km/h)
Rudder	11·39 sq ft (1·06 m²)	Rate of climb at S/L 32,000 ft (9,750 m)/min	
Tailplane	60·37 sq ft (5·61 m²)	T-O run (clean)	2,000 ft (610 m)
		T-O to 50 ft (15 m) (clean)	2,600 ft (792 m)
WEIGHTS AND LOADINGS (F-105F):		Landing from 50 ft (15 m)	4,960 ft (1,510 m)
Weight empty	28,393 lb (12,879 kg)	Landing run, with drag-chute	3,200 ft (975 m)
Max T-O weight	54,000 lb (24,495 kg)	Range with max fuel	
Max landing weight	51,038 lb (23,150 kg)		1,797 nm (2,070 miles; 3,330 km)

FELLABAUM
J. R. FELLABAUM
ADDRESS:
2930 Airport Highway, Toledo, Ohio 43614

Mr Fellabaum has built and flown a side-by-side two-seat light aircraft named the Starfire, of which plans are available to other amateur constructors.

FELLABAUM JRF-22 STARFIRE
The Starfire is a two-seat adaptation of the well-known Loving Love racing aircraft, with redesigned nose and tail unit. Mr Fellabaum began building it in 1961 and it flew for the first time in August 1963. Since then, it has under-gone considerable refinement, one of the latest changes being to reduce the size of the fuel tank to give better over-the-nose visibility.

TYPE: Two-seat amateur-built light aircraft.

WINGS: Cantilever low-wing monoplane of sharply-cranked configuration. Wing section NACA 23015. Wood structure, plywood-covered. Wooden ailerons. No flaps.

FUSELAGE: Welded 4130 steel-tube structure, fabric-covered.

TAIL UNIT: Cantilever wood structure, plywood-covered, except for elevators which have fabric-covered steel-tube structure. Bungee trim system.

LANDING GEAR: Non-retractable tailwheel type. No shock-absorbers. Main wheel tyre pressure 8 lb/sq in (0·56 kg/cm²). Goodyear brakes.

POWER PLANT: One 125 hp Lycoming O-290-D four-cylinder horizontally-opposed air-cooled engine, driving a Met-L-Prop 65 × 70 in two-blade fixed-pitch propeller. Fuel tank in fuse-lage forward of cabin, capacity 24·4 US gallons (92·5 litres).

Fellabaum Starfire, a side-by-side two-seat adaptation of the Loving Love (*Howard Levy*)

ACCOMMODATION: Pilot and passenger side-by-side in enclosed cabin.

EQUIPMENT: Fitted with Narco Simplexer with Omni and full blind-flying panel.

DIMENSIONS, EXTERNAL:
Wing span	26 ft 8 in (8·12 m)
Wing chord at root	4 ft 6 in (1·37 m)
Wing chord at tip	2 ft 8 in (0·81 m)
Length overall	18 ft 0 in (5·49 m)
Height overall	5 ft 3 in (1·60 m)
Wheel track	10 ft 0 in (3·05 m)

AREA:
Wings, gross	101 sq ft (9·38 m²)

WEIGHTS:
Weight empty	804 lb (365 kg)
Max T-O weight	1,450 lb (658 kg)

PERFORMANCE (at max T-O weight):
Max level speed at S/L	135 knots (155 mph; 249 km/h)
Max permissible diving speed	156 knots (180 mph; 290 km/h)
Max cruising speed (75% power) at 8,000 ft (2,440 m)	123 knots (142 mph; 228 km/h)
Econ cruising speed (55% power) at 8,000 ft (2,440 m)	113 knots (130 mph; 209 km/h)
Stalling speed	57 knots (65 mph; 105 km/h)
Rate of climb at S/L	1,500 ft (457 m)/min
Service ceiling	25,000 ft (7,620 m)
T-O run	300 ft (91 m)
Landing run	600 ft (182 m)

FIKE
WILLIAM J. FIKE
ADDRESS:
PO Box 683, Anchorage, Alaska 99501

Mr W. J. Fike, whose 16,000 hours logged as a pilot include thousands of hours of "bush flying" in Alaska, has designed and built four light aircraft since 1929. His Model "B" of 1935 was a tiny parasol-wing single-seat monoplane, powered by a 35 hp Long Harlequin engine and with an empty weight of only 300 lb. In the following year he produced the Model "C" of similar configuration. A later design is the single or two-seat Model "D" high-wing cabin monoplane, of which full details were given in the 1961-62 *Jane's*. Plans of the Model "D" are available to amateur constructors.

Mr Fike has now completed construction of a new aircraft known as the Model "E", with low aspect ratio wings, and all available details follow:

FIKE MODEL "E"

In 1953 Mr Fike began design of an aircraft to evaluate the flight characteristics of a low aspect ratio (3·0) wing of only 9% thickness/chord ratio when applied to a low-power monoplane of high-wing configuration. The wing, of wooden geodetic construction, is so designed that various wingtips may be installed for evaluation following initial flight testing. A standard Piper J-3 tail unit is utilised, but this is modified by limiting the tailplane span to keep within 8 ft (2·44 m) to comply with US highway regulations for towed vehicles.

A secondary object was to develop a low-cost easy-to-build two-seat lightplane. The wing is designed for removal within minutes to enable the aircraft to be housed in an ordinary garage.

Mr Fike's heavy commitments as an airline pilot have been responsible for the extended construction time, but first flight of the Model "E" was scheduled for March 1970.

TYPE: Two-seat high-wing sporting monoplane.

WINGS: Cantilever high-wing monoplane. Wing section NACA 4409. No dihedral. Incidence 2° 15′. No sweepback. All-wood geodetic structure, fabric-covered. Conventional wooden ailerons. No flaps. No trim-tabs.

FUSELAGE: Welded steel-tube structure; fabric-covered.

Fike Model "E" low aspect ratio lightplane (65 hp Continental A65-8 engine)

TAIL UNIT: Cantilever welded steel-tube structure with fabric covering. Variable-incidence tailplane. No trim-tabs in elevators or rudder.

LANDING GEAR: Standard Piper J-3 gear of non-retractable tail-wheel type, with rubber-cord shock absorption. Main wheels and tyres size 8·00 × 4, pressure 15-20 lb/sq in (1·05-1·4 kg/cm²). Goodrich toe-operated hydraulic brakes.

POWER PLANT: 65 hp Continental A65-8 four-cylinder horizontally-opposed air-cooled engine, driving a two-blade fixed-pitch propeller, diameter 6 ft 0 in (1·83 m). One fuel tank in each wing, capacity 12·5 US gallons (47·5 litres). Total fuel capacity 25 US gallons (95 litres). Refuelling point on top of each wing. Oil capacity 1 US gallon (3·8 litres).

ACCOMMODATION: Pilot and passenger seated in tandem in enclosed cabin. Access door on each side of fuselage. Cabin heated and ventilated. Baggage compartment aft of cabin.

DIMENSIONS, EXTERNAL:

Wing span	20 ft 0 in (6·10 m)
Wing chord at root	6 ft 8 in (2·03 m)
Wing chord at tip	5 ft 8 in (1·73 m)
Wing aspect ratio	3·0

Length overall	19 ft 2 in (5·84 m)
Height overall	5 ft 8 in (1·73 m)
Tailplane span	7 ft 11 in (2·41 m)
Wheel track	6 ft 0 in (1·83 m)
Wheelbase	14 ft 2 in (4·32 m)
Passenger doors (2):	
Height	2 ft 7 in (0·79 m)
Width	1 ft 9 in (0·53 m)
Height to sill	2 ft 4 in (0·71 m)
DIMENSIONS, INTERNAL:	
Cabin: length	5 ft 6 in (1·68 m)
Max width	2 ft 0 in (0·61 m)
Max height	3 ft 8 in (1·12 m)
Floor area	10 sq ft (0·93 m²)
Volume	35 cu ft (0·99 m²)
Baggage compartment	12 cu ft (0·34 m²)
AREAS:	
Wings, gross	132 sq ft (12·26 m²)
Ailerons (total)	19·5 sq ft (1·81 m²)
Fin	6·7 sq ft (0·62 m²)
Rudder	6·5 sq ft (0·60 m²)
Tailplane	13·0 sq ft (1·21 m²)
Elevators	10·0 sq ft (0·93 m²)
WEIGHTS (estimated):	
Weight, empty	665 lb (301 kg)
Max T-O weight	1,100 lb (499 kg)

FLAGLOR
FLAGLOR AIRCRAFT
ADDRESS:
1550A Sanders Road, Northbrook, Illinois 60062

The latest of a series of light aircraft designed and built by Mr K. Flaglor is an ultra-light sporting monoplane named the Scooter. Design work began in July 1965, and construction was started in November of the same year. The Scooter was powered originally by an 18 hp Cushman golf-kart engine, and it was with this power plant that the first flight was made in June 1967. Performance was marginal and, as a result, Mr Flaglor replaced the Cushman with a nominal 36 hp (25-28 hp output) Volkswagen engine. Current power plant is a 1,500 cc Volkswagen engine developing 40 hp. When flown to the 1967 EAA meet at Rockford, Illinois, the Scooter won the "Outstanding Ultra-light" and "Outstanding Volkswagen-Powered Airplane" awards. Plans are available to amateur constructors.

FLAGLOR SCOOTER

TYPE: Ultra-light sporting monoplane.

WINGS: High-wing monoplane, braced by wires attached to fuselage and to king-post mounted above centre-section. Wing section NACA 23012. Dihedral 2°. Incidence 3°. Two-spar all-wood structure with wood drag and anti-drag bracing. Aluminium leading-edge and plywood covering. Conventional wooden ailerons. No trim-tabs. No flaps.

FUSELAGE: Wooden structure, plywood-covered in the forward cockpit area, fabric-covered aft. Fuselage of triangular section aft of the wing. Wing centre-section and engine mounting constructed of 4130 steel tube.

TAIL UNIT: All-wooden construction with strut bracing. No fixed fin. No trim tabs.

LANDING GEAR: Non-retractable tail-wheel type. Fixed spring steel main units. Steerable tail-wheel. Main wheels of Go-Kart type, size 4·10 × 3·50-5. Tyre pressure 20 lb/sq in (1·41 kg/cm²). Vespa, Sears motor scooter brakes.

POWER PLANT: One 40 hp Volkswagen 1,500 cc four-cylinder horizontally-opposed air-cooled engine, driving a two-blade Troyer 54-28

Flaglor Scooter ultra-light sporting aircraft (40 hp Volkswagen engine) (*Jean Seele*)

propeller. Single fuel tank in fuselage nose, capacity 5 US gallons (18·9 litres). Filling point on top of fuselage forward of windscreen. Oil capacity 2·5 US quarts (2·37 litres).

ACCOMMODATION: Single seat in cockpit protected by deep windscreen.

DIMENSIONS, EXTERNAL:

Wing span	28 ft 0 in (8·64 m)
Wing chord (constant)	4 ft 2 in (1·27 m)
Wing aspect ratio	6·7
Length overall	15 ft 8 in (4·78 m)
Height overall	7 ft 0 in (2·13 m)
Tailplane span	7 ft 2 in (2·18 m)
Wheel track	4 ft 6 in (1·37 m)
AREAS:	
Wings, gross	115 sq ft (10·68 m²)
Ailerons (total)	12·5 sq ft (1·16 m²)
Rudder	5·6 sq ft (0·52 m²)
Tailplane	10·8 sq ft (1·00 m²)
Elevators	7·7 sq ft (0·72 m²)

WEIGHTS AND LOADINGS:

Weight empty	390 lb (177 kg)
Max T-O and landing weight	650 lb (295 kg)
Max wing loading	5·7 lb/sq ft (27·8 kg/m²)
Max power loading	1·6 lb/hp (0·73 kg/hp)

PERFORMANCE:

Max level speed	78 knots (90 mph; 145 km/h)
Max permissible diving speed	82 knots (95 mph; 153 km/h)
Max cruising speed	69 knots (80 mph; 129 km/h)
Econ cruising speed	56 knots (65 mph; 105 km/h)
Stalling speed	30 knots (34 mph; 55 km/h)
Rate of climb at S/L	600 ft (183 m)/min
T-O run	250 ft (76 m)
Landing run	250 ft (76 m)
Range with max fuel	152 nm (175 miles; 282 km)

FRAKES
FRAKES AVIATION
ADDRESS:
PO Box 159, Angwin, California

FRAKES TURBINE MALLARD

During 1969 Frakes Aviation purchased from Northern Consolidated Airways of Alaska a Grumman Mallard amphibian. This aircraft had been used in 1964 to demonstrate the feasibility of converting from piston engines to turbo-prop engines. The original Pratt & Whitney R-1340 engine was removed from the starboard wing and replaced by a Pratt & Whitney (UACL) PT6A-9 turboprop; the R-1340 engine was retained on the port side and flight tests were carried out with this mixed power plant. After 15 hours of flight testing, during which the conversion was found to be satisfactory, the piston engine was re-installed on the starboard side and the Mallard resumed service with Northern Consolidated Airways.

The Grumman amphibian, last described in the 1951-52 *Jane's*, was acquired by Frakes

Aviation during 1969, and this company has converted the aircraft to turbine power by installing two Pratt & Whitney (UACL) PT6A-27 turboprop engines which are flat-rated at 715 ehp. It flew for the first time in this configuration in September 1969, and Frakes have reported increased performance for this conversion. Standard fuel capacity is 480 US gallons (1,817 litres), with 200 US gallon (757-litre) auxiliary wing tanks.

WEIGHTS:
Max weight   13,500 lb (6,124 kg)
T-O weight with auxiliary wing tanks
                              14,000 lb (6,350 kg)
PERFORMANCE:
Cruising speed 191 knots (220 mph; 354 km/h)
Max rate of climb at S/L 2,000 ft (609 m)/min
Max rate of climb at S/L, one engine out
                              800 ft (244 m)/min
Service ceiling   24,500 ft (7,478 m)
Service ceiling, one engine out
                              11,500 ft (3,515 m)
Water T-O time   16 secs

Frakes Turbine Mallard, a turboprop conversion of the Grumman Mallard

FUNK

D. D. FUNK AVIATION COMPANY, INC
HEAD OFFICE AND WORKS:
Airport Industrial Center, Salina, Kansas 67401
This company was founded in 1950 by Mr Don D. Funk, a former agricultural pilot. It is producing a specialised agricultural aircraft, designated F-23, at the rate of about one a month.

FUNK F-23
Two basic versions of this aircraft are available.
F-23A. With 240 hp Continental W-670 seven-cylinder radial air-cooled engine.
F-23B. With 275 hp Jacobs R-755 seven-cylinder radial air-cooled engine.
The following details apply to both models.
TYPE: Single-seat agricultural monoplane.
WINGS: Cantilever low-wing monoplane. All-metal structure, consisting of wide-span centre-section and two interchangeable outer panels. Dihedral on outer panels only. All four leading-edge sections quickly removable and interchangeable except for minor items. Interchangeable Ceconite-covered ailerons. No flaps.
FUSELAGE: Conventional steel-tube structure. Sides of fuselage covered entirely with quickly removable panels. Fuselage structure designed to absorb impact by progressive collapse.
TAIL UNIT: Cantilever metal structure. Elevators and rudder covered with Ceconite. Interchangeable elevators. Almost all parts of one half of tailplane interchangeable with other half. Wire deflector from cockpit overturn structure to tip of fin.
LANDING GEAR: Non-retractable tail-wheel type. Cantilever main units. Main wheels fitted with nylon-reinforced tyres size 8·50 × 10. Parking brake.
POWER PLANT: One radial engine as shown under model listings above, driving a two-blade metal ground-adjustable propeller. Fuel tanks in wings, total capacity 47 US gallons (178 litres). Oil capacity: F-23A 4·2 US gallons (16 litres), F-23B 4·4 US gallons (16·5 litres).
ACCOMMODATION: Single adjustable seat under large transparent canopy. Seat belts and shoulder harness standard. Steel-tube (4130) overturn structure. No protruding objects in cockpit area. Instrument panel located forward of hopper. Large window which forms starboard side of canopy hinges downward for access. Optional wire deflector for windscreen.
EQUIPMENT: Epoxy glass-fibre hopper in fuselage forward of cockpit, capacity 215 US gallons

Funk F-23B agricultural aircraft (275 hp Jacobs R-755 engine) (*Howard Levy*)

(814 litres). Transland Boom-Master pump standard. Hopper throat size (9½ in × 25 in = 24 cm × 63·5 cm) fits all Transland equipment and most other types of spray-gear. Provision for quick change from liquids to solids and vice-versa. Spray-booms enclosed in wing leading-edge.

DIMENSIONS, EXTERNAL:
Wing span   40 ft 6 in (12·34 m)
Wing chord (constant)   7 ft 0 in (2·13 m)
Length overall:
  F-23A   26 ft 4 in (8·03 m)
  F-23B   27 ft 2 in (8·28 m)
Height overall   8 ft 6 in (2·59 m)
AREAS:
Wings, gross   280 sq ft (26·01 m²)
Ailerons (total)   35·8 sq ft (3·33 m²)
Fin   13·2 sq ft (1·23 m²)
Rudder   13·5 sq ft (1·25 m²)
Tailplane   26·9 sq ft (2·50 m²)
Elevators   13·8 sq ft (1·28 m²)
WEIGHTS AND LOADINGS:
Weight empty, sprayer:
  F-23A   2,250 lb (1,020 kg)
  F-23B   2,280 lb (1,035 kg)
Licenced hopper load   1,500 lb (680 kg)
Max T-O weight   4,300 lb (1,950 kg)
Max wing loading   15 lb/sq ft (73·2 kg/m²)
Max power loading:
  F-23A   17·6 lb/hp (7·98 kg/hp)
  F-23B   15·6 lb/hp (7·08 kg/hp)

PERFORMANCE (at max T-O weight, except where indicated):
Max level speed at S/L:
  F-23A   100 knots (115 mph; 185 km/h)
  F-23B   109 knots (125 mph; 201 km/h)
Never-exceed speed:
  F-23A/B   121 knots (140 mph; 225 km/h)
Cruising speed at S/L:
  F-23A   83 knots (95 mph; 153 km/h)
  F-23B   87 knots (100 mph; 161 km/h)
Working speed:
  F-23A 69-83 knots (80-95 mph; 129-153 km/h)
  F-23B
  69-87 knots (80-100 mph; 129-161 km/h)
Stalling speed, power on:
  F-23A/B   50 knots (57 mph; 92 km/h)
Stalling speed, empty:
  F-23A/B   39 knots (45 mph; 73 km/h)
Rate of climb at S/L:
  F-23A   350 ft (107 m)/min
  F-23B   515 ft (157 m)/min
Service ceiling (empty):
  F-23A   16,500 ft (5,030 m)
  F-23B   19,000 ft (5,800 m)
T-O run:
  F-23A   925 ft (282 m)
  F-23B   850 ft (260 m)
Range with max fuel (75% power):
  F-23A   303 nm (350 miles; 560 km)
  F-23B   260 nm (300 miles; 480 km)

GALAXIE

GALAXIE CORPORATION

ADDRESS:
Box 128, Newtown Square, Pennsylvania 19073
PRESIDENT:
E. W. Glatfelter

Mr E. W. Glatfelter formed this company to continue development of a single-seat lightweight helicopter of his own design, of which details were given in the 1961/62 *Jane's*.

Since that time, extensive mechanical improvements have been made to the aircraft and a flight test programme has been completed, leading to FAA certification of the helicopter which the company designates as the Model G-100. It is one of the few helicopters flying with American-designed and built glass-fibre rotor blades. The rotor controls are conventional in operation but include a pitch-throttle coordination linkage which adds throttle as collective pitch is increased,

thus compensating for the additional power requirements.
Galaxie have also introduced a more powerful version of the above aircraft, designated Model G-100A, with a number of design improvements; this is described separately. Further developments being studied include a two-seat helicopter and the use of small turbine power plants.

GALAXIE MODEL G-100
Design of this helicopter was started in 1956. Construction of the prototype began two years later and it flew for the first time in June 1959. FAA certification was received in February 1968.
TYPE: Single-seat light helicopter.
ROTOR SYSTEM: Two-blade main rotor of teetering type, with servo cyclic control. Fiberdyne (glass-fibre skin, foam core) rotor blades of tapered non-linearly-twisted type, with solidity of 0·0326. Blade section NACA 63₂015. Cyclic and collective pitch control by swashplate and pitch beam. Two-blade teetering tail rotor of glass-fibre construction, with solidity

of 0·1065, driven by shaft and quarter twisted belts in tail pylon. Main rotor may be folded manually. Rotor brake standard.
ROTOR DRIVE: Engine to transmission by multiple V-belts. Multi-plate clutch used for starting and auto-rotation. The transmission uses spiral bevel gears. Main rotor/engine rpm ratio 1:7·11. Tail rotor/engine rpm ratio 1:1·17.
FUSELAGE: Welded 4130 steel-tube structure. Major sections bolted together.
LANDING GEAR: Welded steel-tube skid type.
POWER PLANT: One 65 hp Continental A65-8 four-cylinder horizontally-opposed air-cooled engine, modified to include axial-flow cooling fan which serves also as flywheel. Fuel in single metal tank, aft of main transmission, capacity 3·5 US gallons (13 litres). Refuelling point at top of tail boom. Oil capacity 1 US gallon (3·77 litres).
ACCOMMODATION: Single aluminium bucket seat forward of main rotor drive-shaft. Transparent plastic windscreen fairing. Open sides.
DIMENSIONS:
Main rotor diameter   25 ft 8 in (7·82 m)

Main rotor blade chord (mean) 7½ in (19·05 cm)
Tail rotor diameter   4 ft 0 in (1·22 m)
Distance between rotor centres
                                    15 ft 1½ in (4·61 m)
Length overall, rotors turning
                                    30 ft 0 in (9·14 m)
Length of fuselage   23 ft 2 in (7·06 m)
Width, rotors folded   6 ft 0 in (1·83 m)
Width over skids   6 ft 0 in (1·83 m)
Height overall   7 ft 6 in (2·29 m)
AREAS:
Main rotor blades (each)   9·5 sq ft (0·88 m²)
Tail rotor blades (each)   0·67 sq ft (0·06 m²)
Main rotor disc   520 sq ft (48·3 m²)
Tail rotor disc   12·56 sq ft (1·17 m²)
WEIGHTS AMD LOADINGS:
Weight empty   675 lb (306 kg)
Max T-O weight   880 lb (399 kg)
Max disc loading   1·70 lb/sq ft (8·30 kg/cm²)
Max power loading   13·5 lb/hp (6·12 kg/hp)
PERFORMANCE:
Max level speed at S/L
                        65 knots (75 mph; 120 km/h)
Max diving speed at S/L
                        74 knots (86 mph; 138 km/h)
Max cruising speed at S/L
                        56 knots (65 mph; 105 km/h)
Service ceiling   5,000 ft (1,525 m)
Hovering ceiling in ground effect
                                    5,000 ft (1,525 m)
Hovering ceiling out of ground effect
                                    4,000 ft (1,220 m)
Range with max payload, 10% reserve
                        34 nm (40 miles; 64 km)

GALAXIE MODEL G-100A

The Model G-100A, of which design began in
1969, is a more powerful and much refined development of the G-100. It utilises the basic
dynamic system of the G-100, but has a new and
more streamlined airframe, as shown in the
adjacent drawings.
ROTOR SYSTEM: As for G-100 except servo cyclic
control replaced by direct control to hub.
ROTOR DRIVE: As for G-100 except multi-plate
clutch replaced by over-running clutch. Tail
rotor gear-driven.
FUSELAGE: Welded 4130 steel-tube structure.
TAIL SURFACE: Smal synchronised elevator on
rear fuselage, connected to cyclic control.
LANDING GEAR: As for G-100 except ground
handling wheels provided.
POWER PLANT: One 100 hp Continental O-200-A
four-cylinder horizontally-opposed air-cooled
engine, with power governor. Two metal
fuel tanks, contained within contours of
fuselage, each 7·5 US gallons (28·4 litres)
capacity. Total fuel capacity 15 US gallons
(56·8 litres). Refuelling point at side of aircraft. Oil capacity 1 US gallon (3·77 litres).
SYSTEMS: Electrical system, with engine-driven
generator, to provide power for electric engine
starting, instruments, navigation lights and
nav/com systems.
DIMENSION AND AREAS:
As for G-100 except:
Height to top of rotor hub   6 ft 8 in (2·03 m)
Horizontal elevator area   4·0 sq ft (0·37 m²)

Galaxie Model G-100 single-seat light helicopter (65 hp Continental engine) (*Howard Levy*)

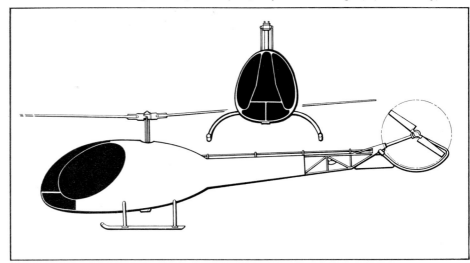

Galaxie Model G-100A, the more refined development of the Model G-100

WEIGHTS AND LOADINGS:
Weight empty   745 lb (337 kg)
Max T-O weight   1,000 lb (453 kg)
Max disc loading   1·92 lb/sq ft (9·37 kg/m²)
Max power loading   10·0 lb/hp (4·54 kg/hp)
PERFORMANCE (estimated at max T-O weight):
Max level speed at S/L
                        78 knots (90 mph; 145 km/h)
Max diving speed at S/L
                        89 knots (103 mph; 166 km/h)

Max cruising speed at S/L
                        69 knots (80 mph; 129 km/h)
Service ceiling   8,000 ft (2,440 m)
Hovering ceiling in ground effect
                                    8,000 ft (2,440 m)
Hovering ceiling out of ground effect
                                    6,400 ft (1,950 m)
Range with max payload, 10% reserve
                        130 nm (150 miles; 243 km)

GATES LEARJET
GATES LEARJET CORPORATION
CORPORATE OFFICES AND AIRCRAFT DIVISION:
Municipal Airport, PO Box 1280, Wichita,
Kansas 67201
STATIC POWER DIVISION:
2001 South Ritchey, Santa Ana, California
92705
GATES AVIATION CORPORATION:
Suite 444, Stapleton International Airport,
Denver, Colorado 80207
JET ELECTRONICS AND TECHNOLOGY INC:
5353 52nd Street, Grand Rapids, Michigan
49508
LEAR JET STEREO INC:
6868 South Plumer Avenue, Tucson, Arizona
85702
AVSCO INC:
Highway 69 and Corum Road, Excelsior
Springs, Missouri 64024
AIRCRAFT DIVISION OFFICERS:
EXECUTIVE VICE-PRESIDENTS:
G. H. B. Gould (Finance and Commercial
Marketing)
Malcolm S. Harned (General Manager)
VICE-PRESIDENTS:
Orrin A. Berthiaume (Manufacturing)
G. B. Doyle (Operations)
Thomas W. Gillespie (Government Marketing)
M. Heppenstall (Commercial Marketing)
Harry W. Johnson (Engineering)
Sandor Kvassay (International Marketing)
Harvey O. Nay (Advanced Technology)
TREASURER: W. H. Webster
SECRETARY: R. C. Troll
Founded in 1960 by William P. Lear Sr, this
company was known originally as the Swiss
American Aviation Corporation, which was form-
ed to manufacture a high-speed twin-jet execu-
tive aircraft known as the Learjet 23 (formerly

SAAC-23). Most of the tooling for production
of this aircraft was completed in Europe and then,
in 1962, all company activities were re-located
at Wichita, Kansas; at the same time the company became known as Lear Jet Corporation.
In 1967 all of Mr Lear's interests in the company
(approximately 60 per cent) were acquired by
The Gates Rubber Company of Denver, Colorado,
and in January 1970 the company name was
changed to Gates Learjet Corporation.

Gates Learjet subsidiaries include Gates Aviation Corporation, of Denver, Colorado; Jet
Electronics and Technology, Inc, of Grand
Rapids, Michigan, which was formed in 1968 to
produce a wide range of aircraft electronic systems and electromechanical equipment; Lear
Jet Stereo, Inc, of Tucson, Arizona, which produces a stereophonic tape player system for use
in automobiles, homes, boats and aircraft; and
Avsco, Inc, of Excelsior Springs, Missouri.

The company announced in 1969 its intention
of developing an advanced version of the Gates
Learjet 25 series, to be powered by two Garrett
AiResearch turbofan engines. Initial deliveries
of this model, which will have a non-stop range
approaching 3,475 nm (4,000 miles; 6,440 km),
are programmed for 1972.

Also in 1969, Gates Learjet released the information of their intention to design and develop
a twin-turbine powered helicopter tailored
especially for the executive transport market.
To be known as the Gates Twinjet, this aircraft
will carry as standard a crew of two and eight
passengers and will have a range of some 350 nm
(400 miles; 645 km) at speeds of up to 156 knots
(180 mph; 290 km/h). An optional commuter
interior arrangement will cater for a pilot and
twelve passengers. Power plant of the Twinjet
will consist of two AiResearch TSE 231-P2400

turboshaft engines, each rated at 474 shp for
take-off and with a continuous rating of 403 shp.
The Gates Twinjet is scheduled to make its first
flight in July 1971, with initial deliveries planned
for late in 1972.
Production of Series 24 and 25 aircraft totalled
five per month at the end of March 1970.

GATES LEARJET 24D
The prototype Lear Jet twin-jet executive
transport flew for the first time on 7 October 1963
and deliveries of production Learjet 23 aircraft
began on 13 October 1964. After a total of 104
of this version had been delivered, it was superseded by the Learjet 24, which was certificated
under Federal Air Regulations Part 25 (formerly
CAR 4B), as have been all subsequent models
produced by the company. Deliveries of the
Learjet 24 began in March 1966, and a total of
80 were built. This was replaced by a developed
version with more powerful engines, known as
the Learjet 24B, which received FAA certification
on 17 December 1968. Some 270 Learjets of all
models had been delivered at the beginning of
1970.
The current version is easily identified externally
by deletion of the non-structural bullet at the
junction of the tailplane and fin, and introduces
a number of refinements. It has been re-designated as the Gates Learjet 24D and all available
details follow:
TYPE: Twin-jet light executive transport.
WINGS: Cantilever low-wing monoplane. Wing
section NACA 64A 109. Dihedral 2° 30'.
Incidence 1°. Sweepback 13° at quarter-chord.
All-metal eight-spar structure with chemically-
milled alloy skins. Manually-operated, aerodynamically-balanced all-metal ailerons. Hydraulically-actuated all-metal single-slotted
flaps. Hydraulically-actuated all-metal spoilers

mounted on trailing-edge ahead of flaps. Trim-tab in port aileron. Balance tabs in both ailerons. Anti-icing by engine-bleed air ducted into leading-edges.

FUSELAGE: All-metal flush-riveted semi-monocoque fail-safe structure.

TAIL UNIT: Cantilever all-metal structure, with electrically-actuated variable-incidence tailplane mounted at tip of swept fin, and with small ventral fin. Conventional manually-operated control surfaces. Trim-tab in rudder. Electrically-heated thermal de-icing of the tailplane leading-edge.

LANDING GEAR: Retractable tricycle type of Cleveland Pneumatic Tool Co design, with twin wheels on each main unit and single steerable nose-wheel. Hydraulic actuation, with back-up pneumatic extension. Oleo-pneumatic shock-absorbers. Main wheels fitted with Goodyear 18 × 5·5 10-ply tyres, pressure 115 lb/sq in (8·08 kg/cm²). Nose-wheel fitted with Goodyear Dual Chine tyre size 18 × 4·4 10-ply rating, pressure 105 lb/sq in (7·38 kg/cm²). Goodyear multiple-disc hydraulic brakes. Anti-skid units.

POWER PLANT: Two General Electric CJ610-6 turbojet engines (each rated at 2,950 lb=1,340 kg st) mounted in pods on sides of rear fuselage. Fuel in integral tanks in wings and wingtip tanks with a total fuel capacity of 840 US gallons (3,180 litres). Oil capacity 1 US gallon (3·75 litres) per engine.

ACCOMMODATION: Two seats side-by-side on flight deck, with dual controls. Up to six passengers in cabin, with one on inward-facing bench-seat on starboard side at front, then two on forward or aft-facing armchairs with centre aisle, and three on forward-facing couch. Toilet and stowage space under front inward-facing seat, which can be screened from remainder of cabin by curtain. Refreshment cabinet opposite this seat. Baggage compartment aft of cabin. With back of rear bench seat folded down, baggage compartment and rear of cabin can be used to carry cargo or stretchers. Table at rear. In full cargo version, the rearward-facing armchair seats are also removed. Two-piece door, with upward-hinged portion and downward-hinged portion with integral steps, on port side of cabin at front. Emergency exit on starboard side.

SYSTEMS: Air-conditioning and pressurisation system, with air-cycle refrigeration system, has differential of 8·77 lb/sq in (0·62 kg/cm²). Windshield primary anti-icing system by engine-bleed air, with alcohol system as back-up.

ELECTRONICS AND EQUIPMENT: Four different nav/com systems, to full airline standard, are available to customer's requirements, comprising Collins, Bendix, Sperry or Export equipment. All have Learjet autopilot as standard.

DIMENSIONS, EXTERNAL:

Span over tip tanks	35 ft 7 in (10·84 m)
Wing chord at root	9 ft 0 in (2·74 m)
Wing chord at tip	4 ft 7 in (1·40 m)
Wing aspect ratio	5·02
Length overall	43 ft 3 in (13·18 m)
Length of fuselage	41 ft 0 in (12·50 m)
Height over tail	12 ft 7 in (3·84 m)
Tailplane span	14 ft 8 in (4·47 m)
Wheel track (C/L shock-struts)	8 ft 3 in (2·51 m)
Wheelbase	16 ft 2 in (4·93 m)
Cabin door:	
Height	3 ft 9 in (1·14 m)
Width	3 ft 0 in (0·91 m)
Emergency exit:	
Height	2 ft 4 in (0·71 m)
Width	1 ft 7 in (0·48 m)

DIMENSIONS, INTERNAL:

Cabin, between pressure bulkheads:	
Length	17 ft 4 in (5·28 m)
Max width	4 ft 11 in (1·50 m)
Max height	4 ft 4 in (1·32 m)
Volume, including baggage compartment	260 cu ft (7·36 m³)
Baggage compartment	40·0 cu ft (1·13 m³)

AREAS:

Wings, gross	231·77 sq ft (21·53 m²)
Ailerons (total)	11·70 sq ft (1·08 m²)
Trailing-edge flaps (total)	36·85 sq ft (3·42 m²)
Spoilers	7·18 sq ft (0·67 m²)
Fin	37·37 sq ft (3·47 m²)
Rudder, including tab	6·85 sq ft (0·64 m²)
Tailplane	54·00 sq ft (5·02 m²)
Elevators	13·66 sq ft (1·27 m²)

WEIGHTS AND LOADINGS:

Weight empty, equipped	6,851 lb (3,107 kg)
Operating weight, empty	7,238 lb (3,283 kg)
Max payload	2,762 lb (1,252 kg)
Max T-O weight	13,500 lb (6,124 kg)
Max ramp weight	13,800 lb (6,260 kg)
Max zero-fuel weight	10,000 lb (4,536 kg)
Max landing weight	11,880 lb (5,389 kg)
Max wing loading	58·2 lb/sq ft (284·1 kg/m²)
Max power loading	2·29 lb/lb st (2·29 kg/kg st)

PERFORMANCE (at max T-O weight):

Max level speed at 31,000 ft (9,450 m)
464,473 knots (545 mph; 877 km/h)
Max diving speed Mach 0·86

Artist's impression of the new Gates Learjet 24C, introduced during 1970

Gates Learjet 25B executive jet transport (two General Electric CJ610-6 turbojet engines) (*M. J. Axe*)

Max cruising speed, at 45,000 ft (13,720 m)
464 knots (534 mph; 859 km/h)
Econ cruising speed at 45,000 ft (13,720 m)
418 knots (481 mph; 774 km/h)
Stalling speed, wheels and flaps down
101 knots (116 mph; 187 km/h)
Stalling speed, clean
128 knots (147 mph; 237 km/h)
Rate of climb at S/L 6,300 ft (1,920 m)/min
Service ceiling 45,000 ft (13,720 m)
Service ceiling, one engine out
26,000 ft (7,925 m)
T-O run 2,914 ft (888 m)
T-O to 35 ft (10·7 m) FAA BFL
3,917 ft (1,194 m)
Landing from 50 ft (15 m) at max landing weight
3,352 ft (1,022 m)
Landing run, at max landing weight
1,881 ft (573 m)
Range with max fuel, 45 min reserve
1,702 nm (1,960 miles; 3,154 km)

GATES LEARJET 24C

This aircraft, which first entered production in 1970, is generally similar to the model 24D, but is a lighter-weight lower-cost version.

The foregoing description of the Learjet 24D applies also the the 24C except in the following details.

POWER PLANT: Total fuel capacity is 715 US gallons (2,706 litres).

WEIGHTS AND LOADINGS:

Weight empty, equipped	6,537 lb (2,965 kg)
Operating weight, empty	6,924 lb (3,140 kg)
Max payload	3,076 lb (1,395 kg)
Max T-O weight	12,500 lb (5,670 kg)
Max ramp weight	12,800 lb (5,806 kg)
Max wing loading	59·93 lb/sq ft (292·6 kg/m²)
Max power loading	2·12 lb/lb st (2·12 kg/kg st)

PERFORMANCE (at max T-O weight):
As for Model 24D except:
Max rate of climb at S/L
6,900 ft (2,103 m)/min
T-O run 2,506 ft (764 m)
T-O to 35 ft (10·7 m) FAA BFL
3,370 ft (1,027 m)
Range with max fuel, 45 min reserve
1,459 nm (1,680 miles; 2,703 km)

GATES LEARJET 25B

First flown on 12 August 1966 as the Learjet 25, this version is 4 ft 2 in (1·27 m) longer than the series 24 aircraft, and will accommodate eight passengers and a crew of two. FAA certification in the air transport category (FAR 25) was obtained on 10 October 1967 and the initial delivery was made in November 1967.

The 1970 version, re-designated Gates Learjet 25B, introduces a number of refinements, and the description of the Learjet 24D applies also to the model 25B, except in the following details:

DIMENSIONS, EXTERNAL:
As for Learjet 24D except:
Length overall 47 ft 7 in (14·50 m)
Wheelbase 19 ft 2 in (5·84 m)

DIMENSIONS, INTERNAL:
As for Learjet 24D except:
Cabin, between pressure bulkheads:
Length 20 ft 7 in (6·27 m)
Volume, including baggage compartment
294 cu ft (8·32 m³)

WEIGHTS AND LOADINGS:

Weight empty, equipped	7,296 lb (3,309 kg)
Operating weight, empty	7,683 lb (3,485 kg)
Max payload	2,317 lb (1,050 kg)
Max T-O weight	15,000 lb (6,803 kg)
Max ramp weight	15,500 lb (7,030 kg)
Max landing weight	13,300 lb (6,032 kg)
Max wing loading	64·7 lb/sq ft (315·9 kg/m²)
Max power loading	2·54 lb/lb st (2·54 kg/kg st)

PERFORMANCE (at max T-O weight):
As for Learjet 24D except:
Max cruising speed at 41,000 ft (12,500 m)
473 knots (545 mph; 877 km/h)=Mach 0·81
Stalling speed, wheels and flaps down, at max landing weight
107 knots (123 mph; 198 km/h)
Max rate of climb at S/L
5,600 ft (1,707 m)/min
Max rate of climb at S/L, one engine out
1,600 ft (488 m)/min
Service ceiling, one engine out
24,500 ft (7,470 m)
T-O run 3,822 ft (1,165 m)
T-O to 35 ft (10·7 m) FAA BFL
5,186 ft (1,580 m)
Landing from 50 ft (15 m) at max landing weight
3,750 ft (1,143 m)
Landing run, at max landing weight
2,287 ft (862 m)
Range, with max fuel, 45 min reserve
1,759 nm (2,026 miles; 3,260 km)

GATES LEARJET 25C

This longer-range version of the basic Learjet 25 entered production in 1970. With the addition of a 210-US gallon (795-litre) fuselage fuel tank, the 25C has a non-stop range in excess of 2,000 nm (2,300 miles; 3,700 km), plus fuel reserve. The cabin of this version is optionally convertible from a four- or eight-seat configuration to a two-bed sleeper compartment. It is otherwise the same as the Learjet 25B, and the description of this aircraft and of the Learjet 24D applies also to the 25C except as detailed below:

DIMENSIONS, INTERNAL:
Volume, including baggage compartment
266 cu ft (7·53 m³)

WEIGHTS:

Weight empty, equipped	7,070 lb (3,207 kg)
Operating weight empty	7,457 lb (3,382 kg)
Max payload	2,543 lb (1,153 kg)

PERFORMANCE (at max T-O weight):
Long-range cruising speed, at 41,000 ft (12,500 m)
441 knots (508 mph; 818 km/h)=Mach 0·77
Max certified operating altitude
45,000 ft (13,716 m)
Range with max fuel, 45 min reserve
2,198 nm (2,532 miles; 4,074 km)

GENERAL AIRCRAFT
GENERAL AIRCRAFT CORPORATION

HEAD OFFICE:
Suite 501, 888 North Sepulveda Boulevard,
El Segundo, California 90245

PRESIDENT:
Dr Lynn L. Bollinger

VICE-PRESIDENTS:
Allan C. Butterworth Jr (Sales and Service)
Joe H. Talley (Engineering)

General Aircraft Corporation has designed a
36 to 40-seat turboprop transport aircraft aimed
primarily at the third-level, commuter and local
airline market. It features advanced high-lift
devices (some under licence from Helio Aircraft
Corporation) for low-speed operation from
unimproved airstrips.

GENERAL AIRCRAFT GAC-100

TYPE: Four-turboprop STOL transport.

WINGS: Cantilever low-wing monoplane. Aerofoil section 23,020 at root, 23,015·5 at tip.
Incidence 3°. Dihedral 7°. Sweepback at
quarter-chord 1° 30'. All-metal two-spar
fail-safe structure of 2024 ST aluminium with
chemically-milled skins. Full-span Fowler-
type double-slotted flaps of aluminium construction. Full-span segmented spoilers.
Trim-tab in trailing-edge of each outboard
flap section. Full-span aerodynamically-
operated leading-edge slats. No ailerons.
Outboard spoiler mixer for roll control. Pneumatic de-icing boots optional.

FUSELAGE: All-metal semi-monocoque fail-safe
structure of circular cross-section, with stringers
and skin of 2024 ST aluminium.

TAIL UNIT: Cantilever all-metal structure of
2024 ST aluminium with small dorsal fin and
swept vertical surfaces. Conventional tailplane, elevators and rudder. Trim-tabs in
rudder and elevators, geared servo-tab in
rudder. Pneumatic de-icing boots optional.

LANDING GEAR: Hydraulically-retractable tricycle type, all units retracting forward. Oleo-
pneumatic shock-absorbers and dual wheels
on each unit. Main wheels and tyres size
29 × 11-10, Type III, pressure 45 lb/sq in
(3·16 kg/cm²). Nose-wheels and tyres size
7·00 × 6, Type III, pressure 38 lb/sq in (2·7
kg/cm²). Goodrich multiple disc brakes. Dual
Hytrol Mk III anti-skid units.

POWER PLANT: Four Pratt & Whitney (UACL)
PT6A-40 turboprop engines, each rated at
850 shp, driving three-blade metal variable-
pitch propellers, diameter 9 ft 0 in (2·74 m).
Fuel contained in four integral wing tanks,
total fuel capacity 1,150 US gallons (4,353
litres). Overwing gravity refuelling points,
central pressure refuelling point in engine
nacelle.

ACCOMMODATION: Provision for crew of two on
flight deck with dual controls. Provision for
third seat on flight deck. Main cabin accommodates 36 passengers as standard, in pairs on
each side of a 20 in (0·51 m) centre aisle, with
seats set at 35 in (0·98 m) pitch. Alternative
seating layout for 40 passengers optional.
Seats track-mounted and foldable for quick
conversion to cargo configuration. Galley and
toilet at rear of cabin. Passenger door at rear
of cabin on port side will be actuated hydraulically or electrically and incorporates an airstair. Service door immediately opposite on

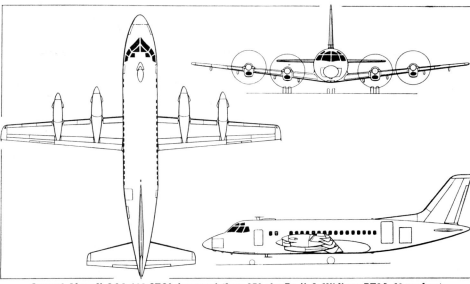

General Aircraft GAC-100 STOL transport (four 850 shp Pratt & Whitney PT6A-40 engines)

starboard side. Two emergency exits on
opposite sides of the cabin, adjacent to leading-
edge of wing. Baggage compartment door aft
of passenger door on port side. Cabin heated
and air-conditioned.

SYSTEMS: AiResearch simple-cycle 'twin pac'
pressurisation system with max differential
of 6·5 lb/sq in (0·46 kg/cm²). Dual 3,000 lb/sq in
(210 kg/cm²) hydraulic systems. Pneumatic
system for flight instruments and optional
de-icing system from engine bleed-air. Electrical system includes four 300A 24-28V DC
starter-generators, two hydraulically-driven
10kVA alternators and one 500VA inverter.
Garrett-AiResearch turbine APU with one
300VA starter-generator to provide electrical
power for engine starting and cabin air-conditioning on the ground. Oxygen system
standard.

ELECTRONICS AND EQUIPMENT: Navigation and
communications equipment to customers'
requirements. Blind flying instrumentation
standard.

DIMENSIONS, EXTERNAL:
Wing span	70 ft 0 in (21·34 m)
Wing chord at root	9 ft 7 in (2·92 m)
Wing chord at tip	3 ft 7 in (1·09 m)
Wing aspect ratio	10·6
Length overall	70 ft 0 in (21·34 m)
Height overall	24 ft 10 in (7·57 m)
Tailplane span	27 ft 6 in (8·38 m)
Wheel track	22 ft 0 in (6·71 m)
Wheelbase	19 ft 3½ in (5·88 m)
Propeller ground clearance	1 ft 6 in (0·46 m)

Passenger door (port, aft):
Height	5 ft 10 in (1·78 m)
Width	3 ft 2 in (0·97 m)
Height to sill	5 ft 7½ in (1·71 m)

Baggage door (port, aft):
Height	4 ft 2 in (1·27 m)
Width	3 ft 2 in (0·97 m)
Height to sill	5 ft 7½ in (1·71 m)

Service door (stbd, aft):
Height	4 ft 0 in (1·22 m)
Width	2 ft 0 in (0·61 m)
Height to sill	5 ft 7½ in (1·71 m)

Emergency exits (two, port and stbd):
Height	4 ft 0 in (1·22 m)
Width	2 ft 0 in (0·61 m)

DIMENSIONS, INTERNAL:
Cabin, excluding flight deck and rear baggage
compartment:
Length	35 ft 3 in (10·74 m)
Max width	8 ft 9 in (2·67 m)
Max height	6 ft 5 in (1·96 m)
Baggage compartment	234 cu ft (6·62 m²)

AREAS:
Wings, gross	461 sq ft (42·8 m²)
Trailing-edge flaps (total)	50 sq ft (4·65 m²)
Spoilers (total)	74 sq ft (6·87 m²)
Vertical tail surfaces	115 sq ft (10·7 m²)
Horizontal tail surfaces	150 sq ft (13·9 m²)

WEIGHTS AND LOADINGS:
Operating weight, empty	15,660 lb (7,103 kg)
Max payload, weight limited	8,340 lb (3,783 kg)
Normal payload	7,200 lb (3,266 kg)
Max T-O weight	26,500 lb (12,020 kg)
Max zero-fuel weight	24,000 lb (10,886 kg)
Max landing weight	26,000 lb (11,793 kg)
Max wing loading	57·5 lb/sq ft (280·7 kg/m²)
Max power loading	7·8 lb/hp (3·54 kg/hp)

PERFORMANCE (estimated at max T-O weight):
Max level speed at 15,000 ft (4,572 m)
254 knots (293 mph; 472 km/h)
Cruising speed at 15,000 ft (4,572 m)
254 knots (293 mph; 472 km/h)
Stalling speed, 50° flaps
62 knots (71 mph; 115 km/h)
Max rate of climb at S/L 2,300 ft (701 m)/min
T-O to 50 ft (15 m), FAR 25, S/L, ISA +
20°C 2,410 ft (735 m)
Landing from 50 ft (15 m), FAR 25, at max
landing weight 2,420 ft (738 m)
Landing run, FAR 25, at max landing weight
1,460 ft (445 m)
Range with max fuel, normal cruising speed
at 15,000 ft (4,572 m)
1,453 nm (1,673 miles; 2,692 km)
Range with normal payload, normal cruising
speed at 15,000 ft (4,572 m)
570 nm (656 miles; 1,055 km)

GENERAL DYNAMICS
GENERAL DYNAMICS CORPORATION

HEAD OFFICE:
1, Rockefeller Plaza, New York, NY 10020

AEROSPACE OPERATING DIVISIONS:
Forth Worth division, Fort Worth, Texas
Pomona division, Pomona, California
Convair division, San Diego, California

PRESIDENT AND CHIEF EXECUTIVE:
Roger Lewis

VICE-PRESIDENTS:
Lloyd Bergeson (General Manager, Quincy
Shipbuilding Division)
Jack L. Bowers (President, Convair Division)
Frank W. Davis (President, Fort Worth
Division)
Max Golden (Contracts)
Roger I. Harris (Chief Counsel)
John T. Hayward
Edward H. Heinemann (Special Projects)
Algie A. Hendrix (Industrial Relations)
Charles F. Horne (President, Pomona Division)
E. J. LeFevre (GD Field Offices)
J. T. MacDonald
George E. Mueller (Programmes and Develop-
ment)
Frank Nugent (Resources)
Joseph D. Pierce (General Manager, Electric
Boat Division)
John A. Sargent (Finance)

SECRETARY: John P. Maguire
TREASURER: Harold K. Pedersen
COMPTROLLER: David L. Thomas

Of the 13 operating units of General Dynamics
Corporation, the three listed above are respons-
ible for its aerospace activities in the United
States. All three were components of the former
Convair Division, which had its origin in the
Consolidated Aircraft Corporation, incorporated
on 29 May 1923.

The activities of the operating divisions may
be summarised as follows:—Convair: manufacture of complete vertical and horizontal tail
surfaces for the Lockheed C-5 military transport;
design and production of a major portion of the
fuselage for the Douglas DC-10 commercial transport; research and development in supersonic and
hypersonic aircraft, portable landing fields and
other restricted projects; design, development,
manufacturing and testing of the Atlas standardised space launch vehicle, the Centaur hydrogen-
fuelled spacecraft for boosting heavy payloads
into orbit and for launching interplanetary probes,
and other design work concerned with space travel;
design and manufacture of oceanographic buoys
for meteorological and oceanographic data
accumulation and transmission, and large navigation buoys for harbour and sealane use.
Pomona:—research, development and production
of Standard and Standard ARM missiles for the
US Navy and of the Redeye ground-to-air missile

system: Fort Worth:—development of the F-111
series of combat aircraft, conversion of B-57's
into RB-57F reconnaissance aircraft, and research
and development work on restricted projects.

Convair division also retains detailed tooling for
high-usage spares for the Convair-Liner 240/340/
440 series of piston-engined transports and
Convair 880 and 990 jet transports, and is manufacturing components for operators of these
types. It is also offering a conversion scheme
under which operators of Convair-Liner aircraft
can have them re-engined with Dart turboprops.
The modified aircraft are designated Convair 600/
640.

Employment figures in January 1970 were
14,000 at Convair, 6,600 at Pomona and 27,700
at Fort Worth

GENERAL DYNAMICS F-111

Following a detailed evaluation of design
proposals submitted by General Dynamics and
Boeing, the US Department of Defense announced
on 24 November 1962 that General Dynamics
had been selected as prime contractor for development of the F-111 tactical fighter (known originally by the designation TFX), with Grumman
Aircraft as an associate. An initial contract
was placed for 23 development aircraft (18
F-111A's for the USAF, five F-111B's for the US
Navy), of which the first were scheduled for delivery within 2½ years. Since then, further orders
have been placed, including 24 F-111C's (similar to

A's) for the Royal Australian Air Force, and reconnaissance and strategic bomber versions for the USAF.

The fleet of swing-wing F-111 aircraft, which now numbers more than 200, has recorded its 50,000th hour of flight.

The 50,000th hour was logged by a US Air Force crew in an F-111A fighter-bomber on a training mission at Nellis Air Force Base, Nebraska.

Several versions of the F-111 are now being developed as follows:

F-111A. USAF two-seat tactical fighter-bomber, with slightly longer nose than that of F-111B to accommodate different electronic equipment. Development models built with two P & W TF30-P-1 turbofan engines; production version has TF30-P-3 engines and Mk I avionics. Manufacture of parts, components and sub-systems began in 1963. First F-111A was completed at GD Fort Worth plant 16 October 1964 and flew for the first time (with wings locked at sweepback of 26°) on 21 December 1964, ten days ahead of schedule and slightly more than two years from announcement of contract. During the second flight of this prototype, on 6 January 1965, complete wing sweep, from the lowest possible sweep of 16° to the highest possible sweep of 72·5°, was accomplished. Initial contracts covered the 18 development aircraft and 141 production models for the USAF, all of which have been delivered. Superseded by F-111E.

The 12th F-111A, first flown on 27 May 1966, was a lightened model incorporating most of the improvements scheduled for the production version. Weight was reduced by 4,000 lb (1,815 kg). Other changes included improved matching of engine and airframe and, in particular, modified inlets to the engine intakes, which improved the stall characteristics of the engine and man-oeuvrability of the aircraft in the Mach 2·2 region, together with new flaps and slats to increase max lift and introduction of the McDonnell crew escape system.

Early in February 1967 the F-111A completed a three-month series of tests of supersonic flying using its TFR (terrain-following radar) system, which constantly scans ahead of the aircraft and from side-to-side. For manual flight, TFR signals are supplied to the pilot's cockpit display; for automatic or electronic flight they are fed into the autopilot for direct control of the aircraft.

During its first 15-minute supersonic dash, on 9 November 1966, an F-111A flew more than 150 nautical miles, half the time in the automatic mode, over uneven terrain that included mountains as high as 8,700 ft (2,650 m). This was the longest low-level flight made at supersonic speed up to that time and also marked the first occasion on which an F-111 had been flown supersonically under electronic control at low altitudes.

The F-111's TFR system is usable day or night to slip beneath enemy radar defences to minimize detection. It automatically checks its own operation and commands the F-111 into a sharp pull-up to a safe altitude if it senses any marginal operation or failure in the system itself.

Two F-111A aircraft demonstrated their long-range capability on 22 May 1967, by flying from the continental United States to two points in Europe, using only internal fuel. The two aircraft departed together from Loring AFB, Maine, and landed separately at Wethersfield Air Force Station, England, and Le Bourget Airport in Paris, France. The flights took 5 hours 23 minutes and 5 hours 54 minutes respectively.

Air Force crew training for the F-111A began in July 1967 at Nellis Air Force Base, Nevada. Deliveries of operationally-configured production F-111As began in October 1967. The first production aircraft made a 1,047-mile (1,685-km) "automatic" flight on TFR from Fort Worth to Nellis at a constant altitude of 1,000 ft (3,048 m) above the ground—a graphic demonstration of the aircraft's low-level penetration capability.

The 474th Tactical Fighter Wing at Nellis is the only one to be equipped with F-111As. Six aircraft from Nellis arrived at the Takhli base in Thailand on 17 March 1968 and made their first operational sorties over Vietnam on 25 March. Two were lost in the next five days.

YF-111A. Strike/reconnaissance fighters completed prior to cancellation of the British government's order for 50 aircraft, under the designation F-111K, have been assigned to the USAF for use in its research, development, test and evaluation programme, with the new designation YF-111A.

F-111B. US Navy version, intended originally for carrier-based fleet defence duties with armament of six Hughes AIM-54 Phoenix air-to-air missiles. Greater wing span and area than F-111A. Powered initially by TF30-P-1 turbofan engines· production models were intended to have more powerful TF30-P-12 engines. First F-111B, assembled by Grumman, flew for the first time

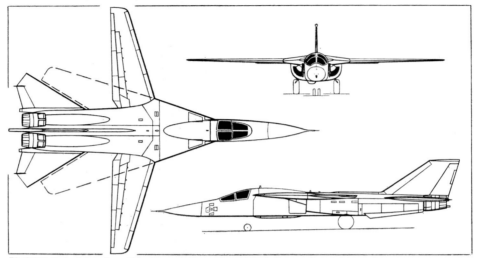

Photograph and drawing of the General Dynamics F-111A, the version of this variable-geometry fighter for USAF Tactical Air Command

on 18 May 1965. The fifth F-111B incorporates the weight-saving, drag-reducing and other improvements made on the twelfth F-111A. Original orders covered the five development aircraft and 24 production models for the US Navy. The sixth aircraft, the first to be fitted with the definitive TF30-P-12 engines, flew on 29 June 1968. It was expected that the seventh F-111B, intended as a test-bed for the Phoenix missile, would also be delivered in August 1968. In July 1968, the F-111B completed successfully limited carrier tests aboard the USS *Coral Sea* off the coast of California. Continued development, production and support of the F-111B was halted by Congress in mid-1968.

F-111C. Strike aircraft. Outwardly similar to FB-111, with Pratt & Whitney TF30-P-3 engines, Mk I avionics, cockpit ejection module and eight underwing attachments for stores. 24 ordered for RAAF. Deliveries deferred.

F-111D. Similar to F-111A, but with more advanced Mk II avionics system, offering improvements in navigation and in air-to-air as well as air-to-surface weapon delivery.

F-111E. Superseded F-111A from 160th aircraft. Modified air intakes to permit removal of flight restrictions above Mach 2·2 and 60,000 ft (18,300 m). A total of 94 F-111E's have been ordered. To be followed by F-111D.

F-111F. Fighter-bomber. Generally similar to the F-111D, but with an avionics system that combines the best features of the F-111E and FB-111A systems, to provide effective tactical avionics at the lowest possible cost. Introduces more powerful TF30-P100 engines, producing 25% more thrust than the basic TF30, and these

are expected to offer a significant improvement in T-O performance, single-engine rate-of-climb, payload capability, acceleration and max speed at low level with use of afterburning. 58 ordered.

F-111K. See YF-111A.

FB-111A. Two-seat strategic bomber version for USAF Strategic Air Command. Requirement for 210 announced by US Secretary of Defense on 10 December 1965, to replace B-52C/F versions of the Stratofortress and B-58A Hustler. Initial contract for 64 signed in Spring of 1967. Subsequently, on 20 March 1969, the US Secretary of Defense stated that FB-111A production would total 76 aircraft. First of two prototypes converted from development F-111A's flew on 30 July 1967. Max load to be 50 × 750-lb bombs, of which two will be carried in internal weapon bay and 48 in twin clusters of three on eight underwing attachments. Full load will be carried with wings swept at 26°, reducing to 38 bombs (six underwing attachments) at 54° of sweep, or 20 bombs at full sweep. Long-span wings. Strengthened landing gear. Increased braking capacity. Mk IIB advanced avionics. TF30-P-7 engines. Ability to carry SRAM missiles.

First FB-111A was delivered to Strategic Air Command at Carswell AFB, Texas, on 8 October 1969. FB-111A Wings will operate from Pease AFB, New Hampshire, and Plattsburgh AFB, New York.

RF-111A. Two-seat reconnaissance version of F-111A for USAF. Cameras, radar and infra-red sensors in fuselage weapon-bay operate through optical windows and radomes on the outboard sides of the reconnaissance pallet. Sensors are operated through a digital computer control

General Dynamics F-111C strike-reconnaissance aircraft for the Royal Australian Air Force

General Dynamics RF-111A reconnaissance aircraft for the USAF

system. Development announced by US Secretary of Defense on 3 December 1965. F-111A No 11 modified as prototype. First flight was made on 17 December 1967.

Factors which were taken into account in selecting General Dynamics as prime contractor included the degree to which weapon system costs could be reduced by maximum use of common equipment and structures in the two versions, utilisation of conventional materials, and similar structural designs and size of the aircraft.

Most revolutionary feature of the F-111 is the use of variable-sweep wings to ensure optimum performance throughout the speed range. The specification called for a maximum speed of about Mach 2·5, capability of supersonic speed at sea level, short take-off capability from rough airfields in forward areas and short landing capability. The F-111 had to be able to fly between any two airfields in the world in one day and to carry a full range of conventional and nuclear weapons including the latest air-to-surface tactical weapons. External stores are carried on four attachments under each wing. The two inboard pylons on each side pivot as the wings sweep back, to keep the stores parallel with the fuselage. The two outboard pylons on each wing are jettisonable and non-swivelling.

General Dynamics have overall responsibility for the F-111 programme, for production of forward and centre fuselage sections and the wings, for final assembly of F-111A's and for flight testing and evaluation of F-111B's. Grumman responsibilities include the aft fuselage sections and landing gear, and, originally, final assembly and flight testing of F-111B's.

Subcontractors on the programme include General Electric Co, for attack radars, flight control systems and portions of the armament system; Westinghouse Electric Corp for electrical generating systems; Litton Industries for the navigation and attack system and astrocompass; Sanders Associates for ECM group; Avco Corp for countermeasures receiving sets; Navigation and Control Division of Bendix Corp for air data computer units; Collins Radio for high-frequency radio and antenna coupler; AiResearch Manufacturing Company for air-conditioning and pressurisation equipment; Texas Instruments for terrain-following radar (not fitted on F-111B); GPL Division of General Precision Inc for Doppler radar; Motorola for X-band transponder; Honeywell for the low-altitude radar altimeter; Textron for the radar homing and warning system; Kaiser Aerospace & Electronics Corp for the F-111B head-up and vertical integrated electronic displays; and Autonetics Division of North American Aviation for Mk II/IIB avionics.

The following details apply to the F-111A and F-111B:

TYPE: Two-seat variable-geometry multi-purpose fighter.

WINGS: Cantilever shoulder wing. Wing section of NACA 63 series, with conventional washout. Sweepback of outer portions variable in flight or on the ground from 16° to 72° 30′. Wing-actuating jacks by Jarry Hydraulics. Five-spar structure, with stressed and sculptured skin panels, each made in one piece between leading and trailing-edge sections, from root to tip. Leading and trailing-edge sections of honeycomb sandwich. Airbrake/lift dumpers above wing operate as spoilers for lateral control at low speeds. Full-span variable-camber leading-edge slats and full-span double-slotted trailing-edge flaps. General Electric flight control system. Span of F-111B increased by "bolt-on" wing-tips.

FUSELAGE: Semi-monocoque structure, mainly of aluminium alloy, with honeycomb sandwich skin. Some steel and titanium. Main structural member is a T-section keel, under the

arms of which the engines are hung. Nose radome of F-111B folds upward to reduce overall length for stowage.

TAIL UNIT: Conventional cantilever sweptback surfaces, utilising honeycomb sandwich skin panels, except for tailplane tips and central area of fin on each side. All-moving horizontal surfaces operate both differentially and collectively to provide aileron and elevator functions. Two long narrow ventral stabilising fins.

LANDING GEAR: Hydraulically-retractable tricycle type. Single wheel on each main leg. Twin-wheel nose unit retracts forward. Main gear is a triangulated structure with hinged legs which are almost horizontal when the gear is extended. During retraction, the legs pivot downward, the wheels tilt to lie almost flat against them, and the whole gear rotates forward so that the wheels are stowed side-by-side in fuselage between engine air intake ducts. Low-pressure tyres on main wheels, size 47 × 18 in on F-111A, 42 × 13 in on F-111B, F-111C and FB-111A. Disc brakes, with anti-skid system. Main landing gear door, in bottom of fuselage, hinges down to act as speed brake in flight.

POWER PLANT: Two Pratt & Whitney TF30 turbofan engines, each giving approx 20,000 lb (9,072 kg) st with afterburning. Fuel tanks in wings and fuselage. F-111B has standard capacity for 16,120 lb (7,310 kg) of fuel. F-111A has additional tankage in compartment aft of cockpit used for electronics in F-111B. Pressure fuelling point in port side of fuselage, forward of engine air intake. Gravity fuel filler/in-flight refuelling receptacle in top of fuselage aft of cockpit. Hamilton Standard hydro-mechanical air intake system with movable shock-cone.

ACCOMMODATION: Crew of two side-by-side in air-conditioned and pressurised cabin. Portion of canopy over each seat is hinged on aircraft centre-line and opens upward. Initial aircraft have conventional ejection seats. Later aircraft (from No. 12) are fitted with a zero-speed, zero-altitude (including underwater) emergency escape module developed by McDonnell Douglas Corp and utilising a 40,000 lb (18,140 kg) st Rocket Power Inc rocket motor. Emergency procedure calls for both crew members to remain in capsule cabin section, which is propelled away from aircraft by rocket motor and lowered to ground by parachute. Air-bags cushion impact and form flotation gear in water. Entire capsule forms survival shelter.

DIMENSIONS:
Wing span:
F-111A, RF-111A:
spread 63 ft 0 in (19·20 m)
fully swept 31 ft 11·4 in (9·74 m)

General Dynamics FB-111A for USAF Strategic Air Command

F-111B, F-111C, FB-111:
spread 70 ft 0 in (21·34 m)
fully swept 33 ft 11 in (10·34 m)
Wing chord at root 6 ft 11 in (2·11 m)
Length overall:
F-111A, RF-111A, F-111C, FB-111
73 ft 6 in (22·40 m)
F-111B
normal 66 ft 9 in (20·35 m)
nose-cone folded 61 ft 8 in (18·79 m)
Height overall:
F-111A, F-111C, FB-111, RF-111A
17 ft 1·4 in (5·22 m)
F-111B 16 ft 8 in (5·08 m)

WEIGHTS (approx):
Max T-O weight:
F-111A 70,000 lb (31,750 kg)
F-111B 68,000 lb (31,000 kg)

PERFORMANCE:
Max speed at height Mach 2·5
Max speed at S/L Mach 1·2
Service ceiling over 60,000 ft (18,300 m)
T-O run under 3,000 ft (915 m)
Landing run under 3,000 ft (915 m)
Range with max internal fuel
over 3,300 nm (3,800 miles; 6,100 km)

GENERAL DYNAMICS/MARTIN RB-57F

Under USAF contract, the Fort Worth division of General Dynamics has converted an initial series of 12 Martin B-57 (licence-built Canberra) tactical bombers into reconnaissance aircraft with the designation RB-57F. The modifications give the aircraft an increased operating ceiling, greater range, increased payload and improved handling characteristics.

The conversion involves almost complete redesign and rebuilding, and General Dynamics are making use of advanced materials, including honeycomb sandwich panels, for the new components. The original wing is replaced by a new three-spar wing of almost double the span and with a marked anhedral. The ailerons are inset at about mid-span and are supplemented by spoilers. New and larger vertical tail surfaces are fitted. All control surfaces have tightly-sealed gaps to reduce drag. There are no flaps.

The standard 7,220 lb (3,275 kg) st Wright J65 turbojets are replaced by two 18,000 lb (8,165 kg) st Pratt & Whitney TF33-P-11 turbofan engines, and there are also two 3,300 lb (1,500 kg) st Pratt & Whitney J60-P-9 auxiliary turbojets in underwing pods. The fuselage fuel tank has been deleted to make way for equipment and all fuel is now carried in the wings outboard of the engines.

There are four underwing hard points for external stores, of which two are used normally to carry the auxiliary turbojets. When these turbojets are not required, all four hard points are available for stores or equipment pods.

A great deal of special equipment is carried, including radar in the fuselage nose and unspecified electronics in the streamwise plastic wingtips. The cockpit layout is unchanged, with ejection seats in tandem for the crew of two. The Lear MC-1 (modified) autopilot is of the type used in the Boeing C-135 transport aircraft.

Delivery of the first RB-57F was made to the USAF's 58th Weather Reconnaissance Squadron at Kirtland AFB, New Mexico, on June 18, 1964, only nine months after design work was started. The aircraft's duties include high-altitude sampling of air for radioactive particles.

DIMENSIONS, EXTERNAL:
Wing span	122 ft 5 in (37·32 m)
Length overall	69 ft 0 in (21·03 m)
Height overall	19 ft 0 in (5·79 m)

AREA:
Wings, gross	2,000 sq ft (185·8 m²)

CONVAIR DELTA DAGGER
USAF designation: F-102

Modification and updating of F-102 fighter aircraft has been a continuing process. Latest modifications include the installation of standby vertical gyro indicators. Radar homing and warning (RHAW) will be incorporated in a limited number of aircraft and equipment complying with the DOD's aircraft identification monitoring systems (AIMS) programme will be installed in the near future under the direction of the San Antonio Air Materiel Area, USAF.

Convair has proposed a Close Air Support Mission re-configuration for this aircraft to provide improved air-to-ground weapon accuracy, maximum use being made of off-the-shelf USAF inventory equipment to effect the modification. The aim is to achieve simplified systems requiring a minimum of maintenance. Improvements would include installation of an internal "Gatling" gun; two additional external pylon stations; increased internal fuel capacity with provision for in-flight refuelling; expanded nav/com equipment and better flight instrumentation. The modifications would allow a large variety of optional weapons to be carried externally.

Details of the F-102 can be found in the 1961/62 *Jane's*.

CONVAIR DELTA DART
USAF designation: F-106

Under contracts awarded by the San Antonio Air Materiel Area of the USAF, F-106 fighter aircraft continue to be updated and modified.

Included in this work are programmes for improved reliability of operating systems (IROS), improved maintainability and reliability (IMRS), and improved mission probability success (IMPS).

Among these improvements are MEISR, which enhances the reliability of the radar system, and RIPS, which deals with reliability of the electrical power distribution/generation system. A feasibility demonstration of an internally mounted "Gatling" gun and a clear-top canopy was conducted successfully in 1969. The USAF is planning modification programmes to incorporate these features to enhance the weapon system's capability to operate in global rôles as well as in continental US defence in conjunction with the USAF advanced airborne warning and control systems (AWACS).

Details of the F-106 can be found in the 1964/65 *Jane's*.

GENERAL DYNAMICS CONVAIR 600/640

The Convair 600 and 640 are, respectively, turboprop conversions of the twin-engined Convair-Liner 240 and 340/440 transports.

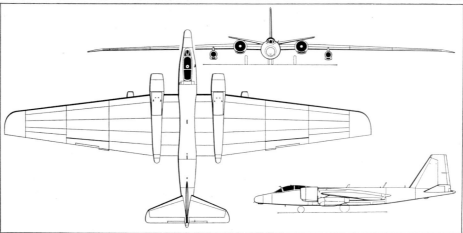

Three-view drawing and photograph (*T. Matsuzaki*) of the General Dynamics/Martin RB-57F high-altitude special reconnaissance aircraft

developed as a joint undertaking by Rolls-Royce of England and the Convair division of General Dynamics.

Conversion to Convair 600/640 standard involves replacing the original piston-engines with two 2,750 shp (3,025 eshp) Rolls-Royce Dart RDa.10 Mk 542-4 turboprops, driving four-blade Dowty Rotol type R-245/4-40-4·5/13 propellers, diameter 13 ft 0 in (3·96 m) for the Convair 600 and 13 ft 4 in (4·06 m) for the Convair 640, and the installation of new gearboxes, nacelles, combustion heaters, cabin air compressor and related cockpit instruments. Customers can choose between buying the kits to carry out modifications themselves or have the work done by an approved modification centre. With interior modifications, it is possible to seat up to 56 persons in Convair 640 aircraft converted from Series 340/440 aircraft.

In passenger versions of the Convair 640 new seating is now available which can be folded quickly against the cabin walls to accommodate cargo.

The Convair 600 has a standard fuel capacity of 1,000 US gallons (3,785 litres) and max capacity of 2,000 US gallons (7,570 litres) with long-range tanks. Corresponding capacities for the Convair

640 are 1,730 US gallons (6,547 litres) and 2,945 US gallons (11,147 litres) respectively.

Included in the modification kit is an AiResearch GTP30-95 APU, driving a 500A DC generator and cabin air compressor for ground air supply and both ground and in-flight electrical power. An enlarged cargo door can also be provided.

The first Convair 600 flew for the first time on 20 May 1965 and received FAA supplemental type approval on 18 November 1965. The Convair 640 received its supplemental type certificate on 7 December 1965. The 600 entered service with Central Airlines on 30 November 1965; the 640 with Caribair on 22 December 1965.

The descriptions of the Convair-Liner 240/340/440 series given in *Jane's* in 1949-59 apply equally to the Convair 600 and 640, except for the details given above.

DIMENSIONS, EXTERNAL:*
Wing span:
600	91 ft 9 in (27·98 m)
640	105 ft 4 in (32·12 m)

Length overall:
600	74 ft 8 in (22·77 m)
640, standard	79 ft 2 in (24·14 m)
640, with nose radome	81 ft 6 in (24·84 m)

General Dynamics Convair 600, a conversion of the Convair-Liner transport in the insignia of Frontier Airlines (*Jean Seele*)

Height overall:
600   26 ft 11 in (8·22 m)
640   28 ft 2 in (8·59 m)

DIMENSIONS, INTERNAL:*
Cabin: Length:
600   33 ft 5 in (10·19 m)
640   36 ft 7 in (11·15 m)
Max width   8 ft 7 in (2·62 m)
Max height   6 ft 7 in (2·00 m)
* Dimensions and areas are unchanged by conversion.

WEIGHTS AND LOADINGS:
Weight empty:
600   28,380 lb (12,872 kg)
640   30,275 lb (13,732 kg)
Max T-O weight:
600   46,200 lb (20,955 kg)
640   55,000 lb (24,950 kg)
Max zero-fuel weight:
600   39,500 lb (17,915 kg)
640   50,000 lb (22,680 kg)

Max landing weight:
600   44,000 lb (19,958 kg)
640   52,500 lb (23,815 kg)
Max wing loading:
600   56·5 lb/sq ft (276 kg/m²)
640   59·8 lb/sq ft (292 kg/m²)

PERFORMANCE (at max T-O weight):
Max level speed at 15,000 ft (4,575 m):
600   268 knots (309 mph; 497 km/h)
640   261 knots (300 mph; 482 km/h)
Max permissible diving speed:
600
234 knots (270 mph; 435 km/h) or Mach 0·550 CAS
640
260 knots (300 mph; 482 km/h) or Mach 0·650 CAS
Max and econ cruising speeds:
Same as max level speed at 15,000 ft
Landing speed, power off, wheels and flaps down:
600   72 knots (83 mph; 134 km/h)

640   73 knots (84 mph; 136 km/h)
Rate of climb at S/L:
600   1,400 ft (427 m)/min
640   1,150 ft (350 m)/min
Rate of climb at S/L, one engine out:
600   440 ft (134 m)/min
640   325 ft (99 m)/min
Service ceiling:
600   24,000 ft (7,315 m)
640   23,000 ft (7,000 m)
FAA T-O distance to 35 ft (10·5 m):
600   4,655 ft (1,419 m)
640   5,245 ft (1,598 m)
Range at 15,000 ft (4,575 m) with long-range tanks, 45 min reserve:
600 at 268 knots (309 mph; 497 km/h)
   1,650 nm (1,900 miles; 3,060 km)
Range at 15,000 ft (4,575 m) with standard fuel, 45 min reserve:
640 at 260 knots (300 mph; 482 km/h)
   1,068 nm (1,230 miles; 1,975 km)

GERONIMO (see under "Seguin Aviation")

GREAT LAKES
GREAT LAKES AIRCRAFT COMPANY
HEAD OFFICE:
PO Box 5974, Cleveland, Ohio 44101
PRESIDENT: H. R. Swack
CHIEF ENGINEER: Andrew Oldfield

Mr Andrew Oldfield designed and built the prototype of a small single-seat sporting biplane, by scaling down the design of the well-known Great Lakes Sport Trainer. The resulting aircraft is known as the Baby Great Lakes. Material kits for building the aircraft and plans of the design are available from Great Lakes Aircraft Company.

There are now more than 250 Baby Great Lakes under construction. At least 20 have been completed, and it is understood that examples are being built in Africa, Australia and Italy. In addition, plans and material kits are available for the full-size Great Lakes Sport Trainer and 140 are at present under construction.

GREAT LAKES BABY GREAT LAKES
TYPE: Single-seat amateur-built sporting biplane.
WINGS: Braced biplane, with N-type interplane struts, double landing and flying wires and N-type centre-section support struts. Wing section modified M6, tapering to USA 27 18 in (46 cm) from tips. Incidence 2° 30′ on top wing, 1° 30′ on bottom wing. Wood structure of spruce spars and Warren truss ribs, with overall fabric covering. Ailerons on lower wings only. No flaps.
FUSELAGE: Welded steel-tube structure, fabric-covered.
TAIL UNIT: Wire-braced welded steel-tube structure, fabric-covered.
LANDING GEAR: Non-retractable tail-wheel type. Oleo main legs with size 5·00 × 4 wheels. Steerable tail-wheel.
POWER PLANT: One 80 hp Continental A80 four-cylinder horizontally-opposed air-cooled engine, driving a two-blade fixed-pitch propeller. Provision for alternative engines of between 50 and 100 hp, and several aircraft now under construction will have 1,500 and 1,600 cc Volkswagen engines. Fuel tank in front fuselage, capacity 12 US gallons (45 litres).
ACCOMMODATION: Single seat in open cockpit.

DIMENSIONS, EXTERNAL:
Wing span: top   16 ft 8 in (5·08 m)
Wing chord (both wings, constant)
   3 ft 0 in (0·91 m)
Length overall   13 ft 9 in (4·19 m)
Height overall   4 ft 6 in (1·37 m)

AREA:
Wings, gross   86 sq ft (7·99 m²)

WEIGHTS (A80 engine):
Weight empty   475 lb (215 kg)
Max T-O weight   850 lb (285 kg)

PERFORMANCE (A80 engine, at max T-O weight):
Max level speed at S/L
   117 knots (135 mph; 217 km/h)
Cruising speed at S/L
   102 knots (118 mph; 190 km/h)
Stalling speed   43·5 knots (50 mph; 81 km/h)
Rate of climb at S/L   2,000 ft (610 m)/min
Service ceiling   17,000 ft (5,200 m)
T-O run   300 ft (91 m)
Landing run (no brakes)   400 ft (122 m)
Max range   217 nm (250 miles; 400 km)

GREAT LAKES SPORT TRAINER
The Great Lakes Sport Trainer was produced with a variety of engines by the original Great Lakes Company, founded on 2 January 1929. Installation drawings for modern Continental, Lycoming, Warner and other engines have been

Mr H. R. Swack's Baby Great Lakes (65 hp Continental engine)

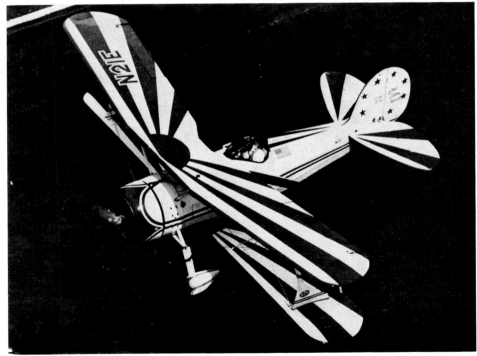
Great Lakes Sport Trainer owned by Mr Harold Krier (185 hp Warner engine)

prepared by Mr Nicholas D'Apuzzo, enabling builders to select versions with engines ranging from 125 to 240 hp. During 1968 installation design for a 200 hp Lycoming IO-360-A1A fuel-injection engine was completed.

In the Spring of 1970 the company was giving serious consideration to starting limited production of the Sport Trainer, but pending a decision, the company is making available to amateur constructors completed fuselages, wing ribs, fuel tanks and tail units.
TYPE: Two-seat amateur-built sporting biplane.
WINGS: Braced biplane, with N-type interplane struts, wire bracing and N-type centre-section support struts. Wing section M-12. Dihedral 3° on upper wing, 2° on lower wing. Sweepback on upper wing 9° 13′. Composite structure,

with spruce spars, metal ribs and overall fabric covering. Ailerons on lower wings only. No flaps or tabs.
FUSELAGE: Welded chrome-molybdenum steel-tube Warren girder structure, with fabric covering.
TAIL UNIT: Wire-braced welded chrome-molybdenum steel-tube structure, fabric-covered. No tabs.
LANDING GEAR: Non-retractable type, with steerable tail-wheel. Divided main legs with spring-oleo shock-absorbers standard. Glass-fibre or cantilever spring steel legs optional. Main wheels size 6·00 × 6. Wheel fairings optional.
POWER PLANT: Any engine in 125-240 hp range

suitable. Data below are for version with 165 hp Franklin horizontally-opposed air-cooled engine. Aluminium or glass-fibre fuel tank in centre-section, capacity 26 US gallons (98·5 litres).

ACCOMMODATION: Basically two seats in tandem in open cockpit. Can be built as high-performance single-seater.

DIMENSIONS, EXTERNAL:

Wing span	26 ft 8 in (8·13 m)
Length overall (165 hp Franklin engine)	20 ft 4 in (6·20 m)
Height overall	7 ft 4 in (2·24 m)

Wheel track	5 ft 10 in (1·78 m)

AREAS:

Wings, gross	187·6 sq ft (17·43 m²)
Ailerons (total)	13·5 sq ft (1·25 m²)
Fin	5·87 sq ft (0·55 m²)
Rudder	6·81 sq ft (0·63 m²)
Tailplane	15·44 sq ft (1·43 m²)
Elevators	10·68 sq ft (0·99 m²)

WEIGHTS:

Weight empty, depending on engine	946-1,025 lb (429-465 kg)
Max T-O weight	1,618 lb (734 kg)

PERFORMANCE (165 hp Franklin engine):

Max level speed at S/L	120 knots (138 mph; 222 km/h)
Max cruising speed	109 knots (125 mph; 201 km/h)
Stalling speed	35 knots (40 mph; 65 km/h)
Rate of climb at S/L	1,200-1,800 ft (365-550 m)/min
Service ceiling	14,000 ft (4,260 m)
T-O run	290 ft (88 m)
Landing run	400 ft (122 m)
Range with max fuel	312 nm (360 miles; 580 km)

GRUMMAN
GRUMMAN CORPORATION

HEAD OFFICE:
South Oyster Bay Road, Bethpage, New York 11714

CHAIRMAN OF THE BOARD AND CHIEF EXECUTIVE OFFICER:
E. Clinton Towl

PRESIDENT:
Llewellyn J. Evans

CHAIRMAN, EXECUTIVE COMMITTEE:
William T. Schwendler

VICE-PRESIDENTS:
Thomas P. Cheatham Jr
John B. Rettaliata (Director of Public Relations)

TREASURER: P. J. Cherry

SECRETARY AND GENERAL COUNSEL: John F. Carr

GRUMMAN AEROSPACE CORPORATION

HEAD OFFICE AND WORKS:
South Oyster Bay Road, Bethpage, New York 11714

CHAIRMAN OF THE BOARD AND CHIEF EXECUTIVE OFFICER:
E. Clinton Towl

PRESIDENT:
L. J. Evans

VICE-CHAIRMAN OF THE BOARD:
William T. Schwendler

SENIOR VICE-PRESIDENT:
Richard Hutton

VICE-PRESIDENTS:
Cregg E. Coughlin
Edward Dalva
Joseph G. Gavin Jr
Robert L. Hall
Ira G. Hedrick
Lawrence M. Mead Jr
Corwin H. Meyer
Robert C. Miller
Edward C. Nezbeda
Gordon H. Ochenrider (Director of Sales)
Michael Pelehach
G. Thomas Rozzi
Charles G. Vogeley
William M. Zarkowsky
A. James Zusi

SECRETARY AND GENERAL COUNSEL: Raphael Mur

TREASURER: Carl A. Paladino

GRUMMAN ALLIED INDUSTRIES, INC

HEAD OFFICE AND WORKS:
600 Old Country Road, Garden City, New York 11530

CHAIRMAN OF THE BOARD:
E. Clinton Towl

PRESIDENT:
Wallace B. Spielman

SENIOR VICE-PRESIDENT:
Robert F. Loar

VICE-PRESIDENTS:
James L. Maxwell
William H. Shaw

SECRETARY AND GENERAL COUNSEL: J. J. Serota

TREASURER-CONTROLLER: Richard P. Segalini

GRUMMAN DATA SYSTEMS CORPORATION

HEAD OFFICE AND WORKS:
South Oyster Bay Road, Bethpage, New York 11714

PRESIDENT:
Peter E. Viemeister

VICE-PRESIDENTS:
James M. Connors
Robert A. Nafis
Burton Stern

SECRETARY: John F. Carr

TREASURER: James M. Pettit

GRUMMAN INTERNATIONAL, INC

HEAD OFFICE AND WORKS:
534 Broad Hollow Road, Melville, New York 11746

PRESIDENT:
Thomas P. Cheatham Jr

EXECUTIVE VICE-PRESIDENT:
Charles B. Kirbow

VICE-PRESIDENTS:
James H. Phillips
Edwin Zolkoski

SECRETARY: Mellor A. Gill

TREASURER: Patrick J. Cherry

MONTAUK AERO CORPORATION

HEAD OFFICE AND WORKS:
South Oyster Bay Road, Bethpage, New York 11714

PRESIDENT:
E. Clinton Towl

VICE-PRESIDENT:
L. J. Evans

SECRETARY: John F. Carr

TREASURER: Patrick J. Cherry

The Grumman Aircraft Engineering Corporation was incorporated on 6 December 1929. Important changes in the corporate structure of the company were announced in 1969, resulting in the formation of Grumman Corporation, a small holding company, with Grumman Aerospace Corporation, Grumman Allied Industries Inc, Grumman Data Systems Corporation, Grumman International Inc and Montauk Aero Corporation as wholly-owned subsidiaries. This re-organisation reflects the wide range of Grumman's current activities.

Grumman's current production types include the A-6 Intruder for the US Navy. For the US Army, the OV-1 Mohawk surveillance aircraft is in production at the Bethpage and Stuart, Florida, factories. Though C-2A Greyhound and E-2A Hawkeye production has ended, a follow-on order for C-2A aircraft is likely and an E-2C version is in the development stage. Grumman was selected as the winner of the VFX fighter competition for a new carrier-based fighter for the US Navy, and has begun development of the new aircraft, now designated F-14A. Its Ag-Cat single-seat single-engined agricultural biplane is being manufactured under licence by Schweizer Aircraft Corporation.

In addition, Grumman is associated with General Dynamics Corporation (which see) in development of the F-111 tactical combat aircraft for the USAF.

On 29 September 1967, Grumman formally opened a new air-conditioned plant with some 260,000 sq ft (24,155 m²) of floor space at Savannah, Georgia. Known as Grumman-Savannah, it accommodates two Gulfstream II corporate aircraft final assembly lines, with production at a rate of three or four aircraft per month, and approximately 1,000 workers are employed there.

Other activities include manufacture of the Apollo Lunar Module and an Orbiting Astronomical Observatory (see "Guided Missiles and Space Vehicles" section) and construction of hydrofoil boats for the US Navy and US Marine Administration.

Grumman employed a total of more than 32,000 people in January 1970.

GRUMMAN G-89 TRACKER
US Navy designations: S-2, TS-2 and US-2

The Tracker is a twin-engined carrier-based anti-submarine search and attack aircraft which is in production for and in service with the US Navy. Also in service are two developments of the Tracker—the C-1A Trader general-utility transport-trainer and E-1B Tracer airborne early warning and fighter direction aircraft—of which details can be found in the 1963-64 Jane's.

The prototype, designated XS2F-1, made its first flight on 4 December 1952, since when Grumman have delivered more than 1,000 S-2's. Export deliveries have been made to the Royal Netherlands and Italian Navies, which have received 26 and 40 S-2's respectively, and to the Argentine Navy (6) and Brazil (12). Sixty have been delivered to the Japanese Maritime Self-Defence Force. Fourteen of the latest S-2E's have been built for the Royal Australian Navy.

The following versions of the S-2 have been produced:

S-2A (formerly S2F-1). Two 1,525 hp Wright R-1820-82 engines. First production model. Supplied also to the Argentine, Japan, Italy, Brazil, Taiwan, Thailand, Uruguay and the Netherlands. About 500 built. Production completed.

TS-2A. Training version of S-2A.

S-2B. Redesignation of S-2A's modified to carry Jezebel acoustic search equipment and Julie acoustic echo ranging system.

S-2C (formerly S2F-2). Developed version to carry larger anti-submarine weapons. An enlarged torpedo bay with asymmetrical extension on port side of fuselage accommodates homing torpedoes. To compensate for increased weight the tail surfaces were increased in area. Sixty built. Most converted into US-2C utility aircraft.

S-2D (formerly S2F-3). Developed version of S-2A ordered in 1958. Increased span. More roomy crew accommodation. Much improved operational equipment and armament. Twice the endurance of S-2A at 200 nm (230 miles; 370 km) radius. Prototype flew on 20 May 1959. Original contracts for 167, for delivery by end of 1963, were increased by a further order for 48 announced in January 1962. Production completed.

S-2E (formerly S2F-3S). Similar to S-2D, but with more advanced ASW electronic equipment, and provision for new types of armament, including nuclear depth charges, AS.12 air-to-surface missiles and Miniguns. Deliveries to VS-41 began in October 1962.

CS2F-1. Canadian production version of S-2A built under licence for Royal Canadian Navy by de Havilland Aircraft of Canada, Ltd. 100 built. Seventeen supplied to Royal Netherlands Navy.

CS2F-2/3. New designations for CS2F-1 aircraft fitted with improved operational equipment.

The following data apply generally to all versions of the S-2.

TYPE: Twin-engined naval anti-submarine aircraft.

WINGS: Cantilever high-wing monoplane. All-metal multi-spar structure. Wings fold upward and inward hydraulically from outboard of the engine nacelles. Fixed leading-edge slots on outer wings. Small ailerons, supplemented by wide-span spoilers on upper surfaces. Long-span slotted flaps. Leading-edge de-icer boots.

FUSELAGE: All-metal semi-monocoque structure.

TAIL UNIT: Cantilever all-metal structure. Rudder split vertically into two sections: forward section actuated hydraulically during take-off, landing and single-engined operation to increase rudder area.

LANDING GEAR: Retractable tricycle type, all units retracting rearward. Twin wheels on nose unit only. Small aft wheel-bumper is extendable but not fully retractable.

POWER PLANT: Two 1,525 hp Wright R-1820-82 WA nine-cylinder air-cooled radial engines, driving three-blade constant-speed metal propellers.

ACCOMMODATION: Crew of four consisting of pilot, co-pilot (who serves as navigator, radio-operator and searchlight-operator), radar operator and MAD operator. Dual controls.

ELECTRONICS AND EQUIPMENT: Equipment of S-2D includes UHF direction finder, LF direction finder, TACAN, APN-122 Doppler radar, APN-117 low-altitude radar altimeter, UHF transmitter/receiver, HF transmitter/receiver, APX 6B and APA 89 IFF, ASA-13 ground position indicator, and auto-pilot. S-2D also has ground track plotter on instrument panel, giving aircraft position and ground track, including Doppler correction for drift and ground speed, target position from Julie computer, sonobuoy location, radar position, MAD mark on ground track and exhaust trail mark on ground track.

OPERATIONAL EQUIPMENT (S-2D): AQA-3 Jezebel passive long-range acoustic search equipment, using sonobuoys; ECM instantaneous electronic countermeasures direction finder; Sniffer passive submarine exhaust trail detector; Julie active acoustic echo ranging by means of explosive charges, automatic target computer and automatic target plotting; retractable ASQ-10 MAD (magnetic anomaly detector) tail "sting"; retractable 75kW X-band 42-in × 20-in search radar under fuselage; 85 million candlepower remotely-controlled searchlight under starboard wing.

ARMAMENT (S-2D): Two homing torpedoes or one Mk 101 depth bomb or four 385-lb depth charges in bomb bay. Six underwing attachments for torpedoes, 5-in rockets, Zuni rockets or 250-lb bombs. Housing for sonobuoys and marine markers in rear of engine nacelles. Fuselage dispenser for 60 underwater sounding charges for echo ranging.

DIMENSIONS, EXTERNAL (S-2E):

Wing span	72 ft 7 in (22·13 m)
Width folded	27 ft 4 in (8·33 m)

Length overall	43 ft 6 in (13·26 m)
Height overall	16 ft 7 in (5·06 m)
Wheel track	18 ft 6 in (5·64 m)

AREAS:
Wings, gross:

S-2A, S-2C, CS2F-1 and 2	485 sq ft (45·1 m²)
S-2D, S-2E	496 sq ft (46·08 m²)

WEIGHTS (S-2E):

Weight empty	18,750 lb (8,505 kg)
Max payload	4,810 lb (2,182 kg)
Max internal fuel	4,368 lb (1,981 kg)
Max T-O weight	29,150 lb (13,222 kg)

PERFORMANCE (S-2E at max T-O weight):

Max level speed at S/L	over 230 knots (265 mph; 426 km/h)
Patrol speed at 1,500 ft (450 m)	130·2 knots (150 mph; 241 km/h)
Stalling speed (landing configuration)	65 knots (74 mph; 119 km/h)
Service ceiling	21,000 ft (6,400 m)
Min T-O run	1,300 ft (396 m)
T-O to 50 ft (15 m)	1,875 ft (572 m)
Ferry range	1,128 nm (1,300 miles; 2,095 km)
Endurance with max fuel, 10% reserves	9 hours

GRUMMAN HAWKEYE
US Navy designation: E-2

The E-2A (formerly W2F-1) Hawkeye is a carrier-borne early-warning aircraft which was flown for the first time on 21 October 1960. It is manned by a crew of five, and carries the AN/APA-143 antenna for its AN/APS-96 long-range radar inside a large revolving saucer-shape radome above its fuselage. This radome revolves in flight at 6 rpm and can be lowered 2 ft (0·61 m) for stowage on board ship. It develops sufficient lift in flight to offset its weight.

Teams of Hawkeyes are able to circle naval task forces in all weathers, and are capable of detecting and assessing any threat from approaching high-Mach-number enemy aircraft early enough to ensure successful interception. The nerve centre of the intercept-control system is the Airborne Tactical Data System (ATDS), consisting of the auto-detection radar, airborne computers, memory and data-link system. ATDS is linked with the Naval Tactical Data System (NTDS), located in fleet headquarters, which processes, organises and displays information obtained from the aircraft, submarines and land and ship-based radar, to provide an overall picture of the tactical situation.

The automatic ATDS is monitored by the Hawkeye's crew, who can be assigned responsibility for controlling carrier-based fighters, so handling the complete process from detection to interception of the enemy.

The first Hawkeye equipped with the full airborne early warning and command electronics system flew on 19 April 1961. By mid-1963 about 20 E-2A's had been built and had completed initial carrier trials. Delivery to the US Navy began officially on 19 January 1964, when the first Hawkeye was accepted at San Diego for use in training air and ground crews of airborne early warning squadron VAW-11. This unit became operational on USS *Kitty Hawk* in 1966. Second Hawkeye unit is VAW-12.

On 20 February 1969, the prototype of a new version of the Hawkeye made its first flight. This is the **E-2B** early-warning aircraft which differs from the E-2A by having a Litton Industries L-304 microelectronic general-purpose computer. A retrofit programme is to update all operational fleet E-2A's to E-2B standard.

Grumman S-2E Tracker in the insignia of the Royal Australian Navy

These E-2B aircraft will be used in conjunction with a third version, designated **E-2C**, which is intended to utilise an advanced form of the Grumman/General Electric-developed AN/APS-111 radar, capable of detecting airborne targets in a land-clutter environment.

A derivative of the E-2A, designated C-2A, was produced for COD (Carrier On-board Delivery) duties with the US Navy and is described separately. The following details apply to the standard production E-2A Hawkeye:

TYPE: Airborne early-warning aircraft.

WINGS: Cantilever high-wing monoplane of all-metal construction. Centre-section is a structural box consisting of three beams, ribs and machined skins. Hinged leading-edge is non-structural and provides access to flying and engine controls. The outer panels fold rearward about skewed axis-hinge fittings mounted on the rear beams, to stow parallel with the rear fuselage on each side. Folding is done through a double-acting hydraulic cylinder. Trailing-edges of outer panels and part of centre-section consist of long-span ailerons and hydraulically-actuated Fowler flaps. When flaps are lowered, ailerons are drooped automatically. All control surfaces of E-2A are power-operated and incorporate devices to produce artificial feel forces. Automatic flight control system (AFCS) can be assigned sole control of the system hydraulic actuators, or AFCS signals can be superimposed on the pilot's mechanical inputs for stability augmentation. Pneumatically-inflated rubber de-icing boots on leading-edges.

FUSELAGE: Conventional all-metal semi-monocoque structure.

TAIL UNIT: Cantilever all-metal structure, with four fins and three rudders. Tailplane dihedral 11°. Full-length trimming surface forward of each rudder. Power control and artificial feel systems as for ailerons. Pneumatically-inflated rubber de-icing boots on all leading-edges.

LANDING GEAR: Hydraulically-retractable tricycle type. Pneumatic emergency extension. Steerable nose-wheel unit retracts rearward. Main wheels retract forward and rotate to lie flat in bottom of nacelles. Twin wheels on nose unit only. Oleo-pneumatic shock-absorbers. Main wheel tyres size 36 × 11 Type VII 24-ply, pressure 260 lb/sq in (18·28 kg/cm²) on ship, 210 lb/sq in (14·76 kg/cm²) ashore. Hydraulic brakes. Hydraulically-operated retractable tail-skid. A-frame arrester hook under tail.

POWER PLANT: Two 4,050 eshp Allison T56-A-8/8A turboprop engines, driving Aeroproducts N41 four-blade fully-feathering reversible constant-speed propellers, diameter 13 ft 6 in (4·11 m). Spinners and blade cuffs incorporate electrical anti-icers.

ACCOMMODATION: Crew of five on flight deck and in ATDS compartment in main cabin. Entry by downward-hinged door, with built-in steps, on port side of centre fuselage.

DIMENSIONS, EXTERNAL (E-2A):

Wing span	80 ft 7 in (24·56 m)
Length overall	56 ft 4 in (17·17 m)
Height overall	18 ft 4 in (5·59 m)
Diameter of AN/APA-143 radome	24 ft 0 in (7·32 m)

AREA:

Wings, gross	700 sq ft (65·03 m²)

WEIGHTS (E-2A):

Weight empty	36,063 lb (16,358 kg)
Max fuel (internal)	12,133 lb (5,503 kg)
Max T-O weight	49,638 lb (22,515 kg)

PERFORMANCE (E-2A at max T-O weight):

Max level speed	over 320 knots (368 mph; 593 km/h)
Cruising speed	274 knots (315 mph; 508 km/h)
Stalling speed (landing configuration)	70 knots (80 mph; 128 km/h)
Service ceiling	31,700 ft (9,660 m)
Min T-O run	1,205 ft (367 m)
T-O to 50 ft (15 m)	2,185 ft (666 m)
Ferry range	1,654 nm (1,905 miles; 3,065 km)

Grumman E-2B early-warning aircraft, developed from the E-2A Hawkeye

Grumman C-2A Greyhound Carrier On-board Delivery aircraft   (*Duane A. Kasulka*)

GRUMMAN C-2A GREYHOUND

The C-2A Greyhound is a derivative of the E-2A Hawkeye, designed specifically to deliver cargo to air groups deployed on carriers of the US Navy. It is compatible with elevators and hangar decks on CVS-10 and CVA-19 carriers, can be launched by catapult, using nose-tow gear, and can make arrested landings.

Many components of the C-2A and E-2A are common, including the complete turboprop power plants, and the Greyhound offers similar all-weather capability to the Hawkeye.

The first of three pre-production C-2A's (one for static testing) flew for the first time on 18 November 1964, and was accepted formally by the US Navy on 2 December 1964. Deliveries to the US fleet began in 1966 and a total of 17 C-2A's have been acquired to supplement C-1's of the Navy's Carrier On-board Delivery force.

Production of the C-2A ended in 1967, but Grumman have announced receipt of an order for 8 C-2A aircraft in the FY 1970 budget. The structural description of the E-2A Hawkeye applies equally to the C-2A Greyhound, with the following differences and additions:

TYPE: Twin-turboprop Carrier On-board Delivery (COD) transport.

WINGS: Incidence 4° at root, 1° at tip.

FUSELAGE: Conventional semi-monocoque light alloy structure. Cargo door, with integral ramp, forms undersurface of rear fuselage.

TAIL UNIT: Basically as for E-2A, but without tailplane dihedral.

LANDING GEAR: Basically as for E-2A, but with stronger nose gear (adapted from that of A-6A Intruder) to cater for higher AUW. Each nose-wheel fitted with 20 × 5·5 Type VII 12-ply tyre. Main wheel tyre pressure 200 lb/sq in (14 kg/cm²) on ship, 165 lb/sq in (11·6 kg/cm²) ashore.

POWER PLANT: Two fuel tanks, total capacity 1,824 US gallons (6,905 litres), occupy entire wing centre-section between the beams and the centre-line and wing-fold ribs. Fuelling point on inboard side of starboard nacelle. Provision for carrying two 300 US gallon (1,135 litre) or 450 US gallon (1,704 litre) external fuel tanks on sides of fuselage, or Douglas D704 or Beech 385 buddy refuelling packs in similar position. Provision for mounting flight refuelling probe above front fuselage. For long-range ferrying, fuel tanks can be supplemented by two 1,000 US gallon (3,786 litre) tanks in main cabin. Oil capacity (usable) 6·2 US gallons (23·5 litres).

ACCOMMODATION: Pilot and co-pilot side-by-side on flight deck, with dual controls. Lavatory and baggage space aft of flight deck. High-strength cargo compartment floor (300 lb/sq ft = 1,465 kg/m²) incorporates flush tracks for attaching tie-down fittings. Cargo door has integral ramp with detachable treadways. Provision for remotely-controlled cargo handling winch. Compartment can be adapted to accept Military Air Transport Command 463L material handling and support system, with choice of either three 108 × 88-in (2·74 × 2·24 m) master pallets or five 88 × 54-in (2·24 × 1·37 m) modular pallets. Alternative payloads include 39 troops in three longitudinal rows of seats or 20 litters and four attendants. Door at front of cabin on port side.

SYSTEMS: Hydraulic system, pressure 3,000 lb/sq in (210 kg/cm²), consists of two independent systems. Both systems supply control surface actuators. One system is also responsible for actuating wing fold system, cargo door, steering damper, arrester hook, brakes, landing gear,

windshield wipers, flaps and auxiliary generator. Air-conditioning system max pressure differential 6·5 lb/sq in (0·46 kg/cm²). Liquid oxygen breathing system, with two 10-litre converters, plus portable unit for cargo or personnel attendant. Primary electrical system supplied by two independent 115/200V 400 c/s three-phase engine-driven generators, each rated at 60kVA. 28V DC secondary sub-system supplied by two independent transformer-rectifiers. Emergency power provided by hydraulically-driven 3kVA AC generator, plus third transformer-rectifier for DC supply. Gas-turbine APU supplies pneumatic power for engine starting.

ELECTRONICS AND EQUIPMENT: Standard equipment includes separate vertical and horizontal attitude control sub-systems, duplicated ID-663 BDHI and ID-387 course indicator, AN/ASW-15 automatic flight control system featuring control wheel steering, heading and altitude hold, and TACAN/VOR radial navigation mode, central air data computer, two VOR receivers, glide slope receiver, marker beacon, receiver, TACAN, UHF and LF ADF's, LORAN, choice of eight receivers and three transmitters in AN/AIC-14 intercommunication and radio control system, AN/APX-46 IFF transponder and AN/APN-141 radar altimeter, Provision for UHF digital data link, automatic carrier landing system, Doppler radar and weather radar.

DIMENSIONS, EXTERNAL:

Wing span	80 ft 7 in (24·56 m)
Wing chord at root	13 ft 0 in (3·96 m)
Wing chord at tip	4 ft 4 in (1·32 m)
Width, folded	29 ft 4 in (8·94 m)
Length overall	56 ft 8 in (17·27 m)
Height overall	15 ft 11 in (4·85 m)
Cargo door:	
Width	7 ft 6 in (2·29 m)
Height	6 ft 6 in (1·98 m)

DIMENSIONS, INTERNAL.

Cargo space: Length	27 ft 6 in (8·38 m)
Width	7 ft 3½ in (2·23 m)
Height	5 ft 6 in (1·68 m)

AREAS:

Wings, gross	700 sq ft (65·03 m²)
Ailerons (total)	62 sq ft (5·76 m²)
Flaps (total)	118·75 sq ft (11·03 m²)
Fins (four, total)	93·02 sq ft (8·64 m²)
Rudders (three, total), including tabs	68·60 sq ft (6·37 m²)
Tailplane	125·07 sq ft (11·62 m²)
Elevators	40·06 sq ft (3·72 m²)

WEIGHTS:

Weight empty	31,154 lb (14,131 kg)
Max payload	10,000 lb (4,535 kg)
Max T-O weight	54,830 lb (24,870 kg)
Max arrested landing weight	44,612 lb (20,236 kg)
Max landing weight ashore	47,372 lb (21,488 kg)

PERFORMANCE (at max T-O weight):

Max level speed at optimum altitude	306 knots (352 mph; 567 km/h)
Stalling speed at max arrested landing weight	78 knots (89 mph; 143 km/h)
Rate of climb at S/L	2,330 ft (710 m)/min
Rate of climb at S/L, one engine out	310 ft (95 m)/min
Service ceiling	28,800 ft (8,780 m)
T-O to 50 ft (15 m)	2,560 ft (780 m)
Landing from 50 ft (15 m) at max arrested landing weight	1,735 ft (530 m)
Combat range at average cruising speed of 297 mph (478 kmh) at 27,300 ft (8,320 m)	1,432 nm (1,650 miles; 2,660 km)

GRUMMAN INTRUDER
US Navy designations: A-6, EA-6 and KA-6

Seven versions of the Intruder have been announced as follows:

A-6A (formerly A2F-1). Basic carrier-borne low-level attack bomber designed specifically to deliver nuclear or conventional weapons on targets completely obscured by weather or darkness. Performance is subsonic, but it is claimed to possess outstanding endurance and to carry a heavier and more varied load of stores than any other US naval attack aircraft.

Five weapon attachment points each have a 3,600 lb (1,633 kg) capacity. Typical weapon loads are thirty 500-lb (225 kg) bombs in clusters of three, or two Martin Bullpup missiles and three 2,000 lb general-purpose bombs.

To free the pilot from the need to consider details which can be performed automatically, and so enable him to focus his attention on immediate tactical decisions, the A-6A employs "DIANE," a Digital Integrated Attack Navigation system.

A Kaiser electronic integrated display system enables the pilot to "see" targets and geographical features at night or in bad weather by means of two viewing screens in the cockpit which provide a visual representation of the ground and air below and in front of the aircraft. Acting upon this information, the pilot is able to pre-select a course of action for his aircraft which can then approach its target, discharge its weapon and leave the target area automatically. A change in plans can be effected easily by the pilot should the tactical situation require it.

The prototype was fitted with hydraulically-actuated tilting tail-pipes, which could be inclined

Grumman A-6A Intruder carrier-based low-level attack bomber

downward to shorten the take-off run; but these were found to be unnecessary for production aircraft.

Competition for the original A-6A contract was conducted from May to December 1957, among eight aircraft companies. Of the 11 designs submitted, Grumman's was adjudged the best on 31 December 1957. The A-6A was developed subsequently under the first "cost plus incentive fee" contract placed by the US Navy. This contract was awarded in March 1959 and, together with a further contract placed in March 1960, covered the delivery of four aircraft in 1960 and four in 1961.

The first A-6A flew on 19 April 1960, and this version entered service officially on 1 February 1963, when the first aircraft was accepted for the US Navy's VA-42 squadron at NAS Oceana. Two more Naval squadrons and one Marine squadron have since been re-equipped with A-6A's. The A-6A Intruder is the only all-weather bomber currently in service with the Navy and Marine Corps in Vietnam.

A-6B. Conversion of the A-6A to provide Standard ARM missile capability. Though primarily an avionics modification, it has three different configurations ranging from limited to full strike capability.

A-6C. Derived from the A-6A but differing externally by carrying electro-optical sensors beneath the fuselage and having a terminal guidance system, providing additional night attack capability.

KA-6D. Grumman modified an A-6A into a flight refuelling tanker demonstrator, with drogue hose, and reel in the rear fuselage. This aircraft flew for the first time on 23 May 1966. The KA-6D production model will be fitted with TACAN and will be able to transfer more than 21,000 lb (9,500 kg) of fuel immediately after take-off or 16,000 lb (7,300 kg) at a distance of 260 nm (300 miles; 500 km) from its carrier base. In addition, the KA-6D could also act as a control aircraft for air/sea rescue operations or as a day bomber. It was planned to modify four A-6's to KA-6D standard during 1969, and the FY 1970 budget requested funding for 20 more conversions.

A-6E. An advanced A-6A featuring multimode radar and an IBM computer similar to that currently being tested in the EA-6B. First flight of an A-6E was made on 27 February 1970. Funds for the first 12 A-6E's were requested in the FY 1970 budget, with deliveries scheduled in the second half of 1971.

EA-6A. First flown in prototype form in 1963, this version retains partial strike capability, but is equipped primarily to support strike aircraft and ground forces by suppressing enemy electronic activity and obtaining tactical electronic intelligence within a combat area. Elements of the A-6A's bombing/navigation system are deleted and the EA-6A carries more than 30 different antennae to detect, locate, classify, record and jam enemy radiation. Externally-evident features include a radome at the top of the tail-fin, hoop-shaped wing-tip aerials and attachment points under the wings and fuselage for ECM pods, fuel tanks and/or weapons.

An initial batch of 12 production EA-6A's was built for the US Marine Corps.

EA-6B. Development of EA-6A for which Grumman received a prototype design and development contract in the Autumn of 1966. Nose is 40 in (1·02 m) longer than that of EA-6A to accommodate an enlarged cockpit housing a crew of four. The two additional crewmen operate the much more advanced electronics. Major sub-contractor is Airborne Instruments, a subsidiary of Cutler-Hammer Corporation, which is responsible for developing the electronic countermeasures system. Prototype EA-6B flew for the first time on 25 May 1968.

The US Administration Fiscal 1969 defence budget allocated a sum of $139 million for the purchase of eight EA-6B's for the US Navy, and funding for 12 additional aircraft was included in the FY 1970 budget request.

Orders for all versions total about 450.

The following details apply to the A-6A:

TYPE: Two-seat carrier-based attack bomber.

WINGS: Cantilever mid-wing monoplane, with moderate sweepback. All-metal structure. Hydraulically-operated almost-full-span leading-edge and trailing-edge flaps, with inset spoilers (flaperons) of same span as flaps (rigged permanently 3° up) forward of trailing-edge flaps. Trailing-edge of each wingtip, outboard of flap, splits to form speed-brakes which project above and below wing when extended. Two short fences above each wing. Outer panels fold upward and inward.

FUSELAGE: Conventional all-metal semi-monocoque structure. Bottom is recessed between engines to carry semi-exposed store. Door-type air-brake on each side of rear fuselage.

TAIL UNIT: Cantilever all-metal structure. All-moving tailplane, without separate elevators. Electronic antenna in rear part of fin immediately above rudder.

Grumman EA-6A electronic counter measures aircraft of the US Marine Corps

Grumman A-6C Intruder with electro-optical sensors beneath the fuselage

Demonstrator prototype of the Grumman KA-6D flight refuelling tanker aircraft

LANDING GEAR: Retractable tricycle type. Twin-wheel nose unit retracts rearward. Single-wheel main units retract forward and inward into air intake fairings. A-frame arrester hook under rear fuselage.

POWER PLANT: Two 9,300 lb (4,218 kg) st Pratt & Whitney J52-P-8A turbojet engines. Provision for up to four external fuel tanks under wings. Removable flight refuelling probe projects upward immediately forward of windshield.

ACCOMMODATION: Crew of two on Martin-Baker Mk GRU5 ejection seats, which can be reclined to reduce fatigue during low-level operations. Bombardier-navigator slightly behind and below pilot to starboard. Rearward-sliding canopy.

DIMENSIONS, EXTERNAL:

Wing span	53 ft 0 in (16·15 m)
Width folded	25 ft 2 in (7·67 m)
Length overall:	
A-6A	54 ft 7 in (16·64 m)
EA-6A	55 ft 3 in (16·84 m)
EA-6B	59 ft 5 in (18·11 m)
Height overall:	
A-6A	15 ft 7 in (4·75 m)
EA-6A, EA-6B	16 ft 3 in (4·95 m)
Height folded (A-6A)	15 ft 10 in (4·82 m)
Tailplane span	20 ft 8½ in (6·31 m)
Wheel track	10 ft 10 in (3·30 m)

AREA:

Wings, gross	529 sq ft (49·15 m²)

WEIGHTS:

Weight empty:	
A-6A	25,684 lb (11,650 kg)
EA-6A	27,769 lb (12,596 kg)
EA-6B	34,581 lb (15,686 kg)

Max internal fuel:	
A-6A	15,939 lb (7,230 kg)
EA-6A	15,857 lb (7,193 kg)
EA-6B	15,728 lb (7,134 kg)
Max external fuel:	
A-6A, EA-6A	10,045 lb (4,556 kg)
EA-6B	8,036 lb (3,645 kg)
Max payload:	
A-6A, EA-6A	18,000 lb (8,165 kg)
EA-6B	4,700 lb (2,132 kg)
Max T-O weight:	
A-6A	60,626 lb (27,500 kg)
EA-6A	56,500 lb (25,628 kg)
EA-6B	58,500 lb (26,535 kg)

PERFORMANCE:

Max level speed:	
EA-6A	538 knots (620 mph; 1,000 km/h)
Normal cruising speed:	
A-6A	417 knots (480 mph; 773 km/h)
EA-6A	418 knots (481 mph; 775 km/h)
Stalling speed (landing configuration):	
A-6A	68·7 knots (79 mph; 126 km/h)
EA-6A	72·1 knots (83 mph; 134 km/h)
Service ceiling:	
A-6A	41,660 ft (12,700 m)
EA-6A	38,960 ft (11,875 m)
Min T-O distance:	
A-6A	1,630 ft (497 m)
EA-6A	2,100 ft (640 m)
T-O to 50 ft (15 m):	
A-6A	2,200 ft (670 m)
EA-6A	2,700 ft (823 m)
Ferry range:	
A-6A	2,800 nm (3,225 miles; 5,190 km)
EA-6A	2,600 nm (2,995 miles; 4,820 km)

GRUMMAN G-134 MOHAWK
US Army designation: OV-1 (formerly AO-1)

The Mohawk is a high-performance two-seat observation aircraft which Grumman have developed for the US Army. The following versions have been announced:—

YOV-1A. Initial batch of nine service test aircraft, of which the first flew on 14 April 1959. Equipment includes ARC-52 UHF, ARC-44 VHF, AIC-12 ICS, ARN-59 ADF, MA-1 compass, APX-6B IFF, ARN-21 VOR/TACAN, ARN-32 marker beacon, KA-30 high-resolution optical photographic system, ARC-39 HF and APA-89 IFF coder.

OV-1A. First 18 production aircraft similar to YOV-1A, but with addition of FD-105 integrated flight system, ARC-55 UHF instead of ARC-52, ARN-30 VOR/TACAN instead of ARN-21, ARN-68 marker beacon instead of ARN-32 and provision for ARC-73 VHF, APX-44 IFF, radar altimeter, ILS, emergency VHF, autopilot, ground track beacon, Doppler and UAS-4 IR. The 19th and subsequent production aircraft have the radar altimeter, ILS, emergency VHF, auto-pilot and ground track beacon installed and have duplicated VOR/TACAN. All versions can carry 52 flares in each of two removable upward-firing pods mounted above the wing roots for night photography.

OV-1B. Different equipment. Similar to second series of OV-1A, but with APS-94 SLAR (side-looking airborne radar) in under-fuselage container and AKT-16 VHF data link. SLAR provides a permanent radar photographic map of terrain on either side of the flight path, on either 4 × 5 in (10 × 12·7 cm) cut film or 70-mm film strip. An in-flight processer enables the observer to see a developed photograph seconds after the film has been exposed. This version has increased wing span and area.

OV-1C. Different equipment. Similar to second series of OV-1A, but with UAS-4 infra-red surveillance equipment installed.

OV-1D. This version can be converted from infra-red to SLAR surveillance capability, and vice versa, in an hour, so combining the duties of the OV-1B and OV-1C. Two 1,160 shp (flat-rated) Lycoming T53-L-15 turboprop engines. Four pre-production prototypes under construction for the US Army.

By the beginning of 1968, more than 300 Mohawks had been delivered. Some of these aircraft are in operational use in Vietnam, with underwing weapons. Production of OV-1B and OV-1C has continued and final deliveries of OV-1A, -1B and -1C versions will make a combined total of 335 aircraft. Current appropriations cover the production of 30 OV-1D's, with an additional 270 planned for completion by the end of 1975.

TYPE: Two-seat army observation aircraft.

WINGS: Cantilever mid-wing monoplane. Wing section NACA 2412. Dihedral 6° 30′. Incidence 1° 30′. Aluminium alloy box-beam structure. Aluminium alloy ailerons and flaps. Full-span leading-edge slats.

FUSELAGE: Aluminium alloy semi-monocoque structure. Forward-opening air-brake on each side, aft of wing.

TAIL UNIT: Cantilever aluminium alloy structure. Central and two end-plate fins and rudders. Trim-tabs in centre rudder.

LANDING GEAR: Retractable tricycle type. Hydraulic retraction, with pneumatic emergency system. Main wheels retract outward into undersides of engine nacelles, nose-wheel rearward into fuselage. Bendix oleo-pneumatic shock-absorbers. Main wheels and tyres size 8·50 × 10, pressure 90 lb/sq in (6·33 kg/cm²). Nose-wheel tyre size 6·50 × 8, pressure 65 lb/sq in (4·57 kg/cm²). Goodyear disc brakes. Provision for wheel/ski gear.

POWER PLANT: Two 1,100 eshp Lycoming T53-L-15 turboprop engines, driving Hamilton Standard three-blade reversible-pitch propellers. Fuel in fuselage tank above wing, with capacity of 297 US gallons (1,125 litres). Provision for one 150 US gallon (567 litre) Aero 1C jettisonable tank under each wing, outboard of engine. Oil capacity 5 US gallons (19 litres).

ACCOMMODATION: Flight compartment seating two side-by-side in nose on Martin-Baker Mk J5 ejection seats. Dual controls, except when electronic surveillance equipment is fitted. Sides of canopy bulged to improve downward visibility. Armouring includes ¼-in (0·64-cm) aluminium alloy cockpit floor, bullet-resistant windshields and removable flak curtains on fore and aft cockpit bulkheads.

EQUIPMENT: Listed in introductory paragraphs above.

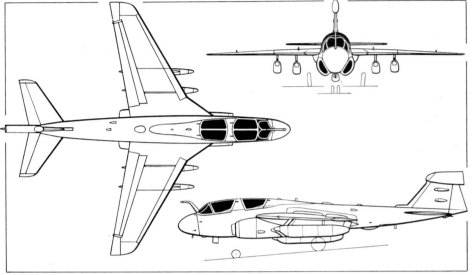

Photograph and three-view drawing of the Grumman EA-6B Intruder four-seat all-weather electronic countermeasures aircraft

DIMENSIONS, EXTERNAL:

Wing span:	
OV-1A, C	42 ft 0 in (12·80 m)
OV-1B	48 ft 0 in (14·63 m)
Wing chord at root	10 ft 6 in (3·20 m)
Wing chord at tip	5 ft 3 in (1·60 m)
Wing aspect ratio	5·35
Length overall	41 ft 0 in (12·50 m)
Height overall	12 ft 8 in (3·86 m)
Tailplane span	15 ft 11 in (4·85 m)
Wheel track	9 ft 2 in (2·79 m)
Wheelbase	11 ft 8¼ in (3·56 m)

AREAS:

Wings, gross:	
OV-1A, C	330 sq ft (30·65 m²)
OV-1B	360 sq ft (33·45 m²)
Ailerons (total)	22·7 sq ft (2·11 m²)
Flaps (total)	43·6 sq ft (4·05 m²)
Fins (total)	41·3 sq ft (3·84 m²)
Rudders (total)	27·5 sq ft (2·55 m²)
Tailplane	66·0 sq ft (6·13 m²)
Elevators	19·0 sq ft (1·77 m²)

WEIGHTS:

Weight empty, equipped:	
OV-1A	9,937 lb (4,507 kg)
OV-1B	11,067 lb (5,020 kg)
OV-1C	10,400 lb (4,717 kg)
Normal T-O weight:	
OV-1A	12,672 lb (5,748 kg)

OV-1B	13,650 lb (6,197 kg)
OV-1C	13,040 lb (5,915 kg)
Max T-O weight:	
OV-1A	15,031 lb (6,818 kg)
OV-1B, C	19,230 lb (8,722 kg)

PERFORMANCE:

Max level speed at 5,000 ft (1,520 m):	
OV-1A, 1C	267 knots (308 mph; 496 km/h)
OV-1B	258 knots (297 mph; 478 km/h)
Max permissible diving speed	390 knots (450 mph; 724 km/h)
Max cruising speed:	
OV-1A	264 knots (304 mph; 489 km/h)
OV-1B	239 knots (275 mph; 443 km/h)
OV-1C	258 knots (297 mph; 478 km/h)
Econ cruising speed:	
All versions 180 knots (207 mph; 334 km/h)	
Stalling speed (landing configuration):	
OV-1A	59 knots (68 mph; 109 km/h)
OV-1B	64 knots (73 mph; 117 km/h)
OV-1C	66 knots (76 mph; 123 km/h)
Rate of climb at S/L:	
OV-1A	2,950 ft (900 m)/min
OV-1B	2,350 ft (716 m)/min
OV-1C	2,670 ft (814 m)/min
Service ceiling:	
OV-1B	30,300 ft (9,235 m)
OV-1C	29,500 ft (9,000 m)
Service ceiling, one engine out:	
OV-1A	13,625 ft (4,152 m)

Grumman OV-1 Mohawk (two 1,100 eshp Lycoming T53-L-15 turboprop engines)

Min T-O run:

OV-1A	475 ft (145 m)
OV-1B	580 ft (177 m)
OV-1C	630 ft (192 m)

T-O to 50 ft (15 m):

OV-1A	922 ft (281 m)
OV-1B	880 ft (268 m)
OV-1C	1,100 ft (335 m)

Landing from 15 ft (15 m):

OV-1A, 1C	787 ft (240 m)
OV-1B	866 ft (264 m)

Landing run:

OV-1A	454 ft (138 m)
OV-1B	540 ft (165 m)
OV-1C	502 ft (153 m)

Max range with external tanks, 10% reserves:

OV-1A	1,220 nm (1,410 miles; 2,270 km)
OV-1B	1,065 nm (1,230 miles; 1,980 km)
OV-1C	1,155 nm (1,330 miles; 2,140 km)

GRUMMAN F-14

US Navy designation: F-14

Grumman announced on 15 January 1969 that it had been selected as winner of the design competition for a new carrier-based fighter for the US Navy. Known as the VFX during the competitive phase of the programme, this aircraft is now designated officially F-14.

Requests for proposals had been sent originally to five aerospace companies on 21 June 1968. One month later, on 17 July, the US Navy awarded contracts to initiate the contract definition phase of the VFX programme. Proposals were requested by 1 October for evaluation by Naval Air Systems Command, and on 17 December the Source Selection Authority announced that the Grumman and McDonnell Douglas entries had been chosen for final consideration.

The two competing designs were then modified to incorporate further technical refinements and were re-submitted to the Naval Air Systems Command in early January 1969. This led to selection of the Grumman design and initiation of the development programme which envisages first flight of the prototype F-14A in early 1971 and initial operational capability with the fleet in 1973.

Emphasis has been placed on producing a comparatively small, lightweight, high-performance aircraft offering a significant advance over the current F-4 Phantom II and the latest Soviet combat aircraft. In terms of airframe design, the F-14 uses advanced constructional techniques and titanium for optimum strength/weight ratio. Structural strength and a high thrust/weight ratio will enable it to combine a maximum speed in excess of Mach 2 with great agility in close-in air-to-air combat. Development time and risk are reduced by use of an already-existing avionics system, a landing gear evolved from that of the A-6 Intruder and proven high-performance engines in the initial version. Armament includes an M61 multi-barrel gun.

The Pratt & Whitney JTF22 advanced technology engine is under development for the F-14B and is expected to produce 28-30,000 lb st (12,700-13,600 kg st). Weighing some 800 lb (363 kg) less than the Pratt & Whitney TF30-P-401 engines which will power the prototype and early production models, it is expected to offer a 30% improvement in fuel consumption over the TF30 engine. It is anticipated that the new engine will be available for installation in the 68th and subsequent production aircraft.

The configuration of the F-14 is unique, with variable-geometry wings, small foreplanes which are extended as the wings sweep back to control centre-of-pressure shift and provide a lower wing loading, leading-edge flaps, and twin outward-canted fins and rudders. The engines are mounted in ducts under the fixed inner wings, with simple inlets and straight-line airflow for maximum efficiency over a wide range of altitudes and Mach numbers. The ducts have multiple-shock ramp systems for good pressure-recovery at high Mach numbers.

The F-14 is designed to fulfil three primary missions. The first of these, fighter sweep/escort, involves clearing contested air-space of enemy fighters and protecting the strike force, with support from E-2 Hawkeye early-warning aircraft, surface ships and communications networks to co-ordinate penetration and escape.

Second mission is to defend carrier task forces via Combat Air Patrol (CAP) and Deck Launched Intercept (DLI) operations. Third role is secondary attack of tactical targets on the ground, supported by electronic countermeasures and fighter escort.

Three versions of the F-14 are currently projected:

F-14A. Initial version, as described in detail below.

F-14B. Airframe and avionics basically the same as those of the F-14A, but powered by Pratt & Whitney JTF22 turbofans. Expected to be capable of acceleration from Mach 0·8 to Mach 1·8 in 1·27 minutes.

F-14C. Development of F-14B, with new avionics and weapons.

Under the initial contracts, Grumman was

Mock-up of the Grumman F-14A carrier-based fighter for the US Navy

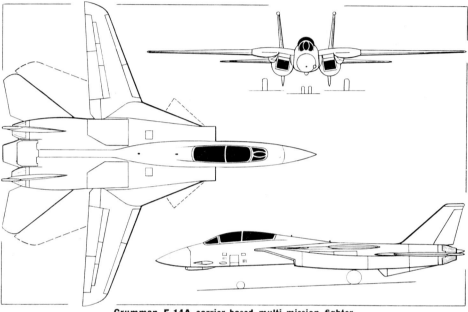

Grumman F-14A carrier-based multi-mission fighter

required to provide the US Navy with a mock-up of the F-14A in May 1969, as shown in the illustration. The contracts include provision of 12 research and development aircraft and an option on 463 F-14A and F-14B production aircraft.

All available details of the F-14A follow:

TYPE: Two-seat carrier-based multi-role fighter.

WINGS: Variable-geometry mid-wing monoplane, with 20° of sweep in the fully-forward position and 68° when fully swept. Wing position is programmed automatically for optimum performance throughout the flight régime, but manual override is provided. A short movable wing section, needing only a comparatively light pivot structure, results from utilisation of a wide fixed centre-section "glove", with pivot points 8 ft 11 in (2·72 m) from the centreline of the airframe. The inboard wing sections adjacent to the fuselage, arc upward slightly to minimise cross-sectional area and wave drag. Small canard surfaces, known as glove vanes, swing out from the leading-edge of the fixed portion of the wing as sweep of outer panels is increased. Stabilisation in pitch, provided by the canard surfaces, leaves the tailplane free to perform its primary control function. Trailing-edge control surfaces extend over almost entire span. Leading-edge flaps.

FUSELAGE: The centre-fuselage section is a simple, fuel-carrying box structure; forward fuselage section comprises cockpit and nose. The aft section has a tapered aerofoil shape to minimise drag, with a fuel dump pipe projecting from the rear. A speed brake is located on the upper surface, between the bases of the vertical tail fins.

View of the Grumman F-14A mock-up showing details of the engine intakes

TAIL UNIT: Twin vertical fins, mounted at the rear of each engine nacelle; a small pod at the top of each houses electronic countermeasures equipment. Outward-canted ventral fin under each nacelle. The all-flying horizontal surfaces have skins of boron-epoxy composite material.

LANDING GEAR: Retractable tricycle type. Twin-wheel nose units retract rearward. Single-wheel main units retract forward and upward. Arrester hook under rear fuselage, housed in small ventral fairing. Nose-tow catapult attachment on nose unit.

ENGINE INTAKES: Straight two-dimensional external compression inlets. A double-hinged ramp extends down from the top of each intake, and these are programmed to provide the correct airflow to the engines automatically under all flight conditions. Each intake is canted slightly away from the fuselage, from which it is separated by some 10 in (0·25 m) to allow sufficient clearance for the turbulent fuselage boundary layer to pass between fuselage and intake without causing turbulence within the intake. Engine inlet ducts and aft nacelle structures will be designed and manufactured by Rohr Corporation. The inlet duct, constructed largely of aluminium honeycomb, is about 14 ft (4·27 m) long, while the aft nacelle structure, of bonded titanium honeycomb, is about 16 ft (4·88 m) in length.

POWER PLANT: Two Pratt & Whitney TF30-P-401 turbofan engines with afterburning, mounted in ducts which open to provide 180° access for ease of maintenance.

ACCOMMODATION: Pilot and missile control officer seated in tandem under a one-piece bubble canopy, hinged at the rear and offering all-round visibility. Provision for internal attachment of armour plate for crew protection.

ARMAMENT: One General Electric M61-A1 Vulcan machine-gun mounted in the port side of forward fuselage. Four Sparrow air-to-air missiles mounted partially submerged in the under-fuselage. Two wing pylons, one under each fixed wing section, will carry both drop tanks and four Sidewinder missiles, the latter being mounted one on either side of each pylon. For Phoenix and later missiles, Grumman has developed a concept in which removable pallets can be attached to the present Sparrow missile positions, the missiles then being attached to the pallets.

ELECTRONICS: Hughes AN/AWG-9 weapons control system.

DIMENSIONS, EXTERNAL:

Wing span: unswept	64 ft 1·5 in (19·54 m)
swept	33 ft 2·4 in (10·12 m)
overswept	32 ft 11·5 in (10·05 m)
Length overall	61 ft 10·6 in (18·86 m)
Height overall	16 ft 0 in (4·88 m)
Tailplane span	32 ft 8·4 in (9·97 m)

WEIGHTS (estimated):

Weight empty	36,000 lb (16,330 kg)
Max T-O weight (with four Sparrow missiles)	53,000 lb (24,040 kg)

GRUMMAN GULFSTREAM II
US Coastguard designation: VC-11A

The decision to start production of this twin-turbofan executive transport was announced by Grumman on 17 May 1965. Since then orders for more than 80 have been received. The first production Gulfstream II (no prototype was built) flew for the first time on 2 October 1966. FAA certification was gained on 19 October 1967, and the first production aircraft was delivered to National Distillers & Chemical Corporation on 6 December 1967. By early February 1969 a

Grumman VC-11A Gulfstream II VIP transport of the US Coast Guard (*S. P. Peltz*)

total of 42 aircraft had been delivered. The current production schedule calls for three aircraft per month during 1969. Custom interiors and avionics, with the exception of the Sperry SP-50G automatic flight control system, which is standard, are installed by the distributors.

A single Gulfstream II operates with the US Coast Guard under the designation **VC-11A.**

TYPE: Twin-turbofan executive transport aircraft.

WINGS: Cantilever low-wing monoplane of all-metal construction. Sweepback 25° at quarter-chord. One-piece Fowler flaps. Spoilers forward of flaps assist in lateral control and can be extended for use as air-brakes. All control surfaces actuated by dual independent hydraulic systems with manual back-up.

FUSELAGE: Conventional all-metal semi-monocoque structure. Glass-fibre nose-cone hinged for access to radar, etc.

TAIL UNIT: Cantilever all-metal structure with tailplane mounted at tip of fin. All surfaces sweptback. Trim-tab in rudder. Powered controls (see under "Wings" above).

LANDING GEAR: Retractable tricycle type, with twin wheels on each unit. Inward-retracting main units. Forward-retracting steerable nose unit. Tyre pressures: nose 80 lb/sq in (5·62 kg/cm²), main 125 lb/sq in (8·79 kg/cm²).

POWER PLANT: Two Rolls-Royce Spey Mk 511-8 turbofan engines (each 11,400 lb=5,171 kg st), mounted in pods on each side of rear fuselage. Rohr target-type thrust reversers form aft portion of nacelles when in stowed position. All fuel in integral tanks in wings, capacity 22,500 lb (10,205 kg).

ACCOMMODATION: Crew of three. Certified for 19 passengers in pressurised and air-conditioned cabin. Large baggage compartment at rear of cabin, capacity 2,000 lb (907 kg). Integral airstair door at front of cabin on port side.

SYSTEMS: Two independent hydraulic systems. All flying controls hydraulically powered, with manual reversion. APU in tail compartment.

DIMENSIONS, EXTERNAL:

Wing span	68 ft 10 in (20·98 m)
Length overall	79 ft 11 in (24·36 m)
Length of fuselage	71 ft 4 in (21·74 m)
Height overall	24 ft 6 in (7·47 m)
Tailplane span	27 ft 0 in (8·23 m)
Wheel track	13 ft 8 in (4·16 m)
Wheelbase	33 ft 4 in (10·16 m)
Passenger door:	
Height	5 ft 2 in (1·57 m)
Width	3 ft 0 in (0·91 m)

Baggage door:	
Height	2 ft 4 in (0·71 m)
Width	2 ft 10 in (0·86 m)
Ventral door:	
Width	1 ft 6 in (0·46 m)
Length	2 ft 4 in (0·71 m)

DIMENSIONS, INTERNAL:

Cabin: Length	33 ft 11 in (10·34 m)
Height	6 ft 1 in (1·85 m)
Volume	1,300 cu ft (36·8 m³)
Baggage compartment	160 cu ft (4·53 m³)

AREA:

Wings, gross	793·5 sq ft (73·72 m²)

WEIGHTS AND LOADING:

Max T-O weight	57,500 lb (26,081 kg)
Max ramp weight	58,000 lb (26,308 kg)
Max landing weight	51,430 lb (23,330 kg)
Max zero-fuel weight	38,000 lb (17,235 kg)
Max wing loading	68 lb/sq ft (332 kg/m²)

PERFORMANCE (at max T-O weight):

Max level speed	Mach 0·83 =
	508 knots (585 mph; 940 km/h)
Max cruising speed	
	491 knots (565 mph; 909 km/h)
Average cruising speed	Mach 0·75
Approach speed	
	134 knots (154 mph; 248 km/h)
Rate of climb at S/L	5,050 ft (1,540 m)/min
Rate of climb at S/L, one engine out	
	880 ft (270 m)/min
Service ceiling	43,000 ft (13,100 m)
Service ceiling, one engine out	
	25,000 ft (7,620 m)
FAA T-O field length	4,070 ft (1,240 m)
FAA landing field length	3,080 ft (939 m)
Range with max fuel	
	3,000 nm (3,460 miles; 5,568 km)

GRUMMAN G-164 AG-CAT/G-164A
SUPER AG-CAT

The Ag-Cat is an agricultural biplane, the prototype of which flew for the first time on 22 May 1957. It is being built in series by Schweizer Aircraft of Elmira, New York, under subcontract from Grumman. First deliveries were made in 1959, and more than 500 were operating in 24 countries by mid-1968.

The Ag-Cat was certificated in the restricted (agricultural) category on 20 January 1959, with a 220-225 hp Continental engine, and received additional approval in this category for patrolling and surveying on 9 April 1962. Other engines for which FAA Type Approval has been received are the 240 hp Gulf Coast W-670-240, 245 hp

Grumman Gulfstream II executive transport owned by the Superior Oil Company
(*Brian M. Service*)

Jacobs L-4M or L-4MB, 275-300 hp Jacobs R-755, 450 hp Pratt & Whitney R-985 and 600 hp Pratt & Whitney R-1340.

The Super Ag-Cat (model G-164A) began with aircraft c/n 401, and is available with either the Jacobs R-755, Pratt & Whitney R-985 or Pratt & Whitney R-1340 engine.

By the end of 1967, Ag-Cats had logged more than one and a half million flying hours in the USA, without a fatal accident.

TYPE: Single-seat agricultural biplane.

WINGS: Single-bay staggered biplane. NACA 4412 (modified) wing section. Dihedral 3°. Incidence 6°. Duralumin two-spar wing structure with duralumin and fabric covering. N-type interplane struts. Duralumin-framed fabric-covered ailerons on all four wings. No flaps.

FUSELAGE: Steel-tube structure, covered with duralumin sheet.

TAIL UNIT: Braced steel-tube structure, covered with fabric.

LANDING GEAR: Non-retractable tail-wheel type. Cantilever spring-steel legs. Cleveland 8·50 × 6·6 wheels and tyres on Ag-Cats of 300 hp and under, 8·50 × 10·0 on Super Ag-Cat. Disc brakes. Super Ag-Cat has brakes of greater capacity. Cleveland steerable spring tail-wheel.

POWER PLANT: One 220 hp Continental W670-6N (R-670-4), W670-16 (R-670-11) or W670-6A (R-670-5) or 240 hp Gulf Coast W-670-240 seven-cylinder radial air-cooled engine or Jacobs R-755 seven-cylinder radial air-cooled engine of 245, 275 or 300 hp, or 450 hp Pratt & Whitney R-985, or 600 hp R-1340 nine-cylinder radial air-cooled engine. Grumman (Sensenich) J5404R/MA96K two-blade ground-adjustable metal propeller optional, except on 450 hp Ag-Cat which has Hamilton Standard two-position or constant-speed two-blade metal propeller with Model 2D30 hub and 6101A-12 blades, or 600 hp Ag-Cat which has a Hamilton Standard Type 12D40 constant-speed propeller, diameter 9 ft 0 in (2·74 m). Fuel tank, usable capacity 46·3 US gallons (174 litres), in upper centre-section. Oil capacity 5 US gallons (19 litres) in 220-300 hp Ag-Cats, 7 US gallons (26·5 litres) in 450 hp Ag-Cats.

ACCOMMODATION: Single open cockpit aft of wings. Optional enclosed canopy. Reinforced fairing aft of cockpit for "turn-over" protection. Forward of cockpit, over CG, is 33 cu ft (0·93 m³) or, optionally, 40 cu ft (1·13 m³) glass-fibre hopper for agricultural chemicals (dry or liquid) with distributor beneath fuselage. Designed to carry 2,000 lb (907 kg) or 247 US gallons (936 litres) chemicals (to requirements of GAM-8).

DIMENSIONS, EXTERNAL:
Wing span   35 ft 11 in (10·95 m)
Wing chord (constant)   4 ft 10 in (1·47 m)
Wing aspect ratio: upper wing   7·81
    biplane-estimated mean   5·29
Length overall:
    W670   24 ft 4 in (7·42 m)
    R-755   24 ft 4¼ in (7·43 m)
    R-985   23 ft 4 in (7·11 m)

Grumman Super Ag-Cat agricultural aircraft (450 hp Pratt & Whitney R-985 engine)

Height overall	10 ft 9 in (3·27 m)
Tailplane span	13 ft 0 in (3·96 m)
Wheel track	7 ft 10 in (2·38 m)
Wheelbase	18 ft 6 in (5·64 m)

AREAS:
Wings, gross	328 sq ft (30·47 m²)
Ailerons (total)	31·5 sq ft (2·93 m²)
Fin	9·0 sq ft (0·84 m²)
Rudder	12·0 sq ft (1·12 m²)
Tailplane	22·8 sq ft (2·12 m²)
Elevators	22·2 sq ft (2·06 m²)

WEIGHTS AND LOADINGS:
Weight empty, equipped, spraying version:
W670-6A, -6N or -16	2,201 lb (999 kg)
W670-240	2,233 lb (1,013 kg)
R-755 (300 hp)	2,239 lb (1,016 kg)
R-985	2,690 lb (1,220 kg)
Certified max T-O weight:
W670-6A, -6N or -16	3,600 lb (1,633 kg)
W670-240, R-755	3,750 lb (1,700 kg)
R-985	4,500 lb (2,040 kg)
Max T-O weight:
R-985	5,300 lb (2,405 kg)
Max power loading:
W670-6A, -6N or -16	16·36 lb/hp (7·42 kg/hp)
W670-240	15·62 lb/hp (7·08 kg/hp)
R-755 (300 hp)	12·50 lb/hp (5·67 kg/hp)
R-985	10·00 lb/hp (4·54 kg/hp)

PERFORMANCE (at certified max T-O weight):
Never-exceed speed:
| Ag-Cat | 114 knots (131 mph; 211 km/h) |
| Super Ag-Cat | 128 knots (147 mph; 237 km/h) |
Abrupt manoeuvre speed:
| Ag-Cat | 89 knots (103 mph; 165 km/h) |
| Super Ag-Cat | 102 knots (117 mph; 188 km/h) |
Working speed:
W670-6A, -6N or -16
    65-74 knots (75-85 mph; 121-137 km/h)
W670-240, R-755
    65-83 knots (75-95 mph; 121-153 km/h)
R-985
    69-87 knots (80-100 mph; 129-161 km/h)
Stalling speed, power off:
W670-6A, -6N or -16
    47 knots (53·5 mph; 86 km/h)
W670-240, R-755
    48 knots (55 mph; 88·5 km/h)
R-985
    59 knots (67 mph; 108 km/h)
Rate of climb at S/L:
W670-6A, -6N or -16	435 ft (132 m)/min
W670-240	600 ft (183 m)/min
R-755	700 ft (213 m)/min
R-985	1,080 ft (329 m)/min
R-1340	1,600 ft (488 m)/min
Rate of climb at 11,000 ft (3,352 m):
R-1340	700 ft (213 m)/min
T-O run:
R-985 (at 5,300 lb = 2,405 kg AUW)
                                                            875 ft (267 m)

GYRODYNE

GYRODYNE COMPANY OF AMERICA, INC
HEAD OFFICE AND WORKS:
St James, Long Island, New York 11780
PRESIDENT AND TREASURER:
Peter J. Papadakos
VICE-PRESIDENTS:
Robert S. Knecht (Plans and Programmes)
Alan H. Yates (Avionics)
A. J. Pappas

SECRETARY: Joseph L. Dorn
The Gyrodyne Company of America, Inc was incorporated in New York State on 7 August 1946. After early research with the single-rotor type of helicopter, it turned to the co-axial rotor configuration in 1949 and this has been a feature of all its subsequent designs.

The major problem of directional control, inherent in early co-axial helicopters, was overcome by development of the Gyrodyne air-drag rotor-tip brake control system.

Under contract to the US Navy Bureau of Naval Weapons, the company developed the XRON-1/YRON-1 Rotorcycle one-man helicopter, of which details can be found in the 1963/64 *Jane's*. Adaptation of the basic Rotorcycle airframe into a pure drone helicopter was accomplished subsequently under Bureau of Naval Weapons contract, as described in the "Drones" section of this edition.

HELICOM

HELICOM INC
ADDRESS:
PO Box 6574, Long Beach, California 90815
PRESIDENT:
Harold E. Emigh
Current products of Helicom Inc are the Commuter Jr helicopter and ground trainer attachment, which are available in the form of plans and kits, as well as in ready-to-fly form.

HELICOM COMMUTER Jr MODEL H-1A
In addition to the standard free-flight model of the Commuter Jr single-seat light helicopter, there is a ground trainer version, mounted via a gimbal on a 500 lb (227 kg) steel plate fitted with casters. The gimbal has stops to prevent the aircraft from striking the ground in any attitude, but the aircraft is free to move 18 in (45 cm) in altitude, to tilt up to 7° in any direction and to rotate through 360°. The weight of the base prevents it from becoming airborne, but the free-swivelling casters on the base permit training in square patterns, quick-stop and other manoeuvres.

Each airframe is tested in free flight before becoming part of the ground trainer device.

The following description applies to the standard Commuter Jr free-flight helicopter.

Helicom SAH-1 Commuter Jr light helicopter built by Mr S. A. Helfferich (*Howard Levy*)

TYPE: Single-seat light helicopter.

ROTOR SYSTEM: Two-blade main rotor of aluminium alloy construction. Blade section NACA 0012. Two-blade aluminium tail rotor. Main rotor/engine rpm ratio 1 : 5. Tail rotor/engine rpm ratio 1 : 1.

FUSELAGE: Open steel-tube structure. Glass-fibre and Plexiglas cabin enclosure at front.

LANDING GEAR: Normally steel-tube skids, with auxiliary ground handling wheels. Tricycle gear optional.

POWER PLANT: One 90 hp Continental C90-12F four-cylinder horizontally-opposed air-cooled engine, mounted vertically aft of seat. Fuel tanks above engine, capacity 12 US gallons (45 litres).

ACCOMMODATION: Single seat in open cockpit. Conventional helicopter controls. Optional equipment includes lights, heater, Nova Star II radio and compartment for 50 lb (23 kg) baggage.

DIMENSIONS, EXTERNAL:
Diameter of main rotor	21 ft 0 in (6·40 m)
Blade chord of main rotor	8 in (20 cm)
Diameter of tail rotor	4 ft 0 in (1·22 m)
Blade chord of tail rotor	4 in (10 cm)
Length overall	24 ft 0 in (7·32 m)
Height overall	7 ft 10 in (2·38 m)
Skid track	5 ft 0 in (1·52 m)

AREA:
Main rotor disc	345 sq ft (32·05 m²)

WEIGHTS AND LOADINGS:
Weight empty, equipped	635 lb (288 kg)
Max T-O weight	950 lb (431 kg)
Max disc loading	2·75 lb/sq ft (13·42 kg/m²)
Max power loading	10·5 lb/hp (4·76 kg/hp)

PERFORMANCE (at max T-O weight):
Max level speed at S/L:
65 knots (75 mph; 121 km/h)
Max rate of climb at S/L 1,670 ft (510 m)/min
Vertical rate of climb at S/L 500 ft (152 m)/min
Hovering ceiling out of ground effect
6,800 ft (2,070 m)
Service ceiling 10,000 ft (3,050 m)
Range with max fuel, 30 min reserve
112 nm (130 miles; 210 km)
Max range, no reserve
147 nm (170 miles; 273 km)

HELIO

HELIO AIRCRAFT COMPANY (a division of General Aircraft Corporation)

HEAD OFFICE:
Hanscom Field, Civilian Terminal Area, Bedford, Massachusetts 01730

WORKS:
Pittsburg, Kansas

CHAIRMAN AND CHIEF EXECUTIVE OFFICER:
Dr L. L. Bollinger

PRESIDENT:
R. B. Kimnach

DIRECTOR OF ENGINEERING:
R. L. Devine

CONTROLLER: J. R. Cray

DIRECTOR ADVANCED PROGRAMMES:
Dr H. I. Flomenhoft

SALES AND PUBLIC RELATIONS
H. A. Wheeler Jr (Asst to the President)

In 1969 the former Helio Aircraft Corporation became a division of General Aircraft Corporation, and was re-named Helio Aircraft Company.

The original company was founded by Dr Otto C. Koppen of the Massachusetts Institute of Technology and Dr Lynn L. Bollinger of the Harvard Graduate School of Business Administration, to develop a light aircraft in the STOL category.

After considerable flight testing of a prototype, converted from a Piper Vagabond light aircraft, Helio designed the four-seat Courier prototype, which first flew in 1953. This was followed quickly by the first five-seat Helio Courier production aircraft, certificated in 1954.

The Courier is an all-metal cantilever high-wing monoplane incorporating full-span automatic leading-edge slats and a high-lift flap system. It received Type Approval on 5 August 1953, and is being produced at Pittsburg, Kansas, in a factory that was acquired by Helio in July 1956.

During 1956, a floatplane version of the Courier was produced, followed early in 1957 by the H-392 Strato-Courier with supercharged engine, in 1958 by the H-395 Super Courier and in 1959 by the Courier Model H-395A. The 4/5-seat Super Courier Model H-395 has been superseded by the six-seat Model H-295, which is now in production together with the lower-powered Model H-250 Courier. Also in production are the six-seat Model H-580 Twin Courier and the 8/11-seat turboprop Model H-550A Stallion. Under development is the 8/11-seat turboprop Model H-634 Twin Stallion.

Helio refers to all its products as C/STOL aircraft, signifying "controlled short take-off and landing".

Over 450 Helio Couriers of all types have been sold in the civilian market and are in service in 38 countries throughout the world. A substantial number are being used by US and foreign military and government agencies.

HELIO H-250 COURIER

The H-250 Courier is generally similar to the H-295 Super Courier, except for its power plant. Design work was started in September 1963 and construction of the prototype began in the following month. First flight took place in May 1964 and the prototype received type approval under FAA CAR 3 in November 1964.

The 1970 version of the Courier includes all the improvements incorporated in the Super Courier. It differs from the Super Courier in the following details:

POWER PLANT: One 250 hp Lycoming O-540-A1A5 six-cylinder horizontally-opposed air-cooled engine, driving a Hartzell two-blade constant-speed propeller, diameter 7 ft 4 in (2·24 m).

DIMENSIONS, EXTERNAL:
As for Super Courier, except:
Length overall	31 ft 6 in (9·60 m)

WEIGHTS AND LOADINGS:
As for Super Courier, except:
Weight empty	1,960 lb (889 kg)
Max power loading (CAR.3)	13·6 lb/hp (6·17 kg/hp)

PERFORMANCE (at max T-O weights indicated):
Max level speed at S/L:
CAR.3	139 knots (160 mph; 257 km/h)
CAR.8	129 knots (148 mph; 238 km/h)

Max permissible speed in dive
164 knots (189 mph; 304 km/h)
Max cruising speed (75% power) at 6,000 ft (1,830 m):
CAR.3	132 knots (152 mph; 245 km/h)
CAR.8	122 knots (140 mph; 225 km/h)

Econ cruising speed (60% power):
CAR.3	116 knots (133 mph; 214 km/h)
CAR.8	105 knots (121 mph; 195 km/h)

Min speed, power on:
CAR.3	27 knots (31 mph; 50 km/h)
CAR.8	34 knots (39 mph; 63 km/h)

Rate of climb at S/L:
CAR.3	830 ft (253 m)/min

Service ceiling:
CAR.3	15,200 ft (4,633 m)
CAR.8	10,000 ft (3,050 m)

T-O run:
CAR.3	420 ft (128 m)
CAR.8	870 ft (265 m)

T-O to 50 ft (15 m):
CAR.3	750 ft (229 m)
CAR.8	1,400 ft (427 m)

Landing from 50 ft (15 m):
CAR.3	520 ft (159 m)
CAR.8	665 ft (203 m)

Landing run:
CAR.3	270 ft (823 m)
CAR.8	355 ft (108 m)

Range with standard tanks:
CAR.3	559 nm (644 miles; 1,036 km)
CAR.8	512 nm (590 miles; 950 km)

Range with optional tanks:
CAR.3	1,118 nm (1,288 miles; 2,073 km)
CAR.8 (including ferry tanks)	
	2,518 nm (2,900 miles; 4,667 km)

HELIO H-295 SUPER COURIER
USAF designation: U-10

The original version of the Super Courier was flown for the first time in 1958 and received FAA Type Approval on 17 November that year. Three were supplied to the USAF for evaluation, under the designation L-28A. Further substantial orders have since been received, some aircraft being assigned to Tactical Air Command for counter-insurgency duties.

The current version of the Super Courier is the Model H-295, with increased seating capacity, as described in detail below. Design and construction of the prototype H-295 began in late 1964 and it flew for the first time on 24 February 1965. FAA certification was received in the following month.

USAF Super Couriers are of three types, as follows:

U-10A. Standard model with fuel capacity of 60 US gallons (227 litres).

U-10B. Long-range version with standard internal fuel capacity of 120 US gallons (454 litres). This version is operating in South-East Asia, South America, and in other parts of the world, on a wide variety of military missions and has an endurance of more than 10 hours. Paratroop doors standard.

U-10D. Improved long-range version with max AUW increased to 3,600 lb (1,633 kg). Standard internal fuel capacity of 120 US gallons (455 litres). Accommodation for pilot and five passengers. In production.

All American Engineering Co improved further the STOL performance of two Couriers for use by an expedition exploring the 14,000 ft (4,270 m) Vilacabamba Plateau in Peru. Modifications included provision for 250 lb (113 kg) st JATO rockets on each side of the fuselage aft of the wing roots and an arrester hook able to stop the aircraft in little more than 100 ft (30 m), using All American's "water twister" arrester gear.

The 1970 commercial version of the Super Courier incorporates as standard a number of improvements, including adjustable seats with reclining backs, improved soundproofing and insulation, a re-designed instrument panel, electrically-operated flaps and large rear picture windows. Electrically-operated elevator trim optional.

The following details refer to the standard commercial Super Courier.

TYPE: Six-seat light STOL personal, corporate and utility monoplane.

WINGS: Cantilever high-wing monoplane. NACA 23012 wing section. Dihedral 1°. Incidence 3°. All-metal single-spar structure. Frise ailerons have duralumin frames and fabric covering and are supplemented by Arc-type aluminium spoilers, located at 15·5% chord on upper surface of each wing and geared to ailerons for control at low speeds. Ground-adjustable tab on ailerons. Full-span automatic all-metal Handley Page leading-edge slats. Electrically-operated NACA slotted all-metal flaps over 74% of span. No anti-icing equipment.

FUSELAGE: All-metal structure. Cabin section has welded steel-tube framework, covered with aluminium; rear section is an aluminium monocoque.

Helio Model H-295 Super Courier six-seat STOL monoplane (295 hp Lycoming GO-480-G1D6 engine)

TAIL UNIT: Cantilever all-metal structure. All-moving one-piece horizontal surface is fitted with trim and anti-balance tabs. Electrically-operated elevator trim optional.

LANDING GEAR: Non-retractable tail-wheel type. Cantilever main legs. Oleo-pneumatic shock-absorbers of Helio design and manufacture on all three units. Goodyear cross-wind landing gear with main wheel tyres size 6·50 × 8, pressure 28 lb/sq in (1·97 kg/cm²). Goodyear 10-in (25-cm) tail-wheel tyre, pressure 40 lb/sq in (2·81 kg/cm²). Goodyear hydraulic disc brakes. Edo 582-3430 floats and Airglass Model LW3600 glass-fibre wheel-skis optional.

POWER PLANT: One 295 hp Lycoming GO-480-G1D6 six-cylinder horizontally-opposed air-cooled geared engine, driving a Hartzell three-blade constant-speed propeller, diameter 8 ft 0 in (2·44 m). Two 30 US gallon (113 litre) bladder-type fuel tanks in wings. Two further 30 US gallon (113 litre) tanks may be fitted to give total fuel capacity of 120 US gallons (455 litres). In addition ferry tanks can be fitted to give a total capacity of 270 US gallons (1,023 litres). Refuelling point above wing centre-section. Oil capacity 3 US gallons (11·4 litres).

ACCOMMODATION: Cabin seats six in three pairs. Front and centre pair of seats individually adjustable. Rear pair comprises double sling seat. FAA standard instrument panel. Special over-strength cabin and seat structure based on Flight Safety Foundation recommendations. Two large doors, by pilot's seat on port side and opposite centre row of seats on starboard side. Baggage compartment aft of rear seats. Second- and third-row seats are removable for carrying over 1,000 lb (454 kg) freight.

ELECTRONICS AND EQUIPMENT: Radio and blind-flying instrumentation to customer's requirements.

DIMENSIONS, EXTERNAL:
Wing span	39 ft 0 in (11·89 m)
Wing chord (constant)	6 ft 0 in (1·83 m)
Wing aspect ratio	6·58
Length overall	31 ft 0 in (9·45 m)
Height overall	8 ft 10 in (2·69 m)
Tailplane span	15 ft 6 in (4·72 m)
Wheel track	9 ft 0 in (2·74 m)
Wheelbase	23 ft 5 in (7·14 m)
Cabin door (fwd, port):	
Height	3 ft 5 in (1·04 m)
Width	2 ft 9½ in (0·85 m)
Height to sill	3 ft 0 in (0·91 m)
Cabin door (stbd, rear):	
Height	3 ft 2½ in (0·98 m)
Width	2 ft 9½ in (0·85 m)
Height to sill	2 ft 2½ in (0·67 m)

DIMENSIONS, INTERNAL:
Cabin: Length	10 ft 0 in (3·05 m)
Max width	3 ft 9 in (1·14 m)
Max height	4 ft 0 in (1·22 m)
Floor area	30 sq ft (2·79 m²)
Volume	140 cu ft (3·96 m²)
Baggage space	15 cu ft (0·42 m²)

AREAS:
Wings, gross	231 sq ft (21·46 m²)
Ailerons (total)	20·7 sq ft (1·92 m²)
Flaps (total)	38·1 sq ft (3·54 m²)
Leading-edge slats (total)	31·3 sq ft (2·91 m²)
Spoilers (total)	1·68 sq ft (0·16 m²)
Fin	15·2 sq ft (1·41 m²)
Rudder	10·6 sq ft (0·99 m²)
Tailplane	37·5 sq ft (3·48 m²)

WEIGHTS AND LOADINGS:
Weight empty	2,080 lb (943 kg)
Max T-O and landing weight (CAR.3)	3,400 lb (1,542 kg)
Max T-O weight (CAR.8 restricted category)	4,420 lb (2,005 kg)
Max wing loading (CAR.3)	14·7 lb/sq ft (71·8 kg/m²)
Max power loading (CAR.3)	11·5 lb/hp (5·22 kg/hp)

PERFORMANCE (at max T-O weights indicated):
Max level speed at S/L:	
CAR.3	145 knots (167 mph; 269 km/h)
CAR.8	135 knots (156 mph; 251 km/h)
Max permissible speed in dive	164 knots (189 mph; 304 km/h)
Max cruising speed (75% power) at 8,500 ft (2,600 m):	
CAR.3	143 knots (165 mph; 265 km/h)
CAR.8	134 knots (154 mph; 248 km/h)
Econ cruising speed (60% power):	
CAR.3	130 knots (150 mph; 241 km/h)
CAR.8	122 knots (140 mph; 225 km/h)
Min speed, power on:	
CAR.3	26 knots (30 mph; 48 km/h)
CAR.8	33 knots (37 mph; 60 km/h)
Rate of climb at S/L:	
CAR.3	1,150 ft (350 m)/min
Service ceiling:	
CAR.3	20,500 ft (6,250 m)
CAR.8	11,000 ft (3,350 m)
T-O run:	
CAR.3	335 ft (102 m)
CAR.8	700 ft (213 m)

Helio U-10D, military long-range version of the Super Courier

T-O to 50 ft (15 m):	
CAR.3	610 ft (186 m)
CAR.8	1,180 ft (360 m)
Landing from 50 ft (15 m):	
CAR.3	520 ft (158 m)
CAR.8	665 ft (203 m)
Landing run:	
CAR.3	270 ft (82 m)
CAR.8	355 ft (107 m)
Range with standard tanks:	
CAR.3	573 nm (660 miles; 1,062 km)
CAR.8	521 nm (600 miles; 965 km)
Range with optional tanks:	
CAR.3	1,198 nm (1,380 miles; (2,220 km)
CAR.8 (including ferry tanks)	2,518 nm (2,900 miles; 4,667 km)

HELIO STALLION MODEL H-550A

Design of the turboprop Stallion was started in July 1963 and construction of the prototype Model HST550 began in November 1963. First flight took place on 5 June 1964 and FAA certification was received in August 1965.

The following details refer to the production version, which is known as the Stallion Model H-550A. It has positive boundary-layer control to enhance STOL performance and a crash-resistant cabin structure, and is designed to operate over a wide speed range to allow flexibility in operation.

TYPE: Eight/eleven-seat general-utility STOL turboprop aircraft.

WINGS: Cantilever high-wing monoplane. Wing section slatted NACA 23012 (constant). Dihedral 1°. Incidence 3°. No sweepback. All-aluminium single-spar structure. Each wing unbolts at side of fuselage. Dacron-covered Frise balanced metal ailerons. NACA high-lift slotted all-metal flaps, electrically-actuated. Arc-type all-metal spoilers at front of wing upper surface, inter-connected with ailerons. Ground-adjustable tab on starboard aileron. Fully-automatic Handley Page full-span leading-edge slats.

FUSELAGE: Aluminium semi-monocoque structure, with welded steel-tube framework forward of pilot's position.

TAIL UNIT: Cantilever all-aluminium structure, with sweptback vertical surfaces. All-moving one-piece horizontal surface with combined trim and anti-balance tab and separate flap trim interconnect tab.

LANDING GEAR: Non-retractable tail-wheel type. Rearwardly-inclined cantilever main legs. Oleo-pneumatic shock-absorbers, designed and manufactured by Helio, on all three units. Goodyear tyres. Main wheels size 7·50 × 10, tyre pressure 22 lb/sq in (1·55 kg/cm²). Steerable tail-wheel with 5·00 × 5 Type II tyre, pressure 55 lb/sq in (3·87 kg/cm²). Goodyear disc brakes. Cross-wind wheels, Edo 59-5250 floats or wheel-ski landing gear available.

POWER PLANT: One 680 shp Pratt & Whitney (UACL) PT6A-27 turboprop engine, driving a Hartzell three-blade reversible-pitch constant-speed propeller, diameter 8 ft 5 in (2·57 m). Fuel tanks in wings, with total capacity of 120 US gallons (455 litres). Provision for two wingtip tanks with total capacity of 104 US gallons (394 litres). Refuelling points above wing. Oil capacity 2·3 US gallons (8·75 litres).

ACCOMMODATION: Pilot and co-pilot or passenger side-by-side at front, on fully-adjustable seats. Nine passengers in three rows, three abreast. Rear three rows of seats can be removed for cargo carrying. Full-length rails in floor for cargo restraint. Jettisonable door on port side of cabin by pilot. Similar door on starboard side optional. Double door, without central pillar on port side of main cabin. Forward section of this door is hinged, rear portion slides. When sliding section is in place, forward section can be used alone as forward-hinged door. When rear (sliding) section is moved aft, the entire double door opening, size 61 in × 43 in (1·55 m × 1·09 m), is available for cargo loading. In the air, the sliding section moves aft to provide a parachuting or cargo-drop doorway. Similar double door on starboard side optional. Doors are non-structural. Hatches in wall of rear cabin enable pieces of freight up to 12 ft (3·65 m) long to be carried. Optional camera hatch size 23 in × 40 in (0·58 m × 1·02 m) in floor. Seats and harness stressed for 15 g. Walls lined with fire-proofing and sound-proofing. Heating and ventilation standard. Provision for carrying external baggage or freight containers on optional underwing racks.

SYSTEMS: Hydraulic system for brakes only. No pneumatic system. 24V electrical system supplied by 150A (optionally 200A) generator.

Helio Stallion Model H-550A (680 shp Pratt & Whitney (UACL) PT6A-27 turboprop engine)

ELECTRONICS AND EQUIPMENT: Radio and blind-flying instrumentation to customer's requirements. Optional items include attachments for two MA4 or Aero 15D bomb-racks under each wing, and two Aero 65A bomb-racks under fuselage.

DIMENSIONS, EXTERNAL:

Wing span	41 ft 0 in (12·50 m)
Wing span over tip-tanks	41 ft 9 in (12·72 m)
Wing chord (constant)	6 ft 0 in (1·83 m)
Wing aspect ratio (without tip-tanks)	6·93
Length overall	39 ft 7 in (12·07 m)
Height overall	9 ft 3 in (2·81 m)
Tailplane span	18 ft 0 in (5·49 m)
Wheel track	9 ft 8 in (2·94 m)
Wheelbase	24 ft 8 in (7·52 m)

Pilot's compartment doors (each):

Height	4 ft 5 in (1·35 m)
Width	3 ft 4 in (1·03 m)
Height to sill (mean)	3 ft 9 in (1·14 m)

Hinged portion of double-door:

Height	4 ft 0 in (1·22 m)
Width	2 ft 7 in (0·79 m)
Height to sill	2 ft 11 in (0·89 m)

Sliding portion of double-door:

Height	3 ft 8 in (1·12 m)
Width	2 ft 7 in (0·79 m)
Height to sill	3 ft 0 in (0·91 m)

DIMENSIONS, INTERNAL:

Cabin: Length	13 ft 6 in (4·11 m)
Max width	4 ft 2½ in (1·28 m)
Max height	5 ft 1¼ in (1·56 m)
Floor area	43·4 sq ft (4·03 m²)
Volume	181·4 cu ft (5·14 m³)

AREAS:

Wings, gross	242 sq ft (22·48 m²)
Wings with tip tanks	248 sq ft (23·04 m²)
Ailerons (total)	20·7 sq ft (1·92 m²)
Trailing-edge flaps (total)	40·32 sq ft (3·75 m²)
Leading-edge slats (total)	38·3 sq ft (3·56 m²)
Spoilers (total)	3·1 sq ft (0·29 m²)
Fin	17·0 sq ft (1·58 m²)
Rudder, including tab	19·62 sq ft (1·82 m²)
Tailplane, including tabs	57·43 sq ft (5·33 m²)

WEIGHTS AND LOADINGS:

Weight empty	2,825 lb (1,281 kg)
Max payload (with 120 US gallons = 454 litres fuel and pilot)	1,325 lb (601 kg)
Max T-O and landing weight	5,100 lb (2,313 kg)
Max wing loading	21·1 lb/sq ft (103·0 kg/m²)
Max power loading	7·5 lb/hp (3·4 kg/hp)

PERFORMANCE (at max T-O weight):

Max level speed at 10,000 ft (3,050 m)	196 knots (226 mph; 364 km/h)
Max permissible speed in dive	197 knots (227 mph; 365 km/h) CAS
Max cruising speed at 10,000 ft (3,050 m)	188 knots (217 mph; 349 km/h)
Econ cruising speed at 10,000 ft (3,050 m)	139 knots (160 mph; 257 km/h)
Min fully-manoeuvrable descent speed, power on	37 knots (42 mph; 68 km/h)
Rate of climb at S/L	1,840 ft (560 m)/min
Service ceiling	28,000 ft (8,530 m)
T-O run	320 ft (98 m)
T-O to 50 ft (15 m)	660 ft (201 m)
Landing from 50 ft (15 m)	750 ft (229 m)
Landing run	250 ft (76 m)

Range with max fuel, allowances for warm-up, taxying, take-off and climb to 10,000 ft only 946 nm (1,090 miles; 1,755 km)

Range with max payload, allowances as above 386 nm (445 miles; 716 km)

HELIO H-580 TWIN COURIER

Design of the original H-500 twin-engined development of the Helio Courier began early in 1958. It flew for the first time in April 1960 and received FAA CAR.3 certification on 11 June 1963. A full description of this version appeared in the 1966/67 *Jane's*.

Work on an improved version of the Twin Courier, designated Helio H-580, began in 1966. Construction of a prototype started in 1969 and the first flight of this aircraft was scheduled for the Summer of 1970, with FAA FAR.23 certification following.

A distinctive feature of the H-580 is location of the engines above and forward of the wing to provide unrestricted lateral visibility and reduce the possibility of damage to the propellers and engine induction systems from debris encountered at unimproved airstrips. An auxiliary aerofoil of 10 in (25 cm) chord is fitted between the engine nacelles.

TYPE: Twin-engined light personal and corporate STOL monoplane.

WINGS: Cantilever high-wing monoplane. Wing section NACA 23012. Dihedral 1°. Incidence 3°. All-aluminium single-spar structure. Fabric-covered Frise metal ailerons. NACA slotted high-lift all-metal flaps, electrically operated. Full-span fully-automatic all-metal Handley Page leading-edge slats. Arc-type aluminium spoilers, located on upper surface at 15·5% chord. Ground-adjustable trim tabs in ailerons. Fixed auxiliary aerofoil between engine nacelles, above wing centre-section, for boundary layer control: section

Artist's impression of Helio Model H-580 Twin Courier (two 290 hp Lycoming IO-540-G1A5 engines)

NACA 4418; aspect ratio 9·78; constant chord of 10 in (25 cm); incidence —10·8°.

FUSELAGE: Cabin section is welded steel-tube structure with aluminium covering. Rear fuselage and nose section are aluminium semi-monocoque structures.

TAIL UNIT: Cantilever all-metal structure. One-piece all-moving tailplane, fitted with two combined trim and anti-balance tabs. Tailplane is interconnected with flaps for trim purposes.

LANDING GEAR: Tricycle type with shock-absorbing tail-skid. Nose-wheel only manually-retracted, rearward, with automatic extension. Oleo-pneumatic nose gear. Cantilever main gear with Helio-designed oleo-pneumatic shock-absorbers. Goodyear main wheels and size 6·50 × 8 six-ply tyres, pressure 51 lb/sq in (3·58 kg/cm²). Goodyear nose-wheel and size 6·00 × 6 eight-ply tyre, pressure 51 lb/sq in (3·58 kg/cm²). Hydraulic brakes.

POWER PLANT: Two 290 hp Lycoming IO-540-G1A5 six-cylinder horizontally-opposed air-cooled engines, driving Hartzell two-blade fully-feathering propellers, diameter 7 ft 4 in (2·25 m). Four bladder-type fuel tanks in wings, with total capacity of 120 US gallons (454 litres), and two wing-tip tanks with total capacity of 104 US gallons (394 litres). Oil capacity 6 US gallons (23 litres).

ACCOMMODATION: Enclosed cabin for pilot and five passengers in three rows of two seats. Front and centre pairs of seats individual, rear seat double. Large door on port side of fuselage provides access to all seats. Similar size emergency or cargo loading door on starboard side. Baggage hold, capacity 10 cu ft (0·28 m³), aft of rear seats. Hold for 10 cu ft (0·28 m³) of baggage in nose. Total of 80 cu ft (2·67 m³) cargo or baggage capacity in cabin if centre and rear rows of seats are removed.

SYSTEMS: Hydraulic system for brakes only.

ELECTRONICS AND EQUIPMENT: Wide range of communications and navigation equipment available to customer's requirements.

DIMENSIONS, EXTERNAL:

Wing span	41 ft 0 in (12·50 m)
Span over tip tanks	41 ft 9 in (12·73 m)
Wing chord (constant)	6 ft 0 in (1·83 m)
Wing aspect ratio	6·93
Length overall	33 ft 6 in (10·21 m)
Height overall	12 ft 4¾ in (3·78 m)
Tailplane span	18 ft 0 in (5·49 m)
Wheel track	9 ft 8 in (2·95 m)
Wheelbase	10 ft 10 in (3·30 m)

Cabin doors (each):

Height	4 ft 0½ in (1·26 m)
Width	5 ft 8 in (1·73 m)
Height to sill	1 ft 9 in (0·53 m)

Baggage door:

Height	7 in (17·8 cm)
Width	9½ in (24·1 cm)
Height to sill	2 ft 8 in (0·81 m)

DIMENSIONS, INTERNAL:
Cabin:

Length	10 ft 0 in (3·05 m)
Max width	4 ft 2 in (1·27 m)
Max height	4 ft 9 in (1·45 m)
Floor area	35 sq ft (3·25 m²)
Volume	155 cu ft (4·39 m³)

AREAS:

Wings, gross	242 sq ft (22·48 m²)
Ailerons (total)	20·7 sq ft (1·92 m²)
Trailing-edge flaps (total)	41 sq ft (3·81 m²)
Leading-edge slats (total)	27·1 sq ft (2·52 m²)
Spoilers (total)	3·1 sq ft (0·29 m²)
Fin	17·0 sq ft (1·58 m²)
Rudder, including tab	19·62 sq ft (1·82 m²)
Tailplane, including tabs	57·42 sq ft (5·33 m²)

WEIGHTS AND LOADINGS:

Weight, empty equipped	3,463 lb (1,571 kg)
Max payload (with 120 US gallons = 454 litres fuel and pilot)	750 lb (340 kg)
Max T-O and landing weight	5,100 lb (2,313 kg)
Max wing loading	21·1 lb/sq ft (103·0 kg/m²)
Max power loading	8·8 lb/hp (3·99 kg/hp)

PERFORMANCE (estimated at Max T-O weight):

Max level speed at S/L	170 knots (196 mph; 315 km/h)
Max diving speed	184 knots (212 mph; 341 km/h)
Max cruising speed at 10,000 ft (3,050 m)	165 knots (190 mph; 306 km/h)
Econ cruising speed at 10,000 ft (3,050 m)	143 knots (165 mph; 266 km/h)
Min speed, power on	29 knots (33 mph; 53 km/h)
Rate of climb at S/L	1,720 ft (524 m)/min
Service ceiling	20,000 ft (6,095 m)
Service ceiling, one engine out	6,500 ft (1,980 m)
T-O run	380 ft (116 m)
T-O to 50 ft (15 m)	780 ft (238 m)
Landing from 50 ft (15 m)	630 ft (192 m)
Landing run	330 ft (101 m)

Range with max fuel (allowances for warm-up, taxiing, T-O and climb to 10,000 ft = 3 050 m) 1,224 nm (1,410 miles; 2,269 km)

Range with max payload (allowance for warm-up, taxiing, T-O and climb to 10,000 ft = 3,050 m) 629 nm (725 miles; 1,167 km)

HELIO MODEL H-634

The Helio Model H-634 is a twin-engined development of the Model H-550A Stallion. Its design was started in January 1966. The first flight of the prototype was scheduled for the Autumn of 1970, with FAA FAR.23 certification anticipated before the end of the year.

Installation of the two Allison 250-B15 turbo-prop engines at the ends of a short stub-wing, extending on either side of the nose, enables the basic airframe to remain generally similar to that of the Model H-550A single-turboprop Stallion. The structural description of this aircraft therefore, applies also to the H-634, except for the following details:

TYPE: Eight/eleven-seat general-utility twin-turboprop aircraft.

WINGS: As H-550A except ground-adjustable tab on starboard aileron only.

LANDING GEAR: As H-550A except no floats available for this model.

POWER PLANT: Two 317 shp Allison 250-B15 turboprop engines, driving Hartzell three-blade fully-feathering constant-speed propellers, diameter 8 ft 0 in (2·44 m). Fuel tankage as for 550A. Oil capacity 3 US gallons (11·36 litres).

ACCOMMODATION: As H-550A except no optional camera hatch, and no provision for external baggage or freight containers.

SYSTEMS: 24V 150A starter/generators on each engine.

ELECTRONICS AND EQUIPMENT: Radio and blind flying instrumentation to customer's requirements. Heated pitot static head standard. Optional attachments for two MA-4 or Aero 15D bomb racks under each wing and for Aero 65A bomb rack under fuselage.

DIMENSIONS, AND AREAS:
As H-550A except:

Wing span	41 ft 0 in (12·50 m)
Wing span over tip tanks	41 ft 9 in (12·73 m)
Length overall	39 ft 8½ in (12·10 m)
Height overall	8 ft 10 in (2·69 m)

WEIGHTS:

Weight empty	2,845 lb (1,291 kg)
Max payload (with 120 US gallons = 454 litres fuel and pilot)	1,300 lb (590 kg)
Max T-O weight	5,100 lb (2,313 kg)

PERFORMANCE (estimated at max T-O weight):
Max level speed, from S/L to 5,000 ft (1,525 m)
182 knots (210 mph; 338 km/h)
Max diving speed
197 knots (227 mph; 365 km/h)
Max cruising speed
178 knots (205 mph; 330 km/h)
Econ cruising speed at 10,000 ft (3,050 m)
156 knots (180 mph; 290 km/h)
Min speed, power on
37 knots (42 mph; 68 km/h)
Rate of climb at S/L   1,900 ft (579 m)/min
Service ceiling   27,000 ft (8,230 m)
Service ceiling one engine out 5,000 ft (1,525 m)
T-O run   335 ft (102 m)
T-O to 50 ft (15 m)   660 ft (201 m)
Landing from 50 ft (15 m) 655 ft (200 m)
Landing run   345 ft (105 m)
Range with max fuel (allowance for warm-up,
taxiing, T-O and climb to 10,000 ft = 3,050 m)
838 nm (965 miles; 1,552 km)
Range with max payload (allowance for warm-
up, taxiing, T-O and climb to 10,000 ft = 3,050
m)   403 nm (465 miles; 748 km)

Artist's impression of Helio Model H-634 (two 317 shp Allison 250-B15 turboprop engines)

HELTON
HELTON AIRCRAFT CORPORATION
HEAD OFFICE AND WORKS:
Falcon Field, Mesa, Arizona 85201

Helton Aircraft Corporation was formed to produce two versions of a two-seat light aircraft
named Lark 95, which has been developed from
the well-known Culver Cadet.

HELTON LARK 95
The Lark 95 is a fully-aerobatic side-by-side
two-seat light aircraft powered by a 90 hp
Continental C90-16F four-cylinder horizontally-
opposed air-cooled engine, driving a McCauley
two-blade fixed-pitch propeller. There are two
versions, as follows:

Lark 95. Basic model, as illustrated. Received FAA type approval in September 1966.

Lark 95A. The fuselage of this version is 2 ft
(0·61 m) longer than that of the Lark 95 and
modified tail surfaces are fitted, without dorsal
fin, to improve aerobatic performance. More
extensive instrumentation, and Nova-Tech radio
are fitted.

Both versions have a non-retractable tricycle
landing gear, fixed wingtip slots and a cockpit
canopy that swings up and rearward for access.
Construction is all-wooden. Dual controls are
optional. Fuel capacity is 19 US gallons (72
litres).

Helton Lark 95 two-seat light aircraft (90 hp Continental C90 engine) *(Henry Artof)*

DIMENSIONS:
Wing span	27 ft 0 in (8·23 m)
Length overall:	
Lark 95	17 ft 0 in (5·18 m)
Lark 95A	19 ft 0 in (5·79 m)

WEIGHT:
Weight empty: Lark 95	940 lb (426 kg)

PERFORMANCE (Lark 95 at max T-O weight):
Max speed at 9,500 ft (2,900 m)
130 knots (150 mph; 241 km/h)
Normal cruising speed
117 knots (135 mph; 217 km/h)
Rate of climb at S/L   1,000 ft (305 m)/min
Range with max fuel
442 nm (510 miles; 820 km)

HUGHES
HUGHES TOOL COMPANY, AIRCRAFT DIVISION
HEAD OFFICE AND WORKS:
Culver City, California 90230
VICE-PRESIDENT AND GENERAL MANAGER:
Rea E. Hopper
VICE-PRESIDENT AND ASST GENERAL MANAGER:
Thomas R. Stuelpnagel
VICE-PRESIDENTS:
Rodney H. Brady (Administration)
Jack E. Leonard (Marketing)
William E. Rankin (Finance)
Charles E. Schaaf (Legal)
DIRECTORS:
W. J. Blackburn (Manufacturing)
E. J. Brandreth (Commercial Sales)
R. E. Brix (Ordnance Engineering)
E. E. Cohen (Material and Helicopter Support
Services)
R. J. Hurley (Contracts Administration)
H. J. Jordan (Industrial Relations)
C. D. Perry (Government Relations)
L. P. Sonsini (Quality Assurance)
R. A. Wagner (Aeronautical Engineering)
F. Weber (Accounting)
PROGRAMME MANAGERS:
R. E. Deyo (Ordnance)
J. N. Kerr (Military Helicopters)
F. C. Strible (Commercial Helicopters)
R. A. Wagner (Hot Cycle/Rotor Wing)
PUBLIC RELATIONS MANAGER:
Harold S. Stall.

The Aircraft Division of Hughes Tool Company
designed and built as a private venture a light
two-seat helicopter known as the Model 269A.
This aircraft was the predecessor of the commercial three-seat Model 300 and US Army
TH-55A primary helicopter trainer, now in production. Also in production are a light observation helicopter, designated OH-6A, and the
Model 500, a commercial version of the same
design.

Current research activities include work on
high-speed and heavy-lift rotor system components, and studies of all types of helicopters.
Hughes had over 3,700 employees in February
1970.

HUGHES MODEL 300
US Army designation: TH-55A
Design and development of the original Hughes
Model 269 two-seat light helicopter began in
September 1955 and the first of two prototypes
was flown 13 months later.
The design was then re-engineered for production, with the emphasis on simplicity and ease
of maintenance. The resulting Model 269A
offered an overall life of over 1,000 hours for all
major components.
Five Model 269A pre-production helicopters
were purchased by the US Army under the
designation YHO-2HU, and completed a highly
successful evaluation programme in the command
and observation rôles.

The Model 269A was then put into production
and deliveries began in October 1961. Production reached the rate of one aircraft each
working day by mid-1963 and 1,175 had been
delivered by April 1968, for both civil and
military use.

A Model 269A owned by Garrett AiResearch
Manufacturing Division of Phoenix, Arizona, has
been re-engined with a 220 shp Garrett AiResearch
TSE 36-1 turboshaft engine and offers greatly
improved performance, including a hovering
ceiling of 14,000 ft (4,265 m).

The design has undergone development and
three commercial and military versions are now
in production, as follows:

Model 300. Three-seat version developed under
the engineering designation 269B. Received

Hughes Model 300C, a developed version of the original Model 300 (190 hp Lycoming HIO-360-D1A engine)

FAA Type Approval 30 December 1963. In production at a rate of one a day by 1964. Hughes engineers have perfected a quiet tail rotor (QTR) for the Model 300, which reduces the sound level of the aircraft by 80%. At cruise rpm, the QTR-equipped version operates at a noise level comparable with that of a fixed-wing light aircraft. QTR has been standard factory-installed equipment on production Model 300's since June 1967, and retrofit kits are available to all Model 269A and 300 owners.

Model 300C. This three-seat version of the Hughes Model 300 was developed under the engineering designation 269C. It is described separately below.

TH-55A. The Hughes 269A was selected by the US Army as a light helicopter primary trainer in mid-1964. The first contract was for 20, under the designation TH-55A. Two follow-up contracts were received in 1965, bringing to 396 the total number of TH-55A's supplied initially to the US Army. A follow-up contract awarded in 1967 called for an additional 396 aircraft and these had all been completed by the end of March 1969.

TYPE: One-, two- or three-seat light helicopter.

ROTOR SYSTEM (all models): Fully-articulated metal three-blade main rotor. Blades are of bonded construction, with constant-section extruded aluminium spar, wrap-around skin and a trailing-edge section. Blade section NACA 0015. Two-blade teetering tail rotor, each blade comprising a steel-tube spar with glass-fibre skin. Blades do not fold. No rotor brake.

ROTOR DRIVE: Vee-belt drive system eliminates need for conventional clutch. Metal-coated and hard-anodised sheaves. Spiral bevel angular drive-shaft. Tail rotor shaft-driven directly from belt-drive. Main rotor/engine rpm ratio 1 : 6.

FUSELAGE: Welded steel-tube structure, with aluminium and Plexiglas cabin and one-piece aluminium tube tail-boom.

TAIL UNIT: Horizontal and vertical fixed stabilisers made up of aluminium ribs and skin.

LANDING GEAR: Skids carried on Hughes oleo-pneumatic shock-absorbers. Two cast magnesium ground handling wheels with 10-in (25 cm) balloon tyres, pressure 60-75 lb/sq in (4·22-5·27 kg/cm²). Model 300 is available on floats made of polyurethane coated nylon fabric, 15 ft 5 in (4·70 m) long and with total installed weight of 60 lb (27·2 kg).

POWER PLANT: One 180 hp Lycoming HIO-360-A1A (HIO-360-B1A in TH-55A) four-cylinder horizontally-opposed air-cooled engine, mounted horizontally below seats. Aluminium fuel tank, capacity 30 US gallons (103·5 litres), mounted externally aft of cockpit. Provision for aluminium auxiliary fuel tank, capacity 19 US gallons (72 litres), mounted opposite standard tank. Oil capacity 2 US gallons (7·5 litres).

ACCOMMODATION: Two seats (TH-55A) or three seats (Model 300) side-by-side in Plexiglas-enclosed cabin. Door on each side. Dual controls optional. Baggage capacity 100 lb (45 kg). Exhaust muff or gasoline-heating and ventilation kits available.

ELECTRONICS AND EQUIPMENT (Model 300): Optional equipment includes King KY 90 radio, welded aluminium Stokes litter kit, cargo rack, external load sling of 600 lb (272 kg) capacity.

ELECTRONICS AND EQUIPMENT (TH-55A): Provision for ARC-524M VHF radio.

DIMENSIONS, EXTERNAL:
Diameter of main rotor	25 ft 3½ in (7·71 m)
Main rotor blade chord	6·83 in (17·35 cm)
Diameter of tail rotor	3 ft 10 in (1·17 m)
Distance between rotor centres	
	14 ft 1 in (4·29 m)
Length overall	28 ft 10¾ in (8·80 m)
Length of fuselage	21 ft 11¾ in (6·80 m)
Height overall	8 ft 2¼ in (2·50 m)
Skid track	6 ft 6½ in (2·00 m)
Cabin doors (each):	
Height	3 ft 8 in (1·12 m)
Width	2 ft 8 in (0·81 m)
Height to sill	2 ft 11 in (0·89 m)

DIMENSIONS, INTERNAL:
Cabin: Length	4 ft 7 in (1·40 m)
Max width	4 ft 3 in (1·30 m)
Max height	4 ft 4 in (1·32 m)
Floor area	13·0 sq ft (1·21 m²)

AREAS:
Main rotor blade (each)	7·1 sq ft (0·66 m²)
Tail rotor blade (each)	0·77 sq ft (0·07 m²)
Main rotor disc	503 sq ft (46·73 m²)
Tail rotor disc	8·70 sq ft (0·81 m²)
Fin	1·22 sq ft (0·11 m²)
Horizontal stabiliser	3·44 sq ft (0·32 m²)

WEIGHTS AND LOADINGS:
Weight empty:		
300		958 lb (434 kg)
TH-55A		1,008 lb (457 kg)
Max certificated T-O and landing weight:		
300, TH-55A		1,670 lb (757 kg)
Max recommended weight (restricted operation):		
300, TH-55A		1,850 lb (839 kg)

Hughes TH-55A light primary training helicopter (180 hp Lycoming HIO-360-B1A engine)

Max disc loading (at certificated AUW):
300, TH-55A	3·3 lb/sq ft (16·1 kg/m²)

Max power loading (at certificated AUW):
300, TH-55A	9·3 lb/hp (4·22 kg/hp)

PERFORMANCE (at max certificated T-O weight):
Max level speed at S/L:	
300	75·5 knots (87 mph; 140 km/h)
TH-55A	75 knots (86 mph; 138 km/h)
Max permissible diving speed:	
300	75·5 knots (87 mph; 140 km/h)
TH-55A	75 knots (86 mph; 138 km/h)
Max cruising speed:	
300	69 knots (80 mph; 129 km/h)
TH-55A	65 knots (75 mph; 121 km/h)
Econ cruising speed:	
300, TH-55A	57 knots (66 mph; 106 km/h)
Max water contact speed (on floats):	
	17 knots (20 mph; 32 km/h)
Max water taxiing speed (on floats):	
	9 knots (10 mph; 16 km/h)
Rate of climb at S/L:	
300	1,140 ft (347 m)/min
TH-55A (mission weight)	1,140 ft (347 m)/min
Service ceiling:	
300	13,000 ft (3,960 m)
TH-55A (mission weight)	11,900 ft (3,625 m)
Hovering ceiling in ground effect:	
300	7,700 ft (2,350 m)
TH-55A	5,500 ft (1,675 m)
Hovering ceiling out of ground effect:	
300	5,800 ft (1,770 m)
TH-55A	3,750 ft (1,145 m)
Range with max fuel no reserve:	
300	260 nm (300 miles; 480 km)
TH-55A	177 nm (204 miles; 328 km)
Endurance with max fuel:	
300	3 hr 30 min
TH-55A	2 hr 35 min

HUGHES MODEL 300C

This is a developed version of the standard Model 300 and introduces a number of improvements to allow an increase in payload of 45 per cent. Construction of the prototype started in July 1968, and this made its first flight in August 1969. Construction of production aircraft started in October 1969 and the first production model flew in December 1969. FAA certification was pending at the time of writing.

The introduction of a more powerful engine and an increase of main rotor diameter have caused a number of related structural changes, including

provision of a larger tail rotor and fin of greater area, while the main rotor mast and tail boom have been lengthened to accommodate the longer and heavier rotor blades.

The description of the standard Model 300 applies also to the Model 300C, except in the following details:

ROTOR SYSTEM: As Model 300 except that limited folding is possible. Tracking tabs on main rotor blades at three-quarters radius.

ROTOR DRIVE: Combination Vee-belt/pulley and reduction gear drive system. Main rotor and tail rotor gear box has spiral bevel right-angle drive. Main rotor/engine rpm ratio 1 : 6·8. Tail rotor/engine rpm ratio 0·97 : 1.

POWER PLANT: One 190 hp Lycoming HIO-360-D1A four-cylinder horizontally-opposed air-cooled engine. Oil capacity 2·5 US gallons (9·5 litres).

ACCOMMODATION: Three persons seated side-by-side on sculptured and cushioned bench seat.

ELECTRONICS AND EQUIPMENT: Optional electronics include King KY95 VHF radio and headsets. Optional equipment includes amphibious floats, litters, cargo rack, external load sling of 600 lb (272 kg) capacity, agricultural spray or dry powder dispersion kits, 19-US gallon (72-litre) auxiliary fuel tank, fire extinguisher, dual luggage case, night flying kit which includes a 70A 28V alternator and nickel-cadmium battery, engine-hour time recorder, external power socket, dual controls, all-weather cover, heavy-duty skid plates, exhaust muffler, main rotor tie-down kit, door lock, outside air temperature gauge, dual oil cooler, tinted glass for cabin windows, gasoline or exhaust manifold cabin heating.

DIMENSIONS, EXTERNAL:
Diameter of main rotor	26 ft 10 in (8·18 m)
Main rotor blade chord	6·75 in (17·1 cm)
Diameter of tail rotor	4 ft 3 in (1·30 m)
Length overall	30 ft 11 in (9·42 m)
Width, rotor partially folded	8 ft 0 in (2·44 m)
Skid track	6 ft 3 in (1·91 m)
Passenger doors (2):	
Height	3 ft 7 in (1·09 m)
Width	3 ft 2 in (0·97 m)
Height to sill	3 ft 0 in (0·91 m)

AREAS:
Main rotor blade (each)	7·55 sq ft (0·70 m²)

Hughes OH-6A Cayuse light observation helicopter (317 shp Allison T63-A-5A turboshaft engine)

Tail rotor blade (each)	0·86 sq ft (0·08 m²)
Main rotor disc	565·5 sq ft (52·5 m²)
Tail rotor disc	14·2 sq ft (1·32 m²)
Fin	2·8 sq ft (0·26 m²)
Horizontal stabiliser	3·44 sq ft (0·32 m²)

WEIGHTS AND LOADING:

Weight empty	1,025 lb (465 kg)
Max payload	680 lb (308 kg)
Max T-O and landing weight	1,900 lb (861 kg)
Max disc loading	3·36 lb/sq ft (16·4 kg/m²)

PERFORMANCE (at max T-O weight):
Max level speed from S/L to 7,000 ft (2,135 m)
91 knots (105 mph; 169 km/h) IAS
Max diving speed
91 knots (105 mph; 169 km/h) IAS
Max cruising speed at 5,000 ft (1,525 m)
87 knots (100 mph; 161 km/h) IAS
Econ cruising speed at 5,000 ft (1,525 m)
87 knots (100 mph; 161 km/h) IAS
Service ceiling 13,200 ft (4,023 m)
Hovering ceiling in ground effect
7,600 ft (2,316 m)
Hovering ceiling out of ground effect
5,200 ft (1,585 m)
Range with max fuel, five min engine warm-up,
econ cruising speed at 5,000 ft (1,525 m), no
reserve 222 knots (255 miles; 410 km)

HUGHES OH-6A
US Army designation: OH-6A (formerly HO-6) Cayuse

This helicopter was chosen for development following a US Army design competition for a light observation helicopter in 1961. Five prototypes were ordered for evaluation in competition with the Bell OH-4A and Hiller OH-5A, and the first of these flew on 27 February 1963.

On 26 May 1965 it was announced that the OH-6A had been chosen, as a result of the evaluation, and an initial order for 714 was placed by the US Army; this was increased by subsequent orders to a total of 1,434, all of which were scheduled for delivery by August 1970. During 1968 production reached a rate of more than 70 aircraft per month and the 1,000th OH-6A was delivered to the Army in March 1969.

In March and April 1966, US Army and civilian pilots set up 23 international records in OH-6A helicopters. Among Class E-1 (covering all classes of helicopters) records established were one for a distance of 2,213 miles (3,561·55 km) in a straight line (California to Florida) non-stop with one pilot, and one for a speed of 171·81 mph (276·506 km/h) over a 15/25-km course.

Full-scale production of the Hughes 500 commercial and 500M international military versions of the OH-6A (which are described separately) began in November 1968.

TYPE: Turbine-powered light observation helicopter.

ROTOR SYSTEM: Four-blade fully-articulated main rotor, with blades attached to laminated strap retention system by means of folding quick-disconnected pins. Each blade consists of an extruded aluminium spar hot-bonded to one-piece wrap-around aluminium skin. Trim-tab outboard on each blade. Main rotor blades can be folded. Two-blade tail rotor, each blade comprising a swaged steel-tube spar and glass-fibre skin covering. No rotor brake.

ROTOR DRIVE: Three sets of bevel gears, three drive-shafts and one over-running clutch. Main rotor/engine rpm ratio 1 : 12·806. Tail rotor/engine rpm ratio 1 : 1·987.

FUSELAGE: Aluminium semi-monocoque structure of pod-and-boom type. Clam-shell doors at rear of pod give access to engine and accessories.

TAIL UNIT: Fixed fin, horizontal stabiliser and ventral fin.

LANDING GEAR: Tubular skids carried on Hughes single-acting shock-absorbers.

POWER PLANT: One 317 shp Allison T63-A-5A shaft-turbine engine, derated to 252·5 shp for take-off and 214·5 shp max continuous rating. Two 50% self-sealing bladder fuel tanks under rear cabin floor, capacity 61·5 US gallons (232 litres). Refuelling point aft of cargo door on starboard side. Oil capacity 1·25 US gallons (4·75 litres).

ACCOMMODATION: Crew of two side-by-side in front of cabin. Two seats in rear cargo compartment can be folded to make room for four fully-equipped soldiers, seated on floor. Crew door and cargo compartment door on each side. Fourteen cargo tie-down points.

ELECTRONICS AND EQUIPMENT: Government furnished electronics and avionics. Sylvania

Hughes Model 500 light helicopter (317 shp Allison Model 250-C18A turboshaft engine)

SLAE avionics package installed in 1969/70 production aircraft. ARC-114 VHF-FM and ARC-116 UHF radios, ARN-89 ADF, ASN-43 gyro compass, ID 1351 bearing-heading indicator and ARC-6533 intercoms are standard. ARC-115 may be substituted for ARC-116.

ARMAMENT: Provision for carrying packaged armament on port side of fuselage, comprising XM-27 7·62 mm machine-gun, with 2,000-4,000 rpm capability, or XM-75 grenade launcher.

DIMENSIONS, EXTERNAL:

Diameter of main rotor	26 ft 4 in (8·03 m)
Main rotor blade chord	6·75 in (17·15 cm)
Diameter of tail rotor	4 ft 3 in (1·30 m)
Distance between rotor centres	15 ft 0¼ in (4·58 m)
Length overall, rotors fore and aft	30 ft 3¾ in (9·24 m)
Length of fuselage	23 ft 0 in (7·01 m)
Height of top of rotor hub	8 ft 1½ in (2·48 m)
Skid track	6 ft 9 in (2·06 m)

Cabin door (fwd, each):

Height	3 ft 11 in (1·19 m)
Width	2 ft 11 in (0·89 m)

Cargo compartment door (each):

Height	3 ft 5 in (1·04 m)
Width	2 ft 10½ in (0·88 m)
Height to sill	1 ft 10½ in (0·57 m)

DIMENSIONS, INTERNAL:
Cabin:

Length	8 ft 0 in (2·44 m)
Max width	4 ft 6 in (1·37 m)
Max height	4 ft 3½ in (1·31 m)

AREAS:

Main rotor blade (each)	7·41 sq ft (0·69 m²)
Tail rotor blade (each)	0·85 sq ft (0·079 m²)
Main rotor disc	544·63 sq ft (50·60 m²)
Tail rotor disc	14·19 sq ft (1·32 m²)
Fin	5·65 sq ft (0·52 m²)
Horizontal stabiliser	7·70 sq ft (0·72 m²)

WEIGHTS AND LOADINGS:

Weight empty, equipped	1,229 lb (557 kg)
Design gross weight	2,400 lb (1,090 kg)
Overload gross weight	2,700 lb (1,225 kg)
Design disc loading	4·4 lb/sq ft (21·48 kg/m²)
Design power loading	9·5 lb/shp (4·31 kg/shp)

PERFORMANCE (at design gross weight):
VNE and max cruising speed at S/L
130 knots (150 mph; 241 km/h)
Cruising speed for max range at S/L
116 knots (134 mph; 216 km/h)
Max rate of climb at S/L (military power)
1,840 ft (560 m)/min
Max rate of climb at S/L (max cont power)
1,250 ft (381 m)/min
Service ceiling 15,800 ft (4,815 m)
Hovering ceiling out of ground effect
7,300 ft (2,225 m)
Hovering ceiling in ground effect
11,800 ft (3,595 m)
Normal range at 5,000 ft (1,500 m)
330 nm (380 miles; 611 km)

Ferry range (1,300 lb = 590 kg fuel)
1,354 nm (1,560 miles; 2,510 km)

HUGHES MODEL 500 AND 500M

These are the commercial and foreign military counterparts of the OH-6A military helicopter.

Although similar in basic design and construction to the OH-6A, the Model 500's have been substantially uprated. The 317 shp Allison Model 250-C18A turbine engine (civil version of the T63-A-5A) is only derated to 278 shp for take-off and has a maximum continuous rating of 243 shp. The certificated gross weight has been increased by 150 lb (68 kg) and the internal volume of the passenger compartment has been increased for executive comfort by rearrangement of a drive system-powered cooling system. The fuel capacity of the Model 500 is 4% greater at 64 US gallons (242 litres). Strengthened landing gear for floats and the ability to accommodate various mission kits are added features. Optional equipment available for the Model 500 includes navigation lights, shatter-proof glass, heating system, radios and intercom, running time meter, attitude and directional gyros, rate-of-climb indicator, inertia reels and shoulder harnesses for pilot and co-pilot, fire extinguisher, dual controls, cargo hook and hoist, auxiliary fuel system, heated pitot tube, extended landing gear, blade storage rack, litter kit, emergency inflatable floats, ground handling wheels and first aid kit. The Model 500 is available in two versions as follows:

Model 500. Commercial helicopter with accommodation for pilot and five passengers or equivalent freight. A deluxe executive interior is available as an optional item.

Model 500M. Military configuration, uprated version of OH-6A. Available to foreign military customers. Four delivered to Colombian Air Force in April 1968. Full production began in November 1968. Twenty-five being delivered to Kawasaki, Japan, under licensing agreement.

DIMENSIONS AND AREAS:
Same as for OH-6A

WEIGHTS:
Weight empty:

500	1,086 lb (492 kg)
500M	1,125 lb (510 kg)
Max T-O weight	2,550 lb (1,157 kg)

PERFORMANCE (at max T-O weight):
Max level speed at 1,000 ft (305 m)
132 knots (152 mph; 244 km/h)
Cruising speed for max range at S/L
120 knots (138 mph; 222 km/h)
Max rate of climb at S/L 1,700 ft (518 m)/min
Service ceiling 14,400 ft (4,390 m)
Hovering ceiling out of ground effect
5,300 ft (1,615 m)
Hovering ceiling in ground effect
8,200 ft (2,500 m)
Range at 4,000 ft (1,220 m):

500	327 nm (377 miles; 606 km)
500M	318 nm (366 miles; 589 km)

HUGO
ADOLPH B. HUGO, Jr
ADDRESS:
7715 East Fourth Street, Tulsa, Oklahoma 74112

Mr Hugo began designing a single-seat sporting biplane named the Hu-go Craft in October 1961. Construction began immediately after and the aircraft flew for the first time on 19 April 1965. It had logged 280 flying hours by December 1969.

Cost was approximately $1,500. At the EAA International Fly-in at Rockford, Illinois, in August 1969, the Hu-go Craft received the award of "Outstanding design, light biplane".

Plans are available to amateur constructors and twelve examples are being built in the United States and Canada.

HUGO HU-GO CRAFT
TYPE: Single-seat amateur-built biplane.
WINGS: Strut-braced biplane, with N-type inter-plane struts and single bracing strut from bottom fuselage longeron to top of rear inter-plane strut on each side. Six-strut cabane. Wing section NACA M-12. Dihedral 3° 30′ (lower wings only). Incidence 2° on both wings. Sweepback 8° on top wing only. Wood structure of aircraft spruce spars and cap-strip and gusset ribs, fabric-covered. Frise-type wooden ailerons on lower wings only. No tabs. No flaps.

FUSELAGE: Welded 4130 steel-tube basic structure with honeycomb formers and aluminium stringers. Fabric covering overall.

TAIL UNIT: Wire-braced welded 4130 steel-tube structure with fabric covering. Fixed-incidence tailplane. No tabs.

LANDING GEAR: Non-retractable type with steerable tail-wheel. Cantilever spring-steel main legs attached to engine mounting, with cut-down Piper Cub wheels, size 5·00 × 4. Tyre pressure 20 lb/sq in (1·41 kg/cm²). Motor scooter brakes.

POWER PLANT: One 65 hp Continental A65-12 four-cylinder horizontally-opposed air-cooled engine, driving a McCauley two-blade fixed-pitch propeller, diameter 5 ft 8 in (1·73 m). Fuel tank in fuselage, capacity 12 US gallons (45·5 litres). Oil capacity 1 US gallon (3·75 litres).

ACCOMMODATION: Single seat in open cockpit. Baggage hold, capacity 15 lb (7 kg), aft of seat.

DIMENSIONS, EXTERNAL:

Wing span: top	17 ft 0 in (5·18 m)
bottom	15 ft 0 in (4·57 m)
Wing chord, constant (both)	3 ft 0 in (0·91 m)
Wing aspect ratio	5·66
Length overall	15 ft 0 in (4·57 m)
Height overall	5 ft 7¾ in (1·72 m)
Tailplane span	6 ft 10 in (2·08 m)
Wheel track	4 ft 6 in (1·37 m)
Wheelbase	11 ft 3 in (3·43 m)

DIMENSIONS, INTERNAL:

Cockpit, max width	1 ft 9 in (0·53 m)
Baggage space	1·5 cu ft (0·04 m³)

AREAS:

Wings, gross	92 sq ft (8·55 m²)
Ailerons (total)	3·75 sq ft (0·35 m²)
Fin	1·25 sq ft (0·12 m²)

Hugo Hu-go Craft single-seat light aircraft (65 hp Continental A65-12 engine) *(Howard Levy)*

Rudder	2·50 sq ft (0·23 m²)
Tailplane	5·06 sq ft (0·47 m²)
Elevators	5·00 sq ft (0·46 m²)

WEIGHTS AND LOADING:

Weight empty	558 lb (253 kg)
Max T-O weight	848 lb (384 kg)
Max wing loading	9·2 lb/sq ft (44·9 kg/m²)

PERFORMANCE (at max T-O weight):

Max level speed at 1,000 ft (305 m)
100 knots (115 mph; 185 km/h)

Max cruising speed (75% power) at 3,000 ft (915 m)	91 knots (105 mph; 169 km/h)
Stalling speed	48 knots (55 mph; 89 km/h)
Rate of climb at S/L	1,000 ft (305 m)/min
Service ceiling	10,000 ft (3,050 m)
T-O run	500 ft (152 m)
T-O to 50 ft (15 m)	1,000 ft (305 m)
Landing from 50 ft (15 m)	1,000 ft (305 m)
Landing run	500 ft (152 m)
Range with max fuel, 45 min reserve	182 nm (210 miles; 338 km)

INTERCEPTOR
INTERCEPTOR CORPORATION
HEAD OFFICE:

1700 Lexington Street, Norman, Oklahoma 73069

This corporation was formed on 18 November 1968 for the purpose of designing, manufacturing, distributing and servicing aircraft for the general aviation market. It has a manufacturing plant at Max Westheimer Field, Norman, Oklahoma.

First aircraft to be produced by this company is the Interceptor 400, an advanced turbine-engined development of what was known originally as the Meyers 200B and was produced subsequently by Aero Commander as their Model 200. Interceptor Corporation has acquired all design drawings, production jigs and tools for this latter aircraft and has re-designed the power plant installation and tail unit. Construction of the prototype started in January 1969 and the first flight was made on 27 June 1969. Deliveries of an initial production batch of five aircraft were scheduled to begin late in 1969, after FAA certification.

INTERCEPTOR 400
TYPE: Four-seat light cabin monoplane.

WINGS: Cantilever low-wing monoplane. Wing section NACA 23015 at root, NACA 23012 at station 62, NACA 4412 at tip. Dihedral 6°. Incidence 2° at root, 2° at station 62, —3° at tip. Sweepback at quarter-chord approx 1°. Root section outboard to station 62 of welded steel-tube construction with aluminium skins. Outer wings are of conventional two-spar flush-riveted light alloy construction. Conventional all-metal ailerons with ground-adjustable trim-tab. All-metal Fowler trailing-edge flaps.

FUSELAGE: All-metal structure. Cabin section of welded steel tube, with overturn structure and light alloy covering. Light alloy semi-monocoque flush-riveted rear fuselage.

TAIL UNIT: Cantilever all-metal structure. Fixed-incidence tailplane. Rudder has ground-adjustable trim-tab. Elevators have controllable trim-tab.

LANDING GEAR: Hydraulically-retractable tricycle type. Nose unit retracts aft, main units inwards. Interceptor oleo-pneumatic shock-absorber struts; single wheel on each unit. Goodyear main wheels and tyres size 7·00 × 6, 6-ply rating, pressure 38 lb/sq in (2·67 kg/cm²). Goodyear nose-wheel and tyre size 5·00 × 5, 6-ply rating, pressure 49 lb/sq in (3·45 kg/cm²). Goodyear caliper drum brakes.

POWER PLANT: One Garrett-AiResearch TPE 331-1-101 turboprop engine, flat rated to 400 shp and driving a Hartzell three-blade feathering and reversible-pitch metal propeller, diameter 7 ft 2 in (2·18 m). Fuel contained in two integral wing tanks, one in each outer wing panel, with total capacity of approx 150 US gallons (568 litres). Oil capacity 1·75 US gallons (6·6 litres).

ACCOMMODATION: Four seats in pairs in enclosed cabin. Door on starboard side, above wing, hinged at forward edge. Baggage compartment aft of cabin with external door on starboard side. Cabin air-conditioned and pressurised.

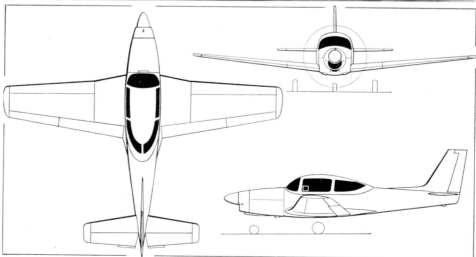

Photograph and three-view drawing of Interceptor 400 light cabin monoplane

SYSTEMS: AiResearch air-cycle air-conditioning and pressurisation by engine-bleed air; max differential 2·75 lb/sq in (0·19 kg/cm²). Pneumatic system for pressurisation control and instruments. Hydraulic system, pressure 1,000-1,300 lb/sq in (70-91 kg/cm²), for operation of flaps, landing gear and passenger step, which retracts simultaneously with landing gear. Electrical power supplied by 200A starter/generator and two 22Ah nickel-cadmium batteries.

DIMENSIONS, EXTERNAL:

Wing span	30 ft 6 in (9·29 m)
Wing chord at root	7 ft 6 in (2·29 m)

Wing chord at tip	3 ft 4 in (1·02 m)		Max width	3 ft 8 in (1·12 m)	Max T-O and landing weight	3,800 lb (1,724 kg)
Wing aspect ratio	5·81		Max height	4 ft 6 in (1·37 m)	Max zero-fuel weight	3,200 lb (1,452 kg)
Length overall	26 ft 11½ in (8·22 m)		Floor area	24 sq ft (2·23 m²)	Max wing loading	23·75 lb/sq ft (115·9 kg/m²)
Tailplane span	12 ft 3 in (3·73 m)		Volume	60 cu ft (1·70 m³)	Max power loading	9·5 lb/hp (4·3 kg/hp)
Wheel track	8 ft 11 in (2·72 m)		Baggage hold	11 cu ft (0·31 m³)		

Wing chord at tip   3 ft 4 in (1·02 m)
Wing aspect ratio   5·81
Length overall   26 ft 11½ in (8·22 m)
Tailplane span   12 ft 3 in (3·73 m)
Wheel track   8 ft 11 in (2·72 m)
Wheelbase (approx)   6 ft 9½ in (2·07 m)
Cabin door (approx):
   Height   3 ft 4 in (1·02 m)
   Width   3 ft 0 in (0·91 m)
Baggage compartment door (approx):
   Height   1 ft 8 in (0·51 m)
   Width   1 ft 11 in (0·58 m)
   Height to sill   2 ft 6 in (0·76 m)

DIMENSIONS, INTERNAL (approx):
Cabin:
   Length   7 ft 3 in (2·21 m)

Max width   3 ft 8 in (1·12 m)
Max height   4 ft 6 in (1·37 m)
Floor area   24 sq ft (2·23 m²)
Volume   60 cu ft (1·70 m³)
Baggage hold   11 cu ft (0·31 m³)
AREAS:
Wings, gross   161·5 sq ft (16·00 m²)
Ailerons (total)   10·8 sq ft (1·00 m²)
Trailing-edge flaps (total)
   22·4 sq ft (2·08 m²)
Fin (approx)   8·94 sq ft (0·83 m²)
Rudder, including tab (approx)
   7·06 sq ft (0·66 m²)
Tailplane   16·4 sq ft (1·52 m²)
Elevators, including tab   17·3 sq ft (1·61 m²)
WEIGHTS AND LOADINGS:
Weight empty   2,200 lb (998 kg)

Max T-O and landing weight 3,800 lb (1,724 kg)
Max zero-fuel weight   3,200 lb (1,452 kg)
Max wing loading   23·75 lb/sq ft (115·9 kg/m²)
Max power loading   9·5 lb/hp (4·3 kg/hp)
PERFORMANCE (at max T-O weight):
Max level speed, above 16,000 ft (4,875 m)
   over 260 knots (300 mph; 483 km/h) TAS
Max diving speed
   269 knots (310 mph; 499 km/h) IAS
Stalling speed, flaps and landing gear down
   55 knots (63 mph; 101 km/h)
Stalling speed, flaps and landing gear up
   66 knots (76 mph; 122 km/h)
Rate of climb at S/L over 2,000 ft (610 m)/min
Service ceiling   24,000 ft (7,315 m)
Range with max fuel, with reserves
   868 nm (1,000 miles; 1,609 km)

ISLAND AIRCRAFT
ISLAND AIRCRAFT CORPORATION
ADDRESS:
   10 Granada Avenue, Merritt Island, Florida 32952
PRESIDENT: LeRoy P. Lopresti
ISLAND AIRCRAFT SPECTRA
Mr LeRoy P. Lopresti, president of Island Aircraft Corporation, is also an employee of Grumman Aerospace Corporation at the Kennedy Space Center. He has designed an advanced light amphibian which he has named Spectra, and a research test vehicle has been built to evaluate water performance. A one-sixth scale radio controlled model has been built and used for flight tests, and this has already demonstrated that the design has good spin recovery qualities. Island Aircraft is currently seeking financial backing to construct two flight test aircraft and one static test vehicle.

Most original feature of the design is the combination engine pylon/T-tail, with the engine mounted at the junction of the fin and tailplane. The majority of small amphibians built previously have had a separate wing-mounted pylon to carry the engine installation and this has imposed a drag penalty. The Spectra's engine installation provides the propeller with protection from spray and permits a tractor installation of the engine with an undisturbed airflow to the propeller. Furthermore, propeller slipstream does not impinge on a large fuselage area, so inducing drag, and the high velocity stream of air flowing over the tail surfaces will provide excellent tail control under all flight conditions. The canted wingtips, which serve also as stabilising floats when the craft is waterborne, increase wing efficiency in flight by providing an endplate effect to inhibit formation of wingtip vortices.

TYPE: Two-seat hydrodynamic test vehicle.
WINGS: Cantilever mid-wing monoplane. All-metal structure with Vultee BT-13 outer wing panels less wingtips. The all-metal wingtips, each of 3 ft 0 in (0·91 m) span, have a flat undersurface and are canted downward 17° 30', serving as stabilising floats for operation on water and as wing extensions in flight. Conventional ailerons with trim-tabs. Trailing-edge flaps consist of Vultee BT-13 outer flap panels.
HULL: Wooden structure of bulkheads and stringers, except for high-strength aluminium

Island Aircraft Spectra light amphibian research test vehicle (*Howard Levy*)

bulkheads in the wing centre-section area to carry wing bending loads. Marine plywood skin, glass-fibre covered. Vertical spray rails. Flight prototypes and production aircraft will have all-metal hull structure. Retractable step in under-surface of hull to eliminate aerodynamic drag in flight and permit step adjustment for varying water conditions. Water-rudder, mounted at rear of fuselage, is of variable area and co-ordinated with the aerodynamic rudder.
TAIL UNIT: Composite cantilever structure with spruce main load-carrying spars and metal control surfaces. The fin houses also a welded steel-tube engine mounting which locates the single engine at the intersection of fin and tailplane.
LANDING GEAR: Research test vehicle has no landing gear, but prototype and production aircraft will have retractable tricycle gear, with main units retracting into the wing. The nose gear will consist of a long leg which will swing out of the top of the nose, travelling through a 270° arc to a suitable position for landing and take-off.
POWER PLANT: Research test vehicle has one 125 hp Lycoming O-290-G four-cylinder horizontally-opposed air-cooled engine, driving a Banks-Maxwell specially carved two-blade fixed-pitch wooden propeller, diameter 6 ft 0 in (1·83 m). Prototype and production aircraft will have a 310 hp engine with reversible-pitch propeller to improve manoeuvrability. Two wing fuel tanks, each of 25 US gallons (94·6

litres). An auxiliary fuselage tank of 40 US gallon (151·4 litre) capacity will provide maximum fuel capacity of 90 US gallons (340 litres).
ACCOMMODATION: Research test vehicle has two seats side-by-side in enclosed cabin. Windshield frame of high strength material to allow minimum frame dimensions to offer maximum visibility; windscreen has single curvature to eliminate distortion. Prototype and production aircraft will have four seats in pairs and a tilt-up canopy similar to that of F-100 Super Sabre. Compartment for 120 lb (54 kg) baggage.
DIMENSIONS, EXTERNAL:
Wing span   32 ft 8 in (9·96 m)
Wing chord at root   5 ft 6 in (1·68 m)
Wing chord at tip   4 ft 0 in (1·22 m)
Length overall (less pitot tube)
   27 ft 10 in (8·48 m)
Height overall   8 ft 11 in (2·72 m)
Tailplane span   14 ft 0 in (4·27 m)
DIMENSIONS, INTERNAL:
Cabin:
   Max width   3 ft 7 in (1·09 m)
WEIGHTS:
Weight empty, equipped   2,800 lb (1,270 kg)
Max T-O weight   3,300 lb (1,496 kg)
PERFORMANCE (estimated, 310 hp engine):
Max level speed 188 knots (217 mph; 349 km/h)
Max cruising speed, 75% power
   165 knots (190 mph; 306 km/h)
Stalling speed   57 knots (65 mph; 105 km/h)
Range with max fuel
   1,042 nm (1,200 miles; 1,931 km)

JANOX
JANOX CORPORATION
HEAD OFFICE:
   PO Box 43, Arcanum, Ohio 45304
GENERAL OFFICE:
   109 West North Street, Arcanum, Ohio 45304
EXPERIMENTAL DEPARTMENT:
   3345 W Kessler-Cowlesville Road, Troy, Ohio 45373
PRESIDENT: Neil A. Nelson
Janox Corporation, manufacturers of reflector landing systems, have acquired Navion Aircraft Corporation of Seguin, Texas. They intend to continue production of the Navion Model H and propose to construct a new factory at Coshocton, Ohio, late in 1970.

Navion Aircraft Corporation was formed by members of the American Navion Society in mid-1965, after acquiring all rights in the North American/Ryan Navion light aircraft. Its first product was a five-seat version of the Navion, of which details follow.

JANOX/NAVION MODEL H
This aircraft is virtually identical with its predecessors of the Rangemaster series (see 1963-64 *Jane's*), but has a more powerful engine, new control wheels and several technical improvements, which have improved performance.
TYPE: Five-seat light aircraft.
WINGS: Cantilever low-wing monoplane. Wing section NACA 4415R at root. NACA 6410R at tip. Dihedral 7° 30'. Incidence 1° at root. —2° at tip. All-metal construction. Metal Frise-type ailerons. Metal slotted flaps. Ground-adjustable tab on starboard aileron.
FUSELAGE: All-metal semi-monocoque structure.

Janox/Navion Model H five-seat light aircraft (285 hp Continental IO-520-B engine)

TAIL UNIT: Cantilever all-metal structure. Ground-adjustable tab on rudder. Trim-tab in each elevator.
LANDING GEAR: Hydraulically-retractable tricycle type. Navion oleo-pneumatic shock-absorbers. Goodyear die-cast magnesium

wheels. Main wheel tyres size 6·50 × 8, pressure 45 lb/sq in (3·16 kg/cm²). Nose-wheel tyre size 6·00 × 6, pressure 30 lb/sq in (2·11 kg/cm²). Goodyear disc brakes.
POWER PLANT: One 285 hp Continental IO-520-B six-cylinder horizontally-opposed air-cooled

engine, driving a McCauley two-blade metal constant-speed propeller. Fuel in 40 US gallon (151 litre) centre main tank and two wing-tip tanks, each of 34 US gallons (129 litres). Total usable fuel capacity 108 US gallons (409 litres).

ACCOMMODATION: Pilot and four passengers, in two pairs of individual seats and single rear seat. Dual controls, head-rests, individual ventilators, and heater-defroster standard. Passenger seats removable for freight carrying. Large forward-hinged door on port side. Baggage space aft of rear seat, with internal and external access, capacity 180 lb (82 kg).

ELECTRONICS AND EQUIPMENT: Standard equipment includes full gyro instrument panel, basic auto-pilot, King KX 160 360-channel transceiver, King KI 201 VOR/LOC converter-indicator, rotating beacon and heated pitot tube.

DIMENSIONS, EXTERNAL:

Wing span	34 ft 9 in (10·59 m)
Wing chord at root	7 ft 2½ in (2·19 m)
Wing chord at tip	3 ft 9½ in (1·15 m)
Wing aspect ratio	6·04
Length overall	27 ft 6 in (8·38 m)
Height overall	8 ft 4 in (2·54 m)
Tailplane span	13 ft 2 in (4·01 m)
Wheel track	8 ft 8½ in (2·66 m)
Wheelbase	approx 5 ft 8½ in (1·74 m)

AREAS:

Wings, gross	184·34 sq ft (17·12 m²)
Ailerons (total)	10·32 sq ft (0·96 m²)
Flaps (total)	29·23 sq ft (2·71 m²)
Fin	6·87 sq ft (0·64 m²)
Rudder	6·05 sq ft (0·56 m²)
Tailplane	28·95 sq ft (2·69 m²)
Elevators	14·10 sq ft (1·31 m²)

WEIGHTS:

Weight empty	1,945 lb (882 kg)
Max T-O weight	3,315 lb (1,504 kg)
Max landing weight	3,150 lb (1,429 kg)

PERFORMANCE (at max T-O weight):

Max level speed	174 knots (200 mph; 322 km/h)
Normal cruising speed	161-166 knots (185-191 mph; 298-307 km/h)
Rate of climb at S/L	1,375 ft (420 m)/min
Service ceiling	21,500 ft (6,550 m)
T-O run	725-925 ft (220-282 m)
Landing run	750-980 ft (230-300 m)
Range with max fuel at econ cruising speed	1,563 nm (1,800 miles; 2,895 km)

KAMAN

KAMAN AEROSPACE CORPORATION
(a subsidiary of Kaman Corporation)

PRESIDENT:
Jack G. Anderson

EXECUTIVE VICE-PRESIDENT AND GENERAL MANAGER:
Robert D. Moses

VICE-PRESIDENTS:
Anthony J. Carbone (Sales)
David W. Demers (Contracts)
James T. King (Administration)
Robert L. Martin (Manufacturing)
W. R. Murray (Test Operations and Customer Service)
Clayton M. Opp (Washington Office)
W. N. Stone (Engineering)

SECRETARY: J. S. Murtha

COMPTROLLER: Jess E. Sweely

PUBLIC RELATIONS MANAGER:
Robert J. Neary

The original Kaman Aircraft Corporation was founded in 1945 by Mr Charles H. Kaman, who continues as President of the Kaman Corporation. Its initial programme was to test and develop a new servo-flap control system for helicopter rotors and the "synchropter" intermeshing rotor configuration.

Production of the HH-43 turbine-powered local base rescue helicopter, the last design embodying both of these concepts, continues on a reduced basis; well over 200 are in service with the USAF and five other services. Details of this helicopter can be found in the 1965-66 *Jane's*. The later UH-2 Seasprite naval utility helicopter, which utilises the servo-flap control system on a conventional single main rotor, is described below. Conversion of UH-2's to twin-engined configuration is under way at the rate of three a month.

In February 1969, Kaman announced development of a twin-turbine medium-size helicopter for commercial and military applications, designated K-700, as well as a high-speed gunship and rescue helicopter based largely on the UH-2C Seasprite, designated K-800, and these new aircraft are also described below.

In recent years, Kaman has diversified its activities considerably and it now operates four plants in Connecticut, located at Hartford, Bloomfield, Windsor Locks and Moosup. Its helicopter production, commercial component and subcontract activities are organised into a single operating unit, as the Kaman Aerospace Corporation. Its capabilities include major production work in the fields of sheet metal, glass-fibre, reinforced honeycomb bonding and chemical milling.

Current production activities of the Kaman Aerospace Corporation on the HH-43 and UH-2 helicopter series includes airframe conversion, the addition of special rescue equipment and manufacture of spare parts for these types. Kaman is an associate contractor with Grumman on the US Navy F-14A, and will construct flaps, spoilers, slats and other control surfaces, as well as providing extensive engineering support to Grumman.

Other major current contracts include the production of components and assemblies for the McDonnell Douglas DC-8, Grumman A-6 and OV-1, and Lockheed C-5, and thrust reversers for the General Electric TF39 turbofan engine.

It is continuing the development of Rotochute rotary-wing devices to control the speed and direction of descent of capsules, vehicles or instrument packages from space and in the atmosphere.

Under a $100,000 contract awarded by the US Naval Air Development Center, Kaman began design studies of a proposed flying ejection seat during 1969. Known as a stowable aircrew vehicle escape rotoseat (SAVER), it was envisaged as a gyroplane with an unpowered rotor.

Subsequently, Kaman announced the award of a $95,000 follow-on contract from the Naval Air Development Center for the design of a full-scale model of SAVER for wind tunnel flight testing. This will involve construction of a full-size SAVER without engine, and tests will demonstrate its aerodynamic characteristics and its capability of deploying stowed rotor blades.

A US Navy programme, at present in the Concept Formulation stage, is aimed at developing a Light Airborne Multi-Purpose System (LAMPS), to utilise helicopters for a variety of missions while operating from, and extending the capabilities of, destroyers and escort vessels. The main task of such helicopters would be anti-submarine warfare (ASW) and cruise missile defence (CMD), but they would be deployed also for general utility operations. Kaman has proposed two helicopters to meet this requirement; the first is designated Sealite, and is intended for deployment on naval destroyers and escort vessels at present in service, which have helicopter deck loading limits of about 6,000 lb (2,720 kg). To overcome this weight limitation Kaman intends to utilise the dynamic system of the UH-2 helicopter, relying upon a small, lighter fuselage, skid landing gear, two Pratt & Whitney (UACL) PT6 (T400-CP-400) turboshaft engines and a three-blade folding rotor with a new rotor hub to keep the maximum gross weight down to 7,900 lb (3,583 kg).

For ASW missions, Sealite would carry one Mk 46 torpedo, MAD equipment, eight sonobuoys, data link, radar, avionics, data processing, missile defence provision and a crew of two. For CMD operation, equipment would be changed to one Sparrow missile, illuminator, electronic countermeasures, data link, radar, avionics, ASW provisions, sensors, and a crew of two.

The second helicopter, designated Sealamp, is intended for deployment on future, heavier destroyers. This is proposed as a conversion of the basic UH-2C, powered by two General Electric T58-GE-10 (or -5) turboshaft engines, incorporating also Kaman's new "101" rotor and simplified controls. It would have a maximum gross weight of 12,800 lb (5,805 kg).

The equipment of this version for ASW operations would duplicate that of Sealite, except that an additional Mk 46 torpedo, more sonobuoys, more extensive radar and avionics, and a third crew member would be carried. For the CMD mission a second Sparrow missile and third crew member would be carried.

Under US Army contract, Kaman is conducting a noise-suppression programme on the HH-43, which at present is claimed to be the world's quietest helicopter.

Kaman is also developing a new helicopter rotor concept, known as controllable twist rotor (CTR) which, if feasible, will permit efficient pitch along the whole blade through its complete rotation. CTR combines features of the Kaman servo-flap and conventional pitch horn controls to increase performance and reduce vibration and structural loads.

Other Kaman Aerospace business interests include long-life self-lubricating aircraft bearings, marketed under the name KA-carb, and automatic packing machinery.

Kaman Corporation announced on 25 March 1968 its intention to establish its four science and technology divisions as a separate wholly-owned subsidiary. Known as Kaman Sciences Corporation, this comprises Kaman Nuclear at Colorado Springs, Colorado; Science Engineering Associates of San Marino, California, active in the fields of oceanography and marine engineering; Kaman AviDyne of Burlington, Massachusetts, experts in structural dynamics, shear blast effects and aeroelasticity; and Kaman System Center.

Other Kaman subsidiaries are AirKaman, Inc, a fixed-base operator at Windsor Locks; AirKaman of Omaha, Inc, a fixed-base operator at Omaha, Nebraska, and Beechcraft distributor for parts of the US mid-west; and AirKaman of Jacksonville, Florida, a fixed-base operator.

The number of people employed by Kaman was 2,800 in January 1970.

KAMAN SEASPRITE

US Navy designation: UH-2 (formerly HU2K-1) and HH-2.

The Seasprite is capable of performing a variety of missions, including all-weather search and rescue, plane guard, casualty evacuation, gun-fire observation, courier service, reconnaissance, personnel transfer, radiological reconnaissance, vertical replenishment, tactical air control, wire-laying, emergency supply and resupply, towing, and operation from small ships. It is equipped with the latest electronic equipment for all-weather navigation, automatic stabilization, auto-navigation, water flotation and in-flight blade tracking. An external cargo hook with 4,000 lb (1,815 kg) capacity is standard equipment.

The prototype Seasprite flew for the first time on 2 July 1959, and the following versions have since been produced for the US Navy:

UH-2A. Initial production version. Entered US Navy service on 18 December 1962, when deliveries began to Helicopter Utility Squadron 2. First shipboard service as HU-2 Detachment 62 on USS *Independence* on 4 June 1963. Total of 88 built.

UH-2B. Development of UH-2A, for operation under VFR conditions. Differs only in the non-installation of certain electronic navigation equipment, although provision for fitting this equipment is retained. Entered shipboard service with Detachment 46 of HU-4, on USS *Albany*, on 8 August 1963. Total of 102 built.

UH-2C. Seasprites were converted to twin-engined configuration, with this designation, under a US Navy contract. Each has two 1,250 shp General Electric T58-GE-8B turboshaft engines in place of the former single T58. Deliveries began in August 1967 and 59 had been delivered by the end of 1969.

HH-2C. Armed and armoured version of the standard UH-2C for search and rescue missions. It differs from the UH-2C by having a chin-mounted Minigun turret, waist-mounted machine-guns, extensive armour around the cockpit and other vital areas, a four-blade tail rotor, dual wheels on the main landing gear and a transmission uprated to 12,500 lb (5,670 kg). The US Navy have ordered 12 of these aircraft as conversions of existing Seasprites.

HH-2D. Announced late in 1969, this version is identical to the HH-2C, except that the armament and armour has been deleted. A total of 31 HH-2D's are currently being retrofitted from earlier single-engine models and first deliveries to the US Navy, at NAS Lakehurst, were scheduled to begin in February 1970.

The K-800 compound gunship, described separately, is based on the HH-2C.

On 2 January 1964 Kaman announced that it had received US Navy contracts covering the installation on Seasprite helicopters of special rescue equipment. The Kaman-developed systems cover three items of new equipment: a rescue boom which swings out and puts the rescue operation in the pilot's field of vision, a ladle net which permits the helicopter to hover and scoop an unconscious man out of the water, and a loud hailer by which the pilot can talk to and direct a victim in the water. The boom and loud hailer, which require minor modification to the UH-2 for installation, were covered in the initial contracts. The company received subsequently contractual coverage for production of the rescue net.

The rescue boom swings out like a long pointer when the pilot lowers the hoist. With it the pilot has the entire rescue operation in his field of vision. Previous techniques demanded co-ordination between the pilot and the crewman operating the hoist. The loud hailer system consists of two speakers mounted in the nose of the helicopter and connected to the pilot's microphone.

The folding rescue net can be stowed in the cabin of the UH-2 and other helicopters, and can be used with either a standard hoist or the Kaman rescue boom. It is lowered under an unconscious man to "ladle" him out of the water. Earlier rescue techniques using standard seat or hook often required that a crewman ride down the line to pick up an unconscious survivor.

Kaman is also producing in quantity a forest-penetrating rescue seat, used widely in Southeast Asia in a variety of helicopters operated by the four US services to recover airmen down in the jungle. Lowered in a cylindrical configuration the device, known as "Sweet Chariot", has spring-loaded seats used during the rescue ascent as well as a plastic "bonnet" that protects the rescuees' heads during recovery from jungle or forest areas. Three persons can be rescued simultaneously.

During 1963, the US Navy initiated a programme to investigate the anti-submarine warfare potential of the UH-2. As a result of a preliminary study and test installation, it was decided to order additional test quantities of specially-equipped UH-2's for operation with the fleet to analyse further the feasibility of a dual anti-submarine/utility rôle.

Kaman announced in October 1968 that they were evaluating the flight characteristics of a UH-2C modified by the addition of stub wings. These wings offer increased fuel storage capacity and serve also to carry a wide range of external stores, including torpedoes, depth charges, grenade launchers, rocket, minigun or machine-gun pods and 60 US gallon (227 litre) auxiliary fuel tanks. As part of this research and development programme, Kaman are also evaluating the lateral stability of the stub-wing UH-2 in flotation, with the wings acting as sponsons. Max range of this version is 377 nm (434 miles; 700 km) when carrying external tanks.

TYPE: Naval all-weather rescue and utility helicopter.

ROTOR SYSTEM: Four-blade main rotor. Three-blade tail rotor on UH-2A, B and C, and four-blade tail rotor on HH-2C, D. Blades of aluminium and glass-fibre construction, with servo-flap controls. Blades folded manually. Main rotor rpm 287.

FUSELAGE: All-metal semi-monocoque structure, with flotation hull housing main fuel tanks. Fixed horizontal stabiliser on tail rotor pylon.

LANDING GEAR: Tail-wheel type, with forward-retracting main wheels and non-retractable tail-wheel. Single wheels on main gear of UH-2A, B, C; dual main wheels on HH-2C and D. Oleo-pneumatic shock-absorbers.

POWER PLANT: One 1,250 shp General Electric T58-GE-8B turboshaft engine on UH-2A and UH-2B. Two similar engines on UH-2C, HH-2C and HH-2D. Normal fuel capacity of 396 US gallons (1,499 litres), including external auxiliary tanks with a capacity of 120 US gallons (454·6 litres).

ACCOMMODATION: Crew of two and up to 11 passengers or four stretcher patients. Can pick up 12 survivors in emergency sea rescue operations.

DIMENSIONS, EXTERNAL:
Diameter of main rotor	44 ft 0 in (13·41 m)
Main rotor blade chord	21·6 in (55 cm)
Diameter of tail rotor	8 ft 0 in (2·44 m)
Length overall	52 ft 2 in (15·90 m)
Length of fuselage	37 ft 8 in (11·48 m)
Length, blades folded	39 ft 7½ in (12·07 m)
Height to top of rotor head	13 ft 6·3 in (4·12 m)
Stabiliser span	9 ft 8 in (2·94 m)
Wheel track	10 ft 10 in (3·30 m)

WEIGHTS:
Weight empty:
UH-2A	6,216 lb (2,819 kg)
UH-2B	6,100 lb (2,766 kg)
UH-2C	7,390 lb (3,351 kg)
HH-2C	8,165 lb (3,703 kg)
HH-2D	7,500 lb (3,401 kg)

Normal T-O weight:
UH-2A/B	8,637 lb (3,917 kg)
UH-2C	9,951 lb (4,514 kg)
HH-2C	12,585 lb (5,708 kg)
HH-2D	10,187 lb (4,620 kg)

Overload T-O weight:
UH-2A/B	10,000 lb (4,535 kg)
UH-2C	11,614 lb (5,268 kg)
HH-2C, D	12,500 lb (5,670 kg)

On 16 May 1968, a UH-2C helicopter, carrying an external load, flew at a gross weight of 13,600 lb (6,169 kg).

PERFORMANCE (at normal AUW, except where indicated):
Max level speed at S/L:
UH-2A/B	141 knots (162 mph; 261 km/h)
UH-2C	136 knots (157 mph; 252 km/h)
HH-2C	135 knots (156 mph; 251 km/h)
HH-2D	146 knots (168 mph; 270 km/h)

Normal cruising speed
132 knots (152 mph; 245 km/h)

Max rate of climb at S/L:
UH-2A/B	1,740 ft (530 m)/min
UH-2C	2,275 ft (693 m)/min
HH-2C	1,980 ft (604 m)/min
HH-2D	2,540 ft (775 m)/min

Service ceiling:
UH-2A/B	17,400 ft (5,300 m)
UH-2C	18,400 ft (5,610 m)
HH-2C	12,300 ft (3,750 m)
HH-2D	17,600 ft (5,365 m)

Hovering ceiling in ground effect:
UH-2A/B	8,700 ft (2,650 m)
UH-2C	18,000 ft (5,485 m)
HH-2C	10,800 ft (3,290 m)
HH-2D	16,900 ft (5,150 m)

Hovering ceiling out of ground effect:
UH-2A/B	5,100 ft (1,555 m)
UH-2C	15,400 ft (4,690 m)
HH-2C	7,700 ft (2,345 m)
HH-2D	14,100 ft (4,300 m)

Kaman HH-2C, armed version of the standard UH-2C, showing twin-wheel landing gear and Minigun installation

Kaman HH-2D, unarmed version of the HH-2C (two 1,250 shp General Electric T58-GE-8B turboshaft engines)

Normal range with max fuel:
UH-2A, B	581 nm (670 miles; 1,080 km)
UH-2C	369 nm (425 miles; 685 km)
HH-2C	341 nm (393 miles; 632 km)
HH-2D	369 nm (425 miles; 685 km)

KAMAN K-700

Kaman announced on 24 February 1969 that its Aircraft Division had begun development and construction of a medium-sized twin-turbine helicopter for commercial and military applications, under the designation K-700. Able to meet both a USAF requirement for a local base rescue helicopter and a civil market requirement for a passenger/cargo transport or air ambulance, the K-700 is substantially a re-designed and re-engined version of the Kaman K-1125 Huskie III, first flown in August 1962 and described fully in the 1963-64 edition of Jane's.

While retaining the intermeshing contra-rotating rotor system of its predecessor, the HH-43B/F, the K-700 has twin engines, dual instrumentation and all-weather flying capability, so offering significant improvements in payload, range, stability and control, and reduced vibration levels.

The K-700 will have the same low downwash and noise characteristics as the HH-43, and the company is currently involved in a programme to further reduce noise level. The absence of a tail rotor permits safe freedom of movement around the aircraft on the ground.

The large unobstructed cabin accommodates two seats and four stretchers, with room for in-flight medical attention. In an all-passenger configuration, a total of twelve persons can be accommodated, or six persons in a VIP layout. Clam-shell doors at the rear of the fuselage facilitate loading outsize or bulky cargo, as well

as making possible straight-in loading of litters.

The power plant comprises a United Aircraft of Canada PT6T-400 Turbo "Twin Pac", consisting of two PT6 turboshaft engines coupled to a common gearbox with a single output shaft. This unit has a take-off rating of 1,800 shp; but less than 1,200 shp are required for normal missions, so this offers more than 600 shp reserve, providing a substantial power safety margin as well as outstanding hot day/altitude performance and single-engine operation.

The streamlined tail assembly has a single high-slung tail-boom and single vertical stabiliser, well clear of rotor downwash. The four rotor blades are of composite construction, the basic structural materials being glass-fibre and Scotch-ply with internal wooden stabilisation. The inboard leading-edges are covered with a highly erosion-resistant estane boot; the outer leading-edges have a stainless steel covering. Blade life is 2,500 hours. Each rotor pylon is inclined outward at 12°30' from the vertical.

For military missions, the K-700 is being designed to incorporate easily such features as lightweight armour, bullet-resistant glass, loud-hailers, personnel hoist, external cargo hook, searchlight and an in-flight operable lightweight fire suppression system with a capacity of 100 US gallons (378 litres).

The following details were available at the time of writing:

DIMENSIONS, EXTERNAL:
Rotor diameter, each	47 ft 0 in (14·33 m)
Width overall, rotors turning	51 ft 5½ in (15·68 m)
Length overall (rotors fore and aft)	58 ft 7 in (17·86 m)

Fuselage length	41 ft 6 in (12·65 m)
Height to top of rotor hubs	12 ft 9 in (3·89 m)
Height over tail	13 ft 4 in (4·06 m)
Wheel track (forward wheels)	6 ft 3½ in (1·92 m)
Wheel track (aft wheels)	8 ft 4 in (2·54 m)

WEIGHTS:

Weight empty	5,600 lb (2,540 kg)
Normal T-O weight	8,400 lb (3,810 kg)
Overload T-O weight	11,000 lb (4,990 kg)

PERFORMANCE (estimated at normal T-O weight, standard day):

Max level speed	122 knots (140 mph; 225 km/h)
Cruising speed	100 knots (115 mph; 185 km/h)
Service ceiling	18,200 ft (5,545 m)
Single-engine ceiling	14,000 ft (4,265 m)
Hovering ceiling, in ground effect	20,200 ft (6,155 m)
Hovering ceiling, out of ground effect	17,500 ft (5,335 m)
Range with normal fuel	364 nm (419 miles; 674 km)
Ferry range	738 nm (850 miles; 1,365 km)

KAMAN K-800

This new Kaman design has been proposed to the US Navy and Air Force as a high-speed gunship and rescue vehicle, with capability for utility missions. It is based on UH-2C Seasprite technology, and draws heavily on the results of the high-speed helicopter research programme which Kaman conducted for the US Army, using a UH-2 fitted with fixed wings and an auxiliary turbojet.

The K-800 would be powered by two General Electric T58-GE-16 turboshaft engines driving four-blade main and tail rotors and a pusher propeller of 10 ft (3·05 m) diameter at the tail. The transmission to the main rotor would be flat rated at 2,400 shp to 95°F, but 3,200 shp would be delivered to the tail propeller. Each turboshaft has a max rating of 1,870 shp. Beechcraft Queen Air wings would be fitted to provide lift in forward flight and so offload the main rotor. The tail rotor would be mounted at the tip of a stabiliser.

Compared with the UH-2, the rotor pylon structure would be greatly reduced in size, by lowering the transmission system into the fuselage. Armament would include an under-nose turret mounting a Minigun and grenade launcher, with provision for underwing rockets and other stores.

The following details were available at the time of writing.

DIMENSIONS, EXTERNAL:

Diameter of main rotor	44 ft 0 in (13·41 m)
Chord of main rotor blades	1 ft 9·6 in (0·55 m)
Diameter of tail rotor	8 ft 2 in (2·49 m)
Length overall	51 ft 7 in (15·72 m)
Length of fuselage	46 ft 0 in (14·02 m)

WEIGHTS:

Weight empty	8,634 lb (3,917 kg)
Normal T-O weight	13,950 lb (6,328 kg)
Overload T-O weight	15,300 lb (6,940 kg)

PERFORMANCE (estimated at normal AUW):

Max level speed at S/L	215 knots (247 mph; 397 km/h)
Normal cruising speed	185 knots (213 mph; 342 km/h)
Max rate of climb at S/L	3,580 ft (1,090 m)/min
Service ceiling	11,850 ft (3,610 m)
Hovering ceiling in ground effect	13,400 ft (4,085 m)
Hovering ceiling out of ground effect	10,500 ft (3,200 m)
Normal range	673 nm (775 miles; 1,247 km)

Model of Kaman K-700 twin-turbine general-purpose helicopter

Artist's impression of Kaman K-800 high-speed gunship and rescue helicopter, based on UH-2C technology

KAMAN SAVER

Combat experience in Vietnam has shown the need to provide aircrew with a means of escape from the vicinity of crashed aircraft. This resulted in Kaman being awarded a contract by the US Naval Air Development Center to carry out concept definition and preliminary design of a flying rescue seat designated AERCAB.

Kaman's proposed vehicle to meet this requirement is a turbofan-powered gyroplane nicknamed SAVER (Stowable Aircrew Vehicle Escape Rotoseat). Work on the programme is being carried out at Bloomfield, with LTV Aerospace Corporation, Vought Aeronautics Division in Dallas, and Continental Aviation and Engineering Corporation, in Detroit, as sub-contractors.

SAVER is basically a gyroplane with an unpowered rotor, having stowable and telescoping blades which, together with its small turbofan engine and controls, will fold into a compact pilot seat for normal use.

In an emergency the pilot would eject from the aircraft as with a conventional ejection seat; but within a second of initiating his escape a small drogue parachute would be deployed to slow the seat and simultaneously withdraw the folded rotor. Within a total elapsed time of four seconds the seat would have become a rotor/glider, and two seconds later, with the turbofan brought up to full power, the seat would become a gyroplane.

Such a vehicle would enable a pilot to make a pinpoint landing within a radius of some 50 nm (57 miles; 92 km) or, by remaining airborne, he could communicate with helicopter rescue crews for a co-ordinated meeting and rescue. Alternatively, the rotor system can be jettisoned and the pilot can make a normal parachute descent from the seat, thus providing a safety backup in the event of malfunction or combat damage.

Kaman has already carried out more than 1,500 air-drops of self-deploying rotor systems that have demonstrated the feasibility of stowed rotor systems capable of deployment at subsonic, transonic and supersonic speeds, and have also demonstrated a 24 ft (7·32 m) diameter rotor system with telescoping blades.

SAVER is being designed to operate from a minimum ejection altitude of 1,000 ft (305 m), and for a minimum safe altitude for autorotative descent of 800 ft (244 m). Stowed in its pilot seat configuration it will measure 1 ft 10 in (0·56 m) in width, 3 ft 2 in (0·97 m) in depth and 4 ft 6 in (1·37 m) in height, and the deployed rotor will be 15 ft 6 in (4·72 m) in diameter. Weight, without pilot, will be 345 lb (156 kg) and the turbofan engine will generate 275 lb (125 kg) st.

Preliminary design parameters call for a range of 50 nm (57 miles; 92 km), speed of 100 knots (115 mph; 185 km/h) and a rate of climb of 1,000 ft (305 m)/min.

It is intended that the SAVER seat will embody automatic flight and homing equipment, an automatic locator beacon, survival kits and restraint harness. Under their contract Kaman will continue to define stowed rotor escape systems and recommend to the Naval Air Development Center the most promising design. LTV Aerospace Corporation are to study the installation and integration of SAVER in A-7 and F-4 aircraft, and Continental Aviation and Engineering Corporation will determine the characteristics of the engine required.

A full-scale unpowered model of SAVER, for wind-tunnel testing, is being built under the latest US Navy contract.

KAMINSKAS
RIM KAMINSKAS

ADDRESS:
312 Camino de las Colinas, Redondo Beach, California 90277

First aircraft designed and built by Mr Kaminskas was a single-seat sporting biplane named the Papoose Jungster I, which is a scaled-down replica of the well-known Bücker Bü 133 Jungmeister.

It was followed by a parasol-wing single-seater named the Jungster II, and sets of plans of both designs are now available to amateur constructors from K and S Aircraft Supply, 4623 Fortune Road SE, Calgary, Alberta.

Mr Kaminskas has since designed another single-seat sporting biplane, with a gull-wing, and this is named Jungster III.

KAMINSKAS PAPOOSE JUNGSTER I

Design of this aircraft was started in April 1959. Construction of the prototype began in December 1959 and it flew for the first time in October 1962. Approximately 175 Jungster I's are known to be under construction and several are already flying.

TYPE: Single-seat sporting aircraft.

WINGS: Braced biplane, with two parallel interplane struts each side and N-struts supporting centre-section each side. Wing section NACA 4413. Dihedral 1° 30′ on top wing, 3° 30′ on lower wings. Incidence 30′ on top wing, 1° 30′ on lower wings. Sweepback 11° at quarter-chord. All-wood two-spar structure of spruce, birch and mahogany plywood, fabric-covered. Wooden Frise ailerons. No flaps or tabs.

FUSELAGE: Spruce truss structure, fabric-covered.

TAIL UNIT: Braced wooden structure of spruce and mahogany ply. Fixed surfaces plywood-covered; rudder and elevators fabric-covered. No tabs.

LANDING GEAR: Non-retractable tail-wheel type. Welded steel-tube main gear, with rubber cord shock absorption. Goodyear main wheel tyres size 500 × 5, pressure 25 lb/sq in (1·76 kg/cm²). Goodyear disc brakes.

POWER PLANT: One 100 hp Lycoming O-235-C four-cylinder horizontally-opposed air-cooled engine, driving a McCauley two-blade fixed-pitch propeller, diameter 5 ft 8 in (1·73 m). Fuel tank in fuselage aft of firewall, capacity 13·5 US gallons (51 litres). Oil capacity 1·5 US gallons (5·75 litres).

ACCOMMODATION: Single seat in open cockpit.

DIMENSIONS, EXTERNAL:

Wing span	16 ft 8 in (5·08 m)
Wing chord, constant (both)	2 ft 8 in (0·81 m)
Wing aspect ratio	6·25
Length overall	16 ft 0 in (4·88 m)
Tailplane span	6 ft 8 in (2·03 m)

AREA:

Wings, gross	80 sq ft (7·43 m²)

WEIGHTS AND LOADINGS:

Weight empty	606 lb (275 kg)
T-O weight, aerobatic	850 lb (385 kg)
Max T-O weight	1,000 lb (455 kg)
Max wing loading	10·6 lb/sq ft (51·75 kg/m²)
Max power loading	8·5 lb/hp (3·85 kg/hp)

PERFORMANCE (at max T-O weight):
Max level speed at S/L
113 knots (130 mph; 209 km/h)
Max cruising speed at S/L
109 knots (125 mph; 201 km/h)
Stalling speed   44 knots (50 mph; 80·5 km/h)
Rate of climb at S/L   1,500 ft (455 m)/min
Service ceiling   13,000 ft (3,960 m)
T-O run   300 ft (91 m)
Landing run   500 ft (152 m)
Range with max fuel
173 nm (200 miles; 320 km)

KAMINSKAS JUNGSTER II

Design of this single-seat parasol-wing monoplane was started in 1962. Construction began
in January 1963 and it flew for the first time in
March 1966. At least 25 were being built by
amateurs in the Spring of 1970.

TYPE: Single-seat amateur-built sporting monoplane.

WINGS: Strut-braced parasol-wing monoplane.
Wing section NACA 2412. No dihedral. Incidence 1°. Sweepback at quarter-chord 15°. All-
wood spruce structure, covered with plywood
and fabric. Frise ailerons. No flaps or tabs.

FUSELAGE: Spruce structure, covered with fabric.

TAIL UNIT: Wire-braced spruce structure. Fixed
surfaces covered with mahogany plywood;
control surfaces fabric-covered. Fixed-incidence tailplane. No tabs.

LANDING GEAR: Non-retractable tailwheel type.
Rubber shock-absorbers adapted from truck
engine mountings. Wheels size 5·00 × 5.
Cleveland hydraulic brakes.

POWER PLANT: One 100 hp Lycoming O-235
four-cylinder horizontally-opposed air-cooled
engine, driving a special two-blade fixed-pitch
propeller, diameter 5 ft 6 in (1·68 m). Fuel tank
forward of cockpit, capacity 18 US gallons
(68 litres). Oil capacity 6 US quarts (5·5 litres).

ACCOMMODATION: Single seat in open cockpit.

DIMENSIONS, EXTERNAL:
Wing span   22 ft 4 in (6·81 m)
Wing chord at root   4 ft 2 in (1·27 m)
Length overall   16 ft 11 in (5·16 m)
Height overall   6 ft 9 in (2·06 m)
Tailplane span   7 ft 9 in (2·36 m)
Wheel track   5 ft 0 in (1·52 m)

DIMENSIONS, INTERNAL:
Cockpit: length   4 ft 0 in (1·22 m)
Max width   1 ft 10 in (0·56 m)

AREAS:
Wings, gross   84 sq ft (7·80 m²)
Ailerons (total)   10·4 sq ft (0·97 m²)
Fin   3·15 sq ft (0·29 m²)
Rudder   4·70 sq ft (0·44 m²)
Tailplane   5·75 sq ft (0·53 m²)
Elevators   7·31 sq ft (0·68 m²)

WEIGHTS AND LOADINGS (Original 180 hp version):
Weight empty   739 lb (335 kg)
Max T-O weight   1,139 lb (517 kg)
Max wing loading   13·5 lb/sq ft (65·9 kg/m²)
Max power loading   6·3 lb (2·85 kg) hp

PERFORMANCE (Original 180 hp version, at max
T-O weight):
Max level speed at S/L
139 knots (160 mph; 257 km/h)
Max permissible diving speed
156 knots (180 mph; 290 km/h) IAS
Max cruising speed up to 10,000 ft (3,050 m)
135 knots (155 mph; 249 km/h)
Stalling speed   48 knots (55 mph; 89 km/h)
Rate of climb at S/L   3,500 ft (1,065 m)/min

KAMINSKAS JUNGSTER III

Design of this single-seat biplane was started in
July 1967 and construction of the prototype began
in the following month. First flight was made
on 1 September 1968. The Jungster III has a
gull-wing upper plane to improve forward
visibility. Mr Kaminskas has since modified the
Jungster III extensively, and it had not been
flight-tested in this new configuration at the time
of writing. The details which follow apply to
the prototype in its original form.

TYPE: Single-seat sport and racing biplane.

WINGS: Strut-braced biplane with upper gull-
wing and lower semi-cantilever wing. Aerofoil
section NACA 64212 at root, NACA 64209 at tip.
Dihedral —2° on top wing, +1° on bottom
wing. Incidence 0° both wings. Sweepback
at quarter chord 7° both wings. Conventional
all-wood structure with plywood skin. No
flaps. Ailerons of wood construction with
plywood skin, on lower wing only. Square
wingtips.

FUSELAGE: All-wood structure of spruce with
fabric covering.

Kaminskas Papoose Jungster I (100 hp Lycoming O-235-C engine) (*Henry Artof*)

Kaminskas Jungster II single-seat light aircraft (100 hp Lycoming O-235 engine) (*Henry Artof*)

Prototype of Kaminskas Jungster III sporting biplane in original form

TAIL UNIT: Cantilever all-wood structure with
plywood skins. Fixed-incidence tailplane. No
trim-tabs.

LANDING GEAR: Non-retractable tail-wheel type.
Main legs of fixed steel-tube bolted to the
firewall. Shock-absorption by rubber in compression. Main wheels and tyres size 5·00 × 5.
Hydraulic brakes.

POWER PLANT: One 125 hp Lycoming O-290
(modified) four-cylinder horizontally-opposed
air-cooled engine, driving a special two-blade
propeller, 5 ft 8 in (1·73 m) in diameter, with
spinner. One fuel tank in each wing, capacity
5·5 US gallons (20·8 litres), and one fuselage
tank, capacity 5·0 US gallons (18·9 litres).
Total capacity 16 US gallons (60·5 litres).

ACCOMMODATION: Single seat in open cockpit.

DIMENSIONS, EXTERNAL:
Wing span   16 ft 0 in (4·88 m)
Wing chord at root (both)   3 ft 0 in (0·91 m)
Wing chord at tip (both)   2 ft 8 in (0·81 m)
Length overall   15 ft 0 in (4·57 m)

Tailplane span   5 ft 4 in (1·63 m)
Wheel track   4 ft 0 in (1·22 m)

AREAS:
Wings, gross   81 sq ft (7·53 m²)
Ailerons (total)   6·3 sq ft (0·59 m²)
Fin   2·18 sq ft (0·20 m²)
Rudder   3·4 sq ft (0·32 m²)
Tailplane   4·0 sq ft (0·37 m²)
Elevators   5·32 sq ft (0·49 m²)

WEIGHTS AND LOADINGS:
Weight empty   550 lb (249 kg)
Max T-O weight   900 lb (408 kg)
Max wing loading   12 lb/sq ft (58·6 kg/m²)
Max power loading   6·5 lb/hp (2·95 kg/hp)

PERFORMANCE (at max T-O weight):
Max level speed at S/L
174 knots (200 mph; 322 km/h)
Max diving speed
213 knots (245 mph; 394 km/h)
Max cruising speed at S/L
156 knots (180 mph; 290 km/h)
Stalling speed   66 knots (75 mph; 121 km/h)

KELEHER

JAMES J. KELEHER

ADDRESS:
4321 Ogden Drive, Fremont, California 94538

In the early 1960's Mr J. Keleher designed and
built a mid-wing sporting monoplane which he
called the Lark. The design was revised in
1963, and the current model, for which plans are
available to amateur constructors, is designated
Lark-1B. All available details follow:

KELEHER LARK-1B

TYPE: Single-seat amateur-built sporting monoplane.

WINGS: Braced mid-wing monoplane with streamline-section Vee bracing struts each side.

x

Wing section NACA 2R₂12. Dihedral 1°. Incidence 4°. All-wood structure of Sitka spruce, with built-up I-beam front spar and ribs, fabric covered. Stressed to 6g plus. Fabric-covered wooden ailerons; no trim-tabs or flaps.

FUSELAGE: Welded steel-tube structure, fabric-covered, stressed to 6 g plus.

TAIL UNIT: Wire-braced welded steel-tube structure with sheet-steel ribs and fabric covering. Adjustable-incidence tailplane. Swept fin. No trim-tabs.

LANDING GEAR: Non-retractable tail-wheel type. Divided main landing gear with shock absorption by rubber cord in fuselage. Cleveland main wheels and tyres size 500 × 5, pressure 20-25 lb/sq in (1·41-1·76 kg/cm²). Cleveland disc brakes. Wheel fairings optional.

POWER PLANT: One 100 hp Continental O-200-A four-cylinder horizontally-opposed air-cooled engine, driving a McCauley two-blade metal propeller, diameter 5 ft 8 in (1·73 m). One galvanised steel fuel tank in the fuselage, aft of the firewall, capacity 15 US gallons (56 litres). Refuelling point on top of cowl, forward of windshield. Oil capacity 1·5 US gallons (5·7 litres).

ACCOMMODATION: Single seat in enclosed cockpit under sliding canopy. Lowered turtle deck and bubble canopy optional. Stowage for 20 lb (9 kg) baggage aft of seat.

DIMENSIONS, EXTERNAL:
Wing span	24 ft 1 in (7·34 m)
Wing chord, constant	4 ft 0 in (1·22 m)
Wing aspect ratio	6
Length overall	17 ft 0 in (5·18 m)
Height overall	5 ft 5 in (1·65 m)

Keleher Lark-1B (75 hp Continental engine) built by Mr Robert Voto of Flint, Michigan
(*Jean Seele*)

Tailplane span	6 ft 6 in (1·98 m)
Wheel track	5 ft 2 in (1·57 m)

AREAS:
Wings gross	82 sq ft (7·62 m²)
Ailerons (total)	9·0 sq ft (0·84 m²)
Fin	3·0 sq ft (0·28 m²)
Rudder	3·5 sq ft (0·33 m²)
Tailplane	8·3 sq ft (0·77 m²)
Elevators	5·2 sq ft (0·48 m²)

WEIGHTS AND LOADINGS:
Weight empty, equipped		688 lb (312 kg)
Max T-O and landing weight		990 lb (449 kg)
Max wing loading	12·07 lb/sq ft (58·9 kg/m²)	
Max power loading	9·9 lb/hp (4·49 kg/hp)	

PERFORMANCE (at max T-O weight):
Max level speed at 2,000 ft (610 m)
  122 knots (140 mph; 225 km/h)
Max diving speed
  143 knots (165 mph; 265 km/h)
Max cruising speed at 2,000 ft (610 m)
  110 knots (127 mph; 204 km/h)
Stalling speed 51 knots (58 mph; 93·5 km/h)
Rate of climb at S/L 1,200 ft (366 m)/min
Service ceiling 16,000 ft (4,875 m)
T-O run 400 ft (122 m)
Landing run 600 ft (183 m)
Range with max payload, no reserves
  260 nm (300 miles; 480 km)

LACEY
JOSEPH L. LACEY
ADDRESS:
7720, E 25th Place, Tulsa, Oklahoma 74129

Mr Lacey designed and built a two-seat light aircraft known as the M-10, of which plans are available. Fifty sets of plans had been sold by early 1967, and many M-10's are known to be under construction by amateurs.

LACEY M-10 MIRACLE OF 10's

Design of the M-10 was started in 1956 and construction began two years later. It flew for the first time on 6 June 1962, after the wings and fuselage had been tested statically with sandbags to 4g conditions.

The M-10 has a unique wing-stowage system in that the wing pivots on a centre point above the cockpit to lie fore and aft. Turning the wing is a simple one-man operation.

TYPE: Two-seat home-built light aircraft.

WINGS: Cantilever high-wing monoplane. Lacey M-10 (modified USA 35-B) wing section. Thickness/chord ratio 11·75%. No dihedral or incidence. Wood structure, with stressed plywood skin and stringers between spars, metal-covered leading-edges and fabric overall. Full-span wooden ailerons, with ground-adjustable tabs. End-plates on tips.

FUSELAGE: Fabric-covered steel-tube structure.

TAIL UNIT: Fabric-covered steel-tube structure. Ground-adjustable tailplane incidence. Ground-adjustable tabs on control surfaces.

LANDING GEAR: Non-retractable tail-wheel type. Main wheels carried on cantilever tapered steel bar legs, with wheels and tyres size 5·00 × 5, pressure 15 lb/sq in (1·05 kg/cm²). Goodyear hydraulic brakes. Tail-wheel and tyre of 3¼ in (8·25 cm) diameter, carried on spring.

POWER PLANT: One 95 hp Continental C90 four-cylinder horizontally-opposed air-cooled engine, driving a McCauley 71-52 two-blade fixed-pitch propeller. Fuel in three tanks in fuselage: front tank of 11 US gallons (41·5 litres), rear tank of 9 US gallons (34·0 litres) and rear seat tank of 27 US gallons (102 litres) capacity. Total fuel capacity 47 US gallons (177·5 litres). Oil capacity 1½ US gallons (5·7 litres).

ACCOMMODATION: Two seats in tandem in enclosed cabin, with dual controls. Fike control system, with hanging sticks on starboard side of cabin, leaving uncluttered floor for sleeping in emergency. Door on starboard side at front, on port side at rear.

DIMENSIONS, EXTERNAL:
Wing span	20 ft 0 in (6·10 m)
Wing chord, constant	5 ft 6 in (1·68 m)
Wing aspect ratio	3·64
Length overall	19 ft 6 in (5·95 m)
Length overall, folded,	
less than	24 ft 0 in (7·31 m)
Height overall	6 ft 9 in (2·06 m)
Width folded	8 ft 0 in (2·44 m)
Tailplane span	8 ft 0 in (2·44 m)
Wheel track	7 ft 6 in (2·29 m)
Wheelbase	15 ft 10 in (4·82 m)
Doors (each):	
Height	3 ft 4 in (1·03 m)
Width	2 ft 4 in (0·71 m)
Height to sill: front	2 ft 0 in (0·61 m)
rear	1 ft 6 in (0·46 m)

For stowage, the wing of the Lacey M-10 pivots on a centre point above the cabin (*Howard Levy*)

Lacey M-10C VW Twin (two 40 hp Volkswagen engines) (*Howard Levy*)

DIMENSIONS, INTERNAL:
Cabin: Length	7 ft 0 in (2·13 m)
Max width	2 ft 0 in (0·61 m)
Max height	3 ft 4 in (1·03 m)
Floor area	14 sq ft (1·30 m²)
Volume	42 cu ft (1·19 m³)

AREAS:
Wings, gross	110 sq ft (10·22 m²)
Ailerons (total)	8·25 sq ft (0·77 m²)

WEIGHTS AND LOADINGS:
Weight empty	622 lb (282 kg)
*Max T-O weight	1,022 lb (464 kg)
Normal max wing loading	
9·25 lb/sq ft (45·16 kg/m²)	
Normal max power loading	
10·75 lb/hp (4·88 kg/hp)	

*The M-10 has been flown at an emergency AUW of 1,236 lb (560 kg)

PERFORMANCE (at normal max T-O weight):
Max level speed at S/L
  109 knots (125 mph; 201 km/h)
Max permissible speed in dive
  130 knots (150 mph; 240 km/h)
Max cruising speed
  104 knots (120 mph; 193 km/h)
Econ cruising speed
  100 knots (115 mph; 185 km/h)
Stalling speed will not stall
Rate of climb at S/L 1,000 ft (305 m)/min
Service ceiling 15,000 ft (4,570 m)
T-O run 1,000 ft (305 m)
T-O to 50 ft (15 m) 1,500 ft (457 m)
Landing from 50 ft (15 m) 1,500 ft (457 m)

Landing run 800 ft (244 m)
Range with max fuel
  998 nm (1,150 miles; 1,850 km)
Range with max payload
  199 nm (230 miles; 370 km)

LACEY M-10C VW TWIN

This aircraft is identical with the M-10 except that the usual single 95 hp engine is replaced by two 40 hp converted Volkswagen engines, mounted at the ends of a stub-wing, on each side of the nose. Construction of a prototype was started in 1966 and it flew for the first time in 1968. Plans are available.

The structural description of the M-10 applies equally to the M-10C, except in the following details:

POWER PLANT: Two 40 hp converted Volkswagen four-cylinder horizontally-opposed air-cooled engines, each driving a Hegy two-blade fixed-pitch propeller, diameter 4 ft 0 in (1·22 m). Fuel and oil as for M-10.

DIMENSIONS:
Same as for M-10.

WEIGHTS:
Weight empty	620 lb (281 kg)
Max T-O weight	1,140 lb (517 kg)

PERFORMANCE (at max T-O weight):
Cruising speed 87 knots (100 mph; 161 km/h)
Rate of climb at S/L 500 ft (152 m)/min
Range with max fuel
  260 nm (300 miles; 480 km)

LAKE

LAKE AIRCRAFT DIVISION OF CONSOLIDATED AERONAUTICS, INC

EXECUTIVE OFFICES:
PO Box 399, Tomball, Texas 77375

SALES OFFICES:
David Hooks Memorial Airport, Tomball, Texas 77375

PRESIDENT:
William A. Thorne.

VICE-PRESIDENT (SALES):
M. L. Alson

SECRETARY: Herbert P. Lindblad

In 1962 Consolidated Aeronautics merged with Lake Aircraft Corporation of Sanford, Maine, as a result of which it operates Lake Aircraft as a division.

It is continuing production of the LA-4 amphibian, which Lake Aircraft developed from the original Colonial C-2 Skimmer IV after purchasing manufacturing rights from Colonial Aircraft Corporation in October 1959. A Lake LA-4 is being used by the Bell Aerospace Company (which see) in the development of an air-cushion landing system.

LAKE LA-4

Design of the original C-1 Skimmer was started in August 1946. Manufacture of the prototype began in January 1947 and it flew for the first time in May 1948. Versions of the Lake LA-4 developed from the improved C-2 Skimmer IV are as follows:—

LA-4P. Prototype. Similar to C-2. First flew in November 1959. FAA certification 21 June 1960.

LA-4. As C-2, but with 4 ft (1·22 m) wing extension, 1 ft (0·30 m) longer ailerons, 1 ft 5 in (0·43 m) longer bow, revised wing-to-fuselage attachment, higher AUW and structural reinforcement. Received Type Approval 26 July 1960. In production.

LA-4A. Two only, prior to LA-4 production. As LA-4, but without the longer bow. Received Type Approval 1 June 1960.

TYPE: Single-engined four-seat amphibian.

WINGS: Cantilever shoulder-wing monoplane with tapered wing panels attached directly to sides of hull. Wing section NACA 4418 at root, NACA 4412 at tip. Dihedral 5° 30′. Incidence 3° 15′. Structure consists of duralumin leading and trailing-edge torsion boxes separated by a single duralumin main spar. All-metal ailerons and hydraulically-operated slotted flaps over 80% of span. No tabs.

HULL: Single-step all-metal structure, with double-sealed boat hull.

Lake LA-4 four-seat amphibian (180 hp Lycoming O-360-A1A engine)

TAIL UNIT: Cantilever all-metal structure. Outboard elevator section separate from inboard section and actuated hydraulically for trimming.

LANDING GEAR: Hydraulically-retractable tricycle type. Consolidated oleo-pneumatic shock absorbers on main gear, which retracts inboard into wings. Long-stroke nose-wheel oleo retracts forward. Goodyear main wheels and tyres, size 6·00 × 6, pressure 35 lb/sq in (2·46 kg/cm²). Goodrich nose-wheel and tyre size 5·00 × 4, pressure 20 lb/sq in (1·41 kg/cm²). Goodyear disc brakes. Nose-wheel is free to swivel 30° either way. Floats are aluminium alloy monocoque structures.

POWER PLANT: One 180 hp Lycoming O-360-A1A four-cylinder horizontally-opposed air-cooled engine mounted on pylon above hull and driving a Hartzell constant-speed pusher propeller, diameter 6 ft 0 in (1·83 m). US Rubber DL10 fuel tank in hull, capacity 40 US gallons (151 litres). Refuelling point above hull. Oil capacity 2 US gallons (7·6 litres).

ACCOMMODATION: Enclosed cabin seating pilot and three passengers. Dual controls. Entry through two forward-hinged windscreen sections. Baggage compartment aft of cabin.

SYSTEMS: Stewart-Warner 940F12 heater. Hydraulic system, pressure 1,500 lb/sq in (105 kg/cm²), for flaps, horizontal trim and landing gear actuation. Engine-driven 12V electrical generator and battery.

ELECTRONICS AND EQUIPMENT: Blind-flying instruments, Narco Mk 12 two-way VHF radio, heater and landing lights optional. Towbar, paddle and anchor.

DIMENSIONS, EXTERNAL:
Wing span	38 ft 0 in (11·58 m)
Wing chord, mean	4 ft 5·1 in (1·35 m)
Wing aspect ratio	8·67
Length overall	24 ft 11 in (7·60 m)
Height overall	9 ft 4 in (2·84 m)

Tailplane span	10 ft 0 in (3·05 m)
Wheel track	11 ft 2 in (3·40 m)
Wheelbase	8 ft 10 in (2·69 m)

DIMENSIONS, INTERNAL:
Cabin: Length	5 ft 2 in (1·57 m)
Max width	3 ft 5½ in (1·05 m)
Max height	3 ft 11½ in (1·32 m)
Floor area	approx 16·5 sq ft (1·53 m²)
Volume	approx 60·0 cu ft (1·70 m³)
Baggage hold	8·5 cu ft (0·24 m³)

AREAS:
Wings, gross	170 sq ft (15·8 m²)
Ailerons (total)	12·5 sq ft (1·16 m²)
Trailing-edge flaps (total)	24·5 sq ft (2·28 m²)
Fin	13·5 sq ft (1·25 m²)
Rudder	8·5 sq ft (0·79 m²)
Tailplane	15·6 sq ft (1·45 m²)
Elevators	8·4 sq ft (0·78 m²)

WEIGHTS AND LOADINGS:
Weight empty, equipped	1,600 lb (726 kg)
Max T-O and landing weight	2,400 lb (1,089 kg)
Max wing loading	14·1 lb/sq ft (68·8 kg/m²)
Max power loading	13·3 lb/hp (6·04 kg/hp)

PERFORMANCE (at max T-O weight):
Max level speed at S/L	117 knots (135 mph; 217 km/h)
Max permissible speed in dive	126·5 knots (146 mph; 235 km/h)
Max cruising speed (75% power)	114 knots (131 mph; 211 km/h)
Econ cruising speed	109 knots (125 mph; 201 km/h)
Stalling speed	45 knots (51 mph; 82 km/h)
Rate of climb at S/L	800 ft (244 m)/min
Service ceiling	14,000 ft (4,270 m)
T-O run on land	650 ft (198 m)
T-O run on water	1,125 ft (343 m)
Landing run on land	475 ft (145 m)
Alighting run on water	600 ft (183 m)
Range with max fuel	542 nm (625 miles; 1,005 km)

LAS

Lockheed L-188 Electra remanufactured by LAS in all-cargo configuration

LOCKHEED AIRCRAFT SERVICE COMPANY
(Division of Lockheed Aircraft Corporation)

HEAD OFFICE AND WORKS:
Ontario International Airport, Ontario, California 91764

Bases:
John F. Kennedy International Airport, Jamaica, New York
Lake Charles, Louisiana
Luke Air Force Base, Arizona
LAS Field Service Operations, Oklahoma City, Oklahoma

SPECIAL DEVICES DIVISION:
Ontario, California

MARINE SERVICES DIVISION:
Ontario, California

PRESIDENT:
Duane O. Wood

EXECUTIVE VICE-PRESIDENT:
C. T. Thum

VICE-PRESIDENTS:
Robert L. Vader (Technical Services and Products)

R. C. Zinn (Maintenance Operations)
K. E. Neudoerffer (Base Manager, LAS—New York)

Lockheed Aircraft Service Company is claimed to be the world's largest independent aircraft maintenance and modification company. It has designed and installed major modifications for such aircraft as the Boeing KC-135 and 707; Douglas C-133; and Lockheed C-130, L-188 Electra, C-121 and L-1649. It has also designed and installed interiors for various transport aircraft.

LAS has diversified into many other fields, including aircraft maintenance training devices, aircraft maintenance recording systems and airborne integrated data systems, marine anti-corrosion systems, aircraft ground support equipment, low-cost housing systems, and special purpose vehicles for marginal terrain usage.

Details of the company's aircraft conversion programme for the Lockheed L-188 Electra is given below.

LOCKHEED ELECTRA CARGO CONVERSIONS

LAS has been remanufacturing Lockheed L-188 Electras in convertible cargo/passenger or pure cargo configurations since 1967.

For either conversion, the airframe is strengthened to increase the zero-fuel weight by 4,000 lb (1,814 kg) to a maximum of 90,000 lb (40,823 kg). The floor structure is replaced completely, permitting either mechanised loading on pallets to a maximum weight of 35,000 lb (15,875 kg), or high-density bulk loading. Customers have the choice of either a lightweight non-structural floor for use with a pallet handling system, or of an extruded aluminium floor for bulk handling. A cargo door 6 ft 8 in (2·03 m) high and 11 ft 3 in (3·43 m) long is provided forward of the wing on the port side of the fuselage. Optionally, a second door of the same height, but 8 ft 3 in (2·51 m) in length, can be provided aft of the wing on the port side.

The convertible Electra Freighter will accommodate 91 passengers, seated five-abreast, on 38 in (91·44 cm) pitch seating, or will permit a combination of passengers and cargo, utilising a movable bulkhead for flexibility with varying loads.

LOCKHEED

LOCKHEED AIRCRAFT CORPORATION

HEAD OFFICE:
Burbank, California 91503
LOCKHEED-CALIFORNIA COMPANY:
Burbank, Palmdale and Van Nuys, California
LOCKHEED-GEORGIA COMPANY:
Marietta, Atlanta and Dawsonville, Georgia
LOCKHEED MISSILES AND SPACE COMPANY:
Sunnyvale, Palo Alto, Santa Cruz and San
Diego, California
LOCKHEED AIRCRAFT INTERNATIONAL, INC:
Los Angeles, California
LOCKHEED AIR TERMINAL, INC:
Burbank California
LOCKHEED ELECTRONICS COMPANY:
Plainfield, New Jersey
LOCKHEED PROPULSION COMPANY:
Redlands, California
LOCKHEED AIRCRAFT SERVICE COMPANY:
Ontario, California
LOCKHEED SHIPBUILDING AND CONSTRUCTION
COMPANY: Seattle, Washington
CHAIRMAN OF BOARD:
Daniel J. Haughton
PRESIDENT:
A. C. Kotchian
EXECUTIVE VICE-PRESIDENTS:
M. Carl Haddon
T. R. May
T. F. Morrow
GROUP VICE-PRESIDENTS:
D. E. Browne
R. J. Osborn
L. E. Root
C. S. Wagner
CORPORATE VICE-PRESIDENTS AND DIVISION
PRESIDENTS:
C. S. Wagner (Lockheed-California Company)
Robert A. Fuhrman (Lockheed-Georgia Company)
D. O. Wood (Lockheed Aircraft Service Company)
A. J. Grant (Lockheed Electronics Company)

L. E. Root (Lockheed Missiles and Space
Company)
W. A. Stevenson (Lockheed Propulsion Company)
CORPORATE VICE-PRESIDENTS:
C. L. Johnson (Advanced Development Projects)
W. A. Pulver (Manufacturing)
W. M. Hawkins (Science and Engineering)
R. I. Mitchell (Commercial Aircraft)
W. G. Myers (Marketing)
V. A. Johnson (Eastern Region)
B. C. Monesmith (Asst to the President)
B. Randolph (Controller)
F. L. Frain (Treasurer)
W. R. Wilson (Public Relations)
R. Donaldson (General Counsel)
R. Smelt (Chief Scientist)
G. C. Prill (New York Office)
C. A. Hofflund (Executive Vice President,
Lockheed-California)
D. M. Wilder (Executive Vice President,
Lockheed-California)
M. M. Egan (European Area)
H. L. Poore (Executive Vice President, Lockheed-Georgia)
W. B. Rieke (Executive Vice President, Lockheed Missiles & Space)
S. W. Burris (Vice President and General Manager, Missile Systems Division, LMSC)
R. R. Kearton (Vice President and General
Manager, Space Systems Division, LMSC)
E. P. Wheaton (Vice President and General
Manager, Research & Development Division,
LMSC)
PRESIDENTS OF SUBSIDIARIES:
D. M. Simmons (Lockheed Air Terminal, Inc)
E. M. Constable (Lockheed Aircraft International, Inc)
A. M. Folden (Lockheed Shipbuilding and
Construction Company)

The original Loughead Aircraft Manufacturing
Co dated from 1913 when the brothers Allan and
Malcolm Loughead began with what was a

forerunner of the true streamlined aeroplane.
Lockheed Aircraft Co, formed in 1926, moved to
Burbank, California, the present site, in 1928.
It was reorganised as Lockheed Aircraft Corporation in 1932.

On 30 November 1943, the Vega Aircraft
Corporation, which had been formed in 1937 as
an affiliate and in 1941 became a wholly-owned
subsidiary of the Lockheed Aircraft Corporation,
was absorbed and the name Vega abandoned.

Lockheed's aircraft and missile activities are
now handled by three separate companies, which
were evolved from the former California, Georgia
and Missiles and Space Divisions in the Summer
of 1961.

The current products of the Lockheed-California
and Lockheed-Georgia Companies are described
below under the individual company headings.

The extensive activities of Lockheed Missiles
and Space Company and Lockheed Propulsion
Company (formerly Grand Central Rocket
Company) are described in the "Guided Missiles"
and "Aero-Engines" sections.

Lockheed has diversified into many fields of
industry since 1959. Following the acquisition
of Stavid Engineering, Inc, it combined this
company and its own Electronics and Avionics
Division into the Lockheed Electronics Company.

Lockheed Air Terminal, Inc (LAT), a wholly-
owned subsidiary, was purchased from United
Air Lines in 1940. LAT manages, operates and
maintains the Hollywood-Burbank Airport, as
well as providing fuelling and related services at
23 other locations in 11 states. Lockheed Aircraft Service Company designs and manufactures
products for the aerospace, marine and construction industries, and Lockheed Aircraft International, Inc, maintains interests in international
joint ventures, licensing programmes and direction of foreign manufacturing operations.

Since March, 1959, Lockheed has also had an
interest in shipbuilding and heavy construction,
following its purchase of the Puget Sound Bridge
and Dry Dock Company (now Lockheed Shipbuilding and Construction Co).

LOCKHEED-CALIFORNIA COMPANY
Burbank, California 91503

Lockheed-California has responsibility for the
land-based P-3 Orion and carrier-based S-3A
naval anti-submarine aircraft, the YF-12A/SR-71
military aircraft, the F-104 Starfighter, and the
AH-56A Cheyenne Advanced Aerial Fire Support
System (AAFSS) combat helicopter.

Also in production is a three-turbofan transport
known as the L-1011 TriStar.

The company's four-year modernisation and
extension programme will be completed in 1970,
and will then have added a total of 1·5 million
sq ft (139,350 m²) of manufacturing, engineering
and office space, at a cost of $100 million.

LOCKHEED STARFIGHTER

**USAF designations: F-104, NF-104, RF-104 and
TF-104**
Development of the F-104 began in 1951 and
versions so far announced are:

XF-104. Two single-seat fighter prototypes
were built under this designation, with Wright
J65-W-6 turbojet engine and afterburner (10,500
lb=4,760 kg st), rearward-retracting nose-wheel
and downward ejection seat. First flight of first
XF-104 was on 7 February 1954, only 11 months
after contract was awarded.

F-104A. Single-seat interceptor. Evaluation
series of 17 ordered, followed by full production.
Basically similar to XF-104, but with air-intake
shock-cones, forward-retracting nose-wheel and
other refinements. General Electric J79-GE-3B
turbojet engine (14,800 lb=6,713 kg st) with
afterburning. Ventral fin for improved stability.
Flap-blowing system and Lockheed in-flight
refuelling equipment with removable probe.
The first production F-104 flew for the first time
on 17 February 1956 and deliveries to the
USAF Air Defense Command began on 26 January 1958. After a period, these aircraft were
withdrawn and issued to American Air National
Guard; these have since been withdrawn again
and placed in storage. A few F-104A's were
converted into QF-104 target drones. Others
serve with the Pakistan Air Force (12, with
J79-GE-11A engines). Delivery of 36 to the
Royal Jordanian Air Force is under way. Total
of 170 built, including 15 YF-104's.

NF-104A. An F-104A fitted with a 6,000 lb
(2,720 kg) st Rocketdyne AR-2 auxiliary rocket-
engine in tail, above jet-pipe, is helping to train
USAF pilots for flight at heights up to 130,000 ft
(39,500 m) at the Aerospace Research Pilots'
School, Edwards AFB, California. Other modifications included the fitting of larger (F-104G
type) fin and rudder, forward extension of the
engine air intake cones to get better pressure

recovery and thrust, and introduction of HTP
reaction jet controls at nose, tail and wing-tips.
Each wing-tip has been extended by 2 ft (0·61 m)
to accommodate the reaction jets. First of
three NF-104A's flew in July 1963.

An NF-104A, piloted by Major R. W. Smith,
USAF, set up an unofficial height record of
118,860 ft (36,230 m) for aircraft taking off under
their own power, in November 1963.

F-104B. Tandem two-seat development of
F-104A, for use as both combat aircraft and
operational trainer. Has same engine, but
considerably greater fin area and fully-powered
rudder. Prototype flew on 7 February 1957.
Some in service with USAF Air Defense Command. Total of 26 built.

F-104C. General Electric J79-GE-7A turbo-
jet engine (15,800 lb=7,165 kg st with afterburning). Fighter-bomber for USAF Tactical Air
Command. Deliveries began on 16 October
1958. Total of 77 built for USAF.

F-104D. Two-seat version of F-104C for
USAF Tactical Air Command. Similar to F-
104B but with power plant, in-flight refuelling
equipment and other modifications introduced
in F-104C. Total of 22 built.

F-104DJ. Similar to F-104D. Lockheed built
20 for Japan Air Self-Defence Force. These
were re-assembled by Mitsubishi.

F-104F. Basically as F-104D, but some equipment changes. Thirty built by Lockheed for
Federal German Air Force. Deliveries began in
1960.

F-104G (Lockheed Model 683-10-19). Single-
seat multi-mission fighter, based on F-104C.
General Electric J79-GE-11A turbojet engine
(15,800 lb = 7,165 kg st with afterburning).
Considerably strengthened structure and different
operational equipment. Lockheed Model C-2
upward-ejection seat. Vertical tail surfaces
enlarged by 25%. Fully-powered rudder. Manoeuvring flaps added to reduce turning radius by
one-third at height of 5,000 ft (1,525 m). Extra
fuel tank interchangeable with fixed armament
of 20-mm Vulcan gun. Larger tyre size than
earlier versions to reduce UCI pressure. First
F-104G flew on 5 October 1960.

A total of 977 were ordered originally from
groups of European manufacturers. One group,
known as Arge Süd and comprising the German
companies of Messerschmitt, Heinkel, Siebelwerke
and Dornier, has produced 210 for the Federal
German Air Forces. A second group, Arge Nord,
made up of the Dutch companies of Fokker and
Aviolanda and the German companies of Hamburger Flugzeugbau and Vereinigte Flugtechnische
Werke, has built 255 for the German Air Force
and 95 for the RNAF, with Fokker handling all

final assembly. The Belgian companies of
SABCA and Avions Fairey have completed a total
of 188, of which 89 were for the German Air Forces
and 99 for the Belgian Air Force. In Italy, Fiat
and Aermacchi have collaborated in the production of 229 for the air forces of Italy (154), the
Netherlands (25) and Germany (50). In November 1968, West Germany announced an order for
an additional 50 F-104G's, to be built under
licence in Europe. In addition to European
production, Lockheed has built 96 F-104G's
for Germany, one each for Italy and Belgium,
and 81 similar F-104G(MAP) aircraft for other
nations participating in the Mutual Assistance
Programme. The first MAP machine flew in
July 1962. Recipients of these aircraft, and
others built by Canadair (see CF-104 entry
below), include Norway, Nationalist China, Spain,
Denmark, Greece and Turkey.

Miss Jacqueline Cochran used an F-104G to set
up three women's speed records in 1964. On
11 May she attained 1,429·30 mph (2,300·234
km/h) over a 15/25-km course. On 1 June she
attained 1,303·18 mph (2,097·266 km/h) over a
100-km closed circuit. And on 3 June she
attained 1,127·40 mph (1,814·368 km/h) over a
500-km closed circuit. The first of these records
remains unbeaten.

RF-104G. F-104G fitted with internal camera
pack for reconnaissance rôle.

TF-104G. (Lockheed Model 583-10-20). Total
of 137 two-seat conversion trainers bearing this
designation were ordered from Lockheed for
the Federal German Air Force, 14 for the Netherlands and 29 for other MAP nations, including
Belgium, Italy and Denmark. They are
equipped with NASARR and full operational
equipment, including the same fittings for underwing and wing-tip stores as the F-104G, with
optional fuselage centre-line bomb rack. Engine
as for F-104G. First TF-104G flew in October
1962. One TF-104G, with civil registration
N10LL, used by Lockheed as demonstrator.

F-104J. Similar to F-104G except for equipment. A total of three were produced by Lockheed
(first flew on 30 June 1961 and was delivered to
Japan in February 1962) and 207 by Mitsubishi
for Japan Air Self-Defence Force, of which the
first 20 were shipped by Lockheed as parts for
assembly in Japan.

F-104N. Astronaut proficiency trainer for
NASA. Three delivered.

F-104S. Developed from F-104G Starfighter,
primarily as interceptor. Powered by General
Electric J79-GE-19 turbojet with redesigned
afterburner, giving 17,900 lb (8,120 kg) st. Nine
external attachments for stores, including rockets,

bombs and Sidewinder missiles. Normal primary armament consists of Raytheon Sparrow air-to-air missiles. Total of 165 being built under licence in Italy for Italian Air Force and the first production model flew in December 1968. Two prototypes built by Lockheed, first of which flew in the second half of 1966. Max speed Mach 2·4.

CF-104. Single - seat strike - reconnaissance aircraft, basically similar to F-104G. Total of 200 built by Canadair for RCAF. Provision for two Sidewinders. Advanced navigation/fire-control system. Lockheed have developed for this version an under-fuselage reconnaissance pod containing four Vinten cameras and Computing Devices of Canada electronic control systems. First production model flew on 26 May 1961. Canadair designation is CL-90. Original RCAF designation was CF-111. Canadair also produced 110 similar aircraft as F-104G (MAP) under contract to USAF for nations participating in Military Aid Programme.

CF-104D. Total of 38 two-seat aircraft ordered from Lockheed by RCAF. First one flew in June, 1961. Original RCAF designation was CF-113.

QF-104. Remotely - controlled recoverable target drone conversion of F-104A for missile evaluation and firing practice.

On all standard versions of the Starfighter an automatic pitch control system is fitted to sense and prevent pitch-up, together with a three-axis autostabilizer. A boundary layer control system (described under "Wings" below) is used to decrease landing speed.

In June 1963, an experimental zero-length launching of a piloted F-104, using a specially-developed Rocketdyne solid-propellant booster rocket, was made successfully at Edwards AFB California.

Details given below refer specifically to the single-seat F-104G version.

TYPE: Single-seat supersonic fighter.

WINGS: Cantilever mid-wing monoplane. Biconvex supersonic wing section with a thickness/chord ratio of 3·36%. Anhedral 10°. No incidence. Sweepback 18° 6′ at quarter-chord. Leading-edge nose radius of 0·016 in (0·041 cm) and razor-sharp trailing-edge. All-metal structure with two main spars, 12 spanwise intermediate channels between spars and top and bottom one-piece skin panels, tapering from thickness of 0·25 in (6·3 mm) at root to 0·125 in (3·2 mm) at tip. Each half-wing measures 7 ft 7 in (2·31 m) from root to tip and is a separate structure cantilevered from five forged frames in fuselage. Full-span electrically-actuated drooping leading-edge. Entire trailing-edge hinged, with inboard sections serving as landing flaps and outboard sections as ailerons. Ailerons are of aluminium, each powered by a servo control system manufactured by Bertea. The control is irreversible and hydraulically-powered, each aileron being actuated by ten small hydraulic cylinders. Trim control is applied to position the aileron relative to the servo control position. An electric actuator positions the aileron trim. Flaps are of aluminium, actuated electrically. Above each flap is the air delivery tube of a boundary layer control system, which ejects air bled from the engine compressor over the entire flap span when the flaps are lowered to the landing position.

FUSELAGE: All-metal monocoque structure. Hydraulically-operated aluminium air-brake on each side of rear fuselage.

TAIL UNIT: T-type cantilever unit with "all-flying" one-piece horizontal tail surface hinged at mid-chord point at top of the sweptback vertical fin and powered by a hydraulic servo. Tailplane has similar profile to wing and is all-metal. Rudder is fully-powered by a hydraulic servo manufactured, like the tailplane unit, by Bertea. Trim control is applied to position the tailplane relative to the servo control position, by means of an electric actuator. Rudder trim is operated by an electric actuator located in the fin. The rudder itself is trimmed in the same way as the tailplane. Narrow-chord ventral fin to improve stability.

LANDING GEAR: Retractable tricycle type. H. M. Loud (Dowty patent) liquid-spring shock-absorbers. Hydraulic actuation. Main wheels raised in and forward. Steerable nose-wheel retracts forward into fuselage on all single-seat models of the F-104, rearward on two-seat models. Main wheel legs are hinged on oblique axes so that the wheels lie flush within the fuselage skin when retracted. Main wheels size 26 × 8·0, with Goodrich tyres size 26 × 8·0 type VIII, pressure 173 lb/sq in (12·16 kg/cm²). Nose-wheel tyre size 18 × 5·5 type VII. Bendix hydraulic disc brakes with Goodyear anti-skid units. Drag parachute of 18 ft (5·50 m) diameter stowed in lower part of fuselage near end of tailpipe.

Lockheed TF-104G of Jagdgeschwader 74 of the Federal German Air Force (*Archiv Redemann*)

POWER PLANT: One General Electric J79 turbojet engine with afterburner (details under series descriptions above). Electrical de-icing elements fitted to air intakes. Most of the aircraft's hydraulic equipment mounted inside large engine access door under fuselage to facilitate servicing. Internal fuel in five bag-type fuselage tanks with total standard capacity of 896 US gallons (3,392 litres) in single-seat models of the F-104, 700 US gallons (2,650 litres) in two-seat models. The capacity quoted for two-seat models includes metal tanks (capacity 122 US gallons = 462 litres) in ammunition, gun and shell-case compartments of fuselage; these are optional and additional to capacity quoted on single-seat models. Provision for external fuel in 2 × 195 US gallon (740 litre) pylon tanks and 2 × 170 US gallon (645 litre) wing-tip tanks. Pressure refuelling of all internal and external tanks through single point on upper port fuselage just forward of air intake duct. Gravity fuelling point for internal tanks aft of pressure refuelling point, with individual gravity fuelling of external tanks. In-flight refuelling can be provided through Lockheed-designed probe-drogue system. Probe, mounted below port sill of cockpit, is removable but when installed is non-retractable. Oil capacity 4 US gallons (15 litres).

ACCOMMODATION: Pressurised and air-conditioned cockpit well forward of wings. Canopy hinged to port for access. Lockheed Model C-2 ejection seat.

SYSTEMS: Air-conditioning package by AiResearch (single-seat) or Hamilton Standard (two-seat), using engine-bleed air. Pressure differential 5 lb/sq in (0·35 kg/cm²). Two completely separate hydraulic systems, using engine-driven pumps operating at 3,000 lb/sq in (210 kg/cm²). No. 1 system operates one side of tailplane, rudder and ailerons, also the automatic pitch control actuator and autopilot actuators. No 2 system operates other half of tailplane, rudder and ailerons, also the landing gear, wheel brakes, speed brakes, nose-wheel steering and constant-frequency electrical generator. Emergency ram air turbine supplies emergency hydraulic pump and 4·5kVA 115/200V electric generator. Electrical system supplied by two engine-driven 20kVA 115/200V variable-frequency (320-520 c/s) generators. Constant-speed hydraulic motor drives 2·5kVA 115/200V generator to supply fixed-frequency AC. DC power supplied by two batteries and an inverter.

ARMAMENT (F-104G): Bomb rack under fuselage for store weighing up to 2,000 lb (907 kg). Under-wing pylons can each carry a 1,000 lb (453 kg) store, fire bomb, rocket pod, Sidewinder air-to-air missile, AGM-12B Bullpup air-to-surface missile or 195 US gallon (740 litres) fuel tank. Provision for two Sidewinders under fuselage and either a Sidewinder or 170 US gallon (645 litre) fuel tank on each wing-tip.

ELECTRONICS AND EQUIPMENT: Integrated electronics system in which various communications and navigation components may be installed as a series of interconnecting but self-sustaining units which may be varied to provide for different specific missions. Equipment includes autopilot with "stick steering", which includes modes for preselecting and holding altitude, speed, heading and constant rate of turn; multi-purpose NASARR radar system; fixed-reticle gunsight; bomb computer; air data computer; dead reckoning navigation device; TACAN radio air navigation system; provision for data link-time division set and UHF radio; lightweight fully-automatic inertial navigation system; and provision for fitting a camera pod under the fuselage for reconnaissance duties.

DIMENSIONS, EXTERNAL (F-104G, TF-104G):
Wing span without tip-tanks	21 ft 11 in (6·68 m)
Wing chord (mean)	9 ft 6·6 in (2·91 m)
Wing aspect ratio	2·45
Length overall	54 ft 9 in (16·69 m)
Length of fuselage	51 ft 3 in (15·62 m)
Height overall	13 ft 6 in (4·11 m)
Tailplane span	11 ft 11 in (3·63 m)
Wheel track	8 ft 10½ in (2·71 m)
Wheelbase: F-104G	15 ft 0½ in (4·59 m)
TF-104G	14 ft 5½ in (4·41 m)

AREAS (F-104G, TF-104G):
Wings, gross	196·1 sq ft (18·22 m²)
Ailerons (total)	9·2 sq ft (0·85 m²)
Trailing-edge flaps (total)	22·7 sq ft (2·11 m²)
Leading-edge flaps (total)	16·2 sq ft (1·50 m²)
Air-brakes (total)	8·25 sq ft (0·77 m²)
Fin	37·7 sq ft (3·50 m²)
Ventral fin	5·9 sq ft (0·55 m²)
Rudder, including tab	5·5 sq ft (0·51 m²)
Tailplane	48·2 sq ft (4·48 m²)

WEIGHTS AND LOADING (F-104G, TF-104G):
Weight empty:	
F-104G	14,082 lb (6,387 kg)
TF-104G	14,181 lb (6,432 kg)
Max armament:	
F-104G	4,800 lb (2,177 kg)
TF-104G	2,744 lb (1,245 kg)
Max T-O weight:	
F-104G	28,779 lb (13,054 kg)
TF-104G	26,364 lb (11,958 kg)
Max ramp weight	29,500 lb (13,381 kg)
Max landing weight (design load factor):	
F-104G	23,000 lb (10,430 kg)
TF-104G	21,500 lb (9,750 kg)
Max wing loading	148 lb/sq ft (723 kg/m²)

PERFORMANCE (F-104G, TF-104G):
Max level speed at 36,000 ft (11,000 m)	
Mach 2·2 = 1,259 knots	(1,450 mph; 2,330 km/h)
Max permissible diving speed	Mach 2·2
Max cruising speed	Mach 0·95
Econ cruising speed	Mach 0·85
Stalling speed 125 knots (144 mph; 232 km/h)	
Rate of climb at S/L	50,000 ft (15,250 m)/min
Service ceiling	58,000 ft (17,680 m)
Zoom altitude	over 90,000 ft (27,400 m)
Time to accelerate to Mach 2·0	3 min
T-O run:	
F-104G at 21,840 lb (9,906 kg) AUW	2,960 ft (902 m)
TF-104G at 18,900 lb (8,573 kg) AUW	2,260 ft (690 m)
T-O to 50 ft (15 m):	
F-104G at 22,840 lb (10,360 kg) AUW	4,600 ft (1,402 m)
TF-104G at 18,900 lb (8,573 kg) AUW	3,500 ft (1,067 m)
Landing from 50 ft (15 m):	
F-104G at 15,900 lb (7,212 kg) AUW	3,250 ft (990 m)
TF-104G at 15,424 lb (6,996 kg) AUW	3,190 ft (972 m)
Landing run:	
F-104G at 15,900 lb (7,212 kg) AUW	2,280 ft (695 m)
TF-104G at 15,424 lb (6,996 kg) AUW	2,215 ft (676 m)
Radius with max fuel:	
F-104G	645 nm (745 miles; 1,200 km)
TF-104G	515 nm (593 miles; 955 km)
Ferry range (excluding flight refuelling):	
F-104G	1,890 nm (2,180 miles; 3,510 km)

LOCKHEED A-11
USAF designations: YF-12A and SR-71

The existence of the Lockheed A-11 was announced by President Johnson on 29 February 1964. At a news conference he stated that this aircraft, developed in conditions of strict secrecy, had already been tested in sustained flight at speeds of more than 2,000 mph (3,200

Lockheed SR-71A strategic reconnaissance aircraft (two Pratt & Whitney J58 turbojet engines with afterburners)

km/h) and at heights in excess of 70,000 ft (21,350 m) at Edwards AFB, California.

Design of the A-11 was started in about 1959, almost certainly to supersede the Lockheed U-2 on long-range high-altitude reconnaissance missions. Like the U-2, it was designed by a team led by C. L. Johnson, Lockheed's Vice-President for Advanced Development Projects, in a restricted building known as the "Skunk Works" at Burbank. About seven A-11's are believed to have been produced by October 1964, with 13 more covered by initial contracts. A further contract for six was placed in the Spring of 1966 to keep the assembly line open in case of any future need for such an aircraft.

President Johnson announced that the then-current flight tests were aimed at determining the A-11's capabilities as a long-range interceptor and the service designation YF-12A was subsequently allocated to it. Five months later, on 24 July 1964, the President revealed that Lockheed were developing a second Mach 3 military aircraft, designated SR-71, as "a long-range advanced strategic reconnaissance plane for military use, capable of world-wide reconnaissance for military operations", and equipped with multiple sensors. He added that it used the same type of engines as the YF-12A.

The four military versions of the A-11 are, therefore, as follows:

YF-12A. Experimental interceptor version of the A-11, displayed publicly for the first time at Edwards AFB on 30 September 1964. No further production anticipated, as any future interceptor version of the A-11 would probably utilise the basic SR-71 airframe.

The pilot and air interception officer of the YF-12A sit on conventional ejection seats in tandem cockpits under individual rearward-hinged canopies. This version has Hughes AN/ASG-18 pulse Doppler fire-control radar in its nose radome, an infra-red sensor at the front of each of the fuselage side fairings, and two missile bays in the undersurface of each of these fairings. The weapon bays are large enough to accommodate eight of the Hughes AIM-47A air-to-air missiles with which the aircraft is armed.

It was announced by Lockheed on 29 December 1969 that two YF-12A's, one belonging to the USAF, were to participate in a joint USAF/NASA flight-test programme, to seek data on altitude-hold at supersonic speeds, boundary layer noise, heat transfer under high speed conditions, propulsion system interactions involving effects of engine intake performance, and other performance and handling characteristics.

The programme is to be conducted in two phases. The USAF is responsible for the first phase, devoted to operational combat research and due to terminate at the end of 1971; the NASA-controlled second phase is expected to begin in mid-1972. A sum of $10 million has been allocated by NASA to finance the programme to the end of 1974.

SR-71A. Strategic reconnaissance aircraft. Fuselage lengthened by comparison with YF-12A. Fuselage side fairings extend forward to nose. No ventral tail-fins. Equipment carried internally ranges from simple battlefield surveillance systems to multiple-sensor high-performance systems for interdiction reconnaissance and strategic systems capable of specialised surveillance of up to 60,000 sq miles of territory in one hour. Described as being substantially heavier and with a longer range than the YF-12A. Crew of two consists of pilot and reconnaissance systems officer. Operational ceiling is over 80,000 ft (24,400 m). Development began in February 1963. First flight of an SR-71 was made on 22 December 1964, and deliveries of operational aircraft to the 9th Strategic Reconnaissance Wing at Beale AFB, California, began in January 1966.

SR-71B. Tandem two-seat training version of SR-71A, with elevated second cockpit aft of

Lockheed YF-12A Mach 3 prototype fighter, mid-1970 holder of the world air speed record
(Duane A. Kasulka)

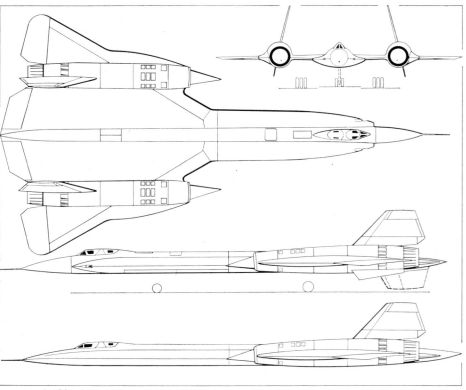

Lockheed YF-12A Mach 3 prototype fighter with additional side view (bottom) of SR-71A reconnaissance aircraft

normal cockpit. Fixed ventral tail-fins reintroduced. First SR-71B delivered to Strategic Air Command's 4200th Strategic Reconnaissance Wing at Beale AFB, California, in early January 1966.

SR-71C. Revised training version, after SR-71B was lost in an accident.

To make possible a cruising speed of Mach 3, the airframe of the A-11 is built almost entirely of titanium and its alloys. The control surfaces consist of an all-moving vertical tail surface above the rear of each engine nacelle, ailerons on the outer wings, and elevators on the trailing-edges between the engine tail-pipes. Except on the SR-71A there is a fixed ventral fin under each engine nacelle and a centrally-mounted ventral fin which folds to port for ground clearance when the landing gear is extended. Also of note is the

considerable camber on the wing-tip leading-edges.

Each main unit of the tricycle landing gear has three wheels. The main units retract inward into the fuselage, the twin nose-wheels forward. The power plant comprises two Pratt & Whitney JT11D-20B (J58) turbojet engines, each with a thrust of 32,500 lb (14,740 kg) with afterburning. A large movable centre-body shock-cone is fitted at the front of each nacelle. At the rear, aft of the four-ring afterburner flame-holder, is a ring of suck-in doors for cooling and area reduction at low speeds, and a variable-area final nozzle.

On 1 May 1965 USAF pilots set up three world records and six international class records in two YF-12A aircraft, from Edwards AFB, California. Col Robert L. Stephens and Lt Col Daniel Andre achieved 2,070·102 mph (3,331·507 km/h) over a 15/25 km course at unlimited altitude, and a sustained height of 80,257·91 ft (24,462·596 m) in horizontal flight. Major Walter F. Daniel and Major Noel T. Warner averaged 1,643·042 mph (2,644·220 km/h) over a 500-km closed circuit. Major Daniel and Capt James P. Cooney averaged 1,688·891 mph (2,718·006 km/h) over a 1,000-km closed circuit, with a 2,000 kg payload, an absolute world record, and qualifying also for records without payload and with a 1,000 kg payload. The 500-km and 1,000-km closed circuit records have since been beaten by the Soviet MiG-23.

DIMENSIONS, EXTERNAL (SR-71A):

Wing span	55 ft 7 in (16·95 m)
Length overall	107 ft 5 in (32·74 m)
Height overall	18 ft 6 in (5·64 m)

LOCKHEED MODEL 185 ORION
US Navy designation: P-3 (formerly P3V-1)

In April 1958 it was announced that Lockheed had been successful in winning with a developed version of the civil Electra four-turboprop airliner a US Navy competition for an "off-the-shelf" ASW aircraft. The two original contracts provided for initial research, development and pre-production activities, while further contracts provided for purchase by the Navy of a standard commercial Electra and its modification, development and testing as a tactical test-bed for anti-submarine warfare systems.

An aerodynamic prototype, produced by modifying the airframe of the third civil Electra, flew for the first time on 19 August 1958. A second aircraft, designated YP-3A (formerly YP3V-1), with full electronics, flew on 25 November 1959.

Three production versions have been announced, as follows:

P-3A Orion. Initial production version for US Navy, with 4,500 eshp (with water injection) Allison T56-A-10W turboprop engines. First P-3A flew for the first time on 15 April 1961. A second production aircraft was flying by October 1961 and deliveries to the US Navy began on 13 August 1962, to replace the P-2 Neptune. By November 1964, a total of 100 had been delivered. Later models (from the 110th aircraft) are known as Deltic P-3A's, as they are fitted with the Deltic system, including more sensitive ASW detection devices and improved tactical display equipment. Production completed.

P-3B Orion. Current production version, with 4,910 eshp Allison T56-A-14 turboprop engines, which do not need water-alcohol injection. Production for US Navy continued through 1967. USN contracts placed by January 1967 covered a total of 210 P-3A's and P-3B's. In addition, five P-3B's were delivered to the Royal New Zealand Air Force in 1966, ten to the Royal Australian Air Force during 1968 and five to Norway in the Spring of 1969. USN P-3B's have been modified to carry Bullpup missiles.

P-3C Orion. Advanced version for the US Navy with the A-NEW system of sensors and control equipment, built around a Univac digital computer, that permits retrieval, transmission and display of tactical data with great speed and accuracy. First flight of this version was made on 18 September 1968 and the P-3C was scheduled to enter into service in 1969.

In June 1963 a standard P-3A Orion, without extra tankage, flew non-stop 6,220 miles (10,010 km) from Van Nuys, California, to Paris in 14 hr 17 min at an average speed of 379 knots (436 mph; 701 km/h).

The following data refer to the current P-3B production version, but are generally applicable to other versions, except for the details noted above.

TYPE: Four-turboprop naval ASW aircraft.

WINGS: Cantilever low-wing monoplane. Wing section NACA 0014 (modified) at root, NACA 0012 (modified) at tip. Dihedral 6°. Inci-

Lockheed SR-71B tandem two-seat training version of this strategic reconnaissance aircraft

dence 3° at root, 0° 30′ at tip. Fail-safe box beam structure of extruded integrally-stiffened aluminium alloy. Lockheed-Fowler trailing-edge flaps. Hydraulically-boosted aluminium ailerons. Anti-icing by engine-bleed air ducted into leading-edges.

FUSELAGE: Conventional aluminium alloy semi-monocoque fail-safe structure. Outside diameter 11 ft 4 in (3·45 m).

TAIL UNIT: Cantilever aluminium alloy structure with dihedral tailplane and dorsal fin. Fixed-incidence tailplane. Hydraulically-boosted rudder and elevators. Leading-edges of fin and tailplane have electrical anti-icing system.

LANDING GEAR: Hydraulically-retractable tricycle type, with twin wheels on each unit. All units retract forward, main wheels into inner engine nacelles. Oleo-pneumatic shock-absorbers. Main wheels have size 40 × 14 type VII 26-ply tubeless tyres. Nose-wheels have size 28 × 7·7 type VII tubeless tyres. Hydraulic brakes. No anti-skid units.

POWER PLANT: Four 4,910 eshp Allison T56-A-14 turboprop engines, each driving a Hamilton Standard 54H60 four-blade constant-speed propeller, diameter 13 ft 6 in (4·11 m). Fuel in one tank in fuselage and four wing integral tanks, with total usable capacity of 9,200 US gallons (34,826 litres). Four overwing gravity fuelling points and central pressure refuelling point. Oil capacity (min usable) 29·4 US gallons (111 litres) in four tanks.

ACCOMMODATION: Normal 12-man crew. Flight deck has wide-vision windows, and circular windows for observers are provided fore and aft in the main cabin, each bulged to give 180° visibility. Main cabin is fitted out as a five-man tactical compartment containing 2½ tons of electronic, magnetic and sonic detection equipment, an all-electric galley and large crew rest area. With minor design changes and removal only of sonobuoy stowage racks, seats can be fitted for approximately 50 fully-equipped combat troops. Alternative VIP seating kit available. Door on port side of rear fuselage.

SYSTEMS: Air-conditioning and pressurisation system supplied by two engine-driven compressors. Pressure differential 5·4 lb/sq in (0·38 kg/cm²). Hydraulic system, pressure 3,000 lb/sq in (210 kg/cm²), for flaps, control surface boosters, landing gear actuation, brakes and bomb-bay doors. Pneumatic system, pressure 3,000/1,200 lb/sq in (210/85 kg/cm²), for ASW store launchers. Electrical system utilises three 60kVA generators for 120/208V 400 c/s AC supply. 24V DC supply. Integral APU with 60kVA generator for ground air-conditioning and electrical supply and engine starting.

ELECTRONICS AND EQUIPMENT: Communications and navigation equipment comprises two ARC-94 HF transceivers, ARC-84 VHF transmitter, two ARC-84 VHF receivers, two ARC-51A UHF transceivers, AIC-22 interphone, TT-264/AG teletypewriter, UNH-6 communications tape recorder, two CU-351 HF couplers, ASN-42 inertial navigation system, APN-153 Doppler navigation system, ASA-47 Doppler air mass computer, ASN-50 AHRS, APN-70 LORAN, ARN-52 TACAN, DF-202 radio compass, ARN-32 marker beacon receiver APN-141 radar altimeter, ARA-25A UHF direction finder, two NVA-22A VOR installations, two HSI, A/A24G-9 true airspeed computer, PB-20N autopilot, ID-888/U latitude/longitude indicator, and APQ-107 radar altitude warning system. ASW equipment includes ASA-16 tactical display, APA-125A radar display, ASR-3 trail detector, two ARR-52A sonobuoy signal receivers, AQA-1 sonobuoy indicator, AQA-5 sonobuoy indicator (Jezebel), ASA-20A sonobuoy recorder (Julie), ASQ-10A magnetic anomoly detector in plastics tail "sting", modified ALD-2B ECM direction finder for detecting and locating electronic emissions from submarines, ULA-2 ECM signal analyser, APX-6 IFF identification, APX-7 IFF recognition, APA-89 IFF coder group, AQH-1(V) tactical tape recorder, ASA-50 ground speed and bearing computer, R-1047/A on top position indicator, TD-441/A intervalometer, PT396/AS ground track plotter, ASA-13 tactical plot board, bearing-distance-heading indicator and K7 364 video decoder. Equipment for day or night photographic reconnaissance. Searchlight under starboard wing.

ARMAMENT: Bomb-bay, 80 in wide, 34·5 in deep and 154 in long (2·03 m × 0·88 m × 3·91 m), forward of wing, can accommodate a 2,000 lb MK 25/39/55/56 mine, three 1,000 lb MK 36/52 mines, three MK 57 depth bombs, eight MK 54 depth bombs, eight MK 43/44/46 torpedoes or a combination of two MK 101 nuclear depth bombs and four MK 43/44/46 torpedoes. There are ten underwing pylons for stores. Two under centre-section each side can carry torpedoes or 2,000-lb mines. Three under outer wing each side can carry respectively (inboard to outboard) a torpedo or 2,000 lb mine (or searchlight on starboard wing), a torpedo or 1,000-lb mine or rockets singly or in pods; a torpedo or 500-lb mine or rockets singly or in pods. Torpedoes can be carried underwing only for ferrying; mines can be carried and released. Search stores, such as sonobuoys and sound signals are launched from inside cabin area. Max total weapon load includes six 2,000 lb mines under wings and a 7,252 lb (3,290 kg) internal load made up of two MK 101 depth bombs, four MK 44 torpedoes, pyrotechnic pistol and 12 signals, 87 sonobuoys, 100 MK 50 underwater sound signals, 18 XI-3A marine markers, 42

Lockheed P-3C Orion anti-submarine patrol aircraft for the US Navy (four 4,910 eshp Allison T56-A-14 turboprop engines)

MK-7 marine markers, two B.T. buoys, and two MK 5 parachute flares.

DIMENSIONS, EXTERNAL:
Wing span	99 ft 8 in (30·37 m)
Wing chord at root	18 ft 11 in (5·77 m)
Wing chord at tip	7 ft 7 in (2·31 m)
Wing aspect ratio	7·5
Length overall	116 ft 10 in (35·61 m)
Height over tail	33 ft 8½ in (10·29 m)
Tailplane span	42 ft 10 in (13·06 m)
Wheel track (C/L shock-struts)	31 ft 2 in (9·50 m)
Wheelbase	29 ft 9 in (9·07 m)
Cabin door:	
Height	6 ft 0 in (1·83 m)
Width	2 ft 3 in (0·69 m)

DIMENSIONS, INTERNAL:
Cabin, excluding flight deck and electrical load centre:	
Length	69 ft 1 in (21·06 m)
Max width	10 ft 10 in (3·30 m)
Max height	7 ft 6 in (2·29 m)
Floor area	658 sq ft (61·13 m²)
Volume	4,260 cu ft (120·6 m³)

AREAS:
Wings, gross	1,300 sq ft (120·77 m²)
Ailerons (total)	90 sq ft (8·36 m²)
Trailing-edge flaps (total)	208 sq ft (19·32 m²)
Fin, with dorsal fin	116 sq ft (10·78 m²)
Rudder, including tab	60 sq ft (5·57 m²)
Tailplane	241 sq ft (22·39 m²)
Elevators, including tabs	81 sq ft (7·53 m²)

WEIGHTS (P-3B):
Weight empty	61,491 lb (27,890 kg)
Max expendable load	18,600 lb (8,435 kg)
Max normal T-O weight	133,000 lb (60,325 kg)
Max permissible weight	142,000 lb (64,410 kg)
Design landing weight	97,000 lb (43,995 kg)

PERFORMANCE (P-3B, at max T-O weight, except where indicated otherwise):
Max level speed at 15,000 ft (4,570 m) at AUW of 105,000 lb (47,625 kg)	
	413 knots (476 mph; 765 km/h)
Econ cruising speed at 25,000 ft (7,620 m) at AUW of 105,000 lb (47,625 kg)	
	345 knots (397 mph; 639 km/h)
Patrol speed at 1,500 ft (450 m) at AUW of 105,000 lb (47,625 kg)	
	200 knots (230 mph; 370 km/h)
Stalling speed, flaps up	
	129 knots (148 mph; 238 km/h)
Stalling speed, flaps down	
	113 knots (130 mph; 210 km/h)
Rate of climb at 1,500 ft (457 m)	
	2,175 ft (663 m)/min
Service ceiling	28,300 ft (8,625 m)
Service ceiling, one engine out	19,000 ft (5,790 m)
T-O run	4,240 ft (1,290 m)
T-O to 50 ft (15 m)	5,550 ft (1,690 m)
Landing from 50 ft (15 m) at design landing weight	2,770 ft (845 m)
Max mission radius (no time on station)	
	2,195 nm (2,530 miles; 4,075 km)
Mission radius (3 hr on station at 1,500 ft = 457 m)	1,675 nm (1,933 miles; 3,110 km)

LOCKHEED S-3A

On 4 August 1969 Lockheed announced the receipt of a $461 million contract from the US Navy to develop a new anti-submarine aircraft under the designation S-3A. It is to be developed by Lockheed in partnership with Vought Aeronautics Division of LTV Aerospace, Dallas, Texas, and Univac Federal Systems Division of Sperry Rand Corporation, St Paul, Minnesota. LTV will design and build the wing, engine pods, tail unit and landing gear, and Univac will supply the digital computer, the heart of the weapon system, which provides high-speed processing of data essential for the S-3A's ASW role. Texas Instruments has been selected to supply several major avionic sub-systems, including a forward-looking infra-red system for night ASW surveillance, AN/ASQ-81 magnetic detection system, AN/APS-116 high-resolution X-band search and detection radar, and scan converter equipment to provide an interface between the APS-116 and the S-3A's central digital computer. Lockheed will build the fuselage, integrate the avionics and be responsible for final assembly at Burbank, California.

The selection of Lockheed-California as contractor for this aircraft follows more than a year of intensive competition between North American Rockwell, McDonnell Douglas, Grumman Aircraft Engineering Corporation, Convair Division of General Dynamics and Lockheed-California Company in conjunction with LTV Aerospace Corporation. Proposals submitted by these five companies in April 1968 were evaluated by Naval Air Systems Command (NASC), and in August 1968 General Dynamics and Lockheed were requested to provide additional contract definition and to make further refinements to their proposals.

The final proposals of these two companies were submitted in late December 1968, and a detailed technical evaluation was carried out by NASC. Prior experience with Navy programmes was taken into consideration, and finally the

Artist's impression of Lockheed S-3A carrier-based advanced anti-submarine aircraft (two General Electric TF34-2 turbofan engines)

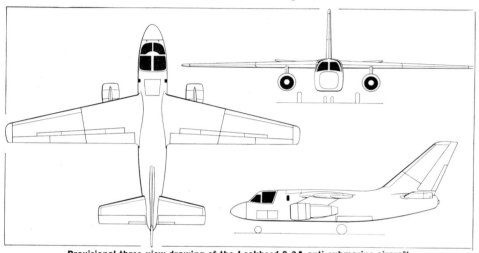

Provisional three-view drawing of the Lockheed S-3A anti-submarine aircraft

Service Selection Authority of NASC awarded the contract to Lockheed-California.

The Lockheed team will be responsible for development, test and demonstration of the aircraft and its weapon systems, with first flight expected early in 1972, and introduction into the fleet scheduled for 1973. The contract price is a ceiling figure, to be funded over a five-year period, and includes production of six research and development aircraft.

The S-3A is intended for operation from aircraft carriers and will have a crew of four, comprising a pilot, co-pilot, tactical operator (Tacco) and acoustic sensor operator (Senso). The pilot will maintain command of the aircraft, while the Tacco formulates strategy and instructs the pilots on the necessary manoeuvres for a successful submarine attack. In addition to flying duties, the co-pilot will be responsible for the non-acoustic sensors (such as radar and infra-red) and navigation: the Senso will control the acoustic sensors.

The development of quieter submarines has led to the design of sonobuoys of increased sensitivity, and advanced cathode ray tube displays will be provided in the S-3A to maintain flexibility of operation with a limited crew. In particular, a cathode ray tube will be utilised to monitor the acoustic sensors. The information formerly stowed in roll form from paper plotters will, instead, be stored in the Univac 1832A computer and become available for instant recall. Other functions of the computer include weapon trajectory calculations and pre-flight navigation. Magnetic anomaly detection (MAD) equipment will be of increased sensitivity, in order to detect submarines at greater depths than is possible at the present time.

Shipboard maintenance will be simplified by the provision of computerised fault-finding equipment, built-in test equipment (BITE), versatile avionic shop test (VAST) compatibility and 30-minute total engine change time. Complete deck-level servicing contributes to the attainment of a 45-minute turnaround time.

The performance characteristics of the S-3A will make possible future design variants, including tanker, utility transport, ASW command and control, and a variety of electronic countermeasures aircraft. To cater for future growth,

the airframe is stressed for a maximum take-off weight of 50,000 lb (22,680 kg) and the fuselage volume is such as to allow for a 50 per cent expansion of avionics equipment.

All available details follow:

TYPE: Twin-turbofan carrier-borne anti-submarine aircraft.

WINGS: Cantilever shoulder-wing monoplane. Sweepback at quarter-chord 15°. All-metal fail-safe structure. Wings fold upward and inward hydraulically, outboard of engine pylons, for carrier stowage. Single-slotted Fowler-type trailing-edge flaps. Hydraulically-powered leading-edge slats, extending from engine pylons to wing-tips. Ailerons augmented by spoilers for roll control. All surfaces hydraulically-powered, with manual reversion in the event of failure of both hydraulic systems.

FUSELAGE: Semi-monocoque all-metal fail-safe structure, incorporating a split bomb-bay with clam-shell doors. Sonobuoy launch tubes in belly. Frangible panel in top of fuselage, just aft of flight deck canopy, is so designed that the two aft crew men (Tacco and Senso) can eject through it in emergency. Avionics bays with external access doors in forward fuselage. MAD boom, extensible in flight, housed in fuselage tail.

TAIL UNIT: Cantilever all-metal structure with swept vertical and horizontal surfaces. Fin and rudder fold downward for carrier stowage. Variable-incidence tailplane. Trim-tabs in elevator and rudder.

LANDING GEAR: Hydraulically-retractable tricycle type. Main units, similar to those of the Vought F-8 Crusader, are fitted with single wheels and retract rearward into wheel wells immediately aft of the split bomb-bays. Nose unit, identical to that of the Vought A-7 Corsair II, with twin wheels and catapult tow bar, retracts rearward into fuselage.

POWER PLANT: Two General Electric TF34-2 high by-pass ratio turbofan engines, in the 9,000 lb (4,082 kg) st class, pylon-mounted beneath the wings. Fuel contained in integral wing tanks, situated inboard of the fold-line. Auxiliary fuel tanks may be carried on under-wing pylons.

ACCOMMODATION: Crew of four. Pilot and co-pilot side-by-side on flight deck with transparent canopy which normally does not open but can be jettisoned in emergency; Tacco and Senso accommodated in aft cabin. All crew on zero-zero ejection seats. Cabin pressurised and air-conditioned. Door for all crew, with integral airstair, in starboard side of lower forward fuselage, hinged to open outward and downward.

SYSTEMS: Dual hydraulic system. SPN-41 all-weather landing system, permitting automatic coupled approaches.

ELECTRONICS: Univac 1832A general-purpose digital computer. ASW sensors include DIFAR (with automatic target classification), CASS, DICASS (upon development), MAD, APS-116 X-band forward-looking radar, ECM, infra-red scanner and a photo system. Navigational equipment will comprise ASN-92 (V) CAINS inertial navigator, Doppler, Air Data System, AHRS, OMEGA, Sonobuoy Reference System, TACAN, UHF/DF and ADF. Communications equipment will consist of dual UHF, Data Link, HF, TACSATCOM provisions and Auto-encryption.

ARMAMENT: Split bomb-bays and underwing pylons will carry torpedoes, depth charges, missiles, mines, rockets or special weapons.

DIMENSIONS, EXTERNAL:
Wing span	68 ft 8 in (20·93 m)
Wing span, wings folded	29 ft 6 in (8·99 m)
Length overall	53 ft 4 in (16·26 m)
Length overall, tail folded	49 ft 5 in (15·06 m)
Height overall	22 ft 9 in (6·93 m)
Height overall, tail folded	15 ft 3 in (4·65 m)

DIMENSIONS, INTERNAL:
Max height	7 ft 6 in (2·29 m)
Max width	7 ft 2 in (2·18 m)

AREA:
Wings, gross	approx 600 sq ft (55·74 m²)

WEIGHTS (estimated):
Weight empty	26,300 lb (11,925 kg)
Max T-O weight	41,000 lb (18,595 kg)
Max landing weight	37,700 lb (17,100 kg)

PERFORMANCE (estimated):
Max level speed
over 430 knots (495 mph; 797 km/h) TAS
Max cruising speed
over 350 knots (403 mph; 649 km/h) TAS
Loiter speed
160 knots (184 mph; 257 km/h) TAS
Stalling speed
84 knots (97 mph; 157 km/h) TAS
Rate of climb at S/L   4,800 ft (1,463 m)/min
Service ceiling   above 35,000 ft (10,670 m)
Ferry range
more than 3,000 nm (3,454 miles; 5,558 km)

LOCKHEED MODEL 186
US military designation: XH-51A

In February 1962, the US Navy and Army awarded Lockheed-California Company a contract to build two high-performance research helicopters, under the designation XH-51A.

These aircraft have a rigid rotor of the kind pioneered by Lockheed on the CL-475 flying test-bed helicopter, described and illustrated in the 1962-63 Jane's. Advantages claimed for the rigid rotor system after two years of private venture flight testing of the CL-475, with both wooden and metal blades, include inherent stability without artificial stabilisation, high manoeuvrability, extremely wide usable CG range, low vibration, ease of control, instrument flight capability, mechanical simplicity and high speed potential.

With the XH-51A Lockheed have achieved an aerodynamic drag value as low as that of a flat plate of only 8 sq ft (0·74 m²) area. External skins are completely flush-riveted and the fuselage is flush-sealed extensively. To reduce further the fuselage drag at high speed the rotor plane is set at a forward tilt of 6° relative to the fuselage datum line. This achieves an optimum balance between fuselage attitude during hovering and high-speed flight attitude. The use of a fully-retractable landing gear has reduced overall drag by some 25%.

To reduce drag around the rotor hub, the control swashplate is mounted at the base of the transmission within the fuselage, and the control rods are brought up through the main rotor shaft.

Features of the rigid rotor design include cantilevered blades with freedom in the feathering axis only, a mechanical stabilising gyro located in series between the blades and the pilot's controls, and a control system utilising a spring cartridge between the pilot's stick and the control gyro to attain the required mechanical motion and force characteristics. The control gyro is mounted as close as possible to the rotor plane to reduce frontal area, and above the rotor to eliminate danger to ground personnel when rotating.

In operation, forward movement of the stick applies a force to the control gyro through the swashplate. This force is in the lateral plane and

the control gyro responds with a nose-down precession. Altering the angle between the plane of the control gyro and the plane of the rotor, the precession introduces cyclic pitch changes in the lateral portions of the rotor disc. The resultant aerodynamic forces on the rotor result in gyroscopic precession in the nose-down direction. As the blades are cantilevered from the hub and mast, which is attached rigidly to the fuselage structure, this produces a nose-down pitch of the entire aircraft. Control in roll is achieved in a similar manner.

If external disturbances, such as wind gusts, move the aircraft and rotor with respect to the control gyro, damping is introduced automatically.

To ensure good autorotative characteristics and transition flares from autorotation, a high ratio of rotor energy to gross weight is utilised in the XH-51. The kinetic energy stored in the rotor is equivalent to the potential energy of the helicopter while hovering at a height of 150 ft (45 m).

In hover, a 1 in (2·5 cm) control displacement in pitch results in a pitch rate of 10 degrees per second for both forward and aft control displacement.

The average time required to reach the maximum pitch rate is approximately 0·8 sec after control displacement. A roll rate of 13 degrees per second per inch of cyclic roll control is obtained in hover for control displacements in either direction. The time to reach the maximum roll rate is approximately 0·7 sec following the initial control input.

There are three versions of the XH-51, which has the Lockheed designation Model 186:

XH-51A. Two original prototypes for US Navy and Army. First one flew for the first time on 2 November 1962. One of these has been withdrawn and placed in storage, and the other converted to XH-51A compound helicopter.

XH-51A Compound. One of the XH-51A's referred to above has been modified for research at higher speeds under a US Army contract. It now has a 2,600 lb (1,180 kg) st Pratt & Whitney J60-P-2 turbojet engine mounted on the port side of the cabin and cantilever mid-set wings spanning 16 ft 11 in (5·16 m). Normal T-O weight is 4,500 lb (2,040 kg). First flight, without using the turbojet, was made in September 1964. During

subsequent flight testing, in June 1967, it attained a speed of 263 knots (302·6 mph; 487 km/h), the fastest recorded for any rotorcraft at that time.

XH-51N. One aircraft only, ordered by NASA in June 1964 and delivered in December 1964. Similar to XH-51A, but with three-blade main rotor and five seats. For advanced flight study at Langley Research Center, Hampton, Virginia. Normal T-O weight 4,000 lb (1,815 kg).

The following details apply to the standard XH-51A.

TYPE: Two-seat research helicopter.

ROTOR SYSTEM: Four-blade rigid main rotor. Blades, manufactured by Parsons Corp, are of stainless steel with bonded aluminium honeycomb core. Two-blade tail rotor of similar construction to main rotor.

ROTOR DRIVE: Main drive-shaft has diameter of 5 in (12·7 cm) to accommodate main rotor controls. Hub is attached to mast by a ring of bolts through a flange and is made of three laminations for fail-safe strength. Transmission, produced by Steel Products Engineering Division of Kelsey-Hayes, produces a gear ratio of 17½ : 1 through single bevel and two carrier sets of gearing. In the planetary gearing, both the sun gear and the planet gearing are free-floating to allow complete self-alignment. Tail rotor drive-shaft is attached to the top of the transmission and extends along the top of the fuselage.

FUSELAGE: Aluminium alloy semi-monocoque structure.

TAIL UNIT: Fixed horizontal stabiliser to compensate for fuselage aerodynamic pitching moment.

LANDING GEAR: Retractable aluminium alloy skids.

POWER PLANT: One 500 shp Pratt & Whitney (UAC) T74 (PT6B) shaft-turbine engine, mounted aft of transmission in mid-fuselage and fed with air from two flush NASA scoops in top of fuselage aft of main rotor mast fairing. Fuel capacity 80 US gallons (303 litres).

ACCOMMODATION: Two seats side-by-side in enclosed cabin, with dual controls. Space for several hundred pounds of flight test instrumentation.

Lockheed XH-51N high-speed rigid-rotor research helicopter

Lockheed XH-51A compound helicopter fitted with an auxiliary turbojet and wings

DIMENSIONS, EXTERNAL:
Diameter of main rotor   35 ft 0 in (10·67 m)
Main rotor blade chord   13·5 in (34·3 cm)
Diameter of tail rotor   6 ft 0 in (1·83 m)
Length overall (rotors fore and aft)
    40 ft 9 in (12·4 m)
Height overall   8 ft 2½ in (2·50 m)
AREA:
Main rotor disc   962 sq ft (89·37 m²)
WEIGHTS:
Weight empty   2,790 lb (1,265 kg)
Payload, excluding pilot   600 lb (272 kg)
Fuel   530 lb (240 kg)
Max normal T-O weight   4,100 lb (1,860 kg)
PERFORMANCE (at max T-O weight):
Max level speed at S/L (to date)
    151 knots (174 mph; 280 km/h)
Cruising speed at S/L
    139 knots (160 mph; 257 km/h)
Max rate of climb at S/L   2,000 ft (610 m)/min
Hovering ceiling in ground effect
    16,000 ft (4,876 m)
Hovering ceiling out of ground effect
    13,000 ft (3,962 m)
Range with max fuel
    225 nm (260 miles; 418 km)

LOCKHEED MODEL 286

The Model 286 is a five-seat utility helicopter, with rigid rotor, almost identical with the Model 186 described above. Two have been built as a private venture, for demonstration flying, and the first of these flew for the first time on 30 June 1965. Since then, the Model 286 has performed loops, rolls and other aerobatic manoeuvres, demonstrating the stability and control offered by the rigid rotor. FAA certification was received in June 1966.

Normal T-O weight of the Model 286 is 4,700 lb (2,130 kg). It is designed for a max speed of 151 knots (174 mph; 280 km/h) but has attained a speed of 179 knots (206 mph; 332 km/h) in a slight descent.

LOCKHEED CHEYENNE
US Army designation: AH-56A

Following a hotly-contested design competition, Lockheed received on 23 March 1966 a US Army contract for engineering development of an Advanced Aerial Fire Support System (AAFSS) helicopter to replace armed helicopters in current use. The contract included funds for the manufacture and testing of ten prototypes, which were subsequently designated AH-56A Cheyenne. All of these had been delivered to the Army by July 1968.

On 7 January 1968, the US Department of Defense gave approval for the production of 375 AH-56A's, but in the Spring of 1969 the US Army cancelled the production portion of the contract. Lockheed are continuing with development of the Cheyenne.

The AH-56A is a two-seat compound helicopter with small low-set fixed wings and a retractable wheel landing gear. The power plant comprises a General Electric T64 shaft-turbine, driving a four-blade rigid main rotor, four-blade tail rotor mounted at the tip of the port horizontal tail surface, and a pusher propeller at the extreme tail.

Planned duties of the AH-56A include escorting troop-carrying helicopters, fire support and anti-tank missions at speeds ranging from hover to more than 217 knots (250 mph; 402 km/h), by day and night in all weathers. Armament can be fired by both crew members, simultaneously or individually.

TYPE: Two-seat compound helicopter for combat duties.

ROTOR SYSTEM: Four-blade gyro-stabilised rigid main rotor with heavy forged titanium hub. Blades, manufactured by Parsons Corp, are of bonded construction, with U-shaped titanium spar, stainless steel skin and aluminium honeycomb core. Blade thickness/chord ratio tapers from 12% at root to 6% at tip. Blades attached to titanium hub extensions by tension/torsion packs made of 39,000 strands of high-tensile steel wire. Main rotor controlled through a universally-gimballed swashplate. Feathering bearings only. Four-blade tail rotor.

ROTOR DRIVE: Main rotor is shaft-driven through double planetary gears, the rotor mast being 11·6 in (29·5 cm) in diameter. Tail gearbox is driven through a drive train coupled to a shaft of 5·5 in (12·71 cm) diameter. Almost entire engine output is fed to tail gearbox in high-speed cruising flight, to drive propeller; only some 300 hp is diverted to the feathered main rotor to reduce windmilling drag. Transmission system is manufactured by Steel Products Engineering Division of Kelsey Hayes Company.

FUSELAGE: Conventional semi-monocoque light alloy structure, built in three sections: nose, centre fuselage and tail-boom.

WINGS: Small low-set cantilever wings, which almost entirely off-load main rotor in high-speed flight. No wing control surfaces. Both wings have pre-set tab deflections.

Lockheed Model 286 five-seat utility helicopter with rigid rotor

Lockheed AH-56A Cheyenne combat helicopter (3,435 shp General Electric T64-GE-16 engine)

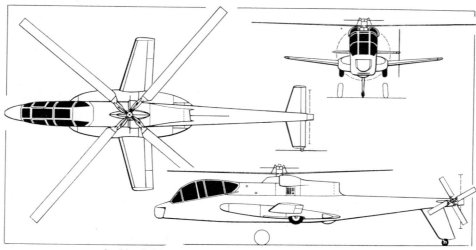

Lockheed AH-56A Cheyenne all-weather combat helicopter

TAIL SURFACES: Fixed cantilever tailplane and ventral fin only. No tail control surfaces.

LANDING GEAR: Tailwheel type, with single wheel on each unit. Main wheels retract rearward into fairings on each side of fuselage. Castoring non-retractable tail-wheel at base of ventral fin. Main gear manufactured by Royal Industries Inc. Brakes on main wheels.

POWER PLANT: One 3,435 shp General Electric T64-GE-16 shaft-turbine engine, driving rotors and tail-mounted Hamilton Standard three-blade variable-pitch propeller, diameter 10 ft 0 in (3·05 m). Fuel tanks in fuselage side and sponsons.

ACCOMMODATION: Pilot and gunner/co-pilot in tandem in enclosed cockpit, with pilot on raised seat to rear. Dual conventional helicopter controls. Access to front seat via upward-hinged canopy-door on starboard side. Rearward-sliding canopy over rear cockpit. Gunner's seat, manufactured by General Electric Co, is mounted on stabilised platform and can swivel through 360°.

ELECTRONICS AND EQUIPMENT: Comprehensive equipment for all-weather flight includes automatic terrain-following radar supplied by Norden Division of United Aircraft Corp, automatic flight control system by Honeywell,

Doppler radar and inertial navigation system by General Precision Laboratories. APU in rear of port landing gear fairing.

ARMAMENT: Nose turret, able to swivel through 180°, mounts interchangeable Aeronutronic XM129 40-mm grenade launcher or 7·62-mm General Electric Minigun. Non-retractable belly turret, able to swivel through 360°, carries an Aeronutronic XM140 30-mm cannon. Two attachments under each wing for Hughes TOW anti-tank missiles, 2·75-in rocket pods, etc. Advanced optical sight system.

DIMENSIONS, EXTERNAL:

Diameter of main rotor	50 ft 4·8 in (15·36 m)
Main rotor blade chord	28·0 in (71·0 cm)
Diameter of tail rotor	10 ft 0 in (3·05 m)
Wing span	26 ft 8½ in (8·14 m)
Length overall	60 ft 0·9 in (18·31 m)
Length, rotors static	54 ft 8 in (16·66 m)
Height overall	13 ft 8½ in (4·18 m)

AREA:

Wings, gross	130 sq ft (12·07 m²)

WEIGHTS:

Weight empty	11,725 lb (5,320 kg)
Design T-O weight	16,995 lb (7,710 kg)
VTOL overload T-O weight	22,000 lb (9,980 kg)
Max overload T-O weight (STOL, ferry mission)	30,000 lb (13,608 kg)

PERFORMANCE (designed, at max T-O weight):

Max level speed at S/L
220 knots (253 mph; 408 km/h)
Max cruising speed at S/L
210 knots (242 mph; 389 km/h)
Max cruising speed at 10,000 ft (3,050 m)
205 knots (236 mph; 380 km/h)
Max rate of climb at S/L 3,420 ft (1,040 m)/min
Service ceiling 26,000 ft (7,925 m)
Hovering ceiling out of ground effect
10,600 ft (3,230 m)
Range at design gross weight, with external fuselage tank, 10% reserve
755 nm (875 miles; 1,400 km)
Ferry range, STOL, 10% reserve
1,640 nm (1,890 miles; 4,650 km)

LOCKHEED L-1011-1 (MODEL 193) TRISTAR

In January 1966, Lockheed-California began a study of future requirements in the short/medium-haul airliner market. The design which emerged, known as the L-1011 (Lockheed Model 193 TriStar), was influenced by the published requirements of American Airlines, who specified optimum payload-range performance over the Chicago-Los Angeles route, coupled with an ability to take off from comparatively short runways with full payload.

The original design centred around a twin-turbofan configuration. Discussions which followed with American domestic carriers led to the eventual selection of a three-engined configuration, and the Rolls-Royce RB.211 high by-pass ratio turbofan was chosen as power plant.

In June 1968 the L-1011 TriStar moved to the production design stage. Construction of the first aircraft began in March 1969, with roll-out scheduled for September 1970, first flight in November 1970 and FAA certification and introduction into service in November 1971.

Two versions of the Lockheed L-1011 have been announced:

L-1011-1. This is the original model, designed for the short/medium-haul airliner market, and which is described in detail below.

L-1011-8. Long-range intercontinental version, announced in September 1969; a committal decision is dependent upon receipt of orders. Described separately.

Orders and options for 181 L-1011-1 aircraft have been received, as follows:

Eastern Air Lines	50
Delta Airlines	24
Northeast Airlines	8
Trans World Airlines	44
Air Holdings	50 (incl 10 for Air Canada, 2 for Air Jamaica)
Finance groups	5

TYPE: Three-turbofan commercial transport.

WINGS: Cantilever low-wing monoplane. Special Lockheed aerofoil sections. Dihedral at trailing-edge: 7° 31′ on inner wings, 5° 30′ outboard. Sweepback at quarter-chord 35°. The wing consists of a centre-section, passing through the lower fuselage, and an outer wing panel on each side. It is of conventional fail-safe construction, with aluminium surfaces, ribs and spars, and integral fuel tanks. Hydraulically-powered aluminium ailerons of conventional two-spar box construction, with honeycomb trailing-edge, in inboard (high-speed) and outboard (low-speed) sections on each wing, operate in conjunction with flight spoilers. The low-speed ailerons extend from approximately 80% of semi-span to within 10 in (25·4 cm) of the wingtips, the high-speed ailerons extend from approximately WBL 387 to WBL 480 on each wing. Double-slotted Fowler trailing-edge flaps, constructed of aluminium and aluminium-honeycomb. Each flap segment consists of a honeycomb trailing-edge, a front spar, ribs, skin panels, carriages,

and tracks mounted on the forward segment to provide for extension and rotation of the aft segment. Four aluminium leading-edge slats outboard of engine pylon on each wing. Each segment is mounted to two roller supported tracks and extends in a circular motion down and forward for take-off and landing. Three Krueger leading-edge flaps inboard of engine pylon on each wing, made of aluminium alloy castings and sheet metal fairings. A sheet metal extension fairing, actuated by a linkage system during flap rotation, forms the forward section of the extended flap. Six spoilers on the upper surface of each wing, two inboard and four outboard of the high-speed aileron, constructed from bonded sheet-metal tapered honeycomb. No trim-tabs. Flight controls fully powered. Each control surface system is controlled by a multiple redundant servo system that is powered by four independent and separate hydraulic sources. Thermal de-icing of wing leading-edge slats by engine-bleed air.

FUSELAGE: Semi-monocoque structure of aluminium alloy. Constant cross-sectional diameter of 19 ft 7 in (5·97 m) for most of the length. Bonding utilised in skin joints, for attaching skin-doublers at joints and around openings to improve fatigue life. Skins and stringers supported by frames spaced at 20-in (0·51-m) intervals. These frames, with the exception of main frames and door-edge members, are 3 in (7·62 cm) deep at the sides of the cabin, increasing progressively to a depth of 6 in (15·24 cm) at the top of the fuselage and below the floor.

TAIL UNIT: Conventional cantilever structure, consisting of variable-incidence horizontal tailplane-elevator assembly and vertical fin and rudder. Primary loads of the fin are carried by a four-spar box-beam structure, with ribs spaced at approx 20-in (0·51-m) centres. The rudder, which is in two segments, comprises forward and aft spars, honeycomb trailing-edges, hinge and actuator back-up ribs, sheet metal formers, box surface panels and leading-edge fairings. Elevators are of similar construction. Truss members for the tailplane centre-section are built up from forged and extruded sections. Outboard of the centre-section, construction is similar to that of the fin box-beam, leading- and trailing-edges. The elevators are linked mechanically to the tailplane actuation gear, to modify its camber and improve its effectiveness. No trim-tabs. Controls are fully powered, the hydraulic servo actuators receiving power from four independent hydraulic sources, under control of avionic flight control system. Control feel is provided, with the force gradient scheduled as a function of flight condition. No de-icing equipment.

LANDING GEAR: Hydraulically-retractable tricycle type, produced by Menasco Manufacturing. Twin-wheel units in tandem on each main gear; twin wheels on nose gear, which is steerable 65° on either side. Nose-wheels retract forward into fuselage. Main wheels retract inward into fuselage wheel-wells. Oleo-pneumatic struts in main and nose landing gear. B. F. Goodrich forged aluminium alloy wheels of split construction. Main wheels carry tubeless tyres size 50 × 20, Type VIII, pressure 150-165 lb/sq in (10·5-11·6 kg/cm²) for short- to medium-range operational weights, 175 lb/sq in (12·3 kg/cm²) for max-range weight. Nose-wheels carry tubeless tyres size 36 × 11, Type VII, pressure 185 lb/sq in (13·0 kg/cm²). Hydraulically-operated brakes, controlled by the rudder pedals. Anti-skid units, with individual wheel skid and modulated control, installed in the normal and alternative braking systems.

POWER PLANT: Three Rolls-Royce RB.211-22-02 three-shaft turbofan engines, each rated at 40,600 lb (18,415 kg) st. Two engines mounted in pods on pylons under the wings, the third mounted in the rear fuselage at the base of the fin. Engine bleed-air is used to anti-ice the engine inlet lips. Two integral fuel tanks in each wing; inboard tank capacity 7,767 US gallons (29,400 litres), outboard tank capacity 3,883 US gallons (14,700 litres). Total fuel capacity 23,300 US gallons (88,200 litres). Pressure refuelling points in wing leading-edges. Oil capacity approx 14·6 US gallons (55·4 litres).

ACCOMMODATION: Crew of 13. First-class and coach mixed accommodation for 244 passengers, with a maximum of 345 in all-economy configuration. Alternative intermediate seating capacities are provided by using eight seat-tracks which permit 6, 8 or 9-abreast seating, with two full-length aisles. Underfloor galley. Seven lavatories are provided, two forward and five aft. Three passenger doors of the inward-opening plug type on each side of the fuselage, one pair immediately aft of flight deck, one pair forward of wing, one pair aft of wing. Two emergency exit doors, on each side of fuselage, at rear of cabin. Baggage and freight compartments beneath floor, able to accommodate eight containers totalling 2,528 cu ft (71·58 m³) and 750 cu ft (21·24 m³) of bulk cargo.

SYSTEMS: Air-conditioning and pressurisation system, using engine-bleed air or APU air combined with air-cycle refrigeration. Pressurisation system maintains equivalent of 8,000 ft (2,440 m) conditions to 42,000 ft (12,800 m). Four independent 3,000 lb/sq in (210 kg/cm²) hydraulic systems provide power for the primary flight control surfaces, normal brake power, landing gear retraction and nose-wheel steering, etc. Electrical system includes four 115/200V 400 c/s generators, one on each engine and one driven by the APU, which is sited in the aft fuselage. APU provides ground and in-flight power, to an altitude of 30,000 ft (9,145 m), producing both shaft and pneumatic power for utilisation by the electric, environmental control and hydraulic systems. Integral electric heaters are used to anti-ice windshields, pitot masts and total temperature probes.

ELECTRONICS AND EQUIPMENT: Standard equipment includes two ARINC 546 VHF communication transceivers, two ARINC 547 VHF navigation systems, two ARINC 568 interrogator units, an ARINC 564 weather radar system, two ARINC 532D air traffic control transponders, partial provision for a dual collision system, three vertical gyros, and full blind-flying instrumentation. Space is provided for future installation of two ARINC 533A HF transceivers and of a dual SATCOM system in accordance with ARINC 546A.

DIMENSIONS, EXTERNAL:

Wing span	155 ft 4 in (47·34 m)
Wing chord at root	34 ft 4 in (10·46 m)
Wing chord at tip	10 ft 3 in (3·12 m)
Wing aspect ratio	6·95
Length overall	177 ft 8½ in (54·16 m)
Height overall	55 ft 4 in (16·87 m)
Tailplane span	71 ft 7 in (21·82 m)
Wheel track	36 ft 0 in (10·97 m)
Wheelbase	70 ft 0 in (21·34 m)
Passenger doors (6):	
Height	6 ft 4 in (1·93 m)
Width	3 ft 6 in (1·07 m)
Height to sill	15 ft 1 in (4·60 m)
Emergency passenger doors (2):	
Height	5 ft 0 in (1·52 m)
Width	2 ft 0 in (0·61 m)
Height to sill	15 ft 1 in (4·60 m)
Baggage and freight compartment doors (forward and centre):	
Height	5 ft 8 in (1·73 m)
Width	5 ft 10 in (1·78 m)
Height to sill	8 ft 7 in (2·62 m)
Baggage and freight compartment doors (aft):	
Height	4 ft 0 in (1·22 m)
Width	3 ft 8 in (1·12 m)
Height to sill	9 ft 7 in (2·92 m)

DIMENSIONS, INTERNAL:

Cabin, excluding flight deck and underfloor galley:

Length	135 ft 5 in (41·28 m)
Max width	18 ft 11 in (5·77 m)
Max height	8 ft 2 in (2·49 m)
Floor area	2,337 sq ft (217·12 m²)
Volume	16,000 cu ft (453 m³)
Baggage holds, underfloor, containerised:	
Volume	2,528 cu ft (71·58 m³)
Freight hold, underfloor, bulk cargo:	
Volume	750 cu ft (21·24 m³)

AREAS:

Wings, gross	3,755 sq ft (348·85 m²)
Ailerons (total)	80 sq ft (7·43 m²)
Trailing-edge flaps (total)	268 sq ft (24·90 m²)
Leading-edge flaps (total):	
Inboard Krueger	70 sq ft (6·50 m²)
Outboard slats	118 sq ft (10·96 m²)
Spoilers (total)	122 sq ft (11·33 m²)
Fin	550 sq ft (51·10 m²)
Rudder	128 sq ft (11·89 m²)
Tailplane	1,282 sq ft (119·10 m²)

WEIGHTS AND LOADING:

Manufacturer's empty weight	208,782 lb (94,703 kg)
Operating empty weight	225,491 lb (102,280 kg)
Max payload	87,811 lb (39,830 kg)
Max T-O weight	409,000 lb (185,552 kg)
Max ramp weight	411,000 lb (186,423 kg)
Max "zero fuel" weight	308,500 lb (139,935 kg)
Max landing weight	348,000 lb (157,848 kg)
Max wing loading	118·5 lb/sq ft (578·5 kg/m²)

PERFORMANCE (estimated, at max T-O weight):

Max level speed at 30,000 ft (9,145 m)
507 knots (583 mph; 939 km/h)
Max diving speed (structural limitations) Mach 0·95 or 435 knots (500 mph; 806 km/h) CAS
Max cruising speed at 35,000 ft (10,670 m)
Mach 0·85
Econ cruising speed at 35,000 ft (10,670 m)
Mach 0·80
Stalling speed (take-off configuration)
129 knots (148 mph; 238 km/h) EAS
Stalling speed (cruise configuration)
166 knots (190 mph; 306 km/h) EAS

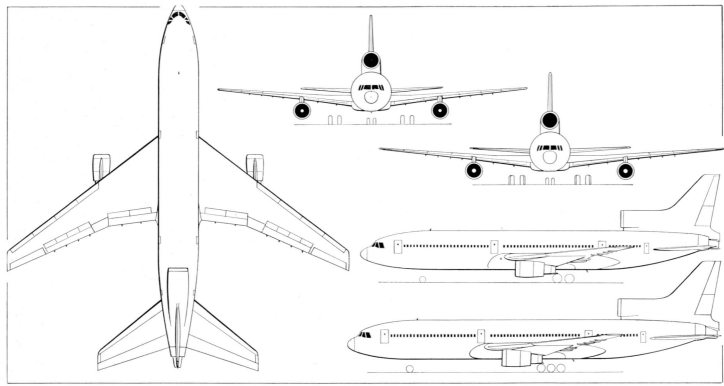

Three-view drawing of the Lockheed L-1011-8 TriStar and head-on and side views (top and centre right) of the L-1011-1

Rate of climb at S/L	2,800 ft (853 m)/min
Service ceiling	35,000 ft (10,670 m)
T-O run	8,394 ft (2,558 m)
T-O to 35 ft (10·7 m)	9,835 ft (2,997 m)
Landing from 50 ft (15 m)	3,895 ft (1,187 m)
Landing run	2,594 ft (790 m)

Range with max fuel and 40,000 lb = 18,145 kg payload at Mach 0·85
3,395 nm (3,915 miles; 6,300 km)
Range with max payload (256 passengers, 5,000 lb = 2,270 kg cargo)
2,850 nm (3,287 miles; 5,290 km)

LOCKHEED L-1011-8
TRISTAR

In September 1969 Lockheed-California announced details of a proposed intercontinental version of the L-1011 TriStar airliner. A decision to proceed to the production stage is contingent upon the receipt of orders.

The L-1011-8 differs from the L-1011-1 in overall size, weights and power plant. The fuselage is lengthened by 3 ft 4 in (1·02 m) by the addition of a constant-section plug aft of the wing trailing-edge. The wing has been enlarged by approximately 20 per cent, to maintain reasonable wing loadings at the higher operating weights, and there are comparable increases in the tailplane span and the height and chord of the vertical stabiliser. A tricycle landing gear arrangement is retained, but each main wheel bogie carries six wheels instead of four, with the centre wheels on each bogie having a wider track.

Basic engine proposed for the -8 TriStar is the Rolls-Royce RB.211-56, rated at 53,500 lb (24,265 kg) st, for delivery in 1973. Eighteen months after entry into service, the same engine could be modified to RB.211-57 rating of 55,000 lb (24,950 kg) st.

The detailed description of the L-1011-1 applies also to the L-1011-8 except for the following:

WINGS: Dihedral at wing reference plane 7° 30′. The high-speed aileron extends from approximately WBL 414 to WBL 510. There are six spoilers on the upper surface of each wing, three inboard of the high-speed aileron and three outboard. Full-span leading-edge slats are utilised, with three slat segments inboard of each engine pylon and four outboard.

LANDING GEAR: The two main gear assemblies will each carry six wheels. Main wheels fitted with tubeless tyres size 49 × 17, Type VII, with reinforced tread, pressure 191 lb/sq in (13·4 kg/cm²) for short/medium-range operational weights, 175 lb/sq in (12·3 kg/cm²) for max-range weights. Nose wheels fitted with tubeless tyres size 40 × 14, Type VII with reinforced tread, pressure 172 lb/sq in (12·1 kg/cm²) for all weights.

POWER PLANT: Three Rolls-Royce RB.211-56 three-shaft turbofan engines, each rated at 53,500 lb (24,265 kg) st. Two integral fuel tanks in each wing; inboard tank capacity 14,400 US gallons (54,506 litres), outboard tank capacity 7,200 US gallons (27,253 litres). Total fuel capacity 43,200 US gallons (163,523 litres).

ACCOMMODATION: Crew of 11. By replacing the aft Type 'I' emergency exits with Type 'A' exits and using 10-abreast high-density seating, a maximum of 400 passengers can be accommodated in a single-class arrangement. Baggage and freight compartments beneath floor, able to accommodate 18 ATA LD-3 containers, totalling 2,844 cu ft (80·53 m³), and 465 cu ft (13·17 m³) of bulk cargo.

ELECTRONICS AND EQUIPMENT: The navigation, communications and radar systems meet ARINC requirements and FAA regulations. Three ARINC standard inertial navigators and two navigation computers form primary navigation system. Two VHF navigation units, containing VOR, ILS and localiser functions, are installed in accordance with ARINC 547. Two DME interrogator units to ARINC 568 are installed together with two ARINC 550 ADF receivers. Two radio altimeters, in accordance with ARINC 552, to provide altitude-above-ground information for pilots, all-weather landing system and the inertial navigation computers. The communications systems consist of three ARINC 566 VHF communications transceivers and two ARINC 533 HF transceivers. ARINC 564 weather radar. Two ARINC 532 air traffic control transponders, two ARINC 565 air data computer systems, an ARINC 542 flight recorder and an ARINC 557 cockpit voice recorder. Space provided for possible future installation of a dual SATCOM system in accordance with ARINC 546A, dual collision avoidance system and an Airborne Integrated Data System (AIDS). An automatic flight control system, an avionic flight control system, a stability augmentation system and an autoland system, when coupled to the navigation, communications and radar systems, provide all-weather take-off, flying and landing capability. The L-1011-8 will be certificated initially to permit FAA Category II all-weather landings. Special equipment includes AFCS mode annunciator panel, and area navigation system.

DIMENSIONS, EXTERNAL:

Wing span	170 ft 0 in (51·82 m)
Wing chord at root	37 ft 10 in (11·53 m)
Wing chord at tip	11 ft 6 in (3·50 m)
Wing aspect ratio	6·91
Length overall	183 ft 5 in (55·91 m)
Height overall	59 ft 5 in (18·11 m)
Tailplane span	79 ft 3 in (24·16 m)
Wheel track	33 ft 6 in (10·21 m)
Wheelbase	70 ft 11½ in (21·63 m)

Passenger doors (2):
As L-1011-1 except:
Height to sill   15 ft 6 in (4·72 m)
Emergency passenger doors (2);
As L-1011-1 except:
Height to sill   15 ft 6 in (4·72 m)

Baggage and freight compartment doors (fwd and centre):
As L-1011-1 except:
Height to sill   9 ft 2 in (2·79 m)

DIMENSIONS, INTERNAL:
Cabin, excluding flight deck:

Length	139 ft 3 in (42·44 m)
Max width	18 ft 11 in (5·77 m)
Max height	7 ft 11 in (2·41 m)
Floor area	2,381 sq ft (221·2 m²)
Volume	16,500 cu ft (467·2 m³)

Baggage holds, underfloor, containerised:
Volume   2,844 cu ft (80·53 m³)
Freight hold, underfloor, bulk cargo:
Volume   465 cu ft (13·17 m³)

AREAS:

Wings, gross	4,180 sq ft (388·3 m²)
Ailerons (total)	187 sq ft (17·37 m²)
Trailing-edge flaps (total)	815 sq ft (75·72 m²)
Leading-edge flaps (total)	392 sq ft (36·42 m²)
Spoilers (total)	277 sq ft (25·73 m²)
Fin	660 sq ft (61·32 m²)
Rudder	188 sq ft (17·47 m²)
Tailplane	1,570 sq ft (145·9 m²)
Elevators (total)	312 sq ft (28·99 m²)

WEIGHTS AND LOADING (estimated):

Max payload	over 100,000 lb (45,355 kg)
Max T-O weight	595,000 lb (269,885 kg)
Max ramp weight	598,000 lb (271,245 kg)
Max "zero fuel" weight	380,000 lb (172,365 kg)
Max landing weight	425,000 lb (192,775 kg)
Max wing loading	142·5 lb/sq ft (695·7 kg/m²)

PERFORMANCE (estimated at max T-O weight):
Max diving speed
Mach 0·95 or 435 knots (500 mph; 804 km/h) CAS
Max cruising speed at 35,000 ft (10,670 m)
Mach 0·88
Econ cruising speed at 35,000 ft (10,670 m)
Mach 0·83
Stalling speed (take-off configuration)
135·5 knots (156 mph; 251 km/h) EAS
Stalling speed (cruise configuration)
161·5 knots (186 mph; 300 km/h) EAS
Rate of climb at S/L   2,500 ft (762 m)/min
Service ceiling at 500,000 lb (226,795 kg) AUW
35,000 ft (10,670 m)
Service ceiling, one engine out, at max landing weight   22,300 ft (6,797 m)
T-O run   9,650 ft (2,941 m)
T-O to 35 ft (10·7 m)   11,300 ft (3,444 m)
Landing from 50 ft (15 m)   5,460 ft (1,664 m)
Landing run   3,790 ft (1,155 m)
Range, with max fuel, Mach 0·85, 31,000 lb (14,060 kg) payload
5,950 nm (6,850 miles; 11,024 km)
Range, with max fuel, Mach 0·83, 31,000 lb (14,060 kg) payload
6,120 nm (7,045 miles; 11,337 km)
Range, with max payload, Mach 0·85
3,970 nm (4,570 miles; 7,354 km)
Range, with max payload, Mach 0·83
4,070 nm (4,685 miles; 7,539 km)

LOCKHEED-GEORGIA COMPANY

86 South Cobb Drive, Marietta, Georgia 30060

Lockheed-Georgia's main building at Marietta covers 76 acres and is believed to be the largest aircraft production plant under one roof in the world. Aircraft in current production on its assembly lines are the C-130 Hercules turboprop transport, the JetStar light jet transport and the C-5 Galaxy heavy logistics transport, the largest aeroplane yet ordered into production anywhere in the world.

Work on the XV-4B Hummingbird II jet-lift research programme has now ended; details of this aircraft may be found in the 1969-70 *Jane's*.

LOCKHEED MODEL 382 HERCULES

USAF designations: C-130, AC-130, HC-130, JC-130, RC-130 and WC-130.
US Navy designations: C-130, EC-130 and LC-130
US Marine Corps designation: KC-130
US Coast Guard designations: EC-130 and HC-130

The C-130 was designed to a specification issued by the USAF Tactical Air Command in 1951. Lockheed was awarded its first production contract for the C-130A in September 1952, and a total of 461 C-130A's and C-130B's was manufactured. Details of these basic versions and their many variants for special duties can be found in the 1967/68 *Jane's*. Later military versions of the C-130 are as follows:

C-130E (Lockheed Model 382-446). Extended-range development of C-130B, with four 4,050 eshp T56-A-7A turboprop engines and two 1,360 US gallon (5,145 litre) underwing fuel tanks. Normal max T-O weight is 155,000 lb (70,310 kg). Take-off at overload gross weight of 175,000 lb (79,380 kg) increases the range and endurance capabilities, with certain operating restrictions at this higher weight. Total of 510 ordered, which includes USAF Tactical Air Command (363), US Navy (12), US Coast Guard (1), Canadian Armed Forces (24), Colombian Air Force (2), Iranian Air Force (28), Turkish Air Force (5), Brazilian Air Force (11), Swedish Air Force (2), Saudi-Arabian Air Force (9), Royal Australian Air Force (12), Argentine Air Force (3), USAF Aerospace Rescue and Recovery Service (14), Libyan Air Force (6), Peruvian Air Force (6) and Norwegian Air Force (6). First C-130E flew on 25 August 1961. Deliveries began in April 1962.

AC-130E. A close-support conversion of the Hercules, armed with four 20-mm multi-barrel cannon and four 7·62-mm Miniguns, was evaluated at Wright-Patterson AFB in the Summer of 1967. Subsequently, LTV was awarded a contract to modify seven aircraft to full AC-130 standard, with guns, searchlight and sensors, including forward-looking infra-red target acquisition equipment and direct-view image intensification sights. In service in Vietnam in 1970.

EC-130E. Special version of C-130E for US Coast Guard.

C-130F (formerly GV-1U). Seven for transport duties with US Navy. Similar to KC-130F, but without underwing pylons and internal refuelling equipment. AUW 135,000 lb (61,235 kg).

WC-130E. Weather reconnaissance version operated by the USAF.

KC-130F (formerly GV-1). Forty-six for US Marine Corps. Deliveries completed in November 1962. Assault transport, basically similar to C-130B, with four 4,050 eshp Allison T56-A-7 turboprops. Equipped for in-flight refuelling to service two jet aircraft simultaneously. Entire refuelling equipment can be quickly and easily installed and removed. Two C-130A's loaned to USMC in the Summer of 1957 for flight refuelling tests. The production tanker version, first flown on 22 January 1960, has a tankage capacity of 3,600 US gallons (13,620 litres) in its cargo compartment. Able to fly 1,000 miles (1,600 km) at cruise ceiling at 340 mph (547 km/h), and transfer 31,000 lb (14,060 kg) of fuel at 25,000 ft (7,620 m) at a refuelling speed of 355 mph (571 km/h) with normal military reserves. Normal crew of five to seven.

C-130H. Basically a C-130E with more powerful engines. T56-A-15 turboprops rated at 4,910 eshp for take-off, but limited to 4,500 eshp. Five delivered to Royal New Zealand Air Force.

HC-130H. Lockheed was awarded two initial contracts in September 1963 for this extended-range air search, rescue and recovery version to be utilised by the Aerospace Rescue and Recovery Service of the USAF for aerial recovery of personnel or equipment and other duties. The US Coast Guard subsequently ordered three. New folding nose-mounted recovery system makes possible repeated pick-ups from ground of persons or objects weighing up to 500 lb (227 kg) including the recoverable gear. Four 4,910 eshp (limited to 4,500 eshp) Allison T56-A-15 turboprop engines, each driving a Hamilton Standard 54H60-91 four-blade constant-speed propeller, diameter 13 ft 6 in (4·11 m). Normal fuel tankage as for C-130E. Provision for installing two 1,800 US gallon (6,814 litres) tanks in cargo compartment. Normal crew of 10, consisting of pilot, co-pilot, navigator, 2 flight mechanics,

Lockheed HC-130P Hercules search and rescue and recovery aircraft (*T. Matsuzaki*)

radio operator, 2 loadmasters and 2 para-rescue technicians, with provision for additional pilot and navigator for long missions. Standard equipment includes four 6-man rafts, two litters, bunks, 16 personnel kits, recovery winches, 10 flare launchers. Total of 66 delivered, of which the first one flew on 8 December 1964.

The recovery system fitted to the HC-130H was designed by the Robert Fulton Company. It involves dropping a personnel kit to the person to be rescued, who puts on a harnessed suit and deploys a 24 ft × 6 ft (7·32 m × 1·83 m) helium-filled balloon on 500 ft (152 m) of nylon line attached to the harness. The HC-130H is flown at 140-160 mph (220-260 km/h) into wind at just under 500 ft (152 m) so that it traps the nylon line in its nose recovery yoke. The balloon breaks away at a weak link in the line and the person to be rescued is pulled off the ground at a force less than that experienced in parachuting. He trails back beneath the fuselage, in such a way that his life-line can be grapnelled from the open cargo ramp and passed over a davit for winching in. The gear is so designed that the possibility of the rescued man striking the aircraft is avoided. Teflon lines from the aircraft's nose to each wing-tip deflect the nylon life-line past the airframe if it misses the yoke.

Live pick-ups have been made successfully from land and water. Recovery of two persons simultaneously has also been accomplished.

C-130K (C.Mk 1). This version is basically a C-130H, modified for use by the Royal Air Force. Much of the electronics and instrumentation are of UK manufacture. Miscellaneous items such as tie-down fittings are also being supplied by the UK. Performance, weights, dimensions and other characteristics are virtually the same as those of the C-130H. Sixty-six delivered for service with RAF Air Support Command. First of these flew on 19 October 1966.

HC-130N. Search and rescue version for recovery of aircrew and retrieval of space capsules after re-entry, using advanced direction-finding equipment. Fifteen ordered for USAF in 1969.

HC-130P. Twenty HC-130H's have been modified into HC-130P's with capability of refuelling helicopters in flight, and for mid-air retrieval of parachute-borne payloads. Modification involves the addition of refuelling drogue pods and associated plumbing. A typical helicopter refuelling mission will involve taking off at an AUW of 155,000 lb (70,310 kg), with 73,600 lb (33,385 kg) of fuel on board, rendezvousing with the helicopters at a radius of 575 miles (925 km), transferring 48,500 lb (22,000 kg) of fuel to the helicopters and returning 575 miles (925 km) to the point of origin.

LC-130R. Basically a C-130H with wheel-ski gear and 4,500 eshp T56-A-16 engines, ordered by the US Navy. Main skis are each approximately 20 ft 0 in (6·10 m) long by 5 ft 6 in (1·68 m) wide. The nose ski is approximately 10 ft 0 in (3·05 m) long by 5 ft 6 in (1·68 m) wide. The total ski installation weighs approximately 5,600 lb (2,540 kg). The main skis have 8° nose-up and nose-down pitch and the nose skis have 15° nose-up and nose-down pitch, to enable them to follow uneven terrain. The load-bearing surfaces of the skis are coated with Teflon plastic to reduce friction and resist ice adhesion. Provision is made for fitting JATO units.

There are also six commercial versions of the Hercules and these are described separately.

The C-130 is able to deliver single loads of up to 14,000 lb (6,350 kg) by the low-level extraction method. This involves making a touch-and-go landing or fly-past 4-5 ft (1·2-1·5 m) above the ground with the rear loading ramp open. The aircraft trails a hook which is attached by cable to the palletized cargo. The hook engages a steel cable on the ground and the cargo is extracted from the aircraft and brought to a stop on the ground in about 100 ft (30 m) by an energy absorption system manufactured by All American Engineering of Wilmington, Delaware. An alternative extraction technique involves deploying a 22 ft (6·70 m) ribbon parachute to drag the pallet from the cabin.

It was announced on 10 December 1969 that two C-130A's are to be modified to launch and control target drone aircraft under a £1 million contract, placed with Lockheed Aircraft Service Company by the US Navy. Modifications include strengthening of the wings, fitment of drone pylons and installation of two launch stations and a three-man tracking and control station in each aircraft. Scheduled for delivery in August 1970, each aircraft will be able to launch and control four drones. (See 1967-68 *Jane's* for details of earlier, similar aircraft).

By January 1970 firm orders for all versions of the C-130 totalled 1,137, of which 1,089 had been delivered.

The following details refer specifically to the standard C-130E, except where indicated otherwise:—

TYPE: Medium/long-range combat transport.

WINGS: Cantilever high-wing monoplane. Wing section NACA 64A318 at root, NACA 64A412 at tip. Dihedral 2° 30'. Incidence 3° at root, 0° at tip. Sweepback at quarter-chord 0°. All-metal two-spar stressed-skin structure, with integrally-stiffened tapered machined skin panels up to 48 ft 0 in (14·63 m) long. Conventional aluminium alloy ailerons have tandem-piston hydraulic boost, operated by either of two independent hydraulic systems. Lockheed-Fowler aluminium alloy trailing-edge flaps. Trim-tabs on ailerons. Leading-edge anti-iced by hot air bled from engines.

FUSELAGE: Semi-monocoque structure of aluminium and magnesium alloys.

TAIL UNIT: Cantilever all-metal stressed-skin structure. Fixed-incidence tailplane. Trim-tabs on elevator and rudder. Elevator tabs use AC electrical power as primary source and DC as emergency source. Control surfaces have tandem-piston hydraulic boost. Hot-air anti-icing of tailplane leading-edge, by engine-bleed air.

LANDING GEAR: Hydraulically-retractable tricycle type. Each main unit has two wheels in tandem, retracting into fairings built onto the sides of the fuselage. Nose unit has twin wheels and is steerable through 60° each side of centre. Oleo shock-absorbers. Tyre pressure 45-95 lb/sq in (3·16-6·68 kg/cm²) depending on mission. Hydraulic brakes with anti-skid units. Retractable combination wheel-skis available.

POWER PLANT: Four 4,050 eshp Allison T56-A-7A turboprop engines, each driving a Hamilton Standard type 54H60 four-blade constant-speed fully-feathering reversible-pitch propeller, diameter 13 ft 6 in (4·11 m). Eight Aerojet-

Lockheed 100-20 civil Hercules (four 4,508 eshp Allison 501-D22A turboprop engines) operated by Red Dodge Aviation   (*Norman E. Taylor*)

General 15KS-1000 JATO units (each 1,000 lb = 455 kg st for 15 sec) can be carried. Fuel in six integral tanks in wings, with total capacity of 6,960 US gallons (26,344 litres) and two underwing pylon tanks, each with capacity of 1,360 US gallons (5,146 litres). Total fuel capacity 9,680 US gallons (36,636 litres). Single pressure refuelling point in starboard wheel well. Fillers for overwing gravity fuelling. Oil capacity 48 US gallons (182 litres).

ACCOMMODATION: Crew of four on flight deck, comprising pilot, co-pilot, navigator and systems manager. Provision for fifth man to supervise loading. Sleeping quarters for relief crew, and galley. Flight deck and main cabin pressurised and air-conditioned. Standard complements are as follows: troops (max) 92, paratroops (max) 64, litters 74 and 2 attendants. As a cargo carrier, loads can include heavy equipment such as a 26,640 lb (12,080 kg) type F.6 refuelling trailer or a 155-mm howitzer and its high-speed tractor. Up to six preloaded pallets of freight can be carried. As a missile carrier can accommodate 3 × Honest John; 2 × Nike-Hercules plus boosters; 2 × Sergeant; 1 × Bomarc or 1 × Matador with, in most cases, related handling and launching equipment. Hydraulically-operated main loading door and ramp at rear of cabin. Paratroop door on each side aft of landing gear fairing.

SYSTEMS: Air-conditioning and pressurisation system max pressure differential 7·5 lb/sq in (0·53 kg/cm²). Two independent hydraulic systems, pressure 3,000 lb/sq in (210 kg/cm²). Electrical system supplied by four 40kVA AC generators, plus one 20kVA auxiliary generator driven by APU. AiResearch gas-turbine APU for engine starting, engine pre-heat, ground air-conditioning and driving air-turbine motor with alternator.

DIMENSIONS, EXTERNAL:
Wing span	132 ft 7 in (40·41 m)
Wing chord at root	16 ft 0 in (4·88 m)
Wing chord, mean	13 ft 8½ in (4·16 m)
Wing aspect ratio	10·09
Length overall:	
all except HC-130H	97 ft 9 in (29·78 m)
HC-130H, recovery system folded	98 ft 9 in (30·10 m)
HC-130H, recovery system spread	106 ft 4 in (32·41 m)
Height over tail	38 ft 3 in (11·66 m)
Tailplane span	52 ft 8 in (16·05 m)
Wheel track	14 ft 3 in (4·35 m)
Wheelbase	32 ft 0¾ in (9·77 m)
Main cargo door (rear of cabin):	
Height	9 ft 1 in (2·77 m)
Width	10 ft 0 in (3·05 m)
Height to sill	3 ft 5 in (1·03 m)
Paratroop doors (each):	
Height	6 ft 0 in (1·83 m)
Width	3 ft 0 in (0·91 m)
Height to sill	3 ft 5 in (1·03 m)

DIMENSIONS, INTERNAL:
Cabin, excluding flight deck:	
Length, without ramp	41 ft 5 in (12·60 m)
Length, with ramp	51 ft 8½ in (15·76 m)
Max width	10 ft 3 in (3·13 m)
Max height	9 ft 2¼ in (2·81 m)
Floor area, excluding ramp	425 sq ft (39·5 m²)
Volume, including ramp	4,300 cu ft (121·7 m³)

AREAS:
Wings, gross	1,745 sq ft (162·12 m²)
Ailerons (total)	110 sq ft (10·22 m²)
Trailing-edge flaps (total)	342 sq ft (31·77 m²)

Fin	225 sq ft (20·90 m²)
Rudder, including tab	75 sq ft (6·97 m²)
Tailplane	381 sq ft (35·40 m²)
Elevators, including tabs	155 sq ft (14·40 m²)

WEIGHTS AND LOADINGS:
Weight empty, equipped:	
C-130E	72,892 lb (33,063 kg)
C-130H	72,892 lb (33,063 kg)
C-130K	72,367 lb (32,825 kg)
Max payload:	
C-130E, H	45,000 lb (20 412 kg)
C-130K	45,525 lb (20,650 kg)
Max normal T-O weight:	
C-130E, H, K, HC-130H, P	155,000 lb (70,310 kg)
Max overload T-O weight:	
C-130E, H, K, HC-130H, P	175,000 lb (79,380 kg)
Max zero fuel weight:	
C-130E, H, K	117,892 lb (53,475 kg)
Max landing weight	130,000 lb (58,970 kg)
Max wing loading:	
C-130E, H, K	89 lb/sq ft (434·5 kg/m²)
Max power loading:	
C-130E	9·6 lb/eshp (4·35 kg/eshp)
C-130H, K	8·6 lb/eshp (3·9 kg/eshp)

PERFORMANCE (at max T-O weight, unless indicated otherwise):
Max level speed:	
C-130E, H, K, HC-130H, P	333 knots (384 mph; 618 km/h)
Max cruising speed:	
C-130E	320 knots (368 mph; 592 km/h)
C-130H, K	326 knots (375 mph; 603 km/h)
HC-130H	318 knots (366 mph; 589 km/h)
Econ cruising speed:	
C-130E, H, K	295 knots (340 mph; 547 km/h)
Stalling speed	100 knots (115 mph; 185 km/h)
Rate of climb at S/L:	
C-130E	1,830 ft (558 m)/min
C-130H, K	1,900 ft (579 m)/min
HC-130H	1,820 ft (555 m)/min
Service ceiling:	
C-130E at 155,000 lb (70,310 kg) AUW	23,000 ft (7,010 m)
C-130H, K at 130,000 lb (58,970 kg) AUW	33,000 ft (10,060 m)
Service ceiling, one engine out at 130,000 lb (58,970 kg) AUW	
C-130E	21,500 ft (6,550 m)
C-130H, K	26,500 ft (8,075 m)
T-O run:	
C-130E	3,800 ft (1,160 m)
C-130H, K, HC-130H	3,580 ft (1,091 m)
T-O to 50 ft (15 m):	
C-130E	5,580 ft (1,700 m)
C-130H, K, HC-130H, P	4,500 ft (1,372 m)
Landing from 50 ft (15 m) at 100,000 lb (45,360 kg) AUW	
C-130H, K	2,700 ft (823 m)
Landing from 50 ft (15 m) at max landing weight:	
C-130E, H, K, HC-130H, P	3,750 ft (1,143 m)
Landing run at max landing weight:	
C-130E, H, K	2,130 ft (650 m)
Range with max payload:	
C-130E, with 5% reserve and allowance for 30 min at S/L	2,101 nm (2,420 miles; 3,895 km)
C-130H, K, with 5% reserve and allowance for 30 min at S/L	2,127 nm (2,450 miles; 3,943 km)
Range with max fuel, including external tanks:	
C-130E with two 1,360 US gallon external	

tanks, 20,000 lb (9,070 kg) payload and reserves of 5% initial fuel plus 30 min at S/L
4,081 nm (4,700 miles; 7,560 km)
C-130H, K with two 1,360 US gallon external tanks, 20,000 lb (9,070 kg) payload and reserves of 5% initial fuel plus 30 min at S/L
4,142 nm (4,770 miles; 7,675 km)

LOCKHEED L 100 SERIES COMMERCIAL HERCULES

Following the production of early C-130 military Hercules aircraft, Lockheed-Georgia decided to offer a commercial version of this heavy transport, since when six models have been offered. Details of these follow:

Model 382. First commercial Hercules with the civil registration N1130E, used for FAA certification and demonstration. FAA Type Certificate for Class A cargo was received on 16 February 1965. Derived from the military C-130E, it was powered by Allison 501-D22 turboprop engines. Converted subsequently to L 100-20 standard, with Allison 501-D22A engines and a fuselage extended by 100 in (2·54 m), it flew for the first time in this configuration on 19 April 1968. Re-registered N50FW, it was delivered to Flying W Airways on 26 December 1969. This model is no longer available.

Model 382B (and L 100). Certificated on 5 October 1965 for Class E cargo, the Model 382B retained all features of the Model 382, while slight differences in cargo loading systems produced the L 100. Operators have included Alaska Airlines, Delta Air Lines, Interior Airways, Pacific Western Airlines, Pakistan International Airlines and Zambian Air Cargoes. This model is no longer available.

Model 382D (L 100-10). Derived from the C-130H, with up-rated Allison 501-D22A engines, this model was offered in August 1967. None was produced.

Model 382E (L 100-20). Certificated on 4 October 1968, this "stretched" version of the Hercules is re-designated L 100-20 and has a 100 in (2·54 m) fuselage extension. It has a 60 in (1·52 m) fuselage plug inserted aft of the forward crew door and a 40 in (1·02 m) plug aft of the paratroop doors, and retains the Allison 501-D22A engines of the Model 382D. Operators include Airlift International, Delta Air Lines, Flying W Airways, Interior Airways, Pacific Western Airlines, Red Dodge Aviation and Southern Air Transport.

Model 382F (L 100-20). Identical to the Model 382E except that it is powered by the lower-rated Allison 501-D22 engines. One aircraft (CF-PWN) in service with Pacific Western Airlines. This model is no longer available.

Model 382G (L 100-30). First proposed in October 1969, this aircraft is generally similar to the Model 382E, but has had the fuselage extended a further 80 in (2·03 m). Rear cargo windows, paratroop doors and provision for JATO have been eliminated. Saturn Airways have ordered three aircraft, and these were scheduled to enter service in December 1970.

The details given for the C-130E apply also to the L 100, L 100-20 and L 100-30 except as follows:

TYPE: Medium/long-range commercial transport.
POWER PLANT: Either four 4,050 eshp Allison 501-D22 or four 4,508 eshp Allison 501-D22A turboprop engines.

DIMENSIONS, EXTERNAL:
Wing span	132 ft 7 in (40·41 m)

Length overall:
L 100	97 ft 9 in (29·79 m)
L 100-20	106 ft 0½ in (32·32 m)
L 100-30	112 ft 8½ in (34·35 m)
Height overall	38 ft 3 in (11·66 m)
Tailplane span	52 ft 8 in (16·05 m)
Wheel track	14 ft 3 in (4·34 m)

Wheelbase:
L 100	32 ft 0¾ in (9·77 m)
L 100-20	37 ft 1¼ in (11·31 m)
L 100-30	40 ft 4¾ in (12·31 m)

Crew door (integral steps):
Height	3 ft 10 in (1·17 m)
Width	2 ft 6 in (0·76 m)
Height to sill	3 ft 5 in (1·04 m)

Rear cargo door:
Height	9 ft 1 in (2·77 m)
Width	10 ft 0 in (3·05 m)
Height to sill	3 ft 5 in (1·04 m)

DIMENSIONS, INTERNAL:
Cabin, excluding flight deck:
Length:
L 100	40 ft 9½ in (12·43 m)
L 100-20	49 ft 1½ in (14·97 m)
L 100-30	55 ft 5¼ in (16·90 m)
Max width	10 ft 3 in (3·12 m)
Max height	9 ft 0 in (2·74 m)
Floor area, ramp	103 sq ft (9·57 m²)

Floor area, excluding ramp:
L 100	413 sq ft (38·37 m²)
L 100-20	499 sq ft (46·36 m²)
L 100-30	563 sq ft (52·30 m²)

Volume, including ramp:
L 100	4,500 cu ft (127·43 m³)
L 100-20	5,307 cu ft (150·28 m³)
L 100-30	5,969 cu ft (169·02 m³)

AREAS:
Wings, gross	1,745 sq ft (162·12 m²)
Ailerons (total)	110 sq ft (10·22 m²)
Trailing-edge flaps (total)	342 sq ft (31·77 m²)
Fin	225 sq ft (20·90 m²)
Rudder, including tab	75 sq ft (6·97 m²)
Tailplane	381 sq ft (35·40 m²)
Elevators, including tab	155 sq ft (14·40 m²)

WEIGHTS AND LOADINGS:
Operating weight, empty:
L 100	67,560 lb (30,645 kg)
L 100-20	70,683 lb (32,060 kg)
L 100-30	72,538 lb (32,903 kg)

Max payload:
L 100	48,534 lb (22,014 kg)
L 100-20	49,317 lb (22,370 kg)
L 100-30	49,462 lb (22,436 kg)

Max "zero fuel" weight:
L 100	116,094 lb (52,664 kg)
L 100-20	120,000 lb (54,430 kg)
L 100-30	122,000 lb (55,337 kg)

Max T-O weight:
L 100, L 100-20, L 100-30	155,000 lb (70,308 kg)

Max ramp weight:
L 100, L 100-20	155,000 lb (70,308 kg)
L 100-30	155,800 lb (70,670 kg)

Max landing weight:
L 100, L 100-20	130,000 lb (58,970 kg)
L 100-30	132,000 lb (59,877 kg)
Max wing loading	88·8 lb/sq ft (433·5 kg/m²)

Max power loading:
L 100	9·6 lb/eshp (4·35 kg/eshp)
L 100-20, L 100-30	8·6 lb/eshp (3·90 kg/eshp)

PERFORMANCE (at max T-O weight):
Max cruising speed at 20,000 ft (6,100 m) at 120,000 lb (54,430 kg) AUW:
L 100	310 knots (357 mph; 575 km/h)
L 100-20, L 100-30	327 knots (377 mph; 607 km/h)

Landing speed:
L 100, L 100-20	126 knots (145 mph; 233 km/h)
L 100-30	127 knots (146 mph; 235 km/h)

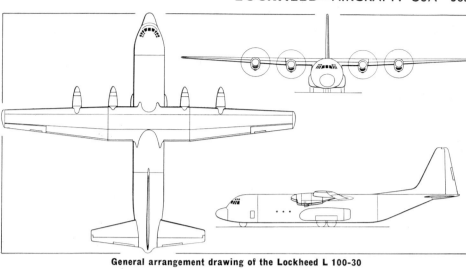

General arrangement drawing of the Lockheed L 100-30

Rate of climb at S/L:
L 100	1,830 ft (588 m)/min
L 100-20, L 100-30	1,900 ft (579 m)/min

FAA T-O field length:
L 100	6,640 ft (2,024 m)
L 100-20, L 100-30	6,000 ft (1,829 m)

FAA landing field length, at max landing weight:
L 100, L 100-20	4,760 ft (1,450 m)
L 100-30	4,830 ft (1,472 m)

Range with max payload, 45 min fuel reserve:
L 100	1,936 nm (2,230 miles; 3,588 km)
L 100-20	2,223 nm (2,560 miles; 4,120 km)
L 100-30	2,058 nm (2,370 miles; 3,814 km)

Range with zero payload, 45 min fuel reserve:
L 100	2,796 nm (3,220 miles; 5,182 km)
L 100-20	4,203 nm (4,840 miles; 7,789 km)
L 100-30	4,194 nm (4,830 miles; 7,773 km)

LOCKHEED MODEL 1329 JETSTAR
USAF designation: C-140

First announced in March 1957, the JetStar is a jet-powered utility transport with normal accommodation for a crew of two and eight or ten passengers. The first prototype, built as a private venture, flew on 4 September 1957, only 241 days after its design was started.

The two prototype JetStars were each powered originally by two Bristol Siddeley Orpheus turbojets, mounted on each side of the rear fuselage. One of them was re-engined in December, 1959, with four Pratt & Whitney JT12 turbojets mounted in lateral pairs in the same position. This power plant was standardised for the production version, which first flew in the Summer of 1960 and received FAA Type Approval in August 1961.

By January 1970, a total of 146 JetStars had been delivered for corporate and private use throughout the world. Twelve have been delivered to foreign customers and two to US government agencies. Production is continuing at the rate of one aircraft per month. In addition, two versions have been delivered to the USAF, as follows:

C-140A. Five for use by the Air Force Communications Service, which is responsible for inspecting world-wide military navigation aids. First delivered in Summer of 1962.

VC-140B. Eleven transport versions for operation by the special air missions wing of MAC. One configuration accommodates a crew of three and eight passengers, the other a crew of three and 13 passengers. First delivered in late 1961.

Early JetStars had JT12A-6 engines, with max continuous rating of 2,400 lb (1,090 kg) st. In the Summer of 1963, these were superseded by JT12A-6A engines, with a max continuous rating of 2,570 lb (1,166 kg) st. The current version, known as the Dash 8 JetStar, flown for the first time in January 1967, has more powerful JT12A-8 turbojets, improved brakes and anti-skid units and a new pneumatic emergency extension system for the landing gear. Structural strength is increased to cater for a higher gross weight. On 6 July 1967 the Type Certificate was amended by the FAA to incorporate the Dash 8 design refinements.

Kits are available to convert earlier JetStars to Dash 8 standard, as described below.

TYPE: Four-jet light utility transport.

WINGS: Cantilever low-wing monoplane. Wing section NACA 63A112 at root, NACA 63A309 (modified) at tip. Dihedral 2°. Incidence 1° at root, —1° at tip. Sweepback at quarter-chord 30°. Conventional fail-safe stressed-skin structure of high-strength aluminium. Bending loads carried by integral skin-stringer extrusion and sheet ribs, shear loads by three beams. Plain aluminium alloy ailerons are mechanically operated with hydraulic boost. Aileron trim-tabs actuated electro-mechanically. Double-slotted all-metal trailing-edge flaps. Hinged leading-edge flaps. No spoilers. Rubber boot de-icers on leading-edge.

FUSELAGE: Semi-monocoque fail-safe structure of aluminium alloy. Hydraulically-operated speed-brake on underside of fuselage aft of pressurised compartment.

TAIL UNIT: Cantilever aluminium alloy structure with tailplane mounted part-way up fin. Fin is pivoted to vary tailplane incidence for trimming. Elevators mechanically operated with hydraulic boost. Rudder mechanically operated with servo assist. Rubber-boot de-icers on leading-edges.

LANDING GEAR: Hydraulically-retractable tricycle type with twin wheels on all units.

Lockheed JetStar light jet transport (four Pratt & Whitney JT12A turbojet engines)

pneumatic shock-absorbers. Main wheel tyres size 26 × 6·6 type VII, pressure 220 lb/sq in (15·5 kg/cm²). Nose-wheel tyres size 18 × 4·4 type VII, pressure 220 lb/sq in (15·5 kg/cm²). Hydraulic brakes with fully-modulated anti-skid units.

POWER PLANT: Four Pratt & Whitney JT12A-8 turbojet engines (each 3,300 lb=1,497 kg st) mounted in lateral pairs on sides of rear fuselage. Thrust reversers fitted. Fuel in four integral wing tanks, total capacity 1,530 US gallons (5,792 litres), and two non-removable external tanks on wings. Total fuel capacity 2,660 US gallons (10,070 litres). Refuelling point on each tank. Oil capacity 6·0 US gallons (23 litres).

ACCOMMODATION: Normal accommodation for crew of two and ten passengers, with wardrobe, galley and toilet aft of cabin and baggage compartments fore and aft. Layout and furnishing can be varied to suit customer's requirements. Door on port side between flight deck and cabin.

SYSTEMS: Air-cycle air-conditioning and pressurisation system, using engine-bleed air. Pressure differential 8·9 lb/sq in (0·63 kg/cm²). Two independent hydraulic systems with engine-driven pumps; pressure 3,000 lb/sq in (210 kg/cm²). Four 28V 300A DC engine-driven starter-generators, three single-phase 115V inverters and two 24V 36Ah batteries. FAA-approved APU available for customer installation on the commercial version.

ELECTRONICS AND EQUIPMENT: Provision for full range of radio, radar and all-weather flying equipment, to customer's specification. Bendix, Collins or Sperry autopilot optional.

DIMENSIONS, EXTERNAL:
Wing span	54 ft 5 in (16·60 m)
Wing chord at root	13 ft 7¾ in (4·16 m)
Wing chord at tip	5 ft 1 in (1·55 m)
Wing aspect ratio	5·27
Length overall	60 ft 5 in (18·42 m)
Length of fuselage	58 ft 9½ in (17·92 m)
Height overall	20 ft 5 in (6·23 m)
Tailplane span	24 ft 9 in (7·55 m)
Wheel track	12 ft 3½ in (3·75 m)
Wheelbase	20 ft 7 in (6·28 m)
Cabin door:	
Height	4 ft 11 in (1·50 m)
Width	2 ft 2½ in (0·67 m)
Height to sill	approx 4 ft 6 in (1·37 m)

DIMENSIONS, INTERNAL:
Cabin, excluding flight deck:
Length	28 ft 2½ in (8·59 m)
Max width	6 ft 2½ in (1·89 m)
Max height	6 ft 1 in (1·85 m)
Volume	850 cu ft (24·07 m³)

AREAS:
Wings, gross	542·5 sq ft (50·40 m²)
Ailerons (total)	24·4 sq ft (2·27 m²)
Trailing-edge flaps (extended, total)	62·6 sq ft (5·82 m²)
Leading-edge flaps (total)	34·0 sq ft (3·16 m²)
Fin	94·0 sq ft (8·73 m²)

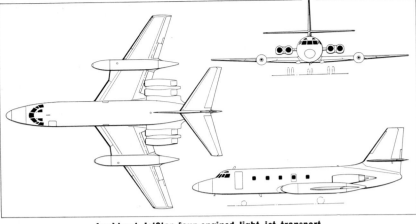

Lockheed JetStar four-engined light jet transport

Rudder, including tab	16·2 sq ft (1·51 m²)
Tailplane	117·8 sq ft (10·94 m²)
Elevators	31·2 sq ft (2·90 m²)

WEIGHTS AND LOADINGS:
Basic operating weight	22,074 lb (10,012 kg)
Max payload	2,926 lb (1,327 kg)
Payload with full fuel	2,604 lb (1,181 kg)
Max T-O weight	42,000 lb (19,051 kg)
Max ramp weight	42,500 lb (19,278 kg)
Max zero-fuel weight	25,000 lb (11,340 kg)
Max landing weight	35,000 lb (15,875 kg)
Max wing loading	77·4 lb/sq ft (377·8 kg/m²)
Max power loading	3·2 lb/lb st (3·2 kg/kg st)

PERFORMANCE (at max T-O weight):
Max level speed at 21,200 ft (6,460 m)
492 knots (566 mph; 911 km/h)
Max permissible diving speed:
below 17,500 ft (5,330 m)
425 knots (490 mph; 788 km/h) IAS
above 17,500 ft (5,330 m) Mach 0·90
Max cruising speed, reduced AUW, at 23,000 ft (7,010 m) 495 knots (570 mph; 917 km/h)
Econ cruising speed, reduced AUW, at 37,000 ft (11,275 m) 440 knots (507 mph; 816 km/h)
Stalling speed, flaps down, at max landing weight 107 knots (123 mph; 198 km/h)
Rate of climb at S/L, at AUW of 38,000 lb (17,235 kg) 5,200 ft (1,585 m)/min
Service ceiling, at AUW of 38,000 lb 37,400 ft (11,400 m)
Service ceiling, one engine out, at AUW of 38,000 lb (17,235 kg) 28,300 ft (8,625 m)
T-O run 3,740 ft (1,140 m)
T-O to 50 ft (15 m) 4,880 ft (1,487 m)
Landing from 50 ft (15 m) 3,770 ft (1,149 m)
Landing run 2,450 ft (747 m)
Range with max fuel, step climb, with 45 min reserve 1,940 nm (2,235 miles; 3,595 km)
Range with max payload, step climb, with 45 min reserve 1,840 nm (2,120 miles; 3,410 km)

LOCKHEED MODEL 500
US military designation: C-5A Galaxy

Design studies for a very large logistics transport for Military Airlift Command (then MATS) began in 1963, when the requirement was for a 600,000 lb (272,200 kg) aircraft known by the designation CX-4. Eventually, this and other requirements evolved into a specification known as CX-HLS (Cargo, Experimental-Heavy Logistics System), calling for an aircraft able to carry a 125,000 lb (56,700 kg) payload 8,000 miles (12,875 km), or twice that payload over shorter ranges. It had to be able to take off from the same 8,000 ft (2,440 m) runways as the C-141 StarLifter and to land on 4,000 ft (1,220 m) semi-prepared runways in combat areas.

Following an initial design competition in May 1964, contracts were awarded to Boeing, Douglas and Lockheed to develop their designs further. By this time, the requirement was for an aircraft with a gross weight of about 700,000 lb (317,500 kg), to which the definitive designation C-5A and the name Galaxy were allocated. Large contracts also went to Pratt & Whitney and General Electric, to finance the development of prototype power plants for the C-5A.

In August 1965, the General Electric GE1/6 turbofan was selected for continued development. In October, Lockheed was nominated as prime contractor for the airframe. Construction of the first C-5A was started in August 1966, and it flew for the first time on 30 June 1968; the first operational aircraft (the ninth C-5A built) was delivered to Military Airlift Command on 17 December 1969. Lockheed-Georgia and the USAF assigned the first eight aircraft to a flight test programme that extended into mid-1970. Present contracts cover the manufacture of 81 for the USAF. About 50% of the work, in terms of payments, is subcontracted.

At the end of 1969 the eight C-5A's assigned

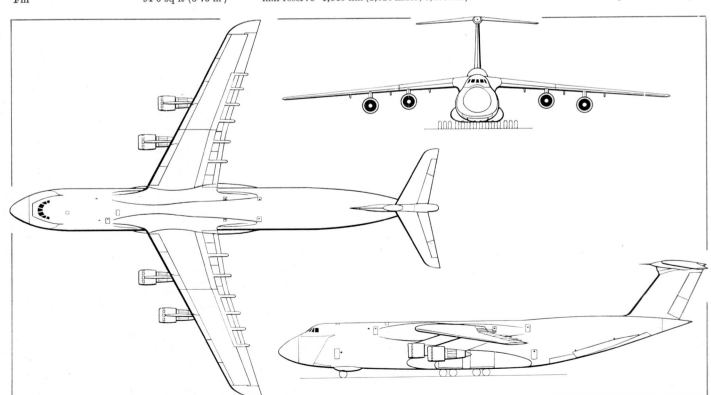

Lockheed C-5A Galaxy four-turbofan long-range military heavy transport

to the flight test programme had completed over 1,850 hours of flight. One take-off was made at a gross weight of 798,200 lb (362,064 kg), constituting an unofficial world record.

Flight refuelling tanker and airborne command post versions of the C-5A are being studied. A commercial version, designated L-500-114MF Galaxy (described separately), is also to be made available.

The following details refer to the standard military C-5A:

TYPE: Heavy logistics transport aircraft.

WINGS: Cantilever high-wing monoplane. Wing section NACA 0012 (mod) at 20% span, NACA 0011 (mod) at 43·7% and 70% span. Anhedral 5° 30′ at quarter-chord. Incidence 3° 30′ at root. Sweepback at quarter-chord 25°. Conventional fail-safe box structure of built-up spars and machined aluminium alloy extruded skin panels. Statically-balanced aluminium alloy ailerons. Modified Fowler-type aluminium alloy trailing-edge flaps. Simple hinged aluminium alloy spoilers forward of flaps. No trim tabs. Sealed inboard slats and slotted outboard slats on leading-edges. Ailerons and spoilers operated by hydraulic servo actuators. Trailing-edge flaps and leading-edge slats actuated by ball screw jack and torque tube system.

FUSELAGE: Conventional semi-monocoque fail-safe structure of skin, stringers and ring-frames, of 7079-T6 and 7075-T6 aluminium alloy and titanium alloy.

TAIL UNIT: Cantilever all-metal structure with tailplane mounted at tip of fin. All surfaces swept; anhedral on tailplane. All components are single-cell box structures with integrally-stiffened aluminium alloy skin panels. Variable-incidence tailplane. Elevators in four sections; rudder in two sections. No trim-tabs. Rudder and elevators operated through hydraulic servo actuators. Tailplane actuated through hydraulically-powered screw-jack. No anti-icing equipment.

LANDING GEAR: Retractable nose-wheel type. Nose unit retracted rearward by hydraulically-driven ball-screws. Main units rotated through 90° and retracted inward via hydraulically-driven gearbox. Single nose shock-strut and four main gear shock-struts are of Bendix oleo-pneumatic dual-chamber type. Four wheels on nose unit. Four main units (two in tandem on each side) each comprise a "triangular footprint" six-wheel bogie made up of a pair of wheels forward of the shock-strut and two pairs aft. All 28 tyres size 49 × 17 type VII 26-ply. Tyre pressures: nose 120 lb/sq in (8·44 kg/cm²), main 155 lb/sq in (10·90 kg/cm²) with in-flight deflation capability. Berylium disc brakes, with fully-modulating anti-skid units.

POWER PLANT: Four General Electric TF39-GE-1 turbofan engines, each rated at 41,000 lb (18,600 kg) st. Twelve integral fuel tanks in wings between front and rear spars, comprising four main tanks (each 3,625 US gallons = 13,721 litres), four auxiliary tanks (each 4,625 US gallons = 17,507 litres) and four extended-range tanks (each 4,000 US gallons = 15,142 litres). Total usable capacity 49,000 US gallons (185,480 litres). Two refuelling points each side, in forward part of main landing gear pods. Flight refuelling capability, via inlet in upper forward fuselage, over flight engineer's station (compatible with KC-135 tanker). Oil capacity 36·4 US gallons (138 litres).

ACCOMMODATION: Normal crew of five, consisting of pilot, co-pilot, flight engineer, navigator and load-master, with rest area for 15 people (relief crew, couriers, etc) at front of upper deck. Initial version has seats for 75 troops on rear part of upper deck, aft of wing box. Provision for carrying 270 troops on lower deck, but aircraft is intended primarily as freighter. Typical freight loads include two M-60 tanks or sixteen ¾-ton lorries; or one M-60 and two Bell Iroquois helicopters, five M-113 personnel carriers, one M-59 2½-ton truck and an M-151 ¼-ton truck; or 10 Pershing missiles with tow and launch vehicles; or 36 standard 463L load pallets. "Visor" type upward-hinging nose, and loading ramp, permit straight-in loading into front of hold, under flight deck. Rear straight-in loading via ramp which forms under-surface of rear fuselage. Side panels of rear fuselage, by ramp, hinge outward to improve access on ground but do not need to open for air-drop operations in view of width of ramp. Provision for Aerial Delivery System (ADS) kits for paratroops or cargo. Two passenger doors on port side, at rear end of upper and lower decks. Two crew doors on port side, at forward end of upper and lower decks. Entire accommodation pressurised and air-conditioned.

SYSTEMS: Electronically-controlled bootstrap air-cycle pressurisation system: pressure differential 8·2 lb/sq in (0·58 kg/cm²). Hydraulic system, pressure 3,000 lb/sq in (210 kg/cm²), supplies flying control and utility systems. Electrical system includes four 60/80 kVA AC engine-driven generators. AiResearch APU to provide pneumatic, hydraulic and electrical power.

ELECTRONICS AND EQUIPMENT: Communications and navigation radio to military requirements. Norden radar. Nortronics inertial navigation system. Special equipment includes electronic Malfunction Detection, Analysis and Recording Subsystem (MADAR) which operates by scanning and analysing over 800 test points.

DIMENSIONS, EXTERNAL:
Wing span	222 ft 8½ in (67·88 m)
Wing chord at root	45 ft 5·3 in (13·85 m)
Wing chord at tip	15 ft 4 in (4·67 m)
Wing aspect ratio	7·75
Length overall	247 ft 10 in (75·54 m)
Length of fuselage	230 ft 7¼ in (70·29 m)
Height overall	65 ft 1½ in (19·85 m)
Tailplane span	68 ft 8½ in (20·94 m)
Wheel track (between outer wheels)	36 ft 0 in (10·97 m)
Wheelbase (c/l main gear to c/l nose gear)	72 ft 11 in (22·23 m)

Crew door (lower deck):
Height	5 ft 11 in (1·80 m)
Width	3 ft 4 in (1·02 m)
Height to sill	12 ft 11 in (3·94 m)

Crew door (upper deck):
Height	5 ft 0 in (1·52 m)
Width	2 ft 6 in (0·76 m)
Height to sill	26 ft 11 in (8·20 m)

Passenger door (lower deck):
Height	6 ft 0 in (1·83 m)
Width	3 ft 0 in (0·91 m)
Height to sill	11 ft 8 in (3·56 m)

Passenger door (upper deck):
Height	5 ft 0 in (1·52 m)
Width	2 ft 6 in (0·76 m)
Height to sill	26 ft 11 in (8·20 m)

DIMENSIONS, INTERNAL:
Cabins, excluding flight deck:
Length:	
upper deck, forward	39 ft 4 in (11·99 m)
upper deck, aft	59 ft 8½ in (18·20 m)
lower deck, without ramp	121 ft 1 in (36·91 m)
lower deck, with ramp	144 ft 7 in (44·07 m)
Max width:	
upper deck forward	13 ft 9½ in (4·20 m)
upper deck, aft	13 ft 0 in (3·96 m)
lower deck	19 ft 0 in (5·79 m)
Max height:	
upper deck	7 ft 6 in (2·29 m)
lower deck	13 ft 6 in (4·11 m)
Floor area:	
upper deck forward,	540 sq ft (50·17 m²)
upper deck, aft	776·1 sq ft (72·10 m²)
lower deck, without ramp	2,300·9 sq ft (213·76 m²)
Volume:	
upper deck, forward	2,010 cu ft (56·91 m³)
upper deck, aft	6,020 cu ft (170·46 m³)
lower deck	34,795 cu ft (985·29 m³)

AREAS:
Wings, gross	6,200 sq ft (576·0 m²)
Ailerons (total)	252·8 sq ft (23·49 m²)
Trailing-edge flaps (total)	991·7 sq ft (92·13 m²)
Leading-edge slats (total)	648·5 sq ft (60·25 m²)
Spoilers (total)	430·7 sq ft (40·01 m²)
Fin	961·1 sq ft (89·29 m²)
Rudder	226·7 sq ft (21·06 m²)
Tailplane	965·8 sq ft (89·73 m²)
Elevators	258·7 sq ft (24·03 m²)

WEIGHTS AND LOADINGS (A=weight for 2·5g, B=weight for 2·25g):
Basic operating weight:	
A, B	325,244 lb (147,528 kg)
Design payload:	
A	220,000 lb (99,800 kg)
B	265,000 lb (120,200 kg)
Max T-O weight:	
A	728,000 lb (330,200 kg)
B	764,500 lb (346,770 kg)
Max ramp weight:	
A	732,500 lb (332,250 kg)
B	769,000 lb (348,800 kg)
Max zero-fuel weight:	
A	545,244 lb (247,318 kg)
B	590,244 lb (267,729 kg)
Max landing weight:	
A, B	635,850 lb (288,416 kg)
Max wing loading:	
A	117·5 lb/sq ft (573·8 kg/m²)
Max power loading:	
A	4·45 lb/lb st (4·45 kg/kg st)

PERFORMANCE (estimated at max T-O weight, except where indicated. A = at 2·5g, B = at 2·25g):
Max level speed at 25,000 ft (7,600 m)	496 knots (571 mph; 919 km/h)
Max permissible diving speed	409·5 knots (472 mph; 760 km/h) CAS or Mach 0·875
Max cruising speed at 30,000 ft (9,150 m) at AUW of 525,000 lb (238,150 kg)	470 knots (541 mph; 871 km/h)
Econ cruising speed at 30,000 ft (9,150 m) at AUW of 675,000 lb (306,175 kg)	466 knots (537 mph; 864 km/h)
Stalling speed, 40° flaps	108 knots (124 mph; 200 km/h) EAS
Rate of climb at S/L	2,300 ft (700 m)/min
Service ceiling at AUW of 615,000 lb (278,950 kg)	34,000 ft (10,360 m)
T-O run:	
A	6,500 ft (1,981 m)
B	7,300 ft (2,225 m)
T-O to 50 ft (15 m):	
A	7,500 ft (2,286 m)
B	8,300 ft (2,530 m)

Lockheed C-5A Galaxy long-range military heavy transport (four General Electric TF39-GE-1 turbofan engines)

Landing from 50 ft (15 m) at max landing
weight   3,500 ft (1,066 m)
Landing run at max landing weight
                               2,350 ft (716 m)
Range with max fuel and 80,000 lb (36,287 kg)
payload, with 5% fuel reserve, plus 30 min
at S/L   5,644 nm (6,500 miles; 10,460 km)
Range with max payload, reserves as above
                 2,560 nm (2,950 miles; 4,745 km)

LOCKHEED MODEL L 500-114ZC

Appreciating that the very large volume and
weight-lifting capability of the C-5 would appeal
to commercial operators, Lockheed began work
on the design of a commercial version, designated
Model L 500, in June 1965. This is basically
similar to the military C-5, but has 52,500 lb
(23,810 kg) st turbofan engines and modified
landing gear. The aft pressure bulkhead
has been moved 34 ft 0 in (10·36 m) aft, providing
substantially more cargo space. Higher take-off
weight and zero-fuel weight, plus the removal of
military equipment, permits carriage of a greater
payload over a longer range than is possible with
the C-5.

A "flying freight train" version, able to airlift
63-111 motor cars, has been proposed. Early in
1969 Lockheed demonstrated to airlines, shippers
and airport operators a Lockheed L 500 cargo
loading simulator, capable of development to a
completely automated rapid loading system.

The description of the C-5 applies also to the
basic L 500-114ZC, except in the following details:

TYPE: Commercial four-turbofan heavy cargo
transport.

LANDING GEAR: Retractable tricycle type.
Hydraulic retraction with electric back-up
system. Nose unit retracts rearward. Main
units rotate through 90° and retract inward via
hydraulically-driven gearbox. Single nose
shock-strut and four Bendix main gear shock-
struts are of oleo-pneumatic dual-chamber type.
Four wheels on nose unit. Four main units
(two in tandem on each side) each comprise a
four-wheel bogie. Main wheel tyres size 56
× 16, pressure 211 lb/sq in (14·8 kg/cm²). Nose-
wheel tyres size 49 × 17, pressure 130 lb/sq in
(9·1 kg/cm²). High-capacity brakes, with
fully-modulating anti-skid units.

POWER PLANT: Four turbofan engines, each
rated at 52,500 lb (23,810 kg) st. Fuel tankage
and capacity as for C-5. Oil capacity is based
on 20-hour duration at maximum oil consumption.

ACCOMMODATION: Normal crew of three, consisting of pilot, co-pilot and flight engineer, with
seats for an observer on the flight deck and
three couriers at front of upper deck. Galley
and toilet facilities are provided between
forward end of upper deck and flight deck.
Aircraft designed for simultaneous power loading through nose, by means of "Visor"-type
upward-opening nose and loading ramp, of three
sticks of pallets or containers into main cargo
compartment, side-loading of 16 pallets through
two cargo doors on port side of upper deck, and
2,000 cu ft (56·6 m³) of bulk cargo at aft end of
main deck, loaded through cargo door at aft
lower port side of fuselage. Main compartment
accommodates 28 pallets or containers, each
8 ft 0 in by 8 ft 0 in by 10 ft 0 in (2·44 m × 2·44 m
× 3·05 m) two-abreast, and 22 suspended containers, each 4 ft 0 in by 10 ft 0 in by 8 ft 0 in (1·22 m
× 3·05 m × 2·44 m). Upper deck forward accommodates 4 pallets, each 7 ft 2 in by 7 ft 4 in by
10 ft 5 in (2·19 m × 2·22 m × 3·19 m) and upper
deck aft 12 pallets of the same dimensions.

ELECTRONICS AND EQUIPMENT: A range of
optional communications and navigation equipment is available.

DIMENSIONS, EXTERNAL:
As for C-5 except:
Length overall   247 ft 10¾ in (76·20 m)
Height overall   66 ft 5 in (20·24 m)
Wheel track (between outer wheels)
                            30 ft 2 in (9·19 m)
Wheelbase (c/l aft wheels to c/l nose gear)
                            85 ft 0 in (25·91 m)
Main cargo doors, port side, to upper hold
(two each):
Height   7 ft 8 in (2·34 m)
Width   10 ft 0 in (3·05 m)
Cargo door, lower port side of aft fuselage:
Height   5 ft 0 in (1·52 m)
Width   4 ft 0 in (1·22 m)
Crew access door:
Height   4 ft 0 in (1·22 m)
Width   2 ft 0 in (0·61 m)

DIMENSIONS, INTERNAL:
Main cargo compartments:
Length   141 ft 0 in (42·98 m)
Width   19 ft 0 in (5·79 m)
Height   13 ft 6 in (4·11 m)
Upper deck forward (excluding flight deck):
Length   30 ft 6 in (9·30 m)
Max width   13 ft 8 in (4·17 m)
Max height   7 ft 9 in (2·36 m)
Upper deck aft:
Length   93 ft 6 in (28·50 m)
Max width   20 ft 3 in (6·17 m)
Max height   7 ft 9 in (2·36 m)
Volume:
Total unitised volume   28,060 cu ft (795 m³)
Bulk volume   2,000 cu ft (56·6 m³)
Total usable volume   30,060 cu ft (851 m³)

WEIGHTS AND LOADINGS:
Basic operating weight 333,264 lb (151,165 kg)
Max payload   319,450 lb (144,900 kg)
Max T-O weight   858,500 lb (389,405 kg)
Max ramp weight   861,500 lb (390,765 kg)
Max zero-fuel weight   652,714 lb (296,065 kg)
Max landing weight   699,000 lb (317,060 kg)
Max wing loading   138·5 lb/sq ft (676·2 kg/m²)
Max power loading   4·09 lb/lb st (4·09 kg/kg st)

PERFORMANCE (estimated, at max T-O weight,
unless otherwise indicated):
Max level speed at S/L
                    350 knots (403 mph; 649 km/h)
Max never-exceed speed at S/L
                    402 knots (464 mph; 743 km/h)
Max cruising speed at 25,000 ft (7,600 m)
                    485 knots (558 mph; 898 km/h)
Econ cruising speed at 28,000 ft (8,534 m)
                    437 knots (503 mph; 810 km/h)
Stalling speed, 40° flaps, at max landing weight
                    112 knots (129 mph; 208 km/h)
Rate of climb at S/L   2,250 ft (686 m)/min
Service ceiling   32,500 ft (9,905 m)
FAR T-O field length   9,500 ft (2,895 m)
FAR landing field length (at max landing
weight)   7,650 ft (2,332 m)
Range with max fuel, with reserve
                 6,956 nm (8,010 miles; 12,890 km)
Range with max payload
                 2,584 nm (2,975 miles; 4,785 km)

LOCKHEED MISSILES AND SPACE COMPANY

Sunnyvale, Palo Alto and Santa Cruz, California.

In addition to its work on missiles and spacecraft, this company has been active in the
development of quiet observation aircraft for the
US Army, and all available details of these aircraft are given below.

It has also been announced that Lockheed
Missiles and Space Company, together with The
Boeing Company and Messerschmitt-Bölkow-
Blohm, of Germany, are to comprise a team to
study a reusable space shuttle transport system.
It is suggested that the use of a shuttle to carry
men and materials into space, returning subsequently to Earth to make a conventional aero-
plane-like landing, could reduce the cost of
putting each pound into orbit by as much as
90%. First test of such a vehicle is expected by
1976.

LOCKHEED Q-STAR

Faced with the military requirement for a
quiet observation aircraft, Lockheed began
studies and development work on quiet aircraft
technology late in 1966. Given the Lockheed
designation QT-2 (quiet thruster, 2-seat), development of this prototype aircraft was helped by
finance from the Advanced Research Projects
Agency, acting through the Army.

The first of two QT-2's built flew for the first
time in August 1967. These two machines were
fitted subsequently with night sensors and taken
to Vietnam for evaluation under operational
conditions. It was reported unofficially that the
QT-2's, introduced during the period of the TET
offensive in 1968, made reconnaissance flights at
an altitude as low as 100 ft (30 m) without being
detected by the enemy.

Little detail of this model is known except that,
like the Q-Star which followed, it was built around
a modified Schweizer SGS 2-32 all-metal sailplane
airframe, powered by a well-silenced engine
driving a large-diameter propeller at low rpm.

The results of early tests were so promising that
long before combat evaluation of the QT-2's,
Lockheed began development of a more advanced
version as a private-venture and this aircraft,
designated Q-Star, flew for the first time in June
1968.

The airframe is essentially that of the Schweizer
SGS 2-32, but in order to carry the extra weight
of the engine and electronic gear the wing has
been strengthened by utilising a more robustly
constructed spar and heavier-gauge wing skins.
The rear fuselage is also strengthened to cater for
a modified tail unit which has had its vertical
surfaces increased by 7 sq ft (0·65 m²). A
conventional non-retractable tail-wheel type
landing gear has been added, and this has a steerable tail-wheel and wheel brakes.

Lockheed Q-Star quiet reconnaissance prototype aircraft

First power plant of the Q-Star was a 100 hp
Continental O-200-A engine. Following early
testing Lockheed sought a quieter engine,
resulting in the installation of a 200 hp Curtiss-
Wright RC 2-60 rotary combustion Wankel
engine, de-rated to 185 hp because of carburettor
limitations. This was the first aircraft to fly in
the USA using this type of engine which, according to Lockheed, not only has a better power/
weight ratio than conventional reciprocating
engines, but is inherently more quite.

The RC 2-60 is liquid-cooled, and a Corvette
radiator is mounted in a box-like structure on the
aircraft's nose to provide the cooling source.
To reduce exhaust noise to a minimum a three-
chamber silencer is used, comprising two large
chambers with a small one between, and the
tail-pipe of the exhaust is mounted to point
skyward. Mounted aft of the cabin, this engine
drives a long propeller shaft through the medium
of a two-stage V-belt-drive reduction system,
giving an engine/propeller-shaft reduction ratio
of 4·34 : 1. The propeller shaft passes over the
top of the cockpit, the forward end being supported by a three-foot (0·91-m) pylon which extends
upward from the aircraft's nose.

Possibly the greatest single reduction in noise
level has come from utilisation of specially-
developed propellers, rotating at speeds as low as

500 rpm. The diameter of experimental propellers has ranged from 7 ft 6 in to 8 ft 4 in (2·29-2·54
m), including three-, four- and six-bladed versions especially made by Ole Fahlin, a former
Lockheed employee.

DIMENSIONS, EXTERNAL:
Wing span   57 ft 1 in (17·40 m)
Length overall   31 ft 0 in (9·15 m)
Tailplane span   10 ft 6 in (3·20 m)
WEIGHT:
Weight equipped   2,166 lb (983 kg)

LOCKHEED YO-3A

Potential of the Q-Star was such that US Army
Aviation Systems Command placed a $2 million
contract with Lockheed in July 1968 for further
development of that aircraft, resulting in a much-
refined version designated YO-3A.

Basis of the design is still the Schweizer SGS
2-32 sailplane, but this has now a low-wing
configuration and the wing roots have been extended forward to accommodate the main wheels
of the landing gear which retract inwards. The
tail unit is little changed, except for the addition
of a larger tail-wheel.

The fuselage has been modified extensively.
The pilot and observer are seated further aft,
with the pilot occupying the rear seat, under a
canopy which has been enlarged considerably.
A heavily-modified 210 hp Continental six-cylinder

horizontally-opposed air-cooled engine is accommodated within the fuselage nose and drives a six-blade wooden propeller. Infra-red equipment is carried for night reconnaissance operations.

No further details were available at the time of writing.

Lockheed YO-3A quiet reconnaissance aircraft (210 hp Continental engine)

LTV

LTV AEROSPACE CORPORATION (A subsidiary of LING-TEMCO-VOUGHT, INC)

HEAD OFFICE:
PO Box 5003, Dallas, Texas 75222

PRESIDENT AND CHIEF EXECUTIVE OFFICER:
Forbes Mann

Vought Aeronautics Company (Division of LTV Aerospace Corporation)

DIVISION HEADQUARTERS:
PO Box 5907, Dallas, Texas 75222

PRESIDENT:
S. Love

VICE-PRESIDENTS:
J. B. Andrasko (Administration)
R. S. Buzard (Engineering)
J. W. Casey (Logistics)
E. F. Cvetko (Manufacturing)
H. H. Hawes Jr (Operations)
Dr W. J. Hesse (Development Programmes)
J. W. Ludwig (Advanced Systems)
J. E. Martin (A-7 Programmes)
L. B. Richardson (Plans and Requirements)
R. F. Ringham (Technical and Logistics)
J. R. Silverman (Controller)

PUBLIC RELATIONS DIRECTOR:
Jack Simon

Vought Aircraft Services Company (a Division of Vought Aeronautics Company)

Vought Helicopter Inc (a Subsidiary of LTV Aerospace)

PRESIDENT: J. R. Silverman

Synetics Company (a Division of LTV Aerospace)
PO Box 6267, Dallas, Texas 75222

PRESIDENT:
D. Gerald M. Munroe

DIVISIONS OF SYNETICS COMPANY
Missiles and Space Division
Kinetics International Division

Kentron Hawaii Ltd (a Subsidiary of LTV Aerospace)
207 Keawe Street, Honolulu, Hawaii 96813

PRESIDENT:
Adrian H. Perry

Subsidiary of Kentron Hawaii Ltd
American Asian International Inc

Service Technology Corporation (a Subsidiary of LTV Aerospace)
2345 West Mockingbird Lane, Dallas, Texas 75235

PRESIDENT:
C. B. Franklin

DIVISIONS OF SERVICE TECHNOLOGY CORPORATION:
Engineering Systems Division
Technical Services Division
Test and Operations Division

LTV Recreation Development Inc (a Subsidiary of LTV Aerospace)
PO Box 947, Steamboat Springs, Colorado 80477

PRESIDENT:
John W. McGuyrt

DIVISIONS OF LTV RECREATION DEVELOPMENT INC
Steamboat Land Company
Mt Werner, Inc

LTV Education Systems Inc (a Subsidiary of LTV Aerospace)
400 Fidelity Union Tower, Dallas, Texas 75201

PRESIDENT:
M. L. Chandler

DIVISIONS OF LTV EDUCATION SYSTEMS INC:
Education Services Division
College Division
Guild Industries Inc
Publishing Division
Abonssie Electronic Systems Inc

International Technovation (a Division of LTV Aerospace)
PO Box 3413, Tyler, Texas 75701

PRESIDENT:
R. J. Phillips

The former Chance Vought Aircraft, Inc, founded in 1917 and a leading producer of aircraft for the US Navy throughout its history, became the Chance Vought Corporation on 31 December 1960. On 31 August 1961, Chance Vought Corporation merged with Ling-Temco Electronics, Inc, to form a new combined company known as Ling-Temco-Vought, Inc. A new Chance Vought Corporation was formed at that time as the aerospace division of LTV.

On 20 October 1963, LTV streamlined its corporate structure and discontinued use of the names of Chance Vought Corporation and Temco Electronics & Missiles Co. The process was carried a stage further in January 1965, when eight of LTV's eleven operating divisions were grouped into three new subsidiary corporations. The three remaining divisions were absorbed later, University Sound Division becoming a part of LTV Ling Altec, Inc, and Continental Electronics and Garland Divisions becoming a part of LTV Electrosystems, Inc. Subsequently, six additional companies have been acquired by LTV Inc. During 1969 there was a further rearrangement of LTV's divisions and subsidiaries, and the company particulars given at the head of this entry detail all divisions and subsidiaries of LTV Aerospace Corporation, which is itself a subsidiary of Ling-Temco-Vought Inc.

The complete LTV group has approximately 128,000 employees, of whom 29,000 were employed by LTV Aerospace Corporation in the Spring of 1970.

Vought Helicopter Inc, a Dallas-based subsidiary of LTV Aerospace Corporation, was formed in July 1969 to sell and support the French Aérospatiale series of Alouette helicopters in the US and Canada. It was announced subsequently, on 28 January 1970, that Vought Helicopters had signed a further agreement with Société Turboméca of France (which see), enabling Vought to sell, service and support Turboméca turbine engines in the US and Canada.

As a division of the LTV Aerospace Corporation, Vought Aeronautics has responsibility for all aircraft work, and sub-contracting. Missiles & Space Division is responsible for manned and unmanned space vehicles and advanced missile systems (see "Missiles" section). LTV Service Technology Corporation handles the establishing and operating of missile and space vehicle test ranges and equipment. Kentron Hawaii, Ltd provides service for missile and space test range operations in the Pacific, and electronic equipment maintenance, repair and calibration service for military and commercial activities in the Pacific.

Vought Aeronautics completed production of the F-8 Crusader fighter early in 1965. It is now modifying Crusaders to new standards and is producing the A-7 Corsair II light attack aircraft for the US Navy and USAF.

It was announced by LTV Aerospace Corporation on 17 December 1969 that The Boeing Company's Vertol Division and Vought Aeronautics Company would cooperate on technology leading to the development of a V/STOL aircraft for the USAF's proposed light intra-theatre transport (LIT) programme, which is in the Concept Formulation phase.

Further development of the XC-142A tilt-wing Tri-Service V/STOL transport, that the LTV-Ryan-Hiller team designed and built for the US armed forces, was ended for economic reasons. The remaining airworthy prototype, full details of which can be found in the 1967-68 *Jane's*, was handed over to NASA in May 1968, for use in an experimental rôle. However, it was announced on 10 April 1970 that this experimental programme had been concluded and that on 4 May 1970 the XC-142A was to be handed over to the USAF at Wright-Patterson AFB, Dayton, Ohio, for permanent exhibition in the Air Force Museum.

On 5 December 1969 LTV Aerospace Corporation announced receipt of a $79,200 contract from the USAF Flight Dynamics Laboratory, for model modification and additional high-speed wind tunnel testing of the air deflection and modulation (ADAM) propulsive-wing turbofan V/STOL strike/reconnaissance aircraft. The ADAM concept full-span model had undergone previously a series of tests at near-Mach 1 speeds, and the new contract is aimed to refine data gained from the earlier tests.

Components produced under sub-contracts include ailerons and flaps for the C-130 Hercules, wing components for the P-3 Orion, the tail section of the Boeing 747, a centre fuselage section for the Boeing SST prototype and the tailplane and elevators for the McDonnell Douglas DC-10. The first completed tailplane for the DC-10 was despatched to McDonnell Douglas at Long Beach, California, on 5 March 1970.

LTV Aerospace Corporation announced on 3 June 1970 that they had withdrawn as a subcontractor to The Boeing Company in their SST programme.

VOUGHT CRUSADER
US Navy designation: F-8

Chance Vought (now Vought Aeronautics Company division of LTV Aerospace Corp) was given a development contract for the F-8 in May 1953 after winning a design competition in which eight airframe manufacturers had participated. The prototype XF-8A Crusader flew for the first time on 25 March 1955, exceeding the speed of sound in level flight. The first production F-8A flew on 20 September 1955, and this version began reaching US Naval operational squadrons in March 1957.

On 21 August 1956 an F-8A set up the first US national speed record of over 1,000 mph (1,600 km/h). Operating under restrictions, it recorded a speed of 1,015·428 mph (1,634·17 km/h) On 16 July 1957 an RF-8A photo-reconnaissance version of the Crusader set up the first supersonic US trans-continental record by flying the 2,445·9 miles (3,936 km) from Los Angeles to New York in 3 hr 22 min 50 sec, at an average speed of 723·52 mph (1,164·39 km/h).

An outstanding feature of the F-8 is its two-position variable-incidence wing. This provides a high angle of attack for take-off and landing, while permitting the fuselage to remain almost parallel to a flight deck or runway for good pilot visibility.

The following versions of the F-8 have been produced:

XF-8A (formerly XF8U-1). Prototype with Pratt & Whitney J57-P-12 turbojet (approx 16,000 lb=7,257 kg st with afterburning).

F-8A (formerly F8U-1). First production version, initially with J57-P-12 turbojet, later aircraft with J57-P-4A (16,200 lb=7,327 kg st with afterburning). Armed with four 20 mm cannon in nose, belly pack of 32 × 2·75-in folding-fin rockets and two Sidewinders on sides of fuselage. AN/APG-30 gunsight-ranging radar. Phased out of production in 1958. Total of 318 built. Designation now changed to **TF-8A.**

F-8B (formerly F8U-1E). Followed F-8A in production from September 1958, with larger nose radome containing AN/APS-67 radar for limited all-weather capability. J57-P-4A turbojet. First flew on 3 September 1958. Total of 130 built. See also **F-8L.**

RF-8A (formerly F8U-1P). Reconnaissance version of -8A which flew for first time on 17 December 1956. Fitted with three CAX-12 trimetrogon cameras and two K-17 vertical cameras in place of cannon and fire-control equipment. Capable of special mapping and charting missions, and night reconnaissance, using internally-stowed photoflash bombs. Fuselage undersurface squared around camera bay. J57-P-4A engine. 144 built. Used extensively for surveillance duties over Cuba in 1962-63. A total of 53 were modified to RF-8G standard in 1965-66. Twenty more modified later.

NTF-8A (formerly F8U-1T). The 74th F-8A was converted into a two-seat fighter-trainer under a US Navy contract. It has a J57-P-20 engine, and ventral fins and afterburner airscoops as on the F-8C. An armament of two 20 mm guns and two Sidewinder missiles is retained, enabling this version to serve as an advanced weapons trainer, with full operational capability. Equipment offered on the NTF-8A includes a flying boom flight refuelling receptacle and a brake-chute to reduce landing distance to 2,700 ft (823 m). The NTF-8A flew for the first time on 6 February 1962.

F-8C (formerly F8U-2). Improved version of F-8A with J57-P-16 turbojet (16,900 lb=7,665 kg st with afterburning), giving higher performance, particularly at altitude. F-8C has improved fire control system and additional radar capabilities. Its armament is the same as that of the F-8A, except that it can carry four Sidewinders, in pairs on each side of the fuselage. Externally the two types are similar, except that the F-8C has two fixed ventral fins under the tail section and two afterburner air-scoops mounted on the tail-cone above the tailplane. First prototype, flown in December 1957, had the new engine only. Second prototype, flown in January 1958, was representative of production aircraft, the first of which flew for the first time on 20 August 1958. First production F-8C delivered to the US Navy on 28 January 1959. First operational squadron (VF-84) formed on 4 April 1959. The 187th and last F-8C was delivered on 20 September 1960. See also F-8K.

F-8D (formerly F8U-2N). Limited all-weather interceptor, capable of speeds approaching Mach 2, for service with US Navy and Marine Corps squadrons. Powered by J57-P-20 turbojet (18,000 lb=8,165 kg st with afterburning). Push-button controls, incorporated in a Vought-developed autopilot, perform many of the pilot's routine tasks such as holding an altitude, holding a heading, selecting a new heading or orbiting over a selected point. F-8D also has improved AN/APQ-83 radar, a later type of Martin-Baker ejection seat, revised internal instrumentation and additional internal fuel capacity, extending its endurance to more than three hours without refuelling. It carries four Sidewinder missiles, in pairs on the sides of its fuselage, in addition to the normal fixed armament of four 20 mm guns. Belly rocket pack deleted. First F-8D flew for the first time on 16 February 1960 and the first production model was delivered to the US Navy on 1 June 1960. Deliveries were completed in January 1962. Total of 152 built. See also F-8H.

F-8E (formerly F8U-2NE). Similar to F-8D, but with higher-performance APQ-94 search and fire-control radar. Nose section more rounded back to cockpit, to accommodate larger radar dish. Improved air duct recovery made possible by rounded shape. AN/AAS-15 infra-red scanner for use with the four Sidewinder air-to-air missiles is mounted above the nose forward of the windshield. The prototype F-8E, a conversion of the second F-8D, flew for the first time on 30 June 1961, followed by the first production F-8E in September 1961. More than 250 built by beginning of 1964. Production has been completed.

In 1962 an F-8E was fitted with two underwing pylons to carry a wide variety of bombs and missiles, to test its suitability for attack duties, as well as interception. Loads carried on these pylons included twelve 250 lb bombs, four 500 lb bombs, two 1,000 lb bombs, two 2,000 lb bombs, or 24 Zuni rockets. Eight more Zunis can replace the four standard Sidewinder missiles on fuselage-side pylons. As a result of the success of these trials, which included a week of deck trials on board the USS *Forrestal* in mid-1963, late-model F-8E's (identified by a bulged top fuselage) were equipped with underwing pylons to carry the full range of attack weapons. The trials aircraft was catapult-launched at an AUW of 34,000 lb (15,420 kg), with full fuel, two 2,000 lb bombs and eight Zunis. See also F-8J.

F-8E (FN). Version of F-8E to equip two French Navy squadrons for service on carriers *Clemenceau* and *Foch*. Main modifications are the incorporation of a boundary layer control system to provide "blowing" of the flaps and ailerons, the introduction of two-stage leading-edge flaps to reduce landing speed on the comparatively small ships, and provision for carrying Matra R.530 air-to-air missiles in addition to Sidewinders. Pratt & Whitney J57-P-20A turbojet engine. Contract for 42 placed in August 1963, through US Navy. Prototype, a converted F-8D, flew on 27 February 1964, and was lost in an accident on 11 April 1964. First production F-8E (FN) flew on 26 June 1964. Last one was delivered in January 1965, bringing to an end the production of new Crusaders.

On 24 March 1969, LTV Aerospace Corporation announced a $1·7 million contract from the French Navy to manufacture new wings and outer panels for an initial batch of 10 F-8E(FN) Crusaders. The new wings, designed for 4,000 flight hours, were supplied minus droops, flaps, ailerons and actuators. They have titanium wing-fold ribs and a thicker skin than standard.

RF-8G. Under a US Navy contract, Vought Aeronautics overhauled and modernised 53 RF-8A photographic-reconnaissance Crusaders to expand their capabilities and extend their service life. Ventral fins and a strengthened wing were fitted, together with fuselage structural reinforcements, a Doppler navigation system and new camera station installations. The modification programme extended through 1965-66, the aircraft being redesignated RF-8G on completion. In 1967 a new contract was negotiated for an additional twenty aircraft, and this programme was scheduled for completion in January 1970.

Vought F-8J Crusader, a remanufactured F-8E with new wings featuring BLC and double leading-edge droops

F-8H. Modernised and remanufactured F-8D, with new extended-service-life wing, addition of attack capabilities identical to those of F-8E/F-8J aircraft, strengthened nose and main landing gear providing an increased carrier landing weight capability, strengthened arresting gear, armament system improvements involving improved fire control computer, expanded missile acquisition envelope and large APQ-94 radar scope. First of 89 F-8H's flew on 17 July 1967.

F-8J. Modified and remanufactured F-8E, incorporating boundary layer control, leading-edge double droops, and larger horizontal tail surfaces for lower landing and catapulting speeds. APQ-124 MAGDARR radar and expanded missile acquisition envelope are added, to provide improvements to the Fire Control System. The F-8J has a new longer-service-life wing identical to that of the F-8H, but also has provision for wing-mounted fuel tanks. The new strengthened landing gear and arresting gear increase carrier landing weight capability. First of 136 F-8J's flew on 31 January 1968.

F-8K. Eighty-seven F-8C's have been modernised and remanufactured with new extended service life wing, wing stores provisions, strengthened fuselage, new nose landing gear, improved lighting and new wiring. This programme was scheduled for completion in the Autumn of 1969.

F-8L. Sixty-three F-8B's have been remanufactured with changes similar to those incorporated in the F-8K's. This programme was scheduled for completion in January 1970.

A total of 375 aircraft have been modernised under the F-8H/J/K/L programme, in the period 1966-70.

The following details apply basically to all versions of the F-8, except for differences detailed above.

TYPE: Supersonic single-seat carrier fighter.

WINGS: Cantilever high-wing monoplane. Thin laminar-flow section. Anhedral 5°. Sweepback 35°. Wing is adjustable to two incidence positions by a hydraulic self-locking actuator. When wing is raised, the ailerons, the flaps and the "dog-tooth" leading-edge are all drooped automatically. Outer wing sections fold upward for carrier stowage. All-metal multi-spar structure with integrally-stiffened aluminium alloy upper and lower skins. Inset aluminium ailerons, inboard of wing fold, are actuated by fully-duplicated hydraulic system and function also as flaps. Small magnesium alloy trailing-edge flaps.

FUSELAGE: All-metal structure in three main assemblies. Both magnesium alloy and titanium are used in the structure, the after section and a portion of the mid-section being of titanium. Ventral speed-brake under centre-fuselage.

TAIL UNIT: Large swept vertical fin and rudder and one-piece horizontal "slab" tail. Tailplane and rudder are actuated by fully-duplicated hydraulic systems.

LANDING GEAR: Hydraulically-retractable tricycle type. Main wheels retract forward into fuselage, nose-wheel aft. Sting-type arrester hook under rear fuselage.

POWER PLANT: One Pratt & Whitney J57 turbojet engine with afterburner. Integral fuel tanks in wings inboard of wing fold. Other tankage in fuselage. Total internal fuel capacity approx 1,165 Imp gallons (5,300 litres). Provision for in-flight refuelling, with retractable probe housed in removable pack on port side of fuselage of F-8A and inside flush panel on RF-8A.

ACCOMMODATION: Pilot on Martin-Baker Mk F7 lightweight ejection seat in pressurised cockpit. Liquid oxygen equipment.

ARMAMENT: Four 20 mm Colt cannon in fuselage nose, with 84 rpg (average) for F-8C/K, F-8H and F-8E/J, and 144 rpg for NTF-8A and F-8F/L. Two Sidewinder missiles (four in F-8C/K, F-8D/H and F-8E/J) mounted externally on sides of fuselage.

DIMENSIONS, EXTERNAL:
- Wing span: 35 ft 8 in (10·87 m)
- Length overall:
  - Except F-8E/J: 54 ft 3 in (16·54 m)
  - F-8E/J: 54 ft 6 in (16·61 m)
- Height overall: 15 ft 9 in (4·80 m)
- Width folded: 22 ft 6 in (6·86 m)
- Tailplane span:
  - except F-8E(FN), F-8J: 18 ft 2 in (5·54 m)
  - F-8E(FN), F-8J: 19 ft 3½ in (5·88 m)
- Wheel track: 9 ft 8 in (2·94 m)

AREA:
- Wings, gross: 375 sq ft (34·84 m^2)

WEIGHT:
- Normal T-O weight:
  - F-8C: 27,550 lb (12,500 kg)
- Max T-O weight: F-8E/J: 34,000 lb (15,420 kg)

PERFORMANCE:
- Max level speed:
  - F-8A and F-8C: over 868 knots (1,000 mph; 1,600 km/h)
  - F-8D, E: nearly Mach 2
- Combat radius:
  - F-8A: 521 nm (600 miles; 965 km)

VOUGHT CORSAIR II

US Military designation: A-7

On 11 February 1964 the US Navy named Ling-Temco-Vought as the winner of a design competition for a single-seat carrier-based light attack aircraft to supplement and eventually replace the A-4E Skyhawk. The requirement was for a subsonic aircraft able to carry a greater load of non-nuclear weapons than the A-4E. To keep costs to a minimum and speed delivery it was decided that the new aircraft should be based on an existing design.

LTV's design study was based on the F-8 Crusader and an initial contract to develop and build three aircraft, under the designation A-7A, was awarded on 19 March 1964; the first flight was made on 27 September 1965.

Since that time a number of versions of the A-7 Corsair II have been introduced as detailed below. They are produced by the Vought Aeronautics Company, an LTV subsidiary, and as the result of a change of company policy are now known as Vought A-7s.

A-7A. Initial attack version for the US Navy, powered by a Pratt & Whitney TF30-P-6 turbofan engine, rated at 11,350 lb (5,150 kg) st, a simplified non-afterburning version of the engine developed for the General Dynamics F-111. The first four were delivered to US Navy Air Test Center, Patuxent River, Maryland, on 13-15 September 1966. Deliveries to user squadrons began on 14 October 1966. The A-7A went into combat for the first time with squadron VA-147 on 4 December 1967, off the USS *Ranger* in the Gulf of Tonkin, and during six months operational service with this squadron only one A-7A was lost in combat. Delivery of 199 A-7A's to the US Navy was completed in the Spring of 1968.

A-7B. Developed version for the US Navy, with TF30-P-8 engine, rated at 12,200 lb (5,534 kg) st without afterburning. First production aircraft flew on 6 February 1968. Last of 196 A-7B's was delivered to the US Navy in April 1969.

A-7C. Projected two-seat version for the US Navy, with TF30 engine and fuselage length of 48 ft 4¼ in (14·73 m).

A-7D. Tactical fighter version for the USAF. First two were powered by TF30-P-8 engine. Subsequent aircraft have an Allison TF41-A-1 (Spey) turbofan engine, rated at 14,250 lb (6,465 kg) st without afterburning. First flight of an A-7D was made on 6 April 1968, and first flight with the TF41 engine on 26 September 1968. Total planned programme calls for 645 aircraft. First A-7D was accepted by the USAF on 23 December 1968. This model is described in detail below.

A-7E. Developed version for the US Navy equipped as a light attack bomber. First 67 aircraft powered by TF30-P-8 turbofan engine, 68th and subsequent aircraft by Allison TF41-A-2 (Spey) turbofan engine rated at 15,000 lb (6,800 kg) st. First flight of an A-7E was made on 25 November 1968 and deliveries began on 14 July 1969. Planned current programme calls for 618 aircraft. Airframe and equipment are virtually identical to those of the A-7D, except that the gas-turbine self-starter is replaced by an air turbine starter. Weight empty approx 18,496 lb (8,389 kg). All major navigation/weapon-delivery equipment is identical to that of the A-7D. Radio navigation aids for the A-7E are as follows: ARN-52 Tacan, ASN-50 UHF-ADF, ARR-69 UHF emergency receiver, APN-154 radar beacon, ARC-51A UHF transceiver, AIC-26 audio amplifier and control, ASW-25 data link and provisions for LORAN. Vought Aeronautics announced on 9 June 1970 that the A-7E had entered combat service in Southeast Asia with Attack Squadron 146 and 147, operating from the aircraft carrier USS *America*.

KA-7F. Proposed carrier-based tanker to replace KA-3B Skywarrior. Drogue and hose reel in fuselage and total internal tankage for 18,600 lb (8,437 kg) of fuel plus four 450-US gal (1,705-litre) drop tanks. Not built.

A-7G. Variant proposed for use by the Swiss Air Force, based on the A-7D with an uprated Allison TF41-A-3 Spey engine.

The following description, which applies in particular to the A-7D, is generally the same for other versions of the A-7 except as detailed above:

TYPE: Subsonic single-seat tactical fighter.

WINGS: Cantilever high-wing monoplane. Wing section NACA 65A007. Anhedral 5°. Incidence —1°. Wing sweepback at quarter-chord 35%. Outer wing sections fold upward to allow best utilisation of revetments at combat airfields. All-metal multi-spar structure with integrally-stiffened aluminium alloy upper and lower skins. Plain sealed inset aluminium ailerons, outboard of wing fold, are actuated by fully-triplicated hydraulic system. Leading-edge flaps. Large magnesium-alloy single-slotted trailing-edge flaps. Spoiler above each wing forward of flaps.

FUSELAGE: All-metal semi-monocoque structure. Large door-type ventral speed-brake under centre fuselage.

TAIL UNIT: Large swept vertical fin and rudder and one-piece horizontal "slab" tailplane set at dihedral angle of 5° 25'. Tailplane and rudder are operated by fully-triplicated hydraulic systems.

LANDING GEAR: Hydraulically-retractable tricycle type, with single wheel on each main unit and twin-wheel nose unit. Main wheels retract forward into fuselage, nose-wheels aft. Main wheels and tyres size 28 × 9-12; nose-wheels and tyres size 22 × 5·5. Sting-type arrester hook under rear fuselage for emergency landings or aborted take-offs. Anti-skid brake system and MLG tyres to minimise aquaplaning.

POWER PLANT: One Allison TF41-A-1 (Rolls-Royce Spey 168-62) turbofan engine, rated at 14,250 lb (6,465 kg) st without afterburning. Engine has self-start capability through the medium of battery-powered electric motor that spins an air-breathing gas-turbine starter. The starter unit includes a turbine-driven compressor that compresses air for combustion, a free-turbine for accelerating the engine to a self-sustaining speed and an integral control system. The engine has self-contained ignition for start/airstart, automatic relight and selective ignition. Integral fuel tanks in wings and additional fuselage tanks. Maximum internal fuel load 9,750 lb (4,423 kg). All fuel tanks lined with polyurethane fire-suppressing foam. Fuselage tanks and all fuel-lines self-sealing. Alternate fuel feed system. Flight refuelling capability of first 16 aircraft met by a probe and drogue system. 17th and subsequent aircraft have boom receptacle above fuselage on port side in line with wing leading-edge. Boron carbide (HFC) engine armour.

ACCOMMODATION: Pilot on Douglas ESCAPAC rocket-powered ejection system, complete with USAF life support system, that provides a fully-inflated parachute three seconds after sequence initiation; positive seat/man separation and stabilisation of the ejected seat and pilot. Boron carbide (HFC) cockpit armour.

SYSTEMS: Triple-redundant hydraulic system for flight controls, brakes and undercarriage retraction. Electrical system includes storage batteries for engine starting and maintenance of ground alert radio communications without need for the engine to be running. Liquid oxygen system. Automatic flight control system provides control-stick steering, altitude hold,

Vought A-7A Corsair II (Pratt & Whitney TF30-P-6 turbofan engine), carrying 300-lb Snakeye bombs

heading hold, heading pre-select and attitude hold. Ram air turbine provides hydraulic pressure and electrical power down to airspeeds below those used in normal landing approaches.

ELECTRONICS AND EQUIPMENT: The primary navigation/weapon-delivery system comprises AN/APQ-126 forward-looking radar which may be utilised for air-to-ground ranging for weapons delivery, ground mapping for navigation or adverse-weather bombing, manual terrain following, circular polarisation to enhance adverse-weather penetration; beacon for use in conjunction with AN/APN-134 rendezvous beacons in other aircraft; direct-view storage tube (DVST) for Walleye or radar presentations; AN/APQ-7 digital computer and head-up display (HUD) by Elliott Automation, UK; AN/ASN-90 inertial measurement system which operates in conjunction with the AN/APQ-126, AN/APQ-7, AN/APN-190 Doppler navigation system and armament system control unit (ASCU); projected moving map display; Laser ranging provisions; and LORAN provisions. Radio communications and navigation systems include FM 622-A VHF radio; AN/ARC-51 BX UHF radio; AN/APR-69 auxiliary UHF receiver; AN/ARA-50 UHF-ADF; AN/APX-72 IFF/SIF transponder; AN/ARN-52 TACAN; AN/ARN-58A ILS, LORAN provisions for AN/ARN-92; AN/APN-141 (V) radar altimeter; AN/APN-154 (V) radar beacon; 'Juliet 28' secure voice coder; RHAW system comprising AN/APR-36 and -37 receivers and ECM systems of the pod type, compatible with the aircraft's internal systems.

ARMAMENT: A wide range of stores can be carried on six under-wing pylons and two fuselage weapon stations. Two outboard pylons on each wing can each accommodate a load of 3,500 lb (1,587 kg). Inboard pylon on each wing can carry 2,500 lb (1,134 kg). Two fuselage weapon stations, one on each side, can each carry load of 500 lb (227 kg). Weapons carried include air-to-air and air-to-ground missiles; general-purpose bombs; rockets; gun pods and auxiliary fuel tanks. In addition, an M-61 Vulcan 20-mm cannon is mounted in the port side of the fuselage. This has 1,000-round ammunition storage and selected firing rates of 4,000 or 6,000 rpm. Strike camera in lower rear fuselage for damage assessment.

DIMENSIONS, EXTERNAL:

Wing span	38 ft 9 in (11·80 m)
Width, wings folded	23 ft 9 in (7·24 m)
Wing chord at root	15 ft 6 in (4·72 m)
Wing chord at tip	3 ft 10¼ in (1·18 m)
Wing aspect ratio	4
Length overall	46 ft 1½ in (14·06 m)

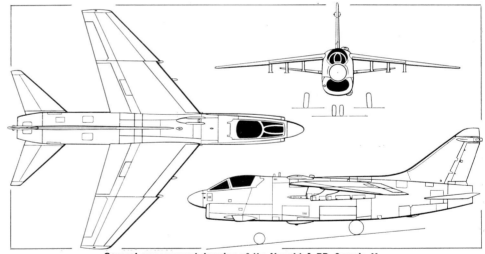

General arrangement drawing of the Vought A-7D Corsair II

Vought A-7D Corsair II, tactical fighter version for the USAF

Height overall	16 ft 0 in (4·88 m)
Tailplane span	18 ft 1½ in (5·52 m)
Wheel track	9 ft 6 in (2·90 m)

AREAS:

Wings, gross	375 sq ft (34·83 m²)
Ailerons (total)	19·94 sq ft (1·85 m²)
Trailing-edge flaps (total)	43·48 sq ft (4·04 m²)
Leading-edge flaps (total)	48·74 sq ft (4·53 m²)
Spoiler	4·60 sq ft (0·43 m²)
Deflector	3·44 sq ft (0·32 m²)
Fin	111·20 sq ft (10·33 m²)
Rudder	15·04 sq ft (1·40 m²)
Horizontal tail surfaces	56·39 sq ft (5·24 m²)
Speed brake	25·00 sq ft (2·32 m²)

WEIGHTS:

Weight empty	approx 18,000 lb (8,165 kg)
Max T-O weight	more than 42,000 lb (19,050 kg)

PERFORMANCE (at max T-O weight):

Max speed	606 knots (698 mph; 1,123 km/h)
T-O run	5,800 ft (1,768 m)
Ferry range	more than 2,450 nm (2,820 miles; 4,538 km)

Vought A-7E Corsair II attack bomber of the USN on board the USS *Independence*

LTV ELECTROSYSTEMS INC

HEAD OFFICE AND WORKS:
PO Box 6030, Dallas, Texas 75222

LTV L45ØF

To meet military requirements for a quiet reconnaissance aircraft, LTV Electrosystems designed and built a test version of a single-seat monoplane designated L45ØF, powered by a turboprop engine. The design provides the capability of carrying data-gathering equipment or electronic relay equipment (similar to that of a communications satellite) to a height of more than 45,000 ft (13,715 m) and offers a 24-hour endurance. Alternatively, the aircraft could be flown unmanned by remote ground control over a radius of 217 nm (250 miles; 402 km).

Development of the L45ØF culminated a $1 million Electrosystems research and development project that originated at its Greenville Division in 1967. The first flight was made during February 1970, and flight testing and overall refinement of the aircraft were scheduled for completion by mid-1970, with initial sales anticipated in 1971. However, the prototype was destroyed during its third flight, on 23 March, after the pilot had escaped by parachute.

Commercial applications of the L45ØF have been considered. Equipped with communications relay systems, such an aircraft could provide economical multiple communications channels between cities in underdeveloped areas of the world.

The basic airframe of the L45ØF prototype was that of a Schweizer SGS 2-32 sailplane; but this was modified extensively by Schweizer, to LTV Electrosystems drawings, to cater for the considerable load increase imposed by the installation of engine, fuel tanks, landing gear and electronics equipment. Modification involved strengthening of the wing spars and areas of the forward and rear fuselage, use of heavier skins, and an increase in the surface area of the fin and rudder. The wing was modified further by the addition of speed-brakes on both upper and lower surfaces. The non-retractable tricycle landing gear, with cantilever spring-steel main legs, was based on that of the Grumman Ag-Cat.

The power plant, mounted in a quick engine-change structure produced by Swearingen Aircraft, consisted of a modified 778 shp Pratt & Whitney (UACL) PT6A-29 turboprop engine, derated to 680 shp and driving a Hartzell three-blade metal propeller. Fuel was contained in wing cells with a combined capacity of 1,800 lb (816 kg) and a single aft fuselage cell containing 100 lb (45 kg), giving a total fuel capacity of 1,900 lb (861 kg). Operating at 45,000 ft (13,715 m), the fuel consumed was estimated to cost about $1·21 per hour, and an alternative version was proposed, equipped with a piston-engine power plant to give greater endurance and increased efficiency at lower altitudes.

The pilot was accommodated beneath a bubble canopy and was provided with conventional flying controls. If the L45ØF were to be operated in unmanned form, under remote control, the bubble canopy could be removed and replaced by an interface unit. For operation in this mode automatic stabilisation equipment would be installed, and the flight test aircraft was intended to be evaluated with a modified Bendix PB-60 autopilot. Complete ground control and monitoring by telemetry would allow control of the aircraft in a variety of modes, including take-off, constant heading/constant

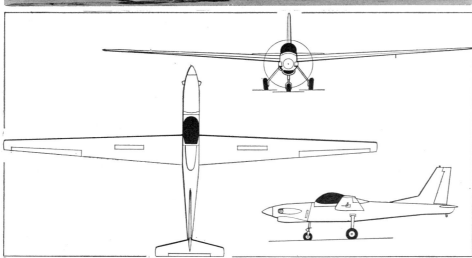

LTV L45ØF with and without cockpit cover fitted, and a three-view drawing

pitch angle, constant altitude/constant heading, constant airspeed/constant heading, reciprocal heading loiter, automatic preset heading and landing. In the event of the loss of command control there would be an in-built automatic destruction capability.

DIMENSIONS, EXTERNAL:

Wing span	57 ft 0 in (17·37 m)
Length overall	29 ft 0 in (8·84 m)

WEIGHTS:

Weight, empty	2,400 lb (1,089 kg)
Payload	350-700 lb (159-318 kg)
Max T-O weight	4,600 lb (2,087 kg)

PERFORMANCE (at max T-O weight):

Cruising speed at 45,000 ft (13,715 m)	91 knots (105 mph; 170 km/h) IAS
Best glide ratio	28:1
Max rate of climb at S/L	2,600 ft (792 m)/min
Service ceiling	52,000 ft (15,850 m)
Range (piloted version)	5,210 nm (6,000 miles; 9,656 km)
Endurance	24-30 hours

McCULLOCH

McCULLOCH AIRCRAFT CORPORATION

ADDRESS:
119 Standard Street, El Segundo, California 90245

PRESIDENT:
L. C. Mattera

VICE-PRESIDENT, ADMINISTRATION:
Paul J. Miller

VICE-PRESIDENT, OPERATIONS:
Norman E. Nelson

This company was formed to design, test and produce light rotating-wing aircraft. It has developed a four-seat tandem-rotor light helicop-

ter known as the 4E, and has developed and is starting production of a two-seat gyroplane known as the J-2, designed originally by Mr D. K. Jovanovich.

McCULLOCH 4E

This tandem-rotor light helicopter is a further development of the JOV-3, MC-4 and YH-30 two-seat helicopters designed by Mr D. K. Jovanovich and tested during the past 18 years. The prototype was, in fact, one of the MC-4C airframes built by the Helicopter Division of McCulloch Motors in 1952 and described in the 1954-55 *Jane's*. It received FAA certification in its current form in 1962.

TYPE: Four-seat tandem-rotor light helicopter.

ROTOR SYSTEM: The two rotors each have three fully-articulated blades of all-metal construction. Blades are built up of an aluminium extrusion and wrap-around skin, bonded together to form fail-safe structures, and are completely interchangeable. Aerofoil section NACA 0015. Blades attached to steel hubs through lag and flapping hinges. Rotor blades fold.

ROTOR DRIVE: Flexible 12-Vee-belt drive between engine and transmission. Only two sets of simple bevel gears used in drive system. Shaft to forward rotor runs above cabin. Rotor/engine rpm ratio 1 : 7.

FUSELAGE: Welded steel-tube structure, covered with light metal skin panels.

TAIL UNIT: Two small fixed stabilising fins.

LANDING GEAR: Non-retractable tricycle type with single wheel on each unit. Oleo-pneumatic shock-absorbers on main units. Goodyear wheels and tyres. Castoring nose-wheel. Provision for fitting skids or floats.

POWER PLANT: One 235 hp Franklin 6A-350 six-cylinder horizontally-opposed air-cooled engine mounted horizontally aft of cabin and removable as a package without disturbing other components. Fuel tank in fuselage. Oil capacity 2 US gallons (7·5 litres).

ACCOMMODATION: Four seats in pairs in enclosed cabin. Four large forward-hinged doors, two on each side of cabin. Dual controls optional. Conventional helicopter controls.

DIMENSIONS, EXTERNAL:
Diameter of rotors (each)　　23 ft 0 in (7·01 m)
Main rotor blade chord, constant
　　　　　　　　　　6·76 in (17·2 cm)
Distance between rotor centres 16 ft 0 in (4·88 m)
Length of fuselage　　　　18 ft 0 in (5·49 m)
Width of fuselage　　　　　4 ft 3 in (1·30 m)
Height overall　　　　　　9 ft 3 in (2·82 m)
Wheel track　　　　　　6 ft 6¾ in (2·00 m)
Wheelbase　　　　　　　7 ft 0 in (2·13 m)

AREA:
Rotor discs (total)　　751 sq ft (69·77 m²)

WEIGHTS:
Weight empty　　　　1,500 lb (680 kg)
Max T-O weight　　　2,400 lb (1,090 kg)

PERFORMANCE (at max T-O weight):
Max level speed at S/L
　　　　78 knots (90 mph; 145 km/h)
Max cruising speed
　　　　69 knots (80 mph; 129 km/h)
Rate of climb at S/L　　800 ft (245 m)/min
Range with max fuel and max payload
　　　　217 nm (250 miles; 400 km)

McCULLOCH J-2

The J-2 is a side-by-side two-seat light autogyro, of which the prototype flew for the first time in June 1962. Initial deliveries were scheduled for mid-1970. The rotor is similar to that of the McCulloch 4E helicopter.

TYPE: Two-seat light autogyro.

ROTOR SYSTEM: One three-blade rotor similar in construction to rotors of McCulloch 4E. Rotor unpowered in flight.

WINGS: Short mid-set cantilever wings, carrying tail-booms and main landing gear. Wing section NACA 0018. Chord 2 ft 6 in (0·76 m). All-metal construction.

FUSELAGE: Aluminium chassis-type structure.

TAIL UNIT: Cantilever all-metal structure, with twin fins and rudders, carried on slim tail-booms.

LANDING GEAR: Non-retractable tricycle type with single wheel on each unit. Oleo-pneumatic shock-absorbers. Cleveland wheels and tyres. Steerable nose-wheel. Wheel fairings optional. Brakes standard.

McCulloch 4E tandem-rotor light helicopter (235 hp Franklin 6A-350 engine)

McCulloch J-2 two-seat autogyro (180 hp Lycoming O-360-A2D engine)

POWER PLANT: One 180 hp Lycoming O-360-A2D four-cylinder horizontally-opposed air-cooled engine, mounted horizontally in rear fuselage and driving a two-blade fixed-pitch pusher propeller, diameter 6 ft 0 in (1·83 m), with spinner. Fuel tanks in wing tips, capacity 26 US gallons (98 litres). Oil capacity 3¾ US gallons (14·2 litres).

ACCOMMODATION: Two seats side-by-side in enclosed cabin. Forward-hinged door on each side. Standard equipment includes nylon safety belts, and enclosed luggage compartment in nose (capacity 2 cu ft = 0·05 m³), with rearward-hinged door on top. Further baggage space (capacity 5 cu ft = 0·15 m³) under seats.

ELECTRONICS AND EQUIPMENT: Standard equipment includes outside air temperature gauge, navigation lights, 60A alternator, battery, de-luxe cabin interior, nylon safety belts and ash tray. Optional equipment includes electric turn and bank indicator, 12-hour clock, dual controls, engine hour indicator, rotating beacon, heater, blower and defroster, and landing light. Optional radio equipment includes Bendix RT221A transceiver and Bendix IN-222A or 223A VOR.

DIMENSIONS, EXTERNAL:
Diameter of rotor　　　　26 ft 0 in (7·92 m)
Main rotor blade chord, constant
　　　　　　　　　　6·76 in (17·2 cm)
Wing chord, constant　　2 ft 6 in (0·76 m)
Wing span　　　　　　11 ft 2 in (3·40 m)
Length overall　　　　16 ft 0 in (4·88 m)
Height overall　　　　　8 ft 3 in (2·51 m)
Wheel track　　　　　6 ft 3 in (1·91 m)
Wheelbase　　　　　　7 ft 0 in (2·13 m)

AREAS:
Rotor disc　　　　　533 sq ft (49·52 m²)
Wings, gross　　33·2 sq ft (3·08 m²) effective

WEIGHTS AND LOADINGS:
Weight empty　　　　950 lb (431 kg)
Max T-O weight　　　1,500 lb (680 kg)
Max disc loading　2·81 lb/sq ft (13·7 kg/m²)
Max power loading　8·06 lb/hp (3·66 kg/hp)

PERFORMANCE (at max T-O weight):
Cruising speed　96 knots (110 mph; 177 km/h)
Landing and T-O speed
　　　　0-26 knots (0-30 mph; 0·48 km/h)
Rate of climb at S/L　800 ft (2,438 m)/min
Service ceiling　　　10,000 ft (3,050 m)
T-O and landing run　75-100 ft (23-30 m)
T-O to 50 ft (15 m)　　500 ft (152 m)
Range with max fuel, with reserve
　　　　217 nm (250 miles; 402 km)

MCDONNELL DOUGLAS
MCDONNELL DOUGLAS CORPORATION

TREASURER: Joseph H. Cinnater
STAFF VICE-PRESIDENTS:
Joseph W. Antonides (Procurement)
O. Ruffin Crow (Corporate Auditor)
Robert L. Hawkins (Auditor, West)
Arthur W. Hyland (Accounting)
Lewis Larmore (Douglas Advanced Research Labs)
Albert E. Lombard (McDonnell Research Labs)
O. Ben Marble (Marketing Communications)
Gilbert D. Masters (Manufacturing)
H. Earle Moore (Quality Assurance)
Anthony J. Piasecki (Financial Planning)
A. Joseph Quackenbush (Corporate Planning)

Laboratories
Douglas Advanced Research Laboratories
5251 Bolsa Avenue, Huntington Beach, California 92647
STAFF VICE-PRESIDENT AND DIRECTOR: Dr Lewis Larmore

MCDONNELL AIRCRAFT COMPANY (A Division of McDonnell Douglas Corporation)
HEADQUARTERS:
Box 516, St Louis, Missouri 63166
PRESIDENT: Sanford N. McDonnell
VICE-PRESIDENTS:
Robert J. Baldwin (Avionics)
Robert H. Belt (Aircraft Engineering)
Alvin L. Boyd (Fiscal Management)
Chester V. Braun (F-4 Programme Manager)
Robert F. Cortinovis (DC-10 Wing Programme)
Garrett C. Covington (General Engineering)
Richard J. Davis (External Relations)
William J. Gamewell (Material)
George S. Graff (Engineering)
Robert C. Little (Marketing)
Donald Malvern (F-15 General Manager)
Nate Molinarro (Personnel)
Madison L. Ramey (Engineering Technology)
John N. Schuler (Contracts)
John F. Sutherland (Product Support)
Sydney C. Wilkinson (Manufacturing)

Production at St Louis continues to be concentrated on various versions of the F-4 Phantom II two-seat twin-engined fighter for the US Navy, USAF and US Marine Corps.

The US Navy's *Blue Angels* flight demonstration team and the USAF's *Thunderbirds* air demonstration squadron began flying the Phantom in 1969. The Phantom is also in service with the Royal Navy and Royal Air Force, the Imperial Iranian Air Force, the Republic of Korea Air Force and the Israeli Air Force.

West Germany gave final approval in late November 1968 for the purchase of 88 RF-4E reconnaissance versions of the Phantom for its air force.

On 1 November 1968, the Japanese Defence Agency also selected the F-4E Phantom interceptor as the mainstay of its defence arm. These aircraft will be built in Japan under a licence agreement, with some components being supplied from St. Louis.

McDonnell have carried out considerable research and development on the technology required for the greater utilisation of beryllium. Under a programme sponsored by the USAF Flight Dynamics Laboratory, they have designed and fabricated a rudder for the F-4 Phantom II, and this was flown for the first time on a USAF YF-4E on 14 May 1968. The weight saving value of beryllium for structural components is demonstrated by comparing the 64 lb (29 kg) weight of a conventional F-4 aluminium rudder with the 42 lb (19 kg) weight of the new rudder.

A flight test programme was undertaken to establish the capability of beryllium structures to perform satisfactorily in service over an extended period of time.

In addition, on 10 September 1968 an RF-4C Phantom made the first flight with a boron composite rudder. On 27 March 1969, McDonnell received a USAF contract to build 50 boron-epoxy composite rudders. Forty-five of these will be retro-fitted on USAF F-4 Phantoms in operational service. The remaining five will be tested to verify unrestricted flight use and to develop and demonstrate environmental protection.

On 23 December 1969, the USAF selected McDonnell Douglas as prime contractor for development and production of the F-15 advanced tactical fighter aircraft.

MCDONNELL DOUGLAS PHANTOM II
US Navy and USAF designations: F-4 and RF-4

The Phantom II was developed initially as a twin-engined two-seat long-range all-weather attack fighter for service with the US Navy. A letter of intent to order two prototypes was issued on 18 October 1954, at which time the aircraft was designated AH-1. The designation was changed to F4H-1 on 26 May 1955, with change of mission to missile fighter. Early production aircraft were to be F4H-1F's with additional external weapon carrying ability. A camera-equipped reconnaissance version was ordered as the F4H-1P.

McDonnell Research Laboratories
Box 516, St Louis, Missouri 63166
STAFF VICE-PRESIDENT AND DIRECTOR: Dr Albert E. Lombard, Jr

McDonnell Douglas Corporation was formed on 28 April 1967, by the merger of the former Douglas Aircraft Company Inc and McDonnell Company. It encompasses both of the original companies and their subsidiaries.

There are four major operating components of the McDonnell Douglas Corporation, as follows:

McDonnell Aircraft Company
See below

Douglas Aircraft Company
See pages 376-385 of this section

McDonnell Douglas Astronautics Company
See "Military Missiles" and "Research Rockets" sections.

McDonnell Automation Company
Box 516, St Louis, Missouri 63166
PRESIDENT: William R. Orthwein, Jr
VICE-PRESIDENT AND GENERAL MANAGER: Robert L. Harmon
Subsidiaries:
Subsidiaries of McDonnell Douglas Corporation include Conductron Corporation, St Charles, Missouri; Hycon Manufacturing Company, Monrovia, California; Douglas Aircraft Company of Canada, Ltd, Malton, Ontario; Douglas United Nuclear, Inc, Richland, Washington; McDonnell Douglas (Japan) Ltd, Tokyo; and McDonnell Douglas Finance Corporation, Santa Monica, California.

At the end of December 1969, McDonnell Douglas employed a total of 107,503 people working in 49 communities in 17 states, Washington, DC, and Canada. Total office, engineering, laboratory and manufacturing floor area was 28,145,355 sq ft.

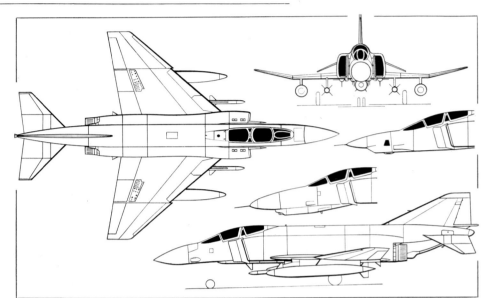

McDonnell Douglas F-4D Phantom II tactical fighter, with additional scrap views of noses of RF-4C (upper) and F-4E (lower)

McDonnell Douglas RF-4C Phantom II multi-sensor reconnaissance aircraft (*Air Portraits*)

The following versions have been developed:

XF4H-1. Prototype, which flew for the first time on 27 May 1958. It was designed for Mach 2 speeds and, in fact, achieved Mach 2·6 during its flight trials.

F-4A (formerly F4H-1F). The 11th production F-4B was equipped for trials in the ground attack rôle under this designation. During one test, it carried a total of twenty-two 500 lb bombs under its fuselage and inner wings. Further F-4B's were subsequently equipped to F-4A standard. After evaluation of this version, the USAF decided to order land-based versions of the F-4A under the designations F-4C and RF-4C.

F-4B (formerly F4H-1). Standard all-weather fighter for US Navy and Marine Corps. Development series of 23 followed by first production models in 1961. First 40 F-4B's were each powered by two General Electric J79-GE-2A turbojets (each 16,150 lb = 7,325 kg st with afterburning). Subsequent aircraft have J79-GE-8's. About 550 built by mid-1965.

RF-4B (formerly F4H-1P). Multi-sensor reconnaissance version of F-4B for US Marine Corps. No dual controls or armament. Reconnaissance system the same as for RF-4C. J79-GE-8 engines. High-frequency single side-band radio. Twelve ordered initially under 1963 fiscal year

budget. First one flew on 12 March 1965. Overall length increased to 63 ft (19·2 m). Production continues in 1970.

F-4C (formerly F-110A). Two-seat fighter for USAF, developed from F-4A, with J79-GE-15 turbojets, cartridge starting, wider-tread low-pressure tyres size 30 × 11·5, larger brakes, Litton type LN-12A/B (ASN-48) inertial navigation system, APQ-100 radar, APQ-100 PPI scope, LADD timer, Lear Siegler AJB-7 bombing system, GAM-83 controls, dual controls and boom flight refuelling instead of drogue (receptacle in top of fuselage, aft of cockpit). Folding wings and arrester gear retained. For close support and attack duties with Tactical Air Command, PACAF and USAFE. Initial orders for 280 under 1962-63 budget. First F-4C flew on 27 May 1963. The last of 583 was delivered to TAC on 4 May 1966. Replaced in production by F-4D.

RF-4C (formerly RF-110A). Multi-sensor reconnaissance version of F-4C for USAF, with radar and photographic systems in modified nose which increases overall length by 2 ft 9 in (0·84 m). Three basic reconnaissance systems are: side-looking radar to record high-definition radar picture of terrain on each side of flight path on film; infra-red detector to locate enemy forces under cover or at night by detecting exhaust

McDonnell Douglas F-4E Phantom II multi-role fighter (two General Electric J79-GE-17 turbojet engines) with M-61A1 multi-barrel gun under nose
(Gordon S. Williams)

gases and other heat sources; forward and side-looking cameras, including panoramic models with moving-lens elements for horizon-to-horizon pictures. Systems are operated from rear seat. HF single side-band radio. Initial series of 24 ordered under 1962-63 budget. This version is replacing all RF-101 aircraft in USAF service. YRF-4C flew on 9 August 1963. First production RF-4C flew on 18 May 1964. Production continues in 1970.

F-4D. Development of F-4C for USAF, with J79-GE-15 turbojets, APQ-109 fire-control radar, ASG-22 servoed sight, ASQ-91 weapon release computer, ASG-22 lead computing amplifier, ASG-22 lead computing gyro, 30kVA generators, and ASN-63 inertial navigation system. First F-4D flew on 8 December 1965. Two squadrons of F-4D's (32 aircraft) have been delivered to the Imperial Iranian Air Force. Production completed.

F-4E. Multi-rôle fighter for USAF, capable of performing air superiority, close-support and interdiction missions. Has internally-mounted M-61A1 20-mm multi-barrel gun, improved (AN/APQ-120) fire-control system and J79-GE-17 turbojets (each 17,900 lb = 8,120 kg st). Increased radius of action is provided by an additional fuselage fuel cell. First production F-4E delivered to USAF for initial testing on 3 October 1967. On 1 November 1968, the Japanese Defence Agency selected the F-4E as the main fighter for the JASDF. These aircraft will be built in Japan under a licence agreement, with some components being supplied from St. Louis.

RF-4E. Multi-sensor reconnaissance version for the Federal Republic of Germany. Generally similar to the RF-4C, it differs by having the J79-GE-17 turbojets of the F-4E and different reconnaissance equipment. Current order for 88 aircraft.

F-4G. Development of F-4B for US Navy, with AN/ASW-21 data link communications equipment. Interim model pending availability of F-4J. In service over Vietnam with Squadron VF-213 from USS *Kitty Hawk* in Spring of 1966. (F-4H designation not used, to avoid confusion with original F4H (see above).)

F-4J. Development of F-4B for US Navy and Marine Corps, primarily as interceptor but with full ground attack capability. J79-GE-10 turbojets. Use of 16½° drooping ailerons and slotted tail give reduced approach speed in spite of increased landing weight. Westinghouse AWG-10 pulse Doppler fire-control system. Lear Siegler AJB-7 bombing system, 30 kVA generators. First F-4J demonstrated publicly on 27 May 1966. In production.

F-4K. Development of F-4B for Royal Navy, with improvements evolved for F-4J plus other changes. The Westinghouse AN/AWG-10 pulse Doppler fire-control radar system has been modified to allow the antenna to swing around with the radome. This "foldable radome" reduces the length of the aircraft, making it compatible with the deck elevators on British aircraft carriers. Two Rolls-Royce Spey RB.168-25R Mk 201 turbofans (each rated at 12,500 lb = 5,670 kg st dry) with 70% reheat. The air intake ducts are 6 in (15·2 cm) wider than on US models to cater for these more powerful engines. Drooped ailerons. Tailplane has reduced anhedral and incorporates a leading-edge fixed slot. Strengthened main landing gear. Nose landing gear strut extends to 40 in (1·02 m), compared to 20 in (0·51 m) on the F-4J, to permit optimum-incidence catapulting. Martin-Baker ejection seats. Weapons include Sparrow air-to-air missiles and Martel air-to-surface missiles. Decision to order this aircraft for the RN taken in February 1964. Initial contracts for two YF-4K's and two F-4K's. First flight 27 June 1966. 24 ordered as Phan-

tom FG. Mk 1. First three aircraft were delivered to the Royal Navy on 25 April 1968 and the Navy's first Phantom training unit, 767 Squadron, was commissioned at RNAS Yeovilton on 14 January 1969, followed by the first operational Phantom unit, 892 Squadron, also commissioned at RNAS Yeovilton, on 31 March 1969.

F-4M. Version for Royal Air Force. Generally similar to F-4K, but with larger brakes and low-pressure tyres of F-4C. Folding wings and arrester gear retained. Orders for F-4K and F-4M expected to total about 174, with up to 50% of the components manufactured in the UK First F-4M flew on 17 February 1967. Deliveries began on 23 August 1968, and in January 1969 crew training was under way with No. 228 Operational Conversion Unit, based at RAF Coningsby. RAF designation is Phantom FGR. Mk 2.

A total of nearly 3,700 F-4's of all models had been built by December 1969. Production was then at the rate of about three per working day.

The Phantom II has set up many official records since December 1959, including World Speed and Height Records of 1,395·108 knots (1,606·48 mph; 2,585·425 km/h) and 98,556 ft (30,040 m) respectively. Records still standing at the time of writing are as follows:

On 28 August 1961, a speed record of 783·92 knots (902·72 mph; 1,452·777 km/h = Mach 1·2) was set up over a hazardous 3-km low-level course (maximum altitude 100 m = 328 ft) by

Lt Hunt Hardisty and Lt E. De Esch in one of the F-4A's. This exceeded the previous (subsonic) record, set up eight years earlier, by over 130 knots (149 mph; 240 km/h).

Between 21 February and 12 April 1962, the following time-to-height records were set up by US Navy pilots in an F-4B:

To 3,000 m (9,840 ft) 34·50 sec
To 6,000 m (19,680 ft) 48·78 sec
To 9,000 m (29,520 ft) 61·68 sec
To 12,000 m (39,360 ft) 1 min 17·14 sec
To 15,000 m (49,200 ft) 1 min 54·54 sec
To 20,000 m (65,600 ft) 2 min 58·50 sec
To 25,000 m (82,000 ft) 3 min 50·44 sec
To 30,000 m (98,400 ft) 6 min 11·43 sec

The following details apply specifically to the F-4B:

TYPE: Twin-engined two-seat all-weather fighter.

WINGS: Cantilever low-wing monoplane. Average thickness/chord ratio 5·1%. Sweep-back 45°. Outer panels have extended chord, giving "dog-tooth" leading-edge, and dihedral of 12°. Centre-section and centre wings form one-piece structure from wing fold to wing fold. Portion that passes through fuselage comprises a torsion-box between the front and main spars (at 15% and 40% chord) and is sealed to form two integral fuel tanks. Spars are machined from large forgings. Centre wings also have forged rear spar. Centre-line rib, wing-fold ribs, two intermediate ribs forward of main spar and two aft of main spar are also made

McDonnell Douglas F-4J Phantom II of the US Marine Corps *(Duane A. Kasulka)*

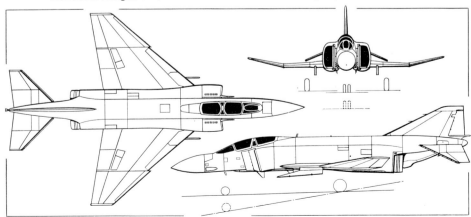

McDonnell Douglas Phantom FG.Mk 1 (F-4K) for the Royal Navy

from forgings. Wing skins machined from aluminium panels 2½ in (6·35 cm) thick, with integral stiffening. Trailing-edge is a one-piece aluminium honeycomb structure. Flaps and ailerons of all-metal construction, with aluminium honeycomb trailing-edges. Inset ailerons limited to down movement only, the "up" function being supplied by hydraulically-operated spoilers on upper surface of each wing. Ailerons and spoilers fully powered by two independent hydraulic systems. Hydraulically-operated trailing-edge flaps and leading-edge flap on outboard half of each inner wing panel are "blown". Hydraulically-operated air-brake under each wing aft of wheel well. Outer wing panels fold upward for stowage.

FUSELAGE: All-metal semi-monocoque structure, built in forward, centre and rear sections. Forward fuselage fabricated in port and starboard halves, so that most internal wiring and finishing can be done before assembly. Keel and rear sections make extensive use of steel and titanium. Double-wall construction under fuel tanks and for lower section of rear fuselage, with ram air cooling.

TAIL UNIT: Cantilever all-metal structure, with 23° of anhedral on one-piece all-moving horizontal surfaces (anhedral on RAF and RN versions is reduced to 15° and leading-edge incorporates a fixed slot). Ribs and stringers of horizontal surfaces are of steel, skin of titanium and trailing-edge of steel honeycomb. Rudder interconnected with ailerons at low speeds.

LANDING GEAR: Hydraulically-retractable tricycle type, main wheels retracting inward into wings, nose unit rearward. Single wheel on each main unit, with tyres size 30 × 7·7; twin wheels on nose unit which is steerable and self-centering, and can be lengthened pneumatically to increase the aircraft's angle of attack for take-off. Brake-chute housed in fuselage tailcone.

POWER PLANT: Two General Electric J79-GE-8 turbojet engines (each 16,500 lb = 7,485 kg st with afterburning). Variable-area inlet ducts monitored by air data computer. Integral fuel tankage in wings, between front and main spars, and in six fuselage tanks, with total capacity of 2,000 US gallons (7,569 litres). Provision for one 600 US gallon (2,270 litres) external tank under fuselage and two 370 US gallon (1,400 litre) underwing tanks. Equipment for probe-and-drogue and "buddy tank" flight refuelling, with retractable probe in starboard side of fuselage.

ACCOMMODATION: Crew of two in tandem on Martin-Baker Mk H5 ejection seats, under individual rearward-hinged canopies. Optional dual controls.

SYSTEMS: Three independent hydraulic systems, pressure 3,000 lb/sq in (210 kg/cm²). Pneumatic system for canopy operation, nose-wheel strut extension and ram air turbine extension. Primary electrical source is AC generator. No battery.

ARMAMENT: Six Sparrow III, or four Sparrow III and four Sidewinder, air-to-air missiles on four semi-submerged mountings under fuselage and two underwing mountings. Provision for carrying alternative loads of up to about 16,000 lb (7,250 kg) of nuclear or conventional bombs and missiles on five attachments under wings and fuselage. Typical loads include eighteen 750-lb bombs, fifteen 680-lb mines, eleven 1,000-lb bombs, seven smoke bombs, eleven 150 US gallon napalm bombs, four Bullpup air-to-surface missiles and fifteen packs of air-to-surface rockets.

ELECTRONICS: Eclipse-Pioneer dead-reckoning navigation computer, Collins AN/ASQ-19 communications-navigation-identification package, AiResearch A/A 24G central air data computer, Raytheon radar altimeter, General Electric ASA-32 autopilot, RCA data link, Lear attitude indicator and AJB-3 bombing system. Westinghouse APQ-72 automatic radar fire-control system in nose. ACF Electronics AAA-4 infra-red detector under nose.

DIMENSIONS, EXTERNAL:

Wing span	38 ft 5 in (11·70 m)
Width, wings folded	27 ft 6½ in (8·39 m)
Length overall	58 ft 3 in (17·76 m)
Height overall	16 ft 3 in (4·96 m)
Wheel track	17 ft 10½ in (5·30 m)

AREA:

Wings, gross	530 sq ft (49·2 m²)

WEIGHTS:

T-O weight (clean)	46,000 lb (20,865 kg)
Max T-O weight	54,600 lb (24,765 kg)

PERFORMANCE:

Max level speed with external stores
over Mach 2
Approach speed 130 knots (150 mph; 240 km/h)
Combat ceiling 71,000 ft (21,640 m)
T-O run (interceptor) 5,000 ft (1,525 m)
Landing run (interceptor) 3,000 ft (915 m)
Combat radius:
interceptor
over 781 nm (900 miles; 1,450 km)

McDonnell Douglas F-4K Phantom of the Royal Navy with braking parachute deployed

ground attack
over 868 nm (1,000 miles; 1,600 km)
Ferry range 1,997 nm (2,300 miles; 3,700 km)

MCDONNELL DOUGLAS F-15

The USAF first requested development funding for a new air superiority fighter in 1965, and in due course design proposals were sought from three airframe manufacturers: Fairchild Hiller Corporation; McDonnell Douglas Corporation; and North American Rockwell Corporation. On 23 December 1969 it was announced that McDonnell Douglas had been named as prime airframe contractor, the first contract calling for the design and manufacture of 20 aircraft for development testing at a total cost of $1,150 million. Funding from the 1970 Fiscal Year budget amounted to $80·24 million for airframe design and engineering, but total FY 1970 funding for the F-15 programme amounted to $175 million. This latter figure included allocations for engine and avionics development. Funding for new armament planned for the F-15 is the subject of a separate budget.

The contract is based on a combination of a cost plus incentive fee and a fixed-price incentive with successive targets. This means that the contractor must attain predetermined stages of development at the proper time and within the estimated cost before being allowed to proceed to the next stage. The USAF determines these stages, relates them to release of finance and decides whether or not the contractor is maintaining a satisfactory rate of progress.

The F-15 will be a single-seat fixed-wing twin-turbofan fighter in the 40,000-lb (18,145 kg) class. Its general configuration is shown in the adjacent illustration. No constructional details are yet available, but it has been stated that the airframe will be composed of considerably more of the advanced lightweight materials such as titanium and boron composites than any previous production aircraft.

Although designed to maintain air superiority, it will also have an air-to-surface attack capability. It will be able to deploy a variety of air-to-air weapons over short and medium ranges, have an internal rapid-firing gun, the ability to seek and destroy enemy aircraft in all weathers, and a maximum speed in excess of Mach 2.

In August 1968 initial engine development contracts were awarded to General Electric and Pratt & Whitney. Two engines, based on a common core but with differing characteristics, were sought to power the USAF's F-15 fighter and the F-14B fleet defence fighter for the US Navy. It was reported in March 1970 that a USAF/USN selection board had recommended Pratt & Whitney as prime contractors, but that this had not, at that time, received final approval from the Defense Secretary. Employing advanced engine technologies and aerodynamics, as well as lightweight materials, it is anticipated that the F-15's thrust-to-weight ratio will be better than 1 : 1.

In November 1968 the USAF awarded contracts to Westinghouse Electric Corporation and Hughes Aircraft Company for competitive development of a new attack radar system. During four years of analysis the USAF considered five possible avionics configurations:

(i) Radar for ranging, an optical computing sight and dive-bombing capability utilising a depressed reticle.

(ii) As above, plus airborne tracking radar for

all-weather capability against airborne targets and semi-active guidance for air-to-air missiles.

(iii) As above, plus expansion of the tracking radar to allow detection of low-flying targets and provide head-up display for aerial combat.

(iv) As above, with expanded radar and onboard computer to provide a degree of capability against ground targets, including the use of laser-guided bombs. In addition, provision of optical means of identifying distant airborne targets.

(v) The most complex configuration, with a multi-purpose radar suitable for blind bombing and aerial combat as well as the foregoing capabilities.

It seems likely that the final system may be a compromise between (iii) and (iv) and it has been suggested that avionics equipment may cost between $1 million and $2 million per aircraft. Flight testing of the two competing avionics systems was scheduled to begin during 1970, aboard two McDonnell Douglas RB-66's, and selection of the prime contractor is expected to take place in October 1970.

It was announced on 5 May 1970 that McDonnell Douglas had awarded a contract worth almost $8.4 million to the International Business Machines Federal Systems Division, Owego, New York, for development and testing of a central computer complex for the F-15. Under the contract, 21 computer units are to be built for ground testing, quality and reliability tests, and flight testing.

A gun development competition has been initiated between General Electric and Philco-Ford Corporation. This weapon is envisaged as a 25-mm high-rate-of-fire gun with caseless ammunition. Pending provision of such a gun, the USAF plans to arm the F-15 with the 20-mm M-61 multi-barrel gun. Advanced weapons are likely to include a short-range air-to-air attack missile, designated AIM-82A, intended as a dog-fight weapon.

The USAF hopes to achieve first flight of the F-15 in 1972, with entry into service in the mid-1970's. It is planned to use 12 aircraft for the contractor's tests necessary to develop the single-seat F-15 and a two-seat trainer version. The remaining 8 aircraft called for in the initial contract would be used in service flight testing to qualify the aircraft for operational use.

MCDONNELL DOUGLAS 188E

This is McDonnell's designation for the French-designed Breguet 941 STOL transport, for which it has licence rights. The production 188E would be built to US military standards, if ordered, with modified rear loading doors that could be opened in flight.

During 1968 McDonnell Aircraft Company completed a successful two-month joint demonstration programme with Eastern Airlines, to evaluate the advantages of STOL aircraft for the high-traffic Washington - New York - Boston air corridors. A further two-month programme in conjunction with American Airlines was undertaken in the Spring of 1969, to evaluate STOL feasibility on short-haul routes in the Middle West. This was followed by a brief programme conducted jointly with the FAA at the National Aviation Facilities Experimental Center, Atlantic City, New Jersey, in connection with an FAA definition of STOLport criteria.

Artist's impression of the McDonnell Douglas F-15 twin-turbofan air-superiority fighter for the USAF

DOUGLAS AIRCRAFT COMPANY (A Division of McDonnell Douglas Corporation)

HEADQUARTERS: 3855 Lakewood Boulevard, Long Beach, California 90801

CHAIRMAN AND CHIEF EXECUTIVE OFFICER: David S. Lewis

PRESIDENT AND CHIEF OPERATING OFFICER: Jackson R. McGowen

EXECUTIVE VICE-PRESIDENT: Wellwood E. Beall

VICE-PRESIDENTS:
Harold Bayer (Product Support)
John C. Brizendine (General Manager DC-10 Programme)
Robert F. Canaday (Military Systems Marketing)
Nathan A. Carhart (Engineering for Military Systems)
Howard W. Cleveland (Manufacturing)
Edward Curtis (Contracts and Pricing)
Warren T. Dickinson (Research and Technology)
Joseph J. Dysart (Product Support and DC-8/9 Programme Management)
James B. Edwards (Assistant to President)
Gilbert G. Fleming (Production)
Charles M. Forsyth (Commercial Marketing)
Thomas Gabbert (Financial Management)
Charles S. Glasgow (Engineering Design and Development)
Robert E. Hage (Engineering)
Harry E. Hjorth (International Commercial Sales)
O. Lee Howser (General Manager Tulsa Division)
Jesse L. Jones (Procurement and Quality Assurance)
John C. Londelius (Flight and Laboratory Development)
Harold E. Showalter (Controller)
Gerald B. Thomas (Domestic Commercial Sales)
Howell L. Walker (Military Systems Division)

CHIEF COUNSEL: John H. Carroll

DIRECTOR, EXTERNAL RELATIONS: Raymond L. Towne

The Douglas Aircraft Company operates plants at Long Beach, Palmdale and Torrance, California and Tulsa, Oklahoma. Total employment in February 1970 was 41,000.

The company is responsible for production of the various versions of the A-4 Skyhawk, the TA-4 trainer, the DC-8, DC-9 and DC-10 commercial jet transports and the DC-8F Jet Trader cargo and cargo-passenger transport, and is engaged in design studies of large commercial transport and space aircraft, in addition to other advanced study programmes. It was responsible for design of the PD-808 light jet executive transport, a description of which appears under the "Piaggio" heading in the Italian section of this edition.

MCDONNELL DOUGLAS DC-8

When Douglas decided to proceed with construction of their first jet transport, the four-engined DC-8, on 7 June 1955, they announced that all projected versions would have the same overall dimensions. They adhered to this policy until 1965, and the first five versions of the DC-8 have an identical airframe, with uniform electrical, hydraulic, control and air-conditioning systems. The intercontinental versions differ from the domestic models only in having extra fuel capacity and the structural modifications needed to carry the additional fuel. The modifications are limited to the use of thicker skin and stronger material within the wing structure, the aft portion of the fuselage and the tailplane. The landing gear is also more robust in the case of the heavier intercontinental versions.

These first five standard-size versions are as follows:

Series 10. Domestic version with 13,500 lb (6,124 kg) st Pratt & Whitney JT3C-6 turbojet engines. The first Series 10 DC-8 flew on 30 May 1958. This version received FAA certification on 31 August 1959 and entered service with United Air Lines and Delta Air Lines on 18 September 1959.

Series 20. Similar to Series 10, but with 15,800 lb (7,167 kg) st Pratt & Whitney JT4A-3 turbojet engines. The first Series 20 DC-8 flew on 29 November 1958 and received FAA certification on 19 January 1960.

Series 30. Long-range intercontinental version. Basically similar to Series 20, with 16,800 lb (7,620 kg) st JT4A-9 or 17,500 lb (7,945 kg) st JT4A-11 turbojet engines, and with increased fuel capacity. The first Series 30 flew on 21 February 1959 and received FAA certification on 1 February 1960.

Series 40. Long-range intercontinental version. Similar to Series 30, but with 17,500 lb (7,945 kg) st Rolls-Royce Conway RCo.12 by-pass turbojet engines. First Series 40 DC-8 flew on 23 July 1959 and received FAA certification on 24 March 1960.

Series 50. Similar to Series 30, but with turbofan engines. Initial production Srs 50 aircraft powered by 17,000 lb (7,718 kg) st Pratt & Whitney JT3D-1 or 18,000 lb (8,172 kg) st JT3D-3 engines. Subsequent production aircraft, known as Model 55, have improved JT3D-3B engines and aerodynamic refinements. Some Srs 30 aircraft have been converted to Series 50 standard. First Series 50 DC-8 flew on 20 December 1960 and received FAA certification on 1 May 1961.

On 23 February 1962 a DC-8 Series 50, with JT3D-3 turbofan engines, set up a distance record for commercial transport aircraft by flying non-stop 7,559 nm (8,705 miles; 14,010 km) from Tokyo to Miami, in 13 hr 52 min. This distance exceeded by nearly 1,476 nm (1,700 miles; 2,730 km) the previous longest flight by a commercial airliner.

A major improvement developed for the above versions of the DC-8 involves the installation of a different leading-edge which changes the wing profile and increases the wing chord by 4%, to reduce drag and improve the speed and range of the DC-8. It is standard on all late-production long-range DC-8's and has been fitted retrospectively to some earlier aircraft.

On 21 August 1961 a DC-8 Series 40 with wings modified in this way became the first jet transport to exceed the speed of sound, in a shallow dive at 40,350 ft (12,300 m). Its true air speed was 579 knots (667 mph; 1,073 km/h=Mach 1·012). On the same flight, it carried the equivalent of its normal payload to a height of 52,090 ft (15,875 m).

Departure from the standardised airframe policy was announced on 5 April 1965 when preliminary details were given of three new and advanced **Super Sixty (Series 60)** versions of the DC-8 as follows:

Super 61. First of the Super Sixty DC-8's, the Super 61 has the same wing and engine pylon structures as the Series 50, but the fuselage is extended by the insertion of a 20 ft 0 in (6·10 m) cabin section forward of the wing and a 16 ft 8 in (5·08 m) section aft of the wing. Accommodation is provided for up to 259 passengers, and cargo space under the floor is increased to 2,500 cu ft (70·80 m³). Powered by four 18,000 lb (8,172 kg) st Pratt & Whitney JT3D-3B turbofan engines. The first Super 61 was completed on 24 January 1966 and made its first flight on 14 March 1966. FAA type approval was received on 2 September 1966. Deliveries began on 26 January 1967 and the Super 61 entered scheduled service on 25 February 1967.

Super 62. This ultra-long-range version of the Super Sixty Series has an extended wing span and a fuselage 6 ft 8 in (2·03 m) longer than that of the standard DC-8. A 3 ft 4 in (1·02 m) cabin section is inserted both fore and aft of the wing, giving standard accommodation for up to 189 passengers. Each wingtip is fitted with a 3 ft 0 in (0·91 m) extension which significantly reduces induced drag under cruise conditions and makes possible an increased fuel tankage. Four Pratt & Whitney JT3D-3B turbofan engines. Engine pods of new design augment thrust and reduce

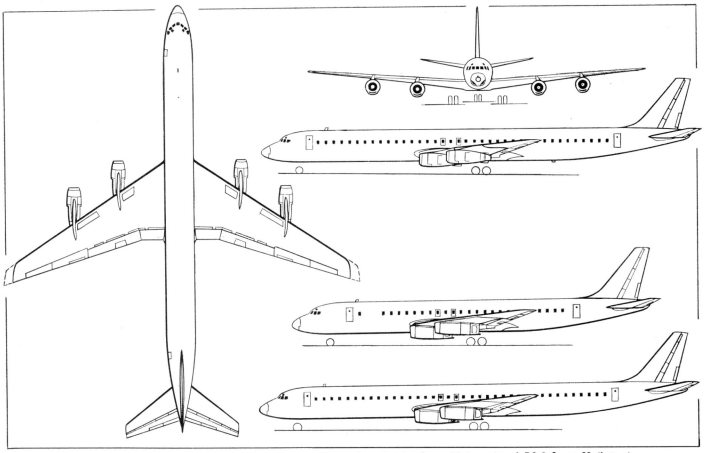

McDonnell Douglas DC-8 Super 61, with additional side elevations of DC-8 Super 62 (*centre*) **and DC-8 Super 63** (*bottom*). **Increased span of Super 62 and 63 is shown dotted in plan view**

McDonnell Douglas DC-8 Super 61 in the insignia of Air Canada (*Brian M. Service*)

drag by ducting by-pass air through the entire length of each nacelle. Redesigned engine pylons reduce interference drag. This version is capable of carrying a full 40,000 lb (18,145 kg) payload non-stop, against prevailing head-winds, from points in central Europe to the West coast of the USA, with ample fuel reserves. The first Super 62 flew for the first time on 29 August 1966. FAA Type Approval was received on 27 April 1967, including qualifiaction for automatic landing approach under Category 2 conditions. First delivery, to SAS, was made on 3 May 1967, and the Super 62 entered scheduled service on 22 May 1967.

Super 63. This developed version combines the long fuselage of the Super 61 with the aerodynamic and power plant improvements of the Super 62, but the majority of Super 63's have JT3D-7 engines of 19,000 lb (8,618 kg) st. Wheel track and tyre size increased The first Super 63, with JT3D-3B engines, flew for the first time on 10 April 1967. FAA Type Approval was received on 30 June 1967 and delivery of the first Super 63 was made, to KLM, on 15 July 1967. It entered scheduled service on 27 July.

All versions of the DC-8 are certificated to carry a spare engine in a streamlined pod under the port wing, inboard of the inner engine. They are also available in cargo or cargo/passenger configurations. These are described separately under the entry for the DC-8F Jet Trader.

Under a USAF contract, Douglas are studying the possibility of producing an Airborne Warning and Control System (AWACS) version of the DC-8 Super 62. This would carry very advanced radar, communications and data-processing equipment, including an over-fuselage rotodome of the kind fitted to the Grumman E-2A Hawkeye.

The following orders and leases for DC-8's had been announced by 1 January 1970:

Series 10

Delta Air Lines	6*
United Air Lines	22**

Series 20

Aeronaves de Mexico	1
Eastern Air Lines	15
National Air Lines	3
United Air Lines	15

Series 30

Japan Air Lines	5

KLM	7
Northwest Orient Airlines	5
Pan American World Airways	19
Braniff (Panagra)	4
Panair do Brasil	2
SAS	7
Swissair	3
UTA	5

Series 40

Air Canada	11
Alitalia	15
Canadian Pacific Airlines	6

Series 50

Aeronaves de Mexico	6
Air Afrique	2
Air Canada	3
Air New Zealand	5
Canadian Pacific Airlines	1
Delta Air Lines	15
Eastern Air Lines	1
Garuda (Indonesia)	1
Iberia	7
Japan Air Lines	10
KLM	9
National Air Lines	6
Philippine Air Lines	2
SAS	2
Swissair	1
Trans Caribbean Airways	2
Trans International Airlines	1
United Air Lines	13
VIASA	2

Super 60 Series

Air Canada	7 (61)
Air Canada	13 (63)
Alitalia	6 (62)
Braniff (Panagra)	6 (62)
Canadian Pacific Airlines	4 (63)
Delta Air Lines	13 (61)
Eastern Air Lines	17 (61)
Eastern Air Lines	6 (63)
Iberia	3 (63)
Japan Air Lines	9 (61)
Japan Air Lines	7 (62)
KLM	9 (63)
National Air Lines	2 (61)
SAS	7 (62)
SAS	5 (63)
Swissair	4 (62)
United Air Lines	30 (61)
United Air Lines	10 (62)

UTA	4 (62)
Viasa	2 (63)
Unannounced (all Series)	13

* All subsequently converted to Srs 50 standard
** Five subsequently converted to Srs 50 standard

A total of 506 DC-8's, including DC-8F's, had been delivered by 1 January 1970.

DC-8F orders are listed separately, under the description of this aircraft.

TYPE: Four-engined jet airliner.

WINGS: Cantilever low wing. Dihedral 6° 30′. Sweepback at quarter-chord 30°. All-metal structure, with three plate-web spars inboard, two plate-web spars outboard forming torsion box, and spanwise stringers riveted to top and bottom skins. Power-operated ailerons in two portions, outer portions being operated from inner portions at low speed only, via torsion-bar springs. Self-coupling manual circuit to tabs on inner ailerons in event of power failure. Two double-slotted flaps on each wing. Spoilers on top wing surface forward of flaps operate on nosewheel contact during landing. Two slots, 6 ft 8 in (2·03 m) and 2 ft 8 in (0·81 m) long respectively, on inboard leading-edge of each wing. Cyclic hot-air anti-icing system.

FUSELAGE: Double circular-section all-metal structure.

TAIL UNIT: Cantilever all-metal structure with 10° of dihedral on tailplane. Hydraulically-operated variable-incidence tailplane. Power-operated rudder with manual standby. Elevators manually-operated through servo-tabs. Cyclic hot-air anti-icing system.

LANDING GEAR: Retractable tricycle type. Nose-wheel unit retracts forward, main units inward into fuselage. Main units are four-wheel bogies, the rear pair of wheels on each bogie being free to swivel in a sharp turn. Goodyear tyres, pressure 131 lb/sq in (9·21 kg/cm²). Dual nose-wheel steerable through steering wheel and rudder pedals. Goodyear disc brakes.

POWER PLANT: Four turbojet or turbofan engines in separate pods, two under each wing (details under "Series" descriptions). All engines fitted with noise suppressors and thrust revers-

McDonnell Douglas DC-8 Super 62, ultra long-range version of the Super Sixty series

McDonnell Douglas DC-8 Super 63F large-capacity long-range all-cargo version of the DC-8 Super Sixty Series

ers for both ground and in-flight operation. All fuel in integral wing tanks with total capacity of 17,600 US gallons (66,528 litres) on Srs 10 and 20, 23,079 US gallons (87,360 litres) on Srs 30 and 40, 23,390 US gallons (88,531 litres) on Srs 50 (JT3D-3B) and Super 61 and 24,275 US gallons (91,881 litres) on Super 62 and 63. Pressure refuelling. Powered fuel dumping at maximum rate of 1,800 US gallons (6,815 litres) per minute.

ACCOMMODATION (Srs 10, 20, 30, 40, 50): Crew of 3-5, plus cabin attendants. Seats for 105-118 persons in first class domestic versions and for 132 in mixed class intercontinental versions, with normal tourist accommodation for 144 and economy class seating for up to 179 in all versions. Mixed-class arrangements to suit requirements of customer. Windows, size 18·5 in × 15 in (0·47 × 0·38 m), correspond with rows of first-class seats. Passenger doors at front and rear of cabin on port side. Servicing doors opposite passenger doors on starboard side. Freight and baggage holds under floor forward and aft of wing, each with two doors on starboard side.

ACCOMMODATION (Super Sixty Srs): See under individual descriptions above. Super 61 has coat room and two galleys at front on starboard side, two galleys at rear on starboard side, galley and coatroom at rear on port side and three toilets aft. Doors as for standard DC-8.

SYSTEMS: Air-conditioning and pressurisation system supplied by engine-driven turbo-compressors, with closed-circuit Freon system by Carrier Corp. Max pressure differential 8·77 lb/sq in (0·62 kg/cm²). Hydraulic system, pressure 3,000 lb/sq in (210 kg/cm²), for landing gear retraction, nose-wheel steering, brakes, flying controls, flaps and spoilers. Electrical system includes four 115/208V three-phase 400c/s AC alternators and four transformer-rectifiers for DC supply.

ELECTRONICS AND EQUIPMENT: Radio and radar to customer's specification. Sperry automatic flight control system, with SP-30 autopilot.

DIMENSIONS, EXTERNAL:
Wing span:
  except Super 62, 63   142 ft 5 in (43·41 m)
  Super 62, 63   148 ft 5 in (45·23 m)
Wing chord, theoretical on C/L
    31 ft 8·8 in (9·67 m)
Wing chord at tip, except Srs 60
    7 ft 3½ in (2·22 m)
Length overall:
  except Super Sixty Series 150 ft 6 in (45·87 m)
  Super 61, 63   187 ft 5 in (57·12 m)
  Super 62   157 ft 5 in (47·98 m)
Height overall:
  except Super 61, 62, 63   42 ft 4 in (12·91 m)
  Super 61, 62, 63   42 ft 5 in (12·92 m)
Tailplane span   47 ft 6 in (14·48 m)
Wheel track, except Super 63 20 ft 10 in (6·35 m)
Wheelbase:
  except Super Sixty Series 57 ft 6 in (17·52 m)
  Super 61, 63   77 ft 7 in (23·65 m)
  Super 62   60 ft 10 in (18·54 m)
Passenger doors (each):
  Height   6 ft 0 in (1·83 m)
  Width   2 ft 10½ in (0·88 m)
Servicing doors (each):
  Height   5 ft 4 in (1·63 m)
  Width   2 ft 9½ in (0·85 m)
Freight hold doors (each):
  Height   3 ft 8 in (1·12 m)
  Width   3 ft 0 in (0·91 m)

DIMENSIONS, INTERNAL:
Cabin, excluding flight deck:
  Length:
    Srs 10, 20, 30, 40, 50   102 ft 1 in (31·11 m)
  Max width:
    Srs 10, 20, 30, 40, 50   11 ft 6 in (3·50 m)
  Max height:
    Srs 10, 20, 30, 40, 50   7 ft 3 in (2·21 m)
  Volume:
    Srs 10, 20, 30, 40, 50 7,617 cu ft (215·7 m³)
    Super 61, 63   10,080 cu ft (285·4 m³)
    Super 62   8,084 cu ft (228·9 m³)
Freight and baggage holds (under floor, total):
    Srs 10, 20, 30, 40, 50   1,390 cu ft (39·35 m³)
    Super 61, 63   2,500 cu ft (70·80 m³)
    Super 62   1,615 cu ft (45·70 m³)

AREAS:
Wings, gross:
  Srs 10. 20, 30, 40, 50, early aircraft
    2,773 sq ft (257·6 m²)
  Srs 10, 20, 30, 40, 50, extended leading-edge
    2,868 sq ft (266·5 m²)
  Super 61   2,884 sq ft (267·9 m²)
  Super 62, 63   2,927 sq ft (271·9 m²)

WEIGHTS AND LOADINGS:
Basic operating weight:
  Srs 10   124,732 lb (56,578 kg)
  Srs 20   127,056 lb (57,632 kg)
  Srs 30 (JT4A-11)   133,803 lb (60,692 kg)
  Srs 40   132,425 lb (60,068 kg)
  Srs 50 (JT3D-3)   132,325 lb (60,020 kg)
  Super 61   148,897 lb (67,538 kg)
  Super 62   141,903 lb (64,366 kg)
  Super 63   153,749 lb (69,739 kg)
Capacity payload:
  Srs 10, 20, 30, 40, 50   34,360 lb (15,585 kg)
  Super 61   66,665 lb (30,240 kg)
  Super 62   47,335 lb (21,470 kg)
  Super 63   67,735 lb (30,719 kg)
Max ramp weight:
  Srs 10   275,000 lb (124,740 kg)
  Srs 20   278,000 lb (126,100 kg)
  Srs 30 (JT4A-11), 40   318,000 lb (144,240 kg)
  Srs 50 (JT3D-3B), Super 61
    328,000 lb (148,775 kg)
  Super 62   338,000 lb (153,315 kg)
  Super 63   353,000 lb (160,120 kg)
Max T-O weight:
  Srs 10   273,000 lb (123,830 kg)
  Srs 20   276,000 lb (125,190 kg)
  Srs 30, 40   315,000 lb (142,880 kg)
  Srs 50 (JT3D-3B), Super 61
    325,000 lb (147,415 kg)
  Super 62   335,000 lb (151,950 kg)
  Super 63   350,000 lb (158,760 kg)
Design landing weight:
  Srs 10   193,000 lb (87,543 kg)
  Srs 20   199,500 lb (90,500 kg)
  Srs 30, 40   207,000 lb (93,900 kg)
  Srs 50 (JT3D-3B)   217,000 lb (98,430 kg)
  Super 61, 62   240,000 lb (108,860 kg)
  Super 63   245,000 lb (111,130 kg)
Max zero-fuel weight:
  Srs 10   165,900 lb (75,250 kg)
  Srs 20   167,500 lb (75,975 kg)
  Srs 30   179,500 lb (81,420 kg)
  Srs 40   177,100 lb (80,330 kg)
  Srs 50 (JT3D-3)   176,500 lb (80,060 kg)
Max wing loading:
  Srs 10   98·5 lb/sq ft (480·9 kg/m²)
  Srs 20   99·6 lb/sq ft (486·3 kg/m²)
  Srs 30, 40, 50   109·2 lb/sq ft (533·2 kg/m²)

PERFORMANCE:
Max recommended cruising speed at 220,000 lb (99,800 kg) AUW at 30,000 ft (9,150 m):

  Srs 10   471 knots (542 mph; 873 km/h)
  Srs 20   503 knots (579 mph; 932 km/h)
  Srs 30 (JT4A-11)
    514 knots (592 mph; 952 km/h)
  Srs 40   509 knots (586 mph; 943 km/h)
  Srs 50 (JT3D-3B)
    504 knots (580 mph; 933 km/h)
  Super 61, 62, 63
    521 knots (600 mph; 965 km/h)
Landing speed at max landing weight:
  Srs 10, 20   129 knots (148 mph; 238 km/h)
  Srs 30, 40, 50
    133 knots (153 mph; 246 km/h)
Rate of climb at S/L:
  Srs 10   1,330 ft (405 m)/min
  Srs 20   2,650 ft (808 m)/min
  Super 61   2,270 ft (692 m)/min
  Super 62   2,240 ft (683 m)/min
  Super 63   2,165 ft (660 m)/min
FAA T-O field length at max AUW:
  Srs 10   9,380 ft (2,860 m)
  Srs 20   8,240 ft (2,510 m)
  Srs 30 (JT4A-11)   9,900 ft (3,020 m)
  Srs 40   9,650 ft (2,940 m)
  Srs 50 (JT3D-3B)   10,560 ft (3,220 m)
  Super 61   9,980 ft (3,042 m)
  Super 62   9,780 ft (2,980 m)
  Super 63   11,500 ft (3,505 m)
FAA landing field length at max landing weight:
  Srs 10, 20   6,400 ft (1,950 m)
  Srs 30, 40   6,800 ft (2,073 m)
  Srs 50   5,620 ft (1,713 m)
  Super 61, 62   6,140 ft (1,870 m)
  Super 63   5,910 ft (1,801 m)
Design range with max payload, normal reserves:
  Super 61   3,256 nm (3,750 miles; 6,035 km)
  Super 62   5,210 nm (6,000 miles; 9,640 km)
  Super 63   3,907 nm (4,500 miles; 7,240 km)
Estimated max range in still air, no reserves:
  Srs 10   3,734 nm (4,300 miles; 6,920 km)
  Srs 20   4,159 nm (4,790 miles; 7,710 km)
  Srs 30 (JT4A-11)
    5,184 nm (5,970 miles; 9,605 km)
  Srs 40   5,297 nm (6,100 miles; 9,817 km)
  Srs 50 (JT3D-3B)
    6,078 nm (7,000 miles; 11,260 km)
  Super 61, zero payload
    6,209 nm (7,150 miles; 11,500 km)
  Super 62, zero payload
    7,381 nm (8,500 miles; 13,675 km)
  Super 63, zero payload
    6,686 nm (7,700 miles; 12,390 km)

MCDONNELL DOUGLAS DC-8F JET TRADER

The DC-8F Jet Trader is a turbofan-engined variant of the DC-8, designed basically as a combination cargo and passenger transport, although an all-cargo model, without cabin windows, is available and has been specified by some operators, including United Air Lines.

The following versions have been announced:
Model 54. This was the basic DC-8F Jet Trader developed from the standard DC-8 Srs 50 and powered by four Pratt & Whitney JT3D-3 turbofan engines (each 18,000 lb = 8,172 kg st). It incorporates all the aerodynamic refinements developed for the DC-8 series. Maximum payload capacity is 95,282 lb (43,219 kg) and the Model 54 can carry its full payload non-stop across the Atlantic in either direction, between New York, London, Copenhagen, Amsterdam and Paris, against Winter head-winds.

Maximum fuel capacity is 23,397 US gallons (88,564 litres).

A typical payload over an operating range of 4,000 miles (6,440 km) is 54 passengers with their baggage, 54,500 lb (24,688 kg) of cargo and normal fuel reserves. However, the bulkhead between the freight and passenger compartments is movable, to permit adjustment of the passenger section to seat 24, 54, 84 or 114 people. In an all-passenger role, 189 economy-class seats can be installed.

In all arrangements, passenger accommodation is to normal tourist or economy class standards, with two entrance doors, a galley and two toilets. Access to the cargo hold is through an upward-hinged forward door which is 3 ft (0·91 m) wider than the largest doors on earlier DC-6A and DC-7F cargo transports. The hold has provision for mechanised quick loading of up to 13 pallets, each 7 ft 4 in × 9 ft (2·24 m × 2·74 m). Pallets are moved through the cabin on rollers and guide rails and locked into place on floor tracks.

A flight crew of four is normally carried, consisting of captain, first officer, flight engineer and navigator, with provision for a load-master's seat at the rear of the flight deck. The crew entry door is on the port side and they have their own galley, wardrobe and toilet on the port side of the flight deck.

The first production DC-8 Model 54 flew on 29 October 1962, was certificated on 29 January 1963 and delivered to Air Canada on 30 January 1963.

Model 55. Basically similar to Model 54, but with increased T-O weight and many detail refinements, including JT3D-3B engines. Received FAA Type Approval on 19 June 1964.

Super 61F/61CF. Cargo-passenger or all-cargo variant of DC-8 Super Sixty Series Super 61, with same long fuselage. Weights and performance as for Super 61 (which see).

Super 62F/62CF. Cargo-passenger or all-cargo variant of DC-8 Super Sixty Series Super 62. Weights and performance as for Super 62 (which see).

Super 63F/63CF. Cargo-passenger or all-cargo variant of DC-8 Super Sixty Series Super 63. First flew on 18 March 1968. Pratt & Whitney JT3D-7 turbofan engines (19,000 lb = 8,618 kg st). Max T-O weight 355,000 lb (161,028 kg). Max landing weight 275,000 lb (124,740 kg). Max all-cargo payload 118,583 lb (53,788 kg). Performance as for Super 63 (which see). Delivery of the first of 12 Super 63CF's ordered by Seaboard World Airlines was made on 21 June 1968.

The following orders and leases for the DC-8F had been announced by 1 January 1970:

Models 54/55

Air Afrique	1
Air Canada	8
Airlift International	2
Canadian Pacific	1
Capitol Airways	3
Flying Tiger	2

Iberia	1
Japan Air Lines	2
KLM	3
Overseas National Airways	2
Philippine Air Lines	1
SAS	1
Seaboard World Airlines	4
Trans Caribbean Airways	4
Trans International Airlines	2
United Air Lines	15
UTA	2

Super 61F/CF

Saturn Airways	2
Trans Caribbean Airways	3
Trans International Airlines	3
Universal	2

Super 62F/CF

Alitalia	2
Braniff	1
Finnair	3
Japan Air Lines	2
SAS	3
Swissair	2

Super 63F/CF

Air Afrique	1
Airlift International	3
American Flyers	2
Capitol Airways	4
Flying Tiger	17
Iberia	1
Overseas International	4
Seaboard World Airlines	12
Trans International	7

DIMENSIONS, INTERNAL AND EXTERNAL (Model 54 and 55):

Same as for DC-8 Srs 50 except for following:

Cargo door (fwd, port):		
Height		7 ft 1 in (2·16 m)
Width		11 ft 8 in (3·56 m)
Cabin:		
Usable cargo capacity		8,810 cu ft (249·5 m³)

WEIGHTS:

Design gross weight:	
Model 54	318,000 lb (144,240 kg)
Max T-O weight:	
Model 54	315,000 lb (142,880 kg)
Model 55	325,000 lb (147,415 kg)
Design landing weight:	
Model 54	240,000 lb (108,860 kg)
Max zero-fuel weight:	
Model 54	224,000 lb (101,600 kg)

PERFORMANCE (Model 54):

Max cruising speed at 220,000 lb (99,790 kg) AUW at 30,000 ft (9,145 m)
 503 knots (579 mph; 932 km/h)
T-O field length 9,450 ft (2,880 m)
Landing field length 7,000 ft (2,135 m)
Max range in still air, with full fuel and zero payload 6,157 nm (7,090 miles; 11,410 km)

MCDONNELL DOUGLAS DC-9
USAF designation: C-9A

Design study data on the DC-9, then known as the Douglas Model 2086, were released in 1962. Preliminary design work began during that year. Fabrication was started on 26 July 1963 and assembly of the first airframe began on 6 March 1964. It flew for the first time on 25 February 1965 and five DC-9's were flying by the end of June 1965. These aircraft were of the basic version now known as the DC-9 Series 10. The full range of DC-9 variants currently available is as follows:

Series 10 Model 11. Initial version, powered by two 12,250 lb (5,556 kg) st Pratt & Whitney JT8D-5 turbofan engines. Max accommodation for 80 passengers at 34 in (86 cm) seat pitch, with normal facilities, or 90 passengers with limited facilities. This version received FAA Type Approval on 23 November 1965 and entered scheduled service with Delta Air Lines on 8 December 1965.

Series 10 Model 15. Generally similar to Srs 10 Model 11 but with 14,000 lb (6,350 kg) st JT8D-1 turbofan engines, increased fuel capacity and increased all-up weight.

Series 20. Developed version for operation in hot climate/high-altitude conditions, combining long-span wings of Series 30 with short fuselage of Series 10. Up to 90 passengers. Two 14,500 lb (6,575 kg) st JT8D-9 turbofans. The Series 20 flew for the first time on 18 September 1968, and was Certificated on 11 December 1968. The first Series 20 was delivered to SAS on the same day and entered commercial service with SAS on 23 January 1969.

Series 30. Developed version with 14,000 lb (6,350 kg) st JT8D-7 turbofans, increased wing span, longer fuselage accommodating up to 105 (normal) or 115 (with limited facilities) passengers, and new high-lift devices including full-span leading-edge slats and double-slotted flaps. First Srs 30 flew for first time on 1 August 1966. First delivery, to Eastern Air Lines, was made on 27 January 1967 and scheduled services began on 1 February 1967.

Series 40. Generally similar to Series 30, but with 14,500 lb (6,575 kg) st JT8D-9 turbofans, increased fuel capacity, longer fuselage accommodating up to 125 passengers, and greater AUW. First flight was made on 28 November 1967 and FAA certification was received on 27 February 1968. The first Series 40 was delivered to SAS on 29 February 1968 and entered commercial service with this airline on 12 March 1968.

All versions are offered in passenger, cargo (**DC-9F**) or convertible (**DC-9CF**) or passenger-cargo (**DC-9RC**) configurations. The cargo and convertible models have a main cabin cargo door measuring 11 ft 4 in (3·45 m) wide and 6 ft 9 in (2·06 m) high. An executive transport version is also offered, with increased fuel, enabling parties of up to 15 persons to be carried non-stop over 3,300 mile (5,300 km) trans-continental and transocean stages. First delivery of an all-cargo model, a DC-9 Srs 30F, was made to Alitalia on 13 May 1968. This model has 4,313 cu ft (122·1 m²) of cargo space in main cabin, plus the

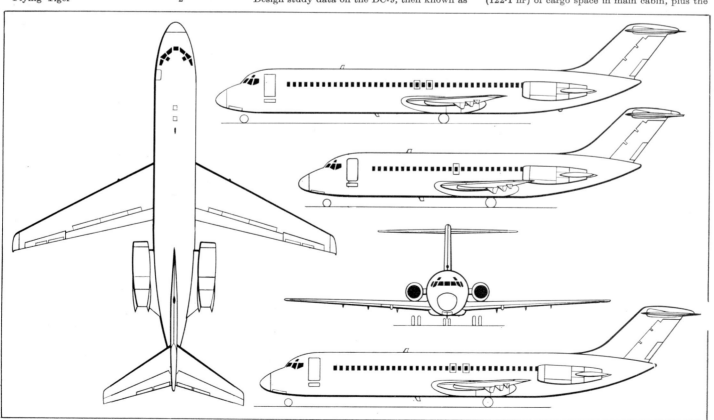

McDonnell Douglas DC-9 Srs 10 transport. Additional side elevations show Srs 30 (*bottom*) **and Srs 40** (*top*)

McDonnell Douglas DC-9 Series 30 in the insignia of Iberia (*Brian M. Service*)

McDonnell Douglas DC-9 Series 10 in the insignia of Saudi Arabian Airlines

underfloor hold, enabling it to carry eight full cargo pallets and two half-pallets with total weight of nearly 40,000 lb (18,144 kg).

There is also a military version of the DC-9, as follows:

C-9A. Aeromedical airlift transport, of which eight were ordered in August 1967 for operation by the 375th Aeromedical Wing of the USAF Military Airlift Command. Essentially an "off-the-shelf" DC-9 Srs 30 commercial transport, but with JT8D-9 engines, the C-9A is able to carry 30 to 40 litter patients, more than 40 ambulatory patients or a combination of the two, together with two nurses and three aero-medical technicians. The interior includes a special-care compartment, with separate atmospheric and ventilation controls. Galleys and toilets are provided fore and aft. There are three entrances, two with hydraulically-operated stairways. The third has an access door 6 ft 9 in (2·06 m) high and 11 ft 4 in (3·45 m) wide, with a hydraulically-operated ramp, to facilitate loading of litters. First C-9A was rolled out on 17 June 1968 and was delivered to the US Air Force at Scott Air Force Base on 10 August 1968.

Orders and leases for the commercial DC-9 announced up to mid-1970, are as follows:

Series 10

Aeronaves de Mexico	9
Air California	2
Air Canada	6
Air West	9
AVENSA	2
Continental Airlines	19
Delta Air Lines	14
Eastern Air Lines	15
Hawaiian Airlines	2
KLM	6
LAV (Venezuela)	1
Ozark Air Lines	6
Saudi Arabian Airlines	3
Southern Airways	6
Standard	2

Swissair	5	
Texas International Airways	7	
Tracy Investment	1	(Executive)
TWA	20	
W. J. Brennen	1	

Series 20

SAS	10

Series 30

Adria	2	
Aero Transporti Italiani	6	
Air Canada	36	
Air Jamaica	2	
Air West	16	
Alitalia	36	
Allegheny Airlines	25	
Ansett-ANA	6	
AVE	1	
Balair	1	
Caribair	3	
Delta Airlines	58	
Dominicana	1	
East African Airways	3	
Eastern Air Lines	72	
Garuda	2	
Hawaiian Airlines	5	
Hugh M. Hefner	1	(Executive)
Iberia	24	
JAT (Yugoslavia)	5	
KLM	16	
Korean Air Lines	1	
Martinair Holland	3	
North Central Airlines	15	
Northeast Airlines	14	
Overseas National Airways	7	
Ozark Air Lines	8	
Pacific Southwest Airlines	2	
Purdue Airlines	2	
SAS	2	
Southern Airways	3	
Sudflug	2	
Swissair	15	
Texas International Airways	4	
Trans-Australia Airlines	6	
Turkish Airlines	4	

Series 40

SAS	24
Unannounced DC-9 orders (all Series)	35

A total of 539 DC-9's had been delivered by 1 January 1970.

Under a then-unique participation plan for major sub-contractors, component manufacturers accepted deferred payment for developing and producing their portions of the aircraft. Each participant used his own capital to finance the engineering, tooling, qualification testing and work in process on the components he produced. Douglas then purchased these components under a firm fixed-price contract covering a specific number of units. Payment was completed upon delivery of the aircraft to airline customers.

First manufacturer to announce participation in this scheme was de Havilland Aircraft of Canada, which produced wings, rear fuselage and tail unit assemblies for the DC-9, until Douglas Aircraft Company of Canada took over responsibility for this work and leased that portion of the de Havilland plant devoted to DC-9 production. Agreements still in being were concluded with Garrett-AiResearch for air-conditioning and ice protection systems, Rohr Corporation for engine pods and thrust reversers, Sperry Phoenix Company for the aircraft's automatic flight control system, Menasco Manufacturing Company for the landing gear, Westinghouse Aerospace Electrical Division for the electric power generating system, Goodyear Tire and Rubber Company for the wheels and brakes, Sundstrand Corporation for constant-speed mechanisms and Hydro-Aire Division of Crane Company for anti-skid braking units.

In June 1966, the FAA certified three Category 2 all-weather landing systems for the DC-9, comprising the Collins FD-108 flight director system, Sperry AD-200 flight director system, and coupled approach utilising the Sperry SP-50A autopilot.

McDonnell Douglas DC-9 Series 40 (two 14,500 lb st Pratt & Whitney JT8D-9 turbofan engines

The following structural details apply to the DC-9 Series 10:

TYPE: Twin-jet short/medium-range airliner.

WINGS: Cantilever low-wing monoplane. Mean thickness/chord ratio 11·6%. Sweepback 24° at quarter-chord. All-metal construction, with three spars inboard, two spars outboard and spanwise stringers riveted to skin. Glass-fibre trailing-edges on wings, ailerons and flaps. Hydraulically-controlled ailerons, each in two sections, outer sections used at low speed only. Wing-mounted speed brakes. Hydraulically-actuated double-slotted flaps over 67% of semi-span. (Leading-edge slats on Srs 20/30/40). Single boundary-layer fence (vortillon) under each wing. Detachable wing-tips. Thermal anti-icing of leading-edges.

FUSELAGE: Conventional all-metal semi-monocoque structure.

TAIL UNIT: Cantilever all-metal structure with hydraulically-actuated variable-incidence tailplane mounted at tip of fin. Manually-controlled elevators with servo-tabs. Hydraulically-controlled rudder with manual override. Glass-fibre trailing-edges on control surfaces.

LANDING GEAR: Retractable tricycle type of Menasco manufacture, with steerable nosewheel. Hydraulic retraction, nose unit forward, main units inward. Twin Goodyear wheels on each unit. Main wheel tyres size 40 × 14. Nose-wheel tyres size 26 × 6·6. Goodyear brakes. Hydro-Aire Hytrol Mk II anti-skid units.

POWER PLANT: Two Pratt & Whitney JT8D turbofan engines (details under individual model listings above), mounted on sides of rear fuselage. Engines fitted with 40% target-type thrust reversers for ground operation only. Standard fuel capacity 2,786 US gallons (10,546 litres) in Srs 10 Model 11, 3,700 US gallons (14,000 litres) in Srs 10 Model 15, 3,679 US gallons (13,925 litres) in Srs 20, 30 and 40.

ACCOMMODATION (Srs 10): Crew of two on flight deck, plus cabin attendants. Accommodation in main cabin for 56-68 first-class passengers four-abreast, or up to 90 tourist class five-abreast. Mixed-class versions include one with 16 first class and 40 tourist seats. Fully-pressurised and air conditioned. Toilets at rear of cabin. Provision for galley. Passenger door at front of cabin on port side, with electrically-operated built-in air-stairs. Optional ventral stairway. Servicing and emergency exit door opposite on starboard side. Under-floor freight and baggage holds, with forward door on starboard side, rear door on port side.

DIMENSIONS, EXTERNAL:

Wing span:	
Srs 10	89 ft 5 in (27·25 m)
Srs 20, 30, 40	93 ft 5 in (28·47 m)
Wing aspect ratio, Series 10	8·25
Length overall:	
Srs 10, 20	104 ft 4¾ in (31·82 m)
Srs 30	119 ft 3½ in (36·37 m)
Srs 40	125 ft 7¼ in (38·28 m)
Height overall:	
Srs 10, 20, 30	27 ft 6 in (8·38 m)
Srs 40	28 ft 0 in (8·53 m)
Tailplane span:	
Srs 10	36 ft 10¼ in (11·23 m)
Wheel track:	
Srs 10, 20, 30, 40	16 ft 6 in (5·03 m)
Wheelbase	
Srs 10, 20	43 ft 8½ in (13·32 m)
Srs 30	53 ft 2½ in (16·22 m)
Srs 40	56 ft 1¼ in (17·10 m)
Passenger door (port, fwd):	
Height	6 ft 0 in (1·83 m)
Width	2 ft 9½ in (0·85 m)
Height to sill	7 ft 2 in (2·13 m)
Servicing door (stbd, fwd):	
Height	4 ft 0 in (1·22 m)
Width	2 ft 3 in (0·69 m)
Height to sill	7 ft 2 in (2·18 m)
Freight and baggage hold doors:	
Height	4 ft 2 in (1·27 m)
Width:	
fwd	4 ft 5 in (1·35 m)
rear	3 ft 0 in (0·91 m)
Height to sill	3 ft 6 in (1·07 m)

DIMENSIONS, INTERNAL:

Cabin (Srs 10): Length	55 ft 9 in (16·99 m)
Max width	10 ft 1 in (3·07 m)
Floor width	9 ft 5 in (2·87 m)
Max height	6 ft 9 in (2·06 m)
Floor area	510 sq ft (47·4 m²)
Volume	3,450 cu ft (97·7 m³)
Carry-on baggage compartment:	
Srs 10, 20	50 cu ft (1·42 m³)
Freight hold (underfloor):	
Srs 10, 20	600 cu ft (17·0 m³)
Srs 30	895 cu ft (25·3 m³)
Srs 40	1,019 cu ft (28·9 m³)

AREAS:

Wings, gross:	
Srs 10	934·3 sq ft (86·77 m²)
Srs 20, 30, 40	1,000·7 sq ft (92·97 m²)
Tailplane:	
Srs 10	275·6 sq ft (25·60 m²)

WEIGHTS AND LOADINGS:

Manufacturer's empty weight:	
Srs 10 Model 11	45,300 lb (20,550 kg)
Srs 10 Model 15	47,750 lb (21,660 kg)
Srs 20	49,900 lb (22,620 kg)
Srs 30	52,935 lb (24,011 kg)
Srs 40	55,690 lb (25,261 kg)
Max space-limited payload:	
Srs 10 Model 11	18,050 lb (8,188 kg)
Srs 10 Model 15	21,381 lb (9,698 kg)
Srs 20	21,885 lb (9,925 kg)
Max weight-limited payload:	
Srs 30	26,156 lb (11,864 kg)
Srs 40	34,195 lb (15,510 kg)
Max T-O weight:	
Srs 10 Model 11	77,700 lb (35,245 kg)
Srs 10 Model 15	90,700 lb (41,140 kg)
Srs 20, 30	98,000 lb (44,450 kg)
Srs 40	114,000 lb (51,710 kg)
Max ramp weight:	
Srs 10 Model 11	78,500 lb (35,605 kg)
Srs 10 Model 15	91,500 lb (41,500 kg)
Srs 20, 30	98,800 lb (44,815 kg)
Srs 40	115,000 lb (52,168 kg)
Max zero-fuel weight:	
Srs 10 Model 11	66,400 lb (30,120 kg)
Srs 10 Model 15	71,400 lb (32,385 kg)
Srs 20	78,000 lb (35,380 kg)
Srs 30	82,000 lb (37,195 kg)
Srs 40	93,000 lb (42,184 kg)
Max landing weight:	
Srs 10 Model 11	74,000 lb (33,565 kg)
Srs 10 Model 15	81,700 lb (37,060 kg)
Srs 20, 30	93,400 lb (42,365 kg)
Srs 40	102,000 lb (46,265 kg)
Max wing loading:	
Srs 10 Model 11	83·2 lb/sq ft (406·2 kg/m²)
Max power loading:	
Srs 10 Model 15	3·24 lb/lb st (3·24 kg/kg st)

PERFORMANCE (at max T-O weight, except where indicated):

Max cruising speed at 25,000 ft (7,620 m):
Srs 10 Model 11 and 15
487 knots (561 mph; 903 km/h)
Srs 20 at 80,000 lb (36,290 kg) AUW
487 knots (561 mph; 903 km/h)

McDonnell Douglas C-9A Nightingale aeromedical transport for USAF Military Airlift Command

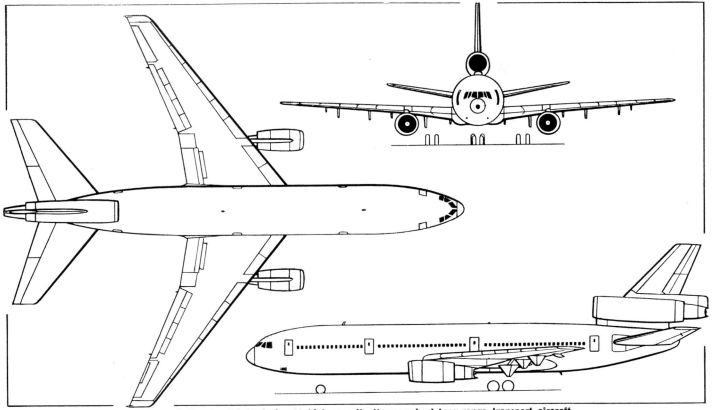

McDonnell Douglas DC-10 Series 30 high-capacity three-engined long-range transport aircraft

Srs 30 491 knots (565 mph; 909 km/h)
Srs 40 487 knots (561 mph; 903 km/h)
Rate of climb at S/L:
Srs 10 Model 11 2,750 ft (838 m)/min
FAA T-O field length:
Srs 10 Model 11 5,300 ft (1,615 m)
Srs 20 5,750 ft (1,750 m)
Srs 30 6,800 ft (2,075 m)
Srs 40 (at 100,000 lb = 45,359 kg AUW)
8,080 ft (2,462 m)
FAA landing field length:
Srs 10 Model 11 4,630 ft (1,411 m)
Srs 20 4,780 ft (1,460 m)
Srs 30 4,920 ft (1,500 m)
Srs 40 4,780 ft (1,456 m)
Range at Mach 0·8, with reserves for 200 nm
(230 mile; 370 km) flight to alternate and
60 min hold at 10,000 ft (3,050 m):
Srs 10 Model 11 at 25,000 ft (7,620 m) with 50
passengers and baggage
864 nm (995 miles; 1,601 km)
Srs 20 at 25,000 ft (7,620 m) with 50 passengers
and baggage
1,213 nm (1,397 miles; 2,250 km)
Srs 30 at 30,000 ft (9,150 m)
1,288 nm (1,484 miles; 2,388 km)
Srs 40 at 25,000 ft (7,620 m)
1,035 nm (1,192 miles; 1,918 km)
Range at long-range cruising speed at 30,000 ft
(9,150 m), reserves as above:
Srs 10 Model 11 with 50 passengers
1,138 nm (1,311 miles; 2,110 km)
Srs 20 with 50 passengers
1,600 nm (1,843 miles; 2,970 km)
Srs 30 1,498 nm (1,725 miles; 2,775 km)
Srs 40 1,463 nm (1,685 miles; 2,710 km)

MCDONNELL DOUGLAS DC-10

In April 1966, American Airlines circulated to
seven airframe manufacturers a statement of the
company's requirements, based on traffic forecasts. They appreciated that increasing airport
congestion would be alleviated by the introduction of commercial transport aircraft of greater
passenger carrying capacity, but considered it
essential that such aircraft should not be restricted to operation from those airports with
very long runways. At that time, they visual-
ised a twin-turbofan aircraft with dimensions
and performance tailored specifically for operation from smaller airports. During the evolu-
tionary period, the major change was a decision
to use three instead of two turbofan engines.

The aircraft which McDonnell Douglas evolved
to meet this specification has been designated
DC-10, an all-purpose commercial transport
able to operate economically over ranges from
260 nm to 5,300 nm (300 to 6,100 miles; 480 to
9,815 km), according to Series, and able to carry
270 mixed-class passengers, or a maximum of
345 passengers in an all-economy configuration.

It is to be produced in three basic versions,
differing primarily in their power plants, as
follows:

Series 10. Initial version, powered by three
General Electric CF6-6 turbofan engines, each
rated at 40,000 lb (18,144 kg) thrust. Intended
for service on domestic routes of 300-3,600

miles (480-5,795 km). Total fuel capacity
22,000 US gallons (83,280 litres).

Series 20. Extended-range version for intercontinental operations, powered by three Pratt
& Whitney JT9D turbofan engines.

Series 30. As series 20, but with three General
Electric CF6-50A turbofan engines, each rated at
49,000 lb (22,225 kg) thrust. Fuel capacity
as for Series 20.

There are also convertible cargo versions,
designated **Series 10F and 30F.** These are
described separately.

At the time of writing, orders and options total
214 aircraft, as follows:

| | | *Firm* | |
	Orders	Options	Series
Air Afrique	2	1	30
Alitalia	4	6	30
American Airlines	25	25	10
National Airlines	9	8	10
Northwest Airlines	14	14	20
Overseas National Airways	3	3	30F
Trans International Airlines	2	2	30F
United Airlines	30	30	10
KLM			
UTA			
SAS	KUSS group	14	22	30
Swissair			

Manufacture of the first aircraft started on 6
January 1969, less than nine months after the
decision to go ahead with this model. Assembly
of this machine, at the McDonnell Douglas plant
at Long Beach, California, began in the Autumn
of 1969, with completion of the first aircraft
scheduled for the summer of 1970, first flight
late in 1970 and initial delivery to an airline in
1971.

McDonnell Douglas announced on 11 June
1970 that the first DC-10 would be rolled out
on 23 July 1970.

The DC-10 manufacturing plan calls for sub-
assemblies and components to be brought together at Long Beach for final assembly. Certain major sub-assemblies will be produced at
other divisions of McDonnell Douglas, the nose
being built at McDonnell Douglas Astronautics
Company, Santa Monica, California; McDonnell
Aircraft Company, St Louis, Missouri is responsible for design and development of the wing,
and production of certain control surface components. Douglas Aircraft Company of Canada,
Ltd., a McDonnell Douglas subsidiary, will build
the wing structure at Malton, Ontario.

Convair Division of General Dynamics Corporation at San Diego, California, has been selected
as sub-contractor for the fuselage, being responsible for five sections totalling 128 ft (39·01 m)
of the 179 ft (54·56 m) fuselage. It is intended
to airlift these complete fuselage sections from
San Diego to Long Beach in Guppy aircraft
manufactured and operated by Aero Spacelines,
Inc, and additional details of this scheme may be
found in that company's entry in this edition.

Other sub-contractors selected for the DC-10
project include Rohr Corporation, Chula Vista,
responsible for engine pods and sound supression;

Aerosystems Division of Howmet Corporation,
Pomana and Montebello, California, main landing
gear units; AiResearch Manufacturing Company,
division of Garrett Corporation, of Los Angeles,
California, and Phoenix, Arizona, auxiliary power
unit and environmental system; Aerospace
Division of Abex Industries of Canada Ltd, Montreal, and Dowty Rotol Division of Dowty Export
Ltd, Gloucester, England, will both build nose
landing units; Vought Aeronautics, a Division of
LTV Aerospace Corporation, Dallas, Texas,
tailplane and elevators; Aerfer Industrie Aero-
spaziale Meridionala, Naples, Italy, upper fin
and rudder; and Mitsubishi Heavy Industries of
Japan the tail-cone and actuators for the main
landing gear doors. Sundstrand Corporation,
Rockford, Illinois, will provide constant-speed
drive mechanisms; Aerospace Electrical Division
of Westinghouse Electrical Corporation, Lima,
Ohio, electrical generating systems; Bendix Corporation's Navigation and Control Division, Teter-
boro, New Jersey, the integrated autopilot-flight
director unit; Amimech Division of Aircraft
Mechanics, Inc, Colorado Springs, Colorado,
crew seats of advanced design; the Aviation
Products Division of Goodyear Tyre and Rubber
Company, Akron, Ohio, wheels and brakes, and
the Flight Systems Division of Sperry Rand Corporation, Phoenix, Arizona, automatic throttle and
speed control system.

The DC-10 is a low-wing monoplane of conventional layout, as can be seen in the accompanying three-view drawing, with 35° sweepback
at 25% chord, and will feature advanced high-
lift wing devices. These, together with large
wing area, will enable the DC-10 to operate with
a full complement of economy class passengers
from small airports over short stage lengths.
Approach speed will be lower than that of current
large jet aircraft.

Power plant will comprise three turbofan
engines (details under Series listings above), two
of which will be mounted on pylons beneath the
wings, while the third is to be installed above the
aft fuselage, at the base of the fin.

Two aisles will run the length of the cabin,
which will be separated into sections by cloakroom dividers. In the first-class section, with
three pairs of reclining seats abreast, the aisles
are 2 ft 7 in (0·78 m) wide. In the coach-class
section, four pairs of seats, with a table between
the centre pairs, will also have two aisles, these
being 1 ft 8 in (0·51 m) wide. One pair of seats
is exchanged for a three-seat unit in the nine-
abreast high-density layout. The 11 in (0·28 m)
by 16 in (0·41 m) cabin windows are 9 in (0·23 m)
apart. Closed compartments within the cabin
will provide storage for passengers' personal
effects. Passenger baggage and other cargo
(in pre-loaded containers) will be accommodated
in a cargo hold in the lower fuselage.

American Airlines plan to embark passengers
by nose-in loading, through bridges similar to
those in current use, and two doors in the forward
section will allow use of both aisles. In all, there
are eight passenger doors.

z

Food will be prepared either in galleys on the passenger deck or in a spacious kitchen on a deck below cabin floor-level, provided with eight high-temperature ovens, refrigerators, storage space for linen, china and other accessories. Serving carts will be taken to cabin level by two electric elevators, to a buffet service-centre, from where stewardesses will serve passengers. To permit quick turn-round at terminals, without interference to passenger movement in the main cabin, the kitchen will be provisioned through the cargo doors at ground level.

The DC-10 will be certificated for operation to Category II weather minima requirements, and a fully-automatic landing system will be evolved concurrently with the basic aeroplane.

The following details were available at the time of writing:

DIMENSIONS, EXTERNAL (Srs 10, 20 and 30):
Wing span:
Srs 10	155 ft 4 in (47·35 m)
Srs 20, 30	161 ft 4 in (49·17 m)

Length overall:
Srs 10, 30	181 ft 5 in (55·29 m)
Srs 20	180 ft 0 in (54·86 m)
Height overall	58 ft 1 in (17·70 m)
Wheel track	35 ft 0 in (10·67 m)
Wheelbase	72 ft 4 in (22·05 m)

Passenger doors (six):
Height	6 ft 4 in (1·93 m)
Width	3 ft 6 in (1·07 m)

Passenger doors (two):
Height	6 ft 4 in (1·93 m)
Width	2 ft 8 in (0·81 m)

DIMENSIONS, INTERNAL (Srs 10, 20 and 30):
Max cabin width	18 ft 9 in (5·72 m)
Cabin height	8 ft 0 in (2·44 m)
Cargo hold, underfloor	3,040 cu ft (86·08 m³)

AREAS:
Wings, including ailerons:
Srs 10	3,550 sq ft (329·8 m²)
Srs 20, 30	3,610 sq ft (335 m²)

WEIGHTS:
Operating weight empty:
Srs 10	230,323 lb (104,476 kg)

Max payload:
Srs 10	80,435 lb (36,484 kg)
Srs 30	110,500 lb (50,122 kg)

Design ramp weight:
Srs 10	413,000 lb (187,331 kg)
Srs 20, 30	533,000 lb (241,765 kg)

Max T-O weight:
Srs 10	410,000 lb (185,970 kg)
Srs 30	555,000 lb (251,744 kg)

Design landing weight:
Srs 10	347,800 lb (157,758 kg)
Srs 30	403,000 lb (182,798 kg)

PERFORMANCE (estimated):
Cruising speed, Srs 10, 20 and 30 in excess of 521 knots (600 mph; 966 km/h)

FAA T-O field length (at max T-O weight):
Srs 10	8,150 ft (2,484 m)
Srs 30	11,160 ft (3,402 m)

FAA landing field length (at design landing weight):
Srs 10	5,350 ft (1,630 m)
Srs 30	5,950 ft (1,813 m)

Max range:
Srs 10	2,171 nm (2,500 miles; 4,023 km)
Srs 30	5,300 nm (6,100 miles; 9,817 km)

MCDONNELL DOUGLAS DC-10F

The DC-10F is a convertible freighter version of the McDonnell Douglas DC-10 high-density commercial transport. Generally similar to the basic DC-10, it is designed for easy conversion to either passenger or cargo configuration. It will be able to carry a payload consisting of 345 passengers and baggage, or 143,000 lb (64,860 kg) of cargo over full intercontinental range; or up to 158,000 lb (71,668 kg) of cargo on domestic transcontinental routes.

Two versions are offered: the DC-10F Series 20 is powered by three Pratt & Whitney JT9D-17 turbofan engines, the Series 30 by three General Electric CF6-50A turbofans. Deliveries of these models will begin in 1973.

In the passenger configuration, interior layout will be generally similar to that of the DC-10, but the DC-10F has been designed to permit overnight conversion to an all-cargo configuration. This entails removal of seats, overhead baggage racks, forward food service centre, cloakrooms and carpeting from the main cabin, and installation of freight loading tracks and rollers, a cargo tie-down system and restraint nets. Coffee service fixtures and lavatories in the aft cabin may also be removed but will be retained normally for regular cargo flights.

The cargo loading system for the DC-10F is based on that in use in the DC-8 Super Sixty Series freighters. A two-channel network of roller conveyors, adjustable guide rails and pallet restraint fittings is installed in the seat tracks in the cabin floor, by use of simple stud and locking pin devices. An 8 ft 6 in × 11 ft 6 in (2·59 m × 3·51 m) cargo door in the side of the fuselage swings upward and allows easy loading of bulky freight.

A total of 27 standard 7 ft 4 in × 9 ft (2·24 m × 2·74 m) cargo pallets or 22 larger pallets measuring 7 ft 4 in × 10 ft 5 in (2·24 m × 3·18 m)

or 8 ft × 10 ft (2·44 m × 3·05 m), can be accommodated in the main cabin. The DC-10F also has 3,040 cu ft (86·08 m³) of cargo space in its two lower baggage compartments for bulk freight or 16 half-size or 8 full-size pallets. The entire cargo loading and restraint system can be stowed in this lower hold, and is thus available for conversion of the aircraft to cargo configuration at any airport.

MCDONNELL DOUGLAS SKYHAWK
US Navy designation: A-4

The Skyhawk is a single-seat lightweight attack bomber which is in production at the Douglas Long Beach works and is in service on board carriers of the US Navy, with land-based Marine Corps squadrons with the air forces of Israel, New Zealand and the Argentine and with the Royal Australian Navy.

The Skyhawk entered production in September 1953 and the maiden flight of the XA-4A prototype, powered by a Wright J65-W-2 engine (7,200 lb = 3,270 kg st), took place on 22 June 1954.

The following versions have been produced:

A-4A (formerly A4D-1). Initial version with Wright J65-W-4 turbojet engine (7,700 lb = 3,493 kg st). First A-4A flew on 14 August 1954, and this version entered service with US Atlantic and Pacific Fleets on 26 October 1956. 166 built. Uprated engines (8,500 lb = 3,855 kg st) fitted progressively to all aircraft.

A-4B (formerly A4D-2). Similar to A-4A but with improved bomb delivery system, provision for carrying Bullpup missiles, automatic dead reckoning navigation computer, flight refuelling capability (both tanker and receiver), dual hydraulic system, stiffer single-surface rudder and powered tail, and Wright J65-W-16A turbojet (7,700 lb = 3,493 kg st). First flight 26 March 1956. 542 built. 50 reconditioned for Argentine Air Force. Uprated engines (8,500 lb = 3,855 kg st) fitted progressively to all aircraft.

A-4C (formerly A4D-2N). Similar to A-4B but longer nose to accommodate additional equipment to improve the all-weather characteristics. New items included advanced autopilot, low-altitude bombing/all-attitude indicating gyro system, terrain clearance radar and angle of attack indicator. First flight 21 August 1958. Deliver-

ies began in December 1959. Production completed in December 1962. 638 built. Uprated engines (8,500 lb = 3,855 kg st) fitted progressively to all aircraft.

A-4E (formerly A4D-5). Increased payload and 27% greater range. Powered by a Pratt & Whitney J52-P-6A turbojet (8,500 kg = 3,855 kg st). Douglas Escapac zero-height 90-knot rocket ejection seat. Five bomb racks can carry 20 separate items weighing up to 8,200 lb (3,720 kg) total. First flight 12 July 1961. Deliveries to US Navy began in November 1962. 500 built.

TA-4E. Original designation of prototypes of TA-4F.

A-4F. Attack bomber with J52-P-8A turbojet (9,300 lb = 4,218 kg st), new lift-spoilers on wings to shorten landing run by up to 1,000 ft (305 m), nose-wheel steering, low-pressure tyres, zero-height zero-speed ejection seat, additional bullet- and flak-resistant materials to protect pilot, and updated avionics. Prototype flew for first time on 31 August 1966. Deliveries to US Navy began on 20 June 1967, and were completed in June 1968.

TA-4F. Tandem two-seat dual-control trainer version of A-4F for US Navy. Pratt & Whitney J52-P-8A turbojet. Douglas Escapac rocket ejection seats. Provision for carrying full range of weapons available for A-4F. First prototype flew on 30 June 1965. Total of 139 ordered for US Navy. Deliveries began in May 1966.

A-4G. Similar to A-4F for Royal Australian Navy. Eight ordered. First delivered on 26 July 1967.

TA-4G. Similar to TA-4F, for Royal Australian Navy. Two ordered. First delivered on 26 July 1967.

A-4H. Designation of version supplied to Israel. Delivery of initial batch of 48 in 1967-68.

TA-4H. Tandem two-seat trainer version of A-4H for Israel.

TA-4J. Tandem two-seat trainer, basically similar to TA-4F. Ordered for US Naval Air Advanced Training Command, under $26,834,000 contract. Some tactical systems deleted, including air-to-air and air-to-surface missile launch equipment. Addition and relocation of certain instruments. J52-P-6 engine standard. Provision for J52-P-8A engine and combat

McDonnell Douglas single-seat A-4K and (above) two-seat TA-4K Skyhawk for the RNZAF

McDonnell Douglas A-4M Skyhawk attack bomber of the US Marine Corps (Pratt & Whitney J52-P-408A turbojet engine)

avionics. Prototype flew in May 1969 and the first four were delivered to the US Navy on 6 June 1969. In production.

A-4K. Similar to A-4F, for Royal New Zealand Air Force. Different radio and tail parachute. Ten ordered. The first of these aircraft were handed over to the RNZAF on 16 January 1970.

TA-4K. Similar to TA-4F, for Royal New Zealand Air Force. Four ordered. The first of these aircraft were handed over to the RNZAF on 16 January 1970.

A-4L. Modification of A-4C with uprated engine, bombing computing system and avionics relocated in fairing "hump" aft of cockpit as on A-4F. Delivery to US Navy Reserve carrier air wing began in December 1969.

A-4M. Basically similar to A-4F, but with J52-P-408A turbojet (11,200 lb = 5,080 kg st), and brake parachute, making possible combat operation from 4,000 ft (1,220 m) fields and claimed to increase tactical effectiveness by 30%. Larger windscreen and canopy. Greater ammunition capacity for 20 mm guns. More powerful generator and self-contained engine starter. First of two prototypes of this version flew for the first time on 10 April 1970. About 50 ordered for US Marines, with deliveries to begin in late 1970.

A-4N. Projected version for US Navy, basically similar to A-4M. Under consideration in mid-1970.

More than 2,400 Skyhawks had been delivered by the Spring of 1970.

Designed to operate from all sizes of aircraft carrier and from short landing fields, the Skyhawk is of such dimensions that it will negotiate the standard aircraft carrier lift without the need for folding wings.

Its several hundred variations of military load can include nuclear weapons and air-to-air or air-to-surface guided missiles.

A Douglas-developed self-contained flight refuelling unit can be carried on the standard bomb shackles to enable the A-4 to operate as a flying "tanker".

The following structural description refers specifically to the A-4F.

TYPE: Single-seat attack bomber.

WINGS: Cantilever low-wing monoplane. Sweep-back 33° at quarter-chord. All-metal three-spar structure. Spars machined from solid plate in one piece tip-to-tip. Hydraulically-powered all-metal ailerons, with servo trim-tab in port aileron. All-metal split flaps. Automatic leading-edge slats with fences. Hydraulically-actuated lift spoilers above flaps.

FUSELAGE: All-metal semi-monocoque structure in two sections. Rear section removable for engine servicing. Outwardly-hinged hydraulically-actuated air-brake on each side of rear fuselage. Detachable nose over Packard-Bell packaged communications and navigation equipment.

TAIL UNIT: Cantilever all-metal structure. Electrically-actuated variable-incidence tail-plane. Hydraulically-powered elevators. Powered rudder with unique central skin and external stiffeners.

LANDING GEAR: Hydraulically-retractable tricycle type, with single wheel on each unit. All units retract forward. Main legs pre-shorten for retraction and wheels turn through 90° to stow horizontally in wings. Menasco shock-absorbers. Hydraulic nose-wheel steering.

POWER PLANT: One 9,300 lb (4,218 kg) st Pratt & Whitney J52-P-8A turbojet engine. Fuel in self-sealing fuselage tank aft of cockpit and integral wing tanks, total capacity 800 US gallons (3,028 litres). Three 300 US gallon (1,136 litres) auxiliary tanks can be carried under wings and fuselage. Large flight refuelling probe on starboard side of nose. Douglas-developed self-contained flight refuelling unit can be carried instead of bomb shackles.

ACCOMMODATION: Pilot on Douglas Escapac 1-C3 zero-speed, zero-altitude lightweight ejection seat.

ARMAMENT: Two 20 mm Mk 12 cannon in wing roots. Provision for several hundred variations of military load, carried externally, including nuclear or HE bombs, air-to-surface rockets, Zuni or Mighty Mouse air-to-air rocket packs, Sidewinder infra-red missiles, Bullpup air-to-surface missiles, ground-attack gun pods, torpedoes, countermeasures equipment, etc. Central rack under fuselage carries up to 3,500

lb (1,588 kg) of stores. Each of the two inboard underwing racks carries 2,250 lb (1,020 kg); each of two outboard underwing racks carries 1,000 lb (450 kg).

DIMENSIONS, EXTERNAL:
Wing span	27 ft 6 in (8·38 m)
Wing chord at root	15 ft 6 in (4·72 m)
Length overall (excl flight refuelling probe):	
A-4A, B	38 ft 4¾ in (11·70 m)
A-4C	39 ft 1¾ in (11·93 m)
A-4E, F, M	40 ft 3¼ in (12·27 m)
TA-4F	42 ft 7¼ in (12·98 m)
Height overall:	
A-4A, B, C, E, F, M	15 ft 0 in (4·57 m)
TA-4F	15 ft 3 in (4·66 m)
Tailplane span	11 ft 3½ in (3·44 m)
Wheel track	7 ft 9½ in (2·38 m)

AREAS:
Wings, gross	260 sq ft (24·16 m²)
Vertical tail surfaces (total)	50 sq ft (4·65 m²)
Horizontal tail surfaces (total)	48·85 sq ft (4·54 m²)

WEIGHTS:
Weight empty:	
A-4A	8,400 lb (3,810 kg)
A-4B	9,146 lb (4,149 kg)
A-4C	9,619 lb (4,363 kg)
A-4E	9,853 lb (4,469 kg)
A-4F, A-4K	10,000 lb (4,535 kg)
TA-4F, A-4M	10,602 lb (4,809 kg)
Normal T-O weight:	
A-4C	17,295 lb (7,845 kg)
Max T-O weight:	
A-4A, B, C	22,500 lb (10,206 kg)
A-4E, A-4F, TA-4F, A-4K, A-4M	24,500 lb (11,113 kg)
A-4F from land base*	27,420 lb (12,437 kg)

export version only: overload condition not authorised by US Navy.

PERFORMANCE (at design T-O weight):
Max level speed	
A-4A	577 knots (664 mph; 1,069 km/h)
A-4B	574 knots (661 mph; 1,064 km/h)
A-4C	564 knots (649 mph; 1,044 km/h)
A-4E	585 knots (674 mph; 1,085 km/h)
TA-4F	586 knots (675 mph; 1,086 km/h)
Max range with external tanks	over 1,736 nm (2,000 miles; 3,200 km)

McKINNON

McKINNON ENTERPRISES, INC

HEAD OFFICE AND WORKS:
Route 1, Box 520, Sandy, Oregon 97055

OWNER AND MANAGER: A. G. McKinnon

McKinnon Enterprises (formerly McKinnon-Hickman Company) entered the aircraft conversion field in 1953 when it undertook the conversion of the Grumman Widgeon twin-engined light amphibian into an executive aircraft. The success of this conversion, which is still being manufactured, led to the development and manufacture of a larger four-engined amphibian, known as the McKinnon G-21, which is a much improved and more luxurious conversion of the Grumman Goose.

Details of the four-engined McKinnon G-21 Goose conversion can be found in the 1966-67 *Jane's*. It has now been superseded by the new turboprop-powered G-21C, D and G, as described below. McKinnon are also offering a minimum conversion scheme by which the standard Goose can be re-engined with turboprops and fitted with any other parts of the G-21C/D conversion specified by the customer.

McKinnon have received official approval for a modification scheme to fit retractable wing-tip floats to standard Goose amphibians. This offers increased cruising speeds, reduced landing speed, better stability on both land and water, and greatly improved accessibility for loading and unloading on water.

Also offered by McKinnon is an officially-approved conversion kit by which the max T-O weight of the standard Goose can be increased by 1,200 lb (545 kg) to 9,200 lb (4,173 kg).

McKINNON G-21C and G-21D TURBO-GOOSE

In these current versions of the G-21, the two normal 450 hp Pratt & Whitney R-985 radial engines of the Goose amphibian are replaced by two 579 eshp Pratt & Whitney (UAC) PT6A-20 turboprop engines, moved further inboard and driving constant-speed and reversible propellers. The internal fuel capacity is increased. Other modifications include the fitting of retractable wing-tip floats, inverted double-slotted flaps, extended radar nose, dorsal fin, one-piece windscreen, larger cabin windows, a new instrument panel, oxygen system, and a 24V electrical system. Landing gear and wing-tip float retraction and flaps are all electrically-operated.

The fully-modified G-21C and D will operate with ease from 2,000 ft (610 m) fields or small lakes, at even the highest altitudes.

The G-21C is fitted out to accommodate from nine to thirteen people, including pilot. The Model G-21D is basically similar except that the bow is extended by 3 ft 0 in (0·91 m), the interior re-designed, the tailplane span increased, a rudder

McKinnon G-21G Turbo-Goose amphibian (two 680 shp Pratt & Whitney (UACL) PT6A-27 turboprop engines)

tab added and the fuel capacity reduced by deletion of the centre-section tank. This version is described below. It received FAA Type Approval in February 1967.

TYPE: Twin-turboprop light amphibian.

WINGS: Cantilever high-wing monoplane. Wing section NACA 23000. Dihedral 2° 30′. All-metal structure with metal covering. Fabric-covered metal ailerons. All-metal inverted double-slotted flaps.

FUSELAGE: All-metal semi-monocoque flying-boat hull with two steps.

TAIL UNIT: Braced all-metal structure.

LANDING GEAR: Retractable tail-wheel type. All wheels retract electrically into hull, with manual extension. Bendix oleo-pneumatic shock-absorbers. Goodyear wheels and double-disc brakes. Retractable wing-tip stabilising floats.

POWER PLANT: Two 579 eshp Pratt & Whitney (UAC) PT6A-20 turboprop engines, driving three-blade constant-speed reversible and fully-feathering propellers. Fuel tanks in wings, total capacity 337 US gallons (1,275 litres).

ACCOMMODATION: Pilot and up to 14 passengers in standard version. Four passengers in bow cabin forward of flight deck, with bow-loading entrance and baggage space in nose. Main cabin, forward of the standard rear door, seats seven people, with four more in a cabin aft of the door. Optional seating for total of 17 persons, including pilot. One baggage compartment, capacity 300 lb (136 kg).

DIMENSIONS, EXTERNAL:
Wing span	50 ft 10 in (15·49 m)
Wing chord at root	10 ft 0 in (3·05 m)
Wing chord at tip	5 ft 0 in (1·52 m)
Wing aspect ratio	6·101
Length overall	39 ft 7 in (12·07 m)
Width of hull	5 ft 0 in (1·52 m)
Tailplane span	19 ft 9 in (6·02 m)
Wheel track	7 ft 6 in (2·29 m)
Wheelbase	17 ft 2 in (5·23 m)

AREAS:
Wings, gross	377·64 sq ft (34·44 m²)
Ailerons (total)	29·64 sq ft (2·75 m²)
Fin	21·20 sq ft (1·97 m²)
Rudder	26·80 sq ft (2·49 m²)
Tailplane	39·48 sq ft (3·67 m²)
Elevators	42·92 sq ft (3·99 m²)
Elevator tab	2·10 sq ft (0·195 m²)

WEIGHTS:
Weight empty, equipped	8,200 lb (3,720 kg)
Max T-O weight	12,200 lb (5,535 kg)
Max landing weight, on land	12,200 lb (5,535 kg)
Max landing weight, on water	12,000 lb (5,445 kg)

PERFORMANCE (at max T-O weight):
Max level speed	191 knots (220 mph; 355 km/h)
Range with max fuel	approx 1,042 nm (1,200 miles; 1,930 km)

McKINNON G-21G TURBO-GOOSE

McKinnon have announced introduction of a new version of the Turbo-Goose, an 8/12-seat conversion of the standard Grumman G-21A, which has been designated as the Model G-21G.

Introduction of more powerful 680 shp Pratt & Whitney (UACL) PT6A-27 turboprop engines, driving Hartzell three-blade metal constant-speed fully-feathering and reversible propellers, has considerably improved the performance, payload and range of this version. Essential modifications to the airframe include a 15 in (0·38 m) nose extension to accommodate radar, metallising treatment of the wings and provision of a wrap-around windshield, retractable wingtip floats, rotating beacon on top of the fin, a small dorsal fin, hull vents and auxiliary wing tanks that increase total fuel capacity to 586 US gallons (2,218 litres). Optional improvements include provision of picture windows for the cabin, a centre main fuel tank of increased capacity, dual landing lights in wing leading-edges, electrically-operated retraction of landing gear and enlargement of the cabin by removing the bulkhead at station 26.

McKinnon have received FAA approval for this new conversion. All available specification details follow:

WEIGHTS:
Weight empty, equipped (approx)
       6,700 lb (3,039 kg)
Max T-O weight 12,500 lb (5,670 kg)
PERFORMANCE (at max T-O weight):
Max operating speed
    205 knots (236 mph; 380 km/h)
Service ceiling 20,000 ft (6,096 m)
Service ceiling, one engine out
      15,000 ft (4,572 m)
Range, with 586 US gallons (2,218 litres) fuel
   1,389 nm (1,600 miles; 2,574 km)

McKINNON TURBOPROP GOOSE CONVERSION

For owners of Goose amphibians who do not require a full conversion of their aircraft to G-21C, D or G standard, McKinnon offer a simple conversion which involves only replacement of the original R-985 piston-engines with two 579 eshp Pratt & Whitney (UACL) PT6A-20 turboprop engines in the original location, driving three-blade constant-speed reversible pitch propellers.

Any of the other modifications incorporated on the G-21C/D can be made on the standard Goose conversion. Speed and take-off performance are comparable with those of the G-21C/D. Range is also comparable after fitment of the optional auxiliary tanks.

WEIGHTS (minimum conversion):
Weight empty, equipped 6,300 lb (2,858 kg)
Max T-O weight 10,500 lb (4,760 kg)
Max landing weight, on land or water
      10,500 lb (4,760 kg)

McKINNON SUPER WIDGEON

The Super Widgeon is an executive conversion of the Grumman Widgeon light amphibian, with the two original 200 hp Ranger six-cylinder in-line inverted engines replaced by two 270 hp Lycoming GO-480-B1D flat-six engines driving Hartzell three-blade fully-feathering propellers. Modifications to the hull and landing gear permit an increase in loaded weight. Extra tanks are provided in the outer wings to increase the fuel capacity from 108 to 154 US gallons (408 to 582 litres). Other new features include picture windows, a modern IFR instrument panel, improved sound-proofing and the provision of an emergency escape hatch. Approval to install retractable floats was obtained in 1960.

The cabin is arranged to accommodate a pilot, co-pilot and three or four passengers.

Well over 50 Widgeons have been converted to Super Widgeon standard by McKinnon, and several retractable float installations have been completed.

DIMENSIONS, EXTERNAL:
Wing span   40 ft 0 in (12·19 m)
Length overall 31 ft 1 in (9·47 m)
Height overall 11 ft 5 in (3·48 m)

McKinnon G-21 Turboprop Goose of the Bureau of Land Management (two Pratt & Whitney PT6A engines) (*Norman E. Taylor*)

McKinnon Super Widgeon, with retractable wingtip floats

WEIGHT:
Max T-O weight 5,500 lb (2,500 kg)
PERFORMANCE (at max T-O weight):
Max level speed at S/L
   165 knots (190 mph; 306 km/h)
Cruising speed at 10,000 ft (3,050 m) (62½% power) 156 knots (180 mph; 290 km/h)
Cruising speed at S/L (70% power)
   152 knots (175 mph; 282 km/h)
Landing speed 54 knots (62 mph; 100 km/h)
Rate of climb at S/L 1,750 ft (534 m)/min
Service ceiling 18,000 ft (5,490 m)
Single-engine ceiling 5,000 ft (1,525 m)
T-O run (land) 600 ft (183 m)
T-O from glassy water 10 seconds
Range with max fuel, reserves for 30 min
   868 nm (1,000 miles; 1,600 km)

MARTIN MARIETTA
MARTIN MARIETTA CORPORATION
AEROSPACE HEADQUARTERS:
Friendship International Airport, Maryland 21240

DENVER DIVISION:
PO Box 179, Denver, Colorado 80201

OFFICERS: See "Missiles" section

Martin Marietta Corporation built two different versions of a manned lifting-body research aircraft, related to its SV-5D Prime (X-23A) unpiloted manoeuverable lifting re-entry vehicle of which details were given in the "Missiles" section of the 1967-68 *Jane's*. Development of the second of these, the SV-5J, has now ended and details of this may be found in the 1969-70 *Jane's*.

MARTIN MARIETTA SV-5P PILOT
USAF designation: X-24A

Martin Marietta has been engaged in lifting-body research and development since 1959, during which time more than two million man-hours have been devoted to engineering design studies, materials investigation and wind-tunnel testing. Its current activities in this field are aimed towards the development of manoeuvring manned re-entry vehicles able to perform as spacecraft in orbit, fly in Earth's atmosphere like aircraft and land at conventional airports.

The small unmanned X-23A (described in the 1967-68 *Jane's*) has proved the aerodynamic characteristics of the design evolved by Martin Marietta. In three flights from orbital altitude and hypersonic speed, the X-23A's stability and manoeuvrability were demonstrated successfully through re-entry conditions down to a speed of Mach 2 and altitude of 100,000 ft. The SV-5P Pilot (PIloted LOw-speed Test aircraft) was ordered by the USAF in May 1966, to begin where the X-23A models ended, by exploring the lower end of the speed scale. Official designation of the SV-5P is X-24A.

Martin Marietta X-24A (SV-5P) rocket-powered lifting-body research aircraft

The X-24A considerably differs in design and flying controls from the two lifting-body research vehicles built for NASA by Northrop. It has a triangular planform and what is described as a "bulbous wedge shape", with flat bottom, rounded top and three vertical fins. Controls consist of two upper flaps (aileron and elevator) and two lower flaps (aileron and elevator) at the extreme rear of the body, and a pair of split rudders on each of the outer tail-fins. The centre tail-fin is fixed.

The lower rudders control the vehicle in yaw. Pitch and roll are controlled by the upper and lower flaps acting as elevons. The upper rudders are not controlled by the pilot but act as trim surfaces, positioning themselves automatically in proportion to the aircraft's speed. All control surfaces are fully powered by irreversible dual hydraulic systems, and have thick trailing-edges. A redundant three-axis stability augmentation system is fitted.

Construction is entirely conventional, using aluminium alloys. The manually-retractable tricycle landing gear consists of a twin-wheel nose unit and single-wheel main units, all rearward-retracting. The pilot sits on a zero-speed, zero-altitude ejection seat, under a jettisonable bubble-type canopy, in a cockpit pressurised at 3·5 lb/sq in (0·25 kg/cm²). He operates conventional stick and rudder/brake pedal controls.

Power plant of the X-24A is an 8,000 lb (3,625 kg) st Thiokol XLR-24A four-chamber regeneratively-cooled turbo-rocket engine. Provision is made for two 500 lb (225 kg) st Bell LLRV optional landing rockets. The cylindrical propellent tanks for the liquid oxygen and ethyl-alcohol-water mixture are housed longitudinally, side-by-side in the centre fuselage. The spherical container of helium gas used to pressurise the tanks is mounted to their rear and immediately forward of the rocket engine.

The X-24A was delivered to the USAF on 11 July 1967 and was sent to Edwards AFB for flight testing on completion of final acceptance tests at Baltimore.

An adapter built by Martin Marietta enables the X-24A to be carried into the air under the wing of the B-52 Stratofortress "mother-plane" used for X-15 launchings. Released at an altitude of about 45,000 ft (13,700 m) and speed of about Mach 0·6, the pilot will ignite the XLR-11 rocket engine, which will boost the X-24A to an altitude of up to 100,000 ft (30,500 m) and speed of Mach 2. From that height and speed, it will be manoeuvred to a landing on Rogers Dry Lake at Edwards AFB. Flare-out will be at a height of about 1,000 ft (305 m), at a speed of 230-345 mph (370-560 kmh). Landing speed will be 160-355 mph (260-575 kmh). Time from launch to touch-down will be approximately 15 minutes (3½ minutes for initial unpowered flights).

During 1969 the X-24A completed successfully nine unpowered flights, and a tenth was scheduled to be made early in 1970. The first powered flight was made by Maj Jerauld Gentry at Edwards AFB on 19 March 1970. Total flight time was 7 min 15 sec with a 2 min 40 sec burn of the Thiokol rocket engine.

Rear view of the X-24A, showing all control surfaces

DIMENSIONS, EXTERNAL:		
Width overall	13 ft 8 in	(4·17 m)
Length overall	24 ft 6 in	(7·47 m)
Height overall	10 ft 4 in	(3·15 m)
AREA:		
Planform	162 sq ft	(15·05 m²)

WEIGHTS AND LOADINGS:	
Min weight, unfuelled	under 6,000 lb (2,720 kg)
Max launching weight, fuelled	approx 11,000 lb (5,000 kg)
Min area loading	36·1 lb/sq ft (176·3 kg/m²)
Max area loading	60 lb/sq ft (293 kg/m²)

MAULE
MAULE AIRCRAFT CORPORATION
HEAD OFFICE AND WORKS:
Spence Air Force Base, Moultrie, Georgia 31768
PRESIDENT: B. D. Maule
VICE-PRESIDENT: Mrs B. D. (June) Maule (Treasurer)
DIRECTOR OF SALES: B. D. Maule (Temporary)
DIRECTOR OF PURCHASING: June Maule (Temporary)

This company was formed to manufacture the Maule M-4 four-seat light aircraft. It transferred to new facilities in Moultrie, Georgia, in September 1968.

MAULE M-4 JETASEN AND ROCKET
Design of the M-4 was started in 1956. Construction of the prototype began in 1960 and it flew for the first time on 8 September 1960. Production began early in 1962 and four basic versions are now available, as follows:

M-4 Jetasen. Basic model with 145 hp Continental O-300-A engine and McCauley fixed-pitch propeller.

M-4 Astro-Rocket. This is a de luxe version of the M-4 Jetasen, powered by a 180 hp engine driving a constant-speed propeller. No performance details of this version were available at the time of writing.

M-4 Rocket. Announced in Autumn of 1964, this version has a 210 hp Continental engine and McCauley constant-speed propeller, giving improved short-field capability and all-round performance increases. Received FAA Type Approval 24 September 1964. Seaplane version became available in 1967, with ability to take off in seven seconds, cruise at over 122 knots (140 mph; 225 km/h) and land at 35 knots (40 mph; 65 km/h).

M-4 Strata-Rocket. Generally similar to Rocket, but powered by 220 hp Franklin 6A-350-C1 engine, driving McCauley constant-speed propeller.

The following structural description refers specifically to the M-4 Rocket, but is generally applicable to the other versions except for the power plant details.

TYPE: Four-seat light aircraft.

WINGS: Braced high-wing monoplane. Streamline-section Vee bracing struts each side. USA 35B (modified) wing section. Dihedral 1°. Incidence 30′. All-metal two-spar structure with metal covering and glass-fibre tips. All-metal ailerons and two-position flaps. Ailerons linked with rudder tab, so that aircraft can be controlled in flight by using only the control wheel in the cockpit. Cambered wingtips standard on all but Jetasen.

FUSELAGE: Welded 4130 steel-tube structure. Covered with glass-fibre, except for metal doors and aluminium skin around cabin.

TAIL UNIT: Wire-braced steel-tube structure, covered with glass-fibre. Trim-tabs in port elevator and rudder. Rudder tab linked to ailerons.

LANDING GEAR: Non-retractable tail-wheel type. Oleo main shock-absorbers. Cleveland main wheels type 0-2000, size 6·00 × 6 4-ply, pressure

Maule M-4 Rocket, showing new cambered wing-tips

22 lb/sq in (1·55 kg/cm²). Maule 1½ P8G steerable tail-wheel. Cleveland hydraulic brakes. Parking brake. Fairings aft of main wheels. Provision for fitting Fli-Lite Model 3000 Mk IIIA or Federal Model A2000A skis, hydraulically-actuated Federal Model C2200H skis, Edo floats, Fleet floats (Rocket only), or over-size tyres.

POWER PLANT: One 210 hp Continental IO-360-A six-cylinder horizontally-opposed air-cooled engine, driving a McCauley two-blade constant-speed propeller, diameter 6 ft 2 in (1·88 m). Two fuel tanks in wings, with total capacity of 42 US gallons (159 litres). Refuelling points in wing leading-edges. Oil capacity 2·5 US gallons (9·5 litres).

ACCOMMODATION: Four persons in pairs in enclosed cabin, with dual controls. Front seats adjustable. Rear bench seat. Forward-hinged doors on each side at front and on port side at rear of cabin. Space for 100 lb (45 kg) baggage aft of rear seat, with external door on port side. Provision for removing passenger seats so that aircraft can be used for cargo, ambulance and agricultural duties. Double cargo door 52 in (1·32 m) wide optional on Jetasen, standard on other models. Cabin heater and windshield defroster.

SYSTEMS: Hydraulic system for brakes. 35A engine-driven generator, 12V battery. 55A alternator on Strata-Rocket.

ELECTRONICS AND EQUIPMENT. Standard equipment on de luxe models (Astro-Rocket, Rocket and Strata-Rocket) includes stall warning system, cabin soundproofing, 8-day clock, cabin steps, tie-down rings, ventilation under dash, navigation lights, landing light, instrument and dome lights, cabin console speaker, cigarette lighter and ashtray. Provision for full range of radio equipment to customer's require-

ments, including Narco and King 1½ systems and ADF. Other optional equipment includes Flite Lite flashing beacons, dual landing lights, blind-flying instrumentation, auto-pilot, carburettor air temperature gauge, heated pitot, glider tow, and dual brakes.

DIMENSIONS, EXTERNAL:		
Wing span, standard tips	29 ft 8 in	(9·04 m)
Wing chord, constant	5 ft 3 in	(1·60 m)
Wing aspect ratio		5·65
Length overall	22 ft 0 in	(6·71 m)
Height overall	6 ft 2½ in	(1·89 m)
Tailplane span	9 ft 8¾ in	(2·97 m)
Wheel track	6 ft 0 in	(1·83 m)
Wheelbase	15 ft 10 in	(4·82 m)
Cabin doors (fwd, each):		
Height	2 ft 9 in	(0·84 m)
Width	2 ft 6 in	(0·76 m)
Height to sill	3 ft 1 in	(0·94 m)
Cabin door (cargo type, rear, stbd):		
Height	2 ft 5½ in	(0·75 m)
Width	4 ft 4 in	(1·32 m)
Height to sill	2 ft 4 in	(0·71 m)

DIMENSIONS, INTERNAL:		
Cabin: Length	8 ft 4 in	(2·54 m)
Max width	3 ft 6½ in	(1·08 m)
Max height	3 ft 10½ in	(1·18 m)

AREAS:		
Wings, gross	152·5 sq ft	(14·17 m²)
Ailerons (total)	14·5 sq ft	(1·35 m²)
Trailing-edge flaps (total)	14·6 sq ft	(1·36 m²)
Fin	11·15 sq ft	(1·04 m²)
Rudder, including tab	5·23 sq ft	(0·49 m²)
Tailplane	12·60 sq ft	(1·17 m²)
Elevators, including tab	14·00 sq ft	(1·30 m²)

WEIGHTS AND LOADINGS:		
Weight empty:		
Jetasen	1,100 lb	(499 kg)
Rocket	1,220 lb	(553 kg)
Strata-Rocket	1,250 lb	(566 kg)

Max T-O and landing weight:
Jetasen   2,100 lb (953 kg)
Rocket, Strata-Rocket   2,300 lb (1,043 kg)
Max wing loading:
Jetasen   13·75 lb/sq ft (67·13 kg/m²)
Max power loading :
Jetasen   14·5 lb/hp (6·58 kg/hp)
PERFORMANCE (at max T-O weight)
Max level speed at S/L:
Jetasen   136 knots (157 mph; 253 km/h)
Rocket   148 knots (170 mph; 273 km/h)
Strata-Rocket
     156 knots (180 mph; 290 km/h)
Max permissible diving speed:
Jetasen   156 knots (180 mph; 290 km/h)
Rocket   182 knots (210 mph; 338 km/h)
Max cruising speed:
Jetasen   130 knots (150 mph; 241 km/h)

Rocket   143 knots (165 mph; 265 km/h)
Strata-Rocket
     156 knots (180 mph; 290 km/h)
Econ cruising speed:
Jetasen   113 knots (130 mph; 209 km/h)
Rocket, Strata-Rocket
     130 knots (150 mph; 241 km/h)
Stalling speed (full flaps):
Jetasen, Rocket, Strata-Rocket
     35 knots (40 mph; 65 km/h)
Rate of climb at S/L:
Jetasen   700 ft (213 m)/min
Rocket, Strata-Rocket   1,250 ft (380 m)/min
Service ceiling:
Jetasen   12,000 ft (3,650 m)
Rocket   18,000 ft (5,500 m)
Strata-Rocket   19,000 ft (5,790 m)

T-O run:
Jetasen   700 ft (213 m)
Rocket   430 ft (131 m)
Strata-Rocket   400 ft (122 m)
T-O to 50 ft (15 m):
Jetasen   900 ft (274 m)
Rocket   650 ft (198 m)
Strata-Rocket   600 ft (183 m)
Landing from 50 ft (15 m):
Jetasen, Strata-Rocket   600 ft (183 m)
Rocket   650 ft (198 m)
Landing run:
Jetasen   450 ft (137 m)
Rocket, Strata-Rocket   500 ft (152 m)
Range with max fuel:
Jetasen   607 nm (700 miles; 1,125 km)
Rocket, Strata-Rocket
     590 nm (680 miles; 1,090 km)

MEYER
MEYER AIRCRAFT
ADDRESS:
5706 Abby Drive, Corpus Christi, Texas 78413

Meyer Aircraft was formed by Mr George W. Meyer, to market plans for the construction by amateurs of a small, fully aerobatic biplane of his own design, known as the Little Toot, which was flown for the first time on 5 February 1957. Several hundred sets of plans have been sold and many Little Toots are now flying.

The prototype, to which the data below apply, has a metal monocoque fuselage and metal tail surfaces; but the plans give details also of an alternative and easier method of making these components, using conventional metal tube construction, with plywood fuselage bulkheads, wood stringers and fabric covering.

Mr Meyer has in the development stage a side-by-side two-seat back-stagger biplane, of which no details are yet available.

MEYER LITTLE TOOT
Following the installation of a sliding cockpit canopy, Mr Meyer's prototype Little Toot has been fitted with improved wheel fairings and low-profile tyres for better streamlining. A 160 hp Lycoming O-320 engine, with full inverted oil system, is to be installed as soon as a new glass-fibre cowling has been made for it.

The following details refer to Mr Meyer's aircraft in its current form, with 90 hp engine.

TYPE: Single-seat sporting biplane.

WINGS: Braced biplane type, with single inter-plane strut each side and two N-type strut NACA 2212 wing section. Sweepback 8° on top wing only. Dihedral 0° on top wing, 2° 30' on lower wing. Incidence (both wings) 2°. All-wood two-spar structure with fabric covering. Fabric-covered metal Frise ailerons on lower wing only. No flaps.

FUSELAGE: All-metal structure, with metal-covered steel-tube construction from rear of cockpit forward, and metal monocoque rear fuselage.

TAIL UNIT: Cantilever all-metal structure. Trim-tab in port elevator.

LANDING GEAR: Non-retractable tail-wheel type. Cantilever spring steel main legs of type fitted to Cessna 140 aircraft. Goodyear wheels and tyres. Goodyear disc brakes. Wheel spats. Steerable tail-wheel.

POWER PLANT: One 90 hp Continental four-cylinder horizontally-opposed air-cooled engine, driving McCauley 72-52 two-blade fixed-pitch propeller. Provision for alternative four-cylinder engines of up to 180 hp. Fuel tank in fuselage, aft of firewall, capacity 18 US gallons (68 litres). Oil capacity 6 US gallons (5·7 litres).

Meyer Little Toot (150 hp Lycoming engine) built by Mr J. D. Mahoney of Clayton, Missouri

ACCOMMODATION: Single seat. Plans show open cockpit, but prototype now has sliding canopy. Space for 30 lb (14 kg) baggage aft of seat.

ELECTRONICS: Aerotech VHF transceiver and Omni.

DIMENSIONS, EXTERNAL:
Wing span (both)	19 ft 0 in (5·79 m)
Wing chord, constant (both)	3 ft 6 in (1·07 m
Wing aspect ratio	5·42
Length overall	16 ft 6 in (5·03 m)
Height overall	7 ft 0 in (2·13 m)
Tailplane span	7 ft 0 in (2·13 m)
Wheel track	6 ft 0 in (1·83 m)

DIMENSIONS, INTERNAL:
Cockpit: Width	2 ft 0 in (0·61 m)

AREAS:
Wings, gross	123 sq ft (11·43 m²)
Ailerons (total)	13·00 sq ft (1·21 m²)
Fin	4·66 sq ft (0·43 m²)
Rudder	3·47 sq ft (0·32 m²)
Tailplane	10·50 sq ft (0·98 m²)
Elevators, with tab	7·25 sq ft (0·67 m²)

WEIGHTS AND LOADINGS (90 hp Continental):
Weight empty	914 lb (415 kg)
Max T-O and landing weight	1,260 lb (572 kg)
Max wing loading	10·20 lb/sq ft (49·8 kg/m²)
Max power loading	13·7 lb/hp (6·22 kg/hp)

PERFORMANCE (at max T-O weight, open cockpit):
Max level speed at S/L:
90 hp Cont	110 knots (127 mph; 204 km/h)
125 hp Lyc	117 knots (135 mph; 217 km/h)
150 hp Lyc	130 knots (150 mph; 241 km/h)

Max permissible diving speed:
     156 knots (180 mph; 290 km/h)
Normal cruising speed:
90 hp Cont	96 knots (110 mph; 177 km/h)
125 hp Lyc	104 knots (120 mph; 193 km/h)
150 hp Lyc	117 knots (135 mph; 217 km/h)

Stalling speed:
90 hp Cont   48 knots (55 mph; 88·5 km/h)
Rate of climb at S/L:
90 hp Cont	1,000 ft (305 m)/min
125 hp Lyc	1,600 ft (490 m)/min
150 hp Lyc	2,000 ft (610 m)/min

Climb to 5,000 ft (1,525 m):
90 hp Cont   5 min 20 sec
Service ceiling:
90 hp Cont   16,500 ft (5,030 m)
T-O run:
90 hp Cont   300 ft (91 m)
T-O to 50 ft (15 m):
90 hp Cont   450 ft (137 m)
Landing run:
90 hp Cont   400 ft (122 m)
Range:
90 hp Cont   304 nm (350 miles; 560 km)

MISSISSIPPI STATE UNIVERSITY
ADDRESS:
Department of Aerophysics and Aerospace Engineering, State College, Mississippi

DIRECTOR, FLIGHT RESEARCH LABORATORIES:
Sean C. Roberts

Mississippi State University's Department of Aerophysics and Aerospace Engineering has been engaged on high-lift boundary-layer control research for several years, under the sponsorship of the US Army and Office of Naval Research. Early flight tests were made with a Schweizer TG-3A glider, which was modified in 1953 in such a way that the boundary layer air was sucked into the wings through about 600,000 hand-drilled perforations.

A Piper L-21 was next fitted with a similar BLC system, which was used during take-off and for minimum speed flying trials. The wing fuel tanks were replaced by a tank in the fuselage, and the original landing gear was replaced by a tricycle gear, with cantilever spring steel main legs. After modification, this aircraft displayed a 42% reduction in take-off distance to 50 ft (15 m), a stalling speed of 28 mph (45 kmh) and a

minimum flying speed of 35 mph (56 kmh) under complete control.

A further series of tests was made with a modified Cessna O-1, of which details were given in the 1961-62 *Jane's*. The results of the programme have been utilised in the development of a STOL research aircraft named the Marvel for the US Army. Initial flight trials of the Marvel wings and other components were made on a test-bed aircraft named the Marvelette, of which a full description can be found in the 1965-66 *Jane's*.

MISSISSIPPI STATE UNIVERSITY MARVEL
US Army designation: XV-11A

The XV-11A Marvel is a STOL research aircraft, with suction-type boundary layer control system, which is under development for the US Army. Construction is largely of glass-fibre, to ensure an extremely smooth surface, and the Marvel has more than one million tiny holes for BLC drilled in its wings and part of the fuselage. The University has produced a special automatic air-turbine-driven drilling machine which can drill these holes at the rate of 5·2 per second, at a spacing of 10 per inch.

Conventional ailerons are fitted, but instead of

flaps the Marvel has a form of warping wing system, which deflects the wing trailing-edges downward to change the camber. The 250 hp Allison T63 shaft-turbine engine is modified to drive a pusher propeller and is mounted in the rear fuselage. It is coupled to the propeller by a long drive-shaft, and the propeller turns inside a glass-fibre shroud-duct which carries flaps for yaw and pitch control. The boundary layer control system suction source is provided by a mixed flow (axial-centrifugal) blower driven from the T63 forward power take-off pad. A "panto-base" type of amphibious landing gear has been developed for this aircraft.

It was hoped to achieve a speed range of 7·25 : 1, with a maximum speed of 252 knots (290 mph; 467 km/h) and landing speed of 35 knots (40 mph; 64 km/h), and a maximum lift coefficient of 5·0. As a first step, the Marvel's wing and ducted propeller were flight tested on the Marvelette test-bed aircraft, as described in the 1965-66 *Jane's*.

The prototype Marvel was built at Parsons Corporation, Traverse City, Michigan, and was completed in the Summer of 1966. It is being used for an extensive flight test programme at the University, under the sponsorship of the US Army Aviation Materiel Laboratories. A total of 77 flying hours had been logged by 18 February 1969. A flight test programme to obtain performance and stability/control data was completed during 1969. A new programme of acoustic research was scheduled to start in the near future at the time of writing.

TYPE: Two-seat STOL research aircraft.

WINGS: Cantilever shoulder-wing monoplane. Wing section NACA 63615 (modified). Dihedral 1° 45'. Incidence 1°. Sweepback at quarter-chord 0°45'. Single-spar structure, with ribs and stressed skin, all of glass-fibre reinforced plastics. Suction boundary layer control effected by means of many small holes drilled in upper surface of wings and ailerons. Sealed ailerons of large chord, constructed of glass-fibre reinforced plastics. No flaps; instead the inboard portion of the wing, from 37% aft, has variable-camber achieved by a form of wing warping.

FUSELAGE: Semi-monocoque structure of glass-fibre reinforced plastics.

TAIL UNIT: Shrouded propeller, with control surfaces forming a cruciform within the shroud. Tailplane extends outboard of shroud. Conventional spar, ribs and stressed skin, constructed of glass-fibre reinforced plastics. Trim tab on elevator.

LANDING GEAR: Non-retractable, with two main wheels in tandem on each leg. Cantilever spring struts built up from reinforced glass-fibre. Tyre size 5·00 × 15, 6-ply. Disc brakes.

POWER PLANT: One 317 shp Allison T63-A-5A turboprop engine, driving an Aeroproducts two-blade variable-pitch propeller, Model 272, with diameter reduced to 5 ft 6 in (1·68 m). Propeller reduction gear limited to 250 shp. Engine is mounted in rear fuselage and is coupled to the pusher propeller by a long drive shaft, the propeller rotating within the tail shroud-duct. Fuel contained in fuselage tank, capacity 37 US gallons (140 litres). Refuelling point on fuselage. Oil capacity 2·5 US gallons (9·5 litres).

ACCOMMODATION: Enclosed cabin seating two, side-by-side, with all round canopy providing excellent visibility. Upward-hinged door on each side of fuselage.

Mississippi State University XV-11A Marvel STOL research aircraft

SYSTEMS: Engine-driven 28V DC generator.

ELECTRONICS AND EQUIPMENT: VHF radio. Blind flying instrumentation standard.

DIMENSIONS, EXTERNAL:
Wing span	26 ft 2½ in (7·99 m)
Wing chord at fuselage c/l	4 ft 10¼ in (1·48 m)
Wing chord at tip	3 ft 2¾ in (0·98 m)
Wing aspect ratio	6·48
Length overall	23 ft 3¾ in (7·10 m)
Height overall	8 ft 8¼ in (2·65 m)
Tailplane span	9 ft 6 in (2·90 m)
Wheel track	6 ft 6 in (1·98 m)
Wheelbase	4 ft 0 in (1·22 m)
Passenger doors:	
Height	2 ft 6 in (0·76 m)
Width	5 ft 2 in (1·57 m)
Height to sill	3 ft 2 in (0·97 m)

AREAS:
Wings, gross	106 sq ft (9·85 m²)
Ailerons (total)	11·13 sq ft (1·03 m²)
Trailing-edge warped	37·80 sq ft (3·52 m²)
Fin	15·58 sq ft (1·45 m²)
Rudder	4·83 sq ft (0·45 m²)
Tailplane	24·04 sq ft (2·23 m²)
Elevators, including tab	8·67 sq ft (0·81 m²)

WEIGHTS AND LOADINGS:
Basic operating weight	1,958 lb (888 kg)
Max T-O weight	2,620 lb (1,188 kg)
Max zero fuel weight	2,379 lb (1,079 kg)
Max landing weight	2,620 lb (1,188 kg)
Max wing loading	24·7 lb/ sq ft (120·5 kg/m²)
Max power loading (propeller limit)	10·5 lb/shp (4·76 kg/shp)

PERFORMANCE:
Max level speed, at 15,000 ft (4,570 m)	195 knots (225 mph; 362 km/h)
Max permissible diving speed	249 knots (287 mph; 461 km/h)
Max cruising speed at 15,000 ft (4,570 m)	187 knots (215 mph; 346 km/h)
Cruising speed for max range, at 15,000 ft (4,570 m)	160 knots (184 mph; 296 km/h)
Stalling speed at S/L	53 knots (60 mph; 97 km/h)
Rate of climb at S/L	1,880 ft (573 m)/min
Service ceiling	15,000 ft (4,570 m)
T-O run	350 ft (107 m)
T-O to 50 ft (15 m)	580 ft (177 m)
Landing from 50 ft (15 m)	950 ft (290 m)
Landing run	480 ft (146 m)
Max range at max weight, 5% reserve, no fuel or range for descent. Fuel flows increased by 5%	230 nm (265 miles; 426 km)

MONG

RALPH E. MONG, Jr

ADDRESS:
1218 North 91st East Avenue, Tulsa, Oklahoma 74115

Mr Ralph Mong is the designer of the Mong Sport light biplane, of which plans are available for amateur construction. At least 50 are known to have been completed and flown successfully.

MONG SPORT

This aircraft is a light single-seat biplane, powered normally by a 65 hp Continental A65 four-cylinder horizontally-opposed air-cooled engine, but with provision for other engines of up to 90 hp. The wings have a wood structure with fabric covering, and the lower wing only has dihedral of 3°. The fuselage and tail unit are fabric-covered welded steel-tube structures. Fuel capacity is 20 US gallons (75·7 litres).

The example illustrated is a standard Sport, owned by Gail Clark of Tulsa, Oklahoma. Mong Sports have achieved notable successes at race meetings. In particular, Dallas Christian of Citrus Heights, California, took first place in the Sport Biplane Class at the Reno, Frederick and Cleveland National Air Races in 1968, with a speed of 175 mph (282 kmh) at Reno.

DIMENSIONS, EXTERNAL:
Wing span	16 ft 10 in (5·13 m)
Length overall	14 ft 1 in (4·39 m)
Height overall	5 ft 6 in (1·68 m)
Wing chord	2 ft 8 in (0·81 m)

AREA:
Wings, gross	80 sq ft (7·43 m²)

Mong Sport owned by Gail Clark of Tulsa, Oklahoma (90 hp Continental engine)

WEIGHTS:
Weight empty	550 lb (249 kg)
Max T-O weight	960 lb (435 kg)

PERFORMANCE (at max T-O weight):
Max level speed at S/L	122 knots (140 mph; 225 km/h)
Cruising speed (with Sensenich 70A54 propeller)	100 knots (115 mph; 185 km/h)

Landing speed	48 knots (55 mph; 89 km/h)
Rate of climb at S/L	1,000 ft (305 m)/min
Service ceiling	13,000 ft (3,962 m)
T-O run	600 ft (183 m)
Landing run	600 ft (183 m)
Range with max fuel	204 nm (350 miles; 563 km)

MOONEY

MOONEY AIRCRAFT CORPORATION (Subsidiary of BUTLER AVIATION INTERNATIONAL INC)

HEAD OFFICE AND WORKS:
PO Box 72, Louis Schreiner Field, Kerrville, Texas 78028

OTHER WORKS:
Route 1, Box 544, Mathis Field, San Angelo, Texas

PRESIDENT AND MEMBER OF THE BOARD:
Ralph M. Harmon

VICE-PRESIDENT, OPERATIONS:
I. B. Jenkins

CHIEF ENGINEER: Phil Furman

INDUSTRIAL RELATIONS MANAGER:
Myron Ligon

SALES MANAGER: Charlie Prince

ASSISTANT SALES MANAGER: Wayne Wilpitz

SALES CO-ORDINATOR: Ron Schupp

TRAFFIC MANAGER AND FOREIGN SALES CO-ORDINATOR: Joe Schmerber

PURCHASING AGENT: Forest Womack

PUBLIC RELATIONS: Loy Furman

Mooney Aircraft, Inc, originated in Wichita, Kansas, in June 1948, where the single-seat Model M18 Mooney Mite was produced until 1952. The company transferred to Kerrville, Texas, in 1953.

In 1954, under new leadership, the company continued to build the Mite and began production of the four-seat Model M-20. By 1964 the M-20 series comprised three aircraft; the Mark 21 (M-20C), Master (M-20D) and Super 21 (M-20E).

On 9 October 1967, Mooney Aircraft concluded

a merger with Alon, Inc, of McPherson, Kansas. Mooney emerged as the surviving corporation and assumed all liabilities and assets of Alon, Inc, including the Pemco Tool and Machine Company in Wichita, Kansas.

Documents completing the sale of the assets of Mooney Aircraft, Inc, and Mooney Corporation to American Electronic Laboratories, Inc, of Colmar, Pennsylvania, were executed on 26 March 1969. Mooney was then renamed Mooney Aircraft Corporation.

On 21 November 1969 Butler Aviation International Inc, and American Electronic Laboratories Inc entered into an agreement whereby the former company acquired 100 per cent stock ownership of Mooney Aircraft Corporation. Mooney now operates as a subsidiary of Butler Aviation International Inc.

Current production models, which are described in detail below, include the new Mooney Cadet (M-10), the Ranger (M-20C), the Chaparral (M-20E), the Executive 21 (M-20F), the Statesman (M-20G), and Mark 22 (M-22).

MOONEY CADET (M-10)

The Mooney Cadet differs from the former Alon Aircoupe principally by having a new single-fin and rudder tail unit and toe-operated brakes. It can be fitted with either of two groups of optional equipment. Group A includes a Brittain turn coordinator, rate of climb indicator, eight-day clock, cigarette lighter, outside air temperature gauge, tinted glass, cabin sunshade, suit hanger, dual-operated toe brakes, four cabin air ventilators, streamlined spinner, rheostat-controlled red instrument light, stall warning horn, tow bar, two-colour paint scheme, communications transceiver whip antenna, navigation receiver antenna, dual controls, improved soundproofing, in-flight adjustable seats, control yoke lock and engine primer system. Group B includes the foregoing plus engine-driven vacuum system with vacuum gauge and regulator, blind-flying instruments, Grimes rotating beacon and Mk VI Summer Air kit.

Production of the Cadet was transferred from the former Alon works in McPherson and Wichita, Kansas, to Mooney's plant in the Spring of 1968. A total of 9 M-10's had been delivered by mid-January 1970.

TYPE: Two-seat light training and sport aircraft.

WINGS: Cantilever low-wing monoplane. Wing section NACA 43013. Dihedral 7°. Incidence 3° 30'. All-metal two-spar structure of aluminium. All-metal ailerons over full span of wings outboard of main landing gear. No flaps or trim-tabs.

FUSELAGE: All-metal construction; forward portion semi-monocoque, rear portion monocoque.

TAIL UNIT: Cantilever all-metal structure with small dorsal fin. Trim-tab on elevator.

LANDING GEAR: Non-retractable tricycle type with steerable nose-wheel. Oleo-pneumatic shock-absorber on nose-wheel gear. Spring steel main landing gear. Oleo-pneumatic shock-absorbers for main gear optional. Main wheels and tyres size 6·00 × 6, pressure 17 lb/sq in (1·20 kg/cm²). Nose-wheel and tyre size 5·00 × 5, pressure 20-30 lb/sq in (1·41-2·11 kg/cm²). Toe-operated brakes. Parking brake.

POWER PLANT: One 90 hp Continental C90-16F four-cylinder horizontally-opposed air-cooled engine, driving a McCauley 7153 two-blade metal fixed-pitch propeller, diameter 5 ft 11 in (1·80 m). Fuel in two wing tanks, each of 9 US gallons (34 litres) capacity and one fuselage tank of 6 US gallons (22·7 litres) capacity. Total fuel capacity 24 US gallons (90·7 litres). Oil capacity 5 US quarts (4·5 litres).

ACCOMMODATION: Enclosed cabin seating two side-by-side under rearward-sliding transparent canopy which can be opened or closed in flight. Cabin heated and ventilated. Optional child's seat at rear of cabin, capacity 90 lb (41 kg) or stowage for 90 lb (41 kg) baggage. Carpeted floor. Cargo tie-down rings.

SYSTEMS: 35A generator, 12V 24Ah battery.

ELECTRONICS: A wide range of VHF transceivers and ADF, glideslope and marker beacon receivers are available to customer's requirements.

DIMENSIONS, EXTERNAL:

Wing span	30 ft 0 in (9·14 m)
Wing chord, constant	5 ft 0 in (1·52 m)
Wing aspect ratio	6·31
Length overall	20 ft 8 in (6·30 m)
Height overall	7 ft 8 in (2·34 m)
Tailplane span	8 ft 2 in (2·49 m)
Wheel track	7 ft 9 in (2·36 m)
Wheelbase	5 ft 0 in (1·52 m)

AREAS:

Wings, gross	142·6 sq ft (13·2 m²)
Ailerons (total)	16·8 sq ft (1·56 m²)
Rudder	5·63 sq ft (0·52 m²)
Elevators, including tab	9·15 sq ft (0·85 m²)

WEIGHTS AND LOADINGS:

Weight empty	950 lb (430 kg)
Max T-O weight	1,450 lb (658 kg)
Max wing loading	10·17 lb/sq ft (49·6 kg/m²)
Max power loading	16·15 lb/hp (7·33 kg/hp)

PERFORMANCE:

Max level speed	102 knots (118 mph; 190 km/h)
Stalling speed	40 knots (46 mph; 74·5 km/h) IAS
Rate of climb at S/L	835 ft (255 m)/min
Service ceiling	15,500 ft (4,725 m)
T-O run, zero wind S/L standard day	334 ft (102 m)
Landing run, zero wind S/L standard day	431 ft (131 m)
Range, including allowances for taxi, climb and 45 min reserves	453 nm (522 miles; 840 km)

MOONEY RANGER (M-20C)

The prototype Ranger (formerly known as Mark 21) flew on 23 September 1961 and the first production model on 7 November 1961. FAA Type Approval was received on 7 November 1961.

Mooney Cadet (M-10) two-seat light monoplane (90 hp Continental C90-16F engine)

The Ranger has as standard equipment the Mooney Positive Control (PC) system which coordinates yaw/roll stability. Developed in association with Brittain Industries, PC employs a sensor in the form of a tilted-axis rate gyro. Any deviation in roll or yaw causes the gyro to emit a mechanical signal to a master vacuum control valve. This valve is connected to the standard vacuum system of the engine and by lines to servo cans. One vacuum servo is located at each aileron for roll control and two in the tail cone to activate the rudder for yaw control. Interconnected control linkages, combined with the sensitivity of the rate gyro, brings pressure on both ailerons and rudder to produce co-ordinated corrective action and restore the aircraft to straight and level flight. PC can be over-ridden by normal control pressures and can be disengaged by depressing a button on the control yoke.

A total of 1,946 M-20C's had been delivered by mid-January 1970.

TYPE: Four-seat cabin monoplane.

WINGS: Cantilever low-wing monoplane. Wing section NACA 63₂-215 at root, NACA 64₁-412 at tip. Dihedral 5° 30'. Incidence 2° 30' at root, 1° at tip. Sweep-forward 2° 29'. Aluminium alloy structure with flush-riveted stretch-formed wrap-around skins. Full-span main spar; rear spar terminates at mid-span of flaps. Sealed-gap differentially-operated aluminium alloy ailerons. Electrically-operated single-slotted aluminium alloy flaps over 70% of trailing-edge. No tabs.

FUSELAGE: Composite all-metal structure. Cabin section is of welded 4130 chrome-molybdenum steel tube with sheet aluminium alloy covering. Rear section is of semi-monocoque construction, with sheet aluminium alloy bulkheads and skin and extruded alloy stringers.

TAIL UNIT: Cantilever aluminium alloy structure, with variable-incidence tailplane. All surfaces covered with wrap-around metal skin. Trim-tab on elevator.

LANDING GEAR: Electrically-retractable levered-suspension tricycle type. Nose-wheel retracts rearward, main units inward into wings. Firestone rubber disc shock-absorbers on main units. Delco hydraulic shock-absorber on nose unit. Cleveland main wheels size 6·00-6 and steerable nose-wheel, size 5·00-5. Tyre pressure (all units) 30 lb/sq in (2·11 kg/cm²). Cleveland hydraulic single-disc brakes on main wheels. Parking brakes.

POWER PLANT: One 180 hp Lycoming O-360-A1D four-cylinder horizontally-opposed air-cooled engine, driving a Hartzell HC-CZYK-1/7666-2 two-blade metal constant-speed propeller, diameter 6 ft 2 in (1·88 m). Two integral fuel tanks with total capacity of 52 US gallons (197 litres) in wing roots. Flush refuelling point above each tank. Oil capacity 2 US gallons (7·5 litres).

ACCOMMODATION: Cabin accommodates four in two pairs of individual seats, front pair with dual controls. Starboard rudder pedals optionally removable to allow more leg-room for passenger. Overhead ventilation system. Cabin heater with adjustable outlets and illuminated control. One-piece wrap-around windscreen. Tinted Plexiglas windows. Starboard front and rear seats removable for freight stowage. Single door on starboard side. Compartment for 120 lb (54 kg) baggage behind cabin, with access from cabin or through outside door on starboard side. Windshield defrosting system standard.

SYSTEMS: Hydraulic system for brakes only. Electrical system includes 60A alternator, 12V 35Ah battery, voltage regulator and warning light, together with protective circuit breakers.

ELECTRONICS: An extensive range of optional equipment is available to customer's requirements, manufactured by Bendix, King, Narco, Ketts and Bonzer. There are, in addition, twelve factory-installed electronic packages available, suitable for amateur or professional needs. Intercom and cabin speaker standard.

Mooney Ranger (M-20C) four-seat light monoplane (180 hp Lycoming O-360-A1D engine)

EQUIPMENT: Standard equipment includes many de luxe features as well as basic instruments, sensitive altimeter, streamlined spinner, and dual controls. Two groups of optional equipment are available. Group A includes two overhead panel floodlights, dry vacuum pump with regulator, communications transceiver whip antenna, navigation receiver antenna, cigarette lighter, assist strap, suit hanger, access step, padded instrument glare shield, alternative instrument panel finishes, sun visors, quick oil drain, hat shelf, Brittain turn co-ordinator with vacuum drive and emergency electric motor, passenger reading light, automatic brightness control for panel lights, removable co-pilot rudder pedals, reclining adjustable front seats, individually reclining removable rear seats, wing jack points, arm rests, ash trays, external tie-down rings and tow bar. Group B includes blind-flying instrumentation, outside air temperature gauge and eight-day clock. Optional items available include all-leather interior trim, alternate static air source, auxiliary power plug, carburettor air temperature gauge, curtains, dual brakes, exhaust gas temperature gauge, set of headrests, Plexring instrument panel lights, polished spinner, rotating beacon, remote indicating compass, full-flow oil filter, strobe lights, Safe Flight SC-100 speed control, white-wall tyres and true airspeed indicator.

DIMENSIONS, EXTERNAL:

Wing span	35 ft 0 in (10·67 m)
Wing chord, mean	4 ft 9¼ in (1·45 m)
Wing aspect ratio	7·338
Length overall	23 ft 2 in (7·06 m)
Height overall	8 ft 4 in (2·54 m)
Tailplane span	11 ft 8 in (3·55 m)
Wheel track	9 ft 0¾ in (2·76 m)
Wheelbase	5 ft 6½ in (1·68 m)
Cabin door:	
Height	3 ft 1¼ in (0·95 m)
Width	2 ft 6½ in (0·78 m)
Height to sill	1 ft 1½ in (0·34 m)
Baggage compartment door:	
Height	2 ft 0 in (0·61 m)
Width	1 ft 7 in (0·48 m)

DIMENSIONS, INTERNAL:

Cabin: Length	8 ft 8 in (2·64 m)
Max width	3 ft 4½ in (1·04 m)
Max height	3 ft 8½ in (1·13 m)
Baggage compartment	13·5 cu ft (0·38 m³)

AREAS:

Wings, gross	167·0 sq ft (15·51 m²)
Ailerons (total)	11·05 sq ft (1·03 m²)
Trailing-edge flaps (total)	17·48 sq ft (1·62 m²)
Fin	7·88 sq ft (0·73 m²)
Rudder	5·01 sq ft (0·46 m²)
Tailplane	21·50 sq ft (2·00 m²)
Elevators	12·02 sq ft (1·11 m²)

WEIGHTS AND LOADINGS:

Weight empty	1,525 lb (691 kg)
Max T-O and landing weight	2,575 lb (1,168 kg)
Max wing loading	15·4 lb/sq ft (75·2 kg/m²)
Max power loading	14·3 lb/hp (6·49 kg/hp)

PERFORMANCE:

Max level speed at S/L
153 knots (176 mph; 283 km/h)

Stalling speed (flaps and wheels down, power off)
50 knots (57 mph; 92 km/h) IAS

Rate of climb at S/L 1,000 ft (305 m)/min

Service ceiling 19,500 ft (5,743 m)

T-O run, zero wind, standard day
815 ft (248 m)

Landing run, zero wind, standard day
595 ft (181 m)

Range, with allowance for taxi, climb and 45 min reserve 869 nm (1,001 miles; 1,610 km)

MOONEY CHAPARRAL (M-20E)

The new Mooney Chaparral is an updated version of the Super-21, which flew for the first time in July 1963, and is generally similar to the current Mooney Ranger (M-20C). It differs by having a more powerful engine and retains the small dorsal fin of the Super-21.

A total of 1,337 M-20E's had been delivered by mid-January 1970.

The description of the Ranger applies also to the Chaparral except in the following details:

POWER PLANT: One 200 hp Lycoming IO-360-A1A four-cylinder horizontally-opposed air-cooled engine, driving a Hartzell two-blade metal constant-speed propeller, diameter 6 ft 2 in (1·88 m). Fuel injection, tuned induction manifold, exhaust gas temperature gauge and ram air boost. Other details as for Ranger.

WEIGHTS AND LOADINGS:

As for Ranger, except:

Weight empty	1,600 lb (725 kg)
Max power loading	12·9 lb/hp (5·85 kg/hp)

PERFORMANCE:

Max level speed at S/L
165 knots (190 mph; 306 km/h)

Stalling speed (flaps and wheels down, power off) 50 knots (57 mph; 92 km/h) IAS

Rate of climb at S/L 1,400 ft (427 m)/min

Service ceiling 21,200 ft (6,460 m)

T-O run, zero wind, standard day
760 ft (232 m)

Landing run, zero wind, standard day
595 ft (181 m)

Range, allowance for taxi, climb and 45 min reserve 838 nm (965 miles; 1,553 km)

Mooney Chaparral (M-20E), a version of the Ranger with 200 hp Lycoming IO-360-A1A engine

Mooney Statesman (M-20G) extended-fuselage version of the Mooney Ranger

MOONEY STATESMAN (M-20G)

This model, introduced during 1968, is basically similar to the Ranger (M-20C), except that it has the longer fuselage of the Executive 21 (M-20F), providing more leg-room and two additional passenger windows, improved sound-proofing and a number of de luxe features, including adjustable seat-backs.

A total of 183 M-20G's had been delivered by mid-January 1970.

The description of the Ranger applies also to the Statesman except in the following details.

DIMENSIONS, EXTERNAL:

Same as for Ranger except:

Length overall	24 ft 0 in (7·32 m)
Wheelbase	5 ft 11½ in (1·82 m)

DIMENSIONS, INTERNAL:

Same as for Ranger except:

Cabin: length	9 ft 6 in (2·90 m)

WEIGHTS:

Weight empty	1,590 lb (721 kg)
Max T-O weight	2,525 lb (1,145 kg)

PERFORMANCE:

Max level speed at S/L
151 knots (174 mph; 280 km/h)

Stalling speed (flaps and wheels down, power off)
53 knots (61 mph; 98·5 km/h) IAS

Rate of climb at S/L 1,100 ft (335 m)/min

Service ceiling 14,600 ft (4,450 m)

T-O run, zero wind, standard day
847 ft (258 m)

Landing run, zero wind, standard day
724 ft (221 m)

Range with allowance for taxi, climb and 45 min reserve 850 nm (979 miles; 1,575 km)

MOONEY EXECUTIVE (M-20F)

This member of the M-20 family of aircraft is basically similar to the Statesman (M-20G), except for installation of a 200 hp Lycoming fuel-injection engine. Differences are noted below.

A total of 1,834 M-20F's had been delivered by mid-January 1970.

POWER PLANT: One 200 hp Lycoming IO-360-A1A four-cylinder horizontally-opposed air-cooled engine, driving a Hartzell two-blade metal constant-speed propeller, diameter 6 ft 2 in (1·88 m). Fuel injection, tuned induction manifold, exhaust gas temperature gauge and ram air power boost. Total fuel capacity 64 US gallons (242 litres).

WEIGHTS AND LOADING:

Weight empty	1,640 lb (743 kg)
Max baggage	120 lb (54 kg)
Max T-O weight	2,740 lb (1,243 kg)
Max wing loading	16·4 lb/sq ft (80·1 kg/m²)

PERFORMANCE:

Max level speed
161 knots (185 mph; 298 km/h)

Stalling speed (flaps and wheels down, power off)
54 knots (62 mph; 100 km/h) IAS

Rate of climb at S/L 1,330 ft (405 m)/min

Service ceiling 18,800 ft (5,730 m)

T-O run, zero wind, standard day
879 ft (268 m)

Landing run, zero wind, standard day
785 ft (239 m)

Range, with allowance for taxi, climb and 45 min reserve 996 nm (1,147 miles; 1,846 km)

Mooney Executive (M-20F) fuel-injection-engined version of the Mooney Statesman

MOONEY MARK 22 (M-22)

First flown on 24 September 1964, the Mark 22 is a pressurised five-seat light aircraft powered by a 310 hp Lycoming turbosupercharged engine which maintains its rated power up to 20,000 ft (6,100 m). It utilises the basic wing of the Ranger and has Mooney's Positive Control (PC) system as standard equipment (described under Ranger entry).

Type approval was received on 26 September 1966 and the first delivery of a production Mark 22 was made on 28 March 1967; a total of 26 of these aircraft had been delivered by mid-January 1970.

TYPE: Five-seat light monoplane.

WINGS: As for Ranger, except incidence 1° 30′ and electrically-actuated double-slotted flaps.

FUSELAGE: Conventional aluminium alloy semi-monocoque structure.

TAIL UNIT: Cantilever aluminium alloy structure, with stretch-formed wrap-around skins. Variable-incidence tailplane. Vacuum-operated rudder trim. Manual elevator trim.

LANDING GEAR: Electrically-retractable tricycle type. Manual emergency gear extension system standard. Steerable nose-wheel retracts rearward, main units inward into wing. Mooney oleo-pneumatic shock-absorbers. Mooney wheels. Nose-wheel tyre size 15 × 6·00 × 6 4-ply rating. Main wheel tyres size 6·00 × 6 6-ply rating. Tyre pressures: nose 42 lb/sq in (2·95 kg/cm²), main 45 lb/sq in (3·16 kg/cm²). Cleveland two-puck hydraulic disc brakes. Optional dual brakes. Parking brakes.

POWER PLANT: One 310 hp Lycoming TIO-541-A1A six-cylinder horizontally-opposed air-cooled turbosupercharged engine, driving a Hartzell two-blade metal constant-speed propeller, diameter 6 ft 8 in (2·03 m). Two integral fuel tanks in wings, forward of main spars, with total capacity of 92 US gallons (348 litres). Refuelling points in top surface of each wing. Oil capacity 3½ US gallons (13 litres).

ACCOMMODATION: Standard seating for four persons in individual reclining seats, with central aisle. Optional fifth seat on port side at rear of cabin. Upward-hinged folding door on starboard side of cabin. Space for 270 lb (122 kg) of baggage aft of second row of seats. Baggage door aft of wing on starboard side. Passenger seats removable for cargo carrying or ambulance work. Cabin heating and ventilation system and windshield defrosting system standard.

SYSTEMS: Pressurisation system, using bleed air from turbocompressor, utilised above 8,000 ft (2,400 m). Max pressure differential 4 lb/sq in (0·28 kg/cm²). Hydraulic brakes only.

Mooney Mark 22 (M-22) pressurised five-seat monoplane (310 hp Lycoming TIO-541-A1A engine)

Electrical system has 12V 70A alternator for supply to landing gear, flaps, step, nose landing light, vent blower, radio blower, etc. Retractable landing light in starboard wing optional.

ELECTRONICS: Provision for wide range of navigation/communications radio, glideslope receiver, DME and transponder to customer's choice. Autopilot optional.

EQUIPMENT: Standard equipment includes all necessary equipment and related instruments for cabin pressurisation and oxygen system; basic instrumentation and many de luxe features are also standard. Optional equipment includes dual controls, dual brakes, blind flying instrumentation, Hobbs hour meter, rotating beacon, G-meter, internally illuminated placards, Ram II audio control, antennae, external power socket, Plex-Ring lighting and eye-ball type dome and map lights.

DIMENSIONS, EXTERNAL:
- Wing span: 35 ft 0 in (10·67 m)
- Wing chord, mean: 4 ft 9¼ in (1·45 m)
- Wing aspect ratio: 7·338
- Length overall: 27 ft 0 in (8·23 m)
- Height overall: 9 ft 10 in (3·00 m)
- Tailplane span: 11 ft 8 in (3·55 m)
- Wheel track: 11 ft 0 in (3·35 m)
- Wheelbase: 8 ft 3 in (2·51 m)
- Cabin door:
  - Height (vertical): 2 ft 10¾ in (0·88 m)
  - Width: 2 ft 9½ in (0·85 m)
  - Height to sill, from wing top surface: 7 in (0·18 m)
- Baggage door:
  - Height: 2 ft 1 in (0·64 m)
  - Width: 1 ft 9¼ in (0·54 m)
  - Height to sill: 2 ft 8¾ in (0·83 m)

AREAS:
- Wings, gross: 166·93 sq ft (15·50 m²)
- Ailerons (total): 11·5 sq ft (1·07 m²)
- Flaps (total): 17·9 sq ft (1·66 m²)
- Fin: 8·14 sq ft (0·76 m²)
- Rudder: 6·9 sq ft (0·64 m²)
- Tailplane: 21·5 sq ft (2·00 m²)
- Elevators: 12·0 sq ft (1·11 m²)

WEIGHTS AND LOADINGS:
- Weight empty: 2,440 lb (1,106 kg)
- Max T-O and landing weight: 3,680 lb (1,670 kg)
- Max wing loading: 22·0 lb/sq ft (107·4 kg/m²)
- Max power loading: 11·88 lb/hp (5·4 kg/hp)

PERFORMANCE:
- Max level speed: 222 knots (256 mph; 412 km/h)
- Stalling speed, wheels and flaps down, power off: 59 knots (67 mph; 108 km/h) IAS
- Rate of climb at S/L: 1,125 ft (340 m)/min
- Service ceiling (max certificated): 24,000 ft (7,300 m)
- T-O run, zero wind, standard day: 1,142 ft (348 m)
- Landing run, zero wind, standard day: 958 ft (292 m)
- Max range, with allowance for climb and 45 min reserve: 1,296 nm (1,493 miles; 2,402 km)

NASA

NATIONAL AERONAUTICS AND SPACE ADMINISTRATION

ADDRESS:
Langley Research Center, Hampton, Virginia

NASA have developed a new wing, called the NASA supercritical wing, as a result of wind-tunnel studies conducted by Dr Richard T. Whitcomb during the past four years. Stated simply, the new wing utilises an aerofoil shape with a flat top and downward cambered rear section, as compared to the curved top and sloped rear section of a conventional wing.

If wind-tunnel measured performance is achieved fully in flight, the new wing could allow highly efficient cruise flight near the speed of sound. In addition to permitting a substantial increase in cruise speed without increase in power, it may significantly reduce the operational cost of subsonic jet transport flight.

When the speed of an aircraft approaches the speed of sound, regions of high supersonic air-flow develop, particularly above the wing. These cause severe local disturbances such as shock-waves and boundary layer flow separation, leading to increased drag, severe buffeting and adverse changes in stability. Subsonic flight operations with current aircraft are normally kept below the speed at which such effects begin to occur, namely Mach 0·8 at a cruising altitude of 35,000 ft (10,670 m). Wind-tunnel and analytical studies indicate that the NASA supercritical wing has the potential of allowing subsonic speeds in excess of Mach 0·95 before the adverse effects become significant.

Swept wings have been employed up to now to delay the rise of the drag force and onset of buffet; but excessive wing sweep increases structural weight, induces problems related to low-speed flight characteristics and can also require increased take-off and landing distances. The supercritical wing shape has been developed to delay substantially the onset of these adverse effects.

The new wing is to be flight tested during 1970 on a modified LTV F-8A Crusader airframe. A request for proposals for detail design and construction of the wing was issued in February 1969 by NASA's Flight Research Center at

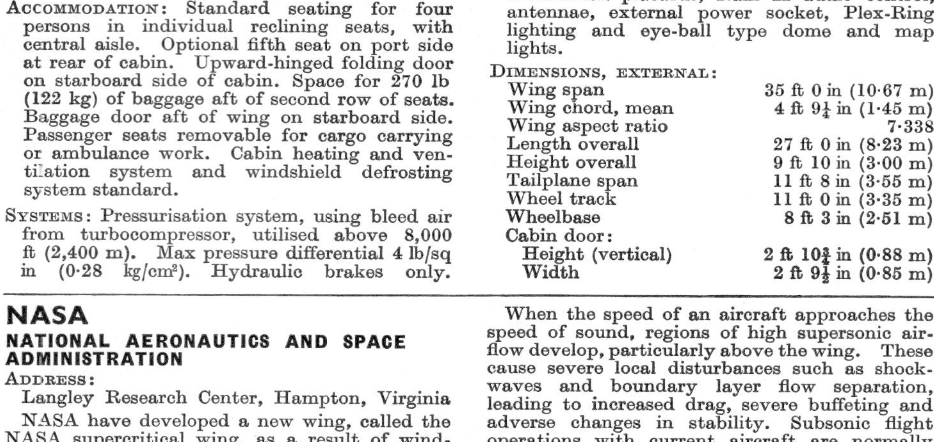

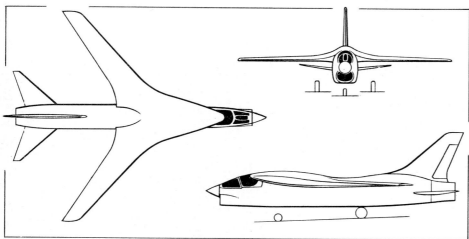

F-8 Crusader fitted experimentally with NASA supercritical wing

Artist's impression of the North American Rockwell/NASA FLEEP

Edwards AFB, California, where the flight tests will be conducted. Award of a fixed-price contract to North American Rockwell Corporation, Los Angeles Division, was announced by NASA in September 1969.

As fitted to the F-8A, the wing will have a span of 43 ft (13·11 m), sweepback of 42·24° at quarter-chord, no anhedral or dihedral, incidence of 1° 30′ at fuselage centre-line, aspect ratio of 6·8 and thickness/chord ratio of 11% at root and 7% at tip. Its area will be 274 sq ft (25·45 m²).

NASA FLEEP

The illustration on page 410 is an artist's impression of the preliminary concept of a Flying Lunar Excursion Experimental Platform (FLEEP) which North American Rockwell Corporation's Space Division is to design and build under contract to NASA's Langley Research Center.

The one-man FLEEP will be flown in Langley's large simulation facility, to test and evaluate the handling qualities and other problems of several design concepts for a vehicle for future travel on the Moon's surface. The cable system attached to the FLEEP during flights in the facility is used to support five-sixths of the vehicle's weight to simulate the reduced gravity on the Moon.

NESMITH
ROBERT E. NESMITH, INC

ADDRESS:
6738, Long Drive, Houston 17, Texas

Mr Robert Nesmith is the designer of a side-by-side two-seat light monoplane named the Cougar, the prototype of which flew for the first time in March 1957. Sets of plans are available to amateur constructors.

Mr Nesmith reported that, by January 1968, more than 2,000 Cougars had been completed and were flying.

NESMITH COUGAR

The data given below apply to the standard Cougar, built according to the plans marketed by Mr Nesmith. Some aircraft now flying incorporate detail modifications. One has a T-tail and at least one other has been completed with folding wings.

TYPE: Two-seat sporting monoplane.

WINGS: Braced high-wing monoplane, with single bracing strut each side. Wing section NACA 4309 (modified). Dihedral 1° 30′. No incidence. All-wood two-spar structure, plywood-covered except for fabric-covered trailing-edge. Ailerons have steel-tube structure, fabric-covered. No flaps.

FUSELAGE: Steel-tube structure, fabric-covered.

TAIL UNIT: Cantilever steel-tube structure, fabric-covered, with comparatively small rudder.

LANDING GEAR: Non-retractable tail-wheel type. Cantilever spring steel main legs. Goodyear main wheels and tyres, size 500 × 5. Brakes. Steerable tail-wheel can be unlocked for 360° castoring on ground.

POWER PLANT: One 115 hp Lycoming O-235 four-cylinder horizontally-opposed air-cooled engine, driving McCauley two-blade fixed-pitch propeller. Alternative engines include the 90 hp Continental C90. Fuel tank in fuselage, capacity 25 US gallons (94·6 litres). Oil capacity 6 US quarts (5·7 litres).

Nesmith Cougar built by Mr Bernard Krenk of Yukon, Oklahoma (*Jean Seele*)

ACCOMMODATION: Two seats side-by-side in enclosed cabin, with dual controls. Space for 90 lb (41 kg) baggage. Provision for radio.

DIMENSIONS, EXTERNAL:

Wing span	20 ft 6 in (6·25 m)
Wing chord (constant)	4 ft 0 in (1·22 m)
Wing aspect ratio	5·16
Length overall	18 ft 11 in (5·76 m)
Height overall	5 ft 6 in (1·68 m)
Tailplane span	6 ft 4 in (1·93 m)
Wheel track	5 ft 2 in (1·57 m)

DIMENSION, INTERNAL:

Cabin: Width	3 ft 2 in (0·96 m)

AREAS:

Wings, gross	82·5 sq ft (7·66 m²)
Ailerons (total)	4·35 sq ft (0·40 m²)
Vertical surfaces (total)	2·80 sq ft (0·26 m²)
Tailplane	4·70 sq ft (0·44 m²)
Elevators	2·36 sq ft (0·22 m²)

WEIGHTS:

Weight empty	624 lb (283 kg)
Max T-O weight	1,250 lb (567 kg)

PERFORMANCE (at max T-O weight):

Max level speed at S/L	169 knots (195 mph; 314 km/h)
Cruising speed (METO) at 7,000 ft (2,130 m)	144 knots (166 mph; 267 km/h)
Econ cruising speed	135 knots (155 mph; 249 km/h)
Stalling speed	46 knots (53 mph; 85 km/h)
Rate of climb at S/L	1,300 ft (395 m)/min
Service ceiling	13,000 ft (3,950 m)
T-O run	450 ft (137 m)
T-O to 50 ft (15 m)	1,100 ft (335 m)
Landing from 50 ft (15 m)	1,000 ft (305 m)
Landing run	350 ft (107 m)
Range with max fuel	651 nm (750 miles; 1,207 km)
Range with max payload	607 nm (700 miles; 1,125 km)

NORTH AMERICAN ROCKWELL
NORTH AMERICAN ROCKWELL CORPORATION

GENERAL OFFICE:
2300 East Imperial Highway, El Segundo, California 90245

CHAIRMAN OF THE BOARD AND CHIEF EXECUTIVE OFFICER:
Willard F. Rockwell Jr

PRESIDENT AND CHIEF OPERATING OFFICER:
Robert Anderson

SENIOR VICE-PRESIDENT:
R. H. Ruud (Aerospace and Systems Office)

CORPORATE VICE-PRESIDENTS:
Dupuy Bateman Jr (Corporate Development)

Wallace W. Booth (Finance)
William H. Cann (Secretary)
H. Walton Cloke (Public Relations and Advertising)
A. B. Kight (International)
John J. Roscia (General Counsel)
Robert W. Smart (Washington DC)
Robert C. Wilson (President, Commercial Products Group)

TREASURER:
Robert D. Krestel

CONTROLLER:
C. E. Ryker

STAFF VICE-PRESIDENTS:
W. A. Davis
H. J. Downes (Corporate Development)
John J. Henry (Corporate Development)

I. Gordon Odell (Corporate Development)
Elmer P. Wohl (Administration)

North American Aviation, Inc, incorporated in Delaware in 1928 and a manufacturer of aircraft of various kinds from 1934, and Rockwell-Standard Corporation of Pittsburgh, Pennsylvania, a manufacturer of automotive components for the last five decades and builder of the Aero Commander line of civilian aircraft, merged on 22 September 1967 to form North American Rockwell Corporation.

The corporation consists of two principal parts: the Aerospace and Systems Divisions (formerly North American Aviation Inc) and the Commercial Products Group (the former Rockwell-Standard Corporation). The constitution and products of each group are detailed hereafter:

AEROSPACE AND SYSTEMS OFFICE

EXECUTIVE OFFICES:
1700, East Imperial Highway, El Segundo, California 90245

PRESIDENT:
John R. Moore

SENIOR VICE-PRESIDENT:
Ralph H. Ruud

VICE-PRESIDENTS:
C. L. Backus Jr, (Central Region Office)
W. L. Clark (Washington DC)
B. F. Coggan (Marketing)
W. E. Fore (Manufacturing)
K. B. Gay (Material)
B. D. Haber (Research and Engineering)
C. E. Hart (Legal)
W. T. Lake (Administration)
C. J. Meechan (Industrial Systems)
H. W. Powell (Programme Monitor)
E. D. Starkweather (Personnel and Industrial Affairs)
F. D. Tappaan (Urban Affairs)
R. K Wilson. (Facilities and Industrial Engineering)

North American Rockwell T-2C Buckeye (two 2,950 lb st General Electric J85-GE-4 turbojet engines)

DIRECTOR, SCIENCE CENTER:
F. J. Morin

Autonetics Division:
3370 Miraloma Avenue, Anaheim, California 92803
PRESIDENT: Donn L. Williams

Columbus Division:
4300 East Fifth Avenue, Columbus, Ohio 43216
PRESIDENT: W. F. Snelling

Los Angeles Division:
5701 West Imperial Highway, Los Angeles, California 90009
PRESIDENT: R. F. Walker

Power Systems Divisions:
6633 Canoga Avenue, Canoga Park, California 91304
PRESIDENT: J. D. Wethe

Atomics International Division:
8900 De Soto Avenue, Canoga Park, California 91304
PRESIDENT: J. J. Flaherty

Rocketdyne Division:
6633 Canoga Avenue, Canoga Park, California 91304
PRESIDENT:
J. D. Wethe (Acting)

Space Division:
12214 Lakewood Boulevard, Downey, California 90241
PRESIDENT: W. B. Bergen

Tulsa Division:
2000 North Memorial Drive, Tulsa, Oklahoma 74151
PRESIDENT: H. W. Todd

Other Plants:
McAlester Plant, McAlester, Oklahoma 74501
Science Center, Thousand Oaks, California 91360
West Virginia Plant, Princeton, West Virginia 24740
Washington Office, 1629 K Street, N.W., Washington, DC 20006

Current aircraft products of the Aerospace and Systems Divisions (formerly North American Aviation Inc) are given below:

The research programmes of the XB-70A Valkyrie and X-15A-2 aircraft have both been terminated. Full details of these aircraft can be found in the 1968-69 *Jane's*.

NORTH AMERICAN ROCKWELL BUCKEYE
US Navy designation: T-2

After a design competition among several leading US manufacturers, North American's Columbus Division was awarded a contract in 1956 to develop and build a jet training aircraft for the US Navy.

Three versions of the aircraft have since been produced, as follows:

T-2A (formerly T2J-1), Initial version, with single 3,400 lb (1,540 kg) st Westinghouse J34-WE-36 turbojet engine, for use throughout the complete syllabus of pilot training, from *ab initio* instruction to carrier indoctrination. There was no prototype, and the first of an initial series of 26 production T-2A's flew on 31 January 1958. A follow-up contract was awarded in 1959 and 217 had been built when production ended in January 1961. Used by US Naval Air Basic Training Command, Pensacola, Florida.

T-2B (formerly T2J-2). To evaluate the potential of the Buckeye airframe, two T-2A's were each re-engined with two Pratt & Whitney J60 turbojets, under US Navy contract, with the designation T-2B. First one flew on 30 August 1962. A US Navy production contract for 10 new T-2B's was announced in March 1964, and has been followed by further contracts, bringing the total on order to 100. The first production T-2B flew on 21 May 1965 and deliveries to the Naval Air Training Command began in late 1965.

T-2C. Generally similar to T-2B, but powered by two General Electric J85-GE-4 turbojet engines, each rated at 2,950 lb (1,339 kg) st. The T-2C entered production late in 1968, following extensive evaluation of J85-GE-4 engines in a T-2B which was re-designated T-2C No 1. T-2C production is an amendment of an existing contract. Current orders call for 84 T-2C's to be delivered by the end of 1970. The first production T-2C flew on 10 December 1968.

The following details apply to the standard T-2B.

TYPE: Two-seat general-purpose jet trainer.

WINGS: Cantilever mid-wing monoplane. Wing section NACA 64A212 (modified). Thickness/chord ratio 12%. All-metal two-spar structure. Interchangeable all-metal ailerons, with hydraulic boost. Large all-metal trailing-edge flaps.

FUSELAGE: All-metal semi-monocoque structure in three main sections: forward fuselage containing equipment bay and cockpit; centre fuselage housing power plant, fuel and wing carry-through structure; and rear fuselage, the undersurface of which has stainless steel skin in way of jet exhausts. Hydraulically-actuated air-brake on each side of rear fuselage.

TAIL UNIT: Cantilever all-metal structure. Each half of tailplane and elevators interchangeable.

Elevators boosted hydraulically. Rudder manually controlled. Trim-tabs in elevators and rudder.

LANDING GEAR: Retractable tricycle type. Oleo-pneumatic shock-absorbers. Hydraulic retraction. Main units retract inward into wings. Nose-wheel retracts forward into fuselage. Main wheels size 24 × 5·5. Nose-wheel size 20 × 4·4. Single-disc hydraulic brakes. Retractable sting-type arrester hook.

POWER PLANT: Two Pratt & Whitney J60-P-6 turbojet engines (each 3,000 lb=1,360 kg st), with jet outlets under rear fuselage. Fuel in main tank over engines with capacity of 387 US gallons (1,465 litres), two wingtip tanks each of 100 US gallons (378 litres) capacity, and two tanks in the inboard sections of the wings, with a combined capacity of 104 US gallons (395 litres). Total fuel capacity 691 US gallons (2,616 litres).

ACCOMMODATION: Pupil and instructor in tandem in enclosed cabin, on rocket-powered ejection seats, under clamshell canopy. Instructor is raised 10 in (0·25 m) above level of pupil and has closed-circuit transistorized TV gunnery instruction monitor to check pupil's accuracy of aim.

ARMAMENT: Optional packaged installations of guns, 100 lb practice bombs, M-5 practice bomb clusters, Type T-1 practice bomb containers, 2·25-in rocket launchers or 2·75-in Mighty Mouse rocket packs.

DIMENSIONS, EXTERNAL:
Wing span, over tip tanks   38 ft 1½ in (11·62 m)
Length overall   38 ft 3½ in (11·67 m)
Height overall   14 ft 9½ in (4·51 m)
Tailplane span   17 ft 11 in (5·46 m)
Wheel track   18 ft 6 in (5·64 m)

AREAS:
Wings, gross   255 sq ft (23·69 m²)
Trailing-edge flaps (total)   45·56 sq ft (4·23 m²)
Fin   27·29 sq ft (2·54 m²)
Rudder   9·01 sq ft (0·84 m²)
Tailplane   42·55 sq ft (3·95 m²)
Elevators   21·00 sq ft (1·95 m²)

WEIGHTS:
Weight empty   8,220 lb (3,728 kg)
Max T-O weight   13,284 lb (6,025 kg)

PERFORMANCE (at max T-O weight):
Max level speed at 25,000 ft (7,620 m)
  469 knots (540 mph; 869 km/h)
Service ceiling   42,000 ft (12,800 m)

NORTH AMERICAN ROCKWELL VIGILANTE
US Navy designations: A-5 and RA-5

After a US Navy design competition, the then North American Aviation, Inc, received a contract to build a small number of prototypes of the A-5 (formerly A3J) twin-jet two-seat carrier-based all-weather combat aircraft in September 1956. Design and development of the aircraft was entrusted to the company's Columbus Division, to which the US Navy awarded a large follow-on production contract in January 1959.

Three versions of the A-5 have been built, as follows:

A-5A (formerly A3J-1). Attack bomber designed to carry nuclear or conventional weapons over a range of several hundred miles at high altitudes, with an over-target speed of Mach 2.

The first of two prototype YA-5A's flew for the first time on 31 August 1958, and a total of 59 A-5A's were delivered to the US Navy. Production was completed in 1963. All remaining A-5A's have been converted to RA-5C configuration.

A-5B (formerly A3J-2). Interim long-range version. Extra fuel tank in shape of hump fairing above fuselage aft of cockpit fairing.

First flown on 29 April 1962. About 20 built. All converted to RA-5C configuration.

RA-5C (formerly A3J-3). Airborne unit of Integrated Operational Intelligence System (IOIS), which includes also an integrated operational intelligence centre on board a carrier or at a shore base. Primarily a reconnaissance version of the Vigilante, with tactical sensory equipment and cameras in ventral fairing, but retaining an attack capability with externally-carried nuclear or conventional weapons. Cameras include vertical, oblique and horizon-to-horizon scanning types. Non-photographic equipment includes side-looking radar and electro-magnetic sensors for intelligence and counter-measures. Data obtained by these reconnaissance systems are fed to a surface-based tactical data system. Airframe similar to A-5B, with hump-back fuel tank, enlarged flaps and drooped leading-edge BLC. Four underwing attachments, each capable of carrying a 400 US gallon (1,514 litre) fuel tank, bomb or missile.

The RA-5C flew for the first time on 30 June 1962. Production models were assigned to VAH-3, training squadron for Heavy Attack Wing One of the US Navy, at Sanford Naval Air Station, in January 1964. Reconnaissance Attack Squadron 5 became operational on USS *Ranger* in the South China Sea by late 1964. Reconnaissance Attack Squadron 7 also equipped with RA-5C's in June 1965, so completing the phase-out of the A-5A from carrier-borne operational units. Heavy Attack Wing One was subsequently re-designated Reconnaissance Attack Wing One, and some seven additional RA-5C-equipped Reconnaissance Attack Squadrons have been formed or converted from other heavy bomber types. In 1968 the Wing was transferred to Albany Naval Air Station, Georgia.

Production of 46 new RA-5C's began early in 1969. The following production details refer specifically to the current production version:

TYPE: Carrier-based tactical reconnaissance aircraft.

WINGS: Cantilever high-wing monoplane. Thickness/chord ratio approximately 5%. Sweep-back 37° 30'. All metal structure with integrally-stiffened machined skins of Alcoa 2020-T6 aluminium-lithium alloy. Hydraulically-operated variable-camber leading-edge, in three sections on each wing, with BLC blowing over outboard two sections. Hydraulically-actuated aluminium spoilers in place of ailerons. Hydraulically-operated flaps. Outer wing panels hydraulically-folded upward for carrier stowage.

FUSELAGE: Semi-monocoque structure, widened aft of cockpit to accommodate engines. Built mainly of aluminium, but with several bulkheads and frames of ultra high-strength steel. Titanium alloy skins and frames are used adjacent to turbojets, and gold coating is applied on certain areas of titanium skins to prevent overheating of structural assemblies. Nose radome folds upward for radar maintenance and carrier stowage.

TAIL UNIT: Cantilever all-metal structure. Tail unit has integrally-stiffened machined skins of Alcoa 2020-T6 alloy on horizontal surface, and 7075-T6 alloy on vertical surface. Aluminium honeycomb structures are used for trailing sections. Both vertical and horizontal surfaces are one-piece structures, swept back at 45° and hydraulically-actuated. Lateral trim is by differential operation of horizontal surfaces. Upper section of fin folds to port for carrier stowage.

LANDING GEAR: Retractable tricycle type of Bendix manufacture, with single wheel on each unit. All units retract hydraulically into fuselage. Oleo-pneumatic shock-absorbers. Main wheels, size 36 × 11, with hydraulic

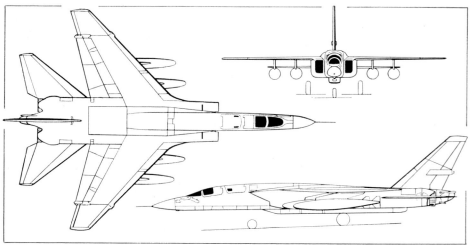

North American Rockwell RA-5C Vigilante naval reconnaissance-attack aircraft

North American Rockwell RA-5C Vigilante of the US Navy (two General Electric J79 turbojet engines) (*Brian M. Service*)

multiple-disc brakes. Steerable nose-wheel, size 26 × 6·6.

POWER PLANT: Current production RA-5C's powered by two General Electric J79-GE-10 turbojets (each rated at 11,870 lb = 5,395 kg st dry, and 17,859 lb = 8,118 kg st with after-burning). Aircraft delivered prior to 1969 equipped with two General Electric J79-GE-8 turbojets (each rated at 10,900 lb = 4,944 kg st dry or 17,000 lb = 7,711 kg st with afterburning). Hydraulically-actuated variable-area intakes. Fuel in three bladder-type tanks in fuselage, three integral tanks in the wing, and two or three (varying with reconnaissance configuration) can-type tanks in the former bomb-bay. Retractable flight refuelling probe on port side of nose. Pressure fuelling points under front and rear fuselage. Provision for four 400 US gallons (1,514 litre) jettisonable tanks under wings.

ACCOMMODATION: Crew of two in tandem under separate rearward-hinging canopies. Advanced rocket-powered type HS-1 ejection seats, developed by NAR Columbus Division, using a drogue parachute to stabilise the seats in an upright position after ejection.

ELECTRONICS AND EQUIPMENT: Equipment includes North American Autonetics REINS (radar equipped inertial navigation system) bombing and navigation system, and automatic flight control system. Auto-pilot provides hold for heading, bank, altitude and Mach number; ability to fly selected track through REINS coupling; and ability to perform selected LABS manoeuvres.

SYSTEMS: AiResearch pressurisation and air-conditioning system. Two 3,000 lb/sq in (210 kg/cm²) hydraulic systems, each supplied by two 15 US gallons/min (58·5 litres/min) engine-driven variable-displacement pumps, one on each engine. Each system provides power for independent flight control systems, and one additionally provides utility hydraulic power for flaps, leading-edge droops, landing gear, nose and fin folding, variable-area intakes, etc. Emergency power by AiResearch ram-air turbine, which also supplies emergency AC electrical power. Two 42kVA engine-driven generators supply 115V 400 c/s AC power. Two transformer-rectifiers provide 28V DC supply.

ARMAMENT: Variety of weapons, including thermonuclear bombs, can be accommodated on underwing attachments.

DIMENSIONS, EXTERNAL:
Wing span	53 ft 0 in (16·15 m)
Span, wings folded	42 ft 5 in (12·93 m)
Length overall	75 ft 10 in (23·11 m)
Length, nose and tail folded	
	68 ft 0 in (20·73 m)
Height overall	19 ft 5 in (5·92 m)
Tailplane span	30 ft 7 in (9·32 m)

AREA:
Wings, gross	769 sq ft (71·44 m²)

WEIGHT (RA-5C):
Max T-O weight (approx)	80,000 lb (36,285 kg)

PERFORMANCE (RA-5C, approx):
Max level speed	Mach 2

NORTH AMERICAN ROCKWELL BRONCO
US Military designation: OV-10

This aircraft was North American's entry for the US Navy's design competition for a light armed reconnaissance aeroplane (LARA) specifically suited for counter-insurgency missions. Nine US airframe manufacturers entered for the competition and the NA300 was declared the winning design in August 1964. Seven prototypes were then built by the company's Columbus Division, under the designation YOV-10A Bronco. The first of these flew on 16 July 1965, followed by the second in December 1965.

A number of modifications were made as a result of flight experience with the prototypes. In particular, the wing span was increased by 10 ft 0 in (3·05 m), the T76 turboprop engines were uprated from 660 shp to 715 shp, and the engine nacelles were moved outboard approximately 6 in (15 cm) to reduce noise in the cockpit.

A prototype with lengthened span flew for the first time on 15 August 1966. The seventh prototype had Pratt & Whitney (UAC) T74 (PT6A) turboprops for comparative testing.

In October 1966 the first production orders for the OV-10A were placed and the first production machine flew on 6 August 1967. The US Marine Corps had a total of 96 in service in September 1969, with 18 of these on loan to the USN, and they were employed on light armed reconnaissance, helicopter escort and forward air control duties. At the same date the USAF had a total of 152 OV-10A's for use in the forward air control rôle, as well as for limited quick-response ground support pending the arrival of tactical fighters.

Production of the OV-10A for the US Services ended in April 1969, but 16 have been ordered for the Thai Air Force, with deliveries to begin towards the end of 1970.

Eighteen **OV-10Bs** have been ordered by the Federal German government for target towing duties. The performance of twelve of these aircraft will be increased by mounting a General Electric turbojet engine above the wing, on a pylon that will be attached to existing hoisting points. Max speed of the jet-boosted version is expected to be 320 knots (368 mph; 593 km/h). The first two examples were scheduled for delivery early in 1970.

The following details apply to the standard production OV-10A.

TYPE: Two-seat multi-purpose counter-insurgency aircraft.

WINGS: Cantilever shoulder-wing monoplane. Constant-chord wing without dihedral or sweep. Conventional aluminium alloy two-spar structure. Manually-operated ailerons, supplemented by manually-operated spoiler forward of outer flap on each wing, for lateral control at low speeds. Hydraulically-operated double-slotted flaps in two sections on each wing, separated by tail-booms.

FUSELAGE: Short pod-type fuselage of conventional aluminium semi-monocoque construction, suspended from wing. Glass-fibre nose-cone.

TAIL UNIT: Cantilever all-metal structure carried on twin booms of semi-monocoque construction. Tailplane mounted near tips of fins. Manually-operated rudders and elevator.

LANDING GEAR: Retractable tricycle type, with single wheel on each unit, developed by Cleveland Pneumatic Tool Co. Hydraulic actuation, nose-wheel retracting forward, main units rearward into tail-booms. Two-stage oleo-pneumatic shock-absorbers. Forged aluminium wheels. Main wheel tyres size 11·00 × 10. Nose-wheel tyre size 7·50 × 10. Hydraulic disc brakes.

POWER PLANT: Two 715 shp AiResearch T76 turboprops, with Hamilton Standard three-blade propellers. Inter-spar fuel tank in centre portion of wing, capacity 258 US gallons (976 litres). Provision for carrying 150 US gallon (568 litre) jettisonable ferry tank on under-fuselage pylon. Refuelling point above tank.

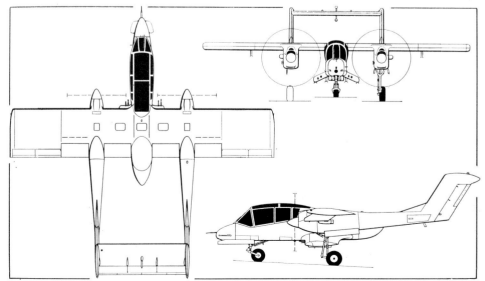

North American Rockwell OV-10A Bronco counter-insurgency combat aircraft

North American Rockwell OV-10A Bronco light armed reconnaissance aircraft of the USAF (two 715 shp AiResearch T76 engines)   (*Gordon S. Williams*)

ACCOMMODATION: Crew of two in tandem, on ejection seats, under manually-operated clamshell canopy. Dual controls standard. Cargo compartment aft of rear seat, with rear-loading door at end of fuselage pod. Rear seat removable to provide increased space for up to 3,200 lb (1,452 kg) of freight, or for carriage of five paratroops, or two stretcher patients and attendant.

ELECTRONICS AND EQUIPMENT: UHF radio standard. Provision for special equipment including Doppler radar and TV reconnaissance systems. Gun-sight above pilot's instrument panel.

ARMAMENT: Four weapon attachment points, each with capacity of 600 lb (272 kg), under short sponson extending from bottom of fuselage on each side, under wings. Fifth attachment point, capacity 1,200 lb (544 kg) under centre fuselage. Two 0·30-in M60C machine-guns carried in each sponson. Provision for carrying one Sidewinder missile on each wing. Max weapon load 3,600 lb (1,633 kg).

DIMENSIONS, EXTERNAL:
Wing span   40 ft 0 in (12·19 m)

Length overall	41 ft 7 in (12·67 m)
Height overall	15 ft 2 in (4·62 m)
Tailplane span	14 ft 7 in (4·45 m)
Wheel track	14 ft 10 in (4·52 m)
Rear loading door: Height	3 ft 3 in (0·99 m)
Width	2 ft 6 in (0·76 m)

AREA:
Wings, gross	291 sq ft (27·03 m²)

DIMENSIONS, INTERNAL:
Cargo compartment	75 cu ft (2·12 m³)
Cargo compartment, rear seat removed	111 cu ft (3·14 m³)

WEIGHTS:
Weight empty	6,969 lb (3,161 kg)
Normal T-O weight	9,908 lb (4,494 kg)
Overload T-O weight	14,466 lb (6,563 kg)

PERFORMANCE (Designed):
Max speed at S/L, without weapons
244 knots (281 mph; 452 km/h)

T-O run:
Normal AUW	740 ft (226 m)

T-O to 50 ft (15 m):
Normal AUW	1,120 ft (341 m)
Overload AUW	2,800 ft (853 m)

Landing from 50 ft (15 m):
Normal AUW	1,220 ft (372 m)

Landing run:
Normal AUW	740 ft (226 m)
Overload AUW	880 ft (268 m)

Combat radius with max weapon load, no loiter
198 nm (228 miles; 367 km)
Ferry range with auxiliary fuel
1,240 nm (1,428 miles; 2,300 km)

NORTH AMERICAN ROCKWELL B-1

Design and development work on the B-1 strategic bomber for the USAF is currently under way at the Los Angeles Division. The USAF hopes to order some 250 of these aircraft to replace the Boeing B-52s now in service. A decision to order the B-1 into production is unlikely before the Summer of 1974.

As now envisaged, this advanced strategic bomber would be powered by four General Electric F101 turbojets of 30,000 lb (13,600 kg) st each, have a maximum speed of approx Mach 2·2 at 50,000 ft (15,240 m), cruising speed of Mach 0·85 and max range without refuelling of 5,300 nm (6,100 miles; 9,800 km).

COMMERCIAL PRODUCTS GROUP

EXECUTIVE OFFICES:
North American Rockwell Building, Pittsburgh, Pennsylvania 15222

PRESIDENT:
Robert Wilson

GENERAL AVIATION DIVISIONS:

EXECUTIVE OFFICES:
5001 North Rockwell Avenue, Bethany, Oklahoma 73008

PRESIDENT:
Richard N. Robinson

VICE-PRESIDENTS:
C. Banks (Acceptance Corp)
F. Fleming (Service Operations)
R. Gayner (Engineering)
W. V. Gres (Operations)
H. Miller (Finance)

DIRECTORS:
A. F. Balaban (Public Relations/Communications)
T. J. Dean (Planning)
R. L. Griesinger (Advertising/Merchandising)
J. B. House (Industrial Relations)

Aero Commander Products Marketing—Bethany, Oklahoma:
D. E. Bradford (Vice-President, Marketing)
Bill Humes (Director, Marketing Administration)
Joe Freeh (Director, Sales)
Ed Blalock (Manager, Customer Service)

Sabreliner Products Marketing—St Louis, Missouri:
F. Fleming (Vice-President, Service Operations)
W. Smiley Jr (Manager, Sales)
H. Dugo (Manager, Service Support)

Bethany Plant:
5001 North Rockwell Avenue, Bethany, Oklahoma 73008

Albany Plant:
One Rockwell Avenue, Albany, Georgia 31702

Los Angeles Plant:
International Airport, Los Angeles, California 90009

St Louis Service Operations:
Lambert Field, St Louis, Missouri 63145
North American Rockwell announced on 30 September 1969 that a new operating unit called

the General Aviation Divisions had been created within the Commercial Products Group, combining the former Aero Commander Division and the Remmert Werner Division. The new operating divisions incorporate all of the corporation's manufacturing, marketing and general aviation aircraft services. They manufacture Sabreliner business jet aircraft and a variety of Aero Commander piston- and turboprop-engined aircraft. In addition, general aviation service support is provided for all types of aircraft through a network of eight fixed base operations in major US cities.

Products of the General Aviation Divisions are described below:

NORTH AMERICAN ROCKWELL SABRELINER
USAF and US Navy designation: T-39

To meet the USAF's "UTX" requirements for a combat readiness trainer and utility aircraft, North American built as a private venture the prototype of a small swept-wing twin-jet monoplane named the Sabreliner. Design work began

on 30 March 1956 and the prototype, powered by two General Electric J85 turbojet engines, flew for the first time on 16 September 1958.

Production of the military versions has been completed and today the Sabreliner is the only business jet in production that has been tested and approved to transport category standard by the FAA and to military specifications by both the USAF and USN.

Two versions are available, as follows:

Series 40. Basic version to carry a crew of two and up to nine passengers. More powerful engines than its predecessors. New brakes with longer life. Three windows instead of two on each side of passenger cabin. Early-model Sabreliners can be modified to Series 40 standard.

Series 60. Generally similar to Series 40, but fuselage lengthened by 3 ft 2 in (0·97 m). Accommodation for crew of two and ten passengers. Five windows on each side of passenger cabin. Early model Sabreliners can be modified to Series 60 standard.

North American Rockwell Sabreliner Srs 40 executive transport (two Pratt & Whitney JT12A turbojets)

A further version is under development, as follows:

Series 70. At the flight test stage in the spring of 1970, this version has a fuselage of deeper section to offer increased headroom in the cabin. It also has square cabin windows and dual wheels on each main landing gear unit. Wings, tail unit and power plant are unchanged.

A total of 150 commercial Sabreliners had been sold by 1 March 1969. The following details refer to the current Series 40 and 60 production versions, built at the General Aviation Divisions Los Angeles plant.

TYPE: Twin-engined jet business transport.

WINGS: Cantilever low-wing monoplane. Sweepback 28° 33'. All-metal two-spar milled-skin structure. Electrically-operated trim-tab in aileron. Electrically-operated trailing-edge flaps. Aerodynamically-operated leading-edge slats in five sections on each wing. Optional full-span pneumatically-operated de-icing boots.

FUSELAGE: All-metal semi-monocoque structure. Large hydraulically-operated air-brake under centre-fuselage.

TAIL UNIT: Cantilever all-metal structure, with flush antennae forming tip of fin and inset in dorsal fin. Moderate sweepback on all surfaces. Direct mechanical flight controls with electrically-operated horizontal tail surfaces. Electrically-operated trim-tab in rudder. Optional full-span pneumatically-operated leading-edge de-icer boots.

LANDING GEAR: Retractable tricycle type. Twin-wheel nose unit retracts forward. Single wheel on each main unit, retracting inward into fuselage. Hydraulic brakes with anti-skid units.

POWER PLANT: Two Pratt & Whitney JT12A-8 turbojet engines (each 3,300 lb=1,497 kg st) in pods on sides of rear fuselage. Integral fuel tanks in wings, with total capacity of 903 US gallons (3,418 litres). Fuselage tank, capacity 160 US gallons (606 litres). Total fuel capacity 1,063 US gallons (4,024 litres).

ACCOMMODATION: Crew of two and 6-10 passengers in pressurised air-conditioned cabin (see descriptions of individual series above). Downward-hinged door, with built-in steps, forward of wing on port side. Emergency exits on starboard side of cabin in the Series 40 and on both sides in the Series 60. Baggage space at front of cabin opposite door in both versions, with adjacent coat rack specified in many interior configurations. Srs 60 has larger lavatory at rear of cabin. With seats removed there is room for 2,500 lb (1,135 kg) of freight.

DIMENSIONS, EXTERNAL:

Wing span	44 ft 5¼ in (13·54 m)
Length overall:	
Srs 40	43 ft 9 in (13·34 m)
Srs 60	48 ft 4 in (14·73 m)
Height overall	16 ft 0 in (4·88 m)
Tailplane span	17 ft 6½ in (5·35 m)
Wheel track	7 ft 2½ in (2·20 m)
Wheelbase:	
Srs 40	14 ft 6 in (4·42 m)
Srs 60	15 ft 10¾ in (4·85 m)
Cabin door:	
Height	3 ft 11 in (1·19 m)
Width	2 ft 4 in (0·71 m)

DIMENSIONS, INTERNAL:

Cabin (excluding flight deck):	
Length:	
Srs 40	16 ft 0 in (4·88 m)
Srs 60	19 ft 0 in (5·79 m)
Max width	5 ft 2½ in (1·59 m)
Max height	5 ft 7½ in (1·71 m)
Volume:	
Srs 40	400 cu ft (11·33 m³)
Srs 60	480 cu ft (13·59 m³)

AREAS:

Wings, gross	342·05 sq ft (31·78 m²)
Ailerons (total)	16·42 sq ft (1·53 m²)
Flaps (total)	40·26 sq ft (3·74 m²)
Slats (total)	36·34 sq ft (3·38 m²)
Fin	41·58 sq ft (3·86 m²)
Rudder	8·95 sq ft (0·83 m²)
Tailplane	77·0 sq ft (7·15 m²)
Elevators	16·52 sq ft (1·53 m²)

WEIGHTS AND LOADINGS:

Basic operating weight, empty:	
Srs 40	9,895 lb (4,488 kg)
Srs 60	10,600 lb (4,808 kg)
Max payload, incl crew:	
Srs 40	2,609 lb (1,180 kg)
Srs 60	2,764 lb (1,254 kg)
Max T-O weight:	
Srs 40	18,650 lb (8,498 kg)
Srs 60	20,000 lb (9,060 kg)
Max ramp weight:	
Srs 40	18,650 lb (8,460 kg)
Srs 60	20,372 lb (9,221 kg)

The Srs 60 "stretched" version of the North American Rockwell Sabreliner

Max landing weight	17,500 lb (7,938 kg)
Max zero-fuel weight:	
Srs 40	12,800 lb (5,798 kg)
Srs 60	13,250 lb (6,010 kg)
Max wing loading:	
Srs 40	53·6 lb/sq ft (261·7 kg/m²)
Srs 60	57·6 lb/sq ft (281·2 kg/m²)
Max power loading:	
Srs 40	3·4 lb/lb st (3·4 kg/kg st)
Srs 60	2·97 lb/lb st (2·97 kg/kg st)

PERFORMANCE (Srs 40 and Srs 60 at max T-O weight):

Max level speed at 21,500 ft (6,550 m)
489 knots (563 mph; 906 km/h) = Mach 0·8
Max permissible diving speed   Mach 0·8
Max cruising speed at 21,500 ft (6,550 m)
489 knots (563 mph; 906 km/h) = Mach 0·8
Econ cruising speed at 39,000-45,000 ft (11,900-13,700 m)   Mach 0·7
Stalling speed:
Srs 40   80 knots (92 mph; 148 km/h)
Srs 60   85 knots (97 mph; 156 km/h)
Rate of climb at S/L:
Srs 40   4,700 ft (1433 m)/min
Service ceiling at AUW of 16,000 lb (7,257 kg)   45,000 ft (13,700 m)
Single-engine ceiling at AUW of 16,000 lb (7.257 kg)   24,000 ft (7,300 m)

FAA runway length for T-O:
Srs 40   4,280 ft (1,305 m)
Srs 60   4,875 ft (1,486 m)
FAA runway length for landing   2,935 ft (895 m)
Range with max fuel, VFR reserves:
Srs 40 over 1,823 nm (2,100 miles; 3,380 km)
Srs 60 over 1,736 nm (2,000 miles; 3,220 km)

AERO COMMANDER LARK COMMANDER

This four-seat high-performance all-metal business/sport/trainer aircraft was designed not only to satisfy the requirements of the sportsman and week-end private pilot, but also those of businessmen who fly their own aircraft on a regular basis. First deliveries of the Lark Commander were made in April 1968.

The basic airframe is similar to that of the earlier Darter Commander (see 1969-70 *Jane's*), which is no longer in production. It differs by having a swept tail fin and rudder, more powerful engine, detail refinements to reduce drag and de luxe furnishing of the cabin.

TYPE: Four-seat light aircraft.

WINGS: Braced high-wing monoplane. Single streamline-section bracing strut each side. All-metal two-spar structure. Three-position manually-operated flaps.

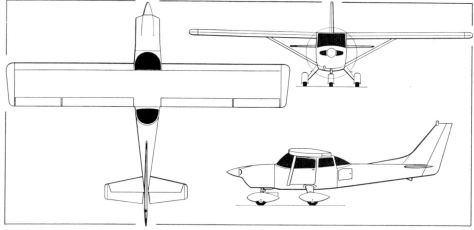

Photograph and general arrangement drawing of the Aero Commander Lark Commander

FUSELAGE: All-metal semi-monocoque rear structure, with cabin section of welded steel-tube construction, covered with light-alloy panels.

TAIL UNIT: Cantilever all-metal structure, with swept vertical surfaces and dorsal fin.

LANDING GEAR: Non-retractable tricycle type. Steerable nose-wheel carried on oleo-pneumatic shock-strut. Cantilever glass-fibre-spring main units. Main wheel tyres size 6·00 × 6. Streamlined wheel fairings standard. Hydraulic disc caliper brakes. Parking brake. Fixed tail-skid to avert damage in tail-down landing.

POWER PLANT: One 180 hp Lycoming O-360-A2F four-cylinder horizontally-opposed air-cooled engine, driving a McCauley 1A170/7660 fixed-pitch metal propeller with spinner. Fuel tank in each wing root, with total capacity of 44 US gallons (166·5 litres). Oil capacity 2 US gallons (7·5 litres).

ACCOMMODATION: Four seats in pairs in enclosed cabin, with 360° visibility. Carpeted baggage compartment aft of seats, capacity 120 lb (54 kg). Forward-hinged door on each side. Separate baggage compartment door on port side. In-flight access to baggage compartment by means of folding rear seat. Heater and windscreen de-froster. Airline-type air vents above seats. Glass-fibre insulation around cabin. Vinyl-covered interior with matching nylon carpeting. Dual wheel-type controls standard.

SYSTEMS: Electrical system includes a 12V 40A alternator and a 12V 35Ah battery.

ELECTRONICS AND EQUIPMENT: Optional items include blind-flying instrumentation and a wide range of nav/com installations. Standard equipment includes navigation lights, landing light (port wing) and rotating beacon.

DIMENSIONS, EXTERNAL:
Wing span	35 ft 0 in (10·67 m)
Length overall	27 ft 2 in (8·28 m)
Height overall	10 ft 1 in (3·07 m)
Tailplane span	10 ft 1·8 in (3·09 m)
Wheel track	7 ft 2 in (2·18 m)
Passenger doors:	
Height	3 ft 3½ in (1·00 m)
Width	2 ft 8½ in (0·82 m)
Baggage door:	
Height	1 ft 3½ in (0·39 m)
Width	1 ft 10 in (0·56 m)

DIMENSIONS, INTERNAL:
Cabin:	
Length	9 ft 10 in (3·00 m)
Max width	3 ft 4 in (1·02 m)
Baggage compartments (2)	15·76 cu ft (0·45 m³)

AREA:
Wings, gross	180 sq ft (16·72 m²)

WEIGHTS AND LOADINGS:
Weight empty	1,532 lb (695 kg)
Max T-O weight	2,475 lb (1,122 kg)
Max wing loading	13·6 lb/sq ft (66·8 kg/m²)
Max power loading	13·6 lb/hp (6·17 kg/hp)

PERFORMANCE (at max T-O weight):
Max level speed at S/L	120 knots (138 mph; 222 km/h)
Max cruising speed, 75% power at 7,500 ft (2,285 m)	115 knots (132 mph; 212 km/h)
Stalling speed, flaps down	51 knots (59 mph; 95 km/h)
Max rate of climb at S/L	718 ft (219 m)/min
Service ceiling	11,100 ft (3,383 m)
T-O run	1,050 ft (320 m)
Landing run	840 ft (256 m)
Range at econ cruising speed (56% power) at 7,500 ft (2,285 m)	486 nm (560 miles; 901 km)

AERO COMMANDER SHRIKE COMMANDER and SHRIKE COMMANDER ESQUIRE

The Aero Commander Shrike Commander is a twin-engined aircraft designed for the business-man-pilot. It is available in two versions:

Shrike Commander. Standard version, as described in detail below.

Shrike Commander Esquire. A de luxe version of the Shrike Commander, with standard accommodation for pilot and five passengers, with a fold-away desk, beverage consoles, stereo units and storage drawers under aft couch seat as standard.

The following details apply to both models:

TYPE: Twin-engined light transport.

WINGS: Cantilever high-wing monoplane. Wing section NACA 23012 modified. Dihedral 4°. Incidence 3° at root, —3° 30′ at tip. All-metal two-spar flush-riveted structure. Frise statically-balanced all-metal ailerons. Hydraulically-operated all-metal slotted flaps. Ground adjustable tab in starboard aileron. Pneumatic de-icer boots optional.

FUSELAGE: All-metal semi monocoque structure with flush-riveted skin.

TAIL UNIT: Cantilever all-metal structure with metal covering on all surfaces and 10° dihedral on tailplane. Trim-tabs in each elevator and rudder. Pneumatic de-icer boots optional.

LANDING GEAR: Retractable tricycle type, with single wheel on each unit. All wheels retract rearward hydraulically, main wheels turning through 90° to stow horizontally in nacelles. Oleo-pneumatic shock-absorbers. Hydraulically-steerable nose-wheel. Goodyear wheels

Aero Commander Shrike Commander Esquire de luxe executive light transport (two 290 hp Lycoming IO-540-E1B5 engines)

and tyres, size 8·50 × 10, 8-ply rating on main units, 6·00 × 6, 6-ply rating on nose unit. Goodyear hydraulic disc brakes.

POWER PLANT: Two 290 hp Lycoming IO-540-E1B5 six-cylinder horizontally-opposed air-cooled engines, each driving a Hartzell HC-C3YR-2/C8468-6R three-blade constant-speed fully-feathering metal propeller, diameter 6 ft 8 in (2·03 m). Bag-type fuel tanks in wings, capacity 156 US gallons (590 litres). Over-wing refuelling. Oil capacity 6 US gallons (22·7 litres). Electrically-heated fuel vents, and propeller anti-icing shoes optional.

ACCOMMODATION: Standard Shrike Commander has four individual seats: two in front with dual controls, and two at rear. Curtains divide pilot's compartment from cabin. Swivel-mounted fresh air vents above each seat, ash trays, window curtains, emergency exit, announcement signs, adjustable heating and fresh air ventilation ports at cabin floor level, double-glazed windows in cabin and a hatbox shelf in aft cabin bulkhead are standard. Optional seating layouts for up to seven persons, some with rear bench seat for two or three. Optional refreshment cabinet for hot and cold drinks. Forward-opening passenger door under wing on port side. Forward-opening door by pilot's seat at front of cabin on port side. All equipment can be removed to permit cabin to be used for freight-carrying. Baggage compartment for 500 lb (227 kg) baggage aft of cabin, with outside door. Windshield wiper and alcohol de-icing system for port side optional. De luxe interior of Esquire is as described above under model listing.

SYSTEMS: Hydraulic system, pressure 1,000 lb/sq in (70 kg/cm²), for landing gear, flaps, brakes and nose-wheel steering. Electrical system includes two 70A alternators and two 35Ah batteries.

ELECTRONICS AND EQUIPMENT: Standard equipment includes flight and engine instrumentation, clock, Janitrol 25,000 BTU cabin heater, rotating beacon, landing lights, reading lights, position lights, vacuum warning lights, instrument lighting system, air filter for vacuum instruments, dual vacuum pumps, electrically-adjustable cowl flap, external power plug, stall warning indicator and alternative static source. Optional equipment includes more advanced instruments, an extensive range of avionics which are available in package form or as individual items, 100A alternators, nickel-cadmium battery, under-fuselage rotating beacon, vertically-adjustable pilot and co-pilot seats with inertia reels and shoulder harnesses, storage drawers under aft couch, cabin and/or cockpit fire extinguishers, low fuel warning light, glass-holders, seat head-rests, lavatory chair for starboard side of aft cabin complete with curtain, 48·3 cu ft (1·37 m³) or 96·6 cu ft (2·74 m³) oxygen system, propeller synchronising equipment, dual relief tubes, sidewall-mounted stereo console, extra seat tracks, polished spinners, cabin table, vent window for co-pilot and wing ice lights.

DIMENSIONS, EXTERNAL:
Wing span	49 ft 0½ in (14·95 m)
Wing chord at root	8 ft 4 in (2·54 m)
Wing chord at tip	2 ft 1½ in (0·65 m)
Wing aspect ratio	9·45
Length overall	36 ft 7 in (11·15 m)
Height overall	14 ft 6 in (4·42 m)
Tailplane span	16 ft 9 in (5·10 m)
Wheel track	12 ft 11 in (3·95 m)
Wheelbase	13 ft 11¾ in (4·26 m)
Crew door (fwd):	
Height	3 ft 10 in (1·17 m)
Width	1 ft 11 in (0·58 m)

Passenger door (aft):	
Height	3 ft 9 in (1·14 m)
Width	2 ft 4 in (0·71 m)
Baggage door:	
Height	1 ft 11½ in (0·60 m)
Width	1 ft 7½ in (0·50 m)

DIMENSIONS, INTERNAL:
Cabin: Length	10 ft 7½ in (3·24 m)
Max width	4 ft 4 in (1·32 m)
Max height	4 ft 5 in (1·35 m)
Volume	177 cu ft (5·01 m³)
Baggage hold	43 cu ft (1·22 m³)

AREAS:
Wings, gross	255 sq ft (23·69 m²)
Ailerons (total)	20·52 sq ft (1·90 m²)
Trailing-edge flaps (total)	21·20 sq ft (1·97 m²)
Fin	24·00 sq ft (2·23 m²)
Rudder, including tab	15·40 sq ft (1·43 m²)
Tailplane	33·06 sq ft (3·07 m²)
Elevators, including tabs	20·54 sq ft (1·91 m²)

WEIGHTS AND LOADING:
Weight empty, equipped	4,635 lb (2,102 kg)
Max T-O and landing weight	6,750 lb (3,062 kg)
Max zero-fuel weight	6,250 lb (2,834 kg)
Max wing loading	26·47 lb/sq ft (129·2 kg/m²)

PERFORMANCE (at max T-O weight):
Max level speed at S/L	187 knots (215 mph; 346 km/h)
Cruising speed (75% power) at 9,000 ft (2,745 m)	176 knots (203 mph; 326 km/h)
Stalling speed, flaps and landing gear down	59 knots (68 mph; 109 km/h)
Stalling speed, clean	68 knots (78 mph; 126 km/h)
Rate of climb at S/L	1,340 ft (408 m)/min
Rate of climb at S/L, one engine out	266 ft (81 m)/min
Service ceiling	19,400 ft (5,913 m)
Service ceiling, one engine out	6,500 ft (1,981 m)
T-O to 50 ft (15 m)	1,915 ft (584 m)
Landing from 50 ft (15 m)	2,235 ft (681 m)
Range with standard fuel at 9,000 ft (2,745 m) at 178 knots (205 mph; 330 km/h) TAS, 45 min reserve	651 nm (750 miles; 1,207 km)
Range, conditions as above, no reserve	782 nm (901 miles; 1,450 km)
Absolute range, standard fuel at 15,000 ft (4,570 m) at 45% power and TAS of 147 knots (170 mph; 274 km/h), no reserve	936 nm (1,078 miles; 1,735 km)

AERO COMMANDER HAWK COMMANDER

The Hawk Commander is a pressurised transport aircraft with an airframe generally similar to that of the Shrike Commander, but it has reduced wing span and is powered by two AiResearch turboprop engines. The prototype flew for the first time on 31 December 1964, and the first production machine followed in April 1965. Deliveries began in May 1966.

The 1970 version introduces eyebrow windows for the flight deck; utilises engine-bleed air for pressurisation, heating and air conditioning; and has new interior and exterior styling.

The description of the Shrike Commander applies also to the Hawk Commander, except in the following details:

WINGS: Span reduced. Incidence at tip 1°. Optional electric trim-tab in aileron.

TAIL UNIT: Tailplane increased in span and area.

LANDING GEAR: Wheelbase increased.

POWER PLANT: Two 605 eshp AiResearch TPE 331-43BL turboprop engines, each driving a three-blade Hamilton Standard 33LF-325 constant-speed reversible-pitch propeller, diameter 7 ft 6 in (2·29 m). Fuel in two bag-type tanks in wings, total capacity 286·5 US gallons (1,086 litres). Optional auxiliary

Aero Commander Hawk Commander 8/11-seat light transport (two 605 eshp AiResearch TPE 331-43BL turboprop engines)

tanks, capacity 51 US gallons (193 litres). Oil capacity 3·75 US gallons (14·25 litres).

ACCOMMODATION: Standard seating for eight persons, on three-place forward-facing bench seat, two rearward-facing single seats and side-facing seat in main cabin, and two adjustable seats on flight deck. Optional seating for up to nine persons. Cabin is fitted with two large picture windows, fold-away work-table, refreshment consoles and lavatory. Baggage compartment aft of rear pressure bulkhead, capacity 500 lb (227 kg).

SYSTEMS: Cabin pressurisation, heating and air-conditioning by engine-bleed air; max pressure differential 4·2 lb/sq in (0·29 kg/cm²). Dual 200A starter-generators and two 22Ah Nicad batteries. Emergency stand-by oxygen system, automatic propeller synchronisation. Foxboro fuel flow system and gauges with digital read-out. Heated fuel vents. Electronically controlled exhaust gas temperature read-out. Engine fire detection system.

ELECTRONICS: A selection of complete IFR systems is available to customer's requirements.

DIMENSIONS, EXTERNAL:

Wing span	44 ft 0¾ in (13·43 m)
Wing chord at root	8 ft 4 in (2·54 m)
Wing chord at tip	2 ft 9 in (0·84 m)
Wing aspect ratio	8·05
Length overall	42 ft 11¾ in (13·10 m)
Height overall	14 ft 6 in (4·42 m)
Tailplane span	19 ft 9½ in (6·03 m)
Wheelbase	17 ft 7¼ in (5·38 m)

AREAS:
As for Shrike Commander, except:

Wings, gross	242·5 sq ft (22·53 m²)
Flaps (total)	20·82 sq ft (1·93 m²)
Tailplane	37·85 sq ft (3·52 m²)

WEIGHTS AND LOADINGS:

Weight empty	5,647 lb (2,561 kg)
Max ramp weight	9,450 lb (4,286 kg)
Max T-O weight	9,400 lb (4,265 kg)
Max zero fuel weight	8,500 lb (3,856 kg)
Max landing weight	9,000 lb (4,080 kg)
Max wing loading	38·8 lb/sq ft (189·5 kg/m²)
Max power loading	8·2 lb/hp (3·72 kg/hp)

PERFORMANCE (at max T-O weight):

Max level speed at 9,000 lb (4,080 kg) AUW
252 knots (290 mph; 467 km/h)
Max cruising speed
241 knots (278 mph; 447 km/h)
Stalling speed, flaps and landing gear down
82 knots (94 mph; 152 km/h)
Stalling speed, flaps and landing gear up
89 knots (102 mph; 164 km/h)
Rate of climb at S/L 2,007 ft (612 m)/min
Rate of climb at S/L, one engine out
484 ft (148 m)/min
Service ceiling 25,600 ft (7,800 m)
Service ceiling, one engine out
10,500 ft (3,200 m)
T-O run 1,706 ft (520 m)
T-O to 50 ft (15 m) 2,016 ft (615 m)
Landing from 50 ft (15 m):
with reverse thrust (estimated)
1,200 ft (366 m)
without reverse thrust 2,504 ft (763 m)
Cruising range with standard fuel at 21,000 ft (6,400 m), 221 knots (254 mph; 409 km/h) TAS, with 45 min reserve
922 nm (1,062 miles; 1,709 km)
Cruising range with max fuel, conditions as above 1,141 nm (1,315 miles; 2,116 km)
Absolute range with standard fuel, conditions as above 1,080 nm (1,244 miles; 2,012 km)
Absolute range with max fuel, conditions as above 1,294 nm (1,491 miles; 2,400 km)

AERO COMMANDER SPARROW COMMANDER

The Sparrow Commander is the smallest of the General Aviation Divisions' three agricultural aircraft, combining 170 US-gallon (643-litre) hopper capacity with low operating cost.

The entire primary structure of the aircraft is coated with Copon, an epoxy resin catalyst paint which is resistant to all known agricultural chemicals.

The Sparrow Commander can be purchased with any type of dispersal equipment required, *i.e.* straight sprayer of either high or low volume, dust dispersal gear, or a quick-change combination dust or spray unit. The units normally offered as optional extras are the Transland Boom Master spray system, StrutMaster spray system with 2-in Simplex pump, invert emulsion spray system, Buckeye bottom loader spray system, Micronair spray system, standard dust spreader, spreader with gate box and agitator, and Transland Swathmaster dry spreader.

TYPE: Single-seat agricultural monoplane.

WINGS: Braced low-wing monoplane. Modified Clark Y wing section. Dihedral 5° 8'. Incidence 0° 20'. Composite structure with spruce wood spars, metal-covered leading-edge and fabric covering on remainder of wing. Multiple steel-tube bracing struts on each side of fuselage. Hoerner wing-tips. Wooden ailerons are fabric-covered. Current version has flaps and drooping ailerons.

FUSELAGE: Steel-tube structure with fabric covering. Removable side-panels.

TAIL UNIT: Wire-braced steel-tube structure with fabric covering. Wire deflector from canopy to fin.

LANDING GEAR: Non-retractable tail-wheel type. CallAir spring shock-absorbers. Cleveland main wheels, with Goodyear tyres, size 8·50 × 6, 6-ply. Scott 8-in (20 cm) steerable tail-wheel. Cleveland toe-actuated brakes. Wire-cutters on main legs.

POWER PLANT: One 235 hp Lycoming O-540-B2B5 six-cylinder horizontally-opposed air-cooled engine, driving a McCauley Type 1A200-DFA9045 two-blade fixed-pitch metal propeller, diameter 7 ft 6 in (2·29 m). Two-position adjustable-pitch McCauley Type 2D34CT-84HF two-blade metal propeller optional, diameter 7 ft 0 in (2·13 m). All fuel in wing tanks, capacity 40 US gallons (151 litres). Oil capacity 3 US gallons (11 litres).

ACCOMMODATION: Single seat for pilot in open-sided cockpit aft of hopper. Side doors on cockpit. Wire-cutters on windscreen. Cabin heater standard. Capacity of standard hopper 22½ cu ft (0·64 m³) or 170 US gallons (643 litres).

SYSTEMS: Electrical system includes 50A 24V alternator and 35Ah battery.

ELECTRONICS: Narco Mk III Omnigator radio and other avionics available as optional extras.

EQUIPMENT: Optional equipment includes night lighting system, landing light in nose cowl and AC full-flow oil filter.

DIMENSIONS, EXTERNAL:

Wing span	34 ft 9 in (10·59 m)
Wing chord, constant	5 ft 2¾ in (1·59 m)
Length overall	23 ft 6 in (7·16 m)
Height overall	7 ft 7 in (2·31 m)
Tailplane span	10 ft 6 in (3·20 m)
Wheel track	6 ft 10 in (2·08 m)
Wheelbase	17 ft 1 in (5·21 m)

AREAS:

Wings, gross	182 sq ft (16·90 m²)
Ailerons (total)	21·4 sq ft (1·99 m²)
Fin	8·6 sq ft (0·80 m²)
Rudder	9·0 sq ft (0·84 m²)
Tailplane	15·8 sq ft (1·47 m²)
Elevators	14·0 sq ft (1·30 m²)

WEIGHTS AND LOADINGS:

Weight empty	1,600 lb (726 kg)
Max payload	1,400 lb (635 kg)
Max T-O weight:	
CAR.3	3,000 lb (1,360 kg)
CAR.8	3,400 lb (1,542 kg)
Max wing loading	16·4 lb/sq ft (80·0 kg/m²)
Max power loading	12·8 lb/hp (5·8 kg/hp)

PERFORMANCE (at CAR.8 max T-O weight, except where indicated):

Max level speed at S/L
103 knots (119 mph; 191 km/h)
Max cruising speed (75% power) at 3,000 lb (1,360 kg) AUW
91 knots (105 mph; 169 km/h)
Normal operating speed
78-87 knots (90-100 mph; 145-161 km/h)
Stalling speed at max T-O weight
53 knots (60 mph; 97 km/h)
Stalling speed as usually landed
35 knots (40 mph; 64 km/h)
Rate of climb at S/L 650 ft (198 m)/min
Service ceiling 14,000 ft (4,265 m)
T-O run 600 ft (183 m)
Landing run 447 ft (136 m)
Range at cruising speed (75% power)
260 nm (300 miles; 483 km)

Sparrow Commander, smallest of Aero Commander's agricultural aircraft (235 hp Lycoming O-540-B2B5 engine)

AA

AERO COMMANDER QUAIL COMMANDER

The Quail Commander is the intermediate model in the Ag Commander series. It differs from the Sparrow Commander only in having a 290 hp Lycoming IO-540-G1C5 six-cylinder horizontally-opposed air-cooled engine and a larger hopper with a capacity of 210 US gallons (795 litres).

Details given for the Sparrow Commander apply also to the Quail Commander, except as shown below:

EQUIPMENT: Optional equipment includes also an alternative retractable landing light in the wing and a rotating beacon.

WEIGHTS:
Max payload	1,600 lb (726 kg)
Max T-O weight (CAR.8)	3,600 lb (1,633 kg)

PERFORMANCE: (at CAR.8 max T-O weight, except where indicated):
Max level speed	104 knots (120 mph; 193 km/h)
Cruising speed (75% power) at 3,000 lb (1,360 kg) AUW	100 knots (115 mph; 185 km/h)
Operating speed	78-87 knots (90-100 mph; 145-161 km/h)
Stalling speed at max T-O weight	54 knots (62 mph; 100 km/h)
Stalling speed as usually landed	35 knots (40 mph; 65 km/h)
Rate of climb at S/L	850 ft (259 m)/min
Service ceiling	16,000 ft (4,875 m)
T-O run	800 ft (244 m)
Landing run at normal landing weight	447 ft (136 m)
Range (at 50% power)	260 nm (300 miles; 483 km)

AERO COMMANDER THRUSH COMMANDER

The Thrush Commander is the largest specially-designed agricultural aircraft in production in the USA at the present time. It has a 600 hp Pratt & Whitney radial engine and carries a 53 cu ft (1·50 m³) hopper able to contain up to 400 US gallons (1,514 litres) of liquid or 3,280 lb (1,487 kg) of dry chemicals. It has corrosion proofing of actuated Copon and is certificated to both CAR Pt 8 and Pt 3 requirements for normal category aircraft.

TYPE: Single-seat agricultural aircraft.

WINGS: Cantilever low-wing monoplane. Two-spar structure of light alloy throughout, except for main spar caps of heat-treated SAE 4130 steel. Leading-edge formed by heavy main spar and flush-riveted nose-skin. Light alloy plain ailerons. Electrically-operated flaps. Wing root sealed against chemical entry.

FUSELAGE: Welded chrome-molybdenum steel-tube structure covered with quickly-removable light alloy panels. Under-fuselage skin of stainless steel.

TAIL UNIT: Wire-braced welded chrome-molybdenum steel-tube structure, fabric-covered. Streamline-section heavy-duty stainless steel wire bracing and heavy-duty stainless steel attachment fittings. Light alloy controllable trim tab in each elevator. Deflector cable from cockpit to fin-tip.

Aero Commander Thrush Commander agricultural aircraft (600 hp Pratt & Whitney R-1340 engine)

LANDING GEAR: Non-retractable tail-wheel type. Main units have rubber-in-compression shock-struts and 27-in wheels with 10-ply tyres. Hydraulic brakes. Parking brakes. Wire cutters on main gear. Steerable, locking tail-wheel size 12·5 × 4·5 in.

POWER PLANT: One 600 hp Pratt & Whitney R-1340-AN-1 nine-cylinder radial air-cooled engine, driving a Hamilton Standard constant-speed two-blade metal propeller. One 52-US gallon (196-litre) integral burst-proof tank in each wing, giving total fuel capacity of 104 US gallons (393 litres). Oil capacity 10·9 US gallons (41·2 litres).

ACCOMMODATION: Single adjustable seat in 40g "safety pod" enclosed cockpit, with steel-tube overturn structure. Downward-hinged door on each side. Tempered safety-glass windshield. Openable windshield optional. Hopper forward of cockpit with capacity of 53 cu ft (1·50 m³) or 400 US gallons (1,514 litres).

SYSTEMS: Electrical system comprises a 50A 24V generator and 35Ah battery.

EQUIPMENT: Standard equipment includes Universal spray system with external 2-in (5-cm) stainless steel plumbing, 2-in (5-cm) Root Model 07 pump with adjustable wooden fan, Ag Commander gate, Transland 2-in (5-cm) valve, Transland quick-disconnect pump mount, 35 nozzles installed, streamlined spray booms with outlets for 70 nozzles 2½-in (6·3-cm) bottom loading system installed in port side. Navigation lights, instrument lights and two rotating beacons. Optional equipment includes Ag Commander high-volume spreader with micro-adjust calibrator, agitator installation, extra-high-density spray configuration with 70 nozzles installed, night working lights including wing-tip turn lights, cockpit fire-extinguisher and ferry fuel system.

DIMENSIONS, EXTERNAL:
Wing span	44 ft 5 in (13·54 m)
Length overall	29 ft 4½ in (8·95 m)
Height overall	9 ft 2 in (2·79 m)
Tailplane span	15 ft 11½ in (4·86 m)
Wheel track	8 ft 11 in (2·72 m)

WEIGHTS AND LOADINGS:
Weight empty	3,700 lb (1,678 kg)
Max T-O weight	6,900 lb (3,130 kg)
Max wing loading	18·4 lb/sq ft (89·8 kg/m²)
Max power loading	10 lb/hp (4·5 kg/hp)

PERFORMANCE: (at CAR.3 max T-O weight, except where indicated):
Max level speed	122 knots (140 mph; 225 km/h)
Cruising speed	96 knots (110 mph; 177 km/h)
Normal operating speed	83-96 knots (95-110 mph; 153-177 km/h)
Stalling speed, flaps up	61 knots (70 mph; 113 km/h)
Stalling speed, flaps down	58 knots (66 mph; 107 km/h)
Stalling speed, at normal landing weight, flaps up	50 knots (57 mph; 92 km/h)
Stalling speed, at normal landing weight, flaps down	48 knots (55 mph; 89 km/h)
Rate of climb at S/L	900 ft (274 m)/min
Service ceiling	15,000 ft (4,570 m)
T-O run	775 ft (236 m)
Landing run, at normal landing weight	500 ft (152 m)
Range (at 50% power)	408 nm (470 miles; 756 km)

NORTHROP

NORTHROP CORPORATION

HEAD OFFICE:
Beverly Hills, California 90212

CHAIRMAN OF THE BOARD, PRESIDENT AND CHIEF EXECUTIVE OFFICER:
Thomas V. Jones

SENIOR VICE-PRESIDENTS:
George F. Douglas (Administration)
Richard E. Horner (Technical)
James D. Willson (Finance and Treasurer)

VICE-PRESIDENTS:
Harrison Van Aken (President, The Hallicrafters Co)
John R. Alison (Customer Relations)
James Allen (Assistant to the President)
Ward B. Dennis (Forward Planning)
Welko E. Gasich (General Manager, Northrop Ventura)
George Gore (General Counsel and Secretary)
James V. Holcombe (Washington, DC)
F. W. Lloyd (General Manager, Northrop Aircraft)
Glenn R. Lord (Marketing)
Frank W. Lynch (General Manager, Electro-Mechanical Division)
J. Grant Macdonnell (Controller)
Ross F. Miller (General Manager, Electronics Division)
Alan C. Morgan (Industrial Relations)
J. M. Ricketts (President, Northrop Carolina)
Frederick Stevens (Diversification)
Joseph A. Waldschmitt (President, Page Communications Engineers, Inc)

ASST SECRETARY: David H. Olson

PUBLIC RELATIONS MANAGER: Charley M. Barr

This company was formed in 1939 by John K. Northrop and others to undertake the design and manufacture of military aircraft. During World War II it built 1,131 aircraft of its own design and was engaged in extensive sub-contract work. It also devoted considerable attention to the design and construction of aircraft of the "Flying Wing" type.

Although continuing its activities in the design, development and production of aircraft, missiles and target drone systems, Northrop has broadened its scope of operation to include electronics, space technology, communications and commercial products. To reflect this changing character of its business, the company changed its name from Northrop Aircraft, Inc, to Northrop Corporation in 1959. In 1969 the name of its former Norair Division was changed to Northrop Aircraft to emphasise this division's prime concern with research, design and manufacture of aircraft. Divisions of Northrop Corporation now include Northrop Aircraft, specialising in aircraft, missiles, astronautic systems and weapon systems management; and Ventura, which is engaged primarily in the design, development and manufacture of spacecraft landing systems and target and surveillance drones. In 1969 the company divided its Nortronics Division into two new operating organisations; the Electronics Division and Electro-Mechanical Division. They handle Northrop activities in the design, development and manufacture of electronic, electro-mechanical and opto-mechanical products and components.

In 1959 Northrop expanded into the field of advanced systems for long-range radio communications with the purchase of Page Communications Engineers, Inc, as a wholly-owned subsidiary. To expand its capabilities in the communications field, Northrop acquired the Hallicrafters Company of Chicago, Illinois, in December 1966. Operating as another wholly-owned subsidiary, Hallicrafters are producing short-wave radio transmitters and receivers and a variety of domestic and military radio equipment.

In 1961 Northrop combined the operations of Acme Metal Molding Co and Arcadia Metal Products in a single organization, Northrop Architectural Systems (a wholly-owned subsidiary).

Northrop Pacific, Inc, was formed from Northrop Architectural Systems in 1969 as a new subsidiary of the company to continue the manufacture of floor panels for commercial aircraft.

To further expand its research and development work, the Northrop Space Laboratories, created in 1962, are now divided into two organisations; the Northrop Corporate Laboratories and the Advanced Systems Department. Current programmes include research and development in such fields as life sciences, bioastronautics, space payloads and space vehicle design.

In January 1963 Northrop and Hawker Siddeley Aviation Ltd announced an agreement for collaboration in the V/STOL strike aircraft field. Under the agreement, Northrop acquired technical know-how and design information on the Hawker Siddeley P.1127 and related aircraft.

On 1 October 1965 Northrop acquired the Amcel Propulsion Co from Celanese Corporation of America. Now known as Northrop Carolina, Inc, a wholly-owned subsidiary, the company develops and produces chemicals, explosives, ordnance, and rocket propulsion devices for the Department of Defense and NASA.

NORTHROP AIRCRAFT
ADDRESS:
3901 West Broadway, Hawthorne, California 90250
CORPORATE VICE-PRESIDENT AND GENERAL MANAGER:
F. W. Lloyd
VICE-PRESIDENTS:
R. P. Jackson (Asst General Manager)
M. Kuska (Engineering)
J. Mannion (Manufacturing and Materiel)
W. E. Woolwine (Military Programmes)

Current production at Northrop's Aircraft Division is centred on major Boeing 747 subcontract work, the T-38A Talon supersonic basic trainer and the related F-5 tactical fighter.

For NASA, Norair has built two lifting body test vehicles, designated M2-F2 and HL-10.

In addition to its main factory at Hawthorne, the Aircraft Division has facilities at Compton, Torrance, El Segundo, Palmdale and Edwards Air Force Base, California.

NORTHROP TALON
USAF designation: T-38

Developed for two years as a private venture, the T-38 supersonic lightweight twin-jet trainer has been in continuous production for the USAF under a series of contracts awarded since May 1956. It is powered by two General Electric J85-GE-5 turbojets, and reproduces the flying characteristics of a supersonic operational fighter aircraft.

The first T-38 flew for the first time on 10 April 1959, and production T-38A's became operational on 17 March 1961. The rate of production of the T-38A is 11 aircraft per month. A total of 1,138 had been ordered at the beginning of 1969, and the 1,000th was delivered to the USAF in January 1969.

NASA is using T-38's as space flight readiness trainers for astronauts and has acquired a total of 24 aircraft; the US Navy is procuring five T-38's from the Air Force Systems Command.

Another customer is the German government, which took delivery of 46 T-38's through the USAF, in 1967, for the advanced training of German student pilots in the USA. These aircraft retain US military insignia.

TYPE: Two-seat supersonic basic trainer.

WINGS: Cantilever low-wing monoplane. Wing section NACA 65A004·8 (modified). Thickness/chord ratio 4·8%. No dihedral or incidence. Sweepback at quarter-chord 24°. Multi-spar aluminium alloy structure with heavy plate machined skins. Hydraulically-powered sealed-gap ailerons at approximately mid-span with aluminium alloy single-slotted flaps inboard. No trim-tabs. Designed to be flown and landed safely using only one aileron. No de-icing system.

FUSELAGE: Aluminium semi-monocoque basic structure with steel, magnesium and titanium used in certain areas. "Waisted" area-rule lines. Two hydraulically-actuated air-brakes on underside of fuselage forward of wheel wells.

TAIL UNIT: Cantilever all-metal structure, with hydraulically-operated rudder and one-piece "all-moving" tailplane. Single spars with full-depth aluminium honeycomb secondary structure. No trim-tabs. Longitudinal and directional stability augmentors installed in series with control system.

LANDING GEAR: Hydraulically-retractable tricycle type with steerable nose-wheel. Emergency gravity extension. Main units retract inward into fuselage, nose-wheel forward. Oleo-pneumatic shock-absorbers. Main wheel tyres size 20 × 4·4, pressure 236 lb/sq in (16·6 kg/cm²). Nose-wheel tyre size 18 × 4·4, pressure 75 lb/sq in (5·27 kg/cm²). Multiple-disc hydraulic brakes.

POWER PLANT: Two General Electric J65-GE-5 turbojets with afterburners (each 2,680 lb = 1,216 kg st dry, 3,850 lb = 1,748 kg with afterburning). Two independent fuel systems, one for each engine. Fuel for starboard engine provided by forward fuselage tank and dorsal tank just aft of rear cockpit. Fuel for port engine provided by centre and aft fuselage tanks. All tanks of bladder type. Total usable capacity 583 US gallons (2,206 litres). No external tanks. Single refuelling point on lower fuselage. Oil capacity 4·7 US quarts (4·5 litres) each engine. Aircraft supplied to NASA have an engine inlet duct lip anti-ice system.

ACCOMMODATION: Pupil and instructor in tandem on rocket-powered ejection seats in pressurised and air-conditioned cockpits, separated by windshield. Separate manually-operated, rearward-hinged jettisonable canopies. Instructor's seat at rear raised 10 in (0·25 m) higher than that of pupil to give improved forward view.

Northrop T-38 Talon two-seat supersonic basic trainer

SYSTEMS: Pressure differential 5 lb/sq in (0·35 kg/cm²). Two separate 3,000 lb/sq in (210 kg/cm²) hydraulic systems, one for flying controls, other for flying controls, air-brakes, landing gear, and nose-wheel steering. No pneumatic system. Two 8·5kVA generators, wide-frequency 320-480 c/s, manufactured by Westinghouse. Two 25A transformer-rectifiers for DC supply.

ELECTRONICS: Magnavox AN/ARC-34X UHF radio. Hoffmann AN/ARN-65 TACAN, Hazeltine AN/APX-64 IFF, Andrea AN/AIC-18 intercom, Collins AN/ARN-58 ILS, Bendix compass system. Integrated instrument panel.

DIMENSIONS, EXTERNAL:

Wing span	25 ft 3 in (7·70 m)
Wing chord (mean aerodynamic)	7 ft 9 in (2·36 m)
Wing aspect ratio	3·75
Length overall	46 ft 4½ in (14·13 m)
Height overall	12 ft 10½ in (3·92 m)
Tailplane span	14 ft 2 in (4·32 m)
Wheel track	10 ft 9 in (3·28 m)
Wheelbase	19 ft 5½ in (5·93 m)

AREAS:

Wings, gross	170 sq ft (15·80 m²)
Ailerons (total)	9·24 sq ft (0·86 m²)
Trailing-edge flaps (total)	19·00 sq ft (1·77 m²)
Fin	41·42 sq ft (3·85 m²)
Rudder, including tab	6·37 sq ft (0·59 m²)
Tailplane	59·00 sq ft (5·48 m²)

WEIGHTS AND LOADINGS:

Max T-O and landing weight	12,050 lb (5,465 kg)
Max zero-fuel weight	7,663 lb (3,475 kg)
Max wing loading	70·9 lb/sq ft (346·2 kg/m²)
Max power loading	1·56 lb/lb st (1·56 kg/kg st)

PERFORMANCE (at max T-O weight, except where indicated):

Max level speed (50% fuel) at 36,000 ft (11,000 m)	above Mach 1·23
Max permissible diving speed	710 knots (818 mph; 1,316 km/h) IAS
Max cruising speed at 36,000 ft (11,000 m)	above Mach 0·95
Econ cruising speed	Mach 0·88
Stalling speed flaps extended (50% fuel)	136 knots (156 mph; 252 km/h) IAS
Rate of climb at S/L (50% fuel)	30,000 ft (9,145 m)/min
Service ceiling (50% fuel)	53,600 ft (16,335 m)
Service ceiling, one engine out (50% fuel)	40,000 ft (12,200 m)
T-O run	2,500 ft (762 m)
T-O to 50 ft (15 m)	3,700 ft (1,128 m)
Landing from 50 ft (15 m) at AUW of 8,850 lb (4,014 kg)	4,500 ft (1,372 m)

Landing run	3,000 ft (914 m)
Range with max fuel, with 600 lb (272 kg) reserve fuel	955 nm (1,100 miles; 1,770 km)

NORTHROP F-5
USAF designation: F-5

This light tactical fighter is similar in design and construction to the T-38 Talon supersonic trainer and utilises a higher-rated version of the J85 turbojets fitted in the Talon. Its design was started in 1955 and construction of the prototype of the single-seat version (then designated N-156C) began in 1958. It flew for the first time on 30 July 1959, exceeding Mach 1 on its maiden flight. Two more prototypes were built and there are several production versions, as follows:

F-5A. Basic single-seat fighter. Two General Electric J85-GE-13 afterburning turbojets. First production F-5A flew in October 1963. Norwegian version has ATO and arrester hook for short-field operation. Total of 569 F-5A aircraft had been ordered by the beginning of 1969.

F-5B. Generally similar to F-5A, but with two seats in tandem for dual fighter/trainer duties. First F-5B flew on 24 February 1964. A total of 90 F-5B's had been ordered by the beginning of 1969.

An F-5B, with General Electric J85-21 engines of 5,000 lb (2,270 kg) st, is being used as a propulsion system test-bed for the projected Northrop F-5-21 fighter. It flew for the first time on 28 March 1969.

F-5A-15. Basically similar to F-5A, but powered by higher-rated (4,300 lb = 1,950 kg st) General Electric J85-GE-15 turbojets with afterburning. Electrically-actuated louvre-doors, on each side of rear fuselage, provide additional air during take-off and flight at speeds below 287 knots (330 mph; 530 km/h). Two-position extending nose-wheel increases angle of attack on ground by 3°, helping to reduce take-off distances by 25%. Prototype, converted as private venture from an F-5A, flew for the first time in May 1965. Offered to USAF Tactical Air Command.

F-5-21. Advanced version of F-5A. Described separately.

CF-5A/D. These are the designations of the versions of the F-5A/B that are being produced for the Canadian Armed Forces. Several improvements have been incorporated in the CF series, including higher thrust engines (J85-CAN-15), and flight refuelling capability. Manufacture and assembly of the 115 aircraft on order is being carried out by Canadair Ltd. The engines are built by Orenda Ltd. The programme was

Northrop F-5B two-seat fighter/trainer of the Air Force of the Republic of Vietnam

initiated in the latter half of 1965 and deliveries will extend to the end of 1970. Maximum speed is in excess of 870 knots (1,000 mph; 1,609 km/h) with a maximum rate of climb of 31,000 ft (9,450 m) min.

Some CF-5 aircraft utilise a reconnaissance nose unit developed by Northrop. The nose houses up to three 70-mm Vinten cameras and contains seven windows. When fitted, it does not limit the aircraft's weapon delivery capabilities.

NF-5A/D. Versions of the F-5 being produced for the Royal Netherlands Air Force with a Doppler navigation system, 275 US gallon (1,040-litre) fuel tanks and manoeuvring flaps. Manufacture and assembly of the 105 aircraft on order are integrated with CF-5 production by Canadair Ltd, with delivery extending to the end of 1971.

RF-5A. Reconnaissance version of the F-5; initial deliveries were made in mid-1968. Its four KS-92 cameras, each with a 100-ft film magazine, can provide forward oblique, trimetrogon and split vertical coverage, including horizon-to-horizon with overlap. Associated equipment includes four light sensors, defogging and cooling systems, a pitot static nose boom and a computer/"J" box, all housed in a nose compartment with forward-hinged clamshell top cover. A total of 69 RF-5A's had been ordered by January 1969.

The F-5A and B were ordered into production by the US government, through the USAF, in October 1962, to meet the defence requirements of allied and friendly nations. Manufacture was under way at a combined rate of 10 aircraft a month by mid-1964. Initial deliveries, beginning April 1964, were made to Williams AFB, Chandler, Arizona, where the USAF Tactical Air Command is training pilots and maintenance personnel of countries that will receive F-5's. The first foreign air force to receive F-5's was the Imperial Iranian Air Force, which put into service its first squadron of 13 aircraft on 1 February 1965. Iran is to have six more squadrons of F-5's. Greece began equipping two squadrons in 1965: Norway received 64 aircraft in 1966-67 with follow-on orders to bring the total to 108. Other nations equipping with F-5's include Canada, Ethiopia, Morocco, Republic of Vietnam, South Korea, Nationalist China, the Philippines, Libya, Netherlands, Spain, Thailand and Turkey. Construcciones Aeronauticas SA (CASA) of Spain is co-operating on production of the 70 Spanish F-5's.

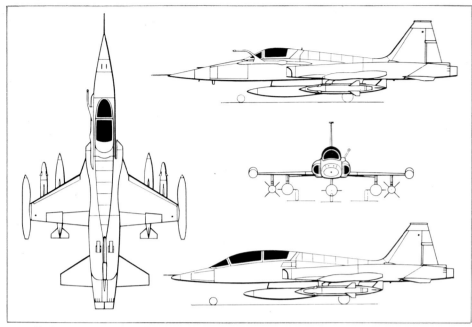

Northrop F-5A supersonic combat aircraft, with additional side elevation of F-5B (*bottom*)

Northrop F-5A's in the service of the Republic of China Air Force

Northrop RF-5A single-seat reconnaissance fighter, showing the reconnaissance nose unit

The USAF has evaluated a squadron of F-5's in Vietnam, where 12 aircraft flew up to 33 sorties a day for a successful trial period as a first-line combat unit.

The F-5 is suitable for a wide range of combat and photographic-reconnaissance duties. It can take off, climb to altitude, complete a mission and return to base on one engine.

Special attention has been paid to simple maintenance. The aft portion of the fuselage is removable to permit quick engine replacement, handling of the engines being facilitated by an overhead track and trolley arrangement in each engine bay. The hydraulic pump and generator and their engine-driven gearbox comprise a packaged unit mounted on the airframe structure.

The basic interception weapons comprise two Sidewinder missiles on wingtip launchers and two 20-mm guns in the fuselage nose. Five pylons, one under the fuselage and two under each wing, permit the carriage of a wide variety of other operational warloads. A bomb of more than 2,000 lb (910 kg) or high-rate-of-fire gun pack can be suspended from the centre pylon. Underwing loads can include four air-to-air missiles, Bullpup

air-to-surface missiles, bombs, up to 20 air-to-surface rockets, gun packs or external fuel tanks. The reconnaissance nose does not eliminate the 20-mm nose gun capability.

The structural description of the T-38 Talon applies also to the F-5A/B, except in the following details:

TYPE: Light tactical fighter and reconnaissance aircraft.

WINGS: Continuous-hinge leading-edge flaps of full-depth honeycomb construction.

LANDING GEAR: Main wheels fitted with tubeless tyres size 22 × 8·5, pressure 85-210 lb/sq in (6-15 kg/cm²). Nose-wheel fitted with tubeless tyre size 18 × 6·5, pressure 60-180 lb/sq in (4·2-12·6 kg/cm²).

POWER PLANT: Two General Electric J85-GE-13 turbojets with afterburning (each with max rating of 4,080 lb = 1,850 kg st and military rating of 2,720 lb = 1,234 kg st). Two internal fuel tanks composed of integral cells with total usable capacity of 583 US gallons (2,207 litres). Provision for one 150 US gallon (568 litre) jettisonable tank on fuselage centre-line pylon, two 150 US gallon (568 litre) jettisonable tanks on underwing pylons and two 50 US gallon (189 litre) wingtip tanks. Total fuel, with external tanks, 1,133 US gallons (4,289 litres). Single pressure refuelling point on lower fuselage. Oil capacity 4·7 US quarts (4·5 litres) each engine.

SYSTEMS: Electrical system includes two 8kVA engine-driven generators, providing 115V 400 c/s AC power, and 24V battery.

ELECTRONICS AND EQUIPMENT: Standard equipment includes AN/ARC-34C UHF radio, PP-2024 SWIA-Missile AVX, AN/AIC-18 interphone, J-4 compass and Norsight optical

sight. Space provision for AN/APX-46 IFF, AN/ARW-77 Bullpup AUX and AN/ARN-65 TACAN. Blind-flying instrumentation not standard.

DIMENSIONS, EXTERNAL:

Wing span	25 ft 3 in (7·70 m)
Wing chord at root	11 ft 3 in (3·43 m)
Wing chord at tip	2 ft 3 in (0·69 m)
Span over tip tanks	25 ft 10 in (7·87 m)
Length overall:	
F-5A	47 ft 2 in (14·38 m)
F-5B	46 ft 4 in (14·12 m)
Height over tail:	
F-5A	13 ft 2 in (4·01 m)
F-5B	13 ft 1 in (3·99 m)
Tailplane span	14 ft 1 in (4·28 m)
Wheel track	11 ft 0 in (3·35 m)
Wheelbase:	
F-5A	15 ft 4 in (4·67 m)
F-5B	19 ft 6 in (5·94 m)

AREAS:

Wings, gross	170 sq ft (15·79 m²)
Ailerons (total)	9·24 sq ft (0·86 m²)
Trailing-edge flaps (total)	19·0 sq ft (1·77 m²)
Leading-edge flaps (total)	12·3 sq ft (1·14 m²)
Fin	35·3 sq ft (3·28 m²)
Rudder	6·1 sq ft (0·57 m²)
Tailplane	33·0 sq ft (3·07 m²)

WEIGHTS AND LOADINGS:

Weight empty, equipped:	
F-5A	8,085 lb (3,667 kg)
F-5B	8,361 lb (3,792 kg)
Max military load	6,200 lb (2,812 kg)
Max T-O weight:	
F-5A	20,576 lb (9,333 kg)
F-5B	20,116 lb (9,124 kg)
Max zero-fuel weight:	
F-5A	14,212 lb (6,446 kg)
F-5B	13,752 lb (6,237 kg)
Max design landing weight	19,857 lb (9,006 kg)

Max wing loading:
  F-5A   121 lb/sq ft (590·8 kg/m²)
  F-5B   118 lb/sq ft (576 kg/m²)
PERFORMANCE (F-5A at AUW of 11,450 lb=
  5,193 kg; F-5B at AUW of 10,840 lb=4,916 kg,
  unless indicated otherwise):
Max level speed at 36,000 ft (11,000 m):
  F-5A   Mach 1·4
  F-5B   Mach 1·34
Max permissible diving speed
        710 knots (818 mph; 1,315 km/h) IAS
Max cruising speed without afterburning, at
  36,000 ft (11,000 m)   Mach 0·96
Econ cruising speed   Mach 0·87
Stalling speed, 50% fuel, flaps extended:
  F-5A   128 knots (147 mph; 237 km/h)
  F-5B   120 knots (138 mph; 223 km/h)
Rate of climb at S/L   28,700 ft (8,750 m)/min
Service ceiling   over 50,000 ft (15,250 m)
Service ceiling, one engine out
                      over 36,000 ft (10,975 m)
T-O run (with two Sidewinder missiles):
  F-5A at AUW of 13,663 lb (6,197 kg)
                              2,650 ft (808 m)
  F-5B at AUW of 13,047 lb (5,918 kg)
                              2,200 ft (671 m)
T-O to 50 ft (15 m) (with two Sidewinder
  missiles):
  F-5A at AUW of 13,663 lb (6,197 kg)
                              3,650 ft (1,113 m)
  F-5B at AUW of 13,047 lb (5,918 kg)
                              3,150 ft (960 m)
Landing from 50 ft (15 m), with brake-chute:
  F-5A at AUW of 9,843 lb (4,464 kg)
                              3,900 ft (1,189 m)
  F-5B at AUW of 9,541 lb (4,327 kg)
                              3,800 ft (1,158 m)
Landing run, with brake-chute:
  F-5A at AUW of 9,843 lb (4,464 kg)
                              2,270 ft (692 m)
  F-5B at AUW of 9,541 lb (4,327 kg)
                              2,200 ft (671 m)
Range with max fuel, with 600 lb (272 kg) reserve
  fuel and 5% service tolerance:
  F-5A, tanks retained
              1,215 nm (1,400 miles; 2,250 km)
  F-5B, tanks retained
              1,220 nm (1,405 miles; 2,261 km)
  F-5A, tanks dropped
              1,359 nm (1,565 miles; 2,518 km)
  F-5B, tanks dropped
              1,363 nm (1,570 miles; 2,525 km)
Combat radius with max payload, allowances
  as above and five minutes combat at S/L:
  F-5A   186 nm (215 miles; 346 km)
  F-5B   195 nm (225 miles; 362 km)
Combat radius with max fuel, two 750 lb (340
  kg) bombs, 600 lb (272 kg) reserve fuel, 5%
  service tolerance and 5 minutes combat at
  S/L:
  F-5A   477 nm (550 miles; 885 km)
  F-5B   486 nm (560 miles; 900 km)
Operational   Hi-Lo-Lo-Hi   reconnaissance
  radius with max fuel, 52-knot (60-mile:
  96-km) S/L dash to and from target and
  allowances as for combat radius with max
  fuel above:
  RF-5A   573 knots (660 miles; 1,060 km)

NORTHROP F-5-21

Under the Improved International Fighter
Aircraft (IIFA) programme, the US government
is seeking a supersonic aircraft as a successor to
the Northrop F-5, of which some 650 are being
supplied under the Military Assistance Programme
to America's allies. Eight airframe companies
have been invited to tender, but since the design
submission has to be based on an existing fighter
aircraft, only four of these companies (LTV,
Lockheed, McDonnell Douglas and Northrop)
are expected to attain the final selection stage.

Northrop proposed an advanced version of the
F-5 early in 1969, before instigation of the IIFA
programme, and an F-5B re-engined with two
General Electric YJ85-GE-21 turbojets flew as
long ago as 28 March 1969. This YF-5B-21
prototype makes Northrop the only contender
for the IIFA contract to have flown a prototype
which will be similar to its final design submission.

The proposed F-5-21 will be powered by two
J85-GE-21 turbojet engines, each of which
produces 5,000 lb (2,267 kg) st. Fuselage modifications to cater for the larger engines allow also
an additional 500 lb (227 kg) of fuel to be carried
internally; and three newly-designed external
tanks, as developed for the NF-5, can be carried,
each of 275-US gallon (1,041-litre) capacity. The
F-5-21 will incorporate also the manoeuvring
flaps, two-position nose gear and auxiliary air
inlet doors developed for the CF-5 and NF-5,
and will have JATO provisions and arrester gear
for short-field operations. Avionics will include
a dead-reckoning navigation system, a small
central computer to help solve fire-control
problems, a small solid-state radar in the nose
to provide air-to-air search and range information,
a lead-computing gunsight to improve accuracy
of the aircraft's two 20-mm cannon, and new
VHF/FM radios. Anti-ice windshield and inlet
duct lips, as developed for the Royal Norwegian
Air Force's version of the F-5, will be available
for aircraft to be used in cold-weather environments.

Northrop YF-5B-21 prototype, an F-5B modified to test the proposed F-5-21 power plant (two General Electric J85-GE-21 turbojet engines)

More than 70 flights with the YF-5B-21
prototype have enabled Northrop to explore the
flight envelope, including altitudes up to 50,000 ft
(15,240 m), a speed of Mach 1·6 and aerial combat
manoeuvres. First flight of a radar-equipped
aircraft was scheduled for April 1970, and if
chosen for the IIFA programme F-5-21's could
be in squadron service in the first half of 1971.

WEIGHTS:
Military payload   7,000 lb (3,175 kg)
Max T-O weight   24,364 lb (11,051 kg)
PERFORMANCE (at max T-O weight):
Max level speed   Mach 1·6
Max rate of climb at S/L
                      35,200 ft (10,729 m)/min
T-O run   5,050 ft (1,539 m)
Ferry range with max fuel, wing tanks jettison-
  ed   2,015 nm (2,320 miles; 3,733 km)

NORTHROP/NASA M2-F2/F3

Under contract to NASA's Flight Research
Center, Northrop built two wingless lifting-body
re-entry research vehicles. One, designated M2-
F2 (now M2-F3—see below), was an Ames
Research Center concept and represents a more
refined metal development of the successful
wooden M2-F1 glider described on pages 249-50
of the 1963-64 *Jane's*. The other, described
separately, is based on a Langley concept and is
designated HL-10.

Both vehicles have a basic delta plan-form and
are D-shaped in cross-section. The fundamental
difference is that in the M2-F2/F3 the straight
side of the D is on top, whereas it forms the
undersurface of the fuselage on the HL-10.

Each vehicle has a conventional semi-monocoque structure for the forward body. The aft
structure is basically a box with side fairings.
Two full-depth keels extend from the cabin to
the base of the vehicle. The box allows for the
provision of non-structural equipment access
doors on the outside and acts also as an isolation
bay for the rocket fuel. The systems in both vehicles use the same components, which are mostly
"off-the-shelf". For example, both aircraft
are fitted with a retractable landing gear comprising a modified North American T-39 nose
unit and Northrop F-5 main legs with T-38 wheels
and brakes. The pilot sits on a modified version
of the F-106 ejection seat in a pressurised cockpit
(differential 10 lb/sq in = 0·70 kg/cm²). All
hydraulic and electrical power is provided by
silver zinc batteries. Cabin air and pressure are
provided by 3,000 lb/sq in (210 kg/cm²) air contained in a tank in each vehicle for free flight,
and in four tanks mounted on the adapter
while the aircraft is being carried by its B-52
"mother-plane". Each vehicle has an 80-
channel PCM instrumentation system for real
time read-out.

The M2-F2/F3 is controlled in pitch by a flap
on the aft lower surface and by two flaps on the
upper aft surface which are used for pitch trim.
These surfaces are also used for roll control.
Flaps on the aft outer face of each fin are used for
yaw control. These surfaces can also be flared
simultaneously to act as speed brakes. Each
flight control surface is actuated by dual 3,000
lb/sq in (210 kg/cm²) hydraulic system actuators.
Stability augmentation is provided in all three
axes.

Unlike the original wooden M2-F1, the M2-F2
was so designed that, after initial unpowered
flight trials, it could be fitted with an 8,000 lb
(3,630 kg) st Thiokol (Reaction Motors) XLR11
liquid-propellant rocket-engine of the kind fitted
initially to the X-15A research aircraft. To
enable it to be air-launched from beneath the
starboard wing of a B-52 Stratofortress "mother-
plane", it was designed to utilise an adapter
under the existing X-15A carrier-pylon.

The M2-F2 was delivered to NASA on 15 June
1965. Following tests in the Agency's full-scale
wind tunnel at Ames Research Center, it made its
first unpowered flight on 12 July 1966, after
release from the B-52 at 45,000 ft (13,700 m).
Its pilot, Mr Milton O. Thompson, made a practice
flare-out at about 25,000 ft (7,600 m) and, after
completing two 90° turns, increased speed to 304
knots (350 mph; 560 km/h) in order to be able to
flare out and slow the rate of descent from 250
ft/sec (76 m/sec) to under 5 ft/sec (1·5 m/sec) for
the landing. Emergency thrusters, fitted for use
during the flare, were not used and the M2-F2
was landed successfully four minutes after release
at about 165 knots (190 mph; 305 km/h) on
Rogers Dry Lake bed, near Edwards AFB,
California.

During these unpowered flights, the rocket
propellant tanks were available for water ballast.
permitting tests over a range of all-up weights.
By the end of 1966, the M2-F2 had completed
its initial programmed series of unpowered flight
tests, having made a total of 14 flights. It was
then fitted with the XLR11 rocket-engine. On
10 May 1967, it was damaged in a wheels-up
landing at Rogers Dry Lake, Edwards AFB,
California, at the end of its 16th flight. Purpose
of the unpowered flight had been to evaluate
the effects of reduction in automatic damping
for roll and yaw before the start of powered
flight trials.

The M2-F2 was completely dismantled, inspected and some components rebuilt. All systems
components were tested prior to re-installation
in the vehicle, which is now designated M2-F3.
It has an additional central vertical fin to improve
yaw control. A reaction control system has also
been added for evaluation of this type of system
in the roll axis. The hydraulically-operated
upper flaps are retained.

Northrop/NASA M2-F2 lifting-body research vehicle photographed in 450 mph powerless flight

The modifications progressed more slowly than anticipated, and first flight in the new configuration was expected during the summer of 1970.

The following details of the M2-F3 are available.

DIMENSIONS:
Max width	9 ft 7 in (2·92 m)
Length overall	22 ft 2 in (6·76 m)
Height overall	8 ft 10 in (2·69 m)

AREA:
Planform area	160 sq ft (14·86 m²)

WEIGHTS:
Max launching weight	9,400 lb (4,265 kg)
Min landing weight	4,700 lb (2,130 kg)

NORTHROP/NASA HL-10

The HL-10 is generally similar in construction to the M-2, except for the basic difference in configuration to which reference is made under the M2-F2/F3 heading above. The two aircraft have almost identical systems and accessories, and each is powered by an XLR11 rocket-engine. The performance of the HL-10 is similar to that of the M2-F3, but its subsonic lift/drag ratio is nearly 4·0. The pilot has a good field of view forward through the transparent nose.

The flying control surfaces of the HL-10 consist of a rudder on the central fin that is split vertically for use as a speed brake, and two very thick blunt-edged elevons, extending the full depth of the vehicle's boat-tail. The outer fin trailing-edges each have two surfaces which can be flared for transonic stability. Each elevon also has a movable flap on the upper surface which can be raised for transonic stability. All the surfaces used for transonic stability are powered by irreversible electric actuators. The rudder speed brakes and elevons are actuated by dual 3,000 lb/sq in (210 kg/cm²) hydraulic system actuators. Stability augmentation is provided in all three axes.

The HL-10 was delivered to NASA on 19 January 1966. After tests in the Ames Research Center wind tunnel and installation of the XLR-11 rocket-engine at Edwards AFB, the HL-10 made its first flight, an unpowered glide test similar to the M2-F2 flights, on 22 December 1966. The vehicle was dropped from under the wing of the B-52 at an altitude of approximately 45,000 ft (13,700 m) and speed of Mach 0·8.

Northrop/NASA HL-10 lifting body research vehicle

The first flight was made by Mr Bruce Peterson of NASA's Flight Research Center, and by 9 December 1968 a total of 14 flights had been made: 11 unpowered, three powered. Powered flights continued during 1969, with speed and altitude being increased progressively towards the maximum capability of the vehicle.

It has been reported that NASA's Flight Research Center is to conduct a series of tests with the HL-10 to gather data on the need for the proposed space-shuttle vehicles to have auxiliary power for use during the landing approach. The Thiokol XLR11 rocket-engine is to be removed and replaced by three Bell hydrogen-peroxide rockets, each of 500 lb (227 kg) st, which can be fired independently to provide the pilot with three thrust levels. It is desirable to know, also, whether auxiliary power should be provided to allow a go-around capability in the event of an aborted landing, but this is not to be evaluated in the proposed series of tests.

Future studies proposed to NASA by Northrop include fitting the HL-10 with the Bell Aero-systems Agena engine of 16,000 lb (7,260 kg) st, which would permit investigation of flight regimes of up to Mach 3·5 or Mach 4.

DIMENSIONS:
Max width	15 ft 1 in (4·60 m)
Length overall	22 ft 2 in (6·76 m)
Height overall	11 ft 5 in (3·48 m)

AREA:
Planform	162 sq ft (15·05 m²)

WEIGHTS:
Max launching weight	9,400 lb (4,265 kg)
Min landing weight	5,300 lb (2,400 kg)
Max landing weight	8,000 lb (3,630 kg)

NSA
NATIONAL SPORT AIRCRAFT

National Sport Aircraft has completed the prototype of a new aerobatic aircraft named the Genie, with a design load factor of plus or minus 9*g*.

NATIONAL SPORT AIRCRAFT GENIE

The prototype Genie is powered by a 200 hp Lycoming IO-360 four-cylinder horizontally-opposed air-cooled engine, but production aircraft will have the new AIO-360-18 fully-aerobatic engine. It is intended that higher-powered models will also be available. Dual controls and instrumentation permit the aircraft to be flown from either the front or rear cockpit. It can also be used for normal sporting aviation at a gross weight of 2,660 lb (1,207 kg).

Flight tests for FAA Type Certification were being carried out during 1969, and initial production of 12-15 aircraft per month was planned; but no recent information has been received from this company.

TYPE: Two-seat aerobatic aircraft.

WINGS: Cantilever low-wing monoplane of all-metal construction.

FUSELAGE: Semi-monocoque all-metal structure.

TAIL UNIT: Cantilever all-metal structure.

LANDING GEAR: Non-retractable tail-wheel type. Cantilever spring steel main gear. Streamlined main-wheel fairings.

POWER PLANT (Prototype): 200 hp Lycoming IO-360 four-cylinder horizontally-opposed air-cooled engine, driving a two-blade propeller.

ACCOMMODATION: Two seats in tandem, under individual upward-hinged transparent canopies. Dual controls and instrumentation standard.

National Sport Aircraft Genie (200 hp Lycoming IO-360 engine) (*Howard Levy*)

DIMENSIONS, EXTERNAL:
Wing span	25 ft 0 in (7·62 m)
Length overall	24 ft 7 in (7·49 m)

AREA:
Wings, gross	116 sq ft (10·78 m²)

WEIGHTS:
Weight empty	1,330 lb (603 kg)
Max T-O weight:	
Aerobatic cat	1,950 lb (884 kg)
Sporting cat	2,660 lb (1,207 kg)

PERFORMANCE (Aerobatic category):
Max level speed	174 knots (200 mph; 322 km/h)
Cruising speed (75% power)	156 knots (180 mph; 290 km/h)
Rate of climb at S/L	1,690 ft (515 m)/min
Service ceiling	over 20,000 ft (6,095 m)
Max range	781 nm (900 miles; 1,445 km)

O'NEILL
O'NEILL AIRPLANE COMPANY, INC

ADDRESS:
791 Livingston, Carlyle, Illinois 62231

PROPRIETOR: Terrence O'Neill

This company was formed by Mr Terrence O'Neill in December 1962, following purchase of the Waco Model W Aristocraft prototype, and became Incorporated in May 1967.

Two derivatives of the Aristocraft have been evolved, the first of which, known as the Model

W Winner, is intended for type certification and production. The second derivative is the Aristocraft II, a version of which plans are available to amateur constructors.

Mr O'Neill also designed and built a small canard-type ultra-light aircraft known as the Pea Pod, and brief details of this appeared in the 1969-70 *Jane's*.

O'NEILL MODEL W WINNER

Design of the original Model W was started by Waco in 1946. Following acquisition of the prototype, Mr Terrence O'Neill has completely redesigned this aircraft, whilst retaining and strengthening the basic structure. The result is aimed at a number of markets, including export to underdeveloped countries, flying clubs, fixed-base operators for charter and light cargo operations, and is suitable also for air camping, flight training and sport parachuting.

Construction of the prototype Model W started in May 1967 and the first flight was made in October 1968. A provisional type certificate was awarded in December 1969, and at the time of writing FAA certification was anticipated in June 1970, with initial deliveries following shortly afterwards.

TYPE: Six-seat light utility aircraft.

WINGS: Braced high-wing monoplane. Aerofoil section NACA 4415. Dihedral 2°. Incidence 3°. No sweepback. All-metal structure with smooth flush-riveted and filled 2024-Tc skin. Full-span plain ailerons. No trim-tabs or flaps.

FUSELAGE: Welded structure of chrome molybdenum steel tube, with metal covering.

TAIL UNIT: Cantilever all-metal structure with swept vertical surfaces. All-moving tailplane with trim-tab combined in anti-servo tab. No trim-tab in rudder.

LANDING GEAR: Non-retractable tricycle type. OAC-designed cantilever glass-fibre strut for main gear, cantilever aluminium strut for castoring nose-wheel. Shimmy damper on nose-wheel. Main wheel tyres size 6·00 × 6, 6-ply rating. Nose-wheel tyre size 6·00 × 6, 4-ply rating. Larger-diameter wheels and tyres optional. Cleveland two-spot disc brakes. Wheel fairings standard. Optional float landing gear under development.

POWER PLANT: One 200 hp Lycoming IO-360-A1B four-cylinder horizontally-opposed air-cooled engine, driving a Hartzell HC2YK constant-speed propeller. Fuel tank in each wing root, capacity 38 US gallons (143·5 litres). Total fuel capacity 76 US gallons (287 litres). Oil capacity 2 US gallons (7·57 litres). Both halves of engine cowling hinge backward for complete access to engine.

ACCOMMODATION: Crew of one or two, with five or four passengers respectively, in enclosed cabin, seated in three pairs side-by-side. Seating quickly removable for conversion to cargo configuration. Cargo payload of 1,300 lb (589 kg) with pilot and minimum fuel. Tie-down shackles at 3 ft (0·91 m) intervals and cargo net standard. Upward-hinged door on each side of forward cabin. Large bubble-hatch on top rear of cabin, hinged at front. Special hatch and/or swing-tail available optionally to facilitate loading of bulky cargo.

SYSTEMS: Hydraulic system for brakes only. Electrical power supplied by 70A engine-driven alternator. External APU socket standard.

ELECTRONICS AND EQUIPMENT: Bertea ML 200 100-channel transceiver with a separate omni head, angle-of-attack indicator and exhaust gas temperature gauge standard. Blind-flying instrumentation optional.

O'Neill Model W Winner (200 hp Lycoming IO-360-A1B engine) (*Jean Seele*)

DIMENSIONS, EXTERNAL:

Wing span	37 ft 6 in (11·43 m)
Wing chord (constant)	5 ft 3 in (1·60 m)
Wing aspect ratio	7·1
Length overall	26 ft 0 in (7·92 m)
Height overall	8 ft 4 in (2·54 m)
Tailplane span	11 ft 7 in (3·53 m)
Wheel track	9 ft 8 in (2·95 m)
Wheelbase	7 ft 0 in (2·13 m)

Passenger doors (port and starboard, forward):

Height (at forward edge)	3 ft 7 in (1·09 m)
Height (at aft edge)	2 ft 5½ in (0·75 m)
Width (at top)	2 ft 4½ in (0·72 m)
Width (at bottom)	2 ft 6 in (0·76 m)
Height to sill	2 ft 1 in (0·64 m)

Bubble hatch:

Length	5 ft 0 in (1·52 m)
Width	3 ft 4 in (1·02 m)
Height above ground at rear	4 ft 9 in (1·45 m)

DIMENSIONS, INTERNAL:

Cabin:

Length, firewall to aft bulkhead	15 ft 0 in (4·57 m)
Max width	4 ft 2 in (1·27 m)
Max height	4 ft 3 in (1·30 m)
Floor area	50·2 sq ft (4·66 m²)
Volume	185 cu ft (5·24 m³)

AREAS:

Wings, gross	190 sq ft (17·65 m²)
Ailerons (total)	42·1 sq ft (3·91 m²)
Fin	18·0 sq ft (1·67 m²)
Rudder	5·5 sq ft (0·51 m²)
Tailplane	30·0 sq ft (2·79 m²)

WEIGHTS AND LOADINGS:

Weight empty	1,750 lb (793 kg)
Max T-O and landing weight	3,300 lb (1,496 kg)
Max wing loading	17·0 lb/sq ft (83 kg/m²)
Max power loading	16·0 lb/hp (7·26 kg/hp)

PERFORMANCE (at max T-O weight):

Max level speed at S/L
    127 knots (147 mph; 237 km/h)
Max diving speed
    178 knots (205 mph; 329 km/h)
Max cruising speed at 7,000 ft (2,135 m)
    109 knots (125 mph; 201 km/h)
Landing speed 43 knots (50 mph; 80·5 km/h)
Max rate of climb at S/L 1,000 ft (305 m)/min
Range, with max fuel at econ cruise speed at 7,000 ft = 2,135 m, no reserves
    751 knots (865 miles; 1,390 km)

O'NEILL ARISTOCRAFT II

The O'Neill Company is marketing plans for the Aristocraft II, and this follows the basic design of the Model W Winner. Suitable for the installation of a variety of engines, gross weight of this version is 2,800 lb (1,270 kg) for engines of less than 230 hp and 3,300 lb (1,496 kg) for engines of 230 to 300 hp. It can be built with either corrugated or conventional wing skins and in addition to normal sport aviation uses can, when correctly rigged, be used for aerobatics. At a gross weight of 2,300 lb (1,043 kg) the wing is stressed to 10g. No further details were available at the time of writing.

ON MARK

ON MARK ENGINEERING COMPANY

HEAD OFFICE AND WORKS:
7929 Hayvenhurst Avenue, Van Nuys Airport, Van Nuys, California 91406

PRESIDENT:
Robert O. Denny

VICE-PRESIDENTS:
L. A. Keithley
W. H. Doheny

SECRETARY-TREASURER: Roy A. Wood

This company was formed in 1954, when Mr R. O. Denny and Mr L. A. Keithley resigned from their former positions as President and Operations Manager respectively of Grand Central Aircraft Company to start their own business.

Main work of On Mark since its formation has been modification, repair and overhaul of Douglas B-26 aircraft. This includes the complete re-manufacture of B-26 airframes to convert them into high-speed civilian executive transports and heavily-armed counter-insurgency combat aircraft. In addition, On Mark is the exclusive licensee of Douglas Aircraft Company in the production of spare parts for the B-26.

Production of the On Mark B-26K Counter Invader has been completed, but full details of this aircraft can be found in the 1967-68 *Jane's*.

As an FAA-approved airframe repair agency, On Mark is engaged in the repair, overhaul and modification of other types of large executive and airline aircraft. Its recent programmes have included the conversion of Stratocruisers into transporters for large rocket boosters, on behalf of Aero Spacelines Inc (which see).

On Mark is organised in two divisions: the Aircraft Division and the Reidon Division which is engaged in the manufacture of close-tolerance resistors. The former Magnatrol Avionics Division, which manufactures electronic filters and transformers, is now a department of the parent Aircraft Division.

No recent information on this company's activities has been received; full details of its B-26 executive conversions may be found in the 1968-69 *Jane's*.

PAC

PACIFIC AIRMOTIVE CORPORATION

HEAD OFFICE:
2940, North Hollywood Way, Burbank, California 91503

CHAIRMAN AND CHIEF EXECUTIVE OFFICER:
John W. Myers

PRESIDENT: Donald C. McMillan

EXECUTIVE VICE-PRESIDENT:
John J. Wittkopf

DIRECTOR OF MARKETING:
Robert H. Cooper

MANAGER, PUBLIC RELATIONS:
Robert E. Smith

AIRCRAFT DIVISION:
3000 North Clybourn Avenue, Burbank, California; 4150 Donald Douglas Drive, Long Beach, California; 3021 Airport Avenue, Santa Monica, California; and Westchester County Airport, White Plains, New York

VICE-PRESIDENT, AIRCRAFT DIVISION:
James L. Barker

Pacific Airmotive's Aircraft and Engineering Center, incorporating the former PacAero Engineering Corporation, provides complete modification, repair, maintenance and overhaul services for business and airline operators on all types of single and multi-engined aircraft. It also designs and installs electronic systems and aircraft cabin interiors to its customers' individual requirements.

PAC is producing, under the name Tradewind, a conversion of the Beechcraft Model 18 which is able to operate at an increased gross weight and is equipped with a single fin and rudder, tricycle landing gear and updated avionics and interior.

On behalf of Allison Division of General Motors, PAC designed, certificated and manufactured the Allison turboprop Convair 580. In 1969 it took over full responsibility for production of this aircraft, but the conversion programme is reported to have been completed early in 1970.

PAC is a distributor for the Dassault/Pan American Falcon business jet, and will install custom interiors and avionics in this aircraft to the individual requirements of customers. It also has responsibility for after-sales servicing and parts support for the Falcon in the United States.

A preliminary agreement with Cessna Aircraft Company has made PAC a sales and service dealer for the new Cessna Citation. A service agreement has been signed with Lear Jet Industries, Inc, for service and support of the Learjet, and during 1968 an agreement was signed with General Aircraft Corporation, under which PAC undertook to manufacture parts of the GAC-100 (which see). PAC has installed executive interiors in Boeing 737's and McDonnell Douglas DC-9's, and continues to produce specialised DC-6 aircraft for flying showrooms and training.

On 24 October 1968 the R. J. Enstrom Corporation, which has been concerned in the development and production of light helicopters, became a member of the Pacific Airmotive group. However, in early 1970, Purex Corporation, which owned PAC, began to reduce its aviation commitments. Further work on the PAC-1 twin-turboprop commuter airliner (see 1969-70 *Jane's*) was abandoned, together with commitments on the GAC-100 programme, and production of Enstrom helicopters was stopped.

PAC TRADEWIND

The Tradewind is virtually a re-manufactured Beechcraft C-45/D18S airframe, incorporating many improvements. These include the installation of a tricycle landing gear, wide-view windscreen, larger cabin windows, air-stair cabin door, increased fuel tankage, redesigned engine cowlings and exhaust stacks and aerodynamically-improved wingtips. Optional extras include wing and tail unit de-icing, propeller anti-icing, oxygen equipment, cabin air-conditioning and fuel injection.

In the current version of the Tradewind, the normal twin fins and rudders are replaced by a single highly-swept fin and rudder. The endplate effect of the original configuration is compensated for by a slight increase in area of both the tailplane and elevator. Controllability is, in general, improved about all three axes. Aircraft single-engine climb and cruise performance show a considerable drag reduction over the original twin-tail configuration.

The standard R-985 engines are fitted with PAC's speed and performance kit. Engine cooling is improved, enabling the engine to be operated continuously at take-off power. In addition, the take-off power of 450 hp can be maintained up to an altitude of 3,700 ft (1,125 m).

The company flight test programme was started on 13 July 1962, and resulted in the award of an FAA Certificate under CAR 3 regulations on 25 March 1963.

TYPE: Twin-engined light transport.

WINGS: Cantilever low-wing monoplane. Wing section NACA 23015 at root, NACA 23012 at tip. Dihedral 6°. Incidence 3° 55′ at root, —20′ at tip. Sweepback at quarter-chord 8° 49′. Welded steel-tube truss basic structure, with aluminium skin. Unslotted Frise aluminium ailerons. Aluminium slotted trailing-edge flaps. Trim-tabs in ailerons. Optional Goodrich pneumatic de-icing of leading-edges.

FUSELAGE: Conventional aluminium semi-mono-coque structure.

TAIL UNIT: Cantilever all-metal structure, with single swept fin and rudder. Trim-tab in rudder and each elevator. No de-icing system.

LANDING GEAR: Fully-retractable tricycle type. Electro-mechanical actuation, all units retracting forward. Standard Beechcraft main oleos; Volpar nose-wheel unit. Goodyear wheels and tyres size 8·50 × 10, pressure 65 lb/sq in (4·57 kg/cm²). Goodyear three-spot disc brakes.

POWER PLANT: Two 450 hp Pratt & Whitney R-985-AN-4 or -14B Wasp Junior radial air-cooled engines, each driving a Hamilton Standard 22D30 two-blade metal propeller. Fuel injection optional. Fuel in six tanks in wings: two main tanks each of 75 US gallons (284 litres), two rear auxiliary tanks each of 25 US gallons (94·5 litres) and two auxiliary tanks each of 100 US gallons (378·5 litres). Total fuel capacity 400 US gallons (1,514 litres). Overwing fuelling. Oil capacity 16 US gallons (60·5 litres) each engine.

ACCOMMODATION: Pilot and up to 10 passengers. Standard layouts known by trade names of Executive, Clubman and Commuter. Airstair door at rear of cabin on port side. Baggage hold in rear fuselage, capacity 300 lb (136 kg).

SYSTEMS: Hydraulic system for brakes only. Pneumatic system for electrically-cycled de-icing, pressure 20 lb/sq in (1·41 kg/cm²). Two 100A electrical generators.

ELECTRONICS AND EQUIPMENT: Optional equipment includes dual communications transceivers and navigation receivers, ADF, glideslope indicator, marker beacon indicator, RCA AVG 55, Bendix RDR-100 or Collins WP103 radar, blind-flying instrumentation, Bendix M-4 autopilot and slaved AIM 400 directional gyro.

DIMENSIONS, EXTERNAL:

Wing span	47 ft 3 in (14·40 m)
Wing chord at root	11 ft 1 in (3·38 m)
Wing chord at tip	3 ft 6 in (1·07 m)
Wing aspect ratio	6·4
Length overall	37 ft 9 in (11·51 m)
Length of fuselage	35 ft 8 in (10·87 m)
Height over tail	13 ft 8 in (4·16 m)

PAC Tradewind, a remanufactured Beechcraft C-45/D18S airframe (*Bob Bryne*)

Tailplane span	15 ft 3 in (4·65 m)
Wheel track	12 ft 10½ in (3·93 m)
Wheelbase	8 ft 9 in (2·67 m)
Passenger door:	
Height	3 ft 10 in (1·17 m)
Width	2 ft 0½ in (0·62 m)

DIMENSIONS, INTERNAL:

Cabin (passenger space only):	
Length	12 ft 4 in (3·76 m)
Max width	4 ft 4½ in (1·33 m)
Max height	5 ft 1 in (1·55 m)
Floor area	50·2 sq ft (4·66 m²)
Volume	230 cu ft (6·5 m³)

AREAS:

Wings, gross	349 sq ft (32·43 m²)
Fin	23·7 sq ft (2·20 m²)
Rudder, including tab	17·7 sq ft (1·64 m²)
Elevators, including tabs	23·5 sq ft (2·18 m²)

WEIGHTS AND LOADINGS:

Basic operating weight	6,500 lb (2,948 kg)
Max payload	2,200 lb (998 kg)
Max T-O weight	10,200 lb (4,627 kg)
Max zero-fuel weight	9,300 lb (4,218 kg)
Max landing weight	9,772 lb (4,433 kg)
Max wing loading	29·2 lb/sq ft (142·6 kg/m²)
Max power loading	11·3 lb/hp (5·13 kg/hp)

PERFORMANCE (at max T-O weight):

Max level speed at S/L	
	208 knots (240 mph; 386 km/h)
Max permissible speed in dive	
	247 knots (285 mph; 458 km/h) IAS
Max cruising speed at 10,000 ft (3,050 m)	
	200 knots (230 mph; 370 km/h)
Econ cruising speed at 10,000 ft (3,050 m)	
	190 knots (219 mph; 352 km/h)
Stalling speed, wheels and flaps down, power on	
	68 knots (78 mph; 126 km/h)
Rate of climb at S/L	1,200 ft (365 m)/min
Service ceiling	17,000 ft (5,180 m)
Service ceiling, one engine out	7,500 ft (2,285 m)
T-O run	2,000 ft (610 m)
T-O to 50 ft (15 m)	2,750 ft (838 m)

Landing from 50 ft (15 m) at max landing weight	
	2,160 ft (658 m)
Landing run	960 ft (293 m)
Range with max fuel and 1,200 lb (545 kg) payload, 45 min reserve	
	1,736 nm (2,000 miles; 3,220 km)
Range with 2,100 lb (950 kg) payload, 45 min reserve	
	955 nm (1,100 miles; 1,770 km)

PAC CONVAIR 580

Conversion of Convair 340/440 aircraft to PAC Convair 580 standard consisted primarily of replacing the existing piston-engines with 3,750 eshp Allison 501-D13 turboprops, driving Aero-products 606 four-blade (steel) constant-speed reverse-pitch propellers with a diameter of 13 ft 6 in (4·11 m). Full details of the associated modifications can be found in the 1969-70 *Jane's*.

DIMENSIONS, EXTERNAL:

Wing span	105 ft 4 in (32·12 m)
Length overall	81 ft 6 in (24·84 m)
Height overall	29 ft 2 in (8·89 m)

WEIGHTS:

Normal max T-O weight	54,600 lb (24,766 kg)
Optional max T-O weight	58,140 lb (26,372 kg)
Max landing weight	52,000 lb (23,587 kg)

PERFORMANCE:

True cruising airspeed at 20,000 ft (6,100 m) at 48,000 lb (21,772 kg) AUW	
	297 knots (342 mph; 550 km/h)
Rate of climb at 5,000 ft (1,525 m)	
	2,050 ft (625 m)/min
CAR single-engine ceiling	14,500 ft (4,420 m)
CAR T-O field length at normal max AUW	
	4,380 ft (1,335 m)
CAR landing field length at max landing weight	
	4,256 ft (1,297 m)
Range with 5,000 lb (2,270 kg) payload, fuel reserves for 130 nm (150 miles; 240 km) and 45 min, zero wind:	
at 54,600 lb AUW	
	1,393 nm (1,605 miles; 2,980 km)
at 58,140 lb AUW	
	2,488 nm (2,866 miles; 4,611 km)

PARSONS-JOCELYN
NICHOLAS E. D'APUZZO

ADDRESS:
704 Booth Lane, Ambler, Pennsylvania 19002

The prototype Parsons-Jocelyn PJ-260 aerobatic biplane was designed by Mr Nicholas E. D'Apuzzo at the request of Mr Rodney Jocelyn, world aerobatic champion in 1950-52, and Capt Lindsey Parsons, a sportsman pilot. It was built by Mr Jocelyn for Capt Parsons and was flown by both pilots at displays throughout the United States, before being sold to another private owner.

Sets of drawings are now available to amateur constructors and three more PJ-260's had been completed by April 1969.

Details of other designs by Mr D'Apuzzo are given under his own name.

PARSONS-JOCELYN PJ-260 and D-295

The standard Parsons-Jocelyn **PJ-260** is a single-seat aerobatic biplane powered by a 260 hp Lycoming engine. However, it can be built as a two-seat sporting aircraft by minor modifications of the fuselage and the installation of a centre-section fuel tank. Alternative engines include the 195 hp Lycoming O-435-1 or O-435-11.

The **D-295** derivative, as illustrated, was built by Mr E. Mahler and Mr L. Webber, and differs from the standard PJ-260 by having a lower wing of reduced span, a modified aileron control system to increase the rate of roll, and wheel fairings. Span of the lower wing is 23 ft 9 in (7·24 m) and total wing area is reduced to 178 sq ft (16·54 m²), increasing max wing loading to 11·2 lb/sq ft (54·7 kg/m²). The aircraft is powered by a 295 hp Lycoming GO-480-G1D6 engine,

Parsons-Jocelyn D-295 aerobatic biplane (295 hp Lycoming GO-480-G1D6 engine)

driving a Hartzell three-blade constant-speed propeller, diameter 8 ft 0 in (2·44 m). Performance is generally similar to that of the standard PJ-260, but stalling speed is increased to 48 knots (55 mph; 88·5 km/h) and service ceiling reduced to 23,000 ft (7,000 m). T-O run is 175 ft (54 m) and T-O to 50 ft (15 m) 475 ft (145 m).

The following details refer to the standard PJ-260, built to Mr D'Apuzzo's plans and similar in all respects to the prototype. Use of a conventional spring steel landing gear, in place of

the glass-fibre legs that were used on the prototype, increases the aircraft's empty weight.

TYPE: Single-seat aerobatic biplane.

WINGS: Conventional braced biplane type. Wing section NACA M12 (modified). Dihedral 30′ on lower wings only. Incidence 2°. Sweepback 9° 15′ on upper wings. Two wood spars, metal ribs, fabric covering. Metal Frise ailerons on all four wings, with fabric covering. No flaps.

FUSELAGE: Steel-tube structure, with aluminium alloy access panels forward of cockpit and fabric covering aft.

TAIL UNIT: Wire-braced fabric-covered steel-tube structure. Trim-tab in starboard elevator.

LANDING GEAR: Non-retractable tail-wheel type. Main legs made from single strut of 3M Scotch-ply glass-fibre. Firestone DFA-180 6·00 × 6 main wheels with 7·00 × 6 tyres, pressure 20 lb/sq in (1·41 kg/cm²). Firestone CFA hydraulic brakes. Wheel spats.

POWER PLANT: One 260 hp Lycoming GO-435-C2 six-cylinder horizontally-opposed air-cooled engine, driving an Aeromatic F-200H-0-93 propeller. Fuel in 33 US gallon (125 litre) main tank and 11 US gallon (41·5 litre) aerobatic tank, both in fuselage. Total fuel capacity 44 US gallons (166·5 litres). Oil capacity 12 US quarts (11 litres).

ACCOMMODATION: Single seat in open cockpit.

DIMENSIONS, EXTERNAL:
Wing span	27 ft 0 in (8·23 m)
Wing chord (constant, both)	3 ft 10 in (1·17 m)
Wing aspect ratio	4·22
Length overall	21 ft 0 in (6·40 m)
Height overall	7 ft 7½ in (2·32 m)
Tailplane span	10 ft 2 in (3·10 m)
Wheel track	6 ft 4 in (1·93 m)

AREAS:
Wings, gross	190 sq ft (17·65 m²)
Ailerons (total)	23·0 sq ft (2·14 m²)
Fin	8·1 sq ft (0·75 m²)
Rudder	7·5 sq ft (0·70 m²)
Tailplane	15·35 sq ft (1·43 m²)
Elevators	14·5 sq ft (1·35 m²)

WEIGHTS AND LOADINGS:
Weight empty	1,300 lb (590 kg)
Max T-O and landing weight	2,000 lb (907 kg)
Max wing loading	10·5 lb/sq ft (51·2 kg/m²)
Max power loading	7·7 lb/hp (3·5 kg/hp)

PERFORMANCE (at max T-O weight):
Max level speed at 1,000 ft (305 m)	148 knots (170 mph; 274 km/h)
Max permissible diving speed	191 knots (220 mph; 354 km/h)
Max cruising speed	130 knots (150 mph; 241 km/h)
Econ cruising speed	120 knots (138 mph; 222 km/h)
Stalling speed	46 knots (52 mph; 84 km/h)
Rate of climb at S/L	2,200 ft (670 m)/min
Service ceiling	24,000 ft (7,300 m)
T-O run	150 ft (46 m)
T-O to 50 ft (15 m)	400 ft (122 m)
Landing from 50 ft (15 m)	650 ft (198 m)
Landing run	350 ft (107 m)
Range with max fuel	434 nm (500 miles; 800 km)

PAYNE
VERNON W. PAYNE

ADDRESS:
8723 E Artessia Boulevard, No 29, Bellflower, California 90706

Mr Vernon Payne is the designer of the Knight Twister, a light sporting biplane of which plans and kits are available for amateur construction. It exists in four main versions and details of each of these are given below.

Under development is a monoplane using the same fuselage and tail unit as the Knight Twister.

KNIGHT TWISTER KT-85

The original prototype of the Knight Twister KT-85 single-seat sporting biplane flew in 1933. Considerable refinement of the design since that time has improved both the appearance and the performance of later models, which have been built in substantial numbers by amateur constructors in the United States and elsewhere.

Standard power plant is a Continental flat-four engine of 85/90 hp, but alternative engines have been fitted by some constructors. Most powerful Knight Twister flown to date is N1B, built by Mr Robert Baber in 1951 and re-engined recently with a 160 hp Lycoming O-320-B by its present owner, Mr W. Nagle. Overall dimensions are standard. Empty weight is 820 lb (372 kg), with a max T-O weight of 1,125 lb (520 kg). Max level speed with the new engine is 152 knots (175 mph; 282 km/h), cruising speed 130 knots (150 mph; 241 km/h), T-O run 350 ft (107 m), and rate of climb over 2,500 ft (762 m)/min.

The following details refer to the standard Knight Twister built from Mr Payne's plans.

TYPE: Single-seat light biplane.

WINGS: Braced biplane type. Wing section NACA M-6. No dihedral. Incidence 1° 30′. All-wood two-spar structure, plywood-covered and with fabric covering overall. Ailerons on lower wings only, of fabric-covered wood construction. No flaps.

FUSELAGE: Steel-tube truss structure with wood stringers and fabric covering.

TAIL UNIT: Cantilever type. Vertical surfaces have fabric-covered steel-tube structure. Horizontal surfaces have plywood-covered wood structure, with fabric covering overall.

LANDING GEAR: Non-retractable tail-wheel type. Cantilever main units. Rubber cord or hydraulic shock-absorption. Wheels size 6·00 × 6 with Goodyear tyres, pressure 5-10 lb/sq in (0·35-0·70 kg/cm²). Goodyear disc brakes.

POWER PLANT: One 90 hp Continental C90 four-cylinder horizontally-opposed air-cooled engine, driving two-blade wood or metal fixed-pitch propeller. Alternatively any other Continental or Lycoming horizontally-opposed four-cylinder engine of 85-145 hp. Fuel tank aft of engine firewall, capacity 18 US gallons (68 litres). Oil capacity 1-1¼ US gallons (3·7-5·7 litres).

ACCOMMODATION: Single seat, normally in open cockpit. Baggage compartment capacity 20 lb (9 kg). Radio optional.

DIMENSIONS, EXTERNAL:
Wing span:	
upper	15 ft 0 in (4·57 m)
lower	13 ft 0 in (3·96 m)
Wing chord (mean, both)	2 ft 1·6 in (0·65 m)
Wing aspect ratio:	
upper	6·87
lower	6·13
Length overall	14 ft 0 in (4·27 m)
Height overall	5 ft 3 in (1·60 m)
Tailplane span	6 ft 0 in (1·83 m)
Wheel track	5 ft 0 in (1·52 m)
Wheelbase	17 ft 2 in (5·23 m)

DIMENSIONS, INTERNAL:
Cockpit: Length	2 ft 3 in (0·68 m)
Width	1 ft 9 in (0·53 m)

AREAS:
Wings, gross	60 sq ft (5·57 m²)
Ailerons (total)	5·00 sq ft (0·46 m²)

N1B, the most powerful Knight Twister yet built (160 hp Lycoming O-320-B engine) (*Howard Levy*)

Fin	2·25 sq ft (0·21 m²)
Rudder	4·35 sq ft (0·40 m²)
Tailplane	5·25 sq ft (0·49 m²)
Elevators	3·75 sq ft (0·35 m²)

WEIGHTS AND LOADINGS (90 hp engine):
Weight empty	535 lb (243 kg)
Max T-O weight	960 lb (435 kg)
Max wing loading	16 lb/sq ft (78 kg/m²)
Max power loading	10·7 lb/hp (4·85 kg/hp)

PERFORMANCE (90 hp engine, at max T-O weight):
Max level speed at S/L	139 knots (160 mph; 257 km/h)
Max cruising speed	122 knots (140 mph; 225 km/h)
Econ cruising speed	109 knots (125 mph; 201 km/h)
Stalling speed	53 knots (60 mph; 97 km/h)
Rate of climb at S/L	900 ft (275 m)/min
T-O run	410 ft (125 m)
T-O to 50 ft (15 m)	1,000 ft (305 m)
Landing from 50 ft (15 m)	1,200 ft (366 m)
Landing run	670 ft (205 m)
Range with max fuel	338 nm (390 miles; 625 km)

SUNDAY KNIGHT TWISTER SKT-125

This developed version of the Knight Twister has a 125 hp Lycoming engine. Increased wing area makes it easier to fly and its name is meant to imply that it is for the "Sunday flyer".

DIMENSIONS, EXTERNAL:
Wing span	19 ft 6 in (5·94 m)
Length overall	15 ft 6 in (4·72 m)
Height overall	5 ft 6 in (1·68 m)

AREA:
Wings, gross	83 sq ft (7·71 m²)

WEIGHTS:
Weight empty	700 lb (318 kg)
Max T-O weight	1,016 lb (461 kg)

PERFORMANCE (at max T-O weight):
Max level speed at S/L	155 knots (178 mph; 286 km/h)
Max cruising speed	144 knots (166 mph; 267 km/h)
Econ cruising speed	132 knots (152 mph; 245 km/h)
Stalling speed	64 knots (73 mph; 118 km/h)
Rate of climb at S/L	1,200 ft (365 m)/min
T-O run	370 ft (113 m)
T-O to 50 ft (15 m)	760 ft (232 m)
Landing run	870 ft (265 m)
Range at max cruising speed with max fuel	307 nm (354 miles; 570 km)

KNIGHT TWISTER KTT-90

The Knight Twister KTT-90 Trainer has the same fuselage, tail unit and landing gear as the KT-85, but is fitted with larger untapered wings. The prototype flew in 1954. Details are as for the KT-85, except for the following:

WINGS: Wing section NACA 25. Incidence 2°.

POWER PLANT: One 90 hp Continental four-cylinder horizontally-opposed air-cooled engine.

DIMENSIONS, EXTERNAL:
As for KT-85, except:
Wing span:	
upper	18 ft 0 in (5·49 m)
lower	16 ft 0 in (4·88 m)
Wing chord (mean):	
upper	2 ft 9 in (0·84 m)
lower	2 ft 6 in (0·76 m)
Wing aspect ratio:	
upper	6·58
lower	6·40

AREAS:
Wings, gross	83 sq ft (7·71 m²)
Ailerons (total)	9·5 sq ft (0·88 m²)

WEIGHTS AND LOADINGS:
Weight empty	575 lb (261 kg)
Normal T-O weight	850 lb (386 kg)
Max T-O weight	1,020 lb (463 kg)
Normal wing loading	10 lb/sq ft (48·8 kg/m²)
Normal power loading	9·5 lb/hp (4·3 kg/hp)

PERFORMANCE (at normal T-O weight):
Max level speed at S/L	126 knots (145 mph; 233 km/h)
Max cruising speed	113 knots (130 mph; 209 km/h)
Econ cruising speed	109 knots (125 mph; 201 km/h)
Stalling speed	44 knots (50 mph; 80 km/h)
Rate of climb at S/L	1,000 ft (305 m)/min
T-O run	325 ft (99 m)
T-O to 50 ft (15 m)	785 ft (239 m)
Landing from 50 ft (15 m)	880 ft (268 m)
Landing run	650 ft (198 m)
Range with max fuel	295 nm (340 miles; 545 km)

KNIGHT TWISTER JUNIOR KT-75

The Knight Twister Junior has the same fuselage, tail unit and landing gear as the KT-85, but its tapered wings have a larger area. The prototype flew in 1947. Details are as for the KT-85, except for the following:

WINGS: Incidence 2°.

POWER PLANT: One Continental or Lycoming four-cylinder horizontally-opposed air-cooled engine of 75-125 hp. Fuel capacity with 75 hp engine 12 US gallons (45 litres).

DIMENSIONS, EXTERNAL:
As for KT-85, except:
Wing span:

upper	17 ft 6 in (5·33 m)
lower	13 ft 6 in (4·11 m)

Wing aspect ratio:

upper	7·78
lower	7·10

AREAS:

Wings, gross	72·8 sq ft (6·76 m²)
Ailerons (total)	6·70 sq ft (0·62 m²)

WEIGHTS AND LOADINGS (75 hp engine):

Weight empty	500 lb (227 kg)
Max T-O weight	890 lb (404 kg)
Max wing loading	12 lb/sq ft (58·6 kg/m²)
Max power loading	7·68 lb/hp (3·48 kg/hp)

PERFORMANCE (75 hp engine at max T-O weight):

Max level speed at S/L	126 knots (145 mph; 233 km/h)
Max cruising speed	113 knots (130 mph; 209 km/h)
Econ cruising speed	104 knots (120 mph; 193 km/h)
Stalling speed	48 knots (55 mph; 89 km/h)
Rate of climb at S/L	900 ft (275 m)/min
T-O run	375 ft (114 m)
T-O to 50 ft (15 m)	910 ft (277 m)
Landing from 50 ft (15 m)	1,020 ft (311 m)
Landing run	625 ft (190 m)
Range with max fuel	247 nm (285 miles; 460 km)

PAZMANY

PAZMANY AIRCRAFT CORPORATION

ADDRESS:
Box 10051, San Diego, California 92110

Mr Ladislao Pazmany, who is Chief Design Engineer for San Diego Aircraft Engineering (a subsidiary of Anadite Corporation), designed a two-seat light aircraft known as the PL-1 Laminar. A prototype, constructed by Mr John Green and Mr Keith Fowler, was flown for the first time on 23 March 1962, the test pilots being Cdr Paul Hayek, USN, and Lieut Richard Gordon, who is best known as one of the Gemini astronauts.

Some 5,000 design hours and 4,000 hours of construction went into the prototype PL-1, which had logged more than 1,200 flying hours by February 1969.

A total of 375 sets of plans and instructions for building the PL-1 were sold, and PL-1's were being built in the USA, Canada, Australia, Norway and other countries in 1969.

Pazmany are no longer marketing plans of the PL-1: instead, plans and instructions for building the improved PL-2 are available to amateur constructors. Several examples of this model are being built and a prototype, built by Mr H. Pio of Ramona, California, made its first flight on 4 April 1969.

Early in 1968 the Aeronautical Research Laboratory of the Chinese Nationalist Air Force, at Taichung, Taiwan, acquired a set of PL-1 drawings. Under the supervision of General K. F. Ku and Colonel C. Y. Lee, personnel of the ARL built a PL-1 in a record time of 100 days. It was flown for the first time on 26 October 1968 and on 30 October was presented to Generalissimo Chiang-Kai-Shek. Extensive flight testing resulted in the decision to utilise the PL-1 as a basic trainer for CAF cadets, and 35 additional aircraft are being constructed during 1970, powered by the 150 hp Lycoming O-320 engine.

PAZMANY PL-1 LAMINAR

An illustration on page 27 shows one of 35 PL-1B's being built by the Aeronautical Research Laboratory of the Nationalist Chinese Air Force, Taiwan. Powered by 150 hp Lycoming O-320 engines, these aircraft are being used by that Air Force as basic trainers.

The details below apply to the prototype PL-1, which was stressed to 9g (ultimate) for aerobatics and to permit the fitting of more powerful engines.

TYPE: Two-seat light aircraft.

WINGS: Cantilever low-wing monoplane. Wing section NACA 63₂615. Dihedral 3°. Incidence —1° 20'. All-metal single-spar structure in one piece, with leading-edge torsion box. Plain piano-hinged ailerons and flaps of all-metal construction. No trim-tabs.

FUSELAGE: Conventional all-metal semi-monocoque structure, with flat or single-curvature skins.

TAIL UNIT: Cantilever all-metal structure. One-piece horizontal surface, with anti-servo tab which serves also as a trim-tab.

LANDING GEAR: Non-retractable tricycle type, with all three oleo-pneumatic shock-absorbers interchangeable. Goodyear wheels and tyres, size 500×5. Tyre pressure 31 lb/sq in (2·18 kg/cm²). Goodyear brakes. Steerable nose-wheel.

POWER PLANT: One 95 hp Continental C90-12F four-cylinder horizontally-opposed air-cooled engine, driving a McCauley Model IA100/MCM 6663 two-blade metal fixed-pitch propeller. Fuel in two glass-fibre wingtip tanks, each of 12·5 US gallons (47 litres) capacity. Total fuel capacity 25 US gallons (94 litres). Oil capacity 5 US quarts (4·5 litres).

ACCOMMODATION: Two seats side-by-side, under rearward-sliding transparent canopy. Dual controls. Space for 40 lb (18 kg) baggage aft of seats. Heater and air scoops for ventilation. VHF radio.

DIMENSIONS, EXTERNAL:

Wing span	28 ft 0 in (8·53 m)
Wing chord (constant)	4 ft 2 in (1·27 m)
Wing aspect ratio	6·7
Length overall	18 ft 11 in (5·77 m)
Height overall	8 ft 8 in (2·64 m)

The first Pazmany PL-1 built by the Nationalist Air Force in the Republic of China

Pazmany PL-2 built by Mr H. Pio (125 hp Lycoming O-290-G engine)

Tailplane span	8 ft 0 in (2·44 m)
Wheel track	8 ft 2½ in (2·50 m)
Wheelbase	4 ft 3 in (1·30 m)

DIMENSIONS, INTERNAL:
Cabin:

Length	4 ft 2 in (1·27 m)
Width	3 ft 4 in (1·02 m)
Height	3 ft 4 in (1·02 m)

AREAS:

Wings, gross	116 sq ft (10·78 m²)
Ailerons (total)	10·54 sq ft (0·98 m²)
Flaps (total)	17·36 sq ft (1·61 m²)
Fin	7·30 sq ft (0·68 m²)
Rudder	3·10 sq ft (0·29 m²)
Tailplane	18·00 sq ft (1·67 m²)

WEIGHTS AND LOADINGS:

Weight empty, equipped	800 lb (363 kg)
Max T-O weight	1,326 lb (602 kg)
Max wing loading	11·4 lb/sq ft (55·7 kg/m²)
Max power loading	14 lb/hp (6·35 kg/hp)

PERFORMANCE (at max T-O weight):

Max level speed at S/L	104 knots (120 mph; 193 km/h)
Max permissible speed in dive	178 knots (205 mph; 330 km/h)
Max cruising speed at S/L	100 knots (115 mph; 185 km/h)
Econ cruising speed at S/L	91 knots (105 mph; 169 km/h)
Stalling speed, flaps down	44 knots (51 mph; 82 km/h)
Rate of climb at S/L	1,000 ft (305 m)/min
Service ceiling	18,000 ft (5,500 m)
T-O run	550 ft (168 m)
T-O to 50 ft (15 m)	784 ft (239 m)
Landing from 50 ft (15 m)	1,100 ft (335 m)
Landing run	175 ft (54 m)
Range with max fuel	521 nm (600 miles; 965 km)

PAZMANY PL-2

Shortly after flight trials of the PL-1 began, Mr Pazmany initiated a complete redesign of the aircraft. The developed design, known as the PL-2, is almost identical with the PL-1 in external configuration. Cockpit width is increased by 2 in (5 cm) and wing dihedral is increased from 3° to 5°. The internal structure is extensively changed, to simplify construction and reduce weight. Suitable Lycoming power plants are the 108 hp O-235-C1, 125 hp O-290-G (ground power unit), 135 hp O-290-D2B or 150 hp O-320-A.

Ten PL-2's are under construction in San Diego. Static tests of every major assembly up to ultimate loads had been made by early 1967. The first PL-2 to be completed was built by Mr H. Pio of Ramona, California, and this aircraft made its first flight on 4 April 1969, piloted by Mr Pio. It has an O-290-G engine.

DIMENSIONS, EXTERNAL:
Same as for PL-1, except:

Length overall	19 ft 3½ in (5·90 m)
Height overall	8 ft 0 in (2·44 m)
Wheel track	8 ft 5½ in (2·60 m)

WEIGHTS:
Weight empty:

108 hp	875 lb (396 kg)
125, 135 hp	900 lb (408 kg)
150 hp	902 lb (409 kg)

Max T-O weight:
108 hp	1,416 lb (642 kg)
125, 135 hp	1,445 lb (655 kg)
150 hp	1,447 lb (656 kg)

PERFORMANCE (at max T-O weight):
Max speed at S/L:
108 hp	120 knots (138 mph; 222 km/h)
125 hp	125 knots (144 mph; 232 km/h)
135 hp	128 knots (148 mph; 238 km/h)

150 hp	133 knots (153 mph; 246 km/h)

Econ cruising speed:
108 hp	103 knots (119 mph; 192 km/h)
125 hp	111 knots (128 mph; 206 km/h)
135 hp	113 knots (130 mph; 209 km/h)
150 hp	118 knots (136 mph; 219 km/h)

Stalling speed (flaps down):
108 hp	45·2 knots (52 mph; 84 km/h)
125, 135, 150 hp	47 knots (54 mph; 87 km/h)

Rate of climb at S/L:
108 hp	1,280 ft (390 m)/min
125 hp	1,500 ft (457 m)/min
135 hp	1,600 ft (488 m)/min
150 hp	1,700 ft (518 m)/min

Range at econ cruising speed:
108 hp	427 nm (492 miles; 790 km)
125 hp	422 nm (486 miles; 780 km)
135 hp	428 nm (493 miles; 792 km)
150 hp	330 nm (381 miles; 610 km)

PiAC
PIASECKI AIRCRAFT CORPORATION

HEAD OFFICE AND WORKS:
Island Road, International Airport, Philadelphia, Pennsylvania 19153
MAYFIELD ELECTRONICS DIVISION:
Mayfield, Pennsylvania 18433
DIRECTORS:
E. R. McLean, Jr
Gerald J. Higgins
Elliott Daland
Donald N. Meyers
Arthur J. Kania
F. K. Weyerhaeuser
F. N. Piasecki
PRESIDENT:
Frank N. Piasecki
VICE-PRESIDENTS:
Donald N. Meyers (Engineering)
James W. Klopp (Asst to the President)
Ernest Summers (Administration and Finance)
CHIEF ENGINEER: Kazimierz Korsak
SECRETARY-TREASURER: Arthur J. Kania
CONTROLLER AND ASST SECRETARY-TREASURER:
A. Raws
INDUSTRIAL ENGINEERING: K. R. Meenen
DIRECTOR MILITARY REQUIREMENTS: H. J. Bird
MAYFIELD PLANT SUPERINTENDENT: S. Russin
PUBLIC RELATIONS MANAGER: Daniel Piazza

The Piasecki Aircraft Corporation was formed in 1955 by Mr Frank Piasecki, who was formerly Chairman of the Board and President of the Piasecki Helicopter Corporation (now the Vertol Division of Boeing).

On 30 March 1959 a major expansion took place with the opening of the Company's Mayfield Electronics Division, equipped for large-scale research, development and production of a wide range of nucleonic, electronic and electromechanical assemblies. This Division has developed and is producing for the US government a banner-type radar-reflective aerial tow target.

PiAC is engaged in vertical lift design research and development under contracts from the US military services. These included a joint Army/Navy contract to provide information and data on the characteristics of compound helicopters at flight speeds in excess of 195 knots (225 mph; 362 km/h) using its Model 16H-1C Pathfinder II prototype, described below.

Following development of the Model 16H-3F Pathfinder III, the company is now working on a nine to fifteen-seat commercial version designated 16H-3J. This aircraft is being developed in collaboration with the Piasecki Aircraft of Canada, Ltd (which see).

PiAC provided engineering assistance to Costruzioni Aeronautiche Giovanni Agusta of Italy in the design and development of the Agusta A.101G transport helicopter, which has the PiAC designation PA-101, and has sales and manufacturing rights in this aircraft.

At its Philadelphia Aerospace Division, PiAC is manufacturing metal and plastics components for missiles, re-entry vehicles, major elements of new surface-to-surface guided weapons, and support equipment. In addition, this Division is engaged on major sub-contract work for several aerospace prime contractors.

PiAC 16H-IC PATHFINDER II

The Pathfinder is a high-speed compound helicopter which utilises a ducted propeller (known as a ring-tail) at the rear to provide directional and anti-torque control by means of vertical vanes in the duct. At a safe height after take-off, increased power is put into the ducted propeller for forward propulsion. In cruising flight the small-span fixed wings off-load the rotor.

In its original form, as the five-seat PiAC 16H-1, the Pathfinder was developed as a private venture and flew for the first time on 21 February 1962. Powered by a 450 shp Pratt & Whitney (UAC) PT6B-2 turboshaft engine, it logged a total of 185 flying hours, during which speeds of up to 148 knots (170 mph; 273 km/h) were attained (see 1965-66 *Jane's*).

In 1964, under contract from the US Army and Navy, PiAC began to modify the Pathfinder to make it capable of attaining speeds of up to 200 knots (230 mph; 370 km/h). Redesignated 16H-1A Pathfinder II, it had a 1,250 shp General Electric T58 turboshaft engine, new drive system and propeller to absorb the increased power, and a 44 ft (13·41 m) diameter rotor in place of the original 41 ft (12·50 m) rotor. The fuselage was lengthened and is spacious enough to accommodate up to eight people.

PiAC 16H-1C Pathfinder II research compound helicopter (1,500 shp General Electric T58-GE-5 turboshaft engine)

Flight trials were resumed on 15 November 1965, when the Model 16H-1A made its initial hovering trials. By May 1966 it had logged more than 40 flying hours under the joint Army/Navy programme, including flight at forward speeds of up to 195 knots (225 mph; 362 km/h). It had shown itself highly manoeuvrable in sideways flight at speeds of 8·7-30 knots (10-35 mph; 15-55 km/h) and had flown backwards at 28 knots (32 mph; 52 km/h). At that time, approximately 20 autorotative flights had been made at speeds between 39 and 100 knots (45-115 mph; 77-185 km/h).

The Pathfinder II is now powered by a 1,500 shp General Electric T58-GE-5 turboshaft engine and has been re-designated Model 16H-1C.

TYPE: Compound helicopter for high-speed research.

ROTOR SYSTEM: Fully-articulated all-metal three-blade main rotor, with folding blades, attached to hub through tension-torsion straps. Anti-torque control by three-blade ducted propeller at tail. Rotor brake fitted.

ROTOR DRIVE: Direct mechanical drive to both main rotor and ducted propeller, via pair of spiral bevels and a single planetary stage. Main rotor/engine rpm ratio 1 : 22·5. Propeller/engine rpm ratio 1 : 2·3.

WINGS: Cantilever low-wing monoplane, of aluminium alloy and honeycomb construction. Aspect ratio 5·3. Wings fold upward manually for stowage on ground. Flaperons (combined ailerons and flaps) fitted.

FUSELAGE: Conventional aluminium alloy and honeycomb semi-monocoque structure. Propeller duct also of aluminium alloy and honeycomb.

LANDING GEAR: Main units retract inward into fuselage. Electrical retraction, with mechanical emergency actuation. Non-retractable fully-castoring tail-wheel. Hydraulic shock-absorbers.

POWER PLANT: One 1,500 shp General Electric T58-GE-5 turboshaft engine.

ACCOMMODATION: Seats for pilot and co-pilot or flight observer side-by-side on flight deck, with two doors on port side. Space provision for up to six passengers in main cabin.

ELECTRONICS AND EQUIPMENT: Radio as required by test programme. Blind-flying instrumentation standard.

DIMENSIONS, EXTERNAL:
Diameter of rotor	44 ft 0 in (13·41 m)
Diameter of propeller	5 ft 6 in (1·68 m)
Length of fuselage	37 ft 3 in (11·35 m)
Width, rotor and wings folded	8 ft 10 in (2·69 m)
Height to top of rotor head	11 ft 4 in (3·45 m)
Wheel track	8 ft 0½ in (2·45 m)
Wheelbase	19 ft 11 in (6·07 m)

DIMENSIONS, INTERNAL:
Cabin: length	11 ft 7 in (3·53 m)
Max width	4 ft 9½ in (1·46 m)
Max height	5 ft 3½ in (1·61 m)

AREAS:
Rotor blade (each)	33 sq ft (3·07 m²)
Rotor disc	1,520 sq ft (141·2 m²)

WEIGHTS:
Weight empty, equipped	5,078 lb (2,303 kg)
Max T-O weight (VTOL)	8,121 lb (3,683 kg)
Max T-O weight (STOL)	11,600 lb (5,261 kg)

Artist's impression of PiAC 16H-3J Pathfinder executive transport (two 690 shp Pratt & Whitney (UACL) PT6B-16 turboshaft engines)

PERFORMANCE (at max T-O weight, VTOL):
Max level speed 182 knots (210 mph; 338 km/h)
Max cruising speed
    171 knots (197 mph; 317 km/h)
Econ cruising speed
    149 knots (172 mph; 277 km/h)
Service ceiling   13,400 ft (4,085 m)
Hovering ceiling in ground effect
    7,200 ft (2,195 m)
Hovering ceiling out of ground effect
    4,800 ft (1,465 m)
T-O run, compound   500 ft (152 m)
T-O to 50 ft (15 m), compound   650 ft (198 m)
Landing from 50 ft (15 m), compound
    500 ft (152 m)
Range with max fuel, STOL, 10% fuel reserve
    1,060 nm (1,221 miles; 1,965 km)
Range with max payload, 10% fuel reserve
    234 nm (270 miles; 430 km)

PiAC 16H-3J PATHFINDER

The illustration on page 427 shows an artist's impression of the Model 16H-3J Pathfinder, with which PiAC hopes to enter the executive aircraft market. Superseding the Model 16H-3H described in the 1968-69 *Jane's*, it will be a compound helicopter structurally similar to the Model 16H-1C Pathfinder II, but having a four-blade main rotor, an enlarged cabin and two 690 shp Pratt & Whitney (UACL) PT6B-16 turboshaft engines, coupled to a common reduction gearbox.

The cabin will accommodate nine to fifteen persons, including the pilot, and will be entered by two large doors on the starboard side, one forward and one aft of the wing. The upper half of these doors will hinge upward and the lower half (with integral airstairs) will hinge downward.

DIMENSIONS, EXTERNAL:
Diameter of rotor   44 ft 2⅔ in (13·49 m)
Length of fuselage   42 ft 9½ in (13·04 m)
Height to top of rotor hub 12 ft 3½ in (3·75 m)

DIMENSIONS, INTERNAL:
Cabin (forward): length 9 ft 1¼ in (2·77 m)
  Max width   4 ft 8 in (1·42 m)
  Max height   4 ft 3 in (1·30 m)
Cabin (aft): length   6 ft 6 in (1·98 m)
  Max width   4 ft 8 in (1·42 m)
  Max height   4 ft 3 in (1·30 m)
AREAS:
Main rotor blade (each)   33 sq ft (3·07 m²)
Main rotor disc   1,520 sq ft (141·21 m²)
WEIGHTS:
Weight empty   5,925 lb (2,687 kg)
Max T-O weight (VTOL) 9,600 lb (4,354 kg)
Max T-O weight (STOL) 10,700 lb (4,853 kg)
PERFORMANCE (estimated):
Max level speed
    165 knots (190 mph; 306 km/h)
Range with standard fuel
    434 nm (500 miles; 800 km)
Range with max fuel
    738 nm (850 miles; 1,365 km)

PIETENPOL
BERNARD H. PIETENPOL

ADDRESS:
  Spring Valley, Minnesota 55975

The prototype of Mr Pietenpol's Air Camper two-seat parasol monoplane flew for the first time in 1929, powered by a 40 hp Ford Model A engine. Plans were published in the magazine *Modern Mechanics and Inventions* in the following year and large numbers of Air Campers, with a wide variety of power plants, were built by amateurs, either from the magazine plans or from kits of parts marketed by Mr Pietenpol.

The original Air Camper was of all-wood construction, with fabric covering, but some examples completed recently and currently being built have a steel-tube fuselage and tail unit. Latest type of power plant fitted by Mr Pietenpol in his own aircraft is a converted Corvair motor-car engine.

The accompanying illustration shows Mr Pietenpol's Air Camper which he has modified by extending the fuselage by 9 in (23 cm), fitting modified Piper J-3 Cub landing gear, strengthening the wings, installation of an 8 US-gallon (30·3-litre) fuselage fuel tank and a 12 US-gallon (45-litre) fuel tank in the wing centre-section. The upper engine mounting on the fuselage has been made larger and a Corvair converted motor-car engine installed.

With this engine Mr Pietenpol's aircraft has a max level speed of 104 knots (120 mph; 193 km/h); max cruising speed of 87 knots (100 mph; 161 km/h); and cruising speed of 65-74 knots (75-85 mph); 121-137 km/h).

JOHN W. GREGA

ADDRESS:
  355 Grand Boulevard, Bedford, Ohio 44014

In addition to the standard Air Camper design, plans of which are obtainable from Mr Pietenpol, a modernised version has been produced by John Grega and Elmer Niebecker, as described below.

GN-1 AIR CAMPER

The prototype of this modernised version of the Air Camper flew for the first time in November 1965. It uses cut-down Piper J-3 Cub wings and bracing struts and J-3 Cub landing gear.

TYPE: Two-seat amateur-built light aircraft.

Air Camper owned by Mr Pietenpol, with Corvair engine and modified airframe

WINGS: Parasol monoplane, with two parallel bracing struts each side and centre-section cabane structure. Pietenpol special wing section. Thickness/chord ratio 9%. No dihedral. Incidence 2°. Fabric-covered two-spar wood structure. Tips may be rounded or square. Plain wooden ailerons with fabric covering. No flaps.
FUSELAGE: Wooden de Havilland truss structure of sitka spruce, covered with birch plywood to back of rear cockpit and fabric on rear fuselage.
TAIL UNIT: Wire-braced wood and steel-tube structure, covered with fabric.
LANDING GEAR: Divided main gear, with spring shock-absorption, modified from Piper J-3 Cub gear. Main wheel tyres size 8·00 × 4, pressure 15 lb/sq in (1·05 kg/cm²). Piper hydraulic brakes. Steerable tail-wheel.
POWER PLANT: One 65 hp Continental A65-8 four-cylinder horizontally-opposed air-cooled engine, driving a two-blade 72/41 metal fixed-pitch propeller. Fuel tanks aft of firewall, capacity 12 US gallons (45 litres), and in top wing centre-section, capacity 6 US gallons (22·5 litres). Oil capacity 1 US gallon (3·75 litres).

ACCOMMODATION: Two seats in tandem in open cockpits.
DIMENSIONS, EXTERNAL:
Wing span   29 ft 0 in (8·84 m)
Wing chord, constant 5 ft 3 in (1·60 m)
Wing aspect ratio   6
Length overall   18 ft 4 in (5·59 m)
Height   6 ft 4 in (1·93 m)
Tailplane span   7 ft 6 in (2·29 m)
Wheel track   5 ft 3 in (1·60 m)
DIMENSIONS, INTERNAL:
Cabin: Max width   1 ft 11 in (0·58 m)
AREA:
Wings, gross   150 sq ft (13·94 m²)
WEIGHT:
Max T-O weight   1,129 lb (512 kg)
PERFORMANCE (at max T-O weight):
Max level speed at S/L
    83 knots (95 mph; 153 km/h)
Max cruising speed at S/L
    69 knots (80 mph; 129 km/h)
Stalling speed 31 knots (35 mph; 56 km/h)
Rate of climb at S/L 600 ft (183 m)/min
T-O run   200 ft (61 m)
Landing run   250 ft (76 m)
Range with max fuel
    347 nm (400 miles; 640 km)

PIPER
PIPER AIRCRAFT CORPORATION

HEAD OFFICE AND WORKS:
  Lock Haven, Pennsylvania 17745
OTHER WORKS:
  Vero Beach, Florida
  Lakeland, Florida
  Piper, Pennsylvania
  Renovo, Pennsylvania
BOARD OF DIRECTORS:
  Nicholas M. Salgo (Chairman)
  Lawrence R. Barnett
  John E. Flick (Secretary)
  C. Leonard Gordon
  William T. Piper Jr
  W. Gordon Robertson
  James J. Rochlis
  David W. Wallace
CORPORATE OFFICERS:
PRESIDENT: William T. Piper Jr
EXECUTIVE VICE-PRESIDENT: Howard Piper
SENIOR VICE-PRESIDENT:
  Charles W. Pool (Finance and Administration)
VICE-PRESIDENTS:
  Walter C. Jamouneau (Chief Engineer)
  Joseph M. Mergen (Operations)

J. Willard Millar (Marketing and New Product Development)
Wallis C. Smith (Sales)
Eugene Stickley (Corporate Planning)
CONTROLLER: Jack J. Cattoni
TREASURER: John Leeson

Piper does not make annual model changes, but incorporates improvements one at a time in production as they become available. Since 1964, when the PA-28-140 Cherokee 140 superseded the PA-22-108 Colt, the entire range of Piper products has been low-wing except for the PA-18 Super Cub. All types in current production are described in detail below.

The main manufacturing centre is at Lock Haven, where average daily production totalled 2 Pawnees, 0·5 Super Cubs, 0·5 Comanches, 2 Twin Comanches, 1·5 Aztecs and 1·25 Navajos in early 1970.

Average daily production at the Vero Beach plant, where the Cherokee series is built, was 12·5 aircraft per day. Vero Beach is responsible for the experimental development of Piper aircraft and also houses the company's Plastics and Electronics Divisions.

Piper operates also two other plants and a third is nearing completion. The first two are at Piper, Pennsylvania, where sheet metal parts are formed, and Renovo, Pennsylvania, which makes plastic components; the third is at Lakeland, Florida.

A Cherokee Six delivered to Kenya in April 1967 was the 10,000th Piper aeroplane delivered overseas, and the 10,000th Cherokee to come off the Vero Beach production line was delivered in August 1967.

Optional equipment on several current types includes an automatic flight system, known as the Piper AutoControl. This operates electrically, obtaining data from the directional gyro and artificial horizon to keep the aircraft in level flight and hold it precisely on a pre-selected course. The installation weighs only 4½ lb. With 3-in gyros installed, Omni and ILS coupler systems can be added to the Auto-Control.

A more advanced flight system is the Piper Alti-Matic lightweight four-control auto-pilot. Its purpose is to hold the aircraft on a selected course and altitude setting; it also permits the pilot to make course and altitude changes by means of the heading and altitude selectors. The AltiMatic is so designed that it is possible to select the desired heading and altitude before take-off and engage the autopilot for automatic flight when a safe height has been reached after take-off. It adds only 10 lb to the equipped weight of an aircraft already fitted with gyro instruments. New Piper 3-in gyros are available, and with these the Omni and ILS coupler may be used. The AltiMatic is also fitted with automatic pitch trim which converts to manual electric pitch trim when the AltiMatic is disengaged. Control is through a toggle switch on the control wheel.

Also available, as an alternative to AutoControl and the AltiMatic, is the Honeywell H-14 autopilot. Offered by Piper as the Altimatic H-14, this is a full three-axis vacuum-operated autopilot with pitch control, course selector, altitude hold and radio coupling to Omni and ILS, and will turn the aircraft automatically to any pre-set heading.

PIPER PA-18 SUPER CUB 150

There are two versions of the Super Cub 150, as follows:

Standard Super Cub 150. As described below.
De luxe Super Cub 150. As Standard model, but with addition of electric starter, generator, battery, navigation lights, sensitive altimeter, tie-down rings, control locks, parking brake and propeller spinner.

The original PA-18 with 90 hp Continental C90-12F engine received FAA Type Approval on 18 November 1949. The PA-18-150, PA-18A-150 agricultural aircraft and PA-18S and PA-18AS seaplanes were all approved on 1 October 1954.

The current international height record in Class C-1-b (aircraft with T-O weight of 500-1,000 kg) is held by Miss C. Bayley of the USA, who climbed to a height of 30,203 ft (9,206 m) in a Super Cub with 125 hp Lycoming engine, on 4 January 1951.

TYPE: Two-seat light cabin monoplane.

WINGS: Braced high-wing monoplane, with steel-tube Vee bracing struts each side. Wing section USA 35B. Thickness/chord ratio 12%. Dihedral 1°. No incidence at mean aerodynamic chord. Total washout of 3° 18'. Aluminium spars and ribs, aluminium sheet leading-edge and aileron false spar, wingtip bow of ash, with fabric covering overall and fire-resistant Duraclad plastic finish. Plain aluminium ailerons and flaps with fabric covering. No trim tabs.

FUSELAGE: Rectangular welded steel-tube structure covered with fabric. Fire-resistant Duraclad plastic finish.

TAIL UNIT: Wire-braced structure of welded steel tubes and channels, covered with fabric. Fire-resistant Duraclad plastic finish. Tailplane incidence variable for trimming. Balanced rudder and elevators. No trim-tabs.

LANDING GEAR: Non-retractable tail-wheel type. Two side Vees and half axles hinged to cabane below fuselage. Rubber cord shock-absorption. Goodrich main wheel tyres, size 800 × 4 four-ply, pressure 18 lb/sq in (1·27 kg/cm²). Steerable leaf-spring tail-wheel by Maule (standard) or Scott (optional 8 in). Goodrich D-2-113 expanding brakes. Tandem-wheel landing gear. Special 36 in (91·5 cm) low-pressure tyres, Federal skis or wheel-skis, or Edo 2000 standard or amphibious floats may be fitted.

POWER PLANT: One 150 hp Lycoming O-320 four-cylinder horizontally-opposed air-cooled engine, driving a two-blade Sensenich metal propeller. Steel-tube engine mounting is hinged at firewall, allowing it to be swung to port for access to rear of engine. One 18 US gallon metal fuel tank in each wing. Total fuel capacity 36 US gallons (136 litres). Refuelling points on top of wing.

ACCOMMODATION: Enclosed cabin seating two in tandem with dual controls. Adjustable front seat. Rear seat quickly removable for cargo carrying. Heater and adjustable cool-air vent. Downward-hinged door on starboard side and upward-hinged window above, can be opened in flight. Sliding windows on port side. Baggage compartment aft of rear seat, capacity 50 lb (22 kg).

ELECTRONICS AND EQUIPMENT: Equipment may be installed for spraying, dusting, fertilising, etc. Optional extras include blind-flying instruments, vacuum system, 8-day clock, metallising and stainless steel control cables, landing light, and Narco Mark III radio.

DIMENSIONS, EXTERNAL:
Wing span	35 ft 2½ in (10·73 m)
Wing chord (constant)	5 ft 3 in (1·60 m)
Wing aspect ratio	7
Length overall:	
landplane	22 ft 7 in (6·88 m)
seaplane	23 ft 11 in (7·28 m)
Height overall:	
landplane	6 ft 8½ in (2·02 m)
seaplane	10 ft 3½ in (3·14 m)
Tailplane span	10 ft 6 in (3·20 m)
Wheel track	6 ft 0½ in (1·84 m)

DIMENSIONS, INTERNAL:
Baggage compartment	18 cu ft (0·51 m³)

AREAS:
Wings, gross	178·5 sq ft (16·58 m²)
Ailerons (total)	18·80 sq ft (1·75 m²)
Trailing-edge flaps (total)	11·50 sq ft (1·07 m²)
Fin	4·66 sq ft (0·43 m²)

Piper PA-18 Super Cub 150 (150 hp Lycoming O-320 engine)

Piper PA-23-250 Aztec D six-seat executive transport (two 250 hp Lycoming IO-540-C4B5 engines)

Rudder	6·76 sq ft (0·63 m²)
Tailplane	15·10 sq ft (1·40 m²)
Elevators	11·70 sq ft (1·09 m²)

WEIGHTS AND LOADINGS (N=normal category; R=restricted, agricultural, category):
Weight empty:	
N landplane	930 lb (422 kg)
N seaplane	1,190 lb (540 kg)
R	930 lb (422 kg)
Max T-O and landing weight:	
N landplane	1,750 lb (794 kg)
N seaplane	1,760 lb (798 kg)
R	2,070 lb (939 kg)
Max wing loading:	
N landplane	10·0 lb/sq ft (48·8 kg/m²)
N seaplane	10·0 lb/sq ft (48·8 kg/m²)
R	11·6 lb/sq ft (56·64 kg/m²)
Max power loading:	
N landplane	11·6 lb/hp (5·26 kg/hp)
N seaplane	11·7 lb/hp (5·31 kg/hp)
R	13·8 lb/hp (6·26 kg/hp)

PERFORMANCE (at max T-O weight: N=normal category; R=restricted, agricultural, category):
Max level speed at S/L:	
N landplane	113 knots (130 mph; 208 km/h)
N seaplane	100 knots (115 mph; 185 km/h)
R	91 knots (105 mph; 169 km/h)
Max permissible diving speed:	
N, R	132 knots (153 mph; 246 km/h)
Max cruising speed (75% power):	
N landplane	100 knots (115 mph; 185 km/h)
N seaplane	89 knots (103 mph; 166 km/h)
R	78 knots (90 mph; 145 km/h)
Econ cruising speed:	
N landplane	91 knots (105 mph; 169 km/h)
R	78 knots (90 mph; 145 km/h)
Stalling speed, flaps down:	
N landplane	38 knots (43 mph; 69 km/h)
N seaplane	37 knots (42 mph; 67 km/h)
R	39 knots (45 mph; 73 km/h)
Rate of climb at S/L:	
N landplane	960 ft (293 m)/min
N seaplane	830 ft (253 m)/min
R	760 ft (232 m)/min
Service ceiling:	
N landplane	19,000 ft (5,795 m)
N seaplane	17,500 ft (5,335 m)
R	17,000 ft (5,180 m)
Absolute ceiling:	
N landplane	21,300 ft (6,492 m)
N seaplane	19,500 ft (5,943 m)
T-O run:	
N landplane	200 ft (61 m)

N seaplane	700 ft (214 m)
R	300 ft (92 m)
T-O to 50 ft (15 m):	
N landplane	500 ft (153 m)
N seaplane	approx 990 ft (300 m)
R	950 ft (290 m)
Landing from 50 ft (15 m):	
N landplane	725 ft (221 m)
N seaplane	730 ft (223 m)
R	875 ft (267 m)
Landing run:	
N landplane	350 ft (107 m)
N seaplane	430 ft (131 m)
R	410 ft (125 m)
Range with max fuel and max payload:	
N landplane	399 nm (460 miles; 735 km)
N seaplane	375 nm (412 miles; 663 km)
R	312 nm (360 miles; 580 km)

PIPER PA-23-250 AZTEC D
US Navy designation: U-11A

This latest version of the Aztec, announced in June 1968, has a completely new instrument panel and interior refinements. It is available in several different models, as follows:

Aztec D. Basic model, as described in detail below.

Custom Aztec D. As basic model, with addition of Piper TruSpeed Indicator in place of standard ASI, glare-ban instrument lighting, full-flow oil filters, alternate static source and curtains, adding 9 lb (4 kg) to empty weight.

Sportsman Aztec D. As Custom model, with addition of Piper External Power and de luxe Palm Beach interior, adding total of 35 lb (16 kg) to basic empty weight.

Professional Aztec D. As Custom model, with addition of Piper External Power, electrical propeller de-icing and pneumatic de-icing boots on wings and tail, adding total of 74 lb (33·5 kg) to basic empty weight.

Turbo Aztec D. Turbocharged version, described separately.

Each of the above versions can be fitted with one of four electronic packages, as follows:

Electronic Group A. Comprises Mk 12 series 90-channel VHF transceiver and 100-channel nav receiver, Mk 12 series 360-channel VHF transceiver and 100-channel nav receiver, two VOA-40 VOR/ILS localiser converter indicators, ADF-T12 series automatic direction finder, marker beacon, Piper AutoControl III with positive heading lock and course selector, anti-static antenna and wicks, Piper Electric Trim, audio amplifier, headset, microphone and radio selector panel, adding total of 54 lb (24·5 kg) to basic empty weight.

Electronic Group B. Same as Group A, but with VOA-50M VOR/ILS localiser converter indicator with glide slope and marker beacon indicator instead of one VOA-40, and addition of UDI-4 series DME with ground speed indication, UGR glide-slope receiver and radio coupler to autopilot, adding total of 71 lb (32 kg) to basic empty weight.

Electronic Group C. Same as Group B, but with second 360-channel transceiver instead of 90-channel transceiver, AT-6A series transponder, Piper AltiMatic III three-axis autopilot and electric trim instead of AutoControl, and glide-slope coupler, adding total of 79 lb (36 kg) to basic empty weight.

Electronic Group D. Comprises radio coupler to auto-pilot, glide-slope coupler, Piper AltiMatic III auto-pilot with automatic electric trim, anti-static antenna and wicks. Two KTR-900 solid-state 380-channel transceivers with KFS-590 channel selector heads, two KNR-600 Omni/Localiser 200-channel nav receivers, KNI-500L integrated Omni/Localiser, glide-slope and marker beacon indicator with automatic light dimming, KNI-500 integrated Omni/Localiser and glide-slope indicator, KGM-690 solid-state marker beacon receiver and solid-state 20-channel glide-slope receiver, KDF-800 digital tune ADF, KNI-580 indicator with manually-rotatable magnetic bearing card, KAA-445 dual audio amplifier, passenger address system, headset, microphone and radio selector panel, adding total of 84 lb (38 kg) to basic empty weight.

Most items covered under model and electronic group listings are available individually and, in addition, a number of items of nav/com equipment are available as options, including the H-14 AltiMatic pilot and RDR-100 radar.

The Aztec received FAA Type Approval as a five-seat aircraft on 18 September 1959, and with six seats on 15 December 1961.

The prototype of a floatplane version of the Aztec was produced as a joint project by Melridge Aviation of Vancouver, Washington, and Jobmaster Company, Inc, of Seattle. Fitted with Edo 4930 floats, this aircraft will take off from calm water in 20 seconds at max T-O weight of 5,200 lb (2,360 kg). Useful load is 1,800 lb (816 kg), permitting a six-passenger load with 120 US gallons (455 litres) of fuel. To simplify docking and loading from either side, a door has been designed for installation on the port side, by the pilot's seat, and is part of the conversion kit which will be offered by Melridge Aviation to permit conversion in the field.

Twenty Aztecs were supplied to the US Navy as "off-the-shelf" utility transports, under the designation U-11A (formerly UO-1). Several South and Central American governments and armed services have also acquired Aztecs, notably the Argentine Army which took delivery of six in 1964.

More than 3,000 Aztecs had been produced by 1 January 1970.

Type: Six-seat twin-engined executive transport.

Wings: Cantilever low-wing monoplane. Wing section USA 35-B (modified). Thickness/chord ratio 14%. Dihedral 5°. Incidence 0° at root, —1° 12′ at mean chord. All-metal stressed-skin structure, with heavy stepped-down main spar, front and rear auxiliary spars, ribs, stringers and detachable wing-tips. Plain all-metal ailerons and hydraulically-actuated flaps. Optional Goodrich de-icing system.

Fuselage: Basic aluminium semi-monocoque structure with welded steel-tube truss around cabin.

Tail Unit: Cantilever all-metal structure with swept fin and all-moving horizontal surfaces. Trim-tab in rudder. Geared anti-servo tab in horizontal surfaces. Optional Goodrich de-icing system.

Landing Gear: Retractable tricycle type. Hydraulic retraction, with CO_2 emergency extension system. Nose-wheel retracts rearward, main wheels forward. Wheel doors enclose landing gear fully when retracted. Electrol oleo shock-absorber struts. Cleveland main wheels, size 600 × 6, with size 700 × 6 8-ply type III tyres. Cleveland steerable nose-wheel, size 600 × 6, with 600 × 6 4-ply type III tyre. Hydraulic disc brakes. Parking brake.

Power Plant: Two 250 hp Lycoming IO-540-C4B5 six-cylinder horizontally-opposed air-cooled engines, each driving a Hartzell HC-E2YK-2RB constant-speed fully-feathering two-blade metal propeller, diameter 6 ft 5 in (1·96 m). Two rubber-cell fuel tanks in each wing. Total fuel capacity 144 US gallons (544 litres); 140 US gallons (530 litres) usable. Refuelling points above wings.

Accommodation: Six persons on two pairs of adjustable individual seats and rear bench seat. Dual controls standard. Individual seat lights and controllable overhead ventilation. Southwind 35,000 BTU heater with six heat outlets and two defrosters. Heated windshield optional. Double windows. Passenger step. Door at front of cabin on starboard side. Emergency exit at rear on port side. Centre and rear seats removable to provide space for stretcher, survey camera or up to 1,600 lb (725 kg) freight. Rear cabin bulkhead removable for stretcher and cargo loading via rear baggage door. Baggage compartments at rear of cabin and in nose, with tiedown fittings, each with capacity of 150 lb (68 kg). Baggage doors on starboard side; rear one enlarged on current aircraft, for stretcher loading. Ash trays, cigarette lighter, coat hooks, complete soundproofing and two sun visors.

Systems: Hydraulic system, pressure 1,150 lb/sq in (81 kg/cm²), for landing gear and flaps. Two 70A 12V alternators. 12V 35Ah battery.

Electronics and Equipment: Standard equipment includes full blind-flying instrumentation, with 3-in pictorial artificial horizon and directional gyro (flight instruments arranged in "T" configuration), flap indicator, stall warning indicator, clock, heated pitot tube, navigation, landing and taxi lights and rotating beacon. Optional items listed under descriptions of individual models above and under electronic groups, plus toe-brakes and altimeter for co-pilot, dual tachometer and hour meter, strobe lights, fire extinguisher and oxygen system with 114 cu ft (3·23 m³) bottle and six outlets.

Dimensions, external:
- Wing span: 37 ft 2½ in (11·34 m)
- Wing chord (constant): 5 ft 7 in (1·70 m)
- Wing aspect ratio: 6·8
- Length overall: 30 ft 2⅝ in (9·21 m)
- Height overall: 10 ft 4 in (3·15 m)
- Tailplane span: 12 ft 6 in (3·81 m)
- Wheel track: 11 ft 4 in (3·45 m)
- Wheelbase: 7 ft 6 in (2·29 m)
- Cabin door: Height: 3 ft 2 in (0·97 m)
  - Width: 2 ft 9 in (0·84 m)
- Baggage compartment door (front):
  - Height: 1 ft 8 in (0·51 m)
  - Width: 2 ft 6 in (0·76 m)
- Baggage compartment door (rear):
  - Height: 2 ft 2 in (0·66 m)
  - Width: 2 ft 9 in (0·84 m)

Dimensions, internal:
- Baggage compartments:
  - front: 17·4 cu ft (0·49 m³)
  - rear: 23·2 cu ft (0·66 m³)
- Max cargo space, incl baggage compartments: 122 cu ft (3·45 m³)

Areas:
- Wings, gross: 207·56 sq ft (19·28 m²)
- Ailerons (total): 8·38 sq ft (0·77 m²)
- Trailing-edge flaps (total): 16·60 sq ft (1·54 m²)
- Fin: 14·80 sq ft (1·37 m²)
- Rudder: 10·30 sq ft (0·96 m²)
- Horizontal surfaces: 39·80 sq ft (3·70 m²)

Weights and Loadings:
- Weight empty (standard): 3,006 lb (1,363 kg)
- Max T-O and landing weight: 5,200 lb (2,360 kg)
- Max wing loading: 25·05 lb/sq ft (122·3 kg/m²)
- Max power loading: 10·4 lb/hp (4·7 kg/hp)

Performance (at max T-O weight):
- Max level speed: 188 knots (216 mph; 348 km/h)
- Max permissible diving speed: 240 knots (277 mph; 446 km/h)
- Normal cruise speed at 4,000 ft (1,220 m): 182 knots (210 mph; 338 km/h)
- Intermediate cruise speed at 6,000 ft (1,830 m): 181 knots (208 mph; 335 km/h)
- Econ cruising speed at 6,400 ft (1,950 m): 177 knots (204 mph; 328 km/h)
- Long-range cruise speed at 10,200 ft (3,110 m): 169 knots (195 mph; 314 km/h)
- Stalling speed, flaps down: 59 knots (68 mph; 109 km/h)
- Rate of climb at S/L: 1,490 ft (455 m)/min
- Single-engine rate of climb at S/L: 240 ft (73 m)/min
- Absolute ceiling: 21,100 ft (6,430 m)
- Single-engine absolute ceiling: 6,400 ft (1,950 m)
- T-O run: 820 ft (250 m)
- T-O to 50 ft (15 m): 1,250 ft (380 m)
- Landing from 50 ft (15 m): 1,250 ft (380 m)
- Landing run: 850 ft (259 m)
- Range with max fuel:
  - Normal cruise speed: 720 nm (830 miles; 1,335 km)
  - Intermediate cruise speed: 1,024 nm (1,080 miles; 1,738 km)
  - Econ cruise speed: 963 nm (1,110 miles; 1,786 km)
  - Long-range cruise speed: 1,050 nm (1,210 miles; 1,947 km)

PIPER PA-23-250 TURBO AZTEC D

The Turbo Aztec D is identical in every way with the Aztec D, described above, except that it has 250 hp Lycoming TIO-540-C1A engines, fitted with the AiResearch turbocharging system. These specially modified engines allow a turbo cruise setting at 2,400 rpm, providing a constant manifold pressure from sea level to 24,000 ft (7,315 m), and result in considerably improved performance.

Standard equipment includes a Piper TruSpeed indicator, glare-ban blue-white instrument lighting, full-flow oil filters, alternate static source, curtains, Piper external power, mixture control indicator, and an oxygen system with 114 cu ft bottle and six outlets.

Weights and Loadings:
- Same as for Aztec D except:
  - Weight empty (standard): 3,193 lb (1,448 kg)
  - Max T-O and landing weight: 5,200 lb (2,360 kg)

Performance (at max T-O weight):
- Same as for Aztec D except:
- Max level speed at 18,500 ft (5,639 m): 220 knots (253 mph; 407 km/h)
- Turbo cruise speed at 12,000 ft (3,655 m): 194 knots (223 mph; 359 km/h)
- Turbo cruise speed at 24,000 ft (7,315 m): 214 knots (246 mph; 396 km/h)
- Intermediate cruise speed at 12,000 ft (3,655 m): 187 knots (215 mph; 346 km/h)
- Intermediate cruise speed at 24,000 ft (7,315 m): 208 knots (239 mph; 385 km/h)
- Econ cruise speed at 12,000 ft (3,655 m): 176 knots (203 mph; 327 km/h)
- Econ cruise speed at 24,000 ft (7,315 m): 195 knots (224 mph; 360 km/h)
- Long-range cruise speed at 12,000 ft (3,655 m): 163 knots (188 mph; 303 km/h)
- Long-range cruise speed at 24,000 ft (7,315 m): 179 knots (206 mph; 332 km/h)
- Max rate of climb at S/L: 1,530 ft (466 m)/min
- Max rate of climb at S/L, one engine out: 260 ft (79 m)/min
- Absolute ceiling: over 30,000 ft (9,145 m)
- Single-engine absolute ceiling: 18,700 ft (5,700 m)
- Range with max fuel:
  - Turbo cruise speed at 12,000 ft (3,655 m): 790 nm (910 miles; 1,464 km)
  - Turbo cruise speed at 24,000 ft (7,315 m): 877 nm (1,010 miles; 1,625 km)
  - Intermediate cruise speed at 12,000 ft (3,655 m): 946 nm (1,090 miles; 1,754 km)
  - Intermediate cruise speed at 24,000 ft (7,315 m): 1,059 nm (1,220 miles; 1,963 km)
  - Econ cruise speed at 12,000 ft (3,655 m): 1,024 nm (1,180 miles; 1,899 km)
  - Econ cruise speed at 24,000 ft (7,315 m): 1,128 nm (1,300 miles; 2,092 km)
  - Long-range cruise speed at 12,000 ft (3,655 m): 1,081 nm (1,245 miles; 2,003 km)
  - Long-range cruise speed at 24,000 ft (7,315 m): 1,198 nm (1,380 miles; 2,220 km)

PIPER PA-24-260 COMANCHE C

The prototype Comanche first flew on 24 May 1956, and the first production aircraft on 21 October 1957.

Only the 260 hp Comanche C was in production in May 1970. It is available in the following models:

PA-24-260 Comanche C. Basic model, as described in detail below. Introduced on 2 June 1969.

PA-24-260 Custom Comanche C. As basic model, with addition of full blind-flying instrumentation, clock, Piper TruSpeed Indicator in place of standard ASI, vacuum system, full-flow oil filter, heated pitot tube, rotating beacon and auxiliary fuel tanks of 30 US gallons (113·5 litres) capacity, adding 31 lb (14 kg) to basic empty weight.

PA-24-260 Sportsman Comanche C. As Custom model, with addition of glare-ban instrument lights, Piper external power, fifth and sixth family seats, Palm Beach de luxe interior and external trim, and curtains, adding 66 lb (30 kg) to basic empty weight.

Turbo Comanche C. First announced on 1 May 1970, this turbocharged version of the Comanche C is described separately.

Each of the above versions can be fitted with one of three electronic packages, as follows:

Electronic Group A. Comprises Piper Auto-Control, Narco Mk 12 90-channel VHF transceiver plus 100-channel nav receiver, Narco VOA-40 VOR/ILS localiser converter indicator, Narco ADF-31 with BFO and tuning meter, microphone, headset, radio selector panel and isolation amplifier, adding 33 lb (15 kg) to basic empty weight.

Electronic Group B. Same as Group A, plus second VOA-40, Piper electric trim, Narco Mk 12 360-channel transceiver plus 100-channel nav receiver, Piper marker beacon indicator, marker beacon receiver, anti-static kit and radio coupling to autopilot, adding total of 57 lb (26 kg) to basic empty weight.

Electronic Group C. Same as Group B, but with Piper AltiMatic autopilot instead of Auto-Control, deletion of Piper electric trim, Narco VOA-50M, instead of second VOA-40, with glideslope and marker beacon indication, UGR series glideslope receiver, glideslope coupling to AltiMatic, UDI-4 series DME with GSI, AT6-A series transponder and Piper noise cancelling microphone and microphone holder, adding total of 92 lb (41·7 kg) to basic empty weight.

Most items covered under model and electronic group listings are available individually. Other optional extras include oxygen system, Bendix ADF T-12, Piper mixture control indicator, alternate static source, Piper external power, headrests in standard interior, right side toe-brakes, adjustable front seats, shoulder harness for standard seats, strobe lights, second altimeter and fire extinguisher.

The Comanche C has the "Tiger Shark" nose cowling developed for the Twin Comanche, improved heating and ventilation system, Sports Power console grouping throttle, propeller and mixture controls, new instrument panel with flight instruments grouped in Tee configuration, resettable switch-type circuit breakers, white instrument lights, ram's-horn control wheel, redesigned rudder trim control and gear-in-transit light. The emergency landing gear extension control is relocated.

Between 18 May and 20 June 1966, Miss Sheila Scott of Britain flew solo 25,231 nm (29,055 miles; 46,760 km) around the world in a standard Comanche B with two additional 65 US gallon (246 litre) fuel tanks in the cabin. This established a new round-the-world speed record in Class 3 and was the longest solo flight around the world to date. Twelve inter-city records were set up en route.

About 50 Comanche C's had been produced by 1 January 1970.

TYPE: Four-seat cabin monoplane.

WINGS: Cantilever low-wing monoplane. NACA 64_2A215 laminar-flow wing section. Dihedral 5°. Incidence 2°. Sweep-forward at quarter-chord 2° 30′. Three-spar aluminium stressed-skin structure. Plastics wingtips. Plain aluminium ailerons. Electrically-actuated single-slotted aluminium flaps.

FUSELAGE: Aluminium semi-monocoque structure.

TAIL UNIT: Cantilever stressed-skin structure, made entirely of aluminium except for steel-tube stub spar. Sweptback vertical surfaces. All-moving one-piece tailplane or stabilator, with anti-servo tab. Trim-tab in rudder.

LANDING GEAR: Electrically-retractable tricycle type, with emergency manual extension. Steerable nose-wheel retracts rearward, main units inward. Piper oleo-pneumatic shock-absorbers. Cleveland wheels size 600 × 6. Tyres, size 6·00 × 6 6-ply rating on main wheels, 6·00 × 6 4-ply rating on nose-wheel. Tyre pressure 42 lb/sq in (2·95 kg/cm²). Cleveland dual-disc hydraulic brakes. Parking brake.

POWER PLANT: One 260 hp Lycoming IO-540 six-cylinder horizontally-opposed air-cooled engine, driving a Hartzell HC82XK1D two-blade metal constant-speed propeller, diameter 6 ft 5 in (1·96 m). Two rubber fuel tanks in wings with total capacity of 60 US gallons (227 litres). Two optional auxiliary tanks in wings with total capacity of 30 US gallons (113·5 litres). Refuelling points above wings. Oil capacity 3 US gallons (11·4 litres).

ACCOMMODATION: Enclosed cabin seating four in two pairs in standard version. Third row of two seats optional. Two rear rows of seats quickly removable to provide space for stretcher, camera or freight. Dual controls, heating and ventilation standard. Forward-opening door at front of cabin on starboard side. Baggage compartment, capacity 250 lb (113 kg), aft of cabin, with door on port side.

SYSTEMS: Hydraulic system for brakes only. Electrical system supplied by 12V 70A engine-driven alternator. 12V 35Ah battery.

ELECTRONICS AND EQUIPMENT: Standard equipment includes heater and defroster, ventilators, navigation and landing lights. Optional equipment as detailed above under individual model and electronic group listings.

DIMENSIONS, EXTERNAL:
- Wing span: 36 ft 0 in (10·97 m)
- Wing chord at root: 7 ft 1 in (2·16 m)
- Wing chord at tip: 3 ft 3 in (0·99 m)
- Wing aspect ratio: 7·28
- Length overall: 25 ft 0 in (7·62 m)
- Height overall: 7 ft 6 in (2·29 m)
- Tailplane span: 12 ft 6 in (3·81 m)
- Wheel track: 9 ft 8 in (2·94 m)
- Wheelbase: 6 ft 6$\frac{5}{8}$ in (1·99 m)
- Baggage compartment door:
  - Width: 1 ft 8 in (0·51 m)
  - Height: 1 ft 8 in (0·51 m)

DIMENSIONS, INTERNAL:
- Cabin: Length: 9 ft 4 in (2·84 m)

AREAS:
- Wings, gross: 178 sq ft (16·53 m²)
- Ailerons (total): 14·0 sq ft (1·30 m²)
- Trailing-edge flaps (total): 20·2 sq ft (1·87 m²)
- Fin: 8·0 sq ft (0·74 m²)
- Rudder: 5·4 sq ft (0·52 m²)
- Tailplane, including tab: 32·5 sq ft (3·04 m²)

WEIGHTS AND LOADINGS:
- Weight empty (standard model): 1,773 lb (804 kg)
- Max T-O weight: 3,200 lb (1,451 kg)
- Max wing loading: 18·0 lb/sq ft (87·9 kg/m²)
- Max power loading: 12·3 lb/hp (5·58 kg/hp)

Piper Turbo Comanche C (260 hp Lycoming IO-540-engine)

PERFORMANCE (at max T-O weight):
- Max level speed at S/L: 169 knots (195 mph; 314 km/h)
- Max permissible diving speed: 197 knots (227 mph; 365 km/h)
- Max cruising speed (75% power) at 6,300 ft (1,920 m): 161 knots (185 mph; 298 km/h)
- Rate of climb at S/L: 1,320 ft (402 m)/min
- Service ceiling: 19,500 ft (5,945 m)
- Absolute ceiling: 21,000 ft (6,400 m)
- T-O run: 820 ft (250 m)
- T-O to 50 ft (15 m): 1,400 ft (427 m)
- Landing from 50 ft (15 m): 1,200 ft (366 m)
- Landing run: 690 ft (210 m)
- Range, 75% power with standard fuel at 6,300 ft (1,920 m): 638 nm (735 miles; 1,180 km)
- Range, 75% power with optional fuel at 6,300 ft (1,920 m): 981 nm (1,130 miles; 1,815 km)
- Range, 65% power with standard fuel at 10,500 ft (3,200 m): 694 nm (800 miles; 1,285 km)
- Range, 65% power with optional fuel at 10,500 ft (3,200 m): 1,063 nm (1,225 miles; 1,970 m)

PIPER TURBO COMANCHE C

On 1 May 1970 Piper announced this turbocharged version of the Comanche C, which offers a significant increase in performance.

Power plant is a 260 hp Lycoming IO-540 six-cylinder horizontally-opposed air-cooled engine. This has a Rayjay turbocharger system which provides boost through dual blowers driven by exhaust gases and brought into operation by a turbo control lever mounted on the pilot's console. Linked to the throttle, this automatically deactivates the turbochargers when the throttle is retarded, and a pressure relief valve provides protection against inadvertent over-boosting.

Standard items of equipment in the Turbo Comanche include a 67 cu ft (1·90 m³) oxygen system with four individual outlets, engine oil cooler, exhaust gas temperature gauge, a higher-capacity cabin heating system and a revised exhaust installation that reduces cabin noise. In other respects the Turbo Comanche C is identical to the Comanche C, described above, except for specification and performance figures which vary as detailed below:

WEIGHTS AND LOADINGS:
- Weight empty: 1,894 lb (859 kg)
- Max T-O weight: 3,200 lb (1,451 kg)
- Max wing loading: 18·0 lb/sq ft (87·9 kg/m²)
- Max power loading: 12·3 lb/hp (5·58 kg/hp)

PERFORMANCE (at max T-O weight):
- Max level speed: 210 knots (242 mph; 389 km/h)
- Max cruising speed at 25,000 ft (7,620 m): 198 knots (228 mph; 318 km/h)
- Intermediate cruising speed at 25,000 ft (7,620 m): 193 knots (222 mph; 357 km/h)
- Econ cruising speed at 25,000 ft (7,620 m): 181 knots (209 mph; 336 km/h)
- Long-range cruising speed at 25,000 ft (7,620 m): 170 knots (196 mph; 315 km/h)
- Stalling speed: 58 knots (67 mph; 107 km/h)
- Max rate of climb at S/L: 1,320 ft (402 m)/min
- Operationally approved service ceiling: 25,000 ft (7,620 m)
- T-O run: 820 ft (250 m)
- T-O to 50 ft (15 m): 1,400 ft (427 m)
- Landing from 50 ft (15 m): 1,200 ft (365 m)
- Landing run: 690 ft (210 m)
- Range at max cruising speed with standard fuel at 25,000 ft (7,620 m): 725 nm (835 miles; 1,343 km)
- Range at max cruising speed with optional fuel at 25,000 ft (7,620 m): 1,087 nm (1,275 miles; 2,052 km)
- Max range at long-range cruising speed, standard fuel at 25,000 ft (7,620 m): 847 nm (975 miles; 1,569 km)
- Max range at long-range cruising speed, optional fuel at 25,000 ft (7,620 m): 1,294 nm (1,490 miles; 2,398 km)

PIPER PA-25 PAWNEE C

The PA-25 Pawnee was developed by Piper's Vero Beach Development Center as a specialised agricultural aircraft for dispersal of chemical dusts and sprays. Special attention was paid to pilot safety, bearing in mind the recommendations of the Crash Injury Research Unit of Cornell Medical College. Thus, the pilot is placed high to ensure a good view, including rearward, during low flying. Extra-strong seat belt and shoulder harness are fitted, and a rounded sheet metal cushion is provided above the instrument panel to prevent the pilot's head from striking the instruments in a severe crash.

The fuselage is designed to fail progressively from the front to reduce the deceleration of the cockpit, and in ordinary low-speed crashes of the kind usually associated with crop-spraying and crop-dusting the pilot's compartment should remain substantially undamaged. The top longerons in the cockpit bay are given a slight outward bulge, so that they would fail outwards in a severe head-on crash. All heavy objects or loads are forward of the cockpit and there is a 10-in space between the metal floor and the bottom of the fuselage to provide additional safety in a relatively flat crash.

The initial production version of the Pawnee had a 150 hp Lycoming engine, but production is now concentrated on the 235 hp or 260 hp Pawnee C, to which the details below apply.

Introduced in January 1967, the "C" has a number of new features. The entire top of the fuselage from the cockpit to the fin can be removed in 60 seconds to provide easy access for inspection and cleaning. A new high-capacity cockpit ventilation system is installed. Ventilating air taken in through an intake in the top of the canopy is used also to lightly pressurise the rear fuselage to keep out dust and chemicals. The engine installation has been modified to permit efficient operation under the most severe hot weather conditions. The landing gear is now fitted with oleo-pneumatic shock-absorbers. A new adjustable pilot's seat is installed and safety exits have been added on both sides of the cockpit.

The first five production Pawnees were delivered in August 1959, with subsequent aircraft leaving the assembly line at the rate of one a day, now increased to two a day. More than 4,000 Pawnees had been produced by 1 January 1970.

TYPE: Single-seat agricultural monoplane.

WINGS: Braced low-wing monoplane, based on wings of Super Cub. Streamlined Vee bracing struts on each side of fuselage, with additional short support struts. Wing section USA 35B (modified). Thickness/chord ratio 12%. Dihedral 7°. Incidence 1° 18′ at mean aerodynamic chord. Wings, ailerons and flaps are all of fabric-covered aluminium construction, with fire-resistant Duraclad plastic finish. No trim-tabs.

FUSELAGE: Basically rectangular-section welded steel-tube structure, with fabric covering and Duraclad plastic finish, except for removable metal under-skin and removable metal top of rear fuselage. Glass-fibre engine cowling.

TAIL UNIT: Wire-braced steel-tube structure with fabric covering and Duraclad plastic finish. Fixed-incidence tailplane. Balanced rudder and elevators. No trim-tabs. Cable from top of cockpit to top of rudder to deflect wires and cables.

LANDING GEAR: Non-retractable tail-wheel type. Oleo-pneumatic shock-absorbers. Main gear has two side Vees and half-axles hinged to centre-line of underside of fuselage. Cleveland 40-61 main wheels, with 8·00 × 6 4-ply tyres, pressure 25 lb/sq in (1·76 kg/cm²). Cleveland type 30-41 toe-actuated hydraulic brakes. Parking brake. Wire-cutters on leading-edge of each side Vee. Scott 8-in (20-cm) steerable tail-wheel, tyre pressure 50 lb/sq in (3·52 kg/cm²).

POWER PLANT: One 235 hp (de-rated) Lycoming O-540-B2B5 six-cylinder horizontally-opposed air-cooled engine, driving two-blade McCauley 1A200/FA84 metal fixed-pitch propeller, diameter 7 ft 0 in (2·13 m), with spinner. Optionally, one 260 hp Lycoming O-540-E engine, with two-blade fixed-pitch propeller or optional constant-speed propeller. Polyurethane rubberised fuel tank in fuselage aft of firewall, capacity 38 US gallons (144 litres), of which

36 US gallons (136 litres) are usable. Oil capacity 3 US gallons (11·4 litres).

ACCOMMODATION: Pilot on adjustable seat in specially-strengthened enclosed cockpit, with steel-tube overturn structure. Heavy-duty safety belt and shoulder harness with inertia reel. Wire-cutter mounted on centre of windshield. Combined window and door on each side, hinged at bottom. Window assemblies jettisonable for emergency exit. Cabin is heated and ventilated. Adjustable cool air vents. Air-conditioning unit optional. A jump-seat can be fitted in the hopper to transport a mechanic or loader between operations. Utility compartment under seat.

SYSTEMS: Electrical system includes 37A alternator and 12V 25Ah battery.

ELECTRONICS AND EQUIPMENT: Standard equipment includes a non-corrosive hopper/tank, installed forward of cockpit and approximately on CG. Volume is 21 cu ft (0·59 m³) or 150 US gallons (568 litres), with capacity for 1,200 lb (544 kg) of dust; quick-change boom brackets, quick-drain gascolator, quick-drain oil sump; quick dump valve to jettison hopper contents in emergency. Spray system uses similar 1-in Simplex centrifugal pump to that on PA-10-A, with spray-bars. The venturi distributor used for dry chemicals gives a total effective swath width of up to 60 ft (18·3 m). Change-over from dust to spray, and *vice versa*, takes less than five minutes. Optional side loading nozzle for liquid chemicals. Other optional equipment includes Narco Mk III Omni-navigation radio with localiser, plus Omni antenna and whip, headphone and microphone, transistorised power supply, full-flow oil filter, control lock, hand fire extinguisher, engine fire extinguisher, landing lights, navigation lights, rotating beacon, electric turn and bank indicator and metallisation.

DIMENSIONS, EXTERNAL:

Wing span	36 ft 2 in (11·02 m)
Wing chord (constant)	5 ft 3 in (1·60 m)
Wing aspect ratio	7·15
Length overall	24 ft 8½ in (7·53 m)
Height overall	7 ft 2 in (2·18 m)
Tailplane span	9 ft 6 in (2·90 m)
Wheel track	7 ft 0 in (2·13 m)
Wheelbase	18 ft 1¼ in (5·52 m)

AREAS:

Wings, gross	183 sq ft (17·0 m²)
Ailerons (total)	19·2 sq ft (1·78 m²)
Trailing-edge flaps (total)	8·4 sq ft (0·78 m²)
Fin	3·8 sq ft (0·35 m²)
Rudder	6·9 sq ft (0·64 m²)
Tailplane	13·0 sq ft (1·21 m²)
Elevators	13·7 sq ft (1·27 m²)

WEIGHTS AND LOADINGS (A=235 hp engine; B=260 hp engine, fixed-pitch propeller; C=260 hp engine, constant-speed propeller):

Weight empty:

A no dispersal equipment	1,420 lb (644 kg)
B no dispersal equipment	1,472 lb (668 kg)
C no dispersal equipment	1,488 lb (675 kg)
A duster	1,479 lb (671 kg)
B duster	1,531 lb (694 kg)
C duster	1,547 lb (702 kg)
A sprayer	1,488 lb (675 kg)
B sprayer	1,540 lb (698 kg)
C sprayer	1,556 lb (706 kg)
Max T-O and landing weight	2,900 lb (1,315 kg)
Max wing loading	15·8 lb/sq ft (77·15 kg/m²)
Max power loading	12·3 lb/hp (5·58 kg/hp)

PERFORMANCE (at Max T-O weight, except where indicated):

Max level speed at S/L:
- A no dispersal equipment 108 knots (124 mph; 200 km/h)
- B, C no dispersal equipment 111 knots (128 mph; 206 km/h)
- A duster 96 knots (110 mph; 177 km/h)
- B, C duster 98 knots (113 mph; 182 km/h)
- A sprayer 102 knots (117 mph; 188 km/h)
- B, C sprayer 104 knots (120 mph; 193 km/h)

Max permissible diving speed
135 knots (156 mph; 251 km/h)

Max cruising speed (75% power):
- A no dispersal equipment 99 knots (114 mph; 183 km/h)
- B no dispersal equipment 100 knots (115 mph; 185 km/h)
- C no dispersal equipment 101 knots (116 mph; 187 km/h)
- A, B, C duster 87 knots (100 mph; 161 km/h)
- A sprayer 91 knots (105 mph; 169 km/h)
- B, C sprayer 92 knots (106 mph; 171 km/h)

Stalling speed, flaps down
53 knots (61 mph; 98 km/h)
Stalling speed at normal landing weight of 1,700 lb (771 kg) 40 knots (46 mph; 74 km/h)

Rate of climb at S/L:
- A no dispersal equipment 700 ft (213 m)/min
- B no dispersal equipment 755 ft (230 m)/min
- C no dispersal equipment 775 ft (236 m)/min
- A duster 500 ft (152 m)/min
- B duster 555 ft (169 m)/min
- C duster 575 ft (175 m)/min
- A sprayer 630 ft (192 m)/min
- B sprayer 685 ft (209 m)/min
- C sprayer 705 ft (215 m)/min

Piper PA-25-235 Pawnee C agricultural aircraft (235 hp Lycoming O-540-B2B5 engine)

Piper PA-28-140C Cherokee two/four-seat light aircraft (150 hp Lycoming O-320 engine)

T-O run:
A no dispersal equipment	785 ft (239 m)
B no dispersal equipment	730 ft (223 m)
C no dispersal equipment	660 ft (201 m)
A duster	956 ft (291 m)
B duster	890 ft (271 m)
C duster	830 ft (253 m)
A sprayer	800 ft (244 m)
B sprayer	740 ft (226 m)
C sprayer	680 ft (207 m)

T-O to 50 ft (15 m):
A no dispersal equipment	1,350 ft (411 m)
B no dispersal equipment	1,250 ft (381 m)
C no dispersal equipment	1,200 ft (366 m)
A duster	1,470 ft (428 m)
B duster	1,420 ft (433 m)
C duster	1,370 ft (418 m)
A sprayer	1,370 ft (418 m)
B sprayer	1,270 ft (387 m)
C sprayer	1,220 ft (372 m)
Max landing run	850 ft (259 m)

Range (75% power) with max fuel:
- A no dispersal equipment
  251 nm (290 miles; 467 km)
- B no dispersal equipment
  247 nm (285 miles; 459 km)
- C no dispersal equipment
  251 nm (290 miles; 467 km)
- A duster 221 nm (255 miles; 410 km)
- B, C, duster 199 nm (230 miles; 370 km)
- A sprayer 234 nm (270 miles; 434 km)
- B, C sprayer 230 nm (265 miles; 426 km)

PIPER PA-28 CHEROKEE SERIES

The Cherokee is a low-cost all-metal low-wing monoplane which is available in 2/4-, four- and 6/7-seat versions. All except the Cherokee Arrow have a non-retractable tricycle landing gear. The Cherokee Arrow gear is retractable.

Only 1,200 parts go into its manufacture, compared with over 1,600 in the four-seat high-wing Tri-Pacer, which preceded it. The first production Cherokee flew on 10 February 1961, and production was at the rate of 12·5 aircraft per day in the Summer of 1969.

Models currently available are the Cherokee 140C (2/4-seat), Cherokee 180E (four-seat), Cherokee Arrow 200 (four-seat, retractable landing gear), Cherokee 235D (four-seat) and Cherokee Six C (6/7-seat). By 1 January 1970, Piper had built more than 5,500 Cherokee 140's; 300 Cherokee 150's; 810 Cherokee 160's; 4,500 Cherokee 180's; 1,500 Cherokee 235's and 1,500 Cherokee Six's.

Descriptions of all current versions follow.

PIPER PA-28-140C CHEROKEE

The original two-seat Cherokee 140, with 140 hp Lycoming engine, was announced in February

1964, primarily as a sporting and training aircraft to replace the Colt, but equally suitable for general transportation use. It received FAA type approval on 14 February 1964.

In the Autumn of 1965 it was superseded by the Cherokee 140-4, convertible into a full four-seater, for four adults. The conversion kit included two separate upholstered seats installed with wing nuts on the raised rear floor over the main spar, two back cushions, seat belts and attachment fittings.

To cater for this additional payload and to improve performance, the engines of all Cherokee 140-4's were rated at 150 hp, whether or not they were equipped as four-seaters. Conversion of existing Cherokee 140's to four-seat use is accomplished by installing the kit and by modifying the propeller to permit the Lycoming O-320 engine to produce 150 hp.

In 1970, the Cherokee 140B was replaced by the Cherokee 140C, which introduces a number of improvements including swingaway sun visors, bigger dynafocal engine mounts to reduce engine noise, extended range of interior and exterior colour trims and Sportsman rallye stripes on the fin. New optional items include Dyna Flair wheel fairings, four airline-type overhead air vents, and six-way adjustable front seats.

The Cherokee 140C is available in the same Custom Executive and Sportsman versions as the Cherokee 180E, with similar equipment and with the same optional electronic packages. An additional optional item, known as the Cruiser package, includes two full-size removable rear seats with ash trays, two additional fresh air vents, de luxe luggage compartment and hat shelf, Palm Beach exterior and wheel speed fairings.

The structural description of the Cherokee 180E also applies to the Cherokee 140C, except for the following details:

TYPE: Two/four-seat sporting and training light aircraft.

POWER PLANT: One 150 hp Lycoming O-320 four-cylinder horizontally-opposed air-cooled engine, driving a two-blade fixed-pitch metal propeller, diameter 6 ft 2 in (1·88 m). Two fuel tanks in wing leading-edges, with total capacity of 50 US gallons (189 litres). Standard fuel capacity of 36 US gallons (136 litres), the remaining tankage for 14 US gallons (53 litres) being regarded as a reserve.

ACCOMMODATION: Two individually-adjustable seats side-by-side in enclosed cabin, with dual controls, are standard. Two rear seats optional (see above). Door on starboard side. Large compartment aft of seats for 200 lb (90 kg) freight or baggage in two-seat version. Cabin heated and ventilated.

DIMENSIONS AND AREAS:
Same as for Cherokee 180E.

WEIGHTS AND LOADINGS:
Weight empty	1,213 lb (550 kg)
Max T-O weight	2,150 lb (975 kg)
Max wing loading	13·4 lb/sq ft (65·5 kg/m²)
Max power loading	14·3 lb/hp (6·50 kg/hp)

PERFORMANCE:
Max speed at S/L*
    123 knots (142 mph; 229 km/h)
Max cruising speed (75% power) at 7,000 ft
    (2,135 m)* 116 knots (133 mph; 214 km/h)
Econ cruising speed (60% power) at 4,000 ft
    (1,220 m)* 100 knots (115 mph; 185 km/h)
Stalling speed, flaps down
    47 knots (54 mph; 87 km/h)
Rate of climb at S/L   660 ft (201 m)/min
Service ceiling   14,300 ft (4,360 m)
T-O run   800 ft (244 m)
Landing run   535 ft (163 m)
Range (75% power at 7,000 ft = 2,130 m,
    36 US gallons fuel)
    455 nm (525 miles; 844 km)
Range (60% power at 4,000 ft = 1,220 m,
    36 US gallons fuel)
    547 nm (630 miles; 1,010 km)
Range (75% power at 7,000 ft = 2,130 m,
    50 US gallons fuel)
    629 nm (725 miles; 1,165 km)
Range (60% power at 4,000 ft = 1,220 m,
    50 US gallons fuel)
    738 nm (850 miles; 1,365 km)
*with optional wheel fairings, which add 3 mph
(5 km/h)

PIPER PA-28-180 CHEROKEE 180E

The Cherokee 180E is available in four different forms, with varying standards of equipment, as follows:

Standard Cherokee 180E. Basic model with dual controls.

Custom Cherokee 180E. As basic model with addition of Piper TruSpeed Indicator, instrument panel light, cabin dome light, navigation, landing and taxi lights, rotating beacon, radio shielding, sensitive altimeter, lighter, coat hook, step and full flow oil filter adding 7 lb (3·2 kg) to basic empty weight.

Executive Cherokee 180E. As Custom model, with addition of blind-flying instrumentation (including new 3 in pictorial gyro horizon and directional gyro, pictorial rate of turn indicator and rate of climb indicator) arranged in "T" configuration, clock, outside air temperature gauge, gyro air filter and vacuum pump, adding 20 lb (9·1 kg) to basic empty weight.

Sportsman Cherokee 180E. As Executive model, with addition of Piper electric trim, external power, and AutoNav tracker for Auto-Flite, adding 30 lb (13·6 kg) to basic empty weight.

Each of the above versions can be fitted with one of four electronic packages, as follows:

Electronic Group A. Comprises VOA-40 VOR/ILS localiser converter indicator; Mark 12 Series 90-channel VHF transceiver with 100-channel VOR/ILS nav receiver; cabin speaker, headset and microphone with jacks, antennae and wiring; and Piper AutoFlite wing levelling stability system, adding 15 lb (6·8 kg) to basic empty weight.

Electronic Group B. Same as Group A, with addition of ADF-31 automatic direction finder, with BFO and tuning meter; Mark 8 90-channel VHF transceiver plus 100-channel VOR/ILS nav indicator replacing VOA-40 and Mark 12 Series transceiver; and Piper AutoNav tracker to AutoFlite, adding 20 lb (9·1 kg) to basic empty weight.

Electronic Group C. Same as Group B, with addition of Mk 12 series 360-channel VHF transceiver plus 100-channel VOR/ILS nav receiver, VOA-4 VOR/ILS localiser converter indicator, Piper Marker Beacon indicator and receiver, transmitter selector switch, and Piper Electric Trim, adding 36 lb (16·3 kg) to basic empty weight.

Electronic Group D. Same as Group C, except for deletion of Mark 8 transceiver and Piper marker beacon indicator, and inclusion of Mark 12 series 90-channel VHF transceiver with 100-channel VOR/ILS nav receiver, VOA-50M VOR/ILS localiser converter indicator with glide slope and marker beacon indicator, UGR series glide slope receiver, and UDI series DME with ground speed indication, adding 56 lb (25·4 kg) to basic empty weight.

Most items covered under model and electronic group listings are available individually. Other optional extras include 57 three-tone Palm Beach external finishes, stainless steel control cables, mixture control indicator, T-12 series ADF, Edo 89-2000 floats, 35Ah battery, Piper AutoControl III, radio coupler to AutoControl III, fire extinguisher, Piper external power, anti-static kit, shoulder strap and inertia reel for front seats, four overhead air vents, adjustable front seats, toe brakes and heated pitot tube.

All versions of the Cherokee 180E can be fitted with the Piper AutoFlite automatic stability system. Weighing less than 4 lb (1·8 kg), this incorporates in the amplifier an electrical rate-gyro with a zero threshold which senses both

Piper PA-28-180 Cherokee 180E four-seat light aircraft (180 hp Lycoming O-360-A3A engine)

Piper PA-28-200 Cherokee Arrow with retractable landing gear (200 hp Lycoming IO-360-C1C engine)

azimuth changes and wing-down condition, and operates the ailerons as required for stability. Automatic pitch control is unnecessary on the Cherokee.

The Cherokee 180E is available in seaplane form (as **PA-28S-180**) with Edo Model 89-2000 floats, having received FAA Type Approval in this form on 10 May 1963.

Low-drag quickly-detachable Sorensen spray-gear can be fitted to the Cherokee D for agri-cultural duties. Available in kit form, the spray-gear consists of a 110 US gallon (416 litre) glass-fibre belly tank, ½-in pump, pipes and boom with openings for 17 nozzles of five different types.

TYPE: Four-seat cabin monoplane.

WINGS: Cantilever low-wing monoplane. Wing section NACA 65₂-415. Dihedral 7°. Incidence 2°. Single-spar wings, plain ailerons and slotted flaps made of aluminium alloy, except for glass-fibre wing-tips. Ailerons and four-position flaps have corrugated skin. Ground-adjustable tab in port aileron.

FUSELAGE: Aluminium alloy semi-monocoque structure. Glass-fibre engine cowling.

TAIL UNIT: Cantilever structure of aluminium alloy, except for glass-fibre tips on fin and tail-plane. Fin and rudder have corrugated metal skin. One-piece all-moving horizontal surface with combined anti-balance and trim tab. Trim-tab in rudder.

LANDING GEAR: Non-retractable tricycle type. Steerable nose-wheel. Piper oleo-pneumatic shock-absorbers. Cleveland wheels and Schenuit tyres, size 6·00 × 6, on all three wheels. Cleveland disc brakes. Parking brake. Toe brakes optional. Wheel fairings standard. Approved for operation on skis.

POWER PLANT: One 180 hp Lycoming O-360-A3A four-cylinder horizontally-opposed air-cooled engine, driving a Sensenich two-blade fixed-pitch propeller, diameter 6 ft 4 in (1·93 m), with spinner. Constant-speed propeller optional. Fuel in two tanks in wing leading-edges, with total capacity of 50 US gallons (189 litres).

ACCOMMODATION: Four persons in pairs in enclosed cabin. Individual adjustable front seats, with dual controls; bench type rear seat. Large door on starboard side. Heater and ventilation. Windshield defrosting. Baggage compartment aft of cabin, with volume of 17 cu ft (0·48 m³) and capacity of 200 lb (90 kg); door on starboard side. Rear seat removable to provide 44 cu ft (1·25 m³) cargo space. Provision for carrying stretcher.

SYSTEMS: Electrical system includes 60A alternator and 12V 25Ah battery.

ELECTRONICS AND EQUIPMENT: Details under

model and electronic group listings above; but standard equipment of all models includes external tie-down points, wing jack points and tow bar.

DIMENSIONS, EXTERNAL:
Wing span	30 ft 0 in (9·14 m)
Wing chord (constant)	5 ft 3 in (1·60 m)
Wing aspect ratio	5·63
Length overall	23 ft 6 in (7·16 m)
Height overall (landplane)	7 ft 3½ in (2·22 m)
Height overall (seaplane)	11 ft 1 in (3·38 m)
Tailplane span	10 ft 0 in (3·05 m)
Wheel track	10 ft 0 in (3·05 m)
Wheelbase	6 ft 2½ in (1·89 m)

AREAS:
Wings, gross	160 sq ft (14·86 m²)
Ailerons (total)	10·60 sq ft (0·99 m²)
Trailing-edge flaps (total)	14·60 sq ft (1·36 m²)
Fin	7·50 sq ft (0·70 m²)
Rudder	4·10 sq ft (0·38 m²)
Tailplane	24·40 sq ft (2·26 m²)

WEIGHTS AND LOADINGS:
Weight empty (Standard):
PA-28-180	1,300 lb (589 kg)
PA-28S-180	1,385 lb (628 kg)

Max T-O weight:
PA-28-180	2,400 lb (1,089 kg)
PA-28S-180	2,222 lb (1,008 kg)

Max wing loading:
PA-28-180	15·0 lb/sq ft (73·2 kg/m²)
PA-28S-180	13·9 lb/sq ft (67·9 kg/m²)

Max power loading:
PA-28-180	13·3 lb/hp (6·04 kg/hp)
PA-28S-180	12·3 lb/hp (5·58 kg/hp)

PERFORMANCE:
Max level speed at S/L:
PA-28-180	132 knots (152 mph; 245 km/h)
PA-28S-180	114 knots (131 mph; 211 km/h)

Max cruising speed (75% power):
PA-28-180 at 7,000 ft (2,135 m)*
    124 knots (143 mph; 230 km/h)
PA-28S-180 at 5,000 ft (1,525 m)
    106 knots (122 mph; 196 km/h)

Stalling speed, flaps down:
PA-28-180	50 knots (57 mph; 92 km/h)
PA-28S-180	49 knots (56 mph; 90 km/h)

Rate of climb at S/L:
PA-28-180	750 ft (229 m)/min
PA-28S-180	640 ft (195 m)/min

Service ceiling:
PA-28-180	16,400 ft (5,000 m)
PA-28S-180	11,000 ft (3,350 m)

Absolute ceiling:
PA-28-180	19,000 ft (5,791 m)

T-O run:
PA-28-180	720 ft (220 m)

Landing run:
PA-28-180   600 ft (183 m)
Range (75% power at 7,000 ft = 2,130 m, 50 US gallons fuel):
PA-28-180   629 nm (725 miles; 1,165 km)
Range (55% power at 10,000 ft = 3,050 m, 50 US gallons fuel):
PA-28-180   660 nm (760 miles; 1,223 km)
PA-28S-180   568 nm (655 miles; 1,054 km)
*with optional wheel fairings, which add 2·6 knots (3 mph; 5 km/h)

PIPER PA-28-200 CHEROKEE ARROW

The Cherokee Arrow is structurally similar to the PA-28-180 Cherokee 180E, but has a retractable landing gear. A fuel-injection engine and constant-speed propeller are standard.

In 1970 both the 180 hp and 200 hp versions of the Cherokee Arrow became designated PA-28-200. Optional equipment and electronics are the same as for the Cherokee 180E.

The tricycle landing gear is retracted hydraulically, with an electrically-operated pump supplying the hydraulic pressure. In addition to the usual "gear up" warning horn and red light, the Cherokee Arrow has an automatic extension system which drops the landing gear automatically if power is reduced and airspeed drops below 91 knots (105 mph; 169 km/h). The sensing system consists of a small probe mounted on the port side of the fuselage. Being located in the propeller slipstream, it can differentiate between a climb with power on and an approach to land with power reduced. A free-fall emergency extension system is also fitted. An "anti-retraction" system guards against premature retraction of the landing gear below an airspeed of 85 mph (137 kmh) at take-off, or accidental retraction on the ground. There is also a manual override lever by which the pilot can hold the landing gear retracted as air speed falls below 105 mph.

The description of the PA-28-180 Cherokee 180E applies also to the Cherokee Arrow, except for the following details:

LANDING GEAR: Retractable tricycle type, with single wheel on each unit. Hydraulic retraction, main units inward into wings, nose unit rearward. All units fitted with oleo-pneumatic shock-absorbers. Main wheels and tyres size 6·00 × 6, four-ply rating. Nose-wheel and tyre size 5·00 × 5, four-ply rating. High-capacity dual hydraulic brakes and parking brake.

POWER PLANT: One 180 hp Lycoming IO-360-B1E four-cylinder horizontally-opposed air-cooled engine, driving a two-blade constant-speed propeller, diameter 6 ft 4 in (1·93 m), with spinner. Optionally, one 200 hp Lycoming IO-360-C1C four-cylinder horizontally-opposed air-cooled engine, driving a two-blade constant-speed propeller, diameter 6 ft 2 in (1·88 m), with spinner. Fuel system as for Cherokee 180E.

DIMENSIONS AND AREAS:
Same as for Cherokee 180E, except:
Length overall   24 ft 2 in (7·37 m)
Height overall   8 ft 0 in (2·44 m)
Wheel track   10 ft 6 in (3·20 m)
Wheelbase   7 ft 5 in (2·26 m)
WEIGHTS AND LOADINGS (A = 180 hp and B = 200 hp engine):
Weight empty:
A   1,420 lb (644 kg)
B   1,459 lb (661 kg)
Max T-O weight:
A   2,500 lb (1,135 kg)
B   2,600 lb (1,179 kg)
Max wing loading:
A   15·6 lb/sq ft (76·17 kg/m²)
B   16·3 lb/sq ft (79·6 kg/m²)
Max power loading:
A   13·9 lb/hp (6·30 kg/hp)
B   13·0 lb/hp (5·9 kg/hp)
PERFORMANCE (at max T-O weight; A = 180 hp and B = 200 hp engine):
Max level speed:
A   148 knots (170 mph; 274 km/h)
B   153 knots (176 mph; 283 km/h)
Max cruising speed (75% power) at optimum altitude:
A   141 knots (162 mph; 261 km/h)
B   144 knots (166 mph; 267 km/h)
Stalling speed, wheels and flaps down:
A   53 knots (61 mph; 98·5 km/h)
B   56 knots (64 mph; 103 km/h)
Rate of climb at S/L:
A   875 ft (265 m)/min
B   910 ft (277 m)/min
Service ceiling:
A   15,000 ft (4,575 m)
B   16,000 ft (4,875 m)
Absolute ceiling:
A   17,000 ft (5,181 m)
B   18,000 ft (5,486 m)
T-O run:
A   820 ft (250 m)
B   770 ft (235 m)
Landing run:
A   776 ft (237 m)
B   780 ft (238 m)
Range with max fuel, 75% power at optimum altitude:

Piper PA-28-235D Cherokee 235D (235 hp Lycoming O-540-B4B5 engine)

A   744 nm (857 miles; 1,379 km)
B   703 nm (810 miles; 1,300 km)
Range with max fuel, 55% power at optimum altitude:
A   864 nm (995 miles; 1,601 km)
B   825 nm (950 miles; 1,525 km)

PIPER PA-28-235D CHEROKEE 235D

The Cherokee 235D retains the basic layout of the Cherokee 180E, and utilises many of the latter's components and systems; but its basic structural members have been strengthened considerably to cater for a more powerful engine and increased gross weight.

The original 235 first flew in prototype form on 9 May 1962, and received FAA type approval on 15 June 1963. The improved 235D, to which the data below apply, was introduced in October 1969.

The power plant is a 235 hp Lycoming O-540-B4B5 six-cylinder horizontally-opposed air-cooled engine, driving a McCauley 1P235 PFA 80 two-blade fixed-pitch metal propeller or optional Hartzell HC-C2YK-1/8468A-4 constant-speed propeller. Normal fuel capacity of 50 US gallons (189 litres) is supplemented by two tanks in the wingtips, containing a total of 34 US gallons (129 litres) of fuel. The tips themselves, made of glass-fibre, extend the wing span by 2 ft 0 in (0·61 m), giving an aspect ratio of 5·97.

The Cherokee 235D has a glass-fibre engine cowling made in two pieces (top and bottom) which can be removed easily to expose the entire engine for servicing. A landing light is incorporated in the nose directly under the propeller spinner and the ram air scoop for the carburettor is offset to accommodate the exhaust system.

In most other airframe details, the Cherokee 235D is similar to the Cherokee 180E, but toe brakes (port side) and wheel fairings are standard equipment. It is available in the same Custom, Executive and Sportsman models as the Cherokee 180E, with similar equipment and with the same optional electronic packages.

The Cherokee 235D is FAA approved to carry a useful load greater than its empty weight. Even the most elaborately-equipped Sportsman model, with full panel, multiple radio and auto-pilot, can carry four 170 lb (77 kg) people, full fuel, oil and 200 lb (90 kg) of baggage and still have some weight allowance to spare. As a result, performance figures are given for both max AUW and an AUW of 2,400 lb (1,089 kg), which includes four 170 lb (77 kg) people, oil and approximately 45 US gallons (170 litres) of fuel.

DIMENSIONS, EXTERNAL:
Same as for Cherokee 180E, except:
Wing span   32 ft 0 in (9·75 m)
Length   23 ft 8½ in (7·22 m)
Height overall   7 ft 1¼ in (2·17 m)
Tailplane span   10 ft 0 in (3·05 m)
Wheel track   10 ft 0 in (3·05 m)
Wheelbase   6 ft 2½ in (1·89 m)

AREAS:
Same as for Cherokee 180E, except:
Wings, gross   171·6 sq ft (15·94 m²)
Tailplane   26·5 sq ft (2·46 m²)

WEIGHTS AND LOADINGS:
Weight empty (standard)   1,467 lb (665 kg)
Max T-O weight   2,900 lb (1,315 kg)
Max wing loading   17·0 lb/sq ft (83 kg/m²)
Max power loading   12·4 lb/hp (5·62 kg/hp)
PERFORMANCE (A = max T-O weight, B = more normal AUW of 2,400 lb = 1,089 kg):
Max level speed at S/L:
A   144 knots (166 mph; 267 km/h)
B   147 knots (169 mph; 272 km/h)
Max cruising speed (75% power) at 7,000 ft (2,130 m):
A   135 knots (156 mph; 251 km/h)
B   138 knots (159 mph; 256 km/h)
Stalling speed, flaps down:
A   53 knots (60 mph; 96·5 km/h)
B   48 knots (55 mph; 88·5 km/h)
Rate of climb at S/L:
A   825 ft (252 m)/min
B   1,250 ft (380 m)/min
Service ceiling:
A   14,500 ft (4,420 m)
B   18,500 ft (5,640 m)
Absolute ceiling:
A   16,500 ft (5,029 m)
B   20,500 ft (6,248 m)
T-O run:
A   800 ft (244 m)
B   600 ft (183 m)
T-O to 50 ft (15 m):
A   1,360 ft (415 m)
B   1,040 ft (317 m)
Landing from 50 ft (15 m):
A   1,300 ft (396 m)
B   1,060 ft (323 m)
Landing run:
A   680 ft (207 m)
B   550 ft (168 m)
Range with max fuel (75% power) at 7,000 ft (2,130 m):
A   812 nm (935 miles; 1,505 km)

Piper PA-32 Cherokee Six C

Range with max fue 55% power) at 10,000 ft
(3,050 m):
A   981 nm (1,130 miles; 1,820 km)

PIPER PA-32 CHEROKEE SIX C

The prototype of the PA-32 Cherokee Six
(N9999W) was flown for the first time on 6
December 1963, followed by the first production
model (N9998W) on 17 September 1964. FAA
Type Approval was received on 4 March 1965.

The original version was a six-seater, but the
model introduced in October 1966 offered an
optional seventh seat. The 1969 Cherokee
Six B introduced increased cabin space, achieved
by moving the instrument panel forward.
Additional shoulder, hip and leg room was provided by moving the seats one inch away from the
fuselage walls. The new features incorporated
in the 1970 Cherokee 140C apply also to the
Cherokee Six C and wheel speed fairings are
standard for both Custom and Executive
versions.

It is available with two alternative power
plants, as follows:

PA-32-260. Basic version with 260 hp Lycoming O-540-E six-cylinder horizontally-opposed air-
cooled engine, driving a two-blade fixed-pitch or
optional constant-speed propeller, diameter
6 ft 10 in (2·08 m).

PA-32-300. More powerful version with 300 hp
Lycoming IO-540-K six-cylinder horizontally-
opposed air-cooled engine, driving a two-blade
constant-speed propeller, diameter 6 ft 8 in (2·03
m). Available also as floatplane, on Edo 3430
floats and with propeller of 7 ft 0 in (2·13 m)
diameter.

Overall dimensions are increased by comparison
with the two/four- and four-seat versions of the
Cherokee, but the basic structural description of
the Cherokee 180E and Cherokee 235D applies
generally to the Cherokee Six C also. It is available in the same Custom, Executive and Sportsman models as the Cherokee 180E, with similar
equipment and with the same optional electronic
packages except that both the 260 hp and 300 hp
versions have been certified with a FluiDyne ski
installation, available as an optional extra.

As part of Piper's continuous research programme, a Cherokee Six was converted into a
three-engined aircraft in 1965, by fitting two
additional Lycoming engines on the wings.
Cruising speed is reported to have been 165 knots
(190 mph; 305 km/h).

It was reported in 1969 that Piper had begun
flight testing a twin-engined version of the
Cherokee Six, with retractable landing gear and
two 180 hp Lycoming O-360-A3A engines, which
may be introduced in 1970.

POWER PLANT: One 260 hp or 300 hp Lycoming
six-cylinder horizontally-opposed air-cooled
engine, driving a two-blade propeller. Two fuel
tanks in inner wings, total capacity 50
US gallons (189 litres). Two auxiliary tanks in
glass-fibre wingtips, with total capacity of 34
US gallons (129 litres). Total standard fuel
capacity, with auxiliary tanks, 84 US gallons
(318 litres). Refuelling point above each tank.
Oil capacity 3 US gallons (11·5 litres).

ACCOMMODATION: Enclosed cabin, seating six
people in pairs. Optional seventh seat between
two centre seats. Dual controls standard. Two
forward-hinged doors, one on starboard side at
front and the other on port side at rear. Space
for 100 lb (45 kg) baggage at rear of cabin, and
another 100 lb (45 kg) forward, between engine
and instrument panel. A set of four pieces
of matched luggage to fit the nose baggage
compartment is provided as standard. Passenger seats easily removable to provide up to
110 cu ft (3·11 m³) of cargo space inside cabin,
or room for stretcher and one or two attendants.
Large optional upward hinged utility door
adjacent to rear door provides loading entrance
nearly 5 ft (1·5 m) wide.

DIMENSIONS, EXTERNAL:
Wing span	32 ft 9½ in (9·99 m)
Length overall	27 ft 8¼ in (8·45 m)
Height overall:	
landplane	7 ft 11 in (2·41 m)
floatplane	11 ft 3½ in (3·44 m)
Tailplane span	12 ft 10½ in (3·92 m)
Wheel track	10 ft 7 in (3·22 m)
Wheelbase	7 ft 10 in (2·39 m)
Cabin door (rear, port):	
Height	2 ft 10 in (0·86 m)
Width	3 ft 1 in (0·94 m)

DIMENSIONS, INTERNAL:
Cabin:	
Length, panel to rear wall	9 ft 11 in (3·02 m)
Max width	4 ft 1 in (1·24 m)
Max height	4 ft 0½ in (1·23 m)
Baggage compartment volume:	
Forward	8 cu ft (0·23 m³)
Aft	20 cu ft (0·57 m³)

AREA:
Wings, gross	174·5 sq ft (16·21 m²)

WEIGHTS AND LOADINGS (FP=fixed-pitch
propeller, CS=constant-speed propeller):
Weight empty, equipped	
PA-32-260C FP	1,688 lb (765 kg)
PA-32-260C CS	1,713 lb (777 kg)
PA-32-260C Skiplane	1,930 lb (875 kg)

Piper PA-30C Twin Comanche C (two 160 hp Lycoming IO-320-B engines)

PA-32-300C	1,789 lb (811 kg)
PA-32-300C Floatplane	2,140 lb (970 kg)
PA-32-300C Skiplane	1,988 lb (901 kg)
Max T-O weight:	
All versions, except PA-32-260C Skiplane	3,400 lb (1,542 kg)
PA-32-260C Skiplane	3,200 lb (1,451 kg)
Max wing loading:	
All versions, except PA-32-260C skiplane	19·5 lb/sq ft (95 kg/m²)
Max power loading:	
PA-32-260C	13·1 lb/hp (5·9 kg/hp)
PA-32-300C Landplane, Floatplane	11·3 lb/hp (5·1 kg/hp)

PERFORMANCE (at max T-O weight, FP=fixed-
pitch, CS=constant-speed propeller):
Max level speed:	
PA-32-260C FP	146 knots (168 mph; 270 km/h)
PA-32-260C CS	144 knots (166 mph; 267 km/h)
PA-32-260C Skiplane	123 knots (142 mph; 229 km/h)
PA-32-300C	151 knots (174 mph; 279 km/h)
PA-32-300C Floatplane	133 knots (153 mph; 246 km/h)
PA-32-300C Skiplane	128 knots (147 mph; 237 km/h)
Max cruising speed (75% power) at optimum altitude:	
PA-32-260C FP	139 knots (160 mph; 258 km/h)
PA-32-260C CS	139 knots (160 mph; 258 km/h)
PA-32-260C Skiplane	116 knots (134 mph; 216 km/h)
PA-32-300C	146 knots (168 mph; 270 km/h)
PA-32-300C Floatplane	128 knots (147 mph; 237 km/h)
PA-32-300C Skiplane	120 knots (138 mph; 222 km/h)
Stalling speed, flaps down:	
Landplane versions	55 knots (63 mph; 102 km/h)
PA-32-260C Skiplane	57 knots (65 mph; 105 km/h)
PA-32-300C Floatplane	58 knots (66 mph; 106 km/h)
PA-32-300C Skiplane	59 knots (67 mph; 108 km/h)
Rate of climb at S/L:	
PA-32-260C FP	760 ft (232 m)/min
PA-32-260C CS	850 ft (260 m)/min
PA-32-260C Skiplane	730 ft (223 m)/min
PA-32-300C	1,050 ft (320 m)/min
PA-32-300C Floatplane	750 ft (229 m)/min
PA-32-300C Skiplane	865 ft (264 m)/min
Service ceiling:	
PA-32-260C FP	13,000 ft (3,960 m)
PA-32-260C CS	14,500 ft (4,420 m)
PA-32-260C Skiplane	12,000 ft (3,660 m)
PA-32-300C	16,250 ft (4,950 m)
PA-32-300C Floatplane	12,100 ft (3,690 m)
PA-32-300C Skiplane	13,000 ft (3,960 m)
T-O run:	
PA-32-260C FP	810 ft (247 m)
PA-32-260C CS	740 ft (226 m)
PA-32-300C	700 ft (213 m)
PA-32-300C Floatplane	1,430 ft (436 m)
T-O to 50 ft (15 m):	
PA-32-260C FP	1,360 ft (415 m)
PA-32-260C CS	1,240 ft (378 m)
PA-32-300C Landplane	1,140 ft (348 m)
Landing from 50 ft (15 m):	
Landplane versions	1,000 ft (305 m)
Landing run:	
Landplane versions	630 ft (192 m)
Range (75% power) basic fuel:	
PA-32-260C	495 nm (570 miles; 917 km)
PA-32-300C	456 nm (525 miles; 845 km)
PA-32-300C Floatplane	395 nm (455 miles; 732 km)
Range (75% power), with auxiliary fuel:	
PA-32-260C	833 nm (960 miles; 1,545 km)
PA-32-300C	764 nm (880 miles; 1,415 km)
PA-32-300C Floatplane	673 nm (775 miles; 1,245 km)
Range (55% power) basic fuel:	
PA-32-260C	607 nm (700 miles; 1,125 km)

PA-32-300C	547 nm (630 miles; 1,015 km)
PA-32-300C Floatplane	468 nm (540 miles; 870 km)
Range (55% power), with auxiliary fuel:	
PA-32-260C	1,016 nm (1,170 miles; 1,780 km)
PA-32-300C	920 nm (1,060 miles; 1,705 km)
PA-32-300C Floatplane	798 nm (920 miles; 1,480 km)

PIPER PA-30C TWIN COMANCHE C

The original four-seat Twin Comanche was
announced in May 1963, as a replacement for
the Apache H. The prototype flew for the first
time on 7 November 1962, followed by the first
production model on 3 May 1963. FAA type
Approval was received on 5 February 1963.
It was superseded in 1965 by the improved four/
six-seat Twin Comanche B, as described in the
1968-69 Jane's.

A new version, designated Twin Comanche C,
was announced in August 1968, and this introduced a number of improvements, including
new instrument panel, new interior and exterior
paint schemes, recessed window curtains and
improvements in the cabin heating and ventilation system.

In addition, the simplified power management
system, introduced by Piper with the Aztec D,
is now recommended for the Twin Comanche C
and Turbo Twin Comanche C.

The Twin Comanche is available in the following
versions.

Standard Twin Comanche C. Basic model, as
described in detail below.

Custom Twin Comanche C. As basic model,
with addition of full blind-flying instrumentation
(new 3 in pictorial gyro horizon and directional
gyro, pictorial rate of turn indicator and
rate of climb indicator), clock, Piper TruSpeed
Indicator in place of standard ASI, dual vacuum
system, full-flow oil filters, dual 70A alternators and heated pitot tube, adding 42 lb (19 kg)
to basic empty weight.

Sportsman Twin Comanche C. As Custom
model, with addition of Piper external power,
glare-ban instrument lights, fifth and sixth family
seats, Palm Beach de luxe interior and external
finish, and curtains, adding 77 lb (35 kg) to basic
empty weight.

Turbo Twin Comanche C. Turbocharged version, described separately.

PA-39 Twin Comanche C/R and **Turbo Twin
Comanche C/R.** Versions with counter-rotating
propellers, described separately.

The above versions of the Twin Comanche C
are available with a choice of electronic packages
as follows:

Electronic Group A. Piper AutoControl III
automatic flight system with heading lock and
course selector, Mark 12 series 90-channel VHF
transceiver plus 100-channel nav receiver, VOA-40
VOR/ILS localiser converter indicator, ADF-31
series ADF with BFO and tuning meter, microphone, headset, radio selector panel and isolation
amplifier, adding 33 lb (14·9 kg) to basic empty
weight.

Electronic Group B. Same as Group A, with
addition of radio coupling to autopilot, Piper
electric trim, Mark 12 series 360-channel VHF
transceiver plus 100-channel nav receiver, a
second VOA-40 VOR/ILS, Piper PM-1 marker
beacon indicator and receiver and anti-static kit,
adding 57 lb (25·8 kg) to basic empty weight.

Electronic Group C. Piper AltiMatic III automatic pilot with pitch control, course and altitude
pre-select and hold and automatic electric trim,
radio coupling to autopilot, glide-slope coupling
to autopilot, Mark 12 series 90-channel VHF
transceiver plus 100-channel nav receiver, Mark
12 series 360-channel VHF transceiver plus 100-
channel nav receiver, VOA-40 VOR/ILS localiser
converter indicator, VOA-50M VOR/ILS localiser
converter indicator with glide-slope, ADF-31
series ADF with BFO and tuning meter, Piper
noise-cancelling microphone, headset, radio select-
or panel, isolation amplifier, anti-static kit,
UDI-4 series DME with GSI, UGR-2 series glide-

slope receiver, Piper marker beacon receiver, glide slope coupling to AltiMatic and AT-6A series transponder, adding 92 lb (41·7 kg) to basic empty weight. Other optional extras include a UAT-1 transponder, Bendix ADF T-12, Mark 12 100-channel transceiver in place of 90-channel, Mark 12 380-channel transceiver in place of 360-channel, VOA-8 in place of VOA-40, VOA-9 in place of VOA-50M, boom microphone with control-wheel button, Piper microphone and microphone holder, dual tachometer and hour meter, starboard toe-brakes, oxygen system, heated windshield, wing and propeller de-icing system, wingtip fuel tanks, alternate static source, mixture control indicator, Piper electric trim and fire extinguisher.

More than 2,000 Twin Comanches had been produced by 1 January 1970.

In a Twin Comanche, Mr Max Conrad set a Class CIe distance record on 24-26 December 1964, by flying 6,841·6 nm (7,878·26 miles; 12,678·83 km) non-stop from Cape Town, South Africa, to St Petersburg, Florida, in 56·8 hours. Carrying 720 US gallons (2,727 litres) of fuel, the aircraft weighed 6,614 lb (3,000 kg) at take-off.

Type: Four-seat twin-engined light aircraft.

Wings: Cantilever low-wing monoplane. Wing section NACA 64_2A215. Dihedral 5°. Incidence 2°. Sweep-forward at quarter-chord 2° 30′. Three-spar aluminium structure. Aluminium ailerons and electrically-operated single-slotted extensible flaps. No trim-tabs. Provision for rubber-boot de-icing system.

Fuselage: Semi-monocoque aluminium structure.

Tail Unit: Cantilever all-metal stressed-skin structure, with one-piece all-flying horizontal surfaces. Combined trim and anti-servo tab in horizontal surfaces.

Landing Gear: Retractable tricycle type, main units retracting inward into wings, nose-wheel rearward. Electric actuation with manual emergency extension. Piper oleo-pneumatic shock-absorbers. Steerable nose-wheel. Cleveland type 40-34 main wheels with Schenuit 6·00 × 6 6-ply tyres. Cleveland type 38501 nose-wheel with Schenuit 6·00 × 6 6-ply tyre. Tyre pressure 42 lb/sq in (2·95 kg/cm²). Cleveland 30-23 brakes.

Power Plant: Two 160 hp Lycoming IO-320-B four-cylinder horizontally-opposed air-cooled engines, each driving a Hartzell HC-E2YL-2/7663-4 constant-speed fully-feathering metal propeller, diameter 6 ft 0 in (1·83 m). Fuel in two main tanks in wings, each of 30 US gallons (113·5 litres) capacity (27 US gallons = 102 litres usable), and two auxiliary tanks in wings, each of 15 US gallons (57 litres) capacity. Standard fuel capacity 90 US gallons (341 litres) of which 84 US gallons (318 litres) are usable. Optional wingtip tanks with total capacity of 30 US gallons (113·5 litres). Max total fuel capacity with wingtip tanks 120 US gallons (454·5 litres). Refuelling points (4) recessed in top of wing. Total oil capacity 4 US gallons (15 litres).

Accommodation: Four persons in pairs in enclosed cabin in standard version. Third row of two seats optional. Dual controls, ash trays, cigarette lighter, cabin speaker, coat hooks, double glazed windows and two sun visors standard. Baggage compartment aft of cabin, capacity 20 cu ft (0·57 m³), with tie-downs and exterior door on port side. Heating, ventilation, windshield defrosting and soundproofing standard. Main cabin door on starboard side, forward of main spar. Rear seats quickly removable for stretcher or cargo installation.

Electronics and Equipment: As listed above. Standard items include landing, navigation, instrument and cabin dome lights and rotating beacon.

Dimensions, external:

Wing span: standard	36 ft 0 in (10·97 m)
over tip-tanks	36 ft 9½ in (11·22 m)
Wing chord at root	7 ft 1 in (2·16 m)
Wing chord at tip	3 ft 3 in (0·99 m)
Wing aspect ratio	7·28
Length overall	25 ft 2 in (7·67 m)
Height overall	8 ft 2⅞ in (2·51 m)
Tailplane span	12 ft 6 in (3·81 m)
Wheel track	9 ft 9½ in (2·98 m)
Wheelbase	7 ft 3⅝ in (2·23 m)
Baggage compartment door:	
Height	1 ft 8 in (0·50 m)
Width	1 ft 8 in (0·50 m)

Areas:

Wings, gross	178 sq ft (16·54 m²)
Ailerons (total)	14·0 sq ft (1·30 m²)
Trailing-edge flaps (total)	21·0 sq ft (1·95 m²)
Fin	9·0 sq ft (0·84 m²)
Rudder	5·9 sq ft (0·55 m²)
Tailplane	32·5 sq ft (3·02 m²)

Weights and Loadings:

Weight empty (Standard)	2,238 lb (1,015 kg)
Baggage	250 lb (113 kg)
Normal max T-O and landing weight	3,600 lb (1,633 kg)
Max T-O weight with wingtip tanks	3,725 lb (1,690 kg)
Normal max wing loading	20·22 lb/sq ft (98·72 kg/m²)
Normal max power loading	11·25 lb (5·10 kg) hp

The Piper PA-39 Twin Comanche C/R

Performance (at max T-O weight):

Max level speed at S/L	178 knots (205 mph; 330 km/h)
Max permissible diving speed	236 knots (272 mph; 438 km/h)
Normal cruising speed	172 knots (198 mph; 319 km/h)
Intermediate cruising speed	170 knots (196 mph; 315 km/h)
Econ cruising speed	163 knots (188 mph; 303 km/h)
Long-range cruising speed	155 knots (178 mph; 286 km/h)
Stalling speed, flaps down, power off	60 knots (69 mph; 111 km/h)
Rate of climb at S/L	1,460 ft (445 m)/min
Rate of climb at S/L, one engine out	260 ft (79 m)/min
Absolute ceiling	20,000 ft (6,100 m)
Absolute ceiling, one engine out	7,100 ft (2,164 m)
T-O run	940 ft (287 m)
T-O to 50 ft (15 m)	1,530 ft (466 m)
Landing from 50 ft (15 m)	1,870 ft (570 m)
Landing run	1,215 ft (370 m)
Range with max standard fuel:	
Normal cruising speed	720 nm (830 miles; 1,335 km)
Intermediate cruising speed	894 nm (1,030 miles; 1,655 km)
Econ cruising speed	963 nm (1,110 miles; 1,785 km)
Long-range cruising speed	1,042 nm (1,200 miles; 1,930 km)

PIPER PA-30C TURBO TWIN COMANCHE C

The Turbo Twin Comanche C is identical in every way with the Twin Comanche C, described above, except that it is powered by 160 hp Lycoming IO-320-C1A engines with Rajay turbochargers. Wingtip fuel tanks, Piper mixture control indicator and an oxygen system are standard on this version, as are all the items listed for the Twin Comanche C Sportsman except for Palm Beach trim and curtains.

Weights and Loadings:

Weight empty	2,384 lb (1,081 kg)
Max T-O weight	3,725 lb (1,690 kg)
Max wing loading	20·9 lb/sq ft (102·0 kg/m²)
Max power loading	11·65 lb/hp (5·28 kg/hp)

Performance (at max T-O weight):

Max level speed at 12,000 ft (3,650 m)	198 knots (228 mph; 367 km/h)
Max level speed at 24,000 ft (7,300 m)	214 knots (246 mph; 396 km/h)
Turbo cruising speed at 12,000 ft (3,650 m)	192 knots (221 mph; 356 km/h)
Turbo cruising speed at 24,000 ft (7,300 m)	208 knots (240 mph; 386 km/h)
Intermediate cruising speed at 12,000 ft (3,650 m)	182 knots (209 mph; 336 km/h)
Intermediate cruising speed at 24,000 ft (7,300 m)	198 knots (228 mph; 367 km/h)
Econ cruising speed at 12,000 ft (3,650 m)	168 knots (193 mph; 311 km/h)
Econ cruising speed at 24,000 ft (7,300 m)	180 knots (207 mph; 333 km/h)
Long-range cruising speed at 12,000 ft (3,650 m)	160 knots (184 mph; 296 km/h)
Long-range cruising speed at 24,000 ft (7,300 m)	168 knots (193 mph; 311 km/h)
Stalling speed, flaps down	60 knots (69 mph; 111·5 km/h)
Rate of climb at S/L	1,290 ft (393 m)/min
Rate of climb at 10,000 ft (3,050 m)	1,160 ft (354 m)/min
Rate of climb at S/L, one engine out	225 ft (69 m)/min
Absolute ceiling	over 30,000 ft (9,150 m)
Single engine absolute ceiling	17,000 ft (5,180 m)
T-O run	990 ft (302 m)
T-O to 50 ft (15 m)	1,590 ft (485 m)
Landing from 50 ft (15 m)	1,900 ft (579 m)
Landing run	1,250 ft (381 m)
Range, with max standard fuel:	
Turbo cruising speed at 12,000 ft (3,650 m)	946 nm (1,090 miles; 1,750 km)
Turbo cruising speed at 24,000 ft (7,300 m)	1,102 nm (1,270 miles; 2,040 km)
Intermediate cruising speed at 12,000 ft (3,650 m)	1,172 nm (1,350 miles; 2,170 km)
Intermediate cruising speed at 24,000 ft (7,300 m)	1,346 nm (1,550 miles; 2,490 km)
Econ cruising speed at 12,000 ft (3,650 m)	1,290 nm (1,485 miles; 2,389 km)
Econ cruising speed at 24,000 ft (7,300 m)	1,450 nm (1,670 miles; 2,685 km)
Long-range cruising speed at 12,000 ft (3,650 m)	1,333 nm (1,535 miles; 2,470 km)
Long-range cruising speed at 24,000 ft (7,300 m)	1,485 nm (1,710 miles; 2,750 km)

PIPER PA-39 TWIN COMANCHE C/R AND TURBO TWIN COMANCHE C/R

It was announced early in February 1970 that Piper had introduced new versions of the PA-30C Twin Comanche C and Turbo Twin Comanche C. These two new aircraft, which have the company designation PA-39, have counter-rotating (C/R) propellers, which Piper claim offer significant advantages. These include transition from climb, cruise and approach speeds without need for trim adjustments; elimination of the so-called critical engine, offering equal climb performance from either engine in an engine-out situation; and improved flight characteristics in all flight conditions due to balanced airflow over each side of the aircraft.

Counter-rotation of the propellers has been achieved by reversing the direction of rotation of the starboard engine. Lycoming engineers effected this modification by reversing certain components of the starboard engine and changing the firing order, so producing a mirror-image of the port engine.

The description of the PA-30C Twin Comanche C and the Turbo Twin Comanche C applies also to the PA-39 Twin Comanche C/R and Turbo Twin Comanche C/R, except for the following performance figures:

Performance (at max T-O weight):

Stalling speed	61 knots (70 mph; 113 km/h)
Service ceiling:	
Twin Comanche C/R	20,000 ft (6,095 m)
Turbo Twin Comanche C/R	25,000 ft (7,620 m)
Service ceiling, one engine out:	
Twin Comanche C/R	7,100 ft (2,165 m)
Turbo Twin Comanche C/R	12,600 ft (3,480 m)
Landing run:	
Twin Comanche C/R	700 ft (213 m)
Turbo Twin Comanche C/R	725 ft (221 m)

PIPER PA-31-300 NAVAJO

First flown at Lock Haven on 30 September 1964, the Navajo was then described as the first of a new Piper series of larger executive aircraft, for corporate and commuter airline service. It is available with normally-aspirated or turbocharged engines, the latter version being known as the Turbo Navajo (described separately). There is also a pressurised version of the Navajo, which is described separately.

Deliveries began on 17 April 1967 and more than 500 Navajos had been produced by 1 January 1970.

The current version of the Navajo introduced an optional nine-seat interior, with cabin ground ventilation fan, in place of standard six/eight-seat interior.

There are three models of the Navajo, as follows:

Standard Navajo. Six individual seats, in pairs, with centre aisle. Rear baggage compartment and wardrobe area. Seventh, eighth and ninth seats optional.

Commuter Navajo. Eight individual seats in pairs. Pilot/cabin divider aft of front pair, with two pilot manual racks, two cabin magazine racks, "no smoking" and "fasten seat belts" signs, aft cabin divider with luggage shelf and ground ventilation fan. Luggage capacity 350 lb (159 kg).

Executive Navajo. Six individual seats, in pairs. Pilot/cabin divider as in Commuter version. Seats in main cabin face each other, with foldaway tables between. Curtained-off area at rear contains refreshment unit, luggage

Piper Turbo Navajo six/nine-seat turbosupercharged executive transport aircraft (two 310 hp Lycoming TIO-540-A engines) (*Air Portraits*)

compartment and shelf, and toilet. Seventh, eighth and ninth seats available in place of refreshment unit and toilet.

Each of the above models may be fitted with one of the following electronic packages:

Electronic Group A. Two Mk 12 series 360-channel VHF transceivers with 100-channel VOR/ILS receiver, VOA-4 VOR/ILS localiser converter indicator, VOA-5 VOR/ILS localiser converter indicator with glide-slope indication, ADF T-12 automatic direction finder, KN 60 DME with ground speed indication, UGR glide-slope receiver, Piper marker beacon, Piper anti-static antennae and wicks, Piper AltiMatic III three-axis autopilot with automatic electric trim, radio coupler to autopilot, TPR 600 transponder, passenger address system, headset, microphone and radio selector panel. Total additional weight 84 lb (38 kg).

Electronic Group B. As Group A, but only one Mk 12 VHF transceiver, no VOA-4, no DME and no TPR 600 transponder. Additional items are second ADF T-12, SA-14R HF transceiver with automatic coupler, microphone replaced by boom microphone with microphone button on control wheel. Total additional weight 97 lb (44 kg).

Electronic Group C. Two KNR-600 remote-mounted omni/localiser 200-channel nav receivers, KGM-690 remote-mounted marker beacon and glide-slope receivers, KAA-445 dual audio amplifier, two KTR-900 remote-mounted 380-channel communications transceivers, KDM-700 DME with digital read-out of distance, ground speed and time to station, DADF-1 series ADF, Bendix RDR-100 weather radar, Piper anti-static antennae and wicks, Piper AltiMatic III autopilot, radio coupler to autopilot, TPR-600 series transponder, passenger address system, headset, microphone and radio selector panel. Total additional weight 137 lb (62 kg).

Other combinations of the above equipment are available optionally, as is the Piper AltiMatic H-4 autopilot, together with an extensive range of radar and radio equipment.

TYPE: Six/nine-seat corporate and commuter airline transport.

WINGS: Cantilever low-wing monoplane. Wing section NACA 63₂415 at root, NACA 63₁212 at tip. 1° aerodynamic twist. 2° 30′ geometric twist. All-metal structure, with heavy stepped-down main spar, front and rear spars, lateral stringers, ribs and stressed skin. Wings spliced on centre-line with heavy steel plates. Flush riveted forward of main spar. Wing-root leading-edge extended forward between nacelle and fuselage. Glass-fibre wingtips. Balanced ailerons are interconnected with rudder. Trim-tab in starboard aileron. Electrically-operated flaps. Pneumatic de-icing boots optional.

FUSELAGE: Conventional all-metal semi-monocoque structure.

TAIL UNIT: Cantilever all-metal structure, with swept-back vertical surfaces. Variable-incidence tailplane. Trim-tabs in rudder and starboard elevator. Optional pneumatic de-icing boots.

LANDING GEAR: Hydraulically-actuated retractable tricycle type, with single wheel on each unit. Manual hydraulic emergency extension. Main wheels and tyres size 6·50 × 10, eight-ply rating, pressure 60 lb/sq in (4·22 kg/cm²). Steerable nose-wheel and tyre size 6·00 × 6, six-ply rating, pressure 42 lb/sq in (2·95 kg/cm²). Toe-controlled hydraulic disc brakes. Main wheel doors close when gear is fully extended.

POWER PLANT: Two 300 hp Lycoming IO-540-M six-cylinder horizontally-opposed air-cooled engines. Turbo-superchargers optional (see Turbo Navajo). Hartzell two-blade extended-hub constant-speed fully-feathering metal propellers, diameter 6 ft 8 in (2·03 m). Propeller de-icing optional. Four rubber fuel cells in wings; inboard cells each contain 55 US gallons

(208 litres), outboard cells 40 US gallons (151·5 litres). Total fuel capacity 190 US gallons (719 litres), of which 188 US gallons (711 litres) are usable. Two-piece glass-fibre engine nacelles.

ACCOMMODATION: Six to nine seats, as described under notes on individual models. Dual controls standard. Thermostatically-controlled Janitrol 45,500 BTU combustion heater, windshield defrosters and fresh air system standard. Double-glazed windows. Electric de-icing and windshield wiper for port side of windshield optional. "Dutch" door at rear of cabin on port side. Top half hinges upward; lower half hinges down and has built-in steps. Luggage compartments in nose, capacity 150 lb (68 kg), and in rear of cabin, capacity 200 lb (91 kg). Cargo door and cockpit door available as optional items.

SYSTEMS: Hydraulic system utilises two engine-driven pumps. 24V electrical system supplied by two engine-driven 50A alternators and 24V 17Ah battery. External power socket standard. Provision for oxygen system.

ELECTRONICS AND EQUIPMENT: Optional electronics described under standard groupings above. Blind-flying instrumentation standard, with optional dual installation for co-pilot. Fire extinguishers, toe-brakes for co-pilot, Piper mixture control indicator, dual 70A alternators, three-bladed propellers and camera provision available optionally. Standard electrical equipment includes navigation, landing, taxying, cockpit, cabin dome and passenger reading lights, two rotating beacons, stall warning light, courtesy lights, cigarette lighter, cabin and cockpit speakers and heated pitot tube.

DIMENSIONS, EXTERNAL:
Wing span	40 ft 8 in (12·40 m)
Length overall	32 ft 7½ in (9·94 m)
Height overall	13 ft 0 in (3·96 m)
Tailplane span	18 ft 1½ in (5·52 m)
Wheel track	13 ft 9 in (4·19 m)
Wheelbase	8 ft 8 in (2·64 m)

DIMENSIONS, INTERNAL:
Cabin: Length	15 ft 10 in (4·83 m)
Height	4 ft 3½ in (1·31 m)

Luggage compartments:
Nose	14 cu ft (0·40 m³)
Aft	16 cu ft (0·45 m³)

AREA:
Wings, gross	229 sq ft (21·3 m²)

WEIGHTS AND LOADINGS:
Weight empty (standard)	3,744 lb (1,698 kg)
Max T-O and landing weight	6,200 lb (2,812 kg)
Max wing loading	27·1 lb/sq ft (132·3 kg/m²)
Max power loading	10·3 lb/hp (4·67 kg/hp)

PERFORMANCE (at max T-O weight):
Max level speed at S/L
  197 knots (227 mph; 365 km/h)
Max cruising speed (75% power) at 6,400 ft
  (1,950 m) 185 knots (213 mph; 343 km/h)
Intermediate cruising speed (65% power) at 10,000 ft (3,050 m)
  180 knots (207 mph; 333 km/h)
Econ cruising speed (55% power) at 14,600 ft (4,450 m) 171 knots (197 mph; 317 km/h)
Econ cruising speed (45% power) at 16,600 ft (5,060 m) 155 knots (178 mph; 286 km/h)
Stalling speed, flaps up
  67 knots (77 mph; 124 km/h)
Stalling speed, flaps down
  61 knots (70 mph; 113 km/h)
Rate of climb at S/L 1,670 ft (509 m)/min
Single-engine rate of climb at S/L
  325 ft (99 m)/min
Service ceiling	16,600 ft (5,060 m)
Single-engine ceiling	6,250 ft (1,905 m)
Absolute ceiling	17,700 ft (5,395 m)
Absolute ceiling, one engine out	
	7,400 ft (2,255 m)

Normal T-O run	1,010 ft (308 m)
Short-field T-O run	790 ft (241 m)
Normal T-O to 50 ft (15 m)	2,120 ft (646 m)
Short-field T-O to 50 ft (15 m)	1,600 ft (488 m)
Normal landing from 50 ft (15 m)	2,150 ft (655 m)
Short-field landing from 50 ft (15 m)	
	1,690 ft (515 m)
Normal landing run	1,725 ft (525 m)
Short-field landing run	1,115 ft (340 m)

Range with max fuel, 45 min reserve:
75% power at 6,400 ft (1,950 m)
  963 nm (1,110 miles; 1,785 km)
65% power at 10,000 ft (3,050 m)
  1,085 nm (1,250 miles; 2,010 km)
55% power at 14,600 ft (4,450 m)
  1,181 nm (1,360 miles; 2,190 km)
45% power at 16,600 ft (5,060 m)
  1,233 nm (1,420 miles; 2,285 km)
Range with max fuel, no reserve:
75% power at 6,400 ft (1,950 m)
  1,107 nm (1,275 miles; 2,050 km)
65% power at 10,000 ft (3,050 m)
  1,215 nm (1,400 miles; 2,250 km)
55% power at 14,600 ft (4,450 m)
  1,311 nm (1,510 miles; 2,430 km)
45% power at 16,600 ft (5,060 m)
  1,346 nm (1,550 miles; 2,490 km)

PIPER TURBO NAVAJO

The Turbo Navajo differs from the Navajo only in having 310 hp Lycoming TIO-540-A engines with turbochargers which provide full sea-level power to 15,000 ft (4,570 m) and 75% power to 23,500 ft (7,150 m). Oxygen system is standard on this version, which has an increased AUW. It is available in the same models as the Navajo and with the same optional electronic packages.

DIMENSIONS AND AREAS:
Same as for Navajo

WEIGHTS AND LOADINGS:
Weight empty (Standard)	3,842 lb (1,742 kg)
Max T-O weight	6,500 lb (2,948 kg)
Max landing weight	6,200 lb (2,812 kg)
Max wing loading	28·4 lb/sq ft (138·7 kg/m²)
Max power loading	10·5 lb/hp (4·76 kg/hp)

PERFORMANCE (at max T-O weight):
Max level speed at 15,500 ft (4,725 m)
  226 knots (260 mph; 418 km/h)
Max cruising speed (75% power) at 23,500 ft
  (7,150 m) 215 knots (247 mph; 397 km/h)
Intermediate cruising speed (65% power) at 24,000 ft (7,300 m)
  201 knots (231 mph; 372 km/h)
Econ cruising speed (55% power) at 24,000 ft (7,300 m) 182 knots (209 mph; 336 km/h)
Econ cruising speed (45% power) at 24,000 ft (7,300 m) 157 knots (181 mph; 291 km/h)
Stalling speed, flaps up
  70 knots (80 mph; 129 km/h)
Stalling speed, flaps down
  62 knots (71 mph; 114 km/h)
Rate of climb at S/L 1,395 ft (425 m)/min
Single-engine rate of climb at S/L
  245 ft (75 m)/min
Service ceiling	26,300 ft (8,000 m)
Single-engine ceiling	15,800 ft (4,800 m)
Absolute ceiling	27,300 ft (8,321 m)
Absolute ceiling, one engine out	
	16,400 ft (5,000 m)
Normal T-O run	1,066 ft (325 m)
Short-field T-O run	890 ft (271 m)
Normal T-O to 50 ft (15 m)	2,270 ft (692 m)
Short-field T-O to 50 ft (15 m)	1,760 ft (536 m)

Landing runs as for Navajo
Range with max fuel, 45 min reserve:
75% power at 23,500 ft (7,150 m)
  972 nm (1,120 miles; 1,800 km)
65% power at 24,000 ft (7,300 m)
  1,207 nm (1,390 miles; 2,235 km)
55% power at 24,000 ft (7,300 m)
  1,302 nm (1,500 miles; 2,415 km)

45% power at 24,000 ft (7,300 m)
            1,346 nm (1,550 miles; 2,495 km)
Range with max fuel, no reserve:
  75% power at 23,500 ft (7,150 m)
            1,128 nm (1,300 miles; 2,090 km)
  65% power at 24,000 ft (7,300 m)
            1,354 nm (1,560 miles; 2,510 km)
  55% power at 24,000 ft (7,300 m)
            1,432 nm (1,650 miles; 2,655 km)
  45% power at 24,000 ft (7,300 m)
            1,467 nm (1,690 miles; 2,715 km)

PIPER PA-31P PRESSURISED NAVAJO

Piper announced on 6 March 1970 that a new pressurised version of the Navajo was to be marketed by the company. Generally similar to the PA-31-300 Navajo and Turbo Navajo already in service, the new version began as a company project in January 1966, and the first prototype was flown in March 1968. From that time to the roll-out of the first production aircraft in March 1970, more than 4,000 hours of flight and ground-testing of the new model had been completed, including 850 hours at altitudes up to 29,000 ft (8,840 m), the aircraft's certificated maximum operating altitude.

There are two models available as follows:

Standard Pressurised Navajo. Six individual seats in pairs. Dividers to separate cabin from flight deck and rear baggage compartment, as well as two additional seats, are available as optional extras.

Executive Pressurised Navajo. Seven individual seats, comprising two crew seats, four reclining chairs facing each other and a fifth passenger seat, food and drink buffet and two fold-away tables as standard. Eighth seat and stereo tape deck optional.

The Navajo's pressurisation system, with a maximum cabin differential of 5·5 lb/sq in (0·38 kg/cm²) provides a sea level cabin atmosphere up to 12,375 ft (3,770 m) and can maintain a cabin altitude of 10,000 ft (3,050 m) up to the aircraft's certificated maximum operating altitude. Special features of this new system includes four sources of pressurised air: engine-bleed air from each of the turbochargers is the main source of supply, and two air pressure pumps, one on each engine, provide a secondary supply adequate to maintain pressurisation at the desired level during engine power changes, and even with throttles closed for descent. A variable rate of change control permits the pilot to select any rate of climb or descent of the cabin altitude from 100 to 1,000 ft (30-305 m)/min to prevent uncomfortably-rapid changes of cabin pressure. A normal rate of change of 500 ft (152 m)/min is programmed into the system.

The cabin environmental control system can be controlled from the flight deck. Cabin temperature is maintained by a thermostat which controls both a 45,000 BTU gasoline heater and a 24,000 BTU Freon-type air conditioner. Cabin air, changed every 90 seconds, is filtered, dehumidified and heated or cooled before being admitted through baseboard outlets that extend the full length of the cabin on both sides. An air recirculation control allows the outside air source to be isolated and cabin air recirculated to prevent intake of exhaust fumes while taxying behind other aircraft. These systems can be operated on the ground for effective cooling or heating with only the starboard engine running. Other changes include introduction of more powerful engines, with an engine-to-propeller rpm ratio of 3 : 2 to provide better propeller efficiency and quieter operation, increased baggage space and a one-piece passenger door with integral airstairs.

The description of the PA-31-300 Navajo applies also to the PA-31P except in the following details:

FUSELAGE: Conventional all-metal semi-monocoque structure with fail-safe structure in the pressurised section.

POWER PLANT: Two 425 hp Lycoming TIGO-541-E1A six-cylinder horizontally-opposed air-cooled turbocharged and geared fuel-injection engines, each driving a three-blade metal constant-speed propeller, diameter 7 ft 9 in

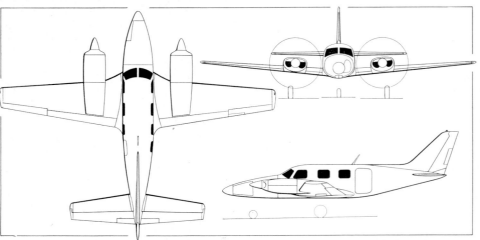

Photograph and general arrangement drawing of the Piper PA-31P Pressurised Navajo

(2·36 m). Fuel contained in four rubber fuel cells in wings; inboard cells each contain 56 US gallons (212 litres), outboard cells each 40 US gallons (151·5 litres). Total fuel capacity 192 US gallons (727 litres) of which 186 US gallons (704 litres) are usable. Two optional 25-US gallon (94·5-litre) transfer cells can be installed in the engine nacelles to provide a maximum fuel capacity of 242 US gallons (916 litres), of which 236 US gallons (893 litres) are usable. All fuel tanks have anti-icing vents.

ACCOMMODATION: Six to eight seats, as described under notes on individual models. One-piece passenger door with integral airstair; when closed the door is secured by seven locking pins. Each seat position has an individual fresh air outlet, reading lamp, head rest, full-length arm rests, ash tray and storage pocket in the seat back. Walk-in baggage compartment aft of cabin, capacity 28 cu ft (0·79 m³), can accommodate 250 lb (113 kg) of luggage. Nose compartment, capacity 14 cu ft (0·40 m³), can hold 150 lb (68 kg) baggage.

DIMENSIONS, EXTERNAL:
Same as for PA-31-300 Navajo except:
Length overall   34 ft 6 in (10·52 m)

WEIGHTS AND LOADINGS:
Weight empty   4,842 lb (2,196 kg)
Max T-O weight   7,800 lb (3,538 kg)
Max wing loading   34·1 lb/sq ft (166·4 kg/m²)
Max power loading   9·18 lb/hp (4·16 kg/hp)

PERFORMANCE (at max T-O weight):
Max level speed
            243 knots (280 mph; 451 km/h)
Max cruising speed, 75% power at 24,000 ft (7,315 m)   231 knots (266 mph; 428 km/h)

Intermediate cruising speed, 65% power at 24,000 ft (7,315 m)
            212 knots (244 mph; 393 km/h)
Econ cruising speed, 55% power at 24,000 ft (7,315 m)   193 knots (222 mph; 357 km/h)
Long-range cruising speed, 45% power at 24,000 ft (7,315 m)
            165 knots (190 mph; 306 km/h)
Stalling speed   72 knots (83 mph; 134 km/h)
Max rate of climb at S/L   1,740 ft (530 m)/min
Maximum operationally approved ceiling
                            29,000 ft (8,840 m)
T-O run   1,440 ft (439 m)
T-O to 50 ft (15 m)   2,960 ft (902 m)
Landing from 50 ft (15 m)   2,700 ft (823 m)
Landing run   1,370 ft (418 m)
Maximum range with maximum fuel, no reserves, at speeds as shown:
Maximum cruising speed at 24,000 ft (7,315 m)
            960 nm (1,105 miles; 1,778 km)
Intermediate cruising speed at 24,000 ft (7,315 m) 1,111 nm (1,280 miles; 2,060 km)
Econ cruising speed at 24,000 ft (7,315 m)
            1,224 nm (1,410 miles; 2,270 km)
Long-range cruising speed at 24,000 ft (7,315 m)
            1,285 nm (1,480 miles; 2,382 km)

PIPER PA-35 POCONO

Announced on 21 March 1967 and flown for the first time on 13 May 1968, the PA-35 Pocono is larger than any aircraft previously built by Piper with accommodation for up to 17 passengers.

At the time of writing Piper had made no decision whether or not to put this model into production. All available details were given in the 1969/70 *Janes'*.

PITTS
PITTS AVIATION ENTERPRISES, INC
ADDRESS:
PO Box 548, Homestead, Florida 33030

One of the best-known US designers of high-performance sporting aircraft, Mr Curtis Pitts is responsible for the Pitts Special biplane, of which detailed construction drawings are available in both single-seat and two-seat versions.

Other designs by Mr Pitts have included the Samson aerobatic biplane of 1945, with 450 hp Wasp engine, and the Pellet and Lil' Monster midget racers.

PITTS S-1 SPECIAL

The original single-seat Pitts Special was designed in 1943-44. Construction of a prototype began in 1944 and it flew in September of that year. One of the most successful early models

was *Little Stinker*, built by Mr Pitts for Miss Betty Skelton, the internationally-known aerobatic display pilot, in 1947, powered by a 90 hp Continental engine. The *Black Beauty* biplane, built by Pitts for Miss Caro Bailey, was of similar design, but powered by a 125 hp Lycoming O-290-D engine. This type of engine is also fitted in *Joy's Toy*, built by Mr D. Case for his daughter Joyce, who has twice won the AAA Women's Aerobatic Championship.

The Pitts Special in which Mr R. Herendeen of Santa Monica, California, won the US National Aerobatic Championship in September 1966 is even more powerful, with a 180 hp Lycoming engine. The same pilot and aircraft also scored top points among the US team entered for the 1966 World Championships in Moscow.

At the US National Aerobatic Championships held in October 1969, Pitts Specials took first and third places, piloted by Mr R. Herendeen and Mr

"Buddy" Head respectively. In the women's unlimited competition at the same event, first place went to another Pitts Special flown by Mary Gaffaney.

The version of the single-seat Pitts Special for which drawings are supplied by Mr Pitts is designed to take a Continental engine of from 65 to 95 hp or a Lycoming engine of up to 170 hp.

The following details of this basic design were supplied by Mr Pitts:

TYPE: Single-seat home-built biplane.

WINGS: Braced biplane type, with single faired interplane strut each side and N-type cabane. Wing section M6. Thickness/chord ratio 12%. Dihedral 0° on upper wing, 3° on lower wings. Incidence 1° 30′ on upper wing, 0° on lower wings. Sweepback at quarter-chord 6° 45′. Wooden structure, with fabric covering. Frise-type ailerons on lower wings only, of similar construction to wings.

FUSELAGE: Welded steel-tube structure, covered with fabric.

TAIL UNIT: Wire-braced steel-tube structure, fabric-covered.

LANDING GEAR: Non-retractable tail-wheel type. Rubber-cord shock-absorption. Cleveland main wheels and tyres, size 5·00 × 5, pressure 30 lb/sq in (2·10 kg/cm²). Cleveland hydraulic brakes. Steerable tail-wheel. Fairings on main wheels.

POWER PLANT: One Lycoming four-cylinder horizontally-opposed air-cooled engine of 100 to 170 hp, driving a Sensenich two-blade metal propeller, diameter 6 ft 0 in (1·83 m). Fuel tank aft of firewall, capacity 20 US gallons (75·5 litres). Oil capacity 2 US gallons (7·5 litres).

ACCOMMODATION: Single seat in open cockpit.

DIMENSIONS, EXTERNAL:
Wing span, upper	17 ft 4 in (5·28 m)
Wing chord (constant, both)	3 ft 0 in (0·91 m)
Wing aspect ratio	5·77
Length overall	15 ft 6 in (4·72 m)
Height overall	5 ft 6 in (1·68 m)
Tailplane span	6 ft 6 in (1·98 m)

WEIGHTS (125 hp Lycoming O-290-D):
Weight empty	640 lb (290 kg)
Max T-O weight	1,050 lb (476 kg)

PERFORMANCE (with 125 hp Lycoming O-290-D, at max T-O weight):
Max level speed at S/L	136 knots (157 mph; 253 km/h)
Max permissible diving speed	188 knots (217 mph; 350 km/h)
Max cruising speed at 8,000 ft (2,440 m)	122 knots (140 mph; 225 km/h)
Stalling speed	50 knots (57 mph; 92 km/h)
Rate of climb at S/L	1,800 ft (550 m)/min
Service ceiling	18,000 ft (5,500 m)
T-O run	240 ft (73 m)
T-O to 50 ft (15 m)	450 ft (137 m)
Endurance with max fuel, no reserve	2 hours 48 min

PITTS S-2 SPECIAL

First flown in 1967, the S-2 is a two-seat version of the Pitts Special. It is similar to the single-seat S-1 in basic configuration and construction, but is slightly larger in overall dimensions, with no attempt at commonality of components. The increased size and power, coupled with aerodynamic changes, give the two-seater improved aerobatic and landing characteristics, and make it extremely stable in rough air conditions. Control responses are better than on the S-1. The ailerons are aerodynamically balanced for higher rate of roll at low speeds, and full vertical rolls can be made with ease. The different wing sections used on the S-2 provide inverted performance equal to conventional flight and facilitate outside loops.

TYPE: Two-seat home-built biplane.

WINGS: Braced biplane type, with single faired interplane strut each side and N-type cabane. Wing section NACA 6400 series on upper wing, 00 series on bottom wings. Wooden structure with fabric covering. Aerodynamically-balanced ailerons on both upper and lower wings.

Pitts S-1 Special (200 hp Lycoming engine) built by Mr Bill Skipper of Greely, Colorado
(Jean Seele)

The two-seat Pitts S-2 Special (180 hp Lycoming O-360-A1A engine) (Howard Levy)

FUSELAGE: Welded steel-tube structure, covered with fabric.

TAIL UNIT: Wire-braced welded steel-tube structure. Fixed surfaces metal-covered, control surfaces fabric-covered.

LANDING GEAR: Non-retractable tail-wheel type. Rubber-cord shock-absorption. Steerable tail-wheel. Fairings on main wheels.

POWER PLANT: One 180 hp Lycoming O-360-A1A four-cylinder horizontally-opposed air-cooled engine, driving a two-blade fixed-pitch propeller.

ACCOMMODATION: Two seats in tandem in open cockpits.

DIMENSIONS, EXTERNAL:
Wing span	20 ft 0 in (6·10 m)
Wing chord (constant, both)	3 ft 4 in (1·02 m)
Length overall	18 ft 3 in (5·56 m)
Height overall	6 ft 2 in (1·88 m)

WEIGHTS:
Weight empty	898 lb (408 kg)
Max T-O weight	1,400 lb (635 kg)

PERFORMANCE (at max T-O weight):
Max level speed at S/L	143 knots (165 mph; 265 km/h)
Cruising speed	113 knots (130 mph; 209 km/h)
Landing speed	48 knots (55 mph; 89 km/h)
Rate of climb at S/L	1,900 ft (580 m)/min
Service ceiling	16,000 ft (4,875 m)
Range with max fuel	390 nm (450 miles; 725 km)

REPPERT
MERLE REPPERT

REPPERT T-AERO

At the time of writing, Mr M. Reppert had almost completed construction of a single-seat sporting aircraft of his own design which he has named the T-Aero. First flight was anticipated before the end of the year.

TYPE: Single-seat homebuilt sporting monoplane.

WINGS: Cantilever shoulder-wing monoplane. All-wood main structure with a single spruce spar and plywood skins. Glass-fibre wingtips.

FUSELAGE: Welded steel-tube structure covered by a glass-fibre shell, moulded in two pieces.

TAIL UNIT: Cantilever T-tail of welded steel-tube construction with plywood skins. Glass-fibre tailplane tips.

LANDING GEAR: Hydraulically-retractable tricycle type. Main units retract outward and upward into wings.

POWER PLANT: One 125 hp Lycoming O-290 four-cylinder horizontally-opposed air-cooled engine, fitted with an augmented exhaust and driving a two-blade metal propeller with spinner. Two-piece laminated glass-fibre engine cowlings.

ACCOMMODATION: Single seat for pilot under transparent bubble canopy.

SYSTEMS: Hydraulic system, supplied by engine-driven hydraulic pump, for landing gear retraction.

DIMENSIONS, EXTERNAL:
Wing span	16 ft 6 in (5·03 m)
Length overall	17 ft 0 in (5·18 m)
Height overall	4 ft 9 in (1·45 m)

AREA:
Wings, gross	68 sq ft (6·32 m²)

Reppert single-seat sporting monoplane (125 hp Lycoming O-290 engine) (Henry Artof)

WEIGHTS (estimated):
Weight empty	750 lb (340 kg)
Max T-O weight	1,000 lb (453 kg)

PERFORMANCE (estimated):
Max level speed	174 knots (200 mph; 322 km/h)
Landing speed	68 knots (78 mph; 126 km/h)
Range	434 nm (500 miles; 805 km)

RICHARD
THE C. H. RICHARD COMPANY

ADDRESS:
2561 West Avenue K, Lancaster, California
93534

Mr C. H. Richard has designed a two-seat high-wing cabin monoplane, designated Richard 125 Commuter; a single-seat mid-wing monoplane, designated Richard 190 Sportplane; as well as a two-thirds replica of the German Focke-Wulf Fw 190-A3 of World War 2. He has formed a company to develop these designs, and to market plans, certain assemblies and kits of parts to amateur constructors. All available details follow:

RICHARD 125 COMMUTER

The prototype Richard 125 Commuter is an all-metal two-seat high-wing monoplane, powered by a 125 hp engine and with no double-curvature skin panels. It was intended to make four different versions available, comprising 125 hp and 180 hp models with either tail-wheel or tricycle landing gear, and to obtain FAA Type Certification for each version. However, Mr Richard announced at the end of April 1970 that an improved version of the Commuter was nearing completion and was scheduled for flight testing during the Summer of 1970. The following details refer to the prototype.

TYPE: Two-seat cabin monoplane.

WINGS: Braced high-wing monoplane with single streamline-section bracing strut each side. Wing has constant chord. All-metal single-spar structure, with skins of 0·032-in thick 2024-T3 aluminium sheet, wrapped chordwise around the leading-edge and flush-riveted. Flaps and ailerons of metal construction. Ailerons mass-balanced. No trim-tabs.

FUSELAGE: All-metal semi-monocoque structure, made in separate centre-section and tail-cone assemblies.

TAIL UNIT: Cantilever all-metal structure. Fixed-incidence tailplane. Elevators and rudder of metal construction, mass-balanced. No trim-tabs.

LANDING GEAR: Non-retractable tail-wheel type. Cantilever steel-tube main gear. Goodyear main wheels and tyres size 5·00 × 5. Hydraulic brakes.

POWER PLANT: One 125 hp Lycoming O-290-G four-cylinder horizontally-opposed air-cooled engine, driving a two-blade fixed-pitch metal propeller, diameter 5 ft 6 in (1·68 m). Engine mounting suitable for a variety of engines up to 250 hp. Fuel contained in fuselage tank, capacity 25 US gallons (94·6 litres). Auxiliary tank containing 25 US gallons (94·6 litres) may also be installed. Later versions will have integral wing fuel tanks of similar total capacity.

ACCOMMODATION: Two seats, side-by-side, in enclosed cabin, with dual controls.

DIMENSIONS, EXTERNAL:
Wing span	25 ft 0 in (7·62 m)
Length overall	19 ft 9 in (6·02 m)
Height overall	5 ft 6 in (1·68 m)

AREAS:
Wings, gross	100 sq ft (9·29 m²)
Ailerons (total)	6·00 sq ft (0·56 m²)
Trailing-edge flaps (total)	6·67 sq ft (0·62 m²)
Fin	4·25 sq ft (0·39 m²)
Rudder	3·00 sq ft (0·28 m²)
Tailplane	14·40 sq ft (1·34 m²)
Elevators	8·00 sq ft (0·74 m²)

WEIGHTS:
Weight empty	805 lb (365 kg)
Max T-O weight	1,500 lb (680 kg)

PERFORMANCE (at max T-O weight):
Max level speed at 5,000 ft (1,525 m)
130 knots (150 mph; 241 km/h)
Cruising speed, 75% power at 5,000 ft (1,525 m)
122 knots (140 mph; 225 km/h)
Stalling speed, flaps up, at 1,500 lb (680 kg) AUW
43·5 knots (50 mph; 80·5 km/h)
Rate of climb at 1,500 lb (580 kg) AUW
900 ft (274 m)/min
Service ceiling, at 1,500 lb (580 kg) AUW
over 15,000 ft (4,570 m)
Range, with 25 US gallons fuel, 30 min reserve
347 nm (400 miles; 640 km)
Range, with 50 US gallons fuel, 30 min reserve
781 nm (900 miles; 1,445 km)

RICHARD 190 SPORTPLANE

The prototype Richard 190 Sportplane is an all-metal single-seat mid-wing monoplane and is stressed for full aerobatic performance. Mr Richard intends to make three versions of the

Richard 125 Commuter two-seat light monoplane (125 hp Lycoming C-290-G engine)

Richard 190 Sportplane single-seat sporting monoplane (100 hp Continental O-200 engine)

Sportplane available; in addition to the mid-wing model described below, there will be low-wing and biplane versions. The following description applies to the prototype 190 Sportplane.

TYPE: Single-seat sporting monoplane.

WINGS: Cantilever mid-wing monoplane. All-metal single-spar structure, with skins of 0·032-in thick 2024-T3 aluminium sheet, wrapped chordwise round the leading-edge and flush-riveted. Flaps and ailerons of metal construction; ailerons are mass-balanced. No trim-tabs.

FUSELAGE: All-metal semi-monocoque structure. Centre fuselage has U-section frames sandwiched between thick (0·040 in) cabin floor and outer skin.

TAIL UNIT: Cantilever all-metal structure with small dorsal fin. Fixed-incidence tailplane. Elevators and rudder of metal construction, mass-balanced.

LANDING GEAR: Non-retractable tail-wheel type. Each main gear strut consists of a tapered hollow box-beam pivoting on a torque tube. Shock-absorption by spring-in-compression, through a tension linkage attached to the torque tube. Hydraulic brakes.

POWER PLANT: One 100 hp Continental O-200 four-cylinder horizontally-opposed air-cooled engine, driving a two-blade fixed-pitch metal propeller, diameter 5 ft 6 in (1·68 m). Engine mounting suitable for a variety of engines up to 250 hp. Fuel contained in wing-tip tanks, total capacity 30 US gallons (113 litres). Internal fuselage tanks optional.

ACCOMMODATION: Single seat for pilot under a Plexiglas transparent canopy, hinged at rear.

DIMENSIONS, EXTERNAL:
Wing span, excluding tip tanks
19 ft 0 in (5·79 m)
Wing chord (constant)	3 ft 9 in (1·14 m)
Wing aspect ratio	5·08
Length overall	16 ft 6 in (5·03 m)
Height overall	5 ft 0 in (1·52 m)
Tailplane span	7 ft 1 in (2·16 m)

AREAS:
Wings, gross	71·5 sq ft (6·64 m²)
Ailerons (total)	4·68 sq ft (0·43 m²)
Trailing-edge flaps (total)	6·67 sq ft (0·62 m²)
Fin	4·62 sq ft (0·43 m²)
Rudder	2·88 sq ft (0·27 m²)
Tailplane	8·30 sq ft (0·77 m²)
Elevators	6·0 sq ft (0·56 m²)

WEIGHTS:
Weight, empty	750 lb (340 kg)
Max T-O weight	1,200 lb (544 kg)

PERFORMANCE:
Max permissible speed
217 knots (250 mph; 402 km/h)
Stalling speed, flaps up
59 knots (67 mph; 108 km/h)

RICHARD FW 190A3

Mr Richard has designed a single-seat aerobatic sportsplane which is approximately a two-thirds replica of the German Focke-Wulf Fw 190-A3 fighter of World War 2. This size has been chosen so that power plants in the 125-200 hp range can be utilised.

The cantilever all-metal wing is of two-spar construction, with aluminium alloy sheet metal skins. The fuselage is of welded steel-tube and is covered by glass-fibre cloth-plastic shells. These shells are cast from a master mould which reproduces characteristic details of the original structure. The fin covering and all wing fairings are cast integrally with the components of the fuselage covering. The cockpit canopy, covers for wing tips, rudder, elevators and ailerons are similar shells.

Landing gear is of the retractable tail-wheel type, with a structure of welded steel tube. Manual retraction is by means of a ratchet-controlled drum windlass, and the main gear can be extended to the down and locked position at any stage of retraction by depressing a ratchet release. Each main strut is spring-loaded to assist automatic extension in an emergency, and incorporates a shock-absorber.

Fuel is carried externally in a replica drop-tank beneath the fuselage and a pair of replica auxiliary tanks wing-mounted outboard of the main landing gear. All fuel tanks are jettisonable.

Drawings, moulded shell covers, material and pre-cut material kits are available to amateur constructors.

RILEY
RILEY TURBO SALES CORPORATION

HEAD OFFICE:
2900 Preston Tower, Dallas, Texas
PRESIDENT: Jack M. Riley
VICE-PRESIDENT: J. Ward Evans
SECRETARY: Edith Roberts

Mr J. Riley, who was responsible for the Riley

55 Twin-Navion conversion scheme in 1952, also designed three improved versions of the Cessna 310, known as the Riley 65, Riley Rocket and Riley Turbo-Rocket; a similar scheme to improve the Hawker Siddeley (DH) Dove, under the name Riley Turbo-Exec 400; and a conversion scheme to re-engine Hawker Siddeley (DH) Heron light transports with Lycoming engines.

No recent information on the company's activities has been received from Riley Corporation, but it is reported that the company is currently producing a conversion of the Cessna 310P, powered by 310 hp Lycoming turbocharged engines, which is known as the Riley Turbo-Stream. Details of the company's earlier products may be found in the 1968/69 Jane's.

RLU

CHARLES ROLOFF, ROBERT LIPOSKY AND CARL UNGER

ADDRESS:
9640 S, 53rd Avenue, Oak Lawn, Illinois

Three members of Corporate Air Transport Inc designed and built a unique light aircraft known as the RLU-1 Breezy. This designation is made up of the initial letters of the surnames of the designers—Charles Roloff, the company's Vice-President, Maintenance, and two pilots, Robert Liposky and Carl Unger.

About 250 sets of plans have been sold to amateur constructors and at least 20 Breezys are now flying.

RLU-1 BREEZY

Described as being of vintage configuration with all modern facilities, such as full radio, instruments and hydraulic brakes, the prototype Breezy is an open three-seat light aircraft powered by a 90 hp Continental engine.

Construction took six months, at a cost of $3,000, including radio. First flight was made in August 1964 and 80 flying hours were logged during the following twelve months.

First Breezy to be built from the published plans was that constructed by Airpark Aero of Santa Rosa, California, for Mr Jack Gardiner of Pandora, Ohio. It differs from the prototype only by having two bucket seats, one of these replacing the usual two-place bench seat behind the pilot.

The following description applies to the prototype Breezy:

TYPE: Three-seat homebuilt parasol-wing monoplane.

WINGS: Strut-braced parasol-wing monoplane. Standard Piper PA-12 wing, with Vee streamline-section bracing struts each side.

FUSELAGE: Triangular-section welded chrome molybdenum steel-tube structure, without any covering.

TAIL UNIT: Welded chrome molybdenum steel-tube braced structure; all surfaces fabric-covered.

RLU-1 Breezy (75 hp Continental engine) built by Mr Joseph Bolk of St Louis, Missouri (*Jean Seele*)

LANDING GEAR: Non-retractable tricycle type. Main wheels and tyres size 600 × 6, 4-ply; nose wheel and tyre size 500 × 5. Cleveland hydraulic brakes.

POWER PLANT: One 90 hp Continental C-90-8F-P four-cylinder horizontally-opposed air-cooled engine, driving a Flottorp 72A50 two-blade pusher propeller. Single fuel tank, capacity 18 US gallons (68 litres), in wing centre-section. Oil capacity 1·25 US gallons (4·5 litres).

ACCOMMODATION: Seats for three in tandem. Pilot on single seat forward, two passengers on bench seat aft.

DIMENSIONS, EXTERNAL:

Wing span	33 ft 0 in (10·06 m)
Length overall	22 ft 6 in (6·86 m)
Height overall	8 ft 6 in (2·59 m)
Wheel track	6 ft 0 in (1·83 m)
Wheelbase	10 ft 0 in (3·05 m)

AREA:

Wings, gross	165 sq ft (15·3 m²)

WEIGHTS AND LOADINGS:

Weight empty	700 lb (317 kg)
Max T-O weight	1,200 lb (544 kg)
Max wing loading	7·27 lb/sq ft (35·5 kg/m²)
Max power loading	13·3 lb/hp (6·03 kg/hp)

PERFORMANCE:

Max permissible speed	91 knots (105 mph; 168·5 km/h)
Cruising speed, 70% power	65 knots (75 mph; 121 km/h)
Stalling speed	26 knots (30 mph; 49 km/h)
Service ceiling	15,000 ft (4,572 m)
T-O run (turf)	450 ft (137 m)
T-O to 50 ft (15 m)	1,100 ft (335 m)
Landing from 50 ft (15 m)	1,100 ft (335 m)
Landing run (turf)	300 ft (91 m)
Range, with max fuel	217 nm (250 miles; 402 km)

ROBERTSON

ROBERTSON AIRCRAFT CORPORATION

HEAD OFFICE AND WORKS:
Bellevue Airfield, 15400 Sunset Highway, Bellevue, Washington 98004

PRESIDENT: James D. Raisbeck

DIRECTOR OF MARKETING: Ralph L. Portner

OPERATIONS MANAGER: Earl Severns

PRODUCTION MANAGER: Henry McKay

Robertson Aircraft Corporation was formed by Mr James L. Robertson, now deceased, who had long been a pioneer in the development of STOL aircraft, having been responsible for the Skycraft Skyshark, Wren 460 and STOL modifications to the IMCO CallAir A-9 and B-1. It has developed a series of STOL conversions for standard Cessna and Piper aircraft, these being chosen because of their rugged design.

ROBERTSON/CESSNA and PIPER STOL CONVERSIONS

The Robertson Cessna conversion, first applied to a Cessna 182, comprises full-span wing leading-edge and trailing-edge high-lift systems which greatly reduce the take-off and landing distances normally required by such aircraft.

The existing ailerons are used as an integral part of the full-span trailing-edge flap system. When the conventional inboard flaps are lowered for take-off or landing, the ailerons droop with them, virtually doubling the wing lift at low speeds, for only a 20% increase in drag. The ailerons retain their differential operation for roll control when drooped.

In addition, the wing is fitted with a full-span distributed-camber leading-edge to provide an optimum spanwise lift distribution for maximum cruise efficiency. The cambered leading-edge also reduces the aerofoil leading-edge pressure peak at high angles of attack, to impart maximum resistance to stall and to provide highly-responsive manoeuvrability at low airspeeds.

To improve controllability at low speeds, stall fences are provided between flaps and ailerons, and to complete the STOL modification the aileron gap is sealed with a strip of aluminium sheet. These modifications permit safe STOL landings and take-offs by even novice pilots.

The new wing high-lift systems have been designed for easy field maintenance. They are designed to be applicable to the following range of Cessna aircraft: Model 172, Model 180, Model 182, Skylane, Model 185 Skywagon, Model 205, Model 206 Super Skywagon, Turbo-System Super Skywagon, Super Skylane and Turbo-System Super Skylane, and Model 210 Centurion and Turbo-System Centurion.

Similar conversions are also offered for the low-wing Piper PA-28-180 Cherokee, PA-28-200 Cherokee Arrow, PA-28-235 Cherokee and PA-32 Cherokee Six.

The Robertson STOL conversion is of particular significance to operators of floatplane versions

Robertson STOL conversion of the Cessna 182, showing drooped ailerons and new cambered wingtips

Robertson STOL conversion of the cantilever-wing Cessna 210, showing stall fence between flaps and ailerons

of the Cessna Model 185. At maximum gross weight, the Robertson STOL 185 lifts clear of the water under S/L standard conditions at 43 mph (69 kmh), opening up vast new areas of operation into previously inaccessible lakes and rivers.

The STOL conversion, as described above, can also be applied to the Cessna Model 337 Super Skymaster and Turbo System Super Skymaster. In addition, these aircraft can be fitted with cambered glass-fibre wingtips to improve lateral/directional stability and take-off and climb performance, belly-mounted vortex generators to improve climb performance when operating on the front engine alone, as well as an elevator boost system to improve power-off flare capability by 30%. The cambered glass-fibre wingtips are available as an option for any model, and the elevator boost system can be applied to any model which does not have a variable-incidence tailplane. A flap dump switch is available for models with electrically-operated flaps, consisting of a

control wheel-mounted switch which allows the pilot to raise the flaps immediately after landing, without having to remove his hand from the throttle. Retraction of the flaps immediately after touch-down increases braking efficiency. Also provided as standard on Cessna 180 models is a manual rudder trim system.

The Robertson STOL conversion can be fitted as a retrospective modification to any of the models detailed above, irrespective of year. Current production of Robertson STOL 180, STOL 182, STOL 185 and STOL 206 totals more than 16 aircraft per month.

Full details of the basic Cessna and Piper airframes are given under that company's heading in this edition, and apply to the Robertson versions except for the added STOL conversions as described. Weights and performance details of the entire range of Robertson STOL conversions for Cessna aircraft are given in the table on page 442; details for the Piper conversions were not available at the time of writing.

CESSNA MODELS	Weight empty equipped lb (kg)	Weight gross lb (kg)	Max level speed knots (mph; km/h)	Max cruising speed knots (mph; km/h)	Stalling speed, wheels and flaps down knots (mph; km/h)	Rate of climb at S/L ft (m)	Service ceiling ft (m)	T-O run ft (m)	T-O to 50 ft (15m) ft (m)	Landing from 50ft (15 m) ft (m)	Landing run ft (m)	Max range nm (miles; km)
Model 172	1,280 (580)	2,300 (1,043)	122 (141; 227)	116 (133; 214)	22 (25; 40·5)	675 (206)/min	13,600 (4,150)	395 (121)	808 (247)	590 (180)	230 (70)	634 (732; 1,178)
Model 180	1,536 (697)	2,800 (1,270)	150 (173; 278)	143 (165; 265)	30 (34; 55)	1,122 (342)/min	19,900 (6,065)	320 (98)	635 (194)	542 (165)	187 (57)	1,083 (1,248; 2,008)
Model 182 and Skylane	1,580 (717)	2,800 (1,270)	152 (175; 282)	146 (168; 270)	31 (35; 57)	1,030 (314)/min	19,300 (5,880)	365 (111)	708 (215)	635 (194)	280 (85)	1,083 (1,248; 2,008)
A185 Skywagon	1,580 (717)	3,300 (1,497)	157 (181; 291)	149 (172; 277)	33 (38; 62)	1,092 (333)/min	17,850 (5,440)	338 (103)	648 (198)	612 (186)	262 (79)	955 (1,100; 1,770)
P206 Super Skylane at 2,600 lb (1,179 kg) AUW	1,730 (785)	2,600 (1,179)	162 (186; 299)	156 (180; 290)	29 (33; 53)	1,605 (489)/min	21,800 (6,645)	221 (67)	431 (131)	405 (123)	202 (62)	1,163 (1,340; 2,156)
P206 Super Skylane at 3,600 lb (1,633 kg) AUW	1,730 (785)	3,600 (1,633)	156 (180; 290)	148 (170; 274)	33 (38; 62)	990 (302)/min	15,400 (4,695)	438 (133)	865 (264)	595 (181)	305 (93)	911 (1,050; 1,690)
TP206 Turbo-System Super Skylane and TU206 Turbo-System Super Skywagon at 2,600 lb (1,179 kg) AUW	1,795 (814)	2,600 (1,179)	181 (208; 335)	172 (198; 319)	29 (33; 53)	1,690 (515)/min	31,100 (9,480)	221 (67)	431 (131)	405 (123)	202 (62)	979 (1,128; 1,815)
TP206 Turbo-System Super Skylane and TU206 Turbo-System Super Skywagon at 3,600 lb (1,633 kg) AUW	1,795 (814)	3,600 (1,633)	195 (202; 325)	163 (188; 302)	33 (38; 62)	1,055 (321)/min	27,100 (8,260)	438 (133)	865 (264)	595 (181)	305 (93)	832 (959; 1,542)
U206C Super Skywagon at 2,600 lb (1,179 kg) AUW	1,730 (785)	2,600 (1,179)	162 (186; 299)	156 (180; 290)	29 (33; 53)	1,605 (489)/min	21,800 (6,645)	192 (58)	382 (116)	405 (123)	202 (62)	1,163 (1,310; 2,156)
U206C Super Skywagon at 3,600 lb (1,633 kg) AUW	1,730 (785)	3,600 (1,633)	156 (180; 290)	148 (170; 274)	33 (38; 62)	990 (302)/min	15,400 (4,695)	398 (121)	779 (237)	595 (181)	305 (93)	911 (1,050; 1,690)
Model 201 Centurion (braced wing)	1,886 (856)	3,300 (1,497)	175 (201; 323)	168 (193; 310)	31 (35; 57)	1,140 (347)/min	20,200 (6,155)	349 (106)	697 (212)	528 (161)	263 (80)	1,137 (1,310; 2,108)
Model 210 Centurion (cantilever wing)	1,975 (896)	3,400 (1,542)	174 (200; 322)	167 (192; 309)	32 (36; 58)	1,020 (311)/min	18,500 (5,640)	307 (94)	609 (185)	543 (165)	263 (80)	1,181 (1,360; 2,189)
T210 Turbo-System Centurion (braced wing)	1,985 (900)	3,300 (1,497)	202 (233; 375)	194 (223; 359)	31 (35; 57)	1,360 (414)/min	31,900 (9,720)	349 (106)	697 (212)	528 (161)	263 (80)	1,133 (1,305; 2,100)
T210 Turbo-System Centurion (cantilever wing)	2,065 (937)	3,400 (1,542)	203 (234; 377)	194 (223; 359)	32 (36; 58)	1,130 (344)/min	30,800 (9,390)	307 (94)	609 (185)	543 (165)	263 (80)	1,220 (1,405; 2,261)
Model 337C Super Skymaster	2,670 (1,211)	4,400 (1,995)	179 (206; 322)	172 (198; 319) at 5,500 ft (1,657 m)	35 (40; 64)	1,260 (384)/min	20,000 (6,100)	418 (127)	728 (221)	728 (221)	340 (104)	1,215 (1,400; 2,253)
Model T337C Turbo-System Super Skymaster	2,815 (1,277)	4,500 (2,041)	208 (239; 385) at 20,000 ft (6,100 m)	175 (201; 323) at 10,000 ft (3,050 m)	36 (41; 66)	1,212 (369)/min	31,700 (9,660)	426 (130)	738 (225)	731 (223)	343 (105)	1,431 (1,648; 2,652)

ROTORMASTER

ADDRESS:
San Diego, California.

ROTORMASTER D5G BOOMERANG

Rotormaster have constructed a small gyroplane known as the Darby D5G Boomerang. Design of this aircraft was begun in December 1960 and construction of the prototype started in June 1963, with first flight following in July 1964. Construction of the first production aircraft began in July 1968, and a total of four Boomerangs had been built at the time of writing.

The Boomerang shown in the accompanying illustration is owned by Mr R. W. Hively of San Diego, California.

TYPE: Two-seat light autogyro.

ROTOR SYSTEM: Single two-blade (optionally three-blade) autorotating rotor of 8H-12 blade section. Structure of each blade comprises a "C" spar and bonded aerofoil skin. Foldable blades, with rotor brake.

FUSELAGE: Built of 2024-T3 light alloy channel sections, with glass-fibre fairing.

TAIL UNIT: Twin fins and rudders of light alloy construction, folded and riveted, with small fixed horizontal surface between them.

LANDING GEAR: Non-retractable tricycle type, with trailing-wheel and spring suspension. Nose-wheel steerable. Main wheels and tyres size 600 × 6, pressure 10 lb/sq in (0·7 kg/cm²). Nose-wheel and tyre size 500 × 5, pressure 10 lb/sq in (0·7 kg/cm²). Internal expanding brakes.

POWER PLANT: Airframe suitable for installation of any Continental or Lycoming horizontally-opposed engine of 65-180 hp, driving a two-blade fixed-pitch wooden pusher propeller, diameter 5 ft 0 in-5 ft 6 in (1·52-1·68 m) according to engine horsepower. Two fuel tanks, each of 6 US gallons (22·7 litres) capacity, one mounted beneath each seat. Total fuel capacity 12 US gallons (45·4 litres). Oil capacity from 1 to 1·5 US gallons (3·8-5·7 litres) according to engine.

ACCOMMODATION: Two seats side-by-side in open cockpit. Radio optional.

DIMENSIONS, EXTERNAL:
Rotor diameter   25 ft 0 in (7·62 m) or 26 ft 0 in (7·92 m)
Rotor blade chord   7 in (17·8 cm)
Length overall   9 ft 0 in (2·74 m)

Rotormaster D5G Boomerang two-seat light autogyro

Width, rotor folded   5 ft 6 in (1·68 m)
Height overall   8 ft 0 in (2·44 m)
Wheel track   5 ft 2 in (1·57 m)
Wheelbase   5 ft 4 in (1·63 m)

WEIGHTS:
Weight empty   400 lb (181 kg)
Max T-O weight   800 lb (362 kg)

PERFORMANCE (at max T-O weight):
Max level speed   104 knots (120 mph; 193 km/h)

Max cruising speed   65 knots (75 mph; 121 km/h)
Econ cruising speed   56 knots (65 mph; 105 km/h)
Max rate of climb at S/L   800 ft (244 m)/min
T-O run   130 ft (40 m)
T-O to 50 ft (15 m)   375 ft (114 m)
Landing from 50 ft (15 m)   100 ft (30·5 m)
Landing run   10 ft (3 m)
Range with max fuel   252-278 nm (290-320 miles; 467-515 km)

ROTORWAY
ROTORWAY, INC
ADDRESS:
244 N Country Club Drive, Suite 205, Mesa, Arizona 85201

Mr B. J. Schramm formed the Schramm Aircraft Company to market, in both ready-to-fly and pre-fabricated component form, a single-seat helicopter of his own design, named the Javelin. Details of this aircraft, which flew for the first time in August 1965, can be found in the 1967-68 *Jane's*.

Since that time, RotorWay Aircraft Inc has been formed to market to amateur constructors plans and kits of components to build Mr Schramms' new Scorpion helicopter, described as a production version of the Javelin. RotorWay offer a comprehensive set of plans, technical advice from their engineers, a complete kit to build the Scorpion, or a series of small progressive kits, allowing the constructor to proceed as finance allows. The company will also supply plans and rotor blades only to those builders wishing to provide their own material and power plant.

ROTORWAY SCORPION
The general appearance of the Scorpion is shown in the accompanying illustration. It is designed to be towable behind a small car.

TYPE: Single-seat light helicopter.

ROTOR SYSTEM: Two-blade semi-rigid main rotor, incorporating Schramm Tractable Control Rotor System. Blade section NACA 0015. Blades, which do not fold, are attached to aluminium rotor hub by retention straps. Two-blade aluminium teetering tail rotor. Swashplate for cyclic pitch control. Cable through rotor shaft to blades for collective-pitch control.

ROTOR DRIVE: Drive from engine to vertical shaft via six Vee-belts. Drive from vertical shaft to main rotor shaft via sprocket chain. Tail rotor driven by Vee-belt from 1st stage of reduction pulleys. Main rotor/engine rpm ratio 1 : 8·36. Tail rotor/engine rpm ratio 1 : 1·92.

FUSELAGE: Basic steel-tube structure of simplified form. Removable glass-fibre body fairing. The small glass-fibre nose cowl and windshield, as shown in the illustration are optional.

TAIL UNIT: Braced steel-tube tail-boom only, to carry tail rotor.

RotorWay Scorpion light helicopter (100 hp Evinrude outboard marine engine)

LANDING GEAR: Main wheels carried on splayed steel-tube, rigidly braced to fuselage. Wheel fairings. Steel nose skid.

POWER PLANT: 100 hp water-cooled Evinrude four-cylinder outboard marine engine mounted aft of pilot's seat. Standard fuel capacity 8 US gallons (30 litres) in tank mounted above drive chain, aft of main rotor shaft. Three optional fuel tanks available, ranging from 5-12 US gallons (18·5-45 litres).

ACCOMMODATION: Single bucket seat in open cockpit. Moulded Plexiglas canopy optional.

EQUIPMENT: Rotor speed, engine speed and air speed indicators and engine temperature gauge.

DIMENSIONS, EXTERNAL:
Diameter of main rotor	19 ft 6½ in (5·96 m)
Main rotor blade chord	7 in (17·8 cm)
Diameter of tail rotor	3 ft 3¼ in (1·01 m)
Length overall	17 ft 1¼ in (5·21 m)
Height to main rotor	6 ft 0 in (1·83 m)
Wheel track	4 ft 4½ in (1·33 m)

WEIGHTS:
Weight empty	450 lb (204 kg)
Max T-O weight	700 lb (317 kg)

PERFORMANCE:
Max level speed at S/L
78 knots (90 mph; 45 km/h)
Cruising speed (70% power)
59 knots (68 mph; 109 km/h)
Max rate of climb at S/L 1,450 ft (442 m)/min
Service ceiling 12,000 ft (3,655 m)
Hovering ceiling in ground effect
6,500 ft (1,980 m)
Hovering ceiling out of ground effect
3,500 ft (1,065 m)
Range with standard fuel, 70% power
91 nm (105 miles; 165 km)

SABEY
RICHARD SABEY
Richard Sabey, former US Naval Air Reserve pilot and now a supervisor in the technical illustrations department of North American Rockwell Corporation's Los Angeles Division, has designed and built a two-seat lightweight cabin monoplane which he has designated SX-1.

Availability of the wings, landing gear and tail unit of a Culver Aircraft Corporation PQ-14 target drone (described in the 1947-48 *Jane's*) induced Sabey to create his own design around these components, although the tail unit has been considerably modified.

When Sabey started high-speed taxying tests on 18 January 1970 he accidently found himself in the air, and stayed there for one circuit to record the first flight of the SX-1 and his own first time at an aircraft's controls for almost 20 years. His aircraft cost about $2,400 to build and occupied 14½ months of spare time.

All available details follow:

SABEY SX-1
TYPE: Two-seat homebuilt sporting monoplane.

WINGS: Cantilever low-wing monoplane. All-wood structure with two laminated spars passing through fuselage, conventional ribs and plywood skin. Plain wooden ailerons with plywood skin. Electrically-operated trailing-edge flaps of similar construction to ailerons. Fixed slots near wingtips.

FUSELAGE: Welded 4130 steel-tube structure covered with ·019 in aluminium skin.

TAIL UNIT: Composite cantilever structure. Fin is original PQ-14 wood structure. Tailplane, rudder and elevator of Sabey's design; tailplane is all-wood and control surfaces all-metal structures. Electrically-operated elevator trim-tab.

LANDING GEAR: Electrically-retractable tricycle type. Main wheels retract inward into wing,

The two-seat Sabey SX-1 uses parts of the Culver PQ-14 target drone

nose-wheel aft. Oleo-pneumatic shock-absorbers on all units. Shimmy-damper on nose unit. Goodyear hydraulic brakes.

POWER PLANT: One 125 hp Lycoming O-290-G4 four-cylinder horizontally-opposed air-cooled engine, driving a two-blade fixed-pitch propeller with spinner. Engine cowling is that of a Cessna 150 modified. Fuel carried in six integral wing tanks, total capacity 26 US gallons (100 litres).

ACCOMMODATION: Two seats side-by-side in enclosed cabin, with rearward-sliding canopy.

SYSTEMS: 12V and 24V electrical system for operating flaps, landing gear, elevator trim, lights, instruments and radio. Hydraulic system for brakes only.

ELECTRONICS: 100-channel VHF transceiver.

DIMENSIONS, EXTERNAL:
Wing span	30 ft 0 in (9·14 m)
Wing chord at root	4 ft 4½ in (1·33 m)
Length overall	21 ft 6 in (6·55 m)
Height overall	7 ft 0 in (2·13 m)

WEIGHTS:
Weight empty	1,273 lb (577 kg)
Max T-O weight	1,820 lb (825 kg)

PERFORMANCE (at max T-O weight):
Max level speed
130 knots (150 mph; 241 km/h)
Max cruising speed
126 knots (145 mph; 233 km/h)
Landing speed 61 knots (70 mph; 113 km/h)
Max rate of climb at S/L 900 ft (274 m)/min
Max range with 30 min reserve fuel
378 nm (435 miles; 700 km)

SALVAY-STARK
SKYHOPPER AIRPLANES, INC
ADDRESS:
17201 McCormick Street, Encino, California 91316

This company was formed by Mr M. E. Salvay, engineering manager of the North American Rockwell Sabreliner programme, and Mr George Stark, to market plans of a light aeroplane named the Skyhopper which they designed and built in

1944-45 and have since developed for amateur construction.

SALVAY-STARK SKYHOPPER
Design of the Skyhopper was begun in the early Spring of 1944 and the prototype flew for the

first time towards the end of March 1945. It was designed to comply with the CAR-04 requirements of the time and has since undergone considerable development and refinement.

Flown initially with a 50 hp engine, after three years the prototype was fitted with a 65 hp Continental A65 flat-four. This was changed in 1956 for an 85 hp Continental C85, and a total of 1,000 hours of flying were logged by this aircraft in the following three years.

Plans of the Skyhopper are available to amateur constructors and many have already been built in the United States, usually with a 65 hp Continental engine.

The aircraft can be built as a side-by-side two-seater, if preferred, and a drawing depicting the necessary design changes for this is included in all sets of plans.

In the two-seater, the width of the fuselage is increased by 14 in (0·36 m), to an inside dimension of 36 in (0·91 m). Few other changes are required, except to the ends of the wing spars, the engine cowling and canopy. The 85 hp engine is recommended for this version, but performance remains adequate with a 65 hp engine, with a loss of approximately 10% in cruising performance compared with the single-seat Skyhopper.

The adjacent illustration shows a two-seat version of the Skyhopper recently completed in Canada.

The following details refer to the standard Skyhopper as built from Salvay-Stark plans.
TYPE: Single-seat or two-seat light monoplane.
WINGS: Cantilever low-wing monoplane. Wing section NACA 23015-23012. All-wood two-spar structure. Leading-edge covered with aluminium sheet; remainder fabric-covered. Statically and dynamically balanced ailerons, fabric-covered. No flaps.
FUSELAGE: Welded steel-tube structure with fabric covering.
TAIL UNIT: Cantilever tailplane and fin have plywood-covered wooden structure. Statically and dynamically balanced rudder and elevators have welded tube structure, with fabric covering.
LANDING GEAR: Non-retractable tail-wheel type. Oil and spring shock-absorbers. Main wheels, size 5·00 × 5. Wheel spats. Steerable tail-wheel.

Two-seat version of the Salvay-Stark Skyhopper built by a Canadian amateur

POWER PLANT: One 65 hp Continental A65 or 85 hp Continental C85 four-cylinder horizontally-opposed air-cooled engine driving two-blade fixed-pitch propeller. Fuel capacity 15 US gallons (56·8 litres).
ACCOMMODATION: Single seat or two side-by-side seats under rearward-sliding canopy. Optional open cockpit. Small baggage space aft of seat.

DIMENSIONS, EXTERNAL:
Wing span:		
Single-seat	25 ft 0 in	(7·62 m)
Two-seat	26 ft 4 in	(8·02 m)
Wing aspect ratio		6
Length overall	18 ft 10 in	(5·74 m)
Height overall	5 ft 3 in	(1·60 m)

AREAS:
Wings, gross:		
Single-seat	100 sq ft	(9·29 m²)
Two-seat	107 sq ft	(9·94 m²)

WEIGHTS:
Weight empty:		
Single-seat	650 lb	(295 kg)
Two-seat	690 lb	(313 kg)

Max T-O weight:		
Single-seat	950 lb	(431 kg)
Two-seat	1,170 lb	(531 kg)

PERFORMANCE (single-seat, 65 hp Continental A65):
Max level speed at S/L		
	113 knots	(130 mph; 209 km/h)
Cruising speed at 7,000 ft (2,135 m)		
	104 knots	(120 mph; 193 km/h)
Stalling speed	39 knots	(45 mph; 72 km/h)
Rate of climb at S/L	700 ft	(213 m)/min
Service ceiling	approx 16,000 ft	(4,875 m)
T-O run	900 ft	(275 m)
Landing run	850 ft	(260 m)
Range with max fuel	300 miles	(480 km)

PERFORMANCE (two-seat, 85 hp Continental C85):
Max level speed at S/L		
	113 knots	(130 mph; 209 km/h)
Cruising speed	100 knots	(115 mph; 185 km/h)
Landing speed	42 knots	(48 mph; 77 km/h)

SCHEUTZOW
SCHEUTZOW HELICOPTER CORPORATION
POSTAL ADDRESS:
PO Box 27, Columbia Station, Ohio 44028
WORKS:
27100 Royalton Road, Columbia Station, Ohio 44028
PRESIDENT: Webb Scheutzow
VICE-PRESIDENT: W. Stuart

This company has been formed by Mr Webb Scheutzow to develop and build a light helicopter incorporating a new type of rotor head in which the blades are carried on rubber bushings.

Initial development of the new head was carried out successfully on a small test-bed helicopter, which was described and illustrated in the 1964-65 *Jane's*. It is now being used on the production-type Scheutzow Model B.

FAA certification tests were continuing in the Spring of 1969 and were scheduled for completion in July 1969. Production procurement has been initiated and an assembly line is being established with the intention of starting deliveries immediately following certification.

SCHEUTZOW MODEL B
Design of this small lightweight side-by-side two-seat helicopter began early in 1964 and construction of three prototypes was started in March 1965. The first of these flew for the first time in 1966 and had completed 14 hours' flying by 26 January 1967. By that date, forward speeds of up to 90 mph (145 kmh) had been attained. Autorotative tests had revealed good power-off handling qualities and the aircraft has proved very stable in hovering flight.

The Model B has a welded steel-tube structure with a completely enclosed metal cabin. The landing gear is of the skid type, with cross-tubes on which the skids are carried.

Power plant is a Lycoming IVO-360-A1A four-cylinder horizontally-opposed air-cooled engine, derated to 165 hp. It drives the two-blade flapping-type main rotor through a centrifugal clutch and multiple V-belt drive system. The conventional two-blade tail rotor is driven through a shaft and bevel gear.

Scheutzow Model B two-seat light helicopter (165 hp Lycoming IVO-360-A1A engine)

The main rotor incorporates Mr Scheutzow's patented "Flexhub", which involves mounting the blades in rubber and so eliminating the need for bearings of any kind in the hub. This is claimed to reduce vibration as well as cost and lubrication requirements. Standard fuel capacity is 22 US gallons (83 litres). A 15-US gallon (56 litre) auxiliary fuel tank is available as an optional accessory, extending range to an estimated 248 nm (285 miles; 458 km).

There is a large baggage compartment aft of the seats, on the centre of gravity, with an outside door on the port side.

DIMENSIONS, EXTERNAL:
Diameter of main rotor	27 ft 0 in	(8·23 m)
Main rotor blade chord	8 in	(20 cm)
Diameter of tail rotor	3 ft 8 in	(1·12 m)
Length overall	31 ft 0 in	(9·45 m)
Length of fuselage	23 ft 8 in	(7·21 m)
Width overall, rotor fore and aft	7 ft 0 in	(2·13 m)
Height overall	8 ft 2 in	(2·49 m)

WEIGHTS:
Weight empty	1,000 lb	(453 kg)
Max T-O weight	1,550 lb	(702 kg)

PERFORMANCE (estimated):
Max level speed at S/L		
	74 knots	(85 mph; 137 km/h)
Max cruising speed		
	69 knots	(80 mph; 128 km/h)
Rate of climb at S/L	1,250 ft	(380 m)/min
Service ceiling	14,000 ft	(4,250 m)
Hovering ceiling in ground effect		
	10,800 ft	(3,290 m)
Hovering ceiling out of ground effect		
	7,200 ft	(2,200 m)
Range with max fuel at max cruising speed		
	145 nm	(168 miles; 270 km)

SEGUIN
SEGUIN AVIATION
HEAD OFFICE AND WORKS:
Seguin, Texas 78155

This company produces a conversion of the 150-160 hp Piper Apache with more powerful engines and many refinements to the structure and equipment. The converted aircraft is named Geronimo after a famous chief of the Apache Indians.

SEGUIN/PIPER GERONIMO
In the standard Geronimo, the original 150-160 hp engines of the PA-23-160 Apache are replaced by two 180 hp Lycoming O-360-A1D four-cylinder horizontally-opposed engines in glass-fibre split nose cowlings and driving Hartzell propellers. Alternatively, two 180 hp Lycoming IO-360-B1B or 200 hp Lycoming IO-360-A1A engines can be installed.

Other new structural items include a one-piece wrap-around windshield, wing-tips of improved aerodynamic form and a 15 in (38 cm) longer streamlined glass-fibre nose-cone. The interior of the cabin is custom-styled for a pilot and four passengers, and the exterior is given a new three-colour finish. Payload is increased by 159 lb (72 kg).

Equipment changes cover the installation of

50A electrical generators, a new instrument panel with dual flying instruments and a Vecto attitude magnetic indicator in which heading and attitude are displayed on a single instrument. The ventilation and heating systems are improved and comprehensive radio is installed.

Standard equipment on the Geronimo includes a Tactair three-axis auto-pilot; a Narco primary radio package made up of a Mk 12 360-channel transceiver and 100-channel nav receiver, VRP-37 VOR antenna, VP-10 communications antenna, VOA-5 VOR/ILS indicator converter and UGR-1 20-channel glideslope receiver; and a Narco secondary radio package made up of a Mk 12 90-channel transceiver with 100-channel nav receiver, VP-10 antenna, VOA-4 converter indicator, ADF-30, MBT-12 marker beacon receiver, Marconi-type marker beacon antenna, headset and microphone.

A total of approximately 50 complete and partial Geronimo conversions had been completed by June 1967, the latest examples with further refinements, including wheel well doors, dorsal fin speed fairings on the nacelles and wing roots and more powerful brakes.

WEIGHT:

Max T-O weight:
3,500 lb AUW Apache	3,684 lb (1,671 kg)
3,800 lb AUW Apache	4,000 lb (1,814 kg)

Current version of the Geronimo conversion of the Piper Apache 160 (*Howard Levy*)

PERFORMANCE (Standard 180 hp Geronimo, at max T-O weight):
Max level speed 189 knots (218 mph; 351 km/h)
Cruising speed (75% power) at 7,000 ft (2,130 m)
181 knots (208 mph; 335 km/h)
Stalling speed, flaps down
48 knots (55 mph; 89 km/h)

Rate of climb at S/L	2,000 ft (610 m)/min
Single-engine rate of climb at S/L	800 ft (244 m)/min
Service ceiling	22,200 ft (6,765 m)
Single-engine ceiling	9,700 ft (2,955 m)
T-O run	600 ft (183 m)
Landing run	750 ft (230 m)

SIKORSKY

SIKORSKY AIRCRAFT, DIVISION OF UNITED AIRCRAFT CORPORATION

HEAD OFFICE AND WORKS:
Stratford, Connecticut 06602

OTHER WORKS:
South Avenue, Bridgeport, Connecticut; and Bridgeport Municipal Airport, Stratford, Connecticut

PRESIDENT:
Wesley A. Kuhrt

VICE-PRESIDENTS:
John A. McKenna (Air Transportation Systems)
Leonard M. Horner (Surface Transportation Systems)
Paul W. Holt (Contract Administration)
James W. Clyne (Marketing and Product Support)
Carlos C. Wood (Engineering)
Oliver B. Chittick (Deputy Programme Manager—German CH-53 Programme)
Robert H. Shatz (Special Projects)

FACTORY SUPERINTENDENT: J. W. Dunn

DIVISION CONTROLLER: James J. Patti

DIVISIONAL AUDITOR: H. W. Engstrom

MARKETING MANAGER, MILITARY: A. K. Poole

MARKETING MANAGER, AIRLINE: E. J. Nesbitt

DIRECTOR, INDUSTRIAL MARKETING: E. E. Gustafson

PUBLIC RELATIONS MANAGER: F. J. Delear

Sikorsky's main plant at Stratford, which has 1,300,000 sq ft of working space, is devoted to production of the S-61 twin-turbine amphibious transport helicopter and its anti-submarine counterpart, the SH-3D, the rear-loading S-61R, the S-62 single-turbine amphibious helicopter, the S-64 Skycrane and the S-65 transport helicopter. The company's original 600,000 sq ft plant at Bridgeport is utilised for detail fabrication, and for overhaul and repair. Employment at both plants totalled slightly more than 9,000 in January 1970.

Research efforts at Sikorsky Aircraft are concentrated currently on advanced heavy-lift helicopters and compounds. Analysis of traffic routes and air terminals used for inter-city services forecast a need for larger and faster VTOL aircraft in the 1970s. To meet such a need, Sikorsky engineers have completed preliminary design of an airline-type S-65, a three-engined 86-passenger compound helicopter with a cruising speed of 250 mph (402 km/h) at 8,000 ft (2,440 m) altitude. A larger S-64, with an 18-ton load capacity, has reached the component test stage, while studies have continued on heavy-lift helicopters of even greater capacity.

Sikorsky's S-65, S-64 and S-61 production helicopters have been fitted with more powerful engines that improved speed, hot-weather, altitude and lifting performances.

Improved versions of the S-65, largest of the company's helicopters, were delivered to the USAF and US Marine Corps during 1969. Two S-65 helicopters were also accepted by the West German government, as the first of an order for 135 aircraft to be built under a US/German co-production programme. Orders for S-65's were also received from the Austrian government, for use as search and rescue vehicles.

A dozen commercial S-61's were delivered in 1969 and Mark II S-61's, with main rotor bifilar absorbers to reduce vibration and other improvements, were produced for the first time. The US Coast Guard's S-61's, with highly sophisticated navigation and rescue equipment, became operational and were delivered to six bases.

Sikorsky UH-34 utility helicopter of the Israel Defence Force (*S. P. Peltz*)

During 1969 the US Army accepted its first two advanced S-64's, with more powerful engines and other improvements, and the commercial S-64 received FAA certification.

In the field of research and development, an experimental compound S-61 continued to provide flight information on components such as blades, engines, wings and control systems, while another S-61, fitted with a six-blade main rotor and ten-blade tail rotor, demonstrated a major reduction in noise levels. Sikorsky's advancing blade concept (ABC), with twin rotor systems on a common axis, was built and prepared for wind tunnel tests. The concept of a telescoping rotor blade was investigated for possible use on a number of different aircraft, and new materials, particularly composites, were tested for weight-saving and strength characteristics. In addition, a new hoist test stand was constructed to evaluate heavy-lift systems more easily.

Production of the S-58 and S-62 has ended, but this may be temporary. A retrofit turbine installation is being offered for the S-58.

Sikorsky licensees are Westland Aircraft Ltd of Great Britain, Gruppo Fratelli Agusta of Italy, Sud-Aviation of France, Mitsubishi Heavy Industries Ltd of Japan, United Aircraft of Canada Ltd and, for co-production of the S-65, the Federal Republic of Germany.

Up to January 1970, Sikorsky had produced a total of 4,850 helicopters, and licensees in Canada, France, Great Britian, Italy and Japan had produced an additional 1,600 helicopters.

SIKORSKY S-58

US Navy designations: LH-34 and SH-34 Seabat
US Army designation: CH-34 Choctaw
US Marine Corps designations: UH-34 and VH-34 Seahorse

The first prototype of this helicopter flew on 8 March 1954, and the first production machine on 20 September 1954.

The following military versions of the S-58 remain in service with the US armed forces:

CH-34A (formerly H-34A) **Choctaw.** Transport and general-purpose helicopter, in service with

US Army. Has been armed experimentally with rockets, etc.

CH-34C (formerly H-34C) **Choctaw.** Similar to CH-34A, but with airborne search equipment.

LH-34D (formerly HSS-1L). Winterised version of Navy Seabat.

UH-34D (formerly HUS-1) **Seahorse.** Utility version for Marines, first ordered on 15 October 1954 and accepted for service in January 1957. Bullpup missiles have been fired experimentally from a UH-34D.

VH-34D (formerly HUS-1Z). VIP transport version of Seahorse.

UH-34E (formerly HUS-1A) **Seahorse.** Version with pontoons for emergency operation from water.

SH-34G (formerly HSS-1) **Seabat.** Anti-submarine version, ordered by US Navy on 30 June 1952 and accepted for service in February 1954.

SH-34J (formerly HSS-1N) **Seabat.** Development of SH-34G for US Navy. This version utilises Sikorsky's automatic stabilisation equipment and is suitable for day and night instrument flying. The changes include (1) incorporation of Ryan-developed AN/APN-97 Doppler and other radar to measure ground speed and altitude accurately; (2) improved flight instrument and cockpit arrangement; (3) addition of automatic engine rpm controls; and (4) introduction of an automatic "hover coupler". With the coupler, which uses the radar to determine ground motion, it is possible for the pilot to place the helicopter on automatic control at 200 ft (60 m) altitude and 92 mph (148 kmh) ground speed and to come automatically to a zero ground speed at a 50 ft (15 m) altitude over a pre-selected spot.

There are three commercial versions of the S-58, of which the S-58B and S-58D passenger-freighters are similar to the H-34. The S-58C scheduled passenger-carrying version has two entrance doors on the starboard side of the cabin. First commercial deliveries of the S-58C were made in 1956-57.

Production of the S-58 series by Sikorsky totalled 1,766 by December 1965, when it terminated temporarily. It re-started subsequently to meet new requirements of the US Military Assistance Programme and an overall total of 1,821 aircraft had been delivered by January 1970, when production had again ended.

In January 1970 Sikorsky Aircraft announced plans to produce and market kits for conversion of the piston-engined S-58 into a twin-turbine helicopter. The turbine version, to be known as the S-58T, is expected to provide increased safety and reliability, greater speed and lifting power, and improved performance at high altitudes on hot days. It also will have lower operating costs than the existing piston engined models.

Sikorsky will deliver FAA-certificated retrofit kits to S-58 operators for their own installation, or will install the kits in the customer's aircraft at the Sikorsky plant. Later, Sikorsky may obtain used S-58s and offer them with the turbine engines installed.

The new turbine powerplant, the Pratt & Whitney (UACL) PT6 Twin Pac, consists of two PT6 free-shaft engines and a combining gearbox, and is certificated by the FAA at an 1,800 hp rating at sea level. Only 1,450 hp is needed by the S-58T in normal service and the excess will provide the reserve of power for altitude operation.

The twin turbines are expected to increase the S-58's payload on a hot day or at high altitudes by up to 3,000 lb (1,360 kg). Alternatively, it will be able to carry the same payload as the piston-engined model to an altitude some 6,000 ft (1,830 m) higher.

On a hot day (95°F/35°C at S/L), the S-58T will be able to hover in ground effect at its allowable gross weight of 13,000 lb (5,900 kg) at 7,500 ft (2,286 m).

Military S-58's have been supplied to the armed forces of the Argentine, Brazil, Canada, Chile, France, Federal Germany, Italy, Japan, the Netherlands and Thailand. In addition, Sud-Aviation delivered 166 S-58's from their works in France and Westland are producing several turbine-powered versions in the UK, under the name Wessex.

TYPE: General-purpose helicopter.

ROTOR SYSTEM: Four-blade all-metal main and tail rotors, both with servo control. Fully-articulated main rotor blades, each made up of a hollow extruded aluminium spar and trailing-edge pockets of aluminium. Each tail rotor blade has an aluminium spar, sheet aluminium skin and honeycomb trailing-edge. Blades of each rotor interchangeable. Main rotor blades fold. Main and tail rotor brakes.

ROTOR DRIVE: Transmission system has 25% fewer parts than in earlier Sikorsky designs, and provides accessory drives for the generator and its blower, primary servo-control hydraulic pump, rotor tachometer and a combining clutch. Steel-tube drive-shafts with rubber couplings. Main gearbox below main rotor, intermediate gearbox at base of tail pylon and tail gearbox behind tail rotor. Main rotor/engine rpm ratio 1 : 11·293. Tail rotor/engine rpm ratio 1 : 1·884.

FUSELAGE: Semi-monocoque structure, primarily of magnesium and aluminium alloys, with some titanium and stainless steel.

TAIL SURFACE: Ground-adjustable stabiliser made of magnesium skin over magnesium and aluminium structure.

LANDING GEAR: Non-retractable three-wheel undercarriage, with tail-wheel towards rear of fuselage. Sikorsky oleo-pneumatic shock-absorber struts. Tail-wheel is fully-castoring and self-centering, with an anti-swivelling lock. Goodyear main wheel tyres size 11·00 × 12, pressure 42 lb/sq in (2·95 kg/cm²). Tail-wheel tyre size 6·00 × 6 6-ply. Toe-operated Goodyear disc brakes. Provision for amphibious gear, pontoons, "doughnut" or pop-out flotation bags.

POWER PLANT: One 1,525 hp Wright R-1820-84B/D nine-cylinder radial air-cooled engine, mounted behind large clam-shell doors in nose of fuselage. Fuel in 113 US gallon (427 litre) forward tank, 70 US gallon (265 litre) centre tank, 31·5 US gallon (119 litre) auxiliary tank and 92 US gallon (348 litre) aft tank. Total internal fuel capacity 306·5 US gallons (1,159 litres). Provision for 150 US gallon (568 litre) external metal tank. Refuelling point on starboard side of fuselage. Oil capacity 10·5 US gallons (40 litres).

ACCOMMODATION: Pilot's compartment above main cabin seats two side-by-side with dual controls. Cabin seats 16-18 passengers on inward-facing troop seats or 12 on airline seats in one or two compartments. Two-compartment version has hinged doors, each cabin seating six in rows of three facing each other. Eight stretchers can be carried. Cabin entrance on starboard side. Sliding windows of pilot's compartment removable in an emergency. Cabin and cockpit are heated and sound-proofed.

SYSTEMS: Air-conditioning by 50,000 or 100,000 BTU heater and 1½ hp Sikorsky blower-defroster. Hydraulic system, pressure 1,250 lb/sq in (88 kg/cm²), for hoist, wheel and rotor

Sikorsky S-61A-4 troop and cargo transport helicopter of the Royal Malaysian Air Force

Sikorsky SH-3A Naval helicopter of the type used for astronaut recovery duties

brakes, clutch, primary and auxiliary servos. 28V DC electrical system. 115V and 26V AC generator, battery and external power supply.

ELECTRONICS AND EQUIPMENT: Optional items include blind-flying instrumentation, ARC-210 VHF, ARC-21A ADF, Collins ILS, HTR-5 HF, cargo sling and military equipment.

DIMENSIONS, EXTERNAL:

Diameter of main rotor	56 ft 0 in (17·07 m)
Diameter of tail rotor	9 ft 6 in (2·90 m)
Distance between rotor centres	33 ft 1 in (10·08 m)
Length overall	56 ft 8½ in (17·27 m)
Length of fuselage	46 ft 9 in (14·25 m)
Width, rotors folded	12 ft 11 in (3·94 m)
Height to top of rotor hub	14 ft 3½ in (4·36 m)
Overall height	15 ft 11 in (4·85 m)
Wheel track	14 ft 0 in (4·27 m)
Wheelbase	28 ft 3 in (8·75 m)
Cabin door:	
Height:	
S-58B	4 ft 0 in (1·22 m)
S-58C	4 ft 8 in (1·42 m)
Width:	
S-58B	4 ft 5½ in (1·36 m)
S-58C	2 ft 5 in (0·74 m)
Height to sill	2 ft 10½ in (0·88 m)

DIMENSIONS, INTERNAL:

Cabin: Length	13 ft 7 in (4·14 m)
Max width	5 ft 0 in (1·52 m)
Max height	5 ft 10 in (1·78 m)
Floor area	65 sq ft (6·04 m²)
Volume	350 cu ft (9·91 m³)

AREAS:

Main rotor blade (each)	35·00 sq ft (3·25 m²)
Tail rotor blade (each)	2·67 sq ft (0·25 m²)
Main rotor disc	2,460 sq ft (228·54 m²)
Tail rotor disc	70·88 sq ft (6·59 m²)
Stabiliser	12·38 sq ft (1·15 m²)

WEIGHTS AND LOADINGS:

Weight empty, equipped:	
CH-34A	7,750 lb (3,515 kg)
UH-34D	7,900 lb (3,583 kg)
SH-34J	8,275 lb (3,754 kg)
S-58	7,630 lb (3,461 kg)
Max normal T-O weight	13,000 lb (5,900 kg)
Max permissible weight	14,000 lb (6,350 kg)
Max disc loading	5·3 lb/sq ft (25·9 kg/m²)
Max power loading	8·53 lb/hp (3·87 kg/hp)

PERFORMANCE (at 13,000 lb = 5,900 kg AUW):

Max level speed at S/L:	
CH-34A	106 knots (122 mph; 196 km/h)
S-58	107 knots (123 mph; 198 km/h)
Max cruising speed:	
CH-34A	84 knots (97 mph; 156 km/h)
S-58	85 knots (98 mph; 158 km/h)
Max rate of climb at S/L	1,100 ft (335 m)/min
Vertical rate of climb at S/L	200 ft (60 m)/min

Service ceiling:	
CH-34A	9,500 ft (2,900 m)
S-58	9,000 ft (2,740 m)
Hovering ceiling in ground effect	4,900 ft (1,490 m)
Hovering ceiling out of ground effect	2,400 ft (730 m)
Range with max fuel, 10% reserve:	
CH-34A	214 nm (247 miles; 400 km)
S-58	243 nm (280 miles; 450 km)

SIKORSKY S-61A, S-61B and S-61F
US military designations: RH-3 and SH-3 Sea King, HH-3A, VH-3A, CH-3B
RCN designation: CHSS-2

Sikorsky's S-61 series of twin-turbine helicopters includes at the present time the following military and commercial variants:

S-61A. Amphibious transport, generally similar to the US Navy's SH-3A. Cabin can accommodate 26 troops, 15 litters, cargo, or 12 passengers in VIP configuration. Rolls-Royce Bristol Gnome H.1200 shaft-turbines available as alternative to standard General Electric T58 engines. Three (plus three SH-3A's) operated by USAF under the designation **CH-3B**, for missile site support and drone recovery duties. Eight delivered to Royal Danish Air Force in 1965, plus a ninth delivered in April 1970, for long-range air-sea rescue duties, with additional fuel tankage. Ten (S-61A-4's) ordered in February 1967 for troop and cargo transport duties with Royal Malaysian Air Force, with deliveries beginning in the Autumn of 1967, and ending in February 1968. The RMAF aircraft are 31-seaters, with rescue hoists and auxiliary fuel tanks as standard equipment. One delivered to Construction Helicopters.

S-61B. Initial production version of S-61, with amphibious capability. In service as the US Navy's standard anti-submarine helicopter, under the designations **SH-3A** (formerly HSS-2) and **SH-3D Sea King.** Difference between the two versions is that the SH-3A has 1,250 shp General Electric T58-GE-8B shaft-turbines, while the SH-3D has 1,400 shp T58-GE-10's and an additional 140 US gallons (530 litres) of fuel. First SH-3D delivered, in June 1966, was one of six aircraft of this type ordered for the Spanish Navy. Forty-one anti-submarine aircraft similar to SH-3A were ordered for the Canadian Armed Forces, with the designation **CHSS-2**. First of these was delivered in May 1963: fifth and subsequent aircraft have been assembled by United Aircraft of Canada Ltd. Four SH-3D's were delivered to the Brazilian Navy in November and December 1969 and January 1970.

The SH-3A is standard equipment in the Japanese Maritime Self-Defence Force. An initial order for 11 was negotiated in 1962, of which the first was delivered by Sikorsky in 1963. The next two aircraft were delivered partially assembled, and Mitsubishi, Sikorsky's Japanese licensee, is assembling the remainder of the total of 83 that have been ordered. Mitsubishi converted two SH-3A's to S-61A standard for use during Antarctic expeditions.

A version of the SH-3D with Rolls-Royce Bristol Gnome shaft-turbine engines and British anti-submarine equipment is being manufactured for the Royal Navy and German Navy by Westland Helicopters Ltd (which see). SH-3D's are also being manufactured by Agusta, Sikorsky's Italian licensee, for the Italian Navy.

Under a contract announced in April 1964, nine SH-3A's have been converted for mine countermeasures duty with the US Navy, under the designation **RH-3A**. This version has two cargo doors, one on each side, instead of one; bubble windows on each side aft of the cargo doors; rear-view mirrors for pilot and co-pilot; and a pivoting tow-tube and hook assembly attached to the fuselage above the tail-wheel. The RH-3A is designed to carry, stream, tow and retrieve a variety of mine countermeasures (MCM) gear. Deliveries were made in 1965, on the basis of three for testing and three each to USN helicopter squadrons on the east and west coasts of the USA, four of these aircraft being assigned for service on board two MCM ships.

A further modified version of the SH-3A, designated **HH-3A**, is being tested by the US Navy as a search and rescue helicopter, with armament, armour and a high-speed rescue hoist. HH-3A conversion kits will be supplied to the Navy's overhaul and repair base at Quonset Point, Rhode Island, where conversions will be carried out.

Eight specially-equipped **VH-3A's** (formerly HSS-2Z), are used by the Executive Flight Detachment which provides a VIP transport and emergency evacuation service for the US President and other key personnel. Two of these aircraft are operated by the US Army and six by the US Marine Corps.

S-61F. Under a two-year Army/Navy research programme, Sikorsky added stub-wings and auxiliary turbojets to a modified SH-3A, to make it capable of speeds exceeding 230 mph (370 kmh). Redesignated S-61F, this experimental high-speed helicopter was also subjected to an extensive drag reduction programme. Its stabilising floats were replaced by a retractable and fully-enclosed main landing gear. A new horizontal stabiliser of increased span, larger tail pylon and fin, and an adjustable rudder were installed. Two Pratt & Whitney J60 turbojets were mounted in pods on each side of the fuselage for forward thrust. The 32 ft (9·75 m) span wings were fitted with full-span flap-ailerons. The fuselage nose was made more rounded and the rear fuselage streamlined. First flight was made on 21 May 1965, and in July 1965, before its fixed wings were fitted, the S-61F attained a speed of 242 mph (390 kmh). Tests were performed with blades of reduced twist and a six-blade rotor, as well as with the standard five-blade rotor. This aircraft was illustrated in the 1966-67 *Jane's*.

S-61L. Non-amphibious civil transport with longer fuselage than S-61A/B. Described separately.

S-61N. Amphibious counterpart of S-61L, with which it is described.

S-61R. Development of S-61B for transport duties with USAF, under the designations **CH-3C** and **E.** Rear loading ramp, new landing gear and other changes. Described separately.

The first version of the S-61 ordered into production was the SH-3A (formerly HSS-2) Sea King amphibious anti-submarine helicopter. The original US Navy contract for this aircraft was received on 23 September 1957, and the prototype flew for the first time on 11 March 1959. Official Navy Board of Inspection and Survey trials began at the Naval Air Test Center, Patuxent River, Maryland, on 8 February 1961, and first deliveries to the Fleet were made in September 1961.

On 6 March 1965, an SH-3A made the first non-stop flight by a helicopter across the North American continent and, in doing so, set a new international straight-line distance record of 1,838 nm (2,116 miles; 3,405 km). The helicopter took off from the aircraft carrier *Hornet* at San Diego, California, and landed on the carrier *Franklin D. Roosevelt* at Jacksonville, Florida, 15 hr 52 min later. Average ground speed was 115·8 knots (133·3 mph; 214·5 km/h). T-O weight was 23,000 lb (10,435 kg), with 1,690 US gallons (6,395 litres) of fuel.

A total of more than 610 military and civil S-61's of all types had been delivered by January 1970.

The following details apply to the SH-3D Sea King, but are generally applicable to the other versions except for accommodation and equipment:

TYPE: Twin-engined amphibious all-weather anti-submarine helicopter.

ROTOR SYSTEM: Five-blade main and tail rotors. All-metal fully-articulated oil-lubricated main rotor. Flanged cuffs on blades bolted to matching flanges on all-steel rotor head. Main rotor blades are interchangeable and are provided with an automatic powered folding system. Rotor brake standard. All-metal tail rotor.

ROTOR DRIVE: Both engines drive through free-wheel units and rotor brake to main gearbox. Steel drive-shafts. Tail rotor shaft-driven through intermediate and tail gearboxes. Accessories driven by power take-off on tail rotor shaft. Additional free-wheel units between accessories and port engine, and between accessories and tail rotor shaft. Main rotor/engine rpm ratio 1 : 93·43. Tail rotor/engine rpm ratio 1 : 16·7.

FUSELAGE: Boat hull of all-metal semi-monocoque construction. Single-step. Tail section folds to reduce stowage requirements.

TAIL SURFACE: Fixed stabiliser on starboard side of tail section.

LANDING GEAR: Amphibious. Land gear consists of two twin-wheel main units, which are retracted rearward hydraulically into stabilising floats, and non-retractable tail-wheel. Oleo-pneumatic shock-absorbers. Goodyear main wheels and tubeless tyres size 6·50 × 10 type III, pressure 70 lb/sq in (4·92 kg/cm²). Goodyear tail-wheel and tyre size 6·00 × 6. Goodyear hydraulic disc brakes. Boat hull and pop-out flotation bags in stabilising floats permit emergency operation from water.

POWER PLANT: Two 1,400 shp General Electric T58-GE-10 shaft-turbine engines. Three bladder-type fuel tanks in hull; forward tank capacity 347 US gallons (1,314 litres), centre tank capacity 140 US gallons (530 litres), rear tank capacity 353 US gallons (1,336 litres). Total fuel capacity 840 US gallons (3,180 litres). Refuelling point on port side of fuselage. Oil capacity 7 US gallons (26·5 litres).

ACCOMMODATION: Pilot and co-pilot on flight deck, two sonar operators in main cabin. Dual controls. Crew entry door at rear of flight deck on port side. Large loading door at rear of cabin on starboard side.

SYSTEMS: Primary and auxiliary hydraulic systems, pressure 1,500 lb/sq in (105 kg/cm²), for flying controls. Utility hydraulic system, pressure 3,000 lb/sq in (210 kg/cm²), for landing gear, winches and blade folding. Pneumatic system, pressure 3,000 lb/sq in (210 kg/cm²), for blow-down emergency landing gear extension. Electrical system includes one 300A DC generators, two 20kVA 115A AC generators and 24V 22A battery. APU optional.

ELECTRONICS AND EQUIPMENT: Bendix AQS-13 sonar with 180° search beam width. Hamilton Standard autostabilisation equipment. Automatic transition into hover. Sonar coupler holds altitude automatically in conjunction with Ryan APN-130 Doppler radar and radar altimeter. Provision for 600 lb (272 kg) capacity rescue hoist and 8,000 lb (3,630 kg) capacity automatic touchdown-release low-response cargo sling for external loads.

ARMAMENT: Provision for 840 lb (381 kg) of weapons, including homing torpedoes.

DIMENSIONS, EXTERNAL:

Diameter of main rotor	62 ft 0 in (18·90 m)
Main rotor blade chord	18·25 in (46·35 cm)
Diameter of tail rotor	10 ft 4 in (3·15 m)
Distance between rotor centres	36 ft 5 in (11·10 m)
Length overall	72 ft 8 in (22·15 m)
Length of fuselage	54 ft 9 in (16·69 m)
Length, tail pylon folded	47 ft 3 in (14·40 m)
Width, rotors folded	16 ft 4 in (4·98 m)
Height to top of rotor hub	15 ft 6 in (4·72 m)
Overall height	16 ft 10 in (5·13 m)
Wheel track	13 ft 0 in (3·96 m)
Wheelbase	23 ft 6½ in (7·18 m)
Crew door (fwd, port):	
Height	5 ft 6 in (1·68 m)
Width	3 ft 0 in (0·91 m)
Height to sill	3 ft 9 in (1·14 m)
Main cabin door (stbd):	
Height	5 ft 0 in (1·52 m)
Width	5 ft 8 in (1·73 m)
Height to sill	3 ft 9 in (1·14 m)

DIMENSIONS, INTERNAL (S-61A):

Cabin: Length	24 ft 11 in (7·60 m)
Max width	6 ft 6 in (1·98 m)
Max height	6 ft 3½ in (1·92 m)
Floor area	162 sq ft (15·1 m²)
Volume	1,020 cu ft (28·9 m³)

AREAS:

Main rotor blade (each)	44·54 sq ft (4·14 m²)
Tail rotor blade (each)	2·46 sq ft (0·23 m²)
Main rotor disc	3,019 sq ft (280·5 m²)
Tail rotor disc	83·90 sq ft (7·80 m²)
Stabiliser	20·00 sq ft (1·86 m²)

WEIGHTS:

Weight empty:		
S-61A	9,763 lb	(4,428 kg)
S-61B	11,865 lb	(5,382 kg)
Normal T-O weight:		
S-61A	20,500 lb	(9,300 kg)
SH-3A (ASW)	18,044 lb	(8,185 kg)
SH-3D (ASW)	18,626 lb	(8,449 kg)
Max T-O weight:		
S-61A	21,500 lb	(9,750 kg)
S-61B	20,500 lb	(9,300 kg)

PERFORMANCE (at 20,500 lb = 9,300 kg AUW):
Max level speed
144 knots (166 mph; 267 km/h)
Cruising speed for max range
118 knots (136 mph; 219 km/h)
Max rate of climb at S/L 2,200 ft (670 m)/min
Service ceiling 14,700 ft (4,480 m)
Hovering ceiling in ground effect
10,500 ft (3,200 m)
Hovering ceiling out of ground effect
8,200 ft (2,500 m)
Range with max fuel, 10% reserve
542 nm (625 miles; 1,005 km)

SIKORSKY S-61L AND S-61N

Although basically similar to the S-61A and B, the S-61L and N commercial transports incorporate a number of changes, including a longer fuselage. Other details are as follows:

S-61L. Non-amphibious configuration. Modified landing gear, rotor head and stabiliser. First flight of the prototype S-61L was made on 6 December 1960, and it received FAA Type Approval on 2 November 1961. Three S-61L's operated by Los Angeles Airways had each exceeded 10,000 flight hours in February 1968.

S-61N. Similar to S-61L, but with sealed hull for amphibious operation and stabilising floats as on SH-3A. First flight of the first S-61N was made on 7 August 1962.

Both models are now offered in the **Mark II** versions, with General Electric CT58-140-2 turboshaft engines, as described below (earlier aircraft have 1,350 shp engines). Passenger accommodation is increased to maximum of 30 in the S-61L and 26 in the S-61N (28 optional); and the Mark II is able to carry 22 passengers on an 86°F day, compared with the former 10. There are six individual cargo bins to speed baggage handling. The rating of the main transmission is increased from 2,300 to 2,500 hp. Other changes include improved vibration damping. Production of 12 S-61L and S-61N Mark IIs is planned for 1970.

Up to January 1970, orders received were as follows:

Ansett-ANA (Australia)	1 S-61N
BEA Helicopters	5 S-61N
Bristow Helicopters	2 S-61N
Brunei Shell	2 S-61N
Canada D.O.T.	1 S-61N
Carson Helicopters	1 S-61N
Elivie (Alitalia)	2 S-61N
Greenlandair	5 S-61N
Helikopter Service (Norway)	3 S-61N
Japan Air Lines	1 S-61N
KLM	2 S-61N
Los Angeles Airways	7 S-61N
Nitto Airways (Japan)	1 S-61N
Okanagan	1 S-61N
Pan American Airways	4 S-61L
San Francisco & Oakland Helicopter Airlines	4 S-61N

On 6 October 1964 the S-61L and S-61N became the first transport helicopters to receive FAA approval for instrument flight operations.

TYPE: Twin-turbine all-weather helicopter airliners.

ROTOR SYSTEM AND ROTOR DRIVE: As for SH-3A/D, S-61A and S-61B, except blades do not fold.

FUSELAGE: All-metal semi-monocoque structure of boat-hull form.

TAIL SURFACE: Stabiliser on starboard side of tail section.

LANDING GEAR (S-61L): Non-amphibious non-retractable tail-wheel type with twin wheels on main units. Oleo-pneumatic shock-absorbers. Goodyear main wheels and tubeless tyres, size 6·50 × 10 type III, pressure 70 lb/sq in (4·92 kg/cm²). Goodyear tail-wheel and tyre, size 6·00 × 6. Goodyear hydraulic disc brakes.

LANDING GEAR (S-61N): Amphibious hydraulically-retractable type. Twin wheels on main units, which retract rearward into stabilising floats. Non-retractable tail-wheel. Each float provides 3,320 lb (1,506 kg) buoyancy and, with the sealed hull, permits operation from water. Shock-absorbers, wheels, tyres and brakes as for S-61L.

POWER PLANT: Two 1,500 shp General Electric CT58-140-2 shaft-turbine engines. Two bladder-type fuel tanks in hull; forward tank capacity 210 US gallons (796 litres), rear tank capacity 200 US gallons (757 litres). Total fuel capacity 410 US gallons (1,553 litres). Additional 244-US gallon (924-litre) tank optionally available for S-61N. Refuelling point on port side of fuselage. Oil capacity 7 US gallons (26·5 litres).

ACCOMMODATION: Crew of three: pilot, co-pilot and flight attendant. Main cabin accommodates up to 30 passengers (22 at 86°F). Standard arrangement has eight single seats and one double seat on port side of cabin, seven double seats on starboard side and one

Sikorsky S-61N twin-turbine amphibious transport helicopter, operated by Elivie, a subsidiary of Alitalia

double seat at rear. Rear seat may be replaced by a toilet. Galley may be installed in forward baggage compartment area on starboard side. Forward half of cabin may be provided with folding seats and tie-down rings for convertible passenger-freight operations. Two doors on starboard side of cabin: main cabin door of air-stair type. Baggage space above and below floor at front, on starboard side of cabin, and below floor in area of air-stair door (aft, starboard side).

SYSTEMS: As for SH-3A, S-61A and S-61B.

ELECTRONICS AND EQUIPMENT: Radio and radar to customer's specification. Blind-flying instrumentation standard.

DIMENSIONS, EXTERNAL:

Diameter of main rotor	62 ft 0 in (18·90 m)
Diameter of tail rotor	10 ft 4 in (3·15 m)
Distance between rotor centres:	
S-61L	36 ft 5 in (11·10 m)
S-61N	36 ft 8 in (11·17 m)
Length of fuselage:	
S-61L	72 ft 7 in (22·12 m)
S-61N	72 ft 10 in (22·20 m)
Width, over landing gear:	
S-61L	14 ft 8 in (4·47 m)
S-61N	19 ft 9 in (6·02 m)
Height to top of rotor hub pitot head:	
S-61L	17 ft 0 in (5·18 m)
S-61N	17 ft 5½ in (5·32 m)
Overall height:	
S-61L	17 ft 0 in (5·18 m)
S-61N	18 ft 5½ in (5·63 m)
Wheel track	
S-61L	13 ft 0 in (3·96 m)
S-61N	14 ft 0 in (4·27 m)
Wheelbase:	
S-61L	23 ft 5½ in (7·15 m)
S-61N	23 ft 11½ in (7·30 m)
Cabin door (Airstair):	
Height	5 ft 6 in (1·68 m)

Width	2 ft 8 in (0·81 m)
Height to sill	3 ft 9 in (1·14 m)
Cargo door:	
Height	5 ft 6 in (1·68 m)
Width	4 ft 2 in (1·27 m)
Height to sill	3 ft 9 in (1·14 m)

DIMENSIONS, INTERNAL:

Cabin: Length	31 ft 11 in (9·73 m)
Max width	6 ft 6 in (1·98 m)
Max height	6 ft 3½ in (1·92 m)
Floor area	approx 217 sq ft (20·16 m²)
Volume	approx 1,305 cu ft (36·95 m³)
Freight hold (above floor)	approx 125 cu ft (3·54 m³)
Freight hold (under floor)	approx 25 cu ft (0·71 m³)

AREAS:

Main rotor blade (each)	40·4 sq ft (3·75 m²)
Tail rotor blade (each)	2·35 sq ft (0·22 m²)
Main rotor disc	3,019 sq ft (280·5 m²)
Tail rotor disc	83·9 sq ft (7·79 m²)
Stabiliser	27·0 sq ft (2·51 m²)

WEIGHTS:

Weight empty:	
S-61L	11,726 lb (5,318 kg)
S-61N	12,224 lb (5,544 kg)
Max T-O weight	19,000 lb (8,620 kg)

PERFORMANCE (at max T-O weight):

Max level speed at S/L	130 knots (150 mph; 241 km/h)
Average cruising speed	122 knots (140 mph; 225 km/h)
Max rate of climb at S/L	1,300 ft (395 m)/min
Service ceiling	12,500 ft (3,810 m)
Hovering ceiling in ground effect	
S-61L	9,000 ft (2,743 m)
S-61N	8,700 ft (2,652 m)
Hovering ceiling out of ground effect	
S-61L	3,900 ft (1,189 m)
S-61N	3,800 ft (1,158 m)

Range with max fuel, 30 min reserve	
S-61L	226 nm (260 miles; 418 km)
S-61N	399 nm (460 miles; 740 km)

SIKORSKY S-61R
US military designations: CH-3 and HH-3

Although based on the SH-3A, this amphibious transport helicopter introduces many important design changes. They include provision of a hydraulically-operated rear ramp for straight-in loading of wheeled vehicles, a 2,000 lb (907 kg) capacity winch for internal cargo handling, retractable tricycle-type landing gear, pressurised rotor blades for quick and easy inspection, gas-turbine auxiliary power supply for independent field operations, self-lubricating main and tail rotors, and built-in equipment for the removal and replacement of all major components in remote areas.

There are four versions, as follows:

CH-3C. Initial order for 22 placed by USAF on 8 February 1963. Two 1,300 shp T58-GE-1 shaft-turbines.

In July 1963, the CH-3C won a competition for a long-range rotary-wing support system for the USAF and further orders followed. Up to January 1970, a total of 133 had been ordered. All those delivered as CH-3C's will be converted eventually to CH-3E or HH-3E standard.

CH-3E. New designation applicable since February 1966, following introduction of uprated engines (1,500 shp T58-GE-5's).

A new pod-mounted turret armament system has been developed for this version, with the weapon located off each sponson, with gunsights at the port and starboard personnel doors. Each pod mounts an Emerson Electric TAT-102 turret, incorporating a General Electric six-barrel 7·62-mm Minigun and an 8,000-round ammunition storage-feed system. Over 180° traverse

Sikorsky S-61R twin-engined amphibious transport helicopter in USAF service

is achieved on each side of the aircraft, to give complete 360° coverage with overlapping fire forward. By January 1970 a total of 83 CH-3E's had been delivered.

HH-3E. For USAF Aerospace Rescue and Recovery Service; orders included in above total. Additional equipment comprises armour, self-sealing fuel tanks, retractable flight refuelling probe, defensive armament and rescue hoist. Two 1,500 shp T58-GE-5 shaft-turbines. By January 1970, a total of 35 HH-3E's had been delivered.

HH-3F. Similar to HH-3E, for US Coast Guard. Advanced electronic equipment for search and rescue duties. No armour plate, armament or self-sealing tanks. Order announced in August 1965. Deliveries began in 1968 and by January 1970 a total of 22 HH-3F's had been delivered.

The first S-61R flew on 17 June 1963, almost a month ahead of schedule, and was followed by the first CH-3C a few weeks later. FAA type approval was received on 30 December 1963, and the first delivery of an operational CH-3C was made on the same day, for drone recovery duties at Tyndall AFB, Florida. Subsequent deliveries have been made to USAF Air Defense Command, Air Training Command, Tactical Air Command, Strategic Air Command and Aerospace Rescue and Recovery Service.

In January 1966, details were announced of a series of flight refuelling trials carried out successfully with a CH-3C at the US Marine Corps Air Station, Cherry Point, NC. Ten experimental contacts were made, with a nose-probe on the CH-3C and a drogue trailed from a USMC KC-130F tanker. The aircraft remained connected for up to five minutes at a time.

On 31 May-1 June 1967, two HH-3E's made the first non-stop transatlantic flights by helicopters, en route to the Paris Air Show. Nine aerial refuellings were made by each aircraft. The 3,708 nm (4,270 miles; 6,870 km) from New York to Paris were flown in 30 hr 46 min.

The following details apply to the current production CH-3E.

TYPE: Twin-engined amphibious transport helicopter.

ROTOR SYSTEM: Five-blade fully-articulated main rotor of all-metal construction. Flanged cuffs on blades bolted to matching flanges on rotor head. Control by rotating and stationary swashplates. Blades do not fold. Rotor brake standard. Conventional tail rotor with five aluminium blades.

ROTOR DRIVE: Twin turbines drive through free-wheeling units and rotor brake to main gearbox. Steel drive-shafts. Tail rotor shaft-driven through intermediate gearbox and tail gearbox. Main rotor/engine rpm ratio 1 : 93·43. Tail rotor/engine rpm ratio 1 : 16·7.

FUSELAGE: All-metal semi-monocoque structure of pod-and-boom type. Cabin of basic square section.

TAIL SURFACE: Horizontal stabiliser on starboard side of tail rotor pylon.

LANDING GEAR: Hydraulically-retractable tricycle type, with twin wheels on each unit. Main wheels retract forward into sponsons, each of which provides 4,797 lb (2,176 kg) of buoyancy and, with boat hull, permits amphibious operation. Oleo-pneumatic shock-absorbers. All wheels and tyres tubeless Type III rib, size 6·50-10, manufactured by Goodyear. Tyre pressure 70 lb/sq in (4·92 kg/cm²). Goodyear hydraulic disc brakes.

POWER PLANT: Two 1,500 shp General Electric T58-GE-5 shaft-turbine engines, mounted side-by-side above cabin, immediately forward of main transmission. Fuel in two bladder-type tanks beneath cabin floor; forward tank capacity 318 US gallons (1,204 litres), rear tank capacity 324 US gallons (1,226 litres). Total fuel capacity 642 US gallons (2,430 litres). Refuelling point on port side of fuselage. Total oil capacity 7 US gallons (26·5 litres).

ACCOMMODATION: Crew of two side-by-side on flight deck, with dual controls. Provision for flight engineer or attendant. Normal accommodation for 25 fully-equipped troops. Alternative arrangements for 30 troops, 15 stretchers or 5,000 lb (2,270 kg) of cargo. Jettisonable sliding door on starboard side at front of cabin. Internal door between cabin and flight deck. Hydraulically-operated rear loading ramp for vehicles, in two hinged sections, giving opening with minimum width of 5 ft 8 in (1·73 m) and headroom of up to 7 ft 3 in (2·21 m).

SYSTEMS: Primary and auxiliary hydraulic system, pressure 1,500 lb/sq in (105 kg/cm²), for flying control servos. Utility hydraulic system, pressure 3,000 lb/sq in (210 kg/cm²), for landing gear, rear ramp and winches. Pneumatic system, pressure 3,000 lb/sq in (210 kg/cm²), for emergency blow-down landing gear extension. Electrical system includes 24V 22A battery, two 20kVA 115V AC generators and one 300A DC generator. APU standard.

ELECTRONICS AND EQUIPMENT (CH-3C): Equipment includes 2,000 lb (907 kg) capacity winch for loading bulk cargo and an 8,000 lb (3,625 kg) capacity cargo sling. Floor incorporates tie-downs and skid strips. Automatic flight control system to stabilise aircraft during typical flight attitudes. Electronics include AN/ARC-34B UHF, TR-4A back-up UHF, AN/ARA-25 UHF direction finder group, AN/ARN-65 TACAN, AN-ARN-58 ILS and marker receiver, AN/ARN-59 LF ADF, AN/AIC-18 intercom, AN-AIC-13 public address system, AN/APX-46 transponder and AN/APN-150 altimeter.

DIMENSIONS, EXTERNAL:
Diameter of main rotor	62 ft 0 in (18·90 m)
Main rotor blade chord	18·25 in (46·35 cm)
Diameter of tail rotor	10 ft 4 in (3·15 m)
Distance between rotor centres	36 ft 10 in (11·22 m)
Length overall	73 ft 0 in (22·25 m)
Length of fuselage	57 ft 3 in (17·45 m)
Width, over landing gear	15 ft 10 in (4·82 m)
Height to top of rotor hub	16 ft 1 in (4·90 m)
Overall height	18 ft 1 in (5·51 m)
Wheel track	13 ft 4 in (4·06 m)
Wheelbase	17 ft 1 in (5·21 m)
Cabin door (fwd, stbd):	
Height	5 ft 4¾ in (1·65 m)
Width	4 ft 0 in (1·22 m)
Height to sill	4 ft 2 in (1·27 m)
Rear ramp:	
Length	14 ft 1 in (4·29 m)
Width	6 ft 1 in (1·85 m)

DIMENSIONS, INTERNAL:
Cabin (excluding flight deck):	
Length	25 ft 10½ in (7·89 m)
Max width	6 ft 6 in (1·98 m)
Max height	6 ft 3 in (1·91 m)
Floor area	approx 168 sq ft (15·61 m²)
Volume	approx 1,050 cu ft (29·73 m³)

AREAS:
Main rotor blade (each)	39·9 sq ft (3·71 m²)
Tail rotor blade (each)	2·35 sq ft (0·22 m²)
Main rotor disc	3,019 sq ft (280·5 m²)
Tail rotor disc	83·9 sq ft (7·80 m²)
Stabiliser	27·0 sq ft (2·51 m²)

WEIGHTS:
Weight empty	13,255 lb (6,010 kg)
Normal T-O weight	21,247 lb (9,635 kg)
Max T-O weight	22,050 lb (10,000 kg)

PERFORMANCE (at normal T-O weight):
Max level speed at S/L	141 knots (162 mph; 261 km/h)
Cruising speed for max range	125 knots (144 mph; 232 km/h)
Max rate of climb at S/L	1,310 ft (400 m)/min
Service ceiling	11,100 ft (3,385 m)
Hovering ceiling in ground effect	4,100 ft (1,250 m)
Range with max fuel, 10% reserve	404 nm (465 miles; 748 km)

SIKORSKY S-62
US Coast Guard designation: HH-52A

Four versions of the S-62 amphibious helicopter have been announced, as follows:

Sikorsky HH-3F search and rescue helicopter for the US Coast Guard

Sikorsky HH-3E of USAF Aerospace Rescue and Recovery Service, with refuelling probe, armour plating, jettisonable fuel tanks and rescue hoist

S-62A. This version incorporates many components of the Sikorsky S-55, including rotor blades, main and tail rotor heads, intermediate and tail gearboxes, shafting, and portions of the flying control and hydraulic systems.

Its empty weight is some 160 lb (72 kg) less than that of the S-55C, largely because it is powered by a 1,250 shp (de-rated to 730 shp) General Electric CT58-110 shaft-turbine, instead of by the latter's heavier piston-engine. Because of this weight saving and the availability of 130 more horsepower, which is maintained for high-altitude or hot weather flight, it can carry a much greater payload than that of the S-55 under all conditions. Full power is available at heights up to 20,000 ft (6,100 m).

First S-62A flew on 14 May 1958, and FAA type approval was received on 30 June 1960. The first delivery was made in the following month to Petroleum Helicopters Inc, to serve off-shore oil-rigs in the Gulf of Mexico.

S-62B. Basically similar to S-62A, but utilising main rotor system of S-58 instead of S-55, with reduced rotor diameter.

S-62C. Commercial and foreign military version of HH-52A.

HH-52A. Ordered for US Coast Guard Service to replace HH-34 for search and rescue duties. First three delivered in January 1963. This version has a 1,250 shp T58-GE-8 engine, automatic stabilisation equipment, towing equipment, and a 4 ft (1·22 m) long rescue platform that folds down from the cabin door and extends over the water, so that a crew member can move out and help survivors aboard after the aircraft has alighted on the water. During evaluation by the Coast Guard, the S-62 operated successfully in 8-10 ft (2·5-3 m) waves.

The S-62 was designed from the start for amphibious operations, so that flotation gear is not required for over-water flights. The bottom of the fuselage is watertight and strengthened to permit landing on either water or snow; and there are two outrigger floats, mounted forward and well away from the fuselage, to resist pitching or rolling during touchdown or while at rest on the water.

Orders for the various versions announced up to January 1970 included the following:

Anchorage Helicopter Service (Alaska)	1
Ansett-ANA	2
Asahi Airlines (Japan)	1
Autair Ltd	1
California Oil Company	2
Canadian Department of Transport	1
Chevron Oil Company	4
ERA Helicopters (Alaska)	1
Freeport Sulphur Co	2
Fuji Airlines (Japan)	1
Grumman Aircraft	1
Helicopter Utilities Ltd (New South Wales)	1
Humble Oil and Refining Company	3
Indian Air Force	2
JASDF (Japan)	3
Johnson & Johnson	1
KLM	1
Mitsubishi (Japan)	2
Naka Nihon Airways (Japan)	1
Nishi-Nihon Airways (Japan)	1
Nitto Airlines (Japan)	1
Petroleum Helicopters	3
Rotor-Aids	5
San Francisco & Oakland Helicopter Airlines	1

Sikorsky S-62 amphibious transport helicopter in service with KLM Noordzee Helikopters

Thailand Dept of Agriculture	2
Thailand Police	2
TPG (Taiwan)	2
United Aircraft Corporation	1
US Coast Guard Service	99
World Wide Helicopters	3

TYPE: Turbine-powered amphibious helicopter.

ROTOR SYSTEM: Three-blade fully-articulated main rotor and two-blade tail rotor. Each blade of the folding main rotor has an extruded aluminium alloy pressurised spar and trailing-edge pockets. Rotor brake standard. Each tail rotor blade is a hollow spar and spacer assembly of aluminium alloy.

ROTOR DRIVE: Steel-tube drive-shafts. Main gearbox below rotor head, intermediate gearbox at base of tail pylon and tail gearbox at top of tail pylon. Main rotor / engine rpm ratio 1:85·757. Tail rotor/engine rpm ratio 1:6·818.

FUSELAGE: Completely amphibious boat hull. Aluminium semi-monocoque structure, with some stainless steel and resin-fabric.

TAIL SURFACE: Horizontal stabiliser on starboard side of tail rotor pylon.

LANDING GEAR: Main units are semi-retractable, being raised hydraulically into the stabilising floats by oleo contraction. Sikorsky oleo-pneumatic shock-absorbers. Goodyear split rim main wheels and tyres, size 6·50 × 10. Non-retractable Goodyear cast aluminium tail-wheel and tyre size 5·00 × 5. Tyre pressure (all) 60-70 lb/sq in (4·22-4·92 kg/cm²). Goodyear hydraulic disc brakes. Emergency flotation bags attached to sponsons.

POWER PLANT: One 1,250 shp General Electric CT58-110-1 (military T58-GE-8) shaft-turbine engine. Fuel in three under-floor tanks; forward tank capacity 92 US gallons (348 litres), main tank capacity 182 US gallons (689 litres), aft tank capacity 138 US gallons (523 litres). Total usable fuel capacity 412 US gallons (1,560 litres). Refuelling point on port side of fuselage. Oil capacity 2·5 US gallons (9·5 litres).

ACCOMMODATION: Crew of two side-by-side on flight deck. Main cabin accommodates 12 fully-equipped troops or 10 airline passengers and baggage. Airline version has three forward-facing seats at rear of cabin, three on port side at front facing inward, two facing forward and two on starboard side facing inward. Door on starboard side of cabin. Internal door between cabin and flight deck. Cabin heated and ventilated.

SYSTEMS: Primary hydraulic system, pressure 1,000 lb/sq in (70 kg/cm²), and auxiliary system, pressure 1,500 lb/sq in (105 kg/cm²), for flying controls, landing gear, rescue hoist and wind-screen wipers. Electrical system includes 28V DC generator, 24V batteries, 26V AC and 115V AC supplies.

ELECTRONICS AND EQUIPMENT: HH-52A has special Coast Guard radio equipment. Optional items include ARC-210, ARC-21, ICS, Collins 618F radio, blind-flying instrumentation, 600 lb (270 kg) capacity rescue hoist, external cargo sling of 3,000 lb (1,360 kg) capacity, auto-stabilisation equipment, rescue platform and sea anchor.

DIMENSIONS, EXTERNAL:
Diameter of main rotor	53 ft 0 in (16·16 m)
Diameter of tail rotor	8 ft 9 in (2·67 m)
Distance between rotor centres	31 ft 4 in (9·55 m)
Length overall	45 ft 5½ in (13·86 m)
Length of fuselage	44 ft 6½ in (13·58 m)
Width, rotors folded	15 ft 9 in (4·80 m)
Height to top of rotor hub	14 ft 2½ in (4·33 m)
Overall height	16 ft 0 in (4·88 m)
Wheel track	12 ft 2 in (3·70 m)
Wheelbase	17 ft 11¾ in (5·48 m)
Cabin door:	
Height	5 ft 0 in (1·52 m)
Width	4 ft 0 in (1·22 m)
Height to sill	3 ft 1½ in (0·95 m)

DIMENSIONS, INTERNAL:
Cabin, excluding flight deck:	
Length	14 ft 0 in (4·27 m)
Max width	5 ft 4 in (1·62 m)
Max height	6 ft 0 in (1·83 m)
Floor area	74·6 sq ft (6·93 m²)
Volume	440 cu ft (12·45 m³)
Baggage hold (fwd, stbd side of cabin)	44 cu ft (1·25 m³)

AREAS:
Main rotor blade (each)	32·5 sq ft (3·02 m²)
Tail rotor blade (each)	3·08 sq ft (0·29 m²)
Main rotor disc	2,206 sq ft (205 m²)
Tail rotor disc	60·1 sq ft (5·58 m²)
Stabiliser	8·21 sq ft (0·76 m²)

WEIGHTS AND LOADINGS:
Weight empty, equipped:	
S-62A	4,957 lb (2,248 kg)
HH-52A	5,083 lb (2,306 kg)
Max useful load:	
S-62A	2,943 lb (1,335 kg)
HH-52A	3,017 lb (1,368 kg)

Sikorsky CH-54B of the US Army—new heavy-lift utility version of the Skycrane, described on page 451

Max T-O weight:
S-62A	7,900 lb (3,583 kg)	
HH-52A	8,100 lb (3,674 kg)	

Max overload T-O weight (sling load):
S-62A	8,000 lb (3,629 kg)	
HH-52A	8,300 lb (3,765 kg)	

Max landing weight:
S-62A	7,900 lb (3,583 kg)	
HH-52A	8,300 lb (3,765 kg)	

Max disc loading:
S-62A	3·58 lb/sq ft (17·48 kg/m²)	
HH-52A	3·67 lb/sq ft (17·92 kg/m²)	

Max power loading:
S-62A	10·8 lb/shp (4·90 kg/shp)	
HH-52A	11·1 lb/shp (5·04 kg/shp)	

PERFORMANCE (at max T-O weight):
Max level speed at S/L:
S-62A	88 knots (101 mph; 163 km/h)	
HH-52A	95 knots (109 mph; 175 km/h)	

Max cruising speed:
S-62A	80 knots (92 mph; 148 km/h)	
HH-52A	85 knots (98 mph; 158 km/h)	

Max rate of climb at S/L:
S-62A	1,140 ft (347 m)/min	
HH-52A	1,080 ft (329 m)/min	

Vertical rate of climb at S/L:
S-62A	300 ft (91 m)/min	
HH-52A	110 ft (33 m)/min	

Service ceiling:
S-62A (FAA limit)	6,600 ft (2,010 m)	
HH-52A	11,200 ft (3,410 m)	

Hovering ceiling in ground effect:
S-62A	14,100 ft (4,295 m)	
HH-52A	12,200 ft (3,720 m)	

Hovering ceiling out of ground effect:
S-62A	4,600 ft (1,400 m)	
HH-52A	1,700 ft (520 m)	

Range with main and aft tanks, 10% reserve:
S-62A	401 nm (462 miles; 743 km)	
HH-52A	412 nm (474 miles; 763 km)	

SIKORSKY S-64 SKYCRANE
US military designation: CH-54

The S-64 is a flying crane helicopter with a useful load of 22,890 lb (10,382 kg) in its initial form. Like the S-60 prototype, described in the 1960-61 *Jane's*, it utilises a modified Sikorsky S-56 rotor system and other components, but is powered by two Pratt & Whitney JFTD12 turboshaft engines.

The S-64 was designed initially for universal military transport duties. Equipped with interchangeable pods, it is suitable for use as a troop transport, and for mine-sweeping, cargo and missile transport, anti-submarine or field hospital operations. Equipment includes a removable 15,000 lb (6,800 kg) hoist, a sling attachment and a load stabiliser to prevent undue sway in cargo winch operations. Attachment points are provided on the fuselage and landing gear to facilitate securing of bulky loads. Pick-up of loads is made easier by the pilot's ability to shorten or extend the landing gear hydraulically.

The first of three **S-64A** prototypes flew for the first time on 9 May 1962 and was used by the US Army at Fort Benning, Georgia, for testing and demonstration. The second and third prototypes were delivered to Federal Germany for evaluation by the German armed forces.

In June 1963, the US Army announced that it had ordered six S-64A's, under the designation CH-54A, to investigate the heavy lift concept, with emphasis on increasing mobility in the battlefield. Delivery of five CH-54A's (originally YCH-54A's) to the US Army took place in late 1964 and early 1965. A sixth CH-54A remained at Stratford, with a company-owned S-64, for a programme leading toward a restricted FAA certification, which was awarded on July 30, 1965. Further US Army orders for some 60 CH-54s have since been placed and deliveries will extend beyond 1971.

Sikorsky CH-53D helicopter of the US Marine Corps

The CH-54A's are assigned to the US Army's 478th Aviation Company. and have performed outstanding service in support of the Army's First Cavalry Division, Airmobile, in Vietnam. The commanding officer of the 478th, Major T. J. Clark, and Chief Warrant Officer U. V. Brown set up three international height records in one of these aircraft in April 1965. They reached an altitude of 21,374 ft (6,515 m) with a 5,000 kg payload, 28,743 ft (8,761 m) with 2,000 kg and 29,340 ft (8,943 m) with 1,000 kg. The last two records remained unbeaten in mid-1969.

On 29 April 1965, a CH-54A of the 478th Company lifted 90 persons, including 87 combat-equipped troops in a detachable van. This is believed to be the largest number of people ever carried by a helicopter at one time.

In Vietnam, Skycranes have transported bulldozers and road graders weighing up to 17,500 lb (7,937 kg), 20,000-lb (9,072-kg) armoured vehicles and a large variety of heavy hardware. They have also retrieved more than 380 damaged aircraft, involving savings estimated at $210 million.

Sikorsky Aircraft has developed an all-purpose van, known as the Universal Military Pod, for carriage by the US Army's CH-54As, and received an order, worth $2·9 million, to supply 22 to the Army. The pods are delivered complete with communications, ventilation and lighting systems, and with wheels to simplify ground handling. They supersede earlier pods which were not certificated to carry personnel.

With a max loaded weight of 20,000 lb (9,072 kg), each pod accommodates 45 combat-equipped troops, or 24 litters, and in the field may be adapted for a variety of uses, such as surgical units, field command posts and communications posts.

Internal dimensions of the pod are: length 27 ft 5 in (8·36 m), width 8 ft 10 in (2·69 m) and height 6 ft 6 in (1·98 m). Doors are provided on each side of the forward area of the pod, and a double-panelled ramp is located aft. The first pod was accepted by the US Army on 28 June 1968, following FAA certification for personnel transport.

A civilian "people pod", known as the XB-1 Skylounge, was built by The Budd Company for an evaluation programme which began in the Spring of 1967, with the pod carried by a Sikorsky-owned S-64. The Skylounge, which seated 23 passengers, was developed for the Los Angeles Department of Airports as a possible means of transporting people speedily between city centre and airport. It could be towed on the ground by a variety of vehicles, enabling passengers to be collected at various points in a city, taken to a central heliport, flown to an airport by helicopter, and towed to a fixed-wing airliner, without changing from one vehicle to another in the process.

On 15 February 1968, Sikorsky announced that it had received an order for two commercial Skycranes, designated **S-64E,** from Rowan Drilling Company, Inc, of Houston, Texas. These were delivered on 18 April 1969, and are being operated by Rowan through a newly-formed subsidiary, Rowan Air Cranes, Inc, in support of oil exploration and drilling operations in Alaska.

FAA certification of the S-64E for civil use was announced in 1969, for the transportation of external cargo weighing up to 22,400 lb (10,160 kg). Further S-64E's are being produced in 1970-71 for commercial sale.

On 4 November 1968 Sikorsky announced that it had received a US Army contract to increase the payload capacity of the CH-54 from 10 to 12½ short tons. The contract called for a number of design improvements to the engine, gearbox, rotor head and structure; altitude performance and hot weather operating capability were also to be improved.

The original JFTD12-4A engines were to be replaced by two Pratt & Whitney JFTD12-5A's, each rated at 4,800 shp, and a new gearbox capable of receiving 7,900 hp from the two engines was to be introduced. Single-engine performance was to be increased, since the new gearbox receives 4,800 hp from one engine, compared with 4,050 hp on the CH-54A.

A new rotor system was to be introduced, utilising a high-lift rotor blade with a chord some 2·5 in (6·35 cm) greater than that of the blades used formerly.

Other changes were to include the provision of dual wheels on the main landing gear, an improved automatic flight control system and some general structural strengthening throughout the aircraft. Gross weight was to be increased from 42,000 lb (19,050 kg) to 47,000 lb (21,319 kg).

Sikorsky S-64E Skycrane helicopter of Rowan Air Cranes, with under-fuselage freight, photographed in Alaska (*Norman E. Taylor*)

Two of the improved flying cranes, designated **CH-54B**, were accepted by the US Army during 1969. They are undergoing rigorous testing at the Sikorsky plant.

Sikorsky plans to obtain FAA certification for the upgraded helicopter, which has the company designation of **S-64F** Skycrane, and offer it on the commercial market. The improvements were introduced into production CH-54's in late 1969, with FAA certification tests to be completed in early 1970.

TYPE: Twin-turbine heavy flying crane helicopter.

ROTOR SYSTEM: Six-blade fully-articulated main rotor with aluminium blades and aluminium and steel head. Four-blade tail rotor with titanium head and aluminium blades. Rotor brake standard.

ROTOR DRIVE: Steel-tube drive-shafts. Main gearbox below main rotor, intermediate gearbox at base of tail pylon, tail gearbox at top of pylon. Main gearbox rated at 6,600 shp on CH-54A and S-64E, 7,900 shp on S-64F.

FUSELAGE: Pod-and-boom type of aluminium and steel semi-monocoque construction.

LANDING GEAR: Non-retractable tricycle type, with single wheel on each unit of CH-54A/S-64A/S, twin wheels on main units of S-64F.

POWER PLANT (CH-54A/S-64E): Two Pratt & Whitney JFTD12-4A (military T73-P-1) turboshaft engines, each rated at 4,500 shp for take-off and with max continuous rating of 4,000 shp. Two fuel tanks in fuselage, forward and aft of transmission, each with capacity of 440 US gallons (1,664 litres). Total standard fuel capacity 880 US gallons (3,328 litres). Provision for auxiliary fuel tank of 440 US gallons (1,664 litres) capacity, raising total fuel capacity to 1,320 US gallons (4,992 litres).

POWER PLANT (S-64F): Two Pratt & Whitney JFTD12-5A turboshaft engines, each rated at 4,800 shp for take-off and with max continuous rating of 4,430 shp. Fuel tanks as for S-64E.

ACCOMMODATION: Pilot and co-pilot side-by-side at front of cab. Aft-facing seat for third pilot at rear of cabin, with flying controls. The occupant of this third seat is able to take over control of the aircraft during loading and unloading. Two additional jump seats available in cab. Payload in interchangeable pods (see above).

DIMENSIONS, EXTERNAL:
Diameter of main rotor	72 ft 0 in (21·95 m)
Diameter of tail rotor	16 ft 0 in (4·88 m)
Distance between rotor centres	
	44 ft 6 in (13·56 m)
Length overall	88 ft 6 in (26·97 m)
Length of fuselage	70 ft 3 in (21·41 m)
Width, rotors folded	21 ft 10 in (6·65 m)
Height to top of rotor hub	18 ft 7 in (5·67 m)
Overall height	25 ft 5 in (7·75 m)
Ground clearance under fuselage boom	
	9 ft 4 in (2·84 m)
Wheel track	19 ft 9 in (6·02 m)
Wheelbase	24 ft 5 in (7·44 m)

AREAS:
Main rotor disc	4,070 sq ft (378·1 m²)
Tail rotor disc	201 sq ft (18·67 m²)

WEIGHTS (CH-54A/S-64E):
Weight empty	19,234 lb (8,724 kg)
Max T-O weight	42,000 lb (19,050 kg)

PERFORMANCE (CH-54A/S-64E at normal T-O weight of 38,000 lb = 17,237 kg):
Max level speed at S/L	
	110 knots (127 mph; 204 km/h)
Max cruising speed	
	95 knots (109 mph; 175 km/h)
Max rate of climb at S/L	1,700 ft (518 m)/min
Service ceiling	13,000 ft (3,960 m)

Hovering ceiling in ground effect
10,600 ft (3,230 m)
Hovering ceiling out of ground effect
6,900 ft (2,100 m)
Range with max fuel, 10% reserve
219 nm (253 miles; 407 km)

SIKORSKY S-65A
US Navy designation: CH-53A Sea Stallion
USAF designations: HH-53B/C
US Marine Corps designation: CH-53D

On 27 August 1962, it was announced that Sikorsky had been selected by the US Navy to produce a heavy assault transport helicopter for use by the Marine Corps. First flight was made on 14 October 1964, and deliveries began in mid-1966.

Designated **CH-53A**, this aircraft uses many components based on those of the S-64A Skycrane, but is powered by two General Electric T64 shaft-turbine engines and has a water-tight hull. A full-size rear opening, with built-in ramp, permits easy loading and unloading, with the aid of a special hydraulically-operated internal cargo loading system and floor rollers.

Typical cargo loads include two Jeeps, or two Hawk missiles with cable reels and control console, or a 105-mm howitzer and carriage. An external cargo system permits in-flight pick-up and release without ground assistance.

The CH-53A is intended to operate under all weather and climatic conditions. Its main rotor blades and tail pylon fold hydraulically for stowage on board ship.

CH-53A's have been serving in Vietnam since January 1967.

On 17 February 1968, a CH-53A, with General Electric T64-16 (modified) engines, flew at a gross weight of 51,900 lb (23,541 kg) carrying 28,500 lb (12,927 kg) of payload and fuel, establishing new unofficial payload and gross weight records for a production helicopter built outside the Soviet Union.

On 26 April 1968, a Marine Corps CH-53A made the first automatic terrain clearance flight in helicopter history and subsequently concluded flight tests of an Integrated Helicopter Avionics System (IHAS). Prime contractor for the IHAS programme was Teledyne Systems Company. Norden Division of United Aircraft Corporation provided the terrain-clearance radar and vertical structure display.

On 23 October 1968, a Marine Corps CH-53A performed a series of loops and rolls, as part of a joint Naval Air Systems Command and Sikorsky flight test programme, aimed at investigating the CH-53A's rotor system dynamics and manoeuvrability characteristics. The helicopter was piloted by Lt Col Robert Guay, USMC, and Byron Graham, Sikorsky experimental test pilot.

Take-off weight of the CH-53A was 27,000 lb (12,247 kg). The rolls were started at a speed of about 140 knots (161 mph; 259 km/h). The rate of roll ranged from 70° to 95° per second. The load factor at the beginning of the roll was 1·6g, and decreased to 0·8g at the inverted position. The load factor at completion varied from 1·8g to 2·7g depending upon the specific roll. Time for the rolls varied from 5·8 to 7·5 seconds, and the speed upon completion was 110 knots (127 mph; 204 km/h).

The loops were begun at about 160 knots (184 mph; 296 km/h) in level flight. The load factor at the start of the loop was 1·2g and increased to 2·5g when the helicopter reached a 50° nose-up position. At the inverted position, the load factor was 0·8g, and upon completion of the loop it was 2·8g. The time for the loops varied from 18 to 25 seconds. Completion speed was 130 knots (150 mph; 250 km/h).

In September 1966, the USAF ordered eight **HH-53B** heavy lift helicopters for its Aerospace Rescue and Recovery Service. The first of these flew on 15 March 1967 and deliveries began in June 1967.

The HH-53B is generally similar to the CH-53A, but is powered by 3,080 shp T64-GE-3 shaft-turbine engines. It has the same general equipment as the HH-3E, including a retractable flight refuelling probe, jettisonable auxiliary fuel tanks and armament.

On 30 August 1968, Sikorsky delivered to the USAF the first **HH-53C** helicopter, an improved version of the HH-53B, with 3,435 shp T64-GE-7 engines, auxiliary jettisonable fuel tanks each of 450 US gallons (1,703 litres) capacity on new cantilever mounts, flight refuelling probe and rescue hoist with 250 ft (76 m) of cable. An external cargo hook of 20,000 lb (9,070 kg) capacity allows the HH-53C to recover Apollo spacecraft. Deliveries will continue through 1970.

The **CH-53D** for the US Marine Corps, the first of which was delivered on 3 March 1969, is an improved version of the CH-53A with two T64-GE-412 or T64-GE-413 engines. The former has a military rating of 3,695 shp, and the latter a maximum rating of 3,925 shp. A total of 64 troops can be carried in a high-density arrangement. An integral cargo handling system makes it possible for one man to load or unload one short ton of palletised cargo a minute. Main rotor and tail pylon fold automatically for carrier operation.

A total of 135 CH-53DG's will serve with the German armed forces. The first of two built by Sikorsky was delivered on 31 March 1969. The next 20 will be assembled in Germany from American-built components. The remainder will embody some 50% components of German manufacture. Israel also has eight CH-53s.

On 10 March 1969, Sikorsky announced an order for two **S-65-Oe** helicopters for rescue duties with the Austrian Air Force in the Alps. The Austrian version, scheduled for delivery in 1970, will carry the same rescue hoist as the HH-53B/C, and fittings for auxiliary fuel tanks, and will be able to accommodate 38 passengers.

The following details refer to the CH-53A:

TYPE: Twin-turbine heavy assault transport helicopter.

ROTOR SYSTEM AND DRIVE: Generally similar to those of S-64A Skycrane, but main rotor head is of titanium and steel, and it has folding blades.

FUSELAGE: Conventional semi-monocoque structure of aluminium, steel and titanium. Folding tail pylon.

TAIL SURFACE: Large horizontal stabiliser on starboard side of tail rotor pylon.

LANDING GEAR: Retractable tricycle type, with twin wheels on each unit. Main units retract into the rear of sponsons on each side of fuselage. Fully-castoring nose unit.

POWER PLANT: Normally two 2,850 shp General Electric T64-GE-6 shaft-turbine engines, mounted in pods on each side of main rotor pylon. The CH-53A can also utilise, without airframe modification, the T64-GE-1 engine of 3,080 shp or the latest T64-GE-16 (mod) engine of 3,435 shp. Two self-sealing bladder fuel tanks, each with capacity of 311 US gallons, housed in forward part of sponsons. Total fuel capacity 622 US gallons (2,354 litres).

ACCOMMODATION: Crew of three. Main cabin accommodates 38 combat-equipped troops on inward-facing seats. Provision for carrying 24 stretchers and four attendants. Roller-skid track combination in floor for handling heavy freight. Door on starboard side of cabin at front. Rear loading ramp.

Sikorsky CH-53D/G built for the German armed forces

DIMENSIONS, EXTERNAL:
Diameter of main rotor	72 ft 3 in (22·02 m)
Diameter of tail rotor	16 ft 0 in (4·88 m)
Length overall, rotors turning	88 ft 3 in (26·90 m)
Length of fuselage, without refuelling probe	67 ft 2 in (20·47 m)
Width overall, rotors folded	15 ft 6 in (4·72 m)
Width of fuselage	8 ft 10 in (2·69 m)
Height to top of rotor hub	17 ft 1½ in (5·22 m)
Overall height	24 ft 11 in (7·60 m)
Wheel track	13 ft 0 in (3·96 m)
Wheelbase	27 ft 0 in (8·23 m)

DIMENSIONS, INTERNAL:
Cabin: Length	30 ft 0 in (9·14 m)
Max width	7 ft 6 in (2·29 m)
Max height	6 ft 6 in (1·98 m)

AREAS:
Main rotor disc	4,070 sq ft (378·1 m²)
Tail rotor disc	201 sq ft (18·67 m²)

WEIGHTS:
Weight empty:	
CH-53A	22,444 lb (10,180 kg)
CH-53D	23,485 lb (10,653 kg)
HH-53B	23,125 lb (10,490 kg)
HH-53C	23,257 lb (10,549 kg)

Normal T-O weight:
CH-53A	35,000 lb (15,875 kg)

Mission T-O weight:
CH-53D	36,400 lb (16,510 kg)
HH-53B	37,400 lb (16,964 kg)
HH-53C	37,466 lb (16,994 kg)

Max T-O weight:
CH-53D, HH-53B/C	42,000 lb (19,050 kg)

PERFORMANCE:
Max level speed at S/L:
CH-53D, HH-53C	170 knots (196 mph; 315 km/h)
HH-53B	162 knots (186 mph; 299 km/h)

Cruising speed:
CH-53D, HH-53B/C	150 knots (173 mph; 278 km/h)

Max rate of climb at S/L:
CH-53D	2,180 ft (664 m)/min
HH-53B	1,440 ft (440 m)/min
HH-53C	2,070 ft (631 m)/min

Service ceiling:
CH-53D	21,000 ft (6,400 m)
HH-53B	18,400 ft (5,610 m)
HH-53C	20,400 ft (6,220 m)

Hovering ceiling in ground effect:
CH-53D	13,400 ft (4,080 m)
HH-53B	8,100 ft (2,470 m)
HH-53C	11,700 ft (3,565 m)

Hovering ceiling out of ground effect:
CH-53D	6,500 ft (1,980 m)
HH-53B	1,600 ft (490 m)
HH-53C	4,300 ft (1,310 m)

Range:
CH-53D, with 4,076 lb (1,849 kg) fuel, 10% reserve at cruising speed and 2 min warming up 223 nm (257 miles; 413 km)
HH-53B/C, with 9,926 lb (4,502 kg) fuel (two 450-US gallon; 1,703-litre auxiliary tanks), which includes 10% reserve and 2 min warmup 468 nm (540 miles; 869 km)

SMITH
MRS FRANK W. (DOROTHY) SMITH

ADDRESS:
1938, Jacaranda Place, Fullerton, California 92633

The late Frank W. Smith built and flew in October 1956 the prototype of a single-seat fully-aerobatic sporting biplane which he designated the DSA-1 (Darn Small Aeroplane) Miniplane. Plans of this aircraft are marketed by Mrs Smith and there were at least 158 Miniplanes flying by May 1969.

Mrs Smith's son has designed a two-seat version of the DSA-1 provisionally designated "Miniplane +1", and all available details of this are given below.

SMITH DSA-1 MINIPLANE

The Smith Miniplane shown in the adjacent illustration is typical of the large number of amateur-built aircraft of this type now flying. Built by Mr C. A. Mejía of Medellín, Colombia, it is of interest as the first homebuilt aircraft to be constructed in Colombia.

Others incorporating various design modifications, have been illustrated in previous editions of *Jane's*.

The following details refer to the standard Miniplane, built according to Frank Smith's original plans.

TYPE: Single-seat sporting biplane.

WINGS: Braced biplane with N-type interplane struts each side and two N-type strut assemblies supporting centre of top wing above fuselage. NACA 4412 wing section. Dihedral 2° on lower wings only. Incidence 0° on top wing, 2° on lower wings. All-wood structure, fabric-covered. Fabric-covered wooden ailerons on lower wings only. No flaps.

FUSELAGE: Welded steel-tube structure, fabric-covered.

TAIL UNIT: Wire-braced welded steel-tube structure, fabric-covered. Adjustable-incidence tailplane.

LANDING GEAR: Non-retractable tail-wheel type. Tripod streamlined-tube main legs. Compression-spring shock-absorbers optional (now fitted on prototype). Goodyear main wheels and tyres, size 7·00 × 4, pressure 20 lb/sq in (1·41 kg/cm²). Goodyear shoe-type brakes. Scott tail-wheel.

POWER PLANT: Designed to take any engine in 65-125 hp category. Prototype has 108 hp Lycoming O-235-C four-cylinder horizontally-opposed air-cooled engine, driving a Sensenich 71-52 two-blade metal fixed-pitch propeller, diameter 5 ft 11 in (1·80 m). Most subsequent aircraft have a 65hp Continental A65, 75 hp Continental A75 or 125 hp Lycoming four-cylinder horizontally-opposed air-cooled engine. Fuel in tank in fuselage, capacity 17 US gallons (64·5 litres). Oil capacity 1·5 US gallons (5·7 litres).

ACCOMMODATION: Single seat in open cockpit. Space for 60 lb (27 kg) baggage.

DIMENSIONS, EXTERNAL:
Span (upper wing)	17 ft 0 in (5·18 m)
Span (lower wing)	15 ft 9 in (4·80 m)

Smith DSA-1 Miniplane built by Mr C. A. Mejía of Medellín, Colombia

Wing chord constant, (both)	3 ft 0 in (0·91 m)
Length overall	15 ft 3 in (4·65 m)
Height overall	5 ft 0 in (1·52 m)
Wheel track	5 ft 0 in (1·52 m)

AREAS:
Wings, gross	100 sq ft (9·29 m²)
Ailerons (total)	10 sq ft (0·93 m²)
Fin	3·02 sq ft (0·28 m²)
Rudder	3·89 sq ft (0·36 m²)
Tailplane	8·22 sq ft (0·76 m²)
Elevators	4·86 sq ft (0·45 m²)

WEIGHTS AND LOADING (prototype):
Weight empty, equipped	616 lb (279 kg)
Max T-O weight	1,000 lb (454 kg)
Max wing loading	10 lb/sq ft (48·8 kg/m²)

PERFORMANCE (prototype, at max T-O weight):
Max level speed at S/L	117 knots (135 mph; 217 km/h)
Max cruising speed	102 knots (118 mph; 190 km/h)
Econ cruising speed	96 knots (110 mph; 177 km/h)
Stalling speed	48 knots (55 mph; 88·5 km/h)
Rate of climb at S/L	1,250 ft (380 m)/min
Service ceiling	13,000 ft (3,960 m)
T-O run	350 ft (107 m)
Landing run	500 ft (152 m)
Endurance with max fuel	2 hr 30 min

SMITH MINIPLANE +1

Mr Donald Smith has designed and is building a two-seat version of the DSA-1 Miniplane. At the time of writing construction of the prototype was well advanced but the aerofoil section of the biplane wings had not been finalised. All available details follow:

WINGS: Braced biplane with conventional forward stagger. Dihedral 2° on lower wings only. Incidence 2° on upper wing, 3° on lower. All-wood structure with spruce spars, fabric-covered. Ailerons on lower wings only, of wood construction, fabric-covered.

FUSELAGE: Welded steel-tube structure, fabric-covered.

TAIL UNIT: Wire-braced welded steel-tube structure, fabric-covered.

LANDING GEAR: Non-retractable tail-wheel type. Tripod streamlined-tube main legs. Rubber bungee shock-absorbers. Cleveland main wheels and tyres, size 6·00 × 6. Cleveland wheel brakes.

POWER PLANT: Designed to take engines in the 100-160 hp category. Prototype will have 125 hp Lycoming four-cylinder horizontally-opposed air-cooled engine, driving a two-blade fixed-pitch propeller. Fuel contained in fuselage tank, capacity 25 US gallons (94·6 litres).

ACCOMMODATION: Two seats in tandem in open cockpit.

DIMENSIONS, EXTERNAL:
Span (upper wing)	20 ft 0 in (6·10 m)
Span (lower wing)	18 ft 6 in (5·64 m)
Wing chord, constant (both)	3 ft 6 in (1·07 m)
Length overall	17 ft 0 in (5·18 m)
Height overall	6 ft 2½ in (1·89 m)
Wheel track	5 ft 6 in (1·68 m)

AREAS:
Wings, gross	128 sq ft (11·9 m²)
Ailerons (total)	12·0 sq ft (1·11 m²)
Fin	4·75 sq ft (0·44 m²)
Rudder	5·75 sq ft (0·53 m²)
Tailplane	11·5 sq ft (1·07 m²)
Elevators	7·25 sq ft (0·67 m²)

WEIGHTS AND LOADINGS:
Weight empty	approx 696 lb (315 kg)
Max T-O weight	1,250 lb (566 kg)
Max wing loading	9·76 lb/sq ft (47·7 kg/m²)
Max power loading	10·0 lb/hp (4·54 kg/hp)

PERFORMANCE (estimated at max T-O weight):
Max level speed at S/L	117 knots (135 mph; 217 km/h)
Cruising speed	104 knots (120 mph; 193 km/h)
Landing speed	52 knots (60 mph; 97 km/h)
Range	312 nm (360 miles; 579 km)
Endurance	more than 3 hours

SMYTH
JERRY SMYTH

ADDRESS:
R.R.4, Huntington, Indiana 46750

In February 1958 Mr J. Smyth began the design of a sporting monoplane, setting out to evolve an aircraft that would be reasonably easy to construct, easy to fly, stressed to 9g for limited aerobatics, of good appearance and offering economic operation. Construction of the prototype began almost nine years later, in January 1967, and occupied two years before completion, at a cost of around $2,500. First flight of what Mr Smyth has named the Model "S" Sidewinder, was made on 21 February 1969, and this aircraft received the "Outstanding Design" award at the 17th EAA fly-in at Rockford, Illinois, in 1969.

Construction has been simplified by utilising a number of standard and readily-obtainable items of equipment. For example, the bubble-canopy is that of a Thorpe T-18, and Wittman landing gear is used. Plans are available to amateur constructors, and Mr Smyth can also supply a glass-fibre nose-wheel fairing and two-piece engine cowling to those constructors who do not wish to mould their own.

SMYTH MODEL "S" SIDEWINDER

TYPE: Two-seat homebuilt sporting monoplane.

WINGS: Cantilever low-wing monoplane. Wing section NACA 64,-612 at root, NACA 64,-210 at tip. Dihedral 4°. Incidence 1° 30′. No sweepback. All-metal structure comprising a centre-section and two outer wing panels. Built-up main spar of ·040-in 2024-T3 aluminium "U"-sections, to which flat aluminium cap strips are riveted; secondary spar is of formed sections. Eleven equally-spaced ribs in each wing panel are made of ·025-in 6061-T4 aluminium. The wing skin, of ·025-in 2024-T3 aluminium, is in three sections: leading-edge, lower and upper skin, and is flush-riveted. Wings filled with epoxy. Simple sealed-gap ailerons of aluminium construction, attached to secondary spar by piano-type hinge. No trim-tabs. No flaps.

FUSELAGE: Welded steel-tube structure with aluminium formers and skin. Electrically-operated speed brake may be fitted in lower fuselage.

TAIL UNIT: Cantilever all-metal structure with swept vertical surfaces. All-moving horizontal surface with electrically-operated anti-servo tab.

LANDING GEAR: Non-retractable nose-wheel type. Wittman cantilever spring steel main gear. Main wheels and tyres size 5·00 × 5, pressure 25 lb/sq in (1·76 kg/cm²). Nose unit carries a 10-in (25·4 cm) diameter tail wheel and smooth tyre, free castoring and non-steerable, pressure 25 lb/sq in (1·76 kg/cm²). Cleveland hydraulic brakes. Glass-fibre fairings on all wheels.

POWER PLANT: Provision for installation of engines from 90-180 hp. Prototype has a 125 hp Lycoming O-290-G four-cylinder horizontally-opposed air-cooled engine, driving a two-blade fixed-pitch aluminium propeller, diameter 5 ft 7 in (1·70 m), with spinner. Fuel tank in fuselage, forward of instrument panel, capacity 17·5 US gallons (66·2 litres). Refuelling point on top of fuselage, forward of windshield. Provision for wingtip tanks. Oil capacity 2 US gallons (7·57 litres).

ACCOMMODATION: Pilot and passenger, seated side-by-side under rearward-sliding bubble canopy. Compartment for 90 lb (40·8 kg) of baggage aft of seats. Cabin heated and ventilated.

SYSTEMS: Hydraulic system for brakes and, optionally, for operation of aerodynamic speed brake. Engine-driven generator provides 35A

Smyth Model "S" Sidewinder, two-seat sporting aircraft (125 hp Lycoming O-290-G engine) (*Jean Seele*)

12V DC for instruments, lights, electrically-operated stabiliser servo-tab and optional electrically-driven hydraulic pump to operate aerodynamic speed brake.

ELECTRONICS: Simple 10-channel VHF communications transceiver.

DIMENSIONS, EXTERNAL:
Wing span	24 ft 10 in (7·57 m)
Wing chord at root	5 ft 0 in (1·52 m)
Wing chord at tip	3 ft 0 in (0·91 m)
Wing aspect ratio	6·85
Length overall	19 ft 4 in (5·89 m)
Height overall	5 ft 5½ in (1·66 m)
Tailplane span	7 ft 7¾ in (2·33 m)
Wheel track	5 ft 7 in (1·70 m)
Wheelbase	4 ft 3 in (1·30 m)
Propeller ground clearance	8 in (20 cm)

DIMENSIONS, INTERNAL:
Cabin:
Length	6 ft 6 in (1·98 m)
Max width	3 ft 2 in (0·97 m)
Max height	3 ft 4 in (1·02 m)
Baggage compartment	9 cu ft (0·25 m³)

AREAS:
Wings, gross	96 sq ft (8·92 m²)
Ailerons (total)	6 sq ft (0·56 m²)

Fin	4·4 sq ft (0·41 m²)
Rudder	2·0 sq ft (0·19 m²)
Horizontal surface	14·1 sq ft (1·31 m²)

WEIGHTS AND LOADINGS:
Weight empty	867 lb (393 kg)
Max T-O and landing weight	1,450 lb (657 kg)
Max wing loading	15·8 lb/sq ft (77 kg/m²)
Max power loading	11·6 lb/hp (5·26 kg/hp)

PERFORMANCE (at max T-O weight):
Max level speed at 2,000 ft (610 m)	161 knots (185 mph; 298 km/h)
Max permissible speed	173 knots (200 mph; 321 km/h)
Max cruising speed, 75% power at 2,000 ft (610 m)	139 knots (160 mph; 257 km/h)
Stalling speed	48 knots (55 mph; 89 km/h)
Max rate of climb at S/L, 32°F (0°C)	1,200 ft (366 m)/min
Max rate of climb at S/L, 75°F (24°C)	900 ft (274 m)/min
Service ceiling	15,000 ft (4,570 m)
T-O run	800 ft (244 m)
T-O to 50 ft (15 m)	2,000 ft (610 m)
Landing from 50 ft (15 m)	2,000 ft (610 m)
Landing run	1,500 ft (457 m)
Range with max fuel, no reserve	369 nm (425 miles; 684 km)

SPEZIO

TONY AND DOROTHY SPEZIO

Mr and Mrs Spezio designed and built a two-seat light aircraft named the Tuholer, of which plans are available to other amateur constructors.

SPEZIO DAL-1 TUHOLER

Named Tuholer because of its two open cockpits, the prototype was built over a period of 2½ years, at a cost of approximately $800. It flew for the first time on 2 May 1961.

Folding wings enable the Tuholer to be kept in a normal home garage and it is towed behind a car on its own landing gear. It can be made ready for flight by two people in about 10 minutes or by one person in 20 minutes.

The adjacent illustration shows a Tuholer built by Mr Erwin Lance of Cuyahoga Falls, Ohio, and which is powered by a 125 hp Lycoming O-290 engine.

TYPE: Two-seat home-built sporting aircraft.

WINGS: Strut-braced low-wing monoplane, with streamline-section Vee bracing strut each side. Clark Y wing section. Dihedral 3°. Incidence 1°. Two-spar spruce structure, with plywood-leading-edge and overall fabric covering. Conventional wooden ailerons. No flaps. Wings fold back along sides of fuselage for stowage.

FUSELAGE: Steel-tube structure with wood stringers and fabric covering.

TAIL UNIT: Braced steel-tube structure, fabric covered. Tailplane incidence adjustable by screw-jack.

LANDING GEAR: Non-retractable tail-wheel type. Rubber-cord shock-absorption. Main units fitted with Shinn aluminium wheels, size 600 × 6, Shinn shoe brakes and wheel fairings. Tyre pressure 40 lb/sq in (2·81 kg/cm²). Steerable tail-wheel.

POWER PLANT: Prototype has a 125 hp Lycoming O-290-G4 four-cylinder horizontally-opposed

Spezio Tuholer (125 hp Lycoming O-290 engine) built by Mr Erwin Lance of Cuyahoga Falls, Ohio (*Jean Seele*)

air-cooled engine converted from a ground power unit. Sensenich two-blade metal fixed-pitch propeller. Glass-fibre fuel tank aft of firewall, capacity 22 US gallons (83·3 litres). Oil capacity 2 US gallons (7·5 litres).

ACCOMMODATION: Two persons in tandem in open cockpits. Small baggage compartment aft of rear seat.

EQUIPMENT: Nova-Tech TR-102 radio.

DIMENSIONS, EXTERNAL:
Wing span	24 ft 9 in (7·55 m)
Wing chord, constant	5 ft 0 in (1·52 m)
Wing aspect ratio	5
Length overall	18 ft 3 in (5·56 m)
Height overall	5 ft 0 in (1·53 m)
Tailplane span	7 ft 0 in (2·13 m)
Wheel track	5 ft 2 in (1·57 m)

AREA:
Wings, gross	115 sq ft (10·7 m²)

WEIGHTS:
Weight empty	810 lb (367 kg)
Max T-O weight	1,400 lb (635 kg)

PERFORMANCE (at max T-O weight):
Max level speed at S/L	130 knots (150 mph; 241 km/h)
Cruising speed	104-113 knots (120-130 mph; 193-209 km/h)
Stalling speed	35 knots (40 mph; 64 km/h)
Rate of climb at S/L	2,000 ft (610 m)/min
Service ceiling	12,000 ft (3,660 m)
T-O run	160 ft (49 m)
Landing run	170 ft (52 m)
Endurance with max fuel	3 hours

SPINKS

M. H. SPINKS SR

ADDRESS:
PO Box 11099, Fort Worth, Texas

Mr Spinks, a manufacturer and airport operator, has designed and built a single-seat aerobatic aircraft which he has called the Akromaster.

Mr Spinks taught himself to fly in 1922 in a homebuilt aircraft that utilised part of a Curtiss Wright JN-4, and now owns a collection of 16 homebuilt and antique aircraft. The Akromaster took twelve months to build and flew for the first time on 28 August 1968.

All available details follow:

SPINKS AKROMASTER

TYPE: Single-seat homebuilt aerobatic monoplane.

WINGS: Cantilever low-wing monoplane of all-metal construction. Conventional ailerons. No flaps.

FUSELAGE: Welded steel-tube structure with fabric covering.

TAIL UNIT: Braced tail unit of all-metal construction.

LANDING GEAR: Non-retractable tail-wheel type. Cantilever spring-steel main gear. Wheel fairings on main wheels.

POWER PLANT: One 200 hp Lycoming IO-360 four-cylinder horizontally-opposed air-cooled fuel-injection engine, driving a two-blade fixed-pitch propeller with spinner.

ACCOMMODATION: Single seat in enclosed cockpit under bubble canopy.

Spinks Akromaster homebuilt aerobatic monoplane (200 hp Lycoming IO-360 engine) (*Howard Levy*)

DIMENSIONS, EXTERNAL:

Wing span	30 ft 0 in	(9·14 m)
Wing chord, constant	5 ft 6 in	(1·68 m)
Length overall	24 ft 0 in	(7·32 m)
Height overall	5 ft 6 in	(1·68 m)

WEIGHTS:

Weight empty	1,300 lb	(589 kg)
Max T-O weight	1,775 lb	(805 kg)

PERFORMANCE (at max T-O weight):

Max permissible speed	243 knots	(280 mph; 451 km/h)
Cruising speed	148 knots	(170 mph; 274 km/h)
Landing speed	48 knots	(55 mph; 89 km/h)
Rate of climb at S/L	3,000 ft	(914 m)/min
T-O run	600 ft	(183 m)
Landing run	800 ft	(244 m)
Range	955 nm	(1,100 miles; 1,770 km)

SPRATT

SPRATT AND COMPANY, INC

ADDRESS:
PO Box 351, Media, Pennsylvania 19063

Mr G. Spratt, formerly a design engineer employed by the Boeing Company and Consolidated Vultee (now known as Convair), has completed more than 30 years' work on developing a two-piece movable-wing control system, which he claims provides improved safety factors compared with the conventional aileron, elevator and rudder control system.

While he was with Consolidated Vultee, Mr Spratt designed a roadable aircraft which featured an earlier version of his wing control system, but this did not enter production. Since that time Mr Spratt has concentrated on perfecting his idea as a private venture.

To flight test the system, Mr Spratt has built a lightweight experimental flying-boat (N910Z) which is constructed almost entirely of molded plastics. In appearance, the hull resembles a

motor boat and can accommodate two persons. The pivoted controllable wings are mounted in a parasol configuration, with inverted-Vee bracing struts on each side: these pivot at their junction with the wings to allow them to move. The butterfly tail unit carries no moving surfaces.

Power plant consists of a modified outboard marine engine, of 60 cu in capacity, which drives a two-blade plastic pusher propeller through an extended drive shaft, which locates the propeller between the butterfly tail surfaces. A small water rudder, interconnected with the control wheel, facilitates manoeuvring on water.

Flying controls are so arranged that the wings are allowed to move freely and collectively in incidence, while their incidence is being controlled differentially by means of a steering wheel. The wings' angle of attack can be adjusted by a separate control, but is best regarded as "fixed" for a particular cruising speed.

Mr Spratt hoped to build a prototype for public demonstration during the Winter of 1969-70.

All available specification and performance details of the test aircraft are given below:

DIMENSIONS, EXTERNAL:

Wing span	24 ft 0 in	(7·32 m)
Length overall	17 ft 0 in	(5·18 m)
Height overall	5 ft 0 in	(1·52 m)
Width of hull	5 ft 0 in	(1·52 m)

WEIGHTS AND LOADINGS:

Weight empty	500 lb	(226 kg)
Max T-O weight	1,000 lb	(453 kg)
Max wing loading	10 lb/sq ft	(48·8 kg/m²)
Max power loading	15 lb/hp	(6·8 kg/hp)

PERFORMANCE (at max T-O weight):

Max level speed	85 knots	(98 mph; 158 km/h)
Max cruising speed	78 knots	(90 mph; 145 km/h)
Max waterborne speed	61 knots	(70 mph; 113 km/h)
Normal T-O speed	43 knots	(50 mph; 80 km/h)
Normal landing speed	36 knots	(42 mph; 68 km/h)
Normal operating ceiling	3,000 ft	(914 m)

STEPHENS

CLAYTON L. STEPHENS

ADDRESS:
2829 Cedar Street, San Bernardino, California 92404

Mr C. L. Stephens has designed a single-seat aerobatic monoplane specifically for homebuilders who wish to own an aircraft for competitive aerobatics. The prototype, designated Model A, was designed for Margaret Ritchie, US National Women's Aerobatic Champion in 1966, and the second machine, the Model B, for Dean S. Engelhardt of Garden Grove, California.

Stressed to +12g and —11g, it is the first US aircraft known to be designed around the Aresti Aerocriptografic System for competitive aerobatics. All control surfaces are fully static-balanced and the entire aircraft comes very close to being aerodynamically symmetrical. Design of the Model A started in July 1966 and construction of the prototype a month later. First flight of this version was made on 27 July 1967, and of the Model B on 9 July 1969. Plans of the Stephens Akro are available to amateur constructors and 33 sets had been sold at the time of writing.

The description which follows applies to the Model A, the prototype of which has since been destroyed. The Model B has wings and ailerons of increased area and reduced fuel tankage.

STEPHENS AKRO

TYPE: Single-seat homebuilt monoplane.

WINGS: Cantilever mid-wing monoplane. Wing section NACA 23012. No dihedral, incidence or sweepback. All-wood two-spar structure. One-piece wing, with solid spar passing through fuselage and positioned by means of removable top longeron sections. Rear spar in two pieces. No internal wires or compression struts. Wing covered with mahogany skin. Plain ailerons have a 4130 steel spar, and spruce ribs and trailing-edge, and are fabric-covered. Ground-adjustable trim-tabs on ailerons, which are statically balanced. No flaps.

FUSELAGE: Welded 4130 steel-tube structure, mostly of 0·75-in outside-diameter tubing, with Ceconite covering.

TAIL UNIT: Wire-braced welded 4130 steel-tube structure with swept surfaces, fabric-covered.

Stephens Akro Model B, built by Dean S. Engelhardt of Garden Grove, California (180 hp Lycoming AIO-360-A1A engine) (*Max Clover*)

Tailplane has variable incidence. Ground-adjustable trim-tab in rudder; controllable trim-tab in elevator. All control surfaces statically balanced.

LANDING GEAR: Non-retractable tail-wheel type. Cantilever spring steel main gear. Goodyear main wheels and tyres size 5·00×5, pressure 28 lb/sq in (1·97 kg/m²). Cleveland disc brakes. Maule steerable tail-wheel. Glass-fibre fairings on main wheels.

POWER PLANT: One 180 hp Lycoming AIO-360-A1A four-cylinder horizontally-opposed air-cooled engine, driving a Sensenich Type 7660 two-blade fixed-pitch metal propeller, diameter 6 ft 4 in (1·93 m), with spinner. Model A has fuel system for prolonged inverted flight, Model B has both fuel and oil system so modified. Model B can also have optional constant-speed propeller. Fuel tank in fuselage, forward of instrument panel. Model A has fuel capacity of 32 US gallons (121 litres), Model B 27 US gallons (102 litres). Refuelling point on top of

fuselage, forward of windshield. Oil capacity 2 US gallons (7·6 litres).

ACCOMMODATION: Single seat for pilot under rearward-sliding bubble canopy. Large window in under-fuselage, forward of control column. Model B has, in addition, a quarter window in each side of the fuselage, beneath the wings. Forced-air ventilation.

SYSTEMS: Hydraulic system for brakes only.

ELECTRONICS: Battery-operated Bayside transceiver.

DIMENSIONS, EXTERNAL:

Wing span	24 ft 6 in	(7·47 m)
Wing chord at root	5 ft 3 in	(1·60 m)
Wing chord at tip:		
A	2 ft 6 in	(0·76 m)
B	3 ft 0 in	(0·91 m)
Length overall	19 ft 1 in	(5·82 m)
Height overall	5 ft 8 in	(1·73 m)
Tailplane span	8 ft 0 in	(2·44 m)
Wheel track	4 ft 6 in	(1·37 m)
Propeller ground clearance	1 ft 1 in	(0·33 m)

AREAS:	
Wings, gross:	
A	49 sq ft (8·73 m²)
B	100 sq ft (9·29 m²)
Ailerons, total:	
A	12 sq ft (1·11 m²)
B	13 sq ft (1·21 m²)
Fin	5 sq ft (0·46 m²)
Rudder, including tab	10 sq ft (0·93 m²)
Tailplane	13 sq ft (1·21 m²)
Elevators, including tab	11 sq ft (1·02 m²)
WEIGHTS AND LOADINGS:	
Weight empty:	
A	850 lb (385 kg)
B	950 lb (431 kg)
Max T-O weight:	
A	1,200 ft (544 kg)
B	1,300 lb (589 kg)
Max wing loading	13 lb/sq ft (63·5 kg/m²)
Max power loading	7 lb/hp (3·18 kg/hp)
PERFORMANCE (at 1,200 lb (544 kg) T-O weight):	
Max level speed at 2,000 ft (610 m)	148 knots (170 mph; 274 km/h)
Max diving speed	191 knots (220 mph; 354 km/h)
Max cruising speed, at 2,000 ft (610 m)	139 knots (160 mph; 257 km/h)
Econ cruising speed, at 2,000 ft (610 m)	109 knots (125 mph; 201 km/h)
Stalling speed	48 knots (55 mph; 89 km/h)
Max rate of climb at S/L	4,000 ft (1,220 m)/min
Service ceiling	22,000 ft (6,705 m)
T-O run	200 ft (61 m)
T-O to 50 ft (15 m)	400 ft (122 m)
Landing from 50 ft (15 m)	1,500 ft (457 m)
Landing run	600 ft (183 m)
Range with max fuel	303 nm (350 miles; 563 km)

STEWARD-DAVIS

STEWARD-DAVIS, INC

HEAD OFFICE:
3200 Cherry Avenue, Long Beach, California 90807

PRESIDENT: F. H. Steward

VICE-PRESIDENT: D. M. Thompson

The cargo landplanes produced by this company utilise the airframe of the Fairchild C-82A/C-119 military transport, with extensive systems changes and fitted with jet-augmentation units of Steward-Davis manufacture, known as Jet-Paks. The aircraft are marketed under the names Skytruck and Jet Packet. Conversion schemes to improve the capabilities of the PBY Catalina amphibian are also available (see 1968/69 *Jane's*.

Steward-Davis acquired from Westinghouse the sole manufacturing rights for the J34-WE-34, J34-WE-36, W340, and 24C-4D turbojets and holds the Type Certificate for the FAA-approved versions of these engines which are incorporated in its Jet-Pak augmentation units. Jet-Paks have been fitted to Fairchild C-119 aircraft of the Indian Air Force and are available for other cargo aircraft.

Steward-Davis developed subsequently a new and improved Jet-Pak fitted with intake duct doors. These doors have excellent aerodynamic characteristics and are used to prevent engine windmilling during periods of non-operation in flight. This new unit is designated Jet-Pak 3402 and is built around a 3,400 lb (1,540 kg) st J34 turbojet engine. The first one built has replaced the 1,000 lb (455 kg) st Jet-Pak fitted some years ago to TWA's C-82A based at Orly Airport, Paris, and used to airlift replacement engines for the airline's fleet of transport aircraft. It is also fitted to the STOLmaster transport manufactured by Steward-Davis for Aircraft International of Santa Monica, California.

Steward-Davis manufactures approved components for the Westinghouse turbojet engines listed above, and is a supplier to the RAAF, French Navy, Indian Air Force, Royal Netherlands Navy, Japanese Self-Defence Force and US Navy. It also overhauls Westinghouse J34 turbojets under French government contract.

STEWARD-DAVIS/FAIRCHILD JET-PAK C-119/R4Q

Development of this jet-augmented conversion of the Fairchild C-119/R4Q military transport was begun in January 1961. Construction of a prototype was started in March 1962 and it flew for the first time in September 1962.

At the present time, no commercial Jet-Pak C-119's are available, but 26 aircraft of the Indian Air Force have been fitted with Steward-Davis Jet-Paks to enable them to operate with higher payloads from high-altitude fields in support of ground forces.

At the request of the Indian Air Force, Steward-Davis has studied the possibilities of a three-jet version of this aircraft, with one Jet-Pak above the centre-section and two more under the wings. The wing units are designed for quick disconnect in the field when one jet unit will suffice.

The following details refer to the standard Jet-Pak C-119/R4Q:

TYPE: Twin-engined cargo and troop transport.

WINGS: Cantilever high-wing monoplane. Wing section NACA 2418 at root, NACA 4409 at tip. Anhedral 7° 46′ on centre-section. Dihedral 1° 30′ outboard of nacelles, measured at 40% chord. Incidence 3° at root, —1° at tip. Sweepback at quarter-chord 3° 51′. Conventional two-spar aluminium alloy structure. Fabric-covered aluminium alloy ailerons, each with trim-tab. NACA slotted aluminium alloy trailing-edge flaps. Thermal de-icing.

FUSELAGE: Aluminium alloy semi-monocoque "pod" structure, of basically-square section, with clam-shell rear loading doors. Seven longitudinal under-floor beams to take floor and tie-down loads.

TAIL BOOMS: Aluminium alloy semi-monocoque structures. Each in two sections, bolted together at leading-edge of tailplane.

TAIL UNIT: Cantilever aluminium alloy structure, with twin fins and rudders. Controllable trim-tabs in elevator and rudders; mechanical servo-tabs in rudders. Thermal de-icing of leading-edges.

LANDING GEAR: Retractable tricycle type, with twin wheels on all three units. Hydraulic actuation, with mechanical emergency release. Hydraulically-steerable nose-wheel. Chicago Pneumatic oleo-pneumatic shock-absorbers. Main wheel tyres size 15·50 × 20 14-ply, pressure 44-82 lb/sq in (3·09-5·77 kg/cm²) depending on AUW. Magnesium nose-wheels with tyres size 9·50 × 16 10-ply. Bendix disc brakes.

POWER PLANT: Two 3,350 hp Wright R-3350-85 or -89 radial air-cooled engines, driving Hamilton Standard Hydromatic or Aeroproducts four-blade constant-speed reversible-pitch propellers. One 3,400 lb (1,542 kg) st Westinghouse J34-WE-36 auxiliary turbojet engine. Fuel in four bladder tanks in wings, each inboard tank of 842 US gallons (3,187 litres) capacity, each outboard tank of 469 US gallons (1,775 litres) capacity. Total fuel capacity 2,622 US gallons (9,924 litres). Refuelling points above wings. Oil capacity 120 US gallons (455 litres).

ACCOMMODATION: Crew of four or five on flight deck, access to which is by a ladder on the port side. Payloads can consist of 67 troops (or 78 in emergencies), 35 stretcher patients or equivalent freight. An electrically-operated monorail is able to discharge up to 20 × 500 lb (227 kg) packages through a hatch in the bottom of the fuselage during air-drop operations. Personnel door forward on port side. Rear clam-shell doors open to full cross-section of hold. Floor is at truck-bed height. Ramps are provided for driving vehicles directly into hold. Small door in each main clam-shell door permits simultaneous jumping of two sticks of paratroops.

SYSTEMS: Individual oxygen supplied for crew-members. Hydraulic system, pressure 3,000 lb/sq in (210 kg/cm²), for landing gear, flaps, brakes, nose-wheel steering, jet starter and jet intake doors. Pneumatic system, pressure 1,600 lb/sq in (112 kg/cm²), for emergency braking. Electrical system includes two engine-driven generators and 36Ah battery. Fairchild APU for auxiliary electrical supply.

ELECTRONICS AND EQUIPMENT: Blind-flying instrumentation standard. Radio and radar to customer's requirements.

DIMENSIONS, EXTERNAL:	
Wing span	109 ft 3¼ in (33·30 m)
Wing chord at root	17 ft 10⅞ in (5·45 m)
Wing chord at tip	8 ft 11 in (2·72 m)
Wing aspect ratio	8·25
Length overall	86 ft 5¾ in (26·38 m)
Length of fuselage	60 ft 6 5/16 in (18·45 m)
Height over tail	26 ft 7¾ in (8·12 m)
Tailplane span	29 ft 3⅝ in (8·93 m)
Wheel track	29 ft 2 in (8·89 m)
Wheelbase	26 ft 3 in (8·00 m)
Rear clam-shell doors:	
Height	8 ft 0 in (2·44 m)
Width	9 ft 2 in (2·79 m)
Height to sill	4 ft 0 in (1·22 m)
DIMENSIONS, INTERNAL:	
Cabin: Length	36 ft 11 in (11·25 m)
Max width	9 ft 2 in (2·79 m)
Max height	8 ft 0 in (2·44 m)
Floor area	353 sq ft (32·8 m²)
Volume	3,150 cu ft (88·2 m³)
AREAS:	
Wings, gross	1,447·24 sq ft (134·4 m²)
Ailerons (total)	120·20 sq ft (11·16 m²)
Trailing-edge flaps (total)	120·00 sq ft (11·15 m²)
Fins, including ventral and dorsal fins	158·20 sq ft (14·70 m²)
Rudders, including tabs	66·22 sq ft (6·15 m²)
Tailplane	58·48 sq ft (5·43 m²)
Elevators, including tabs	113·86 sq ft (10·58 m²)
WEIGHTS AND LOADINGS:	
Weight empty	43,000 lb (19,505 kg)
Max payload	28,500 lb (12,925 kg)
Max T-O weight	77,000 lb (34,925 kg)
Max landing weight	64,000 lb (29,030 kg)
Max wing loading	53·2 lb/sq ft (259·75 kg/m²)
Max power loading	9·33 lb/ehp (4·23 kg/ehp)

Fairchild C-119 transport modified to STOLmaster standard by Steward-Davis on behalf of Aircraft International

PERFORMANCE (at max T-O weight):
Max permissible diving speed
272 knots (314 mph; 505 km/h)
Max cruising speed (70% power):
Piston-engines only
170 knots (196 mph; 315 km/h)
With jet assist
203 knots (234 mph; 377 km/h)
Stalling speed, power off
80 knots (92 mph; 148 km/h)
Rate of climb at S/L   1,200 ft (365 m)/min
Service ceiling   24,000 ft (7,315 m)
Service ceiling, one engine out 9,300 ft (2,835 m)
T-O run   2,750 ft (838 m)
T-O to 50 ft (15 m)   5,250 ft (1,600 m)
Landing from 50 ft (15 m)   5,150 ft (1,570 m)
Landing run   2,215 ft (675 m)
Range with max fuel, 45 min reserve
1,910 nm (2,200 miles; 3,540 km)
Range with max payload, 45 min reserve
390 nm (450 miles; 725 km)

STEWARD-DAVIS/AIRCRAFT INTERNATIONAL STOLMASTER

Steward-Davis Inc has been retained by Aircraft International of Santa Monica, California, to modify Fairchild C-119 aircraft into STOLmaster jet-assisted transports to Aircraft International specification. The jet-assist system to be used is the latest Jet-Pak 3402, built around a Steward-Davis 24C4D (Westinghouse J34) turbojet engine and embodying new quick-attach features which permit each jet pod to be used as a power module. Each Jet-Pak may be removed or installed or interchanged between any aircraft on which simple mounting pads have been incorporated. This enables commercial and military operators of STOLmaster transports to augment the performance of their aircraft in a few minutes by installing one, two or three auxiliary jet pods, as required.

The first C-119 for conversion to STOLmaster standard was flown to Steward-Davis on 9 May 1967. It was scheduled to fly in its new form in July 1967 and was then to leave for a demonstration tour of Central and South America.

The details given above for the Jet-Pak C-119/R4Q apply also to the STOLmaster, except for the following detail changes:

TYPE: Two-to-five-engined cargo and troop transport.

WINGS: High-lift full-span flap system under development.

LANDING GEAR: Anti-skid brake system available.

POWER PLANT: Two permanently-installed 3,250 hp (3,500 hp with water injection) Wright R-3350-89A radial air-cooled engines, each driving a Hamilton Standard Hydromatic or Aeroproducts four-blade constant-speed reversible-pitch propeller. One, two or three 3,400 lb (1,542 kg) st Steward-Davis 24C4D turbojet engines in Jet-Pak 3402 quick-attach pods.

WEIGHTS AND LOADINGS:
Weight empty
41,000-45,290 lb (18,597-20,543 kg)
Max payload 25,000-30,000 lb (11,340-13,608 kg)
Max T-O and landing weight
77,000 lb (34,925 kg)
Max wing loading   53·2 lb/sq ft (259·75 kg/m²)
Max power loading
6·95-11·0 lb/hp (3·15-4·99 kg/hp)

PERFORMANCE (at max T-O weight, with one or more Jet-Paks):
Max permissible diving speed
272 knots (314 mph; 505 km/h)
Max cruising speed (70% power):
Piston-engines only
168-175 knots (194-202 mph; 312-325 km/h)
With Jet-Paks
203-262 knots (234-302 mph; 377-486 km/h)
Stalling speed, power off
92 knots (105 mph; 170 km/h)
Rate of climb at S/L
1,200-2,350 ft (365-716 m)/min
Service-ceiling 24,000-31,000 ft (7,315-9,449 m)
T-O run   1,195-2,150 ft (364-655 m)
T-O to 50 ft (15 m) 1,505-3,040 ft (459-927 m)
Landing from 50 ft (15 m)   3,230 ft (985 m)
Landing run   2,150 ft (655 m)
Range with max fuel, 45 min reserve
1,947-2,596 nm (2,242-2,990 miles; 3,607-4,811 km)
Range with max payload, 45 min reserve
390 nm (450 miles; 724 km)

STEWART
STEWART AIRCRAFT CORPORATION

ADDRESS:
Martin Road, Clinton, New York 13323

Mr Donald Stewart formed this company to market plans of a simple single-seat light aircraft named the Headwind, of which he designed and built a prototype. During 1969 he designed a new wing for the Headwind and this is an integral part of the plans available to homebuilders. A two-seat version, with 60-65 hp engine, is under development.

STEWART HW1.S HEADWIND

Built in only five months, the prototype Headwind flew for the first time on 28 March 1962. It can have an open or enclosed cockpit. The wings can be removed or fitted in about 20 minutes by two people.

The adjacent illustration shows a Headwind built by Mr E. Sampson of Belview, Minnesota, and Mr A. Main of Sioux Falls, South Dakota. Construction took 4 months and cost $500, using parts from Mr E. Anderson's Headwind which was irreparably damaged in an accident, and has a modified Luscombe wing and 65 hp Lycoming O-145-B2 engine. Max T-O weight is 900 lb (408 kg), max speed 125 mph (201 kmh).

At least 16 Headwinds were flying by the Spring of 1970.

The following details apply to Mr Stewart's basic design with the new wing.

TYPE: Single-seat home-built light aircraft.

WINGS: Strut-braced high-wing monoplane, with streamline-section Vee bracing struts each side. Wing section NACA 4415. Dihedral 2°. Incidence 2°. Two spruce spars, steel-tube compression members, drag and anti-drag wires, plywood ribs, fabric covering. Frise-type ailerons of similar construction to wings. No flaps.

FUSELAGE: Welded steel-tube structure, fabric-covered.

TAIL UNIT: Braced steel-tube structure, fabric-covered. Ground-adjustable tailplane incidence. Fixed tabs on rudder and port elevator.

LANDING GEAR: Non-retractable tail-wheel type. Shock-absorption by low-pressure tyres. Hayes main wheels with Goodyear tyres size 8·00 × 4. Tyre pressure 12 lb/sq in (0·84 kg/cm²). No brakes. Steerable tail-wheel.

Modified Stewart Headwind (65 hp Lycoming O-145-B2 engine) *(Howard Levy)*

POWER PLANT: One 36 hp modified Volkswagen 1192 cc motor car engine, driving a specially-made Stewart/Kirk two-blade fixed-pitch propeller, diameter 5 ft 2 in (1·57 m). Fuel tank aft of firewall, capacity 5 US gallons (19 litres). Oil capacity 5 US pints (2·4 litres).

ACCOMMODATION: Single seat in open or enclosed cockpit. No provision for baggage.

DIMENSIONS, EXTERNAL:
Wing span	28 ft 3 in	(8·61 m)
Wing chord constant	4 ft 0 in	(1·22 m)
Wing aspect ratio		7
Length overall	17 ft 9 in	(5·41 m)
Height overall	5 ft 0 in	(1·52 m)
Tailplane span	7 ft 0 in	(2·13 m)
Wheel track	5 ft 0 in	(1·52 m)
Wheelbase	13 ft 6 in	(4·11 m)
Propeller ground clearance	9 in	(23 cm)

AREAS:
Wings, gross	110·95 sq ft	(10·3 m²)
Ailerons (total)	19·36 sq ft	(1·80 m²)
Fin	2·17 sq ft	(0·20 m²)
Rudder	4·77 sq ft	(0·44 m²)
Tailplane	7·00 sq ft	(0·65 m²)
Elevators	9·54 sq ft	(0·89 m²)

WEIGHTS AND LOADING:
Weight empty	437 lb	(198 kg)
Max T-O and landing weight	700 lb	(317 kg)
Max wing loading	6·3 lb/sq ft	(30·8 kg/m²)

PERFORMANCE (at max T-O weight):
Max level speed at S/L
65 knots (75 mph; 121 km/h)
Max permissible speed in dive
86 knots (100 mph; 161 km/h)
Cruising speed   61 knots (70 mph; 113 km/h)
Stalling speed
32-33 knots (36-38 mph; 58-61 km/h)
Rate of climb at S/L   400 ft (122 m)/min
Absolute ceiling   7,000 ft (2,135 m)
T-O run   300 ft (91 m)
T-O to 50 ft (15 m)   1,200 ft (365 m)
Landing from 50 ft (15 m)   1,600 ft (490 m)
Landing run   450 ft (137 m)
Endurance with max fuel, no reserve   2½ hours

STITS
STITS AIRCRAFT SUPPLIES

HEAD OFFICE AND WORKS:
PO Box 3084, 4305 Twining Street, Riverside, California 92509

PRESIDENT: Ray Stits

Between 1948 and 1952 Mr Ray Stits designed, built and tested his original single-seat experimental "midgets". The Stits Junior, a monoplane with a span of 8 ft 10 in (2·69 m) was superseded by the Sky Baby biplane with a span of only 7 ft 2 in (2·18 m). They were described respectively by their designer as the "World's Smallest".

Subsequent Stits designs include the Sky-Coupe, Playboy, Flut-R-Bug and Playmate. These types were intended for construction at home by amateurs and were made available in the form of constructional drawings and raw materials; but Mr Stits has now decided to discontinue the supply of plans and concentrate on the sale of aircraft materials. He has received FAA Supplementary Type Approval for an aircraft covering process which he is marketing under the name "Poly-Fiber". This comprises Dupont Dacron fabric, finished with a new polyurethane dope called Poly-Dope, and will not crack, burn or peel. Details of the Playboy, Flut-R-Bug, Sky-Coupe and Playmate may be found in the 1969-70 *Jane's.*

STOLP

STOLP STARDUSTER CORPORATION

ADDRESS:
4301 Twining, Riverside, California 92509

Mr Louis A. Stolp and Mr George M. Adams designed and built a light single-seat sporting biplane known as the Starduster, which flew for the first time in November 1957. It was followed first by a two-seat version, known as the Starduster Too and, in 1969, by a small single-seat monoplane designated SA-500 Starlet.

These aircraft are licensed in the Home-built category and not intended for series production. However, plans and basic materials for the Starduster, Starduster Too and Starlet are available from Stolp Starduster Corporation, and many have been built by amateurs in the United States.

STOLP-ADAMS SA-100 STARDUSTER

TYPE: Single-seat sporting biplane.

WINGS: Biplane wings of unequal span, with single interplane strut each side. Multiple centre-section bracing struts. Wing section NACA 4412. Dihedral 1° 30' on lower wing only. Incidence 1° 30' on lower wing only. Sweepback on leading-edges of upper wing 6°. Wood structure with fabric covering. Fabric-covered wooden ailerons on lower wings only. No flaps.

FUSELAGE: Welded steel-tube structure with fabric covering.

TAIL UNIT: Welded steel-tube structure with fabric covering.

LANDING GEAR: Non-retractable tail-wheel type. Rubber-cord shock-absorption. Firestone 600 × 6 main wheels and hydraulic brakes.

POWER PLANT: One 125 hp Lycoming O-290-D1 four-cylinder horizontally-opposed air-cooled engine, driving Sensenich Type M74DM61 two-blade metal fixed-pitch propeller. Fuel in one 12 US gallon (45·5 litres) fuselage tank, and one 6 US gallon (22·7 litres) tank in each upper wing. Total fuel capacity 24 US gallons (91 litres). Oil capacity 6 US quarts (5·6 litres).

ACCOMMODATION: Single seat in open cockpit.

DIMENSIONS, EXTERNAL:

Wing span:	
Upper	19 ft 0 in (5·79 m)
Lower	18 ft 0 in (5·49 m)
Wing chord, mean (both)	3 ft 0 in (0·91 m)
Wing aspect ratio	6·33
Length overall	16 ft 6 in (5·03 m)
Height overall	6 ft 0 in (1·83 m)
Tailplane span	7 ft 1 in (2·16 m)
Wheel track	5 ft 0 in (1·52 m)
Wheelbase	12 ft 0 in (3·66 m)

AREAS:

Wings, gross	110 sq ft (10·22 m²)
Ailerons (total)	7·0 sq ft (0·65 m²)
Fin	4·4 sq ft (0·41 m²)
Rudder	6·0 sq ft (0·56 m²)
Tailplane	9·0 sq ft (0·84 m²)
Elevators	7·0 sq ft (0·65 m²)

WEIGHTS AND LOADINGS:

Weight empty, equipped	700 lb (318 kg)
Max T-O weight	1,080 lb (490 kg)
Max wing loading	10 lb/sq ft (48·7 kg/m²)
Max power loading	8·6 lb/hp (3·9 kg/hp)

STOLP SA-300 STARDUSTER TOO

The SA-300 Starduster Too is a slightly enlarged tandem two-seat version of the SA-100 Starduster. The general design and construction of the two types are identical, except that the Starduster Too has ailerons on both top and bottom wings and has wheel fairings as standard equipment. The wing section is M6. Incidence is 1° on the lower wing only; dihedral 1° 30' on the lower wing only.

The design is stressed to take engines in the 125-260 hp range. The prototype has a 180 hp Lycoming O-360-A1A four-cylinder horizontally-opposed air-cooled engine.

The adjacent illustration shows a Starduster Too built by Mr Jack C. Swan of 11205 Rayland Drive, San Fernando, California. It is very considerably modified from the original plans and the most noticeable external change is the provision of retractable main landing gear. An individual hydraulic cylinder is used to actuate each leg, and these receive hydraulic power from a small accumulator which is charged by a hand pump. Power plant comprises a 180 hp Lycoming O-360 engine, driving a Hartzell two-blade constant-speed metal propeller. Fuel capacity of Mr Swan's Starduster is 45·2 US gallons (171 litres), of which 45 US gallons (170 litres) is usable.

Other modifications include a rearward-sliding canopy covering both cockpits, electrically-operated elevator and rudder trim, full IFR

Stolp-Adams SA-100 Starduster (150 hp Lycoming O-320 engine) built by Mr Michael Frey
(Peter M. Bowers)

Modified Stolp SA-300 Starduster Too with enclosed cabin and retractable undercarriage *(Howard Levy)*

Stolp SA-500 Starlet single-seat lightplane (1500 cc Volkswagen engine) *(Jean Seele)*

equipment and increased baggage stowage. Building occupied 3 years at a cost of $4,000.

The following details apply to this aircraft:

WEIGHT:

Max T-O weight	1,950 lb (884 kg)

PERFORMANCE (at max T-O weight):

Max diving speed
182 knots (210 mph; 338 km/h) IAS
Max cruising speed, 75% power at 7,500 ft (2,285 m)
130 knots (150 mph; 241 km/h) TAS
Stalling speed 52 knots (59 mph; 95 km/h) IAS
Max rate of climb at S/L   2,000 ft (610 m)/min
Service ceiling   26,000 ft (7,925 m)
Max range at 91 knots (105 mph; 169 km/h) TAS, 37% power at 2,500 ft (762 m)
720 nm (830 miles; 1,335 km)

STOLP SA-500 STARLET

Few details were available of the new SA-500 Starlet at the time of writing. It is a single-seat swept parasol-wing monoplane. Wing is of wooden construction with spruce spars, plywood web and cap-strip ribs, with Dacron covering. Fuselage is of welded 4130 steel tube with Dacron covering and the tail unit is a braced structure of the same materials. The non-retractable tail-wheel type landing gear has cantilever main legs with wheel fairings. Power plant consists of a 1,500 cc Volkswagen four-cylinder horizontally-opposed air-cooled engine, driving a fixed-pitch two-blade propeller with spinner. Construction occupied three months and cost $1,500. First flight was made on 1 June 1969.

DIMENSIONS, EXTERNAL:

Wing span	25 ft 0 in (7·62 m)
Wing chord	3 ft 0 in (0·91 m)

WEIGHT:

Max T-O weight	750 lb (340 kg)

PERFORMANCE (at max T-O weight):

Cruising speed   78 knots (90 mph; 145 km/h)
Landing speed
48-52 knots (55-60 mph; 89-97 km/h)

STRATO

STRATO ENGINEERING COMPANY INC

ADDRESS:
1843 Empire Avenue, Burbank, California 91504
PRESIDENT: A. M. Kaplan
VICE-PRESIDENT:
Robert L. Libman (Manufacturing)

Strato Engineering Company, incorporated in 1953, has grown progressively to become the largest independent aeronautical engineering (research, analysis, design, testing) company in the USA. It has specialised in providing design, stress analysis, flutter analysis, aerodynamic and basic load testing services.

The company's President, Mr A. M. Kaplan, was employed by Lockheed Aircraft Corporation for 14 years, during which period he was responsible for many major projects, including structural design of the Constellation wings and tail unit. He currently holds appointments as a designated structural, power plant and flight test engineering representative of the FAA.

Strato Engineering has had principal engineering and FAA certification responsibility for a number of important projects, including Boeing B-377 Stratocruiser conversions for Ransa Airlines, Venezuela, and all of Aero Spacelines Guppy aircraft, as well as design and analysis work in connection with C-Air's extended 18-passenger turboprop version of the D.H. Dove, McCulloch's J-2 autogyro, McKinnon's Turbo Goose, Aircraft Hydroforming's Bushmaster 2000

and a cargo door conversion for Lockheed Electras.

The company established a Manufacturing Division at Shafter Airport, near Bakersfield, California, in June 1968. This division is housed in a 40,000 sq ft (3,716 m²) hangar, which can accommodate aircraft with a wing span of up to 120 ft 0 in (36·6 m). Intended originally to build aircraft structures and provide sheet metal

fabrication and upholstery services, its scope has now been widened to include major and minor aircraft repairs, modifications, the manufacture of proprietary items and programmes extending from design to manufacture. The combined services of the two divisions means that Stratos Engineering is able to provide comprehensive design, manufacturing, flight test and FAA certification services.

SUNRISE

SUNRISE AIRCRAFT CORPORATION OF AMERICA

ADDRESS:
8200 Center Drive, La Mesa, California 92041
PRESIDENT: Edgar K. Riddick
VICE-PRESIDENT, DIRECTOR OF RESEARCH AND DEVELOPMENT:
Fred G. Wagner
VICE-PRESIDENT, ADMINISTRATION:
Robert H. Detweiler
SECRETARY-TREASURER:
Robert L. Spears
CHIEF DESIGN ENGINEER: Frank C. Boosman

This company was formed late in 1964 by members of the former Wagner Aircraft Company to continue the development of short-haul transport aircraft using the jet induced lift concept devised by Mr Fred G. Wagner.

SUNRISE S-1600

Design of this twin-turboprop STOL short-haul transport was started in November 1964. The production version is intended to be available in three forms, as follows:

S-1600P. Standard model with seats for 24 passengers.

S-1600C. Cargo transport, with large door aft of wing on port side. Total of 890 cu ft (25·2 m³) unobstructed volume.

S-1600S. High-density commuter transport for 30 passengers.

The prototype is designed in such a way that its interior can be adapted to demonstrate all three of the above models, and it will have the S-1600C cargo door fitted.

Outstanding feature of the S-1600 is its use of a boundary layer control system known as jet induced lift. This involves the installation of spanwise ducts, called "jet-pumps", in the trailing-edge of the wing. The ducts have a slot at each end, and the idea is to suck in boundary layer air at one end and blow it out of the other end over the ailerons and flaps. Flow of the air through the jet-pumps is induced by compressed air from an APU which also makes the aircraft independent of ground services. Multiple JATO-type gas-generators supply the jet-pumps in the event of APU failure.

Jet induced lift is applied also to the tail surfaces of the S-1600.

TYPE: Twin-turboprop STOL short-haul transport.

WINGS: Cantilever high-wing monoplane. Wing section NACA 63₃A418 at root, NACA 63₁A413 at tip. No dihedral. Incidence 2°. Sweep-forward 1° 57′ 48″. Aluminium alloy (2024) sheet and stringer structure. Combined suction-blowing boundary layer control system, obtained with high-pressure high-temperature primary air driving a jet-pump supplied with air from a turbine-driven compressor. An independent emergency system is provided by multiple JATO-type gas generators. Single-slotted statically-balanced blown ailerons of 2024 aluminium alloy faced honeycomb construction, each in two sections. Trailing-edge flaps of similar construction to ailerons, comprising plain suction flaps of 20% wing chord and single-slotted blown flaps of 20% chord. Inboard and outboard ailerons droop with flap deflection. No spoilers or leading-edge slats. Servo-type aileron trim-tabs. All flying controls manually-operated. Anti-icing by heated air.

FUSELAGE: Conventional semi-monocoque structure of 2024 aluminium alloy frames, stringers and skin.

TAIL UNIT: Cantilever two-spar structure of 2024 aluminium alloy, with tailplane mounted near tip of swept vertical surfaces. Tailplane incidence variable by screw-jack. Servo-tab in rudder. Anti-icing of tailplane leading-edge by heated air. Boundary layer control system built into tailplane, as for wings,

LANDING GEAR: Retractable tricycle type with single wheel on each main unit and twin-wheel nose unit. Electro-mechanical retraction, main units inward and upward into fuselage, nose unit forward. Oil spring shock-absorbers. Main wheel tyres size 24 × 7·7 12-ply rating, pressure 105 lb/sq in (7·38 kg/cm²). Nose-wheel tyres size

6·00 × 6 4-ply rating, pressure 20 lb/sq in (1·41 kg/cm²). Multiple disc brakes on main wheels. No anti-skid units. Floats or wheel-skis optional.

POWER PLANT: Two 760 eshp AiResearch TPE-331 or 750 eshp Pratt & Whitney (UAC) PT-6 turboprop engines, each driving a Hartzell (optionally Hamilton Standard) three-blade constant-speed propeller, diameter 8 ft 6 in (2·59 m). Four fuel tanks in belly with total capacity of 290 US gallons (1,098 litres). Two fuel tanks in wings with total capacity of 120 US gallons (455 litres). Total fuel capacity 410 US gallons (1,553 litres). Pressure or gravity refuelling point in port side of fuselage at waist height. Total oil capacity 4 US gallons (15 litres).

ACCOMMODATION: Crew of two on flight deck. Standard version has up to 24 removable or stowable passenger seats, on rails, and movable aft cabin partition for varying cargo space. Nylon tie-down net and straps for cargo. Toilet and carry-on coat/luggage rack on starboard and port sides respectively at front. Optional 30-seat layout with 180 US gallons (682 litres) of belly fuel only. "Dutch" type door at front of cabin on port side; top half hinges upward, bottom half downward, with integral steps. Upward-hinged cargo door on port side of cabin aft of wings. Upward-hinged baggage door on starboard side at rear. Entire accommodation pressurised and air-conditioned.

SYSTEMS: AiResearch air-cycle pressurisation system, differential 4·25 lb/sq in (0·30 kg/cm²). No hydraulic system. Pneumatic system, pressure 250 lb/sq in (17·5 kg/cm²) for boosting brakes. Electrical system includes three 300A 28V DC starter-generators and two 35Ah batteries. AiResearch TPE-331 APU for air-conditioning, pressurisation and jet induced lift system high-pressure air.

ELECTRONICS AND EQUIPMENT: Standard airline communications and navigation systems to customer's specification. Blind-flying instrumentation standard. Provision for Category II and III equipment, long-range navaids and S-band or X-band radar.

DIMENSIONS, EXTERNAL:
Wing span	52 ft 0 in (15·85 m)
Wing chord at root	5 ft 11¼ in (1·81 m)
Wing chord at tip	2 ft 4½ in (0·72 m)
Wing aspect ratio	12·5
Length overall	51 ft 0 in (15·54 m)
Height overall	19 ft 0 in (5·79 m)
Tailplane span	17 ft 0 in (5·18 m)
Wheel track	10 ft 0 in (3·05 m)
Wheelbase	19 ft 2 in (5·84 m)

Passenger door (port, fwd):
Height	5 ft 0 in (1·52 m)

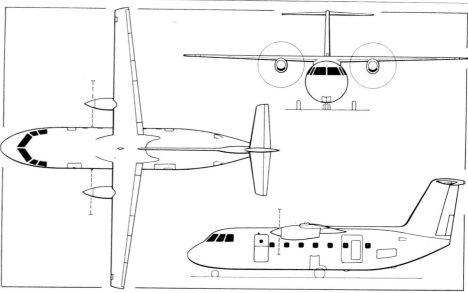

Sunrise S-1600 transport, embodying jet induced lift concept

Width	2 ft 8 in (0·81 m)
Height to sill	2 ft 10 in (0·86 m)

Cargo door (port, aft):
Height	5 ft 0 in (1·52 m)
Width	4 ft 0 in (1·22 m)
Height to sill	2 ft 10 in (0·86 m)

Baggage door:
Height	1 ft 8 in (0·51 m)
Width	3 ft 10 in (1·17 m)

DIMENSIONS, INTERNAL:
Cabin, including fwd luggage and toilet compartments:
Length	25 ft 3¼ in (7·71 m)
Max width	7 ft 0 in (2·13 m)
Max height	6 ft 0 in (1·83 m)
Floor area	124 sq ft (11·53 m²)
Volume	826 cu ft (23·4 m³)
Baggage hold (fwd) volume	32 cu ft (0·91 m³)
Baggage hold (aft) volume	84 cu ft (2·38 m³)

AREAS:
Wings, gross	216·32 sq ft (20·10 m²)
Ailerons (total)	10·24 sq ft (0·95 m²)
Tailing-edge flaps (total)	26·26 sq ft (2·44 m²)
Fin	54·88 sq ft (5·10 m²)
Rudder, including tab	18·11 sq ft (1·68 m²)
Tailplane	36·77 sq ft (3·42 m²)
Elevators	13·23 sq ft (1·23 m²)

WEIGHTS AND LOADINGS:
Weight empty, equipped	7,250 lb (3,289 kg)
Max payload	4,560 lb (2,068 kg)
Max T-O and landing weight	14,250 lb (6,465 kg)
Max zero-fuel weight	11,810 lb (5,357 kg)
Max wing loading	66·0 lb/sq ft (322·2 kg/m²)
Max power loading	9·4 lb/hp (4·26 kg/hp)

PERFORMANCE (estimated at max T-O weight):
Max level speed at 10,000 ft (3,050 m)
287 knots (330 mph; 531 km/h)
Max permissible diving speed
325 knots (375 mph; 603 km/h)
Max and econ cruising speed at 5,000 ft (1,500 m)
269 knots (310 mph; 499 km/h)
Stalling speed:
without flaps 131 knots (150 mph; 241 km/h)
with flaps, no jet induced lift
87 knots (100 mph; 161 km/h)
with flaps and jet induced lift
53 knots (60 mph; 97 km/h)
Rate of climb at S/L	1,630 ft (495 m)/min
Service ceiling	25.800 ft (7,860 m)
Service ceiling, one engine out	13,700 ft (4,175 m)
T-O run	607 ft (185 m)
T-O to 50 ft (15 m)	845 ft (258 m)
Landing from 50 ft (15 m)	850 ft (260 m)
Landing run	390 ft (120 m)

Range with max fuel, 45 min reserve
1,042 nm (1,200 miles; 1,930 km)
Range with max payload, 45 min reserve
651 nm (750 miles; 1,205 km)

SWEARINGEN

SWEARINGEN AIRCRAFT

ADDRESS:
PO Box 32486, San Antonio, Texas 78216
PRESIDENT: Edward J. Swearingen
EXECUTIVE VICE-PRESIDENT AND GENERAL MANAGER: James T. Dresher

VICE-PRESIDENTS:
O. L. Anderson (Marketing)
David B. Daviss (Finance)
Earl E. Morton (Engineering)
Orrin A. Berthiaume (Operations)

PUBLIC RELATIONS MANAGER: Walter H. Kimmell

Swearingen has been engaged in the development of business aircraft for some years and has, among varied activities, built prototypes for other companies, including the Piper Twin Comanche.

The company is now producing four new aircraft of its own design. These are the Merlin IIIB, an eight-seat executive transport, which has superseded the Merlin IIA (described in the

1968-69 *Jane's*); the Merlin III, an improved version of the Merlin IIB; the Merlin IV, which is a corporate version of the fourth model, a 22-seat commuter airliner known as the Metro. Details of these are given below. Swearingen has also announced the forthcoming development and production of a delta-wing transonic business jet, designated SA-28T, with first deliveries scheduled for 1972.

Swearingen marketed improved versions of the Beechcraft Queen Air and Twin-Bonanza, under the names Swearingen 800 and Excalibur 800 respectively. Production of these models has now been taken over by a new division known as Excalibur Aviation, based at Curtis Field, Brady, Texas. This division will also act as sub-contractor on Merlin and Metro production and make avionics installations in export Merlins and airline Metros.

Further expansion of the company's production facilities has taken place during the past year, and they now total 264,239 sq ft under roof on a 26-acre site at San Antonio International Airport. In January 1970 Swearingen had a total of 1,582 employees.

SWEARINGEN 800

The Swearingen modernisation of Queen Air 65's and 80's includes installation of two 400 hp Lycoming IO-720 eight-cylinder engines, driving Hartzell three-blade metal propellers; new engine mountings; new exhaust system; new low-drag engine nacelles; new (or zero-time overhauled and certified) accessories, including Lear-Siegler 90A generators; and Swearingen fully-enclosed wheel-well doors. These modifications qualify the Queen Air 65 for a max T-O weight of 7,900 lb (3,583 kg).

SWEARINGEN EXCALIBUR 800

The Excalibur is basically a series D50 Twin-Bonanza fitted with 400 hp Lycoming IO-720-A1A fuel-injection engines in place of the original 295 hp Lycoming GO-480's. The new engines are housed in low-drag glass-fibre cowlings and have revised exhaust systems. Each drives a fully-feathering Hartzell propeller of 7 ft 6 in (2·29 m) diameter.

Many additional and optional improvements are offered by Swearingen to bring the aircraft to full Excalibur 800 standards. These include the fitting of fairings to enclose the main landing gear when retracted, an increase in total fuel capacity from 180 US gallons (681 litres) to 230 US gallons (870 litres), and refinements to the interior and exterior trim.

Swearingen have in the design study phase a pressurised version of the Excalibur 800.

DIMENSION, EXTERNAL:
Wing span	45 ft 11⅜ in (14·00 m)
Length overall	31 ft 6½ in (9·61 m)
Height overall	11 ft 4 in (3·45 m)

WEIGHT:
Max T-O weight	7,600 lb (3,447 kg)

PERFORMANCE (at max T-O weight):
Max cruising speed (75% power) at 8,300 ft (2,530 m)   213 knots (245 mph; 394 km/h)
Econ cruising speed (55% power) at 10,000 ft (3,000 m)   191 knots (220 mph; 354 km/h)
Stalling speed, wheels and flaps down
72 knots (82 mph; 132 km/h)
Stalling speed, wheels and flaps up
80 knots (92 mph; 148 km/h)
Rate of climb at S/L   1,870 ft (570 m)/min

Swearingen/Beechcraft Queen Air 800 (two 400 hp Lycoming IO-720 engines)

Swearingen Excalibur 800 conversion of the Beechcraft Twin-Bonanza

Single-engine rate of climb at S/L
440 ft (134 m)/min
Service ceiling at AUW of 7,000 lb (3,175 kg)
22,200 ft (6,760 m)
Single-engine ceiling at AUW of 7,000 lb (3,175 kg)   11,800 ft (3,600 m)
Range with max fuel, 30 gallon reserve, at max cruising speed   929 nm (1,070 miles; 1,720 km)
Range with max fuel, 30 gallon reserve, at econ cruising speed
1,120 nm (1,290 miles; 2,075 km)

SWEARINGEN MERLIN IIB

Generally similar to the earlier Merlin IIA, this version, which has the manufacturer's model number SA-26AT, differs in having 665 shp Garrett AiResearch TPE 331-1-151G turboprop engines and a dual pressurisation system providing a differential of 7·0 lb/sq in (0·49 kg/cm²). Standard accommodation is for a crew of two and six passengers, but an alternative layout provides for a maximum of eight passengers.

Seven patented locking devices are used to secure the airstair door, being so designed that when the door is locked in place it becomes an integral part of the airframe structure, allowing airframe loads to pass directly through the door and so avoiding the need for the usual heavy door surround.

Production is at the rate of 6½ units per month, and initial deliveries were made to the Australian

Department of Civil Aviation in June 1968. Current production is for delivery to both domestic and foreign customers, the latter including operators in France, West Germany, Mexico and South Africa.

FAA Type Certification of the Merlin IIB was received on 12 June 1968. A comprehensive icing certification programme was then concluded satisfactorily and FAA Certification under FAR Part 25 was awarded on 14 February 1969, giving the Merlin IIB complete all-weather capability.

TYPE: Eight/ten-seat twin-turboprop executive transport.

WINGS: Cantilever low-wing monoplane. Wing section NACA 23014·1 (modified) at fuselage centre-line, NACA 23012 at tip. Dihedral 7°. Incidence 5° 48′ on centre-line, 1° at tip. Aluminium alloy two-spar structure. All-metal ailerons and electrically-actuated single-slotted trailing-edge flaps. Pneumatic de-icing boots standard.

FUSELAGE: Cylindrical all-metal fail-safe structure, flush-riveted throughout. Glass-fibre honeycomb nose-cap will accommodate an 18-in (45 cm) weather radar antenna.

TAIL UNIT: Cantilever all-metal structure, with sweptback vertical surfaces and dorsal fin. Tailplane dihedral 7°. Pneumatic de-icing

Swearingen Merlin IIB of the British Petroleum Co (*Norman E. Taylor*)

boots on fin and tailplane leading-edges standard.

LANDING GEAR: Retractable tricycle type with single wheel on each unit. Electrical retraction. Main wheel tyres size 8·50 × 10 eight-ply. Nose-wheel tyre size 6·50 × 10 six-ply. Hydraulic disc brakes.

POWER PLANT: Two 665 shp AiResearch TPE 331-1-151G turboprop engines, each driving a Hartzell three-blade fully-feathering reversible-pitch propeller, with automatic synchronisation system. Two integral fuel tanks in wings, with total usable capacity of 386 US gallons (1,461 litres). Anti-icing of air intakes by engine-bleed air.

ACCOMMODATION: Crew of two on flight deck, with dual controls. Bulkhead with sliding door divides flight deck from cabin. Standard accommodation for six persons in pairs in main cabin; front pair in rearward-facing seats. Alternative high-density seating for eight passengers. Centre aisle. Built-in beverage and coffee bar. Bulkhead, with door, separates cabin from aft utility section, which includes the air-stair door on the port side, carry-on baggage space opposite on starboard side, full-height wardrobe and toilet. Emergency exit on starboard side of cabin. Windshield de-icing standard.

SYSTEMS: Air-conditioning and pressurisation system utilises engine bleed air for heating and a freon-cycle refrigeration unit. Pressure differential 7·0 lb/sq in (0·49 kg/cm²). Automatic temperature control. Hydraulic system for brakes only. Emergency oxygen system standard, with outlets at each crew and passenger seat. Electrical power supplied by fail-safe DC system.

EQUIPMENT: Standard equipment includes ash trays, cold and hot air outlet and foot warmer at each crew seat; reading lights, drink holder, ash tray and cold air outlet at each seat location; window blinds, card table, floor lights, entrance and vestibule lights. Second card table optional.

ELECTRONICS: Installed to customer's requirements.

DIMENSIONS, EXTERNAL:

Wing span	45 ft 10½ in (13·98 m)
Wing chord (mean aerodymanic)	
	6 ft 5·8 in (1·98 m)
Wing aspect ratio	7·51
Length overall	40 ft 1¼ in (12·22 m)
Height overall	14 ft 4 in (4·37 m)
Passenger door:	
Height	5 ft 4 in (1·63 m)
Width	2 ft 2 in (0·66 m)

DIMENSIONS, INTERNAL:

Length, including flight deck and rear utility section	20 ft 10 in (6·35 m)
Cabin:	
Length between front and rear bulkheads	10 ft 8 in (3·25 m)
Width	5 ft 2 in (1·57 m)
Height	4 ft 11 in (1·50 m)

AREAS:

Wings, gross	279·74 sq ft (25·97 m²)
Ailerons (total)	13·89 sq ft (1·29 m²)
Trailing-edge flaps (total)	37·80 sq ft (3·51 m²)
Fin	20·49 sq ft (1·90 m²)
Rudder	12·25 sq ft (1·14 m²)
Tailplane	58·10 sq ft (5·40 m²)
Elevator	18·00 sq ft (1·67 m²)

WEIGHTS AND LOADINGS:

Weight empty, equipped	6,450 lb (2,926 kg)
Max ramp weight	10,062 lb (4,564 kg)
Max T-O weight	10,000 lb (4,536 kg)
Max landing weight	9,300 lb (4,218 kg)
Max wing loading	35·8 lb/sq ft (174·7 kg/m²)
Max power loading	7·52 lb/shp (3·41 kg/shp)

PERFORMANCE (at max T-O weight):

Cruising speed at 15,000 ft (4,570 m)	
	256 knots (295 mph; 475 km/h)
Max speed, flaps and wheels down	
	137 knots (158 mph; 254 km/h)
Stalling speed, power off, flaps and wheels down	
	76 knots (87 mph; 140 km/h)
Stalling speed, power off, flaps and wheels up	
	88 knots (101 mph; 163 km/h)
Rate of climb at S/L	2,570 ft (783 m)/min
Rate of climb at S/L, one engine out	
	700 ft (213 m)/min
Service ceiling*	29,900 ft (9,110 m)
Service ceiling, one engine out*	
	12,500 ft (3,810 m)
Maximum operating altitude	
	31,000 ft (9,450 m)
T-O to 50 ft (15 m)	2,600 ft (792 m)
Landing from 50 ft (15 m)	2,200 ft (670 m)
Max range at 236 knots (272 mph; 439 km/h) at 27,500 ft (8,380 m), 45 min reserve	
	1,550 nm (1,785 miles; 2,872 km)

*at 9,400 lb (4,310 kg) AUW with pressurisation system maintaining cabin pressure at 7·0 lb/sq in (0·49 kg/cm²).

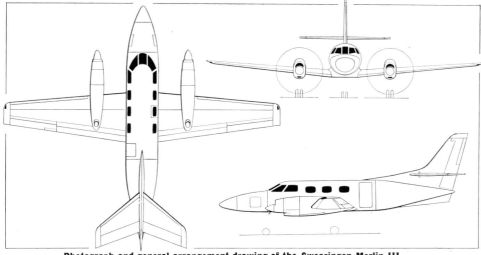

Photograph and general arrangement drawing of the Swearingen Merlin III

SWEARINGEN MERLIN III

The Merlin III is an improved version of the Merlin IIB, from which it differs by having a new tail unit, slightly longer fuselage, and the wings, landing gear and more powerful turboprop engines of the Metro, together with a more sophisticated electrical system.

TYPE: Eight/ten-seat twin-turboprop executive transport.

WINGS: Same as for Metro.

FUSELAGE: Same as for Merlin IIB, except length increased by 2 ft 0·6 in (0·62 m).

TAIL UNIT: Cantilever all-metal structure with sweptback vertical and horizontal surfaces. Dorsal fin with tailplane mounted approximately one-third from base of fin. Small ventral fin. Pneumatic de-icing boots on tailplane leading-edges.

LANDING GEAR: Same as for Metro.

POWER PLANT: Two 840 shp (904 eshp) AiResearch TPE 331-303G turboprop engines, each driving a Hartzell three-blade fully-feathering and reversible metal propeller. Integral fuel tank in each wing, each with capacity of 331·25 US gallons (1,253 litres): total fuel capacity 662·5 US gallons (2,506 litres). Refuelling points in each centre wing panel. Engine inlet de-icing by bleed-air.

ACCOMMODATION: Crew of two on flight deck, with dual controls. Bulkhead with sliding door divides flight deck from cabin. Standard accommodation for six passengers in pairs, with central aisle. Passenger door at rear of cabin on port side with integral airstair. Emergency exit in starboard side of cabin.

SYSTEMS: Same as for Metro except that electrical system comprises two 3kVA engine-driven alternators providing 115 V 400 c/s AC to power gyros, instrumentation and automatic flight control system; auxiliary static inverter; two 300A DC starter/generators with multiple buss bars protected by solid state controls to provide automatic load-shedding and over-voltage protection, which serve as back-up system for instrument flight capability. Automatic engine-start cycle.

DIMENSIONS, EXTERNAL:

Wing span	46 ft 3 in (14·10 m)
Wing chord at root	8 ft 7 in (2·62 m)
Wing chord at tip	3 ft 5 in (1·04 m)
Wing aspect ratio	7·71
Length overall	42 ft 1·9 in (12·85 m)
Height overall	16 ft 8 in (5·08 m)
Wheel track	15 ft 0 in (4·57 m)
Passenger door:	
Height	5 ft 4 in (1·63 m)
Width	4 ft 11 in (1·50 m)

DIMENSIONS, INTERNAL:

Same as for Merlin IIB except:	
Baggage capacity	82 cu ft (2·32 m³)
AREA:	
Wing span	277·50 sq ft (25·78 m²)

WEIGHTS AND LOADINGS:

Weight empty, equipped	7,200 lb (3,266 kg)
Max ramp weight	12,560 lb (5,697 kg)
Max T-O weight	12,500 lb (5,670 kg)
Max zero-fuel weight	9,500 lb (4,309 kg)
Max landing weight	11,500 lb (5,217 kg)
Max wing loading	45·0 lb/sq ft (219·7 kg/m²)
Max power loading	7·44 lb/shp (3·37 kg/shp)

PERFORMANCE (at max T-O weight):

Max cruising speed at 16,000 ft (4,875 m)	
	274 knots (316 mph; 509 km/h)
Econ cruising speed at 28,000 ft (8,535 m)	
	257 knots (296 mph; 476 km/h)
Max permissible speed	
	280 knots (322 mph; 518 km/h)
Max speed, flaps and wheels down	
	200 knots (230 mph; 370 km/h)
Stalling speed, flaps and wheels down	
	85 knots (98 mph; 158 km/h)
Stalling speed, flaps and wheels up	
	98 knots (113 mph; 182 km/h)
Max rate of climb at S/L	2,580 ft (786 m)/min
Max rate of climb at S/L, one engine out	
	504 ft (154 m)/min
Service ceiling	28,000 ft (8,535 m)
Service ceiling, one engine out	
	11,200 ft (3,413 m)
Max operating altitude	31,000 ft (9,450 m)
T-O to 50 ft (15 m), estimated	
	3,480 ft (1,060 m)
Landing from 50 ft (15 m), estimated	
	2,600 ft (792 m)
Range with max fuel at max cruising speed	
	1,710 nm (1,970 miles; 3,170 km)
Range with max fuel at econ cruising speed, 45 min reserve fuel	
	2,353 nm (2,710 miles; 4,361 km)

SWEARINGEN MERLIN IV

The Merlin IV is a corporate version of the Metro commuter airliner to which it is generally similar. It differs principally in its internal configuration which provides accommodation for 12 passengers, a private toilet at the rear of the cabin and a baggage area of 181 cu ft (5·13 m³). Initial deliveries of this version were scheduled for the Summer of 1970.

The description of the Metro applies also to the Merlin IV, except that the systems vary as described for the Merlin III.

DIMENSIONS, EXTERNAL:

Same as for Metro.

The Merlin IV is a corporate version of the Metro

DIMENSIONS, INTERNAL:
Cabin, excluding flight deck, including aft toilet:
Length   25 ft 3 kg (7·70 m)
Baggage compartment:
Length   6 ft 3 in (1·91 m)
Baggage capacity   181 cu ft (5·13 m²)
AREAS:
Same as for Metro
WEIGHTS AND LOADINGS:
Weight empty, equipped   7,700 lb (3,493 kg)
Max ramp weight   12,560 lb (5,697 kg)
Max T-O weight   12,500 lb (5,670 kg)
Max zero-fuel weight   11,000 lb (4,990 kg)
Max landing weight   11,500 lb (5,217 kg)
Max wing loading   45·0 lb/sq ft (219·7 kg/m²)
Max power loading   7·44 lb/shp (3·37 kg/shp)
PERFORMANCE (estimated at max T-O weight):
Max cruising speed at 16,000 ft (4,875 m)
                                265 knots (305 mph; 491 km/h)
Econ cruising speed at 28,000 ft (8,535 m)
                                248 knots (286 mph; 460 km/h)
Max permissible speed
                                280 knots (322 mph; 518 km/h)
Max speed flaps and wheels down
                                200 knots (230 mph; 370 km/h)
Max operating altitude   31,000 ft (9,450 m)
Range with max fuel at max cruising speed
                                1,641 nm (1,890 miles; 3,041 km)
Range with max fuel at econ cruising speed,
45 min reserve fuel
                                2,214 nm (2,550 miles; 4,104 km)

SWEARINGEN MODEL SA-226TC METRO

The Swearingen Metro is basically a 20-passenger airliner, with an easily convertible passenger/cargo interior designed specifically to allow maximum flexibility to operators of commuter airlines. A joint venture of Swearingen Aircraft and the Fairchild Hiller Corporation, the aircraft will be produced at Swearingen's San Antonio factory and marketed by Fairchild Hiller.

Construction of a prototype began in August 1968 and this aircraft flew for the first time on 26 August 1969.

Unlike previous products of this company, and most aircraft currently available to commuter airlines, which are modified, stretched and rebuilt versions of airframes designed originally for corporate use, the Metro is completely new.

TYPE: Twenty-passenger twin-turboprop commuter airliner.

WINGS: Cantilever low-wing monoplane. Wing section NACA 65₂A215 at root, NACA 64₂A415 at tip. Dihedral 5°. Incidence 1° at root, —1°

at tip. Sweepback at quarter-chord 0·9°. All-metal two-spar semi-monocoque fail-safe structure of aluminium alloy. Hydraulically-operated double-slotted trailing-edge flaps. Manually-controlled trim-tab on port aileron. Goodrich pneumatic de-icing boots on wing leading-edges, with automatic bleed-air cycling system.

FUSELAGE: All-metal cylindrical semi-monocoque fail-safe structure of aluminium alloy. Glass-fibre honeycomb nose cap can accommodate a 15 in (38·1 cm) weather radar antenna.

TAIL UNIT: Cantilever all-metal structure with swept-back vertical surface and dorsal fin. Electrically-adjustable variable-incidence tailplane. Manually-controlled rudder-trim. Goodrich pneumatic de-icing boots on tailplane leading-edges, with automatic bleed-air cycling system.

LANDING GEAR: Retractable tricycle type with twin wheels on each unit. Hydraulic retraction, with dual actuators at each unit. All wheels retract forward, main gear into engine nacelles, nose-wheels into fuselage. Ozone Aircraft Systems oleo-pneumatic shock-absorber struts. Nose-wheels steerable. Free-fall emergency extension system. B.F. Goodrich main wheels and tyres, size 18 × 5·5, type VII, pressure 100 lb/sq in (7·03 kg/cm²). General Tire Company nose-wheels and tyres, size 16 × 4·4, type VII, pressure 85 lb/sq in (5·98 kg/cm²). Goodrich self-adjusting hydraulically-operated disc brakes.

POWER PLANT: Two 840 shp (904 eshp) Ai-Research TPE 331-3U-303 turboprop engines, each driving a Hartzell three-blade fully-feathering and reversible propeller with automatic synchronisation. Propeller diameter 8 ft 2 in (2·49 m). Integral fuel tank in each wing, each with capacity of 331·25 US gallons (1,253 litres); total fuel capacity 662·5 US gallons (2,506 litres). Refuelling point in each outer wing panel. Single point refuelling optional. Oil capacity 4 US gallons (15·1 litres). Engine inlet de-icing by bleed air. Electrical propeller de-icing. Automatic fuel heating system to prevent filter icing. Flush-mounted fuel vents.

ACCOMMODATION: Crew of two on flight deck, separated from passenger/cargo area by arm-level curtain. Bulkhead between cabin and flight deck optional. Standard accommodation for 20 passengers seated two-abreast, on each side of a central aisle. Full-length cabin seat tracks. Self-stowing fold-up seats for rapid conversion to cargo or mixed passenger/cargo configuration. Movable bulkhead between passenger and cargo sections. Snap-in carpeting. Self-stowing aisle filler. Tie-down fittings for cargo at 30-in (0·76-m) spacing. Double-pane polarised cabin windows to allow passengers control of external light intensity. Integral-step passenger door on port side of fuselage, immediately aft of flight deck. Large passenger/cargo loading door on port side of fuselage at rear of cabin, hinged at top. Three window emergency exits, one on the port, two on the starboard side. Forward baggage compartment in nose, capacity 45 cu ft (1·27 m³). Rear baggage compartment, aft of cabin in passenger version, capacity 136 cu ft (3·85 m³). Stowage for carry-on luggage. Cabin air conditioned and pressurised. Electrical windshield de-icing. Windshield wipers.

SYSTEMS: AiResearch automatic cabin pressure control system maintains a differential of 7·0 lb/sq in (0·49 kg/cm²). Engine-bleed air heating, dual air cycle cooling system, with automatic temperature control. Independent hydraulic system for brakes. Dual engine-driven hydraulic pumps provide 2,000 lb/sq in (140 kg/cm²) to operate flaps and landing gear. Electrical system supplied by two 200A 28V DC starter/generators. Fail-safe system with overload and over-voltage protection. Redundant circuits for essential systems. Two 25Ah nickel-cadmium batteries for main services. One small nickel-cadmium battery for utility lights only. Engine fire detection system standard. Engine fire extinguisher system optional. Oxygen system of 48 cu ft (1·36 m³) capacity with flush outlets at each seat.

EQUIPMENT: Standard equipment includes individual reading lights and air vents for each

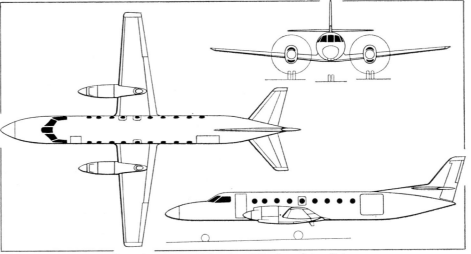

General-arrangement drawing of the Swearingen Metro

Swearingen Metro 20-passenger commuter airliner (two 840 shp AiResearch TPE 331-3U-303 turboprop engines)

passenger, side window de-fog blowers for flight deck, smoke goggles and oxygen masks for crew, electrically-heated pitot heads, ice-free instrument static sources.

ELECTRONICS: Provisions for installation of remotely-mounted or panel-mounted electronics, customer-furnished antennae and Bendix M-4 autopilot. Two flight deck and six cabin speakers standard.

DIMENSIONS, EXTERNAL:
Wing span	46 ft 3 in (14·10 m)
Wing chord at root	8 ft 7 in (2·62 m)
Wing chord at tip	3 ft 5 in (1·04 m)
Aspect ratio	7·71
Length overall	59 ft 4¼ in (18·09 m)
Height overall	16 ft 8 in (5·08 m)
Tailplane span	14 ft 4½ in (4·38 m)
Wheel track	15 ft 0 in (4·57 m)
Wheelbase	19 ft 1½ in (5·83 m)
Passenger door (fwd):	
Height	5 ft 4 in (1·63 m)
Width	2 ft 1 in (0·64 m)
Passenger/cargo door (aft):	
Height	4 ft 3¼ in (1·30 m)
Width	4 ft 5 in (1·35 m)
Height to sill	4 ft 3¼ in (1·30 m)

DIMENSIONS, INTERNAL:
Cabin, excluding flight deck and aft baggage compartment:
Length	25 ft 5 in (7·75 m)
Max width	5 ft 2 in (1·57 m)
Max height (aisle)	4 ft 9 in (1·45 m)
Floor area	140 sq ft (13·01 m²)
Volume	463 cu ft (13·11 m³)

AREAS:
Wings, gross	277·50 sq ft (25·78 m²)
Ailerons (total)	14·12 sq ft (1·31 m²)
Trailing-edge flaps (total)	40·66 sq ft (3·78 m²)
Fin	54·50 sq ft (5·06 m²)
Rudder, including tab	21·27 sq ft (1·98 m²)
Tailplane	75·97 sq ft (7·06 m²)
Elevators	21·27 sq ft (1·98 m²)

WEIGHTS AND LOADINGS:
Design empty weight	7,000 lb (3,175 kg)
Max T-O and landing weight	12,500 lb (5,669 kg)
Max ramp weight	12,560 lb (5,697 kg)
Max wing loading	45·5 lb/sq ft (222·1 kg/m²)
Max power loading	6·92 lb/eshp (3·14 kg/eshp)

PERFORMANCE (estimated):
Max cruising speed at 9,500 ft (2,895 m), at 12,000 lb (5,445 kg) AUW
269 knots (310 mph; 500 km/h)
Long-range cruising speed at 20,000 ft (6,100 m), at 12,000 lb (5,445 kg) AUW
220 knots (253 mph; 407 km/h)

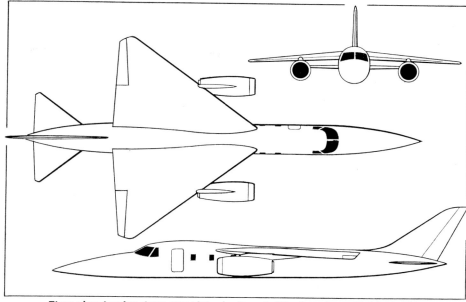

Three-view drawing shows new high-wing layout of the Swearingen Model SA 28T

T-O to 50 ft (15 m) at 12,000 lb (5,445 kg) AUW
2,800 ft (853 m)
Landing from 50 ft (15 m) at 12,000 lb (5,445 kg) AUW
2,500 ft (762 m)
Range at 10,000 ft (3,050 m), with reserves:
VFR mission, 4,350 lb (1,973 kg) payload
99 nm (115 miles; 185 km)
IFR mission, 3,940 lb (1,787 kg) payload
99 nm (115 miles; 185 km)
Range at 25,000 ft (7,620 m), with reserves:
VFR mission, 3,965 lb (1,798 kg) payload
299 nm (345 miles; 555 km)
IFR mission, 3,510 lb (1,592 kg) payload
299 nm (345 miles; 555 km)
Max ferry range (allowance for taxi, T-O, climb, cruise, descent, landing, taxi-in and 45 min reserve fuel 1,498 nm (1,725 miles; 2,780 km)

SWEARINGEN MODEL SA 28T

Swearingen have announced plans for the development of a delta-wing high-speed business jet, to be powered by two AiResearch TFE 731-1 turbofan engines, each rated at 3,500 lb (1,587 kg) st.

Developed from supersonic aircraft studies initiated by Swearingen in 1967, the SA 28T's delta-wing will have a sweepback of 53°, and resembles in some respects the supercritical wing developed by NASA (which see). A delta-tail, mounted low behind the delta-wing, will be of all moving slab design. The flying controls and landing gear will be hydraulically actuated.

In the original design the turbofan engines were to have been pod mounted on each side of the area-ruled fuselage, but wind tunnel tests have indicated excessive drag with this layout. Re-design has raised the delta wing to a high-wing location to permit the engines to be mounted on underwing pylons.

At a gross weight of approximately 13,500 lb (6,123 kg), the seven-seat SA 28T will have a max speed in excess of 500 knots (575 mph; 925 km/h) and range in excess of 2,000 nm (2,300 miles; 3,700 km). A cabin pressure differential of 12 lb/sq in (0·84 kg/cm²) will provide sea level cabin conditions to an altitude of 40,000 ft (12,190 m).

Swearingen's new business jet, which will be marketed by AiResearch Aviation, is scheduled for first flight in 1970, with initial deliveries in 1972. Application for certification under FAR Part 25 has been filed with the FAA.

SZARAZ
ARPAD SZARAZ
ADDRESS:
419 Center Road, Bedford, Ohio 44146
Mr Szaraz markets plans of a two-seat light aircraft of his own design, known as the Daphne SDI-A.

DAPHNE SDI-A
The prototype of this side-by-side two-seat light aircraft was built by Mr James Vidervol and flew for the first time on 4 October 1961. A photograph and brief details of it were published in the 1963-64 Jane's.

At least 26 Daphnes were under construction in January 1970, and two are known to be flying, each powered, like the original prototype, with an 85 hp Continental C85-8 four-cylinder horizontally-opposed air-cooled engine, driving a McCauley 68-54 two-blade metal propeller. One of these, shown in the adjacent illustration, was built by Mr B. D. Darmstadt of Parma, Ohio, over a five-year period at a cost of $2,200 and flew for the first time on 18 June 1965. The other, built by Mr N. Stanich of Berea, Ohio, flew on 28 February 1965, after four years of work, at a cost of $3,000, and differs from the standard design by having full-span ailerons.

Construction of the Daphne SDI-A is conventional, with a braced wooden wing of NACA 4412 (modified) section and steel-tube fuselage and tail unit, all fabric-covered. The engine cowling is of glass-fibre. The non-retractable tail-wheel type landing gear uses cantilever spring steel main legs. Tyre size is 6·00 × 6·16 and hydraulic brakes are fitted. Fuel capacity is 21 US gallons (7·5 litres)

Daphne SDI-A two-seat light aircraft, built by Mr B. Darmstadt

DIMENSIONS, EXTERNAL:
Wing span	26 ft 3 in (8·00 m)
Wing chord (constant)	5 ft 3 in (1·60 m)
Length overall	19 ft 7 in (5·97 m)
Height overall	5 ft 10 in (1·78 m)

AREA:
Wings, gross	130 sq ft (12·08 m²)

WEIGHTS:
Weight empty	825 lb (374 kg)
Max T-O weight	1,350 lb (612 kg)

PERFORMANCE (at max T-O weight):
Max level speed at S/L	129 knots (149 mph; 240 km/h)
Max permissible diving speed	138 knots (160 mph; 257 km/h)
Cruising speed	109-113 knots (125-130 mph; 201-209 km/h)
Stalling speed	39 knots (45 mph; 73 km/h)
Rate of climb at S/L	1,000 ft (305 m)/min
T-O run	300 ft (91 m)
Landing run	300 ft (91 m)
Endurance with max fuel	3 hr 45 min

TELEDYNE RYAN
TELEDYNE RYAN AERONAUTICAL
HEAD OFFICE AND WORKS:
Lindbergh Field, San Diego, California 92112
CHAIRMAN OF THE BOARD:
Robert C. Jackson
PRESIDENT:
Frank Gard Jameson

EXECUTIVE VICE-PRESIDENT:
L. M. Limbach
VICE-PRESIDENTS:
R. A. Ballweg (Washington, DC Office)
R. D. Fields (Finance and Controller)
J. R. Iverson (Electronic and Space Systems)
L. Parma (Administration)
R. R. Schwanhausser (Aerospace Systems)
W. J. Wiley (Plant Operations)

PUBLIC RELATIONS AND COMMUNICATIONS MANAGER:
Robert B. Morrisey
The former Ryan Aeronautical Company was successor to the Ryan Company which produced the aeroplane in which Mr Charles Lindbergh made the first non-stop flight from New York to Paris in 1927. In February 1969, Ryan Aeronautical became a wholly-owned subsidiary

of Teledyne, Inc and in December 1969 the company was re-named Teledyne Ryan Aeronautical.

Its three plants in the San Diego area extend over more than 1,400,000 sq ft, and an average labour force of 5,000 persons is employed.

The current activities of the company fall into two major categories, under the headings of Aerospace Systems and Electronic and Space Systems. The former group is concerned principally with the design, production and field operation of high-performance Firebee aerial jet targets and drone systems, described in detail under the Company's entry in the "Drones" section of this edition.

The Electronic and Space Systems group is responsible for design and production of radar equipment for landing spacecraft and astronauts on the Moon in the Apollo programme; electronic navigation and positioning equipment for aircraft; remote sensors for Earth resources studies; electronic warfare systems; and microwave antennae.

On 8 June 1970 Teledyne Ryan announced that the Brazilian Navy had taken delivery of four Sikorsky SH-3D ASW helicopters equipped with Teledyne Ryan AN/APN-182 Doppler radar navigation equipment.

Teledyne Ryan continues to maintain a strong technical interest in vertical take-off and landing aircraft, but this makes only a minor contribution to the volume of the company's business.

The XV-5B VTOL research aircraft was handed over to NASA for use in its aeronautical research programme, and details of this aircraft may be found in the 1969/70 *Jane's*.

TERMITE
TERMITE AIRCRAFT

Termite Aircraft is marketing plans and kits of pre-fabricated wood components for a single-seat sporting monoplane known as the Termite, which was designed by Mr Wilbur L. Smith. The prototype was flown originally, on 10 February 1957, with a 36 hp Aeronca E-113-C engine, but has since been tested with, successively, a 38 hp Continental A40-5 and a 65 hp Lycoming O-145 engine, both of which are considered suitable for amateur-built Termites.

TERMITE

Many Termites have been built and flown by amateur constructor-pilots in the USA, Canada and elsewhere. The example illustrated was built in Canada and has a 50 hp Continental A50 engine.

The following data apply to the standard Termite, built from Mr Smith's plans.

TYPE: Single-seat sporting monoplane.

WINGS: Braced parasol monoplane, with two parallel streamline-section metal bracing struts each side and six bracing struts between fuselage and centre-wing. Wing section Clark Y. Dihedral 1°. Incidence 2°. All-wood two-spar structure. Aluminium-covered leading-edge. Fabric covering aft of front spar. Fabric-covered wood ailerons.

FUSELAGE: All-wood structure, plywood-covered to rear of cockpit, with fabric covering on rear fuselage.

TAIL UNIT: Wire-braced wood structure, except for steel-tube leading and trailing edges. Fabric-covered.

LANDING GEAR: Non-retractable two-wheel type. Main units of Piper Cub type. Goodyear wheels, size 7·00 × 3. No brakes. Spring-steel tail-skid.

POWER PLANT: One 38 hp Continental A40-5 four-cylinder horizontally-opposed air-cooled engine driving a two-blade wooden fixed-pitch propeller. Alternatively one 65 hp Lycoming O-145 or Continental A65 engine. Fuel tank aft of firewall, capacity 6 US gallons (22·7 litres). Additional 5 US gallon (18·9 litre) wing tank on 65 hp version.

ACCOMMODATION: Single seat in open cockpit.

Termite single-seat amateur-built aircraft (50 hp Continental A50 engine) (*Peter M. Bowers*)

DIMENSIONS, EXTERNAL:

Wing span	23 ft 6 in (7·16 m)
Wing chord, constant	4 ft 2 in (1·27 m)
Length overall:	
A40-5	15 ft 1 in (4·60 m)
O-145, A65	15 ft 9 in (4·80 m)
Height overall	5 ft 9 in (1·75 m)
Tailplane span	6 ft 10 in (2·08 m)
Wheel track	5 ft 2 in (1·57 m)

WEIGHTS:

Weight empty:	
A40-5	432 lb (196 kg)
A65	776 lb (352 kg)
Max T-O weight:	
A40-5	658 lb (298 kg)
A65	976 lb (443 kg)

PERFORMANCE (at max T-O weight):

Max level speed at S/L:	
A40-5	83 knots (95 mph; 153 km/h)
A65	78 knots (90 mph; 145 km/h)
Max cruising speed:	
A40-5	72 knots (83 mph; 133 km/h)
A65	74 knots (85 mph; 137 km/h)
Landing speed:	
A40-5	33 knots (38 mph; 61 km/h)
A65	52 knots (60 mph; 97 km/h)
Rate of climb at S/L:	
A40-5	450 ft (137 m)/min
A65	200 ft (61 m)/min
Service ceiling:	
A65	6,000 ft (1,830 m)
T-O run:	
A65	350 ft (107 m)
Landing run:	
A65	400 ft (122 m)
Range with max fuel:	
A40-5	130 nm (150 miles; 240 km)
A65	277 nm (320 miles; 515 km)

THERMODYNAMIC
THERMODYNAMIC SYSTEMS, INC

ADDRESS: Newport Beach, California

VICE-PRESIDENT: R. G. Smith

Thermodynamic Systems have announced the development of a low-cost steam power plant, and are currently building 25 prototypes in the 150 shp range, which they propose to test for automotive, aviation, industrial and marine applications, as well as for off-road vehicles.

One of these experimental power plants has been installed in a Hughes Model 300 one/three-seat light helicopter, and flight tests of the system were carried out during the Summer of 1969.

Thermodynamic Systems believe that rotary-wing aircraft provide an ideal application for a steam-driven power plant, since they require low output shaft speeds at high torque demand, and quick response to control. One important advantage of steam systems is their ability to store power, providing a power reserve for several minutes in the event of flame-out in the steam generator.

THORP
THORP ENGINEERING COMPANY

ADDRESS:
909, East Magnolia, Burbank, California 91501

This company was founded by Mr John W. Thorp, who is well-known as a designer of light aircraft.

One of his designs, under development since 1946, is the Sky Skooter, of which several examples have flown. A few kits of pre-fabricated parts for this aircraft were produced by Thorp Engineering Company in 1961, but series production was to be undertaken by Tubular Aircraft Products Co of Los Angeles.

A further design by Mr Thorp, of which plans are available, is the T-18 Tiger two-seat all-metal sporting aircraft described below. Several hundred sets of drawings have been sold and many T-18's are flying.

THORP T-18 TIGER

First T-18 to be completed was N9675Z with a 180 hp Lycoming O-360 engine. Built by Mr W. Warwick, it flew for the first time on 12 May 1964 and was illustrated in the 1964-65 *Jane's*. The aircraft illustrated in the 1969-70 *Jane's* was built by Mr Irvin Faur of Princeton, Iowa. Construction occupied six months and cost $2,500. It differs from the standard Thorp plans by having only 2° of wing dihedral, and is powered by a 160 hp Lycoming O-320 engine. Mr Faur's T-18 has an empty weight of 814 lb (369 kg), max T-O weight 1,400 lb (635 kg), max speed 156 knots (180 mph; 290 km/h); cruising speed 130 knots

Thorp T-18 Tiger built by Mr Laurence Larcom of Delaware, Ohio (*Jean Seele*)

(150 mph; 241 km/h), landing speed 59 knots (68 mph; 109 km/h), rate of climb of 2,000 ft (610 m)/min. Take-off run is 300 ft (91 m), landing run 2,000 ft (610 m) and range with max fuel 347 nm (400 miles; 640 km).

The following details apply to the standard Thorp T-18:

TYPE: Two-seat high-performance sporting aircraft.

WINGS: Cantilever low-wing monoplane, with 8° dihedral on outer panels only. All-metal two-spar structure. Normally no flaps, but a flap installation is under design.

FUSELAGE: All-metal structure, without double curvature.

TAIL UNIT: Cantilever all-metal structure.

LANDING GEAR: Non-retractable tail-wheel type. Cantilever main legs. Steerable tail-wheel. Main wheel tyres size 5·00 × 5.

POWER PLANT: One Lycoming or Continental four-cylinder horizontally-opposed air-cooled engine in 108-200 hp category, driving a two-blade fixed-pitch propeller, diameter 5 ft 3 in (1·60 m). Fuel tank aft of firewall, capacity 29 US gallons (110 litres).

ACCOMMODATION: Two seats side-by-side in open cockpit, with dual controls. Space for 80 lb (36 kg) baggage.

DIMENSIONS, EXTERNAL:

Wing span	20 ft 10 in (6·35 m)
Wing chord, constant	4 ft 2 in (1·27 m)
Length overall	18 ft 2 in (5·54 m)
Height overall	4 ft 10 in (1·47 m)
Tailplane span	6 ft 11 in (2·10 m)

AREA:

Wings, gross	86 sq ft (8·0 m²)

WEIGHTS (180 hp Lycoming):

Weight empty	900 lb (408 kg)
Max T-O weight	1,506 lb (683 kg)

PERFORMANCE (180 hp Lycoming):

Max level speed at S/L	174 knots (200 mph; 321 km/h)
Max cruising speed	152 knots (175 mph; 282 km/h)
Stalling speed	57 knots (65 mph; 105 km/h)
Rate of climb at S/L	2,000 ft (610 m)/min
Service ceiling	20,000 ft (6,100 m)
T-O run	300 ft (91 m)
Landing run	900 ft (275 m)
Range with max fuel	434 nm (500 miles; 805 km)

THURSTON

THURSTON AIRCRAFT CORPORATION

HEAD OFFICE AND WORKS:
Box 450, Sanford Airport, Sanford, Maine 04073

PRESIDENT AND CHIEF ENGINEER:
David B. Thurston

TREASURER:
Jason A. Ramsdell

MANAGER, AIRCRAFT SALES:
Stanley Woodward Jnr

PRODUCTION MANAGER:
Theodore J. Greenier

CHIEF PILOT:
Cdr N. J. Vagianos, USN (retd)

Thurston Aircraft Corporation was founded in July 1966 by Mr David B. Thurston, formerly President of Thurston Erlandsen Corporation (TEC). The new company is engaged primarily on the design, development and manufacture of water-based aircraft and related operational improvement devices, and of high-performance water-borne vehicles employing aircraft-type structures.

It is continuing advanced hydrodynamic research studies for the Naval Air Systems Command, Department of the Navy, and has developed for certification a new folding-wing light flying-boat/amphibian, known as the Model TSC-1 which is intended for the sporting and personal aircraft markets.

THURSTON HRV-1

The US Navy has assigned to Thurston Aircraft Corporation the HRV-1 hydro research vehicle described under the "TEC" heading in the 1966-67 *Jane's*. Developed from the original Colonial Model C-2 Skimmer light amphibian (180 hp Lycoming O-360 engine), this aircraft provides the Naval Air Systems Command with the only flying dynamic test-bed capable of extending scale model towing-tank work into full-scale flight investigations and evaluations.

Thurston Aircraft Corporation's first programme for NASC has involved fitting and testing on the HRV-1 a single penetrating supercavitating hydrofoil. Shaped like a shallow Vee, with an included angle of approximately 135°, this hydrofoil spans 17·32 in (44 cm) and is carried on a retractable strut under the hull, well forward of the step.

A major improvement in performance has been achieved with the hydrofoil by comparison with the hydro-ski installations tested previously. While hull bottom pressures are 3-4 lb/sq in (1·4-1·8 kg/cm²) greater with the foil than with skis, they remain well below the values recorded for the basic hull, particularly during rough water operation. In every other design parameter considered, the hydrofoil has been found superior to the hydro-ski.

Extremely great improvement has been noted in the reduction of take-off time and length of run, with approximately half of the gain obtained through increased L/D of the hydrofoil and half due to improved strut ventilation, resulting apparently from interaction with the supercavitating hydrofoil upper-surface blister. Landing impact load factors have consistently approximated one-half of the values obtained with the ski and one-third the magnitude realised with the basic hull.

There is less tendency to either yaw or drop off onto one wing during landing than with the ski. Spray patterns during take-off and landing are considerably reduced by comparison with those experienced with the ski. A considerable weight-saving has also been achieved, the hydrofoil weighing 4·5 lb (2·05 kg) compared with 18 lb (8·2 kg) for the hydro-ski. Including hull structural provisions and instrumented strut, the installed weight of the hydrofoil is 73 lb (33 kg), as against 86 lb (39 kg) for the ski.

The hydrofoil-equipped HRV-1 can land and take off safely in seas three times the wave height permissible with the basic hull. Development work on this project was continuing at the time of writing and consists principally of refining the hydrofoil location and recording performance data.

Thurston Aircraft HRV-1 taking off with hydrofoil at 17-in extension

Thurston Model TSC-1A Teal amphibian (150 hp Lycoming O-320-A3B engine) (*Howard Levy*)

THURSTON MODEL TSC-1A TEAL

The Teal amphibian has been developed to provide a simple, economical and easily-handled two-seat aircraft for cross-country and sporting flying, land and seaplane training and limited business use. The entire structure and covering are of aluminium alloy, except for the bow deck and cabin top skins which are of glass-fibre.

To permit towing on its own landing gear, the Teal can be supplied with removable wings. A flying-boat version, without landing gear, is available and is described separately.

The prototype of the Teal amphibian flew for the first time in June 1968. FAA certification was awarded on 28 August 1969. A production line has been established and four aircraft had been completed at the time of writing.

TYPE: Two-seat cabin monoplane amphibian.

WINGS: Cantilever shoulder-wing monoplane. Wing section NACA 4415. Dihedral 4°. Incidence 4°. All-metal "D-spar" structure. No flaps.

HULL: All-metal semi-monocoque structure, with glass-fibre foredeck and cabin top skins.

TAIL UNIT: Cantilever all-metal structure, with tailplane mounted at tip of fin. Trim-tab on elevator and rudder.

LANDING GEAR: Retractable tailwheel type; manually actuated. Spring steel main struts. Tailwheel integral with water rudder. Main wheels size 6·00 × 6. Tail-wheel size 8·00 × 3·00. Single-disc brakes on main wheels.

POWER PLANT: One 150 hp Lycoming O-320-A3B four-cylinder horizontally-opposed air-cooled engine, driving a Hartzell two-blade constant-speed metal propeller, diameter 6 ft 0 in (1·83 m). All-metal fuel tank in hull, aft of main bulkhead, capacity 25 US gallons (94·6 litres). Oil capacity 2 US gallons (7·5 litres).

ACCOMMODATION: Enclosed cabin seating two persons side-by-side. Baggage compartment behind seats, capacity 230 lb (104 kg). Seat backs fold down for access to baggage compartment and for stand-up fishing from cabin. Door on each side. May be flown with window open. Ventilation system standard.

SYSTEMS: Electrical system has 40A 12V alternator and 12V 25Ah battery. Janitrol heating and defrosting system optional.

EQUIPMENT: Standard equipment includes heated pitot, stall warning indicator, soundproofing, map pockets, ash tray, tinted glass overhead panels, corrosion proofing, anchor, mooring line and paddle. Optional items include dual controls, strobe light, blind flying instrumentation, 8-day clock, outside air temperature gauge and navigation, instrument, landing and cabin lights.

ELECTRONICS: A wide choice of navigation and communication equipment is available to customer's requirements.

DIMENSIONS, EXTERNAL:

Wing span	31 ft 11 in (9·73 m)
Wing chord, constant	5 ft 0 in (1·52 m)
Wing aspect ratio	6·5
Length overall	23 ft 7 in (7·19 m)
Height overall	8 ft 11 in (2·72 m)
Wheel track	8 ft 3 in (2·51 m)

AREAS:

Wings, gross	157 sq ft (14·59 m²)
Ailerons (total)	10 sq ft (0·93 m²)
Fin	10·7 sq ft (0·99 m²)
Rudder	6·8 sq ft (0·63 m²)
Tailplane	15·4 sq ft (1·43 m²)
Elevator	12·6 sq ft (1·17 m²)

WEIGHTS AND LOADINGS:

Weight empty	1,300 lb (589 kg)
Max T-O weight	1,900 lb (861 kg)
Max wing loading	12·1 lb/sq ft (59 kg/m³)
Max power loading	12·7 lb/hp (5·76 kg/hp)

PERFORMANCE:

Max speed at S/L	109 knots (125 mph; 201 km/h)
Cruising speed	94 knots (108 mph; 174 km/h)
Stalling speed	47 knots (54 mph; 87 km/h)
Rate of climb at S/L	1,050 ft (320 m)/min
T-O run on land	400 ft (122 m)
T-O run on water	600 ft (183 m)
Landing run on land	350 ft (107 m)
Landing run on water	450 ft (137 m)
Range, with reserve	347 nm (400 miles; 640 m)

THURSTON MODEL TSC-1 "T-BOAT"

This is the flying-boat version of the Teal. Specifications are as above, except that the landing gear is removed. Useful load and performance are increased as follows:

WEIGHTS:

Weight empty	1,140 lb (517 kg)
Max T-O weight	1,850 lb (839 kg)

PERFORMANCE (estimated):

Max speed at S/L 104 knots (120 mph; 193 km/h)
Max cruising speed (75% power) at 7,500 ft (2,300 m)   109 knots (125 mph; 201 km/h)

TURNER

EUGENE L. TURNER

ADDRESS:
18711 Merridy Street, Northridge, California 91324

SALES MANAGER:
Melva L. Turner

The 1966-67 *Jane's* contains details of a single-seat sporting aircraft designated T-40, which was designed and built by Mr E. L. Turner and flew for the first time on 3 April 1961. This aircraft was modified by Mr Turner and his son into a prototype of the two-seat T-40A and is described below in this form. It was further converted later into another version of the same design, the T-40B, with a tricycle landing gear and other refinements and this also is described.

Plans of these aircraft are available and 124 T-40A's are known to be under construction by amateurs.

TURNER T-40A

The prototype T-40A was produced by conversion of the original T-40. Modification took about four months and the aircraft flew for the first time in this form on 31 July 1966.

The T-40A is small enough to fit in a single-car garage and is transported on a small trailer. It has built-in skids in the fuselage, to protect the pilot in a minor crash landing, and overturn structure.

TYPE: Two-seat sporting aircraft.

WINGS: Cantilever low-wing monoplane. Wing section NACA 65-215. Dihedral 4°. Incidence 1° 30'. All-wood (fir) two-spar structure with mahogany plywood covering. Hoerner low-drag tips. Plain ailerons. Large plain flaps. Wings fold rearward for stowage.

FUSELAGE: All-wood (fir) structure, covered with mahogany plywood. Glass-fibre engine cowling.

TAIL UNIT: Cantilever all-wood (fir) structure with mahogany plywood covering. Horizontal surface of all-flying type with anti-servo tabs. Glass-fibre dorsal fin.

LANDING GEAR: Non-retractable tail-wheel type. Cantilever spring steel main units attached to front spar. Goodyear main wheels and tyres, size 5·00-5, pressure 45 lb/sq in (3·16 kg/cm²). Goodyear brakes.

POWER PLANT: One Continental four-cylinder horizontally-opposed air-cooled engine of 85 to 100 hp, driving a McCauley two-blade fixed-pitch propeller, type 65/57. Fuel tank in front fuselage, capacity 20 US gallons (75 litres). Oil capacity 1 US gallon (3·75 litres).

ACCOMMODATION: Pilot and passenger side-by-side. Each half of transparent canopy is hinged on centre-line of aircraft to form a door, folding in two as it opens upward. Space for 25 lb (11·5 kg) baggage aft of seats.

EQUIPMENT: Prototype has Narco VHT-3 radio.

DIMENSIONS, EXTERNAL:

Wing span	23 ft 6 in (7·16 m)
Wing chord, constant	3 ft 6½ in (1·08 m)
Wing aspect ratio	6·7
Length overall	19 ft 6 in (5·94 m)
Width, wings folded	7 ft 8 in (2·34 m)
Height overall	6 ft 0 in (1·83 m)
Tailplane span	6 ft 5 in (1·96 m)
Wheel track	7 ft 4 in (2·24 m)

DIMENSIONS, INTERNAL:

Cabin: length	5 ft 10 in (1·78 m)
Max width	3 ft 4 in (1·02 m)
Max height	3 ft 3 in (0·99 m)

AREAS:

Wings	84 sq ft (7·80 m²)
Ailerons (total)	6·5 sq ft (0·60 m²)
Flaps (total)	9·9 sq ft (0·92 m²)
Fin	5·8 sq ft (0·54 m²)
Rudder	3·8 sq ft (0·35 m²)
Horizontal tail surfaces	11·34 sq ft (1·05 m²)

Turner T-40A two-seat amateur-built light aircraft, with doors open

Turner T-40B prototype, a conversion of the T-40A with tricycle landing gear

WEIGHTS AND LOADINGS:

Weight empty	828 lb (376 kg)
Max T-O and landing weight	1,310 lb (595 kg)
Max wing loading	15·6 lb/sq ft (76·2 kg/m²)
Max power loading	15·4 lb/hp (7·0 kg/hp)

PERFORMANCE (85 hp engine, at max T-O weight):

Max level speed at S/L	141 knots (162 mph; 261 km/h)
Max diving speed	195 knots (225 mph; 362 km/h)
Max cruising speed at S/L	130 knots (150 mph; 241 km/h)
Econ cruising speed at S/L	120 knots (138 mph; 222 km/h)
Stalling speed, flaps down	49 knots (56 mph; 90 km/h)
Stalling speed, flaps up	54 knots (62 mph; 100 km/h)
Rate of climb at S/L	600 ft (183 m)/min
Estimated service ceiling	12,500 ft (3,800 m)
T-O run	700 ft (213 m)
T-O to 50 ft (15 m)	1,200 ft (365 m)
Landing run	460 ft (140 m)
Range with max payload, 20 min reserve	412 nm (475 miles; 756 km)

TURNER T-40B

This aircraft is basically similar to the T-40A but has a tricycle landing gear and other refinements. Conversion of the prototype started in October 1966 and the first flight was made on 2 March 1969. Flight tests have shown that high-altitude performance with an 85 hp engine is below expectation and it is intended to install a 125 hp engine in the near future.

The description of the T-40A applies also to the T-40B, except in the following details:

WINGS: Wing section NACA 64-212. Fixed leading-edge droop. Double-slotted flaps.

LANDING GEAR: Non-retractable tricycle type. Nose-wheel size 4·1 × 6.

DIMENSIONS, EXTERNAL:
Same as for T-40A, except:

Wing span	22 ft 3 in (6·78 m)
Wing chord at root	4 ft 3 in (1·30 m)
Wing aspect ratio	5·2
Wheel track	7 ft 2 in (2·18 m)
Wheelbase	6 ft 0 in (1·83 m)

AREAS:
Same as for T-40A except:

Wings, gross	96 sq ft (8·92 m²)
Ailerons (total)	6·1 sq ft (0·57 m²)
Trailing-edge flaps (total)	17·8 sq ft (1·65 m²)

WEIGHTS AND LOADINGS:
Same as for T-40A, except:

Wing loading	13·6 lb/sq ft (66·4 kg/m²)

PERFORMANCE (85 hp engine, estimated at max T-O weight):
As for T-40A, except:

Stalling speed, flaps down	43 knots (49 mph; 79 km/h)
Stalling speed, flaps up	51 knots (58 mph; 94 km/h)
Rate of climb at S/L	720 ft (220 m)/min
Service ceiling	14,400 ft (4,400 m)
T-O run	600 ft (183 m)
T-O to 50 ft (15 m)	950 ft (290 m)
Landing run	440 ft (134 m)

VERTIDYNAMICS

VERTIDYNAMICS CORPORATION

HEAD OFFICE:
150 Broadway, New York, New York 10038

WORKS:
ESCOA Corporation, 1818 South 16th Street, Phoenix, Arizona 85034

PRESIDENT: Bruno Nagler
VICE-PRESIDENT: Stephen S. Lush
ATTORNEY: Milton A. Goldiner
PATENTS: A. C. Nolte Jr
PROJECT HEAD: A. P. Kelly
PROGRAMME CONSULTANT: E. K. Liberatore

Vertidynamics Corporation was established in March 1970 as a public corporation, and initial financing was expected to be completed by mid-1970. The company has been formed to develop a combined autogyro-helicopter designed by Bruno Nagler, whose first helicopter was built in Vienna in the early 1930's. Designated VG-2, the new aircraft is similar in configuration to the VG-1, built and flown by Nagler in 1963 and described in the 1964/5 *Jane's*.

VERTIDYNAMICS VERTIGIRO VG-2P

The VG-2P prototype is being constructed from existing components, but the production version, designated **VG-2C**, will use entirely new construction and components.

The Vertigiro has a conventional aeroplane-type fuselage and landing gear, but embodies both a "cold-jet"-driven rotor and a tractor propeller. The rotor can be driven by either a separate turbocompressor or a compressor driven by the tractor engine.

The basic concept was to produce a low-cost high-performance rotorcraft. This is made possible by the type of rotor drive employed and by using the higher installed power for forward flight in autogyro mode. A variable rotor speed is feasible, and the relatively heavy aluminium alloy rotor blades permit sufficient energy to be stored for jump take-offs at loads much higher than those permissible for hovering.

The prototype VG-2P is scheduled to make its first flight early in 1971. It will be powered by a 285 hp (uprated to 320 hp) Continental C-285 TIARA piston-engine, driving either a two-blade variable pitch propeller or a compressor able to deliver 3·2 lb (1·45 kg)/sec of air at a compression ratio of 2·5 absolute. Normal rotor speed for the helicopter mode is 292 rpm, and for the autogyro mode 318 rpm. 400 rpm will be utilised to energise a jump take-off.

The tail unit of the prototype is a cantilever structure with a swept ventral and dorsal fin, conventional tailplane, elevators and rudder. Landing gear is of the fixed tricycle type with fairings on all wheels.

DIMENSIONS, EXTERNAL:
Rotor diameter	36 ft 0 in (10·97 m)
Rotor blade chord	9¼ in (23·5 cm)
Length overall	22 ft 6 in (6·86 m)
Height overall	9 ft 0 in (2·74 m)
Tailplane span	10 ft 2½ in (3·11 m)
Wheel track	6 ft 8 in (2·03 m)
Wheelbase	7 ft 6 in (2·29 m)

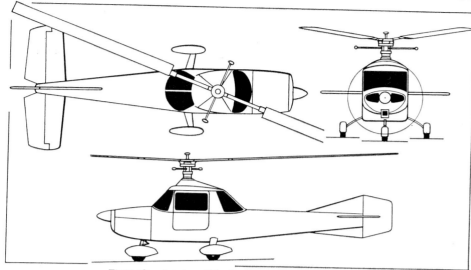

Three-view drawing of the Vertidynamics VG-2P prototype

WEIGHTS:
Empty weight (test purposes)	1,450 lb (657 kg)
Normal T-O weight (test purposes)	1,750 lb (793 kg)
Weight for structural analysis	2,450 lb (1,110 kg)

PERFORMANCE (estimated at normal T-O weight):
Max speed (autogyro)	135 knots (155 mph; 249 km/h)
Max rate of climb (at 69 knots; 80 mph; 129 km/h)	1,850 ft (564 m)/min
Jump height (power off)	39 ft (11·9 m)
Theoretical jump height (powered rotor)	92 ft (28 m)

VERTIDYNAMICS VG-2C

Production version of VG-2P of which two examples will be built for FAA certification. The VG-2C will be a four-seat commercial aircraft, differing from the prototype mainly in having a new rotor system and compressor.

The metal rotor blades, to be built by Parsons Corporation, will have a diameter of 36 ft (10·97 m) and chord of 11·4 in (29 cm). The compressor, of ESCUA Corporation manufacture, will have a rating of 4·4 lb (2 kg)/sec of air at a ratio of 2·5 absolute. Design gross weight is 2,450 lb (1.110 kg).

VOLMER
VOLMER AIRCRAFT
ADDRESS:
104 East Providencia Avenue, Burbank, California

Mr Volmer Jensen, well-known as a designer of sailplanes and gliders, has designed and built a two-seat light amphibian named the Sportsman (formerly Chubasco), which flew for the first time on 22 December 1958, and has since logged over 1,500 flying hours. He is attempting to find a manufacturer who will produce and market the aircraft commercially.

Meanwhile, plans of the Sportsman are being made available to amateur constructors. Over 650 sets had been sold by the Spring of 1970 and approximately 50 Sportsman amphibians are now flying. Some have tractor propellers, but this modification is not recommended by Mr Jensen.

VOLMER VJ22 SPORTSMAN

Typical of Sportsman variants is that built by Mr F. Wallman over a 2 year 10 month period at a cost of $6,000, and with which he won the "Outstanding Amphibian" award, sponsored by Canadair Ltd, at the 1967 EAA fly-in. Changes from standard include a glass-fibre cowling, which encloses completely the 100 hp Continental O-200-B engine, alteration to the tail configuration and the use of a 1940 Stinson 10A control wheel and yoke.

At a gross weight of 1,600 lb (726 kg), Mr Wallman's VJ22 has a max speed of 130 mph (209 kmh), cruising speed of 85 mph (137 kmh) and rate of climb of 600 ft (183 m) min. It flew for the first time on 15 November 1966 and was illustrated in the 1968-69 *Jane's*.

The following details refer to Mr Jensen's prototype.

TYPE: Two-seat light amphibian.

WINGS: Braced high-wing monoplane. Dihedral 1°. Incidence 3°. Wings are standard Aeronca Chief or Champion assemblies with wooden spars, metal ribs and fabric covering, and carry stabilising floats under the tips. Streamline Vee bracing struts each side.

Volmer VJ22 Sportsman built by Mr Fred Wallman of Minneapolis, Minnesota (*Jean Seele*)

FUSELAGE: Conventional flying-boat hull of wooden construction, covered with mahogany plywood and coated with glass-fibre.

TAIL UNIT: Strut-braced steel-tube structure, fabric-covered.

LANDING GEAR: Retractable tail-wheel type. Rubber-cord shock-absorption. Manual retraction. Cleveland wheels and mechanical brakes. Tyre pressure 20 lb/sq in (1·41 kg/cm²). Castoring retractable tail-wheel with integral water rudder.

POWER PLANT: One 85 hp Continental C85 90 hp or 100 hp Continental O-200-B four-cylinder horizontally-opposed air-cooled engine, driving a Sensenich two-blade fixed-pitch pusher propeller. Fuel in a single tank, capacity 20 US gallons (76 litres). Oil capacity 4½ US quarts (4·5 litres).

ACCOMMODATION: Two seats side-by-side in enclosed cabin with dual controls.

DIMENSIONS, EXTERNAL:
Wing span	36 ft 6 in (11·12 m)
Wing chord	5 ft 0 in (1·52 m)
Wing aspect ratio	7·2
Length overall	24 ft 0 in (7·32 m)
Height overall	8 ft 0 in (2·44 m)

AREA:
Wings, gross	175 sq ft (16·3 m²)

WEIGHTS (85 hp):
Weight empty	1,000 lb (454 kg)
Max T-O weight	1,500 lb (680 kg)

PERFORMANCE (85 hp, at max T-O weight):
Max level speed at S/L	83 knots (95 mph; 153 km/h)
Max cruising speed	74 knots (85 mph; 137 km/h)
Stalling speed	39 knots (45 mph; 72 km/h)
Rate of climb at S/L	600 ft (183 m)/min
Service ceiling	13,000 ft (3,960 m)
Range with max fuel, no reserves	260 nm (300 miles; 480 km)

VOLPAR
VOLPAR, INC
HEAD OFFICE AND WORKS:
16300 Stagg Street, Van Nuys California 91406
PRESIDENT: Frank V. Nixon Jr
CHIEF ENGINEER: John R. Mason
PUBLIC RELATIONS MANAGER: R. M. Byrne

Volpar Inc was formed in 1960 to market in kit form a tricycle landing gear modification which is suitable for all models of the Beechcraft Model 18 light twin-engined transport, including the latest Model H18.

The Volpar kit, which has full FAA certification, was designed by Thorp Engineering to require a minimum of modification to the basic airframe. The machined parts are manufactured by Paragon Engineering Corporation, a producer of rocket engine components, tools and dies. The various assemblies were formerly fabricated by Volitan Aviation, Inc, but this company has now merged with Volpar Inc.

As a follow-up to the above modification, Volpar is producing kits to convert the Model 18 to turboprop power, using AiResearch TPE 331 engines. The converted aircraft is known as the Super Turbo 18. Details of this are given below, together with information on a "stretched" version of the same aircraft, known as the Turboliner.

VOLPAR/BEECHCRAFT MODEL 18
The Volpar modification converts the Beechcraft Model 18 to a tricycle landing gear configuration, offering substantially slower approach speeds, greatly improved braking and easier ground handling. Cruising speed is improved, as all three wheels are completely retracted. Furthermore, the aircraft can be kept in hangars with a lower roof clearance, since the overall height is reduced to 9 ft 2 in (2·79 m).

The Volpar kit, which has passed all FAA static tests for a maximum landing weight of 9,772 lb (4,433 kg), utilises basic components of the existing main landing gear. The new nose gear is connected to the existing retraction system, where the tail-wheel connection was removed. The complete modification can be made without removing the wings or stripping any of the wing skin. All cockpit controls and emergency procedures are unchanged, including the instrument panel wheel position indicator. Existing air-stair doors can be retained with only minor modification.

Basically, the modification moves the main landing gear 4 ft 0 in (1·22 m) aft of the original position, attaching it to a welded-tube truss that increases the torsional strength of the centre wing structure by 60% in landing configuration. The nose assembly is completely new and includes a streamlined nose fairing which adds 2 ft 2½ in (0·67 m) to the fuselage length. Space inside the fairing can be used for additional equipment, including a weather radar dish of up to 12 in (30 cm) diameter.

All three wheels are of aluminium and can be fitted with either Goodrich or Goodyear tubed or tubeless tyres, size 8·50 × 10, ten-ply rating. Main wheel tyre pressure 65 lb/sq in (4·57 kg/cm²), nose-wheel tyre pressure 45 lb/sq in (3·16 kg/cm²). Shock-absorption is provided by hydraulic oleo struts of Volpar manufacture. Goodrich multiple disc brakes. All three wheels retract forward in less than eight seconds. On the ground the cabin floor is only 3 ft 6 in (1·07 m) off the ground at the door. Wheelbase is 8 ft 7 in (2·62 m). The aircraft will turn on a 4 ft (1·22 m) radius of the inside wheel and a centering device is incorporated on the shimmy-damper for take off and landing.

The current Mk IV Volpar conversion incorporates Goodrich nine-piston full-circle brakes with twice the braking energy and three times the service life of the two-piston type fitted formerly. The new brakes fit on the original gear and are obtainable from either Volpar or Goodrich.

A total of more than 400 sets of Volpar tri-gear had been delivered by the end of 1969.

VOLPAR/BEECHCRAFT SUPER TURBO 18

The Super Turbo 18 is a Beechcraft Model 18 fitted with the Volpar Mk IV tricycle landing gear described above and re-engined with two 705 eshp AiResearch TPE 331-1-101B turboprop engines, flat rated to 605 eshp. The wing planform is changed, by extending forward the entire leading-edge inboard of each engine nacelle and carrying the new leading-edge line past the nacelle, so increasing the chord and sweepback to a point some distance outboard of the nacelle. The rectangular wingtip panels of the standard Super 18 are replaced by smaller tips which decrease the wing span and maintain the normal leading-edge sweep to the tip.

Installation of TPE 331 engines and Hartzell Model HC-B3TN-5 three-blade reversible-pitch propellers reduces the empty weight, permitting an increase in fuel or payload. Internal fuel capacity is increased by 100 US gallons (379 litres) by installing new integral tanks in the leading-edge immediately outboard of each engine nacelle. These become the main tanks, each delivering fuel directly to the adjacent engine. They increase the maximum fuel capacity to 630 US gallons (2,385 litres), with a normal capacity of 306 US gallons (1,159 litres).

Air-conditioning and heating installations are available, using engine-bleed air. A large cargo door, 5 ft 2 in (1·57 m) wide, with a max height of 3 ft 7 in (1·09 m), can be provided, incorporating the existing air-stair door.

The detailed description of the Turboliner (which follows), applies also to the Super Turbo 18, except that this latter model does not have the "stretched" fuselage.

FAA Supplemental Type Approval of the Super Turbo 18 was received on 17 February 1966. Two were in service with the US Public Health Service at the end of that month and conversion kits are in full production. Customers include

Volpar conversion of the Beechcraft Model 18 with tricycle landing gear

Air Asia of Taiwan, which has been supplied with 15 kits, and a total of 24 had been delivered at the end of 1969.

DIMENSIONS, EXTERNAL:

Wing span	46 ft 0 in (214·0 m)
Length overall	37 ft 5 in (11·40 m)
Height overall	9 ft 7 in (2·92 m)
Wheelbase	8 ft 7 in (2·62 m)

DIMENSIONS, INTERNAL:
Cabin, excluding flight deck:

Length	12 ft 8½ in (3·87 m)
Max width	4 ft 4 in (1·32 m)
Max height	5 ft 6 in (1·68 m)
Volume	260 cu ft (7·36 m³)

WEIGHTS AND LOADINGS:

Weight empty, basic	5,500 lb (2,495 kg)
Max payload	4,786 lb (2,171 kg)
Max T-O weight	10,286 lb (4,666 kg)
Max zero-fuel weight	9,000 lb (4,082 kg)
Max landing weight	9,772 lb (4,433 kg)
Max wing loading	27·51 lb/sq ft (134·3 kg/m²)
Max power loading	8·94 lb/shp (4·05 kg/shp)

PERFORMANCE (at max T-O weight):
Max cruising speed at 10,000 ft (3,050 m)
    243 knots (280 mph; 451 km/h)
Econ cruising speed at 10,000 ft (3,050 m)
    222 knots (256 mph; 412 km/h)
Stalling speed wheels and flaps down, power off
    77 knots (88 mph; (142 km/h)
Stalling speed, wheels and flaps up, power off
    80 knots (92 mph; 148 km/h)

Rate of climb at S/L	1,710 ft (521 m)/min
Service ceiling	26,000 ft (7,925 m)

Service ceiling, one engine out
    14,000 ft (4,265 m)

T-O run	1,665 ft (507 m)
T-O to 50 ft (15 m)	2,380 ft (725 m)
Landing from 50 ft (15 m)	2,107 ft (642 m)
Landing run with reverse thrust	870 ft (265 m)

Range with max fuel at 222 knots (256 mph; 412 km/h), 45 min reserve
    1,884 nm (2,170 miles; 3,492 km)
Range with max payload, 45 min reserve
    400 nm (461 miles; 741 km)

VOLPAR/BEECHCRAFT TURBOLINER

This is a "stretched" 15-passenger version of the Volpar/Beechcraft Super Turbo 18, intended for the third-level airline market. Design was started in August 1966 and construction of the prototype began in December 1966. The

prototype flew for the first time on 12 April 1967 and FAA Certification was granted on 29 March 1968, the Turboliner being approved for operation at a new gross weight of 11,500 lb (5,216 kg).

Hamilton Aircraft in Tucson, Arizona, and American Turbine Corporation in Long Beach, California, are producing the Turboliner under a licence arrangement, and 19 aircraft had been built by 1 January 1970. The first production model was delivered to Ransome Airline of Philadelphia.

TYPE: Twin-turboprop light transport aircraft.

WINGS: Cantilever low-wing monoplane. Wing section NACA 63-015 at station 28·0, NACA 23014 at station 144·5, NACA 23012 at station 260·4. Dihedral 6°. Incidence 5° 20′ at root, 1° at tip. Sweepback 16° 21′ on inner wings, 8° 23′ on outer panels. Steel-truss centre-section spar; remainder of structure aluminium semi-monocoque. Plain differential ailerons and plain trailing-edge flaps of conventional aluminium construction. Trim-tab in port aileron. Optional Goodrich pneumatic de-icing boots on leading-edges.

FUSELAGE: Conventional aluminium semi-monocoque structure.

TAIL UNIT: Cantilever aluminium semi-monocoque structure with twin endplate fins and rudders. Fixed-incidence tailplane. Trim-tabs in rudder and elevators. Optional Goodrich pneumatic de-icing boots on leading-edges.

LANDING GEAR: Volpar electrically-retractable tricycle type. All units retract forward, main wheels into engine nacelles. Volpar hydraulic shock-absorbers. All three wheels size 8·50 × 10 with Goodrich or Goodyear tubeless or tube-type tyres. Main wheel tyre pressure 80 lb/sq in (5·62 kg/cm²); nose-wheel tyre pressure 45 lb/sq in (3·16 kg/cm²). Goodrich multiple-disc brakes.

POWER PLANT: Two 705 eshp AiResearch TPE 331-1-101B turboprop engines, each driving a Hartzell HC-B3TN-5 three-blade reversible-pitch propeller with T10176H blades, diameter 8 ft 0⅝ in to 8 ft 5⅝ in (2·46-2·57 m). Four to

Volpar Super Turbo 18, a conversion of the Beechcraft Model 18 with AiResearch TPE 331 turboprops and Volpar Mk IV tricycle landing gear

Volpar Turboliner, a "stretched" version of the Super Turbo 18 (two 705 eshp AiResearch TPE 331-1-101B engines)

eight fuel tanks in wings, including new integral main tanks in wing leading-edges outboard of nacelles. Normal fuel capacity 306 US gallons (1,159 litres): max capacity 630 US gallons (2,385 litres). Refuelling points in upper surface of wings. Total oil capacity 3 US gallons (11·35 litres).

ACCOMMODATION: Crew of two and up to 15 passengers. Downward-hinged air-stair door on port side at rear of cabin. Optional double-door for freight loading. Seats removable to enable aircraft to be used for freight-carrying. Heating and air conditioning optional. Baggage space aft of cabin and in each wing.

SYSTEMS: Hydraulic system for brakes only. Electrical supply from two 200A starter-generators and two 24V batteries, for landing gear and flap operation, propeller anti-icing, landing lights, radio and lighting.

ELECTRONICS AND EQUIPMENT: Blind-flying instrumentation, radio and radar to customer's specification.

DIMENSIONS, EXTERNAL:

Wing span	46 ft 0 in (14·02 m)
Wing chord at root	13 ft 7·36 in (4·15 m)
Wing chord at tip	3 ft 8·94 in (1·14 m)
Wing aspect ratio	5·67
Length overall	44 ft 2½ in (13·47 m)
Height overall	9 ft 7 in (2·92 m)
Tailplane span	15 ft 0 in (4·57 m)
Wheel track	12 ft 11 in (3·94 m)
Wheelbase	12 ft 7 in (3·84 m)
Passenger door:	
Height	4 ft 0 in (1·22 m)
Width	2 ft 3 in (0·69 m)
Height to sill	3 ft 6 in (1·07 m)

DIMENSIONS, INTERNAL:

Cabin, excluding flight deck:	
Length	19 ft 6 in (5·94 m)
Max width	4 ft 4 in (1·32 m)
Max height	5 ft 6 in (1·68 m)
Floor area	80 sq ft (7·43 m²)
Volume	394 cu ft (11·16 m³)
Freight hold (aft of cabin) volume	
	23 cu ft (0·65 m³)
Freight holds (wings) volume (total)	
	32 cu ft (0·91 m³)

AREAS:

Wings, gross	374 sq ft (34·75 m²)
Ailerons (total)	26·6 sq ft (2·47 m²)
Trailing-edge flaps (total)	28·2 sq ft (2·62 m²)
Fins (total)	16·3 sq ft (1·51 m²)
Rudders (total)	17·28 sq ft (16·05 m²)
Tailplane	38·2 sq ft (35·49 m²)
Elevators, including tab	27·22 sq ft (25·28 m²)

WEIGHTS AND LOADINGS:

Weight empty:	
Cargo version	5,900 lb (2,676 kg)
Airliner	6,600 lb (2,993 kg)
Max T-O weight	11,500 lb (5,216 kg)
Max zero-fuel weight	10,500 lb (4,762 kg)
Max landing weight	11,000 lb (4,989 kg)
Max wing loading	30·75 lb/sq ft (150·1 kg/m²)
Max power loading	10 lb/shp (4·54 kg/shp)

PERFORMANCE (at max T-O weight):

Max level speed at 10,000 ft (3,050 m)	
	243 knots (280 mph; 451 km/h)
Max cruising speed at 10,000 ft (3,050 m)	
	243 knots (280 mph; 451 km/h)
Econ cruising speed at 10,000 ft (3,050 m)	
	222 knots (256 mph; 412 km/h)
Stalling speed, wheels and flaps down, power off	
	80 knots (92 mph; 148·5 km/h)
Stalling speed, wheels and flaps up, power off	
	84 knots (96 mph; 154·5 km/h)
Rate of climb at S/L	1,520 ft (463 m)/min
Service ceiling	24,000 ft (7,315 m)
Service ceiling, one engine out	
	13,000 ft (3,960 m)
T-O run	1,870 ft (570 m)
T-O to 50 ft (15 m)	3,245 ft (989 m)
Landing from 50 ft (15 m)	2,500 ft (762 m)
Landing run	1,040 ft (317 m)
Range with max fuel, 45 min reserve	
	1,802 nm (2,076 miles; 3,340 km)
Range with max payload, 45 min reserve	
	300 nm (346 miles; 556 km)

WACO

WACO AIRCRAFT COMPANY, A SUBSIDIARY OF ALLIED AERO INDUSTRIES, INC

HEAD OFFICE: International Airport, PO Box 16262, San Antonio, Texas 78216

DIRECTOR OF MARKETING:
James R. Frame

WORKS:
PO Box 398, Pottstown, Pennsylvania 19464

Waco is producing versions of the Italian Siai-Marchetti S.205-22 light aircraft, under the designation Waco S220 Vela II, and of the Siai-Marchetti SF.260 with the designation Waco Meteor. It is also marketing a considerably-modified version of the French Socata Rallye Commodore as the Waco M220-4 Minerva.

Scheduled for production late in 1969 was a turbosupercharged version of the Vela II, designated as the Waco TS-250-5 Taurus. Waco intend also to offer a version of the Siai-Marchetti SA.202 Bravo two-seat trainer as the Waco T-2 Meteorite.

WACO S220 VELA II

This five-seat version of the Siai-Marchetti S.205 low-wing monoplane was designed by the Italian company in collaboration with Waco and Franklin (both subsidiaries of Allied Aero Industries). All dimensions are to US standards.

The S220 is being assembled in Waco's plant at Pottstown, Pa. Special features include entrance steps each side, rubber wing walks, electric all gear position indicator and auxiliary mechanical position indicator, full anti-corrosion treatment of interior metal surfaces rocker, circuit-breaker switches, external power socket, carpeted cabin, scratch-proof finish on instrument and switch panels, room for five radios in instrument panel, vernier engine controls, quick oil drain system, exhaust gas temperature monitor and carburettor ice detection system.

Details of the Vela II are as given for the Siai-Marchetti S.205-22/R in the Italian section, except for variations given below.:

Waco Vela II, five-seat version of the Siai-Marchetti S.205 (220 hp Franklin 6A-350-C1 engine)

POWER PLANT: One 220 hp Franklin 6A-350-C1 six-cylinder horizontally-opposed air-cooled engine, driving either a Hartzell or McCauley two-blade constant speed propeller, diameter 6 ft 6 in (1·98 m). Fuel in two wing tanks, with total capacity of 55 US gallons (208 litres). Optional tip tanks available, with a capacity of 18 US gallons (68·1 litres) each. Oil capacity 2 US gallons (7·5 litres).

ACCOMMODATION: Enclosed cabin seating pilot and four passengers. Forward-opening door on each side of fuselage. Stowage for 176 lb (79 kg) baggage.

SYSTEMS: 55A 24V alternator.

EQUIPMENT: Optional equipment includes engine winterisation kit, fire extinguisher, cabin curtains, abrasion boots, static dischargers, Delta skystrobe, electric or vacuum gyros, instrument post lights, and remote compass.

DIMENSIONS, EXTERNAL:

Height overall	9 ft 9¾ in (2·99m)

DIMENSIONS, INTERNAL:

Cabin:	
Length	8 ft 0 in (2·44 m)
Max width	3 ft 11 in (1·19 m)
Max height	4 ft 5 in (1·35 m)

WEIGHTS:

Basic operating weight	1,650 lb (748 kg)
Max T-O and landing weight	
	2,976 lb (1,349 kg)

PERFORMANCE:

Max level speed at S/L	
	155 knots (178 mph; 286 km/h)
Max diving speed	
	178·5 knots (206 mph; 331 km/h)

Max cruising speed, at 6,500 ft (1,980 m)
 148 knots (170 mph; 274 km/h)
Econ cruising speed, at 8,000 ft (2,440 m)
 139 knots (160 mph; 257 km/h)
Stalling speed, flaps up
 48 knots (55 mph; 89 km/h)
Stalling speed, flaps down
 41 knots (47 mph; 76 km/h)
Rate of climb at S/L 1,150 ft (350 m)/min
Service ceiling 18,500 ft (5,640 m)
T-O run 750 ft (229 m)
T-O to 50 ft (15 m) 1,350 ft (410 m)
Landing from 50 ft (15 m) 1,550 ft (470 m)
Landing run 650 ft (198 m)
Range with max payload, 70% power at 6,500
 ft (1,980 m) 20 min reserve
 651 nm (750 miles; 1,205 km)

WACO TS-250-5 TAURUS

Scheduled for initial delivery in late 1969, the Taurus is generally similar to the Vela II (above), but has a turbosupercharged Franklin engine, giving it a max cruising speed of 174 knots (200 mph; 312 km/h) at 30,000 ft (9,150 m) and max range of over 1,042 nm (1,200 miles; 1,930 km) with wingtip tanks.

WACO M220-4 MINERVA

This is a modified version of the four-seat MS 894 Rallye Commodore, with 220 hp Franklin 6A-350-C1 six-cylinder horizontally-opposed air-cooled engine, driving either a McCauley 2A31/C21/84-5-8 or Hartzell HC-C2YF-1B/8459-4 constant-speed propeller.

Details of the Minerva are the same as for the Socata MS 894 Rallye Minerva 220 given in the French section, except for variations noted below:

TYPE: Four-seat light monoplane.

TAIL UNIT: Manually-operated elevator and rudder trim-tabs.

LANDING GEAR: Toe-brakes standard on pilot's side only.

POWER PLANT: Fuel contained in two wing tanks and fuselage header tank, total capacity 45 US gallons (170 litres).

SYSTEMS: Electrical power provided by 55A alternator. 12V 32Ah battery.

DIMENSIONS, EXTERNAL:
Length overall 23 ft 4¾ in (7·13 m)

DIMENSIONS, INTERNAL:
Cabin:
Length 6 ft 8½ in (2·04 m)

AREAS:
Ailerons (total) 33·8 sq ft (3·14 m²)
Trailing-edge flaps (total) 52·0 sq ft (4·83 m²)
Fin 9·55 sq ft (0·89 m²)
Rudder, including tab 9·25 sq ft (0·86 m²)
Tailplane 36·0 sq ft (3·34 m²)
Elevators, including tab 40·0 sq ft (3·72 m²)

WEIGHTS:
Weight empty 1,360 lb (616 kg)
Max T-O weight 2,430 lb (1,102 kg)

PERFORMANCE (at max T-O weight):
Max level speed at S/L
 143 knots (165 mph; 266 km/h)
Cruising speed 129 knots (148 mph; 238 km/h)

Waco Minerva, a modified version of the Socata MS 894 Rallye Commodore

Siai-Marchetti SF.260 with 260 hp Lycoming O-540-E4A5 engine, marketed in the USA as the Waco Meteor

Stalling speed, wheels and flaps down
 44 knots (50 mph; 80·5 km/h)
Rate of climb at S/L 1,020 ft (311 m)/min
Service ceiling 14,800 ft (4,510 m)
Service ceiling at 1,770 lb (803 kg) AUW
 21,800 ft (6,645 m)
T-O to 50 ft (15 m) 875 ft (267 m)
Landing from 50 ft (15 m) 1,148 ft (350 m)
Max range 677 nm (780 miles; 1,255 km)

WACO METEOR

Meteor is the name Waco have given to their version of the Siai-Marchetti SF.260 three/four-seat light cabin monoplane which is being assembled in Waco's plant at Pottstown, Pa. Optional equipment available for the Meteor includes electric or vacuum horizon and directional gyros, outside air temperature gauge, vacuum system with suction gauge, instrument post lights, landing and navigation lights, rotating beacon, heated pitot tube, co-pilot brakes, clock and tow-bar.

A Meteor flown by Mr Harold Fishman set a new FAI class C-1.c record by completing the 204-nm (235-mile; 378-km) flight from Las Vegas, Nevada, to Los Angeles, California, at an average speed of 186 knots (214 mph; 344 km/h).

The detailed description of the Siai-Marchetti SF.260, given in the Italian section, applies also to the Waco Meteor.

WACO T-2 METEORITE

This fully-aerobatic two-seat light aircraft is Waco's version of the Italian Siai-Marchetti SA.202 Bravo (which see). No details are yet available.

WARWICK
WILLIAM WARWICK

ADDRESS:
5726 Clearsite, Torrance, California 90505

The 1960-61 *Jane's* contains details of a single-seat sporting high-wing monoplane named Tiny Champ built by Mr Warwick, who is a laboratory technician employed by the Northrop Corporation. He has since designed, built and flown a single-seat low-wing monoplane named the Bantam, of which plans are available to amateur constructors, as well as a reverse-stagger racing biplane which he has designated W-4. All available details of these two aircraft are given below.

WARWICK BANTAM

First flown in June 1966, the Bantam had logged a total of 90 flying hours by mid-1967. Construction is all-metal, except for tips of the wings, one-piece all-moving tailplane, fin and rudder which are of glass-fibre. The main units of the tricycle landing gear have cantilever spring-steel legs. The nose-wheel is carried on a telescopic strut with a leaf-spring shock-absorber. Fairings are fitted to all three wheels and the cockpit is enclosed by a rearward-sliding bubble canopy. Provision is made for a fully-enclosed retractable landing gear, if required.

Power plant is a 65 hp Lycoming O-145 four-cylinder horizontally-opposed air-cooled engine, driving a two-blade wooden fixed-pitch propeller. Fuel capacity is 11·5 US gallons (43·5 litres). Radio is fitted.

Warwick Bantam single-seat amateur-built lightplane (65 hp Lycoming O-145 engine)
(Peter M. Bowers)

Dimensions, weights and performance figures were not available at the time of writing. Before the canopy was fitted, at an AUW of 760 lb (345 kg), Mr Warwick recorded a cruising speed of 91 knots (105 mph; 169 km/h), stalling speed of 45 knots (52 mph; 84 km/h) and rate of climb of 1,000 ft (305 m)/min.

WARWICK W-4

Design and construction of Mr Warwick's racing biplane began almost simultaneously in June 1968 and the W-4 flew for the first time on 10 September 1969. No performance details were available at time of writing.

TYPE: Single-seat homebuilt racing biplane.

WINGS: Reverse-stagger biplane wings with single streamline section interplane strut each side. All-wood structure. Plain ailerons of wooden construction on lower wings only. No trim-tabs.

FUSELAGE: Slab-sided all wooden structure.

TAIL UNIT: Conventional cantilever structure of wood. No trim-tabs in elevator or rudder.

LANDING GEAR: Non-retractable tail-wheel type. Cantilever spring-steel main gear. Fairings on main wheels.

POWER PLANT: One 125 hp Lycoming O-290-D2 four-cylinder horizontally-opposed air-cooled engine, driving a two-blade fixed-pitch metal propeller with spinner.

ACCOMMODATION: Single seat in open cockpit with small windshield. Pilot's headrest faired into base of fin.

DIMENSIONS, EXTERNAL:
Wing span (both)   16 ft 0 in (4·88 m)
Wing chord, constant (both)   3 ft 0 in (0·91 m)

Warwick W-4 racing biplane (125 hp Lycoming O-290-D2 engine) (*Henry Artof*)

WATERMAN
WALDO D. WATERMAN
ADDRESS: PO Box 6532, San Diego, California 92106.

Mr Waldo D. Waterman, an American pioneer pilot who has been associated with aviation for almost 60 years, has designed and built an unusual single-seat aircraft with pusher propeller. It is Mr Waterman's eleventh original aircraft design and is designated W-11 Chevy Bird. The name reflects the object behind the design, namely to provide a test-bed for a Chevrolet Corvair motorcar engine, which Mr Waterman believes could prove an ideal low-cost power plant for home-builders. Design was started in July 1967 and construction began three months later, with the first flight in July 1968.

By November 1969 the engine had been run for almost 50 hours on the ground, and a total of over 100 hours of flight had been accumulated. Following this period of test the W-11 was converted to a seaplane configuration, as shown in the adjacent illustration, and had completed more than 20 successful flights at the time of writing. The description which follows applies to the W-11 in its original landplane configuration.

WATERMAN W-11 CHEVY BIRD
TYPE: Single-seat high-wing monoplane.

WINGS: Braced high-wing monoplane with Vee bracing struts on each side. Wing section NACA 23012. Dihedral 0°. Incidence 2° 30′. No sweepback. Conventional aluminium alloy structure. Slotted ailerons of aluminium alloy. No trim-tabs. Trailing-edge flaps of aluminium alloy construction.

FUSELAGE: Welded 4130 steel-tube open structure.

TAIL UNIT: Cantilever aluminium alloy structure. Fixed-incidence tailplane. Trim-tab in port elevator.

LANDING GEAR: Non-retractable tricycle type. Cantilever leaf-spring main gear legs. Oleo-pneumatic nose-wheel strut. Goodyear main wheels, nose-wheel and tyres size 6·00 × 6, pressure 40 lb/sq in (2·8 kg/cm²). Goodyear brakes.

POWER PLANT: One 140 hp Chevrolet Corvair motor-car engine, modified for aviation use by

Waterman W-11 Chevy Bird in its new seaplane configuration

provision of special reduction gear, dual ignition system and numerous minor modifications. It drives a McCauley two-blade fixed-pitch pusher propeller, diameter 5 ft 9 in (1·75 m). Fuel contained in two wing tanks, capacity 12·5 US gallons (47·25 litres) each, total capacity 25 US gallons (94·5 litres). Refuelling point on top of wing centre-section. Oil capacity 1½ US gallons (5·6 litres).

ACCOMMODATION: Open seat for pilot, forward of wing. Passenger seat to be added later.

RADIO: Narco Mk III transceiver.

DIMENSIONS, EXTERNAL:
Wing span   30 ft 0 in (9·14 m)
Wing chord, constant   5 ft 2 in (1·57 m)
Wing aspect ratio   6
Length overall   21 ft 5 in (6·53 m)
Height overall   7 ft 6 in (2·29 m)
Tailplane span   9 ft 0 in (2·74 m)

Wheel track   6 ft 6 in (1·98 m)
Wheelbase   8 ft 7 in (2·62 m)
AREAS:
Wings, gross   150 sq ft (13·9 m²)
Ailerons (total)   15 sq ft (1·39 m²)
Trailing-edge flaps (total)   10 sq ft (0·93 m²)
Fin   6 sq ft (0·56 m²)
Rudder   5·5 sq ft (0·51 m²)
Tailplane   15 sq ft (1·39 m²)
Elevators, including tab   18 sq ft (1·67 m²)
WEIGHTS AND LOADINGS:
Weight empty   930 lb (421 kg)
Max T-O weight   1,500 lb (680 kg)
Max wing loading   10 lb/sq ft (48·8 kg/m²)
Max power loading   10·7 lb/hp (4·85 kg/hp)
PERFORMANCE at max T-O weight):
Cruising speed
   65-69 knots (75-80 mph; 121-129 km/h)
Stalling speed   44 knots (50 mph; 80·5 km/h)

WEATHERLY
WEATHERLY AVIATION COMPANY, INC.
HEAD OFFICE AND WORKS:
2304 San Felipe Road, Hollister, California 95023

PRESIDENT: John C. Weatherly

Between January 1961 and the Autumn of 1965, Weatherly Aviation produced 19 Model WM-62C agricultural aircraft. These were conversions of Fairchild M-62 airframes and most were powered by a Continental W670 radial engine, although a few were delivered with Pratt & Whitney R-985 engines.

Weatherly has now developed a new agricultural monoplane, known as the Model 201. This is an outgrowth of the conversion programme, but is somewhat larger than the M-62, with considerable improvements. The prototype received FAA certification early in 1967 and deliveries of production models were scheduled to begin by the Summer of 1968 but were delayed due to the company's involvement in government sub-contract work. No recent information on the state of the production programme has been received.

WEATHERLY MODEL 201
The general appearance of this single-seat agricultural aircraft is shown in the illustration which appears on the following page. It is powered by a 450 hp Pratt & Whitney R-985 radial air-cooled engine. Hopper capacity is 240 US gallons (908 litres) and fuel capacity 45 US gallons (170 litres).

Weatherly Model 201 agricultural aircraft (450 hp Pratt & Whitney R-985 engine)

The fuselage is constructed of chrome-molybdenum steel tubing, internally treated with linseed oil and externally painted with chemical-resisting epoxy paint. All aluminium parts are dipped in a corrosion inhibitor bath prior to priming and epoxy painting. Panels can be removed from the entire fuselage in a few minutes for inspection, maintenance and cleaning. Curved access panels are used to reduce any tendency toward fatigue cracking.

High wing efficiency is claimed to be attained through an arrangement of vortex generators and booster fairing, to direct turbulent boundary-layer flow back to the wing surface. This enables the wing to operate at a higher max lift coefficient and improves aileron effectiveness. The booster fairing serves as a removeable housing for the stainless steel spray-boom. Drag from the spray equipment is reported to be practically nil. Engine mounting is through large rubber bushings to reduce vibration and the engine mount swings out for maintenance.

DIMENSIONS, EXTERNAL:
Wing span   39 ft 0 in (11·89 m)
Length overall   26 ft 7 in (8·10 m)

Height overall	7 ft 11 in (2·41 m)
AREA:	
Wings, gross	248·25 sq ft (23·06 m²)
WEIGHTS:	
Weight empty	2,550 lb (1,157 kg)
Design max weight	3,500 lb (1,588 kg)

Agricultural max weight	4,800 lb (2,177 kg)
PERFORMANCE (at design T-O weight):	
Max level speed at S/L	
	111 knots (128 mph; 206 km/h)
Max permissible diving speed	
	125·5 knots (145 mph; 233 km/h)

Max manoeuvering speed	
	100 knots (115 mph; 185 km/h)
Cruising speed	91 knots (105 mph; 169 km/h)
Stalling speed	51 knots (58 mph; 94 km/h)
Stalling speed (agricultural AUW)	
	60 knots (69 mph; 111 km/h)

WELSH
GEORGE T. WELSH

ADDRESS:
3256 Marber Avenue, Long Beach, California 90808

Mr Welsh designed and built a prototype single-seat light aircraft, known as the Model A Welsh Rabbit, and is building further examples to order. He has since developed a tricycle landing gear version, designated Model B.

WELSH MODEL A WELSH RABBIT

Design of the Welsh Rabbit started on 25 November 1963, and construction of the prototype began in March 1965. FAA Certification in the Experimental category was awarded on 4 November 1965, and first flight of the prototype was made on 12 November 1965. In March 1968 two orders had been received for Model A's.

TYPE: Single-seat light aircraft.

WINGS: Braced high-wing monoplane. Wing section NACA 4412. Dihedral 2°. Incidence 1°. Dacron-covered all-metal two-spar structure. Compression struts of 4130 steel. Wings can be folded for stowage. Conventional all-metal ailerons with corrugated skin. No flaps or tabs.

FUSELAGE: Conventional Warren truss of 4130 steel, stainless steel formers, covered with Dacron fabric.

TAIL UNIT: Conventional steel-tube structure, covered with Dacron fabric. No trim-tabs. Bungee elevator trim to relieve control column pressure.

LANDING GEAR: Non-retractable tailwheel type. Tripod streamlined-tube main legs. Goodyear main wheels and tyres, size 6·00 × 6. Tyre pressure 25 lb/sq in (1·76 kg/cm²). Goodyear hydraulic brakes.

POWER PLANT: One 65 hp Continental A65-8 four-cylinder horizontally-opposed air-cooled engine, driving a McCauley two-blade fixed-pitch metal propeller, diameter 5 ft 2 in (1·57 m). One fuel tank in fuselage, capacity 12 US gallons (45 litres). Refuelling point in front of windscreen on port side of fuselage. Oil capacity 1 US gallon (3·8 litres).

ACCOMMODATION: Single seat in enclosed cockpit. Door in starboard side of fuselage.

RADIO: Battery-operated radio.

DIMENSIONS, EXTERNAL:
Wing span	26 ft 0 in (7·92 m)
Wing chord, constant	4 ft 2 in (1·27 m)
Wing aspect ratio	6·5
Length overall	18 ft 0 in (5·49 m)
Width, wings folded	6 ft 0 in (1·83 m)
Height overall	6 ft 0 in (1·83 m)
Tailplane span	8 ft 0 in (2·44 m)
Wheel track	5 ft 4 in (1·63 m)
Passenger door:	
Height	3 ft 7 in (1·09 m)
Width	2 ft 2 in (0·66 m)
Height to sill	2 ft 0 in (0·61 m)

DIMENSIONS, INTERNAL:
Length	4 ft 0 in (1·22 m)
Max width	2 ft 4 in (0·71 m)
Max height	3 ft 7 in (1·09 m)
Floor area	8·0 sq ft (0·74 m²)

AREAS:
Wings, gross	104·0 sq ft (9·66 m²)
Ailerons (total)	8·4 sq ft (0·78 m²)
Fin	3·2 sq ft (0·28 m²)
Rudder	5·0 sq ft (0·46 m²)
Tailplane	8·0 sq ft (0·74 m²)
Elevators	5·8 sq ft (0·54 m²)

WEIGHTS AND LOADINGS:
Weight empty	600 lb (272 kg)
Max T-O weight	950 lb (431 kg)
Max wing loading	9·1 lb/sq ft (44·4 kg/m²)
Max power loading	14·6 lb/hp (6·6 kg/hp)

PERFORMANCE:
Max level speed at 3,000 ft (915 m)	
	94 knots (108 mph; 174 km/h)
Max cruising speed at 3,000 ft (915 m)	
	85 knots (98 mph; 158 km/h)
Stalling speed	42 knots (48 mph; 77 km/h)
Rate of climb at S/L	500 ft (152 m)/min
Service ceiling	11,500 ft (3,505 m)
T-O run	300 ft (91 m)
T-O to 50 ft (15 m)	480 ft (146 m)
Landing run	500 ft (152 m)
Endurance with max fuel, 30 min reserve	
	3 hours

WELSH MODEL B WELSH RABBIT

The Welsh Model B differs from the Model A by having non-retractable tricycle landing gear, more powerful engine, accommodation for pilot

Model A Welsh Rabbit single-seat homebuilt aircraft (65 hp Continental A65-8 engine)

Welsh Model B conversion of the Model A Welsh Rabbit with tricycle landing gear

and passenger seated side-by-side and fuselage length extended by 7 in (17·8 cm). Wings of this model, which are of slightly increased span, do not fold.

Design and construction of the Model B commenced in March 1968, and the first flight of the prototype was made in November 1968, with FAA Certification in Experimental Category following. Plans are available to amateur constructors and one aircraft is under construction.

The description of the Model A applies also to the model B, except in the following details:

TYPE: Two-seat light aircraft.

LANDING GEAR: Non-retractable tricycle type. Cantilever spring steel main gear. Nose-wheel has oleo-pneumatic strut. All three wheels and tyres size 6·00 × 6, pressure 25 lb/sq in (1·76 kg/cm²). Goodyear hydraulic brakes.

POWER PLANT: One 100 hp Continental O-200 four-cylinder horizontally-opposed air-cooled engine, driving a McCauley two-blade fixed-pitch propeller, diameter 6 ft 0 in (1·83 m). One fuel tank in fuselage, immediately aft of firewall, capacity 13 US gallons (49 litres). Refuelling point forward of windshield on port side of fuselage. Oil capacity 1 US gallon (3·8 litres).

ACCOMMODATION: Pilot and passenger, side-by-side, in enclosed cabin. Access door on starboard side, hinged at forward edge. Baggage compartment aft of passenger seats with internal access, max capacity 25 lb (11 kg).

RADIO: Skycrafters 6-channel radio powered by dry battery.

DIMENSIONS, EXTERNAL:
Wing span	27 ft 0 in (8·23 m)
Length overall	18 ft 7 in (5·66 m)
Height overall	8 ft 3 in (2·51 m)
Passenger door:	
Height	3 ft 3 in (0·99 m)
Width	2 ft 4 in (0·71 m)
Height to sill	2 ft 6 in (0·76 m)
Baggage door:	
Height	2 ft 0 in (0·61 m)
Width	2 ft 4 in (0·71 m)

DIMENSIONS, INTERNAL:
Cabin:	
Length	4 ft 4 in (1·32 m)
Max width	3 ft 5 in (1·04 m)
Max height	3 ft 4 in (1·02 m)
Floor area	15 sq ft (1·39 m²)

AREAS:
Wings, gross	108 sq ft (10·03 m²)
Ailerons, total	8·4 sq ft (0·78 m²)
Fin	3·6 sq ft (0·33 m²)
Rudder	5·0 sq ft (0·46 m²)
Tailplane	8·0 sq ft (0·74 m²)
Elevators	6·0 sq ft (0·56 m²)

WEIGHTS AND LOADINGS:
Weight empty	700 lb (317 kg)
Max T-O weight	1,140 lb (517 kg)
Max wing loading	9·1 lb/sq ft (44·4 kg/m²)
Max power loading	11·4 lb/hp (5·17 kg/hp)

PERFORMANCE (at max T-O weight):
Max level speed at 3,000 ft (915 m)	
	96 knots (110 mph; 177 km/h)
Max permissible diving speed	
	117 knots (135 mph; 217 km/h)
Max cruising speed at 3,000 ft (915 m)	
	87 knots (100 mph; 161 km/h)
Stalling speed	45·5 knots (52 mph; 84 km/h)
Rate of climb at S/L	500 ft (152 m)/min
Service ceiling	11,500 ft (3,505 m)
T-O run	450 ft (137 m)
T-O to 50 ft (15 m)	600 ft (183 m)
Landing from 50 ft (15 m)	500 ft (152 m)
Range with max fuel, 30 min reserve	
	191 nm (220 miles; 354 km)

WHITE

E. MARSHALL WHITE

ADDRESS:
1863 West Street, Anaheim, California 92802

WHITE WW-I DER JÄGER D.IX

Marshall White, a staff engineer of TRW Systems at Redondo Beach, California, has designed an unusual homebuilt aircraft named der Jäger D.IX, which is reminiscent of several German designs, mainly of World War I vintage. The wings are patterned on those of an Albatros D.Va, with the landing gear fairings of the Focke-Wulf Stosser and tail unit of the Fokker D.VII.

Design and construction of the prototype started simultaneously at the beginning of 1969, as Mr White's fifth homebuilt, and first flight of the prototype was made on 7 September 1969.

Plans and kits of materials, as well as some of the more difficult-to-construct parts in finished form, are available to amateur constructors, and a total of 75 der Jäger D.IXs was under construction in February 1970.

The following details apply to the prototype in its original form. At the time of writing it was being re-engined with a 150 hp Lycoming.

TYPE: Single-seat sporting biplane.

WINGS: Forward-stagger single-bay biplane with N-type interplane and centre-section struts. Single streamlined lift strut from each side of lower fuselage to attachment point of forward interplane strut on upper wing. No flying or landing wires. Aerofoil section M-6. Incidence 3° upper wing, 2° lower wing. Spruce spars and plywood ribs, fabric covered. Internal steel-tube bracing. Ailerons in both top and bottom wings. Scalloped trailing-edge to both wings.

FUSELAGE: Welded 4130 steel-tube structure, fabric covered. Aluminium engine cowling.

TAIL UNIT: Wire-braced welded 4130 steel-tube structure, with sheet metal ribs, fabric covered. Balanced rudder and elevator. Ground-adjustable trim-tabs in elevator.

LANDING GEAR: Non-retractable tail-wheel type. Main legs each consist of an "A" frame, welded into the fuselage, with tension springs in the centre-fuselage to cushion landing shock. Main wheels and tyres size 500 × 5. Glass-fibre wheel fairings.

POWER PLANT: One 115 hp Lycoming O-235-C1 four-cylinder horizontally-opposed air-cooled engine, driving a McCauley two-blade metal propeller, diameter 5 ft 6 in (1·68 m). Structure suitable for alternative power plants from 1600cc Volkswagen up to 150 hp. Fuel contained in two tanks, one in upper wing centre-section, capacity 14 US gallons (53 litres), one in fuselage, capacity 10 US gallons (38 litres); total 24 US gallons (91 litres).

ACCOMMODATION: Single seat in open cockpit, with headrest faired into wood or glass-fibre fuselage turtleback.

EQUIPMENT: Two dummy machine-guns mounted on top of fuselage, forward of cockpit. Dummy bomb, carried between legs of main landing gear, can be adapted as oil tank for smoke discharge system.

DIMENSIONS, EXTERNAL:
Wing span, upper .... 20 ft 0 in (6·10 m)

White Der Jäger D.IX homebuilt biplane (115 hp Lycoming O-235-C1 engine)

Wing span, lower	16 ft 0 in (4·88 m)
Wing chord, upper at root	3 ft 6 in (1·07 m)
Wing chord, upper at tip.	4 ft 0 in (1·22 m)
Wing chord, lower (constant)	3 ft 0 in (0·91 m)
Length overall	17 ft 0 in (5·18 m)
Tailplane span	8 ft 0 in (2·44 m)
Wheel track	5 ft 0 in (1·52 m)
Propeller ground clearance	10 in (0·25 m)

AREA:
Wings, gross .... 115 sq ft (10·68 m²)

WEIGHTS:
Weight, empty .... 534 lb (242 kg)
Max T-O weight .... 888 lb (403 kg)

PERFORMANCE (at max T-O weight):
Max level speed at 2,000 ft (610 m)
.... 126 knots (145 mph; 233 km/h)
Max permissible diving speed
.... 152 knots (175 mph; 282 km/h)
Max cruising speed at 2,000 ft (610 m)
.... 116 knots (133 mph; 214 km/h)
Stalling speed ... 47 knots (54 mph; 87 km/h)
Max rate of climb at S/L 2,400 ft (732 m)/min
T-O run .... 150 ft (45·7 m)

WINDECKER

WINDECKER RESEARCH, INC

ADDRESS:
PO Box 6288, Midland, Texas 79701
PRESIDENT: Kenneth M. Smith
CHIEF ENGINEER: W. R. Shackelford
DIRECTOR OF MARKETING:
Edwin H. Magruder Jr

Windecker Research holds an exclusive licence from the Dow Chemical Company for the reinforced plastic aircraft developed since 1960 by Dr Leo Windecker. The plastic material, which Windecker call Fibaloy, was used first to manufacture various parts of an airframe structure, which were then flight tested on existing aircraft of metal construction. Following successful tests, construction of a prototype four-seat low-wing monoplane began in 1965. This aircraft has the name Eagle I, and all available details follow:

WINDECKER ACX-7 EAGLE I

In configuration, the Eagle I is a conventional low-wing monoplane; but Windecker have used reinforced plastics for the construction of the entire airframe. The prototype flew for the first time on 7 October 1967, but after final FAA Certification tests on 19 April 1969 this aircraft was destroyed in an accident. The company's chief test pilot, Mr Bill Robinson, escaped by parachute. A second prototype has been completed and tests for FAA Certification are continuing.

TYPE: Four-seat low-wing monoplane.

WINGS: Cantilever low-wing monoplane. NACA 64A415 wing section. Dihedral 4° 30′. Incidence 2° 30′. No sweepback. Structure of Fibaloy reinforced plastic. Frise-type ailerons of Fibaloy with ground-adjustable trim-tabs. Trailing-edge flaps constructed of Fibaloy.

FUSELAGE: Fail-safe monocoque structure of Fibaloy.

TAIL UNIT: Conventional cantilever structure of Fibaloy. Fixed-incidence tailplane. Trim-tab on starboard elevator.

LANDING GEAR: Retractable tricycle type with single wheel on each unit. Hydraulic retraction, main wheels inboard, nose wheel rearward. Windecker oleo-pneumatic shock-absorbers. Cleveland 6·00 × 6 main wheels, 5·00 × 5 nose wheel; all tyre pressures 45 lb/sq in (3·16 kg/sq cm). Cleveland caliper hydraulic brakes.

POWER PLANT: One 285 hp Continental IO-520-C six-cylinder horizontally-opposed air-cooled engine, driving a McCauley or Hartzell two-blade constant-speed propeller. Optional three-blade propeller. Fuel capacity 86 US gallons (325 litres), in two 43-gallon (162·5 litre) wing tanks. Oil capacity 1·5 US gallons (5·7 litres).

ACCOMMODATION: Four persons in pairs in enclosed cabin. Forward-hinged door on each side of cabin. Compartment aft of rear seats for 120 lb (54 kg), baggage; hatshelf on bulkhead at rear of cabin. Cabin ventilated and heated by ram-air over exhaust.

SYSTEMS: Hydraulic system, pressure 1,500 lb/sq in (105 kg/cm²), for landing gear. 12V 70A alternator. 12 volt battery.

ELECTRONICS AND EQUIPMENT: VHF standard. Various optional equipment.

DIMENSIONS, EXTERNAL:

Wing span	32 ft 0 in (9·75 m)
Wing chord, constant	5 ft 6 in (1·68 m)
Wing aspect ratio	5·82
Length overall	28 ft 6 in (8·69 m)
Height overall	9 ft 0 in (2·74 m)
Tailplane span	11 ft 3 in (3·42 m)
Wheel track	7 ft 0 in (2·13 m)
Wheelbase	6 ft 6 in (1·98 m)
Cabin doors: height	3 ft 0 in (0·91 m)
Width	3 ft 1 in (0·94 m)
Height to sill	1 ft 4 in (0·40 m)

Windecker Eagle 1 lightplane with plastics airframe

DIMENSIONS, INTERNAL:

Cabin: length	9 ft 6 in (2·89 m)
Max width	4 ft 2 in (1·27 m)
Max height	3 ft 6 in (1·07 m)

AREAS:

Wings, gross	176 sq ft (16·35 m²)
Ailerons (total)	15·28 sq ft (1·42 m²)
Trailing-edge flaps (total)	17·96 sq ft (1·67 m²)
Fin	10·18 sq ft (0·95 m²)
Rudder, including tab	6·24 sq ft (0·58 m²)
Tailplane	34·68 sq ft (3·22 m²)
Elevators, including tab	15·14 sq ft (1·41 m²)

WEIGHTS AND LOADINGS:

Weight empty	2,150 lb (975 kg)
Current T-O weight	3,300 lb (1,497 kg)
Design max T-O weight	3,400 lb (1,542 kg)
Max wing loading	19·3 lb/sq ft (94·7 kg/m²)
Max power loading	11·9 lb/hp (5·40 kg/hp)

PERFORMANCE (at design max T-O weight):
Max level speed at S/L
.... 186 knots (214 mph; 344 km/h)
Max cruising speed, 75% power at 6,500 ft
(1,980 m) 181 knots (208 mph; 335 km/h)
Econ cruising speed, 45% power at 10,000 ft
(3,050 m) 152 knots (175 mph; 282 km/h)
Range, at max cruising speed, no allowances,
no reserve fuel 996 nm (1,147 miles; 1,846 km)
Max range, econ cruising speed at 10,000 ft
(3,050 m), no allowances, no reserve fuel
.... 1,327 nm (1,528 miles; 2,459 km)

WING

WING AIRCRAFT COMPANY

HEAD OFFICE:
2550 Skypark Drive, Torrance, California 90509
PRESIDENT: George S. Wing
VICE-PRESIDENT: Harold E. Dale

Wing Aircraft Company was incorporated on 27 June 1966, when it became completely separated from its parent company, Hi-Shear Corporation. Its sales, engineering and executive offices remain unchanged in location at Torrance, California.

WING DERRINGER

Named after the well-known American compact pocket pistol, the Derringer is a twin-engined two-seat high-performance business and sporting aircraft. In its standard form it is fully-equipped for IFR flight.

Design work was started in June 1960, the prototype and subsequent test models being built at the Hi-Shear Corporation factory. The prototype, powered by two 115 hp engines, flew for the first time on 1 May 1962. It was used to prove the design concept and was retired after logging more than 300 flying hours.

The second aircraft, with 150 hp engines, was redesigned to production standards. It flew for the first time on 19 November 1964, but it was lost on an early test flight. A third aircraft was assembled for static structural testing.

A fourth aircraft, with 160 hp engines, flew for the first time on 25 August 1965. Since then all static and flight testing has been completed, and FAA type approval under CAR Part 3 was received on 20 December 1966. A fifth aeroplane is flying as a demonstrator and a sixth is being used to test a turbosupercharged engine installation.

The Derringer utilises manufacturing techniques that are new to the lightplane industry. Butt-jointed flush-riveted chemically-milled and stretch-formed skins are used throughout the airframe. This simplifies the achievement of a flush surface finish and provides integral stiffness, since the skins are left thicker at the points where additional strength is needed. Assembly is simplified as, for example, each wing is formed by a single stretch-formed chemically-milled skin that also acts as an integral fuel tank.

It was reported in March 1970 that production tooling has been completed and that parts and equipment were being stockpiled for early commencement of production.

TYPE: Two-seat twin-engined light aircraft.

WINGS: Cantilever low-wing monoplane. Wing section NACA 65_2-415. Dihedral 6°. Incidence 1°. All-metal two-spar structure of aluminium, except for glass-fibre tips. Conventional ailerons of aluminium with piano-type hinges. Ground-adjustable trim-tab in each aileron. Electrically-actuated slotted trailing-edge flaps. Bungee-type trim control.

FUSELAGE: All-metal semi-monocoque structure of aluminium, except for glass-fibre nose.

Wing D-1 Derringer two-seat light aircraft (two 160 hp Lycoming IO-320-B1C engines)

TAIL UNIT: Cantilever all-metal structure of aluminium with swept vertical surfaces. Tailplane has variable incidence. Electrically operated rudder and elevator trim-tabs.

LANDING GEAR: Retractable tricycle type with single wheel on each unit. Electro-mechanical retraction, nose-wheel forward, main wheels upward into nacelles. Oleo-pneumatic shock-absorbers. Tubeless tyres size 5·00 × 5 on steerable nose-wheel, 6·00 × 6 with low profile on main wheels, pressure 40 lb/sq in (2·8 kg/cm²) on main wheels, 35 lb/sq in (2·5 kg/cm²) on nose-wheel. Cleveland single-disc hydraulic brakes.

POWER PLANT: Two 160 hp Lycoming IO-320-B1C four-cylinder horizontally-opposed air-cooled engines, each driving a Hartzell metal two-blade variable-pitch propeller, diameter 5 ft 6 in (1·68 m). Two integral fuel tanks in leading-edges of outer wings with total capacity of 88 US gallons (333 litres). Refuelling points at wingtips. Total oil capacity 4 US gallons (15 litres). Engine nacelles of glass-fibre.

ACCOMMODATION: Two seats side-by-side under large upward-hinged canopy with opaque top. Tinted windshields and windows. Entry from either side. Dual controls. Cabin heated and ventilated. Baggage compartment capacity 250 lb (113 kg).

SYSTEMS: Electrical system includes two 60A alternators, one 12V 35 Ah battery. Vacuum system for flight instruments only. Hydraulic system for brakes only.

ELECTRONICS AND EQUIPMENT: Fully instrumented and equipped for IFR operation as standard. Transponder, DME, dual nav/com, glide slope, marker beacon, ADF, autopilot, oxygen system etc, optional.

DIMENSIONS, EXTERNAL:

Wing span	29 ft 2 in (8·89 m)
Wing chord, constant	4 ft 2 in (1·27 m)
Wing aspect ratio	7
Length overall	23 ft 0 in (7·01 m)
Height overall	8 ft 0 in (2·44 m)

Tailplane span	10 ft 10 in (3·30 m)
Wheel track	10 ft 10 in (3·30 m)
Wheelbase	5 ft 4½ in (1·64 m)
Propeller ground clearance	8 in (20·3 cm)

DIMENSIONS, INTERNAL:
Cabin:

Length	8 ft 4 in (2·54 m)
Max width	3 ft 6½ in (1·08 m)
Max height	3 ft 10 in (1·17 m)
Floor area	12 sq ft (1·11 m²)
Volume	56 cu ft (1·59 m³)
Baggage hold, volume	25 cu ft (0·71 m³)

AREAS:

Wings, gross	121 sq ft (11·24 m²)
Ailerons (total)	8·00 sq ft (0·74 m²)
Flaps (total)	12·00 sq ft (1·11 m²)
Fin	11·65 sq ft (1·08 m²)
Rudder, including tab	5·18 sq ft (0·48 m²)
Tailplane	18·56 sq ft (1·72 m²)
Elevators, including tab	11·51 sq ft (1·07 m²)

WEIGHTS AND LOADINGS:

Weight empty	2,100 lb (952 kg)
Max T-O weight	3,050 lb (1,383 kg)
Max landing weight	2,900 lb (1,315 kg)
Max wing loading	25·2 lb/sq ft (123 kg/m²)
Max power loading	9·5 lb/hp (4·3 kg/hp)

PERFORMANCE (at max T-O weight):
Max level speed at S/L
201 knots (232 mph; 373 km/h)
Max cruising speed, 75% power at 10,000 ft (3,050 m) 195 knots (224 mph; 360 km/h)
Cruising speed, 65% power at 10,000 ft (3,050 m) 182 knots (210 mph; 338 km/h)
Stalling speed, flaps and wheels down
63 knots (72 mph; 116 km/h)
Rate of climb at S/L 1,700 ft (518 m)/min
Rate of climb at S/L, one engine out
420 ft (128 m)/min
Service ceiling 19,600 ft (5,974 m)
Single-engine ceiling 8,000 ft (2,438 m)
Range with max fuel, 65% power at 10,000 ft (3,050 m), no reserve
1,007 nm (1,160 miles; 1,866 km)

WITTMAN

S. J. WITTMAN

ADDRESS:
Box 276, Oshkosh, Wisconsin 54901

Famous as a racing pilot since 1926, Steve Wittman has designed and built a large number of different racing and touring aeroplanes at Winnebago County Airport, of which he has been manager since 1931.

Of the racers, Bonzo, with which Mr Wittman won the Continental Trophy in 1949, 1950 and 1952, is still flying, and details of this aircraft were given in the 1959-60 *Jane's*.

Most recent Wittman design is the Tailwind side-by-side two-seat light aeroplane. The prototype was built in 1952-53 and proved so successful that sets of plans and pre-fabricated components were made available to amateur builders. By the Spring of 1969, there were 145 Model W-8 Tailwinds flying, including a number built in foreign countries. In January 1968 Mr Wittman's plans were approved by the Australian Department of Civil Aviation.

In 1966, a more powerful six-cylinder Continental engine was installed in a Tailwind redesigned to take the added weight and power. It is designated W-9.

Mr Wittman is currently working on the design of a new aircraft, but no details of this were available at the time of writing.

WITTMAN TAILWIND MODEL W-8

Some Tailwinds have been built with tricycle landing gear and other design changes. One of the most unusual is N314T (illustrated), built by Mr A. C. Occhipinti. Powered by a 125 hp Lycoming O-290-G engine, it has an electrically-retractable main landing gear which gives an improvement in speed of approximately 17·4 knots (20 mph; 32 km/h), for a weight increase of 17-20 lb (8-9 kg).

Wittman Tailwind Model W-8 with retractable landing gear built by Mr A. C. Occhipinti
(Howard Levy)

The following data refer to the standard Tailwind built to Mr Wittman's plans.

TYPE: Two-seat cabin monoplane.

WINGS: Braced high-wing monoplane. Wing section is a combination of NACA 4309 (upper surface) and NACA 0006 (lower surface). Thickness/chord ratio 11·5%. No dihedral. Incidence 1°. Wood structure with plywood and fabric covering. Single bracing strut each side. Ailerons and flaps of steel and stainless steel construction.

FUSELAGE: Steel-tube structure, fabric-covered.

TAIL UNIT: Cantilever structure of steel and stainless steel. Ground-adjustable trim-tabs in control surfaces.

LANDING GEAR: Non-retractable tail-wheel type. Spring steel cantilever main legs. Goodyear 15 × 5 main wheels and tyres, pressure 32 lb/sq in (2·25 kg/cm²). Goodyear brakes.

POWER PLANT: Normally one 90 hp Continental C90-12F four-cylinder horizontally-opposed air-cooled engine, driving a Sensenich or Flottorp two-blade wood fixed-pitch propeller, diameter 5 ft 4 in (1·63 m). Alternative engines are the

85 hp Continental C85, 100 hp Continental O-200, 115 hp Lycoming O-235 or 140 hp Lycoming O-290. One fuel tank of 25 US gallons (94·5 litres) capacity in fuselage. Oil capacity 4·6 US quarts (1·85-2·8 litres).

ACCOMMODATION: Two seats side-by-side in enclosed cabin, with door on each side. Space for 60 lb (27 kg) baggage.

DIMENSIONS, EXTERNAL:
Wing span	22 ft 6 in (6·86 m)
Wing chord, constant	4 ft 0 in (1·22 m)
Wing aspect ratio	5·5
Length overall	19 ft 3 in (5·87 m)
Height overall	5 ft 8 in (1·73 m)
Tailplane span	6 ft 8 in (2·03 m)
Wheel track	5 ft 5 in (1·65 m)

AREAS:
Wings, gross	90 sq ft (8·36 m²)
Ailerons (total)	3·0 sq ft (0·28 m²)
Flaps (total)	7·3 sq ft (0·68 m²)
Fin	4·8 sq ft (0·45 m²)
Rudder	2·3 sq ft (0·21 m²)
Tailplane	5·5 sq ft (0·51 m²)
Elevators	4·8 sq ft (0·45 m²)

WEIGHTS (100 hp Continental engine):
Weight empty	700 lb (318 kg)
Max T-O weight	1,300 lb (590 kg)

PERFORMANCE (100 hp Continental engine at max T-O weight):
Max level speed at S/L
    143 knots (165 mph; 265 km/h)
Max permissible diving speed
    160 knots (185 mph; 297 km/h)
Max cruising speed
    139 knots (160 mph; 257 km/h)
Econ cruising speed
    113 knots (130 mph; 209 km/h)
Stalling speed, flaps down
    48 knots (55 mph; 89 km/h)
Rate of climb at S/L   900 ft (275 m)/min
Service ceiling   16,000 ft (4,876 m)
T-O run   800 ft (245 m)
T-O to 50 ft (15 m)   1,325 ft (405 m)
Landing from 50 ft (15 m)   1,150 ft (350 m)
Landing run   600 ft (183 m)
Range with max payload at 10,000 ft (3,050 m), no reserve:
  at 139 knots (160 mph; 257 km/h)
    521 nm (600 miles; 965 km)
  at 122 knots (140 mph; 225 km/h)
    607 nm (700 miles; 1,125 km)

WITTMAN TAILWIND MODEL W-9

This aircraft was first flown in 1958, as the W-9L Tailwind with tricycle landing gear (see 1965-66 *Jane's*). In 1965 it was fitted with a new wing exactly the same as that used on the W-8 Tailwind. It has more recently been re-engined with a 145 hp Continental O-300 six-cylinder horizontally-opposed air-cooled engine. The structure has been strengthened as necessary to take the extra power and weight, and the landing gear is now of the tail-wheel type.

DIMENSIONS, EXTERNAL:
Same as W-8, except
Length overall	20 ft 0 in (6·10 m)

WEIGHTS:
Weight empty	800 lb (363 kg)

Wittman W-8 Tailwind (135 hp Lycoming O-290-D2 engine) built by Mr Charles Wilford of Naperville, Illinois (*Jean Seele*)

Prototype Wittman Tailwind Model W-9, now fitted with 145 hp Continental O-300-A engine and tail-wheel landing gear (*Howard Levy*)

Max T-O weight	1,420 lb (644 kg)	Landing speed	48 knots (55 mph; 89 km/h)
PERFORMANCE (at max T-O weight):		Rate of climb at S/L	1,400 ft (425 m)/min
Max level speed at S/L		Service ceiling	17,000 ft (5,180 m)
	172 knots (198 mph; 319 km/h)	T-O run	600 ft (183 m)
Max cruising speed		Range with max fuel	
	156 knots (180 mph; 290 km/h)		564 nm (650 miles; 1,045 km)

WOLFORD-WILSON
DALE WOLFORD AND ELMER WILSON
ADDRESS: Route 2, PO Box 154A, Ashland, Ohio

WOLFORD-WILSON SAILWING
Dale Wolford and Elmer Wilson combined forces to design and build a sailwing test vehicle. The forward section of the wing consists of a formed aluminium channel spar with flanged aluminium nose ribs, and aluminium skin is pop-riveted to this structure to form the wing leading-edge and wing tips. The wing trailing-edge consisted originally of a 3/32-in flexible steel cable in tension, but flight tests have shown this to be subject to vertical deflection and steel-tube braces have been added at semi-span to limit this movement. The original Dacron wing covering has been replaced by an extremely light covering, weighing only 6 lb (2·72 kg) to reduce drag, and the trailing-edge cable cambered to maintain chord-wise tension on the wing covering. The "butterfly" type tail unit is composed of tailplane and elevators. The simplest possible wire-braced fuselage structure serves to locate these two structures and provide mountings for a single seat and the fixed tricycle landing gear. A small tail bumper wheel is provided to protect the tail unit.

Preliminary trials consisted of towed test flights, but the aircraft was powered by mounting two 10 hp West Bend industrial engines on outriggers immediately behind the pilot, and these each drive a two-blade fixed-pitch pusher propeller. With these engines the sailwing has a cruising speed of 39 knots (45 mph; 72 km/h) and endurance of 30 min. Flight testing has shown that power with these two engines is very margin-al, and a third engine is to be mounted on a vertical pylon above the wing. An alternative wing is being planned, to see whether the two 10 hp engines would provide adequate power for such a configuration.

Wolford-Wilson Sailwing test vehicle in its original prototype form (*Howard Levy*)

DIMENSIONS, EXTERNAL:
Wing span	29 ft 4 in (8·94 m)
Length overall	18 ft 2 in (5·54 m)

WEIGHT:
Max T-O weight	450 lb (204 kg)

WFI

WORLD FLIGHT INCORPORATED

ADDRESS:
Cuyahoga County Airport, Cleveland, Ohio
44124
PRESIDENT:
James R. Bede

Mr James Bede, president of Bede Aircraft, Inc, formed World Flight Incorporated to concentrate upon the development of his BD-2 aircraft and the detailed preparations for an attempt upon the world's distance record or a round-the-world flight.

WFI BD-2 LOVE ONE

This highly-unorthodox aircraft has been built by Javelin Aircraft Co of Wichita, Kansas, to the design of Mr James Bede, who plans to attempt a round-the-world non-stop flight in it, without the aid of flight refuelling. The aircraft's name "Love One" is an acronym, standing for "Low orbit very efficiently, number one". Fuel cost for the flight will be $230.

The basic airframe is that of a Schweizer 2-32 two-seat all-metal high-performance sailplane, which has been extensively rebuilt into a single-seat, high aspect ratio powered aircraft. The entire wing interior has been sealed to form an integral fuel tank, and there are two further large fuel tanks in the fuselage, aft of the cockpit, near the CG.

Very extensive instrumentation and equipment are fitted. Much of the flight will be made on autopilot. If this should mal-function while the pilot is asleep, causing a change of altitude, a special altitude alert warning system will wake him. NASA has supplied a 25-litre liquid oxygen tank and converter of the type used in the Mercury space-craft. A special Collins transceiver will enable the pilot to keep in contact with the Collins "antenna farm" at Cedar Rapids, Iowa, throughout his flight, which is expected to take between 150 and 170 hours.

The BD-2 flew for the first time on 11 March 1967.

During the period 7-10 November 1969, Mr Bede made a 70 hr 15 min non-stop flight, during which a total distance of 8,974 miles (14,442 km) was covered. Intended as a long-distance trial of the aircraft, it was carried out over a closed circuit bounded by Columbus, Ohio, and Kansas City, Kansas. After eight of a planned nine laps, the flight was terminated due to total failure of the electrical system, by which time Mr Bede had captured three records, already confirmed by the NAA and awaiting FAI ratification. These were for the longest single-

WFI BD-2 Love One, built for an attempted un-refuelled non-stop round the-world flight

engine non-stop non-refuelled solo endurance flight; distance record in closed circuit by piston-engined lightplanes of 3,858-6,614 lb (1,750-3,000 kg); and an absolute closed-circuit distance record for piston-engined aircraft of any class.

Mr Bede's round-the-world flight attempt was scheduled for the Autumn of 1970, to be preceded by one more trial flight.

TYPE: Single-seat experimental aircraft for round-the-world flight.

WINGS: Cantilever mid-wing monoplane. Wing section NACA 63³618 at root, NACA 24012A at tip, and NACA 64⁴221 on tip extensions. Dihedral on main wings. Anhedral on tip extensions. All-metal structure of aluminium alloy, except for tips which are of glass-fibre, each tip holding 12·5 US gallons (47 litres) of fuel. Fabric-covered ailerons. No flaps.

FUSELAGE: All-metal semi-monocoque structure. One-piece glass-fibre engine cowling.

TAIL UNIT: Cantilever all-metal structure, with fabric covering on rudder, metal covering elsewhere. Large dorsal fin. All-moving horizontal surface, with tab.

LANDING GEAR: Jettisonable take-off dolly fitted with three wheels in nose-wheel tricycle configuration. Dolly is fitted with drag-chute to prevent rebound off ground and possible damage to aircraft. Steel and wood skid under belly for landing.

POWER PLANT: One Continental IO-360-C six-cylinder horizontally-opposed air-cooled engine, modified to give 225 hp for take-off and climb and as little as 30 hp at 20,000 ft (6,100 m) for cruising. Engine fitted with special Bendix

magnetos, Champion RHM 38P spark plugs and 60A alternator. McCauley two-blade constant-speed metal propeller. Fuel in integral wing tanks, wingtips and two aluminium tanks in fuselage, with total capacity of 565 US gallons (2,138 litres).

ACCOMMODATION: Single seat under transparent plastic canopy, which hinges to port for access to cockpit.

ELECTRONICS AND EQUIPMENT: Two Bendix 360-channel VHF transceivers, two Bendix T-12C ADF's, Bendix TRPG 600 radar transponder, and Collins 618T-3 single side band HF transceiver. Bendix M-4C autopilot with G-4 slaved compass and automatic altitude hold. Sleep timer and alert system. Change of altitude alert system. Aro Corp liquid oxygen system. Alcor mixture analyser.

DIMENSIONS, EXTERNAL:
Wing span	63 ft 0 in (19·20 m)
Wing aspect ratio	20·7
Length overall	27 ft 7 in (8·40 m)

AREA:
Wings, gross	192 sq ft (17·84 m²)

WEIGHTS:
Weight empty	1,950 lb (885 kg)
Max T-O weight	5,290 lb (2,400 kg)

PERFORMANCE (estimated at max T-O weight):
Max cruising speed	168 knots (194 mph; 312 km/h)
T-O run	4,900 ft (1,495 m)
Range with max fuel	24,750 nm (28,500 miles; 45,865 km)

WOODS

HARRIS L. WOODS

ADDRESS:
3715 Greenleay Street, Raleigh, North Carolina
27606

Mr H. L. Woods, chief engineer of Bensen Aircraft Corporation at Raleigh, has designed and built a total of 13 aircraft and air cushion vehicles, including flex-wing and rotating-wing aircraft, a variety of gliders and the Wager V-1 and ACV No 3 experimental ACV's, described in the 1960-61 and 1962-63 editions of *Jane's* respectively. His latest design to fly, the Woody Pusher two-seat monoplane, of which plans are available to amateur constructors, is described below.

A total of more than 170 Woody Pushers were known to be under construction in February 1969 and 307 sets of plans had been sold at the end of the year.

Mr Woods has built a new ultra-light aircraft during 1969, and this was ready for flight testing in January 1970. Already named the Windy Loo, no other details were available at the time of writing.

WOODS WOODY PUSHER

The prototype Woody Pusher was designed originally with a fuselage of wooden construction, plywood-covered, with fabric covering overall, and was powered by a 65 hp Lycoming engine.

Mr Woods has now redesigned the fuselage and landing gear and increased the engine power as detailed below:

TYPE: Two-seat amateur-built light aircraft.

WINGS: Braced parasol monoplane, with Vee streamline-section main bracing struts each side and multi-strut centre-section cabane structure. Wing section NACA 4412. Two-spar wood structure, with metal leading-edge and fabric covering overall. Fitted with flaps.

FUSELAGE: Welded steel-tube structure with fabric covering.

Woods Woody Pusher prototype in its latest form (*Jean Seele*)

TAIL UNIT: Wire and strut-braced type. Ground-adjustable tab on rudder.

LANDING GEAR: Non-retractable tail-wheel type. Cantilever spring steel main gear. Champion wheels. Wheel fairings on main gear.

POWER PLANT: One 75 hp Continental four-cylinder horizontally-opposed air-cooled engine, driving a two-blade wooden fixed-pitch pusher propeller type LYL 36-68 SEN. Provision for other engines in 65-85 hp range. Fuel tank above wing, forward of engine, capacity 12 US gallons (45 litres).

ACCOMMODATION: Two seats in tandem in open cockpit.

DIMENSIONS, EXTERNAL:
Wing span	29 ft 0 in (8·84 m)
Wing chord	4 ft 6 in (1·37 m)
Length overall	20 ft 5 in (6·22 m)
Height overall	7 ft 0 in (2·13 m)
Tailplane span	7 ft 6 in (2·29 m)

AREA:
Wings, gross	130 sq ft (12·07 m²)

WEIGHTS:
Weight empty	630 lb (285 kg)
Max T-O weight	1,150 lb (522 kg)

PERFORMANCE (at max T-O weight):
Max level speed at S/L	85 knots (98 mph; 158 km/h)
Cruising speed	76 knots (87 mph; 140 km/h)
Stalling speed	39 knots (45 mph; 72 km/h)
Rate of climb at S/L	600 ft (183 m)/min
T-O to 50 ft (15 m)	1,500 ft (457 m)
Landing from 50 ft (15 m)	1,000 ft (305 m)
Endurance with max fuel	2 hr 30 min

WREN
WREN AIRCRAFT CORPORATION

HEAD OFFICE:
Meacham Field, PO Box 4115, Fort Worth, Texas 76106

PRESIDENT:
E. H. Pickering

VICE-PRESIDENT:
Charles Hennigh

DIRECTORS:
James C. Binnion
Gene E. Engleman
James C. Fuller
Marcus Ginsburg
Tom P. Gordon
Wallace Jay
Al W. Mooney
E. H. Pickering

SECRETARY-TREASURER:
Marcus Ginsburg

This company was formed to market a STOL light aircraft known as the Wren 460, based on a design developed by Mr James L. Robertson.

Initial testing of several features of the design was done, under a US Army Transportation Research command contract, on an experimental aircraft known as the Skyshark. Details can be found under the "Skycraft" heading in the 1962-63 *Jane's*.

On 27 May 1968 Wren Aircraft Corporation announced that they had been awarded a contract by the USAF to instal Wren STOL devices on two aircraft, one of which is an Air Force O-2A (military version of the Cessna 337 Super Skymaster). It is hoped that successful test evaluation by the USAF will lead to a follow-on contract for production aircraft.

Wren Aircraft are also marketing a Beta-Control system reversible-pitch propeller for light aircraft, and IPK kits for STOL conversions to the entire range of Cessna aircraft from the Model 150 to Model 210F.

WREN 460

The Wren 460 four-seat STOL light aircraft utilises in its manufacture a new Cessna 182 airframe. This permits production of the Wren at a lower selling price than would otherwise be possible and provides the purchaser with nearly world-wide Cessna parts and service.

The first prototype Wren utilised a 1958 Cessna 182A airframe. Development began in June 1962; first flight was in January 1963, and FAA certification was received on 30 June 1964. By the time of certification, six Wren 460G models (utilising a Cessna 182G airframe) had been produced and delivered, including the certification prototype.

Certification of the Wren 460H (utilising a Cessna 182H airframe) was received in February 1965 and by mid-April 1966, a total of 33 Wrens had been produced. Only new airframes are being used in this programme, in which the Cessna Aircraft Company has offered assistance to Wren Aircraft Corporation.

No changes are made in the power or gross weight of the basic Cessna 182 airframe. Four Wren devices provide the aircraft with its slow flying and STOL capabilities, as follows:

1. Full-span double-slotted flaps are installed. The outer panel of the new flaps, on each wing, operates as both an aileron and a flap in the flaps-extended position. Wing lift coefficient increases from 1·5 to 2·6 as the flaps deflect to their maximum 30° position. A button control on the pilot's control wheel enables the flaps to be retracted instantly on touch-down, for faster braking, without the pilot needing to remove his hands from the wheel or throttle.

2. The basic NACA 2412 wing section nose radius of 1·01 in (2·6 cm) is increased to 1·50 in (3·8 cm) by the use of a sheet metal glove. This postpones wing stalling from the normal 16° angle of attack to 20° and provides a lift coefficient increment of 0·4 independent of flap deflection. The stalling characteristics are extremely docile, with no trace of lateral roll-off.

3. A set of small articulated horizontal control surfaces, known as the Robertson ULS (ultra low speed) nose control system, is mounted

on the nose of the aircraft, immediately aft of the propeller. These control surfaces, each comprising a stabiliser, elevator and tab, are connected permanently to the conventional elevator control system and work in conjunction with this system. They act in the propeller slipstream to augment pitch control in slow-speed flight. The ULS controls serve to reduce the balancing tail download required to trim out the nose-down pitching moment when the flaps are extended, and this provides an increase in the aircraft's total lift.

4. A set of five feathering drag plates, known as "Wren's Teeth", are added to each wing upper surface. These drag plates operate on a harmonic linkage with the ailerons and deflect outward through 60° when the aileron is deflected up. This further decreases lift on the downgoing wing and, more importantly, increases drag on the downgoing wing so that the normal adverse aileron yaw is overcome and the aircraft yaws into rather than away from its turn. Positive and immediate roll response to control deflection is achieved down to an indicated airspeed of 35 mph (56 kmh) in ground effect.

The Wren 460 is unusual in its ability to utilise fully its slow flying capability. At 45-60 mph (72-97 kmh) only 30% power is required and the aircraft can maintain level flight, in level attitude, with no engine heating or cooling problems. At these speeds, it is even more manoeuvrable than at high cruising speeds. At 70 mph (113 kmh), with 20° flaps, the Wren utilises only 21% power, giving a fuel consumption of less than 6 US gallons (23 litres) per hour and endurance of over 15 hours.

Landings under weather conditions of 100 ft (30 m) ceiling and visibility of ¼ mile (or runway visual range of 1,200 ft = 365 m) were approved by the FAA for the Wren 460 in March 1966. Wren Aircraft hopes eventually for removal of all weather minima for this aircraft.

TYPE: Four-seat STOL light aircraft.

WINGS: Braced high-wing monoplane with single streamline-section bracing strut each side. Wing section NACA 2412 (modified) with constant-radius leading-edge cuff (fixed droop). Dihedral 1° 44'. Incidence 0° 55' at root, —3° 8' at tip. All-metal structure. Flaps, ailerons and drag plates described above.

FUSELAGE, LANDING GEAR: As for Cessna 182 (see page 309), except larger wheels and tyres are standard. Main wheels and tyres size 8·00 × 6, pressure 25 lb/sq in (1·76 kg/cm²). Nose-wheel and tyre size 6·00 × 6, pressure 21 lb/sq in (1·48 kg/cm²) standard. Optional nose-wheel tyre size 8·00 × 6 for use on extra-rough or extra-soft landing areas.

TAIL UNIT: As for Cessna 182, but with electrically-actuated automatic trim system, which adjusts tailplane incidence as flaps are raised and lowered, giving reduced landing and take-off runs.

POWER PLANT: As for Cessna 182, but optional Hartzell/Wren Beta reversible-pitch propeller which enables the aircraft to clear a 500 ft (152 m) obstacle and come to a stop in 1,000 ft (305 m).

Wren 460 STOL lightplane showing clearly the ULS nose control system and feathering drag plates

ACCOMMODATION: Four seats in pairs in enclosed cabin, with provision for additional seat for a child. Dual controls optional. Forward-hinged door on each side. Three seats removable for freight carrying. Normal space aft of seats for 120 lb (54 kg) baggage.

DIMENSIONS, EXTERNAL:
Same as for Cessna 182, except:

Wing span	36 ft 7 in (11·15 m)
Wing chord at root	5 ft 4 in (1·63 m)
Wing chord at tip	3 ft 8½ in (1·13 m)
Wing aspect ratio	7·63
Span of ULS surfaces	7 ft 6 in (2·29 m)

DIMENSIONS, INTERNAL:

Cabin: Length	7 ft 9 in (2·36 m)
Max width	3 ft 2 in (0·97 m)
Max height	4 ft 0 in (1·22 m)
Floor area	24 sq ft (2·23 m²)
Volume	71 cu ft (2·01 m³)

AREAS:

Wings, gross	175·4 sq ft (16·30 m²)
Ailerons (total)	16·1 sq ft (1·50 m²)
Trailing-edge flaps, including ailerons (total)	45·7 sq ft (4·25 m²)
Drag plates (total)	3·1 sq ft (0·29 m²)
Fin, including dorsal fin	11·6 sq ft (1·08 m²)
Rudder	7·0 sq ft (0·65 m²)
Tailplane	20·4 sq ft (1·90 m²)
Elevators	15·7 sq ft (1·46 m²)
ULS surfaces	7·0 sq ft (0·65 m²)

WEIGHTS AND LOADINGS:

Weight empty, equipped	1,690 lb (767 kg)
Design min flying weight	1,861 lb (844 kg)
Max T-O and landing weight	2,800 lb (1,270 kg)
Max wing loading	15·96 lb/sq ft (77·92 kg/m²)
Max power loading	12·17 lb/hp (5·52 kg/hp)

PERFORMANCE (at max T-O weight, with automatic trim system):

Max level speed at S/L	139 knots (160 mph; 257 km/h)
Never-exceed speed	167 knots (193 mph; 310 km/h)
Max cruising speed (75% power) at 6,500 ft (1,980 m)	131 knots (151 mph; 243 km/h)
Econ cruising speed at 10,000 ft (3,050 m)	100 knots (115 mph; 185 km/h)
Stalling speed: flaps up, power off	46 knots (52 mph; 84 km/h)
flaps down, power on	27 knots (31 mph; 50 km/h)
Rate of climb at S/L	1,080 ft (330 m)/min
Service ceiling	19,200 ft (5,850 m)
T-O run	270 ft (82 m)
T-O to 50 ft (15 m)	575 ft (175 m)
Landing from 50 ft (15 m)	550 ft (168 m)
Landing run	250 ft (76 m)
Range at max cruising speed, no reserve	757 nm (872 miles; 1,403 km)
Range at econ cruising speed, no reserve	998 nm (1,150 miles; 1,850 km)
Range at 48 knots (55 mph; 89 km/h)	525 nm (605 miles; 975 km)
Endurance at 48 knots (55 mph; 89 km/h)	11 hours

YORK
LEON YORK

Mr Leon York designed a low-wing aerobatic monoplane which he designated York Y-2. It was built jointly by Mr York and Dr David Conoley at a cost of about $2,500. Construction occupied two years and first flight was made in 1966.

The Y-2 is owned by Dr Conoley, and subsequent to first flight he added a rearward-sliding transparent cockpit canopy, wheel fairings and an external power socket. He has also improved the landing gear by adding oleo-spring shock-absorbers and has modified the engine for inverted flight. The Y-2 has been flown by Mr York in three major aerobatic contests, best performance to date being 5th place in an EAA contest held at Dacy, Illinois. An earlier design by Mr York, the June Bug, was described in the 1960/61 *Jane's*.

YORK Y-2

TYPE: Single-seat homebuilt aerobatic monoplane.

WINGS: Cantilever low-wing monoplane. Aerofoil section NACA 23015 at root, NACA 4412 at tip. No dihedral. Incidence 2° 30'. No sweepback. All-wood structure with one-piece I-section spars, plywood ribs and skin, fabric-covered. Plain ailerons of welded steel-tube structure, fabric-covered. No trim-tabs. No flaps.

FUSELAGE: Welded steel-tube structure with sheet aluminium and fabric covering.

TAIL UNIT: Cantilever welded steel-tube structure, with fabric covering. Tailplane incidence ground-adjustable. No trim-tabs.

LANDING GEAR: Non-retractable tail-wheel type. Oleo-spring shock absorbers on main units. Hayes main wheels and tyres, size 5·00 × 4, pressure 24 lb/sq in (1·69 kg/cm²). Goodyear hydraulic brakes. Glass-fibre main wheel fairings.

POWER PLANT: One 125 hp Lycoming O-290-G four-cylinder horizontally-opposed air-cooled engine, driving a Koppers Aeromatic F-200 two-blade propeller, diameter 6 ft 2 in (1·88 m). Fuel contained in two main tanks, capacity 16·2 US gallons (61·3 litres) and one auxiliary tank holding 8·5 US gallons (32·2 litres). Total fuel capacity 24·7 US gallons (93·5 litres). Oil capacity 2 US gallons (7·57 litres).

ACCOMMODATION: Single seat for pilot under rearward-sliding bubble canopy. Cockpit heated.

DIMENSIONS, EXTERNAL:

Wing span	19 ft 8 in (5·99 m)
Wing chord at root	5 ft 8 in (1·73 m)
Wing chord at tip	3 ft 8 in (1·12 m)
Wing aspect ratio	4·5
Length overall	18 ft 6 in (5·64 m)
Height overall	5·0 ft (1·52 m)
Tailplane span	7 ft 6 in (1·52 m)
Propeller ground clearance	1 ft 0 in (0·30 m)

DIMENSIONS, INTERNAL:
Cockpit: length   4 ft 10 in (1·47 m)
   Max width   1 ft 11 in (0·58 m)
   Max height   3 ft 8 in (1·12 m)

AREA:
   Wings gross   84 sq ft (7·80 m²)

WEIGHTS:
   Weight empty, equipped   673 lb (305 kg)
   Max T-O weight   1,040 lb (471 kg)

PERFORMANCE (at max T-O weight):
   Max level speed at S/L
                        126 knots (145 mph; 233 km/h)
   Max cruising speed, at 7,500 ft (2,286 m)
                        122 knots (140 mph; 225 km/h)
   Econ cruising speed
                        113 knots (130 mph; 209 km/h)
   Stalling speed   48 knots (55 mph; 89 km/h)
   Max rate of climb at S/L   1,500 ft (457 m)/min
   Service ceiling   17,000 ft (5,180 m)
   T-O run   600 ft (183 m)
   T-O to 50 ft (15 m)   1,000 ft (305 m)
   Landing run   800 ft (244 m)
   Range with max fuel
                        500 nm (575 miles; 925 km)

York 2 home-built monoplane (125 hp Lycoming O-290 GPU)   (*Howard Levy*)

THE UNION OF SOVIET SOCIALIST REPUBLICS

ANTONOV
OLEG KONSTANTINOVICH ANTONOV

After establishing his reputation with a series of successful glider and sailplane designs, Antonov has now become one of Russia's leading designers of transport aircraft, particularly those types intended for short-field operation.

Details of the current products of his design bureau, which is situated in Kiev, are given hereafter.

ANTONOV AN-2
NATO Code Name: "Colt"

The prototype of this large biplane was designed to a specification of the Ministry of Agriculture and Forestry of the USSR and made its first flight in 1947. It was powered by a 760 hp ASh-21 engine and was known as the SKh-1 (Selskokhozyaistvennyi-1 = agricultural-economic-1). This designation was dropped subsequently and the design went into production as the An-2, with a 1,000 hp ASh-62 engine.

The An-2 is capable of operating out of small airfields and took over most of the duties performed previously by the old Po-2 biplane, such as rescue and ambulance work, passenger and cargo transport, photographic and geophysical survey, forestry patrol and agricultural work and parachute training.

More than 5,000 An-2's were built in 1950-60 for service with the Soviet armed forces, Aeroflot and other civilian organisations. Many were exported, to all of the Socialist States, and to Greece Afghanistan, Mali, Nepal, India and Cuba, and the type continued in production in the Soviet Union in its improved An-2M version, as illustrated. Licence rights were granted to China, where the first locally-produced An-2 was completed in December 1957. Poland also began quantity production of the An-2 in 1960 and has manufactured the An-2P, An-2R, An-2S and An-2W versions, all of which have the original rounded fin and rudder.

The following major versions of the An-2 have been built.

An-2P. Basic general-purpose aircraft. Flight deck seats two side-by-side, with dual controls, and can be fitted with a third seat for a flight engineer. Side windows are bulged to give good downward field of vision. Door between flight compartment and cabin, which accommodates up to 10 passengers on lightweight folding seats, or 14 paratroops or 2,734 lb (1,240 kg) of freight or six stretchers. Standard commercial passenger versions have either seven individual forward-facing armchair seats, with centre aisle, or four two-seat sofas. Cabin is heated and ventilated and has a carpeted floor. Equipment includes cupboards for food, drink and small packages, wardrobe and, at the rear of the cabin, a toilet. A glider-towing hook is included in the standard equipment. In service with Aeroflot, An-2's were still used on more than 2,000 local route stages in 1969-70, handling almost 40% of the airline's passengers; they carried their 100 millionth passenger in 1967.

An-2R. Polish designation for An-2S described below.

An-2S (USSR). Agricultural version of An-2P, fitted with a long-stroke landing gear. This permits the installation of pumping and spraying equipment under the fuselage and wings. A hopper with a capacity of 308 Imp gallons (1,400 litres) of liquid chemicals, or 2,650 lb (1,200 kg)

of dust is mounted inside the main cabin. Spray system has a propeller-driven pump under the fuselage, to discharge liquid through spray-bars at the rate of 1·4-4·0 Imp gallons (6·5-18·0 litres) sec. Dusting and seeding system has a tunnel-type distributor under fuselage. Operating speed is 84-90 knots (96-103 mph; 155-165 kmh), and take-off and landing run 260-330 ft (80-100m). Superseded by An-2M.

An-2S (Poland). Designation of Polish-built ambulance version of An-2P, with accommodation for six stretchers and medical equipment.

An-2M. Latest Soviet agricultural version with more efficient dispensing systems, driven from engine via a gearbox rated at 50 hp. Hopper capacity increased from 308 Imp gallons (1,400 litres) to 431 Imp gallons (1,960 litres). Dispersal rates increased to a maximum of 132 lb/sec (60 kg/sec) for granulated chemicals, 82 lb/sec (37 kg/sec) for dust and 6 Imp gallons (28 litres) sec for liquid chemicals. Swath width 98-102 ft (30-31 m) when dusting, 125-138 ft (38-42 m) during liquid spraying. Air-conditioned cockpit with separate door. Improved engine mounting. Pedal-operated brakes. Main landing gear wheels moved 2·75 in (7 cm) forward to reduce risk of nose-over on landing. Airframe production utilises combination of metal bonding and welding. Can be operated by one-man crew, instead of two specified for earlier versions, and offers 22-27% improvement in operating economy. Identified by larger and more square-cut tail surfaces. Agricultural equipment is quickly removable for carrying passengers in tip-up wall seating, cargo carrying and other duties. Max chemical payload 3,300 lb (1,500 kg). Entered quantity production towards end of 1964. Deliveries began early in 1965.

An-2T. Designation of Polish-built mixed cargo-passenger version, equivalent to Soviet An-2P. Superseded in 1967 by version for passengers only, designated An-2P.

An-2V (design bureau number An-4). Float-plane version of An-2P developed in 1954-55. Floats are 24 ft 7 in (7·5 m) long and, as they have a very shallow draught, the An-2V can be

used in water as little as 2 ft 7½ in (0·8 m) in depth. Pneumatically-operated water rudders are fitted. Usual curved-blade propeller replaced by reversible-pitch Type V514-D9 with straight square-tipped blades. Floats can be fitted to any An-2 to special order. Conversion from wheels to floats can be done by four men in 20 hours, from floats to wheels in 8 hours. Payload of this version is 2,028 lb (920 kg). Polish designation is **An-2W.**

An-2L. Water-bombing version announced in 1966. Similar to An-2V, but adapted to drop water on fires from bottom of each float. Water is taken on board whilst taxying over surface of river or lake. Total water capacity 1½ metric tons. Entered service in Summer of 1969, initially in Siberia and the north-west USSR, to protect forest-land.

An-2ZA (design bureau number An-6). Based on An-2P, with modifications to suit it for high-altitude meteorological research. Has an extra cockpit immediately forward of the fin, from which ice accretion and other weather phenomena may be watched. Powered by an ASh-62 IR/TK engine, with a turbosupercharger mounted externally on the starboard side to maintain 850 hp up to a height of 31,000 ft (9,500 m). Other modifications include deletion of the propeller spinner and use of a longer carburettor air intake. Unslotted ailerons are installed on this aircraft, which is fitted with a glider-towing hook.

The following details apply to the An-2M.

TYPE: Single-engined general-purpose biplane.

WINGS: Unequal-span single-bay biplane. Dihedral, both wings, approx 2° 48′. All-metal two-spar structure, fabric-covered aft of front spar. I-type interplane struts. Drooping ailerons and electrically-actuated automatic slots on upper wings only. Trim-tab in port aileron. Electrically-actuated slotted flaps on all four wings.

FUSELAGE: All-metal stressed-skin semi-monocoque structure of circular section forward of cabin, rectangular in the cabin section and oval in the tail section.

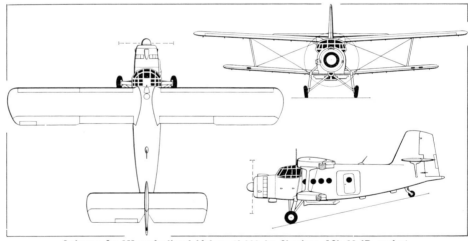

Antonov An-2M agricultural biplane (1,000 hp Shvetsov ASh-62 IR engine)

Antonov An-2M agricultural biplane (1,000 hp Shvetsov ASh-62 IR engine) with under-fuselage dusting gear   *(Novosti)*

Antonov An-10A passenger transport of Aeroflot (four 4,000 eshp Ivchenko AI-20K turboprop engines) taking off from Sheremetyevo Airport, Moscow *(Tass)*

TAIL UNIT: Braced metal structure. Fin integral with rear fuselage. Fabric-covered tailplane. Trim-tabs in rudder and port elevator.

LANDING GEAR: Non-retractable split-axle type with long-stroke oleo shock-absorbers. Main wheel tyres size 800 × 260 mm, pressure 43 lb/sq in (3 kg/cm²). Pneumatic brakes. Self-centering tail-wheel, tyre size 470 × 210 mm. Wheels interchangeable with floats or skis.

POWER PLANT: One 1,000 hp Shvetsov ASh-62 IR nine-cylinder radial air-cooled engine, driving a Type V509-D9 four-blade constant-speed metal propeller. Six fuel tanks in upper wings, with total capacity of 264 Imp gallons (1,200 litres). Oil capacity 26·5 Imp gallons (120 litres).

ACCOMMODATION: Equipped normally for operation by pilot only, in air-conditioned cockpit, separated from main cabin by pressure bulkhead. Side windows of flight deck bulged to give good downward field of vision. Entry via port side of canopy, which hinges upward on centre-line. Dual controls and second seat can be fitted for training or when aircraft is used for other duties. Easily convertible to carry passengers in tip-up wall seating, or for freight transport. Chemical hopper normally installed in cabin. Upward-opening freight door on port side of cabin is removable for parachuting or supply-dropping. Smaller rearward-opening passenger door inset in freight door.

SYSTEMS: 28V electrical system includes a 3,000W engine-driven generator and 30Ah battery.

ELECTRONICS AND EQUIPMENT: Standard equipment includes blind-flying instrumentation, radio and agricultural dusting and spraying gear. Equipment available for special duties includes two fixed semi-automatic AFA-33/50, or one AFA-33/75 and one AFA-18/21, cameras for photographic survey work; Geiger-Müller apparatus, magnetometer, etc, for geological surveying.

DIMENSIONS, EXTERNAL (An-2M):

Span of upper wing	59 ft 8½ in (18·18 m)
Span of lower wing	46 ft 8½ in (14·24 m)
Length overall	42 ft 6 in (12·95 m)
Height overall	13 ft 9¼ in (4·20 m)
Tailplane span	26 ft 3 in (8·00 m)
Wheel track	11 ft 0 in (3·36 m)
Freight door:	
Height	5 ft 5 in (1·65 m)
Width	5 ft 6 in (1·67 m)

DIMENSIONS, INTERNAL:

Cabin: Length	13 ft 5 in (4·10 m)
Max height	5 ft 11 in (1·80 m)
Max width	5 ft 3 in (1·60 m)
Volume	424 cu ft (12 m³)

AREAS:

Wings, gross	765·3 sq ft (71·10 m²)
Horizontal tail surfaces	159·3 sq ft (14·80 m²)

WEIGHTS (An-2M):

Max payload (chemicals)	3,300 lb (1,500 kg)
Max T-O weight	12,125 lb (5,500 kg)

PERFORMANCE (An-2M at max T-O weight):

Max level speed at 5,750 ft (1,750 m)
136 knots (157 mph; 253 km/h)
Econ cruising speed
108 knots (124 mph; 200 km/h)
Operating speed (spraying)
81-87 knots (93-100 mph; 150-160 km/h)
Take-off speed
46-49 knots (53-56 mph; 85-90 km/h)
Landing speed (chemicals discharged)
41 knots (47 mph; 75 km/h)
Rate of climb at S/L:
clean 550 ft (168 m)/min
with spray-gear 395 ft (120 m)/min
Service ceiling 14,270 ft (4,350 m)
T-O run on grass (max) 655 ft (200 m)
Landing run (chemicals discharged)
330 ft (100 m)
Range with max fuel
488 nm (562 miles; 905 km)

ANTONOV AN-6

An improved version of the An-2, with a supercharged ASh-62 radial engine, is reported to have been produced for Aeroflot under the designation An-6. Aircraft operated by Soviet Antarctic expeditions have also been referred to by this designation.

ANTONOV AN-10
NATO Code Name: "Cat"

Design of the An-10 airliner began in November 1955 and the prototype (named "Ukraina") first flew in March 1957. An-10's are used primarily on Aeroflot's domestic services, especially in regions where airfields are small and primitive.

The first prototypes had Kuznetsov NK-4 turboprops, but production aircraft have AI-20's designed by A. G. Ivchenko.

Versions of the An-10 in service are as follows:

An-10. Initial version. One of the prototypes, displayed at Vnukovo Airport, Moscow, in July 1957, had seats for 84 passengers in three cabins, with a "play-room" for children at the rear. This version entered service with Aeroflot in July 1959, on routes from Simferopol, in the Crimea, to Moscow and Kiev.

An-10A. Developed version with fuselage lengthened by 6 ft 7 in (2·0 m) and normal accommodation for 100 passengers. Alternative layouts accommodate 120 or 130 passengers. Details below refer to this type, which entered service with Aeroflot in February 1960. After two months of trials in the Arctic, An-10A airliners are now operating also on skis in the far North of the Soviet Union.

An-12. Specialised freighter version of the An-10A, described separately.

An An-10A, piloted by Alexandre Mitronine and Vladimir Tersky, achieved an average speed of 454 mph (730·616 kmh) over a 500 km closed circuit on 29 April 1961, establishing a speed record for propeller-driven aircraft which had not been beaten by mid-1970.

TYPE: Four-engined passenger transport.

WINGS: Cantilever high-wing monoplane. All-metal two-spar structure in five panels, comprising centre-section, intermediate wings and tip sections, the last with marked anhedral. Manually-operated aerodynamically-balanced ailerons. Double-slotted Fowler flaps in two portions each side, hydraulically-actuated. Electro-thermal de-icing.

FUSELAGE: Stressed-skin semi-monocoque structure of circular section.

TAIL UNIT: Cantilever all-metal structure. Electrically-operated trim-tabs. All controls are manually operated and aerodynamically-balanced. Small stabilising fin under rear fuselage. Electro-thermal de-icing of fin and tailplane. Original auxiliary fins each side on tailplane have been superseded by two large additional ventral fins on current aircraft.

LANDING GEAR: Retractable tricycle type. Hydraulic actuation. Shock-absorbers use nitrogen instead of air and have stroke of 13·4 in (340 mm). Four-wheel bogie on each side retracts into blister on side of fuselage. Hydraulically-steerable dual nose-wheels. Main wheel tyre size 1,050 × 300 mm; pressure 80-95 lb/sq in (5·6-6·7 kg/cm²). Hydraulic disc brakes. Retractable tail bumper. Wheels interchangeable with ski landing gear for Arctic operation.

POWER PLANT: Four 4,000 ehp Ivchenko AI-20K turboprops, driving AV-68 four-blade reversible-pitch propellers, diameter 14 ft 9 in (4·50 m). All fuel in 22 bag-type tanks in wings, total capacity 3,058 Imp gallons (13,900 litres).

ACCOMMODATION (An-10A): Pilot and co-pilot side-by-side on flight deck, with third seat for radio-operator behind in deep well. Navigator in glazed nose compartment. Normal seating

for 100 passengers. Front cabin has toilet on starboard side, opposite two seats, and 24 seats in four rows with centre aisle. Aft of this cabin are a cloakroom, galley-pantry and passenger-entry door on the port side, and cloakrooms and baggage compartment on the starboard side. Then come two small private compartments, each containing five seats. The central cabin has 42 seats in seven rows with centre aisle. Aft of it is a further door and toilet on the port side and cloakroom and toilet on the starboard side. The rear saloon contains 16 seats in four rows and is followed by a tail compartment with six inward-facing seats. In the 130-seat version, three of the rows of seats in the front cabin are seven-abreast, a six-seat compartment replaces the central baggage space and the starboard rear toilet is removed, making room for 63 people in seven-abreast seating in the centre cabin.

SYSTEMS: Entire accommodation air-conditioned and pressurised to differential of 7·1 lb/sq in (0·50 kg/cm²). Hydraulic system operates landing gear retraction, nose-wheel steering, flaps and brakes.

DIMENSIONS, EXTERNAL (An-10A):

Wing span	124 ft 8 in (38·0 m)
Length overall	111 ft 6½ in (34·0 m)
Height overall	32 ft 3 in (9·83 m)
Wheel track	17 ft 9½ in (5·42 m)
Wheelbase	35 ft 6 in (10·82 m)

DIMENSIONS, INTERNAL (An-10A):
Cabin, excluding flight deck:

Width at floor	approx 10 ft 0 in (3·05 m)
Max height	8 ft 2½ in (2·50 m)
Volume	7,840 cu ft (222 m³)
Cargo holds (under floor, total)	1,130 cu ft (32 m³)

AREA:

Wings, gross	1,292 sq ft (120 m²)

WEIGHTS AND LOADINGS (An-10A):

Max payload	32,000 lb (14,500 kg)
Max fuel	22,600 lb (10,250 kg)
Max T-O weight	121,500 lb (55,100 kg)
Max wing loading	88 lb/sq ft (430 kg/m²)
Max power loading	7·2 lb/hp (3·27 kg/hp)

PERFORMANCE (An-10A at max T-O weight):

Max level speed
386 knots (444 mph; 715 km/h)
Max cruising speed at 32,800 ft (10,000 m)
366 knots (422 mph; 680 km/h)
Econ cruising speed at 32,800 ft (10,000 m)
340 knots (391 mph; 630 km/h)
T-O speed
102-113 knots (118-130 mph; 190-210 km/h)
Service ceiling 33,500 ft (10,200 m)
T-O run 2,300-2,625 ft (700-800 m)
Landing run, with reverse pitch
1,640-2,130 ft (500-650 m)
Range with max payload, 60 min reserve fuel
647 nm (745 miles; 1,200 km)
Range with max fuel and 18,600 lb (8,440 kg) payload, no reserves
2,197 nm (2,530 miles; 4,075 km)

ANTONOV AN-12
NATO Code Name: "Cub"

The An-12 is a freight-carrying version of the An-10 with an entirely-redesigned rear fuselage and tail unit. A loading ramp for freight and vehicles is incorporated in the underside of the upswept rear fuselage and can be lowered in flight for air-drop operations. The built-in freight-handling gantry has a capacity of 5,070 lb (2,300 kg). The cargo floor is designed for loadings of up to 307 lb/sq ft (1,500 kg/m²).

The ventral tail-fins fitted to the An-10 are not needed on the An-12. The military version has a tail gunner's position. In the An-12 which Ghana Airways operated for a time, the gunner's position was fitted out as a toilet. In the current commercial version, first demonstrated at the 1965 Paris Air Show, the turret is removed and replaced by a streamlined fairing.

Antonov An-12 rear-loading transport (four 4,000 eshp Ivchenko AI-20K turboprop engines) in the insignia of Bulair (*Aviation Photo News*)

Except for the details noted above, the structural description of the An-10 applies to the An-12, and the two aircraft have the same power plant and fuel capacity. In addition to freight, the An-12 is equipped to carry a crew of five and 14 passengers.

The An-12 is a standard paratroop and freight transport in the Soviet Air Force. Sixteen have been supplied to the Indian Air Force. Others are operated by the air forces of Algeria, Egypt, Indonesia, Iraq and Poland, and by Aeroflot, Polish Air Lines LOT, Bulair and Cubana.

One of the An-12's operated by Aeroflot's Polar aviation service has been used to test skis of an entirely new design. Of unusually wide and deep section, these skis have a shallow curved Vee lower surface, like a flattened version of the planing bottom of a seaplane float. The skis are equipped with braking devices and warming equipment and are claimed to permit landings at prepared fields as well as on virgin snow. Each main ski is supported by a primary oleo strut, with scissor-arm system, and fore and aft secondary oleos to absorb pitching (and possibly rolling) moments. They are to become standard equipment on aircraft used in the Arctic and Antarctic and for winter services.

The following are official Soviet data applicable to the currently-available commercial An-12:

DIMENSIONS, EXTERNAL:
Same as for An-10A, except:
Length overall 108 ft 3 in (33·00 m)

DIMENSIONS, INTERNAL:
Cargo hold:
Length 44 ft 3½ in (13·50 m)
Max width 9 ft 10 in (3·00 m)
Max height 7 ft 10½ in (2·40 m)

WEIGHTS:
Max payload 44,090 lb (20,000 kg)
Normal T-O weight 119,050 lb (54,000 kg)
Max T-O weight 134,480 lb (61,000 kg)

PERFORMANCE (at normal T-O weight):
Max cruising speed
324 knots (373 mph; 600 km/h)
Normal cruising speed at 25,000 ft (7,500 m)
297 knots (342 mph; 550 km/h)
Rate of climb at S/L 1,970 ft (600 m)/min
Service ceiling 33,500 ft (10,200 m)
T-O run 2,790 ft (850 m)
Landing run 2,820 ft (860 m)
Range with 22,050 lb (10,000 kg) cargo, 1 hour
reserve 1,832 nm (2,110 miles; 3,400 km)

ANTONOV AN-14 PCHELKA (LITTLE BEE)
NATO Code Name: "Clod"

The An-14 Pchelka is a twin-engined light general-purpose aircraft, the first prototype of which made its first flight on 15 March 1958.

The two prototypes were each powered by two 260 hp Ivchenko AI-14R radial engines and accommodated six passengers and 330 lb (150 kg) of baggage, or 1,320 lb (600 kg) of freight. They flew originally with a straight tailplane and with V-shape leading-edges on the twin tail-fins. This type of tail unit has been superseded by a dihedral tailplane and rectangular fins of increased area on production aircraft, which also have 300 hp engines, increased wing span and accommodation for a pilot and six to eight passengers, plus baggage.

Production began in 1965 at the Progress Plant at Arsenyev, in the far East of the Soviet Union, for both Aeroflot and the Soviet armed forces. The military version was first seen at the Domodedovo air display in July 1967 and does not appear to differ externally from the civilian passenger version. It serves also with the air force of the German Democratic Republic.

Antonov An-12 transport aircraft fitted with skis which incorporate braking devices and warming equipment

An executive version is available with de luxe accommodation for five passengers and their baggage, with tables between facing seats. All seats are quickly removable to provide an unobstructed cabin for cargo carrying. An ambulance version, which is in production, can accommodate six stretchers, in tiers of three on each side of the cabin, with an attendant. Dual controls are available for pilot training and a variety of equipment can be fitted for geological survey, aerial photography and agricultural duties.

Photographs have been issued showing aircraft No. CCCP-L1053 (with original fins and probably a prototype) equipped for agricultural duties. It has spraybars attached to the aileron-flap brackets under each wing, from the wing tip to a point immediately aft of the wing/bracing strut junction. From there the spraybars run down the bracing strut and along the stub-wings to meet under the fuselage. The chemical tank is housed in the main cabin and the standard rear loading doors are replaced by a larger removable fairing panel. Entry to the flight deck is via a forward-opening door on the starboard side of the nose, hinged on the centre-line of the aircraft.

Great emphasis has been placed on simplicity of servicing and handling, and the An-14 is said to be suitable for operation by "pilots of average skill". It will maintain height on one engine at its maximum T-O weight. Radio, navigation equipment, instrumentation, landing light and de-icing equipment make possible operation at night and in bad weather.

The following data apply to the standard production An-14.

TYPE: Twin-engined light general-purpose aircraft.

WINGS: Braced high-wing monoplane with single streamline-section bracing strut each side. Dihedral 2°. All-metal structure. Entire trailing-edges hinged; each comprising a double-slotted flap, with the slat of the flap extending to the wing-tip and built into the single-slotted aileron as a leading-edge structure. Trim-tab in port aileron. Small stub-wing carries each main landing gear unit and provides lower attachment for bracing strut.

FUSELAGE: Conventional all-metal semi-monocoque pod-and-boom structure.

TAIL UNIT: Cantilever all-metal structure. Twin fins and rudders, mounted at right-angles to the tips of the "dihedral" tailplane, so that

Antonov An-14 Pchelka in Soviet military insignia (*Aviation Week and Space Technology*)

EE

they toe inwards at the top. Trim-tab in each rudder and in port elevator.

LANDING GEAR: Non-retractable tricycle type, with single wheel on each unit. Main units carried on short stub-wings. Wide-tread balloon tyres of same size on all three units. Steerable nose-wheel. Brakes on main wheels. Skis can be fitted for operation from snow, or floats for operation from water.

POWER PLANT: Two 300 hp Ivchenko AI-14RF nine-cylinder radial air-cooled engines, each driving a V-530 two-blade or three-blade variable-pitch propeller, diameter 9 ft 6 in (2·90 m).

ACCOMMODATION: Pilot and one passenger side-by-side on flight deck. Main cabin normally seats six persons in pairs in individual forward-facing armchair seats, each by a large window and with central aisle. Provision for seven seats in main cabin in high-density version. Cabin sound-proofed and provided with heating and ventilation systems. Door from cabin to flight deck. Passengers enter cabin through clam-shell rear doors which form underside of upswept rear fuselage. Chemical tank capacity of agricultural version is 220 Imp gallons (1,000 litres).

DIMENSIONS, EXTERNAL:

Wing span	72 ft 2 in (21·99 m)
Length overall	37 ft 1½ in (11·32 m)
Height overall	15 ft 2½ in (4·63 m)
Tailplane span	16 ft 4¾ in (5·00 m)
Wheel track	11 ft 9¾ in (3·60 m)
Wheelbase	11 ft 11¾ in (3·65 m)
Cabin door:	
Length	6 ft 3 in (1·90 m)
Width	2 ft 9½ in (0·85 m)

DIMENSIONS, INTERNAL:

Cabin, excluding flight deck:	
Length	10 ft 2 in (3·10 m)
Height	5 ft 3 in (1·60 m)
Width	5 ft 0 in (1·53 m)

AREA:

Wings, gross	441 sq ft (41·0 m²)

WEIGHTS:

Max payload	1,590 lb (720 kg)
Max T-O weight	7,935 lb (3,600 kg)

PERFORMANCE (at max T-O weight):

Max cruising speed	102 knots (118 mph; 190 km/h)
Econ cruising speed	95 knots (109 mph; 175 km/h)
Operating speed, agricultural duties	76 knots (87 mph; 140 km/h)
Landing speed	46 knots (53 mph; 85 km/h)
T-O run, from grass	295 ft (90 m)
Landing run, on grass	360 ft (110 m)

RANGES:

with max payload	253 nm (292 miles; 470 km)
with 1,390 lb (630 kg) payload	367 nm (423 miles; 680 km)

ANTONOV AN-22 ANTHEUS
NATO Code Name: "Cock"

Nothing was known of this very large transport aircraft until the first prototype arrived in Paris on 16 June 1965, during the *Salon*. It had flown for the first time on 27 February 1965 and the walls of its main cabin were lined with test equipment, recorders, etc. Four more prototypes and the first production An-22 were flying by mid-

Military version of Antonov An-22 with new nose-mounted radars (*Tass*)

1967. Two of the prototypes were then being operated by Aeroflot on experimental freight services. Three An-22's, in military insignia. took part in the air display at Domodedovo on 9 July 1967, landing batteries of "Frog-3" and "Ganef" missiles on tracked launchers. Series production is under way, for the Soviet Air Force and for Aeroflot, which plans to use the An-22 mainly in under-developed areas of the northern USSR, Siberia and the Far East.

In March 1969, it was announced that an An-22 had made 16 flights to oilfields in the Tyumen region of western Siberia to deliver mobile power stations.

In general configuration, the An-22 is similar to its much smaller predecessor, the An-12, with the outer wing anhedral that has become a characteristic of Antonov designs. It is intended primarily for long-distance transportation of heavy bulk cargoes and civil and military equipment, accompanied by operating personnel.

The military version shown in the upper illustration on this page differs in a number of details from aircraft seen earlier. Its main navigation radar has been moved from under the starboard landing gear fairing to the nose, which now carries two radars, in a thimble-type fairing above the modified nose windows and in a large underfuselage radome. A fairing extends forward from the lower radome and might be fitted with shutters, but its purpose is unknown. One aircraft of this type took part in military manoeuvres at Dvina in NW Byelorussia in early 1970.

A 724-passenger two-deck version, with longer fuselage, reached the design study stage, and brief details of this were given in the 1966-67 *Jane's*. No further development of this version is planned at present. Instead, Antonov's design bureau is reported to be developing an airbus version capable of carrying 300-350 passengers and 66,150 lb (30,000 kg) of freight on a stage length of 1,620 nm (1,865 miles; 3,000 km).

On 26 October 1967, the An-22 set up fourteen payload-to-height records, piloted by I Davydov

and with a crew of seven. It reached a height of 25,748 ft (7,848 m) with a payload of 100,000 kg of metal blocks, qualifying also for records with 35,000, 40,000, 45,000, 50,000, 55,000, 60,000, 65,000, 70,000, 75,000, 85,000, 90,000 and 95,000 kg. Max payload lifted to a height of 2,000 m was 221,443 lb (100,444·6 kg). Take-off run with this load was stated to be just over one kilometre. The flight lasted 78 minutes.

The following details refer to the prototypes. That seen at Paris had flown non-stop from Moscow in 5 hr 5 min (an average of just over 305 knots; 350 mph; 563 km/h) against 43 knot (50 mph; 80 km/h) head-winds, carrying three omnibuses and general cargo.

TYPE: Long-range heavy turboprop transport.

WINGS: Cantilever high-wing monoplane. Marked anhedral on outer panels. All-metal structure, appearing to have three main spars which attach to three strong fuselage ring-frames. Double-slotted trailing-edge flaps.

FUSELAGE: All-metal semi-monocoque structure, with upswept rear fuselage containing loading-ramp/door for direct loading. Retractable jacks support rear fuselage at point where rear loading ramp is hinged.

TAIL UNIT: Cantilever all-metal structure. Twin fins and rudders (each in two sections, above and below tailplane) mounted outboard of mid-span. Tabs in each elevator and in each of the four rudder sections.

LANDING GEAR: Retractable tricycle type, designed to permit off-runway operation. Steerable twin-wheel nose unit. Each main gear consists of three twin-wheel levered-suspension units in tandem, each unit mounted at the bottom of one of the fuselage ring frames that also picks up a wing spar. Main units retract upward into fairings built on to sides of fuselage. Tyre pressure adjustable in flight or on ground to suit airfield surface.

POWER PLANT: Four 15,000 shp Kuznetsov NK-12MA turboprop engines, each driving a pair of four-blade contra-rotating propellers, diameter 20 ft 4 in (6·20 m).

Commercial version of Antonov An-22 Antheus long-range heavy transport aircraft (four 15,000 shp Kuznetsov NK-12MA turboprop engines)

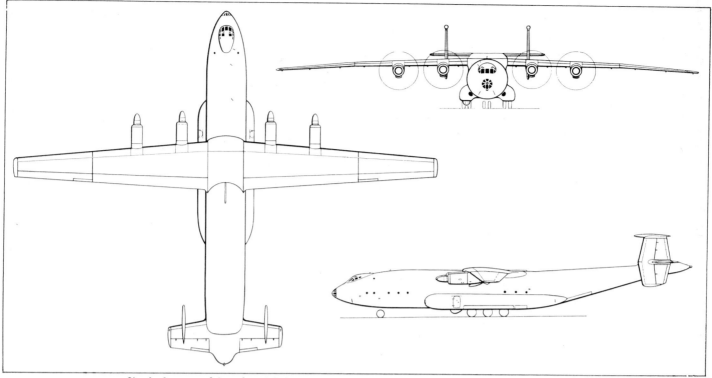

Standard commercial version of Antonov An-22 Antheus four-turboprop long-range heavy transport

ACCOMMODATION: Crew of five or six. Navigator's station in nose. Cabin for 28-29 passengers aft of flight deck, separated from main cabin by bulkhead containing two doors. Uninterrupted main cabin, with reinforced titanium floor, tie-down fittings and rear loading ramp. When ramp lowers, a large door which forms the underside of the rear fuselage retracts upward inside fuselage to permit easy loading of tall vehicles. Rails in roof of cabin for four travelling gantries continue rearward on underside of this door. Two winches, used in conjunction with the gantries, each have a capacity of 5,500 lb (2,500 kg). Door in each landing gear fairing, forward of wheels, for crew and passengers.

ELECTRONICS AND EQUIPMENT: Main navigation radar inside blister under starboard landing gear fairing, forward of wheels, on civil version. Pressurisation equipment and APU in forward part of this fairing. Military version has two radars, in nose "thimble" and under-nose fairings.

DIMENSIONS, EXTERNAL:
Wing span 211 ft 4 in (64·40 m)
Length overall, civil version 189 ft 7 in (57·80 m)
Height overall 41 ft 1½ in (12·53 m)
DIMENSIONS, INTERNAL:
Main cabin: Length 108 ft 3 in (33·0 m)
Max width 14 ft 5 in (4·4 m)
Max height 14 ft 5 in (4·4 m)
AREAS:
Wings, gross 3,713 sq ft (345 m²)
WEIGHTS:
Weight empty, equipped 251,325 lb (114,000 kg)
Max payload 176,350 lb (80,000 kg)
Max fuel 94,800 lb (43,000 kg)
Max T-O weight 551,160 lb (250,000 kg)

PERFORMANCE:
Max level speed 399 knots (460 mph; 740 km/h)
T-O run 4,260 ft (1,300 m)
Landing run 2,620 ft (800 m)
Range with max fuel and 99,200 lb (45,000 kg) payload 5,905 nm (6,800 miles; 10,950 km)
Range with max payload 2,692 nm (3,100 miles; 5,000 km)

ANTONOV AN-24 and AN-26
NATO Code Name: "Coke"

Development of this twin-turboprop transport was started in 1958, to replace piston-engined types on Aeroflot's internal feeder-line routes. It was intended originally to carry 32-40 passengers, but when the prototype flew in April 1960, it had been developed into a 44-seater. It was followed by a second prototype and five pre-production An-24's. Flight trials were stated to be complete in September 1962 and the An-24 entered service on Aeroflot's routes from Moscow to Voronezh and Saratov in September 1963. More than 25 million passengers and 350,000 tonnes of cargo and mail had been carried by Aeroflot An-24's by May 1969.

The An-24 is designed to operate from airfields of limited size, with paved or natural runways. Two were taken to the Antarctic in late 1969, to replace piston-engined Il-14s used previously for flights between Antarctic stations.

Export orders have been received from the following airlines:

Air Guinée 3
Air Mali 2
Balkan Bulgarian Airlines 7
Cubana 6
Interflug (E Germany) 6
Lebanese Air Transport 1*
LOT (Poland) 13
Misrair (United Arab Airlines) 8
Mongolian Airlines 3
Pan African Air Services (Tanzania) 2
Tarom (Romania) 5

*Sold to Misrair and included in latter's fleet of eight.

The An-24 has also been supplied for military service, usually in small numbers, with the air forces of the USSR, Czechoslovakia, Egypt, East Germany, Hungary, North Korea, Poland, the Somali Republic and North Vietnam.

On the prototype, the engine nacelles extended only a little past the wing trailing-edges: production An-24's have lengthened nacelles with conical rear fairings. A ventral tail-fin was also added on production models, more than 100 of which had been built by the Spring of 1966, when the rate of production at Kiev was four a month.

The current production versions are designed for a service life of 30,000 hours and 15,000 landings, and are being produced in a variety of forms, as follows:

An-24V Srs II. Standard version, seating up to 50 passengers. Superseded Srs I (with 2,550 ehp AI-24 engines) in 1968, and described in detail below. Basically as Srs I, powered by two Ivchenko AI-24A turboprop engines, with water injection. Can have crew of up to five (two pilots, navigator, radio operator and, on jump seat, an engineer or cargo handler) on flight deck.

Antonov An-24T local-service transport (two Ivchenko AI-24 turboprop engines) **in the insignia of Air Mali** (*Roger Caratini*)

TG-16 self-contained starter-generator in rear of starboard engine nacelle. Mixed passenger-freight, convertible cargo/passenger, all-freight and executive versions available. Max T-O weight 46,300 lb (21,000 kg).

An-24RV. Generally similar to Srs II version of An-24V, but with a 1,985 lb (900 kg) st Type RU 19-300 auxiliary turbojet engine in starboard nacelle instead of starter-generator. This turbojet is used for engine starting, to improve take-off performance and to improve performance in the air. It permits take-off with a full payload from airfields up to 9,840 ft (3,000 m) above S/L and at temperatures up to ISA+ 30°C. It also ensures considerably improved stability and handling characteristics after a failure of one of the turboprop engines in flight. Max T-O weight is increased by 1,760 lb (800 kg) at S/L ISA and by 4,410 lb (2,000 kg) at S/L ISA +30°C by use of the auxiliary turbojet. An An-24RV was demonstrated at the 1967 Paris Air Show.

An-24T. Generally similar to An-24V Srs II but equipped as specialised freighter, primarily for military duties. Normal crew of five, consisting of pilot, co-pilot, navigator, radio operator and flight engineer. Normal passenger door at rear of cabin is deleted and replaced by a belly freight door at the rear of the cabin. This hinges upward and to the rear, providing a hatchway for cargo loading. An electrically-powered winch, capacity 3,300 lb (1,500 kg), is used to hoist crates through the hatch and runs on a rail in the cabin ceiling to position payload inside cabin. Electrically or manually-powered conveyor, capacity 9,920 lb (4,500 kg), flush with cabin floor. Fewer windows. Folding seats along walls of cabin. Emergency exit hatches in side and in floor at front of cabin. Rear cargo door permits air dropping of payload or parachutists. Provision for stretcher-carrying in air ambulance role. Single ventral fin replaced by twin ventral fins, forming Vee, aft of cargo door. An An-24T was displayed at 1967 Paris Air Show.

An-24RT. Generally similar to An-24T but with Type RU auxiliary turbojet in starboard nacelle, as on An-24RV.

An-24T with enlarged freight door (An-26). Generally similar to An-24RT but with 2,820 ehp AI-24T turboprop engines and a completely redesigned rear fuselage of "beaver-tail" type, embodying a large downward-hinged ramp-door, which can also slide forward under fuselage for direct loading on to cabin floor or for air-dropping of freight. Auxiliary turbojet and electrically-powered mobile winch as on An-24RT. Electrically or manually-operated conveyor, capacity 9,920 lb (4,500 kg), built-in flush with cabin floor. Can accommodate a variety of

Antonov An-24RV, with RU 19-300 auxiliary turbojet in starboard nacelle *(S. P. Peltz)*

motor vehicles including GAZ-69 and UAZ-469 military vehicles, or cargo items up to 59 in (1·50 m) high by 82·6 in (2·10 m) wide. Cargo door width is 7 ft 10½ in (2·40 m). Height of rear edge of cargo door surround above the cabin floor is 4 ft 11 in (1·50 m). Floor sill height is 4 ft 7 in (1·40 m). Max T-O weight of this version is increased to 52,911 lb (24,000 kg). First public demonstration of this version was at 1969 Paris Air Show, where it was referred to as the Antonov An-26 on an identifying board. This example had a bulged observation window aft of the flight deck on port side. It is adaptable for passenger transport and air ambulance duties.

The following description refers to the basic An-24V Srs II, unless otherwise noted, but is generally applicable to all versions except for the detailed differences noted above.

Type: Twin-engined feeder-line transport.

Wings: Cantilever high-wing monoplane, with 2° anhedral on outer panels. Incidence 3°. Sweepback at quarter chord on outer panels 6° 50'. All-metal two-spar structure, built in five sections: centre-section, two inner wings and two outer wings. Wing skin is attached by electric spot-welding. Mass-balanced servo-compensated ailerons, with large trim-tabs of glass-fibre construction. Hydraulically-operated Fowler flaps along entire wing trailing-edges inboard of unpowered ailerons; single-slotted flaps on centre-section, double-slotted outboard of nacelles. Thermal de-icing system.

Fuselage: All-metal semi-monocoque structure in front, centre and rear portions.

Tail Unit: Cantilever all-metal structure, with ventral fin (two ventral fins on An-24T/RT versions). 9° dihedral on tailplane. All controls manually-operated. Trim-tabs in elevators. Trim-tab and spring-tab on rudder. All leading-edges incorporate thermal de-icing system.

Landing Gear: Retractable tricycle type with twin wheels on all units. Hydraulic retraction. Emergency extension by gravity. All units retract forward. Main wheels size 900 × 300-370, tyre pressure 50-71 lb/sq in (3·5-5 kg/cm²). Nose-wheels size 700 × 250, tyre pressure 35·5-50 lb/sq in (2·5-3·5 kg/cm²). Tyre pressures variable to cater for different types of runway. Disc brakes on main wheels. Steerable and castoring nose-wheel unit.

Power Plant (except An-24T with large cargo door): Two 2,550 ehp Ivchenko AI-24A turboprop engines (with provision for water injection; weight of water 150 lb = 68 kg), each driving a Type AV-72 four-blade constant-speed fully-feathering propeller, diameter 12 ft 9½ in (3·90 m). Electric de-icing system for propeller blades and hubs; hot-air system for engine air intakes. Fuel in integral tanks immediately outboard of nacelles, and four bag-type tanks in centre-section, total capacity 1,220 Imp gallons (5,550 litres). Provision for four additional tanks in centre-section. Pressure refuelling socket in starboard engine nacelle. Gravity fuelling point above each tank. Carbon dioxide inert gas system to create fireproof condition inside fuel tanks. Oil capacity 11·5 Imp gallons (53 litres). One

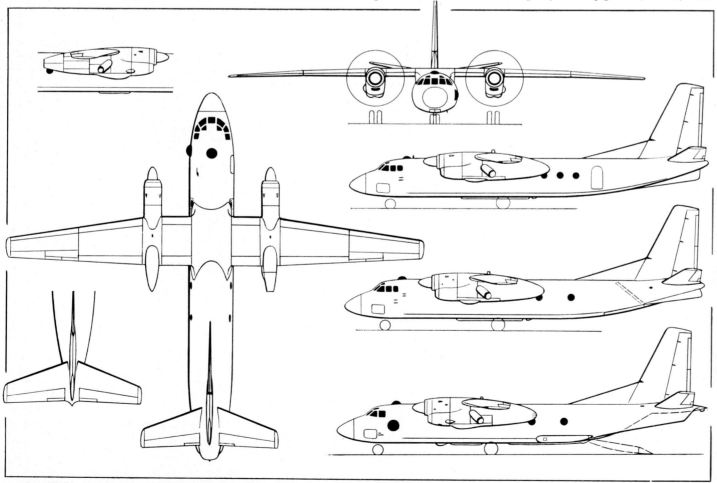

An-24T (An-26) with enlarged freight door, with additional side views of the standard An-24T (centre) and An-24V (top) and scrap views of the auxiliary turbojet engine in the starboard nacelle and the An-24V rear fuselage

Known also as the An-26, this version of the Antonov An-24T convertible passenger/freight transport has an enlarged rear loading ramp-door *(B. M. Service)*

Rear loading door of An-26 lowered as ramp for vehicles (left) and slid forward under fuselage (right) for direct loading into main cabin *(Gordon Swanborough)*

1,985 lb (900 kg) st Type RU 19-300 auxiliary turbojet in starboard nacelle of An-24RV, An-24RT and An-24T (An-26) with enlarged cargo door.

ACCOMMODATION (An-24V/RV): Crew of three (pilot, co-pilot/radio operator/navigator and one stewardess). Provision for carrying navigator, radio operator and engineer. Normal accommodation for 44-50 passengers in air-conditioned and pressurised cabin. Standard layout has baggage and freight compartments on each side aft of flight deck; then the main cabin with 50 forward-facing reclining seats, in pairs at a pitch of 28·3 in (720 mm), on each side of centre aisle and two small sofas for babies (at rear); buffet and stewardess's seat, and toilet, opposite door to rear of cabin; and wardrobes at rear. Passenger door on port side, aft of cabin, is of air-stair type. Door on starboard side for freight hold (front). All doors open inward. The 46-seat version has a removable partition aft of the fifth row of seats, instead of one row of seats. The mixed passenger/cargo version is laid out normally for 36 passengers, with 495 cu ft (14 m³) forward hold for baggage, freight and mail, and rear wardrobe and baggage hold (99 cu ft = 2·8 m³). A typical de luxe or executive layout retains the forward and aft baggage and freight holds of the airliner version but has the main cabin divided into three compartments. The forward compartment contains four pairs of seats, in aft-facing and forward-facing pairs with tables between, and a buffet. Next comes a similar cabin without the buffet, followed by a sleeping compartment, with a sofa, two seats and table. At the rear is the standard toilet compartment opposite the airstair door, and a large wardrobe space.

ACCOMMODATION (An-24T): Provision for crew of up to five, with optional cargo handler. Door at front of cabin on starboard side. Upward-opening cargo door in belly at rear of cabin. Max overall dimensions of cargo packages that can be handled are 43·3 × 59 × 102 in (1·1 × 1·5 × 2·6 m) or 51·2 × 59 × 82·7 in (1·3 × 1·5 × 2·1 m). Toilet (port side) and emergency exit door in belly, immediately aft of flight deck. Folding seats, in two-, three- and four-place units, for 30 paratroops or 38 equipped soldiers along walls of main cabin. Ambulance configuration is equipped to carry 24 stretcher cases and one medical attendant. Cargo loading system includes rails in floor, electric winch, overhead gantry, tie-down fittings, nets and harness. Electric de-icing system for windscreens.

SYSTEMS: Air-conditioning system uses hot air tapped from the 10th compressor stage of each engine, with a heat exchanger and turbo-cooler in each nacelle. Cabin pressure differential 4·27 lb/sq in (0·30 kg/cm²). Main and emergency hydraulic systems, pressure 2,200 lb/sq in (155 kg/cm²), for landing gear retraction, nose-wheel steering, flaps, brakes, windscreen wipers, propeller feathering and, on An-24T, operation of cargo and emergency escape doors. Hand-pump to operate doors only and build up pressure in main system. Electrical system includes two 27V DC starter-generators, two alternators to provide 115V 400 c/s AC supply and two inverters for 36V 400 c/s three-phase AC supply. An-24T has permanent oxygen system for pilot, installed equipment for other crew members and three portable bottles for personnel in cargo hold.

ELECTRONICS AND EQUIPMENT (An-24T): Standard radio equipment includes two R-802V VHF transceivers, R-836 HF transmitter and US-8 receiver, SPU-7 intercom, two ARK-11 ADF, RV-2 radio altimeter, SP-50 ILS with KRP-F glide-path receiver, GRP-2 glide-slope receiver and MRP-56 marker receiver, and RPSN-2AN weather, obstruction and navigation radar. Flight and navigational equipment includes an AP-28L1 autopilot, TsGV-4 master vertical gyro, GPK-52AP directional gyro, GIK-1 gyro compass, two ZK-2 course setting devices, two AGD-1 artificial horizons, AK-59P astro-compass, NI-50BM-K ground position indicator and other standard blind flying instruments, plus three clocks. Optional OPB-1R sight for pinpoint dropping of cargo and determination of navigational data.

DIMENSIONS, EXTERNAL:
- Wing span: 95 ft 9½ in (29·20 m)
- Wing aspect ratio: 11·7
- Length overall: 77 ft 2½ in (23·53 m)
- Height overall: 27 ft 3½ in (8·32 m)
- Width of fuselage: 9 ft 6 in (2·90 m)
- Depth of fuselage: 8 ft 2½ in (2·50 m)
- Tailplane span: 29 ft 9½ in (9·08 m)
- Wheel track (c/l shock-struts): 25 ft 11 in (7·90 m)
- Wheelbase: 25 ft 10½ in (7·89 m)
- Propeller ground clearance: 3 ft 9 in (1·145 m)

Passenger door (port, aft, except on An-24TV):
- Height: 4 ft 7 in (1·40 m)
- Width: 2 ft 5½ in (0·75 m)
- Height to sill: 4 ft 7 in (1·40 m)

Freight compartment door (stbd, fwd):
- Height: 3 ft 7¼ in (1·10 m)
- Width: 3 ft 11¼ in (1·20 m)
- Height to sill: 4 ft 3 in (1·30 m)

Baggage compartment door (stbd, aft, except on standard An-24T):
- Height: 4 ft 7½ in (1·41 m)
- Width: 2 ft 5½ in (0·75 m)

Cargo door (belly, rear, standard An-24T only):
- Length: 9 ft 4 in (2·85 m)
- Width:
  - max: 4 ft 7 in (1·40 m)
  - min: 3 ft 7¼ in (1·10 m)
- Height above ground: 4 ft 1 in to 5 ft 4 in (1·25-1·62 m)

Emergency exit (An-24T, side):
- Height: 1 ft 11½ in (0·60 m)
- Width: 1 ft 7½ in (0·50 m)

Emergency exit (An-24T, under-fuselage):
- Length: 3 ft 9½ in (1·155 m)
- Width: 2 ft 3½ in (0·70 m)

DIMENSIONS, INTERNAL:

Main passenger cabin (50-seater):
- Length: 31 ft 9½ in (9·69 m)
- Max width: 9 ft 1 in (2·76 m)
- Max height: 6 ft 3 in (1·91 m)
- Floor area: 430 sq ft (39·95 m²)

Cargo hold (standard An-24T):
- Length: 51 ft 5½ in (15·68 m)
- Width: 7 ft 1½ in (2·17 m)
- Height: 5 ft 9½ in (1·765 m)
- Volume: 1,765 cu ft (50 m³)

AREAS:
- Wings, gross: 807·1 sq ft (74·98 m²)
- Horizontal tail surfaces (total): 185·5 sq ft (17·23 m²)
- Vertical tail surfaces (total, excluding dorsal fin): 144·0 sq ft (13·38 m²)

WEIGHTS AND LOADINGS:

Weight empty:
- An-24V: 29,320 lb (13,300 kg)
- An-24T: 30,997 lb (14,060 kg)

Basic operating weight:
- An-24T: 32,404 lb (14,698 kg)

Fuel weight:
- An-24T with max payload: 3,968 lb (1,800 kg)
- An-24T for max range: 10,494 lb (4,760 kg)

Max payload (ISA, S/L):
An-24V, An-24RV   12,125 lb (5,500 kg)
An-24T   10,168 lb (4,612 kg)
An-26 (An-24T, large door)
   11,023 lb (5,000 kg)
Max ramp weight:
An-24T   46,540 lb (21,110 kg)
Max T-O and landing weight:
An-24V, standard An-24T, ISA, S/L
   46,300 lb (21,000 kg)
An-24V, standard An-24T, S/L, ISA+30°C
   43,650 lb (19,800 kg)
An-24RV, standard An-24RT, S/L, ISA or
ISA+30°C   48,060 lb (21,800 kg)
An-26 (An-24T, large door), S/L, ISA
   52,911 lb (24,000 kg)
Max wing loading:
An-24V   56·53 lb/sq ft (276 kg/m²)
PERFORMANCE (at max T-O weight):
Normal cruising speed at 19,700 ft (6,000 m)
   243 knots (280 mph; 450 km/h)
Max range cruising speed at 23,000 ft (7,000 m)
   243 knots (280 mph; 450 km/h)

T-O speed:
An-24T   112-115 mph (180-185 km/h)
Landing speed:
An-24V   89 knots (103 mph; 165 km/h) CAS
An-24T
  87-95 knots (100-109 mph; 160-175 km/h)
Rate of climb at S/L:
An-24V   375 ft (114 m)/min
An-24RV   670 ft (204 m)/min
Rate of climb at S/L, one engine out:
An-24V, ISA   275 ft (84 m)/min
An-24V, ISA+30°C, with water injection
   275 ft (84 m)/min
An-24RV, ISA   570 ft (174 m)/min
An-24RV, ISA+30°   295 ft (90 m)/min
Service ceiling:
An-24V, An-24T   27,560 ft (8,400 m)
An-26 (An-24T, large door) 24,935 ft (7,600 m)
Service ceiling, one engine out:
An-24T   9,020 ft (2,750 m)
T-O run:
An-24V   1,970 ft (600 m)
An-24T   2,100 ft (640 m)

Balanced T-O runway:
An-24T, ISA   5,645 ft (1,720 m)
An-24T, ISA+15°C   5,745 ft (1,750 m)
Landing run at AUW of 44,100 lb (20,000 kg):
An-24T   1,903 ft (880 m)
Landing from 50 ft (15 m) at AUW of 44,100 lb
(20,000 kg):
An-24T   5,217 ft (1,590 m)
Range with max payload, with reserves:
An-24V, An-24RV
   296 nm (341 miles; 550 km)
An-24T, An-24RT
   344 nm (397 miles; 640 km)
An-26 (An-24T, large door)
   700 nm (807 miles; 1,300 km)
Range with max fuel:
An-24V, 45 min fuel reserve
   1,293 nm (1,490 miles; 2,400 km)
An-24T, with 3,554 lb (1,612 kg) payload, no
reserves   1,618 nm (1,864 miles; 3,000 km)
An-26 (An-24T, large door), with 3,307 lb
(1,500 kg) payload and 1,280 lb (580 kg)
fuel reserve
   1,348 nm (1,553 miles; 2,500 km)

BERIEV

GEORGI MIKHAILOVICH BERIEV

Beriev is one of a number of Soviet designers about whose early work relatively little is known. He may have studied under Grigorovich, and has been working on water-based aircraft since the late 1920's or early 1930's.

In current production is the Beriev M-12 (Be-12) amphibian, which is in standard service with Soviet Naval Air Force units, presumably as a replacement for the piston-engined Be-6, described in the 1959-60 *Jane's*.

A newcomer at the air display at Domodedovo in July 1967 was the Be-30, a twin-turboprop light transport which is scheduled to go into large-scale service with Aeroflot.

BERIEV Be-30

NATO Code Name: "Cuff"

This 14/15-passenger light transport is intended for large-scale service with Aeroflot, as a replacement for the An-2 on routes which do not justify use of the larger An-24 or where airfields are inadequate for the latter type. It is convertible into a freighter or air ambulance and is described officially as being suitable for geological survey, off-shore and fishery activities, and for use as a sporting or training aircraft.

The Be-30 prototype is reported to have flown for the first time on 3 March 1967, powered temporarily by two 740 hp ASh-21 seven-cylinder air-cooled radial engines. The production version has turboprop engines and was scheduled to enter passenger service with Aeroflot in the Summer of 1970.

TYPE: Twin-turboprop short-haul transport.

WINGS: Cantilever high-wing monoplane. Anhedral on outer panels. Skin panels and spars of main torsion box are described as being made from mechanically- and chemically-milled profile pressings. Detachable leading-edge is of bonded construction. About half of the wing skin consists of thin honeycomb panels stiffened by stringers. Most joints are made by bonding and spot-welding. Double-slotted flaps. Hot-air de-icing system, using engine-bleed air.

FUSELAGE: All-metal semi-monocoque structure, covered mainly with large chemically-milled panels attached by bonding and spot-welding.

TAIL UNIT: Cantilever all-metal structure, with sweptback vertical surfaces. Most skin covering is of thin honeycomb stiffened by stringers. Hot-air de-icing system.

LANDING GEAR: Retractable tricycle type, with single wheel on each unit. Main units retract rearward into engine nacelles. Steerable nose-wheel retracts forward. Low-pressure tyres.

POWER PLANT: Two 950 shp Glushenkov TVD-10 free-turbine turboprop engines, driving propellers of 9 ft 10 in (3·00 m) diameter. Electrical anti-icing system for propeller blades. Provision for interconnecting shaft between engines, to permit drive to both propellers after an engine failure. Engines started electrically from aircraft storage battery or external power source. Four integral fuel tanks in wing torsion box, capacity 2,205 lb (1,000 kg). Hot-air de-icing of engine air intakes.

ACCOMMODATION: Crew of two, or pilot and passenger, side-by-side on flight deck. Electrical anti-icing system for windscreens. Main cabin seats 14 passengers in individual seats (at 29·5 in = 75 cm pitch) on each side of centre aisle. Large polarised window by each seat. Cabin is air-conditioned, with separate ventilator for each passenger. Radio entertainment standard. Compartment for mail and small freight on port side between flight deck and cabin. Carry-on baggage compartment

Beriev Be-30 twin-turboprop STOL transport, designed to replace the An-2 (*Air Portraits*)

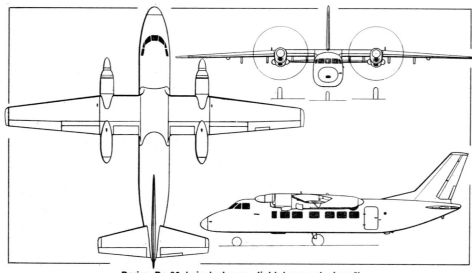

Beriev Be-30 twin-turboprop light transport aircraft

on starboard side, aft of cabin, opposite forward-hinged door, which has a folding stairway. Toilet to rear of cabin. Convertible into all-freight transport or ambulance aircraft with accommodation for nine stretcher cases, six sitting casualties and one medical attendant.

ELECTRONICS AND EQUIPMENT: In addition to standard radio and blind-flying instruments, equipment includes an autopilot and a system that will permit automatic approaches down to an altitude of 165 ft (50 m). A roller-map navigation system is optional.

SYSTEMS: Three-phase AC electrical system supplied by two 16kW 200V generators.

DIMENSIONS, EXTERNAL:
Wing span   55 ft 9¼ in (17·00 m)
Length overall   51 ft 6 in (15·70 m)
Length of fuselage   49 ft 2½ in (15·00 m)
Height overall   17 ft 11 in (5·46 m)
Tailplane span   20 ft 10½ in (6·36 m)
Wheel track   17 ft 0¾ in (5·20 m)
Wheelbase   15 ft 7 in (4·75 m)

DIMENSIONS, INTERNAL:
Passenger cabin:
Length   18 ft 7 in (5·66 m)
Width   4 ft 11 in (1·50 m)
Height   5 ft 11 in (1·82 m)

Beriev Be-30 fourteen-passenger STOL transport (two 950 shp Type TVD-10 turboprop engines) in Aeroflot insignia (*Brian M. Service*)

Baggage hold volume:
Forward	10·6 cu ft (0·3 m³)
Forward (mail)	10·6 cu ft (0·3 m³)
Aft	56·5 cu ft (1·6 m³)

AREA:
Wing area	345 sq ft (32·0 m²)

WEIGHTS:
Normal payload	2,755 lb (1,250 kg)
Max payload	3,307 lb (1,500 kg)
Max T-O weight	12,920 lb (5,860 kg)

PERFORMANCE:
Max cruising speed at 6,500 ft (2,000 m)
    259 knots (298 mph; 480 km/h)
Econ cruising speed
    248 knots (285 mph; 460 km/h)
T-O speed   73 knots (84 mph; 135 km/h)
Landing speed   70 knots (81 mph; 130 km/h)
T-O run   820 ft (250 m)
Runway length required for take-off
    1,805-1,970 ft (550-600 m)
Landing run   430 ft (130 m)
Range with 2,755 lb (1,250 kg) payload and 30 min fuel reserve 323 nm (372 miles; 600 km)
Range with max fuel, payload of 1,984 lb (900 kg) and 30 min fuel reserve
    700 nm (807 miles; 1,300 km)

BERIEV M-12 (Be-12) TCHAIKA (SEAGULL)
Nato Code Name: "Mail"

This twin-turboprop maritime reconnaissance amphibian was displayed publicly for the first time in the 1961 Soviet Aviation Day fly-past at

Latest version of the Beriev M-12 (Be-12) Tchaika maritime patrol amphibian flying-boat, in service with the Red Banner Black Sea Fleet (*Tass*)

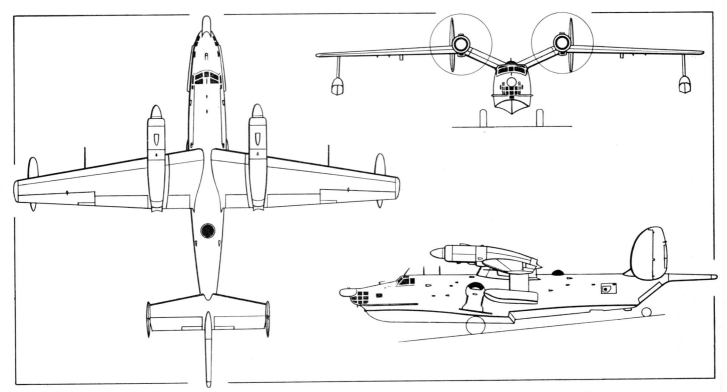

Early version of the Beriev M-12 (Be-12) Tchaika twin-turboprop maritime-reconnaissance amphibian

Early-type Beriev M-12 (Be-12) Tchaika maritime patrol amphibian flying-boat (two 4,000 shp Ivchenko AI-20D turboprop engines)

Tushino Airport, Moscow. Subsequently, during the period 23-27 October 1964, it established six officially-recognised international height records in Class C.3 Group II. Data submitted in respect of these records revealed that the designation of the aircraft was M-12 and the power plant two 4,000 shp Ivchenko AI-20D turboprop engines. The aircraft was also, clearly, able to lift a payload of around 10 tons under record conditions.

The records set up by the M-12 in 1964 were altitude of 39,977 ft (12,185 m) without payload, altitude of 37,290 ft (11,366 m) with payload of 1,000 kg and 2,000 kg, altitude of 35,055 ft (10,685 m) with 5,000 kg payload, altitude of 30,682 ft (9,352 m) with 10,000 kg payload, and maximum payload of 22,266 lb (10,100 kg) lifted to a height of 2,000 m (6,560 ft). In each case, the crew consisted of M. Mikhailov, I. Kouprianov and L. Kuznetsov.

On 24 April 1968, A. Souchko set up a Class C.3 speed record of 298·013 knots (343·169 mph; 552·279 km/h) over a 500-km closed circuit in an M-12. On 9 October 1968, the same pilot set up a speed record of 293·919 knots (338·456 mph; 544·693 km/h) over a 1,000-km circuit and a closed-circuit distance record of 558·599 nm (643·24 miles; 1,035·20 km) in this class.

The M-12 also holds three international records in Class C.2 Group II, for turboprop flying-boats. On 25 April 1968, E. Nikitine set up a 500-km closed-circuit speed record of 305·064 knots (351·290 mph; 565·347 km/h) in an M-12, followed on 12 October 1968 by a closed-circuit distance record of 578·833 nm (666·54 miles; 1,072·698 km) and a speed record of 297·793 knots (342·916 mph; 551·871 km/h) over a 1,000-km closed circuit.

At the 1967 air display at Domodedovo, three M-12's took off from the airport and flew past in formation.

The single-step hull has a high length-to-beam ratio and is fitted with two long strakes, one above the other, on each side of the nose to prevent spray from enveloping the propellers at take-off. There is a glazed observation and navigation station in the nose, with a long radar "thimble" built into it, and an astro-dome type of observation position above the rear fuselage. The nose radar on current aircraft is wider and somewhat flatter in section than that on early M-12's. A long MAD (magnetic anomaly detection) "sting" extends from the tail, and there appears to be an APU exhaust on the port side of the rear fuselage.

The sharply-cranked high-set wing, with non-retractable wingtip floats, is reminiscent of that of the Be-6, and is intended to raise the AI-20 turboprop engines well clear of the water. The

Fuelling a Beriev M-12 (Be-12) Tchaika (two 4,000 shp Ivchenko AI-20D turboprop engines) of the Red Banner Northern Fleet (*Tass*)

cowlings of the turboprops open downward in two halves, so that they may be used as servicing platforms. Propeller diameter is approximately 16 ft (4·85 m). The tail unit, with twin fins and rudders at the tips of a "dihedral" tailplane, is also similar to that of the Be-6.

The tail-wheel landing gear consists of single-wheel main units, which retract upward through 180° to lie flush within the sides of the hull, and a rearward-retracting tail-wheel.

In addition to an internal bomb-bay aft of the step, there is provision for one large and two small external stores pylons under each outer wing panel.

The commentator at Domodedovo said that the unit to which the M-12's belonged was "one of those serving where the country's military air

force began", implying that the aircraft were then in operational service. They have since been identified in standard service at Soviet Northern and Black Sea Fleet air bases and are reported to be operational from bases in Egypt.

DIMENSIONS, EXTERNAL (approx):
Wing span	107 ft 11¼ in (32·9 m)
Length overall	95 ft 9¼ in (29·2 m)
Height overall	22 ft 11½ in (7·00 m)

WEIGHT (estimated):
Max T-O weight	65,035 lb (29,500 kg)

PERFORMANCE (estimated):
Max level speed	329 knots (379 mph; 610 km/h)
Normal operating speed	172 knots (199 mph; 320 km/h)
Max range	2,158 nm (2,485 miles; 4,000 km)

CHKALOV
CHKALOV AERONAUTICAL COLLEGE
ADDRESS: Voronezh

At the suggestion of the Technical Director of the Chkalov Aeronautical College, the students' amateur design group has designed and built a flying scooter. Structural and aerodynamic testing of the prototype was under way in 1969, prior to the start of flight testing.

CHKALOV C-12
TYPE: Single-seat flying scooter.

WINGS: Cantilever low-wing monoplane. Wing section NACA 43012. Dihedral 6°. Incidence 1°. Basic structure of two metal spars; fabric covering. Full-span ailerons. No trim-tabs.

FUSELAGE: Welded steel-tube framework, with fabric covering.

TAIL UNIT: Wire-braced tailplane and full-span horn-balanced elevators are so large that the aircraft is reminiscent of the Mignet tandem-wing configuration. Gap between wing trailing-edge and tailplane leading-edge is 16·45 in (41·8 cm) at root, in plan, but tailplane is placed higher than wings on fuselage, with incidence of 3° 30'; no dihedral. Large vertical fin and rudder. Tail surfaces are each built around a single metal spar, with fabric covering. Ground-adjustable tab in each elevator at root.

LANDING GEAR: Non-retractable tricycle type. Twin wheels, size 210 × 180 mm, on nose unit. Single wheel, size 310 × 350 mm (same as Yak-12 tailwheel), on each main unit.

POWER PLANT: One 28 hp K-750 motor-cycle engine, driving a two-blade wooden propeller, diameter 3 ft 11¼ in (1·20 m). Duralumin fuel tank on each side of fuselage, of same profile as wing-roots.

ACCOMMODATION: Pilot only, sitting astride fuselage on bicycle-type seat, protected by Plexiglas windscreen. Handlebar controls operate elevators and ailerons in same way as normal joystick. Basic flying instruments, electrical and radio switches and fuel valve aft of windscreen.

DIMENSIONS, EXTERNAL:
Wing span	17 ft 8½ in (5·40 m)
Tail unit span	14 ft 5 in (4·40 m)

Length overall	12 ft 1½ in (3·70 m)
Wheel track	3 ft 7½ in (1·11 m)
Wheelbase	3 ft 3½ in (1·00 m)

AREAS:
Wings, gross	72·33 sq ft (6·72 m²)
Horizontal tail surfaces, gross	
	60·06 sq ft (5·58 m²)

WEIGHT:
| Weight empty | 507 lb (230 kg) |

PERFORMANCE (estimated):
Max level speed at S/L	
	56 knots (65 mph; 105 km/h)
Climbing speed	21 knots (24 mph; 39 km/h)
Landing speed	17 knots (20 mph; 31 km/h)
Service ceiling	6,560 ft (2,000 m)
T-O run	50 ft (15 m)
Range 313-334 nm (360-385 miles; 580-620 km)	

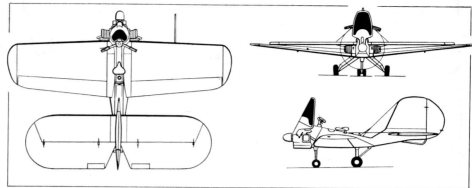

Chkalov C-12 single-seat flying scooter

DEMCHENKO/KHITRY/GUSEV
YURI DEMCHENKO, DMITRY KHITRY, VSEVOLOD GUSEV

In February 1970, it was announced that the three Kiev engineers whose names are listed above had designed a single-seat foldable helicopter named the Tourist, of which all available details follow:

DEMCHENKO/KHITRY/GUSEV TOURIST

The Tourist is a single-seat foldable helicopter which packs into a case for transport. Assembly and preparation for flight take only three minutes, as the rotors and light alloy airframe-chassis are spread by hydraulic pressure. Rubber shock-absorption is employed.

The transport case converts into a seat and seat-back, and the Tourist is powered by a small turbine engine, of the kind used for starting the

engines of large aircraft, mounted to the airframe above the pilot's head and beneath the co-axial, contra-rotating rotors.

Described as being as easy to control as a motor-cycle, the Tourist has a maximum speed of 86 knots (99 mph; 160 km/h). It is said to cruise at a height of several dozen metres above the ground and to need a landing strip only 10 ft (3 m) wide. It is fitted with two-way radio effective over a radius of 50 nm (56 miles; 90 km).

ILYUSHIN

Ilyushin Il-18 turboprop transport in service with United Arab Airlines (four 4,000 eshp Ivchenko AI-20K turboprop engines)

SERGEI VLADIMIROVICH ILYUSHIN

Aircraft designed by Ilyushin and currently in service include the Il-28 twin-jet bomber and the Il-12 and Il-14 piston-engined light transport aircraft, of which details have been given in earlier editions of *Jane's*. The four-turboprop Il-18 transport has been in production and in scheduled service with Aeroflot and other airlines and air forces for many years. It has been followed by a four-jet rear-engined airliner known as the Il-62.

ILYUSHIN Il-18
Nato Code Name: "Coot"

Although the Il-18 is of much the same size as the contemporary Antonov An-10, it is of more sophisticated design and is used on both the international and domestic services of Aeroflot. It was designed originally to carry 75 passengers. The prototype named "Moskva" (Moscow), flew for the first time in July 1957 and was followed by two pre-production models. Production began while these were completing their flight trials, enabling the Il-18 to enter service with Aeroflot on 20 April 1959. In its first ten years of operation by Aeroflot, it carried 60 million passengers and was being utilised on 800 domestic services in the Spring of 1969.

The initial production version was equipped to carry 84 passengers, and could be powered by either Kuznetsov NK-4 or Ivchenko AI-20 turboprops. All aircraft from the 21st built have had AI-20's; a total of 450 had been completed in the Hadinka works, near Moscow, by the Spring of 1966, and production continues.

More than 100 Il-18's have been exported for military and commercial use; foreign civilian operators include the following:

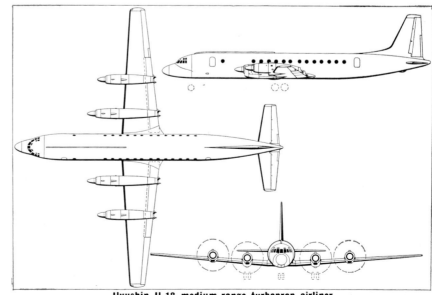

Ilyushin Il-18 medium-range turboprop airliner

Air Guinée	3	Ghana Airways	8*
Air Mali	3	Interflug (E Germany)	16
Air Mauritanie	1	LOT	8
Algerian Government		Malev	8
Balkan Bulgarian Airlines	12	Tarom	12
CAAC (China)	7	United Arab Airlines	3
CSA Czech Airlines	8	Yugoslav Government	1
Cubana	3	*All returned to USSR.	

Ilyushin Il-18 four-engined turboprop transport in the insignia of the Yugoslav Air Force (*N. B. Rivett*)

Military operators include the air forces of Afghanistan, Algeria, China, Czechoslovakia, Poland, the Soviet Union and Yugoslavia, mostly in comparatively small numbers. An anti-submarine version (NATO designation "May") is also in service and is described separately.

All-weather landing systems have been under test on the Il-18 since 1963 and current versions of the aircraft can be fitted with the Polosa automatic landing system, which meets ICAO Cat III specifications.

Current production versions of the Il-18 commercial transport are as follows:

Il-18V. Standard version for Aeroflot, with four 4,000 ehp AI-20K turboprops and fuel capacity of 5,213 Imp gallons (23,700 litres). Accommodation for 110 mixed tourist/economy class passengers, or 90 in all-tourist configuration.

Il-18E. Developed version with 4,250 ehp AI-20M engines. Same fuel capacity as Il-18V. Accommodation can be increased to 122 mixed-class or 110 tourist class in Summer, by deleting coat storage space essential in Winter time.

Il-18D. Generally similar to Il-18E, but with additional centre-section fuel tankage, increasing total capacity to 6,600 Imp gallons (30,000 litres). Increased all-up weight.

The Il-18D is available with a 65-seat layout, equivalent to first-class seating standards. Executive transport versions are also offered.

By the Spring of 1960, the Il-18 had established a total of 12 officially-recognised international records, piloted in each case by Vladimir Kokkinaki. The nine closed-circuit speed-with-payload records have since been beaten by the Tu-114, but the Il-18 retains records for climb to 43,156 ft (13,154 m) with a 10,000 kg payload, on 15 November 1958; climb to 40,915 ft (12,471 m) with a 15,000 kg payload on 14 November 1958; and climb to 39,757 ft (12,118 m) with a 20,000 kg payload on 25 November 1959.

On 6 May 1968, an Il-18 piloted by B. Konstantinov set up speed records of 392·746 knots (452·262 mph; 727·840 km/h) over a 15/25-km course and 380·962 knots (438·7 mph; 706 km/h) over a 100-km closed circuit. Miss L Ulanova and an all-woman crew set up an international straight-line distance record of 4,134·427 nm (4,760·69 miles; 7,661·949 km) on 14-15 October 1967, an altitude record of 44,334 ft (13,513 m) on 20 October 1967, a record for sustained altitude of 42,323 ft (12,900 m) in horizontal flight on 13 June 1969 and a closed-circuit distance record of 4,329·333 nm (4,985·35 miles; 8,023·153 km) on 18-19 June 1969.

TYPE: Four-engined passenger transport.

WINGS: Cantilever low-wing monoplane. Mean thickness/chord ratio 14%. All-metal structure. Three spars in centre-section, two in outer wings. All-metal ailerons are mass-balanced and aerodynamically-compensated, and fitted with spring-tabs. Manually-operated flying controls. Electrically-actuated double-slotted flaps. Electro-thermal de-icing.

FUSELAGE: Circular-section all-metal monocoque structure. The structure is of the fail-safe type, and appears to employ rip-stop doublers around window cut-outs, door frames and the more-heavily loaded skin panels.

TAIL UNIT: Cantilever all-metal structure. Trim-tabs on rudder and elevators. Additional spring-tab on rudder. Manually-operated flying controls. Electro-thermal de-icing.

LANDING GEAR: Retractable tricycle type. Hydraulic actuation. Four-wheel bogie main units, with 930 mm × 305 mm tyres and hydraulic brakes. Steerable (45° each way) twin nose-wheel unit, with 700 mm × 250 mm tyres. Tyre pressures: main 114 lb/sq in (8·0 kg/cm²), nose 85 lb/sq in (6·0 kg/cm²). Hydraulic brakes and nose-wheel steering. Pneumatic emergency braking system, using nitrogen gas.

POWER PLANT: Four Ivchenko AI-20 turboprops (details under individual model listings), driving type AV-68I four-blade reversible-pitch propellers, diameter 14 ft 9 in (4·5 m). Each wing contains ten flexible bag-type fuel tanks in inboard panel and an integral tank in outboard panel, with a total capacity of 5,213 Imp gallons (23,700 litres). The Il-18D has additional bag tanks in centre-section, giving a total capacity of 6,600 Imp gallons (30,000 litres). Pressure fuelling through four international standard connections in inner nacelles. Provision for overwing fuelling. Oil capacity 12·85 Imp gallons (58·5 litres) per engine.

ACCOMMODATION: Crew of five, comprising two pilots, navigator, wireless operator and flight engineer. Flight deck is separated from remainder of fuselage by a pressure bulkhead to reduce the hazards following a sudden decompression of either. Standard 110-seat high-density version has a forward cabin containing 24 seats six-abreast; then, successively, an entrance lobby with two toilets on the starboard side, two large wardrobes in line with the propellers, the main cabin containing 71 seats in six-abreast rows, a galley-pantry opposite the rear door, a rear cabin containing 15 seats five-abreast, and a rear toilet compartment. Deletion of the wardrobes enables two more rows of seats to be installed in the main cabin in Summer, increasing max capacity to 122 seats. In 90-seat configuration, all seating is five-abreast, with 20 passengers in the front cabin, 55 in centre cabin and 15 in rear cabin. Again, two more rows of seats can replace the wardrobes in Summer, increasing the capacity to 100 seats. The 65-seat layout of the Il-18D has 14 seats (5-5-4) in front cabin, 43 seats (4-5-5-5-5-5-5-4) in centre cabin and 8 seats (4-4) in rear cabin. Pressurised cargo holds under floor forward and aft of the wing, and a further, unpressurised, hold aft of the rear pressure bulkhead.

SYSTEMS: Cabin pressurised to max. differential of 7·1 lb/sq in (0·5 kg/cm²). Electrical system includes 8 12kW DC generators and 28·5V single-phase AC inverters. Hydraulic system, pressure 3,000 lb/sq in (210 kg/cm²), for landing gear retraction, nose-wheel steering, brakes and flaps.

ELECTRONICS AND EQUIPMENT: Equipment includes dual controls and blind flying panels, weather radar and ILS indicators, automatic navigation equipment, two automatic radio-compasses, radio altimeter.

DIMENSIONS, EXTERNAL:

Wing span	122 ft 8½ in (37·4 m)
Wing chord at root	18 ft 5 in (5·61 m)
Wing chord at tip	6 ft 2 in (1·87 m)
Wing aspect ratio	10
Length overall	117 ft 9 in (35·9 m)
Height over tail	33 ft 4 in (10·17 m)
Tailplane span	38 ft 8¼ in (11·8 m)
Wheel track	29 ft 6 in (9·0 m)
Wheelbase	41 ft 10 in (12·78 m)

Passenger doors (each):

Height	4 ft 7 in (1·40 m)
Width	2 ft 6 in (0·76 m)
Height to sill	9 ft 6 in (2·90 m)

Freight hold doors (under floor, each):

Height	2 ft 11 in (0·90 m)
Width	3 ft 11 in (1·20 m)

DIMENSIONS, INTERNAL:
Flight deck:

Volume	330 cu ft (9·36 m³)

Cabin, excluding flight deck:

Length	approx 79 ft 0 in (24·0 m)
Max width	10 ft 7 in (3·23 m)
Max height	6 ft 6 in (2·00 m)
Volume	8,405 cu ft (238 m³)

Baggage and freight holds (under floor and aft of cabin: total) 1,035 cu ft (29·3 m³)

AREAS:

Wings, gross	1,507 sq ft (140 m²)
Ailerons (total)	98·05 sq ft (9·11 m²)
Trailing-edge flaps (total)	292·2 sq ft (27·15 m²)
Vertical tail surfaces (total)	193·0 sq ft (17·93 m²)
Rudder	73·52 sq ft (6·83 m²)
Horizontal tail surfaces (total)	299·13 sq ft (27·79 m²)
Elevators (total)	127·0 sq ft (11·80 m²)

WEIGHTS AND LOADINGS:
Weight empty, equipped (90-seater):

Il-18E	76,350 lb (34,630 kg)
Il-18D	77,160 lb (35,000 kg)
Max payload	29,750 lb (13,500 kg)

Max T-O weight:

Il-18V, E	134,925 lb (61,200 kg)
Il-18D	141,100 lb (64,000 kg)
Max wing loading (Il-18D)	93·6 lb/sq ft (457 kg/m²)
Max power loading (Il-18D)	8·38 lb/ehp (3·8 kg/ehp)

PERFORMANCE (at max T-O weight):
Max cruising speed:

Il-18V	351 knots (404 mph; 650 km/h)
Il-18E, D	364 knots (419 mph; 675 km/h)

Econ cruising speed:

Il-18V	324 knots (373 mph; 600 km/h)
Il-18E, D	337 knots (388 mph; 625 km/h)

Operating height:

Il-18D	26,250-32,800 ft (8,000-10,000 m)

T-O run:

Il-18E	3,610 ft (1,100 m)
Il-18D	4,265 ft (1,300 m)

Landing run:

Il-18E, D	2,790 ft (850 m)

Range with max fuel, 1-hour reserve:

Il-18E	2,805 nm (3,230 miles; 5,200 km)
Il-18D	3,508 nm (4,040 miles; 6,500 km)

Range with max payload, 1-hour reserve:

Il-18E	1,728 nm (1,990 miles; 3,200 km)
Il-18D	1,997 nm (2,300 miles; 3,700 km)

ILYUSHIN IL-18 (ASW version)
NATO Code Name: "May"

A few anti-submarine/maritime patrol aircraft based on the Il-18 transport are in service with the Soviet naval air force and have been given the NATO code-name "May". No photographs are yet available.

"May" represents a conversion similar to that by which the US Navy's P-3 Orion was evolved from the Lockheed Electra transport. It has a lengthened fuselage fitted with an MAD tail "sting", other specialised electronic equipment and a weapon-carrying capability.

ILYUSHIN IL-62
NATO Code Name: "Classic"

Announced on 24 September 1962, when the first prototype (CCCP-06156) was inspected by Mr Krushchev, the standard Il-62 is a long-range airliner, with four Kuznetsov turbofan engines mounted in horizontal pairs on each side of the rear fuselage. It accommodates up to 186 passengers and was designed to fly on stages equivalent to Moscow-New York (about 4,155 nm; 4,800 miles; 7,700 km) with more than 150 passengers and reserve fuel.

The Kuznetsov engines were not ready in time for the first flight of the first prototype, which took place in January 1963, with four 16,535 lb (7,500 kg) st Lyulka AL-7 engines installed. This aircraft was followed by a second prototype and three pre-production aircraft. Series production then started at Kazan and Aeroflot introduced the Il-62 on to its Moscow-Montreal service on 15 September 1967, as a replacement for the Tu-114 used previously. Before entering scheduled transatlantic service, the Il-62 had made two proving flights to Canada and more than 50 flights over a 3,640 nm (4,200 mile; 6,750 km) route to the Far East.

Ilyushin Il-62 long-range transport aircraft (four Kuznetsov NK-8-4 turbofan engines) in Aeroflot service *(Martin Fricke)*

The Il-62 inaugurated Aeroflot's new Moscow-New York service in July 1968. It is used on many other routes, including Moscow-Paris and Moscow-Tokyo.

An Il-62 was leased by CSA Czechoslovakian Airlines and was introduced on their Prague-London service on 11 May 1968. CSA announced subsequently that they had placed the first export order for the Il-62, for three aircraft. Delivery of these began in October 1969. Three others began to enter service with the East German airline Interflug in the Spring of 1970, each equipped to carry 150 passengers.

The prototypes had two large blisters under the nose, on each side, over the ends of emergency escape chutes for the pilots. These do not, of course, appear on production Il-62's.

All flying controls are operated manually, but a yaw damper is fitted in the rudder control system. The automatic flight control system is capable of taking over from a height of 650 ft (200 m) after take-off to a similar height during the landing approach. It can maintain a pre-determined speed during climb and descent, and a selected cruising height, and can follow automatically a programmed track under command of the navigation computer.

The IL-62 is designed for an airframe service life of 25,000-30,000 flying hours, including 7,000-8,000 take-offs and landings.

Under development in 1970 was a high-density version designated Il-62M, able to accommodate up to 204 passengers. Brief details of this aircraft are given separately, after the following description of the standard Il-62:

TYPE: Four-turbofan long-range airliner.

WINGS: Cantilever low-wing monoplane. Sweepback 35° at quarter-chord. Extended-chord "dog-tooth" leading-edge on outer two-thirds of each wing. All-metal three-spar structure with end-plate fairings. Each wing fitted with three-section ailerons, electrically-actuated double-slotted flaps and two hydraulically-operated spoiler sections forward of flaps. Trim-tab and spring-loaded servo-tab in each centre-aileron, spring-loaded servo-tab in each inner aileron. Hot-air anti-icing of leading-edges.

FUSELAGE: Conventional all-metal semi-monocoque structure. Frames are duralumin stampings and pressings. Integrally pressed skin

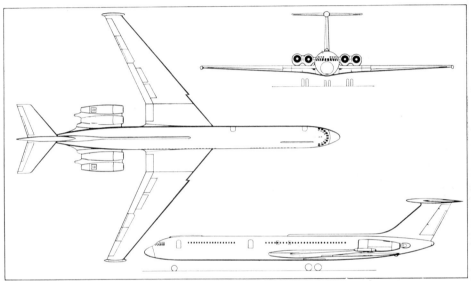

Ilyushin Il-62 long-range four-turbofan airliner

panels at highly-stressed areas. Floors are sandwich panels with foam plastic filler. Nose-cone hinges upward for access to radar. Fuselage width 13 ft 5½ in (4·10 m), height 12 ft 3½ in (3·75 m).

TAIL UNIT: Cantilever all-metal structure, with electrically-actuated variable-incidence tailplane mounted at tip of fin. All surfaces sweptback. Rudder fitted with trim-tab and spring servo tab. Elevators have two automatic trim-tabs and two manual trim-tabs. Hot air leading-edge anti-icing system.

LANDING GEAR: Hydraulically-retractable tricycle type. Twin-wheel hydraulically-steerable nose unit. Emergency extension by gravity. Oleo-nitrogen shock-absorbers on all units. Each main unit carries a four-wheel bogie and retracts inward into wing-roots. Main wheel tyre size 1450 × 450, pressure 135 lb/sq in (9·5 kg/cm²). Nose-wheel tyre size 930 × 305,

pressure 114 lb/sq in (8 kg/cm²). Hydraulic disc brake and inertia-type electric anti-skid unit on each main wheel, supplemented by large tail parachute. Parking brakes. Hydraulic twin-wheel strut is extended downward to support rear fuselage during loading and unloading.

POWER PLANT: Four Kuznetsov NK-8-4 turbofan engines, each rated at 23,150 lb (10,500 kg) st, mounted in horizontal pairs on each side of rear fuselage. Thrust reverser on each outboard engine. Hot-air anti-icing system for engine intakes. Automatically-controlled fuel system, with seven integral tanks extending through entire wing from tip-to-tip. Each engine has its own independent fuel system, with cross-feed. Total fuel capacity 21,998 Imp gallons (100,000 litres). Four standard international underwing pressure refuelling sockets. Eight gravity refuelling sockets.

Ilyushin Il-62 long-range airliner (four Kuznetsov NK-8-4 turbofan engines) in the insignia of Aeroflot *(Tass)*

Total oil capacity 45 Imp gallons (204 litres).

ACCOMMODATION: Crew of five (two pilots, navigator, radio operator and flight engineer) on flight deck. Provision for two supernumerary pilot/navigators. Basic two-cabin layout, and galley, toilet and wardrobe facilities, are unchanged in the three main versions, only the width and pitch of the seats being varied. In the 186-passenger version, there are 72 seats in the forward cabin and 114 in the rear cabin, all six-abreast and all at a seat pitch of 34 in (86 cm). In the 168-seat configuration, increased pitch reduces capacity to 66 in the forward cabin and 102 in the rear cabin. The 114-passenger version has 45 seats in the forward cabin and 69 in the rear cabin, all five-abreast, except for four-abreast rear row by door. A first class/de luxe version for 85 passengers is available, with 45 seats in forward cabin and 40 four-abreast sleeperette chairs with footrests in rear cabin. Passenger doors forward of front cabin and between cabins on port side. Total of five toilets, opposite forward door, between cabins (starboard) and aft of rear cabin (both sides). Electrically powered galley-pantry amidships and wardrobes in each version. Two pressurised baggage and freight compartments under cabin floor, forward and aft of wing. Unpressurised baggage/cargo compartment at extreme rear of fuselage. All compartments have tie-down fittings and rails in floor, and removable nets to restrain cargo.

SYSTEMS: Air-conditioning and pressurisation system maintains sea level conditions up to 23,000 ft (7,000 m) and gives equivalent of 6,900 ft (2,100 m) at 42,600 ft (13,000 m). Pressure differential 9·0 lb/sq in (0·63 kg/cm²). Hydraulic system, pressure 3,000 lb/sq in (210 kg/cm²), for landing gear retraction, nose-wheel steering, brakes, spoilers and windscreen wipers. Three-phase 200/115V AC electrical supply from four 40 kVA engine-driven generators (optional 27V DC system with eight 18kW engine-driven generators). Four transformer-rectifiers and four batteries for DC supply. Electrical windscreen de-icing. Type TA-6 APU in tail-cone.

ELECTRONICS AND EQUIPMENT: Standard equipment includes two-channel autopilot, navigation computer, air data system, HF and UHF radio, VOR/ILS, RMI, Doppler, radio altimeter and weather radar. Polyot automatic flight control system optional.

DIMENSIONS, EXTERNAL:

Wing span	141 ft 9 in (43·20 m)
Length overall	174 ft 3½ in (53·12 m)
Height overall	40 ft 6¼ in (12·35 m)
Tailplane span	40 ft 1½ in (12·23 m)
Wheel track	22 ft 3½ in (6·80 m)
Wheelbase	80 ft 4½ in (24·49 m)
Passenger doors (each):	
Height	6 ft 0 in (1·83 m)
Width	2 ft 9¾ in (0·86 m)
Height to sill	11 ft 8 in (3·55 m)
Emergency exit (galley service) door:	
Height	4 ft 6 in (1·37 m)
Width	2 ft 0 in (0·61 m)
Front cargo hold door:	
Height	4 ft 3½ in (1·31 m)
Width	4 ft 1½ in (1·26 m)
Height to sill	6 ft 3½ in (1·92 m)
Second cargo hold door:	
Height	3 ft 3½ in (1·00 m)
Width	4 ft 1½ in (1·26 m)
Height to sill	6 ft 3½ in (1·92 m)
Third cargo hold door:	
Height	2 ft 3½ in (0·70 m)
Width	2 ft 3½ in (0·70 m)
Height to sill	7 ft 7¼ in (2·32 m)
Rear cargo hold door:	
Height	3 ft 9 in (1·15 m)
Width	3 ft 6 in (1·07 m)
Height to sill	11 ft 10½ in (3·62 m)

DIMENSIONS, INTERNAL:

Cabin:	
Max height	6 ft 11½ in (2·12 m)
Max width	11 ft 5¼ in (3·49 m)
Volume	5,756 cu ft (163 m³)
Total volume of pressure cell	
	13,985 cu ft (396 m³)
Cargo hold volume:	
Underfloor (two, total)	1,380 cu ft (39·1 m³)
Rear fuselage	205 cu ft (5·8 m³)

AREAS:

Wings, gross	3,010 sq ft (279·6 m²)
Ailerons (total)	174·9 sq ft (16·25 m²)
Spoilers (total)	102·7 sq ft (9·54 m²)
Flaps (total)	468·0 sq ft (43·48 m²)
Horizontal tail surfaces (total)	
	430·5 sq ft (40·00 m²)
Vertical tail surfaces (total)	383·2 sq ft (35·60 m²)

WEIGHTS AND LOADING:

Weight empty	146,390 lb (66,400 kg)
Operating weight, empty	153,000 lb (69,400 kg)
Max payload	50,700 lb (23,000 kg)
Max fuel	183,700 lb (83,325 kg)
Max ramp weight	368,000 lb (167,000 kg)
Max T-O weight	357,000 lb (162,000 kg)
Max landing weight	232,000 lb (105,000 kg)
Max zero-fuel weight	206,000 lb (93,500 kg)
Max wing loading	117·2 lb/sq ft (572 kg/m²)

PERFORMANCE (at max T-O weight):

Normal cruising speed
442-486 knots (510-560 mph; 820-900 km/h)
Normal cruising height
33,000-39,400 ft (10,000-12,000 m)
Landing speed
119-129 knots (137-149 mph; 220-240 km/h)
Rate of climb at S/L   3,540 ft (1,080 m)/min
FAR T-O field length:

ISA at S/L	10,660 ft (3,250 m)
ISA+20°C at S/L	12,840 ft (3,915 m)

FAR landing field length:

ISA at S/L	9,185 ft (2,800 m)
ISA+20°C at S/L	9,680 ft (2,950 m)

Range with max payload, 147,050 lb (66,700 kg) fuel, 1-hour fuel reserve
3,612 nm (4,160 miles; 6,700 km)
Range with 176,370 lb (80,000 kg) fuel and 22,050 lb (10,000 kg) payload, 1-hour fuel reserve
4,963 nm (5,715 miles; 9,200 km)

ILYUSHIN IL-62M

This high-density version of the Il-62, able to seat up to 204 passengers, was under development in the Spring of 1970. Dimensionally, it is described as being the same as the standard Il-62, with unchanged wing area; but weights and range are increased, with consequent improvement in operating costs.

WEIGHTS AND LOADING:

Operating weight empty	156,528 lb (71,000 kg)
Max payload	55,116 lb (25,000 kg)
Max T-O weight	363,750 lb (165,000 kg)
Max wing loading	120·8 lb/sq ft (590 kg/m²)

PERFORMANCE (estimated):

Cruising speed
448-486 knots (515-560 mph; 830-900 km/h)
Range with max payload, no reserves
4,480 nm (5,157 miles; 8,300 km)
Range with max fuel and 19,840 lb (9,000 kg) payload, no reserves
5,990 nm (6,900 miles; 11,100 km)

KAI
KHARKOV AVIATION INSTITUTE

A series of light aircraft has been designed and built by students of this institute. Some details of the KAI-17 (or KhAI-17) and KAI-18 were given in the 1962-63 Jane's. A three-view drawing of the KAI-19 single-seat ultra-light monoplane appeared in the 1964-65 Jane's. A photograph and brief details of the KAI-24 two-seat light autogyro can be found in the 1969-70 edition. These aircraft have been followed by the single-seat KAI-22A and two-seat KAI-27 ultra-light helicopters.

KAI-22A

Designed and built at the Kharkov Aviation Institute, this single-seat ultra-light helicopter is powered by a 38 hp two-cylinder motor-cycle engine.

The prototype was displayed in the Exhibition of National Economic Achievements of the USSR in the Summer of 1968, and is shown in the adjacent illustration. It has a welded steel-tube basic structure and a large-diameter tubular boom supporting the two-blade tail rotor. The engine is mounted above and behind the large-diameter non-steerable nose-wheel. It drives a gearbox mounted behind and below the open seat, and a heavy vertical shaft then drives the two-blade main rotor, which has a two-blade stabilising bar at right-angles to it. The tripod support structure for each main wheel incorporates a shock-absorber. Flying controls comprise an overhead cyclic control stick and a collective-pitch lever with twist-grip throttle to the left of the pilot's seat. There do not appear to be any rudder pedals.

A pre-production series of KAI-22As was being built at the end of 1968. An official statement said that they are envisaged as being suitable for pilot training, power-line patrol, fish-spotting and geological survey duties.

DIMENSIONS:

Diameter of main rotor	17 ft 8½ in (5·40 m)
Diameter of tail rotor	3 ft 7¼ in (1·10 m)

WEIGHTS:

Useful load	198 lb (90 kg)
Max T-O weight	485 lb (220 kg)

KAI-22A single-seat ultra-light helicopter, designed at Kharkov Aviation Institute (*Tass*)

PERFORMANCE:

Max speed at 1,650 ft (500 m)
54 knots (62 mph; 100 km/h)
Cruising speed   37 knots (43 mph; 70 km/h)
Service ceiling   6,560 ft (2,000 m)

KAI-27 KHARKOVCHANIN

Displayed in the "Youth Technical Products" section of the National Education Hall of the Soviet National Economy Achievements Exhibition in Moscow, in May 1970, the KAI-27 Kharkovchanin is a side-by-side two-seat light helicopter powered by an M-63 horizontally-opposed two-cylinder motor-cycle engine. It was designed and built by fifth-year students of Kharkov Aviation Institute, one of whom, Miss Zoya Bezuglova, is seen at the controls in the illustration on page 493.

Layout appears to be conventional, with two-blade main and tail rotors and conventional controls comprising an overhead cyclic-pitch control lever, collective-pitch lever by the pilot's left side, and rudder pedals. The structure consists of a flat platform, carrying the bench seat, controls and instrument pedestal at the front, and a tubular support structure at the rear for the power plant, main rotor pylon and tail rotor boom. A tubular skid landing gear is fitted.

The KAI-27 has a T-O weight of 661 lb (300 kg), max speed of 49 knots (56 mph; 90 km/h), ceiling of 6,560 ft (2,000 m) and range of 108 nm (124 miles; 200 km).

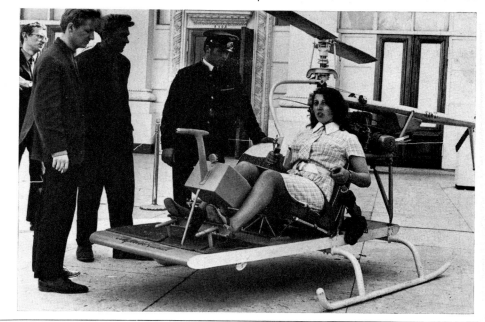

Right: **The KAI-27 Kharkovchanin two-seat light helicopter** (*Tass*)

KAMOV
NIKOLAI I. KAMOV

N. I. Kamov has been a leading Soviet designer of rotating-wing aircraft since the late 1920's and was responsible for the first successful Soviet helicopter, the Red Engineer, in 1929. He became well-known internationally when he designed a series of one-man lightweight helicopters of the "flying motor-cycle" type in the years following World War II.

The Ka-15 and Ka-18 helicopters, developed by Kamov and his design team, under chief engineer Vladimir Barshevskii, were both put into large-scale production and service. Details of them can be found in the 1962-63 and 1963-64 editions of *Jane's* respectively.

The latest Kamov types are the Ka-25 turbine-powered anti-submarine helicopter; a flying-crane version of the same design, designated Ka-25K; and a twin-engined general-purpose helicopter designated Ka-26. All available details of these types follow:

KAMOV KA-25
NATO Code Name: "Hormone"

The prototype of this military helicopter, which was given the NATO code-name "Harp", was first shown in public in the 1961 Soviet Aviation Day fly-past. The two "air-to-surface missiles" carried on outriggers on each side of the cabin on that occasion were dummies and no armament installation of this kind has been seen on production versions of the helicopter, which fulfill a variety of roles and are known to be designated Ka-25. Nato code-name of the production versions is "Hormone".

The Ka-25 follows the familiar Kamov formula with two three-blade co-axial contra-rotating rotors, pod-and-boom fuselage, multi-fin tail unit and four-wheel landing gear. It is powered by two small shaft-turbine engines mounted side-by-side above the cabin, and this has left the cabin space clear for fuel, operational equipment, personnel and payload.

In its anti-submarine version, the Ka-25 operates from ships of the Soviet Navy, including the small carrier *Moskva*. It has a search radar installation in a radome (diameter 4 ft 1 in = 1·25 m) under the nose and a further blister-fairing over equipment mounted at the base of its centre tail-fin.

Aircraft of the Red Banner Black Sea Fleet, based on the *Moskva* have an inflatable pontoon enclosing each wheel of the landing gear, to provide flotation in the event of an emergency landing on the water.

The Ka-25K, described below, is a commercial counterpart of the Ka-25. It can be assumed that the two types are similar in details such as overall dimensions, power plant, weights and performance, except that the military version is a little longer, with an estimated overall length of 33 ft 6 in (10·00 m).

KAMOV Ka-25K
NATO Code Name: "Hormone"

This flying-crane helicopter was shown publicly for the first time at the 1967 Paris Air Show. Instead of the undernose radome of the anti-submarine version of the Ka-25, it has a removable gondola giving an exceptional field of view for the occupant.

One of the pilots occupies this gondola during loading, unloading and positioning of externally-slung cargoes, while the helicopter is hovering. His seat faces rearward, giving him an unobstruct-

Latest version of the Kamov Ka-25 anti-submarine helicopter

Kamov Ka-25K flying-crane helicopter (two 900 shp Glushenkov turboshaft engines) (*S. P. Peltz*)

ed view of the operation, and he is able to control the aircraft by means of a set of dual flying controls fitted in the gondola. This distribution of duty, with one pilot controlling the aircraft during loading and unloading operations and the other pilot controlling it in cruising flight, is claimed to increase the precision and safety of payload handling and to offer a considerable reduction in the overall time required to do a particular job.

The Ka-25K is claimed to combine high payload-to-AUW ratio with good manoeuvrability and minimum dimensions. The rotors, transmission and engines, with their auxiliaries, form a single self-contained assembly, which can be removed in one hour.

TYPE: Twin-turbine flying-crane helicopter.

ROTOR SYSTEM: Two three-blade co-axial contra-rotating rotors. Automatic blade-folding.

FUSELAGE: Conventional all-metal semi-monocoque structure of pod-and-boom type. Detachable gondola under nose.

TAIL UNIT: Cantilever all-metal structure, with central fin, ventral fin and twin end-plate fins and rudders which are toed inward.

LANDING GEAR: Non-retractable four-wheel type. Oleo-pneumatic shock-absorbers. Castoring nose-wheel.

POWER PLANT: Two 900 shp Glushenkov shaft-turbine engines, mounted side-by-side above cabin, forward of rotor drive-shaft.

Accommodation: Crew of two side-by-side on flight deck. Rearward-facing pilot's seat with dual flying controls in under-nose gondola for use during loading and unloading. Main cabin, normally used for freight carrying, contains 12 folding seats for passengers. Rearward-sliding door on each side of flight deck. Large rear-ward-sliding door at rear of main cabin on port side. Hatch-way in cabin floor, with two downward-opening doors, through which sling cable passes from winch on CG.

Electronics and Equipment: Optional equipment includes auto-pilot, navigational system, radio-compass, radio communications installation, and lighting system for all-weather operation by day or night.

Dimensions, external:

Diameter of rotors (each)	51 ft 8 in (15·74 m)
Length overall	32 ft 3 in (9·83 m)
Height to top of rotor head	17 ft 7½ in (5·37 m)
Width over tail-fins	12 ft 4 in (3·76 m)
Wheel track:	
front	4 ft 7½ in (1·41 m)
rear	11 ft 6½ in (3·52 m)
Cabin door: Height	3 ft 7¼ in (1·10 m)
Width	3 ft 11¼ in (1·20 m)

Weights:

Weight empty	9,700 lb (4,400 kg)
Max payload	4,400 lb (2,000 kg)
Max T-O weight	16,100 lb (7,300 kg)

Performance:

Max level speed
119 knots (137 mph; 220 km/h)
Normal cruising speed
104 knots (120 mph; 193 km/h)
Service ceiling 11,500 ft (3,500 m)
Range with standard fuel, with reserves
217 nm (250 miles; 400 km)
Range with max fuel, with reserves
351 nm (405 miles; 650 km)

KAMOV KA-26

NATO Code Name: "Hoodlum"

First details of this twin-engined light helicopter were announced in January 1964, and the prototype flew for the first time in the following year. Kamov described it as an ideal helicopter for agriculture, possessing all the virtues of the Ka-15 (which is used in about a dozen countries) but able to lift three times as much chemical payload, and the Ka-26 entered large-scale service as an agricultural aircraft in the Soviet Union in 1970. It can, however, be used for a wide variety of other duties, including cargo and passenger transport, forest fire-fighting, mineral prospecting, pipeline construction and laying transmission lines.

As can be seen in the three-view drawing, the usual Kamov contra-rotating co-axial three-blade rotor system is retained. The blades are made of glass-textolyte (plastic) materials and are completely interchangeable. They, and the cabin windscreen, are equipped with an anti-icing system, activated automatically by a radio-isotope ice warning device.

The fully-enclosed cabin, with a door on each side, is fitted out normally for operation by a single pilot, but a second seat and dual controls are optional.

The tailplane, with twin fins and rudders, is carried on two slim tail-booms. Short high-mounted stub-wings carry the two podded 325 hp M-14V-26 air-cooled radial piston-engines, designed by I. M. Vedeneev, and the main units of the non-retractable four-wheel landing gear.

The space aft of the cabin, between the main landing gear units and under the rotor transmission, is able to accommodate a variety of interchangeable payloads. For agricultural work the chemical hopper (capacity 1,985 lb = 900 kg) and dust-spreader or spraybars are fitted in this position, on the aircraft's centre of gravity. This equipment is quickly removable and can be replaced by a cargo/passenger pod accommodating six persons, with provision for a seventh passenger beside the pilot. Alternatively, the Ka-26 can be operated with either an open platform for hauling freight or a hook for slinging bulky loads at the end of a cable or in a cargo net.

A version equipped for geophysical survey has flown and is illustrated on this page. It has an electromagnetic pulse generator in the cabin and carries on the port side of the fuselage a mounting for the receiver "bird" which is towed at the end of a cable, beneath the helicopter, when in use. The receiver is lowered by an electric winch and the cable is cut by automatic shears if its traction should exceed the authorised limit.

An aerial survey model is available with an AFA-31-MA camera mounted in the cabin. This aircraft can photograph 2 sq miles (5 km²) per hour at a scale of 1 : 10,000.

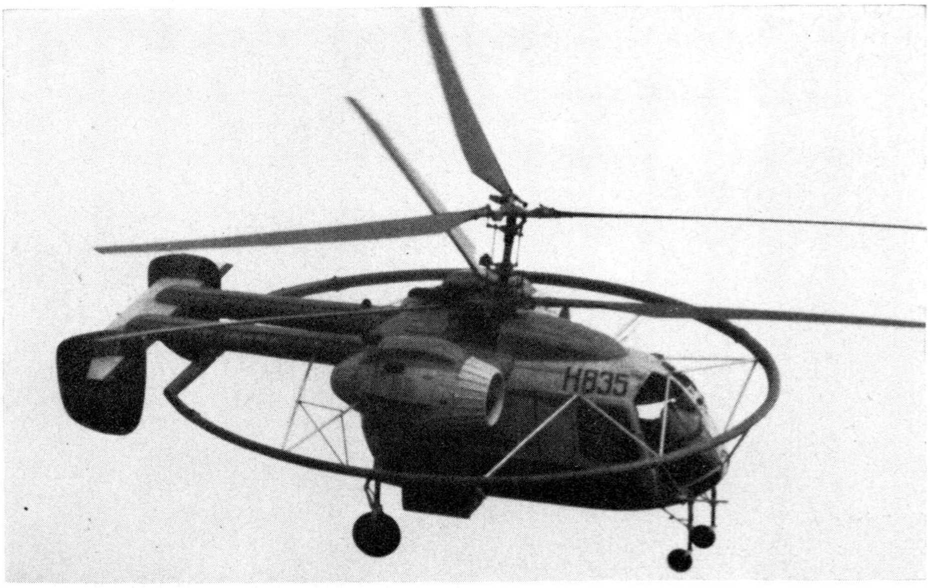

Kamov Ka-26 equipped for geophysical survey duties *(S. P. Peltz)*

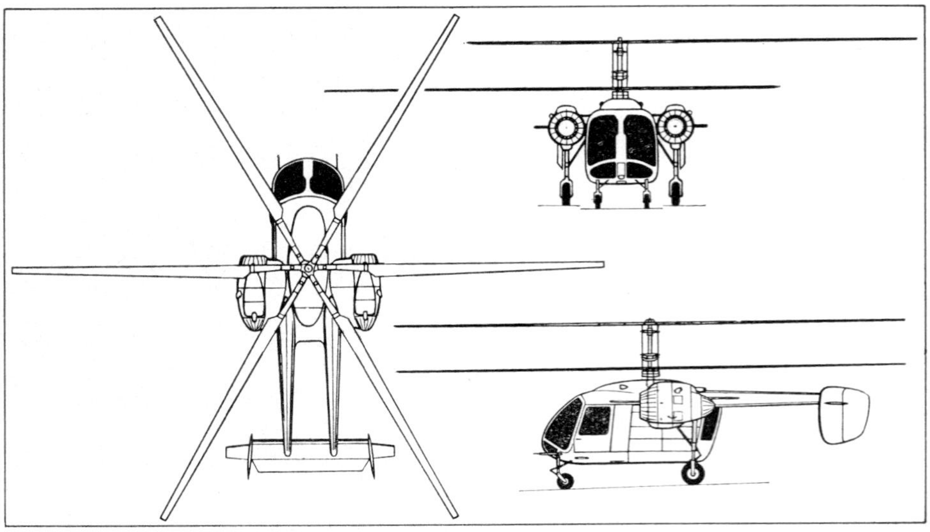

Kamov Ka-26 utility helicopter (two 325 hp M-14V-26 engines)

As an air ambulance, the Ka-26 can carry two stretcher patients, two seated casualties and a medical attendant. A winch, with a capacity of up to 330 lb (150 kg), enables it to be used for rescue duties.

To protect the pilot against toxic chemicals in the agricultural rôle, the cabin is lightly pressurised by a blower and air filter system which ensures that the cabin air is always clean. The flying and navigation equipment are adequate for all-weather operation, by day and night. Both VHF and HF radio are fitted.

Because of its small size and manoeuvrability, the Ka-26 can be operated from platforms on small ships such as whalers and ice-breakers, and a Soviet fishing boat operating in the North Atlantic in early 1970 carried a Ka-26 for fish-spotting duties. This aircraft was equipped with inflated pontoons to permit landing on the water.

In mid-1969, a Ka-26 was tested in Siberia and the north-west USSR in a forest protection version able to deliver six firemen and their equipment speedily to the site of a forest fire.

One of the first export orders for a Ka-26 came from Sweden and this aircraft was delivered in 1970.

Dimensions, external:

Diameter of rotors (each)	42 ft 8 in (13·00 m)
Vertical distance between rotor centres	3 ft 10½ in (1·18 m)
Length of fuselage	25 ft 5 in (7·75 m)
Height overall	13 ft 3½ in (4·05 m)
Width over engine pods	11 ft 11½ in (3·64 m)
Wheel track:	
Main wheels	7 ft 11½ in (2·42 m)
Nose wheels	2 ft 11½ in (0·90 m)
Wheelbase	11 ft 5 in (3·48 m)
Passenger pod door:	
Height	4 ft 7 in (1·40 m)
Width	4 ft 1¼ in (1·25 m)

Dimensions, internal:

Passenger pod:	
Length, floor level	6 ft 0 in (1·83 m)
Width, floor level	4 ft 1¼ in (1·25 m)
Headroom	4 ft 7 in (1·40 m)

Weights:

Operating weight, empty:	
Stripped	4,300 lb (1,950 kg)
Cargo/platform	4,597 lb (2,085 kg)
Cargo/hook	4,519 lb (2,050 kg)
Passenger	4,630 lb (2,100 kg)
Agricultural	4,885 lb (2,216 kg)
Payload:	
Transport, agricultural spraying/dusting	1,985 lb (900 kg)
With cargo platform	2,348 lb (1,065 kg)
Flying crane	2,425 lb (1,100 kg)
Max T-O weight:	
all versions	7,165 lb (3,250 kg)

Performance (at max T-O weight):

Max level speed at S/L
92 knots (106 mph; 170 km/h)
Max cruising speed
81 knots (93 mph; 150 km/h)
Econ cruising speed
49 knots (56 mph; 90 km/h)
Service ceiling 9,840 ft (3,000 m)
Service ceiling, one engine out 1,640 ft (500 m)
Hovering ceiling in ground effect at AUW of 6,615 lb (3,000 kg) 4,265 ft (1,300 m)
Hovering ceiling out of ground effect at AUW of 6,615 lb (3,000 kg) 2,625 ft (800 m)
Range with 7 passengers at 1,600 ft (500 m), 30 min fuel reserve
217 nm (250 miles; 400 km)
Max range with auxiliary tanks
646 nm (745 miles; 1,200 km)
Endurance at econ cruising speed 3 hr 30 min

MiG

MiG-21F ("Fishbed-C") single-seat fighters in service with the Finnish Air Force

ARTEM MIKOYAN AND MIKHAIL GUREVICH

Mikoyan and Gurevich, a mathematician, collaborated in the design of the first of the really-modern Soviet jet-fighters, the MiG-15, which began to appear in squadron service in numbers in 1949.

The MiG-17, a progressive development of the MiG-15, appeared in Soviet squadrons in 1953 or 1954, and was followed into service by the supersonic MiG-19, which appeared in 1955. Descriptions of all three types, and of the E-166 high-speed research aircraft, can be found in previous editions of *Jane's*.

All available details of Mikoyan designs currently in production or under development follow.

MiG-21, E-66, E-76 and E-33
NATO Code Names: "Fishbed" and "Mongol"

This short-range delta-wing fighter was first seen in the Soviet Aviation Day display at Tushino Airport, Moscow, on 24 June 1956. It was identified subsequently as the MiG-21.

The following versions have been identified by unclassified NATO code names:

MiG-21F ("Fishbed-C"). Standard short-range clear-weather fighter, as described below.

MiG-21PF ("Fishbed-D"). Incorporates a number of changes to improve operational capability and performance, including an uprated R-37F turbojet, giving 13,120 lb (5,950 kg) st with afterburning. New forward fuselage of lengthened and less-tapering form, with a larger intake centre-body, presumably housing improved radar to enhance all-weather capability. Pitot boom repositioned above air intake. Two small forward-hinged door-type air-brakes under fuselage in line with wing leading-edge/fuselage juncture. Fairing aft of canopy as on rocket-powered E-66A aircraft referred to below. Cannon armament deleted. Prototype shown at Tushino in 1961 had metal dummy centre-body. In large-scale service with many air forces.

MiG-21FL. Export version of MiG-21PF, as built under licence by Hindustan Aeronautics Ltd in India.

"Fishbed-F". This is the NATO designation of developed aircraft of the MiG-21PF type, which have a number of additional refinements including a sideways-hinged canopy; broader-chord vertical tail surfaces, achieved by extending the leading-edge of the fin; and, in some aircraft, a large dielectric portion at the tip of the fin and an acorn fairing of the type normally associated with a brake-chute at the base of the rudder, above the jet nozzle.

Czechoslovakian journals have referred to aircraft of this type as **"MiG-21SPS"**, signifying the use of blown flaps.

"Fishbed-G". STOL version of MiG-21PF demonstrated in the air display at Domodedovo in July 1967. Described separately.

"Fishbed-J". Latest multi-role version of MiG-21 identified in large-scale service. Equipped Soviet Air Force units in Egypt in 1970. Basically similar to latest "Fishbed-F" but with deeper dorsal fairing above fuselage, giving straight line from top of canopy to fin. This may contain additional fuel tankage. Four underwing pylons, instead of usual two, for a variety of ground attack weapons and stores as alternative or supplementary to air-to-air missiles. Able to carry two underwing fuel tanks and 23 mm gun in underfuselage centre-line pod.

Strengthened wing is claimed to make this version supersonic at sea level.

"Mongol". Two-seat training versions. Generally similar to "Fishbed-C" but with two cockpits in tandem with sideways-hinged (to starboard) double canopy, uprated R-37F (13,120 lb = 5,950 kg st) engine of MiG-21PF and pitot boom repositioned above intake. Cannon armament deleted. Latest models have broad-chord vertical tail surfaces of "Fishbed-F".

When used for record attempts, the training version of the MiG-21 ("Mongol") is designated **E-33** by the Soviet authorities. Records confirmed by the FAI are an altitude of 79,842 ft (24,336 m) set up by Natalya Prokhanova on 22 May 1965, and a sustained altitude of 62,402 ft (19,020 m) in horizontal flight established by Lydia Zaitseva on 23 June 1965.

Alternative designations, allocated by the Soviet authorities to MiG-21's used to set up FAI-recognised world records, are **E-66** and **E-76**.

The basic E-66, in which Col Georgi Mossolov set up a world absolute speed record (since beaten) of 1,288·6 knots (1,484 mph; 2,388 km/h) over a 15/25 km course on 31 October 1959, was powered by a 13,117 lb (5,950 kg) st Type TDR Mk R37F turbojet engine. The E-66A in which the same pilot raised the world height record to

A two-seat training version of the MiG-21, in Czechoslovakian insignia (*Letectvi Kosmonautika*)

MiG-21SPS single-seat fighter of the Czechoslovakian Air Force; this is the version with blown flaps (*Karel Masojidek*)

113,892 ft (34,714 m) on 28 April 1961, from Podmoskovnœ aerodrome, was powered additionally by a 6,615 lb (3,000 kg) st GRD Mk U2 rocket engine. This aircraft took part in the 1961 Tushino display, demonstrating the high rate of climb made possible by its auxiliary rocket-engine. It should not be confused with the short-field take-off demonstration by another MiG-21, using two solid-propellant jettisonable JATO units. This use of JATO was demonstrated by a MiG-21PF during the 1967 air display at Domedodovo Airport.

The E-66A displayed many new features compared with then-standard versions of the single-seat MiG-21 fighter, including a long metal fairing aft of its cockpit canopy, repositioned antennae and a blister fairing above its nose. It also appeared to have twin ventral fins, to each side of the rocket exhaust nozzle (see illustration in 1965-66 *Jane's*).

The E-76, used by Soviet women pilots to establish a series of international speed records, appears to be a standard MiG-21PF. Records confirmed by the FAI are for a speed of 1,112·7 knots (1,281·27 mph; 2,062 km/h) over a 500-km closed circuit by Marina Solovyeva on 16 September 1966, a speed of 485·78 knots (559·40 mph; 900·267 km/h) over a 2,000-km closed circuit by Yevgenia Martova on 11 October 1966, a speed of 1,148·7 knots (1,322·7 mph; 2,128·7 km/h) over a 100-km closed circuit by Miss Martova on 18 February 1967, and a speed of 700·5 knots (806·64 mph; 1,298·16 km/h) over a 1,000-km closed circuit by Lydia Zaitseva on 28 March 1967.

MiG-21's have been supplied to the Afghan, Algerian, Bulgarian, Chinese, Cuban, Czech, Egyptian, Finnish, East German, Hungarian, Indian, Indonesian, Iraqi, North Korean, Polish, Romanian, Syrian, North Vietnamese, Yemeni and Yugoslav Air Forces and are reported to have been ordered by Sudan. The Egyptian air force was reported to have 55 MiG-21C's and 44 MiG-21D's in May 1970, with up to 100 Soviet-operated MiG-21's also based in Egypt for purely defensive operations.

In addition to large-scale production of all versions in the Soviet Union, the MiG-21FL is being built under licence in India by Hindustan Aeronautics Ltd, with an airframe factory at Nasik, Bombay, and turbojet factory at Koraput, Orissa.

A standard MiG-21PF was fitted with a scaled-down replica of the "ogee" delta wing of the Tu-144 supersonic transport, for aerodynamic flight testing and development before the Tu-144 prototype was completed. Known as the "Analogue", this aircraft had no horizontal tail surfaces. It made several dozen research flights, as a result of which modifications were made to the full-size wing. The "Analogue" is illustrated with the Tu-144 prototype on page 517.

The following details refer to the standard MiG-21F ("Fishbed-C") except where stated otherwise.

TYPE: Single-seat delta-wing fighter.

WINGS: Cantilever mid-wing monoplane of delta planform. Sweepback approximately 60°. Slight anhedral. Small boundary layer fence near each wingtip. All-metal construction. Slightly inset ailerons. Large trailing-edge flaps, which are "blown" on the MiG-21 SPS.

FUSELAGE: Circular-section all-metal semi-monocoque structure. Fixed air-intake centre-body. Large dorsal duct fairing along top of fuselage from canopy to fin. Air-brake under centre fuselage of current version. Pitot boom under nose.

TAIL UNIT: Cantilever all-metal structure. All surfaces sharply swept. Conventional fin and hydraulically-powered rudder. No trim-tabs. One-piece all-moving horizontal surface. Single large ventral fin.

LANDING GEAR: Tricycle type, all units of which are housed inside the fuselage when retracted. Forward-retracting steerable nose-wheel and inward-retracting main wheels which turn to stow vertically inside fuselage. High-pressure tyres. Anti-skid system optional. Wheel doors remain open when legs extended. Brake-parachute housed inside small door on port underside of rear fuselage, with cable attachment under rear part of ventral fin.

POWER PLANT: One Type TDR Mk R37F turbojet engine (reported to be a product of the Tumansky design bureau), rated at 9,500 lb (4,300 kg) st dry and 12,500 lb (5,670 kg) st with afterburner in use. Provision for finned external fuel tank, capacity 140-165 Imp gallons (640-750 litres), on under-fuselage pylon. Two jettisonable solid-propellant JATO rockets can be fitted under rear fuselage.

ACCOMMODATION: Single seat. Transparent blister canopy which hinges upward about base of integral flat bullet-proof windscreen. Large blade antenna at rear of canopy (not fitted to MiG-21PF).

ARMAMENT: Originally two long fairings housing 30 mm cannon (600 rpm rate of fire) on undersurface of fuselage. Port fairing blanked off to make room for missile avionics on later aircraft. (Cannon deleted entirely on MiG-21PF). Two "Atoll" air-to-air missiles, similar

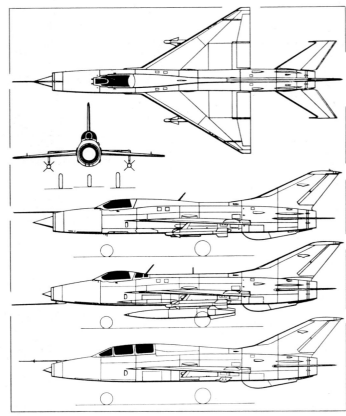

Mikoyan MiG-21PF "Fishbed-D" (upper three-view), with additional side elevations of MiG-21F "Fishbed-C" (beneath it) and two-seat U-MiG-21 "Mongol" (bottom)

STOL version of the MiG-21 ("Fishbed-G") with fuselage intake door open

in configuration and size to US Sidewinder, on underwing attachments. Central attachment for external store under fuselage.

DIMENSIONS, EXTERNAL (estimated):
Wing span	25 ft 0 in (7·60 m)
Length, including nose-probe	55 ft 0 in (16·75 m)
Length, excluding nose-probe	48 ft 10½ in (14·90 m)
Height overall	14 ft 9 in (4·50 m)

WEIGHTS (approx):
T-O weight:
MiG-21F, with full internal fuel and belly tank	16,700 lb (7,575 kg)
MiG-21PF, normal	18,740 lb (8,500 kg)
MiG-21PF, max	20,500 lb (9,300 kg)

PERFORMANCE (MiG-21F, estimated at normal T-O weight):
Max level speed (clean) at 36,000 ft (11,000 m) Mach 2
Max level speed at 36,000 ft (11,000 m) with missiles and under-fuselage fuel tank Mach 1·5
Rate of climb at S/L 30,000 ft (9,150 m)/min
Combat radius (clean)
325 nm (375 miles; 600 km)

PERFORMANCE (MiG-21PF, estimated):
Max level speed at 36,000 ft (11,000 m)
1,152 knots (1,325 mph; 2,136 km/h) = Mach 2·02
Normal cruising speed
520 knots (600 mph; 965 km/h)
Service ceiling	57,400 ft (17,500 m)
Theoretical ceiling	76,350 ft (23,275 m)
Combat radius	302 nm (348 miles; 560 km)
Max range	1,000 nm (1,150 miles; 1,850 km)

MIKOYAN MiG-21 (STOL VERSION)
NATO Code Name: "Fishbed-G"

Three different jet-lift STOL fighters were demonstrated during the air display at Domodedovo on 9 July 1967, which indicates the importance attached by the Soviet Air Force to this technique for increasing the versatility of its tactical units.

One of the three aircraft was a fairly simple adaptation of a standard MiG-21PF, with an additional fuselage section some 4 ft (1·22 m) long inserted aft of the cockpit to house a pair of vertically-mounted lift-jet engines. The air supply for the lift-jets is obtained by raising a rearward-hinged door panel, which forms the top skin of the fuselage when closed. There are longitudinal slots in this upper door and a panel of transverse louvres under the belly of the aircraft, beneath the lift-jets.

The landing gear has a wider track than that of the standard MiG-21 and the main wheels are non-retractable, implying that this aircraft was produced primarily as a lift-jet test vehicle.

MIKOYAN STOL FIGHTER
NATO Code Name: "Faithless"

Second of the Mikoyan STOL fighters demonstrated at Domodedovo on 9 July 1967 was a completely new design, although it follows the delta-wing/swept-tail formula of the MiG-21.

As can be seen in the illustrations on page 497, this aircraft is a single-seater, of larger overall dimensions than the MiG-21 and powered by a single large afterburning turbojet engine, with variable-area nozzle. The fuselage has an ogival nose-cone and is flattened on each side forward of the engine air intakes. These are of the semi-circular type, with half-cone centre-bodies, and there is an additional small inlet door in each intake duct above the wing leading-edge, to provide extra air for the engine at low forward speeds.

The wing is mid-set with the all-moving horizontal tail surfaces positioned a little lower on the rear fuselage. Large area-increasing flaps extend from the inboard end of the inset aileron to the fuselage on each side. No wing fences are fitted.

The main units of the tricycle landing gear each carry a single wheel and retract inward into the air intake fairings. The twin-wheel steerable nose unit retracts rearward and is fitted with a rear mudguard. A cruciform brake-chute is housed in an acorn fairing at the base of the rudder.

Two lift-jet engines are mounted in tandem in the centre fuselage, between the air intake ducts for the propulsion engine. A rearward-hinged trap-type intake box is fitted above them, forming the top surface of the fuselage when closed. There are four rows of longitudinal slots in this upper door and a panel of transverse louvres under the belly of the aircraft, beneath the lift-jets.

No conventional aircraft of this basic design, without a lift-jet installation, has been demonstrated in public. However, the fuselage and tail unit are similar in size and general outline to those of the Mikoyan variable-geometry fighter described below.

This aircraft is unlikely to become a production type.

DIMENSIONS (estimated):
Wing span   30 ft 0 in (9·15 m)
Length overall   60 ft 6 in (18·50 m)

MIKOYAN VARIABLE-GEOMETRY FIGHTER
NATO Code Name: "Flogger"

More advanced of the two variable-geometry fighters displayed at Domodedovo on 9 July 1967, this Mikoyan design is similar in layout to the American General Dynamics F-111, but is a single-seater, powered by a single large after-burning turbojet engine.

Its fuselage and tail unit have much in common with those of the STOL fighter known as "Faithless". The air intake system is, however,

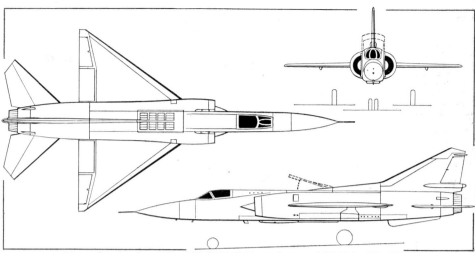

Three-view drawing of the MiG STOL fighter code-named "Faithless" by NATO

This view of "Faithless" shows the louvres in the top of the intake box

Mikoyan STOL fighter, NATO code-name "Faithless", with intake box to lift engines open

Mikoyan variable-geometry fighter with wings fully spread

Mikoyan variable-geometry fighter with wings fully spread

entirely different, resembling that of the McDonnell Douglas F-4 Phantom II, with a basically-rectangular ram intake and a large boundary-layer bleed (splitter) plate each side, forward of the wing-root leading-edge. A large square-cut ventral fin completes a cruciform tail unit, with the all-moving horizontal surfaces mounted high on the rear fuselage. The large tail fin is fitted with a dorsal fin.

The shoulder-mounted wings consist of a comparatively short fixed inner portion and straight-tapered pivoted outer panels. During the demonstration by test pilot Alexander Fedotov at Domodedovo, the wings moved from fully-forward to fully-swept position in about four seconds. When fully swept, there is a larger gap between the wing trailing-edge and tailplane leading-edge than on the F-111.

Other details discernible on photographs include a pair of "blow-in" doors in each air-intake trunk, under the wing-root leading-edge, and a petal-type air-brake on each side of the rear fuselage, under the tailplane. The commentator at Domodedovo credited this aircraft with supersonic speed at ground level and Mach 2 at medium and high altitudes.

DIMENSIONS (estimated):

Wing span:	
fully spread	50 ft 0 in (15·25 m)
fully swept	29 ft 6 in (9·00 m)
Length overall	57 ft 0 in (17·40 m)

MIKOYAN MiG-23 (E-266)
NATO Code Name: "Foxbat"

First news of the existence of this aircraft came in a Soviet claim, in April 1965, that a twin-engined aircraft designated E-266 had set up a 1,000-km closed-circuit speed record of 1,251·9 knots (1,441·5 mph; 2,320 km/h), carrying a 2,000 kg payload. The attempt was made at a height of 69,000-72,200 ft (21,000-22,000 m) by Alexander Fedotov, who had earlier set up a 100-km record in the E-166 (described in 1967-68 *Jane's*).

The same pilot set up a new payload-to-height record of 98,349 ft (29,977 m) with a 2,000-kg payload in the E-266, on 5 October 1967, after a rocket-assisted take-off. This qualified also for the record with a 1,000-kg payload. Photographs of the E-266 issued officially in the Soviet Union identified it subsequently as the new twin-finned Mikoyan single-seat fighter of which four examples took part in the Domodedovo display in July 1967 and which is now known to be designated MiG-23 in the Soviet Air Force.

Its performance in level flight was demonstrated further on 5 October 1967, when M. Komarov set up a speed record of 1,608·83 knots (1,852·61 mph; 2,981·5 km/h) over a 500-km closed circuit. On 27 October, P. Ostapenko set up a 1,000-km closed circuit record of 1,576·00 knots (1,814·81 mph; 2,920·67 km/h) in an E-266, carrying a 2,000 kg payload and qualifying also for records with 1,000 kg payload and no payload.

On three of the aircraft shown at Domodedovo, the cut-off line of the dielectric nose-cone was vertical in side elevation; on the fourth aircraft the nose-cone was covered with paint, giving a sloping cut-off line. This, and detail differences in equipment such as antennae, may indicate that the aircraft were from a pre-production or early production series.

The comparatively low aspect ratio cropped delta wings are mounted high on the fuselage, and have compound leading-edge sweep and anhedral over the entire span. The twin tail fins were almost certainly adopted as being preferable to the single large and tall fin that would otherwise have been essential with such a wide-bodied supersonic design. The fins incline outward, as do the large ventral fins.

The basic fuselage is quite slim, but is blended into the two huge rectangular air intake trunks, which have wedge inlets of the kind used on the North American Rockwell A-5 Vigilante. The inner walls of the intakes are curved at the top and do not run parallel with the outer walls; hinged panels form the lower lip of each intake, enabling the intake area to be varied.

It is likely that the landing gear is a retractable tricycle type, also similar to that of the Vigilante, with the main wheels retracting into the air intake trunks.

The power plant of the MiG-23 consists of a pair of large afterburning turbojet engines (each rated at 24,250 lb = 11,000 kg st), mounted side-by-side in the rear fuselage. To each side of the jet nozzles are low-set all-moving horizontal tail surfaces of characteristic MiG shape.

No pictures of the MiG-23 have yet been released showing it with external stores, and no weapons were visible on the aircraft in the fly-past at Domodedovo. The fact that the commentator referred to these as high-altitude all-weather interceptors confirms the probability that the MiG-23 was designed to intercept fast strike aircraft, possibly with "snap-down" missiles to deal with low-flying raiders. His claim that this

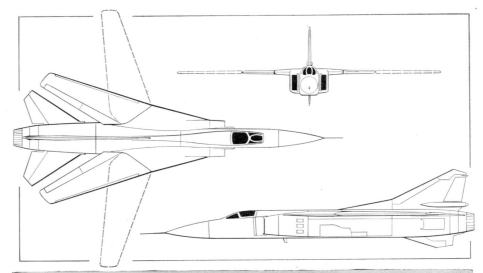

Photo and three-view drawing of the Mikoyan single-seat variable-geometry fighter (NATO Code Name "Flogger")

Mikoyan MiG-23 twin-jet all-weather fighter. The obliquely-painted nose is non-standard (*Tass*)

Mikoyan MiG-23 twin-engined all-weather fighter (NATO Code Name "Foxbat")

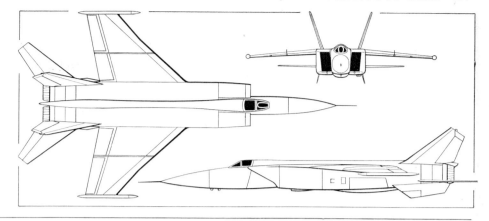

design has a Mach 3 performance is supported by the speed records.

The MiG-23 would also appear to offer some potential in the strike rôle, except at very low altitudes. There is clearly sufficient room between the engines and intake ducts for an internal weapon bay or recessed nuclear weapon, as on the Mirage IV; but the only visible weapon attachments are four underwing hard-points.

DIMENSIONS (estimated):

Wing span	40 ft 0 in (12·20 m)
Length overall	69 ft 0 in (21·00 m)

Mikoyan MiG-23 fighter (NATO Code Name "Foxbat")

MIL
MIKHAIL L. MIL

M. L. Mil was connected with Soviet gyroplane and helicopter development since at least 1930. His achievements were recognised by the award of the Order of Lenin on his 60th birthday in November 1969. He died on 31 January 1970 after a long illness.

His original Mi-1, which was designed in 1949, first flown in 1950 and introduced into squadron service in 1951, was the first helicopter to enter series production in the Soviet Union. It was followed by the developed Mi-3 and by the Mi-4 in a number of variants. All of these types are widely used, in civil and military forms.

The Mi-1 was also produced in Poland, under the designation SM-1.

Subsequent products of Mikhail Mil include the Mi-6, a very large passenger and freight helicopter, the Mi-10 (V-10) and Mi-10K crane versions of the Mi-6, the smaller turbine-powered Mi-2 (V-2) and Mi-8 (V-8) passenger helicopters, and the Mi-12 (V-12), which is the largest helicopter currently flying anywhere in the world. Aviaexport has sold helicopters of Mil design in 38 countries.

All current types are described below, except for the Mi-2, which is built exclusively in Poland.

MIL Mi-2 (V-2)
Described under Polish aircraft industry entry on page 177.

MIL MI-4
NATO Code Name: "Hound"
The Mi-4 is standard equipment in the Soviet armed services, with Aeroflot and with many other civil and military operators throughout the world. Several thousand have been built.

There are three major production variants, as follows:

Mi-4. Basic military version with under-fuselage gondola for navigator. Production said to have started in 1952. Civil freight version is generally similar, with double clamshell rear loading doors.

Soviet films of military exercises, released in 1968, showed a close-support version of the Mi-4, armed with a gun in the front of the under-fuselage nacelle and air-to-surface rockets. A photograph issued in 1970, and reproduced below, shows an ASW version of the Mi-4 with an MAD towed "bird" stowed against the rear of the fuselage pod, an under-nose search radar installation and flares, markers or sono-buoys mounted on the side of the cabin forward of the main landing gear.

Mi-4P. Passenger-carrying version in service with Aeroflot. Has furnished cabin for 8-11 passengers. As an ambulance can carry eight stretchers and medical attendant. This version has square windows instead of the circular windows of the military version, and has no under-fuselage gondola. The wheels are often fitted with spats.

Mi-4S. Agricultural version. Large chemical container in main cabin, capacity 2,200 lb (1,000 kg) of dust or 352 Imp gallons (1,600 litres) spray. Container is fitted with mechanical distributor for dry chemicals, which are spread through bifurcated ducts by hydraulically-actuated fan in duct which replaces the military ventral gondola. Liquids are sprayed from bars mounted aft of main wheels. Rate of spread is up to 4 Imp gallons (18 litres) or 44 lb (20 kg) per sec, with a swath width of 130-260 ft (40-80 m), at forward speed of 32 knots (37 mph; 60 km/h).

All versions are able to be fitted with two large inflatable pontoons, mounted so that the wheels of the landing gear protrude slightly beneath them, for amphibious operation.

In the Spring of 1965, details were given of a series of high-altitude tests made with an Mi-4 fitted with a two-speed supercharger and all-metal main rotor. After engaging the second speed at 15,240 ft (4,650 m), the aircraft climbed to 26,240 ft (8,000 m). It was also operated at an airfield height of 16,400 ft (5,000 m) above S/L.

The following data apply to the standard Mi-4.

TYPE: Single-rotor general-purpose helicopter.

ROTOR SYSTEM: Four-bladed main rotor with hydraulic servo-control, and three-bladed anti-torque rotor at starboard side of tail boom. Main rotor blades were originally tapered, with steel spars and plywood covering; since 1961 they have been of constant-chord all-metal construction. Liquid leading-edge de-icing system.

FUSELAGE: All-metal semi-monocoque structure of pod-and-boom type, with provision for "clam-shell" doors under the tail boom attachment point in freight-carrying version.

LANDING GEAR: Non-retractable four-wheel type. All units fitted with shock-absorbers. Nose-wheels are fully-castoring. Spats optional. Provision for fitting pontoons.

POWER PLANT: One 1,700 hp ASh-82V eighteen-cylinder air-cooled radial engine mounted in fuselage nose.

ACCOMMODATION: Crew of two on flight deck, with under-fuselage gondola for observer in military version. Commercial version carries 8-16 passengers in heated, ventilated and sound-proofed cabin, with door at rear on port side. Aft of cabin are a toilet, wardrobe and compartment for 220 lb (100 kg) of baggage. Ambulance version carries eight stretchers and attendant. Freight version has clam-shell rear doors. Military version carries up to 14 troops, 3,525 lb (1,600 kg) of freight or vehicles such as a GAZ-69 "Jeep," 76 mm anti-tank gun or two motor-cycle/sidecar combinations.

ELECTRONICS AND EQUIPMENT: Radio and instrumentation for night and bad-weather flying are standard equipment.

DIMENSIONS, EXTERNAL:

Diameter of main rotor	68 ft 11 in (21·0 m)
Diameter of tail rotor	11 ft 10 in (3·6 m)
Length of fuselage	55 ft 1 in (16·80 m)
Height overall	17 ft 0 in (5·18 m)
Wheel track (front)	5 ft 0 in (1·53 m)

Anti-submarine version of the Mil Mi-4 operating with the Red Banner Northern Fleet. Note search radar under nose and MAD "bird" mounted to rear of cabin (*Tass*)

Wheel track (rear)	12 ft 6 in (3·82 m)
Wheelbase	12 ft 5 in (3·79 m)
Rear-loading door (freighter):	
Height	5 ft 3 in (1·60 m)
Width	6 ft 1½ in (1·86 m)

DIMENSION, INTERNAL:

Cabin: Volume	565 cu ft (16 m²)

AREA:

Main rotor disc	3,724 sq ft (346 m²)

WEIGHTS:

Max payload	3,835 lb (1,740 kg)
Normal T-O weight	16,535 lb (7,500 kg)
Max T-O weight	17,200 lb (7,800 kg)

PERFORMANCE (at max T-O weight):

Max level speed at 4,920 ft (1,500 m)	
	113 knots (130 mph; 210 km/h)
Econ cruising speed	
	86 knots (99 mph; 160 km/h)
Service ceiling	18,000 ft (5,500 m)
Range with 11 passengers and 220 lb (100 kg)	
baggage	134 nm (155 miles; 250 km)
Range with 8 passengers and 220 lb (100 kg)	
baggage	217 nm (250 miles; 400 km)

MIL MI-6
NATO Code Name: "Hook"

First announced in the Autumn of 1957, the Mi-6 was then the largest helicopter flying anywhere in the world. From it have been evolved the Mi-10 and Mi-10K flying crane helicopters, described separately.

Layout of the Mi-6 is conventional. Clam-shell rear loading doors and folding ramps facilitate the loading of bulky freight and vehicles. Freight can also be carried externally, suspended from a hook on the CG. When the aircraft is operated in this flying crane rôle, the small wings which normally off-load the rotor in flight are removed, permitting an increase in payload.

The stub-wings are also deleted from the fire-fighting version. First demonstrated at the 1967 Paris Air Show, this carries several tons of water in tanks inside its cabin and can either spray this slowly from nozzles or dump it through the hoist cut-out in its belly.

In setting up 14 FAI-recognised records in Class E-1, the Mi-6 has lifted payloads of up to 44,350 lb (20,117 kg). Records still standing in June 1970 included a 100-km closed-circuit speed record of 183·54 knots (211·36 mph; 340·15 km/h), set up by Boris Galitsky on 26 August 1964.

On 15 September 1962 the same pilot, and crew, in an Mi-6 flew at 162·08 knots (186·64 mph; 300·377 km/h) over a 1,000 km circuit, setting up records for speed with no payload, payload of 1,000 kg and payload of 2,000 kg. By averaging 170·33 knots (196·1 mph; 315·657 km/h) on the second 500 km circuit Galitsky also qualified for a no-payload record over this distance.

On 11 September 1962 Vasily Kolochenko and crew of four averaged 153·44 knots (176·69 mph; 284·354 km/h) over a 1,000 km closed circuit, setting a record for speed with a payload of 5,000 kg.

A payload-to-height record still standing to the credit of the Mi-6 was established on 16 April 1959 by R. Kaprelian and N. Lechin, who climbed to 16,027 ft (4,885 m) with a 10,000 kg payload.

Five Mi-6's are reported to have been built for development testing, followed by an initial series of 30 production models. At least one has been supplied to the Indonesian Air Force; many others have been delivered to the Egyptian and North Vietnamese Air Forces.

Six were demonstrated in a tactical missile transport rôle at Tushino in 1961. They landed in two groups of three, after which one helicopter in each group unloaded two dummy field artillery missiles while the others delivered support equipment.

In February 1963, it was announced that an Mi-6 had been adapted to transport the component parts of an oil rig, which was assembled near the town of Zhyrnovsk in the Transvolga steppeland. Other Mi-6's are being used in this flying crane rôle to air-lift drilling rigs to the oilfields of the Tumen region in Siberia.

TYPE: Heavy transport helicopter.

ROTOR SYSTEM: Five-blade main rotor and four-blade tail rotor. Main rotor blades have tubular spars and coincident flapping and drag hinges. Main rotor shaft inclined forward at 5° to vertical. Control via large swashplate. Hydraulically-actuated powered controls. All rotor blades incorporate electro-thermal de-icing system.

FUSELAGE: Conventional all-metal semi-monocoque structure of pod-and-boom type.

WINGS: Two small cantilever shoulder wings, mounted above main landing gear struts, off-load rotor by providing some 20% of total lift in cruising flight. Removed when aircraft is operated as flying crane.

TAIL UNIT: Tail rotor support acts as vertical stabiliser. Variable-incidence horizontal stabiliser, near end of tail-boom, for trim purposes.

Mil Mi-6 helicopter (two 5,500 eshp Soloviev D-25V turboshaft engines) of Aeroflot lowering a four-ton 69 ft (21 m) long TV antenna into position on a tower at Krasnoyarsk (*Tass*)

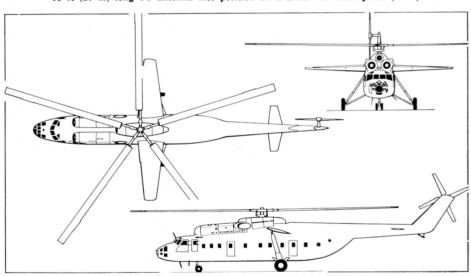

Mil Mi-6 heavy general-purpose commercial helicopter

LANDING GEAR: Non-retractable tricycle type, with steerable twin-wheel nose-unit and single wheel on each main unit. Twin-chamber oleo-pneumatic (high-pressure and low-pressure) main landing gear shock-struts. High-pressure chambers interconnected through overflow system incorporating spring damper, to damp out oscillations at full landing gear loading and so eliminate ground resonance. Main wheels size 1,325 × 480 mm. Nose-wheels size 720-310. Brakes on main wheels. Small tail-bumper under end of tail-boom.

POWER PLANT: Two 5,500 shp Soloviev D-25V (TB-2BM) shaft-turbine engines, mounted side-by-side above cabin, forward of main rotor shaft. Eleven internal fuel tanks, with total capacity of 13,922 lb (6,315 kg), and two external tanks, on each side of cabin, with total capacity of 7,695 lb (3,490 kg). Provision for two additional ferry tanks inside cabin, with total capacity of 7,695 lb (3,490 kg). Automatic fuel-flow control system with manual override. Side panels of engine cowlings are opened and closed hydraulically and are used as platforms for inspection and maintenance of engines and rotor head.

ACCOMMODATION: Crew of five, consisting of two pilots, navigator, flight engineer and radio operator. Equipped normally for cargo operation, with tip-up seats along side walls. When these seats are supplemented by additional seats installed in centre of cabin, 65 passengers can be carried, with cargo or baggage in the aisles.

As an air ambulance, 41 stretcher cases and two medical attendants on tip-up seats can be carried. One of attendant's stations is provided with intercom to flight deck, and provision is made for portable oxygen installations for the patients. Cabin floor is stressed for loadings of 410 lb/sq ft (2,000 kg/m²), with provision for cargo tie-down rings. Rear clam-shell doors and ramps are operated hydraulically. Standard equipment includes an electric winch of 1,765 lb (800 kg) capacity and pulley block system. External cargo sling system for bulky loads. Central hatch in cargo floor. Two passengers doors, fore and aft of main landing gear on port side.

ELECTRONICS AND EQUIPMENT: Standard equipment includes VHF and HF communications radio, intercom, radio-altimeter, radio compass, autopilot, marker beacon, directional gyro and full all-weather instrumentation.

SYSTEMS: Main, stand-by and auxiliary hydraulic systems, each with separate pump mounted on main gearbox. Operating pressure 1,705-2,205 lb/sq in (120-155 kg/cm²). Main 27V DC electrical system, supplied by two 12kW starter-generators, with batteries for 30 min emergency supply. De-icing system and some radio equipment supplied by three-phase 360V 400 c/s AC system, utilising two 90kVA generators. Trolley-mounted APU, consisting of 100 hp AI-8 gas-turbine and 24kW generator, carried on board.

Czechoslovakian troops embarking in Mil Mi-6 helicopter of the Soviet armed forces during exercises, October 1969 (*Tass*)

DIMENSIONS, EXTERNAL:
Diameter of main rotor 114 ft 10 in (35·00 m)
Diameter of tail rotor 20 ft 8 in (6·30 m)
Distance between rotor centres 69 ft $2\frac{1}{2}$ in (21·09 m)
Length overall, rotors turning 136 ft $11\frac{1}{4}$ in (41·74 m)
Length of fuselage 108 ft $10\frac{1}{2}$ in (33·18 m)
Height overall 32 ft 4 in (9·86 m)
Wing span 50 ft $2\frac{1}{2}$ in (15·30 m)
Span of horizontal stabiliser 16 ft $6\frac{1}{2}$ in (5·04 m)
Wheel track 24 ft $7\frac{1}{4}$ in (7·50 m)
Wheelbase 29 ft $10\frac{1}{2}$ in (9·10 m)
Rear loading doors: Height 8 ft $10\frac{1}{4}$ in (2·70 m)
Width 8 ft $8\frac{1}{4}$ in (2·65 m)
Passenger doors:
Height: front 5 ft $7\frac{1}{4}$ in (1·71 m)
rear 5 ft $3\frac{3}{4}$ in (1·62 m)
Width 2 ft $7\frac{3}{4}$ in (0·81 m)
Central hatch in floor: 4 ft 9 in (1·44 m) × 6 ft 4 in (1·93 m)

DIMENSIONS, INTERNAL:
Cabin, at floor: Length 38 ft 6 in (11·73 m)
Max width 9 ft $10\frac{1}{2}$ in (3·01 m)
Max height: at front 6 ft 7 in (2·01 m)
at rear 8 ft $6\frac{1}{4}$ in (2·60 m)

WEIGHTS:
Weight empty 60,055 lb (27,240 kg)
Max internal payload 26,450 lb (12,000 kg)
Max slung cargo 19,840 lb (9,000 kg)
Max T-O weight with slung cargo at altitudes under 3,280 ft (1,000 m) 82,675 lb (37,500 kg)
Normal T-O weight 89,285 lb (40,500 kg)
Max T-O weight for VTO 93,700 lb (42,500 kg)

PERFORMANCE (at max T-O weight):
Max level speed 162 knots (186 mph; 300 km/h)
Max cruising speed 135 knots (155 mph; 250 km/h)
Service ceiling 14,750 ft (4,500 m)
Range with 17,640 lb (8,000 kg) payload 334 nm (385 miles; 620 km)
Range with external tanks and 9,920 lb (4,500 kg) payload 538 nm (620 miles; 1,000 km)
Max ferry range (tanks in cabin) 781 nm (900 miles; 1,450 km)

MIL MI-8 (V-8)

NATO Code Name: "Hip"

This turbine-powered transport helicopter was shown in public for the first time during the 1961 Soviet Aviation Day display. Its overall dimensions are similar to those of the Mi-4, which it supersedes; but the power plant is mounted above the cabin, leaving a clear unobstructed interior, and the Mi-8 (often referred to in the Soviet Union as the V-8) is able to carry a greatly increased payload.

It is in service with both Aeroflot and the Soviet armed forces, appearing in military insignia for the first time at the Domodedovo air show in July 1967. Mi-8's have also been supplied to the Czechoslovakian Air Force.

Five international women's helicopter records for distance and speed in a closed circuit were credited to the Mi-8 in mid-1970.

The original prototype had a single 2,700 shp Soloviev shaft-turbine engine. The second prototype, which flew for the first time on 17 September 1962, introduced the now standard twin-turbine power plant.

Early Mi-8's had a four-blade main rotor, but this was superseded by a five-blade rotor in 1964. In an emergency, the blades and intermediate and tail gearboxes are interchangeable with those of the Mi-4, although this prevents use of the de-icing system, which is electrical in the Mi-8.

The controls of the Mi-8 are hydraulically-powered in the cyclic and collective pitch channels. It is claimed that the autopilot, with barometric height lock, can control all flight modes, including transition.

TYPE: Twin engined transport helicopter.

ROTOR SYSTEM: Five-blade main rotor and three-blade tail rotor. Main rotor shaft inclined forward at 4° 30′ to vertical. All-metal blades. Main rotor blades have flat torsion-box leading-edges. Their drag and flapping hinges are a few inches apart, and they are carried on a machined spider. Controls hydraulically powered. Automatically-controlled electro-thermal de-icing system on all blades.

FUSELAGE: Conventional all-metal semi-monocoque structure of pod-and-boom type.

TAIL UNIT: Tail rotor support acts as small vertical stabiliser. Horizontal stabiliser near end of tail-boom.

LANDING GEAR: Non-retractable tricycle type, with steerable twin-wheel nose unit and single wheel on each main unit. Optional main wheel fairings.

POWER PLANT: Two 1,500 shp Isotov TB-2-117A shaft-turbine engines. Main rotor speed governed automatically, with manual override. Single internal fuel tank, capacity 763 lb (346 kg), and two external tanks, on each side of cabin, with total capacity of 2,433 lb (1,104 kg). Provision for carrying two additional ferry tanks in cabin. Fairing over starboard external tank is extended forward to house optional cabin air-conditioning equipment. Engine cowling side panels form maintenance platforms when open. Total oil capacity 132 lb (60 kg).

ACCOMMODATION: Two pilots side-by-side on flight deck, with provision for a flight engineer's station. Basic passenger version is furnished normally with 28 four-abreast track-mounted seats, a wardrobe and baggage compartment. De luxe version has a saloon, containing a sofa and tip-up table on one side and a table in the centre with three armchair seats around it, plus galley, wardrobe, toilet and baggage compartments. Passenger seats and bulkheads of basic version are quickly removable for cargo-carrying. Standard cargo version has cargo tie-down rings in floor, a winch of 440 lb (200 kg) capacity and pulley block system to facilitate the loading of heavy freight, an external cargo sling system, and 24 tip-up seats along the side walls of the cabin. All versions can be converted for air ambulance duties, with accommodation for 12 stretchers and a tip-up seat for a medical attendant. The large windows on each side of the flight deck slide rearward. The main passenger door is at the front of the cabin on the port side. The rear of the cabin is made up of large clam-shell freight-loading doors, with a downward-hinged passenger airstair door inset centrally at the rear. Hook-on ramps are used for vehicle loading.

ELECTRONICS AND EQUIPMENT: Standard equipment includes VHF radio, four-channel autopilot, autostabilisation equipment, navigation equipment and instrumentation for all-weather flying by day and night, including radio altimeter, radio compass and astro-compass for Polar flying.

Mil Mi-8 (V-8) passenger transport helicopter (two 1,500 shp Isotov TB-2-117A turboshaft engines) in Aeroflot insignia (*Juhani Hakkarainen*)

SYSTEMS: Standard heating system can be replaced by full air-conditioning system. Two independent hydriaulic systems, each with own pump; operating pressure 640-925 lb/sq in (45-65 kg/cm²). DC electrical supply from two 18kW starter-generators and six storage batteries. AC supply for de-icing system and some radio equipment supplied by 30kVA generator. Provision for oxygen system for crew and, in ambulance version, for patients.

DIMENSIONS, EXTERNAL:
Diameter of main rotor 69 ft $10\frac{1}{4}$ in (21·29 m)
Diameter of tail rotor 12 ft $5\frac{1}{2}$ in (3·80 m)
Distance between rotor centres 41 ft 6 in (12·65 m)
Length overall, rotors turning 82 ft $11\frac{1}{4}$ in (25·28 m)
Length of fuselage 60 ft $0\frac{3}{4}$ in (18·31 m)
Height overall 18 ft $4\frac{1}{2}$ in (5·60 m)
Wheel track 14 ft 9 in (4·50 m)
Wheelbase 13 ft $11\frac{3}{4}$ in (4·26 m)
Fwd passenger door:
Height 4 ft $7\frac{1}{2}$ in (1·41 m)
Width 2 ft $8\frac{1}{2}$ in (0·83 m)
Rear passenger door:
Height 5 ft 7 in (1·70 m)
Width 2 ft 9 in (0·84 m)
Rear cargo door:
Height 5 ft $11\frac{1}{2}$ in (1·82 m)
Width 7 ft $8\frac{1}{4}$ in (2·34 m)

DIMENSIONS, INTERNAL:
Main cabin:
Length at floor 17 ft $6\frac{1}{4}$ in (5·34 m)
Width 7 ft $6\frac{1}{2}$ in (2·30 m)
Height 5 ft $11\frac{1}{2}$ in (1·82 m)
Volume: cargo version approx 812 cu ft (23 m³)

WEIGHTS:
Weight empty:
Passenger version 16,352 lb (7,417 kg)
Cargo version 15,787 lb (7,161 kg)
Max payload:
internal 8,820 lb (4,000 kg)
external 6,614 lb (3,000 kg)
Normal T-O weight 24,470 lb (11,100 kg)
T-O weight with 5,510 lb (2,500 kg) of slung cargo 25,195 lb (11,428 kg)
Max T-O weight for VTO 26,455 lb (12,000 kg)

PERFORMANCE:
Max level speed:
Normal AUW 135 knots (155 mph; 250 km/h)
Max AUW 119 knots (137 mph; 220 km/h)
With 5,510 lb (2,500 kg) of slung cargo 97 knots (112 mph; 180 km/h)
Max cruising speed:
Normal AUW 122 knots (140 mph; 225 km/h)
Max AUW 97 knots (112 mph; 180 km/h)
Service ceiling 14,760 ft (4,500 m)
Hovering ceiling in ground effect at normal AUW 5,900 ft (1,800 m)
Hovering ceiling out of ground effect at normal AUW 2,625 ft (800 m)
Ranges:
with 28 passengers, 1,235 lb (560 kg) of cargo, 30 min fuel reserve 194 nm (223 miles; 360 km)
with 6,615 lb (3,000 kg) of cargo 229 nm (264 miles; 425 km)
with ferry tankage 507 nm (584 miles; 940 km)

MIL MI-10 (V-10)

NATO Code Name: "Harke"

This flying crane development of the Mi-6 was first demonstrated at the 1961 Soviet Aviation Day display at Tushino. Above the line of the cabin windows the two helicopters are almost identical, but the depth of the fuselage is reduced considerably on the Mi-10, and the tail-boom is deepened so that the flattened under-surface runs unbroken to the tail. The Mi-10 also lacks the small fixed wings of the Mi-6.

Items which are interchangeable between the Mi-6 and Mi-10 include the power plant, transmission system and reduction gearboxes, swashplate assembly, main and tail rotors, control system and most items of equipment.

The tall long-stroke quadricycle landing gear with wheel track exceeding 19 ft 8 in (6·0 m) and clearance under the fuselage of 12 ft $3\frac{1}{2}$ in (3·75 m) with the aircraft fully loaded, enables the Mi-10 to taxi over a load it is to carry and to accommodate loads as bulky as a prefabricated building.

Use is made of interchangeable wheeled cargo platforms which are held in place by hydraulic grips controllable from either the cockpit or a remote panel. Using these grips without a platform, cargoes up to 65 ft 7 in (20 m) long, 32 ft $9\frac{1}{2}$ in (10 m) wide and 10 ft 2 in (3·1 m) high can be lifted and secured in $1\frac{1}{2}$ to 2 minutes. The cabin can accommodate additional freight or passengers.

A closed-circuit TV system, with cameras scanning forward from under the rear fuselage and downward through the sling hatch, is used to observe the payload and main landing gear, touchdown being by this reference. The TV system replaces the retractable undernose "dustbin" fitted originally.

Mil Mi-10 flying crane helicopter (two 5,500 shp Soloviev D-25V shaft-turbine engines) *(Martin Fricke)*

The power of the Soloviev shaft-turbine engines remains constant up to 9,850 ft (3,000 m) and to an ambient air temperature of 40°C at sea level. The aircraft will maintain level flight on one engine. Full navigation equipment and an autopilot permit all-weather operation, by day and night.

In October 1961 the prototype set up two international helicopter records (since beaten) by lifting a payload of 33,302 lb (15,103 kg) to a height of 7,631 ft (2,326 m). Current international payload-height records in this category are held by the developed Mi-10K, which is described separately.

The following details refer to the standard Mi-10, which is reported to be in service with both Aeroflot and the Soviet armed forces and is also available for export. One was purchased by Petroleum Helicopters (USA) for servicing oil rigs.

TYPE: Heavy flying-crane helicopter.

ROTOR SYSTEM: Same as for Mi-6, except that main rotor shaft is inclined forward at an angle of only 45′.

FUSELAGE: Conventional all-metal semi-monocoque structure.

TAIL UNIT: Same as for Mi-6.

LANDING GEAR: Non-retractable quadricycle type, with twin wheels on each unit. All units fitted with oleo-pneumatic shock-absorbers. Telescopic main legs. Main wheels size 1,230 × 260 mm, each with brake. Levered-suspension castoring nose units. Nose-wheels size 950 × 250. All landing gear struts are faired. The port nose gear fairing incorporates steps to the crew entry door. Despite the height of the gear, the Mi-10 can make stable landing and take-off runs at speeds up to 54 knots (62 mph; 100 km/h).

POWER PLANT: Two 5,500 shp Soloviev D-25V shaft-turbine engines, mounted side-by-side above cabin, forward of main rotor drive-shaft. Single fuel tank, capacity 1,290 lb (585 kg) in fuselage, and two external tanks, on sides of cabin, with total capacity of 12,357 lb (5,605 kg). Provision for carrying two auxiliary tanks in cabin, to give total fuel capacity of 18,210 lb (8,260 kg). Engine cowling side panels (opened and closed hydraulically) can be used as maintenance platforms when open.

ACCOMMODATION: Two pilots and flight engineer accommodated on flight deck, which has bulged side windows to provide an improved downward view. Flight deck is heated and ventilated and has provision for oxygen equipment. Crew door is immediately aft of flight deck on port side. Main cabin can be used for freight and/or passengers, 28 tip-up seats being installed along the side walls. Freight is loaded into this cabin through a door on the starboard side, aft of the rear landing gear struts, with the aid of a boom and 440-lb (200 kg) capacity electric winch. In addition to the cargo platform described above, the Mi-10 has external sling gear as standard equipment. This can be used in conjunction with a winch controlled from a portable control panel inside the cabin. The winch can also be used to raise loads of up to 1,100 lb (500 kg) while the aircraft is hovering on rescue and other duties, via a hatch in the cabin floor.

ELECTRONICS, EQUIPMENT AND SYSTEMS: Generally as for Mi-6, including APU.

DIMENSIONS, EXTERNAL:
Diameter of main rotor 114 ft 10 in (35·00 m)
Diameter of tail rotor 20 ft 8 in (6·30 m)
Distance between rotor centres 69 ft 8 in (21·24 m)
Length overall, rotors turning 137 ft $5\frac{1}{2}$ in (41·89 m)
Length of fuselage 107 ft $9\frac{3}{4}$ in (32·86 m)
Height overall 32 ft 6 in (9·90 m)
Wheel track (c/l shock-struts):
nose wheels 19 ft $8\frac{3}{4}$ in (6·01 m)
main wheels 22 ft $8\frac{1}{2}$ in (6·92 m)
Wheelbase 27 ft $2\frac{1}{2}$ in (8·29 m)
Cargo platform:
Length 28 ft 0 in (8·53 m)
Width 11 ft $7\frac{1}{4}$ in (3·54 m)
Crew door:
Height 4 ft $5\frac{1}{4}$ in (1·35 m)
Width 2 ft $6\frac{3}{4}$ in (0·78 m)
Freight loading door:
Height 5 ft $1\frac{1}{2}$ in (1·56 m)
Width 4 ft $1\frac{1}{2}$ in (1·26 m)
Cabin floor hatch:
Diameter 3 ft $3\frac{1}{2}$ in (1·00 m)

DIMENSIONS, INTERNAL:
Cabin: Length 46 ft $0\frac{3}{4}$ in (14·04 m)
Width 8 ft $2\frac{1}{2}$ in (2·50 m)
Height 5 ft 6 in (1·68 m)
Volume aprox 2,120 cu ft (60 m³)

WEIGHTS:
Weight empty 59,525 lb (27,000 kg)
Max payload on platform, incl platform 33,070 lb (15,000 kg)
Max slung payload 17,635 lb (8,000 kg)
T-O weight with slung cargo 83,775 lb (38,000 kg)
Normal T-O weight 95,790 lb (43,450 kg)

PERFORMANCE:
Max cruising speed with platform cargo 119 knots (137 mph; 220 km/h)
Cruising speed with slung cargo 97 knots (112 mph; 180 km/h)
Service ceiling (limited) 9,850 ft (3,000 m)
Range, standard tanks, 5% reserve:
Slung payload 251 nm (289 miles; 465 km)
Platform payload 231 nm (267 miles; 430 km)
Range, with auxiliary tanks, 5% reserve:
Slung payload 344 nm (397 miles; 640 km)
Platform payload 317 nm (366 miles; 590 km)

MIL MI-10K

First displayed publicly in Moscow on 26 March 1966, the Mi-10K is a development of the Mi-10 with a number of important design changes, most apparent of which is a reduction in the height of the landing gear.

It can be operated by a crew of only two pilots. This is made possible by the provision of an additional cockpit gondola under the front fuselage, with full flying controls and a rearward-facing seat. By occupying this seat, one of the pilots can control the aircraft in hovering flight and, at the same time, have an unrestricted view of cargo loading, unloading and hoisting, which are also under his control.

Mil Mi-10K, the short-landing-gear version of the Mi-10 flying crane helicopter with additional piloting position under nose *(B. M. Service)*

In the Mi-10K, the maximum slung payload is increased to 24,250 lb (11,000 kg) and is expected to go up to 30,865 lb (14,000 kg) when the Soloviev D-25V shaft-turbines can be uprated to 6,500 shp each, in due course. Fuel capacity of the Mi-10K, in standard internal and external tanks, is 1,980 Imp gallons (9,000 litres).

On 26 May 1965 an Mi-10K, piloted by V. Kolochenko, set up an official record in Class E-1 by lifting a payload of 5,000 kg to a height of 23,461 ft (7,151 m). Two days later, G. Alferov, with a crew of three, climbed to a height of 9,318 ft (2,840 m) in an Mi-10K, with a payload of 55,347 lb (25,105 kg). This set up four records (since beaten by the Mil Mi-12), for the greatest payload lifted to 2,000 m and the greatest height achieved with payloads of 15,000, 20,000 and 25,000 kg. The aircraft used may have been the cleaned-up experimental machine, with faired tricycle landing gear, that was illustrated in the 1966-67 *Jane's*.

MIL Mi-12 (V-12)

NATO Code Name: "Homer"

First confirmation of the existence of this aircraft was given in a statement in March 1969 that it had set a number of payload-to-height records which exceeded by some 20% the records established previously by the Mi-6 and Mi-10K.

Flying from an airfield near Moscow on 22 February, the Mi-12 (designated V-12 in the official statement) climbed at a rate of more than 600 ft (180 m) min to an altitude of 9,682 ft (2,951 m) carrying a payload of 68,410 lb (31,030 kg). This represented new records for maximum load lifted to a height of 2,000 m, and height with payloads of 20,000, 25,000 and 30,000 kg. The pilot was V. Kolochenko who, on 6 August 1969, easily beat his own record for payload raised to 2,000 m by lifting 88,636 lb (40,204·5 kg) to a height of 7,398 ft (2,255 m). This also covered new payload-to-height records with 35,000 kg and 40,000 kg. The Mi-12 flew from Podmoskovnoie and carried a crew of six, made up of pilot, co-pilot, navigator, engineer, radio operator and electrician.

The Mi-12 utilises two power-plant/rotor packages similar to those of the Mi-6/Mi-10 series, mounted at the tips of its much-braced high-set wings, which have considerable dihedral and inverse taper to give increased chord from root to tip. The rating of each D-25 engine is stated officially to be 6,500 eshp, and the rotors are opposite-rotating to counter torque.

The general appearance of the Mi-12 is shown in the adjacent illustration of a model that was made for Mikhail Mil. The prototype has twin wheels on each landing gear unit.

DIMENSIONS (estimated):
Span over rotor tips	240 ft 0 in (73 m)
Length of fuselage	200 ft 6 in (61 m)

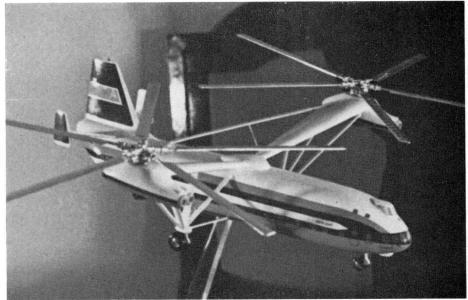

Model of Mil Mi-12 (V-12) helicopter built for the late Mikhail Mil *(Tass)*

Retouched photograph of the Mi-12 (V-12), largest helicopter yet flown. The rotors were not fitted at this stage

MOSCOW AVIATION INSTITUTE

The Students' Design Office of the Sergo Ordzhonikidze Aviation Institute in Moscow is responsible for a small single-seat sporting aircraft named the Kwant, which was displayed outside the People's Education Pavilion at the USSR Economic Achievements Exhibition in Moscow in October 1967.

Earlier, students of this Institute participated in design of the Yak-18 and have also designed and built a number of sailplanes that won awards at exhibitions of work by young people. They are now working on a gyroplane intended for duties such as geological survey and forest fire patrol.

MAI KWANT

As can be seen in the illustration on page 504, this small single-seat aerobatic and sporting aircraft is modelled on the radial-engined fighters of World War II. It is a cantilever low-wing monoplane, with cantilever tail unit, inward-retracting main landing gear and enclosed transparent cockpit canopy. The 300 hp radial engine drives a two-blade propeller. Designed maximum speed is 226 knots (260 mph; 420 km/h).

Kwant single-seat aerobatic aircraft built at the Sergo Ordzhonikidze Aviation Institute

MYASISHCHEV

The developed version of the Myasishchev Mya-4 four-jet maritime reconnaissance bomber known by the official Soviet designation 201-M
(Aviation Week and Space Technology)

VLADIMIR M. MYASISHCHEV

Although Myasishchev's work has been little publicised, he is believed to have been in charge of his own design bureau for many years and to have been responsible for the development of several important types. They include the four-jet Mya-4 bomber (known in the West by the code name of "Bison") which remains in service for maritime reconnaissance and as a flight refuelling tanker carrying a hose-reel unit in its bomb-bay.

The aircraft referred to by the Soviet authorities as the 201-M when it set up a number of officially-recognised records, in 1959, is now identified as a development of the "Bison" and is described briefly below.

Nominated in 1958 as a deputy of the Supreme Soviet, Myasishchev was reported to have designed a new long-range four-jet heavy bomber to replace the "Bison". This aircraft is believed to be the delta-wing type which was allocated the NATO code name of "Bounder" and was described in the 1964-65 *Jane's*. Changing requirements limited "Bounder" to a research rôle.

Myasishchev is engaged on development work connected with supersonic transports.

MYASISHCHEV 201-M
NATO Code Name: "Bison"

Types displayed publicly for the first time in the static park at Domodedovo in July 1967 included the aircraft that was referred to as the 201-M when it set up seven officially-confirmed payload-to-height records in 1959. It has proved to be a development of the familiar Mya-4 ("Bison") long-range strategic bomber, maritime-reconnaissance and flight refuelling tanker aircraft.

Main externally-evident change is to the fuselage nose, which has been extended and redesigned to suit the aircraft better for the duties of shipping and radar reconnaissance. A large search radar, of the kind seen on maritime versions of the Tu-20 and Tu-16, is faired neatly into the new nose, aft of a sturdy flight refuelling probe. As on the

Myasishchev Mya-4 (NATO "Bison") maritime reconnaissance aircraft being "escorted" by Lightnings of No. 74 Squadron, RAF, during a sortie near the UK

standard Mya-4, a prone bombing/observation position, with optically-flat glass panels, is installed below and to the rear of the radar, with further small windows and a domed observation (and probably gunnery aiming) window on each side. Extensive radome and equipment bulges can be seen under the nose and centre fuselage, also as on the standard maritime Mya-4. The tail gun turret is retained.

There is no evidence that this aircraft is a production version.

When the 201-M set up its records, it was said to be powered by four Type D-15 turbojet engines, each rated at 28,660 lb (13,000 kg) st.

The first record was established on 16 September 1959 when, piloted by Nicolai Gorianov and Anatoli Lipko, with a crew of five, the 201-M reached a height of 50,253 ft (15,317 m) with a 10,000 kg payload. On 29 October 1959, piloted by Boris Stepanov and Boris Iumachev, with crew of five, it established a height record of 43,048 ft (13,121 m) with payloads of 35,000, 40,000, 45,000, 50,000 and 55,000 kg, and a record for the greatest payload (121,480 lb=55,220 kg) carried to a height of 2,000 m (6,560 ft).

A further series of records was set up at about the same time by one of the above pilots in an aircraft referred to as the 103-M. This also was described as a mid-wing monoplane with four D-15 engines, and was probably similar to the 201-M.

Flown by Anatoli Lipko, and a crew of seven, the 103-M set up seven speed-with-payload records, by carrying a payload of 59,525 lb (27,000 kg) over a 1,000 km closed circuit at 554·70 knots (638·75 mph; 1,028·664 km/h), on 30 October 1959. The records were for payloads of 1,000, 2,000, 5,000, 10,000, 15,000, 20,000 and 25,000 kg carried over 1,000 km. The records with 1,000 kg and 2,000 kg payload have since been beaten.

The developed version of the Myasishchev Mya-4 four-jet long-range bomber known by the official Soviet designation 201-M   (*Tass*)

SUKHOI
PAVEL OSIPOVICH SUKHOI

Sukhoi is not well-known. He helped to design the ANT-25 and had a share in the construction of the "Rodina" before World War II and his Su-2 attack aeroplane was used in the war. He was also responsible for one of the jet aircraft in the 1947 Soviet Aviation Day display.

Nearly a decade later, on 24 June 1956, there appeared over Tushino new swept-wing and delta-wing fighters from Sukhoi's design team. Both aircraft have since entered squadron service with the Soviet Air Force and its allies and are described briefly below, together with new Sukhoi designs seen for the first time in the 1967 display at Domodedovo.

SUKHOI SU-7B
NATO Code Names: "Fitter" and "Moujik"

This single-seat ground attack fighter was first seen in prototype form during the 1956 Soviet Aviation Day display at Tushino and appeared in formations of up to 21 aircraft at the 1961 Tushino display. It has since become the standard tactical fighter-bomber of the Soviet Air Force and has been supplied to other countries, including Cuba, Czechoslovakia, Egypt, East Germany, Hungary, India, Poland and North Vietnam.

The fuselage and tail unit of "Fitter" appear to be identical with those of the delta-wing "Fishpot". Its wings are swept back at an

Sukhoi Su-7B close-support fighter in Czechoslovakian service (*Letectvi Kosmonautika*)

Sukhoi Su-7B single-seat ground attack fighters of the Indian Air Force

angle of approximately 60° and each is fitted with two boundary-layer fences, at approximately mid-span and immediately inboard of the tip. The wing-root chord is extended, giving a straight trailing-edge on the inboard section of each wing. Very large area-increasing flaps are fitted, extending over the entire trailing-edge of each wing from the root to the inboard end of the aileron.

"Fitter" has attachments for external stores, including rocket packs and bombs (usually two 1,650 lb = 750 kg and two 1,100 lb = 500 kg), under each wing and is usually seen with a pair of external fuel tanks under its centre-fuselage. A 30 mm cannon is installed in each wing-root leading-edge.

The power plant of the standard Su-7 is a TDR R31 turbojet engine, rated at approximately 15,430 lb (7,000 kg) st dry or 22,046 lb (10,000 kg) st with reheat.

Two JATO solid-propellant rockets can be fitted under the rear fuselage to shorten the aircraft's take-off run.

Early production models had the pitot boom mounted centrally above the air intake, but it is offset to starboard on current versions. Another change has been noted in the brake-chute installation. Early aircraft had a single ribbon-type parachute, attached under the rear fuselage. The latest Su-7B's in service have a large fairing, housing twin brake-chutes, at the base of their rudder. The size of the blast panels on the sides of the front fuselage by the wing-root guns has also increased, implying that the cannon now fitted have a higher muzzle velocity or rate-of-fire.

A variant of the Su-7 seen for the first time at Domodedovo is a two-seater, with the second cockpit in tandem, aft of the standard cockpit and with a slightly raised canopy. A prominent dorsal "spine" extends from the rear of the aft canopy to the base of the tail fin. The two-seater was in formation with standard Su-7's. It has the NATO code name **"Moujik"**.

DIMENSIONS, EXTERNAL:
Wing span	29 ft 3½ in (8·93 m)
Length, including probe	57 ft 0 in (17·37 m)
Height overall	15 ft 0 in (4·57 m)

WEIGHTS (approximate):
Normal T-O weight	26,450 lb (12,000 kg)
Max T-O weight	31,965 lb (14,500 kg)

PERFORMANCE (estimated):
Max level speed at 36,000 ft (11,000 m):
clean   944 knots (1,085 mph; 1,750 km/h) = Mach 1·7
with external stores
685 knots (788 mph; 1,270 km/h) = Mach 1·2
Rate of climb at S/L approx
29,900 ft (9,120 m)/min
Service ceiling   49,700 ft (15,150 m)
Combat radius
172-260 nm (200-300 miles; 320-480 km)
Max range   780 nm (900 miles; 1,450 km)

SUKHOI VARIABLE-GEOMETRY SU-7

First of the two variable-geometry aircraft demonstrated at Domodedovo in July 1967 was an adaptation of the Su-7. Described by the commentator as the Soviet Union's first variable-geometry design, it is externally identical with the standard Su-7 except for the movable outer wing panels and associated fences, outboard of the main landing gear.

The movable part of each wing is about 13 ft (4·0 m) long and is fitted with a full-span leading-edge slat. Its entire trailing-edge is also hinged, forming wide-chord slotted ailerons and flaps. The large main fence on each side is square-cut at the front and seems to incorporate attachments for external stores. There appear to be two shorter and shallower fences inboard of the main fence on each side, on the sweptback portion of the centre-section trailing-edge which aligns with the trailing-edge of the outer panel when it is fully swept. The standard flap is retained on the inner portion of the centre-section on each side.

This comparatively simple adaptation of a standard fighter offers improved take-off performance and range, both of which are of vital importance in a tactical combat type. However, with several newer and improved designs already in production, it seems unlikely that the variable-geometry Su-7 will become first-line equipment. The colourful paint-scheme of the aircraft shown at Domodedovo is normally reserved for experimental prototypes and aircraft used by official aerobatic teams.

DIMENSIONS (estimated):
Wing span: spread	41 ft 0 in (12·50 m)
swept	29 ft 6 in (9·00 m)
Length overall, including probe	56 ft 0 in (17·00 m)

SUKHOI SU-9
NATO Code Name: "Fishpot"

When first seen at Tushino during the 1956 Aviation Day display, this single-seat all-weather fighter had a small conical radome

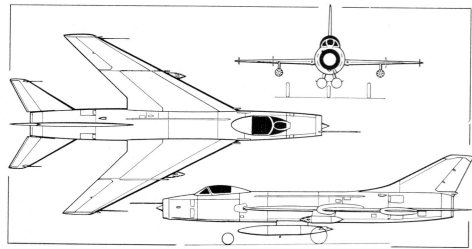

Three-view drawing of the Sukhoi Su-7B close-support fighter

Two-seat version of the Su-7 (rear foreground) seen at the 1967 Domodedovo display; it is code-named "Moujik" (*Aviation Week and Space Technology*)

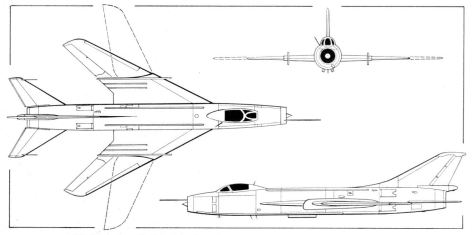

Single-seat variable-geometry aircraft evolved from the Sukhoi Su-7B

Sukhoi variable-geometry research aircraft, based on the Su-7B airframe (*Tass*)

above its engine air intake. This is replaced by a centre-body air intake on the production version, which appears to have a fuselage and tail unit almost identical with those of the sweptwing Su-7.

Examples included in the Tushino display of 1961 carried four of the Soviet Air Force's then-standard radar-homing air-to-air missiles (NATO code-name "Alkali") on underwing attachments, plus two under-fuselage fuel tanks side-by-side. No fixed armament was visible. The latest Su-9's seen at Domodedovo in July 1967, each carried a pair of "Anab" missiles under their wings, one with radar homing head and one with infra-red homing head.

Although the Su-9 is similar to its Mikoyan contemporary, the MiG-21 ("Fishbed"), in general layout, it is a larger and heavier aircraft, with a much more powerful afterburning engine. It is probably less limited in range and all-weather capability than the original MiG-21 and the two types are therefore complementary rather than comparable.

The Su-9 can be identified by its cleaner airframe, and the absence of both a ventral stabilising fin and fairings on the fuselage forward of the wing-root leading-edges. Its pitot boom is mounted above the nose air intake. The cockpit canopy is rearward-sliding, whereas that of the MiG-21 hinges forward about the base of the windscreen or sideways.

The Su-9 has a wide-track tricycle landing gear, with a single wheel on each unit. The main units retract inward into the wings, the nose-wheel forward. Control surfaces appear to be conventional, with a one-piece all-moving tail-plane, carrying the projection at each tip that is found on many Soviet combat aircraft. There are four petal-type air-brakes, in pairs on each side of the rear fuselage.

The current version of the Su-9 has a length-ened nose of less-tapered form and enlarged centre-body. There are also two duct fairings along the top of the centre-fuselage, as on the Su-7B.

As the E-66/E-166 family of aircraft are develop-ments of the MiG-21, it seems logical to assume that their rival in Soviet record attempts, the T-431, should be either an Su-9 or a development of the Su-9. As described on page 524, the T-431 was stated officially to have a 19,840 lb (9,000 kg) st turbojet when it set up a height record in 1959, and a 22,046 lb (10,000 kg) st TRD31 turbojet when it set up a sustained altitude record in 1962.

DIMENSIONS, EXTERNAL (estimated):
Wing span   26 ft 0 in (7·90 m)
Length, including probe   56 ft 0 in (17·0 m)

PERFORMANCE (estimated):
Max level speed at 36,000 ft (11,000 m)
   1,033 knots (1,190 mph; 1,915 km/h) = Mach 1·8

SUKHOI SU-11
NATO Code Name: "Flagon-A"

Ten examples of this new single-seat twin-jet delta-wing fighter participated in the flying dis-play at Domodedovo in July 1967. First to appear was a single black-painted machine, piloted by Vladimir Ilyushin, son of the famous designer and known to be a test pilot for Sukhoi. When a formation of nine similar aircraft appear-ed later, the identity of the design bureau responsible for them was confirmed by the obvious "family likeness" to the Su-9 in the shape of the wings and tail unit.

Sukhoi Su-9 single-seat fighter, armed with two of the missiles code-named "Anab"   (*Novosti*)

Sukhoi Su-11 single-seat tactical fighter (two turbojet engines with afterburners)   (*Tass*)

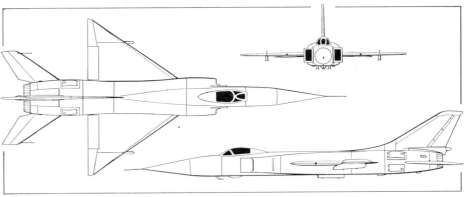

Sukhoi Su-11 single-seat twin-jet all-weather fighter known to NATO as "Flagon-A"

The Sukhoi Su-11 fighter in its STOL version, NATO code-name "Flagon-B"

It seems possible that this new aircraft was developed to meet a Soviet Air Force requirement for a Mach 2·5 interceptor to replace the Su-9 and it has already entered squadron service as a standard first-line type, reportedly under the designation Su-11. A STOL version of it also appeared at Domodedovo and is described separately.

TYPE: Single-seat twin-jet all-weather interceptor.

WINGS: Cantilever mid-wing monoplane, basically similar to those of Su-9. Sweepback approx 53°. No dihedral. All-metal structure. Single boundary-layer fence above each wing at approx 70% span. Large area-increasing flap extends from inboard end of aileron to fuselage on each side.

FUSELAGE: Cockpit section is basically circular with large ogival dielectric nose-cone. Centre fuselage is faired into rectangular-section air intake ducts. Two door-type air-brakes on each side of rear fuselage, forward of tailplane.

TAIL UNIT: Cantilever all-metal structure, with sweepback on all surfaces. All-moving tail-plane, with anhedral, mounted slightly below mid position. Conventional rudder. No trim-tabs.

LANDING GEAR: Tricycle type, with single wheel on each unit. Main wheels retract inward into wings and intake ducts; nose-wheel retracts forward.

POWER PLANT: Two afterburning turbojets, with variable-area nozzles, mounted side-by-side in rear fuselage. Ram-type air intakes, with splitter plates; blow-in auxiliary inlets mid-way between main intake and wing leading-edge in each duct.

ACCOMMODATION: Single seat in enclosed cockpit, with blister canopy.

ARMAMENT: Single pylon for external store under each wing, in line with boundary-layer fence. Normal armament comprises one radar-homing and one infra-red homing "Anab" air-to-air missile. Side-by-side pylons under centre-fuselage for further weapons or external fuel tanks.

DIMENSIONS (estimated):
Wing span   30 ft 0 in (9·15 m)
Length overall   68 ft 0 in (20·5 m)

SUKHOI STOL FIGHTER
NATO Code Name: "Flagon-B"

The Sukhoi prototype STOL fighter demonstrated at Domodedovo in 1967 differs little from the Su-11 twin-jet fighter described above.

Three lift-jet engines are mounted vertically in tandem under two rearward-hinged intake doors in the centre-fuselage, between the air intake trunks. There are longitudinal slots in these doors and transverse louvres in the panels under the fuselage, beneath the lift-jets.

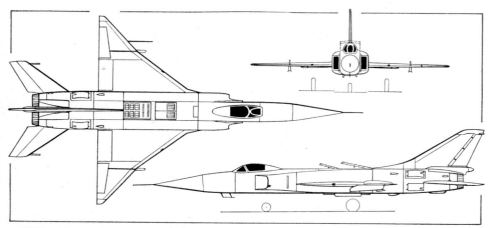

Three-view drawing (provisional) and photograph of the Sukhoi "Flagon-B"

The usual dielectric nose-cone appears to be replaced by a fairing, painted black, with the paint area extending further aft than the normal cut-off line of the dielectric cone. Black triangles forward of the engine air intakes are painted on, perhaps to give the impression of half-cone centre-bodies.

Wing span is increased by about 5 ft (1·5 m),

giving compound sweep at the tips, from a station just outboard of the boundary-layer fence each side. The wing root leading-edge is swept forward, giving increased chord immediately adjacent to the air intake trunk. There is a large scoop on the rear fuselage above each jet nozzle, probably for additional afterburner cooling.

TUPOLEV
ANDREI NIKOLAEVICH TUPOLEV

Andrei Tupolev, who was born in 1888, has been a leading figure in the great Central Aero-Hydrodynamic Institute (TsAGI) in Moscow since it was founded in 1929. He has long been the Soviet Union's outstanding designer and the current products of his design team, described below, range from jet and turboprop transports to the first Soviet supersonic bomber to enter service and the world's first supersonic transport aircraft. Also in production in the Soviet Union are small amphibious aerosleighs of Tupolev design, powered by 150 hp and 260 hp aero-engines and capable of travelling over both water and snow.

TUPOLEV TU-16
NATO Code Name: "Badger"

This Tupolev bomber, from which the Tu-104 airliner was derived, made its first public appearance in some numbers in 1954. In July 1955 a formation of 54 flew over Moscow on Aviation Day, and the Tu-16 has since been standard equipment in the Soviet Air Force and Naval Air Force. About 2,000 are believed to have been built.

Three versions of the Tu-16 are identified by unclassified NATO code-names, as follows:

"Badger-A". Basic bomber with glazed nose and internally-stowed free-fall bombs. In service with Soviet Air Force. Supplied to Iraqi and Egyptian Air Forces. Those supplied originally to Egypt were destroyed in the war of June 1967; but "Badgers" with both Soviet and Egyptian Air Force markings have been seen over units of the US fleet in the Mediterranean in 1968-70. It is possible that they all remain part of the Soviet Naval Air Force and are flown by Soviet crews, from Cairo-West airfield.

"Badger-B". Similar to "Badger-A" but able to carry two swept-wing anti-shipping missiles

Tupolev Tu-16 tanker (lower aircraft in photo) refuelling a Tu-16 reconnaissance bomber of the Soviet Northern Fleet (*Tass*)

(NATO code-name "Kennel") under wings. In service with Soviet Naval Air Force and, since July 1961, Indonesian Air Force (two squadrons). "Kennel" has been followed by the rocket-powered "Kelt" of similar configuration (see "Missiles" section).

"Badger-C". Missile-carrier first seen at 1961 Soviet Aviation Day display. Large stand-off bomb (NATO code-name "Kipper"), similar in configuration to North American Hound Dog, carried under fuselage and stated to be for anti-shipping use. Radar in wide under-nose radome.

Tupolev Tu-16 reconnaissance bomber in Egyptian markings photographed by a US Navy aircraft during a NATO naval exercise in the Mediterranean

Examples of both "Badger-A" and "Badger-C", without missile, have made reconnaissance flights over units of the US Navy at sea in the Atlantic, Pacific and elsewhere, and have been photographed while doing so. The aircraft operate in pairs, with one carrying special electronic equipment in underwing pods.

TYPE: Twin-jet medium bomber.

WINGS: Cantilever high mid-wing monoplane with slight anhedral and with 37° of sweep. Thickness/chord ratio 12½%.

FUSELAGE: All-metal semi-monocoque structure of circular cross-section.

TAIL UNIT: Cantilever all-metal structure, with sweepback on all surfaces. Trim-tabs in rudder and each elevator.

LANDING GEAR: Retractable tricycle type. Twin-wheel nose unit retracts rearward. Main four-wheel bogies retract into housings projecting beyond the wing trailing-edge.

POWER PLANT: Two Mikulin AM-3M turbojet engines, each rated at about 20,950 lb (9,500 kg) at sea level. Fuel in wing and fuselage tanks, with total capacity of approx 10,000 Imp gallons (45,450 litres). Provision for underwing auxiliary fuel tanks and for flight refuelling. Tu-16 tankers trail hose from starboard wing-tip; receiving equipment is in port wing-tip extension.

ACCOMMODATION: Crew of about seven, with two pilots side-by-side on flight deck and navigator in glazed nose ("Badger-A" and "B"). Manned tail position plus lateral observation blisters in rear fuselage under tailplane.

ARMAMENT: Forward dorsal and rear ventral barbettes each containing two 23 mm cannon. Two further cannon in tail position controlled by an automatic gun-ranging radar set. Seventh, fixed, cannon on starboard side of nose. Bomb load of up to 19,800 lb (9,000 kg) delivered from bomb bay about 21 ft (6·5 m) long. Naval versions can carry air-to-surface winged stand-off missiles.

ELECTRONICS AND EQUIPMENT: Radio and radar aids probably include HF and VHF R/T equipment, as well as IFF and a radio-compass and radio altimeter. A radome under the nose of "Badger-A" and "B" contains scanner-type radar.

DIMENSIONS, EXTERNAL:
Wing span	110 ft 0 in (33·5 m)
Length overall	120 ft 0 in (36·5 m)
Height overall	35 ft 6 in (10·8 m)

AREA:
Wings, gross	approx 1,820 sq ft (169 m²)

WEIGHT:
Normal T-O weight approx 150,000 lb (68,000 kg)

PERFORMANCE (estimated at max T-O weight):
Max level speed at 35,000 ft (10,700 m)
510 knots (587 mph; 945 km/h)
Service ceiling 42,650 ft (13,000 m)
Range with max bomb load
2,605 nm (3,000 miles; 4,800 km)
Range at 417 knots (480 mph; 770 km/h) with 6,600 lb (3,000 kg) bombs
3,451 nm (3,975 miles; 6,400 km)

TUPOLEV TU-20 (TU-95)

NATO Code Name: "Bear"

This huge Tupolev bomber was first seen at Tushino in July 1955, and has since been standard equipment in the Soviet Air Force. It has the service designation Tu-20 and design bureau designation Tu-95.

No details of its construction have been released, but the Tu-114 airliner is very similar except for its larger-diameter fuselage. As a

Tupolev Tu-16 bomber carrying two "Kennel" anti-shipping missiles (see also "Missiles" section)

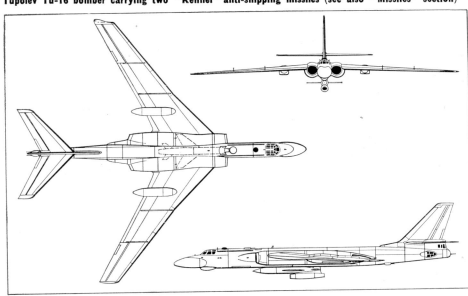

Tupolev Tu-16 with a "Kipper" stand-off bomb under its fuselage

result, the description of the wings, tail unit, landing gear and power plant of the Tu-114 can be taken to apply in general also to the Tu-20, which certainly has the same Kuznetsov NK-12M type of turboprops, each developing 14,795 eshp for take-off.

Three versions have been identified by NATO code-names, as follows:

"Bear-A". Basic bomber, with "chin" radar scanner, dorsal and ventral armament in turrets, and manned tail gun position. Two blisters on rear fuselage, under tailplane, are probably for observation purposes. A braking parachute may be used to reduce landing run.

"Bear-B". First seen in 1961 Soviet Aviation Day fly-past, with new radar equipment, in a wide under-nose radome, and carrying an air-to-surface missile (NATO code-name "Kangaroo"). Now has flight refuelling nose-probe and blister fairing on starboard side of rear fuselage.

What appears at first to be a fairing on the nose of the "Kangaroo" missile is probably a duct leading from the belly of the bomber, through which air is passed to start the missile's turbojet engine.

"Bear-C". First identified when it appeared in vicinity of Allied naval forces during "Exercise Teamwork" in September 1964. Generally similar to "Bear-B", but with large blister fairings on both sides of rear fuselage. Refuelling probe fitted.

"Bear-?". This latest maritime reconnaissance version was photographed extensively when several examples made low passes over US Coast Guard ice-breakers in the Kara Sea in mid-1967. The aircraft differed in detail, but each had an undernose radar scanner in a radome similar in shape to that on the Canadair Argus, a very large under-belly radome, blister fairing on each side of the rear fuselage like Bear-C, nose refuelling

Version of the Tu-20 with additional radomes, first photographed during low passes over USCG ice-breakers in mid-1967

probe, and a variety of other blisters and antennae.

Examples of all versions of "Bear" have made reconnaissance flights over units of the US Fleet at sea and have been photographed by US naval fighters whilst doing so. These photographs first revealed the unidentified streamlined blisters on the sides of the rear fuselage of "Bear-B" and "Bear-C", near the dorsal fin, and that they can be fitted with a flight refuelling probe, mounted above the modified nose.

The dimensions and performance of the Tu-20 should be similar to those of the Tu-114. Its loaded weight is believed to be about 340,000 lb (154,220 kg).

The US Secretary of Defense, Mr Robert McNamara, said in 1963 that the Tu-20 has an unrefuelled range of 7,800 miles (12,550 km) with a 25,000 lb (11,340 kg) bomb-load and an over-target speed of 500 mph (805 kmh) at 41,000 ft (12,500 m).

TUPOLEV Tu-22
NATO Code Name: "Blinder"

First shown publicly in the 1961 Aviation Day fly-past over Moscow, this twin-turbojet bomber is estimated to have a maximum speed of Mach 1·4 at height.

Its wings have some 45° of sweepback on the outer panels, 50° on the inner panels and an acute sweep at the extreme root. They are low-set on an area-ruled fuselage, which has a nose radome and appears to accommodate a crew of two or three in tandem. There is a row of windows in the bottom of the fuselage aft of the nose radome.

The slab tailplane is also low-set, and the large turbojet engines (reported to be rated at 26,000 lb = 11,790 kg st each, with afterburning) are mounted in pods above the rear fuselage, on each side of the vertical fin. The lip of each pod is in the form of a ring which can be extended forward by jacks for take-off. Air entering the ram intake is then supplemented by air injected through the

Another view of one of the Tu-20's photographed from USCG ice-breakers in mid-1967

annular slot between the ring and the main body of the pod.

The original nozzles had a short fluted final section aft of a short fixed section, with an annular space between this and the outer fairing; they have been superseded by new nozzles, with a longer-chord convergent-divergent nozzle inside the outer fairing. These are expected to offer increased thrust and range.

The wide-track four-wheel bogie main landing-gear units retract into fairings built on to the wing trailing-edges. In addition to embodying oleo-pneumatic shock-absorbers, the legs are designed to swing rearward for additional cushion-

ing during taxying and landing on rough runways. The twin-wheel nose unit retracts rearward.

Of the ten Tu-22's shown in 1961, only one carried visible weapons, in the form of an air-to-surface missile (NATO code name "Kitchen"), some 36 ft (11 m) long, semi-submerged in the underside of its fuselage. This aircraft had also a much wider nose radome, and a tail radome above a radar directed turret mounting a single gun.

A total of 22 Tu-22's took part in the 1967 display at Tushino. One was escorted by six MiG-21PF's permitting a more accurate calculation

Tupolev Tu-22 twin-jet supersonic bomber taking off. Note the engine air-intake lips in forward position (*Tass*)

Servicing one of the two tail-mounted engines of a Tupolev Tu-22 supersonic bomber. Aircraft in background is the tandem two-seat training version (NATO "Blinder C") with stepped-up canopy (*Tass*)

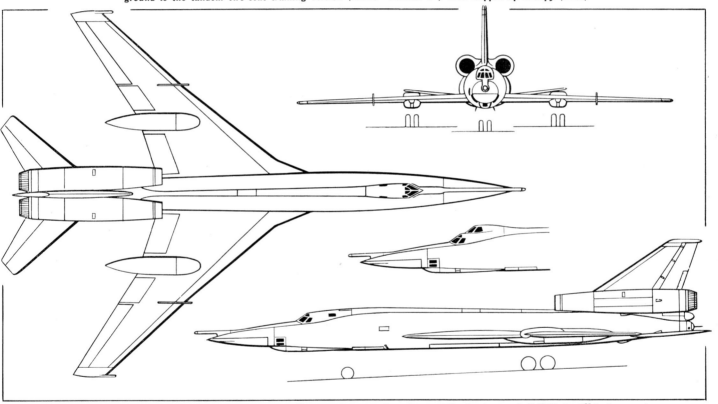

Tupolev Tu-22 twin-jet supersonic bomber ("Blinder A") with additional view of nose of the tandem-cockpit "Blinder C" trainer version

of its overall dimensions than had previously been possible. Most carried "Kitchen" missiles; all had a nose refuelling probe and the wide radome seen on the single missile-armed aircraft in 1961.

The three versions of the Tu-22 identified so far have been given the following NATO code-names:

Blinder A. Basic reconnaisance bomber version, with fuselage weapon-bay for free-fall bombs.

Blinder B. Similar to Blinder A, but equipped to carry the "Kitchen" air-to-surface missile, and with larger radar in nose.

Blinder C. Tandem two-seat training version. Rear pilot sits in raised position, with a stepped-up canopy.

DIMENSIONS (estimated):
Wing span 90 ft 10½ in (27·70 m)
Length overall 132 ft 11½ in (40·53 m)
Height overall 17 ft 0 in (5·18 m)
WEIGHT (estimated):
Max T-O weight 184,970 lb (83,900 kg)

Tupolev Tu-22 ("Blinder A") supersonic bomber (*Tass*)

Three Tupolev Tu-28P all-weather interceptors, code-named "Fiddler", seen at the 1967 Domodedovo display *(Aviation Week and Space Technology)*

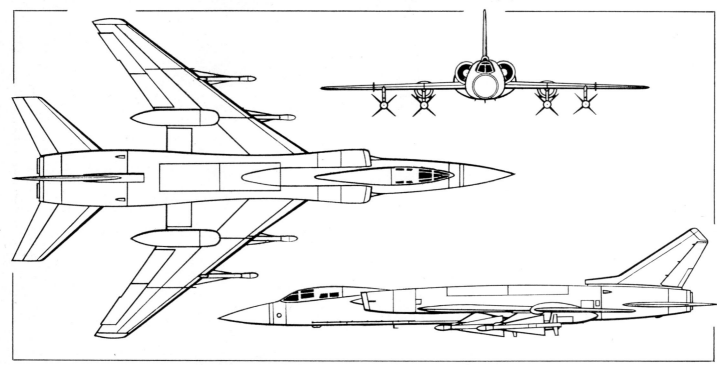

Tupolev Tu-28P twin-jet all-weather interceptor known to NATO as "Fiddler"

PERFORMANCE (estimated):
Max level speed at 40,000 ft (12,200 m)
    800 knots (920 mph; 1,480 km/h) = Mach 1·4
Service ceiling   60,000 ft (18,300 m)
Max range   1,215 nm (1,400 miles; 2,250 km)

TUPOLEV V-G BOMBER
Official US sources are reported to have stated

in the Autumn of 1969 that a new twin-jet variable-geometry ("swing-wing") medium bomber developed by the Tupolev design bureau was being flight tested in the USSR. At least two prototypes are believed to have been completed by that time. Design cruising speed was quoted as Mach 2 and range as more than 1,730 nm (2,000 miles; 3,200 km).

TUPOLEV Tu-28P
NATO Code Name: "Fiddler"

This powerful supersonic twin-jet military aircraft was seen for the first time at Tushino in July 1961 in an interceptor rôle with a large delta-wing air-to-air missile (NATO code-name "Ash") mounted under each wing. It was believed at first to be a product of Yakovlev's design bureau but is now known to be a Tupolev design, with the probable service designation Tu-28P. Its NATO code-name is "Fiddler".

The Tu-28P has a large ogival nose radome and carries a crew of two in tandem. The shoulder intakes for its two afterburning turbojet engines have half-cone shock-bodies, and the jet-pipes are side-by-side in the bulged tail.

The sharply-swept wings are mid-set, with slight anhedral, and have considerably increased chord on the inboard panels, which have both increased sweep and a "straight" trailing-edge. The wide-track main landing gear units, comprising four-wheel bogies, retract into large fairings built on to the wing trailing-edges.

The tail unit is also sharply swept and the two aircraft seen in 1961 were each fitted with two ventral fins. These were missing on the three Tu-28Ps which flew past at Domodedovo in July 1967, as was the large bulged fairing fitted under the fuselage in 1961.

The armament has been doubled since 1961, each aircraft now being equipped to carry two "Ash" missiles under each wing, one usually of the radar homing type and the other of the infra-red homing type. This was confirmed as the standard armament of current first-line service aircraft in a film released in 1969, showing units of the Soviet armed forces taking part in defence exercises.

The span of the Tu-28P has been estimated at

The Tu-28P in its latest form, without under-belly fairing and ventral fins *(Novosti)*

Tupolev Tu-114 long-range passenger transport aircraft (four 14,795 shp Kuznetsov NK-12MV turboprop engines)   *(Novosti)*

about 65 ft (20·0 m), with a max T-O weight of 100,000 lb (45,000 kg). Its performance is believed to include a maximum speed of about Mach 1·75.

TUPOLEV TU-114
NATO Code Name: "Cleat"

The prototype Tu-114 was completed in the Autumn of 1957, at the time of the 40th anniversary of the Russian Revolution, and was named *Rossiya* (Russia) to mark the occasion. Largest and heaviest commercial airliner built up to that time, it was a civil counterpart of the Tu-20 "Bear" bomber, with the same wing, tail unit, landing gear, turboprop engines and other components. Two versions were subsequently put into service, as follows:

Tu-114. Standard version with accommodation for up to 220 passengers. Normal seating is for 170 passengers and the Tu-114 entered service in this form on Aeroflot's Moscow-Khabarovsk route on 24 April 1961. About 20 are believed to be in service.

Tu-114D. Basically similar to Tu-114, but with shorter and slimmer fuselage, apparently of similar size to that of the "Bear". Intended to carry a small number of passengers, mail and urgent freight over very long distances. The normal T-O weight of this version has been reported as 268,800 lb (121,920 kg).

The prototype Tu-114D made a non-stop 4,585 nm (5,280 mile; 8,500 km) flight from Moscow to Irkutsk and back at an average speed of 431 knots (497 mph; 800 km/h) and at altitudes between 33,000 and 40,000 ft (10,000-12,200 m) in the Spring of 1958. The return flight encountered headwinds of up to 108 knots (125 mph; 200 km/h), but sufficient fuel is said to have remained after landing for the aircraft to have flown a further 810-1,080 nm (930-1,240 miles; 1,500-2,000 km).

On 24 March 1960, piloted by Ivan Sukhomlin, a Tu-114 achieved a speed of 470·21 knots (541·45 mph; 871·38 km/h) over a 1,000 km closed circuit, carrying a payload of 25,000 kg. The flight set up eight official records, for speed with payloads of 1,000, 2,000, 5,000, 10,000, 15,000, 20,000 and 25,000 kg and for speed without payload. A second series of eight records was set up on 1 April 1960, when a payload of 25,000 kg was carried over a 2,000 km circuit at 462·60 knots (532·69 mph; 857·277 km/h). The pilot was again Sukhomlin; and he set up a third series of eight records on 9 April 1960, when a 25,000 kg payload was carried over a 5,000 km circuit at 473·35 knots (545·07 mph; 877·212 km/h). Finally, on 21 April 1962, Sukhomlin made a clean sweep of all the distance-with-payload records for propeller-driven aircraft by averaging 397·91 knots (458·2 mph; 737·352 km/h) over a 10,000 km closed circuit, setting up new records for speed without payload and in the 1,000, 2,000, 5,000 and 10,000 kg payload categories.

Two height-with-payload records were set up on 12 July 1961, when a Tu-114 carried a payload of 66,216 lb (30,035 kg) to a height of 39,610 ft (12,073 m). This is a record for height with 25,000 kg and 30,000 kg.

The following data refer specifically to the standard Tu-114.

TYPE: Four-engined long-range airliner.

WINGS: Cantilever low-wing monoplane. Sweepback 35° at quarter-chord. All-metal three-spar structure. All-metal hydraulically-powered ailerons and Fowler flaps. Trim-tabs in ailerons. Spoilers in top surface of wing forward of inboard end of ailerons. Two boundary layer fences on top surface of each wing. Thermal anti-icing system in leading-edges.

FUSELAGE: All-metal semi-monocoque structure of circular section.

TAIL UNIT: Cantilever all-metal structure, with sweepback on all surfaces. Adjustable tailplane incidence. Hydraulically-powered rudder and elevators. Trim-tabs in rudder and each elevator.

LANDING GEAR: Retractable tricycle type. Main units consist of four-wheel bogies, with tyres approx 5 ft (1·50 m) diameter and hydraulic internal-expanding brakes. All units retract rearward, main units into nacelles built on to wing trailing-edge. Retractable tail bumper consisting of two small wheels.

POWER PLANT: Four Kuznetsov NK-12MV turboprop engines, each originally with max rating of approx 12,000 eshp but now uprated to 14,795 eshp and driving eight-blade contra-rotating reversible-pitch Type AV-60N propellers, diameter 18 ft 4½ in (5·6 m). Fuel in wing tanks, with normal capacity of 16,540 Imp gallons (72,980 litres).

ACCOMMODATION: Crew of 10-15, including pilot, co-pilot, one or two navigators, flight engineer, radio operator, and a minimum of three stewards and two cooks. Accommodation for up to 220 passengers, with mainly eight-abreast seating. For long ranges, normal accommodation for 120 passengers in mixed six-abreast and four-abreast seating. Standard 170-seat layout has forward toilets and stewards' seats in compartment between flight deck and front cabin, latter seating 42 persons in six-abreast seats. Next is a small compartment for coat stowage in line with inboard propellers, followed by a centre (restaurant) cabin for 48 persons in six-abreast pullman-type seats; the galley serving compartment; a small compartment containing stairs to the lower-deck kitchen and three seats; four "roomettes," each with two divans or six seats and one folding bunk; the rear cabin containing 54 seats in six-abreast rows; a coat stowage compartment; the entrance compartment with passenger door on port side; port and starboard washing and powder rooms; and finally four toilets. Two electric lifts connect lower-deck kitchen with serving area. Two under-floor pressurised freight holds.

SYSTEMS: Pressurisation and air-conditioning system has max pressure differential of 8·4 lb sq/in (0·59 kg/cm²).

DIMENSIONS, EXTERNAL:
Wing span	167 ft 8 in (51·10 m)
Wing aspect ratio	10·4
Length overall	177 ft 6 in (54·10 m)
Wheel track	44 ft 11½ in (13·70 m)
Wheelbase	67 ft 10½ in (20·69 m)

DIMENSIONS, INTERNAL:
Cabin, including flight deck, toilets, etc:
Length	154 ft 2 in (47·0 m)
Max width	12 ft 10 in (3·92 m)
Max height	7 ft 2 in (2·18 m)
Volume	16,420 cu ft (465 m³)
Freight holds (under floor, total)	2,472 cu ft (70 m³)

AREA:
Wings, gross	3,349 sq ft (311·10 m²)

WEIGHTS AND LOADINGS:
Weight empty	200,620 lb (91,000 kg)
Fuel	134,000 lb (60,800 kg)
Max payload	66,140 lb (30,000 kg)
Normal T-O weight	361,560 lb (164,000 kg)
Max T-O weight	376,990 lb (171,000 kg)
Max landing weight	297,625 lb (135,000 kg)
Max zero-fuel weight	244,100 lb (110,720 kg)
Max wing loading	108·5 lb/sq ft (532 kg/m²)
Max power loading	6·21 lb/hp (2·78 kg/hp)

PERFORMANCE (at max T-O weight):
Max level speed at 26,250 ft (8,000 m)	469 knots (540 mph; 870 km/h)
Max cruising speed at 29,500 ft (9,000 m)	415 knots (478 mph; 770 km/h)
Service ceiling	39,370 ft (12,000 m)
T-O run	8,200 ft (2,500 m)
Landing run	4,595 ft (1,400 m)
Range with max fuel and 33,070 lb (15,000 kg) payload, 60 min fuel reserve	4,828 nm (5,560 miles; 8,950 km)
Range with max payload, 60 min reserve	3,343 nm (3,850 miles; 6,200 km)

TUPOLEV TU-114 (Military Version)
NATO Code Name: "Moss"

An officially-released Soviet documentary film, shown in the West in 1968, included sequences depicting a military version of the Tu-114, carrying above its fuselage a "saucer" type early warning radar of the kind fitted to the US Navy's E-2 Hawkeye. This is a logical development, as the Tu-114 has a larger fuselage of diameter than the military Tu-20, and can accommodate more easily the extensive electronic equipment and large crew required by a long-endurance early-warning and fighter control aircraft.

The general appearance of this aircraft, which has the NATO code-name "Moss", is shown in the illustration below. It can be seen to have a flight refuelling nose-probe, ventral tail-fin and numerous additional antennae and blisters for electronic equipment.

In the AWACS (airborne warning and control system) rôle, "Moss" is probably intended to work in conjunction with advanced interceptors. After locating incoming low-level strike aircraft, "Moss" could direct towards them fighters

The airborne warning and control version of the Tupolev Tu-114, known to NATO as "Moss"

The airborne warning and control version of the Tu-114, known to NATO as "Moss"

armed with "snap-down" air-to-air missiles able to be fired from a cruising height of 20,000 ft (6,100 m) or higher.

TUPOLEV TU-124
NATO Code Name: "Cookpot"

Although similar to the Tu-104 in general configuration, the Tu-124 is 25% smaller and was the first Soviet transport aircraft with turbofan engines.

The prototype flew for the first time in June 1960 and four versions are now in commercial service or available for service.

Tu-124. With accommodation for 44 passengers in three cabins, seating 12, 8 and 24 persons respectively.

Tu-124V. Standard version, seating 56 passengers.

Tu-124K. In this 36-seat version, the forward cabin is furnished to de luxe standard for four persons, with revolving armchair seats, table, desk and other amenities. The centre cabin seats eight persons in facing pairs, with tables. The rear cabin seats 24 persons in the normal four-abreast rows, with two tables between the front pairs of seats.

Tu-124K2. De luxe version for 22 passengers. Forward cabin as in Tu-124K. Centre cabin contains two revolving seats, table and divan. Rear cabin contains eight facing pairs of seats, in four rows, with tables between. There is a small additional pantry and a wardrobe between this cabin and the rear lobby.

Both de luxe versions are easily convertible to standard 56-seat configuration.

The Tu-124 was designed to replace the piston-engined Il-14 on Aeroflot's short/medium routes and entered service on this airline's Moscow-Tallinn route on October 2, 1962. With the new rear-engined Tu-134, it will be Aeroflot's most widely-used intermediate-range airliner.

Three have been delivered to CSA Czech Airlines. Others serve, in small numbers, with the air forces of East Germany, Iraq and India.

TYPE: Twin-engined medium-range transport.

WINGS: Cantilever low-wing monoplane. Sweep-back 35° at quarter-chord. All-metal two-spar construction. Manually-controlled ailerons, with spring tabs. Double-slotted flaps. Spoilers forward of flaps are used as air-brakes to shorten landing run and extend automatically as wheels touch runway. Unswept trailing-edge between landing gear housings and engine nacelles helps to distinguish the Tu-124 from the Tu-104. Hot-air anti-icing system on leading-edges and engine air-intakes.

FUSELAGE: Circular-section all-metal semi-monocoque structure. Large under-fuselage air-brake is used both to steepen angle of approach and to shorten landing run.

TAIL UNIT: Cantilever all-metal structure. Variable-incidence tailplane. Manually-controlled rudder and elevators, each with tab. Electrically-heated leading-edge de-icing system.

LANDING GEAR: Retractable tricycle type. All units retract rearward, in only 6 sec. Main units consist of four-wheel bogies retracting

into fairings built on to wing trailing-edge. Bogie retracts through 180° and is housed inverted. Oleo-pneumatic shock-absorbers. Main wheels size 865 × 280, tyre pressure 92·5 lb/sq in (6·5 kg/cm²). Steerable twin-wheel nose unit, wheel size 660 × 200, tyre pressure 92·5 lb/sq in (6·5 kg/cm²). Disc brakes. Brake-chute in tail is intended mainly for emergency use after engine failure at take-off.

POWER PLANT: Two Soloviev D-20P turbofan engines, each rated at 11,905 lb (5,400 kg) st, in wing-root nacelles. Fuel in 5 rubber-bag tanks and an outboard integral tank in each wing and four centre-section tanks. Total fuel capacity 2,970 Imp gallons (13,500 litres). Oil capacity 16·5 Imp gallons (76 litres).

ACCOMMODATION: Crew of four, comprising two pilots, navigator and stewardess. Provision for radio operator or second navigator on removable seat. In standard 56-seat version, cabin has three compartments, seating 12, 12 and 32 people respectively on rail-mounted reclining seats, all four-abreast in pairs, with centre aisle. Two tables between front pairs of seats in forward cabin. Two doors on port side, one aft of flight deck, the other aft of main cabin. Forward baggage compartment on starboard side opposite door. Buffet-kitchen between forward door and cabin. Wardrobe opposite rear door. Toilet and rear baggage compartment aft of rear door, with external freight loading hatch on starboard side. All doors open inward. Mixed cargo-passenger layouts available.

SYSTEMS: Pressurisation and air-conditioning system max pressure differential 8·1 lb/sq in (0·57 kg/cm²). Hydraulic system, pressure 3,000 lb/sq in (210 kg/cm²), for landing gear, wheel doors, nose-wheel steering, brakes. Main 28V DC electric supply from two 18kW starter-generators. Two standby 55Ah accumulators.

ELECTRONICS AND EQUIPMENT: Standard equipment includes two multi-channel VHF and one HF radio, integrated navigation system including dual ADF and ILS, autopilot and two radio-compasses.

DIMENSIONS, EXTERNAL:

Wing span	83 ft 9½ in (25·55 m)
Length overall	100 ft 4 in (30·58 m)
Height overall	26 ft 6 in (8·08 m)
Tailplane span	32 ft 9½ in (10·00 m)
Wheel track	29 ft 8½ in (9·05 m)
Wheelbase	34 ft 7¼ in (10·55 m)
Passenger doors (port):	
Height	4 ft 3¼ in (1·30 m)
Width	2 ft 3½ in (0·70 m)
Cargo door (stbd):	
Height	2 ft 11½ in (0·90 m)
Width	3 ft 7¼ in (1·10 m)

DIMENSIONS, INTERNAL:

Cabin:	
Length, excluding flight deck	67 ft 11 in (20·70 m)
Max width	8 ft 10 in (2·70 m)
Max height	6 ft 2¾ in (1·90 m)
Volume, including flight deck, toilet, etc:	4,308 cu ft (122 m³)
Baggage compartment (fwd)	212 cu ft (6 m³)
Baggage compartment (aft)	282 cu ft (8 m³)

Tupolev Tu-124 medium-range transport aircraft (two Soloviev D-20P turbofan engines) in the insignia of CSA Czechoslovakian Airlines (*Martin Fricke*)

AREAS:

Wings, gross	1,281 sq ft (119 m²)
Ailerons (total)	76·32 sq ft (7·09 m²)
Flaps (total)	187·51 sq ft (17·42 m²)
Horizontal tail surfaces (total)	
	285·78 sq ft (26·55 m²)
Vertical tail surfaces (total)	117·33 sq ft (10·9 m²)

WEIGHTS:

Empty weight	49,600 lb (22,500 kg)
Manufacturer's max payload	13,228 lb (6,000 kg)
Normal T-O weight	80,470 lb (36,500 kg)
Max T-O weight	83,775 lb (38,000 kg)
Max landing weight	77,160 lb (35,000 kg)
Max zero-fuel weight	52,400 lb (23,770 kg)

PERFORMANCE (at max T-O weight, except where indicated):

Max level speed
524 knots (603 mph; 970 km/h)
Max cruising speed
469 knots (540 mph; 870 km/h)
Econ cruising speed at 33,000 ft (10,000 m) at AUW of 58,000 lb (26,300 kg)
432 knots (497 mph; 800 km/h)

T-O run	3,380 ft (1,030 m)
T-O distance to 33 ft (10 m)	7,000 ft (2,120 m)
Landing run	3,050 ft (930 m)

RANGES (at normal T-O weight, 60 min fuel reserve):

Range with max fuel and 7,715 lb (3,500 kg) payload at econ cruising speed
1,133 nm (1,305 miles; 2,100 km)
Range with max payload at econ cruising speed
660 nm (760 miles; 1,220 km)

TUPOLEV TU-134

NATO Code-Name: "Crusty"

Known originally as the Tu-124A, this aircraft is a rear-engined twin-jet development of the Tu-124. It had completed more than 100 test flights when first details and photographs were released in mid-September 1964. The prototype was followed by five pre-production aircraft and the Tu-134 is now in series production in the factory at Kharkov where the Tu-104 was manufactured. It entered international service on Aeroflot's Moscow-Stockholm route in September 1967 after a period on internal services. Export orders include three for Interflug (E Germany), four for Balkan Bulgarian Airlines, six for LOT (Poland), five for Malev (Hungary) and three for Aviogenex (Yugoslavia). Many of these have been delivered.

The Tu-134 was developed by Tupolev's design team, under the direct leadership of chief designer Leonid Selyakov. Deputy designer Alexandre Arkhangelsky has said that the aircraft can be operated from earth runways. He added that it is equipped for fully-automatic landing and has navigation aids that enable the pilot to land in fog with horizontal visibility down to 165 ft (50 m).

The Tu-134 is designed for a service life of 30,000 flying hours. Airframe overhaul life is 5,000 hours.

Two versions are available, as follows:

Tu-134. Initial version, accommodating 64-72 passengers.

Tu-134A. Fuselage lengthened by 9 ft 5½ in (2·80 m) to accommodate 72-80 passengers and increase baggage space by 71 cu ft (2 m³). Wider seats. Thrust reversers on engines. New radio

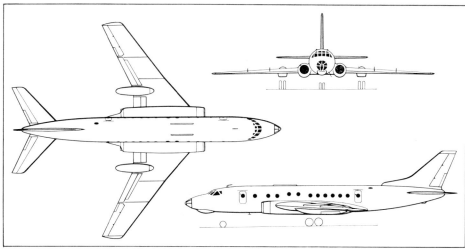

Tupolev Tu-124 medium-range jet airliner

and navigation equipment to international standards. APU for self-contained engine starting and air-conditioning on the ground.

The third aircraft (a Tu-134A) delivered to Aviogenex differs from all Tu-134's and Tu-134A's seen previously in having the usual glazed nose and under-nose radome replaced by a conventional conical nose radome.

The following details apply to both versions.

TYPE: Twin-turbofan short/medium-range transport aircraft.

WINGS: Cantilever low-wing monoplane. Sweepback at quarter-chord 35°. Anhedral 1° 30′. Conventional all-metal two-spar structure. Two-section aileron on each wing, operated manually through geared tabs, and fitted also with trim-tabs. Electro-mechanically-actuated all-metal double-slotted flaps. Hydraulically-actuated spoilers. Hot-air de-icing system.

FUSELAGE: Conventional all-metal semi-monocoque structure of circular section, max diameter 9 ft 6 in (2·90 m). Electro-mechanically-actuated air-brake under fuselage, to steepen angle of approach.

TAIL UNIT: Cantilever all-metal structure, with variable-incidence tailplane mounted at top of fin. Elevators operated manually through geared tabs. Rudder control is hydraulically powered, with yaw damper. Trim-tabs in elevators. Fin leading-edge de-iced by hot air; tailplane leading-edge de-iced electrically.

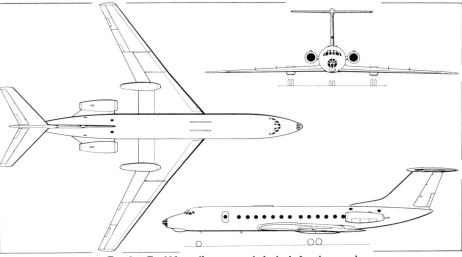

Tupolev Tu-134 medium-range twin-turbofan transport

Tupolev Tu-134 medium-range transport aircraft (two Soloviev D-30 turbofan engines) in service with Malev (*Martin Fricke*)

LANDING GEAR: Retractable tricycle type. All units retract rearward. Main units consist of four-wheel bogies retracting into fairings built onto wing trailing-edge. Oleo-pneumatic shock-absorbers, supplemented by ability of legs to swing rearward to cushion taxying and landing on rough runways. Main wheels size 930 × 305, tyre pressure 85 lb/sq in (6·0 kg/cm²). Steerable twin nose-wheels size 660 × 220, tyre pressure 92·5-100 lb/sq in (6·5-7·0 kg/cm²). Disc brakes and anti-skid units standard. Minimum turning radius 115 ft (35 m).

POWER PLANT: Two Soloviev D-30 turbofan engines, each rated at 14,990 lb (6,800 kg) st, in pods on each side of rear fuselage. Engines with thrust reversers, constant-speed drives and AC generators to be available in 1969-70. Three fuel tanks in each wing, total capacity 3,630 Imp gallons (16,500 litres) when gravity fuelled, 3,520 Imp gallons (16,000 litres) when pressure fuelled. Single-point refuelling socket in starboard wing-root leading-edge. Gravity fuelling point above each tank. Hot-air de-icing system for nacelle intakes. Fire-warning and freon extinguishing system.

ACCOMMODATION (Tu-134): Flight crew of three, consisting of two pilots and a navigator, plus two stewardesses. Mixed-class version accommodates 64 passengers in four-abreast seats, with 17·5 in (0·45 m) centre aisle. 16 first class passengers in front cabin have seats at 36·6 in (93 cm) pitch, with tables between first two rows; 20 tourist class in centre cabin and 28 tourist class in rear cabin. Economy class version accommodates 72 passengers in four-abreast seating, with 44 seats (at 28·35 in = 72 cm pitch) and two tables in forward cabin and 28 seats (at 29·5 in = 75 cm pitch) in aft cabin. In each version there is a galley on the starboard side and baggage compartment and galley on the port side immediately aft of the flight deck, two toilets at the rear and a large baggage and freight compartment aft, in line with the engines. Max loading on floor of freight compartments 82 lb/sq ft (400 kg/m²). The passenger door is on the port side, forward of the front cabin, There are two cargo doors, on the starboard side by the baggage compartments, and an emergency exit on each side over the wing. Crew cabin and canopy observation panel de-iced by electric heater and hot air.

ACCOMMODATION (Tu-134A): Generally similar to Tu-134 except for lengthened cabins. All versions have 28 seats in four-abreast rows in rear cabin. Front cabin seats 44, 48 or 52 passengers, four-abreast, with tables between front two rows. Seat pitch 30 in (76 cm) in all versions.

SYSTEMS: Air-conditioning system, pressure differential 8·10 lb/sq in (0·57 kg/cm²), fed with bleed air from engine compressors. Hydraulic system operating pressure 3,000 lb/sq in (210 kg/cm²). Electrical system includes 27V DC supply from four 12kW starter-generators and two batteries, single-phase 115V 400 c/s AC supply from two inverters and three-phase 36V 400 c/s AC supply. APU to be available in 1969-70. Oxygen available continuously for pilot, from 92-litre bottle with 1-hr supply for other crew members and portable supply for emergency use by passengers.

ELECTRONICS AND EQUIPMENT: Provision for full range of radio and radar communications and navigation equipment, including R-807 HF communications radio, "Lotos" VHF radio, SPU-7 intercom, RO3-1 weather/navigation radar, SOM-64 transponder, AGD-1 remote-reading artificial horizon, AUASP-3 angle-of-attack and g load control unit, KS-8 direction finder, NAS-1A6 navigation system (including "Trassa-A" Doppler), BSU-3P automatic flight control and landing system (including (AP-6EM-3P autopilot) for automatic control in flight and automatic or semi-automatic landing approaches down to 130-200 ft (40-60 m), ARK-11 radio compass, RV-UM low-altitude 0-2,000 ft = 0-600 m) radio altimeter and "Course MP-1" VOR/ILS/SP-50 navigation and landing system.

DIMENSIONS, EXTERNAL:
Wing span	95 ft 1¾ in (29·00 m)
Wing chord at root	28 ft 5 in (8·66 m)
Wing chord at tip	6 ft 3½ in (1·92 m)
Wing aspect ratio	7·3

Length overall:
Tu-134	112 ft 6½ in (34·30 m)
Tu-134A	122 ft 0 in (37·10 m)
Height overall	29 ft 7 in (9·02 m)
Tailplane span	30 ft 2 in (9·20 m)
Wheel track	31 ft 0 in (9·45 m)
Wheelbase	45 ft 8½ in (13·93 m)

Passenger door:
Height	4 ft 3 in (1·30 m)
Width	2 ft 3½ in (0·70 m)
Height to sill	8 ft 6½ in (2·60 m)

Baggage compartment doors:
Height	2 ft 11½ in (0·90 m)
Width: fwd	3 ft 7¼ in (1·10 m)
aft	3 ft 11¼ in (1·20 m)
Height to sill	7 ft 10½ in (2·40 m)

DIMENSIONS, INTERNAL:
Cabin (portion containing seats only):
Length:
Tu-134	45 ft 5½ in (13·85 m)
Width	8 ft 10½ in (2·71 m)
Height	6 ft 5 in (1·96 m)

Floor area:
Tu-134	343 sq ft (31·85 m²)

Volume:
Tu-134	2,073 cu ft (58·7 m³)
Tu-134A	2,400 cu ft (68·0 m³)

Max usable floor area, less flight deck:
Tu-134	506 sq ft (47·00 m²)

Max usable volume, less flight deck:
Tu-134	3,040 cu ft (86·10 m³)

Baggage compartment, Tu-134 (fwd):
Height (mean)	6 ft 1¾ in (1·875 m)
Length (mean)	6 ft 1¾ in (1·875 m)
Width (mean)	4 ft 2½ in (1·28 m)
Floor area	25·8 sq ft (2·4 m²)
Volume	159 cu ft (4·50 m³)

Baggage compartment, Tu-134A (fwd):
Volume	141-212 cu ft (4·0-6·0 m³)

Baggage compartment, Tu-134 (aft):
Height (mean)	5 ft 9 in (1·75 m)
Length (mean)	9 ft 2 in (2·80 m)
Width (mean)	5 ft 9 in (1·75 m)
Floor area	48·4 sq ft (4·5 m²)
Volume	300 cu ft (8·50 m³)

AREAS:
Wings, gross	1,370·3 sq ft (127·3 m²)
Vertical tail surfaces (total)	228·7 sq ft (21·25 m²)
Horizontal tail surfaces (total)	239·0 sq ft (22·20 m²)

WEIGHTS:
Operating weight, empty:
Tu-134	60,627 lb (27,500 kg)
Tu-134A	63,950 lb (29,000 kg)

Max fuel:
Tu-134	28,660 lb (13,000 kg)
Tu-134A	31,800 lb (14,425 kg)

Max payload:
Tu-134	16,975 lb (7,700 kg)
Tu-134A	18,000 lb (8,165 kg)

Max ramp weight:
Tu-134	98,546 lb (44,700 kg)
Tu-134A	104,000 lb (47,175 kg)

Max T-O weight:
Tu-134	98,105 lb (44,500 kg)
Tu-134A	103,600 lb (47,000 kg)

Max landing weight:
Tu-134, standard	88,185 lb (40,000 kg)
Tu-134, emergency	97,000 lb (44,000 kg)
Tu-134A, standard	94,800 lb (43,000 kg)

Max zero-fuel weight:
Tu-134	77,603 lb (35,200 kg)

PERFORMANCE (Tu-134, at T-O weight of 97,000 lb = 44,000 kg unless otherwise stated):
Max cruising speed:
at 36,000 ft (11,000 m)
469 knots (540 mph; 870 km/h)
at 28,000 ft (8,500 m)
485 knots (559 mph; 900 km/h)

Long-range cruising speed at 36,000 ft (11,000 m)
405 knots (466 mph; 750 km/h)

T-O safety speed, one engine out
141 knots (162 mph; 260 km/h)
Approach speed 133 knots (153 mph; 247 km/h)

Landing speed
116-122 knots (134-140 mph; 215-225 km/h)

Stalling speed, wheels and flaps down
103 knots (118 mph; 190 km/h)

Rate of climb at S/L 2,913 ft (888 m)/min
Rate of climb at S/L, one engine out
590 ft (180 m)/min

Service ceiling at AUW of 92,600 lb (42,000 kg)
39,370 ft (12,000 m)

Service ceiling, one engine out, at AUW of 94,800 lb (43,000 kg) 18,375 ft (5,600 m)

T-O run 3,280 ft (1,000 m)

Balanced field length for T-O, FAR standard: at S/L, ISA, max T-O weight
7,152 ft (2,180 m)

Balanced field length for landing, FAR standard: at S/L, ISA, max landing weight
6,726 ft (2,050 m)

Landing from 50 ft (15 m) at AUW of 81,570 lb (37,000 kg) 3,937 ft (1,200 m)

Landing run at AUW of 81,570 lb (37,000 kg): 2,625-2,838 ft (800-865 m)

Ranges, against 27 knots (31 mph; 50 km/h) headwind, 60 min fuel reserve:
with 15,430 lb (7,000 kg) payload at 459 knots (528 mph; 850 km/h) at 36,000 ft (11,000 m) 1,293 nm (1,490 miles; 2,400 km)
with 11,442 lb (5,190 kg) payload at above speed 1,656 nm (1,907 miles; 3,070 km)
with 6,600 lb (3,000 kg) payload at long-range cruising speed 1,888 nm (2,175 miles; 3,500 km)

PERFORMANCE (Tu-134A, at max T-O weight):
Landing run at max landing weight
2,560 ft (780 m)
Range at 405 knots (466 mph; 750 km/h) at 32,800 ft (10,000 m) with reserves for 1 hour flying:
Payload of 18,108 lb (8,215 kg) 1,079 nm (1,243 miles; 2,000 km)
Payload of 8,818 lb (4,000 kg) 1,888 nm (2,175 miles; 3,500 km)

TUPOLEV Tu-144
NATO Code Name: "Charger"

Since this supersonic transport aircraft was first shown in model form at the 1965 Paris Salon de l'Aéronautique, it has undergone considerable development. Its general configuration is similar to that of the Anglo-French Concorde, with an ogival delta wing and large underwing ducts for the four engines. A slight increase in overall dimensions has now given it a greater wing span than the Concorde. In length the two aircraft are almost identical, but the Tu-144 is designed initially to carry fewer passengers than the Concorde, at higher cruising speeds.

According to official Soviet press statements, several prototypes have been built, including a structure test airframe. In addition, an otherwise-standard MiG-21 has been fitted with a scaled-down replica of the Tu-144's ogival wing, in place of both its normal delta wing and horizontal tail surfaces, and is said to have made several dozen research flights, as a result of which modifications were made to the full-size wing.

The first flying prototype of the Tu-144 (CCCP-68001) was assembled and ground-tested at the Zhukovsky Plant, near Moscow, and flew for the first time on 31 December 1968, this being the first flight by a supersonic airliner anywhere in the world. Its landing gear remained extended throughout the 38-minute flight, as it did during the 50-minute second test flight on 8 January 1969. The crew comprised

Tupolev Tu-134A medium-range transport aircraft (two Soloviev D-30 turbofan engines) of Aviogenex, with revised nose configuration *(P. F. Thompson)*

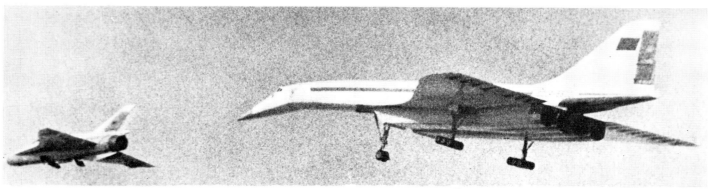

Tupolev Tu-144 in flight, accompanied by the modified MiG-21 "analogue" with scaled-down Tu-144 wing

The prototype Tupolev Tu-144 four-jet supersonic transport, landing at Sheremetyevo Airport, Moscow, with nose in the drooped position (*Tass*)

Eduard Elyan, pilot, Mikhail Kozlov, co-pilot, and two engineers. The pilots sat on upward-ejection seats, and there are two further escape hatches in the top of the fuselage further aft.

On 5 June 1969, the Tu-144 exceeded Mach 1 for the first time, at a height of 36,000 ft (11,000 m), half-an-hour after take-off. Only a slight tremble was said to be discernible as it passed through the transonic region. By 11 May 1970, the prototype had reached a speed of 1,085 knots (1,250 mph; 2,010 km/h) at a height of 54,800 ft (16,700 m). On 26 May it became the first

commercial transport to exceed Mach 2, by flying at 1,160 knots (1,335 mph; 2,150 km/h) at a height of 53,475 ft (16,300 m) for several minutes. The pilot was again Eduard Elyan.

Earlier, at the first public showing of the Tu-144, at Sheremetievo Airport, Moscow, on 21 May, the Deputy Minister for the Aviation Industry, Alexander Kobzarev, said that series production had already started. Export orders will be accepted in 1971.

Construction of the Tu-144 is mainly of VAD-23 light alloy, with extensive use of in-

tegrally-stiffened panels, produced by both chemical milling and machining from solid metal. Stainless steel and titanium are used for the leading-edges, elevons, rudder and under-surface of the rear fuselage, and the aircraft is stated to embody 10,000 parts made of plastics.

The wings have almost a "double-delta" planform, but their aerodynamics are less complicated than those of the Concorde. There is marked conical camber on the highly-swept inner leading-edges, but the tips do not appear to have complex twist. The powered control

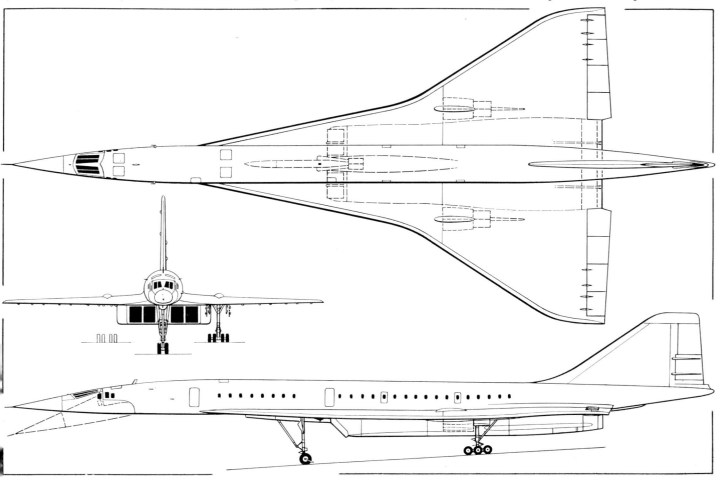

Tupolev Tu-144 supersonic transport (four Kuznetsov NK-144 turbofan engines)

surfaces consist of four separate elevons on each wing and a multi-section rudder.

Each main landing gear unit is fitted with a 12-wheel (three rows of four) bogie, which rotates through 180° as it retracts forward into the wings, outboard of the engine ducts. As the wheels cannot be accommodated entirely within the wing envelope, the landing gear doors embody channels under each longitudinal row of wheels. The twin-wheel steerable nose unit retracts rearward between the engine ducts.

The first flight of the Tu-144 was also the first time that the Kuznetsov NK-144 turbofan engine had been tested in the air. Four NK-144s (each 28,660 lb = 13,000 kg st without reheat) are mounted side by side in the rear of an underwing duct nearly 75 ft (23 m) long. The duct bifurcates into two entirely separate intake trunks, each with a central vertical wall, giving an individual flow of air to each engine. Limited reheat is, or will be, available, raising the static thrust of each engine to 38,580 lb (17,500 kg), but it is intended for use only during take-off under high-temperature conditions and perhaps in cruising flight. Two of the engines are fitted with reverse thrust and a twin brake-parachute is fitted. Fuel capacity is 154,325 lb (70,000 kg).

In service, a flight crew of three will normally be carried. The flight deck windscreen is faired in by a retractable vizor in cruising flight, and the entire nose can be drooped up to 12° for improved visibility during landing.

There are toilet, cloak and baggage compartments between the flight deck and the forward cabin. A galley is positioned between the two cabins and a further large baggage and freight compartment occupies the rear of the fuselage, above the engines. Baggage is intended to be stowed inside this compartment in panniers, which will be unloaded by rolling them back through the pressure bulkhead and down out of the tail. There are no underfloor holds. Up to 121 passengers can be carried, but a 100-seat mixed-class version may be standard initially. In this, the forward cabin accommodates 18 first class seats three-abreast (two one side of the aisle, one on the other side), while the rear cabin has 70 five-abreast and 12 four-abreast tourist class seats.

There are three independent hydraulic systems and two separate systems for pressurisation and air-conditioning. Electronic equipment includes an analogue computer linked to the inertial navigation system (which is supplemented by Doppler), central air data system, auto-pilot and variable-geometry air-intake control system. Approximately 90 per cent of each flight, in scheduled service, will be made under automatic control, with provision for automatic fuel management and blind landing capability.

DIMENSIONS, EXTERNAL:
Wing span   88 ft 7 in (27·00 m)
Length overall, excl probe
                               190 ft 3½ in (58·00 m)
Length overall, incl probe
                               196 ft 10 in (60·00 m)
DIMENSIONS, INTERNAL:
Baggage holds:
Forward   318 cu ft (9 m³)
Aft   565 cu ft (16 m³)
WEIGHT:
Max T-O weight   330,000 lb (150,000 kg)
PERFORMANCE (estimated):
Max cruising speed at 65,000 ft (20,000 m)
             1,350 knots (1,550 mph; 2,500 km/h)
                                          = Mach 2·35
T-O run at AUW of 286,600 lb (130,000 kg)
                                6,235 ft (1,900 m)
Landing run   4,920 ft (1,500 m)
Range with 121 passengers at max cruising
speed   3,508 nm (4,040 miles; 6,500 km)

TUPOLEV TU-154
NATO Code-Name: "Careless"

The three-engined Tu-154, announced in the Spring of 1966, was intended to replace the Tu-104, Il-18 and An-10 on medium/long stage lengths of up to 3,240 nm (3,725 miles; 6,000 km). It will be able to operate from airfields with a class B surface, including packed earth and gravel.

The first of several prototype and pre-production models flew for the first time on 4 October 1968, and entry into service with Aeroflot is scheduled for early 1971. CSA Czech Airlines have already stated that they also plan to operate Tu-154s.

A stretched version, accommodating 250 passengers, is planned.

TYPE: Three-engined medium/long-range transport aircraft.

WINGS: Cantilever low-wing monoplane. Sweepback 35° at quarter-chord. Conventional all-metal three-spar structure; centre spar extending to just outboard of inner edge of aileron on each wing. Five-section slat on outer 80% of each wing leading-edge. Triple-slotted flaps. Four-section spoilers on each wing. Section inboard of landing gear housing serves as air-brake and lift-dumper; two middle sections can be used as air-brakes in flight. Hot-air de-icing of wing leading-edge. Slats are electrically-heated.

FUSELAGE: Conventional all-metal semi-monocoque structure of circular section.

TAIL UNIT: Cantilever all-metal structure, with variable-incidence tailplane mounted at tip of fin. Leading-edges de-iced by hot air.

LANDING GEAR: Retractable tricycle type. Hydraulic actuation. Main units retract rearward into fairings on wing trailing-edge. Each consists of a bogie made up of three pairs of wheels, size 930 × 305, in tandem. Steerable twin-wheel nose unit has wheels size 800 × 225 and retracts forward.

POWER PLANT: Three Kuznetsov NK-8-2 turbofan engines, each rated at 20,950 lb (9,500 kg) st, on each side of rear fuselage and inside extreme rear of fuselage. Standard fuel capacity 9,050 Imp gallons (41,140 litres). Max fuel capacity 10,300 Imp gallons (46,825 litres).

ACCOMMODATION: Flight crew of two pilots and flight engineer; provision for navigator aft of pilot and folding seats for additional pilots or instructors. There are basic passenger versions for 158, 150, 146, 136 and 128 passengers respectively. Each has a toilet at the front (starboard), galley amidships and three toilets aft. Standard economy class version has 54 seats in six-abreast rows, with two tables between front rows, in forward cabin; and 104 seats in six-abreast rows (rear two rows four-abreast) in rear cabin at seat pitch of 29·5 in (75 cm). The tourist class versions carry 146 passengers at a seat pitch of 31·9 in (81 cm) or 136 at a pitch of 34·25 in (87 cm), or 150 passengers at a pitch of 34·25 in (87 cm) with reduced galley facilities. The 128-seat version has only 24 first-class seats, four-abreast at a pitch of 40 in (102 cm), in the forward cabin. There is also an all-cargo version. Passenger doors are forward of front cabin and between cabins on the port side, with service doors opposite. Baggage hold under cabin floor, with two doors. Smaller hold under rear cabin for carrying spare parts or special cargo such as radioactive isotopes.

ELECTRONICS AND EQUIPMENT: Automatic flight control system standard, including automatic navigation on pre-programmed route under control of navigational computer with en-route checks by ground radio beacons (including VOR, VOR/DME) or radar, and automatic approach by ILS to ICAO category II standards. Moving-map ground position indicator, HF and VHF radio, and radar standard.

SYSTEMS: Air-conditioning system pressure differential 9·0 lb/sq in (0·63 kg/cm²). Hydraulic system working pressure 3,000 lb/sq in (210 kg/cm²). Three-phase 200/115V AC electrical system, supplied by three 40kVA alternators. 28V DC system. APU standard.

DIMENSIONS, EXTERNAL:
Wing span   123 ft 2½ in (37·55 m)

Tupolev Tu-154 medium/long-range transport aircraft, photographed during a test flight in November 1969 *(Tass)*

Tupolev Tu-154 medium/long-range transport aircraft (three 20,950 lb = 9,500 kg st Kuznetsov NK-8-2 turbofan engines) *(Tass)*

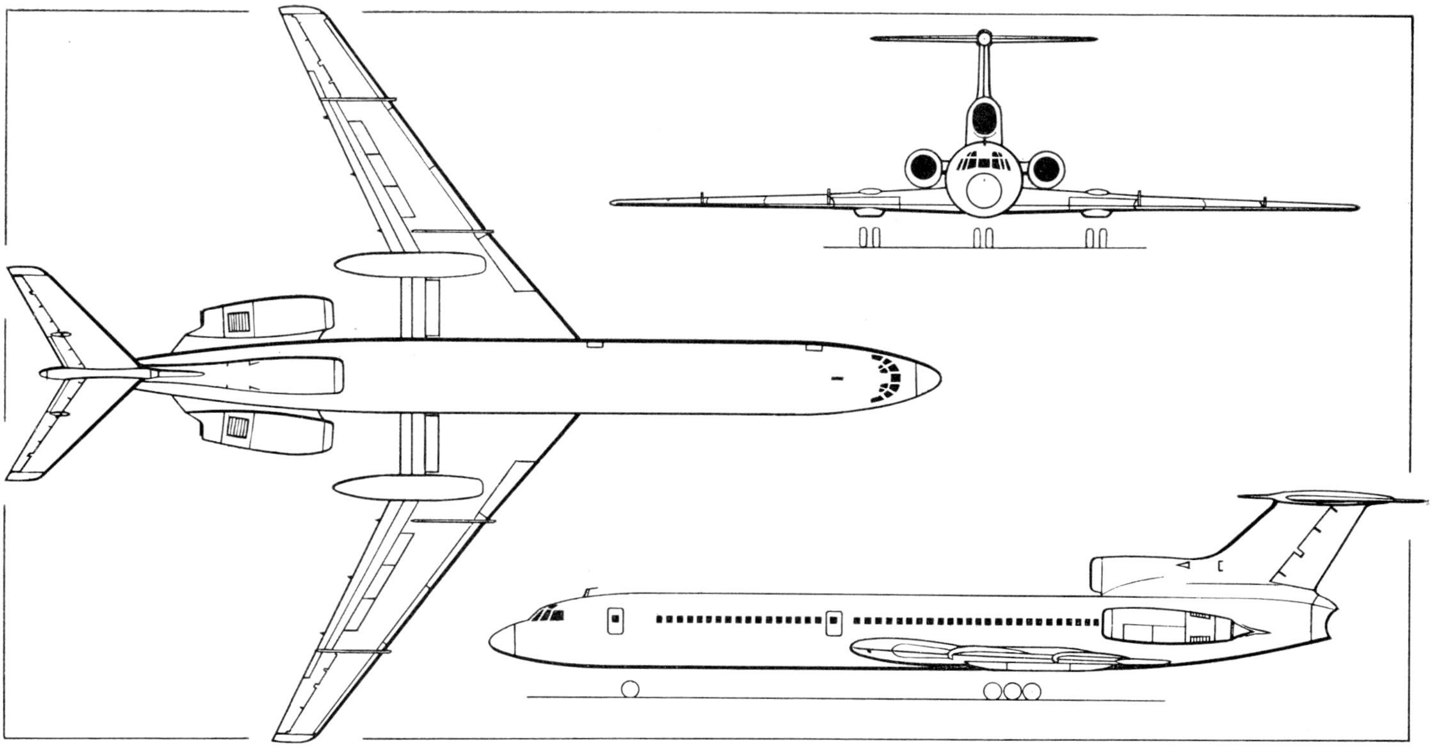

Tupolev Tu-154 medium/long-range transport aircraft (three Kuznetsov NK-8-2 turbofan engines)

Length overall	157 ft 1¾ in (47·90 m)
Height overall	37 ft 4¾ in (11·40 m)
Tailplane span	43 ft 11½ in (13·40 m)
Wheel track	37 ft 9 in (11·50 m)
Wheelbase	62 ft 1 in (18·92 m)
Passenger doors (each):	
Height	5 ft 7 in (1·73 m)
Width	2 ft 7½ in (0·80 m)
Height to sill	10 ft 2 in (3·10 m)
Main baggage hold doors (each):	
Height	3 ft 11¼ in (1·20 m)
Width	4 ft 5 in (1·35 m)

Dimensions, Internal:

Cabin: Width	11 ft 9 in (3·58 m)
Height	6 ft 7½ in (2·02 m)
Volume	5,763 cu ft (163·2 m³)
Main baggage hold	1,342 cu ft (38·0 m³)
Rear underfloor hold	176 cu ft (5·0 m³)

Areas:

Wings, gross	2,169 sq ft (201·45 m²)
Horizontal tail surfaces	436·48 sq ft (40·55 m²)
Vertical tail surfaces	341·43 sq ft (31·72 m²)

Weights:

Operating weight empty	95,900 lb (43,500 kg)
Normal payload	35,275 lb (16,000 kg)
Max payload	44,090 lb (20,000 kg)
Normal T-O weight	185,188 lb (84,000 kg)
Max ramp weight	199,077 lb (90,300 kg)
Max T-O weight	198,416 lb (90,000 kg)
Normal landing weight	149,915 lb (68,000 kg)
Max landing weight	185,188 lb (84,000 kg)
Max zero-fuel weight	139,994 lb (63,500 kg)

Performance (at max T-O weight, except where indicated):

Max level speed: above 36,000 ft (11,000 m) Mach 0·90; at low altitudes 310 knots (357 mph; 575 km/h) IAS

Max cruising speed at 31,150 ft (9,500 m) 526 knots (605 mph; 975 km/h)

Best-cost cruising speed at 36,000-39,350 ft (11,000-12-000 m) 486 knots (560 mph; 900 km/h) = Mach 0·85

Long-range cruising speed at 36,000-39,350 ft (11,000-12,000 m) 459 knots (528 mph; 850 km/h) = Mach 0·80

Approach speed 127 knots (146 mph; 235 km/h)

T-O run at normal T-O weight, ISA 3,740 ft (1,140 m)

Balanced runway length at max T-O weight, FAR standard:

ISA, S/L	6,890 ft (2,100 m)
ISA + 20°C, S/L	7,940 ft (2,420 m)

Landing field length, at max landing weight, FAR standard:

ISA, S/L	6,758 ft (2,060 m)
ISA + 20°C, S/L	7,273 ft (2,217 m)

Ranges at 36,000 ft (11,000 m) with standard fuel, reserves for 1 hour and 6% of total fuel:

at 486 knots (560 mph; 900 km/h), with T-O weight of 84,000 kg and max payload (158 passengers, baggage and 5 tonnes of cargo and mail) 1,360 nm (1,565 miles; 2,520 km)

as above, T-O weight of 90,000 kg 1,867 nm (2,150 miles; 3,460 km)

at 459 knots (528 mph; 850 km/h), with T-O weight of 84,000 kg and max payload as above 1,510 nm (1,740 miles; 2,800 km)

as above, T-O weight of 90,000 kg 2,050 nm (2,360 miles; 3,800 km)

max range with 30,100 lb (13,650 kg) payload 2,850 nm (3,280 miles; 5,280 km)

Ranges at 36,000 ft (11,000 m) with optional centre-wing tanks, reserves as above:

with 19,840 lb (9,000 kg) payload (95 passengers) 3,453 nm (3,977 miles; 6,400 km)

with 14,770 lb (6,700 kg) payload (70 passengers) 3,723 nm (4,287 miles; 6,900 km)

YAKOVLEV

ALEKSANDIR SERGIEVICH YAKOVLEV

Yakovlev is one of the most versatile Russian designers and the recent products of his design bureau have ranged from supersonic long-range fighters to the Yak-24 tandem-rotor helicopter and a variety of training and light general-purpose aircraft. Types in current production or under development are described hereafter.

YAKOVLEV YAK-18

NATO Code Name: "Max"

Standard primary trainer of the Soviet Air Force and civil flying clubs since 1946, the Yak-18 and its developments are also in service in Afghanistan, Albania, Austria, Bulgaria, China, Egypt, East Germany, Hungary, North Korea, Poland and Rumania. The following versions have been produced:

Yak-18. Initial production version with 160 hp M-11FR engine and tail-wheel landing gear. Production completed.

Yak-18U. Modified version of Yak-18 with tricycle landing gear. Main wheels repositioned to an attachment at the rear spar, and retract forward; nose-wheel retracts to rear. Forward part of fuselage lengthened by 18 in (46 cm). Cylinder head covers of the cowling of the M-11FR-1 engine modified to permit a more extensive frontal air entry. Production completed.

Yak-18A. Cleaned-up development of Yak-18U with more powerful Ivchenko AI-14RF engine. Cockpit canopy enlarged. Small dorsal fin extension added. Introduced in 1957 (originally with 260 hp AI-14R engine).

Yak-18P. Single-seat development of Yak-18A for advanced training, including aerobatics. Two versions produced: one with cockpit aft of wing and forward-retracting main wheels, other with cockpit over wing and inward-retracting main wheels. Fuel system for 5 min inverted flying. Longer-span ailerons. Production completed.

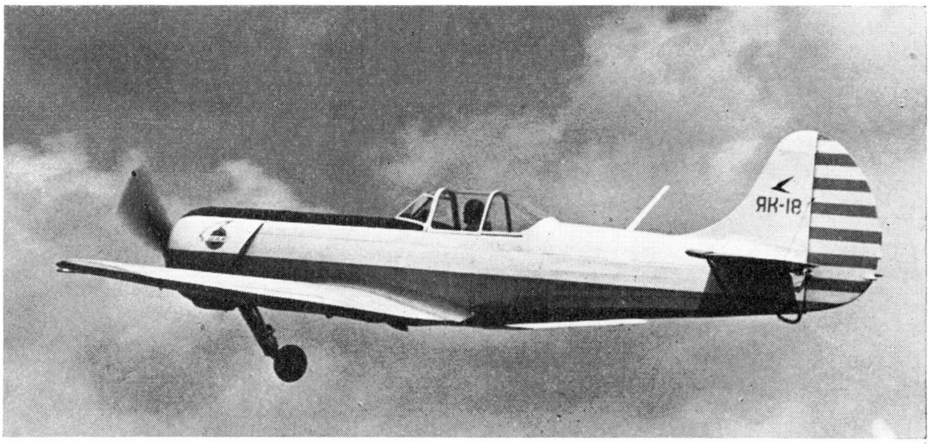

Yak-18PM taking off, with nose-wheel partly retracted *(Tass)*

Yak-18PM. Latest single-seat aerobatic version produced for 1966 World Aerobatic Championships in Moscow, which it won decisively. AI-14RF engine, dihedral reduced, cockpit further aft than on Yak-18P.

Yak-18T. Redesigned four-seat general-purpose cabin version. Described separately.

The following description refers to the Yak-18A and Yak-18PM.

Wings: Cantilever low-wing monoplane. Constant-chord centre-section; tapered outer wings with rounded tips. Dihedral on outer panels 7° 20′ on Yak-18A, 2° on Yak-18PM. All-metal two-spar structure, with metal-covered leading-edge and fabric covering aft of front spar. Longer-span ailerons on Yak-18PM. One-piece pneumatically-actuated trailing-edge flap across centre-section. Forward-hinged air-brake under centre fuselage of Yak-18PM.

FUSELAGE: Steel-tube structure, with metal covering to rear of cockpit and fabric covering on rear section.

TAIL UNIT: Braced metal structure with fabric covering on all surfaces. Trim-tab in rudder and each elevator.

LANDING GEAR: Pneumatically-retractable tricycle type. Rearward-retracting nose unit. Main units retract forward on Yak-18A, the wheels remaining largely exposed to reduce damage in a wheels-up landing. Inward-retracting main units on Yak-18PM, with wheels fully enclosed in centre-section when up. Pneumatic brakes.

POWER PLANT: One 300 hp Ivchenko AI-14RF nine-cylinder radial air-cooled engine, driving a Type V-530 D-35 two-blade wooden variable-pitch propeller, diameter 7 ft 2½ in (2·30 m). Special fuel and oil systems for prolonged inverted flight. Fuel in two tanks in wing roots, with total capacity of 28·5 Imp gallons (130 litres).

ACCOMMODATION: Yak-18A has two seats in tandem beneath continuous canopy, with separate rearward-sliding hoods. Yak-18PM has single cockpit with similar rearward-sliding canopy.

ELECTRONICS AND EQUIPMENT: Both versions have VHF radio as standard. Blind-flying instrumentation, radio-compass, marker beacon receiver and intercom are also standard on Yak-18A.

DIMENSIONS, EXTERNAL:
Wing span:
Yak-18A, -18PM   34 ft 9¼ in (10·60 m)
Length overall:
Yak-18A, -18PM   27 ft 4¾ in (8·35 m)
Height overall:
Yak-18A, -18PM   11 ft 0 in (3·35 m)
AREA:
Wings, gross:
Yak-18A, -18PM   183 sq ft (17·0 m²)
WEIGHTS:
Weight empty:
Yak-18A   2,259 lb (1,025 kg)
Max T-O weight:
Yak-18A   2,910 lb (1,320 kg)
Yak-18PM   2,425 lb (1,100 kg)
PERFORMANCE (at max T-O weight):
Max level speed:
Yak-18A   162 knots (186 mph; 300 km/h)
Yak-18PM   173 knots (199 mph; 320 km/h)
Cruising speed:
Yak-18PM   152 knots (175 mph; 282 km/h)
Rate of climb at S/L:
Yak-18PM   1,970 ft (600 m)/min
T-O run:
Yak-18A   655 ft (200 m)
Yak-18PM   460 ft (140 m)
Landing run:
Yak-18A   820 ft (250 m)
Yak-18PM   427 ft (130 m)
Range with max fuel:
Yak-18A   377 knots (435 miles; 700 km)
Yak-18PM   217 knots (250 miles; 400 km)

YAKOVLEV YAK-18T

This extensively-redesigned cabin version of the Yak-18 was shown for the first time at the 1967 Paris Air Show. It is powered, like the Yak-18A and -18PM, with a 300 hp Ivchenko AI-14RF nine-cylinder radial engine, driving a two-blade variable-pitch propeller. Its braced tail unit and retractable tricycle landing gear, with inward-retracting main wheels and rearward-retracting nose-wheel, are similar in configuration to those of the Yak-18PM.

The wing span has been increased by extending the constant-chord centre-section, and the wing-tips are more square than on other aircraft of the Yak-18 series. The fuselage is entirely new, being built as an all-metal semi-monocoque of square section. Four persons can be carried in pairs in the enclosed cabin, which has a large forward-hinged door on each side. Dual controls, heating and ventilation are standard. The rear bench seat is removable to enable the Yak-18T to be used for cargo-carrying. As an ambulance, it will accommodate the pilot, one stretcher patient and an attendant.

Standard equipment includes ILS, VHF radio, radio-compass, radio-altimeter and intercom.

The Yak-18T is intended to replace the Yak-12 in Aeroflot service.

DIMENSIONS:
Wing span   36 ft 7¼ in (11·16 m)
Length overall   27 ft 4¾ in (8·35 m)
AREA:
Wings, gross   202·4 sq ft (18·80 m²)
WEIGHT:
Max T-O weight   3,571 lb (1,620 kg)
PERFORMANCE:
Max level speed
   162 knots (186 mph; 300 km/h)
Cruising speed   135 knots (155 mph; 250 km/h)

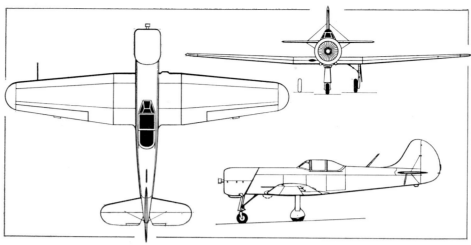

Yakovlev Yak-18PM single-seat aerobatic monoplane

The four-seat Yak-18T (300 hp Ivchenko AI-14RF engine) (*S. P. Peltz*)

T-O run   655 ft (200 m)
Landing run   820 ft (250 m)
Range with max fuel
   over 538 nm (620 miles; 1,000 km)

YAKOVLEV YAK-25/26/27
NATO Code Names: "Flashlight" and "Mangrove"

Four versions of the Yak-25/27 series have been identified by NATO code names, as follows:

Flashlight-A. Original **Yak-25** twin-jet all-weather interceptor, seen in public for the first time at the Tushino display in July 1955. Crew of two in tandem. Radar in rounded nose radome. Armament comprised two 37 mm guns in lower front fuselage and provision for an under-fuselage pack of unguided air-to-air rockets. Powered initially by two AM-5 turbojet engines, for which prototype approval was given in July 1951, with initial flight trials and State Acceptance Trials in 1953. Entered service as standard all-weather fighter of Soviet Air Force in 1955. Changed to Klimov RD-9 turbojets (each 6,175 lb = 2,800 kg st) as **Yak-25F** in 1957. Described in 1963-64 edition of *Jane's*.

Flashlight-B (Yak-25R: Razvedchik = Reconnaissance). Multi-purpose tactical aircraft, which also received prototype approval in July 1951 and had successively AM-5 and RD-9 engines like the basic Yak-25. Shown at 1956 Tushino display. Basically similar to "Flashlight-A", but cockpit canopy redesigned for single occupant and pointed glazed nose, to accommodate a navigator/bomb-aimer. Longer engine nacelles. Extended chord at wing-root leading-edge. Radome under front fuselage.

Flashlight-C (Yak-27). Shown in prototype form at 1956 Tushino display. Improved all-

weather interceptor; basically similar to Yak-25 but with aerodynamic refinements, including pointed nose radome, longer engine nacelles for RD-9 engines with afterburners, and extended chord at wing-root. Seen subsequently with extended wing-tips and drooped extended-chord leading-edge on outer wings as illustrated for "Mangrove". This version is not thought to have entered service in any numbers.

Mangrove (Yak-26). Developed in parallel with Yak-27, embodying the same aerodynamic refinements but with glazed forward fuselage like Yak-25R. Produced in quantity for tactical reconnaissance duties with Soviet Air Force. Same afterburning RD-9 turbojets as Yak-27. Wingtips extended outboard of the now-pointed balancer-wheel fairings (which are in their original position and therefore inset from the new wing-tips). Fixed armament reduced to one 30 mm gun.

The following description refers to "Mangrove".

TYPE: Two-seat tactical reconnaissance aircraft.

WINGS: Cantilever mid-wing monoplane of basically-constant chord. Extended leading-edge on outer wings. Leading-edge has increased sweepback near root, in line with straight portion of trailing-edge; remainder of wing has sweepback of 45°. Single fence on each wing, at inner end of extended chord section. Tab in each aileron. Flaps in two sections on each wing.

FUSELAGE: Circular-section all-metal structure.

TAIL UNIT: Cantilever all-metal structure, with tailplane mid-way up fin. All surfaces swept-back. Small ventral stabilising fin.

LANDING GEAR: Zero-track tricycle type with single steerable nose-wheel and twin-wheel rear

Yakovlev Yak-26 ("Mangrove") tactical reconnaissance aircraft

Two of the Yak-28P ("Firebar") two-seat all-weather interceptors seen at Domodedovo, each armed with two "Anab" missiles
(*Aviation Week and Space Technology*)

unit in line with wing trailing-edge, all retracting aft into fuselage. Small balancer wheel at each wingtip, retracting rearward into streamlined fairing.

POWER PLANT: Two RD-9 turbojet engines, each rated at 8,820 lb (4,000 kg) st with afterburning, in underwing nacelles.

ACCOMMODATION: Pilot on ejection seat under rearward-sliding transparent canopy. Navigator/bomb-aimer in glazed nose compartment.

ARMAMENT: Single 30 mm gun in fairing under starboard side of front fuselage.

DIMENSIONS, EXTERNAL (estimated):
Wing span	38 ft 6 in (11·75 m)
Length overall, including nose-probe	
	62 ft 0 in (18·90 m)
Height	14 ft 6 in (4·40 m)

AREA (estimated):
Wings, gross	340 sq ft (31·5 m²)

WEIGHT (estimated):
Normal T-O weight	25,000 lb (11,350 kg)

PERFORMANCE (estimated):
Max speed at 36,000 ft (11,000 m)	Mach 0·95
Cruising speed at 10,000 ft (3,050 m)	Mach 0·75

YAKOVLEV YAK-28
NATO Code Names: "Brewer", "Firebar" and "Maestro"

First seen in considerable numbers in the 1961 Soviet Aviation Day fly-past were three obvious successors to the Yak-25/27 series described by the commentator as supersonic multi-purpose aircraft. A major change is that these aircraft are shoulder-wing monoplanes, whereas all versions of "Flashlight" and "Mangrove" are mid-wing, and they are in fact entirely new designs, following only the general configuration of the earlier types.

A further important change is that the landing gear of these later aircraft comprises two twin-wheel units in tandem, with the forward unit under the pilot's cockpit and the rear unit moved further aft than on the Yak-25/27, to a point immediately in front of the ventral fin. Wing-tip balancer wheels are retained. The entire wing-root leading-edge has been extended forward and the height of the fin and rudder increased. Tailplane sweep is also increased.

The engines are reported to be similar to the Tumansky Type TDR Mk R37F turbojets fitted in the MiG-21, with intake centre-body shock-cones. Their comparatively short nacelles increase in diameter towards the nozzles, and afterburners are fitted to the current first-line aircraft. A pointed slipper-type external fuel tank can be carried under the leading-edge of each wing, outboard of the engine nacelles.

Three versions of the basic design have been reported, with the following code-names:

Brewer (Yak-28). Two-seat tactical attack version, with glazed nose, corresponding to Yak-26 ("Mangrove") and produced to replace the Il-28 in the Soviet Air Force. Most examples have blister radome under fuselage just forward of wings. Guns semi-submerged in each side of the fuselage on some aircraft, on starboard side only on others. Internal bomb-bay between the under-fuselage radome and the rear main landing gear unit.

Firebar. Tandem two-seat all-weather fighter derivative of Yak-28, corresponding to Yak-27. Nose radome. Internal weapons bay deleted. "Anab" air-to-air missiles under each wing instead of guns. Identified as **Yak-28P** (Perekhvatchik = interceptor) at 1967 Domodedovo display, the suffix "P" indicating that the design had been *adapted* for the fighter role. Example shown in static park had a much longer dielectric nose-cone than the standard operational "Firebars" in the flying display and had two missile pylons under each wing, one for an "Atoll" and the other for an "Anab". This suggested that it was a weapon development aircraft, perhaps for the new Sukhoi "Flagon-A".

Maestro. Trainer version of "Firebar". No details available.

DIMENSIONS (estimated):
Wing span	42 ft 6 in (12·95 m)
Length overall:	
Yak-28	71 ft 0½ in (21·65 m)
Height overall	12 ft 11¼ in (3·95 m)

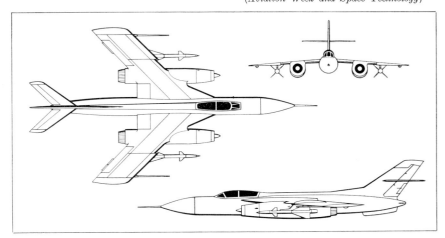

The Yakovlev Yak-28P all-weather fighter, code-named "Firebar"

Yakovlev Yak-28P ("Firebar") two-seat all-weather interceptors, photographed in February 1970 (*Tass*)

The Yakovlev Yak-28 (known to NATO as "Brewer") with underwing auxiliary fuel tanks
(*Miroslav Prucha*)

WEIGHT (estimated):
  Max T-O weight:
    Yak-28P   35,000 lb (15,875 kg)
PERFORMANCE (Yak-28P, estimated):
  Max level speed at 35,000 ft (10,670 m)
    636 knots (733 mph; 1,180 km/h)=Mach 1·1
  Cruising speed 496 knots (571 mph; 920 km/h)
  Service ceiling   55,000 ft (16,750 m)
  Max combat radius 500 nm (575 miles; 925 km)
  Max range 1,040-1,390 nm (1,200-1,600 miles;
    1,930-2,575 km)

YAKOVLEV YAK-?
NATO Code Name: "Mandrake"

Identified at present only by its NATO code-
name of "Mandrake", the Soviet Union's counterpart to the Lockheed U-2 high-altitude reconnaissance aircraft was reported to be operational by
the Spring of 1963.

"Mandrake" is a development of the well-
proven Yak-25, with an existing fuselage married
to a new straight wing of extended span, as shown
in the adjacent three-view drawing. This has
made possible a good high-altitude performance
with a minimum of redesign and has a precedent,
as it was the technique adopted some years ago
by the USAF in evolving the RB-57D special
reconnaissance version of the Martin B-57.

The fuselage is believed to be basically similar to
that of the Yak-25R/26, with a single-seat cockpit
and a new "solid" nose containing reconnaissance
equipment. The zero-track main landing gear
is retained, requiring the provision of housings
for the outrigger wheels on the new wings. The
turbojet engines are possibly a variant of the
Klimov VK-7/VK-9 series, which have already
been used to establish international height records.

DIMENSIONS, EXTERNAL (estimated):
  Wing span   70 ft 6 in (21·50 m)
  Length overall   50 ft 0 in (15·25 m)

YAKOVLEV EXPERIMENTAL VTOL AIRCRAFT
NATO Code Name: "Freehand"

This aircraft is much less refined than the
British Hawker Siddeley Harrier and must be
regarded as a purely experimental design. The
two examples photographed at the air display
at Domodedovo in July 1967 appeared to be
identical. Only one (bearing the number 37
on its nose) took part in the flying programme,
without underwing stores. Photographs of
the other aircraft (No 38) usually show it with
a 16-round rocket pack under each wing.

Code-named "Freehand" by NATO, this
aircraft is clearly subsonic. At Domodedovo,
aircraft No 37 took off vertically, performed a
transition at a height of about 160 ft (50 m),
made a circuit of the airfield, including a high-
speed fly-past, and ended with a 180° hovering
turn before making a vertical landing.

TYPE: Single-seat VTOL research aircraft.
WINGS: Cantilever mid-wing monoplane of
  cropped delta planform. Anhedral from roots.
  Sweepback approx 40° on leading-edges.
  Entire trailing-edge hinged, as flaps and
  ailerons.
FUSELAGE: Wide fuselage of elliptical cross-
  section, with divided ram air intake in nose.
  Two large blister fairings on front fuselage,
  under each engine. Full-width backward-
  hinged door under nose to reduce possibility
  of recirculation into air intakes during take-off
  and landing; this door incorporates small
  separately-hinged centre panels between
  which nose-wheel retracts. Smaller rearward-
  hinged door under centre-fuselage, forward of
  nozzles, prevents undesirable interaction of
  exhaust gases under fuselage, in conjunction
  with two longitudinal strakes forward and

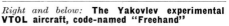
Right and below: **The Yakovlev experimental
VTOL aircraft, code-named "Freehand"**

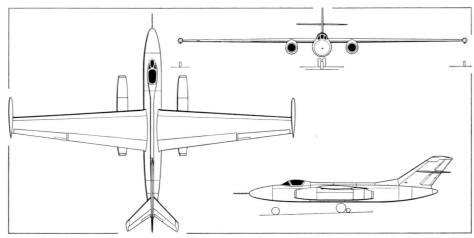
The Yakovlev high-altitude reconnaissance aircraft code-named "Mandrake"

The Yakovlev experimental VTOL aircraft, code-named "Freehand"

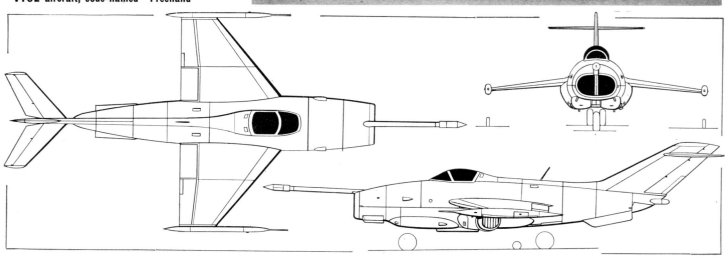

inboard of nozzles. The outboard edges of both doors are bent down in the form of shallow strakes. Double-hinged panel forward of main landing gear unit protects it from hot exhaust gases and is also used as an air-brake.

TAIL UNIT: Cantilever type with tailplane mounted high on fin. All surfaces swept. Fixed-incidence tailplane, with conventional elevators. Trim-tab in rudder. Two large ventral fins, between which is mounted a trapeze-shape telemetry aerial.

LANDING GEAR: Retractable tandem type, consisting of a single forward-retracting nose-wheel and rearward-retracting twin-wheel main unit, with two small balancer wheels which retract forward into the wingtip fairings.

POWER PLANT: Two turbojet engines, mounted side-by-side at bottom of front fuselage and each exhausting through a large-diameter louvred and gridded vectored-thrust nozzle. Bleed-air supply to "puffer-pipe" reaction control nozzles located at the tail, at the end of a massive nose-probe and in each wingtip fairing, for control in hovering and low-speed flight.

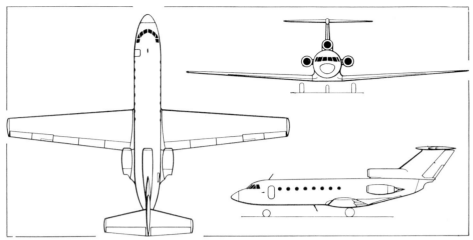

Yakovlev Yak-40 three-turbofan short-haul transport aircraft

Eight-passenger executive transport version of the Yakovlev Yak-40 (three Ivchenko AI-25 turbofan engines) (*Air Portraits*)

ACCOMMODATION: Single seat under sideways-hinged blister canopy. One-piece curved windscreen with no optically-flat panels. Pilot seated high, above power plant.

DIMENSIONS, EXTERNAL (estimated):
Wing span, between centre-lines of wingtip
fairings   27 ft 0 in (8·25 m)
Length overall   57 ft 6 in (17·50 m)
Length of fuselage:
incl nose-probe   51 ft 0 in (15·50 m)
excl nose probe   41 ft 0 in (12·50 m)
Height overall   14 ft 9 in (4·50 m)

YAKOVLEV YAK-40
NATO Code Name: "Codling"

This short-haul jet transport was designed to replace the Li-2 (Soviet-built DC-3) and to operate from Class 5 (grass) airfields. Although comparatively small, it is powered by three turbofan engines, mounted at the tail. The prototype flew for the first time on 21 October 1966 and was followed quickly by four more prototypes. Production was initiated in 1967 and the Yak-40 made its first passenger flight in Aeroflot service on 30 September 1968. It will operate eventually over several thousand short routes.

By April 1970 a total of more than 200 Yak-40s were in service with Aeroflot, some as air ambulances carrying patients to medical centres and to Black Sea convalescent centres. Production of 300 more had been authorised at that time, and these are being built in a factory at Saratov, about 300 miles (500 km) south-east of Moscow, at a current rate of eight per month. Two have been delivered to Aertirrena of Italy, who are also distributors of the Yak-40, and Lineas Aereas La Urraca of Colombia are reported to have ordered four.

Developed versions, on which work is under way, include a "stretched" model, provisionally designated **Yak-40M**, with two 39·4 in (1·0 m) additional cabin sections inserted in the fuselage fore and aft of the wing. These will permit the carriage of 33 passengers with full baggage allowance, or up to 40 persons without baggage. The thrust of each AI-25 turbofan will be increased to 3,850 lb (1,750 kg) to cater for higher weights. Production of this model is scheduled to begin in about 1971-72.

The Yak-40 is designed for a service life of 30,000 hours.

TYPE: Three-turbofan short-haul transport.

WINGS: Cantilever low-wing monoplane. Thickness/chord ratio 15% at root, 10% at tip. No sweepback at quarter-chord. All-duralumin structure consists of a main spar, fore and aft auxiliary spars, ribs and stringers, covered with skin of varying thickness for which chemical milling is utilised. Wing made in two sections, joined at aircraft centre-line. Manually-operated ailerons, each in two sections. Hydraulically-operated plain flaps, each in three sections linked together by perforated plates, reportedly to cater for wing flexing in severe turbulence. Trim-tabs in ailerons. Automatic or manually-controlled hot-air de-icing system.

FUSELAGE: Semi-monocoque duralumin structure of frames, longerons and stringers. Floor of foam plastic with veneer covering. Skin panels spot-welded and bonded in place, then flush-riveted at ends. Diameter of fuselage 7 ft 10½ in (2·40 m).

TAIL UNIT: Cantilever structure of duralumin, with electrically-controlled hydraulically-actuated variable-incidence tailplane mounted at tip of fin. Manually-operated control surfaces. Automatic or manually-controlled hot-air de-icing system.

LANDING GEAR: Hydraulically-actuated retractable type, with single wheel on each unit. Emergency extension by gravity. Main wheels retract inward and are unfaired in flight. Long-stroke oleo-nitrogen shock-absorbers. Main wheel tyres size 1120 × 450, pressure 50-57 lb/sq in (3·5-4·0 kg/cm²). Hydraulically-steerable forward-retracting nose-wheel, with tyre size 720 × 310, pressure 57-64 lb/sq in (4·0-4·5 kg/cm²). Hydraulic disc brakes.

POWER PLANT: Three Ivchenko AI-25 turbofan engines, each rated at 3,300 lb (1,500 kg) st. Fin and boundary layer splitter beneath and forward of intake for centre engine. Thrust reverser under development for this engine, to further improve landing performance. Fuel in integral tanks between front auxiliary spar and main spar in each wing, from outboard of the fuselage to the inner end of the aileron, total capacity 860 Imp gallons (3,910 litres). Type AI-9 turbo-compressor mounted in rear of top engine intake fairing for engine starting. Provision for starting from ground compressed air supply.

ACCOMMODATION: Crew of two side-by-side on flight deck, on adjustable seats with safety belts. Central jump seat at rear may be occupied by third person. Main cabin normally laid out for 24 or 27 passengers in three-abreast rows, with two-chair units on starboard side of aisle. Seat pitch 29·7 in (75·5 cm). Seats fold back against walls when aircraft is used as a freighter. 24-passenger version has large carry-on baggage compartment to rear of cabin, followed by a toilet (starboard) and wardrobe (port). Normal entry via hydraulically-actuated ventral airstair door at rear. Service door on port side of cabin, at front. Provision for carrying up to 33 passengers in high-density version or 8-10 in executive version. Latter has four-seat sofa, armchair seats, conference table and bar in main cabin, with separate compartment aft for four assistants and cabin attendants, and galley. A special door for the flight crew enables them to enter and leave aircraft without disturbing occupants of main cabin. Cabin fully pressurised and air-conditioned; max pressure differential 4·26 lb/sq in (0·3 kg/cm²).

ELECTRONICS AND EQUIPMENT: Full blind-flying instrumentation, HF and VHF communications, radio navigation system, flight director system, autopilot, remote-indicating gyro horizon, dead-reckoning computer, IFF transponder, two radio-compasses, radar altimeter and weather radar, permitting automatic approach, with 165 ft (50 m) cloudbase and 1,650 ft (500 m) visibility minima. A Collins avionics package will be available optionally to Western operators.

SYSTEMS: Hydraulic system, pressure 2,200 lb/sq in (155 kg/cm²), supplied by pumps on centre and port engines, with electrical stand-by pump and emergency hand-pump. Electrical supply from three 18V DC generators and two batteries, with five inverters for 400 c/s AC supply at 115V and 36V.

DIMENSIONS, EXTERNAL:
Wing span   82 ft 0¼ in (25·0 m)
Wing aspect ratio   9
Length overall   66 ft 9½ in (20·36 m)
Height overall   21 ft 4 in (6·50 m)
Tailplane span   24 ft 7¼ in (7·50 m)
Wheel track   14 ft 10 in (4·52 m)
Wheelbase   24 ft 6 in (7·465 m)

Rear cabin door:	
Height	5 ft 8½ in (1·74 m)
Width	3 ft 1 in (0·94 m)
Service door:	
Height	3 ft 11¼ in (1·20 m)
Width	1 ft 9½ in (0·55 m)

DIMENSIONS, INTERNAL:

Cabin: Length	22 ft 0 in (6·70 m)
Max width	7 ft 0¾ in (2·15 m)
Max height	6 ft 0¾ in (1·85 m)

AREA:

Wings, gross	753 sq ft (70 m²)

WEIGHTS AND LOADING:

Operating weight empty	20,600 lb (9,345 kg)
Normal payload	5,070 lb (2,300 kg)
Max payload	6,150 lb (2,790 kg)
Max ramp weight	30,430 lb (13,800 kg)

T-O weight:

with 3,970 lb (1,800 kg) fuel	
	28,990 lb (13,150 kg)
with 6,615 lb (3,000 kg) fuel	
	30,200 lb (13,700 kg)
Max landing weight	29,210 lb (13,250 kg)
Max zero-fuel weight	25,740 lb (11,675 kg)
Max wing loading	40·1 lb/sq ft (195·7 kg/m²)

PERFORMANCE (at max T-O weight):

Max level speed at S/L
324 knots (373 mph; 600 km/h) IAS
= Mach 0·7

Max cruising speed
297 knots (342 mph; 550 km/h)

Best-cost cruising speed
269 knots (310 mph; 500 km/h)

Approach speed	97 knots (112 mph; 180 km/h)
Landing speed	82 knots (94 mph; 150 km/h)
Rate of climb at S/L	2,000 ft (610 m)/min
T-O run	1,115-1,180 ft (340-360 m)
T-O to 35 ft (10 m)	1,310-1,475 ft (400-450 m)

FAR T-O field length, ISA, S/L
1,800 ft (550 m)

Landing run	1,115-1,180 ft (340-360 m)

Yakovlev Yak-40 short-haul transport aircraft (three Ivchenko AI-25 turbofan engines) (*Tass*)

Ranges:
With normal payload at best-cost cruising
speed   540 nm (621 miles; 1,000 km)

With max fuel and 3,140 lb (1,425 kg) payload
at long-range cruising speed
800 nm (920 miles; 1,480 km)

UNIDENTIFIED AIRCRAFT

Hereafter are listed two Russian aircraft concerning which insufficient information is available for positive identification.

1. RV. Two payload-to-height records were established by Vladimir Smirnov, flying an aircraft designated the "RV", in July 1959. A payload of 1,000 kg was lifted to 67,113 ft (20,456 m) and 2,000 kg to 66,188 ft (20,174 m). The records have since been beaten.

The RV was described as a swept mid-wing monoplane with two 8,818 lb (4,000 kg) st Type 37V turbojets. The fact that Smirnov has

since established records in the Yak-30 lends support to the theory that the "RV" was a Yak-25.

A woman's international closed-circuit distance record of 1,347·4 nm (1,551·6 miles; 2,497 km) was claimed by Marina Popovich, wife of cosmonaut Pavel Popovich, flying an RV, in the Summer of 1967.

2. T-431. An aeroplane height record of 94,657 ft (28,852 m) was established on 14 July 1959 by Vladimir Ilyushin flying an aeroplane designated "T-431", with a 19,840 lb (9,000 kg) st TRD turbojet engine, at Podmoskovnœ aero-

drome. The record has since been beaten.

Another short-lived record was set up by Ilyushin in the T-431 on 4 September 1962, when he raised the sustained altitude record to 69,456 ft (21,170 m) over a 15/25 km course at Jukovski-Petrovskoi. The TRD 31 turbojet fitted on this occasion was stated to give 22,046 lb (10,000 kg) st.

Last of the T-431's records, also since beaten, was a speed record of 1,260·9 knots (1,452 mph; 2,337 km/h) set up by Anatoli Koznov over a 500-km closed circuit on 25 September 1962.

It appears likely that the T-431 was a Sukhoi design.

YUGOSLAVIA

GOVERNMENT FACTORIES

All the pre-war Yugoslav aircraft factories were destroyed during the German occupation and it was not until 1945 that the Ikarus plant

at Zemun was sufficiently rebuilt and re-equipped to be able to resume aircraft work. As a nationalised plant it began with the repair and overhaul of Soviet-built Yak-3, Yak-9 and Il-2 Stormovik aircraft belonging to the Yugoslav Air Force.

In August, 1946, the remnants of the former

Ikarus, Rogojarsky and "Zmaj" companies and their surviving technical staffs were incorporated in the national industry and the design and manufacture of aircraft was resumed. Types in current production, or under development, are described below.

SOKO

PREDUZECE SOKO

ADDRESS:

Mostar

GENERAL MANAGER: Dipl-Ing Ivan Sert

ASSISTANT MANAGING DIRECTOR:
Dipl-Ing Stefan Obreht

DIRECTOR, AIRCRAFT FACTORY:
Dipl-Ing Sulejman Gosto

SALES MANAGER: Dedic Drago

Founded in 1951, this company is manufacturing a two-seat jet basic trainer named the Galeb, a single-seat light attack version of the same design named the Jastreb, and a piston-engined lightweight ground attack aircraft known as the Kraguj.

SOKO G2-A GALEB (SEAGULL)

Design of the Galeb was started in 1957. Construction of two prototypes began in 1959 and the first of these flew for the first time in May 1961. Development was carried out in collaboration with the Yugoslav Aeronautical Research Establishments and construction is in accordance with current Military Airworthiness Requirements. Production for the Yugoslav Air Force began in 1963; the current G2-A model embodies several improvements, including an optional cockpit air-conditioning system. The developed G-3 Galeb-3 is described separately.

TYPE: Two-seat jet basic trainer.

WINGS: Cantilever low-wing monoplane. Wing section NACA 64A213·5 at root, NACA 64A212·0 at tip. Dihedral 1° 30′. No incidence. Sweepback at quarter chord 4° 19′. Conventional light alloy two-spar stressed-skin structure, consisting of a centre-section, integral with the fuselage, and two outer panels which

can be removed easily. Manually-operated internally-sealed light alloy ailerons. Trim-tab on port aileron. Hydraulically-actuated Fowler flaps. No de-icing system.

FUSELAGE: Light alloy semi-monocoque structure in two portions, joined together by four bolts at frame aft of wing trailing-edge. Rear portion removable for engine servicing. Two hydraulically-actuated door-type air-brakes under centre-fuselage.

TAIL UNIT: Cantilever light alloy stressed-skin structure. Fixed-incidence tailplane. Rudder and elevators statically and dynamically balanced and manually operated. Trim/balance tab in starboard elevator; balance tab in port elevator.

LANDING GEAR: Hydraulically-retractable tri-

cycle type, with single wheel on each unit. Nose-wheel retracts forward, main units inward into wings. Oleo-pneumatic shock-absorbers manufactured by Prva Petoletka of Trstenik. Dunlop main wheels and tyres size 23 × 7·25-10, pressure 64 lb/sq in (4·5 kg/cm²). Dunlop nose-wheel and tyre size 6·50-5·5 TC, pressure 49·8 lb/sq in (3·5 kg/cm²). Prva Petoletka hydraulic disc brakes.

POWER PLANT: One Rolls-Royce Bristol Viper 11 Mk 22-6 turbojet engine, rated at 2,500 lb (1,134 kg) st. Two flexible fuel tanks aft of cockpits, with total capacity of 1,720 lb (780 kg). Two jettisonable wingtip tanks, each with capacity of 375 lb (170 kg). Refuelling point on upper part of fuselage aft of cockpits. Oil capacity 1⅜ Imp gallons (6·25 litres).

Soko G2-A Galeb two-seat basic training aircraft (Rolls-Royce Bristol Viper 11 turbojet engine)

ACCOMMODATION: Crew of two in tandem on Folland Type 1-B fully-automatic lightweight ejection seats. Separate sideways-hinged (to starboard) jettisonable canopy over each cockpit. Cockpit air-conditioning to special order only.

SYSTEMS: Hydraulic system, pressure 850-1,000 lb/sq in (60-70 kg/cm²), for landing gear, airbrakes and flaps. Separate system for wheel brakes. Pneumatic system for armament cocking. Electrical system includes 6kW 24V generator, 24V battery, and inverter to provide 115V 400 c/s AC supply for instruments. Low-pressure oxygen system, capacity 1.450 litres.

ELECTRONICS AND EQUIPMENT: Blind-flying instrumentation and STR-9Z1 transmitter-receiver standard. Camera can be fitted in rear cockpit.

ARMAMENT: Weapons training version has two 0·50-in machine-guns in nose and underwing pylons for two 110-lb (50-kg) bombs and four 57-mm rockets. Strike version can carry, with the guns, two 220-lb (100 kg) bombs and two 127-mm rockets.

DIMENSIONS, EXTERNAL:

Wing span	34 ft 4½ in (10·47 m)
Span with tip tanks	38 ft 1½ in (11·62 m)
Wing chord at root	7 ft 9 in (2·36 m)
Wing chord at tip	4 ft 7 in (1·40 m)
Wing aspect ratio	5·55
Length overall	33 ft 11 in (10·34 m)
Height overall	10 ft 9 in (3·28 m)
Tailplane span	14 ft 0 in (4·27 m)
Wheel track	12 ft 9 in (3·89 m)
Wheelbase	11 ft 9½ in (3·59 m)

AREAS:

Wings, gross	204·5 sq ft (19·00 m²)
Ailerons (total)	25·40 sq ft (2·36 m²)
Trailing-edge flaps (total)	21·75 sq ft (2·02 m²)
Air-brake	3·66 sq ft (0·34 m²)
Fin	14·42 sq ft (1·34 m²)
Rudder, including tab	6·03 sq ft (0·56 m²)
Tailplane	39·40 sq ft (3·66 m²)
Elevators, including tabs	8·93 sq ft (0·83 m²)

WEIGHTS:

Weight empty, equipped	5,775 lb (2,620 kg)
Max T-O weight:	
Basic trainer (no tip-tanks)	
	7,690 lb (3,488 kg)
Navigational trainer (with tip-tanks)	
	8,439 lb (3,828 kg)
Weapons trainer	8,792 lb (3,988 kg)
Strike version	9,210 lb (4,178 kg)

PERFORMANCE (at normal T-O weight):

Max level speed at S/L	
	408 knots (470 mph; 756 km/h)
Max level speed at 20,350 ft (6,200 m)	
	438 knots (505 mph; 812 km/h)
Max cruising speed at 19,680 ft (6,000 m)	
	394 knots (453 mph; 730 km/h)
Stalling speed:	
Flaps and air-brakes down	
	85 knots (98 mph; 158 km/h)
Flaps and air-brakes up	
	97 knots (112 mph; 180 km/h)
Max rate of climb at S/L 4,500 ft (1,370 m)/min	
Time to 9,840 ft (3,000 m)	2·4 min
Time to 19,680 ft (6,000 m)	5·5 min
Time to 29,520 ft (9,000 m)	10·2 min
Service ceiling	39,375 ft (12,000 m)
T-O run on grass	1,610 ft (490 m)
T-O to 50 ft (15 m)	2,100 ft (640 m)
Landing from 50 ft (15 m)	2,330 ft (710 m)
Landing run on grass	1,310 ft (400 m)
Max range at 29,520 ft (9,000 m), with tip-tanks full	669 nm (770 miles; 1,240 km)
Max endurance at 23,000 ft (7,000 m)	2 hr 30 min

SOKO G-3 GALEB-3 (SEAGULL)

Design of this new, more extensively equipped and more powerful version of the Galeb jet basic trainer was started in April 1969. Construction of the prototype began in November of the same year. It was scheduled to fly for the first time in May 1970 and to be demonstrated at the 1970 Farnborough Display.

The structural descriptions of the G2-A Galeb and J-1 Jastreb apply also the the G-3 Galeb-3, except in the following details.

WINGS: As for J-1 Jastreb.

FUSELAGE: This consists of the cockpit section of the G2-A fuselage and the centre and rear fuselage sections of the J-1 Jastreb. Slight modifications are made as necessary to accommodate new equipment.

TAIL UNIT: As for G2-A, with slight modifications.

LANDING GEAR: Basically as for J-1 Jastreb but adapted for increased energy absorption.

POWER PLANT: One Rolls-Royce Bristol Viper 20-F20 turbojet engine, rated at 3,395 lb (1,540 kg) st. Fuel system as for J-1 Jastreb.

ACCOMMODATION: Unpressurised accommodation for crew of two, as in G2-A, with standard air-conditioning system supplied by Teddington Aircraft Controls Ltd.

SYSTEMS: Teddington air-conditioning system, with air-cycle cooling. Hydraulic and pneumatic systems as for G2-A. DC electrical supply from Rotax BColo7 9kW starter-generator. Main battery is 40Ah SAFT 4080,

Soko J-1 Jastreb single-seat light attack aircraft, developed from the Galeb *(John Blake)*

with 7Ah SAFT 22V07L auxiliary battery. It is possible to start the aircraft engine by means of an internal battery, and a busbar ensures a steady regulated voltage for this purpose. AC power supply from a single-phase 115V 250VA main static inverter, other system components including a single-phase 115V 250VA auxiliary static inverter, a 115V single-phase/115V three-phase phase adapter and 115V/26V transformer. High-pressure oxygen system of 70 cu ft (2,000 litres) capacity, at pressure of 2,200 lb/sq in (150 atm). Hot-air windscreen anti-icing.

ELECTRONICS AND EQUIPMENT: Standard equipment includes Collins 618M-2D VHF transceiver. Optional items include Collins 387C-4 or Elliotts ERSP-34C UHF or VHF/UHF transceiver audio control unit, Collins 51RV-2B VOR/ILS receiver, Collins 51Z-4 marker beacon receiver, Marconi AD370B ADF, Standard Telephones and Cables STR70-P/3 radio altimeter and Collins 313N-2 com/nav control unit. Com/nav control units, ADF control, spherical indicator, course indicator, RMI, radio altimeter indicator, etc, are provided in both cockpits.

ARMAMENT AND OPERATIONAL EQUIPMENT: Machine-guns as on G2-A; rockets and other weapons as on J-1 Jastreb, with provision for wire-guided missiles. A more modern Thompson R-22 gyro gunsight is fitted.

DIMENSIONS, EXTERNAL, AND AREAS:
As for J-1 Jastreb, except:

Length overall	33 ft 11 in (10·34 m)

WEIGHTS AND LOADINGS:

Weight empty, equipped	6,327 lb (2,870 kg)
Max T-O weight	10,582 lb (4,800 kg)

PERFORMANCE (estimated, at max T-O weight except where indicated):

Max level speed at 19,700 ft (6,000 m)	
	448 knots (515 mph; 830 km/h)
Max cruising speed at 16,400 ft (5,000 m)	
	410 knots (472 mph; 760 km/h)
Stalling speed, flaps and air-brakes extended	
	82 knots (95 mph; 152 km/h)
Max rate of climb at S/L 5,120 ft (1,560 m)/min	
Service ceiling	39,370 ft (12,000 m)
T-O run on grass at AUW of 9,745 lb (4,420 kg)	2,790 ft (850 m)
T-O run on concrete at AUW of 9,745 lb (4,420 kg)	2,460 ft (750 m)
T-O to 50 ft (15 m) on grass	3,675 ft (1,120 m)
T-O to 50 ft (15 m) on concrete	3,445 ft (1,050 m)

SOKO J-1 JASTREB (HAWK)

The J-1 Jastreb is a single-seat light attack version of the G2-A Galeb which is in production for the Yugoslav Air Force. The front cockpit of the trainer, with sideways-hinged (to starboard) canopy, is retained, a metal fairing replacing the rear canopy. The engine is the more powerful Rolls-Royce Bristol Viper 531. Other changes include the installation of improved day and night reconnaissance equipment. electronic navigation and communications equipment and, to special order only, a pressurised cockpit and self-contained engine starting. In other respects the airframe and power plant remain essentially unchanged except for some local strengthening and the provision of strong-points for heavier underwing stores.

The details given for the G2-A Galeb apply equally to the J-1 Jastreb, with the exceptions listed below. The developed J-5A and J-5B versions are described separately.

TYPE: Single-seat light attack aircraft.

WINGS: Wing section NACA 64 series. Changed aspect ratio and chord at root.

POWER PLANT: One Bristol Siddeley Viper 531 turbojet engine, rated at 3,000 lb (1,360 kg) st. Capacity of each wingtip tank 485 lb (220 kg). Provision for attaching two 1,000 lb (450 kg) st JATO rockets under fuselage for use at take-off or in flight.

ACCOMMODATION: Pilot only, on Folland Type 1-B fully-automatic lightweight ejection seat. Cockpit pressurisation and air-conditioning to special order only.

SYSTEMS: Electrical system includes 6kW 24V generator and second battery, permitting independent engine starting without ground electrical supply. Capacity of oxygen system 566 litres.

ELECTRONICS AND EQUIPMENT: Provision for assisted take-off rockets. Electronic system for identification purposes to special order only.

ARMAMENT: Three 0·50-in Colt-Browning machine-guns in nose (with 135 rpg). Total of eight underwing weapon attachments. Two inboard attachments can carry two bombs of up to 550 lb (250 kg) each, two clusters of small bombs or two 100-lb (45 kg) photo flares. Other attachments can each carry a 57-mm or 127-mm rocket. Semi-automatic gyro gunsight and camera gun standard.

DIMENSIONS, EXTERNAL:
As for Galeb, except:

Wing span	34 ft 8 in (10·56 m)
Span with tip-tanks	38 ft 4 in (11·68 m)
Wing chord at root	7 ft 3¼ in (2·22 m)
Wing chord at tip	4 ft 7 in (1·40 m)
Wing aspect ratio	5·5
Length overall	35 ft 1½ in (10·71 m)
Height overall	11 ft 11½ in (3·64 m)
Wheelbase	11 ft 10 in (3·61 m)

AREAS:
As for Galeb

WEIGHTS:

Weight empty, equipped	6,217 lb (2,820 kg)
Max T-O weight	10,287 lb (4,666 kg)

PERFORMANCE (T-O and landing runs on concrete):

Max level speed at 19,680 ft (6,000 m) at AUW of 8,748 lb (3,968 kg)	
	442 knots (510 mph; 820 km/h)
Max cruising speed at 16,400 ft (5,000 m), at AUW of 8,748 lb (3,968 kg)	
	399 knots (460 mph; 740 km/h)
Stalling speed, wheels down:	
Flaps and air-brakes down	
	82 knots (95 mph; 152 km/h)
Flaps and air-brakes up	
	94 knots (108 mph; 174 km/h)
Rate of climb at S/L, at AUW of 8,748 lb (3,968 kg)	4,135 ft (1,260 m)/min
Service ceiling, at AUW of 8,748 lb (3,968 kg)	39,375 ft (12,000 m)
T-O run at AUW of 8,748 lb (3,968 kg)	2,300 ft (700 m)
T-O run, rocket-assisted, at max T-O weight	1,325 ft (404 m)
T-O to 50 ft (15 m) at AUW of 8,748 lb (3,968 kg)	3,150 ft (960 m)
T-O to 50 ft (15 m), rocket-assisted, at max T-O weight	1,945 ft (593 m)
Landing from 50 ft (15 m)	3,610 ft (1,100 m)
Landing run	1,970 ft (600 m)
Max range at 29,520 ft (9,000 m), with tip-tanks full	820 nm (945 miles; 1,520 km)

SOKO JASTREB J-5A/J-5B (HAWK)

Two new and more powerful versions of the Jastreb single-seat light attack aircraft were under development in 1970 and are scheduled to be demonstrated publicly at the 1971 Paris Air Show. They have the following designations:

Jastreb J-5A. Powered by Rolls-Royce Bristol Viper 522 turbojet engine, rated at 3,315 lb (1,504 kg) st. Together with use of JATO rockets, as available for all Jastreb versions, this will offer higher average flying speeds, higher rate of climb, shorter take-off run, longer range and 50% greater load-carrying capacity than the J-1.

Jastreb J-5B. Powered by Rolls-Royce Bristol Viper 600 turbojet engine, rated at 4,000 lb (1,814 kg) st. Will offer higher performance in all categories mentioned under J-5A above, and 80% greater load-carrying capacity than J-1.

A new electrical system, already proven by

Bristol Division of Rolls-Royce provides for independent engine starting by two 26Ah 48/24V batteries carried in the aircraft. The Rotax starter-generator is supplemented by a new electrical system offering safer and more reliable operation of instruments and equipment needing a 4,000 c/s 125V AC supply. This is achieved by use of a static inverter in addition to the rotary type, which ensures automatic AC system transfer following failure of the main inverter.

The com/nav installations are improved by installation of a Collins 618 M-2D solid-state fully-transistorised VHF transceiver, with 1,400 channels, 100ms channel switching time and 25W output power; a Marconi AD 370B radio compass; and optional Collins 51Z-4 marker beacon receiver as alternative to the Marconi 6403 unit. Soko are also considering provision of a combined VHF/UHF transceiver as an alternative to the Collins 618 M-2D.

A Teddington Aircraft Controls cockpit air-conditioning system is available, as on the J-1, together with either a low-pressure (147-440 lb/sq in = 10·30 atm) or high-pressure (2,200 lb/sq in = 150 atm) oxygen system.

SOKO P-2 KRAGUJ

This simple lightweight close-support aircraft resurrects a concept pioneered by the American Fletcher Defender in the early 1950s. Easy to fly and simple to build and maintain, it was reported to be in squadron service with the Yugoslav Air Force only two years after the prototype began its flight trials.

TYPE: Single-seat lightweight close-support aircraft.

WINGS: Cantilever low-wing monoplane. Wing section NACA 4415. Dihedral 4°, on outer panels only. No incidence or sweep. All-metal two-spar structure. Light alloy ailerons, with corrugated skin. Manually-operated Type 2H flaps with corrugated skin. Fixed leading-edge slots.

FUSELAGE: All-metal structure of stressed-skin/stringer type, stiffened with frames and bulkheads.

TAIL UNIT: Cantilever all-metal structure, with corrugated skin on control surfaces. Fixed-incidence tailplane. Statically and dynamically balanced elevators. Plastics trim-tab in elevator.

LANDING GEAR: Non-retractable tailwheel type. Oleo-pneumatic shock-absorbers manufactured by Prva Petoletka of Trstenik. Main wheels and tyres size 530 × 185, pressure 50 lb/sq in (3·5 kg/cm²). Tailwheel tyre size 260 × 140, pressure 50 lb /sq in (3·5 kg/cm²). Hydraulic disc brakes manufactured by Prva Petoletka.

Soko P-2 Kraguj lightweight close-support aircraft (340 hp Lycoming GSO-480 engine)

POWER PLANT: One 340 hp Lycoming GSO-480-B1A6 six-cylinder horizontally-opposed air-cooled engine, driving a Hartzell HC-B3Z20-1 three-blade metal constant-speed propeller, diameter 8 ft 0 in (2·44 m). One rubber fuel tank between spars in each inner wing; total fuel capacity 53 Imp gallons (240 litres). Refuelling point above port wing. Oil capacity 3·4 Imp gallons (15·5 litres).

ACCOMMODATION: Single seat in enclosed cockpit. Manually-operated rearward-sliding bubble canopy. Heating and ventilation standard.

SYSTEMS: Hydraulic system for wheel brakes only. Electrical system includes 1·5 kW 30V generator and one 24V 10Ah battery.

ELECTRONICS AND EQUIPMENT: Standard equipment includes STR-9Z1 transmitter-receiver and blind flying instruments.

ARMAMENT: One 7·7-mm machine-gun in each wing (650 rpg), outboard of propeller disc. Total of six underwing weapon attachments. Two inner attachments each carry a bomb of up to 220 lb (100 kg), cluster of small bombs, 33-Imp gallon (150 litre) napalm tank or 12-round rocket pack. Other four attachments each carry a 57-mm or 127-mm rocket.

DIMENSIONS, EXTERNAL:
Wing span	34 ft 11 in (10·64 m)
Wing chord (constant)	5 ft 6½ in (1·69 m)
Wing aspect ratio	6
Length overall	26 ft 0¼ in (7·93 m)
Height overall	9 ft 10 in (3·00 m)

Tailplane span	10 ft 0 in (3·04 m)
Wheel track	7 ft 11 in (2·42 m)
Wheelbase	19 ft 1½ in (5·83 m)

AREAS:
Wings, gross	183 sq ft (17·0 m²)
Ailerons (total)	9·39 sq ft (0·87 m²)
Trailing-edge flaps (total)	32·6 sq ft (3·03 m²)
Fin	15·28 sq ft (1·42 m²)
Rudder	6·18 sq ft (0·57 m²)
Tailplane	29·06 sq ft (2·70 m²)
Elevators, incl tabs	12·59 sq ft (1·17 m²)

WEIGHTS:
Weight empty, equipped	2,491 lb (1,130 kg)
Max T-O weight	3,580 lb (1,624 kg)

PERFORMANCE:
Max level speed at S/L	148 knots (171 mph; 275 km/h)
Max level speed at 5,000 ft (1,500 m)	159 knots (183 mph; 295 km/h)
Max cruising speed at 5,000 ft (1,500 m)	151 knots (174 mph; 280 km/h)
Stalling speed, flaps down, at AUW of 2,857 lb (1,296 kg)	48 knots (55 mph; 88 km/h)
Rate of climb at S/L at AUW of 2,857 lb (1,296 kg)	1,575 ft (480 m)/min
T-O run at AUW of 2,903 lb (1,317 kg)	360 ft (110 m)
T-O to 50 ft (15 m) at AUW of 2,903 lb (1,317 kg)	620 ft (189 m)
Landing from 50 ft (15 m)	1,063 ft (324 m)
Landing run	394 ft (120 m)
Range with max fuel	431 nm (500 miles; 800 km)

UTVA
FABRIKA AVIONA UTVA

HEAD OFFICE AND WORKS:
Pancevo

DIRECTOR GENERAL: Saranovic Marko

SALES MANAGER: Zdravko Rapaic

This concern was responsible for the prototype UTVA-56 four-seat general utility monoplane, which flew for the first time on 22 April 1959 and was described fully in the 1960-61 *Jane's*.

The designers of the UTVA-56, Diploma Engineers Branislav Nikolic and Dragoslav Petkovic, began the work of modifying the design for series production at the beginning of 1960. In particular, they replaced the original 260 hp Lycoming GO-435 engine with a 270 hp Lycoming GO-480. The production version was redesignated UTVA-60 and is described below, together with an agricultural aircraft known as the UTVA-65 Privrednik which utilises the same basic wings.

Also in production is the UTVA-66, a special-purpose version of the UTVA-60 with fixed wing-slots.

Under development are the UTVA-70, a twin-engined six-seat aircraft based on the UTVA-66 airframe, and a light single-engined canard aircraft for private owners and sporting aviation.

UTVA-60

The UTVA-60 is in production and is available in five versions, as follows:

U-60-AT1. Basic four-seat utility version, suitable for use as air taxi, freight transport, liaison and private sporting aircraft.

U-60-AT2. Similar to U-60-AT1, but with dual controls. Suitable for training duties.

U-60-AG. Equipped for agricultural spraying, dusting, top-dressing and seed-sowing duties.

U-60-AM. Ambulance version. Able to accommodate two stretchers, which are loaded through upward-hinged rear cabin canopy. Seat for attendant behind pilot, with drawer for medical equipment.

U-60H. Floatplane version. Generally similar to U-60-AT1, but with 296 hp Lycoming GO-480-G1H6 six-cylinder horizontally-opposed air-cooled engine, driving a Hartzell three-blade constant-speed metal propeller HC-B3Z20-1B/10151 C-5. Strengthened fuselage. Added ventral fin on prototype only. Prototype, which

flew for the first time on 29 October 1961, has Edo floats; production models have BIN-1600 floats designed by Dipl Ing Nikolic. Series production began in mid-1962 and the UTVA-60H is in service for liaison, tourist and ambulance duties. It is available in the same standard -AT1, dual-control -AT2 and -AM ambulance versions as the basic landplane.

In addition, a version equipped with Wild cameras for air survey duties has been built.

The following details apply to all the landplane versions of the UTVA-60.

TYPE: Four-seat general-utility monoplane.

WINGS: Strut-braced high-wing monoplane, with single streamline-section light alloy bracing strut each side. Modified NACA 4412 wing section. Dihedral 2°. Incidence 2° 30′. All-metal single-spar structure. Flaps and ailerons of pure monocoque all-metal construction. Flaps are hydraulically-operated and are linked to ailerons, so that ailerons are drooped 15° when flaps are 40° down. U-60-AG only (optional on U-60-AM) has fixed slots of same span as ailerons.

FUSELAGE: All-metal construction. Nose and cabin of stressed-skin construction. Rear fuselage is a semi-monocoque.

TAIL UNIT: Cantilever all-metal structure. Controllable trim-tab in elevator.

LANDING GEAR: Non-retractable tail-wheel type. Cantilever steel-tube main legs with rubber-in-compression shock-absorption. Wheels and hydraulic disc brakes manufactured by Prva Petoletka. Main wheels size 500 × 180 (620 × 250 on U-60-AG). Tailwheel size 260 × 85. Tyre pressures: main 35·5 lb/sq in (2·5 kg/cm²), tail 28·5 lb/sq in (2·0 kg/cm²). Provision for alternative fitment of floats, floats and wheels in amphibious version, skis or hydraulically-actuated wheel-ski gear.

POWER PLANT: One 270 hp Lycoming GO-480-B1A6 six-cylinder horizontally-opposed air-cooled engine, driving a Hartzell two-blade constant-speed metal propeller HC-A2X20-1B/10133-3. Two metal fuel tanks in wings, total capacity 46 Imp gallons (210 litres). Oil capacity 2·6 Imp gallons (12 litres).

ACCOMMODATION: Enclosed cabin for pilot and three passengers, or pilot, two stretchers and attendant in ambulance version. With passenger seats removed can carry 908 lb (412 kg) of freight. Door on each side of cabin. Rear

canopy hinges upward to form third door, for loading stretchers or freight. Ventilation and heating standard.

ELECTRONICS AND EQUIPMENT: Blind-flying instrumentation standard on U-60-AT and AM, optional on U-60-AG. Standard equipment includes Narco Mk 5 two-way radio and Narco ADF-30 radio-compass. Other navigation, communications and automatic flight control equipment optional. Variety of equipment available for agricultural version, which carries chemicals in either a tank in the cabin or under-fuselage container. Ambulance version can carry parachute-pack of food and medical supplies under fuselage.

DIMENSIONS, EXTERNAL:
Wing span	37 ft 5 in (11·40 m)
Wing chord at root	5 ft 8 in (1·73 m)
Wing chord at tip	3 ft 11½ in (1·21 m)
Wing aspect ratio	1·79
Length overall	26 ft 11½ in (8·22 m)
Height overall	8 ft 11 in (2·72 m)
Tailplane span	11 ft 9½ in (3·60 m)
Wheel track	7 ft 10½ in (2·40 m)
Cabin doors (each):	
Height	3 ft 2½ in (0·98 m)
Width	3 ft 0½ in (0·93 m)
Canopy door:	
Height	1 ft 11½ in (0·60 m)
Width	3 ft 3½ in (1·00 m)

DIMENSIONS, INTERNAL:
Cabin: Length	4 ft 11 in (1·50 m)
Width	3 ft 5 in (1·05 m)
Height	3 ft 11 in (1·20 m)

AREAS:
Wings, gross	194·50 sq ft (18·08 m²)
Ailerons (total)	22·18 sq ft (2·06 m²)
Trailing-edge flaps (total)	24·97 sq ft (2·32 m²)
Fin	12·70 sq ft (1·18 m²)
Dorsal fin	4·74 sq ft (0·44 m²)
Rudder	8·18 sq ft (0·76 m²)
Tailplane	23·68 sq ft (2·20 m²)
Elevators	15·61 sq ft (1·45 m²)

WEIGHTS AND LOADINGS:
Weight empty, equipped:
60-AT1	2,100 lb (952 kg)
60-AG	2,271 lb (1,030 kg)
60-AM	2,174 lb (986 kg)
60H	2,778 lb (1,260 kg)

Normal T-O weight:
60-AT1	3,192 lb (1,448 kg)
60-AG	3,814 lb (1,730 kg)
60-AM	3,267 lb (1,482 kg)

Max T-O weight:
60-AT1	3,571 lb (1,620 kg)
60-AG	3,814 lb (1,730 kg)
60H	3,950 lb (1,792 kg)

Max zero-fuel weight:
60-AT1, AM	3,480 lb (1,580 kg)
60-AG	3,660 lb (1,660 kg)

Max landing weight:
Landplanes	3,527 lb (1,600 kg)
60H	3,950 lb (1,792 kg)

Max wing loading:
Landplanes	16·39-19·58 lb/sq ft (80-95·6 kg/m²)
60H	18·43 lb/sq ft (90 kg/m²)

Max power loading:
Landplanes	11·6-13·14 lb/hp (5·26-5·96 kg/hp)
60H	13·36 lb/hp (6·06 kg/hp)

PERFORMANCE (at max T-O weight):
Max level speed at S/L:
60-AT1, -AT2	136 knots (157 mph; 252 km/h)
60-AG, -AM	128 knots (148 mph; 238 km/h)
60H	119 knots (137 mph; 221 km/h)

Max permissible diving speed:
All versions	161 knots (186 mph; 300 km/h)

Max cruising speed:
60-AT1, -AT2	124 knots (143 mph; 230 km/h)
60-AG, -AM	118 knots (136 mph; 219 km/h)
60H	106 knots (122 mph; 197 km/h)

Econ cruising speed:
60H	99 knots (114 mph; 184 km/h)

Stalling speed:
60AT1, -AT2	39·5 knots (45·5 mph; 73 km/h)
60-AG, -AM	36 knots (41 mph; 66 km/h)
60H	35 knots (40·5 mph; 65 km/h)

Rate of climb at S/L:
60-AT1, -AT2	1,260 ft (385 m)/min
60-AG, -AM	1,200 ft (372 m)/min
60H	824 ft (251 m)/min

Service ceiling:
60-AT1, -AT2	17,060 ft (5,200 m)
60-AG, -AM	16,075 ft (4,900 m)
60H	14,930 ft (4,550 m)

T-O run:
60-AT1, -AT2, -AM	427 ft (130 m)
60-AG	427-640 ft (130-195 m)
60H	1,063 ft (324 m)

T-O to 50 ft (15 m):
60-AT1, AT2, AM	709 ft (216 m)
60-AG	709-1·253 ft (216-382 m)
60H	1,483 ft (452 m)

Landing from 50 ft (15 m):
60-AT1, AT2	673 ft (205 m)
60-AG, -AM	597-673 ft (182-205 m)
60H	1,260 ft (384 m)

Landing run:
60H	761 ft (232 m)

Normal range:
60-AT1,-AT2	420 nm (485 miles; 780 km)
60H	411 nm (474 miles; 762 km)

UTVA-66

This version of the UTVA-60 has been developed for special purposes. It has a Lycoming GSO-480-B1J6 engine, driving a Hartzell HC-B3Z20-1/10151 C-5 propeller. The wings are of the same size as those of the UTVA-60, but have fixed leading-edge slots in line with the ailerons. The tail surfaces are enlarged and the elevator is fitted with both a servo-tab and controllable trim-tab. The shock-absorption capacity of the landing gear has been increased. Fuel tank capacity is increased to 55 Imp gallons (250 litres).

When the UTVA-66 was announced early in 1968, several prototypes had been under flight test for more than one year. Structure testing of the airframe was completed in mid-1968 and the following versions are now available.

UTVA-66. Basic utility version. Can be used for glider-towing.

UTVA-66-AM. Ambulance version, equipped for stretcher carrying.

UTVA-66H. Water-based version on BIN-1600 floats. First flown in September 1968.

DIMENSIONS, EXTERNAL:
Wing span	37 ft 5 in (11·40 m)
Length overall	27 ft 6 in (8·38 m)
Height overall	10 ft 6 in (3·20 m)
Tailplane span	13 ft 4½ in (4·08 m)
Wheel track	8 ft 4¼ in (2·55 m)
Doors as for UTVA-60	

DIMENSIONS, INTERNAL:
As for UTVA-60

AREAS:
As for UTVA-60, except:
Rudder	10·22 sq ft (0·95 m²)
Tailplane	26·00 sq ft (2·42 m²)
Elevators	23·90 sq ft (2·22 m²)

WEIGHTS AND LOADINGS:
Weight empty, equipped:
U-66	2,756 lb (1,250 kg)
U-66H	3,228 lb (1,464 kg)

Max T-O weight:
U-66	4,000 lb (1,814 kg)
U-66H	4,300 lb (1,950 kg)

UTVA-60-AT four-seat utility aircraft (270 hp Lycoming GO-480 engine)

UTVA-60H floatplane (296 hp Lycoming GO-480-G1H6 engine) in Yugoslav Air Force insignia

Max wing loading:
U-66	20·58 lb/sq ft (100·5 kg/m²)
U-66H	22·08 lb/sq ft (107·8 kg/m²)

Max power loading:
U-66	11·79 lb/hp (5·35 kg/hp)
U-66H	12·63 lb/hp (5·73 kg/hp)

PERFORMANCE (at max T-O weight):
Max level speed at S/L:
U-66	124 knots (143 mph; 230 km/h)
U-66H	114 knots (131 mph; 211 km/h)

Max level speed at optimum height:
U-66	135 knots (155 mph; 250 km/h)
U-66H	124 knots (143 mph; 230 km/h)

Max permissible diving speed:
	172 knots (198 mph; 320 km/h)

Max cruising speed at optimum height:
U-66	124 knots (143 mph; 230 km/h)
U-66H	113 knots (130 mph; 210 km/h)

Stalling speed:
U-66	43·5 knots (50 mph; 80 km/h)
U-66H	44·5 knots (51 mph; 82 km/h)

Rate of climb at S/L:
U-66	885 ft (270 m)/min
U-66H	630 ft (192 m)/min

Service ceiling:
U-66	22,000 ft (6,700 m)
U-66H	19,000 ft (5,800 m)

T-O run:
U-66	614 ft (187 m)
U-66H	791 ft (241 m)

T-O to 50 ft (15 m):
U-66	1,155 ft (352 m)
U-66H	1,293 ft (394 m)

Landing from 50 ft (15 m):
U-66	594 ft (181 m)

Landing run:
U-66	899 ft (274 m)
U-66H	637 ft (194 m)

Range with max fuel:
U-66	404 nm (466 miles; 750 km)
U-66H	394 nm (453 miles; 730 km)

UTVA-65 PRIVREDNIK-GO

The Utva-65 Privrednik-GO is a specialised agricultural aircraft designed by Dipl Ing Branislav Nikolic and Dipl Ing Mirko Dabinovic. Design work began in March 1964 and construction of two prototypes was started in June 1964, utilising a number of major components of the UTVA-60, including the basic wings, tail unit and landing gear. The first prototype was completed in the Spring of 1965 and is shown in the illustrations on page 528.

The prototypes have a 270 hp Lycoming GO-480-B1A6 engine. The following details apply to the more powerful version now in production.

TYPE: Agricultural monoplane.

WINGS: Braced low-wing monoplane, with single streamline-section bracing strut each side. Wings are basically identical with those of the UTVA-60, but have increased root chord, span and area.

FUSELAGE: Welded chrome-molybdenum steel-tube structure. Metal skin on sides of forward fuselage and bottom; fabric covering elsewhere.

UTVA-66, a development of the UTVA-60 with Lycoming GSO-480-B1J6 engine

TAIL UNIT: Cantilever all-metal structure, basically similar to that of UTVA-60, but with elevators of increased area.

LANDING GEAR: Non-retractable tail-wheel type. Based on that of UTVA-60. Size 650 × 200 main wheels and size 300 × 125 tail-wheel and tyre. Goodyear hydraulic disc brakes.

POWER PLANT: One 295 hp Lycoming GO-480-G1A6 six-cylinder horizontally-opposed air-cooled engine, driving a two-blade Hartzell HC-A2X20-1B/10133 constant-speed propeller or (for African market) three-blade Hartzell HC-B3Z20-1/10151C-5 constant-speed propeller. One fuel tank in fuselage, capacity 40·5 Imp gallons (185 litres) or 48·5 Imp gallons (220 litres). Oil capacity 3 Imp gallons (13·5 litres).

ACCOMMODATION: Pilot only in enclosed cabin, with a downward-hinged door on each side. Plastic hopper forward of cockpit.

SYSTEM: 24V electrical system.

DIMENSIONS, EXTERNAL:
Wing span 40 ft 1 in (12·22 m)
Wing chord at root 6 ft $3\frac{1}{2}$ in (1·92 m)
Wing chord at tip 3 ft $11\frac{1}{2}$ in (1·21 m)
Length overall 27 ft 9 in (8·46 m)
Height overall 8 ft $6\frac{1}{4}$ in (2·60 m)
Tailplane span 12 ft $7\frac{1}{4}$ in (3·84 m)
Wheel track 8 ft 10 in (2·70 m)

AREAS:
Wings, gross 209 sq ft (19·4 m²)
Horizontal tail surfaces (total) 42·4 sq ft (3·94 m²)

WEIGHTS:
Payload 1,323 lb (600 kg)
Max T-O weight
Normal category, clean 3,225 lb (1,463 kg)
Restricted category, with spraying equipment 4,078 lb (1,850 kg)

PERFORMANCE (at max T-O weight; N= normal category, clean, R= restricted category with spraygear):
Max level speed at S/L:
N 111 knots (128 mph; 206 km/h)
R 95 knots (109 mph; 176 km/h)
Stalling speed, flaps down:
N 43·5 knots (50 mph; 80 km/h)
R 51·5 knots (59 mph; 95 km/h)
Rate of climb at S/L:
N 1,053 ft (321 m)/min
R 462 ft (141 m)/min
T-O run:
N 473 ft (144 m)
R 658 ft (200·5 m)
Landing run:
N 673 ft (205 m)
R at landing weight 637 ft (194 m)

UTVA-65 PRIVREDNIK-IO

At the beginning of 1967, Dipl-Ings Branislav Nikolic, Mirko Dabinovic and Smiljan Cotic began redesigning the Privrednik to make it more suitable for the Western market. The resulting Privrednik-IO has a Lycoming IO-540-K1A5 ungeared engine, driving either a McCauley 1A200/DFA 9046 fixed-pitch propeller or Hartzell HC-C2YF-1 constant-speed propeller. The landing gear is softer, with Goodyear tyres size 7·00-8 Type III on the main wheels and a 10·00-SC electroconducting tailwheel tyre. The hopper is all-plastic. All equipment, parts and instruments conform to A.N. standards and a 12V electrical system is installed.

DIMENSIONS:
As for Privrednik-GO

WEIGHTS:
Weight empty, with agricultural equipment 2,227 lb (1,010 kg)
Max chemical payload 1,543 lb (700 kg)
Max T-O weight 4,123 lb (1,870 kg)

PERFORMANCE (at max T-O weight):
Max level speed 109 knots (125 mph; 202 km/h)
Max permissible diving speed 161 knots (186 mph; 300 km/h)
Stalling speed, flaps down 47·5 knots (55 mph; 88 km/h)

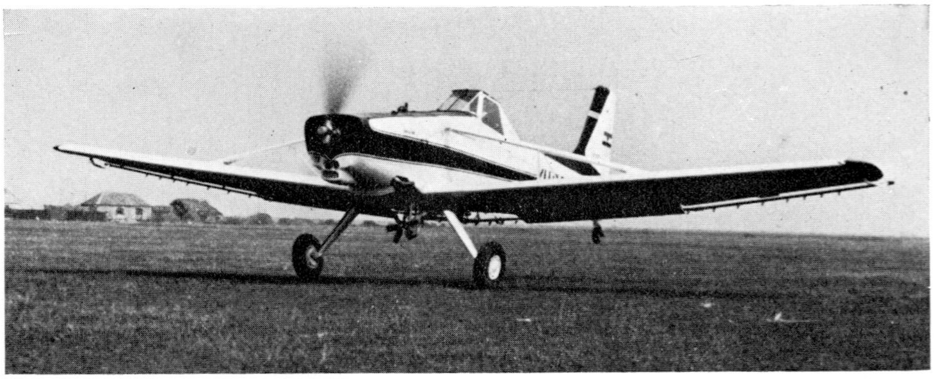

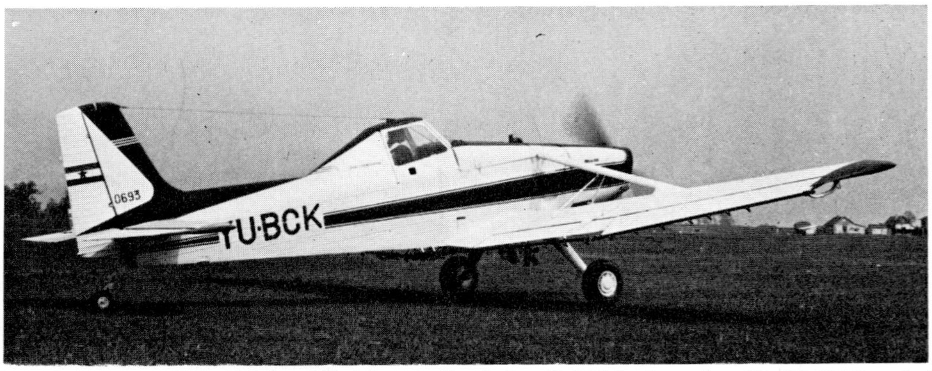

Two views of the UTVA-65 Privrednik-GO agricultural aircraft (295 hp Lycoming GO-480-G1A6 engine)

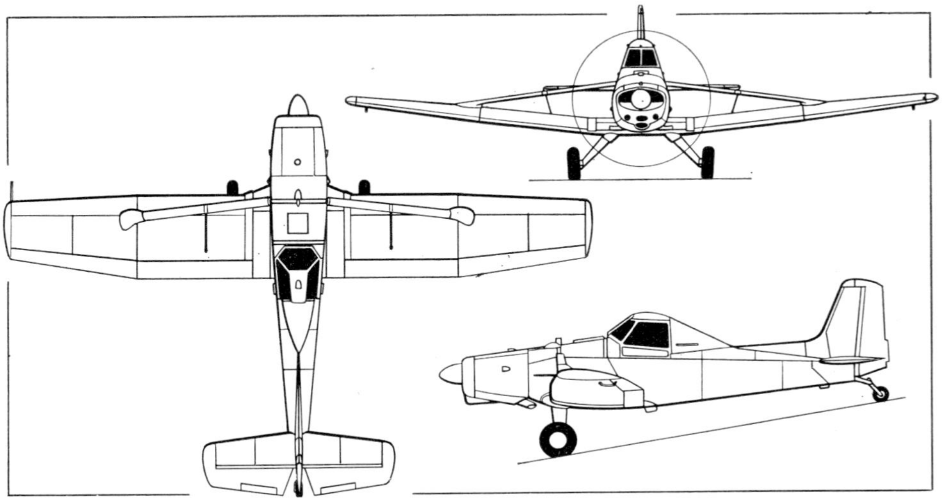

UTVA-65 Privrednik-GO agricultural aircraft

T-O run 755 ft (230 m)
Range, with 40·5 Imp gallons (185 litres) fuel 323 nm (373 miles; 600 km)
Range with auxiliary fuel tank 540 nm (621 miles; 1,000 km)

UTVA-70

The Utva-70 is a twin-engined six-seat utility transport aircraft evolved from the single-engined Utva-66. The basic airframes of the two types are identical; but the Utva-70 has a lengthened cabin, with faired nose, and short sponsons to carry its twin engines.

The prototype, now nearing completion, is powered by two Lycoming GO-480-G1J6 engines. Subsequent models will have two of the new 280 hp Lycoming IGO-268 high-speed engines, and the performance data below apply to this version.

DIMENSIONS, EXTERNAL:
Wing span 37 ft 5 in (11·40 m)
Length overall 27 ft 6 in (8·38 m)
Height overall 10 ft 6 in (3·20 m)
Tailplane span 13 ft $4\frac{1}{2}$ in (4·08 m)
Wheel track 8 ft $4\frac{1}{2}$ in (2·55 m)
Cabin doors (each):
Height 3 ft $2\frac{1}{2}$ in (0·98 m)
Width 3 ft $0\frac{1}{2}$ in (0·93 m)
Canopy door:
Height 1 ft $11\frac{1}{2}$ in (0·60 m)
Width 3 ft $3\frac{1}{2}$ in (1·00 m)

DIMENSIONS, INTERNAL:
Cabin, excluding flight deck:
Length 4 ft 11 in (1·50 m)
Width 3 ft 5 in (1·05 m)

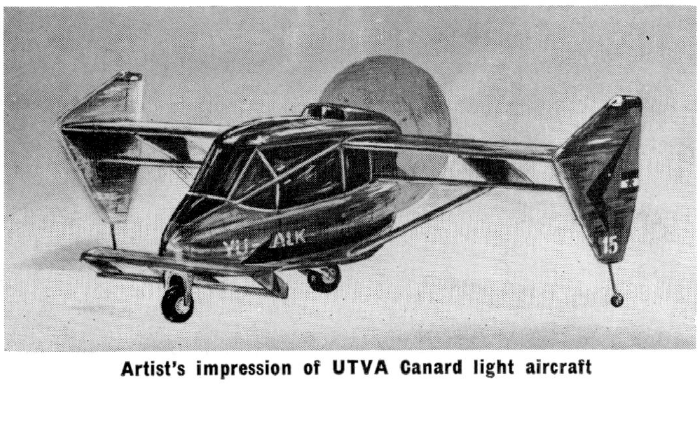

Artist's impression of UTVA Canard light aircraft

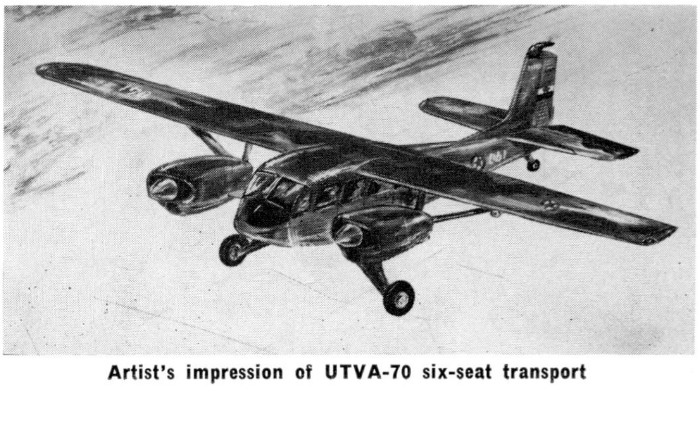

Artist's impression of UTVA-70 six-seat transport

Height	3 ft 11 in (1·20 m)

Flight deck:

Length	3 ft 11 in (1·20 m)
Width	3 ft 11 in (1·20 m)
Height	3 ft 3½ in (1·00 m)

AREAS:

Wings, gross	194·5 sq ft (18·08 m²)
Ailerons (total)	22·18 sq ft (2·06 m²)
Trailing-edge flaps (total)	24·97 sq ft (2·32 m²)
Fin	12·70 sq ft (1·18 m²)
Dorsal fin	4·74 sq ft (0·44 m²)
Rudder	10·22 sq ft (0·94 m²)
Tailplane	26·00 sq ft (2·42 m²)
Elevators	23·90 sq ft (2·22 m²)

WEIGHTS AND LOADINGS:

Weight empty	3,373 lb (1,530 kg)
Max T-O weight	5,070 lb (2,300 kg)
Max wing loading	26 lb/sq ft (127 kg/m²)
Max power loading	9 lb/hp (4·1 kg/hp)

PERFORMANCE (estimated at max T-O weight):

Max level speed at S/L	153 knots (177 mph; 285 km/h)
Max cruising speed at S/L	135 knots (155 mph; 250 km/h)
Stalling speed, flaps down	50 knots (57 mph; 92 km/h)
Rate of climb at S/L	1,280 ft (390 m)/min
Service ceiling	22,650 ft (6,900 m)
Service ceiling, one engine out	8,850 ft (2,700 m)

T-O run	558 ft (170 m)
T-O to 50 ft (15 m)	950 ft (290 m)
Landing from 50 ft (15 m)	900 ft (274 m)
Landing run	360 ft (110 m)
Range with standard fuel and max payload at max cruising speed	540 nm (621 miles; 1,000 km)

UTVA CANARD

This unorthodox single-engined light aircraft is being developed under the design leadership of Dipl-Ing Dimic, for private and sport flying. A one-fifth scale mock-up underwent wind tunnel testing in 1969. First flight of the prototype was scheduled for mid-1970.

In its initial form, the UTVA Canard is a slotted-wing biplane, as shown in the artist's impression on page 528. End-plate fins and rudders span the tips of both wings, and there are narrow-chord staggered biplane canard surfaces at the nose. The landing gear consists of two main wheels in tandem under the cabin nacelle, supplemented by small balancer wheels under the wing-tip fins.

Power plant is a 200 hp Lycoming IO-360-A1A four-cylinder horizontally-opposed air-cooled engine, with the air intakes above the rear of the cabin, driving a two-blade Hartzell constant-speed pusher propeller of 6 ft (1·83 m) diameter.

Fuel capacity is 265 lb (120 kg). The cabin seats three or four persons.

An autogyro version of the UTVA Canard is projected, with a rotating front wing, and a simple modification is being designed to make either version amphibious.

DIMENSIONS, EXTERNAL:

Wing span	22 ft 11¾ in (7·00 m)
Length overall	18 ft 2 in (5·54 m)
Height overall	10 ft 5 in (3·18 m)

AREA:

Wings, gross	150 sq ft (14·0 m²)

WEIGHTS AND LOADINGS:

Weight empty	1,213 lb (550 kg)
Max T-O weight	2,028 lb (920 kg)
Max wing loading	13·45 lb/sq ft (65·7 kg/m²)
Max power loading	10·14 lb/hp (4·6 kg/hp)

PERFORMANCE (estimated):

Max level speed at S/L	124 knots (143 mph; 230 km/h)
Max cruising speed	108 knots (124 mph; 200 km/h)
Stalling speed	43 knots (50 mph; 80 km/h)
Rate of climb at S/L	985 ft (300 m)/min
Service ceiling	12,450 ft (3,800 m)
T-O run	660 ft (200 m)
Landing run	590 ft (180 m)
Range with max fuel	430 nm (500 miles; 800 km)

DRONES
(CORRECTED TO 1 JULY 1970)

AUSTRALIA

COMMONWEALTH OF AUSTRALIA
DEPARTMENT OF SUPPLY
ADDRESS: Constitution Avenue, Canberra, ACT 2600
SECRETARY: A. S. Cooley

GOVERNMENT AIRCRAFT FACTORIES
HEADQUARTERS:
Fishermen's Bend, Melbourne, Victoria 3207
AIRFIELD AND FINAL ASSEMBLY WORKSHOPS:
Avalon, Victoria
MANAGER: G. J. Churcher

The Government Aircraft Factories are units of the Defence Production facilities owned by the Government of the Commonwealth of Australia and operated by the Department of Supply.

Current products include the Jindivik weapons target. Under development is a target drone version of the Ikara anti-submarine missile, known as the Turana.

Jindivik Mk 3B target drone on its take-off trolley

JINDIVIK

The Jindivik continues to be a standard weapons target in Australia and Great Britain.

Up to 1 January 1970 a total of 434 had been ordered, including 194 for Great Britain, 42 for the US Navy and 10 for Sweden. The Royal Australian Navy has ordered a total of 25. Those used in the UK are assembled and equipped to British operational standards by the Guided Weapons Division of British Aircraft Corporation.

Design was begun in March 1948 and construction of the prototype Jindivik Mk 1 was started in December 1950. The prototype flew for the first time on 28 August 1952, and a total of 377 Jindiviks had been delivered by 1 January 1970. The total is made up of 14 Mk 1's, 111 Mk 2's (first flight 11 December 1953), 3 Mk 2A's (first flight 18 September 1958), 76 Mk 2B's (first flight 8 October 1959), 9 Mk 3's (first flight 12 May 1961), 147 Mk 3A's (first flight 10 November 1961) and 17 Mk 3B's (first flight 22 January 1970).

Production of the Mk 3A (known as Mk 103A in Britain) was phased out in 1969 and the Mk 3B is now in production. Deliveries of the Mk 3B (known as the Mk 103B in Britain) began in April 1969. Customers include the UK, Royal Australian Navy and Weapons Research Establishment, Woomera.

The Mk 3B was designed to cater for low-level trials at speeds in excess of 575 mph (925 kmh). In this version, the front fuselage and equipment bay have been redesigned to give greater volume for special trials equipment. This has been made possible by miniaturisation and updating of some of the basic flight equipment.

To meet the higher performance required of the Mk 3B Jindivik, the control systems for the ailerons and elevators have been strengthened and provided with GAF-designed twin-motor servo-motors giving greater torque output. The fin has been strengthened and metal honeycomb used in place of paper honeycomb. Geared tabs are fitted to both the ailerons and elevators, with the latter increased in chord by 50%.

Improvements have also been made to the rear engine steady and rear jet-pipe location in the rear fuselage, to minimise pitch trim requirement. Further optional equipment includes an air-brake fitted under the rear fuselage, which may be used as a dive-brake to reduce descent time from high altitude. Power to actuate the air-brake is supplied from the basic aircraft pneumatic supply.

The air-brake may also be used to control speed when two Jindiviks are flown in close formation. For this purpose a separate pneumatic supply is provided. An in-flight variable fin tab may also be fitted.

Up to 1 January 1970, Jindiviks had flown 2,063 sorties at the RAE, Llanbedr, North Wales, and one particular Mk 3A drone had flown over 160 sorties at Woomera.

The following description applies to the Mk 3B:

TYPE: Pilotless target aircraft.

WINGS: Cantilever mid-wing monoplane. Wing section NACA 64A-106 with modified trailing-edge. Dihedral 2° 30'. Incidence 1°. Multi-spar box structure of aluminium alloy. Spars are Araldite bonded to pre-formed heavy-gauge skins to form inter-spar torsion-box which is utilised as integral fuel tankage. Leading-edge is attached to front spar and rebated skins by Araldite. Trailing-edge box is an Araldite-bonded structure and is riveted to the main

spar box structure, which houses the aileron control system of rods and bell-cranks. Aluminium alloy monocoque flaps and ailerons are hinged to this structure, with continuous piano hinges and three-point pin hinges respectively. Ailerons are fitted with inset geared tab and driven by GAF-designed twin-motor servo motor. Flaps are operated pneumatically.

FUSELAGE: Aluminium alloy semi-monocoque structure, in three main sections: front fuselage, centre fuselage and rear fuselage. Front fuselage carries all control equipment, autopilot and telemetry equipment on three removable trays. A moulded glass-fibre canopy, which lifts off for access to the equipment, forms the ram-type air intake. Rear end of front fuselage and front end of centre fuselage form bay in which all special trials equipment is carried. Centre fuselage also houses landing skid. Rear fuselage carries the engines and jet-pipe.

TAIL UNIT: Cantilever multi-spar tailplane of light alloy bonded with Araldite. Elevators, formed of single wrapped skins stiffened by chordwise flutes and carried on piano hinges, are driven by a GAF-designed twin-motor servo-motor. Inset geared tabs are fitted. Fin consists of light alloy skin bonded to two spars and stabilised by metal honeycomb filling. No rudder; but provision for an in-flight variable trim-tab in fin.

LANDING GEAR: Pneumatically-extended, manually retracted (on ground) central skid. Pneumatic jack acts as shock-absorber. Steel auxiliary skids at wing-tips. See item on "Take-off and landing" below.

POWER PLANT: One Rolls-Royce (Bristol) Viper Mk 201 turbojet engine (2,500 lb = 1,134 kg st). Flexible rubber main fuselage fuel tank, capacity 64 Imp gallons (291 litres), and two integral wing tanks, total capacity 38 Imp gallons (173 litres). Single refuelling point in centre fuselage for all tanks. Wing tanks are pressurised from engine compressor to feed fuselage tank, from where fuel is pumped to the engine. A pressurised fuel recuperator is fitted in this delivery line to cope with negative 'g' conditions. Compressed air is used for starting and throttle is operated by electric actuator through a cam switch box, allowing several fixed rpm engine conditions to be selected in addition to throttle "beep" demands. Oil capacity 1 Imp gallon (4·5 litres).

SYSTEMS: No hydraulic system. Non-regenerative pneumatic system: air stored at 2,000 lb/sq in (140 kg/cm²) in power pack which supplies air to the flap, air-brake and landing skid reduced to 575 lb/sq in (40·5 kg/cm²). If the air-brake is to be used for speed control when two aircraft are formating, a separate air supply system may be fitted as optional equipment. Engine-driven 9kVA alternator delivers 208V AC 3-phase electrical supply at 300-550 c/s. In the event of alternator failure, a 24V DC battery provides limited power for essential control functions.

REMOTE-CONTROL EQUIPMENT: Aircraft is remotely controlled from a ground station. Radio control equipment comprises two receiver/selectors, the second of which may be used as stand-by or destruct, and GAF relay set receiving. Telemetry equipment consists of NIC transducers and Australian-designed transmitter and junction box.

TRIALS EQUIPMENT: Transponders and Microwave reflectors are used for trials of active, semi-active or beam-riding missiles. Heat sources can be fitted to provide low-frequency IR output. Transponders in the X, S, and C bands can be fitted for target acquisition and to enable the Jindivik to be tracked at greater range. Various types of towed target may be fitted, carrying augmentation in the form of transponders, microwave reflectors or infra-red.

RECORDING EQUIPMENT: Cameras fitted with wide-angle lenses are carried in wing-tip pods, with all-round vision capability and are used to film and record the approach path and proximity of missiles fired against the target. Rearward-facing cameras may be used in this role when towed targets are used. Variants are the Mk 5 pod with cameras only and the Mk 8 with cameras, fuel and provision for fitment of microwave reflectors in LE and TE radomes.

TAKE-OFF AND LANDING: Jindivik is mounted on a tubular-framed tricycle take-off trolley. Aircraft/trolley steering is achieved by a servo-controlled nose-wheel which responds to signals from the aircraft's auto-pilot. The aircraft-trolley combination accelerates under normal jet power with flaps retracted and with the aircraft set at a negative incidence. When unstick speed is reached the aircraft is rotated to take-off incidence and flaps are lowered rapidly. Rotation of the aircraft initiates the trolley release system and the aircraft climbs away. At the same time trolley brakes equipped with Dunlop anti-skid devices are applied. When Jindivik is in the approach run, the flaps and skid are selected down for landing. On touch-down, a 'sting' extended below the main skid rotates on impact and initiates rapid retraction of flaps. Fuel supply is terminated by radio command.

DIMENSIONS, EXTERNAL:
Wing span:	
over pods	20 ft 9 in (6·32 m)
with extensions	26 ft 6 in (7·92 m)
Wing chord (constant)	4 ft 0 in (1·22 m)
Wing aspect ratio	6·45
Length overall	26 ft 8·75 in (8·15 m)
Length of fuselage	23 ft 3·75 in (7·11 m)
Height overall, skid extended	6 ft 9·85 in (2·08 m)
Tailplane span	6 ft 6 in (1·98 m)

DIMENSIONS, INTERNAL:
Equipment bays:	
front fuselage	11·46 cu ft (0·32 m³)
centre fuselage	5·24 cu ft (0·15 m³)

AREAS:
Wings, gross:	
standard span	102 sq ft (9·48 m²)
short span	76 sq ft (7·06 m²)
extended span	115 sq ft (10·68 m²)
Ailerons (total)	4·5 sq ft (0·42 m²)
Flaps (total)	11·5 sq ft (1·07 m²)
Fin	7·2 sq ft (0·67 m²)
Tailplane	14·6 sq ft (1·36 m²)
Elevators	4·2 sq ft (0·39 m²)

WEIGHTS AND LOADING:
Weight empty, equipped (min)	2,900 lb (1,315 kg)
Max payload	approx 400 lb (181 kg)
Max T-O and landing weight	3,300-3,650 lb (1,500-1,655 kg)
Max zero-fuel weight	2,500 lb (1,135 kg)
Max wing loading	42·5 lb/sq ft (207·5 kg/m²)

PERFORMANCE:
Max permissible diving speed:
short span at 6,000 ft (1,830 m)
562 knots (647 mph; 1,041 km/h)
40 in (101 cm) extended span, at 37,000 ft
(11,275 m) 500 knots (575 mph; 926 km/h)
80 in (202 cm) extended span, at 45,000 ft
(13,710 m) 470 knots (541 mph; 871 km/h)
Max cruising speed
490 knots (564 mph; 908 km/h)
Econ cruising speed (IAS/EAS)
135 knots (155 mph; 250 km/h)
Stalling speed, flaps up
95 knots (109 mph; 176 km/h)
Rate of climb at S/L   15,000 ft (4,570 m)/min
Service ceiling:

standard span	62,000 ft (18,900 m)
short span	55,000 ft (16,760 m)
extended span	66,000 ft (20,100 m)
T-O run	1,000 ft (305 m)
T-O to 50 ft (15 m)	2,200 ft (670 m)
Landing from 50 ft (15 m)	2,700 ft (823 m)
Landing run	1,500 ft (457 m)

Range with max fuel and max payload, with
280 lb (127 kg) fuel allowance for take-off,
descent and overshoot:
with Mk 8 pods
712 nm (820 miles; 1,320 km)
without Mk 8 pods
442 nm (510 miles; 820 km)

Model of Turana target drone, based on the Ikara anti-submarine missile

TURANA

The Turana is a target drone based on the Ikara missile, described in the "Guided Missiles" section. It is being developed by the Department of Supply to meet a Royal Australian Navy Staff Requirement for a modern gunnery and guided weapons target. The development programme was approved and funded in August 1969.

The programme is well advanced and will include three series of flight trials, the last of which, flown from a ship, will be a service acceptance trial. It is planned that Turana will enter service with the RAN in late 1971.

Government Aircraft Factories are the Co-ordinating Design Authority and Prime Contractor responsible for the airframe, autopilot, engine and fuel system. Guidance and rocket propulsion aspects of the project are sub-contracted to the Weapons Research Establishment/ EMI Electronics (Australia) and Weapons Research Establishment/Ordnance Factory and Explosives Factory Maribyrnong.

TYPE: Pilotless target drone.

WINGS: Cantilever mid-wing tail-less monoplane of cropped delta planform. Wing section modified NACA 64010. Spindle attachment to fuselage, the spindle being also the main spar. Two metal ribs and metal rear spar, the remainder of the wing being of foam-filled glass-fibre. Full-span elevons are operated via a differential mechanical linkage by two electric actuators, one for pitch and one for roll control. The wings are quickly detachable from the fuselage.

FUSELAGE: Aluminium alloy torsion box, with removable glass-fibre fairings, housing the autopilot, fuel tank, engine and various miss distance equipments and transponders. Interface attachments are identical with those of Ikara.

TAIL UNIT: Single vertical fin, of NACA 64010 section, made of chemically-milled aluminium skins and aluminium ribs and spars, with glass-fibre tip and trailing-edge.

POWER PLANT: One Microturbo Cougar 022 turbojet engine of 150 lb (68 kg) st. Stainless steel/air-bag fuel tank of 11·8 Imp gallons

(53 litres) capacity. Air-bag is pressurised from engine compressor. Compressed air is used for starting and the engine speed is controlled by an electronic unit, which forms part of a speed demand loop.

BOOST: Single-nozzle solid-propellant booster motor specially developed for Turana. Nominal burning time 2 seconds; nominal thrust 6,000 lb (2,721 kg). Boost motor is jettisoned at the end of the boost phase. Launching is from the standard Ikara launcher, or from a lightweight portable launcher.

SYSTEMS: All electric. Rechargeable silver-zinc battery pack provides power for all services for over one hour.

CONTROL SYSTEM AND AUTOPILOT: Elevons on the wings are operated symmetrically or differentially by electric actuators. The autopilot includes a displacement gyro sensing roll and pitch, a rate gyro sensing yaw, an air data unit with airspeed and altitude transducers, signal summing and shaping networks and drive amplifiers for the servo system. A pitot-static tube is fitted to the tip of the vertical fin. Height lock and speed lock loops are provided within the drone.

GUIDANCE: Drone is designed to be used initially in conjunction with an adaptation of the Ikara guidance system on board RAN ships. Navigation will be by means of the Ikara tracking receiver and ship's plotting facilities. At a later stage, a simplified guidance system may be provided for other users. Guidance equipment is housed in the vertical fin.

RECOVERY: Command parachute recovery, the parachute being housed on the ejectable nose of the drone. Initial versions of Turana are designed for over-the-water recovery. For use on land, air-bag cushioning will be developed.

TRIALS EQUIPMENT: Drone is intended initially mainly for gunnery practice, for which purpose visual augmentation is provided in the form of a strobe flashing light. Passive radar augmentation is provided by a 7½ in (19 cm) Luneberg lens in the nose and by a ring of corner reflectors from a rearward aspect. Space and

large weight-carrying capacity are available for active augmentation or for other special equipment. Pyrotechnic flares of up to 2½ in (6·3 cm) diameter can be accommodated at the wing-tips. An acoustic miss-distance indication system is being developed. Radioactive MDI or short-running cameras can be provided as an alternative.

OPERATIONS: Typical operation as a service target will begin by boosted launch from a ship and climb (or descent) to the required operational altitude. The height lock can then be engaged, holding the drone to the chosen altitude, and control in azimuth can be exercised to provide a number of presentations, crossing, approaching or receding, for the exercise of guns, short-range or medium/long-range guided weapons. The number of presentations is dependent upon the chosen operating speed and altitude. The flight is concluded by descent to 1,000 ft (305 m), and return to the neighbourhood of the ship, where the parachute is deployed and recovery from the sea is effected.

DIMENSIONS, EXTERNAL:

Wing span	5 ft 0·2 in (1·53 m)
Length	11 ft 3 in (3·44 m)
Height (less boost motor)	3 ft 4 in (1·02 m)
Height (with boost motor)	3 ft 10 in (1·17 m)

DIMENSION, INTERNAL:

Special equipment capacity	1 cu ft (0·028 m³)

AREAS:

Wings, gross	13·2 sq ft (1·23 m²)
Elevons (total)	2·04 sq ft (0·19 m²)
Fin	3·4 sq ft (0·32 m²)

WEIGHTS:

Weight at launch	550 lb (249 kg)
Weight after boost jettison	440 lb (200 kg)
Weight at recovery (empty)	347 lb (157 kg)
Special equipment weight	up to 100 lb (45 kg)

PERFORMANCE (estimated):

Max level speed	over 400 knots (460 mph; 741 km/h)
Service ceiling	33,000 ft (10,000 m)
Max rate of climb at S/L	4,500 ft (1,365 m)/min
Range	347 nm (400 miles; 645 km)
Endurance	60 minutes

BELGIUM

MBLE

MANUFACTURE BELGE DE LAMPES ET DE MATÉRIEL ELECTRONIQUE SA

HEAD OFFICE: 80 rue des Deux-Gares, Bruxelles 7
HEAD OF AERONAUTICAL DIVISION:
A. Colpaert

This company, which employs 5,200 people, has contributed to a number of European aerospace programmes, including those of the F-104G Starfighter, Hawk missile and ELDO space research projects. It has also developed, built

and tested a battlefield surveillance system using an unmanned vehicle named the Epervier, of which details follow.

MBLE EPERVIER

Inspired by a Northrop Ventura primary design, but developed and built entirely in Belgium, the Epervier is a small ramp-launched battlefield surveillance drone, intended to meet NATO specifications.

The airframe, of glass-reinforced plastics, is manufactured under sub-contract by Fairey S A

at Gosselies. The power plant of the X-1 first prototype was a Wankel rotating-piston engine, built by NSU, driving a ducted pusher propeller. This was replaced by a Hirth piston-engine in the X-2 and X-3 versions (see 1967/68 Jane's). A further change of power plant has been made in the current Epervier X-4, which has a Rover TJ125 turbojet engine and has attained much higher speeds than its predecessors. Many trials were made in Belgium and Sardinia during 1968.

The reconnaissance devices which would be

carried by the operational version of the Epervier are those called for in the NATO specifications. The complete system can be mounted on standard types of military vehicles used in forward combat areas and can be operated by three men. A parachute recovery system is fitted to permit re-use of the drone.

DIMENSIONS (X-4):

Wing span	5 ft 7 in (1·70 m)
Length overall	7 ft 0¾ in (2·15 m)
Height overall	2 ft 5½ in (0·75 m)

WEIGHTS (X-4):

Weight empty	214 lb (97 kg)

Fuel	48·5 lb (22 kg)
Payload	44 lb (20 kg)
Max launching weight	306·5 lb (139 kg)

PERFORMANCE:

Cruising speed	186-270 knots (215-310 mph; 350-500 km/h)

Launch of Epervier X-3 drone, with ducted propeller

MBLE Epervier X-4 turbojet-powered surveillance drone

CANADA

CANADAIR

CANADAIR LTD (Subsidiary of General Dynamics Corporation)

HEAD OFFICE AND WORKS:
Cartierville Airport, Montreal, PQ

OFFICERS:
See "Aircraft" section

In addition to its work on piloted aircraft, Canadair has developed a reconnaissance drone system of which all available details follow.

CANADAIR AN/USD/501

The AN/USD/501 short-range reconnaissance drone system is designed for day and night target acquisition and battlefield surveillance. Work on the project was initiated by Canadair in 1959 and development of the drone began in 1961 on a shared cost basis with the Canadian Department of Industry, Trade and Commerce. In 1962, the former British Ministry of Aviation joined with Canada in supporting the project, and the Federal Republic of Germany joined in the development programme in November 1965 as a full one-third partner.

Development of the system is now under the management of the Project Management Branch of the Canadian Department of Supply and Services (formerly the Department of Defence Production). The project management team is located in Ottawa and is staffed with military and civilian personnel from the three participating countries.

The AN/USD/501 is a self-contained mobile system for day and night use by army formations in forward battle areas. The system is based on a simple low-cost drone, powered by a Williams Research turbojet sustainer engine which propels it at a speed approaching Mach 1. Fired from a mobile launcher, with the aid of a booster rocket supplied by Bristol Aerospace and the Royal Ordnance Factory, Bishopton, it follows a pre-selected course and photographs accurately the enemy territory and equipment over which it flies, using a sensor designed and manufactured in Germany by the Zeiss Corporation. The system also employs a Hawk-1 infra-red line-scan sensor supplied by Hawker Siddeley Dynamics of the UK. On completion of a mission, the engine cuts off as the drone approaches the recovery area, guided by a homing beacon, and the drone lands by parachute. Airbags cushion the impact and, after the film has been removed, the drone can be refuelled and prepared quickly for a further mission.

During 1967 teams composed of military personnel from Canada, the UK and Germany successfully completed service engineering trials with the AN/USD/501 at Yuma, Arizona, and service performance trials at Shilo, Manitoba. "Demonstration of Conformance" trials were completed successfully by a tri-partite trials troop of about 75 men in the Autumn of 1969, using production drones.

Canadair AN/USD/501 drone in cruising flight configuration, less booster

Canadair AN/USD/501 short-range surveillance and target acquisition drone system

On one of these flights, the 18th production AN/USD/501 covered a 59-mile (95 km) course in eight minutes and parachuted to earth approximately 100 yards from its homing beacon. Seven subsequent flights, using both types of sensor, included two during which the drone followed a pre-planned course at varying altitudes.

Production is now under way at Canadair on an initial order for 282 drone sets, valued at $67 million, for the three participating partners.

DIMENSIONS, EXTERNAL:

Length overall, excl nose probe:	
with booster	12 ft 2 in (3·71 m)
without booster	8 ft 6½ in (2·60 m)
Body diameter	1 ft 1 in (0·33 m)
Span of wings	3 ft 1 in (0·94 m)
Span of foreplanes	1 ft 7 in (0·48 m)

WEIGHT:

Max launching weight	220 lb (100 kg)

FRANCE

AÉROSPATIALE
SOCIÉTÉ NATIONALE INDUSTRIELLE AÉROSPATIALE

HEAD OFFICE: 37 Bd de Montmorency, Paris 16e

OFFICERS: See "Aircraft" section.

Drones in current production by Aérospatiale (Nord-Aviation) are the CT.20 and supersonic C.30 targets and the R.20 battlefield reconnaissance system. An improved version of the C.30, designated C.30C, is under development.

The earlier CT.10, described in the 1960-61 *Jane's*, is no longer being manufactured, although spares continue to be produced for CT.10's in service. Further work on the Nord 511 "flying platform" reconnaissance system (see 1969-70 *Jane's*) has been abandoned.

AÉROSPATIALE (NORD) CT.20

The CT.20 is a turbojet-powered radio-controlled target of medium performance, which is also used as a tug for a towed target. It is standard equipment for training military units in the use of air-to-air and surface-to-air missiles, in particular the Hawk; and over 1,200 had been ordered by early 1969, by the French, Italian and Swedish Armies and other customers.

On December 30, 1965, Nord received a contract to provide 450 target flights at the new NATO firing range in Crete. The missions are being flown by CT.20 drones, towing Dornier targets (see below), over a three-year period.

The CT.20 is launched from a ramp 32 ft 9½ in (10 m) long and inclined at an angle of 5 degrees to the horizontal. The launching carriage is powered by two powder rockets and, aided by the power of the turbojet engine, the CT.20 attains a speed of 555·9 ft/sec (610 kmh) by the time it reaches its maximum acceleration. The drone then continues to fly under the control of a radio-operator located on the ground or in a "mother" aircraft.

Nine signals can be transmitted: turns to right and left, nose up and down, full throttle, cruising, trace smoke, operate cameras and land. The turning signal controls bank and the turns are executed without reverse yaw. The pitch signals act on the elevators via the auto-pilot. When the landing signal is transmitted, the engine is stopped, the brake parachute opens and, at the end of a delay period, the recovery parachute is released. The descent is made in a level attitude and the impact with the ground is cushioned by an air-bag forward of the centre-section. In the case of radio-control failure the landing sequence occurs automatically.

Low-altitude flight, under barostatic altitude control, can be programmed currently at 300-400 ft (90-120 m). Very low altitude capability is under development.

The CT.20 can be used to tow a type SK3L target produced by Dornier System GmbH of Germany. The target is 3 ft 11¼ in (1·20 m) long, with a fin span of 1 ft 3¾ in (0·40 m) and body diameter of 9·85 in (0·25 m) and is pylon-mounted under the starboard wing of the CT.20 at launch. When towed in flight on a 2,625-3,950 ft (800-1,200 m) cable, it has negligible effect on the CT.20's speed and flight duration is reduced by no more than 15%.

This joint development by Nord and Dornier System overcomes problems resulting from the fact that the performance of modern missiles seldom permits firing of surface-to-air and air-to-air weapons at a target towed by a manned aircraft.

The R.20 reconnaissance drone and M.20 missile, developed from the CT.20, are described separately below and in the "Missiles" section respectively.

TYPE: Turbojet-powered radio-controlled target.

WINGS: Cantilever mid-wing monoplane with medium sweepback. Each wing is made up of two steel-tube spars, aluminium alloy ribs and covering. Lateral control spoilers at wing-tips.

FUSELAGE: In three main sections. Forward section, of aluminium alloy, contains command guidance, auto-pilot, batteries and principal recovery parachute. Central section consists of a structural steel tank divided into two parts, one for fuel and the other containing chemicals for the tracking smoke. Rear fuselage, of aluminium alloy, contains the engine and carries the tail unit. A braking parachute is housed in a cone above the jet nozzle.

TAIL UNIT: "Butterfly" structure of aluminium alloy. Comprises two elevator surfaces controlled simultaneously by a single jack.

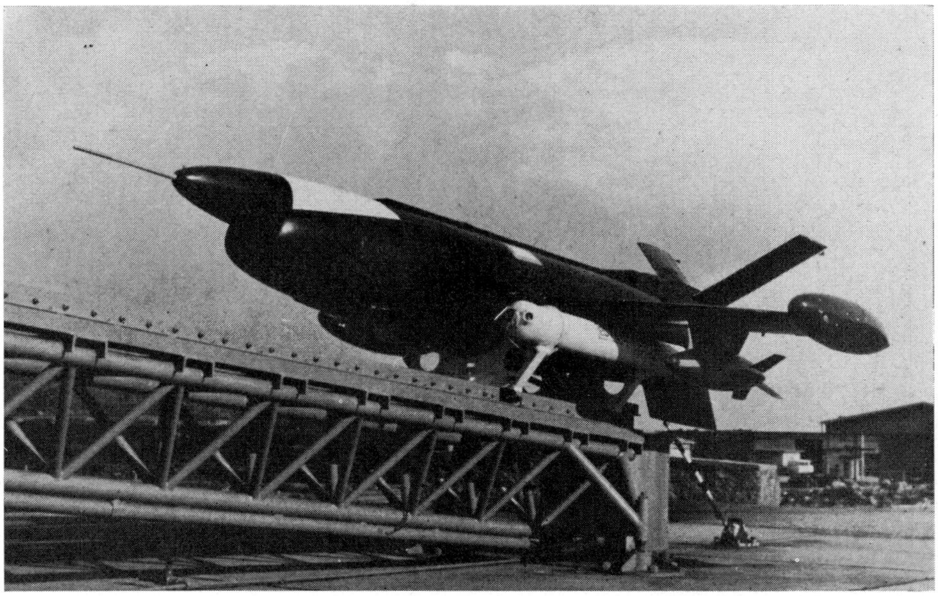

Aérospatiale (Nord) CT.20 drone, with underwing towed target, at the NATO firing range in Crete

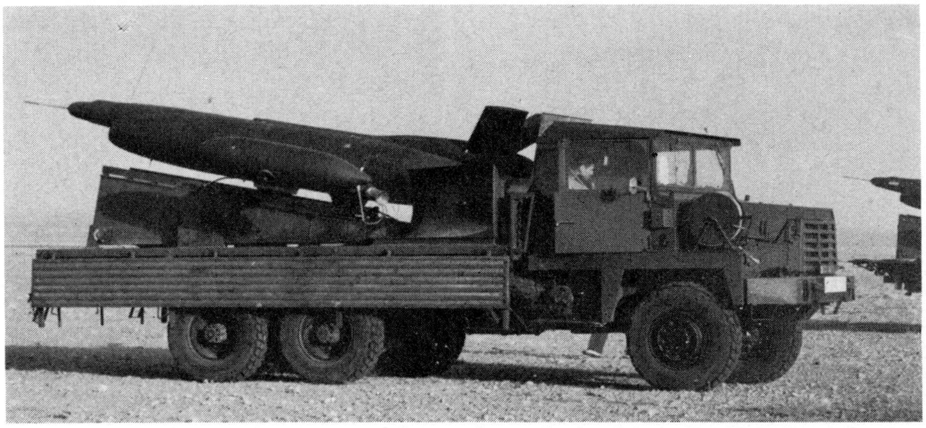

Aérospatiale (Nord) R.20 reconnaissance drone, developed from the CT.20 target

POWER PLANT: One Turbomeca Marboré II (880 lb=400 kg st) turbojet engine in CT.20 Version IV, or Marboré VI (1,056 lb= 480kg st) turbojet engine in CT.20 Version VII.

DIMENSIONS, EXTERNAL:

Wing span	11 ft 9¾ in (3·6 m)
Length overall	17 ft 10½ in (5·45 m)
Body diameter (max)	2 ft 2 in (0·66 m)

AREA:

Wings, gross	33·34 sq ft (3·20 m²)

WEIGHT:

Max launching weight	1,488 lb (675 kg)

PERFORMANCE:

Max speed at 32,800 ft (10,000 m)	
Marboré II	485 knots (560 mph; 900 km/h)
Marboré VI	512 knots (590 mph; 950 km/h)
Time to 32,800 ft (10,000 m)	6 minutes
Service ceiling:	
Marboré II	39,370 ft (12,000 m)
Marboré VI	49,200 ft (15,000 m)
T-O acceleration	7·5 g
Mean endurance	60 minutes

AÉROSPATIALE (NORD) R.20

The Aérospatiale R.20 is a battlefield reconnaissance drone developed from the CT.20 target, to which it is externally similar. It is powered by a Marboré II turbojet and is launched with the aid of two solid-propellent booster rockets from a short ramp on a standard Berliet GB-C8-KT Army lorry. Standard NATO cameras or other surveillance equipment are carried in its nose and in interchangeable wing-tip containers. Two other standard vehicles are used to carry support equipment, including radio control equipment and the antenna system.

When close to its launch-post the R.20 is controlled directly from the ground. Over longer distances, the drone is controlled automatically by an inertial platform and an electronic programmer, enabling it to follow a prearranged flight plan.

It is claimed to offer an over-target accuracy of within 985 ft (300 m) at a distance of 62 miles (100 km) from its launch-site. Average operating height is 3,300 ft (1,000 m), but it can be set to fly higher or lower, as required. It can photograph more than 77 square miles (200 km²) of territory during a single low-altitude sortie, using three synchronised cameras. Data can be sent back during flight by radio link. A special infra-red detector makes possible transmission to the ground of a composite image of an area at night. Flares can be carried for night photography.

After initial testing in 1963, the R.20 was tested under operational conditions in February 1964. It is now in operational use in the French Army and performs routine flights over French training grounds.

DIMENSIONS, EXTERNAL:

Wing span	12 ft 2½ in (3·72 m)
Width, wings folded	4 ft 5 in (1·35 m)
Length overall	18 ft 9 in (5·71 m)
Wing-tip containers:	
Length	6 ft 3 in (1·90 m)
Diameter	1 ft 3¾ in (0·40 m)

WEIGHTS:

T-O weight of drone	1,875 lb (850 kg)
T-O weight with booster	2,425 lb (1,100 kg)
Payload	330 lb (150 kg)

PERFORMANCE:

Operating speed	Mach 0·65
Operating radius at low altitude	
	86 nm (100 miles; 160 km)

AÉROSPATIALE (NORD) C.30

The C.30 target drone is a derivative of the AS.30 tactical missile and is intended mainly to assist in the development testing of surface-to-air weapon systems and in the training of their operators. It carries devices for augmentation of radar reflectivity or infra-red radiation and can simulate either a large bomber aircraft or a missile.

The target is normally air-launched, using standard AS.30 equipment on the carrier-aircraft, and is guided in flight by a pre-set control mechanism. All the equipment associated with its target role is contained in the head, which is recoverable. The aft body, built around a two-stage solid-propellent rocket motor, carries the wings, jet deflectors and control mechanism.

If required, the C.30 can be launched from the ground for very low altitude operations.

First flight development trials were made at Colomb-Béchar in February 1967, using a Canberra of the Bretigny Flight Test Centre as launch aircraft. Launched at varying heights, the C.30 maintained supersonic speed for over 30 miles (50 km) while following a programmed flight path with great accuracy. It is in series production.

DIMENSIONS:

Wing span	3 ft 3½ in (1·00 m)
Length overall	14 ft 11 in (4·55 m)
Max diameter of body	1 ft 1½ in (0·34 m)

WEIGHT:

Launching weight	992 lb (450 kg)
Equipment for drone mission	132 lb (60 kg)

Aérospatiale (Nord) C.30 target, developed from the AS.30 air-to-surface missile

PERFORMANCE:

Endurance, powered cruise	100 seconds
Acceleration (gain of speed over launch vehicle)	
	820 ft (250 m)/sec
Operating height	0–82,000 ft (0–25,000 m)
Mean cruising speed (related to speed and height of launch aircraft):	
Mach 0·7 at 26,250 ft (8,000 m)	Mach 1·4
Mach 0·7 at 39,375 ft (12,000 m)	Mach 1·7
Mach 1·4 at 26,250 ft (8,000 m)	Mach 1·6
Mach 1·4 at 39,375 ft (12,000 m)	Mach 2·1
Mach 1·8 at 26,250 ft (8,000 m)	Mach 1·8
Mach 1·8 at 39,375 ft (12,000 m)	Mach 2·3
Ground launch	Mach 0·95

Range in powered flight:	
Ground launch	15 nm (17·5 miles; 28 km)
Mach 0·7 launch	
	21–27 nm (25–31 miles; 40–50 km)
Mach 1·4 launch	
	27–35 nm (31–40 miles; 50–65 km)
Mach 1·8 launch	
	30–37 nm (34–43 miles; 55–70 km)

AÉROSPATIALE (NORD) C.30C

The C.30C, under study in early 1970, is a new version of the C.30 with improved performance. It will be able to fly at greater altitudes and is intended to offer increased flexibility.

MARCHETTI

SOCIÉTÉ CHARLES MARCHETTI

HEAD OFFICE:
80 avenue de la Grande Armée, Paris 17e

PRESIDENT: Charles Marchetti

This company has undertaken design studies of a variety of rotating-wing aircraft in recent years. Its latest product is a electrically-powered flying platform drone known as the Heliscope, of which details are given below.

Marchetti claims that the basic principles used in the Heliscope project are applicable to other vehicles, including winged aircraft, helicopters and air cushion vehicles, for the driving of compressors, fans, propellers, rotors and other items of equipment.

MARCHETTI HELISCOPE

Developed under contract from the French Ministry of Defence (DRME), the Heliscope is a prototype electrically-powered flying platform which completed its testing early in 1970. It is intended for both military and civilian use, as an unmanned observation and survey platform of exceptionally long endurance.

Basically, the Heliscope consists of two three-blade light alloy fixed-pitch rotors of co-axial contra-rotating design. These rotors are attached respectively to the rotor and stator of a 30kW electric motor located between their hubs.

The power supply for this motor is provided by a generator mounted on the vehicle which serves as the mobile ground station for the drone, and is fed through a cable which runs to the centre of the base of the Heliscope.

Marchetti Heliscope flying platform

When the power is switched on, the rotor and stator of the electric motor, and hence the two rotors, begin to rotate in opposite directions at up to 3,200 rpm and the platform takes off vertically. The system is claimed to offer a high power-weight ratio and to be completely independent of temperature and altitude. The absence of conventional blade root hinges, gears, transmission, swashplate and fuel system is expected to give the Heliscope a service life of 25,000 to 30,000 hours.

DIMENSIONS:

Diameter of rotors (each)	5 ft 3 in (1·60 m)
Height overall	2 ft 11½ in (0·90 m)

WEIGHTS:

Weight empty	121 lb (55 kg)
Electric motor	62 lb (28 kg)
Max T-O weight	286 lb (130 kg)

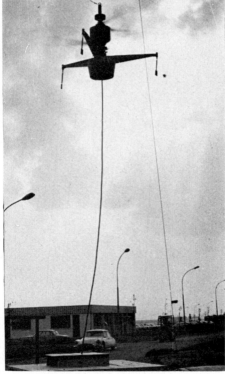

Marchetti Heliscope under test

GERMANY

DORNIER

DORNIER AG

HEAD OFFICE:
Postfach 317, 799 Friedrichshafen/Bodensee

The helicopter division of Dornier AG has developed a mobile drone system, designated Do 32 K Kiebitz.

DORNIER Do 32K KIEBITZ (PEEWIT)

The Do-Kiebitz is a mobile drone system consisting of a tethered rotating-wing platform and a cross-country truck to serve as a ground station. From any point accessible to the truck,

a payload can be stationed by day or night at altitudes of up to 1,000 ft (300 m).

Compressed air to drive the platform's two-blade "cold-jet" rotor is supplied by a KHD T212 turbo-compressor, mounted within the cylindrical light alloy body of the drone. Fuel for the turbine is fed through the tether by means of a pump installed in the ground station, making possible long periods of operation. The rotor turns at 330 rpm.

The platform contains a three-axis autostabiliser which works through the cyclic-pitch control system and compressor exhaust control system. The truck serves as transport vehicle, take-off and landing ramp, and power supply station. An easy-to-operate winch permits the drone to be reeled in and out at a rate of 590 ft (180 m) min. De-icing and a high degree of weather resistance make operations almost independent of weather conditions.

The Do-Kiebitz is intended for use as an emergency transmitter aerial in the long, medium and short-wave bands; as a relay and directional station for TV, VHF and radio communications; for measurement of field strength for localising optimum transmitter positions, photographic survey and reconnaissance, meteorological measurements or radar reconnaissance to detect low-flying objects; and as a directional receiver.

It is being developed under a research contract from the Federal Ministry of Defence.

DIMENSIONS, EXTERNAL:

Diameter of rotor	24 ft 7 in (7·50 m)
Height overall	4 ft 11 in (1·50 m)
Height of body	3 ft 9¼ in (1·15 m)
Body diameter	2 ft 5½ in (0·75 m)

WEIGHTS:

Weight without tether	364 lb (165 kg)
Payload to 655 ft (200 m) ISA	187 lb (85 kg)

PERFORMANCE:

Operational ceiling	1,000 ft (300 m)
Endurance	24 hours

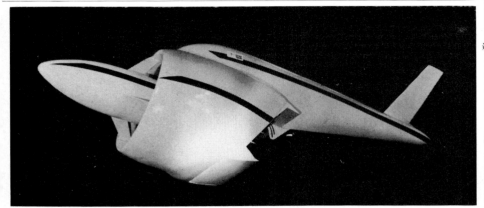

Model of the Dornier System Aerodyne wingless VTOL drone

DORNIER SYSTEM GmbH

HEAD OFFICE:
799 Friedrichshafen/Bodensee

OFFICERS:
See "Research Rockets" section

Current activities of Dornier System GmbH include the development of drones, reconnaissance systems, missiles and air target systems.

The Dornier high-speed tow target system can be carried by a wide variety of aircraft and unmanned target drones. It consists of a fully-automatic towing reel with cable cutter, a launcher to carry the target, and the cruciform-tailed glass-fibre reinforced polyester target itself. After take-off, at a predetermined altitude the tow target is released from its underwing carrier pylon by radio command, and the cable is fully deployed by automatic reeling. The target follows the manoeuvres of the towing aircraft and remains airborne even after it has been penetrated by several bullets.

DORNIER SYSTEM AERODYNE

Development of the Aerodyne wingless high-speed VTOL drone was begun by Dr A. Lippisch in the USA and is being continued by Dornier System GmbH.

The general appearance of the Aerodyne is shown in the adjacent photograph of a model. The prototype, which was constructed in 1969, is powered by a 350 shp MTU 6022 A2 turboshaft engine. Lift and propulsion are generated by a shrouded propeller, the slipstream from which is deflected downward by vanes for vertical take-off and landing. Control is by deflection of the turboshaft exhaust, which emerges at the end of the tail-boom, and vanes in the propeller slipstream.

Dornier Do 32K Kiebitz tethered rotating-wing platform hovering above its truck ground station

Features of the Aerodyne are simplicity, VTOL capability, easy handling and potential usefulness for a variety of duties. First flights of the prototype were scheduled for 1970.

ITALY

METEOR

METEOR SpA COSTRUZIONI AERONAUTICHE ED ELETTRONICHE

MANAGEMENT OFFICE:
29 via Dalmazia, Rome

OFFICERS AND WORKS: See "Aircraft" section

Meteor is developing and producing for the Italian Army, Air Force and Navy several types of propeller-driven radio-controlled drones for operation in the speed range of 215-325 knots (250-370 mph; 400-600 km/h) at heights from sea level to 42,000 ft (13,000 m). It also produces under licence the Northrop MQM-33 drone, as the Meteor 1 (NVM 1), and the Northrop USD-1 surveillance drone. It is collaborating with Aérospatiale of France in production of the CT.20 target drone.

Meteor also manufactures fast radio-controlled boats, ranging in length from 20 to 60 ft (6-18 m) and with a gross tonnage of 5-25 tons.

METEOR 1 (NVM 1)

This is the Northrop MQM-33 target drone, as produced by Meteor under licence. Meteor manufactures components representing about one-third of the total cost of the drone. The solid-propellent booster rocket is a Meteor 8785/CZ unit of 2,860 lb (1,300 kg) st.

Full details of the MQM-33 are given under the Northrop entry.

METEOR P.1

The P.1 is a guided target drone for artillery or missile training. It is available in three versions. The basic model, for contact flying only, is fitted with a 100 hp Meteor Alfa 1 four-cylinder X-type two-stroke air-cooled engine for operation at heights up to 26,000 ft (8,000 m). The second version is basically similar, but has additional equipment for out-of-sight flying. The third version is equipped for out-of-sight flying and has a Meteor Alfa 1/AQ engine, giving 120 hp constant up to 21,325 ft (6,500 m) and permitting operation at heights up to 42,000 ft (13,000 m).

The P.1 is made largely of glass-fibre reinforced polyester resin. Its engine is manufactured from anti-corrosive and special steel and aluminium, with extensive chromium plating. This permits recovery from salt water and re-use. Flotation is ensured by the use of blocks of expanded resin inside the structure.

All Meteor targets are launched normally with the engine running at peak rpm, with the aid of jettisonable solid-propellant JATO rockets. Alternatively, a catapult can be used, or the targets can be air-launched.

For simple in-sight radio control, the operator uses a normal stick control linked to a VHF ground transmitter which emits a five-tone modulated carrier signal. The receiver in the target transforms the signals into seven distinct control operations. Two tones control the elevator, two control the ailerons, and the fifth is used to stop the engine and open the recovery parachute at the end of a flight. The ailerons and elevators are operated by electrical servo controls, those for the ailerons being combined with a gyro which stabilises the target laterally.

In out-of-sight operation, over ranges up to 54-86 nm (62-100 miles; 100-160 km), the stick is replaced by a series of levers for more precise control, and the electronic equipment in the target includes a two-axis automatic stabilisation system. The target's track and altitude are plotted normally by the radar of the gun or missile battery using it, and wing-tip reflectors can be fitted to

Meteor P.1 target drone with wingtip pods and solid-propellant booster

Meteor P.1 target drone on mobile zero-length launcher

amplify the echoes from the target. However, a VHF tracking and tele-control system can be used, in conjunction with a transponder in the target weighing only 4·4 lb (2 kg).

DIMENSIONS, EXTERNAL:
Wing span without wing-tip containers
            12 ft 1 in (3·68 m)
Length overall   11 ft 1½ in (3·39 m)
Height overall   2 ft 1½ in (0·65 m)

WEIGHTS AND PERFORMANCE:
See Table below.

METEOR P.1/R

This is a reconnaissance version of the P.1, first displayed at the 1966 Turin Air Show. It is powered by a 110 hp Meteor Alfa 1 engine, driving a constant-speed propeller, and is launched from a zero-length ramp with the aid of a Meteor 8785/Z solid-propellant booster rocket (3,968 lb = 1,800 kg st).

Control is partially by radio command signals and partially by a pre-programmed guidance system, set up prior to take-off and unaffected by enemy electronic countermeasures. The pre-set guidance system is accommodated in a pylon-mounted container under the starboard wing. A similar container under the port wing houses the reconnaissance camera, manufactured by De Oude Delft of the Netherlands, and can be released in flight for recovery by its own parachute system.

Tracking of the target in flight is by radar, utilising the coded response of a transponder manufactured by Motorola, supplemented by an on-board TV camera. Recovery is by a conventional parachute system.

WEIGHTS:
Useful load   66 lb (30 kg)
Max launching weight   551 lb (250 kg)

PERFORMANCE:
Max level speed
    270 knots (310 mph; 500 km/h)
Service ceiling   30,000 ft (9,150 m)
Operational radius 54 nm (62 miles; 100 km)
Endurance   1 hour

METEOR P.2

The P.2 is generally similar to the P.1 in configuration, method of construction and operation, but is larger and is intended primarily for out-of-sight flying. It is available in two versions, powered respectively by a Meteor Alfa 3AQ four-cylinder X-type two-stroke air-cooled engine rated at 160 hp constant up to 20,000 ft (6,000 m) for operation at heights up to 42,000 ft (13,000 m), or a 320 hp Alfa 5 eight-cylinder two-row engine for operation at heights up to 26,000 ft (8,000 m).

A TV camera and transmitter can be fitted for battlefield surveillance duties over a combat radius of 54 nm (62 miles; 100 km).

DIMENSIONS, EXTERNAL:
Wing span   12 ft 2 in (3·72 m)
Length overall (Alfa 3AQ engine)
          13 ft 1½ in (4·00 m)
Length overall (Alfa 5 engine) 14 ft 6 in (4·42 m)
Height overall   2 ft 3 in (0·68 m)

WEIGHTS AND PERFORMANCE:
See Table.

METEOR P.X

The Meteor P.X is generally similar in layout to other Meteor drones, but is powered by a 72 hp McCulloch O-100-1 four-cylinder horizontally-opposed air-cooled two-stroke engine of the kind utilised in its US counterparts. It is designed for zero-length launching from a tubular-metal ramp, with the assistance of a Meteor 8785 solid-propellant booster rocket.

Guidance is by radio control, via a Meteor RSS 529 fully-transistorised two-axis auto-pilot, with radar tracking of the drone's position. Recovery is by parachute, deployed automatically or on receipt of a signal from the ground.

DIMENSIONS, EXTERNAL:
Wing span without wing-tip containers
            11 ft 8 in (3·56 m)
Length overall   11 ft 4¼ in (3·46 m)
Diameter of fuselage 1 ft 3¾ in (0·40 m)
Span of tail unit   3 ft 11½ in (1·21 m)

PERFORMANCE (at max launching weight):
Max level speed
    194 knots (224 mph; 360 km/h)
Time to reach 20,000 ft (6,000 m) 10 min
Service ceiling   26,500 ft (8,000 m)
Radius of action 86 nm (100 miles; 160 km)
Endurance   1 hour

Meteor P.1/R reconnaissance drone (110 hp Meteor Alfa 1 engine)

Meteor P.X target drone (72 hp McCulloch O-100-1 engine)

METEOR P.1 and P.2 TARGET DRONES

	P.1/100 hp in-sight	P.1/100 hp out-of-sight	P.1/120 hp out-of-sight	P.2/160 hp out-of-sight	P.2/320 hp out-of-sight
Weight without fuel and electronics	293 lb (133 kg)	293 lb (133 kg)	293 lb (133 kg)	407 lb (185 kg)	499 lb (227 kg)
Weight of electronics and gyro guidance equipment	33 lb (15 kg)	55 lb (25 kg)	55 lb (25 kg)	55 lb (25 kg)	55 lb (25 kg)
Launching weight (one-hour flight)	403 lb (185 kg)	425 lb (195 kg)	444 lb (202 kg)	594 lb (270 kg)	818 lb (372 kg)
Max launching weight	462 lb (210 kg)	484 lb (220 kg)	495 lb (225 kg)	880 lb (400 kg)	1,100 lb (500 kg)
Max level speed at S/L (one-hour flight)	215 knots (248 mph; 400 km/h)	215 knots (248 mph; 400 km/h)	226 knots (260 mph; 420 km/h)	242 knots (279 mph; 450 km/h)	323 knots (372 mph; 600 km/h)
Max level speed at 21,325 ft (6,500 m)	178 knots (202 mph; 330 km/h)	178 knots (202 mph; 330 km/h)	296 knots (342 mph; 550 km/h)	296 knots (342 mph; 550 km/h)	270 knots (315 mph; 500 km/h)
Stalling speed	62 knots (71 mph; 115 km/h)	62 knots (71 mph; 115 km/h)	62 knots (71 mph; 115 km/h)	70 knots (80 mph; 130 km/h)	86 knots (99 mph; 160 km/h)
Rate of climb at S/L	2,950 ft/min (900 m/min)	2,950 ft/min (900 m/min)	3,940 ft/min (1,200 m/min)	3,940 ft/min (1,200 m/min)	2,950 ft/min (900 m/min)
Time to 20,000 ft (6,000 m)	10 min	10 min	5 min	4 min 5 sec	10 min

JAPAN

KAWASAKI

KAWASAKI JUKOGYO KABUSHIKI KAISHA
(Kawasaki Heavy Industries Ltd)

HEAD OFFICE:
2-16-1 Nakamachi-Dori, Ikutaku, Kobe

OFFICERS: See "Aircraft" section

In addition to its work on piloted aircraft, Kawasaki is producing a rocket-powered target drone, of which brief details follow.

KAWASAKI KAQ-5

Kawasaki has developed for the Japanese Defence Agency a rocket-powered drone, designated KAQ-5, which is used as an aerial target for air-to-air and surface-to-air missile systems and for determining their effectiveness. Forty-one drones had been delivered to the Japanese Defence Agency by March 1969.

The KAQ-5 has an orthodox high-wing monoplane configuration. It is powered by a slow-burning solid-propellant rocket motor manufactured by Daicel Co, and has a self-contained pre-programmed guidance system.

The KAQ-5 is air-launched from a specially-adapted Lockheed T-33A jet aircraft and is recovered by parachute at the end of its flight. A miss-distance indicator can be fitted.

Kawasaki KAQ-5 target drone (Daicel solid-propellant rocket motor)

DIMENSIONS, EXTERNAL:

Wing span	6 ft 5 in	(1·95 m)
Length overall	11 ft 9½ in	(3·60 m)
Height overall	3 ft 1 in	(0·94 m)
Body diameter	11 in	(0·28 m)

WEIGHTS:

Weight empty	220 lb	(100 kg)
Max launching weight	375 lb	(170 kg)

PERFORMANCE:

Max level speed at 20,000-40,000 ft (6,000-12,000 m)	Mach 0·8
Endurance	8 min

NIPPON DENKI

NIPPON DENKI KABUSHIKI KAISHA (Nippon Electric Company, Ltd)

HEAD OFFICE:
7-15, Shiba Gochome, Minato-ku, Tokyo 108

PRESIDENT:
Koji Kobayashi

Under a technical aid agreement with Northrop Corporation, USA, Nippon Denki is responsible for production under licence and repair of Northrop-Ventura target drones (MQM-36A) for the Japanese Maritime Self Defence Force. Delivery of these drones to the JMSDF began in 1961 and production continues.

UNITED STATES OF AMERICA

BEECHCRAFT

BEECH AIRCRAFT CORPORATION

HEAD OFFICE AND WORKS:
Wichita, Kansas 67201.

OFFICERS: See "Aircraft" section

In addition to manufacturing piloted aircraft, Beech has been designing and producing pilotless target drones of various types since 1955.

BEECHCRAFT MODEL 1001
US Navy designation: MQM-39A (formerly KDB-1)
US Army designation: MQM-61A Cardinal 1025

The Model 1001 pilotless remotely-controlled target drone won a US Navy design competition in 1955 and was the first design by Beech's missile engineering division.

In various versions, the Model 1001 is in service with the US Navy, US Army and in Germany and Switzerland, as an "out-of-sight" target for surface-to-air and air-to-air missiles, rockets and predicted-fire weapons. Production began in 1959 and more than 2,000 had been built by 1 March 1968. The MQM-61A Cardinal version has been used to train the crews of Hawk, Redeye, Chaparral and other missiles and has supported US Army training exercises in Canada, Alaska, Okinawa, Formosa, Korea, Germany, Panama and Hawaii. A total of 4,201 flights had been made from Fort Bliss, Texas, by January 1970.

The Cardinal is used to tow targets and banners and, on its own, to evaluate the accuracy of anti-aircraft missiles and gunfire by means of miss-distance and scoring devices. The Beech-built tow targets have tubular glass-fibre bodies, with cruciform tail-fins, and are equipped with molten infra-red sources when heat-seeking missiles are to be tested. Two targets can be carried under each wing of the Cardinal.

Equipment can be carried by the Model 1001 to give a radar image equivalent to that produced by high-performance aircraft of very much larger size.

TYPE: Pilotless target.

WINGS: Cantilever high-wing monoplane. Wing section NACA 64A-012 at root, NACA 64A-412 at tip. No dihedral. Incidence 3° at root, —30′ at tip. Conventional ailerons.

Beechcraft MQM-61A Cardinal 1025 drone (125 hp McCulloch TC6150-J-3 engine)

FUSELAGE: Cylindrical structure. Recovery drogue parachute in tail-cone.

TAIL UNIT: Cantilever "butterfly" type with included angle of 90°.

POWER PLANT: One 125 hp McCulloch TC6150-J-3 six-cylinder horizontally-opposed air-cooled turbo-supercharged two-stroke engine, driving a two-blade propeller, diameter 4 ft 4 in (1·32 m). Two JATO bottles can be attached under rear fuselage for zero-length launches, accelerating the drone to more than 207 mph (333 kmh) in under two seconds.

GUIDANCE: Radio command.

DIMENSIONS, EXTERNAL:
Wing span over wing-tip containers
12 ft 11½ in (3·95 m)

Wing chord at root	2 ft 7½ in	(0·80 m)
Wing chord at tip	1 ft 8·9 in	(0·53 m)
Length overall	15 ft 1 in	(4·60 m)
Height overall, without JATO	3 ft 3·9 in	(1·02 m)
Diameter of fuselage	1 ft 5¾ in	(0·45 m)
Wing-tip containers:		
Length	4 ft 1 in	(1·24 m)
Diameter	10 in	(0·25 m)

AREAS:

Wings, gross	24·4 sq ft	(2·27 m²)
Ailerons (total)	2·25 sq ft	(0·21 m²)
Fixed tail surfaces (total)	5·38 sq ft	(0·50 m²)
Movable tail surfaces (total)	1·48 sq ft	(0·14 m²)

WEIGHTS:

Launching weight, with JATO	664 lb	(301 kg)
Flight weight	560 lb	(254 kg)

PERFORMANCE:
Max level speed
over 303 knots (350 mph; 560 km/h)
Min operating speed
80 knots (92 mph; 148 km/h)
Service ceiling over 43,000 ft (13,100 m)
Endurance at 25,000 ft (7,600 m) over one hour

BEECHCRAFT MODELS 1019 AND 1072
US Military designation: AQM-37A (formerly KD2B-1)
UK designation: SD.2 Stiletto

Winner of a 1959 US Navy/Air Force design competition, the Beechcraft Model 1019 (US Navy AQM-37A) missile target system is designed to simulate invader aircraft and missile threats, and to provide defence weapon system evaluation and operational crew training. Beech has developed a complete target system, including launcher which is adaptable to a variety of fighter aircraft, test and check-out equipment, handling and servicing equipment and launch aircraft controls, as well as the target vehicle itself. The target is expendable and thus requires no recovery support.

The target provides both active and passive radar augmentation for radar acquisition and lock-on. A chemical flare is provided for missions which require infra-red augmentation. Two optional miss-distance indication systems are available.

Flight termination is normally through aero-dynamic means, but an explosive destructor system is available, to provide additional range safety and operational flexibility. The only procedures required to ready the target for flight are decanning, battery servicing, pre-flight checking out, pressure cartridge inserting and nitrogen pressurizing.

The AQM-37A was launched successfully for the first time on 31 May 1961, at the Naval Missile Center, Point Mugu, California. In subsequent development tests, after being launched at 33,000 ft (10,050 m) from an F-3B Demon, it flew higher and faster than any previous drone developed for target duties. During weapon system training operations at Point Mugu in the Spring of 1965, an AQM-37A, launched from an F-4B at a speed of Mach 1·3 at 47,000 ft (14,300 m), climbed to 91,000 ft (27,750 m) and maintained a speed of Mach 2·8.

The AQM-37A has been operational since 1963 from shore installations and aircraft carriers and is being launched at present from three types of US Navy aircraft, the F-4, F-8 and A-4. A total of more than 1,800 had been delivered by December 1969, including 15 of a modified version to the UK.

The British version, known as Beechcraft Model 1072 and designated SD.2 Stiletto, is substantially re-engineered by Short Brothers and Harland Ltd to meet British requirements, including virtually complete replacement of the radio and radar systems and control system changes. The Stiletto is launched from a Canberra PR.3 aircraft. In a successful first test flight at Llanbedr in September 1968, the drone was released at 55,000 ft (16,750 m) and flew for over 28 nm (32 miles; 52 km) at an average speed of Mach 1·4 before the flight was terminated by a commanded explosive destruct.

In the Spring of 1968, Beech received contracts to modify 10 AQM-37A's for the USAF and three for the US Army, making their electronics and destruct systems compatible with current advanced weapons systems and range requirements of these services. This represents the first use of the AQM-37A by the USAF and Army.

Production of the AQM-37A was transferred from Wichita to Beech's Aerospace Division at Boulder, Colorado, in 1968. It continues under contracts for about 800 placed by the US Navy, extending production to July 1971. Total orders to date cover the delivery of more than

Beechcraft Model 1001 drone carrying a Dornier System towed target under its port wing

2,500 targets, including 20 more Stilettos ordered in November 1969.

TYPE: Supersonic air-launched expendable target drone.

WINGS: Cantilever mid-wing monoplane of cropped delta planform, mounted at rear of fuselage. Modified double-wedge wing section. No dihedral or incidence. Sweepback on leading-edge 76°. Full-span ailerons.

FUSELAGE: Cylindrical centre fuselage, with ogival nose section and tapering rear section over rocket chambers. Under-belly tunnel for rocket-engine cartridge-operated start valves, plumbing, infra-red flare and miss-distance scoring system antenna.

TAIL UNIT: Fixed end-plate fins on each wing-tip. Canard foreplane control surfaces of modified double-wedge section.

POWER PLANT: One Rocketdyne/AMF LR64 P-4 dual-chamber liquid-propellant rocket-engine (631 lb = 286 kg st). Three propellant tanks, for nitrogen pressurant, mixed amine fuel (MAF-4) and IRFNA oxidiser, form integral part of centre-fuselage.

GUIDANCE: Programmed guidance system.

DIMENSIONS, EXTERNAL:

Wing span	3 ft 3¼ in (1·00 m)
Wing chord at root	6 ft 4·1 in (1·93 m)
Wing chord at tip	2 ft 0·6 in (0·62 m)
Length overall	13 ft 6½ in (4·13 m)
Height overall	1 ft 8 in (0·51 m)
Diameter of fuselage	1 ft 1 in (0·33 m)

AREAS:

Wings (exposed)	9·35 sq ft (0·87 m²)
Ailerons (total)	0·95 sq ft (0·088 m²)
Fins (total)	4·20 sq ft (0·39 m²)
Fore-planes (total, exposed)	0·76 sq ft (0·071 m²)

WEIGHT:

Max launching weight	565 lb (256 kg)

PERFORMANCE (rated):

Operating speed	Mach 0·4 to Mach 2·5
Operating height	1,000-80,000 ft (300-24,385 m)
Endurance	15 min

BEECHCRAFT SANDPIPER

It was announced on 29 August 1967 that Beech was developing for the USAF's Armament Laboratory at Eglin AFB a high-performance rocket-powered target drone named the Sandpiper. Designed to simulate a wide variety of aircraft and missiles, the new target is powered by a hybrid engine that uses both solid and liquid propellants.

Phase I of the programme involved verification of the hybrid propulsion system, airframe and components of the Sandpiper system quickly, at minimum cost. To this end, AQM-37A airframes have been used for the initial test vehicles, which are intended to develop and prove the proposed Sandpiper stability and control systems and programmed manoeuvre capabilities.

The first flight test was completed successfully early in 1968; launched from a USAF F-4C Phantom II aircraft, the test model reached a speed of Mach 2 at 49,000 ft (15,000 m) in a five-minute flight over the Gulf of Mexico. Subsequent flights had progressed to Mach 2·5 at 77,000 ft (23,500 m) by mid-1968.

Phase II will cover development of the production model Sandpiper and will establish aircraft compatibility.

In its eventual production form, Sandpiper will have highly-swept cropped-delta wings and canard control surfaces for pitch control. Full-span ailerons will provide roll control, and symmetrical vertical stabilisers will be fitted at each wing-tip.

The engine, produced by United Technology Center, utilises a magnesium compound as the solid propellant and a mixture of nitric oxides as the liquid. The oxidiser is pressure-fed through a low-cost injector into the solid-propellant combustion chambers and is ignited by a conventional pyrotechnic igniter. Thrust is controlled at any desired level from 60 to 300 lb (27-135 kg) by a "dial-a-thrust" unit, set manually before flight; this varies the flow of oxidiser through the injector, using nitrogen to pressurise the oxidiser tank. The system is inherently safe, since neither propellant will burn unless external ignition is applied.

DIMENSIONS:

Length overall	14 ft 8 in (4·47 m)
Body diameter	13 in (33 cm)

WEIGHT:

Launching weight	633 lb (287 kg)

PERFORMANCE (estimated):

Max speed	Mach 4
Ceiling	90,000 ft (22,500 m)

Beechcraft AQM-37A supersonic target drone

Test-bed version of Sandpiper, utilising a modified AQM-37A airframe

DEL MAR
DEL MAR ENGINEERING LABORATORIES
ADDRESS:
International Airport, 6901 Imperial Highway, Los Angeles, California 90045

Del Mar developed a target drone helicopter known as the DH-2C Whirlymite, of which details were given in the 1969-70 *Jane's*. Requirements for this drone were cancelled by the US Army after successful completion of initial operational trials and it is no longer in production. However, it continues to be available.

GYRODYNE
GYRODYNE COMPANY OF AMERICA, INC
HEAD OFFICE AND WORKS:
St James, Long Island, NY 11780
OFFICERS: See "Aircraft" section

Following its successful development of an ultra-light piloted helicopter, Gyrodyne received a US Navy contract to design, develop and produce a small drone helicopter to form the airborne component of the DASH (Drone Anti-Submarine Helicopter) weapon system. As weapon system manager, Gyrodyne is responsible not only for the QH-50 drones, but also for the equipment on board ship for controlling the drones in flight and development of special deck handling equipment, tools, test equipment and technical manuals.

GYRODYNE QH-50
The QH-50 drone is a remotely-controlled lightweight helicopter developed from the Gyrodyne YRON-1 Rotorcycle and capable of all-weather operation. It has a steel-tube chassis with skid landing gear and, in its current operational form, carries a payload of two Mark 44 acoustic homing torpedoes to a "beyond the horizon" radius of operations.

Development of the QH-50 dates from April 1958, when the Department of the Navy authorised Gyrodyne to make minimum modifications to an existing Rotorcycle to make it completely controllable from the ground by means of off-the-shelf and "breadboard" electronic equipment, in order to investigate its suitability as a drone.

Successful completion of this feasibility study led to a follow-on contract on 31 December 1958, for development of a specialised drone helicopter, as the airborne component of the DASH (Drone Anti-Submarine Helicopter) weapon system. Two operational versions of the QH-50 were produced subsequently, as follow:

QH-50C (formerly DSN-3). First production version with 300 shp Boeing T50-BO-8A shaft-turbine coupled directly to transmission, without any form of flexible coupling. CG considerations dictated that the engine should be at the front of the aircraft, balanced by the electronic equipment and tail structure at the rear. This left no room for a safety pilot for initial trials. A solution was found by seating the pilot at the rear of the aircraft, in place of the normal tail assembly, and flying it backwards. Fuel capacity of this version is 35 US gallons (132·5 litres).

An initial series of 10 QH-50C's was ordered. The first one flew with safety pilot aboard on 6 April 1961 and was delivered to the US Navy in July 1961. The first flight of a pure drone QH-50C took place at the NATC, Patuxent River, on 25 January 1962. The Demonstration Programme was completed on 18 July and the Initial Trials Phase of Board of Inspection and Survey Trials at the NATC on 4 September 1962. The initial delivery of production QH-50C drones was made on 15 November 1962. On 7 January 1963, the USS *Buck*, operating off San Clemente Island, California, completed Ships Qualification Trials and became the first US warship to receive operational drone helicopters, which were delivered by flying them from the Island to the ship under radio control.

The shipboard portion of the DASH system includes the target control system, with rotary-wing components, a hangar for two drones, a landing platform and a restraint cable system for moving the helicopters between the hangar and the take-off deck.

For take-off the deck control officer uses a transmitter with manoeuvre stick control of cyclic roll, pitch and flat turns, and knob control of altitude and heading. Digital signals are sent from the transmitter to a relay assembly for assignment to an audio frequency coder. Digital audio command signals are then transmitted by UHF line-of-sight data link. The drone's transistorised FM radio receiver eliminates the carrier frequency and applies the audio frequency to the drone's decoder. The decoder extracts the digital messages, decodes the command information and provides analogue voltages, as well as on/off switch closure for torpedo arming and release mechanisms. The analogue voltages

Gyrodyne QH-50D anti-submarine helicopter drone, without torpedo payload

are combined with sensor inputs from roll, pitch and displacement gyros and altitude control, and then fed to an electronic control amplifier. This in turn controls the pitch, roll, yaw and collective servo clutches in the drone's electro-mechanical actuator.

When the drone helicopter in flight is observed on the radar scope, an integrated transfer of control is made to a second control transmitter in the ship's combat information centre (CIC). The CIC tracks the drone by radar and adjusts course, speed and altitude as necessary to position it over the submarine target whose location is known from sonar information. The CIC controller is then able to actuate the arming and weapon release switches, afterwards returning the drone to the vicinity of the launch-ship.

When the deck control officer sights the returning drone, he takes over control and brings it in for landing. The Landing Assist Device (LAD), described in the 1965-66 *Jane's*, has been eliminated as unnecessary. Good drone controllers, after the ship has been put on the optimum down sea and wind recovery course, can land drones in up to sea state 5.

The QH-50C is designed to attack targets over maximum current and foreseeable sonar ranges.

The DASH system was conceived originally as part of the US Navy's FRAM (Fleet Rehabilitation and Modernisation) Programme, to add 8-10 years of useful life to about 140 World War II destroyers. It has been deployed also on certain types of new anti-submarine ships.

In December 1965 production of the QH-50C was phased out and production of the QH-50D began, but several hundred QH-50C's are still operational.

QH-50D. Final production version, powered by a 365 shp Boeing T50-BO-12 shaft-turbine. Glass-fibre rotor blades with de-icing system. Increased range and payload. Fuel capacity is 52 US gallons (197 litres). Armament comprises two Mk 44 torpedoes, or one Mk 46 torpedo.

By December 1966, a total of 534 QH-50 drones had been delivered to the US Navy and were operational on more than 100 anti-submarine vessels. The Japanese Maritime Self Defence Force was also scheduled to acquire a total of 16 QH-50's.

It is reported that QH-50D's have been used to rescue US aircrew forced down in Southeast Asia, using a TV guidance system monitored by ground-based or airborne controllers.

DIMENSIONS (QH-50C and D):

Rotor diameter (both)	20 ft 0 in (6·10 m)
Length without rotors:	
QH-50C	12 ft 11 in (3·94 m)
QH-50D	7 ft 3½ in (2·22 m)
Height overall	9 ft 8½ in (2·96 m)
Length of skids	5 ft 3½ in (1·61 m)
Width over skids	5 ft 3 in (1·60 m)

AREA:

Rotor disc area	314·2 sq ft (29·20 m²)

WEIGHTS:

Weight empty:	
QH-50C	1,154 lb (524 kg)
QH-50D	1,035 lb (470 kg)
Max T-O weight:	
QH-50C	2,285 lb (1,036 kg)
QH-50D	2,328 lb (1,056 kg)

PERFORMANCE (QH-50C and D):

Max speed	over 80 knots (92 mph; 148 km/h)
Speed for max range	80 knots (92 mph; 148 km/h)
Speed for max endurance:	
QH-50C	50 knots (58 mph; 93 km/h)
QH-50D	55 knots (63 mph; 101 km/h)
Max rate of climb at S/L:	
QH-50C	1,880 ft (573 m)/min
QH-50D	2,810 ft (856 m)/min
Vertical rate of climb at S/L:	
QH-50C	1,410 ft (430 m)/min
QH-50D	2,300 ft (700 m)/min
Service ceiling.:	
QH-50C	16,400 ft (5,000 m)
QH-50D	16,000 ft (4,875 m)
Hovering ceiling in ground effect:	
QH-50C	16,900 ft (5,150 m)
QH-50D	16,300 ft (4,965 m)
Hovering ceiling out of ground effect:	
QH-50C	11,500 ft (3,500 m)
QH-50D	11,300 ft (3,445 m)
Max range, 10% fuel reserve:	
QH-50C	71 nm (82 miles; 132 km)
QH-50D	122 nm (141 miles; 227 km)
Combat radius:	
QH-50C	28 nm (32 miles; 51 km)
QH-50D	47 nm (54 miles; 87 km)
Max endurance, 10% fuel reserve:	
QH-50C	1 hour
QH-50D	1 hr 43 min

NORTHROP

NORTHROP CORPORATION—VENTURA DIVISION

DIVISION HEAD OFFICE:
1515 Rancho Conejo Boulevard, Newbury Park, California 91320

OTHER WORKS:
El Centro, California (test facility)

VICE-PRESIDENTS:
Welko E. Gasich (General Manager)
M. A. Maurer (Manufacturing)
T. E. Flannigan (Marketing)
G. C. Grogan (Technical)
W. F. Sternadel (Finance)

PUBLIC RELATIONS MANAGER: C. R. Ramsey

Northrop Ventura (formerly Radioplane) designs and manufactures pilotless target and surveillance aircraft and related equipment. It produces recovery systems and also manufactures glass-fibre wing fairings for the Boeing 747 transport aircraft. It has diversified into the marine systems field and is under contract to develop an unmanned underwater vehicle as a target in US Navy anti-submarine warfare training.

This organisation undertook the design, development and construction of its first radio-controlled target drone in the mid-thirties. Since then it has become a leader in the field of pilotless aircraft. Over 70,000 drones have been delivered to the US military services and 15 allied nations.

Parachute landing systems designed and produced by Northrop Ventura returned safely to Earth all the US astronauts who accomplished space flight under the Mercury, Gemini and Apollo programmes.

Several important research and development programmes are under way, including landing systems for advanced spacecraft and in the field of composite structures. The division is also producing escape and survival systems for high-speed manned aircraft.

NORTHROP MQM-36

US Navy designation: MQM-36 (formerly KD2R-5)
International designation: KD2R-5

This target drone is currently in use by the US Army Field Forces and Navy as a training device for ground-to-air gunnery and is used as a training target for surface-to-air missiles such as Hawk and Redeye. It has also been supplied to 18 allied nations.

Design of the drone was started in 1946 and the prototype flew for the first time in 1947. Since then more than 45,000 have been built and production continues.

For radar appearance augmentation, two wing-tip reflector pods are optional on the KD2R-5.

The target is surface-launched only, either by catapult or zero launcher. Radio control is utilised, the target being tracked visually and by radar. After completion of its mission, it is recovered by the use of a radio-released parachute. In the event of serious damage by gunfire or loss of radio control or electrical power, the parachute is deployed automatically. The target is designed to be repaired easily if damaged by gunfire.

TYPE: Remotely-controlled aerial target.

WINGS: Cantilever high-wing monoplane. Wing section NACA 23012 at root, NACA 4412 at tip. No dihedral. Incidence 1° at root, —2° at tip. Conventional aircraft aluminium alloy construction. Conventional ailerons servo-operated by type D-9 actuators.

FUSELAGE: Semi-monocoque aluminium alloy structure, with integral steel fuel tanks.

TAIL UNIT: Cantilever aluminium alloy structure. Fixed-incidence tailplane. Elevator servo-operated by type D-9 actuator.

POWER PLANT: One 95 hp McCulloch O-100-3 four-cylinder horizontally-opposed air-cooled two-stroke engine, driving a two-blade fixed-pitch laminated wood propeller, diameter 3 ft 8 in (1·10 m). One steel fuel tank in mid-fuselage, capacity 11·6 US gallons (44 litres). Refuelling point in fuselage forward of wing.

SYSTEMS: Electrical power only, from 28V battery.

ELECTRONICS AND EQUIPMENT: AN/ARW-79 remote flight control system with automatic altitude hold control. Radar or FM type tracking systems or equivalent. Smoke generating, infra-red tow target, night light kits and many other accessories are available to meet the requirements of the individual user.

DIMENSIONS, EXTERNAL:
Wing span	11 ft 6 in (3·50 m)
Wing chord (mean)	1 ft 8·13 in (0·51 m)
Wing aspect ratio	7
Length overall	12 ft 7½ in (3·85 m)
Height overall	2 ft 6 in (0·76 m)
Tailplane span	4 ft 2 in (1·27 m)

AREAS:
Wings, gross	18·7 sq ft (1·74 m²)
Ailerons (total)	1·3 sq ft (0·12 m²)

Northrop KD2R-5 target drone (95 hp McCulloch O-100-3 engine) on its lightweight launcher

Fin	1·8 sq ft (0·17 m²)
Tailplane	3·0 sq ft (0·28 m²)
Elevators	1·4 sq ft (0·13 m²)

WEIGHTS:
Weight empty	271 lb (123 kg)
Max launching weight	360 lb (163 kg)
Max zero-fuel weight	292 lb (133 kg)
Max landing weight	340 lb (154 kg)

PERFORMANCE (at max launching weight):
Max level speed at S/L	175 knots (202 mph; 324 km/h)
Max permissible diving speed	250 knots (288 mph; 463 km/h)
Cruising speed	175 knots (202 mph; 324 km/h)
Stalling speed	58 knots (67 mph; 108 km/h)
Rate of climb at S/L	3,500 ft (1,065 m)/min
Service ceiling	23,000 ft (7,000 m)
Range with max fuel	180 nm (207 miles; 333 km)

NORTHROP FALCONER

This drone was developed originally for the US Army Signal Corps as a tactical battlefield surveillance device. Launched from a zero-length launcher, controlled remotely by radio and tracked by radar, the Falconer (formerly MQM-57A) carries still or TV cameras for surveillance over hostile territory. On reaching a predetermined recovery area the controller who has guided its flight commands parachute recovery. The camera is removed, the film is processed and the prints are delivered to the requesting unit within minutes after recovery.

Design of the Falconer, which is based on the KD2R-5 airframe, was started in 1954 and the prototype flew for the first time in 1955. Production models are in service for day and night photo intelligence and reconnaissance duties with several foreign nations. Flares are carried for night photography. The cameras can be replaced by other sensory systems. All operational equipment is loaded through hatches in the top of the fuselage.

Recovery is by a single-stage 44 ft (13·4 m) extended-skirt parachute, deployed on command or automatically after loss of radio command carrier, or if parachute safety channel ceases to function. The integral keel absorbs the landing impact.

POWER PLANT: One 92 hp McCulloch four-cylinder horizontally-opposed air-cooled two-stroke engine driving a two-blade fixed-pitch laminated wood propeller, diameter 3 ft 8 in (1·10 m). One mid-fuselage steel fuel tank, capacity 5·6 US gallons (21 litres). Provision for two M-3 JATO units for zero-length launching.

SYSTEMS: Electrical power only, from BB-421/USD-1 28V battery.

ELECTRONICS AND EQUIPMENT: Radio command flight control system includes an AN/ARW-79 receiver autopilot. Special equipment includes two 75-mm cameras, flare ejector, radar beacon or passive radar reflector pods and night light identification system.

DIMENSIONS:
Wing span	11 ft 6 in (3·50 m)
Length overall	13 ft 5 in (4·09 m)
Height overall	2 ft 7½ in (0·80 m)

WEIGHTS:
Weight empty	354 lb (161 kg)
Max launching weight	442 lb (200 kg)

PERFORMANCE:
Max level speed at S/L	174 knots (201 mph; 323 km/h)
Service ceiling	15,000 ft (4,570 m)
Endurance at S/L	35 minutes

NORTHROP NV-105 CHUKAR

US Military designation: MQM-74A

This drone was designed to meet requirements for a small lightweight 400-knot target for anti-aircraft gunnery, surface-to-air missile and air-to-air missile training and weapon systems evaluation. It is in production, following receipt of initial US Navy orders for 567 drones.

The general appearance of the MQM-74A is shown in the illustration on page 541. It can simulate the attack modes of missiles or aircraft, including 5° or 10° dive-bombing and strafing. At 400 yards (365 m) range, it appears to a gun crew as a supersonic fighter at 1,000 yards (915 m). Its augmentation is compatible with a variety of weapons systems requirements and it can provide training for the crews of 40-mm, 20-mm and 0·50-in guns or Hawk, Redeye, Chaparral or Nike-Hercules missiles.

Northrop Falconer surveillance drone on its lightweight launcher

TYPE: Turbojet-powered radio-controlled recoverable target.

WINGS: Cantilever shoulder-wing monoplane. No dihedral. Detachable aluminium wings, each with electrically-actuated aileron.

FUSELAGE: Aluminium semi-monocoque structure housing all equipment, power plant and fuel tankage. Nose and tail skins removable for access to electronic components and power plant. Underslung engine air intake duct.

TAIL UNIT: Cantilever aluminium structure of inverted "Y" form, comprising fixed vertical fin, fixed tailplane halves and two electrically-actuated elevators. Tailplane anhedral 30°.

POWER PLANT: Williams Research Corporation Model WR24-6 open-cycle turbojet engine (axial intake, single-stage centrifugal compressor, annular combustion chamber, single-stage axial turbine), rated at 121 lb (55 kg) st at 60,000 rpm. Tank in centre fuselage for JP-4 or JP-5 fuel.

SYSTEMS: Electrical power only, from engine-driven alternator through a rectifier-regulator. 28V nickel-cadmium battery secondary power source used during glide.

CONTROL SYSTEM: Out-of-sight control by automatic stabilisation and command, with radar tracking; in-sight control with visual acquisition aids. Proportional feedback stabilisation and control system for pitch and bank. Engine throttle position, altitude hold initiation and recovery system initiation controlled by audio tone signals. Components include receiver-decoder, control unit assembly and vertical gyro in nose of fuselage, aileron and elevator servos, and altitude hold pressure transducer. Command control antenna in upper forward fuselage.

EQUIPMENT: On-board acquisition and tracking aids include fore and aft Luneberg lenses for passive radar augmentation, IR and a pyrotechnic flash and smoke generating system. Main payload compartment is in front fuselage between control equipment bay and fuel tank.

LAUNCH AND RECOVERY: Zero-length launching by means of two Mk 34 Mod 1 JATO rockets and a ZL-5 launcher. Two modes of command recovery are utilised. Normal method consists of automatic drone pull-up followed by main parachute deployment, and is initiated automatically in emergencies such as interruption of continuous radio signal or loss of parachute command channel. Alternative mode consists of direct main parachute deployment

Northrop MQM-74A (NV-105 Chukar) target drone (Williams Research Corp WR24-6 turbojet)

and is initiated automatically on loss of electrical power. Main parachute, housed in fuselage immediately aft of wing, is a 30 ft (9·15 m) diameter extended-skirt nylon canopy, with automatic disconnect at impact.

DIMENSIONS:
Wing span	5 ft 6¾ in (1·69 m)
Length overall	11 ft 4 in (3·45 m)
Body diameter	1 ft 2 in (0·36 m)
Height overall	2 ft 3¾ in (0·70 m)

WEIGHTS:
Weight empty	252 lb (114 kg)
Max launching weight	317 lb (144 kg)

PERFORMANCE:
Max level speed at S/L
370 knots (427 mph; 760 km/h)
Max level speed at 20,000 ft (6,100 m)
440 knots (507 mph; 815 km/h)
Econ cruising speed at S/L
210 knots (242 mph; 390 km/h)
Rate of climb at S/L   6,300 ft (1,920 m)/min
Service ceiling   40,000 ft (12,200 m)
Range at max speed at S/L
150 nm (173 miles; 278 km)
Range at max speed at 20,000 ft (6,100 m)
224 nm (258 miles; 415 km)
Range at econ cruising speed at S/L
185 nm (213 miles; 342 km)

PHILCO-FORD

PHILCO-FORD CORPORATION (Subsidiary of FORD MOTOR COMPANY)
Aeronutronic Division
HEAD OFFICE:
Ford Road, Newport Beach, California 92663
OFFICERS: See "Missiles" section

In addition to its work on guided missiles, Aeronutronic Division is developing and manufacturing the low-cost rocket-powered LOCAT air target, of which available details follow.

PHILCO-FORD LOCAT II-D

First details of LOCAT (Low Cost Air Target) were released on 24 July 1968. It is an expendable rocket-powered Ballistic Aerial Target System (BATS), made largely of rolled paper tubing of the kind used in the USA to store and ship household carpets. Launched from a ground site, it attains speeds in excess of 345 knots (400 mph; 645 km/h) within two seconds and is intended for use in training gun and guided missile crews to deal with low-flying enemy aircraft. It was designed initially to attain an altitude of 1,000 ft (305 m) with a 10,000 ft (3,050 m) range in a flight time of 17 seconds.

The LOCAT air target is built up of only a small number of major components: a nose-cone made of glass-reinforced plastic, a sustainer motor, a fuselage made of rolled paper tubing, three glass-reinforced plastic fins, and a booster-rocket motor consisting of three 2·75-in folding-fin aircraft rockets of the type used as air armament on some military aircraft. The fuselage is coated with aluminium to provide radar reflectivity for tracking and targeting purposes. An infra-red signature is also provided for compatibility with infra-red homing missile systems.

Assembly of the LOCAT missile, launcher emplacement and target launching can be undertaken by non-specialist army personnel, using common hand tools. Assembly time from delivery of components to the launcher, by truck, until launch is 45 minutes. The target's simplicity has substantially eliminated the need for launch check-out equipment.

The LOCAT air target was developed by Aeronutronic's Air Defense Systems Operation in Anaheim, California; but its performance The first flight of the original version, known as LOCAT II-D, was made 45 days after establishment of requirements. Ninety days after initial design was begun, a demonstration was held for

Philco-Ford LOCAT II-D low cost air target on its launcher

the US Army under live firing operational training conditions at Fort Bliss. Subsequent demonstrations included multiple launches in conjunction with various types of anti-aircraft guns and missiles.

LOCAT air targets were evaluated by the US Army in mid-1968 and in October 1969 Aeronutronic Division received a $100,000 contract from the US Army Missile Command, covering the supply, testing and evaluation of 40 LOCATs. Designated LOCAT II-F, these will differ in certain respects from the II-D version, as described above and below, and are described separately.

DIMENSIONS:
Length overall	15 ft 0 in (4·57 m)
Body diameter	9·6 in (24·4 cm)

WEIGHT:
Launching weight	155 lb (70·5 kg)

PERFORMANCE:
Range limits	2,000-11,000 ft (610-3,350 m)
Altitude limits	300-2,000 ft (90-610 m)
Flight time	4-24 seconds
Speed range	

300-450 knots (345-520 mph; 555-837 km/h)

PHILCO-FORD LOCAT II-F

The LOCAT II-F target is a derivative of the LOCAT II-D intended to meet specific technical requirements of the US Army. It maintains the basic concept of low cost by using the same type of components, including a plastic nose-cone, rolled paper fuselage, wooden wings and aluminium power plant package.

In October 1969, the US Army ordered 40 LOCAT II-F targets and two launchers for test and evaluation. Options for first-year production are included in the contract. Test and evaluation are being conducted at Fort Bliss, Texas.

TELEDYNE RYAN

TELEDYNE RYAN AERONAUTICAL (Subsidiary of Teledyne, Inc)

HEAD OFFICE AND WORKS:
Lindbergh Field, San Diego, California 92112
OFFICERS: See "Aircraft" section

A major production item at Teledyne Ryan's San Diego works for many years has been the Firebee jet-powered target and reconnaissance drone, described in detail below.

The company has other important contracts in the missile and space field, including design and fabrication of radar altimeters, precision antennae and structures for advanced space vehicles.

TELEDYNE RYAN FIREBEE
USAF/US Navy designation: BQM-34A (formerly Q-2C)
US Army designation: MQM-34D

The Firebee is a remotely-controlled high-speed turbojet-powered target drone which was developed as a joint US Air Force/Army/Navy project, with the USAF Air Research and Development Command having technical cognizance of its development.

Glide flight tests of the original version of the Firebee without power were begun in March, 1951, and the first powered flights were made that Summer at the USAF Holloman Air Development Center, Alamogordo, New Mexico. Very large numbers were built eventually for all three US Services and for the RCAF, and full details of these early versions can be found in previous editions of *Jane's*.

Development of the current **BQM-34A** Firebee began on 25 February 1958, with the object of obtaining a much-improved all-round performance. Construction of the prototype started on 1 May and it flew for the first time on 19 December 1958. The first production model flew on 25 January 1960. More than 4,400 have since been produced and the latest contracts extend production through fiscal year 1970. They include a $1 million contract from the Japanese Defence Agency for Firebees for use in training Hawk missile crews.

Remote control methods for the Firebee include a choice of radar, radio, active seeker and automatic navigator, all developed and designed by Teledyne Ryan.

Recent development and operational acceptance of an Increased Manoeuvrability Kit (IMK) for the Firebee give it the capability to perform 5 and 6 *g* turns. This makes it a highly realistic target for the training of pilots in firing missile weapon systems. A Radar Altimeter Low Altitude Control System (RALACS), when added to the Firebee control system, permits precision low altitude flights at 50 ft (15 m) over water and 100 ft (30 m) over land.

The BQM-34A can be equipped with adjustable travelling wave tube amplifiers for use as radar echo enhancers in the L, S, X and C frequency bands. These devices provide realistic radar appearances for all size targets from the smallest fighter to the largest bomber aircraft.

Either air-launching or ground-launching, with the aid of a solid-propellant JATO bottle, can be used; the US Navy has also launched BQM-34A Firebees from ships under way at up to 15 knots. The two-stage parachute recovery system operates automatically in the event of a target hit, loss of radio wave carrier from the remote-control station, engine failure, or upon command by the remote-control operator. To prevent damage by dragging, the recovery system incorporates a disconnect which releases the parachute from the drone on contact with the ground or water.

The **MQM-34D** version used by the US Army has a longer-burning rocket booster for ground launch and extended wings, enabling it to take off at a loaded weight some 1,000 lb (455 kg) greater than the BQM-34A.

In 14 months up to October 1969, such targets, operated by Teledyne Ryan field crews from the Dona Ana Range, New Mexico, had made more than 6,000 target presentations before US Army trainees at Fort Bliss, Texas. Presentations were made to 20 mm Vulcan, 40 mm Duster and quadruple-mounted 0·50 in anti-aircraft gun crews, with a 2 ft × 12 ft (60 cm × 365 cm) banner target towed on a wire cable 500 ft (152 m) behind the Firebee.

A special reconnaissance version of the BQM-34A Firebee, with long-span wings, is being used by America for flights over China and North Vietnam. These drones, of which the Chinese claimed to have destroyed eight by May 1965, are air-launched from C-130A Hercules aircraft based in South Vietnam.

The following details refer to the standard BQM-34A target drone.

TYPE: Remotely-controlled jet target drone.
WINGS: Cantilever mid-wing monoplane. Wing section from leading-edge to ·264 chord NACA 0009·932; from ·264 chord to trailing-edge NACA 63A014·63. Thickness/chord ratio 14%. No dihedral or incidence. Sweepback at quarter-chord 45°. Three-spar aluminium semi-monocoque structure. Single-spar ailerons of magnesium, aluminium and stainless steel, operated by Lear servo-actuators.

Teledyne Ryan BQM-34A Firebee target drone in USAF ground-launch configuration

FUSELAGE: Conventional semi-monocoque structure of aluminium, with chemical-etched components to save weight and simplify sub-assemblies.

TAIL UNIT: Single assembly attached to fuselage by four bolts. All surfaces swept. Fin is multi-spar aluminium monocoque structure. Trim rudder is operated electrically by Bendix actuator. Single-spar aluminium monocoque tailplane. Magnesium elevators powered by Lear servo. Glass-fibre fin-tip houses telemetry antenna. Glass-fibre tailplane-tips house radar echo enhancing antennae.

POWER PLANT: One 1,700 lb (772 kg) st Continental J69-T-29 turbojet engine. Fuel tank integral within forward section of fuselage, capacity 100 US gallons (378 litres). Refuelling point above forward fuselage. Oil capacity 1·5 US gallons (5·75 litres).

SYSTEMS: Electrical power only. 28V DC engine-driven generator, 400 c/s 115V AC inverter and 28V 12·5Ah lead-acid battery.

ELECTRONICS AND EQUIPMENT: R425/ARW-59 (USAF) or AN/DRW-29(USN) radio control receiver. A/A37G-3 flight control system. Dorsett TM-4-31A telemetry system.

DIMENSIONS, EXTERNAL (BQM-34A):
Wing span	12 ft 10 in (3·91 m)
Wing chord (streamwise, constant)	2 ft 9·4 in (0·85 m)
Wing aspect ratio	4·632
Length overall	22 ft 10¾ in (6·98 m)
Height overall	6 ft 8 in (2·03 m)
Tailplane span	7 ft 5 in (2·26 m)

AREAS (BQM-34A):
Wings, gross	36·0 sq ft (3·34 m²)
Ailerons (total)	4·16 sq ft (0·39 m²)

Fin	12·70 sq ft (1·18 m²)
Ventral fin	1·42 sq ft (0·13 m²)
Rudder	0·46 sq ft (0·043 m²)
Tailplane	16·69 sq ft (1·55 m²)
Elevators	6·84 sq ft (0·64 m²)

WEIGHTS AND LOADING (BQM-34A):
Weight empty	1,500 lb (680 kg)
Basic gross weight	2,145 lb (973 kg)
Max launching weight	2,500 lb (1,134 kg)
Max wing loading	69·3 lb/sq ft (338·3 kg/m²)

PERFORMANCE (BQM-34A):
Max level speed at 6,500 ft (1,980 m)
614 knots (707 mph; 1,138 km/h)
Max permissible diving speed   Mach 0·95
Max cruising speed at 50,000 ft (15,250 m) at 1,800 lb (816 kg) AUW
547 knots (630 mph; 1,015 km/h)
Stalling speed, power on, at 1,800 lb (816 kg) AUW   101 knots (116 mph; 187 km/h)
Rate of climb at S/L at 2,200 lb (1,000 kg) AUW
16,000 ft (4,875 m)/min
Operating height range
50 ft to 60,000 ft (15 m to 18,300 m)
Endurance at 50,000 ft (15,250 m)   75 minutes
Flotation time with 25% fuel   24 hours

TELEDYNE RYAN MODEL 166 FIREBEE II
US Navy designation: BQM-34E
USAF designation: BQM-34F

Under contract to the US Navy and USAF, Teledyne Ryan Aeronautical is producing the Model 166 supersonic Firebee II, an advanced development of the BQM-34A Firebee described above. An operational test and evaluation flight programme was completed successfully in August 1969. Production versions of the **BQM-34E** are scheduled for delivery to the US Navy in January 1971. The first **BQM-34F** for the USAF is scheduled for delivery in May 1971.

Teledyne Ryan MQM-34D, the US Army version of the Firebee with Towbee targets on wingtips

The Firebee II will provide aerial target presentations at up to 60,000 ft (18,300 m) at supersonic dash speeds up to Mach 1·5 for a period of 18 minutes. With full fuel load, range time may be extended to 75 minutes. It can be ground- or air-launched, a typical launch aircraft being the US Navy's DP-2E Neptune.

To preserve the supersonic configuration, protuberances beyond the basic airframe lines are avoided by designing the external attachments and antennae to be flush. A nose radome, similar to that of the subsonic Firebee, houses the scoring system and passive augmentation. Directly behind this is the equipment compartment containing electrical and electronic systems, followed by the central fuselage, consisting of the fuel tank and structure for supporting the wing. The inlet and oil tank assembly is slung under the equipment compartment. The inlet duct passes from the inlet opening through the fuel tank to the engine, which is installed in a fuselage half-shell integral with the central fuselage structure. The entire aft portion of the fuselage is a removable sub-assembly which forms the upper shell, covering the engine.

The tail section consists of two all-moving horizontal tail surfaces, used for both roll and pitch control, a vertical fin and rudder. The control surfaces are actuated by an electro-hydraulic actuator unit; this is a self-contained package with two output shafts for the horizontal tail surfaces and one for the rudder, which is used for directional trim and yaw damping.

A tail-cone houses the parachute recovery system, which is similar to that in use in the subsonic Firebee.

A modified Continental J69-T-29 turbojet, designated YJ69-T-406, is fitted. This features a rearrangement of accessories to reduce frontal area, a modified compressor design to uprate thrust, and material changes in the radial compressor to permit supersonic operations at sea level.

Among the unusual design characteristics of the supersonic Firebee are its "clean" wings. No ailerons are used, roll control being achieved by differential deflection of the all-moving horizontal tail surfaces.

Only 263 lb (119 kg) of fuel is carried within the fuselage of the Firebee II, but a further 400 lb (181 kg) may be carried in a jettisonable external fuel pod slung beneath the fuselage. With both tanks, the target will perform subsonic flight missions with similar performance capability, endurance and range to those of the subsonic BQM-34A. For supersonic flights, the external pod is jettisoned.

Bristol Works of the British Aircraft Corporation Guided Weapons Division has licence rights to sell and manufacture the Firebee II. The agreement, announced in September 1968, covers the UK, Australia, France and Denmark.

TYPE: Remotely-controlled supersonic jet target drone.

WINGS: Cantilever mid-wing monoplane. Sweepback 53° at leading-edge. Thickness/chord ratio 3%. Basic structure consists of aluminium honeycomb core, steel skins tapering from 0·10 to 0·012 in (2·5 to 0·3 mm) in thickness, steel leading-edge, machined aluminium trailing-edge and detachable glass-fibre wingtips with glass-fibre honeycomb core. No ailerons.

FUSELAGE: Conventional aluminium semi-monocoque structure. Shear and torsional forces are carried by the skin. Longitudinal members such as side longerons, keel, riser trough and skins carry the fuselage bending loads. Frames, bulkheads and formers shape and hold the skin to its contour. Glass-fibre nose radome.

TAIL UNIT: Sweptback (45°) all-moving horizontal surfaces and sweptback (53°) tapered fin. Aluminium honeycomb cores, with steel skins tapering from 0·10 to 0·016 in (2·5-0·4 mm) in the horizontal tail surfaces, with machined aluminium leading- and trailing-edges, and a steel machined attachment fitting. Fin consists of aluminium honeycomb core, steel skins tapering from 0·145 to 0·035 in (3·7-0·9 mm) in the central section, 0·015 in (0·38 mm) steel forward and aft skins, and aluminium leading- and trailing-edges. The fin tip is a glass-fibre housing for antennae.

Teledyne Ryan BQM-34E supersonic Firebee II target drone leaving ground launcher

Teledyne Ryan BQM-34E Firebee II drone under wing of DP-2E Neptune director aircraft

POWER PLANT: One 1,840 lb (835 kg) st Continental YJ69-T-406 turbojet engine. Internal fuel tank capacity 263 lb (119 kg). External fuel pod capacity 400 lb (181 kg). Oil tank capacity 1·5 US gallons (5·75 litres).

SYSTEMS: Electrical power only. 28V DC engine-driven generator. 400 c/s 115V AC inverter.

ELECTRONICS AND EQUIPMENT: AN/DLQ-2 and -3 ECM equipment, AN/USQ-11A and AN/DRQ-3A missile scoring system, low-altitude radar altimeter, X- and C-band tracking beacons, special low-altitude kit for 50 ft (15 m) altitude. Augmentation includes TWT in S-, C-, and X-band; solid state augmentation in P-band; passive radar reflectors. AN/DRW-29 radio control receiver. Ryan AN/DRW-33 flight control system. Dorsett AN/AKT-21 telemetry system.

DIMENSIONS, EXTERNAL:
Wing span 8 ft 11 in (2·71 m)
Length overall 28 ft 3 in (8·61 m)
Height overall 4 ft 9½ in (1·46 m)
Tailplane span 5 ft 7½ in (1·71 m)

WEIGHTS AND LOADING:
Weight empty:
fuel pod off 1,446 lb (656 kg)
fuel pod on 1,510 lb (685 kg)
Max launching weight (air launch) 2,442 lb (1,108 kg)
Basic design gross weight 2,310 lb (1,048 kg)
Max wing loading 71·8 lb/sq ft (350·5 kg/m²)

PERFORMANCE:
Max speed at 60,000 ft (18,300 m) Mach 1·5
Operating height range 50 to 60,000 ft (15-18,300 m)
Endurance (total time) 75 minutes
Flotation time 24 hours

SAILPLANES

(CORRECTED TO I AUGUST 1970)

ARGENTINA

ALTINGER-BERTONI

AB-1 SUPER ALBATROS

Brief details have been received of this 15-metre sailplane constructed by Ings Altinger and Bertoni in Argentina. The design was initiated in 1957, but before construction of the prototype began in 1960 a considerable re-design was effected. The prototype was nearly completed in late 1962, but for reasons unknown the first flight was not made until early in 1969, and the AB-1 took part in a gliding competition early in 1970.

The wing is of Wortmann FX-1057-816 section and is swept forward 6°. The fuselage is built in two parts, comprising a forward and aft section. Construction is mainly of Epikote 815 balsa/glass-fibre sandwich.

DIMENSIONS:
Wing span	49 ft 2½ in (15·0 m)
Wing aspect ratio	18
Length overall	23 ft 5½ in (7·15 m)

AREAS:
Wings, gross	134·5 sq ft (12·50 m²)

Vertical tail surfaces	10·8 sq ft (1·00 m²)
Horizontal tail surfaces	17·2 sq ft (1·60 m²)

WEIGHTS AND LOADING:
Weight empty	440 lb (200 kg)
Max T-O weight	661 lb (300 kg)
Max wing loading	4·9 lb/sq ft (24 kg/m²)

PERFORMANCE:
Best glide ratio
35 : 1 at 48·6 knots (56 mph; 90 km/h)
Min sinking speed 1·97 ft (0·60 m)/sec
at 37·8 knots (43·5 mph; 70 km/h)

AUSTRALIA

SCHNEIDER

EDMUND SCHNEIDER PTY LTD

HEAD OFFICE AND WORKS:
Parafield Airport, 5106 South Australia
CHIEF DESIGNER:
Harry Schneider

Edmund Schneider Pty Ltd, late of Grunau in Germany, was one of the pioneer sailplane manufacturing companies. It transferred its operations to Australia as a private venture, at the invitation of the Gliding Federation of Australia. Its first project in the Commonwealth was the Kangaroo two-seat sailplane, which flew during 1953, followed by the Grunau Baby 4, Club trainer, Kookaburra and Arrow, described in previous editions of *Jane's*.

The ES 60 Series 2 Boomerang continues to be built to order, and consideration of two design studies has resulted in a decision to build the ES 60B Super Arrow, a development of the ES 60 Series 2 and of the E 59 Arrow, this latter aircraft being described in the 1967-68 *Jane's*.

Two sailplane projects reported in the 1969-70 *Jane's*, the ES 61 and ES 62, have been abandoned. Instead, Schneider are working on a new project, designated ES 63, which is to be a two-seat high-performance machine.

Edmund Schneider Pty Ltd is the sole Australian agent for Schleicher sailplanes (see German section).

SCHNEIDER ES 60 SERIES 2 BOOMERANG

The Boomerang is a single-seat Standard Class sailplane designed for competition flying. The first of two prototypes flew for the first time on 28 November 1964, followed by the second on 24 December. Six similar Series 1 production Boomerangs were completed in 1966, sixteen Series 2 in 1967, and twelve Series 2 in 1968.

The following specification applies to the current production Boomerang Series 2, in which the nose has been lengthened by 2½ in (6·35 cm), the seat-back made adjustable and a larger wheel fitted.

TYPE: Single-seat high-performance sailplane.

WINGS: Cantilever high-wing monoplane. Wing section Wortmann FX-61-184 at root, Wortmann FX-60-126 at tip. Dihedral 1°. Laminated beech spar at 50% chord. Birch-ply covering back to 60% chord; moulded plastics leading-edge and tip "bumpers". Plywood-covered plain wooden ailerons, upper surface hinged. No flaps. Scissor-type air-brakes of metal construction, with epoxy-bonded wooden flanges, at 55% chord.

FUSELAGE: Plywood-covered semi-monocoque structure, with glass-fibre fairings.

TAIL UNIT: "All-flying" cantilever wood tailplane, plywood and fabric covered. Trim-tab in trailing-edge acts also as anti-balance tab. Tailplane halves mount separately onto each side of fin, with automatic spring-loaded bayonet coupling. Plywood-covered fin (height reduced by 3 in = 7·6 cm on Series 2) with fabric-covered wooden rudder. Inset control horns. All surfaces swept 30° at the leading-edges.

LANDING GEAR: Non-retractable mono-wheel type, without forward skid. Spring steel tail-skid. Tost wheel, tyre size 5·00 × 5, with

Second prototype of the Schneider ES 60 Boomerang single-seat Standard Class sailplane
(E. W. Wagner)

Schneider ES 60B Super Arrow high-performance single-seat sailplane

expanding shoe brake. Tyre pressure 35 lb/sq in (2·5 kg/cm²).

ACCOMMODATION: Single seat in enclosed cockpit under sideways-opening Perspex canopy. Lined cockpit, with cushions. Adjustable seat-back and rudder pedals. Locker compartment with separate stowage space for vario flasks, oxygen and radio. Instrument tappings. Instruments to customer's specification. Instrument panel incorporates a bale-out handle.

DIMENSIONS:
Wing span	49 ft 2½ in (15·00 m)
Wing aspect ratio	17·5
Length overall	23 ft 2½ in (7·04 m)
Height over tail	5 ft 0 in (1·52 m)
Tailplane span	8 ft 11 in (2·70 m)
Width at cockpit	1 ft 11¾ in (0·60 m)

AREAS:
Wings (gross)	138 sq ft (12·87 m²)
Air-brakes (total)	5·25 sq ft (0·49 m²)
Tailplane (all-flying)	14·5 sq ft (1·35 m²)

WEIGHTS AND LOADING:
Weight empty	488 lb (222 kg)
Max T-O weight	765 lb (347 kg)
Max wing loading	5·55 lb/sq ft (27·1 kg/m²)

PERFORMANCE (at AUW of 717 lb = 325 kg):
Best glide ratio
30·7 : 1 at 46 knots (53 mph; 85 km/h)
Min sinking speed 2·17 ft (0·66 m)/sec
at 38 knots (44 mph; 71 km/h)
Stalling speed, with brakes
33 knots (37 mph; 59 km/h)

Max speed (smooth air)
122 knots (140 mph; 225 km/h) IAS
Max speed (rough air)
89 knots (103 mph; 166 km/h) IAS
Max aero-tow speed
89 knots (103 mph; 166 km/h) IAS
Max winch-launching speed
61 knots (70 mph; 112 km/h) IAS

SCHNEIDER ES 60B SUPER ARROW

The Super Arrow is a single-seat Standard Class sailplane designed for competition flying, the prototype of which flew for the first time on 22 September 1969, and which was awarded a Certificate of Airworthiness on 31 October 1969. It is essentially the same as the Series 2 Boomerang, but differs in having the conventional tail unit of the E 59 Arrow, with a fixed tailplane mounted at the base of, and forward of, the fin.

The description of the Series 2 Boomerang applies also to the Super Arrow, except as detailed below:

TAIL UNIT: Cantilever wood structure, plywood and fabric covered. Slightly-swept vertical and horizontal surfaces. Spring-loaded elevator trim.

DIMENSIONS:
Tailplane span	9 ft 2¼ in (2·80 m)

AREAS:
Tailplane	10·7 sq ft (0·99 m²)
Elevators	7·10 sq ft (0·66 m²)

WEIGHTS AND PERFORMANCE:
As for Series 2 Boomerang.

AUSTRIA

OBERLERCHNER
JOSEF OBERLERCHNER HOLZINDUSTRIE
HEAD OFFICE:
Egarterplatz 3, Spittal/Drau

This company designed and manufactured sailplanes from 1941 to 1967, during which time it delivered over 4,000, of many types. Its last production model was the single-seat Mg 23 SL, described in the 1967-68 *Jane's*.

Oberlerchner expects to resume the manufacture of sailplanes in due course.

BRAZIL

AB
A. SCHILLER AND A. A. BARROS
Mr A. Schiller and Mr A. A. Barros have designed a two-seat training sailplane known as the AB-1, the prototype of which (PP-ZTE) flew for the first time on 14 August 1965 at the Nova Iguacú Aero Club, Rio de Janeiro. In 1967 it was flight tested extensively by the PAR at São José dos Campos, as a result of which certain modifications were made in 1968.

Also in 1968, the prototype of a new single-seat sailplane, the AB-2, began its flight trials.

AB-1
TYPE: Two-seat training sailplane.

WINGS: Braced high-wing monoplane. Conventional single-spar torsion-box structure of Freijó wood with fabric covering. Wing section NACA 4415 at root, NACA 4412 at tip. Dihedral 2° 30'. Sweep-forward at quarter-chord from root to station 3·12 m 3°, from station 3·12 m to tip 2°. Ailerons of similar construction to wings. Air-brakes on inner wings; upper ones at 58% chord, lower ones at 48% chord.

FUSELAGE: All-metal semi-monocoque structure, with riveted Alclad skin.

TAIL UNIT: Cantilever structure of composite construction. Horizontal surfaces of wood, with plywood covering on tailplane and fabric covering on elevators. All-metal vertical surfaces with Alclad skin.

LANDING GEAR: Non-retractable mono-wheel, diameter 12 in (30 cm), skid and tail-wheel.

ACCOMMODATION: Two seats in tandem, with dual controls. One-piece canopy hinged to starboard.

DIMENSIONS, EXTERNAL:
Wing span	53 ft 9½ in (16·40 m)
Wing chord at root	4 ft 10½ in (1·49 m)

Prototype AB-1 two-seat training sailplane (*Ronaldo S. Olive*)

Wing chord at tip	1 ft 9¼ in (0·54 m)
Wing aspect ratio	13·7
Length overall	27 ft 10 in (8·48 m)
Max width of fuselage	1 ft 11 in (0·58 m)
Tailplane span	11 ft 9¾ in (3·60 m)

AREAS:
Wings, gross	213·4 sq ft (19·83 m²)
Ailerons (total)	20·34 sq ft (1·89 m²)
Air-brakes (total)	6·14 sq ft (0·57 m²)
Fin	7·97 sq ft (0·74 m²)
Rudder	11·30 sq ft (1·05 m²)
Tailplane	15·07 sq ft (1·40 m²)
Elevators	15·07 sq ft (1·40 m²)

WEIGHTS:
Weight empty, equipped	608 lb (276 kg)
Max T-O weight	983 lb (446 kg)

PERFORMANCE:
No details available

AB-2
A prototype of this new single-seat sailplane was being flight tested at the end of 1968. The only available details are as follows:

DIMENSIONS, EXTERNAL:
Wing span	42 ft 8 in (13·0 m)
Length overall	20 ft 6 in (6·25 m)

WEIGHT:
Max T-O weight	573 lb (260 kg)

PERFORMANCE:
Best glide ratio	28 : 1 at 43·4 knots (50 mph; 80 km/h)
Max speed (smooth air)	119 knots (137 mph; 220 km/h)

EMBRAER
EMPRÊSA BRASILEIRA DE AERONÁUTICA S/A

HEAD OFFICE:
Caixa Postale 343, São José dos Campos, São Paulo State

In addition to its work on powered aircraft, this company is also responsible for production of the IPD/PAR-6505 Urupema single-seat high-performance sailplane. All available details of the Urupema are given under the IPD entry in this section.

IPD
INSTITUTO DE PESQUISAS E DESENVOLVIMENTO (IPD), CENTRO TÉCNICO DE AERONÁUTICA (CTA)

HEADQUARTERS:
São José dos Campos, São Paulo

DEPARTAMENTO DE AERONAVES (PAR)
In addition to its work on powered aircraft, this organisation was responsible for the Periquito sailplane (details in 1967-68 *Jane's*) and the Urupema sailplane, of which details follow.

IPD/PAR-6505 URUPEMA
Design of this sailplane was started in 1964 by a group of engineers and students at the Instituto Tecnologico de Aeronáutica (ITA), under the leadership of Mr Guido Pessotti. Construction of the prototype was started in 1965. It flew for the first time on 20 January 1968 and took part later in the year in the World Gliding Championships in Poland. Its flight test programme is now completed and production is being undertaken by Embraer, listed in this section.

TYPE: Single-seat high-performance sailplane.

WINGS: Cantilever shoulder-wing monoplane. Wing section Wortmann FX 05 171 at root, FX 05 121 at tip. Dihedral 3°. Incidence 3°. Sweep-forward at quarter-chord 1° 22'. Wings and ailerons have wood/paper honeycomb/wood sandwich structure. DFS air-brakes at 63% chord and 50% span.

FUSELAGE: Conventional semi-monocoque wood structure. Nose section is of plywood/plastic foam/plywood sandwich.

TAIL UNIT: Cantilever type of wood and honeycomb paper sandwich construction. One-piece all-moving horizontal surfaces, with automatic anti-tab which may be reset to trim.

LANDING GEAR: Non-retractable BF Goodrich mono-wheel, diameter 10 in (25 cm) ahead of CG. Tyre pressure 50 lb/sq in (3·52 kg/cm²). Mechanical brake.

IPD/PAR-6505 Urupema single-seat high-performance sailplane

ACCOMMODATION: Single semi-reclining seat. One-piece removable transparent canopy.

EQUIPMENT: Basic sailplane instrumentation and turn-and-bank indicator standard. Artificial horizon optional.

DIMENSIONS, EXTERNAL:
Wing span	49 ft 2½ in (15·00 m)
Wing chord at root	3 ft 11¼ in (1·20 m)
Wing chord at tip	1 ft 3¾ in (0·40 m)
Wing aspect ratio	18·75
Length overall	24 ft 5¼ in (7·45 m)
Height overall	5 ft 1 in (1·55 m)
Tailplane span	7 ft 2½ in (2·20 m)

DIMENSIONS, INTERNAL:
Cabin: Max width	1 ft 10½ in (0·57 m)
Max height	2 ft 4½ in (0·72 m)

AREAS:
Wings, gross	129·2 sq ft (12·00 m²)
Ailerons (total)	9·69 sq ft (0·90 m²)
Air-brakes (total)	5·17 sq ft (0·48 m²)
Fin	4·31 sq ft (0·40 m²)
Rudder	9·36 sq ft (0·87 m²)
Tailplane	10·76 sq ft (1·00 m²)

WEIGHTS AND LOADING:
Weight empty	507 lb (230 kg)
Max T-O weight	683 lb (310 kg)
Max wing loading	5·33 lb/sq ft (26 kg/m²)

PERFORMANCE:
Best glide ratio	36 : 1 at 51·2 knots (59 mph; 95 km/h)
Min sinking speed	1·3 ft (0·66 m)/sec at 41·7 knots (48 mph; 78 km/h)
Stalling speed	33 knots (38 mph; 61 km/h)
Max speed (smooth air)	137 knots (158 mph; 255 km/h)
Max speed (rough air)	87 knots (100 mph; 160 km/h)
Max aero-tow speed	70 knots (81 mph; 130 km/h)
g limits	+6·25; —4·25

CZECHOSLOVAKIA

OMNIPOL
OMNIPOL FOREIGN TRADE CORPORATION
ADDRESS:
Washingtonova 11, Prague 1
GENERAL MANAGER:
Tomás Marecek, G.E
SALES MANAGER:
Frantisek Rypal, G.E
PUBLIC RELATIONS MANAGER:
Jan Bocek

This concern handles the export sales of the products of the Czechoslovak aircraft industry, including the L-13 Blaník sailplane. A powered version of the Blaník, designated L-13J, was built and flown, but this will not go into production. Brief details of it were given in the 1969-70 *Jane's*.

LET NARODNÍ PODNIK (Let National Corporation)
ADDRESS:
Kunovice, near Uherské Hradiste

In addition to its work on powered aircraft, Let National Corporation manufactures the L-13 Blaník sailplane, of which full details follow.

L-13 BLANÍK

This tandem two-seat all-metal sailplane is designed for training in all categories from elementary to "blind" flying and for high-performance flight. It is fully-aerobatic when flown solo and capable of basic aerobatic manoeuvres when carrying a crew of two.

Design of the Blaník was started in January 1955, and construction of the prototype began in August of the same year. First flight was made in March 1956 and a total of 1,262 had been completed by early 1970.

The L-13J powered version of the Blaník, described in the 1969-70 *Jane's*, will not go into production.

TYPE: Two-seat training sailplane.

WINGS: Cantilever shoulder-wing monoplane, with 5° forward sweep at quarter-chord. Wing section NACA 63_2A615 at root, NACA 63_2A612 at tip. Dihedral 3°. Incidence 4° at root, 1° at tip. All-metal two-spar structure. Main spar forms torsion-box with leading-edge. Each wing secured by three fuselage attachments. Wing-tip "salmons". Ailerons and slotted area-increasing flaps are fabric-covered metal structures. Rectangular light-alloy air-brakes in the upper and lower surfaces of each wing.

L-13 Blaník two-seat training sailplane (*E. W. Wagner*)

FUSELAGE: All-metal semi-monocoque structure of oval cross-section, with riveted skin.

TAIL UNIT: Cantilever all-metal structure. Elevator and rudder fabric-covered. Controllable trim-tab in elevator. Horizontal surfaces fold upward parallel to rudder for transport.

LANDING GEAR: Mechanically-retractable main wheel, type HP-4741-Z, located in lower part of fuselage on centre-line. Wheel manufactured by Rudy Ríjen of Gottwaldov; tyre size 13.8×5.3 in (350×135 mm) by Moravan of Otrokovice, pressure 35.6 lb/sq in (2.5 kg/cm³). Oleo-pneumatic shock-absorber and mechanically-actuated brake.

ACCOMMODATION: Two seats in tandem in part-upholstered cabin, with heat-insulated walls. Upward-opening transparent canopy, hinged on the starboard side, is jettisonable in flight.

EQUIPMENT: Standard equipment includes basic flight instruments on both front and rear instrument panels, tow line and cockpit cover. Optional equipment includes electric gyros, second rate of climb indicator for rear instrument panel, rear compartment blinds for instrument flying instruction, navigation lights and 12V 10Ah battery, water ballast system to increase wing loading for solo flight, skis for operation on snow and a complete set of protective covers.

DIMENSIONS:

Wing span	53 ft 2 in (16·20 m)
Wing chord at root	5 ft 5 in (1·65 m)
Wing chord at tip	2 ft 3½ in (0·70 m)
Wing aspect ratio	13·7
Length overall	27 ft 6½ in (8·40 m)
Height over tail	6 ft 10 in (2·09 m)
Tailplane span	11 ft 3¾ in (3·45 m)

AREAS:

Wings, gross	206·13 sq ft (19·15 m²)
Ailerons (total)	24·87 sq ft (2·31 m²)
Flaps (total)	42·52 sq ft (3·95 m²)
Spoilers (total)	7·00 sq ft (0·65 m²)
Fin	7·58 sq ft (0·70 m²)
Rudder	9·73 sq ft (0·90 m²)
Tailplane	16·79 sq ft (1·56 m²)
Elevators	11·95 sq ft (1·11 m²)

WEIGHTS AND LOADINGS:

Weight empty, standard equipment ±2%	677 lb (307 kg)
Max T-O weight	1,102 lb (500 kg)
Normal wing loading	5·02 lb/sq ft (24·5 kg/m²)
Max wing loading	5·35 lb/sq ft (26·1 kg/m²)

PERFORMANCE (at AUW of 1,102 lb = 500 kg):

Best glide ratio, ±5%	
	28 : 1 at 48 knots (55 mph; 88 km/h) IAS
Min sinking speed	2·69 ft (0·82 m)/sec
	at 44 knots (50 mph; 80 km/h) IAS
Stalling speed 31 knots (35 mph; 55 km/h) IAS	
Max speed (smooth air)	
	136 knots (157 mph; 253 km/h) IAS
Max speed (rough air)	
	78 knots (90 mph; 145 km/h) IAS
Max aero-tow speed	
	76 knots (87 mph; 140 km/h) IAS
Max winch-launching speed	
	65 knots (75 mph; 120 km/h) IAS
g limits	+5; —2·5

FINLAND

FIBERA
OY FIBERA AB
DISPLAY AND SALES OFFICE:
Oy Polykem Ab, Et. Rautatiekatu 10, Helsinki 10

This company specialises in glass-fibre manufacture. Since 1961, it has been engaged in an intensive programme of research into plastics structures and had built a total of 22 examples of an all-plastics sailplane, known as the KK-1 Utu, by mid-March 1970.

FIBERA KK-1 UTU

The original KK-1a prototype Utu was designed and built over a three-year period by engineers of Oy Fibera Ab, to the design of Dipl-Ing Ahto Anttila, to investigate the structural applications of plastics laminates stabilised with polyurethane foam. It flew for the first time on 14 August 1964 and has been followed by further prototypes designated KK-1b, c, d and e, each with structural modifications. The design is stressed for load factors from +8g to —6g.

The following details refer to the latest KK-1e version of the Utu.

TYPE: Single-seat Standard Class sailplane.

WINGS: Cantilever high-wing monoplane. Wing section NACA 63_3618 at root, NACA 63_1612 at tip. Dihedral 2°. Sweep-forward 1° at quarter-chord. Polyester/glass-fibre laminate sandwich shell with foam plastic core, single I-spar and no ribs. Upper-surface-hinged ailerons of glass-fibre reinforced plastic shell construction, with foam plastic stiffening. No spoilers. Trailing-edge drag flaps.

FUSELAGE: Monocoque double-shell structure, with polyester/glass-fibre laminate outer shell and sandwich type inner shell of similar construction to wing.

TAIL UNIT: Cantilever structure, with tailplane mounted at tip of fin. Fin moulded integrally with fuselage. Glass-fibre reinforced plastic shell, stiffened with foam plastic.

Fibera KK-1e Utu Standard Class sailplane

LANDING GEAR: Non-retractable mono-wheel, size 12 × 4, with drum brake.

ACCOMMODATION: Single seat in enclosed cabin.

EQUIPMENT: Normal sailplane instrumentation. Oxygen and radio installed aft of seat.

DIMENSIONS:
Wing span	49 ft 2½ in (15·00 m)
Wing chord at root	3 ft 6¼ in (1·07 m)
Wing chord at tip	1 ft 5 in (0·43 m)
Wing aspect ratio	20
Length overall	21 ft 4 in (6·50 m)
Height overall	4 ft 0 in (1·22 m)

Tailplane span		8 ft 10 in (2·70 m)
Width at cockpit		1 ft 11½ in (0·60 m)

AREAS:
Wings, gross	121 sq ft (11·25 m²)
Ailerons (total)	8·93 sq ft (0·83 m²)
Brakes (total)	9·26 sq ft (0·86 m²)
Fin	4·52 sq ft (0·42 m²)
Rudder	5·38 sq ft (0·50 m²)
Tailplane	7·86 sq ft (0·73 m²)
Elevators	5·27 sq ft (0·49 m²)

WEIGHTS AND LOADING:
Weight empty, equipped	441 lb (200 kg)
Max T-O weight	684 lb (310 kg)
Max wing loading	5·65 lb/sq ft (27·6 kg/m²)

PERFORMANCE:
Best glide ratio
35 : 1 at 43·4 knots (50 mph; 81 km/h)
Min sinking speed 2 ft (0·60 m)/sec
at 40 knots (46 mph; 74 km/h)
Stalling speed 34 knots (39 mph; 63 km/h)
Max speed (smooth air)
135 knots (155 mph; 250 km/h)
Max speed (rough air)
113 knots (130 mph; 210 km/h)
Max aero-tow speed
108 knots (124 mph; 200 km/h)
Max winch-launching speed
81 knots (93 mph; 150 km/h)

IKV
ILMAILUKERHO VASAMA

IKV, the flying club of Vasama, is flying the prototype of the IKV-3 Kotka sailplane designed by Mr Tuomo Tervo and Mr J. Jalkanen, whose earlier designs have included the PIK-16 Vasama and Havukka sailplanes. Design was initiated in December 1964 and construction of the prototype, by flying club members in conjunction with K. K. Lehtovaara Oy, began in mid-1965. It flew for the first time in June 1966 and, on 26 May 1968, piloted by Seppo Hämäläinen, set up a Scandinavian long-distance record of 324 nm (374 miles; 602 km). All available details of this sailplane are given below.

IKV-3 KOTKA

TYPE: Single-seat high-performance sailplane.

WINGS: Cantilever shoulder-wing monoplane. Wing section Wortmann FX-62-K153 at root, FX-60-126 at tip. Sweepback at quarter-chord 0·2°. Single-spar wooden structure with plywood skin and fabric covering overall. Plain ailerons of plastic foam, with plywood skin; trailing-edge flaps of similar construction. Two air brakes in each wing, on the upper and lower surface, of light alloy construction.

FUSELAGE: Conventional wooden structure with nose to trailing-edge of wing glass-fibre-covered and plywood skin aft of the wing.

TAIL UNIT: Cantilever structure of plastic foam; tailplane and fin with plywood skin, rudder and elevators fabric-covered. Tailplane has variable incidence.

LANDING GEAR: Mechanically-retractable mono-wheel, with 15 in (380 mm) diameter tyre. Detachable tail-wheel to facilitate ground handling.

ACCOMMODATION: Single seat in enclosed cabin, with transparent canopy extending to the nose.

IKV-3 Kotka single-seat high-performance sailplane

DIMENSIONS, EXTERNAL:
Wing span	59 ft 8½ in (18·20 m)
Wing chord at root	4 ft 3¼ in (1·30 m)
Wing chord at tip	1 ft 5¾ in (0·45 m)
Wing aspect ratio	19
Length overall	25 ft 5 in (7·75 m)
Tailplane span	11 ft 9¾ in (3·60 m)

AREAS:
Wings, gross	183 sq ft (17·00 m²)
Ailerons (total)	13·3 sq ft (1·24 m²)
Air brakes (total)	3·44 sq ft (0·32 m²)
Trailing-edge flaps (total)	21·5 sq ft (2·00 m²)
Fin	7·53 sq ft (0·70 m²)
Rudder	7·10 sq ft (0·66 m²)
Tailplane	12·8 sq ft (1·19 m²)
Elevators	6·89 sq ft (0·64 m²)

WEIGHTS:
Weight empty (equipped)	749 lb (340 kg)
Max T-O weight	992 lb (450 kg)

PERFORMANCE:
Best glide ratio
38 : 1 at 54 knots (62 mph; 100 km/h)
Min sinking speed 1·74 ft (0·53 m)/sec
at 38 knots (43·5 mph; 70 km/h)
Stalling speed 29 knots (33 mph; 52 km/h)
Max speed (smooth air)
135 knots (155 mph; 250 km/h)
Max speed (rough air)
93 knots (107 mph; 172 km/h)
Max aero-tow speed
86 knots (99 mph; 160 km/h)
Max winch launching speed
81 knots (93 mph; 150 km/h)

PIK
POLYTEKNIKKOJEN ILMAILUKERHO (FLYING CLUB OF THE STUDENT UNION AT THE INSTITUTE OF TECHNOLOGY, HELSINKI)
ADDRESS:
Dipoli, Otaniemi

This club was established in 1931 and has since been engaged mainly in gliding activities. Of the series of gliders designed and constructed, the PIK-7 primary glider, the PIK-5a, b and c intermediate types and the PIK-3a, b and c advanced sailplanes are of particular interest due to the fact that they were accepted as standard types for Finnish Gliding Clubs. The first Finnish two-seat sailplane, the PIK-12, was completed and flown in May 1956.

The first powered aeroplane to be constructed and built in the club was the PIK-11, which flew in March 1953, and the first two-seat aircraft designed and constructed was the PIK-15 which is designed mainly for glider-towing (see "Aircraft" section).

Latest project of the Club was to produce a low-price single-seat sailplane for primary and advanced training in 12 metre and 15 metre class, resulting in completion of the PIK-17a Tumppi and PIK-17b Tintti.

At the beginning of 1970, PIK provided information on the number of gliders constructed to date: 20 PIK-3c; 27 PIK-5c; 1 PIK-11; 4 PIK-12; 6 PIK-15; 55 PIK-16c; 1 PIK-17a and 1 PIK-17b.

PIK-16c VASAMA (ARROW)

The PIK-16 is a single-seat Standard Class sailplane which was designed by Tuomo Tervo, Jorma Jalkanen and Kurt Hedström. The prototype flew on 1 June 1961.

The PIK-16c, described below, has a conventional tail unit instead of the "butterfly" tail of the original version. It was put into production by K. K. Lehtovaara Oy of Hämeenlinna and a total of 55 were built.

TYPE: Single-seat Standard Class sailplane.

WINGS: Cantilever shoulder-wing monoplane. Wing section Wortmann FX-05-188 at root, NACA 63²-615 at tip. Thickness/chord ratio 14% at root. Dihedral 3° 30'. All-wood structure, with 40% of chord formed by shaped box-spar of birch plywood which

PIK-16c Vasama single-seat Standard Class sailplane

takes bending and torsion loads. Nose section of sandwich construction. Aft of spar top surface is plywood-covered, undersurface fabric-covered. Plain ailerons of plywood-covered wooden construction. Spoilers on top and bottom surfaces.

FUSELAGE: Plywood monocoque construction with glass-fibre nose-cap.

TAIL UNIT: Cantilever wood structure. Trim-tab in port elevator.

LANDING GEAR: Non-retractable mono-wheel, size 12 in × 4 in (30·5 cm × 10·2 cm) with brake, and skid.

ACCOMMODATION: Single semi-reclining seat under removable blown Perspex canopy.

DIMENSIONS:
Wing span	49 ft 2½ in (15·0 m)
Wing chord at root	3 ft 6½ in (1·08 m)
Wing chord at tip	1 ft 3½ in (0·40 m)
Height over tail	4 ft 9 in (1·45 m)

Width of cockpit	1 ft 11½ in (0·60 m)
Tailplane span	7 ft 9 in (2·36 m)

AREAS:
Wings, gross	125·9 sq ft (11·70 m²)
Ailerons (total)	10·59 sq ft (0·98 m²)
Spoilers (total)	5·49 sq ft (0·51 m²)

WEIGHTS:
Weight empty, equipped	419 lb (190 kg)
Max T-O weight	661 lb (300 kg)

PERFORMANCE:
Best glide ratio
34 : 1 at 46 knots (53 mph; 85 km/h)
Min sinking speed 1·94 ft (0·59 m)/sec
at 39·5 knots (45·5 mph; 73 km/h)
Max speed (smooth air)
135 knots (155 mph; 250 km/h)
Max speed (rough air)
92 knots (106 mph; 170 km/h)

PIK-17a TUMPPI AND PIK-17b TINTTI

There are two versions of the PIK-17, as follows:

PIK-17a Tumppi. Low-cost single-seat sailplane for primary and advanced training. Designed by Kurt Hedström, Iikka Järvenpää and Juhani Mäkinen to comply with OSTIV requirements for a 12-metre class (mini-Standard Class) sailplane. Construction of prototype was started in June 1964 and it flew on 18 May 1966. Only this single prototype has been built to date.

PIK-17b Tintti. Basically similar to PIK-17a, but modified to conform with OSTIV 15-metre Standard Class specification. Designed by Kurt Hedström, Mauri Määttänen and B-O Lagercrantz. Construction of prototype began in March 1967, for first flight one year later. Only this single prototype has been built to date.

The following description applies to both designs:

TYPE: Single-seat general-purpose sailplane.

WINGS: Cantilever mid-wing monoplane. Wing section Wortmann FX61-163 at root, FX60-126 at tip. Dihedral 17a 2°; 17b 3°. Incidence 2°. No sweepback. D-spar structure, with form-glued shells of birch plywood and ribs of PVC sheet. All-wood inset ailerons hinged at upper edge. No flaps. Glass-fibre trailing-edge airbrakes of centre-hinged flap type, inboard of ailerons.

FUSELAGE: Glass-fibre nose section, back to mid-wing. Conical plywood tube from mid-wing to tail. Inner structure conventional.

TAIL UNIT: Cantilever all-wood structure, with sweptback vertical surfaces and all-moving horizontal surfaces. Combined trim-tabs and stabilizing tabs on horizontal surfaces.

LANDING GEAR: Non-retractable mono-wheel forward of CG. No shock-absorption. Wheel size 12 in × 4 in (30·5 cm × 10·2 cm). Tyre pressure 21·5 lb/sq in (1·50 kg/cm²). Drum-type brake from lightweight motorcycle.

ACCOMMODATION: Single seat under free-blown Plexiglas canopy. Equipment includes ASI, altimeter, two rate-of-climb indicators, electrical turn-and-bank indicator, magnetic compass and oxygen system.

DIMENSIONS:

Wing span:	
17a	39 ft 4½ in (12·00 m)
17b	49 ft 2½ in (15·00 m)
Wing chord at root:	
17a	3 ft 3½ in (1·00 m)
17b	2 ft 11½ in (0·90 m)

PIK-17b Tintti single-seat Standard Class sailplane

Wing chord at tip:			Fin:	
17a	1 ft 7¾ in (0·50 m)		17a	4·41 sq ft (0·41 m²)
17b	1 ft 5¾ in (0·45 m)		17b	4·19 sq ft (0·39 m²)
Wing aspect ratio:			Rudder:	
17a	13·7		17a	6·13 sq ft (0·57 m²)
17b	19·0		17b	6·56 sq ft (0·61 m²)
Length overall	19 ft 2¼ in (5·85 m)		Tailplane:	
Height at fin:			17a	12·38 sq ft (1·15 m²)
17a	4 ft 11 in (1·50 m)		17b	14·00 sq ft (1·30 m²)
17b	5 ft 3 in (1·60 m)			
Tailplane span:			WEIGHTS:	
17a	7 ft 6½ in (2·30 m)		Weight empty:	
17b	9 ft 2 in (2·80 m)		17a	331 lb (150 kg)
			17b	375 lb (170 kg)
AREAS:				
Wings, gross:			PERFORMANCE:	
17a	113 sq ft (10·5 m²)		Best glide ratio (calculated):	
17b	127 sq ft (11·80 m²)		17a	27 : 1
Ailerons (total):			17b	32 : 1
17a	9·04 sq ft (0·84 m²)		Max speed (smooth air):	
17b	9·24 sq ft (0·86 m²)		17a, b	127 knots (146 mph; 235 km/h)
Air brakes (total):			Stalling speed:	
17a	6·89 sq ft (0·64 m²)		17a	32-35 knots (36-40 mph; 58-64 km/h)
17b	7·75 sq ft (0·72 m²)		17b	31-34 knots (35-39 mph; 56-62 km/h)

FRANCE

CARMAM
COOPÉRATIVE D'APPROVISIONNEMENT ET DE RÉPARATIONS DE MATÉRIEL AÉRO-NAUTIQUE DE MOULINS

ADDRESS:
Aérodrome de Moulins-Avermes (Allier)

DIRECTOR: Emile Castanier

This company has extended its work on sailplane repair and maintenance to include the construction of new sailplanes. It began by building under licence the M-100 S, which was designed in Italy by Alberto and Piero Morelli, and which is also being manufactured in Italy by Avionautica Rio at Sarnico (Bergamo). Also in production is the two-seat M-200 by the same designers.

CARMAM M-100 S MÉSANGE (TOMTIT)

The Mésange is a licence-built version of the Italian M-100 S single-seat Standard Class sailplane designed by Alberto and Piero Morelli. The original prototype M-100 S flew for the first time in January 1960 and was followed by 41 production models built in Italy by Aeromere and 85 built by Avionautica Rio by March 1968.

The prototype of the CARMAM-built version obtained its French certificate of airworthiness on 8 February 1963. Deliveries of production models began in June 1963.

The current version, from aircraft No 23 onward, has several improved features including air-brakes of light alloy instead of plastics, a wooden seat and a new metal-framed canopy of Italian manufacture.

TYPE: Single-seat Standard Class sailplane.

WINGS: Cantilever high-wing monoplane. Wing section NACA 63-618 (modified) at root, NACA 63-516 (modified) at tip. Dihedral 2° 30′. Wings swept forward 1° 36′. Single-spar wood structure with leading-edge torsion box. Covered with plywood and fabric. Slotted ailerons of wood construction with fabric covering. Air-brakes consist of three sets of light alloy rotating plates on each wing.

FUSELAGE: All-wood semi-monocoque structure. Single towing hook for both aero and winch launching.

TAIL UNIT: Cantilever all-wood structure, except for fabric covering on rudder and elevators. Elevator trimmer.

CARMAM M-100 S Mésange single-seat Standard Class sailplane (*E. W. Wagner*)

LANDING GEAR: Rubber-sprung nose-skid. Non-retractable mono-wheel, size 300 × 100. Tyre pressure 28·5 lb/sq in (2 kg/cm²). Mechanically-operated disc brake. Tail-skid.

ACCOMMODATION: Single seat in enclosed cockpit, under one-piece transparent plastic canopy.

DIMENSIONS:

Wing span	49 ft 2½ in (15·00 m)
Wing chord at root	4 ft 3 in (1·30 m)
Wing chord at tip	1 ft 6 in (0·45 m)
Wing aspect ratio	17·1
Length overall	21 ft 6 in (6·56 m)
Height over tail	5 ft 3 in (1·60 m)
Tailplane span	9 ft 10 in (3·00 m)

AREAS:

Wings, gross	141 sq ft (13·10 m²)
Ailerons (total)	11·62 sq ft (1·08 m²)
Fin	4·84 sq ft (0·45 m²)
Rudder	5·70 sq ft (0·53 m²)
Tailplane	8·61 sq ft (0·80 m²)
Elevators	8·61 sq ft (0·80 m²)

WEIGHTS AND LOADING:

Weight empty	441 lb (200 kg)
Max T-O weight	694 lb (315 kg)
Wing loading	4·9 lb/sq ft (24 kg/m²)

PERFORMANCE:
Best glide ratio
　32 : 1 at 43·4 knots (50 mph; 80 km/h)
Min sinking speed　2·13 ft (0·65 m)/sec
　at 36·1 knots (41·6 mph; 67 km/h)
Stalling speed　32 knots (36 mph; 58 km/h)
Max speed (smooth air)
　119 knots (137 mph; 220 km/h)
Max speed, air-brakes open
　91 knots (105 mph; 170 km/h)
Max speed (rough air)
　65 knots (75 mph; 120 km/h)
Max aero-tow speed
　81 knots (93 mph; 150 km/h)

CARMAM M-200 FOEHN

Designed by Alberto and Piero Morelli, the M-200 is a two-seat high-performance sailplane developed from the single-seat M-100 S. Except for increases in wing span and overall length, and widening of the fuselage to accommodate two staggered side-by-side seats, the two aircraft are very similar in general appearance and construction.

The first prototype M-200 was built at the CVT, Turin, under a contract from the Aero Club of Italy, and flew for the first time in May 1964. Production has since been undertaken by both CARMAM and Avionautica Rio of Italy (which see).

The description of the M-100 S above applies equally to the M-200, with the following changes:

TYPE: Two-seat high-performance sailplane.

WINGS: Wing section NACA 63-619/15. Airbrakes similar to M-100 S but four sets of rotating plates on each wing.

TAIL UNIT: Dynamically-balanced rudder. Antibalance and trim-tab on elevator.

LANDING GEAR: Wheel size 365 × 150 × 100 mm. Drum brake. Rubber shock-absorbing front and tail skids.

ACCOMMODATION: Two staggered side-by-side seats. Canopy hinged on port side.

DIMENSIONS:
Wing span	59 ft 6½ in (18·15 m)
Wing chord at root	4 ft 10¼ in (1·48 m)
Wing chord at tip	1 ft 5¾ in (0·45 m)
Wing aspect ratio	19
Length overall	24 ft 11¼ in (7·60 m)
Height overall	6 ft 5¼ in (1·96 m)

M-200 Foehn two-seat high-performance sailplane built by CARMAM

Max external width of fuselage	3 ft 3⅜ in (1·00 m)
Tailplane span	12 ft 1½ in (3·70 m)

AREAS:
Wings, gross	188·4 sq ft (17·5 m²)
Ailerons (total)	12·92 sq ft (1·20 m²)
Fin	5·70 sq ft (0·53 m²)
Rudder	8·29 sq ft (0·77 m²)
Tailplane	13·56 sq ft (1·26 m²)
Elevators	13·13 sq ft (1·22 m²)

WEIGHTS AND LOADING:
Weight empty, equipped	760 lb (345 kg)

Max T-O weight	1,257 lb (570 kg)
Max wing loading	6·70 lb/sq ft (32·6 kg/m²)

PERFORMANCE (at AUW of 1,125 lb = 510 kg):
Best glide ratio	32 : 1 at 53 knots (61 mph; 98 km/h)
Sinking speed	8·85 ft (2·70 m)/sec at 81 knots (93 mph; 150 km/h)
Max speed (smooth air)	122 knots (140 mph; 225 km/h)
Max speed (rough air)	81 knots (93 mph; 150 km/h)
Max aero-tow speed	81 knots (93 mph; 150 km/h)

FAUVEL

"SURVOL"-CHARLES FAUVEL

HEAD OFFICE AND WORKS:
30 Chemin de la Roubine, 06- Cannes-La Bocca

Charles Fauvel has been developing and producing for many years a series of tailless sailplanes. The original AV.36 Monobloc single-seater first flew in 1951 and more than 100 were sold to customers in 14 countries before this design was superseded by the improved AV.36 Mk II, the official designation of which is AV.361.

Several powered versions of M Fauvel's designs have been produced. The latest of these, the AV.45 and AV.221, are described below, after the description of the AV.361.

Having been unable to find an entirely suitable engine to power his aircraft, M Fauvel is developing a new 40 hp four-cylinder horizontally-opposed four-stroke engine named the Pygmée, of which details can be found in the "Aero-engines" section. It had been intended to fit this engine in production versions of both the AV.45 and the AV.221 but this had not been done by the Spring of 1970. The prototype AV.45 is being used to flight test a lightweight turbojet power plant.

FAUVEL AV.361

It is known that a total of well over 100 AV.36 and AV.361 sailplanes are flying in 17 different countries. Construction by amateurs continues, especially in the USA and Spain. In France, in 1967, M Gilg of Rouen won the first prize in the amateur-built glider class with his AV.361 at the annual meeting of the Réseau du Sport de l'Air.

TYPE: Single-seat sailplane for competition, cloud and training flying.

WINGS: Cantilever shoulder-wing monoplane. Wing section F₂ 17%. Dihedral 0° on centre-section, 2° 30' on outer wings. Wooden structure, fabric-covered. Ailerons at wing-tips. Elevators in trailing-edge of centre-wing, with large trim-tab in port elevator. Schempp-Hirth retractable air-brakes above and below each outer wing.

FUSELAGE: Short nacelle of wooden construction. Nose is hinged upward to reduce length when the aircraft is transported sideways on a trailer.

TAIL UNIT: No tailplane. Twin fins and rudders inset at junctions of centre-section and outer wings. Rudders fold forward to reduce overall length for transportation on trailer.

LANDING GEAR: Standard gear comprises a flexible rubber-sprung skid. Optional mono-wheel and skid. Bumpers under wingtips.

ACCOMMODATION: Single seat under transparent canopy. Provision for oxygen equipment and radio.

DIMENSIONS:
Wing span	41 ft 10½ in (12·78 m)
Wing chord at root	5 ft 3 in (1·60 m)
Wing aspect ratio	11·4
Length overall	10 ft 8 in (3·24 m)
Length folded	8 ft 1 in (2·46 m)

AREA:
Wings, gross	157 sq ft (14·60 m²)

WEIGHTS:
Weight empty	275 lb (125 kg)
T-O weight	474-569 lb (215-258 kg)

Fauvel AV.361 single-seat sailplane operated by the Aero Club of Dinan

PERFORMANCE:
Best glide ratio	26 : 1 at 44·3 knots (51 mph; 82 km/h)
Min sinking speed	2·43 ft (0·74 m)/sec
Sinking speed at 54 knots (62 mph; 100 km/h)	4·26 ft (1·30 m)/sec
Max speed (smooth air)	119 knots (137 mph; 220 km/h)

FAUVEL AV.44

In July 1940 the prototype of a two-seat tailless monoplane, known as the Fauvel AV.10, was taken by German troops as they swept through France. Powered by a Pobjoy "R" engine, this aircraft was described briefly in the 1938-39 *Jane's*.

An amateur constructor now intends to build a new version of this machine, to be powered by a 100/300 hp engine to provide short take-off capability, and to seat 2 or 3 persons.

It is anticipated that plans will be available later from M Fauvel.

FAUVEL AV.45

The AV.45 is a single-seat tailless self-launching sailplane which first flew on 4 May 1960 with a 35 hp Nelson engine.

In the Summer of 1967 the prototype was re-engined with a Microturbo Éclair turbojet (150 lb = 68 kg st), based on the turbo-starter used for the Olympus engines of the Concorde supersonic airliner. Redesignated AV.45-01R, it completed a programme of flight testing which revealed an outstanding performance (see data below) despite the increased weight of the power plant and necessary fire protection. The jet unit, with its electric starter and long jet-pipe, weighs 80 lb (36·5 kg). The 21 lb (9·5 kg) NiCd battery permits repeated restarts in flight as well as initial ground starting.

During 1970 this engine was to be replaced by an Éclair II turbojet of 172 lb (78 kg) st, and in the Spring of 1970 it was proposed to carry out experiments with another AV.45 powered by a new turbojet engine of 220 lb (100 kg) st.

A second, slightly modified prototype, with 22 hp SOLO engine, was built by Société Aéronautique Normande (SAN) and is representative of the production version, of which several examples are being built by amateurs in France and other countries, including Japan, Spain and Italy.

Changes on the second prototype include the introduction of additional windows under the cockpit canopy, repositioning of the pilot's seat 2·4 in (6 cm) further forward, lengthening of the fuselage by 3·5 in (9 cm), and the installation of larger vertical surfaces, carrying at the bottom small steerable skids, which supersede the under-wing curved wire "bumpers" of the first prototype.

Hoerner wing-tips have also been tested successfully on the AV.45.

The AV.45 is able to take off under its own power, requiring no external launching aids, but retains the excellent performance of an

Fauvel AV.45 single-seat self-launching sailplane

unpowered sailplane. It was planned to replace the present engine with the new 40 hp Pygmée engine developed by M Fauvel (see introductory notes), but this has not, so far, been done.

The following details apply to the second prototype:

TYPE: Single-seat self-launching sailplane.

WINGS: Cantilever shoulder-wing monoplane. Wing section F_2 17%. Dihedral 0° on centre section, 5° 13′ on outer wings. Single-spar wood structure, with plywood leading-edge torsion box and fabric covering aft of spar. Conventional ailerons. Elevators on trailing-edge of centre-wing. Large trim-tab in port elevator. Schempp-Hirth retractable air-brakes above and below each outer wing.

FUSELAGE: Short nacelle of wooden construction, with glass-fibre covering.

TAIL UNIT: No tailplane. Twin fins and rudders inset at junctions of centre-section and outer wings. Wood structure. Fins plywood-cover-ed, rudders fabric-covered.

LANDING GEAR: Tandem two-wheel type. Steerable front wheel, size 300 × 100. Rear wheel, size 380 × 150, with mechanical brake.

POWER PLANT: One 22 hp Hirth SOLO four-cylinder horizontally-opposed two-stroke engine, driving a two-blade wooden fixed-pitch pusher propeller. Normal fuel capacity 3·6 Imp gallons (16·5 litres), with provision for an auxiliary tank of the same capacity.

ACCOMMODATION: Single seat in enclosed cockpit, with sideways-hinged blown plastic canopy.

DIMENSIONS:
Wing span	45 ft 1 in (13·74 m)
Wing chord at root	5 ft 3 in (1·60 m)
Wing chord at tip	1 ft 4 in (0·40 m)
Wing aspect ratio	11·84
Length overall	11 ft 9 in (3·59 m)
Height over tail	6 ft 0 in (1·82 m)
Width of cockpit	2 ft 0 in (0·605 m)

AREAS:
Wings, gross	171·7 sq ft (15·95 m²)
Ailerons (total)	11·11 sq ft (1·03 m²)
Air-brakes (total)	6·72 sq ft (0·624 m²)
Fins (total)	14·85 sq ft (1·38 m²)
Rudders (total)	9·90 sq ft (0·92 m²)
Elevators (total)	14·12 sq ft (1·31 m²)

WEIGHTS:
Weight empty, equipped	476 lb (216 kg)
Max T-O weight	772 lb (350 kg)
Normal loaded weight for gliding	666 lb (302 kg)

PERFORMANCE (standard AV.45):
Best glide ratio, engine stopped, propeller feathered
27 : 1 at 46 knots (53 mph; 85 km/h)
Min sinking speed, engine stopped, propeller feathered, 2·62 ft (0·80 m)/sec at forward speed of 38 knots (43·5 mph; 70 km/h)
Econ cruising speed
69 knots (80 mph; 130 km/h)
Rate of climb at S/L 550 ft (168 m)/min
T-O run 492 ft (150 m)

PERFORMANCE (AV.45-01R with Eclair turbojet):
Best glide ratio, engine stopped
29 : 1 at 46 knots (53 mph; 85 km/h)
Min sinking speed, engine stopped
2·56 ft (0·78 m)/sec
Max level speed at 2,625 ft (800 m)
over 122 knots (140 mph; 225 km/h)
Rate of climb at S/L 785 ft (240 m)/min at 65 knots (75 mph; 120 km/h)
Climb to 9,840 ft (3,000 m) 15 min
T-O from rough grass at max T-O weight
525 ft (160 m)
Endurance at full power with 6·8 Imp gallons (31 litres) of fuel 22 minutes

FAUVEL AV.46

The AV.46 will be a tandem two-seat tailless self-launching sailplane powered by a 40 hp Fauvel Pygmée engine. It is expected to offer a best glide ratio of 30 : 1 with propeller feathered. This project had not been completed at the end of January 1970.

FAUVEL AV.48

Pressure of work on other projects has delayed finalisation of plans for the Fauvel AV.48 to be produced in Germany, but it is expected that this will take place in due course.

In general outline, the AV.48 will bear a strong resemblance to the standard AV.45, but its performance is expected to be substantially better.

The airframe, including the wing, will be constructed entirely of laminated glass-resin plastics. The wing section will be the Wortmann 66H 159, specially designed for flying-wing type aircraft by Dr F. X. Wortmann, on behalf of M Fauvel, and successfully wind-tunnel tested at St Cyr Aerodynamic Laboratory.

The fuselage will have an integral windscreen and has been revised for laminar flow. The vertical tail surfaces will also have a laminar section. The power plant will be a Survol de Coucy Pygmée engine of 40 hp, driving a propeller with two blades that fold back to reduce drag in gliding flight. Nose and main landing gear wheels, in tandem, are retractable.

Microturbo Eclair turbojet installation on prototype Fauvel AV.45-01R

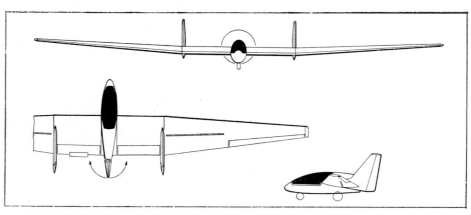

Fauvel AV.48 single-seat self-launching sailplane (40 hp Survol de Coucy Pygmée engine)

DIMENSIONS:
Wing span	52 ft 7 in (16·04 m)
Length overall	12 ft 8 in (3·85 m)
Height overall	6 ft 3½ in (1·92 m)

AREA:
Wings, gross	194·8 sq ft (18·10 m²)

WEIGHTS:
Weight empty, equipped	551 lb (250 kg)
Max T-O weight	838 lb (380 kg)

PERFORMANCE (estimated):
Best glide ratio, propeller folded
34 : 1 at 50 knots (57 mph; 92 km/h)
Min sinking speed 2·23 ft (0·68 m)/sec
T-O run, powered 230 ft (70 m)
Rate of climb, powered 985 ft (300 m)/min

FAUVEL AV.221 and AV.222

The AV.221 side-by-side two-seat self-launching sailplane was developed from the AV.22 tailless sailplane, of which details can be found in the 1960-61 Jane's. It flew for the first time on 8 April 1965.

The AV.221 has a short fuselage, mid-set high aspect ratio wings with slight sweep forward, a single large fin and rudder and non-retractable mono-wheel landing gear, with a small tail-wheel. The prototype is powered by a 39 hp Rectimo 4 AR 1200 conversion of the Volkswagen motor-car engine, mounted conventionally in the nose and driving a fixed-pitch wooden propeller.

The projected production version, designated AV.221B, was to be powered by M. Fauvel's new Pygmée four-cylinder horizontally-opposed four-stroke engine; but this had not been used on the AV.221 at the time of writing and the type will not now go into production.

The landing gear has been completely redesigned since the prototype first flew. The original large-tyred Piper Cub mono-wheel (without shock-absorber) and underwing balancers have been superseded by cantilever main legs, made in one continuous piece of laminated glass-resin plastic, carrying two 330 × 130 wheels with Durable disc brakes. There is no increase in drag from this faired gear and operation from rough fields will be considerably improved.

A version known as the **AV.222**, with a lighter and more simple structure and enhanced performance, is to be made available in plan form for amateur construction.

The following details apply to the prototype AV.221:

DIMENSIONS:
Wing span	50 ft 9½ in (15·48 m)
Wing aspect ratio	11·7
Length overall	15 ft 9 in (4·80 m)

AREA:
Wings, gross	242 sq ft (22·50 m²)

WEIGHTS:
Weight empty	748 lb (339 kg)
Max T-O weight	1,165 lb (528 kg)

PERFORMANCE:
Best glide ratio
25 : 1 at 46 knots (53 mph; 85 km/h)
Min sinking speed:
two crew: 2·95 ft (0·90 m)/sec at 41 knots (47 mph; 75 km/h)
pilot only: 2·62 ft (0·80 m)/sec at 36·5 knots (42 mph; 68 km/h)

Fauvel AV.221 self-launching sailplane

SIREN

SIREN S A

HEAD OFFICE:
13 rue Saint-Honoré, Versailles

WORKS AND AERODROME:
Argenton-sur-Creuse (Indre)

PRESIDENT, DIRECTOR GENERAL:
Emile Gottot

ASSISTANT DIRECTOR GENERAL AND CHIEF ENGINEER:
X. Laguette

SALES AND PUBLIC RELATIONS MANAGER:
J. P. Rajau

Well-known as a manufacturer of aircraft components and equipment, Siren is also producing a single-seat Standard Class sailplane known as the C.30S Edelweiss. Under development is a new single-seat Open Class sailplane designated Edelweiss IV.

SIREN C.30S EDELWEISS

The first of two prototypes of the Edelweiss flew for the first time on 25 September 1962. Both prototypes took part in the 1963 World Gliding Championships in the Argentine, finishing 2nd and 17th in the Standard Class contest.

The first of an initial series of 15 production Edelweiss was completed in January 1965. Six of this series were ordered by the SFA and two of them took part in the Standard Class contest at the 1965 World Gliding Championships. One, piloted by François Henry, won the event, with the other in 7th place. Edelweiss sailplanes also finished 8th and 10th in the Open Class.

The production version does not have the swept-forward wings of the prototype; its ailerons and air-brakes are of shorter span and the fuselage nose is shorter. Fifty had been delivered by 1 March 1968.

TYPE: Single-seat Standard Class sailplane.

WINGS: Cantilever shoulder-wing monoplane. Wing section NACA 64 series, modified as per series 7. Dihedral 3°. Incidence 4°. Single-spar all-wood structure covered with plywood/Klégécel sandwich with a thickness of 8 mm. Only eight ribs, of sandwich construction. Reinforced plastics wing-tips. All-metal unslotted ailerons. Retractable air-brakes in top and bottom surfaces.

FUSELAGE: Moulded plywood/Klégécel sandwich structure, with integral longerons, made in two portions. Laminated plastics nose and tail cones.

TAIL UNIT: "Butterfly" type (included angle 90°) comprising two identical all-moving surfaces, each with a trim-tab. Leading-edges of wooden sandwich construction, remainder fabric-covered.

LANDING GEAR: Non-retractable mono-wheel, size 330 × 130. Castoring leaf-spring tail-skid. Hydraulic brake interconnected with air-brakes.

ACCOMMODATION: Single reclining seat under long transparent canopy, hinged to starboard.

Siren C.30S Edelweiss single-seat Standard Class sailplane (*E. W. Wagner*)

EQUIPMENT: Standard items include ASI, variometer, turn and bank indicator, altimeter, compass, towing attachment and harness. Optional equipment includes covers, barograph, oxygen system, Jaeger altimeter, flight calculator and VHF radio.

DIMENSIONS:

Wing span	49 ft $2\frac{1}{2}$ in (15·00 m)
Wing chord at root	3 ft $7\frac{1}{2}$ in (1·11 m)
Wing chord at tip	1 ft $4\frac{1}{4}$ in (0·42 m)
Wing aspect ratio	18
Length overall	24 ft $7\frac{1}{4}$ in (7·50 m)
Tailplane span	5 ft 10 in (1·78 m)

AREAS:

Wings, gross	133·9 sq ft (12·5 m²)
Tail surfaces (total)	11·85 sq ft (1·10 m²)

WEIGHTS:

Weight empty, equipped	518 lb (235 kg)
Max T-O weight	838 lb (380 kg)

PERFORMANCE:

Best glide ratio	36 : 1 at 51 knots (59 mph; 95 km/h)
Min sinking speed	2·13 ft (0·65 m)/sec at 78 knots (90 mph; 145 km/h)
Stalling speed	approx 35 knots (40 mph; 65 km/h)
Max speed (smooth air)	122 knots (140 mph; 225 km/h)
Max speed (rough air)	86 knots (99 mph; 160 km/h)
Max aero-tow speed	97 knots (112 mph; 180 km/h)

SIREN EDELWEISS IV

Two prototypes of this new Open Class sailplane have been built by Siren. The first of them flew on 9 May 1968, and the flight test programme was continuing at the beginning of 1970. No production is yet planned.

TYPE: Single-seat Open Class sailplane.

WINGS: Cantilever shoulder-wing monoplane. Built in two panels, with sandwich skins and pinch-webbed spars with spruce booms. Wing-tips of reinforced plastic. Unslotted metal ailerons.

FUSELAGE: Completely moulded. Sandwich-type construction with built-in spruce longerons. Nose and tail cones are of laminated plastics.

TAIL UNIT: All-flying horizontal surfaces of delta shape, with trim-tabs. Leading-edge is of sandwich construction and the remainder fabric-covered.

CONTROLS: The ailerons are operated by cables in the fuselage and rods in the wings, the air-brakes by semi-rigid controls in the fuselage and rods in the wings. The elevator, rudder and trim-tabs are operated by semi-rigid controls.

LANDING GEAR: Retractable mono-wheel. Hydraulic wheel brake and air-brakes are linked to operate together.

EQUIPMENT: Can be fitted with full range of modern equipment, including VHF radio and oxygen.

DIMENSIONS:

Wing span	57 ft $4\frac{3}{4}$ in (17·50 m)
Wing aspect ratio	20
Length overall	25 ft 7 in (7·80 m)

AREAS:

Wings, gross	164·68 sq ft (15·30 m²)

WEIGHT:

Max T-O weight	1,058 lb (480 kg)

PERFORMANCE (estimated):

Best glide ratio	40 : 1 at 87 knots (100 mph; 160 km/h)
Min sinking speed	5·58 ft (1·70 m)/sec at 81 knots (93 mph; 150 km/h)
Max speed	129 knots (149 mph; 240 km/h)

WASSMER

WASSMER-AVIATION S A

HEAD OFFICE AND WORKS:
Aérodrome d'Issoire, 63-Issoire

In addition to manufacturing light aeroplanes, as described in the "Aircraft" section, Wassmer have long been famous as builders of gliders and sailplanes. These included the successful Javelot and Super-Javelot single-seat sailplanes and the AV.36 tail-less single-seat sailplane designed by M. Charles Fauvel which are no longer in production. Details of these types can be found in previous editions of *Jane's*.

In current production are the WA-26 Squale and WA-30 Bijave.

WASSMER WA-26 SQUALE

The prototype of this new 15-m single-seat high-performance sailplane flew for the first time on 21 July 1967. Series production started in 1968 and by January 1970 orders for 85 Squales had been placed.

TYPE: Single-seat high-performance sailplane.

WINGS: Cantilever shoulder-wing monoplane. Wing section FX 61 163 at root, FX 60 126 at tip. Dihedral 3°. Orthodox wood construction. Trailing-edge air brakes inboard of ailerons.

FUSELAGE: Reinforced polyester plastics structure of oval section.

TAIL UNIT: Conventional wood structure with fabric covering. All-moving horizontal surfaces, with anti-tab.

LANDING GEAR: Retractable mono-wheel mounted forward of CG. Wassmer size 330 × 130 mm wheel; tyre pressure 28·5 lb/sq in (2 kg/cm²). Satmo hydraulic brake. Optional fixed wheel.

Wassmer WA-26 Squale single-seat high-performance sailplane

ACCOMMODATION: Single semi-reclining adjustable seat under a long flush Plexiglas canopy.

DIMENSIONS:

Wing span	49 ft $2\frac{1}{2}$ in (15·0 m)
Wing chord at root	3 ft $7\frac{1}{4}$ in (1·10 m)
Wing chord at tip	1 ft $3\frac{3}{4}$ in (0·40 m)
Wing aspect ratio	18
Length overall	24 ft $10\frac{3}{4}$ in (7·6 m)
Height over tail	4 ft 9 in (1·45 m)
Tailplane span	9 ft $10\frac{3}{4}$ in (3·0 m)

AREAS:

Wings, gross	135·6 sq ft (12·6 m²)
Rudder	11·84 sq ft (1·1 m²)
Tailplane	16·15 sq ft (1·5 m²)

WEIGHTS:

Weight empty	540 lb (245 kg)
Max T-O weight	833 lb (378 kg)

PERFORMANCE:

Best glide ratio
38:1 at 48·5 knots (56 mph; 90 km/h)

Sinking speed
2 ft (0·61 m)/sec at 39 knots (45 mph; 72 km/h)
2·62 ft (0·80 m)/sec at 54 knots (62 mph; 100 km/h)
3·60 ft (1·10 m)/sec at 65 knots (75 mph; 120 km/h)
6·39 ft (1·95 m)/sec at 81 knots (93 mph; 150 km/h)

Stalling speed at max T-O weight
35 knots (40 mph; 64 km/h)

Max speed (smooth air)
134 knots (155 mph; 250 km/h)

Max speed (rough air)
97 knots (112 mph; 180 km/h)

Max aero-tow speed
81 knots (93 mph; 150 km/h)

g limit 8 (Norme Air 2054)

WASSMER WA-30 BIJAVE

The Bijave is a two-seat advanced training glider, developed from the WA-21 Javelot. The first prototype flew for the first time on 17 December 1958 and the second, improved prototype on 18 March 1960. About 285 had been built by early 1970, with production continuing at the rate of four per month.

TYPE: Two-seat advanced training glider.

WINGS: Cantilever shoulder-wing monoplane. Wing section NACA 63·821 at root, NACA 63·615 at tip. Dihedral 0° at root, 4° 30′ on outer wings. Incidence 4°. Wood structure, with birch plywood covering forward of spar, fabric covering aft of spar. Plain spruce ailerons, fabric-covered. No flaps. Perforated wooden air-brakes, retracting into slots above and below each wing. Wing-tip "salmons".

FUSELAGE: Welded steel-tube structure, covered with fabric and reinforced plastics.

TAIL UNIT: Cantilever wood structure with fabric-covered control surfaces. All-moving one-piece tailplane, with large tab.

LANDING GEAR: Retractable mono-wheel, size 330 × 130. Niemann rubber-ring shock-absorption. Dunlop or Kléber-Colombes tyre, pressure 43 lb/sq in (3 kg/cm^2). SATMO motor-cycle brake. Rubber-sprung wooden nose-skid. Steel tail-skid.

ACCOMMODATION: Two persons in tandem under individual Plexiglas transparent canopies. Equipment can include full range of instruments, compass, oxygen and radio.

DIMENSIONS:

Wing span	55 ft 3 in (16·85 m)
Wing chord at root	4 ft 3 in (1·30 m)
Wing chord at tip	2 ft $5\frac{1}{8}$ in (0·74 m)
Wing aspect ratio	15
Length overall	31 ft 2 in (9·50 m)
Height over tail	9 ft 0 in (2·74 m)
Tailplane span	10 ft 6 in (3·20 m)

AREAS:

Wings, gross	206·7 sq ft (19·20 m^2)
Ailerons (total)	24·11 sq ft (2·24 m^2)
Vertical tail surfaces (total)	17·22 sq ft (1·60 m^2)
Horizontal tail surfaces (total)	28·00 sq ft (2·60 m^2)

WEIGHTS:

Weight empty, with min equipment	639 lb (290 kg)
Max T-O weight	1,102 lb (500 kg)

PERFORMANCE (at max T-O weight):

Best glide ratio
30 : 1 at 46 knots (53 mph; 85 km/h)

Sinking speed:
2·30 ft (0·70 m)/sec at 41 knots (47 mph; 75 km/h)
3·60 ft (1·10 m)/sec at 54 knots (62 mph; 100 km/h)
5·57 ft (1·70 m)/sec at 65 knots (75 mph; (120 km/h)

Stalling speed 33 knots (37 mph; 60 km/h)

Max speed (smooth air)
129 knots (149 mph; 240 km/h)

Max speed (rough air)
81 knots (93 mph; 150 km/h)

Wassmer WA-30 Bijave

Max aero-tow speed
81 knots (93 mph; 150 km/h)

Max winch-launching speed
54 knots (62 mph; 100 km/h)

GERMANY

THE GERMAN FEDERAL REPUBLIC

AKAFLIEG BRAUNSCHWEIG

AKADEMISCHE FLIEGERGRUPPE BRAUNSCHWEIG

ADDRESS:
Technische Universität Braunschweig, 3300 Braunschweig, Pockelstrasse 4

The students of Brunswick University have built a series of high-performance sailplanes. Details of four of the latest are given below.

AKAFLIEG BRAUNSCHWEIG SB-5c DANZIG

The prototype SB-5 flew for the first time on 3 June 1959. Licence production was undertaken by Fa Eichelsdörfer, 86 Bamberg, Hafenstrasse 6, and 15 more had been built by the spring of 1966. The current version, first flown in 1965, is the SB-5c, incorporating a number of design changes, and a total of about 20 have been built.

TYPE: Single-seat Standard Class sailplane.

WINGS: Cantilever shoulder-wing monoplane. Wing section NACA 63_3-618. Dihedral 1° 30′. Incidence 0° 30′. Conventional single-spar wood structure with plywood covering. Wooden ailerons. Schempp-Hirth air-brakes at 50% chord.

FUSELAGE: Plywood monocoque of circular section.

TAIL UNIT: "Butterfly" type, of wooden construction.

LANDING GEAR: Non-retractable unsprung monowheel, size 4·00 × 4, with friction brake. Tyre pressure 28 lb/sq in (2·0 kg/cm^2). Tail-skid.

ACCOMMODATION: Single seat under drawn Plexiglas canopy.

DIMENSIONS:

Wing span	49 ft $2\frac{1}{2}$ in (15·00 m)
Wing chord at root	3 ft $3\frac{1}{4}$ in (1·00 m)
Wing chord at tip	1 ft $7\frac{3}{4}$ in (0·50 m)
Wing aspect ratio	17·3
Length overall	21 ft 10 in (6·65 m)
Tailplane span (horizontal projection)	9 ft $2\frac{1}{4}$ in (2·80 m)
Max width of fuselage	1 ft $11\frac{1}{2}$ in (0·60 m)

AREAS:

Wings, gross	140 sq ft (13·00 m^2)
Air-brakes	4·20 sq ft (0·39 m^2)
Fin (projected)	7·53 sq ft (0·7 m^2)
Rudder (projected)	5·38 sq ft (0·5 m^2)
Tailplane (projected)	10·76 sq ft (1·0 m^2)
Elevators (projected)	7·53 sq ft (0·7 m^2)

WEIGHTS AND LOADING:

Weight empty, equipped	507 lb (230 kg)
Max T-O weight	716 lb (325 kg)
Max wing loading	5·12 lb/sq ft (25·0 kg/m^2)

PERFORMANCE (at max T-O weight):

Best glide ratio
32·5 : 1 at 42 knots (48 mph; 77 km/h)

Min sinking speed
2·07 ft (0·63 m)/sec at 36 knots (41 mph; 66 km/h)

Stalling speed 32 knots (37 mph; 60 km/h)

Max speed (smooth air)
108 knots (124 mph; 200 km/h)

Max speed (rough air)
76 knots (87 mph; 140 km/h)

Max aero-tow speed
59 knots (68 mph; 110 km/h)

Max winch-launching speed
49 knots (56 mph ; 90 km/h)

Akaflieg Braunschweig SB-5c single-seat high-performance sailplane

Akaflieg Braunschweig SB-7 single-seat Standard Class sailplane

AKAFLIEG BRAUNSCHWEIG SB-7 NIMBUS

This Standard Class sailplane, which flew for the first time in October 1962, is a development of the SB-6, which was described in the 1964-65 *Jane's*. It has since been fitted with new horizontal tail surfaces.

A modified version of the SB-7, with increased span, is described and illustrated in the Swiss section under the names of its builders, Paul Kummer and Oskar Wiesendanger.

TYPE: Single-seat Standard Class sailplane.

WINGS: Cantilever shoulder-wing monoplane. Eppler 306 wing section. Thickness/chord ratio 12%. Dihedral 2°. Incidence 1°. Box spar with glass-fibre flanges, covered with diagonally-laid glass-fibre skin, stabilised with balsa. Schempp-Hirth air-brakes at 75% chord.

FUSELAGE: Glass-fibre monocoque, stabilised with balsa.

TAIL UNIT: Cantilever structure of similar construction to wing, with tailplane mounted at tip of fin. One-piece all-moving tailplane, with anti-balance tab.

LANDING GEAR: Retractable unsprung monowheel size 4·00 × 4, with rubber friction brake. Tyre pressure 28 lb/sq in (2·0 kg/cm^2). Tail-skid.

ACCOMMODATION: Single seat under drawn Plexiglas canopy.

DIMENSIONS:

Wing span	49 ft $2\frac{1}{2}$ in (15·00 m)
Wing chord at root	3 ft $0\frac{1}{4}$ in (0·92 m)
Wing chord at tip	1 ft $5\frac{3}{4}$ in (0·45 m)
Wing aspect ratio	19
Length overall	22 ft $11\frac{1}{2}$ in (7·00 m)
Height over cockpit	2 ft 5 in (0·74 m)
Tailplane span	8 ft $2\frac{1}{2}$ in (2·50 m)
Max width of fuselage	1 ft $10\frac{1}{2}$ in (0·57 m)

AREAS:
Wings, gross	127·6 sq ft	(11·85 m²)
Air-brakes	2·05 sq ft	(0·19 m²)
Fin	6·46 sq ft	(0·60 m²)
Rudder	4·31 sq ft	(0·40 m²)
Tailplane	10·75 sq ft	(1·00 m²)

WEIGHTS AND LOADING:
Weight empty, equipped	562 lb	(255 kg)
Max T-O weight	794 lb	(360 kg)
Max wing loading	6·14 lb/sq ft	(30 kg/m²)

PERFORMANCE (at max T-O weight):
Best glide ratio
37·5 : 1 at 49 knots (56 mph; 90 km/h)
Min sinking speed
2·20 ft (0·67 m)/sec at 49 knots (56 mph; 90 km/h)
Minimum speed 40 knots (46 mph; 73 km/h)
Max speed (smooth air)
137 knots (158 mph; 254 km/h)
Max speed (rough air)
97 knots (112 mph; 180 km/h)
Max aero-tow speed
65 knots (75 mph; 120 km/h)
Max winch-launching speed
49 knots (56 mph; 90 km/h)

Akaflieg Braunschweig SB-8 single-seat high-performance sailplane

Akaflieg Braunschweig SB-9 single-seat high-performance sailplane

AKAFLIEG BRAUNSCHWEIG SB-8

The SB-8 flew for the first time on 25 April 1967. It is built mainly of balsa wood/glass-fibre/plastic sandwich.

TYPE: Single-seat high-performance sailplane.

WINGS: Cantilever shoulder-wing monoplane. Wing section Wortmann 62-K-153 at root, 62-K-131 at mid-span, 60-126 at tip. Dihedral 1° 30'. Incidence 1° 30'. Sweep-forward 1° at quarter-chord (straight leading-edge). Balsa and glass-fibre structure. Lower-surface-hinged ailerons, which can be drooped with flaps to give full-span trailing-edge flaps. Schempp-Hirth air-brakes of duralumin.

FUSELAGE: Balsa/glass-fibre structure, contracted aft of wings.

TAIL UNIT: Cantilever structure of balsa and glass-fibre, with tailplane mounted at tip of fin.

LANDING GEAR: Unsprung retractable mono-wheel. Tyre size 380 × 150, pressure 31·5 lb/sq in (2·2 kg/cm²). Manual retraction, via push-strut. Drum-type brake.

ACCOMMODATION: Single semi-reclining seat under small transparent canopy.

DIMENSIONS, EXTERNAL:
Wing span	59 ft 0½ in	(18·00 m)
Wing chord at root	3 ft 2¼ in	(0·97 m)
Wing chord at tip	2 ft 7¾ in	(0·81 m)
Wing aspect ratio		23
Length overall	25 ft 3 in	(7·70 m)
Height over tail	4 ft 11 in	(1·50 m)
Tailplane span	8 ft 10 in	(2·70 m)
Max width of fuselage	1 ft 11½ in	(0·60 m)

AREAS:
Wings, gross	151·8 sq ft	(14·10 m²)
Ailerons (total)	10·23 sq ft	(0·95 m²)
Fin	9·15 sq ft	(0·85 m²)
Rudder	4·85 sq ft	(0·45 m²)
Tailplane	9·80 sq ft	(0·91 m²)
Elevators	4·20 sq ft	(0·39 m²)

WEIGHTS AND LOADING:
Weight empty	485 lb	(220 kg)
Max T-O weight	716 lb	(325 kg)
Max wing loading	4·71 lb/sq ft	(23 kg/m²)

PERFORMANCE (estimated):
Best glide ratio
41 : 1 at 44 knots (51 mph; 82 km/h)
Min sinking speed
1·64 ft (0·50 m)/sec at 37 knots 42 mph; 67 km/h)
Stalling speed 30 knots (34 mph; 55 km/h)
Max speed (smooth air and rough air)
108 knots (124 mph; 200 km/h)
Max aero-tow speed
76 knots (87 mph; 140 km/h)
Max winch-launching speed
65 knots (75 mph; 120 km/h)

AKAFLIEG BRAUNSCHWEIG SB-9 STRATUS

The SB-9 Stratus, which is a development of the SB-8 with increased wing span, flew for the first time on 23 January 1969.

The description of the SB-8 applies also to the SB-9, except in the following details.

WINGS: Incidence 0°. Sweep-forward at quarter-chord 1° 6'. Lift-increasing continuously-variable trailing-edge flaps of elastic glass-fibre construction. Schempp-Hirth air-brakes of duralumin at 50% chord.

DIMENSIONS:
Wing span	72 ft 2 in	(22·00 m)
Wing chord at root	3 ft 2½ in	(0·98 m)
Wing chord, mean	2 ft 3½ in	(0·70 m)
Wing chord at tip	10 in	(0·26 m)
Wing aspect ratio		31·3
Length overall	24 ft 7¼ in	(7·50 m)
Height over tail	4 ft 7 in	(1·40 m)

AREAS:
Wings, gross	167 sq ft	(15·48 m²)
Ailerons (total)	14·3 sq ft	(1·33 m²)
Trailing-edge flaps	18·2 sq ft	(1·69 m²)
Fin	7·75 sq ft	(0·72 m²)
Rudder	6·24 sq ft	(0·58 m²)

WEIGHTS AND LOADING:
Weight empty	692 lb	(314 kg)
Max T-O weight	917 lb	(416 kg)
Max wing loading	5·5 lb/sq ft	(27 kg/m²)

PERFORMANCE:
Best glide ratio
48 : 1 at 46 knots (53 mph; 85 km/h)
Min sinking speed
1·48 ft (0·45 m)/sec at 39 knots (45 mph; 72 km/h)
Stalling speed 33 knots (37 mph; 59 km/h)
Max speed (smooth or rough air)
97 knots (112 mph; 180 km/h)
Max aero-tow speed
65 knots (75 mph; 120 km/h)
Max winch-launching speed
59 knots (68 mph; 110 km/h)

AKAFLIEG DARMSTADT
AKADEMISCHE FLIEGERGRUPPE DARMSTADT EV

ADDRESS:
Technische Hochschule, 61 Darmstadt

The *Fliegergruppe* of Darmstadt University has been designing, building and flying sail-planes for over 40 years. Its first major post-war product was the D-34a single-seat high-performance sailplane, which flew for the first time in 1955. An improved version, designated the D-34b, flew for the first time in the Autumn of 1956. This was described in the 1962-63 *Jane's*, together with the D-34c, first flown in the Spring of 1958, and the D-34d, which flew for the first time in March 1961. A full description of the later D-36 Circe can be found in the 1965-66 *Jane's*. It has been followed by the D-37 powered sailplane.

AKAFLIEG DARMSTADT D-37 ARTEMIS

The D-37 is a power-assisted high-performance sailplane, the prototype of which flew for the first time on 5 August 1969. The Wankel engine, normally completely retracted into the fuselage, can be swung out if necessary to overcome bad weather areas or to return from long-distance cross-country soaring flights. It is not intended to use the engine for self-launching. A drogue parachute (diameter 4 ft 3 in; 1·30 m) can be deployed to permit landings in confined fields.

TYPE: Power-assisted high-performance sailplane.

WINGS: Cantilever shoulder-wing monoplane. Wing section Wortmann FX 66-S-196 at centre-line and FX 66-S-160 at tip. Thickness/chord ratio 19·6% at root, 16% at tip. Dihedral 2°. Incidence 2°. No sweepback at quarter-chord. Wing shell is a glass-fibre/foam Klégécel sandwich structure. Schempp-Hirth-Friess dural air-brakes fitted.

FUSELAGE: Glass-fibre/balsa sandwich shell. Landing gear and engine mounting are attached to steel-tube structure.

Akaflieg Darmstadt D-37 Artemis power-assisted high-performance sailplane

TAIL UNIT: Cantilever structure of glass-fibre/balsa sandwich, with tailplane mounted at tip of fin. No tabs.

LANDING GEAR: Hand-operated retractable mono-wheel, forward of CG, and tail skid. Tost drum brake. Dunlop tyre, pressure 36 lb/sq in (2·5 kg/m²).

POWER PLANT: One air-cooled Wankel F-S KM 914. Weight 62 lb (28 kg). Fuel capacity 8·80 Imp gallons (40 litres).

ACCOMMODATION: Single semi-reclining seat under flush transparent canopy, the rear section of which is removable. Standard instruments. Radio optional.

DIMENSIONS, EXTERNAL:
Wing span	59 ft 0½ in	(18·00 m)
Wing chord at root	3 ft 1¼ in	(0·95 m)
Wing chord at tip	1 ft 0½ in	(0·32 m)
Wing aspect ratio		24·8
Length overall	24 ft 3¼ in	(7·40 m)
Height overall	6 ft 4¾ in	(1·95 m)
Tailplane span	7 ft 3½ in	(2·30 m)

AREAS:
Wings, gross	139·93 sq ft	(13 m²)
Vertical tail surfaces (total)	13·67 sq ft	(1·27 m²)
Horizontal tail surfaces (total)	10·76 sq ft	(1·00 m²)

WEIGHTS AND LOADING:
Weight empty, equipped	661 lb	(300 kg)
Max T-O weight	1,014 lb	(460 kg)
Max wing loading	7·25 lb/sq ft	(35·4 kg/m²)

PERFORMANCE (estimated):
Best glide ratio
42 : 1 at 52 knots (60 mph; 97 km/h)
Min sinking speed
1·84 ft (0·58 m)/sec at 44 knots (51 mph; 82 km/h)
Max cruising speed, with motor
65 knots (75 mph; 120 km/h)
Rate of climb with motor 177 ft (54 m)/min
Max duration, with motor 5 hours

BLESSING

G. BLESSING

ADDRESS:
2051 Hamburg - Ochsenwerder, Ochsenwerder
Landstrasse 23

BLESSING GLEITER MAX

Herr Gerhard Blessing, a well-known German glider pilot, has completed the prototype (D-KOBI) of a two-seat powered glider called the Gleiter Max. As the accompanying illustration shows, the Gleiter Max is a mid-wing monoplane, of pod-and-boom configuration, with large vertical tail surfaces at the top of which the horizontal surfaces are mounted. The two occupants are seated in tandem under a large one-piece transparent canopy which hinges sideways to starboard to provide easy access to both cockpits. Power plant is a 52 hp Porsche engine, which is started electrically and is mounted aft of the rear cockpit, driving a metal two-blade pusher propeller.

DIMENSIONS, EXTERNAL:
Wing span   50 ft 2¼ in (15·30 m)

Blessing Gleiter Max two-seat powered glider (52 hp Porsche engine)

Length overall	23 ft 11½ in (7·30 m)	
WEIGHTS AND LOADING:		
Weight empty	1,058 lb (480 kg)	
Max T-O weight	1,500 lb (680 kg)	
Wing loading	7·54 lb/sq ft (36·8 kg/m²)	

PERFORMANCE (at max T-O weight):
Cruising speed   81 knots (93 mph; 150 km/h)
Min safe speed   38 knots (43·5 mph; 70 km/h)
Rate of climb at S/L   354 ft (108 m)/min
T-O run   820 ft (250 m)

ESPE

GOTTHOLD ESPENLAUB

Gotthold Espenlaub has been working on the design of a twin-engined powered sailplane for two years. Designated the Espe-37T, this new aircraft is being built with the assistance of Peter Kürten and Werner Rüker.

ESPE-37T

TYPE: Two-seat twin-engined powered sailplane.

WINGS: Cantilever high-wing monoplane. Wing section NACA 633-608. Three-piece structure of wooden construction. For transportation the outer sections can be folded back along the sides. Trailing-edge flaps.

FUSELAGE: Steel-tube framework, fabric-covered.

TAIL UNIT: T-tail of wooden construction.

LANDING GEAR: Non-retractable central wheel; manually retractable nose-wheel and electrically-operated lateral supporting wheels.

POWER PLANT: Two 26 hp Hirth F-10 piston-engines, driving 4 ft 3 in (1·30 m) diameter Hoco propellers. Electrical starting.

ACCOMMODATION: Two seats in tandem in enclosed cockpit.

DIMENSIONS:
Wing span	55 ft 0 in (16·76 m)
Wing centre-section width	9 ft 10 in (3·00 m)
Length overall	30 ft 3¾ in (9·24 m)
Height	5 ft 11 in (1·80 m)

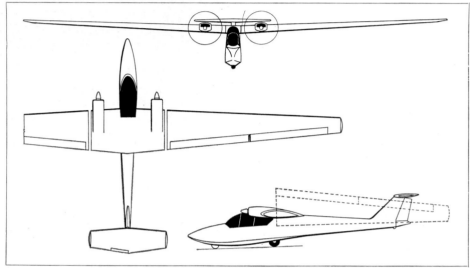

Espe-37T two-seat twin-engined powered sailpane

WEIGHTS:
Weight empty, equipped	926 lb (420 kg)
Max T-O weight	1,433 lb (650 kg)

PERFORMANCE (estimated):
Cruising speed   81 knots (93 mph; 150 km/h)

GLASFLÜGEL

GLASFLÜGEL, ING EUGEN HÄNLE

ADDRESS: 7311 Schlattstall Krs, Nürtingen

This company is responsible for series production of the Standard Libelle, developed from the Hütter H 30 GFK and H 301 of which details appeared in earlier editions of *Jane's*.

Glasflügel has delivered 18 examples of a new version of Björn Stender's BS 1, utilising the same type of all-glass-fibre construction as in the Libelle. It is expanding production to include in its range the high-performance single-seat 17-m Kestrel and a new 18·7-m BS 1b with a three-piece wing.

A new company known as Glasflügel Italiana has been established in Italy to produce in that country sailplanes designed by the parent company.

GLASFLÜGEL STANDARD LIBELLE

The Standard Libelle was developed from the H 301, described in the 1968-69 edition of *Jane's*, to meet the demand for a simple lower-cost glass-fibre sailplane in the Standard Class. The distinctive lines and proportions of the original Libelle have been retained, but terminal velocity dive-brakes have been fitted and a new wing profile utilised to ensure high performance and pleasant handling characteristics without flaps.

A Standard Libelle flown by Per-Axel Persson of Sweden finished in second position in the Standard Class of the 1968 World Gliding Championships in Poland. It is now in quantity production, with deliveries scheduled to begin in November 1970.

TYPE: Single-seat high-performance Standard Class sailplane.

WINGS: Two-piece glass-fibre and balsa sandwich skins, with unidirectional glass-fibre spar caps produced by HH method. Glass-fibre and balsa shear web. Partially mass-balanced ailerons. Flush-fitting terminal velocity dive-brakes.

FUSELAGE: Glass-fibre (not sandwich) monocoque construction.

TAIL UNIT: Glass-fibre and balsa sandwich construction. Automatic elevator connection. Spring trim.

Glasflügel Standard Libelle single-seat high-performance sailplane (*Flight International*)

LANDING GEAR: Retractable or non-retractable mono-wheel, with internal-expanding brake. Interchangeable tail wheel or skid.

ACCOMMODATION: Single seat under large canopy.

EQUIPMENT: Standard items include removable drawer-type instrument panel, built-in VHF antenna, provision for radio and oxygen. Adjustable seat and rudder pedals and inflatable cushions permit seating positions to be changed in flight.

DIMENSIONS:
Wing span	49 ft 2½ in (15 m)
Wing aspect ratio	23·6
Length overall	23 ft 2½ in (7·07 m)
Height over rudder	4 ft 4 in (1·31 m)

AREA:
Wings, gross	102·3 sq ft (9·50 m²)

WEIGHTS:
Weight empty	375 lb (170 kg)
Max T-O weight	640 lb (290 kg)

PERFORMANCE:
Best glide ratio
38 : 1 at 46 knots (53 mph; 85 km/h)
Min sinking speed   1·97 ft (0·60 m)/sec at
46 knots (53 mph; 85 km/h)
Stalling speed   35 knots (40 mph; 64 km/h)
Max speed (smooth air)
135 knots (155 mph; 250 km/h)
Max speed (rough air)
113 knots (130 mph; 209 km/h)

GLASFLÜGEL KESTREL

The Kestrel is currently under development at Glasflügel as an advanced Open Class sailplane. This project was known originally as the "17-metre Libelle", but the design now incorporates many new features and a separate identity was desirable. In addition to proven Libelle features, the Kestrel has a larger cockpit canopy, a new fuselage profile and a T-tail. Deliveries of production Kestrels are scheduled to begin late in 1971.

TYPE: Single-seat high-performance Open Class sailplane.

WINGS: Two-piece glass-fibre and balsa sandwich skins, with unidirectional glass-fibre open caps produced by the HH method. Glass-fibre and balsa sandwich shear web. Partially mass-balanced ailerons and camber-changing flaps. Flush-fitting dive-brakes.

FUSELAGE, TAIL UNIT AND LANDING GEAR: Similar in configuration and construction to those of BS 1b.

DIMENSIONS:
Wing span	55 ft 8½ in (17·0 m)
Wing aspect ratio	25·1
Length overall	21 ft 7¼ in (6·58 m)
Height over rudder	4 ft 4¾ in (1·33 m)

AREA:
Wings, gross	123·7 sq ft (11·50 m²)

WEIGHTS:
Weight empty   463 lb (210 kg)
Max T-O weight   772 lb (350 kg)
PERFORMANCE (estimated):
Best glide ratio
     43 : 1 at 54 knots (62 mph; 100 km/h)
Min sinking speed   1·7 ft (0·52 m)/sec at
     37 knots (43 mph; 70 km/h)
Stalling speed   33 knots (37 mph; 60 km/h)
Max speed (smooth air)
     135 knots (155 mph; 250 km/h)
Max speed (rough air)
     119 knots (137 mph; 220 km/h)

GLASFLÜGEL BS 1

The first of two prototypes of this single-seat high-performance open class sailplane flew for the first time on 24 May 1966. The basic configuration is the same as that of the original BS 1 of Björn Stender, but the structural design has been completely changed and is now similar to that of the Libelle.

Sixteen BS 1's had been built and delivered by Glasflügel by the spring of 1968. Their successes include first place in the 1966 German National and 1967 Swiss National Gliding Competitions.

TYPE: Single-seat high-performance sailplane.

WINGS: Cantilever shoulder-wing monoplane. Wing section Eppler 348K. Double trapezoidal planform. Glass-reinforced plastic/balsa/glass-reinforced plastic sandwich construction. Single spar web, of similar construction to wings, with unidirectional glass-fibre caps, and glass-reinforced plastic ribs, Ailerons linked differentially with high-lift flaps, all partially mass-balanced. Glass-reinforced plastic air-brakes.

FUSELAGE: All-glass-fibre monocoque structure. Glass-reinforced plastic bulkhead strengthening.

TAIL UNIT: Cantilever type, of similar construction to wings, with all-flying tailplane mounted at tip of fin. Spring damping on tailplane.

LANDING GEAR: Retractable main wheel, with drum brake. Tailwheel semi-enclosed in fuselage. Landing with gear up is possible. Releasable tail-chute, diameter 4 ft (1·22 m).

ACCOMMODATION: Semi-reclining seat under long flush transparent canopy which contains clear panel window. Seat back and rudder pedals adjustable.

EQUIPMENT: Standard equipment includes two towing hooks, ventilators, seat pillow with inflatable knee supports, map pocket, head-rest, safety harness, instrument panel, four thermos bottles. Provision for radio and oxygen system.

DIMENSIONS:
Wing span   59 ft 0½ in (18·00 m)
Wing aspect ratio   23
Length overall   24 ft 7 in (7·50 m)
Height over tail unit   4 ft 11 in (1·50 m)
AREA:
Wings, gross   151·7 sq ft (14·10 m²)
WEIGHTS:
Weight empty   684 lb (310 kg)
Max T-O weight   993 lb (450 kg)

Glasflügel Kestrel single-seat high-performance sailplane (*Anne Ince*)

Glasflügel BS 1 single-seat high-performance sailplane

PERFORMANCE (at AUW of 950 lb = 430 kg):
Best glide ratio
     44 : 1 at 51 knots (59 mph; 95 km/h)
Max speed (smooth or rough air)
     135 knots (155 mph; 250 km/h)

GLASFLÜGEL BS 1b

Developed from the BS 1, designed by the late Björn Stender, the BS 1b follows the general lines of the original design but has a new wing section for improved performance in weak lift conditions. The three-piece wing also has a larger span than that of the BS 1, and a new fuselage profile provides more space in the cockpit.

TYPE: Single-seat high-performance Open Class sailplane.

WINGS: Cantilever shoulder-wing monoplane. Three-piece structure, with glass-fibre and balsa sandwich skins and unidirectional glass-fibre spar caps produced by the HH method. Glass-fibre and balsa shear web. Partially mass-balanced ailerons. Camber-changing (high-lift) flaps. Flush-fitting dive-brakes.

FUSELAGE: Glass-fibre monocoque (not sandwich) structure.

TAIL UNIT: Glass-fibre and balsa sandwich construction. Fin has quick-fitting attachment for all-flying tailplane mounted at tip. Tailplane has spring trim.

LANDING GEAR: Retractable main wheel, with drum brake, and tail-wheel. Releasable tail-chute. Approved for wheel-up landing in rough terrain.

DIMENSIONS:
Wing span   61 ft 4 in (18·7 m)
Wing aspect ratio   25
Length overall   24 ft 7 in (7·50 m)
Height over rudder   4 ft 10¾ in (1·50 m)
AREA:
Wings, gross   150·6 sq ft (14·00 m²)
WEIGHTS:
Weight empty   639 lb (290 kg)
Max T-O weight   992 lb (450 kg)
PERFORMANCE:
Best glide ratio
     45 : 1 at 54 knots (62 mph; 100 km/h)
Min sinking speed   1·64 ft (0·5 m)/sec at
     41 knots (47 mph; 75 km/h)
Stalling speed   35 knots (40 mph; 64 km/h)
Max speed (smooth or rough air)
     135 knots (155 mph; 250 km/h)

HIRTH
WOLF HIRTH GmbH
ADDRESS: 7311 Nabern-Teck

HIRTH Hi 26 MOSE II

Wolf Hirth has almost completed the prototype of this two-seat powered sailplane. Design was initiated in January 1968 and construction of the prototype began in August 1969. All available details follow:

TYPE: Two-seat powered sailplane.

WINGS: Cantilever mid-wing monoplane. Wing section Wortmann FX 196. Thickness/chord ratio 19·6%. Dihedral 1° 30′. Wings and ailerons have wood and glass-fibre structure with fabric covering. SHK spoilers.

FUSELAGE: Welded steel-tube structure covered with glass-fibre.

TAIL UNIT: Cantilever structure of glass-fibre and wood with fabric covering. T-type tail with variable-incidence tailplane mounted at top of fin. Trim-tab in horizontal surfaces.

LANDING GEAR: Manually-retractable tricycle landing gear. Centre-fuselage and tail skids for emergency landing.

ACCOMMODATION: Two seats side-by-side under transparent cockpit canopy.

DIMENSIONS:
Wing span   59 ft 0¾ in (18·0 m)
Wing aspect ratio   14·75
Length overall   27 ft 2¾ in (8·30 m)

MBB
MESSERSCHMITT-BÖLKOW-BLOHM GmbH
HEAD OFFICE:
Ottobrunn bei München, München 8
P.O.B. 801220

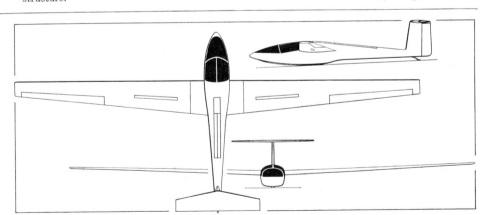

Three-view drawing of Hirth Hi 26 Mose II powered sailplane prototype

Height overall   3 ft 9¼ in (1·15 m)
Tailplane span   12 ft 3½ in (3·75 m)
AREA:
Wings, gross   237 sq ft (22·0 m²)
WEIGHTS AND LOADING:
Weight empty   936 lb (425 kg)
Max T-O weight   1,433 lb (650 kg)
Max wing loading   6·1 lb/sq ft (30 kg/m²)

Details of the Phönix T single-seat high-performance sailplane, built by Bölkow, were given in the 1962-63 *Jane's*. MBB is now producing at the group's Laupheim plant a new sailplane of similar balsa/glass-fibre sandwich construction, named the Phœbus.

PERFORMANCE (estimated):
Best glide ratio
     32 : 1 at 46 knots (53 mph; 85 km/h)
Min sinking speed   2·46 ft (0·75 m)/sec at
     40·5 knots (46·6 mph; 75 km/h)
Stalling speed   34 knots (39 mph; 62 km/h)
Max speed (rough or smooth air)
     135 knots (155 mph; 250 km/h)
Ultimate load factor   8g

L-252 PHŒBUS

The prototype Phœbus, designed by Ings Eppler and Nägele and built by R. Linder, first flew on 4 April 1964. It came third in the Standard Class contest at the 1964 German national gliding championships and 8th in the

1965 World Gliding Championships.

In 1966, production Phœbus came first and third in the South African international championships, and first in the German Championships, and also won the Coupe d'Europe. There are three versions, as follows:

Phœbus A. Standard Class sailplane with 15-m span and non-retractable landing gear. First production model flew on 27 February 1965.

Phœbus B. Similar to Phœbus A, but with retractable landing gear. First production model flew on 13 April 1966.

Phœbus C. Similar to Phœbus B, but with wing span increased to 17 m. First production model flew on 26 April 1967.

A Phœbus C, piloted by Göran Ax of Sweden, finished in second place in the Open Class of the 1968 World Gliding Championships in Poland. A Phœbus A, flown by Rudolf Lindner of West Germany, came third in the Standard Class.

By early 1970, a total of 250 Phœbus sailplanes of all versions had been built.

TYPE: Single-seat high-performance sailplane.

WINGS: Cantilever shoulder-wing monoplane. Eppler 403 wing section. Thickness/chord ratio 15%. Dihedral 2° 45′. Incidence 2°. Sweepback —1·3° at quarter-chord. Glass-fibre/balsa sandwich structure. Schempp-Hirth alloy air-brake at 70% chord on each wing.

FUSELAGE: Glass-fibre/balsa sandwich monocoque structure.

TAIL UNIT: Cantilever structure of glass-fibre/balsa sandwich, with one-piece all-moving tailplane mounted at tip of fin.

LANDING GEAR: Non-retractable or retractable mono-wheel and tail bumper. Continental wheel size 100 × 300, fitted with Zündapp drum brake. Tyre pressure 43 lb/sq in (3 kg/cm²). Provision for drag parachute as optional extra equipment.

Messerschmitt-Bölkow-Blohm Phœbus A single-seat Standard Class sailplane

ACCOMMODATION: Single seat under one-piece transparent canopy. Baggage compartment aft of seat. Provision for extensive instrumentation, radio and oxygen system. Wave trap antenna in rudder.

DIMENSIONS:
- Wing span:
  - A, B — 49 ft 2½ in (15·00 m)
  - C — 55 ft 9¼ in (17·00 m)
- Wing aspect ratio:
  - A, B — 17·1
  - C — 20·55
- Length overall — 23 ft 0 in (6·98 m)
- Height overall — 4 ft 7¼ in (1·40 m)
- Tailplane span — 10 ft 6 in (3·20 m)

AREAS:
- Wings, gross:
  - A, B — 141·5 sq ft (13·16 m²)
  - C — 151·2 sq ft (14·06 m²)
- Ailerons:
  - A, B — 9·25 sq ft (0·86 m²)
  - C — 9·47 sq ft (0·88 m²)
- Air-brakes (total) — 5·59 sq ft (0·52 m²)
- Fin — 6·99 sq ft (0·69 m²)
- Rudder — 6·67 sq ft (0·62 m²)
- Tailplane — 17·2 sq ft (1·60 m²)

WEIGHTS AND LOADING:
- Weight empty:
  - A, B — 474 lb (215 kg)
  - C — 518 lb (235 kg)
- Max T-O weight:
  - A, B — 772 lb (350 kg)
  - C — 825 lb (375 kg)
- Max wing loading — 5·43 lb/sq ft (26·5 kg/m²)

PERFORMANCE:
- Best glide ratio:
  - A, B — 37 : 1 at 49 knots (56 mph; 90 km/h)
  - C — 42 : 1 at 49 knots (56 mph; 90 km/h)
- Min sinking speed at 43·5 knots (50 mph; 80 km/h):
  - A, B — 2·13 ft (0·65 m)/sec
  - C — 1·80 ft (0·55 m)/sec
- Stalling speed:
  - A, B — 33 knots (37 mph; 60 km/h)
  - C — 32 knots (36 mph; 58 km/h)
- Max speed (rough or smooth air) — 108 knots (124 mph; 200 km/h)
- Max aero-tow speed — 97 knots (112 mph; 180 km/h)
- Max winch-launching speed — 65 knots (75 mph; 120 km/h)
- *g* limits — +8; —5·3

RFB

RHEIN-FLUGZEUGBAU GmbH

HEAD OFFICE: 405 Mönchengladbach, P.O.B. 408

RFB SIRIUS

This powered sailplane is claimed to be the first high-performance sailplane in the world of combined metal and glass-fibre construction. Use of a new integrated power system has enabled the aerodynamic qualities of a sailplane to be retained, while making powered take-off from small airfields possible.

The power plant is a fixed low-drag installation, fitted at the centre of gravity and offering a minimum loss of performance during gliding. Compared with a propeller-powered aircraft, third parties are protected from accidents during starting and taxying, and risk of injury to the pilot during heavy landing or when making an emergency exit is much reduced.

The power plant is a Nelson four-cylinder two-stroke engine, developing 48 hp at 4,400 rpm and driving an eight-blade ducted metal fan, coupled directly to the engine. An electrical starter allows easy re-starting in flight. Fuel capacity is 7 Imp gallons (32 litres).

TYPE: Single-seat high-performance powered sailplane.

WINGS: Cantilever mid-wing monoplane. Metal and glass-fibre construction. Trailing-edge flaps variable from —10° to +15°. Orthodox air-brakes.

FUSELAGE: Metal and glass-fibre construction.

LANDING GEAR: Retractable mono-wheel, fitted with brake shoes. Can be landed with wheel retracted.

ACCOMMODATION: Single glass-fibre moulded seat under large side-hinged Perspex canopy.

RFB Sirius single-seat sailplane with ducted-fan auxiliary engine (*Flight International*)

Ventilation tube mounted in the nose of the fuselage delivers controlled ventilating air to the cockpit. Normal instrumentation; space for radio, oxygen equipment and barograph.

DIMENSIONS:
- Wing span — 57 ft 6½ in (17·54 m)
- Wing aspect ratio — 22
- Length overall — 24 ft 1½ in (7·35 m)
- Height — 5 ft 11 in (1·80 m)

AREA:
- Wings, gross — 148·54 sq ft (13·8 m²)

WEIGHTS AND LOADING:
- Weight empty — 639 lb (290 kg)
- Max T-O weight — 882 lb (400 kg)
- Max wing loading — 5·94 lb/sq ft (29 kg/m²)

PERFORMANCE:
- Unpowered:
  - Best glide ratio — 38 : 1
  - Min sinking speed — 2·13 ft (0·65 m)/sec
  - Stalling speed — 35 knots (40 mph; 65 km/h)
- Powered:
  - Max speed — 146 knots (168 mph; 270 km/h)
  - Climbing speed (with engine) — 8·20 ft (2·5 m)/sec
  - Cruising speed — 81 knots (93 mph; 150 km/h)
  - Take-off run — 410 ft (125 m)
  - Fuel consumption, approx — 4·4 Imp gallons (20 litres) per hour

SCHEIBE

SCHEIBE-FLUGZEUGBAU-GmbH

HEAD OFFICE AND WORKS:
August-Pfaltz-Strasse 23, 806 Dachau, near Munich

MANAGER: Dipl-Ing Egon Scheibe

Scheibe-Flugzeugbau-GmbH was founded at the end of 1951 by Dipl-Ing Scheibe, who had previously built a prototype two-seat general-purpose glider known as the Mü-13E Bergfalke in Austria. This aircraft flew for the first time on 5 August 1951 and was the first type produced in quantity by the newly-formed company.

Since then, Scheibe has built several new types of sailplane. Details of those in current production are given below.

Since Scheibe developed the SF-24 Motorspatz in 1957, it has also become the major producer of powered sailplanes in Germany. Currently in production are the SF-25B Falke and SF-27M powered sailplanes, of which details are given after the sailplane entries.

Scheibe has built a total of more than 1,300 aircraft of various types, in addition to many kits for home construction by amateurs. Gliders of Scheibe design are being built under licence by gliding clubs as well as by foreign companies.

SCHEIBE BERGFALKE-III (MOUNTAIN FALCON)

This version of the Bergfalke supersedes the earlier Bergfalke II/55 in production. Like its predecessor, it is a tandem two-seat training and contest sailplane with swept-forward (2°) wings of 14·5% Mü section. It has a steel-tube fuselage and non-retractable landing gear, with main and tail wheels.

The Bergfalke-III has single-spar wooden wings with a dihedral of 3° 30′. Schempp-Hirth air-brakes are fitted.

DIMENSIONS:
- Wing span — 54 ft 5½ in (16·60 m)
- Wing chord at root — 4 ft 11 in (1·50 m)
- Wing chord at tip — 1 ft 11½ in (0·60 m)
- Wing aspect ratio — 15·4
- Length overall — 25 ft 10 in (7·88 m)
- Height over tail — 5 ft 7 in (1·70 m)

AREA:
- Wings, gross — 194·4 sq ft (18·06 m²)

WEIGHTS AND LOADING:
Weight empty, equipped	628 lb (285 kg)	
Max T-O weight	1,025 lb (465 kg)	
Max wing loading	5·33 lb/sq ft (26 kg/m²)	

PERFORMANCE (at max T-O weight):
Best glide ratio		28 : 1
Min sinking speed	2·46 ft (0·75 m)/sec at	
	36·5 knots (42 mph; 68 km/h)	
Stalling speed	32 knots (36 mph; 58 km/h)	
Max speed (smooth air)		
	97 knots (112 mph; 180 km/h)	
Max speed (rough air)		
	76 knots (87 mph; 140 km/h)	
Max aero-tow speed		
	65 knots (75 mph; 120 km/h)	
Max winch-launching speed		
	51 knots (59 mph; 95 km/h)	

SCHEIBE BERGFALKE-IV

The Bergfalke-IV is a developed version of the Bergfalke-III, with a new wing which provides improved performance. Construction of the prototype began early in 1969 and first flight was accomplished a few months later. Five had been built at the beginning of 1970 and production is continuing.

TYPE: Two-seat training and contest sailplane.

WINGS: Cantilever mid-wing monoplane. Wing section Wortmann SO 2 at root, SO 2/1 at tip. Thickness/chord ratio 19·4% at root, 15·8% at tip. Dihedral 3°. All-wood structure. Single laminated beechwood box-spar. Plywood skin, fabric-covered. Ailerons of wooden construction. Schempp-Hirth wooden air-brakes.

FUSELAGE: Welded steel-tube structure. Nose-section covered with a moulded glass-fibre shell, remainder fabric-covered.

TAIL UNIT: Cantilever wooden structure. Tailplane mounted on top of fuselage, forward of fin. Flettner trim-tab on starboard elevator.

LANDING GEAR: Non-retractable mono-wheel and tail-wheel.

ACCOMMODATION: Two seats in tandem beneath a blown Plexiglas canopy.

DIMENSIONS, EXTERNAL:
Wing span	56 ft 5¼ in (17·20 m)
Wing chord at root	4 ft 6¼ in (1·38 m)
Wing chord at tip	1 ft 9¼ in (0·54 m)
Wing aspect ratio	17·4
Length overall	26 ft 3 in (8·0 m)
Height overall	4 ft 11 in (1·5 m)

AREA:
Wings, gross	183 sq ft (17·0 m²)

WEIGHTS AND LOADING:
Weight empty, equipped	661 lb (300 kg)
Max T-O weight	1,102 lb (500 kg)
Normal wing loading	5·7 lb/sq ft (28·0 kg/m²)

PERFORMANCE:
Best glide ratio		
	34 : 1 at 46 knots (53 mph; 85 km/h)	
Min sinking speed	2·23 ft (0·68 m)/sec at	
	41 knots (47 mph; 75 km/h)	
Stalling speed	36 knots (41 mph; 65 km/h)	
Max speed (smooth air)		
	108 knots (124 mph; 200 km/h)	
Max speed (rough air)		
	92 knots (106 mph; 170 km/h)	
Max aero-tow speed		
	76 knots (87 mph; 140 km/h)	
Max winch-launching speed		
	59 knots (68 mph; 110 km/h)	
Ultimate load factor		8g

SCHEIBE L-SPATZ-III (SPARROW)

Compared with the L-Spatz-55, from which it was developed, this lightweight single-seat sailplane has aerodynamic twist on the outer wings to improve stall characteristics, larger air-brakes and tail surfaces, a less-deep fuselage to improve its aerodynamics and appearance, more roomy cockpit, and a newly-introduced trim-tab on the elevator.

TYPE: Single-seat training and competition sailplane.

WINGS: Cantilever high-wing monoplane. 14% Mü wing section. Dihedral 2° 30′. All-wood structure with single box-spar. Plywood-covered leading-edge torsion box; remainder fabric-covered. Air-brakes fitted.

FUSELAGE: Steel-tube fuselage, with rectangular section at front and triangular section at rear. Nose covered with moulded glass-fibre shell. Rear fuselage fabric-covered over wooden formers.

TAIL UNIT: Cantilever wooden structure. Flettner trim-tab in elevators.

LANDING GEAR: Normally fitted with nose-skid and mono-wheel. Optionally, a longer skid can be used, with detachable ground handling trolley.

ACCOMMODATION: Single seat in enclosed cockpit, under blown Plexiglas canopy. Adjustable rudder pedals.

DIMENSIONS:
Wing span	49 ft 2½ in (15·00 m)
Wing aspect ratio	19
Length overall	20 ft 6 in (6·25 m)
Height overall	3 ft 11 in (1·20 m)
Max width of fuselage	1 ft 10¾ in (0·58 m)

AREA:
Wings, gross	125·9 sq ft (11·7 m²)

Scheibe Bergfalke-IV two-seat training and competition sailplane

Scheibe L-Spatz-III lightweight single-seat sailplane

WEIGHTS:
Weight empty	353 lb (160 kg)
Max T-O weight	585 lb (265 kg)

PERFORMANCE:
Best glide ratio		28 : 1
Min sinking speed	2·20 ft (0·67 m)/sec at	
	33·5 knots (38·5 mph; 62 km/h)	
Stalling speed	27 knots (31 mph; 50 km/h)	
Max speed (smooth air)		
	97 knots (112 mph; 180 km/h)	
Max speed (rough air)		
	68 knots (78 mph; 125 km/h)	
Max aero-tow speed		
	68 knots (78 mph; 125 km/h)	
Max winch-launching speed		
	49 knots (56 mph; 90 km/h)	
Ultimate load factor		8

SCHEIBE SF-27 ZUGVOGEL V (MIGRATORY BIRD)

The Scheibe SF-27 Zugvogel V is a single-seat Standard Class sailplane, the prototype of which flew for the first time on 12 May 1964. A total of 120 had been built by January 1970.

TYPE: Single-seat Standard Class sailplane.

WINGS: Cantilever shoulder-wing monoplane. Wing section Wortmann FX 61-184 at root, FX 60-126 at tip. Dihedral 3°. Wooden structure, with laminated beechwood box-spar at about 43% chord. Plywood ribs. Leading-edge torsion box. Outboard half of wing plywood-covered; inboard half covered with plywood to 6 cm behind spar; remainder part-fabric and part-plywood covered. Wooden ailerons, plywood-covered. Schempp-Hirth glass-fibre/metal air-brakes.

FUSELAGE: Welded steel-tube structure. Nose section back to wing trailing-edge covered with moulded glass-fibre shell. Rear section fabric-covered over wooden stringers. Moulded glass-fibre fairing over wing-fuselage junction.

TAIL UNIT: Cantilever wood structure, with all-moving horizontal surfaces. Tailplane covered with plywood and fabric. Fin plywood-covered, rudder fabric-covered. Anti-balance tab in tailplane.

LANDING GEAR: Non-retractable and unsprung mono-wheel ahead of CG, tyre size 4·00 × 4. Wheel brake. No skid. Tailwheel diameter 7·9 in (20 cm).

ACCOMMODATION: Single inclined seat under moulded Plexiglas canopy. Rudder pedals adjustable. Baggage compartment behind seat.

DIMENSIONS:
Wing span	49 ft 2½ in (15·00 m)
Wing chord at root	3 ft 7 in (1·09 m)
Wing chord at tip	1 ft 5½ in (0·44 m)
Wing aspect ratio	18·6
Length overall	23 ft 3½ in (7·10 m)
Tailplane span	8 ft 3¼ in (2·52 m)
Max width of fuselage	1 ft 10½ in (0·57 m)

Scheibe SF-27 Zugvogel V single-seat Standard Class sailplane

AREAS:
Wings, gross	129·9 sq ft (12·07 m²)
Ailerons (total)	10·76 sq ft (1·0 m²)
Air-brakes (total)	4·09 sq ft (0·38 m²)
Fin	5·81 sq ft (0·54 m²)
Rudder	6·67 sq ft (0·62 m²)
Tailplane	16·68 sq ft (1·55 m²)

WEIGHTS:
Weight empty, equipped	474 lb (215 kg)
Normal T-O weight	728 lb (330 kg)

PERFORMANCE (at AUW of 683 lb = 310 kg):
Best glide ratio
34 : 1 at 48 knots (55 mph; 88 km/h)
Min sinking speed 2·10 ft (0·64 m)/sec at
40 knots (46 mph; 74 km/h)
Stalling speed 30 knots (34 mph; 55 km/h)

SCHEIBE SF-25B FALKE (FALCON)

The Falke is a side-by-side two-seat powered sailplane, intended mainly for training. It has good soaring characteristics and does not require ballast when flown solo. Fuel capacity is 8·5 Imp gallons (32 litres). Dual controls are standard. Eighty SF-25B Falke sailplanes had been built by January 1970.

TYPE: Two-seat powered sailplane, particularly suitable for basic and advanced training.

WINGS: Two-piece cantilever low wing of wooden construction, with air brakes. Design developed from the Motorfalke wing.

FUSELAGE: Fabric-covered welded steel-tube structure. Optional tow-hitch for winch launching.

TAIL UNIT: Conventional wooden construction.

LANDING GEAR: Main wheel with brake and aerodynamic fairing; steerable tailwheel; spring outrigger stabilising wheels fitted under each wing.

ACCOMMODATION: Two seats side-by-side in enclosed cabin.

POWER PLANT: One 45 hp Stamo MS 1500 four-cycle horizontally-opposed engine, using Volkswagen and Porsche parts. Normal operating speed about 2,500-3,000 rpm. Starting on the ground and in the air is by means of a pull-cable starter in the cabin.

DIMENSIONS:
Wing span 50 ft 2½ in (15·3 m)
Wing aspect ratio 13·4

AREA:
Wings, gross 188·5 sq ft (17·5 m²)

WEIGHTS AND LOADING:
Weight empty	739 lb (335 kg)
Max T-O weight	1,168 lb (530 kg)
Max wing loading	6·1 lb/sq ft (30 kg/m²)

PERFORMANCE (at max T-O weight):
Max speed at S/L
87 knots (100 mph; 160 km/h)
Cruising speed 69 knots (80 mph; 130 km/h)
Min flying speed 33 knots (37 mph; 60 km/h)

Scheibe SF-25B Falke powered sailplane (45 hp Stamo MS 1500 engine)

Rate of climb at S/L:
1 person	500 ft (150 m)/min
2 persons	400 ft (120 m)/min

T-O run at S/L:
1 person	328-394 ft (100-120 m)
2 persons	492-820 ft (150-250 m)

Best glide ratio 20 : 1
Min sinking speed (engine stopped)
3·1 ft (0·95 m)/sec
Endurance 3 hr 30 min
Range
191-218 nm (220-250 miles; 350-400 km)

SCHEIBE SF-27M

The SF-27M is a single-seat powered sailplane with a retractable power plant which makes it capable of self-powered take-off as well as normal launching by winch or aero-tow. Since the power plant is retractable, the SF-27M has about the same soaring performance as the normal SF-27 Zugvogel V high-performance sailplane. The main difference arises from the additional weight of the engine installation, amounting to approximately 88 lb (40 kg). In addition, the main wheel tyre size is increased to 5·00×5.

The construction of the SF-27M is similar to that of the SF-27. The wings and control surfaces are strengthened internally. The fuselage centre section has also been modified, increasing the overall length to accommodate the engine which, when retracted, lies inside the fuselage behind the wings.

The engine is raised and retracted manually by a crank-driven draw chain-pushrod system, swinging upward and forward into the operating position. The fuselage doors over the engine and propeller bay are automatically opened and closed when the engine is raised or retracted. The whole process is extremely simple, requiring only 3½ turns on the crank, and can be completed in 5 seconds.

The power plant comprises a 26 hp Hirth Solo vertically-opposed four-cylinder engine, driving a propeller of about 53 inches (1·36 m) diameter through a reduction gear of 1:1·86. The engine is started by a hand-operated cable. A specially designed ignition system facilitates easy starting. The fuel tank, capacity 4·4 Imp gallons (20 litres), is mounted in the fuselage behind the pilot.

The first Distance Diamond for a flight in a powered sailplane was issued by the German Aero Club to Willibald Collé, who on 28 July 1968 flew his SF-27M from Elz to Le Rabot airfield, France, a distance of 290 nm (334 miles; 537 km).

Collé launched himself just before 11 am, climbed to a height of approx 3,000 ft (1,000 m), switched off the engine and retracted it. The flight took about 8 hours and was carried out at heights between about 2,500 and 6,000 ft (800 to 1,700 m). A special barograph confirmed that the flight had been made without assistance from the engine.

The value of self-launching was clearly demonstrated on that day, as the winch at the club broke down and only the SF-27M was able to take off.

DIMENSIONS AND AREAS:
As for SF-27, except:
Length overall 23 ft 6 in (7·16 m)

WEIGHTS AND LOADING (approx):
Weight empty, equipped	595 lb (270 kg)
Max T-O weight	849 lb (385 kg)
Wing loading	6·4 lb/sq ft (31·5 kg/m²)

PERFORMANCE (approx):
Best glide ratio
34 : 1 at 48 knots (55 mph; 88 km/h)
Min sinking speed 2·3 ft (0·7 m)/sec
Max powered speed
83 knots (95 mph; 150 km/h)
Stalling speed 32·5 knots (37 mph; 60 km/h)
Rate of climb at S/L approx 395 ft (120 m)/min
T-O run 457-655 ft (150-200 m)
Range 134-161 nm (155-186 miles; 250-300 km)
Endurance 2-3 hours

Scheibe SF-27M single-seat powered sailplane with engine retracted and (right) partially extended

SCHEMPP-HIRTH
SCHEMPP-HIRTH KG

HEAD OFFICE:
Postfach 143, 7312 Kirchheim-Teck
Schempp-Hirth specialises in the production of high-performance Open Class and Standard Class sailplanes.

Production of the SHK Open Class sailplane has now ended and details of this may be found in the 1969-70 *Jane's*. The company's current products are described below.

SCHEMPP-HIRTH CIRRUS

This single-seat high-performance sailplane was designed by Dipl Ing Klaus Holighaus, who was one of the co-designers of the Akaflieg Darmstadt D-36 Circe before joining Schempp-Hirth in 1955. He has utilised the new Wortmann wing section, without flaps, to achieve good low-speed and climb characteristics. Provision for ballast overcomes the slight disadvantage this section has when compared with thinner flapped profiles. Stalling characteristics are good with a thicker wing and Schempp-Hirth claim that weight is saved by comparison with a flapped wing of similar span and aspect ratio.

The first prototype Cirrus flew for the first time in January 1967 with a V tail unit. The second prototype had a conventional tail unit, as fitted to production models.

A Cirrus, flown by Harro Wödl of Austria, won the Open Class of the 1968 World Gliding Championships in Poland.

TYPE: Single-seat high-performance sailplane.

WINGS: Cantilever mid-wing monoplane. Wortmann FX 66 series section. Thickness/chord ratio 19·6% at root, 16% at tip. Dihedral 3° at spar centre-line. Incidence 2°. No sweep at spar centre-line. Wing shell is a glass-fibre/foam sandwich structure, with an all-glass-fibre box spar. Hinged ailerons of glass-fibre/balsa sandwich. No flaps. Schempp-Hirth aluminium alloy air-brakes.

FUSELAGE: Glass-fibre shell, 1·5 mm thick, stiffened with foam rings, secured with resin.

TAIL UNIT: Cantilever structure of glass-fibre/foam sandwich. Tailplane mounted part-way up fin.

LANDING GEAR: Retractable mono-wheel type. Manual retraction. Annular rubber-spring shock-absorber. Tost wheel with Dunlop tyre size 3·50 × 5, pressure 49 lb/sq in (3·45 kg/cm²). Tost drum brake.

ACCOMMODATION: Single semi-reclining adjustable seat. Adjustable rudder pedals. Long flush Plexiglas canopy.

DIMENSIONS:
Wing span	58 ft 2½ in (17·74 m)
Wing chord at root	2 ft 11½ in (0·90 m)
Wing chord at tip	1 ft 2¼ in (0·36 m)
Wing aspect ratio	25
Length overall	23 ft 7¼ in (7·20 m)
Height over tail	5 ft 0 in (1·56 m)
Tailplane span	8 ft 2½ in (2·50 m)

AREAS:
Wings, gross	135·6 sq ft (12·6 m²)
Ailerons (total)	11·2 sq ft (1·04 m²)
Fin	6·8 sq ft (0·63 m²)
Rudder	5·6 sq ft (0·52 m²)
Tailplane	9·7 sq ft (0·90 m²)
Elevators	1·6 sq ft (0·15 m²)

WEIGHTS AND LOADING:
Weight empty, equipped	573 lb (260 kg)
Max T-O weight	882 lb (400 kg)
Max wing loading	6·5 lb/sq ft (31·7 kg/m²)

PERFORMANCE (at AUW of 793 lb = 360 kg):
Best glide ratio
44 : 1 at 46 knots (53 mph; 85 km/h)
Min sinking speed 1·64 ft (0·50 m)/sec at
39 knots (45 mph; 73 km/h)
Stalling speed 33 knots (38 mph; 62 km/h)
Max speed (smooth air)
119 knots (137 mph; 220 km/h)
Max speed (rough air)
119 knots (137 mph; 220 km/h)
Max aero-tow speed
76 knots (87 mph; 140 km/h)
Max winch-launching speed
59 knots (68 mph; 110 km/h)

SCHEMPP-HIRTH STANDARD CIRRUS

Designed by Dipl-Ing Klaus Holighaus, the Standard Class version of the Schempp-Hirth Cirrus entered production during the summer of 1969, following the first flight of the prototype in March 1969.

TYPE: Single-seat high-performance Standard Class sailplane.

WINGS: Cantilever mid-wing monoplane. Wortmann section. Thickness/chord ratio 19·6% at root, 17% at tip. Dihedral 3°. Incidence 3°. Sweepback 1·3° at leading-edge. Wings and ailerons are glass-fibre/foam sandwich structures. Schempp-Hirth aluminium alloy airbrakes.

FUSELAGE: Glass-fibre shell, 1·5 mm thick, stiffened with bonded-in foam rings.

TAIL UNIT: T-tail of glass-fibre/foam sandwich construction. Hinged elevators.

LANDING GEAR: Manually-retractable monowheel standard. Non-retractable faired monowheel optional. Tost wheel with drum brake

Schempp-Hirth Standard Cirrus high-performance sailplane (*Anne Ince*)

and Continental 4·00 × 4 tyre, pressure 50 lb/sq in (3·50 kg/cm²).

ACCOMMODATION: Single seat under long flush Plexiglas canopy. Adjustable rudder pedals.

DIMENSIONS:
Wing span	49 ft 2½ in (15·00 m)
Wing chord at root	3 ft 0½ in (0·93 m)
Wing chord at tip	1 ft 2¼ in (0·36 m)
Wing aspect ratio	22·5
Length overall	20 ft 9¾ in (6·35 m)
Height over tail	4 ft 4¾ in (1·32 m)
Tailplane span	7 ft 10½ in (2·40 m)

AREA:
Wings, gross	107·6 sq ft (10·00 m²)

WEIGHTS AND LOADING:
Weight empty	445 lb (202 kg)
Max T-O weight	728 lb (330 kg)
Max wing loading	6·8 lb/sq ft (33 kg/m²)

PERFORMANCE (estimated):
Best glide ratio
38 : 1 at 46 knots (53 mph; 85 km/h)
Min sinking speed 1·87 ft (0·57 m)/sec at
37·5 knots (43 mph; 70 km/h)
Stalling speed 34 knots (39 mph; 62 km/h)
Max speed (rough or smooth air)
119 knots (137 mph; 220 km/h)
Max aero-tow speed
81 knots (93 mph; 150 km/h)
Max winch-launching speed
65 knots (75 mph; 120 km/h)
g limits 10g

SCHEMPP-HIRTH HS-3 NIMBUS

The HS-3 Nimbus high-performance sailplane was designed and built by Dipl-Ing Klaus Holighaus. The prototype first flew in January 1969.

TYPE: Single-seat high-performance sailplane.

WINGS: Cantilever high-wing monoplane. Wortmann section. Thickness/chord ratio decreases from 17% at root to 15% at tip. Dihedral 2°. Wings, ailerons and flaps are of glass-fibre/foam sandwich construction. No air-brakes.

FUSELAGE: Glass-fibre shell, 2 mm thick. Steel-tube frame for the attachment of wings and landing gear.

TAIL UNIT: Cantilever structure of glass-fibre/foam sandwich. Tailplane mounted part way up fin. Hinged elevators.

LANDING GEAR: Manually-retracted mono-wheel, diameter 14·17 in (360 mm), with drum brake.

ACCOMMODATION: Single seat under long two-piece canopy.

DIMENSIONS:
Wing span	72 ft 2 in (22 m)
Wing chord at root	3 ft 1¾ in (0·96 m)
Wing chord at tip	1 ft 1¾ in (0·35 m)
Wing aspect ratio	30·6
Length overall	23 ft 11½ in (7·30 m)
Height over tail	5 ft 3 in (1·60 m)
Tailplane span	9 ft 0¼ in (2·75 m)

AREAS:
Wings, gross	170 sq ft (15·8 m²)
Tailplane	11·8 sq ft (1·1 m²)

WEIGHTS:
Weight empty, equipped	816 lb (370 kg)
Max T-O weight	1,102 lb (500 kg)

PERFORMANCE:
Best glide ratio
51 : 1 at 49 knots (56 mph; 90 km/h)
Min sinking speed 1·44 ft (0·44 m)/sec at
39 knots (45 mph; 72 km/h)
Stalling speed, 90° flaps
31 knots (35 mph; 56 km/h)
Stalling speed without flaps
32·5 knots (37 mph; 60 km/h)
Max speed (rough or smooth air)
119 knots (137 mph; 220 km/h)
Max aero-tow speed
81 knots (93 mph; 150 km/h)
Max winch-launching speed
59 knots (68 mph; 110 km/h)
g limits 19g

Above: **Schempp-Hirth HS-3 Nimbus single-seat high-performance sailplane**

Left: **Schempp-Hirth Cirrus single-seat high-performance sailplane**

SCHLEICHER
ALEXANDER SCHLEICHER SEGELFLUG-ZEUGBAU

HEAD OFFICE AND WORKS:
6416 Poppenhausen an der Wasserkuppe

This company is one of the oldest manufacturers of sailplanes in the world. Its founder, Alexander Schleicher, was himself winner of the contest for training sailplanes at the 1927 meeting at the famous Wasserkuppe gliding centre. In the same year he built at Poppenhausen a small factory for manufacturing gliders and sailplanes, two of his best-known pre-war products being the Rhönbussard and Rhönadler, designed by Hans Jacobs.

During the war, the factory was engaged on the repair of Baby IIb sailplanes. For a time afterwards it became a furniture factory; but it began producing sailplanes once more in 1951 and the current products of Alexander Schleicher Segelflugzeugbau are described below.

SCHLEICHER Ka 6 E

The prototype Ka 6, designed by Rudolf Kaiser, flew for the first time in November 1955 and many hundreds have since been built, in several versions. The current production model, the Ka 6 E, first flew in the Spring of 1965 and is described below:

TYPE: Single-seat Standard Class sailplane.

WINGS: Cantilever high-wing monoplane. Wing section NACA 63618 at root, a 14% development of NACA 63615 at mid-span and 12% Jukowsky at tip. Dihedral 3°. No incidence. Sweep-forward 1° 12'. Single-spar structure of pine wood and plywood, covered with fabric. Ply-wood-covered wooden ailerons with upper surface hinges. Schempp-Hirth air-brakes.

FUSELAGE: Wooden semi-monocoque structure with plywood covering.

TAIL UNIT: Cantilever type, of similar construction to wings. All-moving horizontal surfaces.

LANDING GEAR: Retractable mono-wheel of Continental manufacture, size 300 × 100, with band-brake. Tyre pressure 28-36 lb/sq in (2·0-2·5 kg/cm²).

ACCOMMODATION: Single seat under blown Plexiglas canopy. Equipment to customer's specification.

DIMENSIONS:
Wing span	49 ft 2½ in (15·00 m)
Wing chord at root	3 ft 11 in (1·20 m)
Wing chord at tip	1 ft 3¾ in (0·40 m)
Wing aspect ratio	18·1
Length overall	21 ft 10 in (6·66 m)
Height over tail	5 ft 3 in (1·60 m)
Tailplane span	9 ft 2¼ in (2·80 m)

AREAS:
Wings, gross	133·5 sq ft (12·40 m²)
Ailerons (total)	8·83 sq ft (0·82 m²)
Air-brakes (total)	3·88 sq ft (0·36 m²)
Fin	5·49 sq ft (0·51 m²)
Rudder	7·10 sq ft (0·66 m²)
Tailplane	10·23 sq ft (0·95 m²)
Elevators	7·10 sq ft (0·66 m²)

WEIGHTS AND LOADING:
Weight empty, equipped	430 lb (195 kg)
Max T-O weight	661 lb (300 kg)
Max wing loading	4·96 lb/sq ft (24·2 kg/m²)

PERFORMANCE (at max T-O weight):
Best glide ratio	approx 32 : 1
Min sinking speed	2·17 ft (0·66 m)/sec
Stalling speed	32 knots (37 mph; 60 km/h)
Max speed, smooth air	108 knots (124 mph; 200 km/h)
Max speed, rough air	75 knots (87 mph; 140 km/h)
Max aero-tow speed	75 knots (87 mph; 140 km/h)
Max winch launching speed	54 knots (62 mph; 100 km/h)

SCHLEICHER K 8 B

Designed by Rudolf Kaiser, the K 8 B was developed from the Ka 6, but features simplified construction throughout. As a result, it is suitable for amateur construction.

The prototype flew in November 1957 and many hundreds have since been built.

TYPE: Single-seat training and sporting sailplane.

WINGS: Cantilever high-wing monoplane. Wing section Gö 533 at root, Gö 532 at tip. Dihedral 3°. Sweep-forward 1° 18'. Single-spar structure of pine and plywood, covered with fabric. Plywood-covered wooden ailerons with upper surface hinges. Schempp-Hirth air-brakes.

FUSELAGE: Steel-tube structure, with fabric covering over wooden formers.

TAIL UNIT: Cantilever type, of similar construction to wing. Optional trim-tab on elevator.

LANDING GEAR: Nose-skid mounted on rubber blocks. Non-retractable and unsprung Continental mono-wheel, size 300 × 100. Tyre pressure 28-36 lb/sq in (2·0-2·5 kg/cm²). No brake.

ACCOMMODATION: Single seat under blown Plexiglas canopy. Equipment to customer's specification.

DIMENSIONS:
Wing span	49 ft 2½ in (15·00 m)
Wing chord at root	4 ft 3 in (1·30 m)
Wing aspect ratio	15·9
Length overall	23 ft 0 in (7·00 m)
Height over tail	5 ft 1¾ in (1·57 m)
Tailplane span	9 ft 2¼ in (2·80 m)

AREAS:
Wings, gross	152·3 sq ft (14·15 m²)
Ailerons (total)	10·76 sq ft (1·00 m²)
Spoilers (total)	3·66 sq ft (0·34 m²)
Fin	6·67 sq ft (0·62 m²)
Rudder	8·07 sq ft (0·75 m²)
Tailplane	10·33 sq ft (0·96 m²)
Elevators	10·12 sq ft (0·94 m²)

WEIGHTS AND LOADING:
Weight empty, equipped	430 lb (195 kg)
Max T-O weight	683 lb (310 kg)
Max wing loading	4·48 lb/sq ft (21·9 kg/m²)

PERFORMANCE (at max T-O weight):
Best glide ratio	25 : 1 at 39·5 knots (45·5 mph; 73 km/h)
Min sinking speed	2·36 ft (0·72 m)/sec at 33 knots (38 mph; 61 km/h)
Stalling speed	28 knots (32·5 mph; 52 km/h)
Max speed, smooth air	102 knots (118 mph; 190 km/h)
Max speed, rough air	70 knots (81 mph; 130 km/h)
Max aero-tow speed	70 knots (81 mph; 130 km/h)
Max winch-launching speed	65 knots (62 mph; 100 km/h)

SCHLEICHER AS-W12

TYPE: Single-seat high-performance sailplane.

WINGS: Cantilever shoulder-wing monoplane, Wortmann wing section. Aspect ratio 25·8.

LANDING GEAR: Retractable mono-wheel.

ACCOMMODATION: Single semi-reclining seat under two-piece canopy.

DIMENSIONS:
Wing span	59 ft 0½ in (18·3 m)
Wing aspect ratio	25·8

AREA:
Wings, gross	140 sq ft (13 m²)

WEIGHTS AND LOADING:
Weight empty	684 lb (310 kg)
Max T-O weight	948 lb (430 kg)
Max wing loading	6·57 lb/sq ft (32 kg/m²)

PERFORMANCE (prototype):
Best glide ratio	47 : 1 at 51 knots (59 mph; 95 km/h)
Min sinking speed	1·6 ft (0·49 m)/sec at 39 knots (45 mph; 72 km/h)

SCHLEICHER AS-K 13

This tandem two-seat training and high-performance sailplane has been developed from the K-7, which is in worldwide use by gliding clubs.

The prototype first flew in July 1966 and by January 1970 a total of 220 AS-K 13's had been built.

Compared with the K-7, the AS-K 13 introduces many improvements, including a large full-blown canopy for all-round visibility, higher performance, improved comfort and a sprung landing wheel for softer touchdowns.

WINGS: Cantilever mid-wing monoplane. Wing section developed from Göttingen 535 and 549. Thickness/chord ratio: 16% at root, 12% at tip. Sweep-forward at quarter-chord 6°. Dihedral 5°. No incidence. Single-spar wood structure, with plywood D-type leading-edge torsion box and fabric covering. Wooden ailerons with fabric covering. Metal air-brakes of Schempp-Hirth type.

FUSELAGE: Welded steel-tube structure with spruce stringers and fabric main covering. Nose made of glass-fibre. Turtle deck aft of canopy is plywood shell.

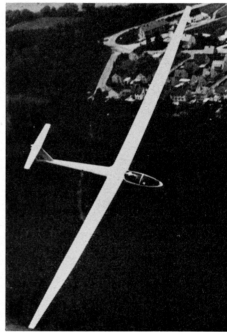

Schleicher AS-W12 single-seat high-performance sailplane

Schleicher K 8 B single-seat training and sporting sailplane

Schleicher Ka 6 E single-seat Standard Class sailplane

Schleicher AS-K 13 two-seat training sailplane   (*Peter M. Bowers*)

TAIL UNIT: Cantilever wood structure. Fixed surfaces plywood-covered. Rear portion of rudder and elevators fabric-covered. Anti-balance and trim-tab in starboard elevator.

LANDING GEAR: Non-retractable sprung mono-wheel, size 5·00 × 5 (350 × 125) with Tost drum brake, mounted aft of CG. Skid in front of wheel and steel tail skid.

ACCOMMODATION: Two seats in tandem under one-piece blown Mecaplex canopy, hinged to starboard. Glass-fibre seat panels. Adjustable rudder pedals.

EQUIPMENT: Aero-tow release in nose. Kombi release at CG. Normal instrumentation; provision for radio and oxygen.

DIMENSIONS:
Wing span	52 ft 6 in (16·00 m)
Wing chord (mean)	3 ft 7 in (1·09 m)
Wing aspect ratio	14·6
Length overall	26 ft 9½ in (8·18 m)
Height over tail	5 ft 3 in (1·6 m)
Tailplane span	9 ft 10 in (3·0 m)

AREA:
Wings, gross	188 sq ft (17·50 m²)
Ailerons (total)	15·93 sq ft (1·48 m²)
Airbrakes (total)	4·62 sq ft (0·43 m²)
Fin	6·45 sq ft (0·60 m²)
Rudder	8·93 sq ft (0·83 m²)
Tailplane	24·22 sq ft (2·25 m²)
Elevators	11·30 sq ft (1·05 m²)

WEIGHTS AND LOADINGS:
Weight empty	640 lb (290 kg)
Max T-O weight	1,060 lb (480 kg)
Wing loading:	
single-seater	4·45 lb/sq ft (21·7 kg/m²)
two-seater	5·61 lb/sq ft (27·4 kg/m²)

PERFORMANCE:
Best glide ratio (two occupants)
28 : 1 at 48·6 knots (56 mph; 90 km/h)
Min sinking speed:
single seater   2·30 ft (0·7 m)/sec
two-seater
2·66 ft (0·81 m)/sec at 35 knots (40 mph; 64 km/h)
Stalling speed   33 knots (38 mph; 61 km/h)
Max speed (smooth air)
109 knots (125 mph; 200 km/h)
Max speed (rough air)
76 knots (87 mph; 140 km/h)
Min flying speed:
single-seater   31 knots (35 mph; 56 km/h)
two-seater   33 knots (38 mph; 61 km/h)
Max aero-tow speed
75·5 knots (87 mph; 140 km/h)
Max winch-launching speed
54 knots (62 mph; 100 km/h)
g limits   4g at safety factor of 2

SCHLEICHER AS-K14

The prototype of the K14, designed by Ing Rudolf Kaiser, flew for the first time on 25 April 1967. A total of 38 had been built by January 1970.

TYPE: Single-seat powered sailplane.

WINGS: Cantilever mid-wing monoplane. Wing section NACA 63-618 at root, a 14% development of NACA 63615 at mid-span and a 12% Jukowsky at tip. Thickness/chord ratios 18% at root, 12% at tip. Dihedral 5°. No incidence. Straight leading-edge. Single-spar orthodox wood and fabric construction. Plywood-covered wooden ailerons, with upper surface hinges. Spoilers on upper surface only.

FUSELAGE: Semi-monocoque wood and plywood construction.

TAIL UNIT: Cantilever type of wood-plywood-fabric construction. All-moving horizontal surfaces.

LANDING GEAR: Manually-retracted mono-wheel, size 5·00 × 5. Tyre pressure 31 lb/sq in (2·2 kg/cm²).

POWER PLANT: One 26 hp Hirth F10 K19 two-stroke engine, driving a Hoffmann feathering propeller.

ACCOMMODATION: Single seat under sideways-hinged blown Plexiglas canopy.

DIMENSIONS:
Wing span	46 ft 11 in (14·30 m)
Wing chord (mean)	2 ft 10¾ in (0·89 m)
Wing aspect ratio	16·2
Length overall	21 ft 8 in (6·60 m)
Height overall	5 ft 3 in (1·60 m)
Tailplane span	9 ft 2¼ in (2·80 m)

Schleicher AS-K14 single-seat powered sailplane (*R. Kaiser*)

Schleicher AS-W15 single-seat Standard Class sailplane

AREAS:
Wings, gross	136·49 sq ft (12·68 m²)
Ailerons (total)	9·25 sq ft (0·86 m²)
Spoilers (total)	3·23 sq ft (0·30 m²)
Fin	5·38 sq ft (0·50 m²)
Rudder	7·10 sq ft (0·66 m²)
Horizontal tail surfaces	17·33 sq ft (1·61 m²)

WEIGHTS AND LOADING:
Weight empty, equipped	540 lb (245 kg)
Max T-O weight	793 lb (360 kg)
Max wing loading	5·85 lb/sq ft (28·6 kg/m²)

PERFORMANCE:
Best glide ratio
28 : 1 at 45 knots (52 mph; 83 km/h)
Min sinking speed
2·46 ft (0·75 m)/sec at 39 knots (45 mph; 72 km/h)
Stalling speed   34 knots (39 mph; 62 km/h)
Max speed (smooth air)
108 knots (124 mph; 200 km/h)
Max speed (rough air)
76 knots (87 mph; 140 km/h)
g limits   4g at safety factor of 2
Rate of climb with engine   8·2 ft (2·5 m)/sec
T-O run with engine 328 ft-393 ft (100 m-120 m)

SCHLEICHER AS-W15

Designed by Gerhard Waibel to meet Standard Class requirements and built by Schleicher, the AS-W15 was first flown in April 1968 and by the end of 1969 a total of 33 had been completed. Production of 5 aircraft per month was planned throughout 1970.

The AS-W15 was first seen in competition flying at the 1968 World Gliding Championships in Poland. Flown by Hans-Werner Grosse of Germany, it was placed tenth in the Standard Class.

The materials and method used in the construction of the AS-W15 are the same as for the AS-W12, but the tailplane is mounted in the conventional position.

TYPE: Single-seat high-performance sailplane.

WINGS: Cantilever shoulder-wing monoplane. Wing section Wortmann FX-61-163 at root/mean and FX-60-126 at tip. Thickness/chord ratios 16·3% at root, 12·6% at tip. Dihedral 2°. No incidence. No sweepback. Structure: glass-fibre Roving spar, glass-fibre/balsa sandwich torsion box. Ailerons of glass-fibre/foam sandwich. Schempp-Hirth air-brakes in separate specially sealed boxes.

FUSELAGE: Glass-fibre/honeycomb sandwich construction.

TAIL UNIT: All moving horizontal surfaces of similar construction to wing. Fin construction same as fuselage and rudder same as ailerons.

LANDING GEAR: Retractable landing gear with central mono-wheel, operated manually through push-pull rods. Dunlop/Continental 400 × 4 tyre, with Tost and own-production internal drum brake. Tyre pressure. 36 lb/sq in (2·5 kg/cm²).

ACCOMMODATION: Single semi-reclining seat. One-piece transparent canopy.

EQUIPMENT: Instrumentation as required.

DIMENSIONS:
Wing span	49 ft 2½ in (15·00 m)
Wing chord at root	3 ft 0 in (0·92 m)
Wing chord at tip	1 ft 3¾ in (0·40 m)
Wing aspect ratio	20·45
Height overall	4 ft 9 in (1·45 m)
Length overall	21 ft 2 in (6·45 m)
Tailplane span	8 ft 7¼ in (2·62 m)
Max width of fuselage	1 ft 10¾ in (0·58 m)

AREAS:
Wings, gross	118·40 sq ft (11·00 m²)
Ailerons (total)	9·14 sq ft (0·85 m²)
Air brakes (total)	4·30 sq ft (0·4 m²)
Fin	6·46 sq ft (0·6 m²)
Rudder	5·17 sq ft (0·48 m²)
Tailplane	12·38 sq ft (1·15 m²)

WEIGHTS AND LOADING:
Weight empty, equipped	460 lb (210 kg)
Max T-O weight	700 lb (318 kg)
Max wing loading	5·92 lb/sq ft (28·9 kg/m²)

PERFORMANCE:
Best glide ratio
38 : 1 at 49 knots (55·9 mph; 90 km/h)
Min sinking speed
1·90 ft (0·58 m)/sec at 39 knots (45 mph; 72 km/h)
Stalling speed   34 knots (39 mph; 63 km/h)
Max speed (smooth or rough air)
119 knots (136·7 mph; 220 km/h)
Max aero-tow speed
78 knots (90 mph; 145 km/h)
Max winch-launching speed
59 knots (68 mph; 110 km/h)
g limits + 6·3; —4·3 with safety factor of 1·5

SCHNEIDER
SEGELFLUGZEUGBAU SCHNEIDER OHG
6073 Egelsbach, Hessen

SCHNEIDER L.S.1
TYPE: Single-seat high-performance Standard Class sailplane.

WINGS: Cantilever shoulder-wing monoplane.

TAIL UNIT: Cantilever T-tail.

ACCOMMODATION: Single semi-reclining seat under large transparent canopy.

DIMENSIONS:

Wing span	49 ft 2½ in (15·00 m)
Wing aspect ratio	23·1
Length overall	22 ft 9 in (6·93 m)
Height overall	4 ft 3¼ in (1·30 m)

AREA:

Wings, gross	104·84 sq ft (9·74 m²)

WEIGHTS AND LOADING:

Weight empty, equipped	414 lb (188 kg)
Max T-O weight	705 lb (320 kg)
Max wing loading	6·57 lb/sq ft (32·0 kg/m²)

PERFORMANCE:

Best glide ratio 43 : 1 at 65 mph (104 kmh)

Min sinking speed
1·70 ft (0·52 m)/sec at 42 knots (48 mph; 78 km/h)

Max speed (smooth or rough air)
119 knots (137 mph; 220 km/h)

Max aero-tow speed 81 knots (93 mph; 150 km/h)

Max winch-launching speed
59 knots (68 mph; 110 km/h)

Schneider L.S.1 high-performance Standard Class sailplane (*Anne Ince*)

VFW-FOKKER
VEREINIGTE FLUGTECHNISCHE WERKE FOKKER GmbH
HEAD OFFICE:

Hünefeldstrasse 1-5, 28 Bremen 1

OFFICERS:

See "Aircraft" section

In addition to its work on powered aircraft, VFW-Fokker is manufacturing a single-seat Open Class sailplane known as the FK-3 at its Speyer works.

VFW-FOKKER FK-3
The FK-3 was designed by Ing Otto Funk and the prototype was manufactured by apprentices in VFW's Speyer plant in the course of their regular training programme. The prototype first flew on 24 April 1968. In its first gliding competition the FK-3, flown by Dr Rolf Spänig, came first in the Open Class of the 1968 Italian Championships. Two FK-3's competing in the Austrian Gliding Championships succeeded in gaining first and second places.

Production started in January 1969 and the first production aircraft were delivered in 1969. Production continues at a rate of 3 to 4 per month.

TYPE: Single-seat Open Class high-performance sailplane.

WINGS: Cantilever shoulder-wing monoplane. Wing section Wortmann 62-K-153. Thickness/chord ratio 15·3%. Dihedral 2·5° at spar centre-line. No incidence. No sweep at spar centre-line. Unusual metal construction, bending loads being carried by a single spar, tapering from a T-section to a U profile. Drag and torsion loads carried by a nose spar of light alloy, transmitting loads to the fuselage fittings. Ribs are of light alloy and foam sandwich, spaced at approx 4 ft 7 in (140 cm) intervals and supporting 0·5 mm thick light alloy skin. Between ribs, foamed honeycomb (Conticell 60) gives additional support to protect the skin from minor damage. All metal is proofed against corrosion. Two-piece camber flaps and Schempp-Hirth air-brakes fitted.

FUSELAGE: Nose section of steel-tube construction covered with a glass-fibre reinforced shell. The narrow-diameter tail-boom is constructed of riveted light metal sheet without frames or stringers. The lower part incorporates a rubbing strip to minimise damage in a rough landing.

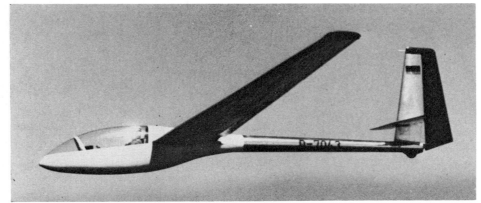

VFW-Fokker FK-3 single-seat all-metal high-performance sailplane

TAIL UNIT: Construction similar to wings. Rudder fabric-covered.

LANDING GEAR: Retractable mono-wheel fitted with cup springs, manually operated. Tost wheel size 300 × 100, with drum brake. Tyre pressure 49 lb/sq in (3·4 kg/cm²). Tail-wheel size 200 × 50.

ACCOMMODATION: Single semi-reclining adjustable seat with head rest. Adjustable rudder pedals. Long Plexiglas canopy is removable, except for small front portion. Optional water ballast in two rubber tanks in wings, each of 5·5 Imp gallons (25 litres) capacity. Central quick-release ballast valve in fuselage aft of landing gear doors.

DIMENSIONS:

Wing span	57 ft 1 in (17·40 m)
Wing chord at root	3 ft 9¾ in (1·16 m)
Wing chord at tip	1 ft 3¾ in (0·40 m)
Wing aspect ratio	22
Length overall	23 ft 7½ in (7·20 m)
Height over tailplane	5 ft 11 in (1·80 m)
Tailplane span	9 ft 2¾ in (2·80 m)

AREAS:

Wings, gross	148·54 sq ft (13·80 m²)
Ailerons (total)	6·67 sq ft (0·62 m²)
Trailing-edge flaps (total)	20·66 sq ft (1·92 m²)
Air-brakes (total)	6·03 sq ft (0·56 m²)
Fin	6·46 sq ft (0·60 m²)
Rudder	6·46 sq ft (0·60 m²)
Tailplane	8·18 sq ft (0·76 m²)
Elevators	5·60 sq ft (0·52 m²)

WEIGHTS AND LOADING:

Weight empty	529 lb (240 kg)

Max T-O weight:

without ballast	816 lb (370 kg)
with 50 kg water ballast	882 lb (400 kg)

Max wing loading 4·71-5·94 lb/sq ft (23-29 kg/m²)

PERFORMANCE:

Best glide ratio
42 : 1 at 48 knots (55 mph; 88 km/h)

Min sinking speed 1·64 ft (0·5 m)/sec at 35 knots (40 mph; 64 km/h)

Stalling speed
27-30 knots (31-34 mph; 50-55 km/h)

Max speed (smooth or rough air)
135 knots (155 mph; 250 km/h)

Max aero-tow speed
76 knots (87 mph; 140 km/h)

Max winch-launching speed
59 knots (68 mph; 110 km/h)

HUNGARY

ESZTERGOM
PESTVIDÉKI GÉPGYÁR ESZTERGOMI GYÁREGYSÉGÉBEN
This factory is producing a single-seat 15-m sailplane known as the Esztergom E-31, of which details are given below. Under development is a new all-metal high-performance sailplane known as the EV-1. Test flying was scheduled to begin in May 1969, but no details were available at press date.

ESZTERGOM E-31
Like its predecessor, the two-seat Góbé (see 1965-66 *Jane's*), the E-31 single-seat training sailplane is of all-metal riveted construction. The prototype, designed by a group of young Hungarian engineers, flew during 1966 and has been followed by a pre-series of five aircraft incorporating various modifications. Production began in 1967.

The prototype utilised wires in its flying control system, but these are replaced by rods in the

Esztergom E-31 single-seat all-metal training sailplane (*Repules*)

production E-31. Special attention has been paid to ensuring quick and easy assembly and dismantling.

TYPE: Single-seat all-metal training sailplane.

WINGS: Cantilever mid-wing monoplane. Single-spar all-metal structure with corrugated skin on nose torsion-box. Some fabric covering aft of spar. Slotted ailerons, DFS air-brakes.

FUSELAGE: Partially metal stressed-skin structure; remainder fabric-covered.

TAIL UNIT: Cantilever all-metal structure.

LANDING GEAR: Non-retractable mono-wheel, with low-pressure tyre, forward of CG. Leaf-spring tail-skid.

ACCOMMODATION: Single adjustable seat under large transparent canopy.

DIMENSIONS:
Wing span 49 ft 1$\frac{3}{4}$ in (14·98 m)
Wing aspect ratio 20
Length overall 24 ft 3$\frac{3}{4}$ in (7·41 m)
Height overall 5 ft 5$\frac{3}{4}$ in (1·67 m)

AREA:
Wings, gross 121·1 sq ft (11·25 m^2)

WEIGHTS:
Weight empty 441 lb (200 kg)
Max T-O weight 705 lb (320 kg)

PERFORMANCE:
Best glide ratio 26-28 : 1
Max speed (smooth air) 135 knots (155 mph; 250 km/h)
Max speed (rough air) 89 knots (102 mph; 165 km/h)
Max aero-tow speed 65 knots (75 mph; 120 km/h)
Max winch-launching speed 59 knots (68 mph; 110 km/h)

INDIA

CIVIL AVIATION DEPARTMENT

TECHNICAL CENTRE, CIVIL AVIATION DEPARTMENT

HEAD OFFICE:
Civil Aviation Department, R. K. Puram, New Delhi 22

DIRECTOR GENERAL: G. C. Arya

WORKS:
Technical Centre, Safdarjung, New Delhi

DEPUTY DIRECTOR GENERAL:
S. Ramamritham

DEPUTY DIRECTOR, RESEARCH AND DEVELOPMENT: K. B. Ganesan

The Technical Centre is the research and development establishment of the Indian Civil Aviation Department. It is equipped with all facilities necessary for the development of design, airworthiness and operational standards, operational research, development testing and standardisation of indigenous aircraft materials, Type Certification of prototype aircraft and equipment, and the scientific investigation of accidents.

Since 1950 the Technical Centre has undertaken the design and development of gliders, under the leadership of S. Ramamritham, utilising predominantly indigenous materials. The first of these gliders, of the open-cockpit primary type, was flown in November 1950. Since then the Technical Centre has built gliders of seven types for service at Civil Gliding Centres in India. These comprise two Model PT-G single-seat open-cockpit primary gliders based on the ESG design, six Model IT-G intermediate training gliders based on the Grunau Baby, two Model AS-1 advanced sailplanes based on the Olympia, five Ashvini tandem two-seat training sailplanes, and prototypes of the Rohini side-by-side two-seat sailplane, the tandem two-seat BS-1 Bharani and the single-seat high-performance Kartik. The Ashvini (described in 1964-65 *Jane's*: production completed), Rohini, Bharani (described in 1965-66 *Jane's*: prototype only to date) and Kartik are original designs.

The Technical Centre is currently engaged on the design and development of another Standard Class sailplane designated HS-I, as a successor to the Kartik II. It does not undertake quantity production of gliders. Complete sets of drawings of the designs developed at the Centre are supplied to interested organisations with permission to manufacture them in series. Two companies in India are manufacturing the Model IT-G3; the Rohini is also being produced by two companies, one of them being Hindustan Aeronautics Ltd at Kanpur.

The Technical Centre has also designed and developed a powered aircraft, the Revathi Mk II, of which details can be found in the "Aircraft" section.

RG-1 ROHINI-I

The Rohini-I is a side-by-side two-seat training sailplane, designed by Mr S. Ramamritham. It flew for the first time on 10 May 1961.

Four prototype Rohini gliders were built at the Technical Centre during the period 1961 to January 1964. Since then 17 production machines have been manufactured by Veegal Engines and Engineering Company of Calcutta, and plans for the production of 86 RG-I's by Hindustan Aeronautics Ltd, Kanpur Division, are nearing completion.

To minimise production and maintenance costs, the tail surfaces, air-brakes and many wing ribs of the Rohini are identical with those of the Ashvini sailplane.

TYPE: Two-seat training sailplane.

WINGS: Braced high-wing monoplane. Single bracing strut each side. Wing section NACA 4418 at root, NACA 4412 (modified) at tip. Dihedral (on top of spars) 1°. Incidence 3° 24′. Two-spar wood structure. Plywood-covered to rear spar, fabric-covered trailing-edge. Plain ailerons of fabric-covered wood construction, with plywood-covered leading-edges. Retractable wooden air-brakes above and below wing on each side.

FUSELAGE: Built as one-piece structure, with integral fin. Forward portion to wing rear spar attachment and rear portion aft of tailplane front attachment bulkhead are plywood-covered wooden semi-monocoque structures. Remaining portion has wooden girder structure, covered with fabric.

Rohini-1 side-by-side two-seat training sailplane

TAIL UNIT: Cantilever wooden structure. Fin plywood-covered. Remainder fabric-covered except for leading-edges and area of tailplane between two root ribs which are plywood-covered. Plywood trim-tab in starboard elevator.

LANDING GEAR: Non-retractable unsprung Dunlop mono-wheel and tyre, size 6·00 × 4, pressure 30 lb/sq in (2·10 kg/cm^2). No brake. Rubber-sprung nose-skid with replaceable steel shoe. Spring steel tail-skid.

ACCOMMODATION: Two seats side-by-side in open cockpit.

DIMENSIONS:
Wing span 54 ft 4 in (16·56 m)
Wing chord at root 5 ft 6$\frac{1}{2}$ in (1·69 m)
Wing chord at tip 2 ft 8$\frac{1}{2}$ in (0·82 m)
Wing aspect ratio 13·2
Length overall 26 ft 9$\frac{1}{2}$ in (8·17 m)
Height over tail 7 ft 7$\frac{7}{8}$ in (2·33 m)
Tailplane span 13 ft 2 in (4·02 m)

AREAS:
Wings, gross 223·3 sq ft (20·76 m^2)
Ailerons (total) 25·00 sq ft (2·32 m^2)
Air-brakes (total) 2·62 sq ft (0·24 m^2)
Fin 5·82 sq ft (0·54 m^2)
Rudder, including tab 11·82 sq ft (1·10 m^2)
Tailplane 21·30 sq ft (1·98 m^2)
Elevators, including tab 17·20 sq ft (1·60 m^2)

WEIGHTS AND LOADING:
Weight empty, equipped 660 lb (300 kg)
Max T-O weight 1,078 lb (490 kg)
Max wing loading 4·83 lb/sq ft (23·60 kg/m^2)

PERFORMANCE (at max T-O weight):
Best glide ratio 22 : 1 at 42 knots (48 mph; 77 km/h)
Min sinking speed 2·85 ft (0·86 m)/sec at 33 knots (38 mph; 61 km/h)
Stalling speed 26 knots (30 mph; 48 km/h)
Max speed (smooth air) 94 knots (108 mph; 174 km/h)
Max speed (rough air) 65 knots (75 mph; 120 km/h)
Max aero-tow speed 61 knots (70 mph; 113 km/h)
Max winch-launching speed 52 knots (60 mph; 96 km/h)

KS-I and KS-II KARTIK

The original prototype KS-I Kartik, designed by Mr S. Ramamritham, flew for the first time on 18 March 1963. Later the same day, after a subsequent winch launch, the first stalling and spinning trials were performed successfully from a height of approximately 6,000 ft (1,800 m). A second prototype was built subsequently.

A distinctive feature of the KS-I Kartik (which was illustrated in the 1964-65 *Jane's*) was the "double-rectangular" wing planform. This minimised the number of different ribs required for a tapered wing, easing production and facilitating close control of accuracy of the aerofoil contours.

A third prototype, designated KS-II Kartik, flew on 4 May 1965. This aircraft introduced a number of major design changes. In particular, it has a conventional tapered wing instead of the "double-rectangular" wing of the KS-I, to permit flight assessment of the relative performance of the two wings. Other changes include a reduction in the height of the cockpit, a slight increase in fuselage length, and modifications to the shape of the aileron leading-edge.

The second, third, fourth and fifth prototypes of the KS-II were test flown during February 1967, March and May 1968 and May 1969 respectively. A sixth prototype was scheduled to fly in 1970. The third and later machines incorporate improvements to the original design, including a reduction in fuselage height, improved forward vision and seating, and larger air-brakes.

The KS-II Kartik was type certificated in 1965.

During the first Indian National Gliding Rally, held in 1967, the Kartik sailplane proved itself by achieving many successes, including the establishment of a national speed record over a 200-km triangular course.

The following details apply to both the KS-I and KS-II:

TYPE: Single-seat high-performance sailplane.

WINGS: Cantilever high-wing monoplane. Wing section NACA 64_3-618. Dihedral 1° 30′. Incidence 0°. Wood structure, with one main spar, one rear spar and a diagonal spar at the root. Plywood-covered torsion-box back to rear spar. Trailing-edge fabric-covered. Plywood-covered wood ailerons on KS-I. Fabric-covered slotted wooden ailerons on KS-II. Retractable wooden air-brakes above and below wing on each side.

FUSELAGE: Semi-monocoque wood structure with plywood covering and glass-fibre nose cap.

TAIL UNIT: Cantilever wood structure. Fin plywood-covered. Remainder fabric-covered except for plywood covering on leading-edges. Plywood trim-tab in starboard elevator.

LANDING GEAR: Non-retractable Palmer/Dunlop unsprung mono-wheel and tyre, size 4·00 × 3·5, pressure 30 lb/sq in (2·10 kg/cm^2). KS-II wheel has drum-type brake, operated by a separate lever mounted on the air-brake operating lever. Rubber-sprung nose-skid with replaceable steel shoe. Tail-skid sprung with tennis balls.

ACCOMMODATION: Single seat under rearward-opening hinged Perspex canopy. Oxygen equipment optional.

DIMENSIONS:
Wing span 49 ft 2$\frac{1}{2}$ in (15·00 m)
Wing chord at root:
KS-I,-II 3 ft 3$\frac{1}{4}$ in (1·00 m)
Wing chord at tip:
KS-I 2 ft 7$\frac{1}{2}$ in (0·80 m)
KS-II 2 ft 1$\frac{1}{4}$ in (0·64 m)
Wing aspect ratio:
KS-I,-II 16·6

Length overall:
KS-I	23 ft 10 in (7·27 m)
KS-II	24 ft 2 in (7·37 m)
Height over tail	7 ft 5 in (2·26 m)
Tailplane span	9 ft 6 in (2·90 m)

AREAS:
Wings, gross	145·7 sq ft (13·54 m²)
Ailerons (total):	
KS-I	13·56 sq ft (1·26 m²)
KS-II	14·21 sq ft (1·32 m²)
Air-brakes (total)	4·68 sq ft (0·43 m²)
Fin:	
KS-I	4·20 sq ft (0·39 m²)
KS-II	5·02 sq ft (0·47 m²)
Rudder	9·60 sq ft (0·89 m²)
Tailplane	13·20 sq ft (1·22 m²)
Elevators, including tab	11·30 sq ft (1·05 m²)

WEIGHTS AND LOADING:
Weight empty, equipped:	
KS-I	467 lb (212 kg)
KS-II	463 lb (210 kg)
Max T-O weight:	
KS-I	661 lb (300 kg)
KS-II	705 lb (320 kg)
Max wing loading:	
KS-I	4·53 lb/sq ft (22·15 kg/m²)
KS-II	4·86 lb/sq ft (23·63 kg/m²)

PERFORMANCE (KS-II at max T-O weight):
Best glide ratio	
	31 : 1 at 41 knots (47 mph; 75 km/h)
Min sinking speed	1·97 ft (0·60 m)/sec at
	35 knots (40 mph; 65 km/h)
Stalling speed	32 knots (36 mph; 58 km/h)
Max speed (smooth air)	
	108 knots (124 mph; 200 km/h)
Max speed (rough air)	
	76 knots (87 mph; 140 km/h)
Max aero-tow speed	
	62 knots (71 mph; 114 km/h)
Max winch-launching speed	
	54 knots (62 mph; 100 km/h)

HS-I

This new Standard Class sailplane has been designed by the Technical Centre of the Civil Aviation Department. It will have a higher aspect ratio wing than the KS-II Kartik, with Wortmann wing sections. A prototype was under construction at the time of writing and was expected to fly for the first time during the Summer of 1970. Only its external dimensions are known at present, and these are quoted below.

TYPE: High-performance Standard Class sailplane.

DIMENSIONS, EXTERNAL:
Wing span	49 ft 2½ in (15·0 m)
Wing aspect ratio	20
Length overall	24 ft 8 in (7·52 m)
Height overall	7 ft 5 in (2·26 m)
Tailplane span	9 ft 6 in (2·90 m)

KS-II Kartik single-seat high-performance sailplane in its latest form

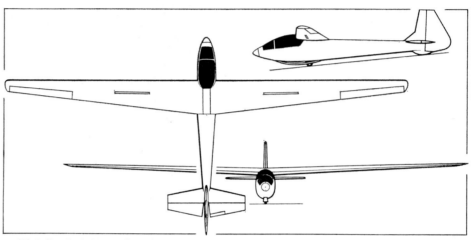

HS-1 Standard Class sailplane designed by the Technical Centre, Civil Aviation Department

ITALY

AVIAMILANO
AVIAMILANO COSTRUZIONI AERONAUTICHE
HEAD OFFICE:
Via Macedonio Melloni 70, Milan

As a result of the death of Ing Mario Vietri, the Aviamilano company is no longer able to continue the production of sailplanes. Pro-duction of the A2 and A3 sailplanes has been taken over by Caproni Vizzola (see below).

CAPRONI VIZZOLA
CAPRONI VIZZOLA COSTRUZIONI AERO-NAUTICHE SpA
HEAD OFFICE: 20122 Milano, Via Durini 24
WORKS: 21010 Vizzola Ticino, Via Montecchio 1
PRESIDENT: Dr Giovanni Caproni
VICE-PRESIDENT:
Rag Achille Caproni di Taliedo

The Caproni company, formed in 1910, is the oldest Italian aircraft manufacturer. It is now engaged in large-scale production of several different types of sailplanes of advanced design.

Production of sailplanes started in 1968 when Caproni Vizzola took over manufacture of the Standard Class Aviamilano A2 and the A3 Open Class version of the same design. Production of these types ended in June 1969 and details of the Standard Class A2 may be found in the 1969-70 *Jane's*.

CAPRONI VIZZOLA CALIF SERIES

Caproni Vizzola are now concerned with the production of a series of sailplanes designed by Carlo Ferrarin and Livio Sonzio. These are as follows:

Calif A-10, A-12, A-14. Single-seat high-performance sailplanes which are basically similar. Six under construction in early 1970.

Calif A-20, A-21. Two-seat high-performance sailplanes. These are basically two-seat versions of the A-12 and A-14 respectively. Sixteen under construction in early 1970.

Calif A-21J. Powered version of the A-21, with adequate power for unassisted take-off.

All available details of the above aircraft are given below.

CAPRONI VIZZOLA CALIF A-10

Design of the Calif series of sailplanes was begun in January 1969, and construction of the

Caproni Vizzola Calif sailplane under construction, showing details of tail unit

prototype started two months later. First flight of the prototype was expected to be made in June 1970, and the first production A-10 sailplane was scheduled to fly in September 1970.

TYPE: Single-seat high-performance sailplane.

WINGS: Cantilever mid-wing monoplane. Wing section Wortmann FX 67-K-170/150 at root, FX 60-126 at tip. Thickness/chord ratio, 17% at root, 12·6% at tip. Dihedral 0° at root, 3° 30′ at a point just outboard of mid-span, 1° 45′ wing outer section to tip. Incidence 0°. Sweepback on leading-edge only outboard of mid-span 4°. Two-piece all-metal single-spar stressed-skin structure. Main spar forms torsion box with leading-edge. Glass-fibre wingtips. Top-hinged partially-balanced differentially-operated plain ailerons of all-metal stressed-skin construction. Automatic connection of controls when wings are assembled. Lower-hinged aerodynamically-balanced trailing-edge flaps/spoilers of all-metal stressed-skin construction, manually operated by a single control, are utilised as camber-changing surfaces in the —8° to +12° range, and as air-brakes when lowered to a 90° position.

FUSELAGE: Low-drag tadpole-shaped fuselage. Monocoque forward section of glass-fibre construction with load-carrying light alloy structure. Narrow-diameter all-metal stressed-skin tail boom.

TAIL UNIT: Cantilever all-metal structure with swept vertical surfaces. All-moving tailplane mounted at the top of the fin. Fin is a single-spar stressed-skin structure. Spring-adjusted tailplane trimming. Automatic control connections during assembly.

LANDING GEAR: Mechanically-retractable mono-wheel, with rubber-in-compression or hydraulic shock-absorption; mechanical up and down lock. Non-retractable steerable tail-wheel for ground handling. Main wheel and tyre size 3·50 × 5, pressure 73·5 lb/sq in (5·17 kg/m²). Mechanically-operated Tost wheel brake.

ACCOMMODATION: Single seat in semi-reclining position in enclosed cabin, under flush transparent canopy.

DIMENSIONS, EXTERNAL:
Wing span	49 ft 2½ in (15·0 m)
Wing chord at root	2 ft 11½ in (0·90 m)
Wing chord at tip	1 ft 0¼ in (0·31 m)
Wing aspect ratio	19·68
Length overall	22 ft 4 in (6·81 m)
Tailplane span	9 ft 5¾ in (2·89 m)

AREAS:
Wings, gross	123 sq ft (11·43 m²)
Ailerons (total)	11·8 sq ft (1·10 m²)
Trailing-edge flaps/ spoilers (total)	26 sq ft (2·42 m²)
Fin	8·07 sq ft (0·75 m²)
Rudder	6·57 sq ft (0·61 m²)
Tailplane	16·6 sq ft (1·54 m²)

WEIGHTS AND LOADING:
Weight empty, equipped	485 lb (220 kg)
Max T-O weight	705 lb (320 kg)
Max wing loading	5·7 lb/sq ft (28 kg/m²)

PERFORMANCE (estimated):
Best glide ratio	41 : 1 at 46 knots (53 mph; 85 km/h)
Minimum sinking speed	1·81 ft (0·55 m)/sec at 40 knots (45·5 mph; 73 km/h)
Stalling speed (flaps up)	34 knots (39 mph; 62·7 km/h)
Max speed (rough and smooth air)	146 knots (168 mph; 270 km/h)
Max aero-tow speed	93 knots (107 mph; 173 km/h)
Ultimate load factor	6g

CAPRONI VIZZOLA CALIF A-12 and A-14

Generally similar to the A-10, these two sailplanes have increased span and wing area, with a resulting increase in performance. The description of the A-10 applies also to the A-12 and A-14, except as detailed below.

WINGS: Same as for the A-10, except that as a result of increased span they are built as three-piece structures.

DIMENSIONS, EXTERNAL:
Same as for A-10 except:
Wing span:	
A-12	58 ft 8 in (17·88 m)
A-14	66 ft 10¼ in (20·38 m)
Wing aspect ratio:	
A-12	23·08
A-14	25·8
Length overall:	
A-14	23 ft 7¾ in (7·21 m)

AREAS:
Same as for A-10 except:
Wings, gross:	
A-12	149 sq ft (13·85 m²)
A-14	173 sq ft (16·10 m²)
Trailing-edge flaps/spoilers:	
A-12	33·6 sq ft (3·12 m²)
A-14	40·8 sq ft (3·79 m²)

WEIGHTS AND LOADING:
Weight empty, equipped:	
A-12	573 lb (260 kg)
A-14	617 lb (280 kg)
Max T-O weight:	
A-12	881 lb (400 kg)
A-14	954 lb (433 kg)
Max wing loading:	
A-14	5·53 lb/sq ft (27 kg/m²)

PERFORMANCE (estimated):
Best glide ratio:	
A-12	45 : 1 at 50 knots (58 mph; 93 km/h)
A-14	49 : 1 at 49 knots (56 mph; 90 km/h)

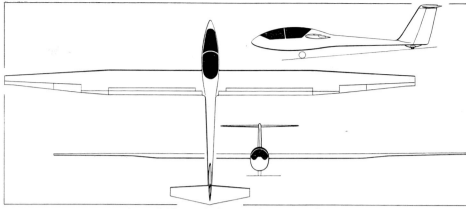

Caproni Vizzola Calif A-10 single-seat sailplane

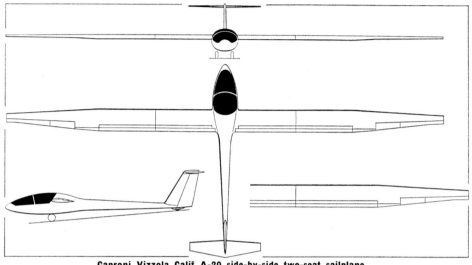

Caproni Vizzola Calif A-20 side-by-side two-seat sailplane

Minimum sinking speed:
A-12	1·54 ft (0·47 m)/sec at 43·4 knots (50 mph; 80 km/h)
A-14	1·31 ft (0·40 m)/sec at 42·6 knots (49 mph; 79 km/h)

Stalling speed (flaps up):
A-12	35 knots (40 mph; 64·4 km/h)
A-14	34 knots (39 mph; 62·4 km/h)

Max speed (smooth and rough air):
A-12, A-14	146 knots (168 mph; 270 km/h)

Max aero-tow speed:
A-12	97 knots (112 mph; 181 km/h)
A-14	96 knots (111 mph; 178 km/h)

Ultimate load factor:
A-12, A-14	6g

CAPRONI VIZZOLA CALIF A-20 and A-21

The A-20 and A-21 are two-seat versions of the A-12 and A-14 respectively. They differ principally by having a wider fuselage to accommodate two side-by-side seats and, as a result of CG shift, a slightly longer fuselage.

The description of the A-10, as modified by the A-12 and A-14 entries, applies also to the A-20 and A-21, except as detailed below.

TYPE: Two-seat high-performance sailplane.

FUSELAGE: As for A-10, except that the forward glass-fibre section is strengthened with bonded plastic foam.

LANDING GEAR: Dual wheels replace mono-wheel of single-seater. Size unchanged.

ACCOMMODATION: Two seats, side-by-side, in enclosed cabin.

DIMENSIONS, EXTERNAL:
Same as for A-12, A-14 respectively except:
Length overall:	
A-20, A-21	25 ft 8¾ in (7·84 m)

AREAS:
Same as for A-12, A-14 respectively, except:
Trailing-edge flaps/spoilers:	
A-20	32·2 sq ft (2·99 m²)
A-21	39·4 sq ft (3·66 m²)

WEIGHTS AND LOADINGS:
Weight empty, equipped:	
A-20	617 lb (280 kg)
A-21	661 lb (300 kg)
Max T-O weight:	
A-20	1,058 lb (480 kg)
A-21	1,146 lb (520 kg)
Max wing loading:	
A-20	7·1 lb/sq ft (34·7 kg/m²)
A-21	6·6 lb/sq ft (32·3 kg/m²)

PERFORMANCE (estimated):
Best glide ratio:	
A-20	42 : 1 at 49 knots (56 mph; 90 km/h)
A-21	45 : 1 at 51 knots (59 mph; 59 km/h)
Min sinking speed:	
A-20	1·80 ft (0·55 m)/sec at 42 knots (48 mph; 77 km/h)
A-21	1·64 ft (0·50 m)/sec at 43·4 knots (50 mph; 80 km/h)

Stalling speed (flaps up):
A-20	38·2 knots (43·9 mph; 70·5 km/h)
A-21	37 knots (42·8 mph; 68·4 km/h)

Max speed (smooth and rough air):
A-20, A-21	146 knots (168 mph; 270 km/h)

Max aero-tow speed:
A-20	97 knots (112 mph; 181 km/h)
A-21	96 knots (111 mph; 178 km/h)

Ultimate load factor 5g

CAPRONI VIZZOLA CALIF A-21J

This is a powered version of the A-21 two-seat sailplane. The description of the A-21 applies also to the A-21J except in the following details:

TYPE: Two-seat powered sailplane.

LANDING GEAR: Mechanically-retractable tail-wheel type. Each main wheel retracts rearward into the fuselage.

POWER PLANT: One Sermel TRS 18 single-spool turbojet engine of 45 lb (100 kg) st or one Microturbo Eclair single-spool turbojet engine of 36 lb (80 kg) st, mounted in the lower fuselage aft of the seats. Fuel contained in two wing tanks, each containing 11 Imp gallons (50 litres). Total fuel capacity 22 Imp gallons (100 litres).

SYSTEMS: Compressed air system for starting TRS 18 engine. Electrical system comprising engine-driven generator and 24V 12Ah nickel-cadmium battery for starting Eclair engine.

WEIGHTS AND LOADING:
Weight empty, equipped	193 lb (427 kg)
Max T-O weight	284 lb (627 kg)
Max wing loading	8·0 lb/sq ft (39 kg/m²)

PERFORMANCE (estimated at max T-O weight):
Best glide ratio	43 : 1 at 58 knots (67 mph; 108 km/h)
Min sinking speed	1·97 ft (0·60 m)/sec at 49 knots (56 mph; 90 km/h)
Stalling speed (flaps up)	41 knots (47 mph; 75·1 km/h)

CVT
CENTRO DI VOLO A VELA DEL POLITECNICO DI TORINO

ADDRESS:
Corso Duca Degli Abruzzi 24, 10129 Turin

OFFICE AND LABORATORY:
Corso Luigi Einaudi 54, 10129 Turin

Gliders built at the CVT have included the CVT-2 Veltro single-seat high-performance sailplane, which set up Italian national records for height and distance. Designed by Alberto and Piero Morelli, it flew for the first time in 1954 and was described in the 1960-61 Jane's.

Subsequent designs by Alberto and Piero

Morelli have included the M-100 S, which is being manufactured under licence in Italy by Avionautica Rio at Sarnico (Bergamo), and in France by CARMAM (which see) as the Mésange; the M-200, which is also being manufactured by CARMAM; and the M-300, of which details follow.

MORELLI M-300

The M-300, designed by Alberto Morelli, is a single-seat high-performance sailplane of which four prototypes are being built at the CVT. It is intended for competition and record flying, as well as for club use, and incorporates many original features. In particular, careful thought has been given to constructional techniques which would simplify eventual series production of the M-300 and reduce labour costs.

The M-300 is of composite metal, wood and plastic construction. The wing spar is made from an H-section extrusion in 7075 aluminium alloy, subsequently machined. The primary wing attachment fittings are of dural, Redux-bonded to the spar. Wing skin is of thick plywood, precured and plastic-reinforced at the leading-edge.

The ailerons and all-moving tailplane are made from extruded sections of aluminium alloy, the thickness of which is reduced by chemical milling. A double-slotted rudder is fitted.

A heavy-duty retractable landing gear is fitted with rubber-in-compression shock-absorbers.

The first M-300 prototype was flown by the French pilot M Rantet in the 1969 "Coup d'Europe—Huit Jours d'Angers", winning the seventh task and gaining an overall 9th final placing.

DIMENSIONS:
Wing span	49 ft 2½ in (15·00 m)
Wing aspect ratio	25

WEIGHTS:
Weight empty	396 lb (180 kg)
Max T-O weight	660 lb (300 kg)

CVT Morelli M-300 single-seat high-performance sailplane

GLASFLÜGEL

GLASFLÜGEL ITALIANA SrL

ADDRESS:
24030 Valbrembo (Bergamo), Via Marconi 11
PRESIDENT:
Dr Ing Sergio Aldo Capoferri
VICE-PRESIDENT:
Dr Ing Mario Moltrasio

TECHNICAL DIRECTOR: Giampaolo Ghidotti

This new company has been established at Valbrembo Airport, where it is accommodated in a factory which occupies an area of 4,300 sq ft (400 m²) and which is insulated and heated to maintain a controlled temperature of 68°F (20°C), essential for work on glass-fibre structures.

Glasflügel Italiana has already assembled eight single-seat Open Class Kestrel sailplanes, details of which may be found under the Glasflügel entry on page 554 of this edition. Three more Kestrels were being assembled in February 1970, and other activities include construction of trailers for road transportation of Kestrel and Libelle sailplanes, repair and maintenance to sailplanes of glass-fibre, wood and metal construction, as well as installation and modification work to sailplanes of all types.

RIO

AVIONAUTICA RIO SpA

ADDRESS:
Piazza Stazione 1, Sarnico, Bergamo
This company has been building under licence since June 1963 the M-100 S single-seat sailplane designed by Piero and Alberto Morelli. Eighty-five had been completed by the end of March 1968, with production continuing. Manufacture of the M-200 two-seater, designed by Morelli, started at the beginning of 1968. Planned production was 10 per year.

Full details of the M-100 S and M-200 are given under the entry for the French licensees, CAR-MAM, on pages 548-9.

SSVV

AEROCLUB VOLOVELISTICO MILANESE, SEZIONE SPERIMENTALE VOLO VELA

ADDRESS:
Viale dell'Aviazione, 65, Milan

DIRECTOR OF SSVV: Felice Gonalba

The SSVV was formed by the Aeroclub Volovelistico Milanese to maintain and repair the club's gliders and to undertake the construction of new aircraft. It concentrated at first on reconditioning Zoegling and Allievo Cantu sailplanes, its first new product being the CVV7 Pinocchio single-seat sailplane.

Subsequently, it built the high-performance single-seat Spillo E.C. 37-53, a small series of the two-seat Urendo E.C. 38-56 and the prototype E.C. 40 Eventuale two-seat training sailplane, all designed by Eng Edgardo Ciani, and the small single-seat Gheppio R.1, designed by Eng Gianfranco Rotondi.

Following the construction of five examples of the Uribel single-seat Standard Class sailplane, the SSVV is now building a small series of the improved Uribel C. This has a completely redesigned wing and a fuselage of reduced cross-section.

From the Uribel C, the SSVV has developed a new Open Class sailplane known as the Crib E.C.41.

Details of the Spillo, Gheppio, Urendo, Eventuale and the original Uribel have appeared in previous editions of *Jane's*. Descriptions of the Uribel C and Crib E.C.41 follow.

SSVV URIBEL C

This latest version of the Uribel, designed by Eng Edgardo Ciani, is very similar in design and construction to the earlier Uribel B. It is a single-seat Standard Class sailplane of all-wood construction. The cantilever shoulder wing has an Eppler 257 section, of 17% thickness/chord ratio, and is plywood-covered; the fuselage is a wooden monocoque, with the cockpit canopy faired completely into the top profile of the nose section. A "butterfly" tail is fitted.

DIMENSIONS:
Wing span	49 ft 2½ in (15·00 m)
Wing aspect ratio	16·2
Length overall	19 ft 6 in (5·94 m)

AREA:
Wings, gross	148·5 sq ft (13·80 m²)

WEIGHTS AND LOADING:
Weight empty	463 lb (210 kg)
Max T-O weight	683 lb (310 kg)
Max wing loading	4·61 lb/sq ft (22·5 kg/m²)

SSVV Uribel C single-seat Standard Class sailplane (*Anne Ince*)

SSVV Crib E.C.41 single-seat high-performance sailplane

PERFORMANCE:
Best glide ratio
    31 : 1 at 41·7 knots (48 mph; 78 km/h)
Min sinking speed   2·17 ft (0·66 m)/sec at
    37·4 knots (43 mph; 70 km/h)

SSVV CRIB E.C.41

This single-seat Open Class sailplane is a development of the Uribel C. It has an all-wood structure, covered with a moulded plywood skin. The wing is similar to that of the Uribel C, with the tips extended; but the fuselage is of new design, with the pilot in a semi-reclining position to permit reduction of the cross-sectional area. The V tail of the Uribel is replaced by a conventional tail unit.

The prototype Crib E.C.41 flew for the first time in December 1966 and three more examples had been built by April 1967.

TYPE: Single-seat high-performance sailplane.

WINGS: Cantilever shoulder-wing monoplane. Wing section Eppler 357. Thickness/chord ratio 17%. Dihedral 2°. Incidence 3°. No sweep. All-wood structure with plywood covering. Upper surface hinged ailerons. No flaps. Light alloy DFS air-brakes.

FUSELAGE: All-wood structure, with moulded plywood skin.

TAIL UNIT: Cantilever all-wood structure. Fixed-incidence tailplane. Trim-tab in elevators.

LANDING GEAR: Non-retractable mono-wheel and nose-skid. Rubber block shock-absorption. Pirelli tyre size 400 × 100, pressure 39 lb/sq in (2·75 kg/cm²). Macchi brake.

ACCOMMODATION: Single semi-reclining seat under long flush sideways-hinged transparent canopy.

DIMENSIONS:
Wing span	57 ft 10½ in (17·64 m)
Wing chord (mean)	2 ft 10·65 in (0·88 m)
Wing aspect ratio	20
Length overall	24 ft 7¼ in (7·50 m)
Height over tail	4 ft 11 in (1·50 m)
Tailplane span	11 ft 1¾ in (3·40 m)

AREAS:
Wings, gross	166·8 sq ft (15·5 m²)
Ailerons (total)	17·22 sq ft (1·6 m²)
Fin	6·78 sq ft (0·63 m²)
Rudder	5·70 sq ft (0·43 m²)
Tailplane	26·37 sq ft (2·45 m²)
Elevators, incl tab	11·41 sq ft (1·06 m²)

WEIGHTS AND LOADING:
Weight empty	606 lb (275 kg)
Max T-O weight	882 lb (400 kg)
Max wing loading	5·22 lb/sq ft (25·5 kg/m²)

PERFORMANCE:
Best glide ratio
    38 : 1 at 48·7 knots (56 mph; 90 km/h)

Min sinking speed	1·97 ft (0·60 m)/sec at 37·8 knots (43·5 mph; 70 km/h)
Stalling speed	33 knots (37·5 mph; 60 km/h)

Max speed (smooth air)	108 knots (124 mph; 200 km/h)
Max speed (rough air)	72 knots (83 mph; 134 km/h)

Max aero-tow speed	72 knots (83 mph; 134 km/h)
Max winch-launching speed	62 knots (71 mph; 115 km/h)

UMBRA

AERONAUTICA UMBRA SpA
HEAD OFFICE AND WORKS:
Via Piave 12, 06034 Foligno
ROME OFFICE:
Via Scarpellini 20, Rome

OFFICERS: See "Aircraft" section
Aeronautica Umbra was founded in 1935 by
Sr Muzio Macchi, former general manager of the
Aeronautica Macchi works at Varese. The Um-
bra factory at Foligno has now been rebuilt and
modernised to provide facilities for the construc-

tion of prototype and production-series aircraft.
This company is manufacturing under licence
the German Scheibe SF-25B Falke powered
sailplane (see page 558) and has acquired exclusive
marketing rights for this aircraft in Italy and
North Africa.

JAPAN

LADCO
LIGHT AIRCRAFT DEVELOPMENT COMPANY, TOKYO

Designer for the Light Aircraft Development
Company (LADCO) is Mr Asahi Miyahara.
Gliding activity in Japan is increasing and
LADCO are now producing two sailplanes per
month, and are developing a powered sailplane.
Current products are described below:

LADCO-KEIHIKOKI SS-1

TYPE: Single-seat Standard Class sailplane.
WINGS: Cantilever shoulder-wing monoplane.
Wing section NACA 63$_4$-421 at root, NACA
63$_2$-615 at tip. The two-piece wing is of
wooden construction, covered with plywood
and fabric. The single box-spar has top
and bottom booms of laminated spruce
covered on both sides by plywood webs.
The leading-edge and the section between the
main and rear spar are covered with plywood.
The ribs are made of spruce and plywood.
DFS type air-brakes are fitted.
FUSELAGE: Tubular steel truss with wooden
stringers and fabric covering. Nose portion
is of moulded glass-fibre.
TAIL UNIT: Cantilever spruce and plywood
structure. Rudder and elevator are fabric-
covered.
LANDING GEAR: Non-retractable mono-wheel
with brake. Nose skid.
ACCOMMODATION: Single seat under blown
Plexiglas bubble canopy.

DIMENSIONS:
Wing span	49 ft 2½ in (15 m)
Wing aspect ratio	20
Length overall	23 ft 5½ in (7·15 m)
Height	5 ft 0 in (1·52 m)

AREAS:
Wings, gross	121·09 sq ft (11·25 m²)
Fin	4·84 sq ft (0·45 m²)
Rudder	6·46 sq ft (0·60 m²)
Tailplane	10·87 sq ft (1·01 m²)
Elevator	8·72 sq ft (0·81 m²)

WEIGHTS AND LOADING:
Weight empty	474 lb (215 kg)
Max T-O weight	705 lb (320 kg)
Max wing loading	5·8 lb/sq ft (28·4 kg/m²)

PERFORMANCE:
Best glide ratio	31·4 : 1 at 46 knots (53 mph; 85·9 km/h)
Min sinking speed	2·30 ft (0·70 m)/sec at 42 knots (48 mph; 76·8 km/h)
	2·36 ft (0·72 m)/sec at 43 knots (50 mph; 80 km/h)
	3·08 ft (0·94 m)/sec at 54 knots (62 mph; 100 km/h)
	4·53 ft (1·38 m)/sec at 65 knots (75 mph; 120 km/h)
Stalling speed	35 knots (40 mph; 65·9 km/h)
Max speed	97 knots (112 mph; 180 km/h)
Max aero-tow speed	70 knots (81 mph; 130 km/h)
Max winch-launching speed	59 knots (68 mph; 110 km/h)

LADCO LSS-02

TYPE: Single-seat high-performance sailplane.
WINGS: Cantilever high-wing monoplane. Wing
section FX-61-184 at root and FX-60-126 at
tip. The three-piece wing is of all-wooden
construction. Box-section mono-spar is completely plywood-covered to increase torsion
resistance. Schempp-Hirth air-brakes.
FUSELAGE: Wooden monocoque structure;
glass-fibre nose section.
TAIL UNIT: Cantilever wood construction.
Plywood-covered tailplane is mounted midway
on fin. Elevator fabric-covered.
LANDING GEAR: Non-retractable mono-wheel in
streamlined pod.
ACCOMMODATION: Single semi-reclining seat
under blown Plexiglas canopy.

DIMENSIONS:
Wing span	57 ft 1 in (17·4 m)
Wing aspect ratio	20
Length overall	25 ft 3 in (7·7 m)
Height overall	4 ft 11 in (1·5 m)

AREAS:
Wings, gross	163·18 sq ft (15·16 m²)
Rudder	6·14 sq ft (0·57 m²)
Tailplane	19·38 sq ft (1·8 m²)

LADCO-Keihikoki SS-1 single-seat Standard Class sailplane

WEIGHTS AND LOADING:
Weight empty	639 lb (290 kg)
Max T-O weight	881 lb (400 kg)
Max wing loading	5·43 lb/sq ft (26·5 kg/m²)

PERFORMANCE:
Best glide ratio	34 : 1 at 47 knots (54 mph; 86·6 km/h)
Min sinking speed	2·10 ft (0·64 m)/sec at 38 knots (44 mph; 71·3 km/h)

Stalling speed	34 knots (39 mph; 62·3 km/h)
Max speed	108 knots (124 mph; 200 km/h)

LADCO MITA III

TYPE: Two-seat training and sporting sailplane.
WINGS: Cantilever shoulder-wing monoplane.
Wing section NACA 63$_3$-618. Three-piece
wing, with constant-chord centre-section and
tapered outer panels. All-wood boxed mono-

LADCO LSS-02 single-seat high-performance sailplane

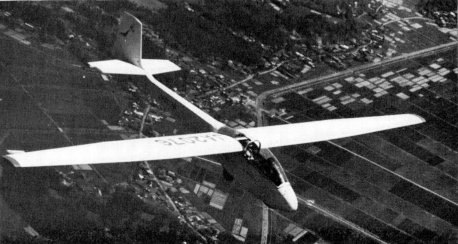

LADCO Mita III two-seat sailplane

spar construction, plywood-covered. Ailerons fabric-covered. Schempp-Hirth air-brakes.

FUSELAGE: Steel-tube frame with wooden stringers and fabric covering. Nose and front section of glass-fibre.

TAIL UNIT: Cantilever type, of wooden construction; rudder and elevator fabric-covered.

LANDING GEAR: Non-retractable mono-wheel with brake and rubber springing.

ACCOMMODATION: Two seats in tandem under two-piece blown bubble canopy.

DIMENSIONS:

Wing span	52 ft 5 in (16 m)
Wing aspect ratio	16·13

Length overall	26 ft 1½ in (7·96 m)
Height	4 ft 2½ in (1·28 m)

AREAS:

Wings, gross	170·82 sq ft (15·87 m²)
Fin	6·03 sq ft (0·56 m²)
Rudder	8·29 sq ft (0·77 m²)
Tailplane	15·50 sq ft (1·44 m²)
Elevators	11·63 sq ft (1·08 m²)

WEIGHTS AND LOADING:

Weight empty	661 lb (300 kg)
Max T-O weight	992 lb (450 kg)
Max wing loading	5·8 lb/sq ft (28·4 kg/m²)

PERFORMANCE:

Best glide ratio
    30 : 1 at 44 knots (51 mph; 82 km/h)

Min sinking speed:
  2·36 ft (0·72 m)/sec at 41 knots (47 mph; 75 km/h)
  2·42 ft (0·74 m)/sec at 43 knots (50 mph; 80 km/h)
  3·05 ft (0·93 m)/sec at 54 knots (62 mph; 100 km/h)
  4·53 ft (1·38 m)/sec at 65 knots (75 mph; 120 km/h)

Stalling speed	34 knots (39 mph; 62 km/h)
Max speed	102 knots (118 mph; 190 km/h)

Max aero-tow speed
  70 knots (81 mph; 130 km/h)
Max winch-launching speed
  59 knots (68 mph; 110 km/h)

YGC
YOKOHAMA GLIDING CLUB

ADDRESS:
6-32 Funakoshi-machi Yokohama, Kanagawa

The Yokohama Gliding Club is flying two sailplanes designed by Mr Osamu Saito; all available details of these follow.

YGC SH-16

TYPE: Two-seat training sailplane.

WINGS: Cantilever high-wing monoplane. Wing section Takatori No II. Thickness/chord ratio 16% at root, 13% at tip. All-wood boxed mono-spar structure with plywood skin. DFS-type air brakes.

FUSELAGE: All-wood monocoque structure.

TAIL UNIT: Cantilever all-wood structure with swept vertical and horizontal surfaces. Tailplane mounted on upper surface of fuselage, forward of fin. Rudder and elevators fabric-covered. Trim-tab in starboard elevator.

LANDING GEAR: Non-retractable mono-wheel and front skid. Wheel brake.

ACCOMMODATION: Two seats in tandem in enclosed cabin. Two-piece transparent canopy supported by wooden frames.

DIMENSIONS:

Wing span	52 ft 11½ in (16·14 m)
Wing aspect ratio	16
Length overall	26 ft 3¾ in (8·02 m)
Height overall	5 ft 3¾ in (1·62 m)

AREAS:

Wings, gross	172 sq ft (16·0 m²)
Air-brakes (total)	5·92 sq ft (0·55 m²)
Vertical tail surfaces (total)	14·0 sq ft (1·30 m²)
Horizontal tail surfaces (total)	23·7 sq ft (2·20 m²)

WEIGHTS AND LOADING:

Weight empty	705 lb (320 kg)
Max T-O weight	1,102 lb (500 kg)
Max wing loading	6·4 lb/sq ft (31·25 kg/m²)

PERFORMANCE (A=two seats occupied, B=one seat occupied):

Best glide ratio:
  A 31·1 : 1 at 50·7 knots (58·5 mph; 94 km/h)
  B 31·1 : 1 at 45·3 knots (52 mph; 84 km/h)

Min sinking speed:
  A 2·40 ft (0·73 m)/sec at 40 knots (46 mph; 74 km/h)
  B 2·13 ft (0·65 m)/sec at 35·6 knots (41 mph; 66 km/h)

Stalling speed:
  A 35·2 knots (40·5 mph; 65 km/h)
  B 30·5 knots (35 mph; 56 km/h)

Max speed (smooth air):
  A, B 86 knots (99 mph; 160 km/h)

Max speed, rough air:
  A, B 81 knots (93 mph; 150 km/h)

Max aero-tow speed:
  A, B 73 knots (84 mph; 135 km/h)

Max winch-launching speed:
  A, B 73 knots (84 mph; 135 km/h)

YGC SH-16S TAKATORI

Few details of this single-seat sailplane are known, but all available information is given below:

TYPE: Single-seat high-performance sailplane.

WINGS: Cantilever shoulder-wing monoplane. Aerofoil section NACA 65₃-418. Aspect ratio 20. All-wood boxed mono-spar structure with

Yokohama Gliding Club SH-16 two-seat training sailplane

Yokohama Gliding Club SH-16S Takatori single-seat high-performance sailplane

plywood skin. Plain trailing-edge flaps at 80% chord. DFS-type air brakes.

FUSELAGE: All-wood monocoque structure.

TAIL UNIT: Cantilever all-wood structure. T-type tail.

LANDING GEAR: Non-retractable mono-wheel, nose-and tail-skid.

ACCOMMODATION: Single seat in semi-reclining position in enclosed cabin under transparent cockpit canopy.

POLAND

SZD
ZAKLADY SPRZETU LOTNICTWA SPORTO-WEGO (Air Sport Factories)

HEAD OFFICE AND WORKS:
Bielsko-Biala 1, vl Cieszynska 325

DIRECTOR:
Mgr Ing Wladyslaw Nowakowski

SALES REPRESENTATIVE:
Motoimport, Warszawa, ul Przemyslowa 26

ZAKLAD DOSWIADCZALNY ROZWOJU I BUDOWY SZYBOWCÓW (Experimental Establishment for Development of Glider Design)

The Instytut Szybownictwa (Gliding Institute), formed officially in April 1946 at Bielsko-Biala, was renamed two years later the Szybowcowy Zaklad Doswiadczalny—SZD (Experimental Glider Establishment). In July 1969 the name was changed again to that shown above, but it retains the well-known initial designation of SZD. This organisation is responsible for the design and development of all Polish gliders and sailplanes. Production plants are situated at Bielsko-Biala, Wroclaw and Jezów. SZD sailplanes have been exported all over the world in substantial numbers.

The current SZD products are described below.

SZD-9bis BOCIAN 1E (STORK)

The original prototype of the Bocian flew for the first time on 11 March 1952. Since then over 320 Bocian sailplanes have been built, in several versions, of which the latest is the Bocian 1E, which first flew on 6 December 1966 and is described below.

The controls, instrument panel and other details have been designed to make the aircraft suitable for sporting flight as well as for school and training duties. Cloud-flying, spinning and basic aerobatics are permitted.

TYPE: Tandem two-seat general-purpose sailplane.

WINGS: Cantilever mid-wing monoplane. Wing section NACA 43018 at root, NACA 43012A at tip. Dihedral 4°. Incidence 2° 30′. Sweepforward 1° 30′ at quarter-chord. Two-spar wood structure, with plywood D-section leading-edge and fabric covering. Slotted ailerons. No flaps. SZD air-brakes inboard of ailerons.

FUSELAGE: Plywood-covered wood structure of oval section.

TAIL UNIT: Cantilever wood structure. Trim-tab in elevators.

LANDING GEAR: Non-retractable mono-wheel and front skid. Shock-absorber fitted. Wheel size 135 × 350, with brake.

ACCOMMODATION: Two seats in tandem under long transparent canopy.

DIMENSIONS:
Wing span	58 ft 4¾ in (17·81 m)
Wing chord at root	5 ft 8¾ in (1·75 m)
Wing chord at tip	1 ft 7·7 in (0·50 m)
Wing aspect ratio	16·2
Length overall	26 ft 10¾ in (8·2 m)
Height overall, excl wheel	4 ft 0¼ in (1·2 m)
Tailplane span	10 ft 2 in (3·1 m)

AREAS:
Wings, gross	215·3 sq ft (20·0 m²)
Ailerons (total)	29·50 sq ft (2·74 m²)
Air-brakes (total)	6·82 sq ft (0·63 m²)
Fin	7·32 sq ft (0·68 m²)
Rudder	8·83 sq ft (0·82 m²)
Tailplane	10·76 sq ft (1·00 m²)
Elevators	16·15 sq ft (1·50 m²)

WEIGHTS AND LOADING:
Weight empty, equipped	794 lb (360 kg)
Max T-O weight	1,191 lb (540 kg)
Max wing loading	5·58 lb/sq ft (27·0 kg/m²)

PERFORMANCE (at max T-O weight):
Best glide ratio
26 : 1 at 43·4 knots (50 mph; 80 km/h)
Min sinking speed 2·69 ft (0·82 m)/sec at
38·3 knots (44 mph; 71 km/h)
Stalling speed 33 knots (37·5 mph; 60 km/h)
Max speed (smooth air)
108 knots (124 mph; 200 km/h)
Max speed (rough air)
81 knots (93 mph; 150 km/h)
Max aero-tow speed
76 knots (87 mph; 140 km/h)
Max winch-launching speed
62 knots (71 mph; 115 km/h)

SZD-30 PIRAT

Designed by Ing Jerzy Smielkiewicz, this single-seat Standard Class sailplane flew for the first time on 19 May 1966. It is suitable for the full range of duties from training to competition flying and is cleared for cloud flying, spinning and basic aerobatics. Production started in 1967 and more than 120 had been built at the beginning of 1970.

TYPE: Single-seat Standard Class sailplane.

WINGS: Cantilever high-wing monoplane. Wing section Wortmann FX61-168 at root, Wortmann FX60-1261 at tip. Dihedral 2° 30′ on outer panels only. No sweep at quarter-chord. Wooden wing, built in three parts. Rectangular centre-section is a plywood-covered multi-spar structure. Tapered outer panels are of single-spar torsion-box construction. Mass-balanced ailerons. Double-plate air-brakes.

FUSELAGE: Plywood monocoque structure, with glass-fibre nose and cockpit floor.

TAIL UNIT: Cantilever wood structure, with tailplane mounted at tip of fin. Tab on trailing-edge of elevator.

LANDING GEAR: Front skid with shock-absorber is easily removable. Non-retractable mono-wheel, size 350 × 135, with band brake.

ACCOMMODATION: Single seat under jettisonable sideways-hinged blown Perspex canopy. Two luggage compartments. Map pockets on each side of cockpit. Provision for radio and oxygen equipment.

DIMENSIONS:
Wing span	49 ft 2½ in (15·00 m)
Wing chord at root	3 ft 4½ in (1·03 m)
Wing chord at tip	1 ft 11½ in (0·60 m)
Wing aspect ratio	16·3
Length overall	22 ft 6 in (6·86 m)
Height overall, excl wheel	3 ft 1¾ in (0·96 m)
Tailplane span	10 ft 2 in (3·1 m)

AREAS:
Wings, gross	148·5 sq ft (13·8 m²)
Ailerons (total)	11·72 sq ft (1·09 m²)
Air-brakes (total)	7·86 sq ft (0·73 m²)
Fin	5·35 sq ft (0·48 m²)
Rudder	8·10 sq ft (0·77 m²)
Tailplane	11·68 sq ft (1·08 m²)
Elevators	7·69 sq ft (0·78 m²)

WEIGHTS AND LOADING:
Weight empty, equipped	575 lb (261 kg)
Max T-O weight	816 lb (370 kg)
Max wing loading	5·49 lb/sq ft (26·8 kg/m²)

PERFORMANCE (at AUW of 750 lb = 340 kg):
Best glide ratio
31·2 : 1 at 45 knots (52 mph; 83 km/h)
Min sinking speed 2·2 ft (0·68 m)/sec at
40·4 knots (46·5 mph; 75 km/h)
Stalling speed 33 knots (37 mph; 59 km/h)
Max speed (smooth air)
135 knots (155 mph; 250 km/h)
Max speed (rough air)
76-89 knots (87-103 mph; 140-165 km/h)
Max aero-tow speed
71 knots (82 mph; 132 km/h)
Max winch-launching speed
74 knots (85 mph; 137 km/h)

SZD-9bis Bocian 1E two-seat general-purpose sailplane (Lorna Minton)

SZD-31 ZEFIR 4

The Zefir 4 is the production development of the Zefir 3, described in the 1968-69 edition of *Jane's*. It first flew on 7 December 1967 and two prototypes had been built by the end of 1968.

A Zefir 4 flown by Jan Wroblewski finished 14th in the Open Class at the 1968 Championships.

TYPE: Single-seat Open Class high-performance sailplane.

WINGS: Cantilever shoulder-wing monoplane. Wing section NACA 66-215-416. Thickness/chord ratio 16%. No dihedral. Incidence 1°. No sweepback. Multi-longeron spar-less wood stressed-skin structure. Double-contour flap-ailerons of wooden construction. VZLU flaps of plywood/balsa sandwich. Double metal air-brakes.

FUSELAGE: Monocoque structure of oval section. Forward portion made of glass-fibre laminate, rear portion of wood.

TAIL UNIT: Cantilever wood structure. All-moving mass-balanced horizontal surfaces with trim-tab. Mass-balanced rudder.

LANDING GEAR: Manually-operated retractable mono-wheel, size 350 × 135; tyre pressure 43 lb/sq in (3 kg/cm²). Rubber shock-absorbers and hand-operated wheel brake. Ribbon-type single-use brake parachute.

ACCOMMODATION: Single fully-reclining seat, with adjustable back-rest and rudder pedals. Side-hinged transparent flush canopy. Oxygen system and radio standard.

DIMENSIONS:
Wing span	62 ft 4 in (19·00 m)
Wing chord at root	3 ft 11¼ in (1·20 m)
Wing chord at tip	1 ft 5¾ in (0·45 m)
Wing aspect ratio	23
Length overall	26 ft 3 in (8·00 m)
Height over tail	7 ft 0 in (2·13 m)
Tailplane span	11 ft 9¾ in (3·60 m)

AREAS:
Wings, gross	169 sq ft (15·70 m²)
Ailerons (total)	13·78 sq ft (1·28 m²)
Trailing-edge flaps (total)	54·90 sq ft (5·10 m²)
Fin	10 sq ft (0·93 m²)
Rudder, including tab	5·17 sq ft (0·48 m²)
Tailplane	18·08 sq ft (1·68 m²)

WEIGHTS AND LOADING:
Weight empty, equipped	985 lb (447 kg)
Max T-O weight	1,213 lb (550 kg)
Max wing loading	7·17 lb/sq ft (35 kg/m²)

PERFORMANCE:
Best glide ratio
42 : 1 at 57·3 knots (66 mph; 106 km/h)

SZD-31 Zefir 4 single-seat high-performance sailplane (J. Roman)

Min sinking speed	2·23 ft (0·68 m)/sec at
	55 knots (63 mph; 102 km/h)
Stalling speed	39 knots (45 mph; 72 km/h)
Max speed (smooth air)	
	129 knots (149 mph; 240 km/h)
Max speed (rough air)	
	108 knots (124 mph; 200 km/h)
Limiting speed for air-brakes	
	129 knots (149 mph; 240 km/h)
Limiting speed for brake-chute	
	118 knots (136 mph; 220 km/h)
Maximum aero-tow speed	
	81 knots (93 mph; 150 km/h)
g limits	+6, —3

SZD-32A FOKA 5 (SEAL)

The Foka 5 has been developed from the Foka SZD-24 series, designed by W. Okarmus and described in detail in previous editions of *Jane's*.

The prototype SZD-24 Standard Foka first flew in May 1960. By the Spring of 1970 a total of more than 270 Fokas had been built, of which 150 had been exported to 17 countries.

The first prototype of the Foka 5 (SP-2504) began its flight test programme on 28 November 1966 and was granted a Polish Certificate of airworthiness on 7 October 1967.

SZD-30 Pirat single-seat Standard Class sailplane (L. J. Bittlestone)

The SZD-32A Foka 5 won first prize at the OSTIV Congress in 1968 as the best Standard Class sailplane. Flown by Edward Makula, a Foka 5 finished in eighth place in the Standard Class at the 1968 World Gliding Championships.

TYPE: Single-seat high-performance sailplane.

WINGS: Cantilever shoulder-wing monoplane. Wing section modified NACA 63₃-618 at root, NACA 4415 at tip. Plywood-covered wing of multi-longeron semi-monocoque construction, with spars in only the inboard portion of each panel. Special SZD plain ailerons of NACA 4415 section, with fabric covering. No flaps. SZD metal air-brakes.

FUSELAGE: Wooden semi-monocoque structure of oval section.

TAIL UNIT: One-piece tailplane of wooden construction mounted at the tip of the swept fin. One-piece elevator. Elevator and rudder are fabric-covered.

LANDING GEAR: Long skid and 350 mm monowheel located under the CG of the empty aircraft. Wheel-brake linked with air-brakes.

ACCOMMODATION: Single fully-reclining seat with adjustable back-rest, under large vacuum-formed forward-opening canopy with ventilation panel on port side. Blind-flying instrumentation standard. Provision for radio and oxygen equipment.

DIMENSIONS, EXTERNAL:
Wing span	49 ft 2 in (14·98 m)
Wing aspect ratio	18·5
Length overall	23 ft 6½ in (7·17 m)
Height overall	5 ft 3½ in (1·61 m)

AREA:
Wings, gross	130·9 sq ft (12·16 m²)

WEIGHTS:
Weight empty, with instruments	565 lb (256 kg)
Max T-O weight	850 lb (385 kg)

PERFORMANCE:
Best glide ratio
36·3 : 1 at 46 knots (53 mph; 85 km/h)
Min sinking speed 2·03 ft (0·62 m)/sec at 41·7 knots (48 mph; 77 km/h)
Min flying speed 37 knots (42 mph; 68 km/h)
Max speed (smooth air) 135 knots (155 mph; 250 km/h)
g limits +10·5, —5·25

SZD-36 COBRA 15

The SZD-36 Cobra 15 is a new single-seat Standard Class high-performance sailplane designed by Ing Wladyslaw Okarmus for use by the Polish team in the 1970 World Gliding Championships.

TYPE: Single-seat high-performance Standard Class sailplane.

WINGS: Cantilever shoulder-wing monoplane. Wortmann wing sections; FX 61-168 at root, FX 60-1261 at tip. Dihedral 2°. Single-spar wooden structure with heavy moulded plywood stressed skin covered with glass-fibre. Water ballast tanks in wing leading-edges. Plain ailerons, hinged at their upper surface and of wooden construction, are mass-balanced. Double-plate air-brakes.

FUSELAGE: All-wood semi-monocoque structure of oval section, covered with plywood and glass-fibre. Aero-tow hook in lower fuselage, forward of mono-wheel.

TAIL UNIT: Cantilever all-wood structure with swept vertical surfaces. T-tail with all-moving mass-balanced tailplane. Trim-tab on tailplane trailing-edge.

SZD-32A Foka 5, the latest T-tail version of this Standard Class sailplane

SZD-36 Cobra 15 single-seat high-performance Standard Class sailplane

LANDING GEAR: Mechanically-retractable monowheel which lies horizontally in bottom of fuselage when retracted. Wheel and tyre size 300 × 125 mm, with brake. Tail-skid.

ACCOMMODATION: Single seat in enclosed cabin under vacuum-formed forward-sliding canopy which can be jettisoned in emergency. Luggage compartment aft of pilot's seat, size 10½ in × 2 ft 4½ in (0·27 × 0·72 m).

EQUIPMENT: Instrumentation includes air speed indicator, altimeter, total energy variometer, rate of climb indicator, turn indicator, artificial horizon and compass. Oxygen system with 0·14 cu ft (4-litre) cylinder in baggage compartment. RS-3A radio.

DIMENSIONS:
Wing span	49 ft 2½ in (15·0 m)
Wing chord at root	3 ft 9¼ in (1·15 m)
Wing chord at tip	1 ft 3 in (0·38 m)
Wing aspect ratio	19·4
Length overall	22 ft 11¼ in (6·99 m)
Height overall	5 ft 2¾ in (1·59 m)
Tailplane span	8 ft 10¼ in (2·70 m)

AREAS:
Wings, gross	125 sq ft (11·6 m²)
Ailerons (total)	6·78 sq ft (0·63 m²)
Air-brakes (total)	8·18 sq ft (0·76 m²)
Horizontal tail surfaces	16·7 sq ft (1·55 m²)
Vertical tail surfaces	11·8 sq ft (1·10 m²)

SZD-39 COBRA 17

The Cobra 17 is a 17-metre wing-span version of the SZD-36 Cobra 15, and is generally the same with the exception of the wing. The description of the SZD-36 applies also to the SZD-39 except in the following details:

TYPE: Single-seat high-performance Open Class sailplane.

DIMENSIONS:
Wing span	55 ft 9¼ in (17·0 m)
Wing chord at root	3 ft 9¼ in (1·15 m)
Wing chord at tip	10¾ in (0·27 m)
Wing aspect ratio	23·56

AREAS:
Wings, gross	132 sq ft (12·27 m²)
Ailerons (total)	7·64 sq ft (0·71 m²)

ROMANIA

The principal Romanian designer of gliders and sailplanes is Prof Iosif Silimon, whose designs are designated with the prefix "IS".

The IS-3 Traian Vuia series of sailplanes, which appeared in several versions, are the most popular of his designs and are in widespread service with Romanian clubs. Details of these types can be found in the 1961-62 *Jane's*.

The later IS-8, IS-10, IS-11, IS-12 and IS-13 were described and illustrated in the 1965-66 *Jane's*.

URMV

URMV-3

ADDRESS:
Sovromtractor, Brasov

In addition to its work on piloted aircraft, this factory has developed the IS-13a sailplane, of which all available details follow.

IS-13a

Brief details have been received of this new Romanian sailplane designed by Ing Iosif Silimon, which was built by URMV-3 and flew for the first time in 1965. No details of construction are known beyond the fact that it is a two-seat high-performance training sailplane with a metal wing.

DIMENSIONS:
Wing span	52 ft 5¾ in (16·0 m)
Length overall	23 ft 3½ in (7·10 m)
Height overall	4 ft 11 in (1·50 m)

AREA:
Wings, gross	138 sq ft (12·8 m²)

WEIGHTS:
Weight empty	595 lb (270 kg)
Max T-O weight	815 lb (370 kg)

PERFORMANCE:
Best glide ratio	35·1
Max permitted speed	97 knots (111·8 mph; 180 km/h)
Stalling speed	36 knots (41 mph; 65 km/h)
Max aero-tow-speed	49 knots (56 mph; 90 km/h)
Max winch-launching speed	49 knots (56 mph; 90 km/h)

SOUTH AFRICA

BEATTY-JOHL

W.A.T. JOHL

ADDRESS:
PO Box 42, Swakopmund, South West Africa

Mr W. A. T. Johl was co-designer, with Mr. P. J. Beatty, of the BJ-2 high-performance sailplane described in the 1962-63 *Jane's*. They have since designed the BJ-3, of which the prototype was built by Performance Sailplanes of Activia Park, Germiston, South Africa, and first flew in 1965.

BEATTY-JOHL BJ-3

Piloted by M. Jackson, the BJ-3 set up an international speed record of 73·01 knots (84·08 mph; 135·32 km/h) over a 500-km triangular course on 28 December 1967.

TYPE: Single-seat high-performance sailplane.

WINGS: Cantilever shoulder-wing monoplane. Wing section NACA 66₁212 at root, NACA

0009-64A-0·8 at tip. Dihedral 1° 28′. Incidence 2°. No sweep. Duralumin basic load-carrying structure, enveloped with foam and with outer protective skin of glass-fibre. Ailerons of foam and glass-fibre. Fowler flaps (40% chord, 80% span) have steel-tube spar, enveloped with foam and covered with glass-fibre. Four sets of double DFS-type air-brakes. Tail parachute-brake.

FUSELAGE: Semi-monocoque structure. Glass-fibre from nose to wing spar; rear fuselage has duralumin skin and stringers.

TAIL UNIT: Cantilever T-type tail unit. Fin and rudder of duralumin. Fixed-incidence tailplane of plywood-covered spruce construction.

LANDING GEAR: Retractable mono-wheel and nose-wheel. Mechanical retraction. Main wheel and tyre, size 6·00 × 6, with drum brake.

ACCOMMODATION: Single seat under rearward-hinged one-piece transparent plastic canopy. Full instrument-flight panel, VHF radio and oxygen fitted.

DIMENSIONS:
Wing span	53 ft 0 in (16·15 m)
Wing chord at root	2 ft 9 in (0·84 m)
Wing chord at tip	1 ft 8 in (0·51 m)
Wing aspect ratio:	
flaps in	20
flaps extended	15·82
Length overall	24 ft 7 in (7·50 m)
Tailplane span	12 ft 1½ in (3·71 m)

AREAS:
Wings, net:	
flaps retracted	132 sq ft (12·26 m²)
flaps extended	172 sq ft (15·98 m²)
Ailerons (total)	13·33 sq ft (1·24 m²)
Flaps	40·0 sq ft (3·72 m²)
Air-brakes (total)	10·0 sq ft (0·93 m²)
Fin	7·5 sq ft (0·70 m²)
Rudder	2·5 sq ft (0·23 m²)
Tailplane	17·36 sq ft (1·61 m²)
Elevators	6·94 sq ft (0·64 m²)

Beatty-Johl BJ-3 single-seat high-performance sailplane

WEIGHT:
Max T-O weight	1,150 lb (522 kg)

PERFORMANCE (estimated):
Best glide ratio	40 : 1 at 70·3 knots (81 mph; 130 km/h)
Min sinking speed	2·2 ft (0·67 m)/sec at 40 knots (46 mph; 74 km/h)
Stalling speed, 30° flap	29 knots (33 mph; 53 km/h)
Max speed (smooth air)	154 knots (177 mph; 285 km/h)
Max speed (rough air)	120 knots (138 mph; 222 km/h)
Max aero-tow speed	120 knots (138 mph; 222 km/h)

BEATTY-JOHL BJ-3A/4

An extensively-modified version of the Beatty-Johl BJ-3, designated BJ-3A, was under construction late in 1968. It is intended to develop further this design by Fritz Johl to produce the BJ-4 for entry in the Open Class at International events.

The BJ-3A combines a new fuselage and tail unit with the existing BJ-3 wings. The new fuselage provides a semi-reclining position for the pilot under a longer flush transparent canopy. The structure is a blend of welded steel tube, riveted duralumin box and glass-fibre shells, and a retractable bicycle landing gear is being fitted.

The original T-tail configuration has been abandoned; in its place a metal all-flying tailplane with anti-balance tab is located on the fuselage centre line aft of a tall high-aspect-ratio fin and rudder, which includes a substantial sub-fin located beneath the centre line.

A unique innovation is the adoption of an external aerofoil flap as a rudder rather than the usual camber-changing flap-type rudder.

These and all other changes are directed towards producing a lighter, more streamlined fuselage with a correspondingly better performance. Control and handling at low speeds should be considerably improved. The flaps are likely to be hydraulically actuated.

SPAIN

STARK
STARK IBÉRICA S A

HEAD OFFICE:
Rosellón 379, Barcelona 13

WORKS AND OFFICERS:
See "Aircraft" section.

Stark Ibérica S A have acquired from Scheibe-Flugzeugbau-GmbH, of Germany, licence rights to manufacture the well-known Bergfalke III and Spatz III sailplanes. The licence agreement includes authorisation to export these aircraft to foreign countries.

Right: **Scheibe Bergfalke III built under licence by Stark Ibérica S A**

SWITZERLAND

FFA
FLUG- & FAHRZEUGWERKE AG

HEAD OFFICE AND WORKS:
Altenrhein, 9422 Staad SG

OFFICERS: See "Aircraft" section

In addition to its work on powered aircraft, FFA is manufacturing a high-performance sailplane named the Diamant, in three versions with differing span.

FFA DIAMANT
The fuselage and tail unit of this all-glass-fibre sailplane were developed at the Swiss Federal Institute of Technology in Zurich under the direction of Prof Rauscher. A prototype fuselage was built in 1962 and flight tested with Ka 6 wings. Since then, three production versions have been evolved, as follows:

HBV-Diamant 15. Original production version with 15-m wings designed by Dipl Ing W. Hütter and built by the Glasflügel company in Germany. Prototype flew on 5 September 1964. Total of 13 built. Production completed.

Diamant 16·5. Generally similar to HBV-Diamant 15, but wings of 16·5 m span, built by FFA. Central control stick instead of side stick of HBV-Diamant.

Diamant 18. Generally similar to Diamant 16·5, but wings of 18 m span, built by FFA.

FFA Diamant 16.5 single-seat high-performance sailplane

Prototype first flew in January 1968. In the 1968 World Gliding Championships in Poland, a Diamant 18 flown by Rudi Seiler of Switzerland came third in the Open Class, followed in fourth position by another Diamant 18 piloted by Alf Schubert of Austria.

The following data apply to the current production Diamant 16·5 and Diamant 18 aircraft.

TYPE: Single-seat high-performance sailplane.

WINGS: Cantilever shoulder-wing monoplane. Wortmann wing section. Glass-fibre balsa sandwich shell without ribs. Mass-balanced ailerons and aerofoil flaps of similar construction to wings. Flap deflection synchronised with partial downward aileron movement. Schempp-Hirth type air-brakes.

FUSELAGE: Monocoque in epoxy-glass-fibre sandwich, with foam inserts.

TAIL UNIT: All-moving one-piece horizontal surface at tip of fin. Trimming by means of spring arrangement in fuselage. Monocoque construction of epoxy-glass-fibre sandwich with foam inserts.

LANDING GEAR: Manually-retractable monowheel with brake. Glass-fibre ring spring shock-absorber. Tyre size 300 × 100. Small nylon tail-wheel (optional tail-skid). Tow release retracts with landing gear.

ACCOMMODATION: Single seat, in semi-reclining position, under sliding transparent canopy. Standard instrument panel for seven instruments, with larger panel optional. Adjustable back-rest and rudder pedals. Provision for radio, oxygen etc. Optional extra is space provision for 130 lb (59 kg) of water ballast.

DIMENSIONS:

Wing span:		
Diamant 16·5	54 ft 2½ in	(16·5 m)
Diamant 18	59 ft 0½ in	(18·0 m)
Wing aspect ratio:		
Diamant 16·5		20·5
Diamant 18		22·5
Length overall	24 ft 9½ in	(7·56 m)
Height over tail	4 ft 5 in	(1·35 m)
Tailplane span	9 ft 6¼ in	(2·90 m)

AREAS:

Wings, gross:		
Diamant 16·5	143 sq ft	(13·3 m²)
Diamant 18	155 sq ft	(14·4 m²)
Tailplane	12·8 sq ft	(1·19 m²)

WEIGHTS AND LOADINGS:

Weight empty, equipped:		
Diamant 16·5	617 lb	(280 kg)
Diamant 18	639 lb	(290 kg)
T-O weight:		
Diamant 16·5	793-904 lb	(360-410 kg)
Diamant 18	815-970 lb	(370-440 kg)
Max wing loading:		
Diamant 16·5	6·3 lb/sq ft	(30·8 kg/m²)
Diamant 18	6·25 lb/sq ft	(30·5 kg/m²)

PERFORMANCE (Diamant 16·5 at AUW of 793 lb = 360 kg; Diamant 18 at AUW of 882 lb = 400 kg):

Best glide ratio:
Diamant 16·5
42 : 1 at 54 knots (62 mph; 100 km/h)
Diamant 18
45 : 1 at 51 knots (59 mph; 95 km/h)

Min sinking speed:
Diamant 16·5
1·8 ft (0·55 m)/sec at 38·2 knots (44 mph; 70 km/h)
Diamant 18
1·7 ft (0·52 m)/sec at 37·3 knots (43 mph; 69 km/h)

Min circling speed:
Diamant 16·5 36·5 knots (42 mph; 67 km/h)
Diamant 18 35·6 knots (41 mph; 66 km/h)

Max speed (smooth air)
129 knots (149 mph; 240 km/h)

KUMMER/WIESENDANGER
PAUL KUMMER AND OSKAR WIESENDANGER

Mr Kummer and Mr Wiesendanger have built at Zurich a modified version of the Akaflieg Braunschweig SB-7 sailplane. The work required about 4,500 man-hours to complete, at a cost of 18,000 Swiss francs, and the first flight was made on 20 May 1967. All available details follow.

KUMMER/WIESENDANGER/AKAFLIEG BRAUNSCHWEIG SB-7

This is an extensively modified Open Class version of the SB-7 Nimbus single-seat Standard Class sailplane designed by Akaflieg Braunschweig. It has a completely new wing of increased span, with an Eppler 417 aerofoil section and thickness/chord ratio of 14%. Trailing-edge air-brakes replace the Schempp-Hirth type fitted to the original German version.

Two prototypes had been completed by mid-1968 and two others are under construction which could see a further increase in wing span to 59 ft 0½ in (18 m). Except for the details noted above and below they are similar to the basic SB-7, described in the German section.

DIMENSIONS:

Wing span	54 ft 2½ in	(16·50 m)
Wing aspect ratio		20·85
Length overall	23 ft 3½ in	(7·10 m)

Kummer/Wiesendanger/Akaflieg Braunschweig SB-7 sailplane (*Peter Wernli*)

Height overall	4 ft 5 in	(1·35 m)
Tailplane span	9 ft 6 in	(2·90 m)

AREAS:

Wings, gross	140·6 sq ft	(13·06 m²)
Tailplane	14·0 sq ft	(1·30 m²)

WEIGHTS AND LOADING:

Weight empty, equipped	589 lb	(267 kg)
Max T-O weight	794 lb	(360 kg)
Max wing loading	5·65 lb/sq ft	(27·6 kg/m²)

PERFORMANCE:

Best glide ratio
43 : 1 at 48·6 knots (56 mph; 90 km/h)
Min sinking speed 1·87 ft (0·57 m)/sec at 41·6 knots (48 mph; 78 km/h)
Stalling speed 34 knots (39 mph; 62 km/h)
Max speed (smooth air)
135 knots (155 mph; 250 km/h)
Max speed (rough air)
86 knots (99 mph; 160 km/h)

NEUKOM
ALBERT NEUKOM
ADDRESS: Klettgauerstrasse 70, Neuhausen

Latest sailplanes built by Mr Neukom are the Standard Elfe, Elfe S-4, Elfe 17, AN-66-2 and AN-66C, of which all available details follow.

NEUKOM STANDARD ELFE

The S-1 prototype of this Standard Class sailplane, which flew for the first time on 1 May 1964, has Vee tail surfaces. The Standard Elfe S-2 has a conventional tail unit, with the tailplane at the base of the fin. The production-type Standard Elfe S-3, first flown in May 1966, has the tailplane mounted part-way up the fin. Eighteen Standard Elfe sailplanes were flying by April 1970.

Piloted by Markus Ritzi, a Standard Elfe gained 2nd place in the 1965 World Gliding Championships. In the Standard Class competition at the 1968 Championships in Poland, an Elfe S-3 piloted by Andrew Smith of the USA came first out of 57 entries, with George Moffat of the USA fourth and Urs Bloch of Switzerland sixth in similar aircraft.

The Standard Elfe S-3 is a cantilever high-wing monoplane, utilising the Wortmann FX wing section. The wing, which is built in three parts, is of plywood-balsa sandwich construction, and is fitted with trailing-edge air-brakes. Fuselage and tail unit are of glass-fibre and plywood sandwich construction. The landing gear comprises a rubber-sprung retractable mono-wheel, size 330 × 130, with brake. The cockpit is fitted with a removable transparent canopy.

DIMENSIONS:

Wing span	49 ft 2½ in	(15·00 m)
Wing aspect ratio		19
Length overall	23 ft 11½ in	(7·30 m)
Height over tail	4 ft 11 in	(1·50 m)
Tailplane span	9 ft 6¼ in	(2·90 m)

AREAS:

Wings, gross	128·1 sq ft	(11·90 m²)
Ailerons (total)	9·15 sq ft	(0·85 m²)
Air-brakes (total)	12·38 sq ft	(1·15 m²)

WEIGHTS AND LOADING:

Weight empty	463 lb	(210 kg)
Max T-O weight	705 lb	(320 kg)
Max wing loading	5·54 lb/sq ft	(26·9 kg/m²)

Neukom Standard Elfe S-3 single-seat Standard Class sailplane (*Dr U. Haller*)

PERFORMANCE:

Best glide ratio
37·5 : 1 at 51·2 knots (59 mph; 95 km/h)
Min sinking speed 2·07 ft (0·63 m)/sec at 41 knots (47 mph; 75 km/h)
Stalling speed 30 knots (34 mph; 55 km/h)
Max speed (smooth air)
130 knots (150 mph; 240 km/h)
Max speed (rough air)
108 knots (124 mph; 200 km/h)

NEUKOM ELFE S-4

This is a developed version of the S-3, from which it differs principally by having a two-piece wing and a more roomy forward fuselage of better aerodynamic form. The prototype was scheduled to fly for the first time in the Spring of 1970, and a total of four were then known to be under construction.

DIMENSIONS:

Wing span	49 ft 2½ in	(15·0 m)
Wing aspect ratio		19
Length overall	23 ft 11½ in	(7·30 m)

AREA:

Wings, gross	127 sq ft	(11·8 m²)

WEIGHTS AND LOADING:

Weight empty	463 lb	(210 kg)
Max T-O weight	705 lb	(320 kg)
Max wing loading	5·5 lb/sq ft	(27 kg/m²)

NEUKOM ELFE 17

The Elfe 17 is a 17-metre version of the S-4, employing the same fuselage, but having a two-piece wing of increased span. One water ballast tank in each wing leading-edge to contain a total of 132 lb (60 kg) water. A braking parachute is carried on this version. A single prototype has been built and this was scheduled to fly for the first time in the Spring of 1970.

DIMENSIONS:

Wing span	55 ft 9¼ in	(17·0 m)
Wing aspect ratio		22·2
Length overall	23 ft 11½ in	(7·30 m)

AREA:

Wings, gross	140 sq ft	(13·0 m²)

WEIGHTS AND LOADING:

Weight empty	529 lb	(240 kg)
Max T-O weight	793 lb	(360 kg)
Max T-O weight with ballast	925 lb	(420 kg)
Max wing loading	5·65 lb/sq ft	(27·6 kg/m²)

NEUKOM AN-66 and AN-66-2

The prototype of this single-seat high-performance sailplane was completed and flew in 1966. Two others have been built with a modified fuselage and are designated AN-66-2.

WINGS: Cantilever shoulder-wing monoplane. Wing section Eppler 441. Wing of sandwich construction, with metal spar. Plain flaps.

FUSELAGE: Forward portion is a glass-fibre sandwich structure, rear portion a wood semi-monocoque.

TAIL UNIT: Vee type.

LANDING GEAR: Retractable mono-wheel.

ACCOMMODATION: Single seat under long flush transparent canopy.

DIMENSIONS:

Wing span	59 ft 0½ in (18·00 m)
Wing aspect ratio	23·2
Length overall	25 ft 3 in (7·70 m)
Height over tail	4 ft 11 in (1·50 m)

AREA:

Wings, gross	150·7 sq ft (14·00 m²)

WEIGHTS AND LOADING:

Weight empty, equipped	635 lb (288 kg)
Max T-O weight	882 lb (400 kg)
Max wing loading	5·86 lb/sq ft (28·6 kg/m²)

PERFORMANCE:

Best glide ratio
45 : 1 at 52 knots (60 mph; 96 km/h)
Min sinking speed 1·64 ft (0·50 m)/sec at
41 knots (47 mph; 75 km/h)

Neukom AN-66-2 single-seat high-performance sailplane (*Dr U. Haller*)

NEUKOM AN-66C

This is a development of the AN-66-2, having the same fuselage, but with an entirely new wing of Eppler section. The wing is of plywood-balsa-plywood sandwich construction, with a single metal spar, and is built in three parts. The centre-section is 21 ft 4 in (6·5 m) in length, the two outer panels each 27 ft 0¾ in (8·25 m) in length. A water ballast tank to contain 132 lb (60 kg) water in the leading-edge of each wing, and Schempp-Hirth air-brakes are fitted. Main interest lies in a newly-designed aerofoil flap which is able to increase the wing

area by about 20%. No details of this were available at the time of writing. A single prototype has been built and this was expected to fly for the first time in March 1970.

DIMENSIONS:

Wing span	75 ft 5½ in (23·0 m)
Wing aspect ratio (flaps in)	33·1
Wing aspect ratio (flaps out)	27·6
Length overall	25 ft 3 in (7·70 m)

AREAS:

Wings, gross (flaps in)	172 sq ft (16·0 m²)
Wings, gross (flaps out)	207 sq ft (19·2 m²)

WEIGHTS AND LOADINGS:

Weight empty	926 lb (420 kg)
Normal T-O weight	1,168 lb (530 kg)
Max T-O weight with ballast	1,433 lb (650 kg)

Wing loading at normal T-O weight:

flaps in	6·8 lb/sq ft (33·1 kg/m²)
flaps out	5·65 lb/sq ft (27·6 kg/m²)

Wing loading at max T-O weight:

flaps in	8·3 lb/sq ft (40·6 kg/m²)
flaps out	6·9 lb/sq ft (33·8 kg/m²)

PERFORMANCE (estimated):

Best glide ratio	50-55 : 1

SCHILLER

ALFRED SCHILLER

ADDRESS:
Rigistrasse 4, CH-8910 Affoltern a.A.

SCHILLER FS-1

This single-seat Standard Class sailplane has been designed and built by Alfred Schiller. Development and construction occupied some 2,500 hours before first flight of the prototype (HB-957) on 27 October 1960.

TYPE: Single-seat Standard Class sailplane.

WINGS: Cantilever mid-wing monoplane. Wortmann wing sections: FX 61-163 at root, FX 61-140 at mid-span and FX 60-126 at tip. Glass-fibre/PVC-foam sandwich shell. Large-span ailerons. Trailing-edge air-brakes.

FUSELAGE: Monocoque glass-fibre polystyrol-foam sandwich structure.

TAIL UNIT: Cantilever structure of polystyrol-foam covered with glass-fibre. Tailplane and elevators mounted at top of fin.

LANDING GEAR: Manually-retractable mono-wheel. Rubber spring shock-absorber. Wheel brake. Small tail skid.

ACCOMMODATION: Single semi-reclining seat under transparent canopy. Seat and rudder-pedals adjustable.

DIMENSIONS:

Wing span	49 ft 2½ in (15·00 m)
Wing aspect ratio	20

Schiller FS-1 single-seat Standard Class sailplane (*F. Maurer*)

Length overall	23 ft 4¾ in (7·13 m)
Height overall	4 ft 8¼ in (1·43 m)
Tailplane span	8 ft 6¾ in (2·61 m)

AREAS:

Wings, gross	124 sq ft (11·5 m²)
Tailplane	14·0 sq ft (1·30 m²)

WEIGHTS AND LOADING:

Weight empty	440 lb (200 kg)
Max T-O weight	683 lb (310 kg)
Max wing loading	5·5 lb/sq ft (27 kg/m²)

PERFORMANCE:

Best glide ratio
40 : 1 at 48·6 knots (56 mph; 90 km/h)
Min sinking speed 1·87 ft (0·57 m)/sec at
40·5 knots (46·6 mph; 75 km/h)
Stalling speed 33 knots (37 mph; 59 km/h)
Max speed (smooth air)
122 knots (140 mph; 225 km/h)
Max speed (rough air)
97 knots (112 mph; 180 km/h)

THE UNITED KINGDOM

BIRMINGHAM GUILD

BIRMINGHAM GUILD LTD

HEAD OFFICE:
Grosvenor Street West, Birmingham 16

SAILPLANE DESIGN LTD

HEAD OFFICE:
12 Ferndale Road, Hereford

BIRMINGHAM GUILD GIPSY 12/15

The Gipsy 12/15 has been designed by L. P. Moore, J. C. Gibson and K. Emslie of Sailplane Design Ltd, to provide a low-cost lightweight Standard/Sports Class sailplane, in which either a medium-performance 12-metre wing or a high-performance 15-metre wing may be fitted to a common fuselage and tail unit. This has been achieved by special attention to structural efficiency (strength and stiffness-to-weight ratio), resulting from efficient wing skin stabilis-ation, with rigid foam cores. Low cost derives from the elimination of taper and of twin-skin sandwich or ribbed forms of construction.

The prototype of the Gipsy 12/15, with a 12-metre wing, was scheduled to fly in early 1970. The 15-metre wing, which will embody performance flaps, is in the design/development stage. Details below apply to the prototype Gipsy 12/15 with the 12-metre wing.

TYPE: Single-seat medium/high-performance

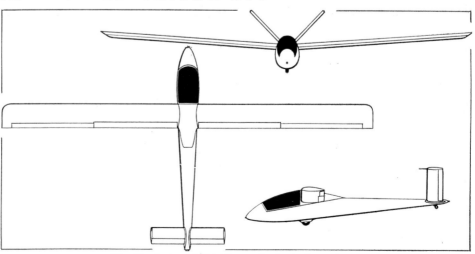

The Birmingham Guild Gipsy 12/15 lightweight sailplane

Wortmann FX61-168 wing section. Thickness/chord ratio 16·8%. Dihedral 3°. No incidence or sweepback. Aluminium alloy

frame and skin with rigid foam stabilisation. Half-span alloy ailerons. Hinged no-lift trailing-edge flaps/air-brakes on inner half-span.

FUSELAGE: Orthodox construction, with a metal-braced glass-fibre cabin and metal monocoque tail-cone of pressed frames, longerons and metal skin, terminating at the rear in a lifting handle.

TAIL UNIT: Vee-tail of relatively high aspect ratio (7). Orthodox metal structure with light alloy frame and skin. Variable incidence. Full-span trim-tabs.

LANDING GEAR: Unsprung fixed wheel forward of CG and leaf-sprung tail-wheel.

ACCOMMODATION: Single seat under large hinged moulded canopy. Standard instrumentation.

DIMENSIONS:
Wing span   39 ft 4 in (12·00 m)

Wing chord, constant	2 ft 3½ in (0·69 m)
Wing aspect ratio	17·15
Length overall	19 ft 8 in (5·95 m)
Height overall	3 ft 11 in (1·19 m)
Tailplane span	10 ft 6 in (3·20 m)

AREAS:

Wings, gross	90 sq ft (8·36 m²)
Ailerons	5·10 sq ft (0·47 m²)
Trailing-edge flaps	5·10 sq ft (0·47 m²)
Tailplane	15·0 sq ft (1·39 m²)

WEIGHTS AND LOADING:

Weight empty, equipped	270 lb (122 kg)
Max T-O weight	520 lb (236 kg)
Max wing loading	5·78 lb/sq ft (28·20 kg/m²)

PERFORMANCE (estimated):
Best glide ratio
31:1 at 47-54 knots (54-62 mph; 87-100 km/h)
Min sinking speed   2·20 ft (0·67 m)/sec at
                                   38·2 knots (44 mph; 71 km/h)
Stalling speed at max AUW
                                   35 knots (40 mph; 64 km/h)

CHARD
KEITH CHARD
ADDRESS:
London Gliding Club, Tring Road, Dunstable, Beds.

Mr Chard, assisted by Mr Frank Jacques and Mr Geoffrey Senior, has built a high-performance Standard Class sailplane named the Osprey, of which details follow.

CHARD OSPREY

The Osprey is, basically, a Slingsby Dart 15 fitted with an entirely new wing, designed by Mr Keith Chard and built at Lasham. The idea was to concentrate on achieving the best possible performance at the high and low ends of the speed range, for competition flying.

First flight of the Osprey was made on 15 May 1966 and it took part in the British National Gliding Championships later that month. As a result of experience gained, the aircraft is undergoing extensive modification, involving change of wing section, increase in wing chord and engineering changes to the tailplane. The new version will be known as the Osprey 2.

The following data apply to the Osprey in its original form, as illustrated.

TYPE: Single-seat Standard Class sailplane.

WINGS: Cantilever shoulder-wing monoplane. Wing section Chard KC-24 at root, KC-29 at mid-span, KC-30 at tip. Thickness/chord ratio 14% throughout. Single-spar structure. Spar has light alloy booms and plywood webs. Wing covered with ³⁄₃₂ in gaboon plywood. Plain shrouded all-wood ailerons. Parallel-rule air-brakes. No flaps.

FUSELAGE: Semi-monocoque spruce structure of elliptical cross-section. Cockpit section covered with glass-fibre, remainder with birch plywood.

TAIL UNIT: Cantilever spruce fin and rudder,

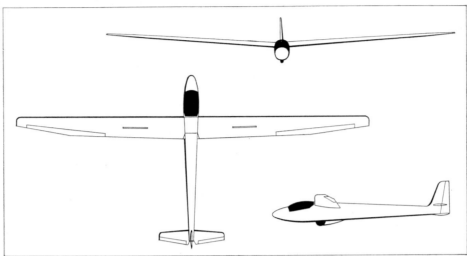

Chard Osprey single-seat Standard Class sailplane

with fabric covering on rudder. All-moving tailplane has light alloy stressed-skin structure, with full-span trim-tabs.

LANDING GEAR: Non-retractable mono-wheel, size 380 × 150, with short forward skid. Tyre pressure 45 lb/sq in (3·15 kg/cm²). Internal expanding brake.

ACCOMMODATION: Single semi-reclining seat under lift-off moulded Perspex canopy. Clear-vision panels.

DIMENSIONS:

Wing span	49 ft 2½ in (15·00 m)
Wing chord at root	3 ft 7 in (1·09 m)
Wing chord at tip	1 ft 4 in (0·41 m)
Wing aspect ratio	18·3
Length overall	25 ft 5 in (7·75 m)
Tailplane span	8 ft 6¾ in (2·61 m)

WEIGHTS:

Weight empty	549 lb (249 kg)
Max T-O weight	790 lb (358 kg)

PERFORMANCE:
Best glide ratio
approx 34:1 at 55 knots (62 mph; 102 km/h)
Min sinking speed   2·1 ft (0·64 m)/sec at
                                   46 knots (53 mph; 85 km/h)
Stalling speed   38 knots (43 mph; 69 km/h)
Max speed (smooth air)
                                   117 knots (135 mph; 217 km/h)
Max speed (rough air)
                                   76 knots (87 mph; 140 km/h)
Max aero-tow speed
                                   76 knots (87 mph; 140 km/h)
Max winch-launching speed
                                   72 knots (83 mph; 133 km/h)

OSBOURN
E. W. OSBOURN

ADDRESS:
17 Everard Road, Bedford, Bedfordshire

OSBOURN/SLINGSBY TWIN CADET

Mr Osbourn has converted a Slingsby Mk 1 Cadet into a powered glider. Modification of the airframe has been minimal, consisting of glass-fibre bonding a web to the forward wing bracing strut on each side, to enable these struts to withstand thrust loads, and the addition of a tubular strut on each side, between the wing root and each forward wing bracing strut.

Power is provided by two 197 cc Villiers 9E single-cylinder two-stroke air-cooled engines, mounted by rubber bushes to the forward wing bracing strut on each side of the aircraft. These standard motor-cycle engines have been modified by removing the gearbox units, and each drives a two-blade fixed-pitch wood propeller, diameter 2 ft 8 in (0·81 m), which is attached directly to the engine crankshaft. A fuel tank of 3 Imp gallon (13·6 litre) capacity is mounted in the fuselage, aft of the pilot's seat. Refuelling point is on the starboard side of the fuselage beneath the wing. Two 6V 8Ah batteries are carried in the fuselage to provide power for the coil ignition system of the engines, which cannot be re-started in flight.

The aircraft made its first flight on 20 September 1969, about seven months after the modifications were started. Flight tests were at an early stage at the time of writing, but Mr Osbourn reported himself satisfied with early trials and commented that single-engine performance was good, the aircraft being just able to maintain height in this condition.

Details of the standard Slingsby (Kirby) Mk 1 Cadet appeared in the 1954-55 *Jane's*.

Osbourne/Slingsby Twin Cadet powered glider (two 197 cc Villiers motor-cycle engines) (*S. MacConnacher*)

WEIGHTS AND LOADINGS:

Weight empty	455 lb (206 kg)
Max T-O weight	657 lb (298 kg)
Max wing loading	3·86 lb/sq ft (18·8 kg/m²)
Max power loading	32·8 lb/hp (14·9 kg/hp)

PERFORMANCE (at max T-O weight):

Max level speed	52 knots (60 mph; 97 km/h)
Max diving speed	53·5 knots (62 mph; 99 km/h)
Max cruising speed	52 knots (60 mph; 97 km/h)

Econ cruising speed
                         35 knots (40 mph; 64 km/h)

Stalling speed	28 knots (32 mph; 52 km/h)
Max rate of climb at S/L	250 ft (76 m)/min
T-O run	330 ft (101 m)
T-O to 50 ft (15 m)	700 ft (213 m)
Landing from 50 ft (15 m)	800 ft (244 m)
Landing run	300 ft (91 m)
Range	about 85 nm (100 miles; 160 km)

SIGMA

OPERATION SIGMA LTD

SIGMA 1

The Sigma 1 is a very high performance sail-plane designed for competition and record-breaking flights. It was intended that it should be used by the British team competing in the 1970 World Gliding Championships, but all drawings and the prototype in construction were destroyed by fire in November 1968. The project was restarted with some difficulty, only to come to a halt again when the company responsible for construction of the prototype went into liquidation in July 1969. This ended any prospect of Sigma 1 being available for the 1970 World Championships. It was hoped, however, that it would be ready to start test flying in September 1970.

The design features a very high aspect ratio wing, fitted with a full-span flap to give both variable area and variable camber. With the flap extended, the circling speeds and sink rate are expected to give as good a rate of climb in weak thermals as those of conventional high-performance sailplanes. With the flap retracted, the high wing loading and low drag should combine to give high glide ratios at high speed. Average cross-country speeds are expected to be some 20% better than the best achieved by current sailplanes.

The Sigma project owes its existence to the support of companies both within and outside the aircraft industry.

TYPE: Single-seat very high performance Open Class sailplane.

WINGS: Cantilever shoulder-wing monoplane. Wortmann FX 67 Sigma wing sections. Thickness/chord ratio 17% flap in, 12·6% flap out. Dihedral 3°. Incidence 0° flap in, 8° 30′ flap out. Sweepback at 45% chord 0°. Light alloy box structure. Conventional ailerons of

steel-tube and glass-reinforced plastics construction, mounted on flap. Full-span trailing-edge flaps of light alloy construction. Light alloy spoilers on upper surface of wing forward of aileron. Light alloy air-brakes of spoiler type on upper surface of wing.

FUSELAGE: Pod and boom type, with welded steel-tube forward structure faired by glass-reinforced plastics pod. Monocoque light alloy tapered boom carries tail surfaces.

TAIL UNIT: Light alloy structure. All-moving horizontal surface mounted high at rear of fin, above rudder. Nearly half of the fin and rudder will project below the rear end of the fuselage, and the under-fin will carry the housing for the retractable tail-wheel. Anti-balance and trim-tab on tailplane.

LANDING GEAR: Dowty-Rotol design. Hydraulically-retractable Tost mono-wheel, with rubber in compression shock-absorption and Dunlop tyre, 15·5 in (39·3 cm) in diameter, pressure 45 lb/sq in (3·2 kg/cm²). Retractable sprung and steerable solid-tyred tail-wheel. Tost brake in main wheel hub.

ACCOMMODATION: Single seat in reclining position under detachable transparent canopy.

DIMENSIONS:
Wing span	68 ft 10¾ in (21·0 m)
Wing chord at root	2 ft 3 in (0·69 m)
Wing chord at tip	1 ft 4·3 in (0·41 m)

Wing aspect ratio	36·2
Length overall	28 ft 10¾ in (8·81 m)
Height overall, excluding tail-wheel	6 ft 0 in (1·83 m)
Tailplane span	8 ft 6 in (2·59 m)

AREAS:
Wings, gross	131·2 sq ft (12·2 m²)
Ailerons (total, including roll spoilers)	19 sq ft (1·77 m²)
Trailing-edge flaps (total)	46 sq ft (4·27 m²)
Air-brakes (total)	6·3 sq ft (0·585 m²)
Fin	8·8 sq ft (0·82 m²)
Rudder	6·7 sq ft (0·62 m²)
Tailplane (including tab)	12·1 sq ft (1·12 m²)

WEIGHTS AND LOADING (estimated):
Weight empty, equipped	1,270 lb (576 kg)
Max T-O weight	1,500 lb (680 kg)
Max wing loading	11·4 lb/sq ft (55·66 kg/m²)

PERFORMANCE (estimated):
Best glide ratio	50 : 1 at 63 knots (72·5 mph; 116·7 km/h)
Stalling speed	36·5 knots (42 mph; 68 km/h)
Max speed (smooth air)	140 knots (161 mph; 259 km/h)
Max speed (rough air)	110 knots (127 mph; 204 km/h)
Max aero-tow speed	110 knots (127 mph; 204 km/h)
Max winch-launching speed	Not permitted
g limits	+5, —3

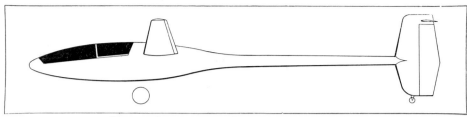

Sigma 1 single-seat very high performance sailplane

SLINGSBY

SLINGSBY SAILPLANES (A Division of Vickers Limited Shipbuilding Group)

HEAD OFFICE AND WORKS:
Kirkbymoorside, Yorkshire YO6 6EZ

MANAGING DIRECTOR: G. E. Burton, BSc, ARCS

GENERAL MANAGER:
W. N. Slater, CEng, AFRAeS

CHIEF ENGINEER:
J. S. Tucker, Dip Tech(Eng), BSc(Eng), CEng, AFRAeS

WORKS MANAGER:
J. A. Goacher

SALES MANAGER:
J. A. Brayshaw, AFRAeS

Slingsby Sailplanes, a division of Vickers Ltd Shipbuilding Group, is a new company formed from the assets of the former Slingsby Aircraft Company Ltd, which went into liquidation in July 1969. As its primary activity, it is engaged in a programme that will lead to production of a complete range of sailplanes and powered sailplanes; but Slingsby is also engaged in the design and manufacture of highly-stressed marine components in composite materials and in carrying out fundamental research into and development of composite materials for general applications.

Present aircraft production is limited to three sailplanes: the Slingsby T.53.C two-seat all-metal sailplane, described below; the 17-metre Glasflügel Kestrel (Slingsby designation T.59) which is being built under licence and is described under the Glasflügel entry in this section; and the Scheibe SF-25B Falke powered sailplane (Slingsby designation T.61), also being built under licence and described under the Scheibe entry in this section. Design and development of a powered version of the T.53 is in progress and it was anticipated that first flight of the prototype would be made in October 1970. The company is also operating a repair and spares service for all sailplanes manufactured by the former Slingsby Aircraft Company.

A special 19-metre version of the Glasflügel Kestrel has been built, and this was flown by Mr G. Burton in the 1970 World Gliding Championships at Marfa.

A total of approximately 120 people were employed by Slingsby in mid-June 1970, but this labour force is to be expanded to fulfil existing orders for 18 T.53's, 57 T.59's and 20 T.61's.

SLINGSBY T.53.C

The former Slingsby Aircraft Company designed and manufactured a two-seat all-metal sailplane known as the T.53.B, and this was

Slingsby T.53.C two-seat all-metal sailplane

Special 19-metre version of the Glasflügel Kestrel built by Slingsby Sailplanes

described in the 1969-70 *Jane's*. The T.53.C is developed from that aircraft and differs mainly in having a structurally re-designed wing, reduced aileron control loads resulting from the use of aileron servo tabs, increased fin and rudder area, revised spring trim system, and improved cockpit layout, seating, ventilation and canopies. Slingsby are also building a specialised version of the T.53 to meet RAF requirements for air cadet training; this is designated **T.53.C(M)**.

Design and prototype construction of the T.53 was initiated by Slingsby Aircraft in 1966 and ARB certification was granted in June 1968. The following description applies to the T.53.C:

TYPE: Two-seat all-metal sailplane.

WINGS: Cantilever shoulder-wing monoplane. Wing section Wortmann FX-61-184. Thickness/chord ratio 18·4%. Dihedral 3°. Incidence 5° 40′. Sweep-forward at quarter-chord 3°. All-metal structure of light alloy. Mass-balanced ailerons with servo tabs. Schempp-Hirth balanced air-brakes on upper and lower surface of each wing, located at 0·346 semi-span, at 65·5% chord on upper surface and 63·2% chord on lower surface.

FUSELAGE: Semi-monocoque structure of light alloy.

TAIL UNIT: All-metal cantilever structure of light alloy. Fixed-incidence tailplane mounted just below the top of the fin. Internal spring-loaded trimmer.

LANDING GEAR: Non-retractable main wheel and nose-wheel. Tail-skid. Main wheel shock-absorption by Armstrong damper units. Tost main wheel size 350 × 150 with Dunlop tyre, pressure 35-40 lb/sq in (2·46-2·81 kg/cm²). Slingsby nose-wheel size 4·00 × 3·5 with Dunlop tyre, pressure 35-40 lb/sq in (2·46-2·81 kg/cm²). Tost expanding caliper brake.

ACCOMMODATION: Two seats in tandem under sideways-hinged transparent canopy. Cockpit ventilated.

EQUIPMENT: Basic instruments on both panels, with dry or wet cell batteries for power, depending on instrumentation required. Oxygen system optional.

DIMENSIONS:
Wing span	55 ft 6 in (17·00 m)
Wing chord, constant	3 ft 6 in (1·07 m)
Wing aspect ratio	15·9
Length overall	25 ft 3 in (7·70 m)
Height overall	4 ft 7¼ in (1·40 m)
Tailplane span	11 ft 2½ in (3·42 m)

AREAS:
Wings, gross	194 sq ft (18·12 m²)
Ailerons (total)	19·05 sq ft (1·77 m²)
Air brakes (total)	7·0 sq ft (0·65 m²)
Fin	17·85 sq ft (1·66 m²)
Rudder	7·35 sq ft (0·68 m²)
Tailplane	25·0 sq ft (2·32 m²)
Elevators	8·75 sq ft (0·81 m²)

WEIGHTS AND LOADING:
Weight, empty (minimum instruments)	780 lb (354 kg)
Max T-O weight	1,250 lb (567 kg)
Max wing loading	6·45 lb/sq ft (31·4 kg/m²)

PERFORMANCE (at max T-O weight):
Max diving speed	130 knots (150 mph; 241 km/h)
Stalling speed	36 knots (41 mph; 66 km/h)

SLINGSBY/GLASFLÜGEL T.59 KESTREL

Construction of the first Slingsby-built Kestrel began in March 1970 and first flight of this aircraft was expected to be made in July 1970, with ARB certification following in August 1970.

SLINGSBY-SCHEIBE T.61 FALKE

Construction of the first Slingsby-built Falke began in April 1970. First flight was scheduled for September 1970, and it was hoped that ARB certification would be granted simultaneously.

THE UNITED STATES OF AMERICA

BRIEGLEB
SAILPLANE ASSOCIATES INC

ADDRESS:
1007 Kirkwall Rd, Azusa, California

PRESIDENT: Charles E. Nickels

Mr William G. Briegleb formed the Sailplane Corporation of America (See 1967-68 *Jane's*) to market gliders of his own design. Since 1 June 1966 all products of this company have been produced by Sailplane Associates Inc.

The BG 12 series of sailplanes are available as complete aircraft, as kits of parts or in the form of plans, for amateur construction. By late 1969 a total of 219 kits and plans had been supplied and about 70 aircraft were known to have been completed.

BRIEGLEB BG 12B

The BG 12 is a single-seat high-performance sailplane, the prototype of which flew for the first time in 1956. All ribs and bulkheads are cut from plywood and construction is similar to that of a model aeroplane.

There have been four versions of this sailplane, as follows:
BG 12. Initial model. First flown in March 1956. One only.
BG 12A. Production version described in 1962-63 *Jane's*. Three-piece wing of NACA 4415R/4406R section. Control system utilised aluminium tubes and castings. First flown in July 1958.
BG 12B. Production model to which details below apply. Two-piece wing with thicker section at root. Welded control system. First production model flew in July 1963.
BG 12BD. This differs from the "B" model described below only in the wing, which is now built with no change in incidence between the root and tip. The control system has an input action at the low speed range that deflects the ailerons upward to give the same effect as "twist".

TYPE: Single-seat high-performance sailplane.

WINGS: Cantilever high-wing monoplane. Wing section NACA 4418R at root, NACA 4406R at tip. Dihedral 1°. Incidence 4° at root, 2° at tip. All-wood structure, with plywood covering. Plywood-covered wooden ailerons and trailing-edge flaps. Flaps used as air-brakes at speeds up to 112 knots (130 mph; 210 km/h).

Briegleb BG 12B single-seat high-performance sailplane (*Peter M. Bowers*)

FUSELAGE: Cut-out plywood bulkheads, spruce longerons, plywood-covered.

TAIL UNIT: Cantilever wooden structure. Ground-adjustable tailplane incidence. No tabs.

LANDING GEAR: Shock-mounted nose-skid and spring tail-skid. Non-retractable unsprung mono-wheel with tyre size 10·50 × 4, manufactured by General Tire & Rubber Co. Tyre pressure 35 lb/sq in (2·46 kg/cm²). Briegleb circumferential brake.

ACCOMMODATION: Single seat under large moulded Plexiglas canopy. Adjustable seat and rudder pedals.

DIMENSIONS:
Wing span	50 ft 0 in (15·24 m)
Wing chord at root	3 ft 9 in (1·14 m)
Wing chord at tip	1 ft 0¼ in (0·31 m)
Wing aspect ratio	17·9
Length overall	21 ft 11 in (6·68 m)
Height overall	4 ft 0 in (1·22 m)

AREAS:
Wings, gross	141 sq ft (13·10 m²)
Ailerons (total)	14·00 sq ft (1·30 m²)
Flaps (total)	13·45 sq ft (1·25 m²)
Fin	2·05 sq ft (0·19 m²)

Rudder	7·00 sq ft (0·65 m²)
Tailplane	10·75 sq ft (1·00 m²)
Elevators	6·15 sq ft (0·57 m²)

WEIGHTS AND LOADING:
Weight empty	500-525 lb (227-238 kg)
Max T-O weight	800 lb (363 kg)
Max wing loading	5·67 lb/sq ft (27·7 kg/m²)

PERFORMANCE:
Best glide ratio	33-34 : 1 at 45 knots (52 mph; 84 km/h)
Min sinking speed	2·26 ft (0·69 m)/sec at 41 knots (47 mph; 76 km/h)
Stalling speed, 70° flap	29 knots (33 mph; 53 km/h)
Stalling speed, without flaps	33 knots (38 mph; 61 km/h)
Max speed (smooth air)	121 knots (140 mph; 225 km/h)
Max speed (rough air)	112 knots (130 mph; 209 km/h)
Max aero-tow speed	112 knots (130 mph; 209 km/h)
Max winch-launching speed	65 knots (75 mph; 121 km/h)

BRYAN
BRYAN AIRCRAFT, INC

HEAD OFFICE AND WORKS:
Williams County Airport, PO Box 566, Bryan, Ohio 43506

This company is producing in kit form the Schreder HP-14 high-performance sailplane, with alternative V-tail or T-tail (HP-14T). The prototype HP-14 flew for the first time on 24 June 1966 and the first T-tail version on 19 May 1968. A total of 89 aircraft had been built or were under construction by the end of April 1969.

Details of earlier designs by Mr Schreder can be found under the "Airmate" heading in the 1965-66 *Jane's*.

BRYAN/SCHREDER HP-14 and HP-14T

Piloted by its designer-builder, Mr R. E. Schreder, the prototype of this sailplane won the 1966 US National Gliding Championships.

The kit marketed by Bryan Aircraft has all skins, ribs and bulkheads formed and welded parts welded ready for assembly.

TYPE: Single-seat high-performance sailplane.

WINGS: Cantilever shoulder-wing monoplane. Wing section Wortmann FX-61-163. Thickness/chord ratio 16·3%. Dihedral 3°. No incidence or sweep. Aluminium structure, with plain aluminium ailerons and manually-operated (optionally hydraulic) flaps. No spoilers. Flaps are used as air-brakes in the 90° down position.

FUSELAGE: Aluminium monocoque structure. Steel-tube frame round cockpit.

TAIL UNIT: "Butterfly" type of aluminium construction; included angle 90° (HP-14) or T-tail (HP-14T).

LANDING GEAR: Manually-retractable main wheel and non-retractable steerable tail-wheel. Hydraulic shock-absorber on main wheel. Good-rich 5·00 × 5 tyre, pressure 30 lb/sq in (2·10 kg/cm²). Rosenhan hydraulic brake and wheel.

ACCOMMODATION: Single semi-reclining (45°) seat. Long transparent Plexiglas canopy, consisting of two fixed pieces and one hinged piece, all removable. Provision for BE 90-channel transceiver and Zep oxygen system.

DIMENSIONS:

Wing span	54 ft 7 in (16·64 m)
Wing chord at root	3 ft 4 in (1·02 m)
Wing chord at tip	1 ft 8 in (0·51 m)
Wing aspect ratio	20
Length overall	23 ft 9½ in (7·25 m)
Height over tail	3 ft 11 in (1·19 m)
Tailplane span (HP-14)	6 ft 4¾ in (1·95 m)

AREAS:

Wings, gross	138·3 sq ft (12·85 m²)
Ailerons (total)	8·0 sq ft (0·74 m²)
Trailing-edge flaps (total)	18·2 sq ft (1·69 m²)
Fixed tail surfaces (total) (HP-14)	8·5 sq ft (0·79 m²)
Movable tail surfaces (total) (HP-14)	7·0 sq ft (0·65 m²)

WEIGHTS AND LOADING:

Weight empty, equipped	464 lb (210 kg)
Max T-O weight	728 lb (330 kg)
Max wing loading	5·26 lb/sq ft (25·2 kg/m²)

PERFORMANCE:

Best glide ratio	39 : 1 at 55 knots (63 mph; 101 km/h)
Min sinking speed	2·0 ft (0·61 m)/sec at 39 knots (45 mph; 72 km/h)
Stalling speed:	
Flaps up	34 knots (39 mph; 63 km/h)
Full flap	26 knots (30 mph; 48 km/h)
Max speed (smooth air)	130 knots (150 mph; 241 km/h)
Max speed (rough air)	104 knots (120 mph; 193 km/h)
Max aero-tow speed	104 knots (120 mph; 193 km/h)
Max winch launching speed	78 knots (90 mph; 145 km/h)
g limit	12

BRYAN/SCHREDER HP-15

The HP-15 was probably the first sailplane to be designed to the new Standard Class Rules, which now permit retractable landing gear and fixed-hinge flaps. As with previous Schreder designs, kits will be made available for HP-15 construction. A production time of 600 hours is estimated for the home-builder using only hand tools, drill, rivet gun and air-compressor.

TYPE: Single-seat high-performance Standard Class sailplane.

WINGS: Cantilever shoulder-wing monoplane. Wing section Schreder 69-180. Dihedral 2°. Incidence 3°. No sweep. Metal construction in which all bending loads are carried by very heavy rolled-to-contour wing skins. Each panel contains only three ribs, a plastic leading-edge, two skins and two bent channel spars; the normal interior structure is replaced by high-quality urethane foam blocks which fill completely the cavity enclosed by the skin and spars. The flaps (+90° to −5°) are simple structures, 4 ft (1·22 m) long, of bent aluminium sheet and triangular prisms, without framing other than a rib at each end. The ailerons are of similar construction. No spoilers.

FUSELAGE: Construction of the HP-15 fuselage is similar to that of the HP-14, except that the 1 in (2·54 cm) square steel-tube cockpit framing has been replaced by aluminium tubing.

TAIL UNIT: "V" tail of aluminium construction. Tail fairings attached permanently to fuselage. Folding of the tail surfaces is accomplished by pulling two lower spring-loaded tapered pins into indents.

LANDING GEAR: Manually-retractable main wheel and non-retractable steerable tail-wheel, as for HP-14.

Bryan/Schreder HP-14T single-seat high-performance sailplane (*Howard Levy*)

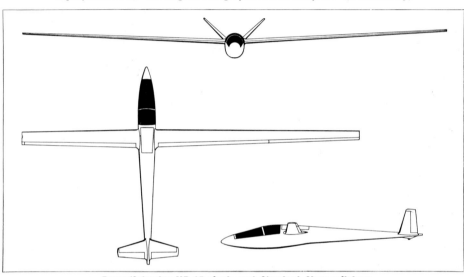
Bryan/Schreder HP-15 single-seat Standard Class sailplane

ACCOMMODATION: Similar to HP-14.

DIMENSIONS:

Wing span	49 ft 2½ in (15 m)
Wing aspect ratio	33
Length overall	23 ft 2½ in (7·07 m)
Height overall	3 ft 9 in (1·14 m)

AREAS:

Wings, gross	75 sq ft (6·97 m²)
Ailerons (total)	4·6 sq ft (0·43 m²)
Flaps (total)	12·4 sq ft (1·15 m²)
Fixed tail surfaces (total)	7·0 sq ft (0·65 m²)
Movable tail surfaces (total)	5·0 sq ft (0·46 m²)

WEIGHTS AND LOADING:

Weight empty	330 lb (150 kg)
Max T-O weight	600 lb (272 kg)
Max wing loading	8 lb/sq ft (39 kg/m²)

PERFORMANCE (estimated):

Best glide ratio	45 : 1 at 48 knots (55 mph; 88 km/h)
Min sinking speed	1·6 ft (0·49 m)/sec at 39 knots (45 mph; 72 km/h)
Stalling speed (no flaps)	39 knots (45 mph; 72 km/h)
Stalling speed (full flap)	31 knots (35 mph; 56 km/h)
Max speed (smooth air)	130 knots (150 mph; 241 km/h)
Max speed (rough air)	99 knots (114 mph; 183 km/h)
Max aero-tow speed	99 knots (114 mph; 183 km/h)
Max winch-launching speed	78 knots (90 mph; 145 km/h)

COWARD
KENNETH COWARD

Mr Coward began the design of a single-seat all-metal sailplane in November 1961, his eighth successful aircraft design, and construction of a prototype started in 1963. Designated as the D-8, plans are available from Pacific Aircraft Co, 5942 Avenida Chamnez, La Jolla, California.

Earlier designs by Mr Coward included the Wee Bee, Honey Bee and Queen Bee light aircraft and the Ryan VZ-3RY-1 VTOL research aircraft.

The adjacent illustration shows the first D-8 built from Mr Coward's plans. Construction was started by Mr Klaus Hill of Salt Lake City, Utah, and was completed by the present owner, Mr John E. Jenista of Vienna, Virginia, at a total cost of $400.

COWARD D-8

WINGS: Cantilever shoulder-wing monoplane. Aerofoil section NACA 4418. Dihedral 0°. Incidence 3°. No sweepback. All-metal one-

Coward D-8 single-seat sailplane built by Mr John E. Jenista (*Howard Levy*)

piece wing with a built-up spar and formed ribs. Simple flap-type all-metal ailerons. No flaps, spoilers, air-brakes, trim-tabs or slots.

FUSELAGE: Monocoque all-metal structure.

TAIL UNIT: Cantilever all-metal structure. Fixed-incidence tailplane. All control surfaces piano-hinged. No trim-tabs.

LANDING GEAR: Non-retractable mono-wheel.

ACCOMMODATION: Single seat under transparent bubble canopy.

DIMENSIONS:

Wing span	32 ft 0 in (9·75 m)
Wing chord (constant)	3 ft 6 in (1·07 m)
Wing aspect ratio	10·0

Length overall	17 ft 0 in (5·18 m)
Height over tail	4 ft 0 in (1·22 m)
Tailplane span	6 ft 8 in (2·03 m)

AREAS:

Wings, gross	100 sq ft (9·29 m²)
Ailerons (total)	16 sq ft (1·49 m²)
Fin	3·5 sq ft (0·33 m²)
Rudder	2·4 sq ft (0·22 m²)
Tailplane	11·1 sq ft (1·03 m²)
Elevators	5·55 sq ft (0·52 m²)

WEIGHTS AND LOADING:

Weight empty, equipped	225 lb (102 kg)
Max T-O weight	460 lb (209 kg)
Max wing loading	4·6 lb/sq ft (22·5 kg/m²)

PERFORMANCE:

Best glide ratio
21·5 : 1 at 52 knots (60 mph; 97 km/h)
Min sinking speed
3·5 ft (1·07 m)/sec at
38 knots (45 mph; 72 km/h)
Stalling speed 30 knots (34 mph; 55 km/h)
Max speed (rough air)
117 knots (135 mph; 217 km/h)
Max aero-tow speed
114 knots (131 mph; 211 km/h)
Max winch-launching speed
65 knots (75 mph; 121 km/h)
g limit 6

KASPER

WITOLD A. KASPER

ADDRESS: 1853 132nd S.E., Bellevue, Washington

Mr Kasper has designed two experimental sailplanes. The first of these is completed and the second was under construction at the beginning of 1970.

KASPER BEKAS-N

Design and construction of this swept-wing tailless sailplane began in 1965, and the first flight was made on 12 April 1968.

WINGS: Cantilever mid-wing monoplane. Wing section NACA 8-H-12. Dihedral 1° 30'. Incidence 8°. Sweepback 15°. Wood and plywood structure. Elevons of wooden construction. Spoilers on fuselage, aft of wing. Rudder, air-brake and trim-tab at each wing tip.

FUSELAGE: All-wood structure, with wooden frames and plywood skin.

LANDING GEAR: Non-retractable mono-wheel. Wheel and tyres size 4 × 8, pressure 72 lb/sq in (5·06 kg/cm²). Nose-skid with rubber shock-absorber. Metal sprung skids at rear of fuselage and each wing tip.

ACCOMMODATION: Single seat under bubble canopy. Pilot's seat adjustable fore and aft in flight to change CG.

DIMENSIONS:

Wing span	49 ft 0 in (14·94 m)
Wing chord (constant)	3 ft 0 in (0·91 m)
Wing aspect ratio	15·0
Length overall	12 ft 1 in (3·68 m)
Height overall	5 ft 0 in (1·52 m)

AREAS:

Wings, gross	165 sq ft (15·33 m²)

Kasper Bekas-N single-seat experimental sailplane (*Peter M. Bowers*)

Elevons (total)	9·48 sq ft (0·88 m²)
Rudders (both)	4·0 sq ft (0·37 m²)

WEIGHTS AND LOADING:

Weight empty, equipped	400 lb (181 kg)
Max T-O weight	650 lb (295 kg)
Max wing loading	3·95 lb/sq ft (19·2 kg/m²)

PERFORMANCE:

Best glide ratio
44 : 1 at 52 knots (60 mph; 97 km/h)
Min sinking speed
2 ft (0·61 m)/sec at 47 knots (54 mph; 87 km/h)
Stalling speed 35 knots (40 mph; 64 km/h)
Max speed (smooth air)
112 knots (129 mph; 208 km/h)
Max speed (rough air)
87 knots (100 mph; 161 km/h)
Max aero-tow speed
85 knots (98 mph; 158 km/h)
Max winch-launching speed
60 knots (69 mph; 111 km/h)

MILLER

W. TERRY MILLER

ADDRESS:
39 McCarty Drive, Furlong, Pennsylvania 18925

Mr Miller is the designer of a high-performance sailplane named the Tern, which is intended for amateur construction. The prototype was constructed in a total of 1,180 working hours and flew for the first time in September 1965.

An improved version, known as the Tern II, has been developed and flew for the first time in August 1968. During 1968 brake parachutes were fitted to the prototype, and two types of parachute are now available for installation in the Tern or the Tern II, comprising a 6 ft (1·8 m) diameter cross parachute (as illustrated) or a 5 ft (1·5 m) diameter guide surface parachute.

Twelve Terns had flown and 96 were under construction by amateurs in Africa, Australia, Canada, S America and the USA by May 1970. At the same date twelve Tern II's were under construction and one has been completed.

MILLER TERN

TYPE: Single-seat high-performance sailplane.

WINGS: Cantilever shoulder-wing monoplane. Wing section Wortmann FX-61-184 at root, Wortmann FX-61-163 at tip. Dihedral 2°. Incidence 2°. No sweep at 50% chord. Two-piece two-spar spruce structure, all plywood covered. Plain ailerons of all-wood construction. No flaps or tabs. Lower-surface dive brakes of wood construction used for glide slope control.

FUSELAGE: Semi-monocoque wood structure. Plastic-reinforced glass-fibre nose. Plywood skin aft of cockpit.

TAIL UNIT: Cantilever all-wood structure, with modified NACA laminar-flow sections. Special hinge-line contouring to reduce drag and increase control effectiveness at large deflections. All control surfaces 60% mass-balanced. No tabs.

LANDING GEAR: Non-retractable mono-wheel forward of CG, in streamlined pod. Skids

Prototype Miller Tern single-seat sailplane with brake-chute deployed

under nose and tail. Wheel and tyre size 5·00 × 4. Brake lever applies pressure directly to tyre.

ACCOMMODATION: Single partially-reclining seat under transparent canopy, centre portion of which hinges sideways for access to cockpit. Standard seven-instrument panel. Space for radio.

DIMENSIONS:

Wing span	51 ft 0 in (15·54 m)
Wing chord at root	3 ft 4 in (1·02 m)
Wing chord at tip	1 ft 10 in (0·56 m)
Wing aspect ratio	20
Length overall	21 ft 3½ in (6·49 m)
Height over tail	5 ft 0 in (1·52 m)
Tailplane span	8 ft 6 in (2·59 m)

AREAS:

Wings, gross	130 sq ft (12·08 m²)
Ailerons (total)	7·60 sq ft (0·71 m²)
Dive-brakes (total)	5·20 sq ft (0·48 m²)
Fin	4·66 sq ft (0·43 m²)
Rudder	5·00 sq ft (0·46 m²)
Tailplane	7·82 sq ft (0·73 m²)
Elevators	6·56 sq ft (0·61 m²)

WEIGHTS AND LOADING:

Weight empty, equipped	475 lb (215 kg)
Max T-O weight	700 lb (318 kg)
Max wing loading	5·4 lb/sq ft (26·36 kg/m²)

PERFORMANCE:

Best glide ratio
36 : 1 at 50·4 knots (58 mph; 93 km/h)
Min sinking speed
2·1 ft (0·64 m)/sec at
41 knots (47 mph; 76 km/h)
Stalling speed 34 knots (39 mph; 63 km/h)
Max speed (smooth air)
104 knots (120 mph; 193 km/h)
Max speed (rough air)
78 knots (90 mph; 145 km/h)
Max aero-tow speed
78 knots (90 mph; 145 km/h)
Max winch-launching speed
61 knots (70 mph; 112 km/h)

MILLER TERN II

This developed version of the Tern sailplane differs from the original model, described earlier, in having a larger wing span. All details are as for Tern except:

DIMENSIONS:

Wing span	55 ft 6 in (18·29 m)
Wing chord at root	3 ft 4 in (1·02 m)
Wing chord at tip	1 ft 8 in (0·51 m)
Wing aspect ratio	22

AREAS:

Wings, gross	140 sq ft (13·01 m²)
Ailerons (total)	9·3 sq ft (0·86 m²)

WEIGHTS AND LOADING:
Weight empty, equipped   550 lb (249 kg)
Max T-O weight   800 lb (363 kg)
Max wing loading   5·72 lb/sq ft (28 kg/m²)

PERFORMANCE (estimated):
Best glide ratio
   38 : 1 at 52 knots (60 mph; 97 km/h)
Min sinking speed   1·95 ft (0·59 m)/sec at
   41·7 knots (48 mph; 77 km/h)

Stalling speed   35 knots (40 mph; 64 km/h)
Max speed (rough air)
   76 knots (88 mph; 142 km/h)
Max aero-tow speed
   76 knots (88 mph; 142 km/h)

SCHWEIZER
SCHWEIZER AIRCRAFT CORPORATION

HEAD OFFICE AND WORKS:
Box 147, Elmira, New York 14902

PRESIDENT AND CHIEF ENGINEER:
Ernest Schweizer

VICE-PRESIDENT AND GENERAL MANAGER:
Paul A. Schweizer

VICE-PRESIDENT IN CHARGE OF MANUFACTURING:
William Schweizer

SALES MANAGER: W. E. Doherty, Jr

TREASURER: Nicholas Haich

SECRETARY: Kenneth Tifft

Schweizer Aircraft Corporation is the leading American designer and manufacturer of sailplanes. Its current products include the SGS 2-33 two-seat general-purpose sailplane, the one-design SGS 1-26 single-seat high-performance sailplane (which is available complete and in kit form for the home builder), the SGS 2-32 two/three-seat high-performance sailplane, and the SGS 1-34 Standard Class single-seat high-performance sailplane.

By agreement with the Grumman Aircraft Engineering Corporation, Schweizer is also manufacturing the Grumman Ag-Cat agricultural biplane, a description of which will be found under the "Grumman" entry. Other sub-contract work includes production of fuselage assemblies for Piper Aircraft Corporation and major structures for Bell Helicopter Company.

About 350 people were employed by Schweizer in 1970.

SCHWEIZER SGS 1-26

Externally similar to the SGS 1-23, described in the 1967-68 *Jane's*. The SGS 1-26 first flew in January 1954 and production of both complete aircraft and kits for the home-builder was under way by November 1954. Further to assist the amateur constructor, all the complicated alignments, welding and assemblies requiring specialised tooling are undertaken by the manufacturer, including a pre-formed aluminium nose-cap and Plexiglas canopy. The design has been granted an Approved Certificate by the FAA. From 300 to 600 man-hours are required for assembly, depending on the experience and skill of the builder.

Nearly 500 SGS 1-26 sailplanes have been built, including kits, and production continues at the rate of more than one a week, the current version being designated SGS 1-26D

TYPE: Single-seat medium-performance sailplane.

WINGS: Cantilever mid-wing monoplane. Dihedral 3° 30'. All-metal structure of aluminium alloy, with metal skin. Fabric-covered ailerons. Balanced dive-brakes immediately aft of spar on each wing.

FUSELAGE: Welded chrome-molybdenum steel-tube framework, covered with fabric.

TAIL UNIT: Cantilever aluminium alloy structure, covered with fabric.

LANDING GEAR: Non-retractable unsprung monowheel, size 4·00-4, with Schweizer brake, aft of rubber-sprung nose-skid. Small solid rubber tail-wheel.

ACCOMMODATION: Single seat under blown Plexiglas canopy. Provision for radio forward of pilot.

EQUIPMENT: Standard equipment includes fresh air vent, wheel cover, seat belt and shoulder harness, air speed indicator and instrument panel.

DIMENSIONS:
Wing span   40 ft 0 in (12·19 m)
Wing aspect ratio   10
Length overall   21 ft 6½ in (6·57 m)
Height overall   7 ft 2½ in (2·21 m)
Tailplane span   7 ft 6 in (2·29 m)

AREAS:
Wings, gross   160 sq ft (14·87 m²)
Spoilers (total)   2·78 sq ft (0·26 m²)

WEIGHTS AND LOADING:
Weight empty   430 lb (195 kg)
Max T-O weight   700 lb (317 kg)
Max wing loading   4·37 lb/sq ft (21·34 kg/m²)

Schweizer SGS 1-26D single-seat medium-performance sailplane

Schweizer SGS 2-32 two/three-seat high-performance sailplane

PERFORMANCE:
Best glide ratio   23 : 1
Min sinking speed   2·6 ft (0·79 m)/sec
Stalling speed   29 knots (33 mph; 54 km/h)
Max permissible speed
   99 knots (114 mph; 183 km/h)
Max aero-tow speed
   99 knots (114 mph; 183 km/h)
Max winch-launching speed
   55 knots (63 mph; 101 km/h)

SCHWEIZER SGS 2-32

The SGS 2-32 has an unusually large "aeroplane-type" cabin capable of carrying one very large or two average-sized passengers in addition to the pilot. The prototype flew for the first time on 3 July 1962. FAA type approval was received in June 1964 and production began immediately. Nearly 75 had been built by March 1970.

The SGS 2-32 sailplane was chosen by Lockheed Missiles & Space Company to form the basic airframe of their YO-3A quiet observation aircraft, and by LTV Electronics for their L450F aircraft.

TYPE: Two/three-seat high-performance and utility sailplane.

WINGS: Cantilever mid-wing monoplane. Wing section NACA 63³618 at root, NACA 43012A at tip. Dihedral 3° 30'. All-metal single-spar structure with metal covering. Fabric-covered metal ailerons. Speed-limiting dive-brakes on upper and lower surfaces.

FUSELAGE: All-metal monocoque structure.

TAIL UNIT: Cantilever metal structure, with all-moving tailplane. Fin metal-covered; control surfaces fabric-covered. Adjustable trim-tab in tailplane.

LANDING GEAR: Non-retractable unsprung monowheel, wheel and tyre size 6·00 × 6, with hydraulic brake, and skid.

ACCOMMODATION: Pilot at front. Seat for one or two persons at rear. Dual controls. Rear control column removable for passenger comfort. Sideways-opening blown Perspex canopy.

EQUIPMENT: Lined cockpit, front and rear cabin air vents, seat belts and shoulder harnesses standard. Optional items include electrical and oxygen systems, radio, special instrumentation, canopy locks, cushions, map cases and wing-tip wheels.

DIMENSIONS:
Wing span   57 ft 1 in (17·40 m)
Wing chord at root   4 ft 9 in (1·45 m)
Wing chord at tip   1 ft 7 in (0·48 m)
Wing aspect ratio   18·05
Length overall   26 ft 9 in (8·15 m)
Fuselage width at cockpit   2 ft 8 in (0·81 m)
Tailplane span   10 ft 6 in (3·20 m)

AREAS:
Wings, gross   180 sq ft (16·70 m²)
Ailerons (total)   14·74 sq ft (1·37 m²)
Dive-brakes (total)   9·76 sq ft (0·91 m²)
Fin   7·86 sq ft (0·73 m²)
Rudder   7·23 sq ft (0·67 m²)
Tailplane   21·88 sq ft (2·03 m²)

WEIGHTS AND LOADINGS (H = high-performance category, U = utility category):
Weight empty, equipped, H, U   850 lb (385 kg)
Max T-O weight:
   H   1,340 lb (608 kg)
   U   1,430 lb (649 kg)
Max wing loading:
   H   7·44 lb/sq ft (36·32 kg/m²)
   U   7·94 lb/sq ft (38·77 kg/m²)

PERFORMANCE (H = high-performance category, U = utility category; at AUW of 1,200 lb = 544 kg):
Best glide ratio
   34 : 1 at 51 knots (59 mph; 95 km/h)
Min sinking speed   2·38 ft (0·72 m)/sec
   at 44 knots (50 mph; 80 km/h)
Stalling speed:
   H   42 knots (48 mph; 78 km/h)
   U   44 knots (50 mph; 81 km/h)
Max speed (smooth air), dive-brakes extended:
   H   130 knots (150 mph; 241 km/h)
   U   122 knots (140 mph; 225 km/h)

Max aero-tow speed
                96 knots (110 mph; 177 km/h)

SCHWEIZER SGS 2-33

The SGS 2-33 was developed to meet the demand for a medium-priced two-seat sailplane for general soaring. The prototype was first flown in the Autumn of 1966 and received FAA Type Approval in February 1967. Production began in January 1967, and 175 SGS 2-33 sailplanes had been built by March 1970.

TYPE: Two-seat general-purpose sailplane.

WINGS: Strut-braced high-wing monoplane. Aluminium alloy structure with metal skin and all-metal ailerons. Dive-brakes fitted.

FUSELAGE: Welded chrome-molybdenum steel-tube structure. Nose covered with glass-fibre, remainder with Ceconite fabric.

TAIL UNIT: Braced steel-tube structure, covered with Ceconite fabric.

LANDING GEAR: Non-retractable Cleveland mono-wheel and 6·00 × 6 tyre, immediately aft of nose skid. Rubber block shock-absorption for skid. Wing-tip wheels optional.

ACCOMMODATION: Two seats in tandem in completely lined cockpit, with dual controls. One-piece canopy. Rear door and window. Standard equipment includes air vent, seat belts and shoulder harness.

DIMENSIONS:
Wing span	51 ft 0 in (15·54 m)
Wing aspect ratio	11·85
Length overall	25 ft 9 in (7·85 m)
Height overall	9 ft 3½ in (2·83 m)

AREAS:
Wings, gross	219·48 sq ft (20·39 m²)
Ailerons (total)	18·24 sq ft (1·69 m²)

WEIGHTS:
Weight empty	600 lb (272 kg)
Max T-O weight	1,040 lb (472 kg)
Max wing loading	4·74 lb/sq ft (23·14 kg/m²)

PERFORMANCE:
Best glide ratio	22·25 : 1

Min sinking speed:
Solo	2·6 ft (0·79 m)/sec
Dual	3·0 ft (0·91 m)/sec

Stalling speed:
Solo	27 knots (31 mph; 50 km/h)
Dual	30·5 knots (35 mph; 57 km/h)
Max speed (smooth air)	85 knots (98 mph; 158 km/h)
Max aero-tow speed	85 knots (98 mph; 158 km/h)
Max winch-launching speed	60 knots (69 mph; 111 km/h)

SCHWEIZER SGS 1-34

Design of this single-seat high-performance Standard Class sailplane, intended to replace the 1-23 series described in the 1967-68 *Jane's*, began in 1967 and construction of the prototype started in the following year. This flew for the first time in the Spring of 1969 and FAA Type Certification was awarded in September 1969. A total of 20 production models had been completed in March 1970.

WINGS: Cantilever shoulder-wing monoplane. Wing section Wortmann FX61-163 at root, Wortmann FX60-126 at tip. Dihedral 3° 30'. Incidence 1° at root, 0° at tip. No sweepback. All-metal aluminium alloy structure. Plain all-metal differential ailerons. Double-flap speed-limiting air-brakes, above and below wing. No flaps, spoilers, trim-tabs or slots.

FUSELAGE: All-metal aluminium alloy semi-monocoque structure.

TAIL UNIT: Cantilever all-metal aluminium alloy structure with swept vertical surfaces. Fixed-incidence tailplane. No trim-tabs.

LANDING GEAR: Non-retractable mono-wheel, with forward skid and auxiliary tail-wheel. Cleveland wheel size 5·00-5, Type III 4-ply tyre. Cleveland wheel brake.

ACCOMMODATION: Single seat under bubble canopy.

Schweizer SGS 2-33 two-seat general-purpose sailplane

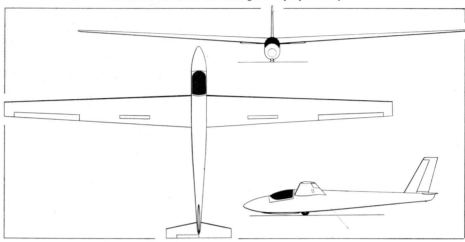

Schweizer SGS 1-34 single-seat Standard Class sailplane

Schweizer SGS 1-34 single-seat high-performance Standard Class sailplane

DIMENSIONS:
Wing span	49 ft 2 in (15·0 m)
Wing chord at root	4 ft 3·63 in (1·31 m)
Wing chord at tip	1 ft 10·13 in (0·56 m)
Wing aspect ratio	16
Length overall	25 ft 9 in (7·85 m)
Height over tail	7 ft 6 in (2·29 m)
Tailplane span	8 ft 6 in (2·59 m)

AREAS:
Wings, gross	151 sq ft (14·03 m²)
Ailerons (total)	10·90 sq ft (1·01 m²)
Fin	5·51 sq ft (0·51 m²)
Rudder	5·18 sq ft (0·48 m²)
Tailplane	13·20 sq ft (1·23 m²)
Elevators	5·88 sq ft (0·55 m²)

WEIGHTS AND LOADING:
Weight empty, equipped	550 lb (249 kg)
Max T-O weight	800 lb (362 kg)
Max wing loading	5·3 lb/sq ft (25·9 kg/m²)

PERFORMANCE:
Best glide ratio	34 : 1 at 45 knots (52 mph; 84 km/h)
Min sinking speed	2·1 ft (0·64 m)/sec at 40 knots (46 mph; 74 km/h)
Max speed (smooth air)	117 knots (135 mph; 217 km/h)
Max aero-tow speed	100 knots (115 mph; 185 km/h)
g limits	+8·33; −5·33

THE UNION OF SOVIET SOCIALIST REPUBLICS

ANTONOV
OLEG KONSTANTINOVICH ANTONOV

Antonov has been well-known as a sailplane designer for many years. Details of his latest known design follows.

ANTONOV A-15

The Antonov A-15 is a single-seat all-metal high-performance sailplane of considerably more refined design than the earlier A-11 and A-13. The prototype flew for the first time on 26 March 1960, since when at least five more have been built. Aerobatics, spinning and cloud flying are permitted.

Four A-15's were entered for the 1965 World Gliding Championships, gaining 13th, 17th, 22nd and 32nd places in the Open Class contest.

TYPE: Single-seat high-performance sailplane.

WINGS: Cantilever mid-wing monoplane, with wingtip "salmons". Wing section NACA 64₃-618 at root, NACA 63₃-616 at tip. Dihedral 1° 30'. Single-spar metal structure, with metal covering. All-metal ailerons. Fowler flaps. Upper-surface spoilers.

FUSELAGE: All-metal monocoque structure.

TAIL UNIT: Cantilever "butterfly" type of all-metal construction, with included angle of 90°.

LANDING GEAR: Retractable sprung mono-wheel. Brake standard.

ACCOMMODATION: Single seat under sideways-opening (to starboard) blown plastic canopy.

Adjustable back-rest and rudder pedals. Provision for oxygen system and radio.

DIMENSIONS:
Wing span	59 ft 0½ in (18·00 m)
Wing chord at root	3 ft 6 in (1·07 m)
Wing chord at tip	1 ft 1½ in (0·34 m)
Wing aspect ratio	26·4
Length overall	23 ft 8 in (7·20 m)
Tailplane span	12 ft 1 in (3·68 m)

AREA:
Wings, gross	132 sq ft (12·3 m²)

WEIGHTS AND LOADING:
Weight empty	705 lb (320 kg)
Max T-O weight	838 lb (380 kg)
Max wing loading	6·47 lb/sq ft (31·6 kg/m²)

PERFORMANCE:
Best glide ratio
    40 : 1 at 54 knots (62 mph; 100 km/h)
Min sinking speed   2·07 ft (0·63 m)/sec at
    48·6 knots (56 mph; 90 km/h)
Min flying speed   35 knots (40 mph; 65 km/h)
Max speed (smooth air)
    135 knots (155 mph; 250 km/h)
Max speed (rough air)
    135 knots (155 mph; 250 km/h)
Max aero-tow speed
    76 knots (87 mph; 140 km/h)
Max winch-launching speed
    65 knots (75 mph; 120 km/h)

Antonov A-15 single-seat high-performance sailplane (*Flight International*)

KAI
KAZAN AVIATION INSTITUTE
Details of the KAI-17 training glider, designed by a team headed by M. P. Simonov, were given in the 1963-64 *Jane's*. Two other sailplanes produced by this team are the KAI-14 and KAI-19, of which descriptions follow.

KAI-14
The KAI-14 conforms to the international Standard Class specification. Construction is all-metal and two versions have been produced.

The first is a competition sailplane, in which the pilot reclines under a long flush transparent canopy and which has a polished metal finish. The second version, intended for series production, has a conventional seat for the pilot and is unpolished.

Two KAI-14's took part in the 1965 World Gliding Championships.

TYPE: Single-seat high-performance sailplane.
WINGS: Cantilever shoulder-wing monoplane, with leading-edges swept forward 2°. Dihedral 4°. All-metal structure, metal-covered. Inset ailerons, each in two sections. Small trailing-edge air-brakes.
FUSELAGE: Pod and boom type, of all-metal semi-monocoque construction.
TAIL UNIT: "Butterfly" type of cantilever all-metal construction.
LANDING GEAR: Non-retractable mono-wheel, size 235 × 110 mm, faired into bottom of fuselage. Tail bumper. Brake linked with air-brakes.
ACCOMMODATION: Single seat under transparent canopy.
DIMENSIONS:
Wing span   49 ft 2½ in (15·00 m)
Length overall   19 ft 1 in (5·82 m)
Tailplane span   7 ft 4 in (2·25 m)
WEIGHT:
Max T-O weight   573 lb (260 kg)
PERFORMANCE:
Min sinking speed   1·90 ft (0·58 m)/sec at
    48·6 knots (56 mph; 90 km/h)
Max permissible diving speed
    135 knots (155 mph; 250 km/h)
Landing speed   43·4 knots (50 mph; 80 km/h)
Max aero-tow speed
    75·6 knots (87 mph; 140 km/h)
Max winch-launching speed
    54 knots (62 mph; 100 km/h)

KAI-19
This highly-advanced single-seat sailplane was designed by a team headed by P. Kamychev, and including M. Simonov and A. Ossokine. All external surfaces are highly-polished to reduce drag.

A two-seat version of the KAI-19 has also been developed; and the international sailplane speed record over a 300-km closed circuit was raised to

KAI-14 single-seat Standard Class sailplane (*Flight International*)

49·946 knots (57·515 mph; 92·562 km/h) in an aircraft of this type by V. Tchouvikov and J. Logvin on 1 August 1964. No details of the two-seater are available and the following data refer to the single-seat KAI-19.

TYPE: Single-seat high-performance sailplane.
WINGS: Cantilever shoulder-wing monoplane. Laminar-flow wing section. All-metal single-spar structure with wing-tip "salmons". Skins are chemically-milled and vary in thickness from 0·8 mm at the root to 0·6 mm at the tip, with the original skin thickness of 1·2 mm retained over the spar caps. All-metal ailerons in two sections on each wing, with sandwich core. Flaps in three sections on each wing, of similar construction to ailerons. "Crocodile" type split air-brakes between flaps and ailerons on trailing-edge of each wing. Provision for 15·5 Imp gallons (70 litres) of water ballast in wings. Weight of complete wing is 379 lb (172 kg).
FUSELAGE: All-metal semi-monocoque structure with max cross-sectional area of 3·88 sq ft (0·36 m²). Weight of fuselage is 80 lb (36 kg). Provision for carrying 14·5 Imp gallons (66 litres) of water ballast in fuselage.
TAIL UNIT: Cantilever all-metal structure with tailplane mounted at tip of fin. Construction similar to that of wings. Tailplane folds down on each side, to lie flat against fin, for transport.

LANDING GEAR: Fully-retractable mono-wheel, fitted with mud-guard. Electrical retraction, with provision for manual actuation. Oleo-pneumatic shock-absorber. Disc brake. Tail bumper.
ACCOMMODATION: Reclining couch for pilot under long transparent canopy. Cabin is ventilated. Provision for radio and oxygen equipment.
DIMENSIONS:
Wing span   65 ft 7¼ in (20·00 m)
Wing aspect ratio   28·6
Length overall   26 ft 1½ in (7·96 m)
Width of fuselage at cockpit 2 ft 1¼ in (0·64 m)
Tailplane span   8 ft 6½ in (2·60 m)
AREA:
Wings, gross   150·70 sq ft (14·00 m²)
WEIGHTS AND LOADINGS:
Weight empty   736 lb (334 kg)
Max T-O weight   913 lb (414 kg)
Max wing loading:
without water ballast 6·04 lb/sq ft (29·50 kg/m²)
with water ballast 8·19 lb/sq ft (40·00 kg/m²)
PERFORMANCE:
Best glide ratio
    45 : 1 at 46 knots (53 mph; 85 km/h)
Min sinking speed   1·94 ft (0·59 m)/sec
Landing speed   41 knots (47 mph; 75 km/h)
Max permissible speed
    135 knots (155 mph; 250 km/h)
Min speed without flaps
    32·2 knots (37 mph; 59 km/h)

VEGA
VEGA-2
The Vega-2 sailplane was designed by Aviation Engineer Valentin Spivak, a graduate of the Kharkov Aviation Institute, and was tested and put into series production during the Summer of 1966.

TYPE: Single-seat high-performance sailplane.
WINGS: Cantilever mid-wing monoplane of all-metal construction. Available as Standard Class 15-m span or with extensions to increase span to 17·5 m.
FUSELAGE: All-metal construction.
TAIL UNIT: "Butterfly" type of all-metal construction.
LANDING GEAR: Main wheel aft of CG in stream-lined pod.
ACCOMMODATION: Single seat under forward-sliding transparent canopy. The oxygen equipment, instruments for all-weather flight and a standard instrument panel are produced as three detachable units, making it possible

Vega-2 single-seat Standard Class sailplane (*Novosti*)

to select the degree of equipment needed for a particular flight.
DIMENSIONS:
Wing span:
standard   49 ft 2½ in (15 m)
extended span   57 ft 4¾ in (17·5 m)

PERFORMANCE:
Max speed (smooth air)
    188 knots (217 mph; 350 km/h)
Best glide ratio:
standard   36 : 1
extended span   41 : 1

YUGOSLAVIA

CENTRE TECHNIQUE VAZDUHOPLOVNO VRSAC

ADDRESS:

Vrsac

Under the technical leadership of Ings Nenad Hrisafovic and Vasilije Stepanovic, this Centre has developed two versions of a tandem two-seat high-performance sailplane named the Cirus.

HS-62 and HS-64 CIRUS

An outstanding feature of the Cirus tandem two-seat high-performance sailplane is its form of wing construction, which helps to ensure an accurate section and smooth surface finish. Instead of covering the wings with thick plywood skin, the constructors of the Cirus have countersunk small individual panels of wood between the ribs and have then covered the complete assembly with a thin veneer. (The designers are now considering the use of glass-fibre instead of veneer.) Wing section is NACA 63·3-618 (modified). Plate-type air-brakes are installed aft of the spar.

Each wing panel has a basic structure of a single wooden main box-spar and trellis ribs with plywood webs. A sweep-forward of 5° 12′ at quarter-chord enables the pilot in the rear cockpit to be placed over the CG without impairing his field of view. The front cockpit can be occupied by a person weighing between 120 and 265 lb (55-125 kg).

A conventional tail unit is fitted, with all-moving horizontal surfaces, fitted with two anti-tabs. The landing gear comprises a non-retractable mono-wheel and tail bumper.

The two versions of the Cirus are characterised by different types of fuselage, as follows:

HS-62. Initial version, first flown on 18 July 1963. Steel-tube fuselage, with fabric covering.

HS-64. Developed version, first flown on 4 January 1965. Plywood-covered wooden monocoque fuselage. Intended as production version.

DIMENSIONS:

Wing span	55 ft 9½ in (17·00 m)
Wing chord at root	5 ft 0¾ in (1·54 m)
Wing chord at tip	2 ft 0¼ in (0·62 m)
Wing aspect ratio	15·73
Length overall	28 ft 11½ in (8·83 m)

AREA:

Wings, gross	197·8 sq ft (18·38 m²)

PERFORMANCE:

Best glide ratio:

HS-62
    28·2 : 1 at 48 knots (55 mph; 88 km/h)

HS-64
    30·7 : 1 at 48·6 knots (56 mph; 90 km/h)

Min sinking speed:

HS-62
    2·69 ft (0·82 m)/sec at 43·4 knots (50 mph; 80 km/h)

HS-64
    2·49 ft (0·76 m)/sec at 40·8 knots (47 mph; 76 km/h)

Stalling speed:

HS-62   37 knots (42 mph; 68 km/h)

HS-64   36 knots (41 mph; 66 km/h)

LIBIS
LETALSKI INSTITUT "BRANKO IVANUS", SLOVENIJA

ADDRESS:

Celovska cesta 258, Ljubljana

In addition to its work on powered aircraft, LIBIS is engaged on the development and manufacture of sailplanes, of which details follow.

LIBIS-17

The LIBIS-17 (formerly KB-17) is a tandem two-seat high-performance training sailplane which is also suitable for flying up to silver and gold "C" standard as a single-seater. It first flew in prototype form in October 1961. The first production model flew in June 1963.

Looping, spinning and cloud flying are permitted in this sailplane.

TYPE: Two-seat high-performance training sailplane.

WINGS: Cantilever high-wing monoplane. Wing section NACA 63₃-618. Dihedral 5°. Incidence 7°. Wooden single-spar structure, with plywood-covered leading-edge torsion box supported by Styrofoam. Remainder of wing fabric-covered. Frise ailerons of wood construction filled with Styrofoam and covered with fabric. Hütter type wooden plate spoilers immediately aft of spar.

FUSELAGE: Welded steel-tube structure, fabric-covered.

TAIL UNIT: Cantilever wooden structure, filled with Styrofoam. All-moving one-piece fin and tailplane, each with servo-tab.

LANDING GEAR: Non-retractable unsprung Borovo main wheel and nose-wheel in tandem. Main wheel size 500 × 180 mm; nose-wheel 300 × 135 mm. Tyre pressure: main 25·5 lb/sq in (1·8 kg/cm²), nose 18·5 lb/sq in (1·3 kg/cm²). LIBIS mechanical brake.

ACCOMMODATION: Two seats in tandem under forward-hinged one-piece blown transparent canopy. Ventilation system. Blind-flying instrumentation, radio and oxygen equipment optional.

DIMENSIONS:

Wing span	55 ft 9 in (17·00 m)
Wing chord at root	5 ft 8½ in (1·74 m)
Wing chord at tip	2 ft 10¼ in (0·87 m)
Wing aspect ratio	13
Length overall	25 ft 1 in (7·64 m)
Height over tail	8 ft 11½ in (2·73 m)
Tailplane span	10 ft 2 in (3·10 m)
Wheelbase	7 ft 2½ in (2·20 m)

AREAS:

Wings, gross	237·9 sq ft (22·10 m²)
Ailerons (total)	20·02 sq ft (1·86 m²)
Spoilers (total)	7·88 sq ft (0·73 m²)
Fin (all-moving)	15·07 sq ft (1·40 m²)
Tailplane (all-moving)	30·14 sq ft (2·80 m²)

WEIGHTS AND LOADING:

Weight empty, equipped	739 lb (335 kg)

LIBIS-17 tandem two-seat high-performance training sailplane

LIBIS-18 single-seat Standard Class sailplane (*Anne Ince*)

Max T-O weight	1,135 lb (515 kg)
Max wing loading	4·77 lb/sq ft (23·3 kg/m²)

PERFORMANCE (at max T-O weight):

Best glide ratio
    27 : 1 at 50·4 knots (58 mph; 93·5 km/h)

Min sinking speed
    2·82 ft (0·86 m)/sec at 41 knots (47 mph; 75 km/h)

Stalling speed   33 knots (37 mph; 59 km/h)

Max speed (smooth air)
    120 knots (138 mph; 222 km/h)

Max speed (rough air)
    78 knots (90 mph; 144 km/h)

Max aero-tow speed
    76 knots (87 mph; 140 km/h)

Max winch-launching speed
    59 knots (68 mph; 110 km/h)

LIBIS-18

The general appearance of this single-seat Standard Class sailplane is shown in the adjacent illustration. Construction is of wood. The tail surfaces consist of a sweptback fin and rudder and all-moving horizontal surfaces with anti-tab.

DIMENSIONS:

Wing span	49 ft 2½ in (15·00 m)
Length overall	22 ft 7½ in (6·90 m)

PERFORMANCE (estimated):

Best glide ratio
    39 : 1 at 37·8 knots (43·5 mph; 70 km/h)

Min sinking speed   1·97 ft (0·60 m)/sec at 34 knots (39 mph; 63 km/h)

Stalling speed   31 knots (35·5 mph; 57 km/h)

MILITARY MISSILES

(CORRECTED TO 1 AUGUST 1970)

AUSTRALIA

COMMONWEALTH OF AUSTRALIA
DEPARTMENT OF SUPPLY

ADDRESS:
Anzac Park West Building, Constitution Avenue,
Parkes, Canberra, A.C.T.2600
SECRETARY: A. S. Cooley

Aircraft Factories
HEADQUARTERS:
Fishermens Bend, Melbourne, Victoria
AIRFIELD AND FINAL ASSEMBLY WORKSHOPS:
Avalon, Victoria
MANAGER: G. J. Churcher
AERONAUTICAL RESEARCH LABORATORIES:
Fishermen's Bend, Melbourne, Victoria
CHIEF SUPERINTENDENT:
Dr J. L. Farrands

Weapons Research Establishment:
Salisbury, South Australia
DIRECTOR: Dr M. W. Woods

In current production are the Ikara anti-
submarine weapon system, described below, and
the Jindivik weapons target, of which details
can be found in the "Drones" section of this
edition.

Information on the upper-atmosphere sounding
rockets developed by the Weapons Research
Establishment can be found in the "Research
Rockets and Space Vehicles" section.

IKARA

Ikara is a long-range anti-submarine weapon
system, conceived and developed by the Australian Department of Supply and Department of
the Navy for the Royal Australian Navy, with
which is it now in operational service. A modified
version, known as the RN Ikara, is under development in Australia and the UK to meet the
requirements of the Royal Navy and will be
deployed first in the new Type 82 guided missile
destroyer.

The basic concept of Ikara is the employment
of a rocket-propelled guided missile which carries
a homing torpedo towards its submarine target
after launch from a surface ship. To ensure that
the missile can be guided to its destination, so
that the torpedo will be dropped in the most
favourable area relative to its target, the system
makes use of a sonar detection equipment fitted to
the surface ship, other surface ships or helicopters
fitted with 'dunking' sonars.

The guided missile consists of a body with
short cropped-delta wings, elevon control surfaces,
and upper and lower vertical tail-fins. It is an
all-weather rapid-reaction weapon of considerable
accuracy, powered by a dual-thrust solid-propellent rocket motor. The payload consists of
an American Type 44 lightweight torpedo, with
an acoustic detection and homing system,
recessed into the under-body of the missile.

Missiles with torpedoes attached are stowed on
board ship in a magazine, a specially-designed

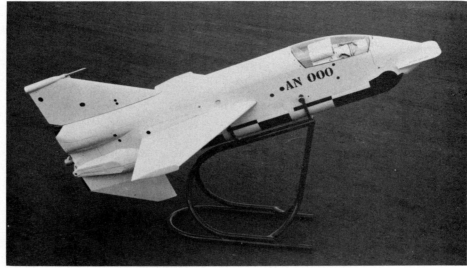
Display model of Ikara long-range anti-submarine missile

handling system enabling them to be loaded
rapidly on to the launcher. In action, data from
ship or helicopter sonar are fed into a prediction
system which calculates where the torpedo must
be dropped to hit the submarine and sends the
necessary signals to the missile through the
radio/radar guidance system. In the Australian
system this function is carried out by a digital
computer and associated peripheral equipment.
On RN Ikara, the Action Data Automation
System (ADA), first developed for HMS Eagle, is
used.

The missile is tracked and guided from the ship
during its flight to the target area. The guidance
system makes it possible to release the torpedo at
the optimum position near the submarine: this is
done by separating the ventral tail fin assembly,
permitting the torpedo which is clamped in place
during launch and cruising flight to be lowered
into the sea by a parachute.

Hawker Siddeley Dynamics leads the UK-based
companies that will provide industrial support
for the RN Ikara weapon system when it has been
accepted into service, and is also the accredited
representative of the Australian government in
Europe for the Ikara weapon system.

A target drone version of Ikara, known as the
Turana, is under development. Details can be
found in the "Drones" section.

DIMENSIONS (approx):
Length overall	11 ft 0 in (3·35 m)
Wing span	5 ft 0 in (1·50 m)

Ikara missile on its launcher on board HMAS
Perth

BRAZIL

BRAZILIAN ARMY

Brazilian Army's 114 mm artillery rockets (*Ronaldo S. Olive*)

COMISSÃO CENTRAL DE MÍSSEIS
A wire-guided anti-tank missile is under
development by the Brazilian Army's Central
Missile Commission. No details may yet be
published, except that it will have a range of
nearly 1·75 nm (2 miles; 3 km).

Brazilian Army's Type 108-R artillery rocket launcher (*Ronaldo S. Olive*)

DEPARTAMENTO DE ESTUDOS E PESQUISAS
TECNOLÓGICAS

Two types of artillery rocket have been developed by the Brazilian Army's Department of Studies
and Technological Research, to replace conven-

tional armament in artillery units. They equip
Rio de Janeiro's 8th Grupo de Artilharia de Costa
Motorisada (8th Group of Motorized Coastal
Artillery).

114 mm ROCKET
This two-stage solid-propellant artillery rocket

has an all-metal cylindrical body with fixed cruciform fins on both stages. The warhead is of the conventional high-explosive type and no guidance system is installed, the rocket being spin-stabilised in flight. The trailer-type five-round launcher is an adaptation of a 40-mm anti-aircraft gun mounting.

DIMENSION:

Length overall	6 ft 6¾ in (2·0 m)

PERFORMANCE (approx):

Max speed	Mach 1·8
Max range	15 miles (25 km)

TYPE 108-R

The Type 108-R is a simple cylindrical artillery rocket with no fins, spin-stabilisation being imparted by the canted nozzles of the solid-propellant rocket motor. The warhead is of a conventional high-explosive type.

Fired from a 16-tube launcher, mounted on a Brazilian-built Willys-Overland vehicle, the 108-R is reported to have a range of 7·5 miles (12 km).

BRAZILIAN NAVY

In partnership with Brazilian private industry, the Navy has developed a number of bombardment rockets which are in standard service.

R-115

This cylindrical metal fin-less surface-to-surface bombardment rocket has been developed and is being produced in quantity by a private company, the Companhia de Explosivos Valparaiba. Its power plant is a 3,082 lb (1,398 kg) st solid-propellant motor with a burning time of 0·5 sec, and it is spin-stabilised by canted nozzles.

The R-115 is deployed operationally by the Navy's Marine Corps, in 12-tube mobile launchers towed by trucks, jeeps and other vehicles. There are plans to equip ships of the Brazilian Navy with this weapon, and the Navy Armament Centre has conducted tests with a launcher for ship-board use.

WEIGHTS:

Propellent weight	6·8 lb (3·1 kg)

Warhead weight	2·97 lb (1·35 kg)
Launching weight	38·6 lb (17·5 kg)

PERFORMANCE:

Max range	4·6 miles (7·5 km)

FA.E. 57

This small air-launched bombardment rocket is intended mainly for training use and is produced by a private company, Indústria Química Mantiqueira. It has a cylindrical body, ogival nose-cone containing the high-explosive warhead, and canted cruciform tail-fins for spin-stabilisation in flight.

FA.E.82 FLECHA (ARROW)

This rocket was developed by the Companhia de Explosivos Valparaiba specifically for launching from helicopters of the Brazilian Navy. Its configuration is similar to that of the FA.E.57, except that it has a more pointed nose-cone and swept leading-edges on its tail-fins. The FA.E.82 is suitable for use against submarines, surface vessels and land targets.

FB.E.127

Similar in basic configuration to the smaller FA.E.82, this weapon also is intended mainly for air-to-surface use from helicopters. It is powered by a solid-propellant motor giving 4,410 lb (2,000 kg) st for 0·95 sec, and is spin-stabilised by canted cruciform tail-fins.

WEIGHTS:

Propellent weight	24·25 lb (11 kg)
Launching weight	110 lb (50 kg)

PERFORMANCE:

Max range	10·5 miles (17 km)

FB.R.127

This fin-less ship-launched bombardment rocket has an ogival nose-cone, housing a high-explosive warhead, and a cylindrical body containing the solid-propellant motor, which develops 4,410 lb the canted nozzles of its motor.

WEIGHTS:

Propellent weight	18·3 lb (8·3 kg)
Launching weight	97 lb (44 kg)

PERFORMANCE:

Max range	6·2 miles (10 km)

FB.E.127 rocket, designed mainly for air-to-surface use from helicopters of the Brazilian Navy *(Ronaldo S. Olive)*

Left:
R-115 rocket multiple launcher for shipboard use *(Ronaldo S. Olive)*

CHINA (PEOPLE'S REPUBLIC)

In a speech before the US Senate Armed Services Committee and the Appropriations Sub-committee, in support of President Nixon's first budget, in February 1970, Defense Secretary Melvin R. Laird said that China was making more rapid progress than any other nation in the field of nuclear weapons, with only a relatively few launchings. This opinion was strengthened by the successful orbiting of China's first Earth satellite on 25 April 1970, as the launch vehicle is assumed to have been based on that country's medium-range ballistic missile (MRBM).

The development of Chinese strategic missiles dates from 16 October 1964, when the first uranium-235 nuclear charge (about 20 kilotons yield) was exploded at Lop Nor in the Sinkiang desert. A second, similar device was exploded on 14 May 1965, almost certainly atop a test tower. The second of three further nuclear tests in 1966, in October, was claimed to have involved delivery of the warhead to a target area by a missile, possibly based on a Soviet MRBM. Since then, and up to September 1969, there have been nine further nuclear test firings in China, according to American reports. Of these, two charges were exploded on a tower and one in an under-ground site, while six were dropped from aircraft. Six of the last eight explosions involved thermo-nuclear charges, that in September 1969 having a yield of about three megatons.

Mr Laird said in February 1970 that China could be expected to deploy its MRBM operationally "at any time" and a force of 80-100 such weapons is expected to be available by the mid-1970s. In addition, it is believed that the Chinese air force may have a small number of twin-jet bombers in service, capable of delivering nuclear bombs. The first test of a nuclear-warhead ICBM is possible during 1970-71, with initial operational capability in 1973-75 and a force of 10-25 ICBMs two or three years later. Mr Laird estimated that 25 missiles, each with a 3-megaton warhead and 40% reliability, would have the potential to cause 11-12 million fatalities in the USA in the absence of an ABM defence system.

In a subsequent statement, Deputy Defense Secretary David Packard said that China was not expected to achieve success in perfecting penetration aids for its strategic missiles. Even to attain a crude capability involving fuel tank fragments would require construction of an extensive radar and instrumentation system to ensure satisfactory in-flight fragmentation of the tanks. A detailed knowledge of the operating characteristics of America's Safeguard ABM system would be a further pre-requisite for even the simplest type of penetration aids.

Estimated range of the first-generation Chinese liquid-propellant ICBM is 5,200 nm (6,000 miles; 9,600 km). A solid-propellant production plant has been established and there is evidence to suggest that a second-generation ICBM, with this type of power plant, is under development.

FRANCE

AÉROSPATIALE
SOCIÉTÉ NATIONALE INDUSTRIELLE AÉROSPATIALE

HEAD OFFICE:
37 Boulevard de Montmorency, 75-Paris 16e

OFFICERS:
See "Aircraft" section

Division Engins Tactiques

EXECUTIVE OFFICE:
2 rue Béranger, 92-Chatillon

The former Nord-Aviation, now part of Aéro-spatiale, was engaged on the design, development and production of guided missiles, pilotless target aircraft and test vehicles for many years, at its Châtillon-sous-Bagneux and Bourges works, and had sold more than 300,000 anti-tank missiles alone by mid-1968. Deliveries had been made to 25 countries.

Information on former Nord-Aviation missiles, now the responsibility of the Division Engins Tactiques of Aérospatiale, is given below, except for the new generation of short-range battlefield weapons being developed in association with Messerschmitt-Bölkow-Blohm of Germany, which are described in the "International" section on pages 592-595.

AÉROSPATIALE (NORD-AVIATION) AS.20

More than 7,000 AS.20 air-to-surface missiles were built by Nord-Aviation for the French Air Force and Navy, to arm the Fiat G91 tactical fighters of the Federal German and Italian Air Forces, and for two other countries.

The AS.20 has a pointed cylindrical body, cruciform wings which are canted to spin-stabilise the missile, and a dual-thrust solid-propellant motor. The booster stage exhausts through two slightly-divergent lateral nozzles, the sustainer through a rear nozzle fitted with jet-deflectors, by which the missile is steered. The main change compared with the earlier AA.20 air-to-surface missile is that a larger warhead, weighing 66 lb (30 kg), was made possible by deletion of the proximity fuze, which is replaced by a contact fuze in this rôle.

The AS.20 is normally guided visually, under radio control, by the pilot of the launch aircraft, tracking being facilitated by flares located at the rear of the missile. It can be adapted to utilise the TCA optical aiming/infra-red guidance system described under the AS.30 entry.

Any aircraft capable of launching the AS.20 at a speed of Mach 0·7 or higher can be equipped with it. A special adaptor makes it possible to fire the AS.20 from aircraft equipped to carry the AS.30 and it can thus be used for training pilots who will use the more powerful weapon operationally.

DIMENSIONS:

Length overall	8 ft 6½ in (2·60 m)
Body diameter	9¾ in (0·25 m)
Wing span	2 ft 7½ in (0·80 m)

WEIGHT:

Launching weight	315 lb (143 kg)

PERFORMANCE:

Speed at burn-out	Mach 1·7
Range (average)	3·75 nm (4·35 miles; 7 km)
Flight time	approx 16 seconds

AÉROSPATIALE (NORD-AVIATION) AS.30

This tactical air-to-surface missile is virtually a scaled-up AS.20, with a similar configuration, two-stage solid-propellant power plant and radio-command guidance system. The only externally-evident change is the introduction of cruciform "flip-out" tail fins, indexed in line with the wings.

The requirements to which the AS.30 was designed included an initial launch range of at least 5·4 nm (6·2 miles; 10 km), with the provision that the launching aircraft should not approach to within 1·6 nm (1·8 miles; 3 km) of the target. A CEP (circular error probability) of less than 33 ft (10 m) was specified and this standard of accuracy has been exceeded by the AS.30. Minimum launching speed is approximately Mach 0·45; there is no limitation for launching at supersonic speeds.

As an alternative to the original manual "steering" system, the AS.30 can utilise the TCA infra-red automatic guidance system evolved by the company's Tactical Missile Department. With this, the pilot has no other task to perform than conventional aiming with his weapon-sight, keeping the target centred in the sight during the flight of the missile. An infra-red tracker is trained constantly on an IR flare on the missile. An axial gyroscope compensates for sight vibration and movement. From data provided by the two devices, deviations of the missile from the correct flight path are detected and corrected by command signals radioed to the missile. Accuracy is claimed to be as great as that achieved by a fully-trained operator controlling the missile by hand.

This automatic guidance system is operational in the French Air Force, which utilises the AS.30 with a 510 lb (230 kg) HE warhead and alternative delay or non-delay fuzes.

Other customers for the AS.30 include the French Navy, the German, Swiss, Israeli and South African air forces and the RAF, which acquired a large number of AS.30's to equip its Canberra tactical bombers.

A total of about 5,500 AS.30's was ordered.

DIMENSIONS:
Length overall	12 ft 9½ in (3·90 m)
Body diameter	1 ft 1½ in (0·34 m)
Wing span	3 ft 3½ in (1·00 m)

WEIGHT:
Launching weight	1,146 lb (520 kg)

PERFORMANCE:
Speed at impact
1,475-1,640 ft/sec (450-500 m/sec)
Range (average)
5·9-6·5 nm (6·8-7·5 miles; 11-12 km)

AÉROSPATIALE (NORD-AVIATION) AS.30L

The AS.30L is a lightweight version of the AS.30, intended to equip aircraft in the class of the Fiat G91 fighter. The body, systems and equipment are largely unchanged, but the wing span is smaller and the launching weight is only 838 lb (380 kg), with a warhead of 253 lb (115 kg). The wings are also mounted further aft.

DIMENSIONS:
Length overall	11 ft 9½ in (3·60 m)
Body diameter	1 ft 1½ in (0·34 m)
Wing span	2 ft 11½ in (0·90 m)

WEIGHT:
Launching weight	838 lb (380 kg)

ENTAC
US Military designation: MGM-32A

Entac (Engin Téléguidé Anti-Char) is a roll-stabilised wire-guided anti-tank weapon intended primarily for infantry use. It was developed by the Direction Technique des Armements Terrestres (DTAT) and is produced in quantity by Aérospatiale (formerly Nord-Aviation). In its Model 58 form, it was adopted by the French Army in 1957, and is now standard equipment also in the armies of Belgium, Canada, the United States, Indonesia, Australia and seven other countries. Orders totalled 130,000 by January 1970, of which 117,000 had been delivered.

The weapon system comprises the missile, fire controller, four-missile launcher, Jeep equipment, and check-out and test equipment. The missile is supplied complete in a polyester water-tight container. A single firing post, manned by one operator, can control and fire 10 missiles. Maximum operator-to-missile distance is 360 ft (110 m).

Entac has a cylindrical body and cruciform wings and is powered by a two-stage solid-propellant rocket motor. It is roll-stabilised and controlled by a spoiler in each wing. The 9 lb (4·1 kg) shaped charge warhead will penetrate more than 25·5 in (650 mm) of steel armour. An inert head can be fitted for practice firing.

DIMENSIONS:
Length overall	2 ft 8½ in (0·82 m)
Body diameter	6 in (0·15 m)
Wing span	1 ft 3 in (0·38 m)

WEIGHTS:
Launching weight	26·9 lb (12·2 kg)

Aérospatiale AS.30 air-to-surface missile on underwing pylon of F-104G Starfighter

Entac anti-tank missile leaving its container-launcher on a Jeep

PERFORMANCE:
Max speed	164 knots (190 mph; 305 km/h)
Range	1,300-6.600 ft (400-2,000 m)

AÉROSPATIALE SS.11 and AS.11 (NORD 5210)
US Military designation: AGM-22A

This line-of-sight wire-guided battlefield missile was developed for use from ground vehicles, helicopters, slow-flying aircraft and light naval vessels. It is normally fired from a launching ramp, but for special applications, such as mountain combat, airborne commando missions and coastal defence, it may be fired from a simplified ground launcher.

Configuration is conventional, with a cylindrical body and swept cruciform wings. The power plant is a two-stage solid-propellant rocket. Directional control is achieved by varying the thrust of the sustainer efflux.

In action the operator acquires the target by means of a magnifying optical device, a special stabilised sight being installed for this purpose in helicopters and ships. As soon as the missile enters his field of vision after launch, the operator passes to it the signals needed to align it with the target, while keeping it above the terrain until target impact. These signals are given by the operator by means of a control stick which makes it possible to send simultaneously up or down and port or starboard commands. The signals are transmitted to the missile over wires. Tracer flares are installed on the rear of the missile for visual reference.

The designation SS.11 is applied to the surface-to-surface version; the AS.11 is the generally-similar air-to-surface version.

Since 1962, the SS.11 B.1 version, using transistorized firing equipment has been in production. It is available with a variety of different warheads, including an inert type for practice, the Type 140AC anti-tank warhead capable of perforating 24 in (60 cm) of armour plate, the Type

140 AP02 explosive warhead (5·72 lb = 2·6 kg of explosive) which will penetrate an armoured steel plate 0·4 in (1 cm) thick at a range of 9,800 ft (3,000 m) and explode about 7 ft (2·1 m) behind the point of impact, and the Type 140 AP 59 high-fragmentation anti-personnel type with contact fuse.

The SS.11 B.1 and similar AS.11 B.1 have been adopted by all three French Services and the armed forces of 18 other countries, including the USA and UK. Orders totalled 145,000 by the beginning of 1970, with production at the rate of 900 per month.

DIMENSIONS:
Length overall	3 ft 11 in (1·20 m)
Body diameter	6½ in (0·16 m)
Wing span	1 ft 7½ in (0·50 m)

WEIGHT:
Launching weight	66 lb (29·9 kg)

PERFORMANCE:
Average cruising speed
313 knots (360 mph; 580 km/h)
Time of flight (propelled)	20-21 sec
Minimum turning radius	
	approx 3,300 ft (1,000 m)
Range	1,650-9,840 ft (500-3,000 m)

AÉROSPATIALE (NORD-AVIATION) HARPON

The Harpon missile has the same characteristics, performance and alternative warheads as the SS.11 B1 but utilises an automatic guidance (Télécommande Automatique, or TCA) system which frees the operator of the task of acquiring the missile and aligning it manually on the target by means of a control stick.

With TCA, all the operator has to do is to aim carefully at the target with an optical sighting device. The missile, after launch, is "captured" by a precision goniometer reacting to infra-red radiation from tracer flares located on the rear of the missile. The reference axis of the goniometer is such as to be accurately parallel to the optical axis. Angular deviation voltages supplied by this device enable a computer to work out the signals that must be transmitted to the missile to get it back on to the line of sight and to keep it there. Signals passed to the missile, over wires, are tied to metric rather than angular deviations. A signal elaboration computer takes this into consideration by injecting range and also makes other, minor adjustments as necessary.

Because no time is lost while the operator acquires the missile after launch, TCA has made it possible to reduce the practical minimum range to about 1,200 ft (400 m). During its flight, the missile remains within less than 3 ft 3½ in (1 m) from a theoretical line which would be parallel to the optical line of sight (i.e. the missile is flown in a "tunnel" slaved to the sighting axis).

The Harpon missile is in production and Aérospatiale is developing TCA guidance equipment suitable for installation on land vehicles, ships, fixed-wing aircraft and helicopters.

Studies and tests have shown that the Harpon can be used with good results as a surface-to-air weapon against frontal attack by low-flying aircraft or helicopters.

AÉROSPATIALE (NORD-AVIATION) SS.12 and AS.12

The surface-to-surface SS.12 and air-to-surface AS.12 are spin-stabilised missiles derived from the SS.11 and with a warhead weighing 66 lb (30 kg), about four times as much as that of the latter, making them suitable for use against fortifications as well as tanks, ships and other vehicles. Available warheads include the type OP.3C which can pierce more than 1·5 in (40 mm) of armour and explode on the other side, the extremely powerful 170 AC anti-tank shaped charge, and a pre-fragmented anti-personnel charge.

The SS.12 and AS.12 employ wire-guidance, the type of control wires used varying with the vehicle carrying the missile—land or sea, aircraft or helicopter. They are operational with the French Army and Navy and have been exported to six countries.

In 1967, Nord-Aviation began adapting the AS.12 missile for use with the TCA automatic guidance system described under the entry for the Harpon missile above. The first application was intended to be on anti-submarine aircraft, followed by adaptation of the system for surface vehicles.

The SS.12/AS.12 has a conventional configuration, with a cylindrical body, cruciform wings and two-stage solid-propellant rocket motor.

The AS.12 arms P-2 Neptune aircraft of the Royal Netherlands Navy, and is carried by the Breguet Alizé and the Breguet Atlantic.

On 15 June 1966, a newly-developed SS.12M "marine" version was demonstrated before 15 naval officers of eight allied countries, embarked on the coastal patrol boat *La Combattante*, off Toulon. Two SS.12M's were fired from a light-weight launcher, with self-contained optical sighting, guidance and control equipment, against a moving target about 3 nm (3·4 miles; 5·5 km) from the ship. Both missiles hit the target within 3 ft (1·00 m) of its centre and about 3 ft (1·00 m) above the waterline. The target was 12 ft (3·65 m) high and 16 ft (5·00 m) long.

The launcher fitted to *La Combattante* is intended specifically to arm high-speed coastal and river patrol boats, giving them a weapon with the effectiveness of a 155-mm artillery shell. It will carry either four SS.11's or two SS.12M's. The special optical sight used with this weapon system was developed by the Puteaux Arsenal, a branch of the Direction Technique des Armements Terrestres, and was produced originally for helicopters, on which it is operational. It has a high degree of magnification and is completely gyro-stabilised to compensate for ship movements.

Panhard armoured car fitted with an N.A.2 turret carrying four Harpon automatically-guided anti-tank missiles

First operational fast patrol boats to be equipped with this type of weapon system are three Vosper Thornycroft FPB's built for the Libyan Navy. The first of these, the *Susa*, completed its trials in mid-1968; it has two four-round launchers to carry SS.12M's for combat use and SS.11's for training.

DIMENSIONS:	
Length overall	6 ft 1·9 in (1·87 m)
Body diameter	7 in (0·18 m)
Warhead diameter	8·25 in (0·21 m)
Wing span	2 ft 1½ in (0·65 m)
WEIGHT:	
Launching weight	167 lb (75 kg)
PERFORMANCE:	
Speed at impact:	
AS.12 (fired at 200 knots; 230 mph; 370 km/h)	
	180 knots (210 mph; 335 km/h)
Time of flight	32 sec
Max range:	
SS.12	19,650 ft (6,000 m)

Aérospatiale SS.12M surface-to-surface missile installation on a Hovercraft

Aérospatiale surface-to-surface wire-guided missiles on the Libyan Navy's *Susa*, a Vosper Thornycroft fast patrol boat
Left: **SS.11M and SS.12M missiles in the upper part of the port launching rack.** *Right*: **General view of the two fixed racks, each able to carry four missiles**

AS.12 in relation to surface
      approx 26,250 ft (8,000 m)
AS.12 in relation to aircraft
      approx 18,000 ft (5,500 m)

AÉROSPATIALE/MESSERSCHMITT-BÖLKOW-BLOHM MILAN, HOT AND ROLAND

See "International" section, pages 592-4.

AÉROSPATIALE (NORD-AVIATION) M.20

The M.20 is a development of the CT.20 target drone and exists in two forms:

SM.20. Surface-to-water (sol-mer) missile.

MM.20. Water-to-water (mer-mer) missile, launched from ships.

Each version is able to deliver a 550 lb (250 kg) warhead over a range of 135 nm (155 miles; 250 km).

The M.20 was developed for use by the Royal Swedish Navy. Further details can be found in the Swedish section under the heading of the Saab company, who are building the M.20 under licence. Its Swedish designation is Saab 08A.

AÉROSPATIALE (NORD-AVIATION) MM-38 EXOCET

Exocet is a surface-to-surface missile designed to provide warships with all-weather attack capability against other surface vessels. It can be fitted in all classes of surface warships, including fast patrol boats, and offers an economical means of defence against missiles like the Soviet "Styx" by attacking the launching vessels rather than attempting to intercept the missiles after launch.

The Exocet missile is in the form of a streamlined body fitted with cruciform wings and cruciform tail control surfaces indexed in line with the wings. Propulsion is provided by a tandem two-stage solid-propellant motor, and the highly-destructive warhead is described as being in the same order as that of a torpedo. The missile is stored in a container which also serves as a launch-tube. The launch-tubes can be installed in fixed positions or on rotatable mountings.

For operation of the weapon system, the launch ship must be fitted with surveillance and target indicating radar, a vertical reference plane gyro and a log, indicating its speed through the water. Also required is a fire control installation comprising a control panel, fire control computer and junction box.

The missile's flight profile consists of a pre-guidance phase (based on systems developed for the now-abandoned AS.33 missile) during which it travels towards the target, whose range and bearing have been determined by the fire control computer and set up in the missile pre-guidance circuits before launch, and a final guidance phase during which the missile flies directly towards the target under the control of its active homing head. Throughout the flight the missile is maintained at a very low altitude (reported to be 2 to 3 metres = 6·5 to 10 ft) by an FM radio altimeter supplied by TRT. Its range is approximately 20 nm (23 miles; 37 km), cruising at high subsonic speed, and Exocet is intended to operate efficiently in an ECM (electronic countermeasures) environment.

No further details are available officially, but Exocet is reported to have a warhead weighing more than 220 lb (100 kg). It uses a modified version of the low-level guidance system developed for the Kormoran missile and a motor similar to that of the Martel missile. Aérospatiale hope to have it ready for service by 1971.

First export order for the Exocet missile is from Greece, which has ordered it as part of the equipment of four new coastal reconnaissance craft.

DIMENSIONS:
Length   16 ft 9½ in (5·12 m)

Aérospatiale AS.12 air-to-surface missile installation on Wasp helicopter

Full-scale mock-up of Aérospatiale MM-38 Exocet ship-to-ship missile (*Flight International*)

Body diameter	1 ft 1½ in (0·344 m)	
Span of wings	3 ft 3½ in (1·004 m)	
Span of fins	2 ft 5¾ in (0·758 m)	
WEIGHT:		
Launching weight	1,587 lb (720 kg)	

PLUTON

The Pluton weapon system is being developed to meet a French Army requirement for a tactical nuclear missile with a minimum range of 5·4 nm (6·25 miles; 10 km) and maximum range of 65 nm (75 miles; 120 km). It consists of a missile and a set of launching equipment developed by Aérospatiale under the programme leadership of the Army's Division des Engins Tactiques. Under the original arrangements, the former Sud-Aviation was responsible for aerodynamic studies, the structure and control system, while Nord-Aviation had responsibility for the guidance system. The dual-thrust solid-propellant motor is being developed by SEP. The weapon will be

Test firing a Pluton tactical missile at the Centre d'Essais des Landes, December 1969

Model of Pluton tactical nuclear missile on its tracked transporter/launcher

installed on and fired from the AMX-30 tank chassis and will be supplied to operational units in two parts—missile and warhead. The missile body's container will be used as the launching ramp. Power of the nuclear warhead has been stated to be in the order of 10-15 kilotons.

Pluton will have a simplified inertial guidance system, related closely to that tested successfully on the experimental AS.33 missile. It will utilise aerodynamic controls, operated by electric actuators. Designed accuracy is "in keeping with the power of the nuclear warhead". Devices will be fitted enabling it to fulfil, on the ground and in flight, the stringent safety regulations demanded by this type of warhead.

The first full-scale firing of Pluton took place in 1969. First unit to deploy it operationally will be the 303rd Groupe d'Artillerie, currently equipped with Honest John. Eventually there will be five such units, each with eight multi-round launchers.

DIMENSIONS:
Length overall	24 ft 10¾ in (7·59 m)
Body diameter	2 ft 1½ in (0·65 m)
Span of fins	4 ft 8 in (1·415 m)

WEIGHT:
Launching weight	5,335 lb (2,420 kg)

Division Systèmes Balistiques et Espace

DIRECTOR: P. M. Usunier

This Division combines, in the ballistic rocket and space fields, the activities of the former SEREB company (see 1969-70 *Jane's*) with some factories and design offices of the Nord-Aviation and Sud-Aviation groups.

All available details of the important SSBS and MSBS missiles, for which the Division has overall technical responsibility, are given below. Its research vehicles are described in the "Research Rockets and Space Vehicles" section.

SSBS

The SSBS (sol-sol balistique stratégique) is a medium-range two-stage solid-propellant missile, with nuclear warhead, that is stored in and launched from an underground silo. It can be maintained at a state of readiness, and preparation for firing and firing are automatic, without human intervention in the launch area. Very quickly after the order to fire, launching of the missile is effected on the simple rapid opening of the silo door.

The responsibilities of the State are assumed by the Direction Technique des Engins. During the research and development phase, SEREB acted as prime contractor for the entire SSBS system. Sub-contracts were awarded to the Direction des Poudres for the solid propellants, Nord-Aviation and SNECMA (through their specially formed Norma group) for the motors and metallic casings, Nord-Aviation for interstage structures and equipment bays, Sud-Aviation and SEPR for the gimballed nozzles and Sud-Aviation for the nose-cone.

The Division Systèmes Balistiques et Espace of Aérospatiale is prime contractor for the entire production SSBS vehicle and retains overall responsibility for design and development of the weapon system.

Early in 1970, it was reported that the French government had decided to reduce the number of operational SSBS missiles from 27, originally planned, to 18. These will equip two squadrons based on the Plateau d'Albion, east of Avignon.

Launch areas are dispersed and hardened to reduce the effects of an enemy attack. Each includes the underground silo in which the missile is maintained in an operational condition and an annex housing the automatic launching equipment and servo mechanisms. The launch areas are controlled from a heavily protected Central Fire Control room (CFC).

Use of such operational sites was not possible for firing trials of the SSBS. These took place at a specially-built experimental and prototype area in the Centre d'Essais des Landes, complete with CFC, silo and assembly buildings for the vehicle and the warhead. Flight trials were conducted in automatic conditions simulating as closely as possible those at an operational site. Launches were made towards a target area in the Azores.

There have been three types of SSBS test vehicle:

S-112. With live first stage and dummy second stage. Used to test full-scale vehicle launching operations from underground silo. Described briefly in 1968-69 *Jane's*.

S-01. Test vehicle with two live stages, used for development of second stage, re-entry and guidance sub-systems.

S-02. SSBS prototype; now operational.

TYPE: Medium-range silo-launched ballistic missile.

FIRST STAGE: Type 902 motor in maraging metal rolled and welded case, containing 35,275 lb (16,000 kg) of solid propellant. Four gimballed nozzles for control.

SECOND STAGE: Type 903 motor with flow-turned Vascojet 1000 casing, containing 22,050 lb (10,000 kg) of solid propellant. Four gimballed nozzles for control.

EQUIPMENT BAY: Houses guidance system,

SSBS in its silo

automatic pilot, functional and sequential equipment.

GUIDANCE: Inertial.

WARHEAD: Nuclear.

DIMENSIONS:
Length overall	48 ft 6½ in (14·80 m)
Body diameter, both stages	4 ft 11 in (1·50 m)

WEIGHT:
Launching weight	70,327 lb (31,900 kg)

PERFORMANCE:
Range	over 1,620 nm (1,865 miles; 3,000 km)

MSBS

The MSBS (mer-sol balistique stratégique) deterrent weapon system is based on the use in the open sea of nuclear-propelled SNLE submarines able to fire while submerged, in 15 minutes, a salvo of 16 missiles equipped with nuclear warheads.

Factors governing the design of the MSBS vehicle included the restrictions on size imposed by installation in a submarine; the necessity to eject the missile from a submerged tube and to begin propulsion just after emersion from the water; and the problem of initial orientation of the missile due to mobility and instability of the launching platform.

As in the case of the SSBS, the responsibilities of the State are assumed by the Direction Technique des Engins, with the Division Systèmes Balistiques et Espace of Aérospatiale acting as prime contractor for the MSBS missile sub-system during the research and development phase. Sub-contracts were awarded to the Direction des Poudres for the solid propellants, the former Nord-Aviation and SNECMA (through their specially formed Norma group) for the motors and metallic casings, Nord-Aviation for the inter-stage structures, Sud-Aviation for the equipment bay and nose-cone, and Sud-Aviation and SEPR for the gimballed nozzles of the first stage and the whole second stage.

Aérospatiale is now prime contractor for the entire production MSBS vehicle and retains overall responsibility for design and development of the missile and of the submarine launch subsystem.

First submarine of the SNLE class, the *Redoutable*, was launched at Cherbourg on 29 March 1967; it was engaged on trials in 1969 and will

Test firing an MSBS ballistic missile

become operational in 1971. The *Terrible* and *Foudroyant* will follow in 1973-75. Initial trials of the MSBS system were conducted from the experimental conventional-powered submarine *Gymnote*, which permits the completely automatic launching of experimental and pre-production missiles under conditions closely simulating those of the SNLE ships.

There have been three types of MSBS test vehicle:

M-112. With live first stage and dummy second stage. Used to test undersea launch operations from the submarine *Gymnote*. Described briefly in 1968-69 *Jane's*.

M-012. Test vehicle with two live stages, used for development of the second stage and the re-entry system.

M-013. MSBS prototype; now operational on board the *Gymnote*.

TYPE: Submarine-launched medium-range ballistic missile.

FIRST STAGE: Type 904 motor in flow-turned Vascojet 1000 casing, containing 22,050 lb (10,000 kg) of solid propellant. Four gimballed nozzles for control.

SECOND STAGE: Rita motor with glass-fibre wound casing, containing 8,820 lb (4,000 kg) of solid propellant. Thrust vector control system in single fixed nozzle.

EQUIPMENT BAY: Houses guidance system, automatic pilot, functional and sequential equipment.

GUIDANCE: Inertial.

WARHEAD: Nuclear.

DIMENSIONS:
Length overall	34 ft 1½ in (10·40 m)
Body diameter, both stages	4 ft 11 in (1·50 m)

WEIGHT:
Launching weight	39,683 lb (18,000 kg)

PERFORMANCE:
No details available.

DTAT
DIRECTION TECHNIQUE DES ARMEMENTS TERRESTRES

ADDRESS:
Caserne Sully, 92-Saint Cloud (Hauts-de-Seine)

DIRECTOR:
L. M. G. Francillon

The Atelier de Construction de Puteaux (APX),

which is part of the DTAT establishment, has been developing for several years a heavy anti-tank weapon known as ACRA. All available details follow.

DTAT ACRA

ACRA (Anti-Char Rapide Autopropulsé) is a semi-automatic weapon which operates on a similar principle to the American Shillelagh. It is fired from a gun on an armoured vehicle and so has a considerable initial velocity before its own integral power plant is fired. This gives it a cruising speed of 970 knots (1,118 mph; 1,800 km/h), which is two or three times higher than current anti-tank missiles, so lessening the time available for reaction by the target.

ACRA is guided along an infra-red director beam emited by a laser. The modular concept of its fire control system enables it to be mounted on various types of armoured vehicle, and the gun/launcher can fire conventional artillery shells as well as ACRA missiles.

Development has progressed very satisfactorily and ACRA is expected to become operational in 1972, with assembly by the Manufacture d' Armes at Saint-Etienne. France hopes to co-operate with other nations in this series production of the missile.

The missile is cylindrical, with a conical nose-cone, four narrow-chord flip-out folding tail-fins for guidance, and four small anti-roll fins for stabilisation.]

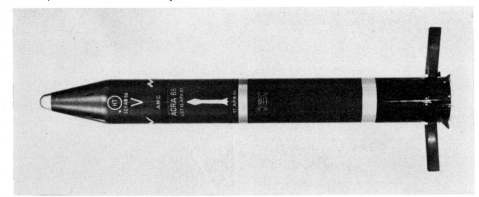

DTAT ACRA heavy anti-tank weapon

LATÉCOÈRE
SOCIÉTÉ INDUSTRIELLE D'AVIATION LATÉ-COÈRE
HEAD OFFICE:
79, Avenue Marceau, Paris XVIe
WORKS:
135, Rue de Périole, Toulouse

This famous French company, dating back to 1917, was best known for its large commercial flying-boats until a few years ago. It is now participating in the construction programme for the Sud-Aviation Caravelle and Concorde transport aircraft and is engaged on the development and manufacture of guided missiles, including the Malafon anti-submarine weapon described below.

LATÉCOÈRE MALAFON
Malafon (MArine, LAtécoère, contre le FONd) is a surface-to-surface or surface-to-underwater anti-submarine weapon. It has an aeroplane configuration and is built around a 21 in (53 cm) acoustic-homing torpedo with a weight of 1,157 lb (525 kg).

The missile is ramp launched with the aid of two solid-propellant boosters with a firing time of three seconds. These jettison after burn-out, by which time the missile has attained a speed of 448 knots (515 mph; 830 km/h), and the remainder of the flight is unpowered. A constant altitude of about 330 ft (100 m) above the water is maintained by a radio-altimeter, the wing incidence being increased progressively to provide the required lift as the speed of the missile falls off.

During this phase, the weapon is guided by a command system, fed with data from the ship's sonar, and utilises a "twist-and-steer" control system. Wing-tip tracking flares assist visual observation of its flight path. At a position some 2,600 ft (800 m) from the predicted location of the target, a tail parachute is streamed, the torpedo is ejected from the airframe by inertia and enters the water, finally homing on to the target.

Development of the Malafon began in 1956 and by May 1959 a total of 21 development launchings had been made, 15 from the ground and six from

Latécoère Malafon Mk 2 surface-to-underwater missile on launcher on board the destroyer *Vauquelin*
(*Ronaldo S. Olive*)

aircraft. Fifty Lat-232 Malafon Mk 1 and Lat-233 Malafon Mk 2 missiles had been delivered by January 1961. In October of that year, the problem of maintaining a correct altitude throughout each flight was overcome and the first launch and guidance test at sea, from the fast anti-submarine vessel *La Galissonnière*, was made successfully in June 1962. Evaluation of the complete weapon system was made with 22 launchings in the first five months of 1964, after which the operational sonar system and artillery-type radar were installed in *La Galissonnière*. Operational testing of current production Malafons took place from this ship during the first half of 1965.

Production of the Malafon continues. It now equips also the missile frigates *Suffren* and *Duquesne*, each of which carries a single launcher and 13 missiles, and five modified T.47 class destroyers and will arm the new corvettes of the "Aconit" class.

DIMENSIONS:
Length	19 ft 8 in (6·0 m)
Span of wings	9 ft 10 in (3·0 m)

WEIGHT:
Launching weight	2,865 lb (1,300 kg)

PERFORMANCE:
Range approx	9·5 nm (11 miles; 18 km)

MARINE FRANÇAISE
DIRECTION TECHNIQUE DES CONSTRUCTIONS NAVALES
ADDRESS:
Ministère d'Etat Chargé de la Défense Nationale, 2, rue Royale, Paris 8e
DIRECTEUR TECHNIQUE DES CONSTRUCTIONS NAVALES:
Ingénieur Général de l'Armement Thiennot
SOUS-DIRECTEUR 'PROGRAMMES AND BUDGET':
Ingénieur Général de l'Armement Baron
CHARGÉ DE PRESSE ET DES RELATIONS EXTÉRIEURES:
J. Favier

The Naval Arsenal at Ruelle is responsible for development and production of the Masurca, a surface-to-air guided weapon to equip medium-tonnage ships of the French Navy.

Following extensive testing on the experimental ship *Ile d'Oléron*, the Masurca is now the main anti-aircraft weapon system of the French frigates *Suffren* and *Duquesne*, each of which carries 48 missiles. It will also arm the cruiser "*Cobbert*" now refitting.

MASURCA
The Masurca (MArine, SUpersonique Ruelle Contre Avions) is a tandem two-stage solid-propellant missile. The first stage, which accelerates the missile to a speed of 2,950 ft (900 m) sec, is a conventional jettisonable booster with four fins indexed in line with those of the second stage.

The second stage has fixed cruciform wings of extremely low aspect ratio and attains a speed of Mach 2·5. Roll stabilisation, yaw and pitch control are achieved by cruciform tail control surfaces indexed in line with the wings.

Masurca Mk 2 twin launcher on the frigate *Suffren*

Warhead weight is 105 lb (48 kg).
There are two versions of this weapon:
Masurca Mk 2 Mod 2. With beam-riding guidance system.
Masurca Mk 2 Mod 3. With self-homing guidance system. Superseding Mod 2 in operational service in early 1970.
In both cases the guidance systems are produced by CFTH/CSF and TRT.
Threat evaluation equipment works in conjunction with radar to establish an order of priority for different targets. It is possible to fire a salvo of two missiles within a few seconds against one or two targets.

DIMENSIONS:

Length with booster	28 ft 2½ in (8·60 m)
Length without booster	17 ft 4½ in (5·294 m)
Body diameter	1 ft 4 in (0·406 m)
Span of wings	2 ft 6 in (0·766 m)
Span of tail fins	4 ft 2 in (1·278 m)
Span of booster fins	4 ft 11 in (1·50 m)
Body diameter of booster	1 ft 10½ in (0·572 m)

WEIGHTS:

With booster, Mod 2	4,387 lb (1,990 kg)
Mod 3	4,585 lb (2,080 kg)
Without booster, Mod 2	1,852 lb (840 kg)
Mod 3	2,050 lb (930 kg)

PERFORMANCE:

Range	over 21 nm (25 miles; 40 km)

MATRA
S A ENGINS MATRA

HEAD OFFICE:
4 rue de Presbourg, 75-Paris XVIe

WORKS:
Avenue Louis Breguet, 78-Vélizy; and 41-Salbris

CHAIRMAN:
Marcel Chassagny

GENERAL MANAGER:
Jean-Luc Lagardere

SALES AND PUBLICITY MANAGER:
Philippe Chassagny

Since 1948, Matra have been engaged in extensive research and experimental work in the guided missile, propulsion and guidance fields.

After prolonged testing on Meteor and Canberra aircraft, the company's type R.510 air-to-air weapon went into small series production for training purposes. Described in the 1958-59 *Jane's*, it was superseded by the fully-developed type R.511 which was manufactured in considerable numbers as a standard weapon of the French Air Force.

The R.511 was followed in turn by the R.530, and further improved weapons are already being developed as armament for the interceptors of the 1970's.

In September 1964, an Anglo-French government agreement was signed, providing for the joint development and production by Matra and Hawker Siddeley of an air-to-surface guided weapon now designated AS.37/AJ.168 Martel. Details of this can be found in the International section.

Matra are also designing on their own, or in collaboration with foreign companies, other missiles to meet current tactical requirements, including the surface-to-air Crotale; a variant of Crotale, known as Cactus, is being evaluated for operation by South Africa.

Matra are responsible for the development and quantity production of launchers for unguided solid-propellent rockets which form standard armament on French fighter and bomber aircraft. A similar launcher for British 2-in rockets, designed by Matra, is manufactured under licence by Thomas French & Sons of Manchester.

Special underwing stores developed by Matra for strike missions include a gun pod, based on the French DEFA 30-mm gun, for fighter and jet training aircraft.

Since 1960, Matra has also been working on retardation systems for bombs under the direction of the Service Technique de l'Aéronautique. The system now in series production and service comprises a cruciform parachute, mechanism to check the release parameters, and nose and tail fuses. It has been used with French SAMP 250 kg and 400 kg bombs since 1966 and is also in service in some ten foreign countries, including West Germany, in certain cases on standard British or US manufactured bombs. It can be used at heights down to 100 ft (30 m).

MATRA R.530

The R.530 air-to-air missile is in quantity production and serves as standard armament on Vautour and Mirage interceptors of the French Air Force, Mirages of the South African, Israeli and Royal Australian Air Forces and F-8E(FN) Crusaders of the French Navy.

Suitable for use at heights from sea level to 69,000 ft (21,000 m), the R.530 is an all-weather missile, with interchangeable semi-active radar and infra-red homing heads. It can be fired at

Matra Crotale/Cactus all-weather surface-to-air missile

the target from any direction, its homing head being sufficiently sensitive not to require firing from astern of the enemy aircraft.

The R.530 has a cylindrical body, with cruciform delta wings, two of which are fitted with ailerons, and cruciform tail control surfaces. It is powered by a two-stage Hotchkiss-Brandt solid-propellent rocket motor (18,740 lb = 8,500 kg st).

There are two types of Hotchkiss-Brandt high-explosive warhead, each weighing 60 lb (27 kg) and fitted with a proximity fuse.

DIMENSIONS:

Length overall	10 ft 9¼ in (3·28 m)
Body diameter	10¼ in (0·26 m)
Wing span	3 ft 7¼ in (1·10 m)

WEIGHT:

Launching weight	430 lb (195 kg)

PERFORMANCE:

Max speed	Mach 2·7
Range	9·5 nm (11 miles; 18 km)

MATRA SUPER 530

No information has yet been made available officially concerning this new air-to-air weapon system, which is intended as armament for the Dassault Mirage F1 interceptors of the French air force. The French technical press has suggested that it will use certain components of the R.530, but will have much improved aerodynamics, electronics and power plant, more than doubling the effective range. It will be an all-weather weapon, with the ability to attack targets flying at an altitude very different from that of the launch aircraft.

MATRA R.550

No information has been released on this new air-to-air weapon system, except that it is intended to meet a French air force requirement for a short/medium-range "dogfight" missile. Development is reported to have been started in 1967 as a private venture and to have continued under official contract since 1968.

MATRA/HSD AS.37/AJ.168 MARTEL
See "International" section, page 594.

CROTALE/CACTUS

On 2 May 1969, the South African Minister of Defence, Mr P. W. Botha, announced that an all-weather surface-to-air weapon system named Cactus was under development by French companies for the South African government, which was financing the programme with some help from the French government.

Matra are responsible for development and manufacture of the missile, which is also known as Crotale in France. It is designed to attack aircraft flying at up to Mach 1·2 at heights as low

as 165 ft (50 m). Reaction time is quoted as six seconds.

Compagnie Electronique Thomson Houston-Hotchkiss Brandt are responsible for the ground equipment, which is designed initially to be fitted into special Hotchkiss vehicles. The developed version for land forces will be air-transportable in aircraft such as the C-130 Hercules and Transall C-160. A semi-mobile or ship-borne installation is feasible.

Integration of the Cactus/Crotale missile with pre-series ground equipment on vehicles began in early 1969, when a number of direct hits or very close misses were achieved against CT.20 jet target drones. Operational evaluation started towards the end of 1969, with initial deliveries of operational systems planned for early 1971 and full production by 1972. It has been ordered by Lebanon as well as South Africa.

The missile is cylindrical in shape, with cruciform canard control surfaces, mounted on the ogival nose-cone and indexed in line with the cruciform fixed tail-fins. Both the control surfaces and the fins have sharply-swept leading-edges. A powerful explosive charge (weight 33 lb = 15 kg) is carried, detonated by infra-red proximity fuse.

Four missiles, in containers, are carried by the Crotale launch vehicle, in ready-to-fire condition. This vehicle also carries a monopulse fire-control radar capable of guiding two missiles simultaneously. The radar tracks each missile with the aid of a transponder mounted on the missile and transmits guidance signals by radio. Acquisition of the missile immediately after launch is facilitated by an infra-red unit which picks up the exhaust heat emission. An optical tracking device is also provided.

The second vehicle required for the Crotale weapon system carries a pulse-Doppler surveillance and target acquisition radar which is reported to have a range of 9·5 nm (11 miles; 18 km) and to be almost impervious to "clutter". The system for evaluating and reacting to signals received is automatic, using an SN-1050 digital computer, and three launch vehicles can be served by a single radar vehicle. Twelve different targets can be tracked simultaneously, and 12 missiles can be fired in pairs at six targets in 11 seconds.

The Crotale missile is believed to have a launching weight of about 165 lb (75 kg) and a range of over 4·3 nm (5 miles; 8 km), which distance it will cover in 16 seconds.

DIMENSIONS:

Length overall	9 ft 4 in (2·84 m)
Body diameter	5·9 in (0·15 m)

Versions of the Matra R.530 air-to-air missile with semi-active radar guidance (*left*) **and infra-red homing head** (*right*)

GERMANY
THE GERMAN FEDERAL REPUBLIC

BODENSEEWERK
BODENSEEWERK GERÄTETECHNIK GmbH
ADDRESS:
7770 Überlingen, Postfach 1120

Bodenseewerk Gerätetechnik (formerly Flug-gerätewerk Bodensee GmbH) was prime contract-or for European production under licence of the American Sidewinder 1A (AIM-9B) air-to-air missile, in collaboration with Société Anonyme Les Forges de Zeebrugge, Belgium; Dansk Industri Syndikat, Glud & Marstrands Fabriker, Jorgen Hoyer's, A/S Wejra and Terma Elektron-isk Industrie of Denmark; Greek Powder &

Cartridge of Greece; Philips Usfa NV of the Netherlands; Kongsberg Vapenfabrikk and Rau-foss Ammunisjonsfabrikker of Norway; Standard Electrica SARL of Portugal and Makina ve Kimya Endüstrisi Kurumu of Turkey.

Since 1965, Bodenseewerk Gerätetechnik has been engaged on a major improvement programme for Sidewinder 1A, of which details follow.

SIDEWINDER
Bodenseewerk Gerätetechnik have developed an improved guidance and control unit for the Sidewinder missile, known by the designation FGW Mod 2. This is intended to increase the

effectiveness of the missile against manoeuvring targets, against targets moving in front of "solid" backgrounds and in bad weather conditions.

The improvement to the infra-red system is achieved by using cooled detectors to increase sensitivity and reduce the effects of background clutter. The tracking rate against manoeuvring targets is increased by using more modern electronic components.

First tests of the FGW Mod 2 units were made in 1966. Production was under way in 1969, for retrospective modification of existing Sidewinder 1A missiles in service with the *Luftwaffe* and other NATO air forces.

MBB
MESSERSCHMITT-BÖLKOW-BLOHM GmbH
HEAD OFFICE AND WORKS:
Ottobrunn bei München
Defence Technology Division
WORKS:
Nabern and Schrobenhausen
OFFICERS:
See "Aircraft" section

In addition to its manufacture of piloted aircraft, MBB is engaged on guided weapon development. Its first product in this field is the BO 810 Cobra wire-guided anti-tank missile, which is in production as a standard weapon for the German army.

In collaboration with Aérospatiale of France, MBB is developing and producing a series of second-generation short-range battlefield missiles named MILAN, HOT and Roland. Also under development is an air-launched anti-shipping missile known as the Kormoran.

MBB is engaged on the development of research rockets and satellites, and is major contractor for the third stage of the ELDO launch vehicle (see "Research Rockets and Space Vehicles" Section).

MESSERSCHMITT-BÖLKOW-BLOHM BO 810 COBRA 2000
The Cobra is a small wire-guided anti-tank missile which can be carried, launched and con-trolled by one man. The complete weapon system comprises the missile, control box and cable links. A distributor is available to permit the connection of up to eight rounds to a single control box and to enable them to be fired selectively in sequence.

The control box is completely self-contained and carries the firing button and control stick. No launcher is required, except for the lid which covers the rear end of the missile during transport and which supports it on the ground.

The Cobra has a cylindrical body of fibre paper and cruciform plastics wings. The integral solid-propellant motor is supplemented by a non-jettisonable solid-propellant booster, mounted under the body. Control is by a spoiler in each wing.

Current version of the missile is the Cobra 2000, its designation indicating an extension of maximum range to 2,000 m. The 5·5 lb (2·5 kg) hollow-charge warhead is designed to penetrate at least 18·7 in (475 mm) of armour plate.

The weapon is fully operational and a total of 120,000 Cobras had been delivered to the German army, and the armed services of other NATO and non-Communist countries, by March 1970.

DIMENSIONS:
Length overall	3 ft 1½ in (0·95 m)
Body diameter	3·9 in (0·10 m)
Wing span	1 ft 7 in (0·48 m)

Messerschmitt-Bölkow-Blohm Kormoran missile under wing of F-104G Starfighter

WEIGHT:
Launching weight	22·5 lb (10·2 kg)
Weight at burn-out	17·6 lb (8·0 kg)

PERFORMANCE:
Max speed	190 mph (306 kmh)
Range	1,310-6,560 ft (400-2,000 m)

MESSERSCHMITT-BÖLKOW-BLOHM KORMORAN
This air-to-surface anti-shipping missile results from a joint development programme by MBB

Messerschmitt-Bölkow-Blohm BO 810 Cobra missile

and the former Nord-Aviation of France, under the design leadership of MBB and financed by the Federal German Government. The programme was covered by the Nord-Aviation designation AS.34.

The general appearance of Kormoran is shown in the adjacent illustration. It has a cylindrical body, fitted with cropped-delta cruciform wings and with cruciform tail control surfaces indexed in line with the wings. Its guidance system employs pre-guidance and homing phases, and enables it to approach the target at a very small height above the water.

The Kormoran can be carried by any aircraft with a modern navigation system and will equip F-104G Starfighters of the German naval air arm.

DIMENSIONS:
Length overall	14 ft 5 in (4·40 m)
Wing span	3 ft 3½ in (1·00 m)

WEIGHT:
Launching weight	1,320 lb (600 kg)

MESSERSCHMITT-BÖLKOW-BLOHM/ AÉROSPATIALE MILAN, HOT AND ROLAND
See "International" section below.

INTERNATIONAL PROGRAMMES

AÉROSPATIALE/MESSER-SCHMITT-BÖLKOW-BLOHM
SOCIÉTÉ NATIONALE INDUSTRIELLE AÉRO-SPATIALE
ADDRESS:
92-Châtillon S/Bagneux, France
MESSERSCHMITT-BÖLKOW-BLOHM GmbH
Defence Technology Division
ADDRESS:
Ottobrunn bei München, 8 München 80, POB 801149, Germany

Aérospatiale and Messerschmitt-Bölkow-Blohm are developing jointly three short-range battle-field weapons known as MILAN, HOT and Roland, for the armed services of France and Federal Germany.

AÉROSPATIALE/MESSERSCHMITT-BÖLKOW-BLOHM MILAN
The MILAN (Missile d'Infanterie Léger ANti-char) wire-guided anti-tank missile is one of the series of weapons being developed jointly by Aérospatiale (formerly Nord-Aviation) of France

Aérospatiale/ MBB MILAN launch and control unit with missile in place

and Messerschmitt-Bölkow-Blohm GmbH of Germany.

It is launched from a tubular container, which is used also for transport and storage. Prior to launch, the tube is placed on the launch and guidance unit, which consists of the firing mechanism, sight, IR goniometer and guidance electronics. MILAN is spin-stabilised in flight by four hinged tail-fins which flick into the extended position as it leaves the end of the launch tube. Its solid-propellant rocket motor has two thrust levels. The TCA automatic guidance system used for MILAN is described in detail under the entry for the Harpon missile on page 586. In brief, during the missile's flight, the operator simply keeps an optical sight trained on the target. The missile is held on course by infra-red guidance.

Over short ranges, MILAN can be used as a recoilless rifle. Studies and testing have also shown that it can be used effectively as a surface-to-air weapon for protection of ground targets against head-on attack by low-flying aircraft and helicopters.

Development testing has been completed and further operational evaluation by French and German military personnel is scheduled to take place during 1970-71.

DIMENSIONS:
Length overall	2 ft 5·5 in (0·75 m)
Body diameter	4·6 in (0·116 m)
Fin span	10·5 in (0·266 m)

WEIGHTS:
Launching weight of missile	13·9 lb (6·3 kg)
Missile and container	24·2 lb (11 kg)
Launcher and guidance unit, with tripod	30 lb (14 kg)

PERFORMANCE:
Max speed	345 knots (400 mph; 640 km/h)
Range	83-6,560 ft (25-2,000 m)

AÉROSPATIALE/MESSERSCHMITT-BÖLKOW-BLOHM HOT

The HOT (High-subsonic, Optically-guided, Tube-launched) is a tube-launched wire-guided anti-tank missile of larger size and with a higher performance than the MILAN. It is being developed jointly by Aérospatiale and Messerschmitt-Bölkow-Blohm; qualification tests were planned as a next step in the current pre-production phase in early 1970.

Like MILAN, it has tail-fins which fold down against the body when it is in its launching tube, and open out to spin stabilise it in flight. The

Aérospatiale/MBB MILAN wire-guided infantry anti-tank missile

Aérospatiale/MBB HOT anti-tank weapon system installed atop a light tracked combat vehicle

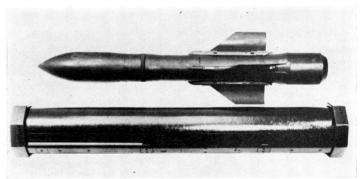
Above: **Aérospatiale/Messerschmitt-Bölkow-Blohm HOT anti-tank missile and tube**
Left: **HOT anti-tank missiles installed on armoured vehicle**

power plant is a two-stage solid-propellant rocket motor. Because of its comparatively high speed, the time of flight to a target is only about half that for the current Nord SS.11. Guidance is by means of the TCA type of optical sighting/infra-red system used for the MILAN. A jet vane control system is used.

Test firings have been made successfully from armoured vehicles and design studies are in hand covering the installation of HOT missiles on various types of helicopters, for both air-to-surface and air-to-air operation. Like Harpon and MILAN, HOT could also be used effectively as a surface-to-air weapon for protection against head-on or nearly head-on attack by low-flying aircraft and helicopters.

DIMENSIONS:
Length overall	4 ft 2 in (1·27 m)
Body diameter	5½ in (0·14 m)
Fin span	1 ft 0¼ in (0·31 m)

WEIGHT:
Launching weight of missile	44 lb (20 kg)
Missile and container	55 lb (25 kg)

PERFORMANCE:
Max speed	545 knots (625 mph; 1,010 km/h)
Range	250-13,100 ft (75-4,000 m)

AÉROSPATIALE/MESSERSCHMITT-BÖLKOW-BLOHM ROLAND

The Roland surface-to-air missile is intended to provide protection against low-flying aircraft and helicopters, flying at speeds up to Mach 1·3, for troops in combat areas. It is tube-launched from a light armoured vehicle, the plastic tube serving also as a storage and transport container.

Roland incorporates the results of independent work on missiles of this type by Nord (SABA, Sol-Air Basse Altitude) and Bölkow (P-250). It underwent firing trials successfully in 1968 and 1969, and both the French and German armoured vehicles intended to deploy Roland were subjected to limited testing by military personnel in early 1969, with the associated Roland ground equipment. Further evaluation is scheduled in 1970-71.

The missile is cylindrical, with cruciform hinged delta wings indexed in line with fixed cruciform foreplanes. It is radio-guided and steered by means of vanes in the efflux from its sustainer motor. A proximity-fused warhead is fitted.

In operation, the missiles will be stowed in their containers in magazines within the launch vehicle. The containers will be brought into the launching position by a hydraulic system which will lift another missile into the firing position each time one is launched.

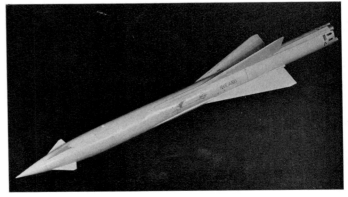
Aérospatiale/MBB Roland low-altitude surface-to-air missile

DIMENSIONS:	
Length overall	
missile	7 ft 10½ in (2·40 m)
tube	8 ft 6½ in (2·60 m)
Diameter:	
missile body	6·3 in (0·16 m)
missile, wings folded	10·24 in (0·26 m)
tube	10·63 in (0·27 m)
Wing span	1 ft 7¾ in (0·50 m)
Length of launch tube	8 ft 6½ in (2·60 m)
WEIGHTS:	
Launching weight of missile	139 lb (63 kg)
Launch tube	26 lb (11·8 kg)
PERFORMANCE (estimated):	
Cruising speed	Mach 1·6
Min range	1,640 ft (500 m)
Max range	19,700 ft (6,000 m)

Below and left:
**Roland twin-launcher
on two different types of
light armoured vehicles**

Target detection in azimuth is performed by a
pulse-Doppler surveillance and search radar on the
launch vehicle. Optical detection of the target
in elevation and target tracking are done manually. After launching, the operator tracks the
target with a periscopic sight, linked to an infra-
red tracking system and a computer which
processes command signals to the missile via a
microwave control link. Details of this type of
guidance system are given under the entry for the
Harpon missile on page 586.

An additional radar guidance device which
will give this weapon all-weather capability,
without requiring any basic modification to either
the missiles or the support equipment, is under
development by Thomson-CSF. The all-weather
version is known as **Roland II**, and is also being
developed as a ship-to-air weapon system. It
retains the clear-weather guidance system for
optimum performance against very low flying
aircraft.

MATRA/HSD

SA ENGINS MATRA, 4 rue de Presbourg, 75-Paris
XVIe, France

HAWKER SIDDELEY DYNAMICS LTD, Manor
Road, Hatfield, Herts, England

Matra and HSD have developed jointly an air-
to-surface precision tactical strike missile known
as Martel, to meet the requirements of the British
and French armed services.

MATRA/HSD AS.37/AJ.168 MARTEL

Martel (Missile Anti-Radar and TELevision) is
a guided air-to-surface missile which can be
fitted with interchangeable heads for TV guidance
or anti-radar homing missions. The British
government has stated that its range is "tens
of miles", giving it a genuine stand-off capability,
and it is designed to function in an ECM (electronic countermeasures) environment.

The anti-radar version of Martel (AS.37) offers
all-weather attack capability against radar antennae in several frequency bands. Depending
on the mission profiles, it can be launched at very
low, medium or high altitudes. It then flies a

homing trajectory into the emitting target source.
This is done without further information or control from the parent aircraft, which can return
to its base immediately after launch.

The television version of Martel (AJ.168) follows
a pre-programmed course immediately after
launch, but the final impact on target is effected
by the weapon operator, who is given a direct
visual picture of the target on a high-brightness
monitor. Command instructions are sent back
from the aircraft to the missile, to control the
field of view of the TV camera in sympathy with
a joystick or similar device in the cockpit. Control signals generated within the missile itself
alter the flight path to bring the axis of the missile
into line with that of the television camera, once
the target has been selected.

A wide variety of initial flight patterns can be
produced to ensure that the TV system has the
best possible opportunity of identifying the
target, with the least possible danger to the
launching aircraft.

Other major companies associated with Martel
are the Marconi Company, who provide the TV
and radio link equipment which forms part of the
guidance system of the TV version, and Electron-

ique Marcel Dassault, who provide part of the
guidance system of the anti-radar version. The
solid-propellant motors are produced by Hotchkiss-Brandt and Aérospatiale (Nord-Aviation).

No other details of Martel may yet be published.
The general appearance of the two versions is
shown in the illustrations below.

The first simulated firings and mock-up launchings were made in the Summer of 1964 and prototypes of both versions were completed in 1965-66.
Development was completed in 1968 with a
highly successful series of firings. Evaluation
was under way in early 1969 and production
orders have been placed.

Martel will arm a variety of aircraft, including
the Hawker Siddeley Buccaneer and Hawker
Siddeley Nimrod operated by the British services,
and the Dassault Mirage III-E, SEPECAT Jaguar
and Breguet Atlantic operated by the French
services.

DIMENSIONS (approx):
Length overall:	
AS.37	13 ft 1½ in (4·00 m)
AJ.168	12 ft 0 in (3·65 m)
Span of wings	3 ft 8 in (1·12 m)
Body diameter	1 ft 3 in (0·38 m)

TV-guidance version of Martel under wing of Sea Vixen trials aircraft

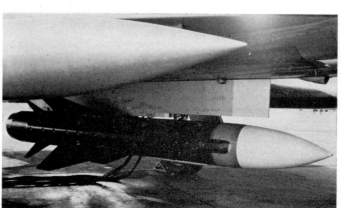

Anti-radar version of Martel under fuselage of Mirage III-E aircraft

ISRAEL

A number of guided missiles and rocket weapons are in service with, or under development for the Israeli armed forces. Some have resulted from development contracts placed with French manufacturers. All available details follow.

"CONCRETE DIBBER" BOMB

The Israeli air force is reported to have used a special rocket-boosted bomb against the runways of Arab airfields, to put them out of action in the early stages of the six-day war in June 1967. Referred to as the "concrete dibber", this bomb was originally the subject of a design study contract placed with Engins Matra of France in 1964; but subsequent development and production are believed to have taken place in Israel.

The original design study, shown in the adjacent illustration, utilised as warhead a standard STA Type 200 bomb, with an explosive charge of 365 lb (165 kg), minus its tail section. The rear part of the weapon consisted of a ring of eight solid-propellant rocket tubes, of which four were arranged to fire rearward as boosters, while the other four (spaced between the boosters) had nozzles firing forward and outward at 20° to function as retro-rockets. A cylindrical container enclosed by the ring of rocket-tubes was used to house a tail parachute-drogue. The retro-rockets were each fitted with a stabilising fin.

After release from an aircraft flying at low level (approx 330 ft = 100 m), this bomb operated in the following sequence: 0·3 seconds after release the retro-rockets fired, followed 0·6 seconds later by opening of the cruciform drogue-chute. This caused the weapon to nose down to its penetration angle of 60/80° relative to the runway surface under attack. Finally, 4·7 seconds after launch, the booster rockets fired, burning away the parachute and increasing the speed of the bomb to about 525 ft (160 m) sec. Total thrust of the four boosters was 16,535 lb (7,500 kg) for 0·9 seconds.

Reports from observers in Egypt suggest that weapons used by the Israeli air force on 5 June 1967 conformed with this general specification. Total weight of the weapon that formed the subject of

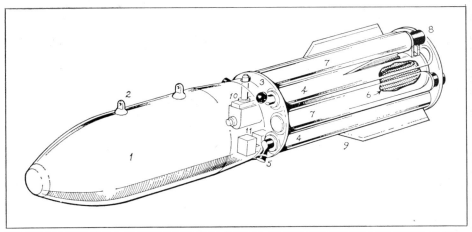

The concrete dibber bomb, as projected by Matra in 1964: (1) warhead: STA Type 200 bomb; (2) two-point mounting; (3) rocket mounting ring; (4) retro-rockets; (5) retro-nozzles; (6) parachute drogue in central container; (7) booster rockets; (8) booster nozzles; (9) stabilising fins; (10) sequential triggering mechanism; (11) igniter batteries (*Flight International*)

the original design study was 1,210 lb (550 kg); its length was 7 ft 10 in (2·39 m). It was intended to be dropped from Vautour and Mirage aircraft flying at speeds of 300-500 knots (350-575 mph; 550-925 km/h).

MD-660

The designation of this two-stage solid-propellant surface-to-surface bombardment missile implies that it has been developed by Avions Marcel Dassault of France, under contract from the Israeli government. Fired from a mobile ramp, it is said to have a designed range of 240 nm (280 miles; 450 km) and to be capable of carrying alternative nuclear or high-explosive warheads.

When details of the MD-660 first appeared, it was suggested that Israel would have suitable nuclear warheads of its own design available by 1970, produced in the Dimona reactor centre near the Dead Sea. Development of the missile itself was said to be more advanced, and firing trials were reported to be under way in the Mediterranean, off Toulon, in the Spring of 1968.

Earlier reports suggested that a missile being developed by Dassault for Israel was designated MD-620, and the name Jericho was associated with a Dassault surface-to-surface weapon project at least five years ago. The designations MD-620 and MD-660 may or may not apply to the same programme.

IAI

ISRAEL AIRCRAFT INDUSTRIES LTD

HEAD OFFICE AND WORKS:
Lod Airport

OFFICERS:
See "Aircraft" section

In addition to its work on manned aircraft, this company has developed for the Israel Navy a ship-to-ship missile named Gabriel, of which first official details were released on 7 May 1970, the 22nd Independence Day of the State of Israel.

IAI GABRIEL

Development of this subsonic ship-to-ship missile was carried out by a group of engineers and technicians of Israel Aircraft Industries in collaboration with the Israeli Navy. The missile and its launching system were designed to a

specific naval requirement and were deployed operationally by the Spring of 1970. Two of the 230-ton "Saar" class gunboats acquired from Chantiers Amiot in 1969 were then displayed, each with two three-round rotating servo-pedestal launchers installed on the after deck, supplemented by two single-round launchers, to each side of the 40 mm gun on the forward deck. The weapon system is equally suitable for use on larger ships.

Research, design and engineering development, manufacture of all parts and components, and all trials of the Gabriel weapon system were conducted by Israeli personnel, over a period of several years. Operational rounds and equipment are ready for service when placed on board ship, requiring no further testing or adjustment.

Gabriel is described as an automatic homing missile, utilising a sophisticated electronic guidance system and delivering a powerful high-ex-

plosive warhead accurately and reliably. It can be used in adverse weather and rough seas, and in an electronic countermeasures environment.

The missile has a cylindrical body, tapering towards the tail. It has cruciform wings of rectangular form, and cruciform tail surfaces indexed in line with the wings. No details of the rocket motor or guidance system are available, but the warhead is known to weigh 330 lb (150 kg).

Each missile is stored, delivered and mounted on board ship in a reinforced glass-fibre container which embodies the launching rail and has a hydraulically-operated door-lid.

DIMENSIONS:
Length overall   11 ft 0 in (3·35 m)
Body diameter   12·8 in (32·5 cm)
Wing span   4 ft 6½ in (1·385 m)
WEIGHT:
Launching weight   882 lb (400 kg)

Above: Gabriel missile leaving its container-launcher during development tests at sea

Right: Container-launcher with lid open, exposing missile for firing

ITALY

CONTRAVES ITALIANA
CONTRAVES ITALIANA SpA

ADDRESS:
via Tiburtina 965, 00156 Rome

SALES MANAGER: Cdr A. Piazzesi, IN (retd)
TECHNICAL ENQUIRIES: Dr Ing D. Bagnini

Contraves Italiana is an associate of the Swiss Oerlikon company and was established to produce in Italy fire control units and guided weapons of Contraves-Oerlikon design. Its current activities include manufacture of the Contraves-Oerlikon Mosquito wire-guided anti-tank missile, and the production of fire control sets, with associated tracking radars, for medium and heavy land-based or ship-borne anti-aircraft guns.

For several years, Contraves Italiana has also participated in international and national space programmes, including the ESRO, ELDO and San Marco projects. FM/FM telemetry packages for the ELDO launch vehicle and telemetry receiving stations have been designed, manufactured and delivered to customers in Europe.

In 1960 Contraves Italiana began building up its own research and development department and subsequently developed a number of new products in the field of guided weapons and associated ground equipment. In particular, it was responsible for the Indigo short-range surface-to-air missile and the Nettuno short-range ship-to-ship missile, both of which are now described under the "Sistel" heading in this section.

Sistel SpA is a new company formed jointly by Contraves Italiana, Finmeccanica, Fiat, SNIA and Montedison, to develop guided weapons and space equipment; and the former missile and space equipment branch of Contraves Italiana is now embodied in Sistel.

Contraves Italiana continues to be responsible for design and manufacture of the ground or ship-borne parts of weapon systems based on the use of Sistel missiles. To confer surface-to-surface missile capability on light naval craft it has developed and manufactured integration kits enabling Sistel Nettuno and Vulcano missiles to be used in naval weapon systems of Contraves design and production, such as the Sea Hunter 2 (Contraves Italiana) or Sea Hunter 4 (Contraves AG).

This company has also designed and manufac-

Contraves-Oerlikon Mosquito wire-guided anti-tank missile system

tured an integration kit to permit the use of Sistel Indigo surface-to-air missiles by anti-aircraft gun batteries utilising either the Super Fledermaus fire control system (designed by Contraves AG, produced by Contraves Italiana) or the CT40-G fire control system (designed and manufactured by Contraves Italiana).

CONTRAVES-OERLIKON MOSQUITO

The Mosquito is a simple wire-guided infantry anti-tank weapon which can be transported and fired by one man, using a joystick-operated control box. It is of conventional design, with a cylindrical glass-fibre body and folding cruciform wings of sandwich construction. Propulsion is by a two-stage solid-propellant rocket motor. In flight the missile is controlled by vibrating spoilers on the trailing-edge of each wing. It is roll-stabilised by a powder-driven gyro.

For storage and transport, a single Mosquito is packed into a container, with its wings in place and only the warhead detached. The complete package, with missile inside, weighs 48·5 lb (22·0

kg). Six Mosquitos can be transported, ready for firing, on a Puch-Haflinger light cross-country vehicle. This weapon has also been mounted on Agusta-Bell 47 helicopters.

Alternative warheads comprise a hollow-charge type capable of penetrating more than 26 in (66 cm) of armour plate or a fragmentation type with splinter density of over six per sq yard at 60 ft (18 m). Weight of the warhead is 9 lb (4 kg).

For training purposes, the Mosquito can be fitted with a parachute recovery system instead of a warhead.

Production of the Mosquito is scheduled to end in 1971.

DIMENSIONS:
Length overall	3 ft 7·7 in (1·11 m)
Body diameter	4·72 in (0·12 m)
Wing span	1 ft 11·6 in (0·60 m)

WEIGHT:
Launching weight	31·0 lb (14·1 kg)

PERFORMANCE:
Cruising speed	178 knots (205 mph; 330 km/h)
Range	1,200-7,800 ft (360-2,375 m)

SIGME
SOCIETÀ GENERALE MISSILISTICA ITALIANA

HEAD OFFICE:
Via Lombardia 31, 00187 Rome

WORKS:
Bosco Faito di Ceccano (Frosinone)
PRESIDENT: Ing C. E. Hidalgo
TECHNICAL MANAGER: Ing F. Rizzi
SALES MANAGER: Com A. Fe'd'Ostiani

ADMINISTRATIVE MANAGER: Dr F. Porzi
This company was formed jointly by Fiat, Finmeccanica and SNIA Viscosa for the manufacture, maintenance and refurbishing of missiles and their systems.

SISTEL
SISTEL—SISTEMI ELETTRONICI SpA

HEAD OFFICE:
via Tiburtina 965, 00156 Rome

MANAGING DIRECTOR:
Dr Ing E. Fagnoni

Sistel—Sistemi Elettronici SpA—has been formed jointly by Montecatini-Edison, Contraves Italiana, Fiat, Finmeccanica and SNIA to develop new products in the missile field. It embodies the former missiles and space equipment branch of Contraves Italiana and is now responsible for the guided missiles that were under development by that branch.

Sistel's current activities include user's trials, with the Italian Army, of the Indigo short-range surface-to-air missile which was tested successfully at the Italian Firing Range in Sardinia, and development and evaluation of the naval Sea Indigo, and the Nettuno and Vulcano surface-to-surface missiles, known originally as Sea Killer

Mk 1 and Mk 2 respectively. FM/FM telemetry packages and telemetry receiving stations are also designed and manufactured by Sistel.

SISTEL INDIGO

This short-range surface-to-air land-based guided weapon has been tested with notable success at the Italian firing range in Sardinia and is being evaluated by the Italian Army.

WINGS: Movable cruciform control surfaces at centre of missile.

BODY: Cylindrical light alloy structure.

TAIL SURFACES: Cruciform stabilising fins, indexed in line with wings.

POWER PLANT: Solid-propellant rocket motor (7,055 lb=3,200 kg st).

GUIDANCE: Command/beam-riding radio command guidance.

CONTROL: Via movable wings.

WARHEAD: High-explosive fragmentation type, detonated by Hawker Siddeley Dynamics infra-red proximity fuse.

DIMENSIONS:
Length overall	10 ft 6 in (3·20 m)
Body diameter	7½ in (0·19 m)
Span of wings	2 ft 7 in (0·79 m)

WEIGHTS:
Launching weight	214 lb (97 kg)
Weight at burn-out	141 lb (64 kg)

PERFORMANCE (approx):
Speed at burn-out	Mach 2·5
Max effective slant range	5·4 nm (6·2 miles; 10 km)
Min effective slant range	0·54 nm (0·6 miles; 1 km)
Ceiling	20,000 ft (6,000 m)

SISTEL SEA INDIGO

This short-range ship-to-air guided weapon is a navalised version of the Indigo. It is intended to utilise an automatic reloading system when installed in ships of more than 500 tons displacement; manual reloading is specified when Sea Indigo is fitted in naval craft of less than 500 tons.

Main features of the missile are similar to those

Sistel Indigo short-range land-based surface-to-air missile

Sistel Nettuno surface-to-surface ship-launched missile

of the Indigo land-based version. Modifications needed to suit it to its new role have been completed, as have the launching systems for both automatic and manual reloading.

SISTEL NETTUNO

This short-range surface-to-surface ship-based guided weapon system, known for a time as Sea Killer Mk 1, has been installed on board the fast patrol boat *Saetta* of the Italian Navy. It is carried in a five-round multiple launcher.

WINGS: Movable cruciform control surfaces at centre of missile.

BODY: Cylindrical light alloy structure.

TAIL SURFACES: Cruciform stabilising fins.

POWER PLANT: Solid-propellant rocket motor (4,410 lb = 2,000 kg st).

GUIDANCE: Beam-rider/radio command/radar altimeter guidance.

CONTROL: Via movable wings.

WARHEAD: High-explosive fragmentation type, with impact/proximity fuse.

DIMENSIONS:
Length overall	12 ft 3 in (3·73 m)
Body diameter	7·87 in (0·20 m)
Span of wings	2 ft 9½ in (0·85 m)

WEIGHTS:
Launching weight	370 lb (168 kg)
Weight at burn-out	260 lb (118 kg)

Nettuno multiple launcher on the fast patrol boat *Saetta*

PERFORMANCE:
Speed at burn-out	Mach 1·9
Max effective range	5·4 nm (6·2 miles; 10 km)
Min effective range	1·6 nm (1·9 miles; 3 km)

SISTEL VULCANO

Known for a time as Sea Killer Mk 2, this two-stage surface-to-surface guided missile is a development of the Nettuno with a heavier warhead and extended range. First flight trials of Vulcano missiles were carried out in mid-1969.

TYPE: Surface-to-surface ship-based guided weapon.

WINGS, BODY, TAIL SURFACES: As for Nettuno. Booster also has stabilising fins.

POWER PLANT: Booster and sustainer are both solid-propellant rocket motors. After burnout, booster is separated by an aerodynamic drag section.

GUIDANCE AND CONTROL: As for Nettuno.

WARHEAD: High-explosive steel penetration shell, with impact/proximity fuse.

DIMENSIONS (approx):
Length overall	14 ft 9 in (4·50 m)
Body diameter	7·87 in (0·20 m)
Span of wings	2 ft 9½ in (0·85 m)

WEIGHT:
Launching weight	approx 530 lb (240 kg)

PERFORMANCE:
Speed	high subsonic
Max effective range	over 10 nm (11·5 miles; 18·5 km)

JAPAN

KAWASAKI

KAWASAKI JUKOGYO KABUSHIKI KAISHA (Kawasaki Heavy Industries Ltd)

HEAD OFFICE:
2-16-1 Nakamachi Dori, Ikuta-ku, Kobe
OFFICERS: See "Aircraft" section

In collaboration with six other companies, Kawasaki has developed and is producing a small anti-tank guided weapon, designated KAM-3D. Details of this are given below.

Since April 1966, Kawasaki has also been prime contractor for an extended-range version of the KAM-3D, designated TAN-SSM.

KAWASAKI KAM-3D (TYPE 64 ATM-1)

Development of this wire-guided anti-tank missile was started in 1957, under a contract awarded by the Technical Research and Development Institute of the Japan Defence Agency. The KAM-3D was adopted as standard equipment of the JGSDF in 1963 after several hundred test rounds had been fired, and has the official designation Type 64 ATM. Trials showed that the missile's velocity control system enables three out of four unskilled operators to hit a target with their first round after completion of a two-week training course with the primary training and field training simulators. Skilled operators can score 19 hits in 20 firings.

The KAM-3D has an orthodox configuration,

Kawasaki KAM-3D wire-guided anti-tank missile on launcher

with a cylindrical metal body and cruciform metal wings incorporating full-span trailing-edge spoilers for control. Propulsion is by a dual-thrust solid-propellant—double base (Nihon Yushi)/composite (Daicel ammonium nitrate/polyurethane)—rocket motor, the booster stage of which accelerates the missile to its cruising speed in 0·8 seconds, after which the sustainer stage maintains this speed. The motor has a casing of rolled and welded AISI 4130 steel and utilises an electrical igniter. Its two stages are rated at 286 lb (130 kg) st and 33 lb (15 kg) st respectively.

The missile can be fired singly or in multiple units by infantry and is also carried by Jeeps and helicopters. It is launched at an elevation of 15°, and the operator controls it via an optical tracking system, using a flare by day and the sustainer rocket exhaust by night as a visual reference. A gyro-stabilisation system is embodied in the missile. A two-man firing team is required, using a push-button control box.

Production continues, the latest order for 275 missiles (195 of them inert rounds) having been placed in the Summer of 1969.

DIMENSIONS:
Length overall	3 ft 4 in (1·02 m)
Body diameter	4·7 in (0·12 m)
Wing span	1 ft 11½ in (0·60 m)

WEIGHT:
Launching weight	34·6 lb (15·7 kg)

PERFORMANCE:
Cruising speed 165 knots (190 mph; 306 km/h)	
Turning radius	820 ft (250 m)
Range	1,150-5,900 ft (350-1,800 m)

KAWASAKI TAN-SSM

This is an extended-range, higher-performance version of the KAM-3D which has been under development since April 1966. It can be used against armoured vehicles on both land and water. The designation TAN-SSM signifies short-range surface-to-surface missile.

MITSUBISHI

MITSUBISHI DENKI KABUSHIKI KAISHA (Mitsubishi Electric Corporation)

HEAD OFFICE:
2-2-3, Marunouchi, Chiyoda-Ku, Tokyo
PRESIDENT: Ken Ohkubo
Since 1921, Mitsubishi Electric has been

responsible for production of a wide range of electrical and electronic products as a sister company of Mitsubishi Heavy Industries. Its recent aerospace products include radar systems, computers, gun-sights, radio equipment and ADF installations.

In 1968, the company was awarded a contract to build the Hawk surface-to-air missile for the Ground Self-Defence Force, under licence from Raytheon (USA). The missiles are scheduled to be delivered to the JGSDF in the period 1968-77.

MITSUBISHI JUKOGYO KABUSHIKI KAISHA (Mitsubishi Heavy Industries, Ltd)

HEAD OFFICE:
Mitsubishi Building, No. 10, 2-chome, Marunouchi, Chiyoda-ku, Tokyo
OFFICERS: See "Aircraft" section

Mitsubishi Heavy Industries is developing and producing air-to-air missiles for the JASDF. It is also manufacturing the Nike-Hercules surface-

to-air missile under licence from McDonnell Douglas Corporation.

Details of its research rockets can be found in the "Research Rockets and Space Vehicles" section of this edition.

MITSUBISHI AAM-1

The AAM-1 is an infra-red homing air-to-air missile which Mitsubishi has developed and is producing for the Japan Defence Agency. It is replacing the Sidewinder on the F-86F and

F-104J interceptors of the JASDF. No details are available.

MITSUBISHI AAM-2

Mitsubishi is developing this missile as a replacement for the AAM-1. It is a collision-course weapon, whereas the AAM-1 is limited to pursuit-course attack. No details are available, except that the Japan Defence Agency has awarded a contract to Nihon Electric Company to cover manufacture of experimental infra-red homing devices for the AAM-2.

NORWAY

A/S KONGSBERG VAAPEN-FABRIKK

HEAD OFFICE AND WORKS: Kongsberg
SALES MANAGER, DEFENCE EQUIPMENT: M. Frihagen
PUBLIC RELATIONS MANAGER: E. Frisvaag

This government-owned company is the only armament manufacturer in Norway. Its products include small arms, guns, rockets and missiles, proximity fuzes, fire control equipment and weapon systems.

A/S Kongsberg Vaapenfabrikk was prime contractor for European production of the Bullpup air-to-surface missile and is the manu-

facturer of the Norwegian-developed Terne anti-submarine system and Penguin anti-ship missile system.

PENGUIN

Penguin is an anti-ship missile system developed by the Norwegian Defence Research Establishment. It can be installed on ships, helicopters and other platforms.

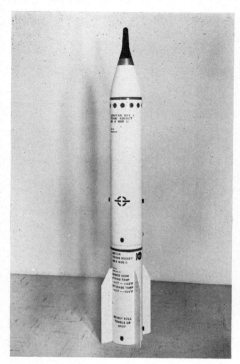

Above: **Six-round launcher for Terne Mk 8 installed on ship**

Left: **Terne Mk 8 anti-submarine missile**

Manufacturing and development rights for the system and missile, which is in production, were assigned to A/S Kongsberg Vaapenfabrikk.

No details have been made available by this company, but a description appeared in the press early in 1970, at the time of the announcement that a joint development contract for the Penguin had been placed by the Norwegian and West German governments. This implied that the missile is powered by a two-stage solid-propellant rocket motor, has cruciform wings and is guided by an inertial system with infra-red terminal homing. The warhead is said to be similar to that of the Bullpup missile for which this company was European prime contractor.

The following specification data appeared in the same report.

DIMENSIONS (approx):	
Length overall	10 ft 0 in (3·05 m)
Diameter of body	11 in (0·28 m)
Span of wings	4 ft 7 in (1·40 m)
WEIGHTS (approx):	
Launching weight	727 lb (330 kg)
Warhead	253 lb (115 kg)
PERFORMANCE (approx):	
Cruising speed	Mach 0·7
Cruising height	200 ft (60 m)
Range	1-10 nm (1·2-12·5 miles; 2-20 km)

TERNE Mk 8

The Terne Mk 8 missile is a rocket-propelled depth charge of cylindrical shape, with an ogival nose-cone and with cruciform stabilising fins at the tail. Propulsion is by two concentric solid-propellant rocket motors, giving this version approximately twice the maximum range of the earlier Mk 7 missile. The Terne is so simple that its warhead, comprising a 110 lb (50 kg) explosive charge, represents more than one-third of the total launching weight. The warhead is detonated by a combined acoustic proximity, impact and time fuse.

The system can be installed on ships of all sizes down to small escort vessels. After the attack sonar has given the range, bearing and depth of the submarine target, a full salvo of six missiles can be fired in five seconds.

The Terne Mk 8, to which the details below apply, is operational on ships of the Norwegian Navy.

DIMENSIONS:	
Length overall	6 ft 4¾ in (1·95 m)
Diameter of body	8·0 in (20·3 cm)
WEIGHT:	
Launching weight	298 lb (135 2 kg)
PERFORMANCE:	
No details available.	

SOUTH AFRICA

First official news of guided weapon development in South Africa was given by the Minister of Defence, Mr P. W. Botha, on 2 May 1969. He announced that both surface-to-air and air-to-air missiles were under development. All available details follow.

CACTUS

Cactus is the South African version of the Matra/CFTH Crotale all-weather surface-to-air weapon system (see page 591). According to the South African Minister of Defence, Mr P. W. Botha, it is being developed by his country in co-operation with the French companies and with the approval of the French government which is helping to finance the programme.

Cactus is intended primarily to attack aircraft flying at speeds up to Mach 1·2 at altitudes down to 165 ft (50 m).

AIR-TO-AIR MISSILE

No details of this missile are available except that it is a purely South African venture, has "some unique characteristics" and had already been tested successfully on a range at St Lucia at the time of Mr Botha's announcement, on 2 May 1969.

SWEDEN

BOFORS
AKTIEBOLAGET BOFORS

HEAD OFFICE AND WORKS:
 Bofors
MANAGING DIRECTOR: P. Odelberg

SALES MANAGER: K. E. Plyhr
PUBLIC RELATIONS MANAGER: N. A. Wahlberg

This world-famous Swedish armament manufacturing concern has been producing unguided air-to-air and air-to-surface rockets for many years. As its first project in the guided missile field it developed as a private venture the Bantam wire-guided anti-tank weapon.

Other missile systems currently in production include multiple launchers for 375 mm anti-submarine rockets with ranges up to 11,100 ft (3,600 m).

Bofors Bantam wire-guided anti-tank missile leaving launcher

Bantam missile being air-launched from an Agusta-Bell 204 helicopter

BOFORS BANTAM

The Bantam is a small wire-guided anti-tank missile, designed for operation by a single infantry soldier.

The cylindrical body and cruciform wings are made largely of glass-fibre reinforced plastics. Control is by vibrating spoilers, in each wing trailing-edge. A two-stage solid-propellant rocket motor is used. The high-explosive warhead weighs 4·1 lb (1·9 kg).

The wings fold at mid-span, making possible the use of a very small carrying container. When the missile is fired from the container the wings unfold and their bent rear corners then cause the missile to rotate in flight.

The total weight of the entire weapon system, including launcher, carrying rack, cable and control unit is 44 lb (20 kg). Time required to set up the missile and fire it is about 25 seconds.

The Bantam continues in large-scale production for the Swedish and Swiss Armies, with which it is standard equipment. The Puch-Haflinger light cross-country vehicle has been adapted easily to carry 12 Bantams, ready for instant use. In this installation the missiles are provided with carrying racks and are therefore available also for use by infantry in combat areas.

The Bantam can also be mounted on the Malmö Mili-trainer light combat aircraft (see page 186), and on helicopters, and a number of missiles have been fired successfully from both types of aircraft.

DIMENSIONS:
Length overall	2 ft 9½ in (0·85 m)
Body diameter	4·3 in (0·11 m)
Wing span	1 ft 3¾ in (0·40 m)

WEIGHT:
Launching weight	16·5 lb (7·5 kg)

PERFORMANCE:
Cruising speed	165 knots (190 mph; 306 km/h)
Range	820-6,600 ft (250-2,000 m)

ROBOTAVDELNINGEN (FMV-F:R)

Swedish Guided Weapons Directorate

ADDRESS:
Försvarets Materielverk, Flygmaterielförvaltningen, Robotavdelningen, S-104 50 Stockholm 80

Since 1 July 1968, the Robotavdelningen has been part of the Air Materiel Department (FMV-F) of the Materiel Administration of the Armed Forces (FMV), which manages all Swedish Army, Navy and Air Force material. It no longer develops guided weapons itself, but is responsible for procuring guided weapons which require development for Swedish use or are to be manufactured under licence in Sweden. Together with the Swedish Research Institute of National Defence (FOA), the Robotavdelningen is also responsible for research in the guided weapon field.

Details are given below of the Robot RB04 which was developed before the change in the function of the Robotavdelningen.

ROBOT RB04

In service since early 1959 as standard armament on the Saab A 32A Lansens of four SwAF attack wings, the RB04 (formerly (Rb 304) is an all-weather powered bomb intended for use against targets at sea. The latest version is intended to equip the new Saab AJ 37 Viggen attack aircraft in due course.

The RB04 was developed to a 1949 specification after firing tests of an earlier experimental missile, designated the type 302, had been made in the previous year from a Saab T.18B piston-engined bomber. Project work on the RB04 began in March 1950 and the first full-scale airframe was flight tested in the spring of 1954. The first complete RB04 was fired from a Saab J 29 fighter on 11 February 1955 and the following versions have since been developed for operational use:

RB04C. Standard version in service at time of writing, as illustrated and described below.

RB04D. Improved version with higher performance, about to be delivered to SwAF attack wings of A 32A aircraft in early 1970.

RB04E. Further improved version intended as primary armament of AJ 37 Viggen, which can carry three, as against two on the A 32A. Described in this section under the entry for the Saab company, which is prime contractor for the RB04E.

TYPE: Air-to-ship guided weapon.

WINGS: Mid-wing cantilever monoplane, mounted at rear of weapon. Ailerons in trailing-edges. Fixed fins at tips.

BODY: Circular-section all-metal structure.

TAIL SURFACES: Tail-first design. Cruciform control surfaces on nose. Fixed fins at wingtips.

POWER PLANT: One solid-propellant rocket motor.

GUIDANCE: High efficiency homing.

CONTROL: Autopilot with pneumatically-driven gyros and pneumatic control surface servos.

WARHEAD: High-explosive. Weight approx 660 lb (300 kg).

DIMENSIONS:
Length overall	14 ft 7½ in (4·45 m)
Body diameter	1 ft 7¾ in (0·50 m)
Wing span	6 ft 8 in (2·04 m)

WEIGHT:
Launching weight	1,320 lb (600 kg)

PERFORMANCE:
No details available, but subsonic

Saab A 32A Lansen two-seat attack fighter armed with two RB04C air-to-surface guided missiles

SAAB

SAAB AKTIEBOLAG

HEAD OFFICE AND WORKS: Linköping

OFFICERS: see "Aircraft" section

In addition to its work on piloted aircraft, Saab is developing a modernised version of the RB04 air-to-ship missile and a new air-to-surface weapon system, designated RB05A. It has also produced in quantity a naval missile system designated RB08A.

Saab is also prime contractor for licence manufacture of two versions of the Hughes Falcon air-to-air missile. These are the RB27 (Hughes designation HM-55), with semi-active radar homing, and the RB28 (HM-58), with infra-red homing. Both versions are carried by the Saab J 35F Draken interceptors of the Swedish Air Force.

SAAB RB04E

Saab is prime contractor for development of this modernised version of the RB04 antishipping missile, on behalf of the Swedish Air Force. Three RB04Es will constitute the most important of the various alternative weapon loads that can be carried by the Saab AJ 37 Viggen attack aircraft.

A description of current versions of the RB04 appears under the "Robotavdelningen" heading in this section of *Jane's*. The modernisation undertaken by Saab on the RB04E involves changes to the missile's structure and guidance system, to increase reliability and target hit capability. The RB04E continues to utilise a solid-propellant rocket motor. No further details may be released.

Saab RB05A missiles

DIMENSIONS:
Length overall	14 ft 7½ in (4·45 m)
Body diameter	1 ft 7¾ in (0·50 m)
Wing span	6 ft 6 in (1·98 m)

WEIGHT:
Launching weight	1,320 lb (600 kg)

PERFORMANCE:
High subsonic cruising speed

SAAB RB05A

The RB05A is a manually-guided supersonic air-to-surface tactical missile for use against targets at sea or on land. It can also be used against aerial targets. Its development began in 1960, when an initial contract was received from what is now the Air Materiel Department of the Materiel Administration of the Armed Forces. It is being developed primarily for use on the AJ 37 Viggen and Sk 60 strike aircraft but can, because of its simplicity, be adapted readily for carriage by other types of aircraft.

The airframe of the RB05A is made of conventional aircraft materials and consists of a pointed cylindrical body with long-chord cruciform wings and aft-mounted cruciform control surfaces. The rocket motor is centrally mounted and is fitted with a tail-pipe which passes through the rear of the body. A solid-propellant dual-thrust motor was fitted initially, but has now been superseded by a pre-packaged liquid-propellant motor supplied by Svenska Flygmotor AB.

The warhead is located in the nose and most of the control equipment is at the rear of the missile.

After launching, the missile is guided by command signals from a pilot-operated joystick transmitted over a micro-wave radio link which is highly resistant to jamming and permits full control at low altitudes over all kinds of terrain. The technique is based on simultaneous observation of the target and the missile, the pilot guiding the weapon so that a tracking flare mounted on its rear end is kept on the line of sight to the target. The high precision of the guidance system and high manoeuvrability of the missile make it possible to attack targets which are some considerable distance to either side of the aircraft's course.

A transverse load factor of at least 10 is regarded as normal: the missile is stressed for a transverse acceleration of 20g. It is designed to be launched from aircraft flying in the speed range of Mach 0·4 to 1·4, at angles of bank up to 45°.

Guidance signals received by the missile are converted by an autopilot to control surface deflections through the medium of four gas-driven actuators, supplied by a solid-fuel gas generator. The autopilot also takes care of roll stabilisation. The roll attitude is controlled with the aid of a roll position gyro.

The very effective proximity-fuzed warhead is of a special design developed by the Swedish Research Institute of National Defence, and is manufactured under sub-contract by the National Defence Factories.

Developed versions of the RB05A fitted with a homing device are envisaged.

Equipment for assembly, testing and servicing forms part of the weapon system, as does the special launching rack on which the missile is carried and the control equipment in the aircraft. The missiles are stored fully assembled in containers, where they can be kept for three years without maintenance or testing.

Training of pilots to utilise the RB05A missile involves the use of different kinds of ground-based and airborne simulators.

DIMENSIONS:

Length	11 ft 7 in (3·52 m)
Body diameter	1 ft 0 in (0·30 m)
Wing span	2 ft 8 in (0·80 m)

WEIGHT:

Launching weight	approx 660 lb (300 kg)

SAAB RB08A

The RB08A is a ship-to-ship or surface-to-ship missile intended to provide an effective defence against invasion from the sea. It was evolved from the Nord CT.20 target drone and reached its present operational design via several intermediate development stages. The first-phase contract was awarded to Saab in 1959. An 86 million Swedish crowns development and production contract was received by Saab, as prime contractor, from the Royal Swedish Navy in 1965 and deliveries were completed by 1970.

Saab RB08A naval missiles under assembly

The RB08A is operated from coastal defence batteries and two naval destroyers (see also Aérospatiale M.20). A drawing of the installation on the destroyer *Halland* has shown how the missiles are stored below deck and transferred by ramp to the launcher immediately aft of the rear funnel.

WINGS: Mid-wing monoplane. Sweep-back 30°. Folding wings, with end-plates and spoilers.

BODY: Cylindrical body.

TAIL SURFACES: Horizontal surfaces comprise conventional tailplane and elevators, with 30° sweep-back and 41° 36′ dihedral. Fin is also swept at 30°.

POWER PLANT: Primary power plant is a Turboméca Marboré IID turbojet. Missile is launched on a carriage powered by two solid-propellant booster rockets.

GUIDANCE: Initial phase stabilised. Terminal homing.

CONTROL: Conventional aerodynamic.

WARHEAD: Special highly-effective Swedish design.

DIMENSIONS:

Length	18 ft 9 in (5·71 m)
Body diameter	2 ft 2 in (0·66 m)
Wing span	9 ft 10½ in (3·01 m)
Span, wings folded	4 ft 5 in (1·35 m)

Saab RB08A missile on ship-board launcher

WEIGHT:

Launching weight	1,985 lb (900 kg)

PERFORMANCE:
No details available.

SWITZERLAND

CONTRAVES-OERLIKON

CONTRAVES AG

ADDRESS:
Schaffhauserstrasse 580, Ch-8052 Zurich

OERLIKON MACHINE TOOL WORKS BUEHRLE & CO

ARMAMENT DIVISION: Zurich

For more than two decades the Contraves and Oerlikon companies have been collaborating in the design and development of guided missile systems on a private venture basis.

Their first major product was the Type 54 liquid-propellant surface-to-air weapon. This was followed by an improved version, designated RSD-58. A training version with parachute recovery system instead of warhead, was designated RSC-57 and was produced in Italy by Contraves Italiana, as the MTG-CI-56, for service as a training weapon at the Italian Air Force firing range on Sardinia.

In current production by Contraves Italiana (which see) is a small surface-to-surface tactical missile known as the Mosquito.

The most recent Contraves-Oerlikon weapon system of which details have been released was the surface-to-air Micon, which was described in the 1969-70 *Jane's*; further work on this system has been suspended. For information on the Zenit sounding rocket, developed jointly with Dornier System GmbH of Germany, see the "Research Rockets" section of this edition.

THE UNITED KINGDOM

BAC

BRITISH AIRCRAFT CORPORATION (HOLDINGS) LTD

HEAD OFFICE:
100, Pall Mall, London, SW1

OFFICERS:
See "Aircraft" section

Under the first stage of the reorganisation of the British Aircraft Corporation, announced in March 1963, the Corporation's guided weapons development and production facilities in English Electric Aviation, Ltd, and Bristol Aircraft, Ltd, were integrated under the management of a new wholly-owned subsidiary known as British Aircraft Corporation (Guided Weapons) Ltd.

On January 1, 1964, the entire aircraft interests of the Corporation, together with its Guided Weapons Division, were integrated into a wholly-owned subsidiary company now named simply British Aircraft Corporation Ltd, as described in the "Aircraft" section. The Guided Weapons Division remains under the management of British Aircraft Corporation (Guided Weapons) Ltd.

BAC and Fairey Engineering, Ltd, own jointly a company named British Aircraft Corporation (AT) Ltd, which took over Fairey Engineering's guided weapons activities in February 1962.

BRITISH AIRCRAFT CORPORATION (GUIDED WEAPONS) LTD

DIRECTORS:
G. R. Jefferson, CBE, BSc, CEng, MIMechE, FRAeS (Chairman and Managing Director)
E. L. Beverley, DFC, ARAeS (Commercial)
J. Cattanach, BSc, CEng (Design)
T. G. Kent, CEng, AMIMechE, AFRAeS (Production)
Lt Col H. Lacy, MBE, BSc (Asst to Chairman and Managing Director)

R. J. Raff, FCA, ACWA (Financial)
D. Rowley, MA, CEng, FRAeS (Executive Director, Electronic and Space Systems)
L. A. Sanson (Sales and Service)
A. T. Slator, MBE, MA, (General Manager, GW Division)
J. McG. Sowerby, BA, CEng, FIEE (Engineering)

SPECIAL DIRECTORS:
E. M. Dowlen, DLC, CEng, DCAe, FRAeS, AFAIAA (Guided Weapons New Project Design)
G. J. Muirhead
R. J. Parkhouse, BSc, CEng, FIProdE
S. A. Smith, MA, CEng, AFRAeS (General Manager, Bristol Works)

SECRETARY:
A. R. Adams, BSc(Econ), FCIS

In addition to its work on the guided weapons, described below, this company is playing a leading part in the design and construction of British satellites, and also produces the highly successful Skylark research rocket. Details of these activities can be found in the "Research Rockets and Space Vehicles" section.

BAC (Guided Weapons) Ltd has a total of 7,000 employees at its Stevenage and Filton works.

BAC VIGILANT

Vigilant is a lightweight one-man-portable anti-tank weapon which was developed originally by Vickers-Armstrongs (Aircraft) Ltd as a private venture, in 1956. The project was subsequently taken over by British Aircraft Corporation at their Stevenage Works and the missile system was adopted for service with the British Army in 1964. It is now in full production for infantry battalions of the British Army, as well as for the Royal Armoured Corps, who mount the missile on Ferret armoured cars. It is also in service with the defence forces of Finland and Kuwait and the National Guard of Saudi Arabia. As well as its prime infantry ground rôle, Vigilant can be mounted on and fired from a wide variety of vehicles.

An advanced velocity control system is used, with a twin-gyro autopilot, which makes the operator's task as simple as possible. Guidance is by an optical line-of-sight command control system, the commands being generated by the operator's thumb movements and transmitted by wire link. A flare is provided to assist tracking, and a monocular optical aid is used when engaging a long-range target.

Short-range capability is achieved by using flap controls rather than spoilers, enabling the missile to turn in a small radius with high manoeuvrability. After a few hours on a training simulator. the average trainee can hit a target with his first missile.

The Vigilant has a 13·2 lb (6·0 kg) warhead of the hollow-charge type and will penetrate at least 22 in (558 mm) of armour plate.

A swivelling launcher, giving a 360° arc of fire, has been developed for Vigilant.

DIMENSIONS:

Length overall	3 ft 6·2 in (1·07 m)
Body diameter	4·5 in (0·11 m)
Wing span	11 in (0·28 m)

WEIGHT:

Launching weight	31·0 lb (14·0 kg)

PERFORMANCE:

Cruising speed	302 knots (348 mph; 560 km/h)
Range	750-5,280 ft (230-1,600 m)

BAC SWINGFIRE

This wire-guided anti-tank weapon is now in service with the Royal Armoured Corps of the British Army. The first reference to it was made officially on 10 August 1962, when the Minister of Defence announced that a new weapon known as Swingfire was under development for the British Army, as an eventual replacement for the Malkara. British Aircraft Corporation (Guided Weapons) Ltd were appointed prime contractors for the weapon, at their Stevenage and Filton Works, on behalf of British Aircraft Corporation (AT) Ltd.

Swingfire was designed and developed initially by Fairey Engineering, Ltd, and probably incorporates features of this company's very advanced Orange William anti-tank missile, work on which was cancelled in 1959.

The appearance of the weapon is shown in the accompanying illustrations. At the front is the warhead, safety and arming mechanism, followed by the motor. The rear section carries cruciform wings, which fold down against the body when the missile is in its launch-tube, and houses the autopilot, wire dispenser and the gimballed motor nozzle by which the missile is steered in flight. The warhead is a hollow charge powerful enough to defeat all known combinations of armour and to destroy the heaviest battle tank.

Swingfire is stored in and launched from a disposable container which hermetically seals it up to the moment of launching. The boxes in turn are housed in armoured bins on the launch vehicle, to ensure protection from small arms and splinter damage in combat. The containers are stowed in the bins at the correct launch attitude, with automatic compensation for vehicle tilt.

The missile's name derives from the fact that it has a firing arc of 90° from a fixed launcher. Since vehicle installations require neither traversing nor elevating gear, it is easy to install the Swingfire weapon system on a wide variety of vehicles. When it is mounted on a traversing turret, targets can be engaged through a full 360° field of view.

Swingfire is claimed to offer a number of significant advances over other types of long-range wire-guided anti-tank missiles. It can be used either in a direct fire rôle or in a separated fire rôle with the operator located more than 160 ft (50 m) from the launch vehicle, which can be concealed behind cover. After launch, Swingfire is programmed automatically into the operator's field of view and is then controlled on to the target by joystick movements. It has a velocity control system. Movements of the joystick adjust the missile heading in azimuth and elevation.

For separated fire, the launch and in-flight

BAC Vigilant wire-guided anti-tank missile leaving its launcher

Swingfire wire-guided anti-tank missile on an FV438 armoured guided weapon carrier

Swingfire and launcher/container, showing foil sealing disc

control equipment is integrated in a single unit mounted on a short tripod for use by an operator in a prone position. It comprises a sight, right-hand joystick and left-hand firing button. Alternative open sighting or 10x magnification are available. Elevating and traversing the sight generates signals which are fed by cable to the programme generator.

The weapon system will be readily adaptable to automatic guidance systems when these are sufficiently developed to offer an improvement over the weapon's current capability. Maximum range is more than 9,800 ft (3,000 m), with a minimum range of less than 500-1,000 ft (150-300 m), depending on whether the operator is sited adjacent to the launcher or separated from it. This short-range target engagement is made possible by a slow launch acceleration and the ability to exercise control from the moment of launch.

Swingfire is in operational service with Royal Armoured Corps units of the British Army,

mounted on a modified FV432 armoured personnel carrier, redesignated FV438. It is also being mounted on the FV712 Ferret scout car and can be installed on a wide variety of other vehicles.

A simple palletised version has been developed to enable missiles to be fired from unmodified load-carrying vehicles and from the ground. In this form, Swingfire is readily air-transportable by both fixed and rotating-wing aircraft.

An air-to-surface version of Swingfire, suitable for launching from helicopters with the aid of a stabilised sight, is being considered for development.

DIMENSIONS:

Length overall	3 ft 6 in (1·07 m)
Max body diameter	6·7 in (0·17 m)
Wing span	14·7 in (0·37 m)

BAC BLOODHOUND
Swedish Air Force designation (Mk 2): RB68

The RAF began to equip with Bloodhound Mk 1 in mid-1958. This version became the RAF's standard home-based surface-to-air guided weapon system, until replaced by the Bloodhound Mk 2, which has a greatly improved performance and is air transportable so that it can be used to reinforce overseas commands. Since the Autumn of 1964, Mk 2 weapons have also been deployed in Singapore. After the projected withdrawal of British Forces from the Far East, these weapon systems will be taken over from the RAF by the Singapore Government. BAC have a contract worth about £10 million for refurbishing and modification of the systems, supply of spares, after-sales services and training of local personnel to operate and maintain the systems.

Mk 1 Bloodhounds were also ordered by Sweden and Australia, while Mk 2 Bloodhounds were ordered in substantial numbers by Switzerland and Sweden. The Swedish system is in a mobile form. Bloodhound has been operational in Switzerland since 1964 and in Sweden since 1965.

Compared with Bloodhound Mk 1, the Mk 2 has more powerful Thor ramjet engines, more

Bloodhound Mk 2 of No. 65 Squadron, RAF, in Far East (*S. P. Peltz*)

Thunderbird Mk 2 surface-to-air missile on launcher

powerful Bristol Aerojet boosters, greater range, better lethality, CW (continuous wave) radar guidance and greater effectiveness at lower altitudes. Trials have shown an interception capability against fast targets at altitudes below 1,000 ft (300 m).

Two CW target-illuminating radars were developed for Bloodhound Mk 2. They are the vehicle-mounted Ferranti Firelight and the longer-range GEC/AEI Scorpion, which can be air-lifted but is more suitable for static sites.

The launcher incorporates its own hydraulic and pneumatic power supplies, and the launch control post is housed in a small air-transportable cabin.

The following details refer specifically to the Bloodhound Mk 2.

TYPE: Surface-to-air land-based guided weapon system.

WINGS: Pivoting mid-wing monoplane type, of double-wedge cross-section, mounted about the CG of the missile. Wings can pivot either together or differentially, providing complete two-axis control, the missile being of the twist-and-steer type.

BODY: Main body is a monocoque structure with light alloy skin, cast magnesium frames and light alloy longerons.

TAIL SURFACES: Fixed mid-set surfaces, of constant chord, in line with wing, at rear end of body.

POWER PLANT: Two Rolls-Royce Bristol Thor ramjets, mounted above and below rear part of body. Kerosene fuel in flexible rubber tank in fore part of body, externally pressurised by ram air from the rear. Four jettisonable solid-propellant wrap-around boosters, with built-on stabilising fins.

GUIDANCE: Semi-active homing type. Receiver in nose picks up reflected radiation from target when latter is illuminated by ground radar. Ferranti Firelight or GEC/AEI Scorpion target-illuminating radar.

WARHEAD: High-explosive with proximity fuse.

DIMENSIONS:

Length with boosters	27 ft 9 in (8·46 m)
Body length	25 ft 2 in (7·67 m)
Max body diameter	1 ft 9½ in (0·546 m)
Wing span	9 ft 3·48 in (2·83 m)

WEIGHTS:
No details available.

PERFORMANCE:
Range   more than 43 nm (50 miles; 80 km)

BAC THUNDERBIRD Mks 1 and 2

Thunderbird is a solid-propellant surface-to-air weapon with semi-active radar homing. The weapon system is entirely mobile, including its power generators and field workshops, and may be transported by air or in standard Army vehicles.

Nos 36 and 37 Anti-Aircraft Regiments of the Royal Artillery were first equipped with Thunderbird Mk 1 in 1960. Their training began at Manorbier, Pembrokeshire, in June 1959 and both Regiments were fully trained by the end of 1960, for services in overseas theatres. No 36 was stationed in Germany and No 37 in the UK.

Each regiment had an establishment of two

batteries, each with eight missile launchers and associated radars and vehicles.

The improved Thunderbird Mk 2 was developed to give increased range, improved low-altitude cover and great resistance to countermeasures, together with improved mobility and air transportability. Like Bloodhound Mk 2, it can utilise either Ferranti Firelight or AEI Scorpion CW target-illuminating radar. Other changes include improved rocket propellants and motor design, the use of larger boosters and tapering of the wing trailing-edges.

Acceptance trials were completed by mid-1964, and Thunderbird Mk 2 began replacing the Mk 1 missiles of No. 36 Regiment at the end of 1965. More recently, Nos 36 and 37 Regiments have been amalgamated to form one large Regiment (No 36), based in the UK but exercising regularly in Germany with the Thunderbird Mk 2.

A quantity of surplus Mk 1 Thunderbirds were delivered to Saudi Arabia in August 1966 and became operational later that year. The planned use of Thunderbird and Rapier missiles by the Libyan armed forces was abandoned following overthrow of the monarchy in that country and a complete revision of its defence programmes.

Details of the Thunderbird 22 air defence system are given separately. The following details refer to Thunderbird 2.

TYPE: Surface-to-air land-based guided weapon.

WINGS: Fixed cruciform wings with 45° sweepback on leading-edges, mounted well back on body. Each machined from piece of light alloy.

BODY: Light alloy stressed-skin tubular structure fabricated in sections from sheet with cast end fittings. Sections are joined by means of quick-release manacle rings.

TAIL SURFACES: Pivoted cruciform tail surfaces of tapered planform, on rear end of body, indexed in line with wings. Each machined from single piece of light alloy.

POWER PLANT: One solid-propellant sustainer in body. Four solid-propellant boosters wrapped around rear part of body, each with large stabilising fin.

GUIDANCE: Semi-active homing.

WARHEAD: High-explosive with proximity fuse.

DIMENSIONS:

Length overall	20 ft 10 in (6·35 m)
Body diameter	1 ft 8¾ in (0·53 m)
Wing span	5 ft 4 in (1·626 m)

WEIGHTS AND PERFORMANCE:
No details available.

BAC THUNDERBIRD 22

Thunderbird 22 is the name given by British Aircraft Corporation to the comprehensive air defence system that they are marketing overseas.

Facilities provided by the complete system include detection and identification of friendly or hostile aircraft, threat evaluation, engagement of low-level and medium-level attacks by Rapier batteries, engagement of medium-level and high-level attacks by Thunderbird batteries and GCI control of fighter aircraft. The units of the system are linked by a comprehensive command communications network.

Operational centre of the system is the Plessey

Radar/Elliott-Automation Nomad missile and fighter control centre. This is a complex data-processing and data-display arrangement built round a high-capacity digital computer. Data inputs to the system come from Marconi tactical control/early warning radar and height-finding radar and from an associated secondary radar (IFF) interrogator responsor and decoder. This information is presented on displays that permit the semi-automatic tracking of targets; and the resultant tracks for hostile targets are stored by the computer and processed to provide advisory information to enable the air defence commander to decide how to meet the threat.

In presenting this information the computer draws on other stored (and periodically updated) data such as weapon availability and state of readiness or interceptor performance and availability.

When the engagement decision is taken, control of the engagement is assumed either by the surface-to-air missile control centre or by the fighter control centre as appropriate. Both centres are located in the Nomad complex and are served by the same radar and computer system; but in other respects their functions and procedures are similar to those of independent GCI or missile control centres (such as the battery command post of Thunderbird 2) except insofar as procedures prior to the engagement decision are concerned.

BAC RAPIER

On 4 September 1964 it was announced that BAC had been awarded a contract for design and development of the ET.316 low-level anti-aircraft guided weapon system, which was subsequently given the name Rapier. The development work was carried out in the Corporation's Guided Weapons Division, at the Bristol and Stevenage works, with such success that BAC was able to announce in June 1967 that production of the weapon for operational use by the British Army and Royal Air Force Regiment had begun. It has been ordered also by the Imperial Iranian Government, whose £47 million contracts, announced in June 1970, cover also technical, maintenance and training support by BAC.

Rapier is a lightweight, highly mobile and low-cost system. With a missile speed in excess of Mach 2 and a very fast reaction time, it can engage helicopters, subsonic and supersonic aircraft from ground level up to several thousand metres, with a high kill probability. It can operate independently or, with suitable planning and communications, in conjunction with other air defence systems.

Main operational units of the system are a launcher trailer, an optical tracker and a power unit. These three units can be disposed in any convenient manner, according to terrain, interconnection being by cable. Once the launcher has been loaded with its four missiles (a two-man job) it can be left unattended and the system operated by one man at the tracker until the missiles have all been fired.

In addition to the missile launch mechanism, the launcher trailer contains a surveillance radar, an IFF interrogator, a hydraulic power pack, a computer and a command transmitter.

When the surveillance radar detects a target the IFF automatically interrogates it to determine whether it is friendly or hostile. If the target is friendly all data on it is cancelled and the radar resumes its search; if it is hostile the tracker operator is alerted by an aural alarm and radar data is used to direct the tracker and the launcher on to the target bearing. The operator carries out a search in elevation, acquires the target optically, and begins to track it, using a joystick control. The launcher follows the tracker in bearing and elevation.

Target position information is processed by the computer and when the target is within system coverage the operator is informed by a lamp signal at the edge of his field of view. He immediately launches a missile.

While the missile flies towards the target the operator continues tracking. A television camera in the tracker, collimated to the tracking telescope, detects flares mounted in the missile tail and measures any deviation from the sightline. These measurements are fed to the computer in the launcher trailer which then causes the command transmitter to transmit correction signals automatically to the missile, in order to bring it on to the tracker/target sightline and maintain it there. Thus the missile is automatically commanded to fly down the optical sightline to impact with the target. It has no proximity fuse.

In normal operational use, the launcher trailer is towed by a long-wheelbase Land-Rover which also carries the tracker, radio equipment, four missiles in sealed containers, and three members of the detachment. A second Land-Rover tows a missile supply trailer carrying nine missiles, also in sealed containers, together with additional equipment and two of the detachment.

The generator set comprises a four-cylinder liquid-cooled petrol engine, driving an alternator. The complete assembly is mounted in a tubular cradle and enclosed in a weatherproof metal casing. Two pneumatic-tyred wheels facilitate ground handling and a pivoted handle is fitted to the forward end. For transit, the wheels are removed and stowed, and the generator set is locked on to a bracket at the rear of the launcher.

For continuous operation the normal detachment strength is five men; but three can deploy and man the system and only one man at a time is needed to operate it after loading. A complete system can be transported in a Chinook helicopter. Alternatively, the launcher can be lifted tactically by a Wessex helicopter, with the tracker, missiles and detachment following as a second lift.

BAC make a special simulator for operator training. They also supply a range of specially equipped repair vehicles for maintaining the system. One of these, the forward repair test vehicle, is a Land-Rover equipped with automatic test equipment suitable for all first-line testing. Two larger vehicles are available for second-line work—one for the electrical and electronic equipment and the other for the optics and hydraulics.

The first firing against a live target was made on 27 April 1967, when a Meteor jet-powered drone, flying at an altitude of 3,000 ft (900 m) at a distance of 10,000 ft (3,000 m) from the Rapier launcher, was destroyed by a direct hit. On a subsequent occasion, a Rapier scored a direct hit on a Rushton towed target, 7 ft (2·13 m) long and 7½ in (19 cm) in diameter, crossing at an altitude of 2,000 ft (610 m) and range of 10,000 ft (3,000 m). The trials programme has since been concluded satisfactorily, and service operators have proved their ability to handle the system and destroy targets.

Further development of the system is planned. The main limitation of the original system is imposed by the need for reasonable visibility conditions for optical target tracking. To overcome this difficulty, BAC have been developing, in conjunction with Elliott Space and Weapon Automation, a radar that will provide guidance when optical tracking is impossible.

The radar tracking system will permit engagement of targets in darkness and poor visibility.

BAC Rapier tracker (foreground) with fire unit in background

BAC Rapier low-level anti-aircraft weapon system fire unit

It will be offered as an "add-on" feature for standard Rapier equipments, so that both optical and radar guidance capability are available.

Design studies have shown that Rapier can be mounted successfully on a variety of tracked armoured vehicles, such as the FV432, M113 and the new German APC Marder. Arrangements are in hand to mount the optical tracker semi-permanently in the launcher-towing Land-Rover. This will enable the tracker to be used from the vehicle, so reducing the "into-action" time and affording weather protection to both tracker and operator. During mobile operations, the tracker will remain mounted in the Land-Rover but, if required, it will be possible to release the modified carrying and handling frame quickly and position the tracker on its tripod in the normal way.

In early 1970, Rapier was scheduled soon to enter service with both the British Army and the Royal Air Force Regiment.

DIMENSIONS:

Launcher: length	13 ft 4 in (4·06 m)
Width	5 ft 8½ in (1·74 m)
Height	5 ft 11½ in (1·82 m)
Missile: length	7 ft 3 in (2·21 m)
Span of wings	1 ft 3 in (0·38 m)
Body diameter	5 in (0·13 m)

BAC SEA WOLF

In the British government's Statement on Defence Estimates in 1967, it was announced that a new close-range surface-to-air guided weapon, designated PX 430, was under development as the next-generation Seacat-type missile for the Royal Navy. In June 1967, BAC's Guided Weapons Division received the contract for design of the PX 430, which was subsequently given the name Sea Wolf. Marconi are contractors for the surveillance radars, target tracking radar, missile gathering and guidance television, data handling and display equipment and command and guidance communications, as well as for management and co-ordination of development of the complete ship-borne system. Vickers are developing the launching system.

Sea Wolf is intended to give ships a greatly improved defensive capability against supersonic anti-ship missiles and aircraft in the 1970's and will be an all-weather weapon. It is also being designed for a surface-to-surface rôle against ships and hovercraft. No other details may be published, except that once a target has been identified as hostile, all phases of the launch and guidance sequence will be carried out automatically, without further manual control.

BAC (AT)
BRITISH AIRCRAFT CORPORATION (AT) LTD

HEAD OFFICE:
100, Pall Mall, London SW1
This company was formed jointly by Fairey Engineering, Ltd, and British Aircraft Corporation in February 1962 to take over Fairey Engineering's guided weapon activities, including development and production of the Swingfire anti-tank missile of which all available details are given in the BAC entry.

As the Australian Government s delegated authority in the United Kingdom for the Malkara anti-tank weapon, it assisted in introducing this missile into service with the British Army.

BAC (AT) is, similarly, the European agent for the Australian Government's Jindivik pilotless target aircraft, and is responsible for assembly, repair and maintenance of Jindiviks used by the Ministry of Technology at target ranges in the United Kingdom.

HSD
HAWKER SIDDELEY DYNAMICS LTD

HEADQUARTERS:
Manor Road, Hatfield, Herts

DIRECTORS:
Sir Arnold Hall, FRS (Chairman)
J. T. Lidbury, FRAeS (Deputy Chairman)
J. F. Robertson, CA

A Stewart Kennedy
G. C. I. Gardiner, CBE, CEng, FRAeS, FIMechE (Managing Director)
M. G. Ash, MBE, FCA (Deputy Managing Director)
G. H. Hough, PhD, CBE, BSc, FRAeS, FIEE (Deputy Managing Director)
Air Chief Marshal Sir Harry Broadhurst, GCB, KBE, DSO, DFC, AFC

C. R. Burgess, MBE, FRAeS, CEng (Sales Director)
J. D. Crane, FCA (Commercial Director)
R. G. Dancey, BA, TD (Personnel Director)
E. D. Dettmer, DFC (Marketing Director)
P. R. Franks, BSc, MSc, FRAeS, MIEE (Technical Director, Electronics)
H. Fuchs, BSc, PhD, CEng, FRAeS, MAIAA, FBIS (Director & Divisional Manager, GW Equipment and Systems)

S. H. Lines, MBE (Works Director)
A. S. Wheate, CA (Financial Director)
C. T. Wilkins (Director & Divisional Manager,
   Space Launchers and Satellites)
PUBLIC RELATIONS MANAGER:
M. K. Hird

HSD air-to-air missiles:
Above: **Firestreaks mounted on a Lightning missile pack**
Right: **Red Tops**

This subsidiary of the Hawker Siddeley Group came into being as a consequence of the reorganisation of the Group on 1 July 1963. It is responsible for the design, development and production of all Hawker Siddeley guided weapons, space-launch vehicles, satellites, propellers, air-conditioning systems, electronic fuel control systems, alternators and static inverter power supply systems, hydraulic and pneumatic systems, automatic check-out systems (TRACE), and electrical and electronic systems.

The company is prime contractor for the Sea Dart ship-to-air/ship-to-surface missile, and has developed jointly with Engins Matra of France the Martel long-range air-to-surface weapon (see "International" section). Both missiles have entered their production phase. Sea Dart will enter service first with the Royal Navy on the new Type 82 destroyer, and Martel will serve with the British and French armed forces.

Hawker Siddeley Dynamics is the British "daughter firm" for the Australian-developed Ikara long-range anti-submarine weapon ordered for the Royal Navy (see Australian section). It also has a major contract for the overhaul and repair of NATO Nike-Ajax and Nike-Hercules missiles.

New projects include a study for Taildog, a highly manoeuvrable short-range air-to-air weapon, and the development and manufacture of an infra-red linescan system which has been ordered for the CL-89 surveillance drone being produced under a joint British, Canadian and West German programme.

In February 1970, it was announced that Hawker Siddeley Dynamics had signed a licence agreement to supply TRW of Redondo Beach, California, with extensive information on tactical guided weapons and systems. It is the third such licence granted to TRW, previous agreements being associated with infra-red technology.

HSD FIRESTREAK

Firestreak is a rear-hemisphere infra-red homing air-to-air weapon which is in service with the RAF and Royal Navy, as standard armament on Hawker Siddeley Sea Vixen and BAC Lightning aircraft.

It has a cylindrical metal body, cruciform wings, and cruciform tail control surfaces indexed in line with the wings. Propulsion is by a solid-propellant rocket motor. The infra-red unit is housed behind a nose-cone made up of flat glass panels. Control is by a proportional navigation system.

In operation, Firestreak is brought close to the target by the infra-red guidance system in its nose. Two rings of infra-red optics mounted further back on the body of the missile then lock on to the target and feed in two continuous series of angular readings to give its bearing and range during the final interception. In this way the 50 lb (22·7 kg) warhead can be detonated at a predetermined range.

A success rate of over 85% is said to have been achieved regularly in trials by the RAF and Royal Navy under all conditions.

Firestreak can be fitted to virtually any interceptor by mounting under the aircraft's fuselage a small "weapon package" in a streamlined container, containing firing equipment that is carried inside the fuselage of the Sea Vixen and Lightning.

DIMENSIONS:
Length overall	10 ft 5½ in (3·19 m)
Body diameter	8¾ in (22·5 cm)
Wing span	2 ft 5½ in 0·75 m)

WEIGHT:
Launching weight	300 lb (136 kg)

PERFORMANCE:
Cruising speed	above Mach 2
Range	0·65-4·3 nm (0·75-5 miles; 1·2-8 km)

HSD RED TOP

Although similar in basic configuration to the Firestreak, and known originally as Firestreak Mk IV, this second-generation infra-red homing air-to-air weapon is radically new and offers greatly enhanced capabilities. It equips the BAC Lightning F.Mk 3 and 6 and T.Mk 5 and Hawker Siddeley Sea Vixen (FAW) Mk 2, on which Firestreaks may also be carried.

Externally apparent changes include wings and control surfaces of increased size and revised shape, for improved manoeuvrability at all altitudes, and a hemispherical nose over the completely new infra-red guidance unit. Weight of the warhead is increased to 68 lb (31 kg).

Internally, the warhead has been moved forward, next to the fuzing system, and the control actuators have been moved aft next to the triangular tail surfaces which they drive. A more powerful rocket motor is fitted and Red Top offers the advantages of interception from any direction, including collision course, whereas Firestreak is a pursuit course weapon.

DIMENSIONS:
Length overall	11 ft 5·7 in (3·50 m)
Body diameter	8¾ in (22·5 cm)
Wing span	2 ft 11¾ in (0·91 m)

WEIGHT:
Not available

PERFORMANCE:
Cruising speed	Mach 3
Range	6 nm (7 miles; 11 km)

HSD/MATRA AJ.168/AS.37 MARTEL

See International section, on page 594.

HSD TAILDOG

Combat experience in Vietnam and other war theatres has emphasised the need for an air-to-air missile which can deal with highly manoeuvring targets when other types of armament would be ineffective. Taildog is the name given to the proposed new missile, which would be complementary to long-range weapons like Red Top.

The project definition phase, funded jointly by the UK Government and Hawker Siddeley, had been completed by early 1970, and the development phase was about to begin. This phase, too, will be jointly funded.

Taildog is being designed from the outset for high reliability, low cost and capability of being installed easily on any type of interceptor or air superiority fighter, strike or reconnaissance aircraft without requiring aircraft modification. Its general appearance is shown in the accompanying illustration.

HSD SEASLUG

Seaslug remains in service on twin launchers on the Royal Navy's "County" class of fleet escort super-destroyers. It is the only long-range guided weapon in use by the RN and the original Mk 1 version achieved a success ratio of 90% against fast high-flying and low-flying target drones, including Canberra U.Mk 10 aircraft at heights in excess of 50,000 ft (15,250 m) during its firing trials.

The Mk 2 version of Seaslug now in service offers longer range, better performance against low-level targets and surface-to-surface capabilities.

TYPE: Surface-to-air and surface-to-surface shipborne guided missile.

WINGS: Fixed cruciform wings of light alloy mounted more than half-way back on body.

BODY: Cylindrical light alloy construction.

TAIL SURFACES: Pivoted cruciform tail surfaces at rear end, indexed in line with wings, are machined light alloy forgings.

POWER PLANT: One ICI solid-propellant sustainer in body. Four solid-propellant boosters wrapped around forward part of body, with blunt noses to assist separation.

GUIDANCE: Beam-riding, provided by ship-borne radar Type 901M. Main contractors are The General Electric Co (guidance) and Sperry Gyroscope Co (control).

WARHEAD: High-explosive with proximity fuse.

DIMENSIONS:
Length overall	20 ft 0 in (6·10 m)
Body diameter	1 ft 4·1 in (0·41 m)
Wing span	4 ft 8·6 in (1·438 m)
Span of tail	5 ft 6·6 in (1·69 m)

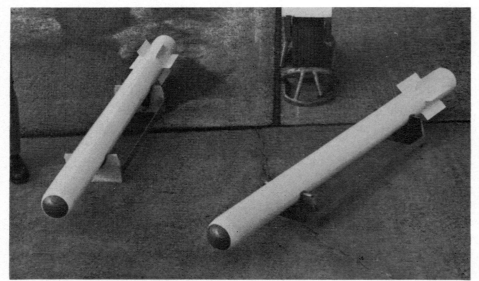

Two mock-up models of the Hawker Siddeley Dynamics Taildog close-range air-to-air missile

Seaslug long-range ship-to-air missile being launched from HMS *Kent*

Hawker Siddeley Sea Dart

WEIGHTS AND PERFORMANCE:
No details available

HSD SEA DART (CF.299)

First news of the development programme for the Sea Dart (originally CF.299) ship-to-air weapon system was given by the British Minister of Defence on 10 August 1962. He stated that it is suitable for installation in ships smaller than those needed to accommodate the Seaslug system but offers an all-round improvement in performance over the earlier weapon. It is an area-defence weapon, capable of intercepting aircraft at both very high and extremely low altitudes, and air- and surface-launched missiles. It is also effective against surface vessels and a helicopter-transportable land-based version is being developed by HSD as a private venture.

Launch-rate is rapid and the weapon system is able to cope simultaneously with many targets.

Sea Dart is a tandem two-stage weapon, with between-stage vents through which the Rolls-Royce Bristol Odin ramjet exhausts before the IMI solid-propellant booster separates.

The body is cylindrical, with a nose intake for the ramjet. Four interferometer aerials surround the intake and are of a new and advanced type equal to a large dish antenna, and overcoming past drawbacks of the interferometer type of antenna. The long-chord cruciform wings and tail control surfaces are indexed in line, as are the forward-folding booster fins. Guidance is by radar semi-active homing, using the Tracker Illuminator Radar Type 909.

Missile systems and warhead are disposed concentrically around the straight-through ramjet duct. Thus, the GEC electronic control system is built in wrap-round form as an integral part of the missile structure but is detachable for servicing.

The ship-borne surveillance radar is by Hollandse Signaalapparaten, small ship control radar by AEI, onboard control system by Sperry, guidance system and test equipment by GEC, surface computer for target selection, data handling, missile launch and in-flight control by Ferranti, twin-round launcher and automatic magazine and loading system by Vickers and proximity fuse by EMI.

Weights and performance figures for Sea Dart are secret, but it is reported to have a range of $14\frac{3}{4}$-$19\frac{1}{2}$ nm (17-22$\frac{1}{2}$ miles; 27-36 km). Test firings began in 1965 and the first production order was announced on 3 November 1967.

Sea Dart will equip the Royal Navy's new Types 82 and 42 guided missile destroyers, each of which will have a twin launcher. The first section of HMS *Sheffield*, first of the Type 42 ships, was laid down in January 1970. HMS *Bristol*, the only Type 82 ship ordered so far, was laid down in November 1967.

Sea Dart will also arm the two Type 42 destroyers ordered for the Argentine Navy in 1970.

DIMENSIONS:
Length overall	14 ft 3½ in (4·36 m)
Body diameter	1 ft 4½ in (0·42 m)
Max span	3 ft 0 in (0·91 m)

SHORT
SHORT BROTHERS AND HARLAND LTD

HEAD OFFICE AND WORKS:
PO Box 241, Queen's Island, Belfast 3, N Ireland

OFFICERS: See "Aircraft" section

Shorts' Missile Systems Division at Castlereagh, Belfast, was responsible for development of the Seacat surface-to-air missile, which has been in large-scale production for the Royal Navy and other customers for many years. A variant known as Tigercat is also in production as a replacement for light guns used by land forces, and an air-to-surface version called Hellcat is under development. Together, Seacat and Tigercat have been sold to 20 user services in 17 nations, and are expected to remain in production into the late 1970's.

The British government has supported continued development of Shorts' man-portable supersonic missile, the Blowpipe, to meet a British Army and Royal Navy requirement for a small anti-aircraft defence weapon. Blowpipe will enter volume production during 1971.

SHORT SEACAT
Swedish Navy designation: RB07

In production and service as the Royal Navy's standard short-range anti-aircraft armament, the Seacat is a small and highly-manoeuvrable weapon for which Shorts were awarded an initial contract in April 1958. A typical launcher, shown in the adjacent illustration, carries four Seacats.

The Royal Navy is using three different fire-control systems. One is the relatively simple Mk 20 visual director, fitted originally on HMS *Decoy* during Seacat trials and now installed in a number of vessels, including the assault ships *Fearless* and *Intrepid* and the destroyers *Caprice* and *Cavalier*. The Mk 21 and Mk 22 radar systems are fitted in a dual installation on the County class of fleet escort super-destroyers, on which Seacat is secondary armament, and singly on Battle and Leander class vessels. Seacat will also arm the new Amazon class frigates, scheduled to enter service in 1973/75.

Seacat has also been ordered for ships of the Royal Australian, Royal New Zealand, Royal

Seacat being fired from HMAS *Yarra*, **third Royal Australian Navy ship to have this weapon system**

Netherlands, Royal Swedish, Chilean, Brazilian, Argentinian, Imperial Iranian, Royal Malaysian, Federal German, Indian, Libyan and Venezuelan Navies. The version operated by the Swedish and Chilean Navies uses an M4/3 radar system produced by NV Hollandse Signaalapparaten of the Netherlands. The Argentine Navy uses a fire control system produced by Nuova San Giorgio, of Genoa, Italy. Australia and Brazil use the Mk 20 director, New Zealand uses the Mk 21 and Mk 22. A number of other directors are in course of development and installation, including one which uses a closed-circuit television aiming system.

A lightweight Seacat missile system, for the defence of small craft such as 100 ft (30 m) fast patrol boats and minesweepers, completed its first live firing test successfully in the Solent in late 1969. Weighing about half as much as the standard four-round system, it utilises a three-round launcher in conjunction with standard Seacat missiles.

During an attack on a ship fitted with a basic Seacat system, the missile aimer, acting on target position information received via the intercommunication system, acquires the target. Binoculars mounted on the head of the manually-operated pedestal director form a combined director and missile aiming sight. When the target comes within range, the aimer starts the firing sequence which fires a missile from the launcher two seconds later.

At a range of approximately 1,000 ft (300 m) the missile appears in the aimer's sight and is guided visually along the line of sight to the target. Fin-mounted flares ensure that the missile is visible all the way. The aimer flies the missile along the line of sight to the target by means of a thumb-operated flight controller. The shipborne guidance and control system translates the flight controller movements into radio commands and transmits them, via an aerial on the top of the launcher, to the missile.

The Seacat system may be employed as an independent weapon or to supplement other armament. Used in conjunction with a fire-control system it offers the added facilities of automatic target acquisition and auto-tracking.

In 1969, Shorts stated that trials had been completed successfully with a system that replaces the optical sighting binocular with a closed-circuit television (CCTV) system produced by Marconi as the 323 series. This enables the aimer to be sited in a much less vulnerable position, and also results in important improvements in efficiency. Further development now in progress includes the use of CCTV for automatic missile tracking operations.

TYPE: Surface-to-air and surface-to-surface close-range weapon.

WINGS: Movable sharply sweptback cruciform wings to provide control in pitch and yaw.

BODY: Basically cylindrical-section all-metal structure, with widened square-section forepart at wing roots.

TAIL SURFACES: Fixed cruciform tail surfaces of rectangular planform, mounted at rear of missile and indexed at 45° to wings. Two carry flares at their tips.

POWER PLANT: Two-stage IMI solid-propellant.

GUIDANCE: Visual or radar command by radio link.

CONTROL SYSTEMS (Royal Navy Seacats): Mark 20: two men accommodated in director unit. One rotates the director so that the second man (the aimer) can pick up the target visually and follow it through binoculars. Launcher is linked in azimuth and elevation with director, so the missile rapidly enters aimer's view field after firing. Aimer guides it on to target by movements of a miniature joystick. Mark 21 and Mark 22: provide radar auto-follow of target, permitting both visual and "dark" firing.

CONTROL SYSTEM (RSwN Seacats): M4/3 one-man radar-controlled director, by NV Hollandse Signaalapparaten, for both visual and "dark" firing.

CONTROL SYSTEM (Argentine Navy): Seacats are integrated with a new fire control system developed by Nuova San Giorgio of Genoa to control both the Seacat launcher and the cruiser's 5-in guns.

WARHEAD: Large high-explosive type, with both contact and proximity fuse.

DIMENSIONS:
Length overall	4 ft 10·3 in (1·48 m)
Body diameter	7·5 in (19·05 cm)
Wing span	2 ft 1·6 in (0·64 m)

WEIGHTS AND PERFORMANCE:
No details available.

The thumb-operated flight controller used with the lightweight version of the Seacat weapon system

SHORT TIGERCAT

This land-based version of Seacat has been ordered for the Royal Air Force Regiment, the Imperial Iranian Air Force, the Jordan Arab Army, Qatar and other customers, and is being evaluated by several countries for the defence of airfields and other land bases. It employs the command link guidance technique perfected for Seacat and can be operated independently or in combination with an existing gunnery system.

Tigercat can be deployed as either a static or mobile defence system. In the mobile mode, the three-round launcher/trailer and the director trailer, with optical sight and launch control gear, are towed by two Land-Rovers or similar vehicles. These also transport the crew, extra missiles, generator and other items, and form the basic fire unit. The Tigercat missile itself is identical with Seacat.

SHORT HELLCAT

Hellcat is a proposed air-launched derivative of the Seacat and Tigercat systems, and uses the same missile. Since Seacat is already the standard ship-to-air and ship-to-ship missile of many navies throughout the world, Hellcat offers considerable savings in procurement spares, maintenance and training costs and, when used on shipborne helicopters, savings in valuable magazine space on board ship. It can be carried by most types of helicopter, and the adjacent illustrations show a typical installation on the Westland Wasp HAS. Mk 1. Hellcat enables these aircraft to attack effectively surface targets such as fast patrol boats, surfaced submarines, hovercraft, road convoys and trains.

Two missiles and their launching beams are mounted on either side of the helicopter on pylons slung from hinged tubular support frames attached to fuselage strong-points. The missiles are

The Tigercat director trailer which houses the missile aimer and all control equipment

Short Tigercat mobile land-based anti-aircraft missile system

Seacat missile leaving lightweight three-round launcher

selected, fired and controlled along the aimer's line-of-sight to the target. The aimer has a gyro-stabilised sight mounted on the cockpit roof through which he views the target and missile. He maintains the two in apparent coincidence until impact by means of demands from a thumb-operated controller which are conveyed to the missile through the radio link.

The controller, which also accommodates the missile selector and firing switch, is mounted on a telescopic tube pivoted off the aimer's seat. A master switch panel is positioned next to the aimer. Other airborne components of the system are the sight amplifier, firing sequence unit, command link shaping and transmitter units. These are all mounted on a common frame and can be rapidly removed, enabling the helicopter's role to be changed quickly. A folding Yagi aerial is fitted on the nose of the helicopter.

One or both missiles can be jettisoned by the pilot or the aimer at any time.

SHORT BLOWPIPE (including SLAM)

Blowpipe is a man-portable supersonic missile system based, like the Seacat and Tigercat, on the command link guidance system. It can be carried by a paratrooper, fired from the shoulder, and air-dropped in a multi-round pack. The system comprises only the missile itself, the canister which serves both for transport and as a launching platform, and the aiming unit attached to the canister, which contains all of the ground equip-

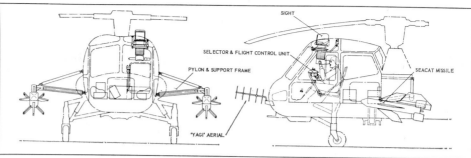

Diagram showing Hellcat, the air-launched version of Seacat, mounted on a Westland Wasp

Firing a Blowpipe man-portable missile

ment. Weight of the complete weapon system, including one Blowpipe missile, is less than 40 lb (18 kg).

Blowpipe can be fired from the ground or from stationary vehicles and can be converted from its transport configuration to operational readiness in 20 seconds. The missile, in its canister, is supported on the operator's shoulder. A monocular sight and thumb joystick are used to guide the missile to its target.

The Blowpipe missile has a slim cylindrical body and pointed ogival nose-cone. Cruciform delta-shape foreplane control surfaces are mounted on the nose-cone and a unique type of cruciform

delta tail-fin assembly is used. It consists of a sliding ring structure, which is positioned near the foreplanes when the missile is in its launch-tube. This enables the diameter of the main part of the tube to be kept down to little more than that of the missile body. As the missile leaves the tube, during launch, the tail-fins engage and lock in place. The larger diameter of the fore-part of the launch-tube is governed by the span of the tail-fin assembly, of which the folding tips flip open on leaving the tube. An infra-red-actuated proximity fuse is fitted.

Firing trials of Blowpipe began in 1965 and advanced development is now being supported by the British government, to meet a British Army and Royal Navy requirement for a small

anti-aircraft defence weapon. The system has been fired successfully from the shoulder by Army personnel. In addition, the Vickers Shipbuilding Group's **SLAM** (Submarine Launched Air Missile) system, based on the Blowpipe missile, had completed preliminary trials by January 1970. Full firing trials for the prototype SLAM missile launcher system were planned for mid-1970, to be followed closely by sea trials.

Other multiple launchers for use on board ships, land vehicles and helicopters, are being developed simultaneously with the basic infantry-man's system.

DIMENSIONS:
Length overall	4 ft 5·1 in (1·35 m)
Body diameter	3 in (7·60 cm)
Span of tail-fins	10·8 in (27·4 cm)

THE UNITED STATES OF AMERICA

BENDIX
THE BENDIX CORPORATION

HEAD OFFICE:
Bendix Center, Southfield, Michigan 48075
CHAIRMAN AND PRESIDENT:
A. P. Fontaine
AEROSPACE SYSTEMS DIVISION-MISHAWAKA
OPERATIONS:
Mishawaka, Indiana
ASSISTANT GENERAL MANAGER: Edmund F. Lapham
PUBLIC RELATIONS MANAGER: William M. Piecuch

Many of the operating divisions of The Bendix Corporation are engaged on missile development and production.

The Aerospace Systems Division is prime contractor for the highly-successful Talos surface-to-air weapon.

The Navigation and Control Division is responsible for the guidance system of the Pershing solid-propellant ballistic missile. The Communications Division produces Talos guidance equipment and radar for fighter and missile control. The company has also supplied electronic or hydraulic systems for the Atlas and Titan ICBM's, Polaris, Nike Hercules, Terrier and Tartar surface-to-air missiles and the USAF's Samos reconnaissance satellites, and the stable platform for the inertial guidance system of the Saturn launch vehicle.

TALOS
US Military designations: RIM-8-G-AAW and RGM-8-H-ARM

Like the RIM-2 Terrier, Talos resulted from the Bumblebee research programme, initiated by the Applied Physics Laboratory of Johns Hopkins University in 1944. The Bendix Corporation's Aerospace Systems Division at Mishawaka, Indiana, is prime contractor, with production continuing in 1970.

Talos is a beam-rider, with semi-active homing head, giving increased accuracy in the final stages of interception. Sperry supply the SPG-49 "lamp" radar installation for this.

First US Navy vessel to deploy Talos operationally was the USS *Galveston*, a guided missile light cruiser (CLG) which fired its first round at sea on February 24, 1959. Six other cruisers have been Talos-armed, including the nuclear-powered guided missile cruiser *Long Beach*, for which a special General Electric handling and launching system has been developed. This incorporates an electronic computing centre, so that the fire controller is able to select either a nuclear or high-explosive Talos from below-deck stores, have it extracted, raised to the launchers and fired automatically.

It has been reported in the press that the *Long Beach* destroyed two MiG fighters using Talos missiles over North Vietnam in the Summer of 1968, with intercepts in the 60 nm (70 miles; 112 km) range.

Talos can be used also as a surface-to-surface weapon.

TYPE: Surface-to-air and surface-to-surface guided weapon.
WINGS: Pivoted cruciform wings mounted at mid-point on body. Hydraulic actuation by Bendix.

Talos ramjet-powered missiles on ship-board launcher

BODY: Cylindrical all-metal structure, mainly of steel.
TAIL SURFACES: Fixed cruciform fins of rectangular planform.
POWER PLANT: Two-stage in tandem. One 40,000 hp Bendix 28 in (710 mm) ramjet sustainer, burning JP-5 fuel. Allegany Ballistics jettisonable solid-propellant booster.
GUIDANCE (both warheads): Initial beam-riding with semi-active homing.
WARHEAD: Choice of nuclear or high-explosive, with proximity fuse.

DIMENSIONS:
Length with booster	38 ft 0 in (11·58 m)
Length without booster	21 ft 0 in (6·40 m)
Body diameter	2 ft 4 in (0·71 m)
Span of wings	9 ft 6 in (2·90 m)

WEIGHT:
Firing weight without booster	3,400 lb (1,542 kg)
Firing weight with booster	7,800 lb (3,538 kg)

PERFORMANCE:
Speed at burn-out	Mach 2·5
Slant range at least 60 nm (70 miles; 112 km)	

BOEING
THE BOEING COMPANY

HEAD OFFICE AND WORKS:
Seattle, Washington 98124

Aerospace Group

OFFICERS: See "Aircraft" section

The Boeing Company's Aerospace Group was reorganised in January 1969, when its major elements, the Space Division and Missile and Information Systems Division were replaced by seven new Divisions and Branches. These are the Aerospace Systems Division, responsible for new product development, some product management and engineering-oriented functional support; the Missile Division, responsible for Boeing's missile products, including the Minuteman intercontinental ballistic missile and AGM-69A SRAM short-range attack missile; Southeast Division, which oversees Boeing activities at Huntsville (Alabama), New Orleans (Louisiana), Boeing Atlantic Test Center at Cape Kennedy (Florida) and Houston (Texas)—these include manufacture of the Saturn IC stage, integration of the Saturn rocket, Saturn launch support and Apollo programme technical integration and evaluation (see "Research Rockets and Space Vehicles" section); Aerospace Operations, providing broad-based support and services for Aerospace Group activities in the Seattle area and surveillance of functional efficiency and quality of the entire group in the fields of manufacturing, quality control, material, administrative services, facilities and industrial relations; ASMS Branch, responsible for work on the US Navy's Advanced Surface Missile System; Spacecraft Branch, responsible for the Burner II programme and advanced space programmes; and Marine Branch, responsible for hydrofoil programmes.

SRAM
US Military designation: AGM-69A (WS-140A)

This supersonic air-to-surface missile will be carried by the General Dynamics FB-111 and the B-52G and H versions of the Boeing Stratofortress. SRAM is intended to be capable of penetrating advanced enemy defence systems and has nuclear capability. It was expected to enter production in mid-1970.

Boeing initiated work on the SRAM (short-range attack missile) concept in December 1963. The USAF request for a weapon system proposal was issued on 30 July 1965, and on 3 November 1965 Boeing and Martin were selected from among five competing companies to proceed with SRAM project definition. The Phase II proposal, in which Boeing defined the SRAM weapon system and proposed to the USAF costs for developing, testing, producing and operating, was submitted on 15 March 1966. On 31 October 1966 the USAF sleected Boeing as prime contractor for the weapon system and awarded the company an initial $142·3 million contract to design and develop SRAM. The USAF also holds firm-priced options to order production of SRAM. These options cover varying quantities of missiles, carrier aircraft equipment and aerospace ground equipment for the carrier aircraft.

As system integration contractor, Boeing, through its Missile and Information Systems Division, is responsible for overall SRAM system performance. The task of marrying the SRAM system to the carrier aircraft is its responsibility, but it is assisted in the flight test programme by General Dynamics/Fort Worth and Boeing-Wichita, in the respective rôles of associate and sub-contractor. The programme is being managed by the Aeronautical Systems Division of the Air Force Systems Command.

Sub-contractors in the SRAM programme are Lockheed Propulsion Company for the LPC-415 restartable solid-propellant two-pulse rocket motor; Kearfott Systems Division of General Precision Inc for the guidance sub-system, Guidance and Controls Division of Litton Industries for the B-52 inertial measurement unit; Autonetics Division of North American Rockwell for the FB-111/B-52 aeroplane computer; Sylvania Electronics for the B-52 radiating site target acquisition system; and Unidynamics Phoenix Division of Universal Match Corporation for the missile safe-arm-fuse sub-system. In addition, International Business Machines have a sub-contract for modifying the bomb-navigation system of the B-52.

Two test launches of SRAM missiles were made from a B-52 in 1969, followed by the first drop of a dummy round from an F-111 later that year. Launches of live rounds from the fifth FB-111A were scheduled to begin in 1970.

Each B-52G and H will carry 20 SRAM's, twelve in four-round underwing clusters and eight in the aft bomb-bay, together with up to four Mk 28 thermonuclear weapons. An FB-111 will carry six SRAM's, four on swivelling underwing pylons and two internally.

Range of each missile is reported to be slightly more than 90 nm (100 miles; 160 km) in the "high mode", 30 nm (35 miles; 55 km) in the "low mode". It will be able to fly "dog-leg"

Test models of the SRAM air-to-surface short-range attack missile

Launching an SRAM missile from an FB-111A test aircraft

courses and its radar "signature" is expected to be no larger than that of a machine-gun bullet.

When SRAM is carried externally, a tail-cone is added for aerodynamic reasons.

DIMENSIONS:

Length overall	14 ft 0 in (4·27 m)
Body diameter	1 ft 5½ in (44·5 cm)

MINUTEMAN
USAF designation: LGM-30 (WS-133A and B)

Designed as a simplified second-generation intercontinental ballistic missile (ICBM), with solid-propellant motors, the Minuteman is a three-stage weapon for launching from hard-pad (i.e. underground) silo sites. Its range is similar to the designed range of the earlier Atlas and Titan liquid-propellant ICBM's but it carries a smaller thermonuclear warhead, reported as one megaton in the initial version.

There are two current operational versions of Minuteman:

LGM-30B (formerly HSM-80A). **Minuteman I.** Equips second, third and fifth wings. Thiokol first-stage motor, with four swivelling nozzles for control purposes. Second-stage motor by Aerojet-General and third-stage by Hercules Inc, each with four nozzles.

LGM-30F (formerly HSM-80B). **Minuteman II** (WS-133B). Became operational with sixth wing at Grand Forks on 7 December 1966, and has since re-equipped fourth wing. With Minuteman III, will eventually replace Minuteman I at all sites. Increased range and azimuth for the missile to provide greater targeting coverage, more sophisticated guidance system capable of pre-storing the locations of a larger number of alternative targets, increased accuracy and larger payload capacity. First-stage and third-stage motors as for Minuteman I. Second-stage motor has single nozzle with liquid-injection thrust-vector control system. First flight of a complete LGM-30F, in September 1964, was successful, as was the first test of the complete operational weapons system from Vandenberg AFB on 18 August 1965.

In addition, a new advanced version is under development, as follows:

LGM-30G Minuteman III. At design, development and evaluation phase in early 1969. USAF has announced that the Minuteman force will eventually be composed of a mix of Minuteman II and III missiles. First-stage Thiokol M.55E motor is the same as that in Minuteman II. Aerojet-General second and third stages. New ogival nose fairing over warhead, which contains multiple individually-targetable re-entry vehicles (MIRV). First test launch on 16 August 1968 was highly successful, the missile travelling from Cape Kennedy to a target zone near Ascension Island in the Atlantic. About 33 further launches were scheduled for 1968-70. All 510 missiles currently authorised are expected to be emplaced by the end of the 1973 fiscal year.

Seventeen companies were invited to tender for Minuteman contracts in the Spring of 1958. Fourteen did so, and Boeing was notified that its bid had been accepted on 10 October 1958. The Aerospace Group is one of six associate contractors, but is in effect the weapon system integrator as it has responsibility for assembling the missile, its test equipment, a large portion of its electronic support equipment, its inter-stage structures and special shipping and storage containers. Boeing also conducts flight testing from Cape Kennedy, Florida, assembles and delivers the complete weapon system to its operational launch complexes and helps train USAF technicians and launch crews in the maintenance and operation of the system.

The inertial guidance system is produced by the Autonetics Division of North American Rockwell. The ablative-type re-entry vehicles normally fitted are the Avco Mk 11 on LGM-30B and General Electric Mk 12 on LGM-30F and G.

Programme management is under the direction of the USAF's Space and Missile Systems Organization (AFSC) with systems engineering and technical direction by TRW Systems Group. Assembly is done at Hill AFB, near Ogden, Utah.

Full-scale firings of tethered XLGM-30A test vehicles at Edwards AFB, beginning on 15 September 1959 with a live first stage only, proved that Minuteman could be fired safely from a simple silo "hole in the ground". The first firing of a pre-production missile took place on 1 February 1961, at Cape Kennedy (then called Cape Canaveral). All three stages fired successfully and the Avco Mk 5 re-entry vehicle impacted

LGM-30G Minuteman III three-stage solid-propellant intercontinental ballistic missile

about 3,735 nm (4,300 miles; 6,900 km) down-range. The second test, on 19 May 1961, was terminated by the Range Safety Officer. The third, on 27 July 1961, was successful.

The first firing of the operational type Minuteman from its underground silo was unsuccessful; but the next five firings were all successful, culminating in a flight of 3,385 nm (3,900 miles; 6,275 km) on 15 February 1962.

The first genuine production Minuteman was assembled at Hill AFB on 12 April 1962. All 800 Minuteman I's had been delivered and were operational by the end of June 1965. They were followed by 200 Minuteman II missiles. All Minuteman I sites are being modernised progressively, by adapting them to take the missile in its Minuteman II or III form, giving a total force of 1,000 high-performance Minuteman missiles.

Minuteman I was deployed in five wings at Malmstrom AFB, Montana; Ellsworth AFB, South Dakota; Minot AFB, North Dakota; Whiteman AFB, Missouri and Warren AFB, Wyoming. The first two flights (total of 20 missiles) became operational in silos at Malmstrom AFB on 11 December 1962, and this base was declared operational with its full complement of 150 missiles (three squadrons) on 3 July 1963. Wing II became operational on 23 October 1963. Wings III and IV became operational in 1964 and Wing V in June 1965. Wing V at Warren AFB has 200 missiles (four squadrons) instead of the usual 150.

Assembly and check-out of Wing VI, the first Minuteman II base, was begun in 1965 and the wing became operational on 7 December 1966. An additional squadron of 50 Minuteman II's was emplaced adjacent to Wing I by 21 April 1967, completing the Minuteman force of 1,000 missiles. Subsequently, Minuteman II missiles replaced Minuteman I at Whiteman AFB and Malmstrom AFB. Re-equipment at Minot AFB was underway in early 1970.

The silo launcher for Minuteman is approximately 80 ft (24·4 m) deep and 12 ft (3·65 m) in diameter, with two underground equipment rooms around the silo casing, extending some 28 ft (8·5 m) below the surface. Surface area of each launch site is 2 to 3 acres. Total area over which Wing I is deployed is stated to be 18,000 sq miles (46,600 km²).

Each flight of 10 launchers has a launch control centre approximately 50 ft (15·25 m) below the surface, in the form of a blast-resistant shock-mounted capsule manned by two Strategic Air Command officers.

It was announced in January 1966 that Boeing was designing an airborne launch control system for Minuteman, for installation in KC-135 airborne command post aircraft, as an alternative to launch control from the underground centres. The qualification testing programme of this system was completed successfully by Boeing in the Autumn of 1966.

DIMENSIONS:
Length overall:
LGM-30B	55 ft 11 in (16·99 m)
LGM-30F, G	59 ft 10 in (18·20 m)
Diameter of first stage	6 ft 0 in (1·83 m)

WEIGHT:
Launching weight (approx):
LGM-30B	65,000 lb (29,500 kg)
LGM-30F	70,000 lb (31,750 kg)
LGM-30G	76,000 lb (34,475 kg)

PERFORMANCE:
Speed at burnout
over 13,000 knots (15,000 mph; 24,000 km/h) =Mach 22·75
Ceiling   approx 600 nm (700 miles; 1,125 km)
Range with max operational load:
LGM-30B 5,470 nm (6,300 miles; 10,130 km)
LGM-30F
    over 6,080 nm (7,000 miles; 11,265 km)
LGM-30G
    over 6,950 nm (8,000 miles; 13,000 km)

CHRYSLER
CHRYSLER CORPORATION
HEAD OFFICE:
341, Massachusetts Avenue, Detroit, Michigan 48231
CHAIRMAN OF THE BOARD:
L. A. Townsend
PRESIDENT: J. J. Ricardo
GROUP VICE-PRESIDENT, DEFENSE-SPACE AND DIVERSIFIED PRODUCTS:
T. F. Morrow
VICE-PRESIDENT, DEFENSE-SPACE GROUP:
W. S. Blakeslee

Defense-Space Group
DEFENSE OPERATIONS DIVISION:
PO Box 757, Detroit, Michigan 48231

MISSILE DIVISION:
PO Box 2628, Detroit, Michigan 48231
SPACE DIVISION:
PO Box 29200, New Orleans, Louisiana 70129
PUBLIC RELATIONS MANAGER: R. B. Heath
Included among Chrysler's current Defense Operations Division programmes is manufacture of the M-60A1E2 combat tank, which is armed with the Shillelagh surface-to-surface guided missile system.

Current work of the Missile Division includes aerospace research and development in electro-optics, re-entry vehicles, guidance and control, materials, and limited warfare. Under USAF contract it is developing an air-to-surface missile designated AGM-80A.

Chrysler Huntsville Space Operations has been selected by the US Army as alternate producer of the TOW anti-tank missile described on page 613.

Chrysler Space Division serves as prime contractor for the Saturn IB launch vehicle for NASA (see "Research Rockets" section).

VIPER
USAF designation: AGM-80A

This air-to-surface weapon is externally similar to the latest version of Bullpup, and uses the same pre-packaged liquid-propellant rocket motor. Its guidance system is new and is of the two-degree-of-freedom inertial type. An aircraft launching the AGM-80A can turn away before impact, as the weapon is detonated at a predetermined height by a radar altimeter.

The AGM-80A is in competition with Martin Marietta's AGM-79A for a USAF contract.

GENERAL DYNAMICS
GENERAL DYNAMICS CORPORATION
HEAD OFFICE:
1, Rockefeller Plaza, New York, NY 10020
AEROSPACE OPERATING DIVISIONS:
Fort Worth division, Fort Worth, Texas
Pomona division, Pomona, California
Convair division, San Diego, California
OFFICERS: See "Aircraft" section

The Pomona division of General Dynamics Corporation is responsible for the Redeye ground-to-air missile system for battlefield use. It also has major contracts to produce the Standard Missile to follow the Terrier and Tartar naval surface-to-air missiles, which have been phased out of production (see 1968-69 Jane's.) and an air-to-surface version known as Standard ARM.

REDEYE
US Army designation: XMIM-43A
Swedish Army designation: RB69

Redeye is a surface-to-air shoulder-fired guided weapon of the "bazooka" type, designed to give combat troops efficient protection against fast low-flying aircraft. Its development began when Convair-Pomona (now Pomona division of General Dynamics) received a "feasibility demonstration" contract in 1958. This was followed in August 1959 by a development contract from the US Army Ordnance Missile Command. An initial production contract was announced in April 1964 and by the Spring of 1968 deliveries to the US Army and Marine Corps had reached the rate of more than 1,000 missiles per month. Redeye now holds a Type A classification with the US Army and Marine Corps. More than 1,000 have been ordered for the Swedish Army and the Australian Army also plans to equip with Redeye.

Deployment of Redeye in US Army units in Europe was completed between January and August 1968. Each armoured, infantry and artillery battalion has a Redeye section composed of one officer, a sergeant and four to six two-man teams.

The complete Redeye weapon system is about 4 ft (1·22 m) long and 2¾ in (7 cm) in diameter, and weighs 29 lb (13·15 kg). The sealed launching tube serves also as a transport container for the missile, which comprises a dual-thrust solid-propellant rocket motor by Atlantic Research Corporation, high-explosive warhead and electronic guidance system of the infra-red homing type.

Both the weapon and its launcher can be carried easily by one man through underbush and over rugged terrain. It is effective at altitudes and ranges commensurate with the defence of Army field positions and Marine Corps amphibious operations, against strafing and bombing aircraft.

On sighting a hostile aircraft, the gunner tracks it in an optical sight. At the same time, he energizes the missile guidance system. A buzzer

Redeye missile being fired by US Marine

located in the launch tube gripstock informs the gunner when the missile is ready to fire. Upon firing, the booster charge propels the missile out of the launch tube. When the missile has cleared the launch tube muzzle by a distance sufficient to protect the gunner from blast effect (about 20 ft = 6 m), the main rocket ignites and propels the missile the rest of the way to its target.

Before and after entering production, Redeye completed a long series of successful firings against a variety of targets, including F9F jet drones and helicopters. Environmental tests included a three-month period of operational trials at Fort Greely, Alaska, in temperatures as low as −40°F, as well as trials in tropical areas.

STANDARD MISSILE
US Navy designations: RIM-66A/67A

This supersonic ship-to-air missile was developed to replace Terrier and Tartar (both described in 1968-69 *Jane's*) on board about 50 destroyers, frigates and escort vessels of the US Navy, with only minor modification to the ship-board launching and control system. It utilises a semi-active homing guidance system.

Standard Missiles are similar in external appearance to Advanced Terrier and Tartar, but offer improved performance and reliability. The RIM-67A two-stage extended-range (ER) version to replace Terrier has a range of more than 30 nm (35 miles; 56 km). The RIM-66A medium-range (MR) Tartar replacement has an integral dual-thrust rocket motor, giving it a range of more than 13 nm (15 miles; 24 km). Both versions have all solid-state electronics, an all-electric control system, with steering accomplished by four independently actuated tail control surfaces, and an adaptive autopilot. Their development was begun under a $13 million contract awarded to General Dynamics/Pomona on 30 December 1964. A follow-on $23·8 million contract was received on 9 July 1965, covering continued development and pilot line production of 100 missiles.

In March 1967, General Dynamics was awarded a six-year $120,651,191 contract for production of the Standard Missile. Under the terms of the contract, General Dynamics is providing the guidance, control and fusing systems. Propulsion and warhead are being produced separately by the Navy Ordnance System Command.

DIMENSIONS:
Length overall:
ER version	over 26 ft (7·92 m)
MR version	over 14 ft (4·27 m)

WEIGHTS:
Launching weight:
ER version	3,000 lb (1,360 kg)
MR version	1,300 lb (590 kg)

STANDARD ARM

It was announced in September 1966 that the US Naval Air Systems Command had awarded a $7·5 million letter contract to Pomona division for initial development of an air-launched weapon that will home on radiation emitted by a ground radar set and destroy the installation with its explosive warhead. Known as Standard ARM (anti-radiation missile), the new weapon utilises an adaptation of the Navy's Standard Missile propulsion system, described above. It is intended to provide a significant increase in capability over existing weapons in countering the threat of enemy radar-controlled anti-aircraft guided missiles and guns.

Contracts worth a further $100 million had been received by March 1970. Several versions of the weapon were scheduled for development. The initial version used the target-seeking head of a Shrike missile. Current models have an improved seeker head and avionics for better target selection, more effective operation against target countermeasures and still greater attack range.

Associated with Pomona division in the Standard ARM development programme are Texas Instruments for the Shrike seeker, Maxson Electronics for the improved seeker head, IBM and Bendix for improved avionics, Aerojet-General for the rocket motor, Grumman (A-6 launch aircraft), Republic Aviation Division of Fairchild Hiller Corporation (F-105 launch aircraft), and Convair division of General Dynamics for aircraft modification.

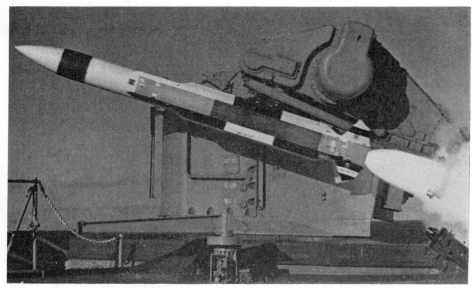
RIM-66A medium-range version of Standard Missile leaving ship-board launcher

RIM-67A extended-range Standard Missiles on ship-board twin launcher

Standard ARM missile under the wing of a Grumman A-6A Intruder

GOODYEAR

GOODYEAR AEROSPACE CORPORATION

HEAD OFFICE:
1210 Massillon Road, Akron, Ohio 44315

Goodyear is engaged on a wide variety of important sub-contract design, development and manufacturing work for US guided weapons and space programmes.

In addition, the company is prime contractor, under the technical direction of the Naval Ordnance Laboratory at White Oaks, Maryland, for a US Navy missile known as Subroc, of which details are given hereafter.

SUBROC
US Navy designation: UUM-44A

Subroc (submarine rocket) is an advanced tactical missile which is designed to be launched from submarines against other submarines. It has a much longer range than earlier anti-submarine weapons and carries a nuclear depth bomb warhead.

The complete weapon system includes equipment to detect targets at long range, compute their course and speed and fire the missiles on an intercept course.

The general configuration of Subroc is shown in the adjacent illustration. It comprises a supersonic ballistic rocket missile which is fired from the torpedo tubes of a submerged submarine. The large solid-propellant tandem booster has four nozzles with jet-deflection, and these make possible changes of course underwater as well as providing guidance during airborne trajectory. The motor ignites underwater when the Subroc is a safe distance from its launch-submarine, which can be moving and need not be pointing towards the target. The missile is propelled upward and out of the water. A lightweight inertial guidance system then directs it toward the target area by means of the thrust vectoring system. At a predetermined range, separation of rocket motor and depth bomb warhead is accomplished by a thrust-reversal and mechanical disconnect system.

After separation, the depth bomb continues on its trajectory under control of its guidance system, which steers the projectile by means of aerodynamic fins. This determines the position and angle of the missile as it re-enters the water. Re-entry is at supersonic speed, but a mitigating device cushions the shock. The depth bomb then sinks and its nuclear warhead explodes.

Development of Subroc was started by Goodyear in June 1958 and the weapon system was fitted first to the advanced nuclear attack submarine *Thresher*. When this vessel was lost in 1963, it was not carrying the Subroc missile. The first series of tests were done from a sister ship, USS *Permit*.

In mid-1965, a series of launchings was made from the USS *Plunger*, in the Pacific, achieving a very successful number of on-target results over the required tactical ranges and depths. The weapon system became operational in late 1965 and will eventually equip about 25 fast nuclear attack submarines.

Major sub-contractors to Goodyear are Librascope Division of General Precision, Inc, for fire control; AiResearch Division of Garrett Corporation for missile control and auxiliary power unit; Aerospace Systems Division of General Precision, Inc, for the stable platform for the guidance system; and Thiokol for the solid-propellant power plant.

DIMENSIONS (approx):
Length overall	21 ft 0 in (6·40 m)
Max diameter	1 ft 9 in (0·53 m)

WEIGHT (approx):
Launching weight	4,000 lb (1,815 kg)

PERFORMANCE (estimated):
Max range	22-26 nm (25-30 miles; 40-48 km)

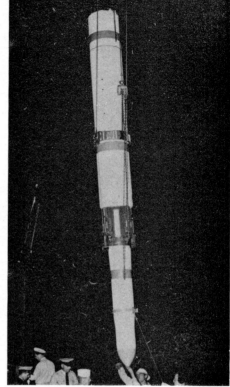

UUM-44A Subroc tactical missile

HONEYWELL
HONEYWELL INC
HEAD OFFICE:
2701 Fourth Avenue South, Minneapolis, Minnesota 55408
CHAIRMAN OF THE BOARD:
James H. Binger
PRESIDENT: Stephen F. Keating

Aerospace and Defense Group
2701 Fourth Avenue South, Minneapolis, Minnesota 55408
VICE-PRESIDENT AND GROUP EXECUTIVE:
W. T. Noll

Aerospace and defence activities of Honeywell Inc are centred in the Aerospace and Defense Group. This was formed in 1957 and consists of three divisions (Aerospace, Ordnance and Systems and Research) and the Marine Systems Center.

Honeywell has contributed to more than 90 per cent of the US space vehicles successfully orbited. It is currently involved in nearly every major civilian and military space effort, both manned and unmanned.

The Ordnance Division is prime contractor for the US Navy's Asroc missile and Mk 46 Mod 1 ASW torpedo. It is a leading producer of missiles, missile warheads, safing, arming and fuzing systems and munitions.

ASROC
US Navy designation: RUR-5A

Asroc is a rocket-assisted anti-submarine ballistic weapon for which Honeywell is prime contractor and weapon system manager, under the technical direction of the US Naval Ordnance Test Station. The original development contract was received from the US Navy Bureau of Ordnance on 2 June 1956 and a production contract was placed in 1959 after successful firing tests. A two-month shipboard evaluation of the weapon system was completed successfully in 1960, on the destroyer-leader USS *Norfolk*.

Asroc became operational on four destroyers in the Summer of 1961, and now equips other destroyers, escort vessels and cruisers. It is also fitted to the Japanese destroyer *Amatsukaze*.

The weapon system consists normally of four parts: an underwater sonar detection device by Sangamo Electric, a Librascope precision fire-control computer, an eight-missile launcher developed by the Universal Match Corporation, and the Asroc missile. Asroc can also be fired from MK-10 Mod 7 and 8 Terrier launchers.

The missile is a ballistic rocket carrying as payload the General Electric Mk 44 Model 0 high-speed acoustic homing torpedo, the Mk 46 Model 0 advanced acoustic homing torpedo in production by Aerojet-General, the Mk 46 Model 1 in production by Honeywell, or a nuclear depth charge developed by the Naval Weapons Center (NWC) and Honeywell. The airframe, which connects the Naval Propellant Plant solid-propellant rocket motor and the payload, consists of two sections, hinged to open like the jaws of an alligator. In flight, a steel band holding the airframe together is severed by a small explosive charge, after which the airframe falls away, leaving the payload to continue its ballistic trajectory. The complete operational sequence is as follows:

In a matter of seconds after sonar detection of a submarine has been made, the computer charts the target's course, range, and speed and the missile launcher turns into firing position. The ship commander then selects the missile with the most appropriate warhead and fires it.

After launching, the missile follows a ballistic trajectory, shedding its rocket motor at a predetermined signal and its airframe shortly before water entry. When the payload is a torpedo, a parachute opens in flight to slow its plunge into the water in the target area.

The Asroc torpedo is activated by the energizing of a sea-water battery after hitting the water and begins acoustical homing search from which it locks onto its target. The Asroc depth charge sinks to a pre-determined depth where it detonates with a large effective kill area.

The range of Asroc is reported to be from one to six miles (1·6-9 km).

DIMENSIONS (approx):
Length	15 ft 0 in (4·57 m)
Diameter	1 ft 0 in (0·30 m)
Span of fins	2 ft 6 in (0·76 m)

WEIGHT (approx):
Firing weight:	1,000 lb (450 kg)

Modified Asroc anti-submarine missile on the Terrier missile launcher of the USS *Belknap*

HUGHES
HUGHES AIRCRAFT COMPANY
HEAD OFFICE:
Culver City, California

Hughes Aircraft began developing an air-to-air weapon for the USAF in 1950, and this weapon has now been in squadron use for many years as the Falcon.

Production of advanced versions of the Falcon continues. In addition, Hughes is developing a new air-to-air missile named Phoenix for the US Navy and is second-source manufacturer of the Walleye glide bomb (described on page 592).

Hughes also manufactures fire-control systems for the majority of USAF and RCAF interceptors.

For the US Army, it has developed and is producing a wire-guided anti-tank missile codenamed TOW.

Hughes is also engaged extensively in space research and communications satellite programmes (see "Research Rockets and Space Vehicles" section).

FALCON
USAF designations: AIM-4A, C and D

First air-to-air guided weapon adopted by the USAF, the basic Falcon in its various forms is standard armament on every US all-weather interceptor.

The latest versions are as follows:

AIM-4D (formerly GAR-2B). "Cross-bred" version, combining improved infra-red homing head of AIM-4G with basic airframe of AIM-4C (see 1969-70 *Jane's*). Arms F-4 fighters of USAF Tactical Air Command as well as F-101 and F-102 fighters of Air Defense Command. Thousands of older Falcons have been converted to AIM-4D standard.

AIM-4H. Conversion of AIM-4D to improve manoeuvrability, particularly in close-in combat, and to permit destruction of target without a direct hit. Modification includes installation of a new warhead and addition of an active optical proximity fuse (AOPF). Latter, installed in quadrants around the missile, emits a pancake beam perpendicular to the missile axis. The fuse uses a solid-state laser which detonates the missile warhead when it comes within range of the target. Development and flight testing of the AIM-4H were covered by a $5·2 million contract awarded by the USAF in December 1969.

These versions of Falcon have a cylindrical body, fixed cruciform nose fins and long-chord cruciform wings with a control surface on the trailing-edge of each wing. Power plant is a 6,000 lb (2,720 kg) st Thiokol M58-E4 solid-propellant rocket motor. An HE warhead is fitted.

DIMENSIONS:
Length overall:	
AIM-4D	6 ft 7½ in (2·02 m)
Body diameter	6·4 in (0·16 m)
Wing span	1 ft 8 in (0·51 m)
LAUNCHING WEIGHT:	
AIM-4D	134 lb (61 kg)
PERFORMANCE (estimated):	
Speed	above Mach 2
Range	5 nm (6 miles; 9 km)

SUPER FALCON
USAF designations: AIM-4F and 4G

Developed from the AIM-4A/C Falcon to arm the F-106 Delta Dart, the Super Falcon has a higher speed and ceiling and greater range than its predecessor.

The airframe has a more pointed nose; wing span and chord are increased and there are no nose fins. The solid-propellant motor is a two-stage Thiokol M46 of 6,000 lb (2,720 kg) st.

Two versions of the Super Falcon are in service, as follows:

AIM-4F (formerly GAR-3A). Introduced in mid-1959. Hughes semi-active radar homing head. Guidance less susceptible to countermeasures. Can be distinguished by short noseprobe. Interim model was AIM-4E.

A selection of missiles currently under development or in production by Hughes. TOW in foreground. Others, left to right, are the AIM-47A, AIM-4F Super Falcon, Walleye, AIM-26A Nuclear Falcon, AGM-65A Maverick, AIM-4D Falcon and XAIM-54A Phoenix

AIM-4G (formerly GAR-4A). Similar to AIM-4F, but infra-red homing guidance. 40 lb (18 kg) HE warhead. Introduced in 1959.

DIMENSIONS:

Length overall:

AIM-4F	7 ft 2 in (2·18 m)
AIM-4G	6 ft 9 in (2·06 m)
Body diameter	6·6 in (0·17 m)
Wing span	2 ft 0 in (0·61 m)

LAUNCHING WEIGHT:

AIM-4F	150 lb (68 kg)
AIM-4G	145 lb (65·7 kg)

PERFORMANCE (estimated):

Speed	Mach 2·5
Range	6 nm (7 miles; 11 km)

NUCLEAR FALCON
USAF designation: AIM-26A and B

The AIM-26A (formerly GAR-11) was the first guided air-to-air missile with a nuclear warhead to enter service and is operational with F-102 fighter squadrons of North American Air Defense Command. It can be carried by the F-102 without modification of the aircraft's weapon mountings or fire-control system.

The airframe is generally similar to that of the Super Falcon but the body is more bulbous There are no nose fins. Power plant is a solid-propellant Thiokol M60. The control and guidance components are similar to those of the AIM-4A.

The AIM-26B (formerly GAR-11A), which entered production in mid-1963, is generally similar to the AIM-26A but has a non-nuclear warhead.

DIMENSIONS (AIM-26A):

Length overall	7 ft 0 in (2·13 m)
Body diameter	11 in (0·28 m)
Wing span	1 ft 8 in (0·51 m)

LAUNCHING WEIGHT:

AIM-26A	203 lb (92 kg)

PERFORMANCE (AIM-26A, estimated):

Speed	Mach 2
Range	4·3 nm (5 miles; 8 km)

AIM-47A FALCON
USAF designation: AIM-47A

This larger derivative of the Falcon series of air-to-air missiles was developed initially as the GAR-9 to arm the abandoned North American F-108 interceptor. It was tested subsequently as armament on the Lockheed YF-12A experimental fighter.

The AIM-47A is an all-weather weapon, utilising infra-red and pulsed Doppler radar guidance. It carries interchangeable high-explosive or nuclear warheads.

The airframe is similar in configuration to that of the Super Falcon, but much larger. Power plant is a Lockheed Propulsion Company storable liquid-propellant rocket motor.

DIMENSION (approx):

Length	12 ft 0 in (3·66 m)

PERFORMANCE (estimated):

Speed	Mach 6

HM-55 and HM-58 FALCON
Swedish Air Force designations: RB27 and RB28

Somewhat similar in appearance to the AIM-26A, but fitted with a high-explosive warhead, the HM-55 forms the standard armament of the Saab J 35F Draken interceptors of the Swedish Air Force and the Dassault Mirage III-S fighters of the Swiss Air Force.

The HM-55 has a Hughes all-weather semi-active radar guidance system, which makes possible attack from any direction, including collision course, and has a launch speed compatible with Mach 2 aircraft. In the Swedish Air Force it is deployed in combination with the HM-58, which is similar to the AIM-4C, with infra-red guidance and forward hemisphere capability. Both missiles have a single-stage solid-propellant motor and a powerful proximity-fused warhead.

The HM-55 and HM-58 are built under licence in Sweden by Saab, as the RB27 and RB28 respectively.

DIMENSIONS (RB27):

Length overall	7 ft 1 in (2·16 m)
Body diameter	11 in (0·28 m)
Wing span	2 ft 0 in (0·61 m)

LAUNCHING WEIGHT:

RB27	262 lb (119 kg)
RB28	134 lb (61 kg)

PERFORMANCE:

Speed	Mach 3
Range	approx 5·4 nm (6·2 miles; 10 km)

PHOENIX
US Navy designation: XAIM-54A (formerly AAM-N-11)

Hughes Aircraft Company received a US Navy development contract for this long-range air-to-air missile, which was intended originally to form the primary armament of the now-abandoned F-111B carrier-based tactical fighter. Phoenix is claimed to have capabilities exceeding those of any air-to-air system yet operational and is now specified as armament for the Grumman F-14A two-seat carrier-based fighter.

Configuration is similar to that of earlier Hughes air-to-air missiles, with a cylindrical body and long-chord cruciform wings; but cruciform tail control surfaces replace the usual wing trailing-edge surfaces.

Phoenix has a solid-propellant rocket motor produced by Rocketdyne. The weapon system consists of the missile itself, AN/AWG-9 advanced radar and missile control system and MAU-48A missile/bomb launcher. Hughes is prime contractor for the entire system, including support equipment. Control Data Corporation has a contract for the central processing portion of the missile control system computer.

A number of innovations in missile design are claimed to provide substantial increases in range, payload, speed and accuracy. The missile is assembled in sections, making it possible to handle it as a complete unit or to break it down for easy shipboard checkout and handling. To minimize maintenance problems, built-in self-test features are incorporated which permit rapid system testing and isolation of faults.

The launch aircraft's AWG-9 weapon control system will be able to lock on an enemy aircraft in any kind of weather and launch the Phoenix missile. The missile will then take over and intercept the target.

The data from the radar is processed by a solid-state, high-speed general-purpose digital computer, the output of which is displayed to the missile control officer in the launch aircraft on two displays; a 10-inch cathode-ray tube and a 5-inch multi-mode storage tube.

Bell UH-1B Iroquois helicopter armed with two pods each containing three TOW missiles. A stabilised sight for tracking targets during missile launchings is visible at right

The long-range high-power pulse Doppler radar has a "look-down" capability that enables it to pick out moving targets from the ground clutter that normally obscures them in a conventional radar. The AWG-9 is also the only air-to-air system with a track-while-scan radar mode that makes it possible to launch up to six missiles and keep them on course while searching for other possible targets.

The first AWG-9 reconfigured for the F-14A fighter was delivered to the US Navy in February 1970, just one year after design began. Extensive use of hybrid circuits and new packaging techniques has enabled its weight to be reduced to less than 1,400 lb (635 kg), compared with 2,000 lb (907 kg) for earlier, less efficient versions. The addition of air combat manoeuvre modes provides improved "dogfight" capability, and it is able to launch all modern naval air-to-air weapons, including Sparrow and Sidewinder missiles, as well as Phoenix. It can also direct the firing of the Vulcan 20 mm cannon.

Flight testing of Phoenix inert rounds began in 1965 from an A-3A Skywarrior launch aircraft and the first powered, unguided flight was made on 27 April 1966. On 8 September 1966, a powered Phoenix development round, with partial on-board guidance system, scored a technical intercept after launch from the A-3A by passing within a specified "miss distance" of a high-speed jet target drone at the US Navy Pacific Missile Range, Point Mugu, California.

The first guided launch of a Phoenix missile from an F-111B fighter, on 17 March 1967, was also successful. On 8 March 1969, in a test of the AWG-9 multiple-launch capability, two Phoenix missiles were fired almost simultaneously from an F-111B test aircraft. The missiles were guided independently towards their respective targets, comprising Firebee drones flying several miles apart over the Pacific. One missile destroyed its target; the other scored a "hit" by passing close enough to the Firebee to have destroyed a full-size aircraft. Flight tests are continuing in 1970.

LAUNCHING WEIGHT: approx 1,000 lb (455 kg)

TOW
US Army designation: XMGM-71A

Hughes Aircraft is prime contractor for development of this high-performance anti-tank missile, the basic characteristics of which are indicated by its name, as TOW is an acronym for Tube-launched, Optically-tracked, Wire-guided.

The TOW system consists of a glass-fibre launch tube, a tripod, a traversing and sighting unit, an electronic package and missiles encased in shipping containers. Total weight of the entire weapon system, including missile, is approximately 200 lb (91 kg), but the launcher and electronics can be broken down into four units for carrying by infantry.

The missile has low aspect-ratio wings and tail control surfaces that remain folded while in the launcher and flick open as the missile leaves the launch-tube. The wings flick forward during extension, the tail surfaces rearward.

TOW is inserted into the rear end of the tube in its container, which forms an extension of the tube. Electrical and mechanical connections to the missile are made automatically during this operation. The solid-propellant motor is designed to give two separate boost periods. It fires first to propel the missile from the launcher. To ensure safety for the operator, the missile then coasts for a period after leaving the mouth of the tube, before the second stage of the booster fires.

The operator guides the missile by keeping the target centred in a telescopic sight. Movement of the sight generates electronic signals to correct the missile's course, the signals being passed through two wires. The tail control surfaces are actuated by a Chandler Evans CACS-2 system using high-pressure stored helium gas to operate four differential piston actuators in matched pairs to control yaw, pitch and roll. The warhead is a high-explosive shaped-charge, developed under the Army Munitions Command, Picatinny Arsenal, New Jersey.

TOW is intended as a heavy assault weapon for use against tanks, armoured vehicles and gun emplacements over ranges of more than one mile. It can be mounted on a variety of ground vehicles, including the M-113 armoured personnel carrier.

To permit use of TOW from helicopters such as the Bell UH-1 Series, Hughes have developed under US Army contract a gyro-stabilised sight that will eliminate the effects of aircraft vibration and manoeuvres. It forms part of the new XM-26 missile-launcher-sight sub-system under development by the US Army Missile Command.

Air-to-surface firing tests of TOW missiles from a UH-1B helicopter have been carried out successfully at Redstone Arsenal, Alabama, with hits on moving tank targets over ranges of more than one mile.

A three-missile TOW pack, under development for helicopter use, is illustrated on page 612.

In mid-September 1965, it was announced that development rounds had scored centre hits on tank-sized targets over ranges greater than one

TOW heavy wire-guided anti-tank weapon system. Normally, the missile is not handled by the launch-crew, being in its cylindrical container when loaded

AGM-65A Maverick air-to-surface missile on underwing launcher of F-4D aircraft. This was the first programmed Maverick, numbered G-6

mile during tests at Redstone Arsenal, Alabama. Both stationary and moving targets were used. Subsequently, successful firings were made from both helicopters and ground launchers.

TOW was ordered into production for the US Army on 29 November 1968, with the award of a $141 million contract to be spread over a three-year period. The missiles are being manufactured in Hughes' missile factory at Tucson, Arizona, the launchers at the company's El Segundo, California plant. They will replace the 106 mm recoilless rifle and the Entac and SS.11 missiles.

MAVERICK
USAF designation: AGM-65A

Development of this air-to-surface missile began in 1966, when Hughes and North American each received a project definition contract to verify preliminary design and engineering studies of the projected weapon and to provide information for development and production contracts.

After evaluation of the results of these contracts, in July 1968, the USAF awarded Hughes a $95 million fixed-price incentive contract to cover development, test and evaluation of Maverick over a three-year period, with options for follow-on production of up to 17,000 missiles.

Maverick is the smallest of four US television-guided missiles currently under development or in operational use. It will be carried by the A-7D, F-4D and F-4E, and is intended for use against pinpoint targets such as tanks and columns of vehicles.

Its general appearance is shown in the adjacent illustrations, including a photograph of full-scale mock-up Maverick missiles in a typical three-round cluster, as will be carried on the wing pylons of USAF aircraft.

Unlike present TV-guided missiles, Maverick is self-homing. The pilot of the launch aircraft selects his target on a high-brightness TV screen in the cockpit, locks the missile guidance system on it and launches the round. Maverick is then homed on the target by an electro-optical device in its nose.

Cluster of three mock-up Maverick missiles on a typical underwing launcher-adapter

The first unguided air launch of the Maverick missile was conducted successfully at Edwards AFB, California, on 15 September 1969. The test was the first of 15 air launches conducted by McDonnell Douglas, with Hughes support, to prove the safe separation of the missile from an F-4 Phantom II throughout the aircraft's flight envelope. On 18 December 1969, a Maverick, complete except for warhead, was launched at medium range from an F-4D in a diving attack against a stripped-down M-41 tank at Holloman AFB, New Mexico. It scored a direct hit in this, its first guided test flight.

DIMENSIONS (approx):
Length overall   8 ft 0 in (2·44 m)
Body diameter   12 in (30 cm)
WEIGHT (approx):
Launching weight   500 lb (227 kg)

LOCKHEED
LOCKHEED AIRCRAFT CORPORATION

HEAD OFFICE AND WORKS:
Burbank, California

OFFICERS: See "Aircraft" Section

LOCKHEED MISSILES & SPACE COMPANY
Sunnyvale, Palo Alto and Santa Cruz, California

The major guided weapon commitments of Lockheed Missiles & Space Company at the present time are concerned with the highly-important Polaris and Poseidon fleet ballistic missiles, which are launched from submerged submarines.

In May 1969 Lockheed Missiles & Space Company announced the formation of an undersea warfare programme organisation to manage submarine missile work and the development of submarines for search and rescue and research. Simultaneously, the company proposed a new non-nuclear submarine tactical missile (STAM) with a stand-off capability as possible armament for future attack submarines. Other current studies include weapon countermeasures and improved missile stowage, launch and delivery techniques.

Advanced research in the field of nuclear rockets is being continued under NASA contract; and many design studies and research programmes connected with space flight are under way (see "Research Rockets and Space Vehicles" section).

POLARIS
US Navy designation: UGM-27

The Polaris combines small size with global range by virtue of the fact that it can be carried and launched by a highly-mobile submarine. It is a solid-propellant two-stage missile which is normally fired while the carrier-submarine is submerged.

Lockheed's Missiles & Space Company began design studies for a weapon of this kind in 1956. During that year, advances in the fields of propulsion, guidance and re-entry vehicle design made possible a missile weighing about one-quarter as much as a land-based IRBM, but with comparable range.

Tests with various types of dummies and vehicles similar in shape to Polaris were made from the Spring of 1957 onward, at Cape Canaveral and from underwater launchers, to develop the launching equipment and technique. It was found that the missile's motors could not be fired in the ship-borne launching tube without unacceptable hazards. The technique adopted initially involved feeding high-pressure air into the tube to force the missile out at a sufficiently high speed to thrust it to the surface of the water; but the current launching system utilises a small Hercules Inc solid-propellant rocket motor for gas steam ejection.

As soon as the missile breaks clear of the surface, its first-stage motor fires and its inertial guidance system stabilises it in the correct trajectory to carry it to the target.

While Lockheed worked on the Polaris missile and Westinghouse on its launching system, the missile's re-entry vehicle and warhead were developed by the use of Lockheed X-17 test vehicles. To save time in constructing a submarine capable of carrying Polaris, the US Navy decided to begin by inserting an additional section, containing vertical launch-tubes for 16 missiles, in the hull of the USS *George Washington*, a nuclear-powered submarine then on the stocks. Subsequent submarines were built from the start as Polaris carriers.

Polaris is now in service in two forms, as follows:

UGM-27B Polaris A2. Developed version, with new second-stage motor. Retains "champagne bottle" configuration of A1. Range 1,500 nm (1,700 miles; 2,800 km). First firing on 10 November 1960 achieved all test objectives. Full production of the A2 began in late 1961 and it became operational on the USS *Ethan Allen* in the Summer of 1962. This version equips a total of 13 submarines. Production was completed in June 1964.

UGM-27C Polaris A3. Further development. Range 2,500 nm (2,875 miles; 4,630 km). 85% new. Top of missile has blunt bullet shape. Size of guidance package reduced by two-thirds.

Both stages have new motors and control systems (see below). First firing on 7 August 1962 was partially successful. Two fully-successful A3 test flights were carried out in February 1963, and the first launch from a submerged submarine, the USS *Andrew Jackson*, was made successfully on 26 October 1963. The A3 became operational on the USS *Daniel Webster* in September 1964. It equipped 23 submarines from the start and has replaced Polaris A1 missiles on the first five ships.

The first shipboard launching of an AX Polaris test missile took place on 27 August 1959, from the US Missile Test (surface) Vessel *Observation Island*. After being "popped" by compressed air, the missile ignited successfully at about 50 ft (15 m).

The first A1-X, with guidance, was launched in January 1960 and on 14 April 1960 a Polaris with a short-burning motor was fired from underwater off the coast of California. A major step forward was made on 20 July 1960 when two A1-X rounds were fired successfully from the *George Washington* while the vessel was submerged at a depth of about 90 ft (27 m). Three months later the second Polaris submarine, USS *Patrick Henry*, fired four missiles in a similar test programme. An A1 missile with nuclear warhead was launched from the USS *Ethan Allen* on 6 May 1962 and exploded on target.

All 41 of the currently authorised US nuclear-powered Fleet Ballistic Missile submarines have been commissioned and are available for operational patrol, each with 16 Polaris missiles. Seven submarines are normally deployed in the Pacific and the remainder in the Atlantic and Mediterranean areas. They operate out of Holy Loch, Scotland; Rota, Spain; Charleston, South Carolina and Apra Harbor, Guam.

It has been stated by the US Navy that each submarine on station in the Atlantic and Mediterranean has all of its missiles ready to fire 95% of the time, 15 rounds available 99·9% of the time and 14 all the time.

The Royal Navy also deploys Polaris A3 on four submarines and has conducted successful firing tests from all of these ships.

A special Ship's Inertial Navigation System (SINS) has been developed by the Autonetics Division of North American Aviation and Sperry to position the launching submarine precisely and so ensure an accurate trajectory for the missile.

The following data apply to the Polaris A2 and A3 series:

TYPE: Underwater-to-surface or surface-to-surface ballistic missile.

WINGS: None.

BODY: Polaris A2 has first-stage casing of thin-gauge steel and second-stage casing of glass-fibre. Polaris A3 has first- and second-stage glass-fibre casings.

TAIL SURFACES: None.

POWER PLANT: In Polaris A2 each of the two stages contains an Aerojet-General solid-propellant motor with four nozzles. First stage uses "jetevators" for missile control; second stage has gimballed nozzles. Polaris A3 has a first-stage Aerojet-General motor with gimballed nozzles and second-stage Hercules Inc motor with a thrust vector control system utilising fluid injection.

GUIDANCE: Inertial system, developed under overall responsibility of Massachusetts Institute of Technology and manufactured by General Electric and Hughes.

WARHEAD: Thermonuclear type in nose-cone developed by Lockheed and Atomic Energy Commission. Yield reported to be about one megaton.

DIMENSIONS (A2 and A3):
Length overall	31 ft 0 in (9·45 m)
Body diameter	4 ft 6 in (1·37 m)

LAUNCHING WEIGHT (A2 and A3):
approx 30,000 lb (13,600 kg)

PERFORMANCE:
Speed at burn-out	Mach 10
Range:	
A2	1,500 nm (1,700 miles; 2,800 km)
A3	2,500 nm (2,875 miles; 4,630 km)

Second Poseidon flight test missile launched at Cape Kennedy, 26 November 1968

POSEIDON C3
US Navy designation: ZUGM-73A

Poseidon is a submarine-launched missile with twice the payload of Polaris but capable of being fired from existing Polaris A3 launch-tubes, with only minor modifications to the tubes. Its increased payload and accuracy, plus the use of multiple and individually-targetable re-entry vehicles (MIRV) are said to make it eight times as effective as Polaris.

Development and production are proceeding under large US Navy contracts. The missile is intended to replace Polaris in 31 of the 41 Fleet Ballistic Missile submarines. Sub-contractors for development of its solid-propellant motors are Hercules Inc (both stages) and Thiokol (first stage). Massachusetts Institute of Technology Instrumentation Laboratory is design agent for the inertial guidance system (which will incorporate post-launch stellar fix), with industrial support from General Electric's Ordnance Department and Raytheon Company's Space & Information Systems Division. Westinghouse Electric Corp is developing the launching and handling system.

Thrust-vector control is provided by a single movable nozzle on each stage, each actuated by a gas generator.

The first flight model of the Poseidon was launched from Cape Kennedy, Florida, on 16 August 1968, with complete success. Fifteen more launches had been made by 4 February 1970, two of them from the surface test firing ship USS *Observation Island*. The fourteenth launch, on 16 December 1969, was the first to be made from this ship. Such launches precede the first tests from a submerged submarine.

First submarine scheduled for retrofit, the USS *James Madison*, entered its assigned shipyard in 1969 for modification of its launch-tubes and outfitting with improved navigational and fire-control systems. She will make her initial Poseidon patrol in 1971.

DIMENSIONS:
Length overall	34 ft 0 in (10·36 m)
Body diameter	6 ft 2 in (1·88 m)

LAUNCH WEIGHT (approx): 65,000 lb (29,500 kg)

PERFORMANCE:
Range	2,500 nm (2,875 miles; 4,630 km)

LTV
LTV AEROSPACE CORPORATION (Subsidiary of LING-TEMCO-VOUGHT, INC)

HEADQUARTERS:
PO Box 5003, Dallas, Texas 75222

Vought Aeronautics Company (Division)
PO Box 5907, Dallas, Texas 75222

Synetics Company (Division)
PO Box 6267, Dallas, Texas 75222

International Technovation (Division)
PO Box 3413, Tyler, Texas 75701

OFFICERS: See "Aircraft" Section.

Missile development and production by the former Chance Vought Corporation (now incorporated in LTV Aerospace Corporation, a subsidiary of Ling-Temco-Vought, Inc) began in 1947 with the Regulus I naval surface-to-surface missile described in the 1961-62 *Jane's*.

Over the years, the company's aerospace divisions have continued to be responsible for a number of important military and research programmes.

Synetics Company division of LTV Aerospace Corporation, formed in 1969, is itself now made up of two divisions. The Missiles and Space Division is responsible for development and production of the Lance field artillery missile,

described below; the Scout launch vehicle (see "Research Rockets" section); components for the NASA Apollo programme and other products of a diversified nature. The second division is Kinetics International, devoted primarily to production of the KID eight-wheel multi-purpose tractor-transporter.

LANCE AND EXTENDED RANGE LANCE (XRL)
US Army designation: XMGM-52B

On 1 November 1962, the US Army announced that Chance Vought (now LTV Aerospace Corporation) would be prime contractor for the

XMGM-52A divisional support missile, known formerly as Missile B and since given the popular name of Lance.

The first contracts covered development and initial production of the missile system, which is intended to replace Honest John and possibly Littlejohn. Lance is transported on a modified M-113-A1 tracked erector/launch vehicle, giving it great mobility, and is able to carry both nuclear and non-nuclear warheads. A similar vehicle carries two more missiles and a hoist to reload the launcher. Both vehicles are produced by FMC Corporation Ordnance Division. An alternative lightweight wheeled launcher produced by Hawker Siddeley Canada is helicopter-transportable and can be dropped by parachute. Only six men are needed to move the missile into position, aim and fire it.

In a launch sequence, the missile is aimed by conventional artillery sighting and laying equipment, fins are attached and the missile elevated as required. A pre-fire tester checks guidance component status, and a portable firing device is unreeled to a safe area by operating personnel. On command, the "FIRE" switch is activated to launch the missile toward its target.

The general configuration of the Lance missile is shown in the accompanying illustration.

It has a Rocketdyne storable liquid-propellant (UDMH and IRFNA) rocket engine composed of two concentrically-mounted engines. The outer one, of high thrust, operates only during the boost phase. The inner, sustainer, engine operates at maximum thrust during the boost phase; when boost is terminated it continues to operate at a lower thrust. Lance is fitted with a simplified inertial guidance system developed by the US Army Missile Command at Redstone Arsenal, Alabama.

Initial procurement of Lance missiles and ground equipment for training was made in the 1965 fiscal year. First launching of the missile was made successfully on 15 March 1965, followed by a second on 15 April at White Sands Missile Range, New Mexico. First launch from an engineering model lightweight launcher was made in July 1965 and the first firing from a self-propelled launcher in August 1965.

Simultaneously with development of the basic Lance, a slightly larger version with an improved Rocketdyne liquid-propellant engine has been

Lance combat ballistic missile on lightweight launcher

under test at White Sands Missile Range. It is reported to have 80-100% greater range than the initial model, but uses the same ground equipment and guidance system. Known as Extended Range Lance (XRL), it is scheduled to become the standard production model.

During 1969, Lance underwent a series of climatic tests. At White Sands it was fired successfully after being chilled to 40° below zero in a refrigerated enclosure. It was also fired successfully after being heated to 140° to simulate desert and tropical conditions. Later, soldiers from Fort Sill, Oklahoma, fired the missile at Fort Greely, Alaska, in a temperature of more than 25° below zero, accomplishing all test objectives.

Lance production will be undertaken by the Missiles and Space Division of Synetics Company, in the Army-owned Michigan Ordnance Missile Plant, at Warren, Michigan. Major subcontractors include American Bosch Arma Corp for the gyroscope, Systron-Donner Corp for guidance components and Garland Division of LTV Electrosystems for power supply and electronics.

DIMENSIONS (approx):
Length	20 ft 0 in (6·10 m)
Body diameter	1 ft 10 in (0·56 m)

WEIGHT (approx):
Launching weight	3,200 lb (1,450 kg)

PERFORMANCE:
Min range	2·6 nm (3 miles; 4·8 km)
Max range	26 nm (30 miles; 48 km)

McDONNELL DOUGLAS
McDONNELL DOUGLAS CORPORATION

HEAD OFFICE AND WORKS:
Box 516, St Louis, Missouri 63166

McDonnell Douglas Astronautics Company
HEADQUARTERS:
5301, Bolsa Avenue, Huntington Beach, California 92646

CHAIRMAN AND CHIEF EXECUTIVE OFFICER:
Charles R. Able

PRESIDENT AND CHIEF OPERATING OFFICER:
Walter F. Burke

VICE-PRESIDENTS:
Lawrence E. Tollefson (Administration)
C. James Dorrenbacher (Advanced Systems and Technology)
John L. Sigrist (Fiscal Management)
Charles W. Hutton (Marketing)
Osmond J. Ritland (General Manager, Launch Operations)

McDonnell Douglas Astronautics Company— Western Division
ADDRESS:
5301 Bolsa Avenue, Huntingdon Beach, California 92646

VICE-PRESIDENT—GENERAL MANAGER:
John P. Rogan

VICE-PRESIDENTS:
Jack L. Bromberg (Deputy General Manager)
Stewart Koepcke (Fiscal Management)
Edward R. Elko (Operations)
Charles S. Perry (Information Systems)
Theodore D. Smith (Space Station Programme)
W. H. Peter Drummond (Development Engineering)

SANTA MONICA PLANT:
3000, Ocean Park Boulevard, Santa Monica, California 90406

VICE-PRESIDENTS:
Thurman W. Stephens (Asst General Manager Safeguard Programme)

LABORATORIES:
Astropower Laboratory, Newport Beach, California 92660
Donald W. Douglas Laboratories, Richland, Washington 99352
Vandenberg Test Center, Vandenberg AFB, California 93437
Kwajalein Test Center
Florida Test Center, Cocoa Beach, Florida 32931

VICE-PRESIDENT, DIRECTOR: William L. Duval
White Sands Field Center, White Sands Missile Range, New Mexico 88002
Sacramento Test Center, Rancho Cordova, California 95670

McDonnell Douglas Astronautics Company— Eastern Division
ADDRESS:
Box 516, St Louis, Missouri 63166

VICE-PRESIDENTS:
Ben G. Bromberg (General Manager)
John F. Yardley (Deputy General Manager)
Raymond L. Pepping (Skylab Programme)
Erwin F. Branahl (Engineering)
Harry W. Oldeg (Fiscal Management)
John F. Aldridge (Consultant)
R. Wayne Lowe (Director, Harpoon Programme)

TI-CO PLANT:
Washington Plaza N, Drawer X, Titusville, Florida 32750

VICE-PRESIDENTS:
Raymond D. Hill (General Manager)
A. Donald Jamtaas (Deputy General Manager)

OFFICERS:
See "Research Rockets and Space Vehicles" section

This company was formed on 26 June 1968, by merging the former Douglas Missile and Space Systems Division and the McDonnell Astronautics Company into a single management structure. It has more than 25,000 employees and operates in facilities with more than 5,000,000 sq ft of floor area at Huntington Beach, Culver City, Newport Beach Santa Monica, El Segundo, Vandenberg and Sacramento, California; Richland and Hanford, Washington; St Louis, Missouri; and Titusville and the Kennedy Space Center, Florida.

In the missile field, McDonnell Douglas Astronautics Company is responsible for development of the Spartan long-range interceptor missile for the US Army's Safeguard Ballistic Missile Defence System, as a principal sub-contractor to Western Electric Company and Bell Telephone Laboratories. It is also developing the Dragon anti-tank missile for the US Army, producing the Genie air-to-air missile for the USAF and working on other projects of a classified nature. Its important space programmes are described in the "Research Rockets and Space Vehicles" section.

DRAGON
US Army designation: XM47

The XM47 Dragon surface attack guided missile system, known originally by the acronym

MAW (Medium Anti-tank/assault Weapon system), is being developed for the US Army by McDonnell Douglas as a weapon light enough to be carried and shoulder-fired by one man yet having a warhead large enough to destroy most armour and other infantry targets encountered on the battlefield. It is superior in range, accuracy and hit probability to the 90 mm recoilless rifle which it will replace.

Dragon employs an automatic command-to-line-of-sight guidance system and consists of a tracker, a recoilless launcher and a missile. The tracker includes a telescope through which the operator sights the target, a sensor device and an electronics package. It is re-usable and is attached to a different launcher for each firing. The launcher is a smooth-bore glass-fibre tube, the aft end of which is enlarged to accommodate a propellant container and breech. It is sealed to form the delivery and storage container and is discarded after firing.

The general appearance of the missile is shown in the illustration on page 616. It has folding fins which flick open as it leaves the launcher, and carries an infra-red flare, wire bobbin, electronics package, gyro battery and warhead. Its solid-propellant propulsion system is unique, consisting of several pairs of small rocket motors mounted in rows around the missile body.

In operation, the infantryman sights the target through the telescopic sight, then launches the missile. While he holds his sight on the target, the tracker senses missile position relative to his line of sight and transmits command signals over wire to the missile. This causes the appropriate rocket motors, or side thrusters, to fire. As commands are transmitted continuously, the side thrusters apply corrective control forces, being fired at appropriate roll angles so that the missile is automatically guided and propelled throughout its flight.

Weight of the Dragon weapon system is approximately 29 lb (13 kg).

The first contract for a one-year exploratory development programme, to prove the feasibility of the concept, was awarded to McDonnell in August 1964. The first in a series of flight demonstration tests was conducted successfully at the company's test range at East St Louis, Illinois, on 13 March 1965. All systems and components worked as required, and the missile hit within inches of the centre of the target. Full-range weapon requirements were demonstrated subsequently at Redstone Arsenal, Alabama, and McDonnell was awarded a development contract as prime contractor for the Dragon missile on 9 March 1966.

This was followed by an engineering-development contract and, in late 1967, the production-engineering phase was begun. Launch-environment testing began at Cape Kennedy in the Summer of 1967, and guided test flights were initiated at Huntsville, Alabama, in the Autumn. In December 1967 the Army announced that a Dragon hit its target with "bull's-eye" accuracy in its first full-range test.

Award to McDonnell Douglas of a contract calling for production engineering and initial production of the Dragon was announced on 28 June 1968. On 5 July that year, the Army announced that the missile hit its target with pinpoint precision in the first of a series of manned, shoulder-fired tests. Previous firings had been unmanned, from a fixed launcher. Five months later the Dragon achieved equal success in its first test against a moving target. The missile is produced at the company's Titusville, Florida, plant.

DIMENSION:
Length overall   3 ft 8½ in (1·13 m)

GENIE
USAF designation: AIR-2A (formerly MB-1)

Genie is an unguided air-to-air rocket missile with a nuclear warhead. Its development was started by Douglas in 1955, as soon as a suitable atomic warhead package had been perfected by Los Alamos Scientific Laboratory, and the first-ever air-to-air firing of a nuclear missile took place on July 19, 1957, when a Genie was released from an F-89J Scorpion interceptor at Indian Springs, Nevada.

In this case the weapon was fired at a height of about 15,000 ft (4,575 m), after which the pilot of the F-89J turned sharply to escape the blast. The missile travelled 2·6 nm (3 miles; 4·8 km) horizontally and was detonated by a signal from the ground. The negligible extent of the fall-out was demonstrated by USAF observers who stood directly under the detonation point for an hour, with no ill effects.

Whilst under development, the AIR-2A was known successively as Ding-Dong and High Card, before entering service as the Genie. A training version, without nuclear warhead, is in use.

McDonnell Douglas AIR-2A Genie nuclear-warhead unguided missile

Genie consists of only four major components: an ogival nose section, a firing mechanism, the nuclear warhead and the motor section with its fins and equipment for attachment to the aircraft. The cruciform tail-fins have movable tips. Genie is powered by an Aerojet-General solid-propellant rocket motor of approximately 36,000 lb (16,330 kg) st.

Thousands of Genies have been delivered to the USAF and production continues at Santa Monica and at Sacramento Test Center. Under separate contracts, McDonnell Douglas has participated in a major Genie improvement programme for development of a new rocket motor with increased shelf-life and improved low-temperature characteristics.

Genie is carried by the F-101B and F-106 interceptors. It is normally fired automatically and detonated by a Hughes fire-control system carried by the launching aircraft. As one of many safety precautions, Genie remains inert in the nuclear sense until it is armed in the air, a few moments before firing.

DIMENSIONS:
Length overall	9 ft 7 in (2·91 m)
Body diameter	1 ft 5·35 in (0·44 m)
Fin span	3 ft 3½ in (1·00 m)

LAUNCHING WEIGHT (approx):   820 lb (372 kg)

PERFORMANCE (estimated):
Speed at burn-out	Mach 3
Range	5·2 nm (6 miles; 9·6 km)

PROJECT UPSTAGE

On 28 June 1968, the Advanced Research Projects Agency (ARPA) awarded the first increment of a planned $25·8 million contract to McDonnell Douglas, to design, develop and flight test an experimental missile configuration known as Project Upstage. It is a follow-on to earlier programmes conducted as part of Project Defender, a continuing series of research experiments in ballistic missile defence systems. Flight tests will be conducted eventually at White Sands Missile Range, New Mexico.

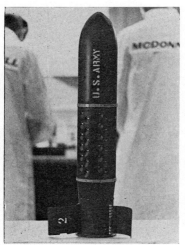

The Dragon medium anti-tank/assault weapon and its man-portable launcher

No further details are available officially, but Upstage is reported to use an advanced propulsion technique to give it adequate manoeuvrability to intercept a manoeuvring re-entry vehicle after its motor has burned out. It is able to carry a nuclear warhead but would be capable of destroying with a high-explosive warhead a non-manoeuvring re-entry vehicle.

Only five test flights of Upstage are funded at present.

SPARTAN
US Army designation: XLIM-49A

In October 1965, the Douglas Aircraft Company was awarded a contract to begin development of what was then called an "improved Zeus", which was to be both longer and heavier than the original version described in the 1966-67 Jane's. This development programme is well underway.

Early in 1967 the improved missile was officially named Spartan. Its role will be essentially the same as that of its predecessor—to provide a long-range defence against ballistic missiles as part of the Safeguard system (see page 625)—but it will have a longer range, described officially as "several hundred miles". Its configuration is shown in the adjacent illustration.

The United States has constructed BMEWS (Ballistic Missile Early Warning System) radar installations in Greenland, England and Alaska, and is developing a satellite system to provide early detection of ICBM's.

The Safeguard system is designed to work with BMEWS or operate independently with its own highly-sophisticated acquisition radars and tracking radars developed by Bell Telephone Laboratories, Western Electric and other contractors.

Within seconds after the approaching ICBM has been picked up by the perimeter acquisition radar (PAR), a Safeguard battery will be assigned to the interception. Tracking radars will lock on the missile as it comes within range. The battery will then follow the complete action through its radar systems and its high-speed computer will calculate flight data to guide the Spartan or Sprint missiles on an interception course towards the oncoming missile.

In the case of Spartan, the missile will have its nuclear warhead triggered at precisely the correct moment to destroy the ICBM re-entry nose-cone before it re-enters the atmosphere. The entire engagement, from detection to destruction, is planned to take place within minutes and can be completely automatic, although human intervention is possible at any stage.

Prime contractor for Spartan is Western Electric Company, under the direction of the Nike X Project Office at Huntsville, Alabama. Bell Telephone Laboratories have research and development responsibility and McDonnell Douglas Astronautics, under the direction of Bell Telephone Laboratories, has responsibility for missile development. Spartan is powered by three Thiokol solid-propellant motors, made up of a first-stage TX-135, second-stage TX-238 and third-stage TX-239.

There was a test firing of a Spartan research and development missile from the Kwajalein Missile Range on 4 June 1969. Although the launch was successful, the missile self-destructed early in its programmed flight and before all the test objectives were completed. Engineers from McDonnell Douglas identified the source of trouble and have taken action to prevent recurrence. The 4 June test flight was the ninth firing of the Spartan missile since March 1968 when the first one was fired. Altogether, there had been 15 launches from Kwajalein by early 1970. Of these, eleven were classed as fully successful, two as partially successful and two as unsuccessful.

DIMENSIONS (approx):
Length overall	55 ft 0 in (16·75 m)
Length of 1st stage	11 ft 0 in (3·35 m)
Length of 2nd stage	16 ft 0 in (4·88 m)

Mock-up of Spartan long-range anti-ballistic missile

MARTIN MARIETTA
MARTIN MARIETTA CORPORATION

CORPORATE HEADQUARTERS:
277 Park Avenue, New York, New York 10017

AEROSPACE GROUP HEADQUARTERS:
Friendship International Airport, Maryland 21240

PRESIDENT AND CHIEF EXECUTIVE OFFICER, MARTIN MARIETTA CORPORATION, AND CHAIRMAN, AEROSPACE GROUP:
George M. Bunker

PRESIDENT, AEROSPACE GROUP:
T. G. Pownall

VICE-PRESIDENTS, AEROSPACE GROUP:
Dr A. C. Hall (Engineering)
C. H. Leithauser (Administration)
H. W. Merrill (Production Operations)
Douglas J. Wishart (Assistant to President)
Joel M. Jacobson (Development)
Melvin A. McCubbin (Controller and Treasurer)
V. R. Rawlings (Baltimore Division)
W. G. Purdy (Denver Division)
G. E. Smith (Orlando Division)
W. W. Quinn (Washington Operations)
K. Jarmolow (Director, Research Institute for Advanced Studies)

DIRECTOR, PUBLIC RELATIONS:
William D. McBride

Current activities of Martin Marietta's Baltimore Division include manufacture of components for a variety of helicopters, fixed-wing aircraft and other aerospace vehicles and ground equipment, as well as operation of an aircraft modification centre. The division also supports joint NASA/USAF flight tests at Edwards AFB of the X-24 wingless manoeuvrable lifting-body research vehicle (see "Aircraft" section).

Space activities are centred in the Denver Division, which produces the Titan III standard space launch vehicle and is integrating contractor to NASA for the Apollo Applications Programme. Research and development activities include design of spacecraft, materials and systems for Earth orbital and planetary missions, and development of manoeuvrable lifting-body vehicles.

Orlando Division produces the Sprint missile system as part of the Safeguard anti-missile defence programme, the Walleye air-to-surface missile and Pershing surface-to-surface intermediate-range missile. Orlando also is engaged in development of the SAM-D missile and the RADA communications system and is supporting the US Army in studies of the Mallard communications system. This Division has extensive laboratories for research, development, test, and evaluation of warheads, materials, special munitions, structures, propellants, lasers, guidance and control, fluidics, reconnaissance devices, digital communications and millimeter wave techniques.

Nuclear Division produces a variety of radio-isotopic power generators for land, sea and sub-sea use. It is developing for NASA the SNAP-19 30W generator, a pair of which will be orbited on the Nimbus advanced weather satellite, and the SNAP-29 which is capable of producing between 200 and 800 watts of electrical power for future space missions.

Basic research is conducted by the Research Institute for Advanced Studies (RIAS), primarily in the fields of physics, biochemistry and materials.

Martin Metals specialises in precision castings for jet turbine blades and development of new high-temperature alloys.

BULLPUP
USAF and Navy designation: AGM-12

Martin Marietta developed the Bullpup air-to-surface tactical guided weapon from design study to flight testing in a period of less than two years, after winning a US Navy competition against 13 other companies. They produced it for several years in their Orlando, Florida, plant for the US Navy, Marine Corps and USAF, with second-source production by the Maxson company. Subsequently, production of the Martin Marietta design was undertaken by Maxson and by an international consortium in Europe with Kongsberg Vaapenfabrikk of Norway as prime contractor, for the armed services of Denmark, Norway, Turkey, Greece and the United Kingdom.

The following versions of Bullpup have been announced:

AGM-12A (formerly ASM-N-7). Initial production version for US Navy. Built around a standard 250 lb (113 kg) bomb and powered by a solid-propellant rocket motor. Carried by strike aircraft flying close support missions and controlled in flight by the pilot, who uses a hand switch to transmit radio command signals to the missile. Became operational on 25 April 1959.

AGM-12B (formerly ASM-N-7A). Bullpup A. Current production version for US Navy with improved high-explosive warhead, extended range control and pre-packaged liquid-propellant rocket motor.

Bullpup A (AGM-12B) under the wing of a Douglas A-4 Skyhawk

Bullpup B (AGM-12C) air-to-surface command-guided missile

AGM-12B (formerly GAM-83A). Current production version for USAF. Basically similar to US Navy version but with modified radio command guidance, permitting pilots to attack targets from an offset position.

AGM-12C (formerly ASM-N-7B). Bullpup B. Version with extended capabilities, developed for US Navy. Thiokol LR62 packaged liquid-propellant motor. Larger conventional warhead. Not to be confused with AGM-12D. Augments, not replaces, Bullpup A.

AGM-12D (formerly GAM-83B). Version with interchangeable nuclear and conventional warheads.

Three AGM-12B Bullpups can be carried by an A-4 Skyhawk and this weapon is also carried by the US Navy's P-3B Orion, A-5 Vigilante, A-6 Intruder and F-8E Crusader. The USAF has deployed the Bullpup with F-100, F-4 and F-105 squadrons.

The Royal Navy selected the AGM-12B Bullpup A as standard strike armament for its Scimitar and Buccaneer aircraft.

The following details refer to the AGM-12B:

TYPE: Air-to-surface guided weapon.

WINGS: Fixed cruciform wings of cropped delta planform, mounted near tail of missile.

BODY: Cylindrical all-metal structure with a boat-tail and ogival nose.

TAIL SURFACES: Tail-first design. Movable cruciform fore-planes of delta planform on nose. Pneumatic actuation.

POWER PLANT: One Thiokol (Reaction Motors) LR58-2 liquid-propellant pre-packaged rocket motor (12,000 lb=5,440 kg st). No booster.

GUIDANCE: Radio-command system. Tracking flares above and below rocket nozzle.

WARHEAD: High-explosive.

DIMENSIONS:
Length:
  AGM-12B   10 ft 6 in (3·20 m)
  AGM-12C   13 ft 7 in (4·14 m)
Body diameter:
  AGM-12B   12 in (0·30 m)
  AGM-12C   18 in (0·45 m)
Span of wings:
  AGM-12B   3 ft 1 in (0·94 m)
  AGM-12C   4 ft 0 in (1·22 m)

WEIGHT:
Firing weight:
  AGM-12B   571 lb (260 kg)
  AGM-12C   1,785 lb (810 kg)
PERFORMANCE:
Cruising speed:
  AGM-12B   Mach 1·8
Range:
  AGM-12B   6 nm (7 miles; 11 km)
  AGM-12C   8·7 nm (10 miles; 16·5 km)

BULLDOG

Texas Instruments are reported to be developing guidance and control packages to adapt the Bullpup air-to-surface missile into a laser-guided weapon known as Bulldog, under a $1·9 million contract from the US Navy. Bulldog will use an electro-optical seeker to home on laser energy reflected from the target when the latter is illuminated by a laser device. It will be flight tested at the Naval Weapons Center, China Lake, California.

BLUE EYE
USAF designation: AGM-79A

This air-to-surface weapon is externally similar to the latest version of Bullpup, and uses the same pre-packaged liquid-propellant rocket engine. Its new guidance system, evolved by Martin Marietta's Orlando Division, is based on an area correlation scanning device in which a vidicon supplies optical data to the guidance system. The launch aircraft can turn away before impact, as the weapon is detonated at a predetermined height by a radar altimeter.

Firing trials of the AGM-79A began late in 1968.

WALLEYE

This 1,100 lb (500 kg) glide bomb has been described by the US Navy as "the most accurate and effective air-to-surface conventional weapon ever developed anywhere". Its official designation is Guided Weapon Mark 1 Mod-O (Walleye) and it was developed at the NOTS (now Naval Weapons Center), China Lake, California. A production contract awarded to Martin Marietta on 21 January 1966 covered production of qualification weapons as well as an initial quantity for operational use, and carried options for continued production in succeeding years. These options were taken up, the work being performed at Orlando Division. In addition, Hughes Aircraft was for a period second source manufacturer, with a scheduled production rate of 300 Walleyes per month.

Walleye is simple in configuration, comprising a torpedo-shaped body with cruciform wings of long-chord short-span cropped-delta form. Control surfaces are hinged to the wing trailing-edges. A ram-air turbine provides the electrical and hydraulic power needed to operate the guidance control system.

Walleye carries a television camera which is focused through remote control by the pilot of the launch aircraft. Once the pilot has focused the camera on the target, with the aid of a TV monitor in the cockpit, the mechanism in the weapon takes over, "watches" the television screen inside the bomb and homes on the target. The pilot is immediately free to take any necessary evasive action. A conventional high-explosive warhead is fitted.

DIMENSIONS:

Length overall	11 ft 3 in (3·43 m)
Body diameter	1 ft 3 in (0·38 m)
Wing span	3 ft 9 in (1·14 m)

PERSHING
US Army designations: XMGM-31A and XMTM-31B

Pershing is a two-stage selective-range ballistic missile system, which is deployed in Europe with the armed forces of the USA and the Federal Republic of Germany.

Development of the weapon system was begun in 1958, by Martin Marietta's Orlando Division, under the technical supervision of the Army Missile Command, Redstone Arsenal, Alabama. The first missile was test fired in 1960 at Cape Kennedy, where Pershing achieved the best test firing record for any weapon system. Since it became operational in 1962, Pershing firings have continued at White Sands Missile Range, to maintain troop proficiency. During 1966 and 1967 the test programme recorded 40 successes in 42 firings, followed by 19 successful firings in 1968 and 14 in 1969.

Pershing is capable of providing Quick Reaction Alert (QRA) fire support for a theatre and general support for a field army. Each battalion is composed of four firing batteries, a headquarters battery, and a service battery.

In the original system, Pershing firing unit equipment was deployed on four XM474 tracked vehicles. One vehicle carried the erector-launcher and missile, less warhead; another carried the programmer-test station and power station; a third carried the radio terminal set; the last one carried the warhead section and azimuth laying equipment. All items were transportable by CH-47 helicopter or C-130 cargo aircraft.

Walleye television-guided glide-bomb missile in production by Martin Marietta

To increase Pershing's rate of fire and system reliability, an improvement programme was begun in 1966, followed by production contracts in 1967, 1968 and 1969. Under this programme, known as Pershing 1-A, the major improvements included provision of a new programmer-test station and a new erector-launcher. There was no change in the missile itself.

The Pershing 1-A system was deployed with US units in late 1969 and early 1970, through a unique logistics programme called SWAP. This involved direct exchange of the new equipment for the old under a contractor-to-troops concept. Units of the Federal Republic of Germany are scheduled for conversion to Pershing 1-A standard soon, also through SWAP channels.

All four vehicles used with the Pershing 1-A weapon system are wheeled and are based on the XM656 five-ton truck. The improved erector-launcher (EL) is an articulated truck and trailer combination, carrying the missile warhead as well as the missile itself, and is capable of paved road or cross-country travel. At the firing site, automatic erection and laying contribute to very

rapid rate of fire. The EL, with missile in place, can be transported by C-130 aircraft.

The other vehicles are a transporter for the improved programmer-test station and power station (PTS/PS), the firing battery control centre (BCC) truck, and the radio terminal set (RTS) vehicle with inflatable antenna.

There are two versions of Pershing:
XMGM-31A (formerly XM-14). Standard operational version.
XMTM-31B (formerly XM-19). Training version.
DIMENSIONS:

Length	34 ft 6 in (10·51 m)
Max body diameter	3 ft 4 in (1·01 m)

WEIGHT:

Launching weight	10,000 lb (4,535 kg)

PERFORMANCE:

Range 100-400 nm (115-460 miles; 185-740 km)

SPRINT

In March 1963, it was announced that Martin Marietta's Orlando Division had been selected to develop the Sprint hypersonic two-stage anti-missile missile after a design study competition in which Douglas and North American had also participated. Martin Marietta thus became a member of the Nike X development team, as a sub-contractor to Bell Telephone Laboratories which have responsibility for system design and development.

Sprint will complement the Spartan missile in the Safeguard anti-ballistic missile defence system. It has the highest acceleration of any US missile, to intercept incoming ICBM warheads at low altitudes.

Pershing 1-A missile on its improved erector-launch trailer. The programmer-test station and power station is at left, mounted on the M656 prime mover

Sprint anti-ballistic missile launch at White Sands Missile Range

As can be seen in the accompanying illustration, Sprint is conical in shape. It is lighter and smaller than Spartan, with solid-propellant rocket motors by Hercules Inc and high-performance guidance and control system components by Western Electric and Honeywell. Command guidance is employed via ground radar, and a nuclear warhead is standard.

In operation, it is "popped" from its vertical underground storage cell by a separate charge placed under it at the time the cell is loaded. Its own motor does not ignite until it is clear of the cell. Fine adjustments in trajectory are made in flight, via radar signals from the ground.

The first Sprint missile was launched successfully at the White Sands Missile Range in November 1965, just 25 months after contract go-ahead. The missile is currently in the advanced test flight phase, and will be integrated with other components of the Safeguard system in test firings at Kwajalein Atoll in the Pacific.

In 38 test firings at White Sands, up to early 1970, Sprint had recorded 19 complete successes, nine partial successes and ten failures.

The first production contract for the Sprint missile was placed in April 1968.

DIMENSIONS:
Length overall	27 ft 0 in (8·23 m)
Diameter across base	4 ft 6 in (1·37 m)

WEIGHT:
Launching weight	7,500 lb (3,400 kg)

NWC
NAVAL WEAPONS CENTER

HEADQUARTERS:
China Lake, California 93555
COMMANDER:
Captain M. R. Etheridge, USN
TECHNICAL DIRECTOR:
H. G. Wilson (Acting)
PUBLIC AFFAIRS OFFICER:
J. T. Bibby

The Naval Weapons Center (formerly US Naval Ordnance Test Station) is located 155 miles northeast of Los Angeles, on the Mojave Desert, and comes under the command of the Chief of Naval Material, Department of the Navy. An additional facility, the Naval Weapons Center Corona Laboratories, is located at Corona, California.

The mission of the Center is to conduct a programme of warfare analysis, research, development, test, evaluation, systems integration and fleet engineering support in naval weapons systems, principally for air warfare, and to conduct investigations into related fields of science and technology.

Chief ordnance developments of the Center are guided missiles, rockets, and aircraft fire-control and bomb-directing systems. Weapons developed at the Center include the 2·75-in folding-fin aircraft rocket, Mighty Mouse; the 11·75-in rocket, Tiny Tim; the 5-in folding-fin aircraft rocket, Zuni; the air-to-air guided missile, Sidewinder; the Snakeye 250/500-lb bomb, with folding dive-brake retardation system to avoid fragmentation damage to the launch aircraft during low-level strikes; the Shrike air-to-surface anti-radar missile; the Walleye glide bomb; and Standard ARM air-to-surface missile. Production of many of these weapons is entrusted to commercial companies under whose entries they are described in *Jane's*.

SIDEWINDER 1A
USAF and Navy designation: AIM-9B (formerly AAM-N-7 and GAR-8) and AIM-9E

One of the simplest and cheapest guided weapons yet produced in quantity, the standard **AIM-9B** Sidewinder air-to-air missile was developed by the NWC and was first fired successfully on 11 September 1953. It was produced in very large numbers by Philco and General Electric, for the US Navy and the USAF, and has been supplied to many foreign air forces, including those of Nationalist China, Australia, Japan, the Philippines, Spain, nine NATO countries and Sweden, the Royal Navy, Royal Canadian and Royal Netherlands Navies.

Licence manufacture was undertaken in Germany by Bodenseewerk, in association with sub-contractors in the Netherlands, Denmark, Norway, Greece, Portugal and Turkey. The first of some 9,000 licence-built rounds on order was delivered on 27 November 1961. Bodenseewerk is engaged currently on a Sidewinder improvement programme (see German section).

Sidewinder is claimed to have fewer than two dozen moving parts and no more electronic components than a domestic radio. It has a cylindrical aluminium body, cruciform control surfaces at the nose and cruciform tail fins. Power plant is a Naval Propellant Plant solid-propellant rocket motor. A 25 lb (11·4 kg) HE warhead is fitted. Guidance is by infra-red homing.

A version modified for improved manoeuvrability has been developed by Philco-Ford for the USAF under the designation **AIM-9E**.

DIMENSIONS:
Length overall	9 ft 3½ in (2·83 m)
Body diameter	5 in (0·13 m)
Fin span	1 ft 10 in (0·56 m)

WEIGHT:
Launching weight	159 lb (72 kg)

PERFORMANCE:
Speed	Mach 2·5
Range	1·75 nm (2 miles; 3·35 km)

SIDEWINDER 1C
US Navy designations: AIM-9C and D (formerly AAM-N-7)

Sidewinder 1C is an advanced model of the Sidewinder with higher speed and greater range capabilities. It was developed by the NWC at China Lake and is now in large-scale production for the US Navy and for the UK. The advanced Mk 36 Mod 5 solid-propellant motors are supplied by Rocketdyne's Solid Rocket division.

This version of Sidewinder has a tapering nose, longer-chord nose fins and greater sweepback on the leading-edges of the tail fins.

There are two versions as follows:

AIM-9C. Version with semi-active radar guidance. In production by Motorola.

AIM-9D. Version with infra-red homing guidance. In production by Raytheon for US Navy and UK. Not yet used by USAF.

DIMENSIONS (AIM-9D):
Length overall	9 ft 6½ in (2·91 m)
Body diameter	5 in (0·13 m)
Fin span	2 ft 1 in (0·64 m)

LAUNCHING WEIGHT:
AIM-9D	185 lb (84 kg)

PERFORMANCE:
Range	over 2 miles (3·5 km)

SHRIKE
US Navy designation: AGM-45A (formerly ASM-N-10)

Known formerly as ARM (anti-radar missile), the Shrike is a supersonic air-to-surface weapon which is intended to home on to enemy radar installations.

Texas Instruments and Sperry Univac produce guidance and control assemblies for Shrike, which has a solid-propellant motor and is armed with a conventional high-explosive warhead. Its general configuration is shown in the illustration on this page.

Delivery to carrier-based attack squadrons of The US Navy began in 1964. Shrike is also being carried by USAF tactical aircraft. An advanced version is under development.

DIMENSIONS:
Length overall	10 ft 0 in (3·05 m)
Body diameter	8 in (20·3 cm)

WEIGHT:
Launching weight	400 lb (182 kg)

PERFORMANCE (estimated):
Max range	8·7 nm (10 miles; 16 km)

Shrike anti-radar missile on underwing rack of a McDonnell Douglas A-4E Skyhawk

Left: **AIM-9B Sidewinder**

Right: **AIM-9C Sidewinder 1C** (*Howard Levy*)

NORTH AMERICAN ROCKWELL
NORTH AMERICAN ROCKWELL CORPORATION
EXECUTIVE OFFICE:
1700 East Imperial Highway, El Segundo, California 90246

OFFICERS: See "Aircraft" section
North American Rockwell's Rocketdyne, Columbus (Ohio) and Autonetics Divisions are playing a major rôle in several important US weapon programmes. Brief details are given below of the Condor air-to-surface weapon which Columbus Division is developing for the US Navy.

CONDOR
US Navy designation: AGM-53A

Condor is being developed by North American Rockwell's Columbus Division, for the Bureau of Naval weapons, as an advanced air-to-surface missile to equip the Grumman A-6 Intruder and LTV A-7 Corsair II.

Layout is conventional, with a cylindrical body, rounded nose, cruciform delta wings and cruciform tail control surfaces indexed in line with the wings. It is powered by a Rocketdyne rocket engine and carries a conventional high-explosive warhead.

Condor is guided to the target by the bombardier in the launch aircraft, who monitors a cockpit display relayed from the missile's television "eye". After launch, the aircraft is free to begin the return flight to the carrier, maintaining control over the flight of the missile until it locks on to the target. A range of up to 35 nm (40 miles; 64 km) has been quoted.

Production is reported to have been deferred because of development delays with the storable hypergolic liquid-propellant engine originally specified. The missile used for the first, successful, air launching test from an F-4 fighter, on 31 March 1970, had a Rocketdyne solid-propellant motor.

AGM-53A Condor air-to-surface missile test round under wing of A-6 Intruder aircraft

PHILCO-FORD

PHILCO-FORD CORPORATION (Subsidiary of FORD MOTOR COMPANY)

Aeronutronic Division

HEAD OFFICE:
Ford Road, Newport Beach, California 92663

DIVISION GENERAL MANAGER:
Louis F. Heilig

DIRECTOR OF TACTICAL MISSILE SYSTEMS OPERATION:
Louis F. Heilig (Acting)

DIRECTOR OF AIR DEFENSE SYSTEMS OPERATION:
Robert O. Case Jr

DIRECTOR OF ORDNANCE AND ELECTROMECHANICAL OPERATION:
Wilbur W. Hawley

DIRECTOR OF ADVANCED DEVELOPMENT OPERATION:
Howard F. Hoesterey

On July 1, 1963, the Aeronutronic Division of Ford Motor Company was transferred to Philco-Ford Corporation, a wholly-owned subsidiary of Ford, and became a division of what is now Philco-Ford's Aerospace and Defense Systems Operations, with headquarters at Newport Beach, California. John B. Lawson is executive Vice-President and General Manager of the Aerospace and Defense Systems Operations. Aeronutronic employs approximately 4,000 people.

Aeronutronic is prime contractor for the US Army's Shillelagh close-support weapon and system contractor for a surface-to-air weapon system named Chaparral, based on the Sidewinder.

CHAPARRAL

In the Spring of 1965, Aeronutronic received a contract from the US Army Missile Command to begin development of Chaparral, a battlefield surface-to-air weapon system adapted from the Sidewinder infra-red homing air-to-air missile.

The Chaparral system utilises the Sidewinder 1C missile, modified for a surface-to-air rôle, and a self-contained firing unit which has four launch rails for missiles in a ready-to-fire condition.

For missions requiring full-tracked mobility, the fire unit is mounted on a modified standard Army M548 self-propelled tracked cargo vehicle, as shown in the illustration on this page. The modified vehicle, designated M730, is amphibious when a "swim kit" is available, will carry a five-man crew, with their combat gear and rations to sustain them in autonomous operations for a minimum of three days, and can travel at up to 40 mph (64 km/h) on the road. It carries four missiles ready to launch and eight more stowed. Time required for re-loading is five minutes. Only one man is required to fire a missile. The others assist him in observing hostile aircraft.

The fire unit is so designed that it may also be trailer-mounted or dismounted from the vehicle in a semi-mobile emplacement.

Two maintenance vans have been developed to support Chaparral. The first, for organisational maintenance, contains equipment and tools for missile and system check-out. The other, for use at support level, contains a sub-assembly

Chaparral surface-to-air weapon system, utilising an adaptation of the air-to-air Sidewinder

test set for testing and repair of the launch and control station sub-assemblies.

Trial firings began in July 1965 from prototype fire units. An initial tooling and production contract followed in April 1966 and Chaparral has been in full-scale production at Aeronutronic's Anaheim, California, Air Defense Manufacturing Plant since then. It forms part of the US Army's new air defence battalions, each of which has two batteries of Chaparrals and two batteries of Vulcan 20 mm guns.

Testing of the Chaparral defence system was initiated by the Army Test and Evaluation Command's Air Defense Board at Fort Bliss, Texas, in the Autumn of 1968. Testing completed to date includes trials in an Arctic environment at Fort Greely, Alaska, and in tropical conditions at Fort Clayton, Panama Canal Zone.

Details of the basic Sidewinder 1C missile can be found under the NWC heading on page 619. In the Chaparral system the missile is aimed by a gunner in the fire unit turret mount, by keeping an optical sight aligned with the target. The missile's own infra-red homing system takes over automatically after launch.

DIMENSIONS:
Length overall   9 ft 6½ in (2·91 m)
Body diameter   5 in (0·13 m)
WEIGHT:
Launching weight   approx 185 lb (84 kg)

SHILLELAGH

US Army designation: MGM-51A (formerly XM-13)

Shillelagh is a lightweight close-support army weapon system, designed to provide greatly increased fire-power against armour, troops and fortifications. It is described as a direct-fire missile, to be launched from a combination gun-launcher carried by a variety of vehicles, including the General Sheridan lightweight air-transportable armoured reconnaissance vehicle, the M60A1E2 medium tank and the forthcoming German/American MBT-70 tank. The gun-launcher can also fire conventional-type ammunition.

Air-to-surface launching from helicopters is also practicable, using an Aeronutronic-developed stabilised sight, already tested on a Bell UH-1B.

Aeronutronic is prime contractor for the missile and its command guidance system.

The Shillelagh follows a line-of-sight from the gunner to a spot pinpointed by the cross-hairs of his optical sight. The gunner has only to keep the cross-hairs on target and Shillelagh follows automatically. The power plant, produced by Amoco Chemicals, is a single-stage solid-propellant rocket motor, and control in flight is by hot gas jet reaction. An Octol shaped-charge warhead is fitted.

The initial research and development contract was awarded to Aeronutronic by the US Army

The Shillelagh close-support missile

in 1959, following an industry-wide competition. The Shillelagh weapon system is managed by the US Army Missile Command, Redstone Arsenal, Alabama. Other government agencies are providing development support for specific components such as the warhead, fusing, propellants and optics.

During development, the Shillelagh underwent a series of tests at White Sands Missile Range, New Mexico, and was test-fired successfully in Arctic temperatures in Alaska and in tropical conditions, with heavy rainfall, at Innisfail, Queensland, Australia. Firing tests against both stationary and moving targets were conducted under a number of different environmental conditions. Subsequently, it went into production in larger numbers than any previous US guided missile.

The first production Shillelaghs and associated vehicle-mounted guidance and control equipment were delivered at the beginning of February 1966. The weapon system entered service with a tank battalion of the US Army at Fort Riley, Kansas, in September 1967, as an integral part of the General Sheridan AFV's equipping the unit, and has since been deployed extensively overseas.

DIMENSIONS:
Length	approx 3 ft 9 in (1·14 m)
Body diameter	5·95 in (152 mm)

WEIGHT:
Firing weight	approx 60 lb (27 kg)

Shillelagh close-support missile leaving combination gun/launcher on General Sheridan AFV

RAYTHEON
RAYTHEON COMPANY

HEAD OFFICE:
141 Spring Street, Lexington, Massachusetts 02173

CHAIRMAN OF THE BOARD:
Charles F. Adams

PRESIDENT:
Thomas L. Phillips

SENIOR VICE-PRESIDENT:
J. F. Alibrandi (General Manager, Missile Systems Division)

VICE-PRESIDENTS:
M. W. Fossier (Asst General Manager, Technical)
Justin Margolskee (Asst General Manager, Operations)
Floyd Wimberly (SAM-D Programme)

DIRECTOR OF PUBLIC RELATIONS:
John F. Campbell

The Raytheon Company, Missile Systems Division, is prime contractor for the US Army's surface-to-air Hawk and US Navy's Sidewinder 1C (described under "NWC" heading) and Sparrow air-to-air weapon systems. It is developing a surface-to-air version of Sparrow as the RIM-7H Sea Sparrow and is prime contractor for development of the important SAM-D surface-to-air missile.

Missile Systems Division is also active in the fields of microminiaturised computers, anti-submarine warfare techniques, advanced avionics systems, phased array radars, lasers and radar systems such as the Missile Site Radar for the Safeguard ABM programme.

SPARROW
US Navy designation: AIM-7E (formerly AAM-N-6B)

The AIM-7E Sparrow, developed by Raytheon Company for the US Naval Air Systems Command, is a radar-homing air-to-air missile with all-weather all-altitude operational capability.

Engineering of the Sparrow weapon system is done at Raytheon's laboratories at Bedford, Mass, and the company's engineering proving site at Oxnard, California. Production of the

Test firing of Sea Sparrow weapon system at sea

missile and its associated systems is centred in plants at South Lowell, Mass, and Bristol, Tenn.

The Sparrow equips McDonnell Douglas F-4 Phantom II aircraft of the US Sixth Fleet in the Atlantic and Seventh Fleet in the Pacific. The F-4 aircraft produced for the USAF are also equipped with the Sparrow missile system and it arms the F-4K and M for the Royal Navy and Royal Air Force respectively. The Lockheed F-104S Starfighters being licence-built in Italy are also Sparrow-armed.

Sparrow has a cylindrical body, pivoted cruciform wings and cruciform tail fins in line with the wings. It is powered by a Rocketdyne Mk 38 Mod 2 solid-propellant rocket motor and uses a Raytheon continuous-wave semi-active radar homing system. A 60 lb (27 kg) HE warhead is fitted.

Advanced versions of the Sparrow, designated AIM-7F and AIM-7G, are under development.

DIMENSIONS:
Length overall	12 ft 0 in (3·66 m)
Body diameter	8 in (0·20 m)
Wing span	3 ft 4 in (1·02 m)

WEIGHT:
Launching weight	450 lb (204 kg)

PERFORMANCE (estimated):
Speed	over Mach 3·5
Range	over 7 nm (8 miles; 13 km)

A Sparrow air-to-air missile being fired from a McDonnell Douglas F-4B Phantom II fighter of the US Navy

SEA SPARROW
US Navy designation: RIM-7H

Sea Sparrow is a ship-launched version of the Sparrow missile for short-range point defence against enemy aircraft and anti-ship missiles.

The missile itself differs little from the air-to-air Sparrow and the specification data given for Sparrow apply equally to Sea Sparrow.

Operational basic systems are installed in ships of the US fleet. In addition, Canada was nearing completion of the development of its Sea Sparrow close-range system in early 1970, with Raytheon Canada Ltd as the prime contractor.

Norway, Denmark, Italy, the Netherlands and the USA have joined together in the development of a NATO Sea Sparrow system. Raytheon is prime contractor and significant portions of the weapon system are being developed by contractors in each European country.

HAWK
US Army designation: MIM-23A (formerly M-3)

The Hawk (Homing All-the-Way Killer) is a comparatively small surface-to-air guided weapon which is effective against aircraft flying at normal tactical combat altitudes down to tree-top level. Modifications have been developed for the Hawk system to extend its capability against ballistic missiles, and procurement of a new version with solid-state guidance package, larger warhead and improved motor was expected to begin in the 1969 fiscal year.

The Hawk's homing system is able to pick out the reflection from a moving target at low altitudes from a mass of signals reflected by ground objects such as hills, buildings and trees.

All components of the missile system are designed to be easily transportable by fixed-wing aircraft, helicopter or land vehicle. Ground support equipment in a standard Hawk battery includes a pulse acquisition radar, a continuous-wave (CW) acquisition radar, a range-only radar, two illuminator radars, a battery control centre, six three-missile launchers and a tracked loader, which can collect the missiles three at a time and deliver them to the triple launchers.

The original trailer-type launcher has been followed in production by a self-propelled tracked triple launcher on an XM727 chassis, to increase system mobility, and some US Army units are being modified to SP (self-propelled) configuration. An SP Hawk platoon consists of three tracked vehicles, each with three missiles on the launcher and each towing an item of ground support equipment.

The Hawk is assembled at the Red River Arsenal, Texarkana, Texas. In the Hawk system, Raytheon supplies the entire guidance package, including CW radars and battery control centre. Northrop is sub-contractor for the wings and elevons, loader and launcher. The M22 E8 solid-propellant rocket motors are produced by Aerojet-General, the warheads by Iowa Ordnance Depot, and transport containers by the Williamson Company.

The weapon has also been manufactured in Europe by a five-nation group of companies which formed the Société Européenne de Téléguidage (SETEL) to co-ordinate the programme. It is being manufactured under licence in Japan by Mitsubishi.

Hawk became operational in the United States in August 1960 and the US Army and Marine Corps have deployed Hawk battalions to Europe, Korea, South Vietnam, Okinawa and the Panama Canal Zone. The weapon has been sold to Sweden, Japan, Israel and Saudi Arabia, and has been supplied under grant aid to Spain, Korea and Taiwan.

In January 1960 a Hawk achieved the first interception and destruction of a ballistic missile by a guided missile when it brought down an Honest John supersonic artillery rocket over White Sands Missile Range. Shortly afterwards, it destroyed a smaller Littlejohn and also intercepted a Corporal.

The following details apply to the standard MIM-23A Hawk, in worldwide service.

TYPE: Surface-to-air guided weapon.

WINGS: Fixed cruciform wings of sharply-swept long-chord planform. Aluminium honeycomb sandwich construction. Hydraulically-actuated elevon control surface on trailing-edge of each wing.

BODY: Cylindrical all-metal structure.

TAIL SURFACES: None.

POWER PLANT: One Aerojet-General M22 E8 two-stage solid-propellant motor, of which the first, rapid-burning portion acts as a booster.

GUIDANCE: Raytheon continuous-wave semi-active radar-homing system.

WARHEAD: High-explosive.

DIMENSIONS:
Length	16 ft 6 in (5·03 m)
Body diameter	1 ft 2 in (0·36 m)
Span of wings	3 ft 11·4 in (1·20 m)

WEIGHT:
Firing weight	1,295 lb (587 kg)

MIM-23A Hawk surface-to-air missiles on new self-propelled triple launcher

PERFORMANCE:
Speed at burn-out	Mach 2·5
Min effective height	less than 100 ft (30 m)
Max effective height	over 38,000 ft (11,600 m)
Max slant range	19 nm (22 miles; 35 km)

SAM-D

Raytheon is prime contractor for this advanced surface-to-air weapon system which is being developed as a potential replacement for Hawk and Nike Hercules in the 'seventies.

The present SAM-D is a follow-on of two earlier study programmes managed by the US Army Missile Command's Research and Development Directorate. Those studies were for weapon systems known as Field Army Ballistic Missile Defense System (FABMDS) and Army Air Defense System for the 1970's (AADS-70).

In January 1965 the SAM-D requirement evolved and a study was begun to provide a defence against high-performance aircraft (both high and low flying) and short-range missiles. Concurrently, a hardware programme aimed at component verification was started. Two independent organisations performed these tests and conducted Concept Formulation Studies.

SAM-D was placed under Project Management at the Army Missile Command in August 1965. The Department of Defense authorised Contract Definition, and the Missile Command issued requests to industry in April 1966 for proposals to conduct Contract Definition. Proposals were received and evaluated by a Source Selection Evaluation Board and CD contracts were awarded in August 1966 to Raytheon Company, Hughes Aircraft Company and Radio Corporation of America.

The winning contractor, Raytheon, was selected after an intensive three-month study at Huntsville, Alabama, and a letter contract was awarded to Raytheon in May 1967 to initiate the first year's advanced development of SAM-D.

Development continued under a FY 1969 contract from the US Army, and the SAM-D system is currently in the advanced development phase. Progress accomplished to date includes completion of wind-tunnel tests, qualification of the propulsion motor through a series of static firings, and proof tests of the "bazooka" launch technique to be used with the operational missile. Principal item on the 1970 schedule is building and firing a number of full-scale test vehicles at White Sands Missile Range.

SAM-D can be deployed as a battery to provide circular defensive coverage or as a fire section to provide coverage over a sector. A fire section will consist of one fire control group and several launchers and may be detached from the major control elements for autonomous operations. A battery in the field will be mounted on approximately twelve vehicles and will include fire control, launcher, battery control, and communications groups.

A fire control vehicle carries a radar, a radar/weapons-control computer, communications, and prime power supply. The multi-function phased array radar will perform all the functions requiring several radars in other systems. It will detect

SAM-D development round leaving its launcher

targets, track them, and track and issue guidance commands to the missile in flight.

The battery control group will coordinate firings within a battery and serve as a communications centre. It houses a computer for handling high data rates, processes and coordinates information between radars and passes on fire-control information.

The launcher will carry six of the supersonic single-stage solid-propellant missiles in launching-shipping containers. Each missile is cradled within a canister supported by teflon-coated launch rails. At launch, the motor blast shatters the rear plastic cover and the missile breaks through the forward plastic cover. The system is capable of firing missiles from their canisters either singly or in close-sequence salvos at selectable azimuths and elevations.

The missile, controlled by four aerodynamic tail surfaces powered by control actuators, can carry either a high-explosive or nuclear warhead. It is segmented into nose, guidance, warhead, motor and control sections. Guidance is by command and semi-active homing.

Principal sub-contractors to Raytheon are Martin Marietta Corporation, Orlando, Florida, for the missile and its shipping/launching canister, and Thiokol Chemical Corporation, Huntsville, Alabama Division, for the propulsion system.

Artist's impression of SAM-D battery combat elements in action

RCA
RADIO CORPORATION OF AMERICA

HEAD OFFICE:
30 Rockefeller Plaza, New York, NY 10020
CHAIRMAN OF THE BOARD, PRESIDENT AND CHIEF EXECUTIVE OFFICER:
Robert W. Sarnoff
CHAIRMAN OF EXECUTIVE COMMITTEE:
Dr Elmer W. Engstrom
SENIOR EXECUTIVE VICE-PRESIDENT:
W. Walter Watts
EXECUTIVE VICE-PRESIDENTS:
Kenneth W. Bilby (Public Affairs)
James R. Bradburn (Information Systems)
Chase Morsey Jr (Operations Staff)
Dr J. Hillier (Research and Engineering)
VICE-PRESIDENT, INTERNATIONAL NEWS AND INFORMATION:
Leslie Slote
RCA is prime contractor for the US Navy's

advanced surface missile system (ASMS) programme, now known as Aegis.

AEGIS

This surface-to-air missile system was conceived as a replacement for weapons currently operational on ships of the US Navy. Contract definition studies were produced by Boeing, General Dynamics and RCA in the Spring of 1969, as a result of which the US Naval Ordnance Systems Command eventually selected RCA as prime contractor for continued development. The programme was allocated $40 million in FY 1970. A sum of $75 million was requested by the US Navy for FY 1971.

The probable configuration of Aegis was shown in a model of RCA's original proposal, of which a photograph was released in early 1969. This model had a cylindrical body with an ogival nose-cone. At the rear of the nose-cone were four small forward-swept surfaces, each with a bullet-shaped antenna at the tip.

Long-span narrow-chord cruciform wings

extended along most of the main body of the missile, to provide lift and stabilisation in flight. Indexed in line with the wings were cruciform tail control surfaces large enough to ensure high-speed manoeuvrability within the atmosphere. Other features of the design included a single-grain dual-thrust solid-propellant rocket motor and a semi-active radar guidance system. The warhead was to be located in the cylindrical fuselage section between the nose-cone and the leading-edges of the wings.

In addition to being prime contractor for Aegis, RCA is responsible for the phased array radar for the weapon system. Bendix is contractor for missile design and support equipment. Raytheon is responsible for the microwave target illuminator and other electronics. Gibbs and Cox will handle integration of the missile system into overall ship design.

No further details are available, except that the Aegis missile will be similar in size to the RIM-66A medium-range Standard Missile.

SPERRY
SPERRY GYROSCOPE COMPANY, DIVISION OF SPERRY RAND CORPORATION

HEAD OFFICE:
Great Neck, New York 11020

Sperry divisions are major contributors to many important US weapon systems. In seaborne equipment, Sperry is a prime contractor in the Polaris programme as Navigation Sub-system Manager; is developing advanced sonar systems for ASW; is producing the Mark 3 Mod 5 SINS (Ships Inertial Navigation System) for a new class of attack submarines, and for Apollo programme tracking vessels, and has developed the SGN-4 inertial navigation system for less-precise requirements.

For space applications, Sperry has produced, under NASA contract, PIP accelerometers for the Project Apollo command module and LM (Lunar Module), and Attitude Reference Units for the Nimbus advanced weather satellite.

Sperry's microcircuit Loran-C radio navigation receiver was selected for use by the Project Apollo recovery aircraft and for the Anglo-French Concorde SST. In addition, Sperry has been awarded a contract to manage NASA's Huntsville Astrionics Laboratory. At Cape Kennedy, the company's new Range Control Center gives the USAF worldwide support for missile and space orbital launches.

Sperry is concerned with design and manufacture of components and sub-systems for guidance and in-flight systems for missiles such as Polaris, Minuteman and Talos, and is developing equipment for a number of advanced missile systems.

The first inertial navigation system for a commercial jetliner was introduced by Sperry. Designated SGN-10, it has been produced for installation in Pan American's fleet of Boeing 707's and in the aircraft of other companies such as MEA, Lufthansa and Alitalia. Sperry's SYP-800 platform is used in a number of fighter aircraft. Its inertial platforms are also fitted in

the B-52, Mirage IV, Mirage III, Lightning and Vulcan.

Serving on military aircraft are Sperry radar systems such as the APN-59 search and tracking radar (C-130, KC-135, C-141 and C-133), APN-150 low-altitude radar altimeter (B-52) and the APN-42A high-altitude radar altimeter.

In advanced avionics, study efforts are currently underway for both the US Navy and Air Force under contract for advanced aircraft. The Navy effort is the Integrated Light Attack Avionics System (ILAAS), and the USAF programme is called Mark II Avionics and is intended to provide improved avionics for the F-111.

Flight controls and instruments range from the SP-50A automatic flight control system for the DC-9 and Boeing 727 and 737 airliners to locator beacons for manned spacecraft. Another recent aviation development is a head-up display.

For precise close air support, Sperry is developing for the US Air Force and Army the Loran-D mobile tactical navigation system.

UNIVAC SALT LAKE CITY
SPERRY RAND CORPORATION

HEAD OFFICE:
322 North 21st West, Salt Lake City, Utah 84116

As its main task, Univac Salt Lake City has responsibility for design, development and production of Univac computer systems and computer peripheral equipment, primarily for use by the US Government. It also continues to design and produce a variety of aerospace products, and was responsible as system prime contractor for the US Army's Sergeant artillery guided missile system. Since 1956, other products have included the Vigilante light anti-aircraft weapon system, MPQ-29 range and beacon tracking system, XM-23 and XM-24 helicopter gun mounts, M-4A1 tank gunfire simulators, and M-5 grenade launchers for the US Army; US Navy Briteye flares for night tactical air and ground operations, and guidance control

radars for the Terrier missile; USAF command and control systems; closed-circuit television systems for use by NASA at Cape Kennedy; a magnetically-inert mechanical fixture used by NASA's Jet Propulsion Laboratory to ready space probes for flight, and "easy-ride" trailers for transport of spacecraft solar panels; and a complete line of fluidic systems for civilian branches of the US Government.

A unique Univac Salt Lake City system is VIPRE-FIRE (Visual Precision Fire Control Equipment), a "hands-off" air-to-ground gun fire-direction system for use in helicopters and fixed-wing aircraft. Under a contract from the US Army, VIPRE-FIRE is being installed on UH-1 helicopters and will control either the XM-21 system (7·62-mm Minigun, plus 2·75-in rockets) or the M-5 system (40-mm grenade launcher).

A lightweight supersonic aerial tow target, the TDU-9/B or Bandito, is produced by Univac Salt Lake City for use by the US Air Force. The

target incorporates an infra-red system, X-band or L-band radars and a dual Doppler scoring system that automatically reports miss-distances of missiles fired at it.

SERGEANT
US Army designation: MGM-29A

The first Sergeant production missile systems were delivered to the US Army in 1961 and became operational in the following year, as replacements for the liquid-propellant Corporal.

More recently, Univac Salt Lake City has been developing advanced ground electronics support equipment for Sergeant. Principal element of the new electronics is a digital computer which consolidates the functions of several items of present equipment. Integration of test functions through use of the computer will ensure that a firing battery can count down and fire a round faster than was previously possible. System mobility is improved by elimination of one semi-trailer van and truck-tractor from each battery.

Following consolidation of the ground electronics equipment, a Sergeant battery can be transported on three semi-trailers and one standard 2½-ton truck.

The Sergeant missile system is deployed with US Army and Federal Republic of Germany forces.

TYPE: Medium-range surface-to-surface field artillery guided weapon.

WINGS: None.

BODY: Cylindrical all-metal structure.

TAIL SURFACES: Fixed cruciform tail-fins of long-chord delta planform, with small control surfaces hinged to trailing-edges and linked to jet-deflectors in the rocket efflux.

POWER PLANT: One Thiokol XM-100 solid-propellant sustainer. No booster.

GUIDANCE: Inertial system by Univac SLC.

WARHEAD: Nuclear or conventional

DIMENSIONS:
Length	34 ft 6 in (10·51 m)
Body diameter	2 ft 7 in (0·79 m)
Span of wings	5 ft 10·2 in (1·78 m)

WEIGHTS:
Firing weight	10,100 lb (4,580 kg)
Weight at burn-out	4,200 lb (1,905 kg)

PERFORMANCE:
Max range	74 nm (85 miles; 135 km)
Min range	24 nm (28 miles; 46 km)

MGM-29A Sergeant surface-to-surface missile system

USAMICOM
US ARMY MISSILE COMMAND

HEADQUARTERS:
Redstone Arsenal, Alabama 35809

This Command retains prime responsibility for the Honest John and Littlejohn surface to-surface unguided artillery rockets, of which descriptions follow.

HONEST JOHN
US Military designation: MGR-1

Honest John is a large-calibre fin-stabilised field artillery rocket, with spin rocket-initiated roll. It can carry either a nuclear or high-explosive warhead and can be fired by fewer than six men if necessary. It is fired from a rail-type launcher.

Development was started by Douglas in mid-1950, under the technical supervision of the Ordnance Missile Laboratories at Redstone Arsenal. Initial tests at White Sands Proving Ground in the following year led to the first production orders and the MGR-1A (formerly M-31) version of Honest John was subsequently built in large numbers by Douglas and Emerson Electric.

An improved version designated MGR-1B (formerly M-50), with slightly smaller airframe and increased performance, followed the MGR-1A into production to meet US Army and NATO requirements. It became operational in 1960.

Honest John is in service with the US Army in Europe and Japan and with other NATO countries, including Britain, Italy (two battalions of 254 rockets each operational), France and Germany.

Three batteries formed by the US Marine Corps have been deactivated, as the missile system proved too unwieldy for amphibious operations.

TYPE: Surface-to-surface unguided missile.

WINGS: None.

BODY: Ogival and cylindrical metal structure.

TAIL SURFACES: Cruciform fixed tail-fins of clipped delta shape, canted to maintain spin of rocket throughout flight.

POWER PLANT: One Hercules M-31A1 single-stage solid-propellant rocket motor. No booster.

GUIDANCE: None. Rocket roll is initiated by Thiokol spin rockets aft of warhead.

WARHEAD: Choice of nuclear or high-explosive.

DIMENSIONS:
Length overall:	
MGR-1A	27 ft 3 in (8·31 m)
MGR-1B	24 ft 9½ in (7·55 m)
Max body diameter	2 ft 6 in (0·76 m)

The MGR-1B version of Honest John on its launch vehicle

MGR-3 Littlejohn surface-to-surface artillery rocket on its launcher

Span of fins:

MGR-1A	9 ft 1 in (2·77 m)
MGR-1B	4 ft 6 in (1·37 m)

Weight:

Launching weight:

MGR-1A	5,820 lb (2,640 kg)
MGR-1B	4,719 lb (2,140 kg)

Performance:

Speed	Mach 1·5

Range limits 4-20 nm (4·6-23 miles; 7·4-37 km)

LITTLEJOHN
US Military designation: MGR-3

Developed "in house" by Army Materiel Command agencies under the direction of the US Army Missile Command, the Littlejohn is a compact, lightweight, highly-mobile surface-to-surface missile system, for use against area targets rather than pin-point targets. It can be fitted with a variety of warheads, including nuclear types, and is well suited to airborne operations.

Composed of the 318 mm MGR-3A (formerly M-15) rocket and the M-34 launcher and ancillary equipment, its total weight is less than 3,000 lb (1,360 kg). Normally towed by a jeep or three-quarter ton truck, the launcher is approximately the width of the Army jeep and 17 ft (5·18 m) long.

Development began in 1956 on the original version of this weapon. In 1957 the development of the current highly-improved version began. Component parts of the weapon were produced by Consolidated Western Steel, Emerson Electric, Hercules Inc, Army Weapons Command, and the Army Munitions Command and its supporting contractors.

Type: Surface-to-surface unguided missile.
Wings: None.
Body: Ogival and cylindrical all-metal structure.
Tail Surfaces: Fixed cruciform tail-fins.
Power Plant: One Hercules single-stage solid-propellant motor.
Guidance: None. Fin stabilised.
Warhead: Nuclear and high-explosive types.
Dimensions:

Length overall	14 ft 5 in (4·40 m)
Body diameter	12·5 in (318 mm)
Span of fins	1 ft 11 in (0·58 m)

Weight:

Firing weight	780 lb (355 kg)

Performance:

Range	over 8·6 nm (10 miles; 16 km)

WESTERN ELECTRIC
WESTERN ELECTRIC COMPANY, INC
General Headquarters:
195 Broadway, New York, NY
Vice-President, Defense Activities Division:
A. P. Clow

Western Electric Company is prime contractor for the Nike series of surface-to-air weapons, which have constituted a major anti-aircraft defence system in the United States since December 1953, when the first Nike Ajax missiles were deployed. Western Electric has worked in association with Bell Telephone Laboratories and McDonnell Douglas in this programme, and the same team, with the addition of Martin Marietta, is now developing America's Safeguard anti-ballistic missile system.

Details of the earlier Nike Ajax and Nike Hercules missile systems, which remain operational in many countries, and are being built under licence in Japan, can be found in the 1964-65 Jane's.

SAFEGUARD BALLISTIC MISSILE DEFENCE SYSTEM

The Safeguard system now being deployed by the US Army is the end product of more than 10 years of ballistic missile defence research and development work by the Army and its contractors. The development programme began in the mid-1950s and was then known as the Army's Nike Zeus project. Under the Nike Zeus programme the Army developed a large acquisition radar, smaller target tracking and missile tracking radars, a discrimination radar to sort real warheads from decoys, and the Zeus long-range interceptor missile. Several prototypes of the radars were built at White Sands Missile Range and the Kwajalein Missile Range (Kwajalein is an atoll, a small group of islands, in the Pacific Ocean, west of Hawaii). Also, a very large number of Zeus test missiles were launched at both ranges.

In 1963 the Nike Zeus programme was superseded by the Nike-X project. Phased array radars, which are extremely fast in operation and can handle numerous targets simultaneously, replaced the conventional less versatile radars and the Sprint missile was added as a close-range interceptor. In 1964, trials began of a test model of the first phased array radar, known as a Multi-function Array Radar (MAR) at White Sands Missile Range. Two phased array radars, the Missile Site Radar (MSR) and the Perimeter Acquisition Radar (PAR) were developed to supplement MAR and are now part of the Safeguard system.

In 1967, a deployment plan was developed to provide light protection for the entire United States, using a small number of strategically located installations. It consisted of long-range PARs located across the northern boundary of the USA and in Alaska, to perform the long-range detection and acquisition function; MSRs with Spartan and, in some cases, Sprint missiles in the continental USA and Alaska; and one MSR with Sprint missiles in Hawaii.

In September 1967, Secretary of Defense McNamara announced a decision to go ahead on this deployment which was known as the Sentinel ballistic missile defence system. The primary purpose of the Sentinel deployment was to provide protection against a possible attack by missiles from China. It also provided a defence against accidental launches, and an option to defend Minuteman ICBM sites.

In February 1969, the Department of Defense reviewed the Sentinel deployment, and in March 1969 President Nixon announced a modified, phased-deployment concept. The name of this modified system is the Safeguard ballistic missile system. The components of the system (ie the radars and missiles) are the same as before, but the manner in which they will be deployed is different.

The Safeguard system is made up basically of two types of radars (the Missile Site Radar and the Perimeter Acquisition Radar); two types of interceptor missiles (the long-range Spartan and the short-range Sprint); and a high-speed computer system which permits men to control the radars and conduct the system's complex engagement planning and execution functions.

An effective defence depends on Safeguard's ability to detect attacking warheads at long ranges. For this purpose, the PAR is designed to detect targets at ranges of over 870 nm (1,000 miles; 1,600 km). The system uses phased array radars, which means that the radar beams are steered electronically from a fixed antenna to search in a particular direction, instead of mechanically rotating the antenna. The beam can be scanned across the sky in a few millionths of a second. When an attacking missile is detected it is tracked by the PAR, which computes the ballistic trajectory and the probable impact point, then relays this information to the appropriate MSR. There the track of the incoming missile is predicted, and the probable point of intercept is computed.

The PAR radar will be housed in a square-shaped concrete structure some 200 ft (61 m) on each side at the base. The structure will be 130 ft (40 m) tall and will be hardened against nuclear effects. Also located with the PAR will be administrative buildings and an underground power plant. The first PAR will be assembled at an operational site.

The other phased array radar employed by the system is the Missile Site Radar (MSR), which has a detection range of several hundred nautical miles. It operates in a manner similar to the PAR but provides much more precise target data, on which the final engagement is based. The MSR also readies the interceptor missiles for launch and guides them to intercept. Generally, Spartan and Sprint missiles are located at the MSR site. The radar building will be about 225 ft (68·5 m) square at the base and 90 ft (27·5 m) high. Only about 40 ft (12 m) of its total height will be above the ground, and both it and its associated power plant will be hardened against nuclear effects. A prototype MSR has been installed at Kwajalein Missile Range, where operational tests are being conducted.

Spartan (see page 616) is a long-range scaled-up version of the Zeus missile, which was fired successfully many times and made several successful interceptions of ICBMs fired from the West Coast of the USA in 1962 and 1963. Zeus also demonstrated successfully a satellite intercept capability.

First fired on 30 March 1968, Spartan is a three-stage, solid-propellant missile, launched from an underground silo. After the first stage is burned out, it separates and the second stage ignites. The missile is guided to its target by the MSR and system computers. The third stage, which is normally outside the atmosphere when used, is ignited on command from the ground. It will carry a nuclear warhead in the megaton range. Development of the warhead is being carried out by the Atomic Energy Commission.

Sprint is a two-stage solid-propellant missile designed to make intercepts at a closer range. It is a very fast missile, and is guided to its target by the MSR and system computers. Sprint is ejected from an underground silo by a gas-propelled piston and its booster ignites once the missile is in the air. It will have a nuclear warhead in the kiloton range (see page 618).

Each MSR and PAR will have large-capacity data processing centres. These computers process and evaluate the vast amount of information accumulated by the radars and provide the means for men to control the system. The data processing centre is composed of computer processors, memory banks, displays, tapes and discs.

The Safeguard system can provide both area defence and terminal defence. Area defence is accomplished by intercepting ICBMs above the atmosphere at ranges of several hundred miles, and hence each site can protect large areas, hundreds of miles across. Terminal defence is a concentrated defence of a small area such as a Minuteman site.

The first element of the Safeguard system to detect an attack would be the PAR. This radar would provide initial track data for alerting Safeguard firing units. The MSR would refine this tracking data and control the flight of Spartan missiles to intercept the incoming ICBMs. The Spartan's kill—a nuclear explosion to destroy or disable the incoming warhead—would occur well out of the atmosphere. The second type of missile, Sprint, would be launched to destroy warheads which penetrated the Spartan defence or which may have been allowed to pass it for sorting purposes. Engagements would be almost entirely automated, except for the necessary human decisions which must be made by command authority. However, all phases of an engagement would be subject to manual human intervention at any time.

The nuclear warheads used in the Spartan and Sprint missiles have elaborate safety devices to prevent a nuclear explosion until after the missile is launched and reaches a safe altitude, at which there can be no damage to people or property.

Specific objectives of the phased Safeguard ballistic missile defence system announced by President Nixon on 14 March 1969 are to safeguard the United States' deterrent system, which has become increasingly vulnerable due to the advances that have been made by the Soviet Union since 1967, when Safeguard's predecessor programme, Sentinel, was first adopted; to offer protection against any attack by the Chinese that can be foreseen over the next 10 years; and to provide protection against an accidental attack of less than massive magnitude, which might be launched by any of the nuclear powers.

The Safeguard system does not provide a massive defence for cities, and for that reason sites have been moved away from major cities.

Two Minuteman bases, at Malmstrom AFB, Montana, and Grand Forks AFB, North Dakota, have been chosen to receive the first two complete systems, with Whiteman AFB, Missouri, scheduled to follow under the FY 1971 procurement programme. Each will deploy an MSR, a PAR, Sprints and Spartans at selected locations around the bases. In addition to the Spartan and Sprint missiles at the MSR, other Sprint missiles will be installed at a few sites located a few miles from the MSR. The equipment at Grand Forks is expected to be in a state of readiness by the end of 1974.

Missile integration tests of the Safeguard system began at Kwajalein in the Spring of 1970. Initial tests were intended to evaluate operation of Spartan and Sprint missiles under the control of the MSR. Later in 1970, missiles from Kwajalein will attempt to intercept Minuteman I ICBMs launched from Vandenberg AFB, California, and Polaris missiles fired at sea.

US MISSILES WITH NO DESIGNATED PRIME CONTRACTOR

AIM-82A

The AIM-82A will be a short-range air-to-air "dog-fight" missile to arm the USAF's McDonnell Douglas F-15 air superiority fighter.

Proposal requests for system definition phase studies were sent to Bendix, Fairchild Hiller, General Dynamics, Grumman, Hughes, Lear Siegler, McDonnell Douglas, Martin, North American Rockwell, Philco-Ford, Raytheon and TRW Systems in February 1970. Two or more of these companies were expected to receive USAF contracts for more detailed studies, in the hope that a firm AIM-82A development proposal could be submitted to the Department of Defense in mid-August 1970, with the names of two contractors selected for competitive development of the missile on a fixed-price basis. A sum of $37·2 million was requested in the FY 1971 budget to cover development of this weapon.

Requirements for the AIM-82A include the ability to attack the target from any angle. No preferred type of guidance is specified and most proposals were expected to be based on either infra-red homing or another form of electro-optical homing such as TV guidance. Meanwhile, the USAF is conducting an independent evaluation of infra-red seekers developed by General Dynamics/Pomona and Philco-Ford, and TV seekers developed by Bendix, Hughes and North American Rockwell.

The TRW Systems proposal will utilise Taildog missile technology acquired under a licence agreement with Hawker Siddeley Dynamics of the UK. In particular, it is expected that this company's design will use the thrust vector control system proposed for the wingless Taildog, instead of the more usual aerodynamic control. The TRW AIM-82A would, however, be larger than Taildog, with a larger warhead detonated by a proximity fuse supplied by Kollsman Instruments. Texas Instruments would contribute the infra-red seeker.

AGILE

Agile is the US Navy counterpart to the AIM-82A (above), to arm the Grumman F-14 fighter. Like the AIM-82A, it is intended to be a highly-manoeuvrable missile, effective at ranges as short as 1,000 yards (915 m). It will, however, be larger than the USAF weapon, with a longer maximum range, and an infra-red guidance system is specified.

Hughes Aircraft already hold a contract for the infra-red seeker. The decision on whether or not to proceed to the next development phase for the Agile weapon system as a whole was expected to be taken in September 1970.

SABMIS

This is the US Navy's projected seaborne anti-ballistic missile system. A sum of $3 million was allocated under the FY 1970 budget to cover early research and development, but was later "frozen" under defence economies demanded by Congress. The US Navy requested $2 million for continued research in FY 1971.

SCAD

The subsonic cruise armed decoy (SCAD) missile is intended as part of the electronic countermeasures systems to be carried by the USAF's projected B-1 bomber, known originally as the advanced manned strategic aircraft (AMSA). Both armed and unarmed (SCUD) versions have been proposed, with an inertial guidance system and, in the armed version, terminal assistance. The power plant will be a small turbojet engine.

A total of $9·1 million was requested for SCAD development in FY 1970. This was increased to $33·6 million in FY 1971.

ULMS

Development of the US Navy's undersea long-range missile system depends to a degree on the outcome of the US/USSR strategic arms limitation talks (SALT). Defense Secretary Laird has described the ULMS as a "priority project I'll carry in my hip pocket". It is intended as a follow-on to the Polaris/Poseidon series of fleet ballistic missiles.

A total of $10 million was allocated for ULMS research and development in FY 1970. The sum requested in FY 1971 was $44 million.

THE UNION OF SOVIET SOCIALIST REPUBLICS

AIR-TO-AIR MISSILES
NATO Code Name: "Alkali"

This first-generation Soviet air-to-air missile is standard armament of the all-weather versions of the MiG-19, which continue in service with the air forces of some of the Soviet Union's allies. It was also carried by the early version of the Su-9 (see page 395 of 1967-68 Jane's).

"Alkali" is a solid-propellant missile, with large delta cruciform wings at the rear and small cruciform foreplanes indexed in line with the wings. There appear to be control surfaces in the trailing-edges of the wings and "Alkali" is believed to employ some form of radar homing. The warhead is carried immediately aft of the foreplanes.

NATO Code Name: "Anab"

First seen as underwing armament on the Yakovlev Yak-28P fighter ("Firebar") in the 1961 Soviet Aviation Day display, "Anab" is now known to be a standard air-to-air missile in the Soviet Air Force. It was carried by both Yak-28 and Sukhoi Su-9 ("Fishpot") interceptors taking part in the 1967 air display at Domodedovo (see pages 521 and 506-7).

"Anab" has a cylindrical body, with small cruciform canard control surfaces indexed in line with very large cruciform tail-fins. Both infra-red and semi-active radar homing versions are operational.

DIMENSIONS (estimated):
Length:
IR version ... 13 ft 5 in (4·1 m)
radar-homing version ... 13 ft 1 in (4·0 m)

NATO Code Name: "Ash"

The code-name "Ash" has been given to the large air-to-air missiles shown under the wings of the Tupolev "Fiddler" on page 512. These missiles have cruciform wings and tail surfaces, indexed in line, and are operational in two versions, which appear to have infra-red and semi-active (or active) radar homing heads respectively.

DIMENSIONS (estimated):
Length:
IR version ... 18 ft 0 in (5·5 m)
radar-homing version ... 17 ft 0 in (5·2 m)

NATO Code Name: "Atoll"

This missile has been seen under the wings of a variety of Soviet aircraft and is standard equipment on home and export versions of the MiG-21 (see pages 495-6). It is almost identical to the American Sidewinder 1A (AIM-9B) in size and configuration and appears to have a similar infra-red guidance system.

The body is cylindrical with cruciform control surfaces near the nose, indexed in line with the fixed cruciform tail-fins. There are no external cable or control conduits.

The triangular control surfaces have a compound sweep averaging about 60° on the leading-edge and 10° on the trailing-edge. They are linked in opposite pairs, with a maximum movement of 20-30°.

Leading-edge sweep on the tail-fins is about 40°, with straight trailing-edges. A small gyroscopically-controlled tab is inset in the trailing-edge of each fin, at the tip, presumably for anti-roll stabilisation but possibly with an added control function.

Nozzle diameter of the solid-propellant motor is 3¼ in (8 cm). Weight and performance of "Atoll" should be very similar to those of Sidewinder 1A.

"Snapper" light anti-tank missiles in firing position on BRDM vehicle (*Tass*)

DIMENSIONS:
Length overall ... 9 ft 2 in (2·80 m)
Body diameter ... 4·72 in (12 cm)
Span of control surfaces ... 1 ft 5¾ in (0·45 m)
Span of tail-fins ... 1 ft 8¾ in (0·53 m)

WEIGHTS AND PERFORMANCE:
No details available.

NATO Code Name: "Awl"

"Awl" is the code-name given to missiles identified so far only as underwing armament on the experimental MiG fighter known as "Flipper" (see 1965-66 Jane's). It has cruciform wings and tail surfaces, indexed in line, and is almost certainly of the radar-homing, or possibly beam-riding, type.

The length of this missile is estimated to be about 16 ft (5·0 m), making it bigger than the American Sparrow IIIB of somewhat similar configuration.

ANTI-TANK MISSILES
NATO Code Name: "Snapper"

This wire-guided anti-tank missile is similar in configuration to Western missiles such as the Bölkow Cobra and Contraves-Oerlikon Mosquito, and employs a similar trailing-edge vibrating spoiler control system.

"Snapper" has a cylindrical body, housing a solid-propellant rocket motor with a nozzle diameter of about 2¼ in (6·5 cm). Spools for the two guidance wires are faired into the body, 180° apart, and the wires have to be screwed into sockets at the ends of right-angle tubular arms, projecting from the guide rail, before launch.

The detachable hollow-charge warhead (11·5 lb = 5·25 kg) is reported to be capable of penetrating 13·7 in (35 cm) of armour, detonation being by a contact fuse at the tip of the sharply-tapered nose-cone. The large cruciform wings each have a vibrating spoiler in a plastic housing inset in the trailing-edge. An additional small spoiler is fitted outboard of the larger one on two wings. The missile is spin-stabilised.

In its initial operational form, "Snapper" was carried on a quadruple launcher mounted on a GAZ-69 light cross-country vehicle. The launcher was pivoted in such a way that the missiles were transported vertically, and then swung down by means of a hand crank to fire rearward over the back of the vehicle. Another crank enabled the operator to traverse the launcher.

GAZ-69/"Snapper" weapon systems of this kind were captured from the Egyptian army by Israeli forces during the Sinai campaign of June 1967. Examination of these has shown that the operator is provided with periscopic binoculars, embodying an illuminated variable-brightness reticle, with which to sight the target. He controls the missile by means of a joystick, keeping it on a line of sight to the target with the aid of tracking flares on two of the wings. Remote firing, at distances up to 165 ft (50 m) from the launcher, is possible.

In the Soviet army, "Snapper" is now deployed usually on a triple-mounting on the BRDM armoured amphibious vehicle, which seems to be the standard Soviet anti-tank missile carrier. The BRDM has four retractable auxiliary wheels under its centre-body, which can be lowered to improve its cross-country capability. Propulsion on water is by means of a screw mounted in a water duct at the rear of the vehicle. (The pear-shaped cover over this duct can be seen in the adjacent photograph of the "Swatter" missile system).

"Snapper's" triple mounting is retractable and the weapons are transported under cover plates which open up when the mounting is raised for firing.

DIMENSIONS:

Length	3 ft 8½ in (1·13 m)
Body diameter	5½ in (0·14 m)
Wing span	2 ft 5½ in (0·75 m)
Wing chord:	
root	1 ft 8 in (0·51 m)
tip	8½ in (0·22 m)

WEIGHT:

Launching weight	49 lb (22·25 kg)

PERFORMANCE:

Cruising speed 175 knots (201 mph; 323 km/h)
Min effective range 1,650-1,980 ft (500-600 m)
Max range 7,650 ft (2,330 m)

NATO Code Name: "Swatter"

Like "Snapper", the "Swatter" is a wire-guided solid-propellant anti-tank missile carried on the BRDM amphibious vehicle. It is of similar size, but has an entirely different configuration and is probably a more advanced weapon in the class of the French SS.11. As can be seen in the adjacent illustration, it is carried on a quadruple launcher and is controlled by elevons on the trailing-edges of the rear-mounted cruciform wings. The two small canard surfaces at the nose are also movable. The motor appears to exhaust through two tubular vents diametrically-opposed between the wings. Two more tubes, projecting rearward from opposite wings, probably contain tracking flares. The blunt nose of "Swatter" may imply the use of a terminal homing system operating via the canard fore-planes.

DIMENSIONS:

Length	3 ft 8 in (1·12 m)
Wing span	2 ft 2 in (0·65 m)

NATO Code Name: "Sagger"

First seen in the VE-Day anniversary parade through Moscow, on 9 May 1965, this anti-tank missile is shown in the upper illustrations on the opposite page. It is a wire-guided solid-propellant weapon, of more compact configuration than "Snapper" and "Swatter", but with an equally-powerful warhead. Its cruciform wings each consist of a swept and fixed inner portion and an unswept outer panel which appears to fold inward for storage and transport.

Six of these missiles are carried by the BRDM vehicle, in clusters of three on a retractable

Close-up of "Sagger" anti-tank missile

launcher. When it extends for firing, the missile system remains protected by the armoured cover plate that encloses it within the vehicle during transport.

A single "Sagger" is rail-mounted above a gun of about 75-mm calibre on a new tracked anti-tank vehicle seen for the first time in a Moscow parade on 7 November 1967. The vehicle appeared to carry a driver, weapons operator and eight soldiers, four of whom sit in each side of an aft compartment which can be totally-enclosed by hinged armoured cover plates.

DIMENSION:

Length	2 ft 6 in (0·76 m)

AIR-TO-SURFACE MISSILES

Three types of air-to-surface missiles were first identified on aircraft which took part in the 1961 Soviet Aviation Day Display. They can be seen mounted on their carrier aircraft in illustrations to the Soviet entries in the "Aircraft" section of this edition and on this page. Descriptions of them follow, together with details of two further air-to-surface weapons identified subsequently.

NATO Code Name: "Kangaroo"

Largest of the air-to-surface missiles first seen in 1961, and known to be operational, was that carried by the Tu-20 ("Bear") and given the NATO code name "Kangaroo". It is a winged missile with an airframe similar in size and shape to a sweptwing turbojet-powered fighter aircraft. The tail unit is conventional, with sweepback on all surfaces. The vertical surfaces, concealed inside the launch-aircraft until the missile is dropped, are of rhomboid form.

What was believed originally to be a radome on the missile's nose was identified subsequently as either a duct through which air can be fed to start the missile's turbojet engine prior to launching or a fairing over the air intake. Radar guidance equipment is carried in the nose of the Tu-20 carrier aircraft. Length of this missile appears to be about 50 ft (15 m).

"Swatter" anti-tank missiles on BRDM amphibious vehicle

Tracked anti-tank vehicle, armed with "Sagger", first seen on 7 November 1967
(Aviation Week and Space Technology)

Latest Soviet anti-tank missile, code-named "Sagger" (Aviation Week and Space Technology)

NATO Code Name: "Kipper"

The missile carried by the Tu-16 ("Badger") in the 1961 Aviation Day Display, and described as an anti-shipping weapon, has a conventional sweptwing aeroplane layout, with an underslung power plant which is almost certainly a turbojet. It appears to be about 31 ft (9·5 m) long. Its performance is likely to be much inferior to that of the more refined and larger American Hound Dog air-to-surface missile of somewhat similar configuration. Radar is carried in the nose of the Tu-16 carrier aircraft. (See drawing on page 509).

NATO Code Name: "Kitchen"

The air-to-surface missile carried semi-sub-

merged in the fuselage of the Tupolev Tu-22 bomber ("Blinder") looks considerably more advanced than the weapons already described. It appears to have stubby delta wings and cruciform tail surfaces. A bulge under the body could be an air intake for its power plant or a radome. The speed of this weapon is probably high. It is about 36 ft (11 m) long.

NATO Code Name: "Kennel"

Two of these air-to-surface winged anti-shipping missiles are carried under the wings of Tu-16's in service with the Soviet Naval Air Force, the Indonesian Air Force and the Egyptian Air Force.

"Kennel" is a turbojet-powered weapon which looks rather like a scaled-down unpiloted version of the MiG-15 fighter aircraft, with a hemispherical radome above its nose air intake. There is further electronic equipment in a pod at the top of the tail-fin. Each wing is fitted with two fences.

"Kennel" spans about 16 ft 0 in (4·9 m) and is about 28 ft 0 in (8·5 m) long. A surface-to-surface version (NATO Code Name "Samlet") is described separately, as is the new rocket-powered version (NATO "Kelt").

NATO Code Name: "Kelt"

In September 1968 a photograph released officially in Moscow showed this air-to-surface missile under the port wing of a Tu-16 bomber. It is externally similar to "Kennel", but the ram air intake and radome of the latter missile are replaced by a hemi-spherical nose fairing, probably housing a larger radar. This implies that "Kelt" is rocket-powered and it may be significant that, unlike "Kennel", it has an under-belly fairing of the kind seen on the rocket-powered "Styx" missile. In other respects the airframes of "Kelt" and "Kennel" appear to be almost identical, but the underwing carrier used with "Kelt" is much larger.

SURFACE-TO-AIR MISSILES

V750VK (SA-2)
NATO Code Name: "Guideline"

This two-stage surface-to-air guided weapon, referred to in the United States as Type SA-2, and allocated the code-name "Guideline" by NATO, was first seen in the 1957 military parade in Moscow and is a standard Soviet air defence missile. It has been exported in considerable numbers to many countries, including Cuba, Egypt, Indonesia, Iraq, North Vietnam and the Warsaw Pact countries.

Examples captured by Israeli forces during the Sinai campaign of June 1967 indicate that the official Soviet designation of the missile is V750VK. The entire weapon system, with radar van and generators, has the designation V75SM. The Zil 157 semi-trailer transporter/erector vehicle has cross-country capability, the inflation pressure of the tyres being adjustable from the cab to suit the terrain. Normal launch angle is 80°.

The original version of "Guideline", which might be termed the Mk 1, was similar to the US Nike Ajax in many design features and the two weapons were probably comparable in performance. The design has undergone several detail changes through the years. For example, the small vanes near the nose were originally rectangular but were changed to a cropped delta shape on the "Mk 2" version, as supplied to Egypt.

Further refinement has led to two improved versions which have been identified in Moscow parades. The latest of these, "Guideline Mk 4", first seen in November 1967, is some 15 in (40 cm) longer than its predecessors. It was claimed by the Moscow commentator to be far more effective than earlier versions and the fact that the enlarged warhead is white-painted may imply that it is of a nuclear type. The small canard surfaces seen on the nose of earlier versions do not appear on the "Mk 4", which has enlarged wings with increased leading-edge sweep. There are no control surfaces on its booster fins.

Examples of "Guideline" captured by Israeli forces are said to have warheads detonated by contact or proximity fuses. Those used in North Vietnam are said to be detonated by command; reports from USAF combat aircrew imply that "Guidelines" used there lack the manoeuvra-

Tupolev Tu-20 ("Bear-B") with "Kangaroo" air-to-surface missile

"Kelt" rocket-powered air-to-surface stand-off missile, developed from "Kennel", under port wing of Tu-16 bomber

bility to intercept high-speed aircraft performing evasive tight turns.

The following details refer to the type ("Mk 2") that was supplied to Egypt:

TYPE: Surface-to-air land-based guided weapon.

WINGS: Fixed cruciform wings mounted well back on body.

BODY: Cylindrical all-metal structure.

TAIL SURFACES: Small movable cruciform tail surfaces at rear of weapon, indexed in line with wings.

POWER PLANT: One liquid-propellant sustainer, using nitric acid and a hydrocarbon fuel as propellants, with burning time of 22 seconds. One in-line solid-propellant booster (burning time 4-5 seconds) fitted with large cruciform fins indexed in line with wings. Control surfaces on trailing-edge of two of the fins.

GUIDANCE: Automatic radio command. Target aircraft tracked by radar, which feeds signals to a computer, from which radio signals to missile are generated. Two sets of four flush strip-antennae, fore and aft of nose fins.

"Kennel" anti-shipping missiles under the wings of a Tupolev Tu-16 bomber of the Indonesian Air Force (see page 627)

WARHEAD: High-explosive, weight 288 lb (131 kg), aft of guidance section.

DIMENSIONS (approx):

Length with booster	35 ft 0 in (10·66 m)
Length without booster	27 ft 0 in (8·25 m)
Body diameter:	
booster	2 ft 2 in (0·66 m)
missile	1 ft 8 in (0·51 m)
Span of wings	5 ft 7 in (1·70 m)
Span of booster fins	8 ft 5½ in (2·58 m)

WEIGHT:

Launching weight with booster	
	approx 5,000 lb (2,270 kg)

PERFORMANCE:

Speed at burn-out	Mach 3·5
Slant range	22 nm (25 miles; 40 km)
Effective ceiling	60,000 ft (18,300 m)

NATO Code Name: "Guild"

Shown publicly for the first time in the parade through Moscow on 7 November 1960, this anti-aircraft missile had no booster unit attached. This may indicate use of a dual-thrust solid-propellant motor.

The control system has also been changed by comparison with "Guideline", and this weapon has movable cruciform foreplane control surfaces, supplemented by small surfaces in the wing trailing-edges. The wings are cruciform, indexed in line with the foreplanes, and of cropped delta planform.

Length of this weapon is about 39 ft (12 m).

SA-3
NATO Code Name: "Goa"

First shown in public in 1964, the two-stage surface-to-air missile code-named "Goa" is compact enough to be carried in pairs on the vehicle that is used as a tractor for the trailer transporters of "Guideline" and "Guild".

It is a two-stage missile, probably intended as the Soviet counterpart of the American Hawk, for short-range defence against aircraft down to very low altitudes. The large-diameter booster is almost certainly of the solid-propellant type, and is fitted with cruciform fins. These are indexed in line with the fixed rear-mounted wings of the second stage, as are the latter's movable foreplane control surfaces.

"Goa" is standard armament on ships of the Soviet Navy. Four destroyers of the *Kynda* class have a twin launcher forward of the cruise missile installation on their fore-deck. The launcher appears to be very similar to that of the American Tartar weapon system. The same missiles and twin launcher are installed on the after deck of two destroyers of the *Kotlin* class. The ten destroyers of the *Kashin* class and two of the *Kresta* class each have two twin launchers, fore and aft.

"Guideline", the Soviet Union's standard surface-to-air missile on its launcher   (*Tass*)

V75SM weapon system, comprising "Guideline" missiles, radar van and generator

Version of "Guideline", with enlarged warhead, first displayed on 7 November 1967
(*Aviation Week and Space Technology*)

Twin launcher for "Goa" surface-to-air missiles on forward deck of a Soviet destroyer   (*Tass*)

Surface-to-air missiles, code-named "Guild", in Moscow parade, 7 November 1969   (*Tass*)

"Goa" is also deployed as a mobile land-based weapon system and is operational in Egypt in this rôle.

DIMENSIONS (approx):

Length overall	20 ft 0 in (6·00 m)
Diameter of second stage	1 ft 6 in (0·45 m)
Diameter of booster	2 ft 3 in (0·70 m)
Span of wings	4 ft 0 in (1·22 m)

New ship-based SAM

The surface-to-air missiles carried on twin launchers on board the helicopter carrier *Moskva* have been referred to as "Goas". This is not so; they are of a new and so far unspecified type.

NATO Code Name: "Gainful"

This compact new surface-to-air weapon system was first shown in public in the Moscow parade of 7 November 1967 and was seen again on May Day 1968. Each unit consists of a tracked transporter, carrying three solid-propellant missiles of simple cylindrical shape, with cruciform wings at about mid-length, indexed in line with cruciform tail-fins. A large duct fairing extends along the side of the missile, from just forward of the wings to just aft of the fins, with a shorter fairing between the wings on top and below. Length of the missile is about 19 ft 6 in (6·0 m), making it rather larger than the American Hawk. It can be assumed to have the same low-altitude rôle as Hawk and was probably not yet operational by mid-1968.

NATO Code Name: "Griffon"

First displayed in a parade through Moscow on 7 November 1963, this large weapon was said to be an anti-missile missile. It appears to be basically two-stage, but the warhead may separate after second-stage burn-out and use an in-built rocket motor for the final stages of interception.

The first-stage booster has a large-diameter solid-propellant motor and is fitted with fixed cruciform fins of cropped delta shape. The second stage has cruciform wings of cropped delta form, each with a small control surface inset in the trailing-edge, extending from near the tip almost to mid-span. Movable cruciform tail control surfaces are indexed in line with the wings.

"Griffon" almost certainly lacks the capability to be effective against strategic ballistic missiles. It is best regarded as a long-range anti-aircraft missile with limited defence capability against tactical ballistic and air-launched missiles.

DIMENSIONS (approx):

Length overall with nose-probe	54 ft 0 in (16·50 m)
Diameter of second stage	2 ft 10 in (0·85 m)
Diameter of booster	3 ft 6 in (1·07 m)
Span of wings	12 ft 0 in (3·65 m)
Span of booster fins	15 ft 0 in (4·57 m)

Top to bottom:

Two-stage solid-propellant surface-to-air missiles, code-named "Goa" (*Novosti*)

"Goa" twin-round launcher on Soviet warship (*Tass*)

Surface-to-air weapon system known to NATO as "Gainful" (*Tass*)

Long-range surface-to-air missile code-named "Griffon", November 1967

NATO Code Name: "Ganef"

This type of surface-to-air missile was displayed for the first time in the 1964 May Day parade through Moscow. As can be seen in the adjacent illustration, the missile is carried on a tracked twin-launcher vehicle and may also have surface-to-surface potential.

The main body of the missile is cylindrical, with a diameter of about 32 in (0·80 m). Control is by means of cruciform tapered all-moving wings on the forward part of the body. Fixed cruciform tail-fins are indexed at 45° to the wings. An annular air intake, with the lengthy warhead section forming a centre-body, implies the use of a ramjet sustainer. Boost is provided by four wrap-round solid-propellant boosters, with canted nozzles and wedge noses to ensure clean separation after burn-out. A command guidance system is used.

En route to the May 1966 Moscow parade, the top tail-fin of some "Ganefs" had been removed and stowed between the rear fuselages, immediately forward of the horizontal tail-fins. They were in place during the parade itself.

"Ganef" is air-transportable on its launch vehicle in the An-22 heavy freight aircraft.

DIMENSIONS (approx):

Length overall	30 ft 0 in (9·15 m)
Body diameter	2 ft 8 in (0·80 m)
Span of wings	7 ft 6 in (2·30 m)
Span of fins	8 ft 6 in (2·60 m)

NATO Code Name: "Galosh"

When this missile was shown for the first time in a Moscow parade on 7 November 1964, it was described by the commentator as an anti-ballistic-missile (ABM) missile. Little is known of "Galosh" itself, as it is largely hidden by the ribbed-skin trailer-container in which it is transported. Four

Ramjet-powered surface-to-air missiles, code-named "Ganef", 7 November 1967 *(Tass)*

"Galosh" anti-ballistic missile system in Moscow parade, 7 November 1969 *(Tass)*

Close-up of the four nozzles of the missile code-named "Galosh" *(Novosti)*

first-stage nozzles are visible inside the forward end of the container, with what appear to be the ends of four guide-rails for loading and/or launching the weapon. The rear end of the container is covered by a spherical cap.

It would clearly be wrong to regard "Galosh" as a mobile missile system. To be effective in an anti-missile rôle, it would need the support of extensive ground equipment, which has not been displayed and is probably static.

US reports have suggested that a total of 67 ABM launch sites have been installed around Moscow, equipped with "Galosh".

The tractor used with this weapon system was also seen for the first time in the 1964 parade and has since become standardised for large Soviet weapon systems. It is used also to haul "Sasin", "Skean", "Savage", "Scrag" and "Scarp" and is, basically, an eight-wheeled vehicle with an overall height of about 10 ft (3·0 m). The "Galosh" container is articulated from a point between the rear pairs of wheels. The other missiles are towed on separate trailers, enabling the tractor to accommodate personnel or equipment aft of the cab and power plant section.

DIMENSIONS OF CONTAINER (approx):

Inside diameter	9 ft 0 in (2·75 m)
Length to bottom of end cap	67 ft 0 in (20·40 m)

NAVAL MISSILES
NATO Code Name: "Styx"

The adjacent illustration depicts a naval surface-to-surface cruise missile which is known as "Styx" to NATO. This missile is standard armament on Soviet fast patrol boats, two being carried by *Komar* class ships and four by *Osa* class vessels, in containers on each side

"Styx" cruise missile being hoisted on board Soviet patrol boat *(Novosti)*

"Styx" surface-to-surface naval missile (*Tass*)

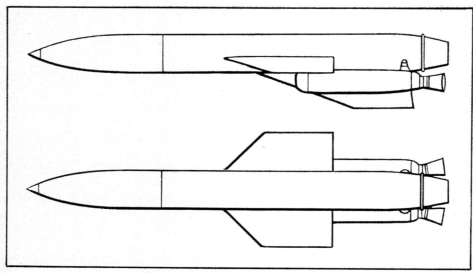

Possible configuration of "Shaddock" cruise missile

of the after deck. At least 125 ships of these classes are believed to serve with the Soviet Navy. In addition, *Komar* class ships are in service with the navies of Algeria (8), the People's Republic of China (3), Cuba (18), Egypt (8), Indonesia (12) and Syria (10). *Osa* class ships have been supplied to Algeria (1), the People's Republic of China (7), Egypt (12), East Germany (12), Poland (12) and Romania (4). All ships of both classes are armed with "Styx". It is believed that the "Styx" missiles used by the Egyptian Navy to sink the Israeli destroyer *Eilat* on 21 October 1967 came from the *Osa* class ships, in harbour at Port Said. Israeli reports credit "Styx" with a radar homing capability.

"Styx" has an aeroplane configuration, with cropped-delta wings, each with an almost-full-span aileron, and three identical tail surfaces, each comprising a fixed stabiliser and trailing-edge control surface. The horizontal tail surfaces have considerable anhedral. Inside its container, "Styx" is carried on a twin-rail launcher, from which it is boosted by a large jettisonable solid-propellant rocket motor, with downward-canted nozzle, mounted under the rear fuselage. The sustainer rocket nozzle is in the tail of the missile, which appears to have a length of about 20 ft (6·10 m) and span of about 8 ft 10 in (2·70 m) and has a range of at least 13 nm (15 miles; 24 km).

Other Cruise Missiles ("Strela")

The six destroyers of the *Krupny* class and two of the *Kanin* class each carry two launchers (one forward, one aft) for an aeroplane-type cruise missile that is larger and more advanced than "Styx". A similar launcher is carried aft by four ships of the *Kotlin* (NATO *Kildin*) class. Nothing is known of this missile, which is often referred to by the name "Strela".

NATO Code Name: "Shaddock"

As in the case of "Galosh", this cruise missile has been seen only within its tanker-like transport vehicle. However, the domed plates which are designed to cover each end of the transport/launch container have been pivoted upward in recent Moscow parades, leaving the ends of the container open. This has revealed a pointed nose-cone at the front and the nozzle arrangement at the rear which is illustrated on this page.

The large basin-shaped top cover probably hides a ramjet or turbojet exhaust nozzle and there are two large JATO units under the rear of the fuselage with what appears to be a ventral fin between them. The wings can be assumed to be of the hinged "flip-out" type, opening out when the missile leaves its launcher.

The accompanying drawing is based on one which appeared in an official East German magazine, but has been modified to reflect known details of the nose and tail shape of "Shaddock". It is possible that the nose has an annular ramjet intake like that of the "Ganef" surface-to-air missile.

Length of the container is about 45 ft (13·75 m) and diameter about 7 ft 6 in (2·25 m). The missile is probably about 40 ft (12 m) long. It cruises at Mach 0·95, or faster, and uses an active radar homing system. Range is in the order of 200 nm (230 miles; 370 km).

Rear view of "Shaddock" missile system, showing nozzle arrangement

(*Aviation Week and Space Technology*)

The surface-to-surface cruise missile system code-named "Shaddock" (*Novosti*)

"Shaddock" is carried as a standard weapon by many Soviet surface ships and submarines. Each of the *Kresta* class of large destroyers carries four in two twin launchers, probably without reload capability. *Kynda* class destroyers each carry four "Shaddock" container/launchers side-by-side on the fore-deck and four more on the after deck, probably with eight further missiles stowed for a second strike.

"Shaddock" submarines include the 25 "E II" class, each with eight missiles; the five "E I" class, each with six missiles; the ten "J" class, each with four missiles; and the converted "W" class, each with one, two or four (longbin) missiles. The "E I" and "E II" class ships are nuclear powered.

Two "Shaddock" missile launchers on a Soviet "W" class submarine

NATO Code Name: "Serb"

First seen in a Moscow parade in November 1964, this ballistic missile was claimed to be capable of underwater launching from submarines. Its general appearance is shown in the adjacent illustration.

"Serb" appears to be a two-stage solid-propellant rocket. When displayed in the November 1967 Moscow parade, the usual cover plate over the base of the missile was removed, revealing the 18 small nozzles of an electrically-detonated cold-gas system by which "Serb" is ejected from its launch-tube.

"Serb", like the earlier "Sark" (see 1967-68 Jane's), is thought to be a research and development version of the first-generation Polaris-type weapon carried by Soviet submarines, which have been seen with from two to eight vertical launch-tubes for ballistic or cruise missiles (see Jane's Fighting Ships).

One ship of this type, the "G" class with three launch tubes, serves with the navy of the People's Republic of China. The missiles are said to have a range of 330 nm (380 miles; 600 km).

DIMENSIONS (approx)
Length overall	33 ft 0 in (10·0 m)
Max diameter	5 ft 0 in (1·5 m)

NATO Code Name: "Sawfly"

First seen publicly in the Moscow parade of 7 November 1967, this weapon is displayed on an articulated trailer towed by a Soviet Navy Type MAZ-537 eight-wheel tractor, and almost certainly represents a research and development model of Russia's second-generation submarine-launched ballistic missile. Considerably larger than the US Poseidon, it probably has a range of at least 1,750 nm (2,000 miles; 3,200 km).

Code-named "Sawfly" by NATO, it appears to be a two-stage solid-propellant missile, with the stage separation point visible mid-way between the front pair of straps securing it to the articulated trailer. The nose-cone fitted to the example displayed was probably unrepresentative of an operational version. Four nozzles were shown at the base of the first stage.

The US Department of Defense estimated that, on 1 September 1969, there were 110 submarine-launched ballistic missiles of all types operational on Soviet nuclear-powered and diesel-powered submarines, compared with 45 one year earlier and with 656 US Polaris missiles available in operational nuclear-powered submarines. Latest type of Soviet nuclear-powered ballistic missile submarine is the "Y" class, equipped with 16 launchers. Several of this class were operational by September 1969 and several more by February 1970. It is estimated that 35-50 "Y" class vessels could be operational by 1974-75.

DIMENSIONS (approx):
Length overall	42 ft 0 in (12·8 m)
Basic diameter	5 ft 9 in (1·75 m)

SURFACE-TO-SURFACE MISSILES
NATO Code Name: "Frog-1"

Soviet counterpart of the US Honest John, this spin-stabilised unguided missile is carried on a tracked vehicle based on the JS 3 amphibious reconnaissance AFV, with enclosed accommodation for the crew. The missile is covered by a heavy ribbed casing, which elevates with it to form a launch-tube. It has been in service since about 1957.

The version of this rocket seen since 1960 has a parallel-sided warhead and six tail fins instead of the original cruciform fins. Soviet commentators have referred to its "high precision and enormously powerful thermo-nuclear warhead".

The NATO code name "Frog" is an acronym for "Free Rocket Over Ground".

TYPE: Surface-to-surface unguided tactical weapon.

WINGS: None.

BODY: Bulbous-nose cylindrical all-metal structure.

TAIL SURFACES: Six fixed tail-fins at rear of missile.

POWER PLANT: One solid-propellant sustainer with seven nozzles. No booster.

GUIDANCE: None. Spin-stabilised.

WARHEAD: Probably choice of nuclear or high explosive.

DIMENSIONS (approx):
Length	31 ft 0 in (9·50 m)
Span of fins	3 ft 3 in (1·0 m)

Submarine-launched missile, code-named "Serb"

Rear end of the R & D submarine-launched missile known as "Serb", showing gas-jets for ejection from launch-tube (Aviation Week and Space Technology)

"Sawfly", the R & D version of Russia's second-generation submarine-launched ballistic missile (Tass)

Surface-to-surface missiles, known as "Frog-1"

WEIGHT (estimated):
Firing weight   6,000 lb (2,700 kg)

PERFORMANCE (estimated):
Range   13 nm (15 miles; 24 km)

NATO Code Name: "Frog-2, 3, 4 and 5"

These unguided spin-stabilised missiles are carried on a tracked vehicle derived from the PT76 amphibious reconnaissance tank. This appears to serve also as the launcher.

The original "Frog-2", illustrated on page 435 of the 1960-61 *Jane's*, was a single-stage missile about 29 ft 6 in (9.0 m) long with a bulbous warhead. It was followed by "Frog-3", illustrated on page 444 of the 1964-65 *Jane's*, which appears to have two stages in tandem and is fitted with a cylindrical bulbous warhead; and "Frog-4" which is similar except that the warhead is no longer bulbous. "Frog-5" is also similar to "Frogs 3 and 4" except for having a different warhead. The following details apply to "Frog-4".

TYPE: Surface-to-surface unguided tactical weapon.

WINGS: None.

BODY: Cylindrical all-metal structure.

TAIL SURFACES: Fixed cruciform tail-fins at rear of missile.

POWER PLANT: Solid-propellant sustainer and booster in tandem. Central nozzle of booster is surrounded by twelve small nozzles.

GUIDANCE: None. Spin-stabilised.

WARHEAD: Probably choice of nuclear or high-explosive.

DIMENSIONS (approx):
Length   33 ft 6 in (10·20 m)
Span of fins   3 ft 6 in (1·05 m)

WEIGHT (estimated):
Firing weight   4,400 lb (2,000 kg)

PERFORMANCE (estimated):
Range   26 nm (30 miles; 50 km)

NATO Code Name: "Frog-7"

First shown in the Moscow Parade of 7 November 1965, this version of "Frog" has reverted to the original single-stage configuration. It should be noted, however, that the main nozzle is surrounded by a ring of smaller nozzles.

"Frog-7" is transported on a different type of erector/launch vehicle, as can be seen in the adjacent illustration, and looks a much more modern and efficient weapon system.

NATO Code Names: "Scud A and B"

Unlike the smaller missiles known as "Frogs", the "Scud" types have movable tail fins, indicating some form of guidance. The original version, known to NATO as "Scud-A", is carried on a tracked vehicle identical with that used for the "Frog-1". The tubular-metal cradle in which it is supported elevates with it into the firing position, ladders embodied in each side of the cradle giving access to the warhead section.

The completely new "Scud-B", carried on a higher-performance wheeled transporter/erector/launch vehicle, was first shown in the November 1965 Moscow parade. Larger than the "A", with an overall length of about 37 ft (11·25 m), it is supported in a similar kind of elevating cradle.
The following details apply to "Scud-A".

TYPE: Surface-to-surface guided weapon.

WINGS: None.

BODY: Cylindrical all-metal structure.

TAIL SURFACES: Cruciform tail-fins, which appear to be movable, at rear of body.

POWER PLANT: One liquid-propellant sustainer. No booster.

GUIDANCE: Type unknown.

WARHEAD: Probably choice of nuclear or high-explosive.

DIMENSIONS (approx):
Length   35 ft 0 in (10·66 m)

WEIGHT (estimated):
Firing weight   10,000 lb (4,500 kg)

PERFORMANCE (estimated):
Speed at burn-out   Mach 5
Range   43 nm (50 miles; 80 km)

Preparing a "Frog-5" two-stage unguided missile for night launching (*Tass*)

Rear view of "Frog-7" missile, showing multiple nozzles (*Aviation Week and Space Technology*)

"Frog-7" unguided tactical missiles, first seen in November 1965

The surface-to-surface weapon system known to NATO as "Scud-B" (*Tass*)

Above: **Two views of "Scud-A" surface-to-surface guided missile systems** (*Tass*)

Right: **"Scud-A" missile systems in a Moscow parade** (*Tass*)

Below: **"Scud-B" tactical surface-to-surface weapon system, on wheeled transporter/erector/ launch vehicle**
(*Aviation Week and Space Technology*)

NATO Code Name: "Scaleboard"

"Scaleboard" is another of the weapons shown for the first time in the military parade to mark the 50th anniversary of the Communist Revolution, on 7 November 1967. Although it is larger in diameter than the "Scuds", its wheeled transporter/launch vehicle is basically similar to that used with "Scud-B". The driver occupies the left-hand cab at the front, with the missile launch operator and his control console in the right-hand cab and seats for at least three other members of the launch crew in the rear of these cabs. A pair of sideways-hinged doors, between the two inner wheels on the left-hand side of the vehicle, give access to control equipment.

In place of the support cradle used with "Scud", this new missile has a ribbed split casing

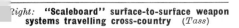

Right: **"Scaleboard" surface-to-surface weapon systems travelling cross-country** (*Tass*)

which encloses it completely and is elevated with it into the firing position. The overall length of "Scaleboard" is estimated to be about 37 ft (11·25 m), the same as "Scud-B". Its maximum range could be of the order of 390 nm (450 miles; 725 km).

NATO Code Name: "Samlet"

"Samlet" is a surface-to-surface version of the air-to-surface jet-powered cruise missile known to NATO as "Kennel" (see page 627). It is known to be in operational service with the armed forces of the Soviet Union, Poland and Cuba, primarily as a coastal defence weapon.

NATO Code Name: "Sandal"/"Shyster"

The original "Shyster" bombardment missile was almost certainly based to a large extent on the wartime German V.2 rocket, incorporating improvements in structure and propellants. First seen in a Moscow parade in 1957, it was always displayed on a mobile transporter, hauled by a tracked vehicle carrying its firing personnel.

A developed version, first seen in 1961 and given the NATO code-name "Sandal", is longer, indicating higher performance than the original version. It can be identified by the flared skirt around its first-stage nozzle and smaller fins.

"Sandal" became a standard intermediate-range ballistic missile in the Soviet armed forces and is used in modified form as a satellite launch vehicle. Weapons of this type were also deployed in Cuba in the Autumn of 1962, but were withdrawn as a result of American/Soviet negotiations.

TYPE: Surface-to-surface guided weapon.
WINGS: None.
BODY: Cylindrical all-metal structure.
TAIL SURFACES: Cruciform tail-fins at rear of body, with movable elevators in trailing-edges and V.2-type control vanes positioned in rocket efflux.
POWER PLANT: One liquid-propellant sustainer. No booster.
GUIDANCE: Type unknown. Reported to be radio-inertial.
WARHEAD: Probably choice of nuclear or high-explosive.
DIMENSIONS ("Sandal", approx):
  Length   68 ft 0 in (20·8 m)
  Body diameter   5 ft 3 in (1·60 m)
WEIGHT ("Sandal", estimated):
  Firing weight   60,000 lb (27,200 kg)
PERFORMANCE ("Sandal", estimated):
  Speed at burn-out   Mach 6·5
  Range   955 nm (1,100 miles; 1,750 km)

NATO Code Name: "Skean"

First seen in a Moscow parade in November 1964, "Skean" is a later development of the "Shyster/Sandal" series of liquid-propellant IRBM's. Although similar in general configuration to its predecessors, it can be identified by the absence of tail-fins and its blunted nose-cone. It is carried on a different trailer, towed by the latest type of heavy tractor vehicle, and has been shown inside silo underground launch facilities in official Soviet films.

The surface-to-surface weapon system known to NATO as "Scaleboard" (*Tass*)

"Samlet" coastal defence missile of the Soviet Red Banner Northern Fleet on launcher (*Tass*)

The surface-to-surface ballistic missile code-named "Sandal"

The liquid-propellant IRBM known by the NATO code-name of "Skean", in the November 1967 parade through Moscow

DIMENSIONS (approx):
Length overall   75 ft 0 in (23·0 m)
Body diameter   8 ft 0 in (2·40 m)
PERFORMANCE (estimated):
Range   1,750 nm (2,000 miles; 3,200 km)

NATO Code Name: "Scamp"

When this weapon was first seen in a Moscow parade on 9 May 1965, it was given the nickname "Iron Maiden" because of the way in which the missile is enclosed in a container made in two halves, split horizontally and hinged. The NATO code-name "Scamp" applies to the complete weapon system, including the tracked erector/launch vehicle. A massive hydraulic jack on each side, at the rear, raises the missile to a vertical position above the firing platform for launching. The hinged container is then opened up and moved away from the missile before the latter is fired.

Soviet official films have revealed the missile to be the two-stage weapon known to NATO as "Scapegoat" and described briefly below. Its role appears to be as a mobile strategic missile, rather like a land-based Polaris, with a claimed range of the order of 2,175 nm (2,500 miles; 4,000 km).

The original type of erector/launch vehicle, illustrated in the 1969-70 *Jane's*, seems to have been superseded by a vehicle similar to that used for the "Scrooge" weapon system. The latest vehicle is shown in the illustration on this page.

"Scamp" systems are reported to have been deployed adjacent to the frontier with China, near Buir Nor in Outer Mongolia.

Right: **The solid-propellant mobile strategic missile system code-named "Scamp"**   (*Tass*)

NATO Code Name: "Scapegoat"

This two-stage solid-propellant IRBM has been identified as the missile carried by the weapon system known to NATO as "Scamp" and described above. It was first displayed openly on a trailer in the November 1967 Moscow parade and appears to comprise the top two stages of the missile code-named "Savage" (see page 639). This gives it an overall length of approximately 35 ft (10·6 m).

Right: **"Scapegoat" missile in place within the container of its "Scamp" transporter/launch vehicle**

NATO Code Name: "Scrooge"

First shown in the Moscow parade of 7 November 1965, this strategic missile is carried, like "Scamp", in a container on a tracked transport/erector/launch vehicle. It is a considerably longer weapon, implying greater range, and is presumably launched from the tubular container as this is not hinged to open up like that of "Scamp".

Photographs have been released showing the tubular container erected into a vertical position for firing. "Scrooge" systems are reported to have been deployed adjacent to the frontier with China, near Buir Nor in Outer Mongolia.

DIMENSIONS (approx):
Length of launch tube   62 ft 0 in (18·90 m)
Diameter of launch tube   6 ft 6 in (2·00 m)
PERFORMANCE (estimated):
Range   3,040 nm (3,500 miles; 5,600 km)

Right: **The mobile strategic missile system known to NATO as "Scrooge", 7 November 1968**   (*Tass*)

First seen in November 1964, this liquid-propellant rocket is code-named "Sasin" *(Aviation Week and Space Technology)*

The three-stage liquid-propellant ICBM code-named "Scrag" *(Aviation Week and Space Technology)*

NATO Code Name: "Sasin"

"Sasin" is a two-stage liquid-propellant long-range rocket which was seen for the first time in a Moscow parade in November 1964. It was towed on a trailer by the standard large eight-wheel tractor vehicle used for other large Soviet missiles, but has not taken part in the most recent parades which may indicate that it is not an operational weapon.

DIMENSIONS (approx):
Length overall	80 ft 0 in (24·40 m)
Max body diameter	9 ft 0 in (2·75 m)

PERFORMANCE (estimated):
Range	5,650 nm (6,500 miles; 10,500 km)

NATO Code-Name: "Scrag"

This liquid-propellant three-stage ICBM was first shown in the Moscow parade on 9 May 1965, when it was stated to be a sister vehicle of the launch vehicle used for the Vostok and Voskhod spacecraft (which see). The stages are separated by truss structures, with no inter-stage fairings.

The first stage has four gimballed nozzles. The second stage appears to have a single very large nozzle and the third stage a single comparatively small nozzle.

There is no evidence to indicate that 'Scrag' is an operational weapon.

The following data are estimated:

DIMENSIONS:
Length overall	120 ft 0 in (36·5 m)
Length of individual stages:	
First	59 ft 0 in (18·00 m)
Interstage	6 ft 0 in (1·80 m)
Second	25 ft 2 in (7·70 m)
Interstage	8 ft 9 in (2·70 m)
Third, including re-entry vehicle	21 ft 0 in (6·40 m)
Nose-cone	8 ft 6 in (2·60 m)
Diameter of individual stages:	
First, at base	9 ft 5 in (2·85 m)
Second	8 ft 9 in (2·70 m)
Third, at base	7 ft 9 in (2·35 m)
Nose-cone, at base	5 ft 0 in (1·50 m)

PERFORMANCE (estimated):
Range	4,350 nm (5,000 miles; 8,000 km)

FOBS (SS-9)
NATO Code Name: "Scarp"

Two examples of this weapon were displayed in the Moscow parade to mark the 50th anniversary of the Communist revolution, on 7 November 1967.

Four days earlier, the then US Secretary of Defense had announced that the Soviet Union appeared to be developing a "space bomb" in the form of a "fractional orbital bombardment system" (FOBS). This was explained as a weapon which could be fired into an orbit about

"Scapegoat" is the missile carried inside the "Scamp" container *(Tass)*

This rocket, being lowered into a silo, is similar in configuration to "Scarp" but differs in important respects from the operational SS-9/FOBS vehicle. It was probably an R & D round

Reported to be designated SS-9 in its ICBM form, this large liquid-propellant weapon is also the launch vehicle for the FOBS "space bomb" (*Tass*)

85 nm (100 miles; 160 km) above the Earth; then, at a given point, and before completion of the first orbit, a retro-rocket would slow the weapon and cause it to drop on its target. Mr McNamara explained that the advantages to the Soviet Union of such a technique for delivering a nuclear warhead are that warning time would be much reduced and the defences could be penetrated from the south; the disadvantages are that FOBS is less accurate and more expensive than the use of an ICBM.

The first launch in the FOBS development programme is believed to have taken place on 25 January 1967 (Cosmos 139) and to have been followed by Cosmos 160 on 17 May and others listed in the satellite table on page 688. Optical sightings of these payloads at the RAE, Farnborough, England, suggest that each is about 6 ft 6 in (2·0 m) long and 4 ft (1·21 m) in diameter.

The Soviet commentator on 7 November 1967 implied that the "space bomb" launcher was included in the parade and this was undoubtedly a reference to this large liquid-propellant vehicle, which has the NATO code name "Scarp". It has been referred to in the American press by the designation **SS-9**, and exists as a standard conventional ICBM as well as being the FOBS launch vehicle. The ICBM has alternative warheads, one of 20/25-megaton yield, the other with three separate re-entry vehicles, each with a yield of five megatons. It is estimated that a simple unguided multiple re-entry vehicle (MRV) of this kind could have become operational in 1969, followed by a multiple independently-targeted re-entry vehicle (MIRV) at any time between late 1970 and 1972, depending on the aims of the current SS-9 test programme. According to US Defense Secretary Melvin R. Laird, US intelligence sources had by early 1970 identified a range of possible future Soviet ICBM re-entry vehicles on launchers.

In basic configuration, "Scarp" looks like a further extension in size, performance and complexity of the "Shyster/Skean" formula. Its first-stage propulsion system is displayed with six nozzles, but a base-plate has prevented detailed study of these. Four vernier nozzles are faired into the periphery of the skirt surrounding the first-stage nozzles.

Only other discernible feature is the bluff cylindrical re-entry body on the nose of the missile. This is probably no more than a test version or a cover for the true re-entry vehicle. The US Department of Defense estimated that a total of 1,060 Soviet ICBMs were deployed on 1 September 1969 (compared with 1,054 US ICBMs), and that more than 275 of these were SS-9s. Total deployment will reach 1,250 by mid-1970 if the rate of increase is maintained, with a potential of more than 2,500 operational ICBMs by the mid-1970s.

One SS-9 fired into the Pacific during the past year delivered an inert MRV warhead over a range of 4,750 nm (5,500 miles; 8,800 km) according to the US Secretary of Defense. Photographs have shown the separate warheads re-entering the atmosphere with about the same dispersal "footprint" as the distances between three typical Minuteman silos.

DIMENSIONS (approx):
Length overall	113 ft 6 in (34·5 m)
Basic diameter	10 ft 0 in (3·0 m)

SS-11

An official announcement in early 1970 suggested that about 670 SS-11 storable liquid-propellant

Right: **The six first-stage nozzles and four verniers of the SS-9/FOBS launch vehicle**

The SS-13 three-stage solid-propellant ICBM, code-named "Savage" (*Tass*)

ICBMs were then deployed operationally in hardened, camouflaged silo launchers in the Soviet Union. No details of the SS-11 are available, but it is being superseded by the solid-propellant SS-13.

SS-13
NATO Code Name: "Savage"

First shown publicly in the parade to mark the 20th anniversary of the end of World War II in Europe, on 9 May 1965, this weapon is a three-stage solid-propellant ICBM in the class of the American Minuteman. The stages each have four nozzles and are separated by a truss structure, as in the case of the larger liquid-propellant "Scrag".

Depending on the efficiency of the propulsion system, the range of "Savage" could be anything from 1,750 to 4,350 nm (2,000-5,000 miles; 2,300-8,000 km). It is replacing the earlier SS-11 storable liquid-propellant ICBM, of which about 900 were deployed at one time.

The two upper stages appear to be used without

the first stage in the missile code-named "Scapegoat" (which see).

DIMENSIONS:
Length overall	66 ft 0 in (20·0 m)
Length of individual stages:	
First	28 ft 6 in (8·70 m)
Interstage	2 ft 8½ in (0·82 m)
Second	13 ft 2½ in (4·00 m)
Interstage	2 ft 6 in (0·75 m)
Third	11 ft 7½ in (3·50 m)
Nose-cone and re-entry vehicle	
	7 ft 6 in (2·30 m)
Body diameter of individual stages:	
First	5 ft 6 in (1·68 m)
Second	4 ft 7½ in (1·40 m)
Third	3 ft 2½ in (0·98 m)
Nose-cone and re-entry vehicle	
	3 ft 2½ in (0·98 m)
Base diameter of individual stages:	
First	6 ft 6 in (2·00 m)
Second	6 ft 2½ in (1·90 m)
Third	4 ft 8½ in (1·40 m)

RESEARCH ROCKETS

AND

SPACE VEHICLES

(CORRECTED TO I AUGUST 1970)

THE ARGENTINE REPUBLIC

FMA
FÁBRICA MILITAR DE AVIONES, INSTITUTO DE INVESTIGACIÓN AERONÁUTICA Y ESPACIAL

ADDRESS:
Guarnición Aérea Córdoba, Córdoba

DIRECTOR OF I.I.A.E.:
Comodoro Aldo Zeoli

HEAD OF SPACE DEVELOPMENT GROUP:
Vicecomodoro Miguel Sanchez Peña

This branch of the Fábrica Militar de Aviones (FMA) is a research and development Institute which, since 1958, has undertaken the design and manufacture of solid-propellant rockets and missiles.

Simultaneously, double-base and composite propellants, payloads for upper atmosphere scientific research, instrumentation, telemetry equipment and other equipment have been developed in its laboratories.

In 1961, the I.I.A.E. conducted the first launching of a sounding rocket produced in the Argentine, the Alfa-Centauro. It has since manufactured a family of Centauro sounding rockets, known as the Alfa, Beta and Gamma. It has also inaugurated the first launching site in Latin America—the C.E.L.P.A. at Chamical, La Rioja (30° 30′ S, 66° W)—and has carried out the first scientific experiments in the Antarctic using vehicles and payloads manufactured in the Argentine Republic. These last launchings were made at Base Matienzo (64° 58′ S, 60° 64′ W).

I.I.A.E. personnel participated in international scientific experiments arranged by the Comisión Nacional de Investigaciones Espaciales (CNIE), using Bélier-Centaure rockets of French manufacture and American-built Nike-Cajuns and Nike-Apaches. It has also collaborated with the national universities in the development of instrumentation and payloads and the planning of scientific experiments.

The characteristics of the most important of the current rockets developed and launched by the I.I.A.E. for upper atmosphere research are as follows:

I.I.A.E. GAMMA-CENTAURO

This two-stage double-base solid-propellant fin-stabilised rocket is the third of the Centauro series. It has been used in the Argentine to initiate investigations in the field of cosmic radiation.

I.I.A.E. Gamma-Centauro two-stage rocket

I.I.A.E. Orion single-stage solid-propellant sounding rockets

DIMENSIONS:
Length overall	8 ft 10·4 in (2·70 m)
Diameter of booster	5·24 in (13·3 cm)
Diameter of second stage	3·66 in (9·3 cm)

WEIGHTS:
Payload	11·0 lb (5·00 kg)
Launching weight	70·5 lb (32·0 kg)

PERFORMANCE:
Max ceiling	24·3 nm (28 miles; 45 km)

I.I.A.E. D.I M.

The D.I.M. (Dart for Meteorological Investigation) consists of a fin-stabilised composite-propellant booster and an unpowered "dart" which can carry a chaff container for wind measurements, or instruments for atmospheric research, to heights of up to 37·8 nm (43·5 miles; 70 km).

DIMENSIONS:
Length overall	8 ft 2½ in (2·50 m)
Diameter of booster	3·94 in (10·00 cm)
Diameter of dart	1·38 in (3·50 cm)

WEIGHT:
Launching weight	55·1 lb (25 kg)
Max payload	7·7 lb (3·50 kg)

PERFORMANCE:
Max ceiling	37·8 nm (43·5 miles; 70 km)

I.I.A.E. ORION II

The Orion II is a single-stage composite-propellant sounding rocket capable of carrying a 55 lb (25 kg) payload to a height of 54 nm (62 miles; 100 km). It is fin-stabilised and has a parachute recovery system for the payload.

Development of Orion II was completed with a series of four launches at the C.E.L.P.A. at Chamical in August-September 1966. Subsequently, three Orion II's were launched at Tartagal (Salta-Argentina) to investigate cosmic radiation during the solar eclipse of November 1966, carrying payloads developed by the I.I.A.E. Radiation Laboratory.

Three more Orion II's were launched at Wallops Island, Virginia, USA, to verify their performance. In one of these launches, the payload descent was slowed by parachute, enabling it to be recovered by helicopter, using the air-snatch technique, at a height of 2,625 ft (800 m) above sea level. This was the first occasion on which a payload had been recovered in the air at Wallops Island.

DIMENSIONS:
Length overall	13 ft 1·6 in (4·00 m)
Body diameter	8·11 in (20·6 cm)

WEIGHTS:
Launching weight	308·6 lb (140 kg)
Payload	55 lb (25 kg)

PERFORMANCE:
Max ceiling	54 nm (62 miles; 100 km)

I.I.A.E. Rigel two-stage sounding rocket

I.I.A.E. RIGEL

Rigel is a two-stage fin-stabilised sounding rocket, able to carry a 66 lb (30 kg) payload to a height of approximately 108 nm (124 miles; 200 km). It consists of an Orion II as its second stage and a solid-propellant first stage. In addition two high-thrust rapid-burning boosters are attached to each side of the first stage at launch, falling away after burn-out.

DIMENSIONS:
Length overall	19 ft 8¼ in (6·00 m)
Body diameter:	
1st stage	10·95 in (27·8 cm)
2nd stage	8·11 in (20·6 cm)

WEIGHTS:
Launching weight	716·5 lb (325 kg)
Payload	66 lb (30 kg)

PERFORMANCE:
Max ceiling approx	118 nm (137 miles; 220 km)

AUSTRALIA

COMMONWEALTH OF AUSTRALIA
DEPARTMENT OF SUPPLY

ADDRESS:
Constitution Avenue, Parkes, Canberra, A.C.T. 2600

SECRETARY: A. S. Cooley

Weapons Research Establishment:
Salisbury, South Australia 5108

DIRECTOR: Dr M. W. Woods

Details are given below of current types of upper atmosphere sounding rockets which have been developed by the Weapons Research Establishment and built in Australia.

HAD

HAD is a two-stage solid-propellant sounding rocket capable of carrying a payload of 20 lb (9 kg) to a height of 69 nm (80 miles; 129 km).

It has been developed primarily for use in upper-atmosphere measurements.

DIMENSIONS:
Length overall	19 ft 6 in (5·94 m)
Length of second stage	8 ft 4 in (2·54 m)
Diameter of second stage	5 in (12·7 cm)
Semi-span of fins	10 in (25·4 cm)

WEIGHTS:
Launching weight, approx	640 lb (290 kg)
Weight of second stage	115 lb (52 kg)

PERFORMANCE:
Max speed (at second-stage burn-out)	2,722 knots (3,135 mph; 5,045 km/h)

HAD two-stage sounding rocket

HAT two-stage sounding rocket

Aero High two-stage sounding rocket

HAT

HAT is a two-stage solid-propellant sounding rocket designed for use in the development of a drop sonde. It carries a payload of 20 lb (9 kg) to a height of 35 nm (40 miles; 64 km).

DIMENSIONS:

Length overall	17 ft 6 in (5·4 m)
Length of second stage	8 ft 4 in (2·54 m)
Diameter of second stage	5 in (12·7 cm)
Semi-span of fins	10 in (25·4 cm)

WEIGHTS:

Launching weight	540 lb (245 kg)
Weight of second stage	115 lb (52 kg)

PERFORMANCE:
Max speed (at second-stage burn-out)
2,545 knots (2,930 mph; 4,715 km/h)

HAT Mk 2

Under development in early 1969, HAT Mk 2 is intended to supersede HAT. It has motors of higher thrust and an improved aerodynamic design, which combine to raise its ceiling to approximately 43 nm (50 miles; 80 km).

AERO HIGH

Aero High is a two-stage solid-propellant sounding rocket developed primarily to carry out "chemical seeding" experiments at altitudes between 54 and 108 nm (62-125 miles; 100-200 km). Observations of glow clouds caused by the sudden release of chemicals are used to determine physical and chemical properties of the upper atmosphere.

The vehicle is capable of carrying a 45 lb (20 kg) payload to a peak height of a little over 113 nm (130 miles; 210 km).

DIMENSIONS:

Length overall	21 ft 6 in (6·56 m)
Length of second stage	10 ft 3 in (3·13 m)
Diameter of second stage	8·3 in (21·1 cm)
Semi-span of fins:	
first stage	20·75 in (52·7 cm)
second stage	16·30 in (41·4 cm)

WEIGHTS:

Launching weight	approx 900 lb (409 kg)
Weight of second stage	260 lb (118 kg)

PERFORMANCE:
Maximum speed at second-stage burn-out
4,340 knots (5,000 mph; 8,050 km/h)

KOOKABURRA

Kookaburra has been designed and is manufactured in Australia to meet the need for a low-cost meteorological sounding rocket. With a ceiling of 42 nm (48 miles; 78 km), it has been used in the development of a drop sonde suitable for transmitting synoptic information to Australian meteorological stations. Payload capacity is 100 cu in (1,650 cc).

DIMENSIONS OF PAYLOAD CONTAINER:

Length overall	14 in (35 cm)
Diameter	3·1 in (7·9 cm)

WEIGHT:

Launching weight	117·5 lb (53·3 kg)

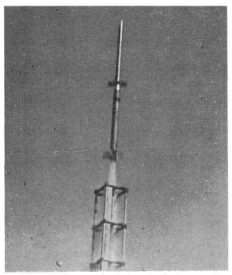

Kookaburra low-cost meteorological sounding rocket

BRAZIL

AVIBRAS
AVIBRAS INDÚSTRIA AERONÁUTICA LTDA

HEAD OFFICE AND WORKS:
Antiga Estrada de Paraibuna, km 118 (CP 229), São José dos Campos, São Paulo

MANAGING DIRECTOR:
Eng Olympio Sambatti

SALES DIRECTOR:
Hely Adilson de Oliveira

SPECIAL CONSULTANT TO BOARD:
Eng João Verdi de Carvalho Leite

This company is engaged in research and development of rockets, propellents, ancillary systems and light aircraft for both civil and military purposes. Details of one of its current rocket programmes follow.

AVIBRAS SONDA-1

The Sonda-1 vehicle is a two-stage solid-propellant sounding rocket, designed to reach heights of up to 37·7 nm (43·5 miles; 70 km). Developed under contract from the Brazilian Ministry of Aeronautics, it has made a series of successful flights and was due to have completed its qualification programme in July 1969.

The first stage, designated Avibras MFB-1, was developed to Min Aero Specification DM-6501. The Avibras MFB-2 second stage is covered by Min Aero Specification DM-6503. The Avibras CP-02 ogival payload container is to Min Aero Specification DM-6601 and has a payload volume of 213·5 cu in (3,500 cc). Both stages have cruciform fins, indexed in line; those on the first stage are rectangular, those on the second stage have swept leading-edges.

DIMENSIONS:

Length:	
MFB-1	3 ft 7·3 in (1·10 m)
MFB-2	5 ft 10·9 in (1·80 m)

Avibras Sonda-1 two-stage sounding rocket being elevated for firing

Body diameter:		WEIGHTS:	
MFB-1 and 2	4·5 in (11·4 cm)	Launching weight:	
		MFB-1	44 lb (20 kg)
Span of fins:		MFB-2	68·3 lb (31 kg)
MFB-1 and 2	13·2 in (33·5 cm)	CP-02 (standard)	11 lb (5 kg)

IPD/PAE

CENTRO TÉCNICO DE AERONÁUTICA INSTITUTO DE PESQUISAS E DESENVOLVIMENTO (IPD)

PAE—Departamento de Assuntos Especiais

ADDRESS:
São José dos Campos, São Paulo State

The PAE—Departamento de Assuntos Especiais (Special Affairs Department) is the branch of the Centro Técnico de Aeronáutica (Aeronautical Technical Centre) in charge of the development and prototype construction of airborne armament, rockets and missiles. Most of its work is classified, but it has been disclosed that the PAE has developed a twin-0·30-in calibre machine-gun mounting for helicopter use, an indigenous 2·75-in folding-fin air-to-ground rocket (now in series production by Brazilian private industry) and a two-stage sounding rocket, the Sonda II.

IPD/PAE SONDA II

The IPD/PAE Sonda II is designed to carry a scientific payload of 66 lb (30 kg) to an altitude of 54 nm (62 miles; 100 km). Both stages have solid-propellant motors, and the first stage has four cropped-delta stabilising fins.

IPD/PAE Sonda II sounding rocket
(Ronaldo S. Olive)

CANADA

BAL

BRISTOL AEROSPACE (1968) LIMITED

HEAD OFFICE AND WORKS:
Winnipeg International Airport, PO Box 874, Winnipeg, Manitoba

VICE-PRESIDENT MARKETING: R. H. May
MARKETING MANAGER: R. J. Bevis

Bristol Aerospace (1968) Limited (BAL) has developed and is manufacturing a series of seven high-altitude sounding rockets known as Black Brants. These vehicles have been designed for upper atmosphere research and have been used successfully by Canadian, United States and European research institutes.

Black Brant rockets have solid-propellant motors, and are designed for simplicity of operation, enabling them to be launched from ranges offering only minimum support facilities.

BAL is able to offer a completely comprehensive service in the sounding rocket field, including propellants, vehicle hardware, recovery systems, electronic components and payload system design and buildup, scientific experiment integration and checkout facilities. Experienced launch crews are available to conduct or support launches at any rocket range.

In addition to the vehicles described below, BAL is continuing its development of new rocket systems. One of these is a low-cost rocket capable of carrying a 9 lb (4·1 kg) payload to a height of 40 nm (47 miles; 75 km).

BLACK BRANT IIIA

Black Brant IIIA is a single-stage fin-stabilised rocket, powered by a 9KS11000 solid-propellant motor. It can carry a nominal gross payload of 110 lb (50 kg) to a height of 89 nm (102 miles; 165 km). The payload compartment is a 5·3 : 1 cone with 10 in (25·4 cm) cylindrical section as standard. The cylindrical section can be lengthened to 50 in (127 cm) if required.

Black Brant IIIA is launched in an overslung position from a Nike launcher or underslung from a boom launcher. Low impact dispersion characteristics suit it for launch from ranges with minimum impact area.

DIMENSIONS:
Length overall (standard configuration)
18 ft 2¼ in (5·54 m)
Body diameter   10·2 in (0·26 m)

WEIGHTS:
Launching weight (less payload) 630 lb (286 kg)
Motor   571 lb (259 kg)

NOMINAL PERFORMANCE:
Altitude with 110 lb (50 kg) gross payload
(Qe = 85°)   89 nm (102 miles; 165 km)
Max acceleration   28 g

BLACK BRANT IIIB

Development of this higher-performance version of Black Brant IIIA was completed during 1968 and six flights were made in 1969. Vehicle hardware and dimensions are identical with those of Black Brant IIIA, with the exception of the motor. The same alternative launchers can be used.

TYPE: Single-stage sounding rocket.
WINGS: None.
BODY: Cylindrical structure. Stainless steel nose section containing payload. Motor casing forms main structural skin and is of AMS 6435 steel. Magnesium aft body and aluminium fins with ablative coating.
TAIL SURFACES: Three fins, equi-spaced around rear of body.
POWER PLANT: Bristol Aerospace Model 12KS-10000 solid-propellant rocket motor.
GUIDANCE: None.
PAYLOAD COMPARTMENT: 5·3 : 1 cone, with 10 in (25·4 cm) cylindrical section as standard. Cylindrical section can be lengthened to 50 in (127 cm) if required.

DIMENSIONS:
Length overall, standard configuration
18 ft 2¼ in (5·54 m)
Body diameter   10·2 in (0·26 m)

WEIGHT:
Launching weight (less payload) 644 lb (292 kg)

NOMINAL PERFORMANCE:
Altitude with 110 lb (50 kg) gross payload
(Qe = 85°)   127 nm (146 miles; 235 km)
Max acceleration   27 g

BLACK BRANT IVA

Black Brant IVA is a two-stage vehicle. It represents the combination of two reliable and successful solid-propellant motors which had already been evaluated fully on the Black Brant IIIA and VA single-stage rockets.

The three-finned first stage of this vehicle utilises the 17·2 in (44 cm) diameter 15KS25000 engine used on the single-stage Black Brant VA; the second stage is generally similar to the production version of Black Brant IIIA, with the same payload capacity, but with a new nozzle and conical stabiliser replacing the fins and aft body of the single-stage vehicle. Stage attachment is accomplished by mounting the nozzle and conical stabiliser of the second stage on to a spigot attached to the first stage. The longitudinal connection between the stages is made by an explosive bolt arrangement. Separation is effected after burn-out of the first stage by timer-induced simultaneous ignition of the connection bolt and deployment of booster drag flaps.

The Black Brant IVA is a simple vehicle which can be assembled in a few hours and may be held at instant launch readiness for many days. It is launched in an underslung position from a rail launcher.

DIMENSIONS:
Length overall (standard configuration)
37 ft 2 in (11·33 m)
Body diameter:
First stage   17·2 in (0·44 m)
Second stage   10·2 in (0·26 m)
WEIGHT:
Launching weight (less payload)
3,330 lb (1,510 kg)
NOMINAL PERFORMANCE:
Altitude with 110 lb (50 kg) gross payload
(Qe = 85°)   448 nm (515 miles; 830 km)
Max acceleration   37 g

BLACK BRANT IVB

This uprated version of Black Brant IVA is

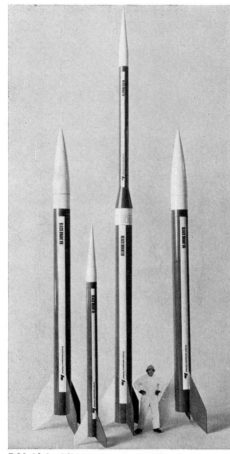

BAL high-altitude research rockets. *Left to right:* **Black Brant VB, Black Brant IIIA, Black Brant IVA and Black Brant VA**

under development, and was scheduled to begin flight testing in 1970. Vehicle hardware and dimensions are identical with those of Black Brant IVA, except that a 12KS10000 solid-propellant motor is used in the second stage. Three low aspect ratio fins may be added to the conical stabiliser to increase stability and so allow payloads up to 60 in (153 cm) long to be flown.
NOMINAL PERFORMANCE:
Altitude with 110 lb (50 kg) gross payload
(Qe = 85°)   507 nm (585 miles; 940 km)
Max acceleration   37 g

BLACK BRANT VA

Black Brant VA is a well-proven single-stage high-altitude research rocket, fitted with three stabilising fins and powered by a 15KS25000 solid-propellant motor. Suitable for carrying very heavy payloads of up to 600 lb (275 kg) to the 67 nm (77 miles; 125 km) region, it offers a smooth ride and combines simplicity with reliability.

Black Brant VA carries its payload in a 4·3 : 1 ogival fairing 6 ft 1 in (1·87 m) long. Cylindrical extensions up to 5 ft 10 in (1·78 m) long may be added. It is launched in an underslung position from a rail.
DIMENSIONS:
Length overall (standard configuration)
26 ft 9 in (8·15 m)
Body diameter   17·2 in (0·44 m)
WEIGHT:
Launching weight (less payload)
2,450 lb (1,111 kg)
NOMINAL PERFORMANCE:
Altitude with 330 lb (150 kg) gross payload
(Qe = 85°)   97 nm (112 miles; 180 km)
Max acceleration   16 g

BLACK BRANT VB

The Black Brant VB single-stage research rocket has the same dimensions and payload space as the Black Brant VA but utilises a different solid-propellant motor, the 26KS20000. It combines a low launch acceleration with high performance and has achieved a 100% success record in its flights to date.
DIMENSIONS:
Length overall (standard configuration)
26 ft 9 in (8·15 m)
Body diameter   17·2 in (0·44 m)
WEIGHT:
Launching weight (less payload)
2,849 lb (1,294 kg)
NOMINAL PERFORMANCE:
Altitude with 330 lb (150 kg) gross payload
(Qe = 85°)   194 nm (223 miles; 360 km)
Max acceleration   14 g

BLACK BRANT VC

Black Brant VC employs the same motor as Black Brant VB, but the tail assembly has been modified and a fourth stabilising fin added to make the vehicle compatible with launch towers at White Sands Missile Range, New Mexico, and Wallops Island, Virginia. The first Black Brant VC was scheduled to be flown late in 1970.
WEIGHT:
Launch weight, less payload 2,888 lb (1,311 kg)
NOMINAL PERFORMANCE:
Altitude with 330 lb (150 kg) payload (Qe = 85°)
183 nm (211 miles; 340 km)
Max acceleration   14 g

SPAR

SPAR AEROSPACE PRODUCTS LIMITED

HEAD OFFICE AND WORKS:
Box 6022, Toronto International Airport, Ontario

DIRECTORS:
Larry D. Clarke (President)
Rolland B. Dodwell (Chairman)
William H. Jackson
Dr Philip A. Lapp (Senior Vice-President)
M. Randolph Wade
Dr Gordon N. Patterson
Charles H. Barrett

DIRECTOR OF SPECIAL PRODUCTS:
John B. Driffield
DIRECTOR OF POWER PRODUCTS:
Terry H. Ussher
DIRECTOR OF MECHANICAL PRODUCTS:
John D. MacNaughton
DIRECTOR OF SALES:
Ralph E. Abbott
DIRECTOR OF MARKETING & PUBLIC RELATIONS:
John C. Ruse

Spar Aerospace Products Limited, formerly the Special Products and Applied Research Division of The de Havilland Aircraft of Canada Limited, was responsible for design and fabrication of the structure of the Alouette I and II, ISIS-1 and ISIS-B spacecraft. In the case of ISIS-1, Spar was also responsible for orbital mechanisms, dynamics analyses, mechanical design, and some of the thermal analysis. All these spacecraft used Spar extendible STEM devices as long sounder antennae. Other STEM

ISIS-1 satellite, photographed just prior to launch

space applications include gravity gradient booms, magnetometer and transponder booms, astronaut mechanical aids and extendible solar panel actuators. Since 1960, over 300 STEM devices have been flown successfully in Canadian, US and European programmes.

ISIS-1

Following on from the successful Alouette I and Alouette II satellites, which have been operating continuously since 1962 and 1965 respectively, the ISIS-1 spacecraft was launched on 29 January 1969 from Vandenberg AFB, using a Thrust Augmented Delta rocket. Weighing

525 lb (238 kg) at launch, the satellite was placed in a polar orbit of 1,889 nm (2,175 miles; 3,500 km) apogee and 269 nm (310 miles; 500 km) perigee. The antenna array used for ionospheric sounding is similar to that of Alouette II, with 240 ft (73 m) crossed dipoles, and equipment includes swept and fixed frequency sounders, VLF receiver and exciter, 136/137 MHz beacon, cosmic noise receiver and five direct measuring experiments in the form of an ion mass spectrometer, a soft particle spectrometer, an energetic particle detector, a spherical electro-static analyser and a langmuir probe.

The form of the satellite is roughly spherical, measuring 42 in (107 cm) in height, 49 in (124·5 cm) in diameter and carrying 11,200 solar cells on 16 flat trapezoidal panels.

ISIS-B

This satellite is very similar to ISIS-1, making use of the same space frame and with, in most cases, identical experiments. The main external differences are deletion of the upper two booms and the addition of an extension on top of the structure to house an auroral scanner. Other new experiments include a photometer and new type of ion mass spectrometer. The orbit for ISIS-B will be circular, at a height of 1,080 nm (1,240 miles; 2,000 km), in a near-polar inclination.

The present plan is to launch ISIS-B in 1971. Both the ISIS-1 and ISIS-B satellite programmes are under the control of the Communications Research Center of the Canadian Government (formerly Defence Research Telecommunications Establishment), with RCA Limited, Montreal, as the prime contractor, and Spar Aerospace Products Ltd as the main subcontractor.

CHINA (PEOPLE'S REPUBLIC)

China launched her first satellite (Norad designation "Chicom 1") on 24 April 1970, and thus became the fifth country to orbit a payload using national resources, following the USSR, USA, France and Japan. Few details have been released; a New China News Agency statement gave the weight of the spacecraft as 380 lb (172 kg), and said that it was injected into a 1,285 × 237 nm (1,480 × 273 mile; 2,382 × 439 km) orbit at an inclination of 68·5°. It is believed to have been launched from the main

Chinese rocket centre near Shuang Cheng Tsu, 500 miles east of the nuclear test establishment of Lop Nor.

No details of any experiments are available, but as a prototype it is probable that only basic vehicle development instrumentation is installed. Signals are transmitted over a cycle time of one minute, on 20.009 MHz, including a 5 sec interval between signals. The first 40 sec of each transmission is devoted to the piece of music "The East is Red". After a 5-sec break, 20 telemetry

data channels then transmit for 10 sec, followed by a further break.

It is widely surmised that the development of the satellite and its launch vehicle have been managed by Dr Tsien Hsue-Shen, a scientist who was employed by the Jet Propulsion Laboratory in California as a member of a rocket design team during World War II. After the war the Doctor worked at the Massachusetts Institute of Technology. He returned to China in 1955.

FRANCE

AÉROSPATIALE

SOCIÉTÉ NATIONALE INDUSTRIELLE AÉRO-SPATIALE

Division Systèmes Balistiques et Espace

EXECUTIVE OFFICE: 6 Quai National, 92-Puteaux

DIRECTOR: P. M. Usunier

The Ballistic Systems and Space Division of Aérospatiale combines the resources of the former SEREB organisation with certain design offices and factories of the Nord- and Sud-Aviation groups. Details of the Division's current range of launch vehicles, research rockets and space vehicles are given below. All available details of its weapon systems can be found in the "Missiles" section of this edition.

A total of 251 Bélier, Centaure, Dragon, Dauphin and Eridan sounding rockets, developed by the former Sud-Aviation company, had been launched by the end of 1969. Launchings took place from 17 firing ranges, including Adelie, the Kerguelen Islands, Kiruna (Sweden), Andoya (Norway), Thumba (India) and Sonmiani (Pakistan).

CORALIE (ELDO Second Stage)

The development programme for Coralie, second stage of the ELDO Europa space launch vehicle, was conducted under the sponsorship of CNES. From the end of 1967, SEREB managed the programme, with Nord-Aviation and LRBA as the main contractors. Prime contractor for development and production is now the Division Systèmes Balistiques et Espace of Aérospatiale.

Coralie is a basically-cylindrical structure, occupied mainly by tanks for the UDMH and nitrogen tetroxide liquid propellants, and with a flared skirt over the four hydraulically-actuated gimballed nozzles which provide control in yaw, pitch and roll. The forward and aft skirts are of sandwich construction.

A small solid-propellant rocket provides the thrust necessary for separation of the first and second stages of the Europa vehicle, before ignition of Coralie's four main engines, which develop a total thrust of 61,730 lb (28,000 kg) *in vacuo*. A sequencer, duplicated for reliability, controls the various stages of operation of the Coralie stage.

A separate gas generator, fed by a tiny proportion of the propellants stored in small auxiliary tanks, is used to pressurise the main propellant tanks and so cause the propellants to flow to the main engines. The UDMH passes through one valve and the nitrogen tetroxide through four valves; the propellants are atomised in the combustion chambers by the injectors.

Stage cut-off is signalled by a system of probes which detects the level of propellants remaining in the tanks.

The Coralie stage performed entirely satisfactorily during the launching at Woomera of Europa F7 on 30 November 1968 and Europa F8 on 3 July 1969.

DIMENSION:
Diameter   6 ft 7·1 in (2·00 m)
WEIGHTS:
Nitrogen tetroxide   14,198 lb (6,440 kg)
UDMH   7,518 lb (3,410 kg)
Structure   4,850 lb (2,200 kg)
PERFORMANCE:
Specific impulse   280 sec
Duration of firing   104 sec

BÉLIER III

The single-stage Bélier is the smallest of the family of upper atmosphere research rockets which Aérospatiale produces. The latest Version III offers increased performance, as the result of the use of a new solid-propellant motor of higher specific impulse and longer burning time. Performance of the two-stage Centaure and Dragon rockets is also improved, as Bélier III forms the second stage of each.

The "Isolane" solid-propellant charge used in Bélier III weighs 507 lb (230 kg). Other components are a rear section fitted with cruciform fins which ensure stability and house the antennae, four external conduits which carry electrical cables between the front and rear sections, and a 12 in (0·305 m) diameter nose-cone making up the scientific payload and recovery package (if required). An initial spin device reduces short-launch dispersion from the 23 ft (7 m) guide rails. No guidance or control system is fitted.

The nose-cone is attached to the body by quick-release clamps, with ejection provision

when in-flight separation is required. An optional destruction device can be incorporated to tear out the front of the nose-cone to stop combustion and unbalance the rocket. This device can be operated by coded remote-control signal.

DIMENSIONS:
Length overall (according to payload)
    12 ft 10 in to 16 ft 8½ in (3·92-5·09 m)
Length of payload section
    3 ft 6½ in to 7 ft 4½ in (1·08-2·25 m)
Body diameter   11¾ in (0·305 m)
Span of fins   2 ft 9¾ in (0·859 m)
Payload capacity   1·0-3·5 cu ft (30-100 litres)
WEIGHTS:
Launching weight, less payload
                        708 lb (322 kg)
Weight at burn-out, less payload
                        202 lb (92 kg)
Payload   66-198 lb (30-90 kg)
PERFORMANCE:
Speed at burn-out at 59,000 ft (18,000 m)
    3,300 knots (3,800 mph; 1,700 m/sec)
Ceiling:
    with 66 lb (30 kg) payload
                        86 nm (99 miles; 160 km)
    with 198 lb (90 kg) payload
                        47·5 nm (55 miles; 88 km)
Time to ceiling:
    with 66 lb (30 kg) payload   195 sec
    with 198 lb (90 kg) payload   147 sec

CENTAURE III

The Centaure III consists of a Bélier III, as described above, with a first-stage tandem booster containing 207 lb (94 kg) of Plastolite solid propellant. The booster is fitted with four tail-fins indexed in line with the fins of the second stage. The two stages are connected by a conical interstage structure housing the separation device. No guidance or control system is employed; but the vehicle is spin-stabilised. The nose-cone, its attachments and optional destruction device are similar to those of the Bélier III.

DIMENSIONS:
Length overall, according to payload
    19 ft 4½ in to 23 ft 2½ in (5·91-7·08 m)

Aérospatiale Centaure research rocket

Length of payload section
  3 ft 6½ in to 7 ft 4½ in (1·08-2·25 m)
Body diameter, first stage   11 in (0·28 m)
Span of fins, first stage   2 ft 9¾ in (0·859 m)
Payload capacity   1·0-3·5 cu ft (30-100 litres)
WEIGHTS:
Launching weight, less payload
                    1,049 lb (476 kg)
Weight at second-stage burn-out, less payload
                    203 lb (92 kg)
Payload   66-242 lb (30-110 kg)
PERFORMANCE:
Speed at burn-out at 91,850 ft (28,000 m)
    3,900 knots (4,495 mph; 2,010 m/sec)
Ceiling:
  with 66 lb (30 kg) payload
                137 nm (158 miles; 255 km)
  with 198 lb (90 kg) payload
                67 nm (77 miles; 125 km)
Time to ceiling:
  with 66 lb (30 kg) payload   255 sec
  with 198 lb (90 kg) payload   184 sec

DRAGON III

The Dragon III is a two-stage research rocket
consisting of a Bélier III vehicle, as described
earlier, and a bonded spiral-wrapped booster
filled with 1,512 lb (686 kg) of Plastolane solid
propellant. Other components are an aft section
carrying cruciform tail fins, an inter-stage structure housing the separation device, and a nose-
cone similar to that of the Bélier III. No guidance or control system is employed, but the

Aérospatiale Dragon sounding rocket

rocket is spin-stabilised at launch. Nose-cone
attachments and optional destruction device are
as for the Bélier III.
DIMENSIONS:
Length overall, according to payload
    23 ft 9½ in to 27 ft 7½ in (7·25-8·42 m)
Length of payload section
    3 ft 6½ in to 7 ft 4½ in (1·08-2·25 m)
Body diameter, first stage   1 ft 9·65 in (0·55 m)
Span of fins   4 ft 3 in (1·30 m)
Payload capacity   1·0-3·5 cu ft (30-100 litres)
WEIGHTS:
Launching weight, less payload
                    2,680 lb (1,216 kg)
Weight at second-stage burn-out, less payload
                    203 lb (92 kg)
Payload   66-242 lb (30-110 kg)
PERFORMANCE:
Speed at burn-out at 220,000 ft (67,000 m)
    6,624 knots (7,628 mph; 3,410 m/sec)
Ceiling:
  with 110 lb (50 kg) payload
                340 nm (391 miles; 630 km)
  with 220 lb (100 kg) payload
                243 nm (280 miles; 450 km)
Time to ceiling:
  with 110 lb (50 kg) payload   420 sec
  with 220 lb (100 kg) payload   360 sec

DAUPHIN

This single-stage research rocket consists of a
solid-propellant motor identical with that used
in the Dragon III booster, filled with 1,512 lb
(686 kg) of Plastolane; an aft section fitted with
cruciform fins; and a nose-cone comprising the
scientific payload, the equipment package
(telemetry antennae, remote-control equipment
and radar transponder), optional recovery system
and optional attitude control system. Nose-cone
attachment and optional destruction device are
as for the Bélier III, but the nose-cone is considerably larger, with capacity for a heavier
payload.
The Dauphin is spin-stabilised at launch, but
has no guidance or control system.
DIMENSIONS:
Length overall, according to payload
    16 ft 5¼ in to 20 ft 4½ in (5·01-6·21 m)
Length of payload section
    6 ft 6¾ in to 10 ft 6 in (2·00-3·20 m)
Body diameter   1 ft 9·65 in (0·55 m)
Span of fins   5 ft 10 in (1·77 m)
Payload capacity   7·0-17·5 cu ft (200-500 litres)
WEIGHTS:
Launching weight, less payload 2,039 lb (925 kg)
Weight at burn-out, less payload 527 lb (239 kg)
Payload   287-551 lb (130-250 kg)
PERFORMANCE:
Speed at burn-out at 46,000 ft (14,000 m)
    3,400 knots (3,915 mph; 1,750 m/sec)
Ceiling:
  with 287 lb (130 kg) payload
                81 nm (93 miles; 150 km)
  with 551 lb (250 kg) payload
                54 nm (62 miles; 100 km)
Time to ceiling:
  with 287 lb (130 kg) payload   186 sec
  with 551 lb (250 kg) payload   151 sec

ERIDAN

This research rocket is made up of two stages,
each identical with the Dauphin, with cruciform
tail fins fitted to both stages. The stages are
connected by a section housing the separation
device. The nose-cone is also similar to that of
the Dauphin. No guidance or control system is
installed, but the Eridan is spin-stabilised at
launch.
Four launches took place at France's Guiana
space centre during 1968 and 1969.

Model of the Eole (FR-2) satellite
(*Flying Review*)

Aérospatiale Dauphin single-stage research rocket

DIMENSIONS:
Length overall, according to payload
    26 ft 3¾ in to 29 ft 10 in (8·02-9·12 m)
Length of payload section
    6 ft 6¾ in to 12 ft 9½ in (2·00-3·90 m)
Body diameter, both stages 1 ft 9·65 in (0·55 m)
Span of fins   6 ft 8½ in (2·05 m)
Payload capacity 7·0-23·7 cu ft (200-670 litres)
WEIGHTS:
Launching weight, less payload
                    4,112 lb (1,865 kg)
Weight at burn-out, less payload
                    529 lb (240 kg)
Payload   287-794 lb (130-360 kg)
PERFORMANCE:
Speed at burn-out
    5,342 knots (6,151 mph; 2,750 m/sec)
Ceiling:
  with 287 lb (130 kg) payload
                237 nm (273 miles; 440 km)
  with 794 lb (360 kg) payload
                121 nm (140 miles; 225 km)
Time to ceiling:
  with 28,710 (130 kg) payload   360 sec
  with 79,410 (360 kg) payload   240 sec

PEOLE and EOLE (or FR-2)

The Eole meteorological research programme
is under the aegis of the CNES and CNRS and is
being conducted in association with NASA. It
involves the use of a satellite to interrogate
hundreds of pressurised meteorological balloons,
in order to track their precise paths and record

Aérospatiale Eridan two-stage research rocket

the pressure and temperature of their environment as they drift at a constant height after release.

First satellite to be launched under the programme, by a Diamant B vehicle in 1970, is **Peole.** It will be followed in 1971 by **Eole** (or **FR-2**), launched by an American Scout vehicle. In each case, this Division of Aérospatiale is responsible for the satellite structure in "nida" light alloy, its thermal control and stabilisation by gravity gradient. Subcontractors are Radio-

technique for the 5920 solar cells and Starec for the 400-460 MHz antennae. Intertechnique and CFTH are prime contractors for satellite/ ground station communications. LCT is prime contractor for satellite/balloon communications.

The Eole satellite has an eight-sided body, with 8 fixed and 8 deployable solar panels extending from the bottom.

Each balloon has a diameter of 13 ft (4 m) and has a series of capsules strung on a cable beneath its envelope. From top to bottom, these capsules

comprise a solar generator, electronic pack, battery, antenna and radar reflector.

SCIENTIFIC SATELLITE D2

The D 2 scientific satellite will carry five CNES experiments and will be orbited by a Diamant B launch vehicle in 1971.

This Division of Aérospatiale is responsible for the lightweight satellite structure, made of "nida" light alloys, MG and AG5, and for some internal sections.

CFTH-HB
COMPAGNIE FRANÇAISE THOMSON HOUSTON —HOTCHKISS BRANDT
Armament Division
ADDRESS:
52, Avenue des Champs Elysées, Paris 8e
WORKS:
Saint Denis, La Ferte St Aubin (Loiret), Tulle (Corrèze)
PRESIDENT:
Ernest Cordier
VICE-PRESIDENT AND GENERAL MANAGER:
Paul Richard

The Armament Division of CFTH-HB, a leading group in the French electronic field, has been engaged in the design and manufacture of mortars and ammunition for the last 40 years. Since 1948 it has also carried out research and development of semi-self-propelled ammunition and solid-propellant rockets, such as the T-10 and the 37-mm and 68-mm SNEB rockets which are in service as a standard armament with a large number of air forces and can be fitted to almost any aircraft in current production.

The Division has designed warheads and solid-propellant rocket motors which currently equip the Matra 510, Matra 530, Matra/HSD Martel and Crotale missiles.

Since 1959, it has developed test tracks, sledges, measuring equipment and fire-control systems, under contract to the DRME. Since 1964, the Division has been prime contractor to the SECT (Firing-Range Equipment Department) for the design and production of sounding rockets, utilising rocket motors of French design already in mass production for military purposes. Details of some of these follow.

MIRE A
Mire A is an auxiliary firing-range rocket that was used initially to train personnel at the Guiana firing range in tracking satellite launch vehicles. Entirely passive, it consists of a 68 mm rocket, with fins and a nose-cone, which is fired from a tube. It has a ceiling of about 20,000 ft (6,100 m), an initial acceleration of under 5g and a radar reflective area of 5·4 sq ft (0·5 m²). Of about 30 delivered by May 1969, two-thirds had been fired. Launching weight of Mire A is 11·5 lb (5·2 kg).

MIRE B
Similar in configuration and purpose to Mire A, this 100 mm rocket is also tube-launched and is capable of carrying either ballast or a ranging beacon. It has a launching weight of 54·7 lb (24·8 kg) and a ceiling of just under 70,000 ft (21,300 m). Most of the ten Mire B's delivered by May 1969 had been fired at the Guiana range. A version equipped with infra-red tracking flares, with a duration of 20 seconds, is under development.

ESUS
Smallest of the current CFTH-HB series of conventional sounding rockets, Esus is intended for low-altitude soundings at heights up to 50,000 ft (15,250 m). It is powered by a 68 mm solid-propellant rocket motor and is fitted with folding cruciform tail-fins to enable it to be launched from a tube. The ogival nose-cone contains instrumentation and the payload separation and parachute-recovery system. Only the payload section is radar-reflective.

An important feature of Esus is that it causes no dangerous fall-out, and is able to be used by the French Meteorological Service and by firing ranges and artillery near inhabited areas.

Four firings had been made by May 1969 and Esus was expected to become operational late in 1969.

EPONA
Epona is used primarily to obtain information on winds at altitudes up to 200,000 ft (60,000 m). The first firing was carried out on 6 March 1968 and the rocket has since become operational. It is composed of two identical 100-mm motors and an inert third stage containing radar reflectors. The first two stages are ignited successively without any intermediate delay, and the third stage is separated on burn-out of the second stage. Payload volume of the third stage is 30·5 cu in (500 cm³).

Epona can be fired in strong winds of up to 28 knots (33 mph; 15 m/sec). When it is required to reach altitudes of no more than 82,000 ft (25,000 m), it can be simplified by using only a single powered stage.

About 20 Eponas had been fired by May 1969.

CFTH-HB sounding rockets: *left to right* **the Epona, Toutatis and Belisama**

DIMENSIONS:
Length overall	14 ft 5½ in (4·406 m)
Body diameter	3·94 in (10 cm)
Wing span	1 ft 2·2 in (360 cm)

WEIGHTS:
Launching weight	135·5 lb (61·5 kg)
Weight, less payload	132·3 lb (60·0 kg)

PERFORMANCE (launch angle of 80°/85°):
Max speed at burn-out	4,660 ft (1,420 m) sec
Peak altitude	220,000 ft (67,000 m)
Max acceleration	157 g
Time of flight	110 seconds

BELISAMA
Developed to obtain meteorological data at an altitude of 54 nm (62 miles; 100 km), Belisama is made up of two solid-propellant stages. The first stage is an Elan motor, with a nominal performance rating of 4,140 daN for 2·5 seconds. The second-stage motor is a 100-mm rocket with a nominal rating of 2·725 daN for 0·9 seconds.

Separation of the first and second stages is achieved by difference in drag at burn-out of the first stage. The speed is then 2,890 ft (880 m) sec. After a period of coasting flight, the second stage is ignited (19 seconds after launch) by which time the speed has fallen to 1,345 ft (410 m) sec. The second stage increases the speed to 4,460 ft (1,360 m) sec. A mechanical timing device causes separation of the payload container once the vehicle has reached its peak altitude. The container splits into two parts and releases the payload which is then lowered by parachute. Payload volume is 183 cu in (3,000 cm³).

After 14 development firings, Belisama is now operational.

DIMENSIONS:
Length overall	13 ft 8 in (4·167 m)
Body diameter:	
1st stage	8·27 in (21·0 cm)
2nd stage	3·94 in (10·0 cm)
Max wing span	2 ft 3½ in (0·70 m)

WEIGHTS:
Launching weight	257 lb (116·6 kg)
Weight, less payload	248·7 lb (112·8 kg)

PERFORMANCE (launch angle 80°/85°):
Max speed at burn-out	4,460 ft (1,360 m) sec
Peak altitude with 13·2 lb (6 kg) payload package	328,000 ft (100,000 m)
Ceiling with 22 lb (10 kg) payload package	265,000 ft (81,000 m)
Max acceleration	143 g
Time of flight	154 seconds

BÉLÉNOS
This two-stage sounding rocket is made up of a 210 mm Thomson-Brandt solid-propellant first-stage motor and a SNECMA Aurore second stage. Its instrument package contains a radio probe and temperature sensor and is recoverable by parachute.

Bélénos is operational.

WEIGHT:
Launching weight with 22 lb (10 kg) nose-cone	300 lb (136 kg)

PERFORMANCE:
Ceiling with 22 lb (10 kg) payload	400,000 ft (122,000 m)

GRANNOS
This two-stage sounding rocket has been developed by CFTH-HB as a private venture, with the assistance of the SECT and the French Army's Solid Propellant Department. It was launched for the first time in the Spring of 1969, from the Ile du Levant, off Hyères, only 4½ months after its design was started.

Grannos is designed to carry a 28·6 lb (13 kg) payload to a height of 500,000-560,000 ft (152,500-170,000 m). Standard instrumentation includes a radio probe and telemetry equipment, with a parachute recovery system.

DIMENSION:
Length overall	16 ft 6 in (5·03 m)

WEIGHT:
Launching weight	388 lb (176 kg)

TOUTATIS
Toutatis is a two-stage solid-propellant semi-self-propelled sounding rocket. It is fired from a 155-mm gun with an initial velocity of 1,640 ft (500 m) sec, the folding tail-fins opening to stabilise it after it has left the barrel. The first-stage 100-mm motor is ignited 13 seconds after launch and burns for 0·9 seconds. After 15 seconds of coasting flight, the second-stage 68-mm motor, which is inside a tube extending from the first stage, is ignited and expelled like a shot from the tube. Its burning time is 0·8 seconds. At the apex of its trajectory, a clockwork mechanism causes ejection of the payload.

The advantage of using a long-barrel smooth-bore gun as a first-stage booster, in this way, is that the speed of the rocket on leaving the barrel is so high that it is virtually unaffected by strong surface winds and maintains a very accurate trajectory.

Three Toutatis firings had been made by May 1969. Most difficult problem that remained to be solved at that time was tracking the second stage.

DIMENSIONS:
Length overall	9 ft 8 in (2·940 m)
Body diameter:	
1st stage	3·94 in (10·0 cm)
2nd stage	2·68 in (6·8 cm)

WEIGHTS:
Launching weight	71·4 lb (32·4 kg)
Weight, less payload	70·1 lb (31·8 kg)

PERFORMANCE (launch angle of 70°/85°):
Max speed at burn-out	4,380 ft (1,335 m)/sec
Peak altitude	279,000 ft (85,000 m)
Time of flight	148 seconds

CNES
CENTRE NATIONAL D'ÉTUDES SPATIALES

ADDRESS: 129 rue de l'Université, Paris 7e
PRESIDENT: J.-F. Denisse
DIRECTOR GENERAL: R. Aubiniere

The CNES is a public establishment, with financial autonomy, charged with a variety of responsibilities in the field of space research. These include collecting all relevant information on the subject; laying down research programmes; assuring the completion of such programmes, either in its own laboratories and technical centres or under research agreements made with other public or private concerns; evaluating the possibilities of international collaboration; and promoting directly or indirectly the publication of scientific works.

Details of two of its current programmes follow:

DIAMANT B

During 1966, studies were made to define ways in which the original Diamant A launch vehicle (see 1969-70 *Jane's*) might be improved, to increase both the weight of payload able to be put into orbit and the size of satellite able to be accommodated.

It was decided to utilise an L 17 stage as the first stage of a new vehicle to be known as Diamant B. The structure for this stage is manufactured by Aérospatiale (Nord) in its Les Mureaux works. It houses guidance and other equipment and a Valois liquid bi-propellant motor, with 17 tonnes of nitrogen peroxide and UDMH propellants. The Valois engine, designed by the LRBA at Vernon and manufactured by the Arsenal of Tarbes, develops 77,160 lb (35,000 kg) st at lift-off and burns for 112 seconds.

The second and third stages are similar to those of Diamant A. The second stage, like the first, is built by Aérospatiale (Nord), which has sub-contracted certain parts to SEP and Matra. The tilt system for control during the ballistic phase and the equipment compartment are supplied by Matra, while the upper parts (including the third stage, its equipment and the nose cone) are produced by Aérospatiale (Sud). SEP supplies the ignition system and the rockets for rotation and separation of the second and third stages. Final assembly of the complete Diamant B is done by CNES at Saint-Médard en Jalles. Aérospatiale (SEREB) are retained by CNES as advisors.

The first launching of a Diamant B was from the French space centre in Guiana on 10 March 1970. It put into orbit the German Dial payload, comprising the MIKA capsule, which was designed to provide data on vehicle performance, and the WIKA scientific satellite. Weights of these two items were 115 lb (52 kg) and 136 lb (61·7 kg) respectively. WIKA was put into an orbit with a perigee of 172 nm (198 miles; 319 km), apogee of 881 nm (1,015 miles; 1,634 km) and inclination of 5·41° to the equator.

Vibration of the first stage of Diamant B prevented the MIKA capsule from operating between the 3rd and 17th seconds of the flight; but otherwise the launch was completely successful. A second launch was scheduled for 24 August 1970, when the payload was to be a satellite known as Peole.

Future versions of Diamant B may utilise an easily-developed fourth stage, giving the potential for putting a 265 lb (120 kg) payload into a circular orbit at an altitude of 870 nm (1,000 miles; 1,600 km).

DIMENSIONS:
Length:	
Overall	77 ft 3 in (23·54 m)
1st stage	46 ft 7½ in (14·21 m)
2nd stage	18 ft 1 in (5·52 m)
Body diameter:	
1st stage	4 ft 7 in (1·40 m)
2nd, 3rd stages	2 ft 7½ in (0·80 m)

WEIGHT:
Launching weight	54,235 lb (24,600 kg)

D-2 SATELLITE

The D-2 is a scientific satellite which carries a five-experiment package for study of the Sun in the ultra-violet region. It has a cylindrical body, 31·5 in (80 cm) in height and 27·5 in (70 cm) in diameter, and four deployable solar panels. The 1,400 solar cells generate 55W and there is a silver-cadmium battery. A pneumatic stabilisation system will maintain a rotational speed of 1 rpm in orbit.

Total weight of the D-2 satellite is 198 lb (90 kg), of which 33 lb (15 kg) is structure.

Sud-Aviation are responsible for the structure, solar panels and antennae; for the telemetry equipment in association with Intertechnique, IER, EMD and Pyral: and for the control system in association with Crouzet, CDC and Sofrair. Thomson Houston/CSF, LCT and Crouzet are providing the command system. Nord-Aviation Matra, Crouzet, Air Equipement and CDC share responsibility for the stabilisation system. SAT, SAFT, Crouzet and EMD are providing the power supply system.

The D-2 satellite is intended to be launched from the Guiana space centre at the end of 1970, by a Diamant B vehicle. It will be put into a circular orbit, at a height of 280 miles (450 km) and inclined at 45° to the equator.

TARAMIS

TARAMIS

Taramis will be the operational version of the experimental Toutatis and is expected to enter service in 1972. It will be an optimised single-stage rocket, designed to carry a payload of 7·7 lb (3·5 kg) to a height of 265,000 ft (81,000 m). Launching weight will be 70 lb (31·7 kg).

LRBA
LABORATOIRE DE RECHERCHES BALISTIQUES ET AÉRODYNAMIQUES

ADDRESS: 27-Vernon

DIRECTOR:
Ing Militaire Général Marchal

The LRBA at Vernon is attached to the Direction Technique des Engins (DTEN), which comes under the authority of the Délégation Ministérielle pour l'Armement. It possesses 721,200 sq ft (67,000 m²) of covered working space and employs about 1,000 persons.

Current activities of the LRBA include research, development and production of propellants, assembly of propulsion systems and manufacture of control and guidance systems for rockets and missiles.

The LRBA was responsible for design and development of the Véronique AGI, Véronique 61/61M and Vesta research rockets, the guidance and propulsion systems of the Emeraude rocket, the first stage of the Diamant A launch vehicle, the second stage of the ELDO Europa 1 launch vehicle and the L 17 first stage of Diamant B.

Véronique AGI research rocket

VÉRONIQUE AGI

The Véronique, designed by the LRBA and produced by the Atelier de Construction de Tarbes, continues to play a major rôle in French rocket research. It was first fired in May 1952, but the initial series of 15 launchings were for development of the vehicle and the first scientific payload was carried in March 1959. By early 1970 a total of more than 80 Véroniques of all kinds had been fired.

Véronique is a single-stage liquid-propellant vehicle which is wire-guided for the first 300 ft (100 m) of its vertical trajectory. At the peak altitude, the nose is separated from the body by a time-switch and can be recovered by parachute.

The propellants consist of nitric acid and any one of a variety of fuels. They are contained in stainless steel tanks and pressure-fed to the engine.

Instruments are carried in the nose compartment, which has a volume of 4·60 cu ft (0·13 m³). Measurements can either be recorded for study

Véronique 61 M in servicing gantry

after the nose section has been recovered, or telemetered to the ground. The two techniques make possible seven and 27 different measurements respectively, using instruments which include radar transponders for tracking, accelerometers, pressure gauges, thermometers and equipment to record radiation.

In other tests, a candle-shape cloud of sodium-potassium is emitted, by means of which the speed and direction of winds can be studied at varying altitudes.

In its original form, the Véronique had a ceiling of 32-35 nm (37-40 miles; 60-65 km), after an engine running time of 32 seconds. The second series were larger, with the motor giving 8,820 lb (4,000 kg) st for 45 seconds, with diesel oil, which raised the ceiling to over 70 nm (80 miles; 130 km).

The current Véronique AGI (Année Géophysique International) uses terebenthine fuel and reached an altitude of 108 nm (124 miles; 200 km), carrying a 132 lb (60 kg) payload, in its first firing at Hammaguir in March 1959.

DIMENSIONS:
Length, with payload	23 ft 11 in (7·30 m)
Body diameter	1 ft 9½ in (0·55 m)
Span of fins	4 ft 5 in (1·35 m)

VÉRONIQUE 61 M

Like Véronique AGI, this version was designed by the LRBA and is produced by the Atelier de Construction de Tarbes. It is longer than earlier versions of Véronique, with a different tail-fin assembly. Its propellant tanks contain 176·5 Imp gallons (803 litres) of nitric acid and 87·5 Imp gallons (397 litres) of terebenthine fuel, sufficient for about 55 sec of combustion. Fuel feed is by gas pressure.

The combustion chamber has a graphite throat of 6·3 in (160 mm) diameter and a nozzle diameter of 13·8 in (350 mm). Expansion ratio is 30·9 : 1. Specific impulse is 198 sec at S/L, 233 sec in space.

For the first 300 ft (100 m) after lift-off, Véronique 61 M is stabilised by four cables attached to its fins by jettisonable cruciform arms and wound on a common drum, the inertia of which prevents deviation by the rocket from its course. The arms are separated by explosive bolts, after which the rocket is stabilised aerodynamically during its trajectory.

A Véronique 61 M was used for the inaugural firing from the French space centre in Guiana on 9 April 1968.

Biological version of Vesta used for studying the behaviour of monkeys under weightless conditions

DIMENSIONS:
Length with payload
  30 ft 4½ in to 37 ft 7 in (9·26 m to 11·45 m)
Length without payload 24 ft 11 in (7·60 m)
Body diameter 1 ft 9½ in (0·55 m)

WEIGHTS:
Empty, without payload or guidance arms
    708 lb (321 kg)
Fuelled, without payload or guidance arms
    4,260 lb (1,932 kg)
Normal payload, including structure
    220-550 lb (100-250 kg)

PERFORMANCE:
Ceiling:
 with 176 lb (80 kg) payload
    183 nm (211 miles; 340 km)
 with 660 lb (300 kg) payload
    108 nm (124 miles; 200 km)

VESTA

Shown in public for the first time at the 1963 Paris *Salon*, Vesta is a single-stage research rocket which has been developed to meet a CNES requirement for a simple vehicle with a higher performance than Véronique. An initial series of 10 is being produced for CNES by the Laboratoire de Recherches Balistiques et Aérodynamiques and several of these have been fired.

The rocket motor has a metal casing and develops 31,680 lb (14,370 kg) st for 56·4 seconds. It runs on terebenthine and nitric acid propellents and has a specific impulse of 192·6 sec at S/L, increasing to 238·5 sec in space.

Vesta uses a similar initial wire-guidance system to that of Véronique.

On March 7 and 13, 1967, Vesta rockets were used for research flights in which the monkeys Martine and Pierrette were subjected to weightlessness experiments at a peak height of 130 nm (149 miles; 240 km). In each case the total payload weight was about 1,985 lb (900 kg), including the cruciform parachutes and air-brakes of the SILAT recovery system.

More recently, this rocket was launched from Kourou, French Guiana, on 8 November 1969, as part of the development programme for Cassiopée and Athalie (stabilised solar lock-on device and micro-accelerometer developed by ONERA) and Cephée.

DIMENSIONS:
Length with payload
 32 ft 9 in to 37 ft 8½ in (10·00 m to 11·50 m)
Body diameter 3 ft 3½ in (1·00 m)
Span of fins 8 ft 0½ in (2·45 m)

WEIGHTS:
Launching weight, without payload
    11,023 lb (5,000 kg)

PERFORMANCE:
Ceiling:
 with 2,200 lb (1,000 kg) payload
    116 nm (133 miles; 215 km)
 with 1,100 lb (500 kg) payload
    197 nm (227 miles; 365 km)

MATRA

S A ENGINS MATRA
HEAD OFFICE:
4 rue de Presbourg, Paris 16e
OFFICERS: See "Missiles" section.

In addition to developing and manufacturing guided missiles, Matra are engaged on a number of research and space programmes.

They are participating in the major French space programmes. Under the overall control of SEREB (now Aérospatiale), they developed the Asterix 1 test satellite (see 1966-67 *Jane's*), the D-1A and D-1C scientific satellites and other equipment for the Diamant project. They collaborated with Hawker Siddeley Dynamics of the UK in developing the ESRO II satellite and, as a member of the MESH consortium (see International section), are prime contractors for ESRO's TD satellite. For the CNES, they are prime contractors for the D-2B satellite, scheduled for launching in 1972.

MATRA/ERNO/SAAB/HSD TD 1 SATELLITE
See "International" section, page 653.

ONERA

OFFICE NATIONAL D'ÉTUDES ET DE RECHERCHES AÉROSPATIALES
ADDRESS:
29-39, Avenue de la Division-Leclerc, 92-Chatillon-sous-Bagneux
DIRECTOR: Prof Raymond Castaing
SALES MANAGER: M. François
PUBLIC RELATIONS MANAGER: Max Salmon

In addition to its normal work as a national research and experimental centre in the service of the entire French aircraft and missile industry, ONERA has designed, built and launched various types of experimental vehicles to obtain basic data in fields such as propulsion and kinetic heating and in connection with scientific research programmes sponsored by the Centre National d'Etudes Spatiales (CNES).

The only rocket currently under development is the Tibère, described below. Details of earlier rockets developed by ONERA can be found in the 1969-70 *Jane's*.

ONERA TIBÈRE

This three-stage solid-propellant rocket is designed especially for studying the electromagnetic phenomena of nose-cones during re-entry at Mach 16, under Project Electre. It can carry a payload of 220 lb (100 kg) to a height of 1,050 nm (1,210 miles; 1,950 km) or 880 lb (400 kg) to 350 nm (400 miles; 650 km). However, in Project Electre, the third stage is fired downwards, so that the height attained is only some 130 nm (150 miles; 240 km).

The first and second-stage rocket motors are produced by SEP as Type 739-2, each with a basic weight of 4,012 lb (1,820 kg), including 2,745 lb (1,245 kg) of propellant. The third stage is similar to the third stage of the Diamant A launcher, with a weight of 1,610 lb (730 kg), including 1,410 lb (640 kg) of propellant.

The first stage, known as BER, has been used extensively on the early Bérénice and Titus rockets. It is stabilised by four small lateral rockets with swivelling nozzles which ignite just before launch and burn as long as the main first-stage motor. This stabilisation system was developed by ONERA and is produced commercially by Aérospatiale.

Stage two is fin-stabilised. Between the second and third stages is installed a Cassiopée lock-on device developed by ONERA. After second-stage burn-out, it points the second/third stage/payload assembly in the correct direction to ensure a zero-angle of attack thrust for stage three during re-entry, when this stage is spun at 360 rpm. Other versions of Cassiopée (now produced industrially by SAGEM for CNES and ONERA) include, besides an inertial aiming accuracy of 1°, a solar or bi-stellar aiming device with an accuracy of 1' and the ability to steer a payload according to a pre-set programme or in several successive pre-set directions in space.

Cassiopée is separated with the second stage of Tibère. After burn-out, the third stage is separated by small retro-rockets when experiments are concerned with only the nose-cone.

The first launching of Tibère was scheduled for the Summer of 1970.

DIMENSIONS:
Length:
 Overall, excluding nose-cone
    39 ft 11½ in (12·175 m)
 First stage 15 ft 4½ in (4·685 m)
 Second stage 15 ft 4¾ in (4·690 m)
 Third stage 6 ft 11 in (2·110 m)
 Nose cone 7 ft 2½ in (2·200 m)
Body diameter:
 First and second stages 1 ft 10 in (0·558 m)
 Third stage 2 ft 1¾ in (0·656 m)

WEIGHTS:
Launching weight, excluding nose-cone
    9,965 lb (4,520 kg)

PERFORMANCE (Qe = 85°):
Max ceiling:
 1,320 lb (600 kg) payload
    225 nm (260 miles; 420 km)
 220 lb (100 kg) payload
    1,050 nm (1,210 miles; 1,950 km)
Range:
 1,320 lb (600 kg) payload
    215 nm (247 miles; 400 km)
 200 lb (100 kg) payload
    675 nm (777 miles; 1,250 km)

ONERA Tibère three-stage research rocket

GERMANY
THE GERMAN FEDERAL REPUBLIC

ASAT
ARBEITSGEMEINSCHAFT SATELLITENTRÄG-ERSYSTEM

ADDRESS:
  8012 Ottobrunn bei München, Postabholfach

ASAT, the Satellite Carrier Advisory Group, is the German national co-ordinating authority for work on the third stage of the ELDO space launch vehicle. It represents a consortium of the major contractors for this stage, Messerschmitt-Bölkow-Blohm GmbH and ERNO Raumfahrttechnik GmbH, who are assisted by a large number of sub-contractors.

ELDO EUROPA 1 THIRD STAGE

The general appearance of the third stage of the ELDO Europa 1 launch vehicle is shown in the adjacent illustration.

It is cylindrical in shape, with a basic structure of welded aluminium alloy tube. Much of the interior is occupied by a spherical propellant tank, divided into two separate compartments by an internal dished bulkhead. The upper compartment contains the Aerozine 50 fuel (a mixture of hydrazine and UDMH in equal proportions); the lower compartment contains nitrogen tetroxide oxidant. The tank is made of titanium alloy and carries the main thrust ring around its equator. The payload is mounted above this ring. Below it are the gimballed main thrust chamber, made of titanium alloy, with two small gimballed vernier motors mounted one on each side. The combustion chamber and throat section of the main thrust chamber are regeneratively cooled; the nozzle is uncooled.

The total thrust of the third stage is given as 5,250 lb (2,380 kg) of which 5,070 lb (2,300 kg) comes from the main engine and 180 lb (80 kg) from the two verniers.

ERNO is responsible for development and production of the main engines, propellant supply

Third-stage assembly for the Europa 1 launch vehicle F8

system, tanks and structure. Messerschmitt-Bölkow-Blohm designed and is producing the glass-fibre reinforced container for pressurised helium, hydraulic system, servo motors for the engines and attitude control system and is responsible for check-out and testing of the engines, in association with the DVL. The vernier engines are being developed, tested and manufactured jointly by the two companies. Ground testing of the complete stage was done by ERNO in collaboration with the DFL.

Developed third stages, using high-energy propellants to permit a large increase in payload, are being studied.

DIMENSIONS:
  Length, base of skirt to satellite mating ring
  12 ft 6·2 in (3·82 m)
  Diameter 6 ft 7·1 in (2·00 m)
WEIGHTS (High orbit):
  Total weight, less payload 7,992 lb (3,625 kg)
  Weight of propellants 6,240 lb (2,830 kg)

DORNIER
DORNIER SYSTEM GmbH (Subsidiary of Dornier GmbH)

HEAD OFFICE AND WORKS:
  Immenstaad/Bodensee
POSTAL ADDRESS:
  Postfach 648, 799 Friedrichshafen/Bodensee
BONN OFFICE:
  Allianzplatz (Heussallee), 53 Bonn
GENERAL MANAGERS:
  Dipl-Ing Donatus Dornier
  Dipl-Ing Dr jur Karl-Wilhelm Schäfer
DEPUTY MANAGING DIRECTOR:
  Dr Bernhard Schmidt
PUBLIC RELATIONS MANAGER:
  Gerhard Patt, Brunhamstrasse 21, 8 München-Neuaubing

Dornier System is a research and development company. Its activities cover an extremely wide technological field, including missiles, drones, reconnaissance systems, air target systems, satellites, upper atmosphere research rockets, payload integration, recovery systems, balloon sondes, attitude stabilisation systems, electronic systems and components, oceanology, solid state physics, materials research, operations research and management consultancy.

Major current programmes include development of the Aeros research satellite, described below.

Dornier System is a leading European contractor for the construction and integration of scientific payloads for rockets and for launch support services. On behalf of ESTeC, the Federal German Ministry for Scientific Research and other agencies, it has produced payloads for Skua, Centaure, Nike-Apache and Black Brant III rockets and prepared them for launching at Kiruna, Sweden, Fort Churchill, Canada and Huelva, Spain. The 30th such payload supplied since 1965 was launched by ESTeC at Kiruna in 1969.

Scientific payloads launched up to that time were designed to investigate meteorite dust and measure cosmic particles, measure wind at high altitude and investigate polar light phenomena.

Dornier System's Astrid single-axis stabilisation system, designed to orientate payloads towards a star or the sun, was employed for the first time in January 1970. A three-axis attitude stabilisation system for rockets and payload containers is under development.

Another Dornier System product is the Resy parachute recovery system, which was first employed on a Skylark sounding rocket launched by ESRO/ESTeC in October 1969 and was scheduled to be fully operational by mid-1970.

AEROS (625-A2) SATELLITE

Following evaluation of several project studies

by German aerospace companies, the Federal Ministry of Education and Science chose Dornier System to develop Germany's second research satellite, the Aeros, early in 1970. This satellite is scheduled to be launched by an American Scout rocket in 1972, for a broad six-month programme of measurements in the upper atmosphere.

The scientific payload for Aeros will consist of an impedance probe and an EUV spectrometer to measure electron density and extreme ultraviolet solar radiation, together with a braking field analyser to measure electron and ion temperatures. The instrument package will be supplemented by a special experiment to measure the neutral atmosphere temperature and the overall density of neutral particles and a mass spectrometer to measure the partial density of ions and neutral particles.

The initial apogee is to be 540 nm (620 miles; 1,000 km), with a perigee of 127 nm (146 miles; 235 km). The apogee will gradually fall in the course of time, but will then be raised to 325 nm (373 miles; 600 km) again after about four months. The correction will be made with the aid of a hydrazine engine. An active magnetic attitude control system will enable the spin-stabilised axis of the body to be aligned to the sun. Solar cells on the face of the Aeros satellite will supply power to operate the equipment on board.

ERNO
ERNO RAUMFAHRTTECHNIK GmbH

ADDRESS:
  28 Bremen 1, Hünefeldstrasse 1-5 (Postfach 1199)
DIRECTORS:
  Dipl-Ing Hans Schneider
  Dr rer pol Rudolf Kappler

This company was formed by Hamburger Flugzeugbau GmbH (now part of MBB) (40 per cent) and Vereinigte Flugtechnische Werke

GmbH (60 per cent) for the joint development of space programmes.

Most of ERNO's current activities are concerned with the ELDO (European Launcher Development Organization) projects, ESRO (European Space Research Organization) projects and the German national space programme.

For the ELDO-A project, ERNO developed and built the third-stage structure and engines, as described under the ASAT heading in this section. It is also participating in ELDO's follow-up programmes.

For ESRO, ERNO is playing a major part in the development of the TD satellite as a member of the MESH consortium (see International section).

ERNO also contributed to the German 625-A1 Azur scientific satellite (see under MBB entry), and is responsible for development and manufacture of the attitude control system for the Intelsat III satellite as subcontractor to the US company TRW, with which it has a technical assistance agreement.

MBB
MESSERSCHMITT-BÖLKOW-BLOHM GmbH
Space Division

HEAD OFFICE AND WORKS:
  Ottobrunn bei München

In addition to its manufacture of piloted aircraft, Messerschmitt-Bölkow-Blohm is engaged on the development of guided weapons (see "Missiles" section), research rockets and satellites, and is major contractor for the third stage of the ELDO launch vehicle (see under "ASAT" entry). It has produced design studies of advanced upper stages for both the ELDO Europa IIID vehicle

and the Thor booster, utilising fluorine and liquid hydrogen propellants.

Preliminary studies of two other projects, the Franco/German Symphonie experimental communications satellite and the German/American Helios solar probe, have been completed. MBB was named as prime contractor for the development and construction of Helios in April 1970.

SPAZ

Under the SPAZ (Slowly-varying absorption, Polar cap absorption, Auroral sub-storm, Zusatzraketenprogramm) research programme,

five payloads are being launched by Black Brant VA sounding rockets from Kiruna, ESRO's launching site in Sweden. The first launch in the series took place on 3 February 1970. The objective is to carry out measurements in the polar light zone, to supplement results obtained by the Azur scientific satellite.

The five SPAZ payloads are divided into three groups, representing three types of experiments. The main purpose of payload version I is to carry out optical measurements using the so-called Ebert-Spectrometer. This payload was designed to be launched into the break-up phase of an Auroral sub-storm.

Two version II payloads, for special measurements of the ultra-violet region, are being launched in the early morning hours, when a slowly-varying absorption phenomenon occurs.

Payloads of version III are equipped with a proton-alpha-particle experiment and are launched when, due to chromospheric eruption on the sun, the polar ionosphere becomes ionised, which results in absorption of electromagnetic waves (PCA).

Nominal weight of each SPAZ payload is 220 lb (100 kg). Peak altitude to which they are being launched is approximately 108 nm (125 miles; 200 km).

HEOS

HEOS-1 (Highly Eccentric Orbit Satellite-1), the third satellite produced for ESRO, was launched from Cape Kennedy on 5 December 1968 by a Thor-Delta vehicle. It was developed over a three-year period by an international team headed by Junkers (now absorbed into MBB). Its payload consists of eight scientific experiments from research institutes in Germany, Great Britain, Italy, France and Belgium, for taking measurements of the interplanetary magnetic field and cosmic radiation.

HEOS is basically a sixteen-sided drum-shape structure, with its sixteen panels covered almost entirely with solar cells. A tripod structure on top of the drum carries instrumentation.

British Aircraft Corporation supplied the satellite's attitude-sensing system and associated electronics. The principle of the system is that, as the spinning satellite rotates, two types of sensors monitor either infra-red or visible light emissions from the Sun and Earth. This information is telemetered back to Earth and enables the satellite's spin rate and attitude to be determined by computation.

HEOS-1 entered an orbit with an inclination of 28·9°, initial perigee of 231 nm (266 miles; 428 km) and initial apogee of 120,000 nm (138,200 miles; 222,400 km). Its spin rate is 10 rpm.

On 18 March 1969 an 18 lb (8·2 kg) capsule containing a mixture of barium and copper oxide was ejected from the satellite at an altitude of 54,120 miles (87,100 km). The ionised cloud subsequently formed was observed from ground stations in Chile, Arizona and Alaska.

In early 1969, ESRO decided to order a follow-up satellite, HEOS-2, based on the HEOS-1 design. HEOS-2 scientific experiments will provide further data on the magnetosphere and the propagation of cosmic rays. The launch into a polar orbit is planned for late 1971.

WEIGHT: 240 lb (109 kg)

DIMENSIONS:
Diameter of body 4 ft 3 in (1·30 m)
Depth of body 2 ft 4 in (0·70 m)

MIKA and DIAL

Within the framework of the French national space programme, the Centre Nationale d'Etudes Spatiales (CNES), with the support of the Bundesministerium für wissenschaftliche Forschung (BMwF), awarded Junkers (since absorbed into MBB) a contract for a 115 lb (52 kg) technological capsule, known as Minikapsel (MIKA), to measure the exact orbit achieved by the Diamant-B launch vehicle.

The objective was almost the same as that planned formerly for the CT-System technological capsule for ESRO (see 1968-69 Jane's), except that a solid-propellant motor was no longer to be tested. Instead, measurements were planned to be made of the dynamic and static behaviour of the Diamant-B vehicle over a period of about one hour.

Within the context of this programme, BMwF and CNES also decided to develop as quickly as possible a German payload for Diamant-B, the complete payload package to be known as DIAL. In addition to the MIKA capsule, it included a 136 lb (61·7 kg) satellite, known as WIKA, which was launched on 10 March 1970

HEOS-1 scientific satellite

Model of DIAL satellite

by the first Diamant-B into an equatorial orbit with an apogee of 881 nm (1,015 miles; 1,634 km), perigee of 172 nm (198 miles; 319 km), inclination of 5·41° to the equator and orbital time of 106 minutes.

The purpose of the DIAL satellite was to investigate the hydrogen geocorona up to an altitude of 1,080 nm (1,240 miles; 2,000 km). The temporal and spatial distribution of geocoronal Ly-H radiation was to be measured, using an ionisation chamber photometer. The intensity of this resonance radiation indicates the degree of concentration of atomic hydrogen in the higher atmosphere. The viewing direction of the photometer—30°, 90° and 150° relative to the satellite's spin axis—was designed to permit determination of the direction and spatial distribution of radiation intensity during the various orbits. Simultaneous measurement of electron density can provide information about possible recombination processes.

Azur satellite undergoing electromagnetic compatibility tests

AZUR SATELLITE

Messerschmitt-Bölkow-Blohm was assigned responsibility for systems management of the programme under which Germany's first research satellite, the Azur, was developed and built by seven German aerospace and electronic companies. It had technical responsibility for the overall satellite system, including the determination of the requirements and specifications for the system and sub-systems. It also assembled and tested the satellite.

Formal agreement for the co-operative programme between the German Ministry for Science and Education and NASA was signed in July 1965. The launch was preceded by a series of sounding rocket launches from various sites, in 1966-67, to check out Azur instrumentation.

Azur itself was launched on 8 November 1969 from the US Western Test Range, into a near-polar orbit with an apogee of 1,697 nm (1,954 miles; 3,145 km), perigee of 207 nm (238 miles; 383 km) and inclination of 102·975°, with an orbital time of 122 minutes. It weighed 157 lb (71 kg), including 37 lb (17 kg) of experiments.

The seven experiments carried by Azur were designed to study the Earth's radiation belt, the aurorae and solar particle events. Special emphasis was placed on measuring the intensity and distribution of protons and electrons in terms of time and location.

The general appearance of the satellite is shown in the accompanying illustration. Sub-system contractors included ERNO for the structure, de-spin mechanism (yo-yo) and boom mechanism; Dornier System for the thermal control sub-system, attitude control and attitude measurement; AEG-Telefunken for the transmitter, receiver, filter and switch, magnetic tape recorder and power supply; Siemens AG for the antenna and diplexar; Standard Elektrik Lorenz AG for the analogue telemetry unit, digital telemetry unit, signal conditioner, command distribution unit and step-down units; and Siemens AG for the electrical ground support equipment.

INTERNATIONAL PROGRAMMES

CIFAS

CONSORTIUM INDUSTRIEL FRANCO-ALLE-MAND POUR LE SATELLITE SYMPHONIE (DEUTSCH-FRANZÖSICHES INDUSTRIE-KONSORTIUM FÜR DEN SATELLITEN SYMPHONIE)

HEAD OFFICE:
12bis Avenue Bosquet, Paris 7e, France

ADMINISTRATOR:
C. Cristofini

This consortium was formed on 25 April 1968 in response to a request from the French and German governments for proposals to develop a telecommunications satellite named Symphonie. Members of the consortium, under the technical, industrial and commercial direction of Société Nationale Industrielle Aérospatiale (Division Systèmes Balistiques et Espace), are Messerschmitt-Bölkow-Blohm, Thomson-CSF, SAT, Siemens-AG and AEG-Telefunken.

SYMPHONIE

The Symphonie telephone/television satellite is

scheduled to be launched from the CNES site in Guiana during 1973, under a joint Franco-German programme. It will be established in geostationary orbit over the South Atlantic, at longitude 15°W, giving coverage of two zones through two elliptical beams, each of 13° × 8°. The first beam will cover Europe, North and Central Africa; the second beam will cover South America and the Eastern parts of North and Central America.

The main body of the Symphonie satellite is a shallow six-sided box, with three deployable panels of solar cells, giving a minimum total power of 177W. Three parabolic and horn telecommunications antennae are mounted above the body. Two transponders provide coverage of the two Earth receiving zones in various combinations. A three-axis stabilisation system and a built-in liquid rocket apogee motor are fitted.

Symphonie is intended for 24-hour use. It will weigh about 500 lb (220 kg) in synchronous orbit.

A model of Symphonie with solar panels folded for launching

CONTRAVES/DORNIER

CONTRAVES AG

8052 Zurich, Schaffhauserstrasse 580, Switzerland

DORNIER SYSTEM GmbH

799 Friedrichshafen, Germany

Contraves and Dornier System have developed jointly and are now producing a high-altitude sounding rocket named Zenit.

CONTRAVES/DORNIER ZENIT

The Zenit sounding rocket is intended for economical scientific research in the lower ionosphere at altitudes between 27 and 162 nm (30-185 miles; 50-300 km). Its solid-propellant motor is derived from that used in a successful guided weapon system. Payload integration is simplified by the modular design of the payload section and by use of standard equipment.

From nose to tail, the Zenit comprises a nose cone, a cylindrical payload section made up of a number of stacked modules clamped together by manacle rings, the main propulsion motor and optional booster. Experimental equipment is housed in the nose cone and the forward modules; standard equipment modules are placed between the experiment modules and the motor. Equipment and instruments are mounted on lightweight boards within each module. Standard modules have lengths of 200, 250 or 300 mm and each type is available plain, with access doors or with ejectable panels. The modules can be used in any combination or number within stability and weight limits.

Zenit was launched successfully for the first time at Salto di Quirra, Sardinia, on 27 October 1967.

TYPE: High-altitude sounding rocket.

NOSE CONE: Alternative plain conical glass-fibre or split jettisonable types, each 5 ft 5 in (1,650 mm) long.

EXPERIMENT MODULE: Experiments that may be carried in Zenit include ionospheric composition, ion concentrations, electron densities, geophysics, aurora borealis, magnetic field measurements, solar rays, X-rays, ultra-violet rays, wave propagation, micrometeorites, meteorology, stellar observations, atomic physics, space medicine. Payload compartment volume approx 110 dm³.

ATTITUDE CONTROL MODULE: This accurately positions the payload section in relation to a chosen object such as a star. The basic Astrid system aligns the longitudinal axis of the spinning vehicle to a predetermined star of magnitude 2, with a maximum error of 5 minutes of arc, and weighs 48·5 lb (22 kg). A higher-accuracy Elliott Brothers three-axis system is available; this is sun or moon orientated and weighs about 110 lb (50 kg).

STANDARD ELECTRONIC MODULE: Contains the power supply, telemetry, magnetometer, programmer or command receiver, distance measuring system, destruct system and various sensors. Module length 7·9 in (200 mm).

RECOVERY MODULE: Housed in a 9·8 in (250 mm) module, the recovery system comprises a 14 ft 9 in (4·5 m) diameter radar-reflective ribbon parachute, twin-cell toroidal soft-landing/flotation bag and location aids. Latter consist of the metalised and coloured parachutes, automatic radio beacon with self-erecting antenna, smoke signal flares and fluorescent dye markers.

POWER PLANT: Single-stage dual-thrust solid-propellant main motor, using high specific impulse grain in lightweight filament-wound case. Burning time 31 seconds. Three fins on rear of motor. Optional jettisonable Cuckoo boost motor, developed by Rocket Propulsion Establishment (UK), burning time 4 seconds. Active booster separation system.

GROUND EQUIPMENT: Ground station is mobile, consisting of rack-mounted units. Command console includes central programmer, time signal generator and external power supply. Check-out circuits are integrated with power supply unit. Telemetry ground station can utilise magnetic tape, multi-channel paper recording or photographic data acquisition and recording system. Zenit can be launched from either a fixed tower or short mobile launcher.

DIMENSIONS:
Length overall:
Unboosted	18 ft 4¼ in	(5·6 m)
Boosted	23 ft 3½ in	(7·1 m)
Body diameter	1 ft 4½ in	(0·42 m)

Launch of single-stage Zenit rocket

LAUNCHING WEIGHTS:
Excluding payload (approx):
Unboosted	1,323 lb	(600 kg)
Boosted	1,852 lb	(840 kg)

PERFORMANCE (Payload = everything forward of motor):
Ceiling with 44 lb (20 kg) payload:
Unboosted	118 nm	(136 miles; 220 km)
Boosted	188 nm	(217 miles; 350 km)

Ceiling with max payload:
Unboosted, 286 lb (130 kg) payload
65 nm (75 miles; 120 km)
Boosted, 551 lb (250 kg) payload
75 nm (87 miles; 140 km)
Peak velocity (approx):
Unboosted	5,250 ft	(1,600 m) sec
Boosted	6,235 ft	(1,900 m) sec
Roll velocity		0-10 rps

Launch acceleration (approx):
Unboosted	6 g
Boosted	8 g

ELDO/CECLES

EUROPEAN SPACE VEHICLE LAUNCHER DEVELOPMENT ORGANISATION

ORGANISATION EUROPÉENNE POUR LA MISE AU POINT ET LA CONSTRUCTION DE LANCEURS D'ENGINS SPATIAUX

ADDRESS:
114 avenue de Neuilly, 92-Neuilly, France
COUNCIL:
Gen R. Aubinière (President 1970, France)
M. B. Gaedke (Vice-President 1970, Germany)
J. Bouha (Vice-President 1970, Belgium)
SECRETARIAT:
SECRETARY GENERAL: R. di Carrobio (Italy)
DEPUTY SECRETARY GENERAL AND DIRECTOR OF FUTURE ACTIVITIES: J. P. Cuasse (France)
ASSISTANT SECRETARY GENERAL (ADMINISTRATIVE DIRECTOR): H. L. Costa (Germany)
TECHNICAL DIRECTOR: Gen P. Girardin (France)
HEAD OF PRESS AND INFORMATION SERVICE:
G. Curtopassi

Although the convention formally establishing this organisation did not come into force until 1 May 1964, ELDO began work in early 1962, to co-ordinate design and manufacture of the European space launch vehicle. The original member countries were the United Kingdom, France, West Germany, Italy, Belgium, the Netherlands and Australia, which is making available the Woomera range for check-out and launching. Observers were Denmark and Switzerland.

Britain has withdrawn from ELDO, but will continue to make the British-developed Blue Streak first-stage rocket available to the organisation commercially until 1976. Blue Streak will continue to be used in the Europa II launch vehicle, but will not be used in the future Europa III.

ELDO EUROPA I and II

The **Europa I** launch vehicle is made up of a British (Hawker Siddeley) Blue Streak first stage, French (Aérospatiale/LRBA) Coralie second stage, and German (ASAT) third stage, with an Italian (Fiat/Aerfer) satellite test vehicle. The Netherlands (PTI) provide long-range telemetry links, including ground equipment, and undertake aerodynamic tests, while Belgium (MBLE)

has responsibility for the down-range ground guidance station.

Details of the individual stages can be found under the entries for "Hawker Siddeley", "Aérospatiale" and "ASAT" in this section.

The first three firings in the initial programme were of the first stage, Blue Streak, alone and were all successful.

The second phase of the trials involved fully representative three-stage vehicles. In the first two, the second and third stages were non-propulsive; both firings were successful. In the next two, F6/1 and F6/2, the second stage was live but the tests were only partially successful since the second stage failed to ignite, due to a fault in the electrical equipment of this stage. A successful separation of first and second stages was, however, obtained and other experiments were carried out satisfactorily. For example, the attitude reference system, which was operational for the first time, functioned satisfactorily.

The eighth firing, designated F7, can be considered to have been 80% successful. The three stages were live and the separation systems between them worked satisfactorily and the engines of the stages ignited correctly. The engines of both first and second stages functioned according to specification, but those of the third stage cut out prematurely with the result that the satellite test vehicle did not go into orbit.

On the ninth firing, on 3 July 1969, the third stage failed to ignite.

The initial programme for the development of Europa I provided for one more firing from the launching site at Woomera in Australia, and this, designated F9, was scheduled for May 1970.

A supplementary programme has been approved under which the Europa I launcher will be modified by the addition of a perigee stage. By embodying in the satellite an apogee motor, this uprated launcher, known as **Europa II**, will be able to put payloads of 375-420 lb (170-190 kg) into geostationary orbit from the ELDO equatorial base in French Guiana. Such payloads would be suitable for telecommunications, meteorology, aerial navigation aid and other practical purposes.

Europa II is expected to serve as launcher for the Franco-German Symphonie satellite and a CETS communications satellite.

Launch of Europa I vehicle F8, Woomera, 2 July 1969

EST

EUROPEAN SATELLITE TEAM

ELLIOTT-AUTOMATION LTD

E-A Space and Advanced Military Systems Ltd
Elliott Space and Weapon Automation Ltd
34 Portland Place, London W.1, England

ASEA Allmänna Svenska Elektriska AB

Västerås, Sweden

DORNIER SYSTEM GmbH

799 Friedrichshafen/Bodensee, Postfach 648, Germany

FIAR-CGE COMPAGNIA GENERALE DI ELETTRICITÀ DIPARTIMENTO ELETTRONICA PROFESSIONALE

Via G. B. Grassi 93, 20157 Milano, Italy

FOKKER-VFW NV

Schiphol-Oost, Amsterdam, Netherlands

THOMSON-CSF

Parc de Rocquencourt, BP 2000, 78-Versailles, France

GENERAL ELECTRIC COMPANY (Consultant)

Valley Forge Space Technology Center, PO Box 8555, Philadelphia, Pennsylvania 19101, USA

EST was formed by Elliott in 1966 to provide ESRO with a European consortium capable of making complete satellites. It was joined subsequently by Dornier System and is still in being for projects planned by ESRO. Leadership of the team would be decided according to programme requirements.

MESH

SA ENGINS MATRA,
4 rue de Presbourg, 75-Paris XVIe, France
ERNO RAUMFAHRTTECHNIK GmbH,
28 Bremen, Hünefeldstrasse 1-5, Germany
SAAB AKTIEBOLAG,
Linköping, Sweden
HAWKER SIDDELEY DYNAMICS LTD
Manor Road, Hatfield, Herts, England
FiAT SpA
Corso Giovanni Agnelli 200, Turin, Italy

This international consortium was formed in September 1966, the word "MESH" being an acronym of the initial letters of the four founder members, listed above. They agreed not only to collaborate in manufacturing programmes, but to submit joint tenders to specifications for space vehicles and satellites issued within and outside Europe.

As a result of one such tender, MESH received in March 1967 a contract to design and develop the TD 1 satellite for the European Space Research Organisation (ESRO). Details of this are given below.

In December 1969, Fiat SpA of Italy, through its Aviation Division, joined MESH as a full member. Fiat has a direct technical exchange agreement with TRW of America, and its membership has strengthened the team considerably.

TD 1 SATELLITE

Largest satellite at present under development in Europe, the TD 1 is intended primarily to study the sun and stellar astronomy in UV, and will be stabilised for certain experiments. Its sun-pointing accuracy will be extremely high during a planned lifetime of six months.

The general appearance of the TD satellite is shown in the adjacent illustration. Its basic launching weight is of the order of 1,000 lb (454 kg). With its four solar panels extended, it will span 15 ft 0 in (4·55 m).

TD 1 satellite with solar panels extended (*Flight International*)

The TD 1 is intended to be orbited in February 1972, using a Delta launch vehicle. It will enter a near-polar orbit at a height of 280 nm (323 miles; 520 km) and will be stabilised by inertia wheels (normal mode) and a pneumatic system (acquisition mode). One axis will be orientated towards the sun, to within 1 minute of arc; another axis will be orientated towards the Earth, within an accuracy of 1°.

Matra is prime contractor for this programme. All member companies of the consortium have agreements with TRW and will benefit from experience gained by this American company in the space field.

Experiments will be provided by the Royal Observatory, Edinburgh, the Utrecht Laboratory, the Saclay Centre for Nuclear Studies, the University of Milan and the Max Planck Institute.

ITALY

ISTITUTO DI COSTRUZIONI AERONAUTICHE CENTRO RICERCHE AEROSPAZIALI, UNIVERSITÀ DEGLI STUDI DI ROMA
ADDRESS:
Via Salaria 851, 00199 Rome
DIRECTOR: Prof Luigi Broglio
DOCUMENTATION OFFICER: Col G. Amoruso

Prof Broglio and his colleagues of the Aerospace Research Centre in Rome are responsible for the San Marco satellites, of which details follow.

SAN MARCO

Launched by an Italian crew, using a NASA Scout booster, from Wallops Island on 15 December 1964, San Marco 1 was designed and built by Italian scientists. It was intended primarily for air-density measurements and functioned in a novel manner, the whole 26-in (66-cm), 254-lb (115-kg) satellite being designed as a dynamometer. Its lightweight outer spherical shell was connected to a heavier inner drum-like structure, carrying the necessary instrumentation, by three flexible links coupled to strain gauges, disposed along three mutually perpendicular axes. The frictional drag due to the very low air densities through which the vehicle travelled acted on the outer shell, the heavy inner core remaining unaffected. This resulted, because of the flexible links, in a relative displacement between the outer shell and the inner body which was measured by the strain gauges along the three axes mentioned

above, the displacement being proportional to the drag. The strain gauge measurements were transmitted to ground stations by telemetry.

A second satellite, the San Marco 2, was launched into an equatorial orbit at sea, off the East Coast of Africa, on 26 April 1967. The launch was effected by a Scout from a mobile base consisting of two floating platforms which were fixed to the sea bed by extensible legs. Like its predecessor, San Marco 2 was intended to obtain continuous measurements of air density, over the Equator, these measurements being of concern because two techniques previously in use gave contradictory results. A second experiment was designed to investigate the properties of the ionosphere which cause interference with long-range radio transmission.

A third satellite, the San Marco C, will be launched into an equatorial orbit in the second half of 1970, from the same mobile base. Apart from the drag balance, it will be equipped with a magnetic attitude control system, two mass spectrometers, and solar panels for rechargeable batteries. Besides continuous measurements of air density, the satellite will report the kinetic temperatures of the main air components in the explored region of the atmosphere.

San Marco C satellite, with half of shell removed to show the inner structure and solar cells

SNIA VISCOSA

DEFENCE AND AEROSPACE DIVISION:
via Lombardia 31, 00187 Rome
FACTORIES:
Colleferro (Rome) and Ceccano (Frosinone)
HEAD OF AMMUNITION BRANCH AND SALES MANAGER: Cdr Walter Auconi

SNIA Viscosa (formerly Bombrini Parodi-Delfino), who have produced gunpowder, high explosives and ammunition since 1913, have been engaged in recent years in research on solid propellants, solid-propellant rocket motors, complete rockets and missiles.

The company possesses all the necessary in-

stallations for the production of double-base solid propellants, from the nitration of glycerine and cotton to the production of grains by extrusion or casting. Composite solid-propellant grains incorporating polybutadiene, polyurethane or polyvinyl polymers as binder are also produced in small and medium sizes, with high specific impulses and outstanding physical and mechanical characteristics.

Complete propulsion units of from 50 to 400 mm diameter, with combustion times ranging from a fraction of a second to 18 seconds, are manufactured by SNIA Viscosa's Defence and Aerospace Division for use in military rockets or missiles.

Two-stage sounding rockets are at an advanced stage of development or under test. A single-stage sounding rocket, especially suited for use in Europe, is also being designed. In addition, the apogee motor for the ELDO Europa II programme has been brought to the final qualification stage, and the design of a new apogee motor is also at an advanced stage.

A major production item is the BPD Type ARF/8M 2-in folding-fin air-to-surface rocket, which can be supplied in honeycomb packs of seven to thirty rounds. Other air-to-air and surface-to-surface rockets are in production or under test, together with advanced anti-tank weapon systems.

STM

CENTRO STUDI TRASPORTI MISSILISTICA (Missile Transport Research Centre)
HEAD OFFICE:
Via Squarcialupo 19-A, 00162 Rome
The STM is developing an upper atmosphere sounding vehicle named the Bora-Sond, of unconventional design.

STM BORA-SOND

The Bora-Sond is designed as a minimum-cost sounding rocket, with a reusable first stage, for probing the atmosphere at heights up to 387,000 ft (118,000 m).

The G.III-P.50 first stage embodies a hot-water propulsion system, using an instant heating process (350°C) of a chemical nature. Such a

system is completely independent of any outside source of energy. There is no flame, no appreciable noise, no internal corrosion problem and no toxic exhaust gas. The whole booster is recoverable by parachute and reusable at least 50 times unless damaged by landing on rocky terrain. A crew of two or three semi-skilled men can service the rocket and launch it, since the system does not come under the regulations governing the handling of explosives and negligible safety precautions are needed.

This stage has a nominal rating of 4,400 lb (2,000 kg) st for two seconds and was completing its static and flight tests, over a temperature range of —50°C to +50°C, in mid-1969.

The T.II-P.300 second stage, under development in 1969, utilises an equally unconventional propulsion system, based on the emission of hydrogen (at above 3,000°C) produced by the combustion of metals into water. The specific impulse, indicated by tests, is in the 300 sec range. Nominal rating is 496 lb (225 kg) st for 29 seconds.

Bora-Sond is launched from a 15 ft (5 m) long rail assembly. Power for ignition of both stages is provided by a ground source, a motion switch firing the sustainer igniter by a delay squib after three seconds of coasting flight between booster burn-out and second-stage ignition. Staging is accomplished by a shear-type interstage adapter. Fin assemblies are set to provide a rate of roll of 10 or 20 rps at burn-out. Payload volume is 366 cu in (6,000 cm³).

DIMENSIONS:
Length: overall   15 ft 1·1 in (4·60 m)

first stage	8 ft 4·8 in (2·56 m)
second stage	5 ft 10·5 in (1·79 m)
payload section	2 ft 3·5 in (0·70 m)
Body diameter:	
first stage	9·6 in (24·5 cm)
second stage	8·6 in (21·9 cm)
Span of fins	2 ft 10·6 in (0·88 m)

WEIGHTS (less payload):

Launching weight	416·7 lb (189 kg)
Weight at first-stage burn-out	209·4 lb (95 kg)
Weight at second-stage ignition	88·2 lb (40 kg)
Weight at second-stage burn-out	39·7 lb (18 kg)
Payload, incl nose-cone and housing.	
	8·8-13·2 lb (4-6 kg)

PERFORMANCE (estimated, with 11 lb = 5 kg payload, at S/L, launch angle of 87°):

Max ceiling	387,000 ft (118,000 m)
Time to max ceiling	180 sec
Altitude at second-stage burn-out	
	52,500 ft (16,000 m)
Max velocity	4,495 ft (1,370 m) sec
Range at max ceiling	70,200 ft (21,400 m)
Altitude at first-stage burn-out	850 ft (260 m)
Velocity at first-stage burn-out	
	690 ft (210 m) sec
Max launch acceleration	13 g

First stage of Bora-Sond sounding vehicle

JAPAN

MITSUBISHI

MITSUBISHI JUKOGYO KABUSHIKI KAISHA (Mitsubishi Heavy Industries, Ltd)

HEAD OFFICE:
Mitsubishi Building, No 10, 2-chome, Marunouchi, Chiyoda-Ku, Tokyo

OFFICERS: See "Aircraft" section

MANAGER, SPACE SYSTEMS DEPARTMENT:
Y. Yokouchi

On June 1, 1964, Shin Mitsubishi Jukogyo, Mitsubishi Zosen (Shipbuilding) and Mitsubishi Nihon Jukogyo were amalgamated as Mitsubishi Jukogyo Kabushiki Kaisha (Mitsubishi Heavy Industries, Ltd). The units known formerly as Shin Mitsubishi and Mitsubishi Zosen, together with Mitsubishi Denki (Electric Machinery) have been engaged since 1955 in the development of missiles and the production of sounding rockets, of which all available details are given below.

Within the framework of Japan's national space programme, Mitsubishi is collaborating with the Science and Technology Agency, Prime Minister's Office, and the Institute of Space and Aeronautical Science, University of Tokyo. It has manufactured the rocket chambers of the Kappa, Lambda and Mu rockets, the attitude control motors of Lambda and Mu, and the launching and assembly tower for the Mu.

For the Japanese Defence Agency, Mitsubishi is developing and producing air-to-air missiles and is manufacturing the Nike-Hercules surface-to-air missile under licence (see "Missiles" section).

MITSUBISHI S-B, S-C, LS-A and LS-C

Mitsubishi has been awarded Science and Technology Agency contracts to develop and test a series of research rockets. First of these were for the S-B and S-C meteorological sounding rockets for observation of the upper atmosphere.

The S-B and S-C are each fitted with a single-stage solid-propellant rocket motor in a fibre-reinforced plastic casing. The S-B is capable of

carrying a payload of 5·1 lb (2·3 kg) to a height of more than 38 nm (44 miles; 70 km); the S-C is designed to carry a 5·5 lb (2·5 kg) payload to a height of more than 43 nm (50 miles; 80 km). At the peak altitude, a radio telemetry and parachute recovery package is released to measure the atmospheric temperature, wind direction and strength.

First launching trials of the S-B were made in 1964. The S-C was launched for the first time in 1969.

First launching of the two-stage LS-A (solid-propellant first stage, liquid-propellant second stage) was made in 1964. Subsequently, Mitsubishi received a follow-on contract for the larger LS-C, which is a research vehicle designed as part of the development programme for the vehicle that will launch an experimental satellite by 1971. First trial launching of the LS-C was made in February 1969.

DIMENSIONS:

Overall length:	
S-B	9 ft 1¾ in (2·778 m)
S-C	9 ft 4¼ in (2·851 m)
LS-A	24 ft 9 in (7·55 m)
LS-C	33 ft 9 in (10·30 m)
Body diameter:	
S-B	6·2 in (0·157 m)
S-C	6·5 in (0·165 m)
LS-A, first stage	13·8 in (0·35 m)
LS-A, second stage	11·8 in (0·30 m)
LS-C, both stages	23·6 in (0·60 m)

WEIGHT:

Launching weight:	
S-B	149 lb (67·8 kg)
S-C	170 lb (77 kg)
LS-A	1,675 lb (760 kg)
LS-C	5,154 lb (2,338 kg)

PERFORMANCE:

Ceiling (80° launch angle):	
S-B	40·5 nm (47 miles; 75 km)
S-C	46 nm (53 miles; 85 km)
LS-A	59 nm (68 miles; 110 km)
LS-C	51 nm (60 miles; 95 km)

S-B research rocket on launcher

NASDA

NATIONAL SPACE DEVELOPMENT AGENCY

ADDRESS:
4-18 Sendagaya, Shibuya-ku, Tokyo

This Agency was established in October 1969, to take over projects initiated by the government's Science and Technology Agency in the space field. It will spend a total of 150 billion yen ($4·2 billion) on the construction and launching of rockets in 1969-74. Initial activities are centred on two large rockets, designated types "N" and "Q".

"N" ROCKET

This four-stage rocket is intended as a launch vehicle for synchronous-orbit satellites. Pre-production models are scheduled to be launched by 1974, with production versions following shortly afterwards. The contract for building the "N" rocket will be awarded to either Mitsubishi or Ishikawajima-Harima Heavy Industries Co.

The "N" rocket is intended to be capable of putting a 264 lb (120 kg) telecommunications satellite into a geostationary equatorial orbit.

Design thrust of its four stages is successively more than 700,000 lb (317,500 kg), 310,000 lb (140,000 kg), 40,000 lb (18,000 kg) and 10,000 lb (4,500 kg).

DIMENSIONS:

Length overall	93 ft 6 in (28·5 m)
Body diameter:	
1st stage	7 ft 6½ in (2·3 m)
2nd stage	7 ft 6½ in (2·3 m)
3rd stage	5 ft 3 in (1·6 m)
4th stage	3 ft 3½ in (1·0 m)

WEIGHT:

Launching weight	239,200 lb (108,500 kg)

"Q" ROCKET

This four-stage rocket will be utilised as launch vehicle for an ionosphere research satellite. Manufacture of the first "Q" rocket was expected to begin in 1970, with the first satellite launching planned for 1972. The first two stages and fourth stage will have solid-propellant motors, the third stage will use liquid propellants. Thrust of the first stage is intended to be about 260,000 lb (118,000 kg), with a second-stage thrust of 95,000 lb (43,000 kg) and third- and fourth-stage

thrusts of 10,000 lb (4,500 kg) each. This would give the "Q" rocket the capability of putting a 187 lb (85 kg) satellite into a circular orbit at a height of 540 nm (620 miles; 1,000 km), or a 616 lb (280 kg) payload into an elliptical orbit with an apogee of 109 nm (125 miles; 200 km).

DIMENSIONS:

Length overall	82 ft 0 in (25 m)
Body diameter:	
1st stage	5 ft 3 in (1·6 m)
2nd stage	5 ft 3 in (1·6 m)
3rd stage	4 ft 7 in (1·4 m)
4th stage	1 ft 11½ in (0·6 m)

WEIGHTS:

Launching weight	113,320 lb (51,400 kg)

NISSAN

NISSAN JIDOSHA KABUSHIKI KAISHA (Nissan Motor Co, Ltd)

HEAD OFFICE:
17-1, 6-chome, Ginza-Higashi, Chuo-ku, Tokyo

SPACE AND AERONAUTICAL DEPARTMENT:
5-1, 3-chome, Momoi, Suginami-ku, Tokyo

PRESIDENT:
Katsuji Kawamata

EXECUTIVE MANAGING DIRECTOR:
Kinzo Amase

DIRECTOR. MANAGER OF SPACE AND AERONAUTICAL DEPARTMENT:
Yasuakira Toda

Nissan Motor Co, Ltd, is the oldest automobile manufacturer in Japan, having been founded in 1918 under the name of Kaishin-sha Motors. It adopted its present name in 1933 and, following its merger with the former Prince Motors, Ltd, on August 1, 1966, is Japan's largest automobile company. The merger has also given Nissan a leading position in the national aerospace industry, as the Space and Aeronautical Division of Prince Motors is now a department of Nissan Motor Co.

Known before and during World War II as Nakajima Aircraft Company, Prince formed its Space and Aeronautical Division as an offshoot of its primary post-war business of automobile manufacture. Today, the Space and Aeronautical Department is responsible for the major share of work on rockets and missiles in Japan.

In the field of military missiles and rockets, the company has been engaged in extensive research and development since 1953. In association with the Technical Research and Development Institute of the Japanese Defence Agency, it has developed many types of air-to-air, air-to-surface and surface-to-surface solid-propellant unguided rockets, several of which are in production, including the "30-rocket", the largest surface-to-surface type in service in Japan.

In addition, this Department has produced many sounding rockets such as Pencil, Baby, Kappa, Lambda and Mu for the Institute of Space and Aeronautical Science, University of Tokyo, and has produced many other research rockets for the Japanese Aerospace Laboratory and Meteorological Agency.

Under contracts from the National Space Development Agency, NASDA (formerly the National Space Development Centre), Nissan has developed a number of rocket motors of the kind that will be used in the projected "Q" and "N" satellite launch vehicles. One of these motors, designated JCR (jet-control rocket), was test fired successfully on the ground in 1967 and performed successfully in test flights from Tanegashima Space Centre in September 1969 and February 1970. The first test firing of a "Q" first-stage motor was scheduled for September 1970.

Nissan's other aerospace research and production activities include work on separation and control mechanisms and static and environmental test equipment.

During 1967, Nissan completed initial experiments in the use of rockets for extinguishing fires.

Details of the important Kappa and early Lambda rockets can be found in the 1963-64 and 1965-66 editions of *Jane's* respectively. Details of the current programmes of Nissan's Space and Aeronautical Division follow.

NISSAN MT-135

This meteorological sounding rocket, developed and produced by Nissan, was evaluated very successfully in comparative tests with the American Arcas rocket at NASA's Wallops Space Flight Station in the Spring of 1967.

The Meteorological Agency of Japan is using an advanced version of the MT-135 for high-altitude study of weather in the Northern part of the country, with weekly launches from July 1970.

NISSAN S-160JA

In support of the Japanese Antarctic Research Expedition (JARE), two S-160JA rockets were fired from Ongul Island, in the South Polar region, in February 1970. Technical staff from Nissan were attached to the Expedition for the launches. The rockets climbed to a height of about 48·5 nm (56 miles; 90 km), providing valuable data on the upper atmosphere in the Antarctic.

The JARE is planning to launch larger rockets, including Kappa-9M, in 1971.

Lambda-4S-5 vehicle for Japan's first successful satellite launch

ADVANCED LAMBDA-4S (AND OSUMI SATELLITE)

Lambda-4S (L-4S), which consists of the three-stage Lambda-3H (L-3H) and a spherical rocket, was intended primarily as a test vehicle for the Mu-4 rocket. It is, however, capable of putting a payload of approximately 40 lb (20 kg) into a 215 nm (250 mile; 400 km) Earth orbit, and an advanced version is being developed with a different orbiting system from the "Gravity Turn" type originally specified.

The fifth launch of an L-4S rocket, on 11 February 1970, from Kagoshima Space Centre, was completely successful and put into an elliptical orbit Japan's first satellite. This consists of the fourth-stage spherical rocket and some sounding devices and is named *Osumi* after the peninsula on which the Space Centre is situated. The success of this experiment is scheduled to be followed by the orbiting of a larger scientific satellite by an Mu-4S rocket.

MU

The first of the Mu series of research rockets (the Mu-1D, described in the 1967-68 *Jane's*) was launched successfully in October 1966. It was followed in August 1969 by the Mu-3D four-stage rocket, with some inert stages. The launching of this rocket was completely successful and provided valuable data for the next vehicle in the series, the Mu-4S, which is intended to put into orbit a 143 lb (65 kg) scientific satellite. The Mu-4S embodies new stabilising devices and was scheduled to be launched for the first time in August 1970.

The Mu-4S will be followed during the next four years by advanced versions designated Mu-4SC, Mu-4SH and Mu-4SS.

The satellites to be orbited by the Mu-4 Series are being developed by the Institute of Space and Aeronautical Science, University of Tokyo.

Mu-3D rocket, predecessor of Mu-4S, on launcher

DIMENSIONS:

Length overall:	
Mu-4S, Mu-4SC	77 ft 5 in (23·6 m)
Mu-4SH	78 ft 9 in (24·0 m)
Mu-4SS	82 ft 0 in (25·0 m)
Body diameter:	
First and second stages	4 ft 8 in (1·42 m)
Third stage	2 ft 9½ in (0·85 m)
Fourth stage:	
Mu-4S, Mu-4SC	2 ft 6¼ in (0·77 m)
Mu-4SH	2 ft 6¾ in (0·78 m)
Mu-4SS	2 ft 7¼ in (0·805 m)

WEIGHTS:

Launching weight, with booster:	
Mu-4S, Mu-4SC, Mu-4SH	86,000 lb (39,000 kg)
Mu-4SS	99,200 lb (45,000 kg)
Weight of booster	6,600 lb (3,000 kg)

POLAND

IL
INSTYTUT LOTNICTWA (AVIATION INSTITUTE)

HEADQUARTERS:
Warsaw 21/Okecie, Al Krakowska 110/114
SCIENTIFIC DIRECTOR:
Dr Czeslaw Skoczylas
HEAD OF TECHNICAL INFORMATION DIVISION:
Jerzy Grzegorzewski, MSc(Eng)

The Aviation Institute (IL) is engaged on aeronautical research, development of power plants, aerodynamic and structural testing, flight testing of fixed-wing aircraft, helicopters and gliders, and development of aviation equipment and materials. It is also responsible for supplying technical information and for standardisation.

The IL has a special production plant responsible for manufacturing prototypes of its designs.

Details of research rockets designed and produced by the IL follow.

METEOR-1

The IL design team, headed by Ing Jerzy Harazny, began work on the Meteor-1 sounding rocket in mid-1962.

Prototype rockets, as well as a launching ramp and ground support equipment, were produced in 1963. Launchings began towards the end of that year, initially on a flat trajectory and later at the steeper angles proposed for operational launches. Trials were completed successfully in April 1965, since when the Meteor-1 has been used by the PIHM (see page 657) for Poland's share of the international programme of upper atmosphere research.

Launches are made from a light transportable ramp and are controlled electrically from a special control console. A mechanical timing device ensures separation of the payload container when the rocket reaches the desired altitude. Separation of the dart begins immediately after engine burn-out, with simultaneous firing of a smoke-trail device, for supplementary observation of the flight path.

There are four versions of this rocket, the original version being designated Meteor-1 and later modified versions Meteor-1A, 1B and 1C. The Meteor-1A carries a single package of hair-like metal needles which drift with the wind when released and can be tracked by ground radar, so indicating the direction and velocity of the wind at high altitudes. Meteor-1B carries two packages of needles which are ejected at different altitudes. Meteor-1C has a longer dart, containing three packages of needles, ejected at different heights. A total of 210 rockets of all types had been built by early 1970.

TYPE: Two-stage sounding rocket.
WINGS: None.
BODY (1st stage): Cylindrical structure. Sheet steel motor casing forms main structural skin.
BODY (2nd stage): Unpowered dart of cylindrical section, housing one or more packages of hair-like needles and pyrotechnic ejection device.
TAIL SURFACES (1st stage): Cruciform fins attached to nozzle clamping ring. Sandwich structure of perforated plywood covered with sheet duralumin, with sharp steel leading-edge blades.
TAIL SURFACES (2nd stage): Cruciform fins in the form of sharp steel plates.
POWER PLANT: Solid-propellant rocket motor with thrust of 3,085 lb (1,400 kg), impulse of 7,055 lb/3,200 kg/sec and burning time of 2·3 sec.
GUIDANCE: None.

The following details refer to the Meteor-1A, except where stated otherwise:

DIMENSIONS:
Length overall:
Meteor-1, 1A, 1B   8 ft 4½ in (2·55 m)
Meteor-1C   9 ft 6 in (2·90 m)
Length of 1st stage   5 ft 9 in (1·75 m)
Length of dart:
Meteor-1, 1A, 1B   2 ft 7 in (0·79 m)
Meteor-1C   3 ft 9 in (1·14 m)
Body diameter:
1st stage   4¾ in (12·0 cm)
dart   1½ in (4·0 cm)
Span of fins:
1st stage   1 ft 4 in (41·0 cm)
dart   4¾ in (12·0 cm)
WEIGHTS:
Launching weight, total   71·6 lb (32·5 kg)
Weight of first stage   61·7 lb (28·0 kg)
Weight at burn-out   32·0 lb (14·5 kg)
PERFORMANCE:
Max speed 2,136 knots (2,460 mph; 3,960 km/h)
Ceiling   114,830 ft (35,000 m)
Time to apogee   80 sec

METEOR-2H

The Meteor-2 prototype version of this single-stage solid-propellant sounding rocket was developed and built by the IL design team for the Polish National Institute for Hydrology and Meteorology (PIHM). Work started in 1965 and the testing of prototype rockets has been under way since 1968.

Meteor-2H is designed to carry a Ramzes telemetry package to a height of 32·3 nm (37·3 miles; 60 km) and eject it on a parachute. The meteor-

IL Meteor-1 meteorological sounding rocket

IL Meteor-2 sounding rocket on launcher

ological instruments, which measure the direction and velocity of wind and air temperature as they descend, were developed by the Rocket and Satellite Research Laboratory of the PIHM.

The 39 ft (12 m) high Type W-120 hydraulically-controlled automatic stationary launcher for Meteor-2H was also designed and built at the IL.

TYPE: Single-stage sounding rocket.
WINGS: None.
BODY: Cylindrical main structure, with conical nose-cone made from sheet steel 0·5 mm thick. Main structural skin formed by 2 mm thick alloy steel sheet motor casing.
FINS: Cruciform tail-fins attached to nozzle ring. Monocoque structures, welded from 0·5 mm steel sheet.
POWER PLANT: Solid-propellant rocket motor with rating of 5,300 lb (2,400 kg) st, impulse of 95,240 lb/43,200 kg/sec and burning time of 18 sec.
GUIDANCE: None.
PAYLOAD COMPARTMENT: In jettisonable nose-cone, volume 305 cu in (5,000 cc).

DIMENSIONS:
Length overall   14 ft 9 in (4·50 m)
Body diameter   1 ft 1¾ in (0·35 m)
Span of fins   4 ft 1¼ in (1·25 m)
WEIGHT:
Launching weight   838 lb (380 kg)
PERFORMANCE:
Max speed at burn-out   Mach 4·2
Ceiling   36·7 nm (42·25 miles; 68 km)

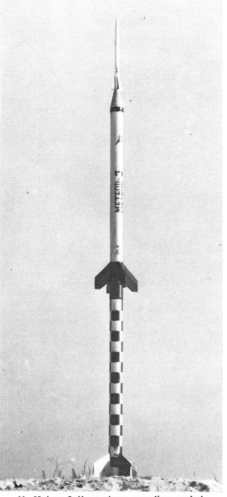

IL Meteor-3 three-stage sounding rocket

METEOR-3

This three-stage meteorological sounding rocket was developed and built for the PIHM in 1967-68 by the IL design team that was responsible for the Meteor-2. It consists of two modified Meteor-1 boosters in tandem, surmounted by a dart which is separated pyrotechnically after burn-out of the second stage.

Meteor-3 is launched from the same Type W-120 launcher as Meteor-2 and was tested in prototype form in 1968-69. Pilot production for the PIHM was started in 1970.

Meteor-3 is intended to measure upper-atmosphere winds by means of hair-like metal needles ejected from the dart at a height of 29·6 nm (34 miles; 55 km).

TYPE: Three-stage sounding rocket.
WINGS: None.
BODY: Same as for Meteor-2.
TAIL SURFACES: Modified geometry and construction. Fins on first stage are of plywood sandwich construction, with steel covering, and have wedge-shaped fore and aft portions. Fins on second stage are of PVC foam sandwich construction with duralumin covering, and have a wedge-shaped fore-part and blunt trailing-edge. Dart fins as on Meteor-1.
POWER PLANT: Each stage as Meteor-1.
GUIDANCE: None.
PAYLOAD COMPARTMENT: In cylindrical portion of dart.

DIMENSIONS:
Length overall   14 ft 1¼ in (4·30 m)
Length of first stage   6 ft 2¾ in (1·90 m)
Length of second stage   6 ft 1¾ in (1·875 m)
Diameter of motors   4·75 in (0·12 m)
Diameter of dart   1·55 in (0·04 m)
Span of fins:
first stage   1 ft 6 in (0·46 m)
second stage   1 ft 4 in (0·41 m)
dart   4·75 in (0·12 m)
WEIGHTS:
Launching weight   143 lb (65 kg)
Weight of first stage   70·5 lb (32 kg)
Weight of second stage   61·7 lb (28 kg)
PERFORMANCE:
Max speed at burn-out   Mach 4·3
Ceiling   35 nm (40·4 miles; 65 km)
Height of needle ejection
                          30 nm (34 miles; 55 km)

PIHM
PANSTWOWY INSTYTUT HYDROLOGICZNO-METEOROLOGICZNY

HEAD OFFICE:
Warszawa 86, ul Podlesna 61
DIRECTOR GENERAL:
Dr Ing Eryk Bobinski
ROCKET SOUNDINGS LABORATORY:
Kraków, ul P Borowego 9

The 1965-66 *Jane's* contained details of a number of sounding rockets which were developed and built jointly by the Experimental Rocket Centre of the Aero Club of Kraków and the Rocket

Soundings Laboratory of the Polish National Institute for Hydrology and Meteorology (PIHM). All meteorological research projects are now undertaken exclusively by the Hydro-Met Institute, which is conducting experiments in accordance with the recommendations of COSPAR and the World Meteorological Organisation.

Rockets used by the PIHM include the Meteor-1, 2 and 3, described under the IL heading, and the Rasko-2, designed and developed by its own staff.

PIHM RASKO-2
Flight tested for the first time in 1964, this unguided rocket has since undergone considerable

development and is used for the artificial modification of clouds. It is a simple solid-propellant rocket, with a cylindrical metal body, cruciform tail surfaces and a chemical payload.

The Rasko-2 was designed by a team led by Dr-Ing J. Walczewski and Ing J. Ksyk.

DIMENSIONS:
Length overall   4 ft 2¼ in (128 cm)
Body diameter   2¼ in (5·7 cm)
Span of fins   10 in (25·3 cm)
WEIGHT:
Launching weight   10 lb (4·5 kg)
PERFORMANCE:
Ceiling   approx 10,000 ft (3,000 m)

SWEDEN

FLYGMOTOR
SVENSKA FLYGMOTOR AB

HEAD OFFICE AND WORKS:
S 461 01 Trollhättan

For several years Flygmotor has been evaluating the possibilities of hybrid rocket engines and their applications in modern missiles and sounding rockets. Several hundred firings have confirmed the inherent advantages of the hybrid concept in terms of handling safety, thrust modulation capabilities and high performance. These feasibility studies and fuel research programmes have enabled Flygmotor to develop a complete sounding rocket system, of which details follow.

FLYGMOTOR SR-1
First shown publicly at the 1969 Paris Air Show, the SR-1 sounding rocket can carry 45 lb (20 kg) of scientific instruments to a height of 97 nm (110 miles; 180 km). It differs from most other research rockets in this category in having a hybrid rocket engine and in being stabilised by an attitude control system which greatly decreases the impact dispersion. It also utilises a new type of smokeless fuel.

In contrast to conventional solid-propellant rocket motors, which are classed as explosive, a hybrid rocket engine is completely safe to handle. The fuel, a plastic-like substance known as Sagaform, and the oxidiser, which is red fuming nitric acid, are kept apart in the rocket casing and react only when brought together at launching. This is effected by using compressed nitrogen to feed the pre-packaged liquid oxidiser into the combustion chamber, where the annular Sagaform charge is ignited spontaneously.

The attitude control system permits small launching sites to be used, with little fear that the rocket will come down in populated areas. It uses steering forces generated by injecting the liquid oxidiser through ports in the exit nozzle and utilizes a pneumatic floating-ball gyroscope

developed by the Research Institute for Swedish National Defence.

TYPE: Scientific sounding rocket.
PAYLOAD CONTAINER: Ogival nose-cone, with total volume of 3,050 cu in (50 litres), housing standard assemblies of power supply, telemetry and attitude control equipment, antennae and scientific experiments. Recovery package optional.
PRESSURISING SYSTEM: Fibre-reinforced resin nitrogen tank between payload container and oxidiser tank, with capacity of 4·4 Imp gallons (20 litres) and working pressure of 3,000 lb/sq in (210 kg/cm²). Fitted with burst-disc to relieve pressure to atmosphere by radio command in emergency.
OXIDISER TANK: Cylindrical centre section of sheet aluminium with welded-on ends and burst-disc. Capacity 16·7 Imp gallons (76 litres) of IRFNA.
COMBUSTION CHAMBER: This section includes the injector, main combustion chamber, turbulence grid with afterburner and exit nozzle. Chamber is lined with annular Sagaform charge (burning time 20 seconds) in case of phenolic-impregnated asbestos to a length of 49·2 in (1,250 mm), with a port diameter of 5·9 in (150 mm). Afterburner is a turbulence-creating device that improves combustion efficiency, made of Refrasil glass-fibre impregnated phenolic resin. Exit nozzle, of Refrasil, has insert of pyrolytic graphite in throat to decrease erosion. Cruciform tail-fins of delta configuration at rear of casing.
DIMENSIONS:
Length overall   16 ft 4¾ in (5·0 m)
Length of payload container 4 ft 5¼ in (1·35 m)
Body diameter   9·85 in (0·25 m)
WEIGHTS:
Launching weight   441 lb (200 kg)
Propellent weight   309 lb (140 kg)
Payload   44 lb (20 kg)

Svenska Flygmotor SR-1 sounding rocket

PERFORMANCE:
Max velocity   Mach 6·5
Ceiling at burn-out   8·6 nm (10 miles; 16 km)
Apogee ceiling   98 nm (113 miles; 182 km)
Time to apogee   202 seconds
Acceleration at launch   6·5 g
Total impulse   294kNs

THE UNITED KINGDOM

BAC
BRITISH AIRCRAFT CORPORATION (GUIDED WEAPONS) LTD

HEAD OFFICE:
100 Pall Mall, London SW1
SALES DIRECTOR: L. A. Sanson
PUBLICITY MANAGER: R. F. Bailey

In addition to its work on guided weapons (see "Missiles" section), this company is heavily engaged in the research rocket and space vehicle field.

In the Spring of 1969, a number of diverse activities handled formerly by its Space, Instrumentation, Industrial, Precision and Microwave Plastics Product Groups were amalgamated under a new Electronic and Space Systems Group (ESS).

ESS is a major contractor to the Hughes Aircraft Company of America in the Intelsat IV telecommunications Satellite programme. It is responsible for the UK.4 (Ariel 4) scientific satellite and Skylark upper atmosphere research rocket. Other products include flight test and accident recording systems for aircraft, automatic test equipment for aircraft, military and industrial applications, precision gyros and inertial guidance equipment for the services and industry, and a wide range of reinforced and plastics products for such applications as aircraft, missiles and ships, and antennae. It also engages in studies of communications systems and research in a number of other branches of advanced technology.

BAC SKYLARK
Skylark sounding rockets have been designed for exploration of the upper atmosphere and to provide platforms for the observation of extra-terrestrial phenomena.

The Skylark was developed originally as a research vehicle for the Royal Aircraft Establishment and for use in a programme of upper-atmosphere research to be undertaken by the Royal Society. It was used during the International Geophysical Year, 1957, its basic design proving so sound and flexible that it has since formed the backbone of British research into

upper-atmosphere phenomena. Over 220 Skylarks had been launched by mid-February 1970. Development of both motors and airframe components has proceeded steadily, and is continuing, so that the new fields of research (particularly astronomical) opened up by use of a stable platform may be exploited fully for many years to come.

BAC is the design authority and industrial agent for Skylark, under contract from the UK government. A complete service is available for users, including design, development and supply of the vehicle assembly, test of payloads, advice to experimenters and design and manufacture of their apparatus, launch preparation and firing, analysis of trajectory and attitude during flight, and delivery of experimental data. This work is centred in the Electronic and Space Systems Group of BAC at Bristol.

The Skylark is a 17·4 in (44-cm) diameter fin-stabilised rocket, comprising a head containing the experiments and instruments, a main Raven motor and, if required, a boost motor. Standard booster is the Cuckoo motor, but the more powerful Goldfinch boost motor was expected to become available in mid-1969.

The head consists of a number of cylindrical body shells and a conical nose-cone. The motors are of a solid-propellant type, and the Raven is available in several Marks with different power outputs. This flexibility allows payloads of anything from 220 to 660 lb (100-300 kg) to be carried to altitudes of from 143 to 54 nm (165-62 miles; 265-100 km). The volume of space available for experiments is about 150 litres.

In order to accommodate experiments and instrumentation assemblies with widely-varying characteristics, the Skylark payload compartment (head) has been designed on a modular basis. Within weight and stability limits, a Skylark head can be assembled from any number of standard cylindrical body sections, with a nose-cone clamped on to form the head structure. Body sections of different lengths, all with a clear 15-in (38-cm) internal diameter, and a variety of nose-

Two-stage Skylark research rocket

cones are available to suit experimental requirements.

A range of attitude control units for Skylark have been designed and manufactured by Elliott

Bros (London) Ltd. These units use nitrogen gas-jets to point the head of the rocket with great accuracy at either the Sun, the Moon or a star, and a magnetometer to control roll. To make best use of available time, payload stabilisation and orientation must be completed as soon as possible after rocket motor separation. The Elliott Sun-pointing ACU performs these operations in less than 30 seconds. Stabilisation of the Skylark payload in this way enables a new range of experiments and observations to be undertaken, in such fields as solar spectroscopy, solar X-ray

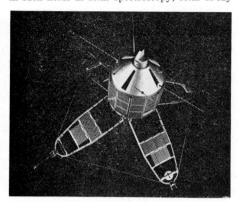

Model of UK.4 scientific satellite

and ultra-violet photography and stellar ultra-violet photography.

A parachute recovery unit is available, consisting of a drogue and main chute which is normally deployed automatically at an altitude of 2 nm (2·35 miles; 3·8 km). The maximum recoverable weight is 400 lb (180 kg) and the unit can be arranged to recover either the experimental equipment or the ACU. A new system is being developed which will allow both the experimental section at the forward end of the head and the ACU at the rear to be recovered.

Standard instruments fitted to Skylark include telemetry on 465 mc/s or IRIG frequencies, magnetometers and accelerometers for attitude determination, a microwave tracker beacon and a Doppler transponder for very precise measurement of trajectory.

On 12 June 1968, a Skylark was launched from the Woomera range carrying the most powerful X-ray telescope yet flown. Built by the X-ray Astronomy Group at Leicester University, the telescope, of 4 sq ft (0·37 m²) overall aperture, made several sweeps across the sky searching for a new type of X-ray star.

Another payload launched from Woomera in late 1968 was the most complex yet carried by a Skylark. It contained experiments from the Universities of London and Birmingham and from the Radio and Space Research Station at Slough, intended to lead to a better understanding of radio propagation in the ionosphere. The package not only had to separate from the rocket but also had to divide into two parts. Flight data then had to be transmitted from one half to the other at a height of 78 nm (90 miles; 145 km).

TYPE: High-altitude research rocket.

WINGS: None.

BODY: Comprises 17 in (43 cm) diameter head secured to motor. Head consists of 5 ft (1·52

m) cone, 7½° semi-angle, and 2 ft 6 in (0·76 m) telemetry bay. Additional sections can be fitted for recovery, or to carry other equipment.

TAIL SURFACES: Three fins of 29 in (0·74 m) span with sweptback leading-edges.

POWER PLANT: One Raven 6A or 8A solid-propellant motor, and optional Cuckoo or Goldfinch solid-propellant booster. Total impulse: Raven 6A 425,000 lb-sec (193,000 kg-sec); Raven 8A 338,000 lb-sec (156,000 kg-sec), Cuckoo 80,000 lb-sec (36,000 kg-sec).

GUIDANCE: Elliott attitude control unit for stabilised rounds.

DIMENSIONS:

Length (nominal)	30 ft 0 in (10·0 m)
Length with booster (nominal)	35 ft 0 in (11·50 m)
Radius of fins	3 ft 2 in (0·97 m)

WEIGHT:

Firing weight, less booster, approx:

stabilised	3,100 lb (1,400 kg)
unstabilised	2,600 lb (1,200 kg)
Head weight	110-550 lb (50-250 kg)

PERFORMANCE:

Raven 6A and Cuckoo 440 lb (200 kg) payload to 121·5 nm (140 miles; 225 km)
Raven 8A, unboosted 260 lb (120 kg) payload to 82·5 nm (95 miles; 150 km)
Time at useful altitude 5-7 minutes

ARIEL 4 (UK. 4) SATELLITE

On 24 February 1969, it was announced that BAC's Electronic and Space Systems Group, at Bristol, had been appointed prime contractor and coordinating design authority for the UK.4 scientific satellite project. The contract was placed subsequently by the Ministry of Technology, acting for the Science Research Council.

The Royal Aircraft Establishment, Farnborough, is the research and development authority, and the Space Research Management Unit of the Science Research Council is responsible for overall management. BAC is responsible for spacecraft design, manufacture, integration and test, handling equipment, ground check-out equipment, launch support, systems engineering, project co-ordination and management.

Associated contractors are GEC (Electronics) Ltd, Portsmouth, for the design and manufacture of power supplies, data handling and telemetry equipment; Ferranti Limited for solar cells; E. Turner Limited for solar cell module assembly and the Atomic Weapons Research Establishment for the recording system.

UK.4 is basically similar to the earlier UK.3 (Ariel 3), described in the 1968-69 *Jane's*, which had completed its 10,000th orbit of the Earth by 25 February 1969. The prototype and development models, in fact, use certain existing UK.3 hardware and test equipment. UK.4 is scheduled to be launched in 1971 by a NASA Scout vehicle into a 297 nm (342 mile; 550 km) circular orbit of the Earth at an inclination of 80°.

The main body of UK.4 is in the form of a polygonal cylinder with a conical top. Four large booms around the base of the satellite provide mountings for some of the experiment sensors, well away from the main body, to reduce the risk of reflection hazards and interferences, and also to provide a convenient platform for mounting the fourth-stage motor of the Scout rocket. After injection into orbit, the booms are deployed to an angle of 65° relative to the spin axis of the satellite.

UK.4 will carry electron temperature and density experiments from the University of Birmingham, VLF and lightning impulse experiments from the University of Sheffield and Radio and Space Research Station, radio-noise joint experiment from the University of Manchester

(Jodrell Bank) and RSRS, and a particle experiment.

X-3 SATELLITE

In aay 1968, the Electronic and Space Systems Group of BAC Guided Weapons Division was awarded a contract by the British Ministry of Technology for the design, development and manufacture of four X-3 satellite structures and associated handling equipment.

The X-3 is one of a series of technological satellites to be launched by the all-British Black Arrow vehicle from Woomera in 1971. It will be placed in a near-Polar orbit, with a perigee of 300 nm (345 miles; 555 km) and an apogee not exceeding 1,000 nm (1,150 miles; 1,850 km), and will rotate at approx 200 rpm. The satellite will weigh about 160 lb (72·5 kg) and will be approx 28 in (71 cm) high by 45 in (114 cm) in equatorial diameter.

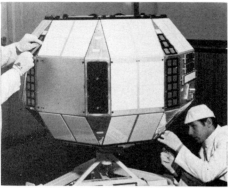

Structural development model (S.1) of X-3 technological satellite

The aims of the satellite are to prove a new PCM telemetry system which will be used in subsequent satellites in the Black Arrow series; to prove new power supply equipment for use in any Black Arrow satellite with an electrical load of less than 30W; to test new thermal control surface finishes and new solar cell assemblies, including ultra lightweight cells and cover materials; and to determine the micrometeoroid flux in the Earth's outer atmosphere.

The satellite consists of eight large and eight small segments attached to a main centre structure which is in the form of a box section. The large segments, or modules, are hinged at their upper ends to provide access to on-board equipments. The small segments, or fillets, form an integral part of the structure, being attached to the main structure at their upper and lower extremities. Four of the modules carry power generating solar cells mounted on their upper, lower and equatorial facets. The other four modules have solar cells mounted on their upper and lower facets only. Two of these modules, diametrically opposed, have the experimental solar cells and associated aspect sensors mounted on their equatorial facets. Four of the eight fillets carry the thermal control surface units on their upper and equatorial facets. These units display the experimental surface finishes.

The spacecraft has four telemetry aerials mounted on its base at 45° to the spin axis.

Major equipment mounted internally includes a telemetry and data handling system, power conditioning system, the Birmingham University micrometeoroid detector, thermal control surfaces electronics and cable form and associated connectors.

BRISTOL AEROJET
BRISTOL AEROJET LTD

HEAD OFFICE AND WORKS:
Banwell, Weston-Super-Mare, Somerset

DIRECTORS:
Dr F. Llewellyn Smith, CBE (Chairman)
W. Strachan, CBE (Managing Director)
C. R. Creighton
R. M. Howarth
G. A. Harrison
W. K. Bachelder (USA)
E. A. Lowe (USA)
J. D. Nichols (USA)
W. L. Gore (USA)
J. M. Beauchamp (USA)

SECRETARY: T. P. Rutter

This company was formed on 1 January 1959, by Aerojet-General Corporation of Azusa, California, and The Bristol Aeroplane Co, Ltd, one of its intentions being to exploit and, where appropriate, manufacture Aerojet-General products in the UK.

Bristol Aerojet specialises in the design, development and production of solid-propellant rocket motor cases, sounding rockets, welded high-pressure gas storage vessels, and equipment for nuclear power reactors and the nuclear energy development industry.

Motor cases manufactured by Bristol Aerojet are used on a wide range of rockets, missiles and drones, including Bloodhound Mk 1 and 2, NATO

Bristol Aerojet Skua meteorological rocket being loaded into its launcher

Bullpup, Rapier, Red Top, Tigercat, Thunderbird, Seacat, Seaslug, AN/USD 501 (CL-89), Jaguar/Jabiru, Petrel, Skua and Skylark. The company also manufactures rockets for NATO, Australia, Canada, France, Germany, Pakistan, Spain and Sweden, as well as the UK; and exclusive processes and equipment are used under licence in Italy by Breda Meccanica Bresciana.

An advanced 18% nickel maraging steel motor case is currently being developed and manufactured for the third (apogee) stage of the UK Black Arrow satellite launch vehicle.

The company is also engaged in the design, development and manufacture of ancillary components for solid-propellant and liquid-propellant rocket motors, and high-pressure gas storage vessels for guided weapons, space vehicles and military and civil aircraft.

Bristol Aerojet has developed two upper atmosphere sounding rockets, named the Skua and Petrel, of which details follow.

BRISTOL AEROJET SKUA

The standard Skua meteorological sounding and upper atmosphere research rocket will lift a payload of 12 lb/500 cu in (5·5 kg/8·2 litres) to a height of 328,000 ft (100 km). Another version, with a shorter motor, can be used for meteorological firings with a wind-finding parachute and temperature-measuring sensor, and lifts the same weight of payload to 256,000 ft (78 km).

Skua rockets use a helically-welded steel motor, with a case-bonded "cigarette-burning" charge which was developed by the Rocket Propulsion Establishment. This gives a long burning time and, thus, maximum thrust at high altitudes. The rocket is fin-stabilised in flight and no guidance system is installed.

An ejection mechanism can be fitted in the rocket to expel the payload instruments at any predetermined time during the flight, and a radar-reflective parachute can be ejected to lower the instruments slowly, and provide a radar target determination of wind speed and height. A small 24-channel telemetry sender, working in the 432·5 to 450 mc/s band, can be fitted into the rocket nose-cone section and can be ejected with the payload instruments. A mobile telemetry receiving station, operating in the 432·5 to 450 mc/s band, is also available.

Skua rockets have been in use by the British Meteorological Office since 1964. Space research groups from British Universities fired Skuas in 1967. Orders have also been received from Australia, Canada, France, Germany, Pakistan, Spain and Sweden.

The launcher consists of a tube 33 ft (10 m) long and 21 in (53 cm) in diameter, which can be carried on a vehicle for mobility or fitted on a

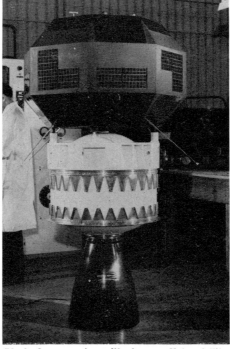

Black Arrow motor with dummy X-3 satellite (described above)

simple static mounting. A boost structure, carrying the small boost motor, runs up inside the launch tube and helps to give the Skua a high launch velocity, with consequent small dispersion.

DIMENSIONS:
Length overall with motor	7 ft 11 in (2·41 m)
Body diameter	5 in (12·7 cm)

WEIGHTS:
Launching weight, including payload	87 lb (39·5 kg)
Weight at burn-out	35 lb (16·0 kg)

PERFORMANCE:
Launch velocity	300 ft (91 m) /sec
Initial acceleration	50 g for 0·2 sec
Burn-our altitude	56,000 ft (17,000 m)
Peak altitude with 11 lb (5 kg) payload	345,000 ft (105,000 m)

Bristol Aerojet Skua (*left*) **and Petrel upper atmosphere sounding rockets**

BRISTOL AEROJET PETREL

This upper atmosphere sounding rocket is larger than Skua, but it is fired from the same launch-tube and uses a similar booster system, with recoverable boost carriage. Its Lapwing motor has been developed by the Rocket Propulsion Establishment. A small telemetry sender, operating in the 432·5 to 450 mc/s band, provides 24 high-speed and 22 low-speed channels.

DIMENSIONS:
Length overall, with motor	9 ft 5 in (2·87 m)
Body diameter	7·5 in (19 cm)
Span of fins	1 ft 8½ in (0·52 m)

WEIGHT:
Launching weight	253 lb (115 kg)

PERFORMANCE:
Mean peak altitude with 30 lb (13·6 kg) payload	514,000 ft (156,600 m)
Launch velocity	360 ft (110 m)/sec

HSD

HAWKER SIDDELEY DYNAMICS LTD

HEADQUARTERS:
Manor Road, Hatfield, Herts
OFFICERS: See "Missiles" section

Hawker Siddeley Dynamics is engaged on many important space research programmes, including manufacture of the ELDO Europa I space launch vehicle and, as a member of the MESH consortium, the TD 1 scientific satellite. Details of these two programmes can be found in the International section.

Other work includes development of the ESRO IV satellite, in association with many international companies. HSD also undertakes sub-contract work on US satellites, such as the manufacture of structures for the Intelsat 3.

Under the terms of an agreement announced in February 1965, HSD and TRW Inc of Los Angeles, USA, are exchanging technical information on satellites and other spacecraft.

HSD's infra-red Linescan System Type 201 is fitted in the Canadair AN/USD 501 battlefield surveillance drone. Similar systems are available for manned reconnaissance aircraft.

HSD BLUE STREAK
(ELDO first stage)

Work on the Blue Streak missile project was started in 1955. Then, the British requirement was for an intermediate-range ballistic missile. Nearly all its flight was to be ballistic, the velocity and direction of the missile being controlled by an autopilot and inertial guidance system during the first three minutes after launch.

To accelerate development, the former de Havilland company, the prime contractor and co-ordinating design authority for the work, entered an agreement for the exchange of information with what is now General Dynamics/Convair of San Diego, USA. A similar agreement was concluded between Rolls-Royce and the Rocketdyne Division of North American Aviation for the rocket engines. Blue Streak was therefore able to take advantage of the experience gained in the design of the Atlas ICBM and space booster.

In April 1960, the Blue Streak missile project was cancelled. The basic missile requirements

were, however, compatible with those of a first-stage satellite launcher and plans were initiated to adapt the missile for a space rôle.

The Anglo-French proposals for a European space launcher, which were issued at the Strasbourg Conference in February, 1961, initiated use of Blue Streak with a French-manufactured second stage and a third stage of German design and manufacture.

This vehicle evolved as the Europa I launcher (see "ELDO" in International section). After launch, for the first 20 seconds of its flight it rises vertically to a height of about 2,000 ft (600 m), and then turns over slowly until the desired trajectory angle, about 30° to the horizontal, is reached. The vehicle's speed at this stage is 2,170 knots (2,500 mph; 4,000 km/h) and its height nearly 16 nm (18 miles; 29 km). Blue Streak then accelerates in a straight climb path until its speed reaches 7,380 knots (8,500 mph; 13,700 km/h) and all its propellants are burned. The time from launch to first-stage burn-out is about 160 seconds, by which time the vehicle is at a height of 43·5 nm (50 miles; 80 km) and 70 nm (80 miles; 130 km) down-range.

After jettison of the Blue Streak booster, the French second stage is designed to increase the speed to 12,600 knots (14,500 mph; 23,335 km/h) and to jettison after burn-out 217 nm (250 miles; 400 km) down-range, at a height of 90 nm (105 miles; 170 km). The third stage then takes over to put the satellite into orbit at 14,750 knots (17,000 mph; 27,360 km/h) for a low circular orbit and 20,850 knots (24,000 mph; 38,625 km/h) for high eccentric elliptic orbits.

With the optimum configuration discussed at Strasbourg, based on Blue Streak uprated to 300,000 lb (136,000 kg) st, the French second stage and a German third stage, a satellite of 2,300 lb (1,040 kg) could be put into a 295 nm (340 mile; 550 km) circular polar orbit or a satellite of 440 lb (200 kg) in a synchronous 19,450 nm (22,400 mile; 36,050 km) orbit.

An improvement in these payload weights could be obtained by using liquid hydrogen/liquid oxygen propulsion in the third stage.

The ELDO development programme for Europa I involves launching twelve development vehicles. By the end of 1969, nine of these had been

launched, the first on 5 June 1964. The first three were solo Blue Streaks. These were followed by two complete Europa vehicles with inert upper stages, the next two with live second stages and the last two with all stages live. One more firing was scheduled at Woomera in mid-1970. The launch site will then be transferred to the operational site in French Guiana, where the last two (PAS) vehicles in the development programme will be launched. These are scheduled for April 1971 and September 1971. The first two fully operational vehicles, F.13 and F.14, will launch the Franco/German Symphonie satellite in June and October 1972.

An illustration of Europa F8 appears under the CECLES/ELDO entry on page 652.

TYPE: Liquid-propellant rocket booster.

WINGS AND TAIL SURFACES: None.

BODY: Cylindrical stainless steel structure. Tank bay structure internally pressurised. Liquid oxygen tank pressurisation 26·5 lb/sq in (1·86 kg/cm²) full, 4·3 lb/sq in (0·30 kg/cm²) empty. Kerosene tank pressurisation 10·25 lb/sq in (0·72 kg/cm²) full, 1·5 lb/sq in (0·105 kg/cm²) empty.

POWER PLANT: Two Rolls-Royce RZ.2 liquid-propellant rocket engines, with max combined thrust of 300,000 lb (136,000 kg).

CONTROL: Hawker Siddeley autopilot controlling gimballing of the engine nozzles.

DIMENSIONS:
Length of Blue Streak	61 ft 6 in (18·75 m)
Overall length of three-stage vehicle	103 ft 0 in (31·4 m)
Body diameter of Blue Streak	10 ft 0 in (3·05 m)

WEIGHTS (Blue Streak booster):
Launching weight	196,200-198,500 lb (89,000-90,040 kg)
Weight at burn-out	13,800 lb (6,260 kg)

ESRO IV

Following its development and manufacture of the successful Iris I (ESRO II) satellite (see 1968-69 *Jane's*), HSD was named as prime contractor for a new satellite, named ESRO IV, for the European Space Research Organisation. This satellite will carry five of the experiments which were originally to be orbited by the TD 2 satellite, deleted from the ESRO programme in 1968.

ESRO IV is scheduled to be launched in September 1972 and will provide scientific information on the neutral particle composition of the upper atmosphere, positive ions, energy and pitch angle distribution of auroral particles, and energy spectrum of 1-100 MeV protons and omni-directional electron and proton fluxes, and will monitor medium-energy solar particles.

Basically, ESRO IV will have a drum-shaped body, covered externally with solar cells and with three folding booms extending from its base in orbit. HSD is responsible for project management, structure, booms and deployment systems, wiring harness, attitude control system, assembly, integration and test, and launch and post-launch

support. Sub-contractors include INTA (Spain) for the spin rate monitor and electronic unit, and battery charge/discharge unit; Terma Electronisic Industria A/S (Denmark) for housekeeping units; Fokker (Netherlands) for solar cell substrates and ground handling equipment; FIAR (Italy) for power system units; Matra (France) for nutation damper units; and Adcole Corporation (USA) for sun sensors and electronics.

Experiment S 45, positive ion probe, will be supplied by Mullard Space Science Laboratory (UK); S 80, quadrapole mass spectrometer, by University of Bonn (Germany); S 94, auroral particle monitor, by Kiruna Geophysical Observatory (Sweden); S 99, solar particle monitor, by Laboratorium voor Ruimte-Onderzoek (Netherlands); and S 103/104, solar particle monitor, by Institut für Extraterrestrische Physik (Germany).

Model of ESRO IV scientific satellite

RAE
ROYAL AIRCRAFT ESTABLISHMENT
ADDRESS:
Farnborough, Hants
DIRECTOR:
Sir Morien Morgan, CB
HEAD OF SPACE DEPARTMENT:
J. E. Twinn, MA, MIEE
HEAD OF WEAPONS DEPARTMENT:
E. G. C. Burt, BSc, MIEE
HEAD OF AERODYNAMICS DEPARTMENT:
Dr D. Küchemann, FRS

The RAE acts as a research, design and development centre in the service of the aerospace industry as a whole. Aerodynamics Department conducts research into all aerodynamic aspects

of low-speed and high-speed flight. Weapons Department covers research on, and assistance in, the development of a wide range of modern weapon systems, including airborne weapons, guided and unguided, and defensive missiles operated from ground and ships. Space Department is concerned with many aspects of space science and technology.

Two major projects described in this issue of *Jane's* are the Black Arrow satellite launch vehicle and the Skylark upper atmosphere research vehicle. Black Arrow is manufactured by Westland Aircraft Ltd, the Gamma 8 first-stage and Gamma 2 second-stage liquid-fuelled engines being supplied by Rolls-Royce Ltd. Bristol Aerojet supply the motor case and nozzle for the Waxwing third-stage solid apogee motor,

developed at the Rocket Propulsion Establishment, Westcott. BAC produce the Skylark rocket, and conduct trials at the Weapons Research Establishment, Woomera Range, Australia.

WESTLAND
WESTLAND AIRCRAFT, LTD
HEAD OFFICE AND WORKS:
Yeovil, Somerset

As a follow-on to its highly successful Black Knight research rocket (see 1965-66 *Jane's*), Westland is now prime contractor for development and manufacture of the Black Arrow satellite launch vehicle.

BLACK ARROW

On 9 September 1964 Mr Julian Amery, then Minister of Aviation, announced a proposal to develop from the successful Black Knight research rocket a small three-stage satellite launch vehicle which was subsequently given the name Black Arrow. An order covering the construction and supply of three such launchers was finally received by Westland Aircraft, Space Department, from the Ministry of Technology, two and a half years later, in March 1967.

Primary purpose of Black Arrow will be to develop and test in space new satellite components which will contribute to communications satellite programmes; it will also be used as a tool for advanced space research of all kinds. Black Arrow may also be suitable as a launch vehicle for some of the future ESRO series of satellites.

It has the potential of putting a 250 lb (113 kg) payload into polar orbit when launched from Woomera, Australia, or about 350 lb (158 kg) if launched easterly from an equatorial site.

A prototype vehicle was completed in time for display at the 1967 Paris Air Show. It consisted of the first two stages of the first vehicle, with a dummy third stage, and was used to determine the resonance characteristics of the complete Black Arrow.

Black Arrow is manufactured at the Osborne, Isle of Wight, works of British Hovercraft Corporation, a Westland subsidiary. Static firing tests are carried out at BHC's Highdown, Isle of Wight, facility, after which each rocket is disassembled and shipped to Australia.

Final assembly and launching of Black Arrow are carried out at Woomera. The first launch, on 28 June 1969, was unsuccessful as the vehicle veered off course and had to be destroyed 65 seconds after lift-off. It was intended to provide data on the performance of the first and second stages, with separation of a dummy third stage. The R1 second launch, on 4 March 1970,

carrying a dummy payload, was completely successful. Separation of the first stage and nose fairings, and spin-up of the payload were accomplished at the predicted times. The second stage and payload impacted some 1,650 nm (1,900 miles; 3,050 km) NW of Woomera, about 15 minutes after launch.

This test proved the structure of all three stages and demonstrated satisfactory performance of the rocket engines in the first and second stages. The performance of all the third-stage systems was also tested, except for the propulsion system.

The third launch, scheduled for later in 1970, is intended to put a test satellite into near-polar orbit.

The first two stages of Black Arrow are directly evolved from Black Knight and use liquid propellants. The third stage has a high-performance solid-propellant motor and is spin stabilised.

The engine of the first stage (Rolls-Royce Bristol Gamma 8) is built up of a cluster of eight thrust chambers derived from successful Black Knight designs. These are fed from a pair of turbo-pumps and can be swivelled in four pairs for control in pitch, yaw and roll. The overall diameter of the tank structure of the first stage is 6 ft 6¾ in (2·0 m). Propellants for both this stage and the second stage are 85% HTP and kerosene. Total thrust of the first stage is 50,000 lb (22,680 kg) at S/L, with a specific impulse of 217·4 lb sec/lb.

The second stage is 4 ft 6 in (1·37 m) in diameter and employs an engine with two thrust chambers (Rolls-Royce Bristol Gamma 2) similar to those in the first stage but with extended nozzles to increase the expansion ratio from 80 : 1 to 350 : 1. These are fully gimballed for flight control. Total thrust of the second stage is 15.300 lb (6,940 kg) in vacuum, with a specific impulse of 265 lb sec/lb.

The payload and third-stage motor are mounted within fairings to protect them from aerodynamic forces and kinetic heating during ascent. These fairings are jettisoned early in the second-stage thrust period, when the rocket leaves the Earth's atmosphere.

The Waxwing solid-propellant third stage represents a continued development of the motor that was used as the second stage of the Black Knight research vehicle and has been developed jointly by the Rocket Propulsion Establishment and Bristol Aerojet.

A fixed-programme form of guidance is used, with a gyro reference system keeping the vehicle

Launch of Black Arrow R1, Woomera, 4 March 1970

to that programme. By the end of the second-stage thrust period the rocket is on the correct flight path to coast up to the desired point in space for orbital injection, which can then be achieved by firing the third stage.

Payloads for Black Arrow include the X-3 satellite (see page 658).
DIMENSIONS:
Overall height   42 ft 9 in (13·03 m)
Body diameter, first stage   6 ft 6¾ in (2·0 m)

THE UNITED STATES OF AMERICA

AEROJET-GENERAL
AEROJET-GENERAL CORPORATION (Subsidiary of the General Tire and Rubber Co)
SPACE DIVISION
ADDRESS:
9200 E Flair Drive, El Monte, California

The Space Division of the Aerojet-General Corporation is responsible for quantity production of the Aerobee series of upper atmosphere research rockets. These are boosted single-stage vehicles capable of carrying scientific payloads to

heights of between 65 and 305 nm (75-350 miles; 120-560 km). They are used by all the US services and by civilian and government organisations in connection with missile and satellite programmes.

Aerobee vehicles are available with a number of accessory sub-systems. A fully flight-tested attitude control system, which utilises residual pressurisation gas, can be used for vehicle de-spin, orientation and up to ten manoeuvres after sustainer burn-out. A yo-yo de-spin system is also available and provides a simple and effective

means for reducing spin rate. Fully-proven payload recovery systems are available.

Also in production, to supplement some versions of Aerobee, is a family of space-probe vehicles known as Astrobees, with the ability to carry scientific payloads to heights of from 173 to 1,563 nm (200-1,800 miles; 322-2,896 km).

Currently under development is a further family of research vehicles, known as Aerobee D, E and F, utilising a newly-developed high-energy long-burning solid propellant.

Aerobees and Astrobees can be launched from

the fixed towers at White Sands (New Mexico), Wallops Island (Virginia), Fort Churchill (Canada) and Natal (Brazil) or from a portable Nike-Ajax rail launcher, as illustrated.

AEROBEE 150 (AEROBEE-HI)

TYPE: Boosted single-stage high-altitude research rocket.

WINGS: None.

BODY: Cylindrical structure. Aluminium nose section containing payload. Optional magnesium extension sections. Propellent tankage section of heat-treated 410 steel. Magnesium tail section.

TAIL SURFACES: Three fins equi-spaced around rear of body.

Aerobee 150 on rail launcher

POWER PLANT: One liquid-propellant gas-pressurised sustainer giving 4,100 lb (1,860 kg) st for 51·8 sec and running on IRFNA and aniline-furfuryl alcohol propellants. One Aerojet type VAM solid-propellant booster (17,400 lb = 7,893 kg, or 20,200 lb = 9,163 kg st) in tandem.

PAYLOAD: 120-400 lb (54-181 kg) in 15 in (38 cm) diameter, 87 in (221 cm) ogive, plus 60 in (152 cm) maximum cylindrical extension.

DIMENSIONS:
Length   30 ft 11 in (9·41 m)
Body diameter   1 ft 3 in (0·38 m)

WEIGHT:
Firing weight, with booster, less payload
     1,908 lb (865 kg)

PERFORMANCE:
Ceiling with 125 lb (56·7 kg) payload
     161·5 nm (186 miles; 300 km)
Max acceleration   11·1 *g*

AEROBEE 150A

Modifications in this version of the Aerobee 150 include transposition of the propellant tanks and the use of four fins instead of three to make the rocket compatible with the Wallops Island launching facility.

AEROBEE 170

This higher-performance version of the Aerobee 150A made a completely successful first flight on 26 October 1968. It carried a 263 lb (119 kg) stellar spectra experiment payload to a height of 139 nm (160 miles; 257 km), and was fitted with yo-yo de-spin, attitude control and recovery systems.

TYPE: Single-stage boosted sounding rocket.

WINGS: None.

BODY AND TAIL SURFACES: Same as for Aerobee 150A.

POWER PLANT: Liquid-propellant gas-pressurised sustainer. Booster is a Nike solid-propellant motor of 48,700 lb (22,090 kg) st.

GUIDANCE: None.

CONTROL: Same as for Aerobee 150.

PAYLOAD COMPARTMENT: Either a 5/1 ogive or 3/1 cone may be used, with up to 60 in (1·52 m) of cylindrical section.

DIMENSIONS:
Length of sustainer   28 ft 3 in (8·61 m)
Length with booster   41 ft 0 in (12·47 m)
Body diameter   1 ft 3 in (0·38 m)
Span of fins   4 ft 0 in (1·22 m)

WEIGHTS:
Firing weight, with booster   3,010 lb (1,370 kg)
Weight, less booster   2,411 lb (1,140 kg)
Weight at burn-out   553 lb (250 kg)

PERFORMANCE (with 250 lb = 113 kg payload):
Speed at burn-out   6,489 ft (1,975 m) sec
Peak altitude   144 nm (166 miles; 267 km)
Max range   185·5 nm (214 miles; 344 km)

AEROBEE 300 (SPAEROBEE)

This member of the Aerobee family of sounding rockets was developed under parallel contracts with the USAF's Cambridge Research Laboratories (AFCRL) and the US Naval Research Laboratory (NRL) during the period of June to October 1958. Five launchings were accomplished at Fort Churchill, Manitoba, Canada, as part of the US International Geophysical Year upper atmosphere research programme, in October, November and December 1958. On 25 October 1958 rocket S/N IGY AA 10·02 carried a 70 lb (31·7 kg) payload package to a slant range altitude of 234 nm (270 miles; 434 km), establishing a new record for Aerobee rockets.

A developed version, for NASA, is the Aerobee 300A which differs in having four fins and was fired for the first time in mid-1960. The following details refer to the Model 300.

TYPE: Two-stage boosted high-altitude research rocket.

WINGS: None.

BODY: Cylindrical structure. First-stage rocket and booster are basic Aerobee 150 power plants. Second-stage solid-propellant motor, in high-strength alloy steel case, and magnesium payload assembly are installed on Aerobee 150 rocket with magnesium extension, in the same manner as a normal Aerobee 150 payload. Flared magnesium transition section with a 14° half-cone angle connects the second-stage motor to the Aerobee 150 first-stage rocket, and also provides aerodynamic stabilisation during the second-stage powered phase of the trajectory.

TAIL SURFACES: First stage and booster assembly has three fins equi-spaced around rear of body.

POWER PLANT: One Aerobee 150 gas-pressurised sustainer as first stage. One modified Aerojet Model 1.8KS-7800 solid-propellant rocket as second stage. One Aerojet VAM solid-propellant booster (17,400 lb = 7,893 kg, or 20,200 lb = 9,163 kg st).

PAYLOAD: Payload assembly, fabricated of aluminium, consists of a 10° half-angle nose-cone extending back to a cylinder, and was designed to provide 1 cu ft (0·028 m³) of usable volume for a nominal 50 lb (22·7 kg) payload. Net payload capabilities are 25-120 lb (11·3-59·5 kg).

DIMENSIONS:
Overall length, with booster 34 ft 7 in (10·54 m)
Length of second-stage assembly
     10 ft 0 in (3·05 m)
Body diameter, sustainer and booster
     1 ft 3 in (0·38 m)
Body diameter, second-stage assembly
     8 in (0·2 m)

WEIGHTS:
Gross weight, with booster, less payload
     2,070 lb (939 kg)

PERFORMANCE:
Ceiling with 50 lb (22·7 kg) payload
     245 nm (282 miles; 454 km)
Max acceleration   63·8 *g*

AEROBEE 300S

This version of the Spaerobee utilizes the Aerobee 170 as the first stage to obtain a significant performance improvement. Details are the same as for the Aerobee 300 (above) except for the following:

TAIL SURFACES: First-stage and booster assembly has four fins equi-spaced around rear of body.

POWER PLANT: One Aerobee 150A gas-pressurised sustainer as first stage. Booster is a Nike solid-propellant motor of 48,700 lb (22,090 kg) st. Second stage is a modified Aerojet Model 1.8KS-7400 solid-propellant rocket. An improved rocket, Model 3KS-7300, may be used as a second stage for a further performance increase.

PERFORMANCE:
Ceiling with 50 lb (22·7 kg) payload:
     1.8KS-7400 motor
         295 nm (340 miles; 547 km)
     3KS-7300 motor 349 nm (402 miles; 647 km)

AEROBEE 350

This new sounding rocket is qualified for scientific use.

TYPE: Single-stage boosted sounding rocket.

WINGS: None.

BODY: Glass-fibre nose, stainless steel tanks, magnesium tail structure.

TAIL SURFACES: Aluminium single-wedge surfaces, with blunt trailing-edge, on main body.

POWER PLANT: Sustainer is made up of four Aerojet-General liquid-propellant rocket motors (each 4,100 lb = 1,860 kg st). Booster is a Nike solid-propellant rocket of 48,700 lb (22,090 kg) st.

GUIDANCE: None.

CONTROL: Cold-gas gyro-stabilised attitude control system manufactured by Aerojet-General.

DIMENSIONS:
Length without booster   38 ft 0 in (11·58 m)
Length with booster   50 ft 4 in (15·34 m)
Body diameter   1 ft 10 in (0·56 m)
Span of fins   7 ft 6 in (2·29 m)

WEIGHTS:
Launching weight, with booster
     6,700 lb (3,040 kg)
Weight, less booster   5,320 lb (2,413 kg)
Weight at burn-out   1,000 lb (454 kg)

PERFORMANCE:
Speed at burn-out   Mach 9·0
Max ceiling   260 nm (300 miles; 480 km)
Ceiling with 500 lb (227 kg) payload
     178 nm (205 miles; 330 km)

ASTROBEE 200

Development of the Astrobee series of high-altitude sounding rockets was started in late 1960 to meet a USAF requirement, through its Cambridge Research Center, for a multi-stage solid-propellant rocket capable of carrying a moderate payload (125 lb = 57 kg) to a height of 173 nm (200 miles; 320 km).

Because of their solid-propellant motors, Astrobees are easier to handle than the earlier series of Aerobees. All are unguided fixed-fin rail-launched vehicles of basically similar design, the main difference being their varying performance capabilities. Provision can be made for payload recovery.

Smallest of the series is Astrobee 200, which has a Nike booster (48,200 lb = 21,860 kg st) as its first stage and an Aerojet 30KS-8000A Alcor as its second stage. The Alcor gives an average of 8,640 lb (3,920 kg) st for 30 sec. The second-stage casing and payload do not separate after burn-out.

The payload compartment has a diameter of 15 in (38 cm) and volume of 8·4 cu ft (0·24 m³), accommodating a payload of 125-250 lb (57-113 kg)

DIMENSION:
Length with booster   28 ft 6 in (8·68 m)

WEIGHT:
Firing weight, with booster, less payload
     2,628 lb (1,192 kg)
Weight at final burn-out, less payload
     274 lb (124 kg)

PERFORMANCE:
Ceiling with max payload
     113 nm (130 miles; 210 km)
Ceiling with min payload
     173 nm (200 miles; 320 km)
Max acceleration   19·2 *g*

ASTROBEE 250

The Astrobee 250 is a single-stage solid-propellant vehicle with Aerojet 28KS-57,000 Junior (52,179 lb = 23,665 kg st for 40 sec) as its main motor, boosted by two Thiokol 1·5KS-35,000 Recruits (each 36,000 lb = 16,330 kg st for 1·6 sec), which are mounted on the sides of the main motor.

The payload compartment has a diameter of 24-31 in (61-79 cm) and volume of 40 cu ft (1·13 m³), accommodating a payload of 400-1,500 lb (182-682 kg).

DIMENSION:
Length   34 ft 2 in (10·41 m)

WEIGHTS (less payload):
Firing weight with boosters, 10,100 lb (4,580 kg)
Weight at final burn-out   2,045 lb (928 kg)

PERFORMANCE:
Ceiling with max payload
     111 nm (128 miles; 206 km)
Ceiling with min payload
     176 nm (203 miles; 326 km)
Max acceleration   15 *g*

ASTROBEE 1500

Largest in the current series of Astrobees, the Astrobee 1500 was first fired in August 1961. The basic vehicle comprises an Aerojet 28KS-57,000 Junior (52,179 lb = 23,665 kg st for 40 sec) as the first stage and an Aerojet 23KS-11,000 Alcor 1B (9,200 lb = 4,180 kg st for 28 sec) as the second stage. Two Thiokol 1·5KS-35,000 Recruits (each 36,000 lb = 16,330 kg st for 1·6 sec) are mounted on the sides of the first stage as boosters.

The payload compartment has a diameter of 20 in (51 cm) and volume of 3·67 cu ft (0·104 m³) accommodating a payload of 50-300 lb (22-136 kg).

After first-stage burn-out the second stage is spin-stabilised prior to separation by four MARC 49A1 (·5KS-180) spin motors. The second-stage casing and payload do not separate after burn-out. A yo-yo de-spin unit is available for payloads requiring low spin rates.

The first flight of the redesigned Astrobee 1500, using the current second-stage motor (Alcor 1B) and a lower second-stage spin rate (5 cps), was made successfully early in 1967. Other successful flights have followed.

DIMENSION:
Length with boosters   34 ft 2 in (10·41 m)

Astrobee 1500 on boom launcher

WEIGHTS (less payload):
Firing weight, with boosters 11,541 lb (5,240 kg)
Weight at final burn-out   140 lb (63 kg)
PERFORMANCE (85° launch angle):
Ceiling with 300 lb (136 kg) payload
          699 nm (805 miles; 1,300 km)
Ceiling with 50 lb (22 kg) payload
          1,597 nm (1,840 miles; 2,970 km)
Max acceleration   41·4 g

AEROBEE D, E AND F

Aerobee D, E and F are the first three of a new family of research vehicles currently under development by Aerojet. They utilise a newly-developed high-energy long-burning solid pro-

pellant which allows optimum delivery of impulse while also providing a more moderate acceleration environment for the scientific payload.

DIMENSIONS:
Length overall:
  Aerobee D   8 ft 4 in (2·54 m)
  Aerobee E   13 ft 5 in (4·09 m)
  Aerobee F   22 ft 6 in (6·86 m)
Body diameter:
  Aerobee D   6 in (15 cm)
  Aerobee E   9 in (23 cm)
  Aerobee F   15 in (28 cm)
LAUNCHING WEIGHT:
  Aerobee D   168 lb (76 kg)
  Aerobee E   599 lb (272 kg)
  Aerobee F   2,670 lb (1,210 kg)
PERFORMANCE (estimated):
Ceiling:
  Aerobee D with 10 lb (4·5 kg) payload
          78 nm (90 miles; 145 km)
  Aerobee E with 50 lb (23 kg) payload
          110 nm (127 miles; 204 km)
  Aerobee F with 250 lb (114 kg) payload
          192 nm (221 miles; 356 km)

NIRO

Niro is a two-stage solid-propellant vehicle for small to medium payloads (40–180 lb = 18–82 kg), which it can carry to the "F" region of the ionosphere. It was developed to meet a USAF requirement for a small and economical vehicle which could provide roll control and good structural stability.

The vehicle consists of a standard Nike M5 booster (2·5DS-59,000), yielding an average thrust of 43,000 lb (19,500 kg) for 3·3 seconds, and a Thiokol Iroquois TE-M-388 second stage delivering 5,500 lb (2,500 kg) of thrust for 7·7 seconds.

Standard diameter (7·75 in) and oversize (9 in) payloads have been flown successfully. Usable volume can be varied up to 4 cu ft (0·113 m³). Both land and water recovery systems are available.

DIMENSIONS:
Length overall, without payload
          21 ft 5 in (6·5 m)
Body diameter:
  first stage   16·5 in (42 cm)

Niro two-stage vehicle on launcher

  second stage   7·75 in (20 cm)

WEIGHTS (less payload):
Launching weight   1,591 lb (723 kg)
at first-stage burn-out   796 lb (362 kg)
at second-stage ignition   278 lb (126 kg)
at second-stage burn-out   95 lb (43 kg)
PERFORMANCE (85° launch angle):
Ceiling with 40 lb (18 kg) payload
          154 nm (178 miles; 287 km)
Ceiling with 180 lb (82 kg) payload
          61 nm (70 miles; 113 km)

ARC

ATLANTIC RESEARCH CORPORATION, DIVISION OF THE SUSQUEHANNA CORPORATION

HEAD OFFICE:
Shirley Highway at Edsall Road, Alexandria, Virginia 22314
PRESIDENT: Emmett H. Bradley
MANAGER, MARKETING: E. A. Painter
DIRECTOR, PUBLIC RELATIONS: Robert Wilson

Missile Systems Division
3333 Harbor Boulevard, Costa Mesa, California 92626
VICE-PRESIDENT AND GENERAL MANAGER:
Robert G. Vande Vrede

Propulsion Division
Shirley Highway at Edsall Road, Alexandria, Virginia 22314
GENERAL MANAGER: Roland C. Webster

The Missile Systems and Propulsion Divisions of this company manufacture solid-propellant upper atmosphere research vehicles which are used by all three US services, NASA, and other government agencies. Other products include the solid-propellant booster and sustainer motors for the Redeye surface-to-air missile and the thrust-vector control system used on the Polaris missile. Also produced are small control rockets for spin, de-spin, stage separation, payload ejection, vernier and related functions on missiles and space probes. Some of these have been used in almost every US satellite or space probe launched to date.

Since 1962, ARC has been under contract to the USAF to provide managerial and technical direction for Project Athena, which includes a series of upper atmosphere and re-entry experiments. The programme is utilising a variety of

existing solid-propellant motors, inter-staged by ARC.

ARCAS

Produced by the Propulsion Division of ARC, Arcas is a small single-stage solid-propellant rocket vehicle that is used primarily to gather meteorological data at an altitude of 35 nm (40 miles; 65 km). It is the standard meteorological rocket of the three US military services, NASA and six foreign countries, and has been used for more flights than all other meteorological rockets combined.

The payload carried most frequently is the Arcasonde 1A, which determines the upper-atmosphere temperature and transmits this information on a 1680 MHz telemetry link, using an AN/GMD-1 or -2 radio theodolite ground receiver. The Arcasonde 1A sensor is a 10-mm diameter bead thermistor, which utilizes immersion techniques, together with a unique method of thermally isolating the thermistor from the heat generated by the T/M portion.

The Arcasonde 4 payload adds a MHz ranging signal to the basic Arcasonde 1A, thus eliminating the need for radar.

Wind information is obtained by tracking the displacement of the parachute/sonde assembly during its descent. The 15 ft (4·57 m) diameter silk parachute is metalized to provide a better radar target.

Approximately 12,000 Arcas vehicles had been flown by March 1970 and launchings continue at the rate of about 2,500 a year. The well-known Meteorological Rocket Network and the Exametnet are consortiums of rocket users that coordinate launchings over a grid extending from Fort Greely, Alaska, to Argentina, with Arcas as the primary vehicle.

The single-stage Arcas is also popular as an upper-atmosphere research vehicle. Payloads

have included cameras, chaff, ozonesondes, ice crystals, inflated spheres for density measurements, biological experiments and a variety of meteorological sondes.

When higher performance is required, several different boosters are used regularly with a version of Arcas called HV-Arcas, fitted with a strengthened fin assembly that incorporates an inter-stage adaptor.

The launcher is a 15 ft (4·57 m) closed-breech tube in which the rocket exhaust is entrapped behind a piston to multiply the normal rocket thrust by a factor of ten. This eliminates the need for the separate booster that is used with other meteorological rockets of similar performance. Elimination of rocket blast on the pad also facilitates the routine ship-board launching of Arcas vehicles.

DIMENSIONS:
Length   7 ft 8·3 in (2·34 m)
Diameter of body   4·45 in (11·3 cm)
Payload volume   310 cu in (5,080 cm³)
WEIGHTS:
Launching weight approx   80 lb (36 kg)
Weight, less payload   64 lb (29 kg)
PERFORMANCE:
Max speed at burn-out
          2,162 knots (2,490 mph; 4,000 km/h)
Peak altitude, with 5 lb (2·27 kg) payload
          300,000 ft (91,440 m)
Max acceleration   30g

SUPER ARCAS

Announced in January 1968, Super Arcas was designed specifically for upper atmosphere research missions requiring heavier payloads and higher performance than are available with Arcas. It has a ceiling of more than 300,000 ft (91,440 m) and provides a simple low-cost means of probing the mesosphere and lower ionosphere.

Super Arcas has a MARC 60A single-stage

Super Arcas single-stage research rocket

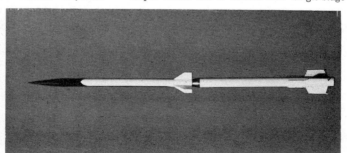

Boosted Arcas II research rocket

solid-propellant rocket motor (370 lb = 168 kg st for 32·6 sec), and can be fired by a two-man crew from the standard Arcas launcher. It can carry payloads of up to 25 lb (11·5 kg) and will accept all of the Arcasonde telemetry packages produced by ARC, as well as specialised instrument payloads. Super Arcas uses the standardised Arcas rocket nose-cone and payload separation equipment, and can be fitted with an optional device for payload separation at other predetermined times after launching. Nominal spin rate at burn-out is 23 rps.

The following specification data are based on a launch angle of 84°, carrying a nominal 12 lb (5·5 kg) payload.

DIMENSION:
Length overall (typical)   8 ft 9·4 in (2·68 m)

WEIGHTS:
Launching weight   95·8 lb (43·5 kg)
Weight at burn-out   40·5 lb (18·4 kg)

PERFORMANCE:
Velocity at burn-out   4,200 ft (1,280 m) sec
Height at burn-out   59,000 ft (18,000 m)
Time to apogee   155 seconds

BOOSTED ARCAS II

Developed by the Propulsion Division of ARC under a company-sponsored programme, Boosted Arcas II is a versatile two-stage vehicle for probing the mesophere and lower ionosphere. Staging is accomplished by a bayonet-type interstage adapter that provides a rigid structure during boost but permits drag-induced stage separation.

Boosted Arcas II is designed for launching from the standard Arcas launcher, with open breech door, or from a 15 ft (4·57 m) long rail. Assembly and launch preparation can be accomplished by a two-man crew.

The first-stage motor is a MARC 42A1 booster, with a nominal rating of 2,740 lb (1,243 kg) st for 3 seconds. Second-stage motor is a MARC 2C1 HV-Arcas, with a nominal rating of 324 lb (147 kg) st for 29 seconds. Payload volume is 305 cu in (5,000 cc).

DIMENSIONS:
Length overall   13 ft 3 in (4·04 m)
Length of booster   5 ft 4·4 in (1·64 m)
Body diameter: both stages   4·5 in (11·4 cm)
Fin span: first stage   13·0 in (33·0 cm)

WEIGHTS (less payload):
Launching weight   135·3 lb (61·4 kg)
at first-stage burn-out   100·0 lb (45·4 kg)
at second-stage ignition   67·5 lb (30·6 kg)
at second stage burn-out   24·4 lb (11·1 kg)
Payload   10-30 lb (4·5-13·6 kg)

PERFORMANCE (at 84° launch angle):
Velocity at burn-out   4,825 ft (1,472 m) sec
Peak altitude
430,000 ft (131,000 m) with 12 lb (5·5 kg) payload
Time to apogee   185 sec
Max acceleration   20 g

SPARROW-HV ARCAS

Developed originally for the Pacific Missile Range Density Probe (DENPRO) programme, by the Propulsion Division of ARC, the Sparrow-HV Arcas has proved a versatile and inexpensive vehicle for probing the mesosphere and lower ionosphere. The vehicle's performance capabilities and reliability have been demonstrated by both US Navy and USAF launchings at several ranges.

Staging is accomplished by a bayonet-type inter-stage adapter that provides structural rigidity during boost, but permits drag-induced stage separation. Fin assemblies are pre-set to provide approximate spin rates of 8 or 15 rps at second-stage burn-out.

Sparrow-HV Arcas two-stage research rocket

Hydra-Iris research rocket, launched from floating, immersed sea platform

The launch system is a 15-ft (4·57 m) long rail assembly designed for mounting on an adjustable-boom launcher of the type available at most launch sites. Assembly and launch preparation require no special handling equipment and can be accomplished by a two-man crew.

First-stage motor is a MK 6 Mod 3 Sparrow C-8. Second-stage motor is a MARC 2C1 HV Arcas with a nominal rating of 324 lb (147 kg) st for 29 seconds.

Power for ignition of both stages is provided by a ground source, a motion switch completing the second-stage firing circuit only after positive booster ignition. A delay squib in the second-stage igniter allows 6 seconds of coasting flight between booster burn-out and second-stage ignition.

DIMENSIONS:
Length overall   12 ft 7·1 in (3·84 m)
Length of booster   4 ft 3·8 in (1·32 m)
Body diameter:
first stage   8 in (20·3 cm)
second stage   4·5 in (11·4 cm)
Fin span, first stage   2 ft 8 in (0·81 m)

WEIGHTS:
Launching weight   206·0 lb (93·5 kg)
at second-stage ignition   67·5 lb (30·6 kg)
at second-stage burn-out   24·4 lb (11·1 kg)

PERFORMANCE (at 84° launch angle):
Peak altitude
570,000 ft (175,000 m) with 12 lb (5·5 kg) payload

SIDEWINDER-HV ARCAS

Developed originally by the Naval Missile Center under the sponsorship of Air Force Cambridge Research Laboratories, the Sidewinder-Arcas vehicle is now in standard use by the USAF, the US Navy, NASA and ESRO for experimentation in the 45/75 mile (75/120 km) altitude range. The Atlantic Research version of this vehicle incorporates modified fins and interstaging to provide increased payload flexibility and improved altitude performance.

Staging is accomplished by a bayonet-type inter-stage adapter that provides structural rigidity during boost, but permits drag-induced stage separation. Fin assemblies are pre-set to provide approximate spin rates of 7 or 15 rps at second-stage burn-out.

The launch system is a 15-ft (4·57 m) long rail assembly designed for mounting on an adjustable-boom launcher of the type available at most launch sites. Assembly and launch preparation require no special handling equipment and can be accomplished by a two-man crew.

First-stage motor is a MK 17 Sidewinder 1A. Second-stage motor is a MARC 2C1 HV Arcas, with a nominal rating of 324 lb (147 kg) st for 29 seconds.

Power for ignition of both stages is provided by a ground source, a motion switch completing the second-stage firing circuit only after positive booster ignition. A delay squib in the second-stage igniter allows 2 seconds of coasting flight between booster burn-out and second-stage ignition.

DIMENSIONS:
Length overall   14 ft 2·5 in (4·33 m)
Length of booster   6 ft 3 in (1·91 m)
Body diameter:
first stage   5·0 in (12·7 cm)
second stage   4·5 in (11·4 cm)

WEIGHTS:
Launching weight   166·3 lb (75·5 kg)
at first-stage burn-out   122·5 lb (55·6 kg)
at second-stage ignition   67·5 lb (30·6 kg)
at second-stage burn-out   24·4 lb (11·1 kg)

PERFORMANCE (at 84° launch angle):
Peak altitude
380,000 ft (116,000 m) with 12 lb (5·5 kg) payload

IRIS

Iris is a solid-propellant single-stage research vehicle capable of carrying 150 lb (68 kg) to 130 nm (150 miles; 241 km) altitude, with very low acceleration forces imposed on the payload.

Its original development by the Propulsion Division of ARC was sponsored by the US Naval Research Laboratory, but sponsorship was transferred during the programme to the Goddard Space Flight Center of NASA. This original programme culminated in May 1962 in four full-scale flights from the 150-ft (45 m)

Aerobee launch tower at the Wallops Island Station of NASA. The configuration included four fins, with a MARC 14B1 seven-rocket cluster for launch boost.

Concurrently, the USAF Cambridge Research Laboratories revised the number of fins to three and procured a number of rockets, while the US Naval Missile Center selected the three-fin Iris for use with their Hydra-launch technique, wherein launch takes place from a floating immersed sea platform. The booster was re-designed into a cluster of three Sparrow military rocket motors.

The Naval Missile Center first flew two test and evaluation Iris vehicles, and has since flown seven more with scientific payloads.

The Hydra technique allows launch from any ocean area free of traffic and accessible by ship. A typical launch sequence involves first the onboard launcher loading and payload checkout, then lowering the vehicle/launcher into the sea, moving the ship to a safe distance and, finally, initiation by radio of the actual launch sequence.

DIMENSIONS:
Length, without booster   19 ft 10 in (6·04 m)
Diameter of body   12·13 in (30·8 cm)
Payload volume   7,860 cu in (0·128 m³)

WEIGHTS:
Launching weight, with booster and payload
    1,870 lb (846 kg)
Payload   100-250 lb (45-115 kg)

PERFORMANCE (with 150 lb = 68 kg payload):
Max speed at burn-out 4,530 mph (7,250 kmh)
Peak altitude (85° launch angle)
    130 nm (150 miles; 241 km)
Max acceleration   12·69g

ATHENA

Athena is used to impact experimental re-entry vehicle payloads on the White Sands Missile

Athena re-entry research vehicle

Range under the advanced ballistic re-entry systems (ABRES) programme. Work on the project by the Missile Systems Division of ARC began in 1962, under a USAF contract. Technical acceptance was received in December 1963 and the first launch was made on 10 February 1964. Sixteen launchings were made in 1968, and 11 in 1969, with further launches planned in the period to the end of 1972.

Depending on the requirement, Athena can have a three- or four-stage configuration, with payload capacity ranging from 50 lb to 250 lb (23-113 kg). It utilises standard solid-propellant rocket motors, including the Thiokol Castor, Thiokol Recruit, Hercules X-259, Thiokol 261 and 23KS11,000. Cruciform fins, indexed in line, are fitted to the first and second stages. Size of the payload compartment is 85 in long by 22 in diameter (216 cm × 56 cm).

Initial Athena launcher offset is adjusted as directed by the output of a ground-based meteorological computer loop. The inputs to this loop are vehicle dynamic characteristics and measured wind profiles to 200,000 ft (61,000 m). The vehicle is spin-stabilized during ascent boost. Ground commands, based upon radar-derived trajectory dispersion data, are generated by a ground-based computer and adjust the pre-set re-entry angle resulting from the control system manoeuvre. The vehicle is re-spun to provide stability during re-entry boost.

Mid-course attitude correction is provided by a Honeywell DHG 138A attitude controller employing two two-degree-of-freedom attitude gyros in a COG orientation.

The velocity package is fired after Athena reaches its apogee of either 850,000 ft (259,000 m) for high-angle re-entry (IRBM) simulation or 600,000 ft (182,900 m) for lower-angle (ICBM) simulation.

DIMENSIONS:
Length overall	51 ft 8 in (15·74 m)
Body diameter, second stage	2 ft 7 in (0·79 m)

WEIGHT:
Max launching weight	16,000 lb (7,260 kg)

PERFORMANCE:
Max speed at re-entry test altitude (nominal)
23,000 ft/sec (7,010 m/sec)
Range (based on current range use)
421 nm (485 miles; 780 km)

ATHENA H

This new and much-enlarged version of the Athena re-entry research vehicle was scheduled to become available for use in 1970. It is large enough to carry a full-scale military re-entry body if required, its max payload being about 1,000 lb (455 kg).

Athena H is available in both two-stage and three-stage configurations, comprising a booster stage and single-stage or two-stage velocity package. After booster burn-out, it will coast to a peak altitude of nearly 1,000,000 ft (305,000 m). During this phase, the velocity package will be re-orientated and re-ignited at the altitude calculated to produce the desired re-entry angle.

The booster can consist of either an Algol IIB or Castor IV solid-propellant motor and four Recruits. The velocity packages can be powered by either a single X259 motor or a 23KS11000 plus a TX261 or X259 motor. A Thiokol M58 is used as the spin motor and the payload is enclosed by clam-shell fairings instead of being accelerated out of its shielding as in the earlier versions of Athena. Payload space is 100 in (254 cm) long in the three-stage model, and 135 in (343 cm) long in the two-stage model, with a diameter of 27 in (68·5 cm).

Thirty Athena H vehicles are expected to be produced under an initial Department of Defense contract.

DIMENSION:
Length overall	60 ft 9 in (18·52 m)

WEIGHT (approx):
Max launching weight	32,000 lb (14,515 kg)

PERFORMANCE (estimated):
Max speed at re-entry test altitude:
100 lb (45 kg) payload 25,000 ft (7,620 m) sec
200 lb (90 kg) payload 23,500 ft (7,160 m) sec

ARGO B-13 NIKE-APACHE

This two-stage rocket, like its predecessor the Nike-Cajun, is used world-wide for scientific research in the ionosphere. As an example of the vehicle's versatility, ARC has successfully adapted it as a ballistic target for tactical surface-to-air missile development. The solid-propellant motors consist of a Nike M-5 first stage and Apache TE307 second stage.

The B-13 Nike-Apache is designed to carry a payload of approximately 60 lb (27 kg), which it will lift to a height of 135 nm (155 miles; 250 km). ARC has available a range of hardware designs to

meet unique requirements. Field and technical support is frequently provided by ARC to assist the experimenter.

ARGO C-22

The Argo C-22 is a three-stage sounding rocket consisting of the first three motors of the four-stage Argo D-4. It is intended primarily to carry net experiment payloads of 150-250 lb (68-113 kg) to altitudes between 109 and 86 nm (125-100 miles; 200-160 km), but can be used for other payload/height combinations.

A wide variety of stage equipment is available to satisfy different performance and experiment requirements.

DIMENSIONS:
Length overall	43 ft 7 in (13·29 m)
Max body diameter	1 ft 10·8 in (0·58 m)
Span of first-stage fins	8 ft 6·9 in (2·61 m)

WEIGHT:
Launching weight	6,950 lb (3,152 kg)

ARGO D-4 JAVELIN

The Argo D-4 is a research vehicle which is able to carry an instrument payload of 50 lb (22·7 kg) to a height of 521 nm (600 miles; 965 km). It is a four-stage vehicle, comprising an Honest John M6, followed by two Nike-Ajax M5 boosters and a final stage designed by the Allegany Ballistic Laboratory and designated X-248. With a payload of 110 lb (50 kg) gross, 62 lb (28 kg) net experiment, a speed of about Mach 13 can be attained.

Argo D-4 is used by NASA, the USAF and other customers.

DIMENSIONS:
Length overall	48 ft 8 in (14·83 m)
Max body diameter	1 ft 10·8 in (0·58 m)
Span of first-stage fins	8 ft 6·9 in (2·61 m)

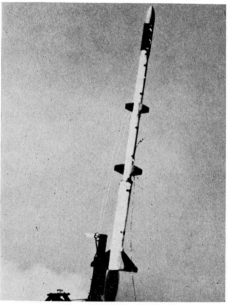

Argo D-4 Javelin four-stage research vehicle

WEIGHT:
Launching weight	7,400 lb (3,355 kg)

SWIK MOD A, B, C & D

The basic SWIK vehicle (MOD A) is a two-stage solid-propellant rocket composed of an XM33-E8 Castor, assisted by two auxiliary XM-19 Recruits, as the first stage and an X-254 Antares second stage.

The SWIK MOD B uses the same first stage, but the X-254 is replaced with the X-259.

The SWIK MOD C & D are also two-stage solid-propellant rockets, each with a TX-354 Castor II, assisted by two auxiliary XM-19 Recruits, as the first stage. An X-254 is used as the second stage of the MOD C, with the X-259 used as the second stage in the MOD D configuration.

All SWIK vehicles follow a ballistic trajectory and can carry net payloads of 100 lb (45 kg) to an altitude in excess of 1,000 nm (1,150 miles; 1,850 km) or 500 lb (225 kg) net payload to an altitude in excess of 700 nm (805 miles; 1,295 km).

DIMENSIONS:
Length overall	35 ft 8 in (10·86 m)
Max body diameter	2 ft 7 in (0·805 m)
Span of first-stage fins	11 ft 8 in (3·57 m)

WEIGHT:
Launching weight	12,824 lb (5,817 kg)

ARGO A-1

The Argo A-1 is a single-stage booster made up of a Sergeant or Castor and two auxiliary Recruit motors. Three were delivered for nose-cone

re-entry tests and all were successful. Seven more were delivered to form the first stage of the two-stage Shotput missile tests.

The A-1 is intended to carry gross payloads of 400-1,200 lb (180-545 kg) to heights between 130 and 95 nm (150-110 miles; 240-180 km).

DIMENSIONS (nominal):
Length overall	31 ft 10 in (9·70 m)
Max body diameter	2 ft 7 in (0·79 m)
Span of first-stage fins	9 ft 10 in (3·00 m)

WEIGHT:
Launching weight	10,400 lb (4,710 kg)

TRAILBLAZER II

Trailblazer II is a four-stage solid-propellant re-entry test vehicle. Two stages are fired upward, two stages downward to achieve a re-entry velocity of 22,000 ft/sec with a 20 lb (9 kg) net payload.

The first stage is a Thiokol Castor TX-33, assisted by two Thiokol Recruit TE-29's, with an LPC Lance second stage, Hercules Altair X-248 third stage and ARC/NASA 15-in spherical fourth stage.

DIMENSIONS:
Length overall	50 ft 0 in (15·24 m)
Max body diameter	2 ft 7 in (0·79 m)
Span of first-stage fins	11 ft 8 in (3·55 m)

WEIGHT:
Launching weight	13,324 lb (6,044 kg)

"MIX OR MATCH"

In addition to its sounding rocket systems, ARC has developed a line of low-cost vehicle hardware components for the user of other systems utilising combinations of standard sounding rockets. Specific component assemblies described below have been flight tested successfully by NASA and the USAF, and this type of "hardware" is sold occasionally to other NATO nations for research purposes.

The Nike adjustable fins and shroud assembly P/N 16151 consists of (1) four diamond cross-section fins, each of 2·5 sq ft (0·23 m²) planform area; (2) mounting structure for fin attachment to motor, including swivel base for continued adjustment; (3) aerodynamic fairing covering the mounting structure; and (4) attachment hardware for installing the assembly. The major features of this assembly are adjustable fins and light weight (75 lb = 34 kg).

The Capache adjustable fins and shroud assembly, P/N 16525, is designed specifically for Cajun Mod I and Apache Mod II rocket motors. It features adjustable-incidence (up to 1°) fins, to provide reliable spin control. Four adjustable flat-plate fins of 1·0 sq ft (0·09 m²) plan area are mounted to a shroud structure which spans the motor/nozzle joint, thereby enhancing the overall load-carrying ability of the vehicle. A fairing is provided for aerodynamic transition from the motor case to the shroud. The fins are fitted with leading-edge "cuffs" for thermal protection. The assembly is provided complete with installation hardware.

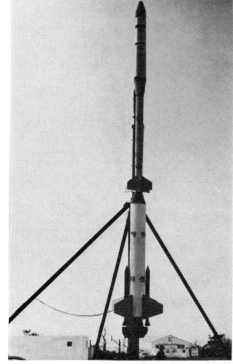

Trailblazer II four-stage re-entry test vehicle

BOEING
THE BOEING COMPANY

HEAD OFFICE AND WORKS:
Seattle, Washington 98124

Aerospace Group
OFFICERS: See "Aircraft" section

Details of the weapon systems developed and produced by Boeing are given in the "Missiles" section. Its current research and space products are described and illustrated below.

BURNER II

Burner II is a low-cost guided solid-propellant upper-stage booster which was developed by Boeing's Spacecraft Branch, at Seattle, under a firm fixed-price contract awarded by the Space Systems Division of the Air Force Systems Command. The initial contract covered one ground test and three flight vehicles. Eleven flight vehicles have subsequently been ordered and delivered.

The general appearance of Burner II is shown in the adjacent illustration. It utilises a Thiokol TE-M-364-2 rocket motor of the kind developed for the Surveyor spacecraft, with 1,440 lb (653 kg) of propellant, a Honeywell guidance system essentially similar to that used on the NASA Scout launch vehicle, and Walter Kidde reaction control system components as used on the Little Joe and Scout boosters and other vehicles. The complete package is suitable for mating to the range of current standard launch vehicles, from Thor to Titan III, and is intended to fill the payload gap between the small Scout and the more complex liquid upper stages. It is able to inject small-to-medium payloads into orbit and then orientate them precisely.

In its first launching, on 15 September 1966, as the upper stage of a Thor vehicle, Burner II put into orbit a secret USAF satellite. By the end of 1969, the Thor/Burner II combination had achieved eight successful launches in eight attempts. The fourth launch placed two scientific satellites, Secor and Aurora, into circular orbits 2,100 nm (2,418 miles; 3,892 km) above the Earth.

Burner II has also been integrated with the Atlas launch vehicle. On the first launch of this combination in 1968, a heat-shield failure precluded mission success.

DIMENSIONS:
Length overall	5 ft 8 in (1·73 m)
Diameter	5 ft 5 in (1·65 m)

BURNER IIA

In August 1969 the USAF's Space and Missile Systems Organisation announced selection of Boeing to develop and manufacture a two-stage version of the Burner II upper-stage booster. The modified upper stage is known as Burner IIA.

A second-stage solid-propellant Thiokol TE-M-442 motor, developing 8,800 lb (3,992 kg) st and with 524 lb (238 kg) of propellant, has been added to the Burner II's 10,000 lb (4,536 kg) st first stage. Burner II sub-systems, including guidance and flight control, reaction control and electrical and communication sub-systems, are mounted on the new stage.

Burner IIA can be utilized with virtually all of the USAF's "family" of space boosters, including Thor, Atlas and Titan III. It can boost larger payloads into Earth orbit than Burner II, or can boost the same sized payload into higher orbits. When teamed with an Atlas booster, Burner IIA will be able to place a satellite in synchronous equatorial orbit. The new stage can also be utilised on missions requiring high-velocity Earth escape speeds.

Boeing's contract called for the manufacture and delivery of six Burner IIA's and one ground test unit, with delivery beginning in June 1970.

S.1C (SATURN V FIRST STAGE)

Boeing manufactures the S.1C first stage of the advanced Saturn V launch vehicle (see page 680) at the Michoud Assembly Facility in New Orleans, Louisiana, under contract to NASA. Its task includes detail design, fabrication, assembly and testing of the S.1C booster, and systems engineering and integration support for the entire Saturn V rocket.

In mid-1967, Boeing was assigned additional responsibilities by NASA for the integration of the Apollo spacecraft and Lunar Module with the three-stage launch vehicle. Boeing also has major ground support tasks for Saturn V launches from Cape Kennedy.

Two S.1C test vehicles and 13 flight stages were ordered initially. Work began on the first Michoud-assembled booster in April 1964 and in April 1965 the first full-thrust one-engine firing of a test vehicle was conducted at Marshall Space Flight Center, Alabama. In August 1965, this test stage completed successfully a 2½-minute full-duration full-thrust firing.

The first Boeing-built flight booster (S.1C-3) was completed in March 1966. It is powered by

Burner II with Secor and Aurora satellites

a cluster of five Rocketdyne F-1 liquid-propellant engines, each generating 1,500,000 lb (680,000 kg) st. Four of the engines are arranged in a square pattern, with gimballed nozzles; the fifth is in the centre, with a fixed nozzle. The structure is of light alloy and includes tankage for 209,000 US gallons (791,124 litres) of RP-1 fuel and 334,500 US gallons (1,266,177 litres) of liquid oxygen. Specification requirement for the S.1C is to lift 1,500,000 lb (680,000 kg) to a height of 35 nm (40 miles; 65 km) at a speed of 5,210 knots (6,000 mph; 9,650 km/h).

DIMENSIONS:
Length overall	138 ft 0 in (42·06 m)
Body diameter	33 ft 0 in (10·06 m)

WEIGHTS:
Launching weight	4,881,000 lb (2,213,985 kg)
Weight less propellants	303,000 lb (137,440 kg)

CHRYSLER
CHRYSLER CORPORATION

HEAD OFFICE:
341, Massachusetts Avenue, Highland Park, Michigan
OFFICERS: See "Missiles" section

Defense-Space Group
DEFENSE OPERATIONS DIVISION:
PO Box 757, Detroit, Michigan 48231
MISSILE DIVISION:
PO Box 2628, Detroit, Michigan 48231
SPACE DIVISION:
PO Box 29200, New Orleans, Louisiana 70129

MANAGER, PLANNING: J. J. Schmidt
MANAGER, PUBLIC RELATIONS: R. B. Heath

Space Division, formed in 1962 to produce the Saturn I first stage, built two S-1 boosters and 12 lighter and more powerful S-1B boosters, and is currently building two more S-1B's. These boosters served as first stages for the two-stage Saturns which successfully orbited satellites and spacecraft ranging from a Pegasus meteoroid technology satellite (S-1 boosted) in May 1965 to the Apollo 7 hardware qualification flight in October 1968. Planned future flights include

experiment payloads in the Apollo Applications Programme. A description of the S-1 can be found in the 1965-66 Jane's.

S-1B (SATURN 1B FIRST STAGE)

The initial type of S-1B booster was 80 ft 2½ in (24·44 m) long and 21 ft 5 in (6·52 m) in diameter, with an empty weight of 93,000 lb (42,200 kg). Later S-1B's have been reduced in weight to about 84,000 lb (38,100 kg). Each is powered by eight up-rated Rocketdyne H-1 engines, giving a total of 1,640,000 lb (743,900 kg) st in current Saturn IB launch vehicles (see page 680).

GENERAL DYNAMICS
GENERAL DYNAMICS CORPORATION

HEAD OFFICE:
1, Rockefeller Plaza, New York, NY 10020
AEROSPACE OPERATING DIVISIONS:
Fort Worth division, Fort Worth, Texas
Pomona division, Pomona, California
Convair division, San Diego, California
OFFICERS: See "Aircraft" section

The Convair division of General Dynamics continues to devote its major efforts to the development and production of Atlas standardised space launch vehicles and the Centaur hydrogen-fuelled spacecraft, but is also engaged on other design work concerned with space travel.

ATLAS

Phase-out of Atlas ICBM's from the US strategic missile force was completed in 1965, and many of the 135 missiles that had been operational at 11 bases, together with five Atlas F sleigh ride missiles, have been and are being converted int launch vehicles.

Thirty-six of them were refurbished and updated under a contract awarded by the US Air Force Space and Missile Systems Organisation (SAMSO) and were used to launch re-entry and upper-stage vehicles for the ABRES (Advanced Ballistic Re-Entry Systems), Nike Target and OAR (Office of Aerospace Research) scientific satellite programmes. The Atlas vehicles allocated to this contract were all of the CGM-16E (Atlas E) and HGM-16F (Atlas F) types (see 1964-65 Jane's for details) and followed 27 CGM-16D (Atlas D) vehicles refurbished earlier for ABRES, Nike Target and OAR missions.

All CGM-16D vehicles have been launched, thereby depleting the Atlas D inventory. Additional Atlas F missiles are now being refurbished under follow-on SAMSO contracts.

Originally, the phased-out Atlas E and F missiles were used to launch nose-mounted re-entry vehicles and side-mounted sub-scale or decoy payloads on sub-orbital missions, and Orbiting Vehicle 1 (OV1) upper stages (manufactured by Convair division of General Dynamics) for orbiting satellites. The versatility of the Atlas E and F launch vehicles has since been increased for sub-orbital missions by the use of a sequential payload delivery system (manufactured by Space and Re-entry Systems Division of Philco-Ford) as an upper stage; and different orbits have been achieved on the same launch by the use of Convair OV1 upper stages (which see). In addition, the Boeing Company's Burner II vehicle is being considered for future orbital missions for the US Air Force.

By mid-October 1969, Atlas had been used as the booster in 140 space missions. It then had a record of 124 successes, including 96 successes in the last 99 missions, and a current record of 47 consecutive successes.

Refurbishment is done at Convair division's Kearny, Mesa plant, San Diego, and includes updating of the telemetry, range safety, electrical, autopilot and engine systems.

Structural and power plant details of the basic retired military missiles are as follows.

BODY: All-metal pressurised structure, largely of thin-gauge stainless steel, forming integral tankage for propellants. Heaviest skin gauge

is less than 0·04 in (0·10 cm) thick. Thinnest section has minimum tensile strength of 200,000 lb/sq in (14,060 kg/cm²). Body is pressurised during ground transport and as propellants are burned in flight, to preserve its shape. Side fairings contain electrical and electronic equipment.

POWER PLANT: One Rocketdyne LR105 liquid-propellant sustainer (57,000 lb = 25,855 kg st) in tail of body, flanked by two Rocketdyne LR89 liquid-propellant boosters (each 165,000 lb = 74,860 kg st). Rocketdyne LR101 vernier motors (each 1,000 lb = 450 kg st) mounted at 90° to boosters, above jettisonable flared "skirt". All five motors fire together for take-off and have the overall designation of MA3 propulsion system. Liquid oxygen and RP-1 propellants in integral tanks. Capacity of upper (Lox) tank 2,503 cu ft (70·88 m³); capacity of lower (RP-1) tank 1,542 cu ft (43·66 m³).

GUIDANCE: Atlas E and F missiles are converted during refurbishment to accept a General Electric Mod 3G guidance system in place of the operational Bosch-Arma inertial system. In-flight guidance commands are furnished from the General Electric Range Tracking Station at Vandenberg AFB, California. This more cost-effective approach has increased the payload-carrying capability of the Atlas on sub-orbital missions by more than 500 lb (227 kg).

DIMENSIONS:
Length overall without payload
	71 ft 3 in (21·72 m)
Body diameter	10 ft 0 in (3·05 m)

WEIGHTS:
Launching weight:

| Atlas E | 270,000 lb (122,470 kg) |
| Atlas F | 269,000 lb (122,000 kg) |

PERFORMANCE:
Ballistic:
Range with 6,000 lb (2,720 kg) payload
5,000 nm (5,750 miles; 9,265 km)
Orbital (Atlas alone):
2,000 lb (907 kg) payload in 100 nm (115 mile;
185 km) Earth polar orbit
Orbital (with upper stages):
Atlas E or F with upper stages such as OV1 or
Burner II can insert varying number of
payloads into various orbits: eg Atlas 107F,
with three OV1s, inserted 27 separate
experiments into four different orbits on
the same launch.

ATLAS SLV-3

The Convair division of General Dynamics
produced for the USAF a total of 56 Atlas
standardised space launch vehicles under the
designation Atlas SLV-3. The contracts covered
design and development of the vehicle, modifications to Atlas space launch pads at the Atlantic
and Pacific missile ranges, and production and
launch of the vehicles.

The SLV-3 consisted of a basic Atlas airframe
and Rocketdyne MA-5 liquid-propellant three-
engine cluster; but the MA-5 engine was up-rated
from 360,000 lb (163,300 kg) st to approximately
390,000 lb (176,900 kg) st equalling the thrust of
the Atlas E and F ICBM's.

Standardized guidance, electrical system, autopilot, tracking, and telemetry kits were provided,
to tailor each space launch vehicle to the mission
and to the launch pad. For example, a General
Electric Model III-G guidance kit was provided
for launches at the Atlantic range, while a GE
Mark II guidance kit was employed for launches
from the Pacific range.

Space launch pads were modified so that
umbilical connections and other points of interface
between the SLV-3 and the launch stand were
identical at both sites.

Formerly, each Atlas booster had to be ear-
marked for a specific mission at least eight months
in advance of delivery date. Its production
then had to be geared to the particular programme and launch pad.

With the SLV-3, the required kits could be
installed on any of the standard launch vehicles
on the production line, as late as 10 weeks prior
to delivery.

The USAF Atlas SLV-3, combined with an
Agena upper stage, was able to put payloads
weighing from 2,000 to 6,800 lb (900-3,085 kg)
into a low Earth orbit. It was launched for the
first time in 1964. From it were developed the
current SLV-3A and SLV-3C launch vehicles
described on this page, and two SLV-3s were
being modified to SLV-3A configuration in early
1970.

ATLAS-AGENA

This general-purpose space vehicle is the Atlas
SLV standardised launcher with an Agena upper
stage produced by Lockheed Aircraft. It is
employed for many programmes, including
military satellite launchings for the USAF, and
scientific launchings for NASA and the USAF.

All Atlas-Agena launchings for the Air Force
take place from a two-launcher complex at Point
Arguello, on the Pacific Missile Range south of
Vandenberg Air Force Base, California. Scientific
missions for NASA are flown from Atlas Complex
12, 13 and 14, Cape Kennedy.

In addition to successful launches of Ranger
lunar probes and Mariner Mars and Venus probes,
Atlas-Agena vehicles have successfully boosted
into orbit the SNAP-10A nuclear reactor satellite,
Vela nuclear detection satellites, OAO and OGO
satellites, and the target vehicles for Gemini
rendezvous flights.

DIMENSIONS:
Overall height:

| Agena B (Ranger) | 104 ft 0 in (31·7 m) |

Length of upper stage:

| Agena B | approx 30 ft 0 in (9·14 m) |

WEIGHT:
Launching weight:

| Atlas-Agena B | 275,000 lb (124,750 kg) |

ATLAS SLV-3A

This uprated version of the SLV-3 is also designed primarily for mating to an Agena upper stage,
with which it can place up to 8,000 lb (3,630 kg)
in low Earth orbit; but it could be used effectively
as a direct ascent vehicle or in conjunction with
other upper stages. Total propellant tank length
is 9 ft 9 in (2·97 m) longer than that of the SLV-3,
increasing usable propellants by about 48,000 lb.
(21,770 kg). Additional helium supply necessitated by the increased tank volume is supplied by
adding two helium storage bottles (total of eight).
Forward tank of the SLV-3A remains tapered,
with a 5 ft (1·52 m) mating ring.

The power plant is uprated, with a sustainer
thrust of 58,000 lb (26,300 kg) and a combined sea
level thrust of 336,000 lb (152,410 kg) from the
boosters.

Atlas-Agena space launch vehicle

The Convair division has developed an advanced
autopilot which can be used on the SLV-3A,
allowing on-the-pad re-targeting. This reduces
re-targeting time to six hours, or to one hour if
new target parameters are known in advance. It
also increases launch availability, because wind
conditions can be offset by varying the programmed pitch profile at the critical altitudes.

Five SLV-3A's were produced under the
initial contract, of which four were to be used in
classified USAF missions. The first of the five
was delivered on 6 October 1967 as the booster
for NASA's Orbiting Geophysical Observatory-E.
Two SLV-3s were being modified to SLV-3A
configuration in early 1970.

ATLAS SLV-3C

The tank of the SLV-3C is 4 ft 3 in (1·30 m)
longer than that of the LV-3C or SLV-3 (OAO),
and is cylindrical instead of in the normal form of
a truncated cone, increasing usable propellant
capacity by approximately 21,000 lb (9,525 kg).
As in the SLV-3A, eight helium storage bottles
supply the increased pressurising medium
necessitated by the increased tank volume.

SLV-3C is intended primarily for use with
Centaur, but is standardised like SLV-3 and
SLV-3A and can be used for other missions by
adding a GE guidance kit and selecting the proper
mission-peculiar kits.

The first of an initial production series of nine
SLV-3C vehicles was delivered to Cape Kennedy
on 30 June 1967 and launched successfully the
Surveyor 5 lunar spacecraft on 8 September 1967.

Under current contract, Convair is producing
six new SLV-3Cs for NASA. These will become
the first stages of Atlas-Centaur launch vehicles
Nos 22 to 27. Planned mission assignments are:

AC-22. Orbiting Astronomical Observatory-C
(OAO-C). The last OAO was launched by AC-16.

AC-23 and **AC-24**. The 1971 Mariner-Mars
orbiters. The 1969 Mars fly-by spacecraft were
launched by AC-19 and AC-20.

AC-25 and **AC-26**. Two Intelsat IV communications satellites.

AC-27. Pioneer F on a Jupiter fly-by mission.

ATLAS SLV-3X

This more powerful Atlas launch vehicle has
been proposed to NASA by the Convair division.
Increased performance is attained primarily by

increasing the tank diameter to 150 in (381 cm)
and using an H-1D rocket engine with a sea-level
thrust of 205,000 lb (92,990 kg) as the sustainer
engine. The larger tank provides an increase in
the propellant load of approximately 120,000 lb
(54,430 kg); the larger sustainer engine in combination with YLR89-NA-7 booster engines
(total of 350,000 lb = 158,750 kg st at sea-level)
yields a total lift-off thrust of 555,000 lb (251,740
kg). The vehicle lengths for the Agena booster
version and the Centaur booster version, as
measured to the upper stage mating station, are
the same as for the SLV-3A and the SLV-3C
respectively.

CENTAUR

Centaur was the first US space vehicle to utilise
liquid hydrogen as a propellant. It is being used
as an upper stage in combination with the Atlas
SLV series of boosters, and is capable of putting

**Atlas-Centaur launch vehicle for Orbiting
Astronomical Observatory**

4½-ton payloads into satellite orbit and of sending
large instrumented probes deep into space.

The original contract for Centaur was awarded
to the former Convair Astronautics and Pratt and
Whitney in November 1958 by the Advanced
Research Projects Agency (ARPA). The prog-
ramme was transferred from ARPA to NASA in
July 1959.

A total of 30 Centaurs had been ordered by
NASA by early 1970, of which 20 had been
launched (see satellite tables in this and previous
editions of *Jane's*). Among the payloads
launched successfully have been the Surveyor
series of lunar spacecraft, the Orbiting Astronomical Observatory, the Mariner-Mars 69
spacecraft and the Applications Technology
Satellite.

Future missions assigned to Centaur include
Orbiting Astronomical Observatories, the Mariner-
Mars 71, the Intelsat IV communications satellit-
es, the Pioneer Jupiter probes, and the Viking
Mars. The Viking Mars will utilise an improved
D-1 version of the Centaur mated to a Titan
vehicle instead of Atlas as a booster.

Centaur is 30 ft (9·14 m) long (70 ft = 21·3 m
with nose fairing attached) and weighs about
37,000 lb (16,780 kg) when fuelled. It is powered
by two Pratt and Whitney RL10A-3 engines,
each of 15,000 lb (6,810 kg) st. Four 50 lb (22·7
kg) st propellant settling, four 3 lb (1·4 kg) st
propellant holding, four 3·5 lb (1·6 kg) st attitude
control and two 6 lb (2·7 kg) st attitude control
motors and rockets are used for velocity trim,
propellant management during coast phase, and

attitude control. Flight events and guidance of both the Atlas and Centaur stages are controlled by a Minneapolis-Honeywell inertial guidance system located on the Centaur upper stage.

The nose section of the Atlas booster used with Centaur is modified to a constant 10 ft (3·05 m) diameter, instead of being tapered as in the Atlas ICBM. Like Atlas, Centaur is fabricated of thin-gauge stainless steel and has no internal braces, being pressurised to maintain cylindrical shape.

DIMENSIONS:

Overall length of Atlas-Centaur
135 ft 0 in (41·15 m)
Length of Atlas first stage 69 ft 5 in (21·16 m)
Diameter of both stages   10 ft 0 in (3·05 m)

ORBITAL VEHICLE ONE (OV1)

The OV1 series of satellites is built for the Air Force Office of Aerospace Research by the Convair division of General Dynamics. Its purpose is to provide versatile and economical space platforms for scientific and technological experiments. The basic configuration of each satellite consists of a cylindrical experiment compartment, 36 in (91·5 cm) long by 27 in (68·5 cm) in diameter, with a faceted solar array attached to each end of the cylinder, making the overall length 54·4 in (138·5 cm). The electronic support systems (command control, telemetry and power conditioning) are mounted under the solar array domes.

Although the satellite may be launched on other vehicles, the primary launch configuration has been an Atlas rocket with one, two or three OV1's mounted in a common fairing on the nose. Each satellite has a secondary propulsion stage,

OV1 satellite leaving Atlas booster 104F in the triple launch on 17 March 1969

with a programmer, autopilot and solid-propellant motor to place it in the desired orbit. Once in orbit the satellite separates from the propulsion unit.

Details of Orbital Vehicles OV1-2 to OV1-19 have been given in previous editions of *Jane's*. They were launched between October 1965 and March 1969.

GENERAL ELECTRIC
GENERAL ELECTRIC COMPANY
MISSILE AND SPACE DIVISION
HEAD OFFICE:

Valley Forge Space Technology Center, PO Box 8555, Philadelphia, Pennsylvania 19101

In addition to developing and producing reentry vehicles for many US missiles and space systems, General Electric's Missile and Space Observatory (OAO). It was also prime contractor for the recoverable Biosatellite spacecraft, of which details were given in the 1969-70 *Jane's*, and continues to be responsible for the gravity gradient test satellite.

NIMBUS

In February 1961, General Electric Company was named contractor for vehicle construction and sub-systems integration for this second-generation weather satellite, including responsibility for the control and stabilisation sub-systems. Other sub-system contractors include RCA Astro-Electronic Products Division for cameras and solar power systems, International Telephone & Telegraph Corporation for infra-red equipment, Radiation Inc for telemetry equipment and California Computer Products Inc for the command system. Prime contractor is NASA's Goddard Space Flight Center.

Initial contracts covered the manufacture of three prototype Nimbus satellites. The first of these was orbited successfully from Point Arguello on 28 August 1964, and returned more than 27,000 excellent photographs during its operational lifetime.

Nimbus 2, launched on 15 May 1966, continued transmitting until 17 January 1969, sending back over 900 horizon-to-horizon pictures of the Earth from the high-resolution IR camera, more than 3,750 horizon-to-horizon shots from the medium-resolution IR camera, and 112,500 close-up photos from the vidicon cameras, transmitted via an automatic picture system, on command, to more than 300 ground stations over an 8,000 hour period.

The next experimental Nimbus satellite (Nimbus-B) had to be destroyed when its launch vehicle veered off course on 18 May 1968. It was replaced by Nimbus 3, launched on 10 April 1969 and described fully in the 1969-70 *Jane's*.

Nimbus 4 was launched on 8 April 1970. Heaviest in the series, with a weight of 1,336 lb (606 kg), it is expected to provide more data than any previous weather satellite. Its primary mission is to continue the experiments conducted by Nimbus 3, by developing and expanding the techniques used to determine the global characteristics of the Earth's atmosphere, with particular emphasis on exploring the vertical profiles of temperature, ozone and water vapour.

The basic Nimbus spacecraft consists of two drum-shape main components, separated by an arrangement of three vee-struts. The larger component (diameter 5 ft = 1·5 m) carries sensors to record cloud cover and other information, and other equipment, and is rimmed with thermal control vanes. The smaller component houses the stabilisation and control system which keeps the larger sensor compartment pointed towards the Earth at all times. Power for the electronics is supplied by solar cells, carried on two large paddles, and storage batteries.

The stabilisation system uses electronic "horizon scanners" and sensors to pick up the Earth's heat radiations. Based on the principle that the Earth is warm and space is cold, the infra-red sensors keep the satellite and its cameras continuously aimed towards the Earth. The system is controlled by a computer which maintains the satellite in its correct attitude, to within one degree in each axis, by means of cold gas jets and inertia wheels.

Spacecraft for Biosatellite primate mission under test

Pitch and roll stability is sensed by the horizon scanners, while a gyroscope effects stability in the yaw axis. The stabilising system also orients the solar paddles.

Nimbus 4 carries three new experiments, three improved versions of earlier Nimbus experiments, and a further three similar to those carried by Nimbus 3.

The new experiments consist of a back-scatter

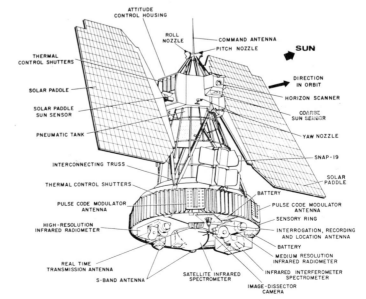

Photograph of Nimbus 4 weather satellite and diagram of Nimbus 3

ultraviolet spectrometer, to monitor the distribution of atmospheric ozone by measuring the intensity of ultraviolet radiation back-scattered in the atmosphere; a filter-wedge spectrometer to measure the vertical distribution of water vapour in the atmosphere; and a selective chopper radiometer designed in the UK and built by Marconi Space and Defence Systems Ltd of Frimley, Surrey, which measures the vertical distribution of temperatures at six levels from cloud-top up to an altitude of 27 nm (31 miles; 50 km).

Nimbus 4 embodies a new attitude control system which provides continuous Earth-pointing to within 1° and permits initial acquisition and re-acquisition of the Earth from any attitude. A gravity gradient attitude control system is fitted as a back-up, consisting of a 45 ft (13·7 m) boom which can be extended on command. The telemetry system allows 512 separate commands to be received, and also enables more data to be transmitted from the satellite.

The advanced Nimbus E and F satellites are scheduled to be launched in 1972 and 1973.

DIMENSIONS:

Height 10 ft 0 in (3·05 m)
Span over solar paddles over 11 ft 0 in (3·35 m)

GRAVITY GRADIENT TEST SATELLITE (GGTS)

This small scientific satellite has been developed by General Electric Company's Missile and Space Division for the USAF. Its purpose is to test

the feasibility of orienting satellites in synchronous or near-synchronous orbits by the gravity gradient method. What this means is that its "double dumb-bell" configuration is intended to take advantage of the principle that space vehicles tend to align themselves with Earth's local vertical along their long axis or minimum moment of inertia.

The 104 lb (47·2 kg) GGTS 1 was launched successfully by a Titan IIIC from Cape Kennedy on 16 June 1966, simultaneously with seven IDCSP communications satellites (see page 676). It entered a near-circular orbit 24,072/24,233 nm (20,905/21,045 miles; 33,643/33,868 km) above the equator. Satellite oscillations were within ±10° about a 15°-from-vertical cross plane bias. Data analysis confirmed that one of the magnetically-anchored viscous dampers was locked due to magnetic debris.

The performance of this satellite demonstrated the feasibility of gravity gradient stabilisation in synchronous orbit. The mission was completed in January 1967, but the spacecraft continued to perform satisfactorily.

A second-generation satellite has been constructed, with a redesigned damper insensitive to magnetic debris, fluid flywheels for rapid damping, and a station-keeping system. The new satellite is expected to damp to ± 3° in 5 days, with ± 4° accuracy during station-keeping propulsion.

Gravity Gradient Test Satellite

GRUMMAN

GRUMMAN AEROSPACE CORPORATION

HEAD OFFICE AND WORKS:
Bethpage, Long Island, New York 11714

OFFICERS: See "Aircraft" section

On 1 July 1969 the former Grumman Aircraft Engineering Corporation changed its name to the Grumman Corporation and established a number of subsidiary corporations. One of the latter, the Grumman Aerospace Corporation, is now charged with the responsibility for production of the Lunar Module (LM) for the Apollo programme and the Orbiting Astronomical Observatory (OAO).

LUNAR MODULE (LM)

On 7 November 1962 it was announced that Grumman had been chosen from nine competing companies to design and produce the Lunar Module (LM) for the Apollo lunar exploration programme. The contract covered manufacture of fifteen flight models and ten test vehicles.

The LM is able to detach from the Apollo

command/service modules in orbit and carry two astronauts down to explore the lunar surface. It is in effect, a two-stage vehicle, each stage being complete with its own liquid-propellant rocket engine. The ascent (upper) stage consists of a pressurised crew compartment, equipment sections and an ascent rocket engine. The descent (lower) stage, to which the landing gear is attached, contains a gimballed, throttleable descent rocket engine and the ALSEP (Apollo Lunar Surface Experiment Package).

The complete LM uses its 9,700 lb (4,400 kg) st descent engine to permit a gentle touchdown on the Moon. After investigating the Moon, the explorers take off in the upper stage, the lower stage serving as a launch platform and remaining on the Moon. They rendezvous again with the command/service modules, jettison the LM and return to Earth.

The LM is a completely self-sufficient spacecraft, equipped with all sub-systems necessary for life support, guidance and navigation, attitude control and communications. The two crew members stand side-by-side, facing two triangular windows that afford forward and downward

vision. They are supported in a harness which provides stability under varying conditions of gravity and helps them to withstand the lunar landing impact. Instrumentation is mounted on a large central panel. Volume of the pressurised cabin is 235 cu ft (6·65 m³).

Sub-contractors include TRW for the lunar descent engine, North American Rockwell, Rocketdyne Division, for the lunar ascent engine, Marquardt for reaction control (RCS) thrusters, Hamilton Standard for environmental control system, Eagle-Pitcher for batteries, RCA for electronic sub-systems, and TRW for abort guidance system. Primary guidance equipment is government furnished.

The first flight vehicle, LM-1, flew unmanned on the Apollo 5 mission. LM-3 flew manned on the Apollo 9 mission and LM-4, LM-5 and LM-6 on the Apollo 10, 11 and 12 missions to the Moon. LM-7 provided the propulsion to return the Apollo 13 spacecraft safely to Earth after the explosion which rendered the Service Module inoperative.

Further details of the Apollo programme can be found on pages 674, 675 and 680.

Apollo 9 lunar module, photographed from command module in orbit

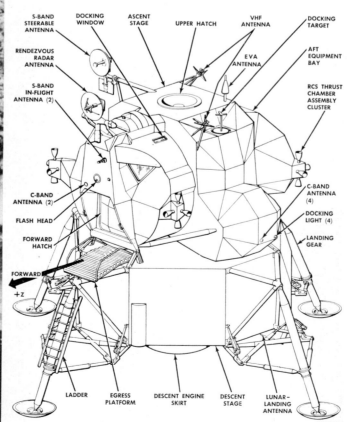

Diagram of Apollo lunar module

DIMENSIONS (legs extended):
Height overall .... 22 ft 11 in (7·00 m)
Width overall .... 14 ft 1 in (4·29 m)
Diameter (diagonally across landing gear)
.... 31 ft 0 in (9·45 m)
Height of ascent stage .. 12 ft 4 in (3·76 m)
Height of descent stage .. 10 ft 7 in (3·24 m)
WEIGHT:
Earth launch weight .... 32,000 lb (14,515 kg)

LUNAR MODULE/APOLLO TELESCOPE MOUNT (LM/ATM)

On 4 November 1968, Grumman announced that it had received a $12·9 million contract from NASA's Marshall Space Flight Center, for modification of Apollo Lunar Module (LM) ascent stages for use in conjunction with the Apollo Telescope Mount (ATM). The ascent stage will serve as the control station for the ATM. The combined LM/ATM will fly in the 1970s as part of NASA's Saturn V Workshop, in which astronauts will stay for prolonged periods, performing solar astronomical experiments.

The contract calls for Grumman to design, develop and manufacture the LM modification, check out the systems and deliver the flight vehicles to NASA. The first flight vehicle (LM-A) is scheduled for delivery by September 1971. The second flight vehicle (LM-B) is scheduled for delivery six months later. The work will be performed at Grumman's Bethpage facility.

The LM/ATM is the first man-operated spacecraft designed for studies of the Sun from above the distorting haze or blanket of the Earth's atmosphere. It consists of a modified LM ascent stage and a structure referred to as the "rack" or ATM, which holds five telescopes to be used in the various solar studies and experiments. Marshall Center is currently developing and building the ATM, and performing the LM/ATM integration.

ORBITING ASTRONOMICAL OBSERVATORY (OAO)

This project was initiated in February 1959, when NASA called a meeting of astronomers interested in an orbiting astronomical observatory (OAO). In August 1959 preliminary specifications for the OAO, drawn up by the NASA Ames Research Center, were distributed to the US industry. Ames engineers also built a prototype full-scale stabilised platform to study problems involved in orientating the satellite. Eleven

Artist's impression of Orbiting Astronomical Observatory satellite

companies submitted formal proposals to meet the final specification drawn up in December, 1959, and in the following October Grumman was chosen as prime contractor and systems manager.

Present contracts call for the manufacture of four flight models of the OAO.

The OAO consists of a standard shell into which one or more separate experiments can be fitted for each flight. The shell is an eight-sided structure of aluminium, measuring 9 ft 10 in (3·00 m) long by 6 ft 8 in (2·03 m) wide, and containing General Electric stabilisation and control equipment, an IBM and Radiation Inc data processing system, telemetry instruments and a command system enabling it to be "locked" on to any selected star by remote control from the ground. Paddles at the sides, with a total area of 264 sq ft (24·4 m²), are covered with more than 108,000 solar cells to generate the power required by the satellite and its payload. Total weight, with about 1,000 lb (450 kg) of payload, is approximately 4,400 lb (1,996 kg).

Astronomical equipment, with reflecting mirrors up to 38 in (0·96 m) in diameter, can be mounted in a 48 in (1·22 m) diameter cylindrical chamber running the full length of the satellite. The cover plate over the end of this chamber is designed to function as a sunshade when open in orbit. Instrumentation varies according to the experiment being conducted, some examples being as follows:

The Smithsonian Astrophysical Observatory is utilising the OAO to orbit four independent electronically-recording telescopic Schwarzschild sensing units, each employing an imaging uvicon system, to map ultraviolet radiation over the entire sky. The University of Wisconsin is providing equipment to measure the brightness of ultraviolet emissions from the stars. NASA's Goddard Space Flight Center proposes to use a 38 in mirror and spectrometer to study emissions from a wide range of celestial bodies. Princeton University Observatory will use a 32 in (81 cm) mirror and spectrometer to study cosmic gas and dust by observing them against the stars.

One of the major advantages offered by the OAO, in addition to its being above the screen of Earth's atmosphere, is that it is potentially stable enough to track a star with an accuracy of one-tenth of a second of arc. The telemetry system transmits experiment results in digital data on wide band, and information on experiments and satellite orientation in real time on narrow band. A memory system can store up to 102,400 items of information for later read-out when the satellite is over ground stations. In addition, an on-board tape recorder permits continuous recording of spacecraft and experiment status data for subsequent playback to ground stations.

The first OAO, designated OAO-1, was launched from Cape Kennedy on 8 April 1966 by an Atlas-Agena. Unfortunately, the spacecraft suffered a power failure and no experiment data were transmitted.

OAO-2, launched on 7 December 1968, contains the Smithsonian and Wisconsin experiments. At the time of launch, mission success was established to occur after thirty days of experiment operation. The design life of the spacecraft was one year. At the time of writing, both of these criteria had been exceeded.

OAO-B was scheduled for launch in the latter part of 1970, followed by OAO-C one year later.

DIMENSIONS:
Overall length, sunshade open 14 ft 1 in (4·29 m)
Length of body .... 9 ft 10 in (3·00 m)
Width of body .... 6 ft 8 in (2·03 m)
Max span over paddles .... 21 ft 2 in (6·45 m)

HUGHES
HUGHES AIRCRAFT COMPANY
HEAD OFFICE:
Culver City, California

Current space programmes for which Hughes Aircraft is prime contractor include development and manufacture of the ATS satellite and a series of communications satellites. The company is also engaged on the investigation and flight testing of experimental ion engines for advanced spacecraft.

The US technical press has reported that Hughes is developing for the USAF a new surveillance satellite to monitor foreign radar activity. Developed under the Air Force's 711 programme, it will be launched by Titan III booster into a highly elliptical orbit in late 1970 or early 1971. Data will be relayed to ground stations for analysis.

Guided weapons currently under development or in production by Hughes are described in the "Missiles" section.

TACOMSAT

The adjacent illustration shows an experimental tactical communications satellite (Tacomsat) that was developed and built by Hughes for the US Army, Navy and Air Force, under the direction of the Air Force Space and Missile Systems Organisation. It is the largest communications satellite yet built, with a weight of approximately 1,600 lb (725 kg). The large 5-element antenna array on top of the satellite consists of helical UHF antennae, each nearly 8 ft (2·4 m) long. Beneath them are two microwave horns, and at extreme top is a bi-conical horn used for telemetry and command. The spacecraft was launched by a Titan IIIC vehicle from Cape Kennedy, into geostationary orbit, on 9 February 1969 and is spin-stabilised at 54 rpm, with the solar panels rotating while the antennae and inner structure remain in a fixed position.

INTELSAT IV

Under a $72 million contract awarded on 18 October 1968, Hughes Aircraft Company became prime contractor for the Intelsat IV satellite. The initial order for four satellites was placed by Communications Satellite Corporation (Comsat) on behalf of the International Telecommunications Satellite Consortium (Intelsat).

Largest communications satellite yet designed, Intelsat IV will be the fifth-generation Hughes satellite to see service since the tiny Syncom 2 was launched in 1963. The others have included the Early Bird, Intelsat 2 (see 1969-70 *Jane's*)

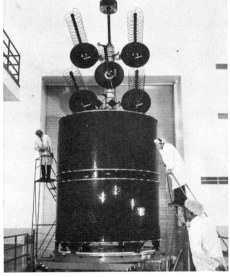

Experimental military tactical communications satellite (Tacomsat)

and several Applications Technology Satellites, all of which are still operating. Hughes is assisted by sub-contractors in the United Kingdom, West Germany, Switzerland, Belgium, Japan, Italy, Sweden, Spain, and France, all of which are member-nations of Intelsat. Northern Electric in Canada is also a sub-contractor.

Intelsat IV is designed to offer communications facilities 25 times greater than those of any satellite now in service. It will be able to carry more than 5,000 two-way telephone calls, transmit 12 simultaneous colour television broadcasts, or handle an infinite variety of different kinds of communications signals.

A unique feature will be the ability to focus power into two "spotlight" beams, 4½° wide, and direct them at any selected areas, thus providing a stronger signal and increased number of available channels in areas of heaviest communications traffic. This is made possible by mounting on the satellite two steerable dish antennae, each 50 in (127 cm) in diameter,

Model of Intelsat IV communications satellite

controlled by command signals from Earth. Two horn antennae, with 17° beams, will provide coverage outside the areas encompassed by the spotlight beams. Electronic switching will enable ground controllers to adjust the amount of power going into each of the two antenna systems. Two Earth-coverage horns (one as a backup) will be used for reception.

Intelsat IV will have 12 broad-band communications channels. Each will have a bandwidth approaching 40 MHz, providing capacity for some 500 communications circuits. Four of the repeaters will serve the Earth-coverage antennae; the other eight will be switched as required to either Earth-coverage or spot-beam antennae.

Solar cells will provide 500W of power. Effective isotropic radiated power (EIRP) at beam centre will be about 36dbw for the spot-beam antennae and 24·3dbw for the Earth-coverage beams. A total of 24 output TWTs will be used (12 for redundancy), each with an output of about 7·5 W.

The satellite will be basically drum-shape. Positioning and orientation control will be provided by a redundant hydrazine system.

The first flight Intelsat IV and its sub-systems will be built and tested at the Hughes space facilities, El Segundo, California, with the member-nation subcontractors participating directly. The second will be assembled and tested at Hughes, but most of its sub-systems will be built by the participating subcontractors. The third and fourth spacecraft will be assembled by British Aircraft Corporation at Bristol, England, using sub-systems furnished by subcontractors. After assembly they will be shipped to Hughes for final testing.

Sub-contractors to Hughes in the Intelsat IV programme are Compagnie d'Electronique Thomson Houston-HB (France), for telemetry and command antennae, planar array antenna, and telemetry and command equipment; Nippon Electric Co (Japan) for repeater F-2; AEG Telefunken (Germany) for repeater F-3; Northern Electric Co (Canada) for repeater F-4; Kolster Iberica SA (Spain) for TWT power supply converters for drivers; Etudes Techniques et Constructions Aérospatiales (Belgium) for battery controller and relay; Svenska Radio AB (Sweden) for solenoid and squib drivers; Contraves AG (Switzerland) for antenna positioning electronics and de-spin control electronics; Selenia SpA (Italy) for Earth coverage—transmit and receive antennae, spot beam communication antennae

and antenna positioner mechanism; British Aircraft Corporation (United Kingdom) for nutation damper, positioning and orientation subsystem, battery pack, structure and harness, sun sensor, and solar panel, with solar cells supplied by Société Anonyme de Télécommunications (France), Ferranti Ltd (United Kingdom) and AEG Telefunken (Germany).

Other participants in the programme include Etudes Techniques et Constructions Aérospatiales (Belgium) for digital portion of systems, test equipment and ground control equipment; Svenska Radio AB (Sweden) for RF portion systems test equipment; and British Aircraft Corporation for handling equipment and spacecraft integration and test.

Intelsat IV is scheduled to be delivered in the second half of 1970 and will be launched into a 19,365 nm (22,300-mile; 35,900-km) synchronous orbit by a Titan IIIB/Agena or Atlas-Centaur vehicle. It is intended to be operational by April 1971.

DIMENSIONS:

Diameter	7 ft 9½ in (2·38 m)
Height of solar drum	9 ft 3 in (2·82 m)
Height overall	17 ft 6 in (5·33 m)

WEIGHTS:

At lift-off	2,452 lb (1,112 kg)
In orbit	1,075 lb (488 kg)

APPLICATIONS TECHNOLOGY SATELLITE (ATS)

Hughes Aircraft announced in March 1964 that it was to develop and produce for NASA five Applications Technology Satellites (ATS) for flights beginning in 1966. The object of the programme was to test several satellite techniques

and devices, particularly spacecraft stabilisation and orientation in high orbits.

ATS has a cylindrical structure, approximately 4 ft 8 in (1·42 m) in diameter, and the five spacecraft in the series varied in length from 4 ft 5 in to 6 ft (1·35-1·83 m), with orbital weights ranging from approximately 650 to 775 lb (295-351 kg). Each was designed to operate in space for a minimum of three years. An Atlas/Agena-D booster was used for the first three launches. The fourth and fifth satellites were launched by Atlas-Centaur vehicles, from Cape Kennedy.

Three types of missions were specified for ATS: (1) A 5,650 nm (6,500 mile; 10,460 km) Earth orbital flight to experiment with the Gravity Gradient stabilisation system. Several long booms extend from the spacecraft to interact with the Earth's gravitation field, to stabilise the satellite and align it with the Earth (ATS-2). (2) Two synchronous 20,410 nm (23,500-mile; 37,820 km) Earth orbital flights with the ATS orbit spin-stabilised to make meteorological communications and navigation investigations (ATS-1 and 3). (3) Two synchronous Earth orbital flights using the Gravity Gradient stabilisation system to make engineering and technological studies (ATS-4 and 5).

Details of the first four ATS spacecraft, launched from Cape Kennedy in 1966-68, can be found in the 1969-70 Jane's.

ATS-5, launched on 12 August 1969, was placed successfully in a near-synchronous orbit. An L-Band communications system is one of 13 experiments carried aboard the ATS-5 to test improved means of locating and tracking aircraft on trans-oceanic flights.

LOCKHEED
LOCKHEED AIRCRAFT CORPORATION
HEAD OFFICE AND WORKS:
Burbank, California
OFFICERS: See "Aircraft" section

Lockheed Missiles and Space Company:
Sunnyvale, Palo Alto and Santa Cruz, California
Lockheed Missiles and Space Company is heavily engaged in both missile work and the design, development and production of satellites and space vehicles. Details of its current space programmes follow.

AGENA
The Lockheed Agena satellite, for which Lockheed was named prime contractor after a design competition in 1956, is a versatile space vehicle which is used normally as the upper stage of a two-stage launcher. It consists of a cylindrical body containing a Bell Aerosystems liquid-propellent rocket engine (16,000 lb = 7,257 kg st) and propellent tanks, telemetry, instrumentation, guidance and attitude control systems. The payload section (nose-cone) can accommodate a wide variety of Earth-orbiting and space probes weighing up to several hundred pounds.

Three versions of the Agena have been announced as follows:

Agena A. Initial version used in Discoverer programme as second stage of Thor-Agena vehicle. Flown for first time in early 1959.

Agena B. Developed version using the new "re-start" version of the Bell Agena rocket-engine. This permits the satellite to change its orbit in space. Used in later Discoverer launchings, and in the now-discontinued Midas programme as second stage of Atlas-Agena. Also used in many civil space programmes, including Ranger, Mariner, Nimbus, Echo, EGO, OAO and POGO.

Agena D. Tested successfully in June, 1962. Can accept a variety of payloads, whereas Agena A and B had integrated payloads. In quantity production. Modified version was used as rendezvous Target Vehicle for Gemini spacecraft.

By the end of 1969, a total of 248 Agena spacecraft applications had been announced, in terms of launches attempted, of which all but 30 had achieved success, with payload injected into orbit. By the same date, a further 45 Agenas had been used as the upper stages of launch vehicles for other spacecraft, with only two recorded failures.

The following details refer to Agena D.

DIMENSIONS:

Length (typical)	23 ft 3 in (7·09 m)
Diameter	5 ft 0 in (1·52 m)

WEIGHTS (typical):

Propellent weight	13,553 lb (6,148 kg)
Vehicle weight empty	1,484 lb (673 kg)
Weight on orbit, less payload	1,277 lb (579 kg)

DISCOVERER
One of the applications of the Agena satellite has been in the USAF's Discoverer programme, in which the Agena carries as part of its payload an ejectable capsule. This capsule was designed to maintain temperature and oxygen sufficient to sustain life in its interior and to be recoverable by parachute.

All launchings in the Discoverer programme are done at Vandenberg AFB. Agena is boosted to near orbital altitude by a modified Thor missile which, after engine burn-out, is separated from the satellite. Agena coasts upwards and positions it-

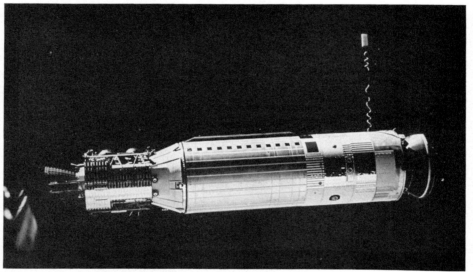

Agena Target Vehicle in orbit

self in a horizontal attitude. The satellite's own engine is then fired to bring it to orbital speed (about 15,600 knots; 18,000 mph; 29,000 km/h). Guidance and altitude control during the coast phase is provided by an infra-red horizon scanner and an inertial reference package. The satellite engine also is gimballed to provide orbit adjustment during the burning period.

Shortly after attaining an orbit and before it has made a complete pass around the Earth, the satellite is programmed to turn itself through 180° in yaw, thus placing the nose section in a rearward-facing position. This is done by cold gas reaction jets which gradually swing the vehicle around. Agena is then stabilized in the rear-facing attitude.

This manoeuvre places the nose section containing the re-entry vehicle and recovery capsule to the rear.

After a pre-determined number of orbits the satellite is tilted 60° downward and stabilized in that position to permit ejection of the nose section. As the satellite swings over the pole and past Alaska, a timer activates the ejection sequence and the re-entry vehicle recovery capsule is separated from the rest of the Agena. A retro-rocket on the nose section fires to slow it down and so permit a gradually curved entry into the Earth's atmosphere. A parachute is deployed and on many occasions an aerial recovery attempt is made.

The first firing, on 28 February 1959, established the satellite in orbit and similar success has been achieved in a high proportion of subsequent Discoverer firings. A major success was obtained with Discoverer 13, as its 300 lb (136 kg) ejected capsule was the first object recovered from orbital flight. An even more striking success was the recovery of the 85 lb (39 kg) Discoverer 14 capsule, which was "snatched" in the air as it descended by a trapeze-like framework towed

behind a C-119 transport aircraft at a height of 8,000 ft (2,450 m), 260 nm (300 miles; 480 km) north-west of Hawaii. This success has since been repeated on many occasions, the latest recoveries being made by Lockheed JC-130B aircraft, which replaced the C-119 for this work.

Details of Discoverers 1 to 38 were given in the 1959-60, 1960-61, 1961-62 and 1962-63 editions of Jane's. Data on subsequent firings has been withheld by the USAF. A high proportion of the unidentified satellites included in the table on pages 681-2 of this edition can be assumed to be Agena vehicles of various kinds.

SAMOS
This reconnaissance satellite is part of an overall USAF satellite system for which Lockheed is prime contractor. Few details are available, but Samos is reported to utilise photographic intelligence equipment by Eastman Kodak in a capsule developed and produced by General Electric and fitted with a parachute and guidance recovery system by Avco and Northrop Ventura. It is intended to be established in a circular polar orbit at a height of 87-260 nm (100-300 miles; 160-480 km). Intelligence data is transmitted by TV, and analysed in greater detail after capsule recovery.

The first launching of a 4,100 lb (1,860 kg) development version, on 11 October 1960, failed to achieve orbit, but Samos 2 was orbited successfully by an Atlas-Agena A booster on 31 January 1961. The third Samos was destroyed in a launch-pad explosion on 9 September 1961.

Details of subsequent launchings are classified, but Samos was believed to be operational by the Summer of 1963, probably in more than one form. One variant, for communications and electronic intelligence, is said to be code-named Ferret.

DIMENSIONS:

Length	22 ft 0 in (6·70 m)
Diameter	5 ft 0 in (1·52 m)

LTV

LTV AEROSPACE CORPORATION (Subsidiary of LING-TEMCO-VOUGHT, INC)
PO Box 5003, Dallas, Texas 75222
Synetics Company
PO Box 6267, Dallas, Texas 75222
PRESIDENT: Dr Gerald M. Monroe
DIVISIONS:
Missiles and Space Division
Kinetics International Division
OFFICERS: See "Aircraft" Section.

Missiles and Space Division of Synetics Company, which is in turn a Division of LTV Aerospace Corporation, is prime contractor for the NASA/DOD Scout launch vehicle, described below, and the US Army's Lance surface-to-surface missile (see "Missiles" section). Its other products include a radiator system used in the Apollo spacecraft command module, and a manned aerospace flight simulator used by Apollo astronauts.

The Division is also engaged in the fields of advanced defence systems, ramjet propulsion systems, electro-optical and other guidance systems, and laser technology.

A pioneer in the extra-vehicular manoeuvering unit field, it developed the USAF's Astronaut Manoeuvering Unit (AMU) and flight demonstration models of the unmanned, radio-controlled Remote Manoeuvering Unit (RMU). Under subcontract to Chrysler, this division produced the fuel and oxidizer containers for the first stage of the Saturn IB space booster.

SCOUT (XRM-91)

Against competition from 12 other companies Chance Vought (now part of LTV Aerospace Corporation) won the major contract for the NASA/Department of Defense Scout four-stage solid-propellant space research vehicle in April 1959. In addition to being responsible for assembly of the overall vehicle, the company developed the nose section and airframe protecting the payload, the inter-stage sections between the various rocket engines, stage separation devices and the jet vanes and fin assemblies.

As prime vehicle contractor, the Missiles and Space Division of Synetics Company performs duties extending from initial assembly and test at the Dallas plant to pre-launch preparation. It also has built the launching towers for the rocket, including a type which permits horizontal checkout of the vehicle and erection to any desired position up to vertical for launch. Launching is possible at any angle from vertical to 20° from vertical.

Scout was designed to make possible space, orbital and re-entry research at comparatively low cost, using "off-the-shelf" major components where possible. Its first stage is the 115,000 lb

(52,160 kg) st Algol IIB (Aerojet Senior) by Aerojet-General; the second stage is the 60,000 lb (27,215 kg) st Castor II by Thiokol; the third stage is the 21,000 lb (9,525 kg) st Antares II (X259) by Hercules Inc's Allegany Ballistics Laboratory; the fourth stage was originally the 3,000 lb (1,360 kg) st Altair (X248) or the more powerful Altair X258, but these have now been superseded by a new UTC stage (see below). Honeywell provide the simplified gyro guidance system. Spin stabilisation of the fourth stage is by LTV Aerospace.

Final assembly of the Scout is done at NASA's Wallops Island facility, Virginia, or at Vandenberg AFB, California, on the Western Test Range, the West Coast launch site for the vehicle.

In the first test, on 1 July 1960, the fourth-stage motor was deliberately not ignited. An entirely successful firing was made on 4 October 1960, when a Scout carried a 125 lb (57 kg) payload to a height of more than 3,125 nm (3,600 miles; 5,800 km).

On 16 February 1961, a Scout became the first solid propellant-vehicle ever to put a satellite into orbit when it was used to launch the Explorer 9 inflatable sphere.

By mid-1962, nine Scouts had been launched, of which six were entirely successful. A second series of 10 Scouts, ordered on 27 June 1962, had more powerful first and third stages, raising the payload for a 260 nm (300-mile; 480 km) orbit from 150 lb (68 kg) to 200 lb (91 kg). Subsequent improvements increased to 230 lb (104 kg) the payload for a 260 nm orbit.

A new version, with an FW-4S fourth stage (6,000 lb = 2,720 kg st) by United Technology Center, was launched for the first time on 10 August 1965, with complete success. In addition to increasing the payload capability to 320 lb (145 kg) in a 260 nm orbit, this new version can be manoeuvred in yaw and can send a 100 lb (45 kg) payload more than 13,900 nm (16,000 miles; 25,750 km) from the Earth.

A fifth-stage velocity package is under development, which will increase the Scout's hypersonic re-entry performance, make possible highly-elliptical deep space orbits and extend the vehicle's probe capabilities to the Sun. A new and larger first stage, the Algol III, is also being developed and will increase the Scout's performance by a further 30 to 35%.

Scouts have been used by NASA for a series of re-entry experiments. In one of these, in 1966, a special 17-in (43 cm) spherical motor was used as a fifth stage to thrust back into the atmosphere at more than 15,600 knots (18,000 mph; 29,000 km/h); a payload designed to provide data on a heat-shield material for nose-caps. Total payload, including the motor, weighed 400 lb (180 kg) at lift-off.

Scout launch from Vandenberg AFB, California

In addition to its use by NASA and the Department of Defense, Scout is used for international programmes, including those of the United Kingdom, Italy, France, Germany and the European Space Research Organisation (ESRO). On 26 April 1967, a Scout inaugurated use of a sea-based platform on the equator, off the east coast of Africa. As space booster for Italy's San Marco programme, it became the first vehicle to orbit a satellite from a launch site at sea.

By March 1970 a total of 92 Scouts had been ordered and 67 had been launched.

DIMENSIONS:
Overall height	72 ft 0 in (21·95 m)
Max body diameter	3 ft 3½ in (1·00 m)

WEIGHT:
Launching weight	37,600 lb (17,055 kg)

MCDONNELL DOUGLAS

MCDONNELL DOUGLAS CORPORATION
HEAD OFFICE AND WORKS:
Box 516, St Louis, Missouri 63166

McDonnell Douglas Astronautics Company
HEADQUARTERS:
5301 Bolsa Avenue, Huntington Beach, California 92646
OFFICERS: See "Missiles" section.

This company was formed on 26 June 1968 by a merger of the former Douglas Missile and Space Systems Division and the McDonnell Astronautics Company into a single management structure. Its guided weapons programmes are described in the "Missiles" section. Details of its current space programmes follow.

THOR

Details of the development, and operational deployment by the RAF, of the Thor IRBM can be found in the 1962-63 edition of this work. The Thor force was disbanded during 1963 and all the missiles were flown back to the United States. Most have been converted into space boosters by McDonnell Douglas. The company is also continuing production of Thors for use as first-stage boosters for the various space launch vehicles described separately below.

Thor has a circular-section aluminium body of lightweight integrally-stiffened design, providing integral tankage for its liquid oxygen and kerosene propellants. There are no tail surfaces.

Propulsion is by a North American Rocketdyne MB-3-III liquid-propellant engine, the chamber of which is gimbal-mounted to provide directional control and stability. Two liquid-propellant vernier engines, on each side of the main engine, provide speed adjustment after main engine burn-out, as required, plus roll stabilisation.

THRUST AUGMENTED THOR (TAT)

Developed for the USAF Space Systems Division, this vehicle is nearly twice as powerful as the standard Thor booster. It consists basically of a standard Thor in which the Rocketdyne MB-3-III liquid-propellant engine is supplemented by three Thiokol TX33-52 solid-propellant rocket motors attached externally to

the lower part of the vehicle's body. This raises the total thrust available at lift-off to 333,000 lb (151,000 kg).

The TX33-52 motors are ignited on the ground, when the liquid-propellant engine approaches lift-off thrust. After burn-out they are jettisoned.

McDonnell Douglas has built 96 Thrust-Augmented Thors for the USAF. The first, launched on 28 February 1963, had to be destroyed when it veered off course. The subsequent record of TAT has been outstanding.

Thrust Augmented Thor is used in conjunction with the Improved Delta Agena B and Agena D upper stages in USAF and NASA space programmes.

THOR-AGENA and TAT-AGENA

This space launch vehicle uses a modified Thor (DSV-2A) as its first-stage booster.

Early firings were made with a Rocketdyne 150,000 lb (68,000 kg) st engine in a type DM1812-3 Thor and a Lockheed-built Agena second stage powered by a Bell 8,500 lb (3,855 kg) st engine. The Rocketdyne engine has since been uprated to 170,000 lb (77,100 kg) st and the latest second-stage Agena D is powered by a Bell liquid-propellant engine developing 16,000 lb (7,257 kg) st.

To improve further the capabilities of Thor-Agena, the USAF began utilising thrust-augmented Thors as first-stage boosters in mid-1963. Overall height of the complete Thor-Agena D vehicle at launching is 82 ft (25 m) and its weight approximately 123,000 lb (55,800 kg). It is able to put a 1,600 lb (725 kg) payload into a 260 nm (300 mile; 480 km) orbit.

LONG TANK THOR

An advanced version of the Thor space booster, known as the Long Tank Thor, made its debut in the Summer of 1966. The length of the liquid oxygen tank was increased and the upper section of the booster was changed from the former conical shape to a cylinder of the same diameter as the rest of the airframe. This increased tankage permits a longer burning time for the main engine, with the result that Long Tank Thor will put 30% heavier payloads in space than Thrust Augmented Thor. Designed burning time

is 216 seconds, compared with 146 seconds for Thrust Augmented Thor.

Main propulsion system is the standard Rocketdyne MB-3-III engine with minor modifications. It is supplemented by three Thiokol TK354-5 Castor II solid-propellant strap-on motors, giving a total thrust for all engines of approximately 330,000 lb (149,700 kg) for take-off.

The USAF has purchased 72 DSV-2L Long Tank Thors from McDonnell Douglas, for use in its space programmes at Vandenberg AFB, California, and for use by NASA at Vandenberg and Cape Kennedy. Fifty-nine had been delivered by February 1970. The first of them was launched successfully as a booster for the Agena D vehicle, on 9 August 1966, putting into orbit a Department of Defense satellite.

A multi-purpose Long Tank Thor is being developed to provide additional performance capability. This configuration provides attachments for six additional solid-propellant strap-on motors, and can be used with three, six or nine such motors.

DIMENSIONS (approx):
Length overall	70 ft 6 in (21·5 m)
Body diameter (constant)	8 ft 0 in (2·44 m)

DELTA, SUPER SIX, THRUST AUGMENTED DELTA (TAD), IMPROVED DELTA AND LONG TANK DELTA (LTD)

In May 1959, Douglas was awarded a prime contract by NASA to develop a three-stage vehicle named Delta, capable of placing a 480 lb (218 kg) payload in a 260 nm (300 mile; 480 km) Earth orbit or of sending a 100 lb (45 kg) payload on deep space probes. The original orders for 12 and 14 Deltas respectively were followed by further contracts in 1963-69, bringing the total to 101.

The following versions of Delta have been produced:

DM-19. The 92 ft (28 m) tall initial version of Delta weighed slightly less than 112,000 lb (50,800 kg). Its flight sequence included 160 seconds of burning time for the 150,000 lb (68,000 kg) st Rocketdyne MB-3-I engine in the

Long Tank thrust-augmented Delta launch vehicle for Intelsat 3 communications satellite

DM-18 Thor, 109 seconds for the 7,500 lb (3,400 kg) st Aerojet-General AJ10-118 second-stage engine and a variable coast period that carried the upper stage to perigee altitude.

The 2,760 lb (1,250 kg) st X248-A5 third-stage engine, manufactured by the Naval Propellant Plant, then fired for 42 seconds, powering the motor casing and the payload into orbit or space. Payload separation was achieved by explosive bolts and a spring mechanism.

DSV-3A. This introduced the DM-21 uprated Thor booster, powered by a 172,000 lb (78,000 kg) st Rocketdyne MB-3-II engine, and could put a 690 lb (314 kg) payload into a 175 nm (200 mile; 320 km) orbit. It was first used to orbit Explorer 14 on 2 October 1962 (13th Delta launch).

DSV-3B. Length of second stage increased by 3 ft (0·91 m) to augment propellant tankage and former BTL 300 guidance replaced by a BTL 600 system. Payload increased to 830 lb (377 kg) in 175 nm (200 mile; 320 km) orbit. First used to orbit Relay I on 13 December 1962 (15th Delta launch).

DSV-3C. New 6,200 lb (2,810 kg) st X258 solid-propellant third stage. Payload increased to 927 lb (421 kg) in 175 nm (200 mile; 320 km) orbit. First used to orbit IMP-A satellite on 26 November 1963.

DSV-3D Thrust Augmented Delta, using Thrust Augmented Thor as first stage. First-stage thrust increased to 333,000 lb (151,000 kg). Able to put 1,270 lb (578 kg) into 175 nm (200 mile; 320 km) orbit. First launching on 19 August 1964, put the Syncom 3 communications satellite into synchronous orbit.

Delta Super Six. This is basically similar to the Thrust Augmented Delta, but has six Castor solid-propellant motors clustered around the base of its first stage instead of the usual three. The additional engines ignite 31 seconds after launch, supplementing the T-O thrust by 150,000 lb (68,000 kg) and making it possible to put an additional 100 lb (45 kg) of payload into synchronous orbit. First Super Six launching, with the Tiros-M satellite, took place in January 1970. Versions of Delta with nine Castor auxiliary rocket boosters are being studied.

DSV-3E Improved Delta. New second stage, with diameter increased from 32 in (0·81 m) to 54½ in (1·38 m), extending burning time from 150 to 400 seconds, and with re-start capability. Payload shroud diameter increased from 33 in

Thrust-augmented Delta launch vehicle for HEOS satellite

(0·85 m) to 65 in (1·67 m). Two- and three-stage versions are available. The two-stage vehicle can put 1,300 lb (592 kg) into a 175 nm (200 mile; 320 km) orbit. The initial third-stage configuration used the Allegany Ballistics Laboratory X258 solid-propellant motor, giving 6,200 lb (2,810 kg) st, which could put 1,530 lb (696 kg) into a 175 nm (200 mile; 320 km) orbit or boost a 225 lb (102 kg) payload to escape velocity. Later versions use either the United Technology Center FW-4D or Thiokol TE364-3 solid-propellant motors, producing 5,700 lb (2,590 kg) or 10,000 lb (4,540 kg) st respectively. The choice of third-stage motor depends upon mission requirements and provides the capability of placing either 1,610 lb (732 kg) or 1,800 lb (818 kg) into a 175 nm (200 mile; 320 km) orbit. Corresponding payload capabilities for escape velocity missions are 300 lb (136 kg) and 410 lb (187 kg) respectively. Eight DSV-3E vehicles were ordered in August 1964, followed by 15 more in July 1965. First used to orbit Geos-A (Explorer 29) on 6 November 1965.

DSV-3L Long Tank Delta. The second stage and payload shroud for this vehicle are as used on the DSV-3E Improved Delta. Two- and three-stage versions are available. Two-stage capability is 2,000 lb (907 kg) into a 200 nm (230 mile; 370 km) circular orbit. Three-stage capability is 750 lb (340 kg) into synchronous transfer orbit or 530 lb (240 kg) to escape velocity. Third-stage motors used for this vehicle are the UTC FW-4D or Thiokol TE364-3. The booster is a version of the DSV-2L Long Tank Thor, with 167,000 lb (75,750 kg) st MB-3-III main engine, supplemented by Thiokol TE354-5 solid-propellant boosters (each 52,000 lb = 23,587 kg) st). The booster propellant tanks are extended 14·4 ft (4·39 m) and are cylindrical over the entire length to permit an increase of 46,200 lb (20,955 kg) of propellant.

The booster is of monocoque waffle pattern aluminium alloy construction. The interstage adapter is of aluminium alloy skin and stringer construction. The second stage is a stainless steel and aluminium alloy monocoque structure and the third stage of high-strength steel alloy. The spin-tables are of monocoque petal magnesium, aluminium alloy and steel. The shroud is a glass-fibre monocoque with aluminium alloy frames.

Guidance and stabilisation during flight are provided by the Thor autopilot and a Bell Telephone Laboratories radio-command guidance system during first and second-stage powered flight, by a McDonnell Douglas flight control system during the second-stage coast period, and

Three-stage Delta launch vehicle for OSO satellite

by spinning up the third stage and payload prior to third-stage powered flight.

DSV-3L Long Tank Delta with multiple solid-thrust Augmentation. Like DSV-3L Long Tank Delta in all respects except that its performance has been increased by the addition of three more (total of six) thrust-augmentation motors. The two-stage payload capability is increased to 2,800 lb (1,270 kg) into a 200 nm (230 mile; 370 km) circular orbit. The three-stage vehicle payload capability is increased to 1,000 lb (450 kg) into a synchronous transfer orbit. Dimensions and weights are as for the DSV-3L Long Tank Delta, except that the firing weight (three-stage) is increased to 230,000 lb (104,500 kg).

Satellites launched by Delta have included many of the Explorer series, Pioneer, Tiros and ESSA weather satellites, Echo I, Orbiting Solar Observatory series, Ariel, HEOS A, Biosatellite, and active communications satellites such as Telstar, Relay, Syncom, Early Bird, Intelsat and Skynet.

DIMENSIONS (DSV-3L):
Length with booster   106 ft 2½ in (32·37 m)
Body diameter   8 ft 0 in (2·44 m)
WEIGHTS (DSV-3L):
Firing weight (3-stage)   200,000 lb (90,720 kg)

Base of first Delta launch vehicle to utilise six thrust-augmentation motors. Used for launch of Tiros-M satellite

Weight, less booster   16,000 lb (7,255 kg)
Weight at 2nd-stage burn-out 4,800 lb (2,175 kg)

S-IVB (SATURN IB SECOND STAGE AND SATURN V THIRD STAGE)

McDonnell Douglas was prime contractor for the S-IVB third stage of the Saturn V launch vehicle used in the Apollo programme. A total of 27 S-IVBs were ordered.

The S-IVB is powered by a single Rocketdyne J-2 liquid oxygen/liquid hydrogen engine of 200,000 lb (90,700 kg) st, and is 58 ft 7 in (17·86 m) tall and 21 ft 8½ in (6·61 m) in diameter. It carries 64,000 US gallons (242,260 litres) of liquid hydrogen and 20,000 US gallons (75,700 litres) of liquid oxygen, and weighs 262,000 lb (118,835 kg) fuelled.

The first flight-type S-IVB was shipped from the McDonnell Douglas Space Systems Center on 30 April 1965. Acceptance firing was successfully accomplished on 8 August at the Sacramento Test Center. The occasion was the first fully-automatic digital computer check-out of a space vehicle. On 26 February, this S-IVB was launched successfully from Cape Kennedy as second stage of NASA's first Saturn IB rocket. Twelve of the stages were ordered subsequently as Saturn IB second stages; the others form the third stage of Saturn V launchers (see page 680).

The first Saturn V configuration S-IVB was used in the Apollo 4 flight on 9 November 1967. The stage's engine was successfully re-started in space for the first time, after coasting in orbit for three hours. This orbital re-start capability is essential to the S-IVB's mission of injecting the Apollo spacecraft on its lunar trajectory on manned flights to the Moon.

SATURN V WORKSHOP (SKYLAB PROGRAMME)

The NASA Skylab programme is to make maximum use of the hardware and techniques developed in the Apollo programme to explore further and extend man's usefulness in space.

The main spacecraft in the Skylab programme is the Saturn V Workshop. This provides an extension of manned space flight capability beyond the Gemini and Apollo flights, by using Saturn/Apollo hardware and the existing skills. Objectives are (1) long-duration flights, (2) Earth-orbit scientific investigations, (3) applications in Earth orbit, and (4) an effective and economical approach to the development of a basis for future

Artist's impression of Saturn S-IVB Orbital Workship, to be launched in 1972

space programmes. Thus, the Workshop fills the development and operational gap between the Apollo Programme and a large permanent station.

The orbital Workshop will be boosted into a 220 nm (253 mile; 407 km) circular orbit by a Saturn V two-stage launch vehicle, in mid to late 1972. It is currently in a hardware design phase; the required boost vehicles are operational and the remaining hardware necessary for the operations is being designed and/or modified, fabricated and qualified.

The Saturn V Workshop is basically a modified S-IVB stage, which will have its 10,000 cu ft (283 m³) hydrogen tank equipped as living and working areas for three astronauts for periods of up to 56 days. McDonnell Douglas Astro-

nautics Company, manufacturer of the S-IVB stage, will outfit the Workshop.

Vital to the operation of the Workshop is the airlock module also being developed by MDAC, at its St Louis facility. This module will provide storage and distribution for environmental gases and electrical power, and perform numerous other service functions.

Purpose of the Workshop is to provide an environment in space in which men can live and work under controlled conditions for extended periods of time, beyond that provided by Gemini and Apollo. The experiments will study the men's physiological and psychological responses in the space environment, and provide more detailed information on their capabilities for extended manned flight.

MARTIN MARIETTA
MARTIN MARIETTA CORPORATION

CORPORATE HEADQUARTERS:
277 Park Avenue, New York, New York 10017

AEROSPACE GROUP HEADQUARTERS:
Friendship International Airport, Maryland 21240

OFFICERS:
See "Missiles" section

The Denver Division of Martin Marietta is working principally on the Titan III family of space launch boosters, and on spacecraft, their systems, and related research.

TITAN III

Titan III is a standard space launch system which provides a high-frequency launch capability for a wide variety of manned and unmanned payloads, ranging from 29,000 lb (13,150 kg) in Earth orbit to 5,000 lb (2,270 kg) for planetary missions such as the exploration of Mars. The Space and Missile Systems Organisation of the Air Force Systems Command has executive management of the programme. Martin Marietta at Denver, Colorado, was named systems integrator for the industry/contractor team on 20 August 1962. Technical direction is assigned to Aerospace Corporation.

Titan III is America's standard heavy-duty space "workhorse" booster and is used for both military and non-military space launch missions. Initial assignments include scientific and communications satellite programmes and NASA's unmanned soft-landing spacecraft for Martian exploration.

Martin Marietta, in addition to its rôle as systems integrating contractor, builds the airframe and is integrating contractor for facilities and launch operations at Cape Kennedy. Aerojet-General Corporation produces the liquid propulsion systems. United Technology Center manufactures the solid-propellant booster motors used in the most powerful model. AC Electronics Division of General Motors Corporation builds the inertial guidance system, which is an adaptation of that used in the Titan II ICBM.

The core section of Titan III consists of elements which provide a high degree of commonality throughout all configurations. It consists of two booster stages evolved from the Titan II ICBM and an upper stage, known as Transtage, that can function both in the boost phase of flight and as a restartable space propulsion vehicle. All stages use storable liquid propellants and have gimbal-mounted thrust chambers for vehicle control.

Titan III exists in three configurations:

Titan IIIB is basically the first two stages of the core section. It can accommodate a variety of specialised upper stages. First launched on 29 July 1966. Series of launches continued through 1969. all with Agena upper stages and classified USAF payloads put into polar orbit.

Titan IIIC consists of the core section of the main airframe, with solid-propellant rocket motors attached to either side to function as a booster stage before ignition of main engines. Later models will have a 15 : 1 expansion ratio engine.

Titan IIID is basically similar to IIIC but has only a two-stage liquid-propellant "core" (without Transtage) and radio guidance instead of the standard inertial guidance. Able to accept a variety of upper stages. Production order placed by USAF in November 1967.

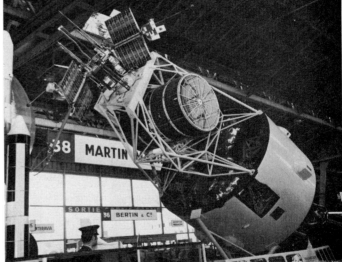

Titan III Transtage, carrying Northrop OV2-5 satellite on nose and cylindrical Lincoln Laboratory LES-6 satellite. Not visible are two small TRW ERS's which complete the payload *(Flight International)*

A Titan IIIC, with a 25 ft long (7·62 m) typical payload fairing and all stages mated, is 130 ft (39·62 m) in height. Future payloads may extend the overall height to more than 150 ft (45·72 m). The first stage of the main airframe (core vehicle) is 71 ft (21·64 m) long and 10 ft (3·05 m) in diameter. Its engines, which use a blend of hydrazine and unsymmetrical hydrazine (UDMH) for fuel, and nitrogen tetroxide as an oxidizer, develop 470,000 lb (213,200 kg) st, since they are ignited at an altitude where efficiency is increased.

The second stage of the core vehicle is 37 ft (11·28 m) tall and 10 ft (3·05 m) in diameter. Its engine uses the same propellants as the first stage and develops 100,000 lb (45,360 kg) st.

The Transtage space propulsion vehicle is 15 ft (4·57 m) tall and 10 ft (3·05 m) in diameter and also uses UDMH/hydrazine and nitrogen tetroxide as propellants. The twin-chamber engine produces 16,000 lb (7,257 kg) of thrust and is

capable of multiple restarts in space, which permits a wide variety of manoeuvres, including change of plane, change of orbit, and transfer to deep space trajectory. Transtage also houses the control module for the entire vehicle, including the guidance system and segments of the flight control and vehicle safety systems.

Titan IIIC's solid-propellant booster motors are each 85 ft (25·91 m) long and 10 ft (3·05 m) in diameter. Each motor is built in five segments and develops more than 1,200,000 lb (544,300 kg) st. Steering for the booster stage is accomplished through a thrust vector control system, which injects nitrogen tetroxide into the engine thrust column.

The Titan III 17-vehicle research and development flight testing programme involved launch of four IIIA's and 13 IIIC's. The first launch of the Titan IIIA occurred on 1 September 1964. Titan IIIC made its maiden flight on 18 June 1965 and had completed ten successful flights by early 1969, putting a total of more than 50 satellites into orbit in the process. Eight more Titan IIIC's were ordered in the Summer of

Titan IIIC standard space launch vehicle putting Hughes tactical communications satellite into near-synchronous orbit, 9 February 1969

1967. These will dispense with special man-rating systems fitted to the initial IIIC's.

Contracts for the period 1964-73 cover production of a total of 95 Titan IIIs.

Viking Orbiter and landing capsule for NASA's Mars 1973 mission

DIMENSIONS: See above.
LAUNCHING WEIGHTS (approx):

Core vehicle	450,000 lb	(204,120 kg)
Titan IIIC	1,500,000 lb	(680,400 kg)

PERFORMANCE (Titan IIIC, approx):
Speed at burn-out:

Solid-propellant boosters		
	4,100 mph	(6,600 kmh)
1st stage	10,200 mph	(16,300 kmh)
2nd stage	17,100 mph	(27,520 kmh)
Transtage	17,500 mph	(28,160 kmh)

VIKING

Viking is the name of the programme under which NASA is proposing to send two unmanned spacecraft to orbit the planet Mars, and two more to make semi-soft landings there in 1975. It replaces the former, more costly Voyager project.

Each of the last two spacecraft will be made up of two modules, known as the Viking orbiter and Viking lander, and will be launched by a Titan IIID-Centaur vehicle. The complete spacecraft will enter a Martian orbit at a minimum height of 1,040 nm (1,200 miles; 1,930 km) above the surface. The lander will then separate and leave orbit, probably by means of a retro-rocket. It will be protected by a heat shield as it decelerates in the Martian atmosphere. A parachute system will be deployed when speed has decreased to about Mach 2, and final touch-down will be cushioned by landing rockets.

Viking orbiter will be developed and built by the California Institute of Technology's Jet Propulsion Laboratory and will be similar in appearance to JPL's 1971 Mariner-Mars orbiters, with a liquid-propellant retro-rocket engine to decelerate the craft into orbit on arrival at the planet. Total launch weight of the complete orbiter/lander is expected to be about 7,000 lb (3,175 kg), of which the orbital insertion engine and fuel will account for 4,000 lb (1,815 kg). The orbiter will have a weight of about 1,200 lb (545 kg) in orbit, of which up to 150 lb (68 kg) will be scientific experiments to record and relay data on the topography and atmosphere of Mars and make possible correlation of orbital and surface data.

Viking lander will be developed and built by an industry team led by Martin Marietta's Denver Division, which will also be responsible for integrating the overall systems. Among sub-contracts announced to date is one awarded in April 1970 to Teledyne Ryan Aeronautical for the development, test and manufacture of nine terminal descent landing radar sets, including test models, spares and flight hardware. This radar will provide measurements of relative velocity to the flight control computer from an altitude of about 17,000 ft (5,200 m) to the touchdown on the Martian surface. Using four beams of microwave energy, the radar will furnish redundant solutions with three-beam pairs.

At separation the lander will weigh about 1,800 lb (815 kg), but will have a touch-down weight of only 400-800 lb (180-360 kg), including some 40 lb (18 kg) of instruments. These will search for living organisms on Mars, investigate the visual and thermal characteristics of the landing area with a camera system, determine whether any water is present on the planet's surface, relay information on atmospheric temperature, pressure, humidity, wind direction and speed, use radio techniques to investigate Mars and its atmosphere, measure the solar ultra-violet flux reaching the Martian surface, and report on the planet's seismic activity.

NORTH AMERICAN ROCKWELL

NORTH AMERICAN ROCKWELL CORPORATION

GENERAL OFFICES:
2300 East Imperial Highway, El Segundo, California 90245
OFFICERS: See "Aircraft" section

The major current products of the North American Rockwell Space Division are the Apollo three-man lunar exploration spacecraft and the S-II second stage of the Saturn V launch vehicle.

S-II SECOND STAGE FOR SATURN V

It was announced on 11 September 1961 that NASA had selected North American's Space and Information Systems Division (now North American Rockwell's Space Division) to develop the S-II second stage for the Saturn V vehicle. This and later contracts cover the production of 15 flight S-II's.

The S-II is powered by five Rocketdyne J-2 engines, running on liquid hydrogen and liquid oxygen propellants and giving a total of 1,125,000 lb (510,300 kg) st.

APOLLO SPACECRAFT

The goal of the Apollo project was to land two men on the Moon by 1970 and return them safely to Earth, using a lunar rendezvous technique. This was achieved in July 1969.

Selection of North American to develop the Apollo three-man spacecraft was announced by NASA on 28 November 1961, after an evaluation of five industry proposals. Contracts to date have covered the production of 20 of the spacecraft, 16 boilerplate versions, 10 full-scale mock-ups, five engineering simulators and evaluators, and two mission simulators.

Design of the Apollo spacecraft is based on the "building block" or modular concept. There are three major components, comprising the Command Module housing the three-man crew; a Service Module housing fuel, electrical power supplies and propulsion units; and the Lunar Module (LM). The Command Module is 10 ft 7 in (3·23 m) high, with a launch weight of about 13,000 lb (5,900 kg). It consists of an inner pressurised compartment of aluminium honeycomb and an outer structure of stainless steel honeycomb with a plastic ablative heat shield coating over the entire outer surface.

The Service Module is 24 ft 9 in (7·54 m) high, with a weight of about 53,000 lb (24,040 kg), and is constructed of aluminium honeycomb. Details of the Lunar Module can be found under the "Grumman" heading in this section. Total weight of the spacecraft is about 95,000 lb (43,100 kg).

North American Rockwell is responsible for design, development and production of the Command and Service Modules. The Massachusetts Institute of Technology's Instrumentation Laboratory is system manager for guidance and control systems, with AC Electronics Division of General Motors Corporation as prime contractor, in association with Raytheon, Sperry and Kollsman-Garrett AiResearch for environmental control, Avco for the heat shield, Northrop-Ventura for parachute recovery, Lockheed Propulsion Company for the escape tower rocket and Rocketdyne for reaction controls. Beech Aircraft Corporation produces the cryogenic storage sub-system installation in the service module, which stores, controls and delivers the oxygen and hydrogen required for life support and electrical power generating equipment. The Service Module engine is supplied by Aerojet-General and has a static thrust of 20,500 lb (9,300 kg).

Preliminary testing of Apollo components and systems, with particular reference to the escape system, was conducted by the use of Little Joe II boosters produced by the Convair division of General Dynamics. The first launch into orbit of a boilerplate Apollo Command Module was made by Saturn SA-6 on 28 May 1964. The first manned orbital flight was delayed by a fire during ground tests of Spacecraft 012, on 27 January 1967, in which astronauts Virgil Grissom, Edward White and Roger Chaffee lost their lives. Details of the Apollo 4, 5, and 6 unmanned flights can be found in the 1968-69 *Jane's*. The Apollo 7, 8, 9, 10 and 11 manned flights were described in the 1969-70 edition. Subsequent missions have been as follows:

APOLLO 12

Apollo 12 was launched at 17.22 BST on Friday 14 November 1969. Lift-off, exactly on time, was made in bad weather and shortly after the launch the Saturn V was struck twice by lightning. Simultaneously an electrical transient caused the fuel cells in the spacecraft to come off line, leaving the electrical loads to be met by the back-up batteries. It also caused the circuit-breaker of the inertial measurement unit to trip and the illumination of "so many warning lights we couldn't read them all" according to Astronaut Conrad. No permanent damage was caused, however, and staging, entry into orbit and the trans-lunar injection operations proceeded as planned.

Crewed by Charles Conrad (Commander), Alan Bean (LM pilot) and Richard Gordon (CM pilot), the mission objectives were to perform selenological inspection and survey in a lunar "sea", deploy an Apollo Lunar-Surface Experiments Package (ALSEP) consistent with a seismic network, develop point-landing techniques, develop man's ability to work in the lunar environment, and obtain photographs of exploration sites. A secondary objective was to examine Surveyor 3 which had landed on 20 April 1967; this required a landing precisely on the selected site in the Ocean of Storms.

The second of two scheduled mid-course corrections included a burn which slowed the craft by 64 ft/sec (19·5 m/sec), and converted the trajectory into a non-free return path. This was done to delay the arrival of the spacecraft at the Moon until the lighting at the selected Site 7 was suitable.

Early on the morning of Monday 17 November the spacecraft reached the Moon and began to swing behind it. The first of two lunar-orbit insertion burns by the SM engine began at 16·52 BST, when the craft was 82 nm (94 miles; 152 km) above the Moon, and placed the craft in a 60 × 169 nm (69 × 195 mile; 111 × 313 km) orbit. Two orbits later the orbit was changed by a second burn to 54 × 66 nm (62 × 76 miles; 100 × 122 km).

On Wednesday morning, at 05·20 BST, the CM/SM undocked from the LM, and the two craft assumed their individual call signs: *Yankee Clipper* for the CM and *Intrepid* for the LM.

To prevent repetition of the landing error in the Apollo 11 mission, a number of refinements were made to the guidance and navigational system. These were eminently successful and a smooth touchdown was accomplished at 07·54 BST, within a few hundred feet of the nominal impact point and within sight of Surveyor 3.

While on the surface, two EVAs were made, each lasting about four hours. During the first EVA the ALSEP was deployed some 600 ft (200 m) from where *Intrepid* had landed. The package was more advanced than the one deployed during the Apollo 11 mission, and was powered by a SNAP-27 generator fueled by a core of radioactive plutonium 238. ALSEP's instruments included a seismometer, solar-wind spectrometer, magnetometer, lunar-atmosphere detector and a lunar-ionosphere detector. A solar-wind experiment was also deployed, as well as the American flag. The only serious mishap was malfunction of the colour TV camera which was to have relayed the EVA to viewers on Earth; this was caused by the camera inadvertently being pointed directly at the sun momentarily while it was being set up.

The purpose of the second EVA, which started at 05.01 BST on Thursday 20 November, was to make a geological survey and to visit Surveyor 3. During the walk, which covered well over a mile (1·6 km), the two astronauts were guided in their choice of rock and soil specimens by a team of geologists relaying their advice directly through the Houston controller. The high point of the EVA was the visit to Surveyor 3 which was lying in a shallow crater some 600 ft. (200 m) from *Intrepid*. From Surveyor, the camera, soil scoop and other parts were retrieved and brought back to Earth for examination.

Lift-off from the Moon took place at 15·26 BST on 20 November and a gentle docking with the CM was achieved at 18.58 BST. At 20·43 BST the LM was undocked and two hours later its engine was fired to cause the craft to crash into the Moon, to provide a calibration moonquake. The shock was recorded by the seismometer, and continued to "ring" for nearly an hour after the impact, some 20 times longer than expected.

The journey back to earth was normal and uneventful, and safe splashdown occurring in the central Pacific at 21·58 BST on Monday 24 November, within sight of the prime recovery ship, USS *Hornet*.

APOLLO 13

Crewed by James Lovell (Commander), Frederick Haise (LM pilot) and James Swigert (CM pilot), Apollo 13 lifted off after a trouble-free countdown at 20·13 BST on Saturday 11 April 1970. James Swigert, a member of the back-up crew, was included in the prime crew only two days before lift-off to replace the original CM pilot, Thomas K. Mattingly, who had been exposed to German measles.

The purpose of the Apollo 13 mission was to

Apollo 9 command module in the water after its splash-down, 13 March 1969

This remarkable photograph shows the lift-off of Apollo 11, on 16 July 1969, carrying the first astronauts to land on the Moon

attempt the first landing in the lunar highlands, the chosen landing site being in an area near the crater Fra Mauro, some 95 nm (110 miles; 180 km) south of the Apollo 12 landing site in the Ocean of Storms. The mission also called for over 33 hours of EVA time and a walk on the surface of two miles (3 km). A third objective was to put the discarded Saturn S-IVB third stage into a lunar-impact trajectory, to obtain readings from the seismometer left behind by Apollo 12; this objective was met satisfactorily, impact occurring on 14 April some 66 nm (76 miles; 120 km) from the Apollo 12 site, with a force equal to 11 tons of TNT.

Initial lift-off and the staging of the S-IC was satisfactory, but the centre J-2 engine of the S-II second stage shut down 2 min 12 sec prematurely. The required orbital speed was obtained by burning the remaining four engines for an extra 34 seconds, and the single J-2 engine of the third S-IVB stage for another 10 seconds longer than planned.

The transposition and docking manoeuvre was completed satisfactorily and the flight continued uneventfully until 04·17 BST on Tuesday 14 April, when a near-catastrophic explosion in the SM occurred. This was caused by one of the oxygen tanks erupting, the explosion blew out a complete side panel, measuring some 13 ft ×

5 ft 6 in (3·96 m × 1·65 m) and rendered the SM useless.

Great ingenuity was then exercised by both ground controllers and the Apollo crew in using the LM as a "lifeboat" to sustain the crew and to permit a return to Earth. The descent engine of the LM was fired four times, first to place the craft on an initial free return trajectory, subsequently to improve the trajectory, and finally to refine the re-entry angle.

At 14·17 BST on Friday 17 April the SM was jettisoned, a procedure fraught with danger as the extent of the damage was still unknown. Explosive bolts were fired to effect separation and small thrusters on the LM were burned to ease the CM/LM gently away from the SM.

At 17·44 BST the crew, now safely installed in the CM, initiated the separation procedure of the LM, *Aquarius*, and it blasted clear of the CM *Odyssey*. Re-entry and parachute deployment were effected normally, the splashdown occurring safely at 19.07 BST on 17 April some 3·5 nm (4 miles; 6 km) from the prime recovery ship, the carrier *Iwo Jima*.

The four-day ordeal, the first major crisis to occur in space, was extensively reported as events took place; the splashdown was watched by an estimated audience of 800 million people throughout the world.

NORTHROP

NORTHROP CORPORATION

HEAD OFFICE:
Beverly Hills, California

Advanced Systems Department

ADDRESS:
Research Park, Palos Verdes Peninsula,
California

VICE-PRESIDENT AND MANAGER:
Dr Vincent W. Howard

DIRECTOR OF MARKETING:
L. K. Jensen

PUBLIC RELATIONS MANAGER:
Roy W. Gregory

Fields in which the Advanced Systems Department is active include space guidance and research studies in the development of space payloads, space optronics and space vehicle design. The Laboratories delivered to the USAF the OV2-1, OV2-3 and OV2-5 satellites, of which details were given in the 1969-70 *Jane's*.

PHILCO-FORD

PHILCO-FORD CORPORATION

SPACE AND RE-ENTRY SYSTEMS DIVISION:
Ford Road, Newport Beach, California 92663

Since late 1965, when an initial $30 million contract was received from the USAF, Philco-Ford Corporation's Space and Re-entry Systems (SRS) Division has been prime contractor for the Re-entry Measurements Programme Phase B (RMP-B). It also designed and built the United Kingdom's Skynet defence communications satellites and the US Department of Defence's IDCSP satellites.

RMP-B PROGRAMME

The Re-entry Measurements Programme Phase B (RMP-B) is a project of the US Department of Defense, on behalf of the Air Force Systems Command's Space and Missile Systems Organisation (SAMSO) and the US Army Nike-X Development Office (NXDO). Its purpose is to determine what happens to advanced missile payloads as they re-enter the Earth's atmosphere from space, to assist development of the US Army's Safeguard and Nike-X anti-ballistic missile defence programmes.

In the RMP-B programme, Atlas-F missiles which have been retired from the USAF's active inventory are used as delivery vehicles for the RMP-B payloads developed by Philco-Ford SRS. Radars at the Kwajalein Missile Range, some 4,350 nm (5,000 miles; 8,000 km) from the launch site at Vandenberg AFB, locate the missile as it arcs over the Pacific towards its target and track each payload to impact.

The cylindrical aluminium payload package, carried on the nose of Atlas-F, is 7 ft 0 in (2·13 m) in diameter and 6 ft 8 in (2·03 m) long, excluding the nose fairing which protects the payload from kinetic heating during launch. The RMP-B package drops off a variety of payloads along its trajectory, deployment being assisted by a twin-chamber solid-propellant rocket motor, with stop/re-start capability, built into the package. The motor is manufactured by Northrop Carolina Inc of Asheville, North Carolina.

Primary target vehicles are carried beneath a glass-fibre fairing. Subscale payloads are in modified launch-tubes of the type used in the ABRES (Advanced Ballistic Re-Entry System) Mod IV programme, for which Philco-Ford SRS was also prime contractor. The overall system is sufficiently versatile to permit the delivery of a wide range of subscale vehicles.

The first in the current series of RMP-B launches was conducted by the 6595th Air Force Test Wing in January 1969. All details are classified, but it was stated that telemetry readings analysed after the flight indicated its complete success.

IDCSP

Seven 100 lb (45·5 kg) satellites were launched on 16 June 1966 by a single Titan IIIC from Cape Kennedy to inaugurate the Initial Defense Communications Satellite Program (IDCSP).

Launched simultaneously with the communications satellites was a Gravity Gradient Test Satellite (GGTS) designed and built by General Electric to test the feasibility of simple, passive stabilisation systems at high altitudes (see page 668).

A further clutch of eight IDCSP satellites, designated Nos. 8 to 15, were launched by a Titan IIIC on 18 January 1967.

Philco-Ford defence communications satellite for British Skynet system

IDCSP: cluster of eight satellites carried by Titan IIIC Transtage

The third launch, on 1 July 1967, placed satellites Numbers 16 to 19 in orbit. A fourth launch, on 13 June 1968, successfully orbited another eight satellites, designated IDCSP 4-1 to 4-8. Each is a 26-faced polyhedron, weighing about 100 lb (45 kg), and about 31 in (80 cm) long by 35 in (90 cm) diameter.

The IDCSP system was declared operational in mid-1967. In early 1970, 26 of the satellites were maintaining the planned objective of providing the Department of Defense with communication links, out of reach of enemy action, to all areas of the Earth.

Prime contractor for the IDCSP satellite is Philco-Ford Corporation.

SKYNET

Britain's Skynet Defence Satellite Communications System is complementary to, and interoperable with, the American IDCSP. The overall Skynet system was designed by Mintech to satisfy MoD requirements. It comprises two

RMP-B payload on Atlas launch vehicle

satellites (procured from and launched by the USA), one operational and one standby, in a closely-defined synchronous orbit above the Indian Ocean, and nine stations (five fixed, two on the assault ships *Fearless* and *Intrepid*, and two air-transportable for rapid deployment).

The satellites were developed and built by Philco-Ford Corporation's Space & Re-entry Systems Division, under a contract managed by the USAF's Space and Missile Systems Organization. Each consists basically of a cylindrical body 54 in (1·37 m) in diameter and 63 in (1·60 m) high overall, with a weight of 535 lb (242·5 kg) at launch and 285 lb (129 kg) in orbit after expending the solid propellant of its apogee boost motor. More than 7,000 solar cells are mounted on eight vertical panels to provide power over the satellite's design operational life of five years.

The Skynet satellite has two channels for receiving, translating, amplifying and retransmitting voice, telegraph and facsimile data originated by the British ground stations.

Skynet 1 was launched by a thrust-augmented Delta vehicle from Cape Kennedy on 22 November 1969. After entering an initial highly-elliptical orbit, its solid-propellant "kick-stage" was fired to put the satellite into synchronous orbit. It was finally manoeuvred into its operational position over the Indian Ocean. The standby Skynet satellite was scheduled to be launched in 1970.

TALLEY

TALLEY INDUSTRIES INC

ADDRESS:
4551 East McKellips Road, PO Box 920, Mesa, Arizona 85201.

DIRECTOR OF MARKETING:
A. P. Kelley

Current products of Talley Industries Inc include sounding rockets, sled propulsion rockets, crew escape systems, missile propulsion motors, and cartridge-actuated devices. Research and development work includes new propellant formulations for advanced applications.

TALLEY PHOENIX 1

Phoenix I is a two-stage unguided solid-propellant ionospheric sounding rocket which was fired for the first time on 21 June 1960.

The first stage comprises a Kiva motor, with heat-treated alloy steel case and cruciform

aluminium alloy tail fins. The second stage is a Hopi motor, with heat-treated alloy steel case and cruciform stainless steel fins.

The ogival nose-cone and cylindrical payload package have an internal volume of 290 cu in (4,750 cm³). A payload of 5 lb (2·25 kg) can be carried to a height of 230 nm (265 miles; 427 km) or 20 lb (9 kg) to 148 nm (170 miles; 274 km).

Phoenix I is launched from a zero-length portable launcher. Full provision is made for telemetry and payload recovery.

DIMENSIONS:

Length of first stage	8 ft 7 in (2·62 m)
Diameter of first stage	6·5 in (16·5 cm)
Diameter of second stage	4·5 in (11·4 cm)
Overall length of vehicle	18 ft 6 in (5·64 m)
Span of fins, first stage	2 ft 0 in (61 cm)
Span of fins, second stage	1 ft 4 in (40 cm)

WEIGHTS:

Firing weight, second stage	83 lb (37·6 kg)

Weight of second stage at burn-out
26 lb (11·8 kg)
Total firing weight, less payload 320 lb (145 kg)

PERFORMANCE:

Velocity at first-stage burn-out
4,000 ft (1,220 m) sec
Velocity at second-stage burn-out
8,750 ft (2,665 m) sec
Max acceleration 148 g

TALLEY HOPI CHAFF DART

This meteorological sounding vehicle consists of a Hopi III first-stage booster, powered by a 2·4KS 5600 solid-propellant motor, and an unpowered chaff-carrying dart second stage of the kind described under the Judi-Dart entry. High-altitude sensors are being developed for this vehicle to give it added capability.

Hopi Chaff Dart is in production.

First and second stages of Talley Phoenix sounding rocket

DIMENSIONS:

Length of first stage	86·1 in (2·19 m)
Length of dart	44·4 in (1·13 m)
Diameter of first stage	4·5 in (11·4 cm)
Diameter of dart	1⅜ in (3·5 cm)
Span of first-stage fins	13⅞ in (35·2 cm)
Span of dart fins	3⅞ in (9·8 cm)

WEIGHTS:

First stage	84 lb (38 kg)
Dart	11 lb (5 kg)

PERFORMANCE:

Ceiling	380,000 ft (115,800 m)
Max velocity	6,100 ft/sec (1,860 m/sec)
Max acceleration	150 g

TALLEY KISHA-JUDI

This two-stage solid-propellant sounding rocket is similar in configuration to Phoenix and has a firing weight of 221 lb (100 kg). Velocity at second-stage burn-out is 3,270 ft/sec (995 m/sec) and it can carry a 16 lb (7·25 kg) payload to a peak altitude of 79 nm (91 miles; 146 km).

TALLEY JUDI CHAFF DART

In quantity production for various US military and government agencies, the Judi-Dart is a meteorological sounding rocket for measurement of winds at altitudes from 100,000 ft (30,500 m) to 250,000 ft (76,200 m). It consists of a Judi I (1·9KS 2150) solid-propellant rocket motor topped by a metal dart. The dart is hollow and houses thousands of hair-like metal objects which are ejected at a pre-determined altitude. The objects, known as chaff, drift with the wind and can be tracked by ground radar, so indicating the direction and velocity of the wind. Alternatively, an instrument package can be used in the dart.

DIMENSIONS:

Length of first stage	63·45 in (1·61 m)
Length of dart	40·25 in (1·02 m)
Diameter of first stage	3·0 in (7·6 cm)
Diameter of dart	1⅜ in (3·5 cm)

WEIGHTS:

First stage	23·8 lb (10·8 kg)
Dart	9·5 lb (4·3 kg)

PERFORMANCE:

Ceiling (nominal)	235,000 ft (71,600 m)
Max velocity	5,100 ft/sec (1,555 m/sec)
Max acceleration	175g

TALLEY JUDI PARACHUTE DART

This meteorological sounding vehicle is identical to the Judi Chaff Dart, except that the dart payload consists of a silverised silk parachute of 7 ft 7 in (2·31 m) diameter, which is ejected pyrotechnically at heights up to a nominal 235,000 ft (71,600 m).

TALLEY JUDI-ROBIN BALLOON DART

This meteorological sounding vehicle is identical to the Judi Chaff Dart, except that the dart payload consists of a balloon, diameter 3 ft 3½ in (1·00 m), with corner reflector, which is ejected at heights up to a nominal 205,000 ft (62,500 m).

TRW
TRW SYSTEMS GROUP

HEAD OFFICE:
1, Space Park, Redondo Beach, California 90278

VICE-PRESIDENT AND GENERAL MANAGER:
Dr Richard D. DeLauer

VICE-PRESIDENT AND DIRECTOR OF MARKETING AND REQUIREMENT ANALYSIS: George E. Solomon

PUBLIC AFFAIRS DIRECTOR: W. M. Millar

Known formerly as TRW/Space Technology Laboratories (STL), and originally as the Guided Missiles Division of Ramo-Wooldridge, TRW Systems Group has provided technical direction and systems engineering for the USAF Atlas/Titan/Minuteman missile programme since 1954. The company has also designed and built 100 spacecraft and scores of major sub-systems. Its recent and current military and civilian contracts have included prime contracts for the NASA OGO and Pioneer, USAF Vela, and international communications satellites, of which brief details are given below.

The company builds the variable-thrust descent engine for the Apollo lunar module (LM) and a variety of low-thrust liquid-propellant and radioisotope thrusters (See "Aero-engines" section). It also produces the LM abort guidance system.

TRW Systems provides NASA with mission analysis and spacecraft systems planning for the Apollo project, and furnishes systems integration and test support for the US Navy's anti-submarine warfare (ASW) programme.

INTELSAT 3

In September 1966, TRW Systems received a contract from the Communications Satellite Corporation, on behalf of the Interim Telecommunications Satellite Consortium (Intelsat), for the development and construction of six satellites for a Global Communications System that was intended to be fully operational by 1970. These satellites follow the first-generation Early Bird and second-generation Intelsat 2 satellites produced by Hughes Aircraft Company (see 1969-70 *Jane's*).

The TRW Intelsat 3 has a diameter of 56 in (142 cm) and overall height of 78 in (198 cm), with a weight of 608 lb (276 kg) before launch and 321 lb (146 kg) in orbit. It operates in a synchronous orbit and is spin-stabilised at a rate of 90-100 rpm. Its capacity is 1,200 telephone channels or 4 TV channels (with 85 ft = 26 m ground dish antenna). Operating life is intended to be five years.

The basic structure of the Intelsat 3 is a magnesium cylinder, which surrounds the apogee motor, and a circular aluminium honeycomb platform which holds sub-system equipment. An outer shell of solar cells surrounds the equipment platform. A directional communications antenna and an omni-directional telemetry and command antenna are mounted above the structure. As the satellite spins clockwise, the communications antenna is mechanically de-spun counter-clockwise at precisely the same speed to keep it pointing always towards the Earth. Launch vehicle is the Long Tank Thrust-Augmented Delta.

Companies participating in the programme with TRW include Bell Telephone Manufacturing of

Intelsat 3 global communications satellite

Belgium (local oscillator and mixer filter), Contraves AG of Switzerland (electrical integration assembly), Engins Matra of France (attitude control electronics), ERNO of Germany (positioning and orientation system), Hawker Siddeley Dynamics of the UK (structure), ITT Federal Laboratories of the USA (communications telemetry and command subsystem), Laboratoire Central des Telecommunications of France (command decoder), Mitsubishi Electric Corporation of Japan (power control unit and equipment converter), SAT of France (solar array), Standard Elektrik Lorenz of Germany (telemetry encoder) and Sylvania Electronic Systems of USA (mechanically de-spun antenna). In addition, Lockheed supplies Earth sensors and Aerojet-General provides the apogee motor for each satellite.

The first four satellites contain components and subsystems of US origin; the fifth and sixth satellites incorporate subsystems manufactured by the international participants. All spacecraft have been assembled, integrated and tested at TRW Systems Group in Redondo Beach, California.

The first Intelsat III was intended to be orbited in September 1968 but was lost when its launch vehicle had to be destroyed. Since then, there have been four successful launches and another launch vehicle failure. There are now two Intelsat IIIs over the Atlantic, one over the Pacific and one over the Indian oceans. One of the satellites over the Atlantic has experienced intermittent difficulties with its communications antenna. It is expected that this satellite will be replaced by a future launching and will become an in-orbit spare.

DEFENSE SATELLITE COMMUNICATIONS SYSTEM, PHASE II

The Phase II Defense Satellite Communications System will utilise synchronous-orbit communications satellites and surface terminals

to provide reliable world-wide circuits for carrying essential military communications. The satellites are under development by TRW Inc for the US Air Force.

Protected against interference, the satellites will be equipped with steerable narrow-beam antennae that focus a portion of the satellite's energy to areas one or two thousand miles (1,600-3,200 km) in diameter. Within these specially illuminated areas, the narrow-beam antennae allow small terminals to be used in place of more costly large terminals. The narrow beams will be designed to be steered in a matter of minutes to different locations on the Earth's surface. The satellites will be designed so that they can be moved in a matter of days to new synchronous orbital positions. In this way antenna coverage will be tailored to fit defence contingency communications all over the world.

ERS

The ERS Environmental Research Satellite is a small spacecraft for conducting scientific and engineering research experiments in space. The satellite was developed by TRW Systems Group in 1961 and the first ERS was launched from Vandenberg AFB in September 1962. Since then, a total of 23 ERS, all launched as piggy-back payloads, have been orbited successfully.

The illustration on page 678 shows the variety of configurations in which ERS satellites can be supplied. They range in weight from 1½ to 44 lb (0·7-20 kg) and generally carry a single experiment.

The most commonly flown ERS has been the octahedron, with eight sides on which triangular solar panels are fastened. The ERS can incorporate many different subsystems. Stabilization can be either spin, passive magnetic, gravity gradient, or active magnetic. Electric power for the satellite is derived from solar cells, often supplemented by rechargeable batteries. VHF transmitters have been employed on all ERS flights for telemetry and tracking beacon signals, and command/receiver systems have been used. Satellite antenna subsystems have included dipole, crossed dipole and monopole. The satellite normally employs a passive thermal control subsystem.

The ERS has been used by NASA to check the manned spaceflight network (TETR-1, launched 13 December 1967, and TETR-2, launched 8

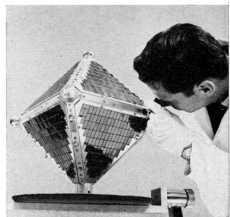

OV5-2 environmental research satellite

November 1968) and by the USAF to conduct experiments concerned with solar cell radiation damage, radiation measurements, surface contact bonding of materials in space, surface friction, zero gravity heat transfer, and solar X-ray and nuclear particle monitoring.

The ERS is one of the most reliable and least expensive active satellites yet produced. The latest configuration is the Prism, which may be used as an earth resources satellite.

ERS satellites are available to any prospective purchaser and can be made to meet any specified dimensions to house space instrumentation.

NUCLEAR DETECTION SATELLITE (VELA AND ADVANCED VELA)

The original Vela spacecraft was designed to detect nuclear explosions in space. It was a 20-sided satellite, with a width of 56 in (1·42 m) and weight of about 510 lb (231 kg). Its payload consisted of a precise 18-detector system to detect X-ray, gamma-ray and neutron emissions, and was provided by Los Alamos Scientific Laboratories. The system could report on nuclear explosions as far away as Venus and Mars.

The first two Vela spacecraft were put into orbit together by an Atlas-Agena on 17 October 1963. They were moved out of their original orbit by a small rocket motor built into each, and put into circular orbits about 58,200 nm (67,000 miles; 107,825 km) above, and on opposite sides of the Earth, well above the outer Van Allen radiation belts. In addition to their primary purpose, they reported bursts of X-rays from the sun.

A second pair of Vela spacecraft was launched successfully on 17 July 1964, with an ERS satellite (see above) making up the surplus payload capacity. The third pair was launched on 15 July 1965, with an ERS variant (ORS II).

Orbital spacing was adjusted by the firing of electro-thermal thrusters on both spacecraft.

Under an advanced Vela programme, TRW developed a larger 730 lb (331 kg) stabilised variant, about 6 ft (1·8 m) in diameter and with payload increased from 90 lb (41 kg) to 155 lb (70 kg). The additional capacity enables the satellite to carry more sophisticated optical and electro-magnetic pulse detectors, capable of detecting

Examples of environmental research satellites developed by TRW for "piggyback" launching

simultaneously with three 20 lb (9 kg) octahedral research satellites (ORS), also built by TRW. The second pair of advanced Velas was launched on 23 May 1969. Last launch in the present programme was to take place in 1970.

OGO

TRW Systems produced for NASA a family of six Orbiting Geophysical Observatories (OGO), each of which was designed to perform simultaneously 20 to 26 different scientific experiments in standardized vehicles. Experiment payload weight was approximately 250 lb (113 kg) and the object of the programme was to help scientists to understand better space phenomena and the potential hazards of manned space travel.

The OGO satellite consisted of a rectangular main body approximately 6 ft (1·83 m) long and 3 ft (0·91 m) square. Two wing-like solar cell "paddles", spanning 20 ft (6·10 m), provided approximately 500W power. Eleven experiment booms folded against the spacecraft body and deployed after launch.

Launches included the EGO eccentric orbit and POGO polar orbit variants. The programme used Atlas-Agena launch vehicles for POGO missions and Thrust-Augmented Thor-Agena boosters for EGO missions.

Details of OGO-1, OGO-2 and OGO-3 can be found in the 1967-68 *Jane's*, OGO-4 in the 1968-69 *Jane's* and OGO-5 in the 1969-70 *Jane's*.

OGO-6 satellite folded for launch

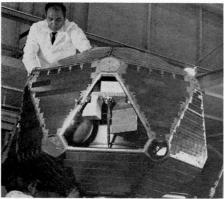

Advanced Vela nuclear detection satellite

Vela nuclear detection satellites with six solar panels removed

nuclear explosions deep into Earth's atmosphere, while retaining space nuclear capabilities out to great distances. The satellite is continuously Earth-oriented and downward-looking in orbit.

The first pair of advanced Velas were launched successfully by a Titan IIIC on 28 April 1967,

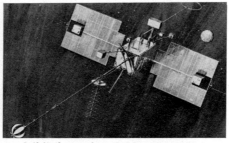

Artist's impression of OGO, the orbiting geophysical observatory

OGO-6. The final OGO was launched into a polar orbit on 5 June 1969. The 1,400 lb (635 kg) spacecraft carries 25 experiments for obtaining data from the Earth's upper atmosphere, ionosphere and the auroral regions.

Information from OGO-6 experiments was designed to improve the understanding of the Earth's environment and the interaction with galactic, interplanetary and solar events. Experiments are being conducted on atmospheric density, electron temperature and density, neutral atmospheric composition, sodium airglow, atmospheric ion concentration and mass, ionosphere ducting, solar X-ray emissions, and low-energy auroral particles.

More than 1,300,000 hours of experimental data had been received from the six OGOs by early 1970, and more than 300 reports and papers had been published concerning the experiments. OGO achievements have included the first observations of protons that are responsible for a ring of current surrounding the Earth during magnetic storms; the first spacecraft global survey of the Earth's magnetic field; first observation of daylight auroras; and the first worldwide map of airglow distribution.

DIMENSIONS:

Length overall, booms extended
$\qquad$ 59 ft 0 in (17·98 m)
Width overall, paddles extended
$\qquad$ 20 ft 0 in (6·10 m)

SOLAR-PIONEER AND TETR-2

The Solar-Pioneer programme aimed at putting five spacecraft in solar orbit to provide data on the interplanetary magnetic field, radio propagation effects of the "quiet Sun", plasma spectrometry, ionization levels and solar high-energy and medium-energy particles. One of the primary objectives was to formulate techniques for predicting solar flares that could be harmful to astronauts on long-duration flights.

Pioneer orbits ranged between 0·8 and 1·2 UA of the Sun; both elliptical and circular orbits were employed within the Earth's ecliptic plane and the spacecraft were spin-stabilised.

The Solar-Pioneer spacecraft consisted of a cylindrical body 35 in (0·89 m) long and 37 in (0·94 m) in diameter, covered with 10,368 solar cells. A command and telemetry antenna extended from the top of the satellite; three booms projected from the vehicle's mid-section, one holding an experiment, one a wobble damper

TETR-2 test and training satellite

and one an orientation nozzle; and an experiment antenna was deployed from the base of the spacecraft. Typical weight (Pioneer 9) was 148 lb (67·1 kg), including 39·5 lb (17·9 kg) of experiments. Spacecraft design stressed the use of non-magnetic materials to assure high accuracy of the magnetic field measurements.

The fourth in this series of spacecraft, Pioneer 9, was launched into solar orbit from Cape Kennedy on 8 November 1968, and complemented Pioneers 6, 7 and 8. It was launched against the direction of the Earth's path round the Sun, to allow it to enter an orbit some 70 million miles (113m km) from the Sun—closer than any of the earlier Pioneers.

Purpose of the craft was to study the Sun during the period of solar activity which reached a peak in the Summer of 1969. Its 39·5 lb (17·9 kg) payload included eight experiments to record solar plasma, energetic particle flux, electric and magnetic fields and micrometeoroid flux.

Data returned were used to help forecast major flares on the solar surface, which might have produced biologically-damaging bursts of high-energy protons, in support of the Apollo programme.

Known as Pioneer D before launch, the spacecraft was built by TRW. It was launched by a Delta vehicle, the second stage of which carried a 40 lb (18 kg) Test and Training Satellite (TETR-2) which was ejected rearward at 3 ft (1 m) sec about one minute after the third stage of the Delta had ignited. The TETR-2 housed a transponder to transmit and receive S-band data signals simulating Apollo spacecraft, and was used in the S-band system checkout and training exercises with the Manned Space Flight Network.

The final launch in the Solar-Pioneer series took place on 27 August 1969. A malfunction in the launch vehicle prevented the spacecraft from being placed in orbit.

PIONEER-JUPITER

TRW has begun to build the first spacecraft which will fly to Jupiter, the largest planet in the solar system. The spacecraft, called Pioneer F, will be launched in 1972. Its journey to Jupiter, some 420,000,000 nm (483,000,000 miles; 777,000,000 km) away, will take from 600 to 800 days.

Pioneer F's mission plan calls for it to pass within approximately 87,000 nm (100,000 miles; 160,000 km) of Jupiter. On board the spacecraft will be photographic equipment to send back to Earth "close-up" pictures during the fly-by. It will also carry experiments to measure the interplanetary environment, obtain data on the Jovian radiation belts and make measurements of the atmosphere of Jupiter in the infra-red, ultra-violet and visible spectra.

TRW is building Pioneer F and a similar craft, Pioneer G (to be launched in 1973), under the direction of NASA's Ames Research Center, Moffett Field, California. The work is being performed at TRW's Space Park facility in Redondo Beach, California.

The Pioneer-Jupiter spacecraft will be spin-

Pioneer-Jupiter scientific spacecraft

stabilised. Each will weigh approximately 500 lb (227 kg) including about 60 lb (27 kg) of scientific experiments. Power will be provided by radio-isotope thermo-electric generators (RTGs), which convert nuclear energy to electricity. The Pioneers will be the first spacecraft to depend wholly on RTGs as a power source.

Data will be returned to ground stations via an Earth-pointing 9 ft (2·75 m) diameter dish antenna on the spacecraft. The data bit-rate near Jupiter will be 512 bits/second.

Launch vehicles for Pioneers F and G will be Atlas/Centaurs.

The two Pioneer-Jupiter missions will give scientists some of the essential information they need to map out "Grand Tour" missions which in the 1970s will fly to several of the outer planets. It is thought now that a sound approach to Grand Tour missions would be to send spacecraft into the gravitational field of Jupiter, using its force to swing the spacecraft out to still more distant planets.

Pioneer F will pass through a large asteroid belt which orbits the Sun at roughly 350,000,000 million miles. The belt contains millions of

Pioneer 9 solar orbiting spacecraft

small pieces of "space debris" travelling at a high velocity. Many are too small to be tracked from Earth but sufficiently large (the size of a fist or larger) to damage or completely decommission a spacecraft on collision. Pioneer F will carry experiments to determine the micrometeoroid hazards of this belt.

UTC

UNITED TECHNOLOGY CENTER (Division of United Aircraft Corporation)

HEAD OFFICE:
PO Box 358, Sunnyvale, California 94088
OFFICERS:
See "Engines" section

KANGAROO

UTC announced on 5 November 1969 that it had received a $110,000 contract to develop a unique new type of rocket vehicle for the US Navy Pacific Missile Range, Point Mugu, California. The contract covers design and construction of several of the rockets for ground test firing at UTC and flight testing at the Pacific Missile Range.

Award of the contract follows completion of a joint study programme by engineers from Point Mugu and UTC. Preliminary design and analysis were under the overall direction of Carl F. Anderson, head of the aero-mechanical branch in the ordnance division at the PMR, while detailed design and performance analysis were conducted at UTC.

Known as Kangaroo, because its second stage and payload are pouched within the solid-propellant booster stage, the production vehicle will be fired prior to manned spacecraft launches and re-entries to investigate the fringes of Earth's atmosphere for unforeseen hazards. Its instrumentation will be capable of detecting and measuring unfiltered cosmic rays and solar radiation, high concentrations of charged particles or heavy meteoroid bombardment.

In conventional meteorological rockets the instrument packages are attached to the nose of the booster, where they are exposed to severe

atmospheric pressures and kinetic heating during flight. This requires heavy interstage structures and payload insulation.

Kangaroo carries its payload in an aerodynamically-designed dart nested in a canister which, although attached to the rocket's forward closure, is partially submerged into the solid-propellant combustion chamber.

At the base of the canister, a small end-burning solid-propellant grain acts as a plug to prevent combustion chamber pressures from pushing the dart forward prematurely. At a pre-determined altitude, the plug consumes itself and chamber pressure is applied to the base of the dart, expelling it from the canister.

As the dart slides forward and out of the canister, it forces open the vehicle's nose fairing and picks up its fin assembly for stabilised flight. After a further pre-determined time, a fuse in the base of the dart fires a booster charge behind a piston which, in turn, ejects the payload into the atmosphere.

Fired from a simple rail launcher, Kangaroo will be capable of sending its instrument package to altitudes of more than 400,000 ft (122,000 m). In addition to its primary task, it could be used to study weather conditions over vast areas, spot the beginnings of storms, and radio warnings to Earth. It could also collect extensive information on the Van Allen radiation belts and their effect on our atmosphere's behaviour as well as on spacecraft.

DIMENSIONS:

Length overall	10 ft 0 in (3·05 m)
Length of dart	4 ft 0 in (1·22 m)
Diameter overall	6½ in (16·51 cm)
Diameter of dart	1⅝ in (4·13 cm)

Kangaroo, showing first and second stage separation

SATELLITES, PROBES AND LAUNCH VEHICLES

The following satellites, probes and launch vehicles are additional to those described under the entries for their prime contractors in the earlier pages of this section. All are listed in the "Guided Missiles and Space Vehicles" index at the back of this edition of *Jane's*.

ESSA

Launched into orbit by NASA for the US Department of Commerce, ESSA is the Tiros Operational Satellite (TOS). The first one, launched from Cape Kennedy on 3 February 1966, was designated ESSA 1 (Environmental Survey Satellite); the responsible office within the Department of Commerce is also known as ESSA

(Environmental Sciences Services Administration). Information gathered by the satellite is being used by the US Weather Bureau to improve daily weather forecasts.

Closely resembling the earlier experimental Tiros satellites, ESSA 1 weighs 305 lb (138 kg) and is 42 in (107 cm) in diameter and 22 in (56 cm) high. In orbit, it rolls like a wheel, so that each of the two cameras on its rim points towards the Earth once in every revolution. In a near-polar, Sun-synchronous orbit, the satellite can observe weather over all the world once each day, photographing a given area at the same local time each day. The two camera systems store

photographs on magnetic tape for transmission to command stations at Fairbanks, Alaska, and Wallops, Virginia. Major contractor for the spacecraft is RCA.

ESSA 2, launched on 28 February 1966, and ESSA 3, launched on 2 October 1966, were almost identical to ESSA 1. ESSA 4 and 5, launched on 26 January and 20 April 1967 respectively, provided additional coverage for the operational Tiros meteorological system. ESSA 6 was launched on 10 November 1967.

ESSA 7, weighing 320 lb (145 kg), was launched on 16 August 1968, to replace ESSA 5. With this satellite, trouble was experienced with one

ESSA, the Tiros Operational System satellite

cf the two Vidicon cameras carried. ESSA 8, similar to ESSA 7, was launched on 15 December 1968. ESSA 9, last of the series, followed on 26 February 1969.

Since the TOS (Tiros Operational System) became operational in February 1966, the ESSA National Environmental Satellite Center has issued many thousands of warnings, based on satellite photographs, to nations threatened by dangerous storms.

MARINER

This is a NASA project covering the design and manufacture of a series of unmanned space-probes for missions to Mars and Venus. The general appearance of one of the latest probes, for which Jet Propulsion Laboratory hold the prime contract, is shown in the accompanying illustration.

Details of the successful missions flown to date by Mariner spacecraft can be found in the 1969-70 *Jane's*. The next scheduled missions will be by two further Mariner Mars spacecraft, which will be launched by Atlas Centaur vehicles in 1971 to orbit Mars. Funds have been requested to equip a back-up Mariner Mars 1969 spacecraft for a close-up photographic fly-by mission to Venus and Mercury in 1973.

OSO

Prime contractor for this Orbiting Solar Observatory satellite is Ball Brothers Research Corporation, with the payload provided by NASA's Ames Research Center and the Universities of California, Minnesota and Rochester. The object is to measure electromagnetic radiation from the sun in the ultra-violet, X-ray and gamma-ray regions of the spectrum and to study time variations of the emissions, unhampered by Earth's atmosphere.

Details of the missions flown by OSO 1 to OSO 5 can be found in the 1969-70 *Jane's*.

OSO electromagnetic radiation satellite

SATURN

The Saturn programme covers production of a series of very large multi-stage launching vehicles, of which development began in late 1958.

Characteristics of the three versions of Saturn are as follows:

Saturn I. Described in 1965-66 *Jane's*. All ten firings successful.

Saturn IB. Development of Saturn I, with S-1B first stage by Chrysler (see page 665) and S-IVB second stage by McDonnell Douglas (see page 673). Able to put payload of 45,000 lb (20,400 kg) into a 120-mile (190 km) orbit. First five flights successful, on 26 February, 5 July and 25 August 1966 and 22 January and 11 October 1968. The fifth launch was the Apollo 7 manned Earth orbital flight.

Saturn V. Three-stage vehicle for manned Apollo lunar flights. S-IC first stage by Boeing (see page 665); S-II second stage by North American Rockwell (see page 674); SIVB third

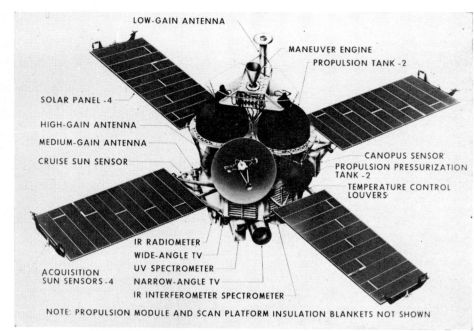

Diagram of JPL unmanned space-probe for the Mariner programme

LOW-GAIN ANTENNA
MANEUVER ENGINE
PROPULSION TANK -2
SOLAR PANEL -4
HIGH-GAIN ANTENNA
MEDIUM-GAIN ANTENNA
CRUISE SUN SENSOR
CANOPUS SENSOR
PROPULSION PRESSURIZATION TANK -2
TEMPERATURE CONTROL LOUVERS
ACQUISITION SUN SENSORS -4
IR RADIOMETER
WIDE-ANGLE TV
UV SPECTROMETER
NARROW-ANGLE TV
IR INTERFEROMETER SPECTROMETER
NOTE: PROPULSION MODULE AND SCAN PLATFORM INSULATION BLANKETS NOT SHOWN

Saturn IB/Apollo 7 launch, 11 October 1968

Saturn V/Apollo 13 launch 11 April, 1970

stage by McDonnell Douglas (see page 673). This version is able to put a payload of 120-140 short tons into Earth orbit or send 50 tons to the vicinity of the Moon. Height with payload 353 ft 5 in (107·7 m). Launching weight 6,100,000 lb (2,767,000 kg). Details of the first two launches (Saturn V/Apollo 4 and 6) can be found in the 1968-69 *Jane's*. The Saturn V/Apollo 8, 9, 10 and 11 missions were described in the 1969-70 edition. Details of the Apollo 12 and 13 flights are given on page 675 of this edition.

SERT 2

SERT 2 was launched on 4 February 1970 by a Thorad-Agena D vehicle from the Western Test Range in California, into a 541-538 nm (623-619 miles; 1,002-996 km) orbit.

The purpose of the Space Electric Rocket Test (SERT) satellite is to test in space two electron-bombardment ion engines. These units, supplied by the Lewis Research Center, generate very low thrust levels compared with the mass of the satellite, but are much more efficient than either conventional chemical or nuclear rockets. Also the thrust generated can be applied for long periods.

The spacecraft itself weighs 3,300 lb (1,500 kg) and consists of the Agena upper stage of the launch rocket, two large solar arrays containing a total of 33,300 individual cells, and a cylinder 40 in (100 cm) long by 59 in (150 cm) in diameter, housing the two ion engines. The solar array has an area of 187·5 sq ft (17·42 m²), the largest yet flown on a NASA satellite, and generates about 1·5kW, of which about 1·0kW is needed to power the ion engines. The propulsion system contains 29 lb (13 kg) of mercury propellant for each engine, sufficient for 9 months' operation at full thrust.

On 10 February 1970 the first ion engine was turned on, initially at 30% thrust, then 80% and finally to its full rated thrust of 0·006 lb (0·0027 kg). It was then shut down and the second engine was brought up to thrust and left on. The minute thrust, providing an acceleration of only 0·000059 ft/sec² (0·000018 m/sec²), is expected to raise the orbit by 52 nm (60 miles; 96 km) over a six-month period.

A sub-orbital test flight of SERT 1 was flown in July 1964.

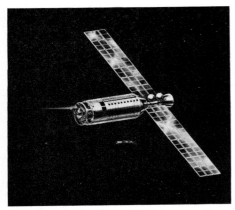

Artist s impression of SERT 2 spacecraft

SKYLAB

NASA's Skylab programme (known formerly as Apollo Applications Programme) is intended to extend the manned space flight capability developed in the Apollo lunar programme with a varied series of manned flights in the period 1972-73. One of the primary elements of the programme will involve orbiting the modified S-IVB Workshop described under the McDonnell Douglas entry on page 673.

Skylab Workshop missions are scheduled to be flown in 1972 and 1973, using Saturn V and Saturn IB launch vehicles. In the first launch, a Saturn V will boost (with its first two stages) a modified S-IVB stage, destined to become the Workshop, into an orbit about 200 nm (230 miles; 360 km) above the Earth. To this S-IVB will be attached an airlock, a special multiple docking structure, and a large solar telescope (the Apollo Telescope Mount, ATM, now being planned by NASA). One or two days later, a Saturn IB will launch a three-man astronaut crew into orbit to rendezvous with the Workshop "cluster."

The S-IVB Workshop will be modified and outfitted on the ground before launch to provide living and working quarters for three astronauts inside the stage's liquid hydrogen tank. Partitions will create separate rooms inside the cylinder; handholds, rails and nets will be attached to the tank walls to help the men control their movements in the absence of gravity; food, water, supplies and experimental equipment will be put into place. The astronauts will then live in the Workshop for up to 28 days of in-space experiments before returning to Earth in their Apollo capsule.

About two months after the first crew returns to Earth, a second three-man crew will be launched by Saturn IB for rendezvous with the Workshop. These men will stay up to 56 days in orbit, using the Workshop and the Apollo Telescope Mount as a manned orbiting solar observa-tory and conducting other scientific tasks. Still another three-man crew will be launched by Saturn IB about two months after the second crew returns to Earth in its Apollo spacecraft. This crew will also live and work in the S-IVB Workshop for up to 56 days before returning to Earth. The Workshop itself is expected to re-main in orbit for up to one year.

TIROS M (ITOS-1)

Tiros M, also known as Improved TIROS Operational Satellite-1 (ITOS-1), was launched from the Western Test Range in California on 23 January 1970. A second-generation oper-ational weather satellite, Tiros M represents a significant improvement over its predecessors (ten Tiros and nine ESSA spacecraft) in that it is capable of mapping the Earth's cloud cover at night as well as by day. A complete scan of the Earth is thus possible in 12 hours rather than just once a day.

The satellite is box-shaped, 14 ft (4·27 m) wide with solar panels deployed, and weighs 682 lb (309 kg.) Instead of spinning, as do ESSA satellites, it is stabilized so that it always faces the Earth. Employing a large spinning flywheel and appropriate electronic circuitry, this stabili-zation system is called "Stabilite".

Picture equipment includes two advanced vidicon cameras, with tape storage, and two automatic picture transmission (APT) cameras. Data from the latter can be picked up by the 500 or so relatively simple APT ground receiving stations located in over 50 countries. Other experiments include a solar proton monitor for solar flare warnings, and a radiometer to measure the Earth's heat balance.

Tiros M was launched, together with a small Australian tracking satellite, by a two-stage Delta-N, with six Castor solid-propellant strap-on boosters. The craft, funded by NASA, was built by RCA. The remaining five craft in the series will be funded by the US Commerce Dep-artment.

US SATELLITES AND SPACECRAFT LAUNCHED SINCE 29 JUNE 1969
Note:—The US Air Force is withholding information on many launchings and this list may be incomplete.
Data in italics are approximate or estimated

Date	Name	Total weight lb	kg	Launch Vehicle	Apogee miles	km	Perigee miles	km	Inclin-ation	Lifetime	Remarks
1969 16 July	Apollo 11 LM 5 (*Eagle*)	33,205	15,062	Saturn V (SA.506)	115 —	185 —	114 —	183 —	32·51° —	Splashdown 24 July	First manned landing on Moon. Crew: N. Armstrong, E. Aldrin, M. Collins. *Eagle*, carrying Armstrong and Aldrin, on Moon 20-21 July
23 July	Unidentified	330	150	*Thor-Burner II*	532	855	489	786	98·8°	80 years	USAF satellite
24 July	Unidentified	—	—	*T-A Thor-Agena D*	137	221	110	177	74·98°	30 days	*USAF recoverable reconnais-sance satellite*
26 July	Intelsat 3E	—	—	T-A Delta	3,353	5,396	169	272	30·33°	30 years	Communications satellite, in unintended parking orbit
31 July	Unidentified	3,300	1,500	*T-A Thor-Agena D*	336	540	287	461	75·02°	6 years	*Reconnaissance satellite*
9 Aug.	OSO-6	638	290	Delta	344	553	305	491	32·96°	20 years	Orbiting Solar Observatory
12 Aug.	ATS-5	—	—	Atlas-Centaur	22,860	36,790	22,230	35,776	2·6°	1 million years	Applications Technology Satellite
22 Aug.	Unidentified	—	—	*Titan IIIB-Agena D*	227	365	83	133	108·0°	16 days	*Manoeuvrable recoverable reconnaissance satellite*
22 Sept.	Unidentified	—	—	*T-A Thor-Agena D*	157	252	111	178	85·03°	20 days	*USAF recoverable reconnais-sance satellite*
	Unidentified	130	59		309	496	304	488	85·16°	2 years	Ejected from above
30 Sept.	Unidentified	7	3	*Atlas-Burner II*						600 years	USAF Calibration target
	Unidentified	4	1·8		580	933	565	909	70·04°	600 years	USAF Calibration target
	Unidentified	125	56							600 years	USAF Gravity-gradient satellite
1 Oct.	Boreas	176	80	Scout	242	389	181	290	85·11°	Down 23 Nov.	ESRO 1B environmental research satellite
24 Oct.	Unidentified	—	—	*Titan IIIB-Agena D*	460	740	85	137	108·04°	15 days	*USAF reconnaissance satel-lite*
8 Nov.	Azur	156	71	Scout	1,957	3,150	240	386	102·96°	100 years	West German satellite (First)
14 Nov.	Apollo 12 LM 6 (*Intrepid*)	33,325	15,116	Saturn V (SA.507)	124 —	199 —	114 —	183 —	32·56° —	Splashdown 24 Nov.	Second manned landing on Moon. Crew: C. Conrad, A. Bean (LM); R. Gordon (CM)
22 Nov.	Skynet 1	284	129	T-A Delta	22,270	35,840	21,560	34,700	2·40°	1 million years	Anglo-US military com-munications satellite
4 Dec.	Unidentified	—	—	*T-A Thor-Agena D*	156	251	99	160	81·48°	Down 10 Jan. 1970	*USAF recoverable reconnais-sance satellite*
1970 14 Jan.	Unidentified	*6,600*	*2,994*	*Titan IIIB-Agena D*	238	383	83	134	109·96°	18 days	USAF satellite
15 Jan.	Intelsat 3F	302	137	Long-tank T-A Delta	22,250	35,808	22,240	35,792	0·9°	Unlimited	1,200-channel communica-tions satellite
23 Jan.	ITOS-I	681	309	Two-stage T-A Delta	921	1,483	892	1,435	102·0°	10,000 years	Advanced Tiros weather satellite
	Oscar 5 (Australis)	39	18		920	1,480	892	1,435	101·96°	10,000 years	Amateur radio communica-tions satellite
4 Feb.	Sert 2	3,300	1,500	T-A Thor-Agena D	623	1,002	619	996	99·13°	700 years	Space Electric Rocket Test satellite
11 Feb.	Unidentified	330	150	*Thor-Burner 2*	543	874	480	773	98·71°	80 years	USAF satellite

US SATELLITES AND SPACECRAFT LAUNCHED SINCE 29 JUNE 1969, contd

Data in italics are approximate or estimated

Date	Name	Total weight lb	kg	Launch Vehicle	Apogee miles	km	Perigee miles	km	Inclin- ation	Lifetime	Remarks
4 Mar.	Unidentified	4,500	2,040	Long-tank T-A Thor-Agena D	160	258	104	167	88·02°	22 days	USAF satellite
	Unidentified	130	59		319	514	274	440	88·14°	18 months	Pickaback satellite ejected from above
20 Mar.	NATO I	258	117	T-A Delta	22,237	35,787	21,394	34,430	2·8°	Unlimited	NATO military communications satellite
8 April	Nimbus 4	1,367	620	Thorad-Agena D	685	1,112	680	1,094	99·89°	1,200 years	Advanced weather satellite
	TOPO 1	40	18		691	1,110	662	1,065	99·76°	1,000 years	US Army geodetic triangulation satellite
8 April	Vela 11	540	245	Titan IIIC	69,696	112,165	69,106	111,215	32·41°	Unlimited	Nuclear test detection satellites. Carry X-ray and particle detectors
	Vela 12	540	245		69,727	112,215	69,286	111,505	32·52°	Unlimited	
11 April	Apollo 13	—	—	Saturn V (SA.508)	—	—	—	—	—	6 days	Crew: J. Lovell, F. Haise, J. Swigert. Went round Moon, but landing cancelled owing to explosion
	LEM 7	—	—		—	—	—	—	—	6 days	Service Module. LM *Aquarius* used as 'lifeboat'
15 April	Unidentified	*6,600*	*2,994*	Titan IIIB-Agena D	241	387	81	130	110·97°	21 days	*Manoeuvrable reconnaissance satellite*
23 April	Intelsat 3G	302	137	Long-tank T-A Delta	22,249	35,807	22,233	35,781	0·7°	Unlimited	Communications satellite. Used own power to achieve synchronous orbit
20 May	Unidentified	—	—	*Long-tank T-A Thor-Agena D*	153	246	101	162	83·00°	28 days	USAF satellite
	Unidentified	—	—		313	504	305	490	83·12°	*2 years*	Ejected from above; has own motor
19 June	Unidentified	*2,000*	*907*	Atlas-Agena D	24,769	39,862	19,686	31,681	9·9°	Unlimited	*USAF early warning satellite*
25 June	Unidentified	*6,600*	*2,994*	Titan IIIB-Agena D	242	388	80	129	108·87°	14 days	*Manoeuvrable reconnaissance satellite*

THE UNION OF SOVIET SOCIALIST REPUBLICS

SOVIET RESEARCH PROJECTS

The information concerning recent research projects contained in the following notes is in almost all cases based on official Soviet news releases.

Full details of earlier Soviet satellites, space-probes and space-craft have appeared in the 1959-60 and subsequent editions of this work, together with descriptions of the A-2 and A-3 research rockets and meteorological rockets which are standard vehicles in constant use.

COSMOS SATELLITES

This series of satellites is continuing the Soviet programme for investigating the upper layers of the atmosphere and outer space, and includes a study of the following subjects: the concentration of charged particles in the ionosphere for the purpose of investigating the propagation of radio waves; corpuscular flows and low-energy particles; the energy composition of the Earth's radiation belts, for the purpose of further evaluating the radiation danger in prolonged space flights; the primary composition of cosmic rays and the variations in their intensity; the Earth's magnetic field; the short-wave radiation of the Sun and other celestial bodies; the upper layers of the atmosphere; the effects of meteoric matter on spacecraft materials; the distribution and formation of cloud patterns in the Earth's atmosphere. In addition, many details of spacecraft construction are being evaluated and refined.

The Mayak radio telemetering system operates on frequencies of around 20·000 and 90·000 megacycles.

The wide terms of reference means that a Cosmos satellite can vary from a small uninstrumented device to a large animal-carrying spacecraft. Cosmos 110, for example, was a sophisticated biological satellite carrying two dogs which were recovered successfully after a record 22 days in orbit at an apogee of 475 nm (547 miles; 880 km).

Cosmos 23 and others of the same type were used for first-stage trials of an electric power generation system. Cosmos 122 and others of its type were used to test the optical and general reliability of equipment.

Solar observation satellite of Cosmos 166/230 series (*Flight International*)

Other Cosmos satellites have been prototype meteorological satellites, preceding the operational Meteor spacecraft (which see).

Cosmos satellites in 49° and 56° orbits survive until natural decay occurs. Observations indicate that these are normally cylindrical in shape, approximately 6 ft (1·83 m) long by 3 ft 6 in (1·05 m) in diameter and weigh about 800 lb (360 kg).

COSMOS 186 and 188

Cosmos 186, launched on 27 October 1967, and Cosmos 188, launched on 30 October 1967, were used for an automatic rendezvous and docking experiment. Both satellites were equipped with special approach systems and docking units. After injection into orbit, Cosmos 186, the "active" partner, carried out a number of complicated manoeuvres, automatically finding its "passive" partner, Cosmos 188, drawing closer and finally docking rigidly. The satellites remained linked for 3½ hours and were then released. After separation the satellites manoeuvred into different orbits by the on-board propulsion systems. Cosmos 186 was recovered successfully after 65 orbits on 31 October and Cosmos 188 on 2 November.

The mission was described officially as marking a further step towards the creation of big scientific space stations and interplanetary spacecraft. The orbits of the two craft were remarkably similar to that of Soyuz 1, which crashed, killing Vladimir Komarov, and led to speculation that Cosmos 186 was an unmanned version of a manned spacecraft.

COSMOS 212 and 213

Cosmos 212, launched on 14 April 1968, and Cosmos 213, launched on 15 April, also docked automatically in space, remaining linked for 3 hours 50 minutes. Cosmos 212 was the "active" satellite and carried a TV camera to transmit pictures of the docking manoeuvre.

Left: **Cosmos 144 meteorological satellite** (*T.A.M.—Air et Cosmos*)

Unidentified Cosmos satellite (*Maurice Allward*)

COSMOS 215

Launched on 19 April 1968, Cosmos 215 is an astronomical observatory carrying eight small telescopes, and was placed in a comparatively low orbit so that it travels below the belts of charged particles surrounding the Earth. The small telescopes have mirrors 2·75 in (70 mm) in diameter, and are designed to observe the radiation of hot stars in various wavebands—from the visible part of the spectrum to the ultra-violet band. In addition, an X-ray telescope registers radiation in the region of the spectrum from 0·5 to 5 angstroms. The field of vision of the telescopes is about 1 degree. Because of this, in order to observe stars with a low intensity of radiation, the satellite's rotation was slowed down by a factor of one hundred, a special magnetic arresting system being used for this purpose.

An article in *Pravda* described the satellite as a first step towards placing a big telescope outside the confines of the Earth's atmosphere.

MILITARY COSMOS

As the table of Soviet satellites on page 688 indicates, there is strong evidence that Cosmos designations are given to Soviet reconnaissance satellites and other types of military spacecraft.

The reconnaissance satellites appear to be 7 ft 6 in (2·3 m) diameter spheres weighing about 7,000 lb (3,175 kg) and are normally launched at a rate of about two a month; the rate rises during periods of tension such as the armed clashes between Soviet and Chinese forces at Damanski Island in March 1969 and the border clash near Western Mongolia in June 1969.

Cosmos reconnaissance satellites are launched from the bases at Plesetsk and Tyuratam, those from Tyuratam being launched into orbits with inclinations of 52°, 65° or, for the majority, 72°. Most eject capsules after 8 days and these are presumably recovered. Some, such as Cosmos 228, have demonstrated the capacity for in-flight frequency changing; others, such as Cosmos 251, 264 and 280, had a small manoeuvring capability for more precise target coverage.

Cosmos 317 appears to have been the first of a new series of operational reconnaissance satellites with an 11-13 day life, instead of the 8 days of early versions. The longer flights could imply that the craft carry a larger film package. If so, the same coverage will be obtained with fewer launches. An unusual characteristic of some of the "longer-life" craft is the ejection of a capsule just before recovery. The ejected capsule goes into a slightly lower orbit, where it remains for several days until it decays naturally.

A number of test vehicles for the Soviet Union's Fractional Orbital Bombardment System have also apparently been given Cosmos designations.

COSMOS LAUNCHER

The vehicle used for the majority of Cosmos satellite launchings employs for first-stage propulsion a four-chamber liquid-propellant rocket engine designated RD-214. In service since 1962, this is a pump-fed engine, burning kerosene and nitric acid, and developing 161,000 lb (73,000 kg) st for lift-off (see "Engines" section).

Depending on the payload to be orbited, the Cosmos launcher is used in two-stage or three-stage form.

Artist's impression of automatic docking of Cosmos 186 and Cosmos 188, showing (1) docking units, (2) self-aligning and search aerials (3) solar cell panels and (4) radio aerials

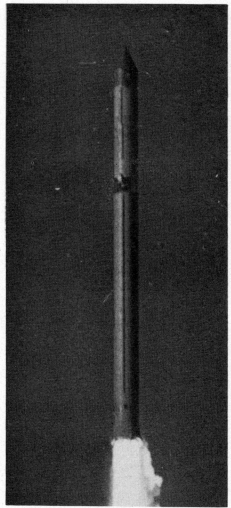

Launch vehicle for Intercosmos 1 communications satellite, 14 October 1969 (*Tass*)

Intercosmos 1 communications satellite with main solar cell panels folded for launch (*Tass*)

Full-scale representation of Molniya 1 communications satellite (*Flight International*)

INTERCOSMOS SATELLITES

Launched on 14 October 1969, **Intercosmos 1** involved the co-operation of seven Socialist countries, Bulgaria, Czechoslovakia, Germany (Democratic Republic), Hungary, Poland, Romania and the USSR. The satellite carries scientific instruments developed and made in Czechoslovakia and Germany as well as in the USSR. Its programme is devoted mainly to research connected with the Sun, and involves simultaneous observations in the seven participating countries into radio-astronomical, ionospheric and optical phenomena.

Instruments on board the satellite are designed to study that part of the spectrum (the extreme ultra-violet and X-ray radiation) which does not reach the surface of the Earth. A Soviet-developed X-ray spectro-heliograph determines where X-ray flares take place on the Sun, and an X-ray polarisation meter determines whether the X-ray radiation is polarised. Other instruments are studying the effects of this radiation on the structure of the upper layers of the Earth's atmosphere.

The programme is directed by a group of specialists from Czechoslovakia, Germany (Democratic Republic) and the USSR, the main solar experiments being supervised by Professor Sergei Mandelshtam.

Intercosmos 2, launched on 25 December 1969, is programmed to study the Earth's ionosphere, concentrations of electrons and positive ions, electronic temperature near the satellite, and the mean electron concentration between the satellite and ground receiving centres. The spacecraft instrumentation was made in Germany (Democratic Republic) and the Soviet Union to designs by scientists of Bulgaria, Czechoslovakia, Germany and the USSR. The Mayak radio transmitter was designed and made in Germany.

LUNA SPACECRAFT

Descriptions of the soft-landing Luna 9 and 13 and lunar-orbiting Luna 10, 12 and 14 spacecraft can be found in the 1968-69 *Jane's*.

Reference to the Luna 15 spacecraft, sent to the Moon at the time of America's Apollo 11 mission, appears in the 1969-70 edition.

METEOR

Meteor is the name given to the Soviet series of first-generation operational meteorological satellites, developed from a number of Cosmos prototypes (described in previous editions of *Jane's*).

The satellites, which provide information about the state of the atmosphere both on the "daylight" and "night" sides of the Earth, are stabilised so that the camera lenses and infra-red instruments always point towards the Earth. The resolving capacity of the cameras is claimed to be three times as good as those used on the US Tiros series of weather satellites.

Information received from Meteors is supplied to the Soviet hydro-meteorological service and to the World Meteorological Service. Cloud cover picture charts are transmitted to Washington, Geneva, Tokyo, Sydney and other foreign weather services.

Meteor 1 was launched on 26 March 1969; Meteor 2 on 6 October 1969; Meteor 3 on 17 March 1970 and Meteor 4 on 28 April 1970. Meteors 2, 3 and 4 were all operating satisfactorily in May 1970 and are placed in orbit in such a way as to pass the same area of the Earth's surface several hours apart.

MOLNIYA

Molniya 1 (Lightning), launched on 23 April 1965, was a communications satellite placed in a highly elliptical orbit designed to provide the longest possible communications sessions between Moscow and Vladivostok. It was the first Soviet communications satellite, and was in the form of a hermetically-sealed cylinder with conical ends, one end containing the correcting engine and a system of micro-jets, and the other end containing solar and Earth-orientation sensors. Six solar battery panels and two parabolic aerials were mounted on the central body. Also attached were the radiation surfaces of the temperature-control system comprising a radiation/refrigerator and a heating panel in the form of a flat ring, which also accommodated solar batteries.

During flight the satellite was orientated with its solar batteries facing the Sun and one of its aerials was directed simultaneously towards the Earth. Signals were transmitted in a relatively narrow beam, ensuring a strong reception at the surface of the Earth. The other aerial was in reserve, and for this to be used the satellite had to be rotated 180° longitudinally.

Other satellites in the Molniya series have included the 1B, launched on 14 October 1965; the 1C, launched on 25 April 1966; the 1D, launched on 20 October 1966; and the 1E, launched on 25 May 1967. The 1B and 1C were used for experimental colour television relays across the USSR and to France.

Molniya 1F, launched on 3 October 1967 and Molniya 1G, launched on 22 October 1967, were used in conjunction with one another for long-distance radio telecommunications, radio telegraphy and TV system experiments.

Molniya 1H, launched on 21 April 1968, is used for transmitting TV programmes to places in the Soviet Far North, Siberia, Far East and Central Asia covered by the Orbita network. Molniya 1J was launched on 5 July 1968, 5 1K on October and 1L on 11 April 1969.

Molniya can handle a television programme, a large number of telephone conversations, still pictures, telegraphic information and other forms of information.

PROTON 4

Proton 4 was launched on 16 November 1968 to continue the programme of research initiated by the earlier series of these craft. Weight of the spacecraft is 17 tons, of which 12½ tons represents equipment and experiments.

The aim of the Proton series is to study the nature of cosmic rays of high and super-high energies, and their inter-action with atomic nuclei. The programme for Proton 4 included studies of the energy spectrum and the chemical composition of cosmic rays. The programme also covers measurements of the possibility of collisions between particles of cosmic rays with the nuclei of the target's hydrogen, carbon and iron, and studies of the dynamics of collisions with the atomic nuclei of targets.

SOYUZ SPACECRAFT

Developed for the Russian Earth-orbital space station programme, Soyuz spacecraft are equipped for missions of up to 30 days duration.

Each spacecraft comprises three basic sections or modules: a laboratory-cum-rest compartment (orbital module), a descent compartment (landing module) and a propulsion and instrument section (service module). The orbital module is mounted on the extreme nose of the craft, and communicates with the landing module via a hermetically-sealed hatch. The orbital and landing modules are pressurised to 14 lb/sq in (1 kg/cm²), have a combined internal volume of 318 cu ft (9 m³) and can accommodate up to four cosmonauts.

The service module contains the main systems for orbital flight, together with a liquid-propellant propulsion system embodying two motors (one a stand-by) each with a thrust of 880 lb (400 kg). These allow mid-course manoeuvres, up to heights of 695 nm (800 miles; 1,300 km), and are used for the de-orbit manoeuvre. Another system provides attitude control. Attached to the service module is a solar-cell array having an area of about 150 sq ft (14 m²).

The landing module contains the parachutes and landing rockets. A back-up parachute system is available in case of failure. The main parachute, preceded by a pilot 'chute, is deployed at 27,000 ft (8,000 m). Retro-rockets, operating at a height of about 3 ft (1 m) above the ground, ensure a landing velocity not exceeding 10 ft/sec (3 m/sec). The aerodynamic design of the landing module permits landing loads to be kept within 3-4 g, although ballistic re-entries, involving loads of 8-10 g can be made if required. The overall length of the craft is about 30 ft (9 m), the diameter of the crew compartments about 7 ft (2·1 m) and the all-up weight about 13,000 lb (6.000 kg).

The Soyuz craft are equipped with an automatic control system for approach and docking manoeuvres, the technique and external aerials being similar to those employed on the Cosmos spacecraft 186 and 188, and 212 and 213.

Details of Soyuz 1 to 5 can be found in the 1969-70 *Jane's*. The following details refer to subsequent spacecraft in the series.

SOYUZ 6, 7 and 8

Soyuz spacecraft 6, 7 and 8 were launched within two days of each other and when in orbit rendezvoused, and carried out several group and individual scientific tasks, including a welding experiment. During the flight the emphasis seemed to be on manual control rather than on automatic procedures and manoeuvres.

Soyuz 6, carrying Lt Col Georgy Shonin (commander) and Valery Kubasov (flight engineer) was launched from the Baykonour complex at 12·10 BST on 11 October 1969. The tasks set for this crew included further development of the spacecraft and its systems, and the assessment of various methods of welding metals under vacuum and weightlessness, using equipment called Vulcan and weighing 110 lb (50 kg). In contrast to previous craft in the series, Soyuz 6 was not equipped for docking. The docking equipment and associated systems, such as the rendezvous radar, had been removed to allow for the increased volume and weight of equipment. The craft also carried a greater fuel load than normal to enable more extensive orbit manoeuvres to be made.

The second launch, of Soyuz 7, took place at 11·45 BST on the following day. This spacecraft was crewed by Lt Col Anatoly Filipchenko (commander), Vladislav Volkov (flight engineer) and Lt Col Victor Gorbatko (research engineer). The programme for Soyuz 7 was to conduct scientific and technical experiments in near-Earth space, to manoeuvre the craft in orbit and to make navigational observations of Soyuz 6 while in formation.

Soyuz 8 was launched at 11·29 BST on 13 October, carrying Vladimir Shatalov (commander) and Alexei Yeliseyev (flight engineer). Shatalov was also named as the overall group commander of the formation.

On 15 October, Soyuz 7 and 8 were manoeuvred to within 1,500 ft (460 m) of one another, this procedure being observed by Soyuz 6. Docking did not take place, although the three craft changed their orbits on 31 occasions.

On 16 October, Kubasov, in Soyuz 6, made the first experiment in molecular or cold welding. For this operation the orbital compartment was depressurised, the operation being remotely controlled from a panel in the command module. After a series of experiments the compartment was repressurised and the samples retrieved. Within a few hours of the experiment, Soyuz 6 re-entered the atmosphere and landed at 10·52 BST, 97 nm (112 miles; 180 km) north-east of Karaganda.

Soyuz 7 landed 83 nm (96 miles; 154 km) north-west of Karaganda at 10·26 BST on 17 October,

Full-scale replica of Proton-4 spacecraft in the Soviet Exhibition of Economic Achievements, Moscow (*Tass*)

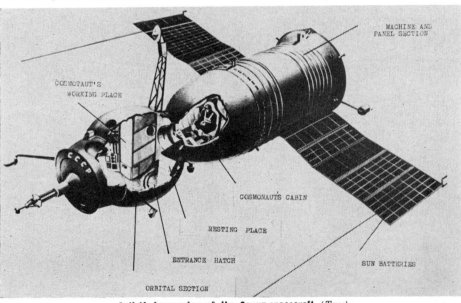

Artist's impression of the Soyuz spacecraft (*Tass*)

Soyuz-5 manned spacecraft on its launch rocket at Baykonour space centre, 15 January 1969
(*Tass*)

followed by Soyuz 8, at 10·10 BST on 18 October, the touch-down point being 78 nm (90 miles; 145 km) north of Karaganda.

The absence of a detailed flight plan of the type issued by America for their manned spaceflight missions makes it difficult to assess the degree of success achieved by the Soyuz group flight. The mission adequately demonstrated the capability of multiple close-spaced launches, indicating that three Soyuz-rated pads are in commission at Baykonour. No docking was achieved during the mission, and this may have implied a failure in this respect. That a docking was part of the programme is reinforced by the fact that Moscow issued officially pictures showing two Soyuz craft linked together during the early stages of the flight.

SOYUZ 9

This Earth-orbiting spacecraft was launched on 1 June 1970, carrying cosmonauts Col Andrian Nikolayev (who took part in the Vostok 3 flight in 1962) and engineer Vitaly Sevastyanov. A primary objective was to study the physical condition of the crew under prolonged periods in space, and Soyuz 9 was not recovered until 20 June, thereby establishing a new record for duration in Earth orbit. Its final descent, under a single parachute, was shown on Soviet television—the first time a Soviet spacecraft recovery had been seen.

SOYUZ LAUNCHER

The vehicle used for launching Soyuz spacecraft appears to be a development of the booster used for launching the Vostok and Voskhod craft, the development consisting of the insertion of some 36 ft (11·8 m) of additional upper staging or sections. To cater for the increased weight and bending moment the inter-stage truss is strengthened. During launch, the Soyuz vehicle is surmounted by an escape tower with three rows of rocket nozzles. Under the projecting domed fairing is a ring of eleven or twelve main nozzles, surmounted by four small vernier nozzles. At the base of the cylindrical section at the top is a ring of still-smaller nozzles of the kind seen around the tail of the "Frog-7" missile on page 634.

Official Soviet reports have stated that this vehicle has a total thrust of around 60 million horsepower, which is three times the power given in 1961 for the Vostok launcher.

VENUS 5

Launched on 5 January 1969, Venus 5 was substantially different from previous Venus spacecraft. Weighing 2,502 lb (1,135 kg), the craft embodied a new altimeter and improved internal electronic equipment. The landing module was extensively redesigned to withstand greater loads (up to 500 g) and higher pressures and temperatures. Based on information on the Venus atmosphere obtained from Venus 4, the area of the parachute was reduced by about two-thirds to reduce the descent time.

A mid-course correction manoeuvre was effected on 14 March and the craft reached the planet Venus on 16 May.

The initial 6·95 miles/sec (11·18 km/sec) velocity of the craft was reduced aerodynamically to 716 ft/sec (218 m/sec), at which speed landing module separation was initiated. While descending through the atmosphere, data on its pressure, density, temperature and chemical composition was returned continuously for a period of 53 minutes. During the descent the craft is also reported to have ejected a pennant displaying a hammer and sickle, and a portrait of Lenin.

VENUS 6

Forming the back-up craft to Venus 5, and of similar construction, Venus 6 was launched on 10 January 1969. It reached the planet Venus on 17 May, ejected its landing module some 185 miles (300 km) from Venus 5, and then transmitted data for about 50 minutes.

VENUS LAUNCHER

Although basically similar in configuration to the launchers used for the Soviet manned spacecraft, the launcher for the Venus probes appears to have elongated first and second stages, giving a considerable increase in propellant tankage.

VOSTOK LAUNCHER

A replica of the launch vehicle used to place in orbit Yuri Gagarin's Vostok 1 spacecraft, on 12 April 1961 was shown publicly for the first time at the 1967 Paris Air Show.

Most interesting technical feature of the vehicle was the use of four tapered liquid-propellant wrap-round boosters, each with four primary nozzles and two verniers. The central sustainer had four primary nozzles and four verniers. Thus, no fewer than 32 rocket chambers were fired simultaneously at take-off. Official Soviet statements have claimed that the total thrust of these engines was 1,323,000 lb (600,000 kg), but this probably represents the figure for thrust in vacuo, the S/L static rating being as much as 20% lower. All primary nozzles were fixed, the verniers being used for control, supplemented by a small delta-shape aerodynamic control surface at the base of each booster.

Display representing orbital space station made up of Soyuz 4 and Soyuz 5 spacecraft, at the Soviet Economic Achievements Exhibition, Moscow (*Tass*)

Soyuz 9 command module just after its return to Earth, 20 June 1970 (*Tass*)

One of the booster engines, designated RD-107, was displayed in sectioned form and is described in the "Aero-Engines" section of this edition. It was stated to utilise liquid oxygen and kerosene propellants and to develop 224,870 lb (102,000 kg) st *in vacuo*.

The first stage of the central sustainer "core" was a slim cylinder which flared out into a larger diameter at the top (or front) end. This unusual geometry allowed the conical boosters to fit snugly against it. The second stage, carrying the spacecraft payload, was attached to the sustainer by a truss arrangement similar to that used on the "Scrag" ICBM. As the basic diameter of the "core" was in the same order as that of "Scrag", it justified official Soviet references to the ICBM as being a sister vehicle of the Vostok launcher.

The second stage was powered by a liquid-propellant engine with a single primary nozzle and four verniers. This bore out the correctness of the original Soviet statement in 1961 that the Vostok launch vehicle had six engines, of which five fired at lift-off.

Designer of the vehicle was the late S. Korolev. It was used for all six Vostok launchings and, with second-stage modifications, for the two Voskhod spacecraft.

At the Paris Air Show, the Vostok launcher was displayed on a large rail-mounted transporter-erector truck of the type reportedly used at the Baikonour cosmodrome from which Russia's manned space launchings are made.

Replica of landing capsule parachuted on to Venus by Venus 5 and 6 spacecraft
(*Flight International*)

DIMENSIONS:
Length overall   124 ft 8½ in (38 m)
Length of second stage, with payload fairing
     32 ft 10 in (10 m)

Close-up of rocket chambers of Vostok launcher *(Maurice Allward)*

Left: **Full-scale mock-up of Venus spacecraft** *(Flight International)*

Length of each booster	62 ft 3½ in (19 m)
Max diameter:	
first-stage sustainer	9 ft 8½ in (2·95 m)
second stage	8 ft 6 in (2·60 m)
boosters (each)	9 ft 10 in (3·00 m)
Overall diameter, over fins	34 ft 0 in (10·3 m)

WEIGHT:
Vostok spacecraft, incl pilot 10,400 lb (4,725 kg)

VOSKHOD LAUNCHER

The first stage of the Voskhod launch vehicle is believed to have been almost identical with that of the Vostok launcher, except that the portion of the core vehicle between the top of the booster and the inter-stage truss structure was cylindrical instead of tapered. This presumably indicated an increase in propellant tankage.

The second stage, in addition to being lengthened to some 20 ft (6 m), is believed to have embodied a twin-chamber rocket engine developing around 308,650 lb (140,000 kg) st.

Replica of Vostok launch vehicle displayed at 1967 Paris Air Show *(Maurice Allward)*

YANTAR 1

Launched by means of a geophysical rocket, Yantar 1 was an automatic ionospheric laboratory embodying a plasma-ion engine powered by argon gas. It has also been used to investigate the possibility of guided flight in the upper layers of the atmosphere at altitudes of 52-220 nm (60-250 miles; 100 to 400 km).

During one reported test, the craft's principal task was to investigate the intricate inter-relations between the ionic jet and the partially ionised low-temperature plasma of the Earth's ionosphere. Measurements were taken of the interaction between the jet and the atmosphere and the results telemetered to Earth. These data make it possible to estimate the electrical potential acquired by the apparatus under the effect of the ionic jet.

The engine was switched on automatically during the test, at an altitude of about 86 nm (100 miles; 160 km). While the craft reached its peak altitude of 215 nm (250 miles; 400 km) and during the descent, the engine was switched on and off 11 times. Measurements taken indicate that the plasma-ion engine developed an exhaust velocity of 21·5 nm/sec (25 miles/sec; 40 km/sec).

Left:
Yantar-1 ionospheric research rocket. Stage at left may be one of the Yantar payloads to study controlled flight in the upper atmosphere *(Tass)*

Right:
Venus launch vehicle inside servicing gantry *(Tass)*

SOVIET SATELLITES LAUNCHED SINCE 20 MAY 1969

Note: The USSR has withheld information on several launchings and this list may be incomplete
Data in italics are approximate or estimated

Date	Name	Total weight lb	Total weight kg	Apogee miles	Apogee km	Perigee miles	Perigee km	Inclination	Lifetime	Remarks
1969										
27 May	Cosmos 283	—	—	956	1,539	130	210	82°	—	Continued Cosmos programme
29 May	Cosmos 284	—	—	191	308	128	206	51·8°	8 days	*Reconnaissance satellite. Recovered?*
3 June	Cosmos 285	—	—	322	518	173	279	71°	—	Continued Cosmos programme
15 June	Cosmos 286	—	—	217	349	128	206	65·4°	8 days	*Reconnaissance satellite. Recovered?*
24 June	Cosmos 287	—	—	166	268	118	190	51·8°	8 days	*Reconnaissance satellite. Recovered?*
27 June	Cosmos 288	—	—	174	281	125	201	51·8°	8 days	*Reconnaissance satellite. Recovered?*
10 July	Cosmos 289	*9,000*	*4,080*	202	325	121	195	65·4°	5 days	*Reconnaissance satellite. Recovered?*
13 July	Luna 15	—	—	—	—	—	—	—	8 days	Tested new automatic navigation systems. Impacted Moon 21 July
22 July	Cosmos 290	—	—	219	352	124	200	65·4°	8 days	*Reconnaissance satellite. Recovered?*
22 July	Molniya 1 M	2,200	998	24,570	39,540	323	520	64·9°	—	Communications satellite
6 Aug.	Cosmos 291	—	—	356	574	95	153	62·3°	34 days	*Fractional Orbital Bombardment System test*
8 Aug.	Zond 7	*6,000*	*2,720*	—	—	—	—	—	6 days	Successfully recovered after orbiting Moon
14 Aug.	Cosmos 292	—	—	488	786	464	747	74°	100 years	*Navigational satellite*
16 Aug.	Cosmos 293	—	—	168	270	129	208	51·8°	12 days	*Reconnaissance satellite. Recovered?*
19 Aug.	Cosmos 294	—	—	216	348	125	202	65·4°	8 days	*Reconnaissance satellite. Recovered?*
22 Aug.	Cosmos 295	900	408	311	500	175	282	71°	Down 1 Dec.	Continued Cosmos programme
29 Aug.	Cosmos 296	—	—	200	322	131	211	65°	8 days	*Reconnaissance satellite. Recovered?*
2 Sept.	Cosmos 297	—	—	207	334	131	211	72·9°	8 days	*Reconnaissance satellite. Recovered?*
15 Sept.	Cosmos 298	—	—	131	211	87	140	50°	*1 orbit*	*Fractional Orbital Bombardment System test*
18 Sept.	Cosmos 299	—	—	193	311	133	214	65°	4 days	*Reconnaissance satellite. Recovered?*
23 Sept.	Cosmos 300	—	—	129	208	118	190	51·5°	4 days	*Lunar satellite failure*
24 Sept.	Cosmos 301	—	—	191	307	122	197	65·4°	8 days	*Reconnaissance satellite. Recovered?*
6 Oct.	Meteor 2	—	—	429	690	391	630	81·2°	60 years	Operational meteorological satellite.
11 Oct.	Soyuz 6	13,000	5,900	144	232	119	191	51·68°	Down 16 Oct.	Crew: G. Shonin and V Kubasov. Conducted welding experiments while in orbit
12 Oct.	Soyuz 7	13,000	5,900	139	224	131	211	51·65°	Down 17 Oct.	Crew: A. Filipchenko, V. Volkov and V. Gorbatko. Rendezvoused with Soyuz 6
13 Oct.	Soyuz 8	13,000	5,900	141	227	125	201	51·65°	Down 18 Oct.	Crew: V. Shatalov and A. Yeliseyev. Rendezvoused with Soyuz 6 and 7
14 Oct.	Intercosmos 1	—	—	398	640	161	260	48·4°	Down Jan 2, 1970	International socialist satellite; studying sun phenomena
17 Oct.	Cosmos 302	—	—	211	340	125	202	65·4°	8 days	*Reconnaissance satellite. Recovered?*
18 Oct.	Cosmos 303	—	—	307	492	175	282	71°	14 weeks	Continued Cosmos programme
21 Oct.	Cosmos 304	—	—	481	774	464	747	74°	100 years	*Navigational satellite*
23 Oct.	Cosmos 305	—	—	127	205	120	193	51·5°	2 days	*Lunar satellite failure*
24 Oct.	Cosmos 306	—	—	206	332	129	208	65°	12 days	*Reconnaissance satellite. Recovered?*
24 Oct.	Cosmos 307	—	—	1,353	2,178	136	220	48·4°	15 months	Continued Cosmos programme
4 Nov.	Cosmos 308	—	—	262	422	174	281	71°	Down 4 Jan '70	Continued Cosmos programme
12 Nov.	Cosmos 309	—	—	226	364	115	185	65·4°	8 days	*Reconnaissance satellite. Recovered?*
15 Nov.	Cosmos 310	—	—	209	336	127	204	65·0°	8 days	*Reconnaissance satellite. Recovered?*
24 Nov	Cosmos 311	—	—	308	496	176	284	71°	12 weeks	Continued Cosmos programme
24 Nov	Cosmos 312	—	—	737	1,187	711	1,145	74°	2,500 years	*Navigational satellite*
3 Dec	Cosmos 313	—	—	171	276	127	204	65·4°	12 days	*Reconnaissance satellite. Recovered?*
11 Dec.	Cosmos 314	—	—	305	491	175	282	71°	14 weeks	Continued Cosmos programme
20 Dec.	Cosmos 315	—	—	345	556	323	521	74°	15 years	*Navigational satellite*
23 Dec.	Cosmos 316	—	—	1,025	1,650	95	154	49·5°	8 months	Purpose unknown
23 Dec.	Cosmos 317	—	—	187	302	130	209	65·4°	13 days	*Reconnaissance satellite. Recovered?*
25 Dec.	Intercosmos 2	—	—	746	1,200	128	206	48·4°	3 months	International socialist satellite, studying ionosphere
1970										
9 Jan.	Cosmos 318	—	—	183	295	128	204	65°	12 days	*Extended flight reconnaissance satellite*
15 Jan.	Cosmos 319	—	—	955	1,537	130	209	82°	—	Continued Cosmos programme
16 Jan	Cosmos 320	—	—	212	342	149	240	48·5°	—	Continued Cosmos programme
21 Jan.	Cosmos 321	—	—	315	507	174	280	71°	—	Continued Cosmos programme
21 Jan.	Cosmos 322	—	—	209	337	124	200	65·4°	8 days	*Reconnaissance satellite*
10 Feb.	Cosmos 323	—	—	207	333	128	206	65·4°	8 days	*Reconnaissance satellite*
20 Feb.	Molniya 1 N	2,200	998	24,342	39,175	302	487	65·3°	—	Communications satellite; first from Plesetsk
28 Feb.	Cosmos 324	—	—	306	492	176	283	71°	—	Continued Cosmos programme
4 Mar.	Cosmos 325	—	—	215	348	128	207	65·4°	8 days	*Reconnaissance satellite*
13 Mar.	Cosmos 326	—	—	244	393	131	212	81·4°	8 days	*Reconnaissance satellite*
17 Mar.	Meteor 3	—	—	643	400	345	555	81·2°	—	Operational meteorological satellite
18 Mar.	Cosmos 327	—	—	531	855	173	279	71°	—	Continued Cosmos programme
27 Mar.	Cosmos 328	—	—	211	340	132	213	72·9°	12 days	Reconnaissance satellite?
3 April	Cosmos 329	—	—	149	240	125	202	81·3°	12 days	*Extended flight reconnaissance satellite*
7 April	Cosmos 330	—	—	340	548	319	514	74·1°	—	—
8 April	Cosmos 331	—	—	216	347	132	213	65°	8 days	*Reconnaissance satellite*
13 April	Cosmos 332	—	—	488	786	469	755	74·5°	15 days	Reconnaissance satellite?
15 April	Cosmos 333	—	—	164	265	135	217	81·4°	—	—
23 April	Cosmos 334	—	—	315	508	174	281	71°	—	Continued Cosmos programme
25 April	Cosmos 335	—	—	258	415	158	254	48·7°	—	
25 April	Cosmos 336-343	—	—	932	1,500	870	1,400	74°	—	First Soviet multiple launch of 8 satellites by a single rocket
28 April	Meteor 4	—	—	—	—	—	—	—	—	Operational meteorological satellite

AERO-ENGINES

(CORRECTED TO I AUGUST 1970)

AUSTRALIA

CAC
COMMONWEALTH AIRCRAFT CORPORATION PTY, LTD

HEAD OFFICE AND WORKS:
304, Lorimer Street, Port Melbourne, Victoria
OFFICERS: See "Aircraft" section

The engine activities of the Commonwealth Aircraft Corporation are centred on licensed-manufacture of the SNECMA Atar 09C and Rolls-Royce Viper 11 turbojets (full descriptions of which appear under the SNECMA and Rolls-Royce entries, respectively, of this edition. These engines power Australian-built Mirage III-O fighters and Australian-built Aermacchi M.B. 326H training aircraft. Overhaul of the Atar, Viper and Rolls-Royce Avon Mks 1, 26 and 109 turbojets is also undertaken.

CAC has been engaged in engine manufacture since 1939 and details of its total production can be found in the 1964-65 *Jane's*.

The Commonwealth Aircraft Corporation-built Viper 11 turbojet (2,500 lb = 1,134 kg st)

The Commonwealth Aircraft Corporation-built Atar 09C turbojet (14,110 lb = 6,400 kg st)

BELGIUM

FN
FABRIQUE NATIONALE D'ARMES DE GUERRE, SA

HEAD OFFICE AND WORKS:
B-4400 Herstal-lez-Liège

FN has now begun licensed-manufacture of the SNECMA Atar 09C turbojet for Belgian-built Mirage 5B fighter-bombers. The production programme is in collaboration with SNECMA and Fairey SA. FN also participates in licensed manufacture of the Rolls-Royce Tyne 21 and 22 turboprops in co-operation with Rolls-Royce, MTU and SNECMA (Hispano Suiza) to power Breguet Atlantic maritime reconnaissance aircraft and Transall C-160 transports. Details of these engines are given under the SNECMA and Rolls-Royce entries, respectively, of this edition.

FN maintains and repairs General Electric J79-GE-11A turbojets which the company produced in association with MAN Turbo (now MTU) in Germany and Fiat in Italy to power F-104G fighters in service with NATO air forces. Other repair and overhaul work concerns Turboméca Marboré 2F turbojets, and the control and accessory components of Orenda 11 turbojets.

In addition, FN manufactures under licence and repairs Steward Davis (ex Boeing) and Caterpillar gas-turbines in the 400 to 500 hp (406-507 cv) range. The Steward Davis/Boeing Models 551 and 553 are turboshaft engines respectively rated at 400 and 490 shp; FN also overhauls and repairs the Boeing 502-12B turbostarter.

CANADA

ORENDA
ORENDA LTD

HEAD OFFICE AND WORKS:
Malton, Ontario
POSTAL ADDRESS:
Box 6001, Toronto International Airport, Ontario
PRESIDENT: F. P. Mitchell
VICE-PRESIDENT: J. Turner
DIRECTOR OF ENGINEERING:
B. A. Avery
OPERATIONS MANAGER: W. G. Eves
MILITARY SALES AND CONTRACTS MANAGER:
D. J. Caple
TREASURER: K. R. Church

Orenda Ltd was formed in November 1966 as a company owned 60 per cent by Hawker Siddeley Canada Ltd and 40 per cent by United Aircraft Corporation, USA, and comprising the former Orenda and Engineering Divisions of Hawker Siddeley, Canada. Main activities of the company are the manufacture of aircraft turbine engines and components, and industrial gas-turbine units.

Current production programmes include licensed manufacture of the General Electric J85-15 turbojet engines for Canadian-built Northrop CF-5 fighters for the RCAF and NF-5 for the Royal Netherlands Air Force. Concurrently, Orenda is overhauling J79-7, J85-CAN-40 and -15 and Orenda turbojet engines. It has spares contracts with Canada, West Germany, the Netherlands, Pakistan, Belgium and South Africa and is engaged in sub-contract work for Pratt & Whitney and other US manufacturers.

Orenda, although associated with United Aircraft of Canada Ltd through the United Aircraft Corporation, operates a fully independent work programme. It does not at present envisage manufacturing aero-engines to its own design, and its future operations will depend on Canadian military requirements.

The Orenda-built J85-CAN-15 turbojet (4,300 lb = 1,950 kg st with afterburning)

ORENDA/GENERAL ELECTRIC J85-15

The version of the J85 being produced by Orenda to power the Canadair-built CF-5 and NF-5 is the J85-CAN-15. Details are the same as for the General Electric J85-GE-15. Deliveries began in 1967.

UACL

UNITED AIRCRAFT OF CANADA LTD

HEAD OFFICE AND WORKS:
PO Box 10, Longueuil, Quebec

PRESIDENT:
T. E. Stephenson

VICE-PRESIDENTS:
R. H. Guthrie (Industrial & Marine Division)
A. C. Kennedy (Personnel)
R. G. Raven (Helicopter & Systems Division)
E. L. Smith (Operations)
E. H. Schweitzer (Product Support)
K. H. Sullivan (Marketing)
V. W. Tryon (Finance)

UACL is a major subsidiary of the United Aircraft Corporation, Connecticut, USA, and was formed originally to manufacture and overhaul reciprocating engines and spare parts designed by UAC's Pratt & Whitney Aircraft Division. In 1957 its activities were enlarged to include design and development of turbine engines and by 1963, when the company's name was changed from Canadian Pratt & Whitney Aircraft Ltd to its present form, its operations had been expanded to embrace the manufacture, overhaul and marketing of products of all Divisions of the United Aircraft Corporation. Today UACL is the prime source of manufacture and spare parts production for all Pratt & Whitney reciprocating engines.

Original turbine work by the company was initiated by the concept and preliminary design of the JT12 (J60) turbojet, development and manufacture of which were taken over subsequently by Pratt & Whitney Aircraft. Design, development and manufacture of the PT6, ST6, PT6T and JT15D series of small turbine aero engines represents 55 per cent of the company's activities.

Research and development programmes underway at UACL include work on high pressure ratio, high efficiency centrifugal compressors; high Mach No, high work axial compressor stages; high work capacity radial turbines for operation at 2,300°F (1,533°K) entry temperature; and very high work output axial turbines.

Owned 90 per cent by the United Aircraft Corporation, the Canadian company achieved a sales turnover in 1969 in excess of $120 million compared with $34 million in 1960. Approximately 40 per cent of sales are linked to defence requirements and three-quarters of all output is exported.

UACL occupies 1,490,000 sq ft (138,455 m²) of space in six plants and employs more than 5,200 persons.

UNITED AIRCRAFT OF CANADA JT15D

Following a comprehensive performance study of small turbofan engines carried out by UACL during 1965, detail design of a definitive engine, the 2,000 lb to 2,500 lb JT15D, was initiated in June 1966. First run of the new turbofan was on 23 September 1967, within eight days of the target set at the start of design. The engine exceeded its rated thrust on its second build in November 1967 and achieved its guaranteed sfc in May 1968. Flight testing of the JT15D in a nacelle under a modified Avro CF-100 test-bed aircraft started on 22 August 1968.

By April 1970, with all phases of the development programme on schedule, eight engines had completed more than 5,000 hr bench testing and 600 hr flight testing, including several 50 hr preflight rating tests and flight to 48,000 ft and Mach 0·8. In 1969 T-O thrust was raised from an initial 2,000 lb to 2,200 lb at an sfc of only 0·504.

Intended to power business aircraft, small transports and counter-insurgency combat aircraft in the 8,000 lb to 12,500 lb AUW category, the JT15D is an advanced technology two-spool front-fan engine having a minimum number of aerodynamic components. Major design objectives were a significant improvement in sfc, and simplicity of construction to ensure low first cost and maintenance costs. Other objectives were low noise levels, ease of handling, and the attainment of airline standards of reliability.

In configuration the engine comprises a single-stage titanium fan without inlet guide vanes, driven by a two-stage LP turbine, a single-stage centrifugal compressor driven by a single-stage HP turbine, and an annular reverse-flow combustion system. The design of the fan is similar to that of the large Pratt & Whitney JT9D turbofan and provides low noise levels, and good foreign-object-damage and flow distortion tolerance. Fan stators and nose bullet are anti-iced.

By-pass ratio ranges from 3 : 1 to 3·3 : 1 depending on rating; mass flow is 82 lb (37·2 kg)/sec, and turbine entry temperatures are moderate. The pressure ratio of almost 10 : 1 benefits from research work by UACL on high pressure ratio, high efficiency centrifugal compressors carried out under contract to the Canadian Government.

A full-length by-pass duct simplifies installation, and airframe-supplied inlet and exhaust ducts may be cantilevered from the engine flanges. The engine may be pod or fuselage mounted from either side. Two main mounts are situated on the intake casing and a single steady mount is located off the fan turbine structure. Port and starboard engines can be interchanged. All controls, including the single-lever fully-compensated fuel control, and accessories are grouped at the bottom of the engine for ease of accessibility.

Initial application for the engine is the new Cessna Citation twin-engined business jet for which Cessna has ordered 2,200 lb JT15D-1s valued at approximately $10 m. Flight-worthy prototype engines were delivered in August 1969 for the Citation's first flight in mid-September. Cessna anticipates selling a minimum of 1,000 Citations during the first ten years of production. Second application is in the prototype Aérospatiale SN 600 Corvette twin-engined business jet for which JT15D-1s were delivered on schedule in September 1969. Other possible applications are the twin-engined Dassault Mystère 10 military communications aircraft, the twin-engined North American Rockwell SabreCommuter, the Beechcraft-Hawker BH.200 and two Beech Aircraft turbofan proposals for 1973—the 18-seat F1 with three JT15Ds and the 24-seat F2 with four JT15Ds.

Civil certification of the JT15D-1 and production deliveries are scheduled for early 1971. The TBO on entry into service is expected to be 1,500 hr. Future thrust growth of the engine is under study.

The following data relate to the JT15D-1:

DIMENSIONS:
Height | 32·97 in (837 mm)

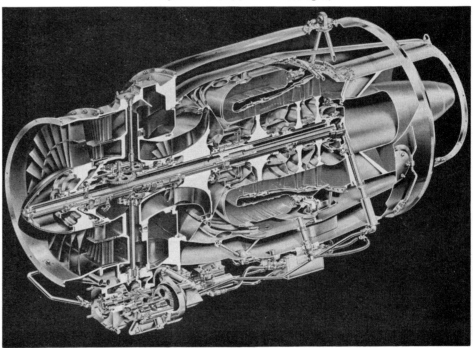

Exhibition mock-up (*above*) **and cutaway drawing** (*below*) **of the United Aircraft of Canada JT15D-1 twin-spool turbofan (2,200 lb = 998 kg st)**

Width	27·55 in (700 mm)
Length overall	60·40 in (1,534 mm)

WEIGHT, DRY:
With standard equipment | 482 lb (219 kg)

PERFORMANCE RATINGS:
T-O	2,200 lb (998 kg) st
Max continuous and climb	2,090 lb (948 kg) st
Cruise	1,980 lb (898 kg) st

FUEL CONSUMPTION:
At T-O rating	0·504
At max continuous and climb ratings	0·503
At cruise rating	0·501

UNITED AIRCRAFT OF CANADA PT6A

The PT6A, UACL's major commercial product, is a lightweight, low consumption free-turbine turboprop. By May 1969 more than 4,300 engines had been ordered, some 2,950 of which had been delivered. With a total flight time of 2,150,000 hr, powering 1,050 aircraft of 62 different types, the PT6 is in service with 540 operators in 48 different countries. With 17 different certificated airframe applications, the PT6A series power 78 per cent of all light twin-turboprop aircraft in the West. Maximum TBO in commuter-type aircraft is 3,000 hr.

An experimental PT6 ran for the first time in November 1959 and flight trials of the turboprop in the nose of a modified Beechcraft 18 began in May 1961. Civil certification of the first production model, the 578 ehp PT6A-6, was granted in late 1963. Progressively higher rated versions have followed in production to power a wide variety of single and twin-engined aircraft, and deliveries are being made at a rate in excess of 100 engines a month. Development, which to date has cost $45 million including $14·5 million from the Canadian Department of Industry, is currently proceeding on models rated up to 1,200 ehp.

Related series of engines include the T74 military turboprop, the PT6B commercial turboshaft, PT6T coupled turboshaft, T400 military coupled engine, and the ST6 series of APU, industrial and marine engines. Technology from the PT6/ST6 family has also been embodied in UACL's new JT15D turbofan.

In December 1968, MAN Turbo acquired an option for licensed manufacture of the PT6A-27 turboprop in Germany.

PT6A-6. Flat rated at 578 ehp (550 shp) at 2,200 propeller rpm to 70°F (21°C), this version received civil certification in December 1963. A total of 350 PT6A-6s were built between then and November 1965. Among aircraft powered by the PT6A-6 are the de Havilland Aircraft of Canada Turbo-Beaver and early DHC-6 Twin Otter Series 100.

PT6A-20. Flat rated at 579 ehp (550 shp) at 2,200 propeller rpm to 70°F (21°C), the -20 offers improved reliability and increases in max continuous, max climb and max cruise power ratings over the PT6A-6. The PT6A-20 was certificated in October 1965. Between then and March 1969 more than 2,300 were built. The PT6A-20 continues in production at a rate of 100 engines a month to power such aircraft as the Beech King Air B90, Beech Model 99 Commuter Liner, Centro Technico de Aeronautica IPD-6504 Bandeirante, de Havilland Aircraft of Canada DHC-6 Twin Otter Series 100 and 200, James Aviation (Fletcher FU-24) conversion, Marshall of Cambridge (Grumman Goose) conversion, Mc-Kinnon G-21C and G-21D Turbo-Goose (Grumman Goose), Pilatus PC-6-B1/H2 Turbo-Porter, Pilatus PC-7 Turbo-Trainer, Piper Navajo and the Swearingen Merlin IIA (which can be re-engined with the PT6A-27).

A further application using the PT6A-20 as a gas generator is the Dornier Do 132 light utility helicopter with hot-gas tip-drive rotor system, development of which is proceeding under a DM9 million German Defence Ministry contract. The turbine exhaust gases are ducted to the rotor head where they pass down the rotor blades to tip jet nozzles.

PT6A-27. Third production version of the PT6A, this version is flat rated at 715 ehp (680 shp) at 2,200 propeller rpm to 71°F (22°C). Its higher ratings are attained by a 12½ per cent increase in mass flow provided by a larger-diameter compressor. The increased airflow enables the higher power to be obtained at lower turbine temperatures than in the PT6A-20. Production began in November 1967 and 175 engines had been delivered by March 1969. Production continues. Applications of the PT6A-27 include the American Turbine Westwind (Beech 18) conversion, Beech Model 97, Beech Model 99A Commuter Liner, projected Beech four-engined light commuter transport, Beech U-21A, de Havilland Aircraft of Canada DHC-6 Twin Otter Series 300, Fairchild Hiller/Pilatus PC-6-B1/H2 Porter, Frakes Aviation (Grumman Mallard) conversion, Israel Aircraft Industries Arava, Let L-410 Turbolet, Pacific Airmotive PAC-1 Commuter-liner, Piper Navajo, projected Saab 1071, Saunders Aircraft ST-27 (de Havilland Heron) conversion and Socata Sherpa.

PT6A-28. Similar to the PT6A-27 and with the same T-O and max continuous ratings, this version has an additional normal cruise rating of 652 ehp available up to 69°F (21°C) corresponding to the max cruise rating conditions of the -27. In addition the max cruise rating of the -28 gives 652 ehp up to the higher ambient of 91°F (33°C). This model, which operates at higher turbine entry temperatures than the -27, is in production for the new Beech Model 100 King Air.

PT6A-29. Company designation for military counterpart of the PT6A-27 which received civil certification in Spring of 1968.

PT6A-30. Rated at 940 ehp, this version has been proposed to power the US Army's new advanced surveillance aircraft (ASA). Features include air-cooled turbine nozzle guide vanes to enable operation at higher turbine entry temperatures.

PT6A-40. This higher mass flow version embodies air-cooled stage-one nozzle guide vanes and a two-stage free turbine (in place of the previous single-stage unit) to give improved power absorption. Length is thus increased by 4 in (100 mm) to 66 in (1,676 mm). The -40 has a T-O rating of 903 ehp (850 shp) at 1,700 to 2,000 propeller rpm, available up to 111°F (44°C). Development is under way for potential applications such as the projected General Aircraft GAC-100 commuter airliner, advanced turboprop commuter aircraft being studied by Beech, and the US Army's ASA project.

PT6A-50. Similar to the PT6A-40 and under development at higher ratings with a longer, higher-ratio reduction gear to give a significantly

The 715 ehp United Aircraft of Canada PT6A-27 free-turbine turboshaft

lower propeller tip speed for quieter operation at T-O. Length is consequently increased to 70 in (1,778 mm). Rating at T-O is 1,088 ehp (1,035 shp) available up to 93°F (34°C) at propeller speeds from 1,210 down to 1,070 rpm. The PT6A-50 is planned to power the projected de Havilland Aircraft of Canada DHC-7 "Quiet STOL" transport.

Other aircraft powered by the PT6A turboprop include the Aircraft of Canada Jobmaster (Beech 18) conversion, Beech MU-8F, Potez 841 and a proposed four-engined search-and-rescue conversion of the Grumman Albatross.

The following data apply generally to the PT6A series:

TYPE: Free-turbine axial-plus-centrifugal turboprop engine.

PROPELLER DRIVE (PT6A-6, PT6A-20, PT6A-27): Two-stage planetary gear train. Ratio 15 : 1. Rotation clockwise when viewed from rear. Drive from free turbine. Flanged propeller shaft. Plain bearings. Higher ratio reduction gear developed for PT6A-50.

AIR INTAKE: Annular air intake at rear of engine, with intake screen. Aircraft-supplied alcohol anti-icing system or inertial separation anti-icing system.

COMPRESSOR: Three axial-flow stages, plus single centrifugal stage. Single-sided centrifugal compressor, with 26 vanes, made from titanium forging. Stainless steel pipe diffuser on PT6A-27. Axial rotor of disc-drum type, with stainless steel stator and rotor blades. The stator vanes (44 first-stage, 44 second-stage, 40 third-stage) are brazed to casing. The rotor blades (32 first-stage, 32 second-stage and 32 third-stage) are dove-tailed to discs. Discs through-bolted, with centrifugal compressor, to shaft. Fabricated one-piece stainless steel casing and radial diffuser. PT6A-27: compression ratio 6·7 : 1, air mass flow 6·8 lb/sec (3·1 kg/sec).

COMBUSTION CHAMBER: Annular reverse-flow type of stainless steel construction, with 14 simplex burners around periphery of chamber. All versions except PT6A-27 have two glow plug igniters, 64° each side of vertical centre-line on lower surface. PT6A-27 has one plug at 64° on starboard side of vertical centre-line and one at 90° on port side.

FUEL SYSTEM: Bendix DP-F2 pneumatic automatic fuel control system. Pneumatic computing section, with automatic inlet air temperature compensation, fuel metering and regulating section, gas generator governor and free turbine governor. PT6A-27 and subsequent models have a dual manifold with seven nozzles per manifold. Maximum fuel pressure 800 lb/sq in (56·25 kg/cm²).

FUEL GRADE: Commercial jet fuels JP-1, JP-4, JP-5, Mil-J-5624. Use of aviation gasolines (Mil-G-5572) grades 80/87, 91/98, 100/130 and 115/145 permitted for a period of up to 150 hours during any overhaul period.

NOZZLE GUIDE VANES: 29 nozzle guide vanes.

TURBINES: Two single-stage axial-flow turbines. LP turbine drives output shaft. Blades (58 first stage, 41 second stage) attached by "fir-tree" roots. PT6A-40 and -50 have stage-one air-cooled nozzle guide vanes, and two-stage power turbine.

BEARINGS: Each main rotor (gas generator and free turbine) supported by one ball and one roller anti-friction bearing.

JET PIPE: Collector duct surrounding free-turbine shaft, exhaust through two ports on horizontal centre-line.

ACCESSORIES: Mounting pads on accessory case (rear of engine) for starter-generator, hydraulic pump, aircraft accessory drive, vacuum pump and tachometer-generator. Mounting pad on the shaft-turbine reduction gear case for propeller overspeed governor, propeller constant-speed control unit and tachometer generator.

All accessories mount on the ends of the engine and do not protrude beyond the major diameter of the engine.

LUBRICATION SYSTEM: One pressure and four scavenge elements in the pump stacks. All are gear type and are driven by the gas generator rotor. Engine has an integral oil tank with a capacity of 2·3 US gallons (8·75 litres). Oil supply pressure is 65 lb/sq in (4·57 kg/cm²).

OIL SPECIFICATION: UACL Spec 202 (7·5 cs vis) (Mil-L-23699, Mil-L-7808 for military engines).

MOUNTING: Turboprop has three-point ring suspension. Turboshaft has two main pads and one steady pad.

STARTING: Electric starter-generator on accessory case.

DIMENSIONS:

Max diameter	19 in (483 mm)

Length, less accessories:

PT6A-6, -20, -27, -28	62 in (1,575 mm)
PT6A-40	66 in (1,676 mm)
PT6A-50	70 in (1,778 mm)
Frontal area	1·95 sq ft (0·18 m²)

WEIGHT, DRY:

PT6A-6	270 lb (122·5 kg)
PT6A-20	275 lb (125 kg)
PT6A-27, -28	289 lb (131 kg)
PT6A-40	363 lb (164 kg)
PT6A-50	454 lb (206 kg)

PERFORMANCE RATINGS:

T-O rating:
See under model listings above.

Max continuous rating:

PT6A-6
525 ehp (500 shp) at 2,200 rpm (available to 65°F/18°C)

PT6A-20
579 ehp (550 shp) at 2,200 rpm (available to 71°F/22°C)

PT6A-27, -28
715 ehp (680 shp) at 2,200 rpm (available to 71°F/22°C)

PT6A-40
903 ehp (850 shp) at 2,000 rpm (available to 111°F/44°C)

PT6A-50
1,009 ehp (960 shp) at 990 to 1,210 rpm (available to 90°F/32°C)

Max climb rating:

PT6A-6	525 eshp (500 shp) at 2,200 rpm (available to 65°F/18°C)
PT6A-20	566 ehp (538 shp) at 2,200 rpm
PT6A-27	652 ehp (620 shp) at 2,200 rpm (available to 69°F/21°C)

PT6A-40
903 ehp (850 shp) at 2,000 rpm (available to 79°F/26°C)

PT6A-50
919 ehp (874 shp) at 990 to 1,210 rpm (available to 78°F/26°C)

Max cruise rating:

PT6A-6	495 eshp (471 shp) at 2,200 rpm
PT6A-20	522 eshp (495 shp) at 2,200 rpm
PT6A-27	652 eshp (620 shp) at 2,200 rpm (available to 69°F/21°C)

PT6A-28
652 ehp (620 shp) at 2,200 rpm (available to 91°F/33°C)

PT6A-40
903 ehp (850 shp) at 2,000 rpm (available to 79°F/26°C)

PT6A-50
919 ehp (874 shp) at 990 to 1,210 rpm (available to 78°F/26°C)

SPECIFIC FUEL CONSUMPTION:

At T-O rating:

PT6A-6	0·65 lb (0·295 kg)/ehp/hr
PT6A-20	0·649 lb (0·294 kg)/ehp/hr
PT6A-26	0·602 lb (0·273 kg)/ehp/hr
PT6A-40	0·591 lb (0·268 kg)/ehp/hr
PT6A-50	0·564 lb (0·255 kg)/ehp/hr

At max continuous rating:

PT6A-6	0·67 lb (0·305 kg)/ehp/hr
PT6A-20	0·649 lb (0·294 kg)/ehp/hr
PT6A-27, -28	0·602 lb (0·273 kg)/ehp/hr

| PT6A-40 | 0·591 lb (0·268 kg)/ehp/hr |
| PT6A-50 | 0·573 lb (0·260 kg)/ehp/hr |

At max cruise rating:

PT6A-6	0·68 lb (0·309 kg)/ehp/hr
PT6A-20	0·670 lb (0·304 kg)/ehp/hr
PT6A-27, -28	0·612 lb (0·277 kg)/ehp/hr
PT6A-40	0·591 lb (0·268 kg)/ehp/hr
PT6A-50	0·587 lb (0·266 kg)/ehp/hr

OIL CONSUMPTION:

| Max | 0·20 lb (0·091 kg)/hr |

UNITED AIRCRAFT OF CANADA T74 TURBOPROP

The T74 is the US designation for military versions of the PT6A turboprop and PT6B turboshaft. The T74 turboprop, which is of the same configuration as the PT6A series, is available with either clockwise or counter-clockwise propeller rotation. Military versions are:

T74-CP-8A. US Navy counterpart of the PT6A-20 with clockwise propeller rotation and rated at 650 shp. Installed in the seventh prototype North American Rockwell OV-10A Bronco twin-engined COIN aircraft (together with T74-CP-10A) which flew in October 1966 for evaluation by the US Navy. Engine is approved by USN Bureau of Naval Weapons.

T74-CP-10A. Same as -8A engine but with counterclockwise propeller rotation. Installed in OV-10A, and approved by USN Bureau of Naval Weapons.

T74-CP-12. Rated at 750 shp, with clockwise propeller rotation.

T74-CP-14. Same as -12 engine but with counterclockwise propeller rotation.

T74-CP-700. US Army counterpart of the PT6A-20. More than 500 T74-CP-700s have been delivered to Beech for 129 U-21A aircraft. These engines are fitted with an inertial separator system developed under Army contract to protect the turboprop against sand and dust ingestion.

T74 (PT6A-27). Retrofitted to some Beech U-21A aircraft operating with US Army in Southeast Asia.

T74 (PT6A-29). Rated at 778 ehp and retrofitted in Beech U-21 aircraft engaged in US Project Crazydog electronic countermeasures operations.

T74 (PT6A-30). Proposed for the US Army advanced surveillance aircraft (ASA).

A further application of the military T74/PT6A is the Helio Stallion HST-550, turbine version of the single-engined Helio U-10 for which FAA certification has been completed.

The following data apply to the military PT6A-29:

DIMENSIONS:

| Diameter | approx 19 in (483 mm) |
| Length | approx 62 in (1,575 mm) |

WEIGHT, DRY:

| With standard equipment | 289 lb (131 kg) |

PERFORMANCE RATINGS:

T-O and max continuous
778 ehp (750 shp) at 2,200 rpm (available to 73°F/23°C)

Max climb or military
726 ehp (700 shp) at 2,200 rpm (available to 73°F/23°C)

Max cruise or normal
714 ehp (688 shp) at 2,200 rpm (available to 73°F/23°C)

SPECIFIC FUEL CONSUMPTION:

At T-O and max continuous ratings
0·598 lb (0·271 kg)/ehp/hr

At max climb or military ratings
0·606 lb (0·275 kg)/ehp/hr

At max cruise or normal ratings
0·608 lb (0·276 kg)/ehp/hr

UNITED AIRCRAFT OF CANADA PT6B

This is the commercial turboshaft version of the PT6A and features a lower ratio reduction gear. Applications include the Lockheed XH-51A and Model 286 rigid-rotor helicopters, the twin-engined Piasecki Model 16H-3H high-speed compound business helicopter (with Piasecki coupling gearbox) scheduled to fly during 1969, and the Nord Aviation 511 transportable unmanned flying platform.

Current production versions of the PT6B are:

PT6B-9. Rated at 550 shp at 6,230 rpm available to 77°F/25°C. Civil certification received in May 1965.

PT6B-16. Rated at 690 shp at 6,230 rpm available to 73°F/23°C for T-O and max continuous ratings. Civil certification was awarded in mid-1967 and production engines became available in October 1967. This version has been selected to power the Nord 511.

Both these engines have a single-stage planetary gear train of 5·3 : 1 reduction ratio. Rotation is clockwise when viewed from the rear. The splined output shaft is mounted in plain bearings.

A twin-engine coupled version of the PT6B is being developed as the T400/PT6T.

DIMENSIONS:

Max diameter	19 in (483 mm)
Length, less accessories, PT6B-9	
	60 in (1,525 mm)
Frontal area	1·95 sq ft (0·18 m²)

WEIGHT, DRY:

| PT6B-9 | 245 lb (111 kg) |
| PT6B-16 | 269 lb (122 kg) |

PERFORMANCE RATINGS:

T-O:
See under model listings above

Max continuous
PT6B-9
500 shp at 6,230 rpm (available to 72°F/22°C)
PT6B-16
690 shp at 6,230 rpm (available to 90°F/32°C)

Max climb
PT6B-9
500 shp at 6,230 rpm (available to 72°F/22°C)

| PT6B-16 | 665 shp at 6,230 rpm |

Max cruise

| PT6B-9 | 485 shp at 6,230 rpm |
| PT6B-16 | 665 shp at 6,230 rpm |

SPECIFIC FUEL CONSUMPTION:

At T-O rating:

| PT6B-9 | 0·665 lb (0·302 kg)/shp/hr |
| PT6B-16 | 0·618 lb (0·280 kg)/shp/hr |

At max continuous rating:

| PT6B-9 | 0·685 lb (0·311 kg)/shp/hr |
| PT6B-16 | 0·618 lb (0·280 kg)/shp/hr |

At max cruise rating:

| PT6B-9 | 0·685 lb (0·311 kg)/shp/hr |
| PT6B-16 | 0·623 lb (0·283 kg)/shp/hr |

OIL CONSUMPTION:

| Max | 0·20 lb (0·091 kg)/hr |

UNITED AIRCRAFT OF CANADA T74 TURBOSHAFT

Military version of the PT6B turboshaft, this variant of the T74 was the first engine in the PT6/T74 series to fly, powering the Hiller Ten-99 in July 1961 developed for the US Marine Assault Helicopter competition. A further installation of the T74 turboshaft was in the twin-engined Kaman K-1125 which first flew in April 1963 as an entrant in the USAF Missile Site Support Helicopter competition.

UNITED AIRCRAFT OF CANADA PT6T TURBO "TWIN PAC"

First run in July 1968, the PT6T Turbo "Twin-Pac" comprises two PT6 turboshaft engines mounted side-by-side and driving into a combining gearbox to provide a single output drive. The engine was launched as a coupled power unit for a new family of twin-engined helicopters based on the Bell Helicopter UH-1 series. First of these, jointly financed by Bell, UACL and the Canadian government, is the 15-seat Bell Model 212, an improved version of the 205A commercial helicopter which first flew with the PT6T-3 in April 1969. Three Model 212s are to be used in the flight test programme.

Installation of the 1,800 shp PT6T-3 in the Model 212, in addition to offering true engine-out capability, provides an additional 300 shp (over the single-engine 205A) and gives enhanced hot day and high altitude performance. The civil certification block test was completed in December 1969 and flight qualified PT6T-3s became available in mid-1970 coincident with certification of the Model 212. Deliveries of the helicopter were to follow in the summer of 1970. Bell has placed orders with UACL for PT6T-3s valued at approximately $8 million (£3·34 million). A PT6T-3 conversion of the Sikorsky S-58 helicopter is under development. First flight was scheduled for the autumn of 1970.

By careful selection of intermediate gear ratios and gear face-width-to-diameter relationships, the PT6T's combining gearbox is of minimum weight for the required overall speed ratio between the gas generators' centre distance and required power transmission capability. Unlike the PT6A, the gas generators of the Turbo "Twin Pac" are mounted with their intakes forward and their exhausts (and combining gearbox) to the rear. The gas generators, which are interchangeable port and starboard, are growth versions of the PT6A-27 and incorporate air-cooled stage-one turbine nozzle guide vanes to enable operation at the higher turbine temperatures required by the engine's higher output.

In the Model 212, the 1,800 shp PT6T-3 is restricted to a T-O rating of 1,250 shp and 1,100 shp for continuous power. In the event of a power section failure, torquemeters in the combining gearbox automatically signal the 'alive' fuel system to bring up the remaining section to demand power. A single-engine 30-minute rating is included for use, at pilot discretion, in such contingencies.

With the advantage of more than 4 million flying hours by PT6A engines in commercial operation, the PT6T-3 is planned to enter service with an initial TBO of 1,600 hr.

The following details relate to the PT6T-3 and describe the main features differing from those of the standard PT6 single engine configuration.

TYPE: Coupled axial-plus-centrifugal free-turbine turboshaft.

SHAFT DRIVE: Combining gearbox comprises three separate gear trains, two input and one output, each contained within an individual sealed compartment and all inter-connected by drive shafts. Overall reduction ratio 5 : 1. Input gear train comprising three spur gears provides speed reduction between power sections and output gearbox. The two drives into the output gearbox are via Formsprag fully-phased overrunning clutches with input third gear forming outer member of clutch, and interconnect shaft forming inner, overrunning member. Output gear train comprises three helical spur gears, i.e. two input pinions meshing with single output gear. Output shaft drives forward between gas generators. Rotation clockwise viewed from front of engine. Hydro-mechanical torquemeter (of PT6 design concept) provided in each interconnect drive shaft, measuring power transmitted by each gas generator as a hydraulic pressure used to control torque balancing (between gas generators) and limiting.

AIR INTAKE: Individual annular intakes with wire mesh debris screens on each gas generator, feeding plenum chamber to compressor. Additional intake inertial particle separator fitted upstream to reduce sand and dust ingestion. High frequency compressor noise suppressed.

FUEL SYSTEM: Basic fuel control as on PT6 with manual back-up fuel system, and dual fuel manifold for cool starts. Automatic power sharing and torque limiting systems. Torquemeters provide signals to Bendix fuel system metering valves to maintain power at level set by pilot's selective-collective control. Fuel heaters.

FUEL GRADES: JP-1, JP-4 and JP-5.

JET PIPE: Single upwards-facing exhaust port on each gas generator.

ACCESSORIES: Starter generator and tacho-generator mounted on accessory drive case at front of each power section. Other accessory drives on combining gearbox, including individual power turbine speed governors and tacho-generators, and provision for blowers and aircraft accessories.

The 1,800 shp United Aircraft of Canada PT6T Turbo "Twin Pac" coupled free-turbine turboshaft

LUBRICATION SYSTEM: Independent lubrication systems on each power section for maximum safety during single-engine operation. Integral oil tanks with provision for remote oil level indication.

OIL SPECIFICATION: MIL-L-7808 and 23699.

STARTING: Electrical, with cold weather starting down to —65°F (—54°C).

DIMENSIONS:
Height	31·6 in (803 mm)
Width	44·4 in (1,128 mm)
Length	65·3 in (1,659 mm)

WEIGHT, DRY:
With standard equipment	617 lb (280 kg)

PERFORMANCE RATINGS:
T-O (5-min):
Total output, at 6,600 rpm	1,800 shp
Single power section only, at 6,600 rpm	900 shp
30-minute power (single power section rating only), at 6,600 rpm	900 shp

Max continuous:
Total output, at 6,600 rpm	1,600 shp
Single power section only, 6,600 rpm	800 shp

Cruise A:
Total output, at 6,600 rpm	1,250 shp
Single power section only, 6,600 rpm	625 shp

Cruise B:
Total output, at 6,600 rpm	1,100 shp
Single power section only, at 6,600 rpm	550 shp
Ground idle, at 2,200 rpm	60 shp max

SPECIFIC FUEL CONSUMPTION:
At T-O and 30 minute ratings (total output)
0·595 lb (0·270 kg)/shp/hr
At max continuous rating (total output)
0·599 lb (0·272 kg)/shp/hr
At Cruise A rating (total output)
0·628 lb (0·285 kg)/shp/hr
At Cruise B rating (total output)
0·653 lb (0·296 kg)/shp/hr

OIL CONSUMPTION:
Max (for both gas generators)
0·4 lb (0·18 kg)/hr

UNITED AIRCRAFT OF CANADA T400

Military version of the PT6T Turbo "Twin Pac", the UACL T400 coupled turboshaft is the first US Navy turboshaft (or turboprop) to be designated under the new US military aircraft turbine engine designation system. The Navy has placed orders with UACL valued at $17,112,445 (£7·43 million) for T400 engines to power 49 Bell AH-1J helicopters, a twin-engined upgraded version of the AH-1G HueyCobra, on behalf of the US Marine Corps and 76 Bell UH-1N Twin Huey helicopters, military counterpart of the Model 212, on behalf of the USAF. Deliveries of the aircraft were scheduled to start in mid-1970.

Another military version of the Model 212, the Bell CUH-1N, has been ordered for the Canadian armed forces. Deliveries of this helicopter are scheduled to begin early in 1971. Another application of the T400 is in the Kaman Sealite

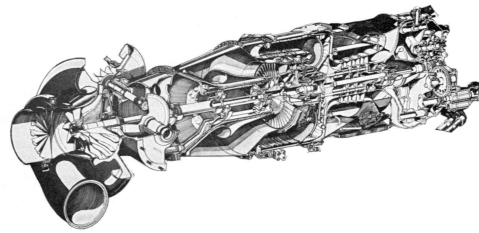

The 850 shp United Aircraft of Canada ST6L-73 free-turbine APU for the Hamilton Standard environmental control system in the Lockheed L-1011 TriStar

helicopter (see US Aircraft section) designed for the US Navy LAMPS role.

For military roles, UACL describe the T400 as producing a minimum infra-red 'signature'.

The following data relate to the T400-CP-400 (PT6T-4) which is of similar construction to the commercial Turbo "Twin Pac" engine.

DIMENSIONS:
Height	32·4 in (823 mm)
Width	40·0 in (1,026 mm)
Length	52·6 in (1,336 mm)

WEIGHT, DRY:
With standard equipment	708 lb (321 kg)

PERFORMANCE RATINGS:
Intermediate, at 6,600 rpm
1,800 shp minimum
Max continuous, at 6,600 rpm
1,530 shp minimum

SPECIFIC FUEL CONSUMPTION:
At intermediate rating 0·603 lb (0·274 kg)/shp/hr
At max continuous 0·612 lb (0·278 kg)/shp/hr

UNITED AIRCRAFT OF CANADA ST6

Directly derived from the PT6 turboprop/turboshaft series, the ST6 is a basic shaft turbine having a wide range of applications in marine, industrial, vehicular and airborne installations. Airborne application is as part of the APU in the Lockheed L-1011 TriStar, where the flat-rated ST6L-73 provides power for the Hamilton Standard integrated environmental system, main engine (Rolls-Royce RB.211 turbofan) starting, and auxiliary electrical power system. A $60 million contract was awarded to Hamilton Standard by Lockheed in July 1968, calling for deliveries of equipment to start in early 1970 as part of an initial requirement for 156 systems.

In the TriStar, the ST6L-73 will provide major improvements in fuel consumption, quietness of

operation and cleanliness of compressed air supply. The ST6L-73 will directly drive a rear-mounted assembly comprising a Hamilton Standard load compressor, and an electrical generator and cooling fan. Initial rating will provide the supply of 385 lb (175 kg)/min of air at 42 lb/sq in abs (2·95 kg/cm²) at 103°F (39°C) ambient with 45 kVA electrical output. (Maximum electrical power obtainable is 90 kVA). Scheduled growth of the ST6L within the same frame size is planned to provide 430 lb (195 kg)/min of air concurrent with 140 hp (104 kVA) for generator drive.

The load compressor air, as well as powering the environmental system, will also be used for pneumatic systems such as the RB.211 engine starters, engine anti-icing, wing de-icing and air turbine motors for driving two of the aircraft's four hydraulic systems.

The following data applies to the ST6L-73:

DIMENSIONS:
Diameter	approx 19 in (483 mm)
Length	approx 52·2 in (1,326 mm)

WEIGHT, DRY:
With standard equipment	300 lb (136 kg)

PERFORMANCE RATINGS:
Max, at 33,000 rpm:
up to 103°F (39°C) at SL static   720 shp
Normal, at 33,000 rpm:
up to 103°F (39°C) at SL static   532 shp

SPECIFIC FUEL CONSUMPTION:
At max rating:
up to 103°F (39°C) at SL static
0·625 lb (0·283 kg)/shp/hr
At normal rating:
up to 103°F (39°C) at SL static
0·670 lb (0·304 kg)/shp/hr

OIL CONSUMPTION:
Max   0·1 lb (0·05 kg)/hr

CZECHOSLOVAKIA

AVIA
AVIA N.P.
ADDRESS: Letnany, Prague 9.

Originally a member of the Czechoslovak Aviation Industry Group, Avia National Corporation was transferred to the Czechoslovak Automotive Industry (CAZ) Group in 1960. The company is at present engaged in series production of the M 337, M 137, M 462RF and Minor 6-III piston-engines, as well as propeller and spare parts manufacture.

AVIA MINOR 6-III

This engine powers the Zlin Z 526 and Zlin Z 526A Akrobat.

TYPE: Six-cylinder inverted in-line air-cooled ungeared, for aerobatic aircraft.

CYLINDERS: Total capacity 364·31 cu in (5·97 litres).

PISTONS: Basically as M 332, but with three compression rings and one grooved scraper ring.

CONNECTING RODS: Aluminium alloy forgings of a different section from those of M 332.

CRANKSHAFT: Six-throw crankshaft, forged from special nitrided chrome-vanadium steel and machined all over. Carried in seven two-piece steel-backed lead-bronze bearings and one ball thrust bearing at the front end.

The 160 hp Avia Minor 6-III six-cylinder air-cooled piston-engine

CRANKCASE: Assembly consists of crankcase itself, upper and front covers. Crankcase has double cross-webs in which crankshaft and camshaft bearings are mounted. All crankcase

parts cast from heat-treated magnesium alloy.
VALVE GEAR: Two parallel interchangeable valves in each cylinder, made from high duty special steel. Valve stems are nitrided. Valves actu-

ated through valve lifters, tappets and rocker arms in oil bath. Steel valve seats pressed into the cylinder head. Camshaft on port side of crankcase, driven from crankshaft through a spur gear.

INDUCTION: Two Walter W45 or W45-AK (aerobatic) down-draught carburettors with manual mixture control and acceleration pump.

FUEL: 72 octane minimum.

IGNITION: Dual shielded ignition. Two Scintilla magnetos OBF 6R 501 Z170 (port) and OBF 6R 701 Z170 (starboard) with automatic sparking advance. Magnetos placed in a hanging position at rear of crankcase. Port magneto driven from camshaft, starboard magneto driven from fuel pump drive. Starboard magneto provided with impulse unit. Sparking plugs 12 × 1·25 mm (PAL L22.90).

LUBRICATION AND PROPELLER DRIVE: Same as for M 332.

ACCESSORIES: Type 2M-50 fuel pump (starboard side of crankcase), Scintilla 24-volt 600-watt generator (port side) and tachometer generator (starboard side) driven by train of spur gears. Tachometer driven by flexible shaft.

STARTING: Walter type P320 electric starter.

MOUNTING: Two engine bearer feet on each side of crankcase, with rubber vibration dampers.

DIMENSIONS:
Overall length, without propeller hub
    49·21 in (1,250 mm)
Overall width, without bearer feet
    17·49 in (445 mm)
Overall height   25·16 in (639 mm)

WEIGHT DRY (including normal accessories):
    279·5 lb (126·8 kg) ±2%

PERFORMANCE RATINGS:
T-O rating   160 hp at 2,500 rpm
Cruising power   125 hp at 2,300 rpm

SPECIFIC FUEL CONSUMPTIONS:
At T-O rating   0·53 lb (240 gr)/hp/hr
At cruising power   0·485 lb (220 gr)/hp/hr

OIL CONSUMPTION:
At T-O rating   0·0044-0·018 lb (2-8 gr)/hp/hr

AVIA M 137

Designed to power light aerobatic, training, sports and single- and multi-engined sports aircraft, the 180 hp M 137 piston-engine is in production for the Zlin Z 526F Trener. The engine also powers the Zlin 42 and 43. The TBO for normal operation is 800 hr, and 600 hr for aerobatic and training applications.

TYPE: Six-cylinder inverted in-line air-cooled ungeared with left-hand rotation.

CYLINDERS: Total capacity 364·31 cu in (5·97 litres). Bore 4 in (105 mm). Stroke 4·625 in (115 mm). Compression ratio 6·3 : 1.

INDUCTION: Low-pressure fuel injection.

FUEL: 72 to 87 octane.

DIMENSIONS:
Length   54 in (1,360 mm)
Width   17·75 in (443 mm)
Height   25 in (628 mm)

WEIGHT (including starter)   302 lb (137 kg)

PERFORMANCE RATINGS:
T-O   180 hp at 2,750 rpm
Max cont   160 hp at 2,680 rpm
Max cruising   140 hp at 2,580 rpm

SPECIFIC FUEL CONSUMPTION:
At max cruise rating   0·437 lb (205 gr)/hp/hr

AVIA M 150 JAWA

The M 150 is a three-cylinder two-stroke engine of inverted air-cooled configuration, rated at 42 hp. Driving a V-120 wooden propeller, the engine provides auxiliary power for the Czech L-13J sailplane and is capable of being stopped and automatically started in flight.

A limited number of M 150s has been built and a 100-hr test programme was successfully completed in February 1969. Full production has yet to be initiated.

Fuel is a petrol-oil mixture using aviation octane ratings of 87 up to 105. Automobile octane fuels may be used for short periods of operation.

CYLINDERS: Total capacity 49·43 cu in (0·810 litres).

WEIGHT:
Including propeller   89·3 lb (40·5 kg)

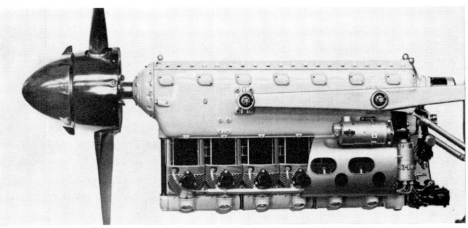

The 180 hp Avia M 137 six-cylinder air-cooled piston-engine

PERFORMANCE RATINGS:
Max T-O   42 hp at 4,500 rpm
Max cont   32 hp at 4,100 rpm
Cruise   28 hp at 3,900 rpm
Ground idling speed   800 rpm

SPECIFIC FUEL CONSUMPTION:
At cruise rating   0·79 lb (360 gr)/hp/hr

AVIA M 332

This 140 hp four-cylinder inverted air-cooled supercharged piston-engine powers the L-40 Meta-Sokol light aircraft.

TYPE: Four-cylinder inverted in-line air-cooled, ungeared, supercharged.

CYLINDERS: Bore 4·13 in (105 mm). Stroke 4·53 in (115 mm). Swept volume 247·87 cu in (3·98 litres). Compression ratio 6·3 : 1. Steel cylinders with cooling fins machined from solid. Cylinder bores nitrided. Detachable cylinder heads are aluminium alloy castings. Cylinder and head assembly attached to crankcase by four studs. Valve seats of special steel. Valve guides and sparking plug bushes of bronze.

PISTONS: Aluminium alloy stampings with graphited surfaces. Two compression rings and two knife-shaped scraper rings in common groove above gudgeon pin. Gudgeon-pins secured by spring-circlips.

CONNECTING RODS: H-section aluminium alloy forgings. Two split big-ends bolted together by two bolts. Steel two-piece liner lead-bronze plated.

CRANKSHAFT: Forged from special chrome-vanadium steel, machined all over. Nitrided crank-pins. Carried in five steel-backed lead-bronze plated slide bearings which are lightly lead-lined, and in one ball-thrust bearing at the front. Terminating in a wedge-shape cone for the propeller hub mounting.

CRANKCASE: Heat-treated magnesium alloy (electron) casting, with top and front covers. Deep-sunk bearing covers forged from aluminium alloy.

VALVE GEAR: Camshaft on the cylinder heads actuates the valves by means of rocker arms. Camshaft driven by vertical shaft and bevel gears. One inlet valve of heat-treated steel, one sodium-filled exhaust valve of austenitic steel with stellite seat. Nitrided valve stems.

IGNITION: Shielded type. Two Scintilla-Vertex Type OBF 4R magnetos with automatic sparking advance or two Palax type LUN 2220 magnetos. Magnetos placed vertically, driven by bevel gears without gear moment dampers. Two PAL L22-62 sparking plugs per cylinder 0·5 × ·07 in (12 × 1·25 mm).

LUBRICATION: Dry sump pressure-feed type. Double gear-type oil-pump with pressure and scavenge stages mounted on rear wall of crankcase. Oil from tank passes through triple filter into pressure stage of oil-pump and then into main channel drilled in crankcase. Pressure control valve adjusted to 3·5-4 atm. Inlet union of main channel provided with oil-pressure gauge connecting pipe. Oil returned from sump by scavenge stage of oil-pump to tank. Special gear-type oil-pump draws oil from cam box and forces it into crankcase from where it flows into sump.

SUPERCHARGER: Centrifugal type mounted on engine rear flange. Driven through a damping rubber coupling from crankshaft. Planetary gear, ratio 7·4 : 1, engaged via band friction clutch. Force feed lubrication of supercharger from main engine lubrication system.

FUEL SYSTEM: Low-pressure injection system. Fuel pump driven from camshaft. Fuel injection nozzles located in front of intake valves. Automatic control in relation to engine manifold pressure. Fuel supplied to

The 42 hp Avia M 150 three-cylinder two-stroke engine for sailplanes

injection pump by fuel pressure pump located in common body with injection pump.

FUEL GRADE: Minimum 72 octane without tetraethyl lead (TEL) or 80 octane, with maximum 0·8 cm³ TEL per litre.

COOLING: Air scoop on port side, designed to provide easy access to sparking plugs and easy removal of scoop and baffles.

STARTING: Electric starter combined with supercharger. Electric motor rotates the starter dog which is engaged by an electro-magnet. Gears and clutch of supercharger serve the starter also.

ACCESSORIES: One 600-watt 24-volt dynamo. Electric rpm transmitter, drive 1 : 1. Propeller control unit. Mechanical tachometer on oil pump, drive 1 : 2.

MOUNTING: Four engine-bearer feet with rubber dampers.

PROPELLER DRIVE: Direct left-hand tractor.

DIMENSIONS:
Length (including supercharger and starter but less propeller boss) 43·4 in (1,102 mm)
Height 24·7 in (628 mm)
Width (with dynamo and electric tachometer) 16·7 in (425 mm)

WEIGHTS:
Dry (with ignition harness, supercharger and starter) 225 lb (102 kg)

PERFORMANCE RATINGS:
T-O rating 140 hp at 2,700 rpm
Rated power 115 hp at 2,550 rpm
Max cruising power at 3,280-6,560 ft (1,000-2,000 m) 100 hp at 2,400 rpm
Normal cruising power 95 hp at 2,400 rpm

SPECIFIC FUEL CONSUMPTIONS:
T-O rating 0·57 lb (0·26 kg)/hp/hr
Rated power 0·475 lb (0·215 kg)/hp/hr
Max cruising power 0·45 lb (0·205 kg)/hp/hr
Normal cruising power 0·43 lb (0·195 kg)/hp/hr

OIL CONSUMPTION: 0·44 lb (0·2 kg)/hr

AVIA M 337

This six-cylinder inverted air-cooled ungeared supercharged engine powers the Morava L-200D light aircraft and is an alternative power unit for the Zlin 42 and 43.

TYPE: Six-cylinder inverted in-line air-cooled, ungeared, supercharged and with direct fuel injection.

CYLINDERS, PISTONS, CONNECTING RODS, VALVE GEAR, SUPERCHARGER, FUEL, LUBRICATION, PROPELLER DRIVE, STARTING AND MOUNTING: Same as for M 332, except: Swept volume 364·31 cu in (5·97 litres). Compression ratio 6·3 : 1.

CRANKSHAFT: Same as for M 332, except six-throw. Seven two-piece steel-backed lead-bronze bearings and one ball thrust bearing at the front end.

CRANKCASE: Same as for M 332. Material is heat-treated magnesium alloy of improved quality.

INDUCTION: Same as for M 332, except for low-pressure injection pump type Yh LUN5152.

IGNITION: Same as for M 332, except magnetos are Palax LUN2221.13 or Scintilla OBF 6R with automatic sparking advance.

ACCESSORIES: Accessories and drives are same as for M 332. Optional hydraulic pump type P6121, with drive transmitter for tachometer.

DIMENSIONS:
Overall length, without propeller boss 55·51 in (1,410 mm)
Width 18·42 in (468 mm)
Height 24·72 in (628 mm)
Frontal area 2·15 sq ft (2,000 cm²)

WEIGHT DRY: 310 lb (140 kg)

PERFORMANCE RATINGS:
T-O rating 210 hp at 2,750 rpm
Rated (climb) power 170 hp at 2,600 rpm
Max cruising power at 3,940 ft (1,200 m) 150 hp at 2,400 rpm

SPECIFIC FUEL CONSUMPTIONS:
At T-O rating 0·595 lb (270 gr)/hp/hr
At rated (climb) power 0·474 lb (215 gr)/hp/hr
At max cruising power at 3,940 ft (1,200 m) 0·43 lb (195 gr)/hp/hr

OIL CONSUMPTION:
At rated power 0·0022-0·013 lb (1-6 gr)/hp/hr

AVIA M 462

This engine powers the Z-37 Cmelák agricultural monoplane.

TYPE: Nine-cylinder air-cooled radial engine.

CYLINDERS: Bore 4·13 in (105 mm). Stroke 5·12 in (130 mm). Swept volume 620 cu in (10·16 litres). Compression ratio 6·35 : 1. Cylinders forged from steel. All surfaces machined. Cylinder bores nitrided. Each cylinder attached to crankcase by eight studs. Cylinder heads are aluminium alloy castings, screwed on to the barrels.

PISTONS: Aluminium alloy forgings. Three compression rings and two scraper rings. First compression ring trapezoidal in cross-section,

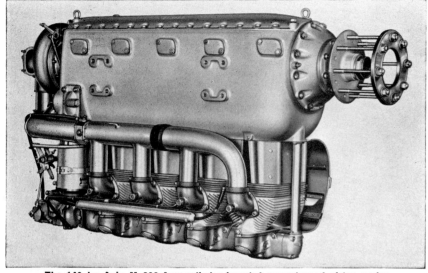

The 140 hp Avia M 332 four-cylinder inverted supercharged piston-engine

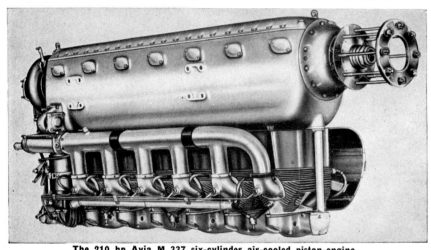

The 210 hp Avia M 337 six-cylinder air-cooled piston-engine

with sliding surfaces chrome-plated. Gudgeon-pin case-hardened and quenched, with conical lightening hole.

CONNECTING RODS: Heat-treated chrome-nickel steel forgings with polished surfaces. Articulated rod ends and master rod gudgeon-pin end have bronze bushes. Master rod main bearing of steel with centrifugally-cast bronze coating of 0·5 mm thickness.

CRANKSHAFT: Single-throw type of chrome-nickel steel. All surfaces machined, heat-treated and polished. Carried in two type 2213 anti-friction bearings. Front bearing is thrust bearing, rear one free.

CRANKCASE: Aluminium alloy forging in two sections.

VALVE GEAR: One inlet and one exhaust valve per cylinder. Both valves of austenitic steel; exhaust valve sodium-cooled. Valve seats of austenitic steel, pressed in and rolled. Cam disc situated in front section of crankcase and driven by spur gears.

The 330 hp Avia M 462 nine-cylinder geared supercharged radial engine

INDUCTION SYSTEM: Mixture fed from super-charger. Low-pressure fuel-injection pump type Yo with closed injection nozzles.

SUPERCHARGER: Single-stage centrifugal type. Spring-loaded, driven by spur gearing. Gear ratio 9·563 : 1.

FUEL: 80 octane minimum.

IGNITION: Four-spark screened ignition system. Two magnetos mounted on accessory drive housing and driven by spur gearing. Two PAL-L 23·81R spark plugs per cylinder.

LUBRICATION: Dry-sump pressure-feed type. Gear-type oil pump with pressure and scavenge stages.

REDUCTION GEAR: Planetary reduction gearing, ratio 0·787 : 1. Hollow shaft for oil supply to hydraulically-actuated variable-pitch propeller.

ACCESSORIES: One 1,500 W generator, type Yo injection pump, electric tachometer drive, type AK 50M air compressor, etc. Accessory drives by spur gearing.

STARTING: Compressed air starting.

MOUNTING: Engine bolted to mounting at eight points through rubber dampers.

DIMENSIONS:
Length overall 39·18 in (995 mm)

Diameter	38·58 in (980 mm)
Frontal area	8·03 sq ft (0·755 m²)

PERFORMANCE RATINGS:
T-O (5 min)	330 hp at 2,450 rpm
Max cont	290 hp at 2,200 rpm
Max rated	255 hp at 2,000 rpm
Max cruise	190 hp at 1,900 rpm

SPECIFIC FUEL CONSUMPTIONS:
At T-O rating	0·606 lb (275 gr)/hp/hr
At max cont rating	0·573 lb (260 gr)/hp/hr
At max rated power	0·562 lb (255 gr)/hp/hr
At max cruise rating	0·485 lb (220 gr)/hp/hr

OIL CONSUMPTION:
At rated power 0·013 lb (6 gr)/hp/hr

MOTORLET
MOTORLET NC
ADDRESS: Prague-Jinonice

GENERAL MANAGER:
J. Janák

ASSISTANTS TO GENERAL MANAGER:
TECHNICAL DIRECTOR: V. Franc
COMMERCIAL DIRECTOR: Dr A. Záruba
ECONOMIC DIRECTOR: Ing J. Svoboda

TECHNICAL & PRODUCTION DIRECTOR: J. Cerveny

HEAD OF DESIGN DEVELOPMENT: Ing V. Popisil

Motorlet National Corporation operates the main aero-engine establishment in Czechoslovakia, based on the former Walter Motoren factory at Jinonice, previously well known for its radial and in-line piston-engines. Today, the Walter name continues in use only as a trade-mark for Motorlet piston-engines.

Motorlet started turbine engine manufacture in 1952 with licenced production of the Russian RD-45 centrifugal turbojet for MiG-15 fighters. Present production activities concern the small M 701 centrifugal turbojet, Czechoslovakia's first indigenous turbine, for the L-29 Delfin trainer, and licenced manufacture of the Ivchenko AI-25 turbofan for the L-39 trainer. Development is also under way on the M 601 turboprop and derivatives of the AI-25.

In addition Motorlet is manufacturing hydraulic instruments, precision castings, automatic regulation and control instruments, and non-aero gas-turbine components.

MOTORLET AI-25 (WALTER TITAN)

Motorlet is licence manufacturing the Ivchenko AI-25 turbofan (which is in service with Aeroflot in the Yakovlev Yak-40 short-haul transport) as the power unit for the new Aero L-39 two-seat basic trainer, which first flew on 4 November, 1968. The Czechoslovak version is also known as the Walter Titan.

The 3,307 lb (1,500 kg) st AI-25 W which powers the L-39 is a modified variant for trainer applications, involving a revised lubrication system and an airflow mixer for the exhaust. A further development version is proposed, designated AI-25 WM, with a two-stage fan and an air-cooled high-pressure turbine. The AI-25 WM is rated at 3,968 lb (1,800 kg) st.

A brief description of the Ivchenko AI-25 is given in the USSR section of this edition.

MOTORLET M 601

Second of Czechoslovakia's small turbine engines to be built, the M 601 is a free-turbine turboprop having a combined axial-and-centrifugal compressor. Designed to power the new Czech twin-engined L-410 light transport aircraft, it is rated at 700 ehp and drives a V508 constant-speed three-bladed propeller with hydraulically-variable pitch.

The first version of the M 601, rated at 550 ehp, ran in October 1967. Development of a revised 700 ehp version, of increased diameter, started during 1968. Until this higher-powered model is certified, the L-410 is being fitted with United Aircraft of Canada PT6A-27 turboprops of 652 ehp. Negotiations have been initiated between UACL and AERO for Czechoslovakian manufacture of the PT6A-27, which is of the same general configuration as the M 601.

TYPE: Free-turbine combined axial-and-centrifugal turboprop.

PROPELLER DRIVE: Reduction gear at front of engine with drive from free-turbine. Reduction ratio 14·9 : 1.

AIR INTAKE: Annular intake at rear of engine, with debris screen, feeds air to compressor plenum chamber.

COMPRESSOR: Two axial stages plus single centrifugal stage. Pressure ratio 6 : 1 at 36,000 rpm gas generator speed and 6·2 : 1 at 37,000 rpm gas generator speed. Air mass flows 6·1 lb/sec (2·75 kg/sec) and 6·8 lb/sec (3·1 kg/sec) respectively.

COMBUSTION CHAMBER: Annular combustor with rotary fuel injection and low-voltage ignition.

COMPRESSOR TURBINE: Single-stage.

The 700 shp Motorlet M601 free-turbine turboprop

POWER TURBINE: Single-stage

FUEL SYSTEM: Low-pressure LUN 6740 system, with single-lever control providing kinematic coupling of gas generator and power turbine speed controls.

FUEL GRADE: LP4 kerosene.

JET PIPE: Collector duct surrounding power turbine shaft. Exhaust through two ports on horizontal centre-line.

ACCESSORIES: Mounting pads on accessory case at rear of engine. Propeller controls mounted on reduction gear case at front of engine.

LUBRICATION SYSTEM: Pressure gear-pump circulation. Integral oil tank and cooler.

OIL SPECIFICATION: Mixture of MK 8 and MS 20 mineral oil; or B3Y synthetic oil.

MOUNTING: Two main pads on compressor intake flange and one steady point at rear of reduction gear case.

STARTING: Electric.

DIMENSIONS:
Diameter (550 ehp version)	12·4 in (314 mm)
Diameter (700 ehp version)	16·9 in (430 mm)
Length (both versions)	60·2 in (1,530 mm)

WEIGHT DRY:
(550 ehp version)	331 lb (150 kg)
(700 ehp version)	298 lb (135 kg)

PERFORMANCE RATINGS:
T-O rating (initial version)	550 ehp
(revised version)	
	700 ehp (available to 77°F/22°C)
Continuous rating (initial version)	517 ehp
(revised version)	
	660 ehp (available to 86°F/30°C)

SPECIFIC FUEL CONSUMPTION:
At T-O rating (initial version)	0·79 lb (0·306 kg)/ehp/hr
(revised version)	0·62 lb (0·280 kg)/ehp/hr

MOTORLET M 701

The M 701 turbojet engine powers the Czechoslovakian L-29 and L-29A Delfin training aircraft. Production is undertaken at the Motorlet factory at Jinonice, near Prague. Manufacture started in 1961 and by the spring of 1969 over 4,500 M 701s had been built. Production of the engine is expected to continue until at least 1972.

All models of the M 701 have the same ratings and differ mainly with regard to TBO, as indicated by their individual designations. The TBOs for the M 701-b150, M 701-c150, M 701-c400 and M 701-c500 are respectively 150, 250, 400 and 500 hr. The M 701-c250 introduced flame tube and turbine improvements, and the M 701-c400 has further improvements in turbine design.

TYPE: Single-shaft centrifugal turbojet.

AIR INTAKE: Annular air intake, with central bullet fairing, at front of engine. De-icing by hot engine-bleed air.

COMPRESSOR: Single-stage centrifugal type.

IMPELLER: Single-sided. Blade-type diffuser. Pressure ratio 4·3 : 1. Air mass flow 37·25 lb/sec (16·9 kg/sec) at 15,400 rpm.

COMBUSTION CHAMBER: Seven straight-flow chambers, interconnected by flame channels. Two igniter plugs in Nos. 2 and 7 chambers.

FUEL SYSTEM: Fuel pump of the LUN 6201.03 multi-plunger type. Baromatic pressure con-

Cutaway Motorlet M 701-c500 turbojet (1,962 lb = 890 kg st)

trol acts on servo-mechanism to vary fuel delivery according to altitude and speed. High-pressure shut-off cock. Max fuel pressure 7·1-14·2 lb/sq in (0·5-1·0 kg/cm²) behind fuel filter, 1,200 lb/sq in (85 kg/cm²) behind fuel pump.

FUEL GRADE: PL-4 to TPD-33-01960 standard, T-1 to GOST-4138-49 standard, or other similar fuels.

TURBINE: Single-stage axial-flow type, with 61 blades. Gas temperature after turbine 680-700°C.

JET-PIPE: Fixed-cone type.

ACCESSORY DRIVES: Drives on engine front casing to fuel pump, 28V generator, hydraulic pump and tachometer. One spare drive.

LUBRICATION SYSTEM: Wet sump type. Sump at bottom of front case. One three-stage gear-type pump. Sump capacity 6 Imp pints (3·5 litres). Normal oil supply pressure 28·5-35·5 lb/sq in (2-2·5 kg/cm²).

OIL SPECIFICATION: OLE-TO to TP 200/074-59 standard, or GOST 982-53.

STARTING: Electric starter.

DIMENSIONS:
Max width   35·28 in (896 mm)

Max height   36·53 in (928 mm)
Length overall   81·38 in (2,067 mm)

WEIGHT:
Weight dry   728 lb (330 kg) + 2·5%

PERFORMANCE RATINGS:
Max T-O   1,962 lb (890 kg) st at 15,400 rpm
Rated power   1,764 lb (800 kg) st at 14,950 rpm
Max cruise rating
                1,587 lb (720 kg) st at 14,500 rpm
Idling   154 lb (70 kg) st at 5,400 rpm

SPECIFIC FUEL CONSUMPTION:
At rated power   1·14

OMNIPOL
OMNIPOL FOREIGN TRADE CORPORATION

ADDRESS:
Washingtonova 11, Prague 1.
Omnipol is responsible for exporting products

of the Czech aviation industry and for supplying information on those products which are available for export.

FRANCE

AÉROSPATIALE
SOCIÉTÉ NATIONAL DE L'INDUSTRIE AÉROSPATIALE
HEAD OFFICE:
37 Boulevard de Montmorency, Paris 16e
OFFICERS: See "Aircraft" section.

This large new grouping of three major companies, formerly Sud-Aviation, Nord-Aviation and SEREB, has resulted in a diverse group which at the time of going to press was still functioning more or less in its constituent parts, although the intention is ultimate total integration. The power plant division is being formed from the former Nord-Aviation, which in mid-1970 retained all its former works, offices and programmes.

Since 1950 the propulsion group of the former Nord company (first SNCA du Nord and later Nord-Aviation) has been engaged at its Châtillon S/Bagneux works on development of ramjet and turbo-ramjet engines suitable for missile and piloted aircraft applications. The company has also conducted significant work on air intakes and exit nozzles for supersonic turbojets.

The Nord Sirius ramjet was developed for use in missiles at sustained speeds between Mach 1·3 and 2·7 at altitudes up to 75,000 ft (23,000 m). The Sirius II, developed for a target missile, had a rating at Mach 2·5 and 50,000 ft (15,000 m) of approximately 2,425 lb (1,100 kg) st. The Sirius II was described in the 1968-69 Jane's.

Sirius III, specially designed for propulsion at Mach numbers between 0·9 and 1·5, was also developed.

The integral ramjet of the Nord Vega test vehicle, described in the "Missiles" section of the 1965-66 Jane's, had the same 2 ft 1·4 in (645 mm) diameter as Sirius, but was capable of operating at speeds up to Mach 4 or 5. At Mach 4 it developed 1,390 lb (630 kg) st at 82,000 ft (25,000 m). Production of Sirius and Vega engines has now been stopped.

The turbo-ramjet arrangement initially studied by Nord consisted of the co-axial installation of a turbojet and a ramjet, with the fixed-geometry air intake and nozzle common to both engines and the combustion chamber of the ramjet surrounding the rear of the turbojet. A system

of this type powered the Nord Griffon II research aircraft in 1959.

Subsequent design and development contracts, mostly on behalf of the USAF, have been directed at evolving an improved dual-cycle engine for propulsion at Mach numbers up to 4·5. An integrated power unit comprising a turbofan and ramjet with variable-geometry intake and nozzle was a significant result of these studies.

Recently within the framework of feasibility studies a turbo-ramjet of such a type, incorporating an existing turbofan, was shown to be adequate for powering a re-usable satellite booster at up to Mach 5-6.

Châtillon has been involved in the design and testing at Saclay of the variable-geometry twin-duct intake of the Concorde, and has also carried out design studies of the new aft thrust-reverser nozzle for this aircraft.

Nord-Aviation, with SNECMA and SEREB, another partner in Aérospatiale, has been a major contractor for both the SSBS and the MSBS (see "Missiles" section) and also pioneered the Norsial type of heat- and noise-resisting light-weight airframe structure.

ARDEM
AVIONS ROGER DRUINE
ADDRESS:
20, Avenue du Général Clavery, Paris (16e)

The late M Roger Druine developed a light aero-engine from the standard Volkswagen motor-car engine. Known as the Ardem 4 CO2, it is particularly suitable for powering the Druine

Turbulent single-seat light aircraft and several versions are being built in Britain by Rollason Aircraft and Engines Ltd of Croydon Airport, Surrey (which see).

FAUVEL
"SURVOL"-CHARLES FAUVEL
HEAD OFFICE AND WORKS:
30 Chemin de la Roubine, Cannes-La Bocca (A-M)

Having been unable to find an entirely suitable engine to power his self-launching sailplanes (see "Sailplanes" section), M Fauvel is developing a new 40 hp four-cylinder horizontally-opposed four-stroke engine named the Pygmée, in collaboration with M E. de Coucy. It is hoped to fit this engine in production versions of both the AV.45 and AV.221 self-launching sailplanes. It is equally suitable as a power plant for conventional light aircraft, single-seat autogyros and small air cushion vehicles.

Bench testing of the Pygmée began early in 1967.

In response to demands for a more powerful version, M Fauvel plans to produce a developed Pygmée, developing 52 hp. This version has a swept volume of 71 cu in (1,160 cc) and operates at the same 2,750 propeller rpm as the 40 hp engine. Weight is slightly higher at 88·2 lb (40 kg) fully equipped. Length is somewhat greater but other dimensions are similar. A 12-volt alternator replaces the previous 6-volt unit. Dual ignition will be available.

DE COUCY "SURVOL" PYGMÉE
TYPE: Four-cylinder horizontally-opposed air-cooled.

CYLINDERS: Bore 2·56 in (65 mm). Stroke 2·68 in (68 mm). Swept volume 55 cu in (900 cc). Compression ratio 9 : 1. Made from AU 4 NT, with cooling fins equivalent to 15 times the surface area of the cylinder and bore. Cylinder bores polished by a process known as "super-finition", not chromed. Design makes this side-valve engine as efficient as an ohv type.

PISTONS: Made of Y alloy and chromium-plated.

CONNECTING RODS: Each made in one piece, from special steel.

CRANKSHAFT: Made from chromed nickel steel. Runs in four roller bearings.

CRANKCASE: Made in two halves, from AS7G. Both halves made in same mould.

VALVE GEAR: One inlet valve and one exhaust valve per cylinder. Nickel bronze valve seats.

IGNITION: One 10 mm spark plug in centre of each cylinder head.

REDUCTION GEAR: Ratio 1 : 2.

STARTING: Bendix Autolite starter mounted above crankcase or, optionally, at rear of engine.

ACCESSORIES: Novi alternator built into rear of engine casing and supplying a 6V battery.

The 40 hp Survol-de Coucy Pygmée engine

DIMENSIONS:
Length overall   19·09 in (485 mm)
Width overall, incl plugs   17·72 in (450 mm)
Height overall   13·39 in (340 mm)

WEIGHT:
With starter   84 lb (38 kg)

PERFORMANCE RATING:
T-O rating
40 hp at 5,500 rpm (2,750 propeller rpm max)

HISPANO-SUIZA
(Société d'exploitation des matériels Hispano-Suiza)
See SNECMA.

LRBA
LABORATOIRE DE RECHERCHES BALISTIQUES ET AÉRODYNAMIQUES
ADDRESS: 27-Vernon (Eure)
DIRECTOR:
Ing Général de 1re Cl de l'Armement Marchal
The principal French Government establishment

for rockets and ballistic flight, LRBA is administered by the Ministère d'Etat Chargé de la Défense Nationale. In addition to its work as development management authority on a wide range of ballistic vehicles (some of which are described in the "Research Rockets and Space Vehicles" section of this annual) LRBA specialises

in the complete development of all kinds of rocket engines, particularly those using liquid propellants. It has been responsible for the entire development of the first three rocket engines described below and is also working on hydrazine rockets for space use and on a large turbopump-fed engine.

Recent photographs depicting current rocket-propulsion activity at LRBA, Vernon. Upper left, Vexin motor; upper centre, Coralie motor for Europa F.7 vehicle; upper right, Valois motor about to begin a test run; lower left, the 40-tonne st turbopump engine in Test Stand No 2; below, hydrazine space thruster rated at 0·2 lb (0·1 kg) st, with measuring tape to give scale in centimetres

LRBA VEXIN

One of the Laboratory's first large liquid-propellant engines, the Vexin provides propulsion for the first stage of the Diamant A satellite launcher. It has a single thrust-chamber, supplied with white fuming nitric acid and turpentine by pressurizing the vehicle tanks from a solid-fuel gas generator. Sea-level thrust is 61,730 lb (28,000 kg). The chamber is machined from refractory steel, contains a throat liner of pyrolitic graphite and has a light-alloy radial propellant injector. The chamber, throat and bell mouth are coated with zirconium oxide. Cooling is provided by a film of fuel over the interior. Flight trajectory control is accomplished by gimballing the chamber about two axes at right angles, by means of two actuating rams supplied from the gas generator with electro-magnetic control. Production of the Vexin has been undertaken by SNECMA.

LRBA CORALIE

This liquid-propellant motor provides propulsion for the second stage of Europa I, the ELDO launch vehicle. It has four thrust chambers each rated at about 15,435 lb (7,000 kg) thrust,

the total thrust amounting to 61,730 lb (28,000 kg). Each chamber is of refractory steel with graphite throat liner, light alloy radial injector and interior coated with zirconium oxide. Propellants are nitrogen peroxide (N_2O_4) and UDMH (unsymmetrical dimethyl hydrazine. The UDMH provides film cooling of the chamber. Two small tanks of the same pair of propellants serve a gas generator which pressurizes the vehicle tanks for propellant supply purposes. Each diametrically opposed pair of chambers is linked together and pivots about a radial axis to provide second-stage vehicle control; they are positioned by Air Equipement oleo-pneumatic jacks, fed with pressurized gas from the generator.

The manufacturing programme for the Coralie motor was entrusted to the Atelier de Construction de Tarbes.

LRBA VALOIS

This is essentially a scale-up of Vexin, incorporating later technology and developed to provide propulsion for the first stage of Diamant B. The single chamber is pressure-fed with N_2O_4 and UDMH, separate tanks of these propellants supplying the gas generator. Chamber construction follows the technique established with Vexin.

Vehicle control again is accomplished by gimballing the thrust chamber about the pitch and yaw axes by means of two gas-pressurized actuating rams with electro-magnetic control. Sea-level thrust is 77,161 lb (35,000 kg).

Production will be assigned to an industrial manufacturer.

LRBA HYDRAZINE MOTORS

For several years the Laboratory has been studying the catalytic decomposition of hydrazine and the application of this reaction to small thrusters for satellites. Studies of chemistry and propulsion hardware have now reached the point where a satisfactory catalyst has been found and test motors built.

Thrust chambers rated at from 0·02 lb (0·01 kg) to 22 lb (10 kg) st have been static-tested, in every case with good results. The motor rated at 0·2 lb (0·1 kg) survived 1,100 starts from cold without damage. The 2 lb (1 kg) motor functioned for a duration of 5,400 seconds, while the 22 lb (10 kg) unit was tested for 2,200 seconds under the same conditions.

Research has shown that the addition of hydrazine nitrate notably depresses the congealing temperature of hydrazine (these thrusters being designed for use after prolonged cold soaking in space) and also improves the specific impulse.

LRBA TURBOPUMP ENGINE

The turbopump engine has simplicity of manufacture and operation as its prime design objectives. As a consequence the engine omits use of gears, jointed high pressure pipes, heat exchangers in the tank pressurization system and lubrication system. The engine comprises two major assemblies, the thrust chamber and turbopump. The thrust chamber features a propellant injection cylinder and is cooled by means of a film of fuel. The thrust chamber wall is fabricated in HS 25 heat resisting alloy and the throat is made of graphite.

The 1,620 hp turbopump comprises a two-stage turbine driving, on the same shaft, the two propellant pumps and a water pump. The propellant pumps supply the UDMH and N_2O_4 propellants from the main tanks through to the turbine and gas generators. In the main gas generator the propellants are supplemented by a flow of water fed from the water tank by the water pump. The ensuing gases are supplied to the turbine, and to the tanks for pressurization purposes. The gases also pass to auxiliary equipment which maintains constant propellant mixture ratio and regulates the thrust chamber combustion zone pressure to ensure thrust build-up following an initial pilot pressure. The exhaust from the turbine is vented to atmosphere via two small thrust nozzles.

The turbopump is rigidly mounted on top of the thrust chamber, the combined assembly being carried on a gimbal mounting (single or double acting) located above the turbopump. The propellant feed pipes to the pumps are flexible to absorb any engine movements.

As the UDMH and N_2O_4 propellants are hypergolic, starting of the turbopump engine involves simply the opening of propellant valves. Ignition is rapid and propellant consumption prior to lift-off is therefore minimised. The gases as used for tank pressurization are inert. As the turbopump and thrust chamber form a single, self-contained assembly, a number of such units may be grouped to meet higher launcher thrust requirements. From a basic single-chamber thrust of 88,200 lb (40 tonnes), multiple engines can be provided to cover a range up to 661,000 lb (300 tonnes).

The turbopump engine has been extensively tested on LRBA's test stands, and has possible application in a variety of French medium-sized launcher vehicles. These include Diamant C with a 440 lb (200 kg) payload using a single chamber; Carmen with payloads up to 1,675 lb (720 kg) using two chambers; and an undesignated vehicle with four or five chambers for placing payloads ranging from 440 lb (200 kg) to 4,400 lb (2 tonnes) in a geo-stationary orbit.

MICROTURBO
MICROTURBO SA
HEAD OFFICE AND WORKS:
Chemin du Pont de Rupé, 31 Toulouse (Haute Garonne)
PRESIDENT DIRECTOR GENERAL:
G. Bayard
MANAGING DIRECTOR:
L. Pech

Microturbo was formed in 1960 by Ateliers SEMCA of Toulouse to produce small gas turbine units, some of which had originally been designed by SEMCA. In its field, Microturbo has specialised in the research, design and development of gas turbine powered starting systems for aircraft main propulsion engines.

Microturbo's initial product, which is still being manufactured, was the Noelle 60 290 free-turbine starter unit for the SNECMA Atar turbojet.

From this unit a range of small gas turbine systems has subsequently been evolved, designed for such duties as APUs, EPUs, GPUs, air conditioning, air turbo-generator and ultra-low thrust turbojets, as well as engine starting. Extensive use is made of basically similar gas generator components to provide cross-feeding of parts manufacture and operating experience.

Significant among the company's current developments are the Emeraude starter APU, and Espadon EPU, for the Concorde supersonic airliner. Microturbo products are licensed in the United Kingdom to Plessey Co Ltd, an agreement which includes joint participation in any future production on behalf of the Concorde programme.

Microturbo employs 240 personnel.

MICROTURBO ATHOS
Derived from the Noelle free-turbine starter, the Athos starting system comprises a basic gas generator unit modified to provide an excess of air which is bled from the combustion chamber and fed to a remotely-positioned air turbine starter with reduction gear. This combines the facility of the Olympie in enabling the drive unit to be mounted direct on the engine and separate from the energy source, with the use of low-temperature (rather than high-temperature) ducting.

The air generator section comprises a single-stage centrifugal compressor of excess air capacity, driven by a two-stage axial turbine and an annular reverse-flow combustion chamber from the rear of which the air is bled, via a bifurcated duct around the curved turbine exhaust duct, to energise the air turbine starter. A butterfly valve in the duct to the air turbine is actuated by combustion chamber pressure. Opening of the bleed valve is thus dependent on correct build-up of pressure within the air generator itself. Microswitches in the air duct prevent the unit starting up if the butterfly valve is not initially closed. The air turbine is a two-stage axial unit driving a two-stage epicyclic gear train and clutch.

Applications of the starter in its 100 hp Athos IV version include the SNECMA TF106 twin-spool turbofan in the Dassault Mirage III-V and the TF306 twin-spool turbofan in the Mirage F2 and G. The 87 hp Athos III was earlier proposed for starting the General Electric J79 single-shaft turbojet in the Lockheed F-104.

The following data relate to the Athos IV.

DIMENSIONS:
Air generator:	
Diameter	11·1 in (282 mm)
Length	34·7 in (882·5 mm)
Air turbine starter and reduction gear:	
Diameter	9·1 in (230 mm)
Length	16·9 in (430·5 mm)

WEIGHTS:
Air generator	55·1 lb (25 kg)
Air turbine starter and reduction gear	31·3 lb (14·2 kg)
Accessories	12·1 lb (5·5 kg)
Total	98·5 lb (44·7 kg)

PERFORMANCE RATING:
Max power, at 2,600 air turbine output rpm
100 hp
FUEL CONSUMPTION:
Per start approx 700 cc

The 100 hp Microturbo Athos air generator and remote air turbine starter system
(Kenneth Fulton)

MICROTURBO COUGAR
This is a new Microturbo turbojet for target drones. Basic rating is 132 lb (60 kg) at a nominal speed of 52,000 rpm for a fuel consumption of 159 lb (72 kg)/hr. Weight is 58·4 lb (26·5 kg). No further details are available.

An earlier engine in the same series was the Microturbo Lynx turbojet, a 1963 project for self-launching sailplanes.

MICROTURBO ECLAIR
Based on the gas generator section of the Microturbo Emeraude starter and APU for Concorde prototypes, the Eclair is an ultra-small single-shaft turbojet designed to power pilotless drones and for use in sailplanes to provide thrust for take-off and climb to altitude. The engine is also capable of in-flight starting to provide powered flight in an emergency. Initial installation was in the Fauvel Aile Volante AV 45-01R single-seat tailless self-launching sailplane which first flew with the Eclair 012-01 in late 1967. With the Eclair, the AV 45 has a max climb rate of 990 ft (302 m)/min and can reach 10,000 ft (3,048 m) in 15 minutes. Other Fauvel projects which may be equipped with the Eclair include the two-seat AV 46 and single-seat AV 48. A further application of the Eclair is in the Caproni Vizzola "Calif" A-21J two-seat sailplane.

Two versions have been developed, the Eclair 1 and Eclair 2 which differ only in their lubrication and starting systems. The following description relates to the Eclair 2.

TYPE: Single-shaft centrifugal turbojet.

AIR INTAKE: Annular intake cast integral with compressor front casing, and supporting impeller/accessory drive shaft bearings, accessory drive gear and nose-mounted electric starter motor.

COMPRESSOR: Single-stage centrifugal unit with two-piece single-sided impeller and radial-plus-axial diffuser. Impeller carried on splined shaft system which extends forward of impeller to provide accessory drive. Main shaft assembly for compressor and turbine is carried on two high-speed ball bearings—one aft of rotating labyrinth seal behind impeller back plate and one on upstream face of turbine disc.

COMBUSTION CHAMBER: Annular reverse-flow with cast outer casing bolted to compressor casing at front and combustor back plate at rear. Four-piece flame tube has three layers of forward-facing skin-cooling slots and single row of air ports near head. Two high energy igniter plugs.

TURBINE: Single-stage axial unit with cast Nimonic alloy inlet nozzle ring and rotor disc with integral blades. Disc through-bolted to main shaft.

JET PIPE: Simple convergent nozzle on parallel-section jet pipe clipped to tapered turbine exhaust duct bolted to combustor back plate. Curved inner exhaust cone. Exhaust gas temperature 1,148°F (620°C).

ACCESSORY DRIVE: Simple spur gear drive from front of impeller extension shaft. Shaft is carried on two ball bearings mounted in intake casing. Drives provided for speed controller and combined fuel-and-oil pump mounted below front of engine. Nose-mounted electric starter motor drives via dog clutch.

FUEL SYSTEM: Fuel supplied by combined fuel-and-oil pump to fuel pressure controller and thence to eight fuel atomizing injectors mounted in combustor back plate. Fuel pressure controller spills back excess fuel to inlet of pump in response to air pressure signal from flyweight-type engine-driven speed governor supplied with compressor delivery air tapping. Compressor air also fed to airspeed safety valve and pneumatic throttle controlling speed, max and idling.

The Microturbo Eclair single-shaft turbojet for self-launching sailplanes (176 lb = 80 kg st)
(Kenneth Fulton)

FUEL GRADES: TR0, TR4 and majority of other jet fuels.

LUBRICATION SYSTEM: Engine-driven fuel-and-oil pump feeds oil to lubrication system via calibration valve and filter. Pressure switch in oil feed line provides warning signal if pressure falls below preset datum. Filter fitted in all oil circuits.

MOUNTING: Forward mounting lugs integral with cast inlet/compressor casing. Aft mounting on rear of combustion chamber.

STARTING: Electrical with nose mounted starter motor supplied by 24-volt sailplane battery.

DIMENSIONS:
Height	approx 12·7 in	(312 mm)
Width, including accessories	19·9 in	(505 mm)
Length overall	23·9 in	(607 mm)

WEIGHT:
	approx 77 lb (35 kg)

PERFORMANCE RATING:
T-O, at 47,000 nominal rpm	176 lb (80 kg)

FUEL CONSUMPTION:
At T-O rating	198 lb (90 kg)/hr

MICROTURBO EMERAUDE
Installed in the prototype Concorde aircraft, the Emeraude was initially intended to provide for starting of the Rolls-Royce/SNECMA Olympus 593 main propulsion turbojets—the unit is mounted on the gearbox of Nos 2 and 4 engines, with cross-bleeding of air enabling Nos 1 and 3 engines to be started also. Subsequently the Emeraude's duties were extended to those of an APU, driving the Olympus 593 accessory gearbox when it is not being driven by the turbojet itself, i.e. for ground check-out purposes or following a main engine failure in flight.

In this additional role, the Emeraude supplies oil to operate the clutch connecting it to the main engine gearbox. This clutch is disengaged in the event of an Olympus 593 failure in flight, enabling the Emeraude to operate as an emergency power unit (EPU), driving the engine-mounted hydraulic pumps for the aircraft flying controls.

On pre-production and production Concordes, the starter and accessory-drive duties of the Emeraude will be performed by individual air turbine starters and the Microturbo Espadon EPU (which see herewith).

The gas generator and accessory-drive section of the Emeraude are the same as those described for the Microturbo Eclair turbojet (which see herewith). The following description refers specifically to the additional power turbine, reduction gearbox and the fuel and lubrication systems.

TYPE: Free-turbine centrifugal gas-turbine starter and APU

POWER TURBINE: Single-stage axial unit overhung from rear on through-bolted shaft carried on two high-speed ball bearings. Turbine shaft is integral with sun gear of first-stage reduction gear to output shaft.

SHAFT DRIVE: Rear-mounted two-stage epicyclic reduction gear with straight spurs providing 7·185 : 1 drive ratio to rear output shaft to

The 167 hp Microturbo Emeraude free-turbine gas-turbine starter and APU for Concorde prototypes *(Kenneth Fulton)*

Olympus 593 accessory gearbox. Bevel gear drive from output annulus gear drives power turbine speed governor via single spur train.

JET PIPE: Bifurcated turbine exhaust duct in ventral position. Flap closes-off ducts when unit shut down. Exhaust gas temperature 1,112°F (600°C).

FUEL SYSTEM: Fuel pumped to Emeraude from secondary tank located inside main engine fuel tank. Fuel supplied to eight atomizing injectors mounted in combustion back plate, via flow controller and solenoid-operated shut-off cock. Fuel control unit determines proportion of fuel spilled back from burner, and is supplied with compressor delivery air pressure signal modified by gas generator and power turbine speed governor. Power turbine speed governed to remain constant while gas generator speed is varied to meet changes in power demand.

FUEL GRADES: TR0, TR4, TR5, DEngRD 2488, 2498, 2482 and 2486.

LUBRICATION SYSTEM: Single gear pump supplies oil, via constant-pressure by-pass valve, to solenoid-operated shut-off valve in supply line to APU drive clutch and to calibrated orifice controlling oil pressure to gas generator and accessory and output reduction gears. Three scavenge gear pumps return oil to main engine oil tank.

MOUNTING: Forward mounting lugs integral with cast inlet/compressor casing. Aft mounting on rear of output reduction gearbox.

STARTING: Electrical with nose-mounted starter motor supplied by 24V aircraft battery.

DIMENSIONS:
Height	approx 17·1 in	(435 mm)
Length	33·4 in	(847·7 mm)

WEIGHT: approx 126 lb (57 kg)
PERFORMANCE RATING:
Starter output power at 47,000 gas generator rpm 167 hp
FUEL CONSUMPTION: 176 lb (80 kg)/hr

MICROTURBO ESPADON

At the request of the airlines, the Microturbo Emeraude starter and APU has been modified for use in pre-production and production Concorde aircraft to undertake combined APU and EPU duties. In this new form the unit is known as the Espadon, and on the ground will operate as an APU for pre-flight check-out of the aircraft flying controls, hydraulics and other systems.

The 167 hp Microturbo Espadon free-turbine gas-turbine EPU for Concorde pre-production and production aircraft (*Kenneth Fulton*)

In ts EPU mode the Espadon, under certain flight conditions, will act as a stand-by power unit, and in the event of an all engine-out emergency, will power the flying controls via duplicate hydraulic pumps. A single Espadon will be mounted in the starboard engine nacelle of the Concorde.

This revised arrangement eliminates the need for mechanical connections and a clutch, and results in a lighter installation. The duty of main engine starting will be undertaken by a separate engine-mounted air turbine starter energised by ground equipment.

In configuration the Espadon comprises the Emeraude gas generator and power turbine, but with a bifurcated direct-ducted air intake to the compressor, and modified output reduction gear to drive port and starboard mounted hydraulic pumps. The jet pipe is a single rearwards-facing circular duct. Power rating and fuel consumption are the same as for the Emeraude but weight is increased to 176 lb (80 kg), height becomes 16·6 in (423 mm), width 23·8 in (604 mm) and length 36·5 in (927 mm).

MICROTURBO GTS 100

The GTS 100 is a gas-turbine starter of 99 hp (100 cv) maximum power output operating at 64,000 rpm. Weighing 70·5 lb (32 kg), the unit has a fuel consumption of approximately 800 cc per start, and is itself started electrically using the aircraft batteries. No application has so far been announced.

MICROTURBO JAGUAR SYSTEM

Combining features of the Saphir air generator and Athos air turbine starter, the Microturbo Jaguar system has been developed for starting the Rolls-Royce Turboméca Adour two-shaft turbofan, two of which power the Anglo-French SEPECAT Jaguar light strike fighter/trainer aircraft. The system comprises an air generator supplying compressed air to 50 hp air-turbine starters mounted direct on the starboard front face of the Adour's HP accessory wheelcase.

The Jaguar starter is also suitable for use in single-engined installations. A related starting system is known as the Microturbo Albatros.

TYPE: Combined air generator and twin air-turbine starter system.

AIR GENERATOR:

AIR INTAKE: Annular intake cast integral with compressor front casing. Intake/compressor casing provides support for impeller extension shaft bearings and nose-mounted electric starter motor. Also houses electric starter reduction gear.

COMPRESSOR: Single-stage centrifugal unit of excess air capacity with two-piece single-sided impeller and radial-plus-axial diffuser. Annular flow splitter at exit to radial diffuser separates proportion of impeller air flow to bleed-air scroll feeding two air turbine starters. Bleed air flow at 51,300 air generator rpm, 55·1 lb (25 kg)/min at 3·22 bars absolute pressure, at ISA SL conditions. Impeller carried on splined shaft system extending forward of impeller to connect with reduction gear from electric starter. Main shaft assembly for compressor and turbine carried on two high-speed ball bearings, one behind impeller back plate and one on upstream side of turbine disc.

COMBUSTION CHAMBER: Annular reverse-flow system with eight atomizing fuel injectors mounted in combustor back plate. Two igniter plugs.

TURBINE: Two-stage axial unit with cast nozzle rings and rotor discs with integral blades. Discs through-bolted to main shaft.

JET PIPE: Curved duct bolted to rear of combustor back plate. Curved inner exhaust cone supported on radial vanes. Exhaust gas temperature 1,148°F (620°C).

MOUNTING: Forward mounting lugs on rear of compressor casing, and rear lugs on combustor back plate.

AIR TURBINE STARTERS:

AIR TURBINE: Single-stage radial inflow unit with intake scroll and axial exit. Single-sided rotor overhung on shaft integral with reduction train sun gear. Shaft supported on high-speed ball bearing either side of sun gear. Inlet air temperature 302°F (150°C) and exhaust 158°F (70°C).

SHAFT DRIVE: Single-stage epicyclic reduction gear of 10 : 1 speed ratio, with annulus gear integral with driving element of Borg Warner centrifugal clutch. Driven element of clutch splined to output shaft in turn splined to main engine wheelcase.

AIR DUCTING: Bleed air duct from air generator supplies air to separate manifolds feeding each air turbine starter unit via electrically-operated on/off air supply valves. Discharge valve upstream of air supply valves permits venting of manifolds to atmosphere to maintain preset delivery air pressure.

FUEL SYSTEM: Combined fuel-and-air pump draws fuel from starter fuel tank (via filter and shut-off cock), and supplies it to eight atomising fuel injectors via distribution unit and pressure switch. Distribution unit determines quantity of excess fuel to spill back to starter tank. Also ensures rapid acceleration without overheating and that adequate power is provided to give minimum main engine start times without overloading the air generator. Speed detection unit on each air turbine starter signals air generator to shut-down to idle when air starter reaches required rpm.

FUEL GRADES: TR0, TR4 and other turbine engine fuels.

LUBRICATION SYSTEM: Air generator has self-contained system comprising oil tank and single-stage of combined fuel-and-oil pump. Oil is supplied by pump to main shaft bearings and to electric starter reduction gear. Oil then drains back to tank. Pressure switch cuts starting cycle if oil pressure too low. Air turbine starters provided with individual oil filling, level and drain caps.

STARTING: With air supply valves and discharge valve closed, electric starter starts air generator

The Microturbo Jaguar air generator and remote twin-air-turbine starter system for the Rolls-Royce Turboméca Adour turbofan powering the SEPECAT Jaguar (*Kenneth Fulton*)

using aircraft 24-28V batteries. Automatic switches terminate start if fuel or oil pressure is low, or if air generator idle speed is not reached. With air generator at correct idle speed, No 1 main engine start switch is closed and air generator accelerates to full speed. With No 1 air supply valve open, air-turbine starter then accelerates up to cut-out speed and air generator then slows back to idle. Air supply valve closes and discharge valve opens. No 2 main engine start switch is then closed and start cycle repeats. Air generator then shuts-down automatically.

DIMENSIONS:
Air generator:
Diameter 11·1 in (282 mm)
Length, excluding exhaust duct 20·6 in (523·4 mm)
Air turbine starter:
Diameter, excluding air inlet 7·2 in (182 mm)
Length, excluding air inlet 11·5 in (292 mm)
WEIGHT:
Air generator 48·9 lb (22·2 kg)
Air turbine starters, 2 off 31 lb (14 kg)
Accessories 26 lb (11·8 kg)
Total 105·8 lb (48 kg)
PERFORMANCE RATING:
Max power at air turbine starter output shaft, at 6,000 rpm 52 hp

MICROTURBO MEON

This is an air generator unit supplying compressed air to an engine-mounted air turbine starter. Its intended application is on General Electric J79-GE-17 turbojets powering Lockheed F-104S fighters of the Italian Air Force. Lockheed is also proposing the Meon to other air forces operating F-104 aircraft, as a self-contained starting system.

MICROTURBO NOELLE

The Noelle gas-turbine starter was the first unit to be marketed by Microturbo when the company entered the small turbine field in 1960. The 60 hp Noelle 60 290 is fitted to SNECMA Atar 08 turbojets powering the Dassault Etendard IV-M and to Atar 09 turbojets powering the Dassault Mirage III and IV. A later version, the Noelle 002 (previously designated Noelle 80) rated at 80 hp, is fitted to more powerful Atar 09 engines powering Mirage III, IV and F1 aircraft. Production of the Noelle system continues today and the unit is in service with the French Air Force, and other national air forces operating Mirage aircraft.

Manufacture of the Noelle 60 and other equipment was licensed to Teddington Aircraft Controls Ltd of Merthyr Tydfil, Wales, in 1961 by Microturbo's founder company, Ateliers SEMCA of Toulouse. Subsequently in 1964 the British licence for all Microturbo units was transferred to the Plessey Dynamics Group of Plessey Co Ltd, Ilford, England. Initial outcome of this second licence arrangement was the Plessey Solent 1 gas-turbine starter, comprising an advanced scaled-down Noelle unit and intended for use in Royal Air Force and Royal Navy McDonnell Douglas Phantoms.

Basic aim of the Noelle unit is to provide a main engine starting system completely self-contained within the aircraft and activated solely by the pilot. As such the starter operates on main engine fuel and is electrically started using aircraft batteries. The Noelle drives the main engine to a speed beyond self-sustaining rpm to avoid any possibility of main engine overheating.

The following description relates to both the Noelle 60 290 and Noelle 002 systems.

TYPE: Free-turbine centrifugal gas-turbine starter.

AIR INTAKE: Annular intake cast integral with compressor front casing, and supporting impeller/accessory drive shaft bearings, accessory drive gear and nose-mounted starter motor. Air enters via ports in conical shroud over intake and starter motor.

COMPRESSOR: Single-stage centrifugal unit with two-piece single-sided impeller and radial-plus-axial diffuser. Impeller carried on splined shaft system which extends forward of impeller to provide accessory drive. Main shaft assembly for compressor and turbine carried on two high-speed ball bearings—one aft of seal behind impeller back plate and one on upstream face of turbine disc.

COMBUSTION CHAMBER: Annular reverse-flow with cast outer casing bolted to compressor casing at front and combustor back plate integral with cast rear support casing. Configuration is conical with increasing diameter to rear to accommodate outward-flared exhaust ducts passing over output reduction gear. Two igniter plugs.

COMPRESSOR TURBINE: Single-stage axial unit with cast inlet nozzle ring and rotor disc with integral blades. Disc retained on splined main shaft by nut on rear face.

POWER TURBINE: Cast nozzle ring and rotor disc with integral blades. Disc retained on splined drive shaft by nut on forward face. Turbine shaft is integral with sun gear of first-stage reduction gear to output shaft.

SHAFT DRIVE: Rear mounted two-stage epicyclic reduction gear with straight spurs. Second-stage annulus gear integral with driving member of roller-type clutch splined to main engine compressor shaft.

JET PIPE: Bifurcated exhaust duct flared to pass over output reduction gear. Ducts pass through ports in starter rear support casing.

FUEL SYSTEM: Electrically-driven fuel pump supplies fuel, via fuel valve and regulator, to atomizing fuel injectors mounted in combustor back plate. Eight injectors for Noelle 60, and ten injectors for higher rated Noelle 002. Compressor delivery air pressure signal supplied to fuel regulator to determine proportion of fuel spilled back from burners to main engine drain pipe.

FUEL GRADES: JP-1, JP-4 and JP-5.

LUBRICATION SYSTEM: Splash lubrication provided for accessory drive gear and output reduction gear. Single-shot total loss lubrication of gas generator main bearings supplied by oil pump, flow being proportional to compressor delivery air pressure.

MOUNTING: Starter bolted direct to main engine intake centre housing via starter rear support casing and output reduction gear casing.

STARTING: Automatic electric starting with nose-mounted starter motor energised by aircraft battery.

DIMENSIONS:
Diameter 12·3 in (312 mm)
Length 26·7 in (678·2 mm)
WEIGHT:
Complete with accessories approx 76·1 lb (34·5 kg)

PERFORMANCE RATINGS:
Max power:
Noelle 60, at 1,500 output rpm   60 hp
Noelle 002, at 1,900 output rpm   80 hp

FUEL CONSUMPTION:
Per start   approx 350 cc

The 80 hp Microturbo Noelle 002 free-turbine gas turbine starter *(Kenneth Fulton)*

MICROTURBO OLYMPIE

From the original Noelle starter, in which the gas generator section, power turbine and output reduction gearbox are mounted as an integral unit, Microturbo developed the Olympie system in which the gas generator is mounted remote from the power turbine assembly but connected by a tubular gas duct. This enables the power turbine and its reduction gear to be mounted on and drive the HP spool of two-shaft engines where it may not be feasible or convenient to locate the complete starter on the engine intake centre housing. A production application for the Olympie has yet to be announced, although the starter has been tested on such engines as the Rolls-Royce Conway, Flygmotor RM8, Rolls-Royce Bristol Pegasus, and Rolls-Royce Napier Gazelle.

Two versions of the starter have been developed, the 80 hp Olympie I derived from the Noelle 002, and the 100 hp Olympie II in turn derived from the Olympie I.

The following data apply to the Olympie I.

DIMENSIONS:
Gas generator only:
Diameter   11·1 in (282 mm)
Length   24·3 in (616 mm)

WEIGHT:
Gas generator   42 lb (19 kg)
Accessories   9·1 lb (4·15 kg)

The 80 hp and 100 hp Microturbo Olympie gas generator and remote gas-turbine starter system *(Kenneth Fulton)*

Power turbine and reduction gear weight varies according to reduction gear ratio and configuration

PERFORMANCE RATING:
Max power, at 1,900 output rpm   80 hp

FUEL CONSUMPTION:
Per start   approx 350 cc

MICROTURBO SAPHIR

The Saphir is an APU providing electrical power and compressed air for cabin conditioning of aircraft both while airborne and on the ground. Two versions of the APU exist, the Saphir 1 (or Saphir 64) which provides air conditioning and 2 to 2·5 kW as optional equipment on the Dassault Mystère 20/Falcons, and Saphir 2 which provides air conditioning and 9kW as standard equipment in the Dassault Falcon F. Further developments of the Saphir are under development for other aircraft applications.

The following description relates to the Saphir 2.

TYPE: Single-shaft gas-turbine APU.

AIR INTAKE: Annular intake cast integral with compressor front casing and enclosed in cylindrical plenum chamber with single opening fed by direct air duct through APU ventilation case. Intake/compressor case provides support for impeller/accessory drive shaft bearings, accessory drive gear and starter-generator.

COMPRESSOR: Single-stage centrifugal unit of excess air capacity with two-piece single-sided impeller and radial-plus-axial diffuser. Annular flow splitter at exit from radial diffuser separates proportion of impeller air flow to bleed air scroll feeding to cabin conditioning system via metering nozzle to prevent surging or overheating. Impeller carried on splined shaft system which extends forward of impeller to provide accessory drive. Main shaft assembly for compressor and turbine is carried on two high-speed ball bearings, one aft of rotating labyrinth seal behind impeller back plate and one on upstream face of turbine disc.

COMBUSTION CHAMBER: Annular reverse-flow, with cast outer casing bolted to compressor casing at front and combustor back plate at rear. Four-piece flame tube has three layers of forward-facing skin-cooling slots and single row of air ports near head. Two high-energy igniter plugs.

TURBINE: Two-stage axial unit with cast nozzle rings and rotor discs integral with blades. Discs through-bolted to main shaft.

JET PIPE: Curved duct bolted to rear of combustor backplate. Curved inner exhaust cone supported on radial vanes. Exhaust gas temperature 1,112°F (600°C).

The Microturbo Saphir single-shaft gas-turbine APU *(Kenneth Fulton)*

ACCESSORY DRIVE: Simple two-stage twin train gear drive from front of impeller extension shaft. Reduction ratio 5·76 : 1. Shaft carried on two ball bearings mounted in intake casing. Single drive provided for nose-mounted DC starter-generator and tacho-generator.

VENTILATION CASE: Complete gas-turbine and starter-generator assembly housed in ventilation case with three air-inlets—one direct into compressor plenum chamber, second direct into case for ventilation purposes, and third ducted direct to starter-generator for cooling air. This last flow in turn induces venting flow from ventilation case.

FUEL SYSTEM: Fuel supplied by remote-mounted electrically-driven combined fuel-and-oil pump to distribution unit embodying filter, servo-valve and fuel pressure switch, and thence to eight fuel atomizing injectors mounted in combustor back plate. Electronic control unit maintains engine and generator speed constant as a function of ambient temperature. This ensures effectively constant bleed air pressure. Control unit also provides automatic starting cycle for APU. Two-way electrical valve downstream of distribution unit determines proportion of fuel spilled back from injector manifold. Servo valve controls secondary flow of fuel to fuel-cooled oil tank.

FUEL GRADES: JP-1, JP-4 and JP-5.

LUBRICATION SYSTEM: Using same oil as main engine, system provides for both lubrication and heat dissipation of bearings and accessory drive gear. Comprises 5·3 pint (3 litre) fuel-cooled oil tank, combined fuel-and-oil pump and filter. Oil from tank pumped, via oil pressure switch, to bearings and accessory gear from whence it drains to oil tank. Switch and tank thermostat stop APU in event of low oil pressure or high oil temperature.

STARTING: Automatic electrical using 28V aircraft battery.

DIMENSIONS:
APU:
Height   approx 16·9 in (429 mm)
Width   approx 15·2 in (385 mm)
Length overall, including exhaust duct
     34·9 in (887·3 mm)
Ventilation case:
Height   24·5 in (622·8 mm)
Width   15·5 in (394 mm)
Length   26·8 in (681·5 mm)

PERFORMANCE RATINGS:
Bleed air flow at 50,500 gas generator rpm using 0·87 in (22·5 mm) diameter air metering nozzle, at 14·7 lb/sq in (760 mm mercury)
     30·4 lb (13·8 kg)/min
Bleed air pressure at 50,500 gas generator rpm
     3·1 bars abs
Electrical output in generator mode   9kW

FUEL CONSUMPTION:
At 50,500 gas generator rpm
     88 to 97 lb (40 to 44 kg)/hr

MICROTURBO SOLENT

Representing the smallest of Microturbo's gas-turbine starters to be built, the Solent is an exceptionally compact unit designed for licensed manufacture by Plessey Co Ltd for use on Rolls-Royce RB.168 Spey military turbofans powering McDonnell Douglas Phantom fighters of the Royal Air Force and Royal Navy. Subsequently the initial Solent 1 unit was superseded by the even smaller Solent 2 capable of more compact installation (see page 727).

PNSM
FOUDRERIE NATIONALE DE SAINT-MÉDARD
ADDRESS:
St. Médard-en-Jalles (Gironde)

Established by Royal Decree in 1679, the Foudrerie Nationale de St. Médard is one of the largest establishments in the Service des Poudres, the state organization administered by the Délégation Ministérielle pour l'Armement which is responsible for all production in France of solid propellant charges for everything from pistol ammunition to an ICBM.

PNSM has a payroll of almost 1,300, of whom 1,000 are organized into skilled groups of civil and military engineers, working in more than 500 buildings dispersed in the pine-forest north-west of Bordeaux.

The establishment probably produces a wider range of solid-propellant rocket charges than any other single organisation in the world. Brief details of some current production motors are given in the accompanying tables. These show that important propellants include all the families of which details have been disclosed outside the Soviet Union. Composite propellants include polybutadiene, polychlorates of vinyl or polyurethane, ammonium perchlorate (with additions such as dispersed aluminium) and numerous other composite propellants, often with 12-15 separate ingredients, as well as the more traditional double-base extruded propellants (type SD) derived from cordite and similar gun propellants which are made very cheaply in sizes up to 200 mm (7·9 in) diameter.

SD motors are used mainly for such applications as anti-tank missiles and take-off boosters. The plastolite/plastolane composites are cast in free blocks, whereas the isolite/isolane/butalite/butalane series are case-bonded permanently into the metal vehicle stage which is also sometimes fabricated by PNSM.

The establishment has test-fired a 57,320 lb (26,000 kg) motor of 78·8 in (2 m) diameter, and at the 1969 Paris Salon exhibited an inert segment weighing approximately 22,000 lb (10,000 kg) and of 118 in (3 m) diameter to demonstrate its capacity to make segments suitable for Titan III-C.

Since 1959 the establishment has been manufacturing the rocket motor of the US Hawk missile under licence, and in turn has licensed the governments of India and Pakistan to make the plastolane motors used in Aérospatiale (Sud-Aviation) sounding rockets.

A completely original way of forming the charge for large motors has been developed which, instead of using a star-centred filling, uses a retractable boring tool (with an extraction duct for the swarf) to machine annular bleed slots around the cast charge. This technique, used on the P.4 and P.6 ballistic-missile stages and on the perigee motor of ELDO-PAS, is described as having the greatest possible simplicity. It reduces the time taken in fabricating the internal profile of the charge to two days, compared with 15 days for methods involving a retractible or fusible mandrel or former. PNSM is at present striving to diversify and to apply its talents and extensive laboratory equipment (which includes a 14 MeV radiographic installation and the largest vibration exciter in Western Europe) to commercial ends.

DATA FOR A SELECTION OF THE MORE IMPORTANT CURRENT PNSM MOTORS

Motor	Application	Total Impulse lb-sec (kg-sec)	Duration (sec)	Diameter in (mm)	Charge Weight lb (kg)
Isolane propellant					
P.16 (Type 902)	SSBS first stage	9,215,350 (4,180,000)	76	59 (1,500)	35,275 (16,000)
P.10 (Type 903)	SSBS second stage	—	—	59 (1,500)	22,050 (10,000)
P10. (Type 904)	MSBS first stage	—	—	59 (1,500)	22,050 (10,000)
P.4 (Rita)	MSBS second stage	2,182,580 (990,000)	55	59 (1,500)	8,820 (4,000)
P.6					
Diamant	Diamant third stage	(295,420 (134,000)	45	25·5 (650)	1,410 (640)
Soleil VE.111	Diamant second stage	1,036,170 (470,000)	36·7	31·5 (800)	4,982 (2,260)
Polka	Masurca boost	352,740 (160,000)	4·6	22 (560)	1,521 (690)
Jacée	Masurca cruise	138,900 (63,000)	26	15·75 (400)	705 (320)
Plastolite/plastolane					
Marie-Antoinette	Matra R. 530	17,635 (8,000)	9	8 (203)	93·7 (42·5)
Vénus	Malafon boost	37,480 (17,000)	2·9	10·8 (275)	203 (92)
Epervier	AS.30 boost	23,600 (10,700)	2	13 (330)	126 (57)
Mammouth	VE.110 test vehicle	811,300 (368,000)	18·2	31·5 (800)	4,210 (1,910)
Stromboli	Aérospatiale Dragon	319,675 (145,000)	16·5	21·6 (550)	1,510 (685)
SD					
ACRA	ACRA missile	—	—	—	—
Entac	Entac missile	—	18·7	2·45 (62)	3·24 (1·47)
Mk 43	2·75 in rocket	—	1·5	2·45 (62)	5·84 (2·65)
CT.20	CT.20 boost trolley	—	2	3·62 (92)	198 (90)

RECTIMO
RECTIMO-SAVOIE AVIATION
OFFICES AND WORKS:

Chamberg, Haute Savoie

Rectimo has manufactured over 240 4 AR 1200 single-ignition derivatives of the Volkswagen four-cylinder air-cooled car engine, which together with the larger 4 AR 1600 are used in the Fournier single-seat RF4D and two-seat RF5 powered gliders. The 40 hp 4 AR 1200 engine has a 1,192 cc cubic capacity, 7 : 1 compression ratio and weighs 136 lb (61·5 kg). Fuel consumption under cruise conditions is 2·4 gallons (11 litres)/hr. The 4 AR 1600 produces 61 hp at T-O and has a cubic capacity of 1,600 cc and an 8 : 1 compression ratio. Weight is 141 lb (64 kg). Both engines have a maximum speed of 3,600 rpm.

SEP
SOCIÉTÉ EUROPÉENNE DE PROPULSION
HEAD OFFICE:

3 avenue du Général de Gaulle, 92-Puteaux (Hauts-de-Seine)

WORKS:

Bordeaux-Le Haillan, Bordeaux-Blanquefort, Melun-Villaroche and Istres

PRESIDENT DIRECTOR GENERAL:

P. Soufflet

Société Européene de Propulsion results from the merger in 1968 of Société d'Etude de la Propulsion par Réaction (SEPR) and the Division Engins-Espace (Space & Missiles Division) of SNECMA. This company specialises in the design and development of all categories of rocket engines and motors for aircraft, missiles, space launchers, and satellites. Its facilities are the largest in Europe devoted to rocket propulsion. Two-thirds of its 1,800 personnel are engineers and technicians engaged in research, development and testing.

Current production engine for aircraft is the SEPR 844 being produced by SNECMA to provide thrust boost for Dassault Mirage III fighters in service with the French Air Force and other national air forces.

SEP produces a wide range of solid-propellant motors as sustainers and boosters for French and European guided and unguided missiles and space launchers. Some 50 different types of motor have been designed since 1950, including four-nozzle configuration for the second stages of Diamant A and B space launchers and the SSBS and MSBS, and the ELDO perigee motor.

The company is also developing two upper-stage liquid oxygen/liquid hydrogen engines designated HM4 and HM7. Other SEP developments include engines using hybrid propellants, fluorine and fluorine compounds, monopropellants, compressed gases, as well as electric 'thrusters'. The company is now applying its missile and space technology to oceanology.

SEPR 844
The SEPR 844, derived from the earlier SEPR 841, is a pump-fed single-chamber rocket engine which delivers a fixed thrust of 3,370 lb (1,530 kg) for 80 seconds for its installation in the Mirage III interceptor. The propellants are nitric acid and JP-1 or JP-4, and are fed by pumps driven by an auxiliary shaft from the turbine power plant of the aircraft in which the rocket is fitted.

The 844 has built-in safety features and is automatic in operation. Extensive use is made of light alloys, even for the oxidant circuit: stainless steel is used for only a few parts of the engine.

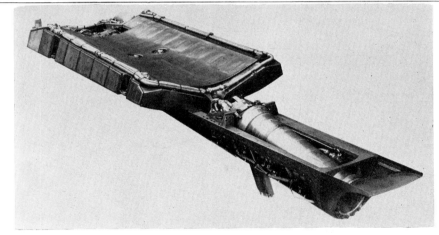

SEPR 844 single-chamber rocket engine (3,370 lb = 1,530 kg st)

Two hundred SEPR 841s and 150 SEPR 844s were in service in Mirage III fighter aircraft of the French and other national air forces in mid-1968. Manufacture of the 844 continues at SNECMA.

DIMENSIONS:

Length	129 in (3·27 m)
Width	43·3 in (1·10 m)
Height	25·6 in (0·65 m)

WEIGHTS:

Dry	200 lb (90 kg)
Total with accessories	500 lb (230 kg)

PERFORMANCE RATINGS:

Max at S/L	3,370 lb (1,530 kg) st
Max at 52,500 ft (16,000 m)	3,700 lb (1,680 kg) st

SPECIFIC IMPULSE:

At S/L	208 s
At 52,500 ft (16,000 m)	228 s

SEP HM4
The HM4 is the smaller of two upper-stage liquid-propellant rocket engines currently being developed by SEP.

TYPE: Liquid-propellant rocket engine.

PROPELLANTS: Liquid oxygen and liquid hydrogen.

THRUST CHAMBER ASSEMBLY: Four-chamber unit of 42 : 1 nozzle area ratio, regeneratively cooled, and with double-wall machined casing in stainless steel and Inconel X750. Operating

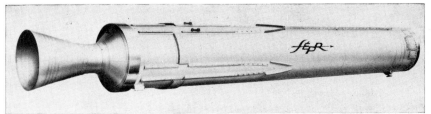

SEPR 739 solid-propellant rocket engine

TYPICAL SEP SOLID-PROPELLANT ROCKET ENGINES

Type	Static Thrust at S/L	Duration of Thrust in sec.	Total Weight	Length	Diameter
SEPR 163	308 lb (140 kg)	37	88 lb (40 kg)	68·7 in (1,745 mm)	5·5 in (141 mm)
SEPR 6854	8,700 lb (3,950 kg)	4	273 lb (124 kg)	101 in (2,560 mm)	8.9 in (226 mm)
SEPR 738	19,300 lb (8,750 kg)	20	2,680 lb (1,206 kg)	155 in (3,942 mm)	23 in (584 mm)
SEPR 739 Used in ONERA Titus	36,520 lb (16,600 kg)	17·5	3,432 lb (1,557 kg)	184·5 in (4,690 mm)	22·7 in (578 mm)
SEPR 7342	61,700 lb (28,000 kg)	4·6	1,870 lb (846 kg)	125·8 in (3,195 mm)	23·2 in (590 mm)
SEPR 299	9,702 lb (4,400 kg)	1·6	126·78 lb (57·5 kg)	42·2 in (1,076 mm)	9·8 in (250 mm)
SEPR 300	220·5 lb (100 kg)	73	115·76 lb (52·5 kg)	43·3 in (1,100 mm)	8·1 in (207 mm)
SEPR ELDO Perigee	8,820 lb (4,000 kg)	45	1,655·9 lb (751 kg)	59 in (1,500 mm)	31·5 in (800 mm)

sequence initiated by hydrogen pre-cooling and pre-opening of hydrogen injection valve. Concentric-tube propellant injection system with central oxygen flow. Pyrotechnic ignition. Combustion pressure 337·8 lb/sq in (23·2 bars) and temperature 5,228°F abs (2,900°K).

THRUST CHAMBER MOUNTING: Chambers hinged around axis concentric with engine axis.

PROPELLANT PUMPS: Axial-plus-centrifugal pumps, co-axial.

PROPELLANT FLOW: Liquid hydrogen flow rate 3·67 lb (1·67 kg)/sec at 580 lb/sq in (40 bars). Liquid oxygen flow rate 18·32 lb (8·33 kg)/sec at 522 lb/sq in (36 bars).

TURBINE: Two-stage axial-flow impulse unit in Inconel X750. Gas inlet temperature, 1,605°F abs (890°K).

GAS GENERATOR: Liquid hydrogen flow rate 0·19 lb (0·088 kg)/sec. Liquid oxygen flow rate 0·17 lb (0·079 kg)/sec. Pyrotechnic ignition.

LUBRICATION SYSTEM: Uses tributyl phosphate spray into gaseous hydrogen.

STARTING: Solid-grain primer.

THRUST CONTROL: Thrust held constant by regulation of turbopump speed via control of gas generator propellant supply.

DIMENSIONS:
Height, overall   45·6 in (1·170 mm)
Diameter, overall   46·5 in (1,220 mm)

WEIGHT, DRY   382·8 lb (174 kg)

PERFORMANCE:
Max thrust   9,080 lb (4,119 kg)
Overall propellant mixture ratio   5 : 1
Specific impulse   412 seconds

SEP HM7

Under development for upper-stage propulsion, the HM7 is a 15,750 lb (7,144 kg) liquid oxygen/liquid hydrogen engine.

TYPE: Liquid-propellant rocket engine.

PROPELLANTS: Liquid oxygen and liquid hydrogen.

THRUST CHAMBER ASSEMBLY: Single-chamber unit of 48 : 1 nozzle area ratio, regeneratively cooled, and of stainless steel tube construction. Operating sequence initiated by hydrogen pre-cooling and pre-opening of hydrogen injection valve. Concentric-tube propellant injection system with central oxygen flow. Pyrotechnic ignition. Combustion pressure

507·5 lb/sq in (35 bars) and temperature 5,405°F abs (3,000°K).

THRUST CHAMBER MOUNTING: Gimballed assembly, turbopump integral with chamber.

PROPELLANT PUMPS: Axial-plus-centrifugal pumps, co-axial.

PROPELLANT FLOWS: Liquid hydrogen flow rate 6·07 lb (2·76 kg)/sec at 942·5 lb/sq in (65 bars). Liquid oxygen flow rate 31·26 lb (14·21 kg)/sec at 754 lb/sq in (52 bars).

TURBINE: Two-stage axial-flow impulse unit in Inconel X 750. Gas inlet temperature 1,605°F abs (890°K).

GAS GENERATOR: Liquid hydrogen flow rate 0·29 lb (0·133 kg)/sec. Liquid oxygen flow rate 0·26 lb (0·12 kg)/sec. Pyrotechnic ignition.

LUBRICATION SYSTEM: Uses tributyl phosphate spray into gaseous hydrogen.

STARTING: Solid grain primer.

THRUST CONTROL: Thrust held constant by regulation of turbopump speed via control of gas generator propellant supply.

DIMENSIONS:
Height, overall   63·06 in (1,617 mm)
Diameter, overall   33·03 in (847 mm)

WEIGHT, DRY   319 lb (145 kg)

PERFORMANCE:
Max thrust in vacuo   15,750 lb (7,144 kg)
Overall propellant mixture ratio   5·15 : 1
Specific impulse   425 seconds

The SEP HM4 liquid oxygen/liquid hydrogen rocket engine for upper-stage propulsion (9,080 lb = 4,119 kg st)

The SEP HM7 liquid oxygen/liquid hydrogen rocket engine for upper-stage propulsion (15,750 lb = 7,144 kg st)

SERMEL

SOCIETE D'ETUDES ET DE RECHERCHES POUR LA MÉCANIQUE, L'ELECTRICITÉ ET L'ELECTRONIQUE, SARL

HEAD OFFICE:
211 Boulevard St Denis, 92 Courbevoie (Paris)
MAIN WORKS:
3bis rue Bernard-Delicieux, 31 Toulouse

Formed in April 1969, this company is staffed mainly by personnel from the aviation industry and is engaged chiefly in research, design and manufacture of aerospace products, particularly small gas-turbines. Its first major products are described below. In addition the SERMEL development programme includes ground auxiliary power units, air-conditioning units, high-performance ventilating fans and compressors and many other products based on fluid dynamics, including hydraulic equipment, fuel and oil systems and gas dynamic devices.

SERMEL TRS 18

The TRS 18 is an exceedingly simple, light-weight turbojet which, with its main accessories, fits within a cylindrical envelope of only 12·5 in (318 mm) diameter (the engine shaft axis lying slightly above the centre of this envelope). The engine has a single-entry centrifugal compressor, folded annular combustion chamber, single-stage axial-flow turbine, nose-mounted electric or air starter and gearbox driving accessories mounted above the intake section. The main shaft is supported in two bearings and the unit is so designed as to be divided rapidly into its major sections to facilitate maintenance.

The TRS 18 has been developed as a completed package with electronic control system and safety devices, and is provided with a fully automatic starting system. If necessary the whole operation of the engine can be controlled by telemetered commands. The TRS 18 can be operated on JP-1, JP-4 or JP-5 fuel and on any

conventional turbojet lubricating oil.

DIMENSIONS:
Diameter of engine   12·005 in (306 mm)
Installational diameter   12·520 in (318 mm)
Length of engine   17·520 in (445 mm)
Length with starter   24·213 in (615 mm)

WEIGHT, DRY:
With 600W electric starter-generator
                         66 lb (30 kg)
With pneumatic starter   60 lb (27 kg)

PERFORMANCE RATINGS (at 59°F=15°C):
Max T-O, SL   220 lb (100 kg) st
Max at SL at 216 knots (250 mph; 400 km/h)
                         190 lb (86 kg) st
Max at 13,100 ft (4,000 m) at 250 mph
                         125 lb (57 kg) st
Max at 40,000 ft (12,000 m) at 250 mph
                         48 lb (22 kg) st

SPECIFIC FUEL CONSUMPTIONS:
Max st, 13,100 ft (4,000 m) at 250 mph   1·45
Max st, 40,000 ft (12,000 m) at 250 mph   1·38

Sermel's first three products: from the left, the TRS 12 turbojet (144 lb = 65 kg st), the TRS 18 turbojet (220 lb = 100 kg st) and the TGS 4 auxiliary power unit which provides bleed air and electrical power

TRS 12

Similar in design to the TRS 18, the TRS 12 is generally smaller and of lower power. It is likewise assembled from easily separated sections and equipped with an electronic control system providing for remote telemetered control of starting, thrust level and shutdown. Design began in April 1969, first run was in July 1969 and development is completed.

DIMENSIONS:
Overall length, with electric starter
    23·27 in (591 mm)
Envelope diameter, concentric with shaft
    12·52 in (318 mm)
Envelope diameter, offset below axis
    11·6 in (295 mm)
WEIGHT (DRY):
  with electric starting 55 lb (25 kg)
  with air starting 49 lb (22 kg)
PERFORMANCE RATINGS (SLS, 59°F = 15°C):
  Max continuous thrust 144 lb (65 kg)
  Max operating altitude 30,000 ft (9,000 m)
FUEL CONSUMPTION:
  At max SLS rating 179 lb (81 kg)/hr

TGS 4

The TGS 4 is a compact auxiliary power unit intended for airborne applications. The basic gas generator, incorporating elements of the TRS 12 and TRS 18, has a single-stage centrifugal compressor and two-stage axial turbine, driving through the compressor shaft to a reduction gearbox on which is mounted a starter/generator and other accessories according to the installation requirement. All units are packaged in a light casing, with a quickly removable panel on each side to provide access for control adjustment and removal of accessories or sections of the gas generator. Equipment includes automatic starting and overspeed control.

DIMENSIONS:
Package length, excluding jet-pipe stub
    25 in (635 mm)
Package overall width 12·8 in (325 mm)
Package height, excluding top connections
    14·4 in (365 mm)
WEIGHT, DRY: 108 lb (49 kg)
PERFORMANCE RATING (SLS, 59°F = 15°C):
  Bleed air flow 55 lb (25 kg)/min

Bleed air pressure 52 lb/sq in abs (3·66 kg/cm²)
Continuous electric power 9 kW at 28V DC
Transient electric power 12 kW at 24V DC
Max altitude for full power 17,000 ft (5,000 m)
Max altitude with limited electrical load
    26,000 ft (8,000 m)
FUEL CONSUMPTION:
  SLS, full load 110 lb (50 kg)/hr

TMS 60

A turboshaft unit rated at 250 hp, the TMS 60 will incorporate the design technology and high performance of the SERMEL turbojets and is expected to set a new standard for light weight and compact design. A turboprop version is likely to be made available, but development has not yet been completed.

SDS 12

The SDS 12 is an air starting system for large twin-engined aircraft main engines. It incorporates one air generator and two type DAS 120 air starters, each with a rating of 120 hp. It is expected to be lighter than any corresponding system and to incorporate advanced control and safety features.

SOCIÉTÉ D'ETUDE DE LA PROPULSION PAR RÉACTION (SEPR) *see Société Européenne de Propulsion (SEP)*

SNECMA

SOCIÉTÉ NATIONALE D'ÉTUDE ET DE CONSTRUCTION DE MOTEURS D'AVIATION

HEAD OFFICE:
150, Boulevard Haussmann, Paris (VIIIe)
PRESIDENT AND DIRECTOR-GENERAL:
  Jacques Edouard Lamy
DEPUTY DIRECTOR GENERAL:
  Henry Wiart
SECRETARY GENERAL:
  Georges Langendorff
SCIENTIFIC DIRECTOR: Raymond Marchal
GENERAL TECHNICAL DIRECTOR: Michel Garnier
INDUSTRIAL DIRECTOR: Michel Viret
DIRECTOR OF "MATÉRIEL EN EXPLOITATION":
  Michel Wartelle
QUALITY CONTROL DIRECTOR:
  Maurice Beguin

ADMINISTRATIVE AND FINANCIAL DIRECTOR, PRESIDENT AND DIRECTOR GENERAL OF CNMP BERTHIEZ: Georges Depallens

PUBLIC RELATIONS DEPARTMENT:
  Raymond Santini
PRESS ATTACHE: Pierre de Saint-Pereuse

Evry-Corbeil Works

RN 446-Nationale 7, 91-Evry-Corbeil
WORKS DIRECTOR: Pierre Enfer

This new facility regroups the turbojet production plant, laboratories for research and development and for quality control, the after-sales service activities, the training centre and various administrative offices.

Billancourt Works:

167, rue de Silly and 68, quai du Point-du-Jour, Boulogne-Billancourt (Seine)

MANAGER: Maurice Florquin

This works, which specialised for many years in the production of piston-engines, is now engaged on repair and overhaul of civil and military turbojets and turbofans, including the SNECMA Atar and Pratt & Whitney J57, JT3C-7, JT3D, JT4 and JT8D.

Gennevilliers Works:

291, avenue d'Argenteuil, Gennevilliers (Seine)
WORKS DIRECTOR: Guy Quintaa

Houses all forge and foundry facilities for SNECMA factories. Also employed on work for private customers in the aviation and other industries.

Suresnes Works:

22, quai Gallieni, Suresnes (Seine)
DIRECTOR, ELECTRONIC DIVISION (ELECMA):
  André Adamsbaum

Houses SNECMA'S electronics division, ELECMA, which develops electronic control systems for gas-turbine engines and various other aerospace electronic equipment.

Blanquefort Works:

MISSILES AND SPACE DIVISION: Jean Bloch

Direction Technique and Melun-Villaroche Test Centre:

Melun-Villaroche (Seine-et-Marne)
TECHNICAL DIRECTOR: Jean Devriese
DIRECTOR OF THE CENTRE: Raoul Dumez

Ground and flight test centre for all SNECMA products.

The Société Nationale d'Etude et de Construction de Moteurs d'Aviation (SNECMA) came into being in 1945, when it took over the production facilities of the Société des Moteurs Gnome et Rhone, Société des Moteurs Renault pour l'Aviation, Société Nationale de Construction de

Moteurs (Lorraine) and the Groupe Etude des Moteurs à Huile Lourde (GEHL). To-day it has 15,500 employees and is devoting the major part of its activities to the development and series production of gas-turbine engines. Major products are the Atar family of military turbojets and, in conjunction with Rolls-Royce, the Olympus 593 turbojet for the Concorde and the M45H turbofan for the VFW 614.

In the Summer of 1959 SNECMA concluded an agreement with the Pratt & Whitney Aircraft Division of United Aircraft Corporation whereby it is licensed to manufacture Pratt & Whitney products and to benefit from the research and development activities of the American company. Products of this agreement include the TF 306C turbofan engine, of which details are given below, together with details of other current SNECMA aero-engines.

SNECMA is also working on equipment to improve the efficiency and versatility of its turbojets, including reheat, variable-area nozzles and jet reversal for braking purposes.

An Electronics Division, named ELECMA, was formed on 1 November 1961.

In December 1968, SNECMA took over Société d'Exploitation des Matériels Hispano-Suiza and its various subsidiaries whose aerospace, nuclear and industrial activities are carried on under the name of the Hispano-Suiza Division of SNECMA.

SNECMA ATAR 09

The Atar 09 exists in four versions as follows:
Atar 09B. Equips the Mirage III-B and III-C, including the aircraft for Israel and South Africa. Air mass flow 150 lb (68 kg) sec. Pressure ratio 5·5 : 1. More than 400 Atar 09B engines have been built.
Atar 09C. Main difference compared with 09B is use of a new compressor, a self-contained starter

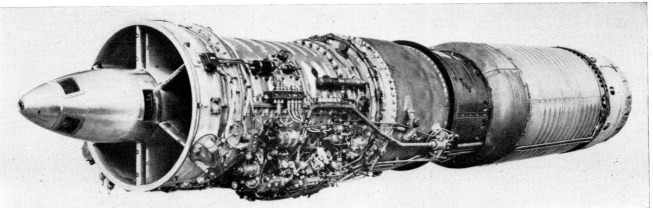

SNECMA Atar 09K turbojet engine (14,770 lb = 6,700 kg st with afterburner)

and an improved overspeed which comes into operation automatically when the aircraft reaches Mach 1·4 and 36,000 ft (11,000 m), giving power equivalent to a sea level thrust of 14,110 lb (6,400 kg) st. The compressor rotor has steel blades on stages 1, 2, 7, 8 and 9 and light alloy blades on stages 3-6: the stator has steel blades on stages 1 and 2 and light alloy blades on stages 3-8. Air mass flow and pressure ratio as for 09B. This engine equips the Mirage III-E and III-R and is in licence production and service in Switzerland and Australia. More than 500 Atar 09C engines have been built.

Atar 09K. Further development to power the Dassault Mirage IV supersonic bomber. Also fitted in Mirage F1 prototype. All-steel compressor with two transonic stages. Air mass flow increased to 158 lb (72 kg)/sec. Overspeed comes into operation at Mach 1·5, giving power at 8,700 rpm equivalent to sea level thrust of 15,430 lb (7,000 kg). More than 270 Atar 09K engines have been built.

Atar 09K-50. Derived from the Atar 09K and intended to power the first batches of the Mirage F1 and Mirage G4 fighters. Designed to offer improved subsonic specific fuel consumption, increased thrust for supersonic acceleration and improved overhaul life. The main improvements are in an entirely redesigned turbine with blades not forged but cast and coated with refractory metal from the vapour phase. This wholly new turbine section includes a section of engine carcase, exit cone and fixed vanes. Stages 1 and 8 of the compressor have been redesigned, resulting in pressure ratio raised from 6 : 1 to 6·5 : 1, coupled with slightly augmented mass flow. The intake section has been revised to accommodate a rearranged accessory-drive system, and the control and electronic equipment has been revised and extended to improve the security of single-engined aircraft. The 09K-50 has done extensive ground and flight testing in Mirage III and F1 aircraft and was homologated for service use following its final 150-hour test at the CEP, Saclay, between 8 September and 24 November 1969.

All Atar 09B, 09C and 09K engines are fitted with an approach control system which adjusts the power of the engine automatically, by varying the nozzle area, during a landing approach, to enable the aircraft to maintain a constant air speed.

DIMENSIONS:
Diameter	40·2 in (1,020 mm)
Length overall:	
Atar 09B	246 in (6,246 mm)
Atar 09C, 09K, 09K50	234 in (5,942 mm)

WEIGHTS:
Dry, complete with all accessories:
Atar 09B	2,970 lb (1,350 kg)
Atar 09C	3,120 lb (1,420 kg)
Atar 09K	3,270 lb (1,485 kg)
Atar 09K-50	3,351 lb (1,520 kg)

SNECMA TF 306 turbofan engine with afterburner (20,506 lb = 9,300 kg st)

PERFORMANCE RATINGS:
Max with afterburner:
Atar 09B, 09C
    13,200 lb (6,000 kg) st at 8,400 rpm
Atar 09K 14,770 lb (6,700 kg) st at 8,400 rpm
Atar 09K-50   15,873 lb (7,200 kg) st

Max without afterburner:
Atar 09B 9,350 lb (4,250 kg) st at 8,400 rpm
Atar 09C 9,430 lb (4,280 kg) st at 8,400 rpm
Atar 09K   10,350 lb (4,700 kg) st
Atar 09K-50   11,023 lb (5,000 kg) st

SPECIFIC FUEL CONSUMPTIONS:
At max rating with afterburner
Atar 09B	2·20
Atar 09C	2·03
Atar 09K	2·15
Atar 09K-50	1·99

At max rating without afterburner:
Atar 09B	1·03
Atar 09C	1·01
Atar 09K	1·04
Atar 09K-50	0·98

OIL CONSUMPTION: 2·64 Imp pints (1·5 litres)/hr

SNECMA ATAR M53

Design started in 1967 on the M53, an advanced derivative of the Atar 09 intended to provide a turbojet of superior performance to present series Atar engines but of simpler and less costly design than the SNECMA TF 306 turbofan. The Super Atar is planned for production delivery to the French Air Force around 1975 to power later batches of the Dassault Mirage F1 and G4. Thrust is in the region of 18,740 lb to 19,840 lb (8,500 to 9,000 kg). The engine is designed for propulsion initially at Mach 2·5 to 2·7 and later at Mach 3 and higher.

SNECMA/TURBOMÉCA LARZAC

This joint design of 2,304 lb (1,045 kg) st turbofan by SNECMA and Turboméca is being developed to power business jets, military liaison aircraft and trainers. A description of the Larzac is given under Groupement Turboméca-SNECMA GRTS on pages 712-713.

SNECMA/ROLLS-ROYCE M45H

This low sfc turbofan is under joint development by SNECMA and Rolls-Royce to power the VFW 614 feederliner. Details of the M45H are given under the International Section, on page 719.

SNECMA/ROLLS-ROYCE OLYMPUS 593

SNECMA is collaborating with Rolls-Royce in the design, development and manufacture of the Olympus 593 turbojet for the Concorde. A description of the engine appears under "Rolls-Royce/SNECMA" in the International section, on page 719.

SNECMA TF 306C

This two-spool turbofan consists of a Pratt & Whitney TF30 engine fitted with a SNECMA-designed afterburner, with convergent nozzle. It powers several supersonic aircraft, including the Mirage F2 and G.

DIMENSIONS:
Diameter	47·0 in (1,200 mm)
Length overall	210 in (5,335 mm)

WEIGHT: Dry   3,880 lb (1,760 kg)

PERFORMANCE RATINGS:
Max with afterburner   20,506 lb (9,300 kg) st
Max without afterburner 11,686 lb (5,300 kg) st

SPECIFIC FUEL CONSUMPTIONS:
At max rating with afterburner	2·6
At max rating without afterburner	0·66

HISPANO-SUIZA DIVISION

WORKS:
Rue du Capitaine Guynemer, 92-Bois Colombes

DIRECTOR:
P. Compagnon

In December 1968, SNECMA acquired Société d'Exploitation des Matériels Hispano-Suiza and the company's activities now continue under the name of Hispano-Suiza Division, SNECMA.

The Hispano-Suiza Division entered the turbojet field by acquiring the licence to build the Rolls-Royce Nene and Tay engines. It produced a total of 1,600 turbojets under this licence.

The Division later acquired a licence to manufacture the Rolls-Royce Tyne turboprop and is producing this engine in series for the Breguet Atlantic and Transall C-160, in collaboration with Rolls-Royce, MAN (Germany) and F N (Belgium). Hispano-Suiza is manufacturing 44% of the components for each engine, Rolls-Royce 20%, MTU 28% and FN 8%. Assembly and testing are done by Hispano-Suiza (RTy.21 for the Atlantic) and MTU (RTy.22 for the Transall). The first production series total 255 RTy.21 and 497 RTy.22 engines.

The first production RTy.21 was accepted officially on 7 April 1965 and by 30 June 1969 a total of 180 Tyne Mk 21 engines and 291 kits for the Tyne Mk 22 had been delivered. Full details of the Tyne can be found under the "Rolls-Royce" entry in the UK section of this work.

Current production also includes the manufacture under contract from SEP of SEPR 844 rocket-engines for the Dassault Mirage III fighter, at the rate of about ten each month. The company is also responsible for repair and overhaul of the Nene, Tay, Verdon and Avon turbojets and Tyne Mk 21 turboprop in service with the French Air Force.

Another important Hispano-Suiza product is the bevel gear control box assembly and flexible drive-shaft for the four-engined Breguet 941 STOL transport. This transmission makes it possible to concentrate all the power on the inner propellers or to operate all the propellers after the failure of any engine.

Under an agreement announced in February 1964, Hispano-Suiza is responsible for the supply, maintenance and general overhaul in Europe of the General Electric CF700-2B turbofan engine which powers the Fan Jet Falcon executive transport, and the CJ610-1 turbojet used in the HFB 320 Hansa.

Hispano-Suiza is to-day devoting a considerable proportion of its facilities to the manufacture of landing gear and hydraulic equipment and accessories. The SO 4050 Vautour, Breguet Alizé and Breguet Atlantic are all equipped with Hispano-Suiza landing gears and complete hydraulic circuits; the SE 210 Caravelle, Mirage III-V and Mirage F1 have Hispano-Suiza landing gears: while the main landing gear of the Concorde airliner is also being developed and built by this company. The Nord 500 has a nose-wheel unit, main gear shock-absorbers, wheels, brakes and transmission system of Hispano-Suiza design and manufacture.

In April 1966 Hispano-Suiza and Hawker Siddeley Dynamics Ltd of the UK signed an agreement under which the two companies are collaborating in the field of aircraft landing gear and related hydraulic equipment.

Hispano-Suiza manufactures Martin-Baker ejection seats under licence. In April 1965 it formed jointly with Martin Marietta Corporation of the USA a company named Société Hispano-Martin to manufacture and sell in Europe products of the Nuclear Division of Martin Marietta, with particular reference to SNAP power generators.

TURBOMÉCA
SOCIÉTÉ TURBOMÉCA

HEAD OFFICE AND WORKS:
Bordes (Pyrénées Atlantiques)

PARIS OFFICE:
1, Rue Beaujon, Paris 8e

PRESIDENT AND DIRECTOR-GENERAL:
J. R. Szydlowski

Turboméca is the leading European manufacturer of small turbine aero engines. Since it first started development of gas-turbines in 1947, the company has developed about 50 different types of power plant of which some 15 have

entered production and ten types have been manufactured under licence in five countries.

By 1 January 1970 10,026 Turboméca engines for fixed and rotary wing applications and aircraft auxiliary duties had been delivered to customers in 81 countries, including France. A further approximately 11,000 engines have been built under licence by Rolls-Royce Ltd in Great Britain, Continental Aviation and Engineering Corporation in the USA, ENMASA in Spain, Hindustan Aeronautics Ltd in India and a state factory in Yugoslavia. Present production rate by Turboméca totals some 110 engines per month.

A new 130,000 sq ft (12,077 m²) extension to the company's factory at Tarnos was commissioned in September 1968, bringing the total covered floor area for Turboméca's three plants at Bordes, Mézières and Tarnos to 1,184,000 sq ft (110,000 m²). In mid-1969 the company employed a total of close on 4,000 people.

In addition Turboméca has a 51 per cent holding in Bet-Shemesh Engines, a new aero-engine factory built in Israel near Jerusalem in conjunction with the Israeli government. The first section of the factory, based on the same layout as Turboméca's Tarnos plant, was officially opened in January 1969. Details of Bet-Shemesh

Engines are given in the Israeli entry of this section on page 721.

A high degree of interchangeability exists among the range of Turboméca turbine engines, Most of them have been described in previous editions of *Jane's* and the entries which follow are concerned with only the more important current types.

In 1967 Turboméca started development of an air-cooled turbine rotor suitable for application to the company's full range of engines. Introduction of this turbine on production engines was initiated in 1969 with the Astazou XVI turboprop, and air-cooled versions of other Turboméca engines are under development.

Two new joint designs of engine are the Rolls-Royce/Turboméca RB.172/T260 Adour augmented turbofan, and the SNECMA/Turboméca M49 Larzac turbofan.

The Société Turboméca was originally formed in 1938 by M. Szydlowski and M. Planiol to develop blowers, compressors and turbines for aeronautical use. M. Szydlowski is president of Turboméca and is also one of four administrators on the board of SNECMA, representing shareholders.

ROLLS-ROYCE TURBOMÉCA RB.172/T260 ADOUR

This joint design of 4,400 lb (1,996 kg) st turbofan by Rolls-Royce and Turboméca is being developed for the SEPECAT Jaguar tactical strike fighter and advanced trainer. A brief description of the Adour is given in the International section on pages 720-721.

TURBOMÉCA ASTAFAN

This is a new low-consumption lightweight turbofan of high BPR, low noise level design which made its first run during the summer of 1969. Comprising the Astazou XIV turboprop power section, operating at constant speed, driving a single-stage variable-pitch fan via gearing, the Astafan has a sea level thrust of 1,570 lb (712 kg) for the exceptionally low sfc of 0·38. By-pass ratio is 6·5 : 1, the highest in use for a commercial engine. Variable-pitch blading facilitates constant speed operation and enables off-loading of the engine during starting.

An application for the Astafan has yet to be announced, but bench development continued at full pace into 1970.

TYPE: Single-shaft turbofan with geared fan.

ENTRY CASING: Annular light alloy entry cowl and fan duct supported on double row of air straightener vanes downstream of fan rotor. Annular intake to gas generator section located at exit to fan duct. Rear casing of secondary intake carries accessories and accessory drives (using arrangement similar to Astazou XIV intake.)

FAN: Single-stage fan with variable-incidence rotor blading overhung at front without entry guide vanes. Drive from gas generator section is via two-stage epicyclic gear train housed in cylindrical casing forming inner wall of fan duct.

COMPRESSOR, COMBUSTION SYSTEM AND TURBINE: Same as Astazou XIV.

JET PIPE: Fixed type with straight frustum inner cone. Extension jet pipe to convergent propulsive nozzle and ejector nozzle at rear of engine pod casing.

ACCESSORIES: Mounted on casing forming rear of secondary air intake.

FUEL SYSTEM: Independent control systems for starting and normal operation. Fuel regulator maintains speed constant with pilot operating single lever controlling fan blade pitch to vary thrust output. Turboméca 'thermic' load limiter controls turbine entry temperature between set limits (using principle of operation similar to that on Astazou XIV).

FUEL GRADES: AIR 3404A, 3405 or 3407A.

LUBRICATION SYSTEM: Pressure lubrication to bearings and reduction gear, with annular engine-mounted oil tank.

STARTING: Automatic electrical starting with compressor blow-off valve and fan in minimum pitch.

DIMENSIONS:
Length overall   84·8 in (2,153 mm)
Max dia over fan cowl   25·7 in (654 mm)

WEIGHT:
Equipped engine   approx 507 lb (230 kg)

PERFORMANCE RATINGS:
T-O   1,570 lb (712 kg) st at 43,000 rpm
Max continuous at 20,000 ft (6,000 m) and 375 mph (600 km/h)
     507 lb (230 kg) at 43,000 rpm

SPECIFIC FUEL CONSUMPTIONS:
At T-O rating   0·38
At max continuous rating   0·63

SNECMA/TURBOMÉCA M49 LARZAC

This joint design of 2,304 lb (1,045 kg) st turbofan by Turboméca and SNECMA is being developed to power business jets, military liaison aircraft and trainers. A description of the Larzac is given under Groupement Turboméca-SNECMA GRTS on pages 711-712.

Turboméca Astafan single-shaft geared front fan engine (1,570 lb = 712 kg st)   (*Kenneth Fulton*)

TURBOMÉCA MARBORE

The Marboré turbojet is the most widely used of Turboméca's range of gas-turbines. By July 1969 more than 4,091 Marboré II engines of 880 lb (400 kg) st had been delivered by Turboméca and a further 10,000 by Continental Aviation in America as the J69. Production of the Marboré IID continues for the Nord CT.20 target drone.

This initial version of the engine was joined in production by the 1,058 lb (480 kg) st Marboré VI with receipt of type approval in June 1962. By July 1969 more than 665 Marboré VI turbojets had been built and production continues under a large French government order awarded in December 1968. Four versions, each with differing accessory arrangements, have been delivered; the Marboré VIC for the Morane-Saulnier Paris II, the Marboré VID for the Aérospatiale M.20 drone, the Marboré VIF for the C.M.170 Super Magister, and the Marboré VIJ for the Morane-Saulnier Paris IA. During 1968, the TBO for the Marboré VIF2 was increased to 1,000 hr.

The Marboré VI is also built under licence in Spain by ENMASA as the Marboré M21. The engine powers the Hispano HA-200E Super Saeta.

A new version of the turbojet announced in May 1969 as being in course of design is the Marboré 8, comprising the Marboré VI with the new Turboméca air-cooled turbine. Take-off rating of this version is 1,323 lb (600 kg). Specific fuel consumption is 1·15.

The following particulars relate to the Marboré VI series.

TYPE: Single-shaft centrifugal-flow turbojet.

AIR INTAKE: Annular sheet metal nose intake bolted to front of light alloy compressor casing.

COMPRESSOR: Single-sided impeller machined from two alloy forgings, shrunk on steel shaft and locked and dowelled to maintain alignment. Externally-finned light alloy compressor casing supports front ball-bearing for rotating assembly in a central housing supported by three streamlined struts. This housing also contains gears for accessory drives. Pressure ratio 3·84 : 1. Air mass flow 21·6 lb (9·8 kg)/sec.

COMBUSTION CHAMBER: Composed of inner and outer sheet metal casings, forming annular flame tube. Air from compressor passes through both radial and axial diffuser vanes and divides into three main flows, two primary for combustion and one secondary. Two primary flows enter combustion zone from opposite ends of chamber, the rear stream through turbine nozzle guide vanes which it cools. Secondary flow enters through outer casing for dilution and cooling of combustion gases. Two torch igniters.

FUEL SYSTEM: Fuel, pumped through hollow impeller shaft, is fed to combustion zone by rotating injector disc around periphery of which are number of vents which act as nozzles. Fuel is vented by centrifugal force, being atomised in the process. Fuel delivery at low thrust settings regulated by by-pass valve.

FUEL GRADE: Air 3405 (JP-1).

NOZZLE GUIDE VANES: Twenty-five hollow sheet steel guide vanes cooled by part of primary combustion air.

TURBINE: Single-stage turbine with thirty-seven blades with fir tree root fittings in steel disc. Bolted to main shaft and tail shaft, latter supported by rear roller bearing for rotating assembly. Gas temperature 613°C at 21,500 rpm.

JET PIPE: Inner and outer sheet metal casings, latter supported by three hollow struts. Inner tapered casing extends beyond end of outer casing to induce air-flow through struts to cool rear main bearing and inner casing.

ACCESSORY DRIVES: Gear casing in central compressor housing with drives for fuel and oil pumps. Connecting shaft to underside of accessories gear case above compressor casing. Accessories include tachometer generator and electric starter. Take-off (4 hp continuous) for remotely-driven accessory box.

LUBRICATION SYSTEM: Pressure type. Single gear-type pump serves front gear casing, two main bearings and rpm governor. Three scavenge pumps return bearing oil to tank *via* cooler. Normal oil pressure 40 lb/sq in (2·8 kg/cm²).

OIL SPECIFICATION: Air 3512 (mineral) or Air 3513A (synthetic).

MOUNTING: Four points, with Silentbloc rubber mountings, two at front and two at rear.

STARTING: Air Equipement 24-volt electric starter or compressed-air starter. Two Turboméca igniter plugs.

DIMENSIONS:
Length with exhaust cone but without tailpipe
     55·74 in (1,416 mm)
Width   23·35 in (593 mm)
Height   24·82 in (631 mm)

WEIGHT (DRY):
Equipped   309 lb (140 kg)

PERFORMANCE RATINGS:
T-O   1,058 lb (480 kg) st at 21,500 rpm
Cruising   925 lb (420 kg) st at 20,500 rpm

SPECIFIC FUEL CONSUMPTIONS:
At T-O rating   1·09
At cruising rating   1·07

TURBOMÉCA ASTAZOU

The Astazou is the major turboprop in the Turboméca range and is in production in its 853 ehp Astazou XIVC and 1,000 ehp Astazou XVI versions to power civil models of the Handley

Turboméca Marboré VIC turbojet engine (1,058 lb = 480 kg st)

Page HP.137 Jetstream and other second-generation business aircraft. These versions are also marketed by Rolls-Royce Turboméca International Ltd under the designations AZ14 and AZ16. By the end of July 1969, 105 Astazou XIVC engines had been built.

The Astazou XIV was certificated by the French airworthiness authorities in October 1968, followed by ARB/FAA certification of the Astazou XIVC and C1 in March 1969. The Jetstream received ARB/FAA certification during the following month. On November 15, 1968, a Pilatus Turbo-Porter STOL aircraft powered by a 585 hp Astazou XIVE achieved a new world altitude record for C1c class aircraft (1,000 to 1,750 kg) with a flight to 44,242 ft (13,485 m).

Current versions of the Astazou are:

Astazou XII: Powers Short Skyvan Series 2 at 690 shp and Pilatus Turbo-Porter PC-6/A1-H2 at 700 ehp.

Astazou XIV (alias AZ14). Developed from Astazou XII. Powers civil Handley Page HP.137 Jetstream at 853 ehp and prototype Dassault MD.320 Hirondelle, which first flew on 11 September 1968, at 870 ehp. Production continues.

Astazou XVI (alias AZ16). Higher rated version of Astazou XIV and is first engine to enter production with new Turboméca air-cooled turbine. Completed French official endurance tests in November 1968 at 1,073 ehp. Being flight tested by CGTM in modified Nord 260 following initial testing in a Morane-Saulnier MS 1500 Epervier. Also flying as AZ16 in prototype Jetstream. Further endurance testing carried out with distilled water injection to provide flat rating performance. On offer as alternative power plant for IAI Arava STOL transport.

Astazou XVIII. Higher rated version of Astazou XVI which first ran early 1969 with T-O rating of 1,220 ehp. Potential application in Astazou XVI installations.

Astazou XX. Under development.

The following description relates to the Astazou XIVC and XVI. Details of the Astazou series of turboshafts are given separately.

TYPE: Single-shaft axial-plus-centrifugal turboprop.

PROPELLER: Hamilton Standard three-bladed single-acting, counterweight type with hydraulically-actuated variable pitch from full negative through to feather position. Emergency hydraulic feathering provided. Diameter to suit individual applications: 8 ft 6 in (2,591 mm) for Handley Page Jetstream.

REDUCTION GEAR: Mounted in tapered cylindrical casing at front of engine, with two-stage epicyclic reduction gear having helical primary gears and straight secondary gears. Reduction ratio 24·115 : 1. Driven from front of compressor and mounted on ball and roller bearings.

AIR INTAKE: Annular air intake at rear of reduction gear casing. Hot air de-icing.

COMPRESSOR: Two-stage axial followed by single-stage centrifugal with single-sided impeller. Two rows of stator blades aft of each axial rotor. Centrifugal stage had radial and axial diffusers. Axial stages have steel discs with integral steel blades. Discs and two-piece steel impeller located on compressor shaft by radial lugs. Shaft carried on ball bearings ahead of stage-one axial disc and ahead of impeller.

COMBUSTION SYSTEM: Reverse-flow annular type with centrifugal fuel injector using rotary atomizer disc. Ignition by two ventilated torch igniters.

TURBINE: Three-stage axial with blades integral with discs. (Air cooling provided for Astazou XVI turbine). Discs attached by curvic couplings and through-bolts. Rotor carried on compressor rear ball bearing and roller bearing aft of stage-three disc supported by struts across turbine exhaust.

JET PIPE: Fixed type with curved inner cone.

ACCESSORIES: Mounted on casing forming rear of air intake. Drive pads provided for starter-generator, oil pump, fuel pump and speed governor, tacho-generator, a.c. generator (optional) and hydraulic pump (optional).

MOUNTING: Trunnion located on each side of turbine casing front flange, plus third trunnion on underside of turbine casing.

FUEL SYSTEM: Automatic constant speed system with propeller Beta-control and Turboméca 'thermic' load limiter and speed governor.

FUEL GRADES: AIR 3404, 3405, or 3407.

LUBRICATION SYSTEM: Pressure lubrication to bearings and reduction gear, with 14 pints (8 litre) oil tank mounted at front of engine.

OIL SPECIFICATION: AIR 3515 or synthetic AIR 3573.

STARTING: Electric.

DIMENSIONS:
Diameter over intake cowl 21·5 in (546 mm)
Overall length, including propeller
80·6 in (2,047 mm)

Turboméca Astazou XIVC turboprop engine, rated at 853 ehp

WEIGHT:
With accessories:
Astazou XIV, XVI   approx 454 lb (206 kg)
Astazou XVIII   approx 452 lb (205 kg)

PERFORMANCE RATINGS:
T-O:
Astazou XIV 853 ehp (800 shp) at 43,000 rpm
Astazou XVI
   1,000 ehp (940 shp) at 43,000 rpm
Astazou XVIII
   1,220 ehp (1,155 shp) at 43,000 rpm
Max continuous:
Astazou XIV 770 ehp (720 shp) at 43,000 rpm
Astazou XVI 867 ehp (810 shp) at 43,000 rpm
Astazou XVIII
   1,130 ehp (1,067 shp) at 43,000 rpm

SPECIFIC FUEL CONSUMPTIONS:
At T-O rating:
Astazou XIV   0·543 lb/shp/hr (248 gr/cv/hr)
Astazou XVI   0·543 lb/shp/hr (248 gr/cv/hr)
Astazou XVIII 0·496 lb/ehp/hr (225 gr/cve/hr)
At max continuous:
Astazou XIV   0·554 lb/shp/hr (253 gr/cv/hr)
Astazou XVI   0·554 lb/shp/hr (253 gr/cv/hr)
Astazou XVIII 0·50 lb/ehp/hr (227 gr/cve/hr)

TURBOMÉCA ASTAZOU TURBOSHAFT

This is the turboshaft series of the Astazou family and is derived from the early second-generation Astazou II turboprop fitted to the Mitsubishi MU-2 and Pilatus Turbo-Porter. By March 1969, 400 Astazou turboshaft engines had been built. The variants are as follows:

Astazou IIA. Rated at 523 shp and powers the Aérospatiale SA 318C Alouette II Astazou helicopter.

Astazou IIN. Original version of turboshaft, powering the Aérospatiale SA 341.

Astazou IIIN. Definitive turboshaft for Anglo-French helicopter programme for Aérospatiale SA 341. Derived from Astazou IIA but with revised profile of turbine using higher temperature alloy to match power needs of Aérospatiale SA 341. In production jointly by Turboméca and Small Engine Division of Rolls-Royce.

Astazou 6. Under design as Astazou III derivative introducing Turboméca cooled turbine. Rated at 730 shp for sfc of 0·593 lb (269 gr)/shp/hr.

The following description relates to the Astazou IIIN except where otherwise indicated.

TYPE: Single-shaft axial-plus-centrifugal turboshaft.

REDUCTION GEAR: Similar to Astazou XIV turboprop. Reduction ratio 7·039 : 1.

AIR INTAKE: Annular air intake at rear of reduction gear casing.

COMPRESSOR: Single-stage axial followed by single-stage centrifugal with single-sided impeller. Two rows of stator blades aft of axial rotor. Otherwise similar to Astazou XIV compressor. Air mass flow 5·5 lb/sec (2·5 kg/sec).

COMBUSTION SYSTEM: Similar to combustor on Astazou XIV.

TURBINE: Similar to Astazou XIV.

JET PIPE: Similar to Astazou XIV.

ACCESSORIES: Mounted on casing forming rear of air intake. Drive pads provide for starter-generator, oil pump, fuel pump and governor, tacho-generator, AC generator (optional).

MOUNTING: At front by flange located at power take-off section, and at rear by two lugs on accessory mounting pad section.

FUEL SYSTEM: Automatic constant speed control with speed governor.

LUBRICATION SYSTEM: Pressure type with gear type pumps. Oil tank of 14 pint (8 litre) capacity mounted at front of engine.

STARTING: Electrical, automatic.

DIMENSIONS:
Height: Astazou IIA   18 in (458 mm)
   Astazou IIIN   18·1 in (460 mm)
Width: Astazou IIA   18·8 in (480 mm)
   Astazou IIIN   18·1 in (460 mm)
Length overall: Astazou IIA 50·0 in (1,272 mm)
   Astazou IIIN   56·3 in (1,433 mm)

WEIGHT:
Bare engine: Astazou IIA   249 lb (113 kg)
   Astazou IIIN   253 lb (115 kg)

PERFORMANCE RATINGS:
Max power, Astazou IIA   523 shp (530 cv)
   Astazou IIIN   592 shp (600 cv)
Max continuous, Astazou IIA   473 shp (480 cv)
   Astazou IIIN   523 shp (530 cv)

SPECIFIC FUEL CONSUMPTIONS:
At max power rating:
Astazou IIA   0·623 lb (283 gr)/shp/hr
Astazou IIIN   0·643 lb (292 gr)/shp/hr
At max continuous rating:
Astazou IIA   0·634 lb (288 gr)/shp/hr
Astazou IIIN   0·659 lb (299 gr)/shp/hr

The 592 shp Turboméca Astazou IIIN turboshaft which powers the SA 341 helicopter

TURBOMÉCA BASTAN

The Bastan turboprop is one of the second generation of Turboméca engines, which are characterised by their two-stage axial-centrifugal compressor. The Bastan VIC rated at 1,055 ehp powers the Aérospatiale N 262 and the 1,000 hp Bastan VID powers the FMA Guarani II. Maximum TBO at the end of 1969 was 1,800 hr in the Nord 262.

By July 1969, Turboméca had built 380 Bastan VIC's, and production continues.

A second version, the Bastan VIIA flat rated at 1,045 shp, is derived from the Bastan VI and powers the N 262 Series C. By July 1969, 14 of these more powerful turboprops had been built.

A new version in course of design during 1969 was the Bastan XVIII with a T-O rating of 1,775 shp. This model introduces the Turboméca cooled turbine to the Bastan range of engines.

The following description relates to both the Bastan VI and VII except for the differences indicated.

TYPE: Single-shaft axial-plus-centrifugal turboprop.

REDUCTION GEAR: Two-stage epicyclic type, inside tapered cylindrical casing at front of engine. Ratio 1 : 21·0957. Propeller shaft carried in ball bearing at front.

AIR INTAKE: Annular intake at rear of reduction gear casing. Outer wall of intake, of triangular cross section, provides mounting for accessories. Front ball bearing for compressor shaft carried by air intake assembly.

COMPRESSOR CASING: Central portion carries rear ball bearing for compressor shaft.

COMPRESSOR: Single axial stage for Bastan VIC, and two axial stages for Bastan VII, followed by single centrifugal stage. Two rows of diffuser vanes between axial stages and two more aft of the centrifugal stage, of which the first is radial and the second axial. On Bastan VII first axial rotor blades are titanium and pin mounted in disc, and second axial rotor blades are light alloy integral with disc. Bastan VIC pressure ratio 5·83 : 1 and air mass flow 10 lb (4·5 kg)/sec. Bastan VII pressure ratio 6·68 : 1 and mass flow 13·1 lb (5·9 kg)/sec.

COMBUSTION CHAMBER: Direct-flow annular type. Usual Turboméca rotary atomiser fuel injection system. Two torch igniters. Gas temperature before turbine 870°C.

TURBINE CASING: Houses combustion chamber and turbine nozzle assembly. Supports engine rear roller bearing at rear end.

TURBINE: Three-stage axial-flow turbine with separate discs. Each turbine preceded by axial-flow nozzle guide vane assembly.

JET PIPE: Annular welded sheet assembly comprising cylindrical outer casing and central bullet fairing.

ACCESSORIES DRIVE: Upper pinion train drives dynamo starter, propeller governor and fuel pump with fuel metering device. Lower gear drives electric tachometer transmitter, fuel pump, 20kVA alternator and landing gear pump. All accessories mounted on intake casing.

MOUNTING: Three attachment points, two lateral, one at bottom of engine.

ENGINE CONTROL: By two governors. One adjusts fuel flow entering engine so that it is maintained at the value set by the power control lever, as a function of the variations of pressure and temperature at the engine air intake. The second governor maintains the propeller rpm at the value set by the rpm control lever, by varying propeller pitch.

STARTING: Automatic starter generator on Bastan VII.

DIMENSIONS:
Height: Bastan VIC	30·53 in (775·5 mm)
Width: Bastan VIC	26·97 in (685 mm)
Diameter: Bastan VII	21·7 in (550 mm)
Length: Bastan VIC	80·1 in (2,034 mm)
Bastan VII	75·2 in (1,911 mm)

WEIGHTS:
Engine only, equipped:
Bastan VIC	687 lb (312 kg)
Bastan VII	approx 816 lb (370 kg)

PERFORMANCE RATING:
T-O and max cont rating: Bastan VIC, at
33,500 rpm   986 shp (1,055 ehp)
T-O: Bastan VII
1,045 shp maintained at sea level to 104°F/
40°C, or at ISA up to 11,975 ft (3,650 m)
Max continuous   1,045 shp

SPECIFIC FUEL CONSUMPTION:
At T-O and max cont rating:
Bastan VIC   0·59 lb (268 gr)/ehp/hr

TURBOMÉCA-AGUSTA TM-251 (TAA 230)

Announced in the Spring of 1964, the TM-251 is the single-shaft turboshaft which powers the Agusta A106 light helicopter, and is sometimes referred to by the Agusta designation TAA 230.

The basic engine is produced by Turboméca and incorporates components developed from parts of the Astazou engine. It has a centrifugal compressor, annular combustion chamber and

The 1,045 shp Turboméca Bastan VII single-shaft turboprop powering the N 262 Series C

two-stage turbine. Mass flow is 4·2 lb (1·9 kg)/sec and pressure ratio 4·1 : 1. To its forward end is bolted a three-stage reduction gearbox, manufactured by Agusta and embodying an automatic hydraulic centrifugal clutch and free-wheel arrangement. The oil filter and pumps are also supplied by Agusta.

By March 1969 five TAA 230s had been built.

DIMENSIONS:
Length overall	46·85 in (1,190 mm)
Max width	14·57 in (370 mm)
Max height	24·80 in (630 mm)

WEIGHT:
Dry, equipped	290 lb (132 kg)

PERFORMANCE:
Max power	354 shp at 43,000 rpm
Rated power	270 shp

SPECIFIC FUEL CONSUMPTIONS:
At max power	0·86 lb (390 gr)/shp/hr
At rated power	0·838 lb (380 gr)/shp/hr

TURBOMÉCA ARTOUSTE IIIB

The Artouste IIIB is a single-shaft turboshaft derived from the Artouste II, and powers the Aérospatiale Alouette III helicopter. It is a member of the second generation of Turboméca engines with a two-stage axial-centrifugal compressor and three-stage turbine. The Artouste IIIB has a pressure ratio of 5·2 : 1. Air mass flow is 9·5 lb/sec (4·3 kg/sec) at 33,300 rpm.

Type approval at the rating given below was received on 25 May 1961, following completion of a 150-hour official type test. By July 1969 a total of 1,026 Artouste IIIBs had been built. Production at Turboméca continues. In addition Artouste IIIBs are being built under licence in India by Hindustan Aeronautics Ltd.

The Artouste IIIB, which powers the Aérospatiale SA 316B Alouette III, obtained FAA certification in March 1962 and in August 1968 similar certification of the Artouste IIC1, C2, C5 and C6, powering the SE 3130 and 313B Alouette II Artouste, was also obtained.

DIMENSIONS:
Length	71·46 in (1,815 mm)
Height	24·68 in (627 mm)
Width	19·96 in (507 mm)

WEIGHT, FULLY EQUIPPED: 400 lb (182 kg)

PERFORMANCE RATINGS:
T-O and max ratings at 113°F (45°C), and at altitudes up to 32,800 ft (10,000 m) and standard atmosphere + 50°F (+10°C)
578 ehp (543 shp) at 33,500 rpm (6,000 output shaft rpm)

SPECIFIC FUEL CONSUMPTION:
0·723 lb (0·328 kg)/ehp/hr

TURBOMÉCA AUBISQUE

This small geared turbofan was developed to power the Saab-105 light multi-purpose jet aircraft

for which an initial series of 300 was ordered. By July 1969 a total of 374 Aubisque 1A engines, rated at 1,635 lb (742 kg) had been constructed for this application.

A new version of the turbofan, the Aubisque 6, ran during the second half of 1969. This model introduces an air-cooled HP turbine, giving the engine a rating of 1,852 lb (840 kg). The sfc is 0·66.

The following details refer to the Aubisque 1A:

TYPE: Single-shaft turbofan engine with geared fan.

AIR INTAKE: Annular intake and central bullet fairing of light alloy, with two support webs in vertical plane. Starter/generator and accessory gear trains in bullet fairing.

ENTRY CASING: Front casing of light alloy, comprising an outer casing and an inner wall which forms the air duct. Lower part of outer casing is extended to provide a mounting for the accessories.

FAN STAGE: Single-stage fan is driven through spur reduction gearing with a ratio of 1 : 2·131839, so that it turns at 15,500 rpm at T-O rating. The front of the casing supports the fan-stage front bearing and carries a row of variable-incidence inlet guide vanes which are provided with thermal de-icing. At the rear of the casing are two rows of straightener vanes and the housing for the rear fan-stage bearing.

CENTRE CASING: This casing divides the airflow into two streams, of which the main stream passes through the compressor, while the outer stream passes through the annular by-pass duct. The inner duct is supported by four streamlined struts and carries the housing for the front bearing of the compressor assembly.

COMPRESSOR: Single axial stage followed by a single centrifugal stage. Two rows of diffuser vanes between the stages and two more aft of the centrifugal stage, of which the first is radial and the second axial. Pressure ratio 6·9 : 1. Air mass flow 49 lb (22·25 kg)/sec.

COMBUSTION CHAMBER: Annular type, with usual Turboméca rotary atomiser fuel injection system.

TURBINE: Two-stage turbine with separate discs and inserted blades. Discs coupled together and to fore and aft shafts by special bolts and curvic couplings. Front shaft is coupled directly to compressor. Rear shaft is carried in rear rotor bearing.

JET PIPE: Inner and outer sheet metal casings, latter supported by three hollow struts, surrounded by annular by-pass air duct.

ACCESSORIES: Provision for tachometer drive, oil pumps (including one for inverted flight), guide-vane controls, fuel pump and regulator, and eventually, a 20kVA alternator.

MOUNTING: Lateral attachment points on each side of entry casing. Main mounting points on lower part of centre casing.

The 543 shp Turboméca Artouste III single-shaft helicopter turboshaft

DIMENSIONS:
Length	90·1 in (2,288 mm)
Width	25·59 in (650 mm)
Height	29·53 in (750 mm)

WEIGHT (DRY):
With full equipment	640 lb (290 kg)

PERFORMANCE RATINGS:
T-O	1,635 lb (742 kg) st at 33,000 rpm
Max cont	1,375 lb (625 kg) st at 32,000 rpm
Cruising	1,100 lb (505 kg) st

SPECIFIC FUEL CONSUMPTION:
At T-O rating	0·618

TURBOMÉCA OREDON IV

This is a new single-shaft turboshaft for light helicopters, derived from the Astazou but of reduced overall dimensions. Maximum power is 420 shp and the engine comprises a two-stage planetary reduction gear of 1 : 9·767 ratio driving, through a centrifugal clutch, a two-stage axial compressor and single-stage centrifugal compressor, an annular combustion system and three-stage axial turbine. The engine control system maintains speed constant at 59,100 rpm (6,051 output rpm) under all operating conditions.

This engine was originally announced in April 1965 as the 350 shp Oredon III, a joint development by Turboméca and Rolls-Royce incorporating a R-R reduction gear. Prototype engines have been built and tested. Development has for the time being been suspended.

An initial application of the Oredon IV is the Wagner Helicopter-Technik Aerocar.

DIMENSIONS:
Overall length	50·3 in (1,279 mm)
Diameter	14·4 in (366 mm)

WEIGHT:
Without accessories	approx 134 lb (61 kg)
Fully equipped, with clutch	approx 240 lb (109 kg)

PERFORMANCE RATINGS:
Max T-O	420 shp at 59,100 rpm
Max continuous	380 shp at 59,100 rpm
Cruise	340 shp at 59,100 rpm

SPECIFIC FUEL CONSUMPTIONS:
At max T-O rating	0·68 lb (253 gr)/shp/hr
At max cont rating	0·71 lb (259 gr)/shp/hr
At cruise rating	0·75 lb (269 gr)/shp/hr

TURBOMÉCA TURMO

The Turmo is a free-turbine engine with both turboshaft and turboprop versions in service.

Each has a gas generator section comprising a single-stage axial plus single-stage centrifugal compressor, annular combuster, and two-stage turbine. The power turbine and transmission system vary according to the engine series. By July 1969, 308 Turmo IIIC₃, C₅ and E₃ geared turboshafts and 70 Turmo IIIC₄ direct-drive turboshafts had been delivered. The main variants of the Turmo are as follows:

Turmo IIIC₃. This version is in production to power the triple-engined SA 321 Super Frelon helicopter. Maximum contingency rating is 1,480 hp.

Turmo IIIC₄. Developed from Turmo IIIC₃ and with a maximum contingency rating of 1,380 shp, this all-weather version is being manufactured jointly by Turboméca and Rolls-Royce to power SA 330 Puma twin-engined helicopters as part of the Franco-British helicopter agreement of October 1967.

Turmo IIIC₅. Similar to Turmo IIIC₃ but with different ratings. The SA 321F and 321J Super Frelon powered by this engine obtained French certification in June 1968.

Turmo IIID. Turboprop version, similar in basic construction to Turmo IIIC series but with output speed limited to 6,000 rpm. Gas generator section is mounted beneath output shaft which is driven by free-turbine. The overhung forward drive leads through a freewheel and dog clutch to the propeller reduction gearbox, which gives a final drive at 1,200 rpm. A drive pad at the rear of the primary gearbox enables the engines of a multi-engined aircraft to be coupled together by spanwise shafting as is employed with the four Turmo IIID₃ turboprops powering the Breguet Br 941S STOL transport.

Turmo IIIE₃. Similar to Turmo IIIC₃ but with different ratings. In production for SA 321 Super Frelon.

Turmo 6. Derived from Turmo IIIC₄. Has rating of 1,677 shp (1,700 cv) and sfc of 0·592 lb/shp/hr (265 gr/cv/hr).

Turmo 10. Derived from Turmo IIIC₃. Has redesigned transmission and additional axial compressor stage to give increased rating of 1,578 shp (1,600 cv) with further potential to 1,775 shp (1,800 cv). Under development for increased-weight versions of civil Super Frelon.

Turmo 16. Derived from Turmo 10 (which it may supersede). Has new Turboméca cooled turbine to give rating of 1,973 shp (2,000 cv) and sfc of 0·536 lb/shp/hr (240 gr/cv/hr). Planned to run before end of 1969.

The following description applies generally to the Turmo IIIC₃, C₄, C₅ and E₃ except where indicated.

TYPE: Free-turbine axial-plus-centrifugal turboshaft.

Turboméca Aubisque 1A turbofan engine (1,635 lb = 742 kg st)

REDUCTION GEAR: Turmo IIIC₃, C₅ and E₃ fitted with rear-mounted reduction gear mounted in bifurcated exhaust duct with rear-facing power take-off shaft. Output shaft from free-turbine drives into high-speed gear of simple helical spur train of 3·53 : 1 reduction ratio. Output shaft also drives reduction gear driving oil cooler fan mounted on front of main reduction gear case. Turmo IIIC₄ is a direct-drive engine.

AIR INTAKE: Annular forward-facing intake, with de-icing in Turmo IIIC₄ and C₅. Centre housing contains forward ball bearing for compressor shaft and bevel gear drive to accessories mounted above and below intake casing.

COMPRESSOR: Single-stage axial followed by single-stage centrifugal with single-sided impeller. Two rows of light alloy stator blades aft of axial stage. Centrifugal stage has steel radial and axial diffusers; impeller located by lugs on turbine shaft. Axial rotor blades, titanium in Turmo IIIC₃, C₅ and E₃ and steel in Turmo IIIC₄, pin-mounted in steel disc with integral shaft. Pressure ratio 5·9 : 1 on Turmo IIIC₃. Air mass flow 13 lb (5·9 kg)/sec. Axial rotor carried on ball bearing ahead of disc and roller bearing aft of disc. Also, ball bearing ahead of impeller.

COMBUSTION SYSTEM: Reverse-flow annular type with centrifugal fuel injector using rotary atomizer disc. Ignition by two ventilated torch igniters.

GAS GENERATOR TURBINE: Two-stage axial unit with integral rotor blades. Discs with curvic couplings through-bolted to compressor shaft. Carried on roller bearing at rear of second-stage disc.

POWER TURBINE: Two stage axial unit in Turmo IIIC₃, C₅ and E₃, and single-stage in Turmo IIIC₄. Blades carried in discs by fir tree roots. Rotor overhung from rear on through-bolted output shaft. Shaft carried on roller bearing at front (at rear of turbine disc) and ball bearing at rear at input to reduction gear.

JET PIPE: Fixed type with lateral bifurcated exhaust duct in Turmo IIIC₃, C₅ and E₃, and single lateral duct on Turmo IIIC₄.

ACCESSORIES: Mounted above and below intake casing with drive pads for oil pump, fuel control unit, electric starter, tacho-generator and, on Turmo IIIC₄, oil cooler fan. Control unit remote drive also provided on Turmo IIIC₄ from bevel gear drive on power turbine output shaft.

MOUNTING: Two lateral supports fitted to lower part of turbine casing at rear flange output shaft protection tube. On Turmo IIIC₄, also on reduction gear case.

FUEL SYSTEM: Fuel control unit for gas generator on Turmo IIIC₃, C₅ and E₃, with speed limiter for power turbine also fitted on E₃. Constant speed system fitted on Turmo IIIC₄ power turbine, with speed limiter also fitted on gas generator.

FUEL GRADE: AIR 3405 for Turmo IIIC₄.

LUBRICATION SYSTEM: Pressure type with oil cooler and 23 pint (13 litre) tank mounted at front of engine on Turmo IIIC₄, with oil tank only around intake casing on Turmo IIIC₃, C₅ and E₃. Oil cooler fan driven by rear-mounted reduction gear case on Turmo IIIC₃,

The 1,380 shp Turboméca Turmo IIIC₄ turboshaft which powers the SA 330 Puma helicopter

The 1,480 hp Turboméca Turmo IIIC₃ turboshaft which powers the Super Frelon helicopter

C$_5$ and E$_3$, and by intake accessory drive gear on Turmo IIIC$_4$.

OIL SPECIFICATION: AIR 3155A, or synthetic AIR 3513, for Turmo IIIC$_4$.

STARTING: Automatic system with electric starter motor.

DIMENSIONS:

Height:
Turmo IIIC$_3$,C$_5$ and E$_3$ 28·2 in (716·5 mm)
Turmo IIIC$_4$ 28·3 in (719 mm)
Turmo IIID$_3$ 36·5 in (926 mm)
Turmo 10   26·8 in (679 mm)

Width: Turmo IIIC$_3$, C$_5$ and E$_3$ 27·3 in (693 mm)
Turmo IIIC$_4$ 25·1 in (637 mm)
Turmo IIID$_3$ 36·8 in (934 mm)

Length:
Turmo IIIC$_3$ C$_5$ and E$_3$ 78·0 in (1,975·7 mm)
Turmo IIIC$_4$ 85·5 in (2,184 mm)
Turmo IIID$_3$ 73·6 in (1,868 mm)
Turmo 10   77·5 in (1,964·7 mm)

WEIGHT, DRY:
Turmo IIIC$_3$, C$_5$ and E$_3$ fully equipped
   655 lb (297 kg)
Turmo IIIC$_4$,equipped engine   496 lb (225 kg)
Turmo IIID$_3$, basic engine   805 lb (365 kg)
Turmo 10, equipped engine   677 lb (307 kg)

PERFORMANCE RATINGS:
T-O: Turmo IIIC$_3$ and E$_3$ 1,480 shp
Turmo IIID$_3$ 1,480 shp
Max contingency: Turmo IIIC$_4$ 1,380 shp
Turmo IIIC$_5$ 1,450 shp
Max emergency: Turmo 10   1,731 shp
T-O and intermediate contingency:
Turmo IIIC$_4$ 1,282 shp
Turmo IIIC$_5$ 1,408 shp
T-O and intermediate emergency, Turmo 10
   1,578 shp

Max continuous:
Turmo IIIC$_3$ and E$_3$ 1,282 shp
Turmo IIIC$_4$ 1,170 shp
Turmo IIIC$_5$ 1,234 shp
Turmo IIID$_3$ 1,282 shp
Turmo 10   1,342 shp

SPECIFIC FUEL CONSUMPTIONS:
At T-O rating:
Turmo IIIC$_3$ and E$_3$ 0·603 lb (274 gr)/shp/hr
Turmo IIID$_3$ 0·616 lb (280 gr)/shp/hr
At max contingency rating:
Turmo IIIC$_4$ 0·625 lb (284 gr)/shp/hr
At max emergency rating:
Turmo 10   0·538 lb (244 gr)/shp/hr
At T-O and intermediate contingency rating:
Turmo IIIC$_4$ 0·640 lb (290 gr)/shp/hr
At T-O and intermediate emergency rating,
Turmo 10   0·550 lb (249 gr)/shp/hr
At max continuous rating:
Turmo IIIC$_3$ and E$_4$ 0·640 lb (290 gr)/shp/hr
Turmo IIIC$_4$ 0·656 lb (294 gr)/shp/hr
Turmo IIID$_3$ 0·640 lb (290 gr)/shp/hr

TURBOMÉCA TURMASTAZOU

A new turboshaft engine, the Turmastazou 14 comprises the Astazou 14 single-shaft turbo-prop with the addition of a free-turbine (Turmo is an abbreviation for 'turbine motoriste' and by implication refers to a free-turbine engine). Development is proceeding and by March 1969 five engines had been built. The Turmastazou is intended for helicopter applications and is also in service with the Orleans-type Bertin Aérotrain. Development is now aimed at more than the 889 shp quoted below.

TYPE: Free-turbine axial-plus-centrifugal turbo-shaft.

POWER DRIVE: Direct at rear of engine. No reduction gear fitted.

AIR INTAKE: Annular forward-facing intake at front of engine feeding direct to compressor inlet.

The 889 shp Turboméca Turmastazou 14 free-turbine turboshaft

The 1,775 shp Turboméca Double Turmastazou 14 coupled free-turbine turboshaft (*K. Fulton*)

COMPRESSOR AND COMBUSTION SYSTEM: Similar to Astazou XIV.

COMPRESSOR TURBINE: Two-stage axial unit with rotor blades integral with turbine discs. Discs through-bolted with curvic couplings.

POWER TURBINE: Two-stage axial unit with rotor blades integral with turbine discs. Discs through-bolted with curvic couplings.

JET PIPE: None fitted as standard.

ACCESSORIES: Mounted on compressor casing behind oil tank. Drive pads fitted for oil pump, tacho-generator, fuel control unit, starter generator, AC generator and hydraulic pump (optional).

FUEL SYSTEM: Automatic control system with constant speed control of free-turbine

LUBRICATION SYSTEM: Pressure type system with gear pump. Oil tank mounted around front of engine.

STARTING: Automatic electrical starting.

DIMENSIONS:
Height   21·7 in (552 mm)
Width   17·3 in (440 mm)
Length overall   53·9 in (1,371 mm)

WEIGHT:
Complete with accessories   341 lb (155 kg)

PERFORMANCE RATINGS:
T-O   889 shp
Max continuous   792 shp

SPECIFIC FUEL CONSUMPTIONS:
At T-O rating   0·52 lb (236 gr)/shp/hr
At max continuous   0·534 lb (242 gr)/shp/hr

TURBOMÉCA DOUBLE TURMASTAZOU

The Double Turmastazou free-turbine coupled turboshaft comprises two Turmastazou turbo-shafts coupled by a combining gearbox to drive a common output shaft. The engine is intended for twin-engined helicopter installations and is specified for a new helicopter by Agusta.

The Double Turmastazou 14 comprises two Turmastazou 14 engines and is under development at 1,775 shp. A higher-powered model, the 2,071 shp Double Turmastazou 16, is derived from this version.

TURBOMÉCA-SNECMA

GROUPEMENT TURBOMÉCA-SNECMA GRTS

OFFICES:
1 Rue Beaujon, Paris 8

ADMINISTRATORS:
R. Florenti
E. Lacrouts

MANAGEMENT CONTROL COMMITTEE:
R. Martin
L. Henrion

FINANCIAL COMMISSARY:
C. Hirt

Announced in March 1969, Groupement Turboméca-SNECMA is a company formed jointly by Société Turboméca and SNECMA to be responsible for the design, development, manufacture, sales and service support of the 2,304 lb (1,045 kg) st Larzac turbofan launched in 1968 as a joint venture by the two companies. Groupement Turboméca-SNECMA has no capital at present and primarily comprises a joint management organisation to produce the new engine. Design, development and manufacture of the Larzac is undertaken jointly at the various works of Turboméca and SNECMA.

SNECMA-TURBOMÉCA LARZAC

This new small turbofan of 1·4 : 1 by-pass ratio is a joint venture by SNECMA and Turboméca

The SNECMA-Turboméca Larzac twin-spool turbofan (2,304 lb=1,045 kg st)
(*Kenneth Fulton*)

to provide a 2,304 lb (1,045 kg) thrust engine suitable for business jets of around 11,000 lb (5,000 kg) take-off weight, military liaison aircraft and trainers. It is intended both to power new designs and to re-engine existing aircraft in these categories. The first of three prototype Larzacs ran in May 1969 and flightworthy engines are scheduled to be available by the end of 1970 with flight testing proceeding during 197₁. Production deliveries are planned to commence in 1972.

The Larzac comprises a two-stage fan and four-stage high-pressure compressor, each rotor being driven by a single-stage turbine. The combustion chamber is annular, with a vaporising fuel injection system. The fan and HP flows are ejected via concentric fixed-area nozzles. Engine and airframe accessories are grouped on a casing under the forward part of the fan duct and are driven by the HP rotor system. Mass flow is 57 lb (26 kg)/sec and pressure ratio 9 : 1.

Initial applications for the Larzac, including as alternative power plant, are the twin-engined Aérospatiale Corvette and Dassault Mystère 10 business jets, and the twin-engined Dassault-Breguet/Dornier Alpha Jet Franco-German basic trainer.

DIMENSIONS:
Diameter 17·3 in (440 mm)
Length 48·8 in (1,240 mm)
WEIGHT: 573 lb (260 kg)
PERFORMANCE RATING:
T-O 2,304 lb (1,045 kg) st at 22,000 HP rpm and 16,500 fan rpm
SPECIFIC FUEL CONSUMPTION:
T-O 0·61

GERMANY
THE GERMAN FEDERAL REPUBLIC

FICHTEL & SACHS
FICHTEL & SACHS AG
OFFICES AND WORKS:
872 Schweinfurt, Postfach 52

Fichtel & Sachs have converted their KM-48 rotary piston-engine for use in sailplane auxiliary propulsion. The 160 cc unit is air-cooled externally and gas-cooled internally, and complete with accessories, gasoline and propeller weighs 22 lb (10 kg). Compression ratio s 8 : 1 and power rating 10 hp (10·1 cv) at 5,000 rpm. The engine has been flown in a single-seat Schleicher Ka 8 sailplane, the maximum level speed of which was 60 mph (96 kmh).

HIRTH
HIRTH MOTOREN KG
ADDRESS:
7141 Benningen Neckar, Kreis Ludwigsburg

HIRTH F 10
This long-established aero-engine company has re-entered the field with a small and efficient four-cylinder horizontally-opposed unit offered in six versions which differ only in propeller reduction gear: sub-type A1a/K1a, propeller shaft above crankshaft, ratio 1·865 : 1, A1b/K1b, above, 2·21 : 1; A1c/K1c, above, 2·58 : 1; A2a/K2a, below, 1·865; A2b/K2b, below, 2·21 : 1; A2c/K2c, below, 2·58 : 1.
TYPE: Four-cylinder horizontally-opposed air-cooled two-stroke.

CYLINDERS: Bore 2·26 in (58 mm). Stroke 2·12 in (54 mm). Capacity 34·78 cu in (570 cc). Compression ratio 8·7 : 1.
INDUCTION: Four Tillotson HC.15A or HC.15B diaphragm carburettors, capable of operating in any attitude. Bing diaphragm fuel pump.
FUEL GRADE: Automatic gasoline (not Super grade) mixed with 1 part in 20 of branded two-stroke lubricating oil.
IGNITION: Bosch SB4V flywheel magneto serving Beru or Bosch 225/14 sparking plug in each cylinder.
PROPELLER DRIVE: Single-stage spur reduction (see sub-type models); direction of rotation, anti-clockwise viewed from rear.

STARTING: Manual pull-cable on recoil starter drum at rear.
DIMENSIONS:
Length overall 19·0 in (483 mm)
Width overall 16·5 in (420 mm)
Height overall 9·1 in (231 mm)
WEIGHT:
Dry, with magneto and fuel pump 55·4 lb (25·2 kg)
POWER RATINGS:
Take-off 26 hp at 5,000 rpm
Max continuous 26 hp
Cruise rating 19 hp at 4,500 rpm
SPECIFIC FUEL CONSUMPTION:
1 lb (0·45 kg)/hp/h

MBB
MESSERSCHMITT-BÖLKOW-BLOHM GmbH
8 Munich 80, POB 801 220
DEVELOPMENT AND PRODUCTION CENTRES:
Ottobrunn bei München; Lampoldshausen; Hamburg; and Bölkow-Apparatebau GmbH at Nabern and Schrobenhausen
OFFICERS: See "Aircraft" section

As noted in the "Aircraft" section, Messerschmitt-Bölkow and Hamburger Flugzeugbau merged in May 1969 to form the MBB Group. The former Bölkow element of this group is engaged in the design and development of a wide variety of medium and high-energy rocket engines and motors. These include liquid bipropellant and monopropellant engines, liquid- and solid-propellant air-augmented rockets, solid-propellant motors for small and medium-size missiles, and hybrid engines. Other activities include thrust augmentation by afterburning, engine casing design, propellant insulation and mounting, and preparatory work towards series production and reliability.

MBB is responsible for development of the liquid-propellant engines for control of the third stage of the ELDO-A satellite launch vehicle Europa 1. Other development of liquid-propellant engines by Bölkow has embraced advanced thermodynamic combustion engines, injection and cooling of engines of low thrust level and engines with high- and medium-energy storable propellants.

Work on the cooling of medium-energy bipropellant engines has led to the development of ultra low-thrust units with outputs well below the 110 lb (50 kg) theoretical minimum thrust level for rockets operating in a vacuum. Cooling of engines with vacuum thrust levels of approximately 88 lb (40 kg), 18 lb (8 kg), 11 lb (5 kg), 7 lb (3 kg) and 2·2 lb (1 kg) has been successfully demonstrated.

These engines, utilizing N₂O₄ and Aerozine 50 hypergolic propellants, are designed for sustained and pulsed operation. This has been assisted by use of a novel propellant injection technique which provides both good performance and combined internal, regenerative and radiation cooling of the combustion chamber.

Other liquid-propellant engines developed by MBB include a 66 lb (30 kg) thrust liquid oxygen/liquid hydrogen engine, an 1,100 lb (500 kg) thrust liquid fluorine/liquid hydrogen engine, an 11,000 lb (5,000 kg) thrust topping cycle engine, a liquid oxygen/liquid hydrogen high-pressure combustion chamber of 30,000 lb (13,600 kg) thrust, and hydrazine monopropellant engines of various thrust levels.

Design, development and manufacture of solid propellant motors has covered units of low and medium thrust output for booster and sustainer roles. By early 1968, Bölkow had performed more than 13,500 tests on solid motors and on hybrid and air-augmented solid and liquid propellants.

MBB TOPPING CYCLE ENGINE
In the course of research work on high-pressure liquid-propellant engines, Bölkow developed a turbopump engine utilizing the topping cycle principle. Since 1963 this throttleable engine has been undergoing tests as a complete unit, incorporating an integral propellant supply system. Using RP-1 and liquid oxygen as its propellants, the engine is rated at 11,000 lb (5,000 kg) st and is the most powerful rocket to be developed in Federal Germany since the war. By March 1968, about 300 tests had been run, amounting to 2 hr 30 min operation. A 30,000 lb (13,600 kg) thrust LH₂/LO₂ high-pressure combustion chamber for high-energy topping cycle engines has been developed since 1968.

MBB MONOPROPELLANT ATTITUDE CONTROL ENGINE
This is a 2·2 lb (1 kg) thrust monopropellant unit, using N₂H₄, which has been developed as a prototype for attitude control engines having a pulse capability. The system has been tested with various catalysts, under both sea level and simulated altitude conditions. By March 1968, a total of 80 tests had been made, totalling 3 hr operation.

MBB RESTARTABLE THROTTLEABLE VERNIER ENGINE
As part of a four-year development programme, a 66 lb (30 kg) prototype liquid oxygen/liquid hydrogen engine has been built, incorporating integral propellant valves and igniter. During simulated altitude tests, an effective specific impulse of 415 sec was achieved, with repeated re-ignition and propellant flow regulation. By March 1968, a total of 150 tests totalling 9 hr 30 min had been run.

MBB HYDROGEN/FLUORINE ENGINES
Since the end of 1965, work has been underway at Bölkow aimed at the development of an 1,100 lb (500 kg) thrust liquid hydrogen/liquid fluorine engine. This has included 50 tests totalling 45 min operation using a model hydrogen/fluorine throttleable engine with a ground level thrust of 48 lb (22 kg). Preliminary basic design studies for the 500 kg engine started at the end of 1967, and static testing of the engine has been in progress at Ottobrunn since March 1969. Chamber pressure is 102 lb/sq in (7·2 kg/cm²) and thrust is variable over a range of ±30 per cent. The first project to be announced using propulsion derived from this engine is the HORA interplanetary vehicle proposed by Dornier in March 1969.

MBB ELDO-A VERNIER ENGINE
An 88 lb (40 kg) thrust bipropellant rocket engine has been under development by Bölkow since 1964 as a vernier engine for the third stage of the ELDO-A satellite launch vehicle, and is now in production. The engine has electro-pneumatic shut-off valves, pressurised helium feed of Aerozine 50 and N₂O₄ propellants, a stainless/Nimonic chamber of 70 : 1 area ratio and combustion temperature of 3,100°C following hypergolic ignition. Dry weight is 4 lb (1·8 kg) and specific impulse 300 sec. Despite a proven total reliability of 97 per cent, with a 90 per cent confidence level over the entire mission required of the ELDO-A launch vehicle, it was prevented by main stage failure of functioning fully in the first two launches of ELDO-A vehicles with live third stages. By March 1968, more than 1,000 tests had been run, totalling over 100 hr operation. Early in 1969 the engine was selected for use as the apogee motor of the Symphonie communications satellite.

MBB LOW-THRUST PULSE ENGINES
Bölkow has built and ground tested 2·2 lb (1 kg) and 7 lb (3 kg) thrust attitude control and vernier engines in a variety of versions, with pulse capability. The 2·2 lb (1 kg) engine, operating with Aerozine 50/N₂O₄ propellants and designed for the attitude control system of long-life satellites such as the Symphonie communications satellite, has been tested over uninterrupted runs of up to 30 min. By March 1968, a total of 80 tests had been made, amounting to 5 hr 30 min operation.

The 7 lb (3 kg) engine, which is to undergo testing during 1968, has integral solenoid-operated propellant shut-off valves. It has been designed for pulse frequencies up to 30 cps.

MBB COBRA BOOSTER AND SUSTAINER MOTORS
Bölkow has delivered 36,000 booster and 26,000 sustainer solid-propellant motors for the Cobra anti-tank weapons system. Both units are of special lightweight construction. The booster has a thrust of 290 lb (133 kg) for a 0·67 sec burning time. corresponding figures for the sustainer motor being 19 lb (8·7 kg) and 19·2 sec. Production of both units continues.

MBB APOGEE MOTOR
This solid-propellant motor is designed to transfer a satellite from an elliptical parking orbit to a synchronous orbit, by provision of a single thrust impulse when at apogee. In this role and others involving the manoeuvring of satellites and upper stages, a propulsion system of minimum weight is required. For this reason the Bölkow apogee motor has a glass-fibre reinforced plastic combustion chamber, and uses a high-performance propellant with advanced mechanical properties. The propellant is case-bonded to the combustion chamber inner wall. Thrust is 3,970 lb (1,800 kg) for a burning time of 22 sec. Overall length is 37·4 in (950 mm), and diameter over the propellant

casing 26·2 in (585 mm).

A similar but larger solid-propellant motor is also being designed by MBB for use as a first-stage motor of a high-altitude research rocket.

Thrust for this is 8,820 lb (4,000 kg) for a burning time of 6 sec.

MBB HYDRAZINE ENGINE

Following preliminary development work during 1967, Bölkow tested a 550 lb (250 kg) thrust hydrazine engine early in 1968. This is understood to be the most powerful hydrazine monopropellant engine yet tested in the West.

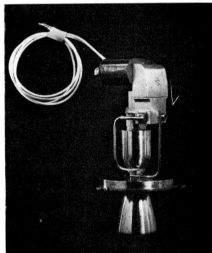

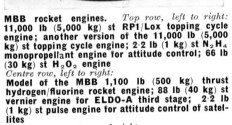

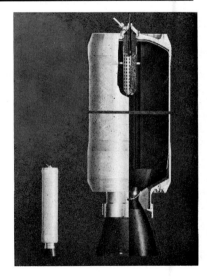

MBB rocket engines. *Top row, left to right:* **11,000 lb (5,000 kg) st RP1/Lox topping cycle engine; another version of the 11,000 lb (5,000 kg) st topping cycle engine; 2·2 lb (1 kg) st N_2H_4 monopropellant engine for attitude control; 66 lb (30 kg) st H_2O_2 engine**
Centre row, left to right:
Model of the MBB 1,100 lb (500 kg) thrust hydrogen/fluorine rocket engine; 88 lb (40 kg) st vernier engine for ELDO-A third stage; 2·2 lb (1 kg) st pulse engine for attitude control of satellites
Bottom row, centre and right:
Apogee motor with glass-fibre reinforced plastic combustion chamber; first-stage engine for high-altitude research rocket with case-bonded propellant

---

MTU
MOTOREN- UND TURBINEN-UNION MÜNCHEN GmbH

HEAD OFFICE AND WORKS:
München-Allach, Dachauer Str 665 (postal address, 8 München 50, Postfach 50 06 40)
DIRECTORS:
Dr Ing Karl Schott (Chairman of the Board)
Rolf Breuning and Dipl Ing Otto Voisard (both acting as representatives of the managements of MTU München and MTU Friedrichshafen)
Dir Ing Karl Adolf Müller and Dr Ing/Dr Ing hc Bruno Eckert (both acting as Managing Director, Development Division)
MTU results from a major rationalisation of the German motive-power industry. In late

1968 the aero-engine activities of Daimler-Benz AG and MAN (MAN Turbo GmbH) were merged under the name Turbo-Entwicklung (as noted in the Addenda to the 1969-70 *Jane's*). On 1 January 1970 the new MTU combine was created. It comprises two elements, MTU München and MTU Friedrichshafen.

MTU München has a nominal capital of DM63 million, and is owned half by Maschinenfabrik Augsburg-Nürnberg AG (MAN) and half by Daimler-Benz AG. This company now manages all the aircraft engine programmes formerly managed by MAN Turbo and Daimler-Benz. These programmes are being concentrated at Munich, and the programmes and staff formerly working on Daimler-Benz aero-engines at

Stuttgart should all have been transferred to Munich by the time this volume appears. The groups which now form MTU München employed 4,491 people on 31 October 1969, and the development staff numbered 900. Covered floor area is 4,865,300 sq ft (452,000 m²).

MTU Friedrichshafen was formerly Maybach Mercedes-Benz Motorenbau GmbH, an 83 per cent affiliate of Daimler-Benz. The latter firm assigned this holding to MTU, so that MTU Friedrichshafen is 83 per cent owned by MTU München, although technically it is a different company. It is engaged in production of high-speed diesels and industrial versions of the MTU aircraft engines; employment is about 5,500 and floor area about 3,767,370 sq ft (350,000 m²).

MTU München holds 40 per cent of the shares of Turbo Union Ltd, an equal percentage being owned by Rolls-Royce and 20 per cent by Fiat (see "International" section, page 721). Turbo-Entwicklung no longer exists.

By far the largest of MTU München's programmes will be its participation, through Turbo Union, in the RB.199 programme for the Panavia MRCA. The company is also developing and testing the RB.193 in collaboration with Rolls-Royce (see "International" section, page 718). The company's own main development activities concern the MTU 6022 turboshaft, described below, and a derivative of this unit under development for MAN AG (half-owner of MTU) for use in heavy road vehicles. Production programmes include licence manufacture of the General Electric J79-MTU-J1K turbojet for 50 new Starfighter aircraft and the General Electric T64-MTU-7 turboshaft for German Sikorsky CH-53D helicopters.

MTU also manufactures parts of the Spey turbofan under sub-contract to Rolls-Royce and is a member of the consortium making the Rolls-Royce Tyne (see Rolls-Royce entry, pages 736-7). MTU is also to share in producing whichever engine is standardized for the Airbus Industrie A 300B (early in 1970 this was the GE CF6-50 series). Servicing and overhaul activities include the J79-11A and -J1K, Tyne, Orenda 10 and 14, Lycoming piston-engines, RB.145 development engines, RB.162 lift-jets, and R-2800 piston-engines. The company holds a licence to manufacture the Pratt & Whitney (UACL) PT6A-27 turboprop.

MTU/ROLLS-ROYCE RB.193

Under development to power the VFW VAK 191B VTOL research aircraft, the 10,163 lb (4,610 kg) st RB.193 twin-spool vectored-thrust turbofan is a joint project with Rolls-Royce. Details of the RB.193 are given in the International section on page 718.

MTU J79

MAN Turbo (now MTU) took over the German licence rights to the General Electric J79 afterburning turbojet from BMW Triebwerkbau who had previously participated in the manufacture of considerable numbers of the engine for European-built Lockheed F-104G Starfighters. In addition to providing an overhaul, repair and maintenance service for licence-built J79-GE-11As, MTU has also developed an improved version of this model under the designation J79-MTU-J1K. The company is to modify J79-GE-11As in service with the German Air Force to the new -J1K standard. Additional engines will be built for 50 new F-104 Starfighters. MTU will also produce J79 components for McDonnell Douglas RF-4E Phantom fighters for the German Air Force.

The J79-GE-11A has a basic T-O rating of 10,000 lb (4,536 kg) st rising with afterburning to 15,800 lb (7,167 kg) st. No rating figures are available from MTU München for the J79-MTU-J1K, although the J79/J1 series of engines developed by General Electric which offer increased thrust, lower sfc and faster acceleration, are rated at 11,870 lb (5,385 kg) st, rising to 17,900 lb (8,120 kg) st with afterburning.

A description of the J79 is given under the General Electric entry in the US section on page 761. Manufacturer's details of the J79 MTU-J1K include the use of a steel compressor rotor and magnesium and steel casings; flame tubes fabricated in Hastelloy; turbine blades in Udimet 700; jet pipe fabricated in Inconel; fuel and oil specification MIL-L-5624 and MIL-7808 respectively; and use of an air supply starter. Technical data for the -J1K include: air mass flow 164 lb (74·4 kg)/sec; compressor pressure ratio 12·1 : 1; diameter 39·2 in (995 mm); length

The MTU J79-MTU-J1K turbojet with afterburner

208 in (5,291 mm); and weight 3,704 lb (1,680 kg). MTU München report the sfc at military rating as 0·84, and 1·97 with afterburning.

MTU TYNE

MTU München is manufacturing the Tyne twin-spool turboprop under licence from Rolls-Royce to power the Breguet Atlantic and Transall C-160, in collaboration with Rolls-Royce, the Hispano-Suiza Division of SNECMA in France and Fabrique Nationale in Belgium. MTU München is manufacturing 28 per cent of the components for each engine and is responsible for assembly and testing of 470 6,100 ehp Tyne RTy.22 engines for the Transall. A description of the Tyne is given under the Rolls-Royce entry in the UK section on pages 736-7.

MTU PT6A-27

Early in 1969 MAN Turbo acquired an option on an exclusive licence to manufacture the Pratt & Whitney (UACL) 715 ehp PT6A-27 turboprop in Germany. MTU München is also participating with UACL in developing the 579 ehp PT6A-20 turboprop in gas generator form for powering the Dornier Do 132 tip-jet helicopter. A description of the PT6A series appears under the UACL entry in the Canadian section on page 692.

MTU T64

MTU München has a licence to manufacture the General Electric T64 free-turbine turboshaft/turboprop. The company has tooled up to participate in manufacture of the 3,925 shp T64-GE-7 turboshaft for powering the Sikorsky CH-53D medium helicopter chosen by the German Army, and production deliveries are to begin in 1970. A description of the T64 is given under the General Electric entry in the US section on pages 767-8.

MTU 6012C, E and L

The basic Model 6012 shaft-turbine engine is a development of the earlier Model 6002 and is suitable for use as a primary power plant for light aircraft and helicopters or as a drive unit for aircraft auxiliary equipment.

There are seven versions as follows:

Model 6012 C1. De-rated 60 hp turboshaft version. Used as APU.

Model 6012 C2. Basic turboshaft version rated at 90 hp. Used as APU.

Model 6012 C3. Turboshaft version rated at 110 hp. Used as APU.

Model 6012 E2. Gas-generator version rated at 90 ehp.

Model 6012 F2. This small turbojet is now no longer in production.

Model 6012 L2. Turbo-compressor based on Model 6012 C2, with an additional radial-type single-stage compressor and a flange-mounted intermediate accessory drive for a tachometer generator, lubricating pump, fuel injection

starting pump, governor and hand-cranked starter support, including magneto. Delivers 1·16 lb (0·53 kg)/sec air-flow at pressure of 37 lb/sq in (2·6 kg/sq cm). Powers the Dornier Do 32 helicopter.

Model 6012 L3. Turbo-compressor developed from Model 6012 C3, with a higher air mass flow of 1·24 lb (0·57 kg)/sec. Powers the Dornier Do 32K Kiebitz rotary-wing platform.

The following details apply to the 6012 C series.

TYPE: Lightweight turboshaft engine.

COMPRESSOR: Single-stage radial compressor. Air mass flow 2·2 lb/sec (0·98 kg/sec). Pressure ratio 3 : 1 at 45,000 rpm.

COMBUSTION CHAMBER: Disc-shaped chamber in annular space between compressor and turbine. Fuel is injected centrifugally by an injection wheel.

TURBINE: Single-stage radial turbine.

JET PIPE: Concentric diffuser. Exhaust gases may be used for heating purposes.

POWER OUTPUT: Via gearbox flanged to the compressor casing. Output shaft speed optional between 2,000 and 8,000 rpm.

GOVERNOR: Fuel-operated hydro-mechanical type, with single-lever master control. Limiting devices for overspeed, exhaust temperature and overload.

LUBRICATION: Dry-sump lubrication system, with gear-type pumps.

STARTING: Hand-crank, hydraulic starter or electrical motor. High-tension ignition.

DIMENSIONS:
Length, with gearbox   27·8 in (706 mm)
Width   16·0 in (407 mm)
Height   16·6 in (422 mm)

WEIGHT (DRY):
Approx   102 lb (46·4 kg)

MTU 6022

This small turboshaft engine powers the Bölkow BO 105 twin-engined light helicopter. There are three main aircraft versions, described hereunder, and a derivative with heat exchangers is under development for automotive applications.

three versions, as follows:

Model 6022 A1. Basic version, rated at 217 shp (220 cv) at 6,000 rpm.

Model 6022 A2. Developed version, rated at 350 shp (355 cv) at 6,000 rpm, which is maintained at temperatures up to 35°C and heights up to 6,500 ft (2,000 m). Powers the prototype BO 105 V3 and successfully completed a 100-hr bench test in the summer of 1968.

Model 6022 A3. Further development, rated at 375 shp (380 cv) at 6,000 rpm, to power production BO 105s. Has air-cooled turbine disc and strengthened reduction gear. Delivery is scheduled for 1971.

The Model 6022 consists of the main shaft, a two-stage radial compressor, a single tubular combustion chamber with fuel nozzle and a three-stage axial turbine. On the 6022 A1 the

The 350 shp MTU 6022 A2 turboshaft engine

The MTU 6012 L air generator (1·16 lb = 0·53 kg air per second)

combustion chamber is longitudinally positioned: on the 6022 A2 it is tangential. The 6022 A2 also has variable inlet guide vanes to the first-stage impeller. To suit the particular installation, the air intake can be arranged on either side of the engine. The reduction gearing is mounted forward of the compressor casing.

All accessories are mounted on the reduction gear casing, including the oil pump, oil cooler, oil reservoir, starter-generator, blower and a governor unit to prevent overspeed or excessive temperatures. A secondary shaft, running parallel with the axis of the engine, has an output rating of 10 shp at 4,200 rpm. The engine will run on JP1, JP4, JP5 or diesel fuel.

Turboprop, airborne APU and ground starter versions of the Model 6022 are projected.

DIMENSIONS:
Diameter	21·25 in (540 mm)
Length overall	45·20 in (1,148 mm)

DRY WEIGHT:
With reduction gearing, without starter:
6022 A1	165 lb (75 kg)
6022 A2	187 lb (85 kg)
6022 A3	198 lb (90 kg)

PERFORMANCE RATINGS:
See above

Former Daimler-Benz engines

MTU 720 (PLT 6)

Although intended primarily as a power plant for light transport and training aircraft and helicopters, the MTU 720 gas-turbine engine has other industrial applications. Development of the engine has been in its turboshaft form.

It has a four-stage axial-flow compressor, followed by a single centrifugal stage, an annular combustion chamber, a two-stage axial-flow compressor turbine and a single-stage axial-flow free power turbine.

Pressure ratio is 5·5 : 1. Max rpm are 21,000 for the gas-generator, 22,000 (normal 18,500) for the free power turbine and 6,100 for the output shaft, which is driven through a single-stage spur gear with a ratio of 3·62 : 1. Air mass flow is 13·5 lb (6·1 kg)/sec. Temperature before turbine is 835°C (1,540°F).

A single-lever control system controls speed and acceleration by regulating the fuel supply, and a governor prevents turbine overspeed.

The MTU 720 was tested in the Stuttgart altitude test facility in 1967 to an equivalent height of 46,000 ft (15,000 m), and was planned to be test flown in a Bell UH-1D helicopter modified for the purpose by Dornier. This work was being performed under a German Ministry of Defence contract.

DIMENSIONS:
Length overall	78·5 in (1,995 mm)
Diameter of combustion chamber	20·3 in (515 mm)

WEIGHT:
Dry, without starter	485 lb (220 kg)

PERFORMANCE RATINGS:
T-O rating
1,330 ehp (1,245 shp + 212 lb = 96 kg st)
Normal rating
1,260 ehp (1,180 shp + 203 lb = 92 kg st)

SPECIFIC FUEL CONSUMPTIONS:
At T-O rating	0·604 lb (270 gr)/ehp/hr
At normal rating	0·610 lb (273 gr)/ehp/hr

MTU DB 721 (PTL 10)

This engine is available in both turboprop and turboshaft versions. It has an eight-stage axial compressor, including one transonic stage, an annular combustion chamber, two-stage axial-flow compressor turbine rotating at 21,000 rpm and a single-stage axial-flow free-power turbine rotating at 18,500 rpm.

Output shaft rpm are 1,400 for the turboprop and 6,000 for the turboshaft. Air mass flow is 22 lb (10 kg)/sec and pressure ratio 6 : 1. Temperature before turbine is 900°C (1,650°F).

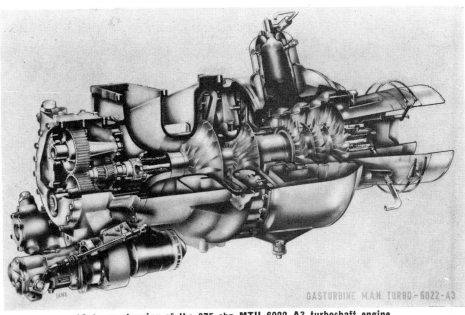

[Cutaway drawing of the 375 shp MTU 6022 A3 turboshaft engine

DIMENSIONS:
Diameter of combustion chamber	19·1 in (485 mm)

Length overall:
Turboprop	105·3 in (2,675 mm)
Turboshaft	91·3 in (2,320 mm)

WEIGHTS:
Dry, without starter:
Turboprop	660 lb (300 kg)
Turboshaft	550 lb (250 kg)

PERFORMANCE RATING:
Nominal rating	2,180 ehp

SPECIFIC FUEL CONSUMPTION:
At normal rating	0·618 lb (276 gr)/ehp/hr

MTU 730 (ZTL 6)

The MTU 730 is a turbofan version of the MTU 720. It differs from the latter only by the addition of a single-stage aft fan driven by the power turbine in modified form.

There are three versions:

MTU 730D. This version has a by-pass ratio of 1·75 : 1, a total air mass flow of 38·0 lb (17·25 kg)/sec and a fan pressure ratio of 1·55 : 1.

MTU 730F. This engine has a by-pass ratio of 5·5 : 1, a total air mass flow of 90·0 lb (40·75 kg)/sec and a fan pressure ratio of 1·295 : 1. The turbine inlet temperature is 875°C (1,610°F) and the air mass flow through the gas generator is 13·75 lb (6·25 kg)/sec.

MTU 730H. A drive for high-speed compound helicopters proposed as an adaptation of the 730F. Modifications to the engine provide for an inter-turbine gas bleed for energizing a remote turbine driving the helicopter rotor. During hover and vertical flight the MTU 730H delivers full gas bleed to the remote turbine for rotorborne flight. Gas is prevented from rotating the engine's aft fan turbine by closing variable-incidence nozzle guide vanes upstream of the power turbine. During transition to forward autogyro flight, the gas flow is switched progressively from the remote turbine to the fan turbine.

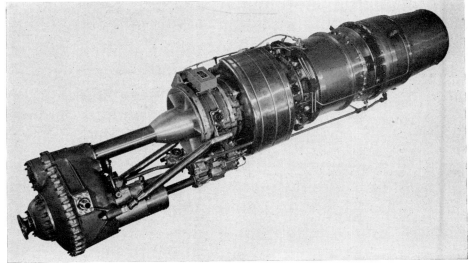

The 2,180 ehp turboprop version of the MTU DB 721 (PTL 10)

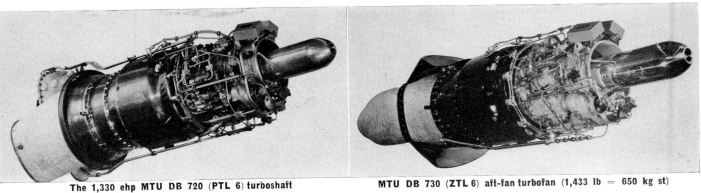

The 1,330 ehp MTU DB 720 (PTL 6) turboshaft   MTU DB 730 (ZTL 6) aft-fan turbofan (1,433 lb = 650 kg st)

At full rotor drive, the MTU 730H develops 1,600 shp, and at full forward thrust, 2,205 lb (1,000 kg).

DIMENSIONS:
Length:
| 730D | 77 in (1,956 mm) |
| 730F | 83·7 in (2,125 mm) |

Width:
| 730D | 23 in (585 mm) |

Height:
| 730D | 27·5 in (698 mm) |

Diameter:
| 730F | 35·4 in (900 mm) |

WEIGHTS:
Dry, without starter:
| 730D | 485 lb (220 kg) |
| 730F | 530 lb (240 kg) |

PERFORMANCE RATINGS:
Nominal rating:
| 730D | 1,433 lb (650 kg) st |
| 730F | 2,205 lb (1,000 kg) st |

SPECIFIC FUEL CONSUMPTIONS:
At nominal rating:
| 730D | 0·65 |
| 730F | 0·44 |

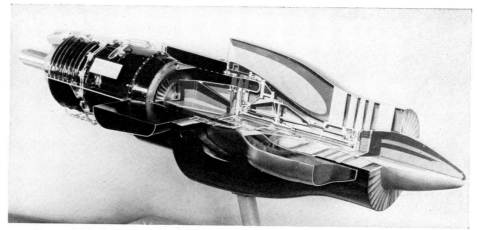

Cutaway MTU DB 730H gas bleed turbofan for high-speed compound helicopter propulsion

---

PIEPER-STARK
PIEPER-STARK MOTORENBAU GmbH

ADDRESS:
Minden/Westf

Pieper-Stark is manufacturing the 45 hp Stamo MS 1500-1 modified Volkswagen four-cylinder air-cooled piston-engine for the Scheibe SF 25B Falke two-seat powered glider. The capacity of this is 1,500 cc, compression ratio 7·2 : 1, length 25 in (640 mm), width 29·3 in (745 mm), height 15·5 in (395 mm), and dry weight 115 lb (52 kg). The MS 1500-1 operates on either 80/86 or 90 octane fuel, and is started by a pull cord.

INDIA

HAL
HINDUSTAN AERONAUTICS LTD

HEAD OFFICE:
Indian Express Building, Bidhana Veedhi, Bangalore 1

OFFICERS: See "Aircraft" section

The Bangalore and Koraput Engine Divisions of HAL comprise the main aero-engine design, development and manufacturing elements of the Indian aircraft industry.

BANGALORE DIVISION

This Division is engaged on a variety of gas-turbine and piston-engines of both indigenous and licensed designs. These include the HJE 2500 turbojet designed by HAL; the Orpheus 701 and 703 turbojets being built under licence from Rolls-Royce Bristol Division to power the Gnat and HF-24 fighter; the Rolls-Royce Dart 531 turboprop being built under licence from Rolls-Royce Aero Engine Division to power the HS 748 transport; the Artouste turboshaft being built under licence from Turboméca to power Alouette helicopters; and the PE 90 and HPE 2 piston-engines designed by HAL. The Bangalore Division also overhauls and repairs Rolls-Royce Avon and HAL Orpheus turbojets and various types of piston-engines, for the Indian Air Force.

HAL HJE-2500

The HJE-2500 is a small turbojet engine which HAL is developing as a potential power plant for production versions of its HJT-16 Mk II basic training aircraft. It is a single-spool design, with a seven-stage compressor driven by a single-stage turbine. All components except the fuel system were manufactured at Bangalore.

The engine ran for the first time on the test bed on 30 December 1966. Further development is now under way.

AIR INTAKE: Made of aluminium-magnesium alloy with three radial struts supporting the main thrust bearing and starter. Inlet guide vanes are fixed type.

COMPRESSOR CASING: Two piece aluminium-magnesium alloy casing with seven rows of aluminium alloy blades and one row of flow straightener vanes.

COMPRESSOR: Built up of seven steel discs mounted on a common drum supported on rear roller bearing and front ball thrust bearing. 410 aluminium alloy rotor blades. Air mass flow 45 lb (20·4 kg)/sec at 12,500 rpm. Pressure ratio 4·2 : 1.

COMBUSTION CHAMBER: Cannular type with seven flame tubes and duplex burners. High-energy ignition system with plugs in tubes 2 and 5.

FUEL SYSTEM: Positive displacement pump with pressure, fuel/air ratio and acceleration control.

FUEL GRADE: DEngRD. 2494.

TURBINE CASING: Nimocast with 65 solid nozzle guide vanes of Nimonic 90.

TURBINE: Single stage with fir-tree root fitting for 103 blades of FV.448. Rear bearing ahead of turbine wheel.

JET PIPE: Fixed nozzle.

CONTROL SYSTEM: Single lever master control.

LUBRICATION: Return-flow system for front bearing and gears. Total loss for centre and rear bearings.

MOUNTING: Spherical joints on sides of delivery casing with steady on compressor casing.

STARTING: Electric starter in nose bullet.

DIMENSIONS:
Length, flange to exit cone	85 in (2,160 mm)
Diameter	26 in (660 mm)
Frontal area	3·66 sq ft (0·34 m²)

WEIGHT DRY:
| | 585 lb (265 kg) |

PERFORMANCE:
T-O rating 2,500 lb (1,135 kg) st at 12,500 rpm

SPECIFIC FUEL CONSUMPTION: 0·98

HAL HPE-2

This is a new 250 hp six-cylinder, horizontally-opposed air-cooled piston-engine of non-super-charged direct drive design. The HPE-2 is intended to power a new agricultural aircraft under development by HAL. The prototype engine is under construction. Cubic capacity is 472 cu in (7·75 litres) and compression ratio 8·7 : 1. The HPE-2 is designed to run on 100/130 octane gasoline and has wet sump, pressure feed lubrication.

DIMENSIONS:
Height	20·1 in (510 mm)
Width	34 in (865 mm)
Length	43·3 in (1,100 mm)

WEIGHT, DRY:
| | 410 lb (186 kg) |

PERFORMANCE RATINGS:
| T-O at 2,625 rpm at S/L | 250 hp |
| Nominal at 2,450 rpm at S/L | 185 hp |

KORAPUT DIVISION

This Division of HAL is located at Orissa and has been created to manufacture the 12,500 lb (5,670 kg) st Type TRD Mk R37F afterburning turbojet being produced in collaboration with Russia to power HAL-built MiG-21 Mach 2 fighters for the Indian Air Force. The engine at present is supplied nearly fully assembled by the Soviet Union. First delivery of the Russian turbojet from Koraput was early in 1969, the engine having also been used to calibrate the Indian test bed.

The Koraput factory is to assume increasing responsibility for the manufacture of the Type R37F and should be largely self-sufficient by 1971. Total expenditure on the new Division, which is already larger than the Bangalore Division, is Rs 350 m (£19·4 m).

INTERNATIONAL PROGRAMMES

ROLLS-ROYCE/ALLISON

ROLLS-ROYCE LIMITED

HEAD OFFICE:
Moor Lane, Derby, England.

THE ALLISON DIVISION, GENERAL MOTORS CORPORATION

HEAD OFFICE:
Indianapolis 6, Indiana, USA

Co-operation between Rolls-Royce and Allison started in November 1958, when the two companies began work on the design and development of high-performance jet engines for commercial and military applications. They have now developed jointly a version of the Rolls-Royce Spey turbofan, under the designation Allison TF41 (see Allison entry), to power advanced versions of the Vought A-7 Corsair II attack aircraft.

Rolls-Royce is marketing the Allison Model 250 shaft-turbine/turboprop engine in five major areas of the world, with an option for exclusive manufacture of the Model 250 in the UK.

Under the terms of a Memorandum of Understanding signed by the US and British governments in October 1965, Rolls-Royce and Allison are also developing jointly an advanced lift-jet engine for use initially in V/STOL fighter aircraft. No details are available except that this engine, the XJ99-RA-1, will have an exceptionally high thrust/weight ratio. No applications have so far been announced other than the now-abandoned EWR-Fairchild US-FRG V/STOL project which was to have been equipped with four retractable fuselage-mounted J99s in addition to two main propulsion lift/cruise turbofans.

ALLISON/ROLLS-ROYCE TF41

(Manufacturers' designations: Rolls-Royce Spey RB.168-62 and -66, Allison Model 912-B3 and -B14)

In August 1966 Allison and Rolls-Royce were awarded a joint $200m contract by USAF Systems Command for the development and production of an advanced version of the RB.168-25 Spey turbofan, to power Vought A-7D Corsair II fighter-bomber aircraft for the USAF. The requirement was to provide an engine offering maximum thrust increase over the TF30-P-6 powering USN A-7As. The amount of the contract was increased to $230m in December 1966, Rolls-Royce's share being about $100m.

Development and production have been undertaken jointly by Rolls-Royce and Allison, with Rolls-Royce supplying parts common to existing Spey variants and Allison, who are manufacturing under licence, being responsible for items peculiar to the new engine. This provides an approximately 50/50 division of manufacturing effort, but with Allison also undertaking assembly, test and delivery.

Design of the RB.168-62 started in June 1966 and, following the award of the USAF contract,

the engine was given the USAF designation TF41-A-1. Major change compared with the RB.168-25 is the move forward of the by-pass flow split into the LP compressor, to give a larger three-stage fan followed by a two-stage IP compressor, all five stages being driven by the two-stage LP turbine. The number of HP compressor stages is reduced from 12 to 11, the HP turbine remaining at two stages. These modifications raise the mass flow to 258 lb (117 kg)/sec and the by-pass ratio from 0·7 : 1 to 0·74 : 1. No afterburner is fitted.

Other design changes compared with the RB.168-25 include omission of the fan inlet guide vanes, the first rotor stage being overhung on a bearing supported by the first-stage stator vanes. The fan and IP compressor are of more modern aerodynamic design, and the HP and LP turbine nozzle throat areas have been increased to pass the additional flow. The HP turbine is of modified aerodynamic design, and an annular exhaust mixer replaces the RB.168-25's chuted design.

First run of the TF41-A-1/RB.168-62, the first at Rolls-Royce, Derby, in October 1967, the first Allison engine following at Indianapolis in March 1968. Development continued ahead of schedule, delivery of the first production TF41-A-1 being made in June 1968.

Ordered in 1968, a second version of the TF41 is the A-2, developed for the US Navy to power the Vought A-7E Corsair. Differences are slight, although the thrust rating is appreciably increased by raising the engine speed. This required re-stressing the disc of the low-pressure turbine and high-pressure compressor. Mass flow is slightly increased, the by-pass ratio being 0·77 : 1. Accessory drives are slightly different and the engine has additional protection against corrosion.

The two current production versions of the TF41 are known to Rolls-Royce as the RB.168-62 and RB.168-66; the corresponding Allison designations are Model 912-B3 and 912-B14. The following description refers basically to the TF41-A-1; where the A-2 differs, the data for that engine are given in brackets.

TYPE: Military turbofan without reheat.

AIR INTAKE: Direct entry, fixed, without intake guide vanes. Nose bullet de-iced by bleed air.

COMPRESSOR: Two-shaft axial. 3 fan stages, 2 intermediate stages on same shaft and 11 high-pressure stages. All rotor blades carried on separate discs. Fan and LP rotor blades of titanium, held by dovetail roots in slots broached in discs which are bolted together through Curvic couplings and similarly attached to the stubshafts. HP rotor blades also of titanium except stages 9, 10 and 11 of stainless steel, the first HP stage being pinned and the remainder being dovetailed into broached slots; discs similarly bolted together but driven through a splined coupling to the shaft. LP rotor carried in 3 roller bearings and HP by 2, with central ball location bearing and inter-

shaft ball bearing. LP casing of steel and aluminium; HP casing of stainless steel, both split at horizontal centre-line. Stainless steel LP stator blades slotted laterally into casing, intermediate stators welded to inner casing sub-assembly rings. HP stator blades of stainless steel, slotted laterally into casing. Overall pressure ratio 20 : 1 (A-2, 21·4 : 1); mass flow 258 lb/sec (117 kg/sec) (A-2, 263 lb/sec; 119 kg/sec). High-pressure compressor pressure ratio, 6·2 : 1; mass flow, 147 lb/sec (67 kg/sec).

COMBUSTION CHAMBER: Tubo-annular, with 10 interconnected Ni-Co alloy flame tubes in steel outer casing. Duple spray atomizing burner at head of each chamber. High-energy 12-joule igniter plug in chambers 4 and 8.

FUEL SYSTEM: Hydromechanical high-pressure system with automatic acceleration and speed control. Emergency manual over-ride of automatic features. Variable-stroke dual fuel pump.

FUEL GRADE: JP-4 (A-2, JP-5).

NOZZLE GUIDE VANES: Two HP stages with air cooling; two LP stages uncooled, but 1st LP blades are hollow and contain air pipes to cool LP turbine rotor. All stators precision cast in Ni-Co alloy.

TURBINE: Impulse-reaction axial type, two HP stages and two LP. All blades forged in Ni-Co alloy; first HP stage blades cooled internally by HP compressor air; remainder have solid blades, all being held by fir-tree roots. HP discs of Inco 901, LP discs of steel. All discs bolted to drive shafts. Temperature before turbine 1,182°C; temperature after turbine 777°C.

JET PIPE: Fixed, heat-resistant steel.

ACCESSORY DRIVES: External gearbox driven by radial shaft from HP system; provision for starter, fuel boost pump, two hydraulic pumps, HP fuel pump, fuel control, HP tachometer, CSD and alternator, permanent-magnet generator, LP fuel pump and oil pumps. Additional low-speed (LS) gearbox, driven from LP shaft, serving LP rotor governor and tachometer.

LUBRICATION SYSTEM: Self-contained, with engine-mounted 2·275 Imp gal tank, fuel/oil heat exchanger and gear type pump; pressure 50 lb/sq in (3·51 kg/cm²).

MOUNTING: Main ball-type trunnions on compressor intermediate casing; rear tangential steady-type at rear of by-pass duct.

STARTING: Integral gas turbine (air turbine).

DIMENSIONS:
Length overall .... 102·6 in (2,610 mm)
Intake diameter .... 37·5 in (953 mm)
Overall height .... 40 in (1,026 mm)

WEIGHT:
Dry 3,252 lb (1,475 kg) (3,308 lb = 1,500·5 kg)

RATING:
Max T-O 14,250 lb (6,463 kg) st up to ISA + 10°C
(15,000 lb = 6,804 kg st up to ISA)

SPECIFIC FUEL CONSUMPTION:
At max T-O rating .... 0·633 (0·664)

Cutaway drawing of the Allison/Rolls-Royce TF41-A-1 (Spey RB.168-62) turbofan (14,250 lb = 6,463 kg st)

ROLLS-ROYCE/KHD

ROLLS-ROYCE LTD
Small Engine Division
HEADQUARTERS:
Leavesden, near Watford, Herts, England

KLÖCKNER-HUMBOLDT-DEUTZ AG
HEAD OFFICE AND WORKS:
5 Köln-Deutz 1, Postfach 440, Germany

Rolls-Royce and KHD are developing jointly a small shaft-turbine, designated T112, which is being utilised first as an auxiliary power unit in the VFW VAK 191B V/STOL fighter. Rolls-Royce Small Engine Division is responsible for the combustion chamber, turbine, exhaust and turbine outer casing. KHD is responsible for the inlet, compressor and diffuser, gearbox and accessories.

ROLLS-ROYCE/KHD T112

The first T112 ran at KHD in September 1967 and a number of engines have since stood up well in elaborate tests. Flight clearance of the engine was completed in December 1969.

TYPE: Single-shaft turboshaft, turbo-compressor, or combined turboshaft and turbo-compressor.

AIR INTAKE: Annular intake, integrally cast in magnesium alloy with three support struts for nose-mounted starter.

COMPRESSOR: Single transonic axial stage, followed by single centrifugal stage with single-sided impeller. Axial stage comprises disc with 19 dovetail root-mounted blades of titanium alloy. Disc is splined to rotor shaft. Casing is a magnesium alloy casting, with 25 chrome-nickel steel stator blades. Impeller is in titanium alloy, with 26 vanes, splined to

Rolls-Royce/KHD T112 APU

rotor shaft. Casing and radial-axial diffuser are in heat-resisting magnesium alloy. Rotor shaft front ball bearing located in rear of impeller. Air mass flow 1·91 lb (0·876 kg)/sec. Pressure ratio 4·96 : 1.

COMBUSTION CHAMBER: Reverse-flow annular type, with 12 vaporising burners. Outer casing and flame tube in nickel-base alloy. One Rotax high-energy igniter.

FUEL SYSTEM: KHD hydro-mechanical control system regulates fuel flow. Max fuel pressure 355 lb/sq in (25 kg/cm²).

FUEL GRADE: ASTM A-1, MIL-J-5624, JP-1, JP-4

TURBINE: Two-stage axial turbine with two disc/drums located by curvic coupling with single tie-bolt. Rotor shaft rear roller bearing located aft of second stage. Steel casing, with

23 cobalt-base alloy nozzle guide vanes per stage. Nickel-base alloy disc/drums, with 29 fir-tree root-mounted rotor blades, also in nickel-base alloy, per stage. Turbine entry temperature 1,223°K.

EXHAUST DUCT: Fixed-area type in nickel-base alloy.

POWER TAKE-OFF: Through single-stage planetary reduction gearbox at rear of engine, with single or multi-shaft outputs.

ACCESSORY DRIVES: Two drives inside gear casing, for fuel pump, and for oil pump and cooling-fuel pump.

AIR OUTLET: Automatic bleed-air delivery valve on compressor casing .

LUBRICATION: Dry sump system. Integral tank with single feed and two scavenge pumps. Oil pressure 28 lb/sq in (2 kg/cm²).

OIL GRADE: MIL-L-7808.

STARTING: Electric starter.

DIMENSIONS:
Length	30·7 in (779 mm)
Height	17·4 in (443 mm)
Width	13·5 in (342 mm)

WEIGHT:
With single output shaft	75 lb (34 kg)
With two output shafts	79 lb (36 kg)

PERFORMANCE RATINGS:
Max cont
142 shp at 64,000 rpm, or 0·48 lb (0·22 kg) bleed air/sec at 63 lb/sq in (4·4 kg/cm²), at ISA
Combined rating
30 shp, plus 0·386 lb (0·175 kg) bleed air/sec at 66 lb/sq in (4·65 kg/cm²) at 64,000 rpm

SPECIFIC FUEL CONSUMPTION:
At max cont rating 0·93 lb (421 gr)/shp/hr

ROLLS-ROYCE/MTU

ROLLS-ROYCE LIMITED
HEAD OFFICE:
Moor Lane, Derby, England

MTU GmbH
HEAD OFFICE:
8 München 50, Germany

Rolls-Royce and MAN Turbo (now MTU München) signed an agreement in 1960 to co-operate on jet-engine development. They are now developing jointly the RB.193 lift-cruise turbofan engine, under contract from the Federal German Ministry of Defence. In addition, MTU is a member of Turbo-Union (the other members being Rolls-Royce and Fiat), the international company developing the RB.199 for the Panavia (MRCA) aircraft, as well as the European consortium producing Tyne turbo-prop engines for the Breguet Atlantic and Transall C-160 aircraft.

ROLLS-ROYCE/MTU RB.193

Design and development of the RB.193 twin-spool vectored-thrust turbofan is being carried out jointly by MTU and Rolls-Royce. This follows the award of a contract from the German Defence Ministry in December 1965 for development of an engine to power the VFW VAK 191B V/STOL strike fighter (now redesignated a research aircraft for the MRCA project).

The VAK 191B has one RB.193 lift/cruise engine and two Rolls-Royce RB.162 lift jets.

First run of the RB.193 was at R-R Derby in December 1967 followed by a further first run at MAN Turbo (now MTU München) on 7 June 1968. A 25-hr endurance test was run at Munich the following month, and by May 1969 six RB.193s were on test under the development programme.

Flight clearance testing of the engine was scheduled for mid-1969 with the first flight RB.193 being delivered to VFW in November 1969. From the beginning of 1970 a total of seven engines were to be available for the RB.193/VAK 191B flight test programmes. First flight of the aircraft is now planned for 1971.

The prime features of the RB.193's design include the use of counter-rotating LP and HP rotors to minimise the engine's resultant gyrocouple; only four main bearings to carry the LP and HP rotors; high percentage air bleed for aircraft stabilisation and control purposes; and the use of a shaft, gear and chain drive mechanism for rotation of the swivelling nozzles. The thrust vectoring system embodies technology derived from Rolls-Royce Bristol Engine Division's Pegasus and BS.100 vectored-thrust turbofans.

The following data relate to the RB.193-12, definitive power unit for the VAK 191B:

TYPE: Twin-spool vectored-thrust turbofan.

AIR INTAKE: Annular forward-facing.

COMPRESSORS: Three-stage LP compressor/fan and two-stage IP compressor on front spool, and six-stage HP compressor on a rear spool, with counter-rotating shafts. Division of air flow to front 'cold' vectored-thrust nozzles at exit from fan. Front stage of fan is overhung, without inlet guide vanes: rotor blades have

Rolls-Royce/MTU RB.193 vectored-thrust turbofan engine (*Kenneth Fulton*)

anti-vibration semi-span snubbers. Fan/IP rotor carried on roller bearing at front supported by first row of stator blades, and ball bearing at rear supported by compressor intermediate casing. HP rotor carried on ball bearing at front and HP conical mainshaft at rear. Fan rotor blades pin-root mounted; remainder of IP and HP blades dovetail/fir tree root mounted. Rotors comprise combined centreless disc and conical drum assemblies. All stator blades tip-shrouded at inner end. Total air mass flow 206 lb (93 kg)/sec, by-pass ratio 1·12 : 1, and overall pressure ratio 16·5 : 1.

COMBUSTION CHAMBER: Annular with atomising fuel injectors. High-energy ignition. Large bleed ports in combustor outer casing for supplying up to 16 per cent of HP air flow for aircraft stabilization and control purposes.

TURBINES: Single-stage HP unit and three-stage LP unit on counter-rotating shafts. HP turbine has air-cooled nozzle guide vanes and rotor blades. All four stages have tip-shrouded rotor blades. Hollow broad-chord nozzle guide vanes for LP stage-one turbine allow passage of spoked support structure for rear main roller bearings—HP bearing aft of HP disc, and adjacent LP bearing located inside centreless hub of LP stage-one disc. LP stages two and three discs overhung.

VECTORED THRUST NOZZLES: Front 'cold' and rear 'hot' nozzles carried on large-diameter swivel bearings with rotating seals. Nozzles have plain interior without cascade vanes, and have external strengthening bands. Four nozzles are mechanically interconnected by tubular shafts with Hooks-type couplings link-

ing round rear of engine to port and starboard nozzles via individual bevel gearboxes and sprocket-and-chain drives at rotating joint of each nozzle. Power for synchronous drive system provided by air motor operating on HP compressor bleed air. Front nozzles fed with fan air via large plenum chamber surrounding IP and HP compressor casings. Rear nozzles fed with exhaust gas via large plenum chamber at rear of engine. Angle of nozzle rotation from horizontal rearwards to 10° ahead of vertical downwards to provide braking thrust. Cold/hot thrust ratio 0·9 : 1.

ACCESSORY DRIVE: Combined spur and bevel gearbox within compressor intermediate case provides shaft drive to external bevel and spur wheelcase on top of fan plenum chamber. Individual drives on wheelcase include fuel and oil pumps with provision also for other accessories.

MOUNTING: Forward trunnions either side of fan plenum chamber, and rear lugs at top of exhaust casing flanges.

LUBRICATION SYSTEM: Oil tank mounted on starboard top of fan plenum casing.

DIMENSIONS:
Intake internal diameter	34·3 in (845 mm)
Length overall	101·4 in (2,575 mm)

WEIGHTS, DRY:
Nominal basic	1,742 lb (790 kg)
Installed engine	2,315 lb (1,050 kg)

PERFORMANCE RATING:
Minimum T-O, ISA SL 10,163 lb (4,610 kg) st

SPECIFIC FUEL CONSUMPTION:
At minimum T-O rating 0·65

ROLLS-ROYCE / SNECMA

ROLLS-ROYCE LTD
BRISTOL ENGINE DIVISION
HEADQUARTERS:
PO Box 3, Filton, Bristol, England

SOCIÉTÉ NATIONALE D'ETUDE ET DE CON-STRUCTION DE MOTEURS D'AVIATION
HEAD OFFICE:
150 Boulevard Haussmann, Paris VIIIe, France

Rolls-Royce Bristol Engine Division and SNECMA are responsible for development and production of the Olympus 593 turbojet engine to power the Anglo-French Concorde supersonic transport. They are also developing the M45 series of advanced turbofan engines for both civil and military use.

M45 SERIES

Collaboration between Rolls-Royce Bristol Engine Division (then Bristol Siddeley Engines, Ltd) and SNECMA on the M45 series of advanced turbofan engines began late in 1964, and a formal agreement was signed in February 1965. First of the series to be built was the M45F demonstrator engine, which ran for the first time in June 1966.

The **M45H** is a series of twin-spool commercial engines in the 7,000 to 10,000 lb (3,175-4,536 kg) thrust class. The **M45H-01**, the first in this series, ran in January 1969 and is under development to power the twin-engined VFW 614 short-haul airliner, on which it is mounted in unique overwing pods. Other versions of the M45H are described later.

Modular construction, using seven modules, has been incorporated to reduce strip time for repair and overhaul. Most major assemblies such as the fan, LP compressor and turbines, and combustion chamber can be removed rapidly and replaced without removing the engine from the aircraft. Internal inspection for 'on-condition' maintenance is possible by means of the intro-scope. In addition magnetic chip-detectors, fine filtration in the oil scavenge line and vibration measuring devices assist in giving early warning of incipient failure.

Low gas velocities should result in noise levels substantially lower than those of current engines. It is also intended that the omission of inlet guide vanes to the fan, and the relatively large fan rotor/stator spacing will provide low compressor noise levels.

The M45H-01, with a take-off thrust of 7,760 lb (3,520 kg), is planned for Type Test in mid-1972, before the VFW 614 receives commercial certification. Subsequently, the engine can be developed to a thrust of the order of 10,000 lb (4,536 kg). Variants currently being discussed with aircraft constructors include:

M45H-04. Uprated version of M45H-01, with take-off rating of 8,190 lb (3,715 kg) st up to ISA+15°C.

M45H-06. Similar to -04, but with extra stage in front of LP compressor. Rating 8,460 lb (3,838 kg) st up to ISA+15°C.

M45H-10. Similar to -04, but with two-stage fan and extra LP turbine stage. Rating 9,500 lb (4,309 kg) st up to ISA+15°C.

The following particulars apply to the M45H-01.
TYPE: Twin-spool turbofan.
AIR INTAKE: Annular, designed to integrate with VFW 614 pod intake and short-length cowl. Mass flow 233 lb/sec (106 kg/sec).
FAN: Single-stage axial unit integral with the LP system. Blades, in titanium, having snubbers at approximately two-thirds of blade height. Inlet guide vanes omitted to reduce icing problems, weight, cost and noise. Fan centrifuging effect and use of snubbers reduce risk of damage from foreign object ingestion. By-pass ratio 2·8 : 1.
LP COMPRESSOR: Five-stage axial unit of constant root diameter, driven by LP turbine. Rotor is of monobloc construction to give smooth running and long life. Fan and LP compressor rotor overhung on LP front shaft carried on bearings supported from compressor intermediate casing. Front bearing (adjacent to stage 1) is main ball thrust unit. Rear bearing (adjacent to stage 5) is roller providing radial location for interconnection of LP front and rear shafts. Fan and LP compressor casing are single ring assemblies giving stiff construction with high degree of circularity. This, together with use of abradable spacer coatings, gives enhanced compressor efficiency through small blade tip clearances. All compressor stators are punched and brazed into stator rings, eliminating stator wear and fretting. Low-pressure air bleed provided to ventilate accessory zone and supply engine and aircraft services. No variable-geometry blading or blow-off valves.
INTERMEDIATE CASING: One-piece casing carrying engine and aircraft accessories, and gearbox. Internally provides support for fan/LP compressor bearings and for HP compressor front bearing. Contains accessory drive gear from **front of HP compressor.**

HP COMPRESSOR: Seven-stage axial unit of constant tip diameter, driven by HP turbine. Rotor uses multi-disc construction with through bolts and curvic couplings. Front stub shaft carried on main ball thrust bearing supported by compressor intermediate casing. Rear HP disc bolted to HP turbine shaft. HP compressor casing and stator mounting as for LP compressor. High-pressure air bleed provided for aircraft cabin air conditioning and, when required, engine nose cowl anti-icing system. No variable-geometry blading or blow-off valves. Overall pressure ratio 18 : 1.
COMBUSTION SYSTEM: Short-length annular chamber with vaporising burners based on half-scale R-R Pegasus 101 chamber.
HP TURBINE: Single-stage axial unit with air-cooled rotor blading. Rear of HP rotor carried on intershaft roller bearing downstream of centreless turbine disc.
LP TURBINE: Three-stage axial unit of constant mean diameter, with centreless discs overhung on rear of LP turbine shaft. Roller bearing, supported by exhaust cone assembly, carries rear of LP turbine shaft adjacent to stage 3 disc.
BEARINGS: Squeeze-film design.
JET PIPE: Plug nozzle type.
FUEL SYSTEM: Dowty hydro-mechanical system. Fuel from first-stage centrifugal pump passes through fuel heater and filter, and thence to second-stage gear pump to main control system and acceleration control. Centrifugal governors on LP and HP shafts cause fuel spill-back in event of more than 2 per cent shaft overspeed.
ACCESSORIES: Engine accessories and engine-driven aircraft accessories are mounted in annulus between gas generator cowling and engine carcase. Accessories mounted directly on engine gearbox and driven from HP compressor. Accessories include fuel heater, engine oil heater, fuel flow meter, LP and HP governors, alternator, constant speed unit, oil tank, air starter, hydraulic and lubricating pumps.
LUBRICATION SYSTEM: Gear-type pressure pump feeds oil to all main bearings, LP and HP drives and accessory gearbox. Oil scavenged from front and rear compartments and from accessory gearbox passes through fuel-cooled oil cooler before returning to tank.
STARTING: Air starter on HP accessory gearbox.
DIMENSIONS:
Fan intake diameter   35·8 in (909 mm)
Overall length   102·4 in (2,600 mm)
WEIGHT:
Maximum, with accessories   1,483 lb (673 kg)
PERFORMANCE RATINGS:
T-O rating:
Sea level ISA   7,760 lb (3,520 kg) st
Sea level ISA+15°C   7,260 lb (3,293 kg) st
Cruise rating:
Mach 0·65 and 20,000 ft (6,100 m) ISA
                               2,745 lb (1,245 kg) st
SPECIFIC FUEL CONSUMPTIONS:
At T-O rating:
Sea level ISA   0·451
Sea level ISA+15°C   0·456
At cruise rating:
Mach 0·65 and 20,000 ft (6,100 m) ISA
                                          0·725

OLYMPUS 593 PROGRAMME
Committee of Directors:
CHAIRMAN: J. E. Lamy
VICE-CHAIRMAN: H. G. Conway
DIRECTORS:
Dr S. G. Hooker
M. Garnier
R. C. Orford
G. Langendorff
C. J. Luby
M. Viret
CO-OPTED MEMBERS:
P. Young
L. Jumelle

Cutaway drawing of Rolls-Royce/SNECMA M45H-01 civil turbofan rated at 7,760 lb (3,520 kg) st

JOINT SECRETARIES:
F. G. Barlow
J. Sollier

The Olympus 593 is being developed jointly by the Bristol Engine Division of Rolls-Royce and SNECMA as the power plant for the Concorde supersonic airliner which made its maiden flight on 2 March 1969. The work is shared on a 60%/40% basis, respectively. Rolls-Royce is developing the gas generator and SNECMA the convergent/divergent exhaust nozzle, thrust reverser, noise suppressor and afterburner system.

Pre-flight Olympus development engines, designated 593D, have been used for bench testing since mid-1964. First of the Olympus 593 flight-type engines made its initial test run in November 1965. At present thrusts up to 38,440 lb (17,436 kg) have been obtained with afterburning in operation. A Vulcan test bed is flying with a single Olympus 593 mounted beneath its fuselage in a representative half-Concorde nacelle. The programme calls for a total of 32,000 hours bench and flight testing, with seven Concorde aircraft, before entry into service.

The initial production Concorde power plant will be the Olympus 602. After two years of service experience these engines will be uprated to the Mk 612, by increasing the rpm and turbine entry temperature and, at the same time deliveries of the Olympus 621 will begin. Incorporated in the Mk 602 are the annular combustion chamber and the zero entry swirl LP compressor. These features not only eliminate smoke but give potential performance improvements and advantages in reliability and maintainability. Bench testing of both these components started in 1969 and test results have proved very satisfactory. The Mk 621 engine, incorporating minor mechanical changes, will have a higher thrust and improved sfc. Further development beyond the Mk 621 is projected.

OLYMPUS 593
TYPE: Axial-flow two-spool turbojet with partial reheat.
AIR INTAKE: One-piece titanium casing, with intake guide vanes mounted tangentially to the LP compressor support bearing. In the Concorde the engine is installed downstream of an intake duct incorporating auxiliary intake and exit door systems and a throat of variable profile and cross-section (see "Aircraft" section).
LP COMPRESSOR: Seven-stage axial-flow type, with all blading and discs manufactured from titanium. Single-piece casing machined from a stainless steel forging.
INTERMEDIATE CASING: Titanium casing, with vanes supporting LP and HP thrust bearings. Drives for engine-mounted aircraft and engine auxiliary drive gearboxes are taken out through the intermediate casing.
HP COMPRESSOR: Seven-stage axial-flow compressor, with first few stages of discs and blading made from titanium. Remaining stages are made from a heat-resistant material due to very high compressor delivery temperatures during supersonic flight. Stainless steel single-piece casing.
DELIVERY CASING: Electro-chemically machined in one piece. Combustion system burner manifold, the burners and the main support trunnions are located around the delivery casing.
COMBUSTION SYSTEM: (Mk 601) Cannular type, with eight flame cans in the annulus formed by an outer and inner casing. Each can is fitted with an air-assisted low-pressure burner.
FUEL SYSTEM. Lucas system, incorporating a mechanically driven first-stage pump and a second-stage pump driven by an air turbine, which is shut down at altitude cruise conditions as cruise fuel requirements can be met by the first-stage pump alone. The first-stage pump also supplies reheat fuel. A fuel-cooled oil cooler

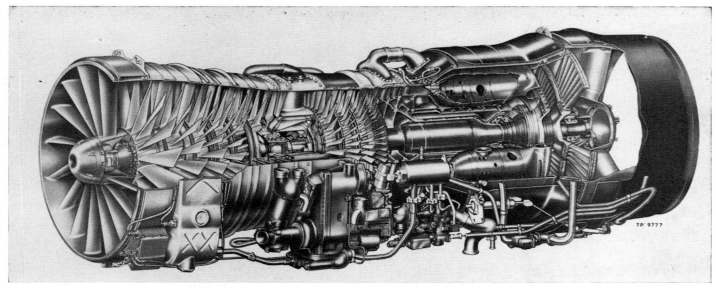

Cutaway illustration of the Rolls-Royce (Bristol Engine Division)/SNECMA Olympus Mk 601, rated at 38,050 lb (17,259 kg) st. This drawing does not include the aircraft inlet and duct nor the afterburner, reverser and nozzle

is incorporated in the system. An Ultra electronic system, with integrated-circuit amplifier, provides combined control of fuel flow and primary-nozzle area. Reheat fuel is controlled by an Elecma electrical control unit.

HP TURBINE: Single-stage turbine, with cooled stator and rotor blading.

LP TURBINE: Single-stage, with cooled blades. LP drive shaft co-axial with HP shaft.

JET-PIPE: Variable primary nozzle, pneumatically actuated, permits maximum LP spool speed and turbine entry temperature to be achieved simultaneously over a wide variation of compressor inlet temperatures.

AFTERBURNER: Single ring sprayer with simple on/off control.

THRUST REVERSER: Two pneumatically-actuated buckets, diverting exhaust gas upward and downward through angled cascades.

SILENCER: Pneumatically-operated retractable lobe system.

SECONDARY NOZZLE: Variable nozzle which controls final exhaust gas expansion, to give greatly increased overall propulsive efficiency at cruise conditions.

ACCESSORY DRIVES: Beneath the compressor intermediate casing are two gearboxes, both mechanically driven off the HP shaft (the LP shaft drives only the N_1 tachometer generator and the LP governor). The LH gearbox drives the main engine oil pressure/scavenge pumps and the first-stage fuel pump. The RH gearbox drives the aircraft hydraulic pumps and CSD/alternator.

LUBRICATION SYSTEM: Closed system, using oil to specification DERD.2497, MIL-L-9236B. Pressure pump, multiple scavenge pumps and return through Serck or Delaney Gallay fuel/oil heat exchanger.

STARTING SYSTEM: The Olympus Mk 601 is started by a SEMCA air-turbine driving the HP spool. A dual high-energy ignition system serves igniters in Nos. 4 and 6 flame cans.

MOUNTING: Main trunnions on horizontal centre-line of the delivery casing, one being fixed and the other allowing slight movement and differential expansion. Front stay from roof of the nacelle picks up on the top of the intake casing.

DIMENSIONS:
Max diameter at intake	47·85 in (1,215 mm)
Length, flange-to-flange	148 in (3,759 mm)
Intake flange to final nozzle	277 in (7,036 mm)

WEIGHTS:
Basic, dry	5,814 lb (2,637 kg)

PERFORMANCE RATINGS:
Nominal take-off thrust, SLS:
Mk 601	38,050 lb (17,259 kg)
Mk 611	38,400 lb (17,418 kg)
Mk 621	38,400 lb (17,418 kg)

ROLLS-ROYCE TURBOMÉCA
ROLLS-ROYCE TURBOMÉCA LIMITED
ADDRESS:
14-15 Conduit Street, London W1, England
DIRECTORS:
J. Szydlowski (Chairman)
Sir David Huddie (Deputy Chairman)
R. Barthelémy
General M. Candelier
E. M. Eltis
A. D. Jackson
C. Martin-Neuville
S. L. Bragg
J. E. B. Perkins
W. Syring

MANAGEMENT COMMITTEE:
CHAIRMAN AND FINANCIAL PROJECT MANAGER:
A. D. Jackson
DEPUTY CHAIRMAN:
General M. Candelier
ENGINEERING PROJECT MANAGER:
G. C. Barlow
DEPUTY ENGINEERING PROJECT MANAGER:
R. Deblache
PRODUCTION PROJECT MANAGER:
C. Martin-Neuville
DEPUTY PRODUCTION PROJECT MANAGER:
J. R. Wheatley
COMMERCIAL PROJECT MANAGER:
W. Clark

DEPUTY COMMERCIAL PROJECT MANAGER:
E. Lacrouts
SALES:
S. Wroath
This company was formed jointly by Rolls-Royce and Turboméca in June 1966 to manage the development and manufacturing programmes for the Adour turbofan engine. This engine is being developed jointly by the two parent companies to power the Anglo-French Jaguar and the Japanese Mitsubishi XT-2 trainer.

ROLLS-ROYCE TURBOMÉCA ADOUR
The Adour is an advanced turbofan engine with a dry take-off thrust range of over 4,400 lb (2,000 kg). In its initial form, to power the

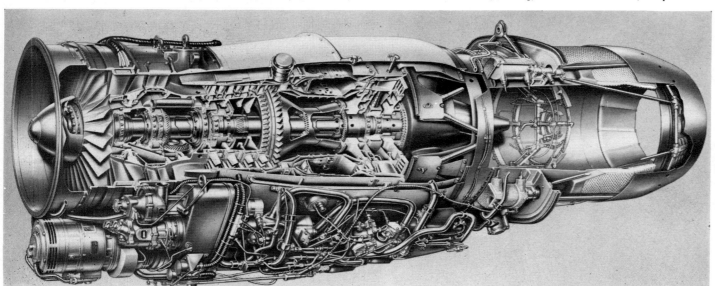

Cutaway illustration of the Rolls-Royce Turboméca Adour two-shaft turbofan for the supersonic SEPECAT Jaguar. This engine has a reheat rating in excess of 6,600 lb (3,000 kg) st

Anglo-French Jaguar dual-rôle supersonic strike/training aircraft, it has a reheat system, giving a 50% increase in static thrust for take-off. Versions without reheat are projected for use in basic military trainer and light strike aircraft. The basic Jaguar engine has the makers' designation RB.172-T-260.

Few details of the Adour are available, but its internal geometry can now be revealed by a cutaway drawing. It has a two-stage low-pressure compressor (fan), five stage-high-pressure compressor, straight-through-flow annular combustion chamber, and single-stage high-pressure and low-pressure turbines. Rolls-Royce describe it as a low-consumption engine with a basic weight of approximately 1,320 lb (600 kg) and by-pass ratio of 1 : 1. It has a self-contained starting system and a design time between overhauls of 1,000 hours.

Bench testing of the Adour began on 9 May 1967, at Derby. The bench development programme is shared equally between Rolls-Royce and Turboméca.

DIMENSIONS:
Intake diameter	22 in (55·9 cm)
Overall length, with reheat	117 in (297 cm)

PERFORMANCE RATINGS:
T-O rating, dry	4,400 lb (1,996 kg)
T-O rating, reheat	over 6,600 lb (3,000 kg)

RRTI
ROLLS-ROYCE TURBOMÉCA INTERNATIONAL SA

HEAD OFFICE:
1 Rue Beaujon, Paris 8e, France

DIRECTOR GENERAL:
Frank Stanton

This company (known formerly as Bristol Siddeley Turboméca International) is owned 50 per cent by Rolls-Royce and 50 per cent by Turboméca. It is responsible for sales and after-sales support of selected engines produced by the parent companies, and in particular the Astazou XIV turboprop engine. RRTI is providing field support of this engine using French and British service representatives. It has entered into an agreement with Rolls-Royce (Canada) under which the latter company provides further field support in North America. Rolls-Royce (Canada) also provide training on the engine at their Montreal engine school. An agreement has been entered into with Airwork Corporation of Millville, New Jersey, under which that company initially holds and distributes spare parts and holds spare engines, and progressively moves from carrying out maintenance and repair of the engines to doing full overhauls. Stocks of spare engines and parts are held by RRTI in France, England and elsewhere as needed.

TURBO-UNION
TURBO-UNION LTD

ADDRESS:
14-15 Conduit St., London W1, England

Formed in October 1969, this international company has been set up to manage the entire programme for the RB.199 engine for the Panavia 100/200 (MRCA) aircraft. Shares are held in the ratio Fiat SpA, 20 per cent; MTU München GmbH, 40 per cent; Rolls-Royce Ltd, 40 per cent. The overall cost of the RB.199 programme, however, will be divided in proportion to the orders placed by the three partner countries, which is at present taken to be: Federal Republic of Germany, 44 per cent; United Kingdom, 44 per cent; Italy, 12 per cent.

TURBO-UNION RB.199
Designed originally by Rolls-Royce Bristol Engine Division, who are design and development leaders, this engine competed with the Pratt & Whitney JTF 16 for the propulsion of the Panavia 100/200 (MRCA-75) aircraft and was announced as the winner after a meeting of the Multi-Role Combat Aircraft Policy Group on 4 September 1969.

A three-shaft augmented turbofan of extremely advanced design, it has a lightweight fan based on that of the Pegasus on a reduced scale, and an advanced reheat system designed for a wider operating envelope than that of any other known reheated turbofan.

Originally, an unofficial report suggested that the sea-level static ratings would be of the order of 9,500 lb (4,300 kg) dry and 16,000 lb (7,260 kg) with maximum augmentation; but the version finally selected is now described as the RB.199-34R, rated at 8,500 lb (3,855 kg) st dry and 14,500 lb (6,577 kg) st with full reheat, and having a net dry weight of some 1,800 lb (816 kg).

Flight-cleared engines will have to be delivered well in advance of the first-flight date for the aircraft of May 1973, and in-service date is 1975 (for the Luftwaffe; the RAF will not receive deliveries until 1976). If the programme proceeds according to plan, the Turbo-Union RB.199 will be the largest engine programme in Europe, running to something in excess of 3,000 engines at a cost of the order of £600 million.

ISRAEL

BET-SHEMESH
BET-SHEMESH ENGINES LTD

OFFICES AND WORKS:
Bet-Shemesh

The first section of a 130,000 sq ft (12,077 m²) new Israeli aero-engine factory, Bet-Shemesh Engines Ltd, near Bet-Shemesh between Tel Aviv and Jerusalem, was officially inaugurated on 15 January 1969. The company is owned 49 per cent by the Israeli government and 51 per cent by Turboméca SA and the works, when complete, will be a replica of Turboméca's factory at Tarnos in France. Some 130 persons are currently engaged at the works and the payroll is planned eventually to rise to around 1,100. Initially Bet-Shemesh is manufacturing turboprop components on behalf of Turboméca. By 1972 or 1973 complete engines—Marboré VI turbojets for Potez CM 170 Super Magister trainers—are intended to be produced.

An associate company of Bet-Shemesh Engines has also been established to produce many of the special small-scale cast items for Israeli-manufactured Turboméca engines and components. Known as Misco-Bet-Shemesh Ltd, the company is owned 25 per cent each by the Israeli government and Turboméca, and 50 per cent by the Howmet Corp of Muskegon, USA. It will utilise the technology and alloys of Howmet in the supply of castings to Bet-Shemesh Engines—as does Microfusion SA, Howmet's French licensee, for Turboméca.

ITALY

ALFA-ROMEO
SOCIETÀ PER AZIONI ALFA-ROMEO

HEAD OFFICE:
Via Gattamelata 45, Milan

AVIATION WORKS:
Pomigliano D'Arco, Naples

This company, famous as an automotive manufacturer, entered the aero-engine industry in Italy in 1925 by acquiring licences for the Jupiter engine from the Bristol Aeroplane Co, Ltd, and the Lynx engine from Armstrong Siddeley Motors, Ltd. In 1930 the company produced its first engine of original design and remained an important manufacturer of piston-engines for Italian aircraft until 1956.

For the following few years, Alfa-Romeo restricted its aviation work to overhaul of Curtiss-Wright R-1820 and R-3350 piston-engines and Wright J65, and Rolls-Royce Dart, Avon and Conway turbine engines. Subsequently, overhaul has also been undertaken of Rolls-Royce Gnome turboshafts, General Electric J85-GE-13A turbojets and T58 turboshafts, and Pratt & Whitney JT3D and JT8D turbofans and PT6 turboprops.

Alfa-Romeo resumed its manufacturing activities by participating in the European production programme for General Electric J79-GE-11A turbojets to power Lockheed F-104G Starfighters built in Europe. To this it has more recently added a role in the international manufacture of the Rolls-Royce Tyne turboprop for the Breguet Atlantic. It is now collaborating with Rolls-Royce in the manufacture and overhaul of Gnome H.1000, H.1200 and H.1400 turboshafts. Recently, a licence agreement has been signed for the manufacture of General Electric T58 turboshafts.

Alfa-Romeo is prime contractor for the manufacture, under General Electric licence, of the J85-GE-13A turbojet to power the Fiat G91Y aircraft. It is also manufacturing the "hot" section of the J79-GE-19 turbojet engines for the new F-104S Starfighters that are being produced in Italy for the Italian Air Force.

Alfa-Romeo is a member of the IRI-Finmeccanica group of companies.

An Alfa-Romeo licence-built General Electric J85-GE-13A turbojet (4,080 lb = 1,850 kg st with reheat)

FIAT

FIAT SOCIETÀ PER AZIONI

AERO-ENGINE WORKS:
Via Nizza 312, Turin

Full details of the present organisation of the Fiat Company are given in the "Aircraft" section of this work.

The Fiat Company was incorporated in 1899 and built its first aero-engines in 1908.

Fiat entered the gas-turbine field after the last war, by undertaking first the licence production of the de Havilland Ghost centrifugal-flow turbojet engine and then, in 1953, the manufacture of parts and assemblies of the Allison J35 turbojet engine for the USAF.

In 1960, Fiat began manufacture of the Orpheus 803 turbojet engine, and overhaul of the Orpheus 801 and 803, under licence from Bristol Siddeley Engines, Ltd. It also produced components and carried out the assembly of General Electric J79 turbojet engines for F-104G Starfighters built in Europe, in collaboration with F.N. of Belgium, BMW of Germany and Alfa-Romeo of Italy.

Its current programmes include production of General Electric J79-GE-19 turbojet engines to power Italian-built F-104S Starfighters, with the assistance of Alfa Romeo, and participation in licence production of the General Electric J85-GE-13A turbojet, for which Alfa Romeo is prime contractor.

Production of the J79-GE-19 turbojet engine has started at the Aero-Engine Works, and several units have already successfully completed the scheduled ground tests.

Fiat is also collaborating with Rolls-Royce (Bristol Engine Division) in the further development of the Viper turbojet for executive and training aircraft.

Fiat is responsible for overhaul and repair of components of the General Electric J47 turbojet engine (European Centre); and the manufacture of component parts of the J65 Sapphire turbojet engine, produced by the Curtiss-Wright Corporation, on behalf of the USAF in Europe.

Fiat further undertakes, for the Italian Air Force and the Italian civil airlines, the overhaul and repair of several types of piston-engines, including the Pratt & Whitney R-985, R-1830 and R-2800; Rolls-Royce Merlin 500; and Curtiss-Wright R-3350 Turbo Compound.

PIAGGIO

INDUSTRIE AERONAUTICHE E MECCANICHE RINALDO PIAGGIO, SpA

HEAD OFFICE:
Viale Brigata Bisagno 14, Genoa (426)
WORKS AND OFFICERS:
See "Aircraft" section.

Following a licence agreement in April 1960, the Aero Engine Division of Piaggio has been manu-facturing Rolls-Royce Bristol Viper 11 turbojets for the Macchi M.B.326 trainer. With successful operation of this licence, including issue of a sub-licence to Atlas Aircraft Corp for Vipers to power South African-built M.B.326 aircraft, a further licence was signed in March 1969. This new agreement provides for Piaggio to manu-facture the 3,360 lb (1,524 kg) st Viper Mks 526 and 540 to power Piaggio-Douglas PD-808 business jets and the M.B.326 trainer.

Piaggio also operates licences for manufacture of the Lycoming T53 turboshaft and GSO-480 and VO-435 piston-engines. Initial production of the turboshaft involved Lycoming supply of "hot end" parts of the T53-L-11 with Piaggio manufacturing the remainder of the engine. During 1968 the company was scheduled to start production of the T53-L-13, both this model and the -11 being for Agusta-Bell 204B and 205 helicopters, among other aircraft.

JAPAN

IHI

ISHIKAWAJIMA-HARIMA JUKOGYO KABUSHIKI KAISHA (Ishikawajima-Harima Heavy Industries Co, Ltd)

HEAD OFFICE:
No 2-1, 2 chome, Ote-Machi, Chiyoda-ku, Tokyo

AIRCRAFT ENGINE DIVISION:
3-5-1, Mukodai-cho, Tanashi-shi, Tokyo

PRESIDENT: Renzo Taguchi

EXECUTIVE VICE-PRESIDENT:
Dr Osamu Nagano

GENERAL MANAGER, AIRCRAFT ENGINE DIVISION:
Tadaaki Mori

On December 1, 1960, Ishikawajima Heavy Industries Co was merged with Harima Shipbuilding Co and now operates as Ishikawajima-Harima Heavy Industries Co.

Its work on turbojet engines dates from June 19, 1956, when the Japanese government approved a licence agreement with the General Electric Company of Cincinnati, Ohio, USA, under which Ishikawajima has been producing spares for the J47-GE-27 turbojet engines which power F-86F Sabre fighter aircraft of the Japanese Air Self-Defence Force.

In February 1960 IHI began the licence manufacture in Japan of J79-IHI-11A turbojet engines for Japanese-built Lockheed F-104J Starfighters. In 1967 the company built a J79 gas generator for use in an 8,000 kW generating set.

The manufacture of the R-R/Turboméca Adour reheat turbofan in Japan under licence agreement was in mid-1970 awaiting government approval. Ishikawajima-Harima Heavy Industries are to make Adours under a licence signed on 3 June 1970. Later in 1970 IHI was expected to start assembling European components; full Japanese production is expected to start before mid-1972.

Also under licensing agreements with General Electric, IHI is producing the T58 shaft-turbine engine as a power plant for helicopters and for other applications, including the propulsion of air-cushion vehicles and hydrofoil boats, and the T64 turboprop engine to power the JMSDF's new PS-1 anti-submarine flying-boat and the Kawasaki P-2J maritime patrol aircraft. In addition the T64 has performed well in a Japanese Navy torpedo boat.

IHI undertakes overhaul and repair of Pratt & Whitney JT8D and General Electric CJ805-23B civil engines, J79, T58, T64 military engines, and Turboméca Artouste, Astazou and Bastan turboshafts and turboprops.

In accordance with the third Five-year Defence Programme of the JASDF the firm was nominated to produce the GE J79-IHI-17 turbojet for the McDonnell Douglas F-4EJ fighter. The first endurance test using a US-built engine, is scheduled for the end of 1970.

Prior to the start of this licence manufacture, in April, 1959, IHI had been responsible for the J3 turbojet engine which had been under development by the Nippon Jet-Engine Company since 1956. This is the only turbojet to have been developed in post-war Japan, and the J3-IHI-7 version is at present installed in Fuji T-1B intermediate jet trainer and Kawasaki P-2J aircraft.

Ishikawajima-Harima J3-IHI-7C turbojet engine (3,080 lb=1,400 kg st)

To follow the J3 series, IHI is developing three engines known as the XJ11, JR-100 and JR-200, which are intended to power V/STOL aircraft.

The Japanese Ministry of International Trade and Industries (MITI) plans to fund a high by-pass ratio turbofan development programme. In support of this venture, IHI has started component studies for the engine and is testing some parts. The programme anticipates development of the turbofan in two stages: the first up to 10,000 lb (4,536 kg) st with an sfc of 0·34, by-pass ratio 7·5 : 1, pressure ratio 22 : 1, turbine entry temperature 1,930°F (1,423°K) and 5·7 : 1 thrust/weight ratio; and the second up to 20,000 lb (9,072 kg) st with an sfc of 0·3, by-pass ratio 8 : 1, pressure ratio 25 : 1, turbine entry temperature 2,370°F (1,573°K) and 6 : 1 thrust/weight ratio.

IHI J3-IHI-7

The J3-IHI-7 is the latest derivative of the J3-1, of which a description appeared in the 1959-60 *Jane's*, under the entry for "Nippon Jet-Engine Company". It is installed on the Kawasaki P-2J aircraft currently under flight test by the JMSDF, and is in production.

Studies are also underway for converting the J3-IHI-7 to an augmented turbofan. Major modifications include the introduction of a shorter combustion chamber, provision for air bleed for aircraft BLC purposes, revised turbine blading, and the addition of an aft-fan and reheat unit.

TYPE: Axial-flow turbojet.

AIR INTAKE: Annular nose air intake. Anti-icing system for front support struts.

COMPRESSOR: Eight-stage axial-flow type, built of Ni-Cr-Mo steel. Rotor consists of a series of discs and spacers bolted on to shaft. Rotor and stator blades of AISI 403 steel. Stator blades brazed on to fabricated base which is fixed in casing with circumferential T-groove. Rotor blades dovetailed to discs. Light alloy casing in upper and lower sections, flange-jointed together. Pressure ratio 4·5 : 1. Air mass flow 56 lb (25·4 kg)/sec.

COMBUSTION CHAMBER: Annular type. AISI 321 steel outer casing. L 605 steel flame tube. Thirty fuel supply pipes located in combustion chamber outer casing and 30 vaporiser tubes located at front of flame tube. Ignition by low-voltage high-energy spark plug in each side of combustion chamber.

FUEL SYSTEM: IHI fuel regulator.

FUEL GRADE: JP-4.

NOZZLE GUIDE VANES: Single row of air-cooled fabricated vanes.

TURBINE: Single-stage axial-flow type. Disc bolted to shaft. Precision-forged blades.

BEARINGS: Rotating assembly carried in front (double ball) and rear (roller) compressor rotor bearings and rear (roller) turbine shaft bearing.

JET-PIPE: Fixed-area type.

ACCESSORY DRIVES: On gearbox under compressor front casing.

LUBRICATION SYSTEM: Forced-feed system for main bearings and gear case. Dry sump. Vane-type positive displacement supply and scavenge pump.

OIL SPECIFICATION: MIL-L-7808.

MOUNTING: Three-point suspension, with one pick-up by a pin on starboard side of compressor front casing and a trunnion on each side of the compressor rear casing.

STARTING: Electrical starter in intake bullet fairing.

DIMENSIONS:
Length, less tailpipe 65·4 in (1,661 mm)
Length overall with rear cone 78·5 in (1,994 mm)
Diameter overall 24·7 in (627 mm)
Frontal area 3·01 sq ft (0·28 m²)

WEIGHT (DRY):
Bare 815 lb (370 kg)
With accessories 948 lb (430 kg)

PERFORMANCE RATING:
T-O 3,080 lb (1,400 kg) st

SPECIFIC FUEL CONSUMPTION:
At T-O rating 1·05

OIL CONSUMPTION:
At normal rating (max)
1·06 Imp pints (0·60 litre)/hr

IHI J3-IHI-8
This engine is an uprated version of the J3-IHI-7 and has completed three 150-hr endurance tests. All details for the J3-IHI-7 apply equally to the J3-IHI-8, with the following exception.

PERFORMANCE RATING:
T-O 3,415 lb (1,550 kg) st at 13,000 rpm

IHI XJ11
The XJ11 is an engine which IHI is developing to follow the J3 series. Design objectives include an especially lightweight structural design, highly-loaded main engine components, simplified fuel and lubrication systems, and thrust/weight ratio of 20 : 1.

IHI JR100
As part of a V/STOL research and development programme, IHI has designed and built a simple 10 : 1 thrust/weight ratio lift jet, designated JR100, under the supervision of the Japanese National Aerospace Laboratory. The prototype engine was completed during 1964, and in the course of 150 hours of testing, including an endurance test in March 1969, some 1,300 starts have been completed. JR100 engines are currently being employed in testing a height control system for a 'soft' landing using the JR100H, and a flying test bed for stability studies using the JR100F.

TYPE: Single-shaft axial-flow lift jet.

AIR INTAKE: Forward-facing annular type.

COMPRESSOR: Six-stage axial unit of 3·9 : 1 pressure ratio and 60·6 lb (27·5 kg)/sec air mass flow.

COMBUSTION CHAMBER: Annular type.

TURBINE: Single-stage axial unit with 1,562°F (1,123°K) entry temperature.

JET PIPE: Fixed area.

FUEL SYSTEM: Hydromechanical system with single master control.

LUBRICATION SYSTEM: Non-return, intermittent oil supply system.

DIMENSIONS:
Diameter 23·6 in (600 mm)
Length overall 38·4 in (975 mm)

WEIGHT, DRY: 347·5 lb (156 kg)

PERFORMANCE RATINGS:
Max T-O:
JR100F 3,180 lb (1,430 kg) st
JR100H 3,360 lb (1,520 kg) st

SPECIFIC FUEL CONSUMPTIONS:
At max T-O rating:
JR100F 1·15
JR100H 1·13

The IHI JR100 lift jet (3,360 lb = 1,520 kg st)

IHI JR200
Following the JR100, IHI designed and built the higher thrust JR200 of improved thrust/weight ratio, under the supervision of the Japanese National Aerospace Laboratory. The design objectives of the JR200 are the same as the JR100 although use is made of a higher air mass flow, smaller combustion chamber and more extensive lightweight materials. The prototype JR200 was completed in the summer of 1966.

An improved version, the JR220 with higher pressure ratio and higher turbine entry temperature, is now under initial development. The prototype JR220 is planned to be built during 1970.

The following details relate to the JR200.

TYPE: Single-shaft axial lift jet.

AIR INTAKE: Forward-facing annular type.

COMPRESSOR: Five-stage axial unit of 4 : 1 pressure ratio and 82 lb (37·2 kg)/sec air mass flow at 12,450 rpm. Air bleed 6·6 lb (3 kg)/sec.

COMBUSTION CHAMBER: Annular type.

TURBINE: Single-stage axial unit with 1,562°F (1,123°K) entry temperature.

JET PIPE: Fixed area.

WEIGHT, DRY: 280 lb (127 kg)

PERFORMANCE RATINGS:
Max, without air bleed 4,585 lb (2,080 kg) st
Max, with air bleed 4,012 lb (1,820 kg) st

The IHI XJ11 high thrust/weight ratio turbojet

The IHI JR200 lift jet (4,585 lb = 2,080 kg st)

SPECIFIC FUEL CONSUMPTIONS:
At max rating, without air bleed 1·13
At max rating, with air bleed 1·17

KAWASAKI
KAWASAKI JUKOGYO KABUSHIKI KAISHA
(Kawasaki Heavy Industries Ltd)

HEAD OFFICE:
38, Akashi-machi, Ikuta-ku, Kobe

WORKS:
Gifu and Akashi

OFFICERS: See "Aircraft" section

Kawasaki's factory at Kobe has been engaged on the repair and overhaul of gas-turbine engines for the US armed forces and the Japan Defence Agency since 1953.

In 1967, with the approval of the Japanese Ministry of International Trade and Industry, it acquired licence rights in the Avco Lycoming T53 shaft-turbine engine, one application for which is in the UH-1B helicopter manufactured in Japan by Fuji.

As a start, engines were shipped complete from the Avco Lycoming works. Stage two involved shipment of unassembled kits of parts for assembly by Kawasaki. Now, Avco Lycoming are shipping partial kits for mating with components produced in Japan by Kawasaki.

The engine being assembled in Japan is known as the Kawasaki KT5311A. It differs only in minor details from the T53-L-11 described in the 1966-67 Jane's.

MITSUBISHI
MITSUBISHI JUKOGYO KABUSHIKI KAISHA
(Mitsubishi Heavy Industries Ltd)

HEAD OFFICE:
Mitsubishi Building, No. 10, 2-chome, Marunouchi, Chiyoda-ku, Tokyo

ENGINE WORKS:
Daiko Plant, Nagoya City

OFFICERS:
See "Aircraft" section

Since 1952 Mitsubishi has been responsible for the repair and overhaul of engines of the Japan Defence Agency and the US Air Force. It is also undertaking licensed manufacture of the Allison T63 turboshaft engine to power Hughes 369 HM helicopters of the Japan Ground Self-Defence Force. Mitsubishi started the T63 programme by assembling US components and is gradually increasing the proportion of its own manufacture.

Ultimately about three-quarters of the whole engine will be made in Japan. A total of 14 engines were to be delivered in the Fiscal year 1968, and the total number to be manufactured in Japan is expected to be 400-500.

Mitsubishi is engaged in the series production of a gas-turbine compressor set of its own design. Designated GCM-1, this is built into the power pack of the starter trolley which supports the Lockheed F-104G aircraft of the Japan Air Self-Defence Force.

POLAND

IL

INSTYTUT LOTNICTWA (Aviation Institute)

HEADQUARTERS:
Warsaw 21 Okecie, Al. Krakowska 110/114

SCIENTIFIC DIRECTOR:
Dr Czeslaw Skoczylas

HEAD OF TECHNICAL INFORMATION DIVISION:
Jerzy Grzegorzewski

The Aviation Institute is an establishment engaged in aeronautical research, aerodynamic tests, strength tests, test flights of aeroplanes, helicopters and gliders, aviation equipment, materials, technical information and standardisation. The Institute has a special manufacturing plant responsible for constructing prototypes to its own design.

IL SO-1

The Aviation Institute designed the SO-1 turbojet to power the Polish TS-11 Iskra (Spark) jet basic trainer. This engine is designed to permit the full range of aerobatics, including inverted flight. Guaranteed overhaul life is 200 hours. Further versions are under development.

TYPE: Single-shaft axial-flow turbojet.

AIR INTAKE: Annular intake casing manufactured as a cast shell. Fixed inlet guide vanes.

COMPRESSOR CASING: Manufactured as a cast shell in two parts, split along horizontal centre-line.

COMPRESSOR: Seven-stage axial-flow compressor. Drum-type rotor built up of disc assemblies, with constant diameter over tips of rotor blades. Carried in ball bearing at front and roller bearing at rear.

COMBUSTION CHAMBER: Annular type with 24 integral vaporisers. Outer casing made of welded steel.

IL SO-1 turbojet (2,205 lb=1,000 kg st), power plant of the TS-11 Iskra (Spark) trainer (*BIIL*)

FUEL SYSTEM: Two independent systems supplied by one pump. Starting system consists of six injectors, with direct injection. Main system consists of twelve twin injectors with outlets towards the vaporisers.

FUEL SPECIFICATION: Paraffin type P-2 or TS-1.

TURBINE: Single-stage axial-flow type. Blades attached to disc by fir-tree roots. Supported in roller bearing at rear.

JET PIPE: Outer tapered casing and central cone connected by streamlined struts. Nozzle area adjusted by exchangeable inserts.

LUBRICATION SYSTEM: Open type for rear compressor and turbine bearings, supplied by separate pumps. Closed type for all other lubrication points, fed by separate pumps.

OIL SPECIFICATION: Type AP-26 (synthetic).

ACCESSARY DRIVES: Gearbox mounted at bottom of air intake casing and driven by bevel gear shaft from front of compressor.

STARTING: 27V starter-generator and bevel gear shaft, driven by aircraft battery or ground power unit, mounted on air intake casing.

DIMENSIONS:
Length overall	84·7 in (2,151 mm)
Width	27·8 in (707 mm)
Height	30·1 in (764 mm)

WEIGHT:
Dry   668 lb (303 kg)

PERFORMANCE RATING:
T-O rating
2,205 lb (1,000 kg) st at 15,600 rpm

SPECIFIC FUEL CONSUMPTION:
At T-O rating   1·045

JANOWSKI

JAROSLAW JANOWSKI

ADDRESS:
Lodz

JANOWSKI SATURN 500

The Saturn 500 has been designed by Mr Janowski and built by Mr S. Polawski for the Janowski J-1 Don Kichote amateur-built aircraft (see "Aircraft" section). The prototype Saturn 500 was built in 1969. This two-cylinder two-stroke engine may be used with tractor or pusher propeller, and is intended for ultra-light aircraft built by amateurs.

TYPE: Two-cylinder two-stroke horizontally-opposed air-cooled.

CYLINDERS: Bore 2·76 in (70 mm). Stroke 2·56 in (65 mm). Swept volume 30·5 cu in (500 cc). Compression ratio 8·5 : 1. Steel barrels with aluminium alloy cylinder heads. Cylinder and head assembly attached to crankcase by four studs.

PISTONS: Of aluminium alloy. Two compression rings and one oil scraper ring.

CONNECTING RODS: Steel forgings.

CRANKSHAFT: Steel counterbalanced shaft, supported in two lead-bronze plain bearings and one ball-thrust bearing at the front.

CRANKCASE: Aluminium alloy case, split in the vertical plane, with front and aft cover.

INDUCTION: Two BVF 28N1 carburettors.

FUEL: Petrol/oil mixture using aviation 90 octane.

IGNITION: Two magnetos. One sparking plug per cylinder M14-250 0·55 in (14 mm).

MOUNTING: Four rubber dampers at rear of crankcase.

25 hp Saturn 500 two-cylinder two-stroke engine designed by Mr Jaroslaw Janowski

PROPELLER DRIVE: Direct tractor or pusher.

DIMENSIONS:
Length overall, with propeller boss
16·93 in (430 mm)
Width, without sparking plugs
20·27 in (515 mm)

WEIGHT, DRY: 59·5 lb (27 kg)

PERFORMANCE RATING:
Max T-O rating   25 hp at 4,000 rpm

SPECIFIC FUEL CONSUMPTIONS:
Max T-O rating   0·70 lb (0·315 kg)/hp/hr
Normal cruising power   0·66 lb (0·300 kg)/hp/hr

PZL

POLSKIE ZAKLADY LOTNICZE

HEADQUARTERS:
Ul. Miodowa 5, Warsaw

SALES REPRESENTATIVE:
Motoimport, Przemyslowa 26, Warsaw

The entire Polish aircraft industry is subordinate to the Zjednoczenie Przemyslu Lotniczego (literally, Union of the Aircraft Industry), the national governing body. Construction on a serial basis is the responsibility of the OKL (Osrodek Konstrukcji Lotniczych) at Warsaw-Okecie.

At the end of World War 2 the Polish industry manufactured Soviet engines under licence: the 125 hp M-11D for the Po-2 and CSS-13, the 160 hp M-11FR for the Junak-2 and -3 and the 575 hp AI-26W (under the designation LIT-3) for the SM-1 and -2 helicopters produced under Soviet licence. An indigenous team headed by Dipl Ing Wiktor Narkiewicz designed the 330 hp WN-3 radial for the TS-8 Bies aircraft. All these have been described in previous editions of *Jane's*.

Today the main engine design team, led by Drozdz, Mirski, Szot and Kotowicz, is administered by the IL, described below. Meanwhile the production of Soviet engines continues, current types being the 1,000 hp ASh-62IR (Polish

Polish-built 260 hp Ivchenko AI-14R piston-engine

Polish-built 1,000 hp Shvetsov ASh-62IR piston-engine

designation, ASz-62IR) for the An-2, the 260 hp AI-14R for the PZL-101 Gawron and PZL-104

Wilga and the 395 shp GTD-350 turboshaft for the Mi-2 helicopter.

SPAIN

ENMASA

EMPRESA NACIONAL DE MOTORES DE AVIACIÓN S.A.

HEAD OFFICE:
Calle Antonio Maura 4, Madrid 14

PRODUCTION PLANT:
Alcalá de Henares, Madrid

PRESIDENT:
Ilmo Sr D. Modesto Aguilera Morente

MANAGING DIRECTOR:
Manuel Ruiz-Constantino Fernández

The Empresa Nacional de Motores de Aviación, which took over the Elizalde organization on 1 January 1952, has produced several different piston-engines of its own design. Details of these can be found in previous editions of *Jane's*.

The first turbojet engine produced by ENMASA was the Marboré II which was built under licence from the French Turboméca company as the Marboré M21.

ENMASA's current aeronautical activities include overhaul and repair of General Electric J47 and J85 and Turboméca M21 turbojet engines in the plant at Alcalá de Henares. The same factory also overhauls and repairs aircraft and engine accessories.

SWEDEN

FLYGMOTOR

SVENSKA FLYGMOTOR AB

HEAD OFFICE AND WORKS: Trollhättan

This company was founded in 1930, as Nohab Flygmotorfabriker AB, and began by building under licence the Bristol Pegasus I aero-engine, under the designation My VI. The name of the company was changed to Svenska Flygmotor AB in 1941 when the company became a member of the Volvo Group, the well-known car manufacturing concern.

Svenska Flygmotor AB holds a licence to build Rolls-Royce Avon engines and is also engaged in research and development work on turbojet engines, ramjet engines and rocket engines.

Its major current programme involves development and production of a licence-built version of the Pratt & Whitney JT8D turbofan engine (Swedish designation RM8) to power the Saab-37 Viggen combat aircraft. It is also engaged in the development of experimental hybrid and liquid-fuel rocket engines, and brief details of some of these are given below.

The company has had a technical collaboration agreement on ramjet development with Bristol Engine Division of Rolls-Royce Ltd since 1957. Details of its RRX-1 ramjet test vehicle were given in the "Missiles" section of the 1964-65 *Jane's*.

FLYGMOTOR RM6C AVON

RM6C is the designation of the licence-built version of the Rolls-Royce Avon 300-series turbojet which Flygmotor is producing to power the Saab-35D, E and F Draken fighters. It is rated at approximately 16,800 lb (7,620 kg) st with its Swedish-developed afterburner in use.

The afterburner has V-type flame-holders with the fuel injection manifold situated at the front of the V. Main fuel injection is made upstream and a smaller quantity is injected into the flame holder. Ignition is by a "hot shot" device. The centrifugal-type fuel pump is driven by air from the engine compressor by means of a single-stage axial-flow turbine, the air supply being controlled by the main engine fuel pressure. Afterburner fuel flow is regulated at the pump outlet by a regulator which ensures a constant pressure ratio over the engine turbine. The jet-pipe has hydraulically-operated two-position clamshell shutters, with an ejector nozzle.

Production of the RM6C will continue for at least two further years, chiefly to meet the needs of the Saab-35XD programme for the Danish Air Force. Manufacture of spares, and general service support, continues for a large number of earlier Avon engines fitted to earlier marks of Draken and to the Lansen.

FLYGMOTOR RM8

The RM8 is a Swedish military version of the Pratt & Whitney JT8D-22 civil subsonic turbofan which Flygmotor has developed to power the Saab-37 Viggen supersonic multi-purpose combat aircraft.

The programme is being undertaken with the assistance of Pratt & Whitney, who supplied Flygmotor initially with three special models of the JT8D-1 able to be fitted with an after-burner for testing in the winter of 1963-64. The first JT8D-22 was put on test on 6 August 1964, and was being run with afterburning by the spring of 1965. Approximately 6,000 hr bench and flight testing had been completed by May 1969, well over half that scheduled for the overall development for the Saab-37.

Development and manufacture of 195 RM8s for the Viggen is covered by a 689 million kroner contract from the Swedish government, the largest single order ever received by Flygmotor. Production, which will absorb 595 million kroner, started in mid-1968 and will continue through to the mid-1970s.

The RM8 is fitted with an afterburner of Flygmotor design, with fully-variable nozzle and thrust-reverser, which gives a 70% increase in thrust, to nearly 26,400 lb (12,000 kg).

Flygmotor have so far devoted almost 4,000,000 man-hours to the development of the RM8, even though compressor and turbine blade profiles are the same as on the JT8D. Apart from this similarity, the RM8 is made up of new parts in different materials and having changed dimensions.

Development has now reached the phase where emphasis is being put on reliability and endurance.

Final preparation of Svenska Flygmotor RM8 reheat turbofans for the Viggen aircraft (26,400 lb = 12,000 kg st with Flygmotor afterburner in operation)

TYPE: Axial-flow two-spool turbofan with reheat.

AIR INTAKE: Annular, with 19 fixed inlet guide vanes.

FAN: Two-stage front fan. Titanium blades.

LP COMPRESSOR: Four-stage axial-flow, integral with fan stages, on inner of two concentric shafts. Blades of titanium. Steel casing.

HP COMPRESSOR: Seven-stage axial-flow on outer hollow shaft. Blades made of special high-temperature alloys of type used for turbine blading. Overall pressure ratio 16 : 1. By-pass ratio approximately 1 : 1. Total air mass flow 320 lb (145 kg)/sec.

COMBUSTION CHAMBER: Cannular type with nine cylindrical flame tubes, each downstream of a single Duplex burner and discharging into a single annular nozzle. Two high-energy spark plugs, each with its own igniter box.

HP TURBINE: Single-stage axial-flow, with cast blades.

LP TURBINE: Three-stage axial-flow, with cast blades. Exit guide vanes after turbine.

AFTERBURNER: Double-skinned to provide duct for cooling air. Outer skin of titanium. Inner skin of special alloys. Two hot-streak igniters. Hydraulically-actuated fully-variable nozzle, using fuel as the operating fluid.

BEARINGS: Main shafts run in total of six bearings.

MOUNTING: Three-point. Main mountings on each side of compressor casing; one under turbine casing.

ACCESSORY DRIVE: Via gearbox, under engine, driven from HP turbine shaft.

SPECIFIC FUEL CONSUMPTION: At T-O rating without afterburning   approx 0·6

FLYGMOTOR HR-4

Flygmotor has been developing small hybrid rocket engines since 1962, under Royal Swedish Air Force Board contracts. Firing tests have been under way since 1963, the latest model on which information has been released being the HR-4. This is a dual-thrust unit of a type that would be suitable to power both sounding rockets and missiles; but no immediate application is envisaged.

Propellants used in the HR-4 are fuming nitric acid oxidiser and a solid-propellant developed by Flygmotor and known as Tagaform. This is basically a polymerised amino resin, with minute quantities of additives that make it hypergolic when used with fuming nitric acid. The casing is of aluminium alloy.

Ignition is initiated by a solid-propellant cartridge at the front of the engine. Expanding gases from this cartridge thrust rearward a piston which forces the oxidiser through an injector into the hollow core of the solid-propellant grain. A diaphragm between the propellants is burst by hydrostatic pressure at the start of this process. The uncooled nozzle has a pyrolytic graphite throat able to withstand the combustion temperature of 5,120°F.

The Swedish-developed afterburner of the RM8

Initial thrust of 380 lb (172 kg) is maintained for 6 seconds, after which a valve-pin attached to the piston reaches a seating in the bulkhead between the two propellants. This results in a decrease of oxidiser flow, by sealing off the main orifice, allowing the oxidiser to enter the combustion chamber only through one or more secondary orifices, and by friction between the stationary valve-pin and the piston. Average thrust for the remaining 10 seconds of firing time is about 75 lb (34 kg).

DIMENSIONS:
Length overall   41 in (105 cm)
Diameter   4 in (10 cm)

WEIGHT:
Fully fuelled   26 lb (12 kg)

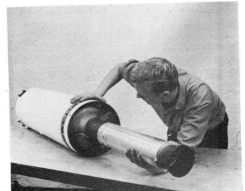

Flygmotor VR-35 pre-packaged liquid-propellant rocket motor

FLYGMOTOR SR-1

A direct scale-up of the HR-4 has produced a larger hybrid propulsion system around which has been designed the SR-1 sounding rocket described in the "Research Rockets and Space Vehicles" section of this annual. Again, fuming nitric acid is pumped down (this time by nitrogen pressure) through a Flygmotor amino-plastic fuel grain. Combustion temperature is 2,830°C, and thrust 3,240 lb (1,470 kg); with total propellant weight of 308 lb (140 kg) the burning time is 20 seconds.

The whole propulsion system is sealed as one package and can be transported without the precautions taken with solid motors (which are classed as explosive). Hybrid motors are considered by Flygmotor to be insensitive to shock, vibration and severe thermal environments.

FLYGMOTOR VR-35

Development of liquid-propellant rocket engines began at Flygmotor in 1951 and the work has now led to a contract from the Royal Swedish Air Board for an engine for the Rb-305 missile to be carried by the AJ 37 Viggen. The VR-35 is a prepackaged motor containing an unspecified fuel and oxidiser. When the liquids come into contact in the combustion chamber they ignite hypergolically. The long blast tube linking the sealed tankage to the propulsive nozzle is called for by the layout of the missile.

THE UNITED KINGDOM

ALVIS
ALVIS LTD
HEAD OFFICE AND WORKS:
Holyhead Road, Coventry CU5 8JH
DIRECTORS:
J. J. Parkes, CBE, CEng, FRAeS (Chairman and Managing)
G. R. Howell, ACWA (Financial)
R. F. Skidmore (Works Director)
W. F. F. Martin-Hurst, CEng, FIMechE
A. B. Smith, MPOA
F. T. Wayne, MA, FCA
SALES AND SERVICE MANAGER, AERO DIVISION:
T. F. Lenton
CHIEF ENGINEER, AERO DIVISION: A. F. Varney

In December 1962, Alvis were appointed a fully-authorised Lycoming overhaul facility by the Avco Lycoming division of Avco Corporation, USA, and are carrying out overhaul and servicing of Lycoming engines in military and civilian service in the United Kingdom. The company's extensive test bed facilities at Baginton Airport are particularly suitable for these engines, in both horizontally and vertically mounted versions.

Alvis also continues to offer an overhaul, reconditioning, spares and "pool" exchange service to operators of the large number of aircraft and helicopters powered by its Leonides and Leonides Major piston-engines, details of which can be found in the 1966-67 *Jane's*.

ROVER GAS TURBINES
HEAD OFFICE AND WORKS:
Holyhead Road, Coventry CU5 8JH
DIRECTORS:
A. B. Smith, MPOA
W. F. F. Martin-Hurst, CEng, FIMechE
J. J. Parkes, CBE, CEng, FRAeS
G. R. Howell, ACWA
R. N. Penny
SALES AND SERVICE MANAGER:
T. F. Lenton
CHIEF ENGINEER: A. F. Varney

The Rover Company was responsible for initial production of the original Whittle-type turbojet engines in 1941-42. Two of its developed engines were taken over by Rolls-Royce and, after further refinement, were produced in quantity as the Welland and Derwent. More recently, Rover developed a series of small gas-turbine engines for industrial applications and as auxiliary power units on aircraft such as the Hawker Siddeley Vulcan and Argosy C.1. They are also used to drive air-cushion vehicles, certain land vehicles and generating sets in oil rigs.

Early in 1968, the aviation activities of Rover Gas Turbines Ltd were transferred to Alvis Ltd at Coventry and all production and development is now centred at the Holyhead Road Works. Rover and Alvis are member companies of British Leyland Motor Corporation.

ROVER TJ.125

This small 114 lb (51·7 kg) st turbojet engine utilises the gas-generator section of the Rover 2S/150A engine and has been developed as a power plant for surveillance drones and similar pilotless aircraft. The single-shaft gas-generator consists of a single-stage centrifugal compressor feeding an annular reverse-flow combustion chamber. Fuel is delivered by a ring of atomizing fuel

Rover TJ.125 turbojet for surveillance drones (114 lb = 51·7 kg st)

injectors, and the gas flow from the combustion chamber is directed to a radial inward-flow turbine. Leaving the eye of the turbine rotor, the gas flow passes to the exhaust nozzle. Auxiliary equipment, comprising a fuel pump and associated governor, is driven from the compressor shaft.

Initial deliveries of TJ.125 engines have been made to MBLE to power the Belgian company's Epervier surveillance drone. Discussions are in progress with other drone manufacturers.

DIMENSIONS:
Length overall — 22 in (558·8 mm)
Max width — 10·625 in (269·9 mm)
Max depth — 12·063 in (306·4 mm)
WEIGHT: — 39 lb (17·7 kg)
PERFORMANCE RATING:
Max thrust at ISA — 114 lb (51·7 kg)
SPECIFIC FUEL CONSUMPTION:
At max rating — 1·31

ROVER 1S/60

The 1S/60 single-shaft turboshaft is installed as an APU in military aircraft. A wide range of accessory equipment and standard reduction gear ratios are available, enabling the engine to be adapted for individual applications. The rotating assembly comprises a single-stage axial-flow turbine. The compressor is housed in a cast aluminium alloy casing, from which air is ducted to a single reverse-flow combustion chamber. Further ducting, in the form of a volute, conveys the high-velocity gas flow from the combustion chamber to the turbine. The compressor housing

The 60 shp Rover 1S/60 APU

carries the engine accessories and power take-off equipment. Two methods of engine starting are available: electric start combining automatic control, and hand start consisting of a completely self-contained system.

DIMENSION:
Length overall — 22·75 in (560·7 mm)

The 103 shp Rover 2S/150A (748) APU

The Rover 2S/150A (801) turbo-compressor

WEIGHT:
With reduction gear, excluding starter
140 lb (63·5 kg)
PERFORMANCE RATING:
Max cont at ISA 60 shp
SPECIFIC FUEL CONSUMPTION:
At max cont rating, ISA 1·5 lb (0·68 kg)/shp/hr

ROVER 1S/90

The 1S/90 turboshaft is similar in configuration to the 1S/60 engine. A turboprop version has been extensively flown in a Chipmunk conversion by Hants & Sussex Aviation.

WEIGHT:
With reduction gear, excluding starter
140 lb (63·5 kg)
PERFORMANCE RATING:
Max cont at ISA 116 shp
SPECIFIC FUEL CONSUMPTION:
At max cont rating, ISA 1·22 lb (0·55 kg)/shp/hr

ROVER 2S/150A (748)

This free-turbine turboshaft is based on the Rover 2S/150A industrial turbine. It has been designed to achieve the highest possible power/weight ratio consistent with reliability and simplicity, and to operate successfully under a wide diversity of conditions. The engine is used as an APU in Hawker Siddeley 748 aircraft.

The 2S/150A consists of a gas-generator and a power turbine section, each incorporating separate rotating parts. The compressor is a single-stage centrifugal unit, feeding an annular reverse-flow combustion chamber. The gas flow from the combustion chamber is directed by a radial inward-flow compressor turbine and thence, via a short duct, to a single-stage axial-flow power turbine. The power turbine drives the output shaft through a 6·818 : 1 ratio reduction gear. Engine accessories include fuel and oil pumps and an electric starter, together with a fully automatic engine control system. The 2S/150A is ARB approved.

DIMENSION:
Length overall 37 in (939·8 mm)

WEIGHT (approx): 160 lb (72·5 kg)
PERFORMANCE RATING:
Max cont 103 shp
SPECIFIC FUEL CONSUMPTION:
At max cont rating 1·2 lb (0·54 kg)/shp/hr

ROVER 2S/150A (801)

This version of the 2S/150A embodies similar components to those used in the Hawker Siddeley 748 application, except that the free power turbine is coupled directly to an auxiliary single-sided centrifugal compressor. The compressed air from this unit is used to start the Rolls-Royce Spey main propulsion engines in the Hawker Siddeley Nimrod (HS.801) maritime aircraft.

DIMENSION:
Length overall 36 in (914·4 mm)
WEIGHT: 154 lb (70 kg)
PERFORMANCE RATING:
88·2 lb air/min at 43·6 lb/sq in (40 kg air/min at 3·06 kg/cm²)
FUEL CONSUMPTION: 137 lb (62 kg)/hr

BUDWORTH
DAVID BUDWORTH LTD

HEAD OFFICE AND WORKS:
Harwich, Essex
DIRECTORS:
D. D. Budworth, MA, CEng, MIMechE, AMINA (Managing Director)
J. Blewitt, MBE, MA
J. M. Budworth

This company entered the gas-turbine field in 1952 when it ran its first small unit used to drive emergency electrical generating and water pumping equipment. Subsequently a series of small gas-turbines has been designed and built, mainly for industrial and instructional duties, but including a number of aircraft installations. Budworth has also engaged in development of a variety of other gas-turbine and aircraft equipment.

BUDWORTH PUFFIN

The Puffin turbo-compressor has been developed initially for helicopter applications, but can also be available in configuration as a turbo-prop or, without the reduction gear, as a turbojet.
TYPE: Centrifugal free-turbine turboshaft/turboprop.
SHAFT DRIVE: Epicyclic and helical spur reduction gear of 16 : 1 ratio. Gears carried on ball and roller bearings.
COMPRESSOR: Single-stage centrifugal unit with RR 58 aluminium alloy single-sided impeller having 13 vanes. Rotor carried on ball and roller bearings. Aluminium compressor casing and radial diffuser. Air mass flow 3·3 lb (1·49 kg)/sec.
COMBUSTION CHAMBER: Annular type with stainless steel air casing and Nimonic 75 flame tube. Vaporising type fuel injectors and high energy ignition.

The Budworth Puffin in its simplest form, without reduction gear, as a turbojet rated at 180 lb (81·7 kg) st

COMPRESSOR TURBINE: Two-stage axial unit with serrated coupling to shaft carried on ball and roller bearings. Rotor blades integral with overhung disc cast in Nimonic PE10. Turbine entry temperature 1,700°F (1,200°K).
POWER TURBINE: Single-stage axial unit with serrated coupling to shaft carried on ball and roller bearings. Rotor blades integral with overhung disc, cast in Nimonic PE 10.
JET PIPE: Fixed.
ACCESSORY DRIVES: Bevel drive at air intake casing with provision for driving pumps.
FUEL SYSTEM: Electronic fuel control system. Max fuel pressure 100 lb/sq in (7·03 kg/cm²).
LUBRICATION SYSTEM: Forced circulation lubrication using gear pumps. Oil tank capacity 4 pints (2·3 litres). Normal oil supply pressure 40 lb/sq in (2·8 kg/cm²).

MOUNTING: Trunnions
STARTING: Electric DC motor at intake end.
DIMENSIONS:
Diameter 15 in (381 mm)
Length 30 in (762 mm)
WEIGHT, DRY
Turboshaft and turboprop:
Basic 100 lb (45·4 kg)
Complete with accessories 130 lb (58·9 kg)
Turbojet:
Basic 70 lb (31·2 kg)
PERFORMANCE RATINGS:
T-O: turbojet 180 lb (81·7 kg) st
Continuous: turboshaft and turboprop 200 hp
SPECIFIC FUEL CONSUMPTION:
At continuous rating, turboshaft and turboprop 0·85 lb (0·39 kg)/shp/hr

CLUTTON
ERIC CLUTTON

ADDRESS:
92 Newlands Road, Shelton, Stoke-on-Trent, Staffs

In order to provide propulsion for his FRED and Easy Too series of light aircraft (see "Aircraft" section) Mr Clutton has been engaged in independent modification of the Volkswagen 1,500 cc engine and intends ultimately to market plans and a conversion kit.

His first conversion involved a geared drive to the propeller by means of a toothed belt. The ratio was 0·5 : 1 and, with the 72 in × 44 in (1,829 mm × 1,118 mm) ex-Cirrus Minor propeller used on FRED Srs 2 the engine speed was held to 3,750 rpm. Despite the fact that the full engine power of 66 bhp was developed only at 4,800 rpm the geared drive resulted in outstanding aircraft performance.

The drive raised the thrust line and provided adequate ground clearance. A second toothed belt from the rear of the crankshaft drove twin Scintex Vertex impulse magnetos, modified to run laterally. Other features included an SU Zenith carburettor with central float chamber and heating provided by hot air drawn at will from an exhaust pipe muff, a tachometer driven from the original distributor shaft and an oil-pressure pick-up in place of the original oil cooler. Engine weight, originally over 200 lb (90·7 kg), was reduced by substituting light alloy castings for certain steel items.

A true geared VW conversion has been under

Close-up of the gearbox on the first Clutton geared 1,500 cc Volkswagen engine

development since 1968, and has been flying since late 1969. The 0·5 : 1 gearbox uses helical automotive gears and is force-lubricated from the engine. Ignition is now by two Lucas SR4 magnetos chain-driven off the clutch end of the crankshaft, and the tachometer is driven from the rear of the gearbox. As the propeller rotates in opposition to the crankshaft, US propellers can

PLESSEY
THE PLESSEY COMPANY LTD

HEAD OFFICE:
Vicarage Lane, Ilford, Essex

Plessey is one of the largest suppliers of electrical and mechanical aerospace equipment. The Plessey Dynamics Group's Mechanical Systems Division, at Titchfield, Fareham, Hants, produces fuel systems for propulsion and lift jets, auxiliary

power units rated at 50 to 200 hp and self-contained gas-turbine starters. The latter were derived originally from designs by Soc Microturbo of France (which see), but these have been further developed by Plessey and produced in quantity for the Spey-engined McDonnell Douglas Phantom. A further design is being developed for the Fiat-Lockheed F-104S. Further development has now resulted in a new unit which starts main engines and can then continue operation in flight as an auxiliary and emergency power unit.

be used and a 68 × 44 in (1,728 mm × 1,118 mm) type is giving good results. The larger propeller accounts for much of the 30 lb (13·6 kg) increase in weight.

Another 1,500 cc VW engine is being converted with a gearbox on the clutch end and the carburettor below the crankcase. This will power Easy Too (see "Aircraft" section).

PLESSEY SOLENT

Known by the manufacturer's designation Solent Mk 2 and by the UK military designation Solent Mk 101, this is an extremely compact gas-turbine starter based on Microturbo technology. Airflow is 1·36 lb (0·62 kg)/sec and the Solent uses the same fuel as the aircraft's main engine: either Avtur 50, Avtag or 8/Avcat. Nominal diameter and length are respectively 8 and 18·25 in (203 and 463 mm) and weight with accessories is 65 lb (29·5 kg). Rated output is a minimum of 65 hp at 63,000 rpm.

ROLLASON

ROLLASON AIRCRAFT AND ENGINES LTD

HEAD OFFICE AND WORKS:
Croydon Airport, Croydon, Surrey

OFFICERS:
See "Aircraft" section

In support of its manufacture under licence of the Druine Turbulent light aeroplane, Rollason Aircraft and Engines Ltd is undertaking the conversion of Ardem 4CO2 power plants for this aircraft, from motor car engines.

A modification introduced on the Rollason version is the use of a Solex side-entry carburettor. This greatly improves the starting characteristics and uses pre-heated air, so that a carburettor heater box is no longer necessary.

Rollason has developed several versions of the Ardem engine, as described below. In addition there are the 45 hp Mark 4 engine, the 55 hp high-compression Mark 5, and the 45 hp Mark X engine which is similar to the Mark 4 and is ARB approved. All three of these variants are of 1,500 cc capacity. The Ardem RTW described in earlier editions of *Jane's* was experimental and not proceeded with.

The firm has now produced a 1,600 cc version, known as the Ardem Mk XI. All these Ardem engines are being installed in Nipper aircraft.

ARDEM 1500cc VERSION

The standard model has a compression ratio of 7·8 : 1 and gives 45 hp at 3,300 rpm for take-off, with a fuel consumption of 3·75 Imp gallons (17 litres)/hr at max rating. In addition, a high-compression version is available, as follows:

CYLINDERS: Bore 3·27 in (83 mm). Stroke 2·72 in (69 mm). Cast steel barrels, light alloy heads. Compression ratio 8·5 : 1.

PISTONS: Aluminium alloy high-compression pistons, each with two compression rings and one scraper ring. Floating gudgeon pins.

CONNECTING RODS: White metal bearings in big-end. Bronze bearings in little-end.

CRANKSHAFT: Runs in four white metal bearings.

CRANKCASE: Magnesium case.

VALVE GEAR: Two valves per cylinder. Camshaft geared to crankshaft.

INDUCTION: Zenith 32 KL P10 carburettor.

FUEL GRADE: 100 octane.

IGNITION: Lucas SR4 magneto mounted below engine, with chain drive. Two Lodge LH spark plugs per cylinder.

LUBRICATION: Wet sump type, with single gear-type pump.

OIL SPECIFICATION: Shell W80.

PROPELLER DRIVE: Direct drive.

ACCESSORIES: SEV 46C fuel pump.

DIMENSIONS:
Length
  16·75 in (426 mm)
Width
  29·50 in (750 mm)
Height
  22·00 in (559 mm)

POWER RATING:
Max rating
  53 hp at 3,600 rpm

FUEL CONSUMPTION:
At max rating
  4·0 Imp gallons
    (18·2 litres)/hr

ARDEM 1600cc VERSION

After extensive testing this engine is now approved and is produced as the Ardem Mk XI. It differs from the Mk X in having cylinders of 3·365 in (85·5 mm) bore and dual ignition.

WEIGHT:
With accessories   158 lb (71·6 kg)

Rollason-converted Ardem 4CO2 engine

POWER RATINGS:
Max rating   55 hp at 3,300 rpm
Cruise rating   35·5 hp at 2,500 rpm

FUEL CONSUMPTION:
At cruise rating 2·75 Imp gallons (12·5 litres)/hr

ROLLS-ROYCE

ROLLS-ROYCE LIMITED

HEAD OFFICE:
Moor Lane, Derby DE2 8BJ

LONDON OFFICE:
14-15 Conduit Street, W1

ESTABLISHED:
March 15, 1906

Rolls-Royce produces a wide range of turbofan, turbojet, turboprop, turboshaft, piston, ramjet and rocket engines. The company employs more than 80,000 people, over 50,000 being engaged on aero-engine production and product support and 18,000 on aero-engine research, design and development. More than 80 per cent of the company's turnover of over £300,000,000 is derived from aero-engines.

Rolls-Royce turbine aero-engines have been chosen by over 200 airlines and 70 armed forces throughout the world. Over 70,000 Rolls-Royce gas turbines have been produced and more than 120 million hours flying experience have been accumulated, three-quarters of these in commercial operation.

Rolls-Royce has six operating divisions, five of which are engaged in aero-engine work—the Aero Engine Division, Bristol Engine Division, Small Engine Division, Industrial and Marine Gas Turbine Division (rocket engines) and the Motor Car Division (light aircraft engine department).

One of the advanced projects now under development is the new generation RB.211 three-shaft turbofan which has been chosen to power

the Lockheed L.1011 TriStar airliner. The RB.211 is rated initially at 40,600 lb (18,416 kg) st, but thrust growth to 60,000 lb (27,216 kg) is envisaged. It is due to go into service in the TriStar in late 1971.

Development continues on the Olympus 593 twin-spool turbojet, four of which power the Anglo/French Concorde supersonic airliner. These engines are developed and produced jointly by the Rolls-Royce Bristol Engine Division and the French company SNECMA.

Other Rolls-Royce commercial turbines include the Trent, Spey and Conway turbofans; Avon and Viper turbojets; Dart and Tyne turbo-props; and Gnome and Nimbus turboshafts. Most of the company's commercial engines also have military applications, an outstanding example being the Spey turbofan which in its differing versions powers RAF and RN Phantom strike fighters, Hawker Siddeley Buccaneer Mk 2 strike aircraft, the Hawker Siddeley Nimrod maritime aircraft, and the LTV A-7D and E Corsair II.

Commercial and military international collaboration and licence agreements have been made with a number of companies in Europe and the United States. Engines involved in these agreements include the TF41 (Allison), Olympus 593 and M45H (both SNECMA), Adour (Turboméca), RB.193 vectored-thrust turbofan (MTU) and the RB.199 (Turbo-Union). The RB.199 is an advanced military turbofan, based on the same three-shaft principle as the company's latest commercial engines. It is being developed by Rolls-Royce Bristol Engine Division, MTU and Fiat, as partners in Turbo-Union, for the Euro-

pean Panavia 100/200 multi-role combat aircraft (MRCA).

A new turboshaft, the BS.360-07, is being developed by Rolls-Royce for the Westland WG.13 multi-purpose helicopter. The BS.360-07, together with the Turmo and Astazou engines on which production is shared with Turboméca, are part of the Anglo/French helicopter programme which is designed to meet the medium and light helicopter requirements of the two countries.

Light aircraft engines of 95, 100, 130 and 145 hp are manufactured under licence from Teledyne Continental Motors. Rolls-Royce also markets the complete Teledyne Continental range (95 to 450 hp) in Europe, Africa, the Indian sub-continent, Australia, New Zealand and certain Far Eastern countries.

The Industrial and Marine Gas Turbine Division is responsible for development and manufacture of a range of rocket engines. These include the RZ.2 and Gamma 2 and 8, which power the Blue Streak first stage of the ELDO satellite launcher, and the RAE/Westland Black Arrow satellite launcher, respectively. This division is also responsible for developing and marketing industrial and marine versions of aero gas turbines which are used as power units for large and small ships, hydrofoils, electricity generating sets, and gas and oil pumping equipment, and for other industrial uses. This division is also responsible for Rolls-Royce marine turbines for air-cushion vehicles. These engines are described in *Jane's Surface Skimmer Systems*.

AERO ENGINE DIVISION

DIRECTORS:
Sir David P. Huddie, BA (Managing Director)
S. L. Bragg, (General Manager, Engineering)
J. F. Bush, BSc, AFRAeS (Engineering Director, Large Transport Engines)
L. G. Dawson, BSc(Eng) (Director of Advanced Engineering)
D. O. Davies, BSc(Eng) (Director of Engineering Projects)
E. M. Eltis, BSc(Eng) (Director of Engineering)
D. Fleming, CBE, BSc(Eng) (General Manager)
A. H. Harvey-Bailey (Director of Production Output)
D. A. Head (Director of Personnel and Administration)
R. M. Kendall (Assistant Managing Director, Market Development)
D. McLean, BSc(Eng), CEng, MIMechE, AFRAeS, (Programme Director, Scottish Projects)

A. C. McWilliams (Production Director)

T. L. Metcalfe, BSc(Eng), CEng, FIMechE, (Director, RB.211 Engineering and Experimental Programmes)

R. Nicholson (Programme Director, RB.211)

A. V. N. Reed (Contracts Director)

J. A. Rigg, FCA (Financial Controller)

P. E. Scarfe (Director and General Manager, Manufacturing)

William T. Seawell (President, Rolls-Royce Aero Engines Inc)

F. O. Thornton, AFRAeS (General Manager, Scottish Group)

J. R. Wheatley, BCom (Production Control Director)

J. Wood, BSc(Eng), AFRAeS, FCASI (Commercial Director)

The Aero Engine Division, largest of the six operating divisions of Rolls-Royce, has works at Derby, Hucknall, Glasgow, Barnoldswick, Dundonald and Sunderland. Principal development and manufacturing programme concerns the RB.211 three-shaft commercial turbofan, power-plant for the Lockheed L.1011 TriStar. Other current programmes include the Trent three-shaft turbofan, Adour military turbofan, (jointly with Turboméca of France), a range of advanced lift/booster engines and military and commercial versions of the Spey turbofan and the Dart turboprop.

ROLLS-ROYCE TURBOMÉCA ADOUR

This joint design of 4,400 lb (1,996 kg) st turbofan by Rolls-Royce and Turboméca is being developed for the SEPECAT Jaguar tactical strike fighter and advanced trainer. A brief description of the Adour is given in the International section on pages 720-721.

ROLLS-ROYCE AVON

The Avon axial-flow turbojet was developed after the war to replace the Nene. It has been in large-scale production both in the United Kingdom and overseas for many years and powers a very large number of military and civil types.

The 100-Series Avons (of which full details can be found in the 1961-62 edition of this work) have a 12-stage compressor and eight individual combustion chambers. The later 200-series and 300-Series (RB.146) engines are of almost entirely new design with higher pressure ratio compressors, cannular combustion chambers and considerably higher thrust.

A series of civil Avon turbojets designated RA.29 has also been developed, based on the military family of engines.

RB.90 AVON 200 SERIES

Current engines in the Avon 200 Series include the following:

RA.24. Military engine. Passed type test at a rating of 11,250 lb (5,103 kg) st in July 1956. Also RA.24R with reheat (14,370 lb = 6,518 kg st).

RA.28. Military engine. First Avon to be type-tested at 10,000 lb (4,540 kg) st.

Avon 200 Series engines currently in service include the Avon Mk 202, 206 and 208 of RA.24 rating, powering the Scimitar, Canberra and Hawker Siddeley Hunter; and Avon Mk 210 and 211 of RA.24R rating powering the BAC Lightning Mks 1, 2, 2A and 4. The Avon Mk 48A of RA.24R rating, is also in licenced production by Svenska Flygmotor under the designation RM5, with Swedish reheat system, for the Saab Draken A, B and C series.

The following details apply to the RA.24 engine:

TYPE: Single-shaft axial-flow turbojet.

AIR INTAKE: Annular casing surrounding starter bullet. Variable-incidence inlet guide vanes, of DTD.171 weldable chrome-nickel austenitic steel, automatically-operated by hydraulic ram. Magnesium intake casing incorporates front bearing housing to which is bolted the starter reduction gear housing. All forward-facing surfaces have compressor bleed anti-icing.

COMPRESSOR: Fifteen-stage axial flow. Rotor blades pinned to rotor discs which are splined to shaft. Discs of Rex 448 or Jessops H.46 stainless steel. Rotor blades are aluminium alloy (stages 1-7) or titanium (stages 8-15). Stator blades are aluminium alloy with tip shrouds (stages 1-4) or titanium (stages 5-15). Compressor shaft on two bearings, one roller (front) and one ball (rear), in two parts with flange forming part of the 15th-stage disc. Front compressor casing in cast magnesium alloy carries stages 1-6 stators; intermediate casing in aluminium alloy carries stages 7-9 stators; fabricated steel outlet casing carries stages 10-15 stators and has eight webs providing eight ducts directing air to the combustion chambers. The webs are hollow and collect hot compressor air for anti-icing and aircraft services.

COMBUSTION CHAMBER: Eight flame tubes mounted within annular chamber, each fitted with Rolls-Royce duplex burners. Interconnecting pipes between each pair of flame tubes. High-energy igniters in Nos. 3 and 6 tubes. Flame tubes of Nimonic 75 and casing of Fortiweld steel.

FUEL SYSTEM: Proportion of main engine flow is fed from upstream of the throttle valve and by-passed to the pump outlet. This forms the proportional circuit which controls main flow under varying conditions of altitude, jet-pipe temperature and engine speed.

NOZZLE GUIDE VANES: Nozzle casing, of cast chrome steel, has two rows of guide vanes, one ahead of each turbine stage. All vanes of C.242.

TURBINE: Two-stage. Turbine shaft coupled to compressor shaft by ball and socket coupling with splined sleeve to transmit torque and supported at rear end by roller bearing. High-pressure blades of air-cooled Nimonic 105, low-pressure blades of Nimonic 100,

Rolls-Royce RB.146 Avon 300-Series turbojet engine (12,690 lb=5,756 kg st)

Rolls-Royce RA.29/6 Civil Avon turbojet engine (12,200 lb=5,533 kg st)

secured to steel discs by "fir tree" roots and locked. All blades shrouded at tips.

EXHAUST SYSTEM: Fabricated in nickel/chromium alloy, flange-bolted to nozzle casing. Exhaust cone carried on four faired struts. Insulation provided on outer casing.

JET PIPE: Dependent on installation. Engines for BAC Lightning have reheat jet pipe with four-position flap-type nozzle driven by pneumatic rams. Light-up by igniter plug.

ACCESSORY DRIVES: Horizontal shaft drive to each side of engine from gear system, driven by main shaft from just aft of centre bearing. External wheel case on starboard side serves lubrication and fuel pump systems; drive on port side serves, through bevel drive, generators or alternators or ancillary gear-box mounted on airframe.

LUBRICATION SYSTEM: Closed circuit system with combined oil tank and sump under compressor casing and fuel-cooled oil cooler on port side. Lubrication of three main bearings, starter reduction gear and ancillary drive system by single pump. Four scavage pumps.

STARTING: By LP air starter motor or iso-propyl-nitrate starter (depending on engine Mk No). Starter mounted in bullet on intake casing.

DIMENSIONS, WEIGHTS AND PERFORMANCE: See table.

RB.146 AVON 300 SERIES

The RB.146 is a development of the RA.24. Its dry rating is 12,690 lb (5,756 kg) st, and reheat is used for all installations. In the BAC Lightning F.6 its rating is 16,860 lb (7,647 kg) st, and 17,110 lb (7,761 kg) st in the Saab Draken. A number of versions of the Avon RB.146 have been produced, including the Mk 60 built under licence by Svenska Flygmotor (as the RM6) with Swedish reheat system, for the Saab Draken D, E and F series; the Mks 301 and 302 powering the Lightning Mks 3, 5 and 6; and the Mk 302C powering the Lightning Mks 53 and 55 (dry and reheat thrusts, 12,100 lb=5,488 kg and 15,680 lb=7,112 kg respectively).

Major differences between the RB.146 and RA.24 are:

AIR INTAKE: Extension ring deleted. Magnesium casing modified to carry intake temperature sensing probe and provision for mating engine to aircraft intake duct. Also carries 'zero' stage stator blades.

COMPRESSOR: Sixteen-stage axial flow by addition of 'zero' stage to RA.24 compressor to give increased air mass flow.

EXHAUST UNIT (except Mk 60): Exhaust cone carried on three struts.

JET PIPE (except Mk 60): Reheat pipe with infinitely variable flap type nozzle driven by screw jacks. Ignition by hot streak from engine.

DIMENSIONS:
Length   138 in (3,505 mm)
Diameter   44 in (1,118 mm)

RA.29 CIVIL AVON

The RA.29 series of civil engines was developed from the military family of Avons, specifically for airline operation, to give long life and low fuel consumption. The mass flow through the engine was increased by means of an additional compressor stage compared with the RA.28, and a high efficiency three-stage turbine is a feature of the design. The civil Avon is in service in the HS Comet 4 and Aérospatiale (Sud-Aviation) Caravelle.

Production versions of the RA.29 are as follows:

RA.29/1. Rated at 10,250 lb (4,650 kg) st. In service in Comet Series 4 and 4C (Mk 524B) and 4B (Mk 525B).

RA.29/3. Rated at 11,400 lb (5,171 kg) st. In service in Caravelle Series III (Mk 527B).

RA.29/6. Entered service in Caravelle Series VI-N (Mk 531B) in February 1961 with rating of 12,200 lb (5,533 kg) st and later in Caravelle VI-R (Mk 533R) with thrust reverser and rating of 12,600 lb (5,715 kg) st.

Both the RA.29/3 and RA.29/6 incorporate a two-position variable-area nozzle (with noise suppressor) for improved cruise performance.

ROLLS-ROYCE AVON AXIAL-FLOW TURBOJET ENGINES

Type	Thrust (Basic S/L rating)	Specific Fuel Consumption (max T-O conditions)	Net Dry Weight	Power/Weight Ratio	Length (with exhaust cone)	Diameter
RA.24 Mk 208 (Sea Vixen)	11,250 lb (5,103 kg)	—	—	—	126·9 in (3,223 mm)	42 in (1,067 mm)
RA.28 Mk 207 (Hunter)	10,150 lb (4,604 kg)	0.88	2,869 lb (1,301 kg)	3.46	123.0 in (3,124 mm)	41.5 in (1,054 mm)
RA.29/1 (Comet 4)	10,250 lb (4,650 kg)	0.786	3,343 lb (1,516 kg)	3.10	126.0 in (3,200 mm)	39 in (991 mm)
RA.29/3 (Caravelle III)	11,400 lb (5,171 kg)	0.853	3,347 lb (1,518 kg)	3.50	126.0 in (3,200 mm)	39 in (991 mm)
RA.29/6 (Caravelle VI)	12,200 lb (5,533 kg) and 12,600 lb (5,715 kg)	0.785 to 0·802	3,488-3,491 lb (1,582-1,583 kg)	3·50-3·65	134.0 in (3,404 mm)	39 in (991 mm)

The RA.29/6 also has an additional "00" compressor stage, making 17 stages in all.

The following details refer specifically to the RA.29/1, but are generally applicable to other versions:

TYPE: Single-shaft axial-flow turbojet.

AIR INTAKE: Annular casing surrounding starter bullet. Variable-incidence inlet guide vanes automatically operated by hydraulic ram. Magnesium alloy intake casing incorporates front bearing housing supported on six tangential struts. Starter motor and reduction gear are mounted in centre of air intake ahead of front bearing. Inlet guide vanes and starter fairing have compressor bleed anti-icing.

COMPRESSOR: Sixteen-stage (seventeen-stage in Avon RA.29/6) axial-flow. Rotor blades pinned to stainless steel discs which are splined to shaft. Stator blades of stainless steel (Stages 0 and 5-8), aluminium alloy (stages 1-4) and titanium or steel (stages 9-15). Rotor blades of aluminium alloy (stages 0-2) and titanium (stages 3-15). First five stages of stator blades (stages 0-4) are tip-shrouded. Compressor shaft mounted on roller bearing at front and ball bearing (rear). Compressor casing in two parts (front part magnesium, rear part aluminium), each split axially into two halves. Last five stages of compressor are housed in fabricated steel casing integral with compressor outlet casing, which directs air into eight ducts, hollow webs between each duct collecting hot compressor air for anti-icing and cabin pressurisation.

COMBUSTION CHAMBER: Eight flame tubes of Nimonic 75 mounted within annular chamber. Combustion system casing of Fortiweld steel.

FUEL SYSTEM: Similar to Avon RA.28.

NOZZLE GUIDE VANES: Nozzle box, of cast chrome steel, carries three rows of guide vanes, one ahead of each turbine stage. All vanes of C.242 cast nickel base alloy.

TURBINE: Three-stage. Turbine shaft, supported at rear end by roller bearing, connected to compressor shaft by screw coupling. Turbine blades of Nimonic alloys, all shrouded at tip and secured to steel discs by fir-tree roots.

EXHAUST UNIT: Of nickel chromium steel, with exhaust cone carried on three faired radial struts. Insulating material in space between two walls of outer casing.

ACCESSORY DRIVES: Horizontal shaft drive to each side of engine from gear system driven by main shaft from just aft of centre bearing. External wheelcase on starboard side serves lubrication and fuel pump systems; drive on port side serves generator or ancillary gear-box according to installation.

LUBRICATION SYSTEM: Closed circuit system with fuel-cooled oil cooler. Combined oil tank and sump under rear compressor casing. Lubrication of three main bearings, starter reduction gear and ancillary drive system by single pump. Five pumps scavenge bearing and drives.

STARTING: By electric starter motor, mounted in bullet in air intake.

DIMENSIONS, WEIGHTS AND PERFORMANCE: See Table.

ROLLS-ROYCE RB.162

The RB.162 is a very simple ultra-lightweight turbojet engine which was initially developed to meet the requirements of the aircraft industries of Britain, France and Federal Germany for a lift-jet unit for V/STOL aircraft. The governments of all three countries contributed to its cost, and special developments needed to make the engine suitable for a particular application will in future be paid for by the country requiring them.

Development of the RB.162 lift-jet series was completed at the end of 1969. Development is continuing on a new version of the engine for use as a take-off booster. By early January 1970 more than 70 RB.162 jets had run, the total number of starts exceeding 38,000 and the number of bench and flight hours exceeding 2,300.

A feature of the RB.162 is the extensive use of low-cost lightweight materials, including glass-fibre reinforced plastics. Although plastics help to give the engine an unprecedented thrust-to-weight ratio of about 16 : 1, they were chosen primarily to reduce production costs.

The engine, by virtue of its compact, lightweight design is also well suited for use as a booster engine for take-off power assistance. With suitable modifications to facilitate operation in the horizontal attitude, a version of the RB.162, the RB.162-86, is in production for the Hawker Siddeley Trident 3B.

The following versions of the RB.162 may be mentioned:

RB.162-1/4. Initial version (-1 has 10% air bleed for stabilisation control). Normal rating of 4,409 lb (2,000 kg) st and emergency rating of 4,718 lb (2,140 kg) st. Bench testing began in January 1962. Preliminary flight clearance test at max power performed in April 1963. Special category test completed in August 1964 demonstrated thrust 2½% above contract figure and sfc 3½% below that specified. This version was described in the 1969-70 *Jane's*.

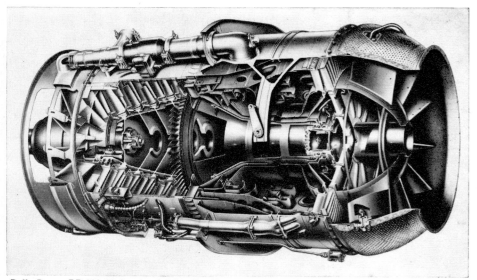

Rolls-Royce RB.162-86 booster jet for the Hawker Siddeley Trident 3B (5,250 lb = 2,381 kg st)

RB.162-30 Series. Specified for virtually all current European V/STOL aircraft, including the Mirage III-V and Do 31. More than 60 had been built for development testing, and for installation in V/STOL aircraft and test rigs, by May 1966.

RB.162-81. Development of RB.162-30 with air-cooled turbine blades to increase rating. Rated at 5,992 lb (2,718 kg) st normal SLS with 8 per cent air bleed; contingency rating 6,010 lb (2,726 kg) st with 13 per cent control air bleed. Developed for VFW VAK 191B V/STOL aircraft.

RB.162-86. Developed for booster applications, with T-O thrust of 5,250 lb (2,381 kg) st. Major features described below. Fitted to Hawker Siddeley Trident 3B. Designed for life of 2,000 take-off cycles, and to meet ARB type-test schedule for booster jets and civil airworthiness requirements. On entering BEA service early in 1971 TBO should be 800 take-off cycles, thereafter increasing at the rate of about 400 per year.

The following details apply to the RB.162-81; particulars of the -86 are given in brackets.

TYPE: Lightweight single-shaft axial-flow lift-jet engine (take-off booster).

AIR INTAKE: Annular type at top of engine, moulded from glass-reinforced composite (grc) with integral fixed inlet guide vanes (-86 vanes, steel). Two pairs of hollow intake struts are moulded integrally with upper and lower portions of nose bullet from grc, and house fuel and oil pipes (-86 hot-air anti-iced).

COMPRESSOR CASING: Made in two halves from grc. Provides mountings for accessories, including throttle and flow control unit, igniter box and oil bottle with visual level scale.

COMPRESSOR: Six-stage axial-flow type. Rotor of aluminium alloy discs and spacers welded together to form a single unit integral with shaft. Stator blades 1-5 grc, 6 steel; all stator blades cast into half casings. Rotor blades, stage 1 (1 and 2) aluminium, 2-6 (3-6) grc; stage 1 pinned, 2-6 dovetailed (dampers at ¾ span on stage 1). Fixed diffuser vanes aft of compressor. Pressure ratio 4·5 : 1; mass flow 85 lb (38·5 kg)/sec.

COMBUSTION CHAMBER: Annular type, inside welded sheet steel casing. Outer flame tube is a continuous drum with perforations for secondary air. Inner flame tube is Nimonic drum carrying 18 equally spaced burners, two starting atomisers and two high-energy igniters 30° each side of vertical section plane. (Casing and turbine stator redesigned to accommodate increased mass flow as result of absence of control air-bleed requirement).

FUEL SYSTEM: Self-contained fuel system consisting of two units. One unit, with a main body cast in magnesium, is housed in the nose bullet and contains the backing pump, gear-type HP fuel pump, acceleration control unit and two datum governors. Second unit is the combined throttle and flow control unit, with main body cast in magnesium, mounted on the compressor casing and incorporating an emergency shut-off cock. Simple form of fuel filtering is included, but fuel system is designed to accept dirty or icy fuel and no provision is made for fuel heating (control system changed to reduce idling speed to reduce fuel consumption and noise during serviceability checks).

FUEL GRADES: JP-1, JP-4.

NOZZLE GUIDE VANES: Hollow air-cooled refractory alloy.

TURBINE: Single-stage axial-flow type. Titanium (steel) disc and hollow air-cooled blades of refractory alloy held by fir-tree roots.

BEARINGS: Only two ball bearings, one between inlet guide vanes and compressor, the other

forward of turbine. Both are single-row, the turbine bearing being for location and the intake bearing making provision for axial expansion.

JET-PIPE: Fixed-area type with outer wall, cone and 12 radial struts. Provision for two-position or infinitely-variable spherical swivelling nozzle, for deflected or vectored thrust (bolted-on pipe and fixed nozzle).

LUBRICATION SYSTEM: One-shot system. Tank with capacity for several starts (1 pint) mounted on compressor casing. Alternatively airframe-mounted tank for a battery of engines. At each start, a single shot of oil is delivered via non-return valves to each bearing by pressurising the tank. Oil from rear bearing drains through exhaust unit. Oil from front bearing is scavenged overboard by an ejector driven by compressor air delivery (detail changes for horizontal installation; tank capacity 6 pints).

MOUNTING: Four equally spaced spherical trunnions, of which any three used; -81 may be swivelled for thrust vectoring.

STARTING: Ground starting by direct air impingement on turbine blades, by air bled from propulsion engines, or by hydraulic starter built into nose bullet. In flight ram air starting is used.

DIMENSIONS:
Height   54 in (1,370 mm)
Diameter   29 in (740 mm)

DRY WEIGHT:
Nominal, with oil and fuel systems
RB.162-81   415 lb (188·2 kg)
RB.162-86   519 lb (236 kg)

PERFORMANCE RATINGS:
See under model listings.

ROLLS-ROYCE RB.202

The first of a new generation of lift-fan engines, the RB.202 is a two-shaft high by-pass-ratio turbofan in the 10,000-20,000 lb (4,540-9,080 kg) st bracket for civil V/STOL operation, where low noise is of prime importance. It is designed for operation in a substantially vertical position, but may be swivelled about a transverse horizontal axis through a limited range for aircraft acceleration and control during the transition.

The high by-pass ratio has been chosen to minimise jet noise. Specific attention has been paid to minimising the noise from the fan and turbine. The fan outlet duct incorporates sound-absorbent materials on the inner and outer walls; further reduction in noise can be obtained by the use of acoustically-lined splitters in the fan outlet duct.

ROLLS-ROYCE/ALLISON XJ99

Based on Rolls-Royce third-generation lift-jet technology, the XJ99 is a joint Rolls-Royce/Allison project for a high thrust/weight, high thrust/volume ratio lift-jet suitable for a wide variety of VTOL and STOL aircraft applications. Development is proceeding under an agreement signed by the American and British governments and the programme is directed by the USAF Aero Propulsion Laboratory and the UK Ministry of Technology. Effort is initially directed at the XJ99 in lift-jet form but it is also adaptable as a gas generator for lift-fans or as a booster engine.

The first XJ99-RA-1 engines ran at R-R, Derby and Allison, Indianapolis early in 1969. The thrust and thrust/weight ratio of the XJ99-RA-1 lift jet are in the region of 9,000 lb (4,082 kg) st and 20 : 1 respectively.

ROLLS-ROYCE/MTU RB.193

This joint design of 10,163 lb (4,610 kg) st vectored-thrust turbofan is being developed by Rolls-Royce and MTU for the VFW VAK 191B V/STOL aircraft. A detailed description of the RB.193 is given in the International section on page 718.

ROLLS-ROYCE RB.211

The RB.211 is an advanced technology three-shaft turbofan of high by-pass ratio, high pressure ratio design spanning the 40,000 lb to 60,000 lb (18,144-27,216 kg) st bracket. The engine was selected by Lockheed Aircraft in March 1968 to power its new L.1011 TriStar three-engined transport. By March 1970 181 TriStars had been ordered, with corresponding orders for the RB.211 amounting to £185 m ($444 m).

Rolls-Royce initiated design studies of three-shaft turbofans in 1961 and a twin-spool engine, the RB.178, was tested in 1967 to provide relevant component and gas generator experience. Among the advantages afforded by a three-shaft layout are its ready use of a high-BPR fan and the availability of a high pressure ratio with fewer compressor and turbine stages. The need for compressor variable stator mechanisms can also be eliminated and the rotating assemblies can be made relatively short and rigid while preserving light construction.

A further unique feature of a three-shaft turbofan is its ability to reduce fan speed—and hence fan noise—on the approach. This is achieved by reducing the area of the final nozzle while maintaining constant thrust by increasing the gas generator rpm.

These characteristics, together with the use of composite materials for selected front-end components, provide the RB.211 with significant advantages over turbofans currently in airline service. Most important of these are a 25 per cent reduction in sfc, improved specific weight, reduced noise levels on take-off and approach, more ready maintenance and repair, and reduced overall operating costs.

For installation of the RB.211 in the Lockheed TriStar, Rolls-Royce is responsible for development and manufacture of the complete integrated propulsion system, comprising (in addition to the engine) the fan airflow reverser, hot stream spoiler, noise reduction nozzle, pod cowlings and related systems, and noise attenuation gear for the fan cowl and turbine exhaust duct.

The engine is divided into seven basic modules. This permits very rapid change of engine parts, and enables service life to be set up for each module rather than for the complete engine. It also facilitates rapid repair, as a damaged or time-expired module can be replaced with the engine installed in the aircraft. Maximum provision is made for in-service monitoring of engine condition and visual inspection on the ground of all engine sections.

The RB.211 combustion chamber is of annular design, giving significant advantages over tubo-annular systems in terms of reduced cost, weight and length, and improved efficiency. The reduced length makes a two-bearing HP system possible, with both bearings located away from the high temperatures of the combustion area. Detailed design of the combustion liner, fuel injection nozzles and fuel control system has been aimed at reducing exhaust contaminants to a minimum. As a result the smoke level of the RB.211 will show a significant reduction compared with turbofans in current service. The proportion of toxic gases in the exhaust will also be well within acceptable levels.

Impingement cooling of the HP turbine blades gives 40°C more cooling than was obtained with the double-pass system used on earlier blades. The cooling air is bled through pre-swirl nozzles, which accelerate the air in the direction of disc rotation. The cooling air passes through the finned interior of the blade and impinges at a high velocity on the inner surface of the leading edge. This results in a high degree of heat transfer from the metal to the air, which is then exhausted through slots in the trailing-edge.

The RB.211 propulsion system for the TriStar incorporates the first of a new generation of Rolls-Royce thrust reversers. The by-pass fan air stream of the RB.211 flows through a three-quarter length duct, thereby creating a requirement for separate deflecting systems for the fan air and exhaust jet. With high by-pass ratio engine such as this (by-pass ratio 5 : 1), the required reverse thrust can be achieved by reversing the fan air stream only and neutralising the thrust of the gas-generator exhaust by the use of a spoiler. Fan stream reversing is achieved by translating rearwards a section of fan cowling, thus uncovering sets of cascades and at the same time closing off the fan duct downstream of the cascades by means of hinged blocker doors.

In order to minimise fan noise, the RB.211 has no inlet guide vanes; the distance between the single-stage fan and its outlet guide vanes is optimised for minimum noise generation, as is

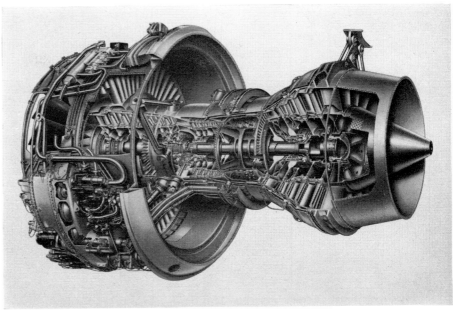

Cutaway drawing of Rolls-Royce RB.211-22 turbofan of 40,600 lb (18,416 kg) st

the numerical ratio of the two rows of blading. The two-position nozzle which is used for fan-slowing consists of four hinged flaps, normally stowed flush with the inside of the jet pipe. When deployed, these reduce the jet nozzle to a rectangle with its major axis vertical. This further reduces noise by preferential radiation.

Additional noise attenuation is achieved by the use of acoustic lining material in the intake, fan and turbine exhaust ducts. Initial development duct linings have reduced noise levels by 6 to 8 PNdB and there are indications that further noise reductions will be produced by current development work. These special linings are products of Short Brothers, who build the complete engine pod for the TriStar.

Bench development work being carried out on the engine includes aerodynamic, performance and strain gauge testing, noise and smoke evaluation and simulated flight cycle endurance running. Ten engines were running at Derby in early March 1970, and two more at the National Gas Turbine Establishment. Engine testing is being supported by considerable rig test work, involving the assessment of different configurations of major components. Flight testing in a modified VC10 began on 6 March 1970. The

planned flight test programme includes a 1,000 hour endurance test under typical TriStar operation.

Production of the RB.211 will involve a major manufacturing programme to a tight time schedule, with a high proportion of the work being sub-contracted by Rolls-Royce. More than 120 British and overseas suppliers of equipment, components and materials are engaged in the programme.

To take full advantage of the new technology embodied in the RB.211, to suit the type of advanced components required, and to increase production capacity, a number of new production facilities are being commissioned. One of these is a precision casting facility which will be the largest of its kind in the world and is based on the most advanced equipment available.

Construction of four new test-beds for production engines, and of a large new test preparation and despatch building was well under way in March 1970. A new manufacturing plant with a floor area of 200,000 sq ft (18,580 m²) for Rolls-Royce Composite Materials Ltd was in March 1970 nearing completion at Avonmouth, near Bristol. It will be used for the production of Hyfil composite material components, and has capacity

Rolls-Royce RB.211-22 advanced technology three-shaft turbofan, rated at 40,600 lb (18,416 kg) st

to meet all the Hyfil requirements of the RB.211 programme.

The **RB.211-22,** the basic engine ordered for the Lockheed L.1011-1, has an initial into-service rating of 40,600 lb (18,416 kg) st in 1971.

RB.211-56. Increased size of RB.211, rated at 53,500 lb (24,267 kg) st with reduced sfc, and designed to meet thrust requirements of long-range Lockheed TriStar versions and large twin-engined aircraft applications. Production propulsion systems to be available for delivery to aircraft manufacturers for entry into service in 1973. Potential growth to 60,000 lb (27,216 kg) st. The RB.211-56 is basically a 1·06 : 1 scaled-up version of RB.211-22 with additional stage on LP turbine driving the fan. Major part of larger gas generator is aerodynamically similar to -22 gas generator thus enabling benefit to be taken of operating experience in early TriStars.

The following description relates to the RB.211-22.

TYPE: Three-shaft axial turbofan.

AIR INTAKE: Annular forward facing.

LP FAN: Single-stage overhung fan driven by LP turbine, the whole rotor assembly being supported on three bearings. Front bearing is large roller, squeeze-film supported behind fan. Axial location of rotor is by intershaft ball bearing in rear end of IP compressor drum. LP turbine supported on roller bearing, squeeze-film mounted in exhaust cone panel. Rotating spinner supported from fan rotor disc, and hot-air anti-iced via central feed-tube within shaft. Hyfil carbon fibre reinforced material used for 25 fan rotor blades, and steel for 70 fan outlet guide vanes. Titanium fan disc bolted with curvic coupling to LP shaft. Aluminium fan casing.

IP COMPRESSOR: Seven-stage compressor rotor driven by IP turbine and supported on three bearings located directly in support panels. Front squeeze-film bearing is roller. Mid bearing at rear of IP compressor is ball bearing providing axial location for IP rotor. Rear bearing is roller, squeeze-film supported in panel between HP and IP turbines. Titanium compressor discs are welded into drum, carrying rotor blades. Aluminium and steel casings carry aluminium and steel stator blades. Single-stage variable inlet guide vanes.

HP COMPRESSOR: Six-stage compressor rotor driven by HP turbine connected by large-diameter shaft and carried on ball location bearing at front and roller bearing squeeze-film mounted in panel behind HP turbine disc. Titanium and steel compressor discs are welded into drum, carrying steel rotor blades. Steel casing carries titanium, steel and Nimonic stator blades. Overall pressure ratio 27 : 1.

COMBUSTION CHAMBER: Fully annular, with steel outer casings and Nimonic flame tube. Downstream fuel injection by 18 airspray burners with annular atomizers. Ignition by starting atomizers and high-energy igniter plugs in Nos 8 and 12 burners.

HP TURBINE: Single-stage axial unit with alloy nozzle guide vanes and Nimonic rotor blades, both rows air-cooled. Impingement-cooled blades mounted in Nimonic disc by fir-tree roots.

IP TURBINE: Single-stage axial unit with Nimonic nozzle guide vanes and Nimonic rotor blades. NGVs are air-cooled. Rotor blades fir-tree mounted in Nimonic disc.

LP TURBINE: Three-stage axial unit with Nimonic rotor blades fir-tree mounted in steel disc.

JET PIPE: Steel jet pipe with two-position nozzle and target type thrust spoiler.

ACCESSORY DRIVES: Radial drive from HP shaft gearbox on fan casing. Accessories driven include integrated-drive generator and (aircraft) hydraulic pumps.

LUBRICATION SYSTEM: Continuous circulation 'dry sump' system with single gear-type pressure pump and multiple gear-type scavenge pumps. Oil tank of 30 pints (17 litres) capacity integral with gearbox.

MOUNTING: Two-point mounting system, Front mount on fan casing takes thrust loads. Rear link mount has provision for expansion of turbine casings. Redundant features incorporated in both mounts for safety.

DIMENSIONS:
Length overall	128·7 in (3,269 mm)
Intake diameter	88·2 in (2,240 mm)

WEIGHT, DRY:
Basic	6,353 lb (2,882 kg)

PERFORMANCE RATINGS:
T-O rating, flat rated to 84°F
40,600 lb (18,416 kg) st
Max cruise rating at 35,000 ft (10,668 m) and Mach 0·85   9,267 lb (4,203 kg) st

SPECIFIC FUEL CONSUMPTION:
At cruise rating at 35,000 ft (10,668 m) and Mach 0·85   0·628

ROLLS-ROYCE RB.163 CIVIL SPEY

Design of the Spey RB.163 began in September 1959, and the first engine ran at the end of December 1960.

Flight testing of two Speys in a Vulcan began on 12 October 1961, and prototype flight trials of the Spey-engined Hawker Siddeley Trident began on 9 January 1962. In July 1962 ARB issued special category approval of the Spey in the Trident pod which involved completion of 150-hour type test to combined UK/US schedule. Civil Speys are in service in the Trident, BAC One-Eleven, Grumman Gulfstream II and F.28 Fellowship.

The civil and military Spey engines are being developed to an integrated programme.

The following versions of the civil Spey have been announced.

Mk 505-5. T-O rating of 9,850 lb (4,468 kg) st at 12,490 rpm, for Hawker Siddeley Trident 1 fleet of BEA.

Mk 506-14. T-O rating of 10,410 lb (4,722 kg) st at 12,530 rpm, for BAC One-Eleven.

Mk 506-14AW. As 506-14, but with water injection to maintain rating to 95°F.

Mk 510-5. T-O rating of 11,000 lb (4,990 kg) st at 12,250 rpm, for Trident.

Mk 511-5, 511-8 and 511-14. T-O rating of 11,400 lb (5,171 kg) st at 12,390 rpm. Mk 511-5 for Trident, Mk 511-8 for Gulfstream II and Mk 511-14 for One-Eleven.

Mk 511-5W and 511-14W. As 511-5 and 511-14 but with water injection to maintain rating to 95°F.

Mk 512-5 and 512-14. T-O rating 11,960 lb (5,425 kg) st in Mk 512-5 for Trident, and 12,000 lb (5,443 kg) st in Mk 512-14 for One-Eleven, in each case at 12,390 rpm. Both engines available with water injection if required.

Mk 512 DW. T-O rating 12,550 lb (5,692 kg) st. Similar to basic Mk 512 but with T-O rating increased by increasing limiting compressor delivery pressure at T-O, with turbine entry temperature maintained by water injection.

Mk 555-15. Lightened and simplified version, reduced rating enabling a number of mechanical features to be deleted. For F.28 Fellowship.

The military versions are described separately. The following details refer specifically to the Spey Mk 505-5, as fitted in the Trident 1 for BEA, except where indicated.

TYPE: Two-spool axial-flow turbofan engine.

AIR INTAKE: Annular type at front of engine, with bleed-air thermal anti-icing.

COMPRESSOR: Axial-flow two-spool type, with four-stage (five-stage on Mks 510, 511 and 512 engines) low-pressure (LP) and twelve-stage high-pressure (HP) compressors. First-stage HP stator vanes are of variable-incidence type. LP compressor is of the drum type, built of aluminium alloy and pinned to shaft. HP compressor is of the disc type, built of aluminium alloy and with first stage bolted to shaft, remaining stages splined to shaft. All stator blades are of aluminium. LP compressor has aluminium blades. HP compressor has blades of aluminium, steel and titanium. Stator blades are slotted into casing. Rotor blades are attached by pins or dove-tailed slots. LP compressor has one-piece aluminium alloy casing. HP compressor has two-piece steel casing. Pressure ratio 16·8 : 1 (15·4 on Mk 555, 16·9 on Mk 506, 18·3 on Mk 510, 19·1 on Mk 512). Air mass flow 203 lb (92·0 kg)/sec (208 lb = 94·5 kg on Mk 506, 206 lb = 93·5 kg on Mk 511). By-pass ratio 1·0 : 1 (0·7 : 1 on Mks 511-512).

COMBUSTION CHAMBER: Cannular type of steel with 10 Nimonic sheet flame tubes. Duplex down-stream burners, one per chamber. High-energy igniters in chambers 4 and 8.

FUEL SYSTEM: Plessey LP fuel pump feeding through fuel-cooled oil cooler and Marston Excelsior fuel heater to LP fuel filter at inlet to Lucas GD-type fuel pump. High-pressure fuel metered by Lucas fuel regulator unit, embodying combined speed and acceleration control and fed through Lucas LP governor and shut-off valve to Duple fuel spray nozzles. Maximum fuel pressure 1,800 lb/sq in (126 kg/cm²).

FUEL GRADE: DERD 2482 or 2486.

WATER INJECTION SYSTEM (applicable to all engines bearing "W" suffix): Water supplied by aircraft-mounted Lucas turbo-pump, fed by air from two or three engines (dependent on aircraft) through engine-mounted automatic shut-off valve to injector passages in fuel spray nozzles (water sprays into primary airflow through flame tube swirlers). Fuel regulator unit incorporates automatic reset, to increase fuel flow and so restore flame temperature reduced by injection of water.

NOZZLE GUIDE VANES: Hollow type cast in nickel-based alloy. HP nozzle guide vanes air-cooled.

TURBINES: Two two-stage axial-flow turbines of which the first HP stage is air-cooled. Turbine discs of creep-resisting ferritic steel, bolted to shaft. Nickel-based alloy blades are attached by fir-tree roots.

BEARINGS: Total of nine bearings. LP compressor is supported in roller bearings, with one ball thrust bearing. HP compressor has front roller bearing and ball thrust bearing. Turbine bearings are all of roller type. Both turbine bearings are flexibly mounted to avoid problems due to vibration.

JET PIPE: Fixed-area type with outer wall and cone of stainless steel sheet.

THRUST REVERSER AND NOISE SUPPRESSOR: Normally an internal clam-shell type reverser (Gulfstream II has target-type, not Rolls-Royce supplied). Six-lobe exhaust suppressor fitted to engines in Trident only.

ACCESSORY DRIVES: Two accessory drives. Port gearbox, driven from LP rotor, carries LP governor and LP tacho. Starboard gearbox, driven from HP rotor, carries LP and HP fuel pumps, fuel regulator, main oil pumps, airflow control rpm signal transmitter, starter and HP tacho. Provision also made on starboard gearbox for aircraft ancillaries such as hydraulic pump, constant-speed drive and generator (One-Eleven has combined constant-speed drive and starter).

LUBRICATION SYSTEM: Self-contained continuous circulation system. Single pressure pump draws oil from tank, feeds it through (fuel-cooled) cooler and HP filter to gearboxes and shaft bearings (front bearing has supplementary pressure and scavenge pumps in nose bullet to ensure positive feed at start-up). Five main scavenge pumps, in casing with pressure pump, return oil from all bearing housings and gearboxes to tank. Total system capacity 24 Imp pints (13·6 litres). Tank capacity 12 Imp pints (6·8 litres). Useable oil 9 Imp pints (5·1 litres). Normal oil supply pressure 35-50 lb/sq in (2·5-3·5 kg/cm²).

OIL SPECIFICATION: DERD 2487.

MOUNTING: Two trunnions, two saddle mountings and one rear mounting.

STARTING: Rotax CT1013 air turbine starter.

Rolls-Royce civil Spey 505 turbofan engine, cut away to show internal details

DIMENSIONS:
  Length, less tailpipe:
    Mk 505, 506, 555   110·0 in (2,795 mm)
    Mk 510, 511   114·6 in (2,911 mm)
  Diameter:
    Mk 505, 506, 555   37·0 in (940 mm)
    Mk 510, 511   37·1 in (942 mm)
WEIGHT, DRY:
  Mk 505-5   2,200 lb (998 kg)
  Mk 506-14   2,257 lb (1,024 kg)
  Mk 506-14AW   2,288 lb (1,038 kg)
  Mk 510-5, 511-5   2,312 lb (1,049 kg)
  Mk 510-5W   2,371 lb (1,075 kg)
  Mk 510-14, 511-14   2,332 lb (1,058 kg)
  Mk 510-14W, 511-14W   2,621 lb (1,188 kg)
  Mk 511-5W   2,317 lb (1,050 kg)
  Mk 511-14   2,332 lb (1,058 kg)
  Mk 511-14W   2,621 lb (1,188 kg)
  Mk 512   2,574 lb (1,168 kg)
  Mk 555-15   2,194 lb (995 kg)
PERFORMANCE RATINGS:
  Max T-O: See under series descriptions
  Max cont:
    Mk 505   9,450 lb (4,286 kg) st at 12,260 rpm
    Mk 506   9,990 lb (4,531 kg) st at 12,385 rpm
    Mk 510   10,540 lb (4,781 kg) st at 12,140 rpm
    Mk 511   10,940 lb (4,962 kg) st at 12,240 rpm
    Mk 512, Mk 512 DW
             11,580 lb (5,253 kg) st at 12,450 rpm
    Mk 555-15 9,470 lb (4,295 kg) st at 11,900 rpm
  Typical cruise rating at 518 mph (834 kmh) at
    32,000 ft (9,750 m):
    All versions   3,070 lb (1,392 kg) st
SPECIFIC FUEL CONSUMPTIONS:
  At T-O rating:
    Mk 505   0·560
    Mk 506   0·563
    Mk 510   0·600
    Mk 511   0·612
    Mk 555-15   0·560
  At max cont rating:
    Mk 505   0·545
    Mk 506   0·556
    Mk 510   0·590
    Mk 511   0·598
    Mk 555-15   0·550
  At typical cruise rating:
    Mk 505   0·763
    Mk 506   0·764
    Mk 510, 511   0·770
OIL CONSUMPTION:
  Max (all Marks) 0·75 Imp pints (0·42 litres)/hr

Rolls-Royce Spey Mk 250 (RB.168-20) military turbofan engine

ROLLS-ROYCE RB.168 MILITARY SPEY

The military Spey RB.168 is fundamentally similar in design to the civil engine, but incorporates modifications to meet the higher-duty conditions of the military rating.

Design of the Spey RB.168-1 started in November 1960; following a contract for prototype development engines, bench testing started in December 1961. During the subsequent month the engine was ordered into quantity production, and flew for the first time in the Hawker Siddeley Buccaneer S.2 strike aircraft in May 1963. The RB.168-1 also powers the Buccaneer S.50 land-based strike aircraft of the South African Air Force.

Major military version of the Spey is the RB.168-25R supersonic engine with reheat. Mainly through the use of an increased turbine entry temperature, the engine has a dry rating of 12,250 lb (5,556 kg) plus a 70 per cent static reheat boost, and powers the McDonnell Phantom FG.1 and FGR.2 fighters. Design of this variant of the Spey started at the beginning of 1964 and the first run was in April 1965. First flight, powering the YF-4K, was on 28 June 1966, followed by the first flight in the YF-4M on 17 February 1967. The RB.168-25R has been in wide-scale production, involving sub-contract component manufacture in many aviation countries in the West, and has been in service with the RN and RAF since early 1969.

The engine used in the Phantom is based closely on the commercial Spey-25, but with stressing and material changes to meet the increased pressure and temperature conditions and flight loads. Major change is the introduction of a robust shaft-and-disc construction for the LP compressor. As with the RB.168-1, use is made of HP compressor bleed air for aircraft BLC purposes. A Plessey gas-turbine starter is fitted. Reheat is fully thrust-modulating from an initial boost, at sea level static, of six per cent. The afterburner incorporates three vee-gutter flame stabilisers, multi-bar fuel injection via four upstream manifolds, self-contained ignition, a fully-variable primary nozzle and a fixed secondary nozzle. Longitudinal movement of the divergent ejector nozzle by six hydraulic rams operates the primary nozzle flaps.

The Spey RB.168-20 Mk 250, closely based on the commercial Spey, powers the Hawker Siddeley Nimrod. Embodying extensive anti-corrosive treatment, this variant provides a higher thrust than its civil counterpart, through operation at higher rpm and higher turbine entry temperature. Provision is made for driving a large alternator, to meet the heavy electrical loads inherent in a maritime reconnaissance aircraft.

Rolls-Royce Spey turbofan engines: foreground, a civil Spey 512 (12,000-12,550 lb=5,443-5,692 kg st); rear, a military Spey 25R (12,250 lb=5,556 kg minimum dry st, not including up to 70 per cent static reheat boost)

ROLLS-ROYCE/ALLISON SPEY TF41

Versions of the Spey are being developed and produced jointly by Rolls-Royce and the Allison Division of General Motors to power USAF and USN versions of the LTV A-7 Corsair II close-support aircraft. These engines, with the designations TF41-A-1 and TF41-A-2, are rated respectively at 14,250 lb (6,463 kg) st and 15,000 lb (6,804 kg) st without reheat. Details of the TF41 are given in the International section, page 717).

ROLLS-ROYCE RB.203 TRENT

The Trent, announced at the 1966 SBAC Display, is the first of a new family of Rolls-Royce three-shaft turbofans for subsonic transport aircraft, known collectively as advanced technology turbofan engines.

Features offered by Rolls-Royce advanced technology engines are claimed to include low noise level, resulting from use of a single-stage independent controllable-speed fan, without inlet guide vanes; low specific fuel consumption, resulting from high compression ratio and high by-pass ratio; simple mechanical construction, with no variable stators or compressor bleed valves; and good engine handling, including rapid response to control and low starting torque.

Some aspects of the advanced technology engine have been under test for many months on a two-spool demonstrator turbofan, which has already shown a 25% better sfc than that of previous-generation turbofans.

The Trent is rated initially at 9,980 lb (4,527 kg) st, flat rated to 90°F/32°C. By-pass ratio is about 3 : 1. Cruising specific fuel consumption is claimed to be 25% lower than that of current turbofans in commercial service. Basic engine weight is 1,776 lb (806 kg).

Bench testing began in December 1967 and the Trent has a full programme of future thrust growth; five per cent more take-off thrust above the minimum rating can be available after two years' service and up to 20 per cent after four years' service, equivalent to an eventual thrust of 12,000 lb (5,443 kg)

ROLLS-ROYCE CONWAY

The Conway turbofan is in service in versions of the Boeing 707 and Douglas DC-8 transports, and also powers the BAC VC10 and Super VC10 airliners. A military version powers the Handley Page Victor Mk 2.

Production versions are as follows:

RCo.11. Type-tested in accordance with the US/UK civil type test schedule at 17,250 lb (7,830 kg) st dry. Produced for Handley Page Victor Mk 2.

RCo.12. Rated at 17,500 lb (7,945 kg) st. For the Boeing 707 (RCo.12 Mk 508) and Douglas DC-8 (RCo.12 Mk 509). Uprated versions of the Mk 508 and Mk 509, carrying the suffix letter "A", are available for the Boeing 707(508A) and DC-8 (509A); these have a T-O rating of 18,000 lb (8,165 kg) st.

RCo.17. Rated at 20,600 lb (9,344 kg) st. In Handley Page Victor Mk 2.

RCo.42. Rated at 20,370 lb (9,240 kg) st. Larger and more efficient LP compressor-turbine assembly. Produced in Mk 540 version for the BAC VC10.

RCo.43. Rated at 21,800 lb (9,888 kg) st. Produced for BAC Super VC10 in Mk 550 version and for RAF VC10 C.1 transports as Mk 301.

TYPE: Two-spool axial-flow turbofan.

AIR INTAKE: Annular, fabricated steel assembly in two circumferentially separate pieces. Forward casing carries nose fairing supported by 19 fixed-incidence hollow steel sheet inlet guide vanes. Rear casing carries LP compressor- or front bearing housing, supported by 31 hollow zero-stage LP stator blades of fabricated steel. Anti-icing is provided by hot air bled from HP compressor outlet casing and fed into inlet guide vanes and zero-stage stators.

LP COMPRESSOR: (RCo.42 and 43) Seven-stage (RCo.42) or eight-stage (RCo.43) axial-flow type, consisting of a drum carrying first four (fan) stages of blades, bolted to rear section of shaft to which are splined the three (RCo.42) or four (RCo.43) intermediate discs. All blades are of aluminium, unshrouded, and are attached to drum or discs by steel pins. The compressor casing consists of three steel rings shrouding the first three rotor stages and an axial split two-piece aluminium casing housing the later stages. The first two rows of stator blades are clamped between the steel casing sections; the remainder are carried in slots in the split casing. All stator blades are of aluminium located by tongue and groove arrangement, and are shrouded at inner ends. Shrouds carry inter-stage seals. LP shaft carried on two roller bearings; axial location by ball thrust bearing inside HP shaft. Air mass flow: RCo.12, 280 lb (127 kg)/sec; uprated RCo.12, 285 lb (129·2 kg)/sec; RCo.42, 367 lb (166·5 kg)/sec; RCo.43, 375 lb (170·1 kg)/sec. Pressure ratio: RCo.12, 14·1 : 1; uprated RCo.12, 14 : 1; RCo.42, 14·8 : 1; RCo.43, 15·8 : 1. By-pass ratio: RCo.12 and 17, 0·3 : 1; RCo.42 and 43, 0·6 : 1; Mk 301 (military VC10), 0·42 : 1.

INTERMEDIATE COMPRESSOR CASING: Magnesium casting housing airflow duct, entry to by-pass and internal wheelcase. Inner casing connected to outer by 8 hollow webs carrying concentric fairing at rear edges to provide airflow separation into by-pass. LP outlet guide vanes located at mouth of airflow duct and HP inlet guide vanes located at rear between inner casing and by-pass intake fairing.

HP COMPRESSOR: Nine-stage axial-flow type, consisting of nine steel discs on two-piece stainless steel shaft. Two sections of shaft connected by bolted flanges. Stage 1 disc located by bolts to flanges of shafts. Stage 2 disc located by shaft connecting bolts. Stages 3-9 discs splined on to shaft. Rotor blades of titanium (stages 1-7) and steel (stages 8-9), attached to discs by hollow steel pins. HP casing of fabricated steel carrying stages 1-8. HP stator blades located by rings attached to casing by set screws. Stator blades of stainless steel. HP shaft carried in front roller bearing and rear ball thrust bearing.

Rolls-Royce Trent three-shaft turbofan (9,980 lb = 4,527 kg st)

COMPRESSOR OUTLET CASING: Fabricated steel casing forming annular airflow duct. Two bell-shaped housings joined by 10 webs. HP compressor outlet guide vanes located at front (small) end of casing and 10 stainless steel flame tube scoops located at rear (large) end.

COMBUSTION SYSTEM: Cannular steel combustion chamber carrying 10 Nimonic flame tubes, interconnected for initial flame spread. Duplex down-stream burners, one per can. High-energy igniter plugs situated in Nos 4 and 7 flame tubes.

NOZZLE BOX: Stainless steel outer casing, supporting inner cone by 10 hollow struts. 10 Nimonic flame tube discharge nozzles at forward end. 3 sets of cast nozzle guide vanes. Stage 1 vanes (HP), located between inner and outer casings, are air-cooled. Second and third stage (LP 1 and 2) vanes are located in outer casing and secured by ring at inner ends.

HP TURBINE: Single-stage. Ferritic steel disc secured to HP shaft by taper bolts. Blades of Nimonic alloy air-cooled, located by fir-tree roots. Roller bearing ahead of turbine disc.

LP TURBINE: Two-stage. Stage 1 disc of steel bolted to LP shaft, extended rearwards to carry steel Stage 2 disc which is located by spigots and supported by roller bearing at tail. Blades of Nimonic alloy located by fir-tree roots.

EXHAUST UNIT: Outer conical member supports LP turbine bearing via ten radial struts. All structural members shielded by ten segments joined by ten streamlined fairings. Entire structure of stainless steel sheet.

BY-PASS DUCT: Two-piece assembly of titanium separated circumferentially. Extends from rear of compressor intermediate casing to end of exhaust unit. Located by flange at forward end and by a serrated ring at rear.

THRUST REVERSAL AND NOISE SUPPRESSION UNIT (Boeing 707-420 installation): Located immediately aft of exhaust assembly. Consists of two ram-operated clam-shell doors which, when closed, direct jet stream toward front via cascade vanes in jet-pipe walls. Reverse thrust equals 50% normal forward thrust. Multi-lobe silencing nozzle fitted immediately aft of thrust reversal unit. No noise suppressor fitted to BAC VC10.

ENGINE MOUNTING (wing): Two trunnions, one each side of compressor intermediate casing. Single suspension point above nozzle box.

ENGINE MOUNTING (pod): Saddle mounts above compressor intermediate casing. Single suspension point above nozzle box.

FUEL SYSTEM: Backing pump delivers LP fuel through heater (hot air) and filter to dual variable-stroke multi-plunger HP pumps. Thence through flow control unit to burners. Lucas flow control unit gives proportional flow and is governed by throttle opening and air intake pressure. Acceleration control unit prevents surge during violent throttle handling. Max fuel pressure (RCo.42) 1,700 lb/sq in (119 kg/cm²).

FUEL GRADE: DERD 2482, American MIL F-5616-Avtur, or DERD 2486, American MIL F-5624C-Avtag.

OIL SYSTEM: Wet sump type. Oil circulated by one pressure and seven scavenge pumps.

OIL GRADE: Civil, Esso Turbo Oil 15 or 35; military, Esso Turbo Oil 35. Sump capacity 24 Imp pints (13·6 litres). Normal oil supply pressure (RCo.42) 40 lb/sq in (2·8 kg/cm²).

ACCESSORY DRIVES: Located in compressor intermediate casing, through bottom three webs to port, starboard and lower wheelcases. Port drive from HP shaft to oil pumps, scavenge pumps, dual fuel pumps, alternator drive and centrifugal breather. Starboard drive from HP shaft to air starter, HP tachometer generator, fuel backing pump, hydraulic pump and scavenge pump. Lower drive from LP shaft to LP tachometer generator.

STARTING (RCo.42): Rotax CT 1012 air turbine starter.

Rolls-Royce Conway RCo.43 turbofan engine with thrust reverser (21,800 lb = 9,888 kg st)

DIMENSIONS:
Length, with exhaust cone:

RCo.11/17	136·0 in (3,454 mm)
RCo.12	132·4 in (3,365 mm)
RCo.42/43	154·0 in (3,912 mm)

Diameter:

RCo.11/12/17	42·0 in (1,067 mm)
RCo.42/43	50·0 in (1,270 mm)

WEIGHTS (DRY):

RCo.11	4,544 lb (2,061 kg)
RCo.42	5,001 lb (2,269 kg)
RCo.43	5,101 lb (2,314 kg)

PERFORMANCE RATINGS:
Max T-O:

RCo.11	17,250 lb (7,830 kg) st
RCo.12	17,500 lb (7,945 kg) st at 9,980 rpm
RCo.17	20,600 lb (9,344 kg) st
RCo.42	20,370 lb (9,240 kg) st at 9,966 rpm
RCo.43	21,800 lb (9,888 kg) st at 10,172 rpm

Max cont rating:

RCo.12	14,625 lb (6,633 kg) st at 9,590 rpm
RCo.42	16,560 lb (7,511 kg) st at 9,575 rpm
RCo.43	17,900 lb (8,120 kg) st at 9,700 rpm

Typical cruise rating at 475 knots (547 mph; 880 km/h) at 36,000 ft (11,000 m):

RCo.12	4,625 lb (2,098 kg) st at 9,240 rpm
RCo.42	5,250 lb (2,380 kg) st at 9,250 rpm
RCo.43	5,345 lb (2,424 kg) st at 9,250 rpm

SPECIFIC FUEL CONSUMPTIONS:
At max T-O rating:

RCo.12 (uprated)	0·735
RCo.42	0·656

At max cont rating:

RCo.12 (uprated)	0·690
RCo.42	0·622
RCo.43	0·605

At typical cruise rating:

RCo.12 (uprated)	0·822
RCo.42	0·840
RCo.43	0·819

OIL CONSUMPTION:
Max (all marks) 0·9 pints/hr (0·51 litres/hr)

ROLLS-ROYCE GAZELLE

The Gazelle is a free-turbine engine which can be mounted in a horizontal, vertical or inclined attitude. It was designed and developed primarily as a helicopter engine and is in current use in the Westland Wessex and Belvedere helicopters.

Design of the Gazelle began in June 1954 and the first unit ran on 3 December 1955, developing its full specified output of 1,260 shp on 14 December 1955. MoA helicopter type approval at 1,650 shp was received in September 1959.

Current versions of the Gazelle are as follows:

Gazelle NGa.13 Mk 161. This has a one-hour rating of 1,410 shp and maximum continuous rating of 1,170 shp. Power-turbine gives opposite rotation to Mk 101 engine, for use in Westland Wessex Mk 1 helicopter with standard Sikorsky transmission. Shaft drive ratio 7 : 1.

Gazelle NGa.13/2 Mk 162. As NGa.13, but with higher turbine entry temperature. Fitted in Wessex Mk 31 helicopters of Royal Australian Navy. Potential one-hour rating of 1,575 shp, flat rated to 1,540 shp. Max cont rating of 1,330 shp.

Gazelle NGa.22 Mk 165. Potential one-hour rating of 1,790 shp, flat rated to 1,600 shp. Basically similar to NGa.13, but re-matched and with increased air mass flow to give higher ratings. Fitted in Wessex Mk 3 helicopter.

Gazelle NGa.22 Mk 165C. Identical to Mk 165, except for having generator instead of alternator. Used in Wessex Mk 31b helicopters of Royal Australian Navy.

TYPE: Free-turbine axial-flow turboshaft engine.

SHAFT DRIVE: Epicyclic reduction gear, incorporating hydraulic torquemeter, driven from free turbine. Ball and roller bearings. Ratios 6 : 1 (NGa.2) or 7 : 1 (all other marks).

AIR INTAKE: Radial type magnesium alloy casting consisting of two discs joined by six radial struts. Anti-icing by hot engine oil circulated through five of the struts and underside of casting, and by hot air through sixth strut. Intake carries row of hollow variable-incidence inlet guide vanes made of beryllium-copper sheet, heated by compressor-delivery air.

COMPRESSOR: Eleven-stage axial. Aluminium-bronze DTD 197A rotor blades secured by fir-tree roots to discs splined to shaft. Discs for stages 1 and 6-11 of Rex 448 stainless steel, remainder are made of aluminium alloy. Rotor shaft of S.106 stainless steel carried in front roller and rear ball bearings. Two-piece casing cast in DTD 5005 (Mks 101, 161 and 162) or RR.450 (Mks 165 and 165C) magnesium alloy, carrying aluminium-bronze (DTD 197A) stator blades mounted in half-rings bolted to casing. Pressure ratio (NGa.2) 6·25 : 1, (NGa.13) 5·90 : 1, (NGa.13/2) 6·10 : 1 (NGa.22) 5·9 : 1. Air mass flow (NGa.2) 16·4 lb (7·44 kg) per sec at 20,100 compressor rpm, (NGa.13) 15·8 lb (7·17 kg) per sec at 19,600 compressor rpm, (NGa.13/2) 16·1 lb (7·30 kg) per sec at 19,900 compressor rpm, (NGa.22) 17·0 lb (7·71 kg) per sec at 19,100 compressor rpm.

COMBUSTION CHAMBERS: Integral type chamber casing, with six flame tubes of Nimonic 75.

Rolls-Royce Gazelle Mk 165 free-turbine helicopter engine (flat-rated at 1,600 shp)

Manufactured by Lucas. One Simplex upstream-injection burner in each chamber. High-energy surface discharge igniter plugs in two chambers.

FUEL SYSTEM: Hydro-mechanical type, compensated for altitude with partial authority rotor speed governor (Mks 161, 162, 165 and 165C only). Fully-variable inlet guide vanes are operated from a fuel pump signal. Manufactured by Lucas.

FUEL GRADE: Normally DERD.2488, 2482, 2494 and 2486. In emergency, DERD.2485, DEF 2401-C and DEF 2402-B may be used, except on Mk 165C.

NOZZLE GUIDE VANES: One row of fixed cast guide vanes for each turbine stage. Material is X40 or G.67, depending on stage and rating.

TURBINE: Two independent axial turbines. Two-stage turbine drives compressor; single-stage turbine drives the reduction gear mounted behind it. First-stage turbine blade material is Nimonic 105 (Mks 101 and 161), Nimonic 108 (Mk 162) and G.67 (Mks 165 and 165C). Third-stage blade material is Nimonic 90 (all Marks). Blades attached by fir-tree roots. Turbine disc material is Rex 448 (compressor turbine) and Rex 535 (power turbine). Compressor turbine shaft is S.106 stainless steel. Power turbine disc and shaft are integral.

JET PIPE: Fixed quadrupled jet pipes of Nimonic 75.

ACCESSORY DRIVES: Through spur gears off lower end of compressor shaft in intake casing. Drive passes through one of radial struts to gear train on upper side of casing, for fuel pump, oil pumps, oil cooler fan (Mks 101, 161 and 162 only) centrifugal breather, tachometer and hydraulic pump (Mks 161, 162, 165 and 165C). On the lower side of the casing, spur gears drive a generator (Mks 161 and 162). Bevel gears drive the generator of the Mk 165C or the CSD and alternator of the Mk 165.

LUBRICATION SYSTEM: Dry sump type, with gear-type pumps. Normal oil supply pressure 80 lb/sq in (5·62 kg/cm²). Oil is fan cooled (Mks 101 and 161), fuel cooled (Mks 165 and 165C) or fuel and fan cooled (Mk 162).

OIL SPECIFICATION: DERD.2487.

MOUNTING: Three struts to pads on main support plate between compressor and combustion chambers. Engine torque reaction mounting on reduction casing.

STARTING: AEI iso-propyl-nitrate starter type QRT12/C3, mounted adjacent to compressor (Mks 101 and 161). Rotax combustion/air starter type CT.0821 (Mks 162, 165 and 165C).

DIMENSIONS:

Overall length	75 in (1,905 mm)
Max diameter	42·5 in (1,080 mm)

WEIGHT (DRY):

NGa.2	928 lb (421 kg) + 2½%
NGa.13	940 lb (426 kg) + 2½%
NGa.22	884 lb (401 kg) + 2½%

PERFORMANCE (nominal):
Max contingency rating (2½ min):

NGa.2	1,610 shp at 3,000 output shaft rpm

Inter contingency rating or one-hour rating:

NGa.2	1,430 shp at 3,000 output shaft rpm
NGa.13	1,410 shp at 2,500 output shaft rpm
NGa.13/2	1,575 shp at 2,500 output shaft rpm
NGa.22	1,600 shp at 2,570 output shaft rpm

Max cont rating:

NGa.2	1,175 shp at 3,000 output shaft rpm
NGa.13	1,170 shp at 2,500 output shaft rpm
NGa.13/2	1,330 shp at 2,500 output shaft rpm
NGa.22	1,400 shp at 2,570 output shaft rpm

SPECIFIC FUEL CONSUMPTIONS:
At max contingency (2½ min) rating:

NGa.2	0·70 lb (0·317 kg)/shp/hr

At inter contingency or one-hour rating:

NGa.2	0·71 lb (0·322 kg)/shp/hr
NGa.13	0·71 lb (0·322 kg)/shp/hr
NGa.13/2	0·685 lb (0·310 kg)/shp/hr
NGa.22	0·68 lb (0·308 kg)/shp/hr

At max cont rating:

NGa.2	0·74 lb (0·336 kg)/shp/hr
NGa.13	0·74 lb (0·336 kg)/shp/hr
NGa.13/2	0·705 lb (0·320 kg)/shp/hr
NGa.22	0·69 lb (0·313 kg)/shp/hr

OIL CONSUMPTION:
Max consumption 1 pint (0·57 litre)/hr

ROLLS-ROYCE DART

Although the design of the Dart began in 1945 the engine has been continuously developed to meet the requirements of civil operators, and the latest versions give over 3,000 eshp. The 5,000th production Dart was completed by Rolls-Royce in January 1967.

In addition to the large number of new aircraft powered by the Dart, General Dynamics' Convair Division and Rolls-Royce offer a turboprop engine modernisation service for twin-engined Convair-Liner transports, based on re-engining the aircraft with two Dart RDa.10. Details can be found under the General Dynamics entry in the US "Aircraft" section.

Ratings, weights and dimensions of current versions are given in the table on page 736.

TYPE: Single-shaft centrifugal-flow turboprop engine.

REDUCTION GEAR: Double reduction gearing with helical high-speed train and final helical gear drive. The two gear trains connected by three layshafts. High-speed pinion driven by an inner shaft system bolted directly onto turbine discs. All gears and propeller shaft carried in roller or ball bearings. Bevel gears from one of the layshafts provide drives to fuel and oil pumps and propeller controller unit. Bevel gear and engaging mechanism on pinion shaft provide drive from starter motor.

AIR INTAKE: Circular intake with annular duct leading to impeller eye of first-stage compressor. Oil tank around intake is cast integral with casing. Secondary air intake supplies air to oil cooler mounted on top of casing.

COMPRESSOR: Two-stage centrifugal-flow compressor. Each impeller has nineteen vanes and steel rotating guide vanes. Mass air flow at maximum rpm 20·5 lb (93 kg)/sec at 5·5 : 1 (RDa.6); 23·5 lb (10·66 kg)/sec at 5·62 : 1 (RDa.7); 27 lb (12·25 kg)/sec at 6·35 : 1 (RDa.10 and 12) pressure ratios respectively.

COMBUSTION CHAMBERS: Seven straight-flow combustion chambers. Flame tubes with fuel atomisers in front end of each tube for downstream injection. High-energy igniter plugs in Nos. 3 and 7 chambers.

FUEL SYSTEM: Single multi-plunger variable-stroke injection pump delivers fuel to burners through flow control unit, which incorporates a filter, throttle valve, shut-off cock and barometric pressure control. Operation of control unit is function of intake pressure and throttle valve pressure drop, thus determining fuel/air ratio for all engine operating conditions. RDa. 10 and 12 have duple fuel system, with pressures of 325 lb/sq in (22·85 kg/cm²) at idle and 900 lb/sq in (63·28 kg/cm²) at T-O. In all other versions, fuel pressure at burners varies from 40 lb/sq in (2·81 kg/cm²) at idling speed to 1,200 lb/sq in (70·3 kg/cm²) at maximum power. Automatically-progressive injection of water/

methanol used to restore take-off power under high ambient temperature conditions. System inter-connected mechanically with throttle lever to ensure that it can only be used at take-off rpm. Fuel filter de-icing by hot air from compressor. Hot-air gate valve fitted to bottom engine mounting.

TURBINE: Two-stage (RDa.3 and 6) or three-stage (RDa.7, 10 and 12) axial-flow turbine. In RDa.3 and 6, the two discs are coupled by a single large annular unit co-axial with single shaft which forms direct drive to compressor. In RDa.7, 10 and 12 first and second stage discs are bolted together by five bolts and all three by further five, while the drive shaft is divided, with inner shaft connecting turbine with reduction gear and outer shaft with compressor. All blades of Nimonic alloy and secured on discs by "fir-tree" type serrated roots.

EXHAUST UNIT: Propeller thrust line co-axial with engine main shaft but exhaust unit has a slight inclination to suit installation. Unit comprises an outer shell which supports an inner cone on three struts enclosed in aerofoil-section fairings to reduce turbulence and straighten gas flow at nozzle. Maximum jet pipe temperature 1,202°F (650°C).

ACCESSORY DRIVES: An accessory gear-box drive is taken from the main-shaft centre-coupling immediately behind compressor through a train of gears to a housing on top of intermediate casing.

LUBRICATION: Entirely self-contained. Integral oil tank (total capacity 25 pints = 14 litres) feeds engine via standpipe and feathering pump through tank base, to ensure feathering possible even after prolonged system oil leak. Gear pump supplies oil to all bearings and reduction-gear jets at nominal pressure of 30 lb/sq in (2·10 kg/cm²) and at nominal flow of 460 Imp gallons (2,091 litres) per hour. Combined delivery from four scavenge pumps returned to tank via oil-cooler on top of intake casing. Pressure and scavenge pumps in single housing and driven by common shaft.

CONTROLS: Only two cockpit controls, a throttle lever for varying power and a high-pressure

The 3,025 ehp Rolls-Royce Dart RDa.10/1 turboprop engine

cock for stopping engine. Throttle valve is interconnected with the propeller controller and high-pressure cock is linked with propeller feathering controls. Blades may be feathered by moving shut-off cock lever past the closed position; depression of an unfeathering button returns blades to fine pitch. Certain Viscount aircraft feature automatic selection into zero pitch, available with the aircraft weight on the landing gear. All other aircraft feature automatic cancellation of ability to come below flight fine pitch when the throttles are advanced to max power with gust locks removed, which is normal for take-off. On landing it is necessary to select manually removal of flight fine stop to permit blades to move down to zero pitch.

MOUNTING: Four feet are provided at 90° on the horizontal and vertical centre-lines of compressor casing, although only three need be

used. Bottom foot for hot-air gate valve. No rear mounting is required, but jet pipe if used requires separate mounting in airframe.

DIMENSIONS, WEIGHTS AND PERFORMANCE: See Table.

ROLLS-ROYCE TYNE

The Rolls-Royce Tyne is an advanced twin-spool high-compression turboprop engine which powers the BAC Vanguard, Canadair Forty Four, Short Belfast military transport, Breguet Atlantic maritime reconnaissance aircraft and Transall C-160 military transport.

The Tyne first ran in April 1955 and began its flight testing in the summer of 1956 in the nose of an Avro Lincoln flying test-bed. It entered service in the Vanguard and Canadair Forty Four in 1961.

The following versions of the Tyne have been produced (see next page).

ROLLS-ROYCE DART TURBOPROP ENGINES

Mark Number	Take-off Guaranteed Minimum Power	Cruising Specific Fuel Consumption (345 mph = 555 kmh) at 20,000 ft = 6,100 m)	Maximum Basic Dry Weight	Gear Ratio	Length (without jet pipe)	Diameter	Remarks
Mk.506 (RDa.3)	1,485 ehp (1,345 shp) at 14,500 rpm	0·645 lb/ehp/hr (0·296 kg/ehp/hr)	1,026 lb (465 kg)	0·106 : 1	95 in (2,413 mm)	37·9 in (963 mm)	Two-stage reduction gear. Standard engine in Viscount 700 Series. 10 ft (3·05 m) diameter propeller.
Mk.510 (RDa.6)	1,670 ehp (1,535 shp) at 14,500 rpm	0·635 lb/ehp/hr (0·288 kg/ehp/hr)	1,106 lb (502 kg)	0·093 : 1	97·6 in (2,480 mm)	37·9 in (963 mm)	For Viscount 700D and 800 Series with 10 ft (3·05 m) diameter propeller.
Mk.511 (RDa.6)	1,740 ehp (1,600 shp) at 14,500 rpm	0·635 lb/hr/ehp) (0·288 kg/he/ehp)	1,088 lb (494 kg)	0·086 : 1	97·6 in (2,480 mm)	37·9 in (963 mm)	For Fokker F.27 Friendship. Same as Mk 510 but 12 ft (3·66 m) diameter propeller.
Mk.514 (RDa.6)	1,860 ehp (1,710 shp) at 14,500 rpm	0·635 lb/hr/ehp (0·288 kg/hr/ehp)	1,114 lb (505 kg)	0·086 : 1	97·6 in (2,480 mm)	37·9 in (963 mm)	Powers Hawker Siddeley 748 Srs 1, With 12 ft (3·66 m) diameter propeller.
Mk.520 (RDa.7)	1,875 ehp (1,700 shp) at 15,000 rpm	0·578 lb/hr/ehp (0·262 kg/hr/ehp)	1,207 lb (548 kg)	0·093 : 1	97·6 in (2,480 mm)	37·9 in (963 mm)	Three-stage turbine, double shafting and new reduction gear. Powers Viscount 806.
Mk.525 (RDa.7/1)	1,985 ehp (1,800 shp) at 15,000 rpm	0·578 lb/hr/ehp (0·262 kg/hr/ehp)	1,227 lb (556 kg)	0·093 : 1	97·6 in (2,480 mm)	37·9 in (963 mm)	De-rated RDa.7/2. Powers Viscount 810 Series.
Mk.526, 527, 528, 530 and 531 (RDa.7/2)	2,100 ehp (1,910 shp) at 15,000 rpm	0·578 lb/hr/ehp (0·262 kg/hr/ehp)	1,235 lb (560 kg)	0·093 : 1	97·6 in (2,480 mm)	37·9 in (963 mm)	Mk 526 for HS Argosy 100 (11 ft 6 in = 3·50 m propeller). Mk 527 for HP Herald (12 ft 6 in = 3·81 m propeller). Mk 528 alternative engine for Fokker Friendship and Fairchild F-27 (11 ft 6 in = 3·50 m propeller). Mk 530 for Viscount 833 (10 ft 0 in = 3·05 m propeller). Mk 531 for HS 748 Srs 2 (12 ft 0 in = 3·66 m propeller).
Mk.529 (RDa.7)	2,180 ehp (1,990 shp) at 15,000 rpm	0·578 lb/hr/ehp (0·262 kg/hr/ehp)	1,235 lb (560 kg)	0·093 : 1	97·6 in (2,480 mm)	37·9 in (963 mm)	Powers Grumman Gulfstream and Fairchild Hiller FH-227. (11 ft 6 in = 3·50 m propeller).
Mk.532 (RDa.7L)	2,280 ehp (2,080 shp) at 15,000 rpm	0·578 lb/hr/ehp (0·262 kg/hr/ehp)	1,237 lb (561 kg)	0·093 : 1	97·6 in (2,480 mm)	37·9 in (963 mm)	Up-rated RDa.7, powers HS 748, Friendship and Argosy 222.
Mk.102 (RDa.8)	2,690 ehp (2,470 shp) at 15,000 rpm	0·578 lb/hr/ehp (0·262 kg/hr/ehp)	1,237 lb (561 kg)	0·093 : 1	97·6 in (2,480 mm)	37·9 in (963 mm)	Powers HS Argosy C. 1.
Mk.550 (RDa.8)	2,450 ehp (2,250 shp) at 15,000 rpm	0·578 lb/hr/ehp (0·262 kg/hr/ehp)	1,237 lb (561 kg)	0·093 : 1	97·6 in (2,480 mm)	37·9 in (963 mm)	Powers HS 748 Model 228.
Mk.542 (RDa.10)	3,025 ehp (2,750 shp) at 15,000 rpm	0·556 lb/hr/ehp (0·252 kg/hr/ehp)	1,366 lb (620 kg) or 1,377 lb (625 kg)	0·0775 : 1	99·49 in (2,527 mm)	37·9 in (963 mm)	Powers NAMC YS-11 and Convair 600.
Mk.201 (RDa.12)	3,245 ehp (2,970 shp) at 15,000 rpm	0·556 lb/hr/ehp (0·252 kg/hr/ehp)	1,387 lb (629 kg)	0·0775 : 1	99·49 in (2,527 mm)	37·9 in (963 mm)	Powers HS Andover C. 1.

RTy.1. Rated at 4,785 ehp minimum for take-off. Cruising specific fuel consumption 0·405 lb (0·184 kg)/ehp/hr.

RTy.11. Rated at 5,325 ehp minimum for take-off. Cruising specific fuel consumption 0·384 lb (0·175 kg)/tehp/hr.

RTy.12. Rated at 5,500 ehp. For Short Belfast (Mk 101) and Canadair 400/CL-44J and CL-44-D (Mk 515/10).

RTy.20. In production by Hispano Suiza (France), MTU (Germany) and FN (Belgium) to power Breguet 1150 Atlantic (Mk 21) and Transall C-160 (Mk 22). Mk 22 engine completed 150-hour type test at T-O rating of 6,100 ehp (5,665 shp) in January 1963.

The following details refer specifically to the Tyne RTy.20, but are generally applicable to all versions:—

TYPE: Two-spool axial-flow turboprop.

REDUCTION GEAR: Double reduction gearing by compound epicyclic train. High-speed pinion driven from forward end of LP shaft with final drive through planet wheel carrier integral with propeller shaft. Ratio 0·064 : 1. Shaft carried in one set of ball bearings and one set of roller bearings. Fixed annulus.

AIR INTAKE: Annular intake surrounds reduction gear housing. Integrally cast in magnesium alloy, with seven hollow support struts. Oil tank of annular form made up by rear wall of air intake casing and fabricated steel shell. Anti-icing by hot oil circulated through struts and by hot air tapped from HP compressor. Electrical de-icing of cowling surrounding intake.

LP COMPRESSOR: Six-stage axial-flow type. Made up from six steel discs, of which 1st (stage 0) disc is integral with shaft and remaining five discs splined to shaft. The 216 light alloy rotor blades are unshrouded and fixed to discs by single pin fixing. Inlet guide vanes and stage 0 stator blades of fabricated hollow construction to provide de-icing by means of air bled off HP compressor. The 431 steel stator blades are secured in casing by tongue and groove location. Steel LP casing in one piece. LP compressor mounted on front roller bearing and rear roller bearing.

INTERMEDIATE COMPRESSOR CASING: Intermediate casing between HP and LP compressors is aluminium alloy casting housing internal wheelcase. Bleed valve mounted on top of casing operates under approach conditions when LP and HP speeds are unmatched.

HP COMPRESSOR: Nine-stage axial-flow type. Made up from nine steel discs splined to shaft. Total of 575 rotor blades of titanium (first seven stages) and steel (last two stages). The 734 steel stator blades are fixed in rings by tongue and groove location. Stator blades are unshrouded. HP casing of centri-cast steel supports stator drum by bolted flanges. HP compressor mounted on front roller bearing and rear ball bearing. Rear bearing also takes thrust from inter-shaft ball bearing mounted slightly ahead of it. Pressure ratio 13·5 : 1. Air mass flow 46·5 lb (21·1 kg)/sec.

COMBUSTION CHAMBER: Ten flame tubes of Nimonic sheet mounted within annular chamber. Combustion system casings of steel. Flame

The 6,100 ehp Rolls-Royce Tyne RTy.20 turboprop engine

tubes contain double twin-flow co-axial burners. Flame tubes 3 and 8 (on engine horizontal centre-line) contain high-energy igniter plugs.

FUEL SYSTEM: Single multi-plunger variable-stroke HP pump delivers fuel to burners via flow control unit. Unit incorporates filter, throttle valves, shut-off cock and barometric pressure sensing device. Operation is a function of air intake pressure and throttle valve pressure drop. Hydro-mechanical governors control overspeeding of LP and HP sections of engine. Fuel anti-icing is by an oil-heated fuel heater between tank and LP pump. Max fuel supply pressure 1,250 lb/sq in (87·88 kg/cm²). Water/methanol is injected on to LP compressor through holes in stage 0 disc.

FUEL GRADE: MIL J5624D, Grade JP-4.

NOZZLE BOX: Centri-cast steel casing, containing 4 stages of nozzle guide vanes. The 50 HP vanes are air-cooled. The three LP stages have 60 hollow blades each. 20 thermocouples are fitted in the leading-edges of the first-stage LP nozzle guide vanes.

HP TURBINE: Single-stage. Steel disc attached to HP shaft by 8 taper bolts. 121 Nimonic blades attached by fir-tree roots. Blades air-cooled and tip-shrouded. HP turbine carried on roller bearing ahead of turbine. Shaft splined to HP compressor shaft. Gas temperature before turbine 1,000°C (1,273°K).

LP TURBINE: Three-stage. Steel discs bolted to each other by 8 bolts. Forward LP shaft is integral with first-stage disc. Stage 3 disc integral with rear LP shaft. All blades of Nimonic, secured by "fir-tree" roots, Stage 1 has 101 tip-shrouded blades. Stage 2 has 106 tip-shrouded blades. Stage 3 has 61 tip-shrouded blades. LP turbine is carried on roller bearings at rear and supported by plain bearing in HP shaft at front. Shaft splined to LP compressor shaft. Gas temperature after turbine 453°C.

EXHAUST UNIT: Fabricated construction, supporting tail bearing from nozzle box outer casing by ten struts with streamlined fairings.

ACCESSORY DRIVES: Internal wheelcase houses two drives. Port wheelcase drive from LP shaft, to accessory gearbox, LP tachometer and LP shaft governor. Starboard wheelcase drive from HP shaft to fuel pumps, HP tachometer, oil pumps and breather, mounting for starter motor.

LUBRICATION: Dry sump type with one pressure and six scavenge spur-gear pumps driven from HP shaft. Tank capacity 46 Imp pints (26·2 litres) including 16 Imp pints (9·1 litres) for feathering reserve. Thermostatically controlled air-cooled oil cooler. Oil supply pressure 45 lb/sq in (3·16 kg/cm²).

OIL GRADE: DERD 2487.

ENGINE MOUNTING: Four mounting feet on engine vertical and horizontal centre-lines, located immediately aft of oil tank.

STARTING: Air starter located on HP wheelcase.

DIMENSIONS (RTy.20):
Overall length   108·724 in (2,762 mm)
Max diameter (over nose cowling) approx
                  55 in (1,400 mm)

WEIGHTS:
RTy.1 Mk 506   2,275 lb (1,032 kg)
RTy.11 Mk 512   2,275 lb (1,032 kg)
RTy.12 Mk 515 (excluding oil coolers)
                2,177 lb (987 kg)
RTy.20 Mk 21, with accessories
                2,391 lb (1,085 kg)

PERFORMANCE RATINGS (RTy.20 Mk 21):
Nominal T-O rating 4,500 shp plus 1,200 lb
                (545 kg) st at 15,250 rpm
Max cont rating 3,995 shp plus 970 lb (440 kg) st
                at 13,500 rpm

SPECIFIC FUEL CONSUMPTION (RTy.20 Mk 21):
At T-O rating   0·485 lb (0·220 kg)/ehp/hr

OIL CONSUMPTION (RTy.20 Mk 21):
Max   1·5 Imp pints (0·85 litres)/hr

BRISTOL ENGINE DIVISION

DIRECTORS:
H. G. Conway, CBE, MA, FRAeS, CEng, FIMechE (Chairman and Managing Director)
F. M. Burns, FCA
Dr S. G. Hooker, CBE, FRS, DPhil, BSc, DIC, ARCSc, FRAeS, CEng, FIMechE (Technical Director)
C. J. Luby, MIPE, AFRAeS (Production Director)
A. D. Cawse, MA (Director—Concorde Engine Support Organisation)
D. E. Collett (General Manager, Bristol)
R. W. F. Farthing, BSc (Eng) (General Manager, Coventry)
L. Haworth, OBE, BSc(Eng), CEng, FIMechE, FRAeS (Director of Design)
P. F. Green, BSc (Director of Engineering)
R. C. Orford, MSc, CPA, CEng, FIEE (Commercial Director)
H. Stringer, OBE
G. F. Pitts, BSc(Eng) London, DLC(Hons), AFRAeS (Personnel and Administration Director)
J. W. H. Hiscocks BSc (Eng), MIMechE, (Director and General Works Manager)
G. M. Lewis, MA, CEng, FRAeS (Director of Advanced Engineering)
J. E. Phipps FCA (Director and Chief Accountant)
P. H. Young, BA, FRAeS (Director and Chief Engineer, Olympus 593)
G. T. Smith, BSc (Eng), CEng, FRAeS (Director of Marketing)

Comprising the former Aero Division of Bristol Siddeley Engines, the Bristol Engine Division has works at Bristol and Coventry. What is likely to become the division's largest programme is the RB.199 military reheat turbofan for the

MRCA aircraft. Other major BED responsibilities include the development of the Olympus 593 turbojet powering the Concorde, and the M45H turbofan powering the VFW 614, both engines in collaboration with SNECMA of France.

ROLLS-ROYCE BRISTOL VIPER

The current versions of the Viper turbojet are as follows:

Viper 11 (Mk 200 Series). Single-shaft seven-stage axial-flow compressor driven by a single-stage turbine. Air mass flow 44 lb/sec (20 kg/sec), type-tested at 2,500 lb (1,134 kg) st and powers the Jindivik Mk 3 target drone, BAC Jet Provost T.Mk 4 and Mk 5, Yugoslav Soko Galeb and Hindustan HJT-16 Mk II Kiran trainers.

The Mk 203 at a thrust of 2,700 lb (1,225 kg) st is used as a boost engine in the HS Shackleton Mk Mk 3.

Viper 22-1. A version of the Viper 11; as well as being produced at Bristol Engine Division, Coventry, is built under licence in Italy by Piaggio for the Aermacchi M.B.326 jet trainer and by the Atlas Corporation of the Republic of South Africa and Commonwealth Aircraft Corporation of Australia for use in the same basic aircraft.

Viper 500 Series. Development of the Viper 11 with increased air mass flow, achieved by the addition of an extra stage in front of the compressor. Major applications are in the Hawker Siddeley 125 and Piaggio-Douglas PD-808 executive transport aircraft (Mk 525, 526) and the BAC 167 Strikemaster (Mk 535), Aermacchi M.B.326G (Mk 540) and Soko Jastreb (Mk 531) training and light ground attack combat aircraft. The HS 125 entered service with Viper 521, rated at 3,120 lb (1,415 kg) st. HS 125s delivered since the beginning of 1966 are powered by Viper 522 engines rated at 3,365 lb

(1,527 kg) st. Soko Jastreb engines assembled in Yugoslavia under terms of Yugoslav Government agreement.

Viper 600 Series. Development of 500 Series for next generation of business jet aircraft and military trainers. Eight-stage axial-flow compressor driven by two-stage turbine in conjunction with a new design annular vaporising combustion chamber. Take-off rating 3,750 lb (1,701 kg) st for commercial applications and 4,000 lb (1,814 kg) st for military applications. Agreement signed with Fiat (Italy) in July 1969 providing for technical collaboration in design, development and ultimate production. Type approval scheduled for February 1971 for entry to service mid-1971.

More than 2,700 Vipers have been delivered to customers in thirty countries, twenty of which have chosen Viper-powered basic training aircraft.

The following details apply to the Viper 500 Series:

TYPE: Single-shaft axial-flow turbojet.

AIR INTAKE: Annular type at front of engine. Anti-icing by hot air tapped from compressor delivery. Air is piped to intake section and divided between nose bullet and guide vanes.

COMPRESSOR: Eight-stage axial-flow. Steel drum-type rotor with disc assemblies. Magnesium alloy casing. Stator blades bonded with resinous compound into diagonal slots in carrier rings: carrier rings attached to casing by means of T-slots. All stator blades and 1st, 2nd and 8th stage rotor blades of steel. Zero-stage and first-stage rotor blades attached by fir-tree roots: Stages 2-7 riveted. Pressure ratio 5·60. Air mass flow 52·7 lb (23·9 kg) sec.

COMBUSTION CHAMBER: Annular type with outer casing and flame tube of heat-resistant steel. Fuel and primary air fed into 24 hook-shape vaporiser tubes whose open ends point upstream and 24 secondary tubes. Electrical ignition.

FUEL GRADE: DERD.2482, 2486 or 2494.

TURBINE: Single-stage axial-flow. Heat-resistant steel disc, attached to shaft by Hirth coupling. Blades attached to disc by fir-tree roots and locking strips.

BEARINGS: Three main bearings: ball thrust type at forward end of compressor, roller bearings at delivery casing and at rear end of combustion chamber inner casing.

JET PIPE: Cone of heat-resisting steel rings butt-welded together.

ACCESSORY DRIVES: Gearbox bolted to bottom of air intake casing and driven from front of compressor by bevel gear shaft.

LUBRICATION SYSTEM: Self-contained, or components in engine pod or on airframe.

OIL SPECIFICATION: Castrol 98, Mobil 2, Esso TJ 15, Esso Extra 274 or Shell ASTO 390.

MOUNTING: Either spherical bearing trunnions each side, or single spherical bearing one side with brackets top and bottom, in each case at engine centre-section. Also jaw type or double spherical bearing at junction of compressor and intake casings, and at joint flange of combustion chamber and exhaust cone.

STARTING: 24-volt starter/generator.

DIMENSIONS:

Max casing diameter:	
All marks	24·55 in (624 mm)
Length overall:	
Viper 22-1	76·5 in (1,943 mm)
Viper 522	85 in (2,159 mm)
Viper 531-540	71·1 in (1,806 mm)
Length of engine to exhaust cone:	
Viper 522	68·72 in (1,746 mm)
Viper 601	71·1 in (1,806 mm)

WEIGHTS (complete engine-change unit):

Viper 22-1	710 lb (322 kg)
Viper 522	815 lb (370 kg)
Viper 531	790 lb (358 kg)
Viper 535-540	780 lb (354 kg)
Viper 601	830 lb (376 kg)

PERFORMANCE RATINGS:

T-O rating:	
Viper 22	2,500 lb (1,134 kg) st at 13,800 rpm
Viper 521	3,170 lb (1,440 kg) st at 13,760 rpm
Viper 522, 535, 540	
	3,365 lb (1,526 kg) st at 13,760 rpm
Viper 531	3,130 lb (1,420 kg) st
Viper 600 (commercial)	3,750 lb (1,700 kg) st
Viper 600 (military)	4,000 lb (1,814 kg) st
Max continuous rating:	
Viper 22	2,160 lb (980 kg) st at 13,100 rpm
Viper 522	2,550 lb (1,157 kg) st at 13,070 rpm
Viper 600 (commercial)	
	3,000 lb (1,361 kg) st at 13,070 rpm

SPECIFIC FUEL CONSUMPTIONS:

Viper 22	1·07
Viper 535, 540	1·009
Viper 22-6	1·07
Viper 531	1·06
Viper 600	0·94

OIL CONSUMPTION:

All versions	1 pint (0·57 litres)/hr

ROLLS-ROYCE BRISTOL ORPHEUS

The Orpheus is a single-spool turbojet engine initiated by Bristol in December 1953 as a private venture. Current versions are as follows:

Orpheus 700 Series

The first of this series was type-tested in November 1956 at a rating of 4,520 lb (2,050 kg) st and with improved altitude performance. The Mk 701, for the HS Gnat fighter, is in service with the air forces of India and Finland and has operated successfully in tropical conditions with air temperatures up to 43°C and 80 per cent humidity, and in sub-arctic conditions at temperatures as low as —34°C. The Mk 701 has been fitted to the Fairchild C-119 transport aircraft of the Indian Air Force in Jet-Pak form as a boost engine.

The Mk 703, rated at 4,850 lb (2,200 kg) st is in service with the Indian Air Force in the Hindustan HF-24 Marut fighter. In all the Indian applications the engine is built under licence at Bangalore, India, by Hindustan Aeronautics Limited (HAL).

Orpheus 800 Series

The first of this series was type-tested in May 1957 at 4,850 lb (2,200 kg) st and at a thrust-weight ratio of 5·9 : 1, the highest figure for any turbojet at that time. The Mk 801 is identical to the 701/703 except for an increased capacity fuel pump and is used in the early Fiat G91s. The Mk 803, rated at 5,000 lb (2,270 kg) st, replaced the Mk 801 in the Fiat G91 and differs mainly in improvements to the compressor. This series engine is built under licence by Fiat in Italy and Klockner-Humboldt-Deutz for the G91 aircraft of the Italian and German Air Forces.

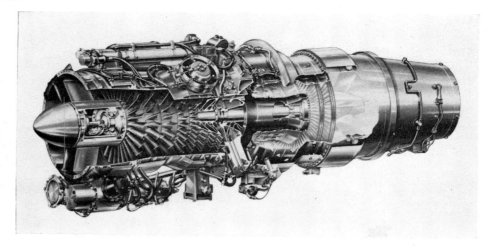

Photograph and (above) cutaway drawing of the Rolls-Royce (Bristol Engine Division) Viper 600 turbojet (3,750-4,000 lb = 1,701-1,814 kg st)

The Mk 805, rated at 4,000 lb (1,814 kg) st, powers the Japanese Fuji TIF2 Trainer.

Orpheus 101

This engine is similar to the 800 series but has an improved turbine and is fully anti-iced. Initially rated at 4,230 lb (1,916 kg) st but subsequently increased to 4,520 lb (2,045 kg) st by increased rpm. It is in service in Gnat trainers of RAF Training Command.

A description of the Orpheus 803 was given in the 1967-68 *Jane's*.

DIMENSIONS:

Diameter	32·4 in (823 mm)
Length:	
Orpheus 701, 703	73·0 in (1,854 mm)
Orpheus 801, 803, 805	75·45 in (1,916 mm)
Orpheus 101	75·50 in (1,919 mm)

WEIGHTS (DRY):

Orpheus 701	860 lb (390 kg)
Orpheus 801, 803, 805	902 lb (409 kg)
Orpheus 101	920 lb (417 kg)

SPECIFIC FUEL CONSUMPTIONS:

At max rating:	
Orpheus 701	1·00
Orpheus 801, 803	1·08
Orpheus 101	1·06

ROLLS-ROYCE BRISTOL/SNECMA M45H

This joint design of turbofan by Rolls-Royce Bristol Engine Division and SNECMA is being developed to power the VFW 614 feederliner. A detailed description of the M45H is given in the International section on page 719.

ROLLS-ROYCE BRISTOL OLYMPUS

The Olympus was the first British turbojet engine of the "two-spool" type. It entered production in 1953 for the Hawker Siddeley Vulcan bomber. The latest supersonic versions are suitable for operation at speeds up to Mach 2·05 at ISA.

Olympus engines equipped with fully-variable reheat have completed a considerable amount of running at thrusts of the order of 38,000 lb (17,237 kg) st.

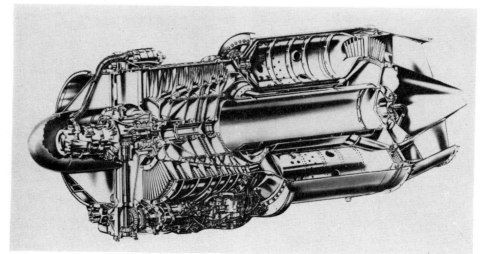

Cutaway drawing of the Rolls-Royce (Bristol Engine Division) Orpheus 800 Series turbojet (5,000 lb = 2,270 kg st)

Versions of the Olympus are as follows:

100 Series. The Mk 101 was the first member of the Olympus family to to into production and at a take-off thrust of 11,000 lb (4,990 kg) st entered service in the Vulcan B. Mk 1 in July 1956. The addition of an extra stage in front of the LP compressor, together with higher operating speed and temperatures, led to the Mk 102 and Mk 104 with take-off thrust increased to 13,500 lb (6,124 kg) st, which also entered service in the Vulcan B. Mk 1. The earlier engines were converted to the Mk 104 standard at overhaul at relatively small cost.

The Olympus 100 series is no longer in service.

Mk 201. A redesigned engine having a five-stage LP compressor and seven-stage HP compressor as with the 100 series, each driven by a single-stage turbine. With a take-off rating of 17,000 lb (7,710 kg) st entered service in the Vulcan B. 2 in July 1960.

The current engine is the Mk 202, and differs from the earlier 201 only in the venting and engine starting systems.

Mk 301. Developed from the 200 series by the addition of an extra stage in front of the LP compressor and at a take-off thrust of 20,000 lb (9,072 kg) st entered service in the Vulcan B. 2 in May 1963. Both 202 and 301 engines are currently in service.

Olympus 593. This engine is being developed jointly by Bristol Engine Division of Rolls-Royce and SNECMA as the power plant for the Concorde supersonic airliner. All available details can be found in the International section, on pages 719-720.

The following data refer to the Olympus 301 but with exception of the number of LP compressor stages and intake support struts will essentially apply to the 200 series.

TYPE: Axial-flow two-spool turbojet.

AIR INTAKE: One-piece magnesium-zirconium casting with 12 radial struts supporting housing for front main bearings. Houses ring of steel inlet guide vanes.

LP COMPRESSOR: Six-stage axial-flow type, made up of six aluminium alloy rotor discs (aluminium blades), five spacer rings, the rotor driving shaft and rotor tail shaft. Compressor driving shaft secured by its integral flange to rear of rotor bolts passing through discs Nos. 4 and 5. Rotor tail shaft splined into rear of driving shaft. Compressor blades secured in discs by fir-tree roots. Casing is a light alloy casting in two sections, split on a horizontal centre-line. Four rows of stator blades (first three in steel) are retained in casing by dove-tail roots.

INTERMEDIATE CASING: Light alloy casting carrying rear LP compressor and front HP compressor bearing, LP exit guide blades and HP entry guide blades. Mounting faces for accessories provided on this casing in two groups.

HP COMPRESSOR: Seven-stage axial-flow type. Construction similar to that of LP compressor but with steel widely used rather than light alloy. The two-piece stator casing, stator blades, rotor discs, and blades are all of steel. Rotor blades are mounted by fir-tree roots in the seven discs, between which are bolted six spacer rings, the whole assembly being contained between the front rotor shaft and the rear rotor centre. Front rotor shaft, carrying compressor front bearing, is bolted to stages 1 and 2. Rear rotor centre, which carries double thrust bearing, bolted to No. 6 spacer ring and No. 7 rotor disc. The cast steel casing is split on the horizontal centre-line. Seven rows of stator blades retained in casing by dove-tail roots.

DELIVERY CASING: Inner and outer casings of welded steel, joined by eight radial struts. Inner wall supports rear bearing of HP compressor. Outer wall carries main engine mounting trunnions.

COMBUSTION CHAMBER: Cannular type, with inner and outer casings forming an annular space which contains eight flame tubes. Outer casing, split along the horizontal centre-line for easy access to flame tubes, is fitted between the delivery casing rear flange and the front flange of the LP turbine casing. When assembled, the outer casing encloses the flame tubes, turbine entry duct, HP turbine stator and HP turbine casing.

FUEL SYSTEM: High-pressure swashplate-type pump feeds duplex burners via air/fuel ratio control, full-range flow control and flow distributor. Governors are provided to limit maximum rotational speed and to control cruising rotational speed.

HP TURBINE: Single-stage. Rotor blades have shrouded tips and are attached to discs by fir-tree roots. Stator blades are precision cast in segments of four and mounted in the sheet steel turbine entry duct, which also supports the downstream end of the flame tubes and is bolted to the HP turbine stator support cone.

LP TURBINE: Single-stage, of similar construction to HP turbine. LP stator blades are fixed at inner ends to an inter-stage seal.

JET PIPE: Fixed type.

ACCESSORY DRIVES: Accessories are mounted in two groups on intermediate casing. One group is driven from LP compressor. Other group, driven from HP compressor, includes fuel pump, oil pressure and scavenge pumps, constant-speed drive and hydraulic pump.

LUBRICATION SYSTEM: Closed system. Main pressure pump feeds bearings through calibrated orifices. Gravity feed to sump, with scavenge pump feed-back, via fuel-cooled oil cooler, to main oil tank.

MOUNTING: Three-point suspension, with trunnions on each side of the HP delivery casing and front mounting bracket at top of LP compressor casing.

STARTER: Rotax air starter on starboard side of intermediate casing.

DIMENSIONS:
Max diameter:

Mk 201	41·75 in (1,060 mm)
Mk 301	44·5 in (1,130 mm)

Length:

Mk 201	126·4 in (3,210 mm)
Mk 301	128·0 in (3,255 mm)

WEIGHTS (DRY):

Mk 201	4,065 lb (1,844 kg)
Mk 301	4,290 lb (1,946 kg)

PERFORMANCE RATINGS:
Max rating:

Mk 201	17,000 lb (7,710 kg) st
Mk 301	20,000 lb (9,072 kg) st

SPECIFIC FUEL CONSUMPTION (max rating):

Mk 301	0·815

ROLLS-ROYCE BRISTOL PEGASUS

The Pegasus is a turbofan engine initially developed under the NATO Mutual Weapons Development Programme. It has found its first application in the Hawker Siddeley P.1127 Kestrel and Harrier V/STOL strike aircraft.

Originally the Pegasus combined major parts of the compressor, combustion system and turbine of the Orpheus turbojet with a new low-pressure assembly. The latter consists of a low-pressure turbine driving a front fan. As the fan and compressor rotate in opposite directions there is little resultant gyroscopic couple. The fan broke new ground in having no intake guide vanes, a feature since adopted on all the latest commercial fan engines.

The inboard portion of the fan functions as a supercharger for the compressor, as in other two-spool turbojets. The outboard portion drives a large mass flow of air through ducts on each side of the engine, whence the air is discharged through a pair of lateral nozzles. The hot gases from the rear of the engine are similarly discharged through lateral nozzles.

All four nozzles can be swivelled to divert the efflux vertically downward and so provide direct lift for VTOL operations, or forward for braking in flight, or to any intermediate position. This makes possible the design of single-engined high-performance VTOL aircraft and of multi-engined VTOL aircraft in which all engines are of the same type, with the whole of the installed thrust available for vertical take-off. Provision is made for tapping off air from the compressor for "puffer-pipe" jet stabilisation systems.

Use of swivelling nozzles also minimises the ground running problems of recirculation, debris

ingestion and ground erosion, which are a major difficulty with fixed lifting engines, because all ground running can be done with the exhaust discharging rearward. Taxying is normal, and a short forward roll at take-off, before the nozzles are deflected downward, ensures that dust and debris are left behind.

By varying the angle of the nozzles, an aircraft powered by the Pegasus can take off vertically or with a short run or with a conventional long run. This offers advantages when developing a new aircraft or training pilots in VTOL flight. In addition, the reserve of power in a normal runway take-off is sufficient for a very large overload.

The Pegasus turbofan ran for the first time in August 1959, and flight trials in the P.1127 prototypes began in October 1960.

The **Pegasus 3,** which powered prototype P.1127 aircraft, was rated at 14,000 lb (6,350 kg) st. The **Pegasus 5,** which powered the tri-partite V/STOL evaluation Kestrels and is fitted to the Dornier Do 31 V/STOL transport, is rated at 15,500 lb (7,030 kg) st. The **Pegasus 6,** with the service designation Mk 101 and rated at 19,000 lb (8,618 kg) st, is in production for RAF Hawker Siddeley Harrier GR. Mk 1 and T. Mk 2 aircraft. The Pegasus 6, which is derived from the Pegasus 5, successfully completed a 150-hr type test at its full design rating in October 1967. Production deliveries started in January 1968 and type approval was obtained ahead of schedule two months later. The Harrier GR.1 has been in RAF service since April 1969.

During 1968 bench running of the higher-thrust **Pegasus 10** started, with testing both at Pegasus 10 rating and at the 21,500 lb (9,752 kg) st rating of the **Pegasus 11.** The Pegasus 11 ran ahead of schedule in August 1969. This version is funded by the British government and is planned to complete type-approval in 1971. The increased thrust of the Pegasus 11 has been obtained by aerodynamic redesign of the fan and by raising the turbine entry temperature.

The Pegasus 11 is interchangeable with the Pegasus 101, and modification of engines from Mk 101 standard to Pegasus 11 standard, under the designation Mk 103 is straightforward. It is anticipated that all RAF Harriers will in due course have their engines modified to Mk 103 standard.

A continuing programme of development is underway further to increase thrust and reduce sfc. Growth to at least 25,000 lb (11,340 kg) st is planned. Additional thrust will be obtained at the front 'cold' nozzles by increasing the fan mass flow through a 2 in (50·8 mm) increase in fan diameter. At the 'hot' rear nozzles increased thrust is to be gained by further raising the turbine entry temperature and by improving component efficiency in the turbine and exhaust system. Improvements in sfc will be made by increasing the overall pressure ratio.

The Bristol Engine Division is also developing a method of reheat suitable for Pegasus-type engines. This system, called plenum chamber burning, consists of burning additional fuel in the cold air ducted to the front pair of nozzles, with a resulting increase in thrust for take-off, transonic acceleration and supersonic flight. The advantage of plenum chamber burning is that a smaller basic engine may be installed in a V/STOL aircraft to achieve a specified performance, with a consequent

Rolls-Royce Bristol Pegasus vectored-thrust turbofan

saving in weight and an improved specific fuel consumption under cruise conditions.

The following data apply specifically to the Pegasus 5:

TYPE: Moderate by-pass ratio vectored-thrust turbofan.

AIR INTAKE CASING: One-piece casting in ZRE magnesium-zirconium alloy.

LP COMPRESSOR: Three-stage overhung fan with snubber anti-vibration surfaces.

INTERMEDIATE CASING: Houses front fan bearing, accessory drives and HP compressor front bearing. All engine-driven accessories are mounted above this casing.

HP COMPRESSOR: Eight-stage compressor with titanium rotor blades throughout.

COMBUSTION SYSTEM: Annular, with low-pressure vaporising burner system.

FUEL SYSTEM: Hydro-mechanical system, comprising plunger pump, HP shut-off cock and overspeed governors.

TURBINES: Two-stage HP turbine and two-stage LP turbine. First stage HP blades are precision-cast and air-cooled by means of internal radial passages. Remaining three rotor stages have solid forged blades.

THRUST NOZZLES: Two steel cold front-thrust nozzles and two Nimonic hot thrust nozzles are actuated by duplicated air motors through system of shafts and chains. Vectored-thrust control is connected directly to the pilot's cockpit.

LUBRICATION SYSTEM: Self-contained, comprising pressure pump and three scavenge pumps, with fuel-cooled oil cooler.

MOUNTING: Conventional three-point suspension, with main trunnions on each side of delivery casing and tie link at rear of turbines.

STARTING: Twin-breech cartridge starter mounted on top of intermediate casing.

DIMENSIONS:
Length overall	98·84 in (2,510 mm)
Diameter, fan casing	48·05 in (1,220 mm)

WEIGHT:
Dry	2,780 lb (1,261 kg)

SPECIFIC FUEL CONSUMPTION:
At max rating	0·613

ROLLS-ROYCE BRISTOL THOR

The Thor was the first ramjet power unit to go into production in Europe, following many hundreds of firings of ramjet development vehicles. Engines of this type are fitted on the BAC Bloodhound surface to-air guided missile which entered service with the Royal Air Force in 1958 and also serves with the Air Forces of Australia, Switzerland, Singapore and Sweden.

Details of the final production Thor BT.3 are classified. The following description applies to an early version.

SMALL ENGINE DIVISION

DIRECTORS:
H. G. Conway, CBE, MA, FRAeS, CEng, FIMechE (Chairman)
J. E. B. Perkins, BSc, AFRAeS, DIC, ACGI, (Managing Director)
K. R. Davies, FRAeS (Director of Engineering)
F. W. Morley, BSc, FRAeS, CEng, FIMechE, MIProdE (Technical Director)
P. A. Norman, BSc, CEng, FIMechE, FRAeS, AMBIM (Marketing Director)
J. R. Thompson, CEng, MIProdE (Production Director)
G. J. Willey, FCA (Financial Controller)

Smallest of the three Rolls-Royce aero-engine divisions, the Small Engine Division is responsible for the design, development and production of all Rolls-Royce small turbines for use as primary power plants in helicopters and fixed-wing aircraft, as airborne APUs and air starters and in other applications. In addition, SED manufactures components of the Turboméca Turmo IIIC₄ and Astazou IIIN under the Anglo/French helicopter agreement. Turmo engines for SA 330 Pumas for the RAF are assembled and tested at Leavesden, the first having run there in February this year. The division anticipates sharing in a run of Astazou engines for the SA 341 Gazelle exceeding 1,000 engines. SED also has marketing rights for the Allison 250 turboshaft and turboprop in the UK and many other non-American countries, and overhauls and manufactures spare parts for the Goblin, Ghost and Gyron Junior turbojets, and the Gipsy, Cirrus and Bombardier light piston aero engines. The Division has works at Leavesden near Watford, Herts, and Hatfield, Herts.

ALLISON MODEL 250

By agreement between the Allison Division of General Motors Corporation and Rolls-Royce, the Small Engine Division is the main distributor for the Allison Model 250 turboshaft and turboprop for the UK and numerous other countries outside North America. The agreement gives Rolls-Royce responsibility for sales and service support in these areas. By January 1970, 340 Model 250 engines had been supplied by the Small Engine Division. The Division is also undertaking the overhaul of Model 250 engines.

A cut-away Rolls-Royce Bristol Thor BT.1 ramjet engine

There is a centre-body intake of the two-shock type, supported by three equi-spaced faired struts, followed by an annular diffuser leading to the combustion system. Behind it is a series of fuel injection rods each with two or three downstream nozzles, and combustion is stabilised by means of baffles. The parallel tailpipe terminates in a convergent/divergent final nozzle which is cooled by means of a ring of apertures surrounding the rear portion of the tail-pipe.

The Thor is designed for external pod mounting and has two mounting brackets, the rear mounting allowing for thermal expansion between the ramjet and the missile or aircraft. Fuel connections are made adjacent to the front mounting bracket.

The fuel system used with the Thor consists of an air-turbine-driven centrifugal pump, a fuel/air ratio control, and a Mach number control to reduce the fuel supply when the selected Mach number is exceeded.

Ignition is achieved by pyrotechnic flares. Complete reliability of ignition of the ramjet unit is essential in a missile or test vehicle which is accelerated from standstill to ramjet-operating speed by booster rockets, and this has been achieved.

A typical 16 in (400 mm) ramjet can develop an effective thrust horsepower at sea level which rises from approximately 25,000 hp (about 6,000 lb=2,720 kg net internal gauge thrust) at Mach 2·0 to about 130,000 hp (about 20,000 lb=9,070 kg net internal gauge thrust) at Mach 3·0.

Details of the Model 250 can be found under the "Allison" heading in the US section.

ROLLS-ROYCE/TURBOMÉCA ARTOUSTE

The Artouste is used widely as an auxiliary power unit in aircraft such as the Handley Page Victor Mk 2, Hawker Siddeley Trident, Canadair Forty Four, Short Belfast and BAC VC10 C.1 for RAF Air Support Command.

By January 1970, 81 commercial and 124 military Artouste APUs had been delivered.

TYPE: Single-shaft open-cycle air-bled turbo-compressor.

AIR INTAKE: Twin forward-facing, mounted at front of engine. Air bled through double-skinned main casing surrounding combustion chamber, from off-take on top of casing.

COMPRESSOR: Single-stage centrifugal.

COMBUSTION SYSTEM: Annular combustion chamber with centrifugal fuel injection.

FUEL SYSTEM: The aircraft main fuel system supplies fuel to an APU fuel system control unit. Fuel from the control unit passes via two torch igniter solenoid valves and a centrifugal cut-off valve to fuel inlet housing.

POWER TURBINE: Two-stage axial-flow turbine.

EXHAUST SYSTEM: Rearward duct tailored to suit aircraft installation.

REDUCTION GEAR: Reduction gearbox for alternator, with ratios available for 6,000 or 8,000 rpm output shaft speeds.

ACCESSORY DRIVES: Drives from rotor shaft are mounted on the upper and lower auxiliary gearboxes, being transmitted through a drive-shaft assembly bolted on to the front of the air intake casing. This assembly also provides the drive to the reduction gearbox. Together, the upper and lower auxiliary gearboxes drive the combined oil pump and filter unit, the starter motor and the fuel control unit.

LUBRICATION: Dry-sump type, including pressure pump, scavenge pump and filters.

STARTING: Electric starter.

DIMENSIONS:
Length (basic engine)	35·2 in (894 mm)
Diameter (maximum)	24·0 in (610 mm)

DRY WEIGHT:
Less accessories, instrumentation, etc	277 lb (125·6 kg)

Effective horsepower falls off with altitude and the same unit would deliver approximately 1,500 hp (about 600 lb=272 kg net internal gauge thrust) at Mach 1·6 at 40,000 ft and 28,000 hp (about 5,000 lb=2,270 kg net internal gauge thrust) at Mach 3 at the same altitude.

The specific consumption of such a power unit would decrease progressively between ground level and the tropopause, remaining constant above this height. At full thrust a specific fuel consumption (based on net internal thrust) of 2·5 would be expected at sea level, falling to 2·3 at the tropopause.

At reduced thrust, specially designed cruise engines can have a specific fuel consumption of between 1·5-1·7.

The Thor BT.2 has an overall diameter of 15·75 in (400 mm) and a length of 103·9 in (2,639 mm). Its thrust and that of the BT.3 may not be published, but the earlier Thor BT.1 was rated at 5,275 lb (2,393 kg) net internal gauge thrust at Mach 2 at sea level.

ROLLS-ROYCE BRISTOL ODIN

The Odin ramjet powers the Hawker Siddeley Sea Dart, which has been developed to meet a Royal Navy and NATO requirement for a medium-range guided weapons system for small warships. The ramjet forms an integral part of the missile body, and gives a longer range and better performance characteristics against fast-manoeuvring targets than a solid-rocket-powered missile. Details of the Odin are classified.

PERFORMANCE AND CONSUMPTION: Variable output shared between shaft power and air-bleed. At 0 shp max air bleed is 2·15 lb (0·98 kg)/sec at 52·5 lb/sq in (3·69 kg/cm²) with fuel consumption of 298 lb (135 kg)/hr. At 125 hp power take-off max air-bleed is 1·45 lb (0·66 kg)/sec at 54·8 lb/sq in (3·85 kg/cm²) with fuel consumption of 310 lb (140 kg)/hr.

ROLLS-ROYCE RS.360 (BS.360)

Under a contract from the Ministry of Technology, the Small Engine Division has designed and is developing a new 900 shp twin-spool free-turbine turboshaft known as the RS.360 (BS.360 when applied to the WG.13 helicopter). The BS.360 gas generator was run in July 1969 and the complete engine in September 1969. Under the designation BS.360-07, the engine is being developed to power the Westland WG.13 helicopter, as one of the three helicopter projects comprising the Anglo/French helicopter programme. The RS.360 is a compact lightweight high-performance engine, taking full advantage of R-R's turbine experience to produce a robust turboshaft which can be handled and maintained easily under service conditions. The full development programme, authorised in November 1969, involves SED in contracts worth about £10 million and extending until 1973.

Choice of a two-spool gas generator eliminates the necessity for variable-geometry components and therefore simplifies the control system. Conservative stressing and thermodynamic loading, and use of proven design and manufacturing techniques, are features which experience has shown to contribute to engine reliability.

The design concept of the engine is based upon seven major modules, each capable of being assembled, tested and released as interchangeable units for service use in the interest of reducing the operator's product-support commitments.

The nine main bearings each have labyrinth seals pressurised by LP compressor air which also cools the bearings and minimises heat transfer to the oil, and oil cooler and fan requirements.

Provision is made for in-flight and on-ground condition monitoring systems. Features include a torquemeter and tacho-generator for power checks, intrascopes to the LP compressor power turbine shaft, combustor and power turbine nozzle guide vanes, and a vibration meter on the power turbine casing.

At its initial rating of 900 shp, the RS.360 will enter service at a conservative power which, together with the use of turbine entry temperatures comparable with R-R's civil turbine experience, is intended to ensure ample margin for power growth.

The following description relates to the initial design of the BS.360-07 engine in front-drive configuration: the turboshaft has also been designed to provide alternative rear-end drive.

TYPE: Twin-spool free-turbine turboshaft.

AIR INTAKE: Annular forward facing.

SHAFT DRIVE: Compact single-stage double-helical reduction gear with rotating planet cage carried by ball bearing at front and roller bearing at rear. Reduction gear mounted within intake casing and driven by power turbine shaft via phase displacement type torquemeter. Gearbox comprises No. 1 module, and power turbine shaft with torquemeter No. 2 module.

LP COMPRESSOR: Four-stage axial unit with rotor carried by roller bearing at front and ball bearing at rear. Stator blades mounted direct in casing. Air intake casing and forward end of compressor casing supported by conical outer casing mounted off compressor intermediate casing. LP compressor and intake case comprise No. 3 module.

INTERMEDIATE CASING: Cast casing forming junction between LP and HP compressors. Carries accessory drive and wheelcase, and provides support for LP ball bearing and HP ball and roller bearings.

HP COMPRESSOR: Single-stage centrifugal unit with single-sided impeller having alternate inducer and radial vanes. Combined radial-and-axial diffuser feeds compressor delivery air to annular combustor. Overall pressure ratio 12·15 : 1.

COMBUSTION CHAMBER: Fully annular reverse-flow combustor with air-atomiser type fuel sprays supplied by external fuel manifold. High-energy ignition box mounted on power turbine/jet pipe case. Combustor outer casing extends forward to compressor conical structure, and rearwards to power turbine outer casing.

HP TURBINE: Single-stage axial unit close-coupled to HP impeller. Tip-shrouded rotor blades and air-cooled nozzle guide vanes based on R-R Dart turboprop technology. Roller bearing downstream of turbine disc carries rear of HP spool. Bearing supported by structure inboard of hollow LP nozzle guide vanes. HP spool (compressor and turbine) with compressor intermediate casing and combustor comprise No. 4 module.

LP TURBINE: Single-stage axial unit with tip-shrouded rotor blades, drives LP compressor. Roller bearing downstream of turbine disc carries rear of LP rotor. This bearing together with power turbine upstream roller bearing are supported by structure inboard of hollow power turbine stage-one nozzle guide vanes. LP turbine and main shaft comprises No. 6 module.

POWER TURBINE: Two-stage axial unit with tip-shrouded rotor blades Thick-section discs have integral stub shafts which abut with centre tie bolt forward to long, small-diameter drive shaft. Discs carried on upstream and downstream roller bearings, latter being supported by four cruciform struts in exhaust duct. Rear of power drive shaft drives output speed governor and overspeed fuel cut-off trip mechanism via spur and bevel gear train in exhaust cone. Power turbine and jet pipe form No. 7 module.

JET PIPE: Short length duct with casing extending forward to combustor rear casing. Four cruciform struts integral with exhaust cone.

ACCESSORY DRIVES: Bevel gear on front of HP compressor shaft drives accessory shaft extending through compressor intermediate casing to spiral bevel gear drive to accessory wheelcase mounted atop intermediate casing. Drives provided for starter generator, fuel pump, oil cooler fan and other accessories. Wheelcase forms No. 5 module.

FUEL SYSTEM: Plessey fuel system with fluidics circuit providing fully automatic control, and power matching for multi-engine installation. Also automatic restoration of power from 'good' engine in event of single engine failure.

LUBRICATION SYSTEM: Optional engine-mounted oil tank and cooler to provide self-contained system. Magnetic chip detectors fitted in each scavenge line.

DIMENSIONS:

Height overall	22·9 in (582 mm)
Width overall	21·7 in (551 mm)
Length overall	43 in (1,092 mm)

WEIGHT DRY:

Net	300 lb (136 kg)

PERFORMANCE RATINGS:

Max contingency (2½ minutes)	900 shp at 6,000 rpm
Max power (1 hour)	830 shp at 6,000 rpm
Max continuous	750 shp

Rolls-Royce BS.360-07 turboshaft engine rated at 900 shp, the version of the RS.360 series under development for the WG.13 helicopter

SPECIFIC FUEL CONSUMPTIONS:

Max contingency	0·489 lb (0·218 kg)/shp/hr
Max power	0·495 lb (0·221 kg)/shp/hr
Max continuous	0·505 lb (0·255 kg)/shp/hr

ROLLS-ROYCE GNOME

Gnome is the name given to the versions of the General Electric T58 shaft-turbine engine which Rolls-Royce has rights to manufacture in England. The first British-built engine ran for the first time on 5 June 1959.

The major difference between the Gnome and the T58 lies in the replacement of the Hamilton Standard fuel supply and control system by a Lucas fuel supply and metering system which receives control signals from an electrical computer designed and built by Hawker Siddeley Dynamics, together with other features to meet the more stringent British requirements. The main gearbox has been partially redesigned, and the materials, starter and ignition system, etc, are of British supply.

The Gnome is the standard power plant for the Westland Whirlwind HAR.Mk 9 and HAR.Mk 10 helicopters for the Royal Navy and Royal Air Force respectively. It powers the civil Westland S-55 Series 3, the Whirlwind HCC.Mk 12 and the S-55 Series 3A and 3Bs of the Ghanaian, Brunei and Brazilian air forces. The Gnome has also been supplied in quantity for the Agusta-Bell 204B and as an alternative power plant for the Boeing-Vertol 107 helicopters for the Royal Swedish Navy and Air Force.

A coupled version of the Gnome is in production for the Westland Wessex HC.Mk 2 for the RAF and Mk 4 of the Queen's Flight, HU.Mk 5 for the Royal Navy, Wessex 50 series, as supplied to Ghana, Iraq and Brunei, and civil Wessex 60 series helicopter. "Marinised" versions are fitted in the BHC SR.N3, SR.N5 and SR.N6 Hovercraft. Since 1967 the latest Gnome H.1400 has been in production for Sea King HAS. 1 helicopters of the Royal Navy.

Four versions of the Gnome turboshaft have been announced. as follows:

H.1000. Initial version, rated at 1,000 shp. Power plant for military Whirlwind HAR.Mk 9, HAR.Mk 10 and HCC.Mk 12, civil S-55 Series 3 and Agusta-Bell 204B. More than 370 Gnome H.1000 engines have been delivered.

H.1200. Uprated version, giving 1,250 shp. Used in Agusta-Bell 204B and Boeing-Vertol 107. Coupled version for Wessex Mks 2, 5, 50 series and 60 comprises two H.1200's driving through a coupling gearbox designed and manufactured by Rolls-Royce. Maximum potential output is 2,500 shp, but the Wessex transmission is limited to 1,550 shp at the rotor head. Should either engine be shut down the other will automatically increase power to the required output, up to the standard maximum H.1200 emergency rating of 1,350 shp. The ratio of the Wessex coupling gearbox is 7·476 : 1.

By January 1970, 723 Gnome H.1200 engines had been delivered for helicopter use, in addition to 70 for air-cushion vehicles.

H.1400. Based on the H.1200, with modified compressor to give increased mass air flow. Turbine diaphragm cooling redesigned to increase temperature capacity and life. Dimensions unchanged. Mounting pads identical to those of H.1200. This version is in production for the Westland Sea King HAS.1 helicopter.

By January 1970 more than 90 Gnome H.1400 engines had been delivered.

The following description refers specifically to the H.1200 turboshaft version.

TYPE: Axial-flow free-turbine turboshaft engine.

AIR INTAKE: Annular forward-facing. Centre housing carrying front main bearing supported by four radial struts. Struts and inlet guide vanes anti-iced with hot compressor bleed air and oil drainage.

COMPRESSOR: Ten-stage axial. Controlled variable incidence for inlet guide vanes and first three rows of stator blades. Integral spool-type rotor assembly with rotor blades secured in dove-tail root fittings. Rotor splined to shaft which is carried on roller bearings at front and ball bearing at rear. Main steel casing split along horizontal centre-line, with stator blades brazed in carrier rings. Pressure ratio 8·12 : 1. Mass air flow 12·55 lb (5·70 kg) per second. A short-length casing interposed between compressor and combustor has radial vanes across compressor outlet to carry main centre bearing.

COMBUSTION SYSTEM: Straight-through annular chamber with outer casing split along horizontal centre-line. Sixteen Simplex-type fuel injectors, eight on each of two sets of manifolds. One Lodge capacitor-discharge high-energy igniter plug.

FUEL SYSTEM: Lucas hydro-mechanical units, comprising variable-stroke multi-plunger pump, flow control unit and throttle working in conjunction with electric control computer and actuator. Also Lucas-manufactured Dynamic Filters type centrifugal filter.

FUEL GRADE: DER 2486, 2494 and 2498.

GAS-PRODUCER TURBINE: Two-stage, coupled to compressor shaft by conical shaft. Extended-root blading with fir-tree attachments. A short-length intermediate casing interposed between gas-producer and power turbines carries power-turbine nozzle guide vanes.

POWER TURBINE: Single-stage free turbine. Extended-root blading with fir-tree attachments. Rotor disc integral with output shaft and overhung from rear on roller bearing on downstream face of disc and ball bearing at rear of shaft. Complete assembly mounted inside exhaust ducting. Power turbine drives reduction gearing via coupling and short shaft.

EXHAUST SYSTEM: Curved exhaust ducting arranged to suit individual applications.

REDUCTION GEAR: Optional double-helical gear providing reduction from nominal 19,500 rpm power turbine speed to either 6,000 or 6,600 rpm at output shaft. Provision for fore and aft power take-off in three positions—top, port and starboard.

ACCESSORY DRIVES: Quill shaft drive through lower intake strut. Fuel and lubrication systems mounted beneath compressor casing. Power take-off shaft up to 100 shp on primary reduction gear casing for separate accessories gear-box.

LUBRICATION: Fully scavenged gear pumps. Serck oil cooler.

OIL SPECIFICATION: Military, DEng RD 2487, Castrol 205 GTO and Esso Turbo Oil 2380. Civil as follows: Aero Shell Turbine Oil 750 and 300, Esso Extra Turbo Oil 274, Esso Aviation Turbo Oil 35, Esso Turbo Oil TJ15, Esso Turbo Oil 35, Castrol 98 and Castrol 98 (UK) gas turbine oil.

MOUNTING: Three forward mounting faces on intake casing. Two rear mounting faces on upper portion of primary gear casing. When no reduction gear fitted, rear mounting face on engine centre-line between branches of bifurcated turbine exhaust duct.

STARTING: Rotax electric starter in nose bullet.

DIMENSIONS:

Length:
H.1000, H.1200 H.1400 (all ungeared)
54·8 in (1,392 mm)
Coupled H.1200 (Wessex) 68·8 in (1,747 mm)

Max height:
H.1000, H.1200, H.1400 (all ungeared)
21·6 in (549 mm)
Coupled H.1200 (Wessex) 40·6 in (1,031 mm)

Max width:
H.1000, H.1200 (ungeared) 18·2 in (462 mm)
H.1400 (ungeared) 22·7 in (577 mm)
Coupled H.1200 (Wessex) 41·7 in (1,059 mm)

WEIGHTS (DRY):
H.1000 (ungeared) 296 lb (134 kg)
H.1200 (ungeared) 314 lb (142 kg)
H.1400 (ungeared) 329 lb (149 kg)
Reduction gearbox 114 lb (51·7 kg)
Coupled H.1200 with coupling gearbox:
for Wessex 930 lb (421·8 kg)
for AB 205 818 lb (371 kg)

PERFORMANCE RATINGS (at free-turbine shaft, at nominal 19,500 free-turbine rpm):

Max contingency rating (2½ min; multi-engine aircraft only):
H.1200 1,350 shp
H.1400 1,500 shp

Max one-hour rating (single engine).
H.1000 1,000 shp
H.1200 1,250 shp
H.1400 1,400 shp

Max cont rating:
H.1000 900 shp
H.1200 1,050 shp
H.1400 1,250 shp

SPECIFIC FUEL CONSUMPTION:

At max contingency rating:
H.1200 0·618 lb (0·280 kg)/shp/hr
H.1400 0·607 lb (0·275 kg)/shp/hr

At max one-hour rating:
H.1000 0·650 lb (0·295 kg)/shp/hr
H.1200 0·624 lb (0·283 kg)/shp/hr
H.1400 0·610 lb (0·277 kg)/shp/hr

At max cont rating:
H.1000 0·670 lb (0·304 kg)/shp/hr
H.1200 0·642 lb (0·291 kg)/shp/hr
H.1400 0·620 lb (0·281 kg)/shp/hr

ROLLS-ROYCE/KHD T112

This joint design of APU by Rolls-Royce Small Engine Division and Klöckner-Humboldt-Deutz is being developed for installation in the VFW VAK 191B V/STOL strike fighter. A detailed description of the T112 is given in the International section on page 718.

ROLLS-ROYCE NIMBUS

The Rolls-Royce Nimbus is a free-turbine turboshaft, which makes use of many design features of well-proven Rolls-Royce/Turboméca engines. It is basically an Artouste with two axial-flow compressor stages added forward of the centrifugal compressor and one axial turbine stage added to the gas-generator. The shaft-drive is taken via a free turbine and a two-stage gearbox.

The Nimbus was first run as a turbojet in July 1958, and as a shaft-turbine in the following month.

In flat-rated form, the Nimbus powers the Westland Scout and Wasp helicopters.

For the Wasp the engine has been "marinised" to combat the effects of salt water ingestion.

TYPE: Free-turbine turboshaft engine.

AIR INTAKE: Annular aluminium alloy casting with three radial struts supporting front ball-thrust bearing.

COMPRESSOR: Two-stage axial-flow compressor, followed by single-sided centrifugal stage. Axial stages have integrally-machined blades and integral stub-shafts and are bolted together. Shaft supported at front in high-speed ball bearing and at rear in high-speed roller bearing. Cast stator blades in inner and outer retainer rings. Stainless steel centrifugal compressor. Pressure ratio 6·5 : 1. Air mass flow 11 lb/sec (5·0 kg/sec).

COMBUSTION CHAMBER: Annular type.

Rolls-Royce Gnome H.1400 free-turbine turboshaft engine rated at 1,500 shp

Rolls-Royce Nimbus free-turbine turboshaft, flat-rated at 710 shp

FUEL SYSTEM: Gear-type pump supplies fuel metered by a mechanically-governed control unit. Fuel is injected centrifugally into flame zone of combustion chamber through radial holes in hollow mainshaft. Starting is by torch igniter.

COMPRESSOR TURBINE: Two-stage axial-flow type, with integrally-machined blades.

POWER TURBINE: Single-stage free turbine of Nimonic, with integrally-machined blades.

REDUCTION GEAR: Helical spur type.

JET-PIPE: Bifurcated type.

ACCESSORIES: Engine-driven auxiliaries and accessories mounted on taper flanges around air intake. Driven by spur gear train from compressor.

LUBRICATION SYSTEM: Gear type compound pressure and scavenge pump, full flow filter and system of oil strainers.

DIMENSIONS:
Installed overall length 73 in (1,854 mm)
Width 38·6 in (980 mm)
Height 34·2 in (868 mm)

WEIGHT:
Dry, less gearbox, approx 390 lb (177 kg)

PERFORMANCE RATINGS:
Max (5 min up to ISA + 30°C) 710 shp
1-hour rating (to ISA + 27°C) 685 shp
Max continuous 600 shp

SPECIFIC FUEL CONSUMPTIONS:
At 5-min rating 0·84 lb (0·381 kg)/hp/hr
At 1-hour rating 0·85 lb (0·385 kg)/hp/hr
At max cont rating 0·89 lb (0·404 kg)/hp/hr

ROLLS-ROYCE T64

Under a licence agreement, the Small Engine Division is enabled to offer British-built General Electric T64 turboprop and turboshaft engines up to and including the 3,400 shp T64-GE-12 model, to power future medium/heavy helicopters and

Rolls-Royce Coupled Gnome H.1200 2,500 shp free-turbine coupled turboshaft for installation in Westland Wessex helicopters

medium-sized propeller-driven STOL aircraft.

Components would be manufactured jointly by Rolls-Royce and General Electric, with complete interchangeability being maintained between British and American engines.

Details of the T64 can be found under the "General Electric" heading in the US section.

INDUSTRIAL AND MARINE GAS TURBINE DIVISION

DIVISIONAL OFFICE:
PO Box 72, Ansty, Coventry CV7 9JR

DIRECTORS:
F. T. Hinkley, BSc, CEng ,FIMechE (Chairman)
R. T. Whitfield, BSc, FInstP (Managing Director)
W. H. Lindsey, MA, CEng, FIMechE, FIMarE, FILocoE (Director of Engineering)
F. T. Blakey, FCWA, FACCA (Commercial Director)

A. H. Fletcher (Director of Marketing)
A. Jubb, BA (Director of Future Projects)
A. V. Cleaver, OBE, CEng, FRAeS, Hon FBIS, Hon FAIAA (General Manager, Rockets)
R. W. F. Farthing, BSc(Eng) London, CEng, FRAeS

The Industrial and Marine Gas Turbine Division was formed in March 1967 at Ansty, near Coventry, Warwickshire, following the acquisition of Bristol Siddeley Engines. The Division comprises the former rocket departments of Rolls-Royce and Bristol Siddeley and is also responsible for the industrial and marine versions

of the company's aero gas-turbines (described in *Jane's Surface Skimmer Systems*).

This Division also operates the government's Spadeadam Rocket Establishment on behalf of the Ministry of Technology.

ROLLS-ROYCE BS.605

The BS.605 is a retractable aircraft assisted take-off rocket. The engine consists of a control system and one or more thrust units, the latter being designed to retract within the aircraft to eliminate any drag penalty after firing. The first assisted take-off with this engine, installed in a

Rolls-Royce BS. 605 retractable rocket boost unit, as used on the Buccaneer S.Mk 50

Buccaneer aircraft, was made on 14 March 1965, and the BS.605 is in service in Buccaneer S.Mk 50 strike aircraft of the South African Air Force.

The BS.605 employs HTP and kerosene propellants, the HTP being contained in an aircraft-installed tank and the kerosene supplied from the normal aircraft system. The propellants are fed directly into he pump via the engine mounting trunnions, and to minimise the overall dimensions the unit pivots on the axis of the turbo-pump which is mounted across the engine.

The turbo-pump and combustion chambers are based on Gamma components. The control system has been designed specifically to avoid the possibility of inadvertent operation, or malfunction of engine components. Engine starting, stopping, lowering and raising operations are performed electro-magnetically. Only when it is in the lowered position can the engine be fired.

The following details refer to the two-thrust-unit version of the BS.605 installed in the Buccaneer aircraft:

DIMENSIONS:
Length overall   42 in (1,067 mm)
Diameter of each thrust unit   12 in (305 mm)
WEIGHT:
Total weight, excluding jacks   367 lb (166 kg)
PERFORMANCE RATING:
Total thrust output   8,000 lb (3,630 kg)

ROLLS-ROYCE GAMMA TYPE 8

Apart from the use of a common suction valve to ensure better synchronisation at start and shut-down, the Gamma Type 8 consists virtually of two Gamma Type 4 engines (see 1968-69 edition of *All the World's Aircraft*). It consists of eight chambers, with four on an inner pitch circle diameter and four on an outer concentric pitch circle diameter. The inner and outer chambers are locked together in pairs to form four thrust units and each thrust unit is swivelled by a common actuator. The four thrust units are swivelled in a manner similar to that adopted for the control of Black Knight, that is, two pairs giving control in pitch, the other two pairs giving control in yaw and all moving together to give control in roll.

The locked pairs are mounted on hollow trunnions through which the propellants are fed, the HTP being supplied at the centre of the vehicle, the fuel at the outside. Two turbo-pumps are employed and two pairs of chambers on each diameter are fed from the same turbo-pump unit. A mixture ratio control and propellant-operated control system similar to those used in the Gamma Type 4 are employed.

The complete installation fits conveniently into a structure 6 ft 6 in (2·00 m) in diameter. It is being developed to provide first-stage propulsion for the Westland Black Arrow launch vehicle.

DIMENSION:
Length of motor bay   58·9 in (1,496 mm)
WEIGHTS:
Dry mass of bare engine   1,147 lb (521 kg)
Mass of engine complete with telemetry and hydraulic systems (excluding bay structure)
           1,220 lb (553 kg)
PERFORMANCE RATING:
Thrust at S/L
   50,000 lb (22,680 kg) + 0·6% —1·25%
SPECIFIC IMPULSE:
at S/L   217·4 sec
in vacuum   250·5 sec

ROLLS-ROYCE GAMMA TYPE 2

The Gamma Type 2 engine is also based on the Gamma Type 4 and adapts a large number of existing components which have been developed to a high state of reliability. The propellants are HTP and kerosene. The two combustion chambers are mounted in gimbals, with the gimbal rings round the throats of the combustion chamber, and can swing in both pitch and yaw planes. Propellants are fed to the chambers through passages in the trunnion assemblies and gimbal rings, thus avoiding the use of high-pressure flexible pipes. The trunnion assemblies are similar to those developed successfully on the Gamma series of engines. A mixture ratio control unit of the same type as used on the Gamma Mk 304 is fitted. The combustion chamber has a nozzle extension to give an expansion pressure ratio of 350 : 1, to obtain improved specific impulse in space.

This engine is specified for the second stage of the Black Arrow launch vehicle.

DIMENSIONS:
Height overall   39 in (990 mm)
Width overall   26 in (660 mm)
Length overall   46 in (1,168 mm)
WEIGHTS:
Dry mass of engine   326 lb (148 kg)
Total engine mass including hydraulic system and jettisoned starting system
           374 lb (170 kg)
PERFORMANCE RATING (estimated):
Max thrust in vacuum
   15,300 lb (6,940 kg) sr ± 0·7
SPECIFIC IMPULSE:
in vacuum   26·5 sec

ROLLS-ROYCE RZ.2 AND RZ.12

Designed and developed by Rolls-Royce, the RZ.2 rocket engine is adapted from the S-3 family of engines manufactured by the Rocketdyne Division of the former North American Aviation Inc, under a technical assistance agreement concluded by the two companies in 1955.

The RZ.2 is the most powerful rocket engine produced in Europe. Two of these engines power the Hawker Siddeley Blue Streak, first stage of the European Launcher Development Organisation (ELDO) satellite launch vehicle, the complete twin-engine installation being designated RZ.12. The RZ.2 was rated originally at a sea level thrust of 137,000 lb (62,125 kg), but engines delivered for flight for several years past have had a higher rating of 150,000 lb (68,040 kg) st.

TYPE: Fixed-thrust single-chamber pump-fed liquid-propellant rocket engine.
PROPELLANTS: Liquid oxygen and kerosene.
THRUST CHAMBER ASSEMBLY: Single chamber. Area ratios: combustion zone/throat 1·8 : 1, final expansion nozzle/throat 8 : 1. Multitubular construction, the longitudinal tubes being brazed together with external circumferential stiffening bands brazed or welded to

Rolls-Royce Gamma Type 8 rocket engine

Rolls-Royce RZ.2 rocket engine

Rolls-Royce Gamma Type 2 rocket engine (15,300 lb = 6,940 kg st)

them. Tubes of nickel. Regenerative cooling by kerosene. Fuel pump total output (except for small amounts used in the gas generator and ignition line) enters a manifold at the injector end and flows down and then up alternate tubes before entering the injector. Plate-type propellant injector, with series of concentric rings brazed to injector body. Alternate rings inject kerosene and liquid oxygen through a number of orifices, a like-on-like injection pattern being employed. Ignition by pyrophoric liquids. Combustion pressure 580 lb/sq in (40·78 kg/cm²) abs. Combustion temperature at maximum S/L rating 3,190°C.

THRUST CHAMBER MOUNTINGS: By gimbal block at dome end of chamber, attached to vehicle structure. Chamber can be gimballed through ± 7° in two planes at right angles for vehicle control purposes.

TURBOPUMPS: Two propellant pump impellers are mounted on a common shaft and driven from the turbine via a two-stage spur reduction gear. Combustion gases from a gas generator drive the turbine. Each pump is of the single-entry fully-shrouded centrifugal type, made of high-strength aluminium alloy. Mass flow: liquid oxygen 416 lb/sec (188 kg/sec), kerosene 189 lb/sec (85·7 kg/sec). Delivery pressures: liquid oxygen 894 lb/sq in (62·85 kg/cm²), kerosene 887 lb/sq in (62·36 kg/cm²).

TURBINE: Two-stage impulse-type with about 5% reaction. Disc of chromium-niobium ferritic steel. Blades of Nimonic 80. Blades attached by fir tree roots. Gas inlet temperature 650°C.

GAS GENERATOR: Mass flow: liquid oxygen 3·4 lb/sec (1·54 kg/sec), kerosene 9·7 lb/sec (4·40 kg/sec). Pyrotechnic igniter.

TURBOPUMP LUBRICATION: Total loss oil system, from pressurised tank. Flow rate 3 Imp gallons (13·6 litres)/min.

STARTING AND STOPPING: Electro-pneumatic control system for valves. Sequential system is fully automatic once start or stop button is pressed. Propellants for starting engine are taken from pressurised ground supply tanks.

THRUST CONTROL: By controlling turbine power and hence pump output. A simple orifice system meters liquid oxygen supply to gas generator.

DIMENSIONS:
Overall height (Blue Streak installation)
approx 10 ft 6 in (3·20 m)
External diameter thrust chamber exit nozzle
44·40 in (1,128 mm)

Rolls-Royce RZ.20, the high-performance liquid-hydrogen rocket engine for spacecraft propulsion for which Rolls-Royce made the thrust chamber, seen test firing at Spadeadam Rocket Test Establishment

WEIGHT:
Total dry weight   1,520 lb (689 kg)
PERFORMANCE:
Nominal thrust at S/L   150,000 lb (68,040 kg)
Overall mixture ratio
2·20 : 1 (oxygen/kerosene) by weight
Specific impulse:
At sea level   248 sec
In vacuum   282 sec

ROLLS-ROYCE RZ.20

Before the UK's withdrawal from the ELDO late in 1968 a contract had been placed in 1966 with Rolls-Royce for an advanced high-energy thrust-chamber for use in an upper stage of the ELDO B vehicle, which was later replaced by the Europa 3. In partnership with the Rocket Propulsion Establishment at Westcott the company carried out extensive component and rig development from 1967, culminating in a completely successful 10-second test of the RZ.20 chamber generating 9,000 lb (4,082 kg) thrust at the Rocket Test Establishment, Spadeadam, in September 1969.

Propellants were liquid oxygen and liquid hydrogen. Rolls-Royce funded the special test installation for this thrust-chamber and has continued to develop high-energy upper-stage propulsion without ELDO funding. Both France (SEP) and Federal Germany (MBB) are now developing replacement systems to a later timescale.

MOTOR CAR DIVISION
(Light Aircraft Engine Department)

Under the terms of a licence agreement signed in 1960 with Teledyne Continental Motors of the United States, Rolls-Royce market Continental light aircraft engines and spare parts throughout the world with the exception of North and South America and certain Far Eastern countries. Four models from the Continental range are manufactured by the Rolls-Royce Motor Car Division at Crewe, and these are described hereunder.

ROLLS-ROYCE CONTINENTAL C90

This is the 95 hp Continental C90 four-cylinder horizontally-opposed air-cooled engine built under licence. Further details are given under the "Teledyne Continental" heading in the US section.

ROLLS-ROYCE CONTINENTAL O-200-A

This is the 100 hp Continental O-200-A four-cylinder horizontally-opposed air-cooled engine, built under licence. Details are given under the "Teledyne Continental" heading in the US section.

ROLLS-ROYCE CONTINENTAL O-240-A

The O-240-A is the first light aircraft engine to be developed by Rolls-Royce in conjunction with Teledyne Continental Motors. The engine had its origins in the United States but, soon after Continental had built and run a prototype, a changed commercial situation and the need to divert engineering resources to other work, especially the new Tiara range, caused Teledyne Continental to cease its active development. Rolls-Royce took over the programme in 1968 with a view to developing the engine specifically for the European market. By the time flight trials began, in July 1969, 300 test bed hours had been logged at Crewe. Certification was completed in January 1970, and production deliveries began in mid-1970. The O-240 is being marketed in the United States by Teledyne Continental.

TYPE: Four-cylinder, horizontally-opposed, air-cooled, carburetted, unsupercharged.

CYLINDERS: Bore 4·438 in (112·5 mm). Stroke 3·875 in (98·4 mm). Capacity 240 cu in (3·933 cc). Compression ratio 8·5 : 1. Cast aluminium alloy finned heads are screwed and shrunk onto forged steel barrels.

PISTONS: Heat-treated aluminium alloy. Two compression rings and one oil control ring above the gudgeon pin, one scraper below. Fully floating, ground steel tube gudgeon pins with pressed in aluminium end plugs.

CONNECTING RODS: Forged steel I-section. Big end bearings are thin steel backed overplated with tin lead alloy. Little end bearings are split bronze bushings.

CRANKSHAFT: Alloy steel forgings, nitrided all over for greater fatigue strength, having three journals running in thin steel backed overplated tin lead alloy bearings.

CRANKCASE: Cast aluminium alloy, split along the vertical centre line.

VALVE GEAR: Two valves per cylinder. Steel inlet valves with hardened tips. Steel exhaust valves with hardened tips faced with stellite 'F'. Valve seats shrunk into position. Camshaft, in centre of crankcase beneath the crankshaft, driven by gear from the crankshaft.

INDUCTION: Float type carburettor with a manual mixture control.

FUEL GRADE: 100/130 octane minimum.

IGNITION: Two 'Slick' type 4001 magnetos on rear of crankcase driven by gears from the camshaft. Two Champion REM 38EC or Lodge RS26-LR 18 mm spark plugs per cylinder.

The 100 hp Rolls-Royce Continental O-200-A (*left*) and 145 hp O-300-D horizontally-opposed air-cooled engines

LUBRICATION SYSTEM: Wet sump. Magnesium crankcase cover houses the engine driven gear type oil pump. An oil pressure relief valve is mounted in the cover. Provision is made for an airframe mounted full flow filter.

PROPELLER DRIVE: Direct drive, clockwise when viewed from the rear. ARP 502 Type 1 flange.

ACCESSORIES: Ford 15 volt 60 amp alternator. Tachometer drive from the oil pump at rear of engine. Fuel pump is operated from an eccentric on the camshaft at front of engine.

STARTING: Prestolite EO 19508 12 volt starter.

MOUNTING: Four rear mounted ring type mounting brackets to which vibration isolators can be attached.

DIMENSIONS:
Length 32·5 in (82·6 cm)
Width 31·4 in (79·8 cm)
Height 28·8 in (73·2 cm)

DRY WEIGHT: including accessories 246 lb (112 kg)

RATINGS:
Take-off 130 hp at 2,800 rpm
Maximum recommended cruise
  97·5 bhp at 2,540 rpm

SPECIFIC FUEL CONSUMPTION:
0·48 lb (0·22 kg)/hp/hr at 2,540 rpm

OIL CONSUMPTION:
Maximum 0·015 lb (0·007 kg)/hp/hr

The 130 hp Rolls-Royce Continental O-240-A engine

ROLLS-ROYCE CONTINENTAL O-300
This is the 145 hp Continental O-300 six-cylinder horizontally-opposed air-cooled engine, built under licence.

Versions currently available include the O-300-C and D, of which full details can be found under the "Teledyne Continental" heading in the US section.

THE UNITED STATES OF AMERICA

AEROJET

AEROJET-GENERAL CORPORATION (Subsidiary of The General Tire & Rubber Company)
CORPORATE EXECUTIVE OFFICES:
9100 East Flair Drive, El Monte, California 91734
AEROJET SOLID PROPULSION COMPANY:
PRESIDENT: Richard F. Cottrell
AEROJET LIQUID ROCKET COMPANY:
PRESIDENT: Ray C. Stiff Jr
AEROJET NUCLEAR SYSTEMS COMPANY:
PRESIDENT: A. L. Feldman
NUCLEAR DIVISION:
NUCLEAR ROCKET OPERATIONS:
Sacramento, California
SAN RAMON FACILITY:
San Ramon, California
PROPULSION DIVISION:
SACRAMENTO FACILITY:
Sacramento, California
DADE FACILITY:
Homestead, Florida
SPACE DIVISION:
El Monte, California
AEROJET-GENERAL INTERNATIONAL (Subsidiary):
El Monte, California
BRISTOL AEROJET LTD (Affiliate):
Weston-Super-Mare, England
(Plus many other operating divisions, subsidiaries and affiliates)
HONORARY CHAIRMAN OF THE BOARD:
A. H. Rude
CHAIRMAN OF THE BOARD:
M. G. O'Neil
VICE-CHAIRMAN OF THE BOARD:
W. E. Zisch
CHAIRMAN OF EXECUTIVE COMMITTEE:
Dan A. Kimball
PRESIDENT:
R. I. McKenzie
EXECUTIVE VICE-PRESIDENT:
L. W. Mullane
SENIOR VICE-PRESIDENTS:
A. L. Antonio
W. L. Gore (Sales)
C. C. Ross (General Manager, Nuclear Division)

Aerojet-General Corporation, a pioneer rocket company formed in 1942 by Dr Theodore von Kármán, is engaged in widely diversified space, defence, industrial and commercial programmes. In addition to being a major producer of solid- and liquid-propellant and nuclear rocket propulsion systems, the company also has strong capabilities in such fields as water desalination and purification, isotope power sources and controlled thermonuclear energy research, microelectronics, automatic materials handling systems, medical technology, waste management and anti-pollution activity, ordnance oceanographic defence systems and manufacture of jet engine components. Employment totalled 18,800 in December 1967.
Applications of the company's solid-propellant rockets include the booster and sustainer motors of the Polaris missile, the second-stage motor of the Minuteman I/II ICBM, the third-stage motor for the Minuteman III, the motors of the Hawk, Tartar and Sparrow, and the first stage of the Scout launch vehicle.

A programme was started during 1967 to develop an advanced version of the USAF 2·75 in (7 cm) air-to-ground rocket, making maximum use of existing hardware. Aerojet is to upgrade the rocket's performance considerably by employing a composite case-hardened solid-propellant.

Aerojet liquid-propellant rockets power the Titan II ICBM, the Titan III launch vehicle, the service module of the three-man Apollo Moon programme, the Improved Delta launch vehicle and the Transtage for Titan III. Several new engines, utilising very high performance fuels, are under development, including a throttling design for space applications.

In February 1970 Aerojet was requested by NASA to submit a proposal for a high-performance propulsion system for use by both stages of a "space shuttle" vehicle combination. NASA also awarded the company a $150,000 contract for studies on modification of test facilities at Marshall Space Flight Center to accommodate shuttle-engine testing. Both stages of a shuttle would use re-startable bell-type liquid-hydrogen engines of 400,000 lb (181,400 kg) st each, clustered into a group on the booster and with two or three on the orbiter. Aerojet considers its experience with the large (1,500,000 lb = 680,400 kg st) M-1 engine built for NASA in 1963 will stand it in good stead in this important competition. It has selected AC Electronics Division of General Motors as first member of its shuttle propulsion team (AC supply control systems for the propulsion systems of the Apollo spacecraft and for the first stage, second stage and transtage of Titan III-C).

Under a contract announced in July, 1961, Aerojet became responsible for first-phase development of the NERVA (Nuclear Engine for Rocket Vehicle Application) nuclear rocket engine, as part of the Rover programme. This portion of the work involves preliminary design of the engine and testing of certain components and was extended under a follow-on contract received in January 1962. The nuclear portion of the work is being done by Westinghouse Electric Corporation, under sub-contract to Aerojet.

In addition Aerojet fabricates spacecraft propellant tankage, including the titanium propellant tanks for the Bell ascent engines of the Apollo Lunar Module. The company was last year additionally charged with making the tanks for the descent stage of Apollo 16 to Apollo 20. The first set of descent-stage tanks was delivered to Grumman ahead of schedule in February 1970. Aerojet engineers have evolved advanced insulation techniques for spacecraft tankage containing liquified gases, and are developing metallic bladders as positive expulsion devices for propellant tanks.

Details of Aerojet's family of Aerobee and Astrobee rocket sounding vehicles and NIRO research rocket are given under the Aerojet-General heading in the "Research Rockets" section.

In October, 1958, the Aerojet-General Corporation and the Bristol Aeroplane Company Ltd of England announced an agreement to form a joint company to be known as Bristol Aerojet, Ltd. This company is devoting its efforts to the development, manufacture, casting and testing of solid-propellant rocket motors.

AEROJET APOLLO ENGINE
Under sub-contract from North American Rockwell, Aerojet's Liquid Rocket Operations developed and is producing the engine that is used to propel the Apollo spacecraft's Service Module. Known as the Service Propulsion System (SPS), the engine is designed to steer the module to the Moon, place it in lunar orbit, eject it from that orbit and bring it back to Earth.

During 1966 the SPS engine, which utilises storable liquid propellants, successfully completed two unmanned flight test launches. The SPS Block II engine, which will be used in the Moon programme, has also been tested. The Block II engine produces 20,000 lb (9,070 kg) st and is 13 ft 4 in (4 m) high. It is designed to operate repeatedly for a total of 12·5 minutes, with a maximum single burn of 10·5 minutes, and is the largest and most powerful ablatively-cooled rocket engine yet developed in the USA.

In November 1967 the SPS engine performed successfully during the Apollo 4 mission. The system fired twice as programmed, first to send the spacecraft to the desired altitude and later to increase its speed to nearly 25,000 mph (40,234 kmh) for a high-speed re-entry to test heat shield capabilities. It has since performed perfectly throughout the lunar missions.

AEROJET TITAN III ENGINES
During 1967 the USAF awarded Aerojet a contract for follow-on production of first-, second- and third-stage liquid-propellant space engines for eight Titan III-C standard space launch vehicles. Together with four of the original 17 research and development Titan III-Cs still remaining to be flown, the eight production models were expected to support mission requirements during 1969 to 1971.

Aerojet also received USAF contracts for the production of first- and second-stage liquid-propellant engines for the Titan III-B and III-D standard space launch vehicles. The Titan III-B and III-D vehicles will be used for unmanned military space missions.

AEROJET TRANSTAGE
Upper-stage engines for the Transtage of the Titan III-C standard space launch vehicle were developed for the USAF by Aerojet's Liquid Rocket Operations. The system has a thrust in the 16,000 lb (7,250 kg) range, uses hypergolic (self-igniting) propellants and has an extremely long burning time, with repeated stop and re-start capability.

The main rôle of Transtage is to switch payloads to new orbits.

AEROJET AJ10-118

The AJ10-118 liquid-propellant (UDMH and IRFNA) engine produces 7,890 lb (3,580 kg) st. It is the propulsion system for the second stage of the Improved Delta launch vehicle.

AEROJET XLR66-AJ-2 ENGINE

A new throttling liquid-propellant rocket engine was announced by Aerojet during 1967. Designated XLR66-AJ-2, it is being developed and tested on behalf of the US Navy. Weighing less than 90 lb (41 kg), the new high-performance engine has already demonstrated its suitability for a wide variety of space tasks, and is claimed to have the most rapid transient thrust response of any rocket in its thrust class.

AEROJET HAWK MOTOR

The single-chamber solid-propellant rocket motor of the Hawk surface-to-air missile was the first dual-thrust dual-grain motor to be mass-produced.

Within its single propellant mass, the motor has an inner core of propellant constituting a short-duration booster grain which launches and accelerates the missile to supersonic speed. When this inner core is consumed, a slower-burning outer core, forming the sustainer portion of the propellant, takes over and keeps the missile at the required velocity.

Aerojet has signed a licensing and technical assistance agreement with SETEL of Paris for the production of Hawk motors, under the European manufacturing programme for this missile.

A new Improved Hawk propulsion system, using an upgraded polyurathene propellant and sprayed liner to give improved propellant-to-case bond, has passed its qualification testing at the US Army Test and Evaluation Command's White Sands Missile Range, New Mexico. More than 100 consecutive Improved Hawk motors have been fired without a failure, and the demonstrated long-life characteristics of the polyurethene propellant have extended the shelf life of the motor to ten years.

AEROJET POLARIS MOTORS

Aerojet was responsible for the solid-propellant rocket motors for both stages of the Polaris A1 fleet ballistic missile.

The first stage grain is 9 ft 2 in (2·79 m) long and 4 ft 5 in (1·35 m) in diameter, and exhausts through four nozzles. Each nozzle is fitted with a curved deflector known as a Jetevator which moves in the efflux to produce offset thrust for control purposes.

The second-stage grain is 3 ft 11 in (1·19 m) long and 4 ft 5 in (1·35 m) diameter and has a similar nozzle arrangement. Both stages have steel cases.

In December 1961, production of the A1 motors was completed and Aerojet switched to production of the first-stage motor for the A2 Polaris. This is similar to the first-stage A1 motor, but 30 in (0·76 m) longer.

Now in production is the first-stage motor for the A3 Polaris, which has a glass-fibre casing and rotating nozzles instead of Jetevator controls.

AEROJET MINUTEMAN MOTORS

Aerojet's Solid Rocket Operations is producing the complete second-stage propulsion system for the Minuteman II ICBM.

This improved motor has a single nozzle with secondary liquid injection for thrust vector control, instead of the four movable nozzles of the Minuteman I motor. Its diameter has been increased.

Aerojet is also engaged in a development and production programme for a third-stage motor for the advanced Minuteman III.

AEROJET SENIOR (ALGOL)

Aerojet Senior produces 115,000 lb (52,160 kg) st for 40 seconds. It is used for first-stage propulsion of the Scout launch vehicle and was clustered

Aerojet-General solid-propellant motor for second stage of Minuteman II ICBM

in the Little Joe II booster for early tests of the Apollo space-craft. The Senior is sometimes given the name of Algol I when used in NASA's Scouts.

An improved version, known as Advanced Senior, or Algol II-A, with a 52% improvement in performance, is also in production for NASA. This version utilises an advanced propellant, new grain design and lightweight plastic nozzle instead of the steel nozzle of Algol I.

NERVA ENGINE

NERVA (Nuclear Engine for Rocket Vehicle Application) does not burn fuel. Liquid hydrogen at —450°F is pumped from a tank through the rocket system and then into the nuclear reactor. Energy from the reactor core instantly heats the hydrogen into a high-temperature gas. It is then expanded rapidly, providing thrust for the rocket. NERVA is a project of the Space Nuclear Propulsion Office, a joint venture of the National Aeronautics and Space Administration and the Atomic Energy Commission.

The present series of tests is focused on the Experimental Engine (XE), first fired on March 20, 1969, at the Nuclear Rocket Development Station at Jackass Flats, Nevada, after many delays brought about by shortage of funds and technical difficulties. Liquid hydrogen from a large cryogenic storage tank is pumped at 75-80 lb/sec through the regenerative cooling jacket of the downward-pointing thrust chamber nozzle, up the sides of the reactor drum and then downwards through the reactor core, which occupies the place of the combustion chamber in conventional rocket engines. Here the liquid flow is violently heated by contact with the walls of numerous tubular fuel elements each consisting of graphite containing a large number of pellets of uranium oxide. Over the length of 41 inches (1·04 m) on its passage through the core the hydrogen is converted from liquid at some —245°C and 900 lb/sq in to gas at 1,990°C and 560 lb/sq in (39·37 kg/cm²). Using the present fuel rods the temperature limit is considered to be about 2,240°C and this is adequate for envisaged interplanetary missions. Using niobium or hafnium carbide the limit might be raised to over 2,900°C. At the present limit the reactor heat output is of the order of 1,100 megawatts and static thrust 50,000-55,000 lb (22,680-24,948 kg). Hot hydrogen bled from the wall of the chamber drives the turbopump.

Aerojet-General is engaged in the design of a flight engine based on the technology of the XE and assuming the same limiting temperature. It would be much lighter in construction, have a thrust of 75,000 lb (34,020 kg) and a specific

XE ground experimental NERVA nuclear rocket engine

impulse of 825 sec. The main advantage of a nuclear rocket is the very high specific impulse that can be obtained by the use of a working fluid of such low atomic weight. Programme cost of a flight engine would be of the order of $500 million for engine development and $600 million for flight stage development. Such an engine, if funded by NASA, could be ready in 1977. It could power a new third stage for the Saturn V, replacing the existing S-IVB.

AEROJET 2.5KS-18000

This solid-propellant rocket motor is used as a booster for the Aerobee Model 100 and Model 150 research sounding rockets. Its designation indicates a thrust of 18,000 lb (8,165 kg).

ALLISON

ALLISON DIVISION, GENERAL MOTORS CORPORATION

HEAD OFFICE AND WORKS:
Indianapolis, Indiana 46206

OTHER WORKS: Cleveland, Ohio

GENERAL MANAGER, ALLISON DIVISION:
Reuben R. Jensen

DIVISIONAL COMPTROLLER:
Frank W. Fleming

MANAGER, PLANT OPERATIONS:
J. E. Knott

DIRECTOR OF ENGINEERING, AEROSPACE:
G. E. Holbrook

GENERAL SALES MANAGER: E. M. Deckman

PLANT MANAGER, AEROSPACE:
H. L. Karsch

The Allison Division of General Motors produces T56 turboprop engines for military and commercial versions of the Lockheed C-130 Hercules transport, and also for the Lockheed P-3B and P-3C Orion anti-submarine aircraft, Grumman E-2A Hawkeye airborne early-warning aircraft and Grumman C-2A Greyhound transport. A commercial counterpart of the T56, the Model 501-D13, powers the Lockheed Electra and Convair 580 airliners.

The Allison T63 small gas turbine powers the Hughes OH-6A and Bell OH-58A light observation helicopters, and its commercial counterpart, the Model 250, powers the Hughes Model 500, the Bell TH-57 SeaRanger, the 206A JetRanger, and the Agusta Bell JetRanger, the Fairchild Hiller FH-1100, MBB BO 105 and VFW H3.

A turboprop version of the Model 250 was certificated in March 1969 for light fixed-wing aircraft applications. In 1966 Allison established

a worldwide distributor organization to provide local service and support for all Model 250-powered equipment.

It was announced in January 1967 that Allison and Rolls-Royce of England would develop and produce jointly a version of the Rolls-Royce Spey turbofan engine, under the designation TF41, to power advanced versions of the Vought A-7 Corsair II aircraft. The TF41 is now in large-scale production for the USAF's A-7D close-support attack aircraft and the US Navy's A-7E carrier-based attack bomber.

The two companies are also collaborating in a joint Anglo-American programme for development of advanced lift-jet engines for V/STOL aircraft. This follows experimental work by Allison on lift-jet research engines of the Model 610 series.

Further details of the Allison/Rolls-Royce programmes can be found in the International section on page 717.

ALLISON MODEL 250
Military designation: T63

The Model 250 is a small shaft-turbine engine in which power is derived from a free power turbine and is delivered through an offset gearbox which includes all accessory drive pads.

The military development contract for the T63 was received by Allison in June 1958 and the engine was first run in the Spring of 1959.

The original T63-A-5, rated at 250 shp, completed a 50-hour preliminary flight rating test in March 1962, prior to the start of its flight test programme in a Bell UH-13R helicopter. The 150-hour military model qualification test was completed in September 1962, with simultaneous completion of tests required for FAA Type Approval. In December 1962, the T63-A-5 was awarded an approved type certificate by the FAA and was accepted by the US Army in a ceremony at Allison.

The T63-A-5A engine, rated at 317 shp, completed its qualification-certification tests in July 1965 and was awarded an FAA type certificate in September 1965. This engine powers the Hughes OH-6A and Bell OH-58A light observation helicopters, the latter being in large-scale production for the US Army.

Also in production, to power the Hughes Model 500, Bell JetRanger and Fairchild Hiller FH-1100 commercial helicopters, is a civil version of the T63 known as the Model 250-C18. This also has a max T-O rating of 317 shp and normal rating of 270 shp.

Delivery of both the military T63-A-5A and commercial Model 250-C18 began in December 1965. A type certificate for the Model 250-B15, a turboprop version of this engine for fixed-wing aircraft, was obtained in March 1969. The B-15 powers the Cessna O-2T, Helio Twin Stallion and H-370 Courier, Robertson STOL series, Siai-Marchetti L-1019 and California Airmotive conversions of the Beech Baron and Bonanza.

Under development are turboshaft and turboprop versions of the T63/Model 250 having a rating of 400 shp. These more powerful engines will be essentially the same size as the 317 shp models except for slight increases in the diameters of the compressor and the power turbine. Dry weight of the 400 shp model will be only 16lb (7·2 kg) greater than that of the 317 shp engine. The 400 shp Model 250-B17 turboprop develops 417 ehp and is specified for the California Airmotive conversion of the Beech Queen Air.

TYPE: Light shaft-turbine or turboprop engine.

COMPRESSOR: Axial/centrifugal compressor with six axial stages and one centrifugal. Axial stages of 17-4 PH cast as single units comprising integral wheels and blades. Compressed air delivered through a vaned diffuser to a collector scroll and thence via two external tubes, one on each side of the engine, to the combustion chamber. Pressure ratio 6·2 : 1. Air mass flow 3 lb (1·36 kg) per second. Compressor assembly bolted to forward face of gear-case.

COMBUSTION CHAMBER: Single can-type chamber at aft end of engine. Single duplex fuel nozzle in rear face of chamber. One igniter.

TURBINES: Two-stage gas-producer turbine and two-stage "free" power turbine. Integrally-cast blades and wheels. Combustion gases after passing through turbines enter exhaust hood in middle of engine where they are collected and exhausted upward. Gas-producer turbine outlet temperature 1,380°F. (750°C). Turbine/combustor assembly, including exhaust collector, bolted to rear face of gear-case.

GEAR CASE: A magnesium casting which forms primary structure of engine and contains all power and accessory gear trains, torque sensor, oil pumps and engine main bearings. Compressor and combustor/turbine assemblies bolted to front and rear faces respectively. One spur gear train engages pinion driven by power turbine shaft and transmits output power to horizontal shaft on centre-line of engine below (in turboprops and optionally on shaft-turbine models, above) compressor turbine output shaft accessible on both front and rear faces of gear-case. Rated shp available at either front or rear spline, or any combination totalling rated power. Second spur gear train engages on gas generator turbine shaft and provides drive for engine accessory pads. Output shaft rpm 6,000, on shaft-turbine version. Turboprop has additional reduction gear to propeller shaft at top front of engine.

CONTROL SYSTEM: Pneumatic-mechanical system consisting essentially of fuel pump and filter assembly, gas producer fuel control and power turbine governor.

FUEL: Primary fuels are ASTM-A or A-1 and MIL-T-5624, JP-4 and JP-5.

LUBRICATION: Dry sump.

OIL SPECIFICATION: MIL-L-7808 and MIL-L-23699.

The 317 shp Allison Model 250-C18 turboshaft engine

The 317 shp Allison Model 250-B15A turboprop engine

DIMENSIONS (T63-A-5A):
(Model 250-B17):

Length	44·6 in (1,132 mm)
Width	19·0 in (483 mm)
Height	22·5 in (572 mm)

WEIGHT DRY (T63-A-5A): 139 lb (63 kg)
(Model 250-B17): 182 lb (82·5 kg)

PERFORMANCE RATINGS (T63-A-5A, S/L static, 59°F conditions):

T-O	317 shp at 35,000 rpm
Military	317 shp
Normal	270 shp
Cruise (90% normal)	243 shp
Cruise (75% normal)	203 shp

SPECIFIC FUEL CONSUMPTIONS (T63-A-5A):

At T-O rating (59°F)	0·697 lb (0·32 kg)/shp/hr
At T-O rating (100°F)	0·740 lb (0·34 kg)/shp/hr
At normal rating (59°F)	0·760 lb (0·34 kg)/shp/hr
At cruise rating (90% normal)	0·725 lb (0·33 kg)/shp/hr
At cruise rating (75% normal)	0·762 lb (0·35 kg)/shp/hr

ALLISON MODEL 501

The Model 501 is the commercial version of the T56 turboprop. Seventy-five per cent of the components in the two engines are interchangeable.

Two versions are currently in service:

501-D13. This engine powers the Lockheed Electra and, under the designation 501-D13D, the Convair 580. The 501-D13 has a propeller reduction gear ratio of 13·54 : 1, the primary step-down being by spur (3·13 : 1) and the secondary by planetary (4·33 : 1). It has been in airline service since 1957 and has a TBO of up to 9,000 hours (reached by Allegheny Airlines).

501-D22A. In service with commercial versions of the Lockheed C-130 transport. This engine is the commercial counterpart of the military T56-A-15, with propeller reduction gear ratio of 13·54 : 1.

DIMENSIONS:
Length:

501-D13	145·2 in (3,688 mm)
501-D22A	146 in (3,708 mm)

Width:

501-D13	30 in (762 mm)
501-D22A	27 in (686 mm)

Height:

501-D13	42 in (1,067 mm)
501-D22A	39 in (991 mm)

WEIGHT (DRY):
With accessories:

501-D13	1,756 lb (797 kg)
501-D22A	1,820 lb (825 kg)

PERFORMANCE RATINGS:
T-O:

501-D13 3,460 shp plus 726 lb (329 kg) st (3,750 ehp) at 13,820 rpm
501-D22A 4,680 ehp at 13,820 rpm

Max cont:

501-D13 3,138 shp plus 705 lb (320 kg) st at 13,820 rpm
501-D22A 4,364 ehp at 13,820 rpm

Max cruising:

501-D13 1,850 shp plus 145 lb (66 kg) st at 13,820 rpm at 406 mph (653 kmh) at 25,000 ft (7,620 m)

SPECIFIC FUEL CONSUMPTIONS:
At T-O rating:

501-D13	0·540 lb (0·245 kg)/ehp/hr
501-D22A	0·502 lb (0·227 kg)/ehp/hr

At max cont rating:

501-D13	0·552 lb (0·25 kg)/ehp/hr
501-D22A	0·512 lb (0·232 kg)/ehp/hr

At max cruising rating:

501-D13	0·458 lb (0·208 kg)/ehp/hr

ALLISON T56

Current versions of the T56 are as follows:

T56-A-7. Rated at 4,050 eshp. Powers the Lockheed C-130B and C-130E Hercules series of aircraft.

T56-A-8. Rated at 4,050 eshp. Powers Grumman E-2A Hawkeye and C-2A Greyhound.

T56-A-9. Rated at 3,750 ehp. Powers the Lockheed C-130A Hercules.

T56-A-10W. Rated at 4,500 eshp with water injection. Powers the Lockheed P-3A Orion.

T56-A-14. Rated at 4,910 eshp. Generally similar to T56-A-15, but seven-point suspension like T56-A-10W and detail changes. In production for P-3B and C Orion. First four delivered to US Navy in August 1965.

The 4,910 ehp Allison T56-A-15 turboprop engine which powers the latest versions of the Lockheed C-130 Hercules transport

T56-A-15. Rated at 4,910 ehp. Introduced hollow air-cooled turbine blades. In production for C-130H, HC-130H, and C-130K Hercules.

Latest orders for the T56 extended production into 1971.

The following details apply to the T56-A-15:

TYPE: Axial-flow turboprop engine.

PROPELLER DRIVE: Combination spur/planetary gear type, primary step-down by spur, secondary by planetary. Overall gear ratio 13·54 : 1. Power section rpm 13,820. Cast magnesium reduction-gear housing. Gearbox assembly supported from power section by main drive shaft casing 28 in (711 mm) long and two inclined struts. Weight of gearbox assembly approximately 550 lb (249 kg) with pads on rear face for accessory mounting.

AIR INTAKE: Circular duct on engine face. Thermal de-icing.

COMPRESSOR: Fourteen-stage axial-flow. Series of fourteen discs with rotor blades dovetailed in peripheries and locked by adjacent discs. Rotor assembly tie-bolted to shaft which runs on one ball and one roller type bearing. Fifteen rows of stator blades, welded in rings. Disc, rotor and stator blades and four-piece cast casing of stainless steel. Compressor inlet area 155·65 sq in (1,004 cm²). Pressure ratio 9·25 : 1. Mass air flow 32·4 lb (14·70 kg)/sec.

COMBUSTION CHAMBER: Six stainless steel cannular-type perforated combustion liners within one-piece stainless steel outer casing. Fuel nozzles in forward end of each combustor liner. Primary ignition by two igniters in diametrically-opposite combustors.

FUEL SYSTEM: High-pressure type. Bendix control system. Water/alcohol augmentation system available.

FUEL GRADE: MIL-J-5624, JP-4 or JP-5.

NOZZLE GUIDE VANES: Hollow air-cooled blades of special high-temperature alloy.

TURBINE: Four-stage. Rotor assembly consists of four stainless steel discs, with first stage having hollow air-cooled blades of special high-temperature alloy, secured in peripheries of discs by "fir-tree" roots. Discs splined to rotor shaft which runs on front and rear roller bearings. Steel outer turbine casing. Gas temperature before turbine 1,970°F (1,076°C).

JET PIPE: Fixed. Stainless steel.

ACCESSORY DRIVES: Accessory pads on rear face of reduction-gear housing at front end of engine.

LUBRICATION SYSTEM: Low-pressure. Dry sump. Pesco dual-element oil pump. Normal oil supply pressure 55 lb/sq in (3·87 kg/cm²).

OIL SPECIFICATION: MIL-L-7808.

MOUNTING: Three-point suspension.

STARTING: Air turbine, gear-box mounted.

DIMENSIONS:
Length:
A-7, A-8, A-10W, A-14, A-15
     146 in (3,708 mm)
A-9   145 in (3,683 mm)
Width:
All versions   27 in (686 mm)
Height:
A-7, A-8, A-15   39 in (991 mm)
A-9   40 in (1,016 mm)
A-10W, A-14   44 in (1,118 mm)

WEIGHT (DRY):
A-7	1,833 lb (831 kg)
A-8	1,887 lb (856 kg)
A-9	1,679 lb (762 kg)
A-10W	1,870 lb (848 kg)
A-14	1,885 lb (855 kg)
A-15	1,825 lb (828 kg)

PERFORMANCE RATINGS:
Max rating:
A-7, A-8	4,050 eshp at 13,820 rpm
A-9	3,750 eshp at 13,820 rpm

A-10W, with water-alcohol injection
    4,500 eshp at 13,820 rpm
A-14, A-15
    4,910 eshp (4,591 shp) at 13,820 rpm

Normal rating:
A-7, A-8, A-10W	3,730 eshp
A-9	3,375 eshp

A-14, A-15
    4,365 eshp (4,061 shp) at 13,820 rpm

SPECIFIC FUEL CONSUMPTIONS:
At max rating:
A-7, A-10W	0·528 lb (0·240 kg)/ehp/hr
A-8	0·531 lb (0·241 kg)/ehp/hr
A-9	0·540 lb (0·245 kg)/ehp/hr
A-14, A-15	0·501 lb (0·227 kg)/ehp/hr

At normal rating:
A-7, A-10W	0·541 lb (0·246 kg)/ehp/hr
A-8	0·544 lb (0·247 kg)/ehp/hr
A-9	0·552 lb (0·250 kg)/ehp/hr
A-14, A-15	0·517 lb (0·234 kg)/ehp/hr

OIL CONSUMPTION:
A-14, A-15   0·35 US gallons (1·3 litres)/hr

AVCO LYCOMING

THE AVCO LYCOMING DIVISION OF AVCO CORPORATION

HEAD OFFICE:
550, South Main Street, Stratford, Connecticut 06497

WORKS:
Stratford, Conn; Charleston, S.C.; and Williamsport, Pennsylvania

PRESIDENT OF AVCO CORPORATION:
James R. Kerr

Stratford Operations:
VICE-PRESIDENTS:
Beverly H. Warren (General Manager)
J. S. Bartos (Assistant General Manager)
L. A. Shadle (Controller)
Paul A. Deegan (Administration)
Dr H. K. Adenstedt (Senior V-P)
Frank T. Dubuque (Factory Operations)
L. H. Sample (Washington Representative)
Michael S. Saboe (Engineering)
Dr F. Haber (Marketing)

Charleston Operations:
Edward A. Burrus (V-P and General Manager)
Edward Blake (Director of Administration)
C. W. Pritchard (Director of Manufacturing)
Jack M. Raymer (Director of Engineering)
Kenneth A. Campbell (Director of Product Assurance)
Harry J. Graham (V-P Operations)

Williamsport Operations:
VICE-PRESIDENTS:
John M. Ferris (General Manager)
Peter J. Goodwin (Assistant General Manager)
F. W. Riddell (Engineering)
E. L. Wilkinson (Manufacturing)

The Avco Lycoming Division is primarily the engine manufacturing division of Avco Corporation. It is producing two families of turbine engines, the T53 and T55 free-turbine units. Industrial and marine versions are available. Development is continuing on the ALF series of turbofans, on the new turboshaft PLT-27 and on the advanced technology LTC4V series.

The Williamsport plant is engaged primarily in the production of the well-known Lycoming series of horizontally-opposed air-cooled reciprocating engines ranging from 115 to 425 hp. Turbocharging will be offered on additional models and the horsepower, in some cases, will be increased. Development efforts are being directed to improvements resulting in lower cost of manufacturing and longer time between overhauls, to help offset increasing labour and material costs. During the past year FAA approval was received on a 425 hp turbocharged version of the Model TIGO-541 six-cylinder geared engine. The turbocharger provides air for cabin pressurization, and the engine also has provisions for a freon compressor for cabin cooling and a torquemeter.

Avco Lycoming is also engaged in extensive missile work and in the development and production of mechanical constant-speed transmissions. It is manufacturing re-entry vehicles for the Minuteman ICBM and components for the Titan III space launch vehicle.

AVCO LYCOMING ALF SERIES

Announced in 1970, these high by-pass ratio turbofan engines are private venture developments which succeed the earlier PLF1A-2 and

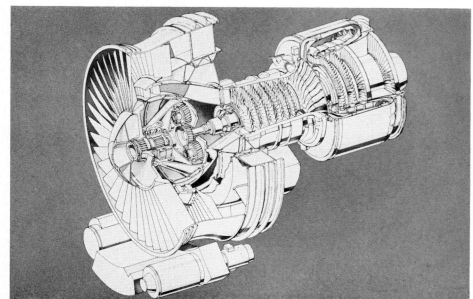

Cutaway drawing of Avco Lycoming ALF 501 high by-pass ratio turbofan (5,800 lb=2,630 kg st)

PLF1C-1 which began bench running during the Winter of 1963-64.

The ALF 501 is a two-spool geared front-fan engine with a by-pass ratio of 6. The engine consists essentially of a front-fan mounted on the forward end of the in-production T55-L-11 turboshaft. The fan airflow is split into two parts with the majority flowing through the by-pass duct and the remainder entering the supercharging stage for the gas generator. The fan is driven by the free power-turbine through a co-axial through-shaft. Take-off rating is 5,800 lb (2,630 kg) st at a specific fuel consumption of 0·417. Dry weight is 1,080 lb (489 kg). Max diameter is 43 in (1,092 mm) and length 52·3 in (1,330 mm).

The ALF 301 is a smaller engine, but is similar in configuration. It employs the T5319A as the "core" and has a by-pass ratio of 5·6. This engine has a take-off rating of 2,600 lb (1,179 kg) st at a specific fuel consumption of 0·450 and has a dry weight of 670 lb (303 kg). Max diameter is 32·5 in (828 mm) and length 50 in (1,260 mm).

AVCO LYCOMING LTC1
Military designation: T53

The T53 is a shaft-turbine with a free power turbine, which was developed under a joint USAF/US Army contract. It had logged over 13 million hours of operation, with every US armed service and in 28 other countries, by January 1970.

Licences for manufacture of the T53 are held by Klöckner-Humboldt-Deutz in Germany, Piaggio in Italy and Kawasaki in Japan. In general these involve the supply of kits of "hot end" parts from Lycoming, with initial production in all three countries being centred on the T53-L-11. All three licensees were in production with the L-13 during 1969.

Versions currently in production or under development are as follows:

T53-L-13. Uprated version of L-11, which it superseded in production in August 1966. Redesigned "hot end" and initial stages of compressor section to provide substantially increased power for hot day and high-altitude performance. Four turbine stages, compared with two in earlier models, and variable-incidence inlet guide vanes combined with redesigned first two compressor stages, permit greater airflow and lower turbine temperatures. This version has atomising combustor to facilitate operation on a wider range of fuels. Powers Bell UH-1C and UH-1D and CUH-1H Iroquois and AH-1G HueyCobra. The **T5313A** commercial version of the T53-L-13 received FAA type certification in Spring 1968 and powers Bell 205A helicopters. Marine and industrial versions are the 1,000 shp **TF12** and 1,250 shp **TF14.**

T53-L-701. Turboprop version of the L-13 incorporating the Lycoming "split-power" propeller reduction gear. Now in production for Grumman OV-1D.

LTC1K-4C. Generally similar to the T53-L-13, but incorporating special seals to allow operation in the attitude range from 105° nose up to 90° nose down. Has 10-minute rating of 1,500 shp and is produced in limited quantity for use in the new Canadair CL-84-1 VTOL aircraft.

T5319A. Latest growth version of T53 turboshaft family. Improvements over L-13 include new gearing, improved cooling of first gas producer turbine nozzle plus air-cooled blades in first turbine rotor. Also incorporates new materials in other turbine stages. Rated at 1,800 shp at take-off. FAA certification imminent.

T5317A. Lower-powered version of -19A with take-off rating limited to 1,500 shp by use of standard L-13 reduction gear.

T5321A. Turboprop version of -19A with "split-power" gear. Uses standard SBAC No. 4 propeller shaft with through-the-shaft oil provisions for use with Dowty-Rotol propeller. Rated at 1,800 shp at take-off.

The following details apply to the T53-L-13 and L-701.

Type: Free-turbine shaft-turbine engine.

Air Intake: Annular casing of magnesium alloy, with 6 struts supporting reduction gearbox and front main bearings. Anti-icing by hot air tapped from engine.

Compressor: Five axial stages followed by a single centrifugal stage. Four-piece magnesium alloy casing with one row of variable-incidence inlet guide vanes and five rows of steel stator blades, bolted to one-piece steel alloy diffuser casing with tangential outlet to combustion chamber. Rotor comprises one stainless steel and four aluminium alloy discs with stainless steel blades and one titanium impeller mounted on shaft supported in forward ball thrust and rear roller bearings. Compression ratio 7·4 : 1. Air mass flow 10·7 lb/sec (4·85 kg/sec) at 25,240 gas producer rpm.

Combustion Chamber: Annular reverse-flow type, with one-piece sheet steel outer shell and annular liner. Twenty-two atomizing fuel injectors.

Fuel Control System: Hydro-mechanical controls for gas generator and for power sections Chandler Evans TA-2S system with one dual

Cutaway drawing of the 1,400 shp Avco Lycoming T53-L-13 turboshaft engine

Avco Lycoming T53-701 (1,451 ehp) turboprop, power plant of the Grumman OV-1D Mohawk

fuel pump. Pump pressure 600 lb/sq in (42 kg/cm²). Main and emergency flow controles Separate interstag air-bleed control.

Fuel Grade: ASTM A-1, MIL-J-5624, MIL-F-26005A, JP-1, JP-4, JP-5, CITE.

Turbine: Four axial-flow turbine stages. Casing fabricated from sheet steel. First two stages, driving compressor, use hollow air-cooled stator vanes and cored-out cast steel rotor blades and are mounted on outer co-axial shaft to gas producer. Second stages, driving reduction gearing, have solid steel blades, and are spline-mounted to shaft.

Exhaust Unit: Fixed-area nozzle. Steel outer casing and inner cone, supported by four radial struts.

Accessories: Electric starter or starter-generator. (not furnished). Bendix-Scintilla TGLN high-energy ignition unit. Two igniter plugs.

Lubrication: Recirculating system, with gear pump with one pressure and one scavenge unit. Filter. Pump pressure 70 lb/sq in (4·9 kg/cm²).

Oil Grade: MIL-L-7808, MIL-L-23699.

Dimensions:

Length overall:

L-13	47·6 in (1,209 mm)
L-701	58·4 in (1,483 mm)

Diameter:

All versions	23·0 in (584 mm)

Weights (Dry):

Less tailpipe:

L-13	549 lb (249 kg)
LTC1K-4C	545 lb (247 kg)
L-701	688 lb (312 kg)

Power Ratings:

Max rating at S/L:

L-13
1,400 shp plus 126 lb (57 kg) st at 20,150 power-turbine rpm

L-701
1,451 ehp (1,400 shp plus 128 lb=58 kg st) at 20,430 rpm

Military rating at S/L:

L-13	1,400 shp
L-701	1,451 ehp

Specific Fuel Consumptions:

At max rating:

L-13	0·580 lb (0·263 kg)/ehp/hr
L-701	0·569 lb (0·258 kg)/ehp/hr

Oil Consumption:

L-13, -701	1·0 lb (450 gr)/hr

AVCO LYCOMING LTC4
Military designation: T55

This engine is based on the T53 design concept but with higher mass flow. It was developed under a joint USAF/US Army contract.

Current production and development versions are as follows:

T55-L-11 (LTC4B-11B). Uprated and redesigned version of L-7, with a second stage added to the compressor turbine, and variable-incidence inlet guide vanes ahead of the compressor. First two compressor stages transonic. New atomising fuel nozzles. Powers CH-47C Chinook, first deliveries having been made in August 1968.

TF25, TF35. Industrial and marine versions of the LTC4; TF25 is rated at 2,000 shp and TF35 is rated at 2,500 shp.

LTC4B-12. Growth version with 4,600 shp maximum power rating (4,370 shp on hot day). Higher turbine entry temperature and increased turbine cooling. Dry weight, 680 lb (308 kg). Now on test.

LTC4R-1. Turboprop version of L-11 with Lycoming "split-power" reduction gear.

The following description applies to the T55-L-11 and LTC4R-1.

Type: Free-turbine gas-turbine engine.

Air Intake: Annular type casing of magnesium alloy with four struts supporting reduction gearbox and front main bearings. Anti-icing by hot air tapped from engine. Provision for intake screens.

COMPRESSOR: Seven axial stages followed by a single centrifugal stage. Two-piece magnesium alloy stator casing with one row of variable inlet guide vanes and seven rows of steel stator blades, bolted to steel alloy diffuser casing to which combustion chamber casing is attached. Rotor comprises seven stainless steel discs and one titanium impeller mounted on shaft supported in forward ball thrust bearing and rear roller bearing. Pressure ratio 8·2 : 1.

COMBUSTION CHAMBER: Annular reverse-flow type. Steel outer shell and inner liner. Twenty-eight fuel burners with downstream injection.

FUEL SYSTEM: Hamilton Standard JFC 31 fuel control system. Gear-type fuel pump, with gas producer and power shaft governors, flow control with altitude compensation and shut-off valve.

FUEL GRADE: MIL-J-5624 grade JP-4, JP-5, MIL-F-46005A or CITE (Combustion Ignition Turbine Engine).

TURBINE: Two two-stage mechanically-independent axial-flow turbines. First turbine, driving compressor, has cored-out cast steel blades, the first stage having air-cooled blades, and is flange-bolted to outer co-axial drive shaft. Hollow stator vanes. Second turbine, driving output shaft, has solid steel blades and is mounted on inner co-axial drive shaft.

EXHAUST UNIT: Fixed-area nozzle, with inner cone, supported by six radial struts.

ACCESSORIES: Electric starter or starter-generator or air or hydraulic starter. Bendix-Scintilla TGLN high-energy ignition unit. Four igniter plugs.

LUBRICATION: Recirculating type. Integral oil tank and cooler on L-11, external tank for 4R-1.

OIL GRADE: MIL-L-7808, MIL-L-23699.

DIMENSIONS:
Length:
T55-L-11	44·03 in (1,119 mm)
LTC4R-1	62·2 in (1,580 mm)

Diameter:
Both versions	24·25 in (616 mm)

WEIGHT (DRY):
T55-L-11	670 lb (304 kg)
LTC4R-1	890 lb (403 kg)

PERFORMANCE RATINGS:
Max rating (10 min):
T55-L-11	3,750 shp
LTC4R-1	3,690 shp plus 285 lb (129 kg) st

Military rating:
T55-L-11	3,400 shp
LTC4R-1	3,344 shp

SPECIFIC FUEL CONSUMPTIONS:
At max T-O and military ratings:
T55-L-11	0·52 lb (0·236 kg)/shp/hr
LTC4R-1	0·52 lb (0·236 kg) eshp/hr

*Flat-rated to unspecified ambient temperature and/or altitude.

AVCO LYCOMING LTC4V SERIES

The Model LTC4V-1 is the first of a new series of advanced technology engines, designed for significant improvements in specific fuel consumption and reduced size and weight. These engines, designated the LTC4V Series, are designed to be scalable in the power range from 4,000 to 10,000 shp.

Based on design studies initiated in 1966, Avco Lycoming has proceeded with the design, fabrication and development of the LTC4V-1, rated at 5,000 shp with a 25 per cent improvement in specific fuel consumption and a power-to-weight ratio approaching 9 : 1. Dry weight of the engine is only 570 lb (258 kg). Following extensive component development of all critical elements from late 1967, initial gas producer testing started in December 1968. Full engine tests began in early 1969, and are proceeding with excellent results.

The basic engine configuration consists of a gas-producer section utilizing a two-spool compressor. The proven reverse-flow annular combustor pioneered by Lycoming is also used on this engine.

Cutaway drawing of the 3,750 shp Avco Lycoming T55-L-11 shaft-turbine engine

The 4,600 shp Avco Lycoming LTC4B-12 shaft-turbine engine

AVCO LYCOMING PLT-27

This entirely new power plant is a private venture regarded as likely ultimately to become very important in scale of output and to replace the T53 as the standard engine in this power class. It is particularly intended to offer severe competition to the General Electric GE12 and Pratt & Whitney ST9. Details remain restricted except for the fact that, despite developing over 1,950 shp with a specific fuel consumption of only 0·43 lb (0·195 kg)/shp/hr, it will be no more than 37 in (939·8 mm) long and weigh only 280 lb (127 kg). Development was continuing at a rapid pace during 1969.

AVCO LYCOMING O-235 and O-290 SERIES

The version of the O-290 Series engine in current production is the O-290-D2C, which differs from the preceding O-290-D2B by having retard breaker magnetos.

TYPE: Four-cylinder horizontally-opposed air-cooled.

CYLINDERS: Bore (O-235-C1B) 4⅜ in (111 mm), (O-290-D2C) 4⅞ in (123·7 mm). Stroke (both) 3⅞ in (98·4 mm). Aluminium alloy head screwed and shrunk on to steel barrel. Cylinder assemblies attached to crankcase by studs and nuts.

PISTONS: Machined from aluminium alloy forgings. O-235 piston has four rings, two compression, an oil regulator and an oil scraper. O-290 has three rings, two compression and one oil regulating. Fully-floating gudgeon-pins with aluminium alloy retaining plugs.

CONNECTING RODS: Forged steel. Copper-lead steel-backed precision type bearings. Bronze bushed little-ends.

The 380 hp Avco Lycoming IGSO-540-A six-cylinder engine

The 425 hp Avco Lycoming TIGO-541-E six-cylinder engine

CRANKSHAFT: One-piece forged chrome nickel molybdenum steel four-throw shaft on four nitrided bearings.

CRANKCASE: Aluminium alloy casting split cn vertical centre-line. Four precision copper-lead steel-backed main bearings.

VALVE GEAR: Two valves per cylinder. Inlet valves of Silchrome No. 1, exhaust valves of AMS 5682 with Stellite-faced heads. Valve seats of AMS 5700 shrunk into head.

INDUCTION: Marvel-Schebler MA-3A and MA-3S1A carburettor with manual altitude control and idle cut-off. Centre zone distribution chamber in oil sump.

IGNITION: Two Bendix Scintilla S4LN magnetos, incorporating a retard breaker.

LUBRICATION: Full pressure wet sump type.

ACCESSORIES: Starter, generator and tachometer drive. Optional drives for fuel pump and vacuum pump can be supplied.

DIMENSIONS, WEIGHTS AND PERFORMANCE: See Table.

AVCO LYCOMING O-320 SERIES

The O-320 is basically the same as the O-290-D2C except for an increase in cylinder bore to 5⅛ in (130 mm) with a corresponding increase in swept volume to 319·8 cu in (5·2 litres), and use of a Marvel-Schebler MA-4SPA carburettor.

It is available in low-compression and high-compression versions for use with 80/87 or 91/96 octane fuels respectively.

For other details see table.

AVCO LYCOMING IO-320 SERIES

The O-320 engines are available as fuel-injected models with both high and low compression. For further details see table.

AVCO LYCOMING O-340 and O-360 SERIES

The O-340 is basically the same as the O-290 except for an increase in stroke to 4⅛ in (105 mm) with a corresponding increase in swept volume to 340·4 cu in (5·58 litres), and use of the larger Marvel-Schebler MA-4-5 carburettor. The O-360, which has the highest rating of any four-cylinder engine certificated for production in America, is the same as the O-340 except for a further increase in stroke to 4⅜ in (111 mm), with a corresponding increase in swept volume to 361 cu in (5·92 litres). Both engines are available in low and high compression versions for use with 80/87 or 91/96 octane fuel respectively.

The VO-360-B1A is the helicopter version of the O-360 arranged for installation with the crankshaft vertical.

The IMO-360-B1B is a fuel-injected single-ignition version of the O-360 for use in unmanned aircraft.

For further details see table.

AVCO LYCOMING IO-360 SERIES

The O-360 is built in two fuel-injection versions: the IO-360-A series with tuned injection, tuned induction and high output cylinders, and the IO-360-B series with continuous-flow port injection and standard cylinders.

AVCO LYCOMING O-435 SERIES

The O-435 Series includes direct-drive, geared, and geared and supercharged models, details of which will be found in the Table. The VO-435-A1F, TVO-435-A1A and TVO-435-B1A are helicopter engines for vertical installation. The TVO-435 engines are equipped with an AiResearch exhaust-driven turbo-supercharger which allows them to maintain rated power to 20,000 ft (6,100 m). The GO-435-C2B2-6 is a geared-drive wet sump engine with a propeller governor drive, mounted on the left side of the propeller reduction-gear housing.

The 310 hp Avco Lycoming TIO-540 six-cylinder engine fitted to the Piper Turbo Navajo

The 400 hp eight-cylinder Avco Lycoming IO-720-A1A engine

TYPE: Six-cylinder horizontally-opposed air-cooled incorporating the major components of O-290.

CYLINDERS: Bore 4⅞ in (123·7 mm). Stroke 3⅞ in (98·4 mm).

PISTONS: Aluminium alloy pistons with two compression and two oil control rings.

CONNECTING RODS: H-section steel forgings with replaceable bearing inserts in big-ends and split bronze bushings in little-ends.

CRANKSHAFT: Machined from chrome nickel molybdenum steel forging. All bearing surfaces nitrided.

CRANKCASE: Aluminium alloy casting split on the vertical centre-line. Additional ball-thrust bearing at forward end of case.

INDUCTION: Marvel-Schebler MA-4-5 or Stromberg PS-5BD single-barrel carburettor attached to bottom of oil sump casting. The distributing zone is submerged in oil. Separate induction pipes lead to inlet valves.

IGNITION: Two Bendix-Scintilla magnetos driven by spur gears from the timing gear.

LUBRICATION: Full pressure type, including valve mechanism. Crankshaft equipped with centrifugal sludge-removers. Pistons, gudgeon-pins and accessory drive gears lubricated by splash.

ACCESSORY HOUSING: Aluminium alloy casting bolted to rear of crankcase and top rear of oil sump. Houses oil pump and geared accessory drives, and provides mounting for starter and generator, fuel pump, tachometer drive and magnetos. Vacuum pump drive optional equipment.

STARTING: Delco-Remy 12-volt automotive type starter. Starter torque applied to crankshaft gear through Bendix-type starter drive.

DIMENSIONS, WEIGHTS AND PERFORMANCE: See Table.

AVCO LYCOMING O-480 SERIES

The O-480 Series is basically the same as the O-435 Series except for an increase in cylinder bore to 5⅛ in (130 mm) and in swept volume to 479·7 cu in (7·8 litres). The geared and normally aspirated engines are available in low and high-compression versions for use with 80/87 or 100/130 minimum octane fuels respectively. The geared and supercharged GSO-480-B Series have a supercharger drive ratio of 11·27 : 1, providing rated power to 8,000 ft (2,440 m) on 100/130 minimum octane fuel. The IGSO-480-A1B6 is similar to the GSO-480 except that it is fitted with direct fuel injection into the eye of the supercharger. High-compression and supercharged engines are provided with internal oil cooling of the pistons as standard equipment. For other details see table.

Right: **the 270 hp Avco Lycoming TVO-435-B1A turbocharged vertical helicopter engine**

Below: **the 200 hp Avco Lycoming IO-360-A1A flat-four engine**

AVCO LYCOMING HORIZONTALLY-OPPOSED PISTON ENGINES

Engine Model	No. of Cylinders	Rated output at Sea Level hp at rpm	Capacity cu in (litres)	Compression Ratio	Fuel Grade	Weight Dry lb (kg)	Overall Length in (mm)	Overall Width in (mm)	Overall Height in (mm)	Gear Ratio†
O-235-C1B	4	115 at 2,800	233 (3·85)	6·75 : 1	80	240 (109)	29·81 (757)	32·00 (812)	22·40 (569)	D
O-290-D2C	4	135 at 2,600 T-O 140 at 2,800	289 (4·75)	7·0 : 1	80/87	263 (119)	29·81 (757)	32·24 (819)	22·68 (576)	D
O-320-A2B and -E2A	4	150 at 2,700	319·8 (5·2)	7·0 : 1	80/87	272 (123)	29·56 (751)	32·24 (819)	22·99 (584)	D
O-320-E2D	4	150 at 2,700	319·8 (5·2)	7·0 : 1	80/87	268 (122)	29·05 (738)	32·24 (819)	22·99 (584)	D
IO-320-B1A	4	160 at 2,700	319·8 (5·2)	8·5 : 1	91/96	285 (129)	33·59 (853)	32·24 (819)	19·22 (488)	D
IO-320-C1A	4	160 at 2,700	319·8 (5·2)	8·5 : 1	100/130	294 (134)	33·59 (853)	32·24 (819)	19·22 (488)	D
LIO-320-B1A	4	160 at 2,700	319·8 (5·2)	8·5 : 1	91/96	292 (133)	33·59 (853)	32·24 (819)	19·22 (488)	D
AIO-320-A1A	4	160 at 2,700	319·8 (5·2)	8·5 : 1	91/96	306 (138)	30·08 (764)	32·24 (819)	20·76 (527)	D
O-360-A1D	4	180 at 2,700	361 (5·92)	8·5 : 1	91/96	284 (129)	29·81 (757)	33·37 (848)	24·59 (625)	D
O-360-A1H	4	180 at 2,700	361 (5·92)	8·5 : 1	91/96	294 (134)	31·82 (807)	33·37 (848)	19·22 (488)	D
O-360-A1F6	4	180 at 2,700	361 (5·92)	8·5 : 1	91/96	294 (134)	30·70 (780)	33·37 (848)	24·59 (625)	D
O-360-A3A	4	180 at 2,700	361 (5·92)	8·5 : 1	91/96	285 (129)	29·56 (751)	33·37 (848)	24·59 (625)	D
AIO-360-A1A	4	200 at 2,700	361 (5·92)	8·7 : 1	100/130	331 (150)	30·08 (764)	34·25 (870)	20·76 (527)	D
HIO-360-D1A	4	190 at 3,200 to 4,200 ft	361 (5·92)	10·0 : 1	100/130	321 (145)	35·28 (894)	34·25 (870)	19·48 (495)	D
HIO-360-A1A	4	180 at 2,900 to 3,000 ft (915 m)	361 (5·92)	8·7 : 1	100/130	315 (143)	33·65 (855)	34·25 (870)	19·48 (495)	D
HIO-360-B1A	4	180 at 2,900	361 (5·92)	8·5 : 1	91/96	290 (132)	32·09 (815)	33·37 (848)	19·38 (492)	D
HIO-360-C1A	4	205 at 2,900	361 (5·92)	8·7 : 1	100/130	322 (146)	31·14 (791)	34·25 (870)	19·48 (495)	D
IO-360-A1A	4	200 at 2,700	361 (5·92)	8·7 : 1	100/130	320 (145)	29·81 (757)	34·25 (870)	21·61 (549)	D
IO-360-B1B	4	180 at 2,700	361 (5·92)	8·5 : 1	91/96	295 (134)	29·81 (757)	33·37 (848)	24·91 (633)	D
IO-360-F1A	4	180 at 2,700	361 (5·92)	8·5 : 1	100/130	303 (137)	32·09 (815)	33·37 (848)	20·70 (526)	D
IVO-360-A1A	4	180 at 2,900	361 (5·92)	8·5 : 1	91/96	300 (136)	30·00 (762)	33·37 (848)	22·95 (583)	D V
TIO-360-A1B	4	200 at 2,575 to 15,000 ft (4,575 m)	361 (5·92)	7·3 : 1	100/130	386 (175)	45·41 (1,153)	34·25 (870)	19·92 (506)	D
HIO-360-A1A	4	200 at 2,700	361 (5·92)	8·7 : 1	100/130	331 (150)	30·08 (764)	34·25 (870)	20·76 (527)	D
VO-435-A1F	6	250 at 3,200 T-O 260 at 3,400	434 (7·1)	7·3 : 1	80/87	399 (181)	34·73 (882)	33·58 (853)	24·13 (612)	D V
TVO-435-B1A	6	220 at 3,200 to 20,000 ft (6,100 m) T-O 270 at 3,200	434 (7·1)	7·3 : 1	100/130	478 (217)	34·73 (882)	33·58 (853)	35·65 (905)	D V
TVO-435-G1A	6	220 at 3,200 to 20,000 ft (6,096 m) T-O 280 at 3,200 to 18,000 ft (5,486 m)	434 (7·1)	7·3 : 1	100/130	465 (211)	34·73 (882)	33·58 (853)	35·67 (906)	D V
IGO-480-A1A6	6	280 at 3,000 T-O 295 at 3,400	479·7 (7·8)	8·7 : 1	100/130	455 (206)	40·76 (1,036)	33·12 (842)	28·02 (712)	0·642 : 1
GO-480-B1D	6	260 at 3,000 T-O 270 at 3,400	479·7 (7·8)	7·3 : 1	80/87	432 (196)	38·64 (981)	33·12 (842)	28·02 (712)	0·642 : 1
GO-480-G1D6	6	280 at 3,000 T-O 295 at 3,400	479·7 (7·8)	8·7 : 1	100/130	437 (198)	38·64 (981)	33·12 (842)	28·02 (712)	0·642 : 1
IGSO-480-A1F6	6	320 at 3,200 to 11,000 ft (3,350 m) T-O 340 at 3,400	479·7 (7·8)	7·3 : 1	100/130	498 (226)	47·56 (1,208)	33·12 (842)	22·44 (570)	0·642 : 1
O-540-A1D5	6	250 at 2,575	541·5 (8·86)	8·5 : 1	91/96	367 (166)	37·22 (945)	33·37 (848)	24·56 (624)	D
O-540-B2B5	6	235 at 2,575	541·5 (8·86)	7·2 : 1	80/87	395 (179)	37·22 (945)	33·77 (858)	24·56 (624)	D
O-540-9	6	305 at 3,200 to 3,000 ft (915 m)	541·5 (8·86)	8·7 : 1	100/130	452 (205)	34·73 (882)	34·70 (880)	25·57 (649)	D V
IO-540-C4B5	6	250 at 2,575	541·5 (8·86)	8·5 : 1	91/96	402 (182)	38·42 (976)	33·37 (848)	24·46 (622)	D
IO-540-D4A5	6	260 at 2,700	541·5 (8·86)	8·5 : 1	91/96	402 (182)	38·42 (976)	33·37 (848)	24·46 (622)	D
IO-540-G1A5	6	290 at 2,575	541·5 (8·86)	8·7 : 1	100/130	443 (201)	38·62 (981)	34·25 (870)	19·60 (498)	D
IO-540-J4A5	6	250 at 2,575	541·5 (8·86)	8·5 : 1	100/130	409 (186)	39·34 (999)	33·37 (848)	24·46 (622)	D
IO-540-K1A5	6	300 at 2,700	541·5 (8·86)	8·7 : 1	100/130	470 (213)	39·34 (999)	34·25 (870)	19·60 (498)	D
IO-540-N1A5	6	260 at 2,700	541·5 (8·86)	8·5 : 1	91/96	428 (194)	38·42 (976)	33·37 (848)	24·46 (622)	D
IO-540-P1A5	6	290 at 2,575	541·5 (8·86)	8·7 : 1	100/130	455 (206)	39·34 (999)	34·25 (870)	19·60 (498)	D
IGO-540-B1C	6	325 at 3,000 T-O 350 at 3,400	541·5 (8·86)	8·7 : 1	100/130	500 (227)	46·38 (1,178)	34·25 (870)	21·66 (550)	0·642 : 1
IGSO-540-A1D	6	360 at 3,200 to 10,500 ft (3,200 m) T-O 380 at 3,400	541·5 (8·86)	7·3 : 1	100/130	540 (245)	48·15 (1,223)	34·25 (870)	28·44 (722)	0·642 : 1
VO-540-B1B3	6	305 at 3,200	541·5 (8·86)	7·3 : 1	80/87	444 (202)	34·73 (882)	34·70 (880)	24·29 (617)	D V
VO-540-B2D	6	Max Continuous 305 at 3,200	541·5 (8·86)	7·3 : 1	80/87	440 (200)	34·73 (882)	34·70 (880)	25·57 (649)	D V
VO-540-C1A	6	305 at 3,200 to 3,000 ft (915 m)	541·5 (8·86)	8·7 : 1	100/130	439 (199)	34·73 (882)	34·70 (880)	25·57 (649)	D V
VO-540-C1C3	6	305 at 3,200	541·5 (8·86)	8·7 : 1	100/130	453 (205)	34·73 (882)	34·70 (880)	25·57 (649)	D V
IVO-540-A1A	6	305 at 3,200 to 3,000 ft (915 m)	541·5 (8·86)	8·7 : 1	100/130	435 (197)	34·73 (882)	34·70 (880)	24·22 (615)	D V
TIO-540-A1A	6	310 at 2,575 to 15,000 ft (4,575 m)	541·5 (8·86)	7·3 : 1	100/130	535 (242)	51·34 (1,304)	34·25 (870)	22·71 (577)	D
TIO-540-C1A	6	250 at 2,575 to 15,000 ft (4,575 m)	541·5 (8·86)	7·2 : 1	100/130	483 (219)	40·38 (1,027)	33·37 (848)	30·33 (769)	D
TIVO-540-A2A	6	305 at 3,200 to 15,000 ft (4,575 m)	541·5 (8·86)	7·3 : 1	100/130	507 (230)	34·73 (882)	34·70 (880)	36·00 (914)	D V
TIO-541-A1A	6	310 at 2,575 to 15,000 ft (4,575 m)	541·5 (8·86)	7·3 : 1	100/130	578 (262)	49·09 (1,247)	34·25 (870)	21·38 (543)	D
TIO-541-E1A4	6	380 at 3,000 to 15,000 ft (4,575 m)	541·5 (8·86)	7·3 : 1	100/130	632 (286)	52·07 (1,320)	35·66 (905)	25·17 (640)	D
TIGO-541-C1A	6	400 at 3,200 to 15,000 ft (4,575 m)	541·5 (8·86)	7·3 : 1	100/130	703 (319)	57·57 (1,462)	34·86 (885)	22·65 (575)	0·667 : 1
TIGO-541-E1A	6	425 at 3,200 to 15,000 ft (4,575 m)	541·5 (8·86)	7·3 : 1	100/130	701 (318)	57·57 (1,462)	34·86 (885)	22·65 (575)	0·667 : 1
IO-720-A1A	8	400 at 2,650	722 (11·84)	8·7 : 1	100/130	597 (271)	46·08 (1,170)	34·25 (870)	22·10 (561)	D

† D=Direct drive; V=Vertical mounting

AVCO LYCOMING O-540 SERIES

The O-540 is basically a direct-drive six-cylinder version of the four-cylinder O-360 with the same bore and stroke and a swept volume of 541·5 cu in (8·86 litres). It is currently available in a high-compression configuration for use with 91/96 minimum octane fuel. A low-compression model for use with 80/87 fuel can be provided and the vertically-mounted VO-540 is in production as a helicopter power plant. The TIVO-540-A1A, equipped with an AiResearch turbo-supercharger, maintains rated power to 17,000 ft (5,180 m). During 1968-1970 computer analysis of engine service records has enabled time between overhaul to be increased by up to 50 per cent. The O-540-B (Cherokee 235) and O-540-E (Comanche and Cherokee Six) are both now cleared at 1,800 hours. For other details see table.

AVCO LYCOMING IO-540 SERIES

A fuel-injection, tuned induction version of the O-540 with high-output cylinders, model IO-540-B1A5, is rated at 290 hp at 2,575 rpm. A geared version of this engine, model IGO-540-B1A, is rated at 350 hp at 3,400 rpm for take-off. The geared and supercharged model IGSO-540-B1A has a supercharger ratio of 11·27 : 1 and provides take-off power to 11,000 ft (3,350 m) altitude on 100/130 minimum octane fuel. The IO-540J (Turbo Aztec) and TIO-540-A (Turbo Navajo) have this year been cleared to operate 1,500 hours between overhauls, and the IO-540C (Aztec), IO-540D (Comanche), IO-540K (Cherokee Six) and IO-540M (Navajo) have been cleared to 1,800 hours. For further details see table.

AVCO LYCOMING TIO-541 SERIES

First engine in this new turbosupercharged six-cylinder series is the TIO-541-A1A, which gives 310 hp to 15,000 ft (4,570 m) and 230 hp to 25,000 ft (7,620 m).

A version with double-scroll blower, to provide cabin pressurisation also, is fitted in the Mooney Mark 22 Mustang business aircraft. For other details, see table.

AVCO LYCOMING IO-720 SERIES

This eight-cylinder version of the IO-540 engine is available and has a rating of 400 hp at 2,650 rpm. For further details see table.

AVCO LYCOMING NEW RANGE

Avco Lycoming, Williamsport, are continuing the development of a new series of high-performance normally-aspirated and turbocharged engines.

BELL

BELL AEROSPACE DIVISION OF TEXTRON INC

HEAD OFFICE AND WORKS:
Buffalo, New York

OFFICERS: See "Aircraft" section

Bell has been engaged in the design, development and production of liquid-propellant rocket engines since 1946.

A single-chamber engine which Bell developed originally to power a nuclear weapon pod to be carried by the B-58 Hustler bomber is now being used in modified form in the Agena space vehicle and provides upper-stage propulsion for numerous spacecraft. The latest version is able to offer multiple re-start capability and was used for the Gemini rendezvous programme. The Agena vehicles used in this programme were also fitted with a Bell-produced secondary propulsion system of 16 lb (7·25 kg) and 200 lb (90 kg) st radiation-cooled rocket motors for fine adjustment of their velocity prior to the docking manoeuvre.

On 28 February 1970, Bell completed 11 years of space use of the Agena series of engines. In that time the Models 8096 and 8247, described hereunder, have been used in almost 300 missions by the US Air Force and NASA with an overall reliability of 99·6 per cent.

Bell reaction controls are used on the Centaur space vehicle and Minuteman III ICBM.

BELL MODEL 8096 AGENA ENGINE

This engine was first developed as the power plant for one of the weapon pods to be carried by the B-58 Hustler supersonic bomber. It is being used in modified form, with gimballed chamber, as the power unit of the Lockheed-built Agena vehicle, forming the second stage of the Thor-Agena, Atlas-Agena and other space vehicles.

During its development the engine has undergone five major modifications, each resulting in an improvement in specific impulse. The present version, designated Model 8096, has a specific impulse of nearly 300 sec, which is more than 10% better than the original version of 1959, an increase equivalent to 500 lb (225 kg) in payload for Earth orbital missions.

The Model 8096 engine is a single-chamber pump-fed engine, running on red fuming nitric acid and unsymmetrical dimethyl-hydrazine (UDMH) hypergolic propellants. It gives 16,000 lb (7,257 kg) st and has re-start capability in space. This feature can be used, for example, to change from a circular to an elliptical orbit.

The Model 8096 engine has the ability to be re-started twice in space. It powers the Agena vehicles used in many US Air Force and NASA programmes, including Ranger, Mariner, Nimbus, Echo 2, Alouette, OGO, POGO, AOSO and OAO.

DIMENSIONS:

Length overall	approx 84 in (2,134 mm)
Nozzle diameter	35 in (889 mm)

WEIGHT: approx 290 lb (132 kg)

PERFORMANCE:

Thrust	16,000 lb (7,250 kg)
Chamber pressure approx 500 lb/sq in (35 kg/cm²)	
Specific impulse	approx 300 sec

BELL MODEL 8247

A modified Model 8096 Agena engine was used

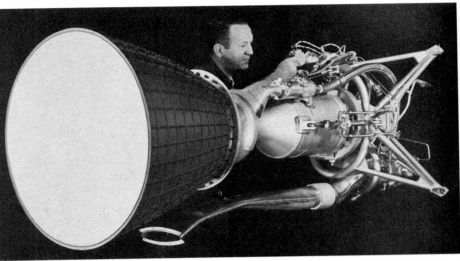

Bell Agena single-chamber liquid-propellant rocket engine

in the Gemini programme to propel the Agena Target Vehicle. This engine was designated Model 8247 and had a multi-restart capability. This capability was called for by NASA's Project Gemini programme, and to meet it the Agena 8096 was used as a basis but with modified starting system, fuel and oxidant valves and changed electrical controls. The turbopump assembly and thrust chamber were essentially unchanged. The classic demonstration of the ability of the 8247 came with Gemini 8. Launched on March 16, 1966, the Agena target vehicle was placed in near-perfect 185-mile circular orbit by a single 186-second burn of the Model 8247. In the three days following the historic first space docking and separation, the Agena engine was fired eight times on command from NASA ground controllers to change the Agena's orbital altitude and plane. One orbital adjustment was correctly made by a minimum impulse burn of less than two seconds' duration.

BELL SECONDARY PROPULSION SYSTEM

The Secondary Propulsion System was developed by Bell for the Agena target vehicle to re-orientate the propellants in the main tanks prior to each space firing of the Agena 8247 engine. A second role was to act as vernier propulsion to effect fine velocity adjustment during docking with Gemini spacecraft. Each Agena target had two SP modules fitting astride its aft rack. Each comprised a storable bi-propellant system containing mixed oxides of nitrogen and UDMH fuel contained in tanks incorporating positive-feed metal bellows to expel the fluids into the appropriate thrust chamber. There were two chambers, both fixed and cooled by radiation. The larger chamber in each module was used for vernier adjustment of vehicle velocity; the smaller chamber was used to initiate propellant feed to the main engine. These small chambers were fabricated in tantalum and tungsten.

DIMENSIONS:

Length	51 in (1,295 mm)

Bell Secondary Propulsion System for Agena target vehicle

Width	35 in (889 mm)
Height	15 in (381 mm)

WEIGHTS:

Dry	129 lb (58 kg)
Gross	304 lb (138 kg)

PERFORMANCE:

Larger chamber thrust	200 lb (91 kg)
Smaller chamber thrust	16 lb (7·3 kg)

DREHER

DREHER ENGINEERING COMPANY

ADDRESS: 1423 Stanford Street, Santa Monica, California 90404

Mr Max Dreher, an aeronautical engineer, has built a series of small turbojet engines over a period of 24 years. The latest one, known as the TJD-76 Baby Mamba, has been mounted on his Prue 215A all-metal 12·0 m sailplane as an auxiliary power plant.

A lighter version is under development and has been designated TJD-76C. Component testing is taking place on the larger TJD-79A Baby Python, described below. This is considered likely to prove much more useful in sailplane applications. So far eight Dreher engines have been built, and manufacture is concentrated on 12 licence-built TJD-76C engines, to be used as research tools, and on the TJD-76C low-cost drone version.

Most of Dreher's effort in the past year has been devoted to the TJD-76 family, but greater attention is about to be paid to the TJD-79. In addition Mr Dreher and his colleagues are making a preliminary study of a two-shaft turbofan in the 200 lb (90·8 kg) st class.

DREHER TJD-76A BABY MAMBA

This very small turbojet engine has a single-stage centrifugal compressor, straight-through-flow annular combustion chamber, with six injectors, and single-stage axial-flow turbine. The shaft runs on two ball bearings. Starting is by compressed air.

Test-bed for the Baby Mamba is a Prue 215A all-metal sailplane, with a span of 39 ft 4½ in (12·00 m) and T-O weight of 605 lb (275 kg). Glide ratio with engine fitted is 28 : 1.

DIMENSIONS:

Length overall	16·3 in (414 mm)
Diameter	6 in (152 mm)

WEIGHTS:

Bare turbojet	17 lb (7·7 kg)
Complete power plant package	25 lb (11·35 kg)

DREHER TJD-76C BABY MAMBA

This new version of the Baby Mamba is lighter and introduces several mechanical and aerodynamic improvements, including a tachometer generator for direct rpm reading.

TYPE: Single-shaft turbojet.

AIR INTAKE: At front. Air flow 1·1 lb (0·50 kg) sec.

COMPRESSOR: Single-stage mixed-flow. Single 17-4 PH stainless steel impeller with sixteen vanes. Splined to shaft and supported in two ball bearings. Mixed-flow two-stage diffuser of 347 stainless steel. Pressure ratio 2·8 : 1.

COMPRESSOR CASING: Of 2024 aluminium alloy and 347 stainless steel.

COMBUSTION CHAMBER: Annular type with Hastelloy X outer casing and flame tube. Vaporising system with fuel-air pre-mix One spark plug in flame tube.

FUEL SYSTEM: Manual with pressurised fuel supply, or electrically-driven fuel pump. Fuel pressure 80 lb/sq in (5·6 kg/cm²). Automatic system for drone applications.

FUEL GRADE: Kerosene or petrol.

NOZZLE GUIDE VANES: Single axial stage, with sixteen investment-cast vanes in Stellite 31. Iron 100.

TURBINE: Single-stage axial-flow, with nineteen integrally-cast blades, of Inconel 713 LC. Gas temperature 1,420°F before turbine, 1,250°F after turbine at continuous cruising power.

JET PIPE: Fixed type, with jet pipe and cone of Hasteloy X.

LUBRICATION: Air-oil mist system with t otal loss, using bleed air equivalent to 2·5 per cent of total mass flow. Capacity 2 US pints (1 litre).

OIL GRADE: MIL-L-7808E (Turbo 15).

MOUNTING: Two rigid connections on diffuser section and one flexible connection on turbine section.

STARTING: Compressed air (150 lb/sq in = 10·5 kg/cm²), via three nozzles driving turbine wheel.

DIMENSIONS:
Length overall .... 16·38 in (416 mm)
Diameter .... 5·94 in (151 mm)

WEIGHT:
Dry .... 13·5 lb (6·1 kg)
Complete powerplant including fuel tank .... 22 lb (10·0 kg)

PERFORMANCE RATINGS:
Max .... 55 lb (25 kg) st
Cont .... 45 lb (20 kg) st

SPECIFIC FUEL CONSUMPTION:
at max rating .... 1·5

OIL CONSUMPTION: at max rating ... 25 cc/min

DREHER TJD-79A BABY PYTHON

Derived from the Baby Mamba, this enlarged unit is still in the component-testing stage, but work on it will shortly be accelerated.

TYPE: Single-shaft turbojet.

AIR INTAKE: At front. Air flow 2·4 lb (1·1 kg)/sec.

Prue 215A sailplane used as flying test-bed for Baby Mamba turbojet

COMPRESSOR: Single-stage, mixed-flow. Precision-cast 356-T-6 aluminium-alloy impeller with 18 vanes. Made in one piece with shaft and supported in ball bearing. Mixed-flow cascade-type diffuser of 321 stainless steel. Pressure ratio 3 : 1.

COMBUSTION CHAMBER: Annular type with Inconel 625 casing and Hastelloy X flame-tube. Vaporising system with fuel/air pre-mix chamber. One spark plug in flame tube.

FUEL SYSTEM: Semi-automatic with pressurised supply or electrically-driven pump; fully automatic feed for drone application.

FUEL GRADE: Petrol or JO-5.

NOZZLE GUIDE VANES: Single axial stage with 18 vanes precision-cast in Stellite 31.

TURBINE: Single-stage axial with disc and 21 blades cast as one unit in Inconel 713 LC. Gas temperature 1,480°F before turbine, 1,290°F behind.

JET PIPE: Fixed type fabricated in Hastelloy X.

LUBRICATION: Air-oil mist, total loss, using bleed air equivalent to 2·5 per cent of total flow. Capacity 2 litres.

OIL GRADE: MIL-L-7808E or Jet-2.

MOUNTING: Two rigid connections on diffuser and one flexible connection on turbine section.

STARTING: Compressed air (150 lb/sq in = 10·5 kg/cm²), via six nozzles driving turbine wheel.

DIMENSIONS:
Length overall .... 25·6 in (650 mm)
Diameter .... 11 in (279·4 mm)

WEIGHTS (estimated):
Dry .... 28 lb (12·7 kg)
Complete with accessories .. 36 lb (16·3 kg)

PERFORMANCE RATING:
Max thrust (S/L, std day) .. 120 lb (54·4 kg)

SPECIFIC FUEL CONSUMPTION:
at max rating .... 1·4

OIL CONSUMPTION:
at max rating .... 40 cc/min

Dreher TJD-76A Baby Mamba turbojet engine

Artist's impression of the Dreher TJD-79A Baby Python turbojet

FRANKLIN

FRANKLIN ENGINE COMPANY, INC
(Subsidiary of Allied Aero Industries, Inc)

HEAD OFFICE AND WORKS:
Syracuse, New York 13208

PRESIDENT AND GENERAL MANAGER:
Roger Swanson

VICE-PRESIDENT SALES, SERVICE: V. J. Mecca
VICE-PRESIDENT ENGINEERING: J. D. Cregan

Known formerly as Aircooled Motors, Inc, this company adopted its present name in 1961 when its assets were purchased by Aero Industries Inc.

The original company produced the first of its very successful series of light horizontally-opposed air-cooled engines in 1938. Up to the outbreak

of war it had placed on the market engines of four and six cylinders ranging in output from 65 to 150 hp.

Until recently, production was restricted to six-cylinder engines in the 150-240 hp category. Now, the range of Franklin products is being broadened as quickly as possible to offer a completely new series of light horizontally-opposed

FRANKLIN HELICOPTER ENGINES

Engine Model	No. and arrangement of cylinders	Capacity cu in (cc)	Compression Ratio	Max T-O rating at sea level hp at rpm	Cruising specific fuel consumption per hp/hr lb (kg)	Fuel Grade	Overall Length in (mm)	Overall Width in (mm)	Overall Height in (mm)	Weight Dry lb (kg)
6V4-200,C32,C33	6 Vert	335 (5,490)	8·5 : 1	200 at 3,100	0·52 (0·235)	91/96	30·67 (779)	31·3 (795)	38·14 (969)	320 (145)
6V-335-A, B	6 Vert	335 (5,490)	8·5 : 1	210 at 3,100	0·54 (0·245)	91/96	30·67 (779)	31·3 (795)	38·14 (969)	320 (145)
6V-335-A1A, A1B	6 Vert	335 (5,490)	7·0 : 1	200 at 3,100	0·52 (0·235)	80/87	30·67 (779)	31·3 (795)	38·14 (969)	320 (145)
6VS-335-A1, B1, A, B	6 Vert	335 (5,490)	7·0 : 1	240 at 3,200 S/L to 13,000 ft (4,000 m)	0·51 (0·23)	100/130	39·73 (1,009)	31·3 (795)	31·8 (965·4)	365 (165·5)
6V-350-A, B	6 Vert	350 (5,735)	10·5 : 1	235 at 3,200	0·46 (0·21)	100/130	30·67 (779)	31·3 (795)		
6A-335-A	6 Horiz	335 (5,490)	8·5 : 1	210 at 3,100	0·54 (0·245)	91/96	30·67 (779)	31·3 (795)	38·14 (969)	307 (139)
6A-335-D	6 Horiz	335 (5,490)	8·5 : 1	200 at 3,100	0·54 (0·245)	100/130	32·1 (795)	31·3 (795)	27·5 (699)	307 (139)
6A-335-D	6 Horiz	350 (5,735)	10·5 : 1	235 at 3,200	0·46 (0·21)	100/130	32·1 (815)	31·3 (795)	27·5 (699)	307 (139)
6A-350-D1	6 Horiz	350 (5,735)	7·0 : 1	200 at 3,200	0·46 (0·21)	80/87	32·5 (768·4)	31·3 (795)	25·3 (642·6)	320 (145)
6A-350-D1A	6 Horiz	350 (5,735)	10·5 : 1	230 at 3,200	0·46 (0·21)	100/130	32·5 (768·4)	31·3 (795)	25·3 (642·6)	319 (144·6)
6AS-335-A, B	6 Horiz	335 (5,490)	7·0 : 1	260 at 3,200 S/L to 10,000 ft (3,050 m)	0·51 (0·23)	100/130	34·5 (877)	31·3 (795)	25·25 (641)	347 (157)

piston-engines for fixed-wing aircraft and heli-copters. Details of current models are given in two tables below.

The 180 hp 6A-335B is FAA approved for use in the Cessna 172 and 175. Owners can have their aircraft re-engined by Franklin or by any certificated aircraft and power plant mechanic.

With the 6A-335B, maximum speed is increased by 10-15 mph (16-24 kmh), and the aircraft will cruise at 142 mph (229 kmh) at 70% power on 80/87 octane fuel.

Franklin is also building the Swiss Saurer turbine APU for Aero Industries Inc.

Right: **The 125 hp Franklin 4A-235-B3**

Right: **The 250 hp Franklin 6AS-350-A**

FRANKLIN FIXED-WING AIRCRAFT ENGINES

Engine Model	No. and arrangement of cylinders	Capacity cu in (cc)	Compression Ratio	Max T-O rating at sea level hp at rpm	Cruising specific fuel consumption per hp/hr lb (kg)	Fuel Grade	Overall Length in (mm)	Overall Width in (mm)	Overall Height in (mm)	Weight Dry lb (kg)
4A-235-B3	4 Horiz	235 (3,850)	8·5 : 1	125 at 2,800	0·49 (0·22)	100/130	29·4 (747)	31·3 (795)	25·1 (638)	240 (109)
4A-235-B	4 Horiz	235 (3,850)	8·5 : 1	130 at 2,800	0·50 (0·227)	100/130	30·5 (775)	31·3 (795)	25·1 (638)	225 (102)
6A-335-B, B1	6 Horiz	335 (5,490)	7·0 : 1	180 at 2,800	0·50 (0·227)	80/87	37·5 (953)	31·3 (795)	25·25 (641)	319 (144·6)
6A-350-C1, C1A	6 Horiz	350 (5,735)	10·5 : 1	220 at 2,800	0·46 (0·21)	100/130	37·5 (953)	31·3 (795)	25·25 (641)	329 (149)
6A-350-C2, C2A	6 Horiz	350 (5,735)	10·5 : 1	215 at 2,800	0·46 (0·21)	100/130	37·5 (953)	31·3 (795)	25·25 (641)	329 (419)
6AS-350-A, A1	6 Horiz	350 (5,735)	7·4 : 1	250 at 2,800	0·50 (0·227)	100/130	43·2 (1,090)	34·2 (869)	38·7 (983)	377 (171)
6A4-165-B3, B4	6 Horiz	335 (5,490)	7·0 : 1	165 at 2,800	0·50 (0·227)	80/87	37·5 (953)	31·3 (795)	25·25 (641)	280 (127)
6A4-150-B3, B4	6 Horiz	335 (5,490)	7·0 : 1	150 at 2,600	0·50 (0·227)	80/87	37·5 (953)	31·3 (795)	22·6 (574)	277 (125·6)

GARRETT-AIRESEARCH
AIRESEARCH MANUFACTURING DIVISION OF ARIZONA (of The Garrett Corporation)

HEAD OFFICE AND WORKS:
Sky Harbor Airport, 402, South 36th Street, Phoenix, Arizona 85034

The Garrett Corporation's AiResearch Manufacturing Division in Phoenix, Arizona, has been called the world's largest producer of small gas-turbines. Development of the first AiResearch small turbines began in 1946 and the division has since produced about 80% of the total of gas-turbine units with power ratings from 30 to 850 hp built in America and Europe. These have been designed primarily to provide ground or airborne auxiliary power for starting and other aircraft services by means of compressed air, shaft power or a combination of compressed air and shaft power.

The first use of AiResearch turbines as prime movers occurred in 1957 when the McDonnell Aircraft Corporation used three GTC85 compressor turbines to power the Model 120 pressure-jet helicopter.

The GTC85 was described in the 1961-62 *Jane's*. It has been followed by the Model 331, the first AiResearch engine designed specifically as an aircraft prime mover.

AiResearch began design and development of the Model 331, as a private venture, in December, 1959, with the object of producing an engine suitable for use as a turboshaft for helicopters and as a turboprop for fixed-wing aircraft.

The first engine, the 500 shp TSE 331 turbo-shaft, was assembled and ready for initial testing by December 1960. Flight tests in a Republic Lark (licence-built Alouette II) helicopter began on 12 October 1961.

A description of the TSE 331 appeared in the 1964-65 *Jane's*. Production is now concentrated on the commercial TPE 331 and military T76 turboprop versions, as described below. The latest engines from the Arizona Division are the TSE 36 for light helicopters, the TSE 231 series, also for helicopters, and the TFE 731 series of turbofan engines for the executive and commuter market. In addition, the AiResearch Los Angeles Division is producing the ATF 3 three-shaft turbofan.

GARRETT-AIRESEARCH TFE 731

Announced in April 1969, the TFE 731 is a two-spool geared front-fan engine designed to confer US coast-to-coast range upon business jet aircraft in the weight category 12,500-15,000 lb (5,670-6,804 kg). Use of a geared fan is expected to confer flexibility in operation and to yield optimum performance both at low altitudes and at up to 50,000 ft (15,250 m).

The engine makes use of a basic core gas-generator developed earlier by AiResearch.

In its original form the TFE 731 had a single-stage fan, an LP compressor with three axial stages, a centrifugal HP compressor, a single-stage HP turbine and a two-stage LP turbine. During the past 18 months the engine has been considerably refined, the fan and duct geometry being redesigned, the LP compressor being redesigned and having four stages, the combustion chamber being much improved and the LP turbine being redesigned with three stages. The resulting engine falls into a higher-power category, 3,500 lb (1,587 kg) st in place of 2,700-3,000 lb.

The by-pass ratio is 2·55 : 1 at 40,000 ft and Mach 0·8. The TFE 731 is planned to have single-lever control and is designed to be capable of using a thrust reverser. The accessory group will be located on the underside, driven from the high-pressure spool. Two features which should reduce exterior noise are the elimination of fan intake guide vanes and the large spacing between the fan blades and the fan stator vanes, added to the basic low noise inherent in a high by-pass ratio.

First applications of the TFE 731 will be to power the Swearingen SA-28T, the Dassault Falcon 10 and the Gates Learjet 26. Component testing began in March 1969; the first engine was due to run in August 1970, FAA Certification is planned for January 1972, and production deliveries are scheduled to start in the first quarter of 1972.

TYPE: Turbofan with two shafts and geared front fan.

AIR INTAKE: Direct pitot, fixed, without guide vanes.

FAN: Single-stage axial titanium fan, with inserted blades. Mounted on a simple shaft supported by a roller bearing, located under the fan disc, and by a ball thrust bearing. The fan shaft is connected directly to the planetary gearbox ring gear.

COMPRESSOR: Low-pressure compressor is the axial compressor developed for the GTCP 660 APU installed in the Boeing 747. It has four stages, each with a separate disc. Rotors and stators have inserted blades and vanes. High-pressure compressor, carried on a separate shaft running at higher speeds, is a development of the centrifugal compressor used on the TPE 331 engine. Overall pressure ratio is 18·9 : 1 at Mach 0·8 at 40,000 ft.

COMBUSTION CHAMBER: Annular combustion chamber of reverse-flow type, with 12 fuel nozzles inserted radially and injecting fuel tangentially.

FUEL SYSTEM: Hydro-electronic, with single-lever control to mechanical and electronic elements.

TURBINE: High-pressure turbine has a single axial stage with inserted blades. Low-pressure turbine has three axial stages, all with inserted blades.

SHAFTING: High-pressure spool consists of HP turbine and HP compressor, mounted on shaft supported by one roller bearing and one ball bearing. This spool drives the accessory gearbox through a tower shaft transfer gearbox system. Low-pressure spool consists of the LP turbine and the LP compressor. It is composed of separate components interconnected by curvic couplings and simply supported on one ball bearing at the compressor end and one roller bearing at the turbine end. LP spool drives the fan shaft through a quill shaft and a planetary gear reduction system. Overall gear ratio is 0·555 : 1.

JET PIPES: Short fan-duct with cool discharge around remainder of engine, facilitating installation of fan reverser. Hot gas pipe at rear, with fixed nozzle of minimum length.

ACCESSORY DRIVES: Accessories driven from HP spool are grouped around underside of the forward section of the fan duct. Pads are provided on the front side of the accessory gearbox for the airframe-type accessories: hydraulic pump, starter-generator or starter-motor and alternators. Pads on the back side of the gearbox drive the engine accessories: fuel control unit and oil pump.

DIMENSIONS:

Intake diameter	28·2 in (716 mm)
Overall width	32·63 in (828 mm)
Overall height	39·07 in (992 mm)
Overall length	52·48 in (1,333 mm)

WEIGHT:

Dry (basic engine)	625 lb (283 kg)

PERFORMANCE RATING:

Max T-O (SLS standard day)	3,500 lb (1,587 kg)
40,000 ft, Mach 0·8, std day	730 lb (331 kg)

SPECIFIC FUEL CONSUMPTIONS:

SLS, standard day	0·49
40,000 ft, Mach 0·8, std day	0·825

GARRETT-AIRESEARCH TSE 36-1

In July 1968 Garrett-AiResearch announced its entry into the helicopter turboshaft market with the 240 shp TSE 36-1, which has completed all FAA tests and was scheduled to be certificated in March 1970.

Derived from the AiResearch GTCP 36 auxiliary power unit, the new turboshaft is of single-shaft design, with a single-stage centrifugal compressor, single combustion chamber, and single-stage radial inflow turbine. Weight is approximately 165 lb (74·8 kg). Approved fuels include jet types A, A-1, B and JP-4, but operation is possible on truck diesel fuel or clean kerosene.

The TSE 36 is intended as a turbine replacement for piston-engines in the 150 to 250 hp range, and is being test flown in Hughes 269A and Enstrom F-28 helicopters. Substitution for the original piston-engine of the Hughes 269A saved 184 lb (83·5 kg) in weight despite the addition of 40 hp. The hover ceiling rose from 6,000 ft to over 14,000 ft.

Throughout the design attention has been paid to robust structure likely to withstand harsh use.

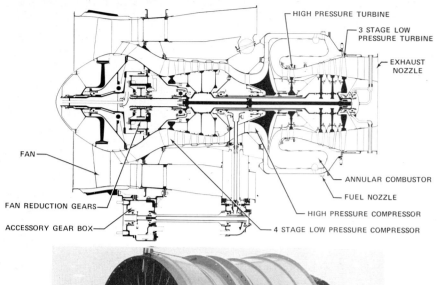

Cross-section (*top*) **and mock-up** (*above*), **of the 3,500 lb (1,587 kg) st Garrett-AiResearch TFE-731 geared front-fan engine**

Prototype engines have survived severe ingestion tests with bolts, ice, slush, rags and sand. AiResearch further claim exceptionally fast response to power change demands. Manual starting is possible.

TYPE: Light turboshaft engine with integral gearbox.

POWER DRIVE: Two-stage reduction, first-stage spur, second-stage helical. Driven through quill shaft from front of compressor.

AIR INTAKE: Free inward radial flow between gearcase and front of compressor.

COMPRESSOR: Single-entry centrifugal stage. Impeller machined from titanium with 17 integral vanes. Driven through splines, registered pivot and tie-bolted. Shaft supported in ball bearing in rear of gearcase and roller bearing in turbine section. Aluminium shroud and stainless-steel compressor housing. Mass flow 2·8 lb (1·27 kg)/sec.

The 240 shp Garrett-AiResearch TSE 36-1 turboshaft for helicopters shown externally (*top*) **and in cutaway form**

COMBUSTION CHAMBER: Single, reverse-flow, with stainless-steel outer casing. Perforated can-type flame tube located tangentially on aft section of turbine plenum. Single spark igniter mounted radially in primary zone and rated for continuous duty.

FUEL SYSTEM: Hydromechanical type. Single spur gear pump, flow divider nozzle, hydraulic on-speed governor and pneumatic overspeed governor, dual-purpose shut-off valve for acceleration, scheduling and normal power.

FUEL GRADES: Jet fuel A, A-1, B, JP-4, JP-5, MIL-T-5624G-1, Avtur ASTM D1655T (emergency, 80 to 145 grade petrol or diesel oil).

NOZZLE GUIDE VANES: Radial inward-flow segments (13), cast in Inco 713C.

TURBINE: Radial inward-flow, precision cast in Inco 713C with integral vanes. Pinned interference fit on main shaft with roller type bearing between turbine and compressor. Gas temperature 1,673°F before turbine, 1,167°F behind.

ACCESSORY DRIVES: AND 20001 Type XI-C, CCW 12,021 rpm; AND 20005 Type XV-B CW 4,193 rpm; on gearcase, tacho-generator, DC starter pad. Additional equipment includes 4% electrically actuated bleed system, hydraulic force-balance torque-sensor, automatic start kit and monopole speed pick-up.

LUBRICATION SYSTEM: Wet-sump type. Gerotor pressure and scavenge pumps, capacity 3-4 quarts (2·8-3·7 litres), pressure 100 lb/sq in (7 kg/cm²).

OIL SPECIFICATION: MIL-L-23699A −40 to 205°F, MIL-L-7808D or 007808F −40 to 175°F.

MOUNTING POINTS: Two on gearbox, one on power section, resilient or rigid.

STARTING: 28V DC starter-generator on 12,000 rpm pad.

DIMENSIONS:
Length	35·9 in (912 mm)
Width	27·9 in (708·7 mm)
Height	21·8 in (553·7 mm)

WEIGHT:
Dry with accessories required for engine to run 178 lb (80·74 kg)

PERFORMANCE RATINGS:
Max take-off	240 shp
Max continuous	220 shp

SPECIFIC FUEL CONSUMPTIONS:
Take-off	0·83 lb (0·376 kg)/shp/hr
Max continuous	0·84 lb (0·38 kg)/shp/hr

OIL CONSUMPTION: Negligible.

GARRETT-AIRESEARCH TSE 231-1

The TSE 231-1 is a 474 shp turboshaft engine for use in advanced helicopters. The first application is to power the Gates Learjet Corporation's Twinjet helicopter.

The engine is of the free-turbine type with front-end drive. The compressor section is scaled down from the compressor of the successful and robust T76-G-10. The combustion section is of the reverse-flow annular type and the turbine section consists of a single-stage axial gas-generator turbine and a single-stage axial power turbine.

TYPE: Free-turbine turboshaft engine with front-end drive.

POWER DRIVE: Two-stage reduction gear: first-stage spur gear and second-stage helical. Output shaft is offset below engine centre-line, driven from power turbine through shafting concentric inside the gas-generator shafting. The power turbine shafting is supported at the power turbine and an inter-shaft bearing. Both shafts rotate in the same direction. The output pad is an internal spline of 1·2 in pitch diameter with fore-and-aft take-off.

AIR INTAKE: Free inward-radial-flow duct between gearcase and front of compressor.

COMPRESSOR: Two-stage centrifugal type. Tandem single-sided titanium impellers are attached to shaft through curvic couplings. First-stage housing of magnesium, second-stage

housing and diffuser of stainless steel. Pressure ratio 8·9 : 1.

COMBUSTION CHAMBER: Annular reverse-flow type with outer case of stainless steel and flame tube of high-temperature stainless steel. Ten radially-mounted simplex nozzles.

FUEL SYSTEM: Hydromechanical control. Two-stage fuel pump: low-pressure pump is ejector type, high-pressure stage is gear type. Control system includes power-turbine governor and gas-generator governor. Provision is made for manual operation.

FUEL GRADES: Jet fuel A, A-1, B, JP-4, JP-5; emergency operation with Avgas 80/87 authorised.

TURBINES: Single-stage gas-generator turbine with individual blades cast in IN 100 and inserted into forged disc. Individual cooled nozzle guide vanes of INCO 713 LC. Power-turbine nozzle is integral casting of INCO 713LC; single-stage rotor is also integral casting of INCO 713 LC.

ACCESSORY DRIVES: Starter/generator pad AND 2001, Type XI-C modified at 12,060 rpm. Designed to accommodate 250A starter.

LUBRICATION SYSTEM: Dry sump system with internal gerotor pressure and scavenge pumps. Normal oil pressure 100 lb/sq in (7 kg/cm²).

OIL SPECIFICATION: MIL-L-23699K, −40°F to 230°F; MIL-L-78080 or 7808F, −40°F to 175°F.

MOUNTING: Three-point suspension on gearcase. Four pads available for choice relative to installation.

DIMENSIONS:
Length	41 in (1,014 mm)
Width	28 in (711 mm)
Height	22·5 in (560 mm)

WEIGHT:
Dry, equipped 171 lb (67·5 kg)

PERFORMANCE RATINGS (SLS, std day):
Take-off	474 shp
Max continuous	403 shp

SPECIFIC FUEL CONSUMPTIONS:
Take-off	0·605 lb (0·27 kg)/shp/hr
Max continuous	0·619 lb (0·28 kg)/shp/hr

OIL CONSUMPTION:
Maximum 0·3 lb (0·14 kg)/hr

GARRETT-AIRESEARCH TPE 331
US Military designation: T76

The first commercial version of this turboprop received FAA type approval in February 1965. In December 1967, two higher-rated additions to the TPE 331 family received FAA approval, the TPE 331-1 rated at 665 shp, and the TPE 331-2 rated at 715 shp, Initial TBOs were established at 1,500 hours and now have been

increased to 2,000 hours. A higher-rated addition, the TPE 331-3, rated at 840 shp, has received FAA certification and is used as the power plant of the Swearingen Metro transport, while a turboshaft verison is flying in the Aviation Specialties S-55T conversion of the Sikorsky S-55 helicopter.

The new models are of the same external dimensions as the basic TPE 331. The higher ratings are attained by means of an increased air mass flow and higher component efficiencies.

Models now in production are the TPE 331-series I and II rated at 575 shp, the TPE 331-1 series rated at 665 shp, the TPE 331-2 series rated at 715 shp, and the TPE 331-3 series rated at 840 shp. Applications include the Japanese Mitsubishi MU-2, Aero Commander Hawk Commander, Fairchild Hiller Porter, Pilatus Turbo Porter, Volpar Super Turbo 18 and Turbo Liner conversions of the Beechcraft 18, Carstedt Jet Liner 600 Dove conversion, Short Skyvan 3, Air Parts (Fletcher) Model 1160, DHC-2 Turbo-Beaver, Conroy Stolifter, Interceptor 400, FMA I.A.58 Pucará, and the Swearingen Merlin IIB and FS-226 Metro.

The military version, designated T76, powers the North American OV-10A Bronco counter-insurgency aircraft and exists in two production configurations.

T76-G-10. Propeller rotates clockwise when viewed from rear of engine. Rated at 715 shp.

T76-G-12. Propeller rotates anti-clockwise when viewed from rear. Rated at 715 shp.

Both of these models of the T76 have a single scoop air intake at the top front of the engine, directly above the gearbox.

The TPE 331 and T76 are of similar frame size, and the following data apply generally to both models.

TYPE: Single-shaft turboprop engine with integral gearbox.

PROPELLER DRIVE: Two-stage reduction gear, one helical spur and one planetary, with overall ratio of 20·865 : 1 or 26·3 : 1. Shaft, driven from single-spool compressor, is carried in ball and roller bearings. Rotation clockwise or anti-clockwise, as required.

AIR INTAKE: Single scoop intake duct at top or bottom of engine, at front. Provision for bleed air de-icing.

COMPRESSOR: Tandem two-stage centrifugal type. Each impeller is single-sided, and is made from titanium. Impellers attached to shaft by curvic couplings. First-stage casing of magnesium, with aluminium diffuser. Second-stage casing and diffuser of stainless steel. Pressure ratio 8·5 : 1 for T76; 8·0 : 1 for TPE 331 series

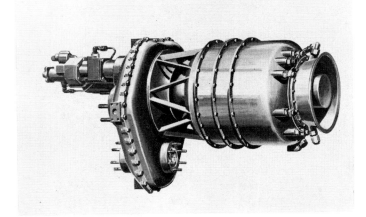

Artist's impression of the Garrett-AiResearch TSE 231 turboshaft engine for helicopters, to be rated at 474 shp

Above: **The Garrett-AiResearch TPE 331 series commercial turboprop engine (all models are similar externally)**
Left: **The 715 shp Garrett-AiResearch T76 military turboprop engine**

I and II; 8·5 : 1 for TPE 331-1; 8·5 : 1 for TPE 331-2; 10·4 : 1 for TPE 331-3.

COMBUSTION CHAMBER: Annular type of high-temperature alloy. High-energy capacitor discharge ignition. Igniter plug on turbine plenum.

FUEL SYSTEM: Woodward or Bendix control system for use with Beta propeller governing control system. Five radial primary nozzles in continuous operation. Ten axial simplex nozzles. Max fuel pressure 600 lb/sq in (42·2 kg/cm²).

FUEL GRADE (TPE 331): Aviation turbine fuels ASTM designation D1655-64T types Jet A, Jet B and Jet A-1; Mil-F-5616-1, Grade JP-1.

FUEL GRADE (T76): Mil-J-5624F(2), Grades JP-4 and JP-5; Mil-G-5572, Grade 115/145.

NOZZLE GUIDE VANES: Axial vanes made from Inco 713C castings.

TURBINE: Three-stage axial-flow type. Discs of first two stages of Inco 100, third stage of Inco 713C, attached to shaft by curvic couplings. Blades cast integrally with disc.

BEARINGS: One ball bearing at compressor end of shaft, one roller bearing at turbine end.

JET-PIPE: Fixed type. Cone and jet-pipe both of stainless steel.

ACCESSORIES: AND 20005 Type XV-B tachometer generator, AND 20002 Type XII-D starter generator, AND 20010 Type XX-A propeller governor and AND 20001 Type XI-B hydraulic pump all mounted on aft face of accessories case.

LUBRICATION SYSTEM: Medium-pressure dry sump system. Gerotor internal gear type pressure and scavenge pumps. Normal oil supply pressure 100 lb/sq in (7·03 kg/cm²). Provision for automatic fuel filter anti-icing.

OIL SPECIFICATION: MIL-L-23699-(1) or MIL-L-7808.

MOUNTING: Five-point suspension. Three pads on aft face of accessories case, two pads at aft end of turbine plenum.

STARTING: Pad for 300 amp starter-generator on aft face of accessory case.

DIMENSIONS (approximate):

Length overall:	
TPE 331	43 to 46 in (1,092-1,168 mm)
T76	44 in (1,118 mm)
Width:	
TPE 331	21 in (533 mm)
T76	19 in (483 mm)
Height:	
TPE 331	26 in (660 mm)
T76	27 in (686 mm)

WEIGHTS:

TPE 331	335 lb (152 kg)
T76-G-10/12	336 lb (152 kg)

PERFORMANCE RATINGS:
T-O rating:

TPE 331 srs I, II	575 shp (605 ehp)
TPE 331-1	665 shp (705 ehp)
TPE 331-2	715 shp (755 ehp)
TPE 331-3	840 shp (904 ehp)
TPE 331-5	715 shp (776 ehp)
Military rating (30 min):	
T76-G-10/12	715 shp (755 ehp)
Max continous rating:	
TPE 331, srs I, II	500 shp (529 ehp)
TPE 331-1	665 shp (705 ehp)
TPE 331-2	715 shp (755 ehp)
TPE 331-3	840 shp (904 ehp)
TPE 331-5	715 shp (776 ehp)
Normal:	
T76-G-10/12	650 shp (690 ehp)
Max cruise rating:	
TPE 331 srs I, II	475 shp (500 ehp)
TPE 331-1	609 shp (648 ehp)
TPE 331-2	650 shp (690 ehp)
TPE 331-3	770 shp (832 ehp)
TPE 331-5	715 shp (776 ehp)

SPECIFIC FUEL CONSUMPTIONS:
At T-O rating:

TPE 331 srs I, II	0·66 lb (0·30 kg)/shp/hr
TPE 331-1	0·61 lb (0·276 kg)/shp/hr
TPE 331-2	0·59 lb (0·268 kg)/shp/hr
TPE 331-3	0·59 lb (0·268 kg)/shp/hr
T76-G-10/12	0·60 lb (0·27 kg)/shp/hr

OIL CONSUMPTION:

Max	0·02 lb (0·009 kg)/hr

AIRESEARCH MANUFACTURING DIVISION OF LOS ANGELES (of The Garrett Corporation)

HEAD OFFICE:
9851 Sepulveda Boulevard, Los Angeles, California 90009

WORKS:
2525 West 190th Street, Torrance, California 90509

GARRETT-AIRESEARCH ATF 3

In May 1968 AiResearch Los Angeles began development testing of a new low-consumption turbofan in the 4,000 lb to 5,000 lb (1,815-2,270 kg) st class. Designated the ATF 3, the engine is designed to power business jets, and utility and commuter aircraft. Through its low sfc—approximately 0·44 at take-off—the ATF 3 is intended to give transcontinental US range to 10/12-seat business aircraft, and the high thrust/weight ratio is planned to meet the needs of VTOL and STOL performance in the 1970s.

The ATF 3 utilises a unique three-shaft layout, involving cross compounding of the intermediate-and low-pressure rotors, and is believed to be the first three-shaft engine to run in the United States.

The arrangement of components allows the fan design to be determined largely independently of the gas generator compresser requirements and permits operation at optimum fan speed. Omission of fan inlet guide vanes, mixing of the gas generator exhaust with the fan air flow, and double reversal of the internal airflow enable the ATF 3 to offer significant reductions in overall noise generation.

By virtue of its three-spool layout, the ATF 3 has approximately 35 per cent fewer parts than a conventional two-spool turbofan of comparable performance. The engine has also been designed to facilitate ease of disassembly and maintenance.

Construction is by a series of major subassemblies which can be removed and replaced without requiring removal of the engine from its airframe. The accessories are accessible by removing the tail cone fairing, and their positioning at the rear of the engine incurs considerably less installed drag.

The ATF 3 is being offered as a bare engine, or completely installed in an AiResearch pod with three-quarter length cowl. Because of its mixed exhaust the combined primary and secondary flows can be deflected together by a single thrust reverser. This consists of a translating cowl section, cascade elements and blocker doors. The cowl assembly is translated fore and aft by screwjacks driven by a pneumatic motor. Aft translation of the cowl exposes the cascade elements and positions the exhaust discharge blocker doors to divert the mixed exhaust flow radially outward through the cascades.

At the start of design of the ATF 3 in early 1966, AiResearch planned the engine for application to VTOL and STOL aircraft in the 1970s. In particular it was intended that by contributing to a high aircraft thrust/weight ratio the new turbofan could be used to re-engine smaller business jets, providing them with STOL capability and increased range.

To minimise the inherent rise in fuel consumption in throttling the engine to around 40 per cent maximum thrust for cruise, cross compounding of the LP and IP components was introduced. This improves the component matching at low powers and is claimed to give the ATF 3 a substantially better part-load sfc than present turbofans.

The ATF 3 is being developed at AiResearch's plant at Torrance, with the company's Phoenix plant also contributing to the programme. Deliveries of the ATF 3 are planned for 1971.

Recent progress at AiResearch Los Angeles with the ATF 3 three-shaft reverse-flow turbofan of 4,050 lb (1,837 kg) st; *left*, assembly of prototype engine No 7; *right*, an ATF 3 on outdoor test

First application of the turbofan is in re-engining the North American Rockwell Sabreliner Series 60 business jet. AiResearch was awarded a $59m contract by North American in October 1968 to supply ATF 3s, nacelles and reversers to replace the aircraft's present Pratt & Whitney JT12A-8 turbojets. The ATF 3 is also scheduled to power the HFB 330 Hansa Fan Jet.

The basic ATF 3 has a sea level static rating of 4,050 lb (1,837 kg) thrust. A 4,000 shp turbo-shaft variant of the engine is also being studied for possible application in the US tri-service heavy-lift helicopter (HLH) project. AiResearch foresee in the long-term a total civil and military market for the ATF 3 family in excess of 2,000 engines.

Testing of full-scale components and complete engines is underway and FAA type certification is scheduled for mid-1971. A new manufacturing facility has been established and an engine assembly and test complex has been constructed to support the development programme. Flight testing will be performed in a Sabreliner. It is planned to achieve a 2,000-hr time-between-overhaul within two years of entering service.

TYPE: Three-shaft axial-flow turbofan.

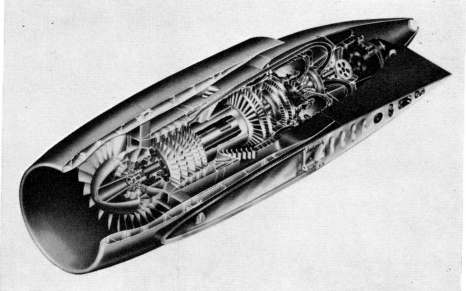

Cutaway of the 4,050-5,000 lb (1,837-2,270 kg) st Garrett-AiResearch ATF 3 three-shaft double-reverse flow turbofan

INTAKE: Direct pitot, fixed type. Total airflow 162 lb/sec (73·5 kg/sec).

LOW-PRESSURE (FAN) SYSTEM: Single-stage titanium fan, driven by three-stage IP turbine. One thrust bearing and one roller bearing support independent LP shaft. By-pass ratio 3 : 1 at take-off.

INTERMEDIATE-PRESSURE SYSTEM: Five-stage titanium axial compressor, each stage having a separate disc, driven by two-stage LP turbine. Airflow is delivered to the rearward-facing HP compressor via eight tubes feeding into an annular duct concentric with the by-pass duct. One thrust bearing and one roller bearing support independent IP shaft.

HIGH-PRESSURE SYSTEM: Single-stage titanium centrifugal compressor, driven by single-stage HP turbine. Airflow at rear of engine is turned through 180° to enter the eye of the single-sided impeller and thence the combustion system. One thrust bearing and one roller bearing support the independent HP shaft. Overall pressure ratio 22-24 : 1.

COMBUSTION SYSTEM: Reverse-flow annular type.

TURBINES: Single-stage HP, three-stage IP and two-stage LP turbines drive, respectively, the HP, fan (LP) and IP compressors. IP and LP turbines have fully shrouded blades. Air-cooled first stage nozzle vanes and HP rotor blades. Exhaust gases turn through 113° via eight ducts with cascades to mix with fan by-pass flow.

FUEL SYSTEM: Electro-mechanical, incorporating a solid-state computer. Manual engine control is provided as a back-up system in case of failure of the primary fuel control.

ACCESSORY DRIVES: Three drive pads on rear-mounted gearbox driven by HP shaft, providing for a hydraulic pump drive, starter/generator drive and one spare. Accessory cooling by fan discharge air which is then exhausted through a separate nozzle at the tip of the fairing.

EXHAUST SYSTEM: Mixed fan and turbine exhaust flow passes to atmosphere through annular nozzle surrounding combustion section.

LUBRICATION SYSTEM: Self-contained hot-tank type; tank integral with gearbox.

MOUNTING: Two-plane pick-up system.

STARTING: 300 or 400 Amp starter-generator.

DIMENSIONS:
Length overall	91·80 in (2,331 mm)
Max diameter	31·95 in (811 mm)

WEIGHT:
Bare, dry	874 lb (396 kg)

PERFORMANCE RATING:
T-O rating (sea level static, standard day):
ATF 3	4,050 lb (1,837 kg) st

SPECIFIC FUEL CONSUMPTION:
At T-O rating (sea level static, standard day)
ATF 3	approx 0·44

GENERAL ELECTRIC
GENERAL ELECTRIC COMPANY AIRCRAFT ENGINE GROUP

HEADQUARTERS:
1000 Western Avenue, West Lynn, Massachusetts 01905

AERO ENGINE WORKS:
Lynn and Everett, Massachusetts; Cincinnati, Ohio; Rutland and Ludlow, Vermont; Hooksett, New Hampshire; and Albuquerque, New Mexico. Also test facilities at Edwards Air Force Base, California and Peebles, Ohio.

VICE-PRESIDENT AND GROUP EXECUTIVE:
Gerhard Neumann

VICE-PRESIDENTS AND GENERAL MANAGERS:

Commercial Engine Division:
Edward E. Hood, Jr

Military Engine Division:
Edward Woll

Aircraft Engine Operating Division:
Fred O. MacFee, Jr

Aircraft Engine Technical Division:
Fred W. Garry

Aircraft Engine Support and Service Division:
Ramond E. Small

MANAGERS:

Group Management Systems Operation:
MANAGER: Robert L. Miles

Group Legal Operation:
COUNSEL & MANAGER: James W. Sack

Group Finance Operation:
MANAGER: Edward F. Roache

Group Business Planning Operation:
MANAGER: Louis E. Schmidt

The General Electric Company entered the gas-turbine field in about 1895. Years of pioneering effort by the late Dr Sanford A. Moss produced the aircraft turbosupercharger, successfully tested at height in 1918 and mass-produced in World War II for US fighters and bombers.

The company built its first aircraft gas-turbine in 1941, when it began development of Whittle-type turbojets, under an arrangement between the British and American Governments.

Since that time, General Electric has produced a series of successful designs. The J47 still powers the Boeing B-47 and the North American F-86 series of aircraft. Its successor, the J79, was the first US production engine capable of powering aircraft at Mach 2 speeds.

Current products of the Aircraft Engine Group include the J79, J85, T58, T64, and TF39 for the military services, and the CT58, CJ610, CF700 and CT64 for the commercial airliner and business aircraft market. General Electric is also developing the CF6 turbofan for the McDonnell Douglas DC-10 three-engined transport and the Airbus Industrie A 300B, the GE4 turbojet for the Boeing 2707-300 supersonic transport, the GE12 turboshaft for the US Army and the TF34 turbofan for the US Navy's Lockheed S-3A anti-submarine aircraft.

In January 1968, as part of a series of major changes to the corporate structure, General Electric's Flight Propulsion Division (one of four divisions forming the company's previous Aerospace and Defence Group), which hitherto had been responsible for all GE's aero-engine work, was promoted to become one of the ten operating groups now comprising General Electric. This change in organisation was aimed at strengthening GE's civil and military aircraft engine activities in the domestic US and international markets.

Elevation of aero-engine work to group status, at corporate level, and the establishment of the Commercial Engine Division as one of the five divisions forming the new Aircraft Engine Group, are further indications of GE's increasing emphasis on civil engine developments. The new group retains the same organisational structure as the former Flight Propulsion Division.

Military Engine Division exercises current programme management of various General Electric military jet engines in production.

The Aircraft Engine Technical Division function encompasses the full engineering spectrum of aircraft propulsion products.

Operating Division involves the manufacture of all Group products, and the logistical and product support of military products.

Support and Service Division contains the Group's marine and industrial business, service shops for engine overhaul and repair as well as other aircraft equipment such as electrical systems and instruments, field service engineering, overseas marketing planning, the General Electric Technical Services Co, Inc, in addition to a number of group-wide support functions.

Commercial Engine Division's engine line includes the GE4 and CJ610 turbojets, CF6 and CF700 turbofan engines, and the CT58 and CT64 turboshaft and turboprop engines.

GENERAL ELECTRIC J85

The following versions of the J85 lightweight turbojet are currently in production or under development:

J85-GE-4. Powers the North American Rockwell T-2C Buckeye trainer.

J85-GE-5. Afterburning version with 6.8 : 1 thrust-to-weight ratio, powers Northrop T-38 Talon supersonic trainer. Non-reheat version powered two VTOL research aircraft, the Bell X-14A and the Ryan XV-5A with wing-mounted GE lift-fans.

J85-GE-13. Higher-powered version with afterburner for Northrop F-5A/B supersonic fighter. As the J85-GE-13A, licence-built by Alfa-Romeo, also powers the Fiat G91Y.

J85-GE-15. Higher-rated version of J85-GE-13, to power CF-5A/B fighters. Manufactured under licence in Canada by Orenda.

J85-GE-17. Higher-rated version powering the Saab 105XT attack/reconnaissance aircraft and Cessna A-37B attack aircraft. Also used as take-off and climb booster for Fairchild C-123K and AC-119K.

YJ85-GE-19. Special vertically-operating version for VTOL aircraft.

J85-GE-21. Higher airflow version with zero-stage to give total of nine compressor stages. To be produced with afterburner for advanced supersonic aircraft (for example, developments of the F-5).

Civil version of the J85 is the CJ610 turbojet, to which the aft-fan CF700 turbofan is closely related.

The following data refer specifically to the J85-GE-5 and 13, except where otherwise stated.

TYPE: Variable-stator axial-flow single-shaft turbojet.

AIR INTAKE: Annular type, surrounding central bullet fairing. Variable-incidence inlet guide vanes, which are anti-iced on J85-GE-5 and -13.

COMPRESSOR: Eight-stage axial-flow type. No shaft, each disc being connected to adjoining disc. Compressor casing in two halves. Pressure ratio approximately 7 : 1. Air mass flow 44 lb/sec (20 kg/sec).

COMBUSTION CHAMBER: Annular type with perforated liner. Twelve duplex fuel injectors. Ports in outer casing facilitate inspection of liner.

TURBINE: Two-stage axial-flow type. Casing is in halves, split horizontally.

AFTERBURNER (J85-GE-5): Afterburner consists of a diffuser and a combustor. A pilot burner with four spray-bars and a main burner of 12 spray-bars are located in the diffuser section. Combustion is initiated by a single igniter plug and is then self-sustained. Nozzle position governs exit area and is regulated automatically by the afterburner control system as a function of turbine exit temperature and throttle lever position.

LUBRICATION: Positive displacement, pressurised recirculating type.

STARTING: Air impingement starter.

DIMENSIONS:
Length overall:
J85-GE-4	40·50 in (1,029 mm)
J85-GE-5 with afterburner	104·6 in (2,657 mm)
J85-GE-13 with afterburner	105·6 in (2,682 mm)
J85-17, YJ85-19	40·5 in (1,039 mm)
J85-21	112·5 in (2,858 mm)

Max diameter:
J85-GE-4	17·7 in (450 mm)
J85-GE-5, 13	21·0 in (533 mm)
J85-17, YJ85-19	17·7 in (450 mm)
J85-21	670 lb (304 kg)

WEIGHT (DRY):
J85-GE-4	404 lb (183 kg)
J85-GE-5	584 lb (265 kg)
J85-GE-13	597 lb (271 kg)
J85-17	398 lb (181 kg)
YJ85-19	389 lb (176 kg)
J85-21	640 lb (290 kg)

PERFORMANCE RATINGS:
Max rating:
YJ85-19	3,015 lb (1,368 kg)

Max rating, with afterburner:
J85-GE-5	3,850 lb (1,748 kg) st
J85-GE-13	4,080 lb (1,850 kg) st
J85-GE-15	4,300 lb (1,950 kg) st
YJ85-19	3,015 lb (1,368 kg) st
J85-21	5,000 lb (2,268 kg) st

Military rating, without afterburner:
J85-GE-4	2,950 lb (1,339 kg) st
J85-GE-5	2,680 lb (1,215 kg) st
J85-GE-13	2,720 lb (1,234 kg) st
J85-17	2,850 lb (1,293 kg) st
YJ85-19	2,950 lb (1,339 kg) st
J85-21	3,500 lb (1,588 kg) st

General Electric J85-GE-13 turbojet (4,080 lb=1,850 kg st with afterburning)

SPECIFIC FUEL CONSUMPTIONS:
At max rating:
YJ85-19 .... 1·0

At max rating, with afterburner:
J85-GE-5 .... 2·20
J85-GE-13 .... 2.22
J85-21 .... 2·13

At military rating, without afterburner:
J85-GE-4 .... 0·98
J85-GE-5, 13 .... 1·03
J85-21 .... 1·00

GENERAL ELECTRIC CJ610

Announced in May 1960, the CJ610 is intended as a power plant for commercial, executive and military aircraft of 12,500-16,500 lb (5,700-7,500 kg) AUW and for heavier four-engined aircraft. It is essentially similar to the basic J85 turbojet, without afterburner, and incorporates an eight-stage axial-flow compressor, annular combustion chamber, two-stage reaction turbine, fixed-area concentric exhaust section and integrated control system. Air mass flow is 44 lb (20 kg)/sec.

By December 1969, a total of 950 CJ610s had accumulated more than 1,000,000 flying hours and the TBO had reached 1,500 hr.

There are six current versions

CJ610-1, CJ610-4. Initial production versions, differing only in accessory gearbox location.

CJ610-5, CJ610-6. Developed versions of -1 and -4 respectively, providing increased T-O thrust.

CJ610-8, CJ610-9. Developed for production deliveries beginning in 1969.

Versions of the CJ610 power the IAI Commodore Jet, Learjet and HFB 320 Hansa twin-jet executive transports.

DIMENSIONS:
Length overall:
CJ610-1, -5 .... 51·1 in (1,298 mm)
CJ610-4, -6 .... 45·4 in (1,153 mm)
CJ610-8 .... 45·4 in (1,153 mm)
CJ610-9 .... 51·1 in (1,298 mm)
Max flange diameter .. 17·7 in (449 mm)

WEIGHT (DRY):
CJ610-1 .... 399 lb (181 kg)
CJ610-4 .... 389 lb (176 kg)
CJ610-5 .... 402 lb (183 kg)
CJ610-6 .... 392 lb (179 kg)
CJ610-8 .... 407 lb (185 kg)
CJ610-9 .... 417 lb (189 kg)

PERFORMANCE RATING (guaranteed):
T-O:
CJ610-1, -4 ...... 2,850 lb (1,293 kg) st
CJ610-5, -6 ...... 2,950 lb (1,340 kg) st
CJ610-8, -9 ...... 3,100 lb (1,406 kg) st
Cruise:
CJ610-1, -4 ...... 2,700 lb (1,225 kg) st
CJ610-5, -6 ...... 2,775 lb (1,260 kg) st
CJ610-8, -9 ...... 2,925 lb (1,327 kg) st

SPECIFIC FUEL CONSUMPTION:
At T-O rating:
CJ610-1, -4 .... 0·99
CJ610-5, -6 .... 0·98
At cruise rating:
CJ610-1, -4 .... 0·97
CJ610-5, -6 .... 0·96
CJ610-8, -9 .... 0·96

GENERAL ELECTRIC CF700
US Military designation: TF37

Developed as a private venture by General Electric, the CF700 is an aft-fan engine suitable for powering military and commercial jet aircraft. It can be tilted while in operation, affording dual lift-cruise capability in VTOL aircraft.

General Electric YJ85-GE-19 turbojet (3,015 lb = 1,368 kg st) for VTOL aircraft

It utilises as its gas generator the CJ610 turbojet and offers a 5·7 : 1 thrust-to-weight ratio in its civil form, as used in the Dassault Mystère 20/Falcon executive transport. FAA certification of the original version was received on 1 July 1964.

The increased performance CF700-2D was certificated in early 1968, with production deliveries immediately following. The CF700-2D has a new design of compressor turbine of higher thermodynamic efficiency. Improved materials were also introduced for other components.

The military version, designated TF37-GE-1, completed its qualification testing in April 1964 and now powers the Bell Lunar Landing Research and Lunar Landing Training Vehicles. It develops slightly more power than the original CF700 and has a thrust-to-weight ratio of 6·5 : 1.

By December 1969, over 500 CF700s had flown some 350,000 hr in service and the TBO had reached 1,500 hr. These engines, together with 950 CJ610 turbojets, power more than 600 business jets, representing more than 50 per cent of all such aircraft in service.

The general description of the J85 turbojet applies also to the CF700, with the following additional assembly.

AFT FAN: Single-stage free-floating fan. By-pass ratio 1·9 : 1. Mass air flow through fan 84·0 lb (38·0 kg)/sec.

DIMENSIONS:
Overall length, compressor nose to tailcone tip .... 58·4 in (1,483 mm)
Max diameter .... 34·7 in (881 mm)
Max diameter less fan .... 17·7 in (449 mm)
WEIGHT (DRY):
CF700-2C .... 725 lb (330 kg)
CF700-2D .... 737 lb (334 kg)
TF37-GE-1 .... 675 lb (306 kg)

General Electric CF700-2D turbofan (4,250 lb = 1,928 kg st)

General Electric CJ610-4 (2,850 lb = 1,293 kg st) and (right) CJ610-5 (2,950 lb = 1,340 kg st) turbojet engines

General Electric GE1/J1A2 supersonic turbojet engine with afterburner

PERFORMANCE RATINGS:
Max T-O:
CF700-2C (flat rated to 86°F)
    4,125 lb (1,895 kg) st
CF700-2D   4,250 lb (1,928 kg) st
TF37-GE-1   4,400 lb (1,995 kg)st
Max continuous:
CF700-2C   4,000 lb (1,814 kg) st
CF700-2D   4,120 lb (1,869 kg) st
Max cruising:
CF700-2C   3,800 lb (1,725 kg) st
CF700-2D   3,910 lb (1,774 kg) st
SPECIFIC FUEL CONSUMPTIONS:
Max T-O:
CF700-2C   0·652
CF700-2D   0·65
Max continuous:
CF700-2C   0·649
CF700-2D   0·65
TF37-GE-1   0·67
Max cruising:
CF700-2C   0·646
CF700-2D   0·64

GENERAL ELECTRIC GE1

This engine introduced General Electric's "core engine" concept. To the basic GE1 gas-generator several components can be added, such as an afterburner, a fan and thrust vectoring devices, to provide specific performance and configurations tailored to specific missions and designs of an aircraft.

The GE1 has been under development since 1963 and is now available for military and commercial applications. It is designed for high gas horse-power and low specific fuel consumption, to produce a power plant with a high thrust-to-weight ratio and a variety of thrust ratings spanning a range up to almost six times the basic gas-generator thrust of 5,000 lb (2,268 kg).

Development time and cost savings are realized because, with the gas generator already fully developed, a specific new aircraft application requires only the development of special "add-on" components. In addition, component standardisation is possible for a wide variety of power plants. This requires a minimum holding of spare parts and makes possible high reliability early in the life of an engine.

The basic GE1 is in the same thrust class as the earlier J47, yet is only 49% as long as its predecessor, with a volume reduction of 79%. Weight and fuel consumption are also greatly reduced.

General Electric has defined seven different configurations of engine embodying the GE1. These comprise an augmented turbofan, with the GE1 energizing a low by-pass ratio fan rotor and spanning a thrust bracket of 15,000 lb to 25,000 lb (6,800-11,300 kg); a cruise fan with the GE1 energizing a remote, high by-pass ratio tip-turbine driven fan and rated at 26,000 lb (11,800 kg); a lift-fan with the GE1 energizing a close-coupled tip-turbine driven high by-pass ratio fan and rated at 27,500 lb (12,500 kg) st; a turboshaft rated at 10,000 shp; an augmented turbofan spanning a thrust bracket of 10,000 lb to 20,000 lb (4,500-9,000 kg), with the GE1 energizing a low by-pass ratio fan rotor and with the full exhaust flow vectored by a single aft nozzle; a turbofan with the GE1 energising a high by-pass ratio fan rotor and rated at 20,000 lb (9,000 kg) st; and an augmented turbofan rated at 7,500 lb (3,400 kg) st. Specific power plants utilizing the GE1 core engine include the GE1/J1A2 turbojet, the GE1/6 high by-pass ratio turbofan used as a ⅔-scale demonstrator for the large TF39 turbofan, and the GE1/10 moderate by-pass ratio turbofan.

DIMENSIONS (basic gas generator):
Length overall   70 in (1,778 mm)
Diameter   24 in (610 mm)

GENERAL ELECTRIC GE1/10

The GE1/10 is an augmented turbofan of moderate by-pass ratio, derived from the GE1

"core engine" described above. Components added to the basic GE1—a fan and augmentor—provide the high gas horse power and thrust/weight ratio and low sfc required for tactical aircraft propulsion. In this role, the GE1/10 is being used as General Electric's demonstrator engine for the company's proposed F400-GE-400/F100-GE-100 joint engine development programme. These augmented turbofans are the F400, proposed for the US Navy's new F-14B air superiority/fleet defence fighter, and the F100 for the USAF F-15 air-superiority fighter. In the event, propulsion of these two fighters has been entrusted to Pratt & Whitney Aircraft.

Designated under the US Department of Defense new engine designation system, the engines are being developed under a competitive Initial Development Phase contract, jointly funded by the USAF and USN, with the Air Force's Aeronautical Systems Division, Wright-Patterson Air Force Base, Ohio, acting as executive agency.

The GE1/10-F400 demonstrator engine has two variable stator stages for the front fan, and a modulating exhaust nozzle. It is approximately 143 in (3,632 mm) long and 38 in (965 mm) in diameter. Turbine entry temperature is in excess of 2,000°F (1,365°K).

GENERAL ELECTRIC GE1/J1A2

The GE1/J1A2 is another derivative of the GE1 "core engine", described above. It is a supersonic afterburning turbojet in the 10,000 lb (4,536 kg) thrust class, offering a high thrust/weight ratio and a substantial improvement in specific fuel consumption by comparison with current engines in its class. It is intended to power advanced combat aircraft.

Few details are available except that the GE1/J1A2 has a 14-stage single-spool compressor, with the first five stator stages and inlet guide vanes variable, an annular combustion chamber, air-cooled turbine, advanced lightweight fully modulating afterburner and guided-expansion convergent-divergent jet nozzle.

DIMENSIONS:
Length overall   140 in (3,556 mm)
Max diameter   24 in (610 mm)

GENERAL ELECTRIC F101

The F101-GE-100 (formerly the GE9) is a new augmented turbofan designed by General Electric for the B-1 strategic bomber (formerly AMSA) competition. All contract performance requirements were met or exceeded by the GE9 engine demonstrator programme under sponsorship of the Aeronautical Systems Division of the US Air Force, Wright-Patterson Air Force Base, Ohio, and that programme is now completed. No details of the F101 are available.

GENERAL ELECTRIC J79

Development of the J79, America's first high-compression variable-stator turbojet, began in 1952. It was flight tested for the first time in 1955 and became the first production Mach 2 engine when it was selected to power the General Dynamics B-58 Hustler bomber. In addition to production by General Electric, versions of the J79 have been or are being manufactured by Orenda of Canada to power the Canadair CF-104/F-104G (MAP), by Ishikawajima-Harima in Japan for the licence-built F-104J and by MAN Turbo of Germany, Fiat of Italy and FN of Belgium for the European-built F-104G. The Italian production team, including Alfa-Romeo, is now engaged on a programme to produce the J79-GE-19, an improved engine similar to the J79-GE-17 but configured for the F-104S Starfighter.

Overall, the International Technical Assistance Programme has been responsible for assembly of more than 2,000 J79 turbojets for the F-104. A total of more than 13,150 J79s had been built by GE and licensees by December 1969.

Derivatives of the J79 have been the CJ805-3 turbojet and CJ805-23 turbofan powering the Convair 880 and 990 Coronado, respectively, as well as the LM1500 industrial and marine gas-turbine.

Versions of the J79 are as follows:

J79-GE-2. Powered early models of the McDonnell F-4A Phantom II and North American A-5A Vigilante. Air mass flow 166 lb (75 kg)/sec. Pressure ratio 12·5 : 1.

J79-GE-3B. Powers the Lockheed F-104A and B Starfighters.

J79-GE-5C. Powers the General Dynamics B-58A Hustler.

J79-GE-7A. Powers the Lockheed F-104C and D Starfighters. Built under licence by Orenda (as J79-OEL-7) for Canadair CF-104.

J79-GE-8. For production versions of F-4B and RF-4B Phantom II and A-5A and RA-5C Vigilante. Air mass flow 169 lb (76·5 kg)/sec. Pressure ratio 12·9 : 1.

J79-GE-10. Advanced version powering North American Rockwell RA-5C and McDonnell Douglas F-4J. Entered production in June 1966, superseding the J79-GE-8. Pressure ratio 13·5 : 1.

J79-GE-11A. For US-built Lockheed F-104G Starfighters. Built under licence in Japan (as J79-IHI-11A), Germany, Italy, Belgium and Canada.

J79-GE-15. Powers McDonnell Douglas F-4C, F-4D and RF-4C for USAF. Similar to J79-GE-8 except for self-contained starting.

General Electric GE1/10 demonstrator engine for the F400-GE-400/F100-GE-100 advanced augmented turbofan development programme

J79-GE-17. Similar to J79-GE-10, but for USAF versions of F-4.

J79-GE-19. Advanced version designed to supersede J79-GE-11A in F-104. Used in F-104S and F-104A. Differs from J79-GE-10/17 only in external characteristics. Guided expansion jet nozzle derived from nozzles of J79-GE-5C and YJ93. Afterburner system provides continuous thrust modulation. Fuel flow can be modulated from 2,700 lb (1,225 kg)/hr to 34,000 lb (15,420 kg)/hr.

The following details cover the basic features of all J79 variants except where otherwise indicated.

TYPE: Variable-stator single-shaft axial-flow turbojet.

AIR INTAKE: Annular type, surrounding central bullet fairing. Struts and inlet guide vanes anti-iced with compressor discharge air. First-stage stator anti-icing on J79-GE-8, -10 and -15.

COMPRESSOR: Seventeen-stage axial-flow. First six stator stages and the inlet guide vanes have variable-incidence. Setting of variable-incidence vanes adjusted by dual actuators moved by engine fuel to achieve optimum air flow angles for each stage at all engine speeds. Rotor, which runs on two bearings, is made from Lapelloy, B5F5 and titanium. All engines have type 403 stainless steel blades and vanes except J79-GE-3B and -7A which have A286 stator vanes at stages 7 to 17 inclusive. Total of 1,260 stator vanes and 1,271 rotor blades. Variable stator vanes have a platform, trunnion and threaded stem arrangement for external attachment to the actuation system linkage. Fixed stator vanes are inserted into T-slots on rear casing. All rotor blades have dovetail roots. Front compressor stator casing is made from a magnesium-thorium casting or Chromolloy forging, depending on engine model. On those engines requiring an intermediate compressor casing this is made of either A286 or 321 SS. All models have a forged and machined rear compressor stator casing, constructed in two halves for ease of assembly and disassembly.

COMBUSTION CHAMBER: Cannular type consisting of 10 combustion cans. Outer casing of Chromolloy, flame tube of Hastelloy. J79-GE-3B, -7A, -11A, -15, -17 and -19 have dual igniters in cans 4 and 5. J79-GE-2, -5C, -8 and -10 have single igniter in can 4.

FUEL SYSTEM: Hydro-mechanical range-governing control system composed of two separate and distinct systems, the main fuel system and afterburner fuel system. Main system is controlled by main fuel control, which is a flow-controlling unit. The afterburner system is controlled by an independent control, also of the flow-controlling type. Automatic acceleration control with exhaust temperature limiting. Gear type main fuel pump. Engine-driven centrifugal afterburner fuel pump.

FUEL GRADE: JP-4 or JP-5.

NOZZLE GUIDE VANES: Three-stage; first with 58 vanes of R41, second with 62 vanes of Hastelloy R235 and R41, third with 44 vanes of A286.

TURBINE: Three-stage axial-flow type. Stages 1 and 2 bolted to shaft, stage 3 integral with aft shaft. J79-GE-8 and -15 have first and second stage wheels of V57 and third stage wheel of A286. All three stages of J79-GE-10, -17 and -19 have intermediate grade V57. J79-GE-2 has all three stages of M308. Other models have all stages of A286. First stage has 148 blades of Udimet 700, second stage has 114 blades of Udimet 500, third stage has 84 blades of M252. All blades attached by fir-tree roots. Lightweight casing of fabricated A286 in two easily-removable halves.

BEARINGS: Three only. Roller in front frame, ball (main thrust) in compressor frame, roller in turbine frame.

JET PIPE: Liner of N155 and L605 with ceramic coating. Jet-pipe of A286.

AFTERBURNER: Short type (max 3,600°F) with fully-variable nozzle of "petal" type. Actuation by hydraulic rams utilising engine lubricating oil. Three-ring, quadrant-burning on all models except J79-GE-3B, -8, -10, -15, -17 and -19, which have core annulus burning with radial spray bars.

ACCESSORY DRIVES: All engine controls and accessories, aircraft hydraulic pumps, generators, alternators and constant-speed drives (as required) are driven by two gearboxes on bottom of engine and a nose inlet gearbox.

LUBRICATION: Dry sump type. Vane type pumps. Sump pressure provided from compressor. Oil cooling from fuel. Sump capacity ranges from 4 to 5 US gallons (15-19 litres). Average normal oil supply pressure 50 lb/sq in (3·5 kg/cm²).

General Electric J79-GE-17 turbojet (17,900 lb=8,120 kg st)

OIL SPECIFICATION: MIL-L-7808, MIL-L-23699.

MOUNTING: Pads provided on front frame and turbine frame for a variety of mounting arrangements, depending on airframe requirements.

STARTING: J79-GE-3B, -5C, -7A and -11A have pneumatic turbine starter mounted on front frame of transfer gearbox. J79-GE-2, -8 and -10 have turbine air impingement starter. J79-GE-15 and -17 have combination cartridge/pneumatic starter on transfer gearbox.

DIMENSIONS:
Length overall:

J79-GE-2, 7A, 11A	207·96 in (5,283 mm)
J79-GE-3B	207·45 in (5,270 mm)
J79-GE-5C	202·17 in (5,136 mm)
J79-GE-8	208·45 in (5,295 mm)
J79-GE-10, 17, 19	208·69 in (5,301 mm)

Diameter at compressor:

J79-GE-2, 7A, 8, 11A, 15	38·3 in (973 mm)
J79-GE-5C	38·0 in (965 mm)
J79-GE-10, 17, 19	39·06 in (992 mm)

Diameter at nozzle:

J79-GE-2, 3B, 7A, 8, 11A, 15	38·31 in (973 mm)
J79-GE-5C	38·0 in (956 mm)
J79-GE-10, 17, 19	39·06 in (992 mm)

WEIGHT (DRY):

J79-GE-2	3,620 lb (1,642 kg)
J79-GE-3B	3,325 lb (1,508 kg)
J79-GE-5C	3,685 lb (1,671 kg)
J79-OEL-7	3,575 lb (1,622 kg)
J79-GE-8	3,672 lb (1,666 kg)
J79-GE-10	3,855 lb (1,749 kg)
J79-GE-11A	3,560 lb (1,615 kg)
J79-GE-15	3,685 lb (1,672 kg)
J79-GE-17, 19	3,835 lb (1,740 kg)

PERFORMANCE RATINGS:
T-O rating, with afterburning:

J79-GE-2	16,150 lb (7,325 kg) st
J79-GE-3B	14,800 lb (6,713 kg) st
J79-GE-5C	15,600 lb (7,076 kg) st
J79-GE-7A, 11A	15,800 lb (7,167 kg) st
J79-GE-8, 15	17,000 lb (7,711 kg) st
J79-GE-10, 17, 19	17,900 lb (8,120 kg) st

Military rating:

J79-GE-2	10,350 lb (4,695 kg) st
J79-GE-3B	9,600 lb (4,355 kg) st

J79-GE-5C	10,300 lb (4,672 kg) st
J79-GE-7A, 11A	10,000 lb (4,536 kg) st
J79-GE-8, 15	10,900 lb (4,944 kg) st
J79-GE-10, 17, 19	11,870 lb (5,385 kg) st

Cruise rating:

J79-GE-2	2,230 lb (1,012 kg) st
J79-GE-3B	2,500 lb (1,134 kg) st
J79-GE-5C	2,450 lb (1,112 kg) st
J79-GE-7A, 11A	2,650 lb (1,202 kg) st
J79-GE-8, 10, 15, 17, 19	2,600 lb (1,179 kg) st

SPECIFIC FUEL CONSUMPTIONS:
At T-O rating:

J79-GE-2	2·00
J79-GE-3B	2·04
J79-GE-5C	2·20
J79-GE-7A, 11A	1·97
J79-GE-8	1·93
J79-GE-15	1·945
J79-GE-10, 17, 19	1·965

At military rating:

J79-GE-2, 3B	0·87
J79-GE-8, 15	0·86
J79-GE-5C, 7A, 10, 11A, 17, 19	0·84

At cruise rating:

J79-GE-2	1·06
J79-GE-3B	1·13
J79-GE-5C	1·01
J79-GE-7A, 8, 15	1·05
J79-GE-10, 17, 19	0·95
J79-GE-11A	1·05

GENERAL ELECTRIC TF34

It was announced in April 1968 that the US Navy Air Systems Command had awarded General Electric a contract for development of the TF34 high by-pass ratio turbofan. This engine is to power the USN's Lockheed S-3A anti-submarine warfare aircraft and was selected in competition with the Allison TF32. Both turbofans had been the subject of USN design contracts awarded in late 1966.

The TF34 is a twin-spool unit in the 9,000 lb (4,082 kg) st category and is being developed by the Aircraft Engine Group's Military Engine Division. Its design utilizes a high by-pass ratio fan, variable-stator compressor, annular combustion chamber, and air-cooled turbine. These features have already been proven in other GE engines, in particular the TF39 turbofan. The TF34 is a "low risk" engine intended

General Electric TF34 ready for installation in a test cell. This high-ratio turbofan engine (unofficially stated to have a thrust in the 9,000 lb = 4,080 kg class) was designed to meet the mission requirements of the Lockheed S-3A anti-submarine aircraft

to meet severe reliability requirements in the arduous carrier-based ASW role within a brief time-scale. The engine operating cycle was based entirely on the US Navy ASW mission and the present four-year development programme is centred wholly on the requirements of the S-3A aircraft. The first engine ran in a test cell at Lynn in April 1969, one month ahead of contract commitment.

Weight, thrust and specific fuel consumption are classified, but the released data enable close approximations to be made. The TF34 has been described as "in the 9,000 lb (4,082 kg) thrust class".

TYPE: Two-shaft high by-pass ratio turbofan for subsonic aircraft.

AIR INTAKE: Plain annular intake. No fixed inlet struts or guide vanes. Small spinner rotates with fan.

FAN: Single-stage fan has blades forged in titanium, with part-span shrouds. Total air-mass flow 338 lb (153 kg)/sec. By-pass ratio 6·2 : 1.

COMPRESSOR: Single axial spool on HP shaft. Total of 14 stages, upstream section having variable stators. First nine stages of titanium, remainder of high-nickel alloy. Total core airflow 47 lb (21·3 kg)/sec.

COMBUSTION CHAMBER: Annular chamber designed for highly efficient and complete combustion with near-zero smoke. Hastelloy chamber liner and front dome providing ports for igniters and vaporizing burners.

TURBINE: Two-stage HP gas generator turbine with convection-cooled rotor blades and stator vanes, the first-stage nozzle vanes having film cooling. Four-stage LP fan turbine with tip-shrouded blades. Turbine entry gas temperature 2,195°F maximum.

FUEL SYSTEM: Integrated hydromechanical control unit with electronic amplifier. Fuel grade JP-4 or JP-5.

ACCESSORY DRIVES: Engine and customer accessories mounted around horseshoe-shaped gearbox, fitting closely around lower half of compressor casing. Radial shaft drive from front of HP shaft. Fan airflow passes outside accessories and over upper half of engine.

LUBRICATION: Enclosed, pressurized system with vent along centre shaft.

DIMENSIONS:
Fan diameter   50 in (1,270 mm)
Basic length   101 in (2,565 mm)

GENERAL ELECTRIC CF6

On 11 September 1967 General Electric announced the endorsement and commitment of corporate funding for the development of the new CF6 turbofan for the forthcoming generation of wide-body transports. From the initial family of 22,000 lb to 36,000 lb (9,979 to 16,329 kg) st CF6 two-shaft engines announced in September 1967 to cover the anticipated thrust requirements of the Lockheed and McDonnell Douglas airbus projects, the CF6 evolved through a series of variants to the CF6/36/6, slack-rated at 39,500 lb (17,917 kg) st and tailored to the propulsion needs of the three-engined McDonnell Douglas DC-10 Series 10 intermediate-range transport. Announcement that this engine had been selected by United Air Lines and American Airlines was made on 25 April 1968.

Basic configuration of the CF6 comprises a new 1¼-stage fan driven by a new five-stage LP turbine energised by a slightly modified TF39 core engine consisting of a 16-stage HP compressor, annular combustor and two-stage turbine. Modifications have been introduced to enable the accessory systems to suit airline installation requirements, while other changes are aimed at enhancing reliability, durability and maintainability.

The construction is modular, featuring easily-removable components that are interchangeable to enable airlines to minimise spare-parts holdings and facilitate sectional overhaul procedures. Provisions have been made for mounting sensors and detection devices to monitor engines during flight. Borescope ports are provided at every compressor and turbine stage, enabling engine checks to be made without disassembly.

The CF6 fan is designed for low noise output and a 30,000 hr operational life. It offers high resistance to erosion and foreign-object damage, and provides inherent foreign material separation capability. Rather than entering the HP compressor inlet, foreign objects are centrifuged into the fan and emerge via the fan nozzle. The fan rotor is designed to meet FAA prime reliability propeller criteria and has substantial speed and stress margins. A blade containment system and automatic engine shut-down system are also provided to enhance safety.

Particular attention has been paid to noise suppression and combustor smoke reduction. A 1-in (25·4-mm) thick glass-fibre sandwich structure developed by GE is incorporated along the outer wall of the fan air duct, from inlet tip to nozzle trailing-edge. Tests were run

Two views of the General Electric CF6-6 turbofan (40,000 lb = 18,144 kg st)

during 1968 on a 42 per cent scale model of the CF6 fan mounted in a simulated DC-10 cowl to check fan noise levels. The TF39 combustor in the core engine has been modified to introduce axial swirlers directing more air through the dome to the burning zone, and improved smoke level has been demonstrated.

The following versions of the engine have been identified.

CF6-6. Initial 40,000 lb (18,144 kg) st version of engine under development for intermediate-range DC-10 Series 10. First ran on 21 October 1968 and 18 days later attained 45,750 lb (20,752 kg) st. Following a series of successful factory and outdoor tests, engine was released for production in February 1969. The second CF6-6, built to the production configuration, first ran in May 1969. By March 1970 a total of 12 engines had run, and flight testing with a single engine hung on the starboard inner pylon of a B-52 had extended to 30,000 ft (9,150 m), Mach 0·896 and 545 knots (621 mph; 1,000 km/h). Delivery of flight test engines to McDonnell Douglas started late in 1969 with aircraft first flight following in September 1970. Certification of the CF6-6 was planned for mid-1970 and the engine is to enter airline service in the DC-10 Series 10 in late 1971.

CF6-50A. Announced by GE in January 1969, the 49,000 lb (22,226 kg) st CF6-50A is a growth version of the CF6-6 to power the intercontinental-range DC-10 Series 30. The increased thrust is achieved by increased flow through the core engine (reducing the by-pass ratio from 6·3 : 1 to 4·6 : 1) and higher turbine entry temperature. A major change is the introduction of two additional core engine booster stages behind the single-stage LP compressor of the CF6-6, with no change in the

turbofan's external dimensions. To provide for flow matching between the two rotors, variable by-pass ratio valves are incorporated between the LP and HP compressors. A two-position turbine exhaust nozzle is fitted to reduce low altitude noise level and improve cruise sfc at altitude. A 41 per cent scale model fan with three-stage compressor and variable by-pass valves started testing in January 1969. The CF6-50A will enter airline service in late 1972 in the DC-10 Series 30. The initial rating will be 47,300 lb (21,455 kg) st, later to be re-rated to 49,000 lb (22,226 kg) st in May 1973. A variant of the CF6-50 series has also been offered for the Airbus Industrie A 300B.

CF6-50B. Planned for availability in May 1974. Higher thrust of 50,000 lb (22,680 kg) st is achieved by slight increase in turbine entry temperature and increased fan speed to give greater flow through core engine.

CF6-50C. Initially rated at 50,000 lb (22,680 kg) st, will be re-rated to give 51,000 lb (23,133 kg) st by May 1975. Higher thrust is provided by a further increase in turbine temperature, with improved cooling of hot-section components.

The following data relate to the CF6-6 with the differing features of the CF6-50 series also detailed.

TYPE: Two-shaft high by-pass ratio commercial turbofan.

AIR INTAKE: Single forward-facing annular configuration.

FAN: Single-stage fan with integrally-mounted single-stage LP compressor (described together as a 1¼-stage fan) both driven by LP turbine. Fan has rotating spinner and omits inlet guide vanes. Blade-containment shroud provided against possible blade failure. The 38 fan rotor blades are individually removable from the thick-section centreless disc bolted to forward conical extension of LP shaft syst-tem. Blade aerofoil has anti-vibration shrouds at $\frac{2}{3}$ span. Fan rotor exit airflow split between LP compressor and fan slipstream. Fan front frame has 12 radial/tangential struts across fan slipstream exit, canted to reduce noise, bolted to core engine inlet which has six radial struts. Front frame provides support for LP and HP rotor front bearings, fan being over-hung ahead of large diameter ball thrust bearing with rear roller bearing ahead of core engine. Fan blades, discs, spool and exit guide vanes of titanium; fan frame and shaft of steel; spinner and fan case of aluminium alloy. Total airflow 1,160 lb/sec (526 kg/sec), fan and LP compressor pressure ratio 1·64 : 1, by-pass ratio 6·25 : 1. Configuration of CF6-50 is similar but with two added LP stages and by-pass valves (described below). No shrouds on fan blade aerofoil. Total airflow 1,178 lb (534 kg)/sec; pressure ratio 1·69 : 1; by-pass ratio 4·3 : 1.

LP Compressor: Single-stage compressor acting as booster to fan flow into core engine. Rotor blades carried on rear rim of tapered drum bolted to rear of fan disc. Stators cantilevered off short-chord shroud ring supported by radial outer struts and radial/tangential inner struts located on fan front frame. Compressor exit flow free to balance between core engine and fan slipstream exit. Configuration of CF6-50 modified to three compressor booster stages carried on flanged rotor drum. Continuous shroud extends to fan front frame with 12 integral by-pass valves located between canted radial struts in fan exit inner casing. These valves maintain proper flow matching between the fan/LP system and core by opening at low power settings to permit LP supercharged flow to bleed into the fan airstream. The doors are closed during take-off and cruise.

HP Compressor: Sixteen-stage compressor of near-constant tip diameter, with inlet guide vanes and first six stator rows having variable incidence. Provision for interstage air-bleed for airframe use and engine cooling. Rotor is of combined drum-and-disc construction with front stage and rear three stages overhung on conical discs providing location on HP front bearing and HP main shaft. All rotor blades held in rabbeted discs and individually replaceable without rotor disassembly. Stages 1-13 blades forged titanium, 14-16 steel. Stages 1-10 discs titanium, 11-16 and aft casing Inconel 718. Casing split on horizontal centreline; stator vanes held in dovetail slots and replaceable after removing half-casing. Stages 1-7 stators titanium, 8 steel, 9-13 titanium, 14-15 steel; inlet guide vanes titanium, outlet guide vanes steel. Double-skin inner casing shrouds the LP main shaft. Outlet frame contains compressor diffuser and incorporates support structure for HP rotor mid-bearings. HP compressor pressure ratio 16·8 : 1, overall cruise pressure ratio 26·6 : 1. Core airflow 183 lb (83 kg)/sec. CF6-50 has 15th and 16th stages removed to pass much greater airflow of 270 lb (122 kg)/sec and reduce pressure and temperature of air entering combustion chamber. Improved materials and strengthened structure in later stages. Overall pressure ratio 29·9 : 1.

Combustor: Fully annular with comprehensive film-cooling. Separable snout, dome and inner/outer skirts, with nozzles, igniter, leads and manifold externally removable. Dome contains ports for two igniters and axial swirler cups for 30 fuel nozzles. Igniters of high-voltage surface-gap type with energy level of 1·5-2 joules, each igniter operated independently. Forged steel nozzles with lever of Hastelloy X. Nozzle and dome designed to minimise smoke, and entrance diffuser has gradual profile to assure low temperature gradient to turbine under all flight conditions. Configuration for CF6-50 is similar but strengthened.

HP Turbine: Two-stage air-cooled turbine with 2,300°F (1,533°K) entry temperature. First-stage rotor blades are film and convection cooled, second stage convection cooled. Rotor blades cast from René 80; discs and forward and rear shafts of Inconel 718. First-stage nozzle guide vanes supported at inner and outer ends, second-stage cantilevered from outer ends, with inner ends carrying inter-stage labyrinth seals. First-stage vanes cast from X40 and film cooled by compressor discharge pressure. Second-stage vanes are cast from René 77 material and are convection cooled. Vanes are welded into pairs to decrease number of gas leakage paths. Thin-section discs with heavy-section centreless hubs are bolted to front and rear conical shafts, including conical and arched inter-disc diaphragms. HP tubular shaft extends through disc hubs to attach to rear conical shafts. Configuration for CF6-50 is similar but introduces improved materials and cooling.

LP Turbine: Five-stage, constant tip-diameter turbine with less than 1,400°F (1,033°K) inlet temperature. Rotor blades tip-shrouded and cast in René 77, not air-cooled. Forward and rear shafts, case and discs of Inconel 718. First-stage nozzle guide vanes supported at inner and outer ends, remaining stages are cantilevered from outer ends, with inner ends carrying inter-stage labyrinth seals. Stages 1-3 guide vanes cast in René 77, stages 4 and 5 cast in René 41. Vanes are cast in pairs and held by dovetails in slots machined in the two half stator casings. Drum and centreless disc construction located on LP rotor by front and rear conical diaphragms attached to third and fourth stage discs. Front diaphragm attached to LP main shaft, rear diaphragm to rear stub shaft. Drive to rotor by means of long fan midshaft. On CF6-50 only the last three stages are unchanged. Stage 1 is eliminated (making four-stage LP turbine) and stage 2 is modified in geometry.

Exhaust Unit (Fan): Fixed-area annular duct with outer cowl and engine cowl forming convergent plug nozzle for fan slipstream.

Exhaust Unit (Turbine): Short-length fixed-area exhaust duct with convergent plug nozzle. On CF6-50, two-position plug nozzle fitted, with aft-translating cowl and plug. Provision for modified exhaust thrust spoiler.

Thrust Reverser (Fan): Annular cascade reverser with blocker doors across fan duct. For reverse thrust, rear portion of fan outer cowl translates aft on rotating ball screws to uncover cascade vanes. Blocker doors (16 off) flush-mounted in cowl on link arms hinged in inner cowl, rotate inwards to expose cascade vanes and block fan duct.

Thrust Spoiler (Turbine): Post nozzle exit, cascade type. Two cascade screens are mounted in vertical plane on fixed pivot aft of turbine exhaust and are enclosed in fairing forming aerofoil-shaped plug. Aft translation of fairing uncovers cascades which open across nozzle exit and divert turbine exhaust radially outward and slightly forward in horizontal plane. Alternative configuration for CF-50 comprises similar design to fan thrust reverser.

Rotor Support System: Eight bearings (four for each rotor) at seven locations. Fan and LP compressor carried on ball thrust bearing (1) behind fan disc and roller bearing (2) at front of LP main shaft, both bearings mounted in fan front frame structure which also supports HP compressor front roller bearing (3). LP turbine carried on roller bearings at front and rear of turbine rotor assembly—rear bearing (7) being mounted in spider structure across turbine exit, and front bearing (6) on major spider structure between HP and LP turbines. HP compressor carried at rear on adjacent roller bearing (4) and ball thrust bearing (5) at interconnection with HP turbine front conical shaft, both bearings being mounted on support structure integral with compressor outlet diffuser.

Accessory Drive: This consists of the inlet gearbox, radial gearbox, radial driveshaft, transfer gearbox, horizontal drive shaft and accessory gearbox. The inlet gearbox is located in the forward sump of the engine. The gearbox transfers energy from the core-engine (HP) rotor to the radial driveshaft located in a housing aft of the bottom vertical strut of the fan frame. The transfer gearbox is mounted on the bottom of the fan frame. Accessory mounting pads are provided on both the forward and aft faces of the gearbox. The engine accessories mounted on the gearbox are starter, fuel pump, main engine control, lubrication pump and tachometer. Pads are also provided for mounting the aircraft hydraulic pumps, constant-speed drive and alternator.

Fuel System: Hydromechanical fuel control system regulates steady-state fuel flow and schedules acceleration and deceleration fuel flow. It also schedules and powers variable-stator vane position. A governor in the Woodward control provides core-engine speed stability during steady-state operation. During transient operation, core-engine fuel flow is scheduled on the basis of throttle position, compressor inlet temperature, compressor discharge pressure and core-engine speed. The fuel control and fuel pump are mounted in the accessory package as an integrated unit which avoids interconnecting high-pressure fuel lines and potential leakage points. This configuration provides a single drive mounting flange. The filter, fuel/oil heat exchanger and control pressurizing valve may be removed individually without removing the entire assembly. The fuel manifold is double-well constructed for safety and mounted on the exterior of the engine. For CF6-50, modified fuel control for by-pass valves and two-position nozzle control fitted.

Fuel Grades: Fuels conforming to the commercial jet fuel specification ASTM-1655-65T, Jet A, Jet A1 and Jet B are authorized. Fuels conforming to MIL-T-5624G2 grades JP-4 or JP-5 are alternatives.

Lubrication System: Dry-sump centre-vented system in which oil is pressure-fed to each engine component requiring lubrication. Oil is removed from the sump areas by scavenge pumps, passed through a fuel/oil heat exchanger and filter to the engine tank. Nominal lubrication system pressure is 20-85 lb/sq in (1·4-6 kg/cm²) above sump reference pressure. All pressure and scavenge pumps and filters are located on the outside of the engine in the lubrication centre forward of the gearbox.

Oil Specification: Conforming to General Electric specification D50TFI-52 classes A&B, equivalent to MIL-L-7808.

Mounting: Main thrust mount located on the inner fan frame; aft flight mount located on the turbine mid frame.

Starting: Air-turbine starter mounted on the front of the accessory gearbox at the through shaft.

Noise Suppression Equipment: Acoustic panels integrated with fan casing, fan front frame and engine inlet cowl.

Dimensions:
- Fan tip diameter 86·4 in (2,195 mm)
- Max width (cold) 93·7 in (2,380 mm)
- Max height (over gearbox) 108 in (3,743 mm)
- Length overall (cold) 193 in (4,902 mm)

Weights, Dry:
- CF6-6:
  - Engine, including sound attenuation materials 7,350 lb (3,334 kg)
  - Thrust reverser and spoiler 1,430 lb (649 kg)
- CF6-50A:
  - Engine, including sound attenuation materials 8,100 lb (3,674 kg)

Performance Ratings:
- Max T-O, flat rated to 84°F (29°C):
  - CF6-6: 40,000 lb (18,144 kg) st at 9,800 core engine rpm and 3,500 fan rpm
  - CF6-50A: 49,000 lb (22,226 kg) st at 10,200 core engine rpm and 3,800 fan rpm (Until May 1973, 47,300 lb=21,555 kg st)
  - CF6-50B (with ideal nozzle; 1,000 lb=454 kg less with real nozzle):
    - 49,000 lb (22,226 kg) st to 84°F (29°C)
    - 50,000 lb (22,680 kg) st to 78°F (26°C)
  - CF6-50C (to 84°F=29°C):
    - 50,000 lb (22,680 kg) with real nozzle
    - 51,000 lb (23,133 kg) with ideal nozzle
- Max altitude and Mach No:
  - CF6-6 and -50 50,000 ft (15,240 m) and Mach 1·0
- Max cruise at 35,000 ft (10,668 m) and Mach 0·85, flat rated to standard day plus 18°F (21°C), with real nozzle:
  - CF6-6 8,800 lb (3,991 kg) st
  - CF6-50A 10,500 lb (4,227 kg) st
- Max continuous at 35,000 ft (10,668 m) and Mach 0·85, flat rated to standard day plus 18°F (21°C):
  - CF6-6 9,550 lb (4,249 kg) st

Specific Fuel Consumptions:
- At max T-O thrust:
  - CF6-6 0·34
  - CF6-50A at 47,300 lb (21,555 kg) st 0·38
- At max cruise thrust:
  - CF6-6 0·635
  - CF6-50A 0·651

Oil Consumption: 2·0 lb (0·9 kg)/hr

GENERAL ELECTRIC TF39

General Electric is supplying the 41,100 lb (18,640 kg) st TF39 turbofan for the Lockheed C-5 Galaxy heavy logistics transport aircraft, under contracts awarded by the USAF Aeronautical Systems Division, Wright-Patterson AFB, Ohio. The contracts cover design, development, qualification and production of the TF39 to power a total of 86 C-5As. Lockheed also contracted with GE to supply the thrust reversers for the engine.

First run of the TF39 was in December 1965, only twelve months after the GE1/6 $\frac{2}{3}$-scale demonstrator was first tested. Development experience with the TF39 has been built up rapidly and by February 1970 some 17,700 hours of bench testing had been accumulated. First flight with the engine installed on the inboard starboard pylon of a modified Boeing B-52E was on 9 June 1967, and at programme completion in August 1969 258 engine operating hours in flight testing had been completed, covering the full C-5 flight envelope to Mach 0·885 and 50,000 ft (15,240 m). Also included in the B-52 programme was a flight demonstrator of an axial-swirler "smokeless" combustion chamber being developed for the TF39. Over 120,000 hours of TF39 component rig and mechanical systems testing had also been run by that time.

By 1970, TF39 engines had successfully completed two series of environmental tests at the Eglin AFB climatic hangar, and altitude performance testing had been completed at the USAF's Arnold Engineering Development Center, Tullahoma, Tennessee. A large crosswind test rig incorporating 13 high-speed fans, built by GE at its Peebles, Ohio, facility, enabled the engine to be tested under wind conditions up to hurricane velocity, severe icing conditions, and sand ingestion. Tests conducted at GE's Evendale, Ohio, facilities included water ingestion; small and large bird ingestion; overspeed and overtemperature; blade containment; simulated service running; and accelerated endurance tests. By mid-1969 two factory engines had each completed more than 1,000 hours of running during simulated service endurance testing designed to accumulate experience ahead of field engine levels.

The TF39 successfully completed its 60-hour Endurance Preliminary Qualification Test (PQT) during November 1967, and its 150-hour Endurance Formal Qualification Test (FQT) during October 1968. Shipment of 24 YTF39 engines for the early C-5 flight programme began in October 1967 and was completed on schedule in June 1968.

General Electric began delivering production Model TF39s in October 1968. At the end of 1969 GE had built 216 TF39 engines, including 165 production TF39 models that averaged 40 lb (18·1 kg) under specification weight. The Formal Qualification, covering over 70 tests and reports on the engine and its components, was approved by the USAF in October 1969.

First flight of the C-5 was accomplished on schedule in June 1968. By mid-February 1970, 710 flights on 12 C-5 aircraft had accumulated 10,128 engine flight hours without an in-flight shutdown caused by the engine. During these flights, aircraft stall investigations were flown at angles of attack in excess of 30° without encountering engine problems. In-flight thrust reverser deployments and engine restarts were routinely accomplished. In addition, the C-5 had reached altitudes of 40,200 ft (12,250 m) and set new take-off and gross weight records including a historic flight with the aircraft weighing 798,200 lb (362,057 kg)—the heaviest flight weight ever recorded.

By early 1970 the TF39 had completed over 32,000 hours of fan engine development testing. By early 1972, the TF39 should have logged 500,000 flight hours and by the end of 1972 about 1,000,000 flight hours.

The TF39 is a twin-spool high by-pass ratio unit, based on new turbofan technology demonstrated by the General Electric GE1/6 high by-pass turbofan during 1964-65. Major features of the TF39 are its exceptionally low sfc, which is 25 per cent lower at cruise than the best of the previous generation of low by-pass ratio turbofans, and its 8 : 1 by-pass ratio, facilitated by the use of an unusual form of 1½-stage 8 ft (2·4 m) diameter fan.

In configuration, the TF39 comprises a 1½-stage fan driven by a six-stage low-pressure turbine, and a 16-stage high-pressure compressor with seven stages of variable stators driven by a two-stage high-pressure turbine. The fan/low-pressure turbine rotor is carried on four bearings, and the high-pressure rotor on three bearings. The combustion chamber is fully annular. Mass flow is 1,549 lb (703 kg)/sec, split approximately 1,377 lb (625 kg)/sec as fan slipstream and 172 lb (78 kg) through the gas generator. Overall pressure ratio 26 : 1, comprising 1·55 : 1 across the fan and 16·8 : 1 across the compressor.

Both the fan duct, which is equipped with a thrust reverser, and the gas generator section are fitted with a fixed annular nozzle, the turbine exhaust having a long streamlined "plug" within the primary nozzle. The oil tank and fuel heater are mounted above the compressor casing on the port side. The main accessory gearbox, with drives for an alternator, fuel pump, oil pumps and tachometer generator, is mounted under the compressor casing. Several bleed air ports are provided.

As a result of the high (8 : 1) by-pass ratio, the by-pass flow ejected by the fan provides 85 per cent of the thrust at take-off. Turbine entry temperature is around 2,300°F, requiring the high-pressure turbine blading to be hollow and air-cooled. The low-pressure turbine blading is solid. To facilitate maintenance, the engine can be disassembled into its three major components; front fan, gas generator and low-pressure turbine. In addition the compressor and low-pressure turbine casing can be split to permit replacement of damaged blades. The fan blades and fuel nozzles can be changed individually.

High corrosion-resistant materials, such as titanium, are used for the larger portion of the fan and compressor, for protection while operating in tropical or coastal areas. All other weather-exposed surfaces of the engine use corrosion resistant alloys or coatings.

Overall the TF39 has been designed for long life in service. Life expectancy of hot-end components such as the combustion chamber and turbine is 15,000 hr. Design life of cold parts is 30,000 hr. TBO on entry into service was 1,000 hours; this figure is expected to be extended progressively to 5,000 hours after two million flight hours.

The 8 ft (2·4 m) diameter fan is of unique 1½-stage design, comprising a front stage of approximately half the blade height of the second stage. The front "½-stage" rotor blading (to which

General Electric TF39 turbofan engine (41,100 lb = 18,640 kg st)

part-span snubber shrouds have been now added), carried on a rotating spinner without inlet guide vanes, rotates inside a stationary flow splitter supported by short-length inlet guide vanes which are mounted by their outer ends on the fan duct. The second-stage rotor blading comprises a row of 3 ft (0·9 m) high fan blades, described by GE as "flades". These have an integral mid-span platform, providing a rotating continuation of the front row flow splitter.

The "flades" are machined from titanium forgings to produce a high-strength lightweight blade with differing inner and outer aerofoil sections designed to satisfy the contrasting aerodynamic requirements of the root and tip. The so-called "split-work" blade is intended to provide a high throughput of air across the fan and supercharge the gas generator section of the engine.

The centrifugal action of the fan stages causes foreign objects to be ejected via the fan exit rather than enter the high-pressure compressor. The robustness and large chord of the fan blades enables them to withstand significant amounts of foreign objects ingestion without damage.

Housed within the 102·5 in (2,600 mm) diameter cowl surrounding the fan section is the fan reverser. This comprises a transverse annulus of reverser cascades which are exposed by rearward movement of the cowl, thus activating simultaneously a ring of "blocker" doors which hinge in to block the normal fan exit annulus. The reverser can be operated in flight on the C-5A's two inboard TF39s with the engines at idle power. During landing, all four reversers can be operated with the engines at take-off thrust. Tests are programmed to prove the reverser's ability to perform 4,000 full-load cycles or operate on the C-5A for at least four years without major repair or overhaul. Useful life will be 14,000 cycles and 30,000 hours of aircraft operation, with reasonable repair.

General Electric announced in April 1968 a new industrial and marine series of gas-turbines under the designation LM2500, based on the gas generator section of the TF39.

DIMENSIONS:
Length, intake flange to turbine exhaust flange
188·4 in (4,785 mm)
Length overall, nose hub to exhaust plug nozzle
324 in (8,230 mm)
Diameter, maximum over fan
100 in (2,540 mm)
WEIGHT (DRY): 7,286 lb (3,304 kg)
PERFORMANCE RATING:
T-O (flat rated to 89·5°F at sea level)
41,100 lb (18,640 kg) st

GENERAL ELECTRIC GE4

In August 1965 it was announced that General Electric and Pratt & Whitney were to be awarded contracts for the design, development and testing of demonstrator engines as competitive power plants for the American supersonic transport programme. The General Electric engine for this Phase II sector of the programme was the GE4, a large medium pressure ratio single-shaft axial turbojet with afterburner, extensively based on GE's J93 and J79 supersonic military turbojet experience.

The first GE4 demonstrator engine ran on 18 July 1966. Two days later it was operated at rated rpm, and on 23 August it achieved its

design thrust of more than 40,000 lb (18,145 kg) without augmentation. With afterburning, the engine produced 52,600 lb (23,860 kg) st on 18 October 1966, some 4 per cent more than was projected for the engine. All three (Block I) demonstrator engines built under the contract were running by the end of that year, and 130 engine test hours had been accumulated.

On 31 December 1966, Boeing and General Electric were selected as winners of the FAA's SST design competition, with responsibility for the airframe and power plant respectively. The prototype stage (Phase III) of the SST programme started on 1 January 1967 and General Electric was awarded a contract for development and fabrication of some 30 prototype and 16 flight test engines, involving 100 hours flight testing in two prototype aircraft starting in 1972.

To meet Boeing's requirement for increased thrust, the 475 lb/sec (215 kg/sec) eight-stage compressor of the Block I engines was modified to a nine-stage design by the addition of a zero stage, giving a Block II engine standard, with other modifications, of 620 lb/sec (281 kg/sec). Rig testing of this larger compressor started in December 1967, and the first Block II engine (GE4-004) ran on 25 March 1968. A thrust of greater than 63,200 lb (26,667 kg) was recorded on 19 September 1968, establishing the GE4 as the world's most powerful aero engine. Unaugmented thrust was 49,100 lb (22,271 kg). Subsequent changes in the design of the Boeing 2707 have not affected the status of the GE4 in the SST programme.

A large new $12m altitude engine test facility (AETF), part of the GE Aircraft Engine Group's $75m three-year improvement programme, was commissioned at Evendale, Ohio, towards the end of 1968 as a major item in a series of new GE4 test and manufacturing facilities. In December that year a Block II engine (GE4-006) was tested in the AETF at simulated conditions of Mach 2·7 and 65,000 ft (19,812 m). By mid-1969, over 800 hr testing of Block I and II engines had been completed including 100 hr in the AETF, 40 hr of which were at a simulated Mach 2·7.

Latest version of the GE4 to be tested in July 1969 was the GE4-006 modified to incorporate a compressor of 2-in (50·8-mm) greater inlet diameter, giving an increased mass flow of 633 lb/sec (287 kg/sec). Aerodynamic changes were also introduced on the compressor's first four stages. Maximum afterburning take-off thrust on test was in excess of 68,000 lb (30,844 kg), reducing, without augmentation, to 54,200 lb (24,585 kg) for an sfc of 0·97 lb/lb/hr. The new standard engine is designated GE4/J5P.

A full GE4 component and systems rig testing programme, extending to over 100,000 hr testing, is also well advanced. Particular emphasis is being given to smoke emission, noise suppression, and engine reliability and ease of maintenance. Component testing has included the various configurations of compressor, initial and improved combustor designs, air-cooled turbine, augmentor and exhaust system and noise suppressor. Power control and lubrication systems have also been individually tested.

Eight Block I and II engines were on test by mid-1969, and Block II engines are being progressively retrofitted with the larger-diameter

General Electric GE4 turbojet (68,600 lb = 31,100 kg st) for the Boeing SST

compressor. A Block I engine is being used on augmentor and noise suppressor tests. The first of a series of factory test engines, No ·009, will go on test early in 1971.

General Electric's share in funding the Phase II prototype stage of the GE4 engine programme through to 1972 is in the region of $86m, including outlays on new R & D facilities. Engine certification (Phase IV) is scheduled for the second quarter of 1976, with entry into commercial operation in the Boeing 2707-300 in 1978. Engine certification and production costs will be additional to those of Phase III. GE do not at present know how the J5P engine can be made to meet expected FAA near-field noise standards.

The following data refer to the current GE4/J5P engine.

TYPE: Single-shaft axial turbojet with afterburner.

INTAKE: Annular, comprising front structural frame with eight radial struts supporting compressor front bearing housing. Downstream of airframe-mounted variable-centrebody intake.

COMPRESSOR: Nine-stage axial single-shaft unit with variable incidence inlet guide vanes and stator vanes, except ahead of stages 2 and 9, giving large stall margin for inlet distortion tolerance. Front and rear groups of stators are individually actuated for starting airflow control and for high airflow capability at supersonic speeds. Rotor construction is combined drum-and-disc with thin-section centreless discs. No 1 disc is overhung on forward conical extension shaft supported by compressor front roller bearing. Rearward conical extension shaft attached to periphery of No 9 disc is supported by centre main ball thrust bearing. Thin-section air tube located on front and rear conical shafts passes through disc centres. Compressor delivery diffuser is integral with mid-section structural **frame** supporting centre main bearing. All stator vanes carried on inner and outer swivel bearings, with inner support rings sealing against rotor inter-disc drums. For reduced weight, rotor blades in stages 1 to 4 are hollow diffusion-bonded titanium alloy, and stages 5 to 9 electro-chemically drilled Inco 718 superalloy. Pressure ratio 12·5 : 1, mass flow 633 lb/sec (287 kg/sec).

COMBUSTOR: Fully annular design of moderately high heat release rate with primary air annulus having axial swirl cups for 42 burners.

TURBINE: Two-stage axial unit with air-cooled cast alloy nozzle guide vanes and rotor blades diffusion-bonded in René 80 alloy. Thin-section centreless discs with arched inter-stage spacers. Rotor blades have fir-tree root fittings and second stage blades are tip-shrouded. Forward conical extension shaft attached to periphery of stage 1 disc locates with compressor rear conical shaft at centre main ball thrust bearing. Rearward tubular shaft extension from stage 2 disc located in rear main roller bearing. Stage 2 nozzle guide vanes cantilever mounted from outer end, with seal on to interdisc spacer at inner end. Turbine entry temperature at T-O in excess of 2,000°F (1,366°K).

EXHAUST SYSTEM: Annular exhaust duct from turbine with rear structural frame, with **radial/tangential** struts, supporting curved centre cone and turbine rear bearing.

AFTERBURNER: Conventional system with four V-gutter flame stabilisers mounted on radial struts in exhaust duct. Two-stage fuel injection enables thrust modulation over full augmentor temperature range. Annular thermal shield protects duct wall between combustion zone and variable nozzle. Fuel supply manifold encased in external annulus around exhaust duct.

EXHAUST NOZZLE AND THRUST REVERSER: Two-stage nozzle with integral thrust reverser. Comprises variable area primary nozzle positioned by hydraulic actuators which also "overtravel" to act as reverser blocker. Long-section secondary shroud includes tertiary air inlet doors which open for low speed operation and can be selectively locked open for reverser operation. Secondary nozzle provides guided expansion of exhaust gases and is pressure-positioned for optimum area ratio. For reverse thrust, primary nozzle translates rearwards to expose thrust reverser ducts (tertiary air inlet doors), closing to form a block, thus directing gases forward through the ducts. Provision also for noise suppression.

FUEL SYSTEMS: Hydromechanical primary engine and afterburner fuel control systems. Fuel grade, Jet A kerosene.

ACCESSORIES: All engine controls and accessories housed in sealed compartments completely surrounding compressor, cooled by normal circulation of fuel to protect from high temperature environment at supersonic cruise. Accessory drive is via bevel gear box in nose cone, driven-off front of compressor. Drive shaft through front frame radial strut at 45°. Starter will be airframe-manufacturer's responsibility. Self-contained 5 US gall = 18·9 litres lubrication oil system.

DIMENSIONS:
Max diameter (over exhaust nozzle)
    90 in (2,286 mm)
Length overall   306 in (7,772 mm)
WEIGHT, DRY (Prototype J5P):
(Dependent on specific installational features)
    13,200 lb (6,000 kg)
PERFORMANCE RATINGS:
Maximum T-O
    68,600 lb (31,100 kg) st at 5,200 rpm
Maximum dry
    51,500 lb (23,300 kg) st at 5,200 rpm
Maximum flight conditions
    Mach 2·7 at 82,000 ft (24,994 m)
Cruise at Mach 2·7 and 65,000 ft (19,812 m)
    15,000 lb (6,804 kg)
SPECIFIC FUEL CONSUMPTIONS:
Take-off   1·77
Maximum dry   1·04

GENERAL ELECTRIC GE12

Under a contract awarded by the US Army Aviation Materiel Laboratories Propulsion Division, General Electric initiated a two-year demonstration programme in August 1967 to design, build and test a new 1,500 shp advanced technology turboshaft. Designated GE12, the engine is being developed by the GE12/TF34 Department of the Aircraft Engine Group's Military Engine Division. During the latter part of 1968 the basic contracts for the GE12 and competing Pratt & Whitney ST9 demonstrator turboshaft were extended to the end of 1969 and additional work was also funded to carry both engine programmes through to 30 April 1970.

At the start of the demonstrator competition in 1967 it was intended that one of the new turboshafts would later be selected to power the Army's projected utility tactical transport system (UTTAS) proposed as a replacement for the present Bell UH-1 family of Army helicopters powered by the Lycoming T53 turboshaft. Budget planning for this has yet to be announced and no other specific application for the GE12, or ST9, has so far been proposed. (Third advanced technology turboshaft competing for the Army's future VTOL requirements is the private venture Lycoming PLT-27 of 1,950 shp.)

The GE12 has been designed to be compatible with the Army's special operating and environmental conditions, and embodies high reliability, simplicity of maintenance, low vulnerability to combat damage, and high performance combined with compact dimensions. Use is made of higher pressure ratios and turbine entry temperatures than with existing small turboshafts to assist in reducing size and weight. Specific fuel consumption of the GE12 is 25 to 30 per cent lower than present turboshafts, and weight is some 40 per cent lower than current helicopter engines of the same power category.

Advanced technology features developed by GE have been extensively applied in the design of the GE12 and full advantage has been taken of programmes completed under previous US Army study and component contracts.

In configuration, the new engine is a front-drive ungeared free-turbine turboshaft with a combined axial-and-centrifugal compressor, annular

Mock-up of the 1,500 shp General Electric GE12 prototype demonstrator turboshaft engine

combustor, two-stage compressor turbine and two-stage power turbine. The complete engine is constructed of major sub-assemblies to facilitate field maintenance through modular replacement or simple replacement of individual components.

The compressor uses advanced materials to provide erosion and corrosion resistance, and embodies special design features to provide inherent robustness. The combustor is of compact, short-length configuration, designed to give reliability and long life. Vaporizing fuel injection is used to reduce susceptibility to fuel contamination and give very low smoke generation and uniform temperature profile into the turbine.

The HP turbine is air-cooled and operates at an entry temperature in excess of 2,000°F. Its materials have been selected to give maximum corrosion resistance. The LP turbine is designed to operate efficiently at part-power levels, especially at 30 and 60 per cent of military rated power. The blades have tip shrouds.

To reduce vulnerability, all external lines and leads are short in length and are grouped compactly for minimum exposure. Self-contained electrical and lubrication systems are fitted. Multiple mounting points allow for ease of installation and the necessary airframe connections have been minimized and are located close to the engine centre-line.

DIMENSIONS:
Length, from intake	38·1 in (967 mm)
Overall length	42 in (1,067 mm)
Diameter	15·8 in (401 mm)
Overall height	21 in (533 mm)

PERFORMANCE RATING:
Military rating	1,500 shp

GENERAL ELECTRIC T58

The T58 is a small free-turbine power-unit which was developed originally by General Electric for the Bureau of Weapons, US Navy. It has been adopted also by the USAF. A civil version, the CT58, was awarded a Type Certificate by the FAA on 1 July 1959 and is described separately.

The engine is intended primarily as a power unit for helicopters. But it may also be developed for small fixed-wing aircraft in the form of a turboprop when combined with propeller reduction gear, as an auxiliary boost unit for large military and commercial aircraft and for marine and industrial use.

Hydro-mechanical constant speed control featured in the T58 maintains essentially constant rotor speed by regulating the engine power automatically, so eliminating the need for speed adjustment by the pilot during normal operation.

Initial flight tests of the T58 were made in a Sikorsky SH-34H, which flew for the first time with two T58s in a nose installation on 30 January 1957.

Rolls-Royce Ltd, are manufacturing the T58 under licence in Great Britain as the Gnome. It is also licenced for manufacture in Italy and Japan. Industrial and marine version of the T58 is the LM100.

Versions currently in service or under development are as follows:

T58-GE-3. Five-minute rating of 1,325 shp. Powers Bell UH-1F.

T58-GE-5. Five-minute rating of 1,500 shp. Powers Sikorsky CH-3E and HH-3E/F.

T58-GE-8B. Rated at 1,250 shp. Powers Boeing-Vertol CH-46A, Kaman UH-2, Sikorsky SH-3A and HH-52A, and Bell X-22A.

T58-GE-10. Rated at 1,400 shp. Powers Sikorsky SH-3D and Boeing-Vertol CH-46D.

T58-GE-16. Rated at 1,870 shp. US military qualified. Introduces air-cooled gas-generator turbine and two-stage power turbine.

TYPE: Free-turbine turboshaft.

AIR INTAKE: Annular intake casing with four hollow radial struts supporting central housing for starter drive clutch and front main roller bearing. Casing and struts anti-iced by air bled from compressor.

COMPRESSOR: Ten-stage axial-flow. Variable-incidence inlet guide vanes. First three of the eleven rows of stator blades also have variable-incidence. One-piece steel construction for last eight stages of rotor hub. Casing divided into upper and lower halves. Pressure ratio 8·4 : 1. Air mass flow 12·4 lb (5·62 kg/sec in T58-GE-3 and 8B, 13·7 lb (6·21 kg)/sec in T58-GE-5, 10 and 16.

COMBUSTION CHAMBER: Annular type. Sixteen fuel nozzles (eight on each of two manifolds) mounted on front of inner liner. One capacitor discharge type igniter, operated only during starting cycle. Dual ignition capability. Outer casing in two halves to facilitate inspection.

The 1,870 shp General Electric T58-GE-16 and (*right*) **1,250 shp T58-GE-8B turboshaft engines**

GAS GENERATOR TURBINE: Two-stage short-chord axial-flow type, coupled directly to compressor by hollow conical shaft. Centre ball thrust bearing, rear roller bearing. Cooling by air bled from compressor. T58-GE-16 has air-cooled first-stage turbine blades.

POWER TURBINE: Single-stage (two-stage in T58-GE-16) axial-flow type, mechanically independent of gas generator turbine. Operated nominally at 19,500 rpm, reduced to 6,000 rpm by reduction gear. Power turbine accessory drive unit and flexible feedback cable provide an Nf speed signal to the control.

TORQUE SENSOR SPEED DECREASER GEARBOX (optional): Gearbox with integral lubrication system. Reduces power speed to 6,000 rpm. Assembly includes an integral torque sensing system.

JET EXHAUST: Two positions (90° left or right) on all versions. T58-GE-16 can also be supplied with downward-ejecting exhaust.

CONTROLS (except T58-GE-10 and -16): Free turbine constant-speed control. Hydro-mechanical controls.

CONTROLS: (T58-GE-10, -16): Integrated hydro-mechanical/electrical power control system for isochronous speed governing and twin-engine load sharing.

ACCESSORY DRIVES: Engine accessories driven partly by the compressor shaft. Airframe accessories mounted on free-turbine reduction gearbox or rotor hub.

DIMENSIONS:
Max width:	
except T58-GE-16	18·8 in (478 mm)
T58-GE-16	20·7 in (526 mm)
Length overall:	
except T58-GE-16	59 in (1,500 mm)
T58-GE-16	63·3 in (1,615 mm)

WEIGHTS (DRY):
T58-GE-3	309 lb (140 kg)
T58-GE-5	335 lb (152 kg)
T58-GE-8B	305 lb (138 kg)
T58-GE-10	350 lb (159 kg)
T58-GE-16	440 lb (200 kg)

PERFORMANCE RATINGS:
Five-minute ratings:
See under model listing above.
Military rating:
T58-GE-3	1,272 shp at 20,960 rpm
T58-GE-5, 10	1,400 shp at 19,500 rpm
T58-GE-8B	1,250 shp at 19,500 rpm
T58-GE-16	1,870 shp at 20,280 rpm
Cruise rating:
T58-GE-3	1,070 shp
T58-GE-5, 10	1,250 shp
T58-GE-8B	1,050 shp
T58-GE-16	1,770 shp

SPECIFIC FUEL CONSUMPTIONS:
At military rating:
T58-GE-3	0·61 lb (0·277 kg)/shp/hr
T58-GE-5, 8B, 10	0·61 lb (0·277 kg)/shp/hr
T58-GE-16	0·53 lb (0·200 kg)/shp/hr
At cruise rating:
T58-GE-3	0·63 lb (0·286 kg)/shp/hr
T58-GE-5	0·61 lb (0·277 kg)/shp/hr
T58-GE-8B	0·64 lb (0·290 kg)/shp/hr
T58-GE-10	0·62 lb (0·281 kg)/shp/hr
T58-GE-16	0·54 lb (0·200 kg)/shp/hr

GENERAL ELECTRIC CT58

The commercial version of the T58 is designated CT58 and was the first US helicopter turbine to receive FAA certification.
Current versions are as follows:

CT58-110. Rated at 1,250 shp (1,350 shp for 2½ min) at 19,500 rpm. Air mass flow 12·5 lb (5·67 kg)/sec. Pressure ratio 8·15 : 1. Weight 315 lb (143 kg).

CT58-140. Rated at 1,400 shp (1,500 shp for 2½ min) at 19,500 rpm. Air mass flow 13·7 lb (6·21 kg)/sec. Pressure ratio 8·4 : 1.

The CT58 powers the Sikorsky S-61 and S-62 and Boeing-Vertol 107 Model II helicopter airliners.

DIMENSIONS:
Max width	16·0 in (406 mm)
Length overall	59·0 in (1,500 mm)

WEIGHT (DRY):
CT58-110	315 lb (143 kg)
CT58-140	340 lb (154 kg)

PERFORMANCE RATINGS:
2½ min rating and normal T-O rating:
See under model listing above.
Cruise rating:
CT58-110	1,050 shp
CT58-140	1,250 shp

SPECIFIC FUEL CONSUMPTIONS:
At normal T-O rating 0·61 lb (0·277 kg)/shp/hr
At cruise rating:
CT58-110	0·64 lb (0·290 kg)/shp/hr
CT58-140	0·62 lb (0·281 kg)/shp/hr

GENERAL ELECTRIC T64

The T64 is a versatile aircraft gas-turbine engine which was initially developed for the US Navy Bureau of Weapons. The basic T64 turboshaft engine becomes a turboprop with the addition of a two-part speed-reduction gearbox.
Current versions include:

T64-GE-7. Direct-drive turboshaft rated at 3,925 shp. Two engines power the Sikorsky CH/HH-53C and German Army CH-53D/G.

T64-GE-412(413). Direct-drive turboshaft. Two engines power the US Navy CH-53D. When designated T64-GE-412 the engine features a military rating of 3,695 shp; when designated T64-GE-413 it is maximum rated at 3,925 shp.

T64-GE-16. Direct-drive turboshaft; powers Lockheed AH-56A helicopter. Flat rated at 3,400 shp, this engine is FAA certificated and planned for the German VFW-Fokker VC 400 tilt-wing transport.

Other T64 engines in service include:

T64-GE-1(-3). Direct-drive turboshaft rated at 3,080 shp. Four engines power the LTV-Hiller-Ryan XC-142A tilt-wing transport and two T64-3s power the Sikorsky HH-53B helicopter.

T64-GE-6. Direct-drive turboshaft rated at 2,850 shp. Two engines power the Sikorsky CH-53A helicopter.

T64-GE-10. Turboprop engine with propeller gearbox above engine centreline; similar to T64-GE-6 and rated at 2,850 eshp. This engine is being produced under licence by Ishikawajima Harima Heavy Industries in Japan for the Shin Meiwa PS-1 flying-boat (four engines) and the Kawasaki P-2J patrol aircraft (two engines).

CT64-GE-820. This turboprop engine is the T64-6 with propeller gearbox and FAA required modifications. Two such engines power the de Havilland of Canada DHC-5 Buffalo and Fiat G.222 medium transports.

All T64s are qualified to operate from 100° nose-up to 45° nose-down. The T64 was designed for extensive growth: current production engines rated at 3,925 shp are a result of growth made possible largely by air cooling of the first-stage gas generator turbine rotor and stator. Eight air-cooling flows within the present turbine configuration are capable of producing up to 4,300 shp. The addition of air-cooling to the second turbine stage provides further horsepower growth beyond 5,000 shp without significant change in external dimensions.

A licence to produce the T64 in the UK is held by Rolls-Royce. Civil versions were awarded a Type Certificate by the FAA on 25 March 1965.

TYPE: Free-turbine turboshaft/turboprop engine.

COMPRESSOR: Fourteen-stage axial-flow. Single-spool steel rotor (titanium compressor in T64-GE-7, 412(413), and -16 only). Inlet guide vanes and first four stages of stator blades are variable. Compressor blades can be removed individually without rotor disassembly. Casing is flanged along the centre-line. Stator blades are removable. Air mass flow (except T-64-7, -16, T64-GE-412(413) 24·5 lb (11·1 kg)/sec; -7, -16, 412(413) 25·6 lb (12·0 kg)/sec. Pressure ratio (except T64-7, -412(413), -16) 12·6 : 1; T64-7, -412(413), -16 13·0 : 1.

COMBUSTION CHAMBER: Annular type. Double fuel manifold feeds twelve duplex-type fuel nozzles with external flow divider. Nozzles mounted on outer diffuser wall of compressor rear frame.

GAS GENERATOR TURBINE: Two-stage axial-flow type, coupled directly to compressor rotor by spline connection.

POWER TURBINE: Two-stage axial-flow type, mechanically independent of gas generator turbine.

REDUCTION GEAR: Remotely-mounted basic reduction gear for turboprop versions is offset and accessible for inspection and replacement. Gear-driven by power turbine, using co-axial shafting through the compressor. Propeller gear ratio 13·44 : 1.

The 2,850 eshp General Electric T64-GE-10 turboprop engine

STARTING: Mechanical.

DIMENSIONS:

Length:

T-64-GE-3, -6, -7, -412(413)	83 in (2·108 mm)
T64-GE-10, -820	113 in (2,870 mm)
T64-GE-16	68 in (1,727 mm)

Width:

T64-GE-3, -6, -7, -412(413), -16	24 in (610 mm)
T64-GE-10, -820	29 in (727 mm)

Height:

T64-GE-3, -6, -7, -412(413), -16	30 in (762 mm)
T64-GE-10	46 in (1,168 mm)

WEIGHTS (DRY):

T64-GE-3, -6	723 lb (328 kg)
T64-GE-7	712 lb (323 kg)
T64-GE-10	1,167 lb (529 kg)
CT64-820-1	1,130 lb (513 kg)
CT64-820-2	1,145 lb (520 kg)
T64-GE-412(413)	710 lb (322 kg)

PERFORMANCE RATINGS:

Max rating (sea level):

T64-GE-3	3,080 shp
T64-GE-10	2,850 ehp at 1,160 output rpm
T64-GE-6	2,850 shp at 13,600 rpm
T64-GE-7, -412(413)	3,925 shp
T64-GE-16 (flat rated at 92°F)	3,370 shp
CT64-820	3,060 ehp

Military rating:

T64-GE-3	2,910 shp
T64-GE-10	2,650 ehp
T64-GE-6	2,690 shp
T64-GE-7, -412	3,695 shp
T64-GE-16 (flat rated at 76°F)	3,400 shp

Max continuous:

CT64-820	2,480 ehp

Cruise rating (at altitude):

T64-GE-3, at 15,000 ft (4,570 m)	1,189 shp at 13,000 rpm
T64-GE-6	1,780 shp at 13,600 rpm
T64-GE-10 at 20,000 ft (6,100 m)	1,915 ehp

SPECIFIC FUEL CONSUMPTION (sea level):

At max rating:

T64-GE-3	0·485 lb (0·220 kg)/shp/hr
T64-GE-10	0·505 lb (0·229 kg)/ehp/hr
T64-GE-6	0·495 lb (0·225 kg)/shp/hr
T64-GE-7, -412, -16	0·476 lb (0·216 kg)/shp/hr

At T-O:

CT-64-820	0·503 lb (0·221 kg)/ehp/hr

At military rating:

T64-GE-3	0·490 lb (0·222 kg)/shp/hr
T64-GE-10	0·500 lb (0·227 kg)/ehp/hr
T64-GE-7, -412, -16	0·479 lb (0·226 kg)/shp/hr

At max continuous:

CT64-820	0·505 lb (0·225 kg)/ehp/hr

GENERAL ELECTRIC LCF-380

This new lift/cruise power plant embodies experience gained with the J85/LF2 lift-fan propulsion system produced by General Electric for the Ryan XV-5A research aircraft (see 1966-67 *Jane's*).

Designed for possible use in subsonic military V/STOL aircraft, the LCF-380 is made up of a non-afterburning J79 turbojet connected to a tip-turbine driven lift/cruise fan of 80 in (203 cm) diameter. During tests in mid-1967, the power plant developed 27,000 lb (12,250 kg) st, equivalent to about 2½ times the output of the basic J79 gas-generator. Thrust/weight ratio was about 10:1, by-pass ratio 6·5:1 and pressure ratio 1·31:1.

A power plant of this type could be installed in a fixed nacelle on the wings or in a rotating pod mounted on the fuselage of a V/STOL aircraft.

General Electric LCF-380 lift/cruise power plant

LPC

LOCKHEED PROPULSION COMPANY

HEADQUARTERS ADDRESS:
PO Box 111, Redlands, California 92373
PRESIDENT:
William A. Stevenson
EXECUTIVE VICE-PRESIDENT:
N. B. Chase
VICE-PRESIDENTS:
J. H. Brown (Administration)
K. H. Jacobs (Diversified Products)
A. H. Von Der Esch (Operations)

Lockheed Propulsion Company is the former Grand Central Rocket Company, which was founded in 1952 as the first major US company devoted entirely to the advancement of solid-propellant rocket development. It became a wholly-owned subsidiary of the Lockheed Aircraft Corporation late in 1961, and a division of Lockheed in February, 1963.

Current programmes include development and qualification of the solid-propellant pulse motor for the USAF short-range attack missile (SRAM), a launch escape motor for NASA's Apollo space-craft, several alternative thrust vector control systems for large solid-propellant motors, and small, variable-thrust motors for attitude control, orbital ejection and re-entry. LPC has also developed and test fired more than 300 hybrid rockets utilising a solid-propellant fuel and liquid oxidiser and with diameters of up to 19 in (0·48 m). This work was done for the US Army.

"Off-the-shelf" solid-propellant rocket motors produced by LPC have been used extensively in recent years as boosters for supersonic research sleds, in sounding and meteorological rockets, for flight control, as drone boosters and in space applications. Current models offer thrusts ranging from 40 lb to over 124,000 lb (18-56,250 kg) for periods of from one to 30 seconds.

LPC developed a "self-eject" launch technique. In this, the solid rocket vehicle ejects itself from a launch tube using low-pressure gas flow from its own first-stage motor. Once out of the tube the motor comes to full thrust automatically. A vehicle weighing more than 300,000 lb (136,078 kg) has been launched successfully by this method.

The company has developed a high-energy smokeless propellant for use in tactical missiles and is studying new techniques for launching rockets from guns. One such concept keeps the rocket vehicle intact while being driven from the barrel by a powder charge. Once out of the nozzle, and while travelling at approximately 3,000 ft (915 m)/sec, the rocket's own motor fires. Such techniques offer a considerable extension of a missile's range.

LPC has developed a family of new solid propellants called polycarbutenes. They are based on polybutadiene prepolymer binder systems (PBAA, PBAN, CTPB, HTPB) and have been characterized to meet a broad spectrum of operational requirements. These propellant systems have been fired with grains weighing up to 364,000 lb (165,108 kg). Solid propulsion units have successfully completed temperature cycling from minus 100 to plus 200° F, random vibration from 20 to 2,000 cycles per second, 10·5 g acceleration, 20 g drop shock, ageing in vacuum and ambient ageing up to seven years. The ballistics of these propellant systems have been tailored to meet broad burning rate requirements, maximum impulse, and low to high pressure exponents for an almost infinite number of solid propulsion design requirements. Physical properties meet complex structural integrity requirements.

LPC also is developing for the USAF solid propellants formulated to provide the high degree of chamber-pressure sensitivity required for controllable-motor applications. Another programme is being conducted under contract to demonstrate the use of fluidically controlled valves (vortex valves) for controllable solid-propellant rocket motors.

LPC has developed and is producing flexible seals, called Lockseals, for use on movable-nozzle thrust-vector control systems. The Lockseal movable joint is composed of alternate layers of rubber and metal in a laminated structure. Lockseal joints also are being produced for commercial applications. The company is conducting propellant structural-integrity programmes under USAF contracts, including a programme to design and fabricate a highly instrumented inert rocket-motor for measurement of missile environments for air-launched rocket applications.

Additionally, and in support of its work on advanced upper-stage rockets, LPC has developed a family of nitrocellulose-base composite propellants (nitroplastisols) of very high specific impulse. Since 1968 research has also been conducted on an advanced monopropellant motor.

LPC is also engaged in fabrication of hardware for the aerospace industry and components for nuclear reactors.

Available details of motors which have aircraft, missile or space vehicle applications are given hereafter.

LPC P16

This is a dual-thrust, triple-pulse controllable solid rocket motor for air launch applications. The pulses, or propellant grains, are arranged in tandem inside the combustion chamber and are fired individually. Units containing as many as 40 pulses have been fired successfully. No further details are available.

LPC-415

This is the propulsion system for the SRAM (Short Range Attack Missile) being developed for the USAF as the AGM-69A. LPC developed and is qualifying the solid-propellant pulse motor for this weapon under sub-contract from Boeing. No details are available.

LPC SR13-LP-1

The XSR13-LP-1 is the 12-in (305 mm) diameter by 58·6-in (1,488 mm) long propulsion system for an advanced air-to-air missile. The qualified motor is being prepared for use in other systems. No other details are available.

LPC-A1 APOLLO MOTOR

This is the launch escape motor which is designed to pull the Apollo spacecraft away from the Saturn booster in the event of an emergency during the launch phase. Fifty-six motors have been fired successfully. A production programme for delivery of additional flight motors is continuing.

Test firing of LPC launch escape motor for Apollo Command Module

Static test-firing of the LPC-415 solid-propellant pulse rocket motor developed and qualified by LPC for the US Air Force's AGM-69A short-range attack missile (SRAM)

DIMENSIONS:
Length overall   185 in (4,700 mm)
Diameter   26 in (660 mm)
WEIGHT: 4,700 lb (2,130 kg)
PERFORMANCE:
Max thrust at S/L   155,000 lb (70,300 kg)

LPC-A2

This is the pitch control motor that is mounted at the forward end of the Apollo escape system. It is fired at the same time as the launch escape motor to push the spacecraft to one side, out of the flight path of the Saturn launch vehicle. This motor also had completed 62 entirely successful firings by early 1970.

DIMENSIONS:
Length   22 in (558 mm)
Diameter   10·5 in (267 mm)
WEIGHT: 51 lb (23 kg)
PERFORMANCE RATING:
Max thrust at S/L   2,522 lb (1,144 kg) for 0·5 sec

LPC HIGH THRUST MOTOR

This high-thrust, short-duration motor was developed and qualified for use in ejecting special payloads from missiles or space vehicles. Similar motors of smaller diameter have been used in tube-launched, shoulder-fired tactical weapons. The high-thrust motor contains a rubber-base PBAN non-aluminized composite fuel with ammonium perchlorate oxidiser, within a 7075 aluminium chamber with a steel nozzle throat. The motor is fired by a low-voltage squib triggered by an electrical pulse; maximum chamber pressure is 4,000 lb/sq in (281 kg/cm²).

DIMENSIONS:
Length overall   10·03 in (255 mm)
Diameter   6·86 in (174 mm)
WEIGHT: 14·5 lb (6·57 kg)
PERFORMANCE:
Max thrust at S/L   30,000 lb (13,607 kg)
Operating time   0·024 sec
Specific impulse   230 sec

LPC M-1

Working under a company-funded programme LPC engaged in static test firings of a rocket engine using an advanced monopropellant. The formulation has not been disclosed but is a liquid, "non-toxic, non-corrosive, reliable and inexpensive", and when used in selected applications, such as reaction control thrusters, "holds great promise when compared to other monopropellant systems based on hydrazine and hydrogen peroxide." The stainless steel test combustion chamber is 6 in (152·4 mm) long and 3·5 in (88·9 mm) diameter. It incorporates a shower-head injector and solid-propellant igniter and thereafter burns at a combustion temperature of 1,204°C. The thrust is regulated by the main propellent control valve.

LPC H 28 HYDAC

The H 28 Hydac sounding rocket utilises PBAA base propellant in a rolled and welded AISI 4130 casing. It has a pyrotechnic igniter.

DIMENSIONS:
Length overall   146·7 in (3,725 mm)
Diameter   9 in (229 mm)
WEIGHT: 557 lb (253 kg)
PERFORMANCE:
Max thrust at S/L   12,500 lb (5,670 kg)
Max thrust at height   13,200 lb (5,990 kg)
Specific impulse   253 sec

LPC J-23 JAVELIN II

The J-23 Javelin II is used for boosting hypersonic sleds. It utilizes a PBAA base propellant in a rolled and welded AISI 4130 casing, with pyrotechnic ignition. The Javelin II gives a guaranteed minimum thrust of 31,000 lb (14,060 kg) for a mean burn time of 1·25 sec.

DIMENSIONS:
Length overall   101·25 in (2,572 mm)
Diameter   9 in (229 mm)
WEIGHT: 341·4 lb (154·9 kg)
PERFORMANCE:
Max thrust at S/L   38,282 lb (17,365 kg)
Max thrust at height   39,700 lb (18,008 kg)
Specific impulse   243 sec

LPC J-33 JAVELIN III

This member of the Javelin family of solid-propellant motors utilises a PBAA base propellant of PBAA and ammonium perchlorate in a rolled and welded AISI 4130 case, with pyrotechnic ignition. The J-33 powers the Javelin III sounding rocket.

DIMENSIONS:
Length overall   103·5 in (2,629 mm)
Diameter   9 in (229 mm)
WEIGHT: 363·3 lb (164·8 kg)
PERFORMANCE:
Max thrust at S/L   19,320 lb (8,763 kg)
Max thrust at height   20,940 lb (9,500 kg)
Specific impulse   239 sec

LPC P2721-77

This is a "solid-solid" propulsion command device for manoeuvring space vehicles. In addition to delivering axial thrust, a gas generator provides hot gases for yaw, pitch and roll control through a valve system interlocking the two combustion chambers. Both axial thruster and gas generator use double-base nitroplastisol propellants.

DIMENSIONS:
Length of axial thruster   30 in (762 mm)
Length of gas generator   60 in (1,524 mm)
Diameter, both components   20 in (508 mm)
PERFORMANCE RATING:
Axial thrust   330 lb (150 kg) for 7½ min

LPC RSVP

RSVP is a command controllable propulsion system capable of unlimited starting, stopping and variation of thrust. The unit, designed for space propulsion applications, employs a solid-propellant grain composed of a pressure-sensitive formulation and a gaseous/liquid hypergolic oxidizer that causes combustion when introduced into the chamber. An RSVP motor was designed for a potential Martian orbit insertion mission.

SPIN/THRUST MOTOR

Avco Corporation, prime contractors for advanced re-entry vehicles for late-model LGM-30 Minuteman missiles, subcontracted to LPC the task of providing a reliable rocket motor capable of imparting either forward thrust or rotational spin (the motors are probably installed either in separate multiple warheads or in decoys or other penetration aids, but LPC cannot comment on this unofficial supposition). The Spin/Thrust motor weighs 2·6 lb (1·18 kg) and imparts a thrust variable from 38 to 800 lb (17-363 kg) over a burn time of 0·15-6·2 sec. The main charge fires through a central nozzle while spin rates of 10·5-19·5 rps (630-1,170 rpm) are imparted by three canted tangential nozzles around the base. To suit the requirements of particular missions the propellant division between thrust and spin can be altered over a wide range, replacing propellant by inert filling if necessary to preserve motor weight and centre of gravity position.

LPC LSM 156-5

When this three-segment solid-propellant motor was fired in 1965 it was the largest flight prototype solid motor tested at that time. It developed about 3,000,000 lb (1,360,000 kg) st and consumed some 700,000 lb (317,500 kg) of polycarbutene propellant in one minute of forced-draught burning. It was the first rocket of this size to be fitted with all major components of a steering system suitable for use in an actual flight.

The LSM 156-5 was made up of a 150-ton 22 ft (6·70 m) long central segment and forward and aft segments of almost equal size. Liquid nitrogen tetroxide, under high pressure, was sprayed through selected injectors in the nozzle expansion cone to create a shock-wave and also to react chemically with the exhaust gases to generate side forces for steering, at right angles to the direction of main gas flow.

This was the fifth consecutive successful firing in the USAF's Large Solid Motor Programme, and the third by LPC.

DIMENSIONS:
Length overall	80 ft 0 in (24·4 m)
Diameter	156 in (3·96 m)

WEIGHT: 850,000 lb (385,500 kg)

PERFORMANCE:
Max thrust at S/L 3,000,000 lb (1,360,000 kg)

LPC LSM 156-6

This monolithic (single-segment) 156 in (3·96 m) solid-propellant motor was the fourth fired by LPC under the USAF's Large Solid Motor Program. It could be considered a potential second stage of a space launch vehicle using a motor like the LSM 156-5, described above, as the first stage. It was filled with a polycarbutene propellant.

DIMENSIONS:
Length overall	34 ft 0 in (10·36 m)
Diameter	156 in (3·96 m)

WEIGHT: 325,000 lb (147,400 kg)

PERFORMANCE:
Max thrust at S/L 1,000,000 lb (453,600 kg)

LPC AA-1 AIR AUGMENTED HYBRID ROCKET

Working under USAF contract, LPC studied an air augmented hybrid rocket system, which augments its propellant supply by inducing air in forward flight. Prime feature of the rocket is a hybrid gas generator, using a liquid oxidiser and solid fuel propellant system. The generator exhausts fuel-rich combustion gases into a rear combustion chamber, where they mix with air rammed in through forward-facing intakes to produce secondary combustion. This results in a large theoretical increase in specific impulse and enhanced performance capabilities.

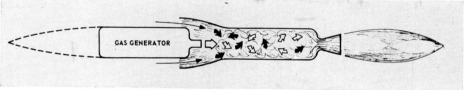

Principle of LPC AA-1 air augmented hybrid rocket

LPC LSM 156-5 flight prototype 156-in solid-propellant motor

MARQUARDT

THE MARQUARDT CORPORATION (a subsidiary of the CCI Marquardt Corporation)

HEAD OFFICE:
16555 Saticoy Street, Van Nuys, California 91046

SUBSIDIARY:
General Applied Science Laboratories Inc, Westbury, Long Island, NY 11591

PRESIDENT:
J. D. Wethe

VICE-PRESIDENTS:
R. E. Fisher (General Manager, Aerospace Products)
H. W. McFarland (General Manager, Rocket Systems)
J. L. Shedd (General Manager, Technical Services)
H. J. Silberstein (General Manager, Systems Engineering)

DIRECTORS:
J. G. Houston (Industrial Relations and Administration)
O. B. McCutcheon (Contracts and Purchases)
T. F. Padden (APL Computing Services)
R. E. Quinn (Finance)
J. E. Zimmermann (Marketing)

PRESIDENT OF GASL:
L. M. Nucci

The Marquardt Corporation was formed in November 1944 to undertake research and development of ramjet engines, and it produced the first American subsonic ramjet in 1945. Since that time the company has diversified into a wide range of industrial products. In addition to aerospace propulsion and ancillary systems, Marquardt is marketing APL/360 (an IBM conversational time-sharing computer language), a marine doppler navigational system and ship's log, base defence systems, weapon delivery systems, warhead safety and arming devices and infantry support systems. GASL, the subsidiary, is supplementing Marquardt's research into electronics, materials, ground transport and traffic control, acoustics, electro-optics, water desalting, medical equipment and air and water pollution.

Marquardt's main business continues to be advanced aerospace propulsion. Flight testing of the LASV (low-altitude supersonic vehicle) powered by integral rocket and ramjet engines for the US Air Force has been completed. Ground test data proved the practicability of the Dual Mode Scramjet (supersonic-combustion ramjet) developed for the US Air Force. This engine operates as a conventional subsonic-combustion ramjet at supersonic flight speeds and as a supersonic-combustion ramjet at hypersonic flight speeds. Marquardt is also developing other, security-classified types of composite rocket/air-breathing propulsion systems for the US Air Force and Navy. These are regarded by the

Sub-scale ground test model of Marquardt ejector ramjet engine

company as likely to lead to a new generation of power plants for supersonic and hypersonic aircraft, missiles and re-usable launch vehicles.

In the field of precision control rockets, Marquardt provides manoeuvring, stabilisation and control propulsion for the Apollo Service Module, the Apollo Lunar Module and the Orbital Workshop, and would have provided similar equipment for the terminated US Air Force Manned Orbiting Laboratory. The company's precision control rockets also served as main propulsion for the five Lunar Orbiters. A complete range of mono-propellant and bi-propellant rockets is now being marketed. The company is continuing to work under contract to the US Navy in the development of an advanced slurry-fuelled rocket system for possible future air-launched missile applications.

Marquardt maintains extensive test facilities at Van Nuys for research and testing of air-breathing and rocket engines. A major propulsion test facility is located at Little Mountain, Utah. A research laboratory at Magic Mountain, California, is used for testing rocket and air-breathing engines, exotic fuels, cryogenic liquids and advanced materials. The subsidiary GASL at Westbury, NY, complements these facilities and can conduct hypersonic propulsion tests. Total land area occupied exceeds 1,100 acres and covered buildings exceed 650,000 square feet (60,400 m²); employment exceeds 1,100.

Marquardt R-4D reaction control engines for the Apollo Service Module

MARQUARDT R-4D

This liquid-bi-propellant rocket reaction control engine has been developed and produced by Marquardt for the Apollo Spacecraft Service Module and Lunar Module (LM).

TYPE: Liquid-propellant reaction control rocket.

PROPELLANTS: Nitrogen tetroxide and monomethyl hydrazine.

THRUST CHAMBER ASSEMBLY: Single chamber. Area ratio 40. Made of aluminium, steel and molybdenum. Radiation cooling. Started by electrical signal to on-off solenoid valves. Hypergolic ignition. Combustion pressure 90 lb/sq in (6·33 kg/cm²). Combustion temperature 5,200°F.

THRUST CHAMBER MOUNTING: Flange bolt circle on injector head.

DIMENSIONS:
- Length overall: 13·5 in (343 mm)
- Height: 6·6 in (168 mm)
- Width: 6·0 in (152 mm)

WEIGHT DRY: 5·0 lb (2·27 kg)

PERFORMANCE RATINGS:
- Max rating at S/L: 63 lb (28·5 kg) st
- Max rating in vacuum: 100 lb (45·5 kg) st

MARQUARDT EJECTOR RAMJET

The ejector ramjet is a composite liquid-propellant rocket/ramjet engine developed by Marquardt under USAF sponsorship. It has potential application to missile propulsion, advanced orbital launch vehicles and advanced "next-generation" aircraft.

This simple lightweight engine is claimed to provide vehicle performance superior to separate rockets and ramjets due to commonality of structure plus rocket thrust augmentation, and to be competitive with more complex turbomachinery at hypersonic flight speeds.

Feasibility of the ejector ramjet was demonstrated in 1964. The sub-scale ground test engine shown in the illustration on page 770 underwent extensive system demonstration and performance testing during 1966. Ejector ramjets could be produced in a broad range of sizes to meet specific applications.

McCULLOCH

McCULLOCH CORPORATION, LOS ANGELES DIVISION

HEAD OFFICE AND MAIN PLANT:
6101, West Century Blvd, Los Angeles, California 90045

PRESIDENT:
Robert P. McCulloch

EXECUTIVE VICE-PRESIDENT:
C. V. Wood, Jr

CHAIRMAN:
Joseph L. Hegener

VICE-PRESIDENTS:
W. B. Burkett (Engineering, World)
Stanley J. Stephenson (Marketing, World)
James L. Dooley (Advance Development)

MANAGER, SPECIAL PRODUCT SALES:
Charles L. Hammond

SECRETARY AND ASSISTANT TREASURER:
J. D. Cavanaugh

McCulloch Corporation produces various gasoline-engined products, making extensive use of high-pressure die casting of aluminium and magnesium.

Since 1943 the company has supplied to the US armed services over 60,000 engines for use in radio-controlled target aircraft and helicopters. The current models are described below.

Amateur builders have for many years been using these target drone engines in their aircraft, and particularly in light autogyros of the Bensen type.

McCULLOCH MODEL 4318A

Military designation: O-100-1

The latest version of this engine has "free-roll" silver-plated bearings on the big end of the connecting rods.

TYPE: Four-cylinder horizontally-opposed air-cooled two-stroke.

CYLINDERS: Bore 3 3/16 in (80·8 mm). Stroke 3⅛ in (79·4 mm). Displacement 100 cu in (1·6 litres). Compression ratio 7·8 : 1. Heat-treated die-cast aluminium cylinders with integral heads, having hard chrome plated cylinder walls. Self-locking nuts secure cylinders to crankcase studs.

PISTONS: Heat-treated cast aluminium. Two rings above pins. Piston pins of case-hardened steel.

CONNECTING RODS: Forged steel. "Free-roll" silver-plated bearings at big end. Small-end carries one needle bearing. Lateral position of rod controlled by thrust washers between piston pin bosses and small end of rod.

CRANKSHAFT: Four-throw one-piece steel forging on four-anti-friction bearings, two ball and two needle, one with split race for centre main bearing.

CRANKCASE: One-piece heat-treated permanent-mould aluminium casting closed at rear end with cast aluminium cover which provides mounting for magneto.

VALVE GEAR: Fuel mixture for scavenging and power stroke introduced to cylinders through crankshaft-driven rotary valves and ported cylinders.

INDUCTION: Crankcase pumping type. McCulloch diaphragm-type carburettor with adjustable jet.

FUEL SPECIFICATION: Grade 115/145 aviation fuel mixed in the ratio 10 parts fuel with one part MIL-O-6082 lubricating oil or 25 parts fuel to one part McCulloch 40/50 SAE two-cycle oil.

IGNITION: McCulloch single magneto and distributor. Directly connected to crankshaft through impulse coupling for easy starting. Radio noise suppressor included. BG type RB 916S spark plugs. Complete radio shielding.

LUBRICATION: Oil mixed with fuel as in conventional two-stroke engines.

PROPELLER DRIVE: RH tractor. Keyed taper shaft.

STARTING: By separate portable gasoline or electric motor with suitable reduction-gear and clutch. Can be started manually by hand-cranking propeller.

MOUNTING: Three mounting lugs provided with socket for rubber mounting bushings.

DIMENSIONS:
- Length: 27·0 in (686 mm)
- Width: 28·0 in (711 mm)
- Height: 15·0 in (381 mm)

WEIGHT (DRY):
- Less propeller hub: 77 lb (34·9 kg)

POWER RATING:
- Rated output: 72 hp at 4,100 rpm

SPECIFIC CONSUMPTION:
- Fuel/oil mixture: 0·90 lb (0·408 kg)/bhp/hr

McCULLOCH MODEL 4318E

The Model 4318E is similar to the Model 4318A, except that it is intended to drive a pusher propeller, for use in the Bensen Model B-8M Gyro-Copter light autogyro. No carburettor is supplied with the engine, but a Carter Model YF 938SA, with main metering rod jet enlarged to No. 42 drill size, has been used successfully.

DIMENSIONS, WEIGHTS AND PERFORMANCE: Same as for Model 4318A.

McCULLOCH MODEL 4318F

This is the same as the Model 4318A except it has a power rating of 92 hp at 4,100 rpm, achieved by enlarged inlet and exhaust ports in the cylinders, together with a modified piston and ring configuration.

McCULLOCH MODEL 6318

Military designation: O-150-2

This six-cylinder development of the Model 4318A has a torsional vibration damper, a medium-pressure continuous fuel-injection system instead of a carburettor and a continuously-variable altitude compensator.

TYPE: Six-cylinder horizontally-opposed air-cooled two-stroke.

CYLINDERS, PISTONS, CONNECTING RODS AND VALVE GEAR: Basically as for Model 4318A. Displacement 150 cu in (2·4 litres). Cylinder has relocated sparking plug position, making possible a reduction of 6 in (15·3 cm) in overall width. Pistons have three rings instead of two.

CRANKSHAFT: Six-throw one-piece steel forging. One ball and four needle bearings, two with split race for centre main bearings.

CRANKCASE: One-piece heat-treated permanent-mould aluminium casting.

INDUCTION: Crankcase scavenging with rotary valves, continuous injection into crankcase, through fixed jets. Fuel supplied and metered by a single-stage Tuthill rotary pump with a McCulloch altitude compensator.

FUEL SPECIFICATION: MIL-F-5572 Grade 115/145 aviation fuel mixed in ratio of 10 to 1 with oil to MIL-O-6082 Grade 1065 or in ratio of 25 to 1 with McCulloch 40/50 SAE two-cycle motor oil.

IGNITION, LUBRICATION, PROPELLER DRIVE, STARTING AND MOUNTING: Same as for Model 4318A.

ACCESSORIES: Alternator pad and auxiliary drive pad on rear cover casting. Both gear-driven.

DIMENSIONS:
- Length: 34·5 in (876 mm)
- Width: 22·0 in (559 mm)
- Height: 12·3 in (312 mm)

WEIGHT (DRY):
- Less propeller hub: 114 lb (51·7 kg)

POWER RATING:
- Rated output: 110 hp at 4,100 rpm

SPECIFIC CONSUMPTION:
- Fuel/oil mixture: 0·85 lb (0·38 kg)/bhp/hr

McCULLOCH 6318K

This is the same as the basic Model 6318 except it has a power rating of 145 hp at 4,100 rpm, achieved by enlarged inlet and exhaust ports in the cylinders, together with a modified piston and ring configuration.

McCULLOCH MODEL TC6150

Military designation: O-150-4A

The Model TC6150 is a turbocharged version of the 6318, to which it is otherwise similar.

The latest O-150-4A version has a pressurised ignition system.

TYPE: Six-cylinder horizontally-opposed air-cooled supercharged two-stroke.

SUPERCHARGER: Exhaust-driven open-end design with radial inflow single-stage turbine and single-stage centrifugal compressor.

DIMENSIONS:
- Length: 44·5 in (1,130 mm)
- Width: 22·0 in (559 mm)
- Height: 17·0 in (432 mm)

WEIGHT (DRY): 142 lb (64·4 kg)

POWER RATINGS:
- Rated output at sea level: 120 hp
- Rated output at 30,000 ft (9,150 m): 86 hp
- Rated output at 40,000 ft (12,200 m): 55 hp

SPECIFIC CONSUMPTION:
- Fuel/oil mixture: 0·80 lb (0·36 kg)/bhp/hr

Above: **The 120 hp McCulloch TC6150 turbocharged engine**

Left: **The 72 hp McCulloch 4318A four-cylinder engine**

NELSON

NELSON AIRCRAFT CORPORATION

HEAD OFFICE:
115 Colonial Manor Road, Irwin, Pennsylvania 15642

PRESIDENT:
Charles R. Rhoades

VICE-PRESIDENT:
Lawrence J. Rhoades

SECRETARY AND TREASURER:
Roy E. Johnson

Nelson Aircraft Corporation, among its many industrial activities, produces to order the Nelson H-63 four-cylinder two-cycle air-cooled engine, which has been certificated by the FAA as a power unit for single-seat helicopters, and is now available also as a power plant for propeller-driven aircraft.

NELSON H-63
US Military designation: YO-65

Developed originally as a power unit for single-seat helicopters, the H-63 is now available in two versions, as follows:

H-63C. Basic helicopter power unit for vertical installation. Certificated by FAA. Supplied as complete power package, including clutch, cooling fan and shroud.

H-63CP. Basically as H-63C, but without clutch, fan and shroud. Intended primarily for installation in horizontal position, with direct drive to propeller. FAA certificated.

Nelson have developed a 42 in (1·07 m) wooden propeller with glass-fibre covering for use with the H-63. It is suitable for either tractor or pusher installation.

TYPE: Four-cylinder horizontally-opposed air-cooled, two-stroke.

CYLINDERS: Bore 2¹¹⁄₁₆ in (68·3 mm). Stroke 2¾ in (70 mm). Total capacity 63 cu in (1·03 litres). Compression ratio 8 : 1. Each cylinder complete is machined from an aluminium alloy casting, the bore being porous-chrome plated for wear resistance. Cylinders bolted to and detachable from crankcase.

PISTONS: Aluminium alloy casting. Two piston rings. Two needle roller bearings pressed in boss. Piston (gudgeon) pin pressed into small end of connecting rod.

CONNECTING RODS: Alloy steel forging. Caged roller bearing at big end.

CRANKSHAFT: Four-throw. Nitralloy shaft on ball and roller bearings.

CRANKCASE: Two-piece case divided on horizontal centre-line. Each half is a magnesium alloy casting.

INDUCTION: Nelson diaphragm-type all-angle fuel control carburettor. Hot-air anti-icing. Fuel/oil mixture valves from crankcase through specially-designed rotary valve driven by crankshaft. Intake to and exhaust from cylinders through ports. Exhaust stacks are of aluminium alloy.

FUEL: 80/87 octane gasoline and SAE 30 paraffin-base oil in 16 : 1 mixture for fuel and lubrication.

IGNITION: Battery-type dual-ignition with automatic retard for starting. Two Champion D-9 or 5 COM spark plugs per cylinder.

LUBRICATION: See under "Fuel".

POWER TAKE-OFF (H-63C): Hollow shaft extension from Salisbury centrifugal clutch output drive.

STARTING: 12V DC Autolite electric motor and Bendix drive.

COOLING (H-63C): Centrifugal aluminium fan and two-piece glass-fibre shrouding designed to maintain all temperatures within acceptable limits on an FAA hot day of 100°F ambient temperature at sea level.

MOUNTING: Four Lord-type mounts, two on each half of crankcase.

DIMENSIONS (H-63C):
Overall length   20·0 in (508 mm)
Overall height   14·8 in (376 mm)
Overall width   23·8 in (605 mm)

WEIGHTS (DRY):
H-63C, with accessories   76 lb (34·5 kg)
H-63CP, with accessories   68 lb (30·8 kg)

POWER RATINGS:
T-O:
H-63C   43 hp at 4,000 rpm
H-63CP   48 hp at 4,400 rpm
Max continuous:
H-63C   43 hp at 4,000 rpm
H-63CP   45 hp at 4,000 rpm

CONSUMPTION:
Fuel/oil
6·3 US gallons (24 litres)/hr at full throttle

The 43 hp Nelson H-63C four-cylinder two-stroke engine

The 48 hp Nelson H-63CP for fixed-wing aircraft

PRATT & WHITNEY

THE PRATT & WHITNEY AIRCRAFT DIVISION OF UNITED AIRCRAFT CORPORATION

HEAD OFFICE AND WORKS:
East Hartford, Connecticut 06108

UAC GROUP VICE-PRESIDENT:
Leonard C. Mallet

DIVISION PRESIDENT:
B. A. Schmickrath

DIVISION EXECUTIVE VICE-PRESIDENT:
B. N. Torell

ASSTS TO DIVISION PRESIDENT:
R. H. Begg
E. L. Davis

ADMIN ASST TO DIVISION PRESIDENT:
R. P. Azinger

DIVISION VICE-PRESIDENTS:
R. T. Horner (Financial Management)
D. Nigro (Production)
R. T. Baseler (Engineering)
W. L. Gorton (Gen Manager, Florida R & D Center)
J. S. Lee (Marketing)
B. J. McNamara (Product Support)

MANAGER, ADVANCED PLANNING:
R. L. Duncan

DIVISION COUNSEL CONTRACTS:
L. J. Daukas

MANAGER PUBLIC RELATIONS:
R. H. Zaiman

DIVISION CONTROLLER:
D. J. Hines

PERSONNEL MANAGER:
F. F. Schirm

GEN MANAGER, TURBOPOWER & MARINE DEPT:
W. J. Closs

GEN MANAGER, OVERHAUL & REPAIR DEPT:
L. Parmakian

PURCHASING MANAGER:
D. L. Brown, Jr

MANUFACTURING MANAGER:
A. L. DeCamillis

Pratt & Whitney, largest of seven Divisions forming the United Aircraft Corporation, has manufactured more than 50,900 military and commercial gas-turbine engines since building its first turboprop in 1947. These engines had accumulated over 200 million flying hours in military and commercial service by the end of March 1970. The Division is a leading supplier of turbofans and turbojets for large and medium transports, and powers the full range of Boeing and Douglas jet airline transports in service today. Pratt & Whitney has also developed the JT9D turbofan which powers the Boeing 747, and will power the McDonnell Douglas DC-10 Series 20.

Details of all current Pratt & Whitney products, including turbofan, turbojet, turboshaft and liquid-propellant rocket engines, appear below.

In addition to its production series of engines, Pratt & Whitney was in February 1970 awarded a contract to develop two versions of its JTF22 demonstrator engine, an advanced reheat turbofan. One version will power the US Navy F-14B fighter and the other the Air Force F-15 fighter. Further demonstrator work includes the JTF20 and ST9, both mentioned on later pages, and the Advanced Turbine Engine Gas Generator programme. The ATEGG programme, funded by the US Air Force, has been active for several years and is continuing to demonstrate the overall, integrated performance of advanced component technology in a full-scale engine.

In March 1970 Pratt & Whitney announced the "Gatorizing" process, for which patents are pending. It enables high-temperature turbine alloys to be forged with ease to extremely close tolerances, in complex configurations and without risk of cracking, using relatively very light forging equipment. Gatorizing has been under development for three years at the Florida R & D Center.

Pratt & Whitney supplied the fuel cell power plants that provide on-board electrical power and drinking water in the Apollo spacecraft.

Licence agreements with SNECMA permit the French company, in which the United Aircraft Corporation has a small financial holding, to manufacture and sell many of Pratt & Whitney's turbine engines, and the division's complete line of piston-engines and spare parts. The Royal Swedish Air Force Board also is licensed to manufacture an afterburning version of the JT8D turbofan engine and its parts. This work is being handled by Svenska Flygmotor (page 725).

Licence agreements for the manufacture of certain of the division's piston-engines or piston-engine parts continue with Commonwealth Aircraft Corporation of Australia; Fiat of Italy; Mitsubishi Heavy Industries of Japan; Metal Leve SA of Brazil; and United Aircraft of Canada Limited. The division has also licensed Ateliers de Constructions Electriques de Charleroi (ACEC) of Belgium to build a free turbine for the industrial J75 engine to be used for electrical peak loading purposes.

Associated companies of the United Aircraft Corporation are United Aircraft of Canada Ltd, a subsidiary of the Corporation, at Longueuil, Quebec, and Orenda Ltd at Malton, Ontario, an associate company owned jointly with Hawker Siddeley Canada Ltd. For Pratt & Whitney, United Aircraft of Canada is now the prime source of manufacture of its piston-engines, and Orenda provides the Division with additional turbine engine production capacity.

Pratt & Whitney has a total of about 45,000 employees at its three main plants at East Hartford and Middletown, Connecticut, and the Florida Research and Development Center, West Palm Beach, Florida.

PRATT & WHITNEY JT12
Military designation: J60

The J60 is a small high-performance turbojet engine which has a nine-stage axial-flow compressor, cannular type combustion section with eight flame tubes and a two-stage turbine. The rotor runs in three bearings. Pressure ratio is 6·5 : 1.

Design studies began in July 1957 and the prototype ran in May 1958. The first prototype (50-hour engine) was delivered in July 1959, with T-O rating of 2,900 lb (1,315 kg). Delivery of production engines, rated at 3,000 lb (1,360 kg), began in October 1960, and 2,032 had been shipped by the end of 1969.

Versions of the J60/JT12 power the Lockheed JetStar, the North American T-39 Sabreliner and the North American T-2B Buckeye trainer. A turboshaft version is the JFTD12, described later.

For details see table.

PRATT & WHITNEY JT8
Military designation: J52

The J52 is a medium-sized turbojet which was designed under the auspices of the US Navy Bureau of Weapons. It powers the Grumman A-6 Intruder naval attack bomber, current versions of the Douglas A-4 Skyhawk, and the North American AGM-28 Hound Dog air-to-surface missile.

The J52 is a two-spool turbojet, with total of 12 compressor stages, a "cannular" type combustion system fed by 36 dual-orifice injectors and mechanically-independent high-pressure and low-pressure single-stage turbines. The latest model in the J52 series, the J52-P-408, is rated at 11,200 lb (5,079 kg) st. Pressure ratio is 14·5 : 1. Several advanced design features are incorporated to achieve the rating increases with a minimum change in engine envelope and weight compared to previous JT8 (J52) models. These include two-position inlet guide vanes and air-cooled first-stage turbine vanes and blades. In addition, the burner cans include features for reduced smoke.

PRATT & WHITNEY JT8D

This turbofan engine was developed as a company-sponsored project to power short/medium-range transport aircraft, including the Boeing 727. United Aircraft's French licencees, SNECMA, designed the complete power plant nacelle, with thrust reverser, used in the Caravelle Super B airliner.

Construction of the JT8D is largely of steel and titanium. An annular by-pass duct runs the full length of the engine, with balanced mixing of the hot and cold air streams in the tail-pipe.

Manufacture of prototype engines began in November 1960 and the first engine run was made in April 1961. Flight testing was carried out initially under a B-45 test-bed aircraft. Prototype engines for airframe testing were delivered to Boeing in 1962. Production deliveries began in the first half of 1963 and 5,236 had been delivered by the end of 1969.

The following versions have been announced:

JT8D-1. Initial version rated at 14,000 lb (6,350 kg) st. Powers Boeing 727-100 and -100C, McDonnell Douglas DC-9-10 and -10F, and Aérospatiale Caravelle 10R.

JT8D-5. Rated at 12,250 lb (5,556 kg) st. Powers McDonnell Douglas DC-9-10.

JT8D-7. Develops 14,000 lb (6,350 kg) st to 84°F at sea level. Specified for Boeing 727-100, -100C and -200, Boeing 737-100, -200 and -200C, McDonnell Douglas DC-9-10, -30 and -30F, Aérospatiale Caravelle 10R and 11R.

JT8D-9. Develops 14,500 lb (6,575 kg) st to 84°F at sea level. Specified for Boeing 737-200 and McDonnell Douglas DC-9-20, -30 and -40. Optional in Boeing 727-200. Deliveries began in July 1967. This version has also been selected to power the Japanese NAMC XC-1 STOL transport.

JT8D-11. Develops 15,000 lb (6,804 kg) st to 84°F at sea level. Specified for McDonnell Douglas DC-9-20, -30 and -40 series aircraft and optional Boeing 727-200. Deliveries began in November 1968.

JT8D-15. Currently under development at rating of 15,500 lb (7,031 kg) to 84°F. FAA certification scheduled for Spring 1971. Selected for Dassault Mercure and improved Boeing 737.

A supersonic military version of the JT8D with afterburning is being developed and manufactured under licence in Sweden by Svenska Flygmotor AB. The Swedish engine, designated RM8, powers the Mach 2 Saab-37 Viggen multi-purpose combat aircraft.

TYPE: Axial-flow two-spool turbofan.

AIR INTAKE: Annular with 19 fixed inlet guide vanes.

FAN: Two-stage front fan. First stage has 30 titanium blades dove-tailed into discs. First-stage blades have integral shroud at about 61% span.

LP COMPRESSOR: Four-stage axial-flow, integral with fan stages, on inner of two concentric shafts. Blades made of titanium. Shaft carried in double ball bearings, either half of each bearing being able to handle the complete loading.

HP COMPRESSOR: Seven-stage axial-flow on outer hollow shaft which, like the inner shaft,

Pratt & Whitney JT12 turbojet engine (3,000 lb = 1,360 kg st)

Pratt & Whitney J52-P-408 turbojet engine (11,200 lb = 5,080 kg st)

Pratt & Whitney JT8D-9 commercial turbofan engine (14,500 lb = 6,575 kg st)

is carried in double ball bearings. One-piece casing. Blades made of steel or titanium. Pressure ratio ranges from 16·2 : 1 on JT8D-1 to 17·5 : 1 on JT8D-11. By-pass ratio 1·1 : 1. Total air mass flow 316 lb (143 kg)/sec.

COMBUSTION CHAMBER: Cannular type with nine cylindrical flame-tubes, each down-stream of a single Duplex burner and discharging into a single annular nozzle.

HP TURBINE: Single-stage axial-flow. Solid blades and guide vanes.

LP TURBINE: Three-stage axial-flow. Solid blades and guide vanes.

DIMENSIONS:
Diameter	42·5 in (1,080 mm)
Length	120·0 in (3,048 mm)

PRATT & WHITNEY JTF10A
Military designation: TF30

Development of this high-compression two-spool turbofan was begun in 1958 as a private venture, and resulted in testing of the first turbofan with afterburning. It was chosen

subsequently as the power plant for the General Dynamics/Grumman F-111 variable-geometry tactical fighter aircraft.

The version used initially in the F-111 was designated TF30-P-1 (JTF10A-20) which provides 18,500 lb (8,392 kg) st with afterburning. It was superseded in the F-111A by the TF30-P-3 (JTF10A-21) which provides the same thrust with reduced sea level supersonic specific fuel consumption. A version developed for the US Navy's now-abandoned F-111B was the TF30-P-12 (JTF10A-27A), a lighter weight and higher thrust model. The F-111D is powered by the TF30-P-9 (JTF10A-36) engine with afterburning rated at 19,600 lb (8,891 kg) st. The FB-111 bomber is equipped with the TF30-P-7 (JTF10A-27D) engine, which is in the 20,000 lb (9,072 kg) thrust class with afterburning. The F-111F will be equipped with the TF30-P-100 (JTF10A-32C) engine, an advanced version with higher thrust. The Vought A-7A and A-7B Corsair II tactical attack aircraft are powered by the TF30-P-6 (JTF10A-8) and TF30-P-8 (JTF10A-9), these being simplified versions without afterburning and rated at 11,350 lb (5,150 kg) and

12,200 lb (5,534 kg) st, respectively. TF30-P-8 engines are being converted to TF30-P-408 (JTF10A-16A) standard, with a thrust rating of 13,400 lb (6,078 kg) st.

In July 1965, the TF30-P-1 completed successfully its official ground tests for military qualification, involving two 150-hour tests, with 12¼ hours of full-power operation in simulated Mach 1·2 flight at sea level. In November 1966, the TF30-P-3 successfully completed a 150-hour military qualification test, with 6·25 hours of simulated Mach 1·2 flight at sea level.

Most recent application of the TF30 is the US Navy's new F-14A fighter project to be powered by the TF30-P-412, a modified version of the TF30-P-12. The TF30-P-412, with a revised form of afterburner nozzle, has a reheat rating in the 20,000 lb (9,072 kg) thrust class.

Afterburning versions of the JTF10 have been developed also by SNECMA in France and one of these, designated TF 106, was fitted in the Mirage III-T experimental test-bed aircraft and the Mirage III-V prototype VTOL fighter.

The SNECMA TF 306 is a TF30 fitted with a SNECMA-designed afterburner. It is used in the Mirage F2 and variable-geometry Mirage G prototypes.

PRATT & WHITNEY JTF22

Stemming partly from the JTF16 demonstrator engine designed in 1965-66, the JTF22 is an advanced-technology military turbofan with afterburner for highly supersonic applications. Basic development has been funded as a demonstrator programme for the US Air Force. In February 1970 the decision was taken to use the JTF22 core engine as the basis of two highly refined power units, one for the Grumman F-14B fighter for the US Navy and the other for the McDonnell Douglas F-15 fighter for the US Air Force. The resulting development and manufacturing programmes are expected to be of profound importance to Pratt & Whitney Aircraft for at least the next 15 years.

The two versions of the engine will differ in more than superficial ways. Each is being tailored exactly to suit the overall mission parameters of the two aircraft, which are far from identical. The gas generator section (core engine) will be the same in both versions but the size of fan (and hence total mass flow and by-pass ratio), afterburner and nozzle and other significant components will not be common. Both engines are described as being "in the 20,000-30,000 lb (9,070-13,610 kg) thrust class".

Internal details of the JTF22 remain classified but a hint was given by a detailed cutaway model of a supersonic reheat turbofan exhibited by Pratt & Whitney to emphasise that such an engine must be designed as an integrated propulsion system from intake to nozzle. The intake had a large axially sliding centrebody, blow-in peripheral flaps and powered exit flaps further aft. Two fan stages preceded variable core entry vanes, a four-stage LP compressor, seven-stage HP compressor with variable stators, single air-cooled HP turbine stage, three-stage LP turbine and variable turbine exit vanes, axially sliding plug in the core nozzle and two sets of variable peripheral flaps in the surrounding secondary fan-duct nozzle; fan-duct reheat was provided by a fuel manifold aligned with the annular combustor of the core.

Announcement of Pratt & Whitney's selection to provide propulsion for these two extremely important aircraft was made on 27 February. The company is developing the JTF22 at its Florida Research and Development Center but will make production engines in Connecticut. The first contract award specifies engineering design and development and the manufacture of 90 engines for use in F-14B and F-15 flight-test programmes. Target price for this work, including initial spares and equipment to support the flight programmes, is $448,162,600. Funding for fiscal year 1970 totals $47,450,000.

PRATT & WHITNEY JTF20

This is an extremely advanced air-breathing power plant optimised for a long-range supersonic-cruise mission at various altitudes. It is being funded as a demonstrator programme for the US Air Force. Details and performance are classified beyond the fact that the JTF20 is an advanced turbofan incorporating "a fan-duct heater system for augmentation". Aspects of this programme are related to the Air Force Advanced Turbine Engine Gas Generator programme. The JTF20 is a candidate engine in the competition to power the B-1A (AMSA) bomber.

PRATT & WHITNEY JT3C
Military designation: J57

Basic design of this two-spool axial-flow turbojet engine began in 1947. The final design was adopted in 1949 and production began in February 1953.

Pratt & Whitney TF30-P-8 military turbofan engine (12,200 lb = 5,534 kg st)

Pratt & Whitney TF30-P-3 turbofan engine with afterburner for the F-111 aircraft

The J57 powers versions of the Boeing B-52 bomber, Boeing KC-135/C-135 series of tanker-transports, three of the USAF's pioneer supersonic fighters, the North American F-100, the McDonnell Douglas F-101, and the Convair F-102, the US Navy's LTV F-8 supersonic ship-board fighter and the McDonnell Douglas A-3 naval attack bomber. The engines used in the fighter aircraft are equipped with afterburners.

Production of the J57 ceased in 1965 after more than 21,000 engines had been built.

The JT3C civil engine powers the Boeing 707-120 (many of which have been re-engined with JT3D turbofans) and 720, and the Douglas DC-8 Series 10, totalling some 150 aircraft. A description of the JT3C-6 was given in the 1967-68 *Jane's*. For data on other versions see table opposite.

PRATT & WHITNEY JT3D
Military designation: TF33

The JT3D is a turbofan version of the J57

turbojet, handling almost 2·5 times more air than the J57 and with pressure ratio ranging from 13 : 1 on the JT3D-1 to 16·1 : 1 on the JT3D-8A. Details of the ratings of the various versions are given in the table opposite.

Evolution from the J57 involved removal of the first three stages of the J57 compressor and replacement by two fan stages. Of considerably larger diameter than the compressor, the fan extends well outside the compressor casing. The third-stage turbine on the J57 was enlarged and a fourth stage added to provide the power necessary to drive the low-pressure compressor rotor and integral fan. A new short discharge duct was designed to exhaust the fan air well forward on the engine nacelle just after it has passed through the fan.

The JT3D produces 50% more take-off and 27% more cruise thrust than the J57, while giving a 13% better cruising specific fuel consumption.

Pratt & Whitney JT3D-3B commercial turbofan engine (18,000 lb = 8,172 kg st)

PRATT & WHITNEY MILITARY AND CIVIL GAS-TURBINE ENGINES

Manufacturers' and civil designation	Military designation	Type	T-O Rating lb st (kg st)	SFC	Weight dry lb (kg)	Diameter in (mm)	Remarks
JT3C-2	J57-P-43WB and -59W	Turbojet	13,750 (6,242)	0·95	3,870 (1,755)	38·90 (988)	Water injection
JT3C-6	—	Turbojet	13,500 (6,124)	0·775	4,234 (1,922)	38·88 (987·5)	Water injection
JT3C-7	—	Turbojet	12,000 (5,443)	0·785	3,495 (1,587)	38·88 (987·5)	—
JT3C-8	J57-P-59W	Turbojet	13,750 (6,242)	0·95	4,320 (1,959)	38·90 (988)	Water injection
JT3C-26	J57-P-20, -20A	Turbojet	18,000 (8,172)	2·35	4,750 (2,156)	38·90 (988)	Afterburning
JT3D-1	—	Turbofan	17,000 (7,718)	0·52	4,130 (1,873)	53·0 (1,346)	Water injection optional
JT3D-2	TF33-P-3	Turbofan	17,000 (7,718)	0·52	3,900 (1,770)	53·0 (1,346)	—
JT3D-3A	TF33-P-5, 9	Turbofan	18,000 (8,172)	0·535	4,170 (1,891)	53·0 (1,346)	—
JT3D-3B	—	Turbofan	18,000 (8,172)	0·535	4,260 (1,932)	53·0 (1,346)	Water injection optional
JT3D-7	—	Turbofan	19,000 (8,615)	0·550	4,260 (1,932)	53·0 (1,346)	Water injection optional
JT3D-8A	TF33-P-7	Turbofan	21,000 (9,525)	0·605	4,650 (2,109)	53·0 (1,346)	—
JT4A-9	—	Turbojet	16,800 (7,620)	0·81	5,050 (2,290)	43·0 (1,092)	—
JT4A-11	—	Turbojet	17,500 (7,945)	0·84	5,100 (2,315)	43·0 (1,092)	—
JT4A-28	J75-P-17	Turbojet	24,500 (11,113)	2·15	5,875 (2,665)	43·5 (1,105)	Afterburning
JT4A-29	J75-P-19W	Turbojet	26,500 (12,030)	2·20	5,960 (2,706)	43·5 (1,105)	Afterburning and water injection
JT8B-1	J52-P-6A	Turbojet	8,500 (3,855)	0·82	2,056 (933)	30·15 (766)	—
JT8B-3	J52-P-8A	Turbojet	9,300 (4,218)	0·86	2,118 (961)	30·15 (766)	—
JT8B-5	J52-P-408	Turbojet	11,200 (5,080)	0·89	2,318 (1,052)	30·15 (766)	—
JT8D-1,-7	—	Turbofan	14,000 (6,350)	0·585	3,156 (1,432)	42·5 (1,080)	—
JT8D-5	—	Turbofan	12,250 (5,556)	0·565	3,156 (1,432)	42·5 (1,080)	—
JT8D-9	—	Turbofan	14,500 (6,575)	0·595	3,218 (1,460)	42·5 (1,080)	—
JT8D-11	—	Turbofan	15,000 (6,804)	0·62	3,310 (1,501)	42·5 (1,080)	—
JT8D-15	—	Turbofan	15,500 (7,031)	0·63	3,310 (1,501)	42·5 (1,080)	—
JT9D-3	—	Turbofan	45,000 (20,412)	0·346	8,608 (3,905)	96·0 (2,438)	Water injection
JT9D-7	—	Turbofan	47,000 (21,310)	0·355	8,770 (3,978)	96·0 (2,438)	Water injection
JT9D-15	—	Turbofan	45,500 (20,630)	0·355	8,430 (3,824)	96·0 (2,438)	—
JTF10A-20	TF30-P-1, -1A	Turbofan	18,500 (8,390) class	2·50	3,869 (1,755)	42·1 (1,069)	Afterburning
JTF10A-8	TF30-P-6	Turbofan	11,350 (5,150)	0·620	2,715 (1,232)	42·1 (1,069)	Non-Afterburning
JTF10A-9	TF30-P-8	Turbofan	12,200 (5,534)	0·630	2,526 (1,146)	42·1 (1,069)	Non-Afterburning
JTF10A-16A	TF30-P-408	Turbofan	13,400 (6,080)	0·64	2,597 (1,178)	42·1 (1,069)	Non-Afterburning
JTF10A-21	TF30-P-3	Turbofan	18,500 (8,390) class	2·50	4,060 (1,842)	42·1 (1,069)	Afterburning
JTF10A-27A	TF30-P-12	Turbofan	20,000 (9,070) class	—	—	—	Afterburning
JTF10A-27D	TF30-P-7	Turbofan	20,000 (9,070) class	—	—	—	Afterburning
JTF10A-27F	TF30-P-412	Turbofan	20,000 (9,070) class	—	—	—	Afterburning
JTF10A-32C	TF30-P-100	Turbofan	20,000 (9,070) class	—	—	—	Afterburning
JTF10A-36	TF-30P-9	Turbofan	19,600 (8,891)	2·61	4,070 (1,846)	42·1 (1,069)	Afterburning
JT11D-20B	J58	Turbojet	30,000 (13,600) class	—	—	—	Afterburning
JT12A-5	J60-P-3, -5, J60-P-6	Turbojet	3,000 (1,362)	0·96	448 (203) 495 (225)	21·9 (556)	—
JT12A-6A	—	Turbojet	3,000 (1,362)	0·96	453 (206)	21·9 (556)	—
JT12A-8	—	Turbojet	3,300 (1,498)	0·995	468 (212)	21·9 (556)	—
JFTD12A-4A	T73-P-1	Free Turbine	4,500 shp	0·690 lb/shp/hr	920 (418)	34·0 (863)	Free-turbine shaft drive
JFTD12A-5A	T73-P-700	Free Turbine	4,800 shp	0·688 lb/shp/hr	935 (424)	34·0 (863)	Free-turbine shaft drive

Flight trials in a B-52 Stratofortress bomber and Boeing 707 airliner began in 1960. The JT3D powers all current versions of these aircraft and of the McDonnell Douglas DC-8. The Lockheed C-141A StarLifter military transport uses the TF33-P-7 version, with an additional stage of compression.

More than 7,900 JT3D turbofans, including converted JT3C engines, had been delivered by the end of 1969.

PRATT & WHITNEY JT4A

Military designation: J75

The J75 was developed between 1951 and 1954 to meet the needs of the supersonic interceptors then under development for the USAF and US Navy. Its general configuration follows that of the smaller J57 in that it is an axial-flow engine with a 15-stage (eight LP and seven HP) two-spool compressor, an annular combustion chamber with eight flame tubes, each with six fuel nozzles, and a three-stage (one HP and two LP) turbine. Control, fuel and lubrication systems are generally similar to those of the JT3 series. The JT4 is a larger engine and incorporated from the beginning many mechanical and aerodynamic improvements which were introduced subsequently into later models of the JT3.

Pratt & Whitney TF33-P-7 turbofan engine (21,000 lb = 9,525 kg st)

Pratt & Whitney J75 military turbojet engine with afterburner (26,500 lb = 12,030 kg st)

The J75-P-19 and P-17 engines for the F-105 Thunderchief and F-106 are approximately 20 ft (6·1 m) long, with afterburner. Pressure ratio is 12 : 1.

The commercial JT4A versions received FAA certification for airline use in March 1957 and power several long-range inter-continental versions of the Boeing 707 and McDonnell Douglas DC-8.

The FT4 is a free-turbine turboshaft used for electricity generation, pumping and marine propulsion. The engine is no longer in production for aircraft use except as spares.

For details of the various versions see table.

DIMENSIONS (JT4A-9):
Max diameter 43 in (1,090 mm)
Overall length 144·1 in (3,680 mm)
WEIGHT DRY (JT4A-9): 5,050 lb (2,291 kg)
PERFORMANCE RATING (JT4A-9):
T-O 16,800 lb (7,620 kg) st at 8,000 rpm
SPECIFIC FUEL CONSUMPTION (JT4A-9):
Normal 0·81

PRATT & WHITNEY JT11
Military designation: J58

The J58 is an advanced single-spool turbojet engine designed for operation at flight speeds in excess of Mach 3·0, and at very high altitudes. It is rated in the 30,000 lb (13,600 kg) st class.

The general configuration of the J58 is shown in the illustration at right. It is fitted with an advanced control system, by Hamilton Standard, which governs automatically the variable intake, fuel supply and variable-area nozzle.

Two J58s (JT11D-20B) form the power plant of the YF-12A and SR-71 versions of the Lockheed A-11 military aircraft, giving them a Mach 3 cruising performance.

A description is still not permitted.

PRATT & WHITNEY JT9D

The JT9D powers the Boeing 747 and has been selected to power the McDonnell Douglas DC-10-20. The first production engine, the JT9D-3, is rated at 43,500 lb (19,730 kg). Water injection is also available, increasing take-off thrust to 45,000 lb (20,410 kg). The engine is a twin-spool turbofan of 6 : 1 by-pass ratio, with an air-mass flow of 1,515 lb (687 kg)/sec, and overall pressure ratio of approximately 22 : 1.

The general configuration of the JT9D is shown in the illustration on the right. There are no inlet guide vanes. The single-stage front fan and three-stage LP compressor are mounted on the same shaft, driven by a four-stage LP turbine. The 11-stage high-pressure compressor is driven by a two-stage turbine, the first stage of which has air-cooled blades. The first two rows of turbine stator blades are also air-cooled and variable stator blading is used at the front of the HP compressor. Titanium is used extensively at the front of the compressor and high-nickel alloys at the rear. Each shaft runs in only two bearings. An annular combustion chamber is used.

The JT9D uses a rotary spinner to improve airflow conditions and has a plug nozzle in the exhaust section.

First run of the JT9D was in December 1966, and first engine flight test, with the engine mounted on the starboard inboard pylon of a Boeing B-52E, was in June 1968. The first flight of the Boeing 747 occurred on 9 February 1969.

Versions of the JT9D include the JT9D-3A model rated at 43,500 lb (19,730 kg) to 80°F, and rated with water injection at 45,000 lb (20,412 kg) to 80°F. First JT9D-3 production engine deliveries were made in April 1969, and this engine was certificated in May 1969. Initial deliveries of JT9D-3 engines with water injection equipment were made in late 1969. The JT9D-7 model is rated at 45,500 lb (20,639 kg) to 80°F, and with water injection is rated at 47,000 lb (21,310 kg) to 86°F. The JT9D-15 model is rated at 45,500 lb (20,639 kg) to 84°F. The JT9D-3A and -7 models power the Boeing 747; the JT9D-15 will power the McDonnell Douglas DC-10-20.

Pratt & Whitney J58 (JT11D-20B) turbojet with afterburner for the Lockheed YF-12A

The Pratt & Whitney JT9D-3 turbofan (43,500 lb = 19,730 kg st) powering the Boeing 747

Additional growth versions are being extensively studied and proposed for the 747B, DC-10 and other aircraft.

DIMENSIONS:
JT9D-3A, -7:
Diameter 95·6 in (2,428 mm)
Length (flange to flange) 128·2 in (3,256 mm)
WEIGHT, DRY:
Guaranteed, including standard equipment:
JT9D-3A 8,608 lb (3,905 kg)
JT9D-7 8,770 lb (3,978 kg)
PERFORMANCE RATINGS:
T-O:
JT9D-3A 43,500 lb (19,731 kg)
JT9D-7 45,500 lb (20,639 kg)
Max continuous:
JT9D-3A 36,400 lb (16,511 kg)
JT9D-7 38,500 lb (17,464 kg)
Max climb:
JT9D-3A 36,400 lb (16,511 kg)
JT9D-7 38,500 lb (17,464 kg)
Max cruise:
JT9D-3A 33,100 lb (15,014 kg)
JT9D-7 35,500 lb (16,103 kg)

SPECIFIC FUEL CONSUMPTIONS:
At T-O rating:
JT9D-3A 0·346
JT9D-7 0·355
At max continuous:
JT9D-3A 0·331
JT9D-7 0·337
At max climb:
JT9D-3A 0·331
JTD9-7 0·337
At max cruise:
JT9D-3A 0·326
JT9D-7 0·332

PRATT & WHITNEY ST9

The ST9 is a new small 1,500 shp direct-drive free-turbine turboshaft being developed in demonstrator form under contract to the US Army Aviation Materiel Laboratories Propulsion Division. In parallel with the competing General Electric GE12 turboshaft, an initial two-year programme covering design, build and development and 100 hours of testing of a complete engine was initiated in August 1967 and extended to continue demonstrator testing through to

30 April 1970. Originally intended application for the competing engines was the Army's utility tactical transport system (UTTAS) but an advanced turboshaft engine in this power class would have many possible uses, not all of them V/STOL.

Pratt & Whitney's extensive experience with small centrifugal compressors, gained via the United Aircraft of Canada PT6A turboshaft and JT15D turbofan, together with research work on behalf of the Canadian government, has been embodied in the new engine. A two-stage centrifugal unit is used to provide what is claimed to be the highest pressure ratio of any small engine. The combustor is of folded annular configuration based on the PT6A design, and both the compressor and power turbines have two stages. Turbine entry temperature is around 2,200° F (1,044°C).

The engine is capable of meeting a wide variety of installation requirements, including front, rear or angled drive, twin-engined coupled drive, horizontal or nose-up or nose-down operating attitudes, and embodies only three electrical and seven mechanical engine-to-airframe connections.

Simple and robust in design, the ST9 is designed for a 5,000-hr life under service operating conditions. As with the GE12, its specific fuel consumption is 20 to 30 per cent below that of existing small turboshafts—in the region of 0·42 lb (0·19 kg)/shp/hr at military rating, rising to around 0·595 lb (0·27 kg)/shp/hr at 60 per cent full load.

DIMENSIONS:
Length	33·1 in (841 mm)
Diameter	18·3 in (465 mm)

WEIGHT:
Approximately	290 lb (132 kg)

PERFORMANCE RATING:
Military rating	1,500 shp

PRATT & WHITNEY JFTD12
Military designation: T73

This free-turbine shaft-turbine engine consists basically of the gas generator of a JT12 turbojet with a two-stage free-turbine added downstream to provide a rear drive. The exhaust is taken out to one side, and in the case of the installation on the Sikorsky S-64 Skycrane helicopter one engine exhausts to port, the other to starboard. Pressure ratio is 6·85 : 1.

There are two current versions:

JFTD12A-1. Rated at 4,050 shp. Powers the S-64A. Development running began in the latter half of 1960 and flight testing began in the Sikorsky S-64 on 9 May 1962.

JFTD12A-4A. Advanced version of the earlier JFTD12A-3; powers the Sikorsky S-64E. Developed under contract to the US Army as the **T73-P-1** to power Sikorsky CH-54A Skycrane heavy-lift helicopters. In production and rated at 4,500 shp.

The 4,050 shp Pratt & Whitney JFTD12A-1 free-turbine engine

JFTD12A-5A. Advanced version of the JFTD12A-4A; powers the Sikorsky S-64F. Developed under contract to the US Army as the **T73-P-700** to power Sikorsky CH-54B Skycrane heavy-lift helicopters. In production and rated at 4,800 shp.

PRATT & WHITNEY RL-10

The RL-10 is an upper-stage space vehicle propulsion unit which offers multiple start capability after coasting periods of hours. The propellants are liquid hydrogen and liquid oxygen, employed in a regenerative cycle, and the current RL-10A-3 version of the engine is rated at 15,000 lb (6,800 kg) st.

First delivery was made in August 1960 for use in NASA's Centaur rocket, the upper stage of which is powered by two RL-10 engines. A six-engine cluster of RL-10A-3 engines powered the S-IV second stage in six of the ten Saturn I vehicles, all of which performed with complete success in their launch programme.

Advanced versions of the RL-10 are under investigation at United Aircraft Corporation's Florida Research and Development Center, including a variable-thrust version. Under a NASA contract, the company has designed and built an RL-10 oxidiser pump using fluorine. This has been tested successfully, showing that a modified RL-10 would be capable of operating with fluorine.

Pratt & Whitney RL-10

ROCKETDYNE

ROCKETDYNE DIVISION OF NORTH AMERICAN ROCKWELL CORPORATION

LIQUID ROCKET DIVISION:
6633 Canoga Ave, Canoga Park, California 91304

SOLID ROCKET DIVISION:
McGregor, Texas

SANTA SUSANA FIELD LABORATORY:
Santa Susana Mountains, Ventura County, California

PRESIDENT:
S. K. Hoffman

EXECUTIVE VICE-PRESIDENT:
C. W. Guy

VICE-PRESIDENTS:
P. H. Milham (Contracts and Pricing)
E. F. Brown (Jet Engine Components Division)
W. J. Brennan (Liquid Rocket Division)
P. J. Fritch (Management Planning and Controls)
D. W. Hege (Marketing)
R. J. Thompson, Jr (Research)
W. J. Cecka Jr (Solid Rocket Division)

Rocketdyne is a division of North American Rockwell, devoted primarily to the design and manufacture of rocket engines for the US Air Force, Army and Navy and the National Aeronautics and Space Administration. It was established as a separate division on 8 November 1955.

On 1 October 1959, Rocketdyne acquired full ownership of the former Astrodyne, Inc, which was formed in 1958 by North American Aviation and Phillips Petroleum Company.

Rocketdyne's work on liquid-propulsion engines is now centred at Canoga Park, California, and work on solid-propulsion engines at McGregor, Texas. Plants at Neosho, Missouri, and Van

Nuys, California, have been closed and their work is now undertaken at Canoga Park.

North American's interest in missile development dates back to 1947, when the company began work on the 14 ft (4·25 m) NATIV research rocket. In 1950, the company built and tested the first high-thrust liquid-propellant engine larger than that of the wartime German V-2 rocket. To-day it is the leading manufacturer of large liquid-propellant rockets in the United States.

Rocketdyne liquid-propellant engines have powered the first stage of the launching vehicles used for the majority of America's satellite and space probe programmes. This leading rôle in space research will continue, as the current and future versions of the Saturn launch vehicle utilise booster stages powered by the 1,522,000 lb st Rocketdyne F-1 and intermediate stages powered by the Rocketdyne J-2, a 230,000 lb (104,325 kg) st liquid hydrogen/liquid oxygen engine.

The SE-8 re-entry control system of the Apollo spacecraft and the SE-9 attitude control system for the Titan III Transtage are produced by Rocketdyne. These systems utilise small liquid-propellant rocket-engines.

Current products of Rocketdyne's Solid Rocket Division include propulsion systems for the US Navy's Sparrow III, Shrike, AIM-9C/D Sidewinder and Phoenix missiles, the Army's Chaparral and Lance missiles, the ullage motor for Saturn V, unique reinforced-grain solid-propellant motors, zero-launch boosters for the Lockheed F-104 fighter-bomber and GQM-15A target drone, and miscellaneous turbine starters and gas generators.

Available details on current Rocketdyne engines are given below. The company is also working on many different types of advanced propulsion techniques for rockets, missiles and spacecraft.

ROCKETDYNE F-1

Research towards an engine in the 1,000,000 lb (453,600 kg) st class began at Rocketdyne in

March 1955, under a USAF contract known as REAP (Rocket Engine Advancement Program).

This programme encompassed a broad range of research and development, directed toward increasing the liquid-propellant engine thrust range. By 1957 Rocketdyne studies had established the feasibility of fabricating a single-chamber liquid-propellant engine that would produce 1,000,000 lb st and studies showed the optimum thrust for such an engine to be 1,500,000 lb (680,000 kg).

The National Aeronautics and Space Administration was assigned the responsibility for development of an engine in the 1,000,000-1,500,000 lb st class on 1 October 1958, and requested competitive proposals from industry. Rocketdyne was named the successful bidder on 17 December 1958, and a contract was entered into with NASA on 9 January 1959. Manufacture of the engine was entrusted to the company's Canoga Park plant.

A cluster of five F-1 engines is used in the S-IC first stage of the Saturn V lunar launch vehicle.

A requirement of the programme was that the design of the engine should be conventional, to take full advantage of present experience and to provide maximum assurance that development schedules and performance targets would be met. As a result the F-1 follows closely the design of engines previously in production by the company, and uses the same liquid oxygen oxidant and RP-1 fuel.

Only eight months after receipt of the contract, in August 1959, Rocketdyne made successful tests of injector patterns in a full-scale uncooled test chamber at thrust levels above 1,000,000 lb (453,600 kg) at its Santa Susana Field Laboratory.

In April 1961, the highest thrust then known to have been achieved by a single engine—1,640,000 lb (744,000 kg)—was developed during a static test of a prototype thrust chamber for the F-1 at the NASA High Thrust Area, Edwards, California. The first test of a complete engine was made on 13 June 1961, when approximately 1,000,000 lb (453,600 kg) of thrust was generated.

The first production F-1 engine was delivered to NASA on 29 October 1963, following a series of four test firings at Edwards to demonstrate its performance. It was flown to Marshall Space Flight Center, Huntsville, Ala, for further testing and for personnel training.

Flight rating tests were completed on 16 December 1964, and the first firing test of a full cluster of five F-1 engines in an S-IC ground-test booster was made successfully on 16 April 1965. The engines generated a total of 7,500,000 lb (3,402,000 kg) st for the 6½-second duration of the test. On 5 August 1965, the full cluster of five engines was run for 150 seconds, equivalent to the time the S-IC stage is required to run during operational launches of Saturn V.

The F-1 completed its qualification tests for manned flight in September 1966. It has since provided propulsion in all of the Apollo flights and will continue to be used in programmes involving the S-IC stage in the next decade. Development of the engine has been under the technical direction of NASA's Marshall Space Flight Center. Current rating is 1,522,000 lb (690,371 kg) st but the engine could be uprated to 1,800,000 lb (816,466 kg) st by direct linear increase in chamber pressure. Extensive tests have proved the ability of the uprated F-1 to perform as predicted, and modifications would include a new turbopump with increased-horsepower turbine and high-head impellers, as well as structural strengthening of the thrust gimbal, nozzle, jacket body, gas-generator valve and duct, turbopump shaft, heat-exchanger shell and turbine exhaust manifold.

NASA has investigated the performance of an Uprated Saturn vehicle (MLV-3B), using these engines in the first stage and having larger tanks in all three stages. Depending on the upper engines used, the MLV-3B would be able to launch payloads 35-50 per cent greater than those of today's Saturn V.

Basic components of the F-1 engine are a tubular-wall regeneratively-cooled thrust chamber assembly, direct drive turbopump, gas generator and required controls.

THRUST CHAMBER: This assembly consists of a tubular-wall chamber, an uncooled nozzle extension, double-inlet oxidizer dome, two fuel valves and a flat-face injector. The basic chamber is formed of high-strength alloy steel tubes which are contoured, stacked and then brazed in a specially designed gas-fired brazing furnace. In operation, fuel flows through alternate tubes the length of the chamber and then returns to an injector feed manifold. Here it is distributed through 32 spokes into the injector, from which it passes through approximately 3,700 holes into the combustion chamber. The cooled portion of the thrust chamber is 11 ft (3·35 m) long, 40 in (1·02 m) in diameter at the throat chamber and 9 ft 6 in (2·90 m) in diameter at the exit.

A unique feature of the chamber is that it provides for attachment of an uncooled extension. This facilitates transport of the engine, since the uncooled extension can be packaged and shipped separately, and makes it possible to attach an uncooled segment to attain an expansion area ratio of 16 : 1.

TURBOPUMP: The turbopump, which weighs 2,800 lb (1,270 kg) and develops 60,000 hp, is able to pump 4,000 lb (1,814 kg) of liquid oxygen and one ton of RP-1 into the combustion chamber each second.

GAS GENERATOR: Gases to run the turbopump are provided by a gas generator which burns fuel-rich liquid oxygen and RP-1. About 2% of the total propellants used in the F-1 are burned in the gas generator, which is regeneratively-cooled by passing fuel through the double-walls of the combustion chamber. The gas generator is partially spherical and about 10 in (0·25 m) in diameter.

CONTROLS: The main controls are two fuel valves and two oxidizer valves mounted on the thrust chamber dome; a gas generator valve; a fuel and oxidizer flow regulator for the gas generator and a four-way solenoid valve, which controls the other valves. The four-way solenoid valve is one of only two components in the engine requiring electrical wiring. The other is the spark exciter which ignites the gas generator.

DIMENSIONS:
Overall height	220·4 in (5,598 mm)
Diameter at nozzle exit	143·5 in (3,645 mm)

WEIGHT:
In flight configuration	18,500 lb (8,391 kg)

PERFORMANCE RATING:
Sea-level thrust	1,522,000 lb (690,367 kg)
Sea-level specific impulse	264·5 sec
Vacuum thrust	1,748,000 lb (792,879 kg)
Vacuum specific impulse	304 sec

ROCKETDYNE J-2

A contract to develop this liquid hydrogen/liquid oxygen rocket engine was received from NASA in 1960. Initial thrust rating (vacuum

Mock-up of Rocketdyne F-1 engine (1,522,000 lb = 690,371 kg st), five of which power the Saturn V lunar launch vehicle

Assembly of Rocketdyne J-2 hydrogen-fuelled engines (230,000 lb = 104,325 kg st)

conditions) was 200,000 lb (90,720 kg), but this was increased progressively first to 225,000 lb (102,000 kg) and then to 230,000 lb (104,325 kg).

The second stage of the Saturn IB launch vehicle is powered by a single J-2. A cluster of five J-2's, developing up to 1,150,000 lb (521,632 kg), powers the S-II second stage of the Saturn V which also has a single J-2 as its third-stage propulsion.

Current contracts are for a total of 152 J-2 engines. Test running began in October 1962, and on 27 November 1963 a J-2 completed successfully a full-duration test firing of 510 seconds at its design thrust. The first delivery of a J-2 to NASA was made on 29 April 1964. Preliminary flight rating tests were completed on 5 November 1964. Re-start capability was demonstrated in a test on 9 December 1964. On 8 August 1965, a flight version of the S-IVB second stage of the Saturn IB, utilising a J-2 engine, was acceptance tested for its full flight duration of 452 seconds. On the following day, a five-engine cluster of J-2s for the S-II second stage of Saturn V was test fired for its flight duration of 390 seconds at full rated power.

The J-2 completed its qualification tests for manned flight in September 1966.

In April 1969 NASA's Marshall Space Flight Center signed an agreement calling for a stretch-out in production to 30 April 1970, at a rate reduced from three engines a month to one.

Basic components of the engine are a tubular-wall regeneratively-cooled thrust chamber, separate turbopumps for each propellant, gas generator and required controls.

THRUST CHAMBER: The basic chamber is formed of stainless steel tubes which are contoured, stacked and then brazed. It is cooled by hydrogen flowing one and a half passes through the tubes, before being injected into the chamber. Injector is designed for gas/liquid. Expansion ratio 27·5 : 1. Chamber gimbals 10° in any direction.

TURBOPUMPS: Two independent single-shaft pumps, with separate two-stage velocity-compound turbines, feed oxygen and hydrogen in ratio of 5·5 : 1 by weight. Single-stage centrifugal liquid oxygen pump. Seven-stage axial-flow liquid hydrogen pump. Rapid initial pump acceleration provided by 4 cu ft (0·11 m³) sphere of gaseous hydrogen, which is recharged automatically between starts. The tank-head start is lit by augmented-spark ignition, and propellant flow rate swiftly builds up to 2,964 US gal/min (11,220 litres/min) of liquid oxygen at 1,107 lb/sq in (778 kg/cm²) abs and 8,584 US gal/min (32,490 litres/min) of liquid hydrogen at 1,247 lb/sq in (7·87 kg/cm²) abs. Thrust level is controlled by fixed orifices, with the propellant utilization valve to by-pass liquid oxygen; electrically controlled propellant valves are triggered for thrust termination.

DIMENSIONS:
Overall height	133 in (3,378 mm)
Diameter at nozzle exit	80 in (2,032 mm)

WEIGHT: approximately 3,480 lb (1,578 kg)

PERFORMANCE RATINGS (VACUUM):
4·5 mixture ratio thrust	180,000 lb (81,646 kg)
4·5 mixture ratio specific impulse	431 sec
5·0 mixture ratio thrust	205,000 lb (92,986 kg)
5·0 mixture ratio specific impulse	428 sec
5·5 mixture ratio thrust	230,000 lb (104,326 kg)
5·5 mixture ratio specific impulse	425 sec
Combustion pressure	780 lb/sq in (3,808 kg/m²)

ROCKETDYNE H-1

The H-1 is a slightly more compact development of the liquid-propellant engine used in the Thor space launch vehicle. In particular the turbo-pump has been repositioned and is now mounted on the side of the chamber instead of on top. It runs on liquid oxygen and RP-1 propellants and the latest version has a new stainless steel tubular-wall thrust chamber.

Eight H-1 engines are clustered to form the first-stage booster of the Saturn IB space vehicle. Those in the first five Saturn IBs were each rated at 200,000 lb (90,720 kg) st. The H-1's in subsequent Saturn vehicles are uprated to 205,000 lb (92,990 kg) st at sea level.

Each engine has its own turbopump, but draws its propellants from common tankage. The chambers of the four outer engines are gimballed to provide directional stability for the booster in flight.

The engines are started with a hypergolic slug igniter, and the booster incorporates a safety device to prevent release of the vehicle unless all engines are functioning correctly.

The contract to develop the H-1 was received in September 1958, and the first engine was delivered to the Army Ballistic Missile Agency in May 1959. Firing tests of the complete Saturn I booster cluster of eight engines began in the Summer of 1960 and the first launching of a Saturn I with dummy top stages, was made on 27 October 1961.

The H-1 was manufactured in Rocketdyne's Canoga Park plant. Over 280 H-1 engines had been delivered by August 1967.

ROCKETDYNE MB-3
USAF designation: LR79

The MB-3 propulsion system was developed originally to power the Thor IRBM, and consisted of an LR79-NA-9 single-chamber liquid-propellant sustainer engine and two verniers to contro missile roll and trim final velocity and directional control after burn-out of the sustainer.

The same basic propulsion system now powers the Thor-Agena, Thor-AbleStar and Delta satellite and space probe launch vehicles.

The design of the LR79 is similar to that of the LR89 and LR105 engines of the MA-2 propulsion system (described in 1966-67 *Janes*), with a gimballed tubular-wall chamber and twin turbopump feed for the liquid oxygen and RP-1 propellants. Engine components have been reduced from 46 in early configurations to 28 in the latest models, following the elimination of airborne start tanks. The rating of the final LR79-NA-11 engine is approximately 170,000 lb (77,100 kg) st for nearly 2½ minutes.

DIMENSIONS:
Overall length	12 ft 0 in (3·66 m)
Nozzle diameter	3 ft 11 in (1·19 m)

WEIGHT (DRY):
Approx	2,000 lb (907 kg)

ROCKETDYNE AEROSPIKE

Illustrated above is a full-scale engineering model of Rocketdyne's Aerospike rocket engine concept, which is expected to provide high performance for future launch vehicles and spacecraft.

The Aerospike has a combustion ring assembled around the upper circumference of a shortened (truncated) centre cone. The model illustrated represents an engine in the 250,000-400,000 lb (113,500-181,500 kg) st class.

A number of Aerospike engines have been hot-fired, using liquid-oxygen/hydrogen and fluorine/hydrogen storable propellants. The programme is being sponsored by NASA and the US Air Force.

Rocketdyne H-1 engine, eight of which power the S-IB first stage of the Saturn IB

Full-scale engineering model of Rocketdyne's Aerospike rocket engine concept

ROCKETDYNE VERNIER ENGINE
USAF designation: LR101

The Rocketdyne low-thrust vernier engine was developed originally as part of the MA-2 propulsion system of the Atlas. It was subsequently added to the MB-3 system of the Thor. In each case two of the engines are used to trim final velocity and to provide roll control.

The vernier is a small gimballed single-chamber engine, operating on liquid oxygen and RP-1 propellants drawn from the missile's main tankage. It utilises an efficient regenerative-cooling system to reduce the normal 5,000°F combustion temperature to a safe level for sustained operation. Gimballing gives approximately 120° movement in roll and 60° in pitch.

Ignition takes place shortly before the missile is launched, but thrust is reduced by approximately 20% for the first few seconds of flight when the verniers are used only to control roll. Subsequently, in the Atlas, they provide adjustment for any thrust variations of the booster engines. In both the Atlas and Thor they continue running for several seconds after sustainer burn-out, to ensure that the vehicles attain their correct attitude in azimuth and elevation.

ROCKETDYNE SE-8

This is an attitude control and stabilization engine for the Apollo spacecraft Command Module. It is used during re-entry into the earth's atmosphere. Two independent and identical sets of six are fitted (one set acting as a back-up) and the propellants are monomethyl-hydrazine and nitrogen tetroxide.

These engines were designed to operate in extremely short bursts. Each gives 95 lb (43 kg) st and has a weight of 8·12 lb (3·68 kg).

Development began in 1962; the first engines were delivered in 1965 and qualification tests were completed in December 1965.

The thrust chamber, including nozzle, consists of a one-piece 45°-oriented high silica fabric, impregnated with phenolic resin. The combustion zone liner is fabricated from the same material, except that the fabric is 6°-oriented. The throat insert is a sintered composite of zirconium diboride, silicon and JTA graphite. The nozzle extensions are also fabricated from the same material as the thrust chamber, except that the fabric is zero-oriented. The nozzle extensions are made in three different lengths and can be scarfed to fit the installation. The chamber is cased in a one-piece stainless-steel jacket with a mounting flange. The jacket is welded to the injector and contains an integral flange for screwed mounting. The stainless-steel injector is all-welded and is attached to the chamber by glass-fibre roving.

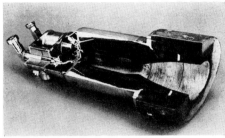

Sectioned Rocketdyne SE-8, the Apollo Command Module reaction control engine

The propellant control valve is a normally-closed rapid-response, solenoid-operated co-axial type of all-welded construction. Propellant shut-off and sealing is by a non-metallic seat and a hard stellite ball. At nominal operating voltage the opening time is 0·007 seconds, and closing time 0·004 seconds. The injector assembly is constructed from machined and forged stainless steel components, assembled and welded together to form a series of internal feed passages and injection orifices. The injection orifice pattern is so designed that 16 unlike doublets impinging on a 45° splashplate are formed, to produce complete propellant mixing and hypergolic ignition.

The SE-8 is 11·65 in (296 mm) long, with a diameter of 5 in (127 mm). Specific impulse is 266 nominal and combustion-chamber pressure and temperature are respectively 138 lb/sq in (9·7 kg/cm²) abs and 5,192°F.

ROCKETDYNE FLEXEM

This new programme, the name of which is derived from "flexible energy management", was initiated by a $2 million US Air Force contract awarded to Rocketdyne in June 1969. Its aim is to provide compact, pre-packaged liquid-propellant engines for advanced air-to-air missiles for use by future US Air Force and Navy fighters, including the F-14 and F-15. The engines would be able to fire in a wide range of combinations of very high thrust booster or long duration sustainer modes to minimise time taken to reach any type of target or to meet other operational requirements. The Air Force, which has responsibility for propulsion of the next generation of air-to-air weapons for both services, regards the programme as one of high priority.

ROCKETDYNE MODEL 16NS-1,000

The 16NS-1,000 was developed as a smokeless JATO unit for the USAF, but has wide applications. It consists of a steel cylinder, closed at the forward end. The igniter is located on the forward end, with the exhaust nozzle and pressure release diaphragm at the aft end. Thrust is transmitted to the aircraft attachment fittings through three mounting lugs welded on the cylinder.

DIMENSIONS:
Length	2 ft 11 in (890 mm)
Diameter	10·5 in (267 mm)

WEIGHTS:
Without propellant	106·6 lb (48·4 kg)
Complete	196·9 lb (89·2 kg)

PERFORMANCE RATING:
1,000 lb (455 kg) st for 16 seconds

ROCKETDYNE MK 25 JATO

The Mk 25 was developed as a standard JATO unit for the US Navy and is used in three forms: Mod 0, with 30° canted nozzle for launching the

A-3 series aircraft; Mod 1, with 15° cant, for boosting the A-4 series; and Mod 2, with straight nozzle, for sled applications. The case is of 4130 steel and the RDS-135 solid propellant burns along inner and outer radii in the form of a sponge-supported cylindrical grain. Performance varies greatly with ambient temperature, a hot day giving much higher thrust for a shorter burn; at 60°F action-time thrust is 4,360 lb (1,977 kg) for 5·41 seconds. The 54 in (1,371 mm) long motor weighs 208 lb (94 kg) filled and 83 lb (37·6 kg) after firing.

ROCKETDYNE M-34 ZEL

The M-34 is a solid-propellant booster rocket which gives 130,000 lb (59,000 kg) thrust for four seconds and is used for zero-length launching of the F-100D Super Sabre fighter aircraft and GQM-15A (formerly KD2U-1) Regulus 2 target drone. Its propellant is ammonium nitrate and it utilizes Rocketdyne's modular design concept in which a series of extruded propellant segments are suspended on longitudinal steel rods and supported by perforated steel plates. This makes it possible to vary the length, shape and number of grains, as required.

Development of the M-34 began under a USAF research and development contract in 1957. Before being used for launching piloted aircraft, the unit had to prove its ability to produce its full rated thrust under split-second timing, along a line of thrust accurate within a fraction of a degree, after being subjected to vibration, salt spray, maximum humidity and temperature conditions ranging from —75 to + 170°F.

The M-34 can accelerate an F-100D from standstill to 275 mph (445 kmh) in under four seconds.

In February 1963, Rocketdyne received a contract from Lockheed Aircraft Corporation to develop a solid-propellent booster rocket for zero-length launching of the F-104G Starfighter. This booster is similar in diameter to the M-34 but is shorter and utilises an improved nitrate propellant in a casing of lighter weight.

ROCKETDYNE RS18

Playing a critical role in the Apollo mission, the RS18 is the Lunar Module Ascent Engine. It has a single fixed thrust chamber, fed with nitrogen tetroxide and unsymmetrical dimethyl hydrazine.

THRUST CHAMBER: The chamber is ablative and has an area ratio of 45·6 : 1. The materials used are Narmco 4065 for the nozzle and 6061 aluminium alloy for the shell, with a C-1554-48 Irish Refrasil inner liner and Narmco 4065 outer liner. Ablative cooling is aided by injector fuel-film cooling. The fuel and oxidizer main propellant valves are mechanically linked and open simultaneously. The oxidizer reaches the combustion chamber 30 milliseconds ahead of the fuel, due to a built-in delay in the fuel duct connecting the fuel valve to the injector. The injector is a one-piece milled body with seven propellant rings which contain electrical-discharge-machined orifices through which the propellants are injected. The injection pattern is unlike doublet orifices with 4·5 per cent of the fuel injected as film coolant. The propellants are hypergolic.

PROPELLANT FEED SYSTEM: This consists of the injector, valve assembly and propellant ducts and elbows. The propellant-valve assembly is a series-parallel design using eight ball-valves to provide greater reliability with minimum pressure drop. Parallel flow paths are provided within the valve assembly for each of the two propellants, with each flow path containing first an isolation valve and secondly a propellant valve. The valves are actuated by means of four pistons, each of which acts through a bell crank to rotate one fuel and one oxidizer ball linked together on a common shaft. Fuel pressure to each of the four actuator pistons is controlled by a three-way solenoid valve. Overboard vents are provided for each solenoid valve, for leakage past oxidizer shaft seals and for fuel piston and shaft seal leakage. The propellant ducts are fabricated of stainless-steel tubing; no flexible joints are used. Propellant flow rates are 4·338 lb (1·97 kg)/sec fuel at 190 lb/sq in (13·35 kg/cm²) abs and 6·941 lb (3·14 kg)/sec oxidizer at 190 lb/sq in (13·35 kg/cm²) abs.

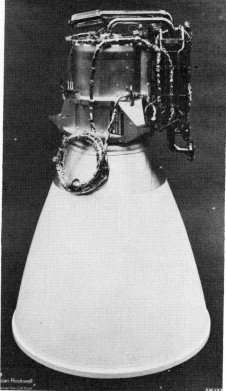

Rocketdyne RS18, the Apollo Lunar Module Ascent Engine (LMAE)

STARTING PROCEDURE: An electrical signal opens the actuation isolation valves (vehicle) and the four engine 3-way solenoid valves. Fuel pressure then passes through each valve to the four actuator pistons. The pressure causes the actuator piston to move and open the fuel and oxidizer ball valves simultaneously. The main propellants then pass through the valve assembly, the propellant ducts and injector to the combustion chamber where they impinge and ignite. The engine develops 90 per cent thrust in 300 milliseconds and shuts down to 10 per cent thrust in 236 milliseconds. The engine is not throttled and operates only at full thrust.

DIMENSIONS:
Overall length	47·21 in (1,199 mm)
Overall height	32·44 in (824 mm)
Overall width	32·44 in (824 mm)

WEIGHT:
Dry weight	171 lb (77·6 kg)

PERFORMANCE:
Max thrust in vacuum conditions
3,500 lb (1,587 kg)
Overall propellant mixture ratio
1·60 (oxidizer : fuel)

Specific impulse   310·3 sec
Combustion pressure
122·3 lb/sq in (8·6 kg/cm²) abs injector end
Combustion temperature   5,074°F

ROCKETDYNE MK 38/39

The Mk 38 solid-propellant rocket motor developed and produced by Rocketdyne for the Sparrow III air-to-air missile was the first to combine a special free-standing propellant charge (grain) with the company's Flexadyne propellant. Based on a carboxy-terminated linear polybutadiene fuel-binder, the new propellant provides a substantial increase in missile performance and has superior physical properties which give it resistance to cracking or tearing at extremely low temperatures.

The development contract for the motor was placed in 1961 and flight tests began successfully 12 months later. Development and qualification of the motor were completed in 22 months. The McGregor plant shortly thereafter, in July 1963, began manufacturing the Mk 39 motor for the AGM-45A Shrike anti-radar missile. This is similar in design and ballistic performance.

ROCKETDYNE MK 36 MOD 5 SIDEWINDER MOTOR

The Solid Rocket Division of Rocketdyne received a development contract for motors for the AIM-9C and AIM-9D advanced versions of the Sidewinder air-to-air missile in 1963. Standard Sidewinder cases were loaded with the company's Flexadyne propellant and tested under temperature extremes ranging from sub-zero to over 300°F. They showed 100% reliability in over 200 firings during development and operational evaluation and first production contracts were awarded in 1964.

Designated Mk 36 Mod 5, the Rocketdyne Sidewinder motor is approximately 72 in (183 cm) long, 5 in (12·7 cm) in diameter and contains 60 lb (27 kg) of Flexadyne propellant.

ROCKETDYNE MK 47

The Mk 47 Mod 0 solid propulsion system for the Navy's AIM-54A Phoenix missile has been under development by the McGregor plant since 1963. The first powered flight was in April 1966, two months after completion of the propulsion system development programme, in the course of which over 60 motors were subjected to such tests as multiple-temperature cycling, shock tests simulating catapult and arrested landings and extensive vibration tests.

The Mk 47 motor utilizes an improved version of Flexadyne, particularly adaptable to Phoenix missile requirements of high volumetric loading, high total impulse and long burning time to provide the long-range missile operational capability required. The propellant has excellent ballistic properties, a 5-10 year shelf life and exhaust characteristics that minimize radar attenuation. Rocketdyne has successfully test fired similar propellant at —75°F in a large research motor after two complete temperature cyclings between —75 and 170°F.

Rocketdyne Mk 47 Mod 0 solid-propellant motor for Hughes AIM-54A Phoenix air-to-air missile

SOLAR

SOLAR (Division of International Harvester Company)

HEAD OFFICE AND WORKS:
2200 Pacific Highway, San Diego, California 92112

PRESIDENT: Herbert Kunzel

Solar manufactures a range of gas-turbine engines which includes the 80-150 hp T62 Titan, the 350 hp Spartan, the 1,100 hp Saturn and the 3,000 hp-range Centaur.

The Titan turbine is used as an auxiliary power unit on every major US military cargo helicopter (which includes the Boeing-Vertol CH-46 and CH-47, Sikorsky CH-3, CH-53 and CH-54) as well

as on several small commercial aircraft and business jets, such as the FH-227, JetStar, Sabreliner, DH.125/BH.125, and Fan Jet Falcon. Titan turbine APUs can provide power for main engine starting, ground air-conditioning and preflight systems checkout. Well over 4,000 Titan APUs have been sold.

The Spartan turbine is used as the prime mover

in Solar's 200kW and 225kW generator sets. Some 200 of these units are in operation, primarily on stand-by duty at telephone exchanges.

The 1,100 hp Saturn is claimed to be used in a wider variety of applications than any other turbine. It has accounted for over 57% of all industrial turbine sales in the 700-5,000 hp range in the US and Canada. It is currently being used to drive such equipment as generators, compressors, pumps and a wide variety of off-highway vehicles, hydrofoils and high-speed boats. Single-shaft or split-shaft versions are available for either continuous duty or standby applications. More than 1,400 Saturns have been sold.

The first application for the Centaur turbine is as the prime mover in Solar's 3,000 hp natural-gas compressor set. Mechanical-drive packages and generator sets powered by the Centaur turbine will enter production in the near future.

Cutaway drawing of the 80-150 shp Solar Titan turboshaft engine

TELEDYNE CONTINENTAL
TELEDYNE CONTINENTAL MOTORS
(Formerly Continental Motors Corporation)
HEAD OFFICE:
12700 Kercheval Avenue, Detroit, Michigan 48215
PRESIDENT:
J. L. Richardson
VICE-PRESIDENTS:
J. E. Smith (Commercial Marketing)
I. W. Nichol (Military Marketing and Engineering)
H. W. Rouse (Operations)
R. Ortiz (Mobile Operations)
W. A. Wiseman (Aeronautical Engineering)
W. E. Lewis (Finance and Treasurer)
DIRECTORS:
Don Fairchilds (Communications)
D. J. Wollenhaupt (Chicago Operations)
E. F. Blackburne (Washington Office)
A. E. Kugler (Getty Street Plant Operation)
C. C. Sharp (Market Street Plant Operation)
H. D. Cox (Aircraft Engine Programmes)
Earl F. Kotts (General Counsel)
K. J. Covey (Plant Manager, Panama City Operation)
H. F. Coleman (Plant Manager, Walterboro Operation)

In 1928, the former Continental Motors Corporation, one of the largest automobile engine manufacturers in the world, produced its first aero-engine, a sleeve-valve air-cooled radial incorporating the Argyll (Burt-McCollum) patents, which had been purchased by the Corporation from the British Argyll Company in 1925.

In 1931 the 38 hp A40 flat-four was put on the market. This was followed by the A50, A65, A75 and A80 series.

The current range of Teledyne Continental light aircraft engines includes horizontally-opposed four- and six-cylinder engines, some with fuel injection, rated between 65 and 375 hp, and details of these are given below.

It has long been known that Teledyne Continental has under development a totally new range of very advanced, high-speed aircraft piston-engines, having a hydrostatic drive to the propeller shaft and rated over a wide range of powers up to 700 hp. These engines have now materialised as the first of the "Tiara" range, on which the company is placing immense reliance for the period from about 1973 onwards. The first of this new family are described in this issue of *Jane's*.

In addition to this wholly new product-line, Teledyne Continental Motors are completing development of a new 425 hp engine in the traditional style.

In October 1960 it was announced that Rolls-Royce Ltd of England had acquired the licence to manufacture and sell certain engines from the complete range of Continental piston-engines throughout the world apart from the Americas and certain countries in the Far East. (See "Rolls-Royce" in UK section).

Continental Aviation and Engineering Division of Teledyne Continental Motors manufactures gas-turbine engines.

CONTINENTAL C90 SERIES
The C90 Series includes the C90-8F which has a flanged crankshaft but does not have provisions for installing either a starter or generator, the C90-12F and -14F which have a flanged crankshaft and Delco-Remy starter and generator, and the -16 which has a vacuum pump adapter.

C90 Series engines have an approved take-off rating of 95 hp at 2,625 rpm.
TYPE: Four-cylinder horizontally-opposed air-cooled.
CYLINDERS: Bore 4$\frac{1}{16}$ in (103·2 mm). Stroke 3$\frac{7}{8}$ in (98·4 mm). Capacity 201 cu in (3·28 litres). Compression ratio 7:1. Externally-finned aluminium alloy head castings, screwed and shrunk permanently on externally-finned steel barrels.

PISTONS: Cam ground aluminium castings. Three compression rings above pin. Top ring chrome-faced. Oil control ring below pin. Holes in groove provided for interior drain. Pins are full floating ground steel tubes with ground aluminium end plugs.
CONNECTING RODS: "I" beam-type, split bronze pin bushings, identical precision inserts (same as main bearings, steel-backed, lead alloy lined).
CRANKCASE: Aluminium alloy.
CRANKSHAFT: Steel alloy forging, with nitrided journals and crankpins for greater strength.
CAMSHAFT: Steel alloy forging.
VALVE GEAR: Exhaust valves are stellite-faced and stem tips are hardened. Bronze valve guides.
GEAR TRAIN: Torque is transmitted to engine components from the crankshaft via gears machined from alloy steel forgings, conforming to SAE specifications.
INDUCTION: Small float-type carburettor with a simplified manual mixture control.
FUEL GRADE: 80/87 octane minimum.
IGNITION: Radio shielded, impulse couples, small or standard size magnetos optional.
LUBRICATION SYSTEM: Magnesium crankcase cover houses the engine-driven gear-type oil pump. An oil pressure relief valve and oil screen are also mounted in the cover.
ACCESSORIES: 12V 20 or 35A alternator standard (12V 60A optional).
For other details, see table.

CONTINENTAL O-200 SERIES
The O-200-A engine is generally similar to the C90 Series engines. It is fitted with a single Marvel-Schebler updraught carburettor, dual Bendix-Scintilla magnetos and Delco-Remy starter and generator.

The O-200-B is similar to the O-200-A, but is designed for pusher installation.
For other details see table.

CONTINENTAL O-300 SERIES
The O-300 is a six-cylinder engine which uses the cylinders of the C90 Series. Equipment includes a Marvel MA-3SPA carburettor and Bendix Scintilla S6LN-21 magneto. General constructional details are otherwise similar to those of the C90 Series. Output is 145 hp.

The A and B Series engines are identical except that there is provision for a controllable-pitch propeller in the latter. The O-300-C has a different propeller flange and, in engines beyond serial No. 21,001, can have a 90° starter drive. This drive, with automatic engagement, is standard on the -D, together with a vacuum-pump drive. The -E differs from the -D in having a governor drive pad and crankshaft provision to supply governor oil to the propeller.

CONTINENTAL IO-346
The IO-346-A is a large-bore four-cylinder engine with a permold crankcase. The accessory case is integral with the crankcase, as with the 470 and 520 series. The IO-346-B incorporates a governor drive pad and crankshaft provision to supply governor oil to the propeller.
TYPE: Four-cylinder horizontally-opposed air-cooled, with fuel injection.
CYLINDERS: Bore 5·25 in (133·35 mm). Stroke 4·00 in (101·6 mm). Capacity 346 cu in (5·67 litres). Compression ratio 7·5 : 1. Forged steel barrels, screwed and shrunk into cast aluminium alloy finned heads.
PISTONS: Heat-treated aluminium alloy. Two compression and one oil control rings above gudgeon pin, one scraper ring below. Fully-floating ground steel tube gudgeon pins with pressed-in aluminium end-plugs.
CONNECTING RODS: Forged steel I-section. Big-end bearings thin-backed steel shelled of tri-metal bronze. Little-end bearings are split bronze bushings.
CRANKSHAFT: Four-throw steel alloy forging, running on four plain shell bearings.
CRANKCASE: Cast aluminium alloy, split along vertical centre plane.
VALVE GEAR: Two valves per cylinder. Steel inlet valves with hardened tips. Steel exhaust valves with hardened tips, faced with Stellite "F". Valve seats shrunk into position.

Top: **The 165 hp Teledyne Continental IO-346 flat-four engine**
Bottom: **The 210 hp Teledyne Continental IO-360 flat-six engine**

Camshaft in centre of crankcase beneath crankshaft, driven by gear from crankshaft. Positive roto-coil exhaust valve rotaters and removable hydraulic tappets.

INDUCTION: Air throttle assembly and intake tubes with Continental low-pressure continuous-flow fuel injection system. Engine-driven rotary-vane fuel pump, fuel mixture control, fuel metering unit, manifold chamber and direct-injection nozzles.

FUEL GRADE: 91/96 octane minimum.

IGNITION: One Bendix-Scintilla S4RN-205 magneto and one Bendix-Scintilla S4RN-201 magneto on top and rear of crankcase, driven by gears from crankshaft. Two Champion RHM-40E 18 mm spark-plugs per cylinder.

LUBRICATION SYSTEM: Wet sump type, with single gear-type pump.

PROPELLER DRIVE: Direct drive, clockwise when viewed from rear. ARP 502 Type I flange.

ACCESSORIES: Delco-Remy 12V alternator at front starboard side of crankcase. Tachometer drive (optional direction of rotation, 0·5 : 1 ratio with crankshaft) driven from oil pump at rear of engine. Fuel pump drive (clockwise, 1 : 1 ratio with crankshaft) at rear of crankcase. Two additional accessory drives (1 : 1 ratio and AND 20000 pads) at rear of crankcase. Optional vacuum pump and propeller governor.

STARTING: Delco-Remy 12V starter.

MOUNTING: Four dyna-focal ring-type mounting brackets at rear of crankcase.

DIMENSIONS, WEIGHTS AND PERFORMANCE: See Table.

SPECIFIC FUEL CONSUMPTION:
0·495 lb (0·225 kg)/hp/hr at 2,450 rpm

SPECIFIC OIL CONSUMPTION:
Max   0·012 lb (0·005 kg)/hp/hr at 2,450 rpm

CONTINENTAL IO-360 SERIES
The IO-360 is a six-cylinder horizontally-opposed air-cooled engine with fuel injection. Design and materials are generally similar to those described for IO-346-A engine, except for number and size of cylinders. Accessories include Harrison oil cooler, two Bendix Scintilla magnetos, propeller governor drive, vacuum

pump and 24V alternator. The IO-360 has a sandcast crankcase, with the accessory case mounted at the rear. The cylinders are shell-moulded.

The IO-360-C has a starter and accessory drive. The TSIO-360-A and -B have a turbocharger pressurised induction system, revised fuel system, starter and accessory drive, scavenge pump and full-flow oil cooler. These engines power the Cessna T337 Super Skymaster.

For further details see Table.

CONTINENTAL O-470 SERIES
Engines in the O-470 series (including the E-185 and E-225) are all basically similar. Following are the main differences in the various versions currently available.

The O-470 family of engines are manufactured in six power ranges, from 225 hp to 310 hp as follows:

225 hp O-470-A, C, E, J and IO-470-J, K.
230 hp O-470-K, L, R.
240 hp O-470-B, G, M, P.
250 hp IO-470-C, G P, R.
260 hp IO-470-D, E, F, H, L, M, N, S, U, V, and TSIO-470-B, C, D.
310 hp GIO-470-A.

The 225 hp and 230 hp models have a compression ratio of 7 : 1, the 240 hp and 250 hp models a ratio of 8 : 1, and the 260 hp models a ratio of 8·6 : 1.

O-470-G. As detailed description below, but with shell-moulded cylinder heads, different mounting and Bendix-Stromberg PSH-5BD automatic altitude-compensating updraught carburettor. Develops 240 hp at 2,600 rpm. 91/96 octane fuel. Weight 432 lb (196 kg).

O-470-J. As detailed description below. Develops 225 hp at 2,550 rpm. Weight 381 lb (173 kg).

O-470-K. Description below refers to this model.

O-470-L. As detailed description below, but with special intake manifold enabling carburettor to be installed approximately 4 in (102 mm) forward of position used on O-470-K. This requires a change in oil sump to provide clearance.

O-470-M. As detailed description below, but with shell-moulded cylinder heads and different mounting. Develops 240 hp at 2,600 rpm. 91/96 octane fuel. Weight 410 lb (186 kg).

O-470-P. Develops 240 hp at 2,600 rpm. 91/96 octane fuel. Weight 432 lb (196 kg).

O-470-R. Develops 230 hp at 2,600 rpm. 80/87 octane fuel. Weight 438 lb (199 kg). Powers Cessna 180, 182 and 188 and Wren 460.

The following description refers specifically to the O-470-K, but is generally applicable to all versions:

TYPE: Six-cylinder horizontally-opposed air-cooled.

CYLINDERS: Bore 5 in (127 mm). Stroke 4 in (101·6 mm). Swept volume 471 cu in (7·5 litres). Compression ratio 7 : 1. Forged steel barrels with integral cooling fins. Heat-treated cast aluminium alloy heads screwed and shrunk on to barrels.

PISTONS: Aluminium. Three rings, two compression and one oil control. Steel gudgeon-pins with circlip retainers.

CONNECTING RODS: Forged steel. Trimetal bronze replaceable type big-end bearings, bronze bushing little-ends.

CRANKSHAFT: One-piece six-throw chrome-nickel-molybdenum steel forging. Outer surfaces nitrided. Four 6th order counter-weights attached to shaft. Five bearings of replaceable shell type.

CRANKCASE: Two-piece heat-treated aluminium casting divided at vertical lengthwise plane through crankshaft, with integral cast accessory section.

VALVE GEAR: Two poppet-type valves per cylinder, one steel inlet and one steel exhaust with stellite seat. Camshaft gear-driven from crankshaft in lower part of crankcase.

INDUCTION: Marvel Schebler MA-4-5 horizontal pressure-type carburettor.

FUEL: 80/87 Octane.

IGNITION: Two Bendix-Scintilla Type S6RN-25 magnetos on top of accessory section. Two Champion RHD-39N spark-plugs per cylinder. Shielded ignition harness.

REPRESENTATIVE TELEDYNE CONTINENTAL HORIZONTALLY-OPPOSED ENGINES

Engine Model	No. of Cylinders	Bore and Stroke in (mm)	Capacity cu in (litres)	Power Ratings hp at rpm Take-off	Power Ratings hp at rpm M.E.T.O.	Comp. Ratio	Dry Weight lb (kg)	Length in (mm)	Width in (mm)	Height in (mm)	Octane No.
C90-16F	4	$4\frac{1}{16} \times 3\frac{7}{8}$ (103·2 × 98·4)	201 (3·28)	95 at 2,625	90 at 2,475	7·0 : 1	186 (84·4)	31·25 (794)	31·5 (800)	24·2 (615)	80/87
O-200B	4	$4\frac{1}{16} \times 3\frac{7}{8}$ (103·2 × 98·4)	201 (3·28)	100 at 2,750	100 at 2,750	7·0 : 1	220 (99·8)	28·53 (725)	31·56 (802)	23·18 (589)	80/87
O-300-A	6	$4\frac{1}{16} \times 3\frac{7}{8}$ (103·2 × 98·4)	301 (4·92)	145 at 2,700	145 at 2,700	7·0 : 1	268 (122)	39·75 (1,011)	31·5 (800)	23·25 (592)	80/87
IO-346-A	4	$5\frac{1}{4} \times 4$ (133 × 101·6)	346 (5·67)	165 at 2,700	165 at 2,700	7·5 : 1	296·5 (134·5)	30·00 (762)	33·38 (848)	22·48 (571)	91/96
IO-360-D	6	$4\frac{7}{16} \times 3\frac{7}{8}$ (112·5 × 98·4)	360 (5·9)	210 at 2,800	210 at 2,800	8·5 : 1	327 (148·3)	34·53 (877)	31·40 (798)	24·33 (618)	100/130
TSIO-360-A	6	$4\frac{7}{16} \times 3\frac{7}{8}$ (112·5 × 98·4)	360 (5·9)	210 at 2,800	210 at 2,800	7·5 : 1	334 (151·5)	35·84* (910)	33·03 (838)	23·75 (603)	100/130
IO-470-D	6	5×4 (127 × 101·6)	471 (7·7)	260 at 2,625	260 at 2,625	8·6 : 1	426 (193·2)	43·31 (1,100)	33·56 (852)	19·75 (502)	100/130
O-470-R	6	5×4 (127 × 101·6)	471 (7·7)	230 at 2,600	230 at 2,600	7·0 : 1	438 (199)	36·03 (915)	33·56 (852)	28·42 (723)	80/87
TSIO-470-D	6	5×4 (127 × 101·6)	471 (7·7)	260 at 2,600	260 at 2,600	7·5 : 1	511 (231·8)	58·07 (1,465)	33·56 (852)	20·25 (514)	100/130
IO-520-A	6	$5\frac{1}{4} \times 4$ (133 × 101·6)	520 (8·5)	285 at 2,700	285 at 2,700	8·5 : 1	471 (213·6)	41·41 (1,053)	33·56 (852)	19·75 (502)	100/130
IO-520-B	6	$5\frac{1}{4} \times 4$ (133 × 101·6)	520 (8·5)	285 at 2,700	285 at 2,700	8·5 : 1	457 (207·3)	39·71 (1,009)	33·58 (853)	26·71 (678)	100/130
IO-520-D	6	$5\frac{1}{4} \times 4$ (133 × 101·6)	520 (8·5)	300 at 2,850	285 at 2,700	8·5 : 1	454 (205·9)	37·36 (949)	35·46 (901)	23·79 (604)	100/130
TSIO-520-B	6	$5\frac{1}{4} \times 4$ (133 × 101·6)	520 (8·5)	285 at 2,700	285 at 2,700	8·5 : 1	483 (219)	58·67 (1,490)	33·56 (852)	20·32 (516)	100/130
TSIO-520-C	6	$5\frac{1}{4} \times 4$ (133 × 101·6)	520 (8·5)	285 at 2,700	285 at 2,700	7·5 : 1	460 (208·7)	40·91* (1,040)	33·56 (852)	20·04 (509)	100/130
TSIO-520-E	6	$5\frac{1}{4} \times 4$ (133 × 101·6)	520 (8·5)	300 at 2,700	300 at 2,700	7·5 : 1	483 (219)	39·75* (1,010)	33·56 (852)	20·74 (527)	100/130
TSIO-520-J	6	$5\frac{1}{4} \times 4$ (133 × 101·6)	520 (8·5)	310 at 2,700	310 at 2,700	7·5 : 1	487·8 (221·3)	39·25 (997)	33·56 (852)	20·32 (516)	100/130
GTSIO-520-C	6	$5\frac{1}{4} \times 4$ (133 × 101·6)	520 (8·5)	340 at 3,200	340 at 3,200	7·5 : 1	557 (252·7)	63·5 (1,612·9)	34·04 (880)	23·1 (587)	100/130
GTSIO-520-D	6	$5\frac{1}{4} \times 4$ (133 × 101·6)	520 (8·5)	375 at 3,400	375 at 3,400	7·5 : 1	550 (250)	64·25 (1,630)	34·04 (880)	26·78 (680)	100/130
Tiara Series											
4-180	4	$4\frac{7}{8} \times 3\frac{5}{8}$ (123·8 × 92·08)	271 (4·44)	180 at 4,000	135 at 3,600	9·0 : 1	264 (120)	33·86 (860)	32·82 (834)	20·85 (530)	100/130
6-285A	6	$4\frac{7}{8} \times 3\frac{5}{8}$ (123·8 × 92·08)	406 (6·65)	285 at 4,000	214 at 3,700	9·0 : 1	354 (161)	41·17 (1,046)	32·82 (834)	20·85 (530)	100/130
T6-285	6	$4\frac{7}{8} \times 3\frac{5}{8}$ (123·8 × 92·08)	406 (6·65)	285 at 4,000	214 at 3,600	8·0 : 1	402 (182)	41·17 (1,046)	32·82† (834)	20·85 (530)	100/130
6-320	6	$4\frac{7}{8} \times 3\frac{5}{8}$ (123·8 × 92·08)	406 (6·65)	320 at 4,400	240 at 4,000	9·6 : 1	354 (161)	41·17 (1,046)	32·82 (834)	20·85 (530)	100/130
T6-320	6	$4\frac{7}{8} \times 3\frac{5}{8}$ (123·8 × 92·08)	406 (6·65)	320 at 4,400	240 at 4,000	8·0 : 1	412 (187)	45·85 (1,165)	32·82 (834)	20·85 (530)	100/130
T8-450	8	$4\frac{7}{8} \times 3\frac{5}{8}$ (123·8 × 92·08)	542 (8·88)	450 at 4,400	338 at 4,000	8·0 : 1	513 (233)	53·16 (1,350)	32·82 (834)	23·45 (596)	100/130

*Not including turbocharger; † with side-mounted turbocharger, 29·95 in (761 mm).

LUBRICATION: Pressure type. Harrison oil-cooler on front of crankcase. Oil filter in crankcase. One impeller type pump. Oil pressure 30-60 lb/sq in (2·1-4·2 kg/cm²).

PROPELLER DRIVE: RH drive. Direct. Flanged propeller shaft. Provision for Hartzell constant-speed propeller.

ACCESSORIES: Delco-Remy generator on accessory section. Drives for vacuum pump and tachometer.

STARTING: Delco-Remy electric starter.

MOUNTING: Four mounting points, one at each lower corner of crankcase.

DIMENSIONS, WEIGHTS AND PERFORMANCE: See Table.

CONTINENTAL IO-470 SERIES

The fifteen engines of this series (IO-470-C-H, J-N and P, R, S, V) are basically similar to the O-470 Series, but feature fuel-injection. Current models in production include the K for the Beech B33 Debonair, L for the Beech B55 Baron and V for the Cessna 310K and 310L.

CONTINENTAL TSIO-470

This engine is basically similar to the IO-470 but has a turbocharger. For details see Table.

CONTINENTAL GIO-470-A

This engine is basically similar to the IO-470, but is geared, with a ratio of 0·750 : 1, and has a compression ratio of 8·6 : 1. Rating is 310 hp at the considerably increased crankshaft speed of 3,200 rpm.

CONTINENTAL IO-520 SERIES

These engines are basically similar to the IO-470, but with cylinders of larger bore. They are manufactured with both sandcast and permold crankcases. Engines with a permold case have an alternator mounting pad at the right front of the crankcase and driven off a face gear attached to the crankshaft. All IO-520 engines are rated at 285 hp METO apart from the IO-520-D, -E, -F and -G which have a take-off rating of 300 hp. IO-520 engines power the Beechcraft Baron S35 Bonanza and B33A Debonair, Navion and Cessna 210. New in 1970 are the generally similar IO-520-J, -K and -L, again rated at 285 hp (-K and -L are cleared to 300 hp at 2,850 rpm at take-off).

The TSIO-520 series are turbocharged. Take-off rating is again 285 hp except for the -E and -G, rated at 300 hp, and the TSIO-520-J rated at 310 hp and equipped with an intercooler and provision for an over-boost valve. These engines power the Cessna 320D, T210 and 210F and Beech Turbo Bonanza.

For other details see Table.

CONTINENTAL GTSIO-520

This is similar to the TSIO-520 range but is geared and uprated. The -C model, rated at 340 hp at 3,200 rpm, powers the Cessna 411; the GTSIO-520-D, rated at 375 hp at 3,400 rpm, powers the Cessna 421.

CONTINENTAL TIARA SERIES

Teledyne Continental Motors is to start production in late 1970 of a comprehensive new range of general aviation piston-engines of air-cooled horizontally-opposed geared design known as the Tiara family. When fully launched the new series will comprise four-, six- and eight-cylinder models spanning a power bracket of 180 to over 500 hp, with fuel injection and turbo-charged versions at each power level. Prime technical features of the new engines are higher specific powers, lower specific weight, smoother and quieter operation and longer service life.

Above: **The 375 hp Teledyne Continental GTSIO-520-D**

Right: **The 310 hp Teledyne Continental TSIO-520-J, power plant of the 1970 Cessna 414**

Design and engineering of the Tiara series was initiated early in 1965 with the object of establishing a completely new generation of aircraft piston-engines. A major $20m development and pre-production test programme was planned, involving 46 prototype engines (initially identified as the GIO-366). By January 1970 these had completed 5,000 hr development testing, 11,000 hr endurance running and 2,000 hr life testing. This programme included 56 type test cycles, and several hundred flight test hours have been completed in a special Beech D18 flying test-bed (with standard Continental TSIO-520s in the wing nacelles and a trial engine in the nose) and in Continental's engineering fleet comprising a Cessna 206, Cessna 175, Cessna Cardinal, Piper Cherokee Arrow and Beechcraft Debonair.

In addition, sample engines have been supplied to major US general aircraft manufacturers for flight evaluation, Environmental testing in California, South Dakota and the central Gulf states has covered the full range of conditions likely to be experienced in service.

FAA certification of all models is scheduled to be completed ahead of production avail-ability. Type tests are being performed using engines equipped with all major accessories, and running a 150 hr cycle with 100 hr at maximum power and 50 hr at selected cruise settings. Models 6-260A and 6-285 received flight certification during 1969 and three further models are scheduled for certification in 1970. Tiara designations comprise a digit indicating the number of cylinders and a dash number indicating power rating; a T prefix is used for turbocharged variants.

Ninety-five per cent of all parts and components comprising the three main series of four-, six-, and eight- cylinder models of the Tiara family are interchangeable on all engines. This major feature of the new series is intended to promote economy of manufacture, reducing spare parts inventories, and simplifying servicing in the field. Standard models of starters, generators, alternators, pumps and other accessory equipment have been extensively tested and certified for use in Tiara engines. A majority of accessories certified are standard off-the-shelf items, obtainable worldwide.

Most significant among the engineering features introduced in the Tiara family is a

The 285 hp Teledyne Continental IO-520-A engine

Right: **Cutaway drawing of the 285 hp Teledyne Continental TSIO-520-B engine**

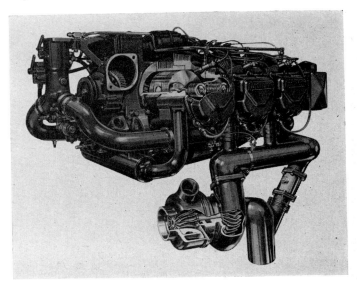

Above: **Teledyne Continental's range of Tiara high-speed piston-engines is going into production in 1970.   Smallest member of the family yet announced is the 4-180 (upper left), rated at 180 hp; the 6-260, of 260 hp, is pictured (upper right) installed in a Piper Cherokee Arrow; turbocharged version of one of the initial production engines is the T6-285 (lower left); the largest Tiara engines have eight cylinders, the 8-380 of 380 hp (lower right) being the naturally-aspirated counterpart of the T8-450**

Below: **Test-bed aircraft flying with Tiara engines: (upper left) Beechcraft Debonair;   (upper right) Piper Cherokee Arrow;   (lower left) Cessna 206; (lower right) Beech 18 with TSIO-520 wing engines and nose-mounted Tiara**

totally new system of torsional vibration control developed by Continental to reduce engine vibration. The new system, designated VTC (vibratory torque control), eliminates the conventional crankshaft pendulum dampers and introduces automatic dual-frequency control which arranges that the propeller drive-shaft is driven either "solidly" or flexibly by a quill shaft.

By this means a major reduction in vibratory torque is achieved in the crankshaft, propeller gearing, propeller and accessory systems. This in turn permits the use of lighter, slower and quieter propellers. Stresses in engine components are also reduced, allowing the use of lighter parts and higher rpm.

The cylinder barrel and cylinder head are of lighter-weight design than hitherto, offering enhanced cooling, lower manufacturing cost and ease of servicing and replacement. The head is a shell-moulded casting providing greater uniformity of dimensions and permitting the use of thinner fins. As a result, the Tiara cylinder design requires approximately a quarter less cooling air pressure than contemporary engines. The crankcase for each of the three series embodies a power section, accessory section and reduction gear section.

As a consequence of operating at higher engine rpm, the camshaft rpm is compatible with that of the propeller. A single pair of spur gears of 2 : 1 ratio drives both the propeller and camshaft. This novel arrangement eliminates the two gears normally required to drive the camshaft, thus saving weight and cost, and the lower-speed propeller is significantly quieter.

Only seven gears instead of the normal 13 are required for the accessory gearing. The train drives seven side-mounted accessories including

the oil pump and, in the turbocharged models, an additional scavenge pump. Hypoid gears provide a right-angle drive from the rear end of the camshaft, facilitating vertical positioning of the accessory section to control overall height.

Common features of all models include a cylinder bore and stroke of 4⅞ in (123·8 mm) and 3⅝ in (92·08 mm) respectively, overhead valves, dual ignition, a Teledyne Continental fuel injection system, a minimum fuel grade of 100/130 aviation gasoline, and a lubrication system having a wet sump of 8 quarts (4·55 litres) capacity with full-flow filtering and using SAE 50 grade oil for sea level ambient conditions above 40°F (4°C) and SAE 30 or 10W-30 below this temperature.

Accessory drives and mounts are provided for a tachometer, two magnetos, a starter, a belt-driven alternator, and a propeller governor. In addition there are two spare drives.

In meeting the design objective of increased power/weight ratio, the four- and six-cylinder models are slightly above one pound per horse-power and the six-cylinder models is below one pound per horsepower. These figures compare with contemporary engines of between 1·5 and 2 lb/hp.

Continental is establishing a highly-automated production line capable of producing 10,000 engines per year. All components for the new Tiara series have been designed to facilitate manufacture using modern, high-speed automated machine tools. This is aimed at minimising the production labour force and assists in achieving engine prices comparable with contemporary engines of the same power bracket.

A product support programme for the Tiara series is already underway, including service

training classes for Teledyne Continental and airframe manufacturers' personnel, and distributors and dealers. Nearly 50 per cent of major components released for production are being allocated to a replacement parts pool for support of Tiara engines worldwide. Some Tiara variants announced to date are as follows (data are included in the table on page 782.)

Model 4-180. Four-cylinder naturally-aspirated engine of 180 hp (182 cv). Flight testing scheduled for late 1970.

Model T6-260. Six-cylinder turbocharged engine of 260 hp (264 cv). Has completed all required development, endurance type and flight tests, and has been granted FAA type certificate. Flown in nose of Beechcraft D18 and Beechcraft Debonair. Initial production engine in Tiara series (with 6-285A).

Model 6-285A. Six-cylinder naturally-aspirated engine of 285 hp (289 cv). Has completed all required development, endurance, type and flight tests, and has been granted FAA type certificate. Service flight testing to 1,000 hr is well advanced, installed in Cessna 206 and Piper Cherokee Arrow. Initial production engine in Tiara series (with T6-260).

Model T6-285. Six-cylinder turbocharged engine of 285 hp (289 cv). Dual rear-mounted turbochargers.

Model 6-320. Six-cylinder naturally-aspirated engine of 320 hp (324 cv).

Model T6-320. Six-cylinder turbocharged engine of 320 hp (324 cv). High-altitude flight testing underway with engine mounted in nose of Beech D18. Service flight testing to 1,000 hr scheduled for summer 1970.

Model T8-450. Eight-cylinder turbocharged engine of 450 hp (456 cv). Has flown in nose of Beech D18.

TELEDYNE CAE

HEAD OFFICE:
1330 Laskey Road, Toledo, Ohio 43601
PRESIDENT: James L. Murray
VICE-PRESIDENTS:
Al Auerbach (Operations)
Henry C. Maskey (Engineering)
Eugene R. Sullivan (Finance)
MARKETING DIRECTOR: Robert P. Schiller

Teledyne CAE (formerly Continental Aviation and Engineering) became a division of Teledyne Inc during 1969. Teledyne CAE has long experience in the design, development and production of gas-turbine engines, and is now devoted exclusively to turbine engine work.

The headquarters for management, marketing, finance, engineering and production has been moved from Detroit and is now housed in the Toledo, Ohio, facility of over 350,000 square feet (32,500 m²). The Neosho, Missouri, facility (also over 350,000 sq ft) overhauls and makes turbine spare parts and gears for turbine engines.

Main turbine engine sales are concerned with the well-established J69 series of engines. A company-sponsored project is currently underway for a new family of turbine engines.

TELEDYNE CAE J69

The J69 was originally the Turboméca Marboré which has been developed to meet American requirements. Four versions are currently available as follows:

J69-T-25. (Teledyne CAE Model 352-5A). Long-life version, which powers the Cessna T-37B trainer and is FAA certificated as the Model CJ69-1025. Its air mass flow is 19·8 lb (9 kg)/sec.

J69-T-29. (Teledyne CAE Model 356-7A). Powers the Ryan BQM-34A subsonic target drone. Max rating of 1,700 lb (771 kg) st at 22,000 rpm. Operational ceiling is 60,000 ft (18,300 m). This is the Continental counterpart to the Turboméca Gourdon turbojet, comprising a Marboré II with the addition of a single-stage transonic axial compressor supercharging the centrifugal stage.

J69-T-41A. Rated at 1,920 lb (871 kg) st.

In production as improved version of J69-T-29 powering special-purpose subsonic target drones.

YJ69-T-406. (Teledyne CAE Model 356-34A). Rated at 1,920 lb (871 kg) st for the US Navy's Ryan BQM-34E supersonic target drone. Initial qualification testing was completed during 1967 and deliveries of production engines began in 1969. The T-406 engine can propel the BQM-34E to Mach 1·5 at 60,000 ft (18,300 m) altitude.

The J69-T-29, YJ69-T-406 and J69-T-41A have a single-stage axial compressor ahead of the standard centrifugal compressor. Combustion system and turbine arrangements are basically the same as on the J69-T-25.

DIMENSIONS (nominal):
Length overall:
J69-T-25   50·00 in (1,270 mm)
YJ69-T-406, J69-T-41A and J69-T-29
     46·25 in (1,175 mm)
Width:
J69-T-25   22·30 in (566 mm)
YJ69-T-406, J69-T-41A and J69-T-29
     22·36 in (568 mm)

DRY WEIGHT:
J69-T-25   364 lb (165 kg)
J69-T-29   340 lb (155 kg)
J69-T-41A   350 lb (159 kg)
YJ69-T-406   360 lb (163 kg)

The J100-CA-100 turbojet engine

The Teledyne CAE J69-T-25 turbojet engine

The J69-T-29 turbojet engine

PERFORMANCE RATINGS:
Max rating:
J69-T-25   1,025 lb (465 kg) st at 21,730 rpm
J69-T-29   1,700 lb (771 kg) st at 22,000 rpm
J69-T-41A   1,920 lb (871 kg) st at 22,000 rpm
YJ69-T-406 1,920 lb (871 kg) st at 22,150 rpm

Normal rating:
J69-T-25   880 lb (400 kg) st at 20,700 rpm
J69-T-29   1,375 lb (625 kg) st at 20,790 rpm

SPECIFIC FUEL CONSUMPTIONS:
At max rating:
J69-T-25   1·14
J69-T-41A, J69-T-29   1·10

YJ69-T-406   1·11
At normal rating:
J69-T-25   1·12
J69-T-29   1·085

TELEDYNE CAE J100-CA-100 (356-28A)
The Model 356-28A has been developed by Teledyne CAE as a power plant for drones and other unmanned aircraft. The engine is derived from the J69 family but has a two-stage transonic axial compressor ahead of the centrifugal stage. The combustion chamber is annular with centrifugal fuel injection. The turbine has two axial stages, each fitted with replaceable blades. Fixed geometry is used throughout, although the engine

is at present operating at altitudes in excess of 75,000 ft (22,860 m).
The J100-CA-100 completed its 18-hour qualification test in June 1968. No details can be given of its applications, but the engine carries the new Department of Defense designation system.

WEIGHT, DRY: 430 lb (193 kg)
PERFORMANCE RATINGS:
Max rating   2,700 lb (1,225 kg) at 20,700 rpm
Normal rating 2,430 lb (1,102 kg) at 20,120 rpm
SPECIFIC FUEL CONSUMPTIONS:
At max rating   1·10
At normal rating   1·08

THIOKOL
THIOKOL CHEMICAL CORPORATION
CORPORATE OFFICE:
Bristol, Pennsylvania 19007
SOLID PROPELLANT ROCKET MOTOR PLANTS:
Elkton, Maryland
Huntsville, Alabama
Marshall, Texas
Brigham City, Utah
PYROTECHNIC AND ORDNANCE PLANTS:
Marshall, Texas
Rockaway, New Jersey
Woodbine, Georgia
CHAIRMAN OF THE BOARD AND CHIEF EXECUTIVE OFFICER:
J. W. Crosby
PRESIDENT:
Dr. H. W. Ritchey
VICE-PRESIDENT AND TREASURER:
A. P. Roeper
GROUP VICE-PRESIDENTS:
R. E. Davis (General Products)
J. S. Jorczak (Industrial/Chemical)
R. L. Marquardt (Economic Development)
J. W. Wiggins (Aerospace)

Organised in 1929, Thiokol Chemical Corporation produced and marketed the first synthetic rubber manufactured in the United States. In 1943, the discovery by Thiokol of liquid polymer, a new type of synthetic rubber, paved the way for the practical development of the "case-bonded" principle of rocket power plant design. The company's polysulphide liquid polymer proved to be the catalyst for the first mass production of efficient solid-propellant rocket motors, as well as for the development of large solid-propellant motors. The firm's operations have now been organized into separate groups to serve widening areas of related products.

The Thiokol Aerospace Group currently operates facilities located at Bristol, Pennsylvania; Elkton, Maryland; Brigham City and Ogden, Utah; Woodbine, Georgia; Rockaway, New Jersey; Huntsville, Alabama; and Marshall, Texas. The major products of these plants include pyrotechnic and ordnance devices, remote environmental sensing equipment, sounding rockets and rocket propulsion systems.

Through its Economic Development Group, Thiokol participates in the challenging socio-economic area. This group provides education and skills training at Clearfield, Utah; Atlanta, Georgia; and Roswell, New Mexico.

A very wide range of interests is vested in the General Products Group: sheet metal and jet engine components at East Granby, Connecticut; spraying equipment and closures in Miami, Florida; medical electronic instruments in Los Angeles, California; synthetic fibres production and weaving capability for the carpet, automotive and bag industries in Waynesboro, Virginia; Toccoa, Georgia; and Paramount, California, as well as in Canada and Scotland; and kitchen cabinets and decorative tiles in San Antonio, Texas.

The Industrial Chemical Group in Trenton, New Jersey, and Moss Point, Mississippi, supplies sealants for automotive, aircraft, construction and marine use, as well as friction materials and laminates in a variety of forms. Its Logan, Utah, plant produces off-highway tracked vehicles used at construction sites, in swamps and by ski resorts.

Available details of some of the more important Thiokol liquid and solid-propellant rocket engines used in manned aircraft, guided missiles and space vehicles are given below.

THIOKOL 156-INCH BOOSTER MOTORS (TU-412, 156-2C1, TU-393, TU-312, TU-562)
Military designations: 156-1, 156-2, 156-7, 156-8, and 156-9
The 156-in (3·96 m) diameter solid-propellant rocket motors were designed primarily to demonstrate feasibility of such very large motors and control systems for possible future missile and space launch applications. The test vehicles were made in both monolithic and segmented configurations, ranging in length from approximately 20 ft (6·1 m) to 100 ft (304·8 m). They produced thrust levels varying from approximately 388,000 lb (176,000 kg) over a 2-minute firing time to 3,250,000 lb (1,477,000 kg) over a 60-second firing time.

Motor cases were manufactured of 18 per cent nickel steel for the 156-1, 156-2 and 156-9 motors. The monolithic case for the 156-7 motor was of glass-fibre reinforced plastic, as was the segmented case for the 156-8 motor.

Propellants for all these motors used polybutadiene acrylonitrile terpolymer binder with ammonium perchlorate oxidizer and aluminium additives. Nozzles for thrust-vector control included external fixed, submerged fixed, external movable and submerged movable types. Hot-gas secondary injection and flexible-bearing thrust-vector control schemes were demonstrated. All necessary technologies for a development programme have been demonstrated, and no further feasibility demonstration effort is currently planned.

THIOKOL TE-260G
The TE-260G rocket motor for the Subroc missile incorporates both directional control and thrust reversal. It consists of a cylindrical case containing the Thiokol propellant charge, a dual forward bulkhead design incorporating a thrust-reversal system, and an aft bulkhead containing four nozzles, each of which is equipped with a jetavator thrust vector control system. Six cable-carrying conduits run the full length of the case on the inside wall to allow guidance signals to be transmitted to the aft vector control system.

The TE-260G employs a composite solid propellant which is bonded to the case wall.

Its principal constituents are polyurethane fuel binder and ammonium perchlorate oxidizer in a propellant system designed to provide a high specific impulse and a low burning rate. Thiokol developed the polyurethane system specifically to meet the Subroc requirements. This motor remained in production during 1969.

THIOKOL TU-122
Military designation: M-55
The TU-122 is the first-stage rocket motor for the solid-propellant Minuteman ICBM. The motor is approximately 25 ft (7·62 m) in length, 5 ft 6 in (1·68 m) in diameter, and weighs about 50,000 lb (22,680 kg). It produces approximately 200,000 lb (90,700 kg) thrust during a 60-second firing time.

The motor case is manufactured from D6AC steel. The composite solid propellant employs a polybutadiene acrylic acid polymer binder with ammonium perchlorate oxidizer and aluminium powder additives. Thrust vector control is achieved through the use of four movable nozzles. Advanced versions continue in production for the LGM-30G; over 1,000 of earlier versions have been delivered.

THIOKOL TU-289
Military designation: SR49-TC-1
The TU-289 solid-propellant rocket motor powers the AIR-2A Genie unguided air-to-air missile. It replaces an earlier motor, and has

Thiokol TU-122, the stage-1 Minuteman motor, on an in-plant transporter at Brigham City

Thiokol TU-289 motor for the Genie air-to-air nuclear rocket, being prepared for static firing at the company's Wasatch Division at Brigham City

an improved propellant which increases the storage life and permits the missile to be deployed in a wide range of environmental temperatures. This motor remains in production.

THIOKOL TX-12
Military designation: XM-100

The XM-100, produced by Thiokol's Longhorn Division, is a solid-propellant rocket motor used in the Sergeant surface-to-surface missile. The case and nozzle are of steel, and an igniter motor is used.

The XM-100 is the production version of the TX-12, developed at Thiokol's Huntsville Division. Production is complete.

THIOKOL TX-131-15
Military designation: XM-51

The TX-131-15 is the solid-propellant rocket motor which launches and boosts the Bomarc IM-99B interceptor missile to cruise speed and altitude. The motor is approximately 18 ft (5,400 mm) in length by 3 ft (910 mm) in diameter, and weighs about 7,800 lb (3,545 kg). It produces approximately 50,000 lb (22,665 kg) thrust during a 30-second firing time.

The motor case is manufactured of AISI 4330 steel. The composite propellant employs a polysulphide polymer binder with ammonium perchlorate oxidizer and aluminium powder additives. A blast tube extends the nozzle aft of the case. Two concentric jetevator rings assist in thrust vector control of the missile during boost. The motor remains in production.

THIOKOL TX-174
Military designation: XM-105

The TX-174 Pershing first-stage motor is a high-performance solid-propellant rocket motor designed for use over a wide temperature range. The case is manufactured of modified AISI H-11 or D6 AC steel. To provide high performance with minimum weight, the nozzle is fabricated largely from lightweight plastic materials. Only the ring used to attach the nozzle to the motor case is of steel.

The motor case is coated on the interior with a thin layer of heat-resistant liner to promote adherence of the case-bonded propellant. Pre-moulded plastic insulation is bonded to the case to protect areas exposed to hot gas flow. The motor is designed for optimum performance at or near sea level, but is readily adaptable to vacuum conditions. Production is complete.

THIOKOL TX-175
Military designation: XM-106

The TX-175 Pershing second-stage motor is a high-performance solid-propellant rocket motor designed for use over a wide temperature range. The case is of modified AISI H-11 or D6AC steel. The cylindrical section is formed in a single piece by spinning from a forged blank. The nozzle is fabricated of lightweight plastic materials, with the exception of the attachment ring, which is steel.

A bond-enhancing coating is applied to the interior of the case to promote adherence of the case-bonded propellant. Plastic insulation is bonded to the interior of the case to protect areas exposed to hot gas flow.

The TX-175 differs from the TX-174 primarily in size and weight and in the incorporation of an impulse system, with three equally-spaced ports, in the head-end. These ports are closed with a retained dome and are fitted with blast tubes. They are used for thrust reversal as required.

The TX-175 motor is designed for optimum performance under near-vacuum conditions, but is readily adaptable to sea-level performance. Production is complete.

THIOKOL TU-223
Military designation: M16E3

The TU-223 solid-propellant rocket motor launches and boosts the Martin B-61B Mace guided missile to flight velocity. The motor is approximately 10 ft (3,040 mm) long by 2 ft (610 mm) in diameter, and weighs approximately 2,900 lb (1,318 kg). It produces approximately 100,000 lb (45,450 kg) thrust over a firing time of approximately 2·5 seconds. The motor case is manufactured of 4130 steel. The polysulphide-polymer-based propellant includes ammonium perchlorate oxidizer and metallic fuel.

THIOKOL TE-M-29 (RECRUIT)

The Recruit was developed for the X-17 re-entry test vehicle. It is especially useful for sounding rockets, sleds and auxiliary boost applications because of its high overall performance. The TE-M-29-1 version was used in the X-17, Project Argus, Project Farside, Trailblazer and Stripi Programmes. Its total loaded weight is 361·5 lb (164 kg); it is 105·28 in (2,674 mm) long and 9 in (229 mm) in diameter. Used with the TE-P-372 pyrogen or TE-I-436 pyrotechnic igniter, it is supplied with 6°, 6·5°, 9°, or 9·5° standard canted adapters. The TE-M-29-2, used in the Project Farside, Little Joe I

Thiokol TX-131-15 (Bomarc M51-U520 booster) being prepared for static test in bay T-6 at Brigham City

The Thiokol TE-M-364-3 rocket engine

and II and Squirt programmes, uses a 4·26 : 1 expansion ratio nozzle. The TE-M-29-3 provides boost to the Athena first stage; it has a 5° 56' canted adapter. The TE-M-29-4 is the retro motor for the S-IVB stage of Saturn V, and the TE-M-29-5 is the retro motor for the S-IV stage of Saturn IB.

THIOKOL TE-M-424 (SATURN S-IC RETRO)

This motor was developed to serve as retrograde propulsion on the S-IC Saturn V first stage. Eight motors are employed for each launch. The TE-M-424 is man-rated because it is used in the Apollo programme. Motor length is 84·3 in (2,141 mm) and diameter is 15·2 in (386 mm). The motor produces 87,800 lb (39,825 kg) thrust for 0·633 seconds. Total motor weight is 504·5 lb (228·8 kg).

Thiokol TE-M-424 rocket motor at Elkton. Eight of these 87,800 lb (39,825 kg) st motors serve as retrograde (braking) propulsion on the Saturn S-IC stage

THIOKOL TE-M-82 (CAJUN)

The TE-M-82-4 is used as the second stage of the Nike-Cajun atmospheric research and target missiles. The motor is 107·98 in (2,743 mm) long and uses an extruded aluminium tube, a forged aluminium headcap and nozzle body, and a head-end insertable pyrogen igniter. It is a cheap, reliable and relatively high-performance motor available off-the-shelf. The TE-M-82-2 version was designed for sled applications. It uses the same loaded case assembly with a nozzle of 7·2 : 1 expansion ratio, closed headcap and pyrotechnic igniter. The TE-M-82-3 was designed for single- or first-stage applications and target missile systems. It uses the basic loaded case and closed headcap with pyrotechnic igniter and 3·61 : 1 expansion ratio nozzle.

THIOKOL TE-M-146 (CHEROKEE)

The TE-M-146 rocket motor was developed for NASA. Its high ratio of thrust to frontal area qualifies it for sled applications, and its configuration makes it particularly adaptable to single-staging, multi-staging or clustering for use in sounding rockets. An example of a clustering application is the second stage of the Squirt vehicle which has a cluster of seven Cherokees.

THIOKOL TE-M-307 (APACHE)

The TE-M-307-3 rocket motor was designed for second-stage applications, and therefore includes a 20-second delay igniter. It is 107·91 in (2,741 mm) long, 6·86 in (174·2 mm) in diameter and is used both as a sounding rocket and as a target missile. The TE-M-307-4 version was designed for single-stage applications. It uses the same loaded case and headcap assembly as the TE-M-307-3 with a 3·32 : 1 expansion ratio nozzle and an instantaneous TE-P-415 pyrogen. It is also used as a sounding rocket and as a target missile.

THIOKOL TE-M-364-2 and 3 (BURNER II and DELTA)

The TE-M-364-2 rocket motor is a 37 in (939·8 mm) diameter spherical main retro-rocket engine designed for the Surveyor and modified for use on the Burner II stage. Modifications consisted of increasing propellant loading to 1,440 lb (653 kg) and strengthening the attachment structure to accommodate higher inertial loads.

The TE-M-364-3 is a Surveyor main retro-rocket engine modified for use as third-stage propulsion on the Improved Delta vehicle. Modifications consisted of again increasing propellant load to 1,440 lb, re-designing the attachment structure to mate with the Delta launch vehicle and changing the diameter to 37·49 in (952·3 mm).

The Thiokol TE-M-364-2 rocket engine

THIOKOL TE-M-442-1 (BURNER IIA)

This motor is spherical, 26·1 in (663 mm) in diameter and 33·05 in (839 mm) long; propellant weight is 525 lb (238 kg) and total motor weight is 576 lb (261 kg). The TE-M-442-1 was developed from the TE-M-442 of 1965 and features a case of titanium instead of steel. It will fly as an additional stage to the standard Burner II launch vehicle, atop the TE-M-364-2 second stage.

Thiokol TE-M-479 rocket engine

Thiokol TE-M-442-1 rocket engine

THIOKOL TE-M-479

The TE-M-479 is a 17·4 in (442 mm) spherical rocket motor developed for NASA's Radio Astronomy Explorer satellite programme. The motor is 27·06 in (687 mm) long and serves as the apogee kick stage which makes the orbit of the spacecraft truly circular. Total motor weight is 173·8 lb (78·8 kg); propellant weight is 153 lb (69·4 kg). High mass-fraction and excellent performance reproducibility characterize this motor for space systems application. The TE-M-479 was first flown in July 1968.

Thiokol TU-223 Mace launch motor

Thiokol TE-M-521 rocket engine

THIOKOL TE-M-521

This 17·5 in (444 mm) diameter and 38·6 in (980 mm) long motor was developed by adding a 6·9 in (175 mm) straight section to the spherical TE-M-479 (RAE) motor. The TE-M-521 has a propellant weight of 247 lb (112 kg) and a total weight of 273·2 lb (123·9 kg). It served to 'circularize' the orbit of the Skynet satellite launched in November 1969. The motor has a titanium case and flight-proven propellant. It was the first flight motor to demonstrate the added-cylindrical-section method of obtaining more total impulse.

Thiokol TE-M-541 rocket engine

THIOKOL TE-M-541/542 (DMU)

This small glass-fibre motor measures 6·2 in (157 mm) in diameter and 14 in (356 mm) long and serves in a classified space application. Using the same hardware, with minor insulation changes, the motor is loaded to either of two configurations: 10·7 lb (4·85 kg), 3,075 lb-sec (1,395 kg-sec) total impulse, 13·2 lb (5·99 kg) total weight (TE-M-541); and 7·2 lb (3·27 kg), 2,050 lb-sec (930 kg-sec) total impulse, 10·6 lb (4·8 kg) total weight (TE-M-542). These motors have an extensive flight history.

THIOKOL TE-M-380 (APOLLO TOWER JETTISON)

The TE-M-380 motor is mounted on top of the Apollo launch escape motor. This 528 lb (239·5 kg) jettison motor, with two canted and skewed nozzles, is used to separate the launch escape tower from the Command Module on each Apollo flight.

THIOKOL TE-M-388 (IROQUOIS)

The TE-M-388 was developed as an outgassing test rocket motor to determine if upper air contamination by rocket exhaust could be reduced. It is currently used as the second stage of the Nike-Iroquois sounding vehicle. Its length is 104·4 in (2,652 mm) and the diameter 7·75 in (197 mm).

THIOKOL TE-M-473 (SANDHAWK)

The Sandhawk TE-M-473 is a high-performance 13 in (330 mm) diameter, 201 in (5,105 mm) long rocket motor designed for sounding rocket use. It features a regressive thrust-time trace, which results in near-constant vehicle acceleration during its 15-second burn time and provides an extremely smooth flight environment. This motor is suited for use in single-stage, two-stage and three-stage vehicle configurations.

THIOKOL TE-M-490-6 (TVC II GAS GENERATOR)

The TE-M-490-6 is used as the energy source for a turbine pump which circulates fluid and simultaneously provides control force through separate reaction nozzles. Measuring 22·375 in (568·3 mm) by 7 in (177·8 mm) this generator is used in the Poseidon second-stage engine, developed for Lockheed Missiles and Space Company.

THIOKOL TE-RC-477 (ROCKET CATAPULT)

The TE-RC-477 is a new and much improved seat ejection propulsion system developed for the US Navy. It is a two-stage (boost-sustain) solid-propellant propulsion system consisting of four major sub-assemblies: mechanical firing mechanism, booster, booster cartridge and sustainer motor. This rocket catapult provides improved control of the thrust axis and yields reliable performance in a -54°C to 71·1°C environment. It has a high-performance hydrocarbon propellant, a rotating nozzle with an expansion ratio of 3·15 : 1 and weighs less than 30 lb (13·6 kg).

TRW
TRW SYSTEMS
HEAD OFFICE:

One Space Park, Redondo Beach, California 90278

TRW developed, built and launched the first mono-propellant hydrazine propulsion system to enter and be started in space. In May 1969 Jet Propulsion Laboratory signed a contract with TRW Systems for a 600 lb (272 kg) thrust hydrazine engine for future Mars soft-landing missions. The engine would have a 5 : 1 thrust range and be capable of firing ten times for a total burn of 500 seconds.

TRW is also testing a broad line of chemical propulsion engines. One of these, the man-rated Lunar Module Descent Engine, has landed astronauts on the Moon. Another engine was built to provide mid-course trajectory corrections for the Mariner '69 missions to Mars.

TRW's propulsion research programmes include low-thrust mono-propellant, bi-propellant, colloid, ion, radio-isotope and electro-thermal engines. In addition, an active research programme in low-cost propulsion technology has been initiated. As part of a US Air Force programme to develop cheaper launch vehicles TRW commissioned a piping manufacturer to build to their design a prototype liquid rocket engine having a sea level thrust of 250,000 lb (113,400 kg). This engine has a single fixed chamber and is constructed of ordinary commercial materials. It was to be static-fired during 1969. Tests of TRW rocket engines are conducted at the company's test site at San Juan Capistrano, California.

TRW LUNAR MODULE DESCENT ENGINE

TRW Systems Group developed and is producing the Lunar Module Descent Engine (LMDE) for NASA's Apollo lunar landing programme. Employed to soft-land astronauts on the Moon, the engine delivers a maximum of 10,500 lb (4,763 kg) of thrust and has a throttle range of 10 : 1. Burning time is longer than 1,000 seconds.

Primary feature of the LMDE is a throttling system that uses the TRW single-element coaxial injector and variable-area cavitating venturi flow control valves. The engine includes an electro-mechanical throttle actuator and mechanically linked quad on-off valves. Mixture ratio, controlled by varying the stroke of the oxidizer flow control valve in relation to the fuel valve, is maintained within close tolerances over a wide range of propellant feed conditions.

The LMDE thrust chamber consists of an ablative combustion chamber and nozzle throat with a radiation-cooled columbium nozzle extension. The ablative sections of the chamber

TRW Mariner '69 mid-course engine

are encased in a continuous titanium shell and jacketed by a lightweight insulating shield.

The LMDE has a height of 93 in (236 cm) and diameter of 59 in (150 cm) at the nozzle exit. It weighs 393 lb (178 kg). The engine successfully completed its qualification test programme in

August 1967, and was initially test fired in orbit during the Apollo 5 mission in January 1968. A total of 101 production LMDE chambers, in titanium and aluminium alloy, was produced for TRW under subcontract by Ryan Aeronautical Co.

TRW Lunar Module Descent Engine

UTC

UNITED TECHNOLOGY CENTER (A division of United Aircraft Corporation)

HEADQUARTERS:
Sunnyvale, California 94088

CHAIRMAN OF UNITED AIRCRAFT CORPORATION
AND CHIEF EXECUTIVE OFFICER:
W. P. Gwinn

CORPORATE PRESIDENT AND CHIEF ADMINISTRA-
TIVE OFFICER:
A. E. Smith

DIVISION PRESIDENT:
B. R. Adelman

DIVISION VICE-PRESIDENTS:
D. Altman
E. Roberts

United Technology Center, a division of United Aircraft Corporation, is engaged in research, development and production of rockets, rocket propellants and advanced propulsion systems. Since its founding over a decade ago, UTC has conducted a continuous programme of rocket technology and is now producing a variety of advanced propulsion systems for both the Department of Defense and the National Aeronautics and Space Administration.

UTC's largest programme is the production of 120 in (3,048 mm) diameter, segmented solid-propellant booster rockets. A five-segment configuration of this motor is used in pairs as the zero (launch) stage of the US Air Force Titan III-C and D space launch vehicles. Operating together, the 86 ft (26·12 m) tall motors produce a thrust of 2,500,000 lb (1,134,000 kg). They are the largest solid rockets now in operational use and account for 80 per cent of the total thrust of the Titan III-C and D. Launched for the first time on 18 June 1965, the boosters completed their flight test programme with 13 consecutive successful launches to 23 May 1969. UTC claim this as the first entirely successful flight test programme for vehicles of such size and power. In the course of it, the boosters helped to launch more than 50 satellites.

Essentially a lengthened version of the five-segment motor, a seven-segment motor was statically test-fired in April 1969. Producing a record 1,400,000 lb (635,020 kg) st, the seven-segment motor was intended for the Titan III-M, later cancelled. A second seven-segment motor was fired in January 1970 and several more firings of the motor are being carried out to flight-qualify certain new components and sub-assemblies for the Titan III-C and -D motors.

Standing 112 ft (34·14 m) tall, these are the most powerful rocket motors outside the Soviet Union, a pair of seven-segment motors producing a combined lift-off thrust of 3,200,000 lb (1,451,500 kg). Each motor has a loaded weight of 700,000 lb (317,510 kg). The US Air Force awarded UTC a $125 million development contract for the seven-segment motor in May 1969.

Late in 1968 UTC initiated a programme to determine the shelf (storage) life of large solid motors. Long experience already indicates that the safe useful life will be at least 10 and possibly 20 years.

UTC produces the versatile FW-4 solid-propellant upper-stage rocket which has attained a series of successes in both military and civil space programmes.

In 1969 UTC also began development of Algol III, a more powerful solid-propellant motor to propel the first stage of future NASA Scout vehicles.

UTC is developing for the US Navy the unique Kangaroo missile described on page 679. The Kangaroo is powered by a solid-propellant motor and contains a novel pressurised gas device to eject the dart payload.

UTC achieved a major advance in rocket propulsion in 1967 with the production and flight testing of America's first hybrid system, designed as a preliminary model for operational use in the Beech Sandpiper target. The Sandpiper is being assessed for development and use in weapons systems evaluation and combat aircrew training and can simulate a wide variety of aircraft and missile threats of the coming decade.

Under contract to the NASA, UTC has also begun a programme to design, fabricate and test a high-performance hybrid rocket engine specifically suited for upper-stage applications. Three successful static tests of the engine were carried out in 1969. Assembled vertically to simulate its flight configuration, the 15 ft 6 in (4·72 m) tall, 45 in (1·14 m) diameter rocket produced a thrust of 11,000 lb (4,985 kg) while operating for burn times of 50 and 15 seconds and a thrust of 8,000 lb (3,625 kg) during a 35-second burn. Its propellant

consisted of a lithium/lithium hydride/polybutadiene solid fuel grain and a liquid fluorine/oxygen oxidiser. Possible uses for the new engine include uprating of the Delta, Atlas/Centaur and Titan/Centaur space launch vehicles.

UTC continued other advances in hybrid rocket technology by designing for the National Aeronautics and Space Administration, under a 20-month, $1+ million contract placed in March 1969, a family of high-energy, upper-stage hybrid rocket engines capable of meeting a wide variety of propulsion requirements for unmanned space missions in the 1970s and beyond.

UTC's activities in liquid rocket development extend from basic propellant chemistry and materials evaluation to the design, production and testing of complete liquid rocket systems. The division has developed a family of high-performance, ablation-cooled, storable engines ranging in size from one 52 in (1·32 m) long and 26 in (0·66 m) in diameter and weighing 72 lb (32 kg) to another 76 in (1·93 m) long and 48 in (1·22 m) in diameter and weighing 185 lb (83 kg). Their propellant is 50/50 hydrazine and UDMH plus nitrogen tetroxide. The nozzles have a shell of glass-fibre and a silica-phenolic liner.

The division has test-fired, under simulated altitude conditions, a liquid engine which demonstrated an efficiency claimed to be higher than any known liquid rocket of comparable size. A new form of injector and a dual manifold provided an improved propellant spray pattern within the ablation-cooled combustion chamber and reduced erosion of the chamber liner. UTC has also fabricated and test fired a small liquid engine with a sugar cube size combustion chamber and a thrust of 0·0005 lb (0·00023 kg).

UTC produces small solid-propellant staging rockets used on the Titan II and the Titan III-C and -D booster stages. Developed for use in separation of the Titan II ICBM stages, the aluminium-encased rockets are about 56 in (1·42 m) long and 6 in (152 mm) diameter. They deliver a thrust of about 4,500 lb (2,041 kg). Propellant is PBAN with aluminium additives and ammonium perchlorate oxidiser. The nozzle has an aluminium housing, asbestos phenolic exit cone and graphite throat. Eight of the 84·5 lb (38 kg) motors are used on each of the 120 in (3 m) diameter solids used in the Titan III-C and -D stage zeros, an aft cluster of four and a forward cluster of four.

A two-fold programme to establish new metal-manufacturing processes for rocket hardware components of tactical weapons was carried out for the US Army Missile Command in 1969. The first step demonstrated that shear forming of advanced steels can produce a rocket casing of light weight and high strength. The second step involved a casting process to fabricate nozzles and motor cases that could be used for tactical weapons. The programme demonstrated that castings of high-strength maraging steel are suitable for fabricating missile-type nozzles and as preforms for shear spinning motor cases.

UTC is at present evaluating several low-cost nozzle insulation materials capable of withstanding the high temperatures encountered in rocket exhausts and the erosive effects of highly-reactive fluids used in steering systems for large solid-propellant rockets. This programme is one of several sponsored by NASA to evaluate relatively inexpensive steering systems for very large solid rockets being considered by the space agency for a variety of launch applications.

A simple and inexpensive device to prevent engine flame-out in tactical rockets from liquid fuel or oxidiser starvation has been demonstrated successfully for the US Naval Air Systems Command. The device, a lightweight, aluminium-spun cylinder for liquids, is forced to collapse in a controlled manner and thus expel its contents into the rocket's combustion chamber, thereby maintaining the flow of propellant.

A unique miniature ballistic test firing range capable of accelerating and measuring the supersonic velocities of particles one-hundredth as large as a grain of sand was developed for work being carried out for the US Army's Research Office. Data obtained from repeated firings is enabling UTC propulsion engineers to study performance losses caused by particles produced during the combustion of metallized solid propellant being expelled through the nozzles of rockets.

The programme to explore the production of sound from fire, reported in the 1969-70 edition, is being carried out for the Air Force Office of Scientific Research. The contract was awarded following the company's discovery that flames can accept electrical impulses and reproduce them as audible sounds with the clarity of a high-fidelity loudspeaker. The technique may prove useful as a means of introducing sound into the combustion chamber of rockets to assess combustion

stability or as a device to take sound recordings of combustion itself.

Completion of a multi-million dollar complex to manufacture metal products ranging in size from small machined parts to large rocket motor cases was announced in February 1970. The new plant has a variety of metal forming and machining equipment as well as a facility for chemical milling. Tooling includes large press and shearing equipment as well as light- and heavy-duty lathe, mill and drill rigs. The facility provides clean rooms for work requiring temperature or other environmental controls and certified welding for items requiring high quality.

UTC 120 in (3,048 mm) SEGMENTED MOTOR

Mass-produced at UTC's Coyote, California, rocket production facility, this 120 in (3,048 mm) diameter solid-propellant rocket motor centre segment is interchangeable with any other centre segment. Its cylindrical metal case is manufactured from high-strength steel (D6AC) and heat

UTC's 1,250,000 lb thrust solid-propellant five-segment, 120 in (3,048 mm) motor, two of which are used on the Titan III-C space launch vehicle

treated to an ultimate strength of 195,000 lb/sq in (13,710 kg/cm²). Less than 0·5 in (12·7 mm) thick, each case is equipped with clevis-type end joints with holes for cylindrical fastening pins. Loaded with propellant, a synthetic rubber (polybutadiene acrylonitrile) with aluminium additives as fuel and ammonium perchlorate as oxidizer, a segment weighs 79,000 lb (35,830 kg). Designed as the basic building

Test firing of a new hybrid rocket engine by UTC. The oxidiser, contained in the spherical tank at the top, is fed through the solid-fuel grain in the cylindrical case and burned there. This engine could be used to up-rate upper stages of the Delta, Atlas-Centaur and Titan-Centaur

block for large solid-propellant booster rockets, the segmented motor can be assembled in from one- to eight-segment configurations with thrusts ranging from 250,000 to 1·5 million pounds (113,400-680,400 kg).

A fully configured motor contains a destruct system, a forward-end ignition system and has its own staging sequence capability. Irrespective of the number of segments used, the 120 in motor can incorporate a steering system in which the hot gas jet is deflected by a strong oblique shockwave created in the flared nozzle exit cone by the injection into an appropriate part of the periphery of a highly-reactive fluid. In 1969 the system was simplified by replacing the two tanks previously needed for fluid and pressurization source by a single tank. At the same time complicated injection initiation valves were replaced by a simple system activated by the hot exhaust gases immediately after ignition and before steering is required, and hydraulic injectant valves were replaced by electric valves. Altogether the new steering system reduces the weight of the Titan III-C booster stage by some 8,700 lb (3,945 kg). The whole system performed well when severely tested in a static firing of a seven-segment motor in January 1970.

UTC has made progress in the development of more efficient and economical means of fabricating the steel motor cases used in the 120 in programme, through production processes known as internal roll extrusion and shear spinning. In the internal roll extrusion process, a 60·5 in by 12 in (1,537 mm by 305 mm) plate was heat-treated, then rolled and welded. After machining, the newly-formed cylinder underwent extrusion, resulting in the first thin-walled rocket case ever formed from HP-9-4 steel, the hardest known material ever to have been extruded. The shear spinning process involved extrusion of a one-piece cylindrical preform over a full-length mandrel by a pair of diametrically-opposed rollers. Beginning as a roll ring forging 45 in (1,140 mm) high, the D6AC steel was stretched to a full height of 129 in (3·28 m). Both techniques reduce production time and result in a more reliable and economical product.

UTC ALGOL III

UTC has begun development of Algol III, a more powerful solid-propellant first stage for NASA's Scout space launch vehicle. Under a contract awarded to UTC by LTV Aerospace Corporation's Missiles and Space Division, prime contractor for the Scout, both development and qualification static firings are being carried out. Thirty feet (9·14 m) tall and 45 in (1·14 m) in diameter, the new UTC solid booster will permit an increase of 40-45 per cent in the Scout's payload weight capability. When loaded with its propellant (PBAN with aluminium additives and ammonium perchlorate oxidiser) Algol III will weigh 30,000 lb (13,605 kg). Its nozzle is fabric-

ated from steel with a graphite cloth-phenolic and silica cloth-phenolic cone liner. Ignition is by a small nose-mounted solid rocket. Producing 130,000 lb (58,965 kg) of lift-off thrust, Algol III will burn for 75 seconds and boost the Scout to an altitude of 30 miles (48 km) before burn-out.

UTC FW-4

The FW-4 is a solid-propellant upper-stage rocket motor which was first used in early 1965 as the top stage of the Thor booster. It is now being flown on the Thor, Atlas F, Scout and Delta launch vehicles. The motor was designed to be interchangeable with existing upper-stage motors on launch vehicles with orbital, probe or re-entry missions, as well as for retro-rocket propulsion in space vehicles. It had placed more than 50 satellites into precise Earth orbit by February 1970.

The FW-4 is 19·6 in (498 mm) in diameter and has an overall length of 58·43 in (1,484 mm). Its case is fabricated from glass-fibre and epoxy resin, with a cylindrical wall thickness of 0·08 in (2·03 mm) and domes with geodesic contours with a nominal wall thickness of 0·03 in (0·76 mm). The igniter and nozzle attachment fittings are fabricated from aluminium, and the aluminium interstage flanges are bonded and riveted to the integrally-wound glass-fibre skirt of the motor case. The standard FW-4 rocket motor has an

UTC FW-4 solid-propellant upper-stage rocket motor

inert weight of 55·5 lb (25·2 kg) and a propellant weight of 605 lb (274 kg), resulting in a motor mass fraction of 0·92. The average motor thrust is 5,620 lb (2,549 kg), with a burn time of 30·5 seconds.

UTC HPS-10

UTC was awarded a contract by Beech Aircraft Corporation in June 1966 to develop a low-cost multi-thrust hybrid rocket propulsion system for the USAF Beechcraft Sandpiper target missile. By the end of 1967 flight testing of the engine, the HPS-10, had started at the Eglin Air Force Base aerial test range over the Gulf of Mexico, with the rocket installed as the propulsion system in a modified AQM-37A target missile.

Development of the HPS-10 engine, including flight certification, is being undertaken by a joint team comprising the USAF Rocket Propulsion Laboratory at Edwards AFB, California, and UTC's Research and Engineering Center at Sunnyvale and its Development, Test and Production Center at Coyote, California. The programme is under the overall direction of the

UTC HPS-10 hybrid rocket engine for Sandpiper target missile

USAF Armament Laboratory, with flight testing being conducted by the Air Force Air Proving Center, both located at Eglin AFB.

A hybrid system, combining both solid and liquid rocket technology, was selected for the HPS-10 as offering the optimum propulsion system able to provide thrust control over a 10 : 1 range, with minimum cost and development time. The Sandpiper utilizes UTC's "Dial-a-Thrust" control which, by governing the rate of oxidiser supply, can provide thrust levels from 60 lb to 300 lb (27 to 136 kg), confering upon the vehicle a multiple-mission capability with a wide variety of flight patterns. Performance is programmed prior to flight by the setting of a single dial. Missile flight can be sustained over a predetermined flight path for up to five minutes, an unusually long burning time for any rocket. The hybrid engine uses Plexiglas plastic with a magnesium compound as its solid fuel and a combination of nitric oxides as its liquid oxidiser. The oxidiser is forced through a low-cost injector into the solid-fuel combustion chamber where it is lit by a pyrotechnic igniter. Capable of sustaining thrust for up to five minutes, the HPS-10 is designed to maintain the Sandpiper in straight and level flight at a range of preselected altitudes up to 80,000 ft (24,384 m) and at speeds up to Mach 3. The HPS-10 has functioned perfectly in three flights to date.

The following details relate to the HPS-10 hybrid propulsion system now being flight tested for the Sandpiper target missile.

Type: Single-chamber hybrid-propellant rocket engine.

Solid-propellant rockets mass-produced by UTC as separation motors for Titan II ICBMs and Titan III-C and -D space launch vehicles

PROPELLANTS: Polymethylmethacrylate/magnesium (90 per cent/10 per cent) solid plastic fuel, MON-25 (a combination of nitric acids) liquid oxidiser.

THRUST CHAMBER ASSEMBLY: Single chamber. Area ratio: 21 : 1. Construction in maraging steel, 200 grade. Heat-sink cooling. Operating sequence: boost followed by sustain. Injection and ignition of liquid oxidiser by gaseous nitrogen pressurization and pyrogen ignition. Combustion pressures: maximum 500 lb/sq in

abs (35·2 kg/cm² abs), minimum 65 lb/sq in abs (4·6 kg/cm² abs). Combustion temperature: 5,700°F (3,131°C).

THRUST CHAMBER MOUNTING: Integral with pre-packaged propulsion system.

PROPELLANT MASS FLOW RATE AND PRESSURE: Variable, depending on thrust level.

STARTING PROCEDURE: Pyrogen ignition, followed by initiation of oxidiser flow.

THRUST CONTROL: Boost thrust on demand,

stepped sustain-thrust by variable-sustain control.

DIMENSIONS:
Length overall   116 in (2·95 m)
Diameter over feed system assembly   13 in (330 mm)
Diameter over thrust chamber assembly   10 in (254 mm)

PERFORMANCE:
Max thrust at 50,000 ft (15,240 m)   500 lb (227 kg)
Overall propellant mixture ratio   1·65 : 1

WILLIAMS
WILLIAMS RESEARCH CORPORATION
ADDRESS: Walled Lake, Michigan.

Sam Williams believed in 1956 that gas turbine technology could be extended down to very small sizes, and that if a small turbojet were made available it would find a market. Accordingly this company began a development programme on the WR2, described below, on a scale of effort and funding reflecting its very limited resources.

The WR2 first ran at a design thrust of 70 lb (31·8 kg) in 1962 and has since been developed into the WR2-6 and WR24-6. The more advanced WR19 uses an aerodynamically similar core, and Williams Research is also building a range of shaft drive engines, all characterized by their very simple design and aerodynamic similarity of their centrifugal compressors, axial compressor and power turbines.

Industrial and automotive engines of 75, 150 and 500 shp have been produced and the first of these, based on the WR2, was also developed for one-man helicopters. Williams Research is now developing, under contract from a private company, an automotive engine with regenerator and, for another company, a shaft-drive engine rated at significantly above 500 shp.

The company is now strong and experienced enough to mount a planned attack on the manned-aircraft market and believes that, as has happened with drone engines, aircraft markets will appear when reliable turbojet and turbofan engines sized between the 430 lb (195 kg) thrust of the WR19 and an upper limit of 2,000 lb (907 kg) st become available.

WILLIAMS WR2 and WR24
Although simple in design, almost to the point of appearing crude, this single-shaft turbojet has shown itself to be an effective power plant for high-subsonic drone aircraft and a suitable base for development of more advanced engines.

Air enters at the eye of a single-sided light alloy centrifugal compressor which handles an air mass flow of 2·2 lb (1 kg)/sec at a pressure ratio of 4·1 : 1. After passing through the diffuser which provides the structural basis for the engine the air divides, part of it flowing radially inwards as primary combustion airflow and the main bulk entering the short outward-radial annular combustor, through dilution apertures around the outer and rear face of the flame tube.

Fuel is sprayed centrifugally through a group of fine holes in the main compressor drive shaft. Surrounding the fuel pipe along the centre-line of the main drive shaft is a cool airflow bled from the diffuser which escapes through holes in the drive shaft to cool the combustion flame and reduce metal shaft and bearing temperatures, the main bearing being behind the compressor. A single igniter is mounted in the chamber at 12 o'clock. The hot gas, at about 1,750°F, then turns inwards and exits rearwards through the single-stage axial turbine and simple jet-pipe.

The two production versions of the WR2 are the WR2-6, fitted to the Canadair AN-USD-501 high-performance battlefield reconnaissance vehicle and the WR24-6 which powers the Northrop NV-105 (US Navy MQM-74A) target drone. The WR2-6 has a variable-area exhaust nozzle and is rated at a maximum of 125 lb (56·7 kg) st at sea level. The following data refer to the WR24-6.

DIMENSIONS:
Overall length: 19 in (483 mm)
Basic diameter over diffuser: 11 in (279 mm)
WEIGHT, DRY: 30 lb (13·6 kg)
RATED THRUST (S/L):   121 lb (55 kg)
SPECIFIC FUEL CONSUMPTION: 1·2

WILLIAMS WR19
To produce this two-shaft turbofan Williams Research used the WR2 as core and added an additional fan, axial compressor and drive turbine on a separate shaft, together with a by-pass duct. The LP turbine is related to those developed for the company's shaft-drive engines.

The WR19 is the power plant used in the Bell Aerosystems Flying Belt (see "Aircraft" section) and is regarded as a particularly strong contender in the US Air Force SCAD (subsonic cruise armed decoy) missile propulsion competition.

Early in 1970 the company received a $1,400,000 contract from the USAF for further development of a turbofan for future decoys. The company is making great efforts to increase the maximum gas temperature, particularly in the WR19 and derived engines. At present the temperature actually used is about 1,750°F, with potential of the present materials (Haynes 31 cobalt-base alloy for inlet guide vanes, Inco 100 for first-stage turbine blades and Inco 713 for other hot parts) limited to about 1,850°F.

Despite the mechanical difficulty of working on such very small components, with turbine rotor disc and blades cast as single units, Williams are experimenting with air-cooled turbine rotor blades and expect soon to be able to operate at gas temperatures higher than 2,000°F. The WR19 would be the first engine offered with cooled blades, and it also continues the company philosophy of using specially developed alternators, governors and other accessories capable of running at the full 60,000 rpm of the main shaft.

AIR INTAKE: Direct pitot type with four struts but no fixed inlet guide vanes. Unlike most WR2 engines the WR19 has a plain annular entry instead of a side intake downstream of an alternator or generator on the nose of the main shaft.

COMPRESSOR: Two-stage metal fan and two-stage axial IP compressor on common shaft leading to HP centrifugal compressor, handed to rotate in opposite direction to minimise gyroscopic couple. Total air-mass flow, about

4·4 lb (2 kg)/sec; overall pressure ratio, 8 : 1; by-pass ratio, approximately 1 : 1.

COMBUSTION CHAMBER: Folded annular type, with fuel sprayed from revolving slinger on HP shaft. Dilution airflow admitted through perforated liner; cooling air injected through two sets of holes in HP shaft. Single igniter mounted diagonally on engine upper centre-line.

FUEL SYSTEM: Fuel fed at low pressure through transfer seal into pipe in HP shaft and ejected at high centrifugally-induced pressure, through calibrated fine orifices drilled radially through HP shaft in line with combustion chamber.

TURBINE: Single-stage axial-flow HP turbine, with Haynes 31 nozzle guide vanes and rotor wheel cast as single unit in Inco IN 100. Two-stage LP turbine, again with both wheels cast as single units, in Inco 713. Provision to be made for air cooling to raise entry gas temperature from 1,750°F to above 2,000°F.

JET PIPE: Mixer unit immediately downstream of LP turbine allows by-pass flow to merge with core gas flow to pass through plain propelling nozzle.

ACCESSORIES: Fuel and control system, filters, oil pump, tacho generator and optional other accessories grouped into flat packages around upper part of fan/IP compressor casing. Starting system, depending on application, drives HP spool.

MOUNTING: Depending on application, main mounting above centrifugal diffuser casing with two double-lug pick-ups on horizontal centre-line at LP turbine casing.

DIMENSIONS:
Length overall: 24 in (610 mm)
Envelope diameter: 12 in (305 mm)
WEIGHT:
Dry, depending on equipment: 61–68 lb (27·6–30·8 kg)
PERFORMANCE RATING:
Max thrust, S/L, static   430 lb (195 kg)
SPECIFIC FUEL CONSUMPTION:
Max thrust, S/L static: 0·7

Williams Research Corporation WR19 two-shaft turbofan engine (430 lb = 195 kg st). Believed to be the smallest turbofan in the world, the WR19 weighs 67 lb (30·4 kg) as shown

---

WRIGHT
CURTISS-WRIGHT CORPORATION, WOOD-RIDGE FACILITY
HEAD OFFICE AND WORKS:
Wood-Ridge, New Jersey
CHAIRMAN OF THE BOARD AND PRESIDENT:
T. Roland Berner

EXECUTIVE VICE-PRESIDENT:
S. D. Brinsfield
VICE-PRESIDENT, ENGINEERING:
A. F. Kossar

The Wood-Ridge facility of Curtiss-Wright Corporation is engaged in the development and manufacture of aircraft components, structural assemblies, nuclear vessels, aerospace propulsion

systems, power transmission systems, subcontract manufacturing, advanced materials and processes, propulsion systems components, aircraft engines, aircraft engine overhaul.

Wright engines continue in world-wide service in fixed-wing aircraft and helicopters, and one of them, the R-1820 Cyclone 9, remains in production. These engines have been described in previous editions of *Jane's*.

THE UNION OF SOVIET SOCIALIST REPUBLICS

AI

A. G. IVCHENKO

The design team headed by general designer Alexander G. Ivchenko until his death in June 1968 is based in a factory at Zaporojie in the Ukraine, where all prototypes and pre-production engines bearing the "AI" prefix are developed and built. Chief designer of the team is Vladimir Lotarev, chief engineer is Tichienko and production director is M. Omeltchenko.

First engine with which Ivchenko was associated officially was the 55 hp AI-4G piston-engine used in the Kamov Ka-10 ultra-light helicopter. He has since progressed, via the widely used AI-14 and AI-26 piston-engines, to become one of the Soviet Union's leading designers of gas-turbine engines.

AI-14

The original 260 hp AI-14R version of this nine-cylinder air-cooled radial engine has been produced in very large quantities, in both the Soviet Union and Poland, to power the Yakovlev Yak-12, PZL-101A Gawron and PZL-104 Wilga 3 utility aircraft. Large numbers of 280 hp AI-14VF engines, fitted with a cooling fan, are also flying in Kamov Ka-15 and Ka-18 helicopters.

Latest version to enter production is the 300 hp AI-14RF, which powers the Antonov An-14 Pchelka twin-engined light transport.

No constructional details of the AI-14RF are available, except that it has a bore of 4⅛ in (105 mm), stroke of 5⅛ in (130 mm) and swept volume of 620 cu in (10·16 litres). It normally drives through 0·787 : 1 ratio planetary reduction gearing, a type AV-14 propeller, although other types can be fitted. A hydraulic friction clutch can be incorporated to provide a 25 hp drive for agricultural equipment.

A further version, designated AI-14F, is under development with a T-O rating of 350 hp.

DIMENSIONS:
Length overall:

AI-14RF	39·45 in (1,002 mm)
AI-14RF with clutch drive	43·58 in (1,107 mm)
AI-14VF	43·03 in (1,093 mm)
Diameter	38·78 in (985 mm)

WEIGHT, DRY:

AI-14RF	478 lb (217 kg)
AI-14RF with clutch drive	496 lb (225 kg)
AI-14VF	534 lb (242 kg)

PERFORMANCE RATINGS:
Max T-O:

AI-14RF	300 hp at 2,400 rpm
AI-14VF	280 hp

Normal:

AI-14RF	285 hp at 2,300 rpm
AI-14VF	235 hp at 2,130 rpm

Cruise:

AI-14RF	188 hp at 1,860 rpm
AI-14VF	160 hp at 2,000 rpm

Econ cruise:

AI-14RF	150 hp at 1,730 rpm

SPECIFIC FUEL CONSUMPTIONS:
At max rating:

AI-14RF	0·584-0·639 lb (265-290 gr)/hp/hr

At normal rating:

AI-14RF	0·584-0·639 lb (265-290 gr)/hp/hr
AI-14VF	0·551-0·617 lb (250-280 gr)/hp/hr

At cruise rating:

AI-14RF	0·463-0·507 lb (210-230 gr)/hp/hr
AI-14VF	0·463-0·496 lb (210-225 gr)/hp/hr

At econ cruise rating:

AI-14RF	0·452-0·496 lb (205-225 gr)/hp/hr

AI-20

Ivchenko's design bureau is responsible for the AI-20 turboprop engine which powers the Antonov An-10, An-12 and Ilyushin Il-18 airliners and the Beriev M-12 Tchaika amphibian.

Six production series of this engine had been built by the spring of 1966. The first four series, of which manufacture started in 1957, were variants of the basic AI-20. They were followed by two major production versions, as follows:

AI-20K. Rated at 3,945 ehp (4,000 ch e). Used in Il-18V, An-10A and An-12.

AI-20M. Uprated version, with T-O rating of 4,190 ehp (4,250 ch e). Used in Il-18D/E, An-10A and An-12. Capable of operation on a wide range of fuels and lubricating oils.

The AI-20 is a single-spool turboprop, with a 10-stage axial-flow compressor, cannular combustion chamber with ten flame tubes, and a three-stage turbine, of which the first two stages are cooled. Planetary reduction gearing, with a ratio of 0·08732 : 1, is mounted forward of the annular air intake. The fixed nozzle contains a central bullet fairing. All engine-driven accessories are mounted on the forward part of the compressor casing, which is of magnesium alloy.

The AI-20 was designed to operate reliably in all temperatures from —60°C to + 55°C at heights up to 33,000 ft (10,000 m). It is a constant-speed engine, the rotor speed being maintained at 12,300 rpm by automatic variation of propeller pitch. Gas temperature after turbine is 560°C in both current versions. TBO of the AI-20K was 4,000

The 280 hp Ivchenko AI-14VF helicopter power plant
(*courtesy of Aviation Magazine International, Paris*)

hours in the spring of 1966; the same life was reached by the -20M in 1968.

In the Il-18 installation, the AI-20 turboprop is supplied as a complete power plant with cowling, mounting and automatically-feathering reversible-pitch four-blade propeller.

WEIGHT, DRY:

AI-20K	2,380 lb (1,080 kg)
AI-20M	2,292 lb (1,040 kg)

PERFORMANCE RATINGS:
Max T-O:

AI-20K	3,945 ehp (4,000 ch e)
AI-20M	4,190 ehp (4,250 ch e)

Cruise rating at 390 mph (630 kmh) at 26,000 ft (8,000 m):

AI-20K	2,220 ehp (2,250 ch e)
AI-20M	2,663 ehp (2,700 ch e)

SPECIFIC FUEL CONSUMPTION:
At cruise rating:

AI-20K	0·472 lb (215 gr)/hp/hr
AI-20M	0·429 lb (195 gr)/hp/hr

OIL CONSUMPTION:

Normal	1·75 Imp pints (1 litre)/hr

AI-24

In general configuration, this single-spool turboprop engine, which powers the An-24 transport aircraft, is very similar to the earlier and larger AI-20. Production began in 1960 and the following data refer to engines of the second series, which were in production in the Spring of 1966.

The basic AI-24 of 2,515 eshp (2,550 ch e) powered the An-24V Series I, and was followed by the AI-24A with provision for water injection, in the main current production versions of the aircraft.

The 300 hp Ivchenko AI-14RF engine (*courtesy of Aviation Magazine International, Paris*)

The more powerful AI-24T of 2,781 eshp (2,820 ch e) with water injection has been introduced to power the An-24T with large rear-loading cargo door. This engine has a cruise rating of 1,627 eshp (1,650 ch e) at 314 mph (505 kmh) at 18,300 ft (6,000 m). It has in-flight vibration monitoring, automatic relief of power overloads and gas temperature behind the turbine and auto-shutdown and feathering.

An annular ram air intake surrounds the cast light alloy casing for the planetary eduction gear, which has a ratio of 0·08255 : 1. The cast magnesium alloy compressor casing carries a row of inlet guide vanes and the compressor stator vanes and provides mountings for the engine-driven accessories. These include fuel, hydraulic and oil pumps, tacho-generator and propeller governor.

The 10-stage axial-flow compressor is driven by a three-stage axial-flow turbine, of which the first two stages are cooled. An annular combustion chamber is used, with eight injectors and two igniters. The tail-pipe comprises a central bullet fairing and fixed outer nozzle carrying 12 thermocouples. Standard propeller is the metal four-blade Type AV-72.

The AI-24 is a constant-speed engine, the speed of the rotor being maintained at 15,100 rpm by automatic variation of propeller pitch. The engine is flat-rated to maintain its nominal output to 11,500 ft (3,500 m). TBO was 3,000 hours in

Ivchenko AI-20K turboprop engine of 3,945 ehp (*courtesy of Aviation Magazine International, Paris*)

The 2,515 ehp Ivchenko AI-24 turboprop engine (*courtesy of Aviation Magazine International, Paris*)

the spring of 1966; by 1968 the later AI-24T had reached 4,000 hours.

DIMENSION:
Length overall .... 95·87 in (2,435 mm)
DRY WEIGHT: .... 1,323 lb (600 kg)
PERFORMANCE RATING:
T-O .... 2,515 eshp (2,550 ch e)
SPECIFIC FUEL CONSUMPTION:
At cruise rating ...... 0·503 lb (0·228 kg)/hp/hr
OIL CONSUMPTION: ..... 1·87 lb (0·85 kg)/hr

AI-25

This is the turbofan that powers the three-engined Yakovlev Yak-40 transport aircraft. Its general appearance is shown in the adjacent illustration.

The AI-25 has a by-pass ratio of 2 : 1 and pressure ratio of 9 : 1. It makes extensive use of titanium, the entire compressor and its casing being of this metal. The Ivchenko bureau also report this engine has an unusual percentage of magnesium alloys and thin-walled structures. Its twin-spool configuration comprises a three-stage fan/LP compressor with pin-fixed blades, eight-stage HP compressor, can-annular combustion system, single-stage HP turbine with cooled stators only, and two-stage LP turbine. Automatic starting is provided by a small AI-9 turbo-compressor unit located behind the centre intake of the Yak-40. This supplies air to an SV-25 compressed air starter mounted on the engine. Equipment includes a self-contained oil system with minimum level indicator, chip detector and vibration meter.

DIMENSIONS:
Length overall .... 76·5 in (1,943 mm)
Width overall .... 32·28 in (820 mm)
Height overall .... 35·24 in (895 mm)
DRY WEIGHT:
Without accessories .... 760 lb (345 kg)

Ivchenko AI-25 turbofan engine (3,300 lb=1,500 kg st)
(courtesy of Aviation Magazine International, Paris)

PERFORMANCE RATINGS:
T-O ..... 3,300 lb (1,500 kg) st at 16,300 rpm
Normal ... 2,470 lb (1,120 kg) st at 15,370 rpm
Cruise ... 977 lb (443 kg) st at 14,470 rpm and
  20,000 ft (6,000 m) and 342 mph (550 kmh)
SPECIFIC FUEL CONSUMPTION:
T-O .... 0·585
Normal .... 0·582
Cruise .... 0·837 at 20,000 ft (6,000 m) and
      342 mph (550 kmh)

AI-26V

The most powerful Ivchenko piston-engine so far announced is the AI-26V, which is used to power the Mi-1 series of helicopters. It is a seven-cylinder radial engine giving 575 hp at 2,200 rpm and has fan cooling.

The AI-26V was built under licence in Poland, with the designation LiT-3, to power the Polish SM-1 and SM-2 helicopters.

ASH
A. D. SHVETSOV

ASH-21

This seven-cylinder radial engine of 730 hp was evolved by Shvetsov from the American Wright R-1300 and has been built in large numbers to power the Yak-11 advanced trainer. A helicopter version has also been produced.

ASH-62

Power plant of the An-2 transport biplane, the ASh-62 is a 1,000 hp nine-cylinder air-cooled radial engine. Several variants have been built, including the ASh-62 IR/TK driving a turbo-compressor to maintain 850 hp up to a height of 31,000 ft (9,500 m).

There are two current versions of the engine, as follows:

ASh-62IR. Standard power plant of all versions of the An-2 except for the new An-2M. Built also in Poland.

ASh-62M. Developed from ASh-62IR to power the An-2M. Fitted with a power take-off shaft, rated at up to 58 hp, to drive agricultural spraying or dusting gear, two electrical generators and the flight deck air-conditioning equipment. Weight of the take-off package is 249 lb (113 kg).

Both versions have a cylinder bore of 6⅛ in (155·5 mm), swept volume of 1,823 cu in (29·87 litres) and compression ratio of 6·4 : 1.

The planetary reduction gear of the ASh-62M has a ratio of 0·637 : 1.

DIMENSIONS (ASh-62M):
Length overall, without power take-off
                   44·50 in (1,130 mm)
Diameter .... 54·13 in (1,375 mm)
DRY WEIGHT (ASh-62M):
Without power take-off ... 1,250 lb (567 kg)
PERFORMANCE RATINGS (ASh-62M: A=with power take-off driving generators and air-conditioning equipment: B=driving also agricultural equipment):
T-O: A .... 1,000 hp at 2,200 rpm

Rated power:
A .... 820 hp at 2,100 rpm
B (75% power) ...... 615 hp at 1,910 rpm
Max cont (90% power):
A .... 738 hp at 2,030 rpm
Cruise:
B (50% power) ...... 410 hp at 1,670 rpm
SPECIFIC FUEL CONSUMPTIONS (corresponding to above ratings):
T-O: A .... 0·661 lb (300 gr)/hp/hr
Rated power:
A .... 0·617-0·661 lb (280-300 gr)/hp/hr
B .... 0·529-0·562 lb (240-255 gr)/hp/hr
Max cont:
A .... 0·573-0·617 lb (260-280 gr)/hp/hr

Cruise:
B .... 0·474-0·507 lb (215-230 gr)/hp/hr

ASH-82T AND ASH-82V

The ASh-82T was developed by Shvetsov from the Pratt & Whitney Twin Wasp design to power the Il-12 and Il-14 twin-engined transports. It has been produced in Russia, Czechoslovakia and East Germany, and the details below were supplied from Germany.

A variant, shown in the adjacent illustration, is the ASh-82V helicopter engine, which powers the Mil Mi-4 and Yakovlev Yak-24. This embodies a cooling fan and a friction clutch in the rotor drive.

Left:
The 1,000 hp Shvetsov ASh-62IR engine *(courtesy of Aviation Magazine International, Paris)*

Right:
The 1,700 hp Shvetsov ASh-82V engine *(courtesy of Aviation Magazine International, Paris)*

Below:
The 1,900 hp ASh-82T fourteen - cylinder radial engine

TYPE: Fourteen-cylinder two-row air-cooled radial, geared and supercharged.

CYLINDERS: Bore 6·12 in (155·5 mm). Stroke 6·10 in (155 mm). Displacement 2,513 cu in (41·2 litres). Nitrided steel barrel with cast aluminium alloy head. Compression ratio 6·9 : 1.

PISTONS: Of forged aluminium. Each piston has three compression rings, one oil scraper ring and one oil seal ring. Upper compression ring of chromium-plated steel, remainder of cast iron. Bearing surfaces graphited. Gudgeon pins secured against axial movement by mushroom heads.

CONNECTING RODS: Master rod and six articulated rods for each row. All rods of forged steel, heat-treated and polished. Bearings of lead-coated bronze.

CRANKSHAFT: Three-piece crankshaft of heat-treated forged chrome-nickel-molybdenum steel. Bearing surfaces nitrided. Supported in three roller bearings.

CRANKCASE: Made up of front housing, six-part centre housing, front and rear supercharger casings, and rear cover, all joined together by set-screws and studs. Centre housing containing cylinders is of steel, all other parts of light alloy. Front housing contains reduction gear and drives for magneto, propeller governor and oil pump.

VALVE GEAR: One inlet and one exhaust valve per cylinder, of heat-resisting steel. Exhaust valves are hollow and sodium-filled. Each row of cylinders has independent valve gear, consisting of camshaft, push-rods, valve levers, springs and valves.

INDUCTION SYSTEM: Direct injection system, with injection pump on rear cover.

FUEL GRADE: Not less than 95 octane.

SUPERCHARGER: Single-stage type. Drive from crankshaft to light alloy impeller through reduction gearing with 7·27 : 1 ratio.

LUBRICATION: Two oil pumps, one for each row.

IGNITION: Two magnetos on front housing. Screened ignition harness.

PROPELLER DRIVE: Provision for four-blade hydraulically-operated constant-speed variable-pitch propeller with fluid de-icing. Reduction gear ratio 54 : 31.

DIMENSIONS:
Diameter   51·18 in (1,300 mm)
Length:
ASh-82T   79·13 in (2,010 mm)
ASh-82V   74·30 in (1,887 mm)

WEIGHT (DRY):
ASh-82T   2,250 lb (1,020 kg)
ASh-82V   2,359 lb (1,070 kg)

PERFORMANCE RATINGS:
T-O (5 min):
ASh-82T   1,900 hp at 2,600 rpm
ASh-82V   1,700 hp at 2,600 rpm
Rated power at S/L:
ASh-82T   1,530 hp at 2,400 rpm
ASh-82V   1,430 hp at 2,400 rpm
Rated power at 5,250 ft (1,600 m):
ASh-82T   1,630 hp at 2,400 rpm
ASh-82V   1,530 hp at 2,400 rpm

FUEL CONSUMPTIONS (ASh-82T):
At T-O rating   1,360-1,444 lb (617-655 kg)/hr
At rated power   959-1,058 lb (435-480 kg)/hr

GDL

ADDRESS: Leningrad

The name of the centre responsible for design of the first-stage engine of the Vostok space launch vehicle, and other rocket engines, was given, in French, at the 1967 Paris Air Show, as the Laboratoire de la Dynamique des Gaz of Leningrad. It was said to have been founded in 1929.

Details of three current major types of engine follow.

GDL RD-107

This four-chamber liquid-propellant rocket engine was developed during 1954 to 1957. The RD-107 and its derivatives have been in use for ten years as launch vehicle first-stage engines for Soviet satellites to the Sun and Moon, and automatic stations launched to the Moon, Venus and Mars. They also powered the Vostok and Voskhod manned spaceship launch vehicles. Their specific impulse and operational reliability are described as being exceptionally high.

TYPE: Four-chamber liquid-propellant rocket engine.

PROPELLANTS: Liquid oxygen and kerosene.

THRUST CHAMBERS: Four primary thrust chambers of double-wall construction, with fabricated corrugations between walls and inner walls of copper or copper-rich alloy. Conical nozzles. All-welded heads. Flat-plate injectors, with concentric rings of tubes in which propellants are pre-mixed before injection. Estimated diameters: throat 6-6·5 in (150-165 mm), nozzle 27 in (685 mm). Combustion pressure 882 lb/sq in (60 atm).

VERNIER CHAMBERS: Two chambers of double-wall construction, with finning between walls. Estimated diameters: throat 3 in (75 mm), nozzle 12 in (305 mm).

TURBOPUMP: One single-shaft turbopump feeding all chambers. Mounted above chambers in tubular frame. Assembly comprises turbine exhaust hood containing coiled heat exchanger, single-sided shrouded centrifugal kerosene pump, double-sided shrouded centrifugal liquid oxygen pump, gearbox, and two auxiliary centrifugal pumps, one of which supplies the mono-propellant gas generator. Fuel lines to main chambers pass through common valve.

PERFORMANCE (in vacuum):
Rated thrust   224,870 lb (102,000 kg)
Specific impulse   314 sec

GDL RD-119

This more modern single-chamber liquid-propellant engine, which has been in use since 1962, forms the second-stage engine of a launch vehicle for Cosmos research satellites. More than 300 of these satellites have been launched, using two-, three-, and four-stage launch vehicles of various types and having lifting capacities ranging from hundreds of pounds to 7·5 tons (7·6 tonnes).

TYPE: Single-chamber liquid-propellant rocket engine.

PROPELLANTS: Liquid oxygen and dimethyl-hydrazine.

THRUST CHAMBER: Single fixed chamber, possibly of tubular-wall construction, with fuel entry above base of nozzle. Estimated diameters: throat 4 in (100 mm), nozzle 37 in (940 mm). Combustion pressure 1,176 lb/sq in (80 atm).

TURBOPUMP: One single-shaft turbopump, driven by monopropellant (hydrazine) gas generator. Exhaust from gas generator taken to multiple auxiliary nozzles for control in roll, pitch and yaw.

PERFORMANCE (in vacuum):
Rated thrust   24,250 lb (11,000 kg)
Specific impulse   352 sec

GDL RD-214

This neat liquid-propellant rocket engine, developed at GDL in 1952-57, has been adopted as the standard first-stage propulsion for launching the Cosmos series of research satellites. It has four thrust chambers, burning nitric acid and kerosene, each chamber being rated at 39,700 lb (18,000 kg) thrust at sea level. Vacuum rating of the engine is 74 tonnes (163,142 lb). The propellants are fed by a single large turbopump group mounted above the chamber group, the fuel being supplied straight to a bolted connection on the welded chamber heads and the nitric acid passing through part-flexible pipes to regeneratively cool the bell mouth chamber nozzle and throat. Chamber pressure is given by

Left: **Exhibition model of the four-chamber RD-107 first-stage rocket engine of the Vostok space launch vehicle** (*TAM Air et Cosmos*)

Below: **The 158,800 lb (72,000 kg) thrust GDL RD-214 rocket engine used to power the first-stage Cosmos launcher**

GDL as 45 kg/cm² (640 lb/sq in) and specific impulse as 246. The four chambers are rigidly fixed to the Cosmos launcher first stage, vehicle control being accomplished by four refractory deflector vanes, one per chamber, mounted on the vehicle skirt control packages and projecting into the rocket exhaust. Several hundred RD-214 engines have been made and flown from Kapustin Yar on non-recoverable Cosmos missions.

GLUSHENKOV

This design bureau had not been named publicly until 1969 when it was revealed as that responsible for the TVD-10 engines fitted in the Beriev Be-30 STOL transport. The TVD-10 is a modern small turboprop in the 950 shp class, supplied to Beriev as a complete neatly-cowled unit with a modern reversing propeller produced specially for this application. The engine air intake is positioned below and behind the spinner but no details of the TVD-10 have yet been made available.

Glushenkov is also believed to be responsible for the 900 shp shaft-turbine engines in the Kamov Ka-25 helicopter.

ISOTOV
S. P. ISOTOV

This designer is responsible for the shaft-turbine engines which power the Mil Mi-2 and Mi-8 helicopters.

GTD-350

The GTD-350 is a free-turbine helicopter power plant. In the version used in the twin-engined Mil Mi-2, the drive is taken from the rear, with the twin jet-pipes of each engine exhausting to port (port engine) and starboard (starboard engine). The GTD-350 can be supplied with downward-facing jet-pipe and with drive from the front, if required. It is in production in both the Soviet Union and Poland. Time between overhauls is 500 hours.

TYPE: Axial/centrifugal-flow free-turbine turbo-shaft engine.

AIR INTAKE: Annular intake casing and inlet guide vanes of stainless steel. Automatic de-icing of inlet guide vanes and central bullet by air bleed from compressor.

COMPRESSOR: Seven axial stages and one centrifugal stage, all of steel, connected together with a tie-bolt. Discs shrunk-fitted to shaft. Blades of axial stages have dove-tail roots. Shaft carried in front roller bearing and rear ball bearing. Pressure ratio 5·9 : 1. Air mass flow 4·83 lb (2·19 kg)/sec at 45,000 rpm.

COMPRESSOR CASING: Horizontally-split aluminium alloy casing, with stator blades brazed to semi-rings. No diffuser blades.

COMBUSTION CHAMBER: Reverse-flow type with air supply through two tubes. Centrifugal duplex single-nozzle burner. Ignition system comprises burner and semi-conductor spark-plug. Eight thermocouples at gas outlet.

FUEL SYSTEM: Includes NR-40T pump governor with shut-off cock, which feeds fuel to burner, controls gas-generator rpm and limits max output; RO-40T power turbine rpm governor, DS-40 signal transmitter controlling bleed valves; and electro-magnetic valve to provide fuel for starting.

FUEL GRADE: TS-1 or TS-2.

COMPRESSOR TURBINE: Single-stage turbine with air-cooled disc. Shrouded blades with fir-tree roots. Precision-cast fixed guide vanes. Turbine casing has metal-graphite insert in plane of blades. Shaft supported in ball bearing at rear. Temperature before turbine 970°C.

POWER TURBINE: Two-stage constant-speed type (24,000 rpm). Shrouded blades with fir-tree roots. Discs bolted together. Stator blades welded to rings. Airflow is again reversed aft of power turbine.

JET PIPES: Two fixed-area jet-pipes.

REDUCTION GEARING: Two sets of gears, with ratio of 0·246 : 1, in cast magnesium alloy casing.

LUBRICATION SYSTEM: Closed type. Gear-type pump with one pressure and four scavenge units. Nominal oil pressure 43 lb/sq in (3±0·5 kg/cm²). Oil cooler and oil tank, capacity 2·75 Imp gallons (12·5 litres), fitted to airframe.

OIL GRADE: B3-W (Synthetic).

ACCESSORIES: STG3 3kW starter-generator, NR-40T governor pump, D1 tachometer generator and oil pumps mounted on reduction gear casing and driven by gas-generator. RO-40T rotating speed governor, D1 tachometer generator and centrifugal breather, also mounted on reduction gear casing, driven by power turbine.

STARTING: STG3 starter-generator suitable for operation at up to 13,125 ft (4,000 m) altitude.

Isotov GTD-350 turboshaft (395 shp = 400 cv)

DIMENSIONS:
Length overall	53·15 in (1,350 mm)
Max width	20·47 in (520 mm)
Max height	24·80 in (630 mm)

DRY WEIGHT:
Less jet pipes and accessories	298 lb (135 kg)

PERFORMANCE RATINGS:
T-O rating (6 min)
395 shp (400 cv) at 94% max gas-generator rpm
Nominal rating (1 hr)
315 shp (320 cv) at 89% gas-generator rpm
Cruising rating (II)
281 shp (285 cv) at 86·5% gas-generator rpm
Cruising rating (I)
232 shp (235 cv) at 83·5% gas-generator rpm

SPECIFIC FUEL CONSUMPTIONS:
At T-O rating	0·805 lb/shp/hr (370 gr/cv/hr)
At nominal rating	0·861 lb/shp/hr (396 gr/cv/hr)
At cruising rating (II)	0·913 lb/shp/hr (420 gr/cv/hr)
At cruising rating (I)	0·978 lb/shp/hr (450 gr/cv/hr)

OIL CONSUMPTION:
Max	0·53 Imp pts (0·3 litres)/hr

TB-2-117

Two shaft-turbine engines designated TB-2-117, of Isotov design, power the Mil Mi-8 transport helicopter. Nothing is known about them, except that each develops 1,500 shp.

M
A. A. MIKULIN
M-11

Very large numbers of M-11 five-cylinder radial engines have been built in the Soviet Union and Poland to power a variety of light aircraft and helicopters. Best-known variants are the 125 hp M-11D and the 160 hp M-11FR which powers the Yak-18 primary trainer.

Swept volume of the M-11 is 525 cu in (8,600 cc). Compression ratio is 5 : 1 in the M-11D and 5·5 : 1 in the M-11FR. Both versions operate on 72 octane fuel.

WEIGHTS:
M-11D	362 lb (164 kg)
M-11FR	397 lb (180 kg)

PERFORMANCE RATINGS:
T-O rating:
M-11D	125 hp at 1,760 rpm
M-11FR	160 hp at 1,900 rpm

Rated power:
M-11D	115 hp at 1,700 rpm
M-11FR	140 hp at 1,760 rpm

SPECIFIC FUEL CONSUMPTIONS:
At T-O rating:
M-11D	0·573-0·639 lb (260-290 gr)/hp/hr
M-11FR	0·551-0·595 lb (250-270 gr)/hp/hr

At rated power:
M-11D	0·551-0·595 lb (250-270 gr)/hp/hr
M-11FR	0·529-0·573 lb (240-260 gr)/hp/hr

RD-3M-500

The basic RD-3M (or AM-3M) single-spool axial-flow turbojet was developed under the design leadership of P. F. Zubets from the original Mikulin M-209 (civil RD-3 or AM-3) engine which

The 125 hp Mikulin M-11D (left) and 160 hp M-11FR radial engines

powered the Tu-16 and Mya-4 bombers and was adapted for Russia's first jet transport, the Tu-104.

The RD-3M-500 was evolved, in turn, from the RD-3M and powers the Tu-104A and Tu-104B commercial transports. It has a simple basic configuration, with an eight-stage axial-flow compressor, annular type combustion system with 14 flame tubes, and a two-stage turbine. The compressor casing is made in front, centre and rear portions, the front casing housing a row of inlet guide vanes. A bullet fairing mounted centrally in the annular ram air intake houses a

type S-300M gas-turbine starter, developing 90-100 hp at 31,000-35,000 rpm. The jet-pipe consists of a central cone and fixed nozzle with an orifice diameter of approximately 33 in (840 mm). Pressure ratio is 6·4 : 1, temperature after turbine 720°C and TBO 1,500 hours in the spring of 1966.

DIMENSIONS:
Length overall	210·23 in (5,340 mm)
Diameter	55·12 in (1,400 mm)

PERFORMANCE RATING:
T-O	20,940 lb (9,500 kg) st

NK
N. D. KUZNETSOV
NK-8

One of the largest Russian civil turbofans known to exist, the NK-8 has been developed through a number of variants, the most powerful of which is the NK-144 supersonic augmented engine for the Tupolev Tu-144 supersonic transport. Basic versions are the 22,273 lb (10,500 kg) thrust NK-8-4 powering the three-engined Tupolev Tu-154 transport aircraft, and the de-rated 20,950 lb (9,500 kg) NK-8-2 powering the first-generation Ilyushin Il-62 four-engined transport.

The engine comprises a two-stage fan and two-stage LP compressor, driven by a two-stage LP turbine, and six-stage HP compressor driven by a single-stage HP turbine. As with all Russian turbofans to date, the NK-8 has a full-length by-pass duct. The following data apply to the NK-8-4.

DIMENSIONS:
Length	201 in (5,100 mm)
Diameter	56·8 in (1,442 mm)

WEIGHTS:
Dry without accessories	4,850 lb (2,200 kg)
Dry with thrust reverser	5,291 lb (2,400 kg)

PERFORMANCE:
T-O rating	22,273 lb (10,500 kg)
Cruise rating at 36,000 ft (11,000 m) and 530 mph (850 km/h)	6,063 lb (2,750 kg)

SPECIFIC FUEL CONSUMPTION:
At cruise rating at 36,000 ft (11,000 m) and 530 mph (850 km/h) 0·78

NK-144

This is the two-spool turbofan installed in the Soviet Union's first supersonic transport aircraft, the Tu-144. It is a development of the NK-8 and the first five pre-production NK-144s completed some 1,500 hours of bench-testing by October 1965. The engine flew in at least one airborne test aircraft before the start of the Tu-144 flight programme in 1968.

The NK-144 has a five-stage fan/LP compressor, eleven-stage HP compressor, annular combustion chamber, single-stage HP turbine and two-stage LP turbine. Air-cooled blades are used in the

HP turbine and titanium is used extensively in construction of the engine. By-pass ratio is reported to be 1 : 1 and pressure ratio 15 : 1. A partial afterburning installation is provided, with a hydraulically-actuated variable-area nozzle. Gas temperature at turbine entry is 1,300°K.

DIMENSIONS:
Length overall	204·7 in (5,200 mm)
Diameter	59 in (1,500 mm)

WEIGHT:
Without jet-pipe, but with afterburner	6,283 lb (2,850 kg)

PERFORMANCE RATINGS:
Max, without afterburning	28,660 lb (13,000 kg) st
Max, with afterburning	38,580 lb (17,500 kg) st

NK-12M

Designed at Kuibishev under the leadership of N. D. Kuznetsov and former German engineers, the NK-12M is the most powerful turboprop engine in the world. In its original form as the NK-12M it developed 12,000 ehp. The later NK-12MV is rated at 14,795 ehp (15,000 ch e) and powers the Tupolev Tu-114 transport, driving four-blade contra-rotating propellers of 18 ft 4 in (5·6 m) diameter. As the NK-12MA, it powers the Antonov An-22 military transport, with propellers of 20 ft 4 in (6·2 m) diameter. A third application is in the Tupolev Tu-20 bomber.

The NK-12M has a single 14-stage axial-flow compressor and the complete rotating assembly weighs about a ton. Compression ratio varies from 9 : 1 to 13 : 1 according to altitude, and variable inlet guide vanes and blow-off valves are provided to facilitate engine handling. A cannular-type combustion system is used: each separate flame tube is mounted centrally on a downstream injector, but all tubes merge at their maximum diameter to form an annular secondary region. The turbine is of the five-stage axial-flow type. Mass flow is reported to be 137 lb (62 kg) sec.

The casing is made in four portions, from sheet steel, and is precision welded. An electric control for variation of propeller pitch is incorporated, to maintain constant engine speed.

DIMENSIONS:
Length   236·2 in (6,000 mm)
Diameter   45·3 in (1,150 mm)

WEIGHT (DRY):   5,070 lb (2,300 kg)

PERFORMANCE RATINGS:
T-O   14,795 ehp (15,000 ch e)
Nominal power   11,836 ehp (12,000 ch e) at
                                          8,300 rpm
Idling speed   6,600 rpm

Kuznetsov NK-8-2 turbofan (20,950 lb = 9,500 kg st)
(*courtesy of Aviation Magazine International, Paris*)

The 14,795 ehp Kuznetsov NK-12M single-shaft turboprop engine (*courtesy of Aviation Magazine International, Paris*)

SOLOVIEV

Engines for which Soloviev's design team is reported to be responsible include the turbofans fitted in the Tupolev Tu-124 and Tu-134 transport aircraft and the shaft-turbine which powers the Mi-6 and Mi-10 helicopters.

SOLOVIEV D-20P

The D-20P is a two-spool turbofan engine, of which two power the Tupolev Tu-124 transport aircraft. It has a three-stage axial fan designed for supersonic airflow, an eight-stage axial-flow high-pressure compressor, single-stage high-pressure turbine, and a two-stage low-pressure turbine driving the fan. To ensure compressor stability and to avoid resonance at low rpm, an automatic control, operated by fuel pressure valves, bleeds air out into the by-pass duct.

A can-annular combustion chamber contains 12 flame-tubes. Fuel injectors are described as being of the twin-channel, twin-flow centrifugal type. No information on methods of construction or materials has been released, except that the HP turbine has cast blades, and a cooled disc and stator blades, while the LP turbine has forged blades. The jet-pipe is of constant cross-section. By-pass ratio is 1 : 1. Pressure ratios are 2·6 : 1 for the fan and 5 : 1 for the HP compressor at nominal rating. Air mass flow is 249 lb (113 kg)/sec. Gas temperature downstream of the turbine is 650°C.

Two gearboxes provide accessory drives for a starter-generator, tachometer, air-compressors, hydraulic pump, oil pump and other controls and instruments. For re-starting in flight, an altitude sensing device meters fuel flow appropriate to height. An automatic fire-extinguishing system is fitted. De-icing of the air intake and inlet guide vanes is by hot air bled from

either the eighth or fourth compressor stage, depending on engine rpm.

Oil pressure is 50-64 lb/sq in (3·4-4·5 kg/cm²). The fan turns at 8,550 rpm at T-O rating and 7,900 rpm at nominal rating. Comparable figures for the HP compressor are 11,700 and 11,170 rpm respectively.

DIMENSIONS:
Length overall   130 in (3,304 mm)
Diameter, bare   38·3 in (976 mm)
WEIGHT (DRY):   3,240 lb (1,470 kg)
PERFORMANCE RATING:
Max T-O rating   11,905 lb (5,400 kg) st
SPECIFIC FUEL CONSUMPTION:
At Mach 0·82 at 32,800 ft (10,000 m)   0·78

Soloviev D-20P turbofan engine (11,905 lb = 5,400 kg st) (*courtesy of Aviation Magazine International, Paris*)

SOLOVIEV D-25V

The D-25V is a free-turbine shaft-turbine engine which powers the Mil Mi-6, Mi-10 and Mi-10K helicopters and was also fitted to the Kamov Ka-22 experimental convertiplane. It is usually referred to officially by the designation **TB-2BM**.

The basic gas-generator consists of a nine-stage axial-flow compressor, cannular combustion chamber containing 12 flame-tubes, and a single-stage axial-flow turbine. A two-stage axial-flow free turbine, aft of the compressor turbine and independent of it, drives the helicopter rotor through a reduction gear and shaft. The reduction gear receives the drive-shafts of two D-25V engines in the standard helicopter power plant, but is so designed that it continues to function if either engine fails. Main rotor/engine rpm ratio is 1 : 69·2 and pressure ratio 5·6 : 1.

The D-25V is flat-rated to maintain rated power to 10,000 ft (3,000 m) or to temperatures up to 40°C at sea level.

DIMENSIONS:
Length overall, bare   107·75 in (2,737 mm)
Length overall with transmission shaft
                              218·0 in (5,537 mm)
WEIGHT, DRY:
With jet-pipe   2,645 lb (1,200 kg)
PERFORMANCE RATINGS:
T-O   5,500 eshp
Rated power   4,700 eshp
SPECIFIC FUEL CONSUMPTION:
At cruise rating at 10,000 ft (3,000 m)
                              0·613 lb (278 gr)/hp/hr

SOLOVIEV D-30

This two-spool turbofan engine powers the Tu-134 twin-engined airliner. The four-stage axial-flow fan/LP compressor is designed for transonic airflow and is driven at up to 8,000 rpm by the two-stage LP turbine. The 10-stage axial-flow HP compressor is driven at up to 11,600 rpm by the two-stage HP turbine, which is air-cooled. A cannular combustion chamber, with 12 flame-tubes, is used. Gas temperature upstream of the turbine is 1,300°K.

Titanium is used extensively in the D-30. In particular, the air intake, first fan stage and the HP compressor are made of titanium alloys.

By-pass ratio is 1 : 1 and overall compression ratio 18·6 : 1. The central portions of this engine are closely similar to those of the earlier D-20.

DIMENSIONS:
Length overall   154·7 in (3,930 mm)
WEIGHT, DRY: 3,350 lb (1,520 kg)
PERFORMANCE RATING:
T-O   14,990 lb (6,800 kg) st
SPECIFIC FUEL CONSUMPTION:
At T-O rating   0·6
At Mach 0·8 at 36,000 ft (11,000 m)   0·77

SOLOVIEV D-30K

Despite its designation, this turbofan engine is very different from the D-30P, described above. It is larger, has a much higher rating, has a by-pass ratio of 2·3 : 1, mass flow of 600 lb/sec (272 kg/sec) and an overall pressure ratio of 20 : 1.

The D-30K has a three-stage axial-flow fan/LP compressor driven by a four-stage LP turbine and an eleven-stage HP compressor driven by a two-stage HP turbine, of which the first stage is cooled. A cannular-type combustion chamber, with 12 flame-tubes, is used.

It is reported that the D-30K may supersede the Kuznetsov NK-8 as the power plant of the Ilyushin Il-62 long-range transport aircraft.

DIMENSIONS:
Length   181·5 in (4,610 mm)
Length with exhaust nozzle   226·7 in (5,760 mm)
Diameter, inside intake   57·3 in (1,455 mm)
Max diameter   61·4 in (1,560 mm)
WEIGHTS:
Dry, without reverser   4,740 lb (2,150 kg)
Dry, with thrust reverser   5,291 lb (2,400 kg)
PERFORMANCE RATINGS:
T-O at ISA   25,350 lb (11,500 kg) st
Nominal (1 hr)   20,944 lb (9,500 kg) st
Max cruise at 36,000 ft and Mach 0·8
                             6,063 lb (2,750 kg) st
SPECIFIC FUEL CONSUMPTION:
At T-O rating   0·49
At nominal rating (1 hr)   0·48
At max cruise at 36,000 ft and Mach 0·8 0·67

Production 5,500 ehp Soloviev D-25V turboshaft engine at the Perm aircraft engine works (*Tass*)

Soloviev D-30 turbofan (14,990 lb = 6,800 kg st) (*courtesy of Aviation Magazine International, Paris*)

Soloviev D-30K turbofan (25,350 lb = 11,500 kg st)
(*courtesy of Aviation Magazine International, Paris*)

VK

V. Y. KLIMOV

VK-1

Led by the late V. Y. Klimov, the Russians developed the Rolls-Royce Nene in much the same way as that by which the Tay was developed from the Nene by both Rolls-Royce and Pratt & Whitney. Without increasing the overall diameter the engine was redesigned internally, to permit about 30 per cent more air to pass through the engine, and to enable it to develop a static thrust of 5,955 lb (2,700 kg) for an engine weight of 2,000 lb (900 kg), as compared with

5,000 lb (2,270 kg) st and 1,715 lb (780 kg) weight of the original Nene.

Known as the VK-1, the redesigned engine powers the MiG-15bis and most production Il-28's. More than 30,000 were built in 1950-56 in Engine Plant No. 45, near Moscow.

The VK-1A which powers the MiG-17 is fitted with an afterburner with which the maximum thrust is 7,590 lb (3,450 kg).

VK-5 (or M-205?)

The VK-5 (sometimes referred to as M-205) is the power-plant of the MiG-19 and Yak-25. Little is known about this power-unit beyond the fact that it is a small-diameter (approximately

32 in = 810 mm) axial-flow turbojet with a rated output of 6,500 lb (2,950 kg) st at sea level. Thrust with afterburner in use is 8,818 lb (4,000 kg).

VK-7 (RD-9F)

It was reported in the autumn of 1961 that this turbojet engine had been offered to India, to power production versions of the Hindustan HF-24 fighter. It is said to be a development of the VK-5 engine used in the MiG-19, and to be comparable in size with the Bristol Siddeley Orpheus BOr.12. It develops 6,700 lb (3,040 kg) st dry and weighs approximately 150 lb (70 kg) more than the BOr.12.

ENGINES OF UNKNOWN DESIGN

1. **Type 37V.** Two Type 37V turbojet engines were fitted to the RV aircraft which set up two payload-to-height records in 1959. Their thrust was given as 8,818 lb (4,000 kg) and they could be the same as the engine listed above under the designation VK-5 or M-205.

2. **Type AL-7PB.** This is the designation of the 14,330 lb (6,500 kg) st turbojet of which two power the Beriev M-10 flying-boat.

3. **Type D-15.** This was given as the designation of the four turbojet engines fitted in the Myasishchev 103-M and 201-M (modified Mya-4) aircraft which set up a number of closed circuit

and payload-to-height records in 1959. At a rating of 28,660 lb (13,000 kg) st, the D-15 is one of the most powerful turbojet engines yet known to have flown.

4. **GRD Mk U2.** The rocket engine fitted to the Mikoyan E-66A aircraft which set up a world height record in April 1961 carries this designation. It develops 6,615 lb (3,000 kg) thrust, presumably at sea level.

5. **R37F.** This is the designation given for the turbojet engine fitted in the Mikoyan E-66 used to set up world speed and height records in 1959-61. Its maximum rating was stated

to be 13,117 lb (5,950 kg) st and the prefix "R" may indicate that it is a reheat version of the Type 37V listed earlier.

6. **TRD Mk P.166/TRD 31.** P.166 is the designation given to the 22,046 lb (10,000 kg) st turbojet fitted in the Mikoyan E-166 aircraft that held the world's absolute speed record. The same rating is quoted for the TRD 31 turbojet fitted in the T-431 aircraft, implying that the designation is related to the aircraft in which the engine is fitted; and the TRD Mk P.166 and TRD 31 are almost certainly versions of the same turbojet. Reheat provides a 50 per cent thrust boost, static.

7. RU-19-300. An auxiliary turbojet of 1,985 lb (900 kg) st for which the only known application is in the Antonov An-24RV transport. Mounted in the rear of the starboard nacelle in place of the TG-16 APU, the RU-19-300 provides additional take-off thrust and also drives an integrally-mounted generator to relieve the aircraft's AI-24T turboprops of supplying electrical power during take-off. This arrangement increases the An-24RV's take-off performance under hot and high conditions, and improves single-engine handling and stability. After take-off, the auxiliary turbojet is shut down and the AI-24Ts coupled mechanically to the engine-mounted generators. In this dual role the RU-19-300 provides 485 lb (220 kg) st for take-off. During flight the auxiliary turbojet is available for use as an APU.

8. Lift Jet. Russian development of lift-jet engines (possibly by modification of existing small turbojets) was demonstrated at the 1967 Domodedovo air show by one Sukhoi and two Mikoyan experimental STOL aircraft.

9. Lift/Cruise Engine. The V/STOL research aircraft ("Freehand") demonstrated at the 1967 Domodedovo air show was powered by a twin-nozzle vectored-thrust propulsion system. The use of a large bifurcated nose intake and only two exhaust nozzles suggests that the installation may make use of two standard turbojets or turbofans fitted with single swivelling nozzles.

10. AI-8. A turbogenerator unit, probably of Ivchenko origin.

11. AI-9. A turbo-compressor unit, probably of Ivchenko origin, installed in the Yak-40 to provide self-contained starting for the Ivchenko AI-25 turbofans.

RU-19-300 auxiliary turbojet (1,985 lb = 900 kg st) installed in Antonov An-24RV to provide take-off boost and electrical supply

ADDENDA

ARGENTINE REPUBLIC

AL-AIRE
TALLERES AL-AIRE SCA

ADDRESS: Aerodromo San Fernando, Provincia Buenos Aires

Talleres Al-Aire SCA undertakes overhaul and repair work, up to fuselage rebuild standard, on light aircraft.

In addition to this work, its premises are currently in use by some of the members of AVEX (which see), who have under development a new aerobatic training aircraft known as the T-11 Cacique, designed by Ing Alfredo Turbay. All known details of this aircraft are given below.

TURBAY T-11 CACIQUE

A group of AVEX members, led by Ing Alfredo Turbay and including Prof Adolfo Yakstas and Sr Norberto S. Cobelo, have begun the development of this two-seat aerobatic and training aircraft as a potential replacement for the obsolete Piper types used by Argentine flying clubs. The original design was by Ing Turbay, but this was subsequently modified and construction of a prototype began in January 1970. Completion was anticipated by mid-1970, with the first flight following shortly afterwards; certification was anticipated by the end of the year, and it was hoped to begin production in 1971. The following description applies to the prototype.

TYPE: Two-seat training and aerobatic aircraft, stressed for $\pm 6g$.

WINGS: Cantilever high-wing monoplane, of laminar-flow profile. Wing section NACA 63₂A415 (modified) at root, NACA 63₁A212 (modified) at tip. Incidence 2° at root, 0° 30' at tip. Dihedral 2° from centre-section. All-metal structure, with glass-fibre wingtip fuel tanks. Ailerons and semi-Fowler flaps on trailing-edge. No tabs.

FUSELAGE: All-metal semi-monocoque structure. Engine cowling metal on prototype, glass-fibre on production version.

TAIL UNIT: Cantilever metal structure, with glass-fibre tips. Sweptback fin and rudder. Tab in elevator.

LANDING GEAR: Non-retractable tricycle type, with glass-fibre cantilever one-piece leg for main units. Steerable nose unit, fitted with maintenance-free polyurethane shock-absorber. Hydraulic brakes.

POWER PLANT: One 100 hp Continental O-200-A four-cylinder horizontally-opposed air-cooled engine, driving a McCauley two-blade fixed-pitch metal propeller. Fuel in two plastic wingtip tanks, total capacity 12·3 Imp gallons (56 litres), and small aerobatic tank for inverted flight. Refuelling point on top of each tiptank.

ACCOMMODATION: Seats for two persons in tandem in fully-enclosed cabin, with access via large door on starboard side. Dual controls fitted.

DIMENSIONS, EXTERNAL:
Wing span	29 ft 6¼ in (9·00 m)
Wing aspect ratio	7·5
Length overall	22 ft 1 in (6·73 m)
Height overall	7 ft 8¾ in (2·36 m)
Fuselage: max width over cowling	2 ft 9¼ in (0·85 m)

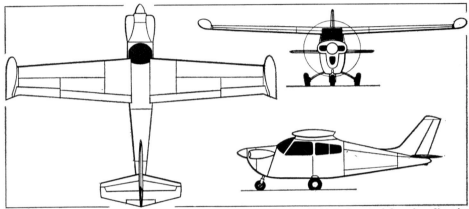

Photograph (*Alex Reinhard*) **and three-view drawing of the Turbay T-11 Cacique training aircraft under construction in Argentina**

Fuselage: max width aft of cowling	2 ft 6 in (0·76 m)

DIMENSIONS, INTERNAL:
Cabin: Length	6 ft 4¾ in (1·95 m)
Max height	4 ft 3¼ in (1·30 m)
Min height	3 ft 8¾ in (1·14 m)

AREAS:
Wings, gross	115·2 sq ft (10·70 m²)
Horizontal tail surfaces (total)	22·4 sq ft (2·08 m²)
Vertical tail surfaces (total)	12·4 sq ft (1·15 m²)

WEIGHTS AND LOADINGS:
Weight empty	751 lb (341 kg)
Max T-O weight (aerobatic)	1,323 lb (600 kg)
Max wing loading	11·5 lb/sq ft (56 kg/m²)
Max power loading	13·23 lb/hp (6 kg/hp)

PERFORMANCE (estimated, at max T-O weight):
Max level speed	122 knots (140 mph; 226 km/h)
Max cruising speed (70% power)	108 knots (124 mph; 200 km/h)
Stalling speed, flaps up	51·3 knots (59 mph; 95 km/h)
Stalling speed, flaps down	42·6 knots (49 mph; 79 km/h)
Rate of climb at S/L	850 ft (259 m)/min
Service ceiling	19,030 ft (5,800 m)
Absolute ceiling	20,670 ft (6,300 m)
T-O run at S/L	377 ft (115 m)
T-O to 50 ft (15 m)	938 ft (286 m)
Landing run	328 ft (100 m)
Range	566 nm (652 miles; 1,050 km)
Endurance	5 hr 15 min

AVEX
ASOCIACION ARGENTINA DE CONSTRUCTORES DE AVIONES EXPERIMENTALES

ADDRESS:
Avenida Centenario 235, 2nd Floor Apartment C, San Isidro, Provincia Buenos Aires

PRESIDENT: Yves Arrambide

AVEX is an Argentine light aircraft association for amateur constructors, similar in concept to the Experimental Aircraft Association in the US. It was formed in 1968 and its members include many people well known among the Argentine aircraft industry, including specialists in most aspects of materials and construction, including the use of glass-fibre and plastics. Ing Alfredo Turbay and Prof Adolfo Yakstas, both members of AVEX, are concerned in the development of the Turbay T-11 Cacique two-seat light aircraft, a prototype of which was built in 1970 at the San Fernando works of Al-Aire (which see).

Among current AVEX activities in 1970 were the completion of a new high-performance all-glass-fibre sailplane, designed by Prof Yakstas and Sr Otto Breithaupt, and the building of a Pazmany PL-2 light aircraft. (Mr Ladislao Pazmany is an Argentine citizen, but is now resident in the United States; a description of the PL-2 appears under the Pazmany heading in the main US section of this edition.)

BASERGA H.B.1

Approval to begin testing the H.B.1 was given in December 1968, when two days of ground handling and taxying tests were carried out. As a result of these tests, modifications were made to the brakes and tailwheel assembly, and the fin and rudder areas were increased, in order to improve directional stability. It was hoped to make the first flight on the third day, but this attempt was prevented by severe bad weather during which the aircraft sustained damage to the wings and the lower part of the fuselage. On the following day Ing Baserga was due to depart for the USA, where he is now resident, and no further attempt to fly the aircraft had been made by mid-1970. The H.B.1 was then in the Al-Aire workshops at San Fernando Aerodrome, where Prof Yakstas hopes eventually to undertake further modification of the design.

CICARELLI

It is now known that the name of the designer of the Cicaré No 1 and No 2 helicopters, described on page 2 of this edition, is Sr Cicaré, and not Cicarelli as was originally believed.

TURBAY

Ing Alfredo Turbay is now a member of AVEX, and is undertaking development of his latest design, the T-11 Cacique light aircraft, at the factory of Al-Aire (which see).

BRAZIL

EMBRAER
EMPRÊSA BRASILEIRA DE AERONÁUTICA SA

HEAD OFFICE AND WORKS:
Caixa Postal 343, São José dos Campos, São Paulo State

PRESIDENT:
Dr Aldo Baptista Franco da Silva Santos

SUPERINTENDENT DIRECTOR:
Lt Col Av Eng Ozires Silva

PRODUCTION DIRECTOR:
Dr Ozilio Carlos da Silva

TECHNICAL DIRECTOR:
Dr Guido Fontegalante Pessotti

INDUSTRIAL RELATIONS DIRECTOR:
Dr Antônio Garcia da Silveira

FINANCIAL DIRECTOR:
Alberto Franco Faria Marcondes

COMMERCIAL DIRECTOR:
Lt Col Renato José da Silva

Embraer was created on 30 December 1969, by Presidential Decree No 66,005, to promote the development of the Brazilian aircraft industry. It has a capital of US $12 million, which is to be increased to $127·28 million over the next six years. The Federal Government of Brazil owns 51% of the shares, the remaining 49% being owned by private shareholders.

The principal current programmes of Embraer are the series production of the IPD-6504 Bandeirante twin-turboprop transport aircraft, production of the IPD-6505 Urupema single-seat sailplane, and licence manufacture of the Italian Aermacchi M.B.326G jet trainer/ground attack aircraft, of which 112 were ordered for the Brazilian Air Force on 29 May 1970. Under development are the IPD-6909 Ipanema agricultural aircraft, and a twin-turboprop medium transport aircraft.

Embraer is responsible for project design work on new prototype aircraft, including all development work previously started at PAR.

EMBRAER IPD-6504 BANDEIRANTE

Brazilian Air Force designation: C-95

The Bandeirante twin-turboprop light transport was developed to a Ministry of Aeronautics specification calling for a general-purpose aircraft capable of carrying out missions such as transport, navigation training and aeromedical evacuation. Its Brazilian design team was, initially, under the leadership of M Max Holste, the well-known French aircraft designer.

Construction of the first prototype was started at the PAR-Departamento de Aeronaves of the Centro Técnico de Aeronáutica in mid-1966. Designated YC-95, and bearing serial number 2130, this aircraft flew for the first time on 26 October 1968, with test pilots Maj Av José Mariotto Ferreira and Eng Michel Cury at the controls. The second prototype (2131) flew for the first time on 19 October 1969, and the basically similar third YC-95 on 26 June 1970. The latter aircraft, registered PP-ZCN, has been purchased by the Comissão Nacional de Atividades Espaciais, and is to be fitted with remote sensors for use in the space agency's Project SERE. The CNAE has an option on two additional production Bandeirantes.

The fourth Bandeirante, which is expected to fly in mid-1971, will be representative of the production version, as depicted in the three-view drawing on page 12 of this edition. It will incorporate a number of design refinements, such as aerodynamically better nose/windshield contours, more streamlined engine nacelles, more powerful engines, five (instead of four) windows, of modified shape, in each side of the fuselage, increased overall length and improved performance.

EMBRAER IPD-6901 IPANEMA

This agricultural aircraft was designed and developed to specifications laid down by the Brazilian Ministry of Agriculture. Design was started in May 1969 by the PAR-Departamento de Aeronaves of the CTA, and construction of a prototype began in November 1969. Responsibility for its development was transferred to Embraer after the creation of this company, on 2 January 1970, and the prototype (PP-ZIP) made its first flight on 30 July 1970.

Subject to the successful completion of flight and other testing, an initial series of 50 production aircraft is to be built: 10 for the Ministry of Agriculture and 40 for sale to private operators.

The correct designation is now understood to be IPD-6901, and not IPD-6909 as previously reported.

TYPE: Single-seat agricultural aircraft.

WINGS: Cantilever low-wing monoplane. Wing section NACA 23015. Dihedral 7° from roots. Incidence 3°. All-metal single-spar structure of 2024 light alloy with all-metal Frise-type ailerons outboard and all-metal slotted flaps (max deflection 45°) on trailing-edge, and detachable leading-edge. No tabs.

Prototype IPD-6901 Ipanema during its first flight on 30 July 1970 *(Ronaldo S. Olive)*

FUSELAGE: Rectangular-section all-metal safe-life structure, of welded 4130 steel tube with removable skin panels of 2024 light alloy. Structure is specially treated against chemical corrosion.

TAIL UNIT: Cantilever two-spar all-metal structure of 2024 light alloy. Slight sweepback on fin and rudder. Fixed-incidence tailplane. Trim-tabs in rudder and starboard elevator.

LANDING GEAR: Non-retractable tail-wheel type, with rubber shock-absorbers on main units. Tail-wheel has tapered spring shock-absorber. Goodyear main wheels and tyres, size 6·50 × 8, pressure 48 lb/sq in (3·4 kg/cm²). Scott tail-wheel, diameter 8 in (20 cm). Goodyear hydraulic disc brakes on main units.

POWER PLANT: One 260 hp Lycoming O-540-H1A5 horizontally-opposed air-cooled engine, driving a McCauley 1A200/FA9041 two-blade fixed-pitch metal propeller, diameter 7 ft 6 in (2·29 m). Integral fuel tank in each leading-edge, with total capacity of 57 Imp gallons (260 litres). Refuelling point on top of each tank. Oil capacity 2·6 Imp gallons (12 litres).

ACCOMMODATION: Single seat for pilot, in fully-enclosed cabin with bottom-hinged window/door on each side.

SYSTEMS: Hydraulic brake actuation. 12V electrical system. Oxygen system optional.

ELECTRONICS AND EQUIPMENT: Standard VFR equipment, including VHF radio transceiver. Standard agricultural equipment includes a 1,212 lb (550 kg) capacity hopper, located in the centre of the CG range and suitable for dust or liquids. Spray booms, when fitted, project slightly aft and below the wing trailing-edges.

DIMENSIONS, EXTERNAL:
- Wing span: 36 ft 9 in (11·20 m)
- Wing chord (constant): 5 ft 3 in (1·60 m)
- Wing aspect ratio: 6·84
- Length overall: 24 ft 4½ in (7·43 m)
- Height overall (tail down): 7 ft 2½ in (2·20 m)
- Fuselage max width: 3 ft 0½ in (0·93 m)
- Tailplane span: 11 ft 4¼ in (3·46 m)
- Wheel track: 7 ft 2½ in (2·20 m)
- Wheelbase: 17 ft 7¼ in (5·20 m)

DIMENSIONS, INTERNAL:
- Cabin: Max length: 3 ft 11¼ in (1·20 m)
  - Max width: 2 ft 9½ in (0·85 m)
  - Max height: 4 ft 4¾ in (1·34 m)

AREAS:
- Wings, gross: 193·75 sq ft (18·00 m²)
- Ailerons (total): 17·21 sq ft (1·60 m²)
- Flaps (total): 24·76 sq ft (2·30 m²)
- Fin: 13·02 sq ft (1·21 m²)
- Rudder: 6·78 sq ft (0·63 m²)
- Tailplane: 32·29 sq ft (3·00 m²)
- Elevators, incl tab: 16·15 sq ft (1·50 m²)

WEIGHTS AND LOADINGS:
- Weight empty, equipped: 1,433 lb (650 kg)
- Max T-O and landing weight:
  - with agricultural equipment: 3,086 lb (1,400 kg)
  - without agricultural equipment: 2,204 lb (1,000 kg)
- Max wing loading: 18·0 lb/sq ft (78 kg/m²)
- Max power loading: 11·9 lb/hp (5·4 kg/hp)

PERFORMANCE (estimated, at max T-O weight, ISA; A = with, B = without agricultural equipment):
- Max level speed at S/L:
  - A: 107 knots (123 mph; 198 km/h)
  - B: 120 knots (138 mph; 222·5 km/h)
- Max permissible diving speed:
  - A, B: 183 knots (211 mph; 340 km/h)
- Max cruising speed:
  - A: 93 knots (107 mph; 173 km/h)
  - B: 108 knots (124 mph; 200 km/h)
- Econ cruising speed:
  - A: 89 knots (103 mph; 165 km/h)
  - B: 98 knots (113 mph; 182 km/h)
- Stalling speed, flaps up:
  - A: 64 knots (73 mph; 117 km/h)
- Stalling speed, flaps down:
  - B: 44 knots (50 mph; 80 km/h)
- Rate of climb at S/L:
  - A: 951 ft (290 m)/min
  - B: 1,988 ft (606 m)/min
- Service ceiling:
  - A: 12,960 ft (3,950 m)
  - B: 22,145 ft (6,750 m)
- T-O run:
  - A: 604 ft (184 m)
  - B: 433 ft (132 m)
- T-O to 50 ft (15 m):
  - A: 971 ft (296 m)
  - B: 1,247 ft (380 m)
- Landing from 50 ft (15 m):
  - A: 1,273 ft (388 m)
  - B: 1,171 ft (357 m)
- Landing run:
  - A: 545 ft (166 m)
  - B: 469 ft (143 m)
- Range with max fuel:
  - B: 646 nm (745 miles; 1,200 km)
- Range with max payload:
  - A: 312 nm (360 miles; 580 km)
- Max endurance:
  - B: 6 hr 45 min

CANADA

DE HAVILLAND CANADA

DHC-4A CARIBOU

Two Caribou have been ordered by Guyana Airways Corporation. The first of these was delivered in June 1970. Three others have been sold to the Sultan of Muscat and Oman's Air Force, for delivery in 1970.

DHC-5 BUFFALO

As reported briefly on page 20 of this edition, a NASA-owned C-8A Buffalo is to be modified as a flying test-bed for the "augmentor wing" concept devised by de Havilland Canada. NASA has selected The Boeing Company for final negotiation of the modification contract, and is also negotiating with the Canadian Department of Industry, Trade and Commerce for joint participation in the development and testing of the Buffalo flight test aircraft, with de Havilland as the Canadian prime contractor. Following delivery of the modified aircraft, NASA, the DITC, de Havilland Canada, Rolls-Royce and Boeing will participate in an estimated 12-month flight test programme to demonstrate and evaluate the augmentor wing concept.

The augmentor wing employs a blown flap system in which the air from a turbofan engine is directed internally along the aircraft wing and expelled rearwards through a slot, so that the air flows between the upper and lower segments of the trailing-edge flap. The slot formed when the flaps are extended rearward is called an ejector duct, and when in use during take-off and landing more than doubles the wing lifting capability. Wind tunnel tests already carried out by de Havilland Canada have shown that an airliner of the Boeing 737 type fitted with this device could operate from 2,000 ft (610 m) runways.

In addition to the wing modifications, the Buffalo flight test aircraft will also be fitted with a power plant incorporating modified Rolls-Royce Spey turbofan engines, designed by DHC and financed by the Canadian government as the Canadian contribution to the programme. DHC and Boeing also have an agreement for co-operation in the further exploitation of the augmentor wing concept for both civil and military applications.

HUNEAULT

JEAN PAUL HUNEAULT

ADDRESS: 95 Deslauriers, Pierrefonds, Quebec

HUNEAULT DHC-1B-2 CHIPMUNK CONTINENTAL

Mr Huneault has now modified his converted Chipmunk (see description on page 25 of this edition) by shortening the main landing gear by 7¼ in (18·4 cm) in the air, as a result of which the max level speed has been increased by about 13 knots (15 mph; 24 km/h). Plans to fit a retractable landing gear have now been abandoned.

Certification of the aircraft in this modified form, with main wheel fairings added, was

Huneault DHC-1B-2 Chipmunk Continental, in latest form with shortened landing gear *(Graham Wragg)*

anticipated in July 1970, and it has been entered for a number of Canadian aerobatic competitions to be held during the year.

DIMENSIONS, EXTERNAL:

Wing span	34 ft 4 in (10·46 m)
Length overall	25 ft 5 in (7·75 m)
Height overall	7 ft 0 in (2·13 m)
Tailplane span	11 ft 11 in (3·63 m)
Wheel track	8 ft 11 in (2·72 m)

WEIGHTS:

Weight empty	1,412 lb (640 kg)
Max T-O and landing weight	2,050 lb (929 kg)

PERFORMANCE (at max T-O weight):

Max level speed at 3,000 ft (914 m)
142 knots (164 mph; 264 km/h)
Max permissible diving speed
180 knots (207 mph; 333 km/h)
Max cruising speed at 3,000 ft (914 m)
125 knots (144 mph; 232 km/h)

Econ cruising speed at 3,000 ft (914 m)
115 knots (132 mph; 212 km/h)

Stalling speed	53 knots (61 mph; 99 km/h)
Max rate of climb at S/L	1,750 ft (533 m)/min
Time to 10,000 ft (3,050 m)	8 min
T-O run	300 ft (91 m)
T-O to 50 ft (15 m)	450 ft (137 m)
Landing from 50 ft (15 m)	700 ft (213 m)

Max range, with reserves
330 nm (380 miles; 611 km)

MONDAIR
MONDAIR AVIATION

ADDRESS: Sherbrooke Airport, PQ

It was announced in mid-1970 that this Canadian company had acquired the rights to manufacture and market the French Gazuit-Valladeau GV 103L two/three-seat light aircraft.

Production aircraft are to be built in a new factory to be erected at Sherbrooke Airport, Quebec, which will employ about 150 people.

A description of the GV 103L, as it was displayed in prototype form at the 1969 Paris Air Show, appears on pages 71-72 of this edition. It is understood that the Canadian production version will incorporate modifications to the wingtips, fin and wheel fairings, and a redesigned instrument panel.

SAUNDERS
SAUNDERS ST-27

The first two ST-27 prototypes, and the third aircraft, are converted from Srs 2 Herons formerly of The Queen's Flight; the conversion facility is also available for the fixed-undercarriage Heron Srs 1.

Delivery of the first ST-27, to a US customer, was scheduled to take place in September 1970.

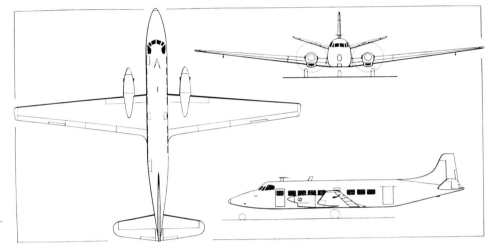

Saunders ST-27 turboprop conversion of the de Havilland Heron transport aircraft

CZECHOSLOVAKIA
AERO
AERO L-39

The second, third and fifth prototypes of the L-39 have been fitted with larger and longer air intakes, with the object of improving the thrust of the Czechoslovak-built AI-25W turbofan engine. The new intake trunks begin immediately aft of the second cockpit, as shown in the adjacent illustration, which also reveals the addition of a rudder trim-tab.

Aero L-39 two-seat jet trainer with modified air intakes

VERNER
VLADA VERNER

ADDRESS: Brandys n/L

VERNER W-01 BROUCEK (BEETLE)

Mr Vladislav Verner, an aircraft engineer, has designed a small single-seat light aircraft which he has named Broucek (Beetle). It is believed to be the first home-built aircraft designed in Czechoslovakia since World War 2, and made its first flight in 1970 piloted by Ing Rudy Duchon, chief pilot of the VZLU.

All known details of the aircraft, which is registered OK-YXA, are given below.

TYPE: Single-seat amateur-built light aircraft.

WINGS: Cantilever low-wing monoplane. Constant-chord wings.

FUSELAGE: Conventional structure of basically rectangular section with rounded top-decking.

TAIL UNIT: Cantilever T-tail with sweptback fin and rudder and constant-chord unswept horizontal surfaces.

LANDING GEAR: Non-retractable tricycle type.

POWER PLANT: One Praga B two-cylinder horizontally-opposed engine, with dual ignition, driving a two-blade propeller.

ACCOMMODATION: Single seat for pilot, under fully-transparent canopy which hinges sideways to starboard to give access to cockpit.

DIMENSIONS, EXTERNAL:

Wing span	20 ft 0 in (6·095 m)
Length overall	16 ft 1 in (4·90 m)
Height overall	5 ft 6 in (1·68 m)

Broucek single-seat light aircraft designed by Mr Vlada Verner (*Karel Masojidek*)

AREA:

Wings, gross	71 sq ft (6·60 m²)

WEIGHT AND LOADINGS:

Max T-O weight	771 lb (350 kg)
Max wing loading	10·85 lb/sq ft (53 kg/m²)
Max power loading	17·2 lb/hp (7·8 kg/hp)

PERFORMANCE (at max T-O weight):

Max level speed 91 knots (105 mph; 170 km/h)

Cruising speed 75 knots (87 mph; 140 km/h)
Landing speed (45° flap)
47 knots (54 mph; 87 km/h)

Rate of climb at S/L	590 ft (180 m)/min
Service ceiling	12,450 ft (3,800 m)
T-O to 80 ft (25 m)	1,476 ft (450 m)
Landing from 80 ft (25 m)	1,476 ft (450 m)
Range	215 nm (248 miles; 400 km)
Endurance	3 hr 30 min

DENMARK

POLYTEKNISK FLYVEGRUPPE (Flying Group of the Technical University, Copenhagen)

ADDRESS: Copenhagen

The Polyteknisk Flyvegruppe is a body of graduates and students of the Technical University of Denmark. It has about 50 members, of whom six form the design team. Its fifth project, which was flown in the Spring of 1970, is known as the Polyt V, and about 15-20 other members took part in its construction.

POLYT V

The Polyt V is designed as a minimum-weight single-seat glider-towing aeroplane, and the prototype (OY-DHP) flew for the first time on 12 April 1970. Construction is almost entirely of wood or glass-fibre, with steel fittings. Suitability for agricultural duties was being considered in 1970.

All known details are given below.

TYPE: Single-seat glider-towing aeroplane.

WINGS: Cantilever low-wing monoplane. Constant-chord wooden box-spar structure, with plywood covering except for leading-edge, which is of glass-fibre. Wide-span ailerons, each having a centrally-located trim-tab. Inboard of each aileron is a mechanically-actuated air-brake/spoiler. These spoilers function similarly to those of a sailplane, and can be deflected to nearly 90°.

FUSELAGE: Plywood-covered wooden box structure.

TAIL UNIT: Cantilever T-tail. All-wood structure with fixed surfaces plywood-covered, control surfaces fabric-covered. All-flying horizontal tail surface, with full-span anti-tab. Trim-tab in rudder.

LANDING GEAR: Non-retractable tricycle type. Nose unit (leg, wheel and shock-absorber) from a Piper Colt, fitted with shimmy damper from a Cessna 172. Main gear legs formed by MFI-designed one-piece semi-circular (9 ft 10 in = 3·00 m diameter) glass-fibre unit, attached to underside of fuselage and providing both lateral and longitudinal shock-absorption. Cessna 172 tyres, size 6·00-6, on all units.

POWER PLANT: One 200 hp Lycoming IO-360-A2B four-cylinder horizontally-opposed air-cooled engine, mounted on a Lord dynafocal mount and driving a Polyteknisk-designed two-blade fixed-pitch propeller, diameter 6 ft 8 in (2·04 m). For cooling the engine during low-speed flight, a fan with 16 plastic blades is mounted in the circular air intake behind the propeller, and is capable of blowing some 3,500 cu ft (99 m³) of air per minute—about four times the normal cooling flow. To prevent excessive cooling (i.e. during diving), the cooling grilles can be closed, and the under-nose cooling flap aft of the cowling closes automatically during a dive. Fuel is contained in two tanks in the wings, total capacity 16·5 Imp gallons (75 litres). Overwing refuelling point in each tank.

ACCOMMODATION: Single seat for pilot under fully-transparent rearward-sliding canopy.

EQUIPMENT: Operational equipment includes an electrical winch in the rear fuselage, which can reel in over 130 ft (approx 40 m) of nylon tow line in 40 sec after sailplane is released. Aircraft can make seven or eight launches an hour.

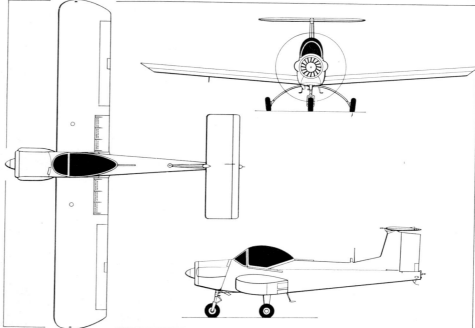

Photograph (*Howard Levy*) **and three-view drawing of the Polyt V prototype glider-towing aircraft**

DIMENSIONS, EXTERNAL:
Wing span	32 ft 0 in (10·50 m)
Wing chord (constant)	4 ft 11 in (1·50 m)
Length overall	20 ft 0 in (6·10 m)
Height overall	8 ft 6½ in (2·60 m)

WEIGHTS AND LOADING:
Weight empty	1,168 lb (530 kg)
Max T-O weight	1,675 lb (760 kg)
Max wing loading	11 lb/sq ft (53·7 kg/m²)

PERFORMANCE (at max T-O weight):
Max speed for manoeuvring	89 knots (102 mph; 164 km/h)
Max permissible diving speed	134 knots (155 mph; 249 km/h)
Stalling speed	44 knots (50 mph; 81 km/h)
Rate of climb at S/L	1,000 ft (305 m)/min
T-O to 50 ft (15 m) with 2-seat glider	800 ft (244 m)

THYREGOD

HARALD C. THYREGOD

ADDRESS: Aktieselskab, DK-6870 Ølgod

Mr Harald Thyregod is the designer of a light, two-seat twin-engined aircraft which he has designated H.T.1. The aircraft was built by Mr Arne Hollaender (Arre, DK-6800, Varde, Denmark) and Mr Arne Smidt, and is known by them as the Hollsmidt 222; it is registered OY-FAI, and is owned by Mr Hollaender.

THYREGOD H.T.1/HOLLSMIDT 222

Design of the H.T.1 was started in 1958, and construction began in 1962. The aircraft was flown for the first time in 1965, but was unable to obtain certification by the Danish Directorate of Civil Aviation at that time. This was primarily due to some unorthodoxy in the method of construction, including the glueing of aluminium skin panels to the wooden fuselage structure, which it was felt might not give adequate strength or durability. However, the aircraft spent several years stored in a barn without any apparent deterioration, and on 1 April 1969 it was granted a limited C of A, allowing it to be flown over fields in the immediate vicinity of Mr Hollaender's farm.

TYPE: Two-seat amateur-built light aircraft.

WINGS: Cantilever low-wing monoplane. Wing section NACA 23012. Wooden structure, with glued aluminium skin. Ailerons and split flaps, of similar construction, on trailing-edge. Trim-tab in aileron. Fixed slot 2 ft 11½ in (0·90 m) from each wingtip.

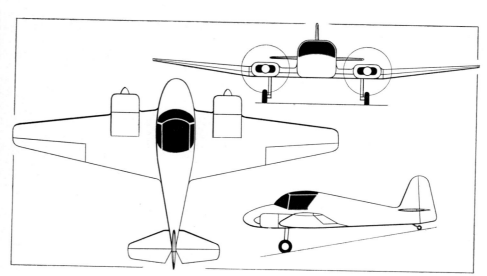

The H.T.1 two-seat light aircraft designed by Mr Harald Thyregod

FUSELAGE: Conventional structure, of wooden frames and longerons with glued aluminium skin.

TAIL UNIT: Cantilever wooden structure with glued aluminium skin. Trim-tab in elevator.

LANDING GEAR: Non-retractable tail-wheel type, with friction-damped steel spring shock absorption on main units. Main wheels and tyres size 4·00-4, pressure 21 lb/sq in (1·5 kg/cm²). Mechanical drum brakes.

POWER PLANT: Two 30 hp Volkswagen engines, each driving a two-blade fixed-pitch wooden propeller of 4 ft 5 in (1·35 m) diameter. Fuel in two tanks, one in each wing, with total capacity of 8·8 Imp gallons (40 litres). Refuelling point above each wing. Oil capacity (total) 1 Imp gallon (5 litres).

ACCOMMODATION: Side-by-side seating for pilot and one passenger in fully-enclosed cabin. One forward-opening door on each side. Cabin heated and ventilated. Space for 44 lb (20 kg) of baggage.

DIMENSIONS, EXTERNAL:

Wing span	29 ft 4¼ in (8·95 m)
Wing chord at root	6 ft 3½ in (1·92 m)
Wing chord at tip	1 ft 11¾ in (0·60 m)
Wing aspect ratio	8
Length overall	17 ft 2¾ in (5·25 m)
Height overall (tail down)	5 ft 5 in (1·65 m)
Tailplane span	8 ft 2½ in (2·50 m)
Wheel track	9 ft 2¼ in (2·80 m)
Propeller ground clearance	8¾ in (0·22 m)
Distance between propeller centres	9 ft 2¼ in (2·80 m)

DIMENSIONS, INTERNAL:

Cabin: Max width	3 ft 5¼ in (1·05 m)
Max height	2 ft 9½ in (0·85 m)

H.T.1/Hollsmidt 222 Danish two-seat homebuilt aircraft, designed by Mr H. Thyregod *(Aero Press)*

AREAS:

Wings, gross	107·6 sq ft (10·00 m²)
Ailerons (total)	16·1 sq ft (1·50 m²)
Trailing-edge flaps (total)	16·1 sq ft (1·50 m²)
Fin	3·23 sq ft (0·30 m²)
Rudder	5·92 sq ft (0·55 m²)
Tailplane	10·8 sq ft (1·00 m²)
Elevators, incl tab	8·07 sq ft (0·75 m²)

WEIGHTS AND LOADINGS:

Weight empty	672 lb (305 kg)
Max T-O weight	1,102 lb (500 kg)
Max wing loading	10·2 lb/sq ft (50 kg/m²)
Max power loading	18·3 lb/hp (8·3 kg/hp)

PERFORMANCE (at max T-O weight):

Max level speed	92 knots (106 mph; 170 km/h)
Max permissible diving speed	161 knots (186 mph; 300 km/h)
Max cruising speed	86 knots (99 mph; 160 km/h)
Econ cruising speed	76 knots (87 mph; 140 km/h)
Stalling speed	36 knots (41 mph; 65 km/h)
Rate of climb at S/L	689 ft (210 m)/min
Rate of climb at S/L, one engine out	98 ft (30 m)/min
T-O run	410 ft (125 m)
T-O to 50 ft (15 m)	820 ft (250 m)
Landing from 50 ft (15 m)	820 ft (250 m)
Landing run	328 ft (100 m)
Max range, no reserves	215 nm (248 miles; 400 km)

FINLAND

HIETANEN
ESKO AND ARI HIETANEN

ADDRESS: Paattistentie 141, Turku 17

Esko and Ari Hietanen have designed and built a single-seat monoplane, powered by a 65 hp Continental piston-engine, and have designated it HEA-23B.

No other details of this aircraft had become available for publication at the time of closing for press.

FRANCE

AÉROSPATIALE

AÉROSPATIALE SE 210 CARAVELLE

Caravelle 12. First flight of the first Caravelle 12 was scheduled for September/October 1970, followed by certification in February 1971. By 25 June 1970 seven of this version had been ordered, with options on a further five.

AÉROSPATIALE N 262

The UK operator Dan-Air took delivery in July 1970 of one N 262, and has an option on a second. This is the first sale of an N 262 to a British operator.

AÉROSPATIALE SN 600 CORVETTE

The prototype Corvette began full-power engine tests and taxying tests on 24 June 1970, and made its first flight on 16 July 1970. Initial flight testing is being carried out with the aircraft fitted with Pratt & Whitney JT15D-1 engines; by April 1971 it is planned to replace these with Larzac turbofan engines (see details on page 44 of this edition).

The prototype Aérospatiale Corvette 6/13-passenger business aircraft, first flown on 16 July 1970

AÉROSPATIALE SA 318C ALOUETTE II ASTAZOU

Sales of the Alouette II included, by mid-1970, a total of 30 to Vought Helicopter Inc for redistribution to civil customers in North America.

AÉROSPATIALE SA 316 ALOUETTE III

Sales of the Alouette III included, by mid-1970, orders for 27 and 50 by Vought Helicopter Inc for redistribution to civil customers in North America. Some aircraft of the second batch are to be assembled in the US by Vought.

AÉROSPATIALE SA 321 SUPER FRELON

The first operational squadron to be equipped with SA 321G helicopters, Flotille 32F, was commissioned at Lanvéoc-Poulmic on 5 May 1970. It will be responsible for patrols in support of *Redoutable* class nuclear submarines entering and leaving their base on the Ile Longue, and will eventually have a strength of 12 SA 321G's. These aircraft can also be operated from the French helicopter carrier *Jeanne d'Arc.*

AÉROSPATIALE/WESTLAND SA 330 PUMA

SA 330 Pumas of the French Army became operational in June 1970, with the *Groupe de l'Aviation Légère* of the 7th French Division at Habsheim Base, Mulhouse, France.

BREGUET

New factory installations at the Breguet works at Toulouse-Colomiers were nearing completion in mid-1970. The activities of Breguet's Toulouse-Montaudran works will also be housed in the new installation, and Toulouse-Colomiers will assume responsibility for assembly of, and acceptance tests for, all Breguet production aircraft. With the new installation, total usable roofed-in area will be increased from 215,278 sq ft (20,000 m²) to 645,834 sq ft (60,000 m²), and the total available works area from 1,399,310 sq ft (130,000 m²) to 2,583,340 sq ft (240,000 m²). Breguet's other works at Biarritz-Anglet and Biarritz-Parme will undertake, respectively, production work and repair and overhaul work on all aircraft built by the Dassault/Breguet group.

DASSAULT

As part of the Mercure production programme, Dassault is building a new factory at Martignas, near Bordeaux. This will be used mainly for manufacturing wings of production Mercures, and will have an initial roofed-in area of 161,459 sq ft (15,000 m²). It is due to begin work in mid-1971.

DASSAULT MILAN

The aircraft referred to on page 62 of this edition as the "first fully-equipped" Milan made its first flight on 29 May 1970, during which it reached a speed of over Mach 1. It flew at Mach 2 during its seventh flight, and subsequent flights included one of 2 hr duration while carrying 374 Imp gallon (1,700 litre) external fuel tanks.

This aircraft is representative of the proposed production version being offered to potential customers, particularly Switzerland, and is designated Milan S-01. It has been modified from a borrowed French Air Force Mirage III-E (to which standard it will eventually be restored), and incorporates features already flight-tested in other members of the Mirage family of combat aircraft.

These include a 15,875 lb (7,200 kg) st Atar 09K-50 afterburning turbojet engine, retractable "moustache" high-lift devices in the nose, increased external stores-carrying capability, moving-map and head-up displays, and an integrated electronic navigation and attack system.

The nav/attack system equipment in the S-01 includes a Crouzet type 91 computer, EMD-72 Doppler radar, SFIM 251, Thomson-CSF LC-101 moving-map display, Thomson-CSF type 31D fire control system, TRT AV-6 radio altimeter, Thomson-CSF LT-102 nose-mounted laser-telemeter range-finder and Thomson-CSF 121RD head-up display. More advanced equipment, including LC-102 moving-map display or Aïda radar range-finder, can be installed in the production version.

DASSAULT MIRAGE F1

The third and last pre-series aircraft, the Mirage F1-04, made its first flight on 17 June 1970. This aircraft is fitted with a complete automatic navigation system.

DASSAULT MIRAGE G

It has been reported that, for financial reasons, it is unlikely that both prototypes of the Mirage G4 (see page 64) will now be completed. The first Mirage G4 (two Atar 09K-50 turbojet engines) was nearing completion in mid-1970, but it was understood at that time that a decision had been taken in principle to complete the second airframe as a smaller, lighter-weight version, powered by two 18,740 lb (8,500 kg) st SNECMA M53 Super Atar engines and designated Mirage G8.

The Mirage G8 would have a max T-O weight in the region of 39,685 lb (18,000 kg), compared with the anticipated 50,700-52,900 lb (23,000-24,000 kg) of the G4, and would fly for the first time in late 1972/early 1973, production aircraft being ready for delivery from 1976.

DASSAULT MYSTÈRE 20/FALCON 20

The first production Falcon F was delivered to the US on 10 June 1970.

By 30 June 1970, total sales of the Mystère 20 and 30 had reached 266, with options on 163 more.

Prototype Dassault Milan S-01 taking off for its first flight on 29 May 1970

DASSAULT MERCURE

In July 1970 the first prototype of the Mercure twin-jet short-range transport was nearing completion, and the second phase of the development programme was being initiated. This phase covers the construction of the second flying prototype and of a static test airframe, and the preparation of drawings and tooling for production aircraft.

French and American certification of the Mercure is scheduled by the end of 1972, with first deliveries to customers following early in 1973.

GAZUIT-VALLADEAU
GAZUIT-VALLADEAU GV 103L

The GV 103L two/three-seat light aircraft is to be built and marketed under licence in Canada by Mondair Aviation (which see, in Addenda section of this edition).

HEINTZ
CHRISTOPHE HEINTZ
ADDRESS: 21-Darois

HEINTZ ZÉNITH

M Heintz is the chief aeronautical engineer of Avions Pierre Robin, and has participated in the design of several of the aircraft currently produced by that company. He has also designed and built his own two-seat light aircraft, which he has named Zénith.

Construction of the Zénith began in October 1968 and was completed in 740 spare-time hours, including time spent on elementary tooling but excluding manufacture of the landing gear, cockpit canopy and glass-fibre wheel fairings, or time spent on welding and engine overhaul. The aircraft, which is registered F-WPZY, flew for the first time on 22 March 1970 and has been granted French CNRA (home-built experimental aircraft) certification.

TYPE: Two-seat all-metal home-built light aircraft.

WINGS: Cantilever low-wing monoplane. Constant-chord wings, of NACA 64A315 (modified) section. Dihedral 6° from roots. Single-spar aluminium alloy structure, with aluminium alloy skin flush-riveted on leading-edge, universal-head rivets elsewhere. Hoerner wing-tips. Aluminium alloy piano-hinged ailerons and electrically-actuated plain flaps on trailing-edge. No tabs.

FUSELAGE: Conventional aluminium alloy stressed-skin structure, of basically rectangular section with rounded top-decking.

TAIL UNIT: Rectangular one-piece all-moving tailplane, with combined trim and anti-servo tabs. Rudder only (no fin), with slight sweepback. Tailplane and rudder are both single-spar structures with ribs and skin of aluminium alloy.

LANDING GEAR: Non-retractable tricycle type, with rubber-block shock absorbers. Manual locking of nose-wheel. All three wheels and tyres size 380 × 150 mm. Hydraulically-actuated drum-brakes on main units. Streamlined glass-fibre fairings over all three wheels and legs.

POWER PLANT: One 100 hp Rolls-Royce/Continental O-200-A four-cylinder horizontally-opposed air-cooled engine, driving a McCauley ECM-72-50 two-blade fixed-pitch metal propeller, diameter 6 ft 0 in (1·83 m). Fuel in single tank in fuselage, aft of passenger seat, capacity 20 Imp gallons (90 litres). Refuelling point in port side of fuselage.

ACCOMMODATION: Side-by-side seating for pilot and one passenger under sideways-opening (to starboard) Plexiglas canopy. Dual controls, with single control column located centrally between seats. Space for 77 lb (35 kg) of baggage aft of seats. Cabin heated and ventilated via ram-type air intake.

SYSTEMS: 12V battery and generator provide power for engine starting, fuel pump and flap actuation.

Photograph and three-view drawing of the Zénith two-seat light aircraft designed and built by M Christophe Heintz

DIMENSIONS, EXTERNAL:			
Wing span	22 ft 11¾ in (7·00 m)	Tailplane span	7 ft 6½ in (2·30 m)
Wing chord (constant)	4 ft 7 in (1·40 m)	Wheel track	7 ft 4½ in (2·25 m)
Wing aspect ratio	5	Wheelbase	4 ft 8 in (1·42 m)
Length overall	20 ft 8 in (6·30 m)	Propeller ground clearance	9¾ in (0·25 m)
Height overall	6 ft 0¾ in (1·85 m)	DIMENSION, INTERNAL:	
		Cabin: Max width	3 ft 3¾ in (1·01 m)

AREAS:
Wings, gross	107·6 sq ft (10·00 m²)
Ailerons (total)	9·26 sq ft (0·86 m²)
Trailing-edge flaps (total)	10·00 sq ft (0·93 m²)
Rudder	7·21 sq ft (0·67 m²)
Tailplane, incl tabs	19·20 sq ft (1·78 m²)

WEIGHTS AND LOADINGS:
Weight empty, equipped	870 lb (395 kg)
Max T-O and landing weight	1,433 lb (650 kg)
Max wing loading	13·3 lb/sq ft (65 kg/m²)
Max power loading	14·33 lb/hp (6·5 kg/hp)

PERFORMANCE (at max T-O weight):
Max level speed at S/L
129 knots (149 mph; 240 km/h)
Cruising speed (75% power) at S/L
116 knots (134 mph; 215 km/h)
Cruising speed (75% power) at 9,000 ft (2,750 m)
122 knots (140 mph; 225 km/h)
Stalling speed, flaps down
46 knots (53 mph; 85 km/h)
Rate of climb at S/L 886 ft (270 m)/min
Service ceiling 15,100 ft (4,600 m)
Range with max fuel, no reserves
485 nm (559 miles; 900 km)

PAYEN
ROLAND PAYEN
ADDRESS: Aérodrome Salis, 94 La Ferté Alais
PAYEN ARBALÈTE (CROSSBOW)
M Payen is at present developing a modified version of this flying-wing aircraft, a brief description of which was given in the 1958-59 *Jane's*.

As can be seen from the accompanying illustration, the principal change of configuration that has been made is that the main landing gear is now designed to retract into the wings, instead of into the lower portions of the out-rigged vertical fins. The original Hirth engine has been replaced by a 180 hp Lycoming horizontally-opposed engine, driving a pusher propeller. Max T-O weight is said to be 1,914 lb (868 kg) and estimated max speed 178 knots (205 mph; 330 km/h). No further details had been received at the time of closing for press, but the aircraft was expected to make its first flight during 1970.

Payen Arbalète flying-wing aircraft (modified), nearing completion at La Ferté Alais
(*P. M. Lambermont*)

ROBIN
The following new models and revised designations were announced in mid-1970:
ROBIN DR 220 "2+2"
This aircraft is now available with a 108/115 hp Lycoming engine, in which form it is designated DR 220/108.
ROBIN DR 300
This basic type designation is now given to the aircraft described on pages 84-85 of this edition as the DR 315 Cadet, DR 330, DR 340 Major, DR 360 Chevalier and DR 380 Prince. New designations of these aircraft, and additional models available in 1970, are as detailed below:

DR 300/108 "2+2". New model, with 108/115 hp Lycoming engine; corresponds to DR 220/108 "2+2" referred to above, but has tricycle landing gear similar to, but larger than, that of DR 300/180.

DR 300/115 Petit Prince. New designation of DR 315 Cadet.

DR 300/130 Acrobat. New designation and name of DR 330. Stressed to +9 and −4·5 g when flown as two-seat aerobatic aircraft, or between +6 and −3 g when flown as four-seat tourer.

DR 300/160 Major and Chevalier. New designation of the former DR 340 and DR 360, both of which now have a 160 hp Lycoming O-320-D

as the standard power plant.

DR 300/180 Prince. New designation of the DR 380.

DR 300/180 R. New version of DR 300/180 Prince, equipped for glider towing as alternative to normal role of four-seat touring aircraft. Towing speed of 48·5-64·75 knots (56-74·6 mph; 90-120 km/h) and max rate of climb of 886 ft (270 m)/min. Power plant as DR 300/180, with Sensenich propeller.

ROBIN HR 100
Production of the HR 100/200 version, with 200 hp Lycoming fuel-injection engine, was under way in mid-1970.

SOCATA
In June 1970 M Henri Ziegler, President of Aérospatiale, disclosed that that company was to lend "heavy support" to its subsidiary, Socata, which was in the process of reorganising in order to expand and develop its marketing network for light aircraft.

As a part of this expansion, Socata has obtained from Britten-Norman Ltd rights to distribute the latter company's BN-2A Islander aircraft in metropolitan France.

SOCATA ST 10 DIPLOMATE
Orders received up to mid-1970 included six for the Brazilian operator Varig, which is the first airline to select the Diplomate for its pilot training programme. The first four aircraft for Varig were delivered in March 1970.

GERMANY
DORNIER
In 1969-70 a German Federal Government committee under Dr Karl Thalau had under consideration six designs submitted by German aerospace companies to meet a requirement for a civil and military V/STOL transport aircraft for service in the late 1970s. These designs included the Dornier Do 231, MBB BO 140 and HFB 600, and the VFW-Fokker VC 400/500, VC 180 and VC 181.

In mid-1970 it was announced that the Do 231 design had been selected by the committee to meet this requirement.

DORNIER Do 231
The Do 231 V/STOL transport project makes extensive use of experience gained during the design, development and flight testing of the Do 31 E experimental VTOL aircraft. It is a cantilever high-wing monoplane, with swept-back anhedral wings and a T-shaped, sweptback anhedral tail unit. It has two Rolls-Royce RB.220 turbofan engines beneath the wings for forward propulsion, and twelve Rolls-Royce RB.202 lift-fan engines mounted in the front and rear fuselage and in two large wingtip pods. The wings have externally blown double-slotted trailing-edge flaps and spoilers inboard of the lift pods, and ailerons outboard.

There are two versions, as follows:

Do 231C. Civil version, designed to accommodate 100 passengers and 4 stewardesses, and having 787·5 cu ft (22·3 m³) of baggage space.

Do 231M. Military transport version. Generally similar to Do 231C, but with modified landing gear and a larger-diameter rear fuselage incorporating a rear-loading ramp-door. A STOL-only version, with increased wing span

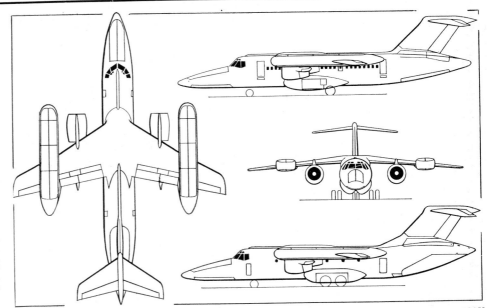

Dornier Do 231C civil V/STOL jet transport, with additional side view (bottom) of the military Do 231M

and area and only six or eight lift-fan engines, has also been projected.

The data below apply generally to both the Do 231C and Do 231M, except as indicated.

LANDING GEAR: Retractable tricycle type, that of the Do 231C having twin wheels on each unit. Main units retract into fairings on lower sides of fuselage. Do 231M gear is generally similar except that entire system has shorter oleos and each main unit consists of two single wheels in tandem, retracting into fuselage fairings of a modified shape.

POWER PLANT: Two Rolls-Royce RB.220 turbofan engines, each developing approx 24,000 lb (10,886 kg) st, are mounted on underwing pylons inboard of the main lift pods and provide power for forward propulsion. For vertical T-O and landing, the Do 231 has a total of twelve Rolls-Royce RB.202 lift-fan engines, each of which develops approx 13,100 lb (5,942 kg) st. Eight of these are contained in two pods, each containing four engines and mounted on the outer wings; two more are installed in the nose of the aircraft and the remaining two in the tail-cone. Each lift engine can be swivelled independently up to 10° forward or 30° rearward. Intake and exhaust doors for lift engines above and below each wing pod, above and below nose, on each side of fin and rudder, and beneath tail-cone. Fuel in integral tanks in wing centre-section, with capacity of 29,983 lb (13,600 kg).

ACCOMMODATION: Do 231C has seating for up to 100 passengers, in a mainly six-abreast layout, with two galleys at front of cabin and two toilets at rear. Passenger doors at front and rear on port side, service doors at front and rear on starboard side. Emergency exit on each side aft of wing trailing-edge. Do 231M can carry a similar number of troops, or such typical loads as three 80 hp Unimog S Army lorries or six 88 × 88 × 100 in (2·24 × 2·24 × 2·54 m) freight pallets.

DIMENSIONS, EXTERNAL:
Wing span 85 ft 3½ in (26·00 m)
Wing aspect ratio 5·63
Distance between c/l of cruise engine pods 32 ft 9¾ in (10·00 m)
Distance between c/l of main lift engine pods 55 ft 9¼ in (17·00 m)
Length overall 118 ft 9¼ in (36·20 m)
Length of fuselage 116 ft 7½ in (35·55 m)
Max width of fuselage 12 ft 4¾ in (3·78 m)
Height overall:
C 31 ft 4 in (9·55 m)
M 32 ft 11¾ in (10·05 m)
Passenger door (Do 231C, fwd, port):
Max height 6 ft 0 in (1·83 m)
Max width 2 ft 10 in (0·86 m)
Passenger door (Do 231C, rear, port):
Max height 6 ft 0 in (1·83 m)
Max width 2 ft 6 in (0·76 m)
Service doors (Do 231C, each):
Max height 5 ft 5 in (1·65 m)
Max width 2 ft 6 in (0·76 m)
Emergency exit doors (Do 231C, each):
Max height 3 ft 0 in (0·91 m)
Max width 1 ft 8 in (0·51 m)

DIMENSIONS, INTERNAL (Do 231M):
Main cabin:
Max length 55 ft 5 in (16·89 m)
Width at floor level 8 ft 2½ in (2·50 m)
Max height 8 ft 2½ in (2·50 m)
AREA:
Wings, gross 1,292 sq ft (120·0 m²)

WEIGHTS:
Design max payload:
C (100 passengers + baggage) 22,530 lb (10,220 kg)
M 22,045 lb (10,000 kg)
Design max T-O weight (VTOL, ISA + 18°C at 1,970 ft = 600 m):
C, M 130,075 lb (59,000 kg)
Design max T-O weight (STOL, ISA + 18°C at 1,970 ft = 600 m):
M 147,490 lb (66,900 kg)

PERFORMANCE:
Max cruising speed at 25,000 ft (7,620 m):
C, M 485 knots (559 mph; 900 km/h)
Max cruising Mach number:
C, M Mach 0·81
Rate of climb at S/L:
C 3,740 ft (1,140 m)/min
M 3,640 ft (1,110 m)/min
Rate of climb at 25,000 ft (7,620 m):
C 1,085 ft (330 m)/min
M 985 ft (300 m)/min
Service ceiling:
C 36,400 ft (11,100 m)
M 35,750 ft (10,900 m)
T-O to 50 ft (15 m), STOL:
C 4,595 ft (1,400 m)
Range with max payload, cruising at 900 km/h at 7,260 m:
C, M 432 nm (495 miles; 800 km)
Max ferry range (VTOL):
C 1,600 nm (1,840 miles; 2,960 km)
M 1,815 nm (2,090 miles; 3,360 km)

KRAUSS (GYROFLUG)

Dipl-Ing Peter Krauss (see pages 98-99) is continuing his activities under the auspices of a new company known as Gyroflug. A new autogyro, the TRS-III, was displayed at the 1970 Hanover Air Show, and a photograph of this aircraft appears on page 99 of this edition. All available details of the aircraft are given below.

GYROFLUG TRS-III

The TRS-III is a single-seat autogyro, of extremely clean aerodynamic appearance and having dependent vertical tail surfaces supported by a curved cantilever boom extending from behind the main rotor head. There are no horizontal tail surfaces. Construction is mainly of glass-fibre reinforced materials, with a duralumin and glass-fibre two-blade main rotor. The cockpit is fully enclosed, and is entered by a trap-door beneath the fuselage. Landing gear is of the non-retractable tricycle type, with cantilever main legs and a steerable nose-wheel.

POWER PLANT: One 65 hp 1,600 cc Volkswagen engine, driving a Hoffmann two-blade pusher propeller of 4 ft 2 in (1·27 m) diameter.
DIMENSION, EXTERNAL:
Rotor diameter 22 ft 11½ in (7·00 m)
PERFORMANCE:
Max level speed 102 knots (118 mph; 190 km/h)
Max rate of climb 885 ft (270 m)/min
T-O run 197 ft (60 m)
Landing run 66 ft (20 m)

MESSERSCHMITT-BÖLKOW-BLOHM

Two new projects, generally similar in appearance to the BO 209 Monsun, have been reported in Germany. These are:

MBB BO 210 TORNADO

Two-seat aircraft, derived from MHK-102 prototype, with fully-retractable tricycle landing gear and 150/160 hp engine.

DIMENSIONS, EXTERNAL:
Wing span 31 ft 2 in (9·50 m)

Length overall 21 ft 0 in (6·40 m)
Height overall 7 ft 2½ in (2·20 m)
WEIGHTS:
Weight empty 1,025 lb (465 kg)
Max T-O weight 1,874 lb (850 kg)
PERFORMANCE:
Endurance 4 hr 30 min

MBB BO 211 TAIFUN (TYPHOON)

Four-seat aircraft, based on BO 210, but slightly larger and having a 180/200 hp engine.

DIMENSIONS, EXTERNAL:
Wing span 32 ft 9½ in (10·00 m)
Wing aspect ratio 7·7
Length overall 22 ft 11½ in (7·00 m)
Height overall 7 ft 6½ in (2·30 m)
AREA:
Wings, gross 145·3 sq ft (13·5 m²)
WEIGHTS:
Weight empty 1,257 lb (570 kg)
Max T-O weight 2,425 lb (1,100 kg)
PERFORMANCE:
Endurance 5 hr

SPORTFLUGZEUG
SPORTFLUGZEUGENTWICKLUNGS GmbH

ADDRESS:
8501 Behringersdorf bei Nürnberg, Am Neubruch 12.
PRINCIPALS:
Ing Jo Hössl
Ing Wolfrum
Flugkapitän Arnold Wagner

This company is responsible for a new single-seat aerobatic light aircraft, of which a prototype was completed early in 1970. The aircraft was evolved primarily to meet the requirements of Flugkapitän Arnold Wagner of Swissair, a well-known aerobatic pilot. In its originally projected form it was known as the Acromaster Mk II, a description of which appears under the "Hirth" heading on page 98 of this edition.

The original design has since been modified slightly, and is now known as the Acrostar Mk II. A prototype (D-EMKB) was completed early in 1970 at the Nabern/Teck factory of Wolf Hirth GmbH, under the guidance of Ing Meder, and took part in the World Aerobatic Championships at Hullavington, England, in July 1970. The Acrostar Mk II is stressed for flying between the limits of +6g and —3g, and is of wooden construction throughout.

All known details appear below.

SPORTFLUGZEUG ACROSTAR Mk II

TYPE: Single-seat light aerobatic aircraft.

WINGS: Cantilever low-wing monoplane. Eppler symmetrical wing section, designed to give similar aerodynamic properties over entire span whether the aircraft is flying inverted or right way up. Epoxy spars and ribs, with plywood covering. Flaps and ailerons are inter-connected to give the effect of full-span ailerons.

FUSELAGE: Conventional semi-monocoque structure.

TAIL UNIT: Conventional cantilever structure, with single fin and balanced rudder. Elevators interconnected with flaps and ailerons.

LANDING GEAR: Non-retractable tail-wheel type, with streamline fairings on main wheels and legs.

The Wagner-designed Acrostar single-seat aerobatic monoplane, built by Wolf Hirth GmbH
(*Flight International*)

POWER PLANT: One 220 hp Franklin 6A-335-C six-cylinder horizontally-opposed air-cooled engine, driving a two-blade Hartzell constant-speed propeller. Fuel and oil systems designed to permit periods of inverted flight. Fuel capacity 159 lb (72 kg). Oil capacity 17·6 lb (8 kg).

ACCOMMODATION: Single seat for pilot under fully-transparent rearward-sliding canopy.

DIMENSIONS, EXTERNAL:
Wing span 26 ft 6 in (8·08 m)
Wing aspect ratio 6·5
Length overall 20 ft 0¼ in (6·10 m)
Height overall 5 ft 10 in (1·78 m)
AREA:
Wings, gross 107·6 sq ft (10·0 m²)
WEIGHTS AND LOADINGS:
Weight empty 1,014 lb (460 kg)
Max T-O weight:
normal 1,543 lb (700 kg)
aerobatic 1,323 lb (600 kg)

Max wing loading:
normal 12·30 lb/sq ft (60 kg/m²)
aerobatic 14·35 lb/sq ft (70 kg/m²)
Max power loading:
normal 7·01 lb/hp (3·18 kg/hp)
aerobatic 6·02 lb/hp (2·73 kg/hp)
PERFORMANCE (estimated, at max normal T-O weight):
Max level speed at S/L 167 knots (193 mph; 310 km/h)
Max permissible diving speed 269 knots (310 mph; 500 km/h)
Max cruising speed at S/L 146 knots (168 mph; 270 km/h)
Landing speed 46-49 knots (53-56 mph; 85-90 km/h)
Max rate of climb at S/L 2,950 ft (900 m)/min
Service ceiling 24,600 ft (7,500 m)
T-O run 328 ft (100 m)
Landing run 590 ft (180 m)
Range 325 nm (375 miles; 600 km)
Endurance 2 hr 30 min

WAGNER SKY-TRAC

The following details supersede those given on page 113 of this edition.

DIMENSIONS, EXTERNAL:
Diameter of rotors (each)	32 ft 9¾ in (10·00 m)
Length overall	23 ft 3½ in (7·10 m)
Length of fuselage	6 ft 10¾ in (2·10 m)
Height overall:	
Sky-Trac 1	11 ft 5¾ in (3·50 m)
Sky-Trac 3	11 ft 9¾ in (3·60 m)
Skid track	7 ft 4 in (2·23 m)

AREA:
Main rotor disc	845·3 sq ft (78·53 m²)

WEIGHTS:
Weight empty:	
Sky-Trac 1	1,764 lb (800 kg)
Sky-Trac 3	2,028 lb (920 kg)
Weight empty, equipped:	
Sky-Trac 1	1,808 lb (820 kg)
Sky-Trac 3	2,072 lb (940 kg)
Max T-O weight (Sky-Trac 1 and 3)	3,307 lb (1,500 kg)

PERFORMANCE (at max T-O weight):
Max level speed at S/L	86 knots (99 mph; 160 km/h)
Max cruising speed	76 knots (87 mph; 140 km/h)
Max rate of climb at S/L	1,180 ft (360 m)/min
Vertical rate of climb at S/L	785 ft (240 m)/min
Service ceiling	12,650 ft (3,860 m)
Max range:	
standard fuel	108 nm (125 miles; 200 km)
auxiliary tank	216 nm (250 miles; 400 km)
Max endurance:	
standard fuel	1 hr 18 min
auxiliary tank	2 hr 30 min

INTERNATIONAL PROGRAMMES

ALPHA JET

On 22 July 1969 the French and German governments announced a joint requirement for a new subsonic basic and advanced training aircraft to enter service with the French and German Armed Forces in the late 1970s. Each government has a potential requirement for about 200 such aircraft, and three designs were studied during the first half of 1970. These were the Franco-German Aérospatiale/MBB E 650 Euro-trainer and Dornier/Dassault-Breguet TA 501 Alpha Jet, and the all-German VFW-Fokker VFT 291.

On 24 July 1970, it was announced that the Alpha Jet design had been selected for development to meet this requirement.

DORNIER/DASSAULT-BREGUET TA 501 ALPHA JET

Dornier AG of Germany and the Dassault-Breguet Group of France have formed the Alpha Jet Company to foster the development of this project, which has German design leadership. The designation is formed by combining those of the former Dornier Do P-375 and Breguet Br 126 jet trainer projects.

The Alpha Jet is a cantilever shoulder-wing monoplane, with anhedral from the wing roots, and the outer wing panels slightly extended to give a "dog-tooth" leading-edge. Wings have ailerons, two-section flaps and spoilers, with a trim-tab in each aileron. Tail unit is all-swept, with the tailplane mounted on the rear fuselage, and trim-tabs in the rudder and each elevator. Accommodation is for two persons in tandem, on zero-zero ejection seats under individual canopies; the rear seat is slightly elevated.

Four prototypes and six pre-series Alpha Jets are to be built. First flight is scheduled for 1972, with first deliveries of production aircraft starting at the end of 1975.

POWER PLANT: Two 2,976 lb (1,350 kg) st SNECMA/Turboméca Larzac turbofans mounted externally on each side of the fuselage.

LANDING GEAR: Retractable tricycle type, with single wheel and low-pressure tyre on each unit.

DIMENSIONS, EXTERNAL:
Wing span	30 ft 0½ in (9·16 m)
Length overall	39 ft 8¾ in (12·11 m)
Height overall	13 ft 5¾ in (4·11 m)
Wheel track	8 ft 11 in (2·71 m)

AREA:
Wings, gross	188·4 sq ft (17·50 m²)

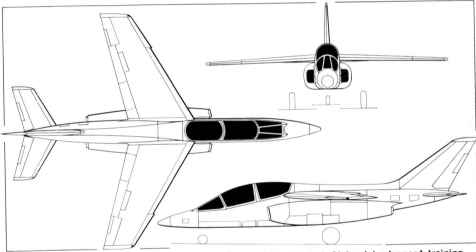

Three-view drawing and photograph of mock-up of the TA 501 Alpha Jet advanced training aircraft

WEIGHT AND LOADINGS:
Max T-O weight	9,634 lb (4,370 kg)
Max wing loading	51 lb/sq ft (249 kg/m²)
Max power loading	1·9 lb/lb st (1·9 kg/kg st)

PERFORMANCE (estimated, at max T-O weight):
Max level speed at 492 ft (150 m)	434 knots (500 mph; 805 km/h)
Max level speed at 29,530 ft (9,000 m)	Mach 0·87
Landing speed	85 knots (98 mph; 158 km/h)
Service ceiling	46,325 ft (14,120 m)
T-O run	1,542 ft (470 m)
Landing run	607 ft (185 m)
Max endurance	approx 2 hr 25 min

CONCORDE

On 12 August 1970 the 002 prototype began a new flight development phase during which it will be flown at speeds up to twice the speed of sound (about 1,216 knots; 1,400 mph; 2,250 km/h).

Modifications carried out in preparation for this phase include replacement of the 32,900 lb (14,925 kg) st Olympus 593-2B engines with 593-3B engines of 34,700 lb (15,740 kg) st; completion of the variable air intake system to its ultimate standard of automatic control; and introduction of automatic rudder control (by engine bleed-air) which becomes operative in the event of engine failure at high supersonic speeds.

It was anticipated that Concorde 002 would achieve Mach 2 within about 25-30 flights. All supersonic test flying will be done at altitudes of more than 36,000 ft (11,000 m) and mainly between 40,000 and 50,000 ft (12,200 and 15,250 m).

PANAVIA

PANAVIA 100 and 200

Following the signing of the necessary agreement by the UK and German Federal governments, it was announced in July 1970 that work was to begin immediately on the prototype construction programme in Britain, Germany and Italy. At that time the Italian government had still to sign the agreement.

SEPECAT

SEPECAT JAGUAR

Preliminary deck trials aboard the French aircraft carrier *Clemenceau* were completed by the M-05 prototype during the period 8-13 July 1970, when twelve catapult launchings and arrested landings were made.

ITALY

AERFER

AERFER/AERMACCHI AM.3C

To clarify the statement on page 128 of this edition, the order for 20 of these aircraft, which was being negotiated in mid-1970, was for a foreign customer and not for the Italian Army.

MERIDIONALI

Prototype EMA 124 helicopter developed by Meridionali from the Agusta-Bell 47
(*Aviation Magazine*)

PARTENAVIA

PARTENAVIA P.64B OSCAR-B

An additional version of this aircraft is now available:

P.64B Oscar-200. Four-seat version, with 180 hp Lycoming O-360-A1A engine.

Prototype of the Partenavia P.68 twin-engined light transport aircraft

JAPAN

ITOH

ADDRESS:
Chofu Airfield, 1060 Nishimachi, Chofu, Tokyo

PRESIDENT: Chusaku Arai

As from 29 May 1970, the C. Itoh Aircraft Maintenance and Engineering Co Ltd (see page 153 of this edition) has been known as:

SHIN NIHON KOKU SEIBI KABUSHIKI KAISHA (New Japan Aircraft Maintenance Co Ltd)

The address of the company under its new title, and the name of its President, are as given above.

Under its former title, Itoh was responsible in 1968-69 for the conversion of some of the aircraft representing Japanese fighters and torpedo-bombers in the film *Tora, Tora, Tora!* The total number of conversions by Itoh were five as 'Zero' (Mitsubishi A6M) fighters (as dummy aircraft) and twelve as 'Kate' (Nakajima B5N) bombers (of which seven were dummies).

The five flyable 'Kates' were all modified from ex-JASDF North American T-6 Texan trainers. Conversion work included a 19¾ in (50 cm) longer nose, with steel tube engine mount, lengthened

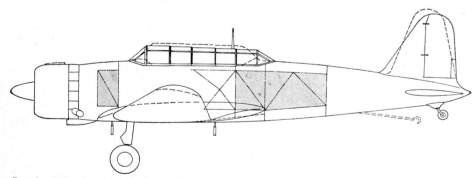

Drawing indicating principal features of the Itoh conversion of T-6 and BT-13 structure to represent the Nakajima B5N torpedo-bomber of World War 2 (*AiReview*)

cowling, propeller spinner, and dummy cowl flap and port-side exhaust; modified windshield; a 6 ft 6¾ in (2·00 m) steel-tube extension of the rear fuselage; replacement of the entire T-6 tail unit by that of a Vultee BT-13 Valiant with re-shaped fin leading-edge; and extension and re-shaping of the wing-tips, wing-root fillets and wing centre-section leading-edge by the use of foam-reinforced plastics.

Work on the conversions began in October 1968, and all five aircraft were completed and delivered in January 1969.

MEXICO

ANAHUAC

FABRICA AVIONES ANAHUAC

ADDRESS: Aeropuerto International, Mexico 9 DF

This company is reported to have under construction the prototype of an agricultural aircraft known as the Tauro. No other details had been received at the time of closing for press.

NETHERLANDS

FOKKER-VFW

FOKKER-VFW F.27 FRIENDSHIP

The following additional version is available:

F.27 Mk 600 RF. Version of Mk 600 for rough-field operation, with special Dowty Rotol landing gear having two-stage oleos with 4 in (10 cm) increase in stroke. Increased overall height and greater propeller ground clearance. First order, for one aircraft, placed by Malaysia-Singapore Airlines.

FOKKER-VFW F.28 FELLOWSHIP

Two Mk 1000 Fellowships were ordered on 4 July 1970 by the German operator Aviaction (Hanseatische Luftreederei GmbH). This brings the total number of Fellowships on order at that time to 33.

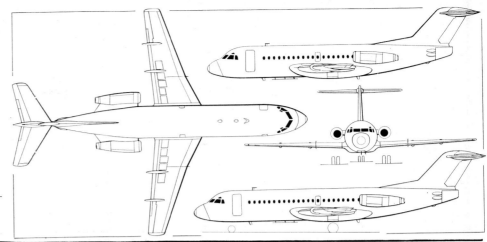

F.28 Mk 2000 Fellowship, with additional side view (top) of the Mk 1000

ROMANIA
IRMA
IAR-822

It now appears probable that the IAR-821, powered by an Ivchenko radial engine and described on page 179 of this edition, will not go into production. It will be superseded by the IAR-822, of which a prototype (YR-MCA) was undergoing flight trials in the early Summer of 1970.

The IAR-822 is powered by a 290 hp Lycoming IO-540 horizontally-opposed engine, and is designed to BCAR Section D requirements; certification was expected by the end of 1970. Production is planned both for Romanian use and for export, and applications of the aircraft, in addition to agricultural duties, include highway de-icing, fire-fighting, aerial survey work, glider towing, and the transport of up to 1,543 lb (700 kg) of mail or other cargo.

The description below applies to the agricultural version, except where otherwise stated.

TYPE: Single-seat agricultural aircraft.

WINGS: Cantilever low-wing monoplane. Wing section NACA 23014. Constant-chord safe-life wings, with 0° dihedral on centre-section and 5° on outer panels. Incidence 5°. Centre-section is a welded steel-tube structure, with metal skin. Outer panels, which are detachable, are of single-spar all-wood construction (Romanian spruce) with birch plywood skin, varnished on the inside and protected externally by a fabric coating. Mechanically-actuated single-slotted all-wood flaps and all-wood ailerons. No tabs.

FUSELAGE: Welded chrome-molybdenum steel-tube truss structure, of basically rectangular section with rounded top-decking. Airtight fabric covering. Fuselage is designed to collapse progressively from the front to decelerate cockpit impact in the event of a crash.

TAIL UNIT: All-wood structure, of similar construction to outer wings. Fixed-incidence braced tailplane, of constant chord and NACA 0012 section, provided with controllable trim-tab on each elevator. Trim-tab on rudder.

LANDING GEAR: Non-retractable tail-wheel type, with main units interchangeable left/right. Main units have oleo-pneumatic shock struts located in the centre-section or, optionally, rubber-in-compression shock struts with friction shock-absorption. Rubber shock strut on tail-wheel. Main wheels and tyres size 600 × 180 mm; self-centering, fully-steerable tail-wheel, size 290 × 100 mm. Hydraulic brakes. Optional ski and float gear under development.

POWER PLANT: One 290 hp Lycoming IO-540-G1D5 six-cylinder horizontally-opposed air-cooled engine, driving a Hartzell HC 92 WK-1D-9349-4-6 two-blade constant-speed metal propeller, diameter 7 ft 3 in (2·20 m). Fuel tank in each outer wing, total capacity 35 Imp gallons (160 litres). Refuelling point above each wing. Optional supplementary fuel system can increase max endurance to 5 hr. Oil capacity 2·5 Imp gallons (11·4 litres).

ACCOMMODATION: Single adjustable seat for pilot, in specially strengthened enclosed cockpit with steel overturn structure. Upward-hinged canopy/door on port side. Cockpit designed to remain intact in a low-speed crash. Provision for fitting jump-seat behind pilot, to accommodate mechanic or loader. Cabin heated and ventilated.

ELECTRONICS: Prototype fitted with mixture of Soviet- and Romanian-designed instrumentation, but provision will be made in production aircraft for western-designed instrumentation to customer's requirements. Standard equipment includes a 24V 30Ah battery, and complete instrumentation for agricultural operation and for long-distance flights between operations. Optional equipment includes Bendix CNS-220 radio with omni, landing and navigation lights, rotating beacon and electrical shielding.

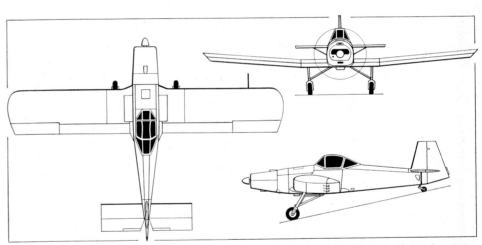

Photograph (*Flight International*) **and three-view drawing of the IAR-822 agricultural aircraft**

OPERATIONAL EQUIPMENT: Chemical is carried in an epoxy-treated duralumin-sheet hopper in forward fuselage, located at the CG point to avoid trim changes as the load is reduced. The hopper, which is loaded through a rubber-sealed door on the top of the fuselage, has an internal volume of 28·25 cu ft (0·8 m³) and can accommodate up to 132 Imp gallons (600 litres) of liquid or 1,323 lb (600 kg) of dry chemicals. The corners are rounded to avoid dust catchment. Prototype fitted initially with boom-and-nozzle spray gear, with windmill-driven centrifugal pump and spray bars giving an effective swath width of over 100 ft (30 m); this can be changed in about 10 min "in the field" for a venturi-type solid chemical distributor giving an effective swath width of over 65 ft (20 m). Rotary atomisers optional. Entire hopper load can be jettisoned in an emergency.

DIMENSIONS, EXTERNAL:

Wing span	42 ft 0 in (12·80 m)
Wing chord (constant)	6 ft 10¾ in (2·10 m)
Wing aspect ratio	6·3
Wing centre-section span	12 ft 1¾ in (3·70 m)
Length overall	30 ft 10 in (9·40 m)
Height overall	9 ft 2¼ in (2·80 m)
Wheel track (average)	8 ft 10¼ in (2·70 m)
Wheelbase	20 ft 1½ in (6·13 m)

AREAS:

Wings, gross	279·86 sq ft (26·00 m²)
Ailerons (total)	30·10 sq ft (2·80 m²)
Flaps (total)	38·75 sq ft (3·60 m²)
Fin	7·32 sq ft (0·68 m²)
Rudder, incl tab	16·00 sq ft (1·49 m²)
Tailplane	27·12 sq ft (2·52 m²)
Elevators, incl tabs	21·31 sq ft (1·98 m²)

WEIGHTS AND LOADINGS:

Weight empty:	
sprayer	2,425 lb (1,100 kg)
duster	2,469 lb (1,120 kg)
Max T-O weight:	
standard	2,755 lb (1,250 kg)
agricultural	4,188 lb (1,900 kg)
Max wing loading	15 lb/sq ft (73·2 kg/m²)
Max power loading	14·4 lb/hp (6·55 kg/hp)

PERFORMANCE (at max T-O weight; A = standard configuration, B = agricultural duster configuration*):

Max level speed at S/L	
A	108 knots (124 mph; 200 km/h)
B	92 knots (106 mph; 170 km/h)
Max cruising speed (75% power):	
A	100 knots (115 mph; 185 km/h)
Crop spraying and dusting speed:	
B	65-86 knots (75-99 mph; 120-160 km/h)
Stalling speed (75% power), flaps up:	
B	49 knots (56 mph; 90 km/h)
Stalling speed (75% power), flaps down:	
A	35·1 knots (41 mph; 65 km/h)
B	40·5 knots (47 mph; 75 km/h)
Rate of climb at S/L:	
A	1,180 ft (360 m)/min
B	690 ft (210 m)/min
Service ceiling:	
A	19,685 ft (6,000 m)
B	14,765 ft (4,500 m)

T-O run, from grass:		Landing from 50 ft (15 m):		Range (standard fuel):	
A	312 ft (95 m)	B	950 ft (290 m)	A	270 nm (310 miles; 500 km)
B	558 ft (170 m)			Endurance (standard fuel):	
		Landing run:		B	3 hr
T-O to 50 ft (15 m):		A	395 ft (120 m)	*performance in spraying configuration is	
B	985 ft (300 m)	B	460 ft (140 m)	higher than that as duster.	

SPAIN
HISPANO

HISPANO HA-220
The following additional structural details are now available:

WINGS: Electrically-operated trim-tab in starboard aileron.

TAIL UNIT: Electrically-operated variable-incidence tailplane.

LANDING GEAR: Pirelli tyre size 19 × 6·00 × 8 on nose-wheel.

POWER PLANT: Fuel in five self-sealing internal tanks, two under cabin floor, one in pressurised rear cabin and two in wings, with total capacity of 195 Imp gallons (886 litres); and two fixed wingtip tanks with total capacity of 141 Imp gallons (644 litres). Overall total fuel capacity 336 Imp gallons (1,530 litres).

ACCOMMODATION: Single seat for pilot in pressurised cabin. Canopy, over cockpit and fuel tank bay, hinges sideways to starboard. Pilot's seat is provided with armoured backplate. Bullet-proof windscreen.

SYSTEMS: Normalair-Garrett pressurisation system. 115/120V 400 c/s AC electrical system.

ELECTRONICS AND EQUIPMENT: Include AN/RTA 51 BX UHF, Bendix DFA 73 ADF, AN/APX 77 IFF, AN/ARN 91 Microtacan, Sperry C-2G Gyrosyn compass, emergency cockpit lighting, oxygen equipment and fire detection equipment.

ARMAMENT AND OPERATIONAL EQUIPMENT: Can be equipped with a variety of guns, rockets and bombs on two under-fuselage and four Hispano or Matra 38 underwing launchers. Maurer type P-2 camera for photographing results of ground attack missions, Maurer type AN-N6 camera gun, and VRM Zeus reflector sight.

SWEDEN
MFI

MFI-11
The photograph shows the prototype MFI-11 nearing completion at the Malmö factory in mid-1970. This aircraft utilises the fuselage of the MFI-9, but has wings of 3 ft (0·90 m) greater span and a 130 hp Rolls-Royce/Continental IO-240 engine in a glass-fibre cowling.

Prototype of the Malmo MFI-11 under construction (*Howard Levy*)

SAAB-SCANIA

Above: **Prototype of the SK 37 two-seat combat trainer version of the Saab Viggen**

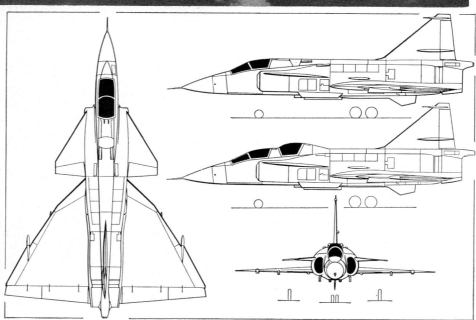

Right: **Saab AJ 37 Viggen, with additional side view (centre) of the two-seat SK 37**

SAAB-37 VIGGEN
The two-seat operational trainer prototype of the Saab-37 Viggen was flown for the first time on 2 July 1970. At that time, flight testing of the single-seat AJ 37 all-weather attack version was nearly completed, and quantity production was under way.

SAAB-105XT
In June 1970, Saab announced brief details of a new version of this aircraft, the **Saab-105XH.** This version, which has been offered to Switzerland, differs from the standard Saab-105XT in having increased armament capability, more advanced avionics, increased fuel capacity and improved high-speed characteristics.

The Saab-105XH is equipped with a built-in 30-mm Aden cannon, installed with a pre-filled magazine holding 100 rounds in a fairing beneath the port side of the centre fuselage. To compensate for the space taken up by this installation, the aircraft has small fixed wingtip fuel tanks, each of 44 Imp gallons (200 litres) capacity. The standard six underwing stores pylons are retained, with increased capacity. Weapons system equipment includes a high-precision bombing delivery system using the Saab BT9R with laser ranging capability, Doppler radar, gyroplatform, and Ferranti ISIS sighting head. A roller map display is specified, and avionics may also include a head-up display.

A drooped wing leading-edge is proposed, to improve combat performance in general and high-speed characteristics in particular. The max T-O weight will be increased by 1,102 lb (500 kg) to 15,430 lb (7,000 kg), and a brake parachute will be installed.

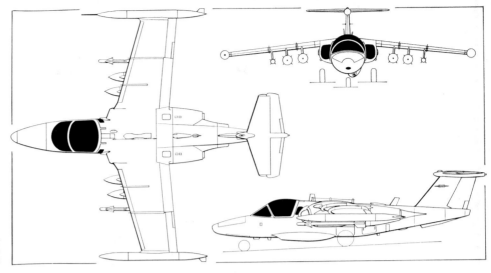

Three-view drawing of the Saab-105XH light attack aircraft

UNITED KINGDOM

BAC

British Aircraft Corporation announced on 6 August 1970 the sale of 10 more BAC One-Eleven jet transports, as under:

Court Line	2 Series 500
Paninternational (Germany)	1 Series 500
Philippine Airlines	4 Series 500
Undisclosed (European independent airline)	3 (Series not disclosed)

These sales bring the number of One-Elevens sold at that date to 200.

BRITTEN-NORMAN

BRITTEN-NORMAN ISLANDER

Two new versions of the Britten-Norman BN-2A Islander twin-engined ten-seat feeder-line transport have recently been announced. The first of these, fitted with two Lycoming IO-540-K1BS engines, each developing 300 hp, is known as the BN-2A/IO-540 Islander and has been evolved for 'hot and high' operations. It completed its tropical trials during July 1970.

The second variant is the Rajay turbocharged Islander, powered by standard Lycoming O-540 engines equipped with turbochargers, and this model is likely to be offered in place of the BN-2S with Rolls-Royce/Continental TSIO-520-E engines which was shown for the first time at Farnborough in 1968.

Recent airframe changes include the optional installation of wing-tip tanks, each providing 20·8 Imp gallons (25 US gallons; 94·5 litres) of additionable usable fuel. The increased aspect ratio this has produced has raised the single-engine ceiling by some 1,000 ft (305 m). Other optional changes comprise the fitting of wider-chord main landing gear leg fairings, drooped wing leading-edge inboard of the engine nacelles, and the improved low-drag engine cowlings. Termed the Speedpak modification, this has increased the single-engine ceiling by almost 2,000 ft (610 m) and raised the cruising speed by between 4 and 5 knots (4·6-5·75 mph; 7-9 km/h). Maximum operational weight has been increased to 6,300 lb (2,857 kg). The drooped leading-edge sections have lowered the stalling speed by 4½ knots (5·2 mph; 8·3 km/h). The Speedpak is available to operators as a kit of parts for on-site embodiment.

Since Constructor's Number 80, all Islanders have been fitted with glass-reinforced plastics doors to the cabin. A side-loading baggage compartment door on the port side is also provided, this, too, being of glass-reinforced plastics.

BN-2A/IO-540 Islander. Standard basic airframe fitted with Lycoming IO-540-K1B5 engines, driving Hartzell two-blade constant-speed feathering propellers, diameter 6 ft 8 in (2·03 m). Flaps are permanently drooped 6° to improve cruise speed flight attitude at maximum weight, and to shift maximum lift to the inner portion of the wing, thus allowing an increase in both all-up weight and zero-fuel weight without increasing wing bending moment. It is believed that this will lead eventually to certification at an all-up weight of 6,500 lb (2,948 kg), without structural modifications.

Rajay Turbocharged Islander. Standard BN-2A Srs 2 aircraft powered by Lycoming O-540 engines equipped with turbochargers developed by Riley-Rajay Corporation of Long Beach,

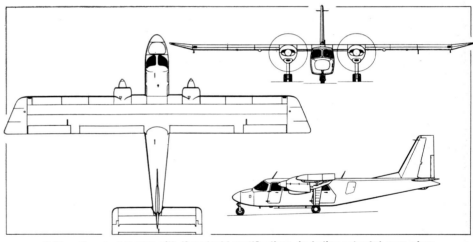

Britten-Norman Islander with 'Speedpak' modifications, including extended-span wings

California, and installed to the order of an Islander user, Jonas Aircraft & Arms Inc.

Latest specification and performance data released by Britten-Norman for the standard BN-2A Islander, the IO-540 Islander and the Rajay Turbocharged Islander are as follows:

DIMENSIONS, EXTERNAL:
Wing span	49 ft 0 in (14·94 m)
Wing span with tip tanks	53 ft 0 in (16·15 m)

AREAS:
Wings, gross	325 sq ft (30·2 m²)
Wings, with tip tanks, gross	337 sq ft (31·25 m²)

WEIGHTS:
Weight empty, with basic equipment:
BN-2A	3,588 lb (1,727 kg)
IO-540	3,738 lb (1,695 kg)
Rajay	3,668 lb (1,664 kg)
Max T-O and landing weight:	
all models	6,300 lb (2,851 kg)
Max zero-fuel weight (FAR):	
all models	5,800 lb (2,631 kg)
Max zero-fuel weight (BCAR):	
all models	6,000 lb (2,722 kg)
Max zero-fuel weight with tip tanks fitted:	
all models	5,930 lb (2,694 kg)

PERFORMANCE (at max T-O weight, ISA):
Cruising speed (75% power):
BN-2A at 7,000 ft (2,135 m)	139 knots (160 mph; 257·5 km/h)
IO-540 at 10,000 ft (3,050 m)	146 knots (168 mph; 270 km/h)
Rajay at 7,000 ft (2,135 m)	147 knots (170 mph; 273·5 km/h)

Cruising speed (65% power):
IO-540 at 20,000 ft (6,100 m)	160 knots (185 mph; 297·5 km/h)

Service ceiling:
BN-2A	16,200 ft (4,950 m)
IO-540	22,000 ft (6,700 m)
Rajay	27,000 ft (8,230 m)

Service ceiling, one engine out:
BN-2A	5,600 ft (1,705 m)
IO-540	7,800 ft (2,375 m)
Rajay	12,500 ft (3,810 m)

T-O run at S/L:
BN-2A	556 ft (169 m)
IO-540	504 ft (153 m)
Rajay	556 ft (169 m)

T-O run at 10,000 ft (3,050 m):
BN-2A	1,065 ft (324 m)
IO-540	895 ft (272 m)
Rajay	640 ft (195 m)

T-O to 50 ft (15 m) at S/L:
BN-2A	1,090 ft (332 m)
IO-540	990 ft (301 m)
Rajay	1,090 ft (332 m)

T-O to 50 ft (15 m) at 10,000 ft (3,050 m):
BN-2A	2,090 ft (637 m)
IO-540	1,760 ft (536 m)
Rajay	1,220 ft (371 m)

Landing distance from 50 ft (15 m) at S/L:
all models	960 ft (292 m)

Landing run at S/L:
all models	449 ft (137 m)

Landing distance from 50 ft (15 m) at 10,000 ft (3,050 m):
all models	1,340 ft (408 m)

Landing run at 10,000 ft (3,050 m):
all models   627 ft (191 m)
Range with max fuel (75% power at 7,000 ft = 2,135 m):
Standard   667 nm (768 miles; 1,236 km)
With tip tanks
          941 nm (1,084 miles; 1,744 km)

Range with max fuel (67% power at 9,000 ft = 2,750 m):
Standard   734 nm (846 miles; 1,361 km)
With tip tanks
      1,038 nm (1,195 miles; 1,922 km)

Range with max fuel (59% power at 13,000 ft = 3,960 m):
Standard   810 nm (933 miles; 1,501 km)
With tip tanks
      1,143 nm (1,317 miles; 2,119 km)

CIERVA

The prototype Cierva Rotorcraft Grasshopper light helicopter, under development at Redhill in June 1970 (*M. Stroud*)

COATES

J. R. COATES

ADDRESS:

The Spinney, Breachwood Green, Hitchin, Herts

Mr Coates has designed and is building a two-seat light aircraft known as the S.A.II Swalesong. All available details are given below:

COATES S.A.II SWALESONG

The Swalesong was designed for sporting and touring purposes and a prototype (G-AYDV) was under construction in mid-1970. First flight was anticipated in late 1970 or early 1971.

Particular attention has been given to achieving a good short-field performance, to enable the aircraft to operate from unprepared surfaces. Drawings for amateur construction will not be made available, but Mr Coates is designing a simplified version, the S.A.III, which will be suitable for home building and will have a choice of wooden or metal construction.

TYPE: Two-seat light aircraft.

WINGS: Cantilever low-wing monoplane. Wing section NACA 23013·5. Dihedral 5° 30'. Incidence 3° 30'. All-wood (spruce) structure, with plywood covering. Frise-type ailerons and slotted trailing-edge flaps, all of plywood-covered wooden construction.

FUSELAGE: Semi-monocoque spruce structure, with plywood covering.

TAIL UNIT: Cantilever structure, with sweptback vertical surfaces. Tailplane incidence adjustable on ground. One-piece fabric-covered wooden elevator, with spring tab.

LANDING GEAR: Non-retractable tricycle type, with spring and rubber shock-absorbers on main units, rubber only on nose unit. Light alloy wheels and same-size 500 × 5 tyres, pressure 17 lb/sq in (1·2 kg/cm²), on all units. Cable-operated drum brakes.

POWER PLANT: One 90 hp Continental C90 four-cylinder horizontally-opposed air-cooled engine, driving a wooden fixed-pitch propeller of 5 ft 2 in (1·52 m) diameter. Fuel in main tank in nose, capacity 14 Imp gallons (64 litres), with 10 Imp gallon (45 litre) reserve tank aft of seats. Refuelling point in front of windscreen. Oil capacity 1 Imp gallon (4·5 litres).

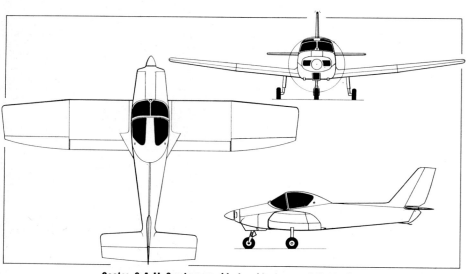

Coates S.A.II Swalesong side-by-side two-seat light aircraft

ACCOMMODATION: Side-by-side seating for pilot and one passenger in fully-enclosed cockpit, access to which is via a front-hinged window on each side. Cabin heated and ventilated.

DIMENSIONS, EXTERNAL:

Wing span	26 ft 5 in (8·05 m)
Wing chord at root	4 ft 9 in (1·45 m)
Wing chord at tip	4 ft 0 in (1·22 m)
Length overall	19 ft 0 in (5·79 m)
Height overall	7 ft 3 in (2·21 m)
Height over cabin roof	5 ft 3 in (1·60 m)
Tailplane span	8 ft 3 in (2·51 m)
Wheel track	6 ft 6 in (1·98 m)
Wheelbase	4 ft 0 in (1·22 m)
Propeller ground clearance	10 in (25 cm)

DIMENSION, INTERNAL:

Cabin: Max length	3 ft 4 in (1·01 m)

AREAS:

Wings, gross	120 sq ft (11·15 m²)
Ailerons (total)	12 sq ft (1·11 m²)
Flaps (total)	14 sq ft (1·30 m²)
Fin	5 sq ft (0·46 m²)
Rudder	6 sq ft (0·56 m²)
Tailplane	10·5 sq ft (0·97 m²)
Elevator, incl tab	9·5 sq ft (0·88 m²)

WEIGHTS AND LOADINGS (designed):

Weight empty	640 lb (290 kg)
Max T-O weight	1,150 lb (521 kg)
Max wing loading	9·5 lb/sq ft (46·4 kg/m²)
Max power loading	12·5 lb/hp (5·67 kg/hp)

PERFORMANCE (estimated at max T-O weight):

Max level speed at 1,000 ft (305 m)
     108 knots (125 mph; 201 km/h)
Max permissible diving speed
     147 knots (170 mph; 273 km/h)
Max cruising speed at 1,000 ft (305 m)
     95 knots (110 mph; 177 km/h)
Econ cruising speed at 1,000 ft (305 m)
     82·5 knots (95 mph; 153 km/h)
Stalling speed   46 knots (53 mph; 86 km/h)
Max rate of climb at S/L   850 ft (260 m)/min
T-O run   450 ft (137 m)
Landing from 50 ft (15 m)   900 ft (274 m)
Landing run   300 ft (92 m)
Range with max fuel
     390 nm (450 miles; 724 km)

GYROFLIGHT

Gyroflight Hornet single-seat light autogyro

HAWKER SIDDELEY

Hawker Siddeley Comet 3B (XP915) of the Blind
Landing Experimental Unit at RAE Bedford.
This aircraft has been used to carry out
experiments with the take-off and landing director
which will be fitted to the Concorde supersonic
transport (*Stephen P. Peltz*)

SHIELD
G. W. SHIELD, BSc
ADDRESS:
    Grammar School, Maple Road, Mexborough,
    Yorkshire WR

    Mr Shield, who is Headmaster of Mexborough
Grammar School, has designed and is building a
light aircraft which he has named Xyla. The

design was begun as a large single-seater, capable
of accommodating a 17-stone pilot and sufficient
fuel for 434-521 nm (500-600 miles; 805-965 km)
flying, yet with aerobatic capability at its max
T-O weight.
    The aircraft, which is registered G-AWPN, is a
cantilever monoplane, with tail-wheel landing
gear, and will be powered by either a 90 hp
Continental or 100 hp Rolls-Royce/Continental

"flat-four" engine. In mid-1970 the fuselage
was almost complete, and installation of the fuel
system and power plant was about to begin.
Completion of the outboard wing panels was
anticipated during the 1970-71 academic year,
after which testing will begin to obtain approval
to operate the aircraft under Permit to Fly or
equivalent C of A regulations.

TAYLOR
    TAYLOR MONOPLANE J.T.1
    The following description applies to the Taylor
Monoplane built by Mr Hugh Beckham of 1920
High, Wichita, Kansas 67203, USA. After its
first flight on 8 August 1964 it flew 270 hours
with its original 1,200 cc Volkswagen engine.
It has recently been refitted with a 1,600 cc
Porsche engine, with which flight testing was
under way in 1970. The details below apply
to it in its latest form.

TYPE: Single-seat ultra-light monoplane.

WINGS: Cantilever low-wing monoplane. Wing
    section RAF 48. Constant chord. Dihedral
    on outer panels 4°. Incidence 2°. Two-spar
    (Douglas fir) wooden structure with spruce
    ribs, comprising centre-section and outer panels.

All-wood sealed, plain top-hinged ailerons.
    Flaps omitted.

FUSELAGE: Conventional plywood-covered wood-
    en (spruce) structure. Wing centre-section
    integral with fuselage.

TAIL UNIT: Cantilever wooden (fir) structure,
    with plywood covering.

LANDING GEAR: Non-retractable tail-wheel type.
    Shock-absorption by simple slip-tube using
    readily-available "die-stripper" springs.
    Wheels and brake assemblies from a Piper
    J-3 Cub, cut down to accept 5·00 × 4 tyres.

POWER PLANT: One 56 hp 1,600 cc Porsche motor-
    car engine, with close-fitting streamlined
    pressure cowling, driving a Hegy propeller of
    4 ft 5 in (1·35 m) diameter. Fuel in fuselage
    tank forward of instrument panel.

ACCOMMODATION: Single seat under transparent
    one-piece canopy opening sideways to star-
    board.

DIMENSIONS, EXTERNAL:
Wing span   21 ft 8 in (6·60 m)
Wing chord (constant)   4 ft 0 in (1·22 m)
Length overall   16 ft 0 in (4·88 m)

PERFORMANCE (at max T-O weight):
Max level speed at S/L
                    121 knots (140 mph; 225 km/h)
Max and econ cruising speed at S/L
                    104 knots (120 mph; 193 km/h)
Stalling speed   42 knots (48 mph; 78 km/h)
Rate of climb at S/L   900 ft (275 m)/min
T-O run   300 ft (92 m)
T-O to 50 ft (15 m)   600 ft (183 m)
Landing from 50 ft (15 m)   800 ft (244 m)

TROJAN
TROJAN LTD
ADDRESS:
    Purley Way, Croydon, Surrey
    It was announced in June 1970 that Trojan is
to manufacture, under licence from AESL of

New Zealand (which see), the Airtourer two-seat
light aerobatic and touring aircraft. It was
expected that production would begin by the
end of 1970, initially from AESL-supplied components but later from UK manufacture. This
will be undertaken in the company's Croydon

factory, and the aircraft will then be transported
by road to Biggin Hill airfield in Kent for final
assembly and test-flying. Glos-Air Ltd of Staverton, Glos, will continue as UK distributor for
the Airtourer.

WESTLAND
    It was announced on 21 July 1970 that West-
land Aircraft Ltd and Sikorsky Aircraft Division

of UAC were negotiating an agreement for a
marketing programme to present the Westland
WG.13 helicopter in the US as the Sikorsky

candidate for the US Navy's LAMPS (Light
Airborne Multi-Purpose System) competition.

USA

BEECH AIRCRAFT CORPORATION

Beech announced on 29 June 1970 that the Chilean Air Force had taken delivery of the first three of nine Beechcraft 99A Airliners, being supplied under a contract worth $7·1 million. Stationed at Quintero Air Base, two of the initial three aircraft have been specially equipped as navigational trainers.

The US Army have ordered 16 Beech **RU-21E** electronic reconnaissance versions of the Beechcraft Model 65-A90 under a contract worth $12·3 million; in addition, 22 more Beech U-21As have been ordered. The Beechcraft Model 65-A90-1 is in service under three US Army designations: **U-21A**, **RU-21A** and **RU-21D**, all of which have Pratt & Whitney PT6A-20 engines, and these three versions all have an AUW of 9,650 lb (4,377 kg). The RU-21D is in service in Vietnam, employed on electronic reconnaissance missions. The Beechcraft Models 65-A90-2 and 65-A90-3 have the US Army designations **RU-21B** and **RU-21C** respectively; both have Pratt & Whitney PT6A-29 engines and an AUW of 10,900 lb (4,944 kg).

Beechcraft RU-21D, with extensive antenna array for unspecified duties   (*Stephen P. Peltz*)

THE BOEING COMPANY

BOEING 707 and 737

On 14 July 1970 it was announced that Iran Air had ordered three advanced Model 737 airliners, one of which will be a 737-200 convertible, for delivery in 1971. Two days later, Alia, the Royal Jordanian airline, announced the purchase of two Model 707-320C airliners, also for delivery in 1971.

BOEING 747

On 2 June 1970 it was announced that the FAA had signed an amendment to the Model 747's Type Certificate, certifying Litton Industries' LTN-51 inertial navigation system as the sole means of navigation and primary attitude source on all models of the 747. This covers not only a triple LTN-51 installation, but also two LTN-51s with one C-IV or one LTN-51 with two C-IVs.

BOEING VERTOL 347

The Vertol Division's Model 347 advanced technology helicopter made its first flight on 27 May 1970. An enlarged version of the CH-47A, it has four-blade main rotors 61 ft 7¼ in (18·78 m) in diameter. Height of the aft rotor pylon is increased by 2 ft 6 in (0·76 m), and the fuselage extended in length by 9 ft 2 in (2·79 m). Retractable landing gear is provided and there are structural provisions for the addition of wings to improve manoeuvrability. Initial flight tests have been made at a T-O weight of 36,000 lb (16,329 kg) and a true airspeed of 172 knots (198 mph; 318 km/h) was attained. It is anticipated that maximum speed will exceed 180 knots (207 mph; 333 km/h) at a max T-O weight of 54,000 lb (24,495 kg).

AWACS

The USAF's airborne warning and control system (AWACS) aircraft will consist basically of a Boeing Model 707 airframe, modified and equipped with extensive sensing, communications, display and navigational devices. The primary use of such an aircraft, deployed by Air Defense Command, will be as a survivable early-warning airborne command-and-control centre for identification, surveillance and tracking of airborne enemy forces and for the command and control of North American Air Defense forces. Similar aircraft operated by Tactical Air Command will be used as airborne command-and-control systems for quick-reaction deployment and initial tactical operations.

The AWACS version of the turbofan Model 707 Intercontinental will be readily identifiable externally by the large saucer-shaped radome above its fuselage and its eight TF 34 engines in podded pairs. The entire cabin area will be devoted to the installation of specialised electronics and communications equipment required for the AWACS rôle.

CALIFORNIA AIRMOTIVE CORPORATION

ADDRESS:
11101 South La Cienega Boulevard, Los Angeles, California 90045

PRESIDENT:
Allen E. Paulson

CALIFORNIA AIRMOTIVE TURBO STAR 402

California Airmotive, which is a sales, servicing and repair organisation for both aircraft and engines, has flown the first of a proposed series of turboprop conversions for light single- and twin-engined aircraft.

Known as the Turbo Star 402, this is a Cessna Model 402 which has had its Continental power plant removed and replaced by two 330 shp Allison 250-B15 turboprop engines, each driving a three-blade constant-speed reversible-pitch metal propeller, with Beta control. The new engines offer a weight saving of 400-600 lb (181-272 kg), adding increased range and payload to the specification of the standard Cessna 402. The turbine power plants, by comparison with the former piston-engines, have increased time between overhauls and lower the cabin noise level.

The prototype Turbo Star 402 conversion by California Airmotive

California Airmotive intends to apply similar conversions to the Beechcraft Bonanza and Twin Baron and Cessna 310, as well as to other popular light aircraft. Conversion kits will be made available to selected modification organisations around the world, on a licensee basis.

CESSNA AIRCRAFT COMPANY
CESSNA MODEL 421 GOLDEN EAGLE

Significant increases in useful load, gross weight and performance were announced by Cessna for their Model 421 Golden Eagle on 28 July 1970. Basically as described on page 320, this latest version of the Golden Eagle has 375 hp Continental GTSIO-520-H engines. All available specification and performance figures are quoted below:

AREA:
Wings, gross   211·65 sq ft (19·66 m²)

WEIGHTS AND LOADINGS:
Weight empty (approximate) 4,359 lb (1,977 kg)
Max T-O weight   7,250 lb (3,289 kg)
Max landing weight   7,200 lb (3,266 kg)
Max wing loading   34·25 lb/sq ft (167·2 kg/m²)
Max power loading   9·67 lb/hp (4·39 kg/hp)

PERFORMANCE (at max T-O weight, unless specified otherwise):
Max level speed at S/L
     207 knots (238 mph; 383 km/h)
Max level speed at 18,000 ft (5,485 m)
     246 knots (283 mph; 455 km/h)

Max cruising speed, 75% power at 10,000 ft (3,050 m)   203 knots (234 mph; 376 km/h)
Max cruising speed, 75% power at 25,000 ft (7,620 m)   234 knots (270 mph; 435 km/h)
Max rate of climb at S/L   1,950 ft (594 m)/min
Max rate of climb at S/L, one engine out
     345 ft (105 m)/min
Service ceiling   31,800 ft (9,692 m)
Service ceiling, one engine out
     15,000 ft (4,572 m)
T-O run   1,838 ft (560 m)
T-O to 50 ft (15 m)   2,325 ft (709 m)
Landing from 50 ft (15 m) at max landing weight
     2,178 ft (664 m)
Landing run, at max landing weight
     720 ft (219 m)
Range, 75% power at 10,000 ft (3,050 m), no reserve fuel:
1,020 lb (463 kg) usable fuel
     804 nm (926 miles; 1,490 km)
1,176 lb (533 kg) usable fuel
     927 nm (1,067 miles; 1,717 km)
1,488 lb (675 kg) usable fuel
     1,173 nm (1,351 miles; 2,174 km)

Range, 75% power at 25,000 ft (7,620 m), no reserve fuel:
1,020 lb (463 kg) usable fuel
     927 nm (1,067 miles; 1,717 km)
1,176 lb (533 kg) usable fuel
     1,068 nm (1,230 miles; 1,979 km)
1,488 lb (675 kg) usable fuel
     1,352 nm (1,557 miles; 2,506 km)
Maximum range, at 10,000 ft (3,050 m), no reserve fuel:
1,020 lb (463 kg) usable fuel
     969 nm (1,116 miles; 1,796 km)
1,176 lb (533 kg) usable fuel
     1,118 nm (1,287 miles; 2,071 km)
1,488 lb (675 kg) usable fuel
     1,414 nm (1,628 miles; 2,620 km)
Maximum range, at 25,000 ft (7,620 m), no reserve fuel:
1,020 lb (463 kg) usable fuel
     1,037 nm (1,194 miles; 1,922 km)
1,176 lb (533 kg) usable fuel
     1,195 nm (1,377 miles; 2,216 km)
1,488 lb (675 kg) usable fuel
     1,513 nm (1,742 miles; 2,803 km)

ECTOR AIRCRAFT COMPANY

ADDRESS:
414 East Hillmont, Odessa, Texas 79760

ECTOR MOUNTAINEER

The Ector Aircraft Company has in production a civil version of the Cessna L-19 Bird Dog (last described in the 1964-65 *Jane's*), to which it has given the name Mountaineer. This is available in two models: the standard Model A, with fixed-pitch propeller; and the Model B, with variable-pitch propeller.

Generally similar to the original Cessna L-19, Ector's Mountaineers are rebuilt completely from new off-the-shelf or serviceable components. The entire airframe is corrosion-proofed with zinc chromate before assembly, mounting brackets for floats are built into the basic airframe and all four side windows can be opened in flight. The rear seat is removable to permit the carriage of cargo. Power plant consists of a 213 hp Continental O-470-11 six-cylinder horizontally-opposed air-cooled engine, driving a two-blade fixed-pitch (optionally variable-pitch) propeller, diameter 7 ft 6 in (2·29 m).

The Mountaineer is already in service with various organisations as a glider tug and for patrol and general-purpose duties: it is also in demand as a sporting aircraft.

Ector Mountaineer civil version of the Cessna L-19 Bird Dog

DIMENSIONS, EXTERNAL:

Wing span	36 ft 0 in (10·97 m)
Length overall	25 ft 9½ in (7·86 m)
Height overall	7 ft 6 in (2·29 m)

WEIGHTS:

Weight empty, equipped	1,450 lb (658 kg)
Max T-O weight	2,300 lb (1,043 kg)

PERFORMANCE (at max T-O weight):

Cruising speed	102 knots (117 mph; 188 km/h)
Stalling speed, flaps up	45 knots (52 mph; 84 km/h)
Stalling speed, 60° flaps	41 knots (47 mph; 76 km/h)
T-O run	355 ft (108 m)
T-O to 50 ft (15 m)	580 ft (177 m)
Landing from 50 ft (15 m)	605 ft (184 m)
Landing run	475 ft (145 m)
Range, max fuel, no reserve	600 nm (692 miles; 1,113 km)

EVANGEL AIRCRAFT CORPORATION

HEAD OFFICE:
PO Box 4500, Orange City, Iowa 51041

EVANGEL 4500

The Evangel Aircraft Corporation has designed and built a twin-engined STOL aircraft which it has designated Evangel 4500. The aircraft is intended specifically for heavy-duty bush operations, and this is reflected in its boxlike fuselage and rugged appearance. Ease of maintenance has been a prime consideration, and surface skins are of 2024-T3 light alloy to permit easy repairs in the field.

Following FAA Certification in July 1970, the Evangel 4500 is in production at a rate of one aircraft per month, and the first was due to be delivered to the Wycliffe Bible Translators in Peru at the time of writing. It is intended to obtain certification for operation on floats or skis, and development of a turbocharged version is planned.

TYPE: Nine-seat light passenger/cargo aircraft.

WINGS: Cantilever low-wing monoplane. Conventional all-metal light alloy structure. Cambered wingtips. Light alloy ailerons and trailing-edge flaps.

FUSELAGE: Rectangular-section all-metal structure.

TAIL UNIT: Cantilever all-metal structure. Large dorsal fin faired into upper surface of fuselage. Dihedral on tailplane. Horn-balanced elevators. Trim-tab in rudder.

LANDING GEAR: Tail-wheel type, main units only retracting into undersurface of wings. Castoring tail-wheel. Wheel brakes.

POWER PLANT: Two 300 hp Lycoming IO-540-K1B5 six-cylinder horizontally-opposed air-cooled fuel-injection engines, each driving a Hartzell two-blade constant-speed fully-feathering metal propeller with spinner. Fuel contained in two wing tanks, total capacity 110 US gallons (416 litres). Refuelling points in upper surface of wings.

ACCOMMODATION: Pilot and eight passengers in enclosed cabin. Cabin doors on each side of fuselage. Large cargo-loading doors on each side of fuselage, aft of wings, permit easy loading of bulky freight.

ELECTRONICS AND EQUIPMENT: Full IFR instrumentation standard, radios to customer's requirements.

DIMENSIONS, EXTERNAL:

Wing span	41 ft 3 in (12·52 m)
Length overall	31 ft 6 in (9·60 m)

Evangel 4500 nine-seat light passenger/cargo aircraft

Height overall	9 ft 6 in (2·90 m)
Tailplane span	14 ft 6½ in (4·43 m)
Wheel track	11 ft 2 in (3·40 m)
Wheelbase	20 ft 4 in (6·20 m)

Cabin doors (fwd):

Height	2 ft 8½ in (0·82 m)
Width	1 ft 9 in (0·53 m)

Cargo doors (aft):

Height	2 ft 11 in (0·89 m)
Width	3 ft 9 in (1·14 m)

AREAS:

Wings, gross	251 sq ft (23·32 m²)
Ailerons (total)	32·0 sq ft (2·97 m²)
Trailing-edge flaps (total)	28·4 sq ft (2·64 m²)
Rudder, including tab	34·2 sq ft (3·18 m²)
Fin	31·5 sq ft (2·93 m²)
Tailplane	62·0 sq ft (5·76 m²)
Elevators	27·5 sq ft (2·55 m²)

WEIGHTS:

Weight empty	3,455 lb (1,567 kg)
Max T-O weight	5,500 lb (2,495 kg)

PERFORMANCE (at max T-O weight):

Max cruising speed, 75% power at 6,000 ft (1,830 m)	158 knots (182 mph; 293 km/h)
Normal cruising speed, 65% power at 10,000 ft (3,050 m)	152 knots (175 mph; 282 km/h)
Econ cruising speed, 55% power	149 knots (171 mph; 275 km/h)
Max rate of climb at S/L	1,500 ft (457 m)/min
Service ceiling	21,030 ft (6,410 m)
Service ceiling, one engine out	7,100 ft (2,164 m)
T-O run	500 ft (152 m)
T-O to 50 ft (15 m)	1,125 ft (343 m)
Landing from 50 ft (15 m)	1,140 ft (347 m)
Landing run	475 ft (145 m)
Range, at normal cruising speed	608 nm (700 miles; 1,126 km)
Range, at econ cruising speed	647 nm (745 miles; 1,199 km)

FAIRCHILD HILLER CORPORATION

Signature of an agreement with California Airmotive Corporation (which see) for the installation of the first large cargo door in an FH-227D Cargonaut has been announced by Fairchild Hiller. This new electrically-operated outward-opening cargo door is 7 ft 7 in (2·31 m) wide and 5 ft 10 in (1·78 m) high, with the lower sill at truck-bed height. The door is to be installed at the forward end of the cabin on the port side, and completion of this first installation is scheduled for May 1971.

Simultaneously, California Airmotive will install all-weather avionics and a new convertible cargo/passenger interior. The cabin conversions consist of providing folding passenger seats, hat-racks and a movable bulkhead.

FAIRCHILD HILLER AC-119K

Weight and performance details of the Fairchild Hiller AC-119K Gunship have been released and are quoted below:

WEIGHTS:

Weight empty	58,282 lb (26,436 kg)
Basic operating weight	60,955 lb (27,649 kg)
Max payload	4,838 lb (2,194 kg)
Max T-O and landing weight	80,400 lb (36,468 kg)

PERFORMANCE (at max T-O weight):

Max level speed, at 10,000 ft (3,050 m)	217 knots (250 mph; 402 km/h)
Max cruising speed at 10,000 ft (3,050 m), with auxiliary turbojets operating	190 knots (219 mph; 352 km/h)
Max cruising speed at 10,000 ft (3,050 m), with auxiliary turbojets inoperative	150 knots (173 mph; 278 km/h)
Stalling speed, wheels and flaps down	88 knots (101 mph; 163 km/h)
Max rate of climb at S/L, one engine out	900 ft (274 m)/min
Service ceiling, one engine out	23,500 ft (7,163 m)
T-O run	1,580 ft (482 m)
T-O to 50 ft (15 m)	1,820 ft (555 m)
Landing from 50 ft (15 m)	1,245 ft (379 m)
Range with max payload	1,720 nm (1,980 miles; 3,186 km)

The Fairchild Hiller AC-119G and AC-119K are operating in Vietnam with the designations "Shadow" and "Stinger" respectively.

GATES LEARJET CORPORATION

It was announced on 17 July 1970 that FAA Certification under FAR Part 25 had been granted for the Learjet Models 24C and 24D. Initial deliveries to customers were scheduled to be made in August 1970.

The Western Gear Corporation of Lynwood, California, has been awarded a contract worth $6 million to produce main rotor transmissions for the Gates Twinjet helicopter. The first complete transmission was scheduled for delivery in September 1970.

LOCKHEED AIRCRAFT CORPORATION

Lockheed announced on 8 June 1970 receipt from the Italian government of a letter of intent to order 14 Hercules transport aircraft. The aircraft, worth $60 million, are scheduled to enter Italian Air Force service during 1971. A reciprocal agreement signed by Lockheed will provide for the Italian aircraft industry to participate as sub-contractors in the L-1011 TriStar programme.

Some estimated specification figures for the Lockheed SR-71A and YF-12A have been reported, and these are given below.

LOCKHEED SR-71A

WEIGHT:
Max T-O weight   170,000 lb (77,110 kg)
PERFORMANCE:
Range, at Mach 3·0 at 78,740 ft (24,000 m)
    2,589 nm (2,982 miles; 4,800 km)

Max endurance, at Mach 3·0 at 78,740 ft (24,000 m)   1 hr 30 min

LOCKHEED YF-12A

PERFORMANCE:
Max speed, short periods only   Mach 3·5
Max speed, long-range cruising   Mach 3·0
Service ceiling   70,000 ft (21,350 m)
Absolute ceiling   88,600 ft (27,000 m)

McDONNELL DOUGLAS CORPORATION

On 1 July 1970 McDonnell Douglas awarded a contract worth about $1·5 million to the Cleveland Pneumatic Co division of Pneumo Dynamic Corporation, Cleveland, Ohio, for the nose and main landing gear for the F-15 air superiority fighter aircraft. This covers landing gear for pre-production testing and the initial phase of the flight test programme, and includes provision of retraction actuators, steering mechanism for the nose gear and swivel mechanism for the main gear.

It has been reported that McDonnell Douglas are investigating the feasibility of mounting a combined infra-red warning device and laser range-finder at the top of one of the F-15's fins. This would alert the pilot of an impending attack from the rear, while the rangefinder would track the enemy aircraft automatically and, at the same time, feed range and tracking data to the F-15's fire control system to permit rapid counter-attack.

On 30 July 1970, a week after the roll-out of the DC-10, McDonnell Douglas announced receipt of 23 new orders and options for their tri-jet airbus. These are detailed below. That of Union de Transports Aériens is a re-order, representing an increase of three aircraft on the original order.

	Orders	Options	Series
Air New Zealand	3	1	30
Continental Airlines	8	8	10
Union de Transports Aériens	4	4	30

Roll-out of the first prototype of the McDonnell Douglas DC-10 high-capacity jet transport aircraft

J. W. MILLER AVIATION INC

HEAD OFFICE:
San Antonio International Airport, San Antonio, Texas

Mr J. W. Miller, a former builder of midget aircraft and a racing pilot has, during the past ten years, produced conversions to improve the appearance and performance of such aircraft as the Piper Apache. The conversions, to which he has given the name of Miller Jet Profiles, involve modifications to clean up the aircraft aerodynamically and the provision of uprated engines; they are available individually or in any combination in kit form, or can be carried out by Miller Aviation at its San Antonio Airport facility.

MILLER JET PROFILE TWIN COMANCHE 200

Latest project of Miller Aviation is the conversion of a Piper Twin Comanche to "Jet Profile" configuration. FAA Certification of the prototype conversion was received just prior to the 1970 Business Aircraft Show at Reading, Pennsylvania, where three firm orders were received.

The modifications are extensive and include installation of two new 200 hp Lycoming IO-360-C1C four-cylinder horizontally-opposed air-cooled fuel-injection engines, each driving a new Hartzell two-blade metal propeller with spinner; provision of square wingtips (with dual flush-mounted navigation lights), offering improved aileron control; an extension to the fuselage nose consisting of a vacuum-formed high-strength glass-fibre honeycomb structure, reducing drag and adding 11 cu ft (0·31 m²) of baggage/electronics capacity; a rudder and aileron interconnect system; a long streamlined dorsal fin, which lowers minimum control speed and improves directional stability; streamlined glass-fibre engine cowlings, extending aft of the trailing-edge

The Miller Jet Profile Twin Comanche 200

flaps and providing an additional 12 cu ft (0·34 m²) of baggage space; an auxiliary integral fuel tank of 19 US gallons (72 litres) capacity in each wing, which also increases the structural strength of the wing and allows an increase of 180 lb (82 kg) in the max T-O weight; a one-piece windshield 0·25 in (0·64 cm) thick, improving visibility and reducing cabin noise level; a dual brake system to improve braking efficiency; and custom three-colour paint schemes and de luxe interior trims.

The resulting aircraft has improved performance by comparison with the standard Piper Twin Comanche, as detailed below:

PERFORMANCE (at max T-O weight):
Max level speed   198 knots (230 mph; 370 km/h)
Max cruising speed   191 knots (220 mph; 354 km/h)
Minimum control speed   72 knots (83 mph; 134 km/h)

Stalling speed, flaps down   60 knots (69 mph; 111 km/h)
Max rate of climb at S/L   1,900 ft (579 m)/min
Max rate of climb at S/L, one engine out   500 ft (152 m)/min
Service ceiling   21,000 ft (6,400 m)
Service ceiling, one engine out   11,500 ft (3,505 m)
T-O run   720 ft (219 m)
T-O to 50 ft (15 m)   1,150 ft (350 m)
Landing from 50 ft (15 m)   1,875 ft (570 m)
Landing run   700 ft (213 m)
Range, 75% power with standard fuel   823 nm (948 miles; 1,525 km)
Range, 65% power with standard fuel   890 nm (1,025 miles; 1,650 km)
Range, 75% power with maximum fuel   955 nm (1,100 miles; 1,770 km)
Range, 65% power with maximum fuel   1,128 nm (1,300 miles; 2,090 km)

NASA

Artists' impressions of (*left*) space shuttle booster returning to Kennedy Space Center landing strip, and (*right*) servicing the orbital section of a space shuttle vehicle

Artist's impressions of the US space shuttle, above, show both booster and orbiter, but the final form may differ considerably as the designs are still in a state of evolution. NASA awarded both North American Rockwell Corporation and McDonnell Douglas Corporation an 11-month

Phase B contract, worth about $8 million in each case, to carry out preliminary design studies. It was reported subsequently that Grumman Aerospace Corporation, Chrysler Corporation and Lockheed Aircraft Corporation had been awarded contracts to study alternative configurations.

NASA believe that if development and production contracts are awarded in August 1971, as scheduled, initial utilisation of the shuttle system, with both stages operating as fully-re-usable vehicles, could be made in 1977.

SIKORSKY AIRCRAFT, DIVISION OF UNITED AIRCRAFT CORPORATION

On 22 July 1970, Sikorsky Aircraft in the USA

and Westland Aircraft Ltd in the UK jointly announced the negotiation of an agreement for a marketing programme in which Sikorsky would

present the Westland WG.13 helicopter (see page 239) in the US as Sikorsky's candidate for the US Navy's LAMPS requirement (see page 366).

SWEARINGEN

SWEARINGEN MERLIN III

The Swearingen Merlin III was awarded FAA

certification on 27 July 1970. Four days earlier, the company announced that the aircraft had been

flown at a true airspeed of 438·5 knots (505 mph; 813 km/h), equivalent to Mach 0·72.

WORLD FLIGHT INCORPORATED

Official FAI confirmation has been received for two records set by James R. Bede in his

BD-2 Love One experimental aircraft in the period 7-10 November 1969. These are for distance in a closed circuit for piston-engined aircraft of any class, and distance in a closed

circuit for piston-engined lightplanes in the 3-858-6·614 lb (1,750 to 3,000 kg) weight catagory, the record-breaking distance recorded being 8,973·18 miles (15,441·26 km).

USSR

First seen at the 1970 World Aerobatic Championships in the UK, the Yak-18PS is similar to the Yak-18PM except for its tailwheel landing gear
(*Flight International*)

SAILPLANES

JAPAN

JEAA (Japan Experimental Aircraft Association, Chapter 306 of EAA International)

JEAA SH-16S

The Japanese Chapter of the EAA has designed a single-seat sailplane of which only very brief constructional details are available. The fuselage is of all-wood monocoque construction, as is the T-type tail unit, which is a cantilever structure. Landing gear comprises a non-retractable mono-wheel with brake. There is accommodation for a pilot only, under a blown Plexiglas canopy.

DIMENSIONS:
Wing span	53 ft 0 in (16·15 m)
Length overall	22 ft 8½ in (6·92 m)
Height overall	4 ft 4¾ in (1·34 m)

AREAS:
Wings, gross	142 sq ft (13·19 m²)
Air brake	5·90 sq ft (0·55 m²)
Horizontal tail surfaces	18·2 sq ft (1·69 m²)

WEIGHTS AND LOADING:
Weight empty	660 lb (299 kg)
Max T-O weight	880 lb (399 kg)
Max wing loading	6·2 lb/sq ft (30·3 kg/m²)

PERFORMANCE:
Best glide ratio
44 : 1 at 54 knots (62 mph; 100 km/h)

Min sinking speed	1·8 ft (0·56 m)/sec at 44 knots (51 mph; 82 km/h)
Stalling speed, flaps up	42 knots (48 mph; 77 km/h)
Stalling speed, flaps down	36 knots (41 mph; 66 km/h)
Max speed (smooth air)	108 knots (125 mph; 201 km/h)
Max speed (rough air)	97 knots (112 mph; 180 km/h)
Max aero-tow speed	73 knots (84 mph; 135 km/h)
Max winch-launching speed	73 knots (84 mph; 135 km/h)

zz

AERO-ENGINES

FRANCE
SNECMA

INTERNATIONAL
ROLLS-ROYCE/SNECMA

Above: **SNECMA Super Atar M53 turbojet in test cell at Melun-Villaroche. First run was made in February 1970; design thrust is approx 20,000 lb (9,080 kg) with reheat**

Rolls-Royce/SNECMA Olympus 593-3 (Mk 601) turbojet (38,050 lb = 17,259 kg st)

ROLLS-ROYCE/SNECMA M45H

New derivatives are announced by Rolls-Royce and SNECMA of the M45H subsonic turbofan for fixed-wing aircraft (page 719). The M57H is a turboshaft engine for helicopters and would have a maximum rating of 8,315 shp. The M57HA, of the same power, would be a forward-drive engine specially adapted for V/STOL aircraft. The THS2000, using the same gas generator as the M57H, would be a turboshaft engine for electricity generation, rail traction and marine applications. The first THS2000 prototype was being constructed in mid-1970, using M45H components.

Right: **Shop assembly of pods for the VFW 614 short-haul jetliner at Rolls-Royce Bristol Engine Division; the engine is the Rolls-Royce/SNECMA M45H-01 rated at 7,760 lb (3,520 kg) st**

ROLLS-ROYCE TURBOMÉCA ADOUR

Although many of the most important data relating to this small two-shaft reheat turbofan remain officially restricted (see "Engines" section, "International programmes," page 720), many new figures have been published in a US journal which visited the French partner, Turboméca. According to *Aviation Week & Space Technology* the basic dry static thrust is 4,620 lb (2,095 kg). This can be raised by the reheat system through any desired augmentation from 30 to 50 per cent, the maximum with full reheat being 6,390 lb (2,900 kg). Pressure ratio is given as 9·6 : 1. Engine weight is stated to be 1,559 lb (707 kg), made up of 983 lb for the basic engine, 370 lb for the afterburner and 206 lb for Jaguar installation sub-assemblies including nozzle fairings and insulation and an intake duct extension. Design time between overhauls is stated to be 1,000 hr but early production engines are not expected to exceed 250 hr.

UK
ROLLS-ROYCE

Right: **Display model of Rolls-Royce RB.202 lift turbofan for VTOL applications; rated thrust 10,000-20,000 lb (4,540-9,080 kg)**

Right: **Rolls-Royce Bristol Viper 600 turbojet (3,750 lb = 1,701 kg st). This engine made its first flight, in an HS 125 test aircraft, on 3 August 1970**

GENERAL INDEX OF AIRCRAFT

Items printed in this type refer to this edition — *Items printed in italics refer to the ten previous editions*

SAILPLANES

MILITARY MISSILES,
RESEARCH ROCKETS & SPACE VEHICLES

AERO ENGINES